WHO'S WHO IN AMERICAN ART

1978

Edited by JAQUES CATTELL PRESS

R. R. BOWKER COMPANY
New York & London

Published by the R. R. Bowker Company
1180 Avenue of the Americas, New York, New York 10036

International Standard Book Number: 0-8352-1036-7
International Standard Serial Number: 0000-0191
Library of Congress Catalog Card Number: 36-27014
Printed and bound in the United States of America

Contents

Advisory Committee vi

Preface vii

Abbreviations ix

Biographies 1

Geographic Index 787

Professional Classifications Index 859

Necrology 937

Advisory Committee

Paul B Arnold, President
National Association of Schools of Art
c/o Department of Art
Oberlin College, Oberlin, Ohio 44074

Mario Cooper, President
American Watercolor Society
1083 Fifth Avenue
New York, New York 10028

Mark Freeman, President
National Society of Painters
in Casein & Acrylic
307 East 37th Street
New York, New York 10016

Kenneth S Friedman, Director
Institute for Advanced Studies
in Contemporary Art
6361 Elmhurst Drive
San Diego, California 92120

Bill Gallo, President
National Cartoonists Society
9 Ebony Court
Brooklyn, New York 11229

Judith Hoffberg, Editor
Umbrella
PO Box 3692
Glendale, California 91201

Konrad Kuchel, Coordinator of Loans
The American Federation of Arts
41 East 65th Street
New York, New York 10021

John J Mahlmann, Executive Director
National Art Education Association
1916 Association Drive
Reston, Virginia 22091

Laurence McGilvery
Rare Art Book Dealer
PO Box 852
La Jolla, California 92037

Margaret Mills, Executive Director
American Academy & Institute of
Arts & Letters
633 West 155th Street
New York, New York 10032

Paul C Mills, Secretary
Association of Art Museum Directors
c/o Santa Barbara Museum of Art
1130 State Street
Santa Barbara, California 93101

Claire Stein, Executive Director
National Sculpture Society
777 Third Avenue
New York, New York 10017

Preface

Who's Who in American Art 1978 contains entries for more than 10,000 living artists, art administrators, art historians, collectors, critics, dealers, art instructors, librarians, patrons, and others prominently active in the world of art residing in or native to the United States, Canada and Mexico. In addition to vital statistics, listings include professional classifications, education and training, information on commissions and work in public collections, exhibitions, personal collections, publications, positions held with museums, schools and art organizations, memberships, interest or research statement, style and technique, media, dealer and preferred mailing address. As a special aid to researchers, the necrology section combines listings from previous editions with notices received since publication of *Who's Who in American Art 1976*. Continued features include the indexing of biographies by geographic location and by professional classification.

This is the first edition published without the sponsorship of The American Federation of Arts. In its stead, the editors have assembled an advisory committee whose responsibilities will include critiquing this edition of both *Who's Who in American Art* and the *American Art Directory,* to provide nominations of qualified artists or organizations not already listed, as well as suggestions for improvement of format and data. In addition, the editors will look to the advisory committee for advice when settling interpretation and criteria problems during compilation of future editions. We are very pleased to have this cooperation and support from these distinguished members of the art community.

Locating current mailing addresses for artists in order to update entries or have questionnaires completed for consideration of inclusion remains a constant problem. The editors are extremely grateful for the assistance of the many galleries, museums, art organizations and individuals who submitted nominations and current addresses for biographees. A number of individuals qualified for inclusion are omitted because forms were not returned and data could not be found in other sources. The editors have also honored specific requests for omission from some artists, and from collectors who do not wish to have their private collections made public information.

For artists, selection has been made on an individual basis, taking into consideration work in public collections, commissions, group and solo exhibitions of an international, national and wide regional scope in noncommercial galleries and museums, plus other pertinent material. The positions and/or activities of other entrants indicate the reason for their inclusion.

All material submitted was carefully edited to established format and proofread. Those whose information is appearing for the first time received a proof for approval prior to publication. While all precautions have been taken to avoid errors, the publishers do not assume and hereby disclaim any liability to any party for any loss or damage caused by errors or omissions, whether such errors or omissions result from negligence, accident or any other cause. In any event, the sole responsibility of the publishers will be the entry of corrected data in a succeeding edition.

Comments and reviews are invited and should be addressed to The Editors, *Who's Who in American Art,* P.O. Box 25001, Tempe, Arizona 85282.

Anita Lee, *Assistant Editor*
Ann Gammons, *Sponsoring Editor*
Anne Rhodes, *Managing Editor*
Steve Nichols, *General Manager*
JAQUES CATTELL PRESS

July 1978

Abbreviations

abstr—abstract(s)
acad—academia, academic, academica, academie, academique, academy
accad—accademia
acoust—acoustic(s), acoustical
actg—acting
addn—addition, additional
adj—adjunct
Adm—Admiral
admin—administration, administrative
adminr—administrator
admis(s)—admission
adv—adviser(s), advisory
advan—advance(d), advancement
advert—advertisement, advertising
aesthet—aesthetics
affil—affiliate, affiliation
agr—agricultural, agriculture
akad—akademi, akademia
Ala—Alabama
Atla—Alberta
Am—America, American
anal—analysis, analytic, analytical
analog—analogue
anat—anatomic, anatomical, anatomy
ann—annual
anthrop—anthropological, anthropology
antiq—antiquary, antiquities, antiquity
antiqn—antiquarian
app—appoint, appointed
appl—applied
approx—approximate, approximately
Apr—April
apt—apartment(s)
arch—archiv, archiva, archivies, archivio, archivo,
archeol—archeological, archeologie, archeologique, archeology
archit—architectural, architecture
Arg—Argentina
Ariz—Arizona
Ark—Arkansas
asn—association
asoc—asociacion
assoc(s)—associate(s), associated
asst(s)—assistant(s)
atty—attorney
Aug—August
auth—author
AV—audiovisual
Ave—Avenue

b—born
BC—British Columbia
bd—board
Belg—Belgian, Belgium
bibliog—bibliografia, bibliographic, bibliographical, bibliography(ies)
bibliot—biblioteca, bibliotek, bibliotheca, bibliothek, bibliotheque
biog—biographical, biography
bk(s)—book(s)
Bldg—Building(s)
Blvd—Boulevard
br—branch(es)
Brit—Britain, British
bull—bulletin
bur—bureau
bus—business
BWI—British West Indies

Calif—California
Can—Canada, Canadian, Canadien, Canadienne
Capt—Captain
Cath—Catholic
CBS—Columbia Broadcasting System
cent—central
Cent Am—Central America
cert—certificate(s), certification, certified
chap—chapter
chmn—chairman
c/o—care of
co—companies, company
Co—County
co-auth—co-author
co-dir—co-director
co-ed—co-editor
co-educ—co-educational
CofC—Chamber of Commerce
Col—Colonel
col(s)—college(s), collegiate
collab—collaboration, collaborative
collabr—collaborator
Colo—Colorado
com—commerce, commercial
comdr—commander
commun—communication(s)
comn(s)—commission(s), commissioned
comnr—commissioner
compos—composition
comt(s)—committee(s)
conf—conference
Cong—Congress, Congressional
Conn—Connecticut
conserv—conservacion, conservation, conservatiore, conservatory
construct—construction
consult—consult, consultant, consultantship, consultation, consulting
contemp—contemporary
contrib—contribute, contributing, contribution
contribr—contributor
conv—convention
coop—cooperating, cooperation, cooperative
coord—coordinate, coordinating, coordination
coordr—coordinator
corp—corporate, corporation
corresp—correspondent, corresponding
coun—council, counsel, counseling
counr—councilor, counselor
Ct—Court
ctr—center
cult—cultural, culture
cur—curator
curric—curriculum
CZ—Canal Zone
Czech—Czechoslovakia

DC—District of Columbia
Dec—December
Del—Delaware
deleg—delegate, delegation
demonstr—demonstrator
dept—department, departmental
develop—development, developmental
dict—dictionaries, dictionary
dig—digest
dipl—diplom, diploma, diplomate, diplome
dir(s)—director(s), directory
dist—district
distribr—distributor
div—division, divisional, divorced
doc—document(s), documentary, documentation
Dom—Dominion
Dr—Doctor, Drive

E—East
econ—economic(s), economical, economist, economy
ed—edicion, edit, edited, editing, edition, editor(s), editorial, edizione
educ—educate, educated, educating, education, educational
elec—electric, electrical, electricity
elem—elementary
emer—emeritus, emeriti
encycl—encyclopedia
eng—engineering
Eng—England, English
environ—environment(s), environmental
equip—equipment
estab—established, establishment
estud—estudante, estudas, estudiante, estudio, estudo

Europ—European
exec(s)—executive(s)
exhib(s)—exhibit(s), exhibition
exped(s)—expedition(s)
explor—exploration(s), exploratory
expos—exposition
exten—extension

fac—faculty
Feb—February
fed—federal
fedn—federation
fel(s)—fellow(s), fellowship(s)
Fla—Florida
for—foreign
found—foundation
Fr—French
Ft—Fort
ft—feet, foot

Ga—Georgia
gen—general, generale
Ger—German, Germany
Ges—Gesellschaft
gov—governing, governor
govt—government, governmental
grad—graduate, graduated
Gt Brit—Great Britain
gym—gymnasium

handbk(s)—handbook(s)
hist—historia, historic, historica, historical, historique, historisch(e), history
HM—Her Majesty
hochsch—hochschule
hon(s)—honor(s), honorable, honorary
hosp(s)—hospital(s), hospitalization
hq—headquarters
Hwy—Highway

Ill—Illinois
illum—illuminating, illumination
illus—illustrate, illustrated, illustration
illusr—illustrator
Inc—Incorporated
incl—include, included, includes, including
Ind—Indiana
indust(s)—industrial, industries, industry
info—information
inst—institut, instituto
inst(s)—institute(s), institution(s)
instnl—institutional, institutionalized
instr(s)—instruct, instruction, instructors
instrnl—instructional
int—internacional, international, internazionale
introd—introduction
ist—istituto
Ital—Italia, Italian, Italiana, Italiano, Italica, Italien, Italienisch, Italienne(s)

J—Journal (title)
Jan—January
jour—journal (descriptive)
jr—junior
juv—juvenile(s)

Kans—Kansas
Ky—Kentucky

La—Louisiana
lab(s)—laboratories, laboratory
lang—language(s)
lect—lecture(s)
lectr—lecturer(s)
lett—letter(s)
lib—liberal
libr—libraries, library, librerio
librn—librarian
lit—literary, literatur, literatura, literature, littera, litterature
Lt—Lieutenant
ltd—limited

mag—magazine
maj—major
Man—Manitoba
Mar—March
Mass—Massachusetts
mat—material(s)
Md—Maryland
med—medical, medicine, medicinal
mem—member(s), membership(s), memoirs
Mem—Memorial
metrop—metropolitan
Mex—Mexican, Mexicano, Mexico
mgr—manager
mgt—management
Mich—Michigan
Minn—Minnesota
Miss—Mississippi
Mo—Missouri
mo—month
mod—modern, moderna, moderne, moderno
monogr—monograph
Mont—Montana
Mt—Mount
munic—municipal, municipalities
mus—musee, museo, museum(s)

N—North
nac—nacional
nat—nationaal, national, nationale, nationalis
naz—nazionale
NB—New Brunswick
NC—North Carolina
NDak—North Dakota
Nebr—Nebraska
Neth—Netherlands
Nev—Nevada
New Eng—New England
Nfld—Newfoundland
NH—New Hampshire
NJ—New Jersey
NMex—New Mexico
Norweg—Norwegian
Nov—November
NS—Nova Scotia
NSW—New South Wales
NY—New York
NZ—New Zealand

Oct—October
off—office, official
Okla—Oklahoma
Ont—Ontario
oper(s)—operation(s), operational, operative
Ore—Oregon
orgn—organization, organizational

Pa—Pennsylvania
Pac—Pacific
Pan-Am—Pan-American
partic—participant, participating
PEI—Prince Edward Island
philos—philosophic, philosophical, philosophy
photog—photographic, photography
photogr—photographer(s)
Pkwy—Parkway
Pl—Place
PO Box—Post Office Box
polytech—polytechnic, polytechnical
Port—Portugal, Portuguese
PQ—Province of Quebec
PR—Puerto Rico
prehist—prehistoric, prehistory
pres—president
Presby—Presbyterian
preserv—preservation
prof—profession, professional, professor professorial
prog(s)—program(s), programmed, programming
proj(s)—project(s), projection(s), projectional, projective
prom—promotion
prov—province, provincial
pub—public
publ—publication(s), published, publisher(s), publishing
pvt—private

Quart—Quarterly
Que—Quebec

Rd—Road
RD—Rural Delivery
rec—record(s), recording
regist—register, registered, registration
registr—registrar
relig—religion, religious
rep—represent, representative
Repub—Republic
res—research
rev—review, revised, revision
RFD—Rural Free Delivery
RI—Rhode Island
Rm—Room
RR—Rural Route
Rte—Route
Russ—Russian

S—South
S Africa—South Africa
S Am—South America, South American
Sask—Saskatchewan
SC—South Carolina
Scand—Scandinavia, Scandinavian
sch(s)—school(s)
scholar—scholarship
sci—science(s), scientific
SDak—South Dakota
sec—secondary
sect—section
secy—secretary
sem—seminar, seminary
Sen—Senator, Senatorial
Sept—September
ser—series
serv—service(s), serving
soc(s)—sociedad, societa, societas, societate, societe, societet, societies, society
Span—Spanish
spec—special
Sq—Square
sr—senior

St—Saint, Street
sta(s)—station(s)
Ste—Sainte
struct—structural, structure(s)
super—superieur, superior, superiore
suppl—supplement, supplemental, supplementary
supt—superintendent
supv—supervising, supervision
Swed—Swedish
Switz—Switzerland
symp—symposium(s)

tech—technical, technique
technol—technologic, technological, technology
tel—telegraph(y), telephone
Tenn—Tennessee
Terr—Terrace
Tex—Texas
transl—translation(s)
translr—translator
treas—treasurer, treasury

Twp—Township

UN—United Nations
undergrad—undergraduate
UNESCO—United Nations Educational, Scientific & Cultural Organization
univ(s)—universidad, universite, universities, university
US—United States
USA—United States Army
USAF—United States Air Force
USMC—United States Marine Corps
USN—United States Navy
USSR—Union of Soviet Socialist Republics

Va—Virginia
var—various
vchmn—vice chairman
Vet—Veteran(s)
VI—Virgin Islands
vis—visiting

vol(s)—volume(s)
vpres—vice president
Vt—Vermont

W—West
Wash—Washington
Wis—Wisconsin
wk—week
WVa—West Virginia
Wyo—Wyoming

yearbk—yearbook
YMCA—Young Men's Christian Association
YMHA—Young Men's Hebrew Association
yr(s)—year(s)
YWCA—Young Women's Christian Association
YWHA—Young Women's Hebrew Association

Who's Who in American Art

A

AACH, HERB
PAINTER, WRITER
b Cologne, Ger, Mar 24, 23; US citizen. Study: Art Acad Cologne, 36-37; Pratt Inst, 41-42; Stanford Univ, 43-44; Escuela di Pintura Y Escultura, Mex, 48-50; Brooklyn Mus Art Sch, 47-48 & 50-51. Work: Boston Mus, Mass; Everhart Mus, Scranton, Pa; Birla Acad, Calcutta, India; Chase Collection; William Penn Mem Mus, Harrisburg, Pa. Exhib: Univ Ill Ann, 61; Childe Hassam Purchase Fund, Acad Arts & Lett, 71; Color Forum/Austin, Univ Tex, 72; one-man shows, Martha Jackson Gallery, 74 & Albright-Knox Mus, 75, Gramercy Fine Arts Gallery, Gramercy Park, NY, 77 & Allentown Art Mus, Pa, 78. Teaching: Pratt Inst, 47-51 & 65-68; Brooklyn Mus; Skowhegan Sch Painting & Sculpture, 69 & 70; assoc prof art & painting, Queens Col, currently. Bibliog: L Finkelstein (auth), Color as system, Craft Horizons, 70. Mem: Color Forum (founder, organizer & bd mem); Col Art Asn; Artists Workshop Club; Intersoc Color Coun; Exp in Art & Technol. Style & Technique: Serialized, sequential color form acrylic painting. Res: All phases of color, phenomenology, perception and fluorescence. Publ: Ed & translr, Goethe's color theory, Van Nostrand Reinhold, 71; contrib ed, J Color & Appearance, 72; auth, articles in Arts, Craft Horizons, Color Eng & many other magazines & journals. Dealer: Martha Jackson Gallery 28 E 69 St New York NY 10021; Aaron Berman Galleries 50 W 57th St New York NY 10019. Mailing Add: 523 E 14th St New York NY 10009

AALUND, SUZY
PAINTER, MINIATURIST
b Long Island, NY. Study: Self-taught. Exhib: One-woman shows, Robert Brooks Gallery, Hyannis, Mass, 72 & 74 & Garden City Galleries, NY, 72 & 74; Nat Arts Club, New York, 72; Painters & Sculptors Soc NJ, Jersey City Mus, 72; Miniature Painters, Sculptors & Gravers Soc, Washington, DC, 73-74; Miniature Art Soc NJ, Nutley, 73-75; plus others. Awards: Second Prize, Oils, Long Beach Art Asn, 72; First Prize, Oils, Nat Miniature Art Show, Miniature Art Soc NJ, 73. Bibliog: Rev in La Rev Mod, 74. Mem: Miniature Art Soc NJ & Fla. Style & Technique: Landscapes and shore scenes, traditional in composition, very realistic in execution; also active in miniature art. Media: Watercolor, Oil, Acrylic. Dealer: Tradewinds Gallery 43-47 W Main St Mystic CT 06355. Mailing Add: 2 Broadway Mystic CT 06355

AARON, EVALYN (WILHELMINA)
PAINTER
b New York, NY. Study: Art Students League; pvt study with Mario Cooper, Motoi Oi, Prof Kawai & Betty Holiday. Exhib: Sumi-e Soc, Nippon Club, 72 & Japan House, 73, New York; Art Fac Show, Great Neck House, NY, 74; Great Neck Pub Libr, 75; one-person shows, Gallery 7 Soho Ltd, Great Neck, 75 & Mirage Gallery, New York, 78. Teaching: Instr sumi-e brush painting, Great Neck Continuing Educ, 64-74; pres & teacher painting, Workshop for Art, Port Washington, NY, 67-73. Awards: Sumi-e Soc Award, Sumi-e Soc Am, 64 & Cup of Consul Gen of Japan, 66; Popular Award, Int Platform Asn, 74. Bibliog: Rhoda Amon (auth), article in Newsday, 11/74; Elizabeth Moore (auth), article in Talent, 5/75; Malcolm Preston (auth), review in Newsday, 8/75. Mem: Artists Equity; Art League of Nassau Co; Sumi-e Soc Am (secy, 62-67, pres, 72-74). Style & Technique: Poetic realism; specialize in Oriental brush painting of landscapes, flowers and still life. Media: Watercolor, Acrylic. Publ: Auth & illusr, Sumi painting, Am Artist Mag, 9/78. Mailing Add: 60 Richards Rd Port Washington NY 11050

AARONS, ANITA
CRAFTSMAN, ART CRITIC
b Sydney, NSW, Australia; Australian & Can citizen. Study: Assoc Sydney Tech Col; East Sydney Tech Col; Nat Art Sch; Columbia Univ, New York, 64. Work: Charlottetown Nat Craft Collection, PEI; Nat Collection Can Craftsmen Guild, Toronto. Comn: Playground Sculpture (Phillip Park), City Coun, Sydney, Australia; Jewelry (neck ornaments), Expo 67 & Can Guild of Crafts. Exhib: 1st World Crafts Conf Exhib, Columbia Univ, 64; Nat Craft Exhib, Toronto, 68; 1st Outdoor Exhib, Sydney; Nat Sculpture Exhib, Melbourne, Victoria. Teaching: Sculptor in charge, East Sydney Tech, 48-49; sculptor in charge, Kindergarten Training Col, Melbourne, 50-54; sculptor in charge, Caulfield Tech Training Col for Sec Arts & Crafts Sch, 54-64; teacher design for crafts, Central Tech, Toronto, 64. Pos: Allied art ed, Architecture Canada, Toronto, 64-70; consult, Art Gallery of Ont, 68-72; demonstr, UNESCO Seminar on Methods. Awards: Canada Council Senior Grant, 71-72. Bibliog: Articles in Encycl Australian Art & Craft Horizons. Style & Technique: Contemporary sculpture and jewelry, rather rich and baroque with strong conceptual image; also designer for furniture and stained glass windows. Media: Silver, Bronze. Mailing Add: 12 Hambly Ave Toronto ON M4E 2R5 Can

AARONS, GEORGE
SCULPTOR
b Lithuania, Apr 6, 96; US citizen. Study: Mus Fine Arts Sch, Boston, Mass; Beaux Arts Inst Design, New York. Work: Mus Art, Ein Harod, Israel; Fitchburg Art Mus, Mass; Musee de St Denis, France; Hilles Libr, Radcliffe Col, Cambridge, Mass; Hillel House, Boston Univ, Mass. Comn: Reliefs, Siefer Hall, Brandeis Univ, Waltham, Mass, 50; reliefs, facade Baltimore Hebrew Congregation Bldg, 56; relief, Combined Jewish Philanthropies Bldg, Boston, 65; commemorative medal, 350th Anniversary, City of Gloucester, Mass, 72; candelabras (6 ft & 5 ft), Temple Israel, Boston, 73. Exhib: 2nd & 3rd Int Exhib Sculpture, Philadelphia Mus, 40 & 49; Inst Contemp Art, Boston, 44; Ann Exhib Contemp Am Sculpture, Whitney Mus Am Art, 57, 59; Mass Inst Technol, Cambridge, 49; Sculpture Ctr, New York, 51; Dallas Mus of Art, Tex, 55; Cleveland Mus Art, Ohio, 55; Albright Art Gallery, Buffalo, 55; Corcoran Gallery of Art, Washington, DC, 55; Mus Fine Arts, Boston, 77; De Cordova Mus, Lincoln, Mass, 77. Awards: Hon mention, Gold Medal Exhib, Archit League NY, 58; R V Steeves Mem, 66 & Gold Medal of Hon, 77, Rockport Art Asn, Mass. Bibliog: Abraham Kampf (auth), Contemporary synagogue art 1945-1965, Union Am Hebrew Congregations, NY; Montreal Expo 67 Internation Exhibition of Contemporary Sculpture, 67; Israel Program for Scientific Translations, Encycl Judaica, 70. Mem: Nat Sculpture Soc; Rockport Art Asn. Style & Technique: Semi-abstract, expressionist, humanist. Media: Wood, Stone & Welded Metals. Mailing Add: Eagle Rd Gloucester MA 01930

ABANY, ALBERT CHARLES
PAINTER, PRINTMAKER
b Boston, Mass, Mar 30, 21. Study: Sch Mus Fine Arts, Boston, M O H Longstreth scholar, 42, dipl, 48; Tufts Univ, BS(educ), 49. Exhib: One-man shows, Carl Siembab Gallery, Boston, 56; Clark Univ, 63; Northeastern Univ, 67; Wessell Libr, Tufts Univ, 71; Art Inst Boston, 72. Teaching: Art teacher drawing & painting, Boston Ctr Adult Educ, 49-51; art teacher drawing, painting, printmaking & art hist, Art Inst Boston, 65-73; art teacher oil & acrylic painting, Brockton Art Ctr, Mass, 75-; art teacher drawing, Danforth Mus Sch, Framingham, 75-77; teacher drawing, painting & hist art, Quincy Jr Col, 75-76. Mem: Col Art Asn Am; Boston Visual Artists Union Inc. Style & Technique: Method of working evolves from the visual stimulus of the medium from which ideas emerge, without direct reference to nature. Media: Oil, Graphics, Mixed Media. Mailing Add: 42 MacArthur Rd Natick MA 01760

ABBATECOLA (ORONZO)
PAINTER, SCULPTOR
b Ceglie del Campo, Bari, Italy, Nov 1, 13. Study: Art & Craft Schs, Bari, Italy; Futurist Schs, Rome; Foothills Col, Los Altos, Calif; Santa Clara Univ; self-taught in art. Work: Marinetti's Futurist Collection, Futurism & Bragaglia's, Rome; Hyde Park Mus, New York; Triton Mus, Santa Clara & Union Bank, Beverly Hills, Calif. Comn: Scale models, Egyptian Mus, 52-54 & murals & dioramas, Rosicrucian Planetarium, San Jose, Calif, 73-74; four paintings, comn by Ralph Meeker, New York; paintings, comn by Dr Arturo B Fallico, San Jose State Univ, Dr Herman Shapiro, Saratoga, Calif & Dr Anthony Gualtieri, Los Gatos, Calif. Exhib: Biennale, Venice, Italy, 36, Quadriennale, Rome, Triennale, Milan & Plastica Murale, Genoa; Int for the Theatre, Vienna, 36. Teaching: Instr art, Rosicrucian Univ, San Jose, 51-74; instr art appreciation, San Jose Dept Adult Educ, 69-71; instr art, Triton Mus, Santa Clara, Calif, 74; pvt art classes, 75- Pos: Owner & operator, Abbatecola Studio, Los Angeles, 40-49; art dir, Rosicrucian Egyptian Mus, San Jose, 50-55; stage dir, Ebell Theatre, Los Angeles, 56-57; asst art dir, Motion Picture Studios, Hollywood, 59-61; art consult, De Metafisica Galleries, Campbell, Calif, 74-77. Awards: For Set Designs, Ital Govt, Rome & Venice, Italy, 35-36; for Theatre Models, Ital Govt, Vienna, Austria, 36; for Murals, Futurism Movement, 37. Bibliog: F T Marinetti (auth), Abbatecola, Rome, 34; art critics, Abbatecola, Rome & Bari, Italy, 35-36; var art critics, Abbatecola, San Francisco, Los Angeles & San Jose, 37-74. Mem: Los Gatos Art Asn (first vpres). Style & Technique: Futuristic; symbolic; metaphysical. Media: Oil. Publ: Contribr, var newspapers & mags, Italy, 35-; contribr, L'Italia, San Francisco, daily, 37-38; contribr, L'Italo Americano, Los Angeles, daily, 40-41; contribr, Rosicrucian Digest, San Jose, monthly, 53-71; contribr, South American Mag, 54-74. Mailing Add: 3095 Greentree Way San Jose CA 95128

ABBE, ELFRIEDE MARTHA
SCULPTOR, ENGRAVER
b Washington, DC. Study: Cornell Univ Col Archit, BFA, 40. Work: Rosenwald Collection, Nat Gallery Art; Mus Fine Arts, Boston; Houghton Libr, Harvard Univ; Sloniker Collection, Cincinnati Art Mus; Mus Fine Arts, Venice, Italy. Comn: The Hunter (large statue), New York World's Fair, 39; oak frieze, Mann Libr, Cornell Univ, 55 & bronze sculptures, Clive McCay Mem, 67; Napoleon (bronze head), McGill Univ Libr; The Illuminator (walnut carving), Sterling Mem Hunt Libr, Carnegie-Mellon Univ, 69. Exhib: Nat Acad Design, New York; San Diego Fine Arts Gallery, 60; Printing in the USA & United Kingdom, London Chappel Exhib, Eng, 63; Int Botanical Artists, Hunt Libr, Carnegie-Mellon Univ, 68; Nat Arts Club, New York, 69 & 70. Awards: Tiffany Fel, 48; Hunt Found Grant, 61; Gold Medal, Nat Arts Club, 70 & Acad Artists Asn, Springfield, Mass, 76. Bibliog: Norman Kent (auth), The Book Art of Elfriede Abbe, Am Artist Mag, 60. Mem: Nat Arts Club; fel Nat Sculpture Soc; Nat Soc of Mural Painters. Media: Wood. Publ: Designed, illus & printed, Garden Spice & Wild Pot-Herbs, Cornell Univ, 55, The American Scholar, 56, Seven Irish Tales, 57 & Significance of the Frontier, 58. Mailing Add: Manchester Center VT 05255

ABBETT, ROBERT KENNEDY
PAINTER
b Hammond, Ind, Jan 5, 26. Study: Purdue Univ, BSc, 46; Univ Mo, BAArt, 48; Chicago Acad Fine Art, 48-50; Am Acad Art, Chicago, 49. Work: Cowboy Hall of Fame & Western Heritage Ctr, Oklahoma City; Diamond M Mus, Snyder, Tex; Genesee Country Mus, Rochester, NY. Comn: Mural, Univ Mo Student Union, 47; portrait of Mrs Roy Larsen, Audubon Soc, Fairfield, Conn, 73; portrait of Jimmy Stewart, Cowboy Hall of Fame,

Oklahoma City, 75; portrait of Silver, comn by Ann Cox Chambers, US Embassy, Brussels, Belg, 77; portrait of Vince Marninaro, comn by A C Soutzos for projected mus of fishing, Boiling Springs, Pa, 77. Exhib: Sporting Art, Brandywine River Mus, Chadds Ford, Pa, 73; Salmagundi Summer Exhib, New York, 73; Convocation Am Artists, Dallas, Tex, 73 & 74; Nat Acad Western Art, Cowboy Hall of Fame, 74 & 75; Grand Cent Galleries Founder's Day Show, New York, 76; Soc Animal Artists Ann Exhib, New York, 77 & 78. Collections Arranged: Sporting Art, Mus Sporting Art, New York, 73; Great American Collection, Union League Club & Civic Arts Found, Chicago, 75; Parker Collection, Tulsa, Okla, 75; Dangerfield Collection, Tex, 76; American West, Continental Bank, Chicago, 76; Stamford Art Found, Tex, 74, 75 & 76. Teaching: Instr introd to media, Silvermine Col, New Canaan, Conn, 59-61; instr drawing, Sisters of Notre Dame, Wilton, Conn, 70 & Washington Art Asn, Conn, 77. Awards: Outstanding Work, Artists & Books, Soc Illusr, 65; Citation of Merit, Soc Illusr Ann Exhib, 66; First Prize, Salmagundi Club, New York, 73. Bibliog: Walter Reed (auth), Outdoor Art of Bob Abbett, Northlight & SW Art, 74; Nick Meglin (auth), Robert Abbett, Am Artist, 7/77; John Pierce (auth), About the artist, Yankee, 11/77. Mem: Soc Illusr; Westport Artists (pres, 67); Soc Animal Artists. Style & Technique: Realistic outdoor scenes, including animals and wildlife, dogs and sporting scenes; portraits in sporting environment. Media: Oil. Publ: Illusr, Great Lives—Great Deeds, Reader's Digest Bks, 64; contribr, The Illustrator in America, Reinhold, 66; contribr, Great American Shooting Prints, Knoff, 72; contribr, Western Art Today, Watson-Guptill, 75; co-auth, Outdoor Paintings of Robert K Abbett, Peacock/Bantam, 76. Dealer: Fred King The Sportsman's Edge 136 E 74th New York NY 10021; Dan May 172 Center St Jackson WY 83001. Mailing Add: Oakdale Farm Bridgewater CT 06752

ABBOTT, DOROTHY I
SCULPTOR
b Thibadoux, La, 32. Study: Tyler Col Fine Arts; Art Stud League; San Francisco State Col, BA; Columbia Univ, MA. Work: Howard Univ, Washington, DC. Exhib: One-woman show, Gallery Madison 90, New York, 73; Silvermine Guild, Conn, 74 & 78; Mickelson Gallery, Washington, DC, 74; Guild Hall, East Hampton, NY, 77; Heckscher Mus, 78; US Info Serv Gallery, Milan, Italy, 78. Mem: Artists Equity; Heckscher Mus; Silvermine Guild Artists. Style & Technique: Abstraction. Media: Marble, Bronze. Mailing Add: Box 369 Skunk Lane Cutchogue NY 11935

ABDALLA, NICK
PAINTER, EDUCATOR
b Albuquerque, NMex, May 24, 39. Study: Eastern NMex Univ, 57-59; Univ Ill, Champaign, 59-60; Univ NMex, BFA, 61, MA, 63. Work: El Paso Mus Art, Tex; Am Tel & Tel Permanent Collection, Ill Bell Tel Syst, Chicago; Fine Arts Mus, Santa Fe; Standard Oil Permanent Collection, Chicago; NC Nat Bank, Davidson. Exhib: 16th Exhib Southwestern Prints & Drawings, Dallas Mus Fine Arts, Tex, 66; 13th, 14th & 18th Ann Sun Carnival Nat Art Exhib, Art Mus El Paso, 68, 69 & 74; First Graphics Ann, Miami Art Ctr, Fla, 73; Los Angeles Print Soc Exhib, Triad Gallery, 73; Nat Print & Drawing Exhib, Davidson Col, NC, 74. Teaching: Asst prof painting & drawing, Univ NMex, 71-; guest artist, Tamarind Inst, Albuquerque, NMex. Awards: First Purchase Award, Nat Print & Drawing Exhib, McCray Gallery, Silver City, NMex, 69; Mus Purchase Award, NMex Biennial Exhib, Mus Fine Arts, Santa Fe, 73; Purchase Award, Nat Print & Drawing Exhib, Davidson Col, NC, 74. Bibliog: Camera Oscura/Camera Lucida: Abdalla and Wood, Artspace Mag, Summer 1977; New Mexico: Open land and psychic elbow room, Art News, 12/77. Style & Technique: Paintings on raw canvas with pastels and acrylics, then sprayed with acrylic for permanence; figurative works. Media: Mixed Media. Dealer: Janus Gallery 116 1/2 E Palace Santa Fe NM 87501; Tally Richards' Gallery Contemp Art One Ledoux St Taos NM 87571. Mailing Add: 515 11th St NW Albuquerque NM 87102

ABDELL, DOUGLAS
SCULPTOR
b Boston, Mass, Mar 16, 47. Study: Syracuse Univ, BFA(sculpture; honors), 70. Work: Corcoran Gallery Art, Washington, DC; H H Thyssen Bornemisza Collection, Lugano, Switz; Univ Notre Dame, Ind; Edwin Ulrich Mus Art, Wichita State Univ, Kans; Davenport Munic Art Gallery, Iowa. Exhib: Artists of Cent NY, Munson-Williams-Proctor Inst, Utica, 70; Ten Artists of Mohawk-Hudson Region, State Univ NY, Albany & Schenectady Mus, NY, 71; Rose Art Mus, Brandeis Univ, Waltham, Mass, 76; one-man exhibs, Graham Gallery, New York, 71 & 72, Andrew Crispo Gallery, New York, 75 & 78 & one-man traveling exhib, The Sculpture of Douglas Abdell (with catalog), Conn Col, New London & St Mary's Col Md, 76, Andrew Crispo Gallery & Edwin Ulrich Mus Art, 77. Awards: Artists & Writers Revolving Fund, Nat Inst Arts & Lett, 71 & 72; Silvermine Award, New Canaan, Conn, 73; Artist Fel, Vt Coun on Arts, 73. Bibliog: John Canaday (auth), rev in New York Times, 72; Grace Glueck (auth), rev in New York Times, 77. Style & Technique: Abstract sculpture. Media: Cast or Welded Bronze. Dealer: Andrew Crispo Gallery 41 E 57th St New York NY 10022. Mailing Add: 135 Beverly Rd Chestnut Hill MA 02167

ABEITA, JIM
PAINTER
b Crownpoint, NMex, Apr 14, 47. Study: Am Acad, Chicago. Exhib: NMex State Fair, 69-74; Gallup Intertribal Ceremonial, NMex, 71, 74, 75 & 76; Heard Mus, Phoenix, Ariz, 73; Scottsdale Nat, Ariz, 73 & 74. Awards: Grand Prizes, Gallup Ceremonial, NMex State Fair & Heard Mus, Phoenix, Ariz. Bibliog: Rick Tanner (auth), American Indians of Abeita—His People, 76. Style & Technique: Simple and direct. Media: Oil. Dealer: Rick Tanner Box 302 Scottsdale AZ 85252. Mailing Add: c/o Rich Tanner Box 302 Scottsdale AZ 85252

ABEL, RAY
ILLUSTRATOR, DESIGNER
b Chicago, Ill, Sept 19, 19. Study: Univ Chicago, AB; Sch of Art Inst Chicago; NY Univ, MA; Art Students League, with Kenneth Hayes Miller & George Grosz. Comn: Aviation (mural frieze), US Army Air Corps Cafeteria, Mitchel Field, NY, 44-45; bk illustrations, McKay, Prentice-Hall, Grolier, Lippincott, Viking & others, 50-; bk jackets, Harper & Row, Putnam, Dodd, Mead, Dutton & others, 50- Exhib: Artists of Chicago & Vicinity, Art Inst Chicago, 43; Nat Acad Design Ann Am Exhib, 42; Ann Exhib Am Art, Mint Mus, Charlotte, NC, 44. Pos: Ed publ, Art Students League, 41-43; art dir, Ray Abel Assoc, 51- Awards: Hon Mention, Ill State Mus Ann Am Art, 41; Hon Mention, Mint Mus Ann Am Art Exhib, 73; Cert of Excellence, Am Observed, Soc Illusr, New York, 72. Mem: Soc Illusr; Art Students League (mem bd control, 41-43 & 46-49). Style & Technique: Black and white, color. Media: Pen and Ink; Wash. Publ: Illusr, Ruth Abel (auth), The New Sitter, Oxford Univ Press, 50; illusr, Mary C Jane (auth), Mystery of Nine-Mile Marsh, Lippincott, 67; illusr, Coal: Energy and Crisis, Harvey House, 74; illusr, Wylie Sypher (auth), Cousins and Circuses, Atheneum, 74; illusr, Bret Hart (auth), The Outcasts of Poker Flat, Listening Libr, 77. Mailing Add: 18 Vassar Pl Scarsdale NY 10583

ABELES, SIGMUND
PRINTMAKER, SCULPTOR
b New York, NY, Nov 6, 34. Study: Pratt Inst; Univ SC, BA, 55; Art Student League; Skowhegan Sch Painting & Sculpture; Brooklyn Mus Sch; Columbia Univ, MFA, 57. Work: Mus Mod Art, New York; Mus Arte, Ponce, PR; Philadelphia Mus Art; Boston Mus Fine Arts; Brit Mus; plus many others. Exhib: Whitney Ann Sculpture & Prints, 67 & Human Concern & Personal Torment, 69, Whitney Mus Am Art, New York; 28 Am Printmakers, Rijksacademie, Amsterdam, Holland, 68; Am Contemp Prints—one, Inst Contemp Art, London, 70; Master Prints of the 20th Century, Boston Mus Fine Arts, 71; plus many other group and one-man shows. Teaching: Swain Sch Design, New Bedford, Mass, 61-64; Wellesley Col, 64-69; Boston Univ, 69-70; Univ NH, 70-; vis artist, Tech Inst for Sculpture, Princeton, NJ, 77. Awards: Grant & Award, Nat Inst Arts & Lett, 65; Sabbatical Grant, Nat Coun Arts & Humanities, 66; Grant for Graphics, Louis Comfort Tiffany Found, 67. Mem: Soc Am Graphic Artists; assoc Nat Acad of Design. Style & Technique: Figurative-realist. Publ: Illusr, Maggie, a girl of the streets, Limited Ed Press, 75. Dealer: Assoc Am Artists Gallery 663 Fifth Ave New York NY 10022. Mailing Add: RFD 1 Rte 107 Northwood NH 03261

ABEYTA, NARCISCO
See Ha-So-De

ABISH, CECILE
SCULPTOR, INSTRUCTOR
b New York, NY. Study: Brooklyn Col, BA. Comn: Boxed Monuments-3 (signed & numbered ed), Multiples, Inc, 69. Exhib: Other Ideas, Detroit Inst Art, 69; 26 Contemporary Women Artists, Aldrich Mus Contemp Art, 71; Bykert Gallery, New York, 71 & 74; Hamburg Kunsthaus, Ger, 72; New York Cult Ctr, 73; Surface Clearance, Inst of Contemp Art, Boston, 74; Michael Walls Gallery, New York, 75; Fine Arts Bldg Gallery, New York, 76; Maps, Mus Mod Art, New York, 77; Alessandra Gallery, New York, 77; Wright State Univ Art Gallery, Ohio, 78; plus others. Teaching: Instr art, Queens Col, NY, Univ Mass, Amherst & Cooper Union, New York. Awards: CAPS Fel, 75; Nat Endowment for Arts Fel, 75 & 77. Bibliog: Mona Da Vinci (auth), Soho Weekly News, 7/75; Deborah Perlberg (auth), Artforum, 4/77; Kenneth Baker (auth), Art in Am, 5/77; plus others. Mem: Col Art Asn Am; Women's Caucus for Art. Style & Technique: Indoor-outdoor on site works; building sculpture is also a political act of taking possession of a surface. Publ: Auth, Surface Clearance (catalog), Inst Contemp Art, Boston, 74; contribr, Proposal for a Fish Flow in Helsinki, 74 & Greek Gifts, 75, Vargen, Stockholm, Sweden; auth, Cecile Abish, Wright State Univ Art Galleries, 78. Mailing Add: 5 E Third St New York NY 10036

ABLOW, JOSEPH
PAINTER, EDUCATOR
b Salem, Mass, Aug 16, 28. Study: Sch Mus Fine Arts, Boston, Paige traveling fel, dipl with highest hons, 51; Bennington Col, BA, 54; Harvard Univ, MA, 55; Fulbright grant, Paris, 58; advan study in painting with Oskar Kokoschka, Ben Shahn, Jack Levine & in design with Gyorgy Kepes. Work: DeCordova Mus, Lincoln, Mass; Univ Mass, Boston; Middlebury Col, Vt; Skowhegan Sch Collection, Maine. Exhib: 62nd Am Exhib, Art Inst Chicago, 57; New Eng Painting, DeCordova Mus, 64; group show, Kunstsalon Wolfsberg, Zurich, Switz, 69; retrospective exhib, Bard Col, 72; one-man show, Princeton Gallery, 71 & Mirski Gallery, 61, 66 & 69. Teaching: Instr, Middlebury Col, 55-58; asst prof, Bard Col, 59-61; asst prof, Wellesley Col, 62-63; chmn div art, Boston Univ, 64-67, prof art, 72-; vis scholar, Mass Inst Technol, 73-; vis artist, Amherst Col, 75-77. Media: Acrylic, Pastel, Watercolor. Dealer: Princeton Gallery Spring St Princeton NJ 08540. Mailing Add: 249 S Pleasant St Amherst MA 01002

ABRAMOVITZ, MR & MRS MAX
COLLECTORS
Mr Abramovitz, b Chicago, Ill, May 23, 08. Study: Mr Abramovitz, Univ Ill, BS, 29; Columbia Univ, MS, 31; Ecole Beaux-Arts, 32-34; Univ Pittsburgh, hon DFA, 61, Univ Ill, 70. Comn: Mr Abramovitz, design of Univ Iowa Art Mus & Krannert Ctr Performing Arts, Univ Ill. Teaching: Mr Abramovitz, assoc prof, Sch Fine Arts, Yale Univ, 39-42. Collection: Contemporary art. Mailing Add: 94 E First St New York NY 10009

ABRAMOWICZ, JANET
PRINTMAKER, SCULPTOR
b New York, NY. Study: Art Students League, with Morris Kantor; Columbia Univ, BA; Accad delle Belle Arti, Bologna, Italy, MFA, with Giorgio Morandi. Work: Wiggins Collection, Boston Pub Libr; Dept of Prints, New York Pub Libr; Albion Col, Mich; Contemporary Art, Mus d'Arte Mod, Bologna; Mus d'Arte Mod, La Spezia, Italy. Collections Arranged: Giorgio Morandi (with catalog), Busch-Reisinger Mus, Harvard Univ, 68. Exhib: Works on Paper, Harvard Sch Design, 74; Weyhe Gallery, New York; Contemporary Miniature Prints Traveling Exhib, Pratt Graphics Workshop, New York, 71; 23rd Nat Exhib of Prints, Libr of Cong-Nat Collection Fine Arts, 73; Abstract Art (sculpture), Boston City Hall, 75. Teaching: Instr, Radcliffe Col, Worcester Art Mus & Accad delle Belle Arti; lectr art hist, Div Educ, Boston Mus Fine Arts, 58-70; lectr printmaking & drawing, Fine Arts Dept, Fogg Art Mus, Harvard Univ, 71- Awards: Fel Printmaking, Radcliffe Inst; MacDowell Colony fel, 75 & 76; Sr Fulbright Fel, Japan, 78. Style & Technique: Sculpture, wood and copper sheeting (three dimensional); etchings, intaglio. Dealer: Weyhe Gallery 789 Lexington Ave New York NY 10021. Mailing Add: 176 Upland Rd Cambridge MA 02140

ABRAMS, HARRY N
PUBLISHER, COLLECTOR
b London, Eng, Feb 23, 05. Study: Nat Acad Design; Art Students League. Pos: Pres, Abbeville Press, Inc. Collection: American and French 20th century paintings, graphic arts and sculpture. Mailing Add: 33 E 70th St New York NY 10021

ABRAMS, HERBERT E
PAINTER, LECTURER
b Greenfield, Mass, Mar 20, 21. Study: Norwich Art Sch, Conn; Pratt Inst, hon grad in illus; Art Student League, with Frank Vincent Du Mond. Work: Portraits, Gov Thomas Meskill, Conn State Libr, Hartford; Gen Creighton Abrams, Gen Bruce Palmer & Gen William C Westmoreland, Chief of Staff Gallery, Pentagon, Washington, DC; Gen William C Westmoreland, West Point Mus. Comn: USAF Insignia, star & tabs on aircraft, 42; portraits, Dr James McCord, Princeton Theol Sem, 70; Gen Anna Mae Hayes, Walter Reed Med Ctr, 71; Dr Phillip Bard, Johns Hopkins Univ, 72 & Dr Thomas B Turner, Turner Auditorium, 74. Exhib: Dallas Mus Fine Arts, 48; one-man shows, Grand Cent Art Galleries, New York, 58, 64 & 68; Okla Mus Art, 69; West Point Libr, 73; Beaufort, SC Mus, 75. Teaching: Lectr & demonstr painting to art orgn & study groups; TV lectr & demonstr, 68, 71, 72 & 74; guest lectr cadets, West Point Mil Acad, 73-74. Awards: Best Still Life, Dr Byron Kenyon Award,

Hudson Valley Art Asn, 68; Best Portrait, 70. Mem: Hudson Valley Art Asn; Art Student League. Media: Oil. Mailing Add: Heartwood Warren CT 06754

ABRAMS, JANE ELDORA
PRINTMAKER, EDUCATOR
b Eau Claire, Wis, Jan 2, 40. Study: Univ Wis-Menomonie, BS, 62, MS, 67; Ind Univ, Bloomington, MFA(with distinction), 71, study with Pozzath & Lowe. Work: Ind Univ; Univ Dallas, Tex; Tex Tech Univ; Tamarind Inst; Univ NMex. Exhib: Pratt Graphics Ctr Traveling Exhib, 72-73; US Info Agency Europ Traveling Exhib, 73-74; Colorprint USA, Tex Tech Univ, 71-75; 25th Boston Printmakers Print Competition, 74; Directors Choice (printmakers), Martha Jackson Gallery, NY, 75; Works on Paper Traveling Exhib, Univ Utah, Salt Lake City, Univ Tex, Houston & Los Angeles Co Mus of Art, Calif, 77; Made in NMex, Mus of NMex, Santa Fe, 77; one-woman show, Rhythms & Reasons, Wellington B Grey Gallery, ECarolina Univ, Greenville, NC, 77. Teaching: Instr art, Univ Wis-Menomonie, 67-69; asst prof art, color, design & intaglio, Univ NMex, 71-; guest artist, Ind Univ, Bloomington, 76. Awards: Guest Artist, Tamarind Inst, 72; Purchase Awards, 5th Ann Calif State Univ; Purchase Award, Tex Tech Univ, 73. Mem: Col Art Asn Am; Woman's Caucus on Art. Style & Technique: Engraving; etching; litho & screenprint, frequently in combination. Media: Intaglio; Litho. Publ: Contribr, Colorprints, USA (slide series), 71-72. Dealer: Martha Jackson 32 E 69th St New York NY 10021; Philadelphia Print Club Philadelphia PA. Mailing Add: 7811 Guadalupe Trail Albuquerque NM 87107

ABRAMS, RUTH
PAINTER
b New York, NY. Study: Columbia Univ; Art Students League; New Sch Social Res; also workshops with Zorach, Archipenko & Harrison. Work: Carnegie Inst Technol; Smith Col Mus Art; Rose A Mus, Brandeis Univ; NY Univ Art Col; Univ Caracas; also in pvt collections, US & SAm. Exhib: Riverside Mus, NY; Art: USA, 58; Critics Choice, 60; Dallas Mus Fine Arts, 63; one-man show, Mus Fine Arts, Caracas, Venezuela, 63, Mass Inst Technol, Cambridge, 64 & 69, Delson-Richter Galleries, Jerusalem, Israel, 76, Contemp Arts Gallery, NY Univ, 77, Amarillo Art Ctr, Tex, 77-78 & Anderson Gallery, Va Commonwealth Univ, Richmond, 77-78; Women Art, 76 & Women Painters & Poets, 77, Visual Arts Coalition, Contemp Arts Gallery, NY Univ; Washington Int Art Show, Delson-Richter Gallery, Washington, DC, 76; 118 Artists, 77 & 10th St Artists at Landmark Gallery, 77-78, Landmark Gallery, New York; plus others. Pos: Art dir, New Sch Social Res Asn, 65-66. Publ: Illusr, Ekistics, Athens, Greece & Arena-Interbuild, London, Eng, 67. Mailing Add: 18 W Tenth St New York NY 10011

ACCONCI, VITO
SCULPTOR
b New York, NY, Jan 24, 40. Study: Holy Cross Col, AB; Univ Iowa, MFA. Work: Mus Mod Art, Paris; Mus Mod Art, New York; Los Angeles Co Mus. Exhib: Information, Mus Mod Art, 70; Software, Jewish Mus, New York, 70; Prospect, Kunsthalle, Dusseldorf, Ger, 71; Sonnabend Gallery, New York, 72, 73, 75 & 76; Documenta 5, Kassel, 72; Eight Contemp Artists, Mus Mod Art, New York, 74; Venice Biennale, Italy, 76; plus others. Teaching: Lectr art theory, Sch Visual Arts, New York, 68-71; instr post-studio art, Calif Inst Art, 76. Bibliog: R Pincus-Witten (auth), Vito Acconci & the conceptual performance, Artforum, 4/72; Alan Sondheim (auth), Vito Acconci: Work 1973-4, Arts, 3/75; Mario Diacono (auth), Vito Acconci: Dal Testo-Azione Al Corpo Come Testo, Out-of-London Press, 76. Publ: Contribr, Conceptual Art, Dutton, 72; contribr, Vito Acconci Issue, Avalanche Mag, 72; auth, Pulse: from my mother, Multiplicata, 72; auth, Ten-Point Plan for Video, Video Art, Harcourt-Brace, 76; auth, Think/Leap/Rethink/Fall, Wright State Univ Press, 77. Dealer: Sonnabend Gallery 420 W Broadway New York NY 10013. Mailing Add: 131 Chrystie St New York NY 10002

ACCURSO, ANTHONY SALVATORE
ILLUSTRATOR, PAINTER
b Brooklyn, NY, Apr 5, 40. Study: Brooklyn Mus Art Sch; Sch Art & Design, New York; Pratt Inst; Sch Visual Arts, New York. Exhib: Bronx Mus Art in coop with Metrop Mus Art, New York, 72; Notre Dame Law Sch, Ind, 73; Harbor Gallery, Long Island, NY, 75; Syracuse Univ, NY, 76; Contemp Courtroom Artists (traveling exhib), Huntsville Mus Art, Ala & Living Arts & Sci Ctr, Lexington, Ky, 76, Mus of Arts & Crafts, Columbus & Mus of Arts & Sci, Macon, Ga, 77, Univ Mus, Miss Law Sch, University & First State Capital Bldg, Little Rock, Ark, 78; Watergate: Am Court-trials (travelling exhib), Galerie Mouffe, Paris, France, 77; Galerie Vallombreuse, Biarritz, Paris, France, 78. Pos: Illusr, Am Mus Natural Hist, New York, 62-64; illusr, Sci Digest, 59; illusr-corresp (trial-courtroom artist), ABC-TV Evening News, Network, Washington, DC, New York, Chicago & Atlanta, 69- & WABC-TV Eyewitness News, Local, NY, 69-; illusr-writer, Am Astrol, Ariz, Horoscope Guide, NY & Astrol, Your Daily Horoscope, NY. Awards: Best Portfolio, Sch Art & Design, 57; Int Salon Award, Biarritz, France, 77. Bibliog: Harry Reasoner (interviewer), Trial Artists, Commentary, ABC-TV News, 74; Dick Cavett (interviewer), On UFO's, Dick Cavett Show, ABC-TV Wide World of Entertainment, 73; UFO's, Do You Believe?, NBC-TV News Documentary, 74. Style & Technique: Rapid life drawing and painting of people, topical and historical events, wildlife, natural history. Media: Pen & ink, with or without watercolor or wash; pencil & charcoal; lino, woodcut. Publ: Illusr, Man's Contact with UFO's, Bantam, 74; illusr, Newsweek, 74-; illusr (motion picture), Mysteries From Beyond Earth, Constantin Films, 75 & NBC-TV Doc, 77; illusr, Contemporary Courtroom Artists , The Today Show, NBC-TV, 76; illusr close-circuit TV hosp-med instructional programming, NY & Calif, 76. Dealer: Harbor Gallery 43 Main St Cold Spring Harbor NY 11724. Mailing Add: 609 45th St Brooklyn NY 11220

ACHEPOHL, KEITH ANDEN
EDUCATOR, PRINTMAKER
b Chicago, Ill, Apr 11, 34. Study: Knox Col, BA; Univ Iowa, MFA. Work: Pennell Collection, Libr of Cong, Washington, DC; Los Angeles Co Mus, Los Angeles, Calif; Art Inst Chicago; Bibliot Nat, Madrid, Spain; Denver Art Mus, Colo; plus 40 others. Exhib: Nat Print Exhib, Libr of Cong, 60, 61, 63 & 69; Seattle Northwest Printmakers Int, 61, 67, 68 & 71; six shows, Philadelphia Print Club Int & Nat Exhibs, 62-75; Brooklyn Mus, 68-74; Achenbach Found for Graphic Art, 75; Am Cult Ctr, Madrid, 77; Grupo Quince, Madrid, 77; Helwan Univ, Cairo, Egypt, 77; Intaglio Invitational, Biella, Italy; 1st Int Print Exhib, Segovia, Spain. Teaching: Instr printmaking, Univ Iowa, 64-67; vis artist printmaking, Univ Wash, summer 67; assoc prof, Pac Lutheran Univ, 69-72; vis artist printmaking, Univ Iowa, 72-73, assoc prof, 73- Awards: Purchase Awards, Pennell Fund, Libr of Cong, 60 & 61; Lynd Ward Prize, 67 & John B Turner Prize, 69, Soc Am Graphic Artists; Philadelphia Print Club, 70. Mem: Soc Am Graphic Artists; Philadelphia Print Club. Dealer: Assoc Am Artists Gallery 663 Fifth Ave at 52nd St New York NY 10022. Mailing Add: 630 W Park Rd Iowa City IA 52240

ACKER, PERRY MILES
PAINTER, EDUCATOR
b Elk Rapids, Mich, Apr 6, 03. Study: With Fred Marshall, Eustace Ziegler & Harry Bonath. Work: Seattle Art Mus; Charles & Emma Frye Pub Art Mus. Exhib: Two Hundred Years of Watercolor Painting in America, Metrop Mus, 67; Am Watercolor Exhib, several times; Northwest Ann, Seattle Art Mus; Northwest Watercolor Exhib, several times. Teaching: Burnley Sch Prof Art, Seattle, 70-74; instr watercolor, Mendocino Art Ctr, Calif, 72-74; instr watercolor, Univ Wash, 74-76 & Univ Idaho, 77. Awards: First Prize, Northwest Marine Exhib, 72; First Prize, Northwest Watercolor Soc, 74; Purchase Award, Northwest Watercolor Exhib, 75. Mem: Am Watercolor Soc; Northwest Watercolor Soc (pres, 60); Puget Sound Group Northwest Painters, Inc (pres, 59); West Coast Watercolor Soc. Style & Technique: Traditional watercolor. Media: Watercolor, Oil & Acrylic. Dealer: Gallery West 4836 Scholls Ferry Rd Portland OR 97225. Mailing Add: 2291 NE 61st St Seattle WA 98115

ACKERMAN, FRANK EDWARD
PAINTER, DESIGNER
b Los Angeles, Calif, Jan 3, 33. Study: Sch Allied Arts, Glendale Col, Calif; Chouinard Art Inst. Work: Univ Utah, Logan; Hunt Collection Fine Art, Fullerton, Calif; Vincent Price Collection, Beverly Hills, Calif. Comn: Antartica Series, USN, Washington, DC, 67; Alaska, Alaskan CofC, 69; Vietnam War Mem, Co Los Angeles, Court of Flags, 73; Gen Omar Bradley, Patriotic Hall, Los Angeles, 75. Exhib: US Embassy Exhib, Acapulco, Mex, 60; US Naval World Tour, 70; Nat Acad Design, New York, 73; one-man show, Brand Libr Fine Arts, Glendale, Calif, 73; Royal Watercolor Soc, London, 75. Teaching: Instr watercolor, Rex Brandt Sch Painting, Corona del Mar, Calif, 55-56; instr painting & watercolor, Creative Arts Prog, Flintridge, Calif, 62-65 & pvt classes, Los Angeles, 61-65. Pos: Illusr, Co of Los Angeles, 56-63; graphic artist, 66-68; head graphic artist, 68-70 & art dir, 70-78; chief exhib, Los Angeles Co Mus Natural Hist, Los Angeles, 78- Awards: Painting of the Year Award, Ebell Club, Los Angeles, 63; Award of Merit, Home Savings & Loan, 64; Watercolor Award, Calif Nat Watercolor Soc, 71. Mem: West Coast Watercolor Soc; State Calif Artist Adv Bd; Calif Nat Watercolor Soc (first vpres & pres, 68-70); Soc of South Pole; Int Inst Arts & Lett, Switz. Style & Technique: Wet into wet, dry brush, transparent, soft real to bold style. Media: Watercolor. Publ: Illusr, Earthquake Report on Los Angeles Co, 73; illusr, End of the Era, 75. Mailing Add: 1323 Columbia Dr Glendale CA 91205

ACKERMAN, GERALD MARTIN
ART HISTORIAN, EDUCATOR
b Alameda, Calif, Aug 21, 28. Study: Univ Calif, BA, 52; Maximilliam Universität, 56-58, with Prof Sedlmayr; Princeton Univ, MFA, 60, PhD, 64, with Prof Lee & Panofsky. Collections Arranged: Thiebaud Figures, Stanford Univ Mus, 65; Gerome, Dayton Art Inst, Minneapolis Art Inst, Walters Art Gallery, Baltimore, 72-73. Teaching: Instr art hist, Bryn Mawr Col, 60-64; asst prof, Stanford Univ, 65-70; assoc prof, Pomona Col, 71-76, chmn art dept, 72-, prof, 76- Mem: Col Art Asn; Deutsche Verein für Kunstwissenschaft. Res: 19th century realism in America and Europe, in particular academic realists such as Jean Leon Gerome and Thomas Eakins; art theory. Publ: Auth, Gerome and Manet, Gazette des Beaux-Arts, 70: 163-176; Lomazzo's treatise on painting, Art Bull, 59: 317-326; Gerome, the academic realist, Art News Ann, 33: 100-107; Thomas Eakins and His Parisian Masters, Gerome and Bonnat, Gazette des Beaux Arts, 72: 235-236; Gerome, exhib catalog, 72. Mailing Add: Art Dept Pomona Col Claremont CA 91711

ACKERMAN, JAMES S
ART HISTORIAN, EDUCATOR
b San Francisco, Calif, Nov 8, 19. Study: Yale Univ, BA, 41; NY Univ, MA, 47, PhD, 52. Teaching: Lectr, Yale Univ, 46 & 49; asst prof hist of art & archit, Univ Calif, 52-56, assoc prof, 56-60; fel, Coun Humanities, Princeton Univ, 60-61; prof fine arts, Harvard Univ, 61- Pos: Pres, Mass Found for Arts & Humanities, 77- Awards: Hon LHD, Kenyon Col, 61; hon DFA, Md Inst Art, 72; hon LHD, Univ Md-Baltimore County, 76. Res: History of architecture; critical and historical theory; interaction of art and science in the period of 1200-1700. Publ: Auth, The Cortile del Belvedere, Vatican City, 54; auth, The Architecture of Michelangelo, 2 vols, Zwemmer, London & Viking, New York, 61, Penguin, rev ed, 71; co-auth, with Rhys Carpenter, Art & Archaeology, Englewood Cliffs, 63; auth, Palladio, Penguin, Eng, 66; co-auth (film), Looking for Renaissance Rome, 77. Mailing Add: Dept Fine Arts Fogg Art Museum Harvard Univ Cambridge MA 02138

ACOSTA, MANUEL GREGORIO
PAINTER, SCULPTOR
b Villa Aldama, Mex, May 9, 21; US citizen. Study: Univ Tex, El Paso; Chouinard Art Inst, Los Angeles; also with Urbici Soler, sculptor. Work: El Paso Mus, Tex; WTex Mus, Lubbock; Time, Inc Collection, New York; also included in Harmsen's Western Collection, Colo. Comn: Pioneer murals (apprenticed with Peter Hurd), WTex Mus, 52; Southwest History (aluminum mural), Casa Blanca Motel, Logan, NMex, 56; fresco mural, First Nat Bank, Las Cruces, NMex, 57; aluminum fresco mural & hist panels, Bank of Tex, Houston. Exhib: Art USA, Mo, 58; Tex Watercolor Soc, Austin, 60; one-man show, Chase Gallery, New York, 62; Am Watercolor Soc, New York, 65. Pos: Adv, Tex Comn Arts & Humanities, 72- Media: Oil; Clay. Publ: Illusr, Cesar Chavez (cover), Time Mag, 69; illusr, Canto y Grito mi Liberacion, Doubleday, 72. Dealer: Baker Collector Gallery 1301 13th St Lubbock TX 79408. Mailing Add: 366 Buena Vista St El Paso TX 79905

ACTON, ARLO C
SCULPTOR
b Knoxville, Iowa, May 11, 33. Study: Wash State Univ, BA, 58; Calif Inst Arts, MFA, 59. Work: San Francisco Mus Art. Exhib: Some Points of View for '62, Stanford Univ, 62; The Artist's Environment: The West Coast, Ft Worth, Tex, 62; Fifty California Artists, Whitney Mus Am Art, New York, 62-63; California Sculpture, Kaiser Ctr, Oakland, Calif, 63; 3rd Paris Biennial, 63; plus many others. Teaching: Univ Calif, Berkeley, 63. Awards: Edgar Walter Mem Prize, San Francisco Mus Art, 61; Second Prize, Richmond Art Asn Ann, 61; Award, San Francisco Art Asn, 64; plus others. Bibliog: Peter Selz (auth), Funk, Univ Calif, Berkeley, 67; Maurice Tuchman (auth), American Sculpture of the Sixties, Los Angeles Co Mus Art, 67. Mailing Add: 63 Bluxome St San Francisco CA 94107

ACUNA, VICTOR MIGUEL
ART DEALER
b Morelia, Mex, Mar 29, 39. Study: St Nicholas Univ, Morelia, BA. Pos: Rep, Contemp Mus Bogota, Colombia; art consult, Festival Cervantino, Guanajuato & Musical Festival of Puebla, Mex; owner, Arvil Art Gallery, Mexico City. Specialty: Contemporary art. Publ: Ed, Toledo/Sahagun, 74; ed, Toledo/Chilambalm, 75. Mailing Add: Hamburgo 241 Mexico DF Mexico

ADAMS, ALICE
SCULPTOR
b New York, NY, Nov 16, 30. Study: Columbia Univ, BFA, 53; Fulbright travel grant, 53-54; French govt fel, 53-54; L'Ecole Nat d'Art Decoratif, Aubusson, France. Work: L'Ecole Nat d'Art Decoratif; Univ Nebr, Lincoln; Wilson Col, Chambersburg, Pa; Hertz Corp, New York; Weatherspoon Gallery, Univ NC, Greensboro. Exhib: Am Abstr Artists Ann, Riverside Mus, New York, 66, 67-68 & 69; Contemp Am Sculpture, Whitney Mus Am Art, 70-71 & 73; Penthouse Gallery Exhib, Mus Mod Art, New York, 71; Am Women Artists, Kunsthaus, Hamburg, Ger, 72; 55 Mercer, NY, 70, 72, 73 & 75. Teaching: Instr sculpture, Manhattanville Col, 61-; asst prof, Calif State Col, Los Angeles, 69. Awards: MacDowall Colony, MacDowall Found, 67. Bibliog: Barbara Kafka (auth), The woven structures of Alice Adams, Craft Horizons, 3/67; Ward Jackson (auth), monograph, color photo, Art Now, New York, 4/69. Mem: Am Abstr Artists (secy, 67). Media: Wood, Metal, Rubber. Mailing Add: 55 Walker St New York NY 10013

ADAMS, ANSEL EASTON
PHOTOGRAPHER
b San Francisco, Calif, Feb 20, 02. Study: Yale Univ, hon DFA, 73. Work: Metrop Mus Art, New York; Mus Mod Art, New York; Victoria & Albert Mus, London, Eng; San Francisco Mus Art; Art Inst Chicago. Exhib: San Francisco Mus Art, 39; Photographs by Ansel Adams, Mus Mod Arts, New York, 44, Metrop Mus Art, 74 & Victoria & Albert Mus, 76; George Eastman House, Rochester, NY, 52. Teaching: Teaching photography at various workshops including, Mus Mod Art, New York, Los Angeles Art Ctr Sch, 40- Pos: Vis mem art comt, Mass Inst Technol, 72-75. Awards: Guggenheim Fels, 46 & 48; John Muir Award, Dept Interior, 63. Bibliog: Robert Katz (dir), Photography: The Incisive Art (5 films for TV), 59; Nancy Newhall (auth), The Eloquent Light, Sierra Club, 63; Ansel Adams (monogr), Morgan & Morgan, 72. Mem: Friends of Photography (pres, 67-74, chmn, 74-75). Media: Black and white photography. Publ: Illusr, Taos Pueblo, 30; auth & illusr, Sierra Nevada: The John Muir Trail, 38; illusr, Yosemite and the High Sierra, 48; contribr, This is the American Earth, 60; ed & illusr, Ansel Adams: Images 1923-1974, 74. Mailing Add: Rte 1 Box 181 Carmel CA 93923

ADAMS, CLINTON
PAINTER, LITHOGRAPHER
b Glendale, Calif, Dec 11, 18. Study: Univ Calif, Los Angeles, BEd, 40; MA, 42. Work: Mus Mod Art, New York; Chicago Art Inst, Ill; Amon Carter Mus Western Art, Ft Worth, Tex; Achenbach Found Graphic Arts, San Francisco, Calif; Grunwald Graphics Art Ctr, Univ Calif, Los Angeles. Exhib: 16th Nat Print Invitational, Brooklyn Mus, 68; Tamarind: Homage to Lithography, Mus Mod Art, New York, 69; 73rd Western Ann, Denver Art Mus, 71; Retrospective Exhibitions: Paintings, 61-71, Roswell Mus & Art Ctr, NMex, 72; Lithographs, Univ NMex Art Mus, 48-72. Teaching: Asst prof painting & lithography, Univ Calif, Los Angeles, 46-54; chmn dept art, Univ Ky, 54-57; chmn dept art, Univ Fla, 57-60; dean col fine arts, Univ NMex, 61-76, prof art, 61- Pos: Assoc dir, Tamarind Lithography Workshop, Los Angeles, 60-61; dir, Tamarind Inst, Albuquerque, 70-; ed, Tamarind Tech Papers, 73- Awards: Purchase Award, 17th Exhib Southwestern Prints & Drawings, Dallas Mus Fine Arts, 67, Nat Print & Drawing Exhib, Northern Ill Univ, 68 & Southwest Biennial, Mus NMex, 72. Bibliog: Van Deren Coke (auth), Clinton Adams, Univ NMex Art Mus, 73. Publ: Co-auth, Tamarind book of lithography: art and techniques, Abrams, 71; auth, Fritz Scholder: Lithographs, NY Graphic Soc, 75; Lithography I, Univ NMex Art Mus, 75. Mailing Add: 1917 Morningside Dr NE Albuquerque NM 87110

ADAMS, GLENN NELSON
PAINTER
b Montreal, PQ, Jan 24, 28. Study: McGill Univ; Montreal Mus Fine Art; Mt Allison Univ, with Alex Colville & L P Harris. Work: Montreal Mus Fine Arts; Can Indust, Ltd; Montreal Star. Exhib: Banfer Gallery, 63 & 64; Galerie Agnes Lefort, 64; Montreal Mus Fine Art, 64; Mt Allison Univ, 74; Gallery One, Moncton, 77. Style & Technique: Precise realism, with a strong emphasis on organization of composition and colors; chiefly man-made subjects. Mailing Add: Box 1541 Sackville NB Can

ADAMS, KATHERINE LANGHORNE
PAINTER, SCULPTOR
b Plainfield, NJ. Study: Art Students League; also studies at Lyme, Conn. Work: Smithsonian Inst, Washington, DC. Comn: Murals in oil for Robert C Hill & Thomas Lamont, Palisades, NY. Exhib: One-man show, Babcock Gallery, NY; invitational group show, Art Inst Chicago, Detroit Mus Art, Buffalo Fine Art Acad & St Louis Mus, plus many others. Media: Oil. Mailing Add: 225 S Lee St Alexandria VA 22314

ADAMS, MARK
DESIGNER, PAINTER
b Fort Plain, NY, Oct 27, 25. Study: Syracuse Univ; with Hans Hofmann & Jean Lurcat, France. Work: Tapestries, Queen of Heaven, Dallas Mus Fine Arts; Phoenix & the Golden Gate, Marina Br, San Francisco Pub Libr; Rose, Santa Rosa-Sonoma Pub Libr, Santa Rosa, Calif; Mounted Policeman (painting), Hall of Justice, San Francisco. Comn: Baptistry, All Saints' Episcopal Church, Carmel, Calif, 68; Man Flying (tapestry), Bank Calif, San Francisco, 68; tapestry, Weyerhaeuser Co, Tacoma, Wash, 71; stained glass, Temple Emanu-el, 72 & St Thomas More Cath Church, San Francisco, 74. Exhib: Int Biennial of Tapestry, Lausanne, Switz, 62 & 65; Collector: Object/Environment, Mus Contemp Crafts, New York, 65; San Francisco Art Inst Ann, San Francisco Mus Art, 65; 400 Years of Tapestry, Norfolk Mus Arts & Sci, 66; one-man retrospective, Calif Palace of Legion of Honor, San Francisco, 70. Media: Tapestry, Stained Glass. Mailing Add: 3816 22nd St San Francisco CA 94114

ADAMS, PAT
PAINTER, INSTRUCTOR
b Stockton, Calif, July 8, 28. Study: Univ Calif, Berkeley, BA, 49; Brooklyn Mus Art Sch, with Max Beckmann & John Ferren; Fulbright fel, France, 56-57. Work: Whitney Mus; Joseph Hirshhorn Mus; Univ Calif, Berkeley; Univ Vt; Univ NC, Greensboro. Exhib: Whitney Mus Painting Ann, 56, 61; Aquarellistes, Mus Mod Art traveling exhib in France, 57; Lyricism in Abstract Art, Am Fedn Arts traveling exhib, 62; Betty Parsons Collection, Finch Col, New York, 68; Color Forum, Univ Tex, Austin, 72; Am Women Artists, Gedok Kunsthaus, Hamburg, Ger, 72; Hassam Invitational, Am Acad of Arts & Lett, 74; New Acquisitions, Hirshhorn Mus, Washington, DC, 74-76; A Bite from the Big Apple, Ind Univ Art Mus, 76; Seven Decades of MacDowell Artists, James Yu Gallery, New York, 76; New in the 70s, Univ Art Mus, Univ Tex, Austin, 77. Teaching: Art fac painting, Bennington Col, 64- Pos: Vis critic painting, Yale Univ, 71-72; grad sem, Queens Col, fall 72. Awards: Yaddo Found Summer Residences, 54, 64, 69 & 70; Painting Award, Nat Coun Arts, 68; Nat Endowment for the Arts grant, 76. Bibliog: Hilton Kramer (auth), Art: Pat Adams paintings, New York Times, 6/22/74; Max Kosloff (auth), Remarks on their medium by four artists, Artforum, 9/75; Martica Sawin (auth), So much to see: Pat Adams new paintings, Arts, 5/76. Media: Oil/Isobutyl Methacrylate, Gouache. Publ: Contribr, Private myth, Tanager Gallery, 61; Art now, 6/72. Dealer: Virginia Zabriskie Gallery 29 W 57th St New York NY 10019. Mailing Add: Bennington Col Bennington VT 05201

ADAMS, ROBERT HICKMAN
PHOTOGRAPHER
b Orange, NJ, May 8, 37. Work: Mus Mod Art, New York; Mus Fine Arts, Houston; Metrop Mus Art, New York; Princeton Univ Art Mus, NJ; Int Mus Photog, George Eastman House, Rochester, NY. Exhib: Photographs by Robert Adams & Emmet Gowin, Mus Mod Art, 71-72; Landscape-Cityscape, Metrop Mus Art, 73-74; 14 American Photographers, Baltimore Mus Art, 75; New Topographics, Int Mus Photog, George Eastman House, 75; Aspects of Am Photog, Univ Mo, St Louis, 76; Castelli Graphics, New York, 76; Target Collection of Am Photog, Mus Fine Arts, Houston, 77; The Great West, Univ Colo, Boulder, 77; Contemp Am Photographic Works, Mus of Fine Arts, Houston, 77. Awards: Nat Endowment Arts Fel Photog, 73 & 77; Guggenehim Found Fel Photog, 73. Bibliog: John Szarkowski (auth), Foreward to, The New West, 74. Publ: Auth & illusr, The New West: Landscapes Along the Colorado Front Range, Colo Assoc Univ, 74; auth, Denver: A Photographic Survey of the Metropolitan Area, Colo Assoc Univ Press, 77; auth, Prairie, Denver Art Mus, 78. Mailing Add: 326 Lincoln St Longmont CO 80501

ADAMS, WILLIAM HOWARD
ART ADMINISTRATOR, COLLECTOR
b Jackson Co, Mo. Study: Univ Mo; Washington & Lee Univ, LLB. Pos: Trustee, Kansas City Art Inst, 56-62; chmn, Mo Coun Arts, 63-65; dir nat prog, Nat Gallery Art; sr fel arts admin, Harvard Inst; bd adv, Dumbarton Oaks, Washington, DC. Collection: Contemporary and primitive art. Publ: Ed, The community and the arts, 64; auth, Politics of art, 67; ed, The eye of Thomas Jefferson, exhib catalog. Mailing Add: 2820 P St NW Washington DC 20007

ADAMY, GEORGE E
EDUCATOR, SCULPTOR
b Manchester, Conn, Apr 19, 25. Study: Univ Conn, BS, 48; NY Univ, MBA, 54, PhD credits, 55; Scarsdale Studio Workshop, 63-65, study with Friedel Dzubas & Knox Martin; Mus of Mod Art, 63-64, study with Ralph Carpentier & Sam Weiner; New Sch for Social Res, 63, study with Mort Borne. Work: Aldrich Mus of Contemp Art, Ridgefield, Conn. Comn: Outdoor acrylic sculpture environment containing five 5ft laminated acrylic discs in an 800 sq ft area, 77 Water St, New York, 69-70. Exhib: Aldrich Mus of Contemp Art, 65; Neuberger Mus, State Univ of NY Col at Purchase, 75; Hudson River Mus, Yonkers, NY. Teaching: Slide lect, demonstrations & exhibs, Face & Body Molding & Casting with Adamate, Plastics as Art Media & Safety & Health Concerns of Artists & Craftspeople, 70-; pvt workshops covering acrylics, polyesters, epoxies, fiberglass, bonded bronze & foams & molds from silicones, urethanes, latex, Adamate, fiberglass, gypsum & films, 70-; lectr plastics & mold-making, State Univ NY Col at Purchase, 73-; vis adj prof plastics & mold-making, Univ Bridgeport, Conn, 75; lectr plastics & mold-making, Elizabeth Seton Col, 74 & Sarah Lawrence Col, 77. Pos: Plastics & mold-making consult to industs & artists. Awards: Yapalater Award, Westchester Art Soc Ann Open Juried Exhib, 74; Best in Show, Mamaroneck Arts Guild Ann Open Juried Exhib, 74; plus numerous others. Bibliog: Luisa Kriesberg & Kathie Beals (authors), articles in Westchester-Rockland newspapers, 63- Mem: Hudson River Contemp Artists, Hudson River Mus (former chmn & prog chmn). Style & Technique: Plastics used as art media. Media: Acrylic, Polyester, Fiberglass, Urethane; Bonded Bronze. Mailing Add: c/o GEA Co 19 Elkan Rd Larchmont NY 10538

ADAN, SUZANNE RAE
PAINTER, INSTRUCTOR
b Woodland, Calif, Feb 12, 46. Study: Calif State Univ, Sacramento, BA & MA, undergrad study with Irving Marcus, grad study with Jim Nutt & Irving Marcus. Exhib: 1970 Drawing Exhib, San Francisco Art Inst, 70; Sacramento Valley Show, San Francisco Art Inst, 70; San Francisco Art Inst Centennial Exhib, San Francisco Mus Mod Art, 71; Candy Store Gallery, Folsom, Calif, 71, 75, 76, 77 & 78; Extraordinary Realities, Whitney Mus Art, New York, 73-74; 7th Nat Drawing & Small Sculpture Show, Del Mar Col Art Gallery, Corpus Christi, Tex, 74; one-woman show, Womanspace, Los Angeles, 74; Fifty Years of Crocker-Kingsley, E B Crocker Gallery, Sacramento, Calif, 75; One Square Foot Environ Exhib, Women's Art Ctr, San Francisco, 76; Clocktower Exhib, Benecia, Calif, 76; Surface and Image, Walnut Creek Civic Arts Gallery, Calif, 76; Candy Store Art Gallery Artists, Am River Col, Sacramento, 76. Teaching: Instr drawing, Am River Col, Sacramento, Calif, 75-76. Awards: Third Place Award, Northern Calif Ann, 66, Ayling Water Award, Kingsley Art Ann, 68 & Purchase Prize, 73, E B Crocker Art Gallery. Mem: Sacramento Regional Arts Coun; San Francisco Mus Mod Art. Style & Technique: Figurative, narrative imagery; heavily textured painting. Media: Oil painting; drawing. Dealer: Adeliza McHugh Candy Store Gallery 605 Sutter St Folsom CA 95630. Mailing Add: 3977 Rosemary Circle Sacramento CA 95821

ADDAMS, CHARLES SAMUEL
CARTOONIST
b Westfield, NJ, Jan 7, 12. Study: Colgate Univ, 29-30; Univ Pa, 30-31; Grand Cent Sch Art, New York, 31-32. Work: Mus Mod Art. Exhib: Fogg Art Mus; Original Drawings, Mus City New York, 56; Pa State Univ Mus, 57; Metrop Mus Art Print Exhib; Nicholls Gallery, New York, 74; plus others. Media: India Ink with Watercolor. Publ: Contribr, New Yorker Mag; auth, Night Crawlers, 57, The groaning Board, 64 & My Crowd, 70, Simon & Schuster; auth, Black Maria, Pocket Books, Inc, 60; auth, The Charles Addams Mother Goose, Harper-Row, 67; plus others. Mailing Add: c/o New Yorker Mag 25 W 43rd St New York NY 10036

ADDISON, CHAUNCEY
See Day, Chon

ADEL, JUDITH
ART DIRECTOR, DESIGNER
b New York, NY, Aug 8, 45. Pos: Assoc art dir, Business Week, 76-; advert & promotional mat for travel agencies & companies. Awards: The One Show, Art Dirs Club, 75; Award of Merit, Soc Publ Desingers, 75; Creativity 76-Editorial Design, Art Direction. Publ: Designer (book jacket), Great Male Dancers of the Ballet, Doubleday & Ballet Guide, Dodd, Mead. Mailing Add: Business Week 1221 Ave of the Americas New York NY 10020

ADELMAN, DOROTHY (LEE) MCCLINTOCK
PRINTMAKER, PAINTER
b Manhattan, NY. Study: Art Student League, with Roberto Delamonico & Michael Ponce de Leon; Westchester Art Workshop, White Plains, NY, with John Ruddley & Stephen Rogers Peck; Silvermine Guild Artists, Inc, New Canaan, Conn. Work: Hudson River Mus; Westchester Art Workshop; in pvt collections throughout US & Israel. Exhib: Yonkers Art Asn, Hudson River Mus, 71-72; Katonah Gallery, NY, 71-72; Greenwich Art Barn, Conn,

72 & 75; Mari Gallery, Mamaroneck, NY, 74; Manhattanville Col, Purchase, NY, 74. Teaching: Instr painting, Am Red Cross, White Plains, 71; instr painting, Westchester Art Workshop, 71-; instr, Elizabeth Seton Col, Yonkers, NY, currently. Pos: Bd mem, White Plains Outdoor Art Exhib, Inc, 70-; coun mem, Katonah Gallery, 70- Awards: Purchase Award, Westchester Art Workshop, 69 & Hudson River Mus, 71; First & Third Award, Mamaroneck Artist Guild, 72; First Award, Westchester Art Soc, 73 & 75. Mem: Art Student League; Mamaroneck Artists Guild; Abraxas. Style & Technique: Exploring the opposites—the gentle embossing next to the strong intaglio technique, using colors that sometimes delight or sometimes cause discord, using organic forms, touching, vibrating with life, creating interactings and tensions among them. Media: Intaglio, Printing. Dealer: Westlake Gallery White Plains NY; Artist Outlet Miami FL. Mailing Add: 36-A E Hill Dr Somers NY 10589

ADKISON, KATHLEEN (GEMBERLING)
PAINTER
b Beatrice, Nebr. Study: With Mark Tobey. Work: Seattle Art Mus; Seattle First Nat Bank; Bank Wash, Tacoma & Spokane; Butler Inst Am Art, Youngstown, Ohio; Cheney Cowles Mus, Spokane. Exhib: Northwest Ann, Seattle, 47-71; El Paso Nat, 60-70; Butler Inst Am Art Ann, 61-69; World's Fair Northwest Artists, Seattle, 62 & 74; Pa Acad Fine Arts 159th Ann, 64; one-person shows, Univ Wash Mus Art, Pullman, 76, Univ Ore Mus Art, Eugene, 77 & Wash State Art Mus, Olympia, 77; Spokane World's Fair Expo 74 Northwest Art, Wash. Teaching: Instr painting, Wash State Univ Exten, 55-67. Awards: Sun Carnival First Prize, El Paso Mus, 61; Dr Fuller Purchase Award, Northwest Ann, 61; Prize for Winter Retreat, Friends Am Art, 69. Media: Oil. Dealer: Gordon Woodside Gallery 803 E Union Seattle WA 98122. Mailing Add: 1203 Overbluff Blvd Spokane WA 99203

ADLER, BILLY (TELETHON)
SCULPTOR, PHOTOGRAPHER
b New York, NY, Sept 5, 40. Study: Univ Pa, BA; Annenberg Sch Commun, MA. Work: Vancouver Art Gallery, BC; Pasadena Mus Art, Calif; Baltimore Mus Art; Mus Mod Art, New York; Whitney Mus Am Art, New York. Awards: Martin Lesuer Achievement Award, 72. Mailing Add: 3666 Barry Ave Los Angeles CA 90066

ADLER, LEE
PAINTER, PRINTMAKER
b New York, NY, May 22, 34. Study: Art Students League, 62-64; Brooklyn Mus Art Sch, 64-65; Pratt Graphics Ctr, New York, 69. Work: Metrop Mus Art, New York; Brit Mus, London; Whitney Mus Am Art, New York; Art Inst Chicago; Corcoran Gallery Art, Washington, DC. Comn: Graham Gallery, New York, 70; Book-of-the-Month Club, 73; New York Times/Quadrangle Books, 73; Hagley Mus, Wilmington, Del, 74. Exhib: Butler Inst Am Art, Youngstown, Ohio, 67, 68 & 77; Childe Hassam Fund Competition, Am Acad Arts & Lett, New York, 68-69; Nat Acad Design, New York, 69; 17th Nat Print Biennial, Brooklyn Mus, 70; Print Acquisitions, Whitney Mus Am Art, 70; one-man shows, Hagley Mus, Wilmington, 74, Inst de Cult Hispanica, Madrid, Spain, 76, Mus Mod Art, Mexico City, 76 & Guadalajara, Mexico, 77 & Mus Contemp Art, Saltillo, Mexico, 76 & Monterrey, Mexico, 76; One Hundred Prints by 100 Artists of Art Students League, 1875-1975, Assoc Am Artists, NY, 75; Mus Mod Art, Sao Paulo, Brazil, 77; plus others. Awards: Grumbacher Award, Jersey City Mus, 68; Burndy Corp Award, 69; Purchase award, Childe Hassam Fund Competition, 69. Bibliog: John Canaday (auth), Lee Adler, New York Times, 12/68; Lee Adler, Arts, 1/69; J G Bowles (auth), Lee Adler, Art News, 3/72. Mem: Audubon Artists; Silvermine Guild Artists; Allied Artists Am; Painters & Sculptors Soc NJ. Style & Technique: Hard-edged, geometric treatment in an abstracted fashion, of a realistic, though specialized visual vocabulary; derived from structure of our high-technology culture. Media: Oil, Silk Screen Printing. Dealer: Heidenberg Gallery 50 W 57th St New York NY 10019; Assoc Am Artists 663 Fifth Ave New York NY 10022. Mailing Add: 168 Clinton St Brooklyn NY 11201

ADLER, MYRIL
PRINTMAKER, PAINTER
b Vilebsk, USSR, Sept 22, 20; US citizen. Study: Brooklyn Mus Art Sch; Art Students League; Theatre Arts Workshop, NY, with Moi Solotaroff; Pratt Graphics Ctr; study with Seong Moy, Michael Ponce de Leon & Ansei Uchima. Work: New York Pub Libr, NY; Hudson River Mus, Yonkers, NY; Mus of Mod Art, Caracas, Venezuela; Univ Calif, Berkeley; Univ RI, Providence; and others. Exhib: 100 Prints, Jewish Mus, New York, 64; First through Fourth Int Miniature Print Shows, traveling throughout US & abroad, 64-71; Salute to 1965, Mus Mod Art, Caracas, Venezuela, 65; Contemp Prints, Mus Mod Art, Warsaw, Poland, 66; Round Tower, Copenhagen, Denmark, 74; one-person shows, Hudson River Mus, Yonkers, 72 & 74 & Katonah Gallery, NY, 72 & 76. Collections Arranged: Assembled, arranged & catalogued exhibs at Briarcliff Pub Libr, Briarcliff Manor, 63-69. Teaching: Organizer & art dir, Hawthorne Cedar-Knolls Sch, Hawthorn, NY, 52-55; instr pvt comprehensive art classes, 55-; instr workshop for teachers, Katonah Gallery, 73-74; instr intensive workshop in printmaking, Truro Ctr for the Arts at Castle Hill, Inc, Mass, summers 75, 76 & 77; organizer & instr mini-workshop in printmaking for adults & children, Katonah Gallery, 75. Awards: First Prize Graphics & Watercolors, Westchester Art Soc, 64; First Prize Graphics & Sculpture, Artists of NWestchester, 68; Hudson River Mus Purchase Award, Yonkers Art Asn, 70. Bibliog: Norman Laliberté (auth), Collage, Montage, Assemblage, History and Contemporary Techniques, Van Nostrand Reinhold, 71; Norman Laliberté and Alex Mogelon (co-authors), The Reinhold Book of Art Ideas, Van Nostrand Reinhold, 77. Mem: Artists Equity, New York; Am Crafts Coun; Nat Asn Women Artists; Yonkers Art Asn (bd dirs, 75-76; secy, 77). Style & Technique: In painting, mixed media, including printed elements and acrylics on carved surfaces; in printing, intaglio etching and illuminated embossments of archetypal themes of varied origin, such as the Kabbalah, Cycladic figure, Tantric imagery and Babushka dolls. Publ: Illusr, Dances of Palestine, B'Nai B'Rith Hillel Foundations, New York, 47. Dealer: Westlake Gallery Ltd 210 E Post Rd White Plains NY 10601; Katonah Gallery 28 Bedford Rd Katonah NY 10536. Mailing Add: 266 Dalmeny Rd Briarcliff Manor NY 10510

ADLER, ROBERT
PAINTER
b New York, NY, Jan 10, 30. Study: Syracuse Univ; Atelier 17, with Stanley Hayter, Paris. Exhib: Silvermine Guild, Conn, 63; Drawings, USA, 65; West Side Artists, Riverside Mus, New York, 66; 2nd Kent Show, Kent State Univ, Ohio, 68; A Sense of Place: the Artist & the American Land, Joslyn Art Mus, Omaha & Sheldon Mem Art Galleries, Lincoln, Univ Nebr. Media: Oil, Ink. Dealer: Poindexter Gallery 24 E 84th St New York NY 10028. Mailing Add: 300 Central Park W New York NY 10024

ADLER, SAMUEL (MARCUS)
PAINTER, EDUCATOR
b New York, NY, July 30, 98. Study: Nat Acad Design, with Leon Kroll & Charles Louis Hinton. Work: Whitney Mus Am Art, New York; Nat Collection Fine Arts, Smithsonian Inst and Joseph H Hirshhorn Mus, Washington, DC; Brooklyn Mus, NY; Munson-Williams-Proctor Inst, Utica; plus others. Exhib: Pa Acad Fine Arts, Philadelphia, var times, 48-68; Univ Ill, var times, 49-71; American Painting Today, Metrop Mus Art, 50; Whitney Mus Am Art Painting Ann, var times, 51-57; Art USA, New York, 62; plus many others, including 23 one-man shows, 48-72. Teaching: Prof art, NY Univ, 48-72; prof art, Univ Ill, 59-60; vis prof art, Univ Ga, 67 & 68. Pos: Pres, New York Chap, Artists Equity Asn, 54-55. Awards: J Henry Schiedt Mem Prize, Pa Acad Fine Arts, 51; Purchase award, Whitney Mus Am Art, 54; Artist in Residence Award, Ford Found, 65. Bibliog: Lee Nordness (auth), Art USA now, Viking Press, 63; Allen Weller (auth), The joys and sorrows of recent American art, Univ Ill Press, 68; Graham Collier (auth), Form, space and vision, 3rd ed, Prentice Hall, 72. Style & Technique: Figurative oils and collage. Media: Oil, Collage. Publ: Illusr, Candide, World Publ, 47; contribr, Education and the imagination, Univ Mich, 58; Education synopsis, NY Univ, 68; Samuel Adler, recent collages, Ga Mus Art, 68; Art Educ Mag, 72. Dealer: Frank Rehn Gallery 655 Madison Ave New York NY 10022. Mailing Add: 226 Lafayette New York NY 10012

ADLER, SEBASTIAN J
MUSEUM DIRECTOR
b Chicago, Ill, Sept 11, 32. Study: Winona State Col, BS; Univ Minn, Duluth. Collections Arranged: Robert Rauschenberg, 71; Roy Lichtenstein 1972; John McLaughlin 1973; Ronald Cooper 1973; Nancy Graves 1973; Innovations 1973; Robert Mangold 1974; Hilla and Bernd Becher 1974; Arman/Selected Works: 1958-1974; Donald Roller Wilson 1974; Jim Dine 1974; Marcia Hafif 1975; Stephen Rosenthal 1975; DeWain Valentine 1975; The Summers Collection, 1975, University of California, Irvine 1965-1975, 1975, Kim MacConnel, 1975, Dennis O'Leary, 1976, Richard Anuszkiewicz, 1976, Patrick Ireland, 1977, The Modern Chair, 1977, Improbable Furniture, 1977, Four Californians, 1977 & Eleanor Antin, 1977, La Jolla Mus of Contemp Art, Calif. Pos: Founder-dir, Nobles Co Art Ctr, 58-60; dir, Sioux Falls Art Ctr, 60-62; asst dir, Wichita Art Mus, 63-64, dir, 64-65; dir, Contemp Arts Mus, Houston, 66-73; dir, La Jolla Mus Contemp Art, 73- Mem: Col Arts Asn; Am Asn Mus; Am Asn Art Mus Dir. Mailing Add: La Jolla Mus Contemporary Art 700 Prospect St La Jolla CA 92037

ADLMANN, JAN ERNST
CURATOR
b Rockland, Maine, Sept 18, 36. Study: Univ Maine, BA(summa cum laude), 59; NY Univ, fel, 59-60, Inst Fine Arts, MA, 64; Univ Vienna, Austrian Govt grant, 61-62; Free Univ Berlin, Ger Govt grant, 63-64; Univ Calif, Berkeley, 65-66. Collections Arranged: Religious Art: From Byzantium to Chagall, Albright-Knox Art Gallery, Buffalo, NY, 64; Art of Venice, Tampa Bay Art Ctr, Fla, 67; 40 Now California Painters, Tampa Bay, 68; Kitsch: The Grotesque Around Us, Wichita Art Mus, Kans, 70 & Max Klinger, A Glove, 71. Pos: Asst cur, Albright-Knox Art Gallery, 64-65; gallery dir, Univ Colo, Boulder, 66-67; dir, Tampa Bay Art Ctr, 67-69; dir, Wichita Art Mus, 69-72; dir, Long Beach Mus Art, Calif, 72-77; adj cur spec proj, Blaeffer Gallery, Univ Houston. Mem: Asn Art Mus Dirs; Am Asn Mus; Western Asn Art Mus (trustee, 76-); Int Coun Mus; Col Art Asn. Publ: Auth, Max Klinger rediscovered, Art News, Vol 71, No 1; auth, Mona Lisa's sweatshirt, ARTgallery, Vol XV, No 8; auth, Kitsch, Mus News, Vol 52, No 1. Mailing Add: 8 Spring St New York NY 10012

ADRIAN, BARBARA (MRS FRANKLIN TRAMUTOLA)
PAINTER, COLLECTOR
b New York, NY, July 25, 31. Study: Art Students League, with Reginald Marsh, 47-54; Hunter Col, 51; Columbia Univ, 52-54. Work: Butler Inst Am Art, Youngstown, Ohio; Univ Southern Ill, Carbondale; City Hall, San Juan, PR. Exhib: Nat Acad Design, New York, 68; Butler Inst Am Art, 70; Gallery Mod Art, New York, 70; Suffolk Mus, Stony Brook, NY, 71; Whitney Mus, 75. Teaching: Art instr painting & drawing, Art Student League, 68- Pos: Art consult, R H Macy, New York, 60-61; Saks Fifth Ave, New York, 60; Doyle Dane & Bernbach, New York, 60. Awards: Benjamin Altman Prize, Nat Acad Design, 68. Bibliog: Edmund Burk Feldman (auth), Art as image and idea, Prentice-Hall. Mem: Life mem Art Student League. Media: Oil. Collection: Reginald Marsh, John Sloan, Will Barnet, Henry Pearson, Rouault, Versalius, Goya, Martin Lewis. Dealer: Coe Kerr Gallery 49 E 82nd St York NY 10021; Capricorn Galleries Washington DC 20014. Mailing Add: 420 E 64th St New York NY 10021

AGAR, EUNICE JANE
EDUCATOR, PAINTER
b Great Barrington, Mass, May 14, 34. Study: Wellesley Col, Mass, BA(art hist), 56; Art Student's League, 57-60, with Thomas Fogarty & Jean Liberte; Jean Liberte Studio, 60-63; Art Student's League, 69, with Edmont Cassarella & Robert Beverly Hale. Exhib: One-person show, Albany Inst of Hist & Art, NY, 67. Teaching: Instr painting, drawing & printmaking, Simon's Rock Early Col, 69-, instr & chmn studio arts, 74- & chmn arts div & studio arts, 75- Pos: Asst ed, Am Artists Mag, New York, 58-60, managing ed, 60-63; dir exhib prog, Simon's Rock Early Col, 70-; bd mem, Southern Berkshire Community Arts Coun, 75-, treas, 76-77. Style & Technique: Expressionist, landscape; reportorial pen and ink drawings. Media: Oil, casein, watercolor and line etching. Mailing Add: RD 1 Box 18 Egremont Plain Rd Great Barrington MA 01230

AGOOS, HERBERT M
COLLECTOR
b Boston, Mass, Dec 12, 15. Study: Harvard Col, AB; also fine arts mus course with Paul Sachs. Collection: 20th century modern art. Mailing Add: 21 Brown Cambridge MA 02138

AGOPOFF, AGOP MINASS
SCULPTOR
b Sliven, Bulgaria; US citizen. Study: Basic art training with Kiril Shivarov & Prof George Nicholov, Varna, Bulgaria; Atelier Damian, Constantza, Roumania; Columbia Univ; Nat Acad Design, with eminent sculptor Charles Keck. Work: Off Commandant, USMC, Washington, DC; Nat Hist Mus, Erevan, Armenia; Diocese, Armenian Church of N & S Am, New York; Hall of Fame for Great Americans, NY Univ; J Edgar Hoover Bur, US Dept Justice, Washington, DC. Comn: Bronze Mem, Rev Dr John Henry House, Thessaloniki, Greece, 34; heroic bronze statue, Gov H Bell, Belton, Tex, 37; Albert Dorne Award Medal for Famous Artists Sch, New York, 64; heroic portrait plaque of John F Kennedy, J F Kennedy Mem, Hyannis, Mass, 64; four large portrait tablets, Dow Chem Co, Midland, Mich, 70. Exhib: Nat Acad Design, 43-; Nat Sculpture Soc, 60-; Hudson Valley Art Asn, 61-; Allied Artists Am, 62-; Am Artists Prof League, 69-; Acad Artists Asn, 77- Awards: Daniel Chester French Medal, Nat Acad Design, 71; Therese & Edwin H Richard Mem Prize, Nat Sculpture Soc, 75; Gold Medal of Hon, Acad Artists Asn, 77. Mem: Nat Acad Design (assoc); Acad

Artists Asn; fel Allied Artists Am; fel Am Artists Prof League; fel Hudson Valley Art Asn; fel Nat Sculpture Soc. Media: Clay, Granite, Bronze. Mailing Add: Summit Dr Denville NJ 07834

AGOSTINELLI, MARIO
PAINTER, SCULPTOR
b Arequipa, Peru, Sept 18, 23; US citizen. Study: Studied in Arg, Brazil, France & Italy. Work: Acad Bellas Artes, Buenos Aires, Arg; Mus Mod Art, Rio de Janeiro; Springfield Mus Art, Mass. Exhib: Allied Artists Am; Butler Inst Am Art; Conn Acad Fine Arts; Knickerbocker Artists; Nat Acad Design, New York; plus others. Awards: Samuel Morse Medal, Nat Acad Design; Gold Medal, Knickerbocker Artists; Gold Medal, Salon Watercolor, Lima, Peru; plus others. Media: Oil. Dealer: Beilin Gallery 655 Madison Ave New York NY 10021. Mailing Add: 423 E 78th St New York NY 10021

AGOSTINI, PETER
SCULPTOR
b New York, NY, Feb 13, 13. Study: Leonardo da Vinci Sch Art, NY. Work: Univ Tex; Univ Calif; Univ Southern Calif; Int Ladies Garment Workers Union; Whitney Mus Am Art. Exhib: Whitney Mus Am Art, 64, 70 & 72; Sculpture of the 60's, Los Angeles, 67; Int Sculpture, Guggenheim Mus, 67 & Toronto, Ont, 68; Nat Inst Arts & Lett, 72; NY State Pavilion, World's Fair; plus others. Teaching: Lectr & summer courses, Columbia Univ, 61-66; prof art, Univ NC, Greensboro, 66-; mem staff, Wagner Col, 68. Awards: Longview Found Purchase Awards, 60-62; Brandeis Univ Creative Arts Award, 64; Guggenheim Fel, 66. Bibliog: Article in Time Mag, 11/13/64. Dealer: Zabriskie Gallery 613 E 12th St New York NY 10009. Mailing Add: 151 Avenue B New York NY 10009

AGUAYO, OSCAR
ART ADMINISTRATOR, GALLERY DIRECTOR
b Tampa, Fla, Sept 23, 25. Study: Univ Okla, BA(govt), 52. Pos: Dir, Latin Quarter Art Gallery, Tampa, 68- Mem: Ridge Art Asn of Winter Haven; Tampa Realistic Artists; Arts Ctr of St Petersburg. Specialty: Contemporary, original art. Mailing Add: c/o Latin Quarter Art Gallery 1509 Eighth Ave Tampa FL 33605

AHL, HENRY C
PAINTER, WRITER
b Springfield, Mass. Study: Harvard Col, with Arthur Pope & Martin Mower, AB; also with Henry Hammond Ahl. Work: Walker Gallery, Bowdoin Col; Farnsworth Mus, Rockland, Maine; Mus Art, Hickory, NC; Ga State Mus, Athens; Vanderpoel Art Collection, Beverly Hills-Chicago, Ill; plus others. Pos: Mem, Ctr for Study of Democratic Inst, Santa Barbara, Calif. Mem: Tommaso Camponella Int Acad Arts & Sci; NShore Arts Asn. Style & Technique: Representational landscape. Media: Oil. Publ: Auth & illusr, Dunes & Beaches of Essex County, Some Common Insects of Massachusetts, A Visit to Orchard House, A Visit to the Old Manse, Edgar Allan Poe; plus others. Mailing Add: RFD Rowley MA 01969

AHLANDER, LESLIE JUDD
CURATOR, ART CRITIC
b New York, NY. Study: Acad Mod, Paris, with Fernand Leger; Pa Acad Fine Arts, dipl, with Henry MacCarter. Exhibitions Arranged: 12 Artists from Latin America (with catalog), 71, After Surrealism (with catalog), 72, Contemporary Religious Imagery (with catalog), 74, Syd Solomon (with catalog), 75, 19th & 20th Century Art, 75, Latin Am Horizons (with catalog), 76 & The Circus in Art (with catalog), 77. Pos: Asst to dir, Mus Mod Art, New York, 41-43; dir exhibs, US Off Educ, Washington, DC, 43-44; chief div visual arts, Pan Am Union, Washington, DC, 44-45; art critic, Washington Post, Washington, DC, 50-63; cur educ, Corcoran Gallery, Washington, DC, 69-70; cur contemp art, John & Mabel Ringling Mus Art, Sarasota, Fla, 71-76; art coordr, Dade Co, Miami, Fla, 76- Awards: Cresson Traveling Scholar, Pa Acad Fine Arts, Philadelphia, 38; Art Critics Award, Col Art Asn Am, 52 & Art Critics Award Hon Mention, 53. Mem: Am Asn Mus; Nat Art Educ Asn; Nat Soc Lit & Arts. Publ: Auth, Doris Leeper, 75. Mailing Add: 441 Cadagua Ave Coral Gables FL 33146

AHLGREN, ROY B
INSTRUCTOR, PRINTMAKER
b Erie, Pa, July 6, 27. Study: Erie Tech Sch; Villa Maria Col (portraiture); Famous Artists Sch, dipl; Univ Pittsburgh, BS; Behrend Col, Pa State Univ; Work: US Info Agency, Washington, DC; Minn Mus Art, St Paul; Seattle Art Mus, Wash; Tex Tech Univ Mus, Lubbock; Butler Art Inst, Youngstown, Ohio. Comn: Ed of serigraphs, Assoc Am Artists, New York, 70; church bulletin cover designs, Lutheran Churches, Erie, 71-72; Int Art Guild, Santa Barbara, 74. Exhib: Nat Acad Design, Nat Galleries, New York, 68-69 & 76; Nat Audubon Artists Ann, 68-69 & 71-72; Nat Arts Club, New York, 68; 21st Nat Exhib Prints, Libr Cong, Washington, DC, 69; NW Printmakers Int Exhib, Seattle, Wash, 69 & 71; Print Club of Albany, NY, 69 & 71; Colorprint USA, Tex Tech Univ, Lubbock, 69, 71 & 75; 164th Ann Exhib, Pa Acad Fine Arts, Philadelphia, 69; Osaka World's Fair, 70; Boston Printmakers, 70-74 & 76; US Info Agency Print Show, Tokyo, Japan, 71; Soc Am Graphic Artists, 71; 40 New Am Prints, US Info Agency Travelling Show, Europe, 71-73; Silvermine Guild of Artists Print Exhib, 76. Teaching: Instr art, Tech Mem High Sch, Erie, 70-; asst prof printmaking, Edinboro State Col, 74. Pos: Assoc, Galerie 8, Erie, 67-75; bd mem, Erie Art Ctr, 70-72. Awards: First Prize (graphics), 11th RI Arts Festival, Providence, 69; Purchase Award, Drawings, USA, Minn Mus Art, St Paul, 70 & 73; Purchase award, Potsdam Univ, 74. Bibliog: Jane Abrams (auth), Educational slide collection, Univ NMex, 71; Lynwood Kreneck (auth), Colorprint USA filmstrip, Tex Tech Univ, 71; Joseph Cain (auth), Corpus Christi Caller, Texas, Iman show rev, 73. Mem: Boston Printmakers; Philadelphia Watercolor Club; Los Angeles Printmaking Soc; Graphics Soc; Erie Art Ctr. Style & Technique: Silk screen stencils, handcut and photo methods, geometric shapes, value modulation and movement, color and shape change, emphasis on illusions. Media: Serigraphy. Publ: Contribr, Showcase sect, Famous Artists Mag, 69, Assoc Am Artists catalog, 71, Ferdinand-Roten catalog, 72. Dealer: Assoc Am Artists 663 Fifth Ave New York NY 10022; Van Straaten Gallery Chicago IL. Mailing Add: 1012 Boyer Rd Erie PA 16511

AHLSKOG, SIRKKA
CRAFTSMAN, SCULPTOR
b Finland, Apr 15, 17. Study: Suolahden Kansanopisto, Finland; Craft Students League, New York. Work: Altanta Art Asn Mus; Norfolk Mus Arts & Sci; Arch Am Art, Smithsonian Inst. Exhib: Cooper Union Mus, 60, 61 & 63; Design Ctr, NY, 60 & 62; one-man show, Columbia Mus Art, SC, 61; Princeton Art Asn, 64; Guild Hall, East Hampton, NY, 67; plus others. Teaching: Instr tapestry weaving, Penland Sch Handicrafts, 56-57; lectr tapestry weaving. Awards: Pen & Brush Club Awards, 57-61 & 63. Mem: Pen & Brush Club; Artist-Craftsmen New York, Del (bd mem). Mailing Add: 414 E 83rd St New York NY 10028

AHLSTROM, RONALD GUSTIN
COLLAGE ARTIST
b Chicago, Ill, Jan 17, 22. Study: Art Inst Chicago, BFA, with Paul Weighart; Univ Chicago; DePaul Univ. Work: Art Inst Chicago; Tacoma Art Mus, Wash; Philbrook Art Ctr, Tulsa; Barat Col Collection, Lake Forest, Ill; Container Corp Am, Chicago. Exhib: 27th Corcoran Biennial, Washington, DC, 61; Chicago & Vicinity Exhib, Art Inst Chicago, 62; 12 Chicago Artists, McCormick Pl Gallery, 62; 50th Northwest Ann, Seattle Art Mus, 64; 6 American Artists, Touchstone Gallery, New York, 73. Awards: Clyde Carr Prize, Art Inst Chicago, 55 & Wm H Bartels Prize, 58; Purchase Prize, 50th Northwest Ann, Ford Found, 64. Bibliog: Meilach & Ten Hoor (auth), Collage and found art, Reinholt Publ, 64 & Collage, trends and technique, 73; H Haydon (auth), article in Chicago Mag, New Chicago Found, 68; Robert Glauber (auth), article in Art Scene Mag, 69. Style & Technique: Abstract, collage, oils, Oils, acrylic on canvas or board. Media: Collage & Acrylic (mixed media). Dealer: Joseph Faulkner Main St Gallery 100 E Walton St Chicago IL 60611; Touchstone Gallery Inc 37 E Fourth St New York NY 10003. Mailing Add: 121 W Park St Lombard IL 60148

AHN, DON C
PAINTER, ART DEALER
b Seoul, Korea, Jan 9, 37. Study: Art Students League; Miami Univ; Seoul Univ, BFA; Pratt Inst, MFA; NY Univ, PhD cand. Work: Mus Mod Art, New York; Dayton Mus Art, Ohio; Evansville Mus, Ind; C W Post Col, Long Island Univ. Exhib: Ohio Regional Show, Dayton, 63; one-man shows, Dayton Mus, 63 & Downey Mus, Los Angeles, 69; Int Print Biennale, Grenchen, Switz, 67 & Mus Mod Art, Tokyo, 71. Teaching: Instr print, C W Post Col, Long Island Univ, 64-68; asst prof painting, NY Inst Technol, 65-77; instr painting, Cooper Union, 66-71. Pos: Art dir, Korea Today, 61; dir, Ahn Tai Chi Studio, New York, 70-; adj instr, Dance Dept, Hunter Col, 74; dir, Lotus Gallery, New York, 74- Awards: First Prize for Painting, Ohio Regional Show, 63; McDowell Asn Fel, 64; First Prize for Print, E Coast Printer, Village Art Ctr, 64. Bibliog: John Canaday (auth), Drawings, New York Times, 12/11/71; Barbara Schwarts (auth), rev in Art News, 12/71; Alvin Smith (auth), rev in Art Int, 12/72. Mem: Am Asn Univ Prof; Col Art Asn Am. Style & Technique: Landscape of Far Eastern styles on canvas using Western and Eastern materials. Specialty: Contemporary art done by minority Asian artists in USA. Interest: Promote arts which synthesize Western visual formality with Eastern spirituality. Collection: Indian, Far Eastern religious sculpture and painting; contemporary Asian artists in New York. Mailing Add: PO Box 301 Canal Sta New York NY 10013

AHRENDT, CHRISTINE
PAINTER
b Dayton, Ohio. Study: Fla State Univ; Ohio Univ; Provincetown Workshop, with Ben Shahn, Will Barnet, Victor Candell & Leo Manso. Exhib: Columbus Gallery Fine Arts, Ohio, 61-65, 69 & 70; Provincetown Art Asn Summer Shows, 62-72; Pa Acad Fine Arts, Philadelphia, 64; Butler Inst Am Art Midyear Show, Youngstown, Ohio, 65 & 74 & Salute the Women, 75; one-man show, E Coast Gallery, Provincetown, 69. Awards: Huntington Galleries Awards, WVa, 62-66; MacDowell Colony Fel, 65, 66 & 71; S M Levy Mem Award, Columbus Art League, 69. Style & Technique: Abstract with expressionist overtones influenced by landscape. Media: Acrylic & Mixed Media. Dealer: Gallery 200 200 W Mound Columbus OH 43215. Mailing Add: 5 Old Peach Ridge Rd Athens OH 45701

AHVAKANA, ULAAQ (LAWRENCE REYNOLD AHVAKANA)
SCULPTOR, GLASS BLOWER
b Fairbanks, Alaska, July 8, 46. Study: Inst Am Indian Arts, Santa Fe, NMex, sculpture with Allen Houser, 66-69; Cooper Union Sch Art, New York, NY, 69-70; RI Sch of Design, Providence, BFA(sculpture/glass). Work: Anchorage Hist & Fine Arts Mus; Port Authority Bldg, New York; Atlantic Richfield Corp, Anchorage; Visual Art Ctr of Alaska. Comn: Wolf Dancer (6ft welded steel sculpture), Inst Am Indian Arts, 69; Dancers (17ft x 4ft welded steel wall relief), Alaska State Ct Bldg, 74; Seal Smooth (17ft x 4ft welded steel sculpture), Calista Corp, Settlers Bay Lodge, Wassilla, Alaska, 76; dedication plaque (2ft x 5ft alder & pine/ivory & metal), NSlope Borough, Barrow, Alaska, 77. Exhib: Scottsdale Invitational, Ariz, 67-68; Heard Mus Invitational, Phoenix, Ariz, 67-69; Native Arts Invitational, Anchorage Hist & Fine Arts Mus, 69-77; Am Art Show, Brooklyn Mus, NY, 71; RI Sch of Design Sculpture Show, Smithsonian Inst Portrait Gallery, Washington, DC, 72; Earth, Fire & Fiber Show & All Alaska Art Show, Anchorage Hist & Fine Arts Mus, 74-76; solo exhib, Governor's Gallery at Alaska State Mus, Juneau, 77. Collections Arranged: Survival/Life & Art of the Alaskan Eskimo (with Nat Endowment of the Arts support), Newark Mus, NJ, Am Fedn of Arts, New York & Bowers Mus, Santa Ana, Calif. Teaching: Artist in residence/glass blowing & sculpture, Community of Barrow, 72-74; artist in residence/sculpture, Visual Art Ctr of Alaska, 75-77; instr sculpture & glass, Inst Am Indian Arts, Santa Fe, NMex, 77- Pos: Mem bd, Visual Art Ctr of Alaska, 75-77; comn mem, Anchorage Hist & Fine Arts Mus, 76-77; mem, Native Arts Task Force, Alaska State Coun on the Arts, 76; pres, Raven's Bones Found, 77- Awards: Grant, Nat Endowment for the Arts, 72-74; Award in Glass, Earth, Fire & Fiber Show, Anchorage Hist & Fine Arts Mus, 74; First in Wood, All-Alaska Juried Art Show, 76; First in Sculpture, Native Arts Invitational, Chevron Corp, 77. Bibliog: Barbara Lipton (auth), Survival/Life & Art of the Alaskan Eskimo, Newark Mus, 77. Style & Technique: Sculptural use of physical forms of the Inupiat people and of their environment; free-form glass work. Media: Stone; Wood; Ivory and Silver; Glass. Publ: Illusr, New World J, Turtle Island Found, Vol 1, Numbers 2 & 3, 77. Mailing Add: Inst of Am Indian Arts 1300 Cerrillos Rd Santa Fe NM 87501

AHYSEN, HARRY JOSEPH
PAINTER, EDUCATOR
b Port Arthur, Tex. Study: Tulane Univ; Univ Houston, BFA; Univ Tex, Austin, MFA. Work: Regent's Room, Univ Tex. Comn: Four Seasons (painting), Huntsville Nat Bank, Tex; Calypso (painting), comn by Moody Col of Marine Sci & Maritime Resources, given to Jacque Costeau by Tex A&M Univ, Bryan, Tex, 72; Am Bank, Huntsville, 75; Bicentinential Huntsville mural (22 ft x 56 ft), 76; 60 ft Sculpture Windmills, Waterwood Corp, 78. Exhib: Miss Nat Exhib, Jackson, 62 & 65; Beaumont Tri-State Ann Art Mus Show, Tex, 63-65; San Antonio Five-State Watercolor Show, Tex, 64; Houston Power & Light Co Exhib, 72; one-man show, Port Arthur, Tex, 70; Southwestern Watercolor Soc Exhib, 72; plus others. Teaching: Asst prof oil painting, Sam Houston State Univ, 63- Awards: Tomaso Campenella Silver Medal, Rome, Italy, 72; Featured Artist, 6th Ann Int Art Show, Brownsville, Tex, 78; Grant Recipient, Hons Exhib, Sam Houston State Univ, 78. Media: Oil, Watercolor. Publ: Auth, Composition Devices for Landscapes, 70; Paul Schumann (monogr), 72. Mailing Add: Dept of Art Sam Houston State Univ Huntsville TX 77340

AICHELE, KATHRYN PORTER
ART HISTORIAN
b Charleston, SC, May 26, 47. Study: Vanderbilt Univ, BA(French), MA(French); Bryn Mawr Col, MA(hist art), PhD(hist art). Teaching: Asst prof hist art, Vassar Col, 75-76 & 78-; asst prof hist art, Fordham Univ, 77- Awards: Fulbright-Hays fel, France, 73-74; Theodore

N Ely res grant, Bryn Mawr Col, 73-74. Publ: Contribr, Benjamin West's chapel of revealed religion, Arts Bull, 76; contribr, Promised Gifts Exhibition, Vassar Col, 77; auth, Studio and Collection, Wharton Esherick Mus, 77. Mailing Add: PO Box 891 Bryn Mawr PA 19010

AIDLIN, JEROME
SCULPTOR, INSTRUCTOR
b Cleveland, Ohio, Aug 6, 35. Study: Cleveland Inst Art, dipl indust design, BFA(sculpture); Carnegie-Mellon Univ; also with William McVey. Work: Cleveland Art Mus; Cleveland Art Asn. Comn: Concrete wall relief, Methodist Hq Bldg, Honolulu, Hawaii; copper wall relief, Cafeteria Bldg, Univ Hawaii, Honolulu, 65; stainless steel relief, Sherwood Refractories, Inc, Cleveland, 68; forged steel sculpture, Ohio Nat Plaza Bldg, Columbus, 76. Exhib: Ceramics & Sculpture Ann, Butler Mus Am Art, Youngstown, Ohio, 62; Young American Craftsmen, Mus Contemp Crafts, NY, 63; Artists of Hawaii Ann, Honolulu Acad Art, 63-65; May Show Ann, Cleveland Mus Art, 62, 66, 67 & 72-74; one-man show, Cleveland Inst Art, 75. Teaching: Chmn sculpture dept, Univ Hawaii, 62-65; instr sculpture, Cleveland Inst Art, 65-, chmn dept, 71- Pos: Staff indust designer, Peter Muller-Munk Assoc, Pittsburgh, 57-60. Awards: Juror's Mention, 62, Wishing Well Purchase, 66 & Spec Jury Mention, 67, May Show, Cleveland Mus Art. Bibliog: Helen Cullinan (auth), Poetic conclusions in metal, Cleveland Plain Dealer, 75; David Parkinson, Jr (auth), Aidlin's sculpture, Sun Press, 75. Style & Technique: Metal forging; metal casting; concrete casting; ceramic sculpture. Media: Forged Steel, Copper; Cast Bronze, Aluminum. Mailing Add: 11141 East Blvd Cleveland OH 44106

AIRD, NEIL CARRICK
GOLDSMITH, DESIGNER
b Dumbarton, Scotland, Mar 13, 45; Can citizen. Study: Glasgow Sch of Art, Scotland, DA(jewelry & silversmithing), 68. Work: Contemp Can Crafts Collection, Ont Crafts Coun. Exhib: One-man shows, Gold & Silver, Agnes Etherington Art Ctr, Queen's Univ, Kingston, Ont, 73, Metalworks, Gallery of Fine Can Crafts, Kingston, Ont, 76 & Frogs, Fish & Fun, Kinnear d'Esterre Gallery, Kingston, Ont, 77; Ont Master Craftsmen, York Univ, Toronto, Ont, 74; Contemp Ont Crafts, Agnes Etherington Art Ctr, Queen's Univ, 76; Ont Crafts 77, Toronto-Dom Ctr, Toronto, Ont, 77; The Crafts Gallery, Toronto, 77; Can Nat Exhib, Toronto, Ont, 77. Collections Arranged: Contemp Can Crafts, Ont Crafts Coun, 75-78; Contemp Ont Craftsmen, Agnes Etherington Art Ctr, Queen's Univ, 76-77; Artisan 78 traveling exhib, Can Crafts Coun, 78-80. Teaching: Master metal arts, St Lawrence Col, Kingston, Ont, 70- Pos: Exec mem, Gallery Asn, Queen's Univ, 70-73; pvt dir crafts, Kingston Arts Coun, 72-74. Awards: Diamonds Int Award, Int Exhib, De Beers, 67; Lipman Co Award, Medium is Metal Exhib, 76; Ont Crafts Coun Award, Ont Crafts 77 Exhib, 77. Bibliog: Students (authors), Tourmaline (film), Queen's Univ Film Dept, 74; Wayne Lilley (auth), Art that wears well, Impetus, Maclean-Hunter Ltd, 6/74; Himel & Lambert (authors), Handmade in Ontario, Van Nostrand Reinhold, 76; Anthony Ibbotson (auth), Profile—Neil Carrick Aird, Crafts Can, Page Publ Ltd, 2-3/77. Mem: Assoc mem Soc NAm Goldsmiths; Metal Arts Guild; Ont Crafts Coun; Can Crafts Coun; World Crafts Coun. Style & Technique: Various techniques of goldsmith, currently light-weight, ultra-thin ciré perdue castings. Media: Precious Metals, Gem Materials; Natural Elements (Wood, Shell and Others). Mailing Add: 293 Victoria St Kingston ON K7L 3Z2 Can

AIROLA, PAAVO
PAINTER, WRITER
b Karelia, Finland; Can citizen. Study: Isaac Grünewald Art Sch, Stockholm, 48; Otte Sköld Art Sch, Sweden; Academie Libre, Stockholm. Work: Nat Gallery, Stockholm; Örebro Mus Fine Art & Hudikswal Art Mus, Sweden; London Art Mus, Ont; Zacks Collection, New York. Exhib: Royal Can Acad Fine Art Ann, 54-61; Toronto Art Gallery, 59; Phoenix Art Mus, 60-64; Galleri Z, Stockholm, 67; Gallerie Raymond Duncan, Paris, 67. Bibliog: Revue Moderne, Paris, 12/64. Mem: Academician Royal Can Acad Fine Arts; Ont Soc Artists; fel Int Inst Arts & Lett; Can Soc Painters in Water Colour. Style & Technique: Purist, colourist, working in oils and watercolours, using classic techniques. Media: Oil, Watercolor. Mailing Add: PO Box 22001 Phoenix AZ 85028

AITSON, MARLAND KONAD
PAINTER, CRAFTSMAN
b Mountain View, Okla, Apr 16, 28. Study: Bacone Col, Muskogee, Okla, AA. Exhib: InterTribal Indian Ceremonials, Gallup, NMex; Scottsdale Indian Arts Nat, Ariz; Philbrook Indian Art Exhib, Tulsa, Okla; Okla Univ Indian Art Traveling Exhib, Europe. Pos: Pres, InterTribal Indian Ceremonial Asn, Gallup, 70-71 & 74-75. Awards: M L Woodard Mem, InterTribal Indian Ceremonial. Style & Technique: Traditional American Indian, two dimensional. Media: Watercolor, Tempera. Mailing Add: 1506 Kit Carson St Gallup NM 87301

AJAY, ABE
PAINTER, SCULPTOR
b Altoona, Pa, Mar 24, 19. Study: Art Student's League; Am Artists Sch. Work: Solomon R Guggenheim Mus, New York; Hirshhorn Mus, Washington, DC; Roy R Neuberger Mus, State Univ NY Col at Purchase; Pa Acad of the Fine Arts, Philadelphia; Johnson Mus of Art, Cornell Univ. Comn: Sculpture edition of 300, J Walter Thompson Co, New York, 68. Exhib: White on White, De Cordova Mus, Lincoln, Mass, 65; Pa Acad of Fine Arts Ann, Philadelphia, 68; Flint Inst of Art, 69; A Plastic Presence, Jewish Mus, New York, Milwaukee Art Ctr & San Francisco Mus of Art, 69; Storm King Art Ctr, Mountainville, NY, 72; Am Acad of Arts & Lett, New York, 73; Roy R Neuberger Mus, 74; Constructivism is Alive, Greunebaum Gallery, New York, Univ NH, Neuberger Mus, 75 & 76; Perspective 1977, Freedman Art Gallery, Albright Col; Conn Painting, Drawing & Sculpture, Carlson Art Gallery, Univ Bridgeport, New Brit Mus Am Art, Cummings Art Ctr, Conn Col, New London, 78. Teaching: Vis artist painting, Univ Minn, Duluth, 69-70; assoc prof visual arts, State Univ NY, Purchase, 73- Bibliog: Irving Sandler (auth), The Poetic Constructivism of of Abe Ajay, Arts Mag, 77. Style & Technique: Constructivist, three-dimensional assemblage & sculpture combined with two-dimensional painted canvas and wood. Media: Plaster; polyester resin & acrylic on canvas. Publ: Auth, The Prize (an exchange of letters with Ad Reinhardt), 71, Working for the WPA, 72 & rev of The New Deal Art Projects & Art for the Millions, by Francis V O'Connor, 72, Art in Am. Dealer: Andre Zarre Gallery 41 E 57th St New York NY 10022. Mailing Add: Walnut Hill Rd Bethel CT 06801

AKAWIE, THOMAS FRANK
EDUCATOR, PAINTER
b New York, NY, Feb 22, 35. Study: Los Angeles City Col, 53-56; Univ Calif, Berkeley, BA(art hist), 59, MA(painting), 63. Work: Milwaukee Art Ctr, Wis; Ithaca Col Art Mus, NY; Oakland Mus, Calif; San Jose Mus of Art, Calif; Williams Col Mus, Williamstown, Mass. Comn: With Shelby Kennedy, filmmaker, Gun Body (humorous film on spray-painting), San Francisco Art Inst, 69. Exhib: Contemp Painting & Sculpture in Am, Krannert Art Mus, Champaign, Ill, 65-69; New York World's Fair, Am Express Pavilion, 65; 1969 Ann Exhib, Whitney Mus Am Art, New York, 69; Alternative Realities, Mus of Contemp Art, Chicago, Ill, 76; Painting & Sculpture in Calif, San Francisco Mus of Mod Art, 76 & Nat Collection of Fine Arts, Smithsonian Inst, Washington, DC, 77; one-man shows, La Jolla Mus of Art, Calif, 67, Calif Palace of the Legion of Hon, San Francisco, 72 & San Jose Mus of Art, Calif, 77. Teaching: Asst prof painting & drawing, Calif Univ, Los Angeles, 65-66; lectr painting & drawing, Univ Calif, Berkeley, 72-73; instr spray-painting & drawing, San Francisco Art Inst, 66- Awards: Los Angeles All-City Exhib Award, City of Los Angeles, Calif, 65; First Prize, Ann Downey Mus Invitational, Calif, 66; First Prize, Jack London Art Exhib, Oakland, Calif, 69. Bibliog: Charles Shere & John Coney (authors), Art of Tom Akawie, KQED-TV, 71. Style & Technique: Precisionistic airbrush and spray gun acrylic paintings of realism and symbolic geometry. Publ: Contribr, Visions, Pomegranate Publ, 77. Dealer: Gallery K 2032 P St NW Washington DC 20036. Mailing Add: 1740 University Ave Berkeley CA 94703

AKSTON, JOSEPH JAMES
COLLECTOR, PATRON
b Warsaw, Poland; US citizen. Study: Sch Foreign Serv, Georgetown Univ. Exhib: One-man exhibs, New York Cult Ctr, NY, 71, 25 Creative Yrs 1946-1971, Norton Gallery & Sch of Art, 72, Palm Beach Galleries, Fla, 72, Corcoran Gallery of Art, Washington, DC, 72, Tapestries, World Trade Ctr, 73 & 77, Bodley Gallery, New York, 76 & Kunst-Atelier 63, Klosters, Switz, 76. Pos: Pres, Arts Mag, New York; pres-founder, Art Voices, S Mag & Art Digest & S Newsletter, West Palm Beach, Fla; mem bd, Creative Arts Comn, Brandeis Univ, Waltham, Mass; exec chmn, Palm Beach Sponsors Comt, Fla; trustee, Mus of African Art, Washington, DC; mem bd dirs, Art Mus of the Palm Beaches, Inc & Norton Gallery & Sch of Art, West Palm Beach, Fla. Awards: Governor's Award for the Arts, State of Fla, Tallahassee, 77. Mem: Life mem Metrop Mus of Art, New York; life mem Soc of the Four Arts, Palm Beach, Fla; life mem Henry Morrison Flagler Mus, Palm Beach, Fla. Interest: Donor, Intetra (monumental outdoor sculpture by Isamu Naguchi) & $1500 for Best Painting Ann Prize to Soc of the Four Arts, Palm Beach, Fla, $1000 for Best Painting Ann Prize to Norton Gallery & Sch of Art, $100,000 Grant to Whitney Mus of Am Art, New York & Grant to produce & publish Contemporary Spanish Art (bk) in conjunction with Contemp Span Painters Exhib, organized by Int Exhibs Found. Collection: Contemporary American, Italian and Spanish paintings, sculptures and tapestries; outdoor sculpture by international artists. Publ: Auth, Beginning of the Beginning, Harry Abrams Inc, New York. Mailing Add: 444 N Lake Way Palm Beach FL 33480

ALAJALOV, CONSTANTIN
PAINTER, ILLUSTRATOR
b Russia, Nov 18, 00; US citizen. Study: Univ Petrograd. Work: Brooklyn Mus; Philadelphia Mus Art; Mus Mod Art, New York; Mus City of New York; Dallas Mus Fine Arts, Tex. Comn: Murals for SS America; The Hands of Leonard Bernstein, 67; sets for Michael Mordkin's Ballet & posters for many theatrical productions. Exhib: Many nat exhibs; one-man shows, Hollywood, Calif, New York, Dallas & Wichita, Kans Teaching: Prof art, Phoenix Art Inst & Archipenko's Ecole Beaux-Arts. Style & Technique: Following the classical tradition. Publ: Illusr, George Gershwin's Song Book, Alice Duer Miller's Cinderella, Out Hearts Were Young & Gay, Nuts in May, Bottoms Up & others; contribr to many nat mag. Mailing Add: 140 W 57th St New York NY 10019

ALAUPOVIC, ALEXANDRA V
SCULPTOR, EDUCATOR
b Slatina, Yugoslavia, Dec 21, 21; US citizen. Study: Acad Visual Arts, Univ Zagreb, sculptor & teaching cert, 48; Acad Visual Arts, Prague, 49; Univ Ill, Urbana-Champaign, 59-60; Univ Okla, MFA, 66. Work: Univ Okla Mus Art, Norman; Okla State Art Col; Continental Fed Savings & Loan, Oklahoma City. Comn: Oklahoma City Libr, 62; Okla Med Res Found Off Bldg, 64; First Unitarian Church, Oklahoma City, 64; busts & pub sculpture, Mercy Health Ctr & Casady Sch, Oklahoma City, 74. Exhib: Exposition Asn Peintres, Graveurs et Sculpteurs de Croatie, Dubrovnik, Yugoslavia, 56; 35th Ann Springfield Art Mus, Mo, 65; On Music, Univ Okla Mus Art, 68; Ann Eight State Exhib of Painting & Sculpture, Oklahoma City, 71; one-man show, Okla Art Ctr, 73. Teaching: Instr drawing, basic form & sculpture, Univ Okla, 64-66; instr sculpture, Okla Sci & Arts Found, Oklahoma City, 69-75; instr sculpture, Oklahoma City Univ, 72- Awards: Jacobson Award, Univ Okla, 64; First Sculpture Award, Philbrook Art Ctr, Tulsa, 70. Mem: The MacDowell Club Allied Arts; Nat Soc Lit & Arts. Style & Technique: Dynamic forces in forms in nature or microstructures express artist's intuitive drive to communicate the concept of universal and organized complexity. Media: Marble, Metals. Dealer: Sales & Rental Gallery Oklahoma Art Ctr 3113 Pershing Blvd Oklahoma City OK 73107; Pickard Art Galleries Inc 541 NW 39 Oklahoma City OK 73118. Mailing Add: 11908 N Bryant Rte 1 Box 167A Oklahoma City OK 73111

ALBERGA, ALTA W
ART HISTORIAN, PAINTER
b Tuscaloosa, Ala. Study: Univ Wichita (Wichita State), Kans, AB, AM; Wash Univ, St Louis, BFA; Univ Ill, Urbana-Champaign, MFA; Art Students League, with Morris Kantor & Robert Beverly Hale. Work: Little Gallery, Wichita State Univ; Univ Ill, Champaign; Gremur Prints, Atlanta, Ga. Comn: Print, Columbia Mus Art, SC, 73; painting, Daniel Int (Construct) Inc, Greenville, SC, 75; portraits, comn by Mrs Howard McCall, Mrs Terry Mills & Mrs Michel de la Villemarque, Greenville, 75. Exhib: One-woman shows, SC State Univ, Orangeburg & Univ SC at Lancaster, 74; SC Artists Guild, Gibbs Gallery, Charleston, 73; Southeastern Ctr Contemp Art, Winston-Salem, SC, 75; Greenville Artists Guild, Greenville Mus Art, SC, 75. Teaching: Instr art hist & drawing, Wichita State Univ, 54-55; instr design, Webster Col, St Louis, 55-61; head visual arts, Presby Col, Clinton, SC, 69-75; lectr, Tri-county Tech Col, Pendleton, SC, 75-; drawing & oil painting, Tempo Gallery & Greenville Co Mus of Art. Pos: Lect on Maya cult, ann meeting, 74. Awards: Richard K Weil Award, City Mus of St Louis, 57; St Louis Artists' Ann Guild, 60; Purchase Prize, print, Columbia Mus, SC, 71. Mem: Artists Equity Asn (pres, St Louis Chap, 61); Art Students League; Southeastern Col Art Conf; SC Artists Guild; Guild of Greenville Artists (bd mem). Style & Technique: Non-objective paintings and abstractions; mostly portraits. Media: Oil, Acrylic. Res: Modern art history. Publ: Auth, Book reviews for Southeastern Col Art Conf publ, 73. Dealer: Garden Gallery Hwy 70 W Raleigh NC 27603. Mailing Add: 11 Overton Dr Greenville SC 29609

ALBERS, ANNI
DESIGNER, GRAPHIC ARTIST
b Berlin, Ger, June 12, 99; US citizen. Study: Bauhaus, Weimar, Ger, dipl; Md Inst Col Art, DFA, 72; York Univ, LLD, 73. Work: Metrop Mus Art & Mus Mod Art, New York; Art Inst Chicago; Victoria & Albert Mus, London; Baltimore Mus Art, Md. Comn: Mem to Nazi victims, comn by List Family for Jewish Mus; Ark Curtain, Dallas. Exhib: Mus Mod Art, New York; Mass Inst Technol, Cambridge; Carnegie Inst Technol, Pittsburgh; Yale Univ Art Gallery, New Haven; Honolulu Acad Art, Hawaii. Teaching: Asst prof art, Black Mountain Col, 33-49; lects, leading univs & mus. Awards: Gold Medal, Am Inst Archit, 61; citation, Philadelphia Col Art, 62; Tamarind Lithography Workshop Fel, Los Angeles, 64. Media: Textile. Publ: Auth, Anni Albers: on designing, Wesleyan Univ Press, 62 & 71; Anni Albers:

on weaving, Wesleyan Univ Press, 65 & 72; Anni Albers: pre-Columbian Mexican miniatures, Praeger, 70. Mailing Add: Orange CT 06477

ALBERT, CALVIN
SCULPTOR, EDUCATOR
b Grand Rapids, Mich, Nov 19, 18. Study: Grand Rapids Art Gallery, with Otto Karl Bach; Art Inst Chicago; Inst Design, with Moholy-Nagy & György Kepes; Archipenko Sch Sculpture; Fulbright advan res grant, 61-62; Tiffany grant, 63 & 65; Guggenheim fel, 66. Work: Metrop Mus, Whitney Mus Am Art & Jewish Mus, New York; Art Inst Chicago; Detroit Inst Arts. Comn: Ark Doors & Candelabra, Steinberg House, Park Ave Synagogue, New York, 54; Outdoor Candelabra, Temple Israel, Tulsa, Okla, 55; Crucifix, Tabernacle & Candlesticks, St Paul's Church, Peoria, Ill, 59; Facade Relief, Congregation Emanuel, Grand Rapids, 74. Exhib: Unknown Political Prisoner Prizewinners, Mus Mod Art, New York & Tate Gallery, London, 53; le Dessin Contemporains aux Etats Unis, Musee Nat d'Arte Moderne, Paris, 54; Whitney Ann Am Artists, 54-68; Univ Ill Contemp Painting & Sculpture, 57 & 65; 20th Century Masters of Drawing, Mus Mod Art, New York, 64. Teaching: Instr sculpture & design, Inst Design, Chicago, 42-46; instr color & drawing, Brooklyn Col, 47-49; prof art & head grad sculpture prog, Pratt Inst, 49- Awards: Nat Inst Arts & Lett Award, 75. Media: Bronze, Fiberglas. Publ: Co-auth, Figure drawing comes to life, 57. Mailing Add: 325 W 16th St New York NY 10011

ALBERTAZZI, MARIO
PAINTER, ART CRITIC
b Bologna, Italy, Dec 9, 20. Study: Istituto Tecnico, Bologna, Italy; Art Student League, New York. Work: Italian Consulate General & Casa Italiana, Columbia Univ, New York. Exhib: Galerie Internationale, 68, Ligoa Duncan Gallery, 69, New York Pub Libr, 69, Caravan House Galleries, 70 & Pacem in Terris Gallery, New York, 71. Pos: Art ed, Il Progresso Italo-Americano, New York, 64-; corresp, Il Giornale d'Italia, Rome, 70- Awards: First Prize (collage), Composers, Authors & Artists Am Nat Contest, 69. Mem: Composers Authors & Artists Am; Burr Artists. Style & Technique: Painter, oils; collage artist. Media: Oil. Mailing Add: 545 W End Ave New York NY 10024

ALBIN, EDGAR A
EDUCATOR, ART CRITIC
b Columbus, Kans, Dec 17, 08. Study: Univ Tulsa, BA; State Univ Iowa, MA; Ariz State Univ; also with Grant Wood, Philip Guston, Donald Mattison & Mauricio Lasansky; Fulbright res grant, India, 54-55. Work: Little Rock Mus Fine Arts, Ark. Exhib: 14th Int Exhib of Northwest Printmakers, Seattle, 42; Mid-Western Artists, Nelson Galleries, Kansas City, 42; Southern Printmakers Circulating Exhib, 42; Tex State Art Asn Int, Elizabeth Ney Galleries, Austin, 43; one-man show, Thayer Mus, Univ Kans, 44. Teaching: Instr art & humanities, Tulsa Pub Schs, Okla, 31-39; assoc prof art hist & studio, Univ Tulsa, 39-47; prof art hist, Univ Ark, 47-62; vis prof, Stetson Univ, 50-52; prof & head dept art, Southwest Mo State Univ, 62-74, emer prof, 74- Pos: Pres, Mo Col Art Asn; mem sem Am insts & cult, Tata Inst, Bangalore, India, 55; auth weekly arts column, Leader & Press, Springfield, Mo, 71- Mem: Am Asn Univ Prof; hon Am Inst Architects; Delta Phi Delta. Res: Asian art and art of the twentieth century. Publ: Co-auth, Syllabus for a basic course in the arts (2 vols) & Syllabus for humanities (2 vols), Univ Ark, 53; auth, Culture of the Orient, Col Art J, summer 55; auth, Howard J Whitlach, sculptor, Art Trends, Madras, India, 1/62; auth, Evan Lindquist Engraver, 1-2/78 & John Walker, Sculptor, 3-4/78, Art Voices/South. Mailing Add: 1332 S Rogers St Springfield MO 65804

ALBRECHT, MARY DICKSON
SCULPTOR, PAINTER
b Dothan, Ala, June 4, 30. Study: Univ Houston; Tex Woman's Univ, BS(sculpture, with hons), 70. Work: Okla Art Ctr Mus, Oklahoma City; Univ Tex Permanent Collection, Arlington; City Dallas Park & Recreation Dept, Tex. Exhib: 13th Nat Exhib Prints & Drawings, Okla Art Ctr, 71; 15th Tex Crafts Exhib, Dallas Mus Fine Arts, 71; Tex Fine Arts Asn State Citation Show, 72, 75 & 76 & 61st Ann Nat Exhib, 72, Laguna Gloria Mus, Austin; 14th Midwest Biennial, Joslyn Art Mus, Omaha, Nebr, 76; Tenth Nat Drawing & Small Sculpture Show, Del Mar Col, Corpus Christi, Tex, 76. Teaching: Sculpture classes, Dallas, Tex, currently. Awards: Juror's choice & circuit merit awards, Tex Fine Arts Asn State Citation Show, 71, 72 & 76; Purchase award, art acquisition comt, Univ Tex, Arlington, 72. Mem: Artists Coalition of Tex (pres). Style & Technique: Very contemporary, abstract and stylized objective. Media: Steel, Bronze, Metal, Plastic. Mailing Add: PO Box 25026 Dallas TX 75225

ALBRECHT, ROBERT A
COLLECTOR, ILLUSTRATOR
b Irvington, NJ, Mar 26, 25. Study: Newark Sch Fine & Indust Art, four yrs; study with James Carlin, four yrs. Work: US Navy Combat Art Collection, Washington, DC; plus numerous pvt collections. Comn: Two murals, Somerset Co Bank & Trust Co, 61. Exhib: US Navy Combat Art Collection, Washington, DC. Teaching: Instr illus & drawing, Newark Sch Fine & Indust Art, NJ, 52-78. Pos: Artist/illusr, Prudential Ins Co, Newark, 46-78; US Navy Combat Artist, Vietnam & elsewhere, 67-78; freelance illusr, numerous outdoor publ, currently. Mem: Navy Combat Artists; Salmagundi Club, New York. Style & Technique: Howard Pyle style. Media: Watercolor, Oil; Pen and Ink. Collection: American Indian and Western art. Mailing Add: 23 Shelly Dr Somerset NJ 08873

ALBRIGHT, IVAN LE LORRAINE
ARTIST
b North Harvey, Ill, Feb 20, 1897. Study: Northwestern Univ, 15-16; Univ Ill, 16-17; Ecole Regionale Beaux-Arts, Nantes, 19; Art Inst Chicago, 20-23, PhD(fine arts), 77; Pa Acad of Fine Arts, Philadelphia, 23; Nat Acad of Design, New York, 24; Mundelein Col, LHD, 69; Lake Forest Col, Ill, PhD(fine arts), 72; Columbia Col, LHD, 69; Lake Forest Col, Ill, PhD(fine arts), 72; Columbia Col, Chicago, PhD(arts), 74. Work: Nat Gallery of Fine Arts, Washington, DC; Metrop Mus of Art, New York; Mus of Mod Art, New York; Guggenheim Mus, New York; Whitney Mus of Am Art, New York; plus many others. Exhib: Carnegie Inst Ints, Pittsburgh, Pa; Pan-Am Int, Baltimore; New York World's Fair; Brussels World's Fair; 20th Century Portraits & Realists & Magic Realistists, Mus of Mod Art, New York; 50 Prints of the Year, 100 Am Prints, The Artist Looks at People & Masterpiece of the Month, Art Inst of Chicago; Corcoran Gallery of Art, Washington, DC; Nat Acad of Design, New York; Whitney Mus of Am Art, New York; one-man retrospective, Art Inst of Chicago, 64; plus many others. Awards: Silver Medal, 30 & Gold Medal, 31, Chicago Soc of Artists; First Medal for Best Painting, 42 & Metrop Mus Prize, 52, Metrop Mus of Art, New York; Silver Medal & Award, Corcoran Gallery of Art, Washington, DC, 55. Mem: Academician Nat Acad of Design; Nat Inst of Arts & Lett; Am Watercolor Soc; fel Pa Acad of Fine Arts; Am Acad of Arts & Lett; plus many others. Dealer: Kennedy Galleries 40 W 57th 5th Fl New York NY 10019. Mailing Add: 47 Elm St Woodstock VT 05091

ALBRIGHT, MALVIN MARR
PAINTER, SCULPTOR
b Chicago, Ill, Feb 20, 97. Study: Univ Ill; Art Inst Chicago; Pa Acad Fine Arts. Work: Corcoran Gallery Art; Toledo Mus Art; Butler Inst Am Art; Univ Ga; Pa Acad Fine Arts; plus others. Exhib: Nat Acad Design; Whitney Mus Am Art; Mus Mod Art; Pa Acad Fine Arts; Carnegie Inst; plus others. Awards: Altman Prize, Nat Acad Design, 42 & 62, Palmer Mem Prize; Corcoran Silver Medal, Washington, DC; Dana Medal, Pa Acad Fine Arts, 65; plus others. Mem: Academician Nat Acad Design; fel Royal Soc Arts; Int Inst Arts & Lett; Nat Sculpture Soc; fel Pa Acad Fine Arts; plus others. Mailing Add: 1500 Lake Shore Dr Chicago IL 60610

ALBRIGHT, THOMAS
ART CRITIC, WRITER
b Oakland, Calif, June 10, 35. Study: Univ Calif, Berkeley, BA. Pos: Art critic, San Francisco Chronicle, 66-; contrib ed, Visuals, Rolling Stone, San Francisco, 68-; San Francisco ed, Art Gallery, Ivoryton, Conn, 70-; San Francisco corresp, Art News, 74- Publ: Auth, San Francisco Rolling Renaissance (catalog), 68; auth, articles in New York Times, 69. Mailing Add: San Francisco Chronicle Art Dept 905 Mission St San Francisco CA 94103

ALBRO, JEANNETTE (JEANNETTE LOUISE CANTRELL)
ART DEALER, COLLECTOR
b Sterling, Colo, June 13, 42. Study: Univ Nebr, Lincoln; Univ Northern Colo, Greeley; John F Kennedy Col, Wahoo, Nebr, BA. Pos: Dir, Bardstown Art Gallery, Ky, 70-; bus mgr, Bardstown Pottery, 70-; organizer/chmn, Bardstown Invitational Art Exhib, 73- Mem: Am Crafts Coun; Art Ctr Asn. Specialty: Oil and watercolor paintings; 20th century stoneware. Collection: Realistic oils and watercolors; graphics (etchings); sculpture; 20th century American pottery. Mailing Add: PO Box 437 Bardstown KY 40004

ALBUQUERQUE, LITA
PAINTER, LECTURER
b Santa Monica, Calif, Jan 3, 46. Study: Univ Calif, Los Angeles, BFA; Otis Art Inst. Work: Newport Harbor Art Mus, Newport Beach, Calif; Assoc Tel & Tel, Chicago; Wells Fargo Bank, Los Angeles; Security Pac Bank, Los Angeles. Exhib: Artists 1976, Marion Koogler Art Mus, San Antonio, Tex, 76; Los Angeles, Mus of Mod Art, Penthouse Gallery, New York, 76 & San Francisco Art Inst, 77; Aesthetics of Graffiti, San Francisco Mus of Mod Art, 78; one-artist shows, Janus Gallery, Venice, Calif, 77, Jack Glenn Gallery, Newport Beach, Calif, 76 & Mus of Univ Calif, Santa Barbara, 78. Teaching: Lectr painting & drawing, Calif State Univ, Los Angeles, 75-77; vis artist painting & drawing, Univ Calif, Santa Barbara, 77-78. Pos: Gallery dir, Gallery 707, Los Angeles, Calif, 73-75; cur, Cedars-Sinai Med Ctr Exhib Comt, Los Angeles, 76-77. Awards: Individual artist fel grant, Nat Endowment for the Arts, 75. Bibliog: Barbara Noah (auth), Lita Albuquerque at Janus, Art in Am, 77; Merle Schipper (auth), Lita Albuquerque, Arts Mag, 78 & Long Beach City Col Catalog, 78. Mem: Los Angeles Inst of Contemp Art. Style & Technique: Abstract paintings dealing with emergence and submersion of form and color; outside environmental work about color. Media: Drawing, Painting. Dealer: Janus Gallery 21 Market St Venice CA 90291. Mailing Add: 19453 Pacific Hwy Malibu CA 90265

ALCALAY, ALBERT S
PAINTER
b Paris, France, Aug 11, 17; US citizen. Study: Studied in Paris & Rome, Italy. Work: Fogg Mus, Harvard Univ; De Cordova & Dana Mus; Mus Mod Art; Boston Mus Fine Arts; Rome Mus Mod Art; plus others. Exhib: Mus Mod Art, 55; Whitney Mus Am Art, 56, 58 & 60; Inst Contemp Art, Boston, 60; Pa Acad Fine Arts, 60; 36 one-man shows, De Cordova Mus, Lincoln, Mass; plus others. Teaching: Lectr design, Carpenter Ctr, Harvard Univ, 59- Awards: Guggenheim Fel, 59-60; prize, Boston Art Festival, 60. Style & Technique: Landscapes and city scape in an abstract manner much like European style. Media: Gouche and Pen & Ink on Rice Paper; Oil, Plexiglas. Mailing Add: 66 Powell Brookline MA 02146

ALCOPLEY, L
PAINTER, GRAPHIC ARTIST
b Ger, June 19, 10; US citizen. Study: Studied in Dresden, Ger. Work: Mus Mod Art, New York; Mus Mod Art, Tokyo; Stedelijk Mus, Amsterdam; Israel Mus, Jerusalem; Nat Gallery Iceland, Reykjavik; plus many others. Comn: Mural, Univ Freiburg, Fed Repub Ger, 58. Exhib: One-man shows, Galerie Bing, Paris, 56, Suermondt Mus, Aachen, WGer, 57 & Stedelijk Mus, 61; Byron Gallery, New York, 64; Israel Mus, 69-70; Retrospective 1944-1977, Kjarvalsstadir, Munic Art Gallery, Reykjavik, Iceland; also many others. Pos: Co-ed, Leonardo, Int J Contemp Artist, 68- Bibliog: Willem De Kooning & Franz Kline (auth), On works of Mr Alcopley, 52; Michel Seuphor (auth), Ecritures-Dessins d'Alcopley, 54; Will Grohmann (auth), Alcopley-Voies et Traces, 61. Mem: Am Abstr Artists; Groupe Espace, Paris. Style & Technique: Painter and printmaker (all media), collage artist, muralist. Media: Oil, Acrylic, Watercolor, Ink. Publ: Auth, Einsichten, drawings by Alcopley to poems by S E Broese, 59; contribr, Art & Thinking, Bokubi Press, Kyoto, Japan, 63; coauth & illusr, Listening to Heidegger and Hisamatsu, 69; illusr, Herman Cherry, auth, Poems of Pain—And Other Matters, Una Ed, New York, 76; illusr, Grete Wehmeyer, auth, Edgard Varèse, Gustav Bosse Verlag, Regensburg, Fed Repub of Ger, 77; plus numerous other publ. Mailing Add: 50 Central Park W New York NY 10023

ALDEN, GARY WADE
ART CONSERVATOR
b Somerville, NJ, May 18, 51. Study: Univ Chicago, 69-73, BA, 73; Oberlin Col, Ohio, 73-76, Intermuseum Conserv Asn Training Prog & study with Richard D Buck, 73-76, cert of conserv, 76. Pos: Conservator, Intermuseum Conserv Asn Intermuseum Lab, Oberlin, 76-77; chief conservator, Balboa Art Conserv Ctr, San Diego, Calif, 77- Mem: Assoc mem Am Inst for Conserv of Hist & Artistic Works; Western Asn of Art Conservators. Interest: Conservation of paintings and polychromed sculpture. Mailing Add: Balboa Art Conserv Ctr PO Box 2107 San Diego CA 92112

ALDRICH, LARRY
ART COLLECTOR
Pos: Chmn & founder, Larry Aldrich Mus Contemp Art, Ridgefield, Conn & founder & pres, SoHo Ctr for Visual Arts, New York, NY, currently. Collection: Contemporary painting and sculpture. Mailing Add: Larry Aldrich Assocs 40 Central Park S Rm 6 New York NY 10019

ALDWINCKLE, ERIC
DESIGNER, PAINTER
b Oxford, Eng, Jan 22, 09; Can citizen. Work: Nat Gallery Can, Ottawa. Comn: Oil, Sunnybrook Hosp, Toronto, 47-48; Heraldy (egg tempera), Oshawa Col, Ont, 53-; Hydro Electric Tempera, York Twp, Toronto, 59. Exhib: Ont Soc Artists, 37-49; New York World's Fair, 39; Nat Gallery, London, 42-43. Teaching: Vprin design, Ont Col Art, 36-42; prin design

& colour, New Sch Design, 44-45. Pos: Art dir, Stratford Festival, Ont, 55-58; art dir, Univ Toronto, 48-53. Awards: Art direction award, Art Dir Club, 49; Can Dollar Award, Govt Can, 71. Bibliog: Paul Arthur (auth), Mural, Can Art Mag, 49; Design-illustration, Graphis (Ger), 50. Mem: Ont Soc Artists; life mem Can Soc Graphic Arts; life mem Arts & Lett Club; Royal Can Acad. Publ: Illusr, Varsity story, 48 & Canada's tomorrow, 54. Mailing Add: 135 Rose Ave Toronto ON Can

ALEXANDER, JOHN E
PAINTER
b Beaumont, Tex, Oct 26, 45. Study: Lamar Univ, BA; Southern Methodist Univ, MFA. Work: Contemp Arts Mus, Houston; Mus Fine Art, Amarillo, Tex; Am Tel Collection, Chicago; Mus Fine Art, Beaumont; Collection, Southern Methodist Univ, Dallas. Comn: Poster, Am Civil Liberties Union, ed of lithographs, 74; poster, Contemp Arts Mus, comn by Dir James Harithas, 75. Exhib: Drawings USA, Springfield, Ill, 70-71; Dallas Mus Art, 72; Artist of the Southwest, Atlanta, Ga, 72; one-man show, Contemp Arts Mus, Houston, 75. Teaching: Instr painting, Univ Houston, 71- Style & Technique: Oil paintings on canvas. Mailing Add: 1810 Portsmouth Houston TX 77098

ALEXANDER, KENNETH LEWIS
CARTOONIST
b Gridley, Calif, June 16, 24. Study: Univ Calif, Berkeley, 42-43; Rutgers Univ, 43-44; Calif Col Arts & Crafts, 46-47. Pos: Free lance com artist, 47-58; ed, Pictorial Living Mag, San Francisco Examnr, 58-63, Sunday art dir, 63-66, ed cartoonist, 66-; TV ed cartoonist, KGO-TV, 68-69. Mem: Soc Am Ed Cartoonist; Am Newspaper Guild; AFTRA. Publ: Co-auth, A Gallery of Great Americans. Mailing Add: 110 Fifth St San Francisco CA 94103

ALEXANDER, MARGARET AMES
ART HISTORIAN
b Sharon, Mass, May 21, 16. Study: Wheaton Col, AB, 38; Inst of Fine Arts, NY Univ, MA, 41, PhD, 58. Teaching: Prof Roman, Early Christian & Byzantine art, Univ Iowa, 62- Pos: Co-dir, Corpus des Mosaiques de Tunisie, Tunis, 68- Mem: Am Asn Univ Women; Archaeol Inst Am; Asn Int Study Antique Mosaics; Int Asn Classical Archaeol; Col Art Asn. Res: Roman and Early Christian mosaics. Publ: Auth of articles on NAfrica, Archaeol, 49-51; co-auth, Quelques Precisions a propos de la Chronologie des Mosaiques d'Utique, La Mosaique Greco-Romaine, Vol II; co-auth, Utique et ses Environs, Fasc 1, 73 & Fasc 3, 76 & ed, Fasc 2, 74, Corpus des Mosaiques de Tunisie. Mailing Add: 9 Forest Glen Iowa City IA 52240

ALEXANDER, PETER
SCULPTOR
b Los Angeles, Calif, Feb 27, 39. Study: Univ of Pa, University Park, 57-60; Univ of London, Eng, 60-62; Univ of Calif, Berkeley, 62-63; Univ of Southern Calif, Los Angeles, 63-64; Univ of Calif, Los Angeles, 64-68, BA, 65 & MFA, 68. Work: Walker Art Ctr, Minneapolis, Minn; Mus of Mod Art, New York; Minneapolis Inst of Art; Joslyn Art Mus, Omaha, Nebr; Los Angeles Co Mus of Art, Los Angeles. Exhib: Small Images, Calif State Col, Los Angeles, 67; West Coast Now, 68 & Am Art, 73, Seattle Art Mus; New Materials-New Methods, Mus of Mod Art, New York, 69; 14 Sculptors: The Indust Edge, Walker Art Ctr, 69; Whitney Mus of Am Art Ann, New York, 69; Highlights: 1968-1969, Larry Aldrich Mus of Contemp Art, Ridgefield, Conn, 69; Am Exhibs, Art Inst of Chicago, 69 & 72; Permutations: Light & Color, Mus of Contemp Art, Chicago, 70; Looking West, Joslyn Art Mus, 70; New Multiple Art, Whitechapel Art Gallery, London, 70; Transparency, Reflection, Light, Space: Four Artists, Univ of Calif, Los Angeles, 70; Documenta 5, Kassel, Ger, 72; Painting & Sculpture in Calif: The Modern Era, San Francisco Mus of Art, 76; Art on Paper, Wentherspoon Gallery, Univ of NC, Greensboro, 76; one-man shows, Akron Art Inst, Ohio, 72, Univ of Calif, Irvine, 75, Bowers Mus, Santa Ana, Calif, 75, Calif State Univ, Long Beach, 76 & Fullerton Col, Calif, 76. Pos: Artist in Residence, Calif Inst of Technol, 70-71 & Calif State Col, Long Beach, 76. Bibliog: Elizabeth Perlmulter (auth), Clear, Cloudy, Smoggy, 1/75 & Dizzy in the Ganzfeld, summer 76, Artnews; Nancy Marmer (auth), Sky Show, Artforum, 2/76; Henry Seldis (auth), Rev in Los Angeles Times, 8/7/77. Mailing Add: PO Box 1124 Topanga CA 90290

ALEXANDER, ROBERT SEYMOUR
EDUCATOR, DESIGNER
b Pittsburgh, Pa, Feb 1, 23. Study: Ad-Art Studio Sch, 41-42; Shrivenham Am Univ, Eng, 45; Carnegie Inst Technol, 47; Univ Ill, BFA, 51; Cranbrook Acad Art, MFA, 52. Comn: Indust designs for FMC Corp, Mich Dept Agr, Recordio Corp, Planet Corp & others. Exhib: Exhib Mich Artists, Detroit Inst Arts, 59, 62 & 72; one-man show, MEA Purchase Award Exhib, 69, 72 & 74; Kresge Art Gallery, Mich State Univ, 73 & 78; 7th Photographic Art Competition, Saginaw Mus, Mich, 77; 3rd Small Paintings Exhib, Gallery North, Mt Clemens, Mich, 77. Teaching: Prof indust design, Mich State Univ, 54- Pos: Artist-designer, James H Matthews Co, Pittsburgh, 46-47; training aids designer, USA, Ft Eustis, Va, 48; automotive designer, Ford Motor Co, Dearborn, Mich, 52-53; independent designer, 55-; univ res grants, 62-65, 67 & 69-78; group leader, design for educ proj, Princeton Univ, 66; gov app mem, Mich Cult Comn, 60-62. First Prize, Int furniture design competition, Nat Cotton Coun, 59; Second Prize, 7th Photographic Art Competition, Saginaw Mus, 77. Bibliog: J Fisher (auth), Education for design, Format Mag, 5/66. Mem: Indust Designers Soc Am. Style & Technique: Relates style and technique to ultimate purpose or message using a wide range of visual and spatial tools. Res: Study of environmental format; photographic study of visual evidence of human response to physical factors such as space, shape and light levels. Publ: Auth, Industrial design, the alumni show, Kresge Art Ctr Bull, 4/75. Mailing Add: Dept of Art Mich State Univ East Lansing MI 48824

ALEXANDER, WILLIAM C
ART ADMINISTRATOR, CERAMIST
b Ada, Okla, Oct 18, 35. Study: Alfred Univ, MFA, 60 with Daniel Rhodes, Robert Turner, Val Cushing & Theodore Randall. Work: Gewerbemuseum, Winterthur, Switz; Kunstgewerbemuseum, Zurich, Switz; Roemermuseum, Augst, Switz; Prieto Mem Collection, Mills Col, Oakland, Calif. Teaching: Prof ceramics, Colo State Univ, 63-77. Pos: Res assoc, Roemermuseum, Augst, 70-71; dir, Sch of Art, Mont State Univ, 77- Mem: Am Crafts Coun (emer trustee); Nat Coun on Educ for Ceramic Arts (mem bd, 67-76, rules chmn, 72-75); World Crafts Coun (adv, NAm sect, 73-76); Nat Coun Art Adminrs. Style & Technique: Revival of Greco-Roman techniques in ceramics; primarily non-functional. Publ: Auth, Wood Firing, Nat Coun Educ for Ceramic Arts, 69 & Studio - Potter, Summer 74; Ceramic Toxicology, Nat Coun Educ for Ceramic Arts, 73, Studio Potter, Spring 74 & Wichita State Univ Ceramics Compendium, 76; A Pottery of the Middle Roman Imperial Period in Augst (monogr), Stiftung Pro Agusta Raurica, Basel, Switz, 75. Mailing Add: Sch of Art Mont State Univ Bozeman MT 59717

ALEXENBERG, MELVIN (MENAHEM)
EDUCATOR, PAINTER
b New York, NY, Feb 24, 37. Study: Queens Col, BS; Yeshiva Univ, MS; Art Students League, with Will Barnet; NY Univ, EdD. Work: Int Sci & Technol Collection, NY. Exhib: One-man show, Adelphi Univ, Oakdale, NY, 67. Teaching: Asst prof visual arts & educ, Adelphi Univ, Oakdale, NY, 65-69, sr lectr educ, Tel Aviv Univ, Israel; assoc prof art & sci, Bezalel Acad Arts & Design, Jerusalem, 70-71; sr lectr art, Haifa Univ, Israel, 70-72; assoc prof art & educ, Columbia Univ, 73-77; assoc prof, Bar Ilan Univ, Israel, 77- Awards: Blue Ribbon, Am Film Festival, 66; Founder's Day Award, NY Univ, 69. Mem: Int Soc for Educ through Art. Style & Technique: Paintings of cellular structures. Media: Encaustic. Res: Relationships between art and science; aesthetic components of creative processes; structural analysis of contemporary art forms. Publ: Auth, Light & Sight, 69; auth, Toward an Integral Structure through Science & Art, 74; auth, Art Teachers as Designers of Alternative Environments for Learning, 75; auth, A Semiotic Taxonomy of Contemporary Art Forms, 75; auth, Aesthetic Creation in Art & Science, 78. Mailing Add: 1015/4 Yeroham Israel

ALF, MARTHA JOANNE
PAINTER, WRITER
b Berkeley, Calif, Aug 13, 30. Study: San Diego State Univ, BA(psychol), MA(painting), 63, with Everett Gee Jackson; Univ Calif, Los Angeles, MFA(pictorial arts), 70, with James Weeks, William Brice & Richard Diebenkorn. Work: Greenville Co Mus Art, SC; Fine Arts Gallery San Diego; Newport Harbor Art Mus, Newport Beach, Calif. Exhib: Three-person show, Fine Arts Gallery of San Diego, 71; Invisible/Visible, Long Beach Mus Art, 72; 8 x 8 plus 4 x 4, 12 Regional Artists, Newport Harbor Art Mus, 75; Whitney Biennial of Contemporary American Art, Whitney Mus Am Art, New York, 75; Current Concerns, Part II, Los Angeles Inst Contemp Art, 75. Teaching: Instr drawing & painting, Los Angeles Harbor Col, Wilmington, Calif, 71-75; instr, Current Art in Los Angeles, Univ Calif Exten, Los Angeles, 71- Pos: Guest cur, Painting: Color Form & Surface (17 Los Angeles Painters), Lang Art Gallery, Scripps Col, Claremont, Calif; sole juror, 15th Ann Show, Palos Verdes Art Mus, Calif, 75. Awards: First Prize, Southern Calif Expos, Del Mar, 67; Second Prize Art Guild Exhib, Fine Arts Gallery San Diego, 67 & 70. Bibliog: Naomi Baker (auth), One man show traces development of artist, San Diego Eve Tribune, 2/20/70; Elaine Lubell (auth), Solo show: Green Mountain Gallery, New York, Arts Mag, 12/73; Melinda Wortz (auth), 8 x 8 plus 4 x 4 at Newport Harbor, Artweek, 6/16/73. Mem: Art Guild of Fine Arts Gallery San Diego (rec secy, 67-68); Los Angeles Inst Contemp Art. Style & Technique: Pencil or oil paint; to record experience of form and color under natural light; romantic realist. Media: Oil Paint on Canvas & Pencil on Paper. Publ: Auth, My interest in women artists of the past, Womanspace J, Vol 1, No 2; auth catalog introd, Painting: Color, Form & Surface, 74; auth, Llyn Foulkes' Portraits, Vol 5, No 18, auth, The Romanticism of Peter Alexander, Vol 5, No 40 & auth, Robert Motherwell in California Collections, Vol 5, No 44, Artweek. Mailing Add: c/o Jack Glenn 260 Newport Ctr Dr Newport Beach CA 92660

ALFORD, GLORIA K
SCULPTOR, PRINTMAKER
b Chicago, Ill, Oct 3, 38. Study: Univ Calif, Berkeley, AB; Art Inst Chicago; Penland Sch Crafts, NC; Columbia Univ; Pratt Graphics Ctr. Work: Elvejem Art Ctr, Univ Wis-Madison; CUNA Art Collection, Madison, Wis. Exhib: Environ-Vision, Nat Competitive Exhib, Everson Mus, Syracuse & NY Cult Ctr, New York, 72; New Talent Show, Gimpel & Weitzenhoffer, New York, 73; In Her Own Image, Philadelphia Mus Art, 74; 19th Ann Print Exhib, Brooklyn Mus, 74; Wis Directions, Milwaukee Art Ctr, 75. Awards: Top Honors, Univ Wis Art Show, Richland Ctr, 72. Style & Technique: Photographic screen printing on fabric combined with low relief sculpture of fabric and surrounding or covering plastic, which is printed on and vacuum formed; life-size sculpture constructed from electronic circuit boards and tied together with copper wire. Dealer: Gimpel & Weitzenhoffer 1041 Madison Ave New York NY 10021. Mailing Add: 435 Meder St Santa Cruz CA 95060

ALHILALI, NEDA
MULTIMEDIA ARTIST, SCULPTOR
b Cheb, Czech, Nov 26, 38. Study: St Martin's Sch of Art, London, Eng; Kunst Akademie, Munich, WGer; Univ of Calif, Los Angeles, BA, 65, MA, 68. Work: Queen Elizabeth II Arts Coun of NZ, New Plymouth; Crocker Art Mus, Sacramento, Calif; Albright Col, Pa; Cypress Col, Calif; Bonaventure Hotel, Los Angeles, Calif. Comn: Tapestry, Albright-Knox Corp, Buffalo, NY, 73 & Fluor Corp, Irvine, Calif, 76; paper structure, Security Pac Bank, Los Angeles, 77; painting, Blue Cross Hq, Los Angeles, 77; paper structures, Hyatt Regency, Chicago, 77. Exhib: Fifth Tapestry Biennale, Lausanne, Switz, 71; Sculpture in Fiber, Mus of Contemp Crafts, New York, 72; Crocker Art Gallery, Sacramento & Fine Arts Gallery of San Deigo, 73; Three-Dimensional Fiber, Govett-Brewster Art Gallery, New Plymouth, NZ & traveling throughout Australia, 74; Fairtree Gallery, New York, 74; Three Sculptors, Riverside Art Ctr & Mus, Calif, 74; Mus of Contemp Art, Chicago, Pac Design Ctr, Los Angeles & Mus of Sci & Indust, Los Angeles, 76; Fiberworks, Cleveland Mus of Art, Ohio, 77; The Americas & Japan—Fiberworks, Nat Mus Mod Art, Tokyo & Kyoto, Japan, 77; one-woman shows, Allrich Gallery, San Francisco & Vanguard Gallery, Los Angeles, 77. Collections Arranged: Fiberworks (cur; auth, catalogue), Lang Art Gallery, Scripps Col, Claremont, Calif, 73; Inaugural Exhib (cur), Mano Gallery, Chicago, 76; Paper Art (cur; co-auth, catalogue), Galleries of the Claremont Cols, 77. Teaching: Asst prof fiber arts, Univ Calif, Los Angeles, 70-77; from asst prof to assoc prof fiber arts, Scripps Col & Claremont Grad Sch, 71- Awards: First Prize & Award of Excellence, Southwest Craftsmen, Dallas Mus of Fine Arts, Tex, 68; First Prize & Award of Excellence, Pac Dimensions, Crocker Art Gallery, 69; Nat Endowment for the Arts grant, 74. Bibliog: Barry Brennan (auth), Character in art..., Eve Outlook, 11/75; Bernard Kester (auth), Paper constructions of Neda Alhilali, Craft Horizons, 2/76; Louisa Kolla (auth), Beach Occurrence of Tongues, pvt publ, 77. Mem: Los Angeles Inst of Contemp Art; Artists Equity Asn; Calif Design; Am Crafts Coun; World Crafts Coun. Style & Technique: Accretive structuring of modular materials; transformation through variety of processes. Media: Mixed Media with Paper and Fabrics. Res: Historic textiles. Dealer: Vanguard Gallery 1317 W Seventh St Los Angeles CA 90017; Allrich Gallery Two Embarcadero Ctr San Francisco CA 94111. Mailing Add: 4727 W Washington Blvd Los Angeles CA 90016

ALICEA, JOSE
PRINTMAKER
b Ponce, PR, Jan 12, 28. Study: Acad Pov, Ponce; Inst PR Cult, with Lorenzo Homar. Work: Philadelphia Mus Art; Mus Mod Art, New York; Libr of Cong, Washington, DC; Boston Pub Libr; Mus Arte Ponce. Comn: Woodcut mural, Inst PR Cult for Guayanilla High Sch, 70. Exhib: 1st Muestra Int Grabado, Barcelona, Spain, 69; 9th & 10th Festival Arte de Cali, Colombia, 69-70; 3rd Int Graphic Biennial, Cracow; 1st & 2nd Biennial Latinamericana Grabado de San Juan, PR, 70-72; 3rd Biennial Int Della Grafica, Florence, Italy, 72; 4th Int Exhib of Drawings, Yugoslavia; 10th & 11th Biennalle Int d'Art, Menton, France; 12th Bienal de Sao Paulo, Brazil; 2nd & 3rd Bienal Int de Grafica, Frechen, Ger. Teaching: Instr printmaking, Escuela Artes Plasticas, San Juan, 67- Pos: Asst to dir, Inst PR Cult Workshop,

58-62, instr, currently; art dir, Revista del Cafe, Ponce. Awards: Prize for Graphic, Ateneo Puertorriqueno, 65; Mildred Boerike Prize, Print Club Philadelphia, 67; Travel Grant, Casa Del Arte, San Juan, 68. Bibliog: E Ruiz de la Mata (auth), The art of Jose R Alicea, San Juan Rev Mag, 7/66 & Graphics by Alicea, San Juan Star, 8/9/70; Gloria Borras (auth), El grabado en la vida de Jose R Alicea, El Mundo, 69. Style & Technique: Woodcut, silkscreen and intaglio. Publ: Illusr, Trovas larenas, 68; auth, Rio grande de Loiza (portfolio of prints), 68; auth, Cancion de Baquine (portfolio of prints), 70; illusr, En las manos del pueblo, 72; illusr, Calambrenas. Dealer: Galeria Coabey Box 1744 San Juan PR 00903. Mailing Add: 911 Campo Rico Ave C Club Rio Piedras San Juan PR 00924

ALIKI (ALIKI BRANDENBERG)
ILLUSTRATOR, WRITER
b Philadelphia, Pa. Study: Philadelphia Mus Col Art, grad. Work: Kerlan Collection, Walter Libr, Univ Minn, Minneapolis; de Grummond Collection, Univ Southern Miss, Hattiesburg; Seattle Pub Libr, Wash; Falvey Mem Libr, Villanova Univ, Pa; Free Libr, Philadelphia. Exhib: Children's Bk Coun Showcase Exhib; Biennale of Illus, Bratislava, Czech, 75; Soc Illusr Exhib, New York, NY; Am Inst Graphic Arts Bk Exhib. Awards: Boys Club of Am Jr Bk Award, 68; First Prize of NY Acad Science's Children's Bk Award, 76. Bibliog: Grace Hogarth (auth), Illustrators of Children's Books, Horn Bk Inc, 78. Media: Gouache, Crayon, Pen and Ink. Publ: Auth & illusr, My Visit to the Dinosaurs, 69, Corn is Maize, 76 & Wild & Wooly Mammoths, 77, Crowell Publ, New York; auth & illusr, Go Tell Aunt Rhody, Macmillan, 74; auth & illusr, At Mary Bloom's, Greenwillow, 76. Mailing Add: 17 Regent's Park Terr London NW 1 7ED England

ALINDER, JAMES GILBERT
PHOTOGRAPHER, MUSEUM DIRECTOR
b Glendale, Calif, Mar 31, 41. Study: Macalester Col, BA; Univ Minn; Univ NMex, MFA, 68. Work: Mus of Mod Art, New York; Bibliot Nat, Paris; Art Inst of Chicago; Int Mus of Photog, George Eastman House, Rochester, NY; Nat Gallery of Can, Ottawa. Exhib: Vision & Expression, Int Mus of Photog, George Eastman House, Rochester, 69; Be-Ing Without Clothes, Hayden Gallery, Mass Inst Technol, Cambridge, 70; The Wider View, 72 & 60's Continuum, 72, Int Mus of Photog, George Eastman House, Rochester; Light & Lens, Hudson River Mus, Yonkers, NY, 73; Photographs of Jim Alinder, The Once Gallery, New York, 74; 20th Century Photog, Pompidou Cult Ctr, Paris, 77; The Great West: Real/Ideal, Univ Colo Galleries, Boulder, 77. Collections Arranged: Wright Morris: Structures & Artifacts, Sheldon Mem Art Gallery, Lincoln, Nebr, 75; Crying for a Vision, 76 & Twelve Photographers: A Mid-America Contemporary Document, 78. Teaching: Assoc prof photog/photog hist, Univ Nebr, Lincoln, 68-77. Pos: Exec dir, Friends of Photog, Carmel, Calif, 77- Awards: Nat Endowment for the Arts fel, 73; Woods Found Fel, 74. Bibliog: Review, Artforum, Vol 12 (1975); N Geske (ed), Photographs, Univ Nebr Press, 77; J Enyeart (ed), Kansas Album, Kans Bankers Asn, 77. Mem: Soc for Photog Educ (ed of Exposure, 73-77; secy, 73-75; vchmn, 75-77; chmn, 77-). Media: Photography. Publ: Co-auth, Crying for a Vision, Morgan & Morgan, 76; auth, On the SPE, Afterimage, 77; auth, Twelve Photographers: A Contemporary Mid-America Document, Mid-Am Arts Alliance, 78; auth, Photographs of Wright Morris, Modern Photog, 78. Mailing Add: PO Box 239 Carmel CA 93921

ALLAN, WILLIAM GEORGE
PAINTER, EDUCATOR
b Everett, Wash, Mar 28, 36. Study: San Francisco Art Inst, BFA. Work: Santa Barbara Mus Art; San Francisco Mus Art; Univ Art Mus, Berkeley; RI Sch Design, Providence; Whitney Mus Am Art, New York. Exhib: Carnegie Int Exhib, Pittsburgh, 57; Continuing Surrealism, La Jolla Mus Art, Calif, 71; Whitney Painting Ann, New York, 72; 70th Am Exhib, Art Inst Chicago, 72; Indianapolis Mus Art Exhib, 72; Whitney Mus Am Art, New York, 73-74; Painting & Sculpture in Calif: The Mod Era, San Francisco Mus Mod Art, 76; Chicago Arts Club, 78. Teaching: Instr painting, Univ Calif, Davis, 65-67; instr painting, Univ Calif, Berkeley, 69; assoc prof art, Calif State Univ, Sacramento, 68- Media: Acrylic, Watercolor. Dealer: Hansen-Fuller Gallery 228 Grant Ave San Francisco CA 94108. Mailing Add: 327 Melrose Mill Valley CA 94941

ALLEN, CLARENCE CANNING
PAINTER
b Cleveland, Ga, Nov 29, 97. Study: Southeastern State Univ, with Dr Allen Berger & Ola Forbes; Art Student League, with George Bridgman & R P R Neilson; San Antonio Art Acad, Tex, with Jose Arpa', Xavier Gonzalez & Rolla Taylor; also with Molly Guion, Dimitri Romanovsky, Charles H Owens & Bettina Steinke. Work: Libr of Pres Truman, Eisenhower & Johnson; portraits: Sen Robert S Kerr, Heritage House, Oklahoma City; Will Rogers, Will Rogers Mem Hosp, Saranac Lake, NY; plus numerous pvt, hist & found collections. Comn: Early and Late Means of Disseminating News (murals), Newspaper Printing Corp, 53; Press Media Symbology, Tulsa Press Club, Okla, 57; Creek Tribe Council Tree (portraits), Tulsa City Hall, 69. Exhib: Giornate Mediche Int, Verona, Italy, 63; La Caricature de Par le Monde, Troisieme Salon Int, Palace Victoria, Montreal, 67; Witte Mus, San Antonio; Philbrook Mus, Tulsa; Lever House, NY. Teaching: Instr graphic art, Cent High Sch, San Antonio, Tex, 24-27; instr fine art & oil painting, Tulsa. Pos: Artist, Los Angeles Times/Mirror, 27; artist, art dir, ed & cartoonist, Tulsa World & Tulsa Tribune, 29-68. Awards: Five nat awards, Freedoms Found, 53, 55, 56, 58, 61 & top nat award, 54. Bibliog: John Chase (auth), Today's cartoon, Hauser Press, New Orleans, 62. Mem: Am Artists Prof League; Nat Soc Mural Painters; Soc Illus; Asn Am Ed Cartoonists; Nat Cartoonists Soc. Style & Technique: Representational, impressionist, soft approach. Media: Oil. Publ: Auth, Sketching, 32; Biographical sketches of prominent Tulsans, 49; Originality, 50; Are you fed up with modern art?, 52; also articles in numerous nat & regional mag. Mailing Add: 1645 E 17th Pl Tulsa OK 74120

ALLEN, CONSTANCE OLLEEN WEBB
PAINTER, JEWELRY DESIGNER
b Camphill, Ala, June 10, 23. Study: George Washington Univ; Inst Allende, San Miguel de Allende, Mex; also with Richard Goetz, Oklahoma City. Comn: 20 Indian Portraits, A C Leftwich, Duncan, Okla, 72. Exhib: Int Art Show, Lawton, Okla, 71; Nat Miniature Art Show, Garden State Plaza, Paramus, NJ, 72; 1st Ann Western Art Roundup-Women Artists Am West, Riverside, Calif, 73; 39th & 41st Ann Miniature Painters, Sculptors & Gravers Soc of Washington, DC, Art Club of Washington, 72 & 74. Teaching: Instr drawing & painting, Univ Sci & Arts of Okla, Chickasha, 74- Awards: First Place for Portrait, Madill Art Festival, Okla, 69; Award of Merit, Lawton-Ft Sill Art Coun, 70; First Place for Pastel, Chickasha Art Guild, Okla, 73. Bibliog: Dick Stoll (auth), Three artists for B Webb Family, 66, A C Leftwich (auth), Indian Hall of Fame, painted by Mrs Webb, 72 & Mrs N H Welch (auth), Mrs Webb has exhibit, 74, Chickasha Daily Express. Mem: Okla Watercolor Asn. Style & Technique: Portraits sketched and painted in pastels, crayons, ink and pencil; jewelry; gold and silver with hand-polished gemstones; landscapes and portraits, pure watercolor; miniatures, watercolor and graphics. Mailing Add: 2009 Carolina Ave Chickasha OK 73018

ALLEN, (HARVEY) HAROLD
PHOTOGRAPHER, ART HISTORIAN
b Portland, Ore, June 29, 12. Study: Art Inst Chicago, 37-41; Univ Chicago, 48-54. Work: Art Inst Chicago; Metrop Mus Art; Chicago Hist Soc; Libr of Cong. Exhib: Photographer's Choice, Ind Univ, Bloomington, 59; Photography in the Fine Arts II, nationally, 60-; Light 7, Mass Inst Technol, 68; New Ground-14 Chicago Photographers, Exchange Nat Bank, Chicago, 72; Chicago Fac, Columbia Col, Chicago, 75; plus others. Teaching: Instr photog, Art Inst Chicago, 48-60 & 66-; instr beginning & documentary photog, Columbia Col, Chicago, 71-72. Awards: Frederick Latimer Wells Professorship, Art Inst Chicago, 71. Mem: Soc Photog Educ. Res: Egyptian Revival art and architecture in Europe and America. Publ: Auth & illusr, Egyptian influences in Wedgwood designs, Seventh Wedwood Int Sem, 62; auth & illusr, Father Ravalli's Missions, The Good Lion, Art Inst Chicago, 72. Mailing Add: 1725 S Desplaines St Chicago IL 60616

ALLEN, JANE ADDAMS
ART EDITOR, ART CRITIC
b Chicago, Ill. Study: Univ Chicago, with Joshua Taylor and Harold Rosenberg, BA & MFA; San Francisco Sch Fine Arts, with Richard Diebenkorn. Collections Arranged: Chicago Like It Is and Was, Centennial Photog Exhib, Chicago State Univ, Chicago Civic Ctr, 69. Pos: Art & photog critic, Chicago Tribune, 71-73; ed, New Art Examiner, 73- Awards: Critics Fel, Nat Endowment for Arts, 75. Bibliog: Joseph Haas (auth), Chicago like it is and was, Panorama, Chicago Daily News, 10/5/69; Sharon Kuzmicz (auth), The new art examiner, Chicago Jour Rev, 11/74. Mem: Chicago New Art Asn (pres, 70-); Col Art Asn; Chicago Artists Coalition. Res: Influence of social, economic, political factors on developing forms in 20th century art. Publ: Auth, Braque, Chicago Tribune Mag, 10/8/72; co-auth, Chicago regionalism, Studio Int, 12/73; auth, Rediscovering Olmsted, Hyde Parker Mag, 12/74. Mailing Add: c/o Chicago New Art Asn 230 E Ohio St Rm 207 Chicago IL 60611

ALLEN, JERE HARDY
PAINTER, EDUCATOR
b Selma, Ala, Aug 15, 44. Study: Ringling Sch Art, Sarasota, Fla, four yr cert, 69, BFA, 70; Univ Tenn, Knoxville, MFA, 72. Work: The Pathenon, Nashville; Mobile Art Gallery, Ala; Liberty Corp, Greenville, SC. Exhib: The 36th Ann Exhib of Contemp Am Painting, Palm Beach, Fla, 74; Mainstreams 76, Marietta, Ohio, 76; 46th Ann, Springfield Art Mus, Mo, 76; NDak Nat, Grand Forks, 77; one-artist show, S/R Gallery, Beverly Hills, Calif, 77. Teaching: Instr drawing, Carson-Newman Col, 71-72; instr painting, Univ Miss, 72- Awards: Tenn Art League Purchase Award, The Pathenon, 74; Award of Distinction, Mainstreams of Marietta Col, 75; Award, Shreveport Nat, Barnwell Art Ctr, La, 75. Mem: Col Art Asn Am. Style & Technique: Figures in oil and mixed media. Media: Oil, Collage. Mailing Add: 1103 S 14th St Oxford MS 38655

ALLEN, LORETTA B
PAINTER, DESIGNER
b Caney, Kans. Study: Fed Arts Schs, Minneapolis; Famous Artists Sch; also with Grace Chadwick, Oklahoma City, Molly Guion & Dimitri Romanofsky, New York. Exhib: Oklahoma City Art Ctr; Tulsa Studio Group, 61 & 62; Osage Co Hist Mus, 69; plus others. Pos: Illusr, children's bks; fashion designer; fashion illusr, local publ. Mem: Am Artists Prof League. Style & Technique: Realistic with abandon, dramatizing the spirit of ballet. Media: Pen & Ink; Pastel, Acrylic. Mailing Add: 1645 E 17th Pl Tulsa OK 74120

ALLEN, MARGARET PROSSER
PAINTER, EDUCATOR
b Vancouver, BC, Jan 26, 13; US citizen. Study: Univ Wash, BA & MFA; also with Alexander Archipenko & Amadee Ozenfant. Work: Pastel, Del Art Mus; mixed media print & carbon pencil drawing, Univ Del Permanent Collection. Exhib: Six exhibs, Northwest Ann, 38-48; over ten exhibs, Del Ann, 42-64; Weyhe Gallery, New York, 47; The Carvings of Sanchi, photog exhib circulated by Smithsonian Inst, 68-72; Univ Del Fac Group Show, Del Art Mus, 72; plus regional & group shows, 65-75. Teaching: Instr design, Univ Del, 42-48, asst prof design, 49-72, assoc prof design, 72- Awards: Hon mention, Wilmington Soc Fine Arts, 47 & First Prize, 49; Popular Prize (one of five), Northwest Ann, 48; Grant, Univ Del, 68. Mailing Add: 119 Briar Lane Newark DE 19711

ALLEN, MARGO (MRS HARRY SHAW)
SCULPTOR, PAINTER
b Lincoln, Mass. Study: Boston Mus Sch Fine Arts; Naum Los Sch Anat, Rome; Venturini Sch Encaustic Painting, Rome; marble carving at Gelli Studio, Querceta, Italy. Work: Dallas Mus Fine Arts, Tex; Mus Mod Art, Mexico City; Calif Palace Legion of Honor, San Francisco; Butler Inst Am Art, Youngstown, Ohio. Columbia Mus of Fine Arts, SC. Comn: 34 terra-cotta reliefs, First Nat Bank, Lafayette, La; bronze eagle, New Iberia Bank, La; USS Constitution (bronze Mem plaque), US Navy; garden fountains, Tex, Mass, Bermuda & others; many portrait commissions in bronze. Exhib: Nat Acad Design, New York; Pa Acad Fine Arts, Philadelphia; Boston Mus Fine Arts; New York Archit League; Addison Gallery Am Art, Andover, Mass. Mem: Nat Sculpture Soc; Nat League Am Pen Women; Ringling Mus; New Eng Asn Contemp Sculpture; Sarasota Art Asn, Fla. Media: Bronze, Terra-Cotta. Mailing Add: 501 Sloop Lane Longboat Key FL 33548

ALLEN, PATRICIA (PATRICIA ALLEN BOTT)
PAINTER, ART CRITIC
b Old Lyme, Conn. Study: With George Burr & Malcolm Fraser; Art Student League, with Ivan Olinsky & Harry Sternberg. Work: Greenville Mus Art, SC; Hickory Mus Art, NC; Bronx Zoo Galleries, New York; Riveredge Found, Calgary; EAfrican Wildlife Soc, Nairobi, Africa. Exhib: Soc Animal Artists Travel & Ann Shows, New York, 55-; Grand Cent Art Galleries, New York, 65-; EAfrican Wildlife Galleries, Nairobi, 71-72; one-man shows, Mex, Burr Galleries, New York, 55 & African Wildlife, Hilton Galleries, Nairobi, 70. Pos: Dir, Burr Galleries, New Yôrk, 50-61; secy & sales, Salmagundi Club, 62-66, in charge sales, Grand Cent Art Galleries, New York, 66-77. Awards: Medal, Fla Fedn Arts, 44; best in show medal, 69 & medal, 70, Gotham Painters. Bibliog: Articles, In: The Standard, 71 & Christian Sci Monitor, 71. Mem: Nat Arts Club; Soc Animal Artists (founder, secy & auth, Newslett, 59-); Am Artists Prof League; Nat Asn Women Artists; Salmagundi Club. Style & Technique: Impressionist, specializing in wildlife. Media: Oil, Watercolor. Publ: Contribr, reviews of art shows, In: The Host, 56-, The Villager, 56-70 & The Pendulum, 59- Dealer: Adler Gallery of Fine Arts 20 E 67th St New York NY 10021. Mailing Add: 151 Carroll St Bronx NY 10464

ALLEN, RALPH
PAINTER, EDUCATOR
b Eng, 1926. Study: Sir John Cass Sch Art & Slade Sch Fine Arts, London. Work: Nat Gallery Can; Art Gallery Toronto; Queen's Univ, Ont; Queen's Park, Toronto; also in pvt collections. Exhib: Montreal, 60; Kingston, 60 & 67; Ottawa, 64; Toronto, 68. Teaching: Lect on Daniel Fowler, Kingston, Ont & Nat Gallery Can, Ottawa, 65; past assoc prof art hist & past dir,

Agnes Etherington Art Ctr, Queen's Univ, Ont. Awards: Jessie Dow Award, Montreal, 59; Can Coun Scholar, 59 & Sr Fel, 68; Baxter Award, Toronto, 60. Mem: Ont Soc Artists; Royal Can Acad Arts. Publ: Auth, Catalogue Permanent Collection of Paintings, Drawings & Sculpture, Agnes Etherington Art Ctr, 68. Mailing Add: 199 Albert St Kingston ON K7L 3V4 Can

ALLEN, ROBERTA
CONCEPTUAL ARTIST
b New York, NY, Oct 6, 45. Work: Mus of Mod Art, New York; Worchester Art Mus, Mass. Exhib: Solo exhibs, John Weber Gallery, New York, 74, 75 & 77 & Galerie Maier-Hahn, Düsseldorf, Ger, 77; Contemp Abstract Art: Works on Paper, Baltimore Mus of Art, 76; New Work/New York, Calif State Univ, Los Angeles, 76; Abstract Drawings, Albright-Knox Art Gallery, Buffalo, NY, 76; Prints in Series: Idea into Image, Brooklyn Mus, NY, 77. Bibliog: Jeff Deitch (auth), Roberta Allen, Arts Mag, 6/77. Media: Drawing; photoworks. Publ: Auth, Partially Trapped Lines, Parasol Press, 75; auth, Pointless Arrows, pvt publ, 76; auth, Pointless Acts, The Collation Ctr, 77; auth, Possibilities, John Weber Gallery & Parasol Press, 77. Mailing Add: c/o John Weber Gallery 420 W Broadway New York NY 10012

ALLEN, TOM, JR
SCULPTOR, DESIGNER
b Havana, Cuba, Jan 23, 27; US citizen. Study: Univ Havana, cert archit; Univ Madrid, cert lit; Royal Acad Fine Arts San Fernando, Spain; Corcoran Sch Art; George Washington Univ, AA. Work: Am Numismatic Soc, New York; Carnegie Mus Natural Hist, Pittsburgh; Metrop Mus Art, New York; Muzeum Sztuki Medalierkiej, Crakow, Poland; World Heritage Mus, Champaign, Ill. Comn: Heroic frieze, Poor Richard Club, Philadelphia, 52; statuary, John Wanamaker, Inc, Philadelphia, 53-55; insignia & medal, Dept Recreation, City Philadelphia, 58; monument, Zool Garden Philadelphia, 74; plus many busts of numerous personalities. Exhib: Metrop State Art Contest, Smithsonian Inst, 51; Nat Sculpture Soc Ann Exhib, 57 & 72; Fidem Int Exhib; Cologne, Ger, 58; artists Equity Exhib, Philadelphia Mus Art, Philadelphia Civic Ctr, 71 & 74; one-man show, Rutgers Univ, 72; Ten Crucial Days, NJ State Mus, Trenton, 76-77. Teaching: Instr art, 20th Army Air Force, Guam, 46; instr arts & crafts, Moyamensing Prison, Philadelphia, 58-59; artisan-instr sculpture, Johnson Atelier, Princeton, 74- Pos: Scenic designer, Valley Forge Music Fair, Pa, 55; art dir, Burroughs Corp, Philadelphia, 56-57; dir advert & promotion, Johnson & Johnson Int, New Brunswick, NJ, 59-62. Awards: First Prize Drawing, Buenos Aires Herald, Arg, 39; Winner Nat Open Competition, Soc Medalists, 70. Mem: Co of Mil Historians; Artists Equity Asn (Philadelphia chap). Style & Technique: Abstract & realistic; murals, sculpture; tutto tondo, bas-relief, intaglio. Media: Forged Stainless Steel; Cast Bas-Relief. Publ: Auth & contribr, numerous How To articles. Mailing Add: RD 3 Box 367 Somerset NJ 08873 Princeton NJ Rd 3 Box 367 Somerset NJ 08873

ALLGOOD, CHARLES HENRY
ART HISTORIAN, PAINTER
b Augusta, Ga, Apr 24, 23. Study: Univ Ga, with Lamar Dodd, Carl Holty, Yasuo Kunyoshi, BFA, MFA; Ecole du Louvre, Paris. Exhib: Painting of the Year, Atlanta, Ga, 63 & 65; Southeastern Art Exhib, Atlanta, 65; Miss Nat Exhib, Jackson, 66; Mid-South Exhib, Memphis, Tenn, 71. Collections Arranged: African Art & Artifacts, 74; Egyptian Art & Artifacts, 75. Teaching: Prof painting, Judson Col, Marion, Ala, 51-55; prof painting, Memphis State Univ, 55- Pos: Dir, E H Little Gallery, Memphis State Univ. Style & Technique: Impressionist. Media: Oil, Transparent Watercolor. Mailing Add: 3886 Healy Rd Memphis TN 38111

ALLING, CLARENCE (EDGAR)
MUSEUM DIRECTOR, CERAMIST
b Dawson Co, Nebr, Jan 28, 33. Study: Washburn Univ, BFA; Ohio State Univ, with Edgar Littlefield; Univ Kans, MFA, with Sheldon Carey. Work: Excelsior Ins Co, New York. Exhib: One-man shows, Mulvane Art Ctr, Topeka, Kans, 63 & Sioux City Art Ctr, Iowa, 63; Area Artists, Sioux City, 63 & 65 & Des Moines, Iowa, 64; two-man show, L'Atelier, Cedar Falls, Iowa, 65; plus others. Pos: Dir, Waterloo Munic Galleries, currently. Awards: Prizes, Designer-Craftsman Show, Lawrence, Kans, 59-61; Purchase award, Ceramic Nat, Everson Mus, Syracuse, NY, 60; Merit award, Sioux City, 65. Mailing Add: c/o Waterloo Munic Galleries 225 Cedar St Waterloo IA 50704

ALLMAN, MARGO
SCULPTOR, PRINTMAKER
b New York, NY, Feb 23, 33. Study: Smith Col; Moore Col Art; Univ Pa; Univ Del; with Reginald Marsh & Hans Hofmann. Work: Del Art Mus, Wilmington; Philadelphia Mus Art. Comn: Travertine sculpture, comn by Mrs Werner Hutz & Family, Kennett Square, Pa, 73, corten steel sculpture, Richard Vanderbilt, Chadds Ford, Pa, 74 & ferro-cement sculpture, Tidewater Publ Co, Centerville, Md, 75. Exhib: Philadelphia Artists Who Have Received Prizes in Recent Years, Philadelphia Mus Art, 62; Philadelphia Women in the Fine Arts, Moore Col Art, ann, 62-68; Nat Biennial, Nat League Am Pen Women, Salt Lake City, 70 & Washington, DC, 72; Margo Allman-Sculptor, Printmaker, Windham Col, Putney, Vt, 73; 7 Delaware Area Sculptors, Univ Del, 75; one-person shows, Haas Gallery of Art, Bloomsburg State Col, Pa, 76 & 77. Pos: Artist mem, Prints in Progress, Philadelphia, 64-66. Awards: Mildred Boericke Prize, 32nd Ann Nat Exhib Woodcuts & Wood Engravings, Print Club Philadelphia, 58; Drawing Prize, 51st Ann Show, Del Art Mus, 65; Best Landscape Painted by Delaware Artist, Wilmington Trust Bank Prize, Del Art Mus, 69. Mem: Del Art Mus; Am Craft Coun; Moore Col Art Alumnae Asn; Print Club, Philadelphia (bd mem, 61-63); Nat League Am Pen Women (art chmn, Diamond State Br, 69-71). Style & Technique: Organic, semi-abstract wood, marble and ferro-cement sculpture; two dimensional related forms in acrylic painting and woodcuts. Media: Wood & Stone; Acrylic Paint-Woodcuts. Publ: Illusr, David Hudson, Glove of Merci (poems), 56 & Adam (poems), 60; illusr, Delaware Engagement Calendar, 69. Mailing Add: RD 1 Box 45B West Grove PA 19390

ALLNER, WALTER H
PAINTER, DESIGNER
b Dessau, Ger, Jan 2, 09; US citizen. Study: Bauhaus-Dessau, with J Albers, V Kandinsky, Paul Klee. Exhib: Mus des Arts Decoratifs, Lausanne, Switz, 74; Expo 74 Spokane World's Fair, Wash, 74; Kunstgewerbemuseum, Zurich, Switz, 74; Castello Sforzesco, Milan, Italy, 74; Galerie Estel, Tokyo, Japan, 74-75; plus others. Pos: Design consult, Johnson & Johnson, New Brunswick, NJ, 54-55; art dir, Fortune Mag, 63-74; design consult, RCA, 65-67; mem hon comt, 5th Int Poster Biennial, Warsaw, Poland, 74. Mem: Alliance Graphique Int (pres US Section, 72-74, int pres, 74-); Nat Endowment Arts. Mailing Add: 110 Riverside Dr New York NY 10024

ALLOWAY, LAWRENCE
EDUCATOR, ART CRITIC
b London, Eng, Sept 17, 26. Collections Arranged: For Solomon R Guggenheim Mus—Morris Louis-Memorial Exhibition, 63, Francis Bacon, 63; Guggenheim International Award Exhibition, 63; William Baziotes-Memorial Exhibition, 65; Barnett Newman: the Stations of the Cross, 66; Jean Dubuffet, 66. Teaching: Instr, Bennington Col, Vt, 61-62; prof art, State Univ NY, Stony Brook, 68-, gallery dir, 77- Pos: Cur, Solomon R Guggenheim Mus, 62-66; art ed, The Nation, 68; assoc ed, Artforum, 72. Awards: Foreign Leader Grant, US State Dept, 68; award for distinction in art criticism, Frank Jewett Mather, 72. Res: 20th century American art and the cinema. Publ: Auth, The metallization of a dream, 64; The Venice Biennale 1895-1968, 68; Christo, 69; Violent America: the movies 1946-1964, 71; American Pop Art, 74. Mailing Add: 330 W 20th St New York NY 10011

ALLRICH, M LOUISE BARCO
ART DEALER
b Ft Monroe, Va, Feb 16, 47. Study: Univ Calif, Davis, BA, 68; Univ Calif, Berkeley, post-grad work art hist & theory. Collections Arranged: Selections from Calif Design, 76, James McManus, New Sculpture, 77, Contemp Japanese Tapestry, 77 & Int Directions in Fiber, 78, Calif State Univ, Fresno. Teaching: Lectr, Calif State Univ, San Francisco & Chico & Alta Col Art, Can; lectr, Am Inst Architects, San Francisco. Pos: Pres, Allrich Gallery, San Francisco, 71-; trustee, Fiberworks Ctr for Textile Arts, Berkeley, 72-; mem design awareness task force, Calif State Design Coun, 73. Mem: San Francisco Art Dealers Asn; Soc for the Encouragement of Contemp Art, Mus Mod Art, San Francisco, Calif. Specialty: Contemporary tapestry, painting and sculpture. Publ: Auth, Center for the Arts, pvt publ, 74; contribr, A look at fiber, Currant Mag, 76. Mailing Add: Two Embarcadero Ctr San Francisco CA 94111

ALLUMBAUGH, JAMES
SCULPTOR, EDUCATOR
b Dallas, Tex, Jan 27, 41. Study: ETex State Univ, BS & MS; NTex State Univ, EdD. Work: Richardson Pub Libr, Tex; Beaumont Art Mus, Tex; Houston Ctr 2, Tex; Tyler Art Mus, Tex. Exhib: Eight State Exhib, Okla Art Ctr, Oklahoma City, 67, 68, 70, 72 & 74; Guiding Hand, Ft Worth Art Mus, Tex, 68; Tex Painting & Sculpture, Dallas Mus of Fine Arts, 68 & 71; SW Fine Arts Biennial, Mus of NMex, Santa Fe, 70 & 74; Delta Art Exhib, Ark Art Ctr, Little Rock, 71, 75 & 77; Artists Biennial, New Orleans Mus of Art, La, 73; Int Print Exhib, Metrop Mus & Art Ctr, Miami, Fla, 75; Ariz Nat, Scottsdale Ctr for the Arts, 76 & 77. Teaching: Fel design, NTex State Univ, 66-68; assoc prof three-dimensional design, ETex State Univ, 68- Pos: Dir, Tex Col Sculpture Symposium, Dallas, 77- Bibliog: Dennis Kowal & Donna Meilach (auth), Sculpture Casting, Crown, 72; Jan Butterfield (auth), The Young Texans, Arts Mag, 72. Mem: Nat Art Educ Asn; Ft Worth Art Mus; Artists Equity (vpres, Dallas chap, 77). Style & Technique: Geometric abstraction. Media: Sculpture. Publ: Illusr (cover illus), 16th Ann Invitational Exhib, Longview Arts Ctr, 74 & 45th Ann Exhib, Springfield Art Mus, 75; auth, Cubes Space and Light, Spiral Enterprises, 77. Mailing Add: 2009 St Francis Dallas TX 75228

ALLWELL, STEPHEN S
SCULPTOR
b Baltimore, Md, Oct 15, 06. Study: Md Inst, Baltimore. Comn: Folksinger, Mrs Robert Lindner, Baltimore, 69; copier, Alan Elkin, Baltimore, 70; Lacrosse, James F Welsh, Baltimore, 71. Exhib: Four shows, Miniature Painters, Sculptors & Gravers Soc, Washington, DC, 67-71; Acad Arts, Easton, Md, 67 & 71; Mariner's Mus Marine Art Exhib, Newport News, Va, 69; Washington Co Mus, Hagerstown, Md, 69; Peale Mus, Baltimore, 70. Awards: Grand Prize Outdoor Exhib, Baltimore Outdoor Art Show, 67; Purchase Award, Metromedia-WCBM, 67; Reese E McLeod Prize Sculpture, Miniature Painters, Sculptors & Gravers Soc, Washington, DC, 69. Bibliog: L'art a l'etranger, La Rev Mod, 7/68. Mem: Artists Equity Asn; fel Md Fedn Art; Alumni Asn Md Inst; Baltimore Art Guild; Rehoboth Art League. Mailing Add: 803 Evesham Ave Baltimore MD 21212

ALMOND, PAUL
FILM MAKER
b Montreal, Can, Apr 26, 31. Study: Bishop's Col Sch, 44-48; McGill Univ; Balliol Col, Oxford, BA & MA. Awards: Liberty Award, Best Can TV Drama Director, 59; Special Award of Merit for Documentary Film, Prague, 63; Canadian Film Awards, Best Motion Picture Director, 70. Bibliog: Janet Edsforth (auth), The Flame Within (a study of Paul Almond's Films), Can Film Inst, 71. Mem: Royal Can Acad Art. Publ: Auth, The Hill (TV play); co-auth, The Broken Sky (TV play); auth, Isabel, Act of the Heart & Journey (films). Mailing Add: 1272 Redpath Crescent Montreal PQ Can

ALONZO, JACK J
ART DEALER, COLLECTOR
b Brooklyn, NY, July 3, 27. Study: Brooklyn Col; NY Univ. Pos: Dir/pres, Alonzo Gallery, 65- Specialty: Contemporary paintings, sculpture, graphics, drawings and others, predominately abstract. Collection: Catholic. Publ: Contribr, Arts Mag, 4/71. Mailing Add: c/o Alonzo Gallery 30 W 57th St New York NY 10019

ALPER, M VICTOR
EDUCATOR, WRITER
b Wilkes-Barre, Pa, Mar 23, 44. Study: Boston Univ, BA; NY Univ, MA & PhD; Harvard Univ. Collections Arranged: Research used as basis for exhibs, The American Character Revealed in Art, 75 & Landscape of the Imagination, 75, Montclair Art Mus-NJ Mus Am Art. Teaching: Instr humanities, NY Univ, 69-73; asst prof humanities, Montclair State Col, 73-77, coordr interdisciplinary lect series, 74-76; vis prof, City Univ New York, 76; guest lectr, Univ Mass. Pos: Lectr, Mus of City of New York, 70-71; contrib ed, Arts Mag, New York, 70-74; partic, Art Critics in Residence Prog, NY Univ, 72; partic, Int Conf on Subsidy of the Arts, New York Cult Ctr, spring 75; dir, Am Hist Photo Arch, New York, 75-77; consult, Newsweek, 75 & Marriott Corp, 77; auth weekly radio series, WGBH, Boston, 76; asst to exec vpres, Rutgers Univ, 77- Mem: Am Asn Univ Prof; Am Fedn Arts; NY State Eng Coun (monogr series ed bd); Nat Acad TV Arts & Sci (1970 Emmy nomination comt, acad coun, 77); Soc Am Historians. Res: Art and culture of the 18th & 19th centuries; interdisciplinary studies; also specialize in American art. Publ: Auth, America's Heritage Trail, 76 & America's Freedom Trail, 76, Macmillan; plus mus catalogues, articles & rev in jours & Mag. Mailing Add: 145 W 79th St Apt 11-C New York NY 10024

ALPERT, GEORGE
PHOTOGRAPHER, GALLERY DIRECTOR
b New York, NY, Apr 3, 22. Study: NY Univ; NC State Col; Stanford Univ; Univ Calif, Berkeley. Work: Il Diaframma, Milan, Italy; Miller-Plummer Collection, Philadelphia. Exhib: One-man shows, Neikrug Galleries, New York, 71, 73, 75 & 77, Everson Mus, Syracuse, NY, 73, Light Gallery, New York, 73, Cameraworks, Los Angeles, Calif, 74, Alfred Stieglitz

Gallery, New York, 74-77, Portogallo Galleries, New York, 74, 76 & 78, Il Diaframma, Milan, Italy, 75, Photographer's Eye, Philadelphia, 77 & Soho Photo Gallery, 78. Teaching: Mem fac creative photog, New Sch for Social Res, New York, 74- Pos: Dir, Soho Photo Galleries, New York, 70-; chmn & pres, Sohophoto Found. Specialty: Photography. Publ: Auth, The Queens, 75 & co-auth, Second Chance to Live: The Suicide Syndrome, 75, Da Capo Press. Mailing Add: 79 W 12th St New York NY 10011

ALPS, GLEN EARL
EDUCATOR, PRINTMAKER
b Loveland, Colo, June 20, 14. Study: Univ Northern Colo, BA; Univ Wash, MFA; Univ Iowa, advanced study with Mauricio Lasansky. Work: Mus Mod Art, New York; Philadelphia Art Mus; Chicago Art Inst; Los Angeles Co Mus Art, Calif; Libr Cong, Washington, DC. Comn: Sculptural panel, Seattle Pub Libr, 60; fountain, Munic Bldg, City of Seattle, 61; wall sculpture, Magnolia Br, Seattle Pub Libr, 64; ed of prints, Washington State Arts Comn, 71; bronze fountain, First Christian Church, Greeley, Colo, 72. Exhib: Twenty Outstanding Printmakers, Univ Ala, 73; 54 Prints by 15 West Coast Artists, Univ Calif, Riverside, 74; Soc Am Graphic Artists Nat Exhib, NY, 74; National Print Show, Cent Wash State Col, 75; Prints & Drawings from the West Coast, Univ Calgary, 75. Teaching: Prof printmaking, Univ Wash, 45-, chmn div, currently. Pos: Treas, Northwest Printmakers, 49-51, pres, 51-53 & 62-64. Awards: Tamarind Fel, Ford Found, 60 & artist-in-residence, 65; Gov Award, 72. Bibliog: Russell O Woody, Jr (auth), Polymer painting and related techniques, Van Nostrand Reinhold, 71; Jules Heller (auth), Printmaking today, Holt Reinhart & Winston, 72. Mem: Col Art Asn; Soc Am Graphic Artists; Am Fedn Arts. Style & Technique: Nonobjective, collagraph. Publ: Auth, The collagraph, 16mm color film. Dealer: Francine Seders Gallery 6701 Greenwood Ave N Seattle WA 98103. Mailing Add: 6523 40th Ave NE Seattle WA 98115

ALSDORF, JAMES W
PATRON, COLLECTOR
b Chicago, Ill, Aug 16, 13. Study: Wharton Sch Finance & Com, Univ Pa. Pos: Chmn, life gov, maj benefactor, mem exec comt & trustee, Art Inst Chicago, also chmn, comn Oriental art, comn primitive art, comn exhibs, vchmn, comn bldgs, comn Buckingham fund & acquisitions, mem comn 20th century paintings & sculpture & comn prints & drawings; mem nat comn, Univ Art Mus, Univ Calif, Berkeley; adv coun, Univ Art Gallery, Univ Notre Dame, Ind, Am Fedn Arts, Mus Contemp Art, Chicago & Field Mus, Chicago; benefactor, Art Asn Indianapolis, John Herron Art Gallery; pres, Alsdorf Found, Chicago, 49- Mem: Gov life mem Chicago Hist Soc; assoc Arch Am Art. Collection: Modern drawings, painting and sculpture; American nineteenth century Trompe l'oeil School; Early Americana and folk art, archaic and classical art. Mailing Add: 301 Woodley Rd Winnetka IL 60093

ALTABE, JOAN BERG
PAINTER, MURALIST
b New York, NY, Apr 27, 35. Study: Hunter Col, BA, 56; advan study of oils with Robert Motherwell, watercolor with William Baziotes, design with Richard Lippold & graphics with Gabor Peterdi. Work: Rassegna Int Arte Mod, Italy; Synagogue Art & Archit Libr of NY. Comn: Six stained glass windows commemorating Genesis, in Situ, Sephardic Synagogue, Long Beach, NY; new flag design, Smithsonian Inst Travelling Exhib, 76-78; Bicentennial mural triptych, Nat Soc Mural Painters Travelling Exhib, 76-78. Exhib: Guild for Relig Archit Exhib, Boston, 76; Mus Mod Art, New York, 76; Int Women's Art Festival, Ford Found, New York, 76; El Paso Mus, Austin, Tex, 76; Va Mus, Richmond, 77; Santa Barbara Mus, Calif, 77; Am Inst of Architects, New York, 77; Oakland Mus, Calif, 77. Bibliog: Articles in Fine Arts Discovery Mag, summer 70, Nassau Star, 2/22/73 & Newsday, 9/21/76. Mem: Artists Equity Asn; Nat Soc Mural Painters (treas, 75-). Style & Technique: Use element of dark and light for 3-D effect in paint; pattern and texture for a 2-D design in stained glass; line in book illustration. Media: Acrylic, Ink, Stained Glass. Publ: Contribr, Fine Arts Discovery Mag, 70; illustr, Translation of Becquer, Gustavo: la Ajorca de Oro, 72; illustr, Translation of Becquer: Las Rimas, 73; ed, National Drawing Anthology, 74; illusr, Leonardo, Int Art J, Autumn 1977. Mailing Add: 421 W Olive St Long Beach NY 11561

ALTERMANN, TONY
ART DEALER
b Dallas, Tex, Aug 10, 40. Study: NTex State Univ, BA & MS. Pos: Dir publicity & pub relations, MGM, Dallas, Tex, 71-73; vpres, Tex Art Gallery, Dallas, 73-78; owner & pres, Altermann Art Gallery, Dallas, Tex, 78- Specialty: Western, wildlife and Americana subjects in all media. Mailing Add: c/o Altermann Art Gallery 2504 Cedar Springs Dallas TX 75201

ALTMAN, HAROLD
PRINTMAKER, EDUCATOR
b New York, NY, Apr 20, 24. Study: Art Students League, 41-42; Cooper Union, 41-47; New Sch Social Res, 47-49; Acad Grande Chaumiere, Paris, 49-52; Black Mountain Col, NC. Work: Mus Mod Art, Metrop Mus Art & Whitney Mus Art, New York; Art Inst Chicago; Nat Gallery Art, Washington, DC; plus many others. Comn: Entire print ed, Mus Mod Art, 60, Soc Am Graphic Artists, 62, Hilton Rockefeller Hotel, 63 & Jewish Mus, NY, 64. Exhib: One-man shows, Martha Jackson Gallery, New York, 58, Art Inst Chicago, 60, San Francisco Mus Art, 61, Sagot Le Garrec Gallery, Paris, 68 & 74 & State Gallery Fine Arts, Istanbul, Turkey, 75; plus many others. Teaching: Asst prof art, NY State Col Ceramics, Alfred Univ, 52-54, Univ NC, Greensboro, 54-56 & Univ Wis-Milwaukee, 56-62; prof art, Pa State Univ, 62-76. Awards: Two Guggenheim Fels, 60-62; Nat Inst Arts & Lett Award, 63; Fulbright Hays Sr Res Fel, 64-65. Bibliog: Articles in New York Times, Los Angeles Times, Vie Des Arts, plus numerous others. Publ: Illusr, The Four Seasons, Pa State Univ, 65. Dealer: Assoc Am Artists 663 Fifth Ave New York NY 10022. Mailing Add: Box 57 Lemont PA 16851

ALTMANN, HENRY S
PAINTER, EDUCATOR
b Manhattan, NY, Dec 4, 46. Study: Pratt Inst, Brooklyn, BFA(art educ), 68; Queens Col, Flushing, NY, MFA(painting), 70; Fulbright fel painting, Fine Arts Acad, Munich, Ger. Work: First Nat Bank New York; Skowhegan Sch Painting & Sculpture, New York. Comn: Three stained glass windows & paintings for rear portal (with Maxine Ann Sorokin), Kehillath Jakob Synagogue, Newton, Mass, 73. Exhib: One-man shows, First St Gallery, New York & Meetinghouse Gallery, Boston, 73; two-person shows, Am Libr, Munich, Ger, 71, Austrian Inst, New York, 72 & Newton City Hall, Mass, 76; Young Realist Show, Harbor Gallery, Cold Spring Harbor, Long Island, NY, 72; plus many others. Teaching: Instr art, Boston Univ, 71-75; instr art, Art Inst Boston, 75- Pos: Exhib chmn, West Roxbury Art Asn, 77-; res comt arch, West Roxbury Hist Soc, 77- Mem: Boston Vis Artists Union (Fair Practic Comt, 73-77). Style & Technique: Figurative realist; landscapes and urban views. Media: Oil, Pastel. Dealer: Crieger Art Assoc 801 Water St Framingham MA 01701. Mailing Add: 61 Perham St West Roxbury MA 02132

ALTMAYER, JAY P
COLLECTOR
b Mobile, Ala, Mar 1, 15. Study: Tulane Univ La, BA & LLB. Pos: Mem, Fine Arts Comt, State Dept. Collection: American paintings mostly dealing with plantation life and workers; paintings by William Aiken Walker, Sully, Rembrandt Peale, Gilbert Stuart, Severn Rosen, Jarvis and others; large collection of precious metal and jewelled historical American presentation swords. Publ: Auth, American presentation swords. Mailing Add: 55 S McGregor St Mobile AL 36608

ALTSCHUL, ARTHUR G
COLLECTOR, PATRON
b New York, NY, Apr 6, 20. Pos: Trustee, Whitney Mus Am Art; fel in perpetuity, Metrop Mus Art; mem gov bd, Yale Art Gallery, New Haven, Conn. Collection: American impressionists and The Eight; cubists and lesser known members of the neo-impressionist, Nabis and Pont-Aven schools. Mailing Add: 55 Broad St New York NY 10004

ALTSCHULER, FRANZ
ILLUSTRATOR, EDUCATOR
b Mannheim, Ger, Oct 2, 23; US citizen. Study: Art Students League; Cooper Union, New York; Inst of Design, Chicago, BFA. Work: Art Inst of Chicago; Standard Oil Co, Chicago; Olivet Col, Mich; Greyhound Co, Phoenix, Ariz; Grant-Jacoby, Chicago. Comn: Design and illustration projects for 36 book publishers and 34 periodicals including 46 books designed or illustrated completely, 1954-78. Exhib: Art Inst of Chicago, 51-53 & 62; Soc of Typographic Arts, 52-77; Art Dir Club of New York, 54-60, 73 & 78; Denver Mus Ann, Colo, 55; Ringling Mus, Fla, 59; Soc of Illusr, 67-78; Ill State Mus, 69. Teaching: Instr drawing, Inst of Design, Chicago, 54-65; asst prof graphic design & illus, Art Inst of Chicago, 73-77 & Morehead State Univ, Ky, 78- Pos: Dir & vpres, Soc of Typographic Arts; secy, Friends of the Inst of Design; mem, 27 Chicago Designers, 58-; chmn planning comt, Urban Renewal, Old Town Triangle Asn, Chicago, 60-67. Awards: Pauline Palmer Prize, Chicago & Vicinity Show, Art Inst of Chicago, 53; Fourth Prize, Asahi Pentax World Photo Contest, Asahi Pentax, 70; First Prize, Watercolor Show, Artists Guild of Chicago, 76. Bibliog: Franz Altschuler/Work, article in Idea Mag, Japan, 75; John Volbrecht (auth), Franz Altschuler/Profile, Creative Communicator, 76. Mem: Arts Club of Chicago; Artists Guild of Chicago (var com); Am Inst of Graphic Arts, New York. Style & Technique: Drawings; watercolors; acrylic and oil painting; collage and constructions. Media: Drawing; Construction. Publ: Illusr, Human Evolution, 74 & Tales of Terror, 75, Rand McNally; illusr, Advise & Consent, The Franklin Libr, 76; illusr, Herbs Spices & Essential Oils, Sphere Mag, 77; illusr, Isabella Wooly Bear Tiger Moth, The Child's World, 78. Dealer: Tria Gallery Ellison Bay WI. Mailing Add: 225 McClure Circle Morehead KY 40351

ALTVATER, CATHERINE THARP
PAINTER
b Little Rock, Ark, July 26, 07. Study: Grand Cent Sch Contemp Arts & Crafts; Art League Long Island, with F Spradling & E Whitney; Nat Acad Fine Arts, with Mario Cooper, Ogden Pleissner, Louis Bouche & Robert Phillips. Work: Museums in US, Europe, Japan & Can; also many pvt collections. Exhib: Nat Acad Design; Nat Arts Club; Audubon Artists, Metrop Mus Fine Arts; Elliott Mus, Stuart, Fla; Reading Mus, Pa; Mus Fine Arts, Mexico City; Royal Soc Watercolor Painters, London. Teaching: Workshops and demonstrations throughout the US. Pos: Pres, Art League Long Island, secy, Hudson Valley Art Asn, treas (1st woman officer), Am Watercolor Soc & treas, Am Artists Prof League, all formerly; instr watercolor, Ark Art Ctr, Little Rock. Awards: Over 70 awards including 20 first prizes. Mem: Am Watercolor Soc; Nat Art League; Allied Artists Am. Style & Technique: Wet in wet technique in both watercolor and oils; impressionistic. Media: Watercolor. Mailing Add: Rte 2 Box 44 Scott AR 72142

ALTWERGER, LIBBY
PAINTER, GRAPHIC ARTIST
b Toronto, Ont, July 13, 21. Study: Ont Col Art. Exhib: Royal Can Acad, 60; Ont Soc Artists, 61; one-man shows, Pascall Gallery, Toronto, 64 & Sonneck Gallery, Kitchener, Ont, 68; Watercolor Nat Gallery, New York, 74. Teaching: Former instr drawing, Ryerson Polytech Inst. Pos: Can exchange artist with Am Watercolor Soc. Awards: Lt Gov Gen Medal, 59; Grand Prix Gold Medal, Int Feminine Culturelle, Vichy, France, 63; Sterling Trust Award for Lithograph, 65; plus others. Mem: Can Soc Graphic Artists; Ont Soc Artists; Can Soc Painters in Water Colour; Can Soc Painter-Etchers & Engravers. Media: Watercolor. Mailing Add: 526 Dovercourt Rd Toronto ON Can

AMAROTICO, JOSEPH ANTHONY
PAINTER, CONSERVATOR
b Bronx, NY, Sept 3, 31. Study: Am Art Sch, New York, with Raphael Soyer; Pa Acad Fine Arts, Philadelphia, with Franklin Watkins, Walter Stuempfig, Hobson Pittman & Theodor Siegl. Work: Pa Acad Fine Arts; George Washington Univ, Washington, DC; Glassboro Col, NJ; Washington, DC, District Court. Comn: Conserv of John Trumbull paintings in the Rotunda, US Capitol, Washington, DC. Exhib: Nat Exhib, Pa Acad Fine Arts, var times, 59-69; Nat Traveling Exhib, Am Fedn Arts, 64; 10th Mary Washington Exhib Mod Art, Fredricksburg, Va, 65; Art for Embassies, US Dept State, Jamaican Embassy, Kingston, 67; Ann Exhib, Butler Inst, Youngstown, Ohio, 69, 70 & 72. Teaching: Instr painting, Pa Acad Fine Arts, 66- Pos: Conservator paintings, Pa Acad Fine Arts, 68-77; tech adv & instr painting mat & techniques, Pa Acad Fine Arts, 77- Awards: Mary Butler Award, Pa Acad Fine Arts Fel Exhib, 62; Painting Prize, Cheltenham Art Ctr, Philadelphia, 68; Endowment Fund Prize, Woodmere Art Ctr, Chestnut Hill, Pa, 72. Mem: Fel Pa Acad Fine Arts (mem bd, 72-); Int Inst for Conserv Hist & Artistic Works. Media: Acrylic on Rag Board or Canvas. Dealer: Pearl Fox Galleries 103 Windsor Ave Philadelphia PA 19126; Mickelson Galleries 709 G St NW Washington DC 20001. Mailing Add: Box 239 Plumsteadville PA 18949

AMATEIS, EDMOND ROMULUS
SCULPTOR
b Rome, Italy, Feb 7, 97; US citizen. Study: Beaux-Arts Inst Design; Acad Julienne; Am Acad Rome, fel, 21-24. Work: Brookgreen Gardens, SC; Hall Am Artists, Columbia Univ. Comn: War Horses, Baltimore War Mem, 27; pediment & metopes, Buffalo Hist Soc, 28; large relief, Kansas City Liberty War Mem, 33; relief & spandrels, Labor & Interstate Com Comn Bldg, 35; Wall of Fame, Ga Warm Springs Found, 52, also numerous medals, garden figures & portraits. Exhib: Biennale Romana Int d'Arte, 23; Nat Acad Design; Philadelphia Mus Art; Philadelphia Acad Fine Arts; Metrop Mus Art. Teaching: Instr sculpture, Sch Am Sculpture, 27; instr sculpture, Columbia Univ, 28-32; instr sculpture, Bennett Sch, 38-40. Awards: Henry O Avery Prize, Archit League NY, 29; James E McClese Prize, Pa Acad Fine Arts, 33. Bibliog: Breving (auth), A sculptor with plastic vision, Int Studio, 26; Ernest Watson (auth), Edmond Amateis, Am Artist, 40; D DeLue (auth), Edmond Amateis, Nat Sculpture Rev, 67. Mem: Nat Acad Design; Nat Sculpture Soc (pres, 42-44); Nat Inst Arts & Lett. Media: Stone,

Bronze, Acrylic. Publ: Auth, A sculptor speaks his mind, Liturgical Arts, 43. Mailing Add: 1620 Fifth St Clermont FL 32711

AMAYA, MARIO ANTHONY
MUSEUM DIRECTOR, WRITER
b Brooklyn, NY, Oct 6, 33. Study: Brooklyn Col, BA(art hist); London Univ, exten courses at Nat Gallery Gt Brit. Exhibitions Organized: Obsessive Image, Inst Contemp Arts, London, 68, British Painting Here & Now for Brit Trade Coun traveling exhib to US, 69; The Sacred & Profane in Symbolist Art & Six Centuries of Treasures for Art Gallery of Ont, 69; Realisms for Montreal Mus Fine Arts & Art Gallery Ont, 70; Eduoard Vuillard for Art Gallery Ont, Calif Palace of Legion of Honor & Art Inst Chicago; French 17th & 18th Century Drawings in North American Collections with Pierre Rosenberg of the Louvre to Ottawa, Toronto, New York & San Francisco, 72; Man Ray Retrospective 1974, New York, London & Rome, with Roland Penrose; Bouguereau 1974, New York & San Francisco. Teaching: Vis prof Symbolism to Surrealism, State Univ NY Buffalo, 71-72; sem on The Exiles (artists who left Paris in '39). Pos: Art critic, London Financial Times, Apollo, Art in Am, London, 57-; Am ed, Connoisseur & Southern ed, Archit Digest; founding assoc ed, About the House, London, 62-68; founding ed, Art & Artists, London, 65-69; contrib ed, Art in Am; chief cur, Art Gallery Ont, 69-72; dir, New York Cult Ctr, 72-; dir, Chrysler Mus, Norfolk, Va, currently. Mem: Col Art Asn Am; Am Mus Asn; Am Asn Mus Dirs. Res: Tiffany Glass, Art Nouveau and Pop Art, 19th century Academic and Symbolist art, Surrealism and contemporary art. Collection: Old Masters, 17 century Italian and 19th century French drawings plus contemporary art. Publ: Auth, Pop as Art, Studio Vista & Viking Press, 65; Art Nouveau, Dutton/Vista Picturebooks, 66; Tiffany Glass, Walker & Co, 67; contribr, Holiday, Nova, Punch, Sunday Times Colour Suppl, Vogue & many others. Mailing Add: Chrysler Mus Mowbray Arch & Olney Rd Norfolk VA 23510

AMBROSE, CHARLES EDWARD
PAINTER, EDUCATOR
b Memphis, Tenn, Jan 6, 22. Study: Univ Ala, BFA, 49, MA, 50. Work: Univ Southern Miss; Carey Col; Biloxi Art Asn; Miss Art Asn; First Nat Bank, Hattiesburg, Miss. Comn: Portrait reliefs, Univ Southern Miss, 58 & portraits, 60; Pat Harrison Waterways Bldg, 65; Carey Col; Miss Archives Bldg, 72. Exhib: Miss Art Asn Ann, 50-; Birmingham Watercolor Soc, 50-; New Orleans Art Asn Ann Spring Exhib, 52-; Edgewater Ann, Biloxi, Miss, 68; Mid-Continent Exhib, Mo, 71; Watercolor USA, Springfield, Mo, 73; 1st Ann Bi-State, Meridian, Miss, 73; Central South, Nashville, Tenn, 75; 17th Dixie Ann, Montgomery, Ala, 75. Teaching: Assoc prof drawing & painting, Univ Southern Miss, 50-70; head art dept, Miss Univ for Women, 70- Awards: First Place Watercolor, Miss Art Asn, 68; First Place Drawing, Edgewater Ann, 70; Purchase Award/Drawing, 1st Ann Bi-State, 73. Mem: Southeastern Col Arts Conf; Nat Coun Art Adminr; Southern Asn Sculptors; Col Art Asn; Miss Art Asn. Media: Watercolor, Oil. Mailing Add: Box 70 Miss Univ for Women Columbus MS 39701

AMEN, IRVING
PAINTER, PRINTMAKER
b New York, NY, July 25, 18. Study: Pratt Inst, scholar, 32-39; study in Paris, 50 & Italy, 53. Work: Mus Mod Art & Metrop Mus, New York; Albertina Mus, Vienna; Victoria & Albert Mus, London; Bibliot Nat, Paris. Comn: Peace Medal (commemorating end of Viet Nam War); Twelve Tribes of Israel (12 stained glass windows 14ft high), comn by Agudas Achim Synagogue, Columbus, Ohio. Exhib: Master Prints, Mus Mod Art, New York; Int Ausstellung Von Holzschnitten, Zurich, Switz; I Mednarodna Graficna Razstava, Ljubljana, Yugoslavia; L V Biannale di Pittura Americana, Bordighera, Italy; Dessins Americains Contemporains, US Info Serv. Teaching: Instr art, Pratt Inst & Univ Notre Dame. Mem: Int Inst Arts & Lett; Int Soc Wood Engravers; Accad Fiorentina delle Arti Disegno; Soc Am Graphic Artists; Am Color Print Soc; plus others. Style & Technique: Free of standard practice in approaching my media, to be abstract or figurative as my mood and inner voice dictate. Media: Oil, Etching, Woodcut. Publ: Print ed, Irving Amen woodcuts 1948-1960, Irving Amen: 1964, Amen: 1964-1968 & Amen: 1968-1970; illusr, Gilgamesh, Ltd Ed Club. Mailing Add:

AMES, ARTHUR FORBES
PAINTER, EDUCATOR
b Tamaroa, Ill, May 19, 06. Study: San Francisco Art Inst. Work: Mus Contemp Crafts, New York, NY; Pasadena Mus, Calif; Calif State Fair, Sacramento; Harvey Mudd Col, Claremont, Calif; Wichita Art Asn, Kans. Comn: Tapestries, Garrison Theater, Univ Ctr, Claremont; enamel mural, Rose Hills, Whittier, Calif; enamel door panels, Emanual Temple, Beverly Hills, Calif; mosaic, Ahmanson Bank, Los Angeles, Calif; mosaic, Apostle Cath Church, Westwood, Calif. Exhib: Syracuse Ceramic Nat, NY, 49, 51 & 54; Brussels World's Fair, Belg; Mus Contemp Crafts; Contemp Arts Exhib, Univ Ill, 52 & 53; Objects USA, Smithsonian Inst & traveling exhib, 69. Teaching: Prof design & head dept, Otis Art Inst, Los Angeles, 54-71. Awards: First Prize for Ferro Enamel, 14th Ceramic Nat, Syracuse, 49; First Prize for Drakenfield, 16th Ceramic Nat, 57; Purchase Award for Painting, Pasadena Mus. Mailing Add: 4094 Olive Hill Dr Claremont CA 91711

AMES, JEAN GOODWIN
DESIGNER, PAINTER
b Santa Ana, Calif, Nov 5, 03. Study: Pomona Col, hon DFA, 75; Art Inst Chicago, grad, 26; Univ Calif, Los Angeles, BE, 31; Univ Southern Calif, MFA, 37. Work: Mus Contemp Crafts, New York; Everson Mus, Syracuse, NY. Comn: Ceramic mural (with Arthur Ames), 56 & enamel mural, 58, Rose Hills Mem Park, Whittier, Calif; ceramic mural (with Arthur Ames), Guarantee Savings & Loan, Fresno, Calif, 58; tapestry designed for Garrison Theater, Claremont, Calif, 64; tapestry designed for Fed Plaza Bldg, Los Angeles, 68. Exhib: French & American Tapestries, Otis Art Inst, Los Angeles & La Jolla Art Ctr, Calif, 61; Mus Contemp Crafts Traveling Exhib, 67; Enamels, Everson Mus Fine Art, Syracuse, NY, 69; Scripps Col, 69- Teaching: Prof drawing & design, Scripps Col & Claremont Grad Sch, 40-69. Awards: First Award, Seventh Nat Decorative Arts & Ceramics, Wichita Art Asn, 52; award for distinguished archit decoration, Am Inst Architects, Southern Calif Br, 56 & 58; woman of the year in art, Los Angeles Times, 58. Mem: Am Crafts Coun. Media: Oil on Canvas. Mailing Add: 4094 Olive Hill Dr Claremont CA 91711

AMES, LEE JUDAH
ILLUSTRATOR, WRITER
b New York, NY, Jan 8, 21. Study: Columbia Univ, with Carnahan. Work: Many pieces, layouts and finished illustrations in Univ Ore & Univ Southern Miss permanent collections. Teaching: Instr comic art, Sch Visual Arts, New York, 48-49; lectr advert art, Dowling Col, 70- Pos: Art dir, Weber Assocs, New York, 47-52; pres, Ames Advert, New York, 53-54; artist-in-residence, Doubleday Publ Co, New York, 55-60; pres, Lee Ames & Zak Ltd, 75- Media: Mixed Media. Publ: Illusr, Exploring chemistry, Doubleday, 58; auth & illusr, Draw, draw, draw, 62, Draw 50 animals, 74, Draw 50 ships and boats and trains and trucks, 75, Draw 50 dinosaurs and other prehistoric animals, 76, Draw 50 Airplanes, Aircraft & Spacecraft, 77, Draw 50 Famous Faces, 78, Doubleday; co-auth & illusr, City street games, Holt, Rinehart & Winston, 63; illusr, Hide and seek A B C, Platt, 71; plus illusr for over 100 addn bks. Mailing Add: 44 Lauren Ave Dix Hills NY 11746

AMES, (POLLY) SCRIBNER
PAINTER
b Chicago, Ill. Study: Univ Chicago, PhB; Art Inst Chicago; Chicago Sch Sculpture, scholar; also with Jose de Creeft & Hans Hofmann, New York; Hans Schwegerle, Munich, Ger. Work: Bronze, Ill State Mus; portrait of singer Povla Frijsh, Town Hall, New York; five panel carving, Univ Chicago High Sch; oil painting, Quadrangle Club, Univ Chicago; Ft Nassau, Asiento Club, Curacao, NWI. Comn: Wood carving, Western Springs First Congregational Church, Ill, 64; portraits of Geraldine Page, 61, Mrs E E Cummings, 68, Maureen Ting-Klein, comn by Richard Klein, 68 & Anne Rothnie, comn by Alan Rothnie, 70. Exhib: One-man shows, Cult Ctr, Neth, WI, 47, Galerie Chardin, Paris, 49, Cercle Univ, Aix-en-Provence, 50 & Esher-Surrey Gallery, The Hague, Holland, 50; also Closson Gallery, Cincinnati & many others. Teaching: Instr art, City & Country Sch, New York, 39-42; instr life class, pvt studio, New York, 39-45; pvt classes in oils, New York & Chicago, 39-68; talks on Greece, educ TV & to var clubs. Pos: Librn, Univ Chicago, 58-59; vol, Recording for Blind, 58-; slide dept, publicity, Art Inst Chicago, 64-65. Awards: Bronze award for Young Satyr and Friend, Ill State Mus, 62. Mem: Arts Club Chicago (bd dir, 57-); Oriental Inst; Chicago Quadrangle Club; Hist Preserv; Contemp Authors. Publ: Auth, two articles, In: Progressive Educ Mag, 41; auth & illusr, Marsden Hartley in Maine, Univ Maine, 72. Mailing Add: 5834 S Stony Island Ave Chicago IL 60637

AMFT, ROBERT
PAINTER, PHOTOGRAPHER
b Chicago, Ill, Dec 7, 16. Study: Art Inst Sch, grad; Oxbow Sch, Saugatuck, Mich, summers. Work: Butler Inst Am Art, Youngstown, Ohio. Exhib: Art USA, New York, 60; one-man show, Welna Gallery, Chicago, 70; Mainstreams, Marietta Col, 74; 75th Artists of Chicago & Vicinity, 74; New Horizons, Chicago, 75. Awards: First Prize (painting), New Horizons, 72 & Spec Award, 75; Renaissance Prize, 75th Artists of Chicago, 74. Mem: Arts Club; Cliff Dwellers (bd dirs). Style & Technique: Spray painting; multiple exposure. Dealer: Joy Horwich 333 E Ontario Chicago IL 60611. Mailing Add: 7340 N Ridge Chicago IL 60645

AMINO, LEO
SCULPTOR, INSTRUCTOR
b Tokyo, Japan, June 26, 11; US citizen. Study: NY Univ; Am Artists Sch, New York. Work: Whitney Mus Am Art & Study Collection, Mus Mod Art, New York; Des Moines Art Ctr, Iowa; Provincetown Mus, Mass; Olsen Found, New Haven, Conn. Exhib: Mus Mod Art, 50, Metrop Mus Art, 51, New York; Whitney Mus Am Art, 56; Jewish Mus, New York, 70; San Francisco Mus Art, Calif, 70. Teaching: Instr sculpture, Black Mountain Col, 46 & 50; instr sculpture, Cooper Union Sch Art, 52-77. Media: Plastic. Dealer: Sculpture Ctr 167 E 69th St New York NY 10021. Mailing Add: 58 Watts St New York NY 10013

AMOR, INES
ART DEALER
b Mexico City, Mex. Pos: Dir, Galeria de Arte Mexicano. Specialty: Since 1935 dealing with the most relevant Mexican artists, all tendencies including contemporary. Mailing Add: Milan 18 Mexico DF Mexico

AMOSS, BERTHE
ILLUSTRATOR, EDUCATOR
b New Orleans, La, Sept 26, 20. Study: Newcomb Col, BA; Univ Hawaii; Kunsthalle Bremen, Ger, three yrs; Acad des Beaux Arts, Antwerp, Belg, one yr. Work: La State Libr; De Grummond Collection, Univ Southern Miss. Teaching: Instr writing & illus children's bks, Tulane Univ, 76- Media: Watercolor. Publ: Auth & illusr, Tom in the Middle, 68 & It's Not Your Birthday, 66, Harper; auth & illusr, The Marvelous Catch of Old Hannibal, 70, Old Hasdrubal and the Pirates, 71, Parents Publ; auth & illusr, The Chalk Cross, Seabury, 76. Mailing Add: 3723 Carondelet St New Orleans LA 70115

AMSDEN, FLOYD T
COLLECTOR, PATRON
b Wichita, Kans, May 25, 13. Study: Univ Kans, BS, 35; Wichita State Univ, post-grad studies in art hist, 73-75. Interest: University collections, Mus Art, Univ Kans & Ulrich Mus Art, Wichita State Univ. Collection: Bronzes, drawing and lithographs by Gerhard Marcks; figure drawings by P Pearlstein, R Diebenkorn, J Beal, W Theibaud, Theodore Roszak, Isabel Bishop, P Modersohn-Becker and others. Mailing Add: 158 N Quentin Wichita KS 67208

AMSTER, SALLY
PAINTER
b New York, NY, Jan 22, 38. Study: Cornell Univ, BFA; Brooklyn Mus Art Sch; Columbia Univ, MFA. Exhib: Centennial House Gallery, Deer Isle, Maine, 63, 64 & 67; The Landscape, Sch Visual Arts, NY, 66; Maine Coast Artists, Rockport, 74, 75 & 77; 118 Artists, Landmark Gallery, NY, 75 & 77; Women in the Arts, NY, 75 & 77; Works on Paper, Brooklyn Mus, NY, 75; Santa Rosa Jr Col, Calif, 76; Landmark Gallery, New York, 77; Olean Pub Libr, NY, 77; State Univ NY, Canton, 77; Richmond Col, City Univ New York, 78; plus other one-person shows. Teaching: Lectr Am art, Soviet Union, 58; vis critic, Wash Univ Sch Fine Arts, 67. Awards: US Rep, First US-USSR Student Exchange, 58; Cornell Univ Fac Medal in Art, Cornell Univ, 59. Mem: Women in the Arts. Style & Technique: Abstract landscape. Media: Oil. Dealer: Prince St Gallery 106 Prince St New York NY 10012. Mailing Add: 470 West End Ave New York NY 10024

ANARGYROS, SPERO
SCULPTOR
b New York, NY, Jan 23, 15. Study: Study with William Zorack, New York, 34-35; asst to Mahonri Sharp Young, This is the Place Monument, Salt Lake City, Utah, 44-47. Comn: Bronze bust, Sheik Khalid ben Mohammed AlQasimi, 70; bronze heroic figure, Pedro Martinez, Knight Comdr of Pope St Sylvester, Agana, Guam, 72; Christ at Resurrection (12 ft bronze), Agana, Guam, 74; bronze portrait of Father Terry, pres, Santa Clara Univ, 77; Jubail commemorative plague, Saudi Arabia, 77; plus many others. Exhib: Nat Acad Design, 38-40, 53-56, 59 & 77; M H De Young Mem Mus, 53 & 62-63; one-man shows, Houston & Corpus Christi, Tex, 68, San Francisco, Calif, 69 & Egyptian Mus, San Jose, Calif, 69; Nat Sculpture Soc Ann, 77; plus many others. Awards: First hon mention, Nat Competition Sculpture, Pomona Co, Calif, 38; first award sculpture, Tenth Ann Nat Exhib, Acad Artists Asn, 59; John Spring Art Founder Award, Nat Sculpture Soc 42nd Ann Exhib, 75. Bibliog: Terence Busch (auth), Spero Anargyros and his 23 ton rock, San Francisco Mag, 11/65; Frederick Whitaker (auth), Spero Anargyros, Sculptor, Am Artist, 2/67; Valerie Shields (auth), Man with a masterful thumb, Spectator, 2/57. Mem: Life mem Art Student League; fel Nat Sculpture Soc; fel Int Inst Arts & Lett; Nat Soc Lit & Arts. Style & Technique:

Representational, specializing in portraits and bas-relief. Media: Bronze, Marble, Stone. Mailing Add: 2503 Clay St San Francisco CA 94115

ANAYA, STEPHEN RAUL
PRINTMAKER
b Los Angeles, Calif, June 29, 46. Study: San Fernando Valley State Col, with Tom Fricano; Univ Calif, Los Angeles, BA; also with David Glines & Raymond Brown. Work: Chicago Inst Art; San Diego State Col; Davidson Col, NC; William Hayes Mem Art Ctr, Univ NC, Chapel Hill; Ga State Univ, Atlanta. Exhib: 4th Ann Nat Print Exhib, San Diego State Col, 71; Davidson Nat Print & Drawing Exhib, Davidson Col, 72; 5th Nat Student Printmakers Exhib, Univ NC, 72; 3rd Nat Print Exhib, Ga State Univ, 72; Nat Print Exhib, Calif Soc Printmakers, Richmond Art Ctr, Calif, 72. Teaching: Teaching asst printmaking, Univ Calif, Los Angeles printmaking, 70-71, assoc 71-74. Awards: Los Angeles Chap Winner, & 4th Nat Print Exhib Prize for Graphics, San Diego State Col, 71; Prize for Graphics, Davidson Nat Print & Drawing Exhib, 72. Mem: Los Angeles Printmaking Soc. Mailing Add: 6309 Canby Ave Reseda CA 91335

ANBINDER, PAUL
ART PUBLISHER, COLLECTOR
b Brooklyn, NY, Apr 19, 40. Study: Cornell Univ, AB, 60; Columbia Univ, grad work, 60-61. Collections Arranged: Cornell Collects (co-organizer), Hudson River Mus, Yonkers, NY, 76-77. Pos: Ed in chief, Shorewood Publ Inc, 64-69; exec ed & vpres, Harry N Abrams Inc, New York, NY, 69-74 & pres, 74-75; dir spec projs, Alfred A Knopf, Random House & ed/vpres, Ballantine Bks, New York, 75. Mem: Col Art Asn; New York Friends of Johnson Mus, Cornell Univ (mem exec coun). Collection: Contemporary American prints and drawings. Mailing Add: 201 E 50 St New York NY 10022

ANDERSEN, WAYNE VESTI
ART HISTORIAN, EDUCATOR
b July 7, 28; US citizen. Study: Univ Calif, BA; Columbia Univ, William Bayard Cutting fel, 61-62, MA & PhD. Teaching: Prof art hist, Mass Inst Technol, 64- Awards: Belg-Am Found CRB Fel, 62; Ford Found Grant Humanities, 62-63; Am Coun Learned Soc Fel. Mem: Col Art Asn Am. Res: Late nineteenth century painting; twentieth century art. Publ: Auth, Cezanne's portrait drawings, 69; auth, Gauguin's paradise lost, 71; auth, American sculpture in process, 75; plus numerous articles in scholarly mags. Mailing Add: Mass Inst Technol 10-461 Cambridge MA 02139

ANDERSON, BRAD J
CARTOONIST
b Jamestown, NY, May 14, 24. Study: Syracuse Univ, BFA, 51. Work: Albert T Reid Col; William Allen White Found, Univ Kans; Complete Collection Grandpa's Boy Original Comic Strips, Syracuse Univ Manuscripts Libr; Birchfield Mus, Buffalo, NY. Exhib: San Diego Fair Fine Arts & Cartoon Exhib; Punch, Brit-Am Exhib, 54; Cartoon Exhib, The Selected Cartoons of 14 Saturday Evening Post Cartoonists; Cartoon Americana, overseas exhib; Birchfield Mus, Buffalo, NY, 76; Albright-Knox Mus, Buffalo, NY, 76; San Francisco Mus of Fine Arts, Calif, 77. Pos: Art dir, Graphic Art Dept, Syracuse Univ, 50-52; free-lance cartoonist, 50-; int syndicated cartoonist, Marmaduke, 54- & Grandpa's Boy, 54- Mem: Mag Cartoonist Guild; Newspaper Comics/Coun. Publ: Illusr, Marmaduke, 55, Marmaduke Rides Agin' & Marmaduke Rides Again, 68; illusr, Marmaduke Rides Again, Marmaduke...Again?, More Marmaduke & Down, Marmaduke!, Scholastic Press, 77; illusr, Marmaduke Digs In, Tempo Publ, 78; illusr, Marmaduke Treasury, Sheed Andrews & McMeel, 78; contribr cartoons, Sat Eve Post, Look Mag & others. Mailing Add: 1439 Pebble Beach Yuma AZ 85364

ANDERSON, DAVID K
ART DEALER, COLLECTOR
b Buffalo, NY, June 26, 35. Pos: Pres & owner, Martha Jackson Gallery, Inc, New York. Mem: Art Dealers Asn Am. Specialty: Art of 20th century since 1945. Mailing Add: 521 W 57th St New York NY 10019

ANDERSON, DAVID PAUL
SCULPTOR, INSTRUCTOR
b Los Angeles, Calif, Feb 3, 46. Study: San Francisco Art Inst; asst to Peter Voulkos, 72-73. Exhib: One-person exhibs, Berkeley Art Ctr, Calif, 72, San Francisco Mus Art, 73, Ruth Braunstein's Quay Gallery, San Francisco, 75 & 78 & Hill's Gallery, Santa Fe, 77. Public Sculpture/Urban Environment, Oakland Mus, Calif, 74; 1975 Biennial Exhib Contemp Art, Whitney Mus, NY, 75. Teaching: Sculpture, Col of Marin, Kentfield, Calif, 75-78 & San Francisco Art Inst, 76-78. Awards: Grant, Soc for Encouragement of Contemp Art, San Francisco Mus, 73; Nat Endowment Arts Fel Grant, 74. Style & Technique: Welded Steel. Mailing Add: 1421 Second St Berkeley CA 94710

ANDERSON, DENNIS RAY
ART DEALER, ART HISTORIAN
b Waynesboro, Va, Mar 8, 47. Study: Va Art Inst & Univ Va, Charlottesville; Greensboro Col, BA, 71; Univ NC, Greensboro, MFA, 72. Collections Arranged: The Gift of American Naive Paintings from the Collection of Edgar William and Bernice Chrysler Garbisch, 48 Masterpieces (auth, catalogue), 75, Chinese Export Porcelain (largest collection of export ever assembled; auth, catalogue), 75 & Three Hundred Years of American Art in the Chrysler Collection, A Catalogue of Selected Paintings (auth), 76, Chrysler Mus at Norfolk, Va; Ernest Lawson Retrospective (auth, catalogue), ACA Galleries, 76, Ernest Lawson and The Eight, American Flower Paintings (1850-1950) (auth catalogue & bk), 78. Pos: Asst to Dir, ACA Galleries. Mailing Add: 51 E 74th St New York NY 10024

ANDERSON, DONALD MYERS
ART WRITER, CALLIGRAPHER
b Bridgewater, SDak. Study: Univ Iowa, MA, study with Phillip Guston & H W Janson; Mexico City Col, Mex. Teaching: Prof watercolor & calligraphy, Univ Wis, 58- Awards: Typographical Excellence Award, Type Dir Club, New York, 71; Cert of Award, Chicago Bk Clinic, 73; Selected for Exhib, Am Inst Graphic Arts, 77. Res: History of writing. Publ: Auth & illusr, Elements of Design, 61 & The Art of Written Forms, 69, Holt, Rinehart & Winston, New York; auth & illusr, All, Calligraphy—Encyclopedia of Library and Information Science, Marcel Dekker, 70; auth & illusr, A Renaissance Alphabet, Univ Wis Press, 71; auth & illusr, Part, Calligraphy—Current Encyclopedia of Britain, W Benton, 74. Mailing Add: Rte 1 Dane WI 53529

ANDERSON, DOUG
ILLUSTRATOR
b NH, Oct 2, 19. Study: New Sch Social Res, New York; Art Students League. Pos: Asst art dir, Crown Publ Co, New York, 72- Publ: Auth, How to Draw with the Light Touch, New Things to Draw & How to Draw Them, Let's Draw a Story & Humorous Drawing Made Easy; illusr, New Yorker Mag, Fortune, Good Housekeeping & many others. Mailing Add: 139 E 27th St New York NY 10016

ANDERSON, GORDON
SCULPTOR, DESIGNER
Study: Univ Wash, BA & MA; with Everett Du Pen, George Tsutakawa, Alexander Archipenko & Glen Alps. Work: St Benedicts Col & pvt collections. Comn: Numerous church, public and private comns. Exhib: Art USA, 58; Madison Square Garden, NY; Bertrand Russell Centenary Show, London, Eng, 73; many others. Teaching: Mem fac, Memphis Acad Arts, Tenn, Seattle Univ, Cornish Sch Allied Arts, Highline Col & various art schs, Wash. Awards: Fel Residence Award, Huntington Hartford Found, Calif; plus others. Style & Technique: Cartoons, murals and illustrations for magazine and local public houses. Mailing Add: 8642 Island Dr S Seattle WA 98118

ANDERSON, GUNNAR DONALD
PAINTER, ILLUSTRATOR
b Berkeley, Calif, Mar 3, 27. Study: Calif Sch Fine Arts, with Clyfford Still; Art Ctr Col Design, BFA, with Lorser Feitelson. Work: Brown-Forman Distillers, Louisville, Ky. Comn: Mrs Robert E Norcross, Tyronza, Ark, 68; Mr & Mrs Meredith Long, Houston, Tex, 71; Mr & Mrs George Weyerhauser, Tacoma, Wash, 72; Mr & Mrs Charlie Rich, Memphis, Tenn; Mr & Mrs Charles Schulz, Calif. Exhib: 5th Winter Invitational, Calif Palace of Legion of Honor, San Francisco, 64; M H de Young Mem Mus, San Francisco, 25th Ann, Soc of Western Artists, 68; Charles & Emma Frye Mus, Seattle, 71; Calif State Fair, Sacramento, 71; Mainstream 72, Grover M Hermann Fine Arts Ctr, Marietta Col, Ohio, 72. Awards: Best figure or portrait, 29th Ann, Soc Western Artists, 71; Third Prize, Calif State Fair, 71; best in fine art, Exhib One, Soc Art Ctr, Alumni, 72. Bibliog: Mrs Linda Hardwick (auth), Collage, educational TV, Memphis Community TV Found, 71-72; TV interview, Memphis, Tenn, 71; Don J Anderson (auth), Paintings of children, Chicago Today, 72. Mem: Soc Western Artists; Soc Art Ctr Alumni; Nat Soc Lit & Arts. Style & Technique: Oil painting and etching using children as main subject matter. Media: Oil. Publ: Illusr, Oscar Lincoln Busby Stokes, Harcourt, Brace & World Inc, 70. Dealer: Conacher Galleries 134 Maiden Lane San Francisco CA 94108. Mailing Add: 4583 Belmont Ct Sonoma CA 95476

ANDERSON, GUY IRVING
PAINTER
b Edmonds, Wash, Nov 20, 06. Study: Pvt classes; Tiffany Found fel. Work: Seattle Art Mus, Wash; Santa Barbara Mus, Calif; Munson-Williams-Proctor Inst, Utica, NY; Univ Ore, Eugene; Smithsonian Inst Nat Collection. Comn: Mural (oil on wood), Seattle Opera House, 62; cement & metal panels, Hilton Inn, Seattle; panel, workers, Edmonds Pub Libr; stone inlay, terrace, Seattle First Nat Bank; mural (oil on canvas), Bank of Calif, Seattle, 74. Exhib: Fine Arts Pavilion, Seattle World's Fair, 62; A University Collects: Oregon, 67-68 & The Drawing Soc Nat Exhib, 70-72, circulated by Am Fedn Arts; 73rd Western Ann, Denver Art Mus, 72; Art of the Pacific NW, Smithsonian Inst Nat Collection; Double Retrospective, Seattle Art Mus, Mod Pavilion & Henry Gallery, Univ Wash, 77. Awards: First Prize, Anacortes Art Festival, Wash, 64; award of merit, Am Inst Archit, Seattle, 65; Guggenheim Fel, 75-76. Bibliog: Holiday Mag, 59; Art in Am, 62; Guy Anderson, Gear Press, Seattle, 65. Style & Technique: Oil wash and mixed media. Media: Oil, Watercolor. Mailing Add: Box 217 La Conner WA 98257

ANDERSON, GWENDOLYN ORSINGER (ORSINI)
ENAMELIST, INSTRUCTOR
b Chicago, Ill, May 31, 12. Study: Univ Calif, Los Angeles, 34-35; Univ Ill, BS, 37; Univ Va, 55. Work: Va Mus Fine Arts, Richmond; Baltimore Mus; Corcoran Gallery Art, Washington, DC; Thomas C Thompson Collection Contemp Am Enamelists, Chicago. Exhib: Creative Craft Biennials, 62, 64 & 70, 9th Int Ceramic Exhib, 63 & Nat League Am Pen Women 22nd Biennial Art Exhib, 64, Smithsonian Inst, Washington, DC; 7th Creative Craft Biennial, Norfolk Mus, Va, 66; 14th Ann Rochester Festival Relig Arts, 72; 1st Va Craftsmen Biennial, Richmond Mus of Fine Arts, 77; Int Shippo (enamel) Exhib, Tokyo, Japan, 78; plus 12 one-man shows, Washington, DC, Va, Md & NC. Teaching: Instr enameling, 1,000 Island Mus Craft Sch, Clayton, NY, 66-67; instr enameling, Am Art Assocs, Washington, DC, 67-; instr enameling, Lake Worth Art League, Fla, winters 73- Pos: Organizer & first pres, Nat Enamelists Guild, 73- Awards: Outstanding Craftsmanship Award, Smithsonian Inst, 56, 60 & 62; First Prize in Ceramics, Corcoran Gallery Art, 57; First Prize in Enamels, Nat League Am Pen Women, 69 & 71; Award, 1st Va Craftsmen Biennial, Richmond Mus of Fine Arts, 77; Second Prize, 30th Creative Crafts Coun, Washington, DC, 76. Mem: Kiln Club, Washington, DC (vpres, 68-69); Nat League Am Pen Women (vpres, 56-58, pres, 58-60); Va Craftsmens Coun; Md Crafts Coun; World Craft Coun. Style & Technique: All forms on enameling on gold, silver, cooper and steel; specializing in cloisonne and champleve; secular and non-secular. Media: Enamel, Watercolor. Dealer: Enamelists' Gallery Torpedo Art Ctr Alexandria VA; Galerie Santiago San Juan PR 00936. Mailing Add: 6520 Ivy Hill Dr McLean VA 22101

ANDERSON, HOWARD BENJAMIN
COLLAGE ARTIST, PHOTOGRAPHER
b Racine, Wis, June 26, 03. Study: Univ Wis-Madison, BA; Art Inst Chicago; Corcoran Gallery Art Sch, Washington, DC. Exhib: 150th Anniversary Exhib Lithography, Print Club Rochester, 48; 69th Ann Exhib Chicago Artists & Vicinity, Art Inst of Chicago, 66; Print Ann, Soc Am Graphic Artists, 50-59, 67-68 & 76; Am-Japanese Contemp Print Exhib, Tokyo, 67; 9th & 11th Union League Art Show, Union League Club, Chicago, 72 & 76; one-man show, Ill Arts Coun Gallery, Chicago. Pos: Package designer, R Loewy & Assocs, Chicago, 45-49; package designer, Cermak Studio, Chicago, 49-55; Mem: Soc Am Graphic Artists; Chicago Soc Artists. Mailing Add: 2725 Devon Ave Chicago IL 60659

ANDERSON, IVAN DELOS
PAINTER, PRINTMAKER
b Yankton, SDak, Feb 13, 15. Study: Yankton Col, BA, with Frederic Taubes, Sergei Bongart, Rex Brandt & Hayward Veal. Work: Libr of Cong, Washington, DC; Los Angeles Co Mus, Los Angeles, Calif; William Cody Mus, Cody, Wyo; Roy Rogers' Mus, Victorville, Calif; Norton Simon's Hunt-Wesson Ctr, Fullerton, Calif. Comn: Serigraph series, Ivan Anderson Children of the World (with Guy Maccoy), 75; portrait of William Boyd, comn by Grace Boyd for Hopalong Cassidy Poster, 76; Catalina Island Poster, comn by Wrigley Catalina Island Hosp, 77; Laguna Beach Poster, comn by City of Laguna Beach, Calif, 77. Exhib: Laguna Beach Mus, 70; Chaffey Mus, Cucamonga, Calif, 71; Laguna Beach Festival Arts, 73-74; Hunt-Wesson, 74; Art-A-Fair, Laguna Beach, 75-78. Awards: Best of Show, Catalina Festival of Arts, 67; Best Portrait of Year Award, Wilshire Ebell Club, 68; Purchase Award, Santa Paula Festival of Arts, 68. Bibliog: John Kingsley (auth), Bringing back those black & white days, Orange Co Illus, 11/76; Phyllis Barton (auth), The difference between painting and pictures, SW Art, 12/76; George A Magnan (auth), Ivan Anderson's impressionistic

serigraphs, Today's Art, 9/77. Mem: Art-a-Fair, Laguna Beach (promotion & publicity adv). Style & Technique: Impressionist painter of children at play. Media: Acrylic; Glazes used in manner of Renoir. Collection: World's largest collection of Will Foster paintings. Publ: Auth, ed & illusr, Creative hairshaping & hairstyling, 47 & Hairstyles for you, 48, privately publ. Mailing Add: 1060 Flamingo Rd Laguna Beach CA 92651

ANDERSON, JAMES P
SCULPTOR, EDUCATOR
b Tulsa, Okla, Mar 30, 29. Study: Eastern NMex Univ, BA, 54; Hardin-Simmons Univ, MA, 60; George Peabody Col, EdD, 64. Work: Zanesville Art Inst, Ohio; Franklin Co Hall of Justice, Columbus, Ohio. Comn: Sculpture (silver, plexiglas, wood), Morehead State Univ, 61; Urschlein XIV (bronze), Muskingum Col, 70; Benjamin Franklin (bronze), Columbus Found, Ohio, 72; Bone Form VI (bronze), Mus Arte Mod, 74; Benjamin Franklin (bronze), Muskingum Col, 74. Exhib: Mainstreams Int, Marietta, Ohio, 69; one-man exhib, Huntington Gallery, Columbus, 71; Ecclesiastical Art, Capital Univ, 72; The Real Thing, Columbus Gallery Fine Arts, 74; X Mostro Int di Sculpture all Aperto, Mus Arte Mod, 74. Teaching: Instr art, Morehead State Univ, 60-62; assoc prof art educ, Tex Tech Univ, 64-65; assoc prof art educ, Western Ky Univ, 65-66; prof & chmn dept art, Muskingum Col, 66-74; prof & chmn dept art, Northern Ariz Univ, 74- Bibliog: C Stebbins (auth), Franklin statue, Muskingum Col Bull, autumn 74; M McGarey (auth), The shaping of a statue, Columbus Dispatch Mag, 5/74. Mem: Assoc Coun Arts; Nat Asn Art Adminr; Col Art Asn Am; Ariz Alliance Arts; Nat Asn Art Educ. Style & Technique: Modeling for bronze and carving in marble; style is from traditional monumental Ben Franklins to modern forms bronze and marble. Publ: Contribr, Franz Cizek, art education's man for all seasons, 10/69 & contribr, Humanism, art educational philosophy in transition, 10/75, Art Educ; contribr, Who shall teach children art, 11/69 & contribr, It's nice to be a pioneer, 12/70, Sch Arts. Dealer: Maxwell Gallery Ltd 551 Sutter St San Francisco CA 94102; Sculptured Arts PO Box 676 Sedona AZ 86336. Mailing Add: 2600 E Seventh Apt 22 Flagstaff AZ 86001

ANDERSON, JEREMY RADCLIFFE
SCULPTOR, EDUCATOR
b Palo Alto, Calif, Oct 28, 21. Study: Calif Sch Fine Arts, cert, 50. Work: Early Morning Hours, Dallas Mus of Fine Arts, Tex; untitled redwood, Pasadena Art Mus; Map No 12, Mus Mod Art, New York; Riverrun, Univ Calif, Berkeley; Serenade for a Broken Heart, Oakland Mus. Exhib: One-man shows, Stable Gallery, New York, 54 & Quay Gallery, San Francisco, 75; one-man retrospective, San Francisco Mus, San Francisco & Pasadena, 66 & 67 & Mus of Contemp Art, Chicago, 75; Funk Show, Univ Calif, Berkeley, 67; American Sculpture of the 60's, Los Angeles Mus, 67. Teaching: Instr sculpture, San Francisco Art Inst, 58-74; Univ Calif, Davis, 74- Awards: I N Walter Sculpture Prize, Calif Sch Fine Arts, 48; Rosenberg Traveling Fel, San Francisco Art Asn, 50. Bibliog: Assignment 4 (film), Arch of KRON-TV, San Francisco, 2/19/62; Gerald Nordland (auth), Jeremy Anderson, introd to catalog, Retrospective, San Francisco Mus, 66; Jose Pierre (auth), Funk art, L'Oeil, No 190, Paris, 10/70. Media: Wood. Publ: Auth, The artist's view, 2, San Francisco Mus, 9/52. Dealer: Ruth Bronstein c/o Quay Gallery 560 Sutter St San Francisco CA 94102. Mailing Add: 534 Northern Ave Mill Valley CA 94941

ANDERSON, JOHN S
SCULPTOR
b Seattle, Wash, Apr 29, 28. Study: Los Angeles Art Ctr, Pratt Inst. Work: Mus Mod Art & Whitney Mus Am Art, New York. Exhib: Int Arts Festival, Providence, RI, 65; Albert A List Show, New Sch Social Res, 65; Cummer Gallery Art, Jacksonville, Fla, 66; seven one-man shows, Allan Stone Gallery, New York, 65-74 & 77. Teaching: Instr sculpture, Pratt Inst, 59-62; instr sculpture, Sch Visual Arts, 68-70; instr sculpture, Cooper Union, 70-; vis sculptor, Univ Conn, 77-78. Awards: Guggenheim Found Grant, 65-66; Mini Grant, NJ State Coun Arts, 72. Dealer: Allan Stone Gallery 48 E 86th St New York NY 10028. Mailing Add: Box 59 School St Asbury NJ 08802

ANDERSON, LENNART
PRINTMAKER, INSTRUCTOR
b Detroit, Mich, Aug 22, 28. Study: Art Inst Chicago, BFA; Cranbrook Acad Art, MFA. Work: Detroit Inst Art; Whitney Mus Am Art; Brooklyn Mus, NY; Hirshhorn Mus, Washington, DC; Mus Fine Arts, Boston. Exhib: Carnegie Inst Mus Art, 64 & 67; Contemp Art USA, Norfolk, Va, 66; Whitney Mus Am Art Ann, 67; Vassar Col, 68; Ravinia Festival, High Park, Ill, 68; plus others. Teaching: Instr, Chatham Col, 61-62; instr, Pratt Inst, 62-64; instr, Swain Sch, New Bedford, Mass, summers 63 & 64; instr, Art Students League; instr, Yale Univ, 67; instr, Skowhegan Sch, 68. Awards: Tiffany Found Grants, 57 & 61; Prix de Rome, 58-61; Raymond A Speiser Mem Prize, Pa Acad Fine Arts, 66; plus others. Dealer: Graham Gallery 1014 Madison Ave New York NY 10021. Mailing Add: 877 Union St Brooklyn NY 11215

ANDERSON, ROBERT RAYMOND
PAINTER, INSTRUCTOR
b Orange, NJ, Nov 9, 45. Study: NJ Inst of Technol, 64-66; State Univ NY, Brockport, BS, 69; Pratt Inst, MFA, 72. Work: Univ Mass, Amherst; Muhlenberg Col, Allentown, Pa; Morris Mus of Arts & Sci, Morristown, NJ; State Univ NY, Brockport; Bloomfield Col, NJ. Comn: Bicentennial painting of Nat Hist Site, 76. Exhib: Discovery, Montclair Mus, Montclair, NJ, 72; Pratt Printers, Brooklyn Mus, 72; New Eng Exhib, Silvermine Guild of Artists, New anan, Conn, 72, 74 & 76; Nat Drawing Show, Univ NDak, Grand Forks, 76; Int Art Exhib, Washington Art 76, Washington, DC, 76; Nat Painting Exhib, Washington & Jefferson Col, Washington, Pa, 77; one-artist shows, Newark Mus, NJ, 75 & NJ State Mus, Trenton, 78. Collections Arranged: Traveling exhib, NJ State Coun on the Arts, 71; 16 Contemp Artists, Hartwick Col, Oneonta, NY, 75; Presence & Absence in Realism, State Univ NY, Potsdam, 76; Viewpoint 76, Morris Mus of Arts & Sci, Morristown, NJ, 76; Contemp Portraits, E R Squibb Gallery, Princeton, NJ, 78. Teaching: Instr painting, Summit Art Ctr, NJ, 74- & Newark Mus, 76- Pos: Treas, Artists Educ & Welfare Fund, 76- Awards: Grand Prize, New Eng Exhib, Silvermine Guild of Artists, 72; fel grant, NJ State Coun on the Arts, 76-77. Bibliog: Ruthann Williams (auth), Bob Anderson: An Artist Evolving, NJ Music & Arts Mag, 74; David Shirey (auth), Exhibit in Newark a Tribute to Jersey Artist, NY Times, 75 & New Realism on View at the Morris Museum, NY Times, 76. Mem: Artists Equity Asn of NJ, Inc (treas, 76-78); Int Asn of Art; Col Art Asn; Assoc Artists of NJ; Alliance for Arts Educ of NJ. Style & Technique: Romantic photorealism. Media: Acrylic. Dealer: James Yu Gallery 393 W Broadway New York NY 10012. Mailing Add: 37 Glenfield Rd Bloomfield NJ 07003

ANDERSON, WILLIAM
SCULPTOR, PHOTOGRAPHER
b Selma, Ala, Aug 30, 34. Study: Ala State Univ, BS(art), 59, study with H L Oubré; Layton Sch Art, BFA, 62, with Burton Blistine; Inst Allende, Guanajuato, Mex, MFA, 68, study with Jesus Mendes. Work: Kiah Mus, Savannah, Ga; DuSable Mus, Chicago; Layton Sch Art, Milwaukee, Wis; Episcopal Day Sch Gallery, Jackson, Miss; Univ NDak Dept Humanities, Grand Forks. Exhib: Sculpture, Atlanta Univ, Ga, 58, Brooks Mem Art Gallery, Memphis, Tenn, 67 & Wright Art Ctr, Delta State Col, Cleveland, Miss, 74; Sculpture & Painting, Milwaukee Mus Art, 62 & Carver Mus, Tuskegee Inst, Ala, 63; Photog, High Mus, Atlanta, 74, Kiah Mus, 77 & Kilby Art Gallery, Montgomery, Ala, 77. Collections Arranged: Day Sch Gallery, Jackson, Miss, 67; Colston Art Gallery for the Performing Arts, Knoxville Col, Tenn, 70; Kiah Mus, 77; William Scarborough House, Savannah, Ga, 77; Dr Benjamin E Mays (photog), Atlanta Univ System, 78; Ft Stewart Air Base, 78. Teaching: Art instr, Univ Wis, 63-64 & Grambling Col, La, 64-65; head dept art, Alcorn A&M Col, Lorman, Miss, 66-69; part-time instr graphics, Univ Tenn, Knoxville, 70-71; art dir sculpture & photog, Savannah State Col, Ga, 71- Pos: Artist-in-residence, Knoxville Col, Tenn, 70-71. Awards: Shouston Gimbel Award for Sculpture, Layton Sch Art, 61-62; Henry Belleman Found Award, Stage Gallery, 66. Bibliog: O C McDavid (auth), Anderson at New Stage, Clarion-Ledger, Jackson, Miss, 2/20/60; William Thomas (auth), The woods and a way of art, Com Appeal, 6/1/69; Margaret DeBolt (auth), A professor's lifestyle, Savannah News/Press, 12/7/75. Mem: Nat Conf Artists; Savannah Art Asn; Ga Art Asn. Style & Technique: Expressionism in sculpture and photography; balance of form and structure in sculpture; incorporation of chiaoscuro in photography. Media: Wood, Stone; Black and White Photographic Prints. Mailing Add: PO Box 20361 Fine Arts Dept Savannah State Col Savannah GA 31404

ANDERSON, WILLIAM THOMAS
PRINTMAKER, PAINTER
b Minneapolis, Minn, Dec 13, 36. Study: Calif State Univ, Los Angeles, with Leonard Edmondson & Bob Fiedler; Chaffey Col; El Camino Col. Exhib: Int Printmaking Exhib, Czech, 72; 10th Int Graphics Exhib, Ljubljana, Yugoslavia, 73; 18th Ann Nat Printmaking Show, Brooklyn Mus, NY, 73; 1st Int Biennial Exhib Graphic Art, Segovia, Spain, 74; In Scapes & Out: Sea, Land, Air, Mind, a Review of Scenery American Style from 1932-1975, Ind State Univ, 75; World Print Competition, San Francisco Mus of Mod Art, 77. Teaching: Assoc prof art, Humboldt State Univ, 67- Media: Silk-screen photo process, air brush, stencil printing and painting on paper and/or Plexiglas. Mailing Add: Box 4181-B Arcata CA 95521

ANDERSON, WINSLOW
DESIGNER, PAINTER
b Plymouth, Mass, May 17, 17. Study: State Univ NY Col Ceramics, Alfred Univ, BFA; Plymouth Pottery, Mass; Hans Hofmann Sch Art, Provincetown, Mass; Pa Acad Fine Arts, Philadelphia; Pratt Graphics Ctr, New York. Comn: Triptych mural, Church of St Mary the Virgin Concert Hall, New York. Exhib: 5th & 11th Ceramic Exhibs, Syracuse Mus Fine Arts, NY, 40 & 46; Guggenheim Mus Ann, NY, 43-46; Kanawha Artists Asn, Charleston, WVa, 50. Pos: Glass designer, Blenko Glass Co, Milton, Va, 46-53; design dir, Lenox China Inc, Trenton, NJ, 53-64, dir dimensional design, 64- Awards: First Prize for African Mask (sculpture), Nat USA Contest, 44; First Prize for Fish (stained glass), Stained Glass Soc Washington, DC, 53; Hon Mention for Spring Flowers (oil painting), Kanawha Artists Asn, Charleston, WVa, 50. Bibliog: Don Wallace (auth), Shaping America's Products, Reinhold Publ Co, 56. Mem: Am Crafts Coun. Style & Technique: Classic to modern. Media: Clay & Glass; Pastel & Oil. Collection: Haitian Primitives. Publ: Auth, Offhand design for offhand glass, Am Ceramic Soc J, 4/49. Mailing Add: 300 W State St Trenton NJ 08618

ANDRADE, EDNA WRIGHT
EDUCATOR, PAINTER
b Portsmouth, Va, Jan 25, 17. Study: Pa Acad Fine Arts, 33-38; Cresson European traveling scholar, Pa Acad Fine Arts, 36-37; Univ Pa Sch Fine Arts, BFA, 37. Work: Philadelphia Mus Art; Pa Acad Fine Arts, Philadelphia; Yale Art Gallery, New Haven; Montclair Art Mus, NJ; Marian Koogler McNay Art Inst, San Antonio, Tex. Comn: Mosiac mural, Columbia Br, Free Libr Philadelphia, 62; marble intarsia mural, Welsh Rd Br, Free Libr Philadelphia, 67; geometric paintings, Smith Kline & French Co, Philadelphia, 68; mobile sculpture, Roxborough Br, Free Libr Philadelphia, 69; granite paving, Salvation Army Div Hq, Philadelphia, 72. Exhib: One-person shows, E Hampton Gallery, New York, 67, Pa Acad Fine Arts, Philadelphia, 67 & Marian Locks Gallery, Philadelphia, 71, 74 & 77; two-person show, Rutgers Univ Art Gallery, New Brunswick, 71; Silkscreen: History of a Medium, Philadelphia Mus Art, 72; 18th Nat Print Exhib, Brooklyn Mus, 72; The Invisible Artist, Philadelphia Mus Art, 73-74; Woman's Work, American Art 1974, Philadelphia Civic Ctr, 74; Philadelphia: 300 Yrs of Am Art, 76, Philadelphia Mus of Art; In This Acad, Pa Acad of Fine Arts, 76; 20th Century Prints, Philadelphia Mus of Art, 77. Teaching: Prof art, Philadelphia Col Art, 57-72, 73-; prof art, Temple Univ, 72-73. Awards: Childe Hassam Mem Purchase Awards, Am Acad Arts & Lett, 67-68; Mary Smith Prize, Pa Acad Fine Arts, 68. Mem: Pa Acad Fellowship; Print Club (mem bd, 72); Artists Equity Asn; Am Color Print Soc; Col Art Asn. Style & Technique: Geometric abstraction. Media: Acrylic, Silkscreen. Dealer: Marian Locks Gallery 1524 Walnut St Philadelphia PA 19102. Mailing Add: 415 S Carlisle St Philadelphia PA 19146

ANDRE, CARL
SCULPTOR
b Quincy, Mass, Sept 16, 35. Study: With Patrick & Maud Morgan; Hollis Frampton; Michael Chapman; Frank Stella. Work: Brandeis Univ; Tate Gallery, London; Mus Mod Art, New York; Albright-Knox Art Gallery, Buffalo; Columbus Gallery Fine Arts, Ohio. Exhib: One-man shows, Stadtisches Mus, Mönchengladbach, 68, Haags Gemeentemuseum, Den Haag, 69, Guggenheim Mus, 70, St Louis Art Mus, 71, Mus Mod Art, New York, 73 & Kunsthalle Bern, Switz, 75. Bibliog: Angela Westwater (auth), Sculpture 1958-1974, Kunsthalle Bern, 75. Style & Technique: Form—structure—place. Mailing Add: Sperone-Westwater-Fischer Inc 142 Greene St New York NY 10012

ANDREJEVIC, MILET
PAINTER
b Petrovgrad, Yugoslavia, Sept 25, 25; US citizen. Study: Sch Appl Arts, Belgrade, Yugoslavia, 41-44; Belgrade Acad Fine Arts, BFA, 50, MFA, 52. Work: Whitney Mus Am Art, New York; Hirshhorn Mus, Washington, DC; RI Sch of Design, Providence; Mus, Univ Tex, Austin; Art Mus, Univ Va, Charlottesville; Allentown Mus; Nicholas Wilder Collection, Los Angeles, Calif. Comn: Portrait, Robert C Scull, New York, NY, 72 & allegorical composition, 73. Exhib: Formalist Exhib, Washington Gallery Mod Art, 63; 28th Biennale, Corcoran Gallery Art, Washington, DC, 63; Am Painting Annuals, 63-65; RI Sch Design, 69 & 70; Green Gallery Revisited, Hofstra Univ, 72; Realism Now, New York Cult Ctr, NY, 72; 76 Jefferson St, Mus Mod Art, New York, 75; Figurative Art in New York—Artists Choice, I St Gallery, New York, NY, 77; Brooklyn Col Art Dept Past & Present, Davis & Long Gallery, New York, NY, 77. Teaching: Instr art hist, NY Univ, 55-56 & instr art hist & lib arts, Exten, 65-66; instr design, Brooklyn Col, 72-74 & instr painting & drawing, 73-76. Awards: Grant, Nat Endowment for the Arts, 76. Bibliog: Donald Judd (auth), articles in Art News, 11/61 & Art Int, 4/63; Paul Katz (auth), Art now, New York, 12/69; Whee K Muller (auth), Iconography of past and present, Arts Mag, fall 72; Claes Oldenburg (auth), Store Days; Hilton Kramer (auth), article in New York Times, 3/13/76. Style & Technique: Post-modernist representational painting. Media: Egg and Oil Tempera; Gouache. Dealer:

Richard Bellamy 333 Park Ave S New York NY 10010. Mailing Add: 35 W 82nd St New York NY 10024

ANDREW, DAVID NEVILLE
PAINTER, EDUCATOR
b Redruth, Eng, Apr 19, 34; Can citizen. Study: Falmouth Sch of Art, 54; Slade Sch of Fine Art, London, 58; study under Patrick Heron & Ben Nicholson. Work: Kettles Yard Mus, Cambridge Univ, Eng; Art Gallery of Ont, Toronto; Burnaby Art Gallery, BC. Exhib: 1st NH Print Ann, Hollis, 73; Ibizagrafic, La Bienal de Ibiza, 74; 11th Biennial of Graphic Art, Ljubljana, Yugoslavia, 75; Imprint, Can Nat Exhib (touring), 76; Brit Int Print Biennale, 76; Premio Int Biella por Incisione, Italy, 76; Int Grafik Biennale, Grenchen, WGer, 76; 9th Burnaby Biennial Print Show, BC, 77. Teaching: Vis artist painting, Portsmouth Col of Art, Eng, 61-70; vis artist painting & print, Bournemouth Col of Art, Eng, 62-69; assoc prof painting & printmaking, Queen's Univ, 71- Pos: External assessor, Croydon Col of Art, Eng, 73; juror, Soc of Can Artists, 74-; dir, Falmouth Summer Sch, Cornwall, Eng, 74-77; adv bd mem, Art Mag, Can, 75- Awards: Purchase Award, Can Cult Exchange to Hawaii, US Comn on Cult & Arts, 74; Horniansky Award, Imprint, Print & Drawing Coun of Can, 76; Purchase Award, 9th Burnaby Biennial Print Show, Burnaby Art Gallery, 77. Mem: Ont Soc Artists; Soc Can Artists; Print & Drawing Coun of Can. Style & Technique: Paint; collage; welding; photomechanical processes in etching, lithography & silk screen printing. Media: Painting; silk screen printing. Dealer: Mira Godard Gallery 22 Hazleton Ave Toronto ON Can. Mailing Add: 399 Victoria St Kingston ON K7L 3Z6 Can

ANDREWS, BENNY
PAINTER, LECTURER
b Madison, Ga, Nov 13, 30. Study: Ft Valley State Col, 48-50; Univ Chicago, 56-58; Chicago Art Inst, BFA, 58. Work: Mus Mod Art, New York; Detroit Inst Art, Mich; Mus African Art, Washington, DC; High Mus, Atlanta; Butler Inst Am Art, Youngstown, Ohio. Exhib: 30 Contemporary Black Americans, Minneapolis Inst Arts, Minn, 68; Martin Luther King Memorial, Mus Mod Art, 69; Afro-Americans: Boston and New York, Mus Fine Arts, Boston, 70; Symbols, Studio Mus Harlem, New York, 71; Artists as Adversary, Mus Mod Art, 71. Teaching: Instr art, New Sch Social Res, 67-70; lectr art, Queens Col, 68-72; Dorne vis prof, Univ Bridgeport, 70. Pos: Co-chmn, Black Emergency Cult Coalition, New York, 69- Awards: John Hay Whitney Fel, 65-66; NY State Creative Arts Prog Awardee, 71; Nat Endowmen for Arts Award, 74. Bibliog: Samella Lewis & Ruth Waddy (auth), Black artists on art, Vol II, Contemp Crafts, 71; Elton Fax (auth), 17 Black artists, Dodd, 71; Barry Schwartz (auth), The new humanism, Praeger, 74. Media: Oil & Collage, Ink. Publ: Illusr, I am the darker brother, Macmillan, 68; auth, On understanding black art, New York Times, 1/21/70; The BECC (Black Emergency Cultural Coalition), Arts Mag, 4/70; To date, M O D E Mag, 4/71. Dealer: ACA Gallery 25 E 73rd St New York NY 10021. Mailing Add: 463 West St New York NY 10014

ANDREWS, MICHAEL FRANK
SYNAESTHETIC EDUCATOR
b Cairnbrook, Pa, Mar 4, 16. Study: Univ Kans, BFA, MS; Ohio State Univ, PhD. Work: Wichita Mus Art, Kans; Univ Kans, Lawrence; Ohio State Univ; Univ Wis-Madison. Exhib: 3rd Int Sculpture Exhib, Philadelphia, 50; Finger Lakes Exhib, Rochester Mem Art Gallery, NY, 69; Sculptors Exhib, Elmira Col, 72; Everson Mus Art, Syracuse, NY, 72; William Rockhill Nelson Art Gallery, Kansas City, Mo, 73. Teaching: Instr sculpture, Univ Kans, Lawrence, 45-48; prof art educ, Univ Southern Calif, 50-52; prof sculpture, Univ Wis-Madison, 52-55; chmn dept synaesthetic educ, Syracuse Univ, 55- Pos: Pres, Kans State Art Teachers Asn, 40-42; vpres, Pac Arts Asn, Los Angeles, 50-52; ed, Synaesthetic Educ, 71. Awards: Sculpture House Award, 53; Wis Salon of Art Award, 54; Design for Hall of Educ Symbol, New York World's Fair, 62. Bibliog: James Schinneller (auth), Art, Search & Self-Discovery; Richard Lowe (auth), Problems in Paradise. Mem: Am Asn Univ Prof; Nat Art Educ Asn (pres, Eastern Region, 60-64); Int Soc Educ Through Art; Creative Leadership Coun, Creative Educ Found; World Orgn Early Childhood Educ. Style & Technique: Expressionistic welding. Publ: Ed, Aesthetic Form & Education, 58, ed, Creativity & Psychological Health, 61 & auth, Creative Education: The Liberation of Man, 65, Syracuse Univ; auth, Creative Printmaking, 64 & Sculpture & Ideas, 65, Prentice-Hall. Mailing Add: 6657 Woodchuck Hill Rd Jamesville NY 13078

ANDREWS, OLIVER
SCULPTOR
Study: Univ Southern Calif; Stanford Univ, BA; Univ Calif, Santa Barbara; also with Jean Helion, Paris, France. Work: Work in many pub & pvt collections. Comn: Stage design, Theatre Group's King Lear, Univ Calif, Los Angeles & Hollywood Pilgrimage Theatre, 64; sculptural lighting fixture, Yale Univ; bronze fountains, W Valley Prof Ctr, San Jose, Calif; water sculpture, Cincinnati Fed Reserve Bank; water sculpture, Civic Ctr, Racine, Wis. Exhib: Santa Barbara Mus Art; Whitney Mus Am Art; San Francisco Mus Art; Taft Mus, Cincinnati; Berkeley Art Ctr; plus many others. Teaching: Prof sculpture, Univ Calif, Los Angeles, 57-; lectr sculpture, mus, schs, art, student & fac groups, radio & TV, 59-78; assoc prof sculpture, San Fernando Valley State Col, 62-63. Awards: Awards, Inst Creative Art, Univ Calif, 67 & 70; winner, Nat Water Sculpture Competition, Odessa, Tex, 76; winner, Int Water Sculpture Competition, Glen Cove, NY, 78. Style & Technique: Water sculptures on a scale from intimate to public; also environments and gardens designed around moving water. Dealer: David Stuart Galleries 807 N La Cienega Blvd Los Angeles CA 90069; A B Closson Jr 401 Race St Cincinnati OH 45202. Mailing Add: 408 Sycamore Rd Santa Monica Canyon CA 90402

ANDREWS, SYBIL (SYBIL ANDREWS MORGAN)
GRAPHIC ARTIST
b Bury St Edmunds, Eng, 1898. Study: Heatherley Sch Fine Art, London, with Henry G Massey; also with Boris Heroys, London. Work: Victoria & Albert Mus, London; Nat Gallery South Australia; Dublin Mus, Ireland; Los Angeles Co Mus Art; Leeds Mus, Eng. Exhib: 200 Years of British Graphic Art, Prague, Vienna & Bucharest, 35-36; Sybil Andrews Exhib Colour Linocut Prints, Vancouver Art Gallery, 48; Primera Expos Arte Sacro Moderno, Buenos Aires, Arg, 54; Print Makers Soc Calif. Teaching: Pvt classes. Awards: G A Reid Award, Soc Can Painter, Etehers & Engravers, 51. Mem: Soc Can Painter, Etchers & Engravers. Media: Oil, Watercolor. Mailing Add: 2131 S Island Hwy Campbell River BC Can

ANDREWS, VICTORIA L
ART DEALER
b Newport News, Va, Feb 23, 50. Study: Sam Houston State Univ, BFA, 68-72; Mexican Field Sch, Puebla, Mex, summer 69 & 70; independent study, Europe, summers 72 & 73. Pos: Assoc dir, Moody Gallery. Specialty: Modern art. Mailing Add: Moody Gallery 2015J W Gray Houston TX 77019

ANDRUS, JAMES ROMAN
PRINTMAKER, PAINTER
b St George, Utah, July 11, 07. Study: Otis Art Inst, Los Angeles; Colorado Springs Fine Arts Ctr; Art Students League; Brigham Young Univ, BA & MA; Columbia Univ; Univ Colo, EdD. Work: Utah State Capitol Collection (three), Salt Lake City; Brigham Young Univ, Provo, Utah; Dixie Col Collection, St George; Provo City Schs Collections; Granite Sch Dist Collection, Salt Lake City. Comn: Mural, St George Temple, Utah, 43; oil painting, Cent Utah Ment Health Ctr, 72; portraits of Charles E Maw & Joseph K Nicoles, Brigham Young Univ, portrait of J C Moffitt, Provo Sch Dist. Exhib: Calif State Fair Exhib, 39; Utah State Inst Fine Arts Exhibs; Boston Mus Ann, Mass; Wichita Print Asn, Kans; Univ Utah Ann, Salt Lake City. Teaching: Spec instr painting, Brigham Young Univ, 40-43, asst prof painting & printmaking, 50-53, prof art, 58-74, emer prof art & educ, 75-, chmn art dept. Pos: Mem, Utah State Fair Art Comt, Salt Lake City; chmn visual arts div, Utah State Inst Fine Arts; mem, Utah State Bd Educ Elem Art Curric. Awards: Fac Award of Merit, Otis Art Inst, 38; Univ Colo Art Fel, 52; Purchase Prizes, Utah State Inst Fine Arts, 45, 50 & 54. Mem: Nat & Western Art Educ Asns; Utah Acad Sci, Arts & Lett; Cent Utah Art Bd. Media: Oil. Mailing Add: 1765 N 651 E Provo UT 84601

ANGEL, RIFKA
PAINTER
b Kalvaria, Russia, Sept 16, 99; US citizen. Study: Art Student League, with Boardman Robinson; also with John Sloan, Alfred Maurer & Emil Ganso; Moscow Art Acad. Work: Honolulu Acad Fine Arts; Chicago Art Inst; Nelson Art Gallery & Mary Atkins Mus Fine Arts, Kansas City, Mo; Brandeis Univ & pvt collections of Laurence S Rockefeller & Bob Dylan. Exhib: Chicago Art Inst, 31, 33, 35 & 39; 16 Cities Exhib, Mus Mod Art, New York, 34; Brooklyn Mus, 37; one-man show & ann, Honolulu Acad, 40-41; one-man shows, Nelson Art Gallery & Mary Atkins Mus Fine Arts, 43; plus many other one-man shows in galleries. Awards: For originality in painting, Art Inst Chicago, 33; City Mus St Louis, 45; Design for Democratic Living, Am Fedn Arts, 48. Bibliog: C J Bulliet (auth), Apples and madonnas, 30; Jacobson (auth), Art of today, Chicago, Stein Publ, 33; F Pratt & B Fizzel (auth), Encaustic—materials and methods, Lear Publ, 49. Mem: Artists Equity Asn New York; fel Int Inst Arts & Lett; Nat Soc Lit & Arts. Media: Encaustic. Mailing Add: 79-81 MacDougal St New York NY 10012

ANGELINI, JOHN MICHAEL
PAINTER, ART DIRECTOR
b New York, NY, Nov 18, 21. Study: Newark Sch Fine & Indust Art; spec studies in Europe, 61. Work: David L Yunich Collection, Bambergers, NJ; Bloomfield Col, NJ; Paterson Main Libr, NJ; Longlines Div, Am Tel & Tel; Morgan Guarantee Trust Co. Exhib: Audubon Artists Nat Ann, Nat Acad Design, New York, 63-74; Nat Arts Club Watercolor Ann, New York, 64; NJ Pavillion, New York World's Fair, 65; Watercolor USA, Nat Ann & Traveling Exhib, Springfield Mus, Mo, 66; NJ Watercolor Soc Ann, Newark, 74; plus many one-man shows in NY & NJ. Pos: Art dir, Berles Carton Co, Inc, Paterson, NJ, 50-; adv bd, NJ Music & Arts, Chatham, 72- Awards: Silver Medal for Watercolor, NJ Watercolor Soc, 63; Medal of Honor for Watercolor, Nat Arts Club, 64; Artist of the Year, Hudson Artists, Inc, NJ, 74. Bibliog: L Pessolano (auth), John Angelini—a profile, 70 & R Williams (auth), John Angelini—A W S, 71, NJ Music & Arts; John Angelini—interview (with R Williams), WDHA-FM New Jersey, 71. Mem: Am Watercolor Soc; Assoc Artists NJ (bd dir, 69-); Audubon Artists; NJ Watercolor Soc (bd dirs, 73-); Allied Artists Am. Style & Technique: Watercolors executed in the wet on wet technique, landscapes, cityscapes and seascapes described as romantic realism. Media: Watercolor, Pencil Rendering. Publ: Contribr, Prize winning watercolors, Book II, 66; contribr, NJ Music & Arts, 70-77; auth, articles, In: Am Artist, 72. Dealer: Gallery Nine 9 Passaic Ave Chatham NJ 07928. Mailing Add: 5 Carey Ave Butler NJ 07405

ANGELO, DOMENICK MICHAEL
SCULPTOR
b Hartford, Conn, May 12, 25. Study: Boston Mus Sch Fine Arts, BFA; Syracuse Univ, MFA; studied with Eduardo Manucci & Fazzini, Rome, Italy, 55-57. Work: Everson Mus, Syracuse, NY; Munson-Williams-Proctor Inst, Utica, NY; Syracuse Univ Gallery; Maxwell Sch, Syracuse Univ. Comn: Garden sculpture, Cole-Capuccilli Architects, Convent-Cloister Garden, Syracuse, 59; bronze centaur, Am Soc Head & Neck Surgery, 66. Exhib: New Visions, Boston Sculptors, Mass, 67; one-man shows, Siembab Gallery, Boston, 68 & Galleria Inquadratura, Florence, Italy, 73; Fiorino Biennale Int D'Arts, Florence, 71; Greater Middletown Art Gallery, NY State Coun Arts, 74. Teaching: Asst prof sculpture, Syracuse Univ, 58-65; sculpture, Boston Mus Sch Fine Arts, 67-69; assoc prof sculpture, Southeastern Mass Univ, 74-76. Pos: Dir art dept, Villa Schifanoia Grad Sch Fine Arts, Florence, 69-73. Awards: Purchase Award, Exhib of Traveling Scholars, Boston Mus, 57; Sculpture Award, Silvermine Guild, 58; Purchase Award, Regional Competition, Everson Mus, 64. Bibliog: Coppini (auth), La mostra a Firenze, 71 & Corrado Marzan (auth), La scultura di Angelo, 73, Il Nazione de Firenze; Patricia Boyd Wilson (auth), Nocturne, Christian Sci Monitor. Style & Technique: Organic contemporary forms; modeling and welding. Media: Bronze, Polyester Resin, Terra-Cotta. Mailing Add: 168 Reed St New Bedford MA 02740

ANGELO, EMIDIO
CARTOONIST, PAINTER
b Philadelphia, Pa, Dec 4, 03. Study: Philadelphia Mus Sch Indust Art. Exhib: Pa Acad Fine Arts; Da Vinci Art Alliance. Teaching: Instr advan art class, Samuel S Fleisher Art Mem, Philadelphia. Pos: Ed cartoonist, (weekly cartoon), The Chestnut Hill Local. Awards: Da Vinci Award, 45, Silver Medals, 58, 60 & 68, Bronze Medal, 61; Charles K Smith Prize, Woodmere Art Gallery, 60; Gold Medal, Philadelphia Sketch Club, 69; plus others. Mem: Da Vinci Art Alliance; fel Pa Acad Fine Arts; Nat Cartoonist Soc; Am Ed Cartoonists. Publ: Producer, short color film of Alighier's, The Inferno, 67; auth, Just be patient, the Time of your Life, Emily and Mabel; plus others. Mailing Add: 7201 Wissachickon Ave Philadelphia PA 19119

ANGELOCH, ROBERT (HENRY)
PAINTER
b Richmond Hill, NY, Apr 8, 22. Study: Art Student League; Acad Fine Arts, Florence, Italy; also with Fiske Boyd. Work: Art Student League; Munson-Williams-Proctor Inst, Utica, NY. Comn: Murals, New York Bd Educ, Kellogg Corp, Brunswick, NJ & Queensboro Pub Libr. Teaching: Supvr, Woodstock Summer Sch, Art Student League, 60-68, instr, Art Student League, 64-; instr, Woodstock Sch Art, 68-; instr, Russell Sage Col, 71-72. Pos: Artist-in-residence, Western Ky Univ, Bowling Green, 74. Awards: Purchase award, Woodstock Art Asn, 64; Jane Peterson Prize, Allied Artists Am, 64; First Prize, Springfield Mus Fine Arts, 68; plus others. Bibliog: S R Day (auth), Creative Woodstock, Mead Mt Press, 66. Mem: Art Student League; Woodstock Artists Asn. Publ: Auth & illusr, Rillet, 65 & Monhegan (bks drawings), 65; auth, Basic oil painting techniques, Pitman, 70; auth, Outdoor sketching, Am Artist Mag, 70. Dealer: Paradox Gallery Woodstock NY 12498. Mailing Add: Box 95 Woodstock NY 12498

ANGLIN, BETTY LOCKHART
EDUCATOR, PAINTER
b Greenwood, SC, Apr 23, 37. Study: Univ Ga, 58, with Lamar Dodd; Col of William & Mary, Williamsburg, Va, BA, 72; additional study with Barclay Sheaks, Leone Cooper & Ferdinand Warren. Work: Hampton Sch Syst, Va; Va Nat Bank Collection; Va Fair Collection; Ft Eustis Collection; Cecil Rawls Mus, Courtland, Va. Comn: Painting, Newport News Shipyard, 72; hist paintings, Hampton City Calendar, 77; four hist paintings, City of Stoney Creek, Va, 78. Exhib: Va Biennial, Va Mus, Richmond, 69 & 71; Irene Leache Show, Chrysler Mus at Norfolk, Va; Mariner's Mus, Newport News, Va, 70; Sears Traveling Exhib; James River Art Exhib, 71; Art Mobile, State Serv Traveling Show, 71; Va Realists Show, Cecil Rawls Mus, 73-74; one-person shows, Pa Arts Asn, Va Wesleyan Col, 72 & Va Beach Arts Asn, 74. Teaching: Guest prof, Va Wesleyan Col, 72 & 74; art resource teacher, Trinity Lutheran Sch, 72-; art teacher, Cecil Rawls Mus, 73-; prof fine arts, Christopher Newport Col, 77- Awards: Spec Award, Tidewater Exhib, Chrysler Mus at Norfolk, Va, 70; Best in Show, Va State Fair, 71; Award, Parthenon, Nashville, Tenn, 76. Mem: Pa Art Asn; Va Beach Art Asn; Tidewater Art Asn. Style & Technique: Waxes, ink and watercolor on rice paper, developed from batik. Publ: Contribr, Barclay Sheaks (auth), Painting with Acrylic from Start to Finish, 74 & Landscape Painting, 74, Davis Publ. Mailing Add: 213 Parkway Dr Newport News VA 23606

ANGUIANO, RAUL
MURALIST, PAINTER
b Guadalajara, Mexico, Feb 26, 15; Mex citizen. Study: Studies with prominent art teachers in Guadalajara; Art Students League. Work: Mus Mod Art, Mex; Mus Mod Art, New York; Mus Art in San Francisco; Royal Mus Art & Hist, Brussels; Arch of Monumental Art Mus, Lund, Sweden. Comn: Three murals, Centro Escolar Revolucion, Ministry of Educ, Mexico City, 37; Birth in the Jungle (mural), Laboratorios Hormona, Mexico City, 62; three murals, Mus Anthorp, Sect of Educ, Mexico City, 63; The Baptism of Christ (mural), Church of San Marcos, Jalisco, Mex, 65; mural, Nat Ballet of Jamaica, Olympia Hotel, Kingston, 70. Exhib: Collective exhib of Mex art, Mus Art, San Francisco, 53; Mus Art, Cincinnati, Ohio, 58; Salon de la Plastica Mex, Mexico City, 69; one-man shows, Mus de Arte Mod, Mex, 71 & Instituto-Italo-Latin-Americano, Rome, Italy, 75. Collections Arranged: Int Biannual Exhib, Tokyo, 57; 29th Biennale Exhib, Venice, 58; Salon Panamericano de Arte, Porto Alegre, Rio Grande do Sul, Brazil, 58. Teaching: Art supvr adult educ, Esmeralda Art Sch, Mex, 42-64; teacher life drawing, Univ Mexico City, 42-69. Pos: Gen secy, Art Teachers Union, Mexico City, 36-38; vpres, Mex Asn Plastic Arts, UNESCO Br, 70- Awards: Gold Medal, First Prize, Salon Panamericano de Arte, Brazil, 58; Dipl Honor, Comt of Int Exhib of Bk of Art, Leipzig, Ger, 60; Commendatore decoration, Pres of Italy, 75. Bibliog: Justino Fernandez (auth), Raul Anguiano, Ediciones de Arte, SAm, 48; Margarita Nelken (auth), Raul Anguiano, Editorial Estaciones, Mex, 58; Jorge Juan Crespo de la Serna (auth), En torno al arte y personalidad de Raul Anguiano, Cuadernos de Bellas Artes, 62. Mem: Soc Europeenne de Cult. Style & Technique: Poetic realism. Media: Oil, Drawing. Publ: Auth, Expedicion a Bonampa: travel diary, Univ Mex, 59; auth, Adventura en Bonampa, Ediciones Novaro, Mex, 68; auth & illusr, Mawarirra, Ediciones Estaciones, Mex, 72. Dealer: B Lewin Galleries 266 N Beverly Dr Beverly Hills CA 90210. Mailing Add: Anaxagoras 1326 Col Narvarte Mexico 13 DF Mexico

ANGULO, CHAPPIE
PAINTER, ILLUSTRATOR
b Mar 3, 28; US citizen. Study: Los Angeles City Col; Univ Calif, Los Angeles; Kahn Art Sch; Esmeralda, Inst Nac Bellas Artes, Mexico City; London Art Ctr. Work: Mus Cultures, Mexico City; Art Mus, Chilpantzingo Guerrero, Mex. Comn: Reproduction murals, Bonampak, 57, Chichen Itza & Tomb 7 Oaxaca, 58, Nat Mus Anthrop, Moneda; reproduction mural, Teotihuacan, Ballet Nac, Mex, 59. Exhib: One-man shows, Olympic Cult Prog, 69, Mus Fronterizo, Juarez, Mex, 71, Age Aquarius, Univ Las Americas, Cholula, 73, La Ciudadela, Monterrey, 74 & Gentes y Lugares Mus de las Cult, Mexico; retrospective, Museo Las Culturas, Mex, 71; La Mujer en la Plastica Bellas Artes, Mexico. Bibliog: M Vazquez (auth), Museo de las Culturas, Inst Nat Antropologia, 65; A Pastrana (auth), El concreto, Arquitectura Arte & Urbanism Mag, 68. Style & Technique: Hard edge and neo-figurative. Media: Mixed. Publ: Illusr, Teotihuacan-un autoretrato cultural, 64; illusr, Tlalmanalli—encontrado en tlatelolco, 66; illusr, Relieves de Chalcatzingo (in press). Mailing Add: A P Postal 1170 Cuernavaca Morelos Mexico

ANHALT, JACQUELINE RICHARDS
ART DEALER
b Kansas City, Mo, Jan 6, 25. Study: Col William & Mary. Pos: Co-owner/dir, Jacqueline Anhalt Gallery, Los Angeles. Mem: Art Dealers Asn Southern Calif (bd mem-treas, 70-74). Specialty: Contemporary paintings and sculpture. Mailing Add: Anhalt-Barnes Gallery 750 N La Cienega Blvd Los Angeles CA 90096

ANKER, SUZANNE C
SCULPTOR
b Brooklyn, NY, Aug 6, 46. Study: Brooklyn Col, BA, study with Ad Reinhardt; Univ Colo, MFA. Work: St Louis Art Mus, Mo; Denver Art Mus, Colo. Exhib: The Hand-made Paper Object, Santa Barbara Mus Art, Calif, 76; New Ways With Paper, Nat Collection Fine Arts, Smithsonian Inst, Washington, DC, 77. Teaching: Asst prof experimental printmaking, Washington Univ, St Louis, 76-78. Mem: Col Art Asn. Style & Technique: Paper casting. Media: Paper, Stone. Mailing Add: 3220 Lafayette Dr Boulder CO 80303

ANKRUM, JOAN
ART DEALER
b Los Angeles, Calif. Collections Arranged: Of Time & the Image, Calif Artists, Phoenix Mus Art, Ariz, 64; People to People, exhib honoring People's Repub China, 72; The Art of African Peoples, private Black Collections, Ankrum Gallery, 73; Calif Artists Exhib, State Capitol Bldg, Sacramento, 75; Morris Broderson Retrospectives, Univ Ariz Mus Art, 75. Pos: Dir, Ankrum Gallery, Los Angeles. Bibliog: H Wurdeman (auth), Los Angeles Galleries, Art in Am, 62; Camilla Snyder (auth), A language without sound, Los Angeles Herald Examr, 5/10/70; Curtis (auth), A woman's place, New York Times, 11/26/71. Mem: Art Dealers Asn Southern Calif (bd mem, 70); Am Fedn Arts. Specialty: West Coast contemporary artists, primarily Californian, ethnic, including Black, Mexican-Indian (Huichol). Publ: Auth & ed, Drawings & Haiku, Janet Lessing, Commun Sci, 65. Mailing Add: Ankrum Gallery 657 N La Cienega ie Blvd Los Angeles CA 90069

ANLIKER, ROGER (WILLIAM)
PAINTER, EDUCATOR
b Akron, Ohio, Jan 27, 24. Study: Cleveland Inst Art, dipl, 47, BFA, 48. Work: Cleveland Mus Art, Ohio; Mus Art, Carnegie Inst, Pittsburgh; Butler Inst Am Art, Youngstown, Ohio; Westmoreland Co Mus Art, Greensburg, Pa; Akron Art Inst. Exhib: Contemporary Drawings from 12 Countries—1945-1952, Art Inst Chicago & traveling to six mus, 52-53; Carnegie Int, 55 & 58; Dessins Americains Contemporains, Strasbourg & travel in France, 56; one-man exhib of 78 works, Westmoreland Co Mus Art, 63; retrospective exhib of 110 works, Temple Univ, Philadelphia, 65. Teaching: Asst prof painting & drawing, Carnegie-Mellon Univ, 48-63; prof painting & drawing, Tyler Sch Art, Temple Univ, 63- Awards: Carnegie Inst Prize, 52 & First Watercolor Prize, 56, Assoc Artists Pittsburgh; Guggenheim Fel, 56. Media: Encaustic, Gouache, Silverpoint. Mailing Add: Dept of Painting & Sculpture Temple Univ Tyler Sch Art Philadelphia PA 19122

ANSPACH, ERNST
COLLECTOR
b Glogau, Ger, Feb 4, 13; US citizen. Study: Univ Munich; Breslau Univ, PhD. Pos: Gen partner, Loeb, Rhoades & Co, Investment Bankers, New York. Mem: Fel in perpetuity Metrop Mus Art, New York; fel Univ Mus, Philadelphia. Collection: African tribal sculpture. Exhibited at Mus Primitive Art, New York, 67-68, Univ Notre Dame, spring 68 & Univ Mus, Philadelphia, 74. Mailing Add: 118 W 79th St New York NY 10024

ANTHONISEN, GEORGE RIOCH
SCULPTOR
b Boston, Mass, July 31, 36. Study: Univ Vt, BA, 61; Nat Acad Design, 61-62; Art Students League, 62-64. Work: Carnegie Hall, New York; Chrysler Mus, Norfolk, Va; Atlanta Univ, Ga. Comn: Bush Hill United Presby Church, Hindman Mem Comt, Alexandria, Va, 74; 8th Cong Dist, Pa House of Rep, Fred Clark Mus, Carversville, 74; Vet Admin, White River Jct, Vt, 75; Washington Sch Psychiat, Washington, DC, 75; Figure of late Sen Ernest Gruening (7ft bronze bronze), Hall of Columns, Capitol Bldg, Washington, DC, 77. Exhib: One-man shows, Hopkins Ctr, Dartmouth Col, Hanover, 66 & Ctr Art Gallery, New York, 69; Nat Acad Design, New York, 70; Allied Artists Am, 70; Nat Sculpture Soc, 72-75; two-man show, M Shacham Gallery, Soho, New York, 77. Awards: James Augustus Suydam Bronze Medal, Nat Acad Design, 68; Sculptor in Residence, Augustus St Gaudens Nat Hist Site, US Dept Interior, 71. Bibliog: Judy Tucker (auth), Bucks Co man sculpts Gershwin, 71 & Artist gets wish for birthday, 10/2/77, Philadelphia Sunday Bull. Mem: Nat Sculpture Soc. Style & Technique: Contemporary realism; modelling in clay. Media: Bronze, Aluminum. Mailing Add: Box 147 Solebury PA 18963

ANTHONY, LAWRENCE KENNETH
SCULPTOR, EDUCATOR
b Hartsville, SC, May 27, 34. Study: Washington & Lee Univ, BA; Univ Ga, MFA; study with Lamar Dodd & Howard Thomas. Work: Brooks Mem Art Gallery, Memphis, Tenn; Vanderbilt Univ Art Dept, Nashville, Tenn; Ark State Univ, Jonesboro; Gibbes Art Gallery, Charleston, SC; SC Art Comn, Columbia. Comn: Menorah form sculpture, Jewish Community Ctr, Memphis, 67; sculpture, Corinthian Broadcasting Co, New York, 71; wall sculpture, CBS-TV, Sacramento, Calif, 72. Exhib: One-man shows, Columbia Mus Art, 66, Brooks Mem Art Gallery, 68 & Vanderbilt Univ, 72 & 74. Teaching: Prof sculpture & drawing, Southwestern at Memphis, 61- Style & Technique: Figurative, expressionistic; repousee and welded and cast metals; wood. Media: Metal, wood and clay. Mailing Add: 2082 Washington Memphis TN 38104

ANTHONY, WILLIAM GRAHAM
PAINTER, DRAFTSMAN
b Ft Monmouth, NJ, Sept 25, 34. Study: Yale Univ, BA, 58, with Josef Albers; San Francisco Art Inst, 59-60; Art Student League, 61; also with Theodoros Stamos. Work: Whitney Mus Am Art, New York; Wallraf-Richartz Mus, Cologne, Ger; Art Inst Chicago; Yale Univ Art Mus, New Haven; Corcoran Gallery Art, Washington, DC; plus others. Exhib: One-man shows, Calif Palace of Legion of Honor, San Francisco, 62 & Fischbach Gallery, New York, 73; group show, Allan Stone Gallery, New York. Teaching: Instr figure drawing, San Francisco Acad Art, 62-63. Pos: Dir, Spectrum Art Gallery, New York, 65-66. Style & Technique: Satirical work. Media: Pencil and oil. Publ: Auth, A new approach to figure drawing, Crown Publ, 65, Odhams, Ltd, Eng, 67 & Bonanza Publ. Dealer: Razor Gallery 464 West Broadway New York NY 10012. Mailing Add: H216 Westbeth 463 West St New York NY 10014

ANTIN, DAVID A
ART CRITIC, WRITER
b New York, NY, Feb 1, 32. Study: Col of the City of New York, 50-55, BA; NY Univ, 64-67, MA, 66. Teaching: Prof visual arts, Univ Calif, San Diego, 68-, chmn dept, 70-72. Awards: Guggenheim Fel, 76-77. Bibliog: Spanos & Kroetsch (ed), Oral tradition & postmodernism, Boundary-2, State Univ NY Binghamton, spring 75; Barry Alpert (ed), Antin/Rothenberg, VORT 7, Eng Dept, Ind Univ, Bloomington, spring 75. Res: Studies in modernism and post modernism; history of art criticism and theory; sociology of art. Publ: Auth, Talking at Pomona, Artforum, 9/72; auth, Talking, Kulchur Press, 72; auth, Television: video's frightful parent, Artforum, 12/75; auth, Talking at the Boundaries, New Directions, 76; auth, Tuning, Alcheringa, winter 78. Mailing Add: PO Box 1147 Del Mar CA 92014

ANTIN, ELEANOR
CONCEPTUAL ARTIST, VIDEO ARTIST
b New York, NY, Feb 27, 35. Study: City Col of New York, BA; Tamara Daykarhanove Sch for the Stage. Exhib: One-woman exhibs, Mus of Mod Art, New York, 73, Everson Mus, Syracuse, NY, 74, Stefanotty Gallery, New York, 75, The Clocktower, New York, 76, M L D'Arc Gallery, New York, 77, Ronald Feldman Fine Arts Gallery, New York, 77, Wadsworth Atheneum, Hartford, Conn, 77 & Whitney Mus of Am Art, New York, 78. Teaching: Visual arts lectr, Univ Calif, Irvine, 74-75; asst prof visual arts, Univ Calif, San Diego, 75-77, assoc prof, 77- Bibliog: John Russell (auth), Eleanor Antin's historical daydream, New York Times, 1/23/77; Kim Levin (auth), Eleanor Antin, Arts Mag, 3/77; Jonathan Crary (auth), Eleanor Antin: a Post-Modern Itinerary, Catalogue Essay, La Jolla Mus, 77. Style & Technique: Post-conceptual; video and performance. Publ: Auth, Reading Ruscha, Art in Am, 11-12/73; auth, Letter to a Young Woman Artist, in: Anonymous Was a Woman, Calif Inst of the Arts, Valencia, 74; auth, Autobiography of the artist as an autobiographer, J Los Angeles Inst Contemp Art, 10/74; auth, Dialogue with a medium, Art-Rite, autumn 74; co-auth (with Cindy Nemser), interview in Art Talk, Scribnners, New York, 75. Dealer: Ronald Feldman Fine Arts New York NY. Mailing Add: PO Box 1147 Del Mar CA 92014

ANTONAKOS, STEPHEN
SCULPTOR
b Greece, Nov 1, 26; US citizen. Work: Whitney Mus Am Art & Mus Mod Art, New York; Milwaukee Art Ctr, Wis; Weatherspoon Art Gallery, Univ NC, Greensboro; Newark Mus, NJ. Exhib: Neon, Fischbach Gallery, New York, 67-70 & 72; Contemp Am Sculpture Ann, Whitney Mus Am Art, 70; Works in Spaces, San Francisco Mus Art, 73; Outdoor Neons, Ft Worth Art Mus, Tex, 74; John Weber Gallery, New York, 74 & 75. Teaching: Vis artist, grad sem, Yale Univ, fall 68; artist-in-residence, sculpture, Univ Wis-Madison, spring 71 &

Fresno State Col, fall 71. Awards: NY State Creative Artists Pub Serv Prog; Individual Artist's Grant, Nat Endowment Arts, 73. Media: Neon. Mailing Add: 420 W Broadway New York NY 10012

ANTONOVICI, CONSTANTIN
SCULPTOR, LECTURER
b Neamt, Romania, Feb 18, 11; US citizen. Study: Fine Arts Acad, Romania; Fine Arts Acad, Vienna, Austria, with Prof Fritz Behn; study with Constantin Brancusi, Paris. Work: Le Salon des Artistes Independants, Paris; Vatican, Roma, Italy; St Joseph, Vienna; Mus Fine Arts, Montreal; Cathedral of St John the Divine, New York. Comn: Monuments of St George, Fine Arts Comt, Vienna, 43 & St Joseph, 47; General De Gaulle, French Army Commandment, Tyrol, Austria, 46; Gen Dwight D Eisenhower, Pres Nixon Collection; Bishop Manning, Cathedral St John the Divine, 54; St Luke, St Luke's Hosp, New York, 55. Exhib: Asn Federative L'Art Libre, Paris, 51; Silver Anniversary, Can Artists Asn, 53; Art Alliance Gallery Am, Philadelphia, 62; NJ Mus Art Ann, 64; Nat Sculpture Soc Ann Exhib, New York, 71-77; Va Mus, Richmond, 77. Awards: Pro Mundi Beneficio medal & dipl, Brazilian Acad, 76; awards for commissions through competitions. Bibliog: Canon West, S T D (auth), The source of courage, The Living Church, 5/12/54; Frank Getlein (auth), Art and artists, Sunday Star, Washington, DC, 7/19/64; Ralph Fabri (auth), Sculpture, Today's Art, 3/70; Constantin Antonovici, Sculptor of Owls, Educ Res Coun Am, 75; plus others. Mem: Nat Soc Lit & the Arts; Nat Sculpture Soc. Style & Technique: Classic and modern. Media: Marble, Bronze, Wood. Mailing Add: 310 W 106th St New York NY 10025

ANTREASIAN, GARO ZAREH
PAINTER, LITHOGRAPHER
b Indianapolis, Ind, Feb 16, 22. Study: Herron Sch Art, BFA; with Stanley William Hayter & Will Barnet. Work: Metrop Mus Art, Mus Mod Art & Guggenheim Mus, New York; Art Inst Chicago; Los Angeles Co Mus Art, Calif. Comn: History of Indiana University, Bloomington, Ind, 54; Lincoln in Indiana (with Ralph Peck), Ind State Off Bldg, Indianapolis, 63. Exhib: Tamarind: Homage to Lithography, Mus Mod Art, New York, 69; Recent Suites, Jewish Mus, New York, 69; US Pavilion, Venice Biennale, Italy, 70; Int Exhib Graphics, Montreal, Que, 71; Brit Int Print Biennale, Bradford, Eng, 72. Teaching: Instr art, Herron Sch Art, Indianapolis, 48-64; prof lithography & art, Univ NMex, 64- Pos: Tech dir lithography, Tamarind Lithography Workshop, Inc, Los Angeles, 60-61; tech dir lithography, Tamarind Inst, Univ NMex, 70-72. Awards: Purchase Awards, Nat Print Exhib, Northern Ill Univ, 68, State Univ NY Albany, 68 & 1st Hawaii Int, Honolulu Acad Arts, 71. Style & Technique: Non-objective, hard edge colorist. Publ: Co-auth, The Tamarind Book of Lithography: Art & Techniques, 71. Dealer: Marjorie Kauffman Graphics The Galleria Houston TX 77056; Alice Simsar Gallery 301 N Main St Ann Arbor MI 48104. Mailing Add: 1520 Los Alamos Dr SW Albuquerque NM 87104

ANTUNG, AHMAD
See Sufi

ANUSZKIEWICZ, RICHARD JOSEPH
PAINTER
b Erie, Pa, May 23, 30. Study: Cleveland Inst Art, BFA, 53; Yale Univ, MFA, 55; Kent State Univ, 56. Work: Corcoran Gallery Art, Washington, DC; Fogg Art Mus, Harvard Univ, Cambridge, Mass; Hirshhorn Mus & Sculpture Garden, Washington, DC; Mus Mod Art & Whitney Mus Am Art, New York. Exhib: Contemporary American Art 1870-1970 Centennial Exhib, Ind State Univ, 70; Pittsburgh Int Exhib Painting & Sculpture, Carnegie Inst, 70; The Structure of Color, Whitney Mus Am Art, New York, 70; Whitney Mus Am Art, New York, 71; Dealer's Choice, New York Cult Ctr, 74; Richard Anuszkiewicz-Recent Paintings, Andrew Crispo Gallery, New York, 74 & 75; Hirshhorn Mus, Washington, DC, 74; Corcoran Biennial, Washington, DC, 75; plus others. Dealer: Andrew Crispo Gallery 41 E 57th St New York NY 10022. Mailing Add: 76 Chestnut St Englewood NJ 07631

ANZURES, RAFAEL
EDUCATOR, ART CRITIC
b Puebla, Mex, June 22, 17. Study: With Ruano Llopis, 36-40; also Gonzalez-Camarena, Mex, 42-55 & Justino Fernandez, Mex, 57; Nat Univ Mex, cert didactics, 74. Comn: Posters, Pemex, Mex, 40-58, mag covers, 46-58. Teaching: Instr drawing, Sch Design & Plastic Arts, Iberoamerican Univ, Mex, 58-61; prof mod & contemp art, Nat Sch Plastic Arts, Nat Univ Mex, 58-, prof hist visual commun, Dept of Graphic Commun, 74- Pos: Dir, Sch Design & Plastic Arts, Iberoamerican Univ, Mex, 59-61; secy, Nat Sch Plastic Arts, Nat Univ Mex, 63-66; secy, Mex Asn Art Critics, 64-70. Awards: Travel & Study Fel, Am Mus of Art & Design & Art Schs, US Govt, 62; Dipl for Educ Work, Nat Univ Mex, 66. Mem: Asn Int des Critiques d'Art, Sect Mex, Paris, France; Asoc Mex de Criticos de Arte. Media: Oil, Tempera. Res: Modern and contemporary art; Mexican painting and sculpture; history of visual communication. Publ: Auth, Critical & aesthetic essays on art in Cuadernos Medicos, 55 & 56; Artes de Mexico, 58 & 61, Mexico en la Cultura, 58 & Novedades, 64. Mailing Add: Privada Luis Mondragon 13 Coyocan Mexico DF Mexico

APARICIO, GERARDO
PAINTER
b Madrid, Spain, 1943. Study: Escuela Bellas Artes; Escuela Artes y Oficios; Escuela Nac Artes Graficas, 63-68. Exhib: II Nac Artes Plasticas, 63; Munic Mus Mataro, Spain, 69; 25th Expos Painting, Casa Siglo SV, Segovia, 70; New Prints, Alonzo Gallery, New York, 70; one-man shows, Galeria Egam, Madrid & Galeria Seiquer, Madrid. Awards: Medella, XII Salon Grabado; First Prize for Printmaking, Expos Bellas Artes, 64. Mailing Add: c/o Alonzo Gallery 30 W 57th St New York NY 10019

APEL, BARBARA JEAN
PRINTMAKER, EDUCATOR
b Falls City, Nebr, June 16, 35. Study: Kansas City Art Inst, BFA, 65; Univ Ill, MFA, 67; study with Lee Chesney, Eugene Tellez & Dennis Rowan. Work: Worcester Art Mus, Mass; Univ Wis, Fond-du-Lac; People's Bank, Providence, RI; Univ Ill, Champaign-Urbana; Art Inst of Boston. Exhib: Surreal Images, De Cordova Mus, Lincoln, Mass, 68; Printmakers' Travelling Show, Brandeis Univ, Waltham, Mass, 68; NW Printmaker's Int Exhib, Seattle Art Mus, Wash, 68; Nat Print Exhib, State Univ NY Col at Potsdam, 68; SAGA, Asn of Am Artists' Gallery, New York, 69; 5th & 7th Ann Art Show, Brockton Art Ctr, Mass, 75 & 77; Boston Visual Artists' Group Show, WBroadway Gallery, New York, 76; New Am Monotypes (travelling exhib), Smithsonian Inst, Washington, DC, 78-80. Teaching: Head, Dept of Printmaking, Art Inst of Boston, 69-, chmn, Fine Arts Dept, 74-75, dir, Summer Sch, 77- Pos: Outside examr, Franconia Col, NH, 72-73. Awards: Louis Black Mem Prize, Boston Printmakers' 20th Ann, Mus Fine Arts, Boston; Tileston & Hollingsworth Prize, Boston Printmakers' 26th Ann, Brockton Art Ctr, Mass, 74; First Prize/All Media, SShore Arts Festival, Cohasset, Mass, 76; Semi-Finalist, Artists' Fel Prog, Mass Arts & Humanities Found, Inc, 77. Mem: Boston Printmakers; Boston Visual Artists' Union (rec secy exec bd, 75-76); Cambridge Art Asn; Copley Soc; Women Exhibiting in Boston. Style & Technique: Monotypes, small scale on copper plates; large expressive etchings, drypoints & engravings on copper plates. Media: Printmaking. Publ: Contribr, Jim Collins (auth), Women Artists in America II, Univ Tenn, 75. Dealer: Impressions Gallery 29 Stanhope St Boston MA 02116. Mailing Add: 235 Rawson Rd Brookline MA 02146

APGAR, NICOLAS ADAM
PAINTER, EDUCATOR
b Gaillon, France, Dec 8, 18; US citizen. Study: Syracuse Univ, 39-41, 55-58, BFA, 58, MFA, 60; Univ Va, cert, 64; also with Louis Bouche, Fletcher Martin, Louis Bosa, Josef Albers & Jean Charlot. Work: Syracuse Univ, NY; Albany Inst Hist & Art, NY; Hyde Collection, Glens Falls, NY; Suksdorf Mem Collection, Hartwick Col, Oneonta, NY; also included in private collections. Exhib: One-man shows, Skidmore Col, Saratoga Springs, 45, Albany Inst Hist & Art, NY, 50 & Randolph-Macon Woman's Col, Lynchburg, Va, 69; State Teachers Col, Albany, 58; Everson Mus Regional, Syracuse, 60. Teaching: Lectr anat, Syracuse Univ, 58-61; asst prof design & drawing, Richmond Prof Inst, 62-67; assoc prof design & drawing, Va Commonwealth Univ, 67-77, prof design & drawing, 77- Style & Technique: Traditional. Media: Oil. Publ: Contribr, Interaction of color, 63; contribr, Search vs research, 71. Mailing Add: 2207 Buford Rd Richmond VA 23235

APPEL, ERIC A
PAINTER, SCULPTOR
b Brooklyn, NY, Dec 26, 45. Study: Pratt Inst, 63-67, BID, 67; Tyler Sch of Art in Rome, 67-68 & Tyler Sch of Art, Temple Univ, Philadelphia, Pa, 67-70, MFA(painting), 70. Exhib: Andrew Carnegie Mansion, New York, 71; 40 Yrs of Am Collage, Buecker & Harpsicords Gallery, New York, 76; St Peter's Col, NJ, 76; producer & dir, The Ecstasy of St Theresa (sculpture with performance), in: Now I Know Why Cannibals Eat Their Enemies—a Consumable Art Event, 112 Greene St Workshop, New York, NY, 77, producer & dir, The Birth of Joy (appliance sculpture with video), in: A Christmas Presence, 78 & Group Indiscriminate, 78; Don't Play With Your Food (performance), Avant-Garde Festival, Inst of Contemp Art, Philadelphia, Pa, 77; Mus of Contemp Crafts, New York, 78. Style & Technique: Multimedia environmental presentations, events and objects dealing in ritual. Media: Paint; Sculpture; Assemblage. Publ: Illusr, Penthouse Mag, 76, Psychology Today Mag, 77, High Times Mag, 77 & MS Mag, 77. Dealer: Kathryn Markel 50 W 57th St New York NY 10014. Mailing Add: 102 Christopher St New York NY 10014

APPEL, KAREL
PAINTER, SCULPTOR
b Amsterdam, Holland, Apr 25, 21. Study: Royal Acad Fine Arts, Amsterdam, 40-43. Work: Tate Gallery, London, Eng; Mus Mod Art, New York, NY; Ctr Nat Art Contemp, Paris, France; Stedelijk Mus, Amsterdam; Mus Fine Arts, Boston, Mass. Comn: Questioning Children (mural), Cafeteria, City Hall, Amsterdam, 49; Garden Hall, Stedelijk Mus, 65; City People (mural), Univ Econ, Rotterdam, Holland, 65; Country People & City People (auth), New Cong House, The Hague, Holland, 67; polychrome statue, Rotterdam Trade Ctr, 73. Exhib: One-man exhib, Studio Fachetti, Paris, 54; Dutch Artists of the Twentieth Century, Stedelijk Mus, 62; Works from the Peggy Guggenheim Foundation, Guggenheim Mus, New York, 69; Karel Apel: Sculpture, Reliefs, Paintings, Kunsthalle, Basel, Switz, 69; Appel's Appels, presented by Rothmans of Pall Mall, Canada, Ltd, museums throughout Canada, 72-73. Awards: UNESCO Prize, 27th Int Biennale, Venice, 54; Int Painting Prize, 5th Sao Paulo Biennale, 59; First Prize for Painting, Guggenheim Internation Exhib, New York, 60. Bibliog: Sir Herbert Read, W Sandberg & Hugo Claus (auth), Karel Appel: Painter, Abrams, 62; Michel Tapie (auth), Karel Appel, Le Grandi Monografie, Fratelli Fabbri Editori, Milano, 68; Simon Vinkenoog (auth), Appel's Oogappels & Het Verhaal van Karel Appel, Brunz & Zoon, Altrecht/Antwerpen, 70. Media: Acrylic; Aluminum, Wood. Publ: Illusr, Appel: a Beast-Drawn Man, 62; auth, Karel Appel over Karel Appel, Triton Press, Amsterdam, 71. Mailing Add: c/o Martha Jackson Gallery 32 E 69th St New York NY 10021

APPEL, KEITH KENNETH
PAINTER, PRINTMAKER
b Bricelyn, Minn, May 21, 34. Study: Mankato State Col, BA, BS & MS. Exhib: Fur Rendezvous Exhib, Anchorage, 61-65; Festival of Music, 63-78; All Alaska Exhib, 64-78; Alaska Centennial, 67; one-man shows, 64, 65, 70, 74-78. Teaching: asst prof art, Univ Alaska, Anchorage, 70-78, assoc prof art, 78- Awards: Alaska Centennial, 67; All Alaska Juried Exhibition Awards, var times, 67-77; Comn, $20,000 Sculpture Competition, Alaska State Art Coun. Mem: Alaska Artists Guild; Alaska State Arts Coun (mem bd); Nat Art Educ Asn. Style & Technique: Contemporary visionary work, sculpture, plastic and enamel painting. Mailing Add: 4705 Malibu Dr Anchorage AK 99503

APPELHOF, RUTH A
ART HISTORIAN, PAINTER
b Washington, DC, Feb 14, 40. Study: Syracuse Univ, BFA(painting & art hist), 65, MFA(art hist), 74, grad studies humanities, 74-77. Work: State Univ NY Col Cortland. Comn: Three paintings, Int Bus Machines Co, New York, 68. Exhib: Regional Exhib, Cayuga Mus, Auburn, NY, 72 & 73; one-person show, State Univ NY Col Cortland, 73; MONY Exhib, Everson Mus, Syracuse, 76-77. Collections Arranged: Cur, New York in Retrospect, Lowe Art Gallery, Syracuse Univ, 76, Bicentennial Exhib, 76 & Prominent Area Artists, 77, Cayuga Co Community Col, Auburn, NY. Teaching: Instr art, Cayuga Co Community Col, 74-77, asst prof art, 77- Pos: Art critic, Syracuse New Times, 74-, Syracuse Guide, 77- Awards: Judges Award, MONY Exhib, Everson Mus, Syracuse, 76; res grant, Peggy Bacon, Syracuse Univ Senate Comt, 76. Mem: Col Art Asn; Women's Art Caucus; Nat Women's Studies Asn; Women in the Arts. Style & Technique: Large canvases, stained, circle & horizontal line. Media: Acrylic, unprimed canvas. Res: Contemporary women in art; iconography and historical contest. Publ: Co-auth with Gene Baro (catalogue), Lee Krasner: Works on Paper, Corcoran Gallery of Art, Washington, DC, 75; auth (travelling exhib catalogue), Jack White, 77-78. Mailing Add: 25 E Lake St Skaneateles NY 13152

APPLE, JACKI (JACQUELINE B)
POST-CONCEPTUAL ARTIST, CURATOR
b New York, NY. Study: Syracuse Univ, 59-60; Parsons Sch Design, 60-63. Exhib: Digging, Martha Jackson West Gallery, New York & Barrington Gallery, Auckland, NZ, 75; Trunk Pieces, 112 Greene St Workshop, New York, 75; Bedtime Stories, Lullabies & Other Lies, 112 Greene St Workshop, 77, Downtown Whitney Mus, 78 & Kansas City Art Inst, 78; Black Holes/Blue Sky Dreams, Kean Col NJ, Union & C Space Gallery, New York, 77; Tracings Performance, Franklin Furnace Archive, New York & Hallwalls, Buffalo, 77; Bk Show, Albright-Knox Art Gallery, Buffalo, 77; Recent Am Narrative, Contemp Arts Mus, Houston, Tex, 77-78; Visual Poetics, Mus Contemp Art, Sao Paulo, Brazil, 77; Heart of Palms, PS 1, 78. Collections Arranged: Notebooks, Workbooks, Scripts & Scores, Franklin Furnace Archive, 77; International Traveling Exhibit of Artists' Books & Audio Tapes for Australia & New Zealand, 78. Pos: Cur exhib, Franklin Furnace Archive, 77- Bibliog: Ann Wooster,

Reviews, Artforum, 76; Lucy R Lippard (auth), Pains & pleasures of rebirth: women's body art, Art in Am, 76 & From the Center: Feminist Essays on Women's Art, Dutton, 76; Deborah Perlberg (auth), rev in Artforum, 2/78. Style & Technique: Installation and performance; narrative; juxtaposition and layering—an interplay of image, object, language, sound and structure. Media: Audiotape, photograph; printed text/books. Publ: Auth, Partitions, privately publ, 76; co-auth, Correspondence with Martha Wilson, 1973-74, Heresides Mag, 77; auth, Tracings, Tracks, 77; Trunk Pieces, Visual Studies Workshop, Rochester, NY, 78. Mailing Add: 161 W 75th St New York NY 10023

APPLEBROOG, IDA H
CONCEPTUAL ARTIST, SCULPTOR
b Bronx, NY. Study: NY State Inst Appl Arts & Sci, 50; Sch of Art Inst Chicago, 65-68. Exhib: Calif S 8, Mus Fine Arts, San Diego, 70; Calif Design XI, Pasadena Art Mus, 71; Invisible/Visible, Long Beach Art Mus, Calif, 72; From the Ceiling—Three Am Sculptors, Max Hutchinson Gallery, New York, 73; one-person shows, Newport Harbor Art Mus, Newport Beach, Calif, 73, Max Hutchinson Gallery, 73 & Inst for Art & Urban Resources, New York, 77; Soho in Berlin, Akademie der Künste, Berlin, WGer, 76; Narrative Art, Contemp Art Mus, Houston, Tex, 78; plus other group and one-person shows. Collections Arranged: Independent Curators Inc (traveling exhib), 78-80; Artwords & Bookworks (int traveling exhib), Los Angeles Inst Contemp Art, 78-79; Art Diary 1978, Milano, Italy, 78; Prints & Illus Bks, Mus Mod Art, New York, 77; Franklin Furnace, New York, 77; Centre for Experimental Art & Commun, Toronto, Ont, 77; Archiv Sohn, Markgröningen, WGer, 77; plus others. Teaching: Teaching asst painting, Sch of Art Inst Chicago, 62-66; instr painting & sculpture, Univ Calif, San Diego, 73-74. Awards: Top Award, Calif S 8, Mus Fine Arts, San Diego, 70. Mem: Col Arts Asn. Style & Technique: Conceptual works including books, videotapes, drawings, stagings and sculpture. Media: Rhoplex on Vellum for Drawings and Stagings. Publ: Auth, The I Am Heathcliffe, says Catherine, Syndrome: Women's Humor, Heresies, 5/77. Mailing Add: 45 Crosby St New York NY 10012

APPLEMAN, DAVID EARL
DESIGNER, PAINTER
b Mansfield, Ohio, May 9, 43. Study: Bob Jones Univ, BA & MA. Work: Bernhardt Industs; Westinghouse Corp; Pee Dee SC State Bank; SC State Art Comn Collection; Sunoco Oil Corp. Comn: Polymer painting (5ft x 5ft), First Fed Bank, Greenville, SC, 73. Exhib: Garden of the Patriots, Cape Coral, Fla, 68; Massilon Mus Ann, Ohio, 70; Hunter Mus of Art Ann, Chattanooga, Tenn, 74; Guild of SC Artists, Gibbes Gallery, Charleston, 74; State Col of Ark, Conway, 75; Mid-S, Parthenon Mus, Nashville, Tenn, 75; Piedmont Painting & Sculpture Exhib, Mint Mus, Charlotte, NC, 77; Greenville Artists Guild, Greenville Mus, SC, 77. Teaching: Prof commun art, Bob Jones Univ, Greenville, SC, 68- Pos: Art dir, Bob Jones Univ Art Agency, 68- Awards: Top Award, Mansfield Guild, Mansfield Mus, 69; Purchase Awards, 16th Guild of SC Artists, Gibbes, Greenville & Florence Mus, 72 & Appalachian Corridors, Charleston Gallery of Sunrise, 74. Mem: Guild of SC Artists (mem bd adv, 75); Greenville Artists Guild; Greenville Art Asn. Style & Technique: Hard-edge polymer painting. Media: Polymer Paint; Collograph Print. Mailing Add: 111 Carmel St Greenville SC 29607

APT, CHARLES
PAINTER
b New York, NY, Dec 10, 33. Study: Pratt Inst, BFA, 56. Work: Chem Bank; Bowery Bank; Celanese Corp; Paine, Webber, Jackson & Curtis, New York. Comn: Painting, Am Stock Exchange, 68. Exhib: Allied Artists Am, New York, 64, 65, 67 & 69; Am Watercolor Soc, New York, 65, 66, 68 & 69; Nat Acad Design, New York, 65, 68 & 73-75; Exposition Intercontinentale, Monaco, France, 66 & 68; Nat Mus Racing Ann, Saratoga, NY, 67. Awards: Best in Show, Saratoga Mus Racing, 67; 2nd Benjamin Altman Award, Nat Acad Design, 68; Le Priz Prince Souverain, Prince Rainier, Monaco, 68. Bibliog: Joan Hess Michael (auth), Charles Apt in Portugal, Am Artist Mag, 4/70. Mem: Assoc Nat Acad Design; Artists Fel; Allied Artists Am. Style & Technique: Realistic in a broad free paint handling technique; direct approach. Media: Oil, Pastel, Watercolor. Dealer: FAR Gallery 22 E 80th St New York NY 10021. New York NY 10021. Mailing Add: 27 W 67th St New York NY 10023

AQUINO, EDMUNDO
PAINTER, PRINTMAKER
b Oaxaca, Mex, June 30, 39. Study: Nat Sch Plastics Art, Nat Univ Mex, Teacher of Fine Arts Degree, 62; Ecole Nat Superieure des Beaux-Arts, Paris, Fr Govt scholar, 67-69; Slade Sch Fine Arts, London, Brit Coun scholar, 69. Work: Nat Libr Paris; Univ Mass Collection; London Co Coun, City Literary Inst London, Eng; Mus Mod Art, Mexico City, Mex; Calif Col Arts & Crafts. Exhib: XVI Interministerial Exhib, Gallery Contemp Art, City of Paris, 68; Int Festival of Painting, Cagnes-Sur Mer, France, 69, 72 & 74; Biennale of Paris, 69; 2nd Brit Int Biennale of Prints, Bradford, Eng, 70; Biennale of Black & White, Lugano, Switz, 72; Mus Mod Art, Mexico City, 77-78. Teaching: Instr drawing & painting & head plastic arts sect, Sch Fine Arts, Oaxaca, Mex, 63-67. Awards: First Prize for Painting, Univ Mus Arts & Sci, Nat Univ Mex, 61; First Prize for Painting & Drawing, Medal awarded by Hotel Monnaie, Paris, at Exhib of Foreign Artists with Fr Govt Scholars, 69; Nat Prize, 6th Int Festival Painting, Cagnes-Sur-Mer, France, 74. Style & Technique: Semi-abstract. Media: Oil, Silkscreen, Lithograph. Dealer: Ines Amor c/o Galeria de Arte Mexicano Milan 18 Mexico 6 DF Mexico. Mailing Add: Apartado Postal 21-031 Coyoacan Mexico 21 DF Mexico

ARAKAWA (SHUSAKU)
PAINTER
b Japan, July 6, 36. Work: Mus Mod Art, New York; Basel Mus, Switz; Walker Art Ctr, Minneapolis; Japan Nat Mus, Tokyo; plus others. Exhib: Documenta IV; Venice Biennial, 70; one-person shows, Kunsthalle, Hamburg, WGer, 72, Mus Mod Art, New York, 74, Univ Wis, Eau Claire, 74 & Art in Progress, Munich, WGer, 74; Painting & Sculpture Today, Indianapolis Mus Art, Ind & Cincinnati Contemp Arts Ctr, Ohio, 74; Wallraf-Richartz Mus, Cologne, WGer, 74; Kennedy Ctr for Performing Arts, Washington, DC, 74; plus others. Awards: DAAD Fel, WBerlin, 72. Bibliog: L Alloway (auth), Introduction to the mechanism of meaning, Bruckman Verlag, 71; N & E Calas (auth), Images & Icons, Dutton, 71; auth, Forgettance, Artsmag, 6/75. Publ: Auth, The Mechanism of Meaning, 71. Mailing Add: 124 W Houston St New York NY 10012

ARBUCKLE, FRANKLIN
PAINTER, ILLUSTRATOR
Mem: Royal Can Acad Arts. Mailing Add: 278 Lawrence Ave E Toronto ON M4N 1T4 Can

ARCHAMBAULT, LOUIS
SCULPTOR, EDUCATOR
b Montreal, Que, Apr 4, 15. Study: Univ Montreal, BA; Ecole des Beaux-Arts de Montreal, dipl ceramics. Work: Nat Gallery Can, Ottawa; Art Gallery Ont, Toronto; Mus Prov Quebec; Mus Int Della Ceramica, Faenza, Italy; Can Imperial Bank Com, Montreal. Comn: Aluminum & terra cotta wall (with Norman Slater), Can Pavilion, Brussels' Expos, 58; six aluminum screens & two pool sculptures, Ottawa Airport, 60; mural sculpture, Place de Arts, Montreal, 63; aluminum sculpture, Toronto Airport, 64; 12 steel sculptures, Can Pavilion, Montreal's Expos, 67. Exhib: Int Sculpture Exhib, Festivals of Gt Brit, London, 51; Milan Triennials, 54 & 57; 28th Venice Biennale, 56; Pittsburgh Int, 58; Int Exhib Contemp Sculpture, Expo 67, Montreal, 67; 11th Middelheim Biennale, 71. Teaching: Prof sculpture, Univ Quebec, 69. Awards: Can Gov & Can Coun Fels, 53, 59, 62 & 69; Allied Arts Medal, Royal Archit Inst Can, 58; Serv Medal, Order Can, 68; Awards, Ministère de l'Education, Québec, 69-71. Bibliog: Flight from tradition, Time Mag, Can ed, 5/5/47; Bill Stephenson (auth), Louis Archambault's wonderful wall, MacLean's, Can, 1/18/58; Guy Robert (auth), Archambault, Vie des Arts, summer 72. Mem: Academician Royal Can Acad Arts. Media: Metal. Mailing Add: 278 Sanford Ave St Lambert PQ J4P 2X6 Can

ARCHER, DOROTHY BRYANT
PAINTER, INSTRUCTOR
b Hampton, Va, Apr 18, 19. Study: Richmond Prof Inst; Kansas City Art Inst, with Wilbur Niewald; Honolulu Acad Art, with John Young. Exhib: Honolulu Acad Arts Ann, Hawaii, 62; Tex Fine Arts Ann, Laguna Gloria Mus, 65 & Tex Fine Arts Invitational, 66; one-woman show, el Inst Relaciones Culturales, Chihuahua, Mex, 69; El Paso Mus, Tex, 71, 73 & 74. Teaching: Instr acrylics, El Paso Mus Art, Tex, 69-70; instr acrylics, pvt nat workshops, 69-; instr acrylics, Carrizo Lodge, Ruidoso, NMex, 69- Pos: Founder, Civic Art Guild, Killeen, 64; fine arts chmn, CofC Festival, Killeen, Tex, 64-66. Awards: Acrylic watercolor, El Paso Art Asn, 70; El Paso Mus Art Award, 73. Bibliog: Barbara Funkhouser (auth), Dorothy Archer—abstract artist, El Paso Times, 70. Style & Technique: Atmospheric non-objective and realistic paintings in heavy impasto. Media: Acrylic, Oil. Dealer: Galeria de Las Artes Box 938 Las Cruces NM 88001. Mailing Add: 8717 Marble Dr El Paso TX 79904

ARCHER, EDMUND
PAINTER
b Richmond, Va, Sept 28, 04. Study: With Nora Houston & Adele Clark, Richmond, Va; with Charles W Hawthorne, Provincetown, Mass; Univ Va; Art Students League, with Allen Tucker & Kenneth Hayes Miller; Acad Colarossi, Paris; independent study, Italy; with Jacques Maroger, New York. Work: Va Mus Fine Arts, Richmond; Mus Fine Arts, Boston; Whitney Mus Am Art; gift of Mrs John D Rockefeller, Jr, Fisk Univ; Corcoran Gallery Art. Comn: Mural, Pub Works Art Proj, Post off, Hopewell, Va, 39; Gov John Garland Pollard (portrait), State of Va, State Capital, 42; Dean Radcliffe Heermance (portrait), Princeton Univ, 46; Dean Charles C Abbott (portrait), Grad Sch Bus Admin, Univ Va, 66; Fred M Carroll (portrait), IBM Corp, IBM Tech Hall of Fame, Yorktown Heights, NY, 68. Exhib: Exhib of Paintings & Sculpture, Century of Progress (Int Expos), Art Inst Chicago, 33-34; Golden Gate Int Expos, Dept Fine Arts, San Francisco, 39; Exhib Contemp Am Painting, New York World's Fair, 40; Am Watercolors, Drawings & Prints, Metrop Mus Art, 52; 131st Ann Exhib, Nat Acad Design, New York, 56. Teaching: Teacher drawing, painting & compos, Corcoran Sch Art, George Washington Univ, 44-68, emer teacher, 68- Pos: Mem bd control, Art Students League, 25; from asst to assoc cur, Whitney Mus Am Art, 30-40. Awards: Corcoran Bronze Medal & Third W A Clarke Prize, Corcoran Gallery Art, 30; Purchase Award, Va Mus Fine Arts, 41; First Prize & Popular Prize, Norfolk Mus Arts & Sci, 50. Mem: Fel Int Inst Arts & Lett, Switz. Mailing Add: 13 S Foushee St Richmond VA 23220

ARCHIE, JAMES LEE
ARTIST
b Orlander, NC, June 14, 24. Exhib: Countee Cullen Libr, New York, 70; 9th Ann Outdoor Afro-Am Art Festival, New York, 72; Westchester Panorama, White Plains, NY, 71; 1st Black Arts Exhib, Albany, NY, 72. Pos: Guest artist, Sunday Gallery traveling art exhib, Westchester Co, 71-72; dir, Creative Community Workshop, New York; decorator, Broadway Producer David Merrick & Actress Leslie Uggams; designer, Apollo Theater, Harlem, NY; dir, Tucker Galleries, New York; vol consult & art therapist to various orgns. Mem: Mus Art; Int Platform Asn; Fed Cult Comn. Mailing Add: 61-15 98th St Rego Park Queens NY 11374

ARCILESI, VINCENT J
PAINTER, INSTRUCTOR
b St Louis, Mo, May 5, 32. Study: Furman Univ, 49-50; Univ Okla, BFA(design), 53; Art Inst Chicago, BFA(painting), 56, MFA, 61. Work: Art Inst Chicago Mus; Ill State Mus, Springfield; Fashion Inst of Technol, New York; Hirshhorn Collection; Kemper Ins, Long Grove, Ill; plus pvt collections. Comn: Mural (oil on canvas), Lake Shore Nat Bank, Chicago, 66. Exhib: 70th Ann, Art Inst Chicago, 67; The American Landscape/1972, Boston Univ, Mass, 72; Visions/Painting & Sculpture, Distinguished Alumni 1945-Present, Sch Art Inst Chicago Gallery, 76; one-man shows, Westbroadway Gallery, New York, 73, 74, 75 & 77; Artists' Choice: Figurative Art In New York, SOHO Ctr for Visual Artists, New York, 76-77; Am 1976 (travelling exhib), Corcoran Gallery, Washington, DC, Wadsworth Atheneum, Hartford, Conn & Fogg Art Mus, Boston, plus others, 76-78; New Realism: New York, Gallery G Fine Arts Inc, Wichita, Kans, 78; plus many other group & one-man shows. Teaching: Assoc prof painting & drawing, Southwest Col, 64-; adj assoc prof painting & drawing, Finch Col, 72-73; adj instr fine arts, Fashion Inst Technol, 74- Pos: Artists comt, Art Rental & Sales Gallery, Art Inst Chicago, 69-72; vis critic, Grad Sch of Painting, Univ Pa, Philadelphia, Spring 1977. Awards: Hon mention, lithography, 34th Ann Okla Artists, 52; hon mention, painting, Festival of Arts, Univ Chicago, 64. Bibliog: Robert Rosenblum (auth), Painting America first, Art in Am, 1-2/76; Hilton Kramer (auth), Back to the land, with a paintbrush, New York Times, 5/76; Hedy O'Beil (auth), Vincent Arcilesi, Arts Mag, 5/77. Mem: Alliance Figurative Artists (prog comt, 72-73); Participating Artists Chicago (exec comt, 67-70); Alumni Asn Art Inst Chicago. Style & Technique: Realistic paintings and drawings from life, primarily nudes in a studio setting and landscapes of mountains, trees and skies. Media: Oil, Graphite. Dealer: Westbroadway Gallery 431 W Broadway New York NY 10012; Capricorn Galleries 8004 Norfold Ave Bethesda MD 20014. Mailing Add: 116 Duane St New York NY 10007

ARCURI, FRANK J
SCULPTOR, PHOTOGRAPHER
b New York, NY, Nov 6, 40. Study: Calif State Univ, Los Angeles, BA, 72, MA, 73. Exhib: 19th Drawing & Small Sculpture Show, Ball State Univ Art Gallery, Muncie, Ind, 73; one-man shows, Paideia Gallery, Los Angeles, 74 & Brand Libr Art Ctr, Glendale, Calif, 75; 51st Ann Nat April Art Exhib, Springville Mus Art, Utah, 75; New Photographics/75, Fine Arts Gallery, Cent Wash State Col, 75. Teaching: Educator, Evening Div Art Dept, East Los Angeles City Col, Calif, currently. Bibliog: Henry Seldis (auth), Art walk, a critical guide to the galleries, Los Angeles Times, 1/11/74; Loretta S Keller (auth), rev in Artweek, 4/26/75. Style & Technique: Anatomical detail made ambiguous by scale change or use of repetitive

pattern; aluminum sand casting or direct stone carving. Media: Metal, Stone; Photography combined with other media. Mailing Add: 1021 E Mooney Dr Monterey Park CA 91754

ARD, SARADELL (SARADELL ARD FREDERICK)
EDUCATOR, PAINTER
b Macon, Ga, Mar 22, 20. Study: Asbury Col, AB(art & speech), 42; Univ Mich, MA, 43; Columbia Univ Teachers Col, DEd(art), 70; Art Students League; Univ Calif, Berkeley. Work: Univ Ill, Edwardsville; Alaska State Mus, Juneau; Alaska Methodist Univ Collection of Alaskan Artists; Univ Alaska. Exhib: Ann All Alaska Art Exhib, 66 & 67; 53rd Ann Exhib Northwest Artists, 67; Alaska 1967 Centennial Exhibiton, 67; one-woman shows, Teachers Col Galleries, Columbia Univ, 68 & 70; Alaska State Mus, 71; Anchorage Hist & Fine Arts Mus, 76; plus others. Teaching: Prof art, Alaska Methodist Univ, 62-73; prof art, Univ Alaska, 73-, actg dean, Col Arts & Sci, 76-77. Pos: Dir arts & crafts prog, European Theater, US Army, 60-62; mem adv bd exhib, Alaska State Mus, 70-71; co-chmn, All Alaska Art Exhib, 71-; vchmn bd dir, Visual Arts Ctr Alaska, 73-; mem bd dir, Mayor's Comn, Fine Arts Mus, Anchorage, 73- Awards: Juror's Choice Award, Ann All Alaska Art Exhib, 66 & First Award for Drawing, 67; Hon Mention, Alaska Centennial Art Exhib, 66. Mem: Nat Art Educ Asn; Col Art Asn. Style & Technique: Abstract expressionist; hard edge. Media: Oil, Acrylic. Publ: Auth, Eskimo art in perspective, Anchorage Mus Publ, 71; Eskimo art today, Alaska J, 72. Dealer: Art Inc Country Village Mall Anchorage AK 99503. Mailing Add: Univ Alaska Col Arts & Sci 3221 Providence Anchorage AK 99504

ARENBERG, MR & MRS ALBERT L
COLLECTORS
b Des Moines, Iowa, Nov 16, 91. Study: Ill Inst Technol, BSEE. Collection: Works by Miro, Giacometti, Soulages, Kline and others. Mailing Add: 1214 Green Bay Rd Highland Park IL 60035

ARIAS-MISSON, ALAIN
VISUAL POET, GRAPHIC ARTIST
b Brussels, Belg, Dec 11, 36; US & Belgian citizen. Study: Harvard Univ, BA(Greek lit; magna cum laude), 59. Work: Stedelijk Mus, Amsterdam; Archief voor Visuele, Concrete en Experimentele Poezie, Dutch Lit Mus, Hague; Archive H Sohm, Markgroningen, Ger; Galleria Schwarz, Millan. Comn: Pamplona Public Poem, Encuentros open air event, Huarte & Pamplona Municipality, 72; Beethoven Public Poem, Beethoven Bicentennial, Fine Arts Div, Municipality of Bonn, Ger, 74. Exhib: Concrete Poesie, Stedelijk Mus, Amsterdam (toured major mus of Europe), 72; Museo di Arte Moderno, Torino, 73; Poesia Visiva, (toured mus of Italy, Ger, Belg), 73; Photographic Supports, Konsthal, Sodertal, Sweden, 76; Art & Language, Toronto, 76; Poeticas Visuais, Museu de Arte Contemporanea da U de Sao Paulo, 77; La Parole en Liberté, Musées de Calais, 78; Art Books, Museo di Bologna, Italy, 78; one-man shows, Tool, Milan, 71, US Cult Ctr, Brussels, 71, Studio Santandrea, Milan, 72, Studio Brescia, Italy, 73 & 74, Il Canale, Venice, 74, Art Fairs, Basle, Brussels & Dusseldorf, 74-75 & Studio 1977, Brescia, 78. Bibliog: Apicella (auth), Poesiva Visiva, Flashart, Milano, 73; M Dachy (auth), Le Poem Publique, Art Vivant, Paris, 74; S H Anderson (auth), When Reality becomes Superfiction, Int Herald Tribune, 5/75. Style & Technique: Visual poems, the complementary or conflictual use of two significant systems, language proper and image (photographic), but image as language as a writing; photo-montage plus handwriting for visual poems; giant linguistic symbols moved and placed throughout cities for public poems. Publ: Co-auth, Projecte Konzepte Aktionen, Dumont Verlag, 74; auth, Confessions of a Murderer, bomber, fascist, rapist, thief, Chicago Rev Press & Swallow, 75; co-ed, Poesia Visiva, Chicago Rev, 76; contribr, Contemporary Artists, St James & St Martins Press, 77; auth, Olé the Public Poem is Me, Arias-Misson, Factotum Press, Italy, 78. Dealer: Sarenco-Galleria 70 Contrada Carmine 19 Brescia Italy 25100. Mailing Add: PO Box 24 Clarksburg NJ 08510

ARISS, HERBERT JOSHUA
PAINTER, ILLUSTRATOR
b Guelph, Ont, Sept 19, 18. Study: Ont Col Art; Can Coun sr fel, 60-61. Work: Nat Gallery Can; Art Gallery Ont; Winnipeg Art Gallery; Vancouver Art Gallery; London Art Gallery, Ont. Comn: Casein, Huron & Erie Co, Chatham, 58; ceramic, John Labatt Brewery, London, 59; multimedia, Sir Adam Beck Sec Sch, London, 67; multimedia, Ont Govt Bldg, Toronto, 68. Exhib: 2nd & 3rd Can Biennial, Ottawa, 64-66; Can Soc Graphic Arts, 70; Can Printmakers, Nat Gallery, Can Int Show, 71; Can Soc Painters in Watercolour, London & New York, 72. Teaching: Instr drawing & painting, Doon Sch Fine Arts, 55-58; head dept art, H B Beal Art Sch, London, Ont, 65- Pos: Pres, Western Art League, 57-60; mem, London Art Gallery Bd, 68-71; dir, London Art Gallery Asn, 69-72; chmn acquisition comt, London Pub Libr & Art Mus, 70-71. Awards: Dirs Purchase Award, Vancouver Art Gallery, 63; Honour Award, Can Soc Painters in Watercolour, 65. Bibliog: Bright lights of London, Time, 68; Barry Lord (auth), How Beal has made London an art centre, Toronto Star, 70; J Bryce (auth), Herb Ariss retrospective, Arts Can, 71. Mem: Ont Soc Artists; Can Soc Painters in Watercolour (vpres, 58-60); Can Soc Graphics Art; Can Group Painters. Publ: Illusr, Contes de nos jours, 56; Lectures variees, 58; La double mort de Frederic Belot, 58; Contes d'Aujour d'hui, 63; War, 71. Mailing Add: 770 Leroy Ave London ON N5Y 4G7 Can

ARKUS, LEON ANTHONY
MUSEUM DIRECTOR
b NJ, May 6, 15. Study: City Col New York, with Townsend Harris. Collections Arranged: 1970 Pittsburgh International, 70-71; Fresh Air Sch, 72; Art in Residence, 73; Twelve Years of Collecting, 74; Celebration, 74-75; Pittsburgh Corporations Collection, 75-76; Pittsburgh Int Series, Pierre Alechinsky, 77. Pos: Asst dir, Mus Art, Carnegie Inst, Pittsburgh, 54-62, assoc dir, 62-68, dir, 68- Awards: Knight Cross of the Order of Dannebrog, Queen Margrethe II of Denmark, 74. Mem: Am Asn Mus; Assoc Artists Pittsburgh (bd mem, 54-); Asn Art Mus Dirs; Pittsburgh Plan for Art (gov, 58-); Century Club; Three Rivers Art Festival (bd mem). Publ: Auth, Three self-taught Pennsylvania artists: Hicks, Kane, Pippin, 66; Carl-Henning Pedersen: paintings, watercolors, drawings, 68; The art of Black Africa, 69; John Kane, painter (catalogue raisonne), Univ Pittsburgh Press, 71. Mailing Add: c/o Mus Art Carnegie Inst 4400 Forbes Ave Pittsburgh PA 15213

ARMAN
SCULPTOR
b Nice, France, 1928; US citizen. Study: Ecole Nat Art Decoratif, BPh; Ecole Louvre. Work: Hirshhorn Mus & Sculpture Garden, Washington, DC; Mus Art Decoratif, Paris; La Jolla Mus, Calif; Louisiana Mus, Danemark; Mod Mus, Stockholm; Kunsthalle, Dusseldorf; plus others. Exhib: Mus Mod Art, Paris, 75; Fort Worth Art Mus, Tex, 75; Des Moines Art Ctr, Iowa, 75; Albright Knox Art Gallery, Buffalo, 75; La Jolla Mus, Calif, 75; plus many others. Teaching: Instr, Univ Calif, Los Angeles, 67-68. Awards: Tokyo Biennel Second Prize, 64; Grand Marzotto Prize, 66. Bibliog: Otto Hahn (auth), Arman, Hatzan, 72; Henry Martin (auth), Arman, Abrams, 73; Arman Selected Activities, Gibson, 75; plus others. Style & Technique: Presentation of man made objects, by the means of accumulation or destruction. Media: Plastic. Mailing Add: 380 W Broadway New York NY 10012

ARMITAGE, FRANK
MEDICAL ILLUSTRATOR, PAINTER
b Melbourne, Australia, Sept 5, 24; US citizen. Study: Ont Col of Art, Toronto, Can; Inst Politecnico Nat, Mexico City, Mex; Chouinard Art Inst, Los Angeles, Calif; asst to Mex muralist David Alfaro Siqueiros, 49. Comn: Returned Soldiers, Sailors, Airmen (mural), Imperial League of Australia, Geelong, 50; mural, Sea World, Fla & Ohio, 71. Exhib: One-man show, Santa Barbara Mus of Art, Calif, 50. Teaching: Lectr visual presentation, Univ Calif, Los Angeles, 74-75; lectr to extend image into time, Chouinard Art Inst. Pos: Graphic consult, Dept of Neuro Sci, Univ of Calif, San Diego, 69-71; principal artist & assoc specialist, Dept of Anat, Univ of Calif, Los Angeles, 71- Awards: Int Award for Mural, Mex, 49. Mem: Acad of Motion Picture Arts & Sci. Style & Technique: Mixed media, multiplane graphics; drawing exploded into different levels, each painted on acetate, lighted independently with colored gels, with results photographed in stills or in motion. Media: Acrylic; Gouache. Publ: Illusr, Life Mag, Time/Life, 71 & Graphis No 165, Walter Herdeg, 73-74; illusr, Central dogma, Biology Today, 72 & Folding Earth (insert), Geology Today, 73, CRM Bks; illusr, Behavioral Neuroscience, Acad Press, 78. Mailing Add: 1807 Ladera Ridge Ojai CA 93023

ARMSTRONG, BILL HOWARD
PAINTER, EDUCATOR
b Horton, Kans, Dec 13, 26. Study: Bradley Univ, Peoria, Ill, BFA(cum laude), 49; Univ Ill, Urbana, MFA, 55, with Abraham Rattner. Work: Brooklyn Mus, NY; San Francisco Mus of Art, Calif; Krannert Mus, Univ Ill, Champaign; Springfield Art Mus, Mo; Albrecht Gallery, St Joseph, Mo. Comn: Sci mural, Ken-Barr Resort, Paducah, Ky, 68; hist mural, Am Bank, Irving, Tex, 75. Exhib: Am Fedn of Arts Int (travelling exhib), 56; 20th & 24th Print Exhib, San Francisco Mus Art, 56 & 59; Butler Inst of Am Art, Youngstown, Ohio, 56-67; PA Acad of Fine Art, Philadelphia, 56-67; 10th Ann Print Exhib, Brooklyn Mus, 59; Soc of Am Graphic Artist Int (travelling exhib), 60; Watercolor USA Nat Exhib, Springfield, Mo, 65-76; Calif Nat Watercolor Soc, Los Angeles, 69-71. Collections Arranged: Watercolor USA Nat Invitational Exhib, 76 (designer catalogue). Teaching: Asst prof painting, Univ Wis, Madison, 56-63; prof watercolor & grpahic design, SW Mo State Univ, 63- Pos: Art adv, Burma Transl Soc, Rangoon, Ford Found, 57-58. Awards: Purchase Awards & Awards, 24th Ann Print Exhib, San Francisco Mus of Art, 59 & 10th Ann Print Exhib, Brooklyn Mus, 59; Philadelphia Watercolor Club, Pa Acad of Fine Arts, 67. Style & Technique: Transparent watercolor; acrylic figure; cultural parody. Mailing Add: RT 5 Box 6 Ozark MO 65721

ARMSTRONG, JANE BOTSFORD
SCULPTOR
b Buffalo, NY, Feb 17, 21. Study: Middlebury Col; Pratt Inst; Art Students League, with Jose De Creeft. Work: Hayden Gallery, Mass Inst Technol; Columbus Gallery Fine Arts, Ohio; New Britain Mus Am Art, Conn; Worcester Polytech Inst, Mass; Columbus Gallery of Arts & Crafts, Ga. Comn: Three marble animals, World of Birds, NY Zool Soc, Bronx, 72; large white marble free-form, Research Triangle Inst, Research Triangle Park, NC, 74. Exhib: One-man shows, Frank Rehn Gallery, New York, 71, 73, 75 & 77. Columbus Mus Fine Arts, Ohio, 72, NC Mus Art, Raleigh, 74, Columbia Mus Art, SC, 75 & Spec Children's Exhib, Dallas Fine Arts Mus, Tex, 78; Critics Choice, Sculpture Ctr, New York, 72. Awards: Gold Medal, Nat Arts Club, New York, 68, 69 & 72 & 74; Coun of Am Artists Soc Prize, Nat Sculpture Soc, New York, 73, bronze medal, 76; Allied Artists Am Gold Medal of Hon, 77. Bibliog: Sandra Satterwhite (auth), Daily Close-Up, New York Post, 11/7/73; Nancy Tobin Willig (auth), JBA comes home to Buffalo, Courier Express Mag, Buffalo, NY, 1/19/75; Diana Loercher (auth), Jane Armstrong—late blooming sculptor, Christian Sci Monitor, 12/19/77. Mem: Sculptors Guild; Nat Sculpture Soc; Allied Artists of Am; Audubon Artists; Nat Asn Women Artists. Style & Technique: Mainly in marble, preferring direct method of carving using varied textures; stress inherent characteristics of a particular stone. Media: Stone. Publ: Auth, Discovery in Stone, Eastwoods Press, 74; auth, From the mountains of Vermont, Nat Sculpture Rev, 74. Mailing Add: High Meadows Studio Manchester Center VT 05255

ARMSTRONG, JOHN ALBERT
ART ADMINISTRATOR, PRINTMAKER
b Billings, Mont, May 14, 43. Study: Eastern Mont Col, BS(art educ); Univ Mont, MFA(painting & printmaking). Work: Bozeman Pub Sch Collection, Mont; Eastern Mont Col, Billings; Univ Mont, Missoula. Comn: Mural (with James Todd), Christ the King Church, Missoula, Mont, 69-70. Collections Arranged: Frank Lloyd Wright, Yellowstone Art Ctr, Billings, Mont, 72; Lee Steen, Yellowstone Art Ctr, Billings, 73; Nick Brigante, Scottsdale Ctr for the Arts, Ariz, 76, Ariz Nat Crafts Exhib, 76, Ariz Nat II Painting Exhib, 77 & Suzanne Klotz-Reilly Environ Exhib, 78. Teaching: Instr art, SDak State Univ, Brookings, 70-71. Pos: Dir, Yellowstone Art Ctr, Billings, 71-74; visual arts cur, Ariz Comn on the Arts, Phoenix, 75-76; visual arts mgr, Scottsdale Ctr for the Arts, 76- Awards: Jurors Award, Young Printmakers, Herron Sch of Art, Indianapolis, Ind, 70; Second Place, Ann Print Competition, NDak State Univ, 70. Mem: Western Asn Art Mus (bd mem, 75); Am Asn Art Mus. Style & Technique: Figurative & social content; collograph. Media: Printmaking; painting. Mailing Add: 7383 Scottsdale Mall Scottsdale AZ 85251

ARMSTRONG, ROGER JOSEPH
PAINTER, CARTOONIST
b Los Angeles, Calif, Oct 12, 17. Study: Pasadena City Col; Chouinard Art Inst; Sueo Serisawa Workshop. Work: City of Santa Fe Springs, Calif; City of Pico Rivera; Banking House of Rothschild, San Francisco; Laguna Beach Art Mus, Calif. Exhib: Nat Watercolor Soc Ann & Traveling Exhibs, 64-69; International Masters of Watercolor, Dalzell-Hatfield Galleries, Los Angeles, 67; one-man shows, Muckenthaler Cult Ctr, 69, Newport Beach Munic Gallery, 70 & Ettinger Gallery, Laguna Beach Sch of Art, 78; Griswold Gallery, Claremont, Calif, 74; Calif 100 Exhib, Laguna Beach Mus Art, 77. Collections Arranged: Three- man exhib, Keith Finch, Edgar Ewing & Robert Frame, 63; West Coast Figurative, 64; First Ann West Coast Sculpture Exhib, 64; plus others. Teaching: Instr drawing & composition watercolor painting, Laguna Beach Sch Art, 65-; instr watercolor, Pasadena City Col; oil painting, Saddlebrook Community Col, Mission Viejo; lectr hist cartooning. Awards: Second Award for Watercolor, First Ann Orange Co Exhib, 63; First Purchase Award, First Ann Pio Pico Art Festival, 68; hon mention, East Meets West Exhib, Calif Nat Watercolor Soc, 72. Bibliog: Raymond Fisher & John Barnard (auths), Roger Armstrong, triple threat artist, World of Comic Art, winter 66-67. Mem: Nat Watercolor Soc; Laguna Beach Art Asn; Los Angeles Art Asn; Nat Cartoonists Soc; Artist's Equity. Style & Technique: Transparent watercolor, non-objective and representational; varying pen and ink styles in cartoon. Media: Watercolor, Ink. Publ: Auth & illusr, All Walt Disney & Warner Bros cartoon comic books, Western Publ, 40-50; illusr, Our country's national parks, Bobbs-Merrill, 41; co-auth & illusr, Ella Cinders comic strip, United Features Syndicate, 50-61 & Napoleon & Uncle Elby, Los Angeles Times Syndicate, 50-60; auth & illusr, Flintstones, Little Lulu & others, Western Publ, 60-72. Mailing Add: 25212 Stockport 90 Laguna Hills CA 92653

ARMSTRONG, THOMAS NEWTON, III
ART ADMINISTRATOR, ART HISTORIAN
b Portsmouth, Va, June 30, 32. Study: Art Students League, summer 53; Cornell Univ Col Archit, BFA(art & planning), 54; Inst Fine Arts, NY Univ, 65-67. Pos: From cur to assoc dir, Abby Aldrich Rockefeller Folk Art Col, Williamsburg, Va, 67-71; dir, Pa Acad Fine Arts, Philadelphia, 71-73; assoc dir, Whitney Mus Am Art, New York, 73-74, dir, 74- Mem: Am Fedn Arts (trustee); Int Exhib Fedn (trustee); Asn Art Mus Dir; Herbert F Johnson Mus Art, Cornell Univ (trustee & mem bd); Alumni Coun, Col Archit Art & Planning, Cornell Univ (comt Alumni Trustees Nominations); Hopkins Ctr, Dartmouth Col (overseer); Creative Arts Award Comn, Brandeis Univ. Mailing Add: 945 Madison Ave New York NY 10021

ARNASON, H HARVARD
ART HISTORIAN, WRITER
b Winnipeg, Man, Apr 24, 09; US citizen. Study: Univ Man; Northwestern Univ, BS & MA; Princeton Univ, MFA. Teaching: Instr art, Northwestern Univ, 36-38; lectr, Frick Col, 38-42; vis assoc prof, Univ Chicago, 47; prof art & chmn dept, Univ Minn, 47-60; Carnegie vis prof, Univ Hawaii, 59. Pos: Sr field rep, Off War Info, Iceland, 42-44, asst dep dir for Europe, Off War Info, 44-45; chief prog planning & eval unit, Off Int Info & Cult Affairs, Dept State, 46-47; US rep, Preparatory Comn, UNESCO, London & Paris, 46; tech adv to US deleg, First Gen Conf UNESCO, 46; dir, Walker Art Ctr, Minneapolis, 51-60; vpres art admin, Solomon R Guggenheim Found, 60-69. Awards: Chevalier, Ordre Arts et Lett, France; Knight, Order St Olav, Norway; Fulbright, Nat Endowment Humanities & Kress Found Fels. Mem: T B Walker Found, Minneapolis (trustee); Solomon R Guggenehim Found (trustee); Joseph H Hirshhorn Mus, Washington, DC (trustee); Int Found Art Res (exec bd & chmn adv comt); plus others. Interest: Modern painting, 19th and 20th centuries; sculpture, 18th to 20th centuries. Publ: Auth, History of Modern Art, Abrams, 68, rev ed, 76, textbook ed, Prentice-Hall, 69; co-auth, Alexander Calder, 69; co-auth, Jacques Lipchitz: My Life in Sculpture, 72; auth, The Sculptures of Houdon, Phaidon Press, & Oxford Univ Press, 75; auth, Robert Motherwell, Abrams, 76; also monogr, catalog & articles on medieval, 18th century & mod art. Mailing Add: River Rd Roxbury CT 06783

ARNAUTOFF, JACOB VICTOR
SCULPTOR, PAINTER
b Coyoacan, Mex, Sept 11, 30; US citizen. Study: San Francisco City Col; Calif Col Arts & Crafts, BFA(indust design); San Francisco State Univ; Calif Inst Fine Arts. Work: Nat Arch, Washington, DC; Kodak Co, New York; Oakland Mus, Cilif. Comn: Docorative permanent screen, Kaiser Hosp, Richmond, Calif, 64. Exhib: Kodak Int Color Competition, New York World's Fair, 64-65; Kingsley Art Club, Sacramento, Calif, 70; Fed Dept Housing & Urban Develop Competitive Exhib, 72. Pos: Dir arts & crafts, Piedmont Recreation Ctr, Calif, 59-63. Awards: Bronze Medallion Spec Award, Kodak Co, 64-65; Int Competition Award, Dept Housing & Urban Develop, 72. Mem: Artists Equity Asn (pres, Northern Calif Chap, 70-72, nat vpres, 72-75). Style & Technique: Abstract-impressionist-realistic; oil on canvas-brush; plastic (acrylic polymer) landscape-figure. Media: Oil; Polymer. Res: Development of art styles in post World War II era in relationship to socio-economic change. Interest: Man's relationship with nature-semi oriental. Collection: Japanese prints; pre-Columbian sculpture; contemporary prints. Publ: Auth catalog, Dept Housing & Urban Develop, 72. Mailing Add: 13902 W Lake Kathleen Dr SE Renton WA 98055

ARNESON, ROBERT CARSTON
SCULPTOR, EDUCATOR
b Benicia, Calif, Sept 4, 30. Study: Calif Col Arts & Crafts, BA(educ), 54; Mills Col, MFA, 58; studied ceramics with Antonio Prieto. Work: Oakland Art Mus; Santa Barbara Mus Art; Univ Calif Art Mus, Berkeley; Nat Mus Mod Art, Kyoto, Japan; E B Crocker Art Gallery, Sacramento. Exhib: Objects USA, Johnson Wax Collection touring US & Europe, 68-73; Human Concern/Personal Torment, Whitney Mus Am Art, 69 & Clay Works, 20 Americans, Mus Contemp Crafts, 71, New York; Contemporary Ceramic Art, Mus Mod Art, Kyoto & Tokyo, 71-72; retrospective, Mus Contemp Art, Chicago & San Francisco Mus Art, 74. Teaching: Instr design, Mills Col, 60-62; prof art, Univ Calif, Davis, 62- Bibliog: Ceramics, Time Mag, 4/26/68; David Zack (auth), The ceramics of Robert Arneson, Craft Horizons Mag, 1/70; Janet Malcolm (auth), On and off the avenue, New Yorker Mag, 9/4/71. Media: Clay, Ceramic. Dealer: Hansen-Fuller Gallery 228 Grant Ave San Francisco CA 94108; Allan Frumkin Gallery 41 E 57th St New York NY 10022. Mailing Add: Art Dept Univ Calif Davis CA 95616

ARNEST, BERNARD
PAINTER, EDUCATOR
b Denver, Colo, Feb 17, 17. Study: Colorado Springs Fine Arts Ctr. Work: Walker Art Ctr, Minneapolis; Minneapolis Inst Arts; Colorado Springs Fine Arts Ctr; Univ Nebr, Lincoln; Univ Ga, Atlanta. Exhib: Whitney Mus Ann Am Painting, New York; Carnegie Int, Pittsburgh; Corcoran Biennial, Washington, DC; Pa Acad, Philadelphia; Univ Ill Ann, Urbana-Champaign; Denver Art Mus; Kraushaar Galleries, New York. Teaching: Assoc prof drawing & painting, Univ Minn, 49-57; prof drawing & painting, Colo Col, 57- Pos: Chief war artist, European Theater Hq, US Army, 44-45; chmn advan placement in art comt, Col Entrance Exam Bd, 69-72. Awards: Guggenheim Fel, 40; int exchange prog, US Dept State, 60. Media: Oil, Acrylic. Dealer: Kraushaar Galleries 1055 Madison Ave New York NY 10028. Mailing Add: 1502 Wood Ave Colorado Springs CO 80907

ARNHEIM, RUDOLF
EDUCATOR, WRITER
b Berlin, Ger, July 15, 04; US citizen. Study: Univ Berlin, PhD, 28; Guggenheim fel, 42-43. Teaching: Mem fac psychol art, Sarah Lawrence Col, 43-68; prof, Harvard Univ, 68-74; vis prof, Univ Mich, 74- Mem: Am Soc Aesthet (pres & trustee); Am Psychol Asn (pres, div arts, 70-72). Publ: Auth, Art and visual perception, Univ Calif Press, 54 & 74; Film as art, 56, Toward a psychology of art, 66, Visual thinking, 69, Entropy and art, 71. Mailing Add: Dept Art Hist Univ Mich Ann Arbor MI 48104

ARNHOLM, RONALD FISHER
DESIGNER, EDUCATOR
b Barre, Vt, Jan 4, 39. Study: RI Sch Design, BFA(graphic design), 61; Yale Univ, MFA(graphic design), 63. Work: Ga Comn Arts Traveling Exhib. Comn: Lobby display for post office (with Herbert Fink), US Postal Serv, Providence, RI, 60; corp design prog, (with Jack MacDonald), Am Tube & Controls, W Warwick, RI, 62; typeface: Jenson Roman, Mergenthaler Linotype Co, Plainview, NY, 64; wall mural, Mead Corp, Atlanta, Ga, 65; typeface: Aquarius series, Visual Graphics Corp, Tamarac, Fla, 70-74. Exhib: Composing Rm Award Typography Exhib, Gallery 303, New York, 63; one-man show, Ga Mus Art, Athens, 65; 45th Ann Art Dir Club New York Ann Exhib, 66; Southeastern Ann, High Mus Art, Atlanta, 67; Typomundus 20/2 Int Typography Exhib, Stuttgart, Ger, 70. Teaching: From instr art to asst prof art, Univ Ga, 63-71, assoc prof art, 71- Pos: Art dir, The Moderator Mag, New Haven, Conn, 62-63. Awards: Composing Room Award for Excellence in Typography, New York, 63; Award of Distinctive Merit, Art Dir Club, New York, 66; Cert of Merit, Typomundus 20/2, 70. Bibliog: Eugene Ettenberg (auth), The Word Paintings of Ronald Arnholm, Am Artist, 11/70; Edward M Gottschall (auth), The Word Paintings of Ronald Arnholm, Typographic, Vol 3, No 3. Mem: Am Inst Graphic Arts. Style & Technique: Word paintings, the image of the painting is directly related to the meaning of the word used; photography. Media: Acrylic, Watercolor. Res: Aspects of visual perception. Mailing Add: Dept of Art Univ of Ga Athens GA 30602

ARNOLD, FLORENCE M
PAINTER
b Prescott, Ariz, Sept 16, 00. Study: Mills Col, degree in music; Univ Southern Calif, BA; Claremont Grad Sch. Work: Long Beach Mus Art; Laguna Mus Art, Calif State Univ, Fullerton; Media Art Gallery, Santa Ana, Calif. Exhib: Gallerias Numero, Florence, Rome, Milan & Prato Venice, 63; Calif Hard-edge Painting, Newport Beach, 64; one-man shows, Long Beach Mus Art, 62-69 & Fresno Art Ctr, 69; Retrospective, Muckenthaler Cult Ctr, 75. Awards: First Prize, Muckenthater Cult Ctr, 67 & 69; First Prize, Orange Co Art Asn, 68; La Mirada Festival Arts Purchase Award, 68. Bibliog: Monogr, Calif State Univ, Fullerton, 69; Nat Archives of Am Art, Smithsonian Inst, Washington, DC; Oral Hist Prog, Fullerton Col, interview published by college. Mem: Los Angeles Art Asn; Muckenthaler Cult Ctr (bd mem, 60-77); Fullerton Cult & Fine Arts Comn; Los Angeles Mus Art (charter mem). Media: Oil on Canvas. Mailing Add: 1136 Valencia Mesa Dr Fullerton CA 92633

ARNOLD, PAUL BEAVER
EDUCATOR, PRINTMAKER
b Taiyuanfu, China, Nov 24, 18; US citizen. Study: Oberlin Col, AB, 40, MA, 41; Cleveland Inst Art; Univ Minn, MFA, 55. Work: Libr Cong, Washington, DC; Cleveland Mus Art, Ohio; Seattle Art Mus, Wash; Baltimore Mus, Md; Dayton Art Inst, Ohio. Comn: Pheasant (color intaglio), Int Graphic Arts Soc, New York, 56; White Peacock (color woodcut), Int Graphic Arts Soc, New York, 57; mural, Gilford Instrument Co, Oberlin, Ohio, 71. Exhib: May Show, Cleveland Mus, 61, 63, 66 & 74; one-man shows, Jersey City State Col, NJ, 66, Miami Univ, Oxford, Ohio, 68, Univ Kans, Manhattan, 70; Contemporary Prints for Collectors, Columbus Gallery Art, Ohio, 75. Teaching: From instr to prof art & chmn dept, Oberlin Col, 41-, Ford Found fac fel prog, 51-52, Great Lakes Cols Asn res grant, 65-66. Awards: Audubon Artists Medal of Honor, 57; Purchase Prize, Ohio Printmakers, 59 & 60 & Cleveland Mus, 63. Mem: Nat Asn Schs Art (bd dir, 70-, vpres, 73-76, pres, 76-); Col Art Asn; Mid-Am Col Art Asn. Style & Technique: Abstract, with emphasis on color organization, primarily Japanese woodblock technique. Media: Woodcut, Intaglio. Publ: Illusr, General chemistry & Laboratory experiments in general chemistry, Campbell & Steiner, 55; co-auth, The humanities at Oberlin, 57; auth, Printmaking today, 4/70 & Silkscreen printing, 12/74, Lalit Kala Contemp, New Delhi, India. Mailing Add: Dept Art Oberlin Col Oberlin OH 44074

ARNOLD, RALPH MOFFETT
PAINTER, EDUCATOR
b Chicago, Ill, Dec 5, 28. Study: Roosevelt Univ, BA; Art Inst Chicago, with Vera Berdich. Work: Whitney Mus Am Art, New York; Fisk Univ, Nashville, Tenn; Rockford Col, Ill; Commonwealth Pa; Ill Bell Tel Co, Chi Chicago. Comn: Wall murals, James House, Arthur Rubloff Realty Co, 71. Exhib: Violence in American Art, Mus Contemp Art, Chicago, 69; American Prints Today, Mus Art, Utica, NY, 70; Afro-American Arts 1800-1969, Mus Philadelphia Civic Ctr, 70; Contemporary Black Artists in America, Whitney Mus Am Art, 71; Cornell Univ, 75. Teaching: Instr painting, Rockford Col, 69-70; asst prof, Barat Col, Lake Forest, 70-; asst prof fine arts, Loyola Univ Chicago, 70-, chmn dept, currently. Pos: Adv bd, Arts & Sales & Rental Gallery, Art Inst Chicago; artist adv bd, Ill Arts Coun. Awards: Artists-in-residence to help underprivileged children, Ill Art Coun, 69. Mem: Arts Club Chicago. Dealer: William Van Straaten 646 N Michigan Ave Chicago IL 60611. Mailing Add: 1858 N Sedgwick St Chicago IL 60614

ARNOLD, RICHARD R
DESIGNER, PAINTER
b Detroit, Mich, July 14, 23. Study: Southwestern Univ; Wayne State Univ, BFA; Cranbrook Acad Art, MFA, with Zoltan Sepeshy; Tulane Univ; Univ Mich. Work: Cranbrook Mus Art; Northwestern Nat Life Ins Collection; Gen Mills Collections; Grey Found; Wayne State Univ. Comn: Mural, Essex Bldg, Minneapolis; designs for Chrysler Corp, Am Motors Corp, Gen Mills Co, Gen Elec Co, Am Standards, Gen Motors Corp, Ford Motor Co, Mich Bell Tel Co, Xerox Corp & others. Teaching: Instr, Univ Wis, 48-51; asst prof, Cornell Univ, 53-56; asst prof, San Jose State Col, 58-60; assoc prof, Rochester Inst Technol, 60-64; prof & head design div, Minneapolis Sch Art, 64-71; vis prof, Univ Victoria, summer 68; prof & chmn art dept, State Univ NY Col Brockport, 71-77; prof art & dir, Sch of Art, Univ of Wash, 77- Mem: Nat Asn Art Adminr. Mailing Add: Sch of Art Univ of Wash Seattle WA 98195

ARNOSKY, JAMES EDWARD
ILLUSTRATOR
b New York, NY, Sept 1, 46. Study: Self taught. Work: Philadelphia Free Libr; Cambridge Pub Libr, Mass. Exhib: Cricket's Traveling Illustrator's Exhib 1 & 2. Bibliog: Article in Jr Lit Guild, New York, 77. Style & Technique: Illustrations in black and white line, scratch broad and watercolor, specializing in outdoor subjects. Publ: Illusr, Swim Little Duck, Atlantic Monthly Press, 75; auth & illusr, I Was Born In A Tree & Raised By Bees, G P Putman's Sons, 76; auth & illusr, Outdoors On Foot, Coward, McCann & Leo, 77; auth & illusr, Nathaniel, Addison-Wesley, 78; illusr, Porcupine Baby, G P Putnam's Sons, 78.

ARON, KALMAN
PAINTER
b Riga, Latvia, Sept 14, 24. Study: Acad Art, Riga; Acad Fine Arts, Vienna, BA. Work: Corcoran Gallery Art; La Jolla Mus Art; Univ Calif, Riverside. Exhib: Los Angeles Co Mus, 56; Denver Art Mus, 60; Fine Arts Houston, 62; Calif Palace of Legion of Honor; O'Hana Gallery, London, Eng, 63; plus others. Awards: Los Angeles Art Asn Awards; Ahmanson Award & Bronze Medal, Los Angeles Co Mus, 62. Mailing Add: 921 N Westmount Dr Los Angeles CA 90069

ARONSON, BORIS
DESIGNER, PAINTER
b Kiev, Russia, Oct 15, 00. Study: State Art Sch, Kiev; Sch of the Theatre, Kiev, with Alexandra Exter; with Herman Struch, Berlin, Ger; Sch Mod Painting, Moscow, with Ilya Mashkov; also study in France. Work: Paintings in pvt collections. Comn: Design, interior for Temple Sinai, Washington, DC; design of Coriolanus for Shakespeare Mem Theatre, Stratford, Eng; sets for more than 100 stage productions incl The Crucible, The Rose Tattoo, The Diary of Anne Frank, Fiddler on the Roof, Judith, Cabaret, Zorba & The Price. Exhib: Tel-Aviv Mus, Israel; Whitney Mus Am Art & Mus Mod Art, New York; Philadelphia Mus Art; retrospective exhib, Storm King Art Ctr, Mountainville, NY; plus many others.

Teaching: Instr stage designing, Pratt Inst Art Sch, 57. Awards: Guggenheim Fel, 50; Ford Found Grant; Tony Awards, 56, 67, 69, 71, 72 & 76. Bibliog: Waldemar George (auth), Boris Aronson et l'art du theatre, Paris, 28. Mem: Ger Art Soc. Publ: Auth, Marc Chagall, 23 & Modern graphic art, 24; illusr, The theatre in life & var children's bks; contribr, Theatre Arts, Show, Vogue & Interior. Mailing Add: 729 Rte 9W Nyack NY 10960

ARONSON, CLIFF
ART DEALER
b Jan 16, 24; US citizen. Pos: Pres, Copenhagen Galleri, Solvang, Calif, 64-; pres, Christopher Galleries, Inc, Palm Springs, Calif, 74-76. Specialty: Contemporary American artists. Mailing Add: c/o Christopher Galleries 1618 Copenhagen Dr Solvang CA 93463

ARONSON, DAVID
PAINTER, SCULPTOR
b Shilova, Lithuania, Oct 28, 23; US citizen. Study: Boston Mus Fine Arts Sch, with Karl Zerbe, cert, 45; Nat Soc Arts & Lett grant, 58; Guggenheim fel, 60. Work: Smithsonian Inst, Washington, DC; Art Inst Chicago; Va Mus Fine Arts, Richmond; Boston Mus Fine Arts; Whitney Mus Am Art, New York. Comn: Great Ideas of Western Man, Container Corp Am, 63. Exhib: Fourteen Americans, Mus Mod Art, 45; Va Mus Fine Arts Biennial, 45; Johnson Collection of American Art (travelled int), 62 & 63; New York World's Fair, 64-65; Nat Collection Fine Arts Opening Exhib, Smithsonian Inst, 65. Teaching: Instr painting, Boston Mus Fine Arts Sch, 43-54; chmn div art, Boston Univ, 54-63, prof art, 62- Awards: Grand Prize, Boston Arts Festival, 52-54; Nat Acad Design, 73, 74 & 75. Bibliog: Article in Time Mag, 11/63; Newman (auth), Wax as art form, 66 & Grossman (auth), Art & tradition, 67, Yosellof. Mem: Academician Nat Acad Design. Media: Encaustic, Bronze. Publ: Auth, Encaustic, Artist Mag, 62; Real & Unreal: the Double Nature of Art, Boston Univ, 67. Mailing Add: 137 Brimstone Lane Sudbury MA 01776

ARONSON, IRENE HILDE
DESIGNER, PAINTER
b Dresden, Ger, Mar 8, 18; US citizen. Study: Eastbourne Sch Art, Eng; Slade Sch Fine Arts, Univ London; Ruskin Sch Drawing, Oxford Univ; Columbia Univ, BFA, 60, MA, 62; Art Student League; Parsons Sch Design; also with Prof Schwabe, Polunin & William S Hayter. Work: Bibliot Nat Print Dept, Paris; Victoria & Albert Mus, London; Brit Mus Print Dept; Mus Mod Art Print Dept & Metrop Mus Art, New York. Exhib: Kunstmuseum, Bern, Switz, 57; Brooklyn Mus, NY & Boston Mus, Mass, 58; Int Print Show, Ljubljana, Yugoslavia, 59; one-woman show, Mus Arte Mod, Mexico City, 59 & Towner Art Gallery, Eastbourne, Eng, 61; Nat Asn of Women Artists, New York, 74-75; Acquisition of Two Linoleumcuts, Nat Collection Fine Arts, Washington, DC, 75. Teaching: Instr art, continuing educ, Bryant Adult Ctr, 54-66; instr art (per diem), New York Jr High Sch, currently. Pos: Asst costume designer, Barnum & Bailey Circus, Broadway, 44. Awards: Gold Medal, Slade Sch Fine Arts, 39; Medal of Honor, Nat Asn Women Artists, 57; plus others. Mem: Nat Asn Women Artists; Asn Univ Women. Publ: Auth, The printmaker, Design Mag, 55; contribr & illusr articles, In: Artist Mag, London sketches, 7/74 & How to make a linocut, 7/75; auth, Setting up a printmaking workshop, Graphic Processes; auth, How to make a lithograph, Am Artist; also illusr of var bks. Mailing Add: 63-20 Haring St Rego Park NY 11374

ARONSON, SANDA
SCULPTOR
b New York, NY, Feb 29, 40. Study: Oswego State Col, BS, 60; study with J De Creeft & Paul Pollaro at New Sch for Social Res, New York; Tulane Univ, New Orleans; Art Students League. Exhib: Exhib Women Artists, Manhattan Community Col, 75; Women Artists/Showing & Sharing, US Mil Acad, West Point, NY, 75; Works on Paper, Brooklyn Mus, NY, 75; Women in the Arts (travelling show), Chatham Col, Pittsburgh, Pa & State Univ NY Binghamton, 76; Four Artists, Women in the Arts Found, New York, 76; Nine/Plus or Minus, US Mil Acad, 77 & The Arsenal, New York, 78. Teaching: Artist-in-residence, NY Found for the Arts, 77- Awards: Hon Mention/Sculpture, Women Artists/Showing & Sharing, US Mil Acad, 76. Bibliog: J L Collins (ed), Women Artists in America, Vol II, Univ Tenn at Chattanooga Press, 75. Mem: Women in the Arts Found (bd mem-at-large, 75-76); Found for the Community of Artists. Style & Technique: Sculpture (primarily in clay), figurative, naturalistic; drawing in line using ink. Media: Clay, pen & ink drawing, woodcuts. Publ: Contribr frontpiece, John Beecher (auth), Hear the Wind Blow, Int Press, 68. Mailing Add: 70 W 95th St New York NY 10025

ARTHUR, JOHN C
CURATOR, GALLERY DIRECTOR
b Arkansas City, Kans, Jan 8, 39. Study: Univ Tulsa, Okla, BA, MA, with Alexandre Hoque. Exhibitions Arranged: Jack Beal (ed, catalogue), Boston Univ Art Gallery, 73; America 1976 (ed, catalogue), US Dept of Interior, 76; Alfred Leslie (ed, catalogue), Boston Mus Fine Arts, 76; Brooke Alexander/A Decade of Print Publishing (ed, catalogue), Boston Univ Art Gallery, 78; Richard Estes (co-auth, catalogue), Boston Mus Fine Arts & New York Graphics Soc, 78. Pos: Cur & gallery dir, Boston Univ Art Gallery, 73- Res: Contemporary American realism and 20th century American prints. Mailing Add: 141 Bay State Rd Boston Univ Boston MA 02215

ARTINIAN, ARTINE
COLLECTOR
b Bulgaria, Dec 8, 07; US citizen. Study: Bowdoin Col, BA & LittD(hon), 66; Harvard Univ, MA, 33; Columbia Univ, PhD, 41. Exhib: (Artinian Collection) Portraits of 19th & 20th Century French Writers, Art Gallery, State Univ NY Col New Paltz, 65; Miguel Covarrubias Drawings of 1930 China, Alliance Francaise, Guadalajara, Mex, 65 & Mex-Am Inst, Mexico City, 78; Drawings by French Writers & Illustrators, var Am cols & univs, 68-74, Auckland City, NZ, Art Gallery, 77 & French Embassy-sponsored tour in US, 78-80; The French Visage, A Century and a Half of French Portraiture and Caricature, Bowdoin Col Mus of Art sponsored tour of New Eng, 69-70; Music in Art, Henry Morrison Flagler Mus, Palm Beach, Fla & var cols & univs, 71; Artists' Letters with Drawings, Seton Hall Univ Libr, 78. Mailing Add: Winthrop House 100 Worth Ave Palm Beach FL 33480

ARTSCHWAGER, RICHARD ERNST
PAINTER, SCULPTOR
b Washington, DC, Dec 26, 24. Study: Cornell Univ, AB; studio study with Amedee Ozenfant. Work: Kunstmus, Basle, Switz; Wallraf-Richartz Mus, Cologne, Ger; Detroit Mus, Mich; Mus Mod Art & Mus Am Art, NY. Exhib: Primary Structures, Jewish Mus, New York, 66; Arp to Artschwager, Bellamy-Goldowsky, New York, 68; When Attitudes Become Form, Kunsthalle, Berne, Switz, 69; Sonsbeek '71, Arnhem/Utrecht, Holland, 71; Documenta, Kassel, Ger, 68 & 72; Venice Biennale, 76. Bibliog: E Baker (auth), Artschwager's mental furniture, Art News, 1/68; Kotte et al (auth), Utrecht, Project 1971, Mus Hedendagse Kunst, Utrecht, Holland, 72. Publ: Auth, The hydraulic door check, Art Mag, 11/67. Dealer: Leo Castelli Gallery 4 E 77 St New York NY 10021. Mailing Add: Box 23 Charlotteville NY 12036

ARTZ, FREDERICK B
ART HISTORIAN, WRITER
b Dayton, Ohio, Oct 19, 94. Study: Oberlin Col, AB, 16; Univ Toulouse, 19; Univ Paris, 22-23; Harvard Univ, PhD, 24; Oberlin Col, LittD, 66; Carthage Col, LittD, 70. Teaching: Instr hist, Antioch Col, 16-17; instr hist, Harvard Univ, 23-24; from asst prof to prof hist, Oberlin Col, 24-66; vis prof, Harvard Univ, 30-31, lectr, summer sch, 31 & 34. Publ: Auth, France under the Bourbon restoration 1814-1830, Russell, 31 & 63; auth, Reaction and revolution: 1815-1832, 35 & 68, Harper-Row; auth, From the Renaissance to romanticism, trends in style in art, literature and music, Univ Chicago Press, 62; auth, Mind of the Middle Ages (rev ed), Knopf, 65; auth, Renaissance humanism 1300-1500 & The enlightenment in France, Kent State Univ Press; plus others. Mailing Add: 157 N Professor St Oberlin OH 44074

ARWIN, KATHLEEN G
ART DEALER
b New York, NY. Study: Ringling Sch of Art, Sarasota, Fla; New York Sch Design, with Werner Drewes. Pos: Co-dir, Arwin Galleries, 58-; mem, Bicentennial Arts Comt, Detroit, 76; mem arts comn, New Detroit, 77- Mem: Founders Soc, Detroit Inst Arts; Am Fed Arts. Specialty: Twentieth century graphics, painting and sculpture. Mailing Add: 222 Grand River W Detroit MI 48226

ARWIN, LESTER B
ART DEALER
b Rochester, NY. Study: Columbia Univ; NY Univ, BS; painting with Carlos Lopez. Teaching: Instr art appreciation, Wayne Co Community Col, 70. Pos: Owner-dir, Arwin Galleries, Detroit. Mem: Am Fedn Arts; Founders Soc, Detroit Art Inst; Mus Mod Art; Mich Acad Sci & Arts. Mem: Detroit Coun for the Arts. Specialty: 20th century paintings, graphics and sculpture. Collection: Reginald Marsh, Burliuk, George Grosz, Rivera, Shahn, Antreasian, Domjan and others. Mailing Add: Arwin Galleries 222 W Grand River at Washington Detroit MI 48226

ASANTE, KWASI SEITU (ROBIN OKEEFFER HARPER)
ART HISTORIAN, PAINTER
b Jackson, Miss, Feb 8, 42. Study: Ctr for Creative Studies, Col Art & Design, Detroit, Mich, 60-65, cert, with Sarkis Sarkisian & Sam Pucci. Work: Johnson Mus, Cornell Univ, Ithaca, NY; Johnson Publ Co, Chicago; Pan African Cong, USA, Detroit. Comn: Mural painting, YMCA, Fisher Br, Detroit, 71; mural painting, comn by Ed Vaughn, Langston Hughes Theater, Detroit, 77; mural painting, Ft Wayne Hist Mus, Detroit, 78. Exhib: Black Arts Festival, Detroit Inst Arts, 68; Midwest Black Artist Exhib, Malcolm X Col, Chicago, 72; Dir in Afro-Am Art, Johnson Mus, Cornell Univ, 74; Jubilee: Afro-Am Artists on Afro-Am, Boston Mus Fine Arts, 75; Black Aesthetics, 200 Yrs of Black Art, Chicago Mus Sci & Indust, 76; Midwestern Black Artists Exhib, Performing Arts Ctr Gallery, Milwaukee, Wis, 76; FESTAC 77, 2nd World Black & African Festival of Arts & Cult, Lagos, Nigeria, 77; Art From a Black Perspective, Am Black Artist Inc, Detroit, 77. Collections Arranged: Black Arts Festival (auth, catalogue), Detroit Inst Arts, 68; Directions in Afro-American Art (auth, catalogue), Johnson Mus, Cornell Univ, 74; Jubilee: Afro-American Artists on Afro-Am (auth, catalogue), Boston Mus Fine Arts, 75; Black Aesthetics, 200 Years of Black Art (auth, catalogue), Chicago Mus Sci & Indust, 76; FESTAC 77, 2nd World Black & African Festival of Arts & Cult (assembled & auth, catalogue), Lagos, Nigeria, 77. Awards: UAW Solidarity First Place, 66; Second Place, Stax Art Award, PUSH EXPO 72; Cert of Recognition, FESTAC 77, US Zonal Comt, 77. Bibliog: Henri Ghent (auth), Quo Vadis Black Art?, Art in Am, 11-12/74; Rosalind Jeffries (auth), Directions in Afro-American Art, Off Univ Publ, Cornell Univ, 74. Mem: Nat Conf Artists; Am Black Artist, Inc. Style & Technique: Realism; objective is to bring out the character of subjects in the environment in which they live. Media: Oil, Acrylic. Res: Relationship between African-American art and African art. Mailing Add: 12069 Cheyenne Detroit MI 48227

ASAWA, RUTH (RUTH ASAWA LANIER)
SCULPTOR, GRAPHIC ARTIST
b Norwalk, Calif, Jan 27, 26. Study: Milwaukee State Teachers Col, with Robert von Neumann; Black Mt Col, with Josef Albers. Work: Mus Mod Art; Whitney Mus Am Art; Chase Manhattan Bank; City of San Francisco; Gov & Mrs Nelson Rockefeller. Comn: Two bronze wire sculpture in fountains, Phoenix Civic Plaza; bronze fountain, Ghirradelli Sq; bronze fountain, Hyatt Hotel, San Francisco Union Sq. Exhib: Whitney Mus Am Art, 55, 56 & 58; Mus Mod Art, 58; San Francisco Mus Art, 54, 63 & 73; one-man shows, de Young Mem Mus, San Francisco, 60 & Pasadena Mus Art, 65; US Info Agency Junk Art Travel Show, 72-73; plus others. Pos: Mem, San Francisco Art Comn, 68-76; co-founder, Alvarado Sch Art Workshop, San Francisco Unified Sch Dist, 68-; mem, Nat Endowment for the Arts Educ Panel, 74-78; mem, Calif Arts Coun, 76-78. Awards: Tamarind fel, 65; Purchase Award, San Francisco Art Festival, 66; Dymaxion Award, 66; plus others. Mailing Add: 1116 Castro St San Francisco CA 94114

ASBEL, JOSEPH
ART DEALER
b Rockville, Conn, Aug 27, 21. Study: Pratt Inst; also with George Podorson. Pos: Dir, Four Winds Gallery, currently. Specialty: 20th century paintings oceana. Mailing Add: Four Winds Gallery Inc 415 Lovell St Kalamazoo MI 49007

ASCH, STAN (STANLEY WILLIAM ASCHEMEIER)
CARTOONIST
b St Paul, Minn, Aug 31, 11. Study: Mills Col, St Paul. Exhib: St Paul Pub Libr, 32, 34. Teaching: Instr cartooning, Univ Minn, 34-37; lectr cartooning, Columbia Univ, 41, Art Students League, 43 & various NY art schs, 49. Pos: Cartoons for the Farmer, Farm, Stock & Home & The Farmer's Wife, St Paul; cartoonist, St Paul Daily News, 31-32; assoc, McClure Newspaper Syndicate, formerly. Mem: Eugene Field Soc; Nat Press Club; Benson Players Club, New York. Mailing Add: 683 Third Ave Apt 1D New York NY 10017

ASCHENBACH, (WALTER) PAUL
SCULPTOR
b Poughkeepsie, NY, May 25, 21. Study: RI Sch Design, 40-41; with Randolph W Johnson, Deerfield, Mass, 42-45; I Marshall, Philadelphia, 46-48. Work: Sculpture on the Highway, Vt Interstate Hwy; Sculpture Park, St Margarethen, Austria; De Cordova & Dana Mus, Lincoln, Mass; Mem Art Gallery, Univ Rochester, NY; Bundy Art Gallery, Waitsfield, Vt. Comn: Forged mild steel crucifix, Trinity Col, Burlington, Vt, 61; corten steel, Bundy Art Gallery, 66; fabricated bronze, Bailey Mem Libr, Univ Vt, Burlington, 63-64; forged steel, Mother Seton, St Josephs Col on the Ohio, Cincinnati, 65. Teaching: Assoc prof art, Univ Vt, 56-

Pos: Trustee, Vt Coun on the Arts, 65-68; coordr, Vt Int Sculpture Symp, 68-; coordr Mill 21, Sculpture Prog, Vt Marble Co, 69-70. Media: Steel, Marble. Mailing Add: Charlotte VT 05445

ASCHER, MARY
PAINTER, PRINTMAKER
b Leeds, Eng; US citizen. Study: New York Sch Appl Design for Women; Hunter Col; Art Students League; also with Will Barnet, Vaclav Vytlacil & Morris Kantor. Work: Norfolk Art Mus, Va; Nat Mus Sports, New York; Bat Yam Mus & Ein Harod L'Osmanut, Israel; Nat Collection Fine Art, Smithsonian Inst, Washington, DC; Butler Inst Am Art, Youngstown, Ohio. Comn: Twelve Women of the Old Testament & Apocrypha, Wizo Bldg, Tel Aviv, Israel. Exhib: American Art in Our Time, Chrysler Exhib, Provincetown, 57; Art USA, Coliseum, 58-59; Exchange Exhib with Japanese Women Artists (Centenary), 60; Exchange Exhib with Argentine Artists (men & women), USIA, 63; 18th New Eng Ann, Silvermine, 67; 30 Yr Retrospective, Nat Arts Club, New York, 73. Teaching: Teacher, dept head, guidance dir & admin asst, var sec sch in NY. Pos: Chaplain, Nat Soc Arts & Lett (Empire State), 72- Awards: Huntington Hartford Found fel, 60; Int Women's Yr Award, 75-76; First Prize/Oil, Womanart Gallery, New York, 77; plus others. Mem: Fel Royal Soc Arts, London; Am Soc Contemp Artists (pres, 73-75); Nat Asn Women Artists (chmn publicity & pub rels, 57-71, ed newslett, 61-69); life mem Art Students League; Am Fedn Arts. Style & Technique: Hard-edge, flat surface, some textural quality, geometric and curved linear forms in abstract and semi-abstract spatial relationships with, at times, realistic forms. Media: Oil, Watercolor, Prints. Publ: Auth, Poetry-painting, 58; contribr, Anthology of Readings for Use in Christian Education & Worship, Word Alive, 69 & News Extra, 71. Mailing Add: 116 Central Park S Apt 10-N New York NY 10019

ASCOTT, ROY
ASSEMBLAGE ARTIST, EDUCATOR
b Bath, Eng, Oct 26, 34. Study: King's Col, Durham Univ, Newcastle upon Tyne, with Victor Pasmore, BA(fine arts with honours). Work: Arts Coun of Gt Brit; Manchester City Art Gallery, Wolverhampton Munic Art Gallery & Univ of Newcastle upon Tyne, Eng; Queen's Univ, Belfast. Exhib: One-man shows, Molton Galleries, London, 64, Hamilton Galleries, London, 67, Angela Flower, London, 70; Int Exhib of Art in Motion, Mod Museet, Stockholm & Stedelijk Mus, Amsterdam, 60; retrospective, Univ Guelph, 72. Teaching: Vis lectr painting, Slade Sch Fine Art, London, 67-70; vis lectr sculpture, St Martin's Sch Art, London, 73-74; vis lectr sculpture, Cent Sch Art, London, 73-74. Pos: Dir groundcourse, Ealing Sch Art, London, 61-64; mem, Nat Adv Coun on Art Educ, Eng, 68-70; pres, Ont Col Art, Toronto, 71-72; vpres & dean col, San Francisco Art Inst, 75-; founder-dir, Ctr for Critical Inquiry, San Francisco Art Inst, 77- Awards: First Prize, John Players Open Painting Competition, Nottingham, Eng, 67. Bibliog: Eddie Wolfram (auth), The Ascott galaxy, Studio Int, 2/68; Gary Dault (auth), The art of Roy Ascott, Arts Canada, spring 72. Mem: Royal Soc Arts, London; Col Art Asn Am. Style & Technique: Analogue structures. Media: Mixed Media. Publ: Auth, Diagram Boxes & Analogue Structures, 63; auth, The construction of change, Cambridge Opinion, 64; auth, Behaviorist art & the cybernetic vision, Cybernetica, 67; Behaviorables & futuribles, Control, 70; auth, The psibernetic arch, Studio Int, 70. Mailing Add: 800 Chestnut St San Francisco CA 94133

ASHBAUGH, DENNIS JOHN
PAINTER
b Red Oak, Iowa, Oct 25, 46. Study: Orange Coast Col, Costa Mesa, Calif, AA, 66; Calif State Col, Fullerton, BA, 68, MA, 69. Work: Rolls Royce Inc, New York; Miami Art Ctr, Fla; Toledo Art Mus, Ohio; Seattle Art Mus, Wash; Owens Corning Inc, New York. Exhib: One-man shows, Galleri Ostergren, Malmo, Sweden, 72, Tower Gallery, Southampton, NY, 73, Whitney Mus Am Art, 75; Gallery Farideh Cadot, Paris, 76, Seattle Mus Art, Wash, 76, Alexander Monett Gallery, Brussels, Belg, 76 & PS 1 Proj Gallery, Long Island, NY, 77; Brockton Art Ctr, 74; Whitney Mus Ann, 75; Rockefeller Arts Ctr, State Univ NY Col, Fredonia, 76; LeGrand Hornu, Le Mons, Belg, 76; Gallery Litho, Tehran, Iran, 76; Hall Walls, Buffalo, NY, 77. Awards: Creative Artists Pub Serv Grant, NY Coun on Arts, 75; Gugenheim Found fel, 76. Bibliog: Marilyn Friedman Hoffman (auth), Unstretched painting (catalog introd), Mass Art Ctr, Brocton, 1/74; Roberta Smith (auth), article in Artforum, 5/75; Bud Hopkins (auth), article in Artforum, 1/76. Style & Technique: Shaped oil paintings on canvas, large scale. Mailing Add: 67 Greene St New York NY 10012

ASHBERY, JOHN LAWRENCE
ART CRITIC
b Rochester, NY, July 28, 27. Study: Harvard Col, BA(Eng lit), 49; Columbia Univ, MA(Eng lit), 51. Pos: Art critic Europ ed, New York Herald-Tribune, Paris, 60-65; Paris corresp, Art News, 64-65; art critic, Art Int, Lugano, Switz, 61-64; ed, Locus Solus, France, 60-62; ed, Art & Lit, Paris, 63-66; exec ed, Art News, 66-72; art critic, New York Mag, 78- Bibliog: David K Kermani (auth), John Ashbery: A Comprehensive Bibliography, Garland, 76. Mailing Add: c/o Georges Borchardt Int 136 E 57th St New York NY 10022

ASHBY, CARL
PAINTER, INSTRUCTOR
b San Rita, NMex, Mar 2, 14. Study: Univ Utah, BS; NY Univ, MA; Grand Cent Sch Art, Atelier 17; also with Morris Kantor. Work: Purdue Univ. Exhib: Pa Ann; Corcoran Gallery, Washington, DC; Whitney Mus Ann, 47 & 49; Libr of Cong Print Show; Tirca Karlis Gallery (collage), 64-75. Teaching: Instr painting, New Sch Social Res, 71- Pos: Owner, Ashby Gallery, 45-48. Mem: Artists Equity Asn; Art Students League (rec-secy, Bd Control, 46). Style & Technique: Expressionist. Media: Oil, Watercolor; Collage. Dealer: Tirca Karlis Gallery Commercial St Provincetown MA 02657. Mailing Add: 18 Cornelia St New York NY 10014

ASHER, BETTY M
COLLECTOR
b Chicago, Ill. Collection: Contemporary art. Mailing Add: 12921 Marlboro St Los Angeles CA 90049

ASHER, ELISE
PAINTER, SCULPTOR
b Chicago, Ill, Jan 15, 14. Study: Art Inst Chicago; Bradford Jr Col; Simmons Col, BS. Work: NY Univ Art Collection; Univ Calif Art Mus, Berkeley; Rose Art Mus. Brandeis Univ; Geigy Chem Corp; First Nat Bank Chicago. Comn: Oil on Plexiglas window, comn by Dr John P Spiegel, Cambridge; cover for Poetry Northwest, autumn-winter 64-65; cover for The Chelsea, No 27, 70; jacket for Stanley Kunitz, The Testing-Tree (poems), Little, Brown, 71. Exhib: One-man retrospective, Bradford Jr Col, 64; one-man shows, The Contemporaries, NY, 66 & Bertha Schaefer Gallery, NY, 73; Lettering, traveling show, Mus Mod Art, New York, 67; The Word as Image, Jewish Mus, New York, 70; Nat Collection of Fine Arts, Washington, DC, 76; Renwick Gallery, Smithsonian Inst, Washington, DC, 76; Univ Duluth, Minn, 77; plus many other one-man & group shows. Bibliog: Ward Jackson (auth), article in Art Now, Vol II, No 4; Natalie Edgar (auth), Poet of plexiglass, Craft Horizons, 10/73; Brian O'Doherty (auth), Elise Asher: ut pictura poesis, Art in Am, 11-12/73. Style & Technique: A painted embodiment of a scriptive language entangled with a fantasy creature-world surface; wall paintings and free-standing structures. Media: Multi-layered densities in Oil & Enamel. Publ: Auth, The Meandering Absolute (poems), 55; contribr six drawing, This Book is a Movie (lang art & visual poetry), 71; contribr, Acrilic for Sculpture & Design, Van Nostrand, 72; contribr, Art: A Woman's Sensibility, Calif Inst Arts, 75. Mailing Add: 37 W 12th St New York NY 10011

ASHER, LILA OLIVER
PRINTMAKER, PAINTER
b Philadelphia, Pa. Study: With Gonippo Raggi, Joseph Grossman & Frank B A Linton; Philadelphia Col Art, grad. Work: Corcoran Gallery Art, Howard Univ & Nat Collection Fine Arts, Washington, DC; Univ Tex, El Paso; City of Wolfsburg, Ger collection. Comn: Oil paintings, two panels, Congregation Rodeph Shalom, Philadelphia, 40; portrait of Dean Dinwoodey, Chmn, Bureau of Nat Affairs, Washington, DC; murals, two rooms, Indian Spring Country Club, Glenmont, Md; portraits, the late Justice Harold H Burton & Hon Cyrus Chyng. Exhib: Pa Acad Fine Arts, Philadelphia; Thomson & Burr Galleries, New York; Green-Field Gallery, El Paso, Tex; Ann Print Exhib, Univ Va; Nat Collection Fine Arts & Franz Bader Gallery, Washington, DC; Retrospective Exhib, Howard Univ, 78; one-woman shows in US, Japan, India, Iran & Pakistan, var times, 51-75. Teaching: Instr art, Howard Univ, 47-51; instr art, Wilson Teachers Col, 53-54; from lectr to prof art, Howard Univ, 61- Awards: Corcoran Gallery Art, 55; Grumbacher Award, 60; Univ Va, 70. Mem: Am Asn Univ Prof; Soc Washington Artists; Soc Washington Printmakers (rec secy, 68-75); Artist Equity Asn (treas, DC Chap, 71-74). Style & Technique: Figurative with limited and reserved color, important use of space in composition. Media: Wood & Linoleum Block, Oil. Mailing Add: 4100 Thornapple St Chevy Chase MD 20015

ASHER, MICHAEL
ARTIST
b Los Angeles, Calif, July 15, 43. Exhib: I am Alive, 67, 24 Young Los Angeles Artists, 71 & Ten Years of Contemp Art Coun Acquisitions, 72-73, Los Angeles Co Mus of Art, Los Angeles; Mini-Things, Lytton Gallery of Visual Arts, Los Angeles, 68; New Work/Southern Calif, Art Gallery, Univ of Calif, San Diego, 68; West Coast Now, Portland Art Mus, Ore, 68; 18'6" x 6'9" x 11'2 1/2" x 47' x 11 3/16" x29' 8 1/2" x 31'9 3/16", San Francisco Art Inst, 69; The Appearing/Disappearing Image/Object, Newport Harbor Art Mus, Newport Beach, Calif, 69; Anti-Illusion: Procedures/Materials, Whitney Mus of Am Art, New York, 69; 557087, Pavilion of the Seattle Art Mus, Wash, 69; Plans & Projects as Art, Kunsthalle, Bern, 69 && traveling to Aktionsraum I, Munich, 69 & as Kunstler machen Pläne, andere auch, to Kunsthaus, Hamburg, 70; Spaces, Mus of Mod Art, New York, 69-70; Art in the Mind, Allen Art Mus, Oberlin Col, Ohio, 71; Documenta 5, Kassel, Ger, 72; 3D into 2D: Drawings for Sculpture, New York Cult Ctr, 73; The Betty & Monte Factor Family Collection, Pasadena Mus of Mod Art, Calif, 73, Recent Works, Gallery 167, Univ of Calif, Irvine, 75; Univ of Calif, Irvine, 65-75, La Jolla Mus of Contemp Art, Calif, 75; Via Los Angeles, Portland Ctr for the Visual Art, Ore, 76; Painting & Sculpture in Calif: The Mod Era, San Francisco Mus of Mod Art, 76; Ambiente, La Biennale di Venezia, Venice, Italy, 76; Michael Asher, David Askevold, Richard Long, Los Angeles Inst of Contemp Art, 77; Fac Exhib, Calif Inst of the Arts, Valencia, 77; Skulptur, Westfalisches Landesmuseum fur Kunst and Kulturgeschickte, Munster, Ger, 77; Los Angeles in the Seventies, Ft Worth Art Mus, Tex, 77; one-man exhib, La Jolla Mus of Art, Calif, 69, Gladys K Montgomery Art Ctr, Pomona Col, Claremont, Calif, 70, Market St Prog, Venice, Calif, 72, Gallery A-402, Calif Inst of the Arts, Valenica, 73, Project Inc, Cambridge Sch, Weston, Mass, 73, Lisson Gallery, London, 73, Heiner Friedrich, Koln, 73, Galleria Toselli, Milano, 73, Claire S Copley, Los Angeles, 74 & 77, Anna Loenowens Gallery, NS Col of Art & Design, Halifax, 74, Otis Art Inst Gallery, Los Angeles, 75, The Clocktower, New York, 76, The Floating Mus, San Francisco, 76, Morgan Thomas Gallery, Santa Monica, Calif, 77 & Van Abbemuseum, Eindhoven, Holland, 77. Mailing Add: 1135 Amoroso Pl Venice CA 90291

ASHEVAK, KENOJUAK
See Kenojuak

ASHTON, DORE
ART CRITIC, ART HISTORIAN
b Newark, NJ, May 21, 28. Study: Univ Wis, BA; Harvard Univ, MA. Teaching: Head dept art & archit hist, Cooper Union, 69- Pos: Assoc ed, Art Digest, New York, 52-54; art critic, New York Times, 55-60; contrib ed, Opus Int, Paris, 65- & Arts Mag, 74- Awards: Mather Award for art criticism, Col Art Asn, 63; Guggenheim Fels, 64 & 69; Ford Found Award, 65. Mem: Int Asn Art Critics (gov bd mem, 60-); Pen Club; Col Art Asn. Res: Modern art. Publ: Auth, The unknown shore, 62; A reading of modern art, 69; The New York school: a cultural reckoning, 72; A Joseph Cornell album, 74; Yes, but..., a critical biography of Philip Guston, 76. Mailing Add: 217 E 11th St New York NY 10003

ASKEVOLD, DAVID
VIDEO ARTIST
b Conrad, Mont, Mar 30, 40. Study: Univ Mont; Brooklyn Mus Sch Art, painting cert; Kansas City Art Inst, BFA(sculpture). Work: Stedelijk van Abbemuseum, Eindhoven, Holland; Mus Contemp Art, Houston, Tex. Exhib: One-man shows, NS Col Art & Design, Mezzanine Gallery, Halifax, 70, John Gibson Gallery, New York, 73, 75 & 77, Art Metropole, Toronto, Ont, 75 & Fine Arts Gallery, Univ Calif, Irvine, 76; Mus Mod Art, New York, 70 & 71; Mus Conceptual Art, San Francisco, Calif, 73; Proj 74, Köln, WGer, 74; Inst Contemp Art, Univ Pa, Philadelphia, 75; Los Angeles Inst Contemp Art, Calif, 77; Documenta, Kassel, WGer, 77; Southland Video Anthology, Long Beach Mus, Calif, 77 & Los Angeles Inst Contemp Art, 77; Story-Narrative Art, Contemp Art Mus, Houston, 77-78. Teaching: Asst prof art, NS Col Art & Design, 68-73; vis lectr studio art, Univ Calif, Irvine, 76-77; spec appt photog & post studio art, Calif Inst Arts, Valencia, 77-78. Awards: Max Beckman Scholar Painting, Brooklyn Mus, 63; Can Coun Arts Bursary Award, 72 & 75. Bibliog: Lucy Lippard (auth), Six Years, Praeger, 73; James Collins (auth), rev in Artforum, 9/74; Alan Sondheim (auth), Individuals, Dutton, 77. Style & Technique: A-logical systems; structural narrative use of video, photography and audio. Media: Film, Audio. Publ: Auth, Werner Lippert, ed, Extra, 75. Dealer: John Gibson Inc 392 W Broadway New York NY 10012; Paul Maenz 23 Lindenstrasse Köln D-500 WGer. Mailing Add: 709 Milwood Ave Venice CA 90291

ASKEW, PAMELA
ART HISTORIAN, WRITER
b Poughkeepsie, NY. Study: Vassar Col, AB, 46; Inst Fine Arts, NY Univ, MA, 51; Courtauld Inst, Univ London, PhD, 54. Teaching: Instr art hist, Vassar Col, 56-57, asst prof, 57-62, assoc prof, 62-69, prof, 69-, chmn dept art, 71-74. Awards: Am Coun Learned Soc Fel Art Hist,

65-66; Fulbright Fel Art Hist, 65-66. Mem: Col Art Asn; Am Soc 18th Century Studies; Renaissance Soc; Friends of Vassar Art Gallery; Atwood Fund (trustee, 75-); Am Asn Univ Prof. Res: Fetti. Publ: Auth, Fetti's martyrdom in the Wadsworth Athenaeum, Burlington Mag, 61; auth, A Melancholy Astronomer by Giovanni Serodine, 65 & auth, The question of Fetti as fresco painter: a reattribution to Andreasi of Frescoes in the Cathedral and Sant 'Andrea at Mantua, 68, Art Bull; auth, The angelic consolation of St Francis of Assisi in post-tridentine Italian painting, J Warburg & Courtauld Insts, 69; auth, Domenico Fetti: parable of the wicked husbandmen, Currier Gallery Art Bull, 73. Mailing Add: Dept of Art Vassar Col Poughkeepsie NY 12601

ASKILD, ANITA (ANITA ASKILD FEINSTEIN)
DESIGNER, WEAVER
b Stockholm, Sweden; US citizen. Study: Konstfack Skolan, Stockholm; Art Students League; also with Hans Hofmann & Sam Feinstein. Work: Mus Contemp Crafts, New York. Comn: Tapestry mural, comn by Architect Tyler Smith, Martha's Vineyard, Mass, 73. Exhib: Stockholm, Sweden, 55 & 57; Young Am, Mus Contemp Crafts, 62; Cape Cod Art Asn, Hyannis, Mass, 67; oné-man shows, Sculpin Gallery, Martha's Vineyard, 70, Tapestry-hangings, 75 & Paintings, 76, Second Story Spring St Soc, New York. Pos: Freelance designer, Gloria Buce, New York, 58-75 & Jack Lenor Larsen, New York, currently; instr textile design, Pratt Inst, 75- Awards: First Prize Painting, Van Dyke Award, Cape Cod Art Asn, 62. Bibliog: Ina Schell (auth), interview in Home Furnishing Daily, 68; D Grover (auth), rev in Craft Horizons, 75. Woven Tapestries, Time-Life Publ, 76. Style & Technique: Abstract; free form color development. Media: Acrylic, Pen & Ink, Yarn. Mailing Add: 311 W 90th St New York NY 10024

ASKIN, ARNOLD SAMUEL
COLLECTOR
b Utica, NY, Aug 21, 01. Study: Yale Univ, BA. Collection: Impressionist and post-impressionist paintings. Mailing Add: Cross River Rd Katonah NY 10536

ASKIN, WALTER MILLER
PAINTER, EDUCATOR
b Pasadena, Calif, Sept 12, 29. Study: Univ Calif, Berkeley, BA & MA; Ruskin Sch Drawing & Fine Art, Oxford Univ. Work: Hellenic Am Union, Athens, Greece; Mus Contemp Art, Chicago; Oxford Mus Mod Art, Eng; San Francisco Mus Art; Tate Gallery, London. Exhib: One-man shows, Santa Barbara Mus Art & La Jolla Mus Art, Calif, 67; Prints by Seven, Whitney Mus Am Art, 70; 3rd Brit Int Print Biennale, Eng, 72; 6th Int Triennial of Coloured Graphic Prints, Switz, 73. Teaching: Prof art, Calif State Univ, Los Angeles, 56-; vis prof art, Univ Calif, Berkeley, 68-69 & Calif State Univ, Long Beach, 74-75. Pos: Bd trustees, Pasadena Art Mus, 63-68; reader in studio arts, ETS, Princeton Univ; bd dir, Los Angeles Inst of Contemp Art, Los Angeles, 77- Awards: Nat Print Exhib Purchase Award, Calif State Univ, San Diego, 68; Senator James Phelan Award, San Francisco Mus Art, 69; Artist Award, Pasadena Arts Coun, 70. Bibliog: Schaad (auth), Realm of Contemporary Still Life Painting, Reinhold, 62; Violante (auth), American Printmakers '74, Graphics Group, 74; Newman (auth), Innovative Printmaking, Crown, 77. Mem: Col Art Asn Am; Los Angeles Inst Contemp Art; Los Angeles Printmaking Soc; Artists for Econ Action. Style & Technique: Screen printing, polychrome wood. Media: Oil, Acrylic. Mailing Add: 846 Bank St South Pasadena CA 91030

ASKMAN, TOM K
PAINTER, EDUCATOR
b Leadville, Colo, Oct 27, 41. Study: Calif Col of Arts & Crafts, BA(educ), BFA; Univ Colo, MFA. Work: City of Seattle, Wash; Cheney Cowles Art Mus, Spokane, Wash; Ft Worth Art Mus, Tex; Mus of Art, Univ Okla, Norman; Mus of Art, Univ Colo, Boulder. Comn: Monument to Art Enigmas, with Lynn Gray, Gary Stoneman & Allegra Berrian Askman, Enigma Art Co, Goose Egg, Wyo, 71. Exhib: New Orelans Mus of Art, La, 71; Addison Gallery of Am Art, Andover, Mass, 71; Minneapolis Art Inst, Minn, 71; Va Mus of Fine Arts, Richmond, 72; Extraordinary Realities, Whitney Mus of Am Art, New York, 73; Springfield Art Mus, Mo, 73-74; Extraordinary Realities, Contemp Arts Ctr, Cincinnati, Ohio, 74; Seattle Art Mus, Wash, 74. Teaching: Instr, Univ Minn, Minneapolis, 68-70; assoc prof, Nicholls State Univ, Thibodaux, La, 70-72 & Eastern Wash Univ, Cheney, 72- Awards: Two awards/painting, 26th Ann Exhib, Cheney Cowles Art Mus, Spokane, 74; Painting Award, 60th Ann NW Artists, Seattle Art Mus, Wash, 74; Two Yr Travelling Exhib, Mus of Art, Univ Ore, 76-78. Bibliog: Mike Walsh (auth), rev in Art Week, Oakland, Calif, 76. Mailing Add: W 524 13th Spokane WA 99204

ASMAR, ALICE
PAINTER, PRINTMAKER
b Flint, Mich. Study: Lewis & Clark Col, BA(magna cum laude); with Edward Melcarth & Archipenko, Univ Wash, MFA; Woolley fel, Ecole Nat Superieure des Beaux-Arts, Paris, with M Souverbie; Huntington Hartford Found residence fels, 61-64. Work: SW Mus, Los Angeles; Franklin Mint, Pa; Bonner Corp, Irvine, Calif; Pub Int Mus, Gabrova, Bulgaria; Levbarg & Weeks, Attys at Law, Austin, Tex. Comn: Channel Island (mural), Joseph Magnin's, 64; California Triptich, Security Pac Nat Bank, Los Angeles, 70. Exhib: Mostra Rappresentativa Nazionale, Biennale Delle Regioni, Ancona, Italy, 68-69; Western Asn Art Mus Circulating Banner Exhib, 70-72; Drawings USA, Minn Mus Art Nat Travel Show, 71-73; one-woman shows, Frye Mus, Seattle, Calif State Capitol, Pasadena Mus, Calif, Cite Univ, Paris & Southwest Mus & Roswell Mus; plus others. Teaching: Asst prof painting & drawing, Lewis & Clark Col, 55-58; instr painting, Lennox Adult Educ, Calif, 63-65. Pos: Eng draftsman, Boeing Aircraft, 52-54. Awards: Menzione Onorevole, Biennale Delle Regione, 68-69; Purchase Award, Seattle Art Mus; First Prize, Southern Calif Expos. Bibliog: Articles in Ariz Hwys Mag, 6/73, Los Angeles Herald Examr, 3/23/75, Seattle Times, 3/28/76 & Los Angeles Times Home Mag, 1/8/78; plus others. Mem: Desert Art Ctr, Palm Springs; Am Fedn Arts; Southwest Mus; Artists Equity; League of the Americas; Los Angeles Co Art Mus; Smithsonian Inst. Media: Casein, Tapestries, Indelible India Ink, Acrylic, Oil. Dealer: Hatfield Dalzell Galleries Ambassador Hotel 3400 Wilshire Blvd Los Angeles CA 90010; Mary Livingston's Gallery Two 1211 N Broadway Santa Ana CA 92701. Mailing Add: 1125 N Screenland Dr Burbank CA 91505

ASOMA, TADASHI
PAINTER
b Iwatsuki, Japan, Apr 28, 23. Study: Saitama Teachers Col, Urawa, MS; Bijitsu Gakko, Tokyo, govt scholar; Grande Chaumiere, Paris, govt scholar; Art Students League. Work: Nelson Gallery, Kansas City; Am Express Co, New York; 3M Co, St Paul, Minn; Andrew Dickson White Mus, Ithaca, NY; Nat Bank, Des Moines, Iowa. Exhib: One-man shows, Mi Chou Gallery, NY, 60, Findlay Galleries, NY, bienially 65-77, Knott Gallery, San Francisco, 70, Alley Gallery, Tex, 72, Elms Gallery, Midland, Tex, 72 & Ginza Matsuya, Tokyo, Japan, 76; Steckler/Haller Galleries, Scottsdale, Ariz. Teaching: Instr art educ, Iwatsuki Jr High Sch, 50-64. Awards: Second Prize, Saitama Bijitsu Ten, 55; Second Prize, Nat Exhib Prof Art, 68. Bibliog: Articles in Art News, Sun New York Times & New York Post, 65, 67 & 69; plus others. Media: Oil. Dealer: Findlay Galleries 984 Madison Ave New York NY 10021. Mailing Add: Philipse Brook Rd Garrison NY 10524

ASTLEY-BELL, RITA DUIS
See Duis, Rita

ASTMAN, BARBARA ANNE
PHOTOGRAPHER, MULTI-MEDIA ARTIST
b Rochester, NY, July 12, 50. Study: Rochester Inst Technol, NY, 70; Ont Col Art, Can, AOCA, 73. Work: Art Gallery of Ont, Toronto; Nat Film Bd, Ottawa, Ont; Agnes Etherington Art Ctr, Kingston, Ont; Ont Arts Coun, Toronto; External Affairs Dept, Ottawa. Exhib: SCAN, Vancouver Art Gallery, BC, 74; Realism, 75, Chairs, 75, Exposure, 75 & Xerography, 76, Art Gallery Ont; Forum, Montreal Mus Art, Que, 76; one-person shows, Nat Film Bd Can, Ottawa, 75 & Sable-Castelli Gallery Ltd, Toronto, 77. Teaching: Instr experimental imagery & photog, Ont Col Art, 75-, instr visual diaries & photog, 76- Awards: Prov Ont Coun of the Arts Grants, 74-77; Can Coun Grants, 76 & 77. Bibliog: Articles in Arts Canada, 73-77; Judith Mewillte (auth), Exploring electrostatic print media, Print Rev, Pratt Graphic Ctr, 77. Style & Technique: Involved in photography, collage, sequence, color Xerox and SX-70. Dealer: Sable-Castelli Gallery Ltd 33 Hazelton Toronto ON M5R 2E3 Can. Mailing Add: 136 Catalpa Rd Rochester NY 14617

ATHENA
PAINTER, SCULPTOR
b Hericlon, Crete, Greece, Nov 24, 28; US citizen. Study: Self-taught. Work: In pvt collections of Aristotle Onassis, Truman Capote, Yul Brynner, Princess Margaret, Mitzi Gaynor, Mrs Bernard Gimbel, Andreas Papandreou, Tasos Papastratos. Exhib: One-woman shows, Sturegalleret, Stockholm, Sweden, 59; US Info Serv, Athens, 60; Kenegis Gallery, Boston, 64; Krasner Gallery, New York, 65, 66 & 72. Mailing Add: 35 W 20th St New York NY 10011

ATIRNOMIS (RITA SIMON)
PAINTER, PRINTMAKER
b New York, June 26, 38. Study: Cornell Univ Sch Archit, BFA; Acad Rome. Work: Joseph H Hirshhorn Mus Art, Washington, DC; Housatonic State Col Mus, Conn. Comn: Dalai Lama Portrait-Mural, The Tibet Ctr, New York, 77-78. Exhib: Inner Spaces-Outer Limits, List Art Ctr, Kirkland Col, NY, 70; Inner Spaces-Outer Limits II, Lerner-Heller Gallery, New York, NY, 72; Reality Plus, James Yu Gallery, New York, NY, 76; Manscapes, Okla Art Ctr, Oklahoma City, 77; Spacescapes, Sid Deutsch Gallery, New York, 77. Pos: Rev ed, Arts Mag, New York, 67-70. Bibliog: First Person, Working Woman, 8/77; L Saphire (auth), Rita Simon, Blue Moon Press, in prep. Style & Technique: Conceptual realist; strong emphasis on spatial ambiguity through spectral color; window shows. Media: Oil; pen and ink. Publ: Auth, Robert Motherwell & Tamarind Workshop and June Wayne, Arts, 68; auth, Surrealism 1970, After Dark, 70. Mailing Add: 414 E 75th St New York NY 10021

ATKINS, BILLY W
ART ADMINISTRATOR, PAINTER
b Puryear, Tenn, Sept 7, 43. Study: Murray State Univ, BS, 67; Sangamon State Univ, MA, 73; Univ Ill, MA, 76. Work: MacMurray Col & Ill Col, Jacksonville. Comn: Sex educ manuals, State of Ill, 74; Ill Jaycees bicentennial pin, 76. Exhib: MacMurray Col, 71; Ill Dept Educ, 74; David Strawn Art Gallery, 74; Ill Col, 76; Galveston Arts Ctr, 77; 59th St Gallery, CEMREL, Inc, St Louis, Mo, 77. Teaching: High sch art teacher in Mo & Ill, 67-75; art educ teacher, MacMurray Col, 73-74; design teacher, Univ Ill, 75-76. Pos: Dir aesthetic educ, Galveston Co Cult Arts Coun, Inc, 76-; dir, The Arts Ctr, 77- Bibliog: Mary King (auth), article in St Louis-Post Dispatch, 77. Mem: Nat Art Educ Asn. Style & Technique: Figurative drawings & paintings accompanied by literary narratives. Media: Drawing; painting. Mailing Add: Galveston Arts Ctr 202 Kempner Galveston TX 77550

ATKINS, GORDON LEE
DESIGNER, ARCHITECT
b Calgary, Alta, Mar 5, 37. Study: Col Archit & Urban Planning, Univ Wash, BArch. Work: Royal Can Acad Art; Nat Gallery Can; Massey Found. Comn: Summer homes, comn by Howard & Gerald Melchin, Windmere, BC, 66; AGT Elbow Park Exchange, Alta Govt Telephones, Calgary, 67; studio, comn by Ed Drahanchuk, Bragg Creek, Alta, 68; Mayland Heights Sch, Calgary Pub Sch Bd, 68; Pinebrook golf & winter club, comn by Wilbur Griffith, West of Calgary, 74-75; Stoney Indian Band Admin Bldg, comn by Chiefs John Snow, Bill McClean & Alvin Two Youngman, Morley, 77. Exhib: Massey Medals Awards, Ottawa, 67; Royal Can Acad Art, Ottawa; Environment '69 & '70, Edmonton & Calgary. Teaching: Archit technol, Southern Alta Inst Technol, 61-63; design, Dept Environmental Design, Univ Calgary, 63; interior design, Mount Royal Col, Calgary, 64-66. Awards: Massey Medal, Massey Found, 67; Award of Excellence, Can Architect Yrbk, 68. Bibliog: Gordon Atkins/architect, compiled & prep by Cult Develop Br, Dept Prov Cult & South Alta, 70. Mem: Alta Asn Archit (pres Calgary chap, 64); Royal Archit Inst Can; academician Royal Can Acad Art. Publ: Contribr, Canadian Architecture 1960-1970; contribr, Can Architect, 67 & 70, Archit Can, 68 & Werk, 69; auth, Plywood World, 70; auth, Investigation North, Arctic Housing Research for Fed Govt, 75. Mailing Add: 1909 17th Ave SW Calgary AB Can

ATKINS, ROSALIE MARKS
PAINTER
b Charleston, WVa, July 21, 21. Study: Mason Sch Music & Fine Arts, Charleston, WVa; Morris Harvey Col, Charleston; workshops with Leo Manso & Victor Candell, Provincetown, Mass; also with Bud Hopkins, Truro, Mass. Work: WVa Arts & Humanities Permanent Collection. Exhib: Allied Artists of WVa Ann Shows, Charleston, 53-78; Exhibition 180 & Exhibition 280, Huntington Galleries, 70 & 72; Appalachian Corridors, Charleston Art Gallery, 72 & 78; Nat League Am Pen Women Ann Show, Washington, DC, 72; Provincetown Art Asn Nat Show, Mass, 72-78; Am Drawing Show, Portsmouth, Va, 76; 39th Ann Exhib Contemp Am Paintings, Four Arts, Palm Beach, Fla, 77. Awards: Selected for traveling show, Art in the Embassies Prog, 70 & Nat League Am Pen Women, 72 & 77; two Purchase Awards, WVa Arts & Humanities, 72. Bibliog: Dorothy Seckler (auth), article in Provincetown Painters; article in Artists/USA, 77-78. Mem: Allied Artists of WVa (vpres, 67); Am Pen Women (pres, Charleston Br, 73-74); Sunrise, Inc; Provincetown Art Asn. Style & Technique: Acrylic-abstract, hard edge. Mailing Add: 1512 Quarrier St Charleston WV 25311

ATKINSON, TRACY
MUSEUM DIRECTOR
b Middletown, Ohio, Aug 10, 28. Study: Ohio State Univ, BFA(summa cum laude), 50; Mex City Col, 50; Univ Pa, 50-55, MA, 51; Bryn Mawr Col, 53. Collections Arranged: Antique

Luster, Albright-Knox Art Gallery, Buffalo, 59; Contemporary American Painting & German Expressionism, Columbus Gallery Fine Arts, Ohio, 61-62. For Milwaukee Art Ctr: Pop Art and the American Tradition, 65, The Inner Circle, 66, Botero, 67, Options & The Bradley Collection, 68, Seymour Lipton & A Plastic Presence, 69, Aspects of a New Realism, 70, Portraits Exhibition, 71 & Six Painters, 72, The Urban River, 73. Pos: Curatorial asst, Albright-Knox Art Gallery, 55-59; asst dir, Columbus Gallery Fine Arts, 59-61, actg dir, 61-62; dir, Milwaukee Art Ctr, 62-76; dir, Wadsworth Atheneum, 77- Mem: Midwest Mus Conf (vpres, Wis, 68-71, exec vpres, 70-71, pres, 71-72); Am Asn Mus; Asn Art Mus Dirs (trustee & 2nd vpres, 72-73); Int Coun Mus; Am Fedn Arts. Publ: Auth, German genre paintings from the Von Schleinitz collection, Antiques Mag, 11/69; David Black, recent work, introd to catalogue for the David Black in Berlin Exhib, 4-5/71; also articles in prof journals, nat art news mags & newspapers. Mailing Add: c/o Wadsworth Atheneum 600 Main St Hartford CT 06103

ATKYNS, (WILLIE) LEE, JR
PAINTER, ART ADMINISTRATOR
b Washington, DC, Sept 13, 13. Work: Phillips Mem Gallery, Washington, DC; Talladega Col, Ala; Rockville Civic Ctr, Md; plus others. Exhib: Annuals, Soc Washington Artists & Landscape Club Washington; Carnegie Inst; Corcoran Gallery Art; Nat Collection Fine Arts; Baltimore Mus of Art; Butler Art Inst, Youngstown, Ohio; Nat Acad of Design, New York; Sweat Mem Mus, Portland, Maine; Hagerstown Mus, Md; Catholic Univ, Washington, DC; Dimmock Gallery, George Washington Univ, Washington, DC; Univ Chicago; Am Univ, Washington, DC. Collections Arranged: Music Themes in Painting, 70-71; Dynamic Liberated Lines, 72- Teaching: Instr painting, Lee Atkyns Studio Sch Art, Washington, DC, 45-68 & summer classes, Puzzletown, Pa, 45-50. Pos: Dir, Lee Atkyns Studio & Gallery of Art, 50-75. Awards: Landscape Club Washington, 54, 56, 60, 62, 68 & 71; Soc Washington Artists, 47-54; Am Artists Prof League, 61. Mem: Soc Washington Artists; Landscape Club of Washington; Artists Equity Asn; Washington Watercolor Club. Style & Technique: Non-objective, highly controlled designed lines giving effect of floating lines in space movements. Media: Acrylic. Specialty: Dynamic Liberated Lines series. Add: c/o Lee Atkyns Puzzletown Art Studio Box 120 RD 2 Duncansville PA 16635

ATLAS, MARTIN & LIANE W
COLLECTORS
b New York, NY. Pos: Liane W Atlas, Mem bd, Washington Print Club, DC, 66-, pres, 71-74. Collection: Prints from Goya to contemporaries; The Avant Garde in Theatre & Art: French Playbill of the 1890's, collected by us, was circulated by the Smithsonian Inst Traveling Exhib Serv for Exhib by Cleveland Mus Art, Clark Mus, Williamstown, Mass & others. Mailing Add: 2254 48th St NW Washington DC 20007

ATLEE, EMILIE DES
PAINTER, INSTRUCTOR
b Bethlehem, Pa, July 6, 15. Study: Spring Garden Inst, Philadelphia; also with Roswell Weidner & Joseph & Gertrude Capolino. Work: United Airlines, Philadelphia Airport; Palasaides High Sch, Bucks Co, Pa; La Salle Col & Franklin Inst, Philadelphia; Del Co Mem Hosp, Drexel Hill, Pa. Comn: Portraits, Libr Univ Del & Berks Co Ct House, Pa. Exhib: One-woman shows, Little Gallery, 63 & Newmans Gallery, Philadelphia, 70; Knickerbocker Artists Ann, New York, 64; Philadelphia Art Teachers Asn, 69-71; Pa 71, Harrisburg Mus, 71. Teaching: Instr, 53-69; instr, Main Line Ctr Arts, Bryn Mawr, Pa, 69-77. Awards: Hon mention, Nat, Ogunquit Art Ctr, 59 & Nat Benedictine Art Awards, 69; Gold Medal, Newtown Sq Arts Festival, 61. Bibliog: Dorothy Grafly (ed), The changing moods of art, Art in Focus, 71. Mem: Artists Equity Asn; Pa Acad Fine Arts; Philadelphia Mus Art; Woodmere Art Gallery; Main Line Ctr Arts. Style & Technique: Realistic—brush or knife glazing, impressionistic and abstract—brush or knife; primarily interested in lighting effects. Media: Oil, Pastel. Dealer: Newman Galleries 1625 Walnut St Philadelphia PA 19103. Add: 2117 Chestnut Ave Ardmore PA 19003

ATTIE, DOTTY
DRAWER
b Pennsauken, NJ, Mar 20, 38. Study: Philadelphia Col Art, BFA, 59; Brooklyn Mus Art Sch, Beckmann fel, 60; Art Students League, 67. Work: Allen Mem Art Mus; Univ Mass, Amherst; Fairleigh Dickinson Univ; IBM Corp. Exhib: One-man shows, Castagno Gallery, 66, AIR Gallery, 72 & 74, AIR Gallery, New York, 76, O K Harris Gallery, New York, Univ Mass, Amherst, Univ Iowa & Manhattanville Col, NY, 77 & Univ RI, 78; Art Acquisitions, Univ Mass, 75; Twentieth Century Drawings, Skidmore Col, New York, 75; Five Americans, Galerie Gerald Piltzer, Paris, 75; Three from NY/Paperworks, Centre Cult Am, Paris, France, 76; Kunsterlinner Int 1877-1977, Berlin & Frankfurt, Ger, 77. Awards: Creative Artists Pub Serv Grant, NY State Coun Arts, 73-74 & 76-77; Nat Endowment on the Arts Grant, 75-76. Bibliog: Francoise Eliet (auth), Five Americans, Art Press, 4/75; Corinne Robins (auth), Dotty Attie: narrative as ordered nightmare, Arts, 11/76; Gloria Orenstein (auth), Dotty Attie, Womanart, Fall 1976. Style & Technique: Small, meticulously rendered drawings, copied from fragments of paintings by Old Masters, put together in sequence to form a kind of narrative. Media: Pencil & Paper. Dealer: AIR Gallery 97 Wooster St New York NY 10012. Mailing Add: 334 E 22nd St New York NY 10010

ATWELL, ALLEN
EDUCATOR, PAINTER
b Pittsburgh, Pa, Oct 19, 25. Study: Cornell Univ, BA, 49 & MFA, 51. Work: Herbert F Johnson Mus Art, Cornell Univ, Ithaca, NY. Comn: Mural, comn by Peggy Mellon Hitchcock, New York, 65; Environment, comn by Reed Erickson, Baton Rouge, La, 68. Exhib: Dusseldorf Mus, Ger, 68; World Cult & Mod Art, Haus Der Kunst, Munich, 72; Willard Gallery, New York, 73; Everson Mus Art, Syracuse, NY, 74; Contemp Reflections, Aldrich Mus Contemp Art, Ridgefield, Conn, 75; plus others. Teaching: From instr art to assoc prof art, 51-64, Cornell Univ, assoc prof art, New York Exten Prog, 64-65; lectr art, NY Univ, 65-66, Manhattan Community Col, 66 & Ithaca Col, NY, 71-; teaching fel art, Inst Allende, Univ Guanajuato, Mex, 73. Awards: Ford Found Fel, India, 53-54; Fulbright Fel, India & Nepal, 61-62; Rockefeller Found Fel, SE Asia, Indonesia & Japan, 62-63. Bibliog: Organizing Comt film, 20th Olympiad, Bavarian Television, 72. Mem: Col Art Asn. Publ: Auth & illusr, Kuo Hsi's Clearing Autumn Skies Over Mountains & Valleys, 72; auth & illusr, Indian Miniature Paintings & The Yama Tanka, Aspen; auth & illusr, Indian art: from multiplicity to unity, Fulbright Newsletter, spring 74. Mailing Add: 432 Tioga St Ithaca NY 14850

AUBIN, BARBARA
PAINTER, INSTRUCTOR
b Chicago, Ill, Jan 12, 28. Study: Carleton Col, BA, 49; Art Inst Chicago, BAE, 54, MAE, 55, George D Brown foreign travel fel, France & Italy, 55-56; Buenos Aires Conv Act grant, Haiti, 58-60. Work: Ill State Mus; Art Inst Chicago; Ball State Univ; Centre d'Art, Port-au-Prince, Haiti. Exhib: Mid-Year Shows, Butler Inst Am Art, Ohio, 61 & 62; Am Drawing Ann, Norfolk Mus Arts & Sci, 63; 10th Ann Nat Prints & Drawings Exhib, Okla Art Ctr, 68; Drawings USA, St Paul Art Ctr, Minn & traveling, 68; Fairweather-Hardin Gallery, Chicago, 75 & 78. Teaching: Asst prof painting, drawing & watercolor, Art Inst Chicago, 60-68; asst prof painting, drawing & design, Loyola Univ (Chicago), 68-71; lectr painting, drawing & design, St Joseph's Col, 71-74; assoc prof painting, drawing & design, Chicago State Univ, 71- Pos: Reporter, Women Artists News, 77 & 78; critic for var publ. Awards: Hon Mention for Dana Medal, Pa Acad Fine Arts, 53; Mich Watercolor Soc Award, 65 & 70; Ill Arts Coun Proj Completion grant, 77. Mem: Col Art Asn Am; Am Asn Mus; Mich Watercolor Soc; Women's Caucus for Art. Style & Technique: Fantasy. Media: Watercolor, Mixed Media. Dealer: Art Rental & Sales Gallery Art Inst of Chicago Michigan & Adams St Chicago IL 60603; Fairweather-Hardin Gallery 101 E Ontario St Chicago IL 60611. Mailing Add: 1322 W Cornelia Chicago IL 60657

AUER, JAMES MATTHEW
ART CRITIC, WRITER
b Neenah, Wis, Dec 2, 28. Study: Writers Inst, Univ Wis-Madison, 49; Lawrence Col, BA, 50. Comn: Writer, dir & photogr, films, Operation Friendship, 59 & Someone Who Cares, 64, Wis Asn Ment Health. Pos: Asst Sunday ed, The Post-Crescent, Appleton, Wis, 60-65, Sunday ed & arts reviewer, 65-72; art ed, Milwaukee Journal, 72- Awards: Award of Merit, State Hist Soc Wis; A Brush with History Award, 62; President's Award, Wis Heart Asn, 66. Mem: Am Asn Sunday & Feature Ed (pres, 71-72); Friends Bergstrom Art Ctr, Neenah (pres, 67-68); City Neenah Munic Found. Publ: The City of Light (play), 61 & Tell It to Angela (play), 70, Attic Theatre, Lawrence Univ; art reviews to various mags including Craft Horizons & Wis Mag Hist. Mailing Add: Milwaukee Journal 333 W State St Milwaukee WI 53201

AULT, LEE ADDISON
COLLECTOR, ART DEALER
b Cincinnati, Ohio, Sept 30, 15. Study: Princeton Univ, 37. Pos: Publ, Art in Am, 57-69; trustee, Skowhegan Sch Painting & Sculpture, 68-78; adv coun, Princeton Univ Art Mus, 66- Collection: 20th century painting and sculpture; primitive art. Mailing Add: Lee Ault & Co 25 E 77th St New York NY 10021

AUSTIN, DARREL
PAINTER
b Raymond, Wash, June 25, 07. Study: Univ Notre Dame; Univ Ore; European Sch Art, with Emil Jaques. Work: Metrop Mus Art & Mus Mod Art, New York; Mus Fine Arts, Boston; Nelson Gallery Art, Kansas City, Mo; Phillips Mem Gallery, Washington, DC. Comn: Four oil panels, Med Col, Univ Ore, 36. Exhib: Whitney Mus, New York; Carnegie Inst, Pittsburgh; City Art Mus, St Louis; Contemp Painting in the US, toured in Latin Am countries; Inst Contemp Art, Boston; also many one-man shows. Awards: Lippincot Award for Figure Oil, Pa Acad Art, 53. Bibliog: Miller (auth), Americans 1942, Mus Mod Art, 42; Bird (auth), Darrel Austin, Art in Am, 43; Darrel Austin, Life Mag, 45. Style & Technique: Palette knives & painting knives. Media: Oil. Dealer: ACA Galleries 25 E 73rd St New York NY 10021; Harmon Gallery Naples FL 33940. Mailing Add: RD 4 Sawmill Hill Rd New Fairfield CT 06810

AUSTIN, JO-ANNE JORDAN
ART DEALER
b Springfield, Ohio, Nov 15, 25. Study: Western Reserve Univ & Cleveland Sch Art, BA(cum laude); Chicago Acad Fine Art; San Diego State Col, MFA. Teaching: Asst & later teacher art for children, Fine Arts Gallery of San Diego, Calif, 53-57; teacher art & English, La Cumbre Jr High, Santa Barbara, Calif, 58-60. Pos: Pub info officer, Fine Arts Gallery of San Diego, 56-57; dir & owner, Austin Gallery, Santa Barbara, Calif, 66-74 & Scottsdale, Ariz, 75- Awards: Bronze Award for Reflections on Oil (film), Int Film & TV Festival of NY, 70 & Chris Award, Columbus Film Festival, 70. Specialty: Paintings, original prints, and sculpture by living artists; diversity of styles. Publ: Reflections on Oil (art/ecology film). Mailing Add: 7103 Main St Scottsdale AZ 85251

AUSTIN, PAT
PRINTMAKER, EDUCATOR
b Detroit, Mich, Mar 17, 37. Study: Univ Mich, AB(Eng), 59; Univ Alaska with Alex Duffs Combs, Jr, 65, MFA, 76; Univ Wash, BFA(art), 71. Work: Evergreen State Col, Olympia; Anchorage Hist & Fine Arts Mus, Alaska; Alaska State Coun Arts, Printmakers Alaska Permanent Collection, Anchorage; Anchorage Borough Sch Dist Permanent Print Collection; Visual Arts Ctr, Permanent Print Collection. Exhib: All Alaska Juried Exhib, Anchorage, 66-69 & 72-75; 50 Years of Alaskan Art, Alaska Methodist Univ Gallery, 67 & Two person exhib, 69; 20 Printmakers Touring Invitational, Wash State Artmobile, 71-72; one-woman show, Migrations of the Moon, Anchorage Hist & Fine Arts Mus, 75. Teaching: Instr art & Eng, Anchorage Borough Sch Dist, 65-69; instr printmaking & drawing, Univ Alaska, 71- Awards: Drawing Award, Alaska Purchase Centennial Exhib, State of Alaska, 67; Printmaking Award, All Alaska Juried Exhib, 69 & 74 & Mel Kohler Award Painting, 75. Bibliog: Connie Godwin (auth), Pat's art is exploring world, Anchorage Daily Times, 11/3/75. Mem: Anchorage Hist & Fine Arts Mus Asn; Anchorage Arts Coun (adv bd vis arts, 75); Visual Arts Ctr. Style & Technique: Aims to effect a visual poem—strong design with highly refined balances using naturalistic imagery in symbolic relations; free combination of all two dimensional media. Media: All techniques of Printmaking; Drawing Collage & Watercolor. Mailing Add: 7030 Apollo Dr Anchorage AK 99504

AUSTIN, PHIL
PAINTER, LECTURER
b Waukegan, Ill, Jan 27, 10. Study: Univ Mich, AB, 33. Work: Ill State Libr, Lincoln Collection, Springfield & Ill State Mus; Wheaton Col Art Collection, Ill. Exhib: Five shows, Am Watercolor Soc Ann, New York, NY, 61-69; Watercolor USA, Springfield, Mo, 72 & 74; Mainstreams, Marietta, Ohio, 72 & 76; Am Artists Prof League Grand Nat, New York, 72; Acad Artists, Springfield, Mass, 72; plus others. Teaching: Guest instr watercolor, Wheaton Col, 63-70; lectr. Pos: Mem staff, Kling Studios, Chicago, 45-50; free lance artist, 50-66. Awards: Merit Award, 3rd Bluegrass Exhib, Louisville, Ky; Hon Mention, Mainstreams '72, Marietta Col, Ohio, 72; Fox Purchase Award, Watercolor USA 74, Springfield, Mo, 74. Bibliog: Phil Austin, watercolorist, Am Artist, 10/71. Mem: Am Watercolor Soc; Nat Watercolor Soc; Midwest Watercolor Soc (vpres, pres-elect, 77-78); Am Artists Prof League. Media: Watercolor. Dealer: Jack Anderson Art Gallery Sister Bay WI 54234; Deer Path Gallery 253 Market Sq Lake Forest IL 60045. Mailing Add: Rte 1 Ellison Bay WI 54210

AUTH, ROBERT R
PAINTER, PRINTMAKER
b Bloomington, Ill, Oct 27, 26. Study: Ill Wesleyan Univ, BFA; Wash State Univ, MFA. Work: Salt Lake Art Ctr, Utah; Col Southern Idaho, Twin Falls; Ricks Col, Rexburg, Idaho;

Boise Gallery Art, Idaho; Wash State Univ. Exhib: Intermountain Painting & Sculpture 4th Biennial, Salt Lake Art Ctr, 69; Fedn Rocky Mountain States Traveling Exhib, 71-72; Inaugural Exhib, Denver Art Mus, Colo, 71; 48th Ann Nat Apr Art Exhib, Springville Mus Art, Utah, 72; Realist Painting: 12 Viewpoints, Minneapolis, 72. Teaching: Instr art, Burley High Sch, Idaho, 60-61; instr art & humanities, Boise High Sch, 61- Pos: From asst supt to supt, Fine Art Div, Western Idaho Fair, 64-; bd dir, Boise Gallery Art, 69-; chmn art curric develop comt, Boise Independent Sch Dist, 71. Awards: Intermountain Painting & Sculpture 4th Biennial Award, 69; 36th Ann Exhib for Idaho Award, 72; Allied Arts Coun Artist of Year Award, 72. Mem: Idaho Art Asn (conf chmn, 68, vpres, 70-72); Boise Art Asn (trustee, 69-). Media: Acrylic. Dealer: Elva Brooks c/o Art Mart 711 S Latah St Boise ID 83705. Mailing Add: 530 Hillview Dr Boise ID 83702

AUTH, SUSAN HANDLER
CURATOR, ARCHAEOLOGIST
b New York, NY, June 25, 39. Study: Swarthmore Col, BA; Univ London; Univ Mich, MA; Am Sch Classical Studies, Athens; Bryn Mawr Col, PhD, 68. Work: Toledo Mus of Art, Ohio, 68; Newark Mus, NJ, 71. Collections Arranged: Myth & Gospel: Art of Coptic Egypt, Newark Mus, 77. Teaching: Asst prof ancient art & archaeol, Dept of Art, Rutgers Univ, Newark, 68-71. Pos: Curatorial asst, Toledo Mus of Art, Ohio, 67; cur of classical collection, Newark Mus, 71- Awards: Am Numismatic Soc Summer Fel, 63; Fulbright Scholar, Greece, 64-65; Res Travel Grants, Rutgers Univ, summer, 69 & Smithsonian Inst, Washington, DC, summer, 71. Mem: Archaeol Inst of Am; Int Asn for the Hist of Glass. Res: Ancient glass; Greek, Roman and Egyptian art and archaeology. Publ: Auth, Ancient Glass at the Newark Museum, from the Eugene Schaefer Collection of Ancient Glass, Newark Mus, 76; auth, var articles, Am J Archaeol, Archaeol & Annales Int d'Etude Hist du Verre. Mailing Add: Newark Mus 43-49 Washington St Newark NJ 07101

AUTH, TONY (WILLIAM ANTHONY AUTH, JR)
EDITORIAL CARTOONIST
b Akron, Ohio, May 7, 42. Study: Univ Calif, Los Angeles, BA(biological illus). Pos: Syndicated ed cartoonist, Philadelphia Inquirer, 71- Awards: Sigma Delta Chi Award, Soc of Prof Journalists, 76; Pulitzer Prize, Columbia Univ Trustees, 76. Bibliog: Stephen Hess & Milton Kaplan (co-auth), The Ungentlemanly Art: A History of American Political Cartoons, MacMillan, 75. Media: Pen and ink. Publ: Auth, Behind the Lines, Houghton-Mifflin, 77. Dealer: Rosenfeld Gallery 113 Arch St Philadelphia PA 19104. Mailing Add: 400 N Broad St Philadelphia PA 19101

AUTRY, CAROLYN (CAROLYN AUTRY ELLOIAN)
PRINTMAKER, INSTRUCTOR
b Dubuque, Iowa, Dec 12, 40. Study: Univ Iowa, Iowa City, BA, 63, MFA, 65; Yale-Norfolk Summer Sch, 62. Work: Libr of Cong, Washington, DC; Philadelphia Mus Art; Worcester Art Mus; Henderson Mus, Univ Colo, Boulder; Calif State Univ, San Diego. Exhib: Libr of Cong Nat Print Exhib, Nat Collection of Fine Arts, Washington, DC, 71, 73, 75 & 77; Boston Printmakers Nat Exhib, 71-77; Philadelphia Print Club Int & Mem Exhib, 72-78; Soc of Am Graphic Artists Exhib, 73, 75, 76 & 77; World Print Competition, San Francisco Mus Art, 73; Miami Graphics Int Biennial, Miami Art Ctr, 73 & 75; Prints Calif, Oakland Mus, 75; Contemp Am Graphics, Santa Barbara Mus, Calif, 75; 11th Int Biennial Graphic Art, Moderna Galerija, Ljubljana, 75; Int Print Invitational, Biella, Italy, 76; Int Graphic Biennale, Frechen, W Ger, 76; Am Graphics, Albion Col, Mich, 78. Teaching: Instr hist & studio, Baldwin-Wallace Col, Berea, Ohio, 65-66; instr art hist, Toledo Mus Art Sch Design, 66- Awards: Louis Black Award, Boston Printmakers Exhib, 71; George Roth Prize, Philadelphia Print Club, 72 & 73; Pennell Fund Award, Libr of Cong Nat Exhib, 71 & 75. Mem: Soc Am Graphic Artists; Calif Soc Printmakers; Boston Printmakers; Philadelphia Print Club. Style & Technique: Etching and aquatint in black and white. Dealer: Jane Haslem Gallery 2121 P St NW Washington DC 20037; ADI Gallery 530 McAllister St San Francisco CA 94102. Mailing Add: 3348 Indian Rd Toledo OH 43606

AUVIL, KENNETH WILLIAM
EDUCATOR, PRINTMAKER
b Ryderwood, Wash, Dec 18, 25. Study: Univ Wash, BA, 50, MFA, 53. Work: Achenbach Found, Palace of Legion of Honor, San Francisco; Seattle Art Mus, Wash; US Embassy, Bonn, Ger; Wichita Art Asn, Kans; Victoria & Albert Mus, London, Eng. Comn: Ed of 170 screen prints, Hilton Collection, New York, 62. Exhib: Northwest Printmakers Int Exhibs, Seattle Art Mus, 53-67 & 70; 4th Biennial di Pittura Americana, Bordighera, Italy, 57; Libr Cong Nat Exhibs, 59, 63 & 66; New Impressions for the Decade, Oakland Art Mus, Calif, 70; Int Print Exhib, Richmond Art Ctr, Calif, 72. Teaching: Prof art & printmaking, Calif State Univ, San Jose, 56- Mem: Northwest Printmakers (pres, 55-56); Calif Soc Printmakers. Publ: Auth, Serigraphy-Silk Screen Techniques for the Artist, Prentice-Hall, 65. Mailing Add: 605 Olson Rd Santa Cruz CA 95065

AVAKIAN, JOHN
PAINTER, INSTRUCTOR
b Worcester, Mass. Study: Yale Univ Sch Art & Archit, BFA & MFA; Boston Mus Sch, grad traveling scholar, dipl(hons) & cert. Work: Kans State Univ; Western Mich Univ; Bucknell Univ; Tulsa Civic Ctr, Okla; White, Weld & Co, Inc, Boston. Exhib: New Talent, New Eng, DeCordova Mus, Lincoln, Mass, 65; 20th Nat Exhib Prints, Libr Cong, Washington, DC, 66; 38th Int Printmakers Exhib, Seattle Art Mus, 67; one-man show, Higgins Wing, Worcester Art Mus, Mass, 71; 21st Ann Int Exhib, Beaumont Art Mus, Tex, 72. Teaching: Instr color & design, Worcester Art Mus Sch, Mass, 65-; instr color & design, Mt Ida Jr Col, 65-, chmn art dept, 66-71, dir art, 72- Awards: William E Brigham Prize, Providence Art Club, 68; Blanche E Colman Found Award, 70; Art Patrons League of Mobile Award, 72. Mem: Col Art Asn Am; Boston Visual Artist's Union; Worcester Art Mus. Style & Technique: Centralized and decentralized geometric configurations in acrylic and serigraph. Dealer: Assoc Am Artist 663 Fifth Ave New York NY 10022. Mailing Add: 43 Morse St Sharon MA 02067

AVEDISIAN, EDWARD
PAINTER
b Lowell, Mass, 1936. Study: Boston Mus Sch Art. Work: Guggenheim Mus, Whitney Mus Am Art & Metrop Mus Art, New York; Los Angeles Mus Art; Pasadena Mus Art; plus others. Exhib: John Powers Collection, Larry Aldrich Mus, 66; Robert Rowan Collection, San Francisco Mus Art, 67; Paintings from Expo '67, Montreal; Boston Inst Contemp Art, 67-68; Painters Under 40, Whitney Mus Am Art, 68; plus others. Teaching: Artist in residence, Univ Kans, 69; instr, Sch Visual Arts, New York, 69-70, Univ Calif, Irvine, 72 & Univ La, 73. Awards: Guggenheim Found Fel, 67; Nat Coun Arts Award, 68. Dealer: Robert Elkon Gallery 1063 Madison Ave New York NY 10028. Mailing Add: 650 Huntington Ave Roxbury MA 02115

AVEDON, RICHARD
PHOTOGRAPHER
b New York, NY, May 15, 23. Study: Columbia Univ. Work: Smithsonian Inst, Washington, DC; Metrop Mus of Art, New York; Mus of Mod Art, New York; Philadelphia Mus of Art, Pa; Minneapolis Inst of Arts, Minn; plus others. Exhib: Family of Man, Mus of Mod Art, New York, 55; Metrop Mus of Art, 59, 60, 63 & 67; Musee Reattu, Arles, France, 65; NY World's Fair, 65-66; Fogg Art Mus, Cambridge, Mass, 67; Rhodes Nat Gallery, Salisbury, Rhodesia, 68; Expo 70, Osaka, Japan; one-man retrospective, Minneapolis Inst of Arts, 70 & Marlborough Gallery, 75; one-man shows, Smithsonian Inst, 62, Mus of Mod Art, New York, 74. Pos: Staff photogr, Harper's Bazaar, 46-65; photogr, French fashions, 47-73; staff photogr, Vogue Mag, 66-70; contribr photogr, Life, Look, Graphis Mag, US Camera Ann; visual consult, Paramount film Funny Face; television consult & advert photogr. Awards: Highest Achievement Medal, Art Dirs Show, 50; One of World's Ten Greatest Photogr, Popular Photog, 58. Mem: Am Soc Mag Photogr. Publ: Co-auth (with Truman Capote), Observations, 59; co-auth (with James Baldwin), Nothing Personal, 64; ed, Diary of a Century, 70; co-auth (with Diane Arbus), Alice in Wonderland, 73. Mailing Add: 407 E 75th St New York NY 10021

AVISON, DAVID
PHOTOGRAPHER
b Harrisonburg, Va, July 13, 37. Study: Mass Inst Technol, ScB, 59; Brown Univ, PhD, 67; Inst of Design, Ill Inst Technol, 74. Work: Exchange Nat Bank, Chicago; Int Mus Photog, George Eastman House, Rochester, NY; Mus Mod Art, New York; Mus Fine Arts, Boston, Mass; Art Inst Chicago. Exhib: New Acquisitions Show, Exchange Nat Bank, Chicago, 74; Am Landscapes (traveling show), DePaul Univ, Chicago, 75; Contemp Color Photog: I, Proctor Art Ctr, Bard Col, Annandale-on-Hudson, NY, 76; 76th Exhib Artists of Chicago & Vicinity & Landscape Photograph, 77, Art Inst Chicago; Panoramic Photog, Grey Gallery, NY Univ, 77; one-man show, Art Inst Chicago, 77. Teaching: Prof photog, Columbia Col, Chicago, 70- Awards: Nat Endowment for the Arts Photogr Award, 77. Bibliog: Gretchen Garner (auth), Organic landscapes, Afterimage, 4/75; David Elliott (auth), Wide view of Chicago, Chicago Daily News, 4/77; Lynne Warren (auth), David Avison, Midwest Art Quart, 4/77. Mem: Soc Photog Educ; Chicago Artists' Coalition. Style & Technique: Straight photographer, exploring the aesthetic possibilities of the wide angle, wide format image. Media: Photography. Interest: Designed and built special panoramic camera. Dealer: Douglas Kenyon Gallery 154 E Erie St Chicago IL 60611; Panopticon, Inc 187 Bay State Rd Boston MA 02215. Mailing Add: 1522 Davis St Evanston IL 60201

AYASO, MANUEL
PAINTER, SCULPTOR
b Riveira, Spain, Jan 1, 34; US citizen. Study: Newark Sch Fine & Indust Arts, cert. Work: Whitney Mus Am Art, New York; Worcester Mus, Mass; Pa Acad Fine Arts, Philadelphia; NJ State Mus, Trenton; Newark Mus, NJ. Exhib: Drawings USA Circulating Exhib, 62 & 64-65; 22nd Int Watercolor Biennal, Brooklyn Mus, NY, 63; El Neo-Humanismo en el Dibujo de USA, Italia y Mexico, Univ Mex, 63; American Painting & Sculpture, Pa Acad Fine Arts, 67; Contemporary American Artists, Nat Inst Arts & Lett, 71; Contemp Am Spiritual Art, Mus Contemp Art, Vatican, Rome, 76. Awards: Tiffany Found Scholar in Painting, 62; Ford Found Purchase Award, 64; Childe Hassam Fund Purchase Award, 71. Mem: Am Fedn Arts. Media: Goldpoint, Mixed Media. Dealer: Forum Gallery 1018 Madison Ave New York NY 10021. Mailing Add: 127 New York Ave Newark NJ 07105

AYCOCK, ALICE
SCULPTOR
b Harrisburg, Pa, Nov 20, 46. Study: Douglass Col, New Brunswick, NJ, 64-68, BA; Hunter Col, New York, 68-71, MA, study with Robert Morris. Work: Mus of Mod Art, New York; Williams Col Mus of Art; Amherst Col Mus; Fr Ministry of Cult. Exhib: 26 Contemp Women Artists, Aldrich Mus, Ridgefield, Conn, 71; Untitled V, Penthouse Gallery, Mus of Mod Art, New York, 72; c 7500 (traveling), Calif Inst of the Arts, Valencia, 73; Interventions in Landscape, Mass Inst of Technol, Cambridge, 74; PROJEKT, Wallraf-Richartz-Mus, Cologne, Ger, 74; Biennale de Paris, Mus of Mod Art, France, 75; Labyrinth (traveling), Watson Gallery, Wheaton Col, Norton, Mass, 75; Otis Art Inst, Los Angeles, Calif, 76; Documenta 6, Kassel, Ger, 77; Drawings for outdoor sculpture: 1946-1977, John Weber Gallery, Amherst Col, Univ of Calif, Santa Barbara, MIT, 77; Metaphor and Illusion, Wright State Univ, 77; Portland Ctr for the Visual Arts, 78; one-woman shows, NS Col of Art & Design, Halifax, 72, Maze, 72, Low Bldg with Dirt Roof, 73 & Walled Trench/Earth Platform/Center Pit, 74, Gibney Farm, New Kingston, Pa, 112 Greene St Gallery, New York, 74-77, Proj Inc, Cambridge, Mass, 74, Williams Col Mus of Art, Williamstown, Mass, 74, Wheaton Col, Norton, Mass, 76, Circular Bldg with Narrow Ledges for Walking, Fry Farm, Pa, 76, Projects: Alice Aycock, Mus of Mod Art, New York, 77, John Weber Gallery, New York, 78 & Univ of RI, Kingston, RI, 78. Teaching: Adj lectr art, Hunter Col, 72-73; artist-in-residence, Williams Col, 74; instr sculpture, Sch of Visual Arts, New York, 77- Pos: Vol asst, Conserv Dept, Guggenheim Mus, New York, 67; cur, Art Hist Slide Libr, Hunter Col, New York, 69-72. Bibliog: Nancy D Rosen (auth), A Sense of Place, Studio Int, 3-4/77; Margaret Sheffield (auth), Mystery Underconstruction, Artforum, 9/77; Stuart Morgan (auth), Interview with Alice Aycock, Arts, 3/78. Style & Technique: Large semi-architectural projects dealing with the interaction of structure, site, materials and the psychophysical responses of the perceiver. Publ: Auth, Four 36-38 Exposures, Avalanche, New York, spring 72; auth, Five Semi-Architectural Projects, c 7500, Valencia, Calif, 73; auth, New York City Orientations, Triquarterly, Evanston, winter 75; auth, Notes on Project for a Simple Network of Underground Wells and Tunnels, Projects in Nature, Far Hills, NJ, 75; auth, Work 1972-1974, In: Individuals: Post-Movement Art in America, E P Dutton & Co, Inc, New York, 76. Dealer: John Weber Gallery 420 W Broadway New York NY 10013. Mailing Add: 62 Greene St New York NY 10012

AYLON, HELENE
PAINTER
b New York, NY. Study: Brooklyn Col, BA(cum laude); with Ad Reinhardt. Work: Whitney Mus Am Art, New York. Comn: Wall painting, Chapel, John F Kennedy Airport, NY, 66; lobby mural, NY Univ Med Ctr, New York, 67. Exhib: Lyrical Abstraction, Whitney Mus Am Art, Aldrich Mus Contemp Art, Phoenix Art Mus & Philadelphia Civic Ctr, 69; Two Generations, Univ Mus, Univ Pa, 70; one-woman shows, Max Hutchinson Gallery, New York, 70-72, Betty Parsons Gallery, New York, 75, Susan Caldwell Gallery, New York, 75, Grapestake Gallery, San Francisco, 76 & Mass Inst Technol, Cambridge, 76; Season's Highlights, Aldrich Mus Am Art, 71; Four Painters, Skidmore Col, Saratoga, NY, 71; plus others. Teaching: Instr painting, Brooklyn Mus & Hunter Col, 72-73; instr, San Francisco State Univ, 73-75. Awards: MacDowell Fel, 72; Nat Endowment Arts Fel, 73 & 74; One of 50 Selected Women, Nat Archives. Bibliog: Grace Glueck (auth), Art: highlights of downtown scene, New York Times, 12/11/70; Gregoire Muller (auth), Materiality and painterliness, Arts Mag, 9-10/71; Carter Ratcliff (auth), New York letter, Art Int, 6/73. Mem: Archit League NY (vpres painting). Style & Technique: Paintings that actually change in

time, after the paintings are finished; oil is applied to paper that is initially impervious to oil and in time the oil gradually seeps through; latest works in natural formations. Media: Paper, Plexiglas, Oil. Mailing Add: 1025 Carleton St Berkeley CA 94710

AYMAR, GORDON CHRISTIAN
PAINTER, ART HISTORIAN
b East Orange, NJ, July 24, 93. Study: Yale Univ, AB, 14; Sch Mus Fine Arts, Boston, 15-17. Work: Yale Univ Art Gallery, New Haven; Addison Gallery Art, Phillips Acad, Mass; Nat Coun Churches, New York; New York Neurol Inst; Photographic Dept Permanent Study Collection, Mus Mod Art, New York. Comn: Portraits, Pres K Towe, Am Cyanamid, New York, 55; Pres W Wheeler, Jr, Pitney Bowes, Stamford, Conn, 58; Dr H S Coffin, Madison Ave Presby Church, New York, 61; Pres L W Wister, South Kent Sch, Conn, 69; Pres J Armstrong, Middlebury Col, Vt, 71. Exhib: Mus Art, Montreal, PQ, 60; Royal Soc Painters in Water Colour, London, Eng, 62; Charles & Emma Frye Art Mus, Seattle, Wash, 64; Nat Acad Design, New York, 68; Am Watercolor Soc, New York, 71. Awards: Awards, Darien Art Show, Conn, 63 & 64, Pomeraug Valley Art League, 75 & Housatonic Art League, 76 & 77. Bibliog: Salon des aquarellistes de New York, Rev Mod, Paris, 62; C R Cammel (auth), American masterpieces in watercolour, New Daily, London, 62; Dorothy Brazier (auth), Crowd enjoys charming picture, Seattle Times, 64. Mem: Am Watercolor Soc (vpres, 63); Washington Art Asn, Conn (trustee, 66); Kent Art Asn (bd dir, 77). Style & Technique: Portrait painting using watercolor for women and children, oil for men. Publ: Auth, The Art of Portrait Painting, 67. Mailing Add: South Kent CT 06785

AYOROA, RODOLFO (RUDY) E
PAINTER
b La Paz, Bolivia, Sept 16, 27. Study: Acad Fine Arts, Cochabamba, Bolivia; Nat Univ Buenos Aires, Arg. Work: Nat Collection Fine Arts, Washington, DC; plus collections in Colombia, Arg, PR, Can & US. Comn: Painting, Pres Palace, La Paz, 52. Exhib: Latin Am Found Arts, San Juan, PR, 69; Coltejer Biennial Art, Medellin, Colombia, 70 & 72; Frostburg Col Mus Art, Md, 71; Biennial Art, Montevideo, Uruguay, 71; Univ PR Mus Art, San Juan, 72; plus many others. Teaching: Lectr art, George Washington Univ & Univ PR. Bibliog: Rafael Squirru (auth), Ayoroa, Americas Mag, 68; E Ruiz de la Mata (auth), Ayoroa, San Juan Star Mag, 2/27/72. Style & Technique: Kinetic light sculpture; architectural design and painting. Mailing Add: 6724 Wilson Lane Bethesda MD 20034

AZACETA, LUIS CRUZ
PAINTER
b Marianao, Cuba, Apr 5, 42; US citizen. Study: Sch of Visual Arts, New York, with Leon Golub, Frank Roth & Michael Loew, 66-69, cert, 69. Work: Cintas Found, Inst of Int Educ, New York; Harlem Art Col, Harlem State Off Bldg, New York. Exhib: Hispanic Art at the World's Fair, Spain Pavillion, New York World's Fair, 65; Int Exhib, Loeb Student Ctr, New York, 67-68; two-person show, New Talent Exhib, Allan Frumkin Gallery, New York, 75; Looking Inside Latin Am, New York Botanical Garden Mus, 76; Bicentennial Exhib, Allan Frumkin Gallery, 76; Latin Excellence, Xerox Corp, Rochester, NY, 77; Artist 77, Union Carbide Bldg, New York, 77; Re-Encuentro Cubano 1977, Dade Pub Libr, Miami, Fla, 77; one-man shows, Crash, l'Atelier Gallery, 71, Love, Odyssey House Gallery, New York, 72, Drawings, Cuban Cult Ctr, New York, 75, Ponce Mus, PR, 76, Inst de Cult Puertoriquena, San Juan, 76 & Allan Frumkin Gallery, Chicago, Ill, 78. Awards: Cintas Found grants, 72-73 & 75-76. Bibliog: Dora Rubiano (auth), Review in ABC Mag, 73; Ivan Acosta (auth), film, 12 Minutos de Cruces y Azacetasos, Cuban Cult Ctr, New York, 73; Paul Stitelman (auth), Review in Arts Mag, 75. Style & Technique: Man in his environment; expressionistic, cartoon-like, black outline. Media: Oil on canvas and tempera on paper. Dealer: Allan Frumkin Gallery 50 W 57th St New York NY 10019. Mailing Add: 32-78 Steinway St Astoria NY 11103

AZARA, NANCY J
SCULPTOR, EDUCATOR
b New York, NY, Oct 13, 39. Study: Finch Col, AAS, 59; Art Students League, sculpture with John Havannes, painting & drawing with Edwin Dickinson, 64-67; Empire State Col, BS(sculpture), 74. Comn: About the Goddess KALI (wood sculpture), Pamela Oline, S France, 77. Exhib: One-woman shows, Women Series, Douglass Col Libr, 72, Cornell Univ, 73, 14 Sculptors Gallery, 76 & Bard Col, 77; group & one-woman exhibs, Sarah Lawrence Col, Bronxville, NY, 73 & 14 Sculptors Gallery, New York, ann, 73-75; Whitney Counterweight, New York, 77; Preparatory Notes, Thinking Drawings, NY Univ, 77; Gallery 10 Ltd, Washington, DC, 77; Orgn of Independent Artists, Fed Bldg, New York, 77; Woman Artists 78, Grad Ctr, City Univ New York. Teaching: Lectr art, Sch Contemp Studies, Brooklyn Col, 73-75, lectr sculpture, 75-76; instr sculpture, Brooklyn Mus Sch, 74-77. Bibliog: Harriet Lyons (auth), Female eroticists, Village Voice, 72; Douglas Davis (auth), Women, women, women, Newsweek, 73; Miriam Brymer (auth), Organic image: women's image, Feminist Art J, 73. Mem: 14 Sculptors Gallery (pres, 74-77); Art Students League; Asn of Artist Run Galleries. Style & Technique: Partially painted, precariously balanced, assembled wood carvings. Media: Wood. Publ: Auth, Artists in their own image, MS Mag, 73. Mailing Add: 46 Great Jones St New York NY 10012

AZUMA, NORIO
SERIGRAPHER, PAINTER
b Kii-Nagashima-cho, Japan, Nov 23, 28. Study: Kanazawa Art Col, Japan, BFA; Chouinard Art Inst, Los Angeles; Art Students League. Work: Nat Collection Fine Arts, Smithsonian Inst, Washington, DC; Whitney Mus Am Art, New York; Philadelphia Mus Art; Brooklyn Mus Art; Art Inst Chicago. Comn: 1500 serigraph prints, IBM Corp, NY, 66. Exhib: Corcoran Biennial, Washington, DC, 63; 3rd Int Triennial Original Graphic, Grenchen, Switz, 64; Mus Mod Art, Tokyo Exhib, 65; Sculpture & Prints, Whitney Mus Am Art, 66; Silkscreen, History of a Medium, Philadelphia Mus Art, 72. Awards: Int Print Show, Seattle Mus Art, 60; Print Exhib, Soc Am Graphic Artists, 68; Print Exhib, Boston Printmakers, 70. Mem: Soc Am Color Prints; Print Club; Soc Am Graphic Artists; Print Coun Am. Style & Technique: Hard edge abstract. Media: Oil. Dealer: AAA Gallery 663 Fifth Ave New York NY 10022; Azuma Gallery 142 Greene St New York NY 10012. Mailing Add: 276 Riverside Dr New York NY 10025

B

BABER, ALICE
PAINTER, PRINTMAKER
b Charleston, Ill, Aug 22, 28. Study: Ind Univ, BA, grad sch; Fontainebleau, France. Work: Corcoran Gallery Art, Washington, DC; San Francisco Mus Art, Calif; Nat Collection Fine Arts, Washington, DC; Whitney Mus Am Art, New York; Mus Mod Art, New York. Exhib: Pinocotheca Mus, Osaka, Japan, 64; Kunstverein Mus, Cologne, Ger, 66; Iran Am Soc, Tehran, Iran, 74; Lowe Gallery, Univ Syracuse, NY, 75; Univ Ala, Birmingham, 75; Am Libr, Brussels, Belg, 75; Santa Barbara Mus Art, Calif, 76; McNay Inst, San Antonio, Tex, 76; Arvil Gallery, Mexico City, 76; Centro Colombo Am, Bogota, Colombia, 77; Centro de Arte Mod, Guadalajara, Mex, 77; plus others. Teaching: Vis artist, Univ Minn, 70-71, Univ Calif, Santa Barbara, fall 71, State Univ NY Col, Purchase, 72-73, Sch Visual Arts, New York, 74-76, New Sch Social Res, New York, 75-77 & Univ Calif, Berkeley, spring 76. Mem: Col Art Asn. Style & Technique: Colorist; lyric abstraction; use of transparencies and circular forms. Media: Oil, Watercolor; Lithography. Publ: Auth, Sonia Delauney, Crafts Horizons, 12/73; auth, Gorky's color, In: Ashile Gorky: Drawings to Paintings, Univ Tex, Austin, 75. Dealer: A M Sachs Gallery 29 W 57th St New York NY 10019. Mailing Add: 597 Broadway New York NY 10012

BACH, DIRK
PAINTER, EDUCATOR
b Grand Rapids, Mich, Nov 27, 39. Study: Univ Denver, BFA(painting), 61, MA(painting), 62; Univ Mich, Ann Arbor, MA(Orient art hist), 64. Work: Denver Art Mus, Colo; Hopkins Ctr Art Galleries, Dartmouth Col, Hanover, NH; Lamont Gallery, Phillips Exeter Acad, NH; Loretto-Hilton Gallery, Webster Col, St Louis, Mo. Comn: Wall reliefs, Denver Art Mus, 62, NH Comn Arts for NH Voc Inst, Berlin, 68 & Grad & Music Schs, Univ NH, 68; St Gaudens Nat Hist Site, Cornish, NH, 72. Exhib: Young New England Painters, John & Mable Ringling Mus Art, Sarasota, Fla, 69; New Eng Drawing Exhib, Addison Gallery, Andover, Mass, 70; one-man touring show, Cloud Mandalas, Landscape Buddhism, Webster Col, Tucson Art Ctr, RI Sch Design & Nat Ctr Atmospheric Res, Boulder, Colo, 71-; New England Drawing Competition, DeCordova Mus, Lincoln, Mass, 74; Saks Galleries, Denver, Colo, 75; Palazzo Cenci, Rome, Italy, 75; Kalamazoo Col, Mich; Newport Art Asn, RI, 76, 77 & 78; RI Sch of Design Mus of Art, Providence, 77. Collections Arranged: One Hundred Years of American Art, 66 & The Rose Art Museum Collection at New Hampshire (with catalog), 69, Scudder Gallery, Durham, NH. Teaching: Asst prof painting, Univ NH, 65-69; asst prof art hist, RI Sch Design, 69-; assoc & lectr, Asian Studies, Brown Univ, 70- Pos: Dir, Scudder Gallery, Univ NH, 65-69; trustee, Arts RI, Providence, 71-; dir Europ honors prog, RI Sch Design, Rome, Italy, 74-75; art critic, The Newporter, 76. Awards: US Nat Defense Lang Grant Mandarin Chinese, 64; Univ NH Cent Univ Res Grant Commemorative Stamp Paintings, 68; Nat Endowment Humanities Travel & Res Grant, Japan, 71. Mem: Col Art Asn Am; Artists Equity Asn; Newport Art Asn; NH Art Asn. Style & Technique: Oil on canvas; assemblage on Masonite; colored pencils and silk screen on colored paper; diagrammatic treatment of landscape forms. Res: Development of Ch'an painting in China; production of cosmic diagrams in the Far East. Collection: Chinese and Japanese hanging scrolls; Tantric Mandalas. Publ: Illusr, A New Way to Paul Klee, Denver Art Mus, 46; contribr, The Painting of Tao Chi, Univ Mich Mus Art, 67; auth, The stamp collection of Dirk Bach, Ramparts, 11/68; auth, Selections From the Oriental Collections, RI Sch Design, 72. Mailing Add: 15 Walnut St Newport RI 02840

BACH, MICKEY (MILTON FRANCIS)
CARTOONIST
b Waconia, Minn, Sept 30, 09. Study: Univ Wis, BA & MS, 33. Pos: Cartoonist & sports art dir, Minneapolis Star J, 35-41 & Chicago Sun, 41-42. Mem: Nat Cartoonists Soc; Gtr Los Angeles Press Club. Publ: Auth, Word-a-Day (syndicated cartoon feature), Publishers-Hall Syndicate. Mailing Add: Publishers-Hall Syndicate 30 E 42nd St New York NY 10017

BACH, OTTO KARL
MUSEUM DIRECTOR, WRITER
b Chicago, Ill, May 26, 09. Study: Dartmouth Col; Univ Paris; Univ Chicago, MA; Univ Denver, hon DH, 55. Pos: Dir, Grand Rapids Art Gallery, 43-44; dir, Denver Art Mus, Colo, 44-74; originator, Living Arts Ctr Pilot Educ Progs, 59- Awards: Extraordinary Serv Cert, City & Co Denver, 55; Am Creativity Award, 61; Chevalier Arts & Lett, 69. Mem: Am Asn Mus; Western Asn Art Mus Dirs; Col Art Asn Am; Int Soc Conserv Mus Objects. Publ: Auth, A new way to Paul Klee, 45, American heritage, 49, Under every roof, 50, Pre Columbian gold, 51 & Life in America; plus others. Mailing Add: 140 Krameria St Denver CO 80220

BACHINSKI, WALTER JOSEPH
SCULPTOR, PRINTMAKER
b Ottawa, Ont, Aug 6, 39; Can citizen. Study: Ont Col of Art, AOCA, 65; printmaking with Frederick Hagen; Univ Iowa, MA(printmaking), 67, printmaking with Mauricio Lasansky. Work: Montreal Mus of Fine Arts, Que; Offizi Gallery, Florence, Italy; Can Coun Art Bank, Ottawa, Ont; Civic Mus, Lugano, Switz; Kitchener-Waterloo Art Gallery, Kitchener, Ont. Comn: 3 bas-reliefs on a humanitarian theme, Univ Waterloo, Ont, 75; bas-relief of seated woman with child, Kitchener Ct House, Ont, 77. Exhib: Three Printmakers, Nat Gallery of Can Travelling Exhib, 68-69; 9th Bienniele of Prints & Drawings, Lugano, Switz, 72; one-man travelling exhib, Mount St Vincent Univ, 73; 4th Int Bienniele of Graphic Arts, Florence, Italy, 74; Bachinski, A Decade (travelling exhib), Kitchener-Waterloo Art Gallery, 76-77. Collections Arranged: Bachinski, Urquart, Weinstein (group exhib), Kitchener-Waterloo Art Gallery, 74; Contemp Can Prints & Drawings, McMaster Univ Art Gallery, 74; Of Human Bondage (travelling exhib), Robert McLaughlin Gallery, Oshawa, Ont, 76; Int Sculptures, Gallery Moos, Toronto, 76; Ont Now, The Art Gallery, Hamilton, Ont, 76. Teaching: Assoc prof drawing & printmaking, Dept of Fine Arts, Univ of Guelph, 67- Awards: Albert Dumochel Prize, Int Exhib of Graphics, Montreal, Que, 71; Merit Prize, 1st Los Angeles Printmaking Soc Ann Exhib, Calif, 73; Premio dell Instituto Bancario Si Paolo di Torino, 4th Int Biennal of Graphic Art, Florence, Italy, 74. Bibliog: Judy Heviz (auth), Review of One Man Exhibition, Art Mag, Summer, 75; Paul Duval (auth), Bachinski, A Decade (exhib catalogue), Kitchener-Waterloo Art Gallery, 76; Sharon Theobald (auth), Bachinski, A Decade, Art Mag, 8-9/77. Style & Technique: Figurative. Media: Drawing; sculpture. Dealer: Gallery Moos 148 Yorkville Ave Toronto ON Can. Mailing Add: 65 Mont St Guelph ON N1H 2A5 Can

BACIGALUPA, ANDREA
DESIGNER, PAINTER
b Baltimore, Md, May 26, 23. Study: Art Students League, painting with Arnold Blanch, summer 49; Md Inst Fine Arts, BFA, 50, painting with Jacques Maroger; Accad de Belli Arti, Florence, Italy, PG, painting with Ottone Rosai, 50-51. Comn: Ceramic mural, Carmelite

Chapel, Santa Fe, NMex, 73; designer & consult, St Laurence Cathedral, Amarillo, Tex, 75; stained glass windows, Good Shepherd Navajo Church, Pinehaven, NMex, 75; conceptual design, St John Neumann Church, Lubbock, Tex, 77; San Lorenzo (bronze), St Lawrence Cathedral, Amarillo, Tex, 77. Exhib: Biarritz, Am Univ, France, 45; Art Students League, 49; one-man show, Mus of NMex, 59; Am House, New York, 60; US Church Archit Guild, Pittsburgh, 61; Gov's Gallery, Santa Fe, NMex, 78. Pos: Dir multimedia, Liturgy in Santa Fe, 70- Awards: Bronze Medallion Fine Arts, Md Inst, 50. Bibliog: Maurice Lavanoux (auth), Liturgy & art, Liturgical Arts, 73; Jack Nelson (auth), Renaissance man, The New Mexican, 74; Clifford Stevens (auth), Sacred arts, Out Sunday Visitor, 74. Style & Technique: Primarily a liturgical designer in all media; multimedia as art form; design of stained glass. Media: Oil; Ceramics. Publ: Auth, Santos & Saints Days, Sunstone Press, 72; auth, The coffeebreak journal (Sunday column), Santa Fe New Mexican, 72-75; auth, Windows-light of the spirit, Stained Glass Quart, 73-74; auth, Liturgy in Santa Fe, Nat Cath Reporter, 75; auth, Journal of an itinerant artist, Our Sunday Visitor, 77. Mailing Add: 626 Canyon Rd Santa Fe NM 87501

BACKUS, STANDISH, JR
PAINTER, MURALIST
b Detroit, Mich, Apr 5, 10. Study: Princeton Univ, AB; Univ Munich. Work: Santa Barbara Mus Art; Utah State Col; San Diego Fine Arts Soc; Nat Watercolor Soc; Los Angeles Mus Art. Comn: Mural, Beckman Instruments, Inc, 55; mosaic mural, Pac War Mem, Corregidor Island, Manila Bay, Philippines, 67-68. Exhib: Los Angeles Mus Art, 38-40; Art Inst Chicago, Ill, 40; IBM Corp; Denver Art Mus; one-man show, Santa Barbara Mus Art; plus others. Teaching: Instr, Univ Calif Exten. Pos: Naval combat artist, Pac area & Japan, 45; off Navy artist, Byrd Exped to South Pole, 55-56. Awards: Prizes, Oakland Art Gallery, 39, Calif Watercolor Soc, 40 & Calif State Fair, 48 & 49. Mem: Nat Watercolor Soc; Am Fedn Arts; fel Int Inst Arts & Lett; Am Watercolor Soc; Los Angeles Art Asn; plus others. Mailing Add: 2626 Sycamore Canyon Rd Montecito Santa Barbara CA 93108

BACON, PEGGY
PAINTER, WRITER
b Ridgefield, Conn, May 2, 95. Study: NY Sch Fine & Appl Art; Art Students League. Work: Metrop Mus Art, Whitney Mus Am Art & Mus Mod Art, New York; Brooklyn Mus; plus others. Exhib: One-man shows, Nasson Col, Maine, 71 & Mus of Art, Ogonquit, Maine, 73; retrospective exhib, Nat Collection Fine Arts, Smithsonian Inst, Washington, DC, 75; plus many other nat exhibs. Awards: Guggenheim Fel, 34; Nat Acad Arts & Lett Award, 44; Butler Inst Am Artists Prize, 55. Mem: Nat Acad Design; Soc Am Graphic Artists; Nat Inst Arts & Lett. Publ: Auth, The Inward Eye, 52; auth & illusr, Good American Witch, Hale, 57; auth, Ghost of Opalina, 57 & auth & illusr, Magic Touch, 68, Little; auth, Oddity, Pantheon, 62; also illusr over 60 bks. Dealer: Kraushaar Galleries 1055 Madison Ave New York NY 10021. Mailing Add: Langsford Rd Cape Porpoise ME 04014

BACOT, HENRY PARROTT
ART HISTORIAN
b Shreveport, La, Dec 13, 41. Study: Baylor Univ, Waco, Tex, BA, 63; La State Univ, Baton Rouge, post grad study, 64-65; fel of the Attingham Park Summer Sch for Study of Great Eng Country Houses, Shropshire, 66; State Univ NY Cooperstown, Scriven Found fel, Cooperstown Grad Progs, MA, 67. Collections Arranged: American Folk Art 1730-1968, 68; Southern Furniture & Silver: The Federal Period 1788- 1830, 68; Louisiana Landscape 1800-1969, 69; Natchez-Made Silver of the 19th Century, 70; Sail & Steam in Louisiana Waters, 71; Louisiana Folk Art, 72. Teaching: Asst prof art hist, La State Univ, 67-, asst prof hist of interior design, 73. Pos: Cur, Anglo-Am Art Mus, Baton Rouge, 67-; hist interiors consult, Kings' Tavern, Natchez, Miss, 71-, Kent Plantation House, Alexandria, La, 71- & Magnolia Mound Plantation House, Baton Rouge, 72-; sponsor, Am Friends of Attingham Summer Sch, 77-; mem, Old State Capitol Comn, 77- Mem: Soc Archit Historians; Am Victorian Soc; Found Hist La (bd mem, 72-74). Res: Fine arts, architecture and decorative arts of the Deep South. Publ: Contribr, Antiques, 67-77; contribr, Antiques Monthly, 68-77; co-auth, Nineteenth century Natchez-made silver, Antiques, 71; contribr, Soc Archit Historians J, 74. Mailing Add: PO Box 20249 La State Univ Baton Rouge LA 70803

BADALAMENTI, FRED
PAINTER, GALLERY DIRECTOR
b Long Island, NY, June 25, 35. Study: Pratt Inst, 53-55; State Univ NY Col, New Paltz, BS, 60, with Carl Holty; Brooklyn Col, MFA, 67; with Philip Pearlstein. Exhib: Parrish Mus, Southampton, NY, 68-70; New York Figurative Painters 1970, Univ NC, 70; New York Figurative Painting & Sculpture Exhib, Univ NH, Swain Sch & Univ NC, 71; Brooklyn Col Art Dept, Past & Present, 1942-1977, Schoekopf Gallery, 77; one-man shows, Suffolk Community Col, New York, 71 & First St Gallery, New York, 76. Teaching: Assoc prof drawing & painting, Brooklyn Col, 67-; vis assoc prof drawing & painting, State Univ NY Col, Stony Brook, 77- Pos: Deputy chmn grad art, Brooklyn Col, 72-; dir, First St Gallery, 78- Awards: Brooklyn Col Grad fel, 65-67. Mem: Col Art Asn. Style & Technique: Realist under classical influences, still life and figurative subjects. Media: Oil on Canvas; Conté Drawing. Mailing Add: 182 Lower Sheep Pasture Rd Setauket NY 11733

BADASH, SANDI BORR
PAINTER, FABRIC DESIGNER
b Hartford, Conn, Mar 2, 36. Study: Lesley Col, BS(educ); Southern Conn State Col, MS(art educ), painting with Howard Fusner & Paul Tedeshi; Paer Sch Art, Yale Univ, summer work with Dean Keller. Exhib: Denver Mus Art Summer Exhib, 70; Woburn Abbey Show, England, 70; one-man shows, Leigh Gallery, Cambridge, Eng, 70, Gallery De Silva, Montecito, Calif, 72, Art Wagon Galleries, Scottsdale, Ariz, 74, Coast Village Gallery, Santa Barbara, Calif, 75 & 77, Lynn Kottler Gallery, New York, 78. Teaching: Art teacher drawing & crafts, Santa Barbar High Sch, 67-69; art supvr, Univ Calif, Santa Barbara, 73-74. Pos: Bd trustees, Santa Barbara Art Asn, 71-72; art dir, Int Art Guild, Santa Barbara, 73-74. Awards: Conn Art Festival, Meriden, 65. Style & Technique: Hard edged montages of interiors and gardens. Media: Oil. Dealer: Art Wagon Galleries 7156 Main St Scottsdale AZ 85251; Coast Village Gallery Santa Barbara CA 93108. Mailing Add: 601 E Anapamo St Apt 325 Santa Barbara CA 93103

BADER, FRANZ
ART DEALER, COLLECTOR
b Vienna, Austria, Sept 19, 03; US citizen. Study: Univ Vienna. Pos: Owner, Wallishussersche Bookshop, Vienna, 39; vpres & gen mgr, Whyte Gallery, Washington, DC, 39-52; pres, Franz Bader Gallery, Washington, DC, 52- Specialty: Contemporary American art, Washington artists, original graphics. Collection: Original graphics, contemporary artists and sculpture. Mailing Add: 2124 Pennsylvania Ave NW Washington DC 20007

BAEDER, JOHN
PAINTER
b South Bend, Ind, Dec 24, 38. Study: Auburn Univ, Ala, AB, 60. Exhib: One-man shows, Hundred Acres Gallery, New York, 72 & 74 & Morgan Gallery, Shawnee Mission, Kans, 73; Gray is the Color, Inst Arts, Rice Univ, 73; Richard Brown Baker Collect, Yale Univ Art Gallery, 75; Realismus und Realitat, Kunsthalle, Darmstadt, Ger, 75. Bibliog: Gregory Battcock (auth), Super Realism, Dutton, 75; D Filipacchi (auth), Les Hyper Realists Americans. Style & Technique: Slide projection, oil paints with brush; etching. Media: Lithography, Oil, Watercolor. Dealer: O K Harris 383 W Broadway New York NY 10012. Mailing Add: 924 Third Ave New York NY 10022

BAEHLER, WALLACE R
ART DEALER, COLLECTOR
b Chicago, Ill. Pos: Owner, Beahler Galleries, Georgetown, Colo, 66- Specialty: Contemporary American artists. Collection: American representational art of the 20th century. Mailing Add: Baehler Galleries PO Box 247 Georgetown CO 80444

BAER, ALAN
ART ADMINISTRATOR
b Philadelphia, Pa, Apr 15, 31. Study: Colby Col, 52. Pos: Chmn & managing dir, Int Art Registry Ltd, London, 70-, chmn & pres, New York, 74- Mem: Int Coun Mus; Am Asn Mus; Int Asn Mus Security Officers; Int Asn Identification. Mailing Add: 111 John St New York NY 10038

BAER, JO
PAINTER, WRITER
b Seattle, Wash, Aug 7, 29. Study: Univ Wash; Grad Fac, New Sch Social Res. Work: Mus Mod Art & Guggenheim Mus, New York; Kölnischer Kunstverein, Köln, WGer; Albright-Knox Art Gallery, Buffalo, NY; Nat Mus, Canberra, Australia. Exhib: Systematic Paintings, Guggenheim Mus, 66; Whitney Mus Am Art Biennial, New York, 67, 69, 73 & 75 & solo show, 75; Documenta IV, Mus Friedericianum, Kassel, Ger, 68; 31st Biennial, Corcoran Gallery Art, Washington, DC, 69; Options and Alternatives, Yale Univ, 73; one-person show, Mus Mod Art, Oxford, Eng, 77; Ft Worth Mus, Tex, 77; Indianapolis Mus, Ind, 77; Chicago Art Inst, 77. Teaching: Instr painting, Sch Visual Arts, New York, 69-70. Awards: Nat Coun Arts Award, 68-69. Bibliog: P Schjeldahl (auth), Jo Baer: playing on the senses, New York Times, 5/14/72; C Ratcliff (auth), Jo Baer: notes on 5 recent paintings, Artforum, 5/72; L R Lippard (auth), Color at the edge, Art News, 5/72. Media: Oil. Publ: Auth, Edward Kienholz: a sentimental journeyman, Art Int, 4/68; auth, Mach bands: art & vision & Xerography & edge-effects (collateral essay), Aspen Mag, fall-winter 70; contribr, Symposium on art & politics, Artforum, 9/70; auth, Fluorescent light culture, Am Orchid Soc Bull, 9-10/71. Dealer: John Weber Gallery 420 W Broadway New York NY 10012. Mailing Add: Smarmore Castle Ardee Co Louth Ireland

BAER, NORBERT SEBASTIAN
EDUCATOR
b Brooklyn, NY, June 6, 38. Study: Brooklyn Col, BSc(chemistry), 59; Univ Wis, MSc(physical chemistry), 62; NY Univ, PhD(physical chemistry), 69. Teaching: Assoc prof conserv, Inst Fine Arts, NY Univ, 69- Pos: Ed adv & assoc ed, Studies in Conservation, J Int Inst for Conserv, 71-; deleg & mem exec comt & chmn educ & training comt, Nat Conserv Adv Coun, 72-; co-chmn, Conserv Ctr, Inst Fine Arts, NY Univ, 75-; mem conserv comt, Nat Endowment for the Arts, 76 & 77; mem adv coun, Int Found Art Res, 76-; chmn ad hoc vis comt, Conserv Analytical Lab, Smithsonian Inst, 77- Mem: Fel Int Inst Conserv; fel Am Inst Conserv (bd dir, 73-76; bd examr for paper conserv, 76-); fel Am Inst Chemists; Am Chemical Soc; Sigma Xi. Res: Application of physico-chemical techniques to the preservation and examination of artistic and historic works. Publ: Co-auth, An evaluation of glues for use in paper conservation, In: Conservation & Restoration of Pictorial Art, Butterworths, London, 76; co-auth, Lining of paintings 1900-1975: an annotated bibliography, Art & Archaeology Tech Abstracts, Vol 14 (1977); co-auth, Chemical investigations on pre-Columbian archaeological textile specimens & Use of the Arrhenius equation in multicomponent systems, Preservation of Paper & Textiles of Hist & Artistic Value, Advances in Chemistry, Vol 164 (1977); co-auth, Application of infrared Fourier transform spectroscopy to problems in conservation: I General principles, Studies in Conserv, Vol 22 (1977): 116-128. Mailing Add: One E 78th St New York NY 10021

BAHM, HENRY
PAINTER
b Boston, Mass, Feb 26, 20. Study: Mass Sch Art, Boston; Boston Mus Fine Arts Sch. Work: Walter P Chrysler Collection; Univ NC; John P Merriam Collection, Boston; Boston Mus Fine Arts; Dillard Collection, SC. Comn: Mural, Foxboro Clubhouse, Mass. Exhib: Los Angeles Co Mus, Los Angeles, Calif, 50; Norfolk Mus, Va, 59; Univ NC, 60; Columbia Mus, SC, 62; Boston Arts Festival, 65. Teaching: Pvt painting classes. Awards: Jordan Marsh Co Award; Purchase Prizes, Cooperstown Art Asn & Univ NC. Mem: Berwick Art Ctr, Pa; DeCordova Mus, Mass; Provincetown Art Asn; Boston Mus Fine Arts & Norfolk Mus; Copley Soc Boston. Mailing Add: 755 Beacon St Newton MA 02159

BAIGTS, JUAN
ART WRITER, LECTURER
b Mexico City, Mexico, Apr 28, 46. Study: Nat Autonomous Univ of Mex. Pos: Art writer, Oaxaca Grafico Newspaper, 64-67; art critic, El Gallo Ilustrado, Cult Sect El Dia, 71-76; art writer, Diorama de la Cult, Excelsior Newspaper, 76-; art lectr, Nat Asn Univs, var cities in Mex, 76- Bibliog: Marco Antonio Acostax (auth), La Joven Narrativa Mexicana, Boletin Bibliog, Secy of Hacienda, 68; Jose Luis Carabes (auth), Entrevista con Juan Baigts, El Informador, Guadalajara, 76; Artistas Plasticos Mexico 1977, Ed Cult, Guadalajara, 77. Res: Study of contemporary Mexicans' primitive art, 1922-1977. Collection: Several works of Mexico's primitive painters and other styles (Rufino Tamayo, Carlos Merida, Maria Izquierdo, Francisto Toledo, Rodolfo Morales, etc). Publ: Auth, El Arte y el Misterio Delser, La Opinión, Torreón, 68; auth, Andy Warhol, El Gallo Ilustrado, El Día, 72; auth, Tamayo, La Estrella Solitaria, Artenoticias Mag, 74; auth, La Pintura de Rodolfo Morales, Catálogo Exposición, 75; auth, La Escultura Sensual de Geles Cabrera, (in press). Mailing Add: General Anaya 139 Esq Div del Norte Mexico 21 DF Mexico

BAILEY, CLARK T
SCULPTOR, EDUCATOR
b Chickasha, Okla, Nov 10, 32. Study: Univ Houston, BFA; Inst Allende, San Miguel de Allende, Mex, MFA; and with Richard Hunt. Comn: Fountain, Mr & Mrs Charles Berry, Casady Sch, Oklahoma City, 70; & smaller works in many pvt collections. Exhib: Nat Acad Design Ann, New York, 67; Nat Sculpture Soc 37th, 38th & 39th Ann, New York, 70-75; Xerox Exhib, Rochester, NY, 71; Reflections—Images of Am, US Info Agency Sponsored Exhib, Europe, 76-77. Teaching: Prof art, Univ Sci & Arts, 58-, chmn art dept. Pos: Staff artist,

Houston Pub Schs, Tex, 54-56; post illusr, US Army, Ft Chaffee, Ark, 56-58. Awards: Mahonri Young Award, Nat Acad Design, 67 & Watrous Gold Medal, 73; C Percival Dietsch Award, Nat Sculpture Soc, 70. Mem: Nat Sculpture Soc; Okla Mus Art. Style & Technique: Realistic; animal forms. Media: Welded Steel. Publ: Contribr, Prize winning sculpture, Allied, 66; contribr, La Rev Mod, 67 & Sculpture Rev, 70-77. Mailing Add: 124 Farris Pl Chickasha OK 73018

BAILEY, JAMES ARLINGTON, JR
PAINTER, RESTORER
b Ft Lauderdale, Fla, May 26, 32. Study: Univ Fla; Univ Denver; Univ Md Overseas Exten, Saudi Arabia; Georgetown Univ, BSFS. Work: Univ NC Mus, Greensboro; Norton Gallery, West Palm Beach, Fla; Princeton Univ, NJ; Mus Contemp Art, Houston; Columbus Mus, Ohio. Exhib: Gulf Coast Regional, Mobile, Ala, 66-68; Max 24 Exhibition, Purdue Univ, Lafayette, Ind, 68-69; Soc Four Arts, Palm Beach, Fla, 69-70; Art for Peace Exhibition, Dainenburg Gallery, New York, 70; Graphikbiennale, Vienna, Austria, 72. Pos: Dir, Fine Arts Res & Investment Div, London Investments Ltd. Awards: Purchase Award, Weatherspoon Mus, Univ NC, 67. Media: Oil. Publ: Contribr, Lo que es y ha sido la pintura, Vanidades, 12/70. Mailing Add: 7719 SW 69th Ave South Miami FL 33143

BAILEY, MALCOLM C W
PAINTER, ILLUSTRATOR
b New York, NY, Aug 18, 47. Study: Pratt Inst, BFA, 69. Work: Mus Mod Art & Whitney Mus Am Art, New York. Exhib: Afro-American Artists since 1950, Brooklyn Col, 69; Whitney Ann Am Painting, 69 & 72 & one-man exhib, 71; Paperworks by 22 Young Artists, Mus Mod Art, New York, 70. Teaching: Adj instr painting, Cooper Union, New York, spring 70. Awards: Fel Award, Yaddo, 69-70 & MacDowell Colony, 70. Bibliog: Barbara Rose (auth), Black artists in America, Art in Am, 70; Grace Glueck (auth), Review of one-man show, Whitney Museum, New York Times, 71. Media: Acrylic, Enamel, Ink, Wash. Publ: Contribr cover, Art Gallery Mag, 70. Mailing Add: 462 Broome St New York NY 10013

BAILEY, OSCAR
PHOTOGRAPHER, EDUCATOR
b Barnesville, Ohio, July 23, 25. Study: Wilmington Col, Ohio, BA; Ohio Univ, Athens, MFA. Work: Int Mus Photog, George Eastman House, Rochester, NY; Hist of Photog Collection, Smithsonian Inst, Washington, DC; New Orleans Mus Art, La; Mus Fine Arts, St Petersburg, Fla; Boston Mus Fine Arts. Exhib: Photog at Mid-Century, Int Mus Photog, George Eastman House, 59; The Sense of Abstraction in Contemp Photog, Mus Mod Art, New York, 60; Photog USA, De Cordova Mus, Lincoln, Mass & George Eastman House, Rochester, NY, 62; Photog in Fine Arts, Metrop Mus Art, New York, 63 & 76; Four Directions in Photog, Albright-Knox Art Gallery, Buffalo, NY, 64; Photog in the 20th Century (contribr), Nat Gallery of Can, Ottawa, 67; Photo-Media, Mus Contemp Crafts, New York, 71; Wider View, Int Mus Photog, George Eastman House, 72; Light & Lens (contribr), Hudson River Mus, Yonkers, NY, 73; Time & Transformation, Lowe Art Mus, Univ Miami, Fla, 75; Photo/Synthesis, Cornell Univ, Ithaca, NY, 76; The Contemp Am S (traveling show, SE Asia & Europ), US Info Agency, 77. Teaching: Prof photog, State Univ NY, Buffalo, 58-69 & Univ S Fla, Tampa, 69- Pos: Founding mem, Soc Photog Educ, 62. Awards: Photog Fel Grant, Nat Endowment for the Arts, 76. Bibliog: John Canaday (auth), New Talent—1960, Art in Am, 60; J Kirk T Varneodoe (ed), Modern Portraits—The Self & Others, Columbia Univ, 76. Style & Technique: Photography, primarily straight silver prints, also photo-constructions, mixed-media and photo manipulation. Publ: Co-auth, Found Objects, State Univ NY, Buffalo, 65; ed, Silver Bullets, Dept Photog, Univ S Fla, 72; contribr, Marcel DuChamp, Mus Mod Art, 73. Mailing Add: 2004 Clement Rd Lutz FL 33549

BAILEY, RICHARD H
SCULPTOR
b Dover, Del, June 24, 40. Study: Del Art Ctr, Wilmington; Art Students League; New Sch Social Res; study in Carrara, Italy; also with Jose DeCreeft, Lorrie Goulet, Leroy Smith & Oya Eraybar. Work: Am Mus Natural Hist, New York; Univ Del. Exhib: Silvermine Guild Artists, New Canaan, Conn; Int Exhib Sculpture, Carrara, Italy; Greer Gallery; one-man show, Del Art Mus, 74; Randall Galleries, New York, 75. Awards: Founders Award, Rehoboth Art League, Del, 71 & 75; Silvermine Guild Award Sculpture, 72 & 73. Style & Technique: Original forms designed and executed from 20th century environment. Mailing Add: RD 1 Box 51 Smyrna DE 19977

BAILEY, WALTER ALEXANDER
PAINTER, WRITER
b Wallula, Kans. Study: Kansas City Art Inst, Mo; Bus Col, Leavenworth, Kans; Fr Inst Lett, dipl; and with John Douglas Patrick, Anthony Angarola, Adolphe Blondheim, Charles A Wilimovsky, Randall Davey, Ross Braught, Thomas Hart Benton & Leon Gaspard. Work: Springfield Pub Libr, Mass; Kansas City Pub Libr, Mo. Comn: Watercolor sketches, Univ Kans, Lawrence, 27 & Univ Tex, Austin, 28; two murals, William Rockhill Nelson Gallery Art, Kansas City, Mo, 35; four murals, Orchestra Promenade, Munic Auditorium Music Hall, Kansas City, 36; mural, East High Sch, Kansas City, 37. Exhib: Louis Comfort Tiffany Guild Exhibs, Anderson Galleries, New York, 26, 27 & 29; Midwestern Art Exhib Ann, Kansas City Art Inst; one-man show, Mexico City, 30; 13th Ann WCoast Paintings Exhib, Charles & Emma Frye Mus, Seattle, Wash, 67; All-City Outdoor Art Festival, Los Angeles, Calif, 68. Teaching: Instr landscape painting, Master Class, Taos, NMex, 27-29, Master Class, Kansas City, Mo, 32-34 & Kansas City Art Inst, 38-39. Pos: Ed art dir, Kansas City Times, 17-27; motion picture story-bd artist, educ films, Douglas Aircraft Co, Santa Monica, Calif, 41-42; scenic artist, motion picture studios, Hollywood, Calif, 43-44; night art dir, Los Angeles Examr, Calif, 50-61; art ed, Los Angeles Herald-Examr, 62-67. Awards: Louis Comfort Tiffany Found fel, 24; Am Inst Fine Arts Fel, 65; Jose Drudis Found Fel, 66; plus others. Bibliog: Sally Sooner (auth), article in, Daily Sun Okla, Oklahoma City, 11/23/30; Allen Charles (auth), article in Art Dig, 36; Howard Burke (auth), article in, Los Angeles Examr, 12/11/59. Mem: Nat Watercolor Soc; Am Inst Fine Arts (pres, 67-68); Calif Art Club (dir, 63 & 66-67); Valley Artists' Guild (vpres & dir, 62-64); Artists of the Southwest, Inc (dir, 68-78); plus others. Style & Technique: Post-impressionist; powerful paintings with rich colors; brush & palette knife technique. Media: Oil, Acrylic. Publ: Contribr, Kansas City Star & Art Dig, 27-28; contribr, Hearst Publ, 50-61; feature writer, South Pasadena Rev, Calif, 72-78. Mailing Add: 1417 12th Ave Los Angeles CA 90019

BAILEY, WILLIAM H
PAINTER
b Council Bluffs, Iowa, Nov 17, 30. Study: Yale Univ, Alice Kimball English traveling fel & BFA, 55, MFA, 57; with Josef Albers. Work: Mus Art, Aachen, Ger; Whitney Mus of Am Art, New York; Speed Art Mus, Louisville, Ky; Kresge Art Ctr, Mich State Univ, East Lansing; Yale Univ Art Mus; plus others. Exhib: One-man show, Kansas City Art Inst, Mo, 67; Realism Now, Vassar Col Art Mus, Poughkeepsie, NY, 68; Twenty-two Realists, Whitney Mus Am Art, New York, 70; one-man shows, Robert Schoelkopf Gallery, New York, 68, 71 & 74 & Galerie Claude Bernard, Paris, 78. Teaching: Prof fine arts, Ind Univ, 62-69; prof art, Yale Univ, 69-, dean sch art, 74-75. Awards: First Prize Painting, Boston Arts Festival, 57; Guggenheim Found Fel Painting, 65. Bibliog: Hilton Kramer (auth), William Bailey & the artifice of realism, New York Times, 10/31/71; Jerrold Lanes (auth), Problems of representation—are we asking the right questions?, Artforum Mag, 1/72; Robert Hughes (auth), The realist as corn god, Time Mag, 1/31/72. Media: Oil. Dealer: Robert Schoelkopf 825 Madison Ave New York NY 10021. Mailing Add: 344 Willow New Haven CT 06511

BAILEY, WORTH
ART HISTORIAN
b Portsmouth, Va, Aug 23, 08. Study: William & Mary Col; Univ Pa, BA. Work: Univ Pa; Valentine Mus Art; Col William & Mary. Comn: Designed Christmas card series; Alexandria Commemorative Stamp, 49. Exhib: Norfolk, Williamsburg & Richmond, Va. Pos: Cur, Jamestown Archaeol Proj, 33-38; cur, Mt Vernon, Va, 38-51; cur consult, Nat Trust Hist Preservation, Washington, DC, 51-56; consult, Our Town 1749-1865, spec exhib, Alexandria Asn, 56; cur, Alexander Hamilton Bicentennial Exhib, US Treas Dept, 57; archit historian, Hist Am Bldgs Surv, Nat Park Serv, Washington, DC, 58-66; ed, Historic Am Bldg Surv Catalog Suppl, 59; historian, Am Bldgs Surv, Wis Archit, 65; fine arts comt, Sully Plantation, Fairfax Co, 63-69. Awards: Norfolk Soc Artists Awards, 26-28; Brookings Inst Ctr Advan Study Fel, 62. Mem: Am Soc Archit Historians; Hist Alexandria Found; Asn Preservation Va Antiq; Va Hist Soc. Publ: Illusr, Christmas with the Washingtons, Seaport in Virginia & George Washington's Alexandria, 49 & 74; auth, Safeguarding a heritage, 63; contribr, With heritage so rich, 66, Encycl Am & var art, antique & hist mag. Mailing Add: 8029 Washington Rd Alexandria VA 22308

BAILIN, HELLA
PAINTER
b Dusseldorf, Ger, Oct 17, 15; US citizen. Study: Berlin Acad, 34, Reimann Sch, Berlin, 36, Newark Sch Fine & Indust Arts, 47 & 52-56. Work: Washington Sch Psychiatry, Washington, DC; Temple Beth Ahm, Springfield, NJ; plus others. Comn: Painting & mural, Marshall Sch, South Orange, NJ, 63; murals, Mennen Prod, Morristown, NJ, 63 & Consol Gas Co, Metuchen, NJ, 63. Exhib: Am Watercolor Soc; Nat Acad Design; Audubon Artists; Watercolor USA; Allied Artists Am. Awards: Ted Kautzky Award, Am Watercolor Soc, 70; David Wuject-Key Mem Prize, Allied Artists Am, 72; Marion de Sola Mendes Award, Nat Soc Painters in Casein & Acrylic, 73. Pos: Pvt instr & demonstr watercolor, portraits & figure painting. Mem: Am & NJ Watercolor Socs; Allied Artists Am; Assoc Artists NJ; Portraits, Inc; plus others. Style & Technique: Figurative expressionist. Mailing Add: 829 Bishop St Union NJ 07083

BAIRD, JOSEPH ARMSTRONG, JR
WRITER, ART DEALER
b Pittsburgh, Pa, Nov 22, 22. Study: Oberlin Col, BA(magna cum laude), 44; Harvard Univ, MA, 47, PhD, 51. Collections Arranged: Numerous exhib, Calif Hist Soc, San Francisco, 62-63, 67-70 & Univ Calif, Davis, 53- Teaching: Instr art hist, Univ Toronto, 49-53; from instr to prof, Univ Calif, Davis, 53-61, lectr, 61- Pos: Cur, Calif Hist Soc, 62-63; art consult, 67-70; cataloguer, Robert B Honeyman, Jr Collection, Bancroft Libr, Univ Calif, Berkeley, 64-65; owner, North Point Gallery, San Francisco. Awards: Calif Hist Soc Merit Award, 62. Mem: Am Fedn Arts; Nat Trust Hist Preserv; Soc Archit Historians. Res: Latin American architecture; California architecture, painting and graphic arts. Collection: Urban art and life in the 19th and 20th century. Publ: Auth, Time's wondrous changes: San Francisco architecture, 1776-1915, Calif Hist, 62; The churches of Mexico, Univ Calif Press, 62; Catalogue of the original paintings, drawings and water colors in the Robert B Honeyman, Jr Collection, Bancroft Libr, Univ Calif, Berkeley, 66; California's pictorial letter sheets, David Magee, San Francisco, 67; Historic lithographs of San Francisco, 72; also compiler & ed several exhib catalogs. Mailing Add: 1830 Mountain View Dr Tiburon CA 94920

BAIRD, ROGER LEE
SCULPTOR, SILVERSMITH
b Washington, DC, May 20, 44. Study: Calif Col Arts & Crafts, BFA, 66, MFA, 68. Work: City of Napa Collection, Calif; City of Walnut Creek Collection, Calif. Comn: Founders Medallion, Calif Col Arts & Crafts, Oakland, Calif, 68. Exhib: One-man show, Richmond Art Ctr, Calif, 65; two-man show, Comara Gallery, Los Angeles, Calif, 65; Sculpture Los Angeles 65, Munic Art Gallery, 65; Zellerbach Mem Competition Art Sculpture, Palace Legion of Honor, San Francisco, 65; Art Inst Centennial Exhib, San Francisco Mus Art, 71. Teaching: Instr jewelry & metal arts, Merritt Col, 66-71; instr jewelry & metal arts, San Francisco City Col, 71- Style & Technique: Casting and carving. Media: Wood; Metal. Mailing Add: 32 Duran Ct Pacifica CA 94044

BAITSELL, WILMA WILLIAMSON
ART ADMINISTRATOR, CRAFTSMAN
b Palmyra, NY, July 5, 18. Study: State Univ NY Col Oswego, BSE & MSE; Syracuse Univ, art teaching cert; Western State Univ, Colo, with Josef Albers, Al Litchenson & Tom Seawell. Work: Sydney Teacher's Col, Newton, Australia; Yamaguchi Univ, Japan. Teaching: Asst prof, State Univ NY Col Oswego, 71-, art supvr, Swetman Learning Ctr, 71- Pos: Art supvr, Phoenix Cent Sch, Phoenix, NY, 60-71; art consult, NY State Dept of Educ, summers, 68-70. Bibliog: John Ritson & James Smith (auth), Creative Teaching of Art in the Elememtary School, Allyn & Bacon, 75. Mem: Int Soc for Educ through Art; Nat Weaver's Asn; Nat Art Educ Asn; NY State Art Teacher's Asn (rules comt chmn, 65-66); Oswego Art Guild (secy, 59; childrens class chmn, 61-71). Style & Technique: Using the five senses and transmitting to work combined with sensitivity in nature. Media: Acrylic. Publ: Auth, Grow a Tiny Garden, Workbasket, 56; auth, Relationship of Intelligence to Art, Arg, SAm Teachers, 58; auth, Relationship of Intelligence to Art, Brazil, SAm Teachers, 69; auth, Crafts for Campers, Maine Campers Asn, 73; auth, Mary's Lamb Comes to School, Search Mag, 76. Mailing Add: RD 4 Box 330 Oswego NY 13126

BAKANOWSKY, LOUIS J
ENVIRONMENTAL ARTIST, DESIGNER
b Norwich, Conn, Oct 8, 30. Work: Harvard Univ; Syracuse Univ; Trinity Col. Comn: Mem structure, Brunswick, Maine, 73. Exhib: View, 60 & Selection, 61, Inst Contemp Art, Boston, Mass; one-man show, Siembab Gallery, Boston, 60; Sculpture, DeCordova Mus, Lincoln, Mass, 64; New England Art Today, Boston, 65; Immanent Domains, Boston, New York & Philadelphia, 77. Teaching: Asst prof design, Cornell Univ, 61-62; prof design, Grad Sch Design, Harvard Univ, 63-, prof & chmn, Dept Visual & Environ Studies, 72- Pos: Designer, Cambridge Seven Assocs, Inc, 62- Awards: Sculpture Prizes, Boston Arts Festival, 58 & Providence Art Festival, 59. Bibliog: Sculpture of Louis J Bakanowsky, Connection Mag, 61; Louis J Bakanowsky, Kenchiku Bunka Mag, 71. Style & Technique: Creation of environmental experiences using space, light and materials. Media: Mixed Media. Mailing Add: 6 Parker St Lexington MA 02173

BAKATY, MIKE
PAINTER, SCULPTOR
b Trenton, NJ, Aug 19, 36. Study: Miami-Dade Jr Col, Fla, AA, 64; Fla Atlantic Univ, BA, 65; Univ Ore, MFA, 69. Work: Colo State Univ, Ft Collins; Miami-Dade Community Col. Comn: Wall sculpture, pvt collection, New York, 73; outdoor monument, Colo State Univ, 75; plus other pvt collections. Exhib: Mike Bakaty, Paley & Lowe Inc, New York, 71-72; Painting & Sculpture Today, 1972, Indianapolis Mus Art, 72; NY Artists, Baltimore Mus Art, Md, 72; Here Comes Tomorrow, Owen Corning Fibreglass Bldg, New York, 73; Mike Bakaty, Mellon Art Ctr, Wallingford, Conn, 74; Am Inst Archit, 74 & Mike Bakaty, Henri Gallery, 74, Washington, DC; plus many others. Teaching: Adj asst prof art, NY Univ, 71-74; asst prof painting, Fla Int Univ, Miami, 73; adj lectr sculpture, Fiorello LaGuardia Community Col, City Univ New York, 73-78, asst prof, 78- Awards: State-wide Touring Exhib, State of Fla, 66; Award for Sculpture, Ft Lauderdale Mus Arts, 66. Bibliog: Barbara Schwartz (auth), Young New York Artists, Crafts Horizons, 72; Julia Busch (auth), A Decade of Sculpture, Assoc Univ Press, 74; Thelma Newman (auth), Plastics as Sculpture, Chilton Bks, 74. Style & Technique: Non-objective fibreglass works. Media: Fibreglass; Graphite. Mailing Add: 295 Bowery New York NY 10003

BAKER, ANNA P
PAINTER, GRAPHIC ARTIST
b London, Ont, June 12, 28. Study: Univ Western Ont, BA; Art Inst Chicago, BFA & MFA. Work: Libr Cong, Washington, DC; London Pub Libr & Art Mus; Cleveland Mus Art; Ball State Teachers Col, Muncie, Ind; Univ Western Ont. Exhib: St Paul, Minn, 62; Philadelphia Art Alliance; Okla Printmakers, 63; DeCordova Mus; Los Angeles, Calif, 66; G W Smith Mus, Springfield, Mass; plus others. Awards: Mr & Mrs Frank Glogan Prize Painting, Art Inst Chicago; Purchase Prize, Cleveland Mus Art; Can Coun Grant, 68. Mem: Can Painters, Etchers & Engravers. Mailing Add: Barton VT 05822

BAKER, DINA GUSTIN
PAINTER
b Philadelphia, Pa, Nov 7, 24. Study: Philadelphia Col Mus Sch Fine Art; Barnes Found, Merion, Pa, with Dr Albert C Barnes & Violet DeMazia; Temple Tyler Sch Fine Art, Philadelphia; Art Students League; Atelier 17, New York. Work: NY Univ; Barnes Found; Philadelphia Art Mus; Butler Mus Am Art, Youngstown, Ohio. Exhib: One-man shows, Roko Gallery, New York, 51 & 58, Angeleski Gallery, New York, 61, Southampton East Gallery, Long Island & New York, 65, Amerika House, Hamburg, Munich & Regensburg, Ger, 74 & Ingber Gallery, New York, 76 & 78; Pa Acad Fine Arts Nat Biennial, Philadelphia; plus many more. Teaching: Instr, Henry St Settlement, 54-55; dir pvt art classes, New York, 60-63. Awards: Barnes Found Award, 42-45; Art Students League Award, 46-47; Edward MacDowell Fel, 59. Bibliog: Allen Ellenzweig (auth), article in Arts Mag, 9/76. Mem: Women in the Arts (publ coordr, 75). Style & Technique: Abstract and figurative technique, always with brushes, rollers, rag, wood and others. Media: Oil on Canvas, Acrylic Watercolor on Paper. Dealer: Barbara Ingber c/o Ingber Gallery 3 E 78th St New York NY 11004. Mailing Add: 88 Eisenhower Dr Cresskill NJ 07626

BAKER, ELIZABETH C
ART EDITOR, CRITIC
b Boston, Mass. Study: Bryn Mawr Col, BA, 56; Radcliffe Col, MA, 58. Teaching: Instr art hist, Boston Univ, 58-59; instr art hist, Wheaton Col, Norton, Mass, 60-61 & Sch of Visual Arts, New York, 68-74. Pos: From assoc ed to managing ed, Art News, 63-73; ed, Art in Am, 73- Mailing Add: c/o Art in America 850 Third Ave New York NY 10022

BAKER, EUGENE AMES
PAINTER, SERIGRAPHER
b Dyersberg, Tenn, Jan 6, 28. Study: Calif Col Arts & Crafts, BA (art educ, high distinction), 51. Exhib: Monterey Co Fair, Calif, 54-62; Laguna Beach Festival Arts, Calif, 56-59; Young Collector's Show, Dallas Mus Fine Arts, Tex, 59; guest artist, Wash State Fair, Puyallup, 64-65; one-man shows, Zantman Art Galleries, Ltd, Carmel, Calif, 70-71. Teaching: Instr arts & crafts, Pac Grove High Sch, Calif, 51-52; instr oil painting & drawing, Monterey Peninsula Col, Calif, 57-62. Pos: Bd dirs, Am Fedn Arts, Carmel, Calif. Awards: Watercolor Award, Laguna Beach Festival Arts, 56 & Monterey Co Fair, 54-57 & 59-62. Bibliog: Carl Martin (auth), Reason & passion, Game & Gossip, 52. Mem: Carmel Art Asn (vpres & treas, themes and rural landscapes painted in stylized realism. Media: Oil, Acrylic, Serigraphy. Dealer: Zantman Art Ltd Sixth & San Carlos Carmel CA 93921; Lyon Art Gallery 459 Geary San Francisco CA Mailing Add: PO Box 335 Carmel Valley CA 93924

BAKER, GEORGE
SCULPTOR
b Corsicana, Tex, Jan 23, 31. Study: Col Wooster; Occidental Col, BA; Univ Southern Calif, MFA. Work: Mus Mod Art & Mus Am Art, New York; Mus 20th Century Art, Vienna, Austria; Forest of Sculptures, Hakone, Japan; San Diego State Col, Calif. Comn: Kinetic fountain, Int Sculptors Symposium, Osaka Worlds Fair, 70; kinetic hanging sculpture, comn by State Calif for San Diego State Col, 72; kinetic sculpture, Nebr Bicentennial Sculpture Proj; kinetic wall sculpture, German Opera, WBerlin, comn by Am CofC for 75th Anniversary, WGer, 78. Exhib: Erlangen, Ger, 68; Mus Mod Art, New York, 68; Whitney Mus Am Art, 68 & 70; Studio Marconi, Milan, Italy, 70; Springer Gallery, Berlin, 75; Munic Art Gallery, Los Angeles, 77; Mekler Gallery, Los Angeles, 77. Teaching: Instr sculpture, Univ Southern Calif, 60-64; asst prof sculpture, Occidental Col, 64-; instr, Schiller Col, Berlin, 71; artist in residence, Berlin, 71-72 & 75 & WTex State Univ, 78. Awards: Int Sculptors Symposium, Osaka, Japan, 69; Berlin Artist in Residence Prog, 71-72 & 75. Bibliog: Articles in, Art & Artists, London, 66, Art in Am, 66 & 67 & Leonardo, fall 75. Style & Technique: Principally kinetic using sheet bronze, aluminum or stainless to produce organic forms; movement induced by water, wind or electric power. Mailing Add: Occidental Col Dept Art 1600 Campus Rd Los Angeles CA 90041

BAKER, GRACE
PAINTER
b Riverdale, NY. Study: Finch Col, BA; and with William Oden-Waller. Work: Mutual Savings & Loan, Williamsburg, Va; plus many pvt collections. Comn: Portrait, Lawrence J Troiano, Riverdale, NY, 66; still life, Blue Ribbon Restaurant, 67; Old Saw Mill, comn by Mr & Mrs Henry Henrici, Williamsburg, 72; Topaz, comn by Holly Patterson, Williamsburg, 72; drawing, Chesapeake Pharmaceut Asn, Va, 73; portrait, comn by Mrs James Shuck, Lanexa, Va, 74. Exhib: Tidewater Artists Asn 21st Biennial, Chrysler Mus, Norfolk, Va, 71; Spec Maritime Exhibs, Newport News, 71 & 72; World Health Day 1972, UN Postage Stamp Design Competition, 71-72; pvt exhib, Bank Hampton Roads, Va, 72; Peninsula Arts Asn Shows, 70-76; Occasion for the Arts, Williamsburg, Va, 76. Awards: Second Place in Oils, Todd Ctr Arts Festival, 72; Cert of Excellence in Oils, Peninsula Arts Asn Mem Exhib, 74; Cert of Merit in Graphics & Oil Technique, Int Biog.Ctr, Cambridge, Eng. Mem: Am Artists Prof League; Int Panel of Artists (design UN stamps); Tidewater Artists Asn; Peninsula Arts Asn. Style & Technique: Smooth, detailed, lifelike realism. Media: Oil. Dealer: Peninsula Arts Asn Gallery Museum Dr Newport News VA 23601. Mailing Add: PO Box 2962 Williamsburg VA 23185

BAKER, JILL WITHROW
ILLUSTRATOR, PAINTER
b Ilion, NY, Oct 12, 42. Study: Baylor Univ, BA, 64; Fla State Univ, with Karl Zerbe; Acad di Belle Arti, Florence, Italy, with Silvio Lofreddo. Work: Merton Collection, Bellarmine Col, Louisville, Ky; Col Educ Collection, Western Ky Univ, Bowling Green; Am Nat Bank Collection, Bowling Green; Goethe House Collection, New York; St Thomas Aquinas Chapel, Bowling Green. Comn: Collages, Cath Church, Bowling Green, 70. Exhib: One-person shows, Western Ky Univ Fine Arts Gallery, Bowling Green, 70, Automation House, New York, 74, Goethe House, New York, 74, Parthenon Mus Fine Arts, Nashville, Tenn, 75, Palazzo Strozzi, Florence, Italy, 75, Ward-Nasse Gallery, New York, 77 & US Info Serv Cult Ctr, Seoul, Korea, 77; Am Painters in Paris, Palais de Congres, City of Paris, France, 76; Bicentennial Heritage Exhib, Rockefeller Ctr, New York, 76; Lever House, New York, 76; Hunter Mus Art, Chattanooga, Tenn, 76; Works on Paper, Mfg Hanover Trust, New York, 77; Avery Fisher Hall, Lincoln Ctr, New York, 78. Pos: Mem bd dir adv coun arts, City of Bowling Green, 74-75; regional rep, SE/Art Mag, 76- Awards: Achievement Award, Bank Am, State of Calif, 60; Achievement Trophy, 60; scholar, Southern Women's Club, 63. Bibliog: Marvin Bowman (auth), Jill Baker Talks About..., Ky Educ Television, 71; Peggy Kirkpatrick (auth), Easier to put thots on canvas, Daily News, 4/74; Karen Wheeless (auth), Jill Baker, an artist who..., Baylor Line Quart, 12/75. Mem: Artists Equity Asn; Artist Referral Telecommun Serv Inc; Southern Ky Guild of Artists & Craftsman (founding mem); Kappa Pi (Baylor chap vpres, 60-63); Northern Fla Guild of Artists & Craftsmen (founding mem). Style & Technique: Surreal collage and oil paintings; pringmaking; blockprints; pen & ink illustrations; realistic figures in oil. Media: Monotype with Ink Drawing. Publ: Illusr, Jim Wayne Miller, auth, The More Things Change, Whipporwill Press, 71; illusr, Lee Pennington, auth, Songs of Bloody Harlan, Westburg Asn Press, 75 & Spring of Violets, Love St Bks, 76; illusr, James T Baker, auth, Under the Sign of the Waterbearer, Love St Bks, 76; illusr, Lee Pennington, auth, I Knew a Woman, Love St Bks, 77. Dealer: Ward-Nasse Gallery 178 Prince St New York NY 10012. Mailing Add: 335 Sumpter Ave Bowling Green KY 42101

BAKER, RALPH BERNARD
PAINTER, EDUCATOR
b Salt Lake City, Utah, Aug 22, 32. Study: Univ Wash, BA & MFA. Work: Munic Collection, City of Seattle, Wash; Univ Alta, Mus Art; Univ Calgary Mus Art; Toronto Dominion Bank; Northwest Collection, Univ Ore Mus Art. Exhib: Northwest Ann, Seattle Art Mus, 59-61 & 71; Univ Centennial Drawing Exhib, Can, 67-68; Artists Alta, Edmonton Art Mus, 66; one-man shows, Univ Ore Mus Art, 72 & Cornish Inst, Seattle, Wash, 77; Artists of Ore, Portland Mus, 72. Teaching: Assoc prof paint & drawing, Univ Calgary, 64-70, asst dean fine arts, 68-70, gallery dir, 67-70; assoc prof paint & drawing, Univ Ore, 70- Awards: Artists Western Wash Award, Woessner Gallery, 59; Gtr Seattle Purchase Award, Bus Orgns, 60; Mus & Art Found Award, 62. Bibliog: Virgil Hammock (auth), Alberta through abstract eyes, Edmonton J, 4/69; David Thompson (auth), Prairie landscapes a force not a scene, Calgary Herald, 1/16/70. Style & Technique: Landscape; flat hard forms; brush and roller. Media: Acrylic, Oil. Mailing Add: Dept of Art Univ of Ore Eugene OR 97403

BAKER, RICHARD BROWN
COLLECTOR
b Providence, RI, Nov 5, 12. Study: Yale Univ, BA, 35; Oxford Univ, Rhodes scholar, 35-38, BA & MA; Art Students League; Hans Hofmann Sch Fine Arts. Exhib: (Richard Brown Baker Collection) RI Sch Design Mus Art, 59, 64 & 73; Yale Univ Art Gallery, 63 & 75; Oakland Univ Art Gallery, Rochester, Mich, 67 & 74; Mus Mod Art, Mexico City, 68; Univ Notre Dame, Ind, 69; Newark Mus, 74; plus others. Pos: Mem comt on art gallery of univ coun, Yale Univ, 62-66 & 71-, mem governing bd, 74-; mem mus comt, RI Sch Design, 66-75; mayoral app, Art Comn of New York, 77. Bibliog: Kenneth B Sawyer (auth), Richard Brown Baker, US collector of modern art, Studio Int, London, 1/65; Paul Gardner (auth), Richard Baker's amazing mini-museum, Art News, 1/78. Mem: Mus Mod Art; life fel Metrop Mus Art; assoc Solomon R Guggenheim Mus; Am Asn Mus; fel Pierpont Morgan Libr. Collection: Recent art in all media (earliest 1940), international in origin, although preponderantly by US artists. Publ: Auth, Notes on the formation of my collection, Art Int, 9/20/61; co-auth, Two in the first row, Art in Am, 10/63. Mailing Add: 1185 Park Ave New York NY 10028

BAKER, SARAH MARIMDA
PAINTER
b Memphis, Tenn, Mar 7, 99. Study: Baltimore Mus of Art; Pa Acad of Fine Arts, fel; Grande Chaumierie, Paris study with Andre Lhote. Work: Pa Acad of Fine Arts, Philadelpphia; Baltimore Mus of Art; Corcoran Gallery of Art, Washington, DC; Phillips Collection, Washington, DC; Norfolk Mus, Va. Exhib: Pa Acad of Fine Arts, Philadelphia, 26; one-person shows, Balitmore Mus of Art, 38 & Phillips Collection, Washington, DC, 77; Retrospective Exhib, Watkins Gallery, Am Univ, Washington, DC, 67 & 74. Teaching: Instr painting & drawing, Bryn Mawr Preparatory Sch, Pa, 29-45; grad instr, St Timothy's Sch, Baltimore & Catonsville, Md, 32-45; prof painting & drawing, Am Univ, Washington, DC, 45-65. Awards: Gold Medal, Pa Acad Fine Arts, 26; Garfinckel Award, Independent Art, Julius Garfinckel, 30. Style & Technique: Traditional. Media: Oil, watercolor, gouache. Mailing Add: 1901 Wyoming Ave NW Washington DC 20009

BAKER, WALTER C
COLLECTOR
Collection: Graphic arts. Mailing Add: 555 Park Ave New York NY 10022

BAKKE, KAREN LEE
FIBER ARTIST, EDUCATOR
b Everett, Wash, Nov 21, 42. Study: Univ Wash; Syracuse Univ, NY, BFA(design), 67, MFA(design), 69. Work: Everson Mus, Syracuse. Exhib: Rochester-Finger Lakes Regional, Rochester Art Mus, NY; Cent NY Regional, Everson Mus, 66, 67 & 71, one-person show, 72; Fabric of the State, Mus of Am Folk Art, New York, 72; Radial 80, Xerox Ctr, Rochester, NY, 74; two-person show, Fabric Forms, Kirkland Art Ctr, Clinton, NY, 76. Teaching: Assoc prof environ arts, Syracuse Univ, 69- Pos: Asst cur, Syracuse Univ Art Collection, 67-69. Awards: Hancock Purchase Prize & One-Person Show Award, Cent NY Regional, Everson Mus, 71. Mem: Am Crafts Coun. Style & Technique: Textile assemblage: textiles combined with metal and photographs developed on fabric; use of traditional techniques in non-traditional manner. Publ: Auth, Sewing Machine as a Creative Tool, Prentice-Hall, 76. Mailing Add: 1136 Cumberland Syracuse NY 13210

BAKKE, LARRY HUBERT
EDUCATOR, PAINTER
b Vancouver, BC, Jan 16, 32. Study: Univ Wash, BA & MFA; Syracuse Univ, PhD, art hist with Laurence Schmeckebier & art educ with Michael F Andrews. Work: Everett Col; Syracuse Univ. Exhib: Figure Painting, Univ BC Fine Arts Gallery, Vancouver, 63; Nat Exhib Small Paintings, Purdue Univ Art Gallery, Ind, 54; The Painter & the Photograph, Univ NMex Art Gallery, Albuquerque, 64-65; 97th Ann, Am Watercolor Soc, New York, 64; Seven Syracuse Artists, Cortland Fine Arts Gallery, NY, 70. Teaching: Vis prof, Univ Victoria, summers, 58-71; instr art hist, drawing & painting, Everett Col, 59-63; from assoc prof to prof aesthetics, painting & synaesthetics, Syracuse Univ, 63-; vis prof, Villa Giglucci, Florence, Italy, summer 68. Awards: First Prize, Northwest Watercolor, Seattle Art Mus, 62; Northwest Painters Award, Puget Sound Group Northwest Painters, 63; First Prize for Painting, Spokane-Northwest Painters, 63. Bibliog: Margaret Harold (auth), Prize-Winning Watercolors, Allied Publ, 63; Van Deren Coke (auth), Painter & the Photograph, Univ NMex, 64; Laurence Schmeckebier (auth), Larry Bakke, Drawings & Paintings, 1957-1969, Syracuse Univ, 69. Mem: Nat Art Educ Asn. Style & Technique: Based on a conceptual approach fusing photographic images and commercial forms with drawing and painting. Media: Oil, Collage. Publ: Co-auth, Washington Education, 62; auth, Creative crafts, 63; auth, New York State Art Teachers Bull, 70; co-auth, Synaesthetic education, 71; auth, Interval, discontinuity, synaesthesia & their relation to the visual arts, Humanities J, 5/73. Mailing Add: 1136 Cumberland Ave Syracuse NY 13210

BAKKEN, HAAKON
ART ADMINISTRATOR, JEWELER
b Madison, Wis, Nov 28, 32. Study: Univ Wis, BSc, 58; Sch for Am Craftsmen, Rochester Inst Technol, MFA, 62. Work: Chalmers Collections, Ont Crafts Coun, Toronto; Sheridan Col Study Collection, Mississauga, Ont. Comn: Bronze door pull, 10 ft high, Ont Crafts Coun, 76; sterling cigar box, Law Soc of Upper Can, Toronto, 74. Teaching: Teaching master metal & jewelry, Sch of Crafts & Design, Sheridan Col, 67-77. Pos: Dir, Sch of Crafts & Design, Sheridan Col, 77- Mailing Add: Sch of Crafts & Design Sheridan Col 1460 S Sheridan Way Mississauga ON L5H 1Z7 Can

BALANCE, JERRALD CLARK
PAINTER, SCULPTOR
b Ogden, Utah, July 20, 44. Study: Univ Utah, Salt Lake City; mainly self-taught. Work: Chrysler Mus at Norfolk, Va; Atlantic City Fine Arts Ctr & Atlantic City Munic Bldg Collection, NJ; Coopers & Lybrand Corp, Washington, DC; Prince Georges Col, Largo, Md. Exhib: Annapolis Fine Arts Found, Md, 72 & 73; 19th Area Exhib, Corcoran Gallery Art, Washington, DC, 74; 14th Md Biennial, Baltimore Mus Art, 74; Five Am Abstract Painters, Northeastern Univ Gallery, Boston, 77; Best of NY—A Survey, Root Art Ctr, Hamilton Col, Clinton, 77; New Talent, 77 & one-man show, 77, Genesis Gallery, New York. Awards: Portsmouth Nat Art Competition Awards in Painting, 71, 72 & 73; Washington Cherry Blossom Festival Nat Art Competition Award in Sculpture, 72. Style & Technique: Abstracted, reduced landscapes with emphasis on the space and color relationships; air-brush, traditional brush, pouring techniques. Media: Oil, Enamel; Plastic. Publ: Contribr, Washington artists, Artists Equity, 72. Dealer: Genesis Galleries Ltd 41 E 57th St New York NY 10022. Mailing Add: 30 Steven Ct Gaithersburg MD 20760

BALAZS-POTTASCH, GYONGYI
PAINTER
b Transylvania, Hungary, Mar 26, 26; US citizen. Study: Hungarian Royal Art Acad; Art Students League. Exhib: One-man shows, Fren Nell Gallery, Tokyo, 69, G'hana Gallery, London, 71, Kulick Gallery, New York, 72, Bruce Mus, Greenwich, Conn, 73 & Ward Nasse Gallery, 75; Third Floor Gallery, New York, 74; Allied Artists Am Ann Exhib, 76; Stampor Art Exhib, 77. Awards: First Prize, Stampor Art Exhib, 77. Style & Technique: Portraits & Surrealist. Media: Oil, Gold Leafing. Dealer: Ward-Nasse Gallery 178 Prince St New York NY 10012 Mailing Add: 22 Brookridge Dr Greenwich CT 06830

BALDESSARI, JOHN ANTHONY
CONCEPTUAL ARTIST
b National City, Calif, June 17, 31. Study: San Diego State Col, BA, 53, MA, 57; Univ Calif, Berkeley, 54-55; Univ Calif, Los Angeles, 55; Otis Art Inst, Los Angeles, 57-59. Work: Mus Mod Art, New York; Basel Mus, Switz; Los Angeles Co Mus Art. Exhib: Konzeption-Conception, Stadtischen Mus, Leverkusen, Ger, 69; Information, Mus Mod Art, New York, 70; Prosepect, Statischen Kunsthalle, Dusseldorf, Ger, 71; Documenta 5, Kassel, Ger, 72; Contemporanea, Rome, 73. Teaching: Asst prof art, Univ Calif, San Diego, 68-70; prof art, Calif Inst Arts, Valencia, 70- Awards: Nat Endowment for Arts Grants, 73-75. Bibliog: James Collins (auth), John Baldessari, Artforum, 10/73. Style & Technique: Photography, video, film. Publ: Auth, Ingres & Other Parables, 72; auth, Choosing: Green Beans, 72; auth, Throwing Three Balls in the Air to Get a Straight Line (Best of 36 Attempts), 73. Dealer: Sonnabend Gallery 420 W Broadway New York NY 10012. Mailing Add: 2405 Third St Santa Monica CA 90405

BALDRIDGE, MARK S
EDITOR, GOLDSMITH
b Lyons, NY, Dec 7, 46. Study: State Univ NY Col, Buffalo, BS(art educ), 68; Cranbrook Acad of Art, Bloomfield Hills, Mich, MFA(metalsmithing), 70; Tyler Sch of Art, Temple Univ, 76. Exhib: 10th Piedmont Crafts Exhib, Mint Mus of Art, Charlotte, NC, 73; Profiles in US Jewelry, 73, Lubbock, Tex, 73; Va Artists 1973, Va Mus of Fine Arts, Richmond, 73; 11th Ann Southern Tier Art & Crafts Show, Corning Glass Mus, NY, 74; Reprise, Cranbrook Acad of Art Mus, Bloomfield Hills, Mich, 75; Objects 75 Designer/Craftsman Show, Grand Junction, Colo, 75; Bicentennial Crafts Exhib, Ind Univ, Bloomington, 76; Marietta Col Crafts Nat, Ohio, 77. Teaching: Instr metal/jewelry, Univ Evansville, 70-72; asst prof metal/jewelry, Longwood Col, 72- Pos: Ed & illusr, Goldsmiths J, 74- Awards: First Prize/Metal, 40th Nat Cooperstown, NY, 75; First Prize, Lake Superior Int, 75; Merit Award, Goldsmiths 77, Phoenix Art Mus, Soc NAm Goldsmiths, 77. Mem: Va Crafts Coun; Soc NAm Goldsmiths. Style & Technique: Metal objects very organic and art nouveauish; cast with some fabrication. Media: Sterling silver and gold, wood and stone. Mailing Add: 1600 Otterdale Midlothian VA 23113

BALDWIN, HAROLD FLETCHER
SCULPTOR, PAINTER
b Lebanon, NH, May 24, 23. Study: Essentially self-taught. Comn: Carved map of Northeastern Seaboard, 200 Mormon Missionaries, Cambridge, Mass, 71; 12 portraits of apostles, comn by Forrest McKerley, Concord, NH, 72; decorative coats of arms, Dean B Smith, Atlanta, Ga, 73; decorative coats of arms, Ned J Nakles, Latrobe, Pa, 74; The Good Samaritan (54 x 18 1/2 inch mahogany plaque), McKerley Med Care Ctr, Concord, NH, 76. Exhib: One-man shows, Concord Pub Libr, NH, 71 & Springfield Art & Hist Soc, Vt, 73; Burlington Mall, Mass, 73; NH Art Gallery, Concord; New Eng Woodcarvers' Asn, Concord Gallery, Mass, 73; Springfield Bicentennial Medallion, Springfield Pub Libr, Vt, 77-78. Style & Technique: Deeply carved bas-relief plaques, mainly hardwood; engraved brass in color. Mailing Add: Baldwin Studios 11 Woodland Dr Springfield VT 05156

BALDWIN, JOHN
EDUCATOR, SCULPTOR
b New York, NY, Jan 28, 22. Study: Pratt Inst, Brooklyn; Chouinard Art Sch, Los Angeles; Escuela Universitaria de Bellas Artes, Instituto Politecnico Nacional & Instituto Allende, Mex, MFA; Ohio Univ, BFA; study with Jean Charlot, David Alfaro Siqueiros, Jose Gutierrez & Rico LeBrun. Work: Butler Inst of Am Art, Youngstown, Zanesville Art Inst & Masselon Mus, Ohio; McAllen Int Mus, Tex. Comn: Bronze scroll, Manchester Col Libr, North Manchester, Ind, 64; Gorsuch Mem Fountain, Bethesda Hosp, Zanesville, 65; Anthony G Trisolini Mem Bronze, Trisolini Gallery, Ohio Univ, 74. Exhib: Zanesville Art Inst, Ohio, 63; LeMoyne Art Found, Tallahassee, Fla, 65; Sioux City Art Ctr, Iowa, 69; Davenport Munic Art Gallery, Iowa, 70; Ft Wayne Art Inst Mus of Art, Ind, 70; McAllen Int Mus, Tex, 73; Mainstreams USA, 74; Ball State 22nd Ann Small Sculpture & Drawing Show, 76. Teaching: Instr lithography, Escuela Universitaria de Bellas Artes, Mex, 48-49; instr painting, Instituto Allende, San Miguel Allende, Mex, 50-59; prof art sculpture, Ohio Univ, 59- Awards: Award for Excellence, Mainstreams USA, 74; Purchase Award, 25th Ann Ceramic & Sculpture Show, Butler Inst, 73. Bibliog: Thelma R Newman, Plastics as an Art Form, Chilton Publ Co, 64. Style & Technique: Semi-abstract figurative sculptures in a variety of media including welded metal, fiberglass, bronze and ceramic. Media: Figure modeling and sculpture techniques; cast bronze and fiberglass. Publ: Auth, Contemporary Sculpture Techniques: Welded Steel and Fiberglass, Reinhold, 67; auth, The Mexican Murals: A Revolution On the Walls, video tape, Ohio Univ Telecommunications Ctr, 77. Mailing Add: Dept of Art Ohio Univ Athens OH 45701

BALDWIN, RICHARD WOOD
ILLUSTRATOR, SCULPTOR
b Needham, Mass, June 8, 20. Study: Pa Acad Fine Arts, with George Harding; also with Harold Von Schmidt. Work: Smithsonian Inst, Washington, DC; Whitney Gallery Western Art. Comn: Murals, comn by USA, 42-45, now in Smithsonian Inst; over 200 medals & coins sculptured for Franklin Mint, 65-75. Pos: Sr master sculptor, Franklin Mint, 70- Awards: Cresson Fel, Pa Acad Fine Arts, 41. Style & Technique: Medalic sculptor; illustrator. Media: Clay & Plaster; Oil & Watercolor. Publ: Illusr bk & periodicals, 46-65. Mailing Add: RD 3 Dutton Mill Rd West Chester PA 19380

BALDWIN, RUSSELL W
INFORMATION ARTIST, GALLERY DIRECTOR
b San Diego, Calif, May 26, 33. Study: San Diego State Univ, BA, 58, MA, 63. Work: Joseph Hirshhorn Collection, Washington, DC; La Jolla Mus Contemp Art, Calif; Santa Barbara Mus Art; Southwestern Col, Chula Vista; Ahmonson Collection, Los Angeles. Exhib: One-man shows, Jefferson Gallery, La Jolla, Calif, 63, Santa Barbara Mus Art, 64, La Jolla Mus Contemp Art, 64 & 73, Jewish Community Ctr, San Diego, 74 & Casat Gallery, La Jolla, 78. Gallery Exhibits Arranged: Objects to Peruse & Use, 68; The Shaped & Formed Canvas, 69; Paintings by John Baldessari, 72; Robert Irwin (installation piece), 75; James Collins, 77; Wayne Thiebaud, 78. Teaching: Assoc prof sculpture & printmaking, Palomar Col, San Marcos, Calif. Pos: Dir, Dwight Boehm Gallery. Awards: First Painting Award, La Jolla Mus Contemp Art, 60; Sculpture Award, Long Beach Mus Art, 63; First Award, Calif-Hawaii Regional, Fine Arts Gallery San Diego, 74. Mem: La Jolla Mus of Contemp Art. Specialty: Information art. Mailing Add: c/o Art Dept Palomar Col San Marcos CA 92069

BALES, JEWEL
PAINTER
b Purcell, Okla, Aug 28, 11. Study: With William B Schimmel, Douglas Greenbowe & others. Work: Alhambra High Sch, Phoenix, Ariz; Mesa City Libr, Ariz; Baptist Hosp, Phoenix. Exhib: Am Watercolor Soc, Nat Acad Design Galleries, New York, 62; Tucson Regional, Art Ctr, Ariz, 63, 66 & 68; Ann, Ariz State Fair, Phoenix; Ann Traveling Exhib, Ariz Watercolor Asn; Open Watercolor Show, Phoenix Art Mus. Awards: First Award for Tree Study, Mesa Art League, 61; People's Choice for Winter Fun, Ariz State Fair, 69; Purchase Award for Winter Fun, Ariz Bank, 69. Mem: Ariz Watercolor Asn (pres, 69-71, treas, 72-78); Ariz Artist Guild (vpres, 64-66); Nat League Am Pen Women (treas, 73-76). Media: Watercolor. Mailing Add: 8122 N Eighth Ave Phoenix AZ 85021

BALKIND, ALVIN LOUIS
FINE ARTS CURATOR
b Baltimore, Md, Mar 28, 21; Can citizen. Study: Johns Hopkins Univ, BA; study at the Sorbonne. Teaching: Assoc prof, Univ BC, 62-73. Pos: Dir fine arts gallery, Univ BC, 62-73; cur contemp art, Art Gallery Ont, 73-75; chief cur, Vancouver Art Gallery, 75- Mailing Add: Vancouver Art Gallery 1145 W Georgia St Vancouver BC Can

BALL, LYLE V
PAINTER, ILLUSTRATOR
b Reno, Nev, Dec 24, 09. Study: Am Watercolor Soc, with Edgar Whitney, New York & with Jack Pellow, Conn; Col of Pacific Union, St Helena, Calif, with Vernon Nye. Work: Nev Legis Bldgs, Carson City; Sparks Fire Dept, Nev; Reno City Hall; Las Vegas Art League; Senate Off Bldg, Washington, DC. Comn: Oil landscapes, comn by Security Nat Bank, Reno, Nev, 65, Settlemeyer Family, Gardnerville, 72, George Mason, 73 & Marvin Humphreys, Reno, 74; Watercolor wildlife, Edward LeBaron Las Vegas, 74. Exhib: Soc Western Artists Ann, DeYoung Mus, San Francisco, 67-70; Death Valley 49ers' Ann Encampment Show, 68-; Artists Prof League, New York, 71- Pos: Gov Appt, Nev State Coun Arts, 71-76. Awards: Best of Show, Nev Day, 77; Silver Medal/Watercolor, Am Indian & Cowboy Artists Show, San Dimas, Calif, 77; First Prize/Mixed Media & Second Prize/Watercolor, Death Valley 49ers Show, 77. Mem: Soc Western Artists, San Francisco; Am Indian & Cowboy Artists; Am Artists Prof League, New York; life mem Nev Art Gallery, Reno (dir, 70-71); charter mem Artists Co-op Reno (past pres). Style & Technique: Western; neo-realism; focus on pioneer days. Publ: Illusr, Ponderosa Country, Stanley W Paher, 72 & Int Turquoise Ann, Int Turquoise Asn, 75. Mailing Add: 181 Bret Harte Ave Reno NV 89502

BALL, WALTER NEIL
PAINTER, EDUCATOR
b Pratt, Kans, Dec 14, 30. Study: Baker Univ, Baldwin City, Kans, BA, 55; Wichita State Univ, Kans, MFA, 57; Ohio State Univ, Columbus, PhD(painting), 68. Work: Evansville Mus Arts & Sci, Ind; NE Mo State Univ, Kirksville; Univ Mont, Dillon; Wichita State Univ. Exhib: Mid-Am Exhib, Nelson-Atkins Gallery, Kansas City, Mo, 58 & 62; two-man show, Sacramento State Col Art Gallery, Calif, 64; E B Crocker Art Gallery, Sacramento, 65; one-man shows, Oshkosh Pub Mus, Wis, 68 & NE Mo State Univ Art Gallery, 77; Lakeview Ctr for the Arts & Sci, Peoria, Ill, 69; Centennial Exhib, Duerksen Fine Arts Ctr, Wichita, Kans, 70; Midwest Biennial, Joslyn Art Mus, Omaha, Nebr, 72; Bates Gallery, Edinboro State

Col, Pa, 72; Mid-States Art Exhib, Evansville Mus Arts & Sci, Ind, 77; Artists of Chicago & Vicinity, Art Inst Chicago, 77; plus many others. Teaching: Instr painting & drawing, Sacramento State Col, 63-65; asst prof painting & drawing, Wis State Univ, Oshkosh, 65-68; assoc prof painting & drawing, Northern Ill Univ, DeKalb, 68- Awards: Hon Mention, Nelson-Atkins Gallery, 62; Juror's First Award, Washington & Jefferson Col, Washington, Pa, 77; Mus Guild Purchase Award, Evansville Mus Arts & Sci, 77. Style & Technique: Abstract, figurative. Media: Oil, Charcoal, Graphite, Lacquer. Mailing Add: 821 Normal Rd De Kalb IL 60115

BALLATORE, SANDRA LEE
ART CRITIC, INSTRUCTOR
b Wausau, Wis, July 31, 41. Study: Southern Ill Univ, BA, 63; Univ Toledo, grad work, 65; Pasadena Art Mus, 72-74; Pasadena City Col, 72-75; Univ Calif, San Diego, currently working on MFA in art criticism. Collections Arranged: Los Angeles 2001, The Image & The Myth Gallery, Calif, 76; Four Solo Shows, Genn Chulick, Valledor & Scott (auth, catalog), Los Angeles Inst Contemp Art, Calif, 76; Miniature (auth, catalog), Calif State Univ Los Angeles, 77. Teaching: Lectr contemp art & West Coast art of the seventies, Univ Calif, Los Angeles, San Francisco Art Inst, Univ Minn & others; instr, North Orange Co Community Col, Calif, 74-77; instr & course planning, Univ Calif, Los Angeles Exten, 76- Pos: Los Angeles ed, Artweek, Oakland, Calif, 75-76. Res: West Coast contemporary art and issues; contemporary miniature art. Publ: Auth, California Clay Rush, Art in Am, 76; auth weekly articles & rev, Artweek, 74-76; auth, Lyn Hershman Solo Exhiibtion Catalog, Melbourne Univ Union Gallery, Parkville, Victoria, Australia, 77; auth, Spagnulo and Redl, Exhibition catalog, Newport Harbor Art Mus, Newport, Calif, 78. Mailing Add: 407 Alta Vista South Pasadena CA 91030

BALLINGER, LOUISE BOWEN
INSTRUCTOR, WRITER
b Palmyra, NJ, Feb 9, 09. Study: Philadelphia Col Art, BFA(art educ), 51; Univ Pa, MS(educ), 61; Pendle Hill; Barnes Found; and painting with Franklin Watkins. Teaching: Cur schs, Pa Acad Fine Arts, 42-48; from assoc dir to dir dept art educ, Philadelphia Col Art, 48-62; instr, Grad Sch Educ, Univ Pa, 62-66, assoc, 66-76. Mem: Philadelphia Art Alliance; Nat Art Educ Asn (coordr & publicity chmn, 65 conf); Comt Art Educ; Eastern Art Asn (mem coun, 64-). Publ: Co-auth, Design: Sources & Resources, 65, auth, Perspective/Space & Design, 69 & co-auth, Sign, Symbol & Form, 72, Van Nostrand Reinhold. Mailing Add: 334 S Camac St Philadelphia PA 19107

BALLOU, ANNE MACDOUGALL
PRINTMAKER
b Winchester, Mass, Apr 27, 44. Study: Abbot Acad; Randolph-Macon Woman's Col, AB(art); Syracuse Univ, grad study in art. Work: Mus Fine Arts, Boston; Va Mus Fine Arts; De Cordova Mus, Lincoln, Mass; Boston Univ; Emmanuel Col. Exhib: 1st Int Graphics Exhib, NH, 73; Boston Printmaker's Nat, 74, 76 & 77; Bradley Nat Print Exhib, 74 & 76; Miami Graphics Biennial, 75; Davidson Nat Print & Drawing Exhib, 75. Awards: First in Graphics, Carl Schurz Ann Art Exhib, NY, 75; Juror's Commendation, Va Mus, 75; Purchase Award, Artists Under 36, De Cordova Mus, 76. Bibliog: Robert Taylor (auth), article in Boston Globe, 9/21/72; Meryle Secrest (auth), article in Washington Post, 4/5/75; Paul Ciano (auth), article in Jewish Advocate, 2/8/78. Mem: Nat Asn Women Artists; Boston Printmakers; Boston Visual Artists Union; Cambridge Art Asn (vpres, 72-73). Style & Technique: Realism which seeks to show the shared space of things visible and things invisible. Media: Serigraphy, Lithography. Dealer: Bernard Pucker c/o Pucker/Safrai Gallery 171 Newbury St Boston MA 02116. Mailing Add: 190 Middlesex Ave Wilmington MA 01887

BALMACEDA, MARGARITA S
EDUCATOR, ART WRITER
b Ponce, PR, Dec 30, 33; US citizen. Study: Manhattanville Col, Purchase, NY, BFA; Immaculate Heart Col, Hollywood, Calif, teaching cert; Cath Univ of PR, Ponce, MEd. Teaching: Lectr art appreciation & art hist, Colegio Regional de Ponce, 73- Pos: Asst dir, Ponce Art Mus, 67-73. Awards: Certificado de reconocimiento por ano Int de la Mujer, Munic of Ponce, 75. Res: Expressionism; Puerto Rican art. Publ: Auth, poems, Tierra y Alma, Ed Ponce de Leon, Spain, 68; auth, El Uso del Museo de Art de Ponce en la Ensenanza del Barroco, Ceiba, 77. Mailing Add: Salud 94 Ponce PR 00731

BALOG, MICHAEL
PAINTER, SCULPTOR
b San Francisco, Calif, Apr 30, 46. Study: Ventura Col, 66-67; Chouinard Art Sch, grad with hons, 59, studied with Stephan Von Huene. Work: Herbert Distel Mus, Bern, Switz; Univ Iowa, Iowa City; Wichita Art Mus, Kans; Joslyn Art Mus, Omaha, Nebr. Exhib: One-man shows, Irving Blum Gallery, Los Angeles, 70, Leo Castelli Gallery, New York, 72 & Jack Glenn Gallery, Newport Beach, Calif, 74; Documenta Five, Kasel, Ger, 72 (via Herbert Distel Mus); Change, Inc, Mus Mod Art, New York, 74. Bibliog: Article in Esquire, 11/74; Barbara Rose (auth), article in Vogue, 12/74; Melinda Wortz (auth), article in Art News, 1/75. Media: Multimedia. Mailing Add: c/o Leo Castelli Gallery 4 E 77th St New York NY 10021

BALOSSI, JOHN
SCULPTOR, PAINTER
b Staten Island, NY, May 28, 31. Study: Columbia Univ, BFA & MA. Work: Mus Mod Art, New York; Finch Col Mus, New York; Chase Manhattan Collection, New York; Ponce Mus, PR; Univ PR Mus, Rio Piedras. Comn: Mural, Student Union Bldg, Univ PR, 69; aluminum wall relief, Inst Puerto Rican Cult, 71; mural, CRUV Pub Housing, Manati, PR, 72. Exhib: Univ PR Mus, 61, 64 & 70; Ruth White Gallery, New York, 66, 68 & 70; Galeria Santiago, San Juan, 66, 69, 73 & 74; Jacques Perrin Gallery, Paris, 67; Am Acad Arts & Lett, New York, 68; 1st, 2nd & 3rd Biennial Grabado, San Juan, PR, 70, 72 & 74; Galeria Rechany, San Juan, 76 & 77; Galeria Manos, San Juan, 77. Teaching: Assoc prof fine arts, Univ PR, Rio Piedras. Bibliog: R Rivera Garcia (auth), John Balossi; escultor, Artes Visuales, 72; Maria Damoni (auth), Las nubes metalicas de John Balossi, Nuevo Dia, 3/4/72; Darcia Moretti (auth), Gente importante, John Balossi, Plus Ultra Educ Publ, 73. Style & Technique: Heightened reality. Media: Aluminum. Dealer: Galeria Santiago 207 Cristo St San Juan PR 00928 Mailing Add: Dept of Fine Arts Univ of PR Rio Piedras PR 00928

BALSLEY, JOHN GERALD
PAINTER, SCULPTOR
b Cleveland, Ohio, Apr 15, 44. Study: Univ of the Americas, 65; Ohio Northern Univ, BA, 67; Northern Ill Univ, MFA, 69. Work: St Louis Mus Art, Mo; Nelson-Atkins Gallery, Kansas City, Mo; Des Moines Art Ctr, Iowa; Joslyn Mus Art, Omaha, Nebr; Univ Iowa Art Mus, Iowa City. Exhib: Cleveland Mus Art, 66-73; one-man shows, Toledo Mus Art, Ohio, 67, Allan Stone Gallery, New York, 72-78, Des Moines Art Ctr, 72, Minneapolis Col Art & Design, 75-76, Univ Wis, Stout, 75 & John Michael Kohler Arts Ctr, Sheboygan, Wis, 78; Violence in Recent Am Art, Mus Contemp Art, Chicago, 68; Am Painting & Sculpture Biennial, Krannert Mus, Urbana, Ill, 69; St Louis Mus Art, 70; Nelson-Atkins Gallery, 70; Joslyn Art Mus, 70-72; Hudson River Mus, Yonkers, NY, 71; Phoenix Art Mus, Ariz, 73; 1973 Accessions, Univ Iowa Mus Art, 74; Painting & Sculpture Today, Indianapolis Mus Art, Ind, 76; Realisms, Ulrich Mus, Wichita State Univ, 76; Chicago Vicinity Show, Art Inst Chicago, 77. Teaching: Asst prof sculpture, Univ Wis-Milwaukee, 76- Awards: Louis Comfort Tiffany Found Grant, 72; Nat Endowment for the Arts Grant, 73; Univ Wis-Milwaukee Grant, 78. Bibliog: Lou Dunkak (auth), Balsley sculptures explore man and machines, Arts, 12/76; Josh Kind (auth), Model art: the intimate enviroment, New Art Examr, Chicago, 1/78; Betty Kaufman (auth), John Balsley at Allan Stone, Art World, New York, 1/78. Mem: Col Art Asn of Am. Style & Technique: Found object sculpture, constructive additive process; abstract and figurative painting. Dealer: Allan Stone Gallery 48 E 86th St New York NY 10028. Mailing Add: 3347 N Bartlett Milwaukee WI 50312

BALTZ, LEWIS
PHOTOGRAPHER
b Newport Beach, Calif, Sept 12, 45. Study: San Francisco Art Inst, BFA, 69; Claremont Grad Sch, MFA, 71. Work: Mus Mod Art, New York; Art Inst Chicago; Int Mus Photog, George Eastman House, Rochester, NY; Libr Cong, Washington, DC; Bibliotheque Nat, Paris, France. Comn: Eight Photographers View of the Nation's Capital in the Bicentennial Year, Corcoran Gallery Art, Washington, DC, 75. Exhib: One-man shows, Castelli Graphics, Leo Castelli Gallery, New York, 71, 73 & 75, La Jolla Mus of Contemp Art, Calif, Baltimore Mus of Art, Md, Galerie December, Dusseldorf, Ger, 76, Sheldon Mem Art Gallery, Lincoln, Nebr & Univ Nebr, 77; Int Mus Photog, Rochester, NY, 72; Corcoran Gallery Art, 74-76; Philadelphia Col Art, 75; Mus Fine Arts, Houston, 76. Awards: Nat Endowment Arts Fel Grant Photog, 73 & individual fel, 76; Guggenheim Mem Found fel in photography. Bibliog: Peter Plagens (auth), Los Angeles, Artforum, 10/71; A D Coleman (auth), Latent image, The Village Voice, 1/72. Publ: Auth, The New Industrial Parks Near Irvine, California, 75. Dealer: Castelli Graphics 4 E 77th St New York NY 10021. Mailing Add: PO Box 366 Sausalito CA 94965

BAMA, JAMES E
PAINTER
b New York, NY, Apr 28, 26. Study: Art Students League, with Frank J Reilly; City Col New York. Work: Smithsonian Inst, Washington, DC; Cowboy Hall of Fame, Oklahoma City; Baseball Hall of Fame, Cooperstown, NY; USAF Acad, Boulder, Colo; Football Hall of Fame, Canton, Ohio. Comn: Portrait of Gary Grant, Cowboy Hall of Fame, Oklahoma City, 74. Exhib: One-man shows, Hammer Galleries, New York, 73, four shows, Cowboy Hall of Fame, 74 & 75, Coe Kerr Gallery, New York & Whitney Mus of Western Art, Cody, Wyo, 78. Bibliog: Larry Roop (auth), James Bama, Wyo Wildlife Mag, & James Bama, Southwest Art Mag, 74; Ian Ballantine (auth), Western Art of James Bama, Bantam, 75. Style & Technique: Very realistic. Media: Oil, Watercolor. Dealer: Coe Kerr Gallery Inc 49 E 82nd St New York NY 10028. Mailing Add: Wapiti WY 82450

BAMBAS, THOMAS REESE
METALSMITH
b Ann Arbor, Mich, Feb 2, 38. Study: Ferris State Col, AA, 60; Cranbrook Acad Art, BFA, 62 & MFA, 64. Work: Johnson Collection, Objects: USA, Smithsonian Inst. Comn: Altar lights, St Johns Episcopal Church, Mt Pleasant, 70 & fount cover, 71; chalis & paten, Grosse Pointe Woods Presby Church. Exhib: The Uncommon Smith, Kohler Arts Ctr, Cheboygan, Wis, 74; The Goldsmith, Renwick Gallery, Smithsonian Inst, 74; Reprise, Cranbrook Acad Art, 75; Forms in Metal, Mus Contemp Crafts, 75; 3rd Biennial Lake Superior Int Craft Exhib, 75. Teaching: Instr art, Interlochen Arts Acad, 64-66; asst prof art, Wichita State Univ, 65-69; prof art & metalsmithing, Cent Mich Univ, 69- Awards: Tiffany Grant, Louis Comfort Tiffany Found, 65; Cash Award for Investigation, Cent Mich Univ, 71 & Cash Award, 75. Bibliog: Lee Nordness (auth), Objects: USA, Viking, 70; art in La Rev Mod, Paris, 72; Seitz & Finegold (auth), Silversmithing, Van Nostrand, 75. Mem: Soc NAm Goldsmiths. Style & Technique: Raised and chased silver and silver and gold hollow ware. Media: Sterling Silver. Res: Exploration of raising and chasing in silver and gold. Mailing Add: 1008 S Arnold Mt Pleasant MI 48858

BAND, MAX
PAINTER, SCULPTOR
b Naumestis, Lithuania, Aug 21, 00; US citizen. Study: Acad Art, Berlin, Ger, 20-22; also in Paris. Work: Mus Luxembourg, Petit Palais, Paris & other Europ mus; Fr Art Inst, Philadelphia; Riverside Mus; Los Angeles Mus Art; Mus Mod Art; plus others. Comn: Sculpture of F D Roosevelt, White House, Washington, DC, 34; Bust of President Roosevelt presented to President Kennedy, White House, 61. Exhib: Art Inst Chicago, 54; Mus Petit Palais, Paris, 55; Calif Palace of Legion of Honor, 56; B'nai B'rith Mus, Washington, DC, 58; Jewish Community Ctr, Long Beach, Calif, 61; also exhibited extensively US & Europe. Teaching: Artist in residence, Univ Judaism, Los Angeles, 64. Publ: Auth, History of Contemporary Art, 35 & Themes from the Bible. Mailing Add: 6401 Ivarene Ave Hollywood CA 90028

BANDEL, LENNON RAYMOND
PAINTER
b Kansas City, Mo, Dec 10, 06. Study: Kansas City Art Inst, with Thomas H Benton & Ross Braught; Dayton Art Inst, with John King & Burroughs; John Huntington Polytech Inst, Cleveland, with Rolf Stoll & F Wilcox. Work: Luxemburg Mus, Europe. Comn: Five portraits of pres, Reorganized Church of Jesus Christ of Latter-Day Saints, 60; six portraits, Hillyard Chem Co, St Joseph, Mo, 70-71; portrait of Joseph Boley, Univ Kans Med Ctr, 71; mural of River Jordan, First Christian Church, Iowa, Kans, 72; Trader's Nat Bank, Kansas City, Mo. Exhib: May Art Show, Cleveland Mus Art, 44-46; Plaza Art Fair, Kansas City, Mo, 56-74; Kansas City Art Inst Alumni Show, 73; Heritage Show, Kansas City Mus Natural Hist, 74. Teaching: Instr portrait, Kansas City Art Inst, 65-71; instr painting & drawing, Jewish Community Ctr, Kansas City, 65-71. Pos: Designer-artist, Hallmark Cards Inc, Kansas City, 27-37; designer-artist, Stanley Mfg Co, Dayton, Ohio, 37-42; artist-art dir, Am Greeting Corp, Cleveland, 42-57. Awards: For Idio, Cleveland Mus Art, 44; for Spring in the Ozarks, Kansas City Mus of Natural Hist, 61 & for Trail of Tears, 64. Mem: Friends of Art, Nelson Gallery, Kansas City. Style & Technique: Realism. Media: Oil, Pastel. Mailing Add: 5327 Rosewood St Mission KS 66205

BANERJEE (BIMAL)
GRAPHIC ARTIST, PAINTER
b Calcutta, India, Sept 4, 39. Study: Indian Col Art, Calcutta, first class hon grad, 55-60; Col of Art, New Delhi, Indian Govt Nat Cult scholar, 65-67; Atelier 17, Paris, French Govt grant, with S W Hayter, 67-69; Ecole des Beaux Arts, Paris, French Govt grant, 67-70; Pratt Inst Exten, New York, inst grants, 69 & 70-72; NY Univ, 76; Columbia Univ, EdM candidate, 76- Work: Mus Mod Art, Paris, France & Barcelona, Spain; Mus Fine Arts, Boston; Univ

Iowa Mus Art, Iowa City; Nat Gallery Mod Art, New Delhi; plus many others. Comn: Mural with five panels, comn by Mario Manto, Levanto, Italy, 68; graphics, New York Graphic Soc, 71; origami-collage graphics, Pratt Inst Exten, 72. Exhib: Triennale-India, Nat Art Acad, New Delhi, 68, 71 & 75; Paris Biennale, Mus Mod Art, Paris, 69; Mus Fine Arts, Montreal, 71; Honolulu Acad Arts, 71 & 73; Brooklyn Mus Biennial, 72-73; Tokyo Biennial, Nat Mus Mod Art, Tokyo & Kyoto, 72-73; Brit Biennale, Bradford City Art Galleries & Mus, Eng, 72 & 76; Joan Miro Int Drawing Prize Contest, Barcelona, Spain, 74 & 75; Rijeka Drawing Biennale, Mus Mod Art, Yugoslavia, 74 & 76; World Print Competition, San Francisco Mus Mod Art, 77; plus many others. Teaching: Art lectr paintings & drawings, Training Col for Teachers of Deaf, Calcutta, 61-65; vis asst teacher graphics, Nat Acad Fine Arts, New York, 69. Awards: Nat Award, Nat Art Acad, New Delhi, 67 & 70; Centre Cult Int, City Univ, Paris, 68; CETA Artists Prog, New York, 77; plus many others. Bibliog: Dona Meilach & Elvie Ten Hoor (auth), Collage & Assemblage, Crown, 73; Ajit K Dutta (auth), bimal BANERJEE, Nat Art Acad J, 9/74; Linda Bryant & Mary Philips (auth), Contextures, 78; plus many others. Style & Technique: Lyrical abstractions involving nature; origami-collages and constructions of various materials and papers; smoke-stain, oil-stain, lead and colored pencil and latex paint on canvas and papers. Media: Rice & Tissue Papers; Stitching & Pencil-Stencil. Publ: Co-auth, I, 63; co-auth, Mine, 64; contribr, Revolutionist Master-Artist Henri Matisse, 70; contribr, Painter Sonia Delaunay, 70; contribr, Metaphysical Master-Artist de Chirico, 72; plus many others. Mailing Add: Atelier 3 147 W 46th St New York NY 10036

BANEY, RALPH RAMOUTAR
SCULPTOR
b Trinidad, West Indies, Sept 22, 29. Study: Brighton Col Art, Eng, 57-62; Univ Md, MFA, 73; also with Kenneth Campbell & Arthur J Ayres. Work: Nat Mus Art Gallery, Trinidad; Cent Bank, Trinidad; Trinidad & Tobago Embassy, London; Univ West Indies; Van Leer Found, Amsterdam, Holland. Comn: Relief sculpture, St Finbar's Church, Trinidad, 66; relief sculpture, Norweg Seamen's Mission, Trinidad, 69; nat coat of arms, Cent Bank Trinidad, 70; mosaic mural (with Vera Baney), Bishop's High Sch, Trinidad, 71; six portrait comns from various individuals. Exhib: Sussex Artists Ann, Eng, 59-61; Sao Paulo Biennial, Brazil, 67 & 69; one-man shows, Sculpture House Gallery, New York 73 & Pan Am Union, Washington, DC, 74; Sculptors Guild Mem Ann, Lever House, New York, 74, 76 & 77. Teaching: Supvr art, Ministry Educ & Cult, Trinidad, 63-71; instr art, Univ Md, 72-75; instr art, Smithsonian Inst, 74-78; asst prof, Dundalk Community Col, 76- Awards: Gold Medal Merit, Govt Trinidad & Tobago, 73; First Prize Sculpture, Ten Md Juried Exhib, Easton Acad Md, 74; First Prize Sculpture, Spanish Am Art Exhib, 74. Mem: Royal Soc Brit Sculptors; Sculptors Guild; Artists Equity Asn; Col Art Asn Am. Style & Technique: Abstract organic forms; carved technique. Media: Wood. Mailing Add: 1112 Sulphur Spring Rd Baltimore MD 21227

BANEY, VERA
CERAMIST, PRINTMAKER
b Trinidad, West Indies, June 6, 30. Study: Brighton Col Art, Eng, 59-62; State Univ NY Col Ceramics, Alfred Univ, 68; Univ Md, 71-75. Work: Nat Mus & Art Gallery, Trinidad; Cent Bank, Trinidad; Hilton Hotel, Trinidad; Naparima Col, Trinidad; Naparima Girls High Sch. Comn: Ceramic cross, Norweg Seamen's Mission, Trinidad, 69; ceramic relief, Alston's Ltd, Trinidad, 70; mosaic mural (with Ralph Baney), Bishop's High Sch, Trinidad, 71; ceramic lamp bases, Hilton Hotel; ceramic sculpture, Cent Bank Trinidad. Exhib: Expo 67, Montreal, 67; one-man show, Trinidad 67 & 69; Commonwealth Inst, London, 74; Sao Paulo Biennial, Brazil, 75; Contemp Crafts Americas, Colo State Univ, 75; 3 Artists from Trinidad, Pan Am Union, Washington, DC, 76. Awards: First Place Ceramics, Univ Md Crafts Guild, 73; Outstanding Young Potter, Creative Crafts Coun 11 Biennial, 74; First Place Ceramics, 2nd Int Art Exhib, Washington, DC, 74. Mem: Artists Equity; Am Crafts Coun; Art League Northern Va. Style & Technique: Handbuilt ceramics; sculptural forms; etching & wood block prints; abstract images. Mailing Add: 1112 Sulphur Spring Rd Baltimore MD 21227

BANISTER, ROBERT BARR
ART DEALER, PAINTER
b Sheridan, Ore, May 10, 21. Study: Univ Ore, BS; Rochester Inst Technol, MA; Western Wash Col; Univ Utah; Univ Ill; Portland State Univ, EdD. Work: Ford Collection, Detroit; Kipplinger Collection, Washington, DC; State Dept Collection, Calif; also in collection of Tomaso Campanella, Rome, Italy. Exhib: Witte Mus Exhib, San Antonio, Tex, 60; Tours of Ford Collection, Rotunda, Detroit, 51-69; Kipplinger Publ, Washington, DC, 69; Rome Int, 69; London Int, 71; plus many others. Collections Arranged: US Army Touring Exhibs, 54-55; Men of Art Guild Nat Touring Exhib. Pos: Art supvr, Ore Pub Schs, Klamath Falls, 48-51; art dir, Hq 5th USA, 51-55, 4th USA, 55-60 & 15th USAF SAC, 60-63; art supvr, Moreno Valley Schs, Calif, 63-71; art dir & owner, Lincoln Art Galleries, Lincoln City, Ore & Sacramento, Calif, 71- Awards: Purchase Award, Witte Mus, 60; Tomaso Campanella Award, Rome, 69; Int Biog Award & Queen's Award, London, 71. Mem: Ore Arts Comn (bd dirs, 72); Arts in Ore Asn (bd, 72); Riverside Fine Arts Guild (pres bd, 68); Moreno Valley Allied Arts Asn (pres bd, 69-71). Media: Oil, Watercolor. Specialty: Paintings of the Northwest. Publ: Auth, Developing Creativity in Children: Grades K through 12, 63-71. Mailing Add: Lincoln Art Galleries 620 NE Hwy 101 Box 424 Lincoln City OR 97367

BANKS, ANNE JOHNSON
SCULPTOR, PRINTMAKER
b New London, Conn, Aug 10, 24. Study: Wellesley Col, BA, 46; Honolulu Sch Art, with Willson Stamper, 48-50; George Washington Univ, with Thomas Downing, MFA, 68. Work: Lyman Allyn Mus, New London; George Washington Univ. Exhib: Virginia Artists 71, Va Mus, Richmond, 71; Fairfax Co Area Exhibs, 71-74; Northern Va Fine Arts Asn Area Exhib, 72-74; one-person shows, Alexandria Art League, 73 & Foundry Gallery, Washington, DC, 78; plus others. Teaching: Lectr art, George Washington Univ, summer 68; instr art, George Mason Col, 68-69; instr art, Northern Va Community Col, 71-72, asst prof art & chmn dept, 73- Awards: Hon Mention, Fairfax Co Area Show, 71; Six Merit Awards, Art League, Alexandria, Va, 71-74; Merit Award, Northern Va Fine Arts Asn, 72. Mem: Northern Va Fine Arts Asn; Alexandria Art League; Graphics Soc; Col Art Asn Am; Smithsonian Inst. Style & Technique: Reliefs & three-dimensional sculpture; abstract. Media: Wood, Plastic, Metal, Silkscreen. Mailing Add: 1104 Croton Dr Alexandria VA 22308

BANKS, VIRGINIA
PAINTER
b Boston, Mass, Jan 12, 20. Study: Smith Col, BA; State Univ Iowa, MA. Work: Seattle Art Mus, Volunteer Park, Wash; IBM Collection, New York; San Francisco Mus Art; Univ Ill, Urbana-Champaign; Univ Ore Mus Art, Eugene. Comn: Portrait of Dr John Hogness (first pres of Inst Med, Acad Arts & Sci). Univ Wash Sch Med, Seattle, 72. Exhib: Pa Acad Fine Arts, Philadelphia, 47-52; Brooklyn Mus, 49-61; American Painting Today, Metrop Mus Art, New York, 50; Young American Painters, Imperial Mus, Tokyo & Osaka, Japan, 51; Jeanne Bucher Gallery, Paris, 53; plus many one-man shows. Teaching: Instr studio & art hist, State Univ Iowa, 42-47; instr studio & art hist, Univ Buffalo, Albright Art Sch & NY State Teachers Col, 47-48; instr studio & art hist, Cornish Art Sch, Seattle, 51-52. Awards: Award, Pepsi-Cola Competition, 48; Hallmark Int Art Award, 49. Bibliog: Lynch (auth), How to Make Collages, Viking, 61; Albe & Peck (auth), Artists of Puget Sound, Metrop Press, 62. Media: Watercolor. Mailing Add: 3879 51st Ave NE Seattle WA 98105

BANNARD, WALTER DARBY
PAINTER, ART CRITIC
b New Haven, Conn. Study: Phillips Exeter Acad; Princeton Univ; Guggenheim Mem Found fel, 68-69. Work: Whitney Mus Am Art, New York; Mus Mod Art, New York; NJ State Mus, Trenton; Dayton Art Inst, Ohio; Albright-Knox Art Gallery, Buffalo, NY; plus many others. Exhib: Six Painters, Albright-Knox Art Gallery, Baltimore Mus Art & Milwaukee Art Ctr, 71; Whitney Mus Ann, New York, 72; Abstract Painting in the 70's, Mus Fine Arts, Boston, 72; Baltimore Mus, 73, Houston Mus, 74; plus many other group & one-man shows. Teaching: Vis critic, Columbia Univ, 68; lectr, Friends Mod Art, Detroit Mus Fine Art, 69; symposium & sem, Princeton Univ, New York Univ, Mus Fine Arts, Boston & others, 66- Pos: Juror, 51st May Show, Cleveland Mus, 69; contrib ed, Artforum Mag, 73-74. Awards: Nat Found Arts Award, 68-69; Purchase Award, NJ State Mus, 71. Bibliog: M Tucker (auth), The structure of color, Whitney Mus Am Art, 71; Canvases brimming with color, Life Mag, 9/24/71; Abstract artmaking in the 70's, Christian Sci Monitor, 4/24/72; plus many others. Publ: Auth, Artist & politics, 9/70, auth, Touch & scale: cubism, Pollock, Newman & Still, summer 71, Nolands new paintings, 11/71 & Caro's new sculpture, summer 72, Artforum; Art Museum & the Living Artist, Prentice-Hall, 75; plus many others. Dealer: Knoedler Gallery 19 W 70th St New York NY 10019. Mailing Add: Box 1157 Princeton NJ 08540

BANNING, JACK (JOHN PECK BANNING, JR)
ART DEALER, LECTURER
b Mt Vernon, NY, June 12, 39. Study: Brown Univ, AB, 61. Pos: Owner, Poster Am, 74- Specialty: American poster art, 1890-1950. Mailing Add: 50 Riverside Dr New York NY 10024

BANTA, MELISSA WIEKSER
ART DEALER, COLLECTOR
b Buffalo, NY, Aug 18, 25. Study: Smith Col, State Univ NY at Buffalo, BA(art hist), MA & PhD(Medieval Eng). Pos: Trustee, Univ Buffalo Found; dir, State Univ NY/AB Creative Assocs; gallery dir, Les Copains Art Ltd, Buffalo. Specialty: Japanese woodblock prints; Indian miniature paintings and drawings; contemporary drawings, watercolors and prints; New Guinea art. Collection: American and European drawings and watercolors; Oriental prints, artifacts and porcelain. Mailing Add: Les Copains Art Ltd 4985 Sheridan Dr Williamsville NY 14221

BANZ, GEORGE
WRITER, ARCHITECT
b Lucerne, Switz, Dec 21, 28; Can citizen. Study: Swiss Fed Inst Technol, Zurich, with S Giedion, dipl archit; Okla State Univ, Stillwater, exchange fel, MS(archit eng). Exhib: Ontario Architecture: the Past, the Present, the Future, Art Gallery of Ont, Toronto, 63; Royal Can Acad of Arts Traveling Exhib, 68. Teaching: Lectr archit design, Dept of Archit, Univ of Toronto, 59-63, asst prof systs aspects of archit design, 71-73. Pos: Spec consult, Ministry of State for Urban Affairs, Ottawa, 72-74. Awards: Massey Award for Archit, V Massey Found & Can Govt, 61 & 67. Mem: Royal Archit Inst of Can; Royal Can Acad of Arts. Res: Systems aspects of urban form, particularly with regard to participatory design processes and the applicability of modern design methods. Publ: Auth, Elements of Urban Form, 70. Mailing Add: 498 St Clair Ave E Toronto ON Can

BARANIK, RUDOLF
PAINTER, INSTRUCTOR
b Lithuania, Sept 10, 20; US citizen. Study: Art Inst Chicago, 46; Art Students League, 47; Acad Julian, Paris, France, 48; and with Fernand Leger, 49-50. Work: Whitney Mus Am Art & Mus Mod Art, New York; Mod Mus, Stockholm, Sweden; New York Univ; Univ Mass. Exhib: Recent Work by Young Americans, Mus Mod Art Traveling Exhib, 55; Whitney Mus Am Art Ann, 58 & 61; Int Anti-War Exhib, Tokyo, Japan, 68; Collage of Indignation, New York Cult Ctr, 70; Am Collages, Mus of Ball State Univ, 71; Nat Inst Arts & Lett, 72; Painting & Sculpture Today, Indianapolis Mus Art, 74; A Patriotic Show, Univ Conn, 76; Rudolf Baranik's Napalm Elegy & Other Works, Wright State Univ Galleries, Dayton, Ohio, 77. Teaching: Vis artist, Ball State Univ, 64; assoc prof, Pratt Inst, 66-76, adj prof art, 77- instr painting, Art Students League, 68- Awards: Childe Hassam Purchase Prize, Nat Inst Arts & Lett, 68, 73 & 77; Am Acad Arts & Lett Award in Art, 73; NY State Creative Artists Pub Serv Award in Painting, 75. Bibliog: Barry Schwartz (auth), New Humanism, Praeger, 74; Martin Ries (auth), interview with Rudolf Baranik, Arts Mag, 2/75; Donald B Kuspit (auth), Rudolf Baranik's uncanny awakening from the nightmare of history, Arts Mag, 2/76. Mem: Artists Equity (bd mem, 60-61); Artists Meeting for Cult Change. Media: Oil, Acrylic. Publ: Co-auth, The Attica Book, 72. Dealer: Lerner Heller Gallery 956 Madison Ave New York NY 10021. Mailing Add: 97 Wooster St New York NY 10012

BARANÓFF, MORT
PRINTMAKER, PAINTER
b Montreal, Que, Mar 8, 23; US citizen. Study: Sch of Art & Design, Montreal Mus of Fine Arts, dipl, 49-52; Los Angeles State Col, BA, 58; Univ Southern Calif, MFA, 59. Work: Dallas Mus of Fine Arts; Cabinet D'Estampes Bibliotheque National de Paris; Denison Univ, Ohio; 3M Co, Minneapolis, Minn; Ft Worth Nat Bank, Tex. Exhib: Ibizagrafica, Musee d'Arte Contemporaneo de Ibiza, Spain, 72-73; 2nd Int Triennial of Colored Graphics, Grenchen, Switz; 4th Int Exhib of Gravure, Ljubljana, Yugoslavia; 5th Nat Exhib Bay Printmakers, Oakland Art Mus, Calif; 11th-15th Southwestern Exhib of Prints & Drawings, Dallas Mus of Fine Arts; 13th & 14th Nat Print Exhibs, Brooklyn Mus; 14th & 16th Ann Exhib Boston Printmakers, Boston Mus Fine Arts; 35th Int Print Exhib NW Printmakers, Seattle. Teaching: Instr art design, drawing & art hist, Univ Mo-Columbia, 59-60; assoc prof art, printmaking & drawing, Univ Tex, 60- Awards: Print & Drawing Prize, Conn Acad of Fine Arts 51st Ann Exhib; Purchase Award, Silvermine Artists Guild, New Canaan, Conn; Purchase Award, 14th Southwestern Print & Drawing Exhib, Dallas Art Mus. Mem: Calif Printmakers. Media: Acrylic paint. Mailing Add: 2307 Tower Dr Austin TX 78703

BARATTE, JOHN J
MUSEUM DIRECTOR
b San Francisco, Calif, Nov 5, 40. Study: Univ Ore, degrees in art hist. Pos: Dir, Carroll Reece Mus, ETenn State Univ; secy, Tenn Arts Comn; adv, Jonesboro Hist Preserv Asn; founder & past pres, Cult Exec Coun, Miami, Fla; current dir, Lowe Art Mus. Mem: Fla Art Mus Dir Asn; SE Mus Conf; Smithsonian Inst; Am Asn Mus; Soc Archit Historians. Publ: Numerous articles and essays ranging in subject from The Artist Craftsman vs the Craftsman

to The Philosophy Behind Environmental Design; contribr, Jr League Mag, Tenn Hist Quart & Inside SEMC. Mailing Add: 1301 Miller Dr Coral Gables FL 33146

BARAZANI, MORRIS
EDUCATOR, PAINTER
b Highland Park, Mich, June 24, 24. Study: Inst Design, Cranbrook Acad Art, Bloomfield Hills, Mich. Work: Gutenberg Mus, Ger; Blue Cross Blue Shield, Chicago, Ill; Gov's State Univ, Ill. Exhib: Art Inst Chicago, 59; Detroit Inst Art, 61; Tacoma Art Mus, Wash, 63; Ill State Mus, 71; Pamlemousse, Chicago, 75; Chicago Gallery, Ill, 76; Zriny-Hayes Gallery, Chicago, 77. Teaching: Prof painting, Univ Ill, Chicago Circle, 69- Media: Oil, Collage. Dealer: Zriny-Hayes Gallery 2044 N Halsted Chicago IL 60640. Mailing Add: 5340 N Magnolia Chicago IL 60640

BARBAROSSA, THEODORE C
SCULPTOR
b Ludlow, Vt, Dec 26, 06. Study: Yale Univ Sch Art & Archit, BFA; hon DFA, Susquehanna Univ, Selingsgrove, Pa, 77; also with Cyrus Dallin, Heinz Warneke & Robert Eberhard. Work: Uncle Sam Monument, Arlington, Md, 77; Susquehanna Univ, 77; Catholic Shrine, Washington, DC, 77. Comn: Many sculptures in stone, Cath Church Assumption, Baltimore, 57; five relief panels, Mus of Sci, Boston; two chapels & ten figures, Cath Shrine, Washington, DC, 62-65; sculptures in stone for St Thomas Episcopal Church, NY, 64 & Washington Cath & Episcopal Churches, 65-75; plus many others. Exhib: Whitney Mus, New York, 40; Nat Sculpture Soc; Nat Acad Design; Allied Artists; Audubon Artists. Awards: Lindsay Morris Mem Prize, Nat Sci Soc, 49; Gold Medal for Sculpture, Allied Artists, New York, 55; Henry Herring Citation for Sculpture, Nat Sculpture Soc, 61 & Hexter Prize, 77. Mem: Fel Nat Sculpture Soc; Audubon Artists; Allied Artists; Int Inst Arts & Lett; assoc Nat Acad Design. Style & Technique: All media. Mailing Add: 12 Randolph St Belmont MA 02178

BARBEE, ROBERT THOMAS
PAINTER, GRAPHIC ARTIST
b Detroit, Mich, Sept 25, 21. Study: Cranbrook Acad Art, BA & MFA; Centenary Col; also in Mex. Work: Butler Inst Am Art, Youngstown, Ohio; Cranbrook Acad Art, Bloomfield Hills, Mich. Exhib: Five shows, Va Mus Fine Arts, Richmond, 53-65 & Traveling Exhibs, 58 & 62; Birmingham Mus Art, 59; Norfolk Mus Art & Sci, 60; Mus Art of Ogunquit, Maine, 62 & 63; Am Fedn Arts, New York, 65; plus others. Teaching: Instr painting & drawing, Univ Va, assoc prof art, 70- Awards: Prizes, Irene Leach Mem Exhib, Norfolk Mus Arts & Sci, 62 & Prize, 64, Thalheimer's Exhib, Richmond, 63. Mailing Add: Dept of Art Univ of Va Charlottesville VA 22903

BARBER, RONALD
ART ADMINISTRATOR
Study: Union Col, Schenectady, NY; Goddard Col, Plainfield, Vt; Univ Without Walls, Skidmore Col, Saratoga, NY. Collections Arranged: Norman Rockwell Retrospective, 5/73; Pa Acad Fine Arts Fel Exhib, 3/74; Woman's Work, 5/74. Teaching: Adj fac painting & photog, Empire State Col, Albany, NY, 70-71. Pos: Dir mus div, Philadelphia Civic Ctr, 72- Mailing Add: Civic Ctr Mus Civic Ctr Blvd & 34th St Philadelphia PA 19104

BARBER, SAMIR
PAINTER
b New York, NY, Apr 9, 43. Study: Art Students League; Nat Acad Design; Cape Sch Art. Work: La Grange Col Collection, Ga; Cape Cod Art Asn, Mass; Shreveport Art Guild, La. Comn: Portrait, comn by Contessa Lydia Guelfi Camaani, Florence, Italy, 72 & portrait, Judge George Finn, Shelton, Conn, 74; painting series, Dunfey's Hyannis Resort, Mass, 75; plus many other portrait comns. Exhib: Shreveport Art Guild, La, 74; Two Flags Festival of Arts, Douglas, Ariz, 74; Tex Fine Arts Asn, Austin, 75; Springville Mus, Utah, 75; Cape Cod Art Asn, 75. Teaching: Teacher portraiture, Cape Cod Art Asn, 74- Awards: Helen Smith Prize, Nat Acad Design, 70; Purchase Prize, La Grange Col, 74; Bronze Medal for Best in Show, Cape Cod Art Asn, 75. Mem: Cape Cod Art Asn; Springfield Art League; Falmouth Art Guild; Allied Artists; Boston Mus Fine Arts. Style & Technique: Portraits, figure compostions and landscapes specializing in color and composition with impressionistic technique. Media: Oil, Pastel. Mailing Add: Main St Cummaquid MA 02637

BARBERA, JOE
CARTOONIST
b New York, NY. Study: Am Inst Banking. Pos: Free lance mag cartoonist; story man, MGM, 37; co-producer with Bill Hanna, Tom & Jerry Cartoon Series; partner, Hanna & Barbera Prod, New York, 57-, producers of Ruff & Reddy, Huckleberry Hound, 58-, Quick Draw McGraw, 59- & Adult Cartoon series, The Flintstones. Awards: Numerous awards for animated cartoons. Mailing Add: 235 Elizabeth St New York NY 10012

BARBOUR, ARTHUR J
PAINTER, WRITER
b Paterson, NJ, Aug 23, 26. Study: Newark Sch Fine & Indust Art; and with Avery Johnson, Syd Brown & James Carlin. Work: US Navy Dept; Marietta Col; Norfolk Mus Arts & Sci; Prudential Life Ins Co; & many pvt collections. Comn: Watercolors, Woman's Day Mag, Ford Motor Co & Essex Chem Corp; mural, Am Artists Christmas Card Group. Exhib: Nat Acad of Design, New York; Am Watercolor Soc, New York; Am Artists Prof League; one-man show, Beaumont Mus Art, Tex, 65; Wolf Gallery, Franklin, NJ, 73; Fritchman Galleries, Boise, Idaho, 74; plus others. Awards: Plainfield Art Asn Awards, 64; Grumbacher Award, NJ Watercolor Soc & Silver Medal, 75; Allied Artists of Am, 72. Mem: Am & NJ Watercolor Socs; Painters & Sculptors Soc NJ; Allied Artists; Nat Soc Painters in Casein & Acrylic. Media: Watercolor. Publ: Auth, Painting Building in Watercolor 73 & auth, Painting the Seasons in Watercolor, 75 & Watercolor: The Wet Technique, Watson-Guptill; plus others. Mailing Add: 29 Voorhis Pl Ringwood NJ 07456

BARD, JOELLEN
PAINTER
b Brooklyn, NY, June 19, 42. Study: Syracuse Univ Art Sch, with Vander Sluis & Robert Goodenough, 59-62; Pratt Inst, BFA(Hon), with Gabriel Laderman, Dore Ashton & Mercedes Matter; Brooklyn Col, MA, painting with Philip Pearlstein, 64-67; Brooklyn Mus Art Sch, Max Beckmann, scholar class, with Reuben Tam, 70-73. Work: Many pvt & corp collections. Exhib: Group juried shows, Brooklyn Mus, 73 & 74; one-man shows, Brooklyn Mus Little Gallery, 73, Gallery 91, Brooklyn, 74-75 & 76 & Pleiades Gallery, New York, 75 & 77. Collections Arranged: Tenth St Days—The Coops of the 50s (cur). Teaching: Art teacher, New York Bd Educ, 64-69. Bibliog: Roger Erickson (auth), Surrealist seamstress, 3/74 & Eileen Blair (auth), Mindscapes, 3/21/75, The Phoenix; David Shirey (auth), Artists forming sobro..., New York Times, 3/75. Mem: Asn of Artist-Run Galleries (publ dir, 75-76, coordr, 76-77); Women in the Arts; Contemp Artists Exhibiting Group (publ dir, 75-); Found for Community of Artists. Style & Technique: Acrylic on sewn and padded canvas; sewn plexiglas collages; abstract, reminiscent of aerial landscapes. Media: Acrylic on Primed & Unprimed Cotton & Linen Canvas & Plexiglas. Dealer: Pleiades/Cloud Gallery 152 Wooster St New York NY 10012; Gallery 91 91 Atlantic Ave Brooklyn NY 11201. Mailing Add: 1430 E 24th St Brooklyn NY 11210

BARDAZZI, PETER
PAINTER
b New York, NY, Mar 5, 43. Study: Pratt Inst, BFA, 67; Yale Univ, MFA, 69; also study art & archit, Asia. Work: Mus Mod Art, New York; Purchase Mus, NY; Corcoran Gallery, Washington, DC; Rockefeller Univ. Exhib: One-man shows, Cordier & Ekstrom Gallery, 71, 72 & 74 & St Mary's Col, Md, 75; Whitney Mus Am Art Painting Ann, 72; Indianapolis Mus Art Painting & Sculpture Today, 72; Am Acad Arts & Lett, 73; Cordier & Ekstrom, 76; Corcoran Gallery, 76; Univ Tex, Austin, 76. Pos: Guest lectr & artist in residence, St Mary's Col, Md, 75. Awards: Fed Work Study Prog Award, 68; Painting Award, New Britain Mus, Conn, 69. Bibliog: J Canaday (auth), articles in, New York Times, 5/31/71 & 2/6/72; J Bell (auth), Arts Mag, 12/74; P Frank (auth), article in Art News Mag, 12/74; plus others. Style & Technique: Abstract. Mailing Add: PO Box 60 Canal St Sta New York NY 10013

BARDIN, JESSE REDWIN
PAINTER, INSTRUCTOR
b Elloree, SC, Mar 26, 23. Study: Univ SC, AB & cert in painting; Art Students League, with Will Barnet & Harry Sternberg, Bernay merit scholar for advan study with Byron Browne & Vyclav Vytlacil; res in mus of US, Europe & Cent Am. Work: Mint Mus, Charlotte, NC; NC Mus, Raleigh; Williams Col Art Mus, Williamstown, Mass; La State Univ, Baton Rouge, La; SC State Art Collection, Columbia Mus Art. Comn: Paintings in bus collections throughout the US. Exhib: 21 Americans, Berlin Acad Art, Ger; Pa Acad Fine Arts Ann, Philadelphia; Butler Inst Am Art, Youngstown, Ohio; 50 Artists-50 States (toured US 2 years, Am Fedn Arts), Burpee Mus, Ill; Contemp SC Artists Tricentennial Exhib, Greenville Co Art Mus, SC, 71; plus numerous other int, nat & regional exhibs. Teaching: Instr & supvr painting, Richland Art Sch, Columbia Mus Art, 56- Awards: Ford Found Purchase Prize, NC State Mus, 60; First Purchase Prize, Hunter Ann, Hunter Gallery Art, 62; First Prize, Springs Mill Art Exhib for NC & SC 3 consecutive years. Bibliog: Jack Morris (auth), Contemporary artists of South Carolina, Greenville Co Mus Art, 70; Adger Brown (auth), South Carolina art, State Newspaper, 71. Mem: Life mem Art Students League; Guild of SC Artists; SC Craftsmen; Columbia Art Asn; Am Craftsmen Coun. Style & Technique: Two and/or three dimensional, based on personal vocabulary of nature and invented forms. Media: Oil on Canvas; Mixed Media. Collection: Contemporary pottery. Mailing Add: 1723 Devine St Columbia SC 29201

BAREISS, WALTER
COLLECTOR
b Tübingen, WGer, May 24, 19. Study: Yale Univ, BS; Columbia Law Sch. Pos: Trustee, Mus Mod Art, New York; trustee, Assocs in Fine Arts, Yale Univ; mem vis comt, Dept Greek & Roman Art, Metrop Mus, New York; mem purchasing comn 20th century art & chmn gallery asn, Bavarian State Mus, Munich, Ger. Collection: Twentieth century art; Greek vases, fifth and sixth centuries, BC. Mailing Add: 60 E 42nd St New York NY 10017

BARETSKI, CHARLES ALLAN
ART LIBRARIAN, ART HISTORIAN
b Mount Carmel, Pa, Nov 21, 18. Study: New York Univ, with Demetrios Tselos, Unified Study Curric scholarships, 35-37; Rutgers State Univ, BA(cum laude), 45; Columbia Univ, BSLS, 46, field res proj on Fine Arts Libr Collections in metrop New York & MSLS, 51; Am Univ, archival dipl, 51, advan archival admin dipl, 55; Univ Notre Dame, MA, 57, PhD, 58; Polish Arts Workshop, Univ Minn Exten, dipl, 60; New York Univ Grad Sch Arts & Sci, MA, 65, PhD, 69. Collections Arranged: International Folk & Handicrafts Exhibitions (series), 54-56; individual exhibs arts & crafts of Spain, Cuba, Port, Ukraine, Poland, PR, Lithuania, Italy, Greece, Iraq, Hungary, WCent Africa, Netherlands & others, 57- Pos: Founder & dir, Inst Polish Cult, Seton Hall Univ, S Orange, 53-54; prof librn, Newark Pub Libr, 38-44, sr art libr asst, 44-47, sr art librn, 48-54, br libr dir, 54-56 & 57-; fac mem, Rutgers State Univ—Newark Col, NJ, 65-66; historian, Polish Arts Club, 76-; chmn permanent archives comt & exec bd mem, Polish Art Info Ctr, Co Col of Morris, Dover, NJ, 77- Bibliog: Herbert S Allen (auth), The good librarian, Ameryka, Vol 38; Dorothy Rowe (auth), Man of letters-the whole alphabet, NJ Music & Arts Mag, summer 53; Marina Antoniou (auth), The romance of the Ironbound: a community within a community, Newark, 1-2/70. Mem: Am Coun Polish Art Cult Clubs (mem Newark Coun & nat archivist-historian, 54-, nat chmn info ctr, 71-74). Res: 19th century American painting; historical school of Polish painting in the 19th century; European folk art of 19th and 20th centuries; history of Polish arts cultural clubs in the US. Publ: Auth, The Karolik Collection: reappraisal & reaffirmation, Art in Am, winter 52; ed, High horizons education program in New York City, 61; auth, Our Quarter Century: History of the American Council of Polish Culture Clubs 1948-1973, 73; plus others. Mailing Add: 229 Montclair Ave Newark NJ 07104

BARGER, RAYMOND GRANVILLE
SCULPTOR
b Brunswick, Md, Aug 27, 06. Study: Carnegie-Mellon Univ, BA; Winchester Fel, Europe; Yale Univ, BFA; Spec Acad Rome, 2 yrs. Work: ETS, Princeton, NJ; Clark Mus, Carversville, Pa; Harmon Galleries, Naples, Fla. Comn: Column of Perfection (65 ft high), H J Heinz Co, New York World's Fair, 39; Fantasy (bronze fountain), Metrop Life Ins Co, 40; Transition, J C Penney, New York, 65; Life Line & Communications, J Mitchelle Collection, New York, 68; Equality (Bicentennial bronze 21 ft x 42 ft), 75-76. Teaching: Teachers, RI Sch Design, 39-40; teacher sculpture, Cooper Union, New York, 40-45. Mem: Nat Sculpture Soc, New York; Archit League of New York. Style & Technique: Abstract constructions. Media: Welded Bronze, Wood & Stone. Mailing Add: The Mill Carversville PA 18913

BARINGER, RICHARD E
PAINTER, DESIGNER
b Elkhart, Ind, Dec 3, 21. Study: Inst Design, Chicago, with Lazlo Moholy-Nagy & Emerson Woelffer, BA, 48; Harvard Univ Grad Sch, with Walter Gropius, BArch, 50, MArch, 51. Work: Busch-Reisinger Mus, Harvard Univ; Coop Ins Co, Manchester, Eng; Pac Indemnity Col, Los Angeles; Univ Mass; Mus Mod Art; plus others. Exhib: Gallery Mod Art, Washington, DC, 63; Mus Mod Art, New York; Ft Worth Art Ctr, Tex; Finch Col, NY, 67; Colgate Univ, 68; plus many others. Teaching: Assoc prof archit, Inst Design, Ill Inst Technol, 55-60; asst prof archit, Columbia Univ, 62-63; vis critic, Univ Pa, 65-66; artist in residence, Inst Design, 66-67. Pos: Pvt practice archit, Chicago, 55-61; pvt practice archit, New York, 61-68; pvt practice archit, VI, 68- Awards: Progressive Architecture Award, Progressive Archit Mag, 57; Award for Residential Design, Am Inst Architects, 58; Archit Rec Award, 58; plus others. Mem: Fel Am Acad Rome; fel Am Inst Architects. Style & Technique: Color field painting in Liquitex on canvas with space as the prime subject matter. Publ: Auth, articles in Progressive Archit, Archit Rec, House & Home, Zodiac, Habitare. Mailing Add: 2-B Herman Hill Star Rt-St Croix Christiansted VI 00820

BARKER, WALTER WILLIAM
PAINTER, WRITER
b Coblenz, Ger, Aug 8, 21; US citizen. Study: Washington Univ, BFA, 48, with Phillip Guston & Max Beckmann; Iowa Univ, with Mauricio Lassansky; Univ Ind, with Alton Pickens & Henry Hope, MFA, 50. Work: Mus Mod Art & Brooklyn Mus, New York; Hirshhorn Collection, Washington, DC; Boston Mus Fine Arts; James Michener Collection, Univ Tex, Austin; Los Angeles Co Mus. Exhib: Int Exhib Mod Graphic Art, Mus Mod Art, New York, 52; Carnegie Int, Pittsburgh, Pa, 56; American Painting, Va Mus Fine Art, Richmond, 62; Schrift und Bild, Stedelijk Mus, Amsterdam, Holland, 63; Painting & Sculpture Today, Herron Inst Art, Indianapolis, Ind, 67; Univ Tex, Austin; Weatherspoon Gallery; Univ NC, Greensboro, 77. Teaching: Lectr art hist, Salem Col, 49-50; instr painting, Washington Univ, 50-62; instr basic found, Brooklyn Mus Sch, 63-66; assoc prof painting, Univ NC, 66- Pos: Spec corresp, St Louis Post-Dispatch, 62-; consult visual arts, St Marks in the Bowery, New York, 63-66; mem vis comt arts, Washington Univ, 68-; chmn NC chap, Save Venice Comt, 69- Awards: New Talent USA Award, 56; spec citation for art rev, Col Art Asn Am, 66; Distinguished Alumnus, Washington Univ, 72. Bibliog: Ernest Smith (auth), Walter Barker, 1958-1968, Webster Col, 68; Joseph Pulitzer, Jr (auth), Walter Barker, Fogg Mus Art, Harvard Univ, 71; Patricia Krebs (auth), On the making of an artist, Greensboro Daily News, 77. Mem: Col Art Asn Am; Max Beckmann Gesellschaft, Munich, Ger (contrib mem, 72-). Res: Max Beckmann's last years in the US. Publ: Auth, Introd to exhib, Max Beckmann in America, Viviano Gallery, 69; contribr, May collection & Max Beckmann, rev in, Arts Mag, 12/1/69; Lucian Krokowski & Max Beckmann, Joseph Pulitzer Collection, Vol 3, 71. Dealer: Betty Parsons Gallery 24 W 57th St New York NY 10019. Mailing Add: Art Dept Univ of NC Greensboro NC 27412

BARNES, CARROLL
SCULPTOR
b Des Moines, Iowa, June 26, 06. Study: Wessington Springs Jr Col, SDak, 27-28; Corcoran Sch Art, Washington, DC, 38; Cranbrook Acad Art, Bloomfield Hills, Mich, scholar with Carl Milles, 40. Work: Duncan Phillips Gallery, Washington, DC; Ft Worth Art Mus, Tex; Los Angeles Co Mus; Fresno Arts Ctr, Calif; Kern Co Pub Libr, Bakersfield. Comn: Paul Bunyan, giant redwood sculpture, Porterville Conv Ctr, Calif, 40; foyer sculpture in lignum vitae & stainless steel, Kern Co Pub Libr, 53; fountain of terrazo & aluminum, Fresno Co Courthouse Pk, 66; sculpture in corten steel, San Francisco Munic Transit Facil, 75; sculpture (mirror polished stainless steel), Nor Cal Savings, Santa Rosa, Calif, 77. Exhib: Mus Mod Art, Washington, DC, 39; Whitney Mus, New York, 40; San Francisco Mus Art, 42 & 49; Santa Barbara Mus Art, Calif, 50 & Palo Alto Cult Ctr, 73. Teaching: Asst prof sculpture, Univ Tex, Austin, 47-48. Awards: Cult Citation, Gov Earl Warren, Calif, 48; Sculpture Prize, Sonoma Co Arts Coun, 73. Bibliog: Am Fedn Art, Mag of Art, 40; Arts: Big redwood carving, Time Mag, 42; Sculptor Carroll Barnes, film, Richard Simpson, PBS/NET of KVIE-TV, Sacramento, Calif. Mem: Sonoma Co Arts Coun. Style & Technique: Abstract-constructivist; developed methods using power tools with laminated wood and tensioning in concrete sculptures. Media: Steel & Concrete; Laminated Alaskan Cedar. Mailing Add: 1450 Tilton Rd Sebastopol CA 95472

BARNES, CURT (CURTIS EDWARD)
PAINTER, INSTRUCTOR
b Taft, Calif, Jan 17, 43. Study: Univ Calif, Berkeley, BA, 64; Pratt Inst, MFA, 66. Exhib: Red River Art Ann, Moorehead, Minn, 67; Chicago Ann, Art Inst of Chicago, 67; New Am Painting, Univ NMex, Albuquerque, 71; Salon Exhib, O K Harris Gallery, New York, 72; Contemporary Reflections, Aldrich Mus of Contemporary Art, Ridgefield, Conn, 75; one-man show, Allesandra Gallery, New York, 76. Collections Arranged: Six Artists, Paterson Col, Wayne, NJ, 75; Group Exhib, Allesandra Gallery, 75. Teaching: Instr painting & drawing, Univ Wis, Stevens Point, 66-67; instr drawing, Parsons Sch of Design, New York, 67-71; asst prof painting, drawing & 20th century art hist, Fordham Univ, 69- Awards: YADDO fel, Saratoga Springs, NY, summer, 76. Bibliog: John Perreault (auth), Catching Up, Soho Weekly News, 3/76; Nancy Grove (auth), Curt Barnes (rev), Arts Mag, 4/76; Joseph Wiltsee (auth), Investing in Young Artists, Bus Wk, 5/76. Style & Technique: Abstract painting incorporating three-dimensional structures on canvas. Media: Acrylic on canvas. Mailing Add: 114 W Houston St New York NY 10012

BARNES, MARY
See Roby, Sara

BARNES, ROBERT M
PAINTER, EDUCATOR
b Washington, DC, Sept 24, 34. Study: Art Inst Chicago, BFA, 56; Univ Chicago, BFA, 56; Columbia Univ, 56; Hunter Col, 57-61; Univ London Slade Sch, Fulbright grants, 61-63. Work: Mus Mod Art & Whitney Mus Am Art, New York; Art Inst Chicago; Pasadena Art Mus, Calif. Comn: Ed lithographs, New York Hilton Hotel, 62. Exhib: Mus Civico, Bologna, 65; Galerie Dragon, Paris, 67; Univ Ill, 67; Kansas City Art Inst, 72; Galeria Fanta Spade, Rome, 72; plus others. Teaching: Instr grad painting, Ind Univ, 60-61; vis artist, Kansas City Art Inst, 63-64; asst prof painting & drawing, Ind Univ, Bloomington, 65-70, prof, Dept Fine Arts, 70- Awards: Copley Found Award, 61. Dealer: Allan Frumkin Gallery 620 N Michigan Ave Chicago IL 60603. Mailing Add: Dept of Fine Arts Ind Univ Bloomington IN 47401

BARNET, WILL
PAINTER, PRINTMAKER
b Beverly, Mass, May 25, 11. Study: Boston Mus Fine Arts Sch, with Phillip Hale, 27-30; Art Students League, with Charles Locke, 30-33. Work: Boston Mus Fine Arts; Whitney Mus Am Art; Metrop Mus Art; Guggenheim Mus; Cincinnati Art Mus; plus others. Exhib: Inst Contemp Art, Boston; Mus Mod Art; Pa Acad Fine Arts, 70; retrospective, Assoc Am Artists, 72; Hirsch & Adler Galleries Inc, 73 & 76; Retrospective, Jane Haslem Gallery, Washington, DC, 77; plus others. Teaching: Instr, Art Students League, 36-; instr, Cooper Union Art Sch, 45-65, prof, 65-; instr, Mont State Col, summer 51; vis critic, Yale Univ, 52 & 53; guid faculty, Famous Artists Schs, 54-; summers, instr, Univ Ohio & Univ Minn, Duluth, 58 & Univ Wash, 63; instr, Des Moines Art Ctr, Iowa, 65; distinguished vis prof, Pa State Univ, 65-66; instr, Pa Acad Fine Arts, 67-; vis prof, Cornell Univ, 68-69. Awards: Third Prize & Purchase Prize, 60, Prize, 61, Corcoran Gallery Art; Walter Lippincott Prize, Pa Acad Fine Arts, 68; Benjamin Altman (figure) Prize, Nat Acad Design, 77. Bibliog: James T Farrell (auth), Paintings of Will Barnet (monogr), Press Eight, New York, 50; Robert Beverly Hale (auth), introd in, Will Barnet-27 paintings completed 1960-1968, New York, 68. Mem: Am Abstr Artists; Nat Acad Design; Century Asn; Soc Am Graphic Artists; life mem Art Students League. Dealer: Hirschl & Adler Galleries Inc 21 E 67th St New York NY 10021. Mailing Add: 43 W 90th St New York NY 10024

BARNETT, EARL D
DESIGNER, PAINTER
b Trenton, Tenn. Study: Cleveland Sch Art, with Henry G Keller, Viktor Schreckengost, Willard Combes, Kenneth Bates & Frank Wilcox. Work: Butler Inst Am Art, Youngstown, Ohio; Grover M Hermann Fine Arts Ctr, Marietta, Ohio. Comn: Six past pres portraits, Bd Dir Room, Benefit Trust Life Ins Co, Chicago, Ill, 64-70; portrait, Hon Robert Downing, Glenville, Ill, 67; past pres portraits, Contracting Plasterers' & Lathers' Int Asn Union Hall, 67-78; portrait, Adm James Ross, Naval Armory, Chicago, 70. Exhib: Five ann, Cooperstown Art Asn, NY, 62-72; four ann, Allied Artists, New York, 64-73; four ann, Butler Inst Am Art, 65-71; Union League Club Ann, Chicago, 67, 68 & 72; Mainstreams, Marietta, 72, 73 & 76; Anderson Winter Show, 73, 74 & 77; Tex Fine Arts Asn Ann, 73 & 76. Pos: Art dir, W L Stensgaard & Assocs, Chicago, 45-47; asst art dir & designer, Kling Studios, Chicago, 48-61; vpres & creative dir, J M Callan Co, Chicago, 61-67; vpres & creative dir, Conway Displays, Inc, Niles, Ill, 67-74; merchandise mgr, NCM Int, Arlington Heights, Ill, 74- Awards: Purchase Prize for Horn & Bell at South Haven, Butler Inst Am Art, 65; Award, Chautaugua Ann, NY, 72; Purchase Prize for Depleted Cord, Mainstreams 73. Mem: Cooperstown Art Asn; Artists Guild Chicago. Style & Technique: Realistic. Media: Oil, Acrylic, Watercolor. Mailing Add: 2221 Prairie Ave Glenview IL 60025

BARNETT, ED WILLIS
PHOTOGRAPHER, WRITER
b Birmingham, Ala, May 8, 99. Study: With Adolf Fassbender, Hon FPSA & Hon FRPS; with Arthur Underwood, Hon PSA & FPSA; with Otto Litzel, FPSA & ARPS. Work: Metrop Mus Art & Mus Mod Art, New York; Birmingham Mus Art; Seattle Art Mus; Mariners Mus, Newport News, Va; Ala Mus Photog, Birmingham. Exhib: One-man shows, Arts Club of Washington, DC, 59, Int Salon, Perigueux, France, 64, Gallery 31, 65 & Jr League Bldg, 68, Birmingham, Birmingham Festival Arts, 73, Kodak Camera Club, Rochester, NY, 75, Birmingham Mus Art, 75, McGuire Mem Mus, Richmond, Ind, 78, Vienna, Austria, 78 & many others; 2 of 50 Best All-Time US Color Prints, Royal Photog Soc, London & mus in Brit, also American Color Show, Kodak Gallery, Grand Cent Sta, New York, 62-63; Photo Europe, Juried, France, Switz & Belg, 65; over 1300 hangings in some 800 exhibs around the world, 54- Pos: Dir, Ala Int Exhib Photog, 62, 73-75; pres, Ala Mus Photog, 74- Awards: Spirit of Detroit Medal, 66; Coupe de la Ville de Perigueux, Syndicat d'Initiative, Perigueux, France, 69; Litzel Gold Medal, 74; plus others. Mem: Fel Photog Soc Am (chmn nat publ comt, 55-57, dir fotos int, 59-66); Fedn Int Art Photog (excellence d'Hon, 71-); hon mem Fedn Nat Soc Photog France; hon mem Austrian Co Photogr; hon mem Cine-Photo Club Perigourdin; hon mem, Salon de Bordeaux. Style & Technique: Full scale (toned) landscapes, buildings, portraits, human interest scenes, nature; line-tone mutations of architecturals, largely chateaux in France. Media: Long range monochrome enlarging papers, matte and textured surfaces; semi-gloss color papers. Publ: Auth & illusr, Perigord—for Pleasure and Pictures, 67; auth, Samuel Chamberlain N A, an Appreciation, 70; auth, New Angles in Exhibitions, 74; auth & illusr, Man Ray in Retrospective, 77 & Shot with Luck, 78. Mailing Add: 4322 Glenwood Ave Birmingham AL 35222

BARNHART, C RAYMOND
ASSEMBLAGE ARTIST, INSTRUCTOR
b Ripley, WVa, June 28, 03. Study: Marshall Univ, AB, 32; Ohio State Univ, MFA, 36; Sch Design, Chicago, with Moholy-Nagy, 38; Black Mt Col, NC, with Josef Albers & Jean Charlot, 44; Inst Politech Nac, Mexico City, with Jose Gutierrez, 48-49, 53 & 55. Exhib: One-man shows, Caravan Gallery, New York, 55, Art Ctr, Louisville, Ky, 63-66, Cleveland Inst Art, 69, Richmond Art Ctr, Calif, 74, Berkeley Art Ctr, Calif, 72, Univ Colo, Univ Stanford, Univ NMex, Univ Ky, Staten Island Mus, NY, plus over 50 one-man exhibs. Teaching: Prof drawing, design, painting & wood sculpture, Univ Ky, 36-68. Awards: Second Prize in Sculpture, Artrium Regional, Santa Rosa, Calif, 71-74 & Best of Show, 73. Bibliog: Rannells-Bayer (auth), The Art of Raymond Barnhart, Univ Ky, 67; Meilach & Ten Hoor (auth), Collage and Assemblage, 73 & Box Art, 75, Crown. Style & Technique: Collages, reliefs and sculpture made from found materials, sometimes called assemblage. Mailing Add: 1947 Burnside Rd Sebastopol CA 95472

BARNWELL, F EDWARD
CURATOR, REGISTRAR
b Abbeville, SC, Nov 10, 21. Study: Univ SC; Erskine Col, AB; Parsons Sch Design with NY Univ, MFA. Collections Arranged: Two Hundred Years of the Arts of France, 65, Nat Southern Sculpture Show & Traveling Exhib, 66-67 & Will Henry Stevens Retrospective Traveling Exhibit, 67, Asheville Art Mus, NC. Teaching: Teaching assoc museology & period furniture, Univ SC, 73- Pos: Cur/librn, Mt Vernon Ladies Asn, Va, 56-62; dir, Asheville Art Mus, NC, 65-68; cur/registrar, Columbia Mus Art & Sci, 69- Mem: Am Asn Mus; Southeastern Mus Asn; Col Art Asn; Registrars Spec Comt. Mailing Add: 1520 Senate St Columbia SC 29201

BARNWELL, JOHN L
PAINTER
b Los Angeles, Calif, Mar 17, 22. Study: Univ Calif, Berkeley, BA; Newark Sch Fine & Indust Art, NJ; Art Students League, with Frank Reilly. Exhib: Painters & Sculptors Soc NJ, 68-75; Knickerbocker Artists, 68; Hunterdon Co Art Ctr State Show, 71; Am Artists Prof League Grand Nat Show, New York, 72-75; Benedictine Art Awards Finalist Show, New York, 72; Jersey City Mus, NJ, 77; Bergen Community Mus, NJ, 77. Awards: Spec Three Man Show Award, Ringwood Manor State Show; Jersey City Mus Asn Award, Painting & Sculptors Soc NJ, 72; Coun Am Artist Socs Award for TBest Traditional Painting in Show, Hudson Artists State Show, 74. Mem: Painters & Sculptors Soc NJ; Salmagundi Club; fel Am Artists Prof League; Miniature Art Soc NJ (pres, 75-); Art Students League. Style & Technique: Realistic style tending toward romantic realism. Media: Oil, Watercolor. Dealer: Piggins Art Gallery 403 Bloomfield Ave Montclair NJ 07042. Mailing Add: 74 Addison Ave Rutherford NJ 07070

BARO, GENE
ART CRITIC, LECTURER
b New York, NY, Jan 12, 24. Study: Univ Fla, 44-49, AB(cult hist), 47, grad study, 47-49. Collections Arranged: Contemporary American and British Graphics, Mod Mus, Belgrade, 67; Color, Form and Image, Detroit Inst Arts, 67; Paul Feeley: A Memorial Retrospective, Guggenheim Mus, New York, 68; 33rd Corcoran Biennial of American Painting, 73. Pos: London corresp, Arts Mag, 63-69 & Art in Am, 65-69; dir, Corcoran Gallery Art, 72 & Bicentennial Exhib, Kennedy Ctr, Washington, DC, 74-75. Res: 20th century American art. Publ: Auth, The Drawings of Claes Oldenburg, 69; contribr, Roy Lichtenstein, 72; auth, Louise Nevelson: Prints, 74. Mailing Add: 150 E 89th St New York NY 10027

BARON, HANNELORE
COLLAGE ARTIST
b Dillingen, Ger, June 8, 26; US citizen. Study: Self-taught. Work: Nat Collection Smithsonian Inst, Washington, DC; Hudson River Mus, Yonkers, NY; Ulster Co Community Col, Stoneridge, NY; plus pvt collections. Exhib: One-person shows, Ulster Co Community Col, 69, Herbert E Feist Gallery, New York, 73, Hudson River Mus, 73; Katonah Gallery, 73, 76 & 77; Kathryn Markel Gallery, 77 & 78. Awards: Nat Asn Women Artists Award, 68; Mus Purchase Award, Hudson River Mus, 72-77; Most Creative Aquarelle, Audubon Artists, 70, 72 & 73. Mem: Audubon Artists; Artists Equity Asn; Hudson River Contemp Artists; Nat Asn Women Artists. Style & Technique: Mixed media collages, using cloth, paper, ink, etchings and watercolor. Dealer: Kathryn Markel Gallery 50 W 57th St New York NY 10019. Mailing Add: 5621 Delafield Ave Bronx NY 10471

BAROOSHIAN, MARTIN
PAINTER, PRINTMAKER
b Chelsea, Mass, Dec 18, 29. Study: Boston Mus Fine Arts Sch, full tuition scholars, dipls with highest hons, 52 & 55; Albert H Whitlin traveling fel, Europe, 52; Tufts Univ, BSEd, 53; Boston Univ, MA(art hist), 58; and with Gaston Dorfinant & S W Hayter, Paris; master teacher grant, NY State Dept Educ, 66, travel grant to India, 73; US Dept Educ Asian studies grant, 70. Work: Mus Mod Art & Metrop Mus Art, New York; Libr Cong, Washington, DC; Lincoln Ctr Mus Performing Arts, New York; Nat Gallery Mod Art, New Delhi, India. Exhib: Boston Printmakers Traveling Exhibs; Soc Am Graphic Artists, New York; First Int Can Graphic Art Exhib, Montreal Mus Fine Art, 71; 1st & 2nd NH Int, 73 & 74; plus one-man shows in Ind, Honolulu & Boston. Teaching: Chmn dept art, Burr's Lane Jr High Sch, Dix Hills, NY 65- Pos: Trustee, Montclair Art Mus, NJ, 59-60; vpres, US comt, Int Art Asn UNESCO, 74- Mem: Boston Printmakers; Soc Am Graphic Artists (pres, 72-74). Style & Technique: Surrealistic. Dealer: Dorsky Gallery 111 Fourth Ave New York NY 10003. Mailing Add: 95 Murray Ave Port Washington NY 11050

BAROWITZ, ELLIOTT
PAINTER, INSTRUCTOR
b Westwood, NJ, Aug 22, 36. Study: Carnegie-Mellon Univ; RI Sch of Design, BFA; San Francisco Art Inst; Univ Cincinnati; Cincinnati Art Acad, MFA. Work: NJ State Mus, Trenton; Rose Mus, Brandeis Univ; Cincinnati Art Mus. Exhib: San Francisco Art Asn Mus, 61; Cincinnati Art Mus, 65; 1st & 2nd Ann Jury Shows, NJ State Mus, 66 & 67; solo exhib, Drexel Univ, 67 & 72; Nat Exhib Philadelphia, 68, group exhib, 70 & Art 75 (commemorating 75 yrs of Drexel Univ); 10 Downtown (The Artists Work in His Studio), 69; Twenty-six by Twenty-six, Vassar Col, 71; The Counterweight, 90 Am Artists, New York, 76; solo shows, Amos Eno Gallery, New York, 76 & 78. Teaching: Assoc prof painting & design, Drexel Univ, Philadelphia, 66-; instr painting & drawing, Portland Sch of Art, Maine, summers, 76 & 77. Bibliog: Interviews with American Artists, Joint Iranian & French TV production, 71. Mem: Artists Tenants Asn; Found for the Commun of Artists (mem bd dirs, 75; chmn bd dirs, 76 & 77). Media: Painting, oil; video; sculpture with acrylic plastic & neon. Publ: Auth, Other Doors of Perception, Chelsea Clinton News, 66; auth, Fashion and Art, Nat Asn of Teachers of Textiles & Clothing, 67; auth, The Rats of Soho, Village Voice, 73; auth, No Where from Noho, Art Workers News, Found for the Commun of Artists, 76; illusr, A Passage of Saint Devil, Duncan McNaughton (auth), Talon Books, 76. Mailing Add: 7 Washington Pl New York NY 10003

BARR, ALFRED HAMILTON, JR
ART HISTORIAN, ART ADMINISTRATOR
b Detroit, Mich, Jan 28, 02. Study: Princeton Univ, AB, 22, univ fel, 22-23, AM, 23, Thayer fel, 24-25, hon LittD, 49; Harvard Univ, PhD, 46; Univ Bonn, hon PhD, 58; Univ Buffalo, hon DFA, 62; Yale Univ, hon PhD, 67; Columbia Univ, hon PhD, 69. Teaching: Instr art, Vassar Col, 23-24; asst dept fine arts, Harvard Univ, 24-25; instr art & archaeol, Princeton Univ, 25-26; assoc prof art, Wellesley Col, 26-29; Mary Flexner lectr, Bryn Mawr Col, 46. Pos: Dir, Mus Mod Art, New York, 29-43, trustee, 39-, vpres bd trustees, 39-43, dir res in painting & sculpture, 44-46, dir mus collections, 47-67, counr bd trustees, 67-; co-ed, Art in Am, 36; chmn, New York Comt, Nat Art Wk, 40; mem adv comt art, Off Coordr Inter-Am Affairs, 40-43; mem adv comt, Inst Mod Art, Boston & Cincinnati Mod Art Soc; ed, Am Painters Series, Penguin Bks (London), 44-45; ed exhib catalog, Mus Mod Art, adv coun, Dept Art & Archaeol, Princeton Univ, 46-; vis comt fine arts, Fogg Art Mus, Harvard Univ, 58-60, chmn, 65-70; bd overseers, Harvard Univ, 64-70. Awards: Chevalier, Legon of Honor, 59; Spec Merit Award for Notable Creative Achievement, Brandeis Univ, 64; Nat Inst Arts & Lett Award for Distinguished Service to Arts, 68; plus others. Publ: Auth, Cubism and Abstract Art, 36; auth, Fantastic Art, Dada, Surrealism, 36; auth, What is Modern Painting, 43; auth, Picasso: Fifty Years of His Art, 46; auth, Matisse: His Art and His Public, 51. Mailing Add: Mus Mod Art 11 W 53rd St New York NY 10019

BARR, DAVID JOHN
SCULPTOR, PAINTER
b Detroit, Mich, Oct 10, 39. Study: Wayne State Univ, BFA & MA. Work: Detroit Inst Arts; Wayne State Univ Alumni Bldg; John Hancock Bldg. Comn: Fairlane Ctr, Dearborn, Mich, 75; nine-part outdoor sculpture, Macomb Col, Warren, Mich, 76; five wall reliefs, Detroit Renaissance Ctr, 77. Exhib: Mich Artists Shows, Detroit, 62-66; Flint Nat, Mich, 66; Evanston Art Ctr, 69; Chicago Contemporary, Herron Mus, Atlanta High Mus & Cranbrook Art Mus, 69; plus several one-man shows. Teaching: Prof sculpture, Macomb Co Col, 64- Awards: Archit Awards, Louis Redstone Assocs, 65 & Albert Kahn Assocs, 65; Mich Found of the Arts Award, 77. Bibliog: Dennis Stone (auth), Young structurists, Midwest Art Scene, 67; Relief makers, Chicago Omnibus, 67; Chicago art, Art News, 68; Michael Greenwood (auth), article in Artscanada, Winter 1976. Style & Technique: Constructed, painted geometric reliefs & sculpture. Media: Masonite, Steel. Publ: Auth, Notes on growth, 69, Notes, 70 & Notes, III, 72, Structurist, 75-76. Dealer: Richard Gray Gallery 620 N Michigan Ave Chicago IL 60611; Donald Morris Gallery Birmingham MI 48012. Mailing Add: 8469 Yale Oak Park MI 48237

BARR, ELIZABETH QUANDT
See Quandt, Elizabeth

BARR, NORMAN
PAINTER
b Melitopol, Russia, Mar 9, 08; US citizen. Study: Nat Acad Design. Comn: Portraits, comn by Dr Harry Barash, Yonkers, NY, 72, Richard Huett, Tarrytown, NY, 72, Mr & Mrs Lester Fuchs, Los Angeles, 73, Dr & Mrs Philip Hennig, New York, 75 & Harry Kerman, Merrick, NY, 75. Exhib: Pepsi-Cola Nat Traveling Exhib, US, 43; Conn Acad Fine Arts, 53; Tupperware Nat Traveling Exhib, US, 56; Eastern States Expos & Mus Fine Arts, Springfield, Mass, 57; Art: USA, New York, 58. Pos: Exec vpres NY chap, Artists Equity Asn, 46-50, mem nat exec comt, 48-50 & regional dir, 49-50; pres, New York Wash Proj for the Arts Artists, Inc, 77- Awards: Honorable Mention, ACA Gallery & Artists Cong, 42; Grumbacher Award, Am Soc Contemp Artists, 57; Bocour Award, Am Soc Contemp Artists, 64. Mem: Am Soc Contemp Artists (bd dir, 66-68). Style & Technique: Cubist-expressionist; oil on canvas; pen and ink, black and color washes. Dealer: Ann Leonard 63 Tinker St Woodstock NY 12498. Mailing Add: 775 Riverside Dr New York NY 10032

BARR, ROGER TERRY
SCULPTOR, PAINTER
b Milwaukee, Wis, Sept 17, 21. Study: Univ Wis; Nat Univ Mex; Pomona Col, BA; Claremont Col, MFA; Jepson Art Inst, Atelier 17. Work: Hirschhorn Mus & Sculpture Garden of Smithsonian Inst, Washington, DC; Pasadena Art Mus; Mus Arte Mod, Sao Paulo, Brazil; Boston Mus Fine Arts; Art Mus Göteborg, Sweden; plus others in pub & pvt collections. Comn: Welded metal fountains, CofC Plaza, Santa Rosa, Calif. Exhib: One-man shows, Felix Landau Gallery, Los Angeles, M H de Young Mem Mus, San Francisco, Galerie Philadelphie, Paris, Esther Robles Gallery, Los Angeles & Feingarten Gallery, New York; Bank of Am World Hq, San Francisco; Int Sculpture Exhib, Mus Rodin, 66 & Mus Toulouse, 67, Paris; Perth Prize for Int Drawing, 73, Australia. plus other one-man & group shows. Teaching: Instr art, Univ Calif, Los Angeles, 50-52; instr art, Calif Sch Fine Arts, San Francisco, 54-56; founding dir, Col Art Study Abroad, Am Ctr Students & Artists, Paris, 58-69; prof, Calif State Univ, Hayward, 69-71; mem art faculty, Santa Rosa Jr Col, currently. Awards: Oakland Art Mus Award, 55; Stanford Univ Purchase Prize, 56; Catherwood Found fel, 56; plus others. Mem: Col Art Asn Am; Am Fedn Arts. Style & Technique: Direct welding of metals and other alloys in a technique related to collage, but in metal and 3-dimensional. Media: Bronze, Corten, stainless steel and other alloys. Dealer: Smith-Andersen Gallery 200 Homer St Palo Alto CA 94301. Mailing Add: 920 McDonald Ave Santa Rosa CA 95404

BARRERES, DOMINGO
PAINTER, EDUCATOR
b Oliva, Valencia, Spain, Feb 23, 41; US citizen. Study: Sch of the Mus of Fine Arts. Work: Worcester Mus, Mass; Addison Gallery of Am Art, Andover, Mass; Minneapolis Inst of Fine Arts, Minn; Brockton Mus, Mass. Exhib: Returned Traveling Scholars Exhib, Mus of Fine Arts, Boston, Mass, 68; Whitney Biennial, Whitney Mus of Am Art, New York, 75; Boston Invitational, Brockton Mus, Mass, 75; For Collectors, Worcester Art Mus, Mass, 77. Teaching: Instr painting, Sch of the Mus of Fine Arts, Boston, 67- Awards: Clarissa Barlett Traveling Grant, Sch of the Mus of Fine Arts, Boston, 65. Style & Technique: Painterly, loose geometrical abstractions in oil and/or acrylic. Media: Oil; Acrylic. Dealer: Sunne Savage Gallery 105 New Bury St Boston MA 02116. Mailing Add: 34 Farnsworth St Boston MA 02210

BARRETT, BARBARA
ART ADMINISTRATOR, PAINTER
b Toronto, Ont, Dec 6, 20. Study: Ont Col of art; Cent Tech Col. Teaching: Instr painting & silkscreen, Toronto Sch of Art, 69- Pos: Dir, Toronto Sch of Art, 69- Mem: Can Artists Representation Ont. Style & Technique: Semi-abstract. Media: Oil, acrylic. Mailing Add: 225 Brunswick Ave Toronto ON M5S 2M6 Can

BARRETT, BILL
SCULPTOR, EDUCATOR
b Los Angeles, Calif, Dec 21, 34. Study: Univ Mich, Ann Arbor, BS(design), 58, MS(design), 59, MFA, 60. Work: Cleveland Mus Art, Ohio; Aldrich Mus Contemp Art, Ridgefield, Conn; Norfolk Mus Art, Va; Lincoln Nat Life Insurance Found; Mercy Col, Dobbs Ferry, NY. Comn: Cast bronze sculpture relief, Mr & Mrs Whitelaw Reid, New York, 59; plaster sculpture, Hanover Col, Ind, 65; welded aluminum sculpture, Class of '42 for Univ Mich Dent Sch, 71; welded aluminum sculpture, Mr & Mrs Gerber, Great Neck, NY, 72. Exhib: Nat Art Inst Show, San Francisco Mus Art, Calif, 64; First Flint Nat Show, Flint Mus Art, Mich, 67; Whitney Mus Am Art Sculpture Ann, New York, 70; NY Cult Ctr, 75; Storm King Art Ctr, New York, 75. Teaching: Assoc prof sculpture, Eastern Mich Univ, 60-68; instr sculpture, Cleveland Art Inst, 63-64; asst prof, City Col New York, 69-76. Mem: Sculptors Guild New York. Media: Aluminum, Bronze. Mailing Add: 11 Worth St New York NY 10013

BARRETT, LENI MANCUSO
See Mancuso, Leni

BARRETT, ROBERT DUMAS
PAINTER, EDUCATOR
b Fulton, NY, Nov 23, 03. Study: Crouse Col Fine Arts, Syracuse Univ, BFA(painting), 25; Augusta Hazard fel grad study abroad, 25; study in Paris, 25-26. Work: El Paso Centennial Mus; Syracuse Univ; Brooklyn Col. Exhib: Syracuse Mus Fine Arts, 25; Oil Paintings, Hotel Barbizon, 43; Oil Paintings of the Southwest, El Paso Centennial Mus, 45; Watercolors, Thomas W Wood Art Gallery, 77; Nat Acad; Am Watercolor Soc Ann, 64- & travelling shows; Allied Artists of Am. Teaching: Prof art, Brooklyn Col, City Univ New York, 32-67. Awards: Louis C Tiffany Found summer guest artist, 27-28; Highest Award Figure Painting, Syracuse Mus Fine Arts Exhib, 25. Mem: Am Watercolor Soc (dir, 66); Allied Artists Am; Hudson Valley Art Asn; Artists Fel (pres, 57-62 & 64-67); Salmagundi Club. Style & Technique: Manipulation of transparent watercolor to achieve light; the poetic mood. Media: Transparent Watercolor; Oil. Mailing Add: RD 1 Morrisville VT 05661

BARRETT, THOMAS R
PAINTER, INSTRUCTOR
b Woodhaven, NY, Feb 17, 27. Study: Wesleyan Univ, BA; Brooklyn Mus Art Sch; Univ NH, MA. Work: DeCordova & Dana Mus, Lincoln, Mass; Portland Art Mus, Maine; Phillips Exeter Acad, Exeter, NH; New Eng Col, Henniker, NH; Kresge Collection, Detroit. Exhib: Metrop Mus Art, 52; Boston Art Festivals, 52-61; DeCordova & Dana Mus, 65 & 68; New England Art, Provincetown & Boston, 70; Currier Gallery Art, 74-77; Art Ctr in Hargate, St Paul's Sch, 76; Univ Maine, Orono, 77. Teaching: Instr painting & art hist & head art dept, St Paul's Sch, Concord, NH. Awards: Currier Gallery Art Award, 60 & 62; City of Manchester Award, NH, 65; DeKalb Award, 72. Mem: NH Art Asn (pres, 68-69); Independent Sch Art Instr Asn (pres, 77-); Boston Visual Artists Union; NH Visual Arts Coalition (secy, 77-); Col Art Asn Am. Style & Technique: Biomorphic expressionist landscapes and figurative painting in direct modes. Media: All painting media. Dealer: Arnold Klein Gallery 4520 N Woodward Royal Oak MI 48072; Cape Split Pl Addison ME 04606. Mailing Add: Eagle Island Sunset ME 04683

BARRIE, ERWIN S
PAINTER
b Canton, Ohio, June 3, 86. Study: Art Inst Chicago. Work: Famous Golf Holes I Have Played (collection of 30 golf paintings), US Golf Asn, Far Hills, NJ; Metrop Golf Asn; also in pvt collections. Exhib: Permanent one-man exhib, The Carolina, Pinehurst, NC; Grand Cent

Galleries, New York. Pos: Former dir & mgr, Grand Central Art Galleries, Inc. Mailing Add: PO Box 206 Greenwich CT 06830

BARRIO, RAYMOND
WRITER, PAINTER
b West Orange, NJ, 1921. Study: Univ Calif, Berkeley, BA, 47; Art Ctr Col Design, Calif, BPA, 52. Work: Boston Printmakers; Philadelphia Color Print Soc. Comn: Print ed, Collectors Am Art, New York, 59 & 60. Exhib: Oakland Art Mus, Calif, 55-60; Am Color Print Soc, Philadelphia, 56-60; San Francisco Mus Art, 56-58; Boston Printmakers, 56-60; Los Angeles Co Mus, 56, 57 & 60; plus over 60 nat exhibs. Teaching: Instr painting & drawing, var Calif cols, 61-75; instr art hist, Foothill Col, currently. Awards: Philadelphia Color Print Soc, 57; Boston Printmakers, 59; San Francisco Mus Art, 66. Bibliog: Zev Pressman (auth), Wet paint (20 min color film), 70; Graphics Group (auth), Calif graphics-1974, Arcadia, Calif, 74. Style & Technique: Abstract expressionist. Media: Acrylic. Res: How-to; art history. Publ: Auth, Experiments in Modern Art, Sterling, 68; auth, Prism, 68, Art: seen, 68, Selections from Walden, 69, Mexico's Art, 75 & Devil's Apple Corps, 76, Ventura Press. Mailing Add: Ventura Press PO Box 1076 Guerneville CA 95446

BARRIO-GARAY, JOSE LUIS
ART ADMINISTRATOR, ART HISTORIAN
b Zaragoza, Spain, Mar 17, 32. Study: Univ Madrid, Professorship(design); Columbia Univ, PhD(art hist); studied with Enrique Lafuente Ferrari, George Collins, Theodore Reff & Meyer Schapiro. Teaching: Asst prof art hist & design, Univ Southern Miss, Hattiesburg, 62-65; preceptor art hist, Columbia Univ, 66-67; asst prof art hist, Univ Wis-Milwaukee, 67-73; dir & assoc prof art hist & criticism, Sch Art, Ohio Univ, Athens, 73-76; prof art hist & criticism & chmn, Dept Visual Arts, Univ Western Ont, London, 76- Pos: Consult, Choice, 68-; foreign corresp in US & Can, Goya, Madrid, 72-; ed-in-chief, Newsletter, Am Soc Hispanic Art Hist Studies, 78- Awards: Var Fels & Grants. Mem: Col Art Asn Am; Univs Art Asn of Can; Nat Coun Art Admis; Am Asn Univ Prof; Can Asn of Univ Teachers. Res: 19th and 20th century European and American art history and criticism; history of Spanish art and architecture. Publ: Auth, Newton Harrison's fourth lagoon: strategy against entrophy, Arts, 11/74; auth, Jose Gutierrez Solana: paintings and writings, 75; auth, George Segal: life and work (in press); auth, George Segel: environments, New Lugano Rev, No 10, 76; auth, Intention, object and signification in the work of Tapies, in: Antoni Tapies: Thirty-Three Years of His Work (exhib catalogue), Albright-Knox Art Gallery, 77; plus exhib catalogues for Milwaukee Art Ctr, The Columbus Gallery of Fine Arts, Marlborough New York, The Inst of Contemp Art, Philadelphia & several other articles & essays. Mailing Add: 950 Woodhaven Ct London ON N6H 4N5 Can

BARRON, ROS
PAINTER, VIDEO ARTIST
b Boston, Mass, July 4, 33. Study: Mass Col Art, BFA; and with Carl Nelson; Radcliffe Inst, Harvard Univ, fel, 66-68. Work: Addison Gallery Am Art, Andover, Mass; Worcester Art Mus; Dartmouth Col Collection; Harvard Univ; Boston Mus Fine Arts; plus others. Comn: Seasons (wall painting), YMCA, Roxbury, Mass, 65; Rainbow, Rocket, Road (wall painting), Lawrence Sch, Brookline, Mass, 67; polarized light painting, comn by SDI, San Francisco, 69; ser wall paintings for Community Ctr, Wilmington, Del, 70; plus others. Exhib: Whitney Ann Am Painting, Salon, 71-72; Ward-Nasse Gallery, NY; Surreal Image, De Cordova Mus; UNESCO Art in Architecture, Rotterdam, Holland; American Painting & Sculpture, US Info Agency Exhib, Europe; plus many others. Teaching: Assoc prof, Univ Mass, Boston. Pos: Dir, Zone, Visual Theater. Awards: Rockefeller Artist-in-TV Grant, WGBH-TV, 68-69, New TV Workshop Grant, 75; NY Found Arts, Inc Award to Zone, 72; Nat Endowment for the Arts Individual Fel, 75-76. Style & Technique: Surreal juxtapositions of space, scale, objects and environments in both painting and video works. Mailing Add: 30 Webster Pl Brookline MA 02146

BARROW, THOMAS FRANCIS
PHOTOGRAPHER, INSTRUCTOR
b Kansas City, Mo, Sept 24, 38. Study: Kansas City Art Inst, BFA(graphic design), 63; Northwestern Univ, film courses with Jack Ellis, 65; Inst Design, Ill Inst Technol, photog with Aaron Siskind, MS, 67. Work: Nat Gallery Can, Ottawa; Mus Mod Art, New York; Int Mus Photog, Rochester, NY; Philadelphia Mus Fine Arts; Fogg Art Mus, Cambridge, Mass. Exhib: The Photograph as Object, Nat Gallery Can, 70; Sharp Focus Realism: A New Perspective, Pace Gallery, New York, 73; Light & Lens: Methods of Photography, Hudson River Mus, Yonkers, NY, 73; one-man show, Light Gallery, New York, 74 & 76; The Extended Document, Int Mus Photog, Rochester, NY, 75; Am Photog: Past & Present, Seattle Art Mus, 76; Contemp American Photog Works, Mus Fine Arts, Houston, 77. Collections Arranged: Figure in Landscape, Int Mus Photog, 69; Light & Substance (with Van Deren Coke), Univ NMex Art Mus, 73. Teaching: Assoc prof photog, Univ NMex, 73- Pos: Asst dir, George Eastman House, Rochester, NY, 71-72; assoc dir, Univ NMex Art Mus, 73-76. Awards: Nat Endowment for the Arts Grant, 73 & 78. Bibliog: Ed, et al (auth), The Art of Photography, Time-Life Bks, 71; Gary Metz (auth), Barrow's Astronaut Drift (slide set), Light Impressions, NY, 72; William Jenkins (auth), The Extended Document, Int Mus Photog, George Eastman House, 74. Mem: Soc Photog Educ (chmn, Rocky Mountain Region, 73). Style & Technique: Manipulated, various toned silver images; various copy machine imagery. Media: Photography. Publ: Auth, A Letter with Some Thoughts on Photography's Future, Album 6, 70; auth, 600 Faces by Benton, Aperture, 15:2; auth, The Camera Fiend, Image, 14:4; contribr, Britannica Encycl Am Art, 73; auth, Three photographers and their books, In: A Hundred Years of Photographic History: Essays in Honor of Beaumont Newhall, 75. Dealer: Light Gallery 724 Fifth Ave New York NY 10019. Mailing Add: Art Dept Univ of NMex Albuquerque NM 87131

BARR-SHARRAR, BERYL
PAINTER, WRITER
b Norfolk, Va. Study: Mt Holyoke Col, BA; Univ Calif, Berkeley, MA; Inst Fine Arts, NY Univ, MA, PhD cand. Exhib: Seven Americans of Paris, Am Cult Ctr, US Embassy, Paris, 62; Maisons Cult Amiens, Bourges, Mus Avignon, Besancon, Montpellier, Nancy & Ste-Etienne, 67; Mus Bourdeux, Menton & le Havre, 68; Sachs Gallery, 73 & Livingstone-Learmonth Gallery, 75, New York. Teaching: Vis lectr painting, Mt Holyoke Col, 68-69; vis lectr art hist, Pratt Inst, 78. Pos: Co-founder, Col Art Study Abroad, Paris, 61, assoc dir, 61-68. Awards: Prix le France pour le jeune peinture, Paris, 64. Style & Technique: Abstract. Publ: Ed, The Artists' & Writers' Cookbook, 61; auth, Wonders, Warriors & Beasts Abounding, Doubleday, 67; auth, Artists en Exil (exhib catalog), Paris Am Ctr, 68; auth, Some aspects of early autobiographical imagery in Picasso's Suite 347, Art Bull, 12/72. Mailing Add: c/o Sharon MacIntosh 412 West End Ave New York NY 10024

BARRY, ANNE MEREDITH
PRINTMAKER, INSTRUCTOR
b Toronto, Ont, Aug 31, 32. Study: Ont Col of Art, 49-54, with Carl Schaefer & Eric Friefield; also printmaking with Nornyansky, 63. Work: St Mary's Univ Art Gallery, Halifax, NS; Toronto Dominion Can Collection; Inco Can Collection, Toronto; Arts & Cult Centre, St John's, Nfld; Norcen Can Collection, Toronto. Comn: Ltd ed seriographs, Knights of Malta, 71, Dow Chemical Co, Can Ltd, 72, Can Soc Crippled Children, 73 & Gallery Fore, Winnipeg, 75; ltd ed collagraphs, Arts Coun, Brantford Art Gallery, 74. Exhib: One-person shows, St Mary's Univ Art Gallery, Halifax, NS, 74, Arts & Cult Centre, St John's, Nfld, 75, travelling exhibs; Twenty-five Women Artists, Art Gallery of Winnipeg, Man, 74; 14th Ann Int Drawing Exhib, Calgary Art Gallery, Alta, 75; Through the Looking Glass, Art Gallery of Ont, Toronto, 75; Int Miniature Print Exhib, Pratt Graphic Gallery, New York, 75 & 77; Biennial Am De Artes Graficas, Mus la Tertulia, Cali, SAm, 76; Japan-Can Print Exhib, Japanese Cult Centre, Toronto, 77. Teaching: Printmaking serigraphy, Mt St Vincent Univ, NS, 74 & 76; printmaking collagraph, Art Gallery of Ont, 76- Pos: Seminar & workshop teacher, Ministry of Cult & Recreation, Ont, 75- Awards: Merit Award, Art Gallery of Brant, 74. Bibliog: K Hofman (auth), A Meredith Barry, Art Mag, 74; J W Graham (auth), Barry Work Lauded, Winnipeg Free Press, 74; J Bonellie (auth), A Meredith Barry: Two Moods, Art Mag, 76. Mem: Print & Drawing Coun of Can; Ont Soc of Artists; Soc of Can Artists (pres, 74-75); Visual Arts Ont (chmn bd, 76-78). Style & Technique: Color, form & textural abstractions; intaglio woodcut; collagraphs in limited fine art editions. Media: Combination of woodcut and collograph print. Publ: Auth, Dateline: Newfoundland, 72 & The Collage Print, Art Mag, 73; co-auth, An Introduction to the Collagraph Print, Ont Ministry of Cult & Recreation, 77; illusr, The Private Eye, pvt publ, 77. Dealer: Gallery Pascal 334 Dundas St W Toronto ON M5T 1G5 Can. Mailing Add: 81 Rameau Dr 7 Willowdale Toronto ON M2H 1T6 Can

BARRY, FRANK (BARRY FRANCIS LEOPOLD)
PAINTER, EDUCATOR
b London, Eng, Apr 16, 13; Can citizen. Study: Ealing Art Sch, London, nat dipl in design (painting), 46-50; Hornsey Art Sch, London, art teachers dipl, 50-51; Sir George Williams Univ, Montreal, MA(art educ), 67-69. Work: McGill Univ; Sir George Williams Univ; Carlton Univ, Ottawa; Central Mortgage & Housing Corp, Ottawa. Exhib: Ontario Centennial Art Exhib, Toronto, 67; one-man show, Galerie Libre, Montreal, 69; L'Exposition des Createurs du Que, Mus d'Art Contemp, Montreal, 71; Soc d'Artistes Prof du Que, Galerie Claude Luce, 74; Intelstat Art Concours, Montreal, 75. Teaching: Art master art & craft, Grammar Sch, UK & High Sch, Montreal, 51-72; asst prof art & art educ, Sir George Williams Univ, 65- Pos: Convener childrens' art exhib, Protestant Sch Bd of Greater Montreal, 64-68. Awards: Brian Robertson Selection, Centennial Exhib Award, Art Inst Ont, 67; Quebec Art Competition Award, Quebec Ministry Cult Affairs, 70, Createurs du Quebec Award, 71. Bibliog: Slides, Frank Barry, Editions Yvan Boulerice, 74. Mem: Nat Soc Art Educ, Eng; Nat Soc Educ Through Art, Montreal (vpres, 67-69); Royal Can Acad Art. Style & Technique: Shaped relief structures in wood, hardboard, canvas. Media: Acrylic. Publ: Auth, School murals are not forever, Sch Arts, 73. Mailing Add: 201 Bedbrooke Ave Montreal PQ Can

BARRY, ROBERT E
ILLUSTRATOR, ART ADMINISTRATOR
b Newport, RI, Oct 7, 31. Study: Acad Fine Art, Munich, Ger; Kunstgewerbeschule, Zurich, Switz; RI Sch Design, BFA & MAT. Work: Kerlan Collection of Children's Literature & Illus, Univ Minn; Klingspor Mus, Frankfurt, Ger; Mus of the Book, San Juan, PR; Mus of the Virgin Islands, St Thomas, VI. Teaching: Instr art, Averett Col, Danville, Va, 67-68; asst prof art, Tex Woman's Univ, Denton, 68-69; assoc prof art/design, Southeastern Mass Univ, North Dartmouth, 69- Pos: Dir, Art Gallery Southeastern Mass Univ, 77- Awards: Am Inst Graphic Arts 50 Books of the Year, 61; Award of Merit, NY Soc Illusrs, 65; New York Times Ten Best Illus Books of the Year, 65. Style & Technique: Author and illustrator of children's books. Publ: Auth/illusr, Faint George, Houghton Mifflin Co, 63; auth/illusr, Mr Willowby's Christmas Tree, 68, The Musical Palm Tree, 71 & The Riddle of Castle Hill, 72, McGraw Hill; auth, Snowman's Secret, Macmillan, 75. Mailing Add: Driftwood Cliff Ave Newport RI 02849

BARRY, ROBERT THOMAS
CONCEPTUAL ARTIST
b New York, NY, Mar 9, 36. Study: Hunter Col, BFA, 57, MA, 63. Work: Stedelijk Mus, Amsterdam, Holland; Van Abbe Mus, Eindhoven, Holland; Kunstmuseum Basel, Switz; Wallraf-Richartz Mus, Cologne, Ger. Exhib: When Attitudes Become Form, Kunsthalle, Bern, Switz & Inst of Contemp art, London, Eng, 69; Op Losse Schroeven, Stedelijk Mus, Amsterdam, 69; Information, Mus of Mod Art, New York, 70; Dokumenta 5, Kassel, Ger, 72; Proj 74, Kunsthalle, Cologne, Ger, 74; solo show, Folkwang Mus, Essen, Ger, 78. Teaching: Asst prof, Hunter Col, 69-77. Pos: Guest artist, Calif Inst of Art, 71 & 76, RI Sch of Design, Providence, 74. Awards: Nat Endowment for the Arts fel grant, 76. Bibliog: Ursula Meyer (auth), Conceptual Art, Dutton, 72; Lucy Lippard (auth), Six Years: The De-Materialization of Art, Praeger, 73; Caolla Gottlieb (auth), Beyond Modern Art, Dutton, 76. Style & Technique: Conceptual art; documentation of ideas with pictures, text and books; projections of words and photographs. Media: Projections, books, printed material. Dealer: Leo Castelli 420 W Broadway New York NY 10013. Mailing Add: 1091 Emerson Ave Teaneck NJ 07666

BARRY, WILLIAM DAVID
CURATOR
b Burlington, Vt, Aug 26, 46. Study: Univ Vt, BA(hist); Univ Vt Mus, Shelburne Mus, Webb Fel, MA. Collections Arranged: George Loring Brown-Landscapes of Europe & America 1834-1880 (co-auth, catalog), Robert Hull Fleming Mus, Herbert F Johnson Mus & Currier Gallery, 73; Sea & Sail (co-auth, catalog), Portland Mus of Art, 74-75; 58 Maine Painters, 1820-1920 (co-auth, catalog), Portland Mus of Art, 76; The Revolutionary McLellans (co-auth, catalog), Portland Mus of Art, 78. Pos: Res asst, Portland Mus of Art, 72-75; cur of res, Portland Mus of Art, 75- Res: Cultural history, 19th century landscape and Maine painters, Colonial and Federal period development. Mailing Add: 111 High St Portland ME 04101

BARSCH, WULF ERICH
PAINTER, PRINTMAKER
b Reudnitz, Ger, Aug 27, 43; US citizen. Study: Werkkunstschule, BFA, 68; Brigham Young Univ, MA, 70, MFA, 71. Work: Utah Mus of Fine Arts; Utah State Div of Fine Arts; San Francisco Mus of Art; Calif Col of Arts & Crafts, Oakland; States Senate, Hamburg, Ger. Exhib: Calif Col Arts & Crafts World Print Competition, San Francisco Mus, 73-76; Mus of Art, Monterey, Calif, 74; Davidson Nat Print & Drawing Competition, Cunningham Arts Ctr, Davidson, Calif, 74-76; Am Acad in Rome, Italy, 76; Smithsonian Inst Travelling Exhib, 77. Teaching: Prof printmaking, Brigham Young Univ, 74- Awards: Award, Calif Col Arts & Crafts World Print Competition, 73; Prix de Rome, Guerin fel, Am Acad in Rome, 75-76.

Style & Technique: Abstract. Media: Lithography; painting, oil. Mailing Add: PO Box 214 Provo UT 84601

BARSCHEL, HANS J
DESIGNER, PHOTOGRAPHER
b Berlin-Charlottenburg, Ger, Feb 22, 12; US citizen. Study: Munic Art Sch; Acad Fine & Appl Art, Berlin, MA, 35. Work: Mus Mod Art; NY Pub Libr; Libr Cong, Washington, DC. Comn: Created graphic arts prog brochure, Rochester Inst Technol, 54, created photo art catalog of new campus art, 75. Exhib: Am Inst Graphic Arts; Art Dir Club, 38, 39 & 50; A-D Gallery, 46; one-man shows, Bevier Gallery, Rochester Inst Technol, 54 & 65; Fac Art Exhibs, 57- Teaching: Prof graphic commun & instr advan design for reproduction, Sch Art & Design, Rochester Inst Technol, 53-76, prof emer commun design, 75- Pos: Free-lance designer, Berlin, Ger & New York, 35-50; art dir, New York Health Dept, 50-52; exp designer for two printing co, Rochester, NY, 52-54; art dir exp jour, Matrix, Rochester Inst Technol; exec mem, Rochester Arts Coun. Awards: Prize, Am Inst Graphic Arts, 38. Style & Technique: Non-objective and abstract paintings and drawings. Media: Graphics. Publ: Auth, A plea for substantialism & Personal reflections on my era, 64; Exploits into the Neo-Cosmos, a search for man's creative sources, 74; Personal recollections: Companion in Hell; Personal philosophy: Neo-Realism; article in NOVUM Mag, Munich, Ger, 2/76. Mailing Add: 37 Hartfeld Dr Rochester NY 14625

BART, ELIZABETH (ELIZABETH BART GERALD)
PAINTER, DESIGNER
b Cleveland, Ohio. Study: Cleveland Inst of Art; study with Hans Hoffmann, Andre Lhote & others. Work: Whitney Mus of Am Art, New York; Brooklyn Mus of Art; Cleveland Mus of Art; Newark Mus of Art, NJ; High Art Mus, Atlanta, Ga. Comn: Foyer, rotundas & staircases, marble, for yacht of William Levitt, Marina di Carrara, Italy, 72. Exhib: Cleveland Mus Art Ann, Ohio, 28-48; Carnegie Inst Int, 31-48; Mus Mod Art, 34; Whitney Mus Am Art Ann, 43 & 74; Corcoran Gallery Art Ann; Everson Mus of Art, Syracuse, NY, 71; Storm King Art Ctr, Mountainsville, NY & Herbert F Johnson Mus of Art, Cornell Univ, Ithaca, NY, 72; one-person retrospective, Washington Art Gallery, Conn, 73; Albright-Knox Art Gallery, Buffalo, 73; Cranbrook Acad of Art Mus, Bloomfield Hills, Mich & Canton Art Inst, Ohio, 74; one-person show, Collages at Cordier and Ekstrom, 77. Style & Technique: Sculpture in precious metals for jewelry; design for fabrics, papers, concrete in architecture; collages. Media: Oil, acrylic & combined oil & acrylic; other media. Dealer: Cordier & Ekstrom 980 Madison Ave New York NY 10021. Mailing Add: Roxbury CT 06783

BARTH, CHARLES JOHN
EDUCATOR, PRINTMAKER
b Chicago, Ill, Nov 27, 42. Study: Chicago State Univ, BEduc; Inst Design, Ill Inst Technol, MS (art educ); Ill State Univ, post grad study. Work: Art Inst Chicago; Philadelphia Mus Art, Pa; Oklahoma Art Ctr, Oklahoma City; Waterloo Munic Gallery, Iowa; Octagon Art Ctr, Ames, Iowa. Comn: Two prints & plates, Okla Christian Col, Oklahoma City, 71. Exhib: Nat Acad Design 146th Ann, New York, 71; Second Ann Mid-Western Graphics Competition & Exhib, Tulsa City-County Libr, Okla, 74; Village Ctr Nat Print Competition & Exhib, Orlando, Fla, 76 & 77; La Grange Nat Competition III, Hawkes Gallery, La Grange, Ga, 77; Eighth Nat Print & Drawing Exhib, Minot State Col, ND, 78. Teaching: Instr art, Lincoln Univ, Jefferson City, Mo, 69-72; assoc prof art, Mt Mercy Col, Cedar Rapids, 72- Awards: Benton Spruance Mem Purchase Award, Black & White Exhib, The Print Club, Philadelphia, 69; Friends of Art Award, 15th Mid-Miss Valley Ann, Davenport Munic Gallery, Iowa, 77; Best in Show, Clay & Fiber Show, The Octagon Art Ctr, Ames, Iowa, 78. Mem: The Print Club, Philadelphia; Cedar Rapids/Marion Fine Arts Coun (mem bd, 77-78). Style & Technique: Imaginary figures in bright color etching. Media: Etching, Collograph. Mailing Add: 1307 Elmhurst Dr NE Cedar Rapids IA 52402

BARTH, FRANCES
PAINTER
b New York, NY, July 31, 46. Study: Hunter Col, BFA & MA. Work: Whitney Mus, New York; Herbert F Johnson Mus, Cornell Univ; Chase Manhattan Bank Collection, New York. Exhib: The New Gallery, Cleveland, 72; Baldessari, Barth, Jackson, Munger, Stephan, Houston Mus Contemp Art, 72; Whitney Biennial Painting, New York, 72 & 73; Three NY Artists, Corcoran Gallery Art, Washington, DC, 73; Susan Caldwell Gallery, New York, 74-76 & 78. Awards: Award, Creative Pub Serv Prog, NY State, 73; Award, Nat Endowment Arts, 74; Guggenheim Found Grant, 77. Bibliog: C Robins (auth), article in Art in Am, 9-10/74; A Kingsley (auth), article in Art Int, summer 74. Style & Technique: Abstract. Mailing Add: New York NY 10002

BARTHOLET, ELIZABETH IVES
ART DEALER, ART CONSULTANT
b New York, NY. Study: Bryn Mawr Col, BA; Grenoble Summer Sch, cert; Harvard Summer Sch, cert. Pos: Art columnist, Cambridge Tribune, Mass, 25-27, Fortune, 29-31; owner/dir, Bartholet Gallery, New York, 57- Mem: Cosmopolitan Club, New York; Appraisers Asn of Am, New York. Specialty: Nineteenth & 20th century American paintings, with emphasis on impressionistic American paintings and The Eight. Publ: Auth, Solving the Problems of Art by Xray, Am Art Mag, 26. Mailing Add: 55 E 76th St New York NY 10021

BARTLE, DOROTHY BUDD
CURATOR, LECTURER
b Caldwell, NJ, May 17, 24. Study: Randolph-Macon Women's Col, BA(art), 45; Columbia Univ, MA(fine arts), 50. Teaching: Instr art, Upsala Col, East Orange, NJ, 48-49; docent art hist, Newark Mus, 51- Pos: Staff mem jr mus, Newark Mus, 51-54, staff mem exhibs dept, 54-63, cur classical, crosses & coin collections, 63-71, cur coin collection, 71- Mem: Am Asn of Mus. Publ: Co-auth, Crosses in the Collection, 60, co-auth, Fires & Firefighters of Newark, 68 & auth, Black Heroes in History, 71, Newark Mus Quart; ed, New Jersey's Money, Kenny Press, 76. Mailing Add: Newark Mus 49 Washington St Newark NJ 07101

BARTLETT, DONALD LORING
SCULPTOR, EDUCATOR
b Quincy, Ill, Sept 20, 27. Study: Univ Tex, with Charles Umlauf, BFA; Cranbrook Acad Art, with Berthold Schiwetz, MFA; also with Bernard Frazier, summer 59. Work: Spiva Art Ctr, Joplin, Mo; Grover M Herman Fine Arts Ctr, Marietta, Ohio; Brooks Mem Art Gallery, Memphis, Tenn; Laguna Gloria Art Mus, Austin, Tex; Mo State Hist Soc, Columbia. Comn: Sculpture, Mo Pavilion, New York World's Fair, 64-65; indoor fountain, Stubbs Brushwood, Lawrence, Kans, 68; sculpture, Boone Co Nat Bank, Columbia, Mo, 71; garden sculpture, Mrs Marguerite Otto, Kansas City, 73. Exhib: Pa Acad of Fine Arts Ann, 60; Audubon Artists, New York, 60; Springfield, Mo, Ann, 61, 65-66 & 69; Ball State Drawing & Small Sculpture, Muncie, Ind, 70 & 74; Mid South Exhib, Memphis, Tenn, 72 & 75. Teaching: Prof sculpture, Univ Mo, 75- Pos: Hon host, 6th Nat Sculpture Conf, Lawrence, Kans. Awards: Fulbright Grant to France, 53-54. Mem: Tex Soc Sculptors. Style & Technique: Synthesis of organic abstract and representational forms; groups of people in environments. Media: Bronze; Epoxy Resin. Mailing Add: 1627 Wilson Ave Columbia MO 65201

BARTLETT, FRED STEWART
ART ADMINISTRATOR
b Brush, Colo, May 15, 05. Study: Univ Colo, AB, 28; Univ Denver, grad study, 32-35; Harvard Univ, Carnegie fel, summer 37. Collections Arranged: Average of 20-25 exhibs per year including biennials Artists West of the Mississippi (odd years) & New Accessions USA (even years). Pos: Docent & actg dir, Denver Art Mus, 32-43; cur painting & asst dir, Colorado Springs Fine Arts Ctr, 43-55, dir, 55-71, dir emer, 71-, hon trustee, 75-; int chmn art dept, Colo Womens Col, 71-72, consult art dept, 72- Mem: Colo Coun Arts & Humanities (bd mem,71-77);Asn Art Mus Dirs (mem, 56-71, hon mem, 71-); Am Asn Mus; US Air Force Acad Fine Arts Panel (chmn, 64-71). Mailing Add: 5440 Manitou Rd Littleton CO 80123

BARTLETT, JENNIFER LOSCH
PAINTER, WRITER
b Long Beach, Calif, Mar 14, 41. Study: Mills Col, BA, 63; Yale Univ, BFA, 64 & MFA, 65, with Jack Tworkov, James Rosenquist, Al Held & Jim Dine. Work: Walker Art Ctr, Minneapolis; Baxter Labs, Deerfield, Ill; Goucher Col, Baltimore; New York Hosps. Exhib: One-woman shows, Reese Palley Gallery, New York, 72, Paula Cooper Gallery, New York, 74, 76 & 77, Saman Gallery, Genoa, Italy, 74 & 78, Garage, London, 75, John Doyle Gallery, Chicago, 75, Dartmouth Col, Hanover, NH, 76, Contemp Art Ctr, Cincinnati, 76, Wadsworth Atheneum, Hartford, Conn, 77 & Univ Calif, Irvine, 78; Seven Walls, Mus of Mod Art, New York, 71 & Maps, Penthouse, 77; Painting Ann, Whitney Mus of Am Art, New York, 72, Contemp Am Drawings, 73, 1977 Biennial Exhib, 77 & 20th Century Am Art from Friends' Collections, 77; Painting & Sculpture Today, Indianapolis Mus of Art, 72; Am Women Artists, GEDOK, Kunsthaus, Hamburg, WGer, 72; 12 group exhibs, Paula Cooper Galleries, New York & Los Angeles, 72-78; Art in Evolution, Xerox Exhib Ctr, Rochester, NY, 73; Conceptual Art, Women's Interart Ctr, New York, 73; Opening Group Exhib, Doyle-Pigman Exhib, Paris, France, 74; 37th Corcoran Biennial, Corcoran Gallery of Art, Washington, DC, 75; Small Scale in Contemp Art, 34th Exhib, Soc Contemp Art, Art Inst of Chicago, 75 & 72nd Ann Exhib, Inst, 76; Soho, Akademie der Kunste, West Berlin, Ger & Louisiana Mus, Humlebaek, Denmark, 76; The Pure Form, Kunstmuseum, Düsseldorf, WGer, 76; Pvt Images: Photographs by Painters, Los Angeles Co Mus of Art, Calif, 77; For the Mind & the Eye, NJ State Mus, Trenton, 77; Documenta VI, Kassel, WGer, 77; Hist Aspects of Constructivism & Concrete Art, Musee d'Art Moderne de la Ville de Paris, 77; Critics' Choice, Lowe Art Gallery, Syracuse Univ & Munson-Williams-Proctor Inst, Utica, NY, 77; plus numerous other group and solo exhibs. Teaching: Instr painting, Univ Conn, 68-72; vis artist, Chicago Art Inst, fall 72; instr painting, Sch Visual Arts, New York, 72- Awards: Fel, Creative Artists Pub Serv, 74; Harris Prize, Art Inst of Chicago, 76. Bibliog: Over 40 articles & reviews in Am & Europ publ, incl Thomas B Hess (auth), At the Whitney: women under wraps, New York Mag, 8/22/77; Vivian Raynor (auth), rev in New York Times, 10/21/77; Peter Frank (auth), rev in Village Voice, 11/7/77; Ellen Lubell (auth), rev in Arts Mag, 12/77; Gerrit Henry (auth), rev in Arts News, 12/77; Viana Conti (auth), Una poesia fatta numero, Corriere Mercantile, Genoa, Italy, 1/20/78; and others. Publ: Auth, Cleopatra I-IV, Adventures in Poetry Press, 71. Mailing Add: c/o Paula Cooper Gallery 155 Wooster St New York NY 10012

BARTLETT, ROBERT WEBSTER
PAINTER, DESIGNER
b Hinsdale, Ill, Dec 14, 22. Study: Art Inst Chicago, 38-39; Art Students League, 43-44. Work: Grumbacher Col; Washington Co Mus Fine Arts; William Penn High Sch, Harrisburg, Pa; Pangborn Co Collection. Comn: Murals, Sullivan High Sch, Chicago, State of Pa & pvt comns. Exhib: Carnegie Mus, Pittsburgh; Army Air Force, Middletown, Pa; many shows, Harrisburg Art Asn & Washington Co Mus Fine Arts. Teaching: Instr painting, Mechanicsburg Art Asn, Pa, 69- Awards: Harrisburg Art Asn Ann, 71. Bibliog: Baker (auth), Visual Persuasion, 64. Mem: Harrisburg Art Asn (pres, 54); Mechanicsburg Art Asn. Media: Oil. Mailing Add: 57 Center Dr Camp Hill PA 17011

BARTLETT, SCOTT
FILM MAKER
b Atlanta, Ga, Nov 4, 43. Study: Ill Inst Technol; Univ Calif, Berkeley; San Francisco State Univ. Work: Mus Mod Art, New York; Chicago Art Inst; Nederlands Filmmuseum, Amsterdam; Oesterriches Filmmuseum, Vienna; Smithsonian Inst, Washington, DC. Exhib: Oberhausen Film Festival, WGer, 69; Whitney Mus Art, New York, 69-73; Ann Arbor Film Festival, Mich & tours, 69-73; Int Independent Filmmakers' Festival, London, 73; Cannes Film Festival, France, 74. Teaching: Film artist in residence, Columbia Univ, summer 72 & 73; film artist in residence, Dartmouth, summer 74; lectr film, San Francisco Art Inst, summer 75. Awards: Guggenheim Fel, 70; Filmmaking Grant, Am Film Inst, 71; Filmmaking Grant, Nat Endowment for the Arts, 72. Bibliog: Gene Youngblood (auth), Expanded Cinema, Dutton, 70; Amos Vogel (auth), Film as a Subversive Art, Random House, 74; Renan & Reveaux (auths), Introduction to American Underground Film, Dutton, 76. Mem: Canyon Cinema Coop (dir, 74); New York, London, Tokyo & Amsterdam Cinema Coop. Style & Technique: Cinemagraphic research in non-verbal vocabulary. Dealer: Serious Business Co 1609 Jaynes St Berkeley CA 94703. Mailing Add: 2042 Green St San Francisco CA 94123

BARTNICK, HARRY WILLIAM
PAINTER, EDUCATOR
b Newark, NJ, July 30, 50. Study: Tyler Sch of Art, Temple Univ, BFA, 72; Syracuse Univ, MFA, 74. Work: Hyde Collection, Glens Falls, NY. Exhib: Samuel S Fleisher Art Mem Gallery, Philadelphia, Pa, 72; Rochester Finger Lakes Exhib, Mem Art Gallery, Univ of Rochester, NY, 73; Everson Regional Exhib, Everson Mus, Syracuse, NY, 74; Atlantic Gallery, Brooklyn, NY, 77. Collections Arranged: Contemporary Drawing Invitational, Ctr for Music, Drama & Art, Lake Placid, NY, 76-77. Teaching: Instr painting & drawing, Lake Placid Sch of Art, 74- Awards: First Prize, Storelli Gallery, Philadelphia, 72; Trustee's Prize, Everson Regional, 74; Creative Artists Pub Serv Grant, 77. Mem: Col Art Asn. Style & Technique: Representational, working from photographs. Media: Oil & Acrylic on Canvas. Mailing Add: 37 Main St Lake Placid NY 12946

BARTON, AUGUST CHARLES
DESIGNER, PAINTER
b Szekesfehervar, Hungary, Nov 15, 97; US citizen. Study: Ludovika Mil Acad, BS; Hungarian Tech Univ; Hungarian Acad Com Arts; Art Students League. Work: Fabric designs for all maj printed fabric mfrs in the US, Can, Eng, Australia, Mex, Holland & Sweden. Exhib: Am Watercolor Soc; Hudson Valley Art Asn; Silvermine Guild Artists. Teaching: Prof art, textile design, Moore Col Art, Philadelphia, Pa, 46-63; lectr, Silvermine Col Art, 62-65; lectr, Philadelphia Col Textiles & Sci, 63- Pos: Pres, Barton Studios, Inc, New York, 31- Mem: Am Watercolor Soc; Silvermine Guild Art; Hudson Valley Art Asn; Textile

Designers Guild Am. Media: Watercolor, Tempera. Publ: Auth, articles in, Women's Wear Daily & college publ. Mailing Add: 110 W 40th St New York NY 10018

BARTON, BRUCE WALTER
PAINTER, EDUCATOR
b Ottumwa, Iowa, Sept 2, 35. Study: San Francisco Art Inst, with Richard Diebenkorn, BFA; San Diego State Univ, MA. Work: San Francisco Art Inst; San Diego State Univ. Exhib: 73rd Ann, Denver Mus; San Francisco Art Inst Ann; Tucson Ann, Ariz; Spokane Ann, Wash; Va Commonwealth Univ; Univ Minn; Artist/Teacher USA, New York. Teaching: Lectr painting, Univ Man, Winnipeg, 66-67; prof art & chmn art dept, Ohio State Univ, Columbus, 67-69; prof art & chmn art dept, Univ Mont, Missoula, 69- Pos: Photogr, Convair/Astronautics, San Diego, 58-59; media specialist, Community Educ Resources, San Diego, 63-64; art dir, Boeing Co, Seattle, 64-65. Awards: Alfred J Wright Award, Ohio State Univ, 69; Educ Grant, Nat Endowment Humanities, US Off Educ & Bur Indian Affairs, 71 & 72. Mailing Add: 108 Crestline Dr Missoula MT 59801

BARTON, ELEANOR DODGE
EDUCATOR
b Willsborough, NY, Jan 23, 18. Study: Vassar Col, AB, 38; Inst Fine Arts, NY Univ, AM, 42; Radcliffe Col Grad Sch, PhD, 52. Teaching: Lectr mod & Baroque sculpture; staff asst, Yale Univ, 40-42; teaching fel, Smith Col, 42-43; instr, 43-48, assoc prof, 48-53; prof art & chmn dept, Sweet Briar Col, 53-71; vis lectr, Wellesley Col, 56-57; vis prof art, Vassar Col, 71; prof art hist & chmn dept, Univ Hartford, 72- Awards: Shirley Farr fel, Am Asn Univ Women, 60-61. Mem: Col Art Asn Am; Renaissance Soc Am; Archaeol Inst Am; Am Asn Univ Women. Publ: Contribr, Marsyas, Collier's Encycl, Encycl World Art, New Cath Encycl & Renaissance Quart. Mailing Add: Dept of Art Hist Univ of Hartford West Hartford CT 06117

BARTON, GEORGIE READ
PAINTER, SCULPTOR
b Summerside, PEI; US citizen. Study: Mt Allison Sch Fine Arts, cert fe arts, 24-27; Art Students League, 29-34, with Frank Vincent Dumond, Edward McCartan & Arthur Lee. Work: Art of the Western Hemisphere, IBM Corp Collection; Bruckner Mus, Albion, Mich; Confederation Art Gallery, Charlottetown, PEI. Exhib: Expos Int, France, Monaco & US, 67-68; Acad Artists Springfield, Mass; Am Artists Prof League, New York; Hudson Valley Art Asn, White Plains, NY; Allied Artists Am, New York, 71- Teaching: Art dir, Ottawa Ladies Col, Ont, 34-40; art dir, St Agnes Sch, Albany, NY, 40-44; pvt classes, 44- Awards: Bronze Medal, IBM Corp, 41; Gold Medal, Hudson Valley Art Asn, 63 & Gold Medal & Citation, 72. Mem: Hudson Valley Art Asn (secy, 58-65, pres, 65-69, first vpres, 69-); Acad Art Asn; Coun Am Artists Socs (dir bd, 66-); Salmagundi Club; fel Royal Soc of Arts; fel Am Artists Prof League (dir nat bd, 64-); Allied Artists Am. Style & Technique: Romantic realism. Media: Oil. Publ: Contribr, Am Artists Prof League Bull, 71. Mailing Add: 3 Hillside Ave Summerside East PE C1N 4H3 Can

BARTON, JEAN L
PAINTER, DESIGNER
b Philadelphia, Pa, Dec 6, 24. Study: Moore Col Art, grad, 48. Work: Gen Foods, Tarrytown, NY; Silver Hill Found, New Canaan, Conn. Exhib: New Canaan Ann Outdoor Art Show, 60-; one & two-women shows, Whitney Shop, biann, 66-; Stamford Art Asn, 70. Teaching: Instr elem & sec art, St Aloysius Sch. New Canaan, 64-74. Pos: Designer, Barton Studios. Inc, New York, 54-, vpres, 60- Awards: Hon mention, New Canaan Outdoor Show, 65, Purchase Pledge, 70. Mem: New Canaan Soc for the Arts; Stamford Art Asn. Style & Technique: Realistic watercolor; textile designs; dress print. Media: Watercolor, Gouache. Mailing Add: 34 Louises Lane New Canaan CT 06840

BARTON, JOHN MURRAY
PAINTER, ART DEALER
b New York, NY, Feb 8, 21. Study: Art Students League; Tschachbasov Sch Art, New York. Work: Metrop Mus Art, New York; Mus Mod Art, Haifa, Israel; Butler Inst Am Art, Youngstown, Ohio; Philadelphia Mus Art, Pa; Bibliotheque Nationale, Paris; plus others. Comn: Murals (with Lumin Martin Winter), New York Bd Educ; History of Money (oil, with Louise August), SC State Bank, Columbia; oil & lacquer mural, Polyclinic Hosp, New York; acrylic on concrete (with Louise August), Gilbert's Hotel, Fallsburgh, NY. Exhib: Numerous nat & regional exhibs. Teaching: Pvt classes at studio on creative expression, 60-65; lectr, creative expression, univ art depts, throughout the East Coast, 60-65. Pos: Pres, John Barton Assocs, Inc, 65-; pres, J M B Publ, Ltd, 68-; pres, Multiple Reproductions, Inc, 70-; secy-treas, Int Assoc Artists, Ltd, 72- Style & Technique: Wood block printing. Specialty: Publisher of original fine art graphics; art shows at colleges, universities, galleries and others. Publ: Illusr, Space aeronautics, Print Mag & Printers Ink. Mailing Add: 915 Broadway New York NY 10014

BARTON, PHYLLIS GRACE
ART WRITER, ART AGENT
b Dubuque, Iowa, Nov 5, 34. Study: Mount St Mary's Col, Los Angeles, BA; Calif State Univ, Long Beach. Pos: Art ed & columnist, Santa Ana Register, Calif, 68-69; antique dealer/appraiser, Artistique, 68-; writer for ann art auction, KCET, Los Angeles, 73- Awards: Award for Excellence, Monograph on Cecil C Bell, 1906-1970, Printing Indust Asn of Am, 77. Mem: Col Art Asn of Am; Women's Nat Bk Asn. Interest: Development of 20th century American art; Oriental arts; children's book illustration. Collection: Picasso, Rouault, Moti, Kyniyoshi, Dali, Kathe Kollwitz, Harold Frank, Marco Sassone, Cecil C Bell, Cecil Aldin, Ira Moskowitz, Peter Max & others. Publ: Auth, Monograph: California Sassone, Italy, 73; auth, Monograph: Cecil C Bell, 1906-1970, McGrew Color Graphics, Kansas City, Mo, 76; auth, Maxfield Parrish-America's Golden Giant, 1/76, Harry Sternberg—A Visual Communicator, 4/77 & The Wyeths—N C, Andrew & Jamie—A Dynasty of Superstars, 5/77, Southwest Art Mag; auth, Monograph: Alexander Dzigurski—His Life and Work, McGrew Color Graphics, Kansas City, 78. Mailing Add: 11030 Kibbins Circle Stanton CA 90680

BARZUN, JACQUES
WRITER, ART CRITIC
b Creteil, France, Nov 30, 07; US citizen. Study: Columbia Col, BA, 27; Columbia Univ, MA, 28 & PhD, 32. Teaching: Instr hist, Columbia Col, 29-38; asst prof hist, Columbia Univ, 38-42, assoc prof hist, 42-45, prof hist, 45-75, retired. Pos: Lit consult, Charles Scribner's Sons, New York, currently. Res: Forty years of study and teaching of intellectual history and culture. Publ: Auth, reviews and articles in Mag of Art, 43-53; auth, articles in Am Scholar, Art Digest & Harper's, 56-; auth, Art—by act of Congress, The Public Interest, fall 65; auth, Museum piece, 1967, Mus News, 4/68; auth, The arts to-day; consolidation or confrontation?, J of Royal Soc Arts, 3/72; auth, The Use & Abuse of Art, Mellon Lectures, Nat Gallery, 73 & Princeton Press, 74. Mailing Add: c/o Charles Scribner's Sons 597 Fifth Ave New York NY 10017

BASHOR, JOHN W
EDUCATOR, PAINTER
b Newton, Kans, Mar 11, 26. Study: Washburn Univ, BA, 49; Univ Iowa, MFA, 53. Work: Rockhill-Nelson Mus, Kansas City, Mo; Washburn Univ, Topeka, Kans; Springfield Art Mus, Mo; Sandzen Mem Mus, Lindsborg, Kans; Kans State Univ, Manhattan. Comn: Murals, Kaw Valley State Bank, Topeka, 64, Bethany Col, Lindsborg, 65 & First Nat Bank, Grand Island, Nebr, 65. Exhib: Mid-Am Ann, Rockhill-Nelson Mus, 56; Nebr Invitational, Univ Nebr, Lincoln, 62; circulating one-man exhib, State of Pa, 62-63; Kansas' Artist, Nat Gov Circulating Exhib, 66; Fedn Rocky Mountain States Circulating Exhib, 68. Teaching: Assoc prof painting & prints, Bethany Col, 54-66; prof painting Mont State Univ, 66- Pos: Dir sch art, Mont State Univ, 66-77. Mem: Mid-Am Col Art Asn; Col Art Asn Am; Mont Art Educ Asn. Media: Acrylic. Mailing Add: Sch of Art Mont State Univ Bozeman MT 59715

BASKERVILLE, CHARLES
PAINTER, MURALIST
b Raleigh, NC, Apr 16, 96. Study: Cornell Univ; Art Students League; Acad Julien, Paris. Work: Nat Fine Arts Collection & Nat Portrait Gallery, Washington, DC; 65 off portraits for USAAF, Pentagon, Washington, DC; Mus of City of New York; Nat Mus Racing, Saratoga Springs, NY. Comn: Mural in relief lacquer, Main Lounge of SS America, 40; mural, Joint Comt Mil Affairs, US Capitol, Washington, DC, 47; Two Tigers (mural), Princeton Univ, 59; Mexican Pavilion (mural), comn by Cornelius Vanderbilt Whitney; Harlequin (mural), comn by Douglas Dillon, Hobe Sound, Fla, 70. Exhib: Carnegie Int, Pittsburgh, Pa, 40; Army Air Force Portraits, Nat Gallery Art, Washington, DC, 45 & Metrop Mus Art, New York, 47; Significant War Scenes, Chrysler Corp Collection, Corcoran Gallery Art, Washington, DC, 49; also 17 one-man shows in New York & Palm Beach. Bibliog: Joe Singer (auth), Painting Women's Portraits & Painting Men's Portraits, Watson-Guptill, 77; Brendan Gill (auth), Here at the New Yorker, Random, 75. Mem: Nat Soc Mural Painters (pres, 3 years); Am Artists Prof League. Style & Technique: Representational, decorative. Media: Oil, Acrylic, Watercolor. Dealer: FAR Gallery 746 Madison Ave New York NY 10021. Mailing Add: 130 W 57th St New York NY 10019

BASKIN, LEONARD
SCULPTOR, GRAPHIC ARTIST
b New Brunswick, NJ, Aug 15, 22. Study: New York Univ, 39-41; Yale Sch Fine Arts, 41-43; Tiffany Found fel, 47; New Sch Social Res, AB, 49, DFA, 66; Acad Grande Chaumiere, 50; Acad Fine Arts, Florence, Italy, 51; Clark Univ, LHD, 66; Univ Mass, DFA, 68. Work: Mus Mod Art; Metrop Mus Art; Brooklyn Mus; Nat Gallery Art, Washington, DC; Fogg Mus Art; plus others. Exhib: New Sch Social Res, 67; Sao Paulo, Brazil; Mus Art Mod, Paris; Yugoslavia; Zurich, Switz; plus others. Teaching: Prof sculpture & graphic arts, Smith Col, 53-74. Awards: Guggenheim Found Fel, 53; Medal, Am Inst Graphic Artists, 65; Medal of Merit Graphic Arts, Nat Inst Arts & Lett, 69; plus others. Bibliog: Herbert Read (auth), article in, A Concise History of Modern Sculpture, 64; Raphael Soyer (auth), article in, Homage to Thomas Eakins, etc, 65; Wayne Craven (auth), article in, Sculpture in America, 68; plus others. Mem: Nat Inst Arts & Lett; William Morris Soc; Am Inst Graphic Artists. Dealer: Kennedy Galleries 20 E 56th St New York NY 10022. Mailing Add: Lurley Manor Lurley Nr Tiverton Devon England

BASS, DAVID LOREN
PAINTER
b Conway, Ark, July 19, 43. Study: Univ NC, Greensboro, MFA; Univ NC, Chapel Hill; Aspen Sch of Contemp Art; Univ Cent Ark, BSE; study with Peter Agostini, Walter Barker, Andrew Martin & Larry Day. Work: Univ Cent Ark, Conway; United Arts Coun Collection, Greensboro, NC; Arts Coun, High Point, NC; Cent NC Sch for the Deaf, Greensboro. Exhib: First Cent South Exhib, Parthenon, Nashville, Tenn, 66; 2nd Ann Cent South Exhib, Parthenon, 67; 37th Ann NC Artists Exhib, NC Mus of Art, Raleigh, NC, 74; Weatherspoon Art Gallery, Greensboro, 75; 15th Ann Hunter Painting & Drawing Exhib, Hunter Mus of Art, Chattanooga, 76; 12th Ann Art on Paper, Weatherspoon Art Gallery, Greensboro, 76; Works on Paper, Montgomery Mus of Art, Ala, 78; 17th Ann Hunter Painting & Drawing Exhib, Hunter Mus of Art, Chattanooga, 78; one-man show, Paintings & Drawings, 1971-1976, works by David Loren Bass, Du Pont Art Gallery, Washington & Lee Univ, 76. Collections Arranged: Drawings & Sculpture by Peter Agostini, Du Pont Art Gallery, 76 & Prints, Dept of Fine Arts, 76, Du Pont Art Gallery, Washington & Lee Univ. Teaching: Instr painting, Washington & Lee Univ, Lexington, VA, 76. Awards: YADDO Residency, Saratoga Springs, NY, 78. Mem: United Arts Coun of Greensboro (bd of dir, 77-); Green Hill Art Gallery Inc (bd of dir, 77-); Weatherspoon Gallery Asn; Southeastern Ctr for Contemp Art; St John's Art Gallery. Style & Technique: Painterly realism. Media: Oil. Dealer: McNeal Gallery 1626 E Blvd Charlotte NC 28203. Mailing Add: 408 S Mendenhall St Greensboro NC 27403

BASS, JOEL
PAINTER
b Los Angeles, Calif, Dec 23, 42. Study: Art Ctr Col of Design, 65-67. Work: Ft Worth Art Ctr; Whitney Mus of Am Art, New York; Albright-Knox Mus of Art, Buffalo; Mus of Mod Art, New York; San Francisco Mus of Art. Exhib: One-man shows, Cusack Gallery, Houston, 74, John Berggruen Gallery, San Francisco, 74, John Doyle Gallery, Chicago, 74, Paris, 75, Galerie Marguerite Lamy Paris, 76 & Kathryn Markel Fine Arts, New York, 77; Uses of Structure in Recent Am Painting, Michael Walls Gallery, San Francisco, 70; Looking West, 1970, Joslyn Art Mus, Omaha, 70; The Structure of Color, Whitney Mus of Am Art, New York, 71; Color & Scale: Eight Contemp Calif Painters, Oakland Mus, 71; The State of Calif Painting, Govett-Brewster Art Gallery, New Plymouth, NZ, 72-73; Southern Calif Attitudes, Pasadena Art Mus, Calif, 72; 1973 Biennial Exhib: Contemp Am Art, 73 & Recent Acquisitions Exhib, 73, Whitney Mus, New York; Printsequence, Mus of Mod Art, New York, 75; Recent Am Etching, Davison Art Ctr, Wesleyan Univ, Middletown, Conn with Nat Mus, Washington, DC, 75. Bibliog: Palmer D French (auth), 3/70 & Jerome Tarshis (auth), 4/71, Artforum; Peter Plagens (auth), From School Painting to a School of Painting in Los Angeles, Art in Am, 3-4/73 & Just Another Rectangle Painter, Artforum, 5/74. Publ: Auth, Verticals & Horizontals, Portfolios of 4 etchings each, with lead collage, 74, ed of 25, printed by Crown Point Press, publ by John Doyle Gallery, Chicago. Mailing Add: 239 S Los Angeles St Los Angeles CA 90012

BASS, JOHN
COLLECTOR, PATRON
b Vienna, Austria, 91. Pos: Dir, Bass Mus Art; adv coun, Dept Art, Hist & Archeol, Columbia Univ. Mem: Am Inst Graphic Arts. Collection: John & Johanna Bass Collection donated to City of Miami Beach which provided a building to house collection; consists of paintings, sculpture, vestments, tapestries and other objects of art; loans and donations of art made to

many museums and universities here and abroad. Mailing Add: Bass Mus of Art 2100 Collins Ave Miami Beach FL 33139

BASS, RUTH GILBERT
EDUCATOR, PAINTER
b Boston, Mass, 38. Study: Radcliffe Col, BA, 60; pvt study with Irving Marantz, Victor Candell, Gabriel Laderman & Maurice Golubov, 60-64; Art Students League, 61-74; NY Univ, MA, 62, PhD, 78. Exhib: One-person show, Brata Gallery, New York, 73; NMex Int Art Show, Eastern NMex Univ, 75; Works on Paper—Women Artists, Brooklyn Mus, NY & Fairleigh Dickinson Univ, 75-76; Woman Is..., Women's Art Ctr, San Francisco, Calif, 76; Shreveport Parks & Recreation Dept Nat 1976, Shreveport, La, 76; Artist's Choice (col & univ traveling exhib), 76-77. Teaching: Lectr, Univ Bridgeport, Conn, 63-64 & Queens Col, NY, 65-66; instr painting, drawing & art hist, Bronx Community Col of City Univ NY, 65-69, asst prof painting, drawing & art hist, 70- Awards: State Univ NY Res Found grant-in-aid for portrait & figure studies, 75-76. Bibliog: Lawrence Campbell (auth), Ruth Bass, Art News, 3/73. Mem: Col Art Asn; Am Asn of Univ Prof; Artists Equity Asn of NY; Inst for the Study of Art in Educ; Nat Art Educ Asn. Style & Technique: Painterly realist; portraits and figure studies. Media: Oil on canvas. Res: Contemporary American realist painting, including painterly realism; phenomenological criticism and aesthetics. Publ: Auth, The Cooper Union Museum, 64 & American Jewelry, From the Gold Rush to Art Nouveau, 66, Art in Am; contribr, McGraw-Hill Dictionary of Art, 69 & auth, Josef Albers, in: B S Myers, auth, Dictionary of 20th Century Art, 74, McGraw-Hill. Mailing Add: 125 E 87th St New York NY 10028

BASSET, BRIAN WILLARD
EDITORIAL CARTOONIST
b Norwalk, Conn, Nov 30, 57. Study: Ohio State Univ, BFA, 78. Work: Art Wood Cartoon Collection, Rockville, Md. Exhib: Retrospective, Ohio State Univ, 78. Pos: Ed cartoonist, Ky Post, summer 74, Ohio State Lantern, 75-78 & Detroit Free Press, 78- Awards: Sigma Delta Chi Region 4 Winner, 75, 76 & 77, Nat Winner, 77. Mem: Asn Am Ed Cartoonists. Style & Technique: Free-wheeling, whimsical style; British School of Humor & Searle & Oliphant School of Style; pen and ink, single panel drawing. Mailing Add: 321 W Lafayette Blvd Detroit MI 48231

BASSET, GENE
POLITICAL CARTOONIST
b Brooklyn, NY, July 24, 27. Study: Univ Mo; Brooklyn Col, BA(design); Cooper Union; Art Students League; Pratt Inst. Work: Syracuse Univ Libr, NY; Wichita State Univ; Univ Mo; Univ Southern Miss. Pos: Polit cartoonist, Honolulu-Star Bull, 61-62, Scripps-Howard Newspapers, Washington, DC, 62- & United Features Syndicate, 72- Awards: Best Ed Cartoon, Population Inst, 74. Mem: Asn Am Ed Cartoonists (pres, 73-74); Nat Cartoonist Soc. Style & Technique: Brush; pen. Media: Ink. Mailing Add: 8106 Birnam Wood Dr McLean VA 22101

BASSIN, JOAN
ART HISTORIAN, EDUCATOR
b St Louis, Mo, Oct 29, 38. Study: Swarthmore Col, BA; Ind Univ, MA & PhD. Teaching: Lectr mod archit, Dartmouth Col, Hanover, NH, 70; instr mod archit & mod sculpture, Kansas City Art Inst, 72-74, asst prof, 74- Mem: Midwest Art Hist Asn; Midwest Victorian Studies Asn; Mo Valley Chap, Soc Archit Historians; Kansas City Landmarks Comn (res priority adv selection comt); Women's Caucus for Art (Kansas City chap pres, 75-77, affirmative action officer, 77-). Res: Eighteenth and nineteenth century English architecture and gardens; architectural competitions in nineteenth century England. Publ: Auth, Continentality: art in mid-America, MS Mag, 78. Mailing Add: 5123 Walnut St Kansas City MO 64112

BASSLER, JAMES W
FIBER ARTIST
b Santa Monica, Calif, Mar 5, 33. Study: Univ Calif, Los Angeles, BA, 63, MA, 69. Work: State Calif, Sacramento; Univ Calif, Los Angeles; Dec Arts & Ceramics Collection, State Kans; Ameron Corp, Los Angeles. Comn: Woven tapestries, Mr & Mrs Benton Sprecker, Beverly Hills, Calif, 76, Hillcrest Country Club, Los Angeles, 77 & Mr & Mrs Arthur Spears, Santa Monica Canyon, Calif, 78. Exhib: Objects Art, Mus Contemp Crafts, New York, 70; Calif Design, Pasadena Mus Art & Pac Design Ctr, 71 & 76; Fabrications, Cranbrook Acad Art, Bloomfield Hills, Mich, 72; Fiber Structures, Denver Art Mus, Colo, 72; Frontiers in Contemp Am Weaving/Fiber, Lowe Mus Art, Univ Miami, Coral Gables, Fla, 76; The Dyer's Art (int traveling exhib), Mus Contemp Crafts, New York, 76-77; erlebt bedacht gestaltet, Handwerksflege in Bayerne, Munich, Ger, 78. Teaching: Prof fiber, Rochester Inst Technol, NY, 73; asst prof fiber, Univ Calif, Los Angeles, 74- Awards: Purchase Awards, Pac Dimensions-Calif Crafts 6, E B Crocker Art Gallery, Sacramento, 69 & 21st Wichita Nat, Wichita Art Asn, 70; Nat Endowment for the Arts Individual Craftsman, 77-78. Mem: Am Crafts Coun; Friends Calif Crafts; Crafts & Folk Art Mus. Style & Technique: Ikat (tie and dye warp), woven on loom. Publ: Contribr, Batik, 72; contribr, Shirley Held, auth, Weaving, A Handbook for the Artist Craftsmen, 78. Mailing Add: 3702 S Weymouth Ave San Pedro CA 90731

BATCHELOR, ANTHONY JOHN
PRINTMAKER, INSTRUCTOR
b Hull, Eng, Sept 3, 44. Study: Brighton Col of Art, Eng, dipl art & design, 67, postgrad printmaking, 67-69; Brit Prix de Rome, Italy, 72-74. Work: S London Gallery, Eng; Glasgow Art Gallery, Scotland; Bradford City Art Gallery, Eng; Ind State Univ; Cincinnati Art Mus, Ohio. Comn: Screen printed ceramic mural, Dept of Music, Ohio Univ, 71. Exhib: Mus of Mod Art, Oxford, Eng, 68; 1st & 3rd Brit Int Print Biennale, Bradford, 68 & 72; Greenwich Theatre Gallery, London, Eng, 69; Brighton Printmakers, ICA Gallery, London, 69; 8th Tyler Nat, Tyler Mus of Art, Tex, 71; Mostra 73 & Mostra 74, Brit Acad, Rome, Italy, 73 & 74; one-man show, Cincinnati, Art Mus, 75; Eight Print- makers, Col of Mount St Joseph, Cincinnati, 77. Teaching: Lectr in chg printmaking, Sunderland Polytechnic, Eng, 69-70; vis asst prof printmaking & basic design, Ohio Univ, Athens, 70-72; instr printmaking & drawing, Art Acad of Cincinnati, 75- Awards: Cash Prize, Northern Arts Print Competition, Eng, Northern Arts Coun, 70; Purchase Award, Colorprint USA, Tex Fine Arts Comn & Tex Tech Univ, 71 & All-Ohio Graphics Biennale, Ohio Arts Coun, 71. Style & Technique: Photo-screen printing, collage & drawing; use of famous paintings from history. Media: Screen-printing; intaglio. Dealer: Zarick Gallery 768 Farmington Ave Farmington CT 06032. Mailing Add: 1306 Michigan Ave Cincinnati OH 45208

BATE, NORMAN ARTHUR
EDUCATOR, PRINTMAKER
b Buffalo, NY, Jan 3, 16. Study: Pratt Inst, BFA, 54; Univ Ill, MFA, 57. Work: Audubon Artists, New York; Univ Maine, Orono; Fogg Mus, Boston; Seattle Art Mus, Wash; also in collection of Dr Marland, Comnr Educ, Washington, DC. Comn: Etchings, 100 prints, Int Graphic Arts Soc, New York, 57, 200 prints, Assoc Am Artists, New York, 58 & 100 prints, Print Club Rochester, NY, 61. Exhib: Peabody Mus, Boston, Mass, 58; Audubon Artists Ann, 59; Libr Cong, Washington, DC, 59; Invitational Printmakers' Show, Rochester Inst Technol, 78; one-man shows, Carnegie Gallery, Univ Maine, 59 & Nazareth Col, Rochester, 64. Teaching: Asst prof drawing, Pratt Inst, 51-55; prof printmaking & illus, Rochester Inst Technol, 57- Awards: Joseph Pennell Award for Etching, Libr Cong, 59; John Taylor Arms Medal & Award for Etching, Audubon Artists, 59; Greene Award for Etching, Albright-Knox Art Gallery, Buffalo, NY, 59. Mem: Can Soc Painter-Etchers & Engravers; Print Club Rochester (pres, 59-61). Publ: Auth & illusr, Who Built the Highway?, 53, Who Built the Bridge?, 54, Who Fishes for Oil?, 55, What a Wonderful Machine is the Submarine, 61 & When Cave Men Painted, 63. Mailing Add: Box 150 RD 2 Geneva NY 14456

BATEMAN, ROBERT MCLELLAN
PAINTER
b Toronto, Ont, Can, May 24, 30. Study: Univ of Toronto, BA(hon); pvt lessons at Toronto Arts & Lett Club from Gordon Payne; five yrs with Carl Schaeffer. Work: Ont Inst for Studies in Educ, Toronto; Dominion Foundaries & Steel Corp Collection, Hamilton, Ont; Devonian Found, Calgary, Alta. Comn: Polar Bear (silver bowl commemorating endangered species), World Wildlife Fund, 76; Super Maple & Blue Jay, Toronto Bd of Trade, 77; Eastern Cougar, Endangered Species Stamp, Can Post Off, 77 & Peregrine Falcon, 78. Exhib: Bird Artists of the World Show, Tryon Gallery, London, Eng, 72; The Acute Image in Can Art, Mt Alyson Univ, NB, 74; Animals in Art, Royal Ont Mus, Toronto, 75; Birds of Prey, Glenbow Inst, Calgary, Alta, 77; Bird Art Exhib, Leigh Yawkey Woodson Art Mus, Wausau, Wis, 77; Queen Elizabeth Jubilee Show, Tryon Gallery, London, 77; one-man show, Endangered Species Show, Tryon Gallery, 75. Teaching: Hd dept of art, Nelson High Sch, Burlington, 59-68 & Lord Elgin High Sch, Burlington, 70-76. Pos: Art consult, Halton Co Bd of Educ, 68-79. Bibliog: J B Falls (auth), Robert Bateman—Canadian Artist, Nature Can, Vol 1, No 1; Manuel Escott (auth), Creatures of the snow, Int Wildlife Mag, 3-4/78; Norman Lightfoot (auth), Images of Nature, Nat Film Bd of Can, 78. Mem: Soc of Animal Artists. Style & Technique: Realism with abstract structure showing a total environment. Media: Acrylic. Publ: Illusr, The Nature of Birds, Natural Hist of Can Series, 74. Dealer: Mill Pond Press Inc 204 S Nassau St Venice FL 33595. Mailing Add: RR 2 Milton ON L9T 2X6 Can

BATEMAN, RONALD C
PAINTER
b Caerphilly, Glamorgan, Wales, July 26, 47; UK citizen. Study: Cardiff Col of Art, predipl, study with Tom Hudson; Swansea Col of Art, SATTC, study with William Price; Tyler Sch of Art, Temple Univ, MFA, study with David Pease & J Moore. Work: Philadelphia Mus of Art; Am Tel & Tel, Basking Ridge, NJ; Museo de Ayuntaimento De Pego, Alicante, Spain. Comn: Three murals, Wistar Inst, Univ of Pa, Philadelphia, 77. Exhib: Int Sommerdstilling, Basel, Switz, 75; Galerie Arnesen Gothersgade 41, Copenhagen, 75; Earth, Art & Water, Welsh Arts Coun, 75; Pego Ayuntamiento Mus Group Exhib, Alicante Province, Spain, 76; Ann Painting Exhib, Cheltenham Art Ctr, Pa, 76; Philadelphia: A Decade, Marian Locks Gallery, Philadelphia, 76; Contemp Artists in Philadelphia, 77; one-man show, Marian Locks Gallery, 77. Awards: Elizabeth Greenshields Mem Found Grant, Can, 72-73 & 74; Primero Primio, Certimen de Pintura, Pascual Hermanos, SA, 76; Mus Purchase, Cheltenham Art Ann, Philadelphia Mus of Art, 76. Style & Technique: Large realistic paintings of gardens, fruit and foliage. Media: Oil over Acrylic Underpainting on Canvas. Dealer: Marian Locks Gallery 1524 Walnut St Philadelphia PA 19102. Mailing Add: 2104 Delancey Pl Philadelphia PA 19103

BATES, BETSEY
ILLUSTRATOR, DESIGNER
b Dobbs Ferry, NY, Nov 29, 24. Study: Beaver Col, BFA(magna cum laude); Barnes Found. Work: Butler Inst of Am Art, Youngstown, Ohio; Fed Reserve Bank, Philadelphia, Pa; Free Libr of Philadelphia; Hahnemann Hosp, Philadelphia; St Charles Borremed Sem, Philadelphia. Comn: Christmas Card, Easter Seal Soc, 74; French street scene mural (25ft x 10ft), comn by Visual Commun for RCA Television Studio, Switz, 77; series of six Collector's Christmas plates (19th century family scenes), Nat Preservation Guild, Washington, DC, 77; 13 paintings of Victorian houses, comn by Tattersfield Design for Washington Hilton, 77; series of collector's Christmas plates (18th century village scenes), Texaco, 78. Exhib: Butler Inst of Am Art, 70, 75 & 76; Philadelphia Art Alliance, 72-77, one-person show, 72; Nat Acad of Design, New York, 72 & 76; Woodmere Gallery, Chestnut Hill, Pa, 73-77, one-person show, 75; Mus of the Philadelphia Civic Ctr, 73, 75 & 78; Print Club, Philadelphia, 74 & 76; Del Art Mus, 75 & 76; Mickelson Gallery, Washington, DC, 76 & 77. Pos: Illusr, Jack & Jill Mag, Curtis Publ, 60-78 & Child Life, Rev Publ, 70-76. Awards: Purchase Prize, Butler Inst of Am Art Ann, 70; Golden Disc Award, Beaver Col, 75; Golden Plum, Ann Show of Artist's Guild of Del Valley, 77. Mem: Philadelphia Art Alliance; Artist's Equity Asn, Philadelphia; Artist's Guild of Del Valley (bd mem, 77). Style & Technique: Bold shapes and strong color to achieve dramatic 3-dimensional effect; selection of abstract patterns from architectural subjects for painting; illustration in decorative, stylized design of figures, animals, etc. Media: Designer's Tempera; Acrylic and Canvas Collage; Silk Screen and Collograph. Publ: Illusr, Needlework Book, Golden-Capitol, 61; illusr, many textbooks for Noble and Noble, Random House and others. Mailing Add: 133 Broadview Rd Springfield PA 19064

BATES, BILL
CARTOONIST
b Eastland, Tex, Jan 6, 30. Study: Tyler Jr Col, AA; Univ Tex. Exhib: One-man show, Gallery Mack, Carmel, Calif, 74; Permanent Exhibs, Gallery Mack & The Gallery of Fine Comic Art, Carmel. Pos: Cartoonist-illusr, San Francisco Examr, 60-64; ed-cartoonist, Fiji Times, Suva, Fiji Islands, 70-72; cartoonist, Serra's Place, Carmel Pine Cone, Calif, 72- Awards: Univ Tex Sr Advert Award, Dr Pepper, 51; First Place for Oil Painting, Air Training Command Art Award, USAF, 53. Bibliog: Robert Miskimon (auth), Perserving Fiji culture with pencil drawings, Carmel Pine Cone, 5/10/75. Style & Technique: Illustration in watercolor; pencil on gesso. Media: Design Markers. Publ: Auth, Ping, 65; illusr, What If, 67; auth & illusr, The Funny Men, 67, The Golf Greats, 69 & Serra's Place, 74. Dealer: Gallery Mack PO Box 4258 Carmel CA 93921. Mailing Add: PO Box 4227 Carmel CA 93921

BATES, GLADYS EDGERLY
SCULPTOR
b Hopewell, NJ, July 15, 96. Study: Corcoran Gallery Sch Art, Washington, DC, 10-16; Pa Acad Fine Arts, 16-21, Cresson European scholar, 20. Work: Pa Acad Fine Arts, Philadelphia, Pa; Metrop Mus Art, New York; NJ State Mus, Trenton. Exhib: A Century of Progress, Art Inst Chicago, 34; Tex Centennial, Dallas, 36; Am Sculpture Exhib, Carnegie Inst, Pittsburgh, 38; Artists for Victory, Metrop Mus Art, New York, 42; Third Sculpture Int, Philadelphia Mus, 49. Awards: George D Widener Gold Medal, Pa Acad Fine Arts, 31; Third Purchase Prize, Artists for Victory, Metrop Mus Art, 42; Nat Asn Women Artists Prize, 48. Mem: Fel Nat Sculpture Soc; Nat Asn Women Artists; Pen & Brush Club; Conn Acad Fine

Arts; Mystic Art Asn. Media: Wood, Stone. Dealer: Stone Ledge Studio Art Galleries Noank CT 06340. Mailing Add: Stonecroft 15 Grove Ave Mystic CT 06355

BATES, KENNETH FRANCIS
ENAMELIST, CRAFTSMAN
b North Scituate, Mass, May 24, 04. Study: Mass Sch Art, BSEduc; also study abroad. Work: Cleveland Mus Art, Ohio; Butler Inst Am Art, Youngstown, Ohio; Arch Am Art, Smithsonian Inst, Washington, DC & branches, 73. Comn: Murals, Campus Sweater Co, Cleveland & Lakewood Pub Libr; ecclesiastical enamels, Washington, DC, Bethesda, Md, Youngstown, Ohio, Univ Notre Dame & others. Exhib: Cleveland Mus Art, 28-61; European traveling exhibs; Smithsonian Inst Traveling Exhib; Nat Syracuse Traveling Exhib; one-man shows, Cleveland, New York, Brooklyn Mus & Art Inst Chicago, 61; plus others. Teaching: Instr & lectr, Cleveland Inst Art, 27-71, emer instr, 71- Awards: Prizes, 29-64 & Silver Medal, 49, 57 & 66, Cleveland Mus Art; Fine Arts Award of Cleveland, 63; first faculty grant for study abroad, 65; plus others. Mem: Fel Int Inst Arts & Lett. Publ: Auth, Enameling, Principles & Practice, 51, Basic Design, Principles & Practice, 60, The Enamelist, 67 & Basic Design, 70, World Publ; auth, articles on enameling, In: Design Mag, Ceramics Monthly, Encycl of the Arts & others. Mailing Add: 7 E 194th St Euclid OH 44119

BATES, MAXWELL BENNETT
PAINTER, LITHOGRAPHER
b Calgary, Alta, Dec 14, 06. Study: Calgary Inst Technol & Art, with Lars Haukaness; Brooklyn Mus Art Sch, with Max Beckmann & Abraham Rattner; Univ Calgary, DUC, 71. Work: Nat Gallery Can, Ottawa; Nat Gallery NZ, Auckland; Art Gallery Winnipeg, Man; Art Gallery Vancouver, BC; Art Gallery Greater Victoria, BC. Exhib: Can Painting, Nat Gallery of Can, 29 & Biennial Exhib, 69; Int Exhib, London, Eng, 37; Can Watercolors & Graphics Today, traveling exhib in US, 59-60; Int Exhib Prints, Tokyo, Japan, 60; Can Painting & Graphics, Mexico City, 61; Retrospective Exhib, Regina Art Gallery, 61; Retrospective Exhib, Winnipeg Art Gallery, 68; Biennial Exhib, Nat Gallery Can, 69; Retrospective Exhib, Vancouver Art Gallery, 71. Awards: Ann Honor Award, Can Soc Painters in Watercolour, 57; Haspel-Seguin Award, Can Soc Graphic Art, 60. Bibliog: Illingworth Kerr (auth), Maxwell Bates—Dramatist, Can Art, 57; John Graham (auth), Maxwell Bates, 12/68 & P K Page (auth), Maxwell Bates, 4/70, Arts Can; Robin Skelton (auth), Maxwell Bates: experience & reality, Malahat Rev, 71; Maxwell Bates, Vie des Arts, 77. Mem: Royal Can Acad Arts; hon mem Can Soc Painters in Watercolour (vpres, 51 & 58); hon mem Alta Soc Artists; hon mem Can Soc Graphic Art; The Limners (pres, 71-). Style & Technique: Expressionist; consistently figurative with the exception of a 1960-61 series. Media: Oil, Watercolor. Publ: Auth, Faraway Flags, Seymour Press, 64; auth, A Wilderness of Days, Sono Nis, 78. Dealer: Bau-xi Gallery 1876 W First Ave Vancouver BC V6J 1G5 Can. Mailing Add: 2071 Stonehewer Pl Victoria BC V8S 2Z8 Can

BATISTA, TOMAS
SCULPTOR, INSTRUCTOR
b Puerto Rico, Dec 7, 35. Study: Taller de Escultura, Inst Cultura Puertorriquena; Escuela Esmeralda, Mexico, DF; Guggenheim Found fel, 62. Work: Mus de Ponce, PR; Mus de Arte, PR, San Juan; Esso Salon Young Artists, Pan Am Union, Washington, DC; Lincoln Med & Ment Health Ctr Collection, Bronx, NY; Inst Cult Puertorriquena, San Juan. Comn: Eugenio Ma de Hostos, Inst Cult Puertorriquena, 67 & Jose Gautier Benitez, 73; Cacique Jayuya, Centro Cult Jayuya, PR, 69; Nemesio R Canales, Inst Cultura, PR, 63. Exhib: Ateneo Puertorriqueno, 57; Mus Univ, PR, 63; Esso Salon Young Artists, Pan Am Union, Washington, DC, 65; one-man shows, Mus de Arte de Ponce, 71 & Inst Cultura, PR, 73. Teaching: Instr modeling, wood & stone carving, Escuela Artes Plasticas, PR, 66- Awards: Second Prize, Esso Salon Young Artists, 65. Style & Technique: Figurative; modern wood carving; stone carving; bronze. Media: Stone, Wood. Mailing Add: Madagascar 765 Country Club R P Puerto Rico PR 00924

BATT, MILES GIRARD
PAINTER, INSTRUCTOR
b Nazareth, Pa, Oct 12, 33. Study: 25 yrs practical exp in commercial art, fine arts, display & sign indust; also with Eliot O'Hara, Ed Whitney, Rex Brandt, Millard Sheets, George Post, Dong Kingman & John Pike. Work: Ford Motor Co (traveling), Dearborn, Mich; Ft Lauderdale Mus Arts; Home Savings & Loan Banking Group, Los Angeles; Southeast Banking Group (statewide), Miami, Fla; Landmark Banking Group, Ft Lauderdale; plus others. Comn: Posters & stage settings, Theatre Wing, Nat Endowment for the Arts, Hollywood, Fla, 75; four paintings, Dade Co Art in Pub Bldg, Miami, Fla. Exhib: Nat Exhib of Contemporary Painting, Soc of the Four Arts, Palm Beach, Fla, var times, 67-78; Miami Metrop Mus Art Ann, 68-74; Watercolor USA, Springfield, Mo, var times, 68-78; Abstract Real-Real Abstract, Louis K Meisel Gallery, NY, 74; A Change of View, Aldrich Mus, Conn, 75; '77 Photo Realists, Hollywood Cult Ctr, Fla & St Petersburg Mus Fine Arts, Fla, 78; plus others. Teaching: Instr watercolor, oil & acrylic, Ft Lauderdale Mus Arts, 69-; instr watercolor, Norton Gallery & Sch Art, West Palm Beach, 70-73; instr watercolor, Miami Art Inst, 74-78. Awards: Purchase Award, Nat Watercolor Soc, Los Angeles, 70, Wisconsin Award, 71 & Creative-West Award, 73; Soc of the Four Arts Akston Award, Nat Exhib of Contemporary Am Painting, 72 & Atwater Kent Award, 73; hors de Concours, 76; plus others. Bibliog: Jeanne Wolf (auth), Miles Batt, in Portrait (30 min film), WPBT-2, Miami, 73; Howard Whitman (auth), Palm Beach has always had the cash-now it gets the culture, Art News, 2/74; Griffin Smith (auth), Why shouldn't a pro win four times in a row, Miami Herald Newspapers, 4/74. Mem: Nat Watercolor Soc, Los Angeles (area rep, 71-75); Am Watercolor Soc; Fla Watercolor Soc (charter mem); Ft Lauderdale Mus Arts; Miami Mus Arts. Style & Technique: Acrylic with air brush, New Realist-Surrealist; watercolor Surrealist-Pop and landscapes. Media: Acrylic on Canvas; Watercolor on Paper. Publ: Auth, Watercolor Workshop, Spain & Portugal, 71; co-auth, Miles Batt: artist, Sunsentinel News, Ft Lauderdale, 10/72; contribr, Fiesta Mag, Ft Lauderdale, 72; contribr, Ford Times Mag, 75-78; contribr, Transparent Watercolor, Davis Publ, 73. Dealer: Hodgell Gallery 48 S Palm Ave Sarasota FL 33577; Miller Gallery 3112 Commodore Plaza Coconut Grove FL 33133. Mailing Add: 301 Riverland Rd Ft Lauderdale FL 33312

BATTCOCK, GREGORY
ART CRITIC, ART HISTORIAN
b New York, NY, July 2, 41. Study: Acad Belle Arti, Rome, Italy; Hunter Col, MA. Teaching: Assoc prof art hist, William Paterson Col, 69- Pos: New York corresp, Art & Artists, London, 69-; assoc ed, Arts Mag, 73-; columnist, Domus, Milan, 74- Bibliog: Pierre Restany (auth), Libres propos sur la nouvelle critique Americaine, Domus, 7/71. Publ: Ed, Trylon & Perisphere Mag; ed, The New Art, 66, ed, Minimal Art, 69, auth, Why Art, 72 & 77, auth, New Ideas in Art Education, 72, ed, Super Realism, 75 & ed, New Artists Video, 78, E P Dutton. Mailing Add: William Paterson Col Wayne NJ 07470

BATTENBERG, JOHN
SCULPTOR, EDUCATOR
b Milwaukee, Wis, 31. Study: Univ Wis, 49; Minn State Col, BS, 54; Ruskin Sch of Fine Art & Drawing, Oxford, Eng; Mich State Univ, MA, 60; Calif Col of Art & Crafts. Work: San Francisco Mus of Mod Art; Tate Mus, London; Oakland Mus, San Jose Mus & Los Angeles Co Mus, Los Angeles, Calif. Exhib: Artists in Maj Mus Collections, Los Angeles, Oakland, Palo Alto, 67; Am Fedn of Arts Travelling Exhib, 68; Mus of Mod Art, Belgrade, 69; Galleria d'Arte Moderna, Milano, 69; Denver Mus of Art, 71; Stanford Univ, 71; Los Angeles Munic Art Gallery, 73; San Francisco Mus of Mod Art, 76. Collections Arranged: 2nd Biennial Am Painting & Sculpture, Pa Acad Art, 60; Am Fedn of Arts Travelling Exhib, 68; Contemp Painting & Sculpture, Ind Mus of Art, 70; The Collectors Show, Crocker Gallery, Sacramento, 71; Sculpture of the Bay Area, James Willis Gallery, San Francisco, 76. Teaching: Instr sculpture, Contra Costa Col, Calif, 64-66; prof art, San Jose State Univ, Calif, 66-67; casting instr sculpture, Calif Col of Arts & Crafts, 77- Bibliog: Aleta Watson (auth), One Step Beyond Printmaking, Marquee, 6/76; Gail Tagashira (auth), He Makes War Not Love, San Jose News, 9/76; Gay Weaver (auth), World Seen Through Sculptors Eyes, Palo Alto Times, 10/76. Style & Technique: Bronze casting. Media: Bronze. Mailing Add: 1950 Manzanita Dr Oakland CA 94611

BATUZ
PAINTER, SCULPTOR
b Budapest, Hungary, May 27, 33; Arg citizen. Study: Self-taught. Work: Mus Mod Art, Buenos Aires; Panamerican Union, Washington, DC; New Brunswick Mus, Can; Bruce Mus, Greenwich, Conn; Mobil Oil Corp; also in pub & pvt collections around the world. Exhib: Nat Mus, Arg; Arg Asn Plastic Artists, 66; Mus Mod Art, Buenos Aires, 67; Wildenstein Gallery, Arg, 70; Orgn Am States, Washington, DC; plus 28 one-man shows. Teaching: Lectr, Art Students League. Bibliog: C Clainman (auth:, article in La Nacion, Arg, 70; Dr R Squirru (auth), Serigrafies de Batuz, Arg, 72; Gumner Climcher (auth), Life of an Artist (film strip), Mass Commun, Inc, 75. Mem: Soc Arg Plastic Artists; Artists Equity Asn. Style & Technique: Abstract painting; silkscreen printmaking. Media: Oil; Concrete & Volcanic Stones. Dealer: Wildenstein Gallery Buenos Aires Argentina; Gruenebaum Gallery 25 E 77th St New York NY 10021. Mailing Add: 4 Beachside Ave Greens Farms CT 06346

BAUERMEISTER, MARY HILDE RUTH
SCULPTOR
b Frankfurt am Main, WGer, Sept 7, 34. Work: Mus Mod Art, Guggenheim Mus & Whitney Mus Am Art, New York; Albright-Knox Art Gallery, Buffalo, NY; Stedelijk Mus, Amsterdam, Holland. Exhib: One-man show, Stedelijk Mus, Amsterdam, 62; Recent Acquisitions, Mus Mod Art, New York, 64; Whitney Mus Am Art Ann, 64-66; European Drawing Show, Guggenheim Mus, 65; Carnegie Int, Pittsburgh, 67-68. Bibliog: Solomon (auth), Mary Bauermeister, Bonino Kotelogue, 64; Fischer (auth), Das werk M Bauermeister, Das Kunstwerk, 65; Pernezky (auth), Mary Bauermeister, Mittelrhein Mus, Koblenz, 72. Media: Wood, Glass, Light. Dealer: Galeria Bonino 7 W 57th St New York NY 10019. Mailing Add: 546 Summer Hill Rd Madison CT 06443

BAUM, HANK
ART DEALER, LECTURER
b New York, NY, July 10, 32. Study: Univ Southern Calif, BA; Los Angeles City Col, AA; New York Sch Printing, printing & related graphic arts degree; Univ Calif, Los Angeles, grad sem, with Dr Lester Longman, also Dr E Maurice Bloch; Calif State Col, Los Angeles, sem with H Glicksman. Teaching: Lectr contemporary graphics & art & artists, Univ Calif, Berkeley, triann & Univ Calif, Los Angeles, biann. Pos: Assoc dir, Tamarind Lithography Workshop, Los Angeles, formerly; exec dir, Atelier Mourlot, New York, formerly; assoc dir, Collectors Press, San Francisco, currently; dir, The Graphics Gallery & Hank Baum Gallery, San Francisco, currently. Mem: Print Coun Am; Am & Calif Printmakers (adv bd mem); Mus Mod Art; Los Angeles Co Mus Art; San Francisco Mus Art. Specialty: Contemporary art; painting, sculpture, drawings, fine original limited edition prints; specializing in Picasso drawings and prints. Collection: Contemporary art. Mailing Add: 3 Embarcadero Ctr San Francisco CA 94111

BAUMBACH, HAROLD
PAINTER, PRINTMAKER
b New York, NY, 05. Study: Pratt Inst; Educ Alliance. Work: Whitney Mus Am Art, New York; Brooklyn Mus, NY; Albright-Knox Art Gallery, Buffalo, NY; Univ Iowa Art Mus, Iowa City; RI Sch Design Mus, Providence. Comn: Five lithograph editions in color, Bank St Atelier, New York, 72. Exhib: Carnegie Int, 47; Ariz Mus Purchase Exhib, Metrop Mus Art, New York, 47; Second Ann Summer Show, Park-Bernet Galleries, New York, 64; one-man show, Univ Iowa Mus, 67; Free Form Exhib, Whitney Mus Am Art, 72; Am Acad Ann, Inst of Arts & Lett, 77. Teaching: Spec lectr art appreciation, Brooklyn Col, 60-66; adj asst prof art appreciation, Long Island Univ, 66-67; vis prof painting, Univ Iowa, summer 67, vis artist, 72-73. Awards: Hon Mention, Pepsi Cola Artists for Victory Competition, 46. Mem: Fedn Mod Painters & Sculptors. Media: Oil. Dealer: Larcada Gallery 23 E 67th St New York NY 10023. Mailing Add: 278 Henry St Brooklyn NY 11201

BAUR, JOHN I H
MUSEUM DIRECTOR, WRITER
b Woodbridge, Conn, Aug 9, 09. Study: Yale Univ, BA, 32, MA, 34. Teaching: Vis lectr Am art, Yale Univ, 51-52. Pos: Supvr educ, Brooklyn Mus Art, NY, cur, 36-52; cur, Whitney Mus Am Art, New York, 52-58, assoc dir, 58-68, dir, 68-74, emer dir, 74- Publ: Auth, Philip Evergood, 60 & Bernaro Reder, 61; co-auth, American Art of Our Century, 61; auth, Revolution & Tradition in Modern American Art, 51 & 67 & Joseph Stella, 71, Praeger; plus others. Mailing Add: Mt Holly Rd Katonah NY 10536

BAVINGER, EUGENE ALLEN
PAINTER, EDUCATOR
b Sapulpa, Okla, Dec 21, 19. Study: Univ Okla, BFA; Inst Allende, Mex, MFA. Work: Addison Gallery Am Art, Andover, Mass; Nelson Gallery, Atkins Mus, Kansas City, Mo; Joslyn Art Mus, Omaha, Nebr; Masur Mus, Monroe, La; Mulvane Art Ctr, Topeka, Kans. Exhib: American Painting Today, Metrop Mus Art, New York, 50; 12 Artists West of the Mississippi, Colorado Springs Fine Art Ctr, Colo, 61; 70th Western Ann Invitational-19 artists, Denver Art Mus, Colo, 64; Fifty Artists from Fifty States, Am Fedn Arts Traveling Exhib, 66; one-man shows, Philbrook Art Ctr, Tulsa, Okla, 65, Sheldon Art Gallery, Lincoln, Nebr, 67, Joslyn Art Mus, Omaha, Nebr, 69, Contemp Arts Found, Oklahoma City, 72, Kans State Univ, Manhattan, 73, Tibor de Nagy Gallery, Houston, Tex, 75 & Tex Christian Univ, Ft Worth, 76; Razor Gallery, New York, 77. Teaching: Prof art, Univ Okla, 47- Awards: Purchase Award, 41st Ann Exhib, Springfield Art Mus, Mo, 71; First Award, 22nd Ann Exhib, Ft Smith Art Ctr, Ark, 72; Purchase Award, 19th Ann, Ark Art Ctr, Little Rock, 76. Mailing Add: 520 Parrington Oval Rm 202 Norman OK 73069

BAXTER, DOUGLAS W
ART DEALER
b Ohio, Nov 3, 49. Study: Oberlin Col, BA(art hist), 72, with Ellen Johnson. Pos: Art dealer, Fischbach Gallery, 73-74; art dealer, Paula Cooper Gallery, New York, 74- Specialty: Contemporary art. Mailing Add: c/o Paula Cooper Gallery 155 Wooster New York NY 10012

BAXTER, IAIN
ENVIRONMENTAL ARTIST, DESIGNER
b Middlesborough, Eng, Nov 16, 36; Can citizen. Study: Univ Idaho, BSc, 59, MEd, 62; Japanese Govt foreign scholar, 61, Can Coun sr grant, 71; Wash State Univ, MFA, 64. Work: Nat Gallery Can, Ottawa; Montreal Mus Fine Arts, Que; Mus Mod Art, New York; Can Coun Art Bank; Univ BC Brock Hall Collection; among others. Comn: Stamp, Can Postal Syst, 71. Exhib: Environmental Work, Edmonton Art Gallery, Alta, 69; N E Thing Co Ltd Sonnabend Gallery, New York, 71; Acts of Venice, Int Univ Arts, Venice, Italy, 71; Cancellation, Richard Demarco Gallery, Edinburgh, Scotland, 71; York Univ Gallery, 73; plus many others. Teaching: Instr art, Pullman Pub Schs, Wash, summer 64; instr, Dept Art Educ, Univ BC, summers 65-66, asst prof fine arts, 64-66; assoc prof & univ resident, Simon Frazer Univ, 66-71; vis prof, Visual Arts Dept, York Univ, 72-73. Pos: Consult, CBC & Data Processing Mgrs Asn, 70; resident artist, King's Col, Cambridge, Eng, 72; co-pres, N E Thing Co Ltd, currently; secy, NE Prof Photog Display Labs Ltd; pres, Eye Scream Parlour Ltd. Awards: Can Centennial Award for Printmaking, 67; Prize for Canadian Artists, Art Gallery Ont, 68; Can Coun Sr Grants, 69, 72 & 73-74; among others. Bibliog: Douglas Davis (auth), Magic of raw life-new photography, Newsweek, 4/24/72; Joyce Zemens (auth), Video activity of N E Thing Co Ltd, ArtsCanada, 73; Vicki Innes (auth), Luxury is..., Can Mag, 74; plus many others. Mem: Academician Royal Can Acad Art. Publ: Co-auth, Squirrels of Idaho, J Idaho Sci, Vol 1 No 1; co-auth, Wildlife of the Northern Rocky Mountains, Naturegraph, 61; Cliches visualized (videotape), 69; North American Time-Zone Photo VSI Simultaneity, 70 & What Is Art?, (in press), N E Thing Co Ltd. Mailing Add: 1419 Riverside Dr North Vancouver BC V7H 1V6 Can

BAXTER, INGRID
GALLERY DIRECTOR
b Spokane, Wash, Feb 10, 38; Can citizen. Study: Univ Idaho, BA, 60. Exhib: In conjunction with N E Thing Co Ltd. Pos: Co-pres, N E Thing Co Ltd, currently. Awards: Outstanding Woman Sr, Univ Idaho, 61. Mailing Add: 1419 Riverside Dr North Vancouver BC Can

BAXTER, PATRICIA HUY
CURATOR
b Washington, DC, Sept 18, 45. Study: Cornell Univ, Ithaca, NY, BA(art hist), Collections Arranged: Southern California Indian Rock Art (with catalog), Sonakinatography, by Channa Davis Horowitz & Joseph Raphael & Carlos Villa, 73; Books by Ed Ruscha, 74. Pos: Chief cur, art gallery, Univ Calif, San Diego in La Jolla, 75- Publ: Auth, Polynesian Ornament, Dimensions of Polynesia, 74. Mailing Add: Univ Calif San Diego La Jolla CA 92037

BAXTER, ROBERT JAMES
PAINTER
b Milwaukee, Wis, Nov 30, 33. Study: Univ Wis, BS(art), 56, MS(painting), 60 & MFA(painting), 60; also with Aaron Bohrod & John Wilde. Work: Univ NC, Greensboro; Wichita Falls Mus & Art Ctr, Tex; Foothill Col, Mountain View, Calif. Exhib: Conn Acad Fine Arts Ann, Wadsworth Atheneum, Hartford, 62-64; Am Drawing Biennial, Norfolk Mus Arts & Sci, 63 & 66; Pa Acad Fine Arts, Philadelphia, 63 & 65; Drawing Soc Am, Art Galleries of Univ Calif, Santa Barbara, 70; one-man show, San Francisco Mus Art, 70; plus others. Teaching: Prof painting, San Diego State Univ, Calif, 62-75. Awards: Howard Penrose Prize, 52nd Conn Acad Fine Arts Exhib, Wadsworth Atheneum; Henry Clay Hofheimer Award, Am Drawing Ann XX, Norfolk Mus Arts & Sci, 63; Grant for Painting, Louis Comfort Tiffany Found, 72. Bibliog: Prof Daniel Mendelowitz (auth), Drawing, 66 & A History of American Art, 70, Holt. Style & Technique: Figurative; minutely rendered. Media: Egg Tempera on Wood Panel; Silverpoint on Gesso Ground. Publ: Contribr, Arts in Society, Univ Wis Exten Div, Vol 3, No 1; In Retrospect, Alfred Sessler. Dealer: Coe Kerr Gallery Inc 49 E 82nd St New York NY 10028. Mailing Add: Via Delle Mantellate 15A Rome 00165 Italy

BAYARD, MARY IVY
ART LIBRARIAN
b Hazleton, Pa, Dec 14, 40. Study: Wilson Col, AB; Drexel Univ, MLS. Pos: Art librn, Tyler Sch of Art, Temple Univ, Philadelphia, Pa, 70- Mem: Art Libr Soc of NAm; Am Libr Asn, Art Section (secy, 73-75); Col Art Asn; Victorian Soc in Am; Nat Trust for Hist Preservation. Res: Chinese porcelains, especially Nanking; interlibrary co-operation. Interest: Decorative arts, architecture. Publ: Auth, articles in Penn Libr Asn Bull, 76. Mailing Add: 3016 Old Arch Rd Norristown PA 19403

BAYEFSKY, ABA
PAINTER, PRINTMAKER
b Toronto, Ont, Apr 7, 23. Study: Cent Tech Sch, Toronto. Work: Nat Gallery Can, Ottawa; Nat Gallery Victoria, Melbourne, Australia; Art Gallery Ont; Libr of Cong, Washington, DC; Hebrew Univ, Jerusalem; plus others. Comn: Mural, Northview Colliate, Toronto; tapestry, Synagogue Ont; mural, Ont Govt Bldg. Exhib: All major Can Art Soc Exhibs & 17 one-man shows. Teaching: Instr, Ont Col Art, 56- Pos: Off war artist, RCAF. Awards: J W L Forster Award, Ont Soc Artists, 57; Can Coun Grant to India, 58; Centennial Citation, Toronto, 67; plus others. Mem: Academician Royal Can Acad Art (coun mem); Can Soc Graphic Art; Can Soc Painters in Water Colour; Can Group Painters. Media: Graphics. Publ: Illusr, Rubaboo, 62, portfolio 18 lithographs, Tales from the Talmud, 63, The Ballad of Thrym, (privately publ), 65 & portfolio colour blockprints, Indian Legends, 68. Mailing Add: 7 Paperbirch Dr Don Mills ON M3C 2E6 Can

BAYER, HERBERT
PAINTER, DESIGNER
b Haag, Austria, Apr 5, 00; US citizen. Study: Real-Gym, Linz, Austria; archit with G Schmidthammer, Linz, 19; with Emanuel Margold, Darmstadt, Ger, 20; wall paintings with Vassily Kandinsky, 21; Bauhaus, Weimar, 21-23. Work: San Francisco Mus Art; Mus Mod Art, Guggenheim Mus; Staatsgemäldesammlungen, Munich; Denver Art Mus; plus many others US & Europe. Comn: Murals, Bauhaus Bldg, Weimar, Commons Bldg, Grad Ctr, Harvard Univ, Elem Sch, Bridgewater, Mass & Health Ctr, Aspen, Colo; designed articulated wall construction for 1968 Olympics, Mexico City; double ascension sculpture, Arco Plaza, Los Angeles; plus others. Exhib: San Francisco Art Mus, 49; Germanisches Nationalmuseum, Nuremberg; Hochsch Bildende Künste, Berlin, 57; Städtische Kunsthalle, Dusseldorf, 60; Marlborough Gallery, New York, 71; plus others. Pos: Master, Bauhaus, Dessau, 25-28; freelance painter, photogr, graphic designer & exhib architect, Berlin, 28-38; art dir, Vogue, Berlin, 29-30; dir, Dorland Studio, Berlin, 28-38, art dir, Dorland Int, NY; consult design, Aspen Inst; chmn dept design, Container Corp Am, 56-65; consult, Atlantic Richfield Co, 65- Bibliog: Included in: George Rickey (auth), Constructivism: Origins & Evolution, Braziller, 67, Hans M Wingler (auth), Graphic Work from Bauhaus, NY Graphic Soc, 68 & Eberhard Roters (auth), Painters of the Bauhaus, Praeger, 69; plus others. Mem: Alliance Graphique Int; Am Abstr Artists; Int Design Conf, Aspen, Colo. Media: Mixed Media. Publ: Auth & designer, Herbert Bayer-Visual Communication, Architecture, Painting, 67; contribr, articles, In: Gebrauchsgraphik, Col Art J, Bauhaus Mag & Linea Grafica; plus others. Dealer: Marlborough Gallery 41 E 57th St New York NY 10022. Mailing Add: 184 Middle Rd Montecito CA 93108

BAYER, JEFFREY JOSHUA
EDUCATOR, SCULPTOR
b New York, NY, Aug 15, 42. Study: Univ NC, Chapel Hill, BA, 64, MFA, 67; NY Univ. Comn: String Quartet (sculpture), Amen, Weisman & Butler Attorneys, New York, 62-65; sculpture collection, comn by Ms Marion McAdoo, Philadelphia, 64. Exhib: One-man shows, Univ SC Art Mus, 75, Vanderbilt Art Gallery, Vanderbilt Univ, Nashville, Tenn, 75, Brooks Mem Art Mus, Memphis, 75, Ark State Univ, 76, Univ WFla, 76 & James Madison Univ, Va, 77; plus many others. Teaching: Assoc prof sculpture & chmn dept art, Univ Ala, Huntsville, 67- Pos: Mem acquisitions comt, City Huntsville Mus Art, 73-75; vpres, Hist Huntsville Found, 75-; nat conf dir, Nat Sculpture Conf, 75 & 77; nat conf dir, Nat Archit Conf, 79. Mem: Southeastern Col Art Conf; Southern Asn Sculptors (pres, 75-); Chicago Sch Archit Found; Friends Cast Iron Archit; Col Art Asn. Style & Technique: Industrial materials and technologies for sculptural use; abstract. Media: Plastic Foams, Sprayed Molten Metalized Surfaces. Publ: Co-auth, 19th Century American Architecture (film series), Ala Educ TV Network, 72-74; auth, Spindle, Shuttle & Dyepot & auth, Metallizing, Nat Handweaver J, 75; auth, Polymer chemistry for the artist, SCLPTR J, 76; auth, Architecture: the World Tribune tower competition, 76. Mailing Add: Univ Ala Dept Art PO Box 1247 Huntsville AL 35807

BAYLISS, GEORGE
PAINTER, ART ADMINISTRATOR
b Washington, DC, Oct 14, 31. Study: Univ Md, BA, 55, with Herman Maril; Cranbrook Acad Art, MFA, 56, with Zoltan Sepeshy; Univ Va; Corcoran Sch Art. Work: Akron Art Inst, Ohio; State Univ NY Col Fredonia; Corcoran Gallery Art. Comn: Rural Elect Transmission, Mus Hist & Technol, Smithsonian Inst, 56-57. Exhib: Corcoran Biennial Contemp Am Painters, 55 & 59; New Accessions USA, Colorado Springs Fine Arts Ctr, 58; 12 Washington Painters, Univ Ky, 60; Four Washington Artists, Corcoran Gallery Art, 61; Drawings USA, circulated by Smithsonian Inst, 62. Teaching: Instr painting & drawing, Sch Akron Art Inst, Ohio, 57-59; instr painting & drawing, Flint Jr Col, Mich, 59-62; asst prof painting & drawing, State Univ NY Col Potsdam, 62-63. Pos: Dean, Parsons Sch Design, New York, 63-67; chmn dept art, State Univ NY Col Fredonia, 67-72; chmn dept art, Univ Mich, 72-74, dean, Sch Art, 74- Awards: Principal Purchase Prize, Corcoran Gallery Art, 55; Award of Merit, South Bend Art Asn, Ind, 56; Bundy Co Prize, Bloomfield Hills Art Asn, 56. Mem: Col Art Asn; Nat Coun Art Adminrs. Style & Technique: Painting, drawing. Media: Oil, Watercolor. Dealer: Zriny Hayes Gallery 2044 N Halsted Chicago IL 30614. Mailing Add: Sch of Art Univ of Mich Ann Arbor MI 48105

BAYNARD, ED
PAINTER
b Washington, DC, Sept 5, 40. Work: Chase Manhattan Bank, New York; Wadsworth Atheneum, Hartford, Conn; Whitney Mus, New York; Inst of Contemp Art, Univ Pa, Philadelphia; Univ Kans, Kansas City. Exhib: New Am Painters, Munson-Williams-Proctor Inst, 71; Landscape, Mus Mod Art, New York, 72; Topography of Nature, Inst of Contemp Art, Philadelphia, 72; Am Drawing 1963-1973, Whitney Mus, New York, 73; Am Drawing, Fine Arts Gallery of San Diego, 77; Drawing Show, Cleveland Mus of Art, 78. Bibliog: Kenneth Wahl (auth), Ed Baynard, Arts Mag, 77. Publ: Illusr, Somewhere in Ho, Buffalo Press, 72; illusr (cover & frontispiece), Paris Rev, 74; illusr (cover), Miami, Donnes, 75; auth (interview), Arlene Slavin & Ed Baynard, NY Arts J, 76. Mailing Add: c/o Willard Gallery 29 E 72nd St New York NY 10021

BAZ, MARYSOLE WÖRNER
PAINTER, SCULPTOR
b Aug 17, 36. Study: Primaria y Secundaria, Mex. Work: Anexo Catalogo; Mus of Morelin, Mex; Mus of Israel, Jerusalem. Exhib: 24 one-woman shows in Mex & US, 55-70; Galeria Mer-Kup, Mexico DF, 71 & 73; Palace of Fine Arts, Nat Inst Fine Arts, Mex, 72; Paliforum Cult, Siguieros (painting & sculpture), Mex, 73; Woman, Creator & Theme of Art, Mus Mod Art, Chapultepec, Mex, 75. Awards: Dipl, Asn Mex Theater Critics for Scenography of Atila, 73. Mem: Galeria Mer-Kup, Mex. Style & Technique: Impressionist and expressionist, figurative-abstract. Media: Oil & Acrylic; Stone & Bronze. Mailing Add: Ciceron 721 Mexico 5 DF Mexico

BEACH, WARREN
PAINTER
b Minneapolis, Minn, May 21, 14. Study: Phillips Acad, Andover, Mass; Yale Univ, BFA, 39; Univ Iowa, MA, 40; Harvard Univ, MA, 47. Work: Addison Gallery Am Art, Andover; Columbus Gallery Fine Arts, Ohio. Exhib: Art & Artists Along the Mississippi, 41; one-man shows, Minn State Fair, 41 & Grace Horne Gallery, Boston, Mass, 45; one-man retrospective, Telfair Acad Arts & Sci, Savannah, Ga, 75; Trend House Gallery, Tampa, Fla, 75. Teaching: Dean, Columbus Art Sch, 47-49. Pos: Dir exten serv, Walker Art Ctr, Minneapolis, 40-41; asst art mus, Addison Gallery Am Art, 46-47; asst dir, Columbus Gallery Fine Arts, 47-55; dir, Fine Arts Gallery San Diego, 55-69. Mem: Addison Gallery Am Art; Am Asn Mus; Yale Art Alumni Asn; Harvard Art Alumni Asn; Fine Arts Soc San Diego. Mailing Add: 3740 Pio Pico St San Diego CA 92106

BEAL, GRAHAM WILLIAM JOHN
CURATOR, LECTURER, HISTORIAN
b Stratford-on-Avon, Gt Brit, Apr 22, 47. Study: Manchester Univ, BA, 69; Courtauld Inst, London Univ, MA, 71. Collections Arranged: Made in California (with catalog), 73; La Pintura (with catalog), 75; Joe Goode, Recent Paintings, 76; Charles Parsons Collection, 77. Pos: Acad asst, Sheffield City Art Galleries, 72-73; art historian & gallery dir, Univ SDak, 73-74; gallery dir, Washington Univ, 74-77; cur, Walker Art Ctr, 77- Mailing Add: Walker Art Ctr Vineland Pl Minneapolis MN 55408

BEAL, JACK
PAINTER
b Richmond, Va, June 25, 31. Study: Norfolk Div, Col William & Mary & Va Polytech Inst, 50-53; Art Inst Chicago, 53-56, with Briggs Dyer, Isobel Mackinnon & Kathleen Blackshear. Work: Whitney Mus Am Art, New York; Walker Art Ctr, Minneapolis; Art Inst Chicago;

San Francisco Mus Fine Arts; Del Mus, Wilmington. Comn: The Hist of Labor in Am (murals), US Labor Bldg, Washington, DC, 75-77. Exhib: Ann exhibs, Allan Frumkin Gallery, New York; Galerie Claude Bernard, Paris; Ten-Yr Retrospective, Boston Univ, Va Mus & Mus of Contemp Art, Chicago, 73-74; Print Retrospective, Madison Art Ctr & Art Inst of Chicago, 77-78. Dealer: Allan Frumkin Gallery 50 W 57th St New York NY 10019 & 620 N Michigan Ave Chicago IL 60611. Mailing Add: 67 Vestry St New York NY 10013

BEAL, MACK
SCULPTOR
b Boston, Mass, Apr 20, 24. Study: Harvard Univ, BS, 46; grad study, Dept of Art, Univ NH, Durham; apprentice to master blacksmith Joe Tucker, Milford, NH. Work: Addison Gallery Am Art, Phillips Acad, Andover, Mass; New Eng Ctr, Univ NH, Durham; Worcester Art Mus, Mass; Permanent Exhib, Symp Lindabruun, Bad Voslau, Austria. Exhib: Currier Gallery Art, Manchester, NH, 70-76; Inst Contemp Art, Boston, Mass, 70-73; Plymouth State Teachers Col, NH, 71 & 76; Worcester Art Mus, Mass, 72 & 73; Hopkins Ctr, Dartmouth Col, Hanover, NH, 73; Addison Gallery Am Art, Phillips Acad, Andover, Mass, 74; Goethe Inst, Boston, Mass, 74; Danforth Mus, Framingham, Mass, 75; Berkshire Mus, Pittsfield, Mass, 75; Greenville Mus Art, SC, 75; Univ Mus, Southern Ill Univ, Carbondale, 76. Pos: Dir, The Sculptors Workshop, Somerville, Mass, 70-76. Mem: NH Art Asn; NH League of Craftsmen; Boston Visual Artists Union; Ogunquit Art Asn; Artist Blacksmith Asn NAm (dir, 76 & 77). Style & Technique: Contemporary abstract sculpture; direct work in granite, marble—sometimes in combination with iron, bronze or stainless steel—using current industrial technique as well as traditional 17th and 18th century forge disciplines. Dealer: NH Art Asn West Bridge St Manchester NH 03105. Mailing Add: Dundee Rd Jackson NH 03846

BEALL, DENNIS RAY
PRINTMAKER, EDUCATOR
b Chickasha, Okla, Mar 13, 29. Study: Oklahoma City Univ; San Francisco State Univ. Work: Achenbach Found for Graphic Arts, San Francisco; San Francisco Mus Art; Mus Mod Art, New York; Libr Cong, Washington, DC; Philadelphia Mus. Comn: Lone Star (ed 20, collagraph), C Troup Gallery-Codex Press, Inc, Dallas, 66; Emblem V (ed 75, relief & etching), Univ Calif, Berkeley Mus, 67; Emblem VI (ed 50, collagraph), San Francisco Mus Art, 67; Miz Am (ed 20, etching), Hansen-Fuller Gallery, 68; Ars Medicus (ed 20, etching & screen print), San Francisco Art Comn, 71. Exhib: San Francisco Mus Art, 60-65 & 67; 2nd & 3rd Int Trienale, Grenchen, Switz, 61 & 62; 1963 Paris Bienale, 64; 14th & 15th Nat, Brooklyn Mus, 64 & 65; Original Prints, Calif Palace of Legion of Honor, San Francisco, 64; 4th Biennial Int, Pasadena Art Mus, 64; Art in the Embassies Prog, US Dept State, Oakland Art Mus, Calif, 66; NY Ann, Whitney Mus Am Art, 66-67; one-man show, Achenbach Found Graphic Arts, 68-69; Cincinnati Art Mus, 73; 1st Bienal Int, Segovia, Spain, 73; 11th Biennial Graphic Art, Ljubljana, Yugoslavia, 75. Teaching: Prof art, San Francisco State Univ, 65- Awards: Purchase Awards, Ultimate Concerns, Ohio Univ, Athens, 63, 25th & 26th San Francisco Art Festivals, 71 & 72 & 5th Ann Graphics Competition, De Anza Col, Cupertino, Calif, 76. Bibliog: Leonard Edmondson (auth), Etching, Van Nostrand, Reinhold, 73; Mimi Jacobs (auth), Arts—Interview, Pac Sun, 2/74. Mem: Calif Soc Printmakers (past chmn). Media: Intaglio; screen print. Dealer: Suzy R Locke & Assoc 4014 Lakeshore Dr Oakland CA 94610. Mailing Add: 106 Industrial Ctr Bldg Sausalito CA 94965

BEALL, JOANNA
PAINTER, SCULPTOR
b Chicago, Ill, Aug 17, 35. Study: Yale Sch of Fine Art, with Josef Albers, 53-57; Sch of the Art Inst of Chicago, 57. Work: Included in pvt collections of Howard & Jean Lipman, New York, Julien Levy, Conn, William Copley, New York, H C Westermann, Conn, plus others. Comn: Sculpture (wood), comn by B H Freidman, New York, 63. Exhib: Under 35, New Britian Mus of Am Art, Conn, 68; Extraordinary Realities, Whitney Mus of Am Art, New York, 73; Wadsworth Atheneum Group Exhib, Hartford, Conn, 73; Univ Calif Riverside Group Exhib, 73; Extraordinary Realities, Everson Mus of Art, Syracuse, NY, 74; Visions, Art Inst of Chicago, 76; one-woman shows, James Corcoran Gallery, Los Angeles, Calif, 74 & Rebecca Cooper Gallery, Washington, DC, 75; plus others. Pos: Practicing prof artist. Bibliog: New Talent USA, Art in Am, New York, 64; Melinda Wortz (auth), The World of Joanna Beall, Art Week, Los Angeles, 74; Dennis Adrian (auth), Visions, Art Inst of Chicago, 76. Style & Technique: Surrealist landscapes in oil and watercolor, also sculpture in wood. Media: Oil, Watercolor. Dealer: James Corcoran Gallery 8223 Santa Monica Blvd Los Angeles CA 90046. Mailing Add: Box 28 Brookfield Center CT 06805

BEALL, KAREN F
CURATOR
b Washington, DC. Study: Am Univ, BA; Johns Hopkins Univ. Exhib Arranged: EEuropean Prints of the 1960s, 70; The Graphic Landscape: 15th Century to the Present, 71. Pos: Asst to cur of prints, Libr of Cong, 64-67, specialist fine prints, 67-68, cur fine prints, 68- Awards: Res grant, Am Philos Soc, 67. Mem: Print Coun of Am; Col Art Asn. Publ: Auth, articles on John Singer Sargent, Rembrandt van Rijn, Max Beckmann, Street Cry prints, Nicholas Toussaint-Charlet, Rockwell Kent & others in Libr of Cong Quart & Philobiblon, 66-78; co-auth with Alan Fern, The Pembroke Album of Chiaroscuro Woodcuts, Libr of Cong Quart J, 69; auth, American Prints in the Library of Congress, Johns Hopkins Press, 70; auth, Cries and Itinerant Trades, Hauswedell Verlag, 75. Mailing Add: Prints & Photog Div Libr of Cong Washington DC 20540

BEALMER, WILLIAM
GALLERY DIRECTOR, EDUCATOR
b Atlanta, Mo, Sept 9, 19. Study: Northeast Mo State Teachers Col, BSc; Univ Colo, MFA; Chicago Inst Design; Des Moines Art Ctr; Univ Iowa. Exhib: Univ Colo Art Ctr; Des Moines Art Ctr; Sioux City Art Ctr; Joslyn Art Mus, Omaha, Nebr; Art Dept, Grinnell Col & Iowa State Col. Teaching: Assoc prof art, Northern Ill Univ, 70- Pos: Spec consult, many univs, schs, filmmakers, TV, art confs & other orgns & insts; asst supt & state supvr art educ, Springfield, Ill; dir educ, Springfield Art Asn, currently. Mem: Nat Art Educ Asn (pres, 69-71); Int Soc Educ Through Art; Ill Educ Asn; Nat Educ Asn; Am Craftsmen's Coun; plus others. Mailing Add: Springfield Art Asn 700 N Fourth Springfield IL 62702

BEAM, PHILIP CONWAY
ART ADMINISTRATOR, EDUCATOR
b Dallas, Tex, Oct 7, 10. Study: Harvard Col, AB, 33; Courtauld Inst, Univ London, cert, 36; Harvard Univ, MA, 43, PhD, 44. Teaching: Asst prof art, Bowdoin Col, 39-46, assoc prof, 46-49, prof, 49-, chmn dept, 49-, Henry Johnson prof art & archaeol, 58-; vis prof Wesleyan Univ, summers 60 & 69; lectr, Shelburne Mus, summers 67 & 70; vis prof art, Univ Vt. Pos: Dir, Bowdoin Col Mus Art, 39-64, cur, Winslow Homer Collection, 67-; consult, World of Winslow Homer, Time-Life Bks, 66, consult, World of John Singleton Copley, currently. Mem: Am Asn Univ Prof; Am Asn Mus; Maine Art Comn (chmn, 54-55); Col Art Asn Am. Publ: Auth, The Language of Art, Ronald, 58; auth, The Art of John Sloan, 62 & Winslow Homer at Prouts Neck, 66, Little; contrib ed, A Dictionary of the Visual Arts, NY Graphic Soc, 73; Winslow Homer, McGraw-Hill, 75. Mailing Add: 41 Spring St Brunswick ME 04011

BEAMAN, RICHARD BANCROFT
PAINTER
b Waltham, Mass, June 28, 09. Study: Exeter; Harvard Univ, SB, 32; Union Theol Sem, MDiv, 35; Eliot O'Hara Sch Watercolor Painting; Univ Calif, Berkeley; Mass Inst Technol, with Gyorgy Kepes. Work: Carnegie Inst Mus Art; Westmoreland Co Mus Art; Art Complex Mus. Comn: Fused stained glass murals, Hilton Hotel, Rivers Suite, Pittsburgh, Pa, 59; fused stained glass windows, Wayne State Univ Col Educ, Detroit, 60; fused stained glass wall, Provident Inst for Savings, Prudential Ctr, Boston, Mass, 60's; fused stained glass window, Trinity Church, East Liverpool, Ohio, 61; fused stained glass wall, Commonwealth Bank, Trust Dept, Pittsburgh, 61. Exhib: Regional Shows, New York, Philadelphia, Washington, DC, Los Angeles, Pittsburgh & Westmoreland, Pa, 33-72; Carnegie Inst Int, Pittsburgh, 59; one-man shows, Carnegie Inst & Pittsburgh Plan for Art, 62-78. Teaching: Asst prof art, Univ Redlands, 39-55; Stickney lectr painting, Calif Inst Technol, 48-50; prof painting & art hist, Carnegie-Mellon Univ, 55-74. Pos: Pres, Assoc Artists Pittsburgh, 62. Awards: Purchase Prize, Westmoreland Co Mus Art, 62; Purchase Prize, Carnegie Inst, 63; Louis Comfort Tiffany Award, 65. Mem: Pittsburgh Plan for Art (pres, 64-68). Style & Technique: Color field related to landscape. Media: Acrylic. Publ: Auth, The cubist witch, SAtlantic Quart, 49; auth, Vitrail reconsidered, Stained Glass Mag, fall 67. Dealer: Pittsburgh Plan for Art 1251 N Negley Ave Pittsburgh PA 15206. Mailing Add: Penryn Lane Rockport MA 01966

BEAMENT, HAROLD
PAINTER
b Ottawa, Ont, July 23, 98. Study: Osgoode Hall Law Sch, Toronto, Barrister-at-law; Ont Col Art. Work: Nat Gallery Can, Ottawa; Arch Can, Ottawa; Montreal Mus Fine Arts, PQ; Quebec Provincial Mus, PQ; Art Gallery Hamilton, Ont. Comn: Designed Canadian Eskimo ten-cent stamp, 55-67. Exhib: Brit Empire Exhib, Wembley, Eng, 24-25; Expos Art Can, Mus Jeu Paume, Paris, France, 27; Traveling Southern Dominions of British Empire, 36; A Century of Canadian Art: Tate Gallery, London, Eng; Canadian War Art, Nat Gallery Eng, 44; all arranged by Nat Gallery Can; McGill Univ; Queens Univ; Art Gallery London, Ont, Seagram Cities of Can. Teaching: Instr painting, Montreal Mus Fine Arts, 36-37; instr painting, NS Col Art, 62-63. Awards: Jessie Dow Prize, Montreal Mus Fine Arts, 36; Can Govt Medal, 67. Mem: Academician Royal Can Acad Arts (secy-treas, 60-61, vpres, 62-63, pres, 64-67). Style & Technique: Generally representational, occasionally nonfigurative work. Media: Oil. Publ: Auth, articles in, The Studio (London), 11/15/24 & 2/46. Mailing Add: 1160 St Matthieu St 410 Montreal PQ Can

BEAMENT, TIB (THOMAS HAROLD)
PAINTER, INSTRUCTOR
b Montreal, PQ, Feb 17, 41. Study: Fettes Col, Edinburgh, Scotland, O level cert; Ecole Beaux-Arts, Montreal, dipl; Acad Belle Arti, Rome, Italian Govt grant; Ecole Beaux-Arts, Montreal, postgrad studies & teaching cert; Sir George Williams Univ, MA(art educ); also in graphic studios of Shirly Wales, France; Richard Lacroix, Albert Dumouchel & Atelier 838, Montreal. Work: Tate Gallery, London; Mus Mod Art, New York; Mus Rio de Janeiro; Nat Gallery Can, Ottawa; Art Inst Chicago. Comn: Decorative Trees (mural), Holiday Inn, Montreal, 65. Exhib: 4th Biennial Paris, France, 65; Int Exhib Northwest Printmakers, Seattle, Wash, 65; 1st Biennial Graphics, Crakov, Poland, 66; Int Exhib Graphics, Montreal, 71; Int Art Fair, Basel, Switz, 74. Teaching: Dir art dept, Edgars & Cramps Sch, Montreal, 67-; lectr drawing, McGill Univ, 74-; lectr design, Concordia Univ, 76- Awards: Can Coun grant, 66; Spec Mention, Price Fine Arts Awards, 70; Elizabeth T Greenshields Found Grant, 71 & 75. Mem: Royal Can Acad of Arts; Print & Drawing Coun Can. Style & Technique: Subjects based on nature with an almost surreal feeling about them. Media: Pencil. Dealer: Walter Klinkhoff Gallery 1200 Sherbrooke St W Montreal PQ Can; Roberts Gallery 641 Yonge St Toronto ON Can. Mailing Add: 121 Lewis Ave Montreal PQ Can

BEAN, JACOB
CURATOR
b Stillwater, Minn, Nov 22, 23. Study: Harvard Univ. Teaching: Adj prof, Inst Fine Arts, NY Univ. Pos: Charge Mission, Cabinet Dessins, Mus Louvre, Paris, France, 56-60; cur drawings, Metrop Mus Art, 62-; assoc ed, Master Drawings, 63- Publ: Auth, Les Dessins Italiens de la Collection Bonnat, Bayonne, 60; auth, 100 European Drawings in the Metropolitan Museum of Art, 64; co-auth, Drawings in New York Collections I, The Italian Renaissance, 65, Drawings in New York Collections II, The Seventeenth Century in Italy, 67 & Drawings in New York Collections III, The Eighteenth Century in Italy, 71. Mailing Add: Metrop Mus of Art Fifth Ave at 82nd St New York NY 10028

BEAR, MARCELLE L
COLLECTOR, PAINTER
b Chicago, Ill, Jan 13, 17. Study: Chicago Acad & Am Acad, Chicago, two yrs; Ecole des Arts Decoratifs, Paris, France, one yr; Art Inst of Chicago, two yrs with Elliot O'Hara, John Caceres, Peterdi, W M Parker, M Ponce De Leon, A Daschaes, K Kerslake. Work: Jacksonville Art Mus, Fla; Wright State Univ, Dayton, Ohio; Ira Koger Corp Collection; Leonard Bocour Collection; Glidden Organics Corp Collection. Comn: Mural, comn by Mrs Ruth Ullrick, Mandarin, Fla, 56; Painting, comn by Ben Jones, Universal Marion Corp, Jacksonville, 62; carved doors, Temple Ahavath Chesed, Jacksonville, 64 & 66; painting, comn by Duckett, Hubbard, Duckett, Mason & Dow, 69; painting, comn by George Dickerson, Sutton Place, Jacksonville, 72. Exhib: 10th Ann Drawing & Print, San Francisco Mus of Art, 46; 14th New Yrs Show, Butler Art Inst, Youngstown, Ohio, 46; group, one-man, two & three-man exhibs, Jacksonville Art Mus, 46-49; Nat, Lowe Gallery, Coral Gables, Fla, 63; Artists of Gulf States & Tex, Delgado, New Orleans, 63, 64 & 67; South Coast, Ringling Mus, Sarasota, Fla, 63; Everhart Mus, Scranton, Pa, 64; Dulin Art Gallery, Knoxville, Tenn, 64; Mint Mus, Charlotte, NC, 64, 66 & 68; Hunterdon Co, Clinton, NJ, 63; Hunter Gallery, Charlotte, NC, 64 & 65; Metrop Mus & Art Ctr, Miami, Fla, 77; SEAS Nat, Panama City, Fla, 77. Teaching: Instr painting, Santa Maria Jr Col, Calif, 45; instr painting, Southside Womans Club, Jacksonville, two yrs & Jacksonville Art Mus, one yr. Pos: Bd, Jacksonville Art Mus, 48-76; treas, Fla Artist Group, 75-79. Awards: Best in Show, Jacksonville Art Mus, 48-49, Fla Fedn of Women Clubs, 64 & Jacksonville Fair, 61-66. Mem: Jacksonville Art Mus (charter mem); Fla Artists Group. Style & Technique: Abstract, sculptural, sometimes semi-hard edge, free. Media: Oi; Acrylic. Collection: Contemporary, graphics, small sculpture, paintings, American, European, Japanese, some ceramics. Dealer: Jack Bear c/o Reddi-Arts Gallery 1037 Hendricks Ave Jacksonville FL. Mailing Add: 1200 San Amaro Rd Jacksonville FL 32207

BEARD, MARION L PATTERSON
EDUCATOR, PAINTER
b Vincennes, Ind. Study: Ind State Univ, BS(art); Syracuse Univ, MFA. Exhib: Nat Asn Women Artists Ann, New York; Am Watercolor Soc, New York Watercolor Club; Hoosier

Art Salon, Indianapolis; Nat Prof Exhib Ann, Ogunquit, Maine; one-man show, H Lieber Art Gallery, Indianapolis. Teaching: Art supvr, Vincennes City Schs, 36-; supvr art educ, Vincennes Community Schs Corp, 55-; art critic teacher, Ind State Univ, 57-; art critic teacher, Ind Univ, 61-62; prof painting, Adult Educ Art Dept, Vincennes Univ & Ind Univ, 51-; prof painting, Vincennes Univ Educ Ctr, 51- Awards: First Award, Margaret George Bridwell Mem Watercolor Award & First Award, William H Block Co Watercolor Award, Hoosier Art Salon; William E Tirey Mem Watercolor Award, Wabash Valley Artists. Mem: Nat Asn Women Artists; Ind Artists Club; Int Platform Asn; Indianapolis Mus Art. Mailing Add: Rte 1 Vincennes IN 47591

BEARD, RICHARD ELLIOTT
PAINTER, EDUCATOR
b Kenosha, Wis, June 13, 28. Study: Univ Wis-Madison, BS & MA; Ohio State Univ, PhD. Work: Ohio State Univ; Univ Ky; Defiance Col. Exhib: Butler Inst, Youngstown, Ohio, 62; Cincinnati Artists in Vicinity 63; one-man show, Distelheim Gallery, Chicago, 68; Rockford Ann, Ill, 74; Purdue Univ, 74; Chicago Artists & Vicinity, Chicago Art Inst, 77. Teaching: Asst prof art, Maryville Col, 52-61; asst instr art, Ohio State Univ, 61-63; vis prof art, Univ Ky, 63-64; assoc prof art, Wis State Univ, Stevens Point, 64-66; prof art, Northern Ill Univ, 66- Awards: Merit Prize Drawing, Nat Print & Drawing, Knoxville, Tenn, 62; Catalog Prize, Cincinnati Artists & Vicinity Show, 63; Best Painting in Show, Kenosha Art Asn, 66. Mem: Col Art Asn; Mid Am Col Art Asn. Style & Technique: Painterly, somewhat expressionistic. Media: Oil, Acrylic, Chalk. Dealer: Am Print & Drawing De Kalb IL 60115; Washington Gallery 500 E Washington St Frankfort IN 46041. Mailing Add: 730 W Taylor DeKalb IL 60115

BEARDEN, ROMARE HOWARD
PAINTER
b Charlotte, NC, Sept 2, 14. Study: NY Univ, BS, 35; Art Students League, 36-37; Columbia Univ, 43; Sorbonne, cert, 51. Work: Mus Mod Art, New York; Whitney Mus, New York; Newark Mus, NJ; Albright Mus, Buffalo, NY. Exhib: One-man shows, Corcoran Gallery, Washington, DC, 66, Mus State Univ NY, Albany, 68, Univ Calif Mus Art, Berkeley, Calif, 71; Cordier-Ekstrom Gallery, New York, 61-77; one-man retrospective, Mus Mod Art, 71; Alpert Web Gallery, Paris, 75. Teaching: Vis lectr African & Afro-American art & cult, Williams Col, 69. Pos: Dir, Cinque Gallery, New York, 69- Bibliog: Dore Ashton (auth), Romare Bearden-projections, Quadrom 17, 65; Art of Romare Bearden, Abrams, NY. Mem: Black Acad Art & Lett; Am Inst Arts & Lett. Publ: Co-auth, Painters Mind, Crown, 69; co-auth, Six Black Masters of American Art, Doubleday, 72. Dealer: Cordier & Ekstrom Inc 980 Madison Ave New York NY 10021. Mailing Add: 357 Canal St New York NY 10013

BEARDSLEY, BARBARA H
CONSERVATOR
b New York, NY, Mar 30, 45. Study: Elmira Col, BA; Univ Wis, cert in Europ Study Prog; Univ NMex, grad studies; State Univ NY, Cooperstown, MA(conserv), cert advan standing, study with Kecks; study with Louis Pomerantz; McCrone Res Inst. Comn: Cleveland Mus of Art; I Tatti, Harvard Univ, Florence, Italy; Currier Gallery, Manchester, NH; William Hayes Fogg Art Mus, Cambridge, Mass; Taft Mus, Cincinnati, Ohio. Collections Arranged: Mary Lester Field Collection of Santos, Albuquerque, NMex, 70; Harwood Collection, Span Colonial Art, Taos, NMex, 71. Pos: Conservator, Intermuseum Conserv Assoc Lab, Oberlin, Ohio, 73-75; conserv intern, Newberry Libr, Chicago, 74-75; guest lectr conserv methods, State Univ NY, Cooperstown, 75-77; conservator (six locations), New Eng Coun, Am Asn of Mus, 75-76; chief conservator, Art Conserv Lab, Inc, 75- Bibliog: K Schaal (auth), New Life for Old Masters, NH Profiles, 10/77; J Dueland (auth), Barbara Beardsley's Barn, Christian Sci Monitor, 1/78. Mem: Am Asn of Mus; Int Coun of Mus; fel Am Inst for Conserv of Hist & Artistic Works; Nat Conserv Adv Coun (rep, 76-); Am Inst for Conserv (dir, 76-). Res: Polarizing pigment analysis, material studies, art history research, Spanish Colonial Santos. Publ: Auth, The Field Collection of Santos, Univ NMex Art Mus Bull, 70; auth, The Adaptation of an Examination Microscope, Am Inst for Conserv Bull, 72; auth, Basic Guide to a Healthy Collection, Art Conserv Lab, rev ed, 76. Mailing Add: Dudley Homestead Raymond NH 03077

BEARMAN, JANE RUTH
PAINTER, ILLUSTRATOR
b Minneapolis, Minn. Study: Univ Minn, BA(fine arts); Minneapolis Inst Arts; Walker Art Ctr, Minneapolis; Chicago Art Inst; Am Acad Art; Montclair Col, NJ. Work: Temple Beth Shalom, Livingston, NJ; Adath Jeshuran Synagogue, Minneapolis; YMCA, Livingston, NJ. Comn: Painting, Congregation Beth Torah, Orange, NJ, 68; Sclauo Serum Inst, Siena, Italy, 69; painting, Wells Labs, Jersey City, NJ, 75; Torah cover (needlepoint design), Knesses Israel Congregation, Pittsfield, Mass, 77; paintings, Allied Commodities Corp, Minneapolis, 77. Exhib: State Exhib, Montclair Mus, NJ, 61-; Audubon Artists, Nat Acad Arts Gallery, New York, 65-; NJ Printmakers, Newark Mus, 65; Painters & Sculptors Soc Jersey City Mus, 65-; 30 Artists in Watercolor & Casein, NJ State Mus, Trenton, 69; NJ Watercolor Soc, Morris Co Mus; Nat Asn Women Artists, Nat Acad, New York, 68-70; Painters & Sculptors Soc, Nat Arts Club, New York, 73-; NJ Watercolor Soc, 63-77; NJ Coun Arts Traveling Exhib, 70; one-person shows, Brandeis Univ, Hallmark Gallery, Kansas City, Univ NMex, Loyola Univ, Chicago, & Carver Mus, Calif. Teaching: Teacher painting & life drawing, YM-YWHA of Metrop NJ-West Orange, 63-; instr art hist, Seton Hall Univ, 70-72. Pos: Fashion illusr, Dayton Co, Minneapolis, 37-41; art dir, Dept Training, New York, 41-45; free lance illusr books & mag, New York, 45-60. Awards: First in Graphics, Montclair Mus Ann, Russel T Mount, 61; Yelen Award Watercolor, Nat Asn Women Artists Ann Exhib, Mary Yelen, 70; Medal of Honor, Painters & Sculptors Soc, 73. Bibliog: Interview, First Estate—Religion in Review, Dr Russell Barbara, NBC Channel 4, 77. Mem: Nat Asn Women Artists; NJ Watercolor Soc; Painters & Sculptors Soc NJ (mem jury, 73); Artists Equity (mem bd). Style & Technique: Abstract and semi-abstract or figurative collage, realistic collage. Publ: Auth & illusr, Happy Chanukah, Union Am Hebrew Congregation, 43 & Passover Party, 46; auth & illusr, Jonathan, Jonathan-David Co, 65 & David, 65; contribr, T Newman (auth), Contemporary Decoupage, Crown, 72 & Paper as Art & Craft, 73; auth & illusr, The Eight Nights, Union Am Hebrew Congregation, 78. Mailing Add: 30 Spier Dr Livingston NJ 07039

BEASLEY, BRUCE
SCULPTOR
b Los Angeles, Calif, May 20, 39. Study: Dartmouth Col; Univ Calif, Berkeley, BA. Work: Mus Mod Art & Solomon R Guggenheim Mus, New York; Los Angeles Co Mus Art, Los Angeles; Musee d'Art Moderne, Paris, France; Univ Art Mus, Berkeley. Comn: Apolymen (cast acrylic sculpture), State Calif, 70; cast acrylic sculptures, US Govt-GSA Art in Pub Places, San Diego, Calif, 76 & City of San Francisco, Calif, 77; metal sculptures, City of Eugene, Ore, 74 & Miami Int Airport, Fla, 78. Exhib: Art of Assemblage, Mus Mod Art, New York, 61; Biennale de Paris, Musee d'Art Moderne, 63; Selected Acquisitions, Solomon R Guggenheim Mus, 66; A Plastic Presence, Jewish Mus, New York & Milwaukee Art Ctr, San Francisco Mus Art, 69-70; American Sculpture in Perspective, Sheldon Art Gallery, Univ Nebr, 70. Awards: Andre Malraux Purchase Award, Biennale de Paris, 63; Frank Lloyd Wright Mem Purchase Award, Marin Mus Asn, 65; Purchase Prize, San Francisco Arts Festival, 67. Bibliog: The crystal clear scene, Time Mag, 2/9/68; Shipley & Weller (auth), Contemporary American Painting & Sculpture, Univ Ill, 69; Hotaling (auth), The age of Lucite dawns in Sacramento, Art News 5/70. Style & Technique: Abstract; large & small scale. Media: Acrylic Plastic, Metal. Dealer: Andre Emmerich Gallery 41 E 57th St New York NY 10022; Hansen-Fuller Gallery 228 Grant Ave San Francisco CA 94108. Mailing Add: 322 Lewis St Oakland CA 94607

BEATTIE, GEORGE
ART ADMINISTRATOR, PAINTER
b Cleveland, Ohio, Aug 2, 19. Study: Cleveland Inst Art, 38-41. Work: Whitney Mus Am Art, New York; Montclair Mus, NJ; High Mus of Atlanta Mem Arts Ctr, Ga; Mead Painting of the Year; Larry Aldrich Collection, Conn. Comn: Murals, History of Agriculture in State of Georgia, State Agr Bldg, Atlanta, 56 & History of Middle Georgia, Fed Post Off Bldg, Macon, Ga, 68. Exhib: Mead Painting of the Year, 55 & 61; Int Drawing Ann, Uffizi Loggia, Florence, Italy, 57; Fulbright Exhib, Rome, Italy, 57; Smithsonian Traveling Exhib, 58-59; Art USA, 59. Teaching: Head creative drawing, Ga Inst Technol Sch Archit, 57-67. Pos: Exec dir, Ga Coun for the Arts, 67-75; dir pub serv in art, Ga State Univ, 75- Awards: Nat Inst Arts & Lett Grant, 55; Fulbright Grant to Italy, 56-57; artist, Link Archaeol Exped to Israel, 60 & Sicily, 62. Bibliog: Nina Kaiden & Bartlett Hayes (auth), Artist & advocate, Renaissance Ed, 67. Mem: Atlanta Mem Arts Ctr, High Mus (mem bd sponsors); Arts Festival Atlanta, Inc (Hon life mem bd trustees). Media: All media. Mailing Add: 857 Woodley Dr NW Atlanta GA 30318

BEATTY, FRANCES FIELDING LEWIS
ART HISTORIAN, ART CRITIC
b New York, NY, Nov 23, 48. Study: Vassar Col, BA; Columbia Univ, MA(art hist), MPhil(art hist), with Meyer Schapiro & Theodore Reff. Teaching: Instr surrealism, Renaissance & 19th & 20th century art hist & lit, Ramapo Col, NJ, 74; instr art hist, Columbia Col, 74-76. Pos: Sr ed, Art/World, 76- Awards: Noble Found Fel, Columbia Univ, 72; Vassar Col Fel for Dissertation Res, 75; Columbia Univ Grant for Dissertation Studies, 77. Res: Work of Andre Masson in the 1920s and its relation to surrealist poetry and prose. Publ: Co-auth (catalogue), Louise Nevelson, Centre Nat d'Art Contemporain, Paris, 74; auth, rev in Art in Am, 75; contribr (catalogue), Andre Masson, Mus Mod Art, New York, 76. Mailing Add: 46 E 92nd St New York NY 10028

BEAUCHAMP, JOHN R
INSTRUCTOR, PAINTER
b Denver, Colo, Nov 19, 23. Study: Colorado Springs Fine Arts Ctr; Cranbrook Acad of Art, Bloomfield Hills, Mich, BFA; Hans Hofmann Sch of Art. Work: Mus of Mod Art, New York; Whitney Mus of Am Art, New York; Carnegie Inst Int, Pittsburgh; Hirshhorn Mus & Sculpture Garden, Washington, DC; Denver Art Mus. Exhib: Walker Art Ctr, Minneapolis, 53; Carnegie Int, Carnegie Inst of Technol Mus of Art, Pittsburgh, 58 & 61; Whitney Mus of Am Art, 61-63, 65, 67 & 69; Mus of Mod Art, New York, 62; Artists Abroad, Inst of Int Educ, New York, 69; Ten Independents, Solomon R Guggenheim Mus, New York, 72. Teaching: Instr painting, Brooklyn Col, 73 & Sch of Visual Arts, 74-76. Awards: Fulbright Grant, 59; Nat Found of Arts Grant, 66; Guggenheim Found Fel, 74. Bibliog: Scott Burton (auth), Paint the devil, Art News, 66. Mem: Artists Equity. Style & Technique: Oil on canvas. Media: Oil and Graphite. Dealer: Sindin Gallery 1035 Madison Ave New York NY 10021. Mailing Add: 463 West St 346 New York NY 10014

BEAUCHEMIN, MICHELINE
PAINTER, WEAVER
b Longueuil, PQ, Oct 24, 31. Study: Ecole Beaux Arts Montreal; Ecole Beaux Arts, Paris, with Zadkine; also with Tatsumura & Kawashima, Kyoto, Japan. Work: Nat Art Gallery, Ottawa; Montreal Mus Fine Arts; Quebec Mus Fine Arts; Malton Int Airport, Toronto; Montreal Star. Comn: Tapestry, Place Arts, Salle Wilfrid Laurier, Montreal, 63; tapestry, Ont Prov Govt, Queens Park, 68; stage curtain tapestry, hand woven, Opera House, Nat Art Ctr, Ottawa, 69; tapestry, Sci & Humanities Bldg, York Univ, 70; tapestry, Can Pavilion, Expo 70, Osaka, Japan, 70. Exhib: 1st Nat Can Craft Exhib, Ottawa, 57; Brussels World's Fair, 57; solo exhibs, Montreal Mus Fine Arts, 60 & Nihon Bashi Gallery, Tokyo, 68; retrospective solo, Ctr Cult Can, Paris, 71. Awards: Silver Medal, Gov Gen Can, 67; Can Coun Award, Can Govt, 72. Bibliog: Claude Gauvreau (auth), L'itineraire de l'ange, Cult Vivante No 3, 67; Michel Mercier (producer), Femme d'aujoud'hui (TV film), 71; Claude Lyse Gagnon, Au mur, Vie Arts, 72. Mem: Royal Can Soc Arts (mem coun, 71). Media: Wool, Acrylics, Metallic Threads. Publ: Illusr & auth, Minstra, Can Arts, 59; illusr covers, Vie Arts, 59 & Can Arts, 59; Fin d'une enfance, Marie Claire Blais, Chatelaine, 63. Mailing Add: 22 Chemin du Roy Les Grondines Cte Portneuf PQ G0A 2Y0 Can

BEAUDOIN, ANDRE EUGENE
PRESS MANUFACTURER, PHOTOGRAPHER
b Calais, France, Apr 11, 20; US citizen. Study: Ecole des Arts de Metiers, Paris, France, machine design & metallurgy; Brown Univ, photog. Pos: Owner, designer & constructor of etching & lithographic presses for artist printmakers, Am-French Tool Co, 69- Interest: Presses are now in over 150 universities and workshops in North America and Europe, including Rhode Island School of Design, University of Massachusetts, Amherst, Indiana University, Bloomington, University of New Mexico, Iowa University, Iowa City and workshops of Vermont, Leonardo Lasansky of Minnesota, Richard Upton of Connecticut, David Bombeck of Vermont, Alice Vaccino of New York and Vivian Berman of Massachusetts. Mailing Add: Rte 117 Coventry RI 02816

BEAUMONT, MONA M
PAINTER, PRINTMAKER
b Paris, France; US citizen. Study: Univ Calif, Berkeley, BA & MA; grad study, Fogg Mus, Harvard Univ, Cambridge, Mass; spec study with Hans Hoffman, New York. Work: Oakland Mus Art, Calif; City & Co San Francisco; Hoover Found; The Grey Found, Washington, DC; Bulart Found, San Francisco. Exhib: Textile/Design Exhib, Mus Mod Art, New York, 45; San Francisco Mus Mod Art, 45, 47-49, 54, 57 & 68; San Francisco Art Inst, 58, 62-66 & 74, traveling exhib, 64 & 65; Calif Painters & Sculptors 35 & Under, Univ Calif, Los Angeles, 59; Regional Painters, de Young Mem Mus Art, San Francisco, 62; Regional Gallery Artists, Stanford Univ Art Mus, 66; Print & Drawing Ann, Richmond Art Ctr, Va, 68; Bell Tel Print/Drawing, Chicago, 69; one-person shows, Calif Palace of Legion of Honor, San Francisco, 64, San Francisco Mus Art, 68 & Palo Alto Cult Ctr, Calif, 77; Los Angeles Co Mus Art, 73. Awards: Purchase Award, US Artists Tour of Asia, Grey Found, 63; Ackerman Award, San Francisco Woman Artists Ann, 68; Purchase & One-Person Show Awards, San Francisco Art Festival Ann, 66 & 75. Bibliog: Margarita Nelken (auth), Mona Beaumont at Proteo, Novedades, 9/60; Bernard Nebout (auth), Mona Beaumont & Art of the Pacific,

Paris-Normandie, 2/66; Andrew De Shong (auth), Works on Paper—San Francisco Art Inst, Art Week Mag, 11/74. Mem: Soc Encouragement Contemp Art; Bay Area Graphic Arts Coun. Style & Technique: Hard-edge linear emphasis on abstract elements of mass and volume, seeking formalization of logic and movement from complex, stable-appearing relationships. Media: Murals in Acrylic; Mixed-Media Drawing. Publ: Contribr, articles in Artforum, 5/64 & 12/64; contribr, Frankenstein, San Francisco Chronicle, 66 & 67. Mailing Add: 1087 Upper Happy Valley Rd Lafayette CA 94549

BEAVER, FRED
PAINTER, LECTURER
b Eufaula, Okla, July 2, 11. Work: Philbrook Art Ctr, Tulsa, Okla; Gilcrease Mus Art & Hist, Tulsa; Heard Mus, Phoenix, Ariz; Five-Tribes Mus, Muskogee, Okla. Comn: Indian Dancers, Thunderbird Motel, Oklahoma City, 57; Indian Dancers, 23rd & May Ave Bank, Oklahoma City, 59; Seminole Indian Life, Arts & Crafts Ctr, Bur Indian Affairs, Washington, DC, 61; Indian Outlook, Durwood Indian Church, Ardmore, Okla, 63. Exhib: American Indian Paintings Exhibs, Tulsa, 47- & Heard Mus, 63-71; Indian Paintings, Scottsdale, Ariz, 65-71; Art Gallery, Fresno, Calif, 65-75; Five-Tribes Mus exhibs, 67-71; Regional Art Show, Tulsa, 70; Okalii Seminole Art Ctr, Dania, Fla, 74-75. Pos: Judge Indian paintings, Philbrook Art Ctr, Tulsa, Okla, 57, 63 & 78. Awards: Trophy, Waite Phillips Found, Tulsa, 63; Heritage Award, Indian Heritage Found, Muskogee, 68; Drawing Award, Murray Col, Tishomingo, Okla, 70. Bibliog: Dorothy Dunn (auth), American Indian Painting; article in Indian Art, SDak Rev, 69; plus others. Media: Watercolor. Publ: Illusr, Creek-Seminole Spirit Tales, 71; contribr, Southeastern Indians, 75; contribr, J Highwater (auth), Songs from the Earth, 77. Mailing Add: Sycamore Bay West Star Rte Box 97 Checotah OK 74426

BECHTLE, C RONALD
PAINTER
b Philadelphia, Pa, Nov 14, 24. Study: ETenn Univ; Tyler Sch Fine Arts, Temple Univ; Fleisher Mem, Sch Indust Art; also with Benton Spruance, 52-53. Work: Munson-Williams-Proctor Inst, Utica, NY; Denver Art Mus, Colo; Santa Barbara Mus Art, Calif; Columbus Gallery Fine Art, Ohio; Nat Collection Fine Arts. Exhib: Pa Acad Fine Arts Regional, 65 & 69; one-man shows, Panoras Gallery, New York, 66, Santa Barbara Mus Art, 67, Miami Mus Mod Art, Fla, 68 & Philadelphia Art Alliance, 73, Stohelli Gallery, 74 & E Tenn Univ, 77. Pos: Pres, Group 55, 56-57; pres, Philadelphia Abstract Artists, 57-63. Mem: Artists Equity; Mus Mod Art, New York; Am Fedn Arts; Col Art Asn Am. Style & Technique: Nonrepresentational form highly dependant on drawing and transparent color. Media: Watercolor, Gouache. Publ: Auth, Information theory of art, Mensa J, 61. Mailing Add: Apt 12B 26 Strawberry Hill Ave Stamford CT 06902

BECHTLE, ROBERT ALAN
PAINTER
b San Francisco, Calif, May 14, 32. Study: Calif Col Arts & Crafts, BA & MFA; Univ Calif, Berkeley. Work: Whitney Mus Am Art, New York; Mus Mod Art, New York; Neue Gallerie, Aachen, Ger; Univ Calif Art Mus, Berkeley; San Francisco Mus Art. Exhib: Realism Now, Vassar Col Art Gallery, 66; Contemp Am Painting, Whitney Mus Am Art, New York, 67 & 73, 22 Realists, 70 & 30 Yrs of Am Art, 77; Aspects of a New Realism, Milwaukee Art Ctr, Wis, 68; Radical Realism, Mus of Contemp Art, Chicago, 71; Amerikanischer Fotorealismus, Wurttemburgischer Kunstverein, Stuttgart, Ger, 71; Documenta 5, Kassel, Ger, 72; Photo Realism, Serpentine Gallery, London, Eng, 73; Ein Grosses Jahrzehnt Amerikanischer Kunst, Kunstmuseum Luzern, Switz, 73; Am Art, Seattle Art Mus, Wash, 73; Ekstrem Realism, La Mus, Humlebaek, Denmark, 73; Tokyo Biennale, 74; Image, Form & Color: Recent Paintings by 11 Americans, Toledo Mus of Art, Ohio, 75; Super Realism, Baltimore Mus, Md, 76; Painting & Sculpture in Calif: The Mod Era, San Francisco Mus of Mod Art, 76; Am 1976, Corcoran Gallery of Art, Washington, DC, 76; Aspects of Realism/Du Realisme, Rothmans of Can Ltd, Montreal, 76-77; Illusion & Reality, Australian Gallery Dirs Coun, 77-78; Representations of Am, Pushkin Fine Arts Mus, Moscow, USSR, 78; plus others. Teaching: Prof printmaking, Calif Col Arts & Crafts, 57-; guest artist, Univ Calif, Davis, 66-68; prof art, San Francisco State Univ, 68- Awards: James D Phelan Award in Painting, 65; grant, Nat Endowment for the Arts, 77. Bibliog: U Kultermann (auth), Radical realism, New York Graphic Soc, 72; W Seitz (auth), The real and the artificial: painting of the new environment, Art in Am, 11-12/72; G Battcock (auth), Super Realism, A Critical Anthology, Dutton, 75; plus others. Dealer: O K Harris Gallery 383 W Broadway New York NY 10012. Mailing Add: 850 Mendocino Ave Berkeley CA 94707

BECK, CURT WERNER
ART CONSERVATOR, ART EDITOR
b Halle/Saale, Ger, Sept 10, 27; US citizen. Study: Univ of Munich; Tufts Univ, BS(chemistry), 51; Mass Inst of Technol, PhD(organic chemistry), 55. Teaching: From instr to prof chemistry, Vassar Col, Poughkeepsie, NY, 57- Pos: Co-ed, Art & Archaeology Tech Abstracts, 66-; section editor dealing with applications of chemistry to art hist & archaeology, Chemical Abstracts, 67- Mem: Fel Int Inst for Conservation of Hist & Artistic Works; fel Am Inst for Conservation of Hist & Artistic Works; fel Royal Soc of Arts. Res: Archaeological chemisty of organic materials, including resins, fats, oils and waxes. Publ: Ed, Archaeological chemistry, Am Chemical Soc, 74. Mailing Add: Skidmore Rd LaGrange Pleasant Valley NY 12601

BECK, DOREEN
EDITOR, WRITER
b Medomsley, Durham, Eng, Mar 12, 35; US & UK citizen. Study: Leicester Univ Col, Univ London, BA(hons in French), 57; NY Univ, film prod; NY Sch Visual Arts, screen writing with Andrew Sarris. Pos: Researcher & writer, MD Med Newsmag; ed & writer, UN; research, ed & writing, BBC, World Bk Enc (int ed), The Observer, Thames & Hudson, Julian Press, Ved Mehta & New Yorker; ed, NY Hosp/Cornell Med Ctr Ann Report. Publ: Co-auth, Everything in its Place (30 min training film), NJ Community Action Training Group, 69; auth, Britain: An Enduring Heritage (script for 3-part filmstrip), 69; auth, Book of Bottle Collecting, 73; auth, Book of American Furniture, 73; auth, Country & Western Americana, 75; plus var Fr transl including articles in Atlas Mag. Mailing Add: 100 W 57th St New York NY 10019

BECK, MARGIT
PAINTER, EDUCATOR
b Tokay, Hungary. Study: Inst Fine Arts, Oradea Mare, Roumania; Art Students League. Work: Whitney Mus Am Art, New York; J B Speed Mus, Louisville, Ky; Washington Co Mus Fine Arts, Hagerstown, Md; Lyman Allyn Mus, New London, Conn; Norfolk Mus Arts & Sci, Va; plus others. Comn: Portrait of Bayonne (oil), NJ Jewish Community Art Ctr, 72. Exhib: Corcoran Gallery Art Biennial, 65; four shows, Pa Acad Fine Arts Ann, 57-68; Whitney Mus Am Art Ann, 58-61; four shows, Brooklyn Mus Int Watercolor Biennial, 59-67; Art Inst Chicago, 60-61; Childe Hassam Fund Exhib, Am Acad of Arts & Lett, 60, 62 & 66-71; Ann Exhib of Candidates for Grants, Nat Inst of Arts & Lett, New York, 60, 66-68; plus other group & one-woman exhibs. Teaching: Lectr art, Hofstra Univ, 66-67; asst prof art, New York Univ, 67-; adv & tutor art hist, Empire State Col, 74- Awards: Henry Ward Ranger Purchase Award, 65 & Edwin Palmer Award, 75, Nat Acad Design; Childe Hassam Purchase Award, Am Acad Arts & Lett, 68, 70 & 71; Medal of Hon, 68 & 72 & Stephen Hirsh Mem Award, Audubon Artists; plus others. Bibliog: Sharon Theobold (auth), Homes of distinguished Nassau artists, Mag Nassau, 6/74; John Gruen (auth), Margit Beck (monogr), Soho News, 3/3/75; Jeanne Paris (auth), Margit Beck (monogr), Long Island Press, 3/30/75; plus others. Mem: Artists Equity (exec bd mem, 65-70); Audubon Artists (vpres, 66-70); Nat Acad Design; Col Art Asn Am. Style & Technique: Semi-abstract lyrical landscapes, seeing the earth from great heights. Media: Oil, Ink. Dealer: Babcock Galleries 22 E 67th St New York NY 10021. Mailing Add: 22 Florence St Great Neck NY 11023

BECK, ROSEMARIE (ROSEMARIE BECK PHELPS)
PAINTER, EDUCATOR
US citizen. Study: Oberlin Col; Columbia Univ; NY Univ. Work: Whitney Mus Am Art; Vassar Col Mus; State Univ NY Col New Paltz; Hirshhorn Collection; Nebr Art Mus. Comn: Mural painting, Rotron Mfg Co, 58. Exhib: Pa Acad Fine Arts; Nat Inst Arts & Lett; Whitney Mus Am Art; Art Inst Chicago; eleven one-man shows, Peridot Gallery; one-man show, Poindexter Gallery, New York. Teaching: Lectr painting, Vassar Col, 57-58, 61-62 & 63-64; lectr painting, Middlebury Col, 58-60 & 63; asst prof painting, Queens Col, 68- Awards: Ingram-Merrill Grant, 67. Media: Oil. Dealer: Poindexter Gallery 24 E 84th New York NY 10028 Mailing Add: 6 E 12th St New York NY 10003

BECK, STEPHEN R
PAINTER, EDUCATOR
b Salt Lake City, Utah, Dec 28, 37. Study: Univ Utah, BFA; Cranbrook Acad Art, MFA. Work: Cranbrook Acad Art Galleries, Bloomfield Hills, Mich; Kingswood Sch-Cranbrook, Bloomfield Hills; Salt Lake Art Ctr; Utah Mus Fine Arts, Salt Lake City; Univ Utah. Exhib: US Senate Bldg, Washington, DC, 65; Mich Ann, Detroit, 65; Western Regional Biennial, Salt Lake City, 71; Westminster Col Exhib, Salt Lake City, 71; 73rd Ann Western, Denver, Colo, 71. Teaching: Instr drawing & painting & admin asst, Univ Utah, 68-75; asst prof drawing & painting, Westminster Col, 75-77. Pos: Mem adv comt, Utah State Inst Fine Arts, Salt Lake City, 70- Awards: Purchase Awards, Salt Lake Art Ctr, 70 & 72. Style & Technique: Abstract; air brush & paint gun. Media: Acrylic Lacquer. Mailing Add: c/o Max Hutchinson Gallery 127 Greene St New York NY 10012

BECKER, BETTIE (BETTIE GERALDINE WATHALL)
PAINTER
b Peoria, Ill, Sept 22, 18. Study: Univ Ill, BFA; Art Students League, with John Carroll; Art Inst Chicago, with Lewis Ritman; Inst Design, Ill Inst Technol, with Hans Weber. Work: Witte Mem Mus, San Antonio, Tex; Union League Club, Chicago, Ill. Comn: Mural (with Frank Wiater), Talbot Materials Testing Lab, Univ Ill, Urbana, 40. Exhib: Drawings USA, St Paul, Minn, 66-68; one-woman show, Crossroad's Gallery, Art Inst Chicago, 73; Festival de Arte de las dos Banderas, US-Mexico, Douglas, Ariz, 72; Critic's Choice, Art Inst Chicago, 72; Union League Civic & Arts Found Exhibs, 67, 72 & 74; Print & Drawing Exhib, Artist's Guild, Chicago, 76; 36th NE Wis Art Ann, Neville Mus, Green Bay; plus many others. Awards: Newcomb Prize, Univ Ill Col Fine & Appl Arts, 40; First Prize for Print, Chicago Soc Artists, 67, 71 & 74; H Barry McCormick Purchase Prize, Union League Club, 74; plus others. Mem: Chicago Soc Artists (rec secy, 68-77); Alumni Asn Art Inst Chicago; Wis Arts Coun; Peninsula Arts Asn; Artist's Guild of Chicago. Style & Technique: Naturalistic, using simplest of visual haiku statements. Media: Collage, Acrylic. Publ: Auth, Life with Liberty, 43; illusr, Sat Rev Lit, 48, New York Times, 48, Chicago Tribune, 48 & 49 & Evanston Rev, 68. Mailing Add: Juddville Rd Fish Creek WI 54212

BECKER, CHARLOTTE (MRS WALTER COX)
ILLUSTRATOR, PAINTER
b Dresden, Ger; US citizen. Study: Cooper Union; Indust Arts Night Sch; Art Students League. Mem: New York Camera Club. Media: Oil. Interest: Painted over a thousand magazine covers, art calendars and art prints, all of children; painting restoration. Publ: Auth & illusr, Hello Judy Stories, 50, Stories for Fun, 50, Unlike Twin Series, 52 & Three Little Steps Series, 52, Scribner; auth & illusr, A Chimp in the Family, Messner; also many other children's bks. Mailing Add: Pine Plains NY 12567

BECKER, HELMUT JULIUS
PRINTMAKER
b Castor, Alta, Can, Feb 24, 31; Can citizen. Study: Univ Sask, BA, with distinction, 54; Univ Wis-Madison, Can Amateur Hockey Asn Scholar, 54-55, MA(art educ), 55; Acad of Fine Arts, The Hague, with W J Rozendaal. Work: Burnaby Art Gallery, BC; Sask Arts Bd, Regina; Univ Calgary, Alta; Univ Regina, Sask; Banff Sch of Fine Arts, Alta. Exhib: One-man show Can Art Gallery, Calgary, 70; Burnaby Biennial, 73; Can Soc of Graphic Art, 74; Calgary Graphics Exhib; two-man show, London Pub Libr & Mus, Ont, 74. Teaching: Printmaking, NS Col Art & Design, Halifax, 64-65 & Univ Calgary, 66-71; asst prof printmaking, Univ Western Ont, London, 71- Awards: Can Govt Overseas Award Scholar, 55-56; Can Coun Grant, 70. Bibliog: Shirley Raphael (auth), Calgary workshop, Vie des Arts, 70; Electro-hydraulic printing press, Art Mag, 71. Mem: Can Soc Graphic Art (pres, 74-75); Univ Art Asn of Can; Can Artists Representation. Style & Technique: Abstract to non-objective colour expressions evolving from light phenomena; metaphysical overtones of photo processed images vs the non-objective. Media: Relief, Intaglio & Lithography with Handmade Paper. Res: Designed and constructed large electro-hydraulic printing press for lithography, intaglio and relief; research in the handmaking of paper and experimental application of special handmade papers for painting, drawing and printmaking. Mailing Add: Dept Visual Art Univ Western Ont London ON N6A 5B8 Can

BECKER, MARTIN EARLE
PUBLISHER, PATRON
b Boston, Mass, May 21, 35. Study: RI Sch of Design & Mass Inst of Technol. Pos: Exec publ, Art Voices/South & Art Digest/South Newsletter, West Palm Beach, Fla, 77- Mem: Eclectic Found (chmn bd). Mailing Add: 200 S Dixie Hwy West Palm Beach FL 33401

BECKER, NATALIE ROSE
PAINTER
b Philadelphia, Pa. Study: Fleisher Art Mem, Philadelphia; Temple Univ, AA(bus admin); Pa Acad Fine Arts; Art Students League with Robert Phillip & Henry Gasser. Work: Fine Arts Galleries, Carnegie Inst; Bloomfield Col. Exhib: Allied Artists Am, Nat Acad Design, New York, 72, 73 & 74 & Audubon Artists of Am, 73, 75 & 78. Teaching: Instr drawing & painting, Union Col, Cranford, NJ. Awards: Leon Lehrer Mem Award Landscape, Allied Artists Am, 72; Grumbacher Award of Merit, Catharine Lorillard Wolfe Art Club, 72; Grumbacher Award, Nat Arts Club, 75. Mem: Salmagundi Club, New York; Pen & Brush Club; Catharine Lorillard Wolfe Art Club; fel Am Artists Prof League (trustee, NJ chap, 75). Style &

Technique: Oil landscapes; impressionistic style. Media: Oil, Watercolor. Mailing Add: 97 Barchester Way Westfield NJ 07090

BECKLEY, BILL
POST-CONCEPTUAL ARTIST
b Hamburg, Pa, Feb 11, 46. Study: Kutztown State Col, Pa, BFA; Tyler Sch of Art, Temple Univ, MFA, with Steven Greene & Italo Scanga. Work: Mus Mod Art, New York. Exhib: Proj Pier 18, 71 & Seven, 73, Mus Mod Art, New York; Narrational Imagery: Beckley, Ruscha, Warhol, Univ Mass, Amherst, 76; Venice Biennale, Italy, 76; San Francisco Art Mus, Calif, 76; Documenta, Kassel, WGer, 77; Three Artists Using the Photograph, Alta Col Art Gallery, Calgary, 77; Narrative Art, Mus Contemp Art, Houston, Tex, 77; New Art For Jimmy Carter, Ga Art Mus, Athens, 77; Art of the 70s, PS 1, New York, 77; one-man shows, Gallery G7, Bologna, Italy, John Gibson, New York, Konrad Fischer, Dusseldorf & Daniel Templon, Paris, 78. Teaching: Instr, Sch Visual Arts, 71- Bibliog: Barbara Radice (auth), article in Data, Milano, Italy, 4/76; Jane Bell (auth), article in Arts Mag, 5/76; Eric Cameron (auth), Bill Beckley's Lies, Artforum, 2/77. Style & Technique: Post-conceptual artist using photographs and text. Dealer: Hans Mayer Grabbeplatz 2 4000 Dusseldorf WGer. Mailing Add: 155 Wooster St New York NY 10012

BECKMANN, ROBERT OWEN
PAINTER, MURALIST
b Philadelphia, Pa, Mar 20, 42. Study: Col Wooster, BA, 64; Univ Iowa, with Byron Burford, David Proctor, Herbert Katzman, MA & MFA, 67. Work: Denver Art Mus, Colo; Univ Iowa; Western Ill Univ; Idaho State Univ. Comn: Symbiosis (with Doug Jones, Robert Behrens & Jack Edwards), Friends of Contemp Art, Denver, 72; murals, Lynn Co Courthouse, Nev, 76, City Hall Annex, Downtown Fire Alarm Sta & Whipple Ctr for Arts, Las Vegas, 77. Exhib: Cent South Exhib, Parthenon, Nashville, Tenn, 68; Ill Painters II, Ill Arts Coun, Traveling Exhib, 70-72; 73rd Ann Exhib, Artists Chicago & Vicinity, Art Inst Chicago, 71; Colorado-Nebraska Exchange 1973, Joslyn Mus, Omaha & Friends of Contemp Art, Denver, 73; one-man shows, Joseph Magnin Gallery, Denver, 74 & Boise Gallery of Art, Idaho, 76; Ten Artists (travelling exhib), Western Asn Art Mus, 77-78. Teaching: Instr studio art, Univ Southern Ala, 67-68; instr life drawing, Northern Ill Univ, 68-71; instr art hist, Kendall Col, summer 69; instr art, Univ Nev, Las Vegas, 77-78. Pos: Organizer for western slope, Col Chatauqua, Colo Coun for the Arts, 72; artist in residence, Artrain, 73; Artist in Nat Endowment Arts in the Schs Prog, Idaho, 74-75 & Nev, 76 & 77-78; proj dir/res artist, Community Murals Proj, Las Vegas, 77-78. Awards: Laura Slobe Mem Prize, Art Inst Chicago, 71; Western States Arts Found Fel, 76. Bibliog: Patricia Raymer (auth), Climb aboard the Artrain, Am Educ, 12/73; Duncan Pollock (auth), rev in arts now, Rocky Mountain News, Denver, 9/22/74; Jean Morrison (auth), Project murals, Nevadan, 4/24/77. Style & Technique: Large exterior wall murals. Media: Latex, Acrylic. Publ: Auth, A portrait of the artist as a human being, rev, Chicago Literary Rev, summer 68. Dealer: Thompson Gallery 2020 N Central Phoenix AZ 85004. Mailing Add: 594 Sierra Vista A-17 Las Vegas NV 89109

BEDNARZ, ADELE
ART DEALER
b Minneapolis, Minn. Study: Concordia Col, Morehead, Minn, Pub Sch Music & Art & McPhail Sch Music, Minneapolis. Teaching: Supvr music & art, Fairmont, Minn, 32-34. Pos: In charge catalogues & reproductions, Art Inst Chicago, 36-46; owner & dir, Adele Lawson Galleries, Chicago, 46-54 & Adele Bednarz Galleries, Los Angeles, 55- Mem: Art Dealers Asn Chicago, 46; Art Dealers Asn Southern Calif (secy, 71-73 & vpres, 75-); Los Angeles Co Mus Art; Mus Mod Art, New York. Specialty: Contemporary art including paintings, sculpture and graphics. Mailing Add: 902 La Cienega Blvd Los Angeles CA 90069

BEDNO, EDWARD
DESIGNER, EDUCATOR
b Chicago, Ill, Mar 8, 25. Study: Art Inst Chicago, BFA; Inst Design, Ill Inst Technol, MS. Exhib: Art Dirs Clubs, Chicago, New York, Detroit, Cincinnati, Indianapolis & Los Angeles; Soc Typographic Arts; Libr of Cong, Washington, DC; US Info Agency; Am Inst Graphic Arts; plus others. Teaching: Instr, Northwestern Univ, Evanston, 51-52; instr, Inst Design, Ill Inst Technol, 57, lectr, 60-64, asst prof, 64-67, assoc prof, 67-71; assoc prof, Va Commonwealth Univ, 71-, dept chmn, 71-73. Pos: Pres, Bedno Assocs, Chicago, Ill; lectr. Awards: Midwest Film Festival, Art Dirs Club Chicago; Nat Endowment for the Arts. Mem: Soc Typographic Arts. Publ: Contribr, photog essay, Am Heritage Mag, 64; retrospective article, Commun Arts Mag, 70; contribr, res article, Visible Language, 72; contribr, Print Mag, 76. Mailing Add: 8505 Academy Rd Richmond VA 23229

BEEBE, MARY LIVINGSTONE
ART ADMINISTRATOR
b Portland, Ore, Nov 5, 40. Study: Bryn Mawr Col, Pa, BA, 62. Collections Arranged: Numerous exhibitions at the Portland Center for the Visual Arts, since July 73. Pos: Mus apprentice, Portland Art Mus, 63-64; asst to registr & secy, Mus Fine Arts, Boston, 65-66; secy & curatorial asst, Fogg Art Mus, Harvard Univ, 66-67; prodr, Am Theater Co, Portland, 69-71; dir, Portland Ctr Visual Arts, 73-; bd mem, Henry Gallery, Univ Wash, Seattle. Mem: Western Asn Art Mus (bd mem). Mailing Add: Portland Ctr for Visual Arts 117 NW Fifth Ave Portland OR 97209

BEELER, JOE (NEIL)
PAINTER
b Joplin, Mo, Dec 25, 31. Study: Univ Tulsa; Kans State Univ, BFA; Art Ctr Sch, Los Angeles. Work: Gilcrease Mus, Tulsa, Okla; Nat Cowboy Hall of Fame, Oklahoma City; Mont Hist Soc, Helena; Phoenix Art Mus; Five Civilized Tribes Mus, Muskogee, Okla. Exhib: One-man shows, Gilcrease Mus, 61, Mont Hist Soc, 61, Nat Cowboy Hall of Fame, 63, Heard Mus, Phoenix, 68 & C M Russell Mus, Great Falls, Mont, 70; Cowboy Artist of Am Ann Show, 66-77. Awards: Best of Sculpture, Cowboy Artist Show, 67, Silver Medal/Sculpture, 69-74, Colt Award for Best Over All of Show, 71 & Silver Medal/Drawing, 74. Bibliog: Jeff Dykes (auth), 50 Great Western Illustrators, Northland Press, 75. Mem: Cowboy Artist of Am (one of four founding mem, pres, 70-71). Style & Technique: Realistic view point-strong on story telling quality. Media: Oil, watercolor; bronze; pastel. Res: Western Americana. Collection: Many American artists. Publ: Auth, Cowboys and Indians, Univ Okla, 67; illusr, Ben Green, Last Trail Drive through Downtown Dallas, 72; contribr, Abrams & Pat Broder, Bronzes of the American West, 74; auth, Joe Beeler Sketch Book, Northland Press, 75; illusr, Cowboy in Art, World Pub, 69. Dealer: Shriver Gallery Taos NM 87571. Mailing Add: Box 989 Sedona AZ 86336

BEELKE, RALPH G
EDUCATOR
b Buffalo, NY, Dec 16, 17. Study: Buffalo Sch Fine Arts, dipl; Columbia Univ, MA, 47, EdD, 52. Teaching: Instr art, pub schs & cols, 40-52; head dept art, State Univ NY Col Fredonia, 51-56; head dept creative arts, Purdue Univ, 62-72 & 77-, prof art & design, 72-76. Pos: Ed, Eastern Arts Asn Bull, 55-57; specialist educ in arts, Off Educ, Dept Health, Educ & Welfare, Washington, DC, 56-58; exec secy art educ, Nat Art Educ Asn, Washington, DC, 58-62; ed, Art Educ J & Western Arts Asn Bull, 58-62. Awards: Art Educator of Yr, Nat Art Educ Asn, 63. Mem: Col Art Asn Am; Nat Art Educ Asn (pres, 65-67); Am Soc Aesthet & Art Criticism. Publ: Contribr, Sch Arts Mag, 55-62; auth, Curriculum Development Art Education, 62; co-auth, Spectrum of Music & Related Arts, 74. Mailing Add: 304 Hollowood Dr West Lafayette IN 47906

BEER, KENNETH JOHN
EDUCATOR, SCULPTOR
b Ferndale, Mich, May 4, 32. Study: Wayne State Univ, BA & MA. Work: Detroit Inst of Art; Thalhimers & First Merchants Bank, Richmond & Va Beach Art Ctr, Va. Comn: Campus libr relief, Eastern Mennonite Col, Harrisonburg, Va, 69; James Madison Mem (cast bronze), James Madison Univ, Harrisonburg, 77. Exhib: Ann Mich Artists, Detroit Inst of Art, 55-62; Va Artists Biennial, Va Mus, Richmond, 65, 67 & 73; Southern Sculpture, Mint Mus, Charlotte, NC, 65 & Birmingham Mus, Ala & Columbus Mus, Ga, 66; solo exhib, Columbia Mus, SC, 69 & Va Mus, 73; Drawing & Sculpture Ann, Ball State Univ Art Gallery, 74 & 76. Teaching: Assoc prof sculpture, James Madison Univ, Harrisonburg, 61- Awards: Whitcomb Prize, Mich Artists Ann, Detroit Inst of the Arts, 61; Best in Show, Thalhimers Invitational, 66; Distinction Award, Va Artists Biennial, Va Mus, 73. Style & Technique: Work in all permanent materials; mostly metals by direct means, and casting. Media: Bronze, steel. Publ: Auth, Sanctum, The Emergence of a Form, Studies & Res Bull of Madison Col, 64. Dealer: Yeatts Gallery 364 Walnut Ave SW Roanoke VA 24016. Mailing Add: Rt 1 Box 343 Bridgewater VA 22812

BEERMAN, HERBERT
PAINTER, EDUCATOR
b Newark, NJ, Nov 8, 26. Study: Rutgers Univ; Univ Miami, AB; Sch Design, Yale Univ, BFA, with Josef Albers. Exhib: One-man shows, Artists Gallery, New York, Krasner Gallery, New York, Seton Hall Univ & Saratoga Springs, NY; Newark Mus; Fairleigh Dickinson Univ; plus others. Teaching: Lectr contemp art, Rutgers Univ, Seton Hall Univ & Cornell Univ; instr painting, Arts Workshop, Newark Mus; from instr color theory & 2-D design to prof art, Sch Art & Design, Pratt Inst, 60- Awards: MacDowell Fel, 58, 59 & 61; Prize, Saratoga Centennial, 63; Yaddo Fel, 63 & 64. Mailing Add: Sch of Art & Design Pratt Inst Brooklyn NY 11205

BEERMAN, MIRIAM H
PAINTER
b Providence, RI. Study: RI Sch Design, BFA; Art Students League, with Yasuo Kuniyoshi; New Sch Social Res, with Adja Yunkers; Atelier 17, Paris, with Stanley Hayter. Work: Whitney Mus Am Art, New York; Brooklyn Mus; Andrew Dickson White Mus, Cornell Univ, Ithaca, NY; New Sch Social Res. Exhib: The Humanist Tradition in Contemp Am Painting, New Sch Social Res, 68; Am Drawings of the Sixties, New Sch Art Ctr, 69; Am Acad Arts & Lett, New York, 69; Douglass Col for Women, New Brunswick, NJ, 76; Morris Mus, Morristown, NJ, 76; Montclair Art Mus, NJ, 76; Images of Horror & Fantasy, Bronx Mus, NY, 77; Women Artists 78, Grad Ctr, City Univ New York, 78; one-woman exhibs, Long Island Univ, Brooklyn, NY, 65, Newport Art Asn, RI, 65, Chelsea Gallery, New York, NY, 69, Benton & Bowles, New York, NY, 70, Graham Gallery, New York, 72 & 77, The Enduring Beast, Brooklyn Mus, NY, 71-72, Discovery Art Gallery, Clifton, NJ, 74 & 78, Montclair Art Mus, NJ, 74, Cathedral Mus at Cathedral of St John the Divine, 77 & Montclair State Col, NJ, 78; plus numerous other group & solo exhibs. Teaching: Adj asst prof, Queensborough Community Col, City Univ New York, 72-; instr, Jersey City State Col, 73-75; instr, Montclair Mus Art Sch, 74- Awards: Fulbright Grant, 51-53; Award, 11th RI Arts Festival, 69; Creative Artists Pub Serv grant, NJ State Coun Arts, 74; Award, Millay Colony for the Arts, Austerlitz, NY, 76; Childe Hassam Purchase Award, Am Acad of Arts & Lett, 77; Award, Ossabaw Island Proj, Ga, 78. Bibliog: Gene Thornton (auth), The critical people (rev & anal), 10/27/68 & 1/26/69; The new grotesques, Time Mag, 6/13/69; Barry Schwartz (auth), The New Humanism, Art in a Time of Change, Praeger. Media: Drawing, Painting, Collage. Publ: Ed & illusr, The Enduring Beast, Doubleday, 72. Dealer: Graham Gallery 1014 Madison Ave New York NY 10021. Mailing Add: 6 Macopin Ave Upper Montclair NJ 07043

BEERY, ARTHUR O
PAINTER
b Marion, Ohio, Mar 4, 30. Work: Butler Inst Am Art, Youngstown, Ohio; Erie Art Ctr, Pa; Lessco Data, New York; J M Katz Collection, Pa. Comn: Murals of Athens, Greece, Monte Carlo, Stromboli, Rock of Gibralter & Charleston, SC for US Navy Minecraft Base, Charleston, 54. Exhib: Pa Acad Fine Arts, Philadelphia, 68; Butler Inst Am Art, 68, 70, 72 & 73; Watercolor USA, Mo, 71 & 75; Tex Art Asn, 72 & 75; Contemp Am Art, Paris, France, 72; plus others. Awards: Butler Inst Am Art Award, 68 & 74; Richard P Stahl Award, Watercolor USA, 71; Columbus Ohio Art Festival Best of Show, 73; plus others. Mem: Mansfield Fine Arts Guild, Ohio; Columbus Art League, Ohio. Style & Technique: Images painted with dots of color over harmonizing colored background; and topological abstracts with Mobius stripe. Media: Oil, Acrylic, Watercolor. Mailing Add: c/o Cernuschi Galleries 5 E 57th St New York NY 10022

BEERY, EUGENE BRIAN
PAINTER
b Racine, Wis, Oct 13, 37. Study: Layton Sch Art, Milwaukee, Wis, 57-61; Univ Wis-Milwaukee, 60-61; Art Students League, 62. Work: Ill Tel & Tel, Chicago; Marine Bank, Milwaukee. Exhib: Recent Figure Painting USA, Mus Mod Art, New York, 61; Wis Painters & Sculptors, War Mem, Milwaukee, 64; Spirit of the Comics, Philadelphia Mus Mod Art, 71; conceptual art exhibs, 557,087, Seattle, Wash & 955,000, Vancouver, BC, 72; Whitney Biennial of Am Art, New York, 75; La Mammelle Art Space, San Francisco, 77; Northwestern Artists Workshop, Portland, Ore, 77. Awards: Cash Award, Max Ernst, 62; William & Noma Copley Found Award for Painters, Chicago, 63. Bibliog: An answers only no questions interview with a famous art world personality, La Mammelle—Art Contemp, spring 77. Style & Technique: Oil and Acrylic on Canvas, Logoscape; two dimensional visual percussion. Publ: Auth, A Nice Painting Book, 77. Mailing Add: 1301 San Rafael Dr Petaluma CA 94952

BEGGS, THOMAS MONTAGUE
FINE ARTS CONSULTANT, PAINTER
b Brooklyn, NY, Apr 22, 99. Study: Pratt Inst; Art Students League; Yale Univ, BFA; Ecole Am Beaux-Arts, Fontainebleu, France; Harvard Univ, Carnegie scholar, 28-29. Work: Portrait of Jasper Newton Field, Redlands Univ. Comn: Club Room Overmantle, Miami Realty Bd, Fla, 26; Guild Hall Overmantle, Claremont Congregational Church, Calif, 28; Mem Court Bench, Pomona Col, 33. Exhib: Los Angeles Co Fair, 27; Ebell Club, Los

Angeles, 37; Washington Watercolor Club, 48. Collections Arranged: Weather in Art, Pomona Col Art Gallery, 46; Pictorial Art of the American Indian, Nat Collection Fine Arts, 49; Art & Magic in Arnhem Land, 50 & Art & Archaeology of Vietnam, 59, Smithsonian Inst. Teaching: Prof art & head dept, Pomona Col, 26-47. Pos: Dir, Nat Collection Fine Arts, Smithsonian Inst, 48-64, spec asst to secy fine arts, 65. Awards: Fed Repub Ger Travel Grant, 54; Gold Medal for Advan Am Art, Am Artists Prof League, 63. Media: Oil, Tempera. Publ: Auth, Artist in residence, Parnassus, 12/40; auth, The golden brush of Kristian Krekovic, Am Mag Art; auth, Harriet Lane Johnston & the National Collection of Fine Arts, Smithsonian Report for 1954, 55. Mailing Add: 6540 Hitt Ave McLean VA 22101

BEHL, MARJORIE
PAINTER
b Pocahontas, Ark. Study: Layton Art Inst, Col William & Mary; Calif Col Arts & Crafts; Univ Calif Workshop; Old Dom Univ; also with George Post & Charles Sibley. Work: Alfred Khouri Collection, Walter Chrysler Mus, Norfolk, Va; Valentine Mus, Richmond, Va; Univ Va Permanent Collection, Charlottesville, Va; Borden Chem Co, Smith-Doughlas Div, Virginia Beach, Va; Pub Sch Purchase Collection, Norfolk, Va. Exhib: One of Three Rotating Show, Va State Mus, Richmond; Soc Western Artists, M H De Young Mem Mus, San Francisco, 64; Tidewater Artists Asn Show & Am Drawing Biennial, Norfolk Mus, Va, 64; one-man show, Norfolk Mus, 66; State of Fla Watercolor Show, Sarasota Art Mus, 72; plus many others. Teaching: Instr art, Norfolk Col Sch, Norfolk High Schs & Jewish Community Ctr, Norfolk, 63-67; lectr, Tidewater Art Asn, Women's Club & others, 60-64. Awards: First Prize Watercolor, Ark State Watercolor Exhib, 57; First Prizes in Watercolor, Va Beach Boardwalk Show, 57-68; First Prize for Watercolor, Tidewater Artists Asn Bi-ann, 65. Mem: Sarasota Art Asn; Tidewater Artists Asn Bi-ann, 65. Mem: Sarasota Art Asn; Tidewater Artists Asn (bd mem, 60-64, chmn Azalea Festival, 57-60); Soc Western Artists. Media: Watercolor, Oil. Mailing Add: Villa 13 6308 Midnight Pass Rd Sarasota FL 33581

BEHL, WOLFGANG
SCULPTOR, EDUCATOR
b Berlin, Ger, Apr 13, 18; US citizen. Study: Acad Fine Art, Berlin; RI Sch Design. Work: Pa Acad Fine Arts, Philadelphia; Addison Gallery Am Art; Conn Gen Ins Co; New Britain Mus Am Art; Cornell Univ. Comn: Welded menorah & eternal light, Temple Beth Sholom, Manchester, Conn, 64; bronze tabernacle & processional cross, Church of the Resurrection, Wallingford, Conn, 66; Reredos, Immanuel Lutheran Church, Attleboro, Mass, 69; woodcarving of monument, Elemer Nagy Millard Auditorium, Univ Hartford, 75; welded sculpture, Town of Bloomfield, Conn, 76; plus others. Exhib: Plastics USA, Soviet Union, 60; Carnegie Inst Int, Pittsburgh, 64; Fogg Art Mus, Harvard Univ, Cambridge, 66; Hemisfair 68, San Antonio, Tex, 68; Retrospective, New Britain Mus, 68. Teaching: Asst prof sculpture & drawing, William & Mary Col, 45-53; prof sculpture, Univ Hartford, 55- Awards: Sculpture Awards, Conn Acad Fine Arts, 61, 63 & 64; Nat Inst Arts & Lett Grant, 63; Ford Found Purchase Award, 64. Bibliog: Eye to Eye (film), WGBH TV, Boston, 71. Mem: Nat Sculpture Ctr (chmn adv bd, 68-); Sculptors Guild (dir, 72). Style & Technique: Figurative, expressionist; wood sculpture is laminated of selected pieces and carved. Media: Wood, Bronze, Stone. Dealer: Genesis Gallery 41 E 57th St New York NY 10022; Bienville Gallery, 539 Bienville New Orleans LA 70130. Mailing Add: Charlemont MA 01339

BEINEKE, DR & MRS J FREDERICK
COLLECTORS
Dr Beineke, b Decatur, Ind, Apr 5, 27. Collection: African and South Pacific art; Japanese woodblock prints; ancient art, ethnographica, old graphic art and modern Far East art. Mailing Add: West St Litchfield CT 06759

BEITZ, LESTER U
PAINTER, ILLUSTRATOR
b Buffalo, NY, May 11, 16. Study: Art Inst Buffalo; and with Charles S Bigelow. Work: In pvt collections only. Comn: Murals, Officer's Club, Royal Air Force Sta, Fairford, Eng & Enlisted Men's Club, Schilling Air Force Base, Salina, Kans, 62; also recent oils, frontier subjects, comn by pvt collectors of Western art. Style & Technique: Portrayal of the American West. Publ: Auth & illusr, A Treasury of Frontier Relics; auth, Overlooked Treasures, Barnes, 75; contribr, articles, illus & features on frontier Americana, In, Real West, Desert, Western Dig, Argosy, Ford Times & var other mag. Mailing Add: 2407 Audubon Pl Austin TX 78741

BEJAR, FELICIANO
SCULPTOR, PAINTER
b Jiquilpan, Mex, July 14, 20. Work: Mus Arte Mod, Mexico City, Mex; Birmingham City Mus, Eng; Herron Mus, Indianapolis, Ind; Mus Arte Mod, Sao Paulo, Brazil; Mus Fine Art, Montreal, PQ. Comn: Series of 8 paintings, Roussel Labs, Mexico City, 67; series of 300 Magiscope sculpture in plastic, J Walter Thompson Co, New York, 71; series of 13 Magiscope sculptures in crystal, Carborundum Co, Niagara Falls, NY, 72 & 74; Magiscope sculpture, Banco Nac de Mexico, Palacio De Iturbide, Mexico City, 72; crystal sculpture, Nac de Cobre, Mexico City, 75; plus others. Exhib: One-man shows, Magiscopes, Bertha Schaefer Gallery, New York, 66, 68, 71 & 74, World of Feliciano Bejar, City Mus, Sheffield, Eng, 66, Mus Arte Mod, Mexico City, 70 & 75, Magiscopes, 1964-1970, Grosvenor Gallery, London, Eng, 70; one-man retrospective, Galerie Valentin, Zurich, Switz, 72. Bibliog: Nelkin, Fernandez, Xirau & De La Maza (auth), Feliciano Bejar 1947-1962, Nat Inst Fine Arts, Mexico City, 62; Ian Hugo (dir), Through the Magiscope (film), 68; Martin Foley (auth), Barry Undazo, Felicano Bejar in the Crystal Forest, Mexico, 75; plus others. Awards: Sculpture Prize, Salon de la Plastica Mexicana, Nat Inst Fine Arts, Mex, 73. Mem: Salon Plastica World Crafts Coun, New York. Media: Crystal, Plastic. Interest: Inventor of special form of optical sculpture using lenses and prisms and other reflective and refractive forms in plastic and crystal, given generic name of Magiscopes. Publ: Illusr, Inscriptions, Ainle Press Mex, 75. Dealer: Martin Foley c/o Antiguo Camino a Acapulco 369 San Angel Mexico 20 DF Mexico. Mailing Add: Apartado Postal 20-029 Mexico 20 DF Mexico

BEKER, GISELA
PAINTER
b Zoppott, EGer; US citizen. Study: Kunstinstitut, Rostock, EGer, 48-50; with Rudolf Kroll (of Bauhaus Sch), Dusseldorf, WGer. Work: Everson Mus, Syracuse, NY; Palm Springs Mus, Calif; Arts & Sci Ctr, Baton Rouge, La; plus others. Exhib: One-woman show, Huntsville Art Mus, 74, Arts & Sci Ctr, Baton Rouge, La, 75 & Wilkes Col, Wilkes Barre, Pa, 75; Mus Mod Art, Paris, France, 74; NY Univ, 76; Chrysler Mus of Norfolk, Va; New Orleans Mus Art, La; Phoenix Art Mus, Ariz; plus others. Awards: First Prize, Nat Soc Painters, NY, 73; Gold Medal, Int Exhib Painters & Sculptors, Paris, 74; Silver Medal (watercolor), Grand Prix Humanitaire de France, Paris, 75. Bibliog: The feminist movement in art, Southwest Art, 7/74; Gisela Beker art Arts & Science Center, Arts Mag, 2/75; Gregory Battcock (auth), Why Art, Dutton, 77. Dealer: Findlay Gallery 984 Madison Ave New York NY 10021. Mailing Add: 530 E 72nd St New York NY 10021

BELFIORE, GERARDO
PAINTER, INSTRUCTOR
b Italy, Jan 15, 14; US citizen. Work: Philadelphia Mus Art; Atwater Kent Mus, Philadelphia Art Alliance; Woodmere Art Gallery; Pa Hist Soc, Philadelphia. Exhib: Pa Acad Fine Arts, 40; Boston Mus Art, 41; Nat Acad Design, 44; Libr of Cong, 44; Philadelphia Mus Art, 73; Nat Exhib of Italian-Am Artists in US, Stone Park, Ill, 77. Teaching: Instr printmaking, Main Line Ctr of the Arts, Philadelphia, 72-73; instr watercolor, Community Arts Ctr Wallingford, Pa, 74- Awards: The Woodmere Prize, Woodmere Art Gallery, 62; Watercolor Prize, Regional Watercolor Exhib, Philadelphia Art Alliance, 66; Gold Medal, Ann Exhib, Da Vinci Art Alliance, 71-73. Mem: Philadelphia Watercolor Club; Woodmere Art Gallery; Da Vinci Art Alliance; Community Arts Ctr of Wallingford; Main Line Ctr of Arts, Haverford, Pa. Style & Technique: Realism to nonobjective; pioneered in Monoscreen, a new print technique based on silk screen process, and stratascape, a three dimensional collage made with plywood, glue impasto and acrylics. Media: Watercolor, Mixed Media, Acrylic. Publ: Illusr, Pennsylvania Cavalcade, 42; contribr, Charette, 63. Mailing Add: 6234 Chelwynde Ave Philadelphia PA 19142

BELING, HELEN
SCULPTOR, INSTRUCTOR
b New York, NY, Jan 1, 14. Study: Nat Acad Design, 30-37, with Paul Manship & Lee Lawrie; Art Students League, 44-45, with William Zorach. Work: Butler Inst Am Art, Youngstown, Ohio; Hirshhorn Mus, Washington, DC; Norfolk Mus Arts & Sci, Va; St Lawrence Univ, Canton, NY; George Jr Repub, Freeville, NY. Comn: Eternal Light (brass), Jewish Community Ctr, White Plains, NY, 57; Menorah (bronze), Temple Israel, Waterbury, Conn, 59; Eternal Light (bronze), Temple B'nai Jacob, Woodbridge, Conn, 61; Candelabra Room (ceramic), Pleasant Valley Home, West Orange, NJ, 62; Exodus (wall relief), Temple Emanu-el, Yonkers, NY, 66. Exhib: Nine one-man shows, Pa Acad Fine Arts, 50-66; Metrop Mus Art Sculpture Exhib, 51; Sculptors Guild Ann, 54-77; St Louis Mus, Mo; Everson Mus, Syracuse, NY; Whitney Mus Am Art, 55; Univ Ill, 57. Teaching: Instr sculpture, Westchester Art Workshop, White Plains, 50-66 & 77-78; instr, NY Univ, 61-62; instr sculpture, Col New Rochelle, 70-71. Awards: Sculpture Award, Sabena Airline Int Competition, 53; Medals of Honor, Nat Asn Women Artists, 58 & 68 & Audubon Artists, 65; finalist, Sculpture Competition, New Orleans, 75. Mem: Nat Asn Women Artists (chmn sculpture jury, 68-70); Sculptors Guild (pres, 72-74); Fine Arts Fedn (vpres, 74-77). Style & Technique: Mainly abstract; some figurative. Media: Reinforced Fiber Glass, Welded Stainless Steel, Bronze. Dealer: Sculpture Ctr 167 E 69th St New York NY 10021. Mailing Add: 287 Weyman Ave New Rochelle NY 10805

BELKIN, ARNOLD
PAINTER, MURALIST
b Calgary, Alta, Dec 9, 30. Study: Vancouver Art Sch, 45-47; Nat Polytech Inst, Mex, 47-50; asst to David Alfaro Siqueiros, 51. Work: Mus Arte Mod, Mexico City; Phoenix Art Mus, Ariz; Betzalel Nat Mus, Jerusalem, Israel; Gen Motors Collection, Austin, Tex; Kresge Int Collection, Detroit, Mich. Comn: Mural, Fed Penitentiary, Mexico City, 61; Gov Sch Handicapped Children, Mex, 63; Jewish Community Cult Ctr, Mex, 67; portable mural, Mex Pavillion, Expo' 67, Montreal; mural, Humanities Bldg, Lock Haven State Col, 71. Exhib: Guggenheim Int Award Exhib, New York, 64; Biennale des Jeunes, Paris, 65; Mexico, The Emergent Generation, Univ Tex Art Mus, Austin, 67; 2nd Latin Am Graphics Biennale, San Juan, PR, 72; 3rd Biennale, Medellin, Colombia, 72. Teaching: Asst prof mural techniques, Univ of the Americas, Mex, 54-60; vis instr painting, Pratt Inst, 67-71. Awards: Theatre Design Award, Mex Theater Critics, 61; Nat Purchase Prize for painting, Salon de la Plastica Mex, 63; Purchase Prize, 2nd Graphics Biennale, San Juan, 72. Bibliog: Henry Seldis (auth), article in Los Angeles Times, 67; Raquel Tibol (auth), Secuencia y consecuencia de A Belkin, Excelsior, Diorama de la Cult, 71. Mem: Salon de la Plastica Mex, Salon de Los Independientes, Mex, Mus Latino Am, New York (co-organizer, 71). Media: Acrylic. Publ: Co-auth, Nueva Presencia—a humanist manifesto, 61. Dealer: Richard Lerner 789 Madison Ave New York NY 10021. Mailing Add: 135 Hudson St New York NY 10013

BELL, ALISTAIR MACREADY
PRINTMAKER, PAINTER
b Darlington, Eng, Oct 21, 13; Can citizen. Work: Nat Gallery Can, Ottawa, Ont; Mus Mod Art, New York; Victoria & Albert Mus, London, Eng; Mus Ugo Carpi, Italy. Vancouver Art Gallery, BC. Exhib: 1st Int Biennial Graphics, Tokyo & Osaka, Japan, 57; 3rd Int Exhib Graphics, Lubljana, Yugoslavia, 59; 6th Bianco e Nero, Lugano, Switz, 60; Recent Prints, Canada, Mus Mod Art, 67; 1st Int Triennial of Contemp Xylography, Carpi, 69; plus others. Awards: Can Coun Sr Arts Fel, 59, Sr Arts Award, 67. Mem: Royal Can Acad Art; Can Soc Graphic Art; Soc Can Painter-Etchers & Engravers. Media: Woodcut, Watercolor. Dealer: Bau-Xi Gallery 3003 Granville St Vancouver BC Can. Mailing Add: 2566 Marine Dr West Vancouver BC V7V 1L4 Can

BELL, CHARLES S
PAINTER
b Tulsa, Okla, Feb 2, 35. Comn: Spieser Collection, 74. Exhib: Tokyo Biennial, 74; New Realism, Wadsworth Atheneum, 74; Butler Inst Am Art, 75; Rothman's Int Realism Exhib, Can, 76-77; Jacksonville Mus, Fla, 77; Sewall Gallery, Rice Univ, Houston, 77; Tulane Univ, La, 78. Bibliog: Articles in Illus London News, 1/75, Chicago Tribune, 76 & Jacksonville J, 2/77. Style & Technique: Photo realism. Media: Oil on Canvas. Mailing Add: c/o Louis K Meisel 141 Prince St New York NY 10012

BELL, COCA (MARY CATLETT BELL)
PAINTER
b Weleetka, Okla, Sept 26, 24. Study: Univ Okla, BA(lang); painting with Milford Zornes, Edith & Richard Goetz & Charles Reid; drawing with Don Coen & Robert Kaupelis. Comn: Oil painting, Gov Mansion, Oklahoma City, 70. Exhib: 14th Ann Eight State Exhib, Okla Art Ctr, 72; 34th Okla Artists Ann, Philbrook Art Ctr, Tulsa, 74; 61st Ann Exhib, Allied Artists of Am, New York, 74; 150th Ann Exhib, Nat Acad Design, New York, 75; Watercolor USA, Springfield Art Mus, Mo, 75; 18th Ann Eight State Exhib, 76, four-man show, 77 & two-man show, 78, Okla Art Ctr, Oklahoma City; Distinguished Artists of Okla Exhib, Midwestern Gov's Conf, 77. Awards: Hon mention, 2nd Ann, Okla Art Guild, 73; Fourth Award, 10th Ann Southwestern Watercolor Soc Regional Exhib, 73; Second Award Watercolor 74, Okla Watercolor Asn, 74. Mem: Philbrook Art Ctr; Okla Art Ctr; Okla Watercolor Asn; Okla Art Guild. Style & Technique: Impressionistic. Media: Watercolor, Oil. Mailing Add: 2 Colony Lane Oklahoma City OK 73116

BELL, EVELYN BEHNAN
PRINTMAKER, PHOTOGRAPHER
b Detroit, Mich, Mar 30, 38. Study: Wayne State Univ, BFA, 60; Univ Mich, MFA, 62. Work: Detroit Inst Art; Dayton Art Inst, Ohio; Nelson Gallery Art, Kansas City, Mo; Silvermine Guild, New Canaan, Conn; Okla Art Ctr; plus others. Exhib: 164th Ann Exhib, Pa Acad Fine

Arts, 69; 23rd Nat Exhib Prints, Smithsonian Inst, 73; 1974/75 Michigan Focus Exhibition; 15th Nat Bradley Print Show, Peoria, Ill, 75; Contemporary American Graphics, Old Bergen Art Guild Traveling Exhibs, ann; plus numerous others. Teaching: Teacher metalcraft, drawing & photog, Bryan Community Ctr, Yellow Springs, Ohio, 74-77. Awards: Purchase Awards, Ann Exhib of Prints & Drawings, Okla Art Ctr, 69 & All Ohio Graphics & Photog Biennial, 75; Cash Merit Award, 18th Ann Print & Drawing Exhib, Okla Art Ctr, Oklahoma City, 76. Mem: Soc Am Graphic Artists. Style & Technique: Recent work combines printmaking and photography techniques. Media: Woodcut, intaglio & natural and urban environment. Media: Woodcut. Plastic Engraving; Black & non-silver photography. Dealer: The Little Gallery Springfield Art Asn 107 Cliff Park Rd Springfield OH 45504. Mailing Add: PO Box 271 Yellow Springs OH 45387

BELL, JAMES M
ART ADMINISTRATOR
Study: NTex State Univ, BA; Stephen F Austin Univ, MA. Pos: All level art supvr, Pub Sch Syst, Texarkana, Ark, 66-68; asst educ cur, Wichita Art Mus, Kans, 68-70; dir, Abilene Fine Arts Mus, Tex, 70-73; dir, Tampa Bay Art Ctr, 73- Mailing Add: Tampa Bay Art Ctr 320 N Blvd Tampa FL 33606

BELL, LARRY STUART
SCULPTOR
b Chicago, Ill, Dec 6, 39. Study: Chouinard Art Inst, Los Angeles, 57-59, with Robert Irwin, Richards Ruben, Robert Chuey & Emerson Woelfer. Work: Nat Collection Fine Arts; Mus Mod Art, New York; Whitney Mus Am Art, New York; Tate Gallery, London, Eng; Gallery New S Wales, Australia. Exhib: Southern Calif Painting & Sculpture Ann, Los Angeles Co Mus Art, Los Angeles, 59; Mus Mod Art, New York, 65; 8th Bienal de Sao Paolo, Mus de Arte Mod, Sao Paolo, Brazil, 65; Jewish Mus, New York, 66; Contemp Am Sculpture & Prints Ann Exhib, Whitney Mus Am Art, 66; Guggenheim Mus, New York, 67; one-man shows, Stedelijk Mus, Amsterdam, Holland, 67, Pasadena Art Mus, Calif, 72, Oakland Mus, Calif, 73, Ft Worth Art Mus, Tex, 75, Santa Barbara Mus Art, Calif, 76 & Art Mus STex, 76; Los Angeles 6, Vancouver Art Gallery, BC, 68; Walker Art Ctr, Minneapolis, 68; Documenta 64, Kassel, WGer, 68; Kompas 4—WCoast USA, Stedelijk Van Abbe-Mus, Eindhoven, The Netherlands, 69; three-man show, Tate Gallery, London, 70; 11 Los Angeles Artists, Hayward Gallery, London, 71; USA WCoast, Kunstverein, Hamburg, WGer, 72; Detroit Inst Arts, Mich, 73; Sculpture: Am Directions 1945-1975, Nat Collection Fine Arts, Smithsonian Inst, Washington, DC, 75; Painting & Sculpture in Calif: The Mod Era, San Francisco Mus Mod Art, 76 & Smithsonian Inst, 77. Teaching: Instr sculpture, Univ SFla, Tampa, Univ Calif, Berkeley & Univ Calif, Irvine, 70-73. Awards: Copley Found, 62; Guggenheim Mus Fel, 70; Nat Endowment for the Arts Grant, 75. Bibliog: Barbara Rose (auth), Los Angeles, The Second City, Art in Am, 1-2/66 & American Art Since 1900, Thames & Hudson, London, 67; Peter Plagens (auth), Larry Bell Reassessed, Artforum, 10/72; Henry J Seldis (auth), article in Los Angeles Times, 10/21/73. Style & Technique: Light transmission characteristics through glass panes. Media: Light. Mailing Add: PO Box 1778 Taos NM 87571

BELL, PETER ALAN
PAINTER, ART CRITIC
b Grantham, UK, Apr 21, 18. Study: Univ Cape Town; Rhodes Univ, SAfrica, BA(fine art) & UED, 52. Work: Confederation Art Ctr, Charlottetown, P E I; Dalhousie Univ Art Gallery, Halifax, NS; Erindale Col, Univ Toronto, Ont; Univ NB, Fredericton; Nat Gallery SAfrica, Cape Town. Comn: Banner, Confederation Ctr, Charlottetown; mural, Post Off, Truro, NS, 77; Opus Series, Mem Univ, Nfld. Exhib: Van Riebeck Festival, Cape Town, 53; Quinquennial Exhib SAfrican Art, 70; Atlantic Province Art Circuit Biennial, 70-71; Eastern Province Art Exhib, Port Elizabeth, SAfrica; var one-man shows, SAfrica & Can. Collections Arranged: Centennial Sculpture Proj, St John's, Nfld, 67; Graphics SAfrica, Can tour, 67-68; Christopher Pratt, Retrospective, Can tour, 70-71; Greetings from the Artist, 70- Teaching: Head, Ndaleni Art Sch, Richmond, SAfrica, 59-63; art specialist, Mem Univ Nfld, 63. Pos: Cur, Mem Univ Art Gallery, 63-72; artist in residence, 72-78, art critic, Eve Telegram, St John's, 73- Mem: Can Soc Graphic Arts; Can Soc Painters in Water Colour; Soc Can Painter-Etchers & Engravers; Can Print Soc. Style & Technique: Hard-edge, romantic, exuberant tropical fantasy. Media: Oil, Acrylic, Watercolor; Serigraphy. Mailing Add: Box 14 Site 79 Marine Dr St John's NF Can

BELL, PHILIP MICHAEL
ART ADMINISTRATOR, ART HISTORIAN
b Toronto, Ont, Dec 31, 42. Study: Univ Toronto, BA & MA(fine art). Collections Arranged: Image of Canada, Public Archives Can, 72, W H Coverdale Collection of Canadiana, 73, Western Odyssey, Drawings by S P Hall, 74 & Quebec and Its Environs, Drawings by J P Cockburn (with catalog), 75. Teaching: Instr Can art hist, Queen's Univ, Kingston, Ont, 75-76. Pos: Cur paintings, drawings & prints, Public Archives Can, Ottawa, Ont, 68-73; dir, Agnes Etherington Art Ctr, Queen's Univ, currently. Awards: Governor-General's Award for Non-Fiction for Painters in a New Land, Can Coun, 74. Res: 19th century Canadian art. Publ: Auth, Image of Canada, 72; auth, Painters in a New Land, 73; ed, Braves and Buffalo, Paintings by A J Miller, 73. Mailing Add: 133 Munro St Toronto ON Can

BELL, R MURRAY
COLLECTOR
Study: Univ Alta; Osgoode Hall Law Sch, Toronto. Collection: Chinese ceramics, with special interest in blue and white Chinese porcelain. Mailing Add: 134 Forest Hill Rd Toronto ON Can

BELLAMY, RICHARD
ART DEALER
Pos: Pres, HEGD Co. Mailing Add: 333 Park Ave S New York NY 10010

BELLE, ANNA (ANNA BELLE BIRCKETT)
PAINTER
b Crescent, Okla. Study: Cent State Univ, Edmond, Okla; also with John Pike, Robert E Wood, Mel Crawford, Merlin Enabnit, John Pellew, Edgar Whitney, Gene Dougherty & Jack Vallee. Exhib: Eight Okla Mus Art Ann; Southwestern Watercolor Soc, Dallas; one-man shows, Roadrunner Gallery, Raton, NMex, 74, Ponca City, Okla, Owens Gallery & Wilson Gallery, Oklahoma City, 74 & 75; A Gallery, Taos, NMex; Seths' Canyon Rd Gallery, Santa Fe, NMex; M Gallery, Tulsa, Okla. Teaching: Instr watercolor, Okla Mus Art, 73-74. Pos: Dir Okla Mus Art, 67-75; judge, Int Show, Lawton, Okla, 72 & El Reno Open Exhib, 73 & 74. Mem: Okla Mus Art (dir, pres, vpres, secy & treas); Southwestern Watercolor Soc (vpres, 69; pres, 70); Okla Watercolor Soc (secy, 74-75), Okla City Art Guild. Style & Technique: Watercolor, oils, representational in style. Dealer: Owners Gallery 5 Santa Fe Plaza Oklahoma City OK 73102. Mailing Add: 417 NW 41st Oklahoma City OK 73118

BELSHE, MIRELLA MONTI
SCULPTOR, ART HISTORIAN
b Tuscany, Italy, July 28, 28; US citizen. Study: Univ Hawaii, MA(Eastern art), 67, MFA, 69. Work: Bronze sculpture, Hawaii State Found Purchase, 69 & plexi-light sculpture, 72; bronze-plexi sculpture, AMFAC Collection, Honolulu, 71. Comn: Bronze sculpture, Waimea Kohala Airport, Hawaii Dept Transportation, 72. Exhib: Hawaii Craftsmen Ann, 66-; Honolulu Artists Ann, 68-; Hawaii Painters & Sculptors League Ann, 70-; Northwestern Regional, Oakland, Calif, 70; one-man show, Contemporary Arts, Honolulu, 71. Teaching: Assoc prof educ & art, Univ Hawaii, 69- Pos: Comnr, Mayor Comn Art & Cult, 71- Awards: First Prize Sculpture, Univ Art Festival, 68; First Prize Over All Categories, Easter Art Festival, 70 & Second Prize Sculpture, 72. Mem: Hawaii Painters & Sculptors League (exhib chmn, 71); Hawaii Craftsmen (vpres & pres, 71-72); Art Educr Asn (vchmn, 70-71, secy, 72). Media: Bronze, Plexiglas, Aluminum. Res: Sculpture of the Nara Period; Japanese primitive art; early Hawaiian art. Mailing Add: Dept of Art Univ Hawaii at Manoa Honolulu HI 96822

BELZ, CARL IRVIN
MUSEUM DIRECTOR
b Camden, NJ, Sept 13, 37. Study: Princeton Univ, BA, 59, MFA, 62, PhD, 63. Teaching: Asst prof mod art, Mills Col, Oakland, Calif, 65-68; asst prof mod art, Brandeis Univ, 68-74, lectr mus studies, 74- Pos: Dir, Mills Col Art Gallery, 65-68; dir, Rose Art Mus, Brandeis Univ, 74- Publ: Auth, The Story of Rock, Oxford, 69; auth, Paul Cezanne, McGraw-Hill, 73; auth, Rohm/Sproat, Mus of Fine Arts, Boston, 74; auth, Painted in Boston, Inst of Contemp Art, Boston, 75; auth, Mitchell Siporin: A Retrospective, Brandeis Univ, 76. Mailing Add: Rose Art Mus Brandeis Univ Waltham MA 02154

BENDA, RICHARD R
PAINTER
b Chicago, Ill, Sept 22, 34. Study: Chicago Acad Fine Arts, Art Inst Chicago. Work: Mus Mod Art, Mexico City, Mex; Columbia Col, Ill; Borg Warner Corp Collection, Chicago; Ill State Mus, Springfield; Ill Bell Tel Collection, Chicago. Comn: 14 Stations of the Cross, oil paintings, St Patrick's Church, Elkhart, Ill, 68; Conference (acrylic & collage painting), Blue Cross Asn, Chicago, 70; St John's Church, Lostant, Ill. Exhib: New Horizons in Painting & Sculpture, North Shore Art League, Winnetka, Ill, 68-75; 20th Ann Exhib Knickerbocker Artists, Nat Arts Club, New York, 70; Bertrand Russell Centenary Exhib, London, Eng; Fr Inst Latin Am Gallery, Mexico City, 71; Arts Club Chicago, 72-76; plus others. Awards: Hon Mention Awards, Ill State Fair, Springfield, 69-71; A I Friedman Award, Painters in Casein Soc, New York, 69; First Prize, Nat Juried Exhib, Slidell, La, 70. Mem: NShore Art League; Audubon Artists Soc, New York; Arts Club Chicago. Style & Technique: Mood, thought or desire as subject matter. Media: Acrylic, Collage. Publ: Contribr, The journal, 12/67, 11/68 & 12/68; contribr, La Rev Mod, Paris, 7/68; contribr, Art Scene Mag, 1/69; contribr, Signature Mag; contribr, Vision Mag, Mexico City, 11/71. Dealer: Verzyl Gallery 377 Ft Salonga Rd Rte 25A Northport NY 11768; Cain Galleries Oak Park IL 60303. Mailing Add: c/o Verzyl Gallery 377 Ft Salonga Rd Rte 25A Northport NY 11768

BENDELL, MARILYN
PAINTER, INSTRUCTOR
b Grand Ledge, Mich, Sept 19, 21. Study: Am Acad Art; and with Arnold E Turtle & Pierre Nuyttens. Work: Principia Col, St Louis; Saginaw Mus, Mich; Hadley Sch for Blind, Winnetka, Ill; Huntington Mus Fine Arts, WVa. Comn: Juggler of Notre Dame, comn by Sen Schuch, Saginaw Mus, 50; portrait of founder Principia Col, comn by William E Morgan, St Louis, 58; portrait of Helen Keller, Hadley Sch for Blind, 58; portrait of Mrs Paul Schulze, comn by Paul Schulze, Chicago, Ill, 60; David & Kim, Huntington Mus Fine Arts, 65. Exhib: Chicago Galleries, Ill, 55; Ill State Fair, Springfield, 58; 16th Ann Mem Exhib, Acad Artists Asn, Springfield, Mass, 64; Famous Florida Artists, Frank Oehlschlaeger Galleries, Sarasota, 64 & 65; Acad Artists Asn Nat Show, Springfield, 72. Teaching: Instr portrait, figure & still life, Longboat Key Art Ctr, Fla, 52-68; instr still life, Oak Park-River Forest Art League, Ill, 57-59; instr portrait, figure & still life, Cortez Art Sch, Fla, 68-74; pvt art classes, 74- Awards: Popular Award for Bus Stop, Ill State Fair, 61; First in Portrait for Jeri, Springfield Mus Fine Arts, 64 & First in Portrait & Figure, Portrait of a Young Woman, 70. Bibliog: Edith Weigle (auth), Wonderful world of art, Chicago Tribune 8/17/58; W C Burnett (auth), Two art shows reviewed, Sarasota Herald Tribune, 64; Charles Benbow (auth), She reflects her colorful oil paintings, St Petersburg Times, 11/13/71. Mem: Brown Co Art Gallery Asn; fel Royal Soc Arts; Am Artists Prof League; Acad Artists Asn, Springfield; Sarasota Art Asn. Style & Technique: Contemporary impressionism. Media: Oil. Dealer: Lester Kierstead Henderson Galleries 712 Hawthorne Monterey CA 93940. Mailing Add: PO Box 5 Longboat Key FL 33548

BENDER, BEVERLY STERL
SCULPTOR, DESIGNER
b Washington, DC, Jan 14, 18. Study: Knox Col, BA; Art Students League; Sculpture Ctr, New York; Mus Natural Hist, New York. Work: James Ford Bell Mus Natural Hist, Minneapolis. Comn: Memorial, Mrs Disco, Mystic Seaport, Conn, 69. Exhib: Nat Sculpture Soc, New York, 65, 70 & 72; Nat Arts Club, New York, 69-77; Smithsonian Inst, Washington, 70 & 71; one-man shows, Grist Mill Gallery, Chester, Vt, 74 & Southern Vt Art Ctr, Manchester, 75; Metrop Mus of Art, New York, 77. Pos: Artist & designer, Johns-Manville, New York, 43-72. Awards: First Prize, Beaux Arts, 64; Gold Medal, Catharine Lorillard Wolfe, 69; Founders Prize, Pen & Brush Club, 75. Mem: Soc Animal Artists (treas, 74-78); Southern Vt Art Ctr; Catharine Lorillard Wolfe Art Club; Knickerbocker Artists; Pen & Brush Club (bd dirs, 65-67, 69 & 70). Style & Technique: Traditional; realistic; animals. Media: Stone, Wood. Mailing Add: RD 3 Pound Ridge NY 10576

BENDER, BILL
PAINTER
b El Segundo, Calif, Jan 5, 20. Work: US Air Force Acad, Colorado Springs, Colo; US Navy, Pensacola, Fla; Pentagon, Washington, DC; Living Desert Asn, Palm Desert, Calif; Visitors Ctr, Death Valley, Calif. Exhib: Death Valley 49'er Art Exhib, 50-78; Catalina Festival of Art, 62-78; Mountain Oyster Contemp Western Art Show, Tucson, Ariz, 72-78; Tex Cowboy Reunion & Art Exhib, Stamford, 74-78; Tex Art Classic, Ft Worth, 77-78. Awards: Artists' Artist Award & First Place Award, Chriswood Gallery 70 & 20th Ann Death Valley Exhib, 70; Best of Show, 19th Ann Catalina Festival Art, 77; Second Place, 27th Ann Death Valley Exhib, 77. Bibliog: Ed Ainsworth (auth), Painters of the desert, Desert Mag, 60; Art & artists, Desert Art Ctr, 65; Ed Ainsworth (auth), The Cowboy in Art, World Publ, 69. Mem: Am Indian & Cowboy Artists (vpres); Life mem & fel, Am Inst Fine Arts; Cowboy Hall Fame; hon life mem, Mountain Oyster Club, Tucson; hon tailhook airdale, USS Lexington; Death Valley 49ers Inc (dir). Style & Technique: Portrayal of the West, playing lights against darks. Media: Oil, Watercolor. Publ: Illusr, Christmas cards, stationery & calendars, Leanin' Tree Publ, 60-75; illusr, Beakoning Desert, Prentice-Hall, 62; auth & illusr, My Friend John, Los Angeles Westerners, 70; auth & illusr, Day I Clumb Down from the Horse, Brand Bk 3, San Diego Westerners, 73. Mailing Add: Star Rte Box 154 Oro Grande CA 92368

BENDIG, WILLIAM CHARLES
PAINTER, PUBLISHER
b Corry, Pa, Dec 1, 27. Study: Trinity Col; Chelsea Sch Art, Univ London, with Ceri Richards; pvt study in Greece & Italy. Work: Trinity Col, Hartford, Conn. Exhib: Essex Art Asn, 56-61; New York City Ctr, 57; Springfield Art League, 57; Mystic Art Asn, 57-58 & 61; Riverside Mus, New York, 60. Teaching: Instr painting, drawing & art hist, Brunswick Sch, Greenwich, Conn & Cheshire Acad, Conn; lectr art hist, mediaeval art & archit, Trinity Col, 65. Pos: Juror of exhibs, Silvermine Guild, Chautauqua Art Ctr & Va Beach Regional; publ, Art Gallery, 57- Mem: Essex Art Asn (vpres, 59-61); Mediaeval Acad Am. Mailing Add: Hollycroft Ivoryton CT 06442

BENEDICT, NAN M
PAINTER, EDUCATOR
b Lynchburg, Va, July 27, 37. Study: Pratt Inst, BFA, 59, MFA, 61. Comn: Mural, New York City Pub Libr Syst, 69. Exhib: Pratt Inst Faculty Exhibs, 61, 62, 68 & 71; Detroit Art Inst, 63; Brooklyn Mus, 63 & 72; Manhattan Ctr, 71; one-woman show, Pacem in Terris, New York, 75; Lotus Gallery, 76; O'Henry Gallery, 76; Manufacturers Hanover, 78. Teaching: From instr to prof art, Pratt Inst, 61-, actg dir grad progs, 70-71, chmn grad art, 71- Mem: Am Asn Univ Prof. Style & Technique: Realistic imagery in oil paintings and mixed printmaking techniques. Mailing Add: 183 Steuben St Brooklyn NY 11205

BENEDIKT, MICHAEL
WRITER, ART CRITIC
b New York, NY, May 26, 35. Study: NY Univ, BA; Columbia Univ, MA. Teaching: Vis prof writing, Sarah Lawrence Col, Bronxville, NY, 69-74; assoc prof writing, Hampshire Col, Amherst, Mass, 73-75; vis prof writing, Vasser Col, 76-77 & Boston Univ, 77-78. Pos: New York corresp, Art Inst, Zurich, Switz, 65-67; ed assoc, Art News, New York, 63-72. Res: Surrealist poetry-art relationships; late 19th century French painting, particularly impressionists and Nabis. Publ: Auth, The continuities of Pierre Bonnard, 64 & The visionary French, 68, Art News; contribr, New York letter, Minimal Art (anthology), 68; auth, Notes on Yoko Ono, Art & Artists, 72; ed, The Poetry of Surrealism, Little, 75; also translr of art-related texts. Mailing Add: 59 Bay State Rd Boston MA 02215

BENGE, DAVID PHILIP
CERAMIST, DESIGNER
b Santa Monica, Calif, Sept 6, 36. Study: Univ Calif Los Angeles, study with Laura Andreson, 66-68; Univ of Southern Calif, MFA, study with Carlton Ball & Susan Peterson, 68. Exhib: 25th Ceramic Nat, Everson Mus of Art, Syracuse, NY, 68; Southwest, 71 & NMex, 72, Crafts Biennial, Mus of Int Folk Art, Santa Fe, NMex; Biennial Exhib, Mus of Albuquerque, NMex, 73; Ceramics-NMex, 74, Univ of Albuquerque, 74; Smithsonian Inst, Washington, DC, 75; Contemp Arts of the Southwest, Univ of NDak, Grand Forks, 76; Crafts 7 Biennial, Mus of Albuquerque, 77. Awards: Architects Prize, 25th Ceramic Nat, Syracuse Soc of Architects, 68; Purchase Prize, Mus of Int Folk Art, Santa Fe Arts Guild, 70 & Crafts & Biennial, Albuquerque Designer Craftsmen, 77. Style & Technique: Fine art porcelain and stoneware functional pottery, striving for a union of beauty and function, with excellent design and high quality, presently moving toward architectural tile and ceramic assemblage. Dealer: Hills Gallery of Contemp Art 110 W San Francisco St Santa Fe NM 87501. Mailing Add: Rte 3 Box 108A Santa Fe NM 87501

BENGLIS, LYNDA
SCULPTOR, PAINTER
b Lake Charles, La, Oct 25, 41. Study: Yale Norfolk summer fel, 63; Newcomb Col, Tulane Univ, with Ida Kohlmeyer, Pat Trivigno, Zolton Buki & Halrold Carney, BFA, 64; Brooklyn Mus Art Sch, Max Beckman scholar, 65, with Rubin Tam. Work: Detroit Inst Arts, Mich; Ft Worth Art Ctr, Tex; Lannan Found, Palm Springs, Fla; Walker Art Ctr, Minneapolis, Minn; Milwaukee Art Ctr, Wis. Comn: Latex rubber corner piece, Univ RI, Kingston, 69; Rouge, polyurethane foam corner piece, Vera List, Byram, Conn, 70; Adhesive Products, pigmented polyurethane foam, Walker Mus, Minneapolis, 71; Totem, pigmented polyurethane foam, Hayden Gallery, Mass Inst Technol, Boston, 71. Exhib: One-woman shows, Paula Cooper Gallery, New York, 70, 71, 74 & 75, Hansen-Fuller Gallery, San Francisco, 72, 73, 74 & 77, Tex Gallery, 74 & 75 & Margo Leavin Gallery, Los Angeles, 77. Teaching: Asst prof painting & sculpture, Univ Rochester, 70-72; asst prof sculpture, Hunter Col, 72- Bibliog: Ann McIntoche (auth), Lynda Benglis paints with foam (video tape), Mass Inst Technol, 71-72; Klaus Kertess (auth), On Lynda Benglis, Studio Arts, 5-6/72; Robert Pincus-Witten (auth), The frozen gesture, Artforum, 11/74; Lucy Lippard (auth), You can go home again, five from Louisiana, Art in Am, 7-8/77. Dealer: Paula Cooper Gallery 96-100 Prince St New York NY 10012. Mailing Add: 222 Bowery St New York NY 10012

BENGSTON, BILLY AL
PAINTER
b Dodge City, Kans, June 7, 34. Work: Mus Mod Art, New York; Art Inst Chicago; Los Angeles Co Mus Art; Whitney Mus Am Art, New York; Ft Worth Art Ctr Mus, Tex; Guggenheim Mus, New York. Exhib: Chicago Biennial Painting Exhib, Art Inst Chicago, 63 & 72; 8th Biennial, Sao Paulo, Brazil, also shown Smithsonian Inst, 65; Whitney Ann Painting Exhib, Whitney Mus Am Art, 67 & 69; retrospective, Los Angeles Co Mus Art, 68; Kompas IV, Stekelijk van Abbemuseum, Eindhoven, Holland, 69. Pos: Founder, Artist Studio, Venice, Calif, 60. Awards: Nat Found Arts Grant, 67; Tamarind Fel, Tamarind Lithography Workshop through Ford Found, 68; Guggenheim Found Fel, 75. Bibliog: Fidel Danieli (auth), Billy Al Bengston's Dentos, 5/67 & Peter Plagens (auth), Billy Al Bengston's new paintings, 3/75, Artforum. Media: Mixed Media. Publ: Co-auth, Business cards, Heavy Indust Publ, 68; auth, Late fifties at the Ferus, Artforum, 1/69; auth, Los Angeles artists' studios, Art in Am 11-12/70. Mailing Add: Artist Studio 110 Mildred Ave Venice CA 90291

BENGTZ, TURE
MUSEUM DIRECTOR, PAINTER
Study: In Finnish Schs & Sch Mus Fine Arts, Boston, Mass, dipl; Slade Sch, London, Eng; Fontainebleau, Paris, France; Paige traveling scholar to Europe, summers 33-37; Tiffany Found fels, 40-41. Work: Mus Fine Arts, Boston; Addison Gallery, Andover, Mass; Libr Cong, Washington, DC; Seattle Art Mus, Wash; Cincinnati Art Mus, Ohio; plus many other pub & pvt collections. Comn: Design of stained glass window, 12th century church, Finland, 68. Exhib: Nat Acad Design, New York; Brooklyn Mus, New York; Chicago Art Inst; Palace of Legion of Honor, San Francisco; Am Fedn Arts Watercolor Traveling Show, Australia, India & Japan; plus many other one-man shows, group exhibs & traveling exhibs. Teaching: Instr drawing & painting, Sch Mus Fine Arts, Boston, 34-38, instr artistic anat, 38-39, instr graphic arts, 39-41, head drawing & graphic arts dept, 41-69; demonstr & lectr drawing & anat, WGBH-TV, 57-60; lectrs & demonstrations drawing, composition, anat, painting & printmaking, US & abroad. Pos: Tech illusr radar equip, Raytheon Corp, Waltham, Mass, 41-45; mus dir, Art Complex, Inc, Duxbury, Mass, 69-76. Awards: Palmer Mem Prize, Nat Acad Design, 44; Boston Mus Prize, Boston Printmakers, 65, Boston Printmakers Prize & Gendrot Prize, 69; plus many others. Media: Oil, Watercolor. Publ: Illusr, White Squaw, Heath. Mailing Add: Art Complex Inc PO Box 1411 Duxbury MA 02332

BENHAM, ROBERT CHARLES
PAINTER
b Gloucester, Mass, June 29, 13. Study: Bucksport Acad, Maine; also with Paul Strisik. Exhib: Allied Artist, Nat Acad, New York; Salmagundi Club, New York; Rockport Art Asn; Springfield Mus Fine Arts; Butler Mus, Ohio. Teaching: Instr art, Gloucester High Sch. Awards: Curtis News Award, 69; Aldro Hibbard Award, 74; Harriet Preston Award, 74. Bibliog: Herb Rugoff (auth), Some notions on oceans, 69 & Painting fog, 75, Palette Talk. Mem: Rockport Art Asn; North Shore Art Asn; Allied Artist of Am; Acad Artists, Springfield; Salmagundi Club, New York. Style & Technique: Realistic with impressionistic approach. Media: Oil. Mailing Add: 4 Harbor Rd Bass Rocks Gloucester MA 01930

BENJAMIN, KARL STANLEY
PAINTER, INSTRUCTOR
b Chicago, Ill, Dec 29, 25. Study: Northwestern Univ; Univ Redlands, BA, 49; Claremont Grad Sch, MA, 60. Work: Whitney Mus Am Art, New York; Los Angeles Co Mus Art; San Francisco Mus Art; Wadsworth Atheneum, Hartford, Conn; Nat Collection Fine Arts, Smithsonian Inst, Washington, DC. Exhib: Four Abstract Classicists (West Coast Hard-Edge), Los Angeles Co Mus & San Francisco Mus Art, also shown Inst Contemp Art, London, Eng, 59; Purist Painting, Am Fedn Arts Traveling Exhib, shown at Andrew Dickson White Mus, NY, Walker Art Ctr, Minneapolis, Minn, Speed Mus, Louisville, Ky & others, 60; Geometric Abstraction in America, Whitney Mus Am Art, 62; The Responsive Eye, Mus Mod Art, New York, 65; 30th & 35th Ann Exhib Am Painting, Corcoran Gallery, Washington, DC, 67 & 77; Pac Cities Exhib, Auckland, New Zealand, 71; Painting & Sculpture in Calif: The Mod Era, San Francisco Mus of Mod Art & Nat Collection of Fine Arts, Smithsonian Inst, Washington, DC, 76-77; Los Angeles Hard Edge: The Fifties & the Seventies, Los Angeles Co Mus of Art, Los Angeles, 77. Style & Technique: Hard edge. Media: Oil on canvas. Dealer: Tortue Gallery 2917 Santa Monica Blvd Santa Monica CA 90403. Mailing Add: 675 W Eighth St Claremont CA 91711

BENN, BEN
PAINTER
b Russia, Dec 27, 84. Study: Nat Acad Design, 04-08. Work: Metrop Mus Art & Whitney Mus Am Art, New York; Hirshhorn Mus & Sculpture Garden, Washington, DC; Baltimore Mus Art, Md; Kroller-Mueller Found, The Hague, Holand; Univ Minn, Minneapolis; Sheldon Mem Art Gallery, Univ Nebr, Lincoln. Exhib: The Forum Exhibition of Modern American Painters, Andersen Galleries, New York, 16; Abstract Painting in America, Whitney Mus Am Art, New York, 35; American Painting Today, Metrop Mus Art, New York, 50; The Decade of the Armory Show: New Directions in American Art 1910-1920, Friends of Whitney Mus Am Art Travelling Exhib, 63-64; Exhibition of Contemporary Artists Eligible for Awards, Am Acad Arts & Lett, New York, 71. Awards: J Henry Schiedt Award, Pa Acad Fine Arts 147th Ann Exhib, 52; Carol H Beck Gold Medal, Pa Acad Fine Arts, 66; Peabody Waite Award, Am Acad Arts & Lett, 71. Bibliog: Leslie Katz (auth), Ben Benn, Arts Yearbook III, 59; Dorothy Adlow (auth), Ben Benn Exhibition: Part I, Christian Sci Monitor, 2/18/63; Sidney Geist (auth), Letters to the Editors, Arts Mag, 5-6/63. Style & Technique: Lyrical expressionist; subjects are still life, landscapes and the figure. Dealer: Babcock Galleries 805 Madison Ave New York NY 10021. Mailing Add: Apt 4A 110 W 96th St New York NY 10025

BENNETT, DON BEMCO
PAINTER, PRINTMAKER
b McGlaughlin, SDak, Jan 8, 16. Study: Univ Wash; Edison Voc Sch, Seattle; also with the late Eliot O'Hara. Work: Cheney-Cowles Fine Arts Mus, Spokane, Wash; Ford Motor Co Collection of Am Art, Dearborn, Mich. Exhib: 4th Ann Art Exhib, Merchant Seamen of United Nations, Corcoran Gallery, Washington, DC, 46; US Info Agency Exhib Contemp Am Artists, Worldwide traveling exhib, 60; Craftsman Competition, Pac Northwest Painters, Fry Mus, Seattle, 68; 15th Ann Exhib, Acad Artists Asn, Mus Fine Arts, Springfield, Mass, 64; Am Natural Hist Art Show, James Ford Bell Mus, Univ Minn, Minneapolis, 71. Awards: First Place in graphics, Acad Artists Asn, 64; Top Twenty Award, Craftsman Press, Seattle, 68; Second Place Award, Representational Watercolor, 28th Ann Exhib Idaho Artists Boise Art Asn. Mem: Graphics Soc. Style & Technique: Representational landscape, wildlife and wildflower subjects in watercolor, oil, acrylic, color lithographs and monotype. Media: Watercolor (transparent), Oil, Acrylic, Lithography. Publ: Auth & illusr, Ford Times Mag, 58- Mailing Add: PO Box 105 Sun Valley ID 83353

BENNETT, HARRIET
PAINTER
b New York, NY. Study: Art Students League, with Robert Brackman & Byron Browne; Brooklyn Mus, with Minna Citron; New Sch Social Res; Pratt Graphic Art Ctr; YWCA Craft Ctr. Work: Five paintings, Inst High Fidelity, New York; also incl in many pvt collections. Exhib: One-man shows, Marino Gallery, New York, 58, Condon Riley Gallery, New York, 59, Cichi Gallery, Rome, Italy, 62, Galerie de l'Univ, Paris, France, 62 & Woodstock Gallery, London, Eng, 65. Awards: Falmouth Artists Guild Award, 62; Int Women's Slide Exhib Award, 75-76. Bibliog: Mario Federici (auth), Harriet Bennett's paintings, Brochure, Rome, 1/62; Enrico Centardi (auth), Harriet Bennett, Voce Del Sud, Rome, 2/3/62; Raymond Charmet (auth), Fusion in light, Arts, Lettres, Spectacles du, Paris, 9/6/62. Mem: Artist's Equity Asn of New York, Inc; Women's Interart Ctr, New York. Media: Oil. Mailing Add: PO Box 3738 Grand Cent Sta New York NY 10017

BENNETT, JAMIE
JEWELER, INSTRUCTOR
b Philadelphia, Pa, Oct 6, 48. Study: Univ Ga, BBA & BFA; State Univ NY New Paltz, MFA. Work: Univ Ga. Exhib: Goldsmith 74, Renwick Gallery, Smithsonian Inst & Minn Mus Art, 74; Baroque 74, Mus Contemp Crafts, New York, 74; Precious Metals, Lowe Art Mus, Miami, Fla, 75; L'Art de Email, Limoges, France, 75; Jewelers USA, Calif State Univ, Fullerton, 76; Am Enamelists, Elements Gallery, Greenwich, Conn, 76; Metalsmith, Phoenix Art Mus, Ariz, 77; Schumk-Tendenzen, Schumk Mus, Pforzheim, Ger, 77; Nat Metal Invitational, Humboldt State Univ, Arcata, Calif, 77. Collections Arranged: Six at Univ Tex, Arlington, group exhib & symp, 77; Enamelists, Established & Emerging, Chastain Arts Ctr, 77. Teaching: Instr metal, Bradley Univ, Peoria, Ill, 74-76; asst prof metal & drawing, Memphis Acad Art, Tenn, 76- Pos: Artist-in-residence, Kohler Art Ctr, Sheboygan, Wis, 74; vis artist, Penland Sch Crafts, 74, 76 & 77, Fla Int Univ, 77 & Colo Mountain Col, 77. Awards: Nat Endowment for the Arts, Craftsmen's fel, 75; First Place, Nat Ring Competition, Univ Ga, 77. Bibliog: Sandy Ballatore (auth), Jewelers USA, 3/76 & Enamelists, 11/76, Art News; Lisa Hammel (auth), Enameling, New York Times, 12/76. Mem: Soc NAm Goldsmiths. Style & Technique: Fabricated metal and cloisonne enamel; wall relief and wearables. Media:

Precious metals; enamels. Publ: Contribr, Jewelry Making, Prentice Hall, 74; contribr, The Box Book & The Mirror Book, Crown, 76. Mailing Add: 1995 Central Memphis TN 38104

BENNETT, RAINEY
PAINTER
b Marion, Ind, July 26, 07. Study: Univ Chicago, PhB, 30; Art Inst Chicago; Am Acad Art; Art Students League; George Grosz-Maurice Stern Sch. Work: Metrop Mus Art, New York; Cranbrook Mus; Art Inst Chicago & many pvt collections. Comn: Mural, Peoples Gas Co, Century Progress, Chicago, 33; mural, Post Off, Dearborn, Mich, 37, Rushville, Ill, 38 & Naperville, Ill, 41; 13 panel mural, Neil House, Columbus, Ohio, 39; watercolors in Venezuela for Standard Oil Co, comn by Nelson Rockefeller, Brazil, Arg, Bolivia, Peru & Ecuador. Exhib: Downtown Gallery, New York; Art Inst Chicago; Cleveland Mus; Toledo Mus; Whitney Mus; Mus du que de Paume, Paris. Pos: Free-lance writer, 31-33; supvr, Fed Art Proj, Chicago, 35-38. Mailing Add: 5761 Dorchester Ave Chicago IL 60637

BENNEY, ROBERT
PAINTER, ILLUSTRATOR
b New York, NY. Study: Cooper Union; Nat Acad Design; Grand Cent Art Sch; Art Students League; also with Harry Wickey, Frank A Nankivell, Harry Sternberg & Harvey Dunn. Work: Corcoran Gallery Art, Washington, DC; USN, USA, USAF & USMC Art Collections, Washington, DC; de Young Mus Art, San Francisco; Mariners Mus Art, Newport News, Va; Chrysler Collection, Detroit Mus, Mich; plus others. Comn: Paintings, Am Sugar Refining Co, New York, 52-55; paintings of hist events, Reader's Digest, 64-; Vietnam combat art, USMC, 68-70; plus others. Exhib: Nat Gallery Art, Washington, DC; Metrop Mus Art, New York; de Young Mus; Brooklyn Mus; Corcoran Gallery Art; Fine Arts Gallery, San Diego; Portland Art Mus, Ore; Art Asn Montreal, Que; Norfolk Mus Arts & Sci; Dallas Mus Fine Arts, Tex; La Jolla Art Ctr, Calif; plus others. Teaching: Instr painting, drawing & compos, Sch Visual Arts; instr illus, Pratt Inst, 49-52; assoc prof fine & com art, Dutchess Co Col, 64-73. Awards: First Award, Philadelphia Mus Art, Pa; Gold Medal, Chicago Art Dirs Club; Cert Commendation Fine Arts, USN, 74. Mem: Soc Illusr; Artists Equity Asn; life mem Art Students League; Artists & Writers Asn; Appraisers Asn Am. Style & Technique: Realism. Media: Oil, Acrylic, Watercolor; Etching, Aquatint. Publ: Illusr, Reader's Digest, True, Argosy & many others; contribr, Life's Picture History of World War II, Our Flying Navy—Men Without Guns, Life of Joshua & others. Mailing Add: 50 W 96th St New York NY 10025

BENNO, BENJAMIN G
PAINTER, SCULPTOR
b London, Eng, June 2, 01; US citizen. Study: Mod Sch, New York, 12-16, with Robert Henri & George Bellows; Sch Archit & Beaux Arts New York, 14-17, with Solon Borglum, John Gutzon de la Mothe Borglum & others; Guggenheim fel, Europe, 32-33. Work: Fogg Mus Art, Cambridge, Mass; Brooklyn Mus Art, NY; Baltimore Mus Art, Md; San Francisco Mus Art, Calif; also in many pvt collections in US & Europe. Exhib: Pastels from the Years 1930-1959, Collector's Gallery, New York, 59; Poetic Image I, Paintings with Group, Amel Gallery, New York, 61; Drawings from the Years 1926-1961; Greer Gallery, New York, 62; Poetic Image II, Paintings & Drawings with Group, Amel Gallery, 62; retrospective, Paintings & Drawings from the Years 1933-1961, Mont State Univ, Missoula, 64; plus many others. Teaching: Instr drawing & painting, Brooklyn Children's Mus, 41-42; pvt classes in drawing & painting, 48-55; instr advan painting, Mont State Univ, summer 64. Bibliog: Gertrude Stein (auth), Everybody's autobiography, William Heineman, Ltd, London & Toronto, 37; Henry Miller (auth), Chez Benno, London Bull, 6/38; Waldemar George (auth), Le salon de surindependents, Arts & Metiers Graphique, 1/1/39; incl in, Letters of Alice B Toklas, edited by Edward Burns, 73. Mem: Nat Soc Lit & Arts. Media: Drawing, Painting, Sculpture. Mailing Add: Kheel Tower Apt 2D 315 Seventh Ave New York NY 10001

BENOIT, JEAN
SCULPTOR, CONCEPTUAL ARTIST
b Que, Can, Aug 27, 22. Study: Ecole des Beaux-Arts, Quebec, 38-42; self-taught as artist; influenced by life and writings of Alfred Jarry, Jacques Rigaud & Jacques Vache; Musee de i'Homme, Paris, Ethnography, 51-54. Exhib: Exposition Int du Surrealisme, Galerie Daniel Cordier, Paris, 59; Surrealist Intrusion in the Enchanters Domain, D'Arcy Galleries, New York, 60; Exposition Surrealiste, Galleria Schwarz, Milan, 61; Xle Exposition In du Surrealism, Galerie de l'Oiel, Paris, 66; Exposica Surrealista, Museo de Bellas Artes, Sao Paulo, Brazil, 67; Exposition Surrealiste Princip Slasti, Brno, Czechoslovakia, 68. Teaching: Prof, Ecole des Beau-Arts, Quebec, 38-42. Bibliog: Roger Cardinal & Robert Stuart Short (auths), Surrealism: Permanent Revelation, London, 70; Jose Pierre (auth), Ils Habitent au Choc, Vie des Arts, Montreal, autumn 75. Publ: Illusr, Rapaces (cover), Paris, 60; illusr, L'Avanguardia Internazionale, Milan, 62; illusr, La Pierre de la Folie (cover), Paris, 63; illusr, Envers L'Ombre, Paris, 65; illusr, L'Archibras No 1-3 & 6, Paris, 4/67, 3/68 & 12/68. Mailing Add: 15 rue Saint Louis-enl'Isle Paris 4 France

BENSINGER, B EDWARD, III
COLLECTOR
b Chicago, Ill, Nov 27, 29. Study: Yale Univ, BA; Grad Sch Bus, Univ Southern Calif, MBA. Pos: With Bensinger Enterprises, Beverly Hills, Calif; with Brunswick Corp, Chicago, Ill, formerly; with Bache & Co, Beverly Hills, currently. Collection: Beckmann & Corot; Pieter Mondriaan; 18th century Indian prints. Mailing Add: 1540 N Lake Shore Dr Chicago IL 60610

BENSON, ELAINE K G
ART DEALER, WRITER
b Philadelphia, Pa, Apr 30, 24. Study: Univ Pa, BA, 44. Teaching: Coordr fashion fields, Philadelphia Col Art, 63-64. Pos: Dir pub rels, Philadelphia Col Art, 57-64; dir, Benson Gallery, 65-; co-dir summer art prog, Southampton Col, 67-69. Mem: Am Fedn Art. Specialty: Contemporary European and American paintings, sculpture and fine crafts. Publ: Criticism and articles on art and artists in Craft Horizons, On the Sound and others. Mailing Add: Benson Gallery PO Box AJ Bridgehampton NY 11932

BENSON, GERTRUDE ACKERMAN
WRITER, ART CRITIC
b Romania, Aug 6, 04. Study: Hunter Col, BA; NY Univ Inst Fine Arts, MA; Princeton Univ, Carnegie fels art & archaeol, 28-30, year abroad, 30-31. Teaching: Asst prof humanities, Philadelphia Col Art, 60-63. Pos: Feature writer & critic, New York Times, 31-57, Philadelphia Bull, 49-64, Philadelphia Inquirer, 50-, Drexel Univ, 64-70 York Times, Drexel Univ & Thomas Jefferson Univ, 71; art ed, Philadelphia Inquirer, 50-57. Publ: Auth, Greco-Roman influence on Utrecht Psalter, Art Bull, 31; Exploding the Van Gogh myth, Mag Art, 35; La tour & le Nain, Mag Art, 35; Lewis Carroll, New York Times Mag, 57; interviews with Marin, Jacob Epstein, DeKooning, Stuart Davis, Lipchitz, Knaths, Rouault, Nolde, Calder, Watkins Shahn & many others; also many articles & book reviews in nat mag & newspapers. Mailing Add: Rittenhouse Claridge Philadelphia PA 19103

BENSON, MARTHA J
GALLERY DIRECTOR, SCULPTOR
b Kansas City, Mo, July 30, 28. Study: Univ Kansas City; Baker Univ, BA; spec study Kans Univ, Iowa State Univ & Utrecht, Holland. Comn: Downtown supergraphic proj, 73-74 & bicentennial mural proj, 76, Ames, Iowa; five wood-assemblage panels, St David's Episcopal Church, Ames, 75; six wood-assemblage panels, Chapel, Mary Greeley Hosp, Ames, 77; Ross Hall sculpture proj, Iowa State Univ, Ames. Exhib: Lithuanian Book Plates, 70, Twelve Dutch Potters, 71, Three Chilean Printmakers, 73, Technol & the Artist-Craftsman-A Nat Crafts Exhib, 73-75, The Artists of San Miguel, 74-75, The Octagon Art Ctr, Ames; plus others. Pos: Dir, The Octagon Art Ctr, Ames, 68- Awards: Theta Sigma Pi Award, Woman Behind the News, 70; Recognition Award: One of Five Outstanding Women Art Dirs, Iowa Women's Caucus, 76. Bibliog: Annabelle Liu (auth), Martha Benson-A Profile, Craft Connection, 75. Style & Technique: Wood assemblage sculpture. Media: Wood. Mailing Add: 928 Garfield Ames IA 50010

BENSON, ROBERT FRANKLIN
PAINTER, INSTRUCTOR
b Arcata, Calif, Apr 3, 48. Study: Humboldt Co Schs, Indust Arts Scholar, 65; Humboldt State Univ, Art Dept Scholar, 70 & BA, 71; Univ Ill, Creative & Performing Arts Fel, 72; Univ Ill, Champaign-Urbana, MFA, 73; also with Morris Graves, 73. Exhib: Univ NMex Art Gallery, Albuquerque, 72; Print & Drawing Exhib, Univ Ky Art Gallery, 72; Dallas Summer Arts Festival, North Park Ctr, Dallas, 73; Thesis Exhib, Krannert Mus Lobby, Champaign, Ill, 73; Six from Northwest Coast, Henry Galleries, Univ Wash, Seattle, 75; one-man show, Lindhurst Gallery, Univ Southern Calif, Los Angeles, 76; Humboldt Artists, Ankrum Gallery, Los Angeles, 77. Teaching: Asst oil painting, Univ Ill, Champaign, spring 71; instr studio courses, Col of the Redwoods, Eureka, Calif, 78- Style & Technique: Oil, watercolor and acrylic mixed on paper, of abstract images with landscape forms, done outside on location. Dealer: Humboldt Cult Ctr 422 First St Eureka CA 95501. Mailing Add: 541 First Ave Blue Lake CA 95525

BENSON, S PATRICIA (MCMAHON)
PRINTMAKER
b Philadelphia, Pa, July 27, 41. Study: Mich State Univ, BFA, 63, with John DeMartelly; Fla State Univ, BFA, 67, with Arthur Deshaies. Work: Brooklyn Mus, New York; Achenbach Found, Calif Palace of Legion of Honor, San Francisco; Anchorage Fine Arts Mus, Alaska; Cincinnati Mus Art; US Info Serv, 14 prints in var embassies. Exhib: One-person shows, Fla State Univ, 67, Reed Col, Portland, Ore, 72 & Univ Maine, Orono, 75; Libr of Cong Nat Print Exhib, 69; Potsdam Nat Print Exhib, NY, 69-72; Four Printmakers, San Francisco Mus Art, 71; Am Grafika, Belgrade, Yugoslavia & Eastern Europ tour, 71; Oversize Prints, Whitney Mus, New York, 71; Patricia Benson Prints, travel exhib thru SAm, US Info Serv, 72-75; Univ Hawaii, Hilo, 76-77; Talent USA, Jacksonville Art Mus, Fla, 76. Teaching: Instr printmaking, Fla State Univ, 67-69; asst prof printmaking, Sonoma State Col, Calif, 70-71; head etching dept, San Francisco Art Inst, 71-74. Awards: Calif Soc Printmakers, Achenbach Found, San Francisco, 72; Purchase Awards, 15th Ann NDak Print & Drawing Exhib, 72 & Anchorage Fine Art Mus Print Exhib, Alaska, 73. Bibliog: Prints of Patricia Benson (film), Stewart Lippe, 73; article in Artforum, 4/71. Style & Technique: Etching, engraving and Lucite relief intaglio embossing. Dealer: Assoc Am Artists 663 Fifth Ave New York NY 10011. Mailing Add: PO Box H Alfred ME 04002

BENTHAM, DOUGLAS WAYNE
SCULPTOR
b Rosetown, Sask, Apr 16, 47. Study: Univ Sask, BA & advan degree in fine arts. Work: Sask Arts Bd, Regina, Sask; Edmonton Art Gallery, Alta; Art Gallery Windsor, Ont; Univ Sask, Saskatoon; Univ Calgary, Alta. Comn: Outdoor sculpture (corten steel), Nat Sci Libr, Ottawa, comn by Govt Can Dept Pub Works. Exhib: One-man shows, Regina Pub Libr Art Gallery, 70 & 73, Edmonton Art Gallery, 73; Saskatchewan-Art & Artists, Norman Mackenzie Art Gallery, Regina, 71; West 71, Edmonton Art Gallery; Mendel Art Gallery, Saskatoon, 69, 70 & 72; Kingston Spring Exhib, Ont, 72; Waddington Galleries, Montreal, 74; Saskatoon Pub Art Gallery, 74; Glenbow-Alta Art Gallery, 75; Art Gallery of York Univ, Toronto, 76. Awards: For work in sculpture, Sask Arts Bd, 69; Can Coun Arts Bursaries, 70-71 & 72-73; Purchase Award for Sculpture, West '71, Edmonton Art Gallery, 71. Bibliog: Karen Wilkin (auth), The prairies, a limited view, Can Forum 54, 1/75; Terrence Heath (auth), Bentham's recent sculpture, Winter 75-76 & David Burnett (auth), Three Toronto Reviews, Winter 76-77, Artscanada. Mem: Royal Can Acad Arts. Mailing Add: RR 2 Dundurn SK Can

BENTLEY, CLAUDE
PAINTER, MURALIST
b New York, NY, June 9, 15. Study: Northwestern Univ; Art Inst Chicago. Work: Univ Ill, Metrop Mus Art; Denver Art Mus; Art Inst Chicago; Ill State Mus; plus others. Comn: Murals, 3600 Lake Shore Dr Bldg, Chicago, Ill; comn as design consult, Plaza del Lago Shopping Ctr, Winnetka, Ill. Exhib: Corcoran Gallery Art; San Francisco Mus Art; Whitney Mus Am Art; Art Inst Chicago; Sarasota Art Asn; plus others. Awards: John G Curtis Jr Award, 63; Old Orchard Art Fair Award, 63; Purchase Award, Ill State Mus, 63; plus others. Bibliog: Literary Times, 4/65; Creating art from anything, Meilach, 68. Style & Technique: Perceptual abstraction; colors applied flat and hard-edged; generally simplified forms refer to geometric shapes and often present dual or single motifs. Media: Acrylic. Collection: African, oceanic and pre-Columbian art. Dealer: Hokin Gallery Inc 200 E Ontario St Chicago IL 60611. Mailing Add: 878 Ridge Rd Highland Park IL 60035

BENTON, FLETCHER
SCULPTOR
b Jackson, Ohio, Feb 25, 31. Study: Miami Univ, BFA. Work: Whitney Mus Am Art, New York; Hirshhorn Mus, Washington, DC; San Francisco Mus Mod Art, Calif; Univ Art Mus, Berkeley, Calif; Rockefeller Collection, New York; plus others. Comn: IBM Corp, Morgan Hill, Calif; Taubman Corp, Ann Arbor, Mich; Univ Calif, Los Angeles; Ohio Nat Bank, Columbus; Lakeside Mall, Sterling Heights, Mich. Exhib: Univ Ill, 67 & 69; HemisFair '68, San Antonio, Tex; Whitney Mus Am Art Sculpture Ann, 68 & 73; Lytton Art Ctr, Los Angeles, 68; Electric Art, Univ Calif, Los Angeles, 69; Albright-Knox Art Gallery, Buffalo, NY, 69 & 71; San Francisco Mus Art, 70 & 76; Int Mus Fine Arts, Osaka, Japan, 70; Stanford Univ Mus, Calif, 70 & 71; Galeria Bonino, Rio de Janiero, Brazil, 73; de Saisset Mus, Univ Santa Clara, Calif, 75; Nat Collection Fine Arts & Renwick Gallery, Washington, DC, 76; Univ Minn, Minneapolis, 76; John Berggruen Gallery, San Francisco, 77; plus others. Teaching: Instr, Calif Col Arts & Crafts, 59; instr, San Francisco Art Inst, 64-68; prof art, San Jose State Univ, 68- Bibliog: Peter Selz (auth), article in Directions in Kinetic Sculpture, Univ Calif, Berkeley, 66; George Rickey (auth), Constructivist Tendencies, 71; Tracy Atkinson (auth), article in Directions I: Options 1968, Milwaukee Art Ctr, 68. Dealer: John

Berggruen Gallery 228 Grant Ave San Francisco CA 94108. Mailing Add: 1072 Bryant St San Francisco CA 94103

BENTON, SUZANNE E
SCULPTOR, ART WRITER
b New York, NY, Jan 21, 36. Study: Queens Col, New York, BA(fine arts), 56; studies in New York at Art Students League, Columbia Univ, NY Univ, Brooklyn Col, Brooklyn Mus Art Sch & Mus Mod Art; Silvermine Col Art, Conn. Work: Oakton Community Col, Ill; Nat Mus Mod Art, New Delhi, India; Birla Acad, Calcutta, India; Tokyo Sch Fine Arts, Japan; Deree Pierce Col, Athens, Greece. Comn: Sculptured theatre sets, Viveca Lindfors I Am A Woman Theatre Co, 73; The Sun Queen, large-scale bronze sculpture & Throne of the Sun Queen, bronze & corten steel, Art Park, Lewiston, NY, 75. Exhib: Metal Masks Sculpture for the Performing Arts, Mus of Performing Arts, Lincoln Ctr, New York, 71; US Info Agency Group, throughout Eastern Europe, 71-75; Metal Mask and Ritual Sculpture, Mus Art, Sci & Indust, Bridgeport, Conn, 73; Touching Ritual, Wadsworth Atheneum, Hartford, Conn, 75; one-person shows, Hanguk Ilbo Auditorium, Seoul, Korea, 75, US Info Agency, New Delhi, India, 76, Chemould Gallery, Bombay, India, 76 & Hellenic Am Union, Athens, Greece, 76; Expo 74, Spokane, Wash, 74. Teaching: Instr welded sculpture, Brookfield Craft Ctr, Brookfield, Conn, 72-73. Pos: Convener-coordr, Arts Festival-Metamorphosis I, New Haven, Conn, 69-70 & Conn Feminists in the Arts, 69-72; producer-dir, Four Chosen Women, New York, 72. Awards: Susan B Anthony Award, Eastern Regional Conf, Nat Orgn Women, 72; Sculpture Award Number One, Conn Artists, Stamford Mus, Conn, 76. Bibliog: Henry Michaud, Masks (film), SDA Prod, Can, 76-77; Carman Kagal (auth), The Masks of Suzanne Benton, SPAN, US Info Serv, India, 6/77; Ivan Kostka, Masks that Bare a Woman's Soul, Statesman Ltd, India, 77. Mem: Artists Equity; Am Crafts Coun; Now Women in the Arts (nat coordr, 73-76); hon mem Nat Korean Sculptress Asn. Style & Technique: Modern with an affinity to ancient art; sculptures which evolve organically through the use of welding metal techniques; mask rituals from similar techniques examine lifestory and ancient tales from a contemporary woman's view; masks are open and manipulated. Media: Welded metal sculpture; mask ritual, workshops & performances using sculptured metal masks. Publ: Contribr, Masks, Face Coverings and Headgear, Can Nostrand Reinhold, 73; contribr, Woman in the Year 2000, Arbor House, 74; auth, The Art of Welded Sculpture, Van Nostrand Reinhold, 75; illusr, Women Artists in America, Collins, 75; contribr, Survivor's Box, Possum Press, 77. Mailing Add: 22 Donnelly Dr Ridgefield CT 06877

BENTON, WILLIAM
COLLECTOR
b Minneapolis, Minn, Apr 1, 00. Pos: Owner, Encycl Britannica & subsids, Praeger Publ, Inc & Phaidon Press, Ltd; hon trustee, Wadsworth Atheneum. Mem: Life fel Metrop Mus Art; Mus Mod Art, New York (mem int coun & bus comt for arts). Collection: Twentieth century American art including Reginald Marsh, Ivan Albright, Bellows, Levine, Benton and many others; widely exhibited, and donated to universities, colleges and museums. Mailing Add: 342 Madison Ave New York NY 10017

BENTOV, MIRTALA
SCULPTOR
b Kharkov, USSR, Apr 29, 29; US citizen. Study: Boston Mus Sch, cert; Grande Chaumière, Paris, France, with Zadkine; École Arts Décoratifs, Paris, with Couturier; Tufts Univ, BFA. Work: Park Synagogue Mus, Cleveland, Ohio; Universalist Unitarian Church, Brighton, Mass; Ford Motor Co, Detroit, Mich; Tufts Univ; Harvard Univ. Comn: Medal for Sixth Cong, Int Soc Hemat, 56; portraits of two founders, Missionary Order of Maryknoll, NY, 62; portrait of Roman Jakobson, Slavic Depts of Harvard Univ & Mass Inst Technol, 69; portrait of Pres Milton Grahm, Grahm Jr Col, Boston, 70. Exhib: One-person shows, Pucker-Safari Gallery, Boston, Mass, 69, 72 & 78, Salem State Col, Mass, 71, Tufts Univ, Medford, Mass, 72, Regis Col, Weston, Mass, 74, Univ Mich, Ann Arbor, 76, Niagara Falls Art Gallery & Mus, Can, 76, Nicholas Roerich Mus, New York, 77, Duxbury Art Complex Mus, Mass, 78 & Attleboro Mus, Mass, 78. Awards: Second Prize Sculpture, Boston Art Festival, 56; Boston Mus Sch Albert Whitin Traveling Scholar, 57; Prize, Providence Art Club, 72. Mem: Boston Visual Artists' Union. Style & Technique: Expressionistic work in direct wax cast by lost wax process. Media: Bronze. Publ: Auth (Mirtala Kardinalovska), Poems (in Russian), Madrid, 72 & Rainbow Bridge (in Ukrainian), New York, 76; auth, Thought-Forms, Branden Press, Boston, 75. Dealer: Pucker-Safrai Gallery 171 Newbury St Boston MA 02116. Mailing Add: 241 Glezen Lane Wayland MA 01778

BENTZ, HARRY DONALD
ART ADMINISTRATOR, PAINTER
b Robesonia, Pa, Dec 2, 31. Study: Kutztown State Col, 53; Pa State Univ, with Hobson Pittman, 58; Lehigh Univ, 68; watercolor portraiture with Lester Stone. Work: Bank of Pa, Reading; Farmer & Merchants Bank of Hagerstown, Md. Comn: Two murals, Spec Educ Ctr, Reading Sch Dist, 62; 15 display units, Daniel Boone Homestead, Birdsboro, Pa, 63. Exhib: Pa Art Educ Exhib, William Penn Mem Mus, 54; Washington Co Mus of Fine Arts Exhib, 65-67; Second Ann Watercolor Exhib, Millersville State Col, 76. Teaching: Prof painting, Shippensburg State Col, 70- Pos: Art teacher, Columbia High Sch, 55-60; art supervisor, Reading Sch Dist, 60-71; chmn dept art, Shippensburg State Col, 71- Awards: Hayes Art Materials Award, 43rd Ann Cumberland Valley Exhib, 75; Purchase Award, 43rd Ann Cumberland Valley Exhib, Farmers & Merchants Bank, 75; First Prize, Huntingdon Co Arts Festival, Huntingdon Co Arts Coun, 76. Mem: Nat Art Educ Asn; Pa Art Educ Asn; Cumberland Valley Arts Coun. Style & Technique: Watercolor with tissue paper in semi abstract manner. Media: Watercolor, Oil. Mailing Add: RD 5 Shippensburg PA 17257

BENY, ROLOFF
PHOTOGRAPHER, WRITER
b Medicine Hat, Alta, Jan 7, 24. Study: Banff Sch Fine Arts, scholar, 39; Trinity Col, Univ Toronto, BA & BFA, 45; State Univ Iowa fel, 46-47, with Mauricio Lasansky, MA & MFA, 47; Columbia Univ; Inst Fine Art, NY Univ, scholar, 47-48; study & travel in Europe, 48-49 & 51-52; Guggenheim fel for printmaking & painting, 53; Univ Lethbridge, LLD, 72. Work: Nat Gallery Can, Ottawa, Ont; Art Gallery of Ont, Toronto; Mus Mod Art, New York; Milione Gallery, Milan, Italy, Redfern Gallery, London, Eng; plus many other pub & pvt collections. Comn: Photographic murals, Nesbitt-Thomson, Toronto-Dominion Bank Ctr, 67; Image Canada (38 photo-murals), comn for Fed Pavilion of Expo, Montreal, 67; The Renaissance (photo exhib), Ontario Music Educ Asn & Govt Ont Coun Arts, 68; Island-Ceylon (book with John Lindsay), Govt Ceylon, 71; Persia—Bridge of Turquoise, Empress of Iran, 75. Exhib: Ont Soc Artists Show, Art Gallery Toronto, 45; 32nd Nat Exhib, Soc Am Etchers, Gravers, Lithographers, New York, 47; Second Nat Print Ann Exhib, Brooklyn Mus, NY, 48; Exhib Current Am Prints, Dept Fine Arts, Carnegie Inst, 48; Nat Gallery Can, Ottawa; Palace of the Legion of Honor, San Francisco; San Francisco Mus; Libr of Cong, Washington, DC; Dallas Mus of Fine Art, Tex; plus many other group & one-man shows. Awards: Int Prize for Design for The Thrones of Earth & Heaven, Leipzig Book Fair, 58; Award for Comite des Arts Graphiques Francais, 65; Gold Medal for World's Finest Book for Japan in Colour, Int Bk Fair, 68, Can Gold Medal, 67 & Can Coun Award, 68. Bibliog: Merle Shain (auth), Roloff Beny in Rome, Chatelaine, 5/7/70; Kay Kritzwiser (auth), Roloff Beny: Breathtaking odyssey, Toronto Globe & Mail, 5/1/71; Arnold Edinborough (auth), Superb camera art of Roloff Beny, Financial Post, 5/22/71. Mem: Life mem Royal Can Acad. Publ: Co-auth, The Thrones of Earth & Heaven, 58, A Time of Gods, 62, Pleasure of Ruins, 64, To Every Thing There is a Season, 67, Japan in Colour, 67 & In Italy, 74; plus others. Mailing Add: 432 13th St S Lethbridge AB Can

BENZ, LEE R
PRINTMAKER, WATERCOLORIST
b Neponset, Ill. Study: Bradley Univ, BA & MA; Salzburg Col, Austria. Exhib: One-man shows, Colorprint USA, 72, Lakeview Collector's Gallery, 74, Metamora Court House, 74, Prix de Paris, 74, Bradley Nat Print Show, 75 & Westminster Hall, 76. Teaching: Prof printmaking, design & sculpture, Ill Cent Col, 69- Awards: Printmaking Salon of 50 States Award, NY, 74; Rennick Award, Peoria, 74, 76 & 77; Purchase Award/Printmaking, Quincy, Ill, 77. Mem: Peoria Art Guild; Lakeview Ctr; Nat Soc Lit & Arts; Int Soc of Artists; Ill Art League. Style & Technique: Wide variation of objective expression from impressions to highly organized abstraction depending on media. Media: Intaglio, Serigraph, Watercolor. Dealer: Peoria Art Guild 1831 N Knoxville Peoria IL 61604; Lakeview Ctr 1125 Lake St Peoria IL 61604. Mailing Add: 1125 Fon Du Lac Dr East Peoria IL 61611

BEN-ZION
PAINTER, SCULPTOR
b Ukraine, July 7, 97; US citizen. Work: Mus Mod Art, Metrop Mus Art & Whitney Mus Am Art, New York; Art Inst Chicago; Jewish Mus, New York; plus others. Exhib: Advancing American Art, State Dept Traveling Show, 47; Bezalel Mus, Jerusalem, Israel, 57; A Retrospect, Jewish Mus, New York, 59; Whitney Mus Am Art Rev, 60-61; Collector's Choice, Denver Art Mus, Colo, 61; Retrospective, Mus of Haifa, 75. Teaching: Instr painting, Cooper Union, 43-50; instr painting, Ball State Univ, summer 56; instr painting, Univ Iowa, summer 59. Bibliog: Ralph Pearson (auth), The Modern Renaissance in American Art, Harper & Row, 54; Emery Grossman (auth), Art & Tradition, Thomas Yoseloff, 67. Media: Oil, Watercolor; Ironwork. Publ: Eight Portfolios of Etchings. Mailing Add: 329 W 20th St New York NY 10011

BERAHA, ENRIQUE MISRACHI
ART DEALER
b Skopjle, Yugoslavia, Sept 11, 25. Study: Nat Univ Mex, Law degree; Escuela Artes del Libro, Mexico City; Nat Univ Mex Sch Philos. Pos: Dir, Galeria Arte Misrachi; publ art bks. Specialty: Modern art, especially Mexican. Publ: Ed, Sequeiros, 64; ed, Tamayo, 65; ed, Siqueiros escultopintura, 68; ed, Francisco Zuniga, 69; ed, Jose Luis Cuevas, His World, 69. Mailing Add: Genova 20 Mexico DF Mexico

BERD, MORRIS
PAINTER, EDUCATOR
b Philadelphia, Pa, Mar 12, 14. Study: Philadelphia Col Art; Univ per Strangeri, Perugia, Italy, cert. Work: Lancaster Courthouse Collection, Pa; Philadelphia Mus Art; Pa Acad Fine Arts, Philadelphia; Philadelphia Col Art; Arco Collection, Los Angeles; plus others. Comn: History of Oil (mural), Sun Oil Co, Franklin Inst; History of Architecture (mural), Gimbel Bros, Philadelphia. Exhib: Many Pa Acad Fine Arts Ann & Philadelphia Mus Art Regionals; also over 15 one-man shows, incl Wilcox Gallery, Swarthmore Col, 73; Marion Locks Gallery, 75 & Pa State Univ Mus Art, 75; Drawing Exhib, Beaver Col, 76; Sketch Bk Exhib, Philadelphia Col Art, 77. Teaching: Prof painting, Philadelphia Col Art, 36-76, co-chmn dept, 50-71. Awards: Gimbels Mural Award, 52; Silver Medal, YMHA Jubilee Show; Katzman Prize, Philadelphia Print Club, 62. Style & Technique: Realistic or neorealistic. Media: Oil, Acrylic. Mailing Add: 350 Howarth Rd Media PA 19063

BERDICH, VERA
PRINTMAKER, PAINTER
b Chicago, Ill. Study: Art Inst Chicago, BA, 46, hon PhD, 77. Work: Chicago Art Inst Print & Drawing Collection; Rosenwald Collection; Libr Cong Prints, Washington, DC; Mus Mod Art; Univ Chicago Print Libr. Comn: Symphonic Metamorphosis (100 prints), Ravinia Festival, 69; 25 prints for Ill Arts Coun, 73. Exhib: Prints, Yamada Gallery, Kyoto, Japan, 59; Int Exchange Prints (France); Prints & Paintings, San Francisco Mus Art, 63; one-man show, Graphic Works, Art Inst Chicago, 66; Prints, Carnegie Mellon Univ, 67; Kennedy Galleries, New York, 73. Teaching: From assoc prof to prof etching, Art Inst Chicago, 46-; instr printmaking, Univ Chicago, 57-58. Awards: Frank G Logan Second Prize, 62, First Prize, 64, John G Curtis Prize, 66, Logan Prize, 77, Art Inst Chicago. Mem: Sch Art Inst Chicago Alumni Asn; Am Asn Univ Prof; Nat Soc Lit & Arts. Style & Technique: Surreal; phantastic. Media: Intaglio. Mailing Add: Art Inst of Chicago Michigan Ave at Adams Chicago IL 60603

BEREN, STANLEY O
PATRON
b Parkersburg, WVA, Feb 1, 20. Study: Harvard Col, AB, 41, Harvard Univ, MBA, 43. Pos: Pres, Wichita Art Mus Mem Found Inc, 68, chmn bd, Wichita Art Mus, 70-72, mem bd, 72-; mem adv bd, JFK Ctr, 70- Mem: Am Asn Mus; Int Coun Mem. Interest: Special interest in raising funds for accessions for Wichita Art Mus. Collection: Modern painting and pre-Columbian artifacts. Mailing Add: 257 N Broadway Wichita KS 67202

BERG, BARRY
PAINTER, MAIL ARTIST
b Glendale, Calif, May 13, 47. Study: Univ Calif, Irvine, BA(studio art, cum laude), 75 & grad study in art educ with Ed Bereal, 76. Work: Nat Art Gallery, Wellington, NZ; Uniart Gallery, Elblag, Poland; Univ Waterloo, Ont, Can; Univ Mass, Amherst; San Diego State Univ, Calif. Comn: Exterior wall murals (with Mesa Alternative Sch; 9ft x 35ft), 76 & (16ft x 96ft), 77, Newport Mesa Unified Sch Dist. Exhib: Univ Calif, Irvine, 65-75; La Jolla Mus of Contemp Art, Calif, 75; All Calif Exhib, Laguna Beach Mus of Art, Calif, 76; Sign/Symbol, Nat Art Gallery, Wellington, NZ, 77; Circle 77, Uniart Gallery, Elblag, Poland, 77; All of the Above, Witchita Art Mus, Kans, 77; Winter Show, Los Angeles Co Mus, Los Angeles, 77; CS/PG all Media Show, Muckerthaler Cult Ctr, Fullerton, Calif, 77; Not Clay Invitational, Univ Mass, Amherst, 77; Summer Attraction, TJB Gallery, Newport Beach, Calif, 77; Artwords and Bookworks, Los Angeles Inst of Contemp Art, 78; one-man show, Southern Exposure, Arnold Gallery, Newport Beach, Calif, 76. Teaching: Art facilitator, Mesa Alternative Sch, Costa Mesa, Calif, 75-77. Pos: Dir, TJB Gallery, Newport Beach, 77; advert art dir, Surfing Mag, San Clemente, Calif, 78- Bibliog: Martha Spellman (auth), Barry Berg: Environmental references, 11/76 & Gerard Haggarty (auth), Winter show at the Los Angeles County Museum, 12/77, Artweek. Style & Technique: Paintings and drawings of environmental references; art as communication on a global basis through mail art. Media: Latex, Oil; Mail.

Publ: Auth, Problems, privately publ, 78. Dealer: TJB Gallery 1535-B Manrovia Newport Beach CA 92663. Mailing Add: 237-B La Paloma San Clemente CA 92672

BERG, PHIL
COLLECTOR, PATRON
b New York, NY, Feb 15, 02. Study: Col Textiles & Sci, Pa, BS. Mem: Los Angeles Co Mus of Art (trustee); Southwest Mus (trustee); Soc Am Archaeol; Am Anthrop Asn; Explorers & Adventurers Club. Specialty: Archaeological activities include excavations in Meso-America, Mesopotamian Valley and elsewhere; over 400 major pieces of art donated to the Los Angeles County Museum of Art and other museums. Collection: Material covers the history of art from Sumerian worshipper figures until Miro. Publ: Auth, Man Came This Way, 71; auth, Museums and People, 73; auth, Now It Can Be Told, 76. Mailing Add: 10939 Chalon Rd Los Angeles CA 90024

BERG, SIRI
PAINTER, INSTRUCTOR
b Stockholm, Sweden; US citizen. Study: Inst Art & Archit, Univ Brussels; Pratt Graphics Ctr, New York. Work: Chase Manhattan Bank, New York; Union Dime Savings Bank, New York; Carter Orgn, New York; Ted Bates Advert, Stockholm, Sweden; Univ Ala, Birmingham. Exhib: Three New Women Painters, East Hampton Gallery, New York, 70; one-person shows, Phoenix Gallery, New York, 72 & 74, Debel Gallery, Ein Kerem, Israel, 75, US Cult Ctr, Jerusalem, 76 & Hansen Galleries, New York, 77; Ward-Nasse Gallery, New York, 74; Year of the Woman, Bronx Mus Arts, New York, 75; Va Mus Fine Art, Richmond, 75; Contemp Reflections 76-77, Aldrich Mus, Ridgefield, Conn, 77; Magic Circle Exhib, Bronx Mus, New York, 77; plus others. Teaching: Instr, Col New Rochelle, 74-; color theory workshop, New Sch-Parsons Sch of Design, 77- Pos: Dir art prog, Riverdale Ment Health Clin, Bronx, NY, 66- Mem: Nat Asn Women Artists. Style & Technique: Geometric, pure and relational nonobjective painting; flat painted surfaces. Publ: Auth, Therapeutic art programs around the world; Uses of art in educational day treatment center, Am J Art Ther, 70. Mailing Add: 530 W 236th St Bronx NY 10463

BERG, THOMAS
PAINTER
b Cheyenne, Wyo, Feb 10, 43. Study: Univ Wyo, BA, 66, MA, 68, MFA, 72. Work: El Paso Mus Art, Tex; Univ Wyo Mus Art, Laramie; Kansas City Art Inst, Mo; Delta State Univ, Cleveland, Miss; Sublette Co Libr Collection, Pinedale, Wyo. Comn: Group mural with NY Correspondence Sch Vancouver, Nat Res Libr, Ottawa, Can, 73. Exhib: 23rd Nat Print & Drawing Show, Smithsonian Inst, Washington, DC, 73; A Pictorial Hist of the World, Kansas City Art Inst, 75; two-man show, with Shepherd, Yellowstone Art Ctr, Billings, Mont, 76; 55 Mercer Gallery, New York, NY, 77; The Am Landscape, El Paso Mus, Tex, 77; Ten Artists, Western States Arts Found Touring Show, Mus in Idaho, NDak, NMex, Wis, Utah, Wash & Ariz, 77-79. Collections Arranged: Conception, direction & hanging of US Mail, the first US int invitational show of Mail Art, Univ Maine, Augusta, 73. Teaching: Instr art, Point Park Col, Pittsburgh, Pa, 69-71; vis lectr painting, Univ Wyo, Laramie, summer, 77. Pos: Vis lectr, Univ Rochester, 71; artist-in-residence, Univ Maine, Augusta, 72-73, Wyo Artists in Schs Prog, 73-76 & Delta State Univ, Cleveland, Miss, 76. Awards: $5000 Visual Arts fel Wyo, Western States Arts Found, Denver, 76-77. Style & Technique: Multiple image paintings using flat subject matter (postcards, photographs, mag photographs); Wyo landscapes. Media: Oil. Mailing Add: 519 S Fifth St Laramie WY 82070

BERGE, CAROL
LECTURER, WRITER
Study: NY Univ; Columbia Univ; New Sch, 8 yrs. Teaching: Vis lectr contemp cult, Thomas Jefferson Col, Allendale, Mich, 75-76; assoc prof lit, Univ Southern Miss. Pos: Ed, Miss Rev, 77-78. Awards: NY State Coun Arts Grants for Ctr Mag, 71-75; Creative Artists Pub Serv Grant in Fiction, NY State Coun, 74. Mem: PEN Am; MacDowell Colony Fels; Authors' League & Guild; Popular Cult Asn. Res: Art, cinema, astrology, theatre, contemporary culture, fiction and anti-fiction (the New Writing). Publ: Auth, Ikon, the work of Meredith Monk, Phoebe Neville & Co, 68; auth, Film culture, the work of filmmaker Harry Smith, 69; auth, article in J Inst Contemp Art, 75. Mailing Add: c/o Rhoda Weyr William Morris Agency 1350 Ave of Americas New York NY 10019

BERGE, HENRY
SCULPTOR
b Baltimore, Md, May 29, 08. Study: Md Inst Fine Arts; Rhinehart Sch Sculpture with J Maxwell Miller. Work: Portrait head & 2 portrait reliefs, Hagerstown Mus Fine Arts; approx 300 portrait heads for figures in 12 waxworks mus in US & Can. Comn: Portrait relief, Joseph D Baker, Mem Tower, City Park, Frederick, Md, 41; large tympanum relief, Angel of Truth, First Unitarian Church, Baltimore, Md, 55; portrait reliefs, Henrietta & Jacob Blaustein, Oheb Shalom Temple, Baltimore, 63; hundreds more. Exhib: Baltimore Mus Art, 40; Nat Acad Design, New York, NY; Pa Acad Fine Arts; Nat Sculpture Soc Ann, Lever House, New York, 68-75; Rhinehart Sch Sculpture 75th Anniversary, Baltimore, 71. Mem: Fel Nat Sculpture Soc; Charcoal Club, Baltimore; Md Inst Fine Arts Alumni Asn. Style & Technique: Traditional. Media: Plastolene. Mailing Add: 5 Merrymount Rd Baltimore MD 21210

BERGEN, SIDNEY L
ART DEALER
b New York, NY, Sept 27, 22. Study: Alfred Univ. Pos: Owner & dir, ACA Galleries, New York. Mem: Art Dealers Asn Am. Specialty: Early 20th century and contemporary American and European art. Mailing Add: ACA Galleries 25 E 73rd St New York NY 10021

BERGER, JASON
PAINTER, PRINTMAKER
b Malden, Mass, Jan 22, 24. Study: Boston Mus Fine Arts Sch, 42-43; Univ Ala, 43-44; Boston Mus Fine Arts Sch, 46-49; Ossip Zadkine Sch Sculpture, Paris, France, 50-52. Work: Mus Mod Art; Chase Manhattan Bank, New York; Smith Col Mus Art; Guggenheim Mus Art; Brandeis Univ; plus others. Exhib: Carnegie Inst Mus, 54 & 55; Recent Drawings USA, Mus Mod Art, 56; Pa Acad Fine Arts, 62; Silvermine Guild; Providence Art Festival, RI, 69; plus others. Teaching: Instr painting, Boston Mus Fine Arts Sch, 55-69; vis prof, State Univ NY Buffalo, 69-70; instr painting, Art Inst Boston, 73- Awards: Grand Prize, 55 & First Prize, 61, Boston Art Festival; Boston Mus Fine Arts Sch Traveling Fel; Purchase Prize, Sheraton-Boston Hotel, 65; plus others. Style & Technique: Naturistic. Media: Oil, Watercolor; Woodcut. Publ: Illusr, Foundation Course in French, 56. Mailing Add: 40 University Rd Brookline MA 02146

BERGER, JERRY ALLEN
CURATOR
b Buffalo, Wyo, Oct 8, 43. Study: Univ Wyo, BA(psychology), 65, BA(art), 71, MA(art hist), 72. Pos: Cur collections, Univ Wyo Art Mus, Laramie, 72- Mailing Add: Univ of Wyo Art Mus Box 3138 Univ Sta Laramie WY 82071

BERGER, OSCAR
GRAPHIC ARTIST
b Presov, Eperjes, Czech, May 12, 01; US citizen. Work: Libr of Cong & Nat Portrait Gallery, Washington, DC; Metrop Mus Art, New York; also pvt collections & mus. Comn: Graphics, Paul Poiret, Paris, 24; design, League of Nations, Geneva, 26; posters, Brit Transport & Gen Post Off, London, 38; curtain design, Palladium, London; mag pages (San Francisco Conf of UN), New York Times, London Daily Telegraph, King Features Syndicate, 45. Exhib: One-man show, Gallery of Mod Art, New York Cult Ctr, 68. Bibliog: Geoffrey Holme (auth), Caricature of today, The Studio, London, 28; Oscar Berger, France Dimanche, Paris, 48; Norman Kent (auth), Famous faces by Oscar Berger, Am Artist, 63. Mem: Nat Press Club, Washington, DC; Nat Regist Indust Art Designers. London. Style & Technique: Drawings and portrait caricatures, drawn from life including world celebrities. Media: Pencil, Ink. Publ: Auth, A La Carte, 48; auth, Aesop's Foibles, 49; auth, Famous Faces, 50; auth, My Victims, 52; auth, The Presidents, 68. Mailing Add: 120 Central Park S New York NY 10019

BERGERE, RICHARD
ILLUSTRATOR, PAINTER
Study: NY Univ, BS; Columbia Univ, MA; Art Students League; Parsons Sch. Publ: Designer & illusr, From Stones to Skyscrapers, 60, Automobiles of Yesteryear, 62 & Homes of the Presidents, 62, Dodd; designer & illusr, When Will My Birthday Be?, McGraw, 62; designer & illusr, The Story of St Peter's, 66; plus others. Mailing Add: 143-28 41st Ave Flushing NY 11355

BERGGRUEN, JOHN HENRY
ART DEALER
b San Francisco, Calif, June 18, 43. Study: San Francisco State Col, AB, 67. Pos: Pres & owner, John Berggruen Gallery, San Francisco, 70- Mem: Soc Encouragement Contemp Art; Art Dealers Asn Am; San Francisco Art Dealers Asn. Specialty: Paintings, drawings and original prints of the 20th century. Mailing Add: 228 Grant Ave San Francisco CA 94108

BERGLING, VIRGINIA CATHERINE (MRS STEPHEN J KOZAZCKI)
ART BOOK DEALER, PUBLISHER
b Chicago, Ill, Nov 6, 08. Work: Books in large libraries throughout the world; also used as texts for designers' schools. Mem: Miami Art League; Brit Heraldry Soc, London. Res: All phases of technical art and design. Interest: Genealogy and heraldic art; coats of arms. Publ: Ed, Art monograms & lettering, 20th ed, 64; ed, Ornamental designs & illustrations, 4th ed, 64; ed, Art alphabets & lettering, 9th ed, 67; ed, Heraldic designs & engravings, Illus Manual Rev, 66; ed, style charts for gen jewelry & silverware engraving; plus others. Mailing Add: 1150 NE 110th St Miami FL 33161

BERGUSON, ROBERT JENKINS
PAINTER, EDUCATOR
b Blossburg, Pa, Dec 6, 44. Study: Corning Community Col, NY, AA, 64; Univ Iowa, Iowa City, BA, 67, MA, 68, MFA, 70. Work: Norfolk Mus Arts & Sci, Va; Univ NDak Art Gallery, Grand Forks; Univ Iowa Sch Art Gallery, Iowa City; Hunter Mus Art, Bluff View, Chattanooga, Tenn. Exhib: XXIII Am Drawing Biennial, Smithsonian Traveling Exhib Serv, Norfolk Mus Arts & Sci, Va, 69; 11th Midwest Biennial, Josyln Mus Art, Omaha, Nebr, 70; Am Artist Biennial, New Orleans Mus Art, La, 71 & 73; All Media Art Exhib, Assistance League, Houston, Tex, 76; 19th Ann Delta Art Exhib, Little Rock Art Ctr, Ark, 76; 18th Dixie Ann, Works on Paper Exhib, Montgomery Mus Fine Arts, Ala, 77; 16th Hunter Ann Painting & Drawing Exhib, Hunter Mus Art, Bluff View, Tenn, 77. Teaching: Asst prof painting & drawing, La Tech Univ, Ruston, 70-76, assoc prof, 77- Awards: Purchase Award, XXIII Am Drawing Biennial, Norfolk Art Mus, 69 & 13th NDak Exhib Prints & Drawings, Univ NDak, 70; Merit Award, 16th Hunter Mus Art, Lincoln-Davies, Inc, Bluff View, Chattanooga, Tenn, 77. Style & Technique: Calligraphic; mixed media. Media: Enamel & latex; ink. Mailing Add: 1211 Robinette Dr Ruston LA 71270

BERKMAN, AARON
PAINTER, GALLERY DIRECTOR
b Hartford, Conn, May 23, 00. Study: Hartford Art Sch; Mus Art Sch, Boston; Yaddo Found fel; Huntington Hartford Found fel. Exhib: Kaufman Art Gallery, New York, NY, 60 & 63; Bercone Galleries, New York, 70 & 75; one-man show, Audubon Artists, 71; Audubon Artists, 71-78. Teaching: Instr & lectr art, 92nd St YMHA Art Ctr, New York, 43-65. Pos: Art dir, 92nd St YMHA Art Ctr, 55-65; art dir, Bercone Studios, New York, 67- Mem: Artists Equity; Audubon Artists. Style & Technique: Semiabstract form derived from naturalistic observation and inspiration. Media: Acrylic, Oil, Watercolor. Publ: Auth, Art & Space, 49; auth, Amateur standing, monthly column in Art News, 55-61; auth, The Functional Line in Painting, 57. Dealer: Bercone Galleries 1305 Madison Ave New York NY 10028. Mailing Add: 230 E 88th St New York NY 10028

BERKON, MARTIN
PAINTER
b Brooklyn, NY, Jan 30, 32. Study: Brooklyn Col, BA; New York Univ, MA; Pratt Inst. Work: Aldrich Mus Contemp Art. Exhib: One-man shows, Brooklyn Mus, NY, 58, Smolin Gallery, New York, 62, 20th Century W Gallery, 67, Soho Ctr for Visual Artists, New York, 74 & Genesis Gallery, New York, 78; Butler Inst Am Art Ann Midyear Show, 65, 67 & 69; Contemporary Reflections, 73-74, Aldrich Mus Contemp Art, Ridgefield, Conn, 74 & 75; New Brit Mus, Conn, 74; Flint Inst, 75; Oakland Univ, Calif, 75; Am Fedn Arts Traveling Exhib, 75-76. Teaching: Instr elements of design, Fairleigh Dickinson Univ, 66-67; instr drawing & painting, City Col New York, 68-69; guest lectr, Middlebury Col, 77. Bibliog: Grace Glueck (auth), Art notes, New York Times, 12/1/74; E F Perlmutter (auth), Aldrich Museum, Art News, 12/74. Awards: Patron's Prize, Nat Soc Painters in Casein, 65. Mem: Col Art Asn Am. Style & Technique: Chromatically rendered organic forms in deep space. Media: Oil, Gouache. Dealer: Genesis Galleries 41 E 57th St New York NY 10022. Mailing Add: 51-25 Van Kleek St Elmhurst NY 11373

BERKOWITZ, HENRY
PAINTER, DESIGNER
b Brooklyn, NY, Feb 5, 33. Study: Brooklyn Mus Art Sch, with Sidney Simon; Workshop Sch Advert & Ed Art; Sch Visual Arts, New York. Work: Gutenberg Mus, Main, Ger. Exhib: Berkshire Mus, Pittsfield, Mass, 71; Galeries Raymond Duncan, Paris, 74; Art Festival Thours, France, 74; Parrish Art Mus, 75; Surindependants, Paris, 75; plus others. Pos: Asst art dir, Pyramid Publ, New York, 63-77. Awards: Award of Merit, New York Coliseum, 70; Am Vet Soc for Artists Award for an Abstract Work of Art, 72; Palmas de Oro, Int Art Festival, Paris, 74; plus others. Mem: Am Vet Soc Artists; Huntington Art League; Berkshire Art Asn; Awixa Pond Art Asn; Shore Arts Asn. Style & Technique: Abstract, traditional

nonobjective work in all media. Dealer: Ligoa Duncan Gallery 1045 Madison Ave New York NY 10021. Mailing Add: 11701 NW 29th Manor Sunrise FL 33323

BERKOWITZ, LEON
PAINTER
b Philadelphia, Pa. Study: Univ Pa, BFA; George Washington Univ, MA; Art Students League; Corcoran Gallery Art Sch; Mexico City Univ; Acad Grande Chaumiere, Paris, France; Acad Bella Arti, Florence, Italy. Work: Wadsworth Atheneum, Hartford, Conn; Mus Fine Arts, St Petersburg, Fla; Everson Mus Art, Syracuse, NY; Mus Mod Art, New York; Des Moines Art Ctr, Iowa. Comn: Murals, Harris Nat Trust, Chicago, 75. Exhib: Contemporary Imagery in American Art, Ringling Mus, Sarasota, Fla; Corcoran Mus, Washington, DC, 73, Everson Mus, Syracuse, 74, Atelier Chapman Kelley, Dallas, Tex, 75; Phillips Gallery, Washington, DC, 77; Chicago Arts Club, 77; Middendorf-Lane Gallery, Washington, DC, 77; plus others. Teaching: Prof art, Corcoran Sch Art, 68- Pos: Co-founder & dir, Workshop Ctr rts, Washington, DC, 47-55. Awards: Purchase Prize, Second Flint Invitational, 70; Nat Found Arts & Humanities Grant, 71. Style & Technique: Light and color primary concern. Media: Oil. Dealer: Middendorf-Lane Gallery 2014 P St NW Washington DC 20036; Atelier Chapman Kelley 2526 Fairmount Dallas TX 75201. Mailing Add: 2003 Kalorama Rd NW Washington DC 20009

BERLANT, TONY
ARTIST
b New York, NY, Aug 7, 41. Study: Univ Calif, Los Angeles, MA(painting) & MFA(sculpture). Work: Whitney Mus Am Art, New York; Art Inst Chicago; Los Angeles Co Mus Art; Philadelphia Mus Art; Wichita Mus Art, Kans. Exhib: One-man shows, Fourcade & Droll Inc, New York, 74, Whitney Mus Am Art, New York, 74, James Corcoran Gallery, Los Angeles, 75, Kind Gallery, Chicago, 75 & Polly Friedlander Gallery, Seattle, 75. Style & Technique: Collage and sculpture. Dealer: Fourcade & Droll Inc 36 E 75th St New York NY 10021. Mailing Add: 2802 Second St Santa Monica CA 95060

BERLIN, BEATRICE WINN
PRINTMAKER, PAINTER
b Philadelphia, Pa, May 27, 22. Study: Fleisher Art Mem, Philadelphia; Moore Col Art; Philadelphia Col Art; printmaking with Sam Maitin & Victor Lasuchin. Work: Philadelphia Mus Art; Brooklyn Mus Art; Lessing J Rosenwald, Jenkintown, Pa; Grunwald Col, Univ Calif; New York Pub Libr Print Collection; plus others. Exhib: Nat Acad Design Ann, New York, 65 & 66; Pa Acad Fine Arts Ann (watercolor & prints), 65, 67 & 69; Libr of Cong 21st Nat Print Show, 69; Print Club Philadelphia Ann Int, 69, 73 & 75; one-woman show, Philadelphia Print Club, 70. Awards: First Prize, Cheltenham Art Ctr Print Show, 70; Purchase Prize, Lebanon Valley Col, 73; Best in Show, Ocean City Boardwalk, NJ, 73. Bibliog: Wenniger (auth), Collograph-Printmaking, Watson-Guptill, 75. Mem: Am Color Print Soc; Philadelphia Watercolor Soc; Artists Equity Asn; San Francisco Women Artists; Philadelphia Print Club. Style & Technique: Abstract embossed prints in collograph technique and nature studies in etch and drypoint, occasionally work in other print media. Dealer: Assoc Am Artists 663 Fifth Ave New York NY 10022. Mailing Add: 1526 Ninth St Alameda CA 94501

BERLIND, ROBERT
PAINTER
b New York, NY, Aug 20, 38. Study: Columbia Col, BA, 60; Sch Art & Archit, Yale Univ, BFA, 62, MFA, 63. Exhib: Kultureel Centrum, Venlo, Neth, 67; one-man show, Maison de la Cult, L'Isle of Sorgire, Vaucluse, France, 69 & Green Mountain Gallery, New York, 72; Minneapolis Inst Art Biennial, Minn, 70; Yale at Norfolk Summer Prog Show, Norfolk, Conn, 72. Teaching: Asst prof, Minneapolis Sch Art, 64-66 & 69-70; asst prof art hist & humanities, Haarlem, Neth, 66-68; assoc prof & dir grad studies, NS Col Art & Design, 76- Media: Oil on Canvas. Mailing Add: NS Col Art & Design Duke St Halifax NS B3J 3J6 Can

BERLYN, SHELDON
PAINTER, PRINTMAKER
b Worcester, Mass, Sept 6, 29. Study: Worcester Art Mus Sch, cert, 50; Yale Norfolk Summer Art Sch, 50; Art Acad Cincinnati with Herbert Barnett, 54-55. Work: Worcester Art Mus, Mass; E B Crocker Art Gallery, The Art Mus City Sacramento, Calif; Dayton Art Inst, Ohio; Mohawk Valley Community Col, Utica, NY; State Univ NY Brockport Gallery Collection; plus numerous pvt & corp collections. Exhib: One-man shows, Dana & Decordova Mus, Lincoln, Mass, 55 & Schuman Gallery, Rochester, NY, 65-66 & 70; Western NY Exhib, Albright-Knox Art Gallery, Buffalo, NY, 58-66 & 77 & one-man show, 76; Drawings Above the Pa Line, Roberson Ctr Arts, Binghamton, NY, 68; American Drawings, Moore Col Art, Philadelphia, 68; Begegnung-Mass Inst Technol, Auslands Inst, Dortmund, WGer, 76. Teaching: Instr drawing, Worcester Art Mus Sch, Mass, 56-57; assoc prof painting & drawing, State Univ NY Buffalo, 58- Awards: Stephen Wilder Traveling Fel, Cincinnati Mus Asn, 55-56; State Univ NY Res Found Fel, 66-68; Sattler Award Painting, Western NY Exhib, Albright-Knox Art Gallery, 60 & Reeb Award Drawing, 64. Style & Technique: Geometric abstraction, paintings, constructions, serigraphs, drawings, strong emphasis on interlocking forms and color interaction. Media: Painting, Constructions; Serigraphs. Dealer: Oxford Gallery 267 Oxford St Rochester NY 14607; Dubose Gallery 2950 Kirby Dr Houston TX 77006. Mailing Add: 813 Richmond Ave Buffalo NY 14222

BERMAN, AARON
ART DEALER, COLLECTOR
b New York, NY, Nov 21, 22. Study: Brooklyn Col, BA; Columbia Univ, MA; Bezalel Acad, Jerusalem, dipl painting & sculpture, with Itzhak Danziger. Teaching: Lectr contemp art, New Sch for Social Res, New York, 76- Pos: Art dir mod & contemp art, Spencer Enterprises, New York, 57-; art consult & appraiser, United Jewish Appeal, New York, 69- & Am Friends Haifa Univ, Israel, 73- Mem: Am Fedn of Arts; Brooklyn Mus Art Sch (bd trustee, 73). Specialty: Modern and contemporary art with emphasis on abstract expressionism; abstract figurative expressionism. Collection: Flemish period to modern and contemporary American and European art, 19th and 20th centuries. Mailing Add: 50 W 57th St New York NY 10019

BERMAN, ARIANE R
PAINTER, PRINTMAKER
b Freeport, Danzig, Mar 27, 37; US citizen. Study: Hunter Col, BFA, 59; Yale Univ, scholar, 59-62 & MFA, 62; Am Asn Univ Women & Fondation Etats-Unis grants, Ecole Beaux Artes, 62-63; and with Stanley William Hayter & lithography with Jacques Desjobert. Work: Metrop Mus Art; Philadelphia Mus Art, Pa; Philadelphia Art Alliance; US Info Agency via Am Color Print Soc Exhib; Am Petrol Inst, Washington, DC. Comn: Painting, Seventeen Mag, 71; painting, Shipley Sch, Bryn Mawr, Pa, 71; painting, Charles E Ellis Col, Newtown Square, Pa, 71; plus others. Exhib: Several one-man shows, incl Fontana Gallery, 63, 71 & 74, Eileen Kuhlik Gallery, New York, 71 & 73, Butler Inst Am Art 36th Ann, 72, Gallery Art Helioart, Rome, 74; Munson Gallery, Conn, 75; Ward-Nasse Gallery, New York, 75-77; plus many group exhibs. Pos: Chairperson Fulbright grants in painting, Nat Screening Comt, 78, juror, 77. Awards: Painting Prize, Yale Univ Sch Fine Arts, 62; Gold Medal & Purchase Prize, Philadelphia Art Alliance, 73; Catherine Lorillard Wolfe Arts Club Gold Medal, 73; plus others. Bibliog: Cover story in, Host Mag, 73; plus articles in many periodicals. Mem: Am Color Print Soc; Nat Asn Women Artists; Silvermine Guild Artists; Philadelphia Art Alliance; Yonkers Art Asn. Style & Technique: Figurative, using large flat areas of color for both mood and abstraction of design. Media: Acrylic, Serigraphs. Dealer: Assoc Am Artists 663 Fifth Ave New York NY 10022; Ward-Nasse Gallery 131 Prince St New York NY 10012. Mailing Add: 161 W 54th St New York NY 10019

BERMAN, BERNARD
COLLECTOR
b Pennsburg, Pa, Aug 28, 20. Mem: Am Asn Mus, Washington, DC (trustee); Allentown Art Mus, Pa (pres bd trustees, 71-). Collection: German Expressionist, Italian sculpture, American artists. Mailing Add: 2830 Gordon St Allentown PA 18104

BERMAN, FRED J
PAINTER, PHOTOGRAPHER
b Milwaukee, Wis, Nov 3, 26. Study: Milwaukee State Teachers Col, BS; Univ Wis-Madison, MS. Work: Norton Mus Art, Fla; Elvejhem Art Ctr, Madison, Wis; Ft Lauderdale Mus, Fla; Milwaukee Art Ctr. Exhib: Walker Art Ctr Biennials, Minneapolis, Minn, 47, 51, 54, 56 & 62; 6th Biennial Contemp Am Paintings, Va Mus of Fine Arts, Richmond, 48; Pa Acad Fine Arts Ann, Philadelphia, 51, 52 & 53; Am Watercolors, Drawings & Prints, Metrop Mus of Art, New York, 52; Corcoran Biennials, Corcoran Gallery Art, Washington, DC, 53, 55 & 59; Am Exhib, Art Inst Chicago, 54 & 57; Whitney Ann, 59 & Young Am, 60, Whitney Mus Am Art, New York; Venice Biennale, Italy, 56; San Francisco Mus Art Ann, 60 & 65; Summer Exhib, Royal Acad Art, London, 67; one-man exhibs, Milwaukee Art Ctr, 51 & 64, Tyler Sch Art, Pa, 75, Brown Univ, 75, Palo Alto Cult Ctr, Calif, 76 & Bristol Art Mus, RI, 77. Teaching: Instr painting & printmaking, Layton Sch Art, Milwaukee, Wis, 49-60; prof design & drawing, Univ Wis-Milwaukee, 60- Awards: Milwaukee Art Inst Award, Milwaukee Art Ctr, 47, 52, 53, 54 & 56; Joseph Eisendrath Award, Chicago & vicinity, Art Inst Chicago, 50; Wis Union Top Purchase Award, Wis Salon Art, Univ Wis-Madison, 67. Style & Technique: Semi-abstract landscapes, interiors, urban themes and ambiguous images. Media: Oil, charcoal; color photography. Dealer: Bradley Galleries 2562 N Downer Ave Milwaukee WI 53211. Mailing Add: 2321 E Belleview Pl Milwaukee WI 53211

BERMAN, MURIEL MALLIN
COLLECTOR, PATRON
b Pittsburgh, Pa, June 21, 24. Study: Univ Pittsburgh; Carnegie-Mellon Univ; Pa Col Optom; Cedar Crest Col; Muhlenberg Col. Teaching: Lects on African art and its origins, American, French, Picasso, Wyeth, fakes, forgeries and reproductions. Pos: Mem, Pa Coun Arts; hon chmn, Bucks Co Collectors Art Show, New Hope, Pa, 66; co-chmn, Episcopal Diocese Bicentennial Art Comn, 71; numerous other govt, civic & educ positions. Mem: Art Collectors Club Am; Am Fedn Arts; Friends Whitney Mus Am Art; Arch Am Art, Detroit; Mus Mod Art, New York; plus many others. Interest: Collection on loan, Art in the US Embassies Program; founder and donor, Carnegie-Berman College Art Slide Library Exchange; Berman Circulating Traveling Art Exhibitions, colleges and museums in the East. Collection: Early 20th century American modern, pop and op art; Eskimo, Japanese, Aboriginal Australian, French and African. Mailing Add: 20 Hundred Nottingham Rd Allentown PA 18103

BERMAN, NANCY MALLIN
MUSEUM DIRECTOR, ART HISTORIAN
b Philadelphia, Pa, Oct 20, 45. Study: Wellesley Col, BA, 67; Hunter Col; Hebrew Union Col; Calif Sch of Masters; Jewish Theol Sem, New York. Pos: Cur, Lester Francis Avnet Collection, New York, 67-68; cur, Judaica Dept, Jewish Mus, New York, 68-72; cur, Skirball Mus, Hebrew Union Col, Los Angeles, 72-77, dir, 77- Res: Jewish art, especially the development of the Hanukah Lamp in relation to prevailing architectural styles. Mailing Add: 3077 University Ave Los Angeles CA 90007

BERMAN, PHILIP I
COLLECTOR, PATRON
b Pennsburg, Pa, June 28, 15. Study: Ursinus Col, LLD, 68; Lehigh Univ, LHD, 69. Pos: Pres, Philip & Muriel Berman Found; chmn vis comt, Fine & Creative Arts, Lehigh Univ, 66-; many other positions in bus, govt, educ, civic & art activities. Awards: First Ann Am Jewish Comn Pa, Del, Md Region Award; Distinguished Serv Award, Allentown CofC; Outstanding Civic Leaders Am Award, 68; plus others. Mem: Life fel Metrop Mus Art, New York; Aspen Ctr Contemp Art; Am Fedn Arts; Art Collectors Club Am; Arch Am Art; plus many other art mus & asns. Interest: Collections on traveling exhibitions and temporary loan in the US; many paintings on permanent loan to civic and educational institutions in Lehigh Valley area; participant in Art in the Embassies Program. Collection: American, French and Japanese art. Mailing Add: 20 Hundred Nottingham Rd Allentown PA 18103

BERMAN, REBECCA ROBBINS
GALLERY DIRECTOR, PAINTER
b Pittsburgh, Pa. Study: Univ Pittsburgh; Divine Prov Acad. Work: Carnegie Inst Mus Art, Pittsburgh. Pos: Exec dir, Pittsburgh Plan for Art, 60- Awards: Purchase Prize, Best of Show & Jury Distinction, Assoc Artists. Style & Technique: Space-oriented minimal art. Media: Craypas; Oil. Specialty: Non-profit organization for professional artists. Mailing Add: 808 Morewood Ave Pittsburgh PA 15213

BERMAN, STEVEN M
PAINTER, PRINTMAKER
b Chicago, Ill, Jan 18, 47. Study: Kansas City Art Inst, BFA, 70; Chicago Art Inst, MFA, 72. Work: House of Culture, Moscow, USSR; Wichita Art Mus, Kans; Playboy Enterprises, Chicago; Western Ill Univ, Macomb; Kansas City Art Inst, Mo. Exhib: One-man shows, Phyllis Kind Gallery, Chicago & Chicago Art Inst, 72 & Rebecca Cooper Gallery, Washington, DC, 77; Extraordinary Realities, Whitney Mus Am Art, New York, 73-74; Mid Am Five, Nelson Mus Art, Kansas City, 74; The Small Scale in Contemporary Art, Chicago Art Inst, 75. Teaching: Instr painting & drawing, Wichita State Univ, 72-76, asst prof painting & drawing, 76-77. Awards: Ryerson Traveling Fel Grant, Chicago Art Inst, 72; Renaissance Prize for painting, 73; St Louis Art Mus Prize for painting, 74. Bibliog: Ivan Karp (auth), Olympics of Art, New York, 74; B J Smith (auth), Festured artist, Cimarron Review, Okla State Univ, 75; Peter Frank (auth), The Small Scale in Contemporary Art, Chicago Art Inst, 75. Mem: Wichita Fine Arts Coun (vchmn, 75-76); Wichita Artist Guild (bd mem, 75-76). Style & Technique: Fantasy landscapes, optical color misture theory; surreal qualities with humorous overtones; small in scale. Media: Acrylic on Masonite Board; Lithography. Publ: Illusr, A sporting life, Playboy Mag, 1/76, Italian issue, 2/76. Dealer: Rebecca Cooper

Gallery 2130 P St NW Washington DC 20037. Mailing Add: 9343 Oak Park Ave Morton Grove IL 60053

BERMAN, VIVIAN
PRINTMAKER
b New York, NY, Aug 28, 28. Study: Cooper Union, BFA; Art Students League; Brandeis Univ, with Mitchell Siporin. Work: Libr Cong, Washington, DC; Wiggin Collection, Boston Pub Libr, Mass; Pa Acad Art; De Cordova Mus, Lincoln, Mass; Hopkins Art Ctr, Dartmouth Col. Exhib: Boston Printmakers Ann, 68-75; Libr Cong Nat Print Exhib, 70; Davidson Nat Print & Drawing Competition, Davidson Col, 72-73; 18th Nat Print Exhib, Brooklyn Mus, 73; Nat Exhib Collagraphs, Pratt Graphic Ctr, New York, 75. Awards: Award for Graphics, Springfield Mus Art, 69; Purchase Award, Libr Cong Pennel Fund, 70; Purchase Award, Nat Print Show, Western NMex Univ, 71; plus others. Mem: Cambridge Art Asn (exec bd mem, 68-70); Boston Visual Artists Union; Boston Printmakers (exec bd mem, 69, pres, 70-75); NH Art Asn; Graphics Soc. Style & Technique: Semi-abstract and sometimes surreal style; collagraph and combination collagraph and serigraph, lithograph and others. Dealer: Ainsworth Gallery 42 Bromfield St Boston MA 02108; Assoc Am Artists 663 Fifth Ave New York 10022. Mailing Add: 11 Barberry Rd Lexington MA 02173

BERMUDEZ, EUGENIA M
See Dignac, Geny

BERMUDEZ, JOSE YGNACIO
SCULPTOR, PAINTER
b Havana, Cuba, Aug 6, 22; US citizen. Study: With Roberto Diago, Havana, Cuba, 52-53; Bell Voc Sch, Washington, DC, 61. Work: Mus Mod Art, New York; Corcoran Gallery Art, Washington, DC; Mus Bellas Artes, Caracas, Venezuela; Philadelphia Mus Art; Mus Mod Art, Cali, Colombia. Comn: Metal Relief 1961, First Americana Ann Mural Competition, 61. Exhib: New Media-New Form I & II, Martha Jackson Gallery, New York, 60; Corcoran Gallery Art, Washington, DC, 61; Mus Bellas Artes, Caracas, 67; Sculptures & Drawings, Pyramid Galleries, Washington, DC, 70; 3rd Biennial Art Coltejer, Medellin, Colombia, 72; Fountain at Scottsdale Civic Ctr Mall, Ariz, 76. Pos: Asst visual arts, Cult Dept, Orgn Am States, Washington, DC, 53-58, chief graphic serv div, 58-71. Awards: Fourth Prize for Painting, 6th Ann Art Exhib, Havana, 53; Second Prize, 9th Festival Art, Cali, 69; Cintas Fel Found Fel, New York, 69-70. Bibliog: L J Ahlander (auth), article in Washington Post, 7/29/62; T Alvarengo (auth), Imagen, Arte y Technologia, 71. Media: Metal. Dealer: Pyramid Galleries Ltd 2121 P St NW Washington DC 20037. Mailing Add: 4109 E Via Estrella Phoenix AZ 85028

BERNARD, DAVID EDWIN
PRINTMAKER, EDUCATOR
b Sandwich, Ill, Aug 8, 13. Study: Univ Ill, BFA; Univ Iowa, MFA; and with Mauricio Lasansky & Humbert Albrizio. Work: Pennell Collection, Libr Cong, Washington, DC; Mid-Am Collection, Nelson Gallery, Atkins Mus, Kansas City, Mo; Otis Art Inst, Los Angeles, Calif; Free Pub Libr, Philadelphia, Pa; Joslyn Mus, Omaha, Nebr. Comn: Mural (steel & wood), Duerksen Fine Art Ctr, Wichita State Univ, 57; free standing tree symbol (steel), Camp Fire Girls Orgn, Wichita Art Mus, Kans, 60; sculpture (steel, wood & brass), Irene Vickers Baker Children's Theatre, Wichita; pair of standing tree shapes, Art Asn Wichita, 71-72. Exhib: God and Man in Art, Am Fedn Arts Traveling Exhib, 57; First Ann, Otis Art Inst, 61; two-man traveling print exhib, Inst Cult Mexicano-Norte Americano, Guadalajara & five cities in Mex, 63; Univ Nebr Print Exhib, Sheldon Art Gallery, Lincoln, 67; one-man exhib prints, Philbrook Art Ctr, Tulsa, Okla, 67. Teaching: Instr art prog, Maryville Col, 46-48; prof printmaking, Wichita State Univ, 49- Awards: Purchase Award for Hombre y Toro (intaglio), Pennell Collection, Libr Cong, 53; Purchase Award for Calvary (colored intaglio), Mid-Am Ann, Nelson Gallery, 55; Purchase Award for La Mer (colored intaglio), 10th Kans Artists Ann, Wichita Art Mus, 64. Mem: Soc Am Graphic Artists; Calif Soc Printmakers; Artists Guild Wichita (pres, 56); Mid-Am Col Art Asn; Wichita Art Mus Mem. Style & Technique: Symbolic realism. Media: Intaglio, Collagraph. Publ: Auth, The collagraph print, Artists Proof, 62; illusr, A West Wind Rises, 62 & Sun City, 64, Univ Nebr Press. Mailing Add: 2243 N Yale Ave Wichita KS 67220

BERNARD, FELIX S
ART DEALER
b Vienna, Austria, Dec 7, 19; US citizen. Study: Akademie der Darstellenden Kunst, Vienna; Univ Calif, Berkeley, MBA. Pos: Owner, Bernard Galleries, Walnut Creek & Laguna Beach, Calif. Awards: First Prize Norma Award, Gallery for Outstanding Newspaper Advert, 77. Specialty: Publishers of the serigraphs of Marco Sassone; decorative antique graphics. Mailing Add: c/o Bernard Galleries 1489 E Newell Ave Walnut Creek CA 94596

BERNAY, BETTI
PAINTER
b New York, NY, Sept 21, 26. Study: Pratt Inst; Nat Acad Design, New York, with Louis Bouche; Art Students League, with Frank Mason; also with Robert Brackman. Work: Circulo Amistad, Cordoba, Spain; Columbus Mus Arts & Crafts, Ga; Columbia Mus Art, SC; Andre Weil Collection, Paris. Comn: Painting, pres of Renault, Madrid, Spain, 64; painting, Children Have No Barriers, IOS Found, Geneva, 69; paintings, Macaws, Seacost E Bldg, Miami Beach, Fla, 69 & mural, Sandy Cove, S Bldg, 70. Exhib: One-man shows, Columbus Mus Arts & Crafts, 60, Columbia Mus Art, 60, Andre Weil Gallery, 60 & 63 & Mus Malaga, Spain, 65; Salas Munic, San Sebastian, Spain, 58; Circulo de Bellas Artes, Madrid, Spain, 59; Mus of Mod Art, Paris, France, 63; Salon des Artistes Independants, Grand Palais, Paris, 63; Salon Populiste, Mus Mod Art, Paris, 63; Mus of Bella Artes, Malaga, Spain, 65; Bacardi Gallery, Miami, Fla, 67; Metrop Mus & Art Ctr, Miami, 75; Rosenbaum Gallery, Palm Beach, Fla, 77; plus many others. Awards: Artistic Merit Medal, City of New York, 42; Prix de Paris, 58; Medal of Honor, Mus Bellas Artes, Malaga, 65. Mem: Artists Equity Asn; Am Artists Prof League; Nat Asn Painters & Sculptors Spain; Soc Artistes Français; Prof Artists Guild; Women's Caucus for Art; Soc Artistes Independants. Style & Technique: Realistic interpretations with simplicity and sincereity. Media: Oil. Mailing Add: 5001 Collins Ave Miami Beach FL 33140

BERNE, GUSTAVE MORTON
COLLECTOR
b New York, NY, Mar 4, 03. Study: Columbia Col, AB, Columbia Law Sch, LLB. Pos: Pres, Long Island Jewish Med Ctr, NY. Collection: French impressionists. Mailing Add: 9 Beech Ln Great Neck NY 11024

BERNECHE, JERRY DOUGLAS
EDUCATOR, PAINTER
b Greentown, Ind, July 24, 32. Study: John Herron Art Sch, BFA, 56, studies painting and printmaking with Garo Antreasian; Ohio Univ, MFA, 59, study with Robert Friemark. Work: Butler Mus Am Art, Youngstown, Ohio; Springfield Art Mus, Mo; Canton Art Mus & Massillon Mus, Ohio; Mo State Hist Soc, Columbia. Exhib: Drawing USA Nat, Walker Art Mus, 62; Mid-Am Nat Exhib, Butler Mus Art, 62-64; Chautauqua Exhib Art, NY, 65-67; Springfield Regional Exhib, 66-75; Watercolor USA Nat, Springfield, 73-74. Teaching: Instr art, Cooper Art Sch, Cleveland, Ohio, 62-65 & Mont State Univ, Bozeman, 65-66; assoc prof drawing & painting, Univ Mo, Columbia, 66- Awards: Mrs E J Bellinger Award, Chautauqua Nat Exhib, 65 & 67; Watercolor Purchase Award, Watercolor USA, 73. Style & Technique: Representational with emphasis on broad color areas. Media: Oil and Printmaking. Mailing Add: 3708 Oakland Rd Columbia MO 65201

BERNSTEIN, BENJAMIN D
COLLECTOR
b New York, NY, June 24, 07. Pos: Patron, Whitney Mus; mem, Philadelphia Art Alliance; mem bd trustees, Pa Acad Fine Arts. Mem: Life mem Am Fedn Arts; Metrop Mus Art; fel Philadelphia Mus Art; Mus Mod Art, New York; Buten Mus of Wedgewood. Collection: Large collection of contemporary oils, gouache, drawings, prints and sculpture including a great many Cobra works; large colltions of art from New Guinea, Africa, and American Indian art. Mailing Add: 1824 Delancey Pl Philadelphia PA 19103

BERNSTEIN, GERALD
PAINTER, RESTORER
b Indianapolis, Ind, Aug 25, 17. Study: John Herron Art Inst; Art Students League, with George Bridgman & Yasuo Kuniyoshi; NY Univ, BA, Inst Fine Arts, MA. Work: Staten Island Inst Arts & Sci. Exhib: Staten Island Inst Arts & Sci Ann, 50-78; Pietrantonio Gallery, New York, 59-62; one-man show, Kade Gallery, Wagner Col, 73; Metrop Mus, 75; Avery Fisher Hall, Lincoln Ctr, 75. Collections Arranged: Artist Look at Nature, Surveys of American Painting & one-man & group exhibs, Staten Island Mus, 50-56. Teaching: Artist in residence, Staten Island Community Col, 70-71. Pos: Cur art, Staten Island Mus, 50-56; owner & dir, Island Art Ctr, Staten Island, 58- Awards: First Prize for Watercolor, Edison Art Ctr, 68; First Prize, Staten Island Mus Spring Exhib Weissglass Awards, 69; Dennen Award, Snug Harbor Community Gallery, 77. Style & Technique: Semi-abstract motifs deriving from edge of the sea. Media: Oil, Watercolor. Mailing Add: 1639 Richmond Rd Staten Island NY 10304

BERNSTEIN, JOSEPH
COLLECTOR, PATRON
b New Orleans, La, Feb 12, 30. Study: Univ Ala, BS(bus admin), 52; Tulane Law Sch, 57. Pos: Pres, Orleans Gallery, 67-69. Interest: Younger artists in New Orleans area; collecting their work providing sustenance; gifts to New Orleans Mus of Art & Rose Art Mus, Brandeis Univ. Collection: Works of Francis Bacon, Mark Rothko, J DuBuffet, G Oreano, P Guston, J Rosenquist, F Stella, A Warhol & J Rosati. Mailing Add: 5705 St Charles Ave New Orleans LA 70115

BERNSTEIN, JUDITH
PAINTER, LECTURER
b Newark, NJ, Oct 14, 42. Study: Pa State Univ, BS & MS; Yale Univ Sch Art & Archit, BFA & MFA. Work: Mus Mod Art, New York; Int Mus Erotic Art, San Francisco; Univ Colo Mus, Boulder; Int Mus Erotic Art, San Francisco. Exhib: 1st Int Exhib Erotic Art, Konsthall, Sweden & Kunstmuseum, Denmark, 68; one-person shows, AIR Gallery, New York, 73 & Univ Colo Mus, Boulder, 76; Erotica, Allan Stone Gallery, New York, 73; Warren Benedek Gallery, New York, 73; Five Americans a Paris, Galerie Gerald Piltzer, Paris, 75; Yr of the Women, Bronx Mus of Arts, NY, 75; Contemp Women: Consciousness & Content, Brooklyn Mus, NY, 77. Teaching: Pratt Inst; Rutgers Univ; asst prof fine arts, State Univ NY Stony Brook, 74-; vis slide lectr on own work and contemp women artists, 72- Awards: Elizabeth Canfield Hicks Mem Scholar, Yale Univ Sch Art & Archit, 64-67; Individual Artists Fel Grant, Nat Endowment Arts, 74-75. Bibliog: Jay Jacobs (auth), Etcetera-Judith Bernstein, Art Gallery, 6/74; Jeremy Gilbert-Rolfe (auth), Judith Bernstein, Artforum, 6/74; Cindy Nemser, (auth), Four artists of sensuality-Antin, Benglis, Bernstein, Wilke, Arts Mag, 3/75. Mem: Col Art Asn Am (Women's Caucus); Nat Soc Lit & Arts. Style & Technique: Large charcoal drawings of phallic/screws; architectural scale. Mailing Add: 45 E Broadway New York NY 10002

BERNSTEIN, SYLVIA
PAINTER, SCULPTOR
b Brooklyn, NY, Apr 11, 18. Study: Nat Acad Design; and with Arthur Covey, Gifford Beal, Sidney Dickinson, Charles Hinton, Carl Anderson & Leon Kroll. Work: New Brit Mus Am Art, Conn; Corcoran Gallery of Art, Washington, DC; Adlai Stevenson Mem Inst, Chicago; Univ Maine, Orono; Norfolk Mus, Va; Va Mus Fine Arts, Richmond. Exhib: 21st Nat Watercolor Biennial, Brooklyn Mus, 61; Childe Hassam Fund Paintings Exhib, Am Acad Arts & Lett, 61; Contemporary American Drawings, Smithsonian Inst Traveling Exhib, 66-67; 200 Years of Watercolor Painting in America, Metrop Mus Art, New York, 67 & Philadelphia Art Alliance Watercolor Painting in America, 67; Philadelphia Art Alliance Watercolor Show, 71-72. Awards: Zimmerman Mem Award for Most Distinguished Entry, Philadelphia Watercolor Club, 62; Medal of Honor for Watercolor, 63 & Medal of Honor for Oils, 74, Nat Asn Women Artists; Medal of Honor for Watercolor, Nat Arts Club. Mem: Nat Asn Women Painters (chmn watercolor jury, bd dirs); Philadelphia Watercolor Soc; Am Watercolor Soc; Audubon Artists; NY Soc Women Artists. Style & Technique: Subjective lyrical imagery in painting; figurative and semi-abstract in sculpture. Media: Watercolor, Oil. Mailing Add: 8 Circle Rd Scarsdale NY 10583

BERNSTEIN, THERESA
PAINTER, ART HISTORIAN
b Philadelphia, Pa. Study: Pa Acad Fine Arts; Art Students League. Work: Metrop Mus Art; Brooklyn Mus; Harvard Univ; Phillips Art Gallery, Washington, DC; Nat Mus, Smithsonian Inst. Comn: First Orchestra in America, Treas Dept for Mannhein, Pa, 40; portrait of Prof David Lyons, Harvard Univ Biblical Mus Fac, 54; portrait of Prof Robert Pheiffer, Harvard Univ, 56; portrait of Henrietta Szold, Founder of Hadassan, comn by mem of family, 59. Exhib: Exhib Am Painters, Metrop Mus Art, New York, 50; Carnegie Inst, Pittsburgh; Biennial Am Art, Corcoran Gallery Art, Washington, DC; Nat Mus, Smithsonian Inst, Washington, DC, 56; New York Ann, Nat Acad Design. Teaching: Dir summer art course, Gloucester, Mass, 32-69. Awards: Shilliard Gold Medal, Plastic Club, 25; Jeanne d'Arc Medal, Fr Inst Arts & Lett, 29; John A Johnson Award, North Shore Arts Asn, 71. Bibliog: Dorothy Adlow (auth), article in Christian Sci Monitor, 29; E A Jenell (auth), articles in New York Times, 45 & Menorah J, 48. Mem: Nat Asn Women Artists (jury awards, 38-59); Audubon Artists Am (mem jury, 50-); Soc Am Graphic Artists; Allied Artists Am; New York Soc Women Artists (dir, 28-). Media: Oil, Aquarelle, Graphics. Res: Graphic art; American art. Publ: Auth, William Meyerowitz, 58 & auth, History of Jewish Artists, 58, Zukenft; auth, History-Cape Ann artists, Gloucester Times, 70; auth, History North Shore Arts Association,

72; auth, History New York Society of Women Artists, 72. Mailing Add: 54 W 74th St New York NY 10023

BERNSTEIN, WILLIAM JOSEPH
DESIGNER, GLASSBLOWER
b Newark, NJ, Dec 3, 45. Study: Philadelphia Col Art, BFA, 68; Penland Sch, NC, craftsman in residence, 68-70. Work: Mint Mus Art, Charlotte, NC; Nat Collection Fine Art, Washington, DC; Craft & Folk Art Mus, Los Angeles; R J Reynolds Collection, Winston-Salem, NC; Contemporary Glass 1976 Microfiche Collection, Corning Mus, NY. Exhib: American Glass Now, Toledo Mus Art, Ohio, 72; Fun & Fantasy for Children, Xerox Corp, Fairtree Gallery, Xerox Hall, Rochester, NY, 73; Baroque '74, Mus Contemp Crafts, New York, 74; In Praise of Hands, 1st World Crafts Exhib, Toronto, Can, 74; Craft Multiples, Renwick Gallery, Smithsonian Inst, Washington, DC, 75; Philadelphia Mus of Art, 77; Am Crafts in the White House, White House, Washington, DC, 77. Awards: Nat Endowment Arts Fel, 74; Louis Comfort Tiffany Found Grant, 75. Bibliog: R L Grover (auth), Contemporary Art Glass, Crown Publ, 75; F Kulasiewicz (auth), Glassblowing, Watson-Guptill, 75; Design in Modern Interiors, article in Studio Vista, 75. Style & Technique: Design and direct work in free blown glass of both functional and sculptural pieces. Mailing Add: Box 73 AA Rte 5 Burnsville NC 28714

BERRESFORD, VIRGINIA
PAINTER, MURALIST
b New Rochelle, NY. Study: Teacher's Col, Columbia Univ, with Charles Martin; Acad Mod, Paris, France, with Ozenfant. Work: Whitney Mus Am Art, New York; Detroit Mus, Mich; Columbus Gallery Fine Arts, Ohio. Comn: Juliet by Moonlight (mural), comn by Katharine Cornell, Assoc Hall, Vineyard Haven, Mass. Exhib: World's Fair, 39; Pa Acad Fine Arts; Mus Mod Art, New York; Brooklyn Mus, NY; Art Inst Chicago; plus many other group & one-woman shows. Style & Technique: Simplified smooth forms in landscape and still life; emphasis on composition; free, simplified brushwork based on Oriental technique. Media: Oil, Watercolor. Dealer: E Ives Bartholet 55 E 76th St New York NY 10021. Mailing Add: RFD Vineyard Haven MA 02568

BERRY, GLENN
PAINTER, EDUCATOR
b Glendale, Calif, Feb 27, 29. Study: Pomona Col, BA(magna cum laude); Art Inst Chicago, BFA & MFA. Work: Storm King Art Ctr, Mountainville, NY; Joseph H Hirshhorn Collection, Washington, DC; Kaiser Aluminum & Chem Corp, Oakland, Calif; Palm Springs Desert Mus, Calif; Calif State Univ, Humboldt. Exhib: Phelan Awards Exhib & Artists Behind Artists, Calif Palace of Legion of Honor, San Francisco, 67; one-man shows, Ingomar Gallery, Eureka, Calif, 68, Ankrum Gallery, Los Angeles, 70, Esther Bear Gallery, Santa Barbara, Calif, 71 & Humboldt State Univ, 75; Six Northern Calif Artists, Henry Gallery, Univ Wash, 75; two-man show, Humboldt Cult Ctr, Eureka, Calif, 77; Mural, Griffith Hall, Humboldt State Univ, Arcata, Calif, 78. Teaching: Prof painting, Humboldt State Univ, 56- Style & Technique: Surreal. Media: Acrylic, Oil. Dealer: Ankrum Gallery 657 N La Cienega Blvd Los Angeles CA 90069. Mailing Add: Dept of Art Humboldt State Univ Arcata CA 95521

BERRY, WILLIAM DAVID
ILLUSTRATOR, SCULPTOR
b San Mateo, Calif, May 20, 26. Study: Art Ctr Sch of Los Angeles, 43; Sch of Allied Arts, Glendale, Calif, 47-50; Univ Alaska, 71. Work: Anchorage Hist & Fine Arts Mus, Alaska. Comn: Murals, Fairbanks Mem Hosp, 72 & Fairbanks North Star Borough Pub Libr, 78. Exhib: An Exhib of Bird Paintings: William D Berry & Robert V Clem, Los Angeles Co Mus, 57; one-man shows, Univ Alaska Mus, Fairbanks, 68 & Anchorage Hist & Fine Arts Mus, 70; Am Natural Hist Art Show, James Ford Bell Mus Natural Hist, Minn, 71. Teaching: Instr life drawing, Tanana Valley Community Col, Fairbanks, 75-77, instr animal drawing, 76-77. Bibliog: Reginald A Emmert (auth), Bill Berry: artist of the Far North, Alaska J, Vol 1 (summer 71); feature prog, Bill Berry, Alaskan Artist, KUAC Television, Univ Alaska, Fairbanks, 72. Style & Technique: Representational and illustrative: chiefly wildlife and figure. Media: Watercolor, Charcoal Pencil; Bronze. Publ: Illusr, Mammals of Los Angeles Co, Los Angeles Co Mus, 59; co-auth & illusr, Mammals of the San Francisco Bay Region, Univ Calif Press, 59; auth & illusr, Buffalo Land, 61 & Deneki, an Alaskan Moose, 65, Macmillan; illusr, Animals of the North, Harper & Row, 66. Dealer: Gloria Fischer The Artworks 3055 College Rd Fairbanks AK 99701. Mailing Add: Miller Hill SR Box 20063 Fairbanks AK 99701

BERTHOT, JAKE
PAINTER
b Niagara Falls, NY, Mar 30, 39. Study: New Sch for Social Res, New York, Work: Brandeis Univ, Waltham, Mass; Va Mus Fine Arts, Richmond; Whitney Mus Am Art, New York; Aldrich Mus Contemp Art, Ridgefield, Conn. Exhib: One-man exhib, O K Harris Gallery, New York, 70, 72 & 75, Portland Ctr for the Visual Arts, Ore, 72, Galerie de Gestlo, Hamburg, Ger, 73 & 77, Daniel Weinberg, San Francisco, 75, David McKee Gallery, New York, 76; group exhib, Ann, Whitney Mus Am Art, 69 & 73, Recent Acquisitions, 71, Continuing Abstraction in Am Art, 74; Contemp Drawings, Chicago Art Inst, 71; Highlights of the 1970-71 Season, Aldrich Mus, Ridgefield, Conn, 71; Eight New York Painters, Univ Calif Art Mus, Berkeley, 72; Paris Biennale, France, 73; Recent Abstract Painting, Pratt Inst, Brooklyn, NY, 74; Corcoran Biennial, Corcoran Gallery, Washington, DC, 75; Fundamental Painting, Stedelijk Mus, Amsterdam, 75; Venice Biennale, US Pavilion, 76; From Women's Eyes, Rose Art Mus, Brandeis Univ, Mass, 77; New Acquisitions Show, Mus Mod Art, New York, 77; plus others. Bibliog: Kasha Linville (auth), Jake Berthot at O K Harris, Art in Am, 1/73; Dore Ashton (auth), Peinture, Peinture-O, Painterly Painting, Plural, 9/73 & Jake Berthot, Arts, 6/74; Peter Plagens (auth), Peter and the Pressure Cooker, Artforum, 6/74. Dealer: Daivd McKee Gallery 140 E 63rd St New York NY 10021. Mailing Add: 66 Grand St New York NY 10013

BERTOIA, HARRY
SCULPTOR, GRAPHIC ARTIST
b San Lorenzo, Italy, Mar 10, 15; US citizen. Study: Arts & Crafts Sch, Detroit, Mich; Cranbrook Acad Art, Bloomfield Hills, Mich, 37-42. Work: Va Mus Fine Art; San Francisco Mus Art; Mus Mod Art; Dallas Pub Libr, Tex; Denver Art Mus; plus others. Comn: Sculptural screens, Gen Motors Tech Ctr, Detroit, Mfrs Trust Bank, NY & Mass Inst Technol Chapel; bronze sculpture, View of Earth from Space, Dulles Airport, Washington, DC, 62; copper & bronze fountain piece, Civic Ctr, Philadelphia, 67; plus others. Exhib: Mus Nonobjective Art, New York; circulating exhib, Smithsonian Inst; Whitney Mus Am Art; Mus Mod Art; Int Sculpture Exhib, Battersea Park, London, Eng. Awards: Gold Medal, Archit League NY, 55; Gold Medal, Am Inst Architects, 56; Graham Fel, 57. Bibliog: Wayne Craven (auth), Sculpture in America, Crowell, 68; Eduard Trier (auth), Form & Space: Sculpture in the 20th Century, Praeger, 68; plus others. Media: Copper, Bronze. Dealer: Fairweather-Hardin Gallery 101 E Ontario St Chicago IL 60611; Staempfli Gallery 47 E 77th St New York NY 10021. Mailing Add: RD1 Barto PA 19504

BERTONI, DANTE H
PAINTER, ILLUSTRATOR
b New York, NY, Nov 13, 26. Study: Parson's Sch Design, New York, Advert Design Cert, 51; Art Students League, with Bernard Klonis, 52-54; NY Univ, 60. Work: US Navy Combat Art Collection, Washington Naval Yard, DC; Forbes Mag Collection, New York; Hotel DuPont Collection, Wilmington, Del; Mutual Benefit Life Ins Co Collection, New York. Comn: Sea Mule (illus), Lederle Labs, Am Cyanamid Co, Wayne, NJ, 71; Atomic Submarine Base, New London, Conn, Rear Adm L R Geis, US Navy, 70, Exotic Dancer (exercise), Rear Adm William Thompson, 71, Oper Homecoming & Endsweep, Capt D M Cooney, 73; Proceedings (cover illus), US Naval Inst, Annapolis, Md, 72. Exhib: Am Watercolor Soc, NY, 55-; Nat Acad Fine Arts, 56-; Nat Arts Club, 60-; Salmagundi Sketch Club, 55-; US Navy Combat Art Exhibit Travel Show, Washington Navy Yard, DC, 70- Pos: Asst art dir, J Walter Thompson, New York, 51-57; graphics designer, Lippencott & Margulies Co, 62-63; package designer, Reigel Paper Co, 64-66; artist, Equitable Bag Co, 72- Awards: Spec Award for watercolor, Long Beach Art Asn, 70; NACAL Gold Medal, Louis E Seley, 72; Grand Prize Washington Sq Outdoor Art Exhib, Lufthansa Air Lines, 73. Bibliog: Mary O'Flaherty (auth), Artist pictures way through Navy activity, New York News, 11/14/71. Mem: Am Watercolor Soc, New York; Salmagundi Sketch Club (vchmn NACAL, 70); US Naval Inst, Annapolis, Md; Long Beach Art Asn, NY; Am Vet Soc Artists, New York. Style & Technique: Representational realist; traditional transparent wet-on-wet through dry-on-dry glazes, augmented with brush stroking, puddling, wiping, sponging, palette-knifing and scraping. Dealer: Chadd's Ford Gallery Inc Rte 1 & 100 Chadd's Ford PA 19317. Mailing Add: 52-02 Eighth Ave Brooklyn NY 11220

BERZON, IRENE GROSS
See Gross, Irene

BESNER, J JACQUES
SCULPTOR, EDUCATOR
b Vaudreuil, Que, Can, Sept 28, 19. Study: Teachers' Col, Univ Montreal, Que, 42; study of archit, Int Corresp Sch, Chicago, Ill. Work: Phoenix Art Mus, Ariz; Bhirla Mus, Calcutta, India; Mus d'Art Contemporain & Thomas More Inst, Montreal, Que; Winston Collection, Dearborn, Mich. Comn: Monumental kinetic piece (stainless steel), Avnet Corp, New York; aluminum mural, Aluminum Co Jamaica-Kingston, 72, 12 ft by 8ft piece, Aluminum Co Can Ltd, Montreal, 76, 16 ft by 9 ft piece, Chromasco-Timminsco Inc Montreal, 76 & 30 ft by 15 ft piece, Montreal Metro-Aqueduct Sta, 77. Exhib: Montreal Mus Fine Arts, Can, 64; Jeune Sculpture, Rodin Mus, Paris, 65; Mus d'Art Contemporain, Montreal, Que, 65-68; Pagani Found, Milan, Italy, 68; Rose Fried Gallery, New York, 68; Nat Cult Ctr, Ottawa, Ont, 70; Que Pavilion, Expo 70, Osaka, Japan, 70; Int Arts Fair, Basel, Switz, 73. Collections Arranged: Stratford Festival, Ont, Can, 76; Salon de l'Acier, Brussels, Belg, 68; Pagani Found, Milan, Italy, 68; 20 Years of Que Sculpture, Mus Rodin, Paris, 70. Teaching: Part-time prof, Visual Arts Ctr, Montreal, 69-71 & Saydie Bronfman Ctr, Montreal, 71-73; prof sculpture, Dawson Col, Montreal, 73-75; chmn dept visual arts, Univ Que, Trois Rivieres, 75- Pos: Dir visual arts (Man the Creator), Expo 67, Montreal, Que, 64-67; dir, Maison des Arts la Sauvegarde, Montreal, 67-69. Awards: Rothman's Award, Rothman's of Pall Mall, Stratford, Ont, 65; Que Competition Award, Mus Art Contemporain, Montreal, Cult Affairs, Que, 66; Thomas More Award, Thomas More Inst, Montreal, 69 Bibliog: F Sigouin (auth), Critique, Le Figaro, Paris, 66; Paul Gladu (auth), Monograph, Que Sculptors' Asn, 68; L Levesque (auth), pictorial article, Vie des Arts Mag, Montreal, 71. Mem: Arts Club, Montreal; Prof Artists Asn Que. Style & Technique: Constructivist style including kinetics. Media: Aluminum, stainless steel, copper alloys, plastic. Mailing Add: 212 Sacrement St Montreal PQ H2Y 1W8 Can

BESON, ROBERTA (ROBERTA BESON HILL)
PAINTER, ART ADMINISTRATOR
b Minneapolis, Minn. Study: Univ Minn; Orange Co Jr Col, Newport Beach, Calif, with Stan Parkhouse; and with Pruett Carter & D Logan Hill. Pos: Cur & mgr, D Logan Hill Fine Art Gallery, Carmel, Calif, 67- Media: Oil. Mailing Add: 23222 Caminito Andreta Laguna Hills CA 92653

BESSEMER, AURIEL
MURALIST, ILLUSTRATOR
b Grand Rapids, Mich, Feb 27, 09. Study: Western Reserve Acad, scholar, 24-27; Columbia Univ, Columbia Univ Club scholar, 27-30; Master Inst United Arts, Roerich Mus scholar, 31-33, with Howard Giles; Nat Acad Design, 27-30, with Arthur Covey & Leon Kroll; Art Students League; State Univ NY, 49; George Washington Univ; Wilson Teacher's Col. Comn: Southern Tapestry (mural), Post Off, Winnsboro, SC, 37-38; Life in the Southern Cotton Belt (mural), Post Off, Hazlehurst, Miss, 38-39; six murals, Post Off, Arlington, Va, 39-40; six murals, Wabash Railroad parlor cars, 49; twelve murals, Pa Railroad parlor cars, Congressionals NY to Washington run, 51-52; plus many other murals & portraits. Exhib: One-man shows at 16 art ctrs in the US incl Pub Libr, Washington, DC, City Hall, Asheville, NC, Art Ctr, Raleigh, NC, Currier Gallery, Manchester, NH & Bowdoin Col Mus Fine Arts, Brunswick, Maine, 35-43. Teaching: Instr art, Nat Art Sch, Washington, DC, 45-46; instr art, Jean Morgan Art Sch, New York, 47-49, Roerich Acad Arts, 48-52 & Pan Am Art Sch, 49-51; instr art, Catan-Rose Art Inst, Forest Hills, NY & Montclair Sch Art, NJ, 50; also lectr on & relig; pvt art classes, 63-70; artist-illusr, Summit Lighthouse, Colorado Springs, 72- Pos: Art gallery dir, Gallery Mod Masters, 36-42; spec asst to dir, Univ Sci & Philosophy, Waynesboro, Va, 62. Awards: Maximillian Toch Prize, Nat Acad Design, 30; first hon mem, Chaloner Prize, 32; Dipl & Silver Medal, Tommaso Campanella Int Acad Rome, 70, Gold Medal, 72; plus others. Bibliog: Marian Slater (auth), Auriel Bessemer—artist, philosopher, poet, Voice Universal, 11/62; article in, Georgetown Times, SC, 10/8/64; Margaret Odom (auth), Internationally known artist will teach at YWCA, Columbia Rec, 10/6/66. Style & Technique: Contemporary, with synthesis of historical, classical and romantic influences. Media: Oil. Publ: Illusr, Climb the Highest Mountain, 72, Light from Heavenly Lanterns, 73 & Cosmic Consciousness, 75, Summit Lighthouse. Mailing Add: 1801 NE 58th St Ft Lauderdale FL 33308

BESSER, ARNE CHARLES
PAINTER
b Hinsdale, Ill, May 11, 35. Study: Univ NMex; Art Ctr Sch, Los Angeles, with John Audobon Tyler and Lorser Feidelsson. Comn: Portrait of Mr Aldrich, Chmn Bd, Chemical Bank, 68; painting, comn by Stuart M Speiser, 73. Exhib: Lowe Art Mus, Coral Gables, Fla, 74; Pa State Mus Art, University Park, 74; Butler Inst Am Art, Youngstown, Ohio, 75; Louis K Meisel Gallery, New York, 75; Baltimore Mus Art, 75. Awards: Butler Inst of Am Art Medal of Merit, Today's Art Mag, 75. Style & Technique: Photo realism. Media: Oil on

Canvas, Watercolor. Mailing Add: c/o Louis K Meisel Gallery 141 Prince St New York NY 10012

BETANCOURT, R ARENAS
SCULPTOR
b El Uvital, Antioquia, Colombia, SAm, Oct 23, 19. Study: Fine Arts Inst, Medellin, 38; Fine Arts Faculty Nat Univ, Bogota, 39-41; San Carlos Acad, Mexico City, 44; La Esmerelda Art Sch, Mex City, 47-48. Work: Nat Corn Comn, Mex. Comn: Painted concrete sculpture, Hospital, Social Security Tower, Mex, 52; bronze sculpture, Univ Autonoma de Mex, 53, Ministry Pub Communications, Mex, 54 & Mex Embassy, Santiago, Chile, 58; forged bronze, Mus Aquiles Zerdan, Puebla, Mex, 62. Exhib: Young Artists of Mex, Chapultepec Park, Mex, 48; Soc of Promotion of Plastic Arts, Inst of Fine Arts, Mex, 48; Exhib of Mex Arts, San Antonio, Tex, 59; Exhib of Mex sculpture, Alameda Cent, Mex, 60; First Interamerican Biennial, Mex, 62; Fourth Sculpture Biennial, Mex, 69; one-man shows, Municipal Salon, Fredonia, 28 & Gallery, Cent Colombo-Am, Bogota, 76. Teaching: Prof drawing, Univ Antioquia, Medellin, 42; prof sculpture, Indust Inst Pascudl Bravo, Medellin, 42-43; prof drawing & sculpture, Worker's Univ, Mex City, 52; prof & founder Artisans Sch, La Ciudadela, Mex, 54-55. Pos: Asst to sculptor Ramon Elias Betancourt, Medellin, 38; asst to sculptor Bernado Viceo, Bogota, 39-41; asst to sculptor Romulo Rozo, Merida, Yucatan, Mex, 45; art adv, Antioquia Univ, Medellin Minister Counselor, Colombia Embassy, Rome, Italy, 66-67. Awards: First Prize in sculpture, for monument to commemorate Battle of May 5th in Puebla, Mex, 62; Cross of Boyaca, for serv to nation, 66; Nat Prize for Plastic Arts of Colombia 72. Bibliog: Orvin Evans Myers (auth), Mod Mex Archit, 50; Margarita Nelken (auth), Contemp Mex Sculpture, 51; Antonio Luna Arroyo (auth), Panorama of Plastic Arts. Mem: Colombian Asn of Writers & Artists; Mex Soc for Plastic Arts; Realistic Artists League, Prauge. Publ: Auth, Chronical of Error of Love and of Death (autobiography), Colcultura, Colombia, 76. Mailing Add: Carrera 72 No 29-27 Medellin Colombia

BETENSKY, ROSE HART
PAINTER, ART ADMINISTRATOR
b New York, NY. Study: Painting with Josef Presser. Exhib: Nat Acad Galleries, New York, 60-77; Royal Acad, Edinburgh, Scotland, 63; Norfolk Mus of Arts & Sci, Va, 64; Cult Inst of Tolsa, Guadalajara, Mex, 65; Palazzo Vecchio, Florence, Italy, 72. Pos: Pres, New York Soc of Women Artists, 69-70, Nat Asn of Women Artists, 70-72 & Am Soc of Contemp Artists, 77- Awards: Lillian Cotton Prize, Nat Asn of Women Artists, 70 & Charlotte Orndorff Prize, 72; Windsor Newton Award, Am Soc of Contemp Artists, 76. Mem: Audubon Artists; Nat Asn of Women Artists; New York Asn of Women Artists; Am Soc of Contemp Artists; Prof Artists Guild of Long Island (vpres, 63). Style & Technique: Abstract in acrylic on paper; acrylic on canvas. Media: Acrylic. Mailing Add: 66 Hayloft Lane Roslyn Heights NY 11577

BETTERIDGE, LOIS ETHERINGTON
SILVER & GOLDSMITH, LECTURER
b Drummonville, Que, Nov 6, 28. Study: Ont Col Art, 47-48; Univ Kans, BFA, 51; Cranbrook Acad Art, MFA, 57. Work: Ont Craft Coun Permanent Collection, Toronto; Nat Mus Natural Sci, Ottawa. Comn: Stations of the Cross, bronze, Marymount Col, Sudbury, Ont, 58; baptismal font & processional Cross, St Christopher's Church, Burlington, 61; communion set, Christ Church Cathedral, Vancouver, 74; bronze sculptures, Int Bus Machines, Can, 75 & Can Nuclear Asn, Ottawa, 76. Exhib: First Nat Fine Crafts Exhib, Nat Gallery, Ottawa, 57; Can Abstract Art, Commonwealth Inst Gallery, London, Eng, 67; Craft Dimensions Can, Royal Ont Mus, Toronto, 69; Jewellery 71, Art Gallery Ont, Toronto, 71; Profile 74, Soc NAm Goldsmiths, Humber Col, Toronto, 74; Reprise, A Retrospective, Cranbrook Acad Art, Mich, 75; Contemp Ont Crafts, Agnes Etherington Gallery, Kingston, Ont, 77; Metalsmiths, Soc NAm Goldsmiths, Phoenix Art Mus, Ariz, 77. Collections Arranged: Metal Four, Craft Gallery, Toronto, 74; Visual Arts Survey Exhib, Ottawa, 75. Teaching: Lectr design, metal & weaving, Univ Guelph, Ont, 57-61; vis lectr & workshop leader, var NAm cols & univs, 69- Pos: Mem bd, Ont Crafts Coun, 72-73, crafts chmn & vpres, Visual Arts Ottawa Region, 74-77 & mem spec projs comt, Can Crafts Coun, 77; mem adv bd visual arts, Algonquin Col Appl Art & Technol, 78. Awards: Commendations (2), De Beers Int Diamond Ring Competition, London, 66; Citation Distinguished Prof Achievement, Univ Kans, 75. Mem: Ont Crafts Coun (mem bd, 72-73); Soc NAm Goldsmiths; Can Crafts Coun (mem spec projs comt, 77); Visual Arts Ottawa Region (crafts chmn & vpres, 74-77). Style & Technique: Raised vessels, chasing & repousee bas relief. Media: Silver, Gold. Publ: Auth, The Function of the Artist in Canada, Ont Crafts Coun Rev, 58; auth, The Techniques of Chasing and Repousse, Crafts Can, 75. Mailing Add: 33 Lockhart Ave Ottawa ON K2A 3R1 Can

BETTIGA, FLOYD HENRY
EDUCATOR, PAINTER
b Grizzley Bluff, Calif, May 31, 32. Study: Santa Rosa Col, 50; Humboldt State Univ, BA, 54, MA, 64. Work: Am Toy Co, Oakland, Calif; Congressman Don Clausen, Calif; Humboldt State Univ. Exhib: Am House, Ger, 56; Phelan Awards, Palace Legion Honor, San Francisco, 61; NCA Show, Crocker Gallery, Sacramento, 61; Calif Jr Col Exhib, 71; Henry Galleries, Seattle, 75. Teaching: Prof art, Col Redwoods, 65- Awards: Purchase Award, Humboldt Arts Coun, 66; Painting Award, Redwood Art Asn, 74. Mem: Humboldt Arts Coun; Nat Trust Hist Preservation; Redwood Art Asn (pres, 72-73). Style & Technique: Contemporary. Media: Watercolor. Dealer: Humboldt Cult Ctr Eureka CA 95501. Mailing Add: PO Box 56 Bayside CA 95524

BETTINSON, BRENDA
EDUCATOR, PAINTER
b King's Lynn, Eng, Aug 17, 29; US citizen. Study: St Martins Sch Art, London, 46-48; Cent Sch Arts & Crafts, London, 48-50, Nat Dipl in Design, 50; Acad de la Grande Chaumiere, Paris, 51; Ecole Pratique des Hautes Etudes, Sorbonne, 51-53, Eleve Titulaire, 52. Comn: Soc for Renewal of Christian Art, New York; St Anselm's Abbey, Washington, DC; St Mary's Benedictine Abbey, Morristown, NJ; Dominican House of Studies, Washington, DC; Our Lady of Grace Monastery, New Guilford, Conn. Exhib: 4th Biennial Art Exhib, Detroit, Mich, 64; Comn on Worship & Fine Arts, Bridgeport, Conn, 65; Int Exhib Relig Art, Nat Arts Club, New York, 66; Cranbrook Acad Art, Detroit, 69; Episcopal Ctr, Chicago, 71; plus numerous one-man shows. Teaching: Prof art & coordr, Arts Prog, Pace Univ, 63-; lectr art, Katonah Gallery, NY, 72-75. Pos: Art ed, Riverside Radio WRVR-FM, New York, 61-65; mem art comt, Contemporary Christian Art Gallery, New York, 63-; consult, Soc for Renewal of Christian Art, 69- Awards: Gold Medal, Nat Arts Club, New York, 66. Bibliog: The Beginning (film), Columbia Univ Press, 62. Style & Technique: Large panels dealing with major iconographical themes of Christian art in a contemporary idiom. Media: Oil or Acrylic on Masonite. Publ: Auth, Patron of the Living Arts, America, 63; auth, Maurice Lavanoux, Crusador Extraordinary, Sign Mag, 75. Dealer: Contemporary Christian Art Gallery 1060A Lexington Ave New York NY 10021. Mailing Add: 150 Pleasant Ave Pleasantville NY 10570

BETTMANN, OTTO LUDWIG
ART HISTORIAN
b Leipzig, Ger, Oct 15, 03; US citizen. Study: Univ Leipzig, PhD, 27, MS in LS, 32. Exhib: Bettmann Panopticon Exhib, New York, 63. Teaching: Adj prof Am studies, Fla Atlantic Univ, 74. Pos: Assoc ed, C F Peters Co, Leipzig, 27-28; ed, Axel Juncker Publ, Berlin, 28-30; cur rare bks, State Art Libr, Berlin, 30-33; founder & pres, Bettmann Archive, Inc, 36- Awards: Award of Merit, Inst Graphic Arts, 67, 68 & 71. Bibliog: Friedof Johnson (auth), One million pictures, Am Artist, 67; Reliving the bad old days, Newsweek, 12/2/74; John F Baker (auth), Living in the past with Dr Otto Bettmann, Publ Weekly, 11/25/74. Mem: Am Inst Graphic Arts; Fr Inst; Am Fedn Arts. Res: Pictorial documentation of all aspects of cultural history. Publ: Auth, A pictorial history of medicine, 56; co-auth, Our literary heritage, 56; co-auth, Pictorial history of music, 60; auth, The good old days-they were terrible, 74; auth, The Bettmann Portable Archive, 67, A Word From the Wise, 77 & The Bettmann Archive Picture History of the World, 78. Mailing Add: 136 E 57th St New York NY 10022

BETTS, EDWARD HOWARD
PAINTER, EDUCATOR
b Yonkers, NY, Aug 4, 20. Study: Art Students League; Yale Univ, BA, 42; Univ Ill, MFA, 52. Work: Fogg Mus Art, Cambridge, Mass; Butler Inst Am Art, Youngstown, Ohio; Va Mus Fine Arts, Richmond, Va; Univ Rochster Mem Art Gallery, NY; Indianapolis Art Mus, Ind. Exhib: Five Corcoran Biennials, Washington, DC, 47-59; American Painting Today-1950, Metrop Mus Art, New York, 50; Int Watercolor Exhibs, Brooklyn Mus, NY, 53, 55 & 61, Watercolor USA, Springfield Art Mus, Mo, 63-71 & 74-75. Teaching: Prof painting, Univ Ill, Champaign, 49- Awards: Silver Medal of Honor, Am Watercolor Soc, 53 & 59; First Altman Landscape Prize, Nat Acad Design, 57, 59 & 66; Purchase Award, Childe Hassam Purchase Fund Exhib, 66. Bibliog: A S Weller (auth), Edward Betts, Art in Am New Talent Issue, 2/55. Mem: Nat Acad Design; Am Watercolor Soc; life mem Art Students League. Media: Semi-abstract; representational. Media: Acrylic, Watercolor. Publ: Auth, Edward Betts discusses his lacquer paintings, 3/55 & Painting in polymer & mixed media, 10/64, Am Artist Mag; Master Class in Watercolor and Acrylics, Watson-Guptill, 75; auth, Creative Landscape Painting, Watson-Guptill, 78. Dealer: Midtown Galleries 11 E 57th St New York NY 10022. Mailing Add: 804 Dodds Dr Champaign IL 61820

BEVLIN, MARJORIE ELLIOTT
PAINTER, WRITER
b The Dalles, Ore, May 9, 17. Study: Univ Colo, BFA; Univ Wash, Col of Archit; NY Univ, MS; also with Jimmy Ernst, 56. Comn: Two murals (6 ft x 24 ft), Otero Jr Col, La Junta, Colo, 55. Exhib: Scottish-Am Women's Exhib, Edinborough Royal Gallery, 63; Nat Acad Design, New York, NAWA Ann, 63-71; Brit Women's Exhib, Liverpool, 64; 8th Ann Prix de Deauville, France, 72; Prix de Rome, 72. Teaching: Founding chmn fine arts, Otero Jr Col, 55-67. Pos: Dir & founder, Ark Valley Sch Arts Festival, 56-75. Awards: Selectionee de Jury, Prix de Deauville, 72. Mem: Nat Asn Women Artists (mem chmn, 73-75); Delta Phi Delta (vpres Rho Chap, 38). Style & Technique: Multiple imagery with symbolic color. Media: Mixed Watercolor & Acrylic, Oil. Res: All areas of design and the application of natural elements and principles in the artist's work. Publ: Auth, Design Through Discovery, Holt, Rinehart & Winston, Inc, 63, 2nd ed, 70, 3rd ed, 77; contribr, Junior Col Journal, Colorado State Art Asn. Mailing Add: Star Rte 95 Eastsound WA 98245

BEYDLER, GARY EARL
SCULPTOR, PHOTOGRAPHER
b Los Angeles, Calif, Sept 3, 44. Study: Calif State Univ, Long Beach, BA; Univ Calif, Irvine, MFA. Work: Newport Harbor Art Mus, Newport Beach, Calif. Exhib: One-man show, Newspace Gallery, 74; 24 from Los Angeles, Los Angeles Munic Art Gallery, 74; Sense of Reference, Art Gallery, Univ Calif, San Diego & Eight Los Angeles Artists, San Francisco Art Inst, Calif, 75; New Am Filmmakers, 2 series & Biennial of Contemp Am Art, Whitney Mus Am Art, NY, 75. Awards: Nat Endowment Arts Grant, 75. Mem: Los Angeles Inst Contemp Art. Style & Technique: Installation sculpture and films. Dealer: Newspace Gallery 5051 Melrose Los Angeles CA 90038. Mailing Add: 3724 Wasatch Los Angeles CA 90066

BEYEH, KIN-YA-ONNY
See Gorman, Carl Nelson

BHALLA, HANS
PAINTER, ART HISTORIAN
Study: Cranbrook Acad Art, MFA; Columbia Univ. Work: Pub & pvt collections in US, Europe, Can, India, Jamaica & Japan. Exhib: 37th Int Exhib, Northwest Printmakers; Seattle Art Mus, Wash; 15th Nat Print Exhib, Brooklyn Mus, New York; Boston Mus Fine Arts, Mass; Butler Inst Am Art, Youngstown, Ohio; plus many others. Teaching: Lectr mod art, Middlebury Col, Cedar Crest Col, Ursinus Col & Fordham Univ; lectr Afro-Am art, Columbia Univ; from asst to assoc prof painting & printmaking, Talladega Col, 63-67; assoc prof art & chmn dept, Spelman Col, 67- Pos: Coordr, Coord Art Prog, Atlanta Univ Ctr Cols, currently; assoc dir & consult, Spelman/Atlanta Area Faculty Sem in India, 73 & 74; nat bd mem, Creatadrama Educ Ctr, Environ Drama Art Consults, 75. Awards: Grant, Atlanta Univ Corp, 70; IBM Faculty Fel, 71; Grant, Bd Home Missions, United Church Christ, New York, 71 & 74. Mem: Col Art Asn Am; Am Asn Mus; Mus Mod Art; Am Asn Univ Prof. Media: Collage. Mailing Add: Dept of Art Spelman Col Atlanta GA 30314

BHAVSAR, NATVAR PRAHLADJI
PAINTER
b Gothava, India, Apr 7, 34. Study: Bombay State Higher Art Exam, India, AM, 58, Govt Dipl Art, 59; Gujarat Univ, India, BA, 60; Univ Pa, MFA, 65, John D Rockefeller III Fund fel, 65-66; Guggenheim fel, 75-76. Work: Whitney Mus Am Art, New York; Mass Inst Technol, Cambridge; Metrop Mus Art, New York; Boston Mus Fine Arts, Mass; Australian Nat Gallery, Canberra; plus others. Exhib: 7th Int Print Exhib, Mod Gallery Ljubljana, Yugoslavia, 67; Painting & Sculpture Today, Indianapolis Mus Art, Ind, 70; Whitney Mus Am Art Painting Ann, 70-71; Two Generations of Color Painting, Inst Contemp Art, Univ Pa, Philadelphia, 70; Beautiful Paintings & Sculpture, Jewish Mus, New York, 70. Teaching: Art instr, Univ RI, spring semesters 67-69. Bibliog: Christopher Andreae (auth), Painters philosophy, goal beyond objects, Christian Sci Monitor, 1/24/70; Carter Ratcliff (auth), article in, Art Int, 10/72; Elwyn Linn (auth), article in Art Int, Vol 21 (April 1977). Media: Dry Pigment, Acrylic. Dealer: Max Hutchinson Gallery 138 Greene St New York NY 10012. Mailing Add: 131 Greene St New York NY 10012

BIALA, JANICE
PAINTER
b Biala, Poland, Oct 18, 03; US citizen. Study: Nat Acad Art, New York; Art Students League. Work: Whitney Mus, New York; Centre Contemp Art, Paris, France; Duncan Phillips Collection, Washington, DC; Mus Cantonal de Lausanne, Switz; Mus Nat, Oslo,

Norway. Exhib: Bignou Gallery, New York, 42; Jeanne Bucher Gallery, Paris, 46; Stable Gallery, New York & Le Point Cardinale, Paris, 61. Bibliog: Biala paints a picture, Art News, 56; Chefs—d'oeuvre de l'art, Hachette, 65; Dora Vallier (auth), Biala, Pour l'Art, 60 & Repères la Peinture en France...1870-1970, Alfieri & Lacroix. Style & Technique: Figurative. Mailing Add: 8 Rue du General Bertrand Paris France

BIANCO, PAMELA RUBY
PAINTER
b London, Eng, Dec 31, 06; US citizen. Study: Guggenheim fel for creative painting abroad, 30. Work: Mus Mod Art & Chase Manhattan Bank, New York; Queens Col; New York Pub Libr; Hirshhorn Mus Art, Washington, DC. Exhib: One-woman exhibs, Leicester Galleries, London, 19-20, Anderson Galleries, New York, 21, Knoedler Galleries, New York, 24, Graham Gallery, New York, 69 & 76 & Santa Barbara Mus Art, 70. Bibliog: J B Manson (auth), Drawings of Pamela Bianco, Studio, 11/25/20; Louis Untermeyer (auth), Drawings of Pamela Bianco, Century Mag, 7/22; Joseph Stella (auth), Pamela Bianco, An appreciation, Playboy, 25. Media: Oil. Publ: Illusr, Flora, William Heinemann, London, 20; illusr, Natives of Rock, Francesco Bianco, 25; illusr, Skin Horse, George H Doran, 27; auth & illusr, Beginning with A, Oxford Univ, 47; auth & illusr, Valentine Party, Lippincott, 54. Dealer: Graham Gallery 1014 Madison Ave New York NY 10021. Mailing Add: 428 Lafayette St New York NY 10003

BIBERMAN, EDWARD
PAINTER, LECTURER
b Philadelphia, Pa, Oct 23, 04. Study: Univ Pa, BS(econ); Pa Acad Fine Arts, Philadelphia. Work: Butler Inst Am Art, Youngstown, Ohio; Mus Pa Acad Fine Arts; Mus Fine Art, Houston, Tex; Brandeis Univ, Waltham, Mass; Los Angeles Co Mus, Los Angeles. Comn: Wall murals, Fed Bldg, Los Angeles, 37 & 40 & Venice, Calif, 39. Exhib: 46 Under 35, Mus Mod Art, New York, 30 & Mural Projs Exhib, 32; var ann exhibs, Whitney Mus Am Art, New York, 30-40, Los Angeles Co Mus Art, 36-65 & Los Angeles Munic Art Gallery, 71. Teaching: Instr drawing, Art Ctr Sch Design, 38-50; lectr art hist, Univ Calif, Los Angeles, Irvine & San Diego Campuses, 67- Awards: Lambert Fund Purchase Prize, Pa Acad Fine Arts, 30; Tupperware fel, Orlando, Fla, 57; Los Angeles City Ann Award, 68. Mem: Nat Soc Mural Painters. Style & Technique: Figurative painter, mostly oil on gesso panels; serigraphs, glue and tusche, positive technique. Publ: Auth, The Best Untold, Blue Heron Press, 54; Time & Circumstance, Ritchie, 68. Dealer: Gallery 2 1634 Tower Grove Dr Beverly Hills CA 90210. Mailing Add: 3332 Deronda Dr Los Angeles CA 90028

BICE, CLARE
ART ADMINISTRATOR, PAINTER
b Durham, Ont, Jan 24, 09. Study: Univ Western Ont, LLD, 62; Art Students League; Can Govt fel for study in France, 52-53. Work: Imperial Oil Collection; Seagram Collection; Nat Gallery Can, Ottawa, Ont. Exhib: Royal Can Acad Arts, major Can cities, 40-70; Ont Soc Artists, Toronto, 40-70. Collections Arranged: Canadian Painting 1850-1950; Young Contemporaries (Canada), 50-65; Annual Western Ontario Exhibitions, 40-72. Pos: Cur, London Art Mus, Ont, 40- Awards: Can Coun Sr Arts Fel, 62-63; Can Coun Fel for Writing, 72-73. Mem: Can Art Mus Dirs Orgn (pres, 66-68); Royal Can Acad Arts (pres, 67-70); Ont Soc Artists. Media: Oil. Publ: Auth-illusr, Jory's Cove, 41, Across Canada, 48, The Great Island, 54, A Dog for Davie's Hill, 57 & Hurricane Treasure, 65. Mailing Add: 1010 Wellington St London ON N6A 3T4 Can

BICKFORD, GEORGE PERCIVAL
COLLECTOR
b Berlin, NH, Nov 28, 01. Study: Harvard Col, AB, 22, Harvard Law Sch, LLB, 26. Teaching: Lectr Indian hist & cult, Cleveland Col, 48-50. Pos: Trustee & vpres, Cleveland Inst Art, Ohio, 55-; vpres & trustee, Cleveland Mus Art, 57-; trustee, Am Comt S Asian art. Mem: Am Asn Mus; Am Oriental Soc; Am Asn Asian Studies; Harvard Univ (vis comt, dept fine arts). Collection: East Indian antiquities. Mailing Add: 2247 Chestnut Hills Dr Cleveland OH 44106

BIDDLE, JAMES
ART ADMINISTRATOR, COLLECTOR
b Philadelphia, Pa, July 8, 29. Study: Princeton Univ, BA, 51. Pos: Cur, Am Wing, Metrop Mus Art, 63-67; pres, Nat Trust Hist Preservation, Washington, DC, 67-; trustee, Corcoran Gallery Art. Mem: Drawing Soc (pres); Am Fedn Arts (trustee); White House Hist Asn (bd dirs). Mailing Add: 2425 Wyoming Ave Washington DC 20008

BIDDLE, LIVINGSTON LUDLOW, JR
ART ADMINISTRATOR
b Bryn Mawr, Pa, May 26, 18. Study: Princeton Univ, AB, 40. Pos: Dep chmn, 65-67, liaison dir, 74-78, chmn, Nat Endowment for the Arts, Washington, DC, 78-; chmn div of arts, Liberal Arts Col, Fordham Univ, Lincoln Ctr, New York, 67-70. Mem: Int Coun Fine Arts Deans. Mailing Add: 2914 P St NW Washington DC 20007

BIDNER, ROBERT D H
PAINTER, ART DIRECTOR
b Youngstown, Ohio, Mar 14, 30. Study: Cleveland Inst Art, BFA, 53. Work: Nat Collection Fine Arts, Washington, DC; Andrew Dickson White Mus Art, Cornell Univ, Ithaca, NY; Butler Inst Am Art, Youngstown; Nat Acad Design, New York; Am Acad of Arts & Lett, New York. Comn: Murals, Bd Educ, Cleveland, Ohio, 53, William A Stenson, Greenwich, Conn, 69 & Fordham Univ, New York, 70. Exhib: Mid-Year Shows, Butler Inst Am Art, 51-55, 72, 74-75 & 77; 25th Biennial Exhib, Corcoran Gallery Art, Washington, DC, 57; Dark Mirror, Am Fedn Arts, New York, 64-65; Contemporary American Artists, Westmoreland Co Mus Art, Pa, 69; Art in Embassies Prog, US State Dept, Washington, DC, 69-78. Pos: Asst arf dir, G M Basford, Inc, New York, 57-58; art dir, Fuller Smith & Ross, Inc, New York, 58-66; art dir, Ted Bates & Co, Inc, New York, 66-78. Awards: Purchase Award, Nat Acad Design, 56; Medal for a Creative Painting, Allied Artists Am, 66; Third Medal Purchase Award, Butler Inst Am Art, 74. Bibliog: Jerry Flint (auth), feature article in Esquire Mag, 11/77; Vivien Raynor (auth), article in New York Times, 11/77; Marilyn Pearl (auth), rev in Art News Mag, 1/78. plus others. Style & Technique: Sharp realism in which nature and/or man-made objects are the starting point; paintings have strong surrealistic overtones without being impossible. Technique of underpainting and glazing with a slow build up of opaques and impastos is used. Dealer: Far Gallery 32 E 80th St New York NY 10021. Mailing Add: 559 First St Brooklyn NY 11215

BIEDERMAN, CHARLES (KAREL JOSEPH)
SCULPTOR
b Cleveland, Ohio, Aug 23, 06. Study: Art Inst Chicago, 26-29; Minneapolis Col Art & Design, hon DFA, 73. Work: Tate Gallery, London, Eng; Kröller-Müller Mus, Otterlo, Holland; Albright-Knox Art Gallery, Buffalo; Dallas Mus of Fine Arts, Tex; Univ EAnglia, Norwich, Eng; Minneapolis Inst Arts. Comn: Three constructionist pieces, Interstate Med Clin, Red Wing, Minn, 40; work in pub plaza, Nat Endowment Arts, Red Wing, 71. Exhib: One-man shows, Arts Club, Chicago, Ill, 41 & Gallery 12, Minneapolis, 71; retrospectives, Walker Art Ctr, Minneapolis, 65, Hayward Gallery, London, 69 & Minneapolis Inst Arts, 76. Awards: Ford Found Purchase Award, 64; Nat Coun Arts Grant, 66; Nat Endowment for Arts Award, 73. Bibliog: Jan van der Marck (auth), Charles Biederman & the structurist direction in art, Feistbundel F vanderMeer, 66; Leif Sjoberg (auth), London ahead of New York?, Studies in the 20th Century, 71. Media: Spray painted aluminum. Publ: Auth, Art as the evolution of visual knowledge, 48; auth, Letters on the new art, 51; auth, The new Cezanne, 58; auth, Dialogue II, creative or conditioned vision, Faber, 68; auth, A note on new arts, Studio Int, 70. Mailing Add: Rte 2 Red Wing MN 55066

BIELER, ANDRE CHARLES
PAINTER, PRINTMAKER
b Lausanne, Switz, Oct 8, 96; Can citizen. Study: Art Students League, Woodstock, with Charles Rosen & Eugene Speicher; Acad Ranson, Paris, France, with Paul Serusier & Maurice Denis; also execution of frescoes with Ernest Bieler, Switz. Work: Nat Gallery Can, Ottawa; Mus Quebec, PQ; Montreal Mus Fine Art, PQ; Agnes Etherington Art Ctr, Queen's Univ, Kingston, Ont; Art Gallery Ont, Toronto. Comn: Saguenay: People & Hydro-Electric Development, Shipshaw (on aluminum panels), Aluminum Co Can, 48; Rehabilitation (oil on canvas glued to wall), Vet Welfare Serv, Ottawa, 55; Scenes de Quebec (oil on canvas attached to wall), Procter & Gamble, Pointe Claire, PQ, 57; aluminum foil, plaster & aluminum plates, comn by Aluminum Labs, Tokyo Aluminum Co, Japan. Exhib: A Century of Canadian Art, Tate Gallery, London, Eng, 38; Int Watercolour Exhib, Chicago, Ill, 39; Golden Gate Int Exhib Contemp Art, San Francisco, Calif, 39; one-man retrospective, Andre Bieler-50 Years 1920-1970, 11 cities, 70-71; Int Exhib Graphics, Montreal Mus Fine Arts & Traveling Exhib, 71- Teaching: Resident artist & prof art hist, appreciation & painting, Queen's Univ, 36-63. Pos: Dir, Agnes Etherington Art Ctr, 57-63. Awards: J W L Forster Award, Ont Soc Artists, 57; C W Jeffery Award, Can Soc Graphic Art, 64; Centennial Medal, Can Govt, 67. Bibliog: M Barbeau (auth), Painters of Quebec, Toronto Press, 46; Frances K Smith (auth), A Canadian artist in the market place, Can Collector, 2/71. Mem: Academician Royal Can Acad Arts; Ont Soc Artists; Can Soc Graphic Art; Can Group Painters; Can Soc Painters in Watercolour. Style & Technique: Primarily people at work and at play against rural landscape. Media: Acrylic, Oil. Collection: French Canadian furniture and artifacts; Canadian and European paintings. Publ: Ed, Kingston Conf Proc, 41; contribr, Can Art, IX: 70-71; auth, Twelve Pines Press (monogr), Agnes Etherington Art Ctr, 72. Dealer: Walter Klinkhoof 1200 Sherbrooke W Montreal PQ Can; Wallack Galleries 202 Bank St Ottawa ON Can. Mailing Add: Shipyards 33 Ontario St No 621 Kingston ON K7L 2Y2 Can

BIELER, TED ANDRE
EDUCATOR, SCULPTOR
b Kingston, Ont, July 23, 38. Study: Sculpture with Ossip Zadkine, Paris, 53; tapestry with Jean Lurcat, St Cere, France, 54; Slade Sch Art, London, Eng, printmaking, 54; Cranbrook Acad Art, BFA, 61. Work: Montreal Mus Fine Arts; Can Coun, Ottawa; Univ Toronto; Agnes Etherington Art Centre, Queen's Univ, Kingston; McMaster Univ; York Univ. Comn: Concrete relief walls, News & Admin Bldg, Expo '67, 65; modular wall reliefs, Health Sci Ctr, McMaster Univ, 68-71; Star-Cross'd (sculpture ballet set), comn by Brian MacDonald, Ottawa, 73; stainless steel sculpture, Forensic Sci Bldg, Govt Ont, 75; aluminum tetrahedra sculpture, Portsmouth Harbour, Kingston, Govt Can, 75; sculpture for Govt of Can Bldg, comn by Macy Dubois & Shore Tilbe Henschel Irwin, Architects, Toronto, 77; cast aluminum relief sculpture for Wilson Sta, comn by Spadina Subway Line, Toronto, 78; and others. Exhib: One-man shows, Isaacs Gallery, Toronto, 64, York Univ, 77 & Univ of Rochester, 77; Centennial Sculpture Exhib, Toronto City Hall, 67; Can Govt Pavilion, Expo '67, Montreal, 67; Can Artists '68, Art Gallery Ont, Toronto, 68; A Plastic Presence, Jewish Mus, New York & Milwaukee Art Ctr, 70; Fac Exhib, York Univ, Downsview, 70, 75 & 76, Signs & Symbols, Art Gallery of Ont Traveling Show, 71, Artario 72, numerous locations, 72, Sculpture Stratford, The Gallery Stratford, 76 & Rehearsal, Harbourfront Art Gallery, Toronto, 77. Teaching: Assoc prof sculpture, York Univ, 70- Awards: Allied Arts Medal, Royal Archit Asn Can, 69. Bibliog: L Sabbath (auth), Sculpture in Canada, 62 & H McPherson (auth), Scope of Sculpture in '64, 64, Can Art; William Withrow (auth), Canadian Sculpture, Graph, Montreal, 67. Mem: Royal Can Acad Arts (mem coun, 75-77); Int Sculpture Ctr, Lawrence, Kans (vchmn adv bd); Toronto Karma Kargyu Centre (mem bd dirs). Style & Technique: Sculpture independant and integrated in architecture; large scale in wood, concrete, plastics and metals. Mailing Add: Glenstreams RR1 Locust Hill ON L0H 1J0 Can

BIER, JUSTUS
MUSEUM DIRECTOR, WRITER
b Nürnberg, Ger, May 31, 99; US citizen. Study: Univs Munich, Erlangen, Jena & Bonn, 18-24; Univ Zurich, PhD, 24; Duke Univ, DFA, 70; Louisville Univ, DHL, 72. Teaching: Lectr, Tilmann Riemenschneider, Franconian & 20th century sculpture; docent & instr art hist, Munic Univ, Nürnberg, 25-30; asst prof art hist & actg head dept fine arts, Univ Louisville, 37-41, assoc prof, 41-46, prof, 46-60; vis prof, Free Univ Berlin, 56; vis prof, Univ Southern Calif, 59; Fulbright lectr & vis prof, Univ Wurzburg, 60-61; vis prof, Univ Tex, Austin & Univ Wis-Milwaukee, 75. Pos: Dir & cur, Kestner-Gesellschaft Art Inst, Hanover, Ger, 30-36; founder & dir, Mus Vorbildliche Serienprodukt, Hanover, 30-36; critic & art ed, Courier-J, Louisville, Ky, 44-53; dir, Allen R Hite Art Inst, 46-60; critic & art ed, Courier-J, 54-56; dir, NC Mus Art, Raleigh, 61-70, dir emer, 70-, cur res, 70-72, cur sculpture, 72-74, consult, 74- Awards: Guggenheim Fel, 53-54 & 56-57; Fulbright Award, 60-61; Commander's Cross, Fed Ger Repub, 73. Mem: Col Art Asn Am; Am Soc Aesthet; assoc Int Asn Art Critics; Am Fedn Arts; Am Asn Univ Prof; plus others. Publ: Auth, Tilmann Riemenschneider, 48 & 73; contribr, Art Bull, Art in Am, Art Quart, Gazette Beaux-Arts; plus others. Mailing Add: 201 Peartree Rd Raleigh NC 27610

BIERK, DAVID CHARLES
PAINTER, GALLERY DIRECTOR
b Appleton, Minn, June 9, 44. Study: Calif Col Arts & Crafts; Humboldt State Univ, BA & MA, study with Tom Knight, Norman Griffin & Larry Giray. Work: Humboldt State Col; Sir Sanford Fleming Col; Brampton Pub Libr & Art Gallery; Can Postal Mus. Comn: Portrait of David Sutherland, Sir Sanford Fleming Col Comt Arts, 75; Robert Service Commemorative Stamp, Can PO, 76. Exhib: Aspects of Realism, Walter Moos Gallery, Toronto, 75; New Tale Art, Marlboro Goddard Gallery, Toronto, 75; Ont Now, Art Gallery Hamilton, 76; Forum 76, Montreal Mus Fine Arts, 76; Brampton Pub Libr & Art Gallery, 77. Collections Arranged: Monument to Miniature, 75; Artspace Steps Out, Ont prov, 76; Artspace Inaugural Exhib, Peterborough, 77. Teaching: Painting master art & admin, Sir Sanford Fleming Col, 74-77. Pos: Adv comt mem, St Lawrence Col, visual & creative arts comt; partic artist, Art Gallery Ont & Ont Arts Coun Creative Artists; founder & exec dir, Artspace, 74- Awards: Arts grant, Can Coun, 75; Best in Show, Sir Sanford Fleming Col Invitational Art Exhib, 75; Artists grant, Ont Arts Coun, 75, 76 & 77. Bibliog: James Purdie (auth), Toronto Globe & Mail, 75; Annie Thurlow, Arts Mag, 76. Mem: Art Gallery of

Peterborough (mem bd dirs); Can Artists Representation Ont. Style & Technique: Realism; photo silkscreen; photography. Dealer: Nancy Poole Studio Hazelton Ave Toronto ON M5R 2E5 Can. Mailing Add: 430 Donegal St Peterborough ON K9H 4L6 Can

BIESER, NATALIE
PAINTER
b Grand Junction, Colo, Dec, 14, 48. Study: Chouinard Art Sch, Los Angeles; Calif Inst Arts, BFA, 70. Work: Va Mus Art, Richmond; Whitney Mus Am Art, New York. Exhib: Document V, 1972, Kassel, Ger, 72; one-woman show, Nancy Hoffman Gallery, New York, 72, 74, 75 & 77 & Baum-Silverman Gallery, Los Angeles, 77; Biennial Contemp Am Art, Whitney Mus Am Art, 73; Watercolors & Related Media by Contemp Californians, Baxter Art Gallery, Calif Inst of Technol; Both Kinds: Contemp Art from Los Angeles, Univ Art Mus, Berkeley, 75. Style & Technique: Wall pieces, composed of balsa wood, thread, glass beads, graphite and watercolors. Dealer: Nancy Hoffman 429 W Broadway New York NY 10012. Mailing Add: 350 Sunset Ave Venice CA 90291

BIGELOW, CHANDLER, II
PAINTER
b Boston, Mass, Sept 16, 37. Study: Trinity Col, BA, 59; portraiture with Robert Cormier, Boston, 59-60. Work: St Lawrence Univ, Canton, NY; Cornell Univ; Wichita State Univ, Kans; Univ Kans, Lawrence; Hamilton Col; many pvt collections. Exhib: One-man shows, Wickersham Gallery, New York, 67, 69 & 71 & Panoras Gallery, New York, 73; Parrish Mus Art, Southampton, NY, 66; Hammond Art Mus, Katonah, NY, 68; Doll & Richards Gallery, Boston, 69; plus others. Style & Technique: Impressionist and abstract landscape. Media: Oil on Canvas and/or Board. Mailing Add: 203 W 23rd St New York NY 10011

BIGGER, MICHAEL DINSMORE
SCULPTOR, INSTRUCTOR
b Waukegan, Ill, Oct 10, 37. Study: Miami Univ, Ohio, BFA(archit); RI Sch Design, MFA(sculpture). Work: Evansville Mus Arts & Sci, Ind; Oakland Mus Art, Calif; Atlantic Richfield Corp, Los Angeles, Calif; Taft Mus, Cincinnati, Ohio; Embarcadero Ctr, San Francisco, Calif. Comn: Monumental sculpture, Cincinnati Zoological Soc, 69; five works (steel), State of Maine Arts & Humanities Coun, 70; ten large paintings, Bunker Hill Community Col, Boston, 73; two stainless steel wall works, Vassar Col, Poughkeepsie, NY, 74-75; monumental sculpture, Thompson Provincial Bldg, Thompson, Man, 77. Exhib: Conn Acad Fine Arts, Wadsworth Atheneum, Hartford, 67; Sculpture, Painting & Contemp Technol, Berkeley Art Ctr, Calif, 68; Ann Exhib Contemp Sculpture, Whitney Mus Am Art, New York, 68; Structured Art, 69 & Outdoor Sculpture, 69, DeCordova Mus, Lincoln, Mass; Pub Sculpture/Urban Environ, Oakland Mus Art, Calif, 74; Drawings for Monumental Sculpture, Cleveland Mus Art, 77; Sculpture on the Prairies, Winnipeg Art Gallery, Man, 77. Collections Arranged: New Eng Sculpture Traveling Exhib, 73; Max Wasserman Collection, Boston, Mass, 74-75. Teaching: Tech instr sculpture, RI Sch Design, Providence, 69-70; instr, 3-D Design, Atlanta Sch Art, Ga, 70-71; chmn dept sculpture, Univ Man, Winnipeg, 75- Awards: Judges Award, 10th Ann RI Sch Design Arts Festival, Providence, 68 & Ball State Drawings & Small Sculpture, Muncie, Ind, 69; Olivetti Awards, 20th & 23rd Ann New Eng Exhib, Silvermine Guild Artists, Conn, 69 & 72. Bibliog: Artist-at-Work (film), Merrimack Valley Art & Humanities Coun, 74; article in Financial Post Mag, 76. Mem: Artists' Equity Asn Inc; Can Artists Representation. Style & Technique: Abstract expressionism-constructivism; welded steel, industrial forms. Media: Steel. Mailing Add: 656 St Mary's Rd Winnipeg MB R2M 3M4 Can

BIGGERS, JOHN THOMAS
EDUCATOR, PAINTER
b Gastonia, NC, Apr 13, 24. Study: Hampton Inst, 41-46; Pa State Univ, BS & MS(art educ), 48, DEduc, 54. Work: Houston Mus Fine Arts; Dallas Mus Fine Arts; Reader's Digest Collection; Tex Southern Univ; Golden State Mutual Life Ins Co. Comn: Seasons of Want and Plenty; Afro-American Folklore; Contribution of Negro Women; Web of Life; Birth from the Sea. Exhib: Tex Contemp Artist, M Knoedler & Co, New York, 52; Regional & Nat Drawing Soc Exhib, Houston & New York, 65; one-man show, Houston Mus Fine Arts, 68; Tex Painting & Sculpture, the 20th century, six Tex mus & galleries, 71-72; Reflections: the Afro-Am Artist, Benton Conv Ctr, Winston-Salem, NC, 72. Teaching: Distinguished prof painting, drawing & art hist, Tex Southern Univ, Houston, 49-, head art dept. Pos: Mem, Houston Fine Arts Comn, 68-72 & Tex Fine Arts Comn, Houston, 70-73. Awards: Art Fel in Africa, UNESCO, 57. Bibliog: Cedric Dover (auth), American Negro Art, New York Graphic Soc, 60; Ralph E Shikes (auth), The Indignant eye, Beacon Press, 69; Elton Fax (auth), 17 Black Artists, Dodd, Mead, 71. Mem: Fel Int Inst Arts & Lett; Tex Col Art Asn; Tex Fine Arts Soc; Nat Soc Mural Painters; Pa State Grad Club in Art Educ. Style & Technique: Lithography, mixed media; expressionistic. Media: Conte Crayon; Oil and Tempera Mixed. Res: African art and culture. Publ: Auth, Ananse, Web of Life in Africa, 69; illusr, Good earth, Readers' Digest Series, 66; illusr, I Momolu, Crowell Co, 66; illusr, Cross timbers, Univ Tex, 66; contribr, Afro-American Art, Van Nostrand Reinhold Co, 72. Mailing Add: 3338 Prospect St Houston TX 77004

BILLECI, ANDRE GEORGE
SCULPTOR, EDUCATOR
b New York, NY, Dec 2, 33. Study: State Univ NY Col, Alfred, BFA(ceramics; cum laude), 60, MFA(ceramic art), 61. Work: Corning Mus of Glass, NY; Lannan Found, Palm Beach, Fla; Australian Coun for the Arts, Sydney; Galleries Nat de Prague, Czech; Mus für Kunsthandwerk, Frankfurt, Ger. Exhib: Toledo Glass Nat 1st-3rd, Toledo Mus of Art, Ohio, 66, 68 & 72; one-man shows, Lowe Art Ctr, Syracuse Univ, NY, 68, Mus of Contemp Crafts, New York, 70, John Nelson Bergstrom Art Ctr, Neenah, Wis, 72, Corning Mus of Glass, 72 & Pilkington Glass Mus, St Helens, UK, 73; Objects USA, Johnsons Wax Collection (traveling exhib), 69-77; Reflections, Long Beach Mus of Art, Calif, 71; Int Glass Sculpture, Lowe Art Mus, Univ Miami, Coral Gables, Fla, 73; Am Craftsmen in Glass, Australian Coun for the Arts, Sydney, 74; Glas I Gladge, Sweden, Denmark & Finland, 74-75; New Am Glass, Huntington Galleries, WVa, 76; Mod Glas aus Am, Europ & Japan, Mus für Kunsthandwerk, Frankfurt & Kunstgewerbemus, Berlin, Ger, 76; Glassmaking & Purchase Exhib, Corning Mus of Glass, 76. Teaching: Assoc prof sculpture/glass, State Univ NY Col, Alfred, 61- & Summer Sch, Sheridan Col of Applied Arts & Technol, Toronto, Ont, 71. Pos: Mem bd dirs, NY State Craftsmen, Ithaca, 70-72; artist-in-residence, Blenko Art Glass Co, Milton, WVa, 71 & Steuben Glass Co, Corning, NY, 72; founding trustee, Naples Mill Sch of Arts & Crafts, NY, 72-74. Awards: Purchase Award, Toledo Glass Nat II, Toledo Mus of Art, Ohio, 68. Media: Glass; mixed media. Publ: Auth, Electric Melting Unit for Covered Melting, Corning Mus of Glass, 76. Mailing Add: Thurston Studio RD 1 Campbell NY 14821

BILLINGS, HENRY
PAINTER, ILLUSTRATOR
b Bronxville, NY, July 13, 01. Study: Art Students League. Work: Whitney Mus Am Art; William Allen White Libr, Kans State Teachers Col. Comn: Painting, Ford Motor Co, New York World's Fair, 38; paintings comn by US Treas Dept Fine Arts Div for Saranac Post Off, NY, 37, Medford Post Off, Mass, 38, Wappinger Falls Post Off, NY & Columbia Court House, Tenn, 40. Exhib: Carnegie Inst, Pittsburgh, Pa, 47; Whitney Mus Ann, 32, 37 & 40. Teaching: Vis lectr painting, Bard Col, 35-53; instr painting, Art Students League, 40; instr painting, Art Students League Summer Sch, Woodstock, NY, 60-61. Pos: Designer, United Neighborhoods, Inc, 75th Anniversary Exhib, 59-61; consult, UNICEF Photo Exhib, New York World's Fair, 64. Media: Oil. Publ: Auth & illusr, Construction Ahead, 50, All Down the Valley, 52 & Bridges, 55, Viking Press. Mailing Add: RFD 3 North Haven Sag Harbor NY 11963

BILLMYER, JOHN EDWARD
CRAFTSMAN, EDUCATOR
b Denver, Colo, Aug 17, 12. Study: Univ Denver; Kirkland Sch Art; Case Western Reserve Univ, BA & MA; also study abroad. Work: Cleveland Mus Art; Denver Art Mus. Exhib: Cleveland Mus Art; Denver Art Mus, 47-68 & Metrop Show, 52-67; five shows, Syracuse Mus Fine Art, 48-56; Wichita Mus Art, 51, 55 & 57; Colorado Springs Fine Arts Ctr, 60; plus others. Pos: Retired univ prof, current artist & art historian. Mem: Denver Art Mus (trustee, 62-71); Col Art Asn Am. Mailing Add: 7301 E Placita Sinaloa Tucson AZ 85710

BIMROSE, ARTHUR SYLVANUS, JR
CARTOONIST
b Spokane, Wash, Mar 18, 12. Study: San Francisco Art Inst Col, 31; Univ Ore, 33. Work: State Hist Soc, Mo; Wayne State Univ; Libr Cong. Pos: Free-lance commercial artist, 34-37; staff artists, Oregonian, Portland, 37-39, ed cartoonist, 49- Awards: Freedoms Found Award, 52, 61 & 65. Mem: Asn Am Ed Cartoonist. Mailing Add: 1632 SW Westwood Ct Portland OR 97201

BINAI, PAUL FREYE
PAINTER, ART CURATOR
b Lancaster, Pa, July 3, 32. Study: Indiana Univ, AB & MFA, with Alton Pickens & Leo Steppat; Yale Univ; John Herron Art Inst; Ecole Fontainebleau, Paris, France, Walter Damrosch fel for study in painting, 62. Work: Purdue Univ Art Ctr; Miami Mus Mod Art. Exhib: Palais Fontainebleau, France, 62; Am Fedn Arts, 64-65; Akron Art Inst, 64; one-man shows, Miami Mus Mod Art, Ligoa Duncan Gallery, New York & Raymond Duncan Gallery, Paris, 64; plus many others. Teaching: Instr art & design, Purdue Univ, 60-64; instr art, Akron Art Inst, 64-68. Pos: Asst cur graphic arts, Detroit Inst Art, 71-75, cur, Mus Art, Carnegie Inst, Pittsburgh, Pa, 75- Awards: Purdue Univ Res Found Grant, 61. Mem: Col Art Asn Am; Am Asn Mus. Mailing Add: Mus Art Carnegie Inst Pittsburgh PA 15213

BINFORD, JULIEN
PAINTER, SCULPTOR
b Richmond, Va, Dec 25, 08. Study: Emory Univ; Art Inst Chicago, with Boris Anisfeld; Ryerson traveling fel for France & Spain. Work: Boston Mus Fine Arts; Springfield Art Mus, Mass; New Britain Mus, Conn; Phillips Gallery, Washington, DC; Va Mus Fine Arts, Richmond. Comn: Seven mural panels in banking room, Greenwich Savings Bank, 3 W 57th St New York, one mural panel, Greenwich Savings Bank, 14th St at 6th Ave, New York; mural panel in lobby, Va State Libr, Richmond; church panel (mural) behind rostrum, Shiloh Baptist Church, Fine Creek, Va; mural panel for libr, Thomas Jefferson High Sch, Richmond. Exhib: Salon Tuileries, Paris, France; Carnegie Inst Int, Pittsburgh; Int Watercolor Show, Chicago Art Inst; Pa Acad Fine Arts, Philadelphia, Corcoran Gallery Art Biennial, Washington, DC. Teaching: Prof art, Mary Washington Col, Univ Va, 46-62, 64-72, emer prof, 72- Pos: Artist corresp, Life Mag, 44-46; chmn, Int Exhib Contemp Art, Mary Washington Col, Univ Va, 55-66. Awards: Springfield Mus Art Purchase Award, 42; Purchase Award, Buck Hill Falls Art Asn, 46; Childe Hassam Fund Purchase, Am Acad Arts & Lett, 74. Bibliog: River Jordan Mural, Life Mag, 42; Harry Salpeter (auth), Julien Binford, Esquire, 44; Elizabeth Binford (auth), Julien Binford, Am Artist Mag, 53. Style & Technique: Reexamination of nature. Media: Oil, Mixed Media, Marbles, Beeswax. Publ: Paintings for hist record of New York Harbor at War, Life Mag, 44. Dealer: Midtown Galleries 11 E 57th St New York NY 10022. Mailing Add: PO Box 187 Powhatan VA 23139

BINGHAM, MRS HARRY PAYNE
COLLECTOR
Collection: Paintings. Mailing Add: 834 Fifth Ave New York NY 10021

BINGHAM, LOIS A
ART ADMINISTRATOR, LECTURER
b Iowa Falls, Iowa, July 8, 13. Study: Oberlin Col, scholar, BA & MA; Sch Fine Arts, Yale Univ, scholar; Inst d'Art & Archeol, Univ Paris, Carnegie grant for grad study. Collections Arranged: More than 200 exhibs arranged & supervised incl Nation of Nations, to inaugurate Berlin Cong Hall, 54, Modern Painting & Sculpture, Moscow, 59 & biennial exhibs at Sao Paulo, Venice, Santiago, New Delhi & Paris, 61- Teaching: Lects, Medici: Patrons of Art, Index of Am Design, Dutch Painting, Manuscripts of the Middle Ages & Duccio's Maestra, Nat Gallery Art. Pos: Staff, Nat Gallery Art, 43-48, assoc cur educ, 48-54; chief fine arts div, exhib br, US Info Agency, 54-65; chief, Int Art Prog, Smithsonian Inst, Nat Collection Fine Arts, Washington, DC, 65-72, chief, Off of Exhibs Abroad, 72-76, chief, Off of Prog Support, 76- Publ: Auth, How to look at works of art, Nat Gallery Art; auth, Highlights of American painting, Care, NY; contribr, Favorite paintings from The National Gallery of Art. Mailing Add: Nat Collection Fine Arts Smithsonian Inst Washington DC 20560

BINNING, ROBIN
PRINTMAKER, SCULPTOR
b Rosset, North Wales, Dec 16, 09. Study: Plymouth Sch Art, Eng; also with Leon Underwood. Work: Kungliets Kunstmuseet, Stockholm; Imp War Mus, London; Arthur M Sakler Collection, New York. Comn: Reliefs, Hilton Hotels, Inc, 67; Altars, lecterns, font, etc, Church St Dominic, Barbados, 72. Exhib: St George's Gallery, London, 53 & 55; Penwith Soc, St Ives, Corwall, 53 & 57; Neutida Englska Gafisk, Stockholm, 56; NW Printmakers Int, Seattle Wash, 56 & 57; one-man show, Bristol Mus Art, RI, 71. Teaching: Teacher sculpture, workshop, Bowdoin Col, 71; prof sculpture, New Eng Sch Art, 72-78; guest lectr Putnam Sculptures, Princeton Univ, 75. Awards: Giles Mem Bequest Prize, 56. Mem: Fel MacDowell Colony. Style & Technique: Abstract; carving & fabricating. Media: Stone; Sheet Aluminum. Dealer: Nielsen Gallery Newbury St Boston MA 02116. Mailing Add: 30 Ipswich St Boston MA 02215

BIRCKETT, ANNE BELLE
See Belle, Anna

BIRDMAN, JEROME M
ART ADMINISTRATOR, EDUCATOR
b Philadelphia, Pa, Dec 4, 30. Study: Temple Univ, BS, 56; Univ Ill, Urbana, AM, 57, PhD, 70. Pos: Dean, Col Fine Arts, Univ Nebr, Omaha, 73- Mailing Add: Col of Fine Arts PO Box 688 Univ of Nebr Omaha NE 68101

BIRDSALL, BYRON
PAINTER
b Buckeye, Ariz, Dec 18, 37. Study: Seattle Pacific Col, BA; Stanford Univ, MA. Work: Anchorage Hist & Fine Arts Mus; Jean Haydon Territorial Mus, Pago Pago, Am Samoa. Comn: Painting, Alaska Bank of Com, Anchorage, 76; paintings, Alyeska Pipeline Co, Anchorage, 77; paintings, RCA, Anchorage, 77. Exhib: All Alaska Watercolor Exhib, Alaska Watercolor Soc, 75-77; Anchorage Hist & Fine Arts Mus, 76; All Alaska Exhib, Anchorage Hist & Fine Arts Mus, 78; also many one-man shows. Teaching: Instr, Makerere Univ, Kampala, Uganda, 66-70; feature prog, art dir, KVZK Television, Pago Pago, Am Samoa, 72-73 & Graphix West Advertising Agency, Anchorage, Alaska, 75-76. Awards: Alaska Arts & Crafts League First Prize in Watercolor; Alaska Watercolor Soc First Prize, 76 & Second Prize, 77, Alaska Watercolor Show. Bibliog: Jeanne Abbott (auth), Footloose artist find inspiration in Alaska, Anchorage Daily News, 4/77; Lana Johnson (auth), Watercolorist forsakes his palm trees, Anchorage Times, 11/77. Mem: Alaska Watercolor Soc (pres, 76); Alaska Artists Guild. Style & Technique: Landscapes in watercolor. Media: Watercolor. Dealer: Artique Gallery 314 G St Anchorage AK 99501; The Gallery 817 W 7th Ave Anchorage AK 99501. Mailing Add: 4057 Brentwood Dr Anchorage AK 99502

BIRELINE, GEORGE LEE
PAINTER, EDUCATOR
b Peoria, Ill, Aug 12, 23. Study: Bradley Univ, BFA, 49; Univ NC, MACA, 52. Work: Everson Mus, Syracuse, NY; NC Mus Art, Raleigh; Mint Mus, Charlotte; Duke Univ Mus, Durham. Comn: Wall mural relief, Mecklenberg Co Off Complex, 61; decorative solar screen, bank bldg, SC, 63 & NCNB Bldg, Charlotte, 65; outdoor environ sculpture cast concrete, Mecklenburg Co Libr, Albemarle, 71. Exhib: Post Painterly Abstraction, Los Angeles Co Mus Art, 64; one-man shows, Andre Emmerich, 64, 65 & 67; Contemporary American Painting & Sculpture, Univ Ill, 65; 4th Int Young Artists, USA & Tokyo, 67; Retrospective, NC Mus Art, 76. Teaching: Vis lectr design & painting, Univ NC, Chapel Hill, 65-66; assoc prof design, Sch Design, NC State Univ. 57-75. Awards: First Purchase Awards, NC Mus Art, Artists Ann, 56, 57 & 64; Nat Coun on Arts Grant, 67-68; Guggenheim Found Grant for painting, 68-69. Bibliog: M Fried (auth), rev in Art Int, 64; L Lippard (auth), rev in Art Int, 65 & Art Forum, 67. Style & Technique: Color field, emphasis on color, brush and stain; later work: trompe l'oeil watercolor, polymer, oil; spatial illusion. Media: Oil, Watercolor; Colored Pencil. Mailing Add: 228 East Park Dr Raleigh NC 27605

BIRKIN, MORTON
PAINTER
b Philadelphia, Pa, Apr 27, 19. Study: Philadelphia Mus Col of Art, with Earl Horter, 36-40; Tyler Col Art, Temple Univ, with Franklin Watkins, Boris Blai, BFA, 45 & MFA, 51; NY Univ, with Hale Woodruff, 55-58. Work: Wurlitzer Mus, Taos, NMex; Philadelphia Pub Schs; Philadelphia Mus Art; Bruce Payne Collection, Time Life Bldg, New York. Comn: Mural, Dept of Navy, Mexico City, 39; mural, Reptile Rm, Philadelphia Zool Gardens, 40; mural, Recreation Rm, Aberdeen Proving Grounds, Ft Meade, Md, 41. Exhib: Pa Acad Fine Arts, 47; Brooklyn Mus Nat Exhib, 51; Metrop Mus Art, New York, 52; Emily Lowe Award Competition Exhib, 52; NJ State Exhib, Ringwood State Park, 69; Nat Am Drawings, Portsmouth Mus, Va, 76; Smithsonian Inst Travelling Exhib, 77-79. Teaching: Instr painting & drawing, Temple Univ, 42-48; instr painting & drawing, Philadelphia Mus Art, 43-49; instr painting, Mus Mod Art, Amagansatt, NY, 62-63; instr painting & drawing, Rockland Community Col, Suffern, NY, 70- Awards: Wurlitzer Nat Fel Painting, Wurlitzer Found, 58 & 67; First Prize Oils, NJ State Exhib, 69. Mem: Nat Art Educ Asn. Style & Technique: Poetic landscapes. Media: Oil, Watercolor. Mailing Add: 13-34 Sunnyside Dr Fair Lawn NJ 07410

BIRMELIN, AUGUST ROBERT
PAINTER, PRINTMAKER
b Newark, NJ, Nov 7, 33. Study: Cooper Union Art Sch; Yale Univ, BFA & MFA. Work: Mus Mod Art; San Francisco Mus Art; Whitney Mus, New York; Sheldon Mem Gallery, Lincoln, Nebr; Mus Contemp Art, Nagaoka, Japan; plus others. Exhib: Indianapolis Mus Art, 72; Art Gallery, Pa State Univ, 73; Art Mus, Kalamazoo, Mich, 74; Nat Acad Design, New York, 74; Whitney Mus, New York, 75; plus 7 one-man shows. Teaching: Instr, Yale Summer Sch, 60; prof art, Queens Col, New York, 64-; instr, Columbia Univ, summers 65 & 66; instr, Skowhegan Sch Painting, 67. Awards: Fulbright Grant, London, 60-61; Fel Award, Am Acad Rome, 61-64; Childe Hassam Purchase Award, Nat Inst Arts & Lett, New York, 71; Louis Comfort Tiffany Found Grant, 73. Style & Technique: Representational. Dealer: Terry Dintenfass Inc 18 E 67th St New York NY 10021. Mailing Add: 176 Highwood Ave Leonia NJ 07605

BIRNBAUM, MILDRED
GALLERY DIRECTOR, PAINTER
b New York, NY. Study: NY Univ; Columbia Univ; Manhattanville Col; New York Sch Design; studies with Leo Manso, Anthony Toney & Marvin Horowitz. Work: Am Can Co, Armonk, NY; Court Gallery, Lincoln Ctr, New York. Exhib: El Paso Mus, Tex, 71; Sarah Lawrence Col Mus, Bronxville, NY, 75; Hudson River Mus, Yonkers, NY, 76; The Nat Acad Design, New York, 76-77; Univ Conn, Stamford, 77. Pos: Gallery dir, Greenwich Art Barn, Conn, 70-, vpres, 72- Awards: Best in Show, Westchester Art Soc, 72-73. Mem: Nat Asn Women Artists; Conn Art Resources; Yonkers Art Asn; Greenwich Art Soc; Greenwich Art Coun. Mailing Add: Brynwood Lane Greenwich CT 06830

BIRNBERG, GERALD H
ART DEALER
b New York, NY, Oct 15, 31. Study: Syracuse Univ, NY, BA. Collections Arranged: 100 Years of American Drawings, Prince Arthur Galleries, Toronto, Ont, 77. Pos: Co-owner, Prince Arthur Galleries, 76- Specialty: Nineteenth and 20th century international art; concentration on 20th century figurative expressionism, including the work of Leonard Baskin, Will Barnet, Ben Shahn, Bruno Lucchesi, Francoise Gilot and Jack Levine. Mailing Add: Prince Arthur Galleries 33 Prince Arthur Ave Toronto ON M5B 1B2 Can

BIRNBERG, RUTH CARREL
ART DEALER
b Buffalo, NY, Mar 8, 33. Study: Univ Buffalo, NY, BA. Collections Arranged: 100 Years of American Drawings, Prince Arthur Galleries, Toronto, Ont, Can, 77. Pos: Co-owner, Prince Arthur Galleries, 76- Specialty: Nineteenth and 20th century international art; concentration on 20th century figurative expressionism such as that of Leonard Baskin, Will Barnet, Ben Shahn, Bruno Luccheso, Francoise Gilot and Jack Levine. Mailing Add: Prince Arthur Galleries 33 Prince Arthur Ave Toronto ON M5R 1B2 Can

BISCHOFF, ELMER NELSON
PAINTER, EDUCATOR
b Berkeley, Calif, July 9, 16. Study: Univ Calif, Berkeley, BA, 38, MA, 39. Work: Mus Mod Art & Whitney Mus Am Art, New York; Art Inst Chicago; New Sch Art Ctr, New York; San Francisco Mus Art. Exhib: Whitney Mus Am Art Ann Exhib Contemp Am Painting, 59; Recent Painting USA: The Figure, Mus Mod Art, New York, 62; '54 to '64, Painting & Sculpture of a Decade, Tate Gallery, London, Eng, 64; Pittsburgh Int Exhib Contemp Painting & Sculpture, 67; Osaka World's Fair, 70. Teaching: Instr painting & drawing, San Francisco Art Inst, Calif, 46-52, 56-63; prof painting & drawing, Univ Calif, Berkeley, 63- Awards: Ford Found Grant, 59; Nat Inst Arts & Lett Grant, 63. Style & Technique: Figurative. Media: Oil, Acrylic. Dealer: Staempfli Gallery 47 E 77th St New York NY 10021; Charles Campbell Gallery 647 Chestnut St San Francisco CA 94133. Mailing Add: 2571 Shattuck Ave Berkeley CA 94705

BISGYER, BARBARA G (BARBARA G COHN)
SCULPTOR
b New York, NY, June 7, 33. Study: Sarah Lawrence Col; Sculptors & Ceramic Workshop, New York; also indust design with R R Kostellow. Work: US Info Agency Permanent Collection, US Embassy; Larry Aldrich Mus Contemp Art. Exhib: Princeton Univ, 69; First Nat City Bank, New York, 68-70; Young Sculptors for Channel 13, 70; Lever House, 70-72; Union Carbide, 71; plus other group & one-man shows. Awards: Medal for Creative Sculpture, 68 & Today's Art Medal, 71, Audubon Artists; Merit Award for Outstanding Design & Craftsmanship in Sculpture, Artist Craftsmen New York, 71. Bibliog: Candidates for fame, Cue Mag, 64; articles in, Art News, 66 & 68 & Today's Art, 71. Mem: Artists Craftsmen New York (mem bd gov, 64-69 & 72-, exhib chmn, 67-69); Mamaroneck Artists Guild (vpres, 72-73); New York Soc Women Artists (exhib chmn, 72-73); Am Soc Contemp Artists. Style & Technique: Figurative; abstract. Media: Wax, Stone, Welded Steel. Dealer: Environment Gallery 205 E 60th St New York NY 10022. Mailing Add: 50 Lake Rd Rye NY 10580

BISHOP, BARBARA LEE
EDUCATOR, PRINTMAKER
b Roanoke, Va, Sept 9, 30. Study: Longwood Col, BS(art educ), 60; Univ NC, Greensboro, MFA, 62; Am Ctr Students & Artists, study with Misch Kohn, 65; Teachers Col, Columbia Univ, cert doctoral cand, 68-74; Penland Sch Crafts, 76. Work: Phillip Morris, Inc, USA & First & Merchants Bank, Richmond, Va; Gen Elec Co, Salem, Va; Hayes, Seay, Mattern & Mattern, Roanoke, Va. Comn: Varied Publ, Longwood Col, Farmville, Va, 65-; gallery flyers, Yeatts, Gallery, Roanoke, Va, 75-77; banner, Roanoke Fine Arts Ctr, Va, 77. Exhib: Arts Festival VII, VIII & IX Southeastern Drawing & Painting Shows, Jacksonville, Fal, 64-66; Eastern Regional Drawing Exhib, Philadelphia Mus Art, Pa, 65; The Print in Am/Nat Print Show, Peabody Col, Nashville, Tenn, 66; Soc Am Graphic Artists 50th Ann Exhib, New York, 69; Va Photogrs, 71, 73 & 75 & Va Designers, 76, Va Mus Fine Arts, Richmond; Ann Print & Drawing Exhib, Winston-Salem Gallery Contemp Art, 72; Va Artist, Int Women's Arts Festival, New York, 75; 21 one- woman shows, Va, NY, Alaska, NC & Pa, 62-77. Collections Arranged: Thomas Sully, 73 & Thomas Sulley and His Contemporaries, 78, Bedford Gallery, Longwood Col, Farmville, Va. Teaching: Prof printmaking & photog & chmn dept art, Longwood Col, Farmville, Va, 65- Pos: Proj dir, Thomas Sully Gallery, Longwood Col, 72-; mem cert rev & arts assessment comt, Va Dept Educ, 73-77; mem educ for arts comt, Va Mus Fine Arts, 74-; visual arts consult, Va Comn Arts & Humanities, 73- Awards: Second Prize, 17th Ann Southeastern Exhib, High Mus Art, Atlanta, Ga, 62; Purchase Award, Roanoke Fine Arts Ctr Sidewalk Exhib, S H Heironimus Co, Va, 64; Cert Distinction, Va Photogrs 71, Va Mus Fine Arts, Richmond, 71. Mem: Roanoke Fine Arts Ctr (mem bd dirs, 71-74); Nat Art Educ Asn (mem states assembly, 71-73); Va Art Educ Asn (pres, 71-73, mem exec comt, 73-75); Nat Coun Arts Adminrs; Southeastern Graphics Coun. Style & Technique: Abstract natural forms; landscape. Media: Photo silk-screen and intaglio; black and white still photog. Publ: Co-auth article, To Open Eyes, Art Educ J, Nat Art Educ Asn, 71; auth, Through Search: The Finding and Maintaining of Identity Through the Design of Nature by Imprinting and Embossing, Lock Haven Rev, Lock Haven Col, 73; contribr, Virginia Elementary Art Curriculum Guide, Va Dept Educ, 75; guest art columnist, Penland Sch of Crafts, Roanoke Times, 76. Dealer: Yeatts Gallery 426 Walnut Ave Roanoke VA 24016; Harold Decker Galleries Norfolk & Virginia Beach, Va. Mailing Add: Rte 3 Box 568-B Farmville VA 23901

BISHOP, BENJAMIN
PAINTER, EDUCATOR
b New York, NY, Feb 10, 23. Study: Art Students League, 45-47; Univ Nebr, BFA; NY Univ Inst Fine Arts, 50-51; Columbia Univ; Univ Calif, Berkeley, MA, 65. Work: Norfolk Mus Art & Sci, Va; State Univ NY Col Potsdam; Univ Mass, Amherst; Syracuse Univ Mus; State Univ NY Binghamton. Exhib: Drawing Soc Nat Exhib, 65, circulated by Am Fedn Arts, 65-66; Monterey Peninsula Chap of Am Fedn of Arts, 66; Alonzo Gallery, New York, 67-69; Mari Gallery, Woodstock, NY, 68; Monterey Peninsula Mus; First St Gallery, New York, 77. Teaching: Instr art, Memphis Acad Art, Tenn, 47-48; instr art, Vassar Col, 51; instr art, Univ Mo-Columbia, 52-54; instr art, Santa Catalina Sch Girls, Monterey, Calif, 64-65; prof art, State Univ NY Col New Paltz, 65- Awards: Delta Pi Delta Award, Joslyn Art Mus, 48; First Prize for Drawing, Monterey Co Fair, Calif, 65; Childe Hassam Fund Purchase Award, Am Acad Arts & Lett, 68. Media: Oil. Dealer: Alonzo Gallery 26 E 63rd St New York NY 10021. Mailing Add: Rte 1 Box 450B High Falls NY 12440

BISHOP, BUDD HARRIS
MUSEUM DIRECTOR
b Canton, Ga, Nov 1, 36. Study: Shorter Col, Ga, AB, 58; Univ Ga, MFA, 60, with Lamar Dodd & Howard Thomas; Arts Admin Inst, Harvard Univ, 70. Collections Arranged: Tenn State Collection of Sculpture; The Collection of Hunter Mus of Art. Teaching: Lectr art hist, Vanderbilt Univ, 61-62; art dir children's prog, Ensworth Sch, Nashville, Tenn, 61-64; lectr art surv, Univ Chattanooga, 67-68. Pos: Dir creative serv, Transit Advert Asn, New York, 64-66; exec dir, Hunter Mus Art, 66-76; dir, Columbus Gallery of Fine Arts, Ohio, 76- Mem: Am Asn Mus; Midwest Mus Conf; Tenn Asn Mus (pres, 71-); Asn of Art Mus Dirs; Ohio Mus Asn. Res: Early Tennessee artists; early Southern American painting. Mailing Add: 545 City Park Ave Columbus OH 43215

BISHOP, ISABEL (MRS HAROLD G WOLFF)
PAINTER, ETCHER
b Cincinnati, Ohio, Mar 3, 02. Study: Wicker Art Sch, Detroit, Mich; New York Sch Appl Design for Women; Art Students League; Moore Inst, hon DFA. Work: Metrop Mus Art & Whitney Mus Am Art, New York; Boston Mus Fine Art, Mass; Des Moines Art Ctr, Iowa; Philips Mem Gallery, Washington, DC. Comn: Mural for post off in New Lexington, Ohio,

US Govt Sect Fine Arts. Exhib: Venice Biennials; Pittsburgh Int; Nat Exhib Prints, Brooklyn Mus; one-man shows, Berkshire Mus, Pittsfield, Mass & Midtown Galleries, New York. Teaching: Instr figure painting & drawing, Art Students League, 35-37; instr art, Skowhegan Sch Painting & Sculpture, 56 & 58. Mem: Am Soc Graphic Artists (vpres, 69-72); Nat Arts Club; Audubon Artists; Royal Soc Arts, London. Dealer: Midtown Galleries 11 E 57th St New York NY 10022. Mailing Add: 355 W 246th St New York NY 10471

BISHOP, JAMES
PAINTER
b Neosho, Mo, Oct 7, 27. Study: Syracuse Univ, New York, BA, 46-50; Wash Univ Sch of Fine Arts, St Louis, Mo, 51-54; Black Mountain Col, study with Esteban Vicente, 53; Columbia Univ, 55-56. Work: San Francisco Mus of Art. Exhib: Salons des Realites Nouvelles, Paris, 62-65; Ten Americans, Amerika Haus, Berlin, 66; Albright-Knox Art Gallery, Buffalo, NY, 67; Corcoran Gallery, Washington, DC, 67; Painting Ann, Whitney Mus of Am Art, New York, 67; San Francisco Mus of Art, Calif, 68; Director's Choice, Dallas Mus of Fine Arts, Tex, 70; Art on Paper, Weatherspoon Gallery, Univ of NC, Greensboro, 71; Works on Paper, Art Lending Serv; Mus of Mod Art, New York, 74; Tendances Actuelles de la Nouvelle Peinture Americaine, Musee d'Art Moderne de la Ville de Paris, 75; The Vogel Collection, The Clocktower, Inst for Art and Urban Resources, New York & the Inst of Contemp Art, Philadelphia, Pa, 75; Recent Drawings (traveling), Am Fedn of the Arts, 75; Europa-Americo, Galleria d'Arte Moderno, Bologna, Italy, 76; Recent Acquisitions, Musee de Grenoble, France, 76; Project Studio 1, Inst for Art & Urban Resources, New York, 76; Opening Exhib, Drawing Ctr, New York, 77; The McCrory Collection, Zurich Munstmuaeum, Switz, 77; one-man shows, Fischback Gallery, New York, 66, 68, 70 & 72, The Clocktower, Inst for Art & Urban Resources, New York, 73; Annemarie Verna Gallery, Zurich, Switz, 76 & Galerie Jean Fournier, Paris, France, 76; plus many others. Teaching: Instr, Cooper Union, 69-70, Carnegie-Mellon Inst, 71 & Sch of Visual Arts, New York, 72. Pos: Ed assoc, Art News, 69-72. Awards: Guggenheim Found Fel, 70. Bibliog: Phyllis Derfner (auth), New York Letter, Art Int, 9/73; John Russell (auth), Review of James Bishop drawings at Rosa Esman, 4/20/74 & Inaugural Show, the Drawing Ctr, 1/21/77, New York Times; Joseph Dreiss (auth), Reviews, Arts Mag, 6/74. Mailing Add: 5 Lispenard St New York NY 10013

BISHOP, MARJORIE CUTLER
PAINTER
b Melrose, Mass. Study: Art Students League; New Sch Social Res; and with Guy Pene du Bois, Moses Soyer, Sol Wilson & Valero, Paris, France. Work: Walker Art Ctr, Minneapolis, Minn; Photo Researchers, Inc, New York. Exhib: Carnegie Inst, Pittsburgh, Pa, 45; Pa Acad Fine Arts, Philadelphia, 45; Audubon Artists, New York, 47, 52 & 54; Hecksher Mus, Huntington, NY & Guild Hall, Easthampton, NY, 65; State Univ NY Col, Stony Brook, 78; plus many one-man shows in New York & Long Island. Teaching: Instr creative painting & art hist, Bishop Art Studio, Oldfield, NY, 56- Pos: Art Coun, Suffolk Mus, Stony Brook, NY, 61-65. Awards: Purchase Prize, Walker Art Ctr, 45; Exhib Award, St Paul-de-Vence, France, 53. Style & Technique: Semi-abstract. Media: Oil, Sand. Publ: Women Artists in America: 18th Century to the Present. Dealer: Gallery North North Country Rd Setauket NY 11733. Mailing Add: Flax Pond Woods Setauket NY 11733

BISHOP, ROBERT CHARLES
MUSEUM DIRECTOR, ART WRITER
b Readfield, Maine, Aug 25, 38. Study: Univ Mich, Ann Arbor, PhD(Am cult), 76. Teaching: Lectr Am decorative arts, Univ Mich, Ann Arbor, 75-77. Pos: Cur furniture, Henry Ford Mus, Dearborn, Mich, 69-71, mus ed, 71-77; dir, Mus of Am Folk Art, New York, 77- Mem: Am Asn Mus; Metrop Mus of Art Connoisseur Club; Midwest Mus Conf; Victorian Soc; Impresario Cult Soc (pres, 75-76). Publ: Auth, Centuries and Styles of the American Chair, 1640-1970, 72, How to Know American Antique Furniture, 73, American Folk Sculpture, 74, New Discoveries in American Quilts, 75 & co-auth, A Gallery of Amish Quilts, 76, Dutton. Mailing Add: 213 W 22nd St New York NY 10011

BISONE, EDWARD GEORGE
PAINTER, ILLUSTRATOR
b Buffalo, NY, Nov 19, 28. Study: Univ Buffalo, with Seymour Drumlevitch. Exhib: 27th Ann, 62 & 37th Ann Mid-Year Show, Butler Inst Am Art, Youngstown, Ohio, 73; 99th Ann Exhib, Am Watercolor Soc, New York, 66; Ann Drawing & Small Sculpture Show, Ball State Univ, Muncie, Ind, 70; 145th Ann Exhib, Nat Acad Design, New York, 70; 35th Ann Western NY Art Show, Albright Knox Art Gallery, Buffalo, 75; 22nd Nat Ann Drawing & Small Sculpture Show, Ball State Univ Art Gallery, Muncie, Ind, 76; Am Drawings 1976 Nat Exhib, Portsmouth Community Arts Ctr, Va, 76; State of NY Images/Shapes Show, Clinton Co Govt Ctr, NY, 76. Awards: First Prize Painting, Burnhams Gallery Sight & Sound, 63; Tony Sisti Award, Leisureland Show, 68; First Prize Graphics, McAlpine United Presby Church, 72. Bibliog: Discussed in La Rev Mod, Paris, France, 67; Art Rev Mag, 68. Mem: Artists Equity Asn; Nat Soc Lit & Arts. Style & Technique: Combination of figurative and abstract images. Media: Mixed Media. Publ: Auth, Art Notebook, Vol 1, No 2; illusr, Tour the World of Cooking in 15 Minutes, 72. Dealer: Jerel Gallery & Framery Snyder NY 14226. Mailing Add: 79 Williamstowne N Apt 5 Cheektowaga NY 14227

BISSELL, CHARLES OVERMAN
CARTOONIST
b Nashville, Tenn, June 29, 08. Pos: Lithographic artist, 24-45; ed cartoonist & mem staff, Nashville Tennessean, 43-; art dir, Sunday Mag, 45-70. Awards: Cartoon Award, Nat Headliners Club, 63; Distinguished Serv Award, Sigma Delta Chi, 64; Pub Serv Award, Nat Safety Coun, 66. Mem: Asn Am Ed Cartoonists; Nat Cartoonist Soc. Publ: Creater cartoon feature Bissell's Brave New World, 62. Mailing Add: 4221 Farrar A Nashville TN 37215

BISSELL, PHIL
CARTOONIST, ILLUSTRATOR
b Worcester, Mass, Feb 1, 26. Study: Sch Practical Art, Boston, Mass; Art Instr Inc, Minneapolis, Minn, grad. Work: Baseball Hall Fame, Cooperstown, NY; Basketball Hall Fame, Springfield, Mass; Football Hall Fame, Canton, Ohio; Hockey Hall Fame, Toronto, Can; Swimming Hall of Fame, Ft Lauderdale, Fla; plus others. Comn: New Eng Patriots (Nat Football League) insignia. Exhib: Southern Calif Expo, 64; Nat Cartoonists Soc, New York, 71 & Washington, DC, 72; Man & His World, 9th Int Salon Cartoons, Montreal, PQ, 72. Mem: Nat Cartoonists Soc. Media: Ink, Tempera. Awards: Best Ed Cartoons of Yr, 74 & 75; Scarlet Quill Award for Outstanding Coverage of Intercollegiate Athletics, 76. Mailing Add: PO Box 305 Rockport MA 01966

BITTERS, JEAN RAY
See Laury, Jean Ray

BITTNER, HANS OSKAR
PAINTER, ILLUSTRATOR
b Breslau, Ger, Jan 25, 05; US citizen. Study: Breslau Kunstschule; Munich Acad. Work: Collection of Crown Prince William of Ger; Breslau Kunst Mus; Breslau Art Galleries; also in pvt collections. Exhib: Ill Festival Art, Chicago, 64; Three Main Libr, Chicago; Chicago Chap Artists Equity Asn; Rockford Col, Kenosha Col & Univ Wis-Stevens Point; work also exhibited on ABC & NBC. Pos: Glass & display designer, Goldblatt Stores, Chicago, 30-35; commercial artist, Vogue Wright, 35-45; artist & designer, Wilding Picture Studio, 52-68. Awards: Several Second Place & Hon Mentions, Palette & Chisel Acad & Munic Art League, Chicago; Col Frank Chesrow Gold Medal, Chicago, 72. Mem: Palette & Chisel Acad (dir, 68-); Munic Art League (dir, 69-); Artist Guild Chicago. Mailing Add: 10357 Loma Blanca Dr Sun City AZ 85351

BJORKLUND, LEE
PAINTER, EDUCATOR
b Wadena, Minn, June 20, 40. Study: Univ Minn, Minneapolis, BA, 69 & MFA, 73. Work: Walker Art Ctr, Minneapolis; Univ Gallery, Univ Minn; Fed Reserve Bank & First Nat Bank, Minneapolis; Amerada Hess Corp, New York; WTCN-Metromedia, Golden Valley, Minn. Exhib: One-man show, Univ Gallery, 71; Introduction: Seven Young Artists, Walker Art Ctr, 72; Six Young Artists, Foster Gallery, Univ Wis, Eau Claire, 72; An Int Cyclopedia of Plans & Occurrences, Va Commonwealth Univ, 73; Walker Art Ctr, 75; Minneapolis Inst of Arts, 76; Hanson-Cowles Gallery, Minneapolis, 76. Teaching: Instr studio art, Univ Minn, 70-72; instr studio art, Minn Mus Art Sch, St Paul, 72-73; asst prof studio art, Minneapolis Col Art & Design, 73-78, chmn basic studies div, 75-78. Pos: Visual arts coordr, Minn State Arts Bd, Minneapolis, 74-75. Awards: Studio Arts Student Scholar, Univ Minn, 67; Minn State Arts Coun Fel Grant, 72. Bibliog: Mike Steele (auth), Practitioners explore the modern art mystique, Minneapolis Tribune, 5/18/75. Mem: Twin Cities Metrop Arts Alliance; Walker Art Ctr; Minneapolis Soc Fine Arts. Style & Technique: Painterly abstraction. Media: Polyester Resin, Powder & Metallic Pigments. Dealer: Hanson-Cowles Gallery 331 Second Ave N Minneapolis MN 55401. Mailing Add: 2742 Bryant Ave S Minneapolis MN 55408

BLACK, DAVID EVANS
SCULPTOR
b Gloucester, Mass, May 29, 28. Study: Skowhegan Sch, Maine, summer 49; Wesleyan Univ, AB, 50; Ind Univ, Bloomington, 53, with Karl Martz & George Rickey. Work: Neue Nat Galerie, West Berlin, Ger; Addison Gallery Am Art, Mass; Dayton Art Inst; Butler Inst Am Art, Youngstown, Ohio; Ind Univ. Comn: Ceramic reliefs for apt bldgs, Lane & Neil Aves, Columbus, Ohio, 61; ceramic sculpture, Hardesty Village, Columbus, 65; outdoor sculptures in transparent Lexan & steel, Neue Nat Galerie Sculpture Ct, 72, Miami Univ, Ohio, 73 & Credit Life Insurance Co, Springfield, Ohio, 75. Exhib: One-man shows, Contemp Gallery, New York, 67, Amerika-Haus, West Berlin, 71; Nat Gallery, WBerlin, Ger, 77 & Lehmbruck Mus, Duisberg, Ger, 77; Plastics Presence, Jewish Mus, New York, Milwaukee Art Ctr, Wis & San Francisco Mus Art, 69-70; Alloway Selects, Columbus Gallery Fine Arts, 77. Teaching: Prof sculpture, Ohio State Univ, 54- Pos: Mem artists in residence prog, Berlin & WGer Govt, 70-71. Awards: Fulbright Grant to Italy, 62-63; Nat Arts Coun Award, 66. Bibliog: David Black, Sculptor, Ohio State Univ TV Ctr, 67; Tracy Atkinson (auth), David Black, recent work & George Rickey (auth), David Black, Art Int, 12/72. Media: Plastic, Metal. Publ: Auth, Transparent sculpture, Ohio State Univ Arts, 2/72. Mailing Add: Dept of Art Ohio State Univ Columbus OH 43210

BLACK, FREDERICK (EDWARD)
PAINTER
b Providence, RI, May 24, 24. Study: Univ NMex, BS, BA & MA. Work: Univ NMex; Roswell Art Mus; Long Beach Mus Art. Exhib: Phoenix Art Mus, 63; Univ Ill Biennial Invitational; one-man shows, Calif Palace of Legion of Honor & Paul Rivas Gallery, Los Angeles, 65; Whitney Mus Am Art Invitational; plus many others. Collections Arranged: Arts of Southern California (series contemp art), organized by Long Beach Mus Art, circulated by Western Asn Art Mus, 62-65; period & contemp exhibs, NMex State Art Mus; Tucson Art Ctr. Teaching: Vis prof art, Univ Colo, summers 60 & 61; prof art, Univ Ariz Exten, 60-61; vis prof art, Otis Art Inst, summers 65 & 66; vis prof art hist, Univ Calif, Los Angeles, 65; vis prof art hist, Calif State Col, Long Beach, summer 66; assoc prof art, Univ Albuquerque, 66-69. Pos: Dir, State Art Mus, Santa Fe, NMex; dir, Tucson Art Ctr, Ariz; adv prof painting, Art Ctr Sch, Los Angeles; state & regional art juror, 61-64; dir, Long Beach Mus Art, 61-66; mem fine arts adv bd, Albuquerque City Comn, 70- Awards: First Prize, Providence Art Club, 53; nominee for New Talent, Art in Am, 58. Mem: Western Mus League (past pres); Long Beach Arts Coun (pres); Artists Equity Asn; Am Asn Mus; Western Asn Art Mus. Media: Oil, Acrylic. Publ: Contribr, bk revs, NMex Quart, 53 & 64; contribr, Director's choice, Art in Am, 62; auth, Long & Evangel, Craft Horizons, 3-4/70. Mailing Add: 7300 Arroyo Del Oso Ave NE Albuquerque NM 87109

BLACK, LISA
PAINTER
b Lansing, Mich, June 19, 34. Study: Univ Paris, Sorbonne, dipl, 55; Univ Mich, BA, 56. Exhib: New Haven Paint & Clay Club Art Exhib, Conn, 71 & 72; Art Asn Newport 60th & 61st Am Ann Exhib, Newport, RI, 71; Springfield Art League 53rd Nat Exhib, Mass, 72; 32nd Ann Art Exhib, Cedar City, Utah, 72; 15th Nat Exhib Am Art, Chautauqua, NY, 72. Awards: William Holland Drury Prize, Art Asn Newport 60th Am Ann, 71; Second Award Graphics, Springfield Art League Nat, 72; First Award Graphics, Easter Seal Salute to Arts, Westport, 74. Mem: Artists Equity; Westchester Art Soc; Stamford Art Asn; New Haven Paint & Clay Club; Yonkers Art Asn. Style & Technique: Abstract. Media: Acrylic. Mailing Add: 17 Brushy Hill Rd Darien CT 06820

BLACK, MARY CHILDS
ART HISTORIAN, CURATOR
b Pittsfield, Mass. Study: Univ NC, Greensboro, BA; George Washington Univ, MA; Cath Univ Am. Collections Arranged: Edward Hicks, Abby Aldrich Rockefeller Folk Art Collection, 60, Erastus Salisbury Field (with catalog), 63, plus traveling & spec exhibs, 57-65; Ammi Phillips (co-auth, catalog), Mus Am Folk Art, 68, Limners of the Upper Hudson, 69, plus other major exhibs; City of Promise, Jewish Life in New York, New York Hist Soc, 70; Audubon's Birds of America, Series of Nine Special Bicentennial Exhibitions, 76 & 77; plus all known original watercolors and other major exhib. Pos: From registr to cur & dir, Abby Aldrich Rockefeller Folk Art Collection, Williamsburg, Va, 57-65; dir, Mus Am Folk Art, New York, 65-70; cur painting & sculpture, New York Hist Soc, 70- Mem: Am Asn Mus. Res: American folk art subjects c 1640 to 1840. Publ: Co-auth, American Folk Painting, 66; co-auth, What's American in American Art, 71; Old New York in Early Photographs, 73; American Advertising Posters of the 19th Century, 76. Mailing Add: 149 W 94th St New York NY 10025

BLACK, MARY MCCUNE
CURATOR, PAINTER
b Broadwell, Ohio, Feb 14, 15. Study: Ohio Univ, BS(educ), 37, MFA, 58; Amagansett Sch Art, Sarasota, Fla; workshop study with Charles Burchfield, William Thon, Aaron Bohrod, Paul Sample, Elliot O'Hara & Hilton Leech. Work: FMC Corp; McJunkin Corp; Kanawha Co Pub Libr; Art in Embassies Prog; Lutheran Church, Parkersburg, WVa. Comn: Three murals for pediatric ward, Charleston Gen Hosp Auxiliary, WVa, 53. Exhib: Ohio Valley Regional, Ohio Univ, 45; Huntington Galleries Regional, 54; Intermont Col Regional, Bristol, Va, 57; Nat League Am Pen Women, Tulsa, Okla, 68 & Smithsonian Inst, Washington, DC, 63. Collections Arranged: Permanent collection exhibition; Fiber & Fabrics; Collectors Exhibition of Kanawha Valley. Teaching: Instr art, Sandusky Jr High Sch, 37-39; instr painting, adult prog, Kanawha Co Bd Educ, 58-64; instr art, Valley Day Sch, 60-63; instr painting, YMCA & Charleston Art Gallery, 63-68. Pos: Dir, Charleston Art Gallery Sunrise, 63-75, cur fine arts of Sunrise, 75-77. Mem: Am Asn Mus; Allied Artists WVa (pres, 58-59); Nat League Am Pen Women (pres, Charleston Br, 59-60, state pres, 74-); WVa Art Educ Asn; Southeastern Mus Asn. Style & Technique: Abstract. Media: Watercolor. Mailing Add: Charleston Art Gallery 755 Myrtle Rd Charleston WV 25314

BLACK, SHIRLEY
PAINTER
b New York, NY, June 20, 21. Study: Art Students League, with E Yaghijian, G Grosz, M Glasier & Morris Kantor; Phillips Mem Gallery, Washington, DC, 42; Columbia Univ Teachers Col, with Arthur Young, 56-57; Mus Mod Art, with Zoltan Hecht, 57-58; Nat Acad Design, with Federico Castellon & Mario Cooper. Work: Alfred Univ, NY; Bridgeport Univ, Conn; Marine Midland Trust Co Rochester, NY; Mt Holyoke Col, South Hadley, Mass. Exhib: Butler Inst Am Art, Youngstown, Ohio, 57; The Importance of the Small Painting, Nordness Gallery, New York, 60; The Fifth Season, Alonzo Gallery, New York, 69; Am Watercolor Soc, Nat Acad Sch Fine Arts, New York, 70-71; Philbrook Mus, Tulsa, Okla, 71; two-artist show, Bell Gallery, Greenwich, Conn, 77; one-artist shows, Alonzo Gallery, 69, 71 & 76, Alfred Univ, Rochester, NY, 70 & Alfred, NY, 70 & Univ of Bridgeport, Conn, 71. Bibliog: Martha B Scott (auth), Watercolors of Shirley Black bring some response as poetry, Bridgeport Sunday Post, 10/17/71. Mem: Silvermine Guild Artists. Media: Watercolor. Mailing Add: c/o Alonzo Gallery 30 W 57th St New York NY 10019

BLACKBURN, LENORA WHITMIRE
COLLECTOR
b Midland, Tex, Aug 21, 04. Study: Univ Tex, Austin, BA, 27; also grad study. Mem: Mobile Art Asn; Art Patrons League of Mobile. Interest: Exhibiting collection for groups and giving lectures on artists. Collection: Old Masters including Titian, Ghirlandaio, Rubens, Van der Helst, Bol, Franz van Mieris, Van Dyck, Constable, Turner, Watteau, Ingres, Vigee-Lebrun, Gainsborough, Richard Wilson, Bonington, Alma-Tadema, T Rousseau, Daubigny, Jules Breton, Eugene Isabey; H W Pickersgill; John F Herring, Sr, Claude Monet, Rouault, Sir Alfred East and many others. Americans including Charles Wilson Peale, Inness, Sully, Eakins, William Marshall (Lincoln's portrait of which Marshall made an engraving), Bierstadt, Blakelock, Robert Henri, John Sloan, Childe Hassam, Alexander Wyant, George Phippen, Peter Hurd, Joe Rader Roberts, Harold I Hopkinson, Carl J Smith, Joanne Hennes, Travis Keese, Kensett, Cropsy, Thomas Moran, Frederic Waugh, Emil Carlson, George Luks, Potthast, John Carroll, Guy Wiggins, Grandma Moses, Porfirio Salinas, Endre Szabo, G Harvey, A D Greer, Mario Larrinaga, Van Driest, Lester Parisch, Vannerson, Raul Gutierrez, Americo Makk, Vives Atsara; plus many others. Mailing Add: 4505 N Sunset Dr Mobile AL 36608

BLACKBURN, MORRIS (ATKINSON)
PAINTER, PRINTMAKER
b Philadelphia, Pa, Oct 13, 02. Study: Pa Acad Fine Arts; and with Arthur B Carles, Jr. Work: Pa Acad Fine Arts; Philadelphia Mus Art; NJ State Mus, Trenton; Mus NMex, Santa Fe; Libr Cong, Washington, DC. Exhib: Pa Acad Fine Arts Ann, 30-72; 39 one-man shows, 30-75; plus many exhibs, Nat Acad Design, Am Watercolor Soc & Audubon Artists. Teaching: Instr painting, Philadelphia Mus Art, 45-72; instr painting, drawing & graphics, Pa Acad Fine Arts, 52- Awards: Guggenheim Fel, 52; Watercolor Medal, Philadelphia Watercolor Club, 69; Percy M Owens Prize, Fellowship Pa Acad Fine Arts, 72. Bibliog: Henry Pitz (auth), Morris Blackburn, Am Artist Mag, 11/70; Portrait of a painter (film), Philadelphia Mus Art. Mem: Philadelphia Watercolor Club (mem bd & chmn exhib comt, 69-71 & hon vpres); Am Watercolor Soc; Audubon Artists; Allied Artists Am; Fellowship Pa Acad Fine Arts. Style & Technique: Abstract realism; mixed oil-tempera technique. Media: Oil, Watercolor; Gouache, Sumi. Mailing Add: 2104 Spring St Philadelphia PA 19103

BLACKETER, JAMES RICHARD
PAINTER, ART DEALER
b Laguna Beach, Calif, Sept 23, 31. Study: Santa Ana Col; also with Bennett Bradbury. Exhib: Laguna Beach Invitational Marine Show, Calif, 59; Los Angeles Co Fair Invitational Exhib, Pomona, Calif, 60; Hunt-Wesson Foods Show, Fullerton, Calif, 72. Teaching: Pvt classes oil painting, 60- Pos: Art dir, Fed Sign & Signal Corp, Los Angeles, 58-60, Santa Ana, 60-72; owner, The Studio (art gallery), Laguna Beach. Awards: Laguna Beach Art Asn Awards, 51, 58, 59 & 60; Festival of Arts Award, 58; Ebell Club Los Angeles Award, 60. Mem: Laguna Beach Art Asn (secy, 60); Am Inst Fine Arts; Laguna Beach Festival Arts, Showcase 21. Media: Oil. Specialty: Marine oil paintings. Mailing Add: 2260 Glenneyre St Laguna Beach CA 92651

BLACKMUN, BARBARA WINSTON
EDUCATOR, ART HISTORIAN
b Merced, Calif, June 29, 28. Study: Univ Calif, Los Angeles, BA(fine arts), Honors, 49, two teaching credentials, PhD prog art hist, at present; Ariz State Univ, MA(art hist), 71. Teaching: Lectr art hist & chmn art subject bd, Univ Malawi, Limbe, Malawi, Africa, 67-69; instr art hist, San Diego Mesa Col, Calif, 71-, chmn dept visual arts, 76- Pos: Founding dir, Univ Arts Workshop, Malawi, Africa, 68-69; co-dir, Nat Craft & Fabric Show, Malawi, Africa, June 69; co-founder & chmn, Pub Arts Adv Coun, Co of San Diego, 76- Mem: Col Art Asn; Archaeol Inst Am (prog chmn, San Diego chap, 76-); San Diego Fine Arts Gallery (mem prog comt, Educ Coun, 75- & mem bd, African Arts Comt); Art Historians Southern Calif. Res: The Nyau masks of the Maravi and their significance in African art. Publ: Co-auth, Masks of Malawi, Summer 72 & auth, Maravi Nchawa Mask, Autumn 75, African Arts. Mailing Add: 9850 Ogram Dr La Mesa CA 92041

BLACKWELL, JOHN VICTOR
ART HISTORIAN, EDUCATOR
b Yale, Okla, Oct 25, 19. Study: James Millikin Univ, BA; State Univ Iowa, MA, MFA & PhD. Teaching: Prof art, Univ Nebr, Omaha. Res: Medieval art history. Mailing Add: Univ of Nebr Dept of Art 60th & Dodge Sts Omaha NE 68101

BLACKWELL, THOMAS LEO
PAINTER
b Chicago, Ill, Mar 9, 38. Work: Guggenheim Mus, New York. Exhib: Human Concern-Personal Torment, Whitney Mus Am Art, New York, 69; Whitney Mus Am Art Painting Ann, 72; New Realism, Lowe Mus, Univ Miami, Fla, 72; New Painting, Indianapolis Mus Art, Ind, 72; Sharp Focus Realism, Sidney Janis Gallery, 72; Hyperrealistes Americains, Galerie 4 Movements, Paris, 72; Jacksonville Art Mus, Fla, 77; Recklinghausen Mus, Ger, 77; Nat Air & Space Mus, Smithsonian Inst, Washington, DC, 77-78. Bibliog: John Russell (auth), To, Blackwell, New York Times, 2/8/75; Carlo Lamagna (auth), Tome Blackwell's new paintings, Art Int, Vol 20 (Dec 1976); William Zimmer (auth), article in Arts Mag, 3/77. Media: Oil. Mailing Add: c/o Louis K Meisel Gallery 141 Prince St New York NY 10012

BLACKWOOD, DAVID (LLOYD)
PAINTER, PRINTMAKER
b Wesleyville, Nfld, Nov 7, 41. Study: Ont Col Art, Toronto, 59-64. Work: Nat Gallery Can; Nat Gallery Australia; Art Gallery Ont; Montreal Mus Fine Arts; NB Mus. Exhib: Int Graphics, Montreal Mus Fine Arts, 71; 1st Norweg Biennial, Fredrickstad, 72; Biennial Int de l'Estampe, Paris, France, 73. Teaching: Art master, Trinity Col Sch, Port Hope, Ont, 63-75; artist in residence, Univ Toronto, 69-75. Awards: Ingres Medal, Govt France, 63; Purchase Award Can Biennial, Nat Gallery Can, 64; Hornansky Award Int Graphics, Montreal Mus Fine Arts, 71. Bibliog: Rex Bromfield (auth), David Blackwood (film), CBC, 72; Farley Mowat (auth), Survivor, Wake of the Great Sealers, McClelland (Can) & Little Brown (US), 73; Blackwood (film), NFB, 75. Mem: Royal Can Acad Art. Style & Technique: Single and group figures in landscape and marine environment. Dealer: Gallery Pascal 334 Dundas St W Toronto ON Can. Mailing Add: 22 King St Port Hope ON Can

BLADEN, RONALD
SCULPTOR
b Vancouver, BC, July 13, 18. Study: Vancouver Art Sch; Calif Sch Fine Arts. Work: Mus Mod Art; Los Angeles Co Mus Art. Exhib: Whitney Mus Am Art, 66 & 68; Guggenheim Mus Art, 67; Corcoran Gallery Art, 67; Minimal Art, The Hague, 68; Documenta, Kassel, 68; plus others. Awards: Rosenberg Fel, Nat Arts Coun, San Francisco. Dealer: Sculpture Now Inc 142 Greene St New York NY 10012. Mailing Add: 5 W 21st St New York NY 10010

BLAGDEN, ALLEN
PAINTER
b New York, NY, Feb 21, 38. Study: Hotchkiss Sch; Yale Univ Summer Art Sch; Cornell Univ, BFA. Work: Berkshire Mus, Pittsfield, Mass; Garvan Collection, Peabody Mus, New Haven, Conn. Comn: Portrait, Hotchkiss Sch, Lakeville, Conn, 70; plus many pvt portrait comns. Exhib: Silvermine Guild Artists, Conn, 67; St Gaudens Mus, NH, 67; Wadsworth Atheneum, Hartford, Conn, 68; Albright-Knox Art Gallery, Buffalo, NY, 69; Lenox Hill Hosp Benefit Exhib, Gimbel's East, New York, 72; plus six one-man shows. Teaching: Instr painting, Hotchkiss Sch, 68-69. Pos: Illusr, dept ornith, Smithsonian Inst, Washington, DC, 62-63. Awards: Allied Artist Award, 63; Century Club Art Prize, 71. Mem: Century Asn, New York. Style & Technique: Realistic watercolors in dry brush technique. Dealer: Frank Rehn Gallery 655 Madison Ave New York NY 10021. Mailing Add: Salisbury CT 06068

BLAGDEN, THOMAS P
PAINTER
b Chester, Pa, Mar 29, 11. Study: Yale Univ, BA, 33; Pa Acad Fine Arts, 33-35; spec study with Henry Hensche & George Demetrios. Work: Addison Gallery Am Art, Andover, Mass; Wadsworth Atheneum, Hartford, Conn; Albany Inst Hist & Art, NY; Berkshire Mus, Pittsfield, Mass; Chrysler Mus, Provincetown, Mass. Exhib: Pa Acad Fine Arts, Philadelphia, 38; Corcoran Gallery Art, Washington, DC, 41; Metrop Mus Art, New York, 50; Am Acad Arts & Lett, NY, 61; Loeb Drama Ctr, Harvard Univ, Cambridge, Mass, 71; one-man show, Berkshire Mus, 77 & 18 other one-man exhibs, incl nine in New York (Milch Galleries & others), St Gaudens Mus, New Britain Mus, Americanart & others. Teaching: Instr art, Hotchkiss Sch, Lakeville, Conn, 35-56. Awards: Purchase Prize, Wadsworth Atheneum & Berkshire Mus. Mem: Century Club, New York; Conn Watercolor Soc. Style & Technique: Realistic and semi-abstract landscapes and figure paintings in oils, watercolors and acrylics. Mailing Add: Lime Rock Rd Lakeville CT 06039

BLAHOVE, MARCOS
PAINTER
b Ukraine, Apr 22, 28; US citizen. Study: Acad Vicente Puig, Buenos Aires, Arg; Nat Acad Design, New York. Work: Nat Collection Fine Arts & Portrait Gallery, Smithsonian Inst, Washington, DC; Navy Combat Art Collection, Washington, DC; Weatherspoon Art Gallery, Univ NC, Greensboro; Southampton Col, Long Island Univ, NY; Salmagundi Club, New York. Comn: Portrait of Aaron Copland, comn by Mrs F Copland, New York, 72, Lt Barbara A Allen, comn by NACAL, 74 & Bill Koghler, comn by Salmagundi Club, New York, 74. Exhib: Fine Arts Festival, Parrish Art Mus, Southampton, NY, 71; Artists Exhib, Southampton Col, NY, 71; Art on Paper, Weatherspoon Art Gallery, Univ NC, Greensboro, 74; Contemporary Portraits by American Painters, Lowe Art Mus, Coral Gables, Fla, 74. Awards: Purchase Prize, Artists Exhib, Southampton Col, NY, 71; Eliot Liskin Award, Salmagundi Club, 72; Fine Arts Comn Purchase Award, Am Drawings 76, Portsmouth Mus, 76. Bibliog: Lois Miller (auth), Marcos Blahove at the heart of his subject, Am Artist, 7/73. Mem: Salmagundi Club, New York. Style & Technique: Portraits, figures in watercolor, oil painting, palette knife technique. Publ: Co-auth, with Joe Singer, Painting Children in Oil, Watson-Guptill, 78. Dealer: Attic Art Gallery 402 East Lake Dr Greensboro NC 27401. Mailing Add: 4908 Manning Dr Greensboro NC 27410

BLAI, BERT
INSTRUCTOR, CERAMIC ARTIST
b Baltimore, Md. Study: Tyler Sch Art, Temple Univ, BFA; with Rudy Staffel, Raymond Gallucci, Toshieko Takieuzi & Karen Karns. Exhib: Philadelphia Civic Ctr, 70; Paley Libr, Temple Univ, 71; DuCret Sch Art, North Plainfield, NJ, 71; Widener Col, Chester, Pa, 72; Glassboro State Col, NJ, 74. Teaching: Instr, Ocean Co Col, 68-69; instr, DuCret Sch Art, 69-72; artist in residence ceramics, Glassboro State Col, 72- Mem: Hon mem Pa Guild Craftsmen; Am Craftsmen Asn; Artists Equity Asn; hon life mem Long Beach Island Found of Arts & Sci, NJ. Style & Technique: Individualized ceramic creations, privately researched and applied glazes. Media: Pottery Clay, Glazes. Interest: Emphasis on teaching and inspiring students to become deeply involved in personal creativity. Mailing Add: Fourth & High Aves Melrose Park PA 19126

BLAI, BORIS
SCULPTOR, LECTURER
b Russia, July 24, 98; US citizen. Study: Imperial Acad Russia; Ecole Beaux-Arts, Paris, France; student of Rodin, France; Glassboro State Col, LLD, 75. Work: Rhythm of the Sea

(bronze), Philadelphia Mus Art, Pa; busts of all five presidents & other portraits, Temple Univ, Philadelphia; busts of Frank Lloyd Wright & Pres Spivey, Fla Southern Col, Lakeland; also in many pvt collections. Exhib: First Open Air Show, Rittenhouse Square, Philadelphia, 27; Chicago Art Inst, 32; Philadelphia Art Alliance, 37; Philadelphia Acad Ann, 40; retrospectives, Long Beach Island Found Arts & Sci, NJ, 68 & Harcum Jr Col, Bryn Mawr, Pa, 69. Teaching: Dir & instr art, Oak Lane Country Day Sch, 27-30; founder, prof art & dean, Tyler Sch Fine Arts, Temple Univ, 30-60, emer dean, 60-; dean, DuCret Sch Art, Plainfield, NJ, 69-72; founder, Blai Sch of Fine Arts, Melrose Park, Pa, 72- Pos: Founder & hon pres, Long Beach Island Found Arts & Sci, 49-; artist in residence, Glassboro State Col, 72- Awards: Page One Award, Newspaper Guild Greater Philadelphia, 60; Philadelphia Art Alliance Medal, 60; Samuel S Fels Medal, Fels Jr High Sch, 62. Bibliog: Dr Millard E Gladfelter & Dr Herman S Gunderheimer (auth), The Stella Elkins Tyler School of Fine Arts of Temple University, 53; Louis A deFuria (auth), Boris Blai...sculptor, educator, NJ Music & Arts Mag, 10/70. Media: Bronze, Wood, Stone. Publ: Auth, The arts in education, Educ & the Exceptional Child, 35; auth, The future of art in America, Dept of Art Educ Bull, 41; auth, Your happiness is in your hands, Am Mag, 40 & Reader's Dig, 40 & 62. Mailing Add: Fourth & High Ave Melrose Park Philadelphia PA 19126

BLAINE, NELL
PAINTER
b Richmond, Va, July 10, 22. Study: Richmond Prof Inst, 39-42; Hans Hofmann Sch Fine Arts, 42-43; Atelier 17, etching & engraving with William S Hayter, 45; New Sch Social Res, 52-53. Work: Whitney Mus Am Art, New York; Brooklyn Mus, NY; Mus Mod Art, New York; Va Mus Fine Arts, Richmond; Univ Art Mus, Univ Calif, Berkeley; plus many others. Comn: Two murals, landscapes & cityscapes of Paris, Revlon, Inc, New York, 58. Exhib: The Women, Art of This Century, Peggy Guggenheim Gallery, New York, 45; American Abstract Artists Ann, 44-57; Stable Gallery Ann, 50-59; CAPS-GANYS sponsored retrospective, 55-73, traveling, NY, 73-74; plus 31 one-woman shows & many other group shows. Teaching: Instr landscape & studio, Great Neck Pub Sch Adult Prog, 56; instr, Great Lakes Col Asn, New York, 70, 72-75. Pos: Ceramic artist, Warner Prins Co, New York, 48-49; costume & set designer for dancers, Midi Garth & E Goff, New York, 49-54; art dir, United Jewish Appeal, New York, 50; set designer, Artists Theatre, New York, 55. Awards: Va Mus Fine Arts fels for painting, 43 & 46; Hallmark Int Award, 60; CAPS grant, 72. Bibliog: Lawrence Campbell (auth), Blaine paints a picture, Art News Mag, 5/59; Homage to Nell Blaine, Art News Mag, 12/59; James R Mellow (auth), The flowering summer of Nell Blaine, New York Times, 10/11/70. Mem: Artists Equity Asn. Style & Technique: Direct perception of nature employing a free, untheoretical use of color and paint. Media: Oil, Watercolor. Publ: Co-auth, Prints/Nell Blaine - Poems/Kenneth Koch, 53; illusr, In memory of my feelings, Mus Mod Art, 68; auth, Getting with Lester & Mondrian in the forties, Jazz & Painting, 72; contribr, A sense of place—the artist & the American landscape, 72; illusr, Loves aspects, 75. Dealer: Poindexter Gallery 24 E 84th St New York NY 10028. Mailing Add: Apt 8A 210 Riverside Dr New York NY 10025

BLAIR, CARL RAYMOND
PAINTER, EDUCATOR
b Atchison, Kans, Nov 28, 32. Study: Univ Kans, BFA, 56; Kansas City Art Inst; Sch Design, MFA, 57. Work: Mint Mus Art, Charlotte, NC; Greenville Co Mus Art, SC; Greenville Col, Ill; SC Arts Comn, Columbia; Clemson Univ, SC. Exhib: 33rd Butler Ann Painting Exhib, Youngstown, Ohio; Soc Four Arts, Palm Beach, Fla; Piedmont Painting & Sculpture Exhib, Charlotte, 65; Appalachian Corridors I, Charleston, WVa, 68; Int Platform Asn, Washington, DC, 71. Teaching: Prof drawing & painting, Bob Jones Univ, 57-; summer sch, Kansas City Art Inst & Greenville Co Mus Art. Pos: Co-founder & pres, Hampton III Gallery, Taylors, SC. Awards: Piedmont Painting & Sculpture Exhib, Mint Mus Art, 65; Appalachian Corridors I, SC Arts Comn, 68; Int Platform Asn, 68. Bibliog: La Revue Moderne, Paris, France, 65-68; Jack A Morris, Jr (auth), Contemporary artists of South Carolina, 70. Mem: SC Artists Guild (adv bd, 57-); Int Platform Asn; Greenville Artists Guild (pres, 71-); SC Arts Comn (acquisitions comt, 69-). Media: Oil. Dealer: Hampton III Gallery Ltd Gallery Ctr Taylors SC 29687. Mailing Add: 1 Oakleaf Rd Greenville SC 29609

BLAIR, HELEN (HELEN BLAIR CROSBIE)
SCULPTOR, ILLUSTRATOR
b Hibbing, Minn, Dec 29, 10. Study: Mass Sch Art, with Cyrus Dallin; Boston Mus Sch; Archipenko Sch Art, with Archipenko. Comn: Plaques of Dr Waring, Colo Med Sch, 69 & of Dr Porter, Porter Mem Hosp, Denver, 70; plaque of Robert Ledbettor, Rome, Ga. Exhib: One-man shows, Ardan Studios, New York, 34, Portraits, Inc, New York, 41-42, Vose Galleries, Boston, 44, St Paul Art Ctr, Minn, 62 & Martin Gallery, Phoenix, 73-74. Teaching: Instr art educ, Boston Univ, 37-40. Bibliog: K S Thompson (auth), Figurines step into a new role, Boston Transcript, 34; Peter Martin (auth), Moulder of youth, Am Mag, 46; Marjorie Barrett (auth), Helen Blair's little people, Denver Post, 70. Mem: Artists Equity Asn; Nat Arts & Lett Soc; Ariz Artists Guild. Style & Technique: Slightly rough impressionistic technique in bronze using two-tone patina. Publ: Illusr, Jeanne-Marie, 34, Great Day in the Morning, 46, Assorted Sisters, 47, House Under the Hill, 49 & Hetly & the Grand Deluxe, 51, Houghton Mifflin. Dealer: Portraits Inc 41 E 57th St New York NY 10022; Art Wagon Gallery 7156 Main St Scottsdale AZ 85251. Mailing Add: 1919 E Claremont St Phoenix AZ 85016

BLAIR, JEANETTE ANNE
PAINTER
b Buffalo, NY, Sept 21, 22. Study: Art Inst Buffalo. Work: Butler Inst Am Art, Youngstown, Ohio. Exhib: Butler Inst Am Art Ann, 54, 56 & 70; Cooperstown Art Asn Ann, NY, 69 & 70; La Watercolor Soc Ann, Baton Rouge, 70-72; Arena 75, Binghamton, NY, 75; Chautauqua Inst Ann, NY, 75. Awards: Buffalo Soc Artists Award, Buffalo Savings Bank, 68; Arena 75 Purchase Award, Louis N Picciano & Sons, Binghamton, 75; Judges Award, Cooperstown Art Asn Ann, NY, 77. Mem: Buffalo Soc Artists (coun, 70-73); Patteran Art Soc, Buffalo. Style & Technique: Landscapes in watercolor; figure and landscape in oil. Dealer: Gallery Without Walls 460 Franklin St Buffalo NY 14202. Mailing Add: RD 1 Olean Rd Holland NY 14080

BLAIR, ROBERT NOEL
PAINTER, SCULPTOR
b Buffalo, NY, Aug 12, 12. Study: Sch of Mus Fine Arts, Boston, Mass. Work: Metrop Mus Art, New York; Butler Inst Am Art, Youngstown, Ohio; Munson-Williams-Proctor Inst, Utica, NY; State Univ NY Col Buffalo; Ford Motor Co Collection, Dearborn, Mich. Comn: Sermon on the Mount (oil, tempera), US Army Chapel, Ft McClellan, Ala, 43; Open Hearth (oil), Bethlehem Steel Plant, Lackawanna, NY, 47; Olean in 1890's (two tempera panels), Olean House, NY, 61; Venetian Feast (oil panel), Lakeview Hotel, NY; fountain with three figures (fiberglass-epoxy sculpture), Dr & Mrs Hal Meisburger, Patchen, NY, 62-65. Exhib: Corcoran Biennial, Corcoran Gallery Art, Washington, DC, 47; Watercolor Int, Art Inst Chicago, Ill, 48; Pa Acad Fine Arts Nat, Philadelphia, 48; Butler Art Inst Nat & Metrop Mus Art Watercolor Nat, 53; one-man retrospective, Community Tribute Exhibition, State Univ NY Col Buffalo, 66; plus 30 one-man shows. Teaching: Instr painting, Art Inst Buffalo, 38-55, Albright Art Sch, 55 & State Univ NY Col Buffalo, 71. Pos: Dir, Art Inst Buffalo, 46-49. Awards: Guggenheim Fels, 46 & 51; Watowsky Prize, Art Inst Chicago, 48; First Watercolor Prize, Butler Inst Am Art, 53. Mem: Patteran Soc, Buffalo; Buffalo Soc Artists. Style & Technique: Free style. Media: Watercolor, Oil, Acrylic. Res: Expansion of technical possibilities in painting. Publ: Illusr, St Lawrence Seaway, 57; illusr, Ford Times Mag, 58-61; illusr, Am Artist Mag, 66; illusr, Jeannie's world, 66; illusr & auth, Watercolorists at work, 71. Mailing Add: RD 1 Olean Rd Holland NY 14080

BLAKE, JOHN CLEMENS
PAINTER, SCULPTOR
b East Greenwich, RI, Jan 11, 45. Study: Carnegie Inst of Technol, Pittsburgh, 63-67, BA, 67; Royal Col of Art, London, 67-69, MA, 69. Awards: Fulbright, New York, 68; Arts Coun Award for filmmaking, London, 74. Dealer: Robert Self Gallery 50 Earlham St London W C 2 England. Mailing Add: 103 B Earls Court Rd London W 8 England

BLAKE, PETER JOST
ARCHITECT, CRITIC
b Berlin, Ger, Sept 20, 20; US citizen. Study: Univ London, 38; Regent St Polytech, Sch Archit, London, 39; Univ Pa, 41; Sch of Archit, Pratt Inst, BArch, 49. Teaching: Vis critic/lectr, var US & Ger cols & univs. Pos: Writer, Archit Forum, New York, 42-43, assoc ed, 50-54 & 58-61, managing ed, 61-64, ed, 64-72; cur archit & design, Mus Mod Art, New York, 48-50; partner, Peter Blake & Julian Neski, 58-61; partner, James Baker & Peter Blake, Architects, New York, 64-72; ed-in-chief, Archit Plus, New York, 72-75; chmn, Sch Archit, Boston Archit Ctr, Mass, 75- Awards: Howard Myers Award Archit Jour, 60; Citation for Design Am Archit Exhib Sent to Iron Curtain Countries, 58; Medal Hon & Award Merit, Am Inst Architects, 68-69; Archit Critic's Medal, Am Inst Archit, 75; and others. Mem: Fel Am Inst Architects (mem comt aesthet, 65-66, juror, 68-69, mem urban design comt, 69); Archit League New York (vpres archit, 66-68, mem scholar & awards comt, 68-69, pres, 71-72); Int Design Conf, Aspen, Colo (bd dirs, 65-70); Regional Plan Asn (mem comt second regional plan). Publ: Auth, Master Builders, Knopf, 60; auth, God's Own Junkyard: Planned Deterioration of America's Landscape, Holt, Rinehart & Winston, 64; auth, Form Follows Fiasco—Why Modern Architecture Hasn't Worked, Atlantic Monthly Press & Little, Brown & Co, 77; also contribr articles pop mags & newspapers. Mailing Add: 85 East India Wharf No 30G Boston MA 02110

BLAKELY, JOYCE (CAROL)
PAINTER, INSTRUCTOR
b New Orleans, La, July 1, 29. Study: Delgado Art Mus; S Ga Col; also with Bill Hendrix, St Simon's Island; also with John Pellew, Zoltan Szabo & Edmond J Fitsgerald. Comn: Boatscape, First Presby Church, Hendersonville, NC, 72; River Jordan Mural, Green River Baptist Church, 72; seven NC landscapes, Pardee Hosp, Hendersonville, NC, Fletcher Hosp, NC & Bank of NC; murals, Cedar Spring Baptist Church, Mountain View Baptist Church & NJ Sch Dept. Exhib: Sovereign Exhibs, Hendrix Gallery, St Simon's Island, 69-70, Winston-Salem, NC & London, Eng, 70, Williamsburg, Va, 71 & Myrtle Beach, SC, 71; USS Hope Exhib, Butler Inst Am Art, 72; B Russell Contemp Art Exhib, Rotunda Gallery, London, 72. Teaching: Instr oil painting, Opportunity House, Hendersonville, NC; pvt instr. Mem: Nat League Am Pen Women (state pres, 74-76); League Pen Women Asheville, NC (secy, 72-74 & 76-78, pres, 74-76); Henderson Art League, NC (past pres, bd mem, 72-78). Media: Oil. Mailing Add: Rte 1 Zirconia NC 28790

BLAKESLEE, SARAH (SARAH BLAKESLEE SPEIGHT)
PAINTER
b Evanston, Ill, Jan 13, 12. Study: Corcoran Sch Art; Pa Acad Fine Arts; Cresson Europ traveling scholars; also with Catherin Critcher. Work: Pa Acad Fine Arts; Nat Acad Design; Jackson Libr & Scotland Neck Libr, NC; Inst Govt, Univ NC, Chapel Hill; Greenville Art Ctr, NC. Comn: Portraits, ECarolina Univ, Greenville & St Mary's Col, Raleigh; portraits, still life & landscapes in many pvt collections. Exhib: Art Inst Chicago Ann, 39 & 40; Corcoran Gallery Art Biennial, 40; Pa Acad Fine Arts Ann, Philadelphia; Nat Acad Design Ann; NC Mus Art Collectors Exhib, 68. Teaching: Instr art, Lankenau Sch, Philadelphia, 52-61; instr art, var art ctrs, NC, 61- Awards: Mary Smith Prize, Pa Acad Fine Arts, 41; First Prize, Woodmere Art Gallery, Chestnut Hills, Philadelphia, 56; First Prize & Gold Medal, Penn-Nat-Ligonier Pa, 61. Media: Oil. Dealer: Hines Gallery of Art Rocky Mount NC 27801. Mailing Add: 508 E Ninth St Greenville NC 27834

BLAMEUSER, MARY FLEURETTE
PAINTER, INSTRUCTOR
b Skokie, Ill. Study: Art Inst Chicago; Univ Colo; Columbia Univ; Clarke Col, BA; State Univ Iowa, MA; Georgio Cini Found fel, Venice, Italy, 65; watercolor with Nöel Quinn & Edgar Whitney. Work: Wichita Art Asn, Kans. Comn: Mosaic mural, Sisters of Charity, Wichita, 61, bronze tabernacle, 63. Exhib: Contemporary, State Univ Iowa, Iowa City, 48; Wichita Women Artists, 57; Kans Watercolor Soc Exhib, Wichita, 70-77; Kans Cult Arts Comn Traveling Show, 71-72; one-person shows, Graphics Art, Wichita Art Asn, 73 & Sally Hershberger Gallery, 77; Wichita Art Mus, Kans; Century II Gallery, 77; St Capitol, Topeka, 78. Teaching: Instr sec art, Holy Angels Acad Milwaukee, Wis, 33-45; instr sec art, Bishop Conaty Mem High Sch, Los Angeles, Calif, 45-56; instr art educ & painting, Clarke Col, Dubuque, Iowa, 51 & 58; instr sec art, Mt Carmel Acad, Wichita, 56-70; instr, Kapaun-Mt Carmel High Sch, 70-74. Pos: Chmn art educ, Archdiocese Los Angeles, 46-56; mem, Diocesan Liturgical Art Comn, Wichita, 64-; active comt, Scholastic Art Awards, Kans Regional, 69-75. Awards: Watercolor Award, Wichita Women Artists, 57; Kans Watercolor Award, 72. Bibliog: S M Cathlin (auth), Story of a mosaic, Vista, Sisters of Charity, 63; John Simoni (auth), Nun exhibits sensitivity, Wichita Eagle & Beacon, 5/9/65; Connie Close (auth), Nun finishing mosaic mural, Wichita Eagle, 65. Mem: Artists Guild of Wichita; Wichita Women Artists; Wichita Art Asn; Wichita Art Mus Mem; Kans Watercolor Soc (bd mem publicity, 70-74). Style & Technique: Vigorous, naturalistic, semi-abstract, poetic, reverent. Media: Watercolor, Oil, Lithography, Mosaics. Dealer: Wichita Art Mus 619 Stackman Dr Wichita KS 67203; Wichita Art Asn 9112 E Central Wichita KS 67206. Mailing Add: 8506 E Central Ave Wichita KS 67206

BLANC, PETER (WILLIAM PETERS BLANC)
SCULPTOR, PAINTER
b New York, NY, June 29, 12. Study: Harvard Univ, BA; St John's Univ, LLB; Corcoran Sch Art; Am Univ, MA. Work: Va Mus Fine Arts, Richmond; Ft Worth Art Ctr, Tex; NY Univ; Tweed Mus, Duluth, Minn. Exhib: 14 one-man shows, 50-74; Southampton Col Artist's Exhib, 71; Ashawagh Hall, Springs, NY, 71-76; Artists Equity Asn & Artists New York 75, Union Carbide Exhib Hall, New York, 75; Jewish Community Ctr, Englewood, NJ, 75; Art Guild, New York, 76; Baltimore Mus of Art, Md; Brooklyn Mus, NY; Corcoran Gallery, Washington, DC; Fogg Art Mus, Cambridge, Mass; Mus of Santa Fe, NMex; Nat Collection

of Arts, Washington, DC; Va Mus of Fine Arts, Richmond, Va; Whitney Mus of Am Art, New York. Teaching: Pvt classes in painting & drawing, 47-54; instr painting & drawing, Am Univ, 50-53. Awards: First Prize for Drawing, Corcoran Gallery Art, 59; Special Award, Washington Watercolor Club, 52; Hon Mention, Soc Washington Artists, 53. Mem: Artists Equity Asn New York (bd dir, 63-71). Media: Wood. Publ: Auth, Artist & the atom, Mag of Art, 51. Dealer: Elaine Benson Gallery Bridgehampton NY 11932. Mailing Add: 161 W 75th St New York NY 10023

BLANCHARD, CAROL
PAINTER, GRAPHIC ARTIST
b Springfield, Mass, Aug 29, 18. Study: Colby Jr Col; Art Students League; Painter's Workshop, Boston. Work: Pasangrahn, St Martin, BWI; Bay Roe, Jamaica, BWI; San Miguel Allende, Mex; also in pvt collections. Comn: Illusr, Christmas cards, UN. Exhib: Art Inst, Zanesville, Ohio, 50; Carnegie Inst, Pittsburgh, 51-59; Univ Ill, 53; Walker Art Ctr, Minneapolis, 60; Kalamazoo Inst Art, Mich; plus others. Awards: Award, Carnegie Inst Art, 51-53 & 59 & Art Dirs Club, 55 & 56; Benedictine Art Award Creative Arts, 67 & 68; plus others. Publ: Illusr, Always Ask a Man; illusr, seven bks by Mary Stolz; illusr, Village Voice, Women's Wear Daily & other newspapers. Mailing Add: 375 Bleecker St New York NY 10014

BLANCHE, MARILYN
See Lynch, Jo

BLANKFORT, DOROTHY
COLLECTOR
Study: Bates Col; Cornell Univ. Mem: Los Angeles Co Mus (exec bd contemp art coun). Collection: Chiefly contemporary American. Mailing Add: 1636 Comstock Ave Los Angeles CA 90024

BLANKFORT, MICHAEL
COLLECTOR
b New York, NY, Dec 10, 07. Pos: Mem bd trustees, Los Angeles Co Mus Art. Collection: Contemporary American art. Mailing Add: 1636 Comstock Ave Los Angeles CA 90024

BLATAS, ARBIT
PAINTER
b Kaunas, Lithuania, Nov 19, 08. Study: Acad Julien, Paris & self taught. Work: Mus Nat de Jeu de Paume, Paris; Mus Grenoble, France; Nat Mus Lithuania; Mus Mod Art, New York & Paris, France; Metrop Mus Art. Exhib: World's Fair Expo, Paris, 37; Galerie Bernheim Jeune, Prix Paul Guillaume, 38; Herschl & Adler Galleries, New York, 57; Marcel Marceau, New York, 58; Carnegie Inst, Rochester, NY, 59; plus numerous others. Mailing Add: 50 W 56th St New York NY 10019

BLATTNER, ROBERT HENRY
PAINTER, ILLUSTRATOR
b Lynn, Mass, Dec 8, 06. Study: Mass Col Art, BS(educ). Teaching: Instr design, Boston Univ, 37-38; instr design, Col New Rochelle, 39-41. Pos: Illusr, Christian Sci Monitor, 34-42; art dir, Marschalk & Pratt Advert Agency, 43-45; art dir, Reader's Dig, 45-71, consult art dir, 77- Awards: Soc Illustrators Award of Merit, 71. Mem: Soc Illustrators; Art Dirs Club (pres, 60-61); Am Inst Graphic Arts (dir, 58-59); hon mem Am Watercolor Soc. Media: Watercolor. Mailing Add: Loch Lane Port Chester NY 10573

BLAUSTEIN, ALFRED H
PAINTER, PRINTMAKER
b Bronx, NY, Jan 23, 24. Study: Cooper Union Art Sch, grad fine arts; Prix de Rome fel, 54-57. Work: Whitney Mus Am Art, New York; Metrop Mus Art, New York; Chicago Art Inst; Libr Cong, Washington, DC; Pa Acad Fine Arts, Philadelphia. Comn: Drawing assignment, Life & Brit Overseas Food Corp, Tanzania, EAfrica, 48-49; fresco mural, S Solon Meeting House, Maine, 53; painting assignment, Fortune Mag, 70. Exhib: Four shows, Pa Acad Fine Arts, 51-67; Metrop Mus Art, 50 & 66; Carnegie Inst Int, Pittsburgh, 52 & 64; Whitney Mus Am Art Ann, 53 & 57; six shows, Brooklyn Mus Print Ann, 57-70; plus many one-man shows. Teaching: Lectr fine arts, Yale Univ, 59-62; prof fine arts, Pratt Inst, 59-; instr printmaking, Pratt Graphic Ctr, 64-69. Awards: Am Acad Arts & Lett Grant in Painting, 58; Guggenheim Fel Painting, 58, Printmaking, 61. Mailing Add: 141 E 17th St New York NY 10003

BLAZ, GEORGIA LEE
CRAFTSMAN, PAINTER
b Albuquerque, NMex, Sept 25, 47. Study: Univ NMex, 65-67; Univ Idaho, 67-68. Exhib: Las Aranyas, Mus Albuquerque, 74; Phoenix Art Mus Biennial, Ariz, 74; Mus Int Folk Art Biennial, Santa Fe, NMex, 74; 40th Ann Nat Art Exhib-Cooperstown Art Asn, NY, 75; one-man show, Hill's Gallery, Santa Fe, 75. Awards: Award of Merit, Crafts V, Mus Albuquerque, 73; Award of Merit, Las Aranas, 74. Style & Technique: Large hangings that are sewn paintings using textiles instead of paint to achieve the designs. Dealer: Hill's Gallery 110 W San Francisco St Santa Fe NM 87501. Mailing Add: 1612 Quapaw St Santa Fe NM 87501

BLAZEJE, ZBIGNIEW
SCULPTOR, PAINTER
b Barnaul, USSR, Jan 2, 42; Can citizen. Study: Royal Conserv Music, Toronto. Work: Art Gallery Ont, Toronto; Norman McKenzie Art Gallery, Regina, Sask; Confedn Art Gallery, Charlettetown, PEI; Hart House, Univ Toronto; Sir George William Univ, Montreal, PQ. Comn: Structrual sculpture, Libr-Ross Bldg, York Univ, 72. Exhib: 10th Winnipeg Show, Winnipeg Art Gallery, Man, 65; Canadian Art, Art Gallery Can Pavillion Expo 67, Montreal, 67; Sculpture 67, City Hall Toronto, 67; Electric Art, Univ Calif, Los Angeles Art Gallery & Phoenix, Ariz, 69; Sensory Perceptions Traveling Exhib, Art Gallery Ont, 70-71. Teaching: Instr environ, Ont Col Art, 70-; instr environ, New Sch Art, Toronto, 71-72. Awards: Can Coun Jr Grants, 66, 67 & 69. Bibliog: H Malcomson (auth), Sculpture in Canada, Artforum, 10/67; G M Dault (auth), In the galleries Toronto, Artscanada, 6/71; Electric Gallery plus 3, McCurdy-Bursell Films, Toronto, 4/72. Dealer: Electric Gallery 272 Avenue Rd Toronto ON Can. Mailing Add: 75 Boulton Ave Toronto ON Can

BLAZEY, LAWRENCE EDWIN
DESIGNER, PAINTER
b Cleveland, Ohio, Apr 6, 02. Study: Cleveland Inst Art, grad, 24; Slade Sch, Univ London, with Prof Tonks, 26; Cranbrook Acad, Bloomfield Hills, Mich, with Mia Grotell, 53. Work: Cleveland Mus Art; Butler Inst Am Art, Youngstown, Ohio; City of Cleveland Munic Art Collection. Comn: Big Band Hall of Fame (mural), Holiday Inn Composers Showcase, Cleveland, 75. Exhib: Int Watercolor Show, Chicago Mus Art, 37; Ohio Valley Oil & Watercolor Show, Ohio Univ, 50; Everson Mus Nat Ceramic, Syracuse, NY, 50-54; Int Art Benefit, Cleveland, 70; Ann Nat Watercolor Show, Butler Inst Am Art, 72-73. Teaching: Instr ceramics, John Huntington Polytech Inst, Cleveland, 51-54; instr ceramics, Baycrafters, Bay Village, Ohio, 60-63. Pos: Vpres & dir design, Designers for Indust Inc, Cleveland, 42-52. Awards: Prizes in Painting, Cleveland Mus Art May Show, 37-45; Butler Inst Am Arts Ceramic Prizes, 69-70; Hon Mention/Painting, Beck Cult Ctr, Lakewood, Ohio, 77. Mem: Cleveland Soc Artists (pres, 45); Indust Designers Soc Am; Baycrafters (trustee, 63); Ohio Designer Craftsmen. Style & Technique: Pure watercolor painting on the spot in representational style of landscapes. Media: Ceramics, Graphics, Watercolor, Acrylic. Mailing Add: 537 Juneway Dr Bay Village OH 44140

BLEDSOE, JANE KATHRYN
ART HISTORIAN, ART ADMINISTRATOR
b Independence, Mo, Sept 9, 37. Study: Calif State Univ, Long Beach, BA(art hist) & cert mus studies. Collections Arranged: Dir & Cur, Maria Poveka, American Potter (with catalog), 74; cur, Masterworks in Modern Sculpture from the Collection of Ben C Deane (with catalog), 75; Anna A Hills, American Impressionist, 76. Pos: Asst dir gallery, Calif State Univ, Long Beach, 74- Res: Southwestern American Indian ceramics, 19th and 20th centuries. Mailing Add: 6449 Fairbrook Long Beach CA 90815

BLEIFELD, STANLEY
SCULPTOR, INSTRUCTOR
b Brooklyn, NY, Aug 28, 24. Study: Albert C Barnes Found, Meryon, Pa, 42-43; Tyler Sch Art, Temple Univ, BFA, 49, BS(educ), 49, MFA, 50. Work: Temple Univ, Philadelphia, Pa; Tampa Bay Art Ctr, Fla; Pa State Mus, Philadelphia; Westmoreland Mus, Pa; New Brit Mus of Am Art, Conn. Comn: The Prophets (relief), Vatican Pavilion, New York World's Fair, 64; Magic Carpet (relief), Pub Libr, Kokomo, Ind, 69; Mediterranean Landscape (relief), Washington, DC, 72; Family of Acrobats, Orlando, Fla, 73; Family at Play, Richmond, Va, 75. Exhib: One-man shows, Peridot Gallery, New York, 63, 65 & 68 & Kenmore Galleries, Philadelphia, 67; Am Fedn Arts, 66-67; IFA Galleries, Washington, DC, 68 & 71; FAR Gallery, New York, 71, 73 & 77; New Britain Mus Am Art, 74; Reflections, Images of Am, US Info Agency Travelling Exhib, 76-77. Teaching: Asst prof art, Southern Conn State Col & Western Conn State Col, 53-63; instr sculpture, Silvermine Guild, New Canaan, Conn, 63-66; dir sculpture, Bleifeld Studio, Westport, Conn, 66- Pos: Fel, Tyler Sch Fine Arts, 64-; ed bd, Nat Sculpture Rev, 70. Awards: John Gregory Award, 64 & Bronze Medal, 70, Nat Sculpture Soc; Tiffany Found fel, 65 & 67. Bibliog: A sculptor hails the Bible, Life Mag, 6/28/63; article in, Am Artist Mag, 72. Mem: Nat Sculpture Soc. Style & Technique: Representational. Media: Bronze. Publ: Illusr, A Day at the County Fair, 60 & Elly the Elephant, 62. Dealer: FAR Gallery 746 Madison Ave New York NY 10021; Sandra Wilson Galleries 1756 Broadway Denver CO 80202. Mailing Add: 27 Spring Valley Rd Weston CT 06883

BLEVINS, JAMES RICHARD
ART ADMINISTRATOR, EDUCATOR
b Feb 1, 34; US citizen. Study: David Lipscomb Col, BA, 56; George Peabody Col, MA, 60, PhD, 70; Univ Calif, Los Angeles, 75. Pos: Chmn, Div Humanities, Ind State Univ, 69-; mem bd dirs, Evansville Mus, 70-, chmn, Fine Arts Comt, 76-; chmn, Ohio River Arts Festival, 72. Mem: Evansville Arts & Educ Coun (vpres, 73, chmn long-range planning, 76). Mailing Add: 801 SE Third St Evansville IN 47713

BLIZZARD, ALAN
PAINTER, EDUCATOR
b Boston, Mass, Mar 25, 29. Study: Mass Sch Art, Boston, with Lawrence Kupferman; Univ Ariz, with Andreas Andersen; Univ Iowa, with Stuart Edie, James Lechay & Byron Burford. Work: Brooklyn Mus, NY; Metrop Mus Art, New York; Art Inst Chicago; Denver Art Mus, Colo, La Jolla Mus Art, Calif. Exhib: Many exhibs in leading mus, cols, univs & art ctrs. Teaching: Vis asst prof, Univ Okla; asst prof, Univ Calif, Los Angeles; prof art, Scripps Col & Claremont Grad Sch. Mailing Add: Dept of Art Scripps Col Claremont CA 91711

BLOCH, E MAURICE
ART HISTORIAN, EDUCATOR
b New York, NY. Study: NY Univ Sch Archit, BFA; Harvard Univ; NY Univ Inst Fine Arts, MA & PhD; Nat Acad Design; Art Students League, with Brackman; Belg-Am Educ Found fel, 51. Teaching: Lectr, Univ Mo, 43-44; lectr, NY Univ, 44-45; lectr, Univ Minn, Minneapolis, 46-47; asst prof & cur, Cooper Union, 49-55; prof Am art, hist prints & hist drawings & dir, Grunwald Ctr Graphic Arts, Univ Calif, Los Angeles, 56- Awards: Founders Day Award of Achievement, NY Univ, 57; Western Heritage Ctr Award, 68. Mem: Print Coun Am; Univ Calif, Los Angeles Art Coun (bd dirs); Tamarind Inst, Univ NMex, Albuquerque (bd dirs); life mem Art Students League; Art Historians Southern Calif. Res: American art of the 18th and 19th centuries; history of European and American drawings and graphic arts. Publ: Auth, George Caleb Bingham: evolution of an artist and a catalogue raisonne, Vols I & II, 67; auth, articles in, Gazette Beaux Arts, New York Hist Soc Quart, Connoisseur, Art in Am & others. Mailing Add: 2253 Veteran Ave Los Angeles CA 90064

BLOCH, MILTON JOSEPH
ART ADMINISTRATOR, MUSEUM DIRECTOR
b Bronx, NY, Apr 4, 37. Study: Pratt Inst, Brooklyn, NY, BID, 58; Univ Fla, Gainesville, MFA, 61. Collections Arranged: Three Centuries of Art in New Jersey, 71; New Jersey Arts & Crafts; The Colonial Expression, 73; American Crafts, Nat Endowment Humanities, 75. Teaching: Instr art & chmn dept, Lake Sumter Col, Fla, 61-63. Pos: Dir, Pensacola Art Ctr, Fla, 64-66; dir, Mus Sci & Natural Hist, Little Rock, Ark, 66-68; dir, Monmouth Mus, Lincroft, NJ, 69-76; dir, Mint Mus, Charlotte, NC, 76- Mem: Am Asn Mus; Southeastern Mus Conf; NC Arts Coun; Asn of Art Mus Dirs. Publ: Series of six articles on improvised exhibiton design, Mus News, 66-68. Mailing Add: 501 Hempstead Pl Charlotte NC 28207

BLOCK, ADOLPH
SCULPTOR, INSTRUCTOR
b New York, NY, Jan 29, 06. Study: Beaux Arts Inst Design; Fontainebleau Sch Fine Arts; also with Hermon MacNeil & Sterlin Calder. Work: Bryant High Sch, New York; Bayonne Pub Libr, NJ; Queens Voc High Sch, NY; Beth-El Hosp, Brooklyn, NY; Garfield Restaurant, NY; plus others. Comn: Panels, Nat Shrine Immaculate Conception, Washington, DC; bronze mem portrait panel, Dr Franz J Kallmann, Columbia-Presby Med Ctr, NY, 67; Washington Irving Medal, 68 & Simon Newcomb Medal, 70, NY Univ Hall of Fame Series; Nathan Hale Coin Medal, Nat Commemorative Soc, 69; plus others. Exhib: Nat Acad Design; Pa Acad Fine Arts; Archit League NY; Nat Sculpture Soc; Whitney Mus Am Art; plus others. Teaching: Instr sculpture, Nat Acad Design, 59- Pos: Deleg to Fine Arts Fedn, 54-60; dir, Fine Arts Fedn New York, 54-62; Nat Sculpture Soc deleg, Int Coun Plastic Arts, 58-62; ed, Nat Sculpture Rev, 58-76; vpres, Int Coun Plastic Arts, 60-63. Awards: Lindsay Morris Prize Medals, 58, Herbert Adams Mem Medal & Citation, 61, Silver Medal, 67 & Award for Most

Notable Serv, 70, Nat Sculpture Soc; plus others. Mem: Academician Nat Acad Design; fel Nat Sculpture Soc (rec secy, 53-55, secy, 56-58), chmn mem comt, 56-62, first vpres, 59-62, pres, 63-65); Allied Artists Am; Fontainebleau Alumni Asn. Media: Bronze. Mailing Add: 319 W 18th St New York NY 10011

BLOCK, AMANDA ROTH
PAINTER, PRINTMAKER
b Louisville, Ky, Feb 20, 12. Study: Smith Col; Univ Cincinnati; Art Acad Cincinnati; Art Students League; Herron Sch Art, Ind Univ-Purdue Univ, Indianapolis, BFA; and with Garo Antreasian. Work: J B Speed Mus, Louisville, Ky; Cincinnati Art Mus, Ohio; Brooklyn Mus, NY; Tucson Mus of Art, Ariz; Philadelphia Mus Art, Pa. Exhib: American Sculpture Show, Chicago Art Inst, Ill, 41; Soc Am Graphic Artists Show, 67-; Philadelphia Print Club; Watercolor, Drawing & Print Biennial, Pa Acad Fine Arts, Philadelphia, 69; Butler Inst Am Art, Youngstown, Ohio; Bus & Corp Collect, Indianapolis Mus of Art, Ind, 77. Teaching: Lectr lithography & drawing, Herron Sch Art, 69- Awards: Katherine Mattison Watercolor Award, Indianapolis Mus Art, 63; Watercolor Award, Indiana Artists Exhib, Sheldon Swope Art Gallery, 64; Ben & Beatrice Goldstein Award, Soc Am Graphic Artists Exhib, Kennedy Gallery, New York, 71. Mem: Philadelphia Print Club; Soc Am Graphic Artists. Style & Technique: Figurative. Media: Acrylic, Oil; Serigraph, Lithograph. Dealer: Editions Limited Gallery 919 Westfield Blvd Indianapolis IN 46220; Washington Gallery Frankfort IN 46041. Mailing Add: 6000 Spring Mill Rd Indianapolis IN 46208

BLOCK, HERBERT LAWRENCE
See Herblock

BLOCK, HUNTINGTON TURNER
ART INSUROR
b Washington, DC, Oct 8, 24. Study: Princeton Univ, AB. Pos: Chartered Property Casualty Underwriter, Huntington T Block Insurance. Interest: Insuror of more than 150 museums across the United States; administrator of insurance program for members of Art Dealers Association of America; specialist in fine arts insurance for museums, dealers and art collectors. Mailing Add: 2101 L St NW Washington DC 20037

BLOCK, IRVING ALEXANDER
PAINTER, EDUCATOR
b New York, NY. Study: NY Univ, BS; Nat Acad Design; Acad Grande Chaumiere, Paris, France. Work: Hirshhorn Mus & Sculpture Garden, Washington, DC; San Diego Fine Arts Gallery, Calif; Storm King Mountain Art Ctr, NY; Univ Mass Art Collection, Amherst; Victoria & Albert Mus, London, Eng. Comn: Mural, Am Med Asn, Med Bldg, New York World's Fair, 39; murals, comn by US Treas Dept, Post Off Bldgs, Batesburg, SC, 40 & Wakefield Sta. Exhib: Los Angeles Co Art Mus, Metrop Mus Art, New York, Colorado Springs Art Ctr, La Jolla Mus & others, 40-; one-man shows, Ankrum Gallery, Los Angeles, 68-78; Inaugural Exhib, Hirshhorn Mus, Washington, DC, 75. Teaching: Prof art, Calif State Univ, 63- Awards: Third Int Art Film Festival Award, 57; Hirshhorn Found Grant in Painting, 69; Calif State Univ Outstanding Prof Award, 70. Bibliog: C Perkins (auth), Irving Block, Artforum, 5/63; taped biog interviews, Arch Am Art, 66; V Shears (auth), California painters in oil, Am Artist, 5/68. Mem: Hon mem Acad Int Tommaso Campanella, Rome. Style & Technique: Figurative. Publ: Co-auth, dir & producer (films), Rembrandt, Poet of Light, 53, Goya, 55 & World of Rubens, 57. Dealer: Ankrum Gallery 657 N La Cienega Blvd Los Angeles CA 90069. Mailing Add: 3880 Carpenter Ave Studio City CA 91604

BLOCK, JOYCE
CALLIGRAPHER, INSTRUCTOR
b Chicago, Ill. Study: Univ Calif, Los Angeles, BA; Teachers Col, Columbia Univ, MA; Tenshin Calligraphy Res Inst, Tokyo, with Kakei Fujita. Exhib: Ann calligraphy exhib, Nihon Shodo Bijutsuin, Tokyo, 63-, Yokohama Shodo Renmei, 68-75 & Gen Nichi Sho Ten, 70-76; Western NMex Univ, 67; Japanese Calligraphy of Joyce Block, Lynn Kottler Galleries, New York, 71; East of Athens, Ohio, 74; Things Japanese, Waianae, Hawaii, 75. Teaching: Instr, Dept Defense Overseas Dependents Schs, Italy, 58-60, Yokohama, Japan, 60-, Kinnick Mid Sch, 70- Mem: Nat Educ Asn. Style & Technique: Classical Chinese calligraphy; combination of various styles with English translations of Hebrew and Japanese/Chinese characters. Mem: Nat Asn Retired Teachers; Nat Asn Retired Fed Employees. Media: Sumi Ink. Mailing Add: Box 412 Fleacts Detachment FPO Seattle WA 98761 Yokohama Japan Box 412 Fleacts Detachment FPO Seattle WA 98761

BLOCK, MR & MRS LEIGH B
COLLECTORS
Mr Block, b Chicago, Ill, Apr 7, 05. Study: Mr Block, Univ Chicago. Pos: Mr Block, chmn bd, Art Inst Chicago; trustee, Northwestern Univ, Evanston; hon life trustee, Orchestral Asn of Chicago; trustee, Joseph H Hirshhorn Mus & Sculpture Garden, Washington, DC. Awards: DHA, Kenyon Col, Gambier, Ohio; Chevalier of Legion of Honor, France. Mem: Mr Block, Art Collectors Club. Mailing Add: 30 W Monroe St Suite 1170 Chicago IL 60603

BLODGETT, ANNE WASHINGTON
PAINTER
b New York, NY, Apr 17, 40. Study: Smith Col, BA, 61; Boston Mus Sch Fine Arts, 61-62; Cambridge, Eng, Sch of Fine Arts, 64; also with George Demetrios, Boston, 63. Work: Berkshire Mus, Pittsfield, Mass; Fitzwilliam Col Collection, Cambridge. Comn: Large landscape paintings, comn by Mr & Mrs George Rowe, New York, 71, Mr Charles D Ravenel, SC, 72 & Mr Lawson Bernstein, New York, 74. Exhib: One-woman shows, Berkshire Mus, 71, Caravan House Gallery, New York, 71 & 74 & Medici Gallery, London, 73; New Grafton Gallery, London, 72; Pioneer Gallery, Cooperstown, NY, 74. Style & Technique: Lyrical, semi-abstract, subtle use of collage. Media: Oil and/or collage. Mailing Add: 930 Park Ave New York NY 10021

BLODGETT, PETER
SCULPTOR, EDUCATOR
b New York, NY, June 5, 35. Study: RI Sch Design, BFA(painting), 60; study with Conte Prof Carlo Alberto Petrucci, Rome, Italy, 61; Sch Mus Fine Arts, Boston, 67; RI Sch Design, MFA(sculpture), 73. Exhib: Mus RI Sch Design, 73; Am Crafts Coun Gallery, New York, 73; The Goldsmith, Renwick Gallery, Smithsonian Inst, Washington, DC, 74 & Minn Mus Art, 74; Brockton Art Ctr, Mass, 75; Visual Arts Gallery, Pensacola, Fla, 75; The Metalsmith, Phoenix Mus Art, 77; Blacksmiths, Bowling Green, Ohio, 77; Master Craftsmen, Mus Fine Arts, Boston, 78. Collections Arranged: Amulets & Talismans, New York, 73. Teaching: Artist-in-residence & head dept, Marlboro Col, Vt, 62-63; instr metals & form design, RI Sch Design, Providence, 72-74; instr metals workshop, Haystack Mt Sch, Deer Isle, Maine, 74; instr metals, Sch of Mus Fine Arts, Boston, 74- Pos: Mgr pavilion, Southern Vt Art Centre, Manchester, 62-64; head designer, Wuersch Assoc, Fall River, Mass, 64-67. Awards: Merit Award, The Goldsmith, Renwick Gallery, Smithsonian Inst, 74; Hon Mention, The Metalsmith, Phoenix Mus Art, 77. Bibliog: M Chamberlain (auth), Jewelry Techniques, Watson-Guptill, 76; Ralph Turner (auth), Modern Jewelry, A Critical assessment, Van Nostrand, 76. Mem: Am Crafts Coun; Soc NAm Goldsmiths. Style & Technique: Graphic, sculptural, visually direct statements which can be worn, used or carried about, with a strong sense of design. Media: Precious & Non-Precious Materials; Silver, Gold, Brass, Titanium. Dealer: Helen Drutt Gallery 1625 Spruce St Philadelphia PA 19103; Mary Brenda Cortell Harckus Krakow Gallery 7 Newbury St Boston MA 02116. Mailing Add: 72 1/2 John St Providence RI 02906

BLOOM, DONALD STANLEY
PAINTER
b Roxbury, Mass, Sept 3, 32. Study: Mass Col Art, BFA, 53; Art Students League, 53-55, with Barnet, Levi & Trafton; Inst Allende, San Miguel Allende, Mex, MFA, 57. Work: New Brunswick Pub Libr, NJ; NJ Food Coun; Fairleigh Dickinson Univ, Madison, NJ; Montclair State Col, NJ; Rutgers Univ. Comn: Mural (ceramic in concrete), Judge Raymond del Tufo, Newark, NJ, 64. Exhib: Whitney Ann Am Painting, Whitney Mus Am Art, New York, 60; Silvermine Guild Ann, New Canaan, Conn, 63; Audubon Artists Ann, Nat Acad Galleries, New York, 63; NJ Pavilion, New York World's Fair, 65; Springfield Watercolor Asn Traveling Show, Mo, 65. Teaching: Instr painting & collage, Morris Co Art Asn, NJ, 60-68; instr painting, Bloomfield Col, 65-66; dist chmn art dept, Piscataway Schs, NJ, 66-; instr watercolor, Summit Art Ctr, 74. Awards: Guggenheim Fel Creative Painting, 61; Silvermine Guild Award, 63; Huntington Hartford Found Fel, 64. Bibliog: E Genauer (auth), rev in, New York Herald Tribune, 9/61; J Beck (auth), rev in, Art News, 10/61; V Raynor (auth), rev in, Arts, 10/61. Mem: Assoc Artists NJ; Art Educators NJ. Media: Oil, Watercolor. Publ: Auth, We learned about color & design, Sch Arts Mag, 58; illusr, Seventeen Mag, 61; illusr, Country & Western Issue, Billboard Mag, 63; auth, Batik in the classroom & Woodcuts by children, 72 & Two for one, 75, Instructor. Dealer: Lawrence Gallery 901 Westport Rd Kansas City MO 64111; Lillian Kornbluth Gallery Fair Lawn NJ 07410. Mailing Add: 31 Dexter Rd East Brunswick NJ 08816

BLOOM, HYMAN
PAINTER
b Riga, Latvia, Apr, 1913. Study: West End Community Ctr, Boston, Mass, study with Harold Zimmerman; Harvard Univ, study with Denman W Ross. Work: Harvard Univ; Hirshhorn Mus & Sculpture Garden, Smithsonian Inst, Washington, DC; Kalamazoo Inst of Arts, Mich; Mus of Mod Art, New York; Whitney Mus of Am Art, New York. Exhib: Americans 1942, Mus of Mod Art, New York; Mus of Fine Arts, Boston; Whitney Mus of Am Art, New York; two-man show, Univ Calif Los Angeles; one-man shows, Stuart Gallery, Boston, 45, Inst of Contemp Art, Boston, Whitney Mus of Am Art, 68, Univ of Conn, 69 & Terry Dintenfass Inc, 72 & 75; Retrospective, Albright-Knox Art Gallery, Buffalo, NY, 54. Teaching: Instr, Wellesley Col, 49-51 & Harvard Univ, 51-53. Style & Technique: Dense built-up, jeweled surface. Dealer: Terry Dintenfass Inc 50 W 57th St New York NY 10019. Mailing Add: 1426 Cambridge St Cambridge MA 02139

BLOOM, JASON
ART DEALER, CURATOR
b White Plains, NY, Jan 21, 47. Pos: Dir, Dorsky Galleries, New York, 73-77; pres, Jason Bloom Res & Provenance/Dealer of Fine Works of Art, 77- Mem: Appraisers Asn of Am. Res: Research and provenance investigations for private collectors. Specialty: Nineteenth and twentieth century European and American art. Mailing Add: 416 W 20th St New York NY 10011

BLOOMGARDEN, JUDITH MARY
ART LIBRARIAN
b Brooklyn, NY, Jan 29, 42. Study: Inst of Archaeol, Univ of London, 61-62; Elmira Col, BA, 63; Sch of Fine & Applied Art, Boston Univ, grad work, 63-64; Dept of Art Hist & Archaeol, Columbia Univ, grad work, 64-66; Sch of Libr & Info Sci, Pratt Inst, MLS, 69. Pos: Libr asst, Elmira Col Libr, 62-63, Boston Univ, Sch of Educ Libr, 64 & Fine Arts Libr, Columbia Univ, 65; sr cataloguer, Mus of Mod Art Libr, New York, 66-70; libr consult, New York State Coun on the Arts, 69-71; head of tech servs, Art & Archit Libr, Yale Univ, 71-; consult, Comt for the Preservation of Archit Records, NY, 77- Mem: Art Libr Soc of NAm; Conn Archit Records & Drawings Survey (vpres, bd dirs); Nat Arts Club; Nat Trust for Hist Preservation; Soc for the Preservation of New England Antiquities. Mailing Add: c/o Yale Art & Archit Libr Box 1605A Yale Station New Haven CT 06520

BLOS, MAY (ELIZABETH)
ILLUSTRATOR, PAINTER
b Sebastopol, Calif, May 1, 06. Study: Univ Calif, Berkeley, AB(cum laude), 26; also with Perham Nahl, Eugen Neuhaus, M Heymann & Hans Hoffman, Munich. Comn: Murals, Migration of Molluscs, 68 & display, Carboniferous, 71, Paleontology Dept, Univ Calif, Berkeley (with help of staff). Exhib: Hunt Botanical Libr, Carnegie Inst Technol, Pittsburgh, Pa, 63 & 77; Canessa Gallery, San Francisco, Calif, 70; Univ Calif, Berkeley, 71; Lawrence Hall Sci, Berkeley, 75; Int Botanical Artists, Hunt Botanical Libr, Carnegie Inst Technol, Pittsburgh, 77. Pos: Adv, Am Indian Artists, San Francisco, 68-77, Hayward, 75- Mem: Oakland Mus Asn; United Bay Area Coun Am Indians; Ethnic Guild, Oakland Mus. Style & Technique: Line and stipple in ink technique, with emphasis on design potentialities of forms in nature. Media: Tempera, Acrylic. Illusr, Cambrian Invertebrate Restorations, var publ, 67-78; illusr, diplay maps for seismology, Univ Calif, Berkeley, 70-71. Mailing Add: 29 Live Oak Rd Berkeley CA 94705

BLOS, PETER W
PAINTER, INSTRUCTOR
b Munich, Ger, Oct 29, 03; US citizen. Study: State Acad Art, Munich, with Groeber & von Stuck; also French schs, Paris. Work: Oakland Art Mus, Calif; Wilshire Methodist Church, Los Angeles, Calif. Comn: Portraits of faculty members, Univ Calif, Berkeley, 62-75; portrait of Dr R Bahner, former dir Nat Archives, Washington, DC, 77. Exhib: Nat Acad Design, 41; Oakland Mus Art; East Bay Artist Asn, 70; Soc Western Artists Ann, San Francisco, Calif, 55-71; Rosicrucian Art Gallery, San Jose, Calif, 63 & 77-78; Haggin Gallery, Pioneer Mus, Stockton, Calif, 67, Walnut Creek Civic Arts Ctr, 75. Teaching: Instr portraits & figures, Walnut Creek Civic Arts Ctr, 62- Pos: Adv, United Am Indian Artists, San Francisco, 68-70, Redwood City, 75- Awards: Klumpke Figure Painting Award, Soc Western Artists, 41 & 70; Gold Medal, Oakland Mus, 51; Second Prize for Oils, Springville Invitational, Utah, 69. Mem: Oakland Mus Asn; Oakland Art Asn; East Bay Artists Asn; Soc Western Artists; United Bay Area Coun Am Indians. Style & Technique: Humanistic. Media: Oil, Acrylic. Collection: Navaho rugs, Indian baskets and paintings. Mailing Add: 29 Live Oak Rd Berkeley CA 94705

BLUHM, NORMAN
PAINTER
b Chicago, Ill, Mar 28, 20. Study: Ill Inst Technol; and with Mies Van der Rohe. Work: Dallas Mus Fine Arts, Tex; Dayton Art Inst, Ohio; Mus Mod Art, New York; Whitney Mus of Am Art, New York; Corcoran Gallery, Washington, DC; plus others. Exhib: Carnegie Inst, 58; Am Abstract Image, Guggenheim Mus, 61; Two Decades Am Painting, Mus Mod Art, 66; Large Scale Am Painting, Jewish Mus, 67; one-man shows, Leo Castelli Gallery, 57 & 60, Corcoran Gallery Art, 69 & 77, Martha Jackson Gallery, 70-74, Everson Mus, 73, Vassar Col, 74 & Contemp Arts Mus, Houston, Tex, 76. Media: Oil. Dealer: Martha Jackson Gallery 32 E 69th St New York NY 10021. Mailing Add: PO Box 729 Millbrook NY 12545

BLUM, SHIRLEY NEILSEN
ART HISTORIAN
b Petaluma, Calif, Oct 14, 32. Study: Stockton Col, AA; Univ Chicago, MA; Univ Calif, Los Angeles, PhD. Teaching: Instr, Univ Calif, Riverside, 62-73; Dana Prof fine arts, Colgate Univ, 73-74. Awards: Distinguished Teaching Award, Univ Calif, Riverside, 69; Nat Endowment Humanities Fel, 74. Mem: Col Art Asn (bd mem, 76-); Friends of the Neuberger Mus (bd mem, 78-). Publ: Co-auth, Jawlensky & the Serial Image, 66, Cubist Circle, 70 & Early Netherlandish Triptychs: a study in patronage, 69, Univ Calif. Mailing Add: Div Humanities SUNY Purchase NY 10577

BLUMBERG, BARBARA GRIFFITHS
PAINTER, INSTRUCTOR
b Wheelersburg, Ohio, Dec 30, 20. Study: Stratford Col, Danville, Va; Marshall Univ; also with Fletcher Martin, Elliott O'Hara, Leo Manso & Victor Caudall. Work: Charleston Art Gallery Permanent Collection, WVa; WVa Col Grad Studies; WVa State Capitol Bldg; FMC Corp, New York; Kanawaha Co Libr, Charleston. Comn: Mural, Marshall Univ, 57; tapestry, WVa State House, 70; painting, comn by Gov Hulette Smith, 71; tapestry, T F Goldthorpe Collection, Fla, 73. Exhib: 280, Huntington, WVa, 54-74; Int Fabric Exhib, Asher Gallery, London, Eng, 68; Fabric Structures, one-man nat touring exhib, 69; Appalachian Corridors, Fabric Sculpture, 70; Norfolk Biennial Drawing & Graphics, Va, 70- Teaching: Instr creative expression, WVa Col Grad Studies, Institute, WVa, 69-; instr painting & drawing, Charleston Art Gallery, 70-; instr painting & drawing, Univ Hawaii, Honolulu, 70-71. Pos: Guest artist, Maine, 68-69 & Bowling Green, Ohio, 70-71; consult, State WVa, 72-75. Awards: Purchase Award for Dark Quarters, Huntington, WVa, 70, for Sun Dance, Ala Moana Art Festival, Honolulu, 72 & for Hill Patterns, Allied Artists WVa, 74-75. Bibliog: Bill Bellinger (auth), Art with a purpose, WVa Illus, 70; Connie Shearer (auth), Full page life style, Charleston Gazette, 71. Mem: Nat Asn Am Pen Women (pres, 69); Allied Artists WVa (vpres, 70); Provincetown Art Asn, Mass; East Coast Gallery, Mass. Style & Technique: Abstract expressionist painting; free form weavings and stitchery. Media: Watercolor, Oil, Soft Sculpture, Fabric. Res: Extensive research, writing and application of art therapy; art for mentally retarded and physically handicapped. Publ: Auth, Creative approach to mental retardation, WVa Sch J, 61; illusr & contribr, Inklings, Nat Asn Am Pen Women, 72-; illusr & contribr, Art & Develop Disabilities J, 74. Mailing Add: 1422 Wilkie Dr Charleston WV 25314

BLUMBERG, RON
PAINTER, INSTRUCTOR
b Reading, Pa. Study: Nat Acad Design; Art Students League; Acad Grande Chaumiere, Paris, France. Work: Los Angeles Co Mus, Calif; Calif Executive Mansion, Sacramento; Bart Lytton Collection, Los Angeles. Exhib: One-man shows, Esther Robles Gallery, Los Angeles, 58, Raymond Burr Galleries, Los Angeles, 62-63, Dallas North Galleries, Tex, 66, Cowie Galleries, Los Angeles, 70 & Rosequist Galleries, Tucson, Ariz, 71. Teaching: Pvt classes painting & drawing, 50- Pos: Cult chmn, Westwood CofC, West Los Angeles, 69-73. Awards: J Coun Prize & Purchase Award, Los Angeles Co Mus Art, 50; Calif Watercolor Soc Award, 63; award, Inland VI, San Bernardino, 71. Mem: Artists for Econ Action (pres, 74-75); Los Angeles Art Asn; Artists Equity Asn. Style & Technique: Contemporary landscape and figure painting; palette knife technique. Media: Oil, Watercolor. Mailing Add: 974 Teakwood Rd Los Angeles CA 90049

BLUME, PETER
PAINTER
b Russia, Oct 27, 06; US citizen. Study: Educ Alliance Sch Art, 19-24; Art Students League; Beaux Arts Acad Art. Work: Boston Mus Fine Arts; Columbus Gallery Fine Arts; Mus Mod Art; Metrop Mus Art; Whitney Mus Am Art; plus others. Comn: Murals, US Post Off, Cannonsburg, Pa, Rome, Ga & Geneva, NY. Exhib: Boston Mus Fine Arts; Whitney Mus Am Art; Metrop Mus Art; Mus Mod Art; Kennedy Galleries; plus many others. Awards: Guggenheim Fel, 32 & 36; Prizes, Carnegie Inst, 34; Nat Inst Arts & Lett Grant, 47. Bibliog: Lloyd Goodrich & I H Baur (auth), American Art of Our Century, Whitney Mus Am Art, 61; George A Flanagan (auth), Understanding and Enjoying Modern Art, Crowell, 62; plus others. Mem: Assoc Nat Acad Design; Nat Inst Arts & Lett; Am Acad Arts & Lett. Mailing Add: Rte 1 Box 140 Sherman CT 06784

BLUMENTHAL, FRITZ
PAINTER, PRINTMAKER
b Mainz, Ger, June 16, 13; US citizen. Study: Univ Wuerzburg. Work: Metrop Mus Art, New York; Nat Gallery Art, Nat Collection of Fine Arts & Smithsonian Inst, Washington, DC; Stedelijk Mus, Amsterdam; Victoria & Albert Mus, London, Eng; Yale Univ Art Gallery, New Haven, Conn; plus many others. Comn: Prog cover designs, Gtr Middletown Arts Coun, NY State Coun Arts in collection of Mus Performing Arts at Lincoln Ctr, New York Pub Libr. Exhib: One-man shows, Gutenberg Mus, 64, Kunstverein Ulm, 65 & Herbert E Feist Gallery, New York, 72; Print Club, Philadelphia, 60 & 72; Traveling Exhib, Pratt Graphics Ctr, 74-76; plus many others. Awards: First Prize Painting, Nantucket Artists Asn, 61. Bibliog: Dr Werner Spanner (auth), Fritz Blumenthal, Das Neue Mainz, 64; La Liberte & Mogelon (co-auths), The Art of Monoprint, Van Nostrand, 74; plus many others. Style & Technique: Casein, oil painting and monoprints; oil on Japanese rice paper. Mailing Add: 30 Wickham Ave Middletown NY 10940

BLUMENTHAL, MARGARET M
DESIGNER
b Latvia, Sept 7, 05. Study: Berlin, Ger, with B Scherz & Bruno Paul. Exhib: Monza, Italy; Metrop Mus Art; Pratt Inst Gallery. Pos: Indust & textile designer, 43-; freelance designer & stylist, Libbey-Owens Co, Fallani & Cohn Co, Drulane Co, Toscony Fabrics, Franco Mfg Co, Colortex Co & Astorloid Soc. Media: Textiles. Mailing Add: 689 Columbus Ave New York NY 10025

BOAL, SARA METZNER
PAINTER, INSTRUCTOR
b Wheeling, WVa, Jan 10, 96. Study: Wellesley Col, BA; Cornell Univ; Columbia Univ; and with M A Rasko, Richard Marwede, Dmitri Romanovsky & Carle Blenner. Work: Libr, Barnesville, Ohio & Wheeling, WVa; Starr Mus, Albion, Mich; Wellesley Col, Mass; Hammond Mus; Hispanic Mus. Comn: Many pvt commissions. Exhib: Academic Artists of Springfield, Mass, Springfield Mus Art, 55; Fifty American Artists, Schoneman Gallery Art, New York; Belgian Pavilion, New York World's Fair, 64-66; Catharine Lorillard Wolfe Art Club, Nat Acad Design, 69-71; Burr Artists, Metrop Mus Art, New York. Teaching: Pvt classes in art. Awards: Norbury Mem Prize, Catharine Lorillard Wolfe Art Club, 53; Kramer Montgomery Medal of Honor, Ogunquit Art Studio, 59; First Prize in Landscape, Ahde Arzt Gallery, Soc Composers, Authors & Artists, 69. Mem: Catharine Lorillard Wolfe Art Club (pres, 65-68); Composers, Authors & Artists Am (pres, NY Chap, 70-72); life fel Royal Soc Arts; Nat Arts Club New York; Salmagundi Club NY. Media: Oil. Publ: Auth, Sketches of the Alps, 60, Sketches of Greece, 63, Sketches of New York, 65, Sketches of Japan, 67 & Sketches of Segovia, 71. Mailing Add: 246 Corona Ave Pelham NY 10803

BOARDMAN, SEYMOUR
PAINTER
b Brooklyn, NY, Dec 29, 21. Study: City Col New York, BS, 42; Art Students League; Ecole Beaux Arts, Paris, France; Acad Grande Chaumiere, Paris; Atelier Fernand Leger, Paris, 46-52. Work: Whitney Mus Am Art; Guggenheim Mus; Walker Art Ctr, Minneapolis, Minn; Santa Barbara Mus Art; New York Univ; plus others. Exhib: Whitney Mus Am Art, 55, 61 & 67; Nebr Art Asn, 56; Kunsthalle, Basel, Switz, 64; Santa Barbara Art Mus, 64; Albright-Knox Gallery, Buffalo, NY, 67; Andrew Dickson White Mus of Art, Cornell Univ, 71; one-man shows, Galerie Mai, Paris, 51, Martha Jackson Gallery, New York, 55 & 56, Stephen Radich Gallery, New York, 60, 61 & 62, A M Sachs Gallery, New York, 65, 67 & 68 & Dorsky Gallery, New York, 72; plus others. Awards: Longview Found Award, 63; Guggenheim Fel, 72. Media: Acrylic, Oil. Mailing Add: 234 W 27th St New York NY 10001

BOBICK, BRUCE
PAINTER, EDUCATOR
b Clymer, Pa, Oct 25, 41. Study: Indiana Univ Pa, BS, 63, MS, 67; Univ Notre Dame, MFA, 68. Work: Ill State Mus, Springfield; Mt Mercy Col, Cedar Rapids, Iowa; Western Ill Univ, Macomb; Springfield Art Mus, Mo; Laura Musser Art Mus, Muscatine, Iowa. Exhib: Watercolor USA Ann Exhib, Springfield Art Mus, Mo, 68-77; Ann Nat Watercolor Soc Exhibs; 61st & 64th Ind Artists Exhib, Ind Mus Art, Indianapolis, 68 & 73; Nat Exhib Watercolor Soc of Ala, Birmingham Mus Art, 69-77; 71st & 74th Ann Open Watercolor Exhib, Nat Arts Club, New York, 69 & 72; 164th Ann Am Watercolors, Prints & Drawings, Pa Acad Fine Arts, Philadelphia, 69; 145th & 146th Ann, Nat Acad Design, New York, 70 & 71; 35th Ann Exhib Contemp Am Paintings, Soc Four Arts, Palm Beach, Fla, 73; New Horizons in Art, Chicago, 73 & 76; 12th & 14th Midwest Biennial Exhib, Joslyn Art Mus, Omaha, Nebr, 72 & 76; 17th Hunter Ann Exhib Paintings & Drawings, Hunter Mus Art, Chattanooga, Tenn, 78; 2nd Ann Exhib Southern Watercolor Soc, Columbus Mus Arts & Sci, Ga, 78. Teaching: Assoc prof art, Western Ill Univ, 68-76 & WGa Col, 76- Awards: Purchase Award, Ill State Mus, 71; Watercolor Soc Award, 74; Watercolor USA Purchase Award, 75. Mem: Nat Watercolor Soc; Pittsburgh Watercolor Soc. Media: Watercolor. Res: Study of communication between artist and viewer. Mailing Add: Chateau A-3 Hays Mill Rd Carrollton GA 30117

BOBROWICZ, YVONNE P
INSTRUCTOR, FIBER ARTIST
b Maplewood, NJ, Feb 17, 28. Study: Cranbrook Acad of Art; Study with Anni Albers; with Paolo Soleri at Haystack. Comn: Woven wall, comn by Louis I Kahn, Kimball Mus, Ft Worth Tex, 72; rm divider, Chemistry Bldg, Univ of Pa Bank, Philadelphia, 76; woven wall hanging, Savings & Loan Bank, Pittsburgh, Pa, 77. Exhib: Detroit Art Mus, Mich, 50; Southwest La State, 51; Walker Art Ctr, Minneapolis, Minn, 53; Wichita Art Mus, Kans, 54; Mus of Contemp Crafts, New York, 60; Philadelphia Mus of Art, 63 & 300 yrs of Philadelphia Art, 76; Civic Ctr Mus of Philadelphia, 67-73; Univ of Pa Mus, Philadelphia, 75. Teaching: Lectr textiles & weaving, Drexel Univ, Philadelphia, 66-; instr weaving, Peters Valley, Leyton NY, summers 72 & 76. Pos: Decorative arts comt, Philadelphia Mus of Art, 75-; Exhib designer, Philadelphia Guild of Handweavers, 61-65, prog chmn, 62-64. Awards: First Prize, Los Angeles County Fair, 51; Honorable Mentions, Am Craft Coun, New York & Art Alliance, Philadelphia. Bibliog: Articles in Handweaver Mag, 60- Mem: Am Craft Coun; World Craft Coun. Style & Technique: Woven hangings and forms, two and three dimensional, extensive texture. Media: Thread (fiber or metal). Publ: Contribr, Rugmaking, Golden Bks, 72; contribr, Hooked and Rya Rugs, Van Nostrand Reinhold, 74; contribr, Am Rugs and Carpets, William Morrow, 78. Dealer: Helen Drutt 1625 Spruce St Philadelphia PA 19103. Mailing Add: 2312 Spruce St Philadelphia PA 19103

BOCCIA, EDWARD EUGENE
PAINTER
b Newark, NJ, June 22, 21. Study: Pratt Inst Art Sch, NY; Art Students League; Columbia Univ, BS & MA. Work: City Art Mus St Louis; Denver Art Mus; Univ Mass; St Louis Univ; State Hist Soc Mo; plus others. Comn: Stained glass, Clayton Inn, Mo; four wall paintings, First Nat Bank, St Louis; Stations of the Cross, Old Cathedral, St Louis; mural, Stations of the Cross & stained glass windows, Newman Chapel, Washington Univ, St Louis; religious drawings & 14 mural paintings, Temple Brith Sholom Kneseth Israel, St Louis; plus others. Exhib: One-man shows, Drury Col, 65, Gallery Tournabuoni, Florence, Italy, 71 & Fontbonne Col, St Louis, Mo, 76; traveling exhib, sponsored by Mo State Coun Arts, 68; Southern Ill Univ, 75; Fine Arts Salon, Milwaukee, Wis, 75; Italian Am Artists in USA, Stone Park, Ill, 77; Washington Univ Sch of Fine Arts Ann Fac Show, Steinberg Gallery, Washington, Univ, DC; plus others. Teaching: Dean, Columbus Art Sch, Ohio, 48-51; guest instr, Univ Sask, summer 60; guest instr, Webster Groves Col, summer 65; prof fine arts, Washington Univ. Awards: Ital Govt Fel Award Res & Painting in Italy, 58-59; Bronze Medal, Temple Israel, St Louis, 62; Hon Mention, Kirkwood United Methodist Church, Mo, 75. Style & Technique: Figure and figure compositions; linear volumetric via color and chiaroscuro; epic symbolic (non-abstract). Publ: Contribr, St Louis Post-Dispatch & Washington Univ Mags. Mailing Add: 600 Harper Ave Webster Groves MO 63119

BOCHNER, MEL
CONCEPTUAL ARTIST, ART WRITER
b Pittsburgh, Pa, 40. Study: Carnegie Inst of Technol, Pittsburgh, BFA(painting & philos), 62. Work: Los Angeles Co Mus Art, Calif; Mus Nat d'Art Mod, Paris, France. Exhib: Monuments, Mus Contemp Crafts, New York, 67; Art by Tel, Mus Contemp Art, Chicago, 69; Plans & Proj, Kunsthalle, Bern, Switz, 69; 057, 087, Seattle Art Mus, Wash, 69; Info, Mus Mod Art, New York, 70 & 71; Documenta 5, Kassel, WGer, 72; Am Drawings: 1963-1973, Whitney Mus Am Art, New York, 73; Art & Image in Recent Art, Art Inst Chicago, 74; one-man shows, Visual Arts Gallery, New York, 66, Bykert Gallery, New York, 68, Yale

Univ Gallery, New Haven, Conn, 69, 112 Greene St Gallery, New York, 71, Mus Mod Art, New York, 71, Sonnabend Gallery, New York, 71, 72 & 75 & Univ Calif, Berkeley, 75. Teaching: Instr, Sch Visual Arts, New York, 65. Bibliog: Lucy R Lippard (auth), Ultra-conceptual art, Art Int, Laugano, 3/68; B Boice (auth), Axiom of indifference, Arts Mag, New York, 4/73; R McDonald (auth), Mel Bochner, Artweek, 9/74. Publ: Auth, Background is not the margin, Art in Process, 69; auth, Ten Misunderstandings: A Theory of Photography, New York, 70; auth, No thought exists, Arts Mag, 4/70; auth, Excerpts from speculation, Artforum, 5/70; auth, Mental exercise: No 1 counting, Data, 2/72. Dealer: Sonnabend Gallery 924 Madison Ave New York NY 10021. Mailing Add: c/o School of Visual Arts 209 E 23rd St New York NY 10012

BOCK, WILLIAM SAUTS-NETAMUX'WE
ILLUSTRATOR, PAINTER
b Sellersville, Pa, Sept 18, 39. Study: Philadelphia Col of Art, BFA(illus), spec study with Robert Riggs; Lutheran Sem, Philadelphia, MA(theology). Comn: Watercolor series of Am cities, comn by Marriott Corp for reproduction in many cities & 3-dimensional art (Indian Mexican) & murals, Marriott Camelback Inn, Phoenix, Ariz, 69-70; watercolor for Christmas card, Book of the Month Club, New York, 71 & 74; Olympic designs for Plexiglas etching, McDonalds, Willow Grove, Pa, 75. Awards: Honored by Exhib for Illustrations for Crusader King, Am Inst of Graphic Arts, New York, 74; Monthly Choice Award for Illustrations for Malcolm Yucca Seed, Philadelphia Children's Reading Round Table, 78. Bibliog: Mr & Mrs Philip Berman (interview), Berman Collection, Pub Television, Allentown, Pa, 69; B A Bergman (auth), The First Aristocrats, Sunday Bull, Philadelphia, 2/75; Gerry Wallerstein (auth), William Sauts-Netamux'we Bock, Record Keeper of the Lenape, Bucks Co Panorama Mag, 1/76. Mem: Philadelphia Children's Reading Round Table. Style & Technique: Realistic to surrealistic, very detailed, precise, clear, built upon light and dark foundation; subject of paintings, Lenape Indian cosmos, vision, religion; size ranges from miniature to mural. Media: Pen & Ink; Watercolor, Acrylic. Publ: Illusr, Wolf Hunt, Little Brown, 70; illusr & auth, Coloring Book of the First Americans, Lenape Indian Drawings, Middle Atlantic Press, 74; illusr, Tom Sawyer, Field Enterprizes, World Bk, 75; illusr, Of Whales & Wolves, Lothrop, Lee, 78; illusr, White Fang (film strip), Spoken Arts, 78. Mailing Add: 252 E Summit St Souderton PA 18964

BODE, ROBERT WILLIAM
DESIGNER, PAINTER
b New York, NY, Nov 20, 12. Study: Sch Fine & Appl Arts, Pratt Inst; also with Ogden Pleissner. Comn: Designs for US postal stamps, Johnny Appleseed, Davy Crockett & Energy Conservation. Pos: Exec art dir, Kudner Agency, 51-57; creative art supvr, J Walter Thompson, 57-67. Awards: Art Dirs Awards; Am Watercolor Soc; Hudson River Valley Awards. Mem: Am Watercolor Soc; Soc Illusr; Art Dirs Club. Mailing Add: 8 McClelland Pl Chappaqua NY 10514

BODEM, DENNIS RICHARD
MUSEUM DIRECTOR
b Milwaukee, Wis, July 27, 37. Study: Wabash Col, BA, 59; Grad Sch, Univ Wis-Madison, 59-61. Pos: Dir, Jesse Besser Mus, 75- Mem: Thunder Bay Arts Coun (mus liaison); Bd Mich Coun for the Arts (mem, Mus Rev Comt); Mich Mus Asn (treas). Interest: Representative works of outstanding US, Midwest and Michigan artists of the late 19th and 20th centuries for museum collection. Mailing Add: 491 Johnson St Alpena MI 49707

BODNAR, PETER
PAINTER, EDUCATOR
b Andrejova, Czech, Nov 27, 28; US citizen. Study: Flint Inst Arts, Mich, 41-44; Western Mich Univ, BS, 51; Mich State Univ, MA, 56. Work: Dallas Mus; Isaac Delgado Mus, New Orleans; Ft Worth Art Mus; Lakeview Ctr for Arts, Peoria, Ill; De Waters Art Ctr, Flint. Exhib: One-man retrospectives, Isaac Delgado Mus, 66, Ill Art Coun Galleries, Chicago, 71 & Newport Harbor Art Mus, Newport Beach, Calif, 74; Spirit of the Comics, Inst Contemp Art, Univ Pa, 69; one-man show, Lakeview Ctr for Arts, Peoria, 72. Teaching: Asst prof art, State Univ NY Col Plattsburgh, 56-58; asst prof art, Univ Fla, 60-62; prof painting, Univ Ill, Urbana-Champaign, 62- Pos: Vis artist, Bradley Univ, spring 70; vis artist, Southern Methodist Univ, Dallas, 72, artist in residence, summer workshop, Taos, NMex, 72; vis artist, Univ Southern Calif, 74. Awards: Tamarind Lithography Workshop, Inc Grant, 64; Univ Ill Fel, Ctr for Advan Study, 67-68; Nat Endowment for Arts Fel, 75- Bibliog: Hiram Williams (auth), Notes for a Young Painter, Prentice-Hall, 65; Franz Schulze (auth), rev in Art Int, summer 67; Daniel Wells (auth), rev in Chicago Tribune, summer 71. Style & Technique: Surrealist. Media: Oil, Acrylic. Publ: Contribr, Strung Out with Elgar on a Hill, 70; contribr, Portrait: Converse, 75. Mailing Add: c/o Delahunty Galleries 2611 Cedar Springs Dallas TX 75204

BODO, SANDOR
PAINTER, SCULPTOR
b Szamosszeg, Hungary, Feb 13, 20; US citizen. Study: Col Fine & Appl Art, Budapest, Hungary. Work: (Restoration works) President Andrew Jackson Home in the Hermitage, Nashville, Tenn; President James K Polk Mus, Columbia, Tenn; Tenn State Mus, Nashville; Tenn Fine Arts Ctr, Nashville. Comn: Bronze reliefs, Hungarian Reformed Fedn Am, 65; portrait of Andrew Jackson, Royal Palace, Copenhagen, Denmark, 71. Exhib: Nat Housing Ctr, Washington, DC; Butler Inst Am Art, Youngstown, Ohio; Nat Acad Galleries, New York; Smithsonian Inst, Washington, DC; Brooks Mem Art Gallery, Memphis, Tenn. Pos: Self-employed artist & art restorer. Awards: Gold Medal of Honor for Watercolor, Am Art Week Exhib, 61; Gold Medal of Honor for Sculpture, Nat Arts Club, New York, 63 & Gold Medal of Honor for Oil Painting, 66. Mem: Fel Am Artists Prof League; Nat Arts Club; Allied Artists Am. Mailing Add: Bodo's Art Studio 6513 Hwy 100 Nashville TN 37205

BODOLAI, JOSEPH STEPHEN
FILM MAKER, SCULPTOR
b Youngstown, Ohio, May 11, 48. Study: Allegheny Col, BA, 70; Univ Manchester, with Alistair Smith; King's Col, Univ Cambridge, 68, with Sir Francis Warner. Comn: Tableaux, Cliche Guild of Can, Toronto, 72. Exhib: Thrill Factory, D W Griffith Film Festival, Louisville, Ky, 70; Univ Film Asn Film Festival, 71; Art Gallery Ont, Toronto, 72; Entertainment from the Thrill Factory, A Space, Toronto, 72; Electric Poetry, York Univ, Toronto, 72. Pos: Cur contemp art, The Electric Gallery, Toronto, 71- Awards: Foster P Doane Prize, Allegheny Col, 70. Mem: Alliance Technol & Art. Media: Film, Tape, Contemporary Materials. Publ: Contribr, Essays on Kinetic Art, The Electric Gallery, 72; contribr, Leonardo, Paris & London, 72. Dealer: A Space 85 St Nicholas St Toronto ON Can. Mailing Add: 24 Hazleton Ave Toronto ON M5R 2E2 Can

BOE, ROY ASBJÖRN
ART HISTORIAN, EDUCATOR
b Fredrikstad, Norway, Sept 27, 19; US citizen. Study: Univ Minn, BS, 41 & MA, 47; Univ Oslo, Fulbright fel, 50-51; NY Univ, grad fel, 49-50, PhD, 70; Moorhead State Col, fac res grant, 72-73. Teaching: Instr art hist, Univ Minn, 46-47, 55-56; asst prof art hist, La State Univ, 56-57; asst prof art hist, Pa State Univ, 57-60; assoc prof art hist, Univ Miss, 60-66, chmn dept art, 61-64; assoc prof art hist, Moorhead State Univ, 67- Mem: Col Art Asn Am; Norweg-Am Hist Asn; Am Asn Univ Prof. Res: 19th and 20th century European and American art; northern European art; Edvard Munch; artists of American western frontier; panoramas. Publ: Auth, Edvard Munch's murals for the University of Oslo, Art Quart, 60; auth, Edvard Munch og J P Jacobsen's Niels Lyhne, Oslo, 60; auth, The panoramas of the Mississippi, Miss Quart, 63. Mailing Add: 1106 Fifth Ave S Moorhead MN 56560

BOEDEKER, ARNOLD E (BOEDIE)
ILLUSTRATOR, PAINTER
b Sheboygan, Wis, June 5, 93. Study: Art Inst Chicago; and with John Pike, Edgar Whitney, Jerry Farnsworth, Don Stone, Tom Nichols, Dong Kingman, Millard Sheets, Rex Brandt, Caude Croney, Robert E Wood, John Pellew & George Post. Work: Canton Art Inst; Massillon Art Mus; Akron Art Inst; Cuyahoga Valley Art Ctr; Drawing Room Gallery. Exhib: Mainstreams, Marietta, Ohio, 72-73 & 75-76, Am Watercolor Soc; Butler Inst Am Art; Wichita Centennial Exhib; Canton Art Inst; Massillon Art Mus; plus many others. Pos: Art dir, Goodyear Tire & Rubber Co, Akron, Ohio, 15-61. Awards: Pres Award for Monhegan Coast Guard Station, Grand Nat Am Artists Prof League Exhib, 74; First Place Award, Cuyahuga Vallery Art Ctr Ann, 75-77; Gumbacher's Artist Award, Grand Nat, Grand Cent Gallery, Am Artist Prof League, 77. Mem: Am Artists Prof League; Akron Soc Artists (pres, 66-68); Cuyahoga Valley Art Ctr (trustee, 61-78, pres, 62-63). Media: Watercolor, Oil, Acrylic. Mailing Add: 2965 Silver Lake Blvd Cuyahoga Falls OH 44224

BOESE, ALVIN WILLIAM
RESEARCHER, COLLECTOR
b St Paul, Minn, Mar 24, 10. Pos: Mgr dept devoted to res & develop improved surfaces for artists, 3M Co, St Paul. Collection: Mainly contemporary American art, all media except sculpture. Mailing Add: 803 Lincoln Ave St Paul MN 55102

BOEVE, EDGAR GENE
EDUCATOR, PAINTER
b Marshalltown, Iowa, Sept 27, 29. Study: J Franklin Sch of Prof Arts, Inc, New York, cert; Calvin Col, Grand Rapids, Mich, AB; Univ Mich, Ann Arbor, MSD. Work: Calvin Theological Seminary Grand Rapids, Mich; Dordt Col, Sioux Center, Iowa; Catholic Info Ctr, Lansing, Mich. Comn: Sculpture, mural, Holland Church, Mich, 66; sculpture, Unity Sch, Hudsonville, Mich, 68; sculpture, Pine Rest Hosp, Cutlerville, Mich, 74 & 77; banners, Woodland Church, Grand Rapids, Mich, 75; mural, Holland Church, Mich, 76. Exhib: Detroit Art Inst, Mich, 65; Kresge Art Ctr, East Lansing, Mich, 68; Kalamazoo Art Ctr, Mich, 72; Grand Rapids Art Mus, Mich, 75. Teaching: Prof art hist, Calvin Col, Grand Rapids, Mich, 58- Awards: First Prize, 63 & 70 & Second Prize, 73, Christian Art Show, Peace Lutheran. Mem: Midwest Col Art Conf; Col Art Asn. Style & Technique: Painting on gold leaf & on Japanese tea chest paper. Media: Painting. Res: Art education. Publ: Auth, Childrens Art and the Christian Teacher, Nat Union Christian Sch, Concordia, Mo, 67, 2nd ed, 77; illusr, Youth Hymnal, Eerdmans, 68; illusr, The Touch of His Hand, World Home Bible, 76; illusr, The Gifted Church, Home Mission, Can Relig Conf, 77. Mailing Add: 9468 Whispering Sands Dr West Olive MI 49460

BOGAEV, RONNI (RONNI BOGAEV GREENSTEIN)
LECTURER, PAINTER
b Philadelphia, Pa. Study: Hussian Sch Art; portrait painting with Lazar Raditz. Work: Ft Lauderdale Mus Arts, Fla; Le Moyne Art Found, Tallahassee; Temple Beth Am, Miami; Bleemer & Levine Art Found, Miami; Tallahassee State Bank. Comn: Six mag covers, Adult & Child, Didactic, Inc, Chicago, 69; portrait, comn by John McMullan, Knight Newspaper, 72; portrait, comn by Karl Katz, Cur, Metrop Mus Art, New York, 74. Exhib: Major Fla Artists Exhib, Harmon Gallery, Naples, Fla, 72; Piedmont Painting & Sculpture, Mint Mus, Charlotte, NC, 73; Contemporary Portraits by American Artists, Lowe Mus, Miami, 74; Miami Deals, Metrop Mus & Art Ctr, Fla, 74; New Talent, ACA Gallery, New York, 74. Awards: Hortt Mem Purchase Award, Ft Lauderdale Mus Arts, 66; Temple Beth Am First Prize Painting, 72; Hilton Leech Mem Award, Fla Artist Group, 75; Hilton Leech Mem Award, 76; Best in Show Award, 15th Ann Maj Fla Artists Exhib, 78. Bibliog: Ted Krail (auth), Artist's mini memoir, Miami Beach Sun Mag, 68; Griffin Smith (auth), The artists of Miami, Tropic Mag, Miami Herald, 72; Mary Jo Hall (auth), Woman's Way, Channel 11 TV, 75. Mem: Lowe Mus; Metrop Mus & Art Ctr; Fla Artists Group, Inc. Style & Technique: Realist, sable brush painting. Media: Oil, Pencil. Dealer: Harriet Griffin Gallery 850 Madison Ave New York NY; Genesis Gallery Ltd 41 E 57th St New York NY. Mailing Add: 3845 Park Ave Miami FL 33133

BOGARIN, RAFAEL
PRINTMAKER
b El Tigre, Venezuela, Jan 20, 46. Study: Cristobal Rojas, Caracas, Venezuela, BA, 66; Pratt Graphics Ctr, New York, 70-71, study with Michael Ponce de Leon; Blackburn Workshop, New York, 71-73. Work: Mus of Fine Arts, Caracas; White House, Caracas; Corcoran Gallery of Art, Washington, DC; Chase Manhattan Bank, New York; Mus of Mod Art, New York. Comn: Three-floor-high mural, comn by Venezuelan Govt, Venezuelan Consulate, New York, 74. Exhib: One-man shows, Colegio Medico, Caracas, 66, Venezuelan Am Ctr, Caracas, 66, Galeria Portobello, Venezuela, 70 & First Nat Bank of Louisville, Ky, 77, Galeria Venezuela, New York, 78; Nat Salon of Plastic Arts, Caracas, 66-68; Bibliot Luis Angel Arango, Bogota, Colombia, 69; Chile Bienal, Santiago, 72; Espoletto Festival, Italy, 73; Semana Cult, Miami Libr, Fla, 73; Young Artists, Union Carbide Bldg, New York, 74. Teaching: Prof plastic arts, Sch of Plastic Arts, 67-70; prof plastic arts, Sch of Arts & Sci, Caracas, 69-70; asst etching/intaglio, Pratt Graphic Ctr, New York, 71- Awards: Roma Prize, Salon de Arte Venezoland, Italian Govt, 68; Hon Mention, Young Artists Salon Venezuela Inst of Fine Arts, 71. Bibliog: Calvin J Goodman (auth), Master Printers and Print Workshops, Am Artists, 10/76. Style & Technique: Geometric design and graphic techniques. Mailing Add: 14 W 17th St 5th Floor New York NY 10011

BOGART, GEORGE A
PAINTER
b Duluth, Minn, Oct 30, 33. Study: Univ Minn, Duluth, BA; Univ Wash, MFA; also with Fletcher Martin, Philip Evergood & Dong Kingman. Work: Delgado Mus Art, New Orleans, La; Ill State Univ; Washburn Univ, Topeka, Kans; Okla State Collection. Exhib: Delgado Mus Art, 61 & 64; New York World's Fair, 64; Dallas Mus Fine Arts, 64 & 65; Okla Art Ctr, 75; Amarillo Art Mus, 75; plus others. Teaching: Instr, Univ Wash; prof art, Univ Tex, Austin; prof art, Pa State Univ, State College; prof art, Univ Okla. Awards: Purchase Prizes, Ill State

Univ, Normal, 69, Prize, Washburn Univ, 71 & Amarillo Art Mus, 75. Style & Technique: Large acrylic paintings. Publ: Contribr, Southwestern Art; illusr, George Bogart drawings and paintings, 67. Mailing Add: 138 Page St Norman OK 73069

BOGART, RICHARD JEROME
PAINTER
b Highland Park, Mich, Oct 30, 29. Study: Art Inst Chicago, grad, 52; Univ Ill, 54; Black Mountain Col, NC, 56. Exhib: Riverside Mus, New York, 64; The American Landscape, A Living Tradition, circulated by Am Fedn Arts, Peridot Gallery, New York, 68; Poindexter Gallery, New York, 73-77; Conn Painting, Drawing & Sculpture Exhib, 78; one-man shows, Poindexter Gallery, New York, 68-70 & Meredith Long & Co, Houston, Tex, 77. Bibliog: Alan Gussow (auth), A sense of place—the artist & the American land, Sat Rev Press. Media: Oil. Dealer: Poindexter Gallery 24 E 84th St New York NY 10028. Mailing Add: RFD 2 Monroe CT 06468

BOGDANOVIC, BOGOMIR
PAINTER, LECTURER
b Senje, Yugoslavia, Aug 20, 23. Study: Belgrade Univ, with Prof S Strala, Prof A Samojlov. Work: Mus Anchorage, Alaska; Presidential Palace, Indonesia; New York Times. Exhib: One-man shows, Quadrangle Gallery, Dallas, 67-74; Pa Acad Fine Arts, Philadelphia; Nat Acad Fine Art, Am Watercolor Soc & Kennedy Galleries, New York. Pos: Guest artist & demonstr for various art asns. Awards: Charles Dana Medal, Pa Acad Fine Arts, 63; Silver Medal, Am Watercolor Soc, 71; Gold Medal, Franklin Mint, 73. Mem: Am Watercolor Soc; Audubon Artists; Allied Artists of Am; Knickerbocker Artist; hon mem South-Western Watercolor Soc. Style & Technique: Figure, landscape, still life. Media: Oil, Pastel Watercolor. Mailing Add: 9 West St Warwick NY 10990

BOGGS, FRANKLIN
PAINTER, EDUCATOR
b Warsaw, Ind, July 25, 14. Study: Ft Wayne Art Sch, Ind; Pa Acad Fine Arts. Work: Abbott Labs; US War Dept; US Post Off, Newton, Miss; Mayo Clin, Rochester, Minn; Merchants & Savings Bank, Janesville, Wis; plus others. Comn: Mural, Voc Sch, Janesville, 61; concrete murals, Yates Am Mach Co, Madison, Wis, 61, Univ Wis Math Bldg, 62 & Cancer Res Bldg, Madison, 63, Univ Wis-Milwaukee, 64 & Cutler-Hammer Off Bldg, Milwaukee, 65; plus others. Exhib: Pa Acad Fine Arts. Collections Arranged: Supvr assembling, American Indian Exhibition. Teaching: Prof & artist in residence, Beloit Col, 45-, chmn art dept, 55-71; lectr Am Indian Exhib, Finland & Sweden, 58-59. Pos: Illusr, Tenn Valley Auth, 40-44; war artist, 44. Awards: Gimbels Wis Exhib Prize, 52; Milwaukee J Prize, Freedom of the Press Exhib; Fulbright Res Grant to Finland, 58; plus others. Publ: Illusr, Men Without Guns; army med paintings reproduced in art mags. Mailing Add: Dept of Art Beloit Col Beloit WI 53511

BOGGS, JEAN SUTHERLAND
MUSEUM DIRECTOR, ART HISTORIAN
b Negritos, Peru, June 11, 22; Can citizen. Teaching: Asst prof art, Skidmore Col, 48-49; asst prof art, Mt Holyoke Col, 49-52; assoc prof art, Univ Calif, 54-62; Steinberg prof hist art, Washington Univ, 64-66. Pos: Dir, Nat Gallery Can, 66- Awards: Officer of the Order of Can. Mem: Am Asn Mus (mem coun, 69-); Can Art Mus Dirs Asn; Asn Art Mus Dirs (trustee); fel Royal Soc Can. Publ: Auth, Portraits by Degas, 62, Drawings by Degas, 66, The National Gallery of Canada, 71; The last thirty years, Picasso 1881-1973, 73. Mailing Add: Elgin at Slater Ottawa ON Can

BOGGS, MAYO MAC
SCULPTOR, EDUCATOR
b Ashland, Ky, Mar 22, 42. Study: Univ Ky, with Mike Hall, BA(art); Univ NC, Chapel Hill, with Robert Howard, MFA(sculpture). Work: NC Nat Bank, Charlotte; Spartanburg Bank, SC; Huntington Galleries, WVa. Comn: Fountain sculpture, Charles Lea Ctr for Handicapped, Spartanburg, SC, 73; garden sculpture, Spartanburg Arts Coun, 75. Exhib: Midstates Sculpture, Lexington, Ky, 69; 9 in 69, Peabody Mus, Nashville, Tenn, 69; 1969 Regional Fine Arts Biennial, J B Speed Mus, Louisville, 69; Southeastern How, Gallery Contemp Arts, Winston-Salem, NC, 70; SC Artists Ann, Gibbes Gallery, Charleston, SC, 71-72. Teaching: Asst prof sculpture & chmn dept, Converse Col, Spartanburg, SC, 70-; guest artist, Penland Sch Crafts, NC, 74. Awards: John W Oswald Res & Creativity Award, Univ Ky, 69; Kathryne Amelia Brown Fac Award, Converse Col, 72. Mem: Spartanburg Artists Guild. Style & Technique: A transition from non-objective to more objective recognizable image. Media: Steel Construction, Bronze and Aluminum Casts. Mailing Add: Rte 4 Box 199 Gaffney SC 29340

BOGHOSIAN, VARUJAN
SCULPTOR, EDUCATOR
b New Britain, Conn, June 26, 26. Study: Vesper George Sch Art, Boston; Yale Univ Sch Art & Archit, BFA & MFA. Work: Mus Mod Art & Whitney Mus Am Art, New York; Addison Gallery Am Art, Andover, Mass; Worcester Mus, Mass; Currier Gallery Art, Manchester, NH. Exhib: One-man shows, Stable Gallery, 63-66 & Cordier & Ekstrom, 69, 71, 73, 75, 77 & 78, New York. Teaching: Prof sculpture, Dartmouth Col, 68- Awards: Fulbright Grant, 53; sculptor-in-residence, Am Acad Rome, 67; Nat Inst Arts & Lett Award, 72. Bibliog: Dore Ashton (auth), article, In: Studio Int, 4/65; article, In: Time Mag, 2/9/70. Media: Constructions. Dealer: Cordier & Ekstrom Inc 980 Madison Ave New York NY 10021. Mailing Add: Dept of Art Dartmouth Col Hanover NH 03755

BOGORAD, ALAN DALE
ILLUSTRATOR
b Brooklyn, NY, July 29, 15. Study: Pratt Inst, AA, 34. Work: Pentagon, Washington, DC; Air Force Mus, Wright-Patterson Field, Dayton, Ohio. Exhib: Alwin Gallery, London; Diogenes Galleries, Athens; Col New Rochelle; Great Neck Libr, NY; Soc Illusr, New York. Awards: Honorable Mention for Mark Cross covers, Soc Illusr, 61-62 & for Birds of Peace, Marymount Show Union Carbide Bldg, New York, Col, 74. Bibliog: Mona Moffitt (auth), article in Athens Post, 73; article in People, Places & Parties, Fall 1977; also articles in Graphis & Art Direction Mag. Mem: Soc Illusr; Graphic Artists Guild; Artist's Fel. Style & Technique: Painter in acrylics in a distinctive transparent color treatment of figure compositions and non-objectives; collages. Media: Acrylic and/or Paper Collage. Publ: Ed, It's Fun to Draw & Junior's Fun to Draw. Dealer: Phyllis Lucas Gallery 981 Second Ave New York NY 10021. Mailing Add: 320 E 42nd St New York NY 10017

BOGUCKI (EDWIN ARNOLD BOGUCKI)
SCULPTOR, PAINTER
b Racine, Wis, July 5, 32. Study: Wis Art Acad; also with Christopher Thompson, Baltimore, Md; Leon Pescheret, Whitewater, Wis & Alex Dzigurski, Chicago. Work: Pvt collections, Don Ford, Fla, Douglas Marshall, Tex, Count Federico Zichy-Thyssen, Buenos Aires, Arg, Wayne Van Veet, Colo, Woodson K Woods, Hawaii, Robert Q Sutherland, Kans & Dale Robertson, Calif; pub collections, Ft Wayne Mus of Art, Ind. Comn: Portraits, comn by Mrs Parker Poe, Harrodsburg, Ky, 64; bronze & painting, comn by James F Lewis, Jr, Charlottesville, Va, 65-73, Mrs Guilbert Humphrey, Cleveland, 70, Daniel C Gainey, Owatonna, Minn, 71-75 & Phil Witter, Baton Rouge, La. Ga Rageyma (bronze), Arabian Horse Registry, Denver, 74. Style & Technique: Modern classic with kinetic realism; non geometric motion; accurate representations with balanced motion; paintings reflect use of as many natural colors as possible. Dealer: Troy's Cowboy Art Gallery 7106 Main Scottsdale AZ 85251. Mailing Add: 8110 Foley Rd Racine WI 53402

BOHAN, PETER JOHN
ART HISTORIAN, PAINTER
b New York, NY. Study: Bristol Univ, 47-48; Rensselaer Polytech Inst, BEng, 50; Columbia Univ, 54-55; Yale Univ, MA, 57; Courtauld Inst Art, Univ London, Fulbright scholar, 58-59; Yale Univ, PhD, 61; State Univ NY, Res Fel Archit & Urban Planning, Europe, 69-70. Exhib: 32nd Regional Exhib, Albany Inst Hist & Art, 67; 1st State Univ NY Artists Exhib, Albright-Knox Art Gallery, Buffalo & traveling exhib, 67-68; 19th Ann New Eng Exhib, Albany Inst Hist & Art, 69; Convocation of the Arts, State Univ NY, Albany & traveling exhib, 69. Collections Arranged: American Gold 1700-1860, Yale Univ Art Gallery, 63; From Victor Hugo to Jean Cocteau (French portrait drawings), 65 & First Intercollegiate Student Exhibition, 66, State Univ NY Col New Paltz Art Gallery; plus others. Teaching: Asst prof art hist, Southern Conn State Col, 62-63; prof art hist, State Univ NY Col New Paltz, 63- Pos: Asst cur, Garvan Collection, Yale Univ Art Gallery, 59-63; dir, Col Art Gallery, State Univ NY Col New Paltz, 63- Awards: Perkin-Elmer Prize in Painting, Silvermine Guild Artists Ann, 68. Mem: Soc Archit Historians. Media: Acrylic Resins. Res: Architecture and design, 1870-1930. Publ: Auth, American gold, 1700-1860, Yale Univ Art Gallery, 63; auth, From Victor Hugo to Jean Cocteau, New Paltz Col Art Gallery, 65; auth, Early American gold, Antiques, 12/65; auth, First New Paltz intercollegiate student exhibition, New Paltz Col Art Gallery, 66; auth, Early Connecticut silver, 1700-1840, Wesleyan Univ, 70. Mailing Add: Hist of Art Dept State Univ NY New Paltz NY 12561

BOHLEN, NINA (CELESTINE EUSTIS BOHLEN)
PAINTER
b Boston, Mass, Mar 5, 31. Study: Radcliffe Col, BA, 53, drawing & painting with Hyman Bloom. Exhib: Boston Arts Festival, 62; Goldberg Collection, Boston Mus Sch, 63; Brockton Mus, Mass, 69; Westmoreland Mus, Pa, 73; Animal in Art, Far Gallery, New York, 74; Candidates for Awards Exhib & Exhib of Recipients of Awards, Am Acad of Arts & Lett, 77; one-person shows, Swetzoff Gallery, Boston, 57, Siewab Gallery, Boston, 59, Shore Gallery, Boston, 65, Tragos Gallery, Boston, 68 & Boston Atheneum Libr, 71, 74 & 75. Teaching: Pvt instr drawing & painting, 73-77. Awards: Am Acad Arts & Lett Award in Art, 77. inspiration. Media: Drawing; Painting; Monotype. Mailing Add: 55 Hagen Rd Newton MA 02159

BOHNEN, BLYTHE
PAINTER
b Evanston, Ill, July 26, 40. Study: Smith Col, BA; Boston Univ, BFA; Hunter Col, MA. Work: Aldrich Mus Contemp Art, Ridgefield, Conn; Allen Art Mus, Oberlin Col, Ohio; Dallas Mus Fine Arts, Tex; McCrory Corp, New York; Whitney Mus Am Art, New York. Exhib: Penthouse, Mus Mod Art, New York, 72; Painting and Sculpture Today, Indianapolis Mus Art, Ind, 72; New American Abstract Painting, Vassar Col Mus, 72; American Women Artists, Kunsthaus, Hamburg, Ger, 72; Wadsworth Atheneum, Hartford, Conn, 75. Teaching: Lectr, Metrop Mus Art, 67-72; instr, Stockton State Col, NJ, 73-75. Bibliog: Carter Rat Ratcliff i (auth), The Whitney annual, Art Forum, 4/72; Kenneth Baker (auth), New York commentary, Studio Internation, 5/72; Susan Heineman (auth), rev in Art Forum, 9/74. Style & Technique: Study of forms created by gesture and motion in various media. Media: Acrylic, Graphite. Dealer: A I R Gallery 97 Wooster St New York NY 10012. Mailing Add: 833 Broadway New York NY 10003

BOHROD, AARON
PAINTER, EDUCATOR
b Chicago, Ill, Nov 21, 07. Study: Art Inst Chicago; Art Students League, with John Sloan. Work: Art Inst Chicago; Corcoran Gallery Art, Washington, DC; Metrop Mus Art, New York; Philippines Mus Art, Manila; Whitney Mus Am Art, New York. Exhib: Art Inst Chicago Int Watercolor Exhibs, 32-40; Guggenheim Found Exhib, 36-38; Carnegie Inst Int Exhib, 36-38 & 40; Artists for Victory Exhib, Metrop Mus Art, 42; Pa Acad Fine Arts, 42; Nat Acad Fine Arts Exhibs, 53-72; plus many others. Teaching: Artist in residence, Southern Ill Univ, Carbondale, 41-42; artist in residence, Univ Wis-Madison, 48- Pos: Artist war corresp, US Corps Engr & Life Mag, 42-45. Awards: Clark Prize & Silver Medal, Corcoran Gallery Art; Artist for Victory Exhib Prize, Metrop Mus Art; First Logan Prizes, Art Inst Chicago, 37 & 45. Bibliog: Harry Salpeter (auth), Bohrod: Chicago's gift to art, Esquire Mag, 40; article in Life Mag, 41; plus others. Publ: Auth, A Pottery Sketch Book, 59, A Decade of Sill Life, 66 & Wis Sketches, 75, Univ Wis. Dealer: Oehlschlaeger Galleries 107 E Oak Chicago IL 60611. Mailing Add: 4811 Tonyawatha Trail Madison WI 53716

BOIGER, PETER
SCULPTOR
b Altoetting, Ger, Apr 24, 41; US citizen. Study: Apprenticeship & study with Hans Frank & August Buttler, Munich, Ger, 59-64; Mills Col. Work: E B Crocker Art Gallery, Sacramento; Storm King Art Ctr, Mountainville, NY. Comn: Cosmic Fugue (granite relief), Pac Tel Co, Old Courthouse Sq, Santa Rosa, Calif, 73-74; Space Fugue (sculpture aluminum & Plexiglas), Amax Aluminum Co, San Mateo, Calif, 74; Great Eye (granite sculpture), City Napa, Calif, 75. Exhib: Oakland Mus, Calif, 70; San Francisco Mus Art, 70-72; one-man shows, William Sawyer Gallery, San Francisco, 71, St Mary's Col Art Gallery, Morage, Calif, 72 & E B Crocker Art Gallery, Sacramento, 74; plus many others. Awards: Award Graphic Design, City of Munich, 62. Bibliog: Joan Palm (auth), Open caves and floating forms, Oakland Tribune, 8/8/71; Charles Johnson (auth), Peter Boiger: sculpture in a high tradition, Sacramento Bee, 9/8/74. Style & Technique: Organic abstraction; abstracted figuratism. Media: Cast Bronze, Carved Wood, Stone. Dealer: Humboldt Gallery 37 W 57th St New York NY 10019; James Willis Gallery 109 Geary St San Francisco CA 94108. Mailing Add: 332 Lewis St Oakland CA 94607

BOLINGER, TRUMAN
SCULPTOR
b Sheridan, Wyo, Dec 3, 44. Study: Sheridan Jr Col; Colo Inst of Art; Art Students League. Work: NC Mus of Art, Raleigh; Minn Hist Soc, Minneapolis; First Fed Savings & Loan Art Dept, Phoenix, Ariz. Exhib: Solon Borglum Mem Sculpture Exhib, Cowboy Hall of Fame, Oklahoma City, Okla, 75; Mus of the SW, Midland, Tex, 75; John Selmon Mem Art Exhib, Stamford, Tex, 76 & 77. Bibliog: Ann Patterson (auth), Truman Bolinger, In Wyo, 6/74; Gordon Milhone (auth), Sensitivity in Bronze, SW Art, 11/74; Claudia Reinhardt (auth), Truman Bolinger, Artists of the Rockies, summer 76. Style & Technique: Realism, western

subject matter. Media: Wax. Dealer: Hammer Galleries 51 E 57th New York NY 10022. Mailing Add: 355 E Mountain View Dr Sheridan WY 82801

BOLINSKY, JOSEPH ABRAHAM
SCULPTOR, EDUCATOR
b New York, NY, Jan 17, 17. Study: Columbia Univ, MA; Stourbridge Col Art, Eng; Skowhegan Sch Painting & Sculpture, with Jose de Creeft; Iowa Univ, MFA. Work: Newark Mus Art, NJ; Tel Aviv Mus Art, Israel; State Univ NY Col Buffalo. Comn: Carved ark doors & welded menorah, Sons Jacob Synagogue, Waterloo, Iowa, 52; three welded forms & facade, Dr Diamond Med Ctr, Waterloo, 60; cast bronze group of six figures, Jewish Community Fedn Bldg, Cleveland, Ohio, 66; bronze screen, St Mary's Hosp, Rochester, NY, 70; carved ark doors, Temple Shaarey Zedek, Amhurst, NY, 71. Exhib: Des Moines Art Ctr, Iowa, 52; Western NY Regional, Albright-Knox Gallery, Buffalo, NY, 59; Art on Paper, Skowhegan Sch Painting & Sculpture, 69; Rochester Festival of Religious Art, NY, 70; Our Legacy of Art in Western New York, Charles Birchfield Ctr, 72. Teaching: Instr sculpture, Univ Northern Iowa, 49-54; prof sculpture, State Univ NY Col Buffalo, 54-; vis sculptor, Stanislaus State Univ, summer 71. Awards: First Prize for Stone Carving, Des Moines Art Ctr, 52; First Prize for Stone Carving, Albright-Knox Gallery, 59; Award for Bronze Casting, Rochester Festival of Religious Art, 70. Mem: Patteran Art Asn, Buffalo. Media: Bronze, Stone, Wood. Publ: Contribr, Jewish form symbolism, Ethos Mag, 58; demonstr, Carved Sculpture (film), US Info Serv, 68. Dealer: Gallery West 311 Bryant St Buffalo NY 14222. Mailing Add: 10 Ames Ave Tonawanda NY 14150

BOLLES, JOHN S
ART DEALER, COLLECTOR
b Berkeley, Calif, June 25, 05. Study: Univ Okla, BS; Harvard Univ, MArch. Pos: Owner & dir, Bolles Gallery, 58- Awards: Artists Equity Award, Artists Equity Asn & Calif Coun Architects, 50. Mem: Am Inst Architects; Calif Coun Architects (pres, 46); San Francisco Art Inst (chmn bd, 61-64). Specialty: Contemporary, mostly California and the West Coast art. Collection: Contemporary, includes Dove, Soulage, Hoffman, Olivera and many others; gifts to University of Oklahoma Museum and Oakland Museum, California. Publ: Auth, La Iglesia, Chichen Itza Yucatan, 65; auth, Las Momjas, Chichen Itza Yucatan, Univ Okla Press, 77; auth, var archaeol reports for Carnegie Inst & Oriental Inst, Univ Chicago. Mailing Add: 14 Gold St San Francisco CA 94133

BOLLEY, IRMA S
PAINTER, DESIGNER
b Turku, Finland; US citizen. Study: Mass Col Art, dipl; Kean Col, NJ; Art Student League; spec study with Jerry Farnsworth, F D Greenbowe & Joe Jones. Exhib: 32nd Ann NJ State Exhib, Montclair Mus, 63; Exhibition of Finnish-American Art, Riverside Mus, New York, 64; 9th Westfield Art Asn Ann, Union Col, Cranford, NJ, 70; Crafts for Fun and Function, Union Carbide Corp, New York (courtesy McCalls Needlework & Crafts), 70; Art from New Jersey, NJ State Mus, Trenton, 71. Pos: Art dir, Gray Advert Agency, New York, 41-44; designer-consult, needlework & crafts, McCall Pattern Co, 49-72. Awards: First Prize for oil, Waiting, Finlandia Found, 63; First Prize for mixed media, Growth, Summit Art Ctr, 68 & Beneath the Earth, Westfield Art Asn, 70. Bibliog: Irma Bolley, designer-artist, McCall Publ, 65; Peggy Ann Darbie (auth), Leisure crafts appeal to young, Courier News, Plainfield, NJ, 9/24/69; Randy Stiles (auth), The joys of creation, Scene Publ, 3/70. Mem: Nat Asn Women Artists; NJ Watercolor Soc; Summit Art Ctr. Style & Technique: Traditional; transparent watercolor. Media: Watercolor. Publ: Contribr, articles, In: McCall Needlework & Crafts, 68-72; Hot iron transfer kit with booklet, Needle Arts Soc. Mailing Add: 79 Redmont Rd Watchung NJ 07060

BOLLINGER, WILLIAM
CONCEPTUAL ARTIST
b Brooklyn, NY, 39. Study: Brown Univ, Providence, RI, 57-61. Exhib: Sound, Light, Silence: Art that Performs, Nelson Gallery of Art, Kansas City, Mo, 66; Ben Berns, Bill Bollinger, Clark Murray, Bykert Gallery, New York, 66; Contemp Am Artists, Univ Ill, Urbana, 67; Rejective Art, Am Fedn Art, New York, 67; Cool Art, Aldrich Mus Contemp Art, Ridgefield, Conn, 68; Bollinger, Hart, Marsden, Saret, Tuttle, Wilson, Bykert Gallery, New York, 68; Kunstmarkt, Cologne, Ger, 68; Nine at Leo Castelli, Leo Castelli Gallery, New York, 68; Six Kuenstler, Galerie Ricke, Cologne, 69; Op Losse Schroeven/Square Tags in Round Holes, Stedelijk Mus, Amsterdam, Holland; Anti-Illusion: Procedures/Material, 69 & Ann, 69 & 73, Whitney Mus Am Art, New York; Info, Mus Mod Art, New York, 71; Sculpture in the Fields, Storm King Art Ctr, Mountainville, NY, 74; Drawings, Univ RI, 74; one-man shows, Bianchini Gallery, New York, 66, Bykert Gallery, New York, 67 & 69, Galerie Ricke, Cologne, 68, O K Harris Gallery, New York, 72 & 74, 10 Bleecker St Gallery, New York, 72 & Bard Col, 73; Retrospective, Bennington Col, 73. Bibliog: Rev in Arts, New York, 4/72 & Artforum, New York, 10/72; N Foote (auth), Rev in Art in Am, 75. Dealer: O K Harris Works of Art 383 W Broadway New York NY 10013. Mailing Add: c/o Bykert Gallery 24 E 81st St New York NY 10028

BOLMGREN, DONNA HOLLEN
EDUCATOR, PAINTER
b Willmar, Minn, May 28, 35. Study: Univ Minn, BS(in art educ), 57; Univ Pittsburgh, 58; Carnegie-Mellon Univ, 59. Work: Pvt collections. Exhib: Assoc Artists of Pittsburgh, Carnegie Mus, 68-75; Gallery Upstairs, Arts & Crafts Ctr of Pittsburgh, 70; William Penn Mus, Harrisburg, Pa, 71-73; Ogleby Mus, Wheeling, WVa, 72; Butler Mid-Year Nat, 73. Teaching: Instr design, Arts & Crafts Ctr, 70-, instr painting, 73-; instr design & painting, Sweetwater Art Ctr, currently. Awards: South Hills Art League Award, 67-72 & 74; Pittsburgh Soc of Artists Award, 68, 69 & 71; Harrisburg Arts Festival Award, 73. Mem: Assoc Artists of Pittsburgh (pres, 74-); Pittsburgh Soc of Artists; South Hills Art League (pres, 69-71); Renaissance Ctr for the Arts (bd mem, 70-). Style & Technique: Abstract impressionism to abstract expressionism. Media: Acrylic, Mixed Media. Dealer: Helen Vargo 133 Lee St Apt 712 Carnegie PA 15106. Mailing Add: 1371 Stoltz Rd Bethel Park PA 15102

BOLOMEY, ROGER HENRY
SCULPTOR, ART HISTORIAN
b Torrington, Conn, Oct 19, 18; US & Swiss citizen. Study: Acad Bella Arte, Florence, Italy, 47; Univ Lausanne, 47-48; Calif Col Arts & Crafts, Oakland, 48-50. Work: Mus Mod Art & Whitney Mus Am Art, New York; Oakland Mus, Calif; Los Angeles Co Mus, Calif; Univ Calif Mus Art, Berkeley. Comn: Aluminum sculpture, Southridge Mall, Milwaukee, Wis, 70; two reliefs, Mutual of NY, Syracuse, 71; aluminum sculpture, Eastridge Mall, San Jose, Calif, 71; two bronze sculptures, S Mall Proj, Albany, 71; cor-ten steel sculpture, Lehman High Sch, Bronx, 71-72. Exhib: Carnegie Inst Int, Pittsburgh, 64; Whitney Mus Am Art Sculpture Ann, 64; Quatriene Exposition Suisse Sculpture, Bienne, Switz, 66; Contemporary American Paintings & Sculpture, Univ Ill, Urbana, 67; American Sculpture, Univ Nebr, Lincoln, 70. Teaching: Assoc prof art, Herbert H Lehman Col, 68-75; chmn dept art, Calif State Univ, Fresno, 75- Awards: First Prize & Purchase Award, Bundy Art Mus Sculpture Int, Waitsfield, Vt, 63; Sculpture Prize, San Francisco Art Inst 84th Ann, 65; Res Found Award, City Univ NY, 70. Mem: San Francisco Art Inst; Am Fedn Arts. Style & Technique: Sculpture designed for specific architectural or other environments. Media: Steel, Aluminum. Mailing Add: 4014 N Van Ness Blvd Fresno CA 93704

BOLOTOWSKY, ILYA
PAINTER, EDUCATOR
b St Petersburg, Russia, July 1, 07; US citizen. Study: Col St Joseph, Constantinople, Turkey, cert, 23; Nat Acad Design, dipl, 30. Work: Mus Mod Art, Solomon R Guggenheim Mus, Whitney Mus Am Art & Chase Manhattan Bank Collection, New York; Hirshhorn Collection, Washington, DC; plus many others. Comn: Abstract mural, comn by Works Progress Admin, Williamsburg Housing Proj, NY, 36-37; mural, comn by Works Progress Admin, Hall of Med Sci, New York World's Fair, 38-39; mural, comn by Works Progress Admin, Men's Day Room, Hosp for Chronic Dis, Welfare Island, NY, 41; abstr murals, Cinema I Lobby, New York, 63; abstr mural, N Cent Bronx Hosp, 74; plus many others. Exhib: The Classic Spirit in XX Century Art, Janis Gallery, New York, 64; The 1930's Painting & Sculpture in America, Whitney Mus Am Art, 68; The Nonobjective World, 1924-1939, Gallerie Jean Chauvelin, Paris, Annalee Jude Fine Art, London, Galleria Milano, Italy & others, 71; one-man show, Guggenheim Mus, New York, 74; plus many others. Teaching: Prof painting & drawing, Black Mountain Col, 46-48; assoc prof painting, drawing & design, Univ Wyo, 48-57; prof painting, drawing & design, State Univ NY Col New Paltz, 57-65; prof painting, drawing & design, Southampton Col, 65-74, retired, 74. Awards: First Hallgarten Prize for painting, Nat Acad Design, 29 & 30; First Prize for film, Metanoia, Midwest Film Festival, Univ Chicago, 63; Abstr Painting Award, Nat Inst Arts & Lett, 71. Bibliog: Lawrence Campbell (auth), Squaring the circle and vice-versa, Art News, 2/70; Knute Stiles (auth), Ilya Bolotowsky, Artforum, 3/70; Robert M Ellis (auth), Ilya Bolotowsky—paintings and columns art museum, Univ NMex, 70. Mem: Am Abstr Artists (co-founder, charter mem, former pres); Fedn Mod Painters & Sculptors (co-founder, charter mem, former vpres); Fine Arts Fedn NY (bd dirs); Nat Soc Mural Painters; Audubon Soc. Media: Oil, Acrylic, Wood, Metal. Publ: Co-auth, An interview of Naum Gabo, Harvard Univ Press & Wittenborn, 55; auth, Metanoia (film), Grove Press, 63; auth, A Russian-English dictionary of painting, Telberg Book Co, 65; auth, On neoplasticism and my own work, Leonardo, 6-7/69. Dealer: Grace Borgenicht Gallery 1018 Madison Ave New York NY 10021. Mailing Add: Box 1661 John St Sag Harbor NY 11963

BOLSTER, ELLA S
DESIGNER, WEAVER
b Helena, Mont, Dec 8, 06. Study: Mont State Univ; art metalwork with Alexander Bick, Colo State Univ; handweaving with Mary Meigs Atwater, Univ Mont; handweaving gold brocades, Nat Col Arts & Crafts, Tehran, Iran; pottery with Pieter Grueneveld, The Hague, Neth; handweaving with Anni Albers, Haystack Mountain Sch Crafts, Maine. Work: Handwoven formal tablecloth, Wichita Art Mus, Kans. Comn: Handwoven altar hanging, pulpit antipendium, burse & veil, St Mary's Episcopal Church, Arlington, Va, 62; plus several individual handweaving & stitchery commissions. Exhib: Int Textile Exhib, Greensboro, NC, 54; Fiber, Clay, Metal, St Paul Gallery & Sch Art, Minn, 55; Decorative Arts & Ceramics Exhib, Wichita, 55-57; Contemp Handweaving, Univ Nebr Art Gallery, Lincoln, 61; Textiles by Outstanding Am Designer-Weavers, Univ Gallery Fine Art, Lafayette, La, 61; plus many others including one-man shows. Teaching: Instr art metalwork, Mont State Univ, summer 44; instr canvaswork & macrame, Univ Ariz, Tucson, summer 71 & 72; also traveling lectr, Weavers' Guild, east & midwestern states & other orgns throughout the US. Awards: Purchase Prize, Ann Nat Exhib, Wichita Art Asn, 55; First in Fiber, St Paul Gallery & Sch Art, 55; First in Textiles, Nat League Am Pen Women Biennial Exhib, Smithsonian Inst, Washington, DC, 64, Miami, 74; plus many others, 54- Bibliog: Mickey Gates Maker (auth), Her weaving is a creative art, Alpha Gamma Delta Quart, 58; Mary Alice Smith (auth), Ella Bolster, experiments in many techniques, Handweaver & Craftsman Mag, 61; Opal Johnston (auth), Weaver magna cum laude, Southwest Art Scene Mag, 68; plus many others. Mem: Hon life mem Designer Weavers of Washington; Am Craftsmen's Coun; Nat League Am Pen Women; Nat Art Bd. Style & Technique: Contemporary and experimental. Mailing Add: 17610 Conestoga Dr Sun City AZ 85373

BOLTON, JAMES
PAINTER, LECTURER
b Corpus Christi, Tex, June 13, 38. Study: Univ NMex, BFA, 65 & MA, 67. Work: Univ NMex Art Gallery, Albuquerque; Yale Univ Art Gallery; Am Tel & Tel, New York; Downey Mus Art, Calif; Achenbach Found for Graphic Arts, San Francisco. Exhib: Ann Exhib Contemp Am Painting, Whitney Mus Am Art, 67; 18th Nat Print Exhib, Brooklyn Mus, 72; West Coast Artists, Museo de Bellas Artes, Caracas, Venezuela, 73; California's Representation, Santa Barbara Mus Art, 73; 4th Int Exhib Original Drawings, Mus Mod Art, Rijeka, Yugoslavia, 74. Teaching: Vis lectr painting & drawing, Univ NMex, 71-74; vis lectr painting & drawing, Calif State Col, Stanislaus, 74-75, San Jose State Univ, 76 & Tex Tech Univ, 77-78. Awards: Travel Grant, Nat Found Arts & Humanities, 66; Guest Artist, Tamarind Inst, Albuquerque, 71. Style & Technique: Realist, still-life. Media: Watercolor, Oil on Canvas, Pencil on Paper. Dealer: Hank Baum Gallery One Embarcadero Ctr San Francisco CA 94111. Mailing Add: 21 S Park San Francisco CA 94107

BONACKER, JOYCE SYBIL
PAINTER, ART DEALER
b Jerseyville, Ill, Feb 9, 32. Study: Springfield Art Mus; Drury Col, Southwestern Mo State Univ; also with Ed Whitney, Siegfried Reinhardt, Bill Armstrong, Charles Kinghan & others. Work: Sch of the Ozarks, Point Lookout, Mo; Drury Col, Springfield, Mo; Springfield Art Mus; Springfield Community Ctr; Empire Bank. Exhib: 17 State Regional Exhib, Springfield Art Mus, Mo, 69-72 & 76; 5th Ann Tulsa Regional, Okla, 71; Ann Mid-South Exhib, Memphis, Tenn, 71-72; Watercolor USA, Springfield Art Mus, 72-73; Ala Watercolor Soc, Birmingham, 73; Am Contemp Art & Crafts, Slide Libr, Fla, 73; Rocky Mountain National Watermedia, Denver, Colo, 74; Chautauqua 17th Nat, Chautauqua, NY, 74; NMex Int, E NMex Univ, Portales, 75; Southern Watercolor Soc, Nashville, Tenn, 77 & Columbus, Ga, 78. Teaching: Instr, Springfield Art Mus, 75- Pos: Co-owner, Park Central Gallery, Springfield, Mo, 72- Awards: First Place, Arts Coun of Tulsa, 71; Watercolor USA Purchase Award, Southwest Mo Mus Assoc, 72; Watercolor USA Cash Award, Am Watercolor Soc, 73. Mem: Ala Watercolor Soc; Southern Watercolor Soc; Midwest Watercolor Soc; Int Soc of Artists. Style & Technique: Mystical abstracted figures and calligraphy in ambiguous space, inspired by dreams and magic practices. Media: Acrylic, Pencil. Mailing Add: 802 Maplewood Springfield MO 65807

BONAMARTE, LOU
PAINTER, DESIGNER
b New London, Conn, Jan 18, 33. Study: Mitchell Col; also with John Pike & Frank Reilly. Work: Slater Mem Mus, Norwich, Conn. Comn: Yuletide watercolors, Gen Dynamics Corp, 66 & 68; watercolor illus, Combustion Eng, 72. Exhib: Acad Artist Asn, Springfield, Mass,

71-72; Am Watercolor Soc, 72, Knickerbocker Artist, Nat Arts Club, 72, New York; Allied Artists Am, 73-74; Rockport Art Asn, 74. Awards: Prize for watercolor, Salmagundi Club, New York, 71, 72, 73 & 74; Herb Olson Award, Am Watercolor Soc, 74; Charles H Cleaves Award, Rockport Art Asn, 74. Mem: Nat Soc Lit & Arts; Salmagundi Club; Am Artists Prof League; Allied Artists Am; Rockport Art Asn. Style & Technique: Realist. Media: Watercolor. Publ: Illusr, Mike's world your world, Educ Ventures Inc, 71; illusr, Let's give a party, Am Educ Publ, 72; illusr, introd to Psychology, Dodd Mead & Co. Mailing Add: 62 Norwood Ave New London CT 06320

BOND, ORIEL EDMUND
ILLUSTRATOR, PAINTER
b Altus, Okla, July 18, 11. Study: Rockford Col, exten courses with Marquis E Reitzel, Einar Lundquist & Alice McCurry. Work: Works in private collections only. Exhib: Six shows, Rockford Art Asn, Ill, 56-63; Ill State Fair, Springfield, 59-61; Sovereign Exhibs Ltd, Winston-Salem, NC & Williamsburg, Va, 70; Am Artists Prof League, New York, 71 & 72. Pos: Chief artist, J L Clark Mfg Co, Rockford, 38-77. Awards: Popular Award, Ill State Fair, 59; First Place Display Award, Trading Post Days, Rockton, 72; First Place & Popular Award, Colonial Village Mall, 72. Mem: Fel Am Artists Prof League; Nat Soc Lit & Arts. Media: Oil and Polymer. Mailing Add: 7816 Bond Dr The Ledges Roscoe IL 61073

BOND, ROLAND S
COLLECTOR
b Van Alstyne, Tex, Dec 25, 98. Pos: Trustee, Dallas Mus Fine Arts. Collection: Paintings by contemporary French and American artists. Mailing Add: 4600 Brookview Dr Dallas TX 75220

BONET, JORDI
SCULPTOR, MURALIST
b Barcelona, Spain, May 7, 32; Can citizen. Work: Exterior sculpted mural, Orthogenic Sch, Univ Chicago; sculpted ceramic mural, Queen's Park Bldg, Toronto; cast aluminum doors, Nat Art Ctr, Ottawa; five cast aluminum sculptures, Expo '67, Place des Nations, Montreal; sculpted cement walls, Grand Theatre Quebec. Comn: Ceramic mural, Trade Bank & Trust Co, New York, 63; cast aluminum mural, Charleston Nat Bank, WVa, 66; sculpted aluminum mural, Pac Gas & Elec Co, San Francisco, 71; ceramic mural, Zale Corp, Dallas, 71; ceramic mural, Continental Bank, Chicago, 72. Exhib: Can Govt Exhib, Triennial Milan, Italy, 68; Nat Art Gallery, Ottawa, 69; Am Inst Archit IRAIC Conv, Chicago, 69; Mus Rodin, Paris, 70; Exhib Quebec Pavilion, Expo 70, Osaka, Japan, 70. Awards: Drawing Award, Spring Salon, Montreal Mus Fine Arts, 59; Sculpture Award, Abramowitz Chap of Hadassah, 63 & 65; Allied Arts Medal, Royal Archit Inst Can, 65. Bibliog: J Folch-Ribas (auth), The Sign & the Earth, 64; Guy Robert (auth), L'infinie a Remplir, 71 & Bonet, 75; Paul Vezina (auth), Jordi Bonet, Film Off, Quebec, 72. Mem: Royal Can Acad Arts; Asn Prof Artists Quebec; Art Guild Quebec. Media: Cast Aluminum, Bronze, Fired Clay, Cement, Plastic. Mailing Add: Manoir Campbell Mont St Hilaire PQ Can

BONEVARDI, MARCELO
PAINTER, SCULPTOR
b Buenos Aires, Arg, May 13, 29. Work: Mus Mod Art, United Nations, Guggenheim Mus & Brooklyn Mus, New York; Mus d'Art Contemporain de Montreal, Can. Awards: Int Award, 10th Bienal de Sao Paulo, Brazil, 69. Style & Technique: Constructions. Media: Mixed. Mailing Add: 799 Greenwich St New York NY 10014

BONGART, SERGEI R
PAINTER, INSTRUCTOR
b Kiev, Russia. Study: Kiev Art Acad. Work: Theater Mus, Kiev, Russia; Nat Acad Design, New York; Tretyakov Gallery, Moscow; State Mus of Ukrainian Art, Kiev; Mus of Russian Art, Kiev, Russia. Exhib: Charles & Emma Frye Art Mus; Los Angeles Co Mus Art, Calif; Nat Acad Design & Metrop Mus Art, New York; M H De Young Mem Mus, San Francisco. Teaching: Instr drawing & painting, Sergei Bongart Sch Art, Santa Monica, Calif, 49- Awards: Grand Nat Gold Medal, Am Artists Prog League, New York, 59; Silver Medal of Honor, Am Watercolor Soc, 69; Winslow Home Award, Watercolor USA, 74. Bibliog: Janice Lovoos (auth), The paintings of Sergei Bongart, Am Artist, 9/62; Nancy Kalis (auth), Sergei Bongart: romantic realist with a Russian soul, Art Rev, 69; Wendon Blake (auth), Complete guide to acrylic painting, Watson-Guptill, 71. Mem: Nat Acad Design; Nat Acad Western Art; Am Watercolor Soc; Royal Soc Arts; Soc Western Artists. Media: Oil, Acrylic. Publ: Contribr, Joe Singer, auth, Painting Men's Portraits, Watson-Guptill, 77. Mailing Add: 533 W Rustic Rd Santa Monica CA 90402

BONGIORNO, LAURINE MACK
ART HISTORIAN
b Lima, Ohio, Apr 17, 03. Study: Oberlin Col, AB, 25; Radcliffe Col, PhD, 30. Teaching: Asst prof art hist, Wellesley Col, 30-42, assoc prof art hist, 42-44; lectr art hist, Oberlin Col, 55-66. Pos: Ed, Allen Art Mus Bull, 50-67. Res: Italian Renaissance sculpture; Giotto. Publ: Auth, Notes on art of Silvestro dell'Aquila, 42 & Date of altar of madonna in S M del Soccorso, 44, Art Bull; A Fifteenth century stucco & art of Verrocchio, Allen Art Mus Bull, 62; Theme of old and new law in Arena Chapel, Art Bull, 68; Umbrian statue of Saint Sebastian, Allen Art Mus Bull, 71; auth, Fruits of Idealism, Apollo, 76. Mailing Add: 19 N Park St Oberlin OH 44074

BONI, DELMAR
PAINTER, INSTRUCTOR
b Safford, Ariz, Apr 28, 48. Study: Inst Am Indian Arts, AFA(painting); Col of Santa Fe, BA(visual arts). Work: Inst Am Indian Arts Mus Gallery Honor Collection; Philbrook Indian Art Ctr; Pima Com Col. Comn: Painting, Am Jr Col Bd, Washington, DC, 72; poster, SW Asn Indian Affairs, Santa Fe, NMex, 75. Exhib: Philbrook Indian Art Show, Tulsa, Okla, 75; NMex Biennal Fine Art, Santa Fe, 75; Santa Fe Armory for the Arts, Santa Fe, NMex, 77; one-man show, One with the Earth, Inst Am Indian Arts, Santa Fe, 76. Teaching: Instr silk-screen, Inst Am Indian Art, 74-75; instr various media, Santa Fe Preparatory Sch, 77-78. Pos: Bd dir, SW Asn Indian Affairs, 77- Awards: Purchase Award, Philbrook Art Ctr, 75. Bibliog: Jamake Highwater (auth), Song From the Earth, New York Graphic Soc, 76. Dealer: Los Lalonos Gallery Santa Fe NM 87501. Mailing Add: Country Club Apts No 46 Airport Rd Santa Fe NM 87501

BONINO, ALFREDO
ART DEALER
b Naples, Italy, July 29, 25. Pos: Pres, Galeria Bonino, Buenos Aires, Arg, 45-, Rio de Janeiro, Brazil, 52 & New York, 61- Mem: Mus Mod Art, New York, Rio de Janeiro & Buenos Aires; Solomon R Guggenheim Mus. Specialty: Contemporary art. Mailing Add: 48 Great Jones St New York NY 10012

BONTECOU, LEE
ASSEMBLAGE ARTIST, SCULPTOR
b Providence, RI, Jan 15, 31. Study: Bradford Jr Col, with Robert Wade; Art Students League, with William Zorach & John Hovannes, 52-55. Work: Stedelijk Mus, Amsterdam, Holland; Albright-Knox Art Gallery, Buffalo, NY; Chase Manhattan Bank, New York; Art Inst of Chicago; Corcoran Gallery of Art, Washington, DC; Mus Mod Art & Whitney Mus Am Art, New York. Exhib: Whitney Ann, 61, 63, 64 & 66, Sculpture Ann, 68, Whitney Mus Am Art; The Art of Assemblage, 61, Americans 1963, 63-64 & The 1960s, 67, Mus Mod Art, New York; 6th Sao Paulo Biennial, 61; 1963, 63, Sculpture-A Generation of Innovation, Art Inst Chicago, 67; Corcoran Gallery Art, Washington, DC, 63; Mixed-Media & Pop Art, Albright-Knox Art Gallery, 63; Documenta III, Kassel, WGer, 64; Carnegie Inst of Technol, 70; Works on Paper, Univ NC, 71; Am Drawings: 1970-1973, Yale Univ, 73; one-man shows, Ileana Sonnabend Gallery, Paris, 65, Stadticshes Mus Leverkusen, Ger, 68, Mus Boymans-Van Beuningen, Rotterdam, Holland, 68; Kunstverein, Berlin, 68 & Mus Contemp Art, Chicago, 72; Retrospective, Mus Boymans-Van Beuningen, Rotterdam, 58. Teaching: Instr, Brooklyn Col, 71-75. Awards: Fulbright Fel, Rome, 57 & 58; L C Tiffany Grant, 59; Award, Corcoran Gallery Art, Washington, DC, 63. Dealer: Leo Castelli Inc 420 W Broadway New York NY 10012. Mailing Add: PO Box 1290 East Hampton NY 11937

BONY, JEAN VICTOR
EDUCATOR, ART HISTORIAN
b Le Mans, France, Nov 1, 08. Study: Univ Paris, licence & agregation in hist, 33; study of hist of art with Henri Focillon, 29-33. Teaching: Lectr art hist, French Inst, London, 46-61; Slade Prof Fine Art, Cambridge Univ, Eng, 58-61; prof art hist, Univ Calif, Berkeley, 62- Mem: Soc Francaise Archeol; Royal Archaeol Inst (vpres, 55-61); Col Art Asn; Soc Archit Historians; hon fel Soc of Antiquaries, London. Res: Romanesque and Gothic architecture, particularly in France and England. Publ: Co-auth, French Cathedrals, Thames & Hudson, 51; ed, H Focillon, auth, The Art of the West in the Middle Ages, Phaidon Press, 63; auth, French Gothic Architecture of the 12th and 13th Centuries, Univ Calif Press, (in press). Mailing Add: Dept of Art Hist Univ of Calif Berkeley CA 94720

BOOKATZ, SAMUEL
PAINTER, SCULPTOR
b Philadelphia, Pa, Oct 3, 10. Study: Cleveland Inst Art; Boston Mus Sch Art; Harvard Univ; Acad Grande Chaumiere & Colarossi, Paris; Am Acad Rome; also with Oskar Kokoschka Chaim Soutine & Ivan Mestrovic. Work: Corcoran Gallery Art, Phillips Gallery & Smithsonian Inst, Washington, DC; Cleveland Mus Art, Ohio; Norfolk Mus Art & Sci, Va. Comn: Portraits of Pres & Mrs F D Roosevelt, 41; murals, comn by US Govt, US Naval Hosp, Norfolk, Va & San Diego, Calif, 42-45; murals, Govt Turn Key Housing for Aged, Prince George's Co, Md & Della Ratta Off Bldg, Bethesda, Md, 71; portrait, Gov David L Lawrence, Pa, 65; portrait of Joseph H Hirshhorn, Hirshhorn Mus & Sculpture Garden, Washington, DC, 78. Exhib: One-man shows, Cleveland Mus Art, 40 & Corcoran Gallery Art, 46; Pa Acad Fine Arts, Philadelphia, 52; Va Mus Art, Richmond, 55; Baltimore Mus Art, Md, 60. Teaching: Dir art, Samuel Bookatz Sch Art, Washington, DC, 45- Pos: Govt artist & White House artist, 41-43. Awards: William Page Award & Prix de Rome Award in the Arts, Boston Mus, 37; Inst Allende Fel, 54; Ford Found Grant, 62. Style & Technique: Varied from realism to abstract. Mailing Add: 2700 Q St NW Washington DC 20007

BOOKBINDER, JACK
PAINTER, PRINTMAKER
b Odessa, Ukraine, Jan 15, 11; US citizen. Study: Univ Pa, BS(in educ); Pa Acad Fine Arts; Tyler Sch Art, Temple Univ, MFA; hon DFA, Moore Col Art, Philadelphia, 76. Work: Pa Acad Fine Arts, Philadelphia; Philadelphia Mus Art; Libr Cong & Nat Gallery Art, Washington, DC; Yale Univ Art Gallery, New Haven, Conn. Comn: Mosaic mural (with Frederick Geasland), Church of the Redeemer, Bryn Mawr, Pa, 64; painting of Hahnemann Med Col, Squibb Pharmaceut Co, 66. Exhib: One-man shows, Nessler Gallery, New York & Gross McLeaf Gallery, Philadelphia, 76; Retrospective, William Penn Mem Mus, Harrisburg, Pa, 74; 100 American Water Colorists Exhibition, Royal Acad Arts, London, 62; American Printmakers Abroad, US State Dept Exhib, 62; Two Hundred Years of American Watercolors, Metrop Mus Art, 66; Fifty American Watercolorists, Mexico City, 68; Retrospective, William Penn Mem Mus, Harrisburg, Pa, 74. Teaching: Lectr art, Barnes Found, Merion, Pa, 36-44; lectr art, Univ Pa, 47-59; lectr art, Pa Acad Fine Arts, 49-61. Pos: Consult dept educ, Philadelphia Mus Art, 45-46; spec asst to dir of art educ, Sch Dist Philadelphia, 46-59, dir of art educ, 59-77. Awards: Morris Katzman Award, Philadelphia Print Club, 74; Juv Diabetes Found Super Achiever Award, 76; Purchase Award, Bradley Univ Nat Print Exhib, 77. Bibliog: Henry Pitz (auth), Jack Bookbinder, painter and educator, Am Artists Mag, 3/61. Mem: Artists Equity Asn; Philadelphia Watercolor Club; Audubon Artists; Nat Soc Painters in Casein & Acrylic; Am Watercolor Soc; Allied Artists Am. Style & Technique: Romantic realist. Media: Oil, Casein, Lithography. Publ: Auth, Invitation to the arts & The gifted child, his education in the Philadelphia Public Schools; auth, History of sculpture & Art in the life of children, Compton's Encycl. Dealer: Newman Galleries 1625 Walnut St Philadelphia PA 19103; Jane Haslem Gallery 2121 P St NW Washington DC 20037. Mailing Add: 323 S Smedley St Philadelphia PA 19103

BOONE, MARY
ART DEALER
b Pa, Oct 29, 51. Collections Arranged: Group show, Tex Gallery, Houston, 77; New Work/New York, Los Angeles, Calif, 77; Painting 75/76/77, Sarah Lawrence Col, Bronxville, NY, 77; Am Found for the Arts, Miami, Fla & Contemp Arts Ctr, Cincinnati, Ohio, 77; Painting, Hal Bromm Gallery, New York, 77. Pos: Dir, Mary Boone Gallery. Specialty: Contemporary art. Mailing Add: 420 W Broadway New York NY 10012

BOOTH, BILL
EDUCATOR
b Wallins Creek, Ky, June 20, 35. Study: Cumberland Jr Col, Williamsburg, Ky, 5[illegible] Eastern Ky State Univ, Richmond, AB, 60; George Peabody Col, Nashville, Tenn, MA, 64, EdS, 65; Univ Ga, Athens, PhD, 70. Teaching: Instr art appreciation, George Peabody Col, 63-65; asst prof art hist, Wis State Univ, Oshkosh, 65-68; prof art hist & head dept, Morehead State Univ, Ky, 70- Mem: Col Art Asn; Cumberland Col Alumni Asn (pres & vpres, 62-63); Am Fedn Arts. Res: Frank Duveneck, 1848-1919. Mailing Add: UPO Box 714 Morehead State Univ Morehead KY 40351

BOOTH, CAMERON
PAINTER
b Erie, Pa, Mar 11, 92. Study: Art Inst Chicago, 12-17; also with Andre L'Hote, Paris, 27 & Hans Hofmann, Munich, Ger, 28. Work: Minneapolis Art Inst, Minn; Guggenheim Mus, New York; Walker Art Ctr, Minneapolis; Butler Mus Am Art, Youngstown, Ohio; Univ Minn, Minneapolis. Exhib: Five shows, Carnegie Inst Int, 23-64; 16 American Cities, Mus Mod Art, New York, 33; retrospective, Am Fedn Arts, 61; American Abstract Expressionists,

Imagists, 62; Art Across America, Mead Corp, 65. Teaching: Instr drawing & painting, Minneapolis Sch Art, 22-28; instr drawig & painting, Art Students League, 44-48; instr drawing & painting, Queens Col, 46-47; instr drawing & painting, Univ Minn, 48-60; vis artist, Univ Calif, Berkeley, 57-59. Awards: John Simon Guggenheim Mem Found Fel, 40. Bibliog: Booth (monogr), Am Fedn Arts, 61. Mem: Fedn Mod Sculptors & Painters. Style & Technique: Traditional. Media: Oil. Dealer: Osborne Gallery 1074 Grand Ave St Paul MN 55105. Mailing Add: 3408 Park Terr Minneapolis MN 55406

BOOTH, GEORGE WARREN
PAINTER, ILLUSTRATOR
b Omaha, Nebr. Study: Ohio Univ, teaching fel, with L C Mitchell, AB & MA; Chouinard Sch of Art, with Pruett Carter; John Huntington Polytech, with Carl Gaertner. Exhib: Nat Acad of Design, Am Watercolor Soc & Allied Artists of Am, New York; Calif Watercolor Soc, Los Angeles & San Francisco Mus of Art. Pos: Art dir, J Walter Thompson Co, New York, 48-59. Awards: Gold Medal & Kerwin H Fulton Medal, Art Dir Club of New York, 54; Grand Award, 100 Best Posters of the Year, Outdoor Advert Asn of Am, 54. Bibliog: Edward L Bowen (auth), George Warren Booth, The Blood-Horse, 12/74; Linette Albert (auth), George Warren Booth: the thoroughbred scene, Am Artist, 7/75. Mem: Soc Illusr. Style & Technique: Specializing in the thoroughbred racing scene, polo, foxhunting. Media: Acrylic, Watercolor, Oil. Dealer: Petersen Galleries 9433 Wilshire Blvd Beverly Hills CA 90212; Venable-Neslage Galleries 1742 Connecticut Ave NW Washington DC 20009. Mailing Add: 314 E 41st St New York NY 10017

BOOTH, JUDITH GAYLE
CURATOR
b Pawhuska, Okla, Nov 18, 42. Study: Cent State Univ, Edmund, Okla, BA; Univ Mo, Columbia; Univ NMex, Albuquerque, MA. Pos: Cur, Tamarind Inst, 71-72, asst dir & cur, 72-76, asst dir, 76- Mailing Add: 1109 57th St NW Albuquerque NM 87105

BOOTH, LAURENCE OGDEN
SCULPTOR, ARCHITECT
b Chicago, Ill, July 5, 36. Study: Stanford Univ, BA, 58; Mass Inst Technol, BArch, 60. Work: Sch Social Sci, Univ Chicago. Exhib: Young Structurists, Ore & Chicago, 68; one-man show, Kansas City Libr, 68; Black & White, Kouler Gallery, Chicago, 70; Beloit Col, 71; Group 5, Chicago, 71-75; Richard Gray Gallery, 76; Chicago 7 Architects, Walter Kelly Gallery & Richard Gray Gallery, 77. Teaching: Instr archit, Univ Ill, Chicago Circle, 69-71. Bibliog: Amy Goldin (auth), Vitality vs greasy kid stuff, Art Gallery Mag, 72. Mem: Ill Arts Coun. Media: Plexiglas, Felt, Steel. Publ: Auth, Spiritual content of order, Arc Mag, 68; auth, Review of Stanley Tigerman sculpture, Art Scene Mag, 69. Mailing Add: 553 W Fullerton Chicago IL 60614

BOOTHE, POWER ROBERT
PAINTER
b Mar 12, 45; US citizen. Study: Colo Col, BFA, 67; Whitney Mus, independent study prog, 67-68. Work: Guggenheim Mus; Hirshhorn Mus; Chase Manhattan Bank; New York Bank for Savings. Exhib: Theodoron Award Show, 71, Art of this Decade, 74 & New Acquisitions, 75, Guggenheim Mus, New York; Painting Endures, Inst of Contemp Art, Boston, 75; one-man exhibs, A M Sachs Gallery, 73, 74, 76 & 77, Pvt Images, Los Angeles Co Mus of Art, Calif, 77 & Painting Show, PS1 Gallery, Brooklyn, NY, 77. Awards: Nat Endowment Arts Grant, 75. Bibliog: Barbara Thompson (auth), Power Boothe at Sachs, Art in Am, 3-4/75; Allen Ellenzweig (auth), Power Boothe, Arts Mag, 12/77; Hal Foster (auth), Power Boothe, Artforum, 12/77. Style & Technique: Paintings built up of overlapping layers of paint. Media: Acrylic, Oil. Mailing Add: 49 Crosby St New York NY 10012

BOPP, EMERY
PAINTER, EDUCATOR
b Corry, Pa, May 13, 24. Study: Pratt Inst Art Sch, NY; Yale Sch Painting & Design, with Josef Albers & William de Kooning, BFA; NY Univ; Rochester Inst Technol, MFA. Work: Addison Gallery Am Art, Andover, Mass; Greenville Co Mus Art, SC; SC Arts Comn Collection. Exhib: Bob Jones Univ, 62-64; Butler Inst Am Art Exhib, 66; Birmingham Mus Art, 66; Southeastern Exhib, Atlanta, Ga, 67; Greenville Co Mus Art, 68; plus others. Teaching: Chmn div art, Bob Jones Univ, 55- Awards: Purchase Award, Hunter Gallery Art, Chattanooga, Tenn, 65; Merit Award, Southeastern Exhib, Atlanta, 67; Purchase Award, Greenville Co Mus Art, 68. Mem: Southeastern Col Art Conf; Guild SC Artists; Col Art Asn Am; Cooperstown Art Asn, NY. Mailing Add: Div of Art Bob Jones Univ Greenville SC 29614

BORCOMAN, JAMES
CURATOR
b Ontario, Can, Jan 17, 26. Study: Univ NB, BA; Univ BC, Vancouver; State Univ NY Buffalo, MFA; hist photog with Beaumont Newhall & Nathan Lyons. Collections Arranged: Goodridge Roberts Retrospective, 1969, Nat Gallery Can, 69, Four 19th Century Canadian Photographers, 70 & Photographs from the Collection, 75; The Photograph as Object traveling show (with catalog), 69; Nathan Lyons: Notations in Passing traveling exhib (with catalog), 72; Charles Nègre (with catalog), Ottawa, 76; Brit Photographs from the Collection, 1844-1914, 76; Recent Acquisitions, 77; The Painter as Photogr: D O Hill, Charles Nègre, Auguste Salzmann (with monograph), 78. Teaching: Part time lectr hist photog & photog workshop, Univ Ottawa, Ont, 71-75. Pos: Educ officer, Nat Gallery Can, 60-66, dir educ dept, 66-69 & cur photographs, 67- Awards: Prize for Distinguished Achievement in Photog Hist, Photog Hist Soc of NY; Seal of City of Arles, France; Bronze Medal, Leipzig Bk Fair. Bibliog: Peter Bunnell (auth), The National Gallery photographic collection, An inquiry into the aesthetics of photography (series), Artscanada, 75. Mem: Soc Photog Educ; hon mem Asn Charles Nègre, France. Res: Prior to 1969, Canadian art; from 1969 on, history of photography. Publ: Purism vs pictorialism, some notes on photographic aesthetics, An inquiry into the aesthetics of photography (series), Artscanada, 75; auth, Notes on the early use of combination printing, In: 100 Years of Photographic History, 75. Mailing Add: Nat Gallery Can Ottawa ON Can

BORDEAUX, JEAN LUC
ART HISTORIAN, CURATOR
b Laval, France, Feb 13, 38. Study: Univ Paris, Fac Sci, PCB, 60; Mus Nat d'Art Mod, Paris, study of museology with Jean Cassou, 58-60; Iowa State Univ, BS(journalism), 64; Ariz State Univ, MA(art hist), 66; Univ Calif, Los Angeles, PhD(art hist), 70. Exhib: Exhib Organized & Curated: Cartoons from the Jerome K Muller Collection, 72, Baroque Masters from the J Paul Getty Mus, 73, Greek & Roman Portraits from the J Paul Getty Mus, 73, Art of India, Selections from the Heeramaneck, 74, Hans Burkhardt Retrospective (1928-1973), 73, First Calif Sculpture Invitational (State Grant), 74, Charles Garabedian Retrospective (1963-74), 74, Mark Tobey (prints), 75, DeWain Valentine: Camera Obscura, 75, A Collection without Walls: Problems in Connoisseurship, 76, Fundamental Aspects of Modernism (1908 Picasso to F Bacon—Swiss pvt collection), 77, Fifth Nat Los Angeles Printmaking Soc, 78, Harry Callahan Retrospective with MOMA, 78, Calif State Univ, Northridge. Teaching: Instr art hist, Univ Calif, Los Angeles, 69-72; prof art hist, Calif State Univ, Northridge, 69- Pos: Art critic & writer, Connaissance des Arts, 55-; lectr, J Paul Getty Mus, Malibu, Calif, 67-68, asst cur paintings, 69-72; dir, Fine Arts Gallery, Calif State Univ, Northridge, 72-; guest cur, Calif Palace of the Legion of Honor, San Francisco, 75. Awards: Kress Fel, Louvre, Hermitage & Pushkin Mus (France & Soviet Union), 70-71. Mem: Col Art Asn; Art Hist from Southern Calif; Western Asn Am Mus. Res: French painting from 17th to early 19th centuries. Interest: Contemporary art. Publ: Auth, articles in Burlington Mag, Gazette des Beaux Arts, Art Int, Art in Am, J of J Paul Getty Mus & Am Art Rev; co-auth with Prof Jiri Frel, Rodin's Rodin, The Maryhill Collection, J Paul Getty Mus, 76. Mailing Add: 640 Kingman Ave Santa Monica CA 90402

BOREN, JAMES ERWIN
PAINTER, LECTURER
b Waxahachie, Tex, Sept 26, 21. Study: Kansas City Art Inst & Sch Design, BFA & MFA; Univ Kansas City. Work: Nat Cowboy Hall of Fame, Oklahoma City; Diamond M Found, Snyder, Tex; Read Mullin Mus, Phoenix, Ariz; Rockwell Mus, Corning, NY. Comn: Many pvt comns. Exhib: Two-man show, Nat Cowboy Hall of Fame, 69; one-man show, Tex Art Gallery, Dallas, 69-78; Cowboy Artists of Am, Nat Cowboy Hall of Fame, 70-72 & Phoenix Mus, Ariz, 73-78; Whitney Mus, Cody, Wyo, summer 73; Mont Hist Soc, Helena, 73. Collections Arranged: National Cowboy Hall of Fame Permanent Collection; Joe Beeler, Cowboy Artists of Am Ann Show, 65, Necolai Fechin, 68, Harry Jackson, 68 & Frank Hoffman, 69. Teaching: Art instr, St Mary Col, Kans, 51-53. Pos: Concept illusr, Martin-Marietta Co, Denver, Colo, 56-64; art dir, Nat Cowboy Hall of Fame, 65-69. Awards: Excellence Award, Soc Tech Writers & Publ, 64; First Place Watercolor, Cowboy Artists Am Ann, Nat Cowboy Hall of Fame, 68-71 & Phoenix Art Mus, 73 & 76; First Place/Mixed Media, Cowboy Artists of Am Competition, 73. Bibliog: Watercolor demonstration, Channel 4, Oklahoma City, 69; Dean Krakel (auth), James Boren a Study in Discipline, Northland Press, 69; Joe M Dealey, Jr (auth), The treasured West of James Boren, Southwest Scene, Dallas Morning News, 9/17/72. Mem: Cowboy Artists Am (secy-treas, 69-70, pres, 73-74, dir, 74-75). Style & Technique: Various media in a realistic manner with slightly impressionistic style; basic modern concepts of design and composition. Media: Watercolor, Oil. Publ: The Cowboy in Art, 68; illusr, James Boren: A Study in Discipline, Northland Press, 69; illusr, Harmsen's Western Americana, 71; illusr, Ariz Hwys, 12/73; illusr, How Come I Wrote a Book, 74; illusr, Royal B Hassrick, auth, Western Painting Today, Watson-Guptill, 75. Mailing Add: PO Box 533 Clifton TX 76634

BORETZ, NAOMI
PAINTER, EDUCATOR
b New York, NY. Study: Art Students League; Boston Mus Sch; Rutgers Univ; City Col New York, MA(fine arts), 71. Work: Joslyn Art Mus, Omaha, Nebr; Nanuet Nat Bank, NY; Hove Mus Art, Sussex, Eng; Glasgow Mus, Scotland; Dundee Mus, Scotland. Exhib: One-woman shows, Contemporary Artists, Westminster Arts Coun, London, 72, Nicholas Roerich Mus, New York, 75 & Hudson River Mus, 75; Awards Exhib, Brooklyn Mus Art, 72; Contemporary Am Watercolorists, Bard Col, 73; Randolph-Macon Woman's Col, Va, 77; Katonah Gallery, NY, 78; Queen's Col, New York, 78; plus many one-woman exhib in US & Eng & many group shows. Teaching: Instr watercolor, City Col New York, 68-71 & Princeton Art Asn, 72-73; asst prof art & dir art prog & art hist, Rider Col, Lawrenceville, NJ, 73- Awards: Watercolor Award, Brooklyn Mus Art, 71; Fel, Va Ctr for Creative Arts, 73 & 75; Fel, Ossabaw Proj Found, 75. Bibliog: Ian Woodcock (auth), rev in Arts Mag, London, 7/72; Cantilevers, article in arts column, Staffordshire Sentinel, Eng, 7/72; Brit Broadcasting Co Radio interview, 72-73; plus others. Mem: Col Art Asn Am; Free Painters & Sculptors Gt Brit. Style & Technique: Large canvases, brushwork; abstracts in dry technique, sometimes mixed media. Media: Acrylic, Watercolor. Publ: Illusr, Perspectives of New Music, 74 & 75; contribr articles in Leonardo, 76- Dealer: Harry Smith Esq c/o Pentagon Gallery Staffordshire England. Mailing Add: 15 Southern Way Princeton NJ 08540

BORGATTA, ISABEL CASE
SCULPTOR, EDUCATOR
b Madison, Wis, Nov 21, 21. Study: Smith Col, 39-40; Yale Univ Sch Fine Arts, BFA, 44; New Sch Social Res, 44-45; Studio of Jose de Creeft, 44-45; Art Student League, 46. Work: Wadsworth Atheneum, Hartford, Conn; Yeshiva Univ, New York; Krannert Mus, Univ Ill, Champaign; Norfolk Mus, Va; Benton Mus, Univ Conn. Comn: Mem sculpture, City New Rochelle Pub Schs, 72; Book-of-the-Month Club Limited Editions, 75. Exhib: Pa Acad Fine Arts Ann, Philadelphia, 49-55; Whitney Mus Am Art, 51-52; Hudson River Mus, 60-61; retrospective, Briarcliff Col Mus, 71; one-woman shows, Frank Rehn Gallery, 68, 71, 74 & 77, New York Cult Ctr, 73, Brooklyn Mus, 75, Gen Elecric Hq, 77 & Benson Gallery, 78; Ingber Gallery, 77; plus many others. Teaching: Instr art, Halsted Sch, Yonkers, NY, 45-49; lectr sculpture, City Col New York, 60-71; assoc prof, Col New Rochelle, 73-78, prof, 78- Awards: First Prize for sculpture, Hudson River Mus, 60; Jacques Lipchitz Award, 61; Edward MacDowell Fels, 68, 73 & 74; Yaddo Fel, 71 & 72. Bibliog: Mark van Doren (auth), The sculptures of Isabel Case Borgatta, Galerie St Etienne Brochure, 54; William D Allen (auth), Borgatta's marbles, Arts Mag, 68; James R Mellow (auth), article in New York Times, 74. Mem: Sculptors League; Women in the Arts; Artists Equity; Sculptors Guild. Style & Technique: Large stretch knit sculptures, stuffed & stretched over tempered masonite. Media: Stone, Wood. Dealer: Frank Rehn Gallery 655 Madison Ave New York NY 10022. Mailing Add: 617 West End Ave New York NY 10024

BORGATTA, ROBERT EDWARD
PAINTER, EDUCATOR
b Havana, Cuba, Jan 11, 21; US citizen. Study: Nat Acad Design, 34-37; NY Univ, Sch Archit & Allied Arts, BFA, 40, Inst Fine Arts, 46-53; Yale Univ Sch Fine Arts, MFA, 42. Work: Norfolk Mus, Va; Ford Found. Comn: Mural & sculpture, Gutman Assocs, New York; stained glass design, Temple Emanu-el, Yonkers, NY, 60. Exhib: Audubon Artists Ann, 53-72; Whitney Mus Am Art Prizewinners Show, 54; Schettini Gallery, Milan, Italy, 57; Corcoran Gallery of Art, 68; one-man shows, Babcock Galleries, 64 & 68 & Southern Vt Art Ctr, 77. Teaching: Prof painting & drawing, City Col New York, 47- Awards: Tiffany Fel, 42; Emily Lowe Found Award, 57; Newman Medal, Nat Soc Painters in Casein, 69. Bibliog: American artists in Italian exhibit, Valligia Diplomatica, 10/57; An artist in his studio, House Beautiful, 3/60; John Canaday (auth), review in New York Times, 3/15/69. Mem: Audubon Artists; Am Watercolor Soc; Nat Soc Painters in Casein. Media: Oil, Marble. Dealer: Babcock Galleries 805 Madison Ave New York NY 10051. Mailing Add: 56 E 11th St New York NY 10003

BORGENICHT, GRACE (GRACE BORGENICHT BRANDT)
ART DEALER, COLLECTOR
b New York, NY, Jan 25, 15. Study: Columbia Univ, MA, 37; also with Andre Lhote, Paris, 34. Pos: Dir & owner, Grace Borgenicht Gallery, 51- Specialty: Contemporary American

painting and sculpture. Collection: Cezanne, Matisse, Picasso, de Kooning, Bonnard, Mondrian, Degas, Vuillard, Avery, Leger, de Rivera. Mailing Add: 1018 Madison Ave New York NY 10021

BORGLUM, JAMES LINCOLN DE LA MOTHE
SCULPTOR, PHOTOGRAPHER
b Stamford, Conn, Apr 9, 12. Study: With father 12 years and in Europe, 29-31. Comn: Statue, Our Lady of Loreto, La Bahia Mission, Goliad, Tex; statue of Gladys Porter, founder of Gladys Porter Zoo, Bronswville, Tex; statue of St Francis, Rockport, Tex; designed carving of world's largest-known ruby (22,000 karat), Ada Wilson, Corpus Christi, Tex. Exhib: Color photog exhib in salon at Milwaukee, Rochester, NY & New York. Pos: With, Mt Rushmore Nat Mem, Black Hills, SDak, 32-, in-chg of measurement and enlarging models, 34-38, appt supt, Mem Comn, 38, appt to complete Mem following father's death, 40, mem, Comn, 60-; tech adv, carving world's largest known sapphires in likeness of Washington, Jefferson & Eisenhower. Mem: Mt Rushmore Nat Mem Soc (trustee). Publ: Cover for This Week & Sat Eve Post; auth, My Father's Mountain, 65; co-auth, with June Zeitner, Mt Rushmore, Borglums Unfinished Dream, North Plains Publ, 76; auth, Mt Rushmore, The Story Behind the Scenery, K C Publ, 77. Mailing Add: Box 908 La Feria TX 78559

BORGO, LUDOVICO
ART HISTORIAN
b Naples, Iltaly, Aug 30, 30; US citizen. Study: Wash Univ, BA; Harvard Univ, PhD. Teaching: Asst prof Renaissance art, Wash Univ, St Louis, Mo, 66-69; assoc prof Renaissance art, Brandeis Univ, Waltham, 69- Publ: Auth, The Works of Mariotto Albertinelli, Garland, 76. Mailing Add: 5 Solon St Wellesley MA 02181

BORIS, BESSIE
PAINTER
b Johnstown, Pa. Study: Art Student League, 40-42; study with George Grosz & Vaclav Vytlacil. Work: Mills Col, New York; Norfolk Mus Arts & Sci, Va; Univ Mass, Amherst; NY Univ Collection; Chase Manhattan Bank, New York. Exhib: Corcoran Gallery of Art, Washington, DC, 49; Inst Contemp Art, Boston, 51; Mills Gallery, New York, 60; Cober Gallery, New York, 60, 61, 63, 65 & 68; Pa Acad Fine Arts Ann Drawing Show, 63 & 69; Am Acad Arts & Lett, Childe Hassam Show, New York, 70-72 & 76; Babcock Gallery, New York, 70; Image Gallery Stockbridge, Mass, 71, 76 & 77; Touchstone Gallery, New York, 76. Awards: First Painting Award, Butler Inst Am Art, 46; First Prize Purchase Award, Mo Valley Artists, Mulvane Mus, 48; Dana Watercolor Medal, Pa Acad Fine Arts, 61; plus others. Bibliog: Articles in Chrysalis, 51 & The Insiders, vol 4, La State Univ Press, 60. Style & Technique: Expressionist style in mixed media. Media: Acrylic, Ink, Pastel. Mailing Add: Box 187 Stockbridge MA 01262

BORN, JAMES E
SCULPTOR
b Toledo, Ohio, Nov 16, 34. Study: Toledo Mus Sch, cert; Univ Toledo, BA; Univ Iowa, Iowa City, MFA. Work: Univ Iowa, Iowa City. Exhib: San Diego Fine Arts Mus, Calif, 65; All-Mich II, Flint Art Inst, 75; 22nd Drawing & Sculpture Exhib, Ball State Univ, Muncie, Ind, 76; 9th Biennial Michiana, S Bend Art Ctr, Ind, 76; Sculpture & Ceramics Exhib, Butler Inst Am Art, Youngstown, Ohio, 76; 19th Ann Mich Exhib, Midland Art Ctr, 78; 24th Drawing & Sculpture Show, Ball State Univ, 78; one-man shows, State Univ Calif, Humboldt, 63, Calif Western Univ, San Diego, 65, State Univ Calif, Stanislaus, 65 & Cent Mich Univ, 69 & 77. Teaching: Asst prof sculpture, painting, design & drawing, Univ Calif at Humboldt, Arcata, 62-64 & Calif Western Univ, San Diego, 64-65; asst prof sculpture, design & painting, Univ Calif at Stanislaus, Turlock, 65-68; assoc prof sculpture, Cent Mich Univ, Mt Pleasant, 68-76, acting chmn, 72-74, prof sculpture, 76- Awards: Third Prize Painting, 13th Ann Exhib, SW Tex Univ, San Marcos, 76; First Prize Sculpture, 41st Nat, Cooperstown, NY, 76. Mem: Col Art Asn; Mid-Am Art Asn; Southern Sculptors Asn. Style & Technique: Bronze sculpture using the lost wax casting process. Media: Bronze. Mailing Add: 502 S University Mt Pleasant MI 48858

BORNE, MORTIMER
SCULPTOR, PAINTER
b Poland; US citizen. Study: Art Student League; Nat Acad Design; Ecole Beaux Arts. Work: Chromatic wood sculpture, Munic Mus Ramat-Gan, 70 & Bar-Ilan Univ, 73, Israel; oil paintings, Univ Judaism Mus, Los Angeles; color drypoints, Nat Gallery Art & drypoints, Libr Cong, Washington, DC; drypoints & color drypoints, Metrop Mus Art, New York. Exhib: One-man shows, Spec Exhib of Drypoints, Corcoran Gallery Art, Washington, DC, 41, drypoints, Mus Fine Arts, Montreal, Can, 42, Color Drypoints—A New Medium, US Nat Mus, Smithsonian Inst, Washington, 44 & color drypoints, Currier Gallery, Manchester, NH. Teaching: Lectr art, New Sch, New York, 45-67. Awards: Talcott Prize, 39 & Noyes Prize, 43, Soc Am Etchers. Bibliog: Leila Mechlin (auth), The art world, Washington Sun Star, 12/10/44; H M (auth), Mortimer Borne and a note on color prints, New York Pub Libr Bull, 5/44; The chromatic wood sculpture of Mortimer Borne, Nat Hist, 11/70. Style & Technique: Originator of color drypoint, chromatic wood sculpture, convex canvas painting, constructive woodcut; various degrees of representation and abstraction. Publ: Auth, Idiomatic specialization, 52; auth, Modern art goes below the surface, Rotarian, 10/60; auth, New art techniques, 69 & auth, Chromatic versus polychrome sculpture, 71 & Convex canvas painting, 74, Leonardo Mag. Dealer: Tappan Zee Art Ctr Nyack NY 10960. Mailing Add: 107 S Broadway Nyack NY 10960

BORNSTEIN, ELI
EDUCATOR, SCULPTOR
b Milwaukee, Wis, Dec 28, 22. Study: Univ Wis, BS, 45 & MS, 54; Art Inst Chicago; Univ Chicago, 43; Acad Montmartre of Fernand Leger, Paris, 51; Acad Julien, Paris, 52. Work: Walker Art Ctr, Minneapolis, Minn; Nat Gallery Can, Ottawa. Comn: Aluminum construction, Sask Teacher's Fedn, Saskatoon, 56; structurist relief, Univ Sask, Saskatoon, 58; structurist relief, Int Air Terminal, Winnipeg. Exhib: Retrospective 1941-1964, Mendel Art Gallery, Saskatoon, 64; one-man shows, Kazimir Gallery, Chicago, 65 & 67; Nat Gallery Can Biennial, Ottawa, 67; 2nd Int Biennial, Medellin, Colombia, 70; Can Cult Centre, Paris, France, 76; Glenbow-Alta Inst, Calgary, 76. Teaching: Instr drawing, painting & sculpture, Milwaukee Art Inst, 43-47; instr design, Univ Wis, 49; prof art, Univ Sask, 50-, head dept art, 63-71. Pos: Ed, The Structurist, 60- Awards: Allied Arts Medal, Royal Archit Inst Can, 68; hon mention, 2nd Int Biennial Exhib, Medellin, Colombia, 70; Gov Gen's Queen Elizabeth Silver Jubilee Medal, 77. Publ: Auth, articles, In: The Structurist No 1-14; auth, Structurist art and creative integration, Art Int, 67; auth, Notes on structurist process, DATA, directions in art, theory and aesthetics, Faber & Faber, Ltd, 1968; auth, Notes on structurist vision, Can Art Today, Studio Int, 69; auth, Toward an organic art, 71, The color molecule in art, 73-74 & Art Toward Nature, 75-76. The Structurist. Mailing Add: Box 378 Univ of Sask Saskatoon SK Can

BOROCHOFF, (IDA) SLOAN
PAINTER
US citizen. Study: High Mus Art, 39; Univ Ga, 39-40; Ga State Univ, 40; Chicago Sch Interior Decorating, dipl, 66; Atlanta Art Inst, 68. Work: Ga Inst Technol, Vet Admin & Lovett Sch, Atlanta; The Temple, Tucson, Ariz; Nat Acad Eng, Washington, DC. Comn: Noah's Ark (print), Atlanta Jewish Welfare Fedn, 71; painting, Am Art Campaign, Atlanta, 72. Exhib: One-woman shows, Dzikalas Gallery, 61, Ga Inst Technol Student Ctr & Lovett Sch Show, 71 & 75; 3rd Nat Art Competition, B'nai B'rith Woman, 65 & Int Platform Asn Art Exhib, 71, Washington, DC. Teaching: Lectr, schs & pvt parties, 70- Pos: Vpres, Designs Unlimited, Inc, Atlanta, 64-; chairwoman, Dogwood Festival Nat Juried Art Show & Childrens Art Show; columnist, Profile, A Synagogue Mag & Northside Neighbor Newspapers; pres, Sloan Borochoff Gallery; auth & artist, Atlanta Playhouse Theatre Ltd, 75- Awards: Award for Three Boats, Sandy Springs Jr Woman's Club, 71; Award for Designs in Art, Scottdale Enterprises, Inc, 72; Leading Lady, Atlanta JC Singles, 76. Mem: Atlanta Col Arts; Atlanta Artists Club; Atlanta Writers Club; Atlanta Music Club (co-ed newslett, 70-); Atlanta Press Club; Womans CofC (chmn fine arts comt). Style & Technique: Miscellaneous printmaker and painter. Media: Oil. Publ: Auth, Story prints, 69-71; auth, Story graphics, 71 & 75. Mailing Add: 3450 Old Plantation Rd NW Atlanta GA 30327

BOROFSKY, JON
PAINTER
b Boston, Mass, 42. Study: Carnegie Mellon Univ, BFA, 64; Ecole de Fontainbleau, summer 64; Yale Sch Art & Archit, MFA, 66. Exhib: Wadsworth Atheneum, Hartford, Conn, 66; 557, 087, Seattle Art Mus & Vancouver Art Gallery, 70; Autogeography, Whitney Mus Am Art, New York, 75; Int Tendencies 72-76, Venice Biennale, Italy, 76; Soho, Akademie der Kunste, West Berlin & La Mus, Humlebaek, Denmark, 76; one-man shows, Paula Cooper Gallery, New York, 75 & 76, Wadsworth Atheneum, 76, Univ Calif, Irvine, 77, Protetch-McIntosh Gallery, Washington, DC, 78. Teaching: Instr, Sch Visual Arts, New York, 69-77; instr, Calif Inst Arts, Valencia, 77- Bibliog: Lucy Lippard (auth), Six Years: The Dematerialization of the Art Object from 1966 to 1972, Praeger, New York, 73 & Jonathan Borofsky at 2,096,974, Artforum, 11/74; Mark Rosenthal (auth), Jon Borofsky, Matrix 18, Wadsworth Atheneum, 4-5/76. Mailing Add: c/o Paula Cooper Gallery 155 Wooster St New York NY 10012

BOROS, BILLI (MRS PHILIP BISACCIO)
PAINTER, WRITER
b New York, NY. Study: Art Student League, with Edwin Dickinson, Reginald Marsh & Iver Rose; Aviano Acad Art. Work: Private collections only. Exhib: Studio 41, the Cortile; Nat Arts Club, 65; Am Artists Prof League, 65-67; Nat Art League, 69; Catharine Lorillard Wolfe Art Club, 66 & 69; plus others. Pos: Publ, Art Times, 58-60, 63-64; dir, Grafton Potter Art Gallery, 70- Awards: Catharine Lorillard Wolfe Art Club Award, 69; Am Artist's Prof League Award, 77. Mem: Am Art Prof League; life mem Art Student League. Publ: Auth, Boros' Hall (monthly column), Grafton Potter Art Gallery, 71- Mailing Add: 101 W 78th St New York NY 10024

BORSTEIN, ELENA
PAINTER, LECTURER
b Hartford, Conn, Feb 5, 46. Study: Skidmore Col, BS; Univ Pa, BFA & MFA. Work: Am Acad Arts & Lett; Univ Idaho Mus; Neuberger Mus; Albright Col. Exhib: Contemporary Reflections, Aldrich Mus Art, Ridgefield, Conn, 74; Hassam Purchase Fund Exhibit, Am Acad Arts & Lett, New York, 75; Year of the Woman, Bronx Mus, 75; Point of View, Portland Mus Art, Maine, 75; 14 Am Artists, Corcoran Gallery/Aarhus Kunstmuseum Traveling Exhib, 77; City Univ New York Grad Ctr, 77; WCA Group Show, Bronx Mus, 77; Allessandra Gallery, New York, 77; André Zarre Gallery, New York, 77; Albright Col, Pa, 77; one-woman shows, Soho 20 Gallery, New York, 74-75, Max Protetch Gallery, Washington, DC, 76 & André Zarre Gallery, New York, 78. Teaching: Lectr painting & photog, York Col, City Univ New York, 70- Pos: Art consult, Aarhus Kunstmuseum, Denmark, 74-75. Awards: Childe Hassam Purchase Award, Am Acad Arts & Lett, 75. Mem: Assoc mem Soho 20 Gallery; André Zarre Gallery; Col Art Asn (mem, Women's Caucus). Style & Technique: Architectural spaces in acrylics and pastels. Mailing Add: 487 Broadway New York NY 10013

BOSA, LOUIS
PAINTER
b Codroipo Udine, Italy, Apr 2, 05; US citizen. Study: Acad Delle Belle Arte, Venice, Italy; Art Students League. Work: Metrop Mus, New York; Whitney Mus, New York; Notre Dame Univ Mus; Butler Mus, Ohio; Univ Ill. Exhib: Acad Art & Lett, 48; Univ Ill, 49; Hallmark Int Competition, 49, 55 & 58; Nat Acad Design, 54, 60 & 61. Teaching: Instr painting, Art Students League, 39-51; instr painting, Parsons Sch Design, NY, 3 years; prof advan painting, Cleveland Inst Art, Ohio, 54-69. Awards: Portraits of Am Award, Pepsi Cola, 44; Acad Arts & Lett Award, 48; Los Angeles Co Fair Award, 48. Bibliog: Life follows artist home to Italy, Life Mag, 50-51; Paul Cummings (auth), Contemporary American Artists, St Martin's Press, 66; Edmund Feldman (auth), Arts as Image & Idea, Prentice-Hall, 67. Mem: Nat Acad Design NY; Audubon Artist NY (bd dirs); Art Students League. Style & Technique: A personal style with modern shapes; exten- sive use of palette knife in oils and uses of glazes and acrylics. Media: Oil, Acrylic. Dealer: Frank Oehlschlaeger Gallery 107 E Oak Chicago IL 60611; Harmond Gallery 1258 Third St S Naples FL 33940. Mailing Add: Lonely Cottage Dr Upper Black Eddy PA 18972

BOSIN, BLACKBEAR
PAINTER, DESIGNER
b Anadarko, Okla, June 5, 21. Work: Wichita Art Mus, Kans; Wichita Art Asn; Philbrook Art Ctr, Tulsa, Okla; Heard Mus, Phoenix; Whitney Gallery of Western Art, Cody, Wyo. Comn: Sculpture design for city, Kans Gas & Elec, Wichita, 69; mural, comn by Schafer, Schirmer & Eflin for Farmers Credit Land Bank, Wichita, 72; painting, Southern Plains Mus, Anadarko, 72. Exhib: Festival of Arts, White House, Washington, DC, 65; Whitney Gallery of Western Art, 66; Nat Indian Ann, Philbrook Art Ctr, 67; Heard Mus, 67; Wichita Art Asn, 71. Awards: Grand Award, Philbrook Art Ctr, 59-63; Waite Phillips Special Indian Artists Award, 67. Bibliog: Articles in Life Int, 60 & Newsweek; Lilian Westphal (auth), article in Woche, 72. Mem: Wichita Artists Guild (vpres, 63-66); Wichita Advert Asn. Media: Watercolor, Gouache, Acrylic, Charcoal. Res: American Indian in the Great Plains Region. Collection: American Indian artifacts. Mailing Add: 710 W Douglas Wichita KS 67203

BOSTELLE, THOMAS (THEODORE)
PAINTER, SCULPTOR
b West Chester, Pa, Nov 16, 21. Work: Del Art Mus; West Chester State Col; Southeast Nat Bank, West Chester; Hist Soc West Chester; Butler Inst Am Art, Youngstown, Ohio; plus other work in private collections. Comn: Portraits for private collectors. Exhib: Over 50 one-man shows, Bianchini Gallery, 57-60; Selected Artists, 63; Carspecken-Scott, Wilmington, Del, 75; retrospectives, George Washington Univ, 69, Del Art Mus, 73 &

Woodmere Art Gallery, Philadelphia, 77. Teaching: Instr drawing & painting, Fleisher Art Mem, 52-55; instr, Wilmington Soc Fine Arts, 56-77; pvt classes, 60- Pos: Aesthetic adv, One world or none & Stuff for stuff (documentaries), Phillip Ragan Assocs, 47-49. Awards: Four Christian Brinton First Prize Awards & three NC Wyeth First Prize Awards, 46-72. Bibliog: Clint Collins (auth), Wilmington News-J, 4/11/72; Robert Winthrop (auth), feature in Brandywine Bugle, 3/75; article in Today Mag, Philadelphia Inquirer, 11/13/77. Media: Oil, Wood. Dealer: Franz Bader Inc 2124 Pennsylvania Ave NW Washington DC 20037; Aeolian Palace Gallery Box 8 Pocopson PA 19366. Mailing Add: 408 1/2 E Lancaster Ave Downingtown PA 19335

BOSTICK, WILLIAM ALLISON
PAINTER, CALLIGRAPHER
b Marengo, Ill, Feb 21, 13. Study: Carnegie Inst Technol, BS; Cranbrook Acad Art, with Zoltan Sepeshy; Detroit Soc Arts & Crafts, with John Foster; Wayne State Univ, MA(art hist); Berlitz Sch Lang. Work: Detroit Inst Arts, Mich; Evansville Mus Arts & Sci, Ind; Cranbrook Acad Art Mus, Detroit; Detroit Pub Libr; Wayne State Univ, Detroit. Comn: 32 calligraphic panels on wood, 11 calligraphic lecterns & 1 large calligraphic quotation (with Christopher Bostick), Cath Cemeteries of Chicago for Resurrection Mausoleum, Justice, Ill, 71. Exhib: Exhib Mich Artists, Detroit Inst Arts, 36-63; Pepsi-Cola Exhib, 45; Scarab Club Gold Medal Exhib, 47-77; Mich Water Color Soc, 48-76; Mich Acad Sci, Arts & Lett Art Exhib, 55-65. Collections Arranged: Mich Artists Ann, Detroit Inst Arts, 47-57. Teaching: Instr drawing, Wayne State Univ, 46-47; instr calligraphy, Detroit Soc Arts & Crafts Art Sch, 61-63; instr hist of the book, Wayne State Univ Grad Sch, 62-67; instr calligraphy, Grosse Pointe War Mem, 73- Pos: Typographer & graphic designer, Evans-Winter-Hebb, Detroit, 36-37; exec secy, Founders Soc, Detroit Inst Arts, 46-60; adminr & secy, Detroit Inst Arts, 46-76; ed, Midwest Mus Quart, 59-60. Awards: Garelick's Gallery Purchase Prize, Mich Artists Exhib, 63; Scarab Gold Medal, Scarab Club Detroit, 62 & 68; Knight, Order of Ital Solidarity; Chevalier, French Order of Arts & Lett. Mem: Scarab Club Detroit; Midwest Mus Conf; Am Inst Graphic Arts; Am Asn Mus; Int Coun Mus. Style & Technique: Cityscapes, most especially old architecture; watercolor over pen line and also hand-colored lithographs of historic buildings. Media: Watercolor, Acrylic. Publ: Illusr, Many a watchful night, 45; co-auth, The amphibious sketch, 45; auth & illusr, England under GI's reign, 46; illusr, The mysteries of Blair House, 48; plus articles in Mus News. Dealer: Arwin Galleries 222 W Grand River Detroit MI 48226. Mailing Add: 9340 W Outer Dr Detroit MI 48219

BOSTWICK, MR & MRS DUNBAR W
COLLECTORS
Collection: Paintings. Mailing Add: 113 E 77th St New York NY 10021

BOTERF, CHESTER ARTHUR (CHECK)
PAINTER, LECTURER
b Ft Scott, Kans, Apr 27, 34. Study: Univ Kans, BA, 59; Art Student League; Hunter Col, 63-64; Columbia Univ, MFA, 65. Work: Mus Mod Art, Chase Manhattan Bank & Columbia Univ, New York; Larry Aldrich Mus, Ridgefield, Conn; Des Moines Art Ctr, Iowa; plus others. Exhib: Des Moines Art Ctr, 68; Indianapolis Mus Art, Inc, 68-69; Finch Col, 71, Recent Acquisitions, Mus Mod Art, 71, New York; one-man shows, Tibor DeNagy Gallery, New York, 67, 68 & 70, Rice Univ, Houston, 74 & John Bernard Myers Gallery, New York, 71, 73 & 74. Teaching: Lectr design & drawing, Hunter Col, 65-71; Brooklyn Mus Art Sch, 73; vis assoc prof fine arts, Rice Univ, Houston, 73-75, assoc prof art, 76- Pos: Dir, Sewall Art Gallery, Rice Univ, 77- Media: Acrylic. Mailing Add: 46 MacDougal St New York NY 10012

BOTERO, FERNANDO
SCULPTOR
b Madelin, Colombia, 32. Study: Acad San Fernando, Spain, 53; Prado Mus, Madrid, 54; Univ Florence, Italy, art hist with Roberto Longhi. Work: Mus d'Arte Mod del Vaticano, Rome; Mus de Arte Contemp, Madrid; Mus de Arte Mod, Bogota, Colombia; Mus Mod Art, New York; Guggenheim Mus, New York. Exhib: Biennale of Barcelona, Spain, 55; 29th Biennale di Venezia, Italy, 58; 5th Biennale of Sao Paulo, Brazil, 59; Recent Acquisitions, Mus Mod Art, New York, 61; Selection from the Carnegie, Hudson Gallery, Detroit, Mich, 65; The Emergency Decade, Guggenheim Mus, 66; 5th Biennale of Paris, France, 67; Twelve Artists from Latin Am, Ringling Mus Art, Sarasota, Fla, 71; one-man shows, Bibliot Nac, Bogata, Colombia, 59, Staatliche Kunsthalle, Baden-Baden, WGer, 66, Milwaukee Art Ctr, Wis, 67, Galerie Juana Mordo, Madrid, 68, Ctr for Inter-Am Relations, New York, 69, Marlborough Gallery, New York, 72-74 & Overzichtstenroonstelling, Bogata, 73; Retrospective (touring WGer), Staatliche Kunsthalle, Baden-Baden, WGer, 70. Bibliog: Fernando Botero at Marlborough, Artsmag, 4/72; Un falso ingenuo: Botero, Goya, Madrid, 1/73; G R Hocke (auth), Fernando Botero: a continent under the magnifying glass, Art Int, Lugano, 12/74. Style & Technique: Exaggerated human forms in the elaborately decorative costumes and colors of South American peasant art; use of anti-natural devices common to native art or primitive painters. Mailing Add: c/o Marlborough Fine Arts 40 W 57th St New York NY 10019

BOTHMER, BERNARD V
CURATOR, ART HISTORIAN
b Ger, Oct 13, 12; US citizen. Collections Arranged: Egyptian Sculpture of the Late Period, 700 BC to AD 100, 60; Art from the Age of Akhenaten, 73. Teaching: Adj prof fine arts, Grad Sch Arts & Sci, NY Univ, 60- Pos: From asst to asst cur, Dept Egyptian Art, Mus Fine Arts, Boston, 46-56; assoc cur ancient art, Brooklyn Mus, 56-64, cur ancient art, 64-72, cur Egyptian & class art, 73- Mem: Am Res Ctr in Egypt; Egypt Explor Soc; Archaeol Inst Am; Col Art Asn Am. Res: Ancient Egyptian portraiture, Egyptian sculpture of the late period. Publ: Co-auth, The Pomerance collection of ancient art, 66; ed, Wilbour monographs, Vols I-VII, 68-74; co-auth, Brief guide, Dept Ancient Art, Brooklyn Mus, 70 & 74. Mailing Add: c/o Brooklyn Mus 188 Eastern Pkwy Brooklyn NY 11238

BOTHMER, DIETRICH FELIX VON
ART HISTORIAN, ART ADMINISTRATOR
b Eisenach, Ger, Oct 26, 18; US citizen. Study: Friedrich Wilhelm Univ, Berlin, Ger; Oxford Univ, dipl class archaeol; Univ Chicago; Univ Calif, PhD. Teaching: Adj prof Greek art, Inst Fine Arts, NY Univ, 65- Pos: Asst cur, Dept Greek & Roman Art, Metrop Mus Art, 46-51, assoc cur, 51-59, cur, 59-73, chmn, 73- Awards: Guggenheim Fel, 67. Mem: Archaeol Inst Am; Soc Promotion Hellenic Studies; Vereinigung der Freunde antiker Kunst; Deutsches Archaol Inst. Res: Greek and Roman art and archaeology. Publ: Auth, Ancient art from New York private collections, 60; co-auth, An inquiry into the forgery of the Etruscan terra cotta warriors, 61; auth, Corpus Vasorum Antiquorum USA, Fascicule 12, 63 & co-auth, Fascicule 14, 73, Fascicule 16, 75 & Fascicule 19, 78; co-auth, Greek vase painting, 72. Mailing Add: 373 Centre Island Rd Oyster Bay NY 11771

BOTHWELL, DORR
PAINTER, PRINTMAKER
b San Francisco, Calif, May 3, 02. Study: Calif Sch Fine Arts & Rudolph Schaeffer Sch Design, San Francisco; Univ Ore; Abraham Rosenberg fel for art study abroad, 49-51. Work: Metrop Mus Art & Whitney Mus Am Art, New York; Fogg Mus, Cambridge; Victoria & Albert Mus, London; Bibliotheque Nat, Paris. Exhib: Pittsburgh Int, 52 & 58; 3rd Bienale, Sao Paulo, Brazil; Meltzer Gallery, New York, 58; one-man shows, De Young Mem Mus, 58 & 63 & Bolles Gallery, 72, San Francisco; Bali Seen, 76 & All Kinds of Cats, 77, Bay Window Gallery, Mendocino, Calif; Thirty Yrs of Am Printmaking, Brooklyn Mus, NY, 77; Falkirk Mus, San Rafael, Calif, 77. Teaching: Instr design, Calif Sch Fine Arts, 44-48; instr design, Parsons Sch Design, New York, 52; instr design, Calif Sch Fine Arts, 53-58; instr design, San Francisco Art Inst, 59-61; instr, Mendocino Art Ctr, 61-; instr, Ansel Adams Photog Workshop, Yosemite Nat Park, Calif, 64-; Summer in Mendocino, Univ Calif, Santa Cruz, 76-77. Mem: Mendocino Art Ctr. Style & Technique: Evocative semi-recognizable. Media: Oil, Acrylic. Publ: Co-auth, Notan dark-light design, Van Nostrand Reinhold, 68, transl into Danish, 77. Mailing Add: PO Box 27 Mendocino CA 95460

BOTKIN, HENRY
PAINTER, WRITER
b Boston, Mass. Study: Mass Sch Art; Art Student League. Work: Metrop Mus Art, Mus Mod Art & Whitney Mus Am Art, New York; Phillips Mem Gallery, Washington, DC; Walter P Chrysler Jr Collection. Exhib: One-man shows, Phillips Mem Gallery, 37, Art Club Chicago, 38, Riverside Mus, 61, Syracuse Univ, 71; 69 one-man shows plus many other group shows. Pos: Art adv to leading collectors. Awards: Nat Inst Arts & Lett Grant, 65; 3 Purchase Awards, Acad Arts & Lett, 67, 74 & 75. Mem: Artists Equity Asn (pres NY chap, 52-53); Group 256, Provincetown, Mass (pres, 55-56); Am Abstr Artists (pres, 54-55); Fedn Mod Painters & Sculptors (pres, 57-61, 68-69); fel Int Asn Plastic Arts & Lett. Media: Oil, Collage. Dealer: Frank Rehn Gallery 655 Madison Ave New York NY 10021. Mailing Add: 56 W 11th St New York NY 10011

BOTT, H J
SCULPTOR, ASSEMBLAGIST
b Greeley, Colo, Dec 28, 33. Study: Art Ctr Sch Los Angeles; Inst Fine Arts, NY Univ; Art Students League; Kunstakademie-Dusseldorf, Bamberg-Kunstschule, Ger, MBK, 55. Work: Kunsthalle der Garten, Dusseldorf; Dallas Mus Fine Arts, Tex; Bundy Outdoor Mus, Waitsfield, Vt; Cooperstown Art Mus, NY; plus others. Comn: 5' bas relief (bronze), Anglo-Tex Soc, London, Eng, 60; six 4' stylized heads, Olin-Mathieson Chem Corp, New Haven Conn, 62; 12' stainless flight form, US Air Force Acad, Colo, 64; Southland Corp, Dallas, Tex, 73; Univ Houston, 76; plus many others. Exhib: One-man shows, Dusseldorf Kunsthalle & Univ Heidelberg, Ger, 56, ADG Arts Inc, New York, 64, Galleria Sonnason, Nueva Laredo & Mexico City, 67-69, Beaumont Art Mus, Tex, 75, Barnwell Mus & Sculpture Garden, Shreveport, La, 75, Amarillo Art Ctr, Tex, 76, Works, San Jose, Calif, 77 & Frank C Smith Fine Arts Ctr, Tex A&I Univ, 67 & 78; Calif Palace of the Legion of Honor, San Francisco, 60 & 63; Minn Mus Fine Art, St Paul, 62 & 67; Atkins Mus Fine Arts, Kansas City, Mo, 62; San Diego Fine Arts Gallery, Calif, 63; Pa Acad of Fine Arts, Philadelphia, 66; Tex Invitational Sculpture, Dallas, 75 & 76; Alessandra Gallery, New York, 77; plus many others. Pos: Artist in residence, Joint Art Ventures Group, Loft-on-Strand, Inc, Galveston, Tex, 69-; art ther consult, Gulf-Coast Regional Ment Health-Ment Retardation Ctr, Tex, 73- Awards: Plastik Reisestipeduim, Museen der Stadt Koln, Ger, 56; Premier Les Plus Sculpture, Prix De Paris, France, 65; Beck Award, Tex Tri-Ann Painting & Sculpture, Dallas Mus of Fine Arts, 76. Bibliog: Tom Livesay & John Norton (co-auths), H J Bott sculpture, Longview Mus & Arts Ctr, 10/73; Robert M Murdock & Richard Van Buren (co-auths), The drawings & sculpture of H J Bott, pvt Houston Monogr publ, 2/77; Charlotte Mosev (auth), Squaring off, Art News, 4/77. Dealer: Alessandra Gallery 20 W 57th St New York NY 10019; Bienville Gallery 228 Decatur St New Orleans LA 70130. Mailing Add: c/o Loft-on-Strand Gallery 2218 1/2 B Galveston TX 77550

BOTT, MARGARET DEATS
See Deats, Margaret

BOTT, PATRICIA ALLEN
See Allen, Patricia

BOTTINI, DAVID M
SCULPTOR
b Santa Clara, Calif, June 1, 45. Study: Calif State Univ, San Jose, BA, 69, MA, 70. Work: De Saisset Mus, Univ Santa Clara; Oakland Mus; Calif State Univ, San Jose; San Jose City Col Permanent Collection. Comn: Sculpture, M & M Robert Bernard, Lafayette, Calif, 70; sculpture, Oakland Mus, 74. Exhib: One-man shows, De Saisset Mus, Univ Santa Clara, 70, Arleigh Gallery, San Francisco, 71, Esther Robles Gallery, Los Angeles, 72 & William Sawyer Gallery, San Francisco, 75; Oakland Mus, 76. Awards: Outdoor Painting Award, Aristocrat Trailers, 68; Contemp Art Comt Ann Artist Award, Oakland Mus, 75. Bibliog: Thomas Albright (auth), San Francisco, NY Gallery Mag, 70; Charles Shere (auth), An informed conservatism trend, Oakland Tribune, 73; Alfred Frankenstein (auth), Oakland Art Steps Outdoors, San Francisco Chronicle, 74. Style & Technique: A non-objective constructivist working with painted fabricated steel. Media: Steel, Stainless Steel. Dealer: William Sawyer Gallery 3045 Clay St San Francisco CA 94115 Mailing Add: 246 Caselli Ave San Francisco CA 94114

BOTTO, RICHARD ALFRED
PAINTER, INSTRUCTOR
b Union City, NJ, May 5, 31. Study: Pratt Inst, cert, 56, AS(appl sci), 58, with Walter Klett, Charles Mazoujian, Walter Murch, Stephen Peck & Edgar Whitney; Art Student League & Woodstock, NY, with Frank Reilly. Comn: Last Supper (mural), St Paul's Convent Chapel, 74. Exhib: Nat Acad Design, 71, Allied Artists Am, 72 & Am Artists Prof League, 72, New York; Hudson Valley Art Asn, White Plains, NY, 72; State Exhib, NJ State Mus, Trenton, 72. Teaching: Instr fine art, Frank Reilly Sch Art, New York, 64-68. Pos: Pres, Hudson Artist Inc, Jersey City, 66-68, chmn bd, 69-; pres, Reilly Sch Art, New York, 67-68; chmn dept fine arts, Jersey City Mus, 68-69; founder-dir, Renaissance Sch Art, NJ, 74. Awards: Best-in-Show Medal, Jersey City Mus, 67; Gerald Lubeck Prize, Allied Artists Am, 71; Gold Medal, Grand Nat, Am Artists Prof League, 72. Mem: Allied Artists Am; Am Artists Prof League; Hudson Valley Art Asn; Painters & Sculptors Soc NJ; Hudson Artists. Media: Oil. Mailing Add: 138 Union Pl Ridgefield Park NJ 07660

BOTWINICK, MICHAEL
MUSEUM DIRECTOR
b New York, NY, Nov 14, 43. Study: Rutgers Col, BA, 64; Columbia Univ, MA, 67. Collection: Coordr exhib, The Year 1200, Metrop Art Mus, NY, 69-70 & Masterpieces of 50 Centuries, 71. Pos: Asst cur, Medieval Art & the Cloisters, Metrop Mus Art, New York, 69, assoc cur, 70, asst cur in chief, 70-71; asst dir art, Philadelphia Mus Art, 71-74; dir,

Brooklyn Mus, 74- Mem: Col Art Asn; Asn Art Mus Dirs. Mailing Add: Brooklyn Mus 188 Eastern Pkwy Brooklyn NY 11238

BOUCHARD, LORNE HOLLAND
PAINTER, ILLUSTRATOR
b Montreal, PQ, Mar 19, 13. Study: Drawing with W M Barnes; also with Prof Felix, Ecole Beaux-Arts, Montreal. Work: Mus Fine Arts, Montreal; Quebec Prov Mus, PQ; Tom Thomson Mem Mus & Art Gallery, Owen Sound, Ont; also in pvt collections in Can, US, Eng & Brazil. Comn: Numerous pvt comns from advert agencies for large painting for bd rms of Can Iron, Nordair, Seagrams, Hewitt Equipment Co & others. Exhib: First group show, 31, two-man show, 62, Montreal Mus; Royal Can Acad Arts Ann Exhib & Traveling Shows, 40-70; one-man shows, Continental Galleries, Montreal, 40-49 & 52-55, Walter Klinkhoff Gallery, Montreal, eight times, 60-71; four-man show, Ont Mus Art, London, 62. Awards: Award of Merit, Advert & Ed Art Exhib, Art Dirs Club, Montreal, 56; First Prize, Montreal Hadassah Exhib, 59; Hon Mention, Price Fine Arts Award, Montreal, 70. Bibliog: Magic of the mountains, 60 & The Mackenzie river-Mississippi of the North, 63, Week End Mag; Alex Mogelon (auth), Art profile: Lorne Bouchard, Montrealer Mag, 4/68; John Basset (producer), An Artist's Impression of the Arctic-Lorne Bouchard (film), Nat Can TV, 69. Mem: Academician Royal Can Acad Arts. Media: Oil. Publ: Illusr, Trapping is My Life, 70. Dealer: Walter Klinkhoff Gallery 1200 Sherbrooke St W Montreal PQ Can. Mailing Add: 2021 Lakeshore Dr Baie-d'urfe PQ H9X 1P9 Can

BOUCHER, TANIA KUNSKY
ART DEALER, PAINTER
b Vilno, Lithuania, Feb 17, 27; US citizen. Study: City Col New York, BS; Univ Pa, MS; Univ Del, BA; also with Tom Bostelle. Exhib: Del Art Mus, 66-68; Franz Bader Gallery, Washington, DC, 70-74; one-woman shows, Westtown Friends Sch, 71 & Univ Del, 73; Carspecken Scott Art Gallery, Wilmington, Del, 74. Teaching: Instr, Westtown Friends Sch, Pa, 64-69; art teacher, West Chester Adult Night Sch, 70-72. Pos: Dir, Aeolian Palace Gallery, Pocopson, Pa, 74- Awards: First Drawing Award, Chester Co Art Asn, 67; First Painting Award, Del Art Mus, 68; Judges Award, Old York Rd Art Guild, 69. Bibliog: H Aizupitis (auth), exhib critique & interview, Daily Local News, West Chester, Pa, 10/23/68; B Ogram (auth), interview, Kennett News, 74. Media: Oil, Etching. Specialty: Contemporary painting and sculpture. Mailing Add: Box 182 Mendenhall PA 19357

BOUGHTON, WILLIAM HARRISON
PAINTER, EDUCATOR
b Dubuque, Iowa, Feb 19, 15. Study: Univ Iowa, BA, 43; Univ Calif, Berkeley, MA, 45; James Phelan Fel (foreign travel & independent study), 45-47; Far East & Near East, 70-71; with Earl Loran, Fletcher Martin, Grant Wood, Emil Ganso, Lester Longman, Worth Ryder, Stephen Peper, H W Janson & Shaefer-Simmern. Work: New York Schs; Luxury Liners, SS Constitution & SS Independence; Am Embassy, Paris; Libr Cong, Washington, DC; Fla State Univ Gallery. Comn: Mural, Student Union, Lamar Univ, 55 & sculpture, Quadrangle, 57. Exhib: Serigraphies Americaines, Paris, 53; Dix Peintres Americaines, Paris, 54; L'aquarelles Contemporarines Aux Etats Unis, France, 55; Kunst Uit Amerika, Breda, Neth, 57; L'arte Grafica, Villa Giula, Rome, 57. Teaching: Asst prof art, Fla State Univ, 47-54; head art dept, Lamar Univ, 54-70, prof art, 54-77. Awards: Elected mem & Silver Medal, Int Acad Arts, Tommaso Campanella, Rome, 70. Bibliog: F Dugas (auth, Texas professor has shown his work world wide, Facets, Tex Fine Arts Soc, 71. Mem: Nat Serigraph Soc; Col Art Asn; Am Color Print Soc; Beaumont Art Asn. Style & Technique: Semi-abstract with strong emphasis on form and structure; oil media, alla prima technique. Media: Oil. Publ: Auth, Maskoid and the silk screen, Art Mat Trade News, 50; Maskoid stencil technique, Fla Newspaper News & Radio Dig, 50. Dealer: Meredith J Long Galleries 2323 San Felipe Rd Houston TX 77019. Mailing Add: PO Box 376 El Prado NM 87529

BOULTON, JACK
ART ADMINISTRATOR
b Columbus, Ind, 44. Study: Col Design, Archit & Art, Univ Cincinnati, BS, 67, MA, 70. Collections Arranged: Richard Hamilton, Kent State Univ, 71; Urban Walls, Cincinnati, 71-72; Alternative Landscape: Christo, Steir, Richardson, 72; Cincinnati Union Terminal Exhib (with catalogue), 73; Rafael Ferrer (with catalogue), 73; Twentieth Century Am Folk Art: Hemphill Collection, 73; Chris Burden, 74; Ann Wilson, 74; Bochner/LeVa/Rockburne/Tuttle (with catalogue), 75; Jackie Winsor Sculpture (with catalogue), 76. Teaching: Lectr, Univ Cincinnati, Columbus Gallery of Fine Arts & Wright State Univ, 76 & New Orleans Mus & Whitney Mus of Am Art, 77. Pos: Dir, Contemp Arts Ctr, Cincinnati, 72-76; US comnr, Sao Paulo Bienal, 75; chmn, Ohio Arts Coun-Visual Arts Panel, 76; assoc dir, Int Exhibs Comt, Am Fedn of Arts, Washington, DC, 77-; trustee, The New Mus, New York, NY, 77- Awards: Corbett Award, Cincinnati, 76. Mailing Add: Int Exhibs Comt 1521 New Hampshire Ave NW Washington DC 20036

BOULTON, JOSEPH L
SCULPTOR, DESIGNER
b Ft Worth, Tex, May 26, 96. Study: Nat Acad Design; Art Students League; Beaux-Arts Inst Design; apprentice to Herman A MacNeil. Work: Ft Worth Mus Art; Southern Plains Indian Mus, Anadarko, Okla; NJ State Mus, Trenton; Mus Fine Arts, Springfield, Mass; Detroit Art Inst Mus; plus many other pub & pvt collections. Comn: Coins and medals for Med Soc, State of Pa, Am Acad Gen Practice, Pa, Franklin Mint, Polish-Am Asn & others; series of American wildlife, Am Sculpture Soc, Westport, Conn; plus many plaques and busts. Exhib: Many shows, Hudson Valley Art Asn, 51-68; Nat Acad Design, New York, 53; Allied Artists Am; Arts & Crafts Asn, Meriden, Conn, 68 & 70; Silvermine Guild, New Canaan, Conn, 71; plus many others. Awards: Anna Hyatt Huntington Award, Hudson Valley Art Asn, 54, 56 & 68; Arts & Crafts Asn Awards, 68 & 70; Olivetti Award, Silvermine Guild, 71; plus many others. Mem: Nat Sculpture Soc; Allied Artists Am; Painters & Sculptors Soc NJ; Acad Artists Asn; Royal Soc Arts. Mailing Add: 43 Old Hill Rd Westport CT 06880

BOURAS, HARRY D
SCULPTOR, PAINTER
b Rochester, NY, Feb 13, 31. Study: Univ Rochester, BA, 51; Univ Chicago, 55-56. Work: Mus Mod Art, New York; Art Inst Chicago; Mus Fine Arts, Rochester, NY; Ishibashi Mus, Tokyo, Japan; Palais Beaux Artes, Brussels, Belg. Exhib: Five shows, Am Exhib, Art Inst Chicago, 58-72; Art of Assemblage, Mus Mod Art, New York, 66; Corcoran Ann, Washington, DC, 66 & 68; Beyond Illustration, Rotunda Bella Besana, Milan, Italy, Gemeentemuseum, Arnhem, Holland, Kunstverein, Munich, Ger, Mus Mod Art, Tokyo & others, 71-73. Teaching: Artist in residence, Univ Chicago, 62-64; artist in residence, Columbia Col, Chicago, 64- Awards: Pauline Palmer Award, Art Inst Chicago, 62 & Logan Gold Medal for Sculpture, 65; Guggenheim Found Fel, 71-72. Bibliog: William Seitz (auth), Art of Assemblage, Simon & Schuster, 66; M Kirby (auth), Happenings, Dutton, 69; Meilach & Selden (auth), Direct Metal Sculpture, Crown, 69; plus reviews in nat art mag. Media: Steel, Concrete; Acrylic, Oil. Mem: Arts Club Chicago. Publ: Contribr, The Arts and the Public, Univ Chicago, 67; auth, Burlington Diner (film), Film Group, 68. Dealer: Noah Goldowsky 1080 Madison Ave New York NY 10021; B C Holland 260 Ontario St Chicago IL 60611. Mailing Add: 814 Sheridan Evanston IL 60202

BOURDON, DAVID
ART CRITIC
b Glendale, Calif, Oct 15, 34. Study: Columbia Univ, BS. Pos: Art critic, Village Voice, New York, 64-66 & 74-77; asst ed, Life Mag, New York, 66-71; assoc ed, Saturday Rev of Arts, New York, 72, Smithsonian Mag, Washington, DC, 72-74 & Arts Mag, New York, 73- Publ: Auth, Christo, Abrams, 72. Mailing Add: 30 Fifth Ave New York NY 10011

BOURGEOIS, LOUISE
SCULPTOR
b Paris, France; US citizen. Study: Lycee Fenelon, Paris, Baccalaureate, 32; Sorbonne, 32-35; Ecole du Louvre, 36-37; Acad des Beaux-Arts, 36-38; Acad de la Grande Chaumiere, 37-38; Atelier Fernand Leger, 38. Work: Mus Mod Art & Whitney Mus Am Art, New York; NY Univ; Mus RI Sch Design, Providence; Harvard Univ, Cambridge, Mass. Exhib: The New American Painting & Sculpture, The First Generation, Mus Mod Art, 69; La Biennale de Carrara, Italy, 69; L'Art Vivant aux Etats Unis, Fondation Maeght, Vence, France, 69; American Sculpture, Univ Nebr, Lincoln, 70; Whitney Biennial, 73; Sculpture: Am Directory 1945-75, Washington, DC, 75. Teaching: Instr sculpture, Pratt Inst, 64-65; instr sculpture, Brooklyn Col, 63 & 68; field fac sculpture, Goddard Col, 71- Bibliog: Daniel Robbins (auth), Sculpture by Louise Bourgeois, Art Int, 10/64; William Rubin (auth), Some reflections on the work of Louise Bourgeois, 4/69; J P Marandel (auth), Louise Bourgeois, 12/71. Media: Wood, Latex, Plastic & Marble. Mailing Add: 347 W 20th St New York NY 10011

BOUSSARD, DANA
SCULPTOR
b Salem, Ore, Feb 7, 44. Study: St Mary's Col; Art Inst Chicago; Univ Chicago; Univ Mont, BFA, MFA, 68. Work: Am Mus Contemp Crafts, New York; Univ Ore. Comn: Altar hanging banner, Newman Ctr Church, Missoula, Mont, 70, vestment, 71; vestment, St Francis Church, Missoula, 71; portrait of Art Longpre family, Seattle, 71; portrait of Mr Evans, comn by family, Seattle, 72. Exhib: Face Coverings, Mus Contemp Crafts, New York, 71; Deliberate Entanglements of UCLA, Portland, Ore, 72; San Francisco Mus Art, 74; Fine Art Gallery, London, Eng, 75; Xerox Exhib, Fairtree Gallery, New York, 75; plus others. Teaching: Instr design, Univ Mont, 70-71; instr fabric, Factory Visual Arts Workshop, 71 & 72; instr fabric, Arts & Crafts Soc, Portland, 72; artist in sch, Nat Endowment Arts, 74-75. Pos: Mem steering comt, Artist in Schs Res Survey, Nat Endowment Arts, 75- Awards: Western States Arts Found Grant, 75. Bibliog: Lee Snow (auth), Soft Jewelry & Body Ornaments, Simon & Schuster, 73. Mem: Am Crafts Coun (mem at large); Friends of the Crafts, Seattle; Mont Arts Coun (adv coun visual art). Style & Technique: Drawing, figures in mixed and oil wash and silver point collage; fabric sculpture with Plexiglas and wood frame, banners and free standing. Media: Fabric. Dealer: Fountain Gallery 115 SW Fourth Ave Portland OR 97204; William Sawyer Gallery 3043 Clay St San Francisco CA 94115. Mailing Add: No 358 Choteau MT 59422

BOUTIS, TOM
PAINTER
b New York, NY, Aug 25, 22. Study: Cooper Union, New York, BFA, 48; Skowhegan Sch Painting & Sculpture, summer 51. Work: Art Inst Chicago: Cibi-Geigy Collection, Ardsley, NY; Canton Art Inst, Ohio; Colby Col. Comn: Drawings, New York Hilton Collection Am Art, 62. Exhib: One-man shows, Zabrieskie Gallery, New York, 55, Area Gallery, New York, 59 & 60 & Landmark Gallery, New York, 73, 75 & 77; Drawings Exhib, Uffizzi Mus, Florence, Italy, 57; Selected Painters of Soho, Lehigh Univ Mus, 74; Cibi-Geigy Collection, Summit Art Mus, NJ, 74. Teaching: Artist in residence painting, Summer Art Prog, Cooper Union, 69. Awards: Fulbright Grant, US-Ital Govts, 55-57; NY State Coun for the Arts Award, 75; Nat Endowment for the Arts, 76. Style & Technique: Colorist and lyrical abstraction. Media: Collage. Dealer: Landmark Gallery 469 Broome New York NY 10013. Mailing Add: 162 E 82nd St New York NY 10028

BOVA, JOE
SCULPTOR, CERAMIST
b Houston, Tex, June 1, 41. Study: Univ Houston, BFA, 67; Univ NMex, MA, 69. Work: Greenville Co Mus, Greenville, SC; State of Tenn, Tenn Art Comn, Nashville; State of La, Old State Capitol Galleries, Baton Rouge; Miami Univ Gallerie, Oxford, Ohio; McAllen Mus, Tex. Exhib: Young Americans, 69 & The Great American Foot, 78, Mus of Contemp Crafts, New York; 7th-10th Ann Piedmont Crafts, Mint Mus, Charlotte, NC, 69-72; 12th Midwest Biennial, Joslyn Mus of Art, Omaha, 71; Artists of the Southeast & Tex, New Orleans Mus of Art, 72; 35 Artists of the Southeast, High Mus of Art, Atlanta, 77; The Whitewater Ann, Univ Wis, 77; Objects of Play, Pa State Univ, 78. Teaching: Asst prof design & ceramics, Nicholls State Univ, Thibodaux, 69-71; assoc prof ceramics & sculpture, La State Univ, Baton Rouge, 71; instr ceramics, Penland Sch of Crafts, 74 & 77. Bibliog: Jacob Eleasari (auth), Clay artists, Eleasari & Hahn Films, Nashville, 75; Paul Donhauser (auth), History of American Ceramics, Kendall/Hunt, Dubuque, Iowa, 78. Mem: Am Crafts Coun (state rep, 72-75 & southeast region chmn, 73-77); Nat Coun on Educ of the Ceramic Arts (prog chmn & mem bd, 76); La Crafts Coun (mem bd & exhibs chmn, 71-77). Style & Technique: Figurative, human and animal—Neo Dada/Post Pop/Funk; naturalistic, handbuilt and modeled from slabs, extrusions and pottery wheel forms. Media: Ceramic. Dealer: Bienville Gallery 228 Decatur New Orleans LA 70130. Mailing Add: 644 Camelia Baton Rouge LA 70806

BOVE, RICHARD
PAINTER, EDUCATOR
b Brooklyn, NY, Oct 21, 20. Study: Pratt Inst, BFA; Art Students League; Brera Acad, Milan, Italy. Exhib: Am Acad Design, New York; Philadelphia Mus Art; Corcoran Gallery Art, Washington, DC; Whitney Mus Art & Metrop Mus Art, New York. Teaching: Instr painting, Art Students League, 55-65; chmn dept painting, Pratt Inst, 70-74, prof painting, Grad Sch, 73- Awards: Nat Acad Design Award; Louis Comfort Tiffany Found Award; Fulbright Fel, Italy. Style & Technique: Constructions, collage; oil and water based pigments. Media: Concrete, Plastics. Mailing Add: 180 Emerson Pl Brooklyn NY 11205

BOWATER, MARIAN
ART DEALER, COLLECTOR
b Emmons, Minn, Sept 5, 24. Study: Study with Gustavous Adolphus. Pos: Owner, Bowater Gallery. Mem: Art Dealers Asn of Southern Calif. Specialty: Late 19th to 20th century American paintings. Collection: American impressionists and English Old Masters. Mailing Add: Bowater Gallery 8485 Melrose Pl Los Angeles CA 90069

BOWEN, HELEN EAKINS
PAINTER
b Bluefield, WVa. Study: Univ Alaska; Art Students League; Nat Acad Sch Fine Arts; with Raymond Huit, Paris & Jose de Creeft, Hugh Gumpel, Marshall Glasier & Vincent Malta. Work: Finch Col Mus Art; Chrysler Mus, Norfolk, Va; Gibbes Art Gallery, Charleston, SC; Syracuse Mus of Art, NY. Exhib: Catherine Lorillard Wolfe Art Club, New York, 64; Am Artists Prof League, New York, 67; Nat Arts Club Gallery, New York, 68; one-man show, Gibbes Art Gallery, 69; Allied Artists Am, Nat Acad Design Galleries, New York, 70. Pos: Mem adv coun, Sch Visual & Performing Arts, Syracuse Univ, 71- Awards: Mark Trafton Fowler Fel, 63; Louis Jambor Mem Award, 64; James A Suydam Bronze Medal, 66. Mem: Life mem Art Students League; Mus Mod Art, New York; Gibbes Art Gallery; Metrop Mus Art. Media: Oil, Watercolor, Polymer. Mailing Add: 40 Waterside Plaza Apt 8B New York NY 10010

BOWER, GARY DAVID
PAINTER
b Dayton, Ohio, May 10, 40. Study: Ohio State Univ, BA(philos), 62 & MFA(painting), 65. Work: Whitney Mus Am Art, New York; Allen Art Mus, Oberlin, Ohio; Akron Art Inst; Dayton Art Inst; Walker Art Ctr, Minneapolis. Exhib: Four Painters, Leo Castelli Warehouse Gallery, New York, 69; Whitney Mus Ann, 70; one-man shows, O K Harris Gallery, New York, 69 & 72, Univ Ky, 71 & Akron Art Inst, 72. Teaching: Staff critic painting, Dept Educ, Whitney Mus Am Art, 68-74. Awards: James Broadus Award, Chicago Art Inst, 67; Achievement in Painting, Ohio State Fair, 70. Style & Technique: Naturalistic and non objective propositions with brush and palette knife. Media: Oil & Acrylic on Canvas. Dealer: New Gallery Bellflower Rd Cleveland OH 44106. Mailing Add: Box 34 Charlotteville NY 12036

BOWERS, CHERYL OLSEN
PAINTER, LECTURER
b Berkeley, Calif, Sept 11, 38. Study: San Francisco Art Inst, MFA(with honors); Univ Calif, Berkeley with Fred Martin, Bob Hudson, Harold Paris & Peter Plagens. Work: Univ Mus, Univ Calif, Berkeley; Univ Mus, Bellingham, Wash; Tamarind Lithographic Inst, Albuquerque. Exhib: Nat Drawing Exhib, Potsdam, NY, 73; Davidson Nat Print & Drawing, NC, 73; Women From Permanent Collection, Univ Mus, Berkeley, 73; Biennial, Whitney Mus Am Art, New York, 75; San Francisco Mus Art, 75. Teaching: Lectr painting, Calif State Univ, Hayward, 75; vis lectr painting, Univ Calif, Berkeley, 75- Awards: Tamarind Lithographic Inst Fel, 72; SECA Award, Soc Creative Arts, San Francisco, 75. Style & Technique: Abstract realism, large, thinly painted acrylic, rhoplex on linen, unstretched, work on floor. Dealer: Malvina Miller 1150 Union St San Francisco CA 94109. Mailing Add: c/o Malvina Miller 1150 Union St San Francisco CA 94109

BOWERS, LYNN CHUCK
PAINTER
b Philadelphia, Pa, Dec 21, 32. Study: Art Students League; New Sch Social Res. Work: Mus Mod Art & Chase Manhattan Bank, New York. Exhib: Martha Jackson Gallery, 67; Rose Fried Gallery, 69; Whitney Mus Am Art, 69-70; Mus Fine Art, Boston, 70; Dorsky Gallery, 70. Bibliog: Charles Childs (auth), Artist-caught between two worlds, Time Union, 67; Tuesday Magazine Artist, NY & Boston, Oakland Tribune, 70. Style & Technique: Watercolors of sea and clouds; acrylic painting of clouds with brushes and newspaper. Media: Acrylic, Watercolor. Mailing Add: Heinz-Heimweg Darmstadt West Germany

BOWIE, WILLIAM
SCULPTOR
b Youngstown, Ohio, Feb 15, 26. Study: Youngstown Univ; Bethany Col. Work: Skyline of New York, New York Bank Savings; Globe-Wernicke Showroom, New York; Hertz Skyctr Airport, Huntsville, Ala; Brown & Williamson Tobacco Corp, Louisville, Ky; Glass Container Div, Owens-Ill, Scarsdale, NY. Comn: Exec off, Am Brands, Inc, New York; Brooklyn Col Student Ctr; Honeywell, Inc, Framingham, Mass; Irving Trust Co, Caracas, Venezuela, Frankel Rare Book Room, Univ Houston Libr. Exhib: Meltzer Gallery; George Jensen's; Am House; Sculpture Exhib, Butler Inst Am Art, 65; For Your Home, Krannert Art Mus, Univ Ill; Symposium 66, Purdue Univ, 66; plus many others. Pos: Judge Sculpture Exhib, Butler Inst Am Art, 66. Awards: Purchase Award, Sculpture Exhib, Butler Inst Am Art, 65; Good Design Award, Purdue Univ, 66; spec award outstanding merit in craftsmanship, Artist-Craftsmen New York. Media: Metal. Mailing Add: c/o Sculpture Studio Inc 441 Lafayette St at 8th St New York NY 10003

BOWLER, JOSEPH, JR
PORTRAIT ARTIST, ILLUSTRATOR
b Forest Hills, NY, Sept 4, 28. Study: Charles E Cooper Studios, New York; Art Students League. Work: Sanford Low Collection, Hartford Mus; Soc of Illusr Permanent Collection; US Air Force Permanent Collection. Comn: Portraits, Rose Kennedy, Rose Kennedy Wing, Albert Einstein Hosp, 71, President Nixon, Time Mag, Man of the Yr, (unpublished), 72, Francis Hipp, Liberty Corp, 74, Dr Peter LaMotte, Hilton Head Hosp, 75 & Patty Hearst, Good Housekeeping, 77. Exhib: Ann Exhib of Published Work for 1977, Soc of Illusr, 78. Teaching: Instr painting, Parsons Sch of Design, New York, 68-72. Pos: Free lance illusr & portrait painter, 50- Awards: Artist of the Yr 1967, Artists' Guild of New York. Bibliog: Don Holden (auth), Joe Bowler, Illustrator, Am Artist, 11/67; Cory SerVaas (auth), Artist in the White House, Saturday Evening Post, summer 72; Betty Lynn Compton (auth), Joe Bowler transforms photographs into reality, The State, Columbia, SC, 2/22/76. Mem: Soc of Illusr. Style & Technique: Portraits and illustrations for national magazines as well as private, institutional and corporate commissions; realistic. Media: Oil. Mailing Add: 9 Baynard Cove Rd Hilton Head Island SC 29928

BOWLES, THOMAS ANDREW, III
ART ADMINISTRATOR, ART HISTORIAN
b Decatur, Ala, Nov 2, 39. Study: Vanderbilt Univ; Univ Okla; Otis Art Inst; Kokoshka Sch, Salzburg, Austria with Alfred Hrdlichka, Leonard McMurray & Francisco Nieva. Collections Arranged: The Arts of Ludwig, II (with catalog); Works of Ricardo de Villodas; McKinney & Hall Lithographs & Chas Bird King & collection of Huntsville Mus Art. Pos: Stage designer, Nat Theaters, Madrid, 67-68; art historian & restorer, Schlosser Verwaltung, Munich, 69-70; dir Huntsville Mus Art, 75- Mem: Hon Kappa Pi. Style & Technique: Plastics-optical properties; kinetic portrait sculpture in terra-cotta. Res: 19th century, the technical history of light used as an art medium. Interest: 19th century paintings. Collection: Works of Ricardo de Villodas and other 19th century artists; musical instruments; early Italian print. Publ: Auth, Ricardo de Villodas, a critical biography, 75. Mailing Add: 700 Monroe St SE Huntsville AL 35801

BOWLING, FRANK
PAINTER
b Bartica, Guyana, Feb 29, 36; US & Guyanese citizen. Study: Slade Sch Fine Art, Univ London; ARCA. Work: Contemp Art Soc, Tate Gallery, London; NJ State Mus, Trenton; Mus Mod Art & Whitney Mus, New York; Mus Fine Arts, Boston; RI Mus. Exhib: One-man shows, Grabowski Gallery, London, 62-63, Whitney Mus, 71, Centre Inter-Am Rel, New York, 73 & Noah Goldowsky Gallery, 73-74; Obssive Immage, Int Exhib, Inst Contemp Art, 68; Whitney Ann, 69-72; Artist Immigrants to Am 1876-1976, Hirshhorn Mus, Washington, DC; William Darby Gallery, London, Eng, 75-77; Tibor de Nagy Gallery, New York, 75-76 & 78. Awards: Silver Medal for Painting, Royal Col Art, 62; Painting Prize, Richard Demarco Gallery, Edinburgh, Scotland, 67; Guggenheim Fel, 67 & 73. Style & Technique: Abstract. Media: Acrylic, Oil. Dealer: Tibor de Nagy Gallery 29 W 57th St New York NY 10019. Mailing Add: PO Box 318 Canal St Sta New York NY 10013

BOWLING, JACK
SILVERSMITH, PRINTMAKER
b Bonham, Tex, July 5, 03. Study: With Charlie Phillips, Tex, 10-20; Fleischer Art Mem Sch, Philadelphia, 30; Honolulu Art Acad, 32-35; also with Millard Sheets & Elliot O'Hara, 45; Barnes Found, 64-66. Work: Libr Cong, Washington, DC; Mus Art, Colombo, Ceylon; Honolulu Acad Art; plus many churches & pvt collectors. Comn: Silver cross with ivory, Dogwood Emanuel Episcopal Church, Wilmington, Del, 58; metal mural (gold on lead), First Baptist Church, Bonham, Tex, 59; silver basin, Diocese of Pa, Philadelphia, 60; metal pewter seagulls, Christ First Presby Church, Hempsted, NY, 73; processional cross with dogwood, Mem Chapel, Valley Forge Park. Exhib: One-man shows, Honolulu Acad Arts, 35; Newport Art Asn, RI, 45 & Colombo, Ceylon & Singapore, Manila, 46; Yesterdays Crafts by Craftsmen of Today, William Penn Mem Mus, Harrisburg, Pa, 72. Awards: Best Ecclesiastical Art, Guild Relig Archit, 59; Best in Show, Int Platform Asn, 71; Best if Gold or Silver, Woodmere Art Gallery, Philadelphia, 62, 63, 67 & 68. Mem: Woodmere Art Asn; Philadelphia Art Alliance; Philadelphia Print Club; Guild Relig Archit; Stained Glass Asn Am. Style & Technique: For silver, simple lines, unadorned almost colonial; prints, black & white representational, academic, economy of line. Publ: Illusr, Naval Acad Log, 23-27, Book of Navy Songs, Doubleday, 27 & Naval Inst Proc, 27. Mailing Add: 1920 Ringgold Pl Philadelphia PA 19146

BOWLT, JOHN
ART HISTORIAN, EDUCATOR
b London, Eng, Dec 6, 43. Study: Univ Birmingham, Eng, BA, 65 & MA, 66; Moscow Univ, USSR, 66-68; Univ St Andrews, Scotland, PhD, 71. Teaching: Lectr Russian, Univ St Andrews, Scotland, 68-69; asst prof Russian, Univ Kans, Lawrence, 70-71; assoc prof Russian art & lang, Univ Tex, Austin, 71- Awards: Brit Coun Scholar for Moscow Univ, USSR, 66-68; Woodrow Wilson Nat Fel, 71; Fel Nat Humanities Inst, Yale Univ, 77-78. Mem: Assoc de Cent Francais d'Art et d'Histoire d'Europe Orientale; Am Asn Advan Slavic Studies. Res: Russian art and architecture of 18th, 19th and 20th centuries. Publ: Auth, Art, politics, money, Art in Am, 3-4/75; auth, Pavel Filonov, a alternative tradition? Art J, spring 75; auth, The Russian Avant-garde, Theory & Criticism 1902-34, Viking, 76; auth, Russian Art 1875-1975: A Collection of Essays, 77; translr, Benedikt Livshits: The One-and a Half-Eyed Archer, 77. Mailing Add: Dept of Slavic Lang Univ Tex Box 7217 Austin TX 78712

BOWMAN, BRUCE
PAINTER, ART WRITER
b Dayton, Ohio, Nov 23, 38. Study: San Diego City Col, Calif, AA; Calif State Univ, Los Angeles, BA & MA; Univ Calif, Los Angeles. Exhib: Calif State Univ, Los Angeles, 68; Santa Paula Ann Exhib, Calif, 69-70; 1st Nat Automotive Art Exhib, San Bernardino, Calif, 69; Cypress Col, Calif, 77; Designs Recycled Gallery, Fullerton, Calif, 77. Teaching: Instr art, West Los Angeles Col, Culver City, 69-; instr art, Cypress Col, 76-77. Pos: Mem, Art Testbook Comt, Los Angeles City Schs, 71-72, mem, Art Curric Comt, 72-73, chmn art dept, 75-76. Mem: Los Angeles Mus of Art; Nat Art Educ Asn; Calif Art Educ. Style & Technique: Work with shaped canvases. Media: Acrylic. Res: Contemporary art forms and techniques. Publ: Auth, articles in Arts & Activities Mag, Design Mag & Sch Arts Mag; auth, Shaped Canvas, 76 & Toothpick Sculpture & Ice Cream Stick Art, 76, Sterling. Dealer: Designs Recycled Gallery 619 N Harbor Blvd Fullerton CA 92632. Mailing Add: 3870 Rambla Orienta Malibu CA 90265

BOWMAN, DOROTHY (LOUISE)
PAINTER, PRINTMAKER
b Hollywood, Calif, Jan 20, 27. Study: Chouinard Art Inst, with Rico Lebrun & Jean Charlot; Jepson Art Inst, Los Angeles; Otis Co Art Inst, Los Angeles; Webster Col, St Louis, scholar for BFA. Work: Brooklyn Mus; Mus Mod Art; Libr Cong; Los Angeles Co Mus Art; De Cordova & Dana Mus. Comn: Ed serigraphs, Int Graphics Art Soc, New York, 58-69; Hilton Hotel, New York, 62; panels of stained glass, Methodist Church, San Luis Obispo, 67, now at Webster Col, St Louis, Mo. Exhib: Brooklyn Mus Nat Print Show, 54-62; Boston Mus Print Ann, 60; Mus Arte Mod, Sao Paulo, Brasil, 61; 50 American Printmakers, Am Fedn Arts Traveling Show, Japan & Moscow, 64; Manila Hilton Art Ctr, Philippines, 71. Awards: Many awards, Brooklyn Mus Print Shows, Libr Cong Nat Print Shows & Boston Mus Shows, 54-71. Bibliog: Enciclopedia internazionale degli artisti, 70; Bruce Cody (auth), Modern American printmaking. Mem: Western Serigraphic Soc. Style & Technique: Serigraphy: opaque and transparent colors plus callage-agraphy. Dealer: Oscar Salzer PO Box 36523 Los Angeles CA 90036. Mailing Add: Star Rte No 1 Ste Genevieve MO 63670

BOWMAN, JEAN (JEAN BOWMAN MAGRUDER)
PAINTER, ILLUSTRATOR
b Mt Vernon, NY, Sept 27, 17. Study: Grand Cent Art Sch, with Jerry Farnsworth; Nat Acad Design, with Leon Kroll; also with Scott Carbee, Boston. Work: Mus of Racing, Saratoga Springs, NY; plus over 350 paintings in pvt collections. Comn: Horse & equestrian portraits, including landscape & archit for Paul Mellon, Richard K Mellon, Queen Elizabeth II, Robert Kleberg, Walter Chrysler & Walter Jeffords. Exhib: Knoedler Gallery, New York; Horse Painters of the World, Tryon Gallery, London, Eng, 69; one-man shows, Vose Galleries, Boston, 40, Scott & Fowles, New York, 52, Grand Cent Galleries, New York, 53 & Ackermann's, London, 68. Mem: Grand Cent Galleries; Soc Animal Artists; Portraits Inc. Publ: Illusr, Maryland Horse, 40-45; illusr, British Race Horse, 54; illusr, Know About Horses, 60; illusr, Spur of Virginia, 70-72; illusr, Chronicle of the Horse. Dealer: Ackermann Gallery 3 Old Bond St London England. Mailing Add: 2705 34th Pl NW Washington DC 20007

BOWMAN, JEFF RAY
ART ADMINISTRATOR, EDUCATOR
b Oneida, Ky, Sept 5, 43. Study: Eastern Ky Univ, AB, 65; Ball State Univ, MA, 69, EdD(art, admin, coun psychol), 71. Teaching: Art instr, Jackson Co Sch Syst, McKee, Ky, 65-66; asst & doctoral fel, Dept Art & Teachers Col, Ball State Univ, 68-71; prog chmn art educ, Univ Houston, 71-74; prof & chmn dept art, Univ Southern Miss, 74- Pos: Consult student asn,

Tex Art Educ Asn & Sch Corps, Ind, Tex & Miss, 71-75; juror art exhib, Tex & Miss, 71-75; mem, Southern Asn Eval Team, 72-; mem develop comt, Tex Art Educ Asn, 73-; mem selection team, Tex Demonstration Schs, 73-; guest lectr, Art & Pub Sch Groups, Tex & Miss, 73-75; coordr workshops, Alliance Arts Educ, Miss, 75. Mem: Nat Art Educ Asn; Ky Guild Artists & Craftsmen; Hattiesburg Civic Arts Coun. Publ: Co-auth, Parochial Education Within the Diocese of Fort Wayne-South Bend, Ind, Phase I, Educ Serv Assocs, Muncie, 70; auth, Meeting the needs, Art Teacher, fall 74. Mailing Add: 312 Third Ave Hattiesburg MS 39401

BOWMAN, KEN
PAINTER
b Denver, Colo, Mar 28, 37. Study: Univ Colo; Art Inst Chicago, BFA, 63. Work: Utah Mus Fine Arts, Salt Lake City; Univ Art Mus, Berkeley, Calif. Exhib: One-man exhibs, Tibor de Nagy Gallery, Inc, New York, 70 & 72; Art on Paper, Weatherspoon Gallery, Univ NC, 71; 3rd Biennial Art, Medellin, Colombia, SAm, 72; Painting and Sculpture Today 1972, Indianapolis Mus Art, Ind, 72. Media: Acrylic Polymer, Collage. Mailing Add: c/o Tibor de Nagy Gallery Inc 29 W 57th St New York NY 10019

BOWMAN, RICHARD
PAINTER
b Rockford, Ill, Mar 15, 18. Study: Art Inst Chicago, 38-42; Univ Iowa, MFA, 49. Work: San Francisco Mus Art; Oakland Mus; Stanford Univ; Univ Tex Mus; Santa Barbara Art Mus; Recent Acquisitions, Mus of Am Art, New Britain, Conn; plus others. Exhib: Retrospectives, Stanford Univ, 56 & San Francisco Mus Art, 61; Whitney Mus Am Art, 62; one-man show, San Francisco Mus Art, 70 & retrospective (1943-1972); Roswell Mus & Art Ctr, NMex, 72; plus others. Teaching: Instr, NPark Col, 44-46; instr, Chicago Art Inst Sch, 44-47; instr, State Univ Iowa, 47-49; instr, Stanford Univ, 49-50 & 57, 58 & 61; instr, Univ Man, 50-54. Awards: Ryerson Travelling Fel, Art Inst Chicago, 42; prizes, Montreal, 52 & Winnipeg Art Gallery, 53; hon mention, Oakland Art Mus, 55; artist-in-residence grant painting, Roswell Mus & Art Ctr, 72; plus others. Mailing Add: 178 Springdale Way Redwood City CA 94062

BOWMAN, RUTH
EDUCATOR, ART HISTORIAN
b Denver, Colo, June 14, 23. Study: Bryn Mawr Col, AB; NY Univ Inst Fine Arts, MA; Harvard Univ Inst Arts Admin, cert. Exhibitions Arranged: The New York Painter, A Century of Teaching: From Morse to Hofmann, Marlborough-Gerson Gallery, 67, A University Collects (tour with Am Fedn Arts), 65-68 & Twentieth Century Painting and Sculpture from the NY Univ Art Collection, Hudson River Mus, 71; Murals Without Walls, Newark Airport Murals of Arshile Gorky, Newark Mus, 78-79. Teaching: Adj asst prof art hist, Sch Continuing Educ, NY Univ, 65-70, adj asst prof art hist, Sch Educ, 70-73, lectr art, Washington Sq Col, 72-73 (Sunrise Semester-CBS); also many free lance courses & lects on mod art; radio & TV weekly-WNYC. Pos: Asst cur, Jewish Mus, 62-63; cur & dir, NY Univ Art Collection, 63-74; consult educ prog, Guggenheim Mus, 69-72; dir educ, Los Angeles Co Mus Art, 74-75. Awards: Nat Endowment for Arts Grant, 75. Mem: New York Cult Coun (chmn, visual arts comt, 71-74); Bank St Col Educ (adv comt, 71-73); Am Asn Mus (vpres); Am Fedn Arts; Col Art Asn; Coun for Arts at Mass Inst Technol; Craft & Folk Art Mus, Los Angeles (trustee). Res: 19th and 20th century American and European art and architecture. Publ: Auth, catalog introd, The thirtieth anniversary exhibition, American Abstract Artists, 66; auth, Double exposure (catalog), Am Fedn Arts, 69; auth, Nature, the photograph and Thomas Anshutz, Col Art Asn J, fall 73; auth, The artist as model: portrait of David Wilson Jordan by Thomas Anshutz, Univ Kans Register, fall 73. Mailing Add: 10701 Wilshire Blvd Los Angeles CA 90024

BOWNE, JAMES DEHART
MUSEUM DIRECTOR, ART HISTORIAN
b Philadelphia, Pa, Mar 5, 40. Study: George Washington Univ; Corcoran Sch of Art; Sandhills Community Col, Southern Pines, NC, AA, 68; ECarolina Univ, Greenville, NC, AB, 70; Univ NC, Chapel Hill, MA, 72. Collections Arranged: Reflections of Our Heritage—The Art of the American Indian, 9/76, 20th Century German Expressionist Prints, 11/76, Collectors Choice Exhibition, 12/76 & Annual Wabash Valley Exhib, 3/77, Sheldon Swope Art Gallery, Terre Haute, Ind; plus numerous others. Teaching: Instr drawing/painting, Lauren Rogers Libr & Mus of Art, Laurel, Miss, 73-75. Pos: Dir-cur Lauren Rogers Libr & Mus of Art, 73-75; dir, Sheldon Swope Art Gallery, 75- Mem: Am Asn of Mus; Col Art Asn; Assoc Coun of the Arts; Midwest Mus Conf; Asn of Ind Mus. Res: Reception of German expressionism in America between the World Wars (MA thesis). Publ: Contribr, A Medieval Treasury From Southeastern Collections, Univ NC, Chapel Hill, 71. Mailing Add: 63 S 20th St Terre Haute IN 47803

BOWRON, EDGAR PETERS
CURATOR, ART HISTORIAN
b Birmingham, Ala, May 27, 43. Study: Colgate Univ, AB, 65; Univ Pa, 65-66; Inst Fine Arts, NY Univ, AM, 69; Metrop Mus Art, Ford Found fel, 68-69, cert mus training, 69. Collections Arranged: Art in 18th Century Rome, 71 & cur in charge, J Paul Getty Collection Exhib (with catalog), 72, Minneapolis Inst Arts, Minn; Masters of Italian Painting 76 & Renaissance Bronzes in the Walters Art Gallery, 78, Baltimore, Md. Pos: Educ lectr, Metrop Mus Art, 69-70; registr, Minneapolis Inst Arts, 70-73; cur Renaissance & baroque art, Walters Art Gallery, 73-; fac, Peabody Inst, Johns Hopkins Univ, 73- Awards: Ford Found Mus Training Fel, 66-69; Nat Endowment Arts Fel, 75-76; Nat Endowment for the Humanities Grant (proj dir), 77-78. Mem: Col Art Asn Am; Am Eighteenth Century Soc. Res: Roman painting, 17th and 18th centuries. Publ: Auth, Scarsellino's nymphs at the bath, 70 & Vasari's portrait of six Italian poets, 71-73, Minneapolis Inst Arts Bull; articles & rev in Minn Inst Arts Bull, Apollo, Walters Art Gallery Bull, J Walters Art Gallery & Mus News. Mailing Add: Walters Art Gallery 600 N Charles Baltimore MD 21201

BOXER, STANLEY (ROBERT)
SCULPTOR, PAINTER
b New York, NY, June 26, 26. Study: Brooklyn Col; Art Student League. Work: Chase Manhattan Bank & Guggenheim Mus, New York; Cornell Univ Johnson Mus; Ciba-Geigy Corp, NY; Albright-Knox Mus, NY. Exhib: One-man shows, paintings, Andre Emmerich Gallery, Zurich, Switz, 75 & New York, 75-78, paintings, Galerie Wentzel, Hamburg, Ger & Tibor de Nagy Gallery, New York, 71-75, Mus Fine Arts, Boston, 77 & Edmonton Mus, Alta, Can, 77, sculpture, Pa Acad Fine Arts, Philadelphia, 76. Awards: John S Guggenheim Mem Found Fel, 75. Bibliog: Jeanne Siegel (auth), article and cover, Art Spectrum, 2/75; Hilton Kramer (auth), rev in NY Times, 75; article in Studio Int, 6-7/75. Style & Technique: Abstract artist. Dealer: Watson/de Nagy Gallery Texas Inc 1106 Berthea Houston TX 77006; Andre Emmerich Gallery Inc 41 E 57 St New York NY 10022. Mailing Add: 37 E 18th St New York NY 10002

BOYCE, GERALD G
EDUCATOR, PAINTER
b Embarrass, Wis, Dec 29, 25. Study: Wis State Col, BS; Milwaukee Art Inst; Am Guatemalan Inst, Guatemala City; Univ Iowa, MFA; Univ Ill; study & res, Brit Mus & Courtauld Inst, London. Work: Evansville Col; St John's Univ; Wabash Col; Minot Col; Univ Iowa. Exhib: Los Angeles Co Mus; San Francisco Mus Art; Art Inst Chicago, 54; Mus Mod Art, New York, 56; Corcoran Gallery Art, Washington, DC, 71. Teaching: Prof art hist & studio, Ind Cent Col, 50-; lectr art hist, DePauw Univ, 68- Pos: Consult, Ind Bell Tel Co, 67-70; consult, US Post Off Dept, 72. Awards: First Prizes, Ind Artists Club, St John's Univ Nat & Minot Col Show, 71. Mem: Nat Col Art Conf; Am Crafts Coun. Style & Technique: Silverpoint medium. Media: Mixed Media. Mailing Add: RR1 Box 239A Morgantown IN 46160

BOYCE, RICHARD
SCULPTOR
b New York, NY, June 11, 20. Study: Mus Fine Arts Sch, Boston, William Paige grant, 49, Bartlett grant, 56. Work: Whitney Mus Am Art, New York; Joseph H Hirshhorn Found; Mus Art, RI; Addison Gallery Am Art, Andover, Mass; Harvard Univ, Cambridge, Mass. Comn: Andromeda Fountain, comn by Dr & Mrs Morton Grossman, Los Angeles, 64. Exhib: Univ Ill, 55 & 67; Art Inst Chicago, 60; Pa Acad Fine Arts, Philadelphia, 64; The New Vein, Smithsonian Inst European Traveling Exhib, 68-69; The Partial Figure in Art, Baltimore Mus Art, 70. Teaching: Asst prof painting, Wellesley Col, 53-62; lectr design, Boston Univ, 59-61; lectr sculpture, Univ Calif, Los Angeles. Dealer: Silvan Simone Gallery 11579 Olympic Blvd Los Angeles CA 90064. Mailing Add: 1419 W Washington Blvd Venice CA 90291

BOYCE, WILLIAM G
MUSEUM DIRECTOR, EDUCATOR
b Fairmont, Minn, July 25, 21. Study: Univ Minn, Minneapolis, BS, 49, MEd, 52; Mills Col, 54-55. Collections Arranged: Cataloged the George P Tweed Memorial Art Collection; Dedicatory Exhibition Honoring Mrs Alice Tweed Tuohy; Tweed at Twenty Exhibition; A University Collects-Tweed Gallery Traveling Exhib; David Ericson Exhibition; plus many others. Teaching: Prof art, Univ Minn, Duluth, 70- Pos: Ed cur, Tweed Gallery, Univ Minn, Duluth, 57-65, assoc dir, 65-69, dir, Tweed Mus Art, Univ Minn, Duluth, 69- Mem: Life mem Nat Educ Asn; Minn Art Educ Asn (pres, 63-65); Midwest Mus Conf (Minn vpres, 67-70); Am Asn Mus; Am Asn Univ Prof. Publ: Auth, David Erickson (monogr), Edgewater Press, 63; also many catalogs. Mailing Add: 2700 Minnesota Ave Duluth MN 55802

BOYD, DONALD EDGAR
PHOTOGRAPHER, ART DEALER
b Sparta, Ohio, Feb 20, 34. Study: Ohio State Univ, BFA(cum laude), 56; Harvard Univ, with Mirko Basadella, MAT, 61; Univ Iowa, MFA, 66; with Elliot Offner & Robert Laurent; Hobart Welding Sch, with Richard Stankiewicz, 68; SC Educ TV, with Stan Vanderbeek & Jack Perlmutter, 74; also with Dick Higgins & Alison Knowles, 76. Work: Dayton Art Inst, Ohio. Exhib: Boston Arts Festival, Mass, 62 & 64; Blossom Music Ctr Sculpture, Kent, Ohio, 71 & 73; Spring Mills Traveling Show, 74; SDak Biennial, 75; plus nine one-man shows. Teaching: Asst prof sculpture & drawing, Kenyon Col, 66-72; artist-in-residence, SC Arts Comn, 73-74; asst prof sculpture & design, SDak State Univ, 74-78. Awards: First Prize, First Ann Nat Slide Competition, Univ Buffalo, 69; Purchase Prize for sculpture, Dayton Art Inst, 69; Biddle Award, Mansfield, Ohio Art Ctr, 69. Bibliog: R Stevens (auth), Donald Boyd, La Rev Mod, 1/63; Meilach (auth), Small wood objects, 75. Mem: Fluxus West (dir); Southern Asn of Sculptors (regional vpres); Found Community Artists. Style & Technique: Natural materials for themselves, color and texture in an art context. Media: Leather, Intermedia. Publ: Eclat, int art quart, 68-72; producer, Electronic Gallery, SC Educ TV & Nat Endowment for the Arts, 75. Dealer: Ecart 6 rue Plantamour CH1201 Geneva Switzerland. Mailing Add: Cameo Photo Ctr & Gallery 124 N LBJ San Marcos TX 78666

BOYD, JAMES HENDERSON
PRINTMAKER, SCULPTOR
b Ottawa, Ont, Dec 16, 28. Study: Art Student League, with Wil Barnet; Nat Acad Design; Contemporaries Graphic Workshop, with M Ponce de Leon. Work: Nat Gallery Can, Ottawa; Mus Mod Art, New York; Victoria & Albert Mus, London, Ont; Lugano Art Mus; Sorsbie Art Gallery, Nairobi, SAfrica. Comn: Carved doors, Centennial Libr, Campbellton, NB, 67 & 72; carved doors, Pub Serv Alliance Bldg, Ottawa, 69; entrance sculpture, Can Pavilion, Osaka World's Fair, 70; mural, MacDonald Bldg, Univ Ottawa, 73. Exhib: Cincinnati Biennial of Prints, 62; 1st Biennial of Prints, Santiago, Chile, 63; 8th Int Black & White Exhib, 64; Tokyo Biennial of Prints, 64; Centennial Art Exhib, Toronto, 67. Teaching: Resident artist, Univ Western Ont, 67-69; prof printmaking, Ont Col Art, 71-, head dept, 70-71; prof painting, Munic Art Ctr, Ottawa, 70-72; prof visual arts dept, Univ Ottawa, 73- Pos: Hon cur, Univ Western Ont, 67-69; adv, Visual Arts Ottawa, 74- Awards: Purchase Award, 8th Int Black & White Exhib, 64; First Prize, 1st Nat Print Exhib, Burnaby, BC; Venezuela Prize, best foreign artist, 2nd Biennial of Prints, Santiago, Chile, 65. Mem: Fel & life mem Int Inst Arts & Lett; Can Graphic Art Soc. Dealer: Isaacs Gallery Yonge St Toronto ON Can. Mailing Add: PO Box 2400 Sta D Ottawa ON K1P 5W5 Can

BOYD, JOHN DAVID
EDUCATOR, PRINTMAKER
b London, Ark, Jan 22, 39. Study: Calif State Univ, Long Beach, with Richard Swift, BA; Cranbrook Acad Art, with Lawrence Barker, MFA. Work: Tex Tech Univ; Ga State Univ; Univ NC, Chapel Hill; State Univ NY Col Potsdam; Springfield Art Mus, Mo. Exhib: Seattle Print Int, Wash, 68, 69 & 71; Ann Drawing & Small Sculpture Exhib, Ball State Univ, 69, 70 & 77; Printmakers 20 Invitational, State Univ NY Col Oneonta, 72; 5th Nat Print & Drawing Exhib, Minot State Col, 75; 24th Nat Exhib Prints, Libr Cong, 75; 16th Bradley Nat Print & Drawing Exhib, Bradley Univ Sch of Art, Peoria, Ill, 77. Teaching: Asst prof printmaking & drawing, Wichita State Univ, 72- Style & Technique: Representational; lithography, intaglio, relief painting. Mailing Add: 2641 Garland Wichita KS 67204

BOYD, KAREN WHITE
WEAVER, TAPESTRY ARTIST
b Akron, Ohio, Sept 8, 36. Study: Kent State Univ, BA(art educ), 58 & MA(studio art), 64; Tyler Sch Art, Temple Univ, MFA(weaving), 75. Comn: Woven tapestries, Dept Spec Educ, Murray State Univ, 75. Exhib: Regional Craft Biennial, J B Speed Mus, Louisville, Ky, 70; Mid-States Craft Exhib, Evansville Mus, Ind, 73; Nat Fiber Design Show, Calif Polytech State Univ, San Luis Obispo, 75. Teaching: Asst prof weaving & textiles, Murray State Univ, 67- Awards: Juror's Award, Ted Hallman, Nat Fiber Design Show, 75. Mem: Ky Guild Artists & Craftsmen; Handweaver's Guild Am. Style & Technique: Tapestry sculptures woven in various materials; emphasis on engineering aspect of loom construction; multi-layers locked on loom. Dealer: Rodney Beck Coffee Trees Gallery Walnut St Louisville KY 40200. Mailing Add: 211 S 16th St Murray KY 42071

BOYD, LAKIN
EDUCATOR, PRINTMAKER
b Athens, Ala, Aug 27, 46. Study: Univ Ala, BFA, 68 & MA, 70; Pratt Graphic Ctr, 70-71, intaglio with Michael Ponce de Leon. Work: Oscar Wells Mem Mus, Birmingham, Ala; Univ Ala, Tuscaloosa; Ala Arts Comn; Univ of the South; Pratt Graphic Ctr Print Collection, New York. Exhib: Nat Student Printmakers Travel Exhib, 68; 13th Dixie Ann, 72; one-man shows, Univ Ala & Judson Col, 73; 14th Ann Reece Regional, 74. Teaching: Asst prof graphics & art hist, Ala A&M Univ, Huntsville, 71- Awards: Purchase Award, Birmingham Art Asn, 67; Fulbright Grant to Belg & The Netherlands, 75. Mem: Southeastern Col Art Conf; Am Asn Univ Prof; Nat Art Educ Asn; Am Crafts Coun (Ala state rep); Ala Art Educ Asn. Style & Technique: Intaglio print; presently combining photo-etching with color viscosity printing. Media: Intaglio; Lithography. Mailing Add: 426 Eustis Ave SE Huntsville AL 35801

BOYER, JACK K
MUSEUM DIRECTOR, CURATOR
b Van Houten, NMex, Sept 2, 11. Pos: Dir & cur, Kit Carson Home & Mus, Taos, NMex, 54- Mem: Am Asn Mus; Archaeol Soc NMex; NMex State Hist Soc; Clearing House Western Mus. Mailing Add: Kit Carson Mem Found Old Kit Carson Rd Taos NM 87571

BOYLAN, JOHN LEWIS
PAINTER, PRINTMAKER
b Cleveland, Ohio, Oct 8, 21. Study: Oberlin Col, 39-42; Cleveland Inst Art, 42; Univ NMex, BFA, 47; Art Students League, 47-50; study with Vaclav Vytlacil, Morris Kantor, Harry Sternberg & Will Barnet. Work: Metrop Mus Art, New York; New York Pub Libr; Roswell Mus, NMex; Univ Pa Art Mus. Exhib: One-man show, Roswell Mus, 59 & 66; Soc Am Graphic Artists, 50 & 71; Royal Soc Painter-Etchers & Engravers, London, 54 & 56; Japan Print Soc, Tokyo, 67. Teaching: Dir painting & design, Roswell Mus Art Sch, 50-51; instr painting & design, Inst Am Indian Art, Santa Fe, NMex, 66-, actg head fine arts, 74-75. Pos: Mem bd control, Art Students League, 48-50; cur, Old Lincoln Co Mem Comn, Lincoln, NMex, 52-65. Awards: Award of Merit, Am Asn State & Local Hist, 60. Mem: Soc Am Graphic Artists; Artists Co-op Gallery (co-dir, 75). Style & Technique: Abstract; watercolor, etching, lithograph. Media: Oil, Acrylic; Woodcut, Metal Plate Lithograph. Mailing Add: PO Box 2181 Santa Fe NM 87501

BOYLE, KEITH
PAINTER, EDUCATOR
b Defiance, Ohio, Feb 15, 30. Study: Ringling Sch Art, Sarasota, Fla; Univ Iowa, BFA. Work: San Francisco Mus Art & Stanford Univ Mus, Calif; Mead Paper Corp, Atlanta, Ga; Nat Fine Arts Collection, Washington, DC; Oakland Mus, Calif. Exhib: Current Bay Area Art, Stanford Univ Mus, 64; The Colorists, San Francisco Mus Art, 65; Drawings by 100 American Artists, Ann Arbor, Mich, 65; A Century of California Painting, 1870-1970, 70; Looking Westward, Joslyn Art Mus, Omaha, Nebr, 70; Retrospective Exhib of Paintings: 1965-1977, San Jose Mus of Art, Calif, 78. Teaching: Prof painting & drawing, Stanford Univ, 62- Mailing Add: 515 Newell Rd Palo Alto CA 94303

BOYLE, RICHARD J
MUSEUM DIRECTOR, WRITER
b New York, NY, June 3, 32. Study: Adelphi Univ, BA; Oxford Univ, with Edgar Wind & John Pope-Hennessy; Art Student League, with Will Barnet. Collections Arranged: John Twachtman Retrospective, 66, Laser Light: A New Visual Art, 69, The Early Work of Paul Gauguin, 71 & Robert S Duncanson: A Centennial Exhibition, 72, Cincinnati Art Mus; American Paintings from Newport, Wichita Art Mus, 69. Pos: Cur, Int Art Found, Newport, RI, summer 62; dir, Middletown Fine Arts Ctr, Ohio, 63-65; cur painting, Cincinnati Art Mus, 65-73; dir, Pa Acad of Fine Arts, 73-; art comn chmn, Redevelop Authority, Philadelphia. Awards: Benjamin Franklin Fel, Royal Soc of Art, London, Eng. Mem: Asn Art Mus Dir; Nat Trust Hist Preservation. Res: Late nineteenth and twentieth century painting, especially late nineteenth century American painting. Publ: Co-auth, Rediscovery: Thomas Cole's voyage of life, Art in Am, 67; auth, From Hiram Powers to laser light, Apollo, 71; contribr, French impressionists influence American impressionists, Lowe Art Mus, Fla, 71; contribr, Genius of American painting, Weidenfeld & Nicolson, 73; auth, American impressionism, 74. Mailing Add: c/o Pa Acad Fine Arts Broad & Cherry St Philadelphia PA 19102

BOYLEN, MICHAEL EDWARD
CRAFTSMAN, ART ADMINISTRATOR
b Stoughton, Wis, Dec 12, 35. Study: Yale Univ, AB(hist), 58, with Josef Albers; Sch for Am Craftsmen, pottery with Frans Wildenhain; Univ Wis, MS, MFA, with Harvey K Littleton. Work: Corning Mus of Glass, NY; Cleveland Mus of Art, Ohio; Mus für Kunst und Gewerbe, Hamburg, Ger; Victoria & Albert Mus, London; Chrysler Mus at Norfolk, Va. Exhib: Nat Ceramic Exhib, Everson Mus, Syracuse, NY, 64 & 68; Toledo Glass Nat Exhib, Toledo Mus of Art, Ohio, 66 & 68; New Am Glass, Dallas Mus of Fine Arts, Tex, 67; Smithsonian Inst Travelling Exhib, 68-69; Del Art Mus, Wilmington, 71 & 75; one-man shows, Fleming Mus, Univ Vt, Burlington, 75; Bergstrom Mus, Neenah, Wis, 76; Corning Mus of Glass, NY. Teaching: Instr ceramics, Cleveland Inst of Art, Ohio, 66; lectr design & ceramics, Lyndon State Col, Lyndonville, Vt, 67-76. Pos: Pres, Vt Coun on the Arts, Vt State Arts Agency, 74-76, vpres, 76-77. Awards: L C Tiffany Found grant, 65. Bibliog: Clemens Kalischer (auth), Glass—Michael Boylen, Vt Life Mag, 72; R & L Grover (auths), Contemporary Art Glass, Crown, 75; Paul Hollister (auth), Hollister on Glass, Acquire, 12/76. Mem: Glass Art Soc. Style & Technique: Decorative and sculptural using the transparency of glass for multiple layers of color and producing forms within forms. Media: Blown glass; clay. Publ: Auth, Studio Glass in Perspective, Studio Potter, 73 & 74 Crafts Ann, NY State Craftsmen, 74. Dealer: Contemp Art Glass Group 806 Madison Ave New York NY 10021. Mailing Add: RFD 2 West Burke VT 05871

BOYNTON, JAMES W
PAINTER, PRINTMAKER
b Ft Worth, Tex, Jan 12, 28. Study: Tex Christian Univ, BFA & MFA. Work: Dallas Mus Fine Arts; Mus Fine Arts, Houston; Witte Mem Mus; Tex Fine Arts Asn; Ft Worth Art Ctr; plus others. Exhib: San Francisco Mus Art, 52, 62 & 69; Mus Mod Art, 56, 62 & 69; Whitney Mus Am Art, 57-58 & 67-68; Tex Pavillion HemisFair, San Antonio, 68; Los Angeles Mus Art, 69; Tamarind: A Renaissance of Lithography (traveling exhib), Int Exhib Found, Washington, DC, 71-72; plus others. Teaching: Instr, Univ Houston, 55 & 57; instr, San Francisco Art Inst, 60 & 62; instr, Univ NMex, summer 63; instr, Houston Mus Sch, 68-69; instr, Northwood Inst, Dallas, 68-69; instr, Univ St Thomas, Tex, 69-70. Awards: Tamarind Workshop Fel, 67; Awards, Beaumont Art Mus & Oklahoma City Art Ctr, 68; plus others. Bibliog: Douglas MacAgy (auth), James Boynton (monogr), Barone Gallery Inc, 59. Media: Graphic. Dealer: Atelier Chapman Gallery 2526 Fairmont St Dallas TX 75201. Mailing Add: 3723 Albans St Houston TX 77005

BOZ, ALEX (ALEX BOZICKOVIC)
PAINTER, LECTURER
b Sarajevo, Yugoslavia, July 8, 19; US citizen. Study: Univ Belgrade, BFA, 43; Belgrade Acad Fine Arts, 43-50; Belgrade, 48-50. Work: Contemp Mus Art, Rijeka, Yugoslavia; Contemp Mus Art, Novisad, Yugoslavia; City of Bremen, WGer; Bell Tel Co, Chicago; City Hosp, Bremen. Comn: Murals, Zopas Corp, Rome, Italy, 53 & City Planning Comn, Bremen, WGer, 55. Exhib: One-man shows, Los Angeles, Milwaukee, Chicago, New York, Toronto & Europe, 52-72; Kunsthall Exhib, Bremen, 55; Gallery Boheme, Copenhagen, Denmark, 55; Old Orchard Festival, Chicago, 59-67; Art Inst Chicago, 60. Teaching: Prof art, Rijeka, Yugoslavia, 50-52; instr painting & printmaking, Americana Art Ctr, Northfield, Ill, 65-68. Awards: Awards from Gallery Boheme, Copenhagen, 55 & Old Orchard Festival, Chicago, 66. Media: Casein, Oil. Mailing Add: c/o Americana Galleries 271 Waukegan Rd Northfield IL 60093

BRACH, PAUL HENRY
PAINTER
b New York, NY, Mar 13, 24. Study: State Univ Iowa, BFA, 48, MFA, 49. Work: Mus Mod Art; Whitney Mus Am Art; St Louis Mus; Los Angeles Co Mus of Art, Los Angeles; Smith Col Mus; plus others. Exhib: Corcoran Gallery, 59; Contemporary American Painting and Sculpture, Univ Ill, 65; For Eyes and Ears, Cordier-Ekstrom Gallery, 65; Art in Progress, Finch Col Art Mus, 65; An Environment for Faith, San Francisco Mus Art, 65; Andre Emmerich Gallery, New York, 74; Cirrus Gallery, Los Angeles, 75; Benson Gallery, Bridgehampton, NY, 75; Lerner Heller Gallery, New York, 78; plus others. Teaching: Mem fac, Univ Mo, 49-51, New Sch Social Res, 52-55, NY Univ, 54-56, Parsons Sch Design, 56-67, Cooper Union, 60-62 & Cornell Univ, 65-67; prof art & chmn dept, Univ Calif, San Diego, 67-69; dean sch art, Calif Inst Art, 69-75; chmn div arts, Lincoln Ctr Campus, Fordham Univ, 75- Pos: Fel, Tamarind Lithog Workshop, Los Angeles, 64; artist in residence, Am Fedn Arts, Albuquerque, 65. Mem: Col Art Asn. Publ: Auth, John Mandel, Arts, 9/75; auth, rev in Artforum, 10/76 & Art in Am, 3-4/78. Mailing Add: 393 W Broadway New York NY 10012

BRACKMAN, ROBERT
PAINTER, EDUCATOR
b Odessa, Russia, Sept 25, 98. Study: Francisco Ferrer Sch; Nat Acad Design; also with George Bellows & Robert Henri. Work: Metrop Mus Art, New York; Whitney Mus Am Art, New York; Colonial Williamsburg; West Point Acad Collection; plus others. Comn: Portraits of Gen Charles Lindbergh, Mr & Mrs John D Rockefeller, Jr, Hon Herbert H Lehman, John Foster Dulles, Gen Nathan F Twining & many others. Exhib: Nat Acad Design, New York; Audubon Artists, New York; Allied Artists Am, New York; Pa Acad Fine Arts, Philadelphia; Art Inst Chicago; plus many others. Teaching: Instr art, Art Students League. Awards: N Grumbacher Purchase Prize, Audubon Artists Exhib, 60; Adolph & Clara Obrig Prize, Nat Acad Design, 60, Andrew Carnegie Prize, 65 & Gold Medal of Honor, 66; plus many others. Bibliog: Peyton Boswell (auth), Modern American Painter; Homer St Gaudens (auth), Art and Artist. Mem: Royal Soc Arts, London, Eng; Nat Acad Design; Am Watercolor Soc; Audubon Artists; Int Soc Arts & Lett; plus many others. Mailing Add: Noank CT 06340

BRADBURY, ELLEN A
CURATOR, ART HISTORIAN
b Louisville, Ky, Feb 26, 40. Study: Univ NMex, BA & MA, 66; Yale Univ; Univ Vienna, Austria, 60. Collections Arranged: African Oceanic Art, American Indians, North and South; shows arranged: Black Kingdoms, Art of the Benin and Ashanti; catalogued: Meso American Collections. Teaching: Instr art hist, Univ NMex, 65-66. Pos: Res asst, Minneapolis Inst Art, 69-70, asst registrar, 70-72, registrar, 72-75 & curator primitive art, 75- Mem: Col Art Asn; Am Asn Mus. Res: Shirts worn in ghost dances by North American Indians. Publ: Co-auth, Moi Kavakava, Minneapolis Inst Arts Bull, LX:76-81; auth, Black Kingdoms, African Arts, 75; co-auth, The Minneapolis Inst Art Ijo screen, Minneapolis Inst Art Bull; auth (catalogue), I Wear the Morning Star, American Indian Ghost Dance. Mailing Add: Minneapolis Inst Arts 2400 Third Ave S Minneapolis MN 55404

BRADFORD, HOWARD
PRINTMAKER, PAINTER
b Toronto, Ont, July 14, 19; US citizen. Study: Chouinard Art Inst, Los Angeles; Jepson Art Inst, Los Angeles; Calif Sch Fine Arts, San Francisco. Work: Philadelphia Mus Fine Arts; Boston Mus Fine Arts; Bibliotheque Nat France; Los Angeles Co Mus; New York Pub Libr. Comn: Print editions (100), Dallas Mus Fine Arts, 53, Hilton Hotel, New York, 64 & Assoc Am Artists, New York, 67-69; Brentanos: Print Editions 1977-78. Exhib: Libr Cong Nat Print & Drawing Exhib, 51; Brooklyn Mus Print Ann, 52; Dallas Mus Fine Arts Nat Print Exhib, 53; 60 American Printmakers, US Info Serv, Europe, 56; Carmel Art Asn, Calif, 72 & 76. Awards: Birds by Beach (serigraph), Libr Cong, 51 & Dallas Mus Fine Arts, 53; Guggenheim Fel Creative Printmaking, 60. Mem: Am Color Print Soc; Western Serigraph Inst, Los Angeles; Carmel Art Asn. Style & Technique: Organic abstraction. Media: Silk Screen; Acrylic. Dealer: Oscar Salzer 448 N Detroit St Los Angeles CA 90036. Mailing Add: 684 Alice St Monterey CA 93940

BRADLEY, DOROTHY
ART DEALER, PAINTER
b Wild Rose, Wis, Oct 21, 20. Study: Milwaukee State Teachers Col; Oshkosh State Teachers Col, cert elem educ; Layton Art Sch, Milwaukee, with Gerrit Sinclair. Work: Milwaukee Pub Libr, Wis. Exhib: Watercolor USA, St Louis, 63; Wis Painters & Sculptors, Milwaukee, 65; one-woman shows, Rahr-West Mus, Manitowoc, Wis, 71, Allis Art Libr, Milwaukee, 71, Oshkosh Pub Mus, Wis, 72 & Wustum Mus, Racine, Wis, 72. Pos: Dir, Bradley Galleries, Milwaukee, 60- Style & Technique: Watercolor, transparent acrylic and stained canvas. Media: Watercolor. Specialty: Wisconsin artist and art of Haiti. Mailing Add: c/o Bradley Galleries 2565 N Downer Ave Milwaukee WI 53211

BRADLEY, MRS HARRY LYNDE
COLLECTOR
Collection: Contemporary art. Mailing Add: 2115 W Brown Deer Rd Milwaukee WI 53217

BRADLEY, IDA FLORENCE
PAINTER, INSTRUCTOR
b Johnstown, Pa, Oct 24, 08. Study: Puzzletown Art Sch, with Lee Atkyns; Art League Ligonier Valley, with Lucile Banks & Ralph Reynolds, Ind. Work: Watercolor, Govt Bldg; painting, Penelec Elec Co; First Methodist Church; painting, Pitt Col. Comn: Three oils, Bethlehem Steel Corp, Johnstown, 58. Exhib: Allied Artists Johnstown, 40-; Am Artists Prof League, New York, 72; Johnstown Area Arts Coun, 72; Arts Assocs, Johnstown, 72. Teaching: Instr painting, pvt sch, 45- Awards: Best of Show, Allied Artists Johnstown, 53, Best Watercolor Prize, 59; Best of Show, St Vincent Col, 71. Mem: Allied Artists Johnstown

(mem bd dir, 60-70); Am Artists Prof League; Johnstown Area Arts Coun; Arts Assocs. Media: Watercolor. Mailing Add: 2139 Pitt Ave Johnstown PA 15905

BRADLEY, PETER ALEXANDER
PAINTER, ART DEALER
b Connellsville, Pa, Sept 15, 40. Study: Cranbrook Acad Art, Bloomfield, Mich, 63; Soc Arts & Crafts, Detroit; Yale Univ. Work: Mus Mod Art, New York; Metrop Mus Art, New York. Comn: Sculpture, de Menil Found, Houston, 71. Exhib: American Print Makers, US Info Agency, circulated in USSR, 66; Some American History, Rice Univ, Houston, 71; Deluxe Show, Houston, 71; Toward Color and Field, Mus Fine Arts, Houston, 71; one-man show, Andre Emmerich, New York, 71-75. Teaching: Instr printing, Franconia Col, currently. Pos: Art dealer, Perls Gallery, New York, 64-; guest cur, Deluxe Show, 71. Bibliog: Simone Swan (auth), The Deluxe Show (catalog), De Menil Publ, 71; E A Carean (auth), Toward Color and Field, Mus Fine Arts, 71; John Canady (auth), Peter Bradley, New York Times, 6/3/72. Specialty: 20th century modern masters; French paintings. Dealer: Andre Emmerich 41 E 57th St New York NY 10022. Mailing Add: 20 Main St Littleton NH 03561

BRADSHAW, GLENN RAYMOND
PAINTER, EDUCATOR
b Peoria, Ill, Mar 3, 22. Study: Ill State Univ, BS, 47; Univ Ill, MFA, 50. Work: Butler Inst Am Art, Youngstown, Ohio; Springfield Art Mus, Mo; Pasadena Mus, Calif; El Paso Mus, Tex; Ill State Mus, Springfield. Exhib: 200 Years of Watercolor Painting in America, Metrop Mus Art, New York, 66-67; A View of Contemporary Watercolor, Cleveland Inst Art, Ohio, 68; Watermedia '70, Univ Colo, Boulder, 70; Contemp Images in Watercolor, Akron Art Inst, Ohio, 76; Watercolor USA Bicentennial, Springfield Mus Art, Mo, 76. Teaching: Prof art, Univ Ill, 52- Awards: John Young Hunter Award, 73 & Ed Whitney Prize, 74, Am Watercolor Soc Ann; Arches Paper Co Prize, Nat Watercolor Soc Ann, 74, First Prize, 77. Bibliog: E Reep (auth), The content of watercolor, Van Nostrand Reinhold, 69; Kent & Meyer (auth), Watercolorists at work, Watson-Guptill, 72; E Betts (auth), Master Class in Watercolor, Watson-Guptill, 75. Mem: Am Watercolor Soc; Nat Watercolor Soc; Nat Soc Painters in Casein & Acrylic. Media: Watercolor, Collage. Dealer: Tower Park Gallery 4709 N Prospect Peoria Heights IL 61614. Mailing Add: 906 Sunnycrest St Urbana IL 61801

BRADSHAW, LAWRENCE JAMES
INSTRUCTOR, PAINTER
b St Paul, Kans, Sept 21, 45. Study: Kans State Col, Pittsburg, BFA, MA with Reed Schmickle; Ohio Univ, MFA with William Kortlander, Dana Loomis, Gary Pettigrew. Work: Whitesitt Gallery, Kans State Col, Pittsburg; Akron Art Inst, Ohio; Siegfried Gallery, Ohio Univ, Athens; New Gallery, Univ Nebr, Omaha; Eisenberg Art Gallery, Omaha. Comn: Posters, Union Oil Co of Calif, Honolulu, Hawaii, 67; 20 waterfowl ilus, Henry Doorly Zoo, Omaha, 75; logo & stationary, Riverfront Forum, Metrop Area Planning Agency, Omaha, 75; logo, Metrop Arts Coun, Omaha, 76. Exhib: Thirteenth Mid-West Biennial Exhib, Joslyn Art Mus, Omaha, 74; 17th Nat Printing Exhib, Greater Fall River Art Mus, Mass, 74; All-Ohio Biennial Exhib, Dayton Art Inst, Ohio, 74; 1st & 2nd Am Contemp Arts & Crafts Ann, Palm Beach, Fla, 74 & 75; 44th & 45th Ann Exhib, Springfield Art Mus, Mo, 74 & 75; 37th Ann Fall Show, Sioux City Art Ctr, Iowa, 75; Nebr 75 Exhib, Joslyn Art Mus, Omaha, 75; Midlands Bicentennial Exhib, Omaha & Lincoln, 76. Collections Arranged: The City as Art, Akron Art Inst Summer Students' Show, 73; Regional Artists' Group Exhib, 74, Charles Schmidt One-Man Drawing, 75, Omaha Collector's Exhib (auth, catalogue), 75, Abraham Kamberg Collection of Bauhaus Prints, 75, Univ of Nebr Collection, 75 & Univ Design Students' Show, 75-76, Univ Nebr Art Gallery, Omaha. Teaching: Instr life-drawing, painting & silkscreen, Akron Art Inst, Ohio, summer 73; asst prof drawing, design & painting, Univ Nebr at Omaha, 73- Pos: Designer, CBS-TV, Hollywood, Calif, 67-69; production artist, Writers' Serv, Hollywood, 68-69; fac adv, Art Student Forum, Dept of Art & dir, Art Gallery, 74-75, Univ Nebr, Omaha. Awards: Purchase Award, CBS-TV Artist's Show, Hollywood, 67; Cash Award, Drawing & Prints Ann, Col of St Mary's, 76; Hon Mention, Midlands Bicentennial, Area Artists of Omaha, Nebr Arts Coun, 76. Bibliog: Bidez Embry Moore (auth), St Mary's Exhib, Omaha World Herald Newspaper, 76. Mem: Nat Col Art Asn of Am; Mid-Am Col Art Asn; Nebr Art Asn; Joslyn Art Mus; Metrop Arts Coun (visual arts rep, 76-77). Style & Technique: Abstract/surrealistic pencil and acrylic paintings. Media: Pencil; acrylic. Publ: Auth, The Gird as a Compositional/Design Factor in Painting, Kans State Col, 73; illusr, Painting with Acrylics, Van Nostrand-Reinhold, 74; illusr, Only You Can Unlock the Door, Am Cancer Soc, 75; illusr, Riverfront: The Humanist Speaks, Univ Nebr, 75. Dealer: Betty Hiller The New Gallery 133 S Elmwood Rd Univ Nebr Omaha NE 68101. Mailing Add: 5607 Howard Omaha NE 68106

BRADSHAW, ROBERT GEORGE
PAINTER, EDUCATOR
b Trenton, NJ, Mar 13, 15. Study: Princeton Univ, AB; Columbia Univ, MA. Exhib: NJ State Mus; Am Watercolor Soc; Boston Mus Fine Art; Cape Ann Soc Mod Art; New York World's Fair, 65; plus others. Teaching: Lectr art appreciation & hist; prof art, Douglass Col, Rutgers Univ, New Brunswick, 46-, actg chmn dept art, 64-65. Awards: Hons art & archaeol, Princeton Univ, 37; Prize, NJ Watercolor Soc, 59 & Montclair Art Mus, NJ, 63. Mem: NJ Watercolor Soc; Hunterdon Co Art Ctr. Style & Technique: Realism to free brush expression. Media: Watercolor, Acrylic. Mailing Add: 48 Hilltop Blvd East Brunswick NJ 08816

BRADY, CHARLES MICHAEL
PAINTER
b New York, NY, July 27, 26. Study: Art Student League, 48-51, with John Groth & Morris Kantor. Work: Six works in Irish Arts Coun Collection, Dublin; Northern Ireland Arts Coun; NW Trust; Northern Bank Finance Corp; Bank of Ireland Collection. Exhib: Living Art, Dublin, 59-71; Royal Hibernian Acad, Dublin, 65; Pa Acad Fine Arts, Philadelphia, 67; Harrison S Morrison Exhib, Newport, RI, 68; Figurative Image, Wexford & Trinity Col, Dublin, 74; Sommer Show, Picadilly Gallery, London, Eng, 76; two-person show, Caldwell Gallery, Dublin, 77; one-man show, Keys Gallery, Londonderry, Eng, 77. Teaching: Artist-instr graphics, dept archit, Col Technol, Dublin, 70-71; lectr painting, Nat Col Art, Dublin, 75-78. Awards: Player-Wills Third Prize, 66; Douglas Hyde Gold Medal, Oireachtas Art Exhib, Dublin Univ, 73. Mem: Life mem Art Student League; United Arts Club (hon chmn artist group, 71), Dublin. Style & Technique: Figurative subjects, objects inside and outside, sometimes compared with Morandi. Media: Oil. Dealer: Tom Caldwell Gallery Dublin & Belfast Ireland. Mailing Add: One Royal Terr W Dun Laoghaire Ireland

BRAGAR, PHILIP FRANK
PAINTER, PRINTMAKER
b New York, NY, May 10, 25. Study: Esmeralda Sch Painting & Sculpture, Mexico City, 54-59, with Raul Anguiano, Carlos Orozco Romero, Alfonso Ayala & Ignacio Aguirre. Work: New York Pub Libr; Pasadena Art Mus, Calif, NJ State Mus, Trenton; Los Angeles Co Mus Art, Los Angeles, Calif; Newark Publ Libr, NJ. Comn: Illusr poem in El Corazon Cae Fuera del Camino, Armando Zarate (auth), Mexico, 63; illusr, Americans Under Mexican Law, Dr Oswaldo Schon, Mexico City, 71. Exhib: Contemp Am Graphic Art, Terrain Gallery, New York, 65; Language of Prints, Newark Pub Libr, 69; 4th Am Biennial, Santiago de Chile, Chile, 70; Pan Am Graphic Art Exhib, Cali, Colombia, 70; Graphic Art Collection of Gen Motors, Mex-NAm Inst Cult Relations, Mexico City, 71; Int Exhib Painting, Univ de las Americas, Puebla, 72; Homage to Pablo Picasso, Mus Fine Arts, Mexico City, 73; 1st Biennial of Art, Morelia, Michoacan, Mex, 74; one-man shows, Galeria Antonio Souza, Mexico City, 68, Galeria Pecanins, Mexico City, 69 & 73; Ninteen Yrs of Woodcut Prints, Galeria Pecanins, 78. Teaching: Instr drawing, painting, design & prints, US Int Univ, 70-75, dir art dept, 70-75. Bibliog: Toby Joysmith (auth), Philip F Bragar—On the edge of chaos, The NEWS, 10/2/66; Duchamps (auth), Mexican landscape was made for painting, says Bragar, Excelsior, 5/16/73; Raquel Tibol (auth), Sixty woodcut prints by Philip Bragar, article in Proceso, 4/10/78. Style & Technique: German expressionistic painting and woodcut prints. Media: Oil. Dealer: Galeria Pecanins Hamburgo 103 Mexico DF Mex. Mailing Add: Atlixco 159-6 Colonia Condesa Mexico 11 DF Mexico

BRAIDEN, ROSE MARGARET J
ART HISTORIAN, ILLUSTRATOR
b Los Angeles, Calif, Nov 25, 23. Study: Study: Mt St Mary's Col, Los Angeles, BFA; Calif Col of Arts & Crafts, Oakland, MFA; Long Beach State, study printmaking with Dick Swift; Univ of Southern Calif; Univ Calif at Los Angeles. Work: Mt St Mary's Col, Libr & Gallery, Los Angeles. Comn: St Bernard's Church, stained glass windows, Glendale; Design for wall mural, St Lawrence Church, 65; stained glass work, Roger Darricannene Studios, 69; portraits, Univ Calif, Northridge, 76; bk illus, comn by Steve Pouliot, Banner & Assoc, 78. Exhib: Etchings, Long Beach State Gallery, 68; Drawings, Art Gallery, Ojai, Calif, 69; Retrospective, Ten Yrs of Work, Brooks Inst Gallery, 76; Drawings, 76 & Icons, 77, Faulkner Gallery, Santa Barbara, Calif. Teaching: Instr painting, Bishop Montgomery High Sch, 58-68; prof art hist, Mt St Mary's Col, 68-70. Pos: Chmn art dept, Bishop Montgomery High Sch, 58-68; judge, Nat Scholastic 64-67; chmn photog art dept, Brooks Inst of Photog, 70-; gallery dir, Brooks Inst of Photog, 74- Bibliog: Ann Vail Van Horn (auth), Iconography & Icons of the Spirit, News & Rev, 78; Pauline Combe (auth), An artist, Santa Barbara Mag, 11/78. Mem: Univ Calif Santa Barbara, Friends of the Libr; Soc of Photographic Educators; Artist Mem of Religious Guild, Am Inst of Archit. Style & Technique: Works calligraphically, in lettering, drawings & egg tempera. Media: Ink & Pencil; Egg Tempera. Res: Greek & Russian Icon. Dealer: Kay Thackery c/o The Poster Anacapa & De La Guerra Santa Barbara CA 93105. Mailing Add: 2929 Paseo Tranquillo Santa Barbara CA 93105

BRAINARD, JOE
GRAPHIC ARTIST, PAINTER
b Salem, Ark, Mar 11, 42. Work: Colorado Springs Fine Arts Ctr, Colo; Harvard Univ; Liason Films Inc; Mus Mod Art, New York; Utah Mus Fine Arts, Salt Lake City. Exhib: In Memory of My Feelings: Frank O'Hara, Mus Fine Art, Richmond, 68; White on White, Mus Contemp Art, Chicago, 72; Seven Young Artist, Corcoran Gallery Art, Washington, DC, 72; New Am Graphic Art, Harvard Univ, 73; Am Drawing: 1970-1973, Yale Univ, 73; Am Drawings, Tyler Sch Art, Temple Univ, Philadelphia, 73; one-man shows, Fischbach Gallery, 71, 72 & 74, Sch Visual Arts, New York, 72, New York Cult Ctr, 72 & Utah Mus Fine Arts, 73. Teaching: Instr, Cooper Union, 67-68. Awards: Copley Found Grant. Dealer: Fischbach Gallery 29 W 57th St New York NY 10019. Mailing Add: 8 Greene St New York NY 10013

BRAINARD, OWEN
PAINTER, EDUCATOR
b Kingston, NY, June 9, 24. Study: Columbia Univ, 46, with Dong Kingman; Syracuse Univ, BFA, 48, with Stephen Peck; State Univ NY Albany, 51; Syracuse Univ, with Fred Haucke, MFA, 52. Work: Iowa Art Educ Asn; Fort Collection Am Art; Chicago Pub Libr; Univ Ryukyus, Okinawa; Mich State Univ. Comn: Mosaic wall mural, Everett High Sch, Lansing, Mich, 59. Exhib: Walker Art Ctr Biennial, Minneapolis, 53; Regional Art Today, Joslyn Mus, Omaha, 57; Art: USA, Madison Sq Garden, NY, 58; 16th Nat Print Exhib, Libr Cong, 58; 3rd Nat Print Exhib, New Canaan, Conn, 60; plus many others. Teaching: Asst prof design & painting, Drake Univ, 52-57; prof painting & serigraphy, Mich State Univ, 57- Pos: Free-lance designer & illusr, Lincoln-Mercury Times Mag, Iowa Children's Home Soc, Mich State Univ Publ & others, 49- Awards: Iowa Artists Ann Award, 55; Western Mich Ann Award, Friends of Art, 60; Midland Art Asn Ann Award, 62. Mem: Col Art Asn; Nat Soc Arts & Lit; Screen Printing Asn Int. Style & Technique: Lyrical abstraction, semi-sculptural forms. Media: Acrylic. Publ: Serigraphy: art and industry (in press). Dealer: 420 Gallery Union St Traverse City MI 49684. Mailing Add: 321 Kresge Art Ctr Mich State Univ East Lansing MI 48824

BRAITSTEIN, MARCEL
SCULPTOR, EDUCATOR
b Charleroi, Belg, July 11, 35; Can citizen. Study: Ecole Beaux-Arts Montreal, dipl; Inst Allende, San Miguel Allende, Mex. Work: Montreal Mus Fine Arts, PQ; Art Gallery Ont, Toronto; Winnipeg Art Gallery, Man; Confederation Ctr, PEI. Comn: Sunscreen, comn by Architect L Lapierre, Firemen's Bank, Montreal, 65; monument to Rt Hon A Meighen, comn by Dept Pub Works, Can Govt, 69. Exhib: Quebec Prov Competition, Quebec, 59; Spring Show, Montreal Mus Fine Arts, 61; Vermont USA, Bundy Art Gallery, 66; Panorama of Quebec Sculpture, Mus Rodin, Paris, France, 70; 1st Int Biennial Small Sculpture, Budapest, Hungary, 71. Teaching: Prof sculpture, Ecole Beaux-Arts Montreal, 65-69; prof sculpture, Univ Quebec, Montreal, 69-73 & 75-; prof, Mt Allison Univ, 73-75. Awards: Sculpture Prizes, Quebec Govt, 59; Sculpture Prize, Montreal Mus Fine Arts, 61. Bibliog: Guy Robert (auth), Marcel Braitstein, Vie des Arts, Montreal, 62; E H Turner (auth), Sculpture in Canada, Can Art, 62; Jean Simard (auth), Marcel Braitstein, Sculpteur (Monogr), Quebec Sculptors Asn, 69. Mem: Quebec Sculptors Asn (vpres, 69-71); Royal Can Acad Arts. Style & Technique: Figurative, symbolic and surrealistic; combines soft sculpture and welded steel. Media: Welded Steel, Bronze, Stainless Steel. Mailing Add: PO Box 385 Hudson Heights PQ Can

BRAKHAGE, JAMES STANLEY
FILM MAKER, LECTURER
b Kansas City, Mo, Jan 14, 33. Pos: Lectr film, US & Europe, 55-; lectr film hist, Art Inst Chicago, 69- Awards: Avon Found, 65-69; Rockefeller Found, 67-69; Nat Endowment Arts, 74 & 75. Bibliog: Eisenstein/Brakhage issue, Artforum Mag, 1/73; P Adams Sitney (auth), Visionary Film, Oxford Univ, 74; Parker Tyler (auth), Underground Film, Grove Press, 73. Mem: Film-Makers Co-op, New York; Canyon Cinema Co-op Sausalito; London Film-Makers Co-op; Cooper Cinestes Independantes, Montreal. Publ: Auth, Metaphors on Vision, 63; auth, A Moving Picture Giving & Taking Book, 71; auth, The Brakhage Lectures, 72; auth, Seen, 75; auth, Film Biographies, 77. Mailing Add: Box 170 Rollinsville CO 80474

BRALEY, JEAN DUFFIELD
PRINTMAKER, PAINTER
b Wilkesboro, NC. Study: Univ Calif, San Diego BA(with distinction); Pratt Graphics Ctr, New York; Art Students League; La Reparata Graphic, Florence, Italy; Sch Prof Art, New

York. Work: Riverside Mus, Calif; Libr Cong, Washington, DC; NZ Embassy, Washington, DC; R J Softwears Computer Co, San Diego, Calif; Bullocks Retail Co, San Diego. Comn: Wall paintings, Glendale Fed Bank, San Diego, 75; two intaglio ed in color, Orr's Graphic Ctr, San Diego, 76 & three intaglio ed in color, 77; wall paintings, Calif First Bank, San Diego, 77. Exhib: Smithsonian Inst Mus, Washington, DC, 68 & 69; La Jolla Contemp Mus, Calif, 74-76; Fine Arts Gallery Mus, San Diego, 74-77; Riverside Mus, Calif, 75-78, one-person show, 77; Calif-Hawaii Biennial, San Diego, 76; Palace Fine Arts, Mexico City, 76; 50 Calif Printmakers Nat Tour, 76 & 77; Soc Am Graphic Artists, New York, 77. Teaching: Instr design & drawing, Luther Rice Col, Franconia, Va, 70-71; instr advan oil, San Diego Community Col, 71-78. Pos: Prof illusr, publ & advert agencies, New York & Washington, DC, 50-68; chmn art dept, North Shores Community Col, San Diego, 73-74; vchmn, Docents, Fine Arts Gallery Mus, San Diego, 74-75. Awards: Third Prize, Annapolis Ann Regional, 68; Hon Mention, Ajax Nat Traveling Exhib, 69; Awards, SW Ann Regional, Washington, DC, 68-70. Bibliog: Reva Prell (auth), Women's Art Festival, N Co Living Mag, San Diego, 4/76; Cur of Educ (auth), Printmaking Processes (film), Fine Arts Gallery, San Diego, 11/76; Gay Fall (auth), Art You Can Bank On, Applause, San Diego Mag of the Arts, 1/78. Mem: Artists Equity Asn San Diego (founder, 72, pres, 73 & 74); N Bergin Art League, NJ; Calif Art Comn (consult, 75); Lawyers for Creative Arts, San Diego (founder, 77, mem bd, 77 & 78). Style & Technique: Figurative and landscape expressionist. Media: Intaglio/embossing; Palette Knife Oil Painting. Dealer: Knowles Art Gallery 7420 Girard Ave La Jolla CA 92037. Mailing Add: 519 Stratford Ct Del Mar CA 92014

BRAMLETT, BETTY JANE
ART ADMINISTRATOR, PAINTER
b Augusta, Ga. Study: Converse Col, Spartanburg, SC, BA; Univ NC, Chapel Hill; Columbia Univ, MA; Univ SC, Columbia, doctoral candidate. Work: SC State Collection, Columbia; Spartanburg Arts Ctr Gallery, SC; Springs Mills Res & Develop Bldg, SC; C S Nat Bank Collection, Columbia, SC; Greenville City Hall Collection, SC. Exhib: Sixth Ann Piedmont Painting & Sculpture Exhib, Mint Mus of Art, Charlotte, NC, 65; Sculpture Show, Univ SC, Columbia, 66; Savannah Art Asn Print & Drawing Competition, Telfair Acad, Ga, 68; 6th Ann Nat Art Exhib, Tyler, Tex, 69; Appalachian Corridors Exhib 2, Charleston Art Gallery of Sunrise, WVa, 70; one-woman show, The Gallery, Spartanburg, 70; three-woman show, Tryon Arts Ctr, NC, 70; Painting Show, Furman Univ, Greenville, SC, 71; El Paso's 17th Nat Sun Carnival Art Exhib, El Paso Art Mus, Tex, 72; 25th Ann SC Artists Exhib, Gibbes Art Gallery, Charleston, 72; Painting Show, Erskine Col, Due West, SC, 73; 41st Ann Show, Greenville Mus of Art, SC, 77. Teaching: Instr art hist & art educ, Univ SC, Columbia, 69-73. Pos: Art Supvr, Spartanburg Co Sch Dist 7, 59-; arts comnr, SC Arts Comn, 77-80. Awards: Cash Award/Painting, Appalachian Corridors Exhib 2, 70 & Spartanburg Bank & Trust Ann, 73; Best-in-Show & Cash Award/Painting, Spartanburg Art Asn, 76. Bibliog: Jack Bass (auth), Porgy Comes Home, World Publ, 70; Seth Vining (ed), article in Tryon Daily Bull, NC, 70; Bramlett's Art Goes on Display, Spartanburg Herald-J, 70. Mem: Greenville Artists Guild; SC Watercolor Soc; SC Artists Guild (pres-elect, 77); SC Art Educ Asn (pres-elect, 77); Nat Art Educ Asn. Style & Technique: Abstract watercolor and mixed media painting using staining and pouring as a technique on paper with rice papers. Media: Watercolor, acrylic. Publ: Auth, Glass on Glass, Sch Arts, Vol 62 (Apr 63); auth, Spartanburg's Adventure in Art, Vol 18 (Apr 67) & A Federal Program Can be Successful, Vol 3 (Spring 73), SC State Dept; auth, Elementary Art Media, 73 & co-auth, Elementary Art Aids, 73, Spartanburg Co Sch Dist 7. Mailing Add: 375 Forest Ave Spartanburg SC 29302

BRAMS, JOAN
PAINTER, SCULPTOR
b Montreal, PQ, Mar 30, 28; US citizen. Study: Ont Col Art. Comn: Southeastern Banking Corp, Fla; Sanwa Bank, New York; Norton Simon Inc, New York. Exhib: Ft Lauderdale Mus Arts, Fla; Columbia Mus Art, SC; Birmingham Mus Art, Ala; John Herron Mus Art, Indianapolis, Ind; Worcester Art Mus, Mass; Ind Cent Col, Indianapolis; Mountain View Col, Ind; Palm Beach Col, Fla; plus others. Bibliog: Articles in La Revue Mod des Arts, France, 71, Art News, 74 & 1/78 & Arts Mag, 10/77. Media: Bronze; acrylic with aggregates on wood or fibre. Dealer: Contemp Gallery 2425 Cedar Springs Dallas TX 75201; Gallery 99 1135 Kane Concourse Bar Harbour FL 33154. Mailing Add: 324 Eden Rd Palm Beach FL 33480

BRAMSON, PHYLLIS HALPERIN
PAINTER, INSTRUCTOR
b Madison, Wis, Feb 20, 41. Study: Yale Summer Art Sch, Norfolk, Conn, 62; Univ Ill, Champaign, BFA, 63; Univ Wis, Madison, MA, 64; Art Inst of Chicago, MFA, 73. Work: Univ Wis, Madison. Exhib: Chicago & Vicinity Show, Art Inst Chicago, 74; The Object as Poet, Renwick Gallery, Smithsonian Inst, Washington, DC, 76 & Mus Contemp Crafts, New York, 77; Papermaking as Art, SITES, Smithsonian Inst, 78; Marianne Deson Gallery, Chicago, 78; one-person show, Monique Knowlton Gallery, New York, 77. Teaching: Instr drawing & painting, Columbia Col, Chicago, 72-; vis artist drawing, Univ Ill, 75. Awards: Vilas fel, Univ Wis, 64; Nat Endowment for the Arts craft grant, 76. Style & Technique: Contemporary symbolist, emphasis on figurative images; hand-cast paper sculpture. Media: Clay, pastel, found objects and gouache; drawing and cast paper sculpture. Dealer: Monique Knowlton Gallery 19 E 71st St New York NY 10021; Marianne Deson Gallery 226 E Ontario Chicago IL 60611. Mailing Add: 300 Flora Ave Glenview IL 60025 Chicago IL

BRANDENBERG, ALIKI
See Aliki

BRANDFIELD, KITTY
PAINTER
b London, Eng; US citizen. Study: Nat Acad Design; Art Students League; also London, Paris & Mex. Work: Jewish Mus, New York; Am Watercolor Soc; Parish Mus, Southampton, NY. Comn: Philbrook Mus, Tulsa, Okla, 64; Bath & Tennis Club, Westhampton, NY, 69; Baccarat Glass Exhib, New York, 73; Episcopal Church, Southampton, NY, 75; Hunter Col, 75. Exhib: Am Watercolor Soc, 60, 62 & 63; Nat Acad Design, 63; Cord Gallery, Southampton, 67; Jewish Mus, 69; Parish Mus, 74. Pos: Stylist & designer, Americana, New York, 55-60 & Covington Fabrics, 65-68; designer record jackets, Triton Record Prod Inc, currently. Awards: First Prizes (oil, watercolor), Fire Island Art Asn, 52-56; Prize for Drawing, Nat Acad Design, 54; First Prize, Ann Competition, Tulsa, Okla, 64. Bibliog: Alice Marriott (auth), Critique of current work, Tulsa News, 64; Gordon Ragoff (auth), monogr, Yale Univ, 68; B Kaiser (auth), Program Notes, Former Jewish Mus Cur, 69. Style & Technique: Contemporary romantic realist; Turneresque approach to the sea; profound and intense understanding of man in his city environment. Media: Oil, Watercolor; Clay, Wood. Dealer: Environment Gallery 205 E 60th St New York NY 10022. Mailing Add: 231 W 22nd St New York NY 10011

BRANDT, FREDERICK ROBERT
PRINTMAKER, MUSEUM EXHIBITION DIRECTOR
b Paterson, NJ, June 7, 36. Study: Pa State Univ, BA, 60, MA, 63. Work: Chrysler Mus, Norfolk, Va; Va Polytech Inst & State Univ, Blacksburg, Va; Richmond Humanities Ctr, Va; St Mary's Hosp, Richmond; Retreat for the Sick, Richmond. Comn: Slide-tape pub permanent presentations for Agecroft Hall, Richmond, 69 & Stratford Hall, Va, 72. Exhib: 20th Irene Leache Biennial Exhib, Chrysler Mus, Norfolk, 70; Virginia Artists 1971, Va Mus Fine Arts, Richmond, 71; one-man show, Va Mus Fine Arts, Richmond, 72; Virginia Artists 1973, Va Mus Fine Arts, Richmond, 72; 16th Dixie Ann, Montgomery Mus Fine Arts, Ala, 74. Collections Arranged: William Hogarth, 67; Art Nouveau (contribr, catalog), 71; Francisco Goya: Portraits in Paintings, Prints and Drawings (contribr, catalog), 72; Nell Blaine (contribr, catalog), 73; Picasso: Paintings and Prints, 74; Jose Puig, 74; American Pewter, 76; American Marine Painting, 76. Pos: Interpretation asst, gallery div, Va Mus Fine Arts, 60-61; teaching asst, Pa State Univ, 61-63; asst prog dir, Va Mus Fine Arts, 63-77, assoc cur, 77-; cur, Sydney & Frances Lewis Collection, 72- Awards: Juror's spec mention for prints, 9th Dixie Ann, Montgomery Mus Fine Arts, 68; Purchase Award, 20th Irene Leache Biennial Exhib, 68; Cert of Distinction, Va Artists 1971, Va Mus Fine Arts, 71. Mem: Am Asn Mus; James River Mus Conf; Va Hist & Mus Fedn (bd mem). Media: Silkscreen. Publ: Auth various articles in antique periodicals, 71-72. Dealer: Harold Decker Galleries 318 N 24th St Richmond VA 23223; 8471 Chesapeake Blvd Norfolk VA 23518. Mailing Add: 3207 Monument Ave Richmond VA 23221

BRANDT, GRACE BORGENICHT
See Borgenicht, Grace

BRANDT, REXFORD ELSON
PAINTER, PRINTMAKER
b San Diego, Calif, Sept 12, 14. Study: Univ Calif, Berkeley, AB(art), 36; Stanford Univ, 38. Work: San Diego Fine Arts Gallery, San Francisco Mus Art & Los Angeles Co Mus Art, Calif; Currier Gallery Am Art, Andover, NH; Nat Acad Design Galleries, New York. Comn: Metropolitan Aqueduct, portfolio for Fortune Mag, 37; scraffiti tile murals (with William O Payne), Corona del Mar State Beach Park, 65; San Diego County, Calif, portfolio for Copley Found, La Jolla, Calif, 68; carved wall relief (with John Svenson), Irvine Coast Country Club, 68; murals, Southern Calif First Nat Bank, Newport, 69. Exhib: Int Watercolor Exhib, Chicago Art Inst, 36 & 37; one-man shows, Los Angeles Co Mus of Art, 39 & 41, Calif Palace of the Legion of Honor, San Francisco, Crocker Gallery of Art, Sacramento, 40 & 60, Santa Barbara Art Mus, Major Retrospective, Laguna Beach Art Mus, 67, San Diego Fine Arts Gallery, Faulkner Gallery of Art, Santa Barbara & Southern Methodist Univ, Dallas, Tex; Nat Gallery Art, Washington, DC, 41; Royal Soc Painters in Watercolour, London, 62; Am Watercolor Soc Ann, 60-75; Nat Acad Design Ann, 62-75; plus many others. Teaching: Dir of Brandt Painting Workshops, Corona del Mar, Calif, also in Europe & Mex, 46- Awards: First Prize, Calif Watercolor Soc, 38 & 70; Samuel F B Morse Medal, Nat Acad Design Ann, 68 & 70; Bronze Medal, Am Watercolor Soc, 70. Bibliog: Norman Kent (auth), Seascapes and landscapes, Am Artist, 56; Ernest Watson (auth), Composition in Landscape and Still Life, Watson-Guptill, 59; Cynthia Lindsay (auth), The Natives Are Restless New Am Libr, 60. Mem: Am Watercolor Soc; Nat Acad Design; plus many regional soc. Style & Technique: Expressionist-geometric style, direct technique. Media: All Media. Publ: Auth, Watercolor landscape, 63, The artists' sketchbook and its uses, 66, San Diego, land of the sundown sea, 69, Watercolor Technique & Methods, 77 & West Coast Sketches, 78. Challis Gallery 1370 S Coast Blvd Laguna Beach CA 92652. Mailing Add: 405 Goldenrod Corona del Mar CA 92625

BRANDT, WARREN
PAINTER
b Greensboro, NC, 1918. Study: Pratt Inst, 35-38; Wash Univ, BFA(hons); with Philip Guston & Max Beckmann; John J Milliken traveling fel; Univ NC, Greensboro, MFA. Work: Chase Manhattan Bank; Chrysler Mus; Nat Collection Fine Arts, Smithsonian Inst; James Michener Collection; plus many other public & pvt collections. Exhib: Metrop Mus Watercolor Exhib; Am Fedn Arts; Whitney Mus Am Art; Artists by Artists, New Sch Social Res, 67 & Drawings of the Sixties, 69; one-man retrospective, Allentown Art Mus, 69; plus many others. Teaching: Head dept art, Salem Col, 49-50; instr art, Pratt Inst, 50-51; instr art, Guilford Col, Greensboro, 52-54; chmn dept art, Univ Miss, 57-59; instr, Southern Ill Univ, 59-61; dir, New York Studio Sch, 67- Bibliog: Kenneth Sawyer (auth), Notes on the painter, Warren Brandt, Art Int, 66; Herman Cherry (auth), Brandt, the mystery of the commonplace, Art News, 68; Jay Jacobs (auth), The French touch, Art Gallery, 72. Media: Oil. Publ: Auth, Painting With Oils, Van Nostrand Reinhold, 71. Mailing Add: c/o Fischbach Gallery 29 W 57th St New York NY 10022

BRANSBY, ERIC JAMES
MURALIST, EDUCATOR
b Auburn, NY, Oct 25, 16. Study: Kansas City Art Inst, Mo, with Thomas Hart Benton & Fletcher Martin, Cert Painting & Printmaking; Colorado Springs Fine Arts Ctr & Colo Col, with Boardman Robinson & Jean Charlot, BA & MA(mural painting); Yale Univ, with Josef Albers & Carol Meeks, MFA(painting). Work: Colorado Springs Fine Arts Ctr; Mo State Hist Soc Collection, Columbia; Brigham Young Univ Gallery. Comn: Mural (casein tempera), Cossett Rotunda, Colo Col, 50; mural (polymer tempera), USAAF Acad Planetarium, Colorado Springs, 60, Rockhurst Col, 68, Western Ill Univ, 65, Univ Mo-Kansas City, 75; twelve paneled mural, Munic Bldg, Sedalia, Mo; many others. Exhib: Nat Soc Mural Painters Traveling Exhib, Moscow, Russia, 63; Libr Cong Print Ann, 50; one-man show, Colorado Springs Fine Arts Ctr, 67; Nat Ctr Fine Arts, Washington, DC, 73; Joslyn Mus Biennial, Omaha, 72. Teaching: Instr drawing, Colorado Springs Fine Arts Ctr, 58-63; asst prof drawing & painting, Western Ill Univ, 63-65; assoc prof drawing, painting & printmaking, Univ Mo-Kansas City, 65-70, prof, 70- Awards: Edwin Austen Abbey Found Fel for Mural Painting, 52; Kansas City Asn Trusts & Founds, 70; Veatch Award, Univ Mo, 78. Mem: Phi Kappa Phi; Col Art Asn; Am Asn Univ Prof; Nat Soc Mural Painters. Style & Technique: Special optical problems in murals keyed to particular viewing angles; linear-planar, cubist, futurist. Media: Fresco; Polymer Tempera. Res: Design analysis of Piero della Francesca's mural cycle in the Church of San Francesco at Arezzo, Italy, Mailing Add: Dept of Art Univ of Mo Kansas City MO 64110

BRANSKY, MIRIAM (MIRIAM ANN GILDEN)
ART DEALER, PAINTER
b New York, NY, June 25, 36. Study: Md Inst of Art, cert; spec study with Jaques Maroger. Comn: Seven walls, Fifth Floor, comn by State of Md, Univ Md Hosp, Baltimore, 75. Exhib: Peale Mus, Baltimore, 57; Am Drawing Show, Tidewater, Va, 77. Pos: Dir, Jerry Gilden Gallery, 59- Awards: Second Prize, St John's Church, Md, 62; Cert of Merit, Villa Julie Col, Carroll Br Pen Women's Guild, 78. Style & Technique: Realist. Media: Oil; Drawing. Specialty: American contemporary realism. Mailing Add: c/o Jerry Gilden Gallery 303 Reisterstown Rd Baltimore MD 21201

BRANSOM, (JOHN) PAUL
PAINTER, ILLUSTRATOR
b Washington, DC, July 26, 85. Exhib: Retrospective exhib, Woodmere Art Gallery, Chestnut Hill, Philadelphia, 63. Awards: Hon DA, Weber State Col, Ogden, Utah, 74; Benjamin West Clinedinst Mem Medal, 76. Mem: Am Watercolor Soc; Salmagundi Club; Soc Animal Artists; Am Artists Prof League. Publ: Illusr, Call of the wild, spec ed, 12, Wind in the willows, 13 & An argosy of fables, 21; illusr, Wilderness champion: the story of a great hound, 44, Wolf king, 49 & Phantom deer, 54, Lippincott; illusr, Wilderness champion, G&D, 70; also illusr over 40 bks. Mailing Add: 15 W 67th St New York NY 10023

BRASELMAN, LIN EMERY
See Emery, Lin

BRATCHER, DALE
PAINTER
b Rockport, Ky, Jan 10, 32. Study: Univ Louisville, BCE, MCE. Work: Citizens Fidelity Bank & Trust Co, Louisville, Ky; Island Creek Coal Co, Lexington, Ky; Athens Plastic Co, Tenn; Courier-J, Louisville; Avondale Shipyards Inc, New Orleans, La; and others. Comn: Paintings, Lewisport Sch & Lewisport City Hall, Ky, 77; Pate House, Hancock Co, Ky, 77. Exhib: Cent S Art Exhib, Parthenon, Nashville, Tenn, 70-75 & 77; Mid-States Art Exhib, Evansville Mus of Arts & Sci, Ind, 70-76; Exhib for Corp Collecting, 71 & Exhib for Corp Collecting II, 77, J B Speed Art Mus & Citizens Fidelity Bank, Louisville; Salutes to the Arts, On the Mall, Louisville, 73; Watercolor Soc of Ala Exhib, Birmingham Art Mus, 73-75; Nat Show Chautauqua Exhib of Am Art, Chautauqua Inst Art Gallery, NY, 73, 75 & 76; Watercolor USA Nat Competition, Springfield Art Mus, Mo, 74; Nat Art Round-Up, Las Vegas Art Mus, Nev, 74; Ky Bicentennial Art Exhib (traveling exhib), Ky, 74-75; Ann Nat Art Exhib, Springville Art Mus, Utah, 74 & 76; Eight State Ann, J B Speed Art Mus, Louisville, 74 & 77; Ann Piedmont Graphics Exhib, Greenville Co Mus of Art, SC, 75; Mid-States 5th Ann Travelling Exhib, Evansville Mus of Art, Ind, 75-76; Ann Open Exhib of Watercolor, Okla Mus of Art, Oklahoma City, 76; Mainstreams, Grover M Hermann Fine Arts Ctr, Marietta, Ohio, 76; W & J Nat Painting Show, Washington & Jefferson Col, Washington, Pa, 77; Barn-A Vanishing Landmark, Sioux Falls, SDak & Springfield Art Mus, Mo, 77; Fresh Paint, Ky Arts Comn Travelling Exhib, 77-79; one-man exhib, Dobame Gallery, Cleveland, Ohio, Parthenon, Nashville, 74 & WHAS Gallery, Louisville, 77. Awards: Purchase Award, Ky Painters Invitational, Phelps Dodge Commun Co, Elizabethtown, Ky, 75; Cash Award/Traditional Style Painting, Nat Jury Show, Chautauqua Exhib of Am Art, NY, 75; Cash Award, Greater New Orleans Int Art Exhib, 77. Mem: Watercolor Soc of Ala; Ky Watercolor Soc; Tenn Art League; Southern Watercolor Soc. Media: Egg tempera and watercolor. Dealer: Allen House Gallery 1419 E Washington Louisville KY 40206. Mailing Add: 655 Upland Rd Louisville KY 40206

BRAUER, CONNIE ANN
DESIGNER, METALSMITH
b Denver, Colo, May 4, 49. Study: Colo State Univ, BFA, 71; Inst of Europ Studies, Vienna, Austria, 71; Rochester Inst of Technol, 72-73. Exhib: All-Colo Show, Denver Art Mus, 74; Metals Invitational (travelling exhib), ECoast & Australia, 75-76; Hot Rocks in Bizarre Settings, Denver, 75 & 77; Small Sculptures Nat, Cypress Col, Calif, 76; Profile of US Jewelry, Tex Tech Univ Mus, Lubbock, 77; Copper, Brass & Bronze Exhib, Univ Ariz, Tucson, 77; Cloisonne, The Artists' Canvas, Aaron Faber Gallery, New York, 77. Awards: First Prize, Jewish Community Ctr Christmas Show, Denver, 76; Cash Award, Copper, Brass & Bronze Exhib, Univ Ariz, Tucson, 77. Bibliog: Carol Hoffman (auth), Connie Brauer, Colorado Artist Craftsman, 1/77; Adina Wingate (auth), Copper, Brass & Bronze, Craft Horizons, 8/77. Mem: Am Craft Coun; Colo Artist Craftsman; Enamel W Guild. Style & Technique: Fabricated metals and enamel, both wearable and sculptural. Media: Cloisonne enamel; fabricated silver, gold, copper & brass. Publ: Contribr cover photograph, Small Sculptures Nat catalogue, Cypress Col, 76. Mailing Add: 3710 S Huron Englewood CO 80110

BRAUNSTEIN, H TERRY
MIXED-MEDIA ARTIST
b Washington, DC, Sept 18, 42. Study: Carnegie grant, l'Ecole des Beaux Arts, France, 62; Univ Mich, Ann Arbor, BFA, 64; Pratt Graphic Art Ctr, New York, 65; Md Inst Art, Baltimore, MFA, 68. Exhib: One-person shows, St John's Col Gallery, Annapolis, Md, 65, Washington, DC, 74, Wash Proj for the Arts Gallery, Washington, DC, 76; Corcoran Gallery of Art, Washington, DC, 65; AIR Gallery, New York, 73, Bicentennial Exhib, 73, Paperworks, Washington Gallery of Art, 74 & Corcoran Gallery of Art, 74, Washington, DC; Anderson Gallery, Richmond, Va, 75; Bronx Mus, NY, 76; Foundry Gallery, 76 & The Book as Art II, Fendrick Gallery, 77, Washington, DC; Mint Mus Art, Charlotte, NC; Art Assocs, Lake Charles, La, 77; The Art Ctr, Waco, Tex, 77; The Artist's Bk, Mandeville Art Gallery, San Diego, Calif, 77. Teaching: Instr, Prince Georges Community Col, Largo, Md, 71-74; mem video prog, Long Beach Mus Art, Calif, 74-75; instr, Washington Women's Art Ctr, 76- & Northern Va Community Col, Annandale, 76- Publ: Contribr, Women Artists Newsletter, summer 76. Mailing Add: 317 Fifth St SE Washington DC 20003

BRAUNSTEIN, RUTH
ART DEALER
b Minneapolis, Minn. Collections Arranged: California Era, Update (cur), Huntsville Art Mus, Ala. Pos: Dir, Braunstein/Quay Gallery, San Francisco, 61-75 & Quay Ceramics Gallery, 76- Mem: San Francisco Art Dealers Asn (pres, 75-77). Specialty: Contemporary art: sculpture, painting and drawing; ceramic sculpture, mostly California artists. Mailing Add: 560 Sutter St San Francisco CA 94102

BRAVMANN, RENE A
ART HISTORIAN, EDUCATOR
b Marseilles, France, Dec 10, 39; US citizen. Study: Cleveland Mus Art, 57-61; Western Reserve Univ, BA, 61; Univ Wis, 61-63; Ind Univ, MA(fine arts), PhD, 63-71. Teaching: Asst prof art hist, Univ Wash, Seattle, 68-72, assoc prof, 72-76, prof, 77-, chmn African studies, 69-75. Awards: Ford Found Fel, Am Coun Learned Socs, 66-68; Post-doctoral Res Grant, Soc Sci Res Coun, 72-73; Am Philos Soc Grant, 74. Publ: Auth, West African Sculpture, 70 & auth, Open Frontiers: The Dynamics of Art in Black Africa, 73, Univ Wash; auth, The diffusion of Ashanti political art, chap, In: African Art & Leadership, 72; auth, Islam & Tribal Art in West Africa, Cambridge Univ, 74; auth, An urban way of death, African Arts, Vol 8, No 3. Mailing Add: Sch of Art Univ of Wash Seattle WA 98195

BRAWLEY, ROBERT JULIUS
EDUCATOR, PAINTER
b Brainerd, Minn, Apr 29, 37. Study: Cent Wash Col; Univ Wash; San Francisco Art Inst, BFA, 63, MFA, 65; Acad de Belli Arti, Florence, Italy; study with Frank Lobdell & Richard Diebenkorn. Work: Tyler Sch of Art; Temple Univ; Pioneer Mus, Stockton, Calif; San Francisco Art Inst, Calif; Richmond Art Ctr, Calif. Exhib: Am Drawing 1969, Tyler Sch of Art, 69; Beyond the Actual W Coast Realism, Pioneer Mus, 71; From Photograph to Painting, Five Bay Area Realists, San Francisco Mus of Art, 73; Formalist & Personal Art of Bay Area, Six Bay Area Artists, St Mary's Col, 75. Teaching: Asst prof painting & drawing, Acad of Art Col, San Francisco, 69-72; asst prof aesthetics & painting, Lone Mountain Col, San Francisco, 72- Pos: Dir, Acad of Art Col, 69-72; chmn art dept & dir grad studies in art, Lone Mountain Col, 72- Awards: Fulbright, US Govt grant to Italy, 65-66. Mem: Calif Asn of Fine Arts Deans. Style & Technique: Realist tradition-color and pattern. Media: Oil; Watercolor. Mailing Add: Box 597 El Verano CA 95433

BRECHER, SAMUEL
PAINTER, PRINTMAKER
b Boryslaw, Austria; US citizen. Study: Cooper Union; Nat Acad Design; spec study with Charles W Hawthorne, Provincetown, Mass & New York. Work: Metrop Mus Art, New York; Walker Art Ctr, Minneapolis; Newark Mus Art, NJ; Tel Aviv Mus & Ein Harod Mus, Israel; Smithsonian Inst, Washington, DC. Exhib: Nat Acad Design, New York, 24-46; one-man shows, ACA Gallery, 35, Hudson Walker Gallery, 38 & 40, Kraushaar Gallery, 42 & 44, Babcock Gallery, 49 & 51 & Merrill Gallery, 62; American Art Today, New York World's Fair, 39; Directions in American Painting, Carnegie Inst, Pittsburgh, Pa, 41 & 44; Sawdust and Spangles, San Francisco Mus Art, Calif, 42; Brooklyn Mus, NY, 44; 4th Biennial Exhib Contemp Am Paintings, Va Mus Fine Arts, Richmond, 44; Rochester Mem Art Mus, NY, 51-55; New Brit Art Mus, Conn, 51; 23rd Biennial Exhib, Corcoran Gallery Art, Washington, DC, 53; Staten Island Mus Arts & Sci, 56 & 61. Teaching: Instr painting, Newark Sch Fine & Indust Art, 46-74. Awards: First Prize in oil painting, Salmagundi Club, 50; prize in oil painting, 14th Ann Audubon Exhib, 56; First Prize, 8th Ann Exhib Nat Soc Casein Painters, 62. Bibliog: Charles Z Offin (auth), Cape Cod on canvas, Pictures on Exhib, 1/42; Zelda Ormont (auth), Samuel Brecher, artist, Caravan, 11/46; Howard Devree (auth), Portrait of Staten Island, New York Times Mag, 1/13/57. Mem: Audubon Artists; Allied Artists; Nat Soc Casein Painters; NJ Painters & Sculptors Soc. Media: Oil. Mailing Add: 124 W 23rd St New York NY 10011

BRECHT, GEORGE
CONCEPTUAL ARTIST, ASSEMBLAGE ARTIST
b Blomkest, Miss, Mar 7, 24. Study: Philadelphia Col of Pharmacy & Sci, Pa, BSc, 50; New Sch for Social Res, New York, with John Cage, 58-59. Work: Mus Mod Art, New York; Stadtisches Mus, Monchengladbach, Ger, Arch Sohm, Margroningen, Ger; Fluxus W Collection, San Diego, Calif. Comn: Music and sets, James Waring Dance Co, New York. Exhib: Art in Motion, Mod Mus, Stockholm & Stedelijk Mus, Amsterdam, 61; The Art of Assemblage, Mus Mod Art, New York, 61; The Popular Image, Washington Gallery of Mod Art, DC, 63; Mixed-Media & Pop Art, Albright-Knox Art Gallery, Buffalo, NY, 63; Black, White & Gray, Wadsworth Atheneum, Hartford, Conn, 64; Eleven from the Reuben Gallery, Guggenheim Mus, New York, 65; Poems to be Seen, Paintings to be Read, Mus Contemp Art, Chicago, 67; Publications by Hansjorg Mayer, Gemeentemuseum, The Hague, Netherlands, 68; La Cedille Qui Sourit, Stadtisches Mus, Monchengladbach, Ger, 69; Superlimited, Jewish Mus, New York, 69; Kunst Nach Planen, Kunsthalle Bern, Switz, 69; Pop Art, Hayward Gallery, London, Eng, 69; Art by Tel, Mus Contemp Art, Chicago, 69; Art in the Mind, Allen Art Mus, Oberlin Col, Ohio, 70; Sun IV, Mus Fodor, Amsterdam, 70; Dusseldorf Artists, Gallery House, London, 72; Documenta 5, Kassel, WGer, 72; one-man shows, Toward Events, Reuben Gallery, New York, 59, Life of George Washington, Cafe au Go Go, New York, 64, The Bk of the Tumbler on Fire, Fischbach Gallery, New York, 65, Galleria Schwarz, Milan, 67 & 69, Galerie Rudolf Zwirner, Cologne, 69, Galerie Hansjorg Mayer, Stuttgart, 69 & Los Angeles Co Mus Art, Los Angeles, Calif, 69. Teaching: Res fel, Leeds Col Art, Eng, 68-69. Pos: Founder, Sight Unseen J, Leeds, Eng, 68-69. Bibliog: Allan Kaprow (auth), Assemblage, Environments & Happenings, New York, 66; Barbara Rose (auth), The Value of Didactic Art, New York, 8/67; Jasia Reichardt (auth), Non-games, Studio Int, Lugano, 3/68. Publ: Auth, Chance imagery, Collage, Palermo, Italy, 12/64; auth, Dances, events & other poems, Something, Vol 1 (1965); auth, From the Brecht/Lovell Motto board, Big Venus, London, 69; co-auth (with Patirck Hughes), Vicious Circles & Infinity, New York, 75. Dealer: Arturo Schwarz via Gesu 17 Milan 20121 Italy. Mailing Add: Wildenburgstrasse 9 5 Cologne-Sülz West Germany

BRECKENRIDGE, BRUCE M
CERAMIC ARTIST, EDUCATOR
b Chicago, Ill, Oct 29, 29. Study: Wis State Col-Milwaukee, BS, 52; Cranbrook Acad Art, Bloomfield Hills, Mich, MFA, 53; Acad Grande Chaumier, Paris, 56. Work: Elvehjem Art Ctr, Univ Wis-Madison; Westum Mus, Racine, Wis. Exhib: Objects as Objects, Mus Contemp Crafts, New York, 68 & Coffee Tea and Other Cups, 71; National Ceramics Invitational Exhibition, Nelson Gallery Atkins Mus, Kansas City, 69; National Ceramics Invitational, Scripps Col, 71; The Plastic Earth, John Michael Kohler Arts Ctr, Sheboygan, Wis, 73. Collections Arranged: Richmond Art Ctr, Calif, 59-61; Mus Contemp Crafts, New York, 65-66. Teaching: Instr ceramics, Brooklyn Mus Art Sch, 65-68; prof art-ceramics, Univ Wis-Madison, 68- Pos: Asst dir, Richmond Art Ctr, 59-61; installation asst, Mus Mod Art, New York, 64-65; asst dir, Mus Contemp Crafts, New York, 65-66. Media: Ceramics. Publ: Auth, New ceramic forms, 65, Wisconsin designer-craftsman, 69, Don Reitz exhibition, 70 & National invitational exhibition II, glass, 71, Craft Horizons. Mailing Add: Univ Wis Art Dept 455 N Park Madison WI 53706

BRECKENRIDGE, JAMES D
ART HISTORIAN
b New York, NY, Aug 8, 26. Study: Cornell Univ, BA; Princeton Univ, MFA & PhD. Teaching: Lectr art hist, Johns Hopkins Univ, 57-59; vis prof art hist, Univ Pittsburgh, 60-61; prof art hist, Northwestern Univ, 61-, chmn dept, 64-74. Pos: Cur, Corcoran Gallery Art, 52-55; cur, Baltimore Mus Art, 55-60. Awards: Res Fel, Am Coun Learned Socs, 59-60; Sr Fel, Nat Endowment for Humanities, 70-71; Inst for Advan Study Mem, 74-75. Mem: Int Ctr Medieval Art (dir, 72-); Col Art Asn Am (dir, 67-71); Medieval Acad Am (counr, 75-78); US Nat Comt for Byzantine Studies; fel Royal Numismatic Soc; fel Royal Soc Arts; fel Am Numis Soc. Res: History of portraiture. Publ: Auth, Likeness: a conceptual history of ancient portraiture, 69. Mailing Add: Dept Art Hist Northwestern Univ Evanston IL 60201

BREDER, HANS DIETER
SCULPTOR, VIDEO ARTIST
b Herford, Ger, Oct 20, 35; US citizen. Study: Hochschule fuer Bildende Kunste, Hamburg, Ger, with Willem Grimm, asst to sculptor, George Rickey. Work: Cleveland Mus, Ohio; Joseph H Hirshhorn Collection, Washington, DC; Whitney Mus of Am Art, New York; Mus of Art, State Univ NY Col, Purchase; Mus of Art, Iowa City. Comn: Three outdoor sculptures, City of Hanover, Ger, 71. Exhib: Plastica Galeria de Arte, Buenos Aires, 66; one-man show, Richard Feigen Gallery, New York, 67; Directions 1: Options, Mus of Contemp Art, Chicago, 68; La Jolla Mus of Art, Calif, 69; Gallery Marcel Liatowitsch, Basel, Switz, 72; Max Hutchinson Gallery, New York, 72; Int Cult Centrum, Antwerpen, Belg, 76; Signals, Mus of Mod Art, New York, 77. Teaching: Assoc prof multimedia, Univ Iowa, Iowa

City, 66-77. Pos: Co-dir, Corroboree: Gallery of New Concepts, Univ Iowa, Iowa City, 77- Bibliog: George Rickey (auth), Constructivism—Origins & Evolution, George Braziller, 68; R G Dienst (auth), Deutsche Kunst: Eine Neue Generation, Dumont Schauberg, Ger, 70; Michael Kirby (auth), Hybrids, Drama Rev, 73. Media: Sculpture, video. Publ: Co-auth, Speculum, Ctr for New Performing Arts, 73; co-auth, Participatory Art and Body Sculpture with Mirrors, Leonardo: Art, Sci & Technol, 74. Mailing Add: 502 Brown St Iowa City IA 52240

BREDLOW, TOM
DESIGNER, BLACKSMITH
b Pontiac, Mich, Oct 18, 38. Study: Tex A&M Col, BA(math). Comn: Grilles, door hardware, fireplace accessories, weathervanes, gates, railings, tables & chandeliers, pvt residences in US & Mex, 64-; gates, railings, candlestick & flower stands, Washington Cathedral, 68-; Barrio-Historico (grilles, gates, doors, railings, downspouts), comn by H Kelley Rollings, Tucson, 70-; hand rails, comn by Harriet Hubbell, Hubbell House (SW Span Craftsmen), Santa Fe, NMex, 71. Exhib: One-man show, Boyer Gallery, Tucson, 68 & 70; 3rd-5th Ann Western Art Show, Mountain Oyster Club, Tucson, 72-74; Iron-Solid Wrought, Mus Southern Ill Univ, Mus Contemp Crafts, New York & Smithsonian Inst, Washington, DC, 76-77. Teaching: Guest lectr hist archaeol, Univ Ariz, speaker-demonstr, Ironworking Conv, var times. Pos: Owner & sole craftsman, Bredlow's Blacksmith Shop, Tucson, 64- Style & Technique: Forged iron gates, furniture, animals and figures; cut and welded steel store fronts, grilles, gates, figures, animals. Publ: Auth, Stagecoach, Frontier Times, summer 60; auth, Anvils and coal smoke, Old West, winter 66. Mailing Add: 1827 E Limberlost Tucson AZ 85719

BREED, CHARLES AYARS
SCULPTOR, EDUCATOR
b Paw Paw, Mich, Jan 31, 27. Study: Western Mich Univ, BS; Univ Wis, MA. Work: Midland Ctr Arts, Mich. Comn: 12 Stations of the Cross, Indian River Cath Church, 55; Cross (glass & brass), Mem Presby Church, Midland, Mich, 57; window panels (plastic), William Dixon Home, Midland, 60; Eternal Flame (Plexiglas), Temple Beth El, Spring Valley, NY, 66; Icon Screen (polyester), Hellenic Orthodox Church, Bloomfield Hills, Mich, 68. Exhib: Craftsman USA 66, Mus Contemp Crafts, New York, 66, Plastic as Plastic Nat Invitational, 68; Made of Plastic Nat Invitational, Flint Inst Art, Mich, 68; Exhib 70, Columbus Art Gallery, Ohio, 70; First Biennial Int Small Sculpture Exhib, Budapest, Hungary, 71. Teaching: Dir art, Nat Music Acad, 58-62; assoc prof art & chmn dept, Delta Col, 62- Pos: Bd dirs, Awareness Inc, Lansing, Mich, 62-64; bd dirs, Midland Art Coun, Mich, 65-68; bd dirs, Midland Ctr Arts, 67-72; mem, Coun Arts, Lansing, 71-72. Awards: Res Fel, Dow Found, 61; Nat Merit Award, Mus Contemp Crafts, New York, 66; Outstanding Teacher Year, Bergstein Found, 67. Bibliog: Jack Brickhouse (auth), Everything is Double in Paw Paw, Paramount Films, 48; Curtis Bessinger (auth), Where does the design of a house begin, House Beautiful, 1/62; John Krafft (auth), Plastic as plastic, Detroit News Sunday Mag, 66. Mem: Life mem Nat Educ Asn; Mich Art Educ (treas, 55, pres, 56); Am Craftsmen Coun; Mich Coun Ar Media: Plastic. Publ: Auth, Plastic as a new art form, House Beautiful, 2/62; co-auth, Plastic-the visual arts in crafts, Crafts & Craftsmen, 67. Dealer: Lee Nordness Galleries 236 E 75th St New York NY 10021. Mailing Add: 4202 Sherwood Ct Midland MI 48640

BREER, ROBERT C
SCULPTOR, FILM MAKER
b Detroit, Mich, Sept 30, 26. Study: Stanford Univ, BA. Work: Mus Mod Art, New York; Mod Mus, Stockholm, Sweden; Anthology Film Archives, New York; Mod Art Mus, Krefeld, Ger; Centre Beaubourg, Paris, France. Comn: Design for Pavilion, Expo '70, Japan, Pepsi-Cola Co, 70; kinetic sculpture, IBM Plaza, Pittsburgh Arts Fete, 74. Exhib: New York & London Film Festivals, 64-71; Salon des Galeries Pilotes, Lausanne, Switz, 66; The Machine as Seen at the End of the Mechanical Age, Mus Mod Art, New York, 68; Plans and Projects as Art, Kunsthalle, Berne, Switz, 70; Kinetics-Arts Coun of Gt Brit, Hayward Gallery, London, 70; Albright-Knox Art Gallery, Buffalo, NY, 71; Yale Univ, 73; Cannes Film Festival, 74; Mus Mod Art, New York; plus others. Teaching: Vis instr kinetics, Cooper Union, 71-75. Pos: Mem bd dirs, Filmmakers Coop, New York, 67-72 & 75- Awards: Creative Film Found Award, 59; Oberhausen Film Festival Award, Femme, 69; Film Culture Independent Film Award, 72. Bibliog: Noel Burch (auth), The films of Robert Breer, Film Quart, 59; Adrienne Mancia & William Van Dyke (auth), Four artists as film makers, Art in Am, 1/67; Calvin Tompkins (auth), Onwards and upwards with the arts, New Yorker, 10/70. Style & Technique: Film and kinetic sculpture. Mailing Add: Ludlow Lane Palisades NY 10964

BREESKIN, ADELYN DOHME
ART ADMINISTRATOR
b Baltimore, Md, July 19, 96. Study: Bryn Mawr Col; Radcliffe Col; Sch Fine Arts, Boston; Goucher Col, hon LittD, 53; Washington Col, hon DFA, 61, Wheaton Col, 63, Hood Col, 66, Morgan State Col, 66; Md Inst, 75. Teaching: Instr art, McCoy Col, Johns Hopkins Univ, 37-50; lectr, US & abroad; also radio & TV appearances; Am specialist lect tour of Orient, State Dept, 64-65. Pos: Cur prints & drawings, Baltimore Mus Art, 30-, gen cur, 38, actg dir, 42, dir, 47-62; art consult & cur contemp art, Nat Col Fine Arts, Smithsonian Inst, 66-74, consult, 74- Awards: Star of Solidarity for promoting intercultural betterment, Ital Govt, 54. Mem: Am Asn Mus Dirs; Print Coun Am (secy); Int Graphic Arts Soc; Am Fedn Arts (trustee, 60-74). Mailing Add: Rm 256 Nat Collection Fine Arts Smithsonian Inst Washington DC 20560

BREIGER, ELAINE
PAINTER, PRINTMAKER
b Springfield, Mass. Study: Art Student League; Cooper Union, cert fine arts; spec master printing with Krishna Reddy. Work: Brooklyn Mus, NY; Libr of Cong, Washington, DC; Honolulu Acad of Art, Hawaii; Chase Manhattan Bank, New York; De Cordova Mus, Lincoln, Mass. Comn: Print of etching & acrylic painting for Great Ideas of Western Men series, Container Corp Am, 70. Exhib: Glaser Gallery, La Jolla, Calif; Contemp Gallery, Dallas; Leslie Rankow Gallery, New York; Martha Jackson Gallery, New York, 74; Pace Gallery, New York, 76; Source Gallery, San Francisco, Calif, 77. Teaching: Instr techniques etching & intaglio printing, 92nd St YMHA-YMHA, New York, 71-76, chmn dept art, 72-76; color etching, Sch of Visual Arts, New York, 77- Pos: Mgr, Printmaking Workshop, 68-70. Awards: Creative Arts Pub Serv fel, 74; Nat Endowment for the Arts grant, 75. Media: Acrylic, Oil. Dealer: Pace Gallery 32 E 57th St New York NY 10022 Mailing Add: 20 E 14th St New York NY 10003

BREININ, RAYMOND
PAINTER, SCULPTOR
b Vitebsk, Russia, Nov 30, 10. Study: Chicago Acad Fine Arts, with Uri Penn. Work: Metrop Mus Art; Mus Mod Art; Brooklyn Mus; Art Inst Chicago; Phillips Collection, Washington, DC; plus others. Comn: Costumes & settings, Ballet Theatre's Undertow; murals, Winnetka High Sch, Ill, State Hosp, Elgin, Ill, US Post Off, Wilmette, Ill & Ambassador E Hotel, Chicago; plus others. Teaching: Artist in residence, Univ Southern Ill; instr art, Univ Minn; instr, Breinin Sch Art, Chicago; instr painting & drawing, Art Students League; instr, Nat Acad Design, New York. Awards: Prizes, Art USA, 58, Art Inst Chicago (seven) & Pa Acad Fine Arts (two); plus others. Bibliog: Rosamond Frost (auth), included in: Contemporary Art: The March of Art from Cezanne Until Now, Crown, 42; Emily Genauer (auth), included in: Best of Art, Doubleday, 48; plus others. Mem: Nat Acad Design. Mailing Add: 121 Inwood Rd Scarsdale NY 10583

BREITENBACH, EDGAR
ART HISTORIAN
b Hamburg, Ger, June 26, 03. Study: Univ Munich, 21-22; Univ Hamburg, 22-27, PhD, 27; Univ Berlin, libr dipl, 29. Teaching: Vis lectr, Mills Col, 37-41. Pos: Res assoc, Fine Arts Ctr, Colorado Springs, 42-43; monuments officer, Rep to Berlin, 45-55; prints & photographs div, Libr Cong, 56-73, hon consult, 73- Mem: Col Art Asn Am. Publ: Auth, Speculum Humanae Salvationis, Strassburg, 30; auth, Santos, the religious folk art of New Mexico, 43; The American poster, 67. Mailing Add: 3223 Coguelin Terr Chevy Chase MD 20015

BREITENBACH, WILLIAM JOHN
SCULPTOR, DRAFTSMAN
b Milwaukee, Wis, Jan 21, 36. Study: Univ Wis-Milwaukee, BS, 62 & MS, 65; Stephen F Austin State Univ, MFA, 71. Work: Brentwood Col, NY; Del Mar Col, Corpus Christi, Tex; Stephen F Austin State Univ, Tex. Comn: Sculptural fountain, William Robert Murfin, Houston, 72; plywood wall sculpture, Performing Arts Ctr, Sam Houston State Univ, Huntsville, Tex, 76. Exhib: 49th Regional Exhib, R S Barnell Art Ctr, Shreveport, La, 72; 5th Ann Del Mar Col Drawing & Small Sculpture Show, 71; Creative Collab, Rice Univ, Houston, 72; 9th Monroe Ann, Masur Mus Art, Monroe, La, 72; Southwest Graphics Invitational, Mex-Am Cult Exchange Inst, San Antonio, Tex, 72. Teaching: Supvr elem art, South Door Co Sch Dist 1, Brussels, Wis, 62-65; asst prof art educ & drawing, Sam Houston State Univ, 65- Awards: First Prize in sculpture, 5th Ann Exhib, Del Mar Col, 71; Merit Award for creative collab, Rice Univ, 71. Mem: Tex Art Educ Asn; Nat Art Educ Asn. Style & Technique: Symbolic approach using primitive and erotic motifs abstracted and simplified. Media: Cast Aluminum, Fabricated Plywood; India Ink. Publ: Auth, Art education and the modern age, Tex Trends in Art Educ, 68. Dealer: Sol Del Rio Gallery 1020 Townsend San Antonio TX 78209. Mailing Add: Box 2023 Sam Houston State Univ Huntsville TX 77341

BREITHAUPT, ERWIN M
EDUCATOR, ART HISTORIAN
b Columbus, Ohio, Nov 12, 20. Study: Miami Univ, BFA; Ohio State Univ, MA & PhD; Oak Ridge Inst Nuclear Studies. Exhib: Design of the Future, Mus Mod Art, New York, 54 & Merchandise Mart, Chicago, 55. Collections Arranged: F L Wright Centennial Exhib, 66. Teaching: Assoc prof art hist & design, Univ Ga, 47-62; prof art & chmn dept art hist & design, Ripon Col, 62- Awards: Gen Educ Bd Fel, Rockefeller Found, 51; Severy Award, 65 & Uhrig Award, 69, Ripon Col. Mem: Col Art Asn. Res: Area of the art institution and creativity. Publ: Auth, A new approach to art education, 56; auth, The basic art course at Georgia, 57; co-auth, An institutional approach to aesthetics, 59; contribr, The creative life of man, 70. Mailing Add: Dept Art Ripon Col Ripon WI 54971

BREJCHA, VERNON LEE
GLASSBLOWER, INSTRUCTOR
b Ellsworth, Kans, Jan 30, 42. Study: Ft Hays State Col, BA & MS; Univ Wis-Madison, MFA with Harvey K Littleton. Work: Corning Mus of Glass, NY; Mus of Contemp Crafts, New York; Krannert Art Mus, Univ Ill, Champaign; Wichita Art Mus, Kans; Bergstrom Art Mus, Neenah, Wis; plus others. Comn: 24 Award Mugs, Mutual of New York Ins Co, Chicago Off, 72. Exhib: Non-Silver Photog (photographs on glass), Chicago Art Inst, 71; The Craftsman, St Louis Art Mus, Mo, 72; Lake Superior Nat, Tween Mus, Duluth, Minn, 72 & 77; Southeastern Invitational, Greenville Mus, SC, 74; Glass Invitational, Bergstrom Art Mus, Neenah, 76; New Am Glass, Huntington Galleries, WVa, 76; Glass Art Soc Exhib, Corning Mus of Glass, NY, 76; one-man show, Sheldon Mem Mus, Lincoln, Nebr, 78. Collections Arranged: Glass 73, Design Ctr, Iowa State Univ, Ames; Secrets of Light, New York, 75; Exhib of Glass, Honolulu, 76; Tenn Bicentennial Art Exhib, Tenn Mus, Nashville, 76; Contemp Art Glass, New York, 76. Teaching: Asst prof glass, ceramics & sculpture, Tusculum Col, Greenville, Tenn, 72-76; asst prof design glass, Univ Kans, 77- Awards: First Place Purchase, Ceramics Northwest, C M Russell Mus, Great Falls, Mont, 70; Cash Award, Miss River Show, Brooks Mem Art Gallery, Memphis, 75; Purchase Award, Tenn Bicentennial Art Exhib, State of Tenn, 76. Bibliog: Frank Kulasiewicz (auth), Glassblowing, Watson-Guptill, 74; Polly Rothenberg (auth), The Complete Book of Creative Glass Art, Crown, 74; Lelia Daw (auth), Vernon Brejcha, Craft Horizons, 75. Mem: Am Crafts Coun; Nat Coun on Educ for the Ceramic Arts (glass panel chmn, 77); Glass Art Soc; Kans Artist-Craftsmen Asn. Style & Technique: Blown glass wall sculptures, statements about prairie life and farming. Media: Hot glass and mirrors. Publ: Auth, Throw the Lid First, Ceramics Monthly, 70; auth, Fritz in East Tennessee, Glass Art Mag, 74; contribr, The Complete Book of Creative Glass Art, Crown, 74; contribr, Crafts & Craftsmen of the Tennessee Mountains, Summit Press. Mailing Add: 2403 Ridge Ct Lawrence KS 66044

BRENDEL, BETTINA
PAINTER, LECTURER
b Luneburg, Ger; US citizen. Study: Hamburg, Ger, BA, 40; Kunstschule Schmilinsky, Hamburg, 41-42; Landes Hochschule Bildende Künste, Hamburg, 45-47, with Erich Hartmann; Univ Southern Calif, 55-58; New Sch Social Res, 68-69. Work: San Francisco Mus Art, Pasadena Art Mus, Long Beach Mus Art & La Jolla Art Mus, Calif. Exhib: Esther Robles Gallery, Los Angeles, 57, 60 & 61; Los Angeles Co Mus Ann, Los Angeles, 55, 57, 59 & 61; Long Beach Mus, Calif, 58; La Jolla Art Mus, Calif, 62; Pasadena Art Mus, Calif, 62; Intern Ctr, Torino, Italy, 64; 58th Ann, San Francisco Mus Art, 66; On Mass and Energy, Santa Barbara Mus Art, 66; Spectrum Gallery, New York, 67; A Study Exhibition, Downey Mus Art, 75; Women Artists, Santa Monica Col Art Gallery, Calif, 77. Teaching: Instr, The Emergence of Mod Painting, Univ Calif, Los Angeles, 58-61, lectr art, Exten, spring 76. Awards: Award, La Jolla Art Mus, 58 & 59; Long Beach Mus Art, 60; First Purchase Award, San Francisco Mus Art, 66. Bibliog: Michel Tapie (auth), Musee manifeste, Fratelli Pozzo Editori, Torino, 62; Constance Perkins (auth), article in Art Forum, 4/62; H Von Breton (auth), article in Santa Barbara News Press, 2/66. Mem: Col Art Asn Am; Los Angeles Co Mus of Art; Artists for Econ Action. Res: Theoretical physics and its relation to the arts. Style & Technique: Large abstract paintings depicting the overall pattern of linear vibrations in subatomic energy fields. Media: Acrylic. Publ: Auth, The painter and the new physics, Art J, fall 71; auth, The influence of atomic physics, Leonardo Mag, 73. Mailing Add: 1061 N Kenter Ave Los Angeles CA 90049

BRENDER A BRANDIS, GERARD WILLIAM
PRINTMAKER, ILLUSTRATOR
b Maarn, Neth, May 13, 42; Can citizen. Study: McMaster Univ, BA(fine arts), 65; study with Norma Waters, Rosemary Kilbourn. Work: Nat Gallery, Ottawa; Art Gallery of Hamilton; London Pub Libr & Art Mus, Ont; Art Gallery of Brant; Ont Inst Studies Educ. Exhib: Int Miniature Prints, Pratt Graphics Ctr, New York, 68; Allied Arts Ctr, Calgary, Alta, 69; Art Gallery Hamilton, 69-73; Royal Can Acad, 70; Soc Wood Engravers & Relief Printers, London, Eng, 71-77; mini-traveling show, Art Gallery, Gallery Ont, 77; two-man show with David Blackwood, Sarnia Pub Libr & Art Gallery, 74. Teaching: Instr botanical art, Royal Botanical Gardens, Hamilton, Ont, 70-77. Bibliog: Films, Wood Engraving & Making Books by Hand, Nelvana Productions, Can Broadcasting Corp, 74. Mem: Print & Drawing Coun Can; Soc Wood Engravers & Relief Printers, Eng; Alcuin Soc, Vancouver, BC; Ont Crafts Coun. Style & Technique: Wood engraving, lino cut, drawing; realistic. Publ: Ed & illusr, A Miscellany of Prints and Poems, 70, illusr, Pekoo, The Cat Who Talks/Pikou, let Chat qui Parle, 71, Mingling Uneasy, 74, Notes From Stone Voices, 76 & Larkspur and Lad's Love, 77, Brandstead Press. Dealer: Merton Gallery 68 Merton St Toronto ON M4S 1A1 Can. Mailing Add: Progreston Rd Carlisle ON L0R 1H0 Can

BRENNAN, FRANCIS EDWIN
ART DIRECTOR, EDITORIAL CARTOONIST
b Maywood, Ill, July 14, 10. Study: Univ Wis; Art Inst Chicago. Pos: Chief of graphics & exhib, OWI, 42-45; secy, Am Fedn Arts; assoc art dir, Life Mag & Int Ed Fortune Mag; picture ed, Life Picture Hist World War II; art adv to ed in chief, Time Inc; ed cartoonist syndicated by Newsweek Int Ed Serv, currently. Awards: Order Merite Commercial, France, 50; Legion Honor, France, 60. Mailing Add: Hampton House 123-35 82nd Rd Kew Gardens NY 11415

BRENNER, LEONARD J
PAINTER
b Newark, NJ, Nov 20, 23. Study: Art Students League, with C Holty, V Vatlacil, John Corbino; Acad Grand Chaumiere, Paris. Work: Guggenheim Mus, New York; NY Univ; Syracuse Univ; Cornell Univ; Notre Dame Univ. Exhib: Salon de l'Art Libre, Paris, 52; Am Embassies of World, 67; 7 Decades of Modern Art, Guggenheim Mus, 67 & Selection from Permanent Collection, 75; New Jersey Artists, Newark Mus, 68. Style & Technique: Abstract; suggestive of nature (landscape). Media: Oil, Watercolor. Mailing Add: 27 E 22nd St New York NY 10010

BRENNER, MABEL
PAINTER
b New York, NY, Mar 27, 06. Study: With Fred Patrone, Fla; Boston Univ, with Vincent Ferrini & Sydney Hurwitz; also with Victor Candell, New York & Provincetown. Work: Goddard Mem Hosp; Chaim Gross Collection; North Easton Savings Bank. Exhib: One-woman shows, Cape Cod Art Asn, 63, Robert Brooks Studio, Hyannis, 69, Attleboro Art Mus, Mass, 66, Norton Br, North Easton Savings Bank, 75 & North Easton, 78, Stonehill Col, North Easton, 77 & others; Attleboro Art Mus, 75; Avon Libr, Mass; 1620 Gallery, Plymouth, Mass. Awards: Award, Brockton Art Asn, 60; Award, South Shore Art Festival, 70; Award, Lutheran Church Exhib, 71. Mem: Brockton Art Asn (vpres, 60-); Attleboro Art Mus; Fuller Mem, Brockton Art Ctr; Copley Art Soc; Cape Cod Art Asn. Style & Technique: Expressionist. Media: Oil, Tempera, Acrylic. Mailing Add: c/o Edouard Du Buron Gallery 50 Wapping Rd Rte 106 Kingston MA 02364

BRESCHI, KAREN LEE
SCULPTOR
b Oakland, Calif, Oct 29, 41. Study: Calif Col Arts & Crafts, BFA, 63; Sacramento State Univ, 60-61; San Francisco State Univ, MA, 65. Work: Oakland Mus, Calif; Crocker Art Gallery, Sacramento; San Francisco Mus Art. Exhib: Fac Show Sculpture, San Francisco Art Inst, 73, Ceramic Sculpture, 74; Ceramics Invitational, Hoffman Gallery, Sch Arts & Crafts Soc Portland, 73; Ceramics Show, Philadelphia Sch Art, 74; Ceramics & Glass Shows, Oakland Art Mus, 74; Clay, Whitney Mus, New York, 74; plus many others. Teaching: Instr sculpture, San Francisco Art Inst, 71-; instr sculpture, San Francisco State Univ, 74- Awards: First Place for Painted Flower, Oakland Art Mus, 62; Women's Archit League Award, Crocker Art Mus, 63; Award, Calif State Fair, 63. Mem: West/East Bag. Style & Technique: Surreal figurative. Media: Clay. Dealer: Allan Frumkin Gallery 41 E 57th St New York NY 10022. Mailing Add: c/o Quay Gallery 560 Sutter St San Francisco CA 94102

BRESLIN, WYNN
PAINTER, SCULPTOR
b Hackensack, NJ, Nov 6, 33. Study: Syracuse Univ, 50; Ohio Wesleyan Univ, BFA, 54; Univ Del, MFA, 60. Work: Univ Del Fine Arts Collection, Newark; Syracuse Univ Fine Arts Collection; Maine Collection, Haystack Sch Art, Deer Isle; Collection of the Pres, Salisbury Col Art, Md; Del Trust Co, Wilmington. Comn: Teacher & Child (sculpture), Immanuel Episcopal Church, Wilmington, Del, 70; landscape painting, First Fed Savings & Loan, Wilmington, 73. Exhib: Del Art Mus Regional Shows, 56-75; Benedictine Art Awards, Am Fedn Arts, 67; Woodmere Art Gallery, Philadelphia, 73-75; Philadelphia Art Alliance, 74; Catharine Lorillard Wolfe Art Club, Nat Arts Club, 74. Teaching: Art instr, Del Pub Schs, 54-63; art instr, Del Art Mus, 56-63; instr adult pvt classes, 63-67; art instr, Tatnall Sch, 64. Awards: Benedictine Art Award, Am Fedn Arts, 67; First Prize Watercolor, Nat Orgn Women Art Exhib, Wilmington, 73; Ethel M Schnader Art Prize, Woodmere Art Gallery, Philadelphia, 74. Bibliog: From an artistic viewpoint, Univ News, Univ Del, 67. Mem: Nat League Am Pen Women (treas, Diamond State Br, 72-74); Wilmington Soc Fine Arts (educ comt, 73-75); Coun Del Artists; Woodmere Art Gallery; Rehoboth Art League. Style & Technique: Oils, abstracted landscapes with brush in individualized style; watercolors, combinations of fluid landscapes with calligraphic style. Media: Oil, Watercolor. Mailing Add: 470 RD 2 Terrapin Ln Newark DE 19711

BRETTELL, RICHARD ROBSON
ART HISTORIAN
b Rochester, NY, Jan 17, 49. Study: Yale Univ, BA & MA, PhD, 76. Collections Arranged: Four Directions in Modern Photography (auth, catalogue), Yale Art Gallery, 73; The Drawings of Camille Pissarro (auth, catalogue), Norton Gallery Art, West Palm Beach, Fla, 76 & (co-auth, catalogue), Ashmolean Mus, Oxford, Eng, 79. Teaching: Asst prof hist of art, Univ of Tex, Austin, 75- Res: French drawing, printmaking & painting, 1800-1914; American architecture of the 19th century; landscape painting, history of photography 1839-1900. Publ: Auth, Historic Denver, Architects & Architecture 1858-1893, Hist Denver, 74. Mailing Add: Dept of Art Univ of Tex Austin TX 78712

BREVERMAN, HARVEY
PAINTER, PRINTMAKER
b Pittsburgh, Pa, Jan 7, 34. Study: Univ Pittsburgh; Carnegie Inst Technol, with Samuel Rosenberg & Balcomb Greene & BFA; Ohio Univ, MFA. Work: Whitney Mus Am Art, New York; Albright-Knox Art Gallery, Buffalo; Baltimore Mus, Md; Philadelphia Mus, Pa; Mus of Mod Art, New York. Comn: Bronze relief edition, comn by NY State Soc Pathologists, 74; Bronze relief, Temple B'rith Kodesh, Rochester, 74; tapestry, Temple Beth Zion, Buffalo, 75. Exhib: American Painting Biennial, Corcoran Gallery Art, Washington, DC, 63; Brooklyn Mus Biennial, New York, 64; New Talent-65, Assoc Am Artists Galleries, New York, 65; 2nd & 3rd Brit Int Print Biennial, Bradford, Eng, 70 & 72; 2nd Norweg Int Print Biennale, Fredrickstad, 74; 35 Yrs in Retrospective, Butler Inst Am Art, Youngstown, Ohio, 71; Contemp Graphics—Major Acquisitions, Albright-Knox Art Gallery, Buffalo, NY, 71; Three Artists, Mod Mus Art, Oxford, Eng, 74; Honolulu Acad of Arts, 75; Paintings for the Embassies, US State Dept, Belgrade, Yugoslavia, 76; Selected Drawings from Can Mus Collections, Rodman Hall Arts Centre, St Catharines, 77; Auslands Inst, Dortmund, WGer, 77; 8th Int Art Fair, Basel, Switz, 77; Two by Twenty, Kalamazoo Inst Art, Mich, 78. Teaching: Prof art, State Univ NY Buffalo, 61-; artist-in-residence, State Acad Fine Arts, Amsterdam, Neth, 65-66; vis artist, Oxford Univ Ruskin Sch Fine Arts, Eng, summer 74 & 77. Awards: Tiffany Found Grant, 62; Creative Artists Pub Serv Grant, 72; Nat Endowment Arts Fel, 74-75. Style & Technique: Figurative expression. Dealer: FAR Galleries Inc 746 Madison Ave New York NY 10021; Assoc Am Artists 663 Fifth Ave New York NY 10022. Mailing Add: 76 Smallwood Dr Buffalo NY 14226

BREWER, DONALD J
MUSEUM DIRECTOR, ART HISTORIAN
b Los Angeles, Calif, July 22, 25. Study: Univ Calif, Santa Barbara, BA, 50; special study with Donald J Bear, Santa Barbara, 48-50. Collections Arranged: Henry Moore Sculpture and Drawing, 63; The Work of Louis I Kahn, 65; The Reminiscent Object—Harnett, Peto & Haberle, 65; Beyond the Actual—Contemporary California Realism, 70; Other Landscapes and Shadow Land, San Francisco Visionary Painting (with catalog), 71. Teaching: Instr 20th century art, Univ Calif Exten, 55-64; instr mus & gallery world, Fresno State Col, 68-70; instr art of collecting art, Pioneer Mus, Stockton, Calif, 71- Pos: Registr, cur & dir, La Jolla Mus Art, Calif, 51-68; dir art galleries, Fresno State Col, 68-70; dir, Pioneer Mus & Haggin Galleries, 70-71; dir, Univ Art Galleries, Univ Southern Calif, 71- Mem: Western Asn Art Mus (vpres, 62). Publ: Co-auth, John Marin & Marsden (exhib catalog), 66, auth, Georges Rouault (exhib catalog), 66 & auth, The Louis & Charlotte Bergman Collection (exhib catalog), 67, La Jolla Mus Art; auth, Reality and Deception (exhib catalog), Univ Southern Calif, 75. Mailing Add: Art Galleries Univ Southern Calif Los Angeles CA 90007

BREWSTER, MICHAEL
SCULPTOR, EDUCATOR
b Eugene, Ore, Aug 15, 46. Study: Sao Paulo Grad Sch, Brazil, dipl, 64; Pomona Col, Claremont, Calif, BA, 68, with John Mason & David Gray; Claremont Grad Sch, MFA, 70, with David Gray & Mowry Baden. Exhib: New Art in Orange Co, Newport Harbor Art Mus, Newport Beach, Calif, 72, Inside a Long Wave, Sounds Show, Newport Harbor Art Mus, 75 & Los Angeles in the Seventies, Ft Worth Mus Art, Tex, 77; one-man shows, Narrow Open Spaces, The Roger Wong Gallery, Los Angeles, 76, Synchromesh, An Acoustic Sculpture, La Jolla Mus Contemp Art, 77, Inside, Outside, Down & Soliloquies, Baxter Art Gallery, Calif Inst Technol, 77, An Acoustic Sculpture & a Clicker Drawing, Artists Space, New York, 77 & Concentrate/Break-Up, CARP, San Francisco, 77. Teaching: Instr sculpture, drawing & painting, Pomona Col, 71-73; asst prof sculpture, drawing & painting, Dept Fine Arts, Claremont Grad Sch, 73- & chmn dept, 75. Awards: Artists fel, Nat Endowment for the Arts, 76. Bibliog: Melinda Wortz (auth), Installations—Michael Brewster, Los Angeles Inst Contemp Arts J, 1-2/78. Style & Technique: Installation artist, using sound to generate acoustic sculptures and drawings, documented by visual drawings and photographs. Media: Sound; Electronic Light; Pen & Ink; Photography. Dealer: Jean Milant Cirrus Gallery Ltd 708 N Manhattan Pl Los Angeles CA 90038. Mailing Add: 11 Navy St Venice CA 90291

BREZIK, HILARION
PAINTER, EDUCATOR
b Houston, Tex, Aug 5, 10. Study: Univ Notre Dame, BFA, MA & MFA. Comn: Stage sets for Beautiful Dreamer, New Moon & The Golden Trail, Student Theater, Cathedral High Sch, Indianapolis, Ind, 37-40; God Bless America (three walls), Recreation Rm, St Charles Boys Home, Milwaukee, Wis, 41; Winter Wonderland (painting), Dining Hall, Boysville of Mich, Clinton, 54; Signs of Zodiac (mural), Mary Moody Northern Theater, St Edward's Univ, Austin, Tex, 72. Exhib: Wis Art Asn, Milwaukee Mus Art, 43; Tex Fine Arts Asn, Laguna Gloria Mus, Austin, 61; Brothers of Holy Cross Biennial, St Edward's Univ, Austin, 63-69; Art Dept, Univ Notre Dame, Ind, 71; Watercolor Exhib, Elizabeth Ney Mus, Austin, 72. Collections Arranged: Brothers of Holy Cross Nat Exhib Biennial, Austin, 61-69. Teaching: Assoc prof watercolor & art hist, St Edward's Univ, 67- Pos: Ed, The South West Rev, Austin, 58-68; dir, St Edward's Univ Exhib Prog, 67- Awards: Hon mention, Wis Art Asn, 43. Mem: Am Fedn Arts; Tex Asn Schs Art. Media: Watercolor. Publ: Auth, A man from Texas sees a parade, Christian Art Quart, Vol II, No 3; auth, Art and the Catholic artist, Assoc St Joseph, Vol XXVI, No 4 & Vol XXVII, No 1; illusr, The happy heart, Dujarie Press. Mailing Add: Dept Art St Edward's Univ Austin TX 78704

BRIANSKY, RITA PREZAMENT
PAINTER, PRINTMAKER
b Grajewa, Poland, July 25, 25; Can citizen. Study: Montreal Mus Fine Arts, with Jacques de Tonnancour; also with Alexandre Bercovitch, Montreal; Ecole Beaux-Arts Montreal; Art Students League. Work: Vancouver Art Gallery, BC; Art Gallery Hamilton, Ont; London Art Mus, Ont; Willistead Art Gallery, Windsor, Ont; Lambton Col, Sarnia, Ont. Exhib: 2nd Int Biennial Exhib of Prints, Tokyo & Osaka, Japan, 60-61; Salon Int Femme Vichy, France, 60-61; UNICEF Int, UN, New York, 65; 7th Calgary Graphics Exhib Centennial Show, Alta, 67; 4th Biennial Exhib Prints, Invitational Sect, Burnaby, BC, 67. Awards: Third Prize, 1st & 2nd Nat Exhib Prints, Burnaby, BC, 60 & 63; Dipl Honneur, Salon Int Femme Vichy, 61; Can Coun Grant, 62 & Arts Award, 67. Bibliog: E Kilbourn (auth), 18 print-makers, Can Art, 61. Mem: Soc des Artistes Prof du Que. Publ: Illusr, Rubboo Reader, 68; illusr, Grandmother Came From Dworitz, Tundra Bks, Montreal, 69; illusr, Ten Etchings from Wm Shakespeare's Sonnets, 72; illusr, On Stage Please, Mcclelland & Stewart, Toronto, 77. Dealer: West End Art Gallery 1358 Greene Ave Montreal PQ Can. Mailing Add: 2284 Regent Ave Montreal PQ Can

BRICE, WILLIAM
PAINTER, EDUCATOR
b New York, NY, Apr 23, 21. Study: Chouinard Art Inst; Art Student League. Work: Metrop Mus Art; Whitney Mus Am Art; Mus Mod Art; Los Angeles Mus Art; Santa Barbara Mus Art. Exhib: Va Mus Fine Arts, 66; Des Moines, 67; one-man shows, Univ Calif, San Diego, Dallas Mus Fine Arts & San Francisco Mus Art, 67; plus others. Teaching: Prof art, Univ

Calif, Los Angeles, 53- Awards: Awards, Los Angeles, 47 & Los Angeles City Exhib, 51. Bibliog: Nathaniel Pousette-Dart (auth), included in: Paintings, watercolors, lithographs, Clayton Spicer Press, 46. Mem: Artists Equity Asn. Mailing Add: 427 Beloit St Los Angeles CA 90049

BRIGADIER, ANNE
PAINTER, LECTURER
b New York, NY. Study: Art Student League, with Kimon Nicolaides & Morris Kantor; also with Rudolph Ray; study in France, Italy & Spain. Work: Syracuse Univ Mus, NY; NC Mus Art, Raleigh; Univ Md, Baltimore; Finch Col Mus, New York; Newark Mus Art, NJ; plus others. Exhib: Eastern States Exhib of Contemp Painting, Springfield Mus Fine Arts, Mass, 60; solo shows, ROKO Gallery, 61-66; one-woman show, 30 Collages, 1954-1964, Mansfield State Col, Pa, 64; Mus Mod Art Lending Serv, Libr, New York, 66-68; Philadelphia Mus Art Lending Serv, Pa, 70-72; Provincetown Artists, Everson Mus, Syracuse, NY, 77; plus others. Teaching: Pvt classes & lect demonstrations in collage. Awards: Oil Painting Award, November Woods, Cape Cod Art Asn, 57. Bibliog: F Crotty (auth), Why try to imitate the past says noted Provincetown artist, Worcester Sun Telegram, 11/9/58, Provincetown Advocate, 11/13/58 & Interior Design Mag, 10/58. Mem: Am Fedn Arts; Provincetown Art Asn (hon vpres, 65-70, trustee, 58-64 & 71-). Media: Oil, Acrylic, Collage, Encaustic. Publ: Auth & illusr, Collage, a complete guide for artists, Watson-Guptill, New York & London, 11/70. Dealer: Roko Gallery 90 E Tenth St New York NY 10003. Mailing Add: 69 Fifth Ave New York NY 10003

BRIGGS, ERNEST
PAINTER
b San Diego, Calif, Dec 24, 23. Study: Calif Sch Fine Arts, San Francisco, with Clyfford Still, David Park & Mark Rothko, 47-50. Work: Carnegie Inst, Pittsburgh; Mich State Univ, East Lansing; Rockefeller Inst, New York; Whitney Mus Am Art; San Francisco Mus Art; also in pvt cols. Exhib: Carnegie Inst, 61; Dallas Mus Fine Arts, 61 & 62; San Francisco Mus Art, 62 & 63; Jewish Mus, New York, 67; Yale Art Gallery, 68; plus others. Teaching: Instr drawing & painting, Univ Fla, 58; instr, Pratt Inst, New York. Dealer: Alonzo Gallery 26 E 63rd St New York NY 10021. Mailing Add: 128 W 26th St New York NY 10010

BRIGGS, JUDSON REYNOLDS
PAINTER
b Philadelphia, Pa, May 17, 06. Study: Art Inst Chicago; Art Students League. Work: Mus Mod Art, New York; Maison Cult, France; Mus Bellas Artes, Caracas, Venezuela; Mex Am Cult Inst, Mexico City; UN Bldg, New York; plus many others. Exhib: Metrop Mus Art, New York; Mus Mod Art Traveling Exhib; one-man shows, Nat Gallery Sect & Sala Int Friendship, 57, Palacio Bellas Artes, Mex; Paris Exhib, sponsored by Picasso, Malraux & Leger, Maison Club, 38; Spanish Children's Milk Fund World Tour, 38; plus many others. Teaching: Instr graphic arts, New York Sch Fine & Indust Arts, 36; dir painting, Artes Contemporaneos, Cuernavaca, Mex; instr drawing, Sch Archit, Univ Morelos; instr, St Mary's Univ, Tex; instr, San Antonio Jewish Community Ctr; instr, Our Lady of the Lakes Col; pvt instr. Bibliog: Enrique Gaul (auth), book, Ed Arte Universal. Mailing Add: c/o Fairmont Gallery 6040 Sherry Lane Dallas TX 75225

BRIGHT, BARNEY
SCULPTOR
b Shelbyville, Ky, July 8, 27. Study: Davidson Col; Univ Louisville; Art Ctr, Louisville, Ky. Work: J B Speed Art Mus, Louisville; Milwaukee Art Ctr, Wis; Childrens Art Gallery, Louisville; Univ Ky, Lexington; Libr Bldg, Jeffersonville, Ind; represented in 250 pvt collections, over 25 pub sculptures. Comn: Sculpture for Old Stag Distillery, Frankfort, Ky, 65; The Louisville Clock, Louisville, Ky; sculpture at WAVE Garden, WAVE Inc, Louisville; sculpture of Dean A C Russell, Univ Louisville Law Sch; plus many others. Exhib: Friendship Exhib, France, 58; Sculpture Today, John Herron Art Inst, Indianapolis, 61; Tri-State Exhib, Evansville Mus Arts & Sci, Ind, 62; Parrish Art Mus, South Hampton, NY, 70; Suffolk Co Mus, Stony Brook, NY, 71. Style & Technique: Figurative bronzes. Media: Bronze, Other Metals. Mailing Add: 2031 Frankfort Ave Louisville KY 40206

BRIGHTWELL, WALTER
PAINTER
b Del Rio, Tex, July 14, 19. Study: Art Student League, with Frank Dumond. Work: US Navy Combat Art Collection, Washington, DC. Comn: Mural, West Side Savings Bank, New York, 57. Exhib: Mus Marine, Paris, 63; Allied Artists Am, Nat Acad Design, 66, Am Watercolor Soc, 69 & Coun Am Artists Socs, 66, New York; Ft Lauderdale Mus Arts, Fla, 69. Awards: George Burr Gold Medal, Nat Arts Club, New York, 59; Gwynne Lennon Award, Salmagundi Club, New York, 63; Purchase Award, Am Watercolor Soc, 66. Mem: Allied Artists Am; Am Watercolor Soc (dir, 69-71); Artists Fel (corresp secy, 63-69); Salmagundi Club (art chmn, 63-67); Grand Cent Art Galleries. Style & Technique: Traditional. Media: Oil, Watercolor. Dealer: Grand Central Art Galleries 40 Vanderbilt Ave New York NY 10017. Mailing Add: 946 Reef Lane Vero Beach FL 32960

BRIMHALL, MARY JANE
MUSEUM DIRECTOR
b Brasov, Romania; Sept 9, 44; US citizen. Study: Univ Calif, Riverside, BA(Eng lit), 67, Davis, BA(art), 68, Berkeley, MA(art hist), 72. Pos: Dir, Copper Village Mus & Arts Ctr, 74- Mailing Add: Copper Village Mus & Arts Ctr PO Box 29 Anaconda MT 59711

BRINK, GUIDO PETER
PAINTER, SCULPTOR
b Dusseldorf, WGer, Jan 8, 13; US citizen. Study: State Acad Fine Arts, Dusseldorf; Acad Beaux Arts-Metiers Art, Paris. Work: Busch-Reisinger Mus, Harvard Univ, Cambridge, Mass; Ministry Cult, NRhine Prov, WGer; Inland Steel Corp, Chicago; Transworld Art Corp, New York; Art Ctr & Performing Art Ctr, Milwaukee, Wis. Comn: Sculpture fountain, Milwaukee Co Zoo, 68; hanging sculpture, Tippecanoe Libr, Milwaukee, 68; perforated metal screen, E Side Libr, Milwaukee, 69; wall relief, Supersteel Prod Inc, Milwaukee; sculpture (aluminum with baked enamel), Frank W Ladky Assoc, Inc, Milwaukee. Exhib: Art in Architecture, Archit League New York Int, 53; Sculptures of Painters, Fairweather-Hardin Gallery Int, Chicago, 59; Nat Painting & Sculpture Show, Butler Inst Am Art, Youngstown, Ohio, 60; 22nd Watercolor Biennial Int, Brooklyn Mus, NY, 63; Int Outdoor Sculpture Exhib, Mus Arte Mod, Milan, Italy, 70; two-man show, Transworld Art Corp, New York, 78. Teaching: Instr painting, Layton Sch Art & Design, Milwaukee, 55-, chmn, Sophomore Comprehensive Study Prog, 72-; founder & pres, Milwaukee Sch of Fine Arts, 74-76. Awards: Layton Sch Art & Design Fel, 61; Award of Merit, Am Inst Architects, 70; Nat Merit Award, Indust Perforators Asn, Chicago, 70. Bibliog: M Graham (auth), Sculpture & engineering, Milwaukee Eng Mag, 1/67; M Fish (auth), Guido Brink, Wis Architects Mag, 68; M Kirkhorn (auth), Modern artist abandons his studio for a factory, Milwaukee J, 69. Mem: Wis Painters & Sculptors; Art Ctr, Milwaukee; Friends of Art, Milwaukee Art Ctr. Dealer: Irving Galleries 400 E Wisconsin Ave Milwaukee WI 53202; Transworld Art Corp 600 Fifth Ave New York NY 10020. Mailing Add: 2827 N Farwell Ave Milwaukee WI 53211

BRINKERHOFF, DERICKSEN MORGAN
ART HISTORIAN, EDUCATOR
b Philadelphia, Pa, Oct 4, 21. Study: Taft Sch, dipl, 39; Williams Col, BA(art), 43; Yale Univ, MA(art hist), 47; Univ Zurich, 48-49; Harvard Univ, PhD(fine arts), 58. Teaching: Instr art hist, Brown Univ, Providence, 52-55; from instr to assoc prof art hist, RI Sch Design, Providence, 52-59; assoc prof art hist, Pa State Univ, University Park, 61-62; assoc prof art hist, Tyler Sch Art, Temple Univ, 62-65; assoc prof art hist, Univ Calif, Riverside, 65-67, prof art hist, 67- Awards: Cash Prize, Am Numismatic Soc, New York, 52; Sr Fel Classical Studies, Am Acad Rome, 59-61. Mem: Col Art Asn Am; Riverside Art Asn (trustee, 68-72, mem exhib comt, 71-). Publ: Contribr, Ptolemais, City of the Libyan Pentapolis, Oriental Inst Publ, 69; auth, New examples of the Hellenistic statue group, The Invitation to the Dance, and their significance, Am J Archaeol, 65; auth, A Collection of Sculpture in Classical & Early Christian Antioch, 70; contribr, Studies Presented to G M A Hanfmann, 71. Mailing Add: Dept of Art Hist Univ of Calif Riverside CA 92521

BRISTOW, WILLIAM ARTHUR
PAINTER, EDUCATOR
b San Antonio, Tex, Feb 1, 37. Study: Univ Tex, BFA, 58; Univ Fla, MFA, 60; also with Clinton Adams, Ernest Briggs & George Lockwood. Work: Dallas Mus Fine Art; Houston Mus Fine Art; San Antonio Art League; WTex Mus, Lubbock; Longview Jr League, Tex. Comn: Migration (aluminum fountain sculpture), US Govt, HemisFair, San Antonio, 68; steel sculpture fountain, Turbine Support Co, San Antonio, 69; Communication Is (mural), Sid Richardson Commun Ctr, Trinity Univ, 72; tapestry mural (10'x54') & tapestry (11'x22'), Frost Nat Bank, San Antonio. Exhib: Southwest Print & Drawing Soc, Dallas Mus Fine Art, 60, Tex Ann, 60-63; Small Painting, Tour Gallery Assoc, Albuquerque, NMex, 62; Painting in the Southwest, Okla Art Ctr, Oklahoma City, 62; Artist of the Year, San Antonio Art League, Witte Mus, 65. Teaching: Instr painting & drawing, Univ Fla, Gainesville, 58-60; assoc prof painting & drawing, Trinity Univ, San Antonio, 60-, chmn dept design & drawing, 65- Awards: Purchase Prize, Tex Ann, Houston Mus Fine Art, 62; First Prize Southwest Print & Drawing, Mrs Edwin B Hopkins Fund, Dallas Mus, 64; Mus STex Prize for Sculpture, Coca Cola Bottling Co, 66. Mem: Col Art Asn Am. Style & Technique: Abstracted aspects of nature, landscape. Media: Oil, Oil Wash Over Gesso. Publ: Illusr, Animal Tales of the West, 74. Dealer: Dorothy Katz Sol del Rio Gallery 1020 Townsend Ave San Antonio TX 78209. Mailing Add: 344 Wildrose Ave San Antonio TX 78209

BRITSKY, NICHOLAS
PAINTER, EDUCATOR
b Weldirz, Ukraine, Dec 11, 13; US citizen. Study: Yale Univ, BFA; Syracuse Univ; Cranbrook Acad Art; Fulbright fel to Italy, 56-57; Portugal, 65-66. Work: Evansville Mus, Ind; Ford Motor Co Collection, Dearborn, Mich; Univ Ill, Chicago; Prudential Life Ins Co, New York; Springville Mus, Utah; also 65 in pvt collections. Comn: Bronze grille, Bell Tel Co, Waterloo, Iowa, 40; mosaic tile mural, Allen Park High Sch, Galesburg, Ill, 54; com mural, E B Evans Co, Philadelphia, 64; painting for print reproduction, Donald Art Co, Mamaroneck, NY, 65; mural decoration, St Boniface Church, Seymour, Ill, 78. Exhib: Denver Mus, Colo, 51, 53 & 55; Butler Inst Am Art, Youngstown, Ohio, 52-54; Nat Acad Design, New York, 60; Evansville Mus, 61, 67 & 68; Mainstreams USA, Marietta Col, Ohio, 69-72. Teaching: Emer prof art, Univ Ill, 39- Awards: Critics Award in painting, Marietta Col, 71; First Prize (watercolor), Ohio Univ; First Prize, Springville Mus Art, Utah, 74. Mem: Am Fedn Arts. Style & Technique: Flexible-conservative, in communicative content which exploits the media. Media: Oil, Casein, Watercolor. Publ: Contribr, Encycl Slavonica, Philos Press, 49; illusr, Ford Times Mag, 64. Dealer: Grand Central Galleries 40 Vanderbilt Ave New York NY 10017. Mailing Add: Dept Art Univ Ill Champaign IL 61820

BRITT, AL
PAINTER, EDUCATOR
b Cuthbert, Ga, Nov 16, 34. Study: Ala State Col, BA & BS, 59; Univ Mex, Mexico City (pre-hispanic art workshop), 64; Univ NMex, MFA, 65; Univ Ghana, Lagon (African art), 70; Univ Nigeria, Lagos (African studies), 71; Fla State Univ, PhD, 74. Work: Atlanta Univ, Afro-Am Collection; Oakland Mus, Calif; Dusable Mus Afro-Am Hist, Chicago. Comn: Mixed media sculpture, (Dr & Mrs V J Kiah), Kiah Mus, Savannah, Ga, 71; Historical Wall, Savannah State Col, 72. Exhib: Smith Mason Gallery, Washington, DC, 71; Expo 72, San Francisco; Expo 73, Chicago; Nat Conf Artists Exhib, 50-75. Collections Arranged: Southern Univ, New Orleans; Savannah State Col; Itta Bena; Ala State Univ, Montgomery. Teaching: Head art dept, Mo State Penitentiary, 65; prof & head dept, Savannah State Col, Ga, 69-75; prof & head dept art, Ala State Univ, Montgomery, 75- Pos: Art demonstr, cols, univ, churches & art ctrs, 50-74. Awards: First Prize, At Last (painting), Crystal Caves, Birmingham, Ala, 62; Society Wheels, Atlanta Univ, 67 & Poverty Toy Chest (sculpture), 68. Mem: Nat Art Educ Asn; Nat Conf Artists (regional dir, 70-73); Col Arts Asn; Creative Artist Asn; Ga Art Educ Asn. Style & Technique: Abstract expressionism; drip. Media: Paint; Junk. Res: A survey of Afro-American art and a study of drawings by five-year olds. Collection: Afro-Am artists. Publ: Contribr, Black Artist on Art, 69; contribr, Black Dimensions in Contemporary Art, 71; contribr, An American History, Appleton, 72; contribr, Afro American Art, 73; contribr, Atlanta Univ Bull. Mailing Add: Dept of Art Ala State Univ Montgomery AL 36101

BRITT, SAM GLENN
EDUCATOR, PAINTER
b Ruleville, Miss, Sept 26, 40. Study: Memphis Acad Art, BFA; Univ Miss, MFA; Cape Cod Sch Painting, Provincetown, Mass, with Henry Hensche. Work: Union Bldg, Delta State Univ, Munic Art Gallery, Jackson, Miss; Winterville Mounds, Greenville, Miss. Comn: Drawing depicting the life style of ancient Indians, Winterville Mounds Mus, Miss, 67; four-paneled screen (oil), comn by Mrs Stanley Levingston, Ruleville, 71. Exhib: Nat Painting Exhib, Jackson, 64; Mid-South Exhib, Memphis, 64 & 71; Two Plus Two Gallery, New Orleans, 75; Nat Small Painting Exhib, Hadley, Pa, 74; Mid-South Biennial, Memphis, 75; one-man show, Gov's Mansion, Jackson, Miss; plus others. Teaching: Instr drawing & painting, Delta State Univ, 66-73, asst prof, 73-; pvt instr, Clarksdale, Miss, 73- Awards: Second Prize, Nat Painting Exhib, 64; Second Prize for Painting, Greenwood Arts Festival, 71; Most Outstanding Work, Nat Small Painting Exhib, Hadley, 74. Bibliog: Ed Phillips (auth), Finding God's beauty in a simple world, Delta Scene Mag, 75. Style & Technique: Influence of light on color as seen on varied kinds and times of days, demonstrated through proper proportion of color in proper relationship according to the light source. Media: Oil. Mailing Add: Box 3236 Delta State Univ Cleveland MS 38733

BRITTON, EDGAR
SCULPTOR
b Kearney, Nebr, Apr 15, 01. Study: Univ Iowa, 18-20; also with Grant Wood, 20-24. Work: Doors & tower, United Bank Denver, Colo; column, Fed Ctr Bldg, Denver; Orpheus, Colorado Springs Libr, Colo; Genesis, Antlers Plaza, Colorado Springs; The Family, Denver Gen Hosp. Comn: Frescoes for Chicago Heights & Deerfield Shields High Schs, Works Proj Admin, 35; frescoes, Lane Tech High Sch, Chicago, 37; frescoes, 39 & frescoes for Waterloo Post Off, Iowa, 40, US Dept Interior Fine Arts Comn. Exhib: Opening show, 72 & one-man show, 72, Denver Art Mus; one-man & group shows, Fine Arts Ctr, Colorado Springs. Teaching: Instr painting, Fountain Valley Sch Boys, Colo; instr painting, Colorado Springs Fine Arts Ctr. Pos: Pres, Artists Equity, Colorado Springs; mem, Fine Arts Comn City & Co Denver, 67-71; mem, Arts & Humanities, 67-68. Awards: Anne Evans Mem Prize for painting, Denver Art Mus, 48; First Prize for Painting, Pasadena Art Inst, 49; Award, Denver Chap, Am Inst Architects, 71. Mem: Allied Sculptors Colo. Media: Bronze. Dealer: Britton Gallery 2309 W Main St Littleton CO 80120. Mailing Add: Edgar Britton Studio 2309 W Main St Littleton CO 80120

BROADD, HARRY ANDREW
PAINTER, ART HISTORIAN
b Chicago, Ill, Feb 17, 10. Study: Univ Chicago, PhB, 30; Columbia Univ, AM, 31; Art Inst Chicago; Univ Mich, PhD, 46. Exhib: Int Exhib Watercolors, Art Inst Chicago, 32; Artists of Chicago & Vicinity Show, Art Inst Chicago, 33, 36 & 37; Mich Artists Exhib, Detroit Inst Arts, 46; one-man retrospective, 1931-1961, Philbrook Art Ctr, Tulsa, Okla, 61. Teaching: Asst prof art & art educ, Eastern Mich Univ, 37-47; prof art hist, Univ Tulsa, 47-67; prof art hist, Northeastern Ill Univ, 67-77. Mem: Col Art Asn Am; Nat Art Educ Asn; Ill Art Educ Asn. Style & Technique: Semi-abstract. Media: Oil, Acrylic. Publ: Auth, Music as a stimulus to design & Literature as a stimulus to expression, Design, 35; auth, articles on graphic arts, block printing & others, In: World Bk Encycl, 62; auth, Sandpaper lithographs, 69 & Art appreciation and history/who needs it?, 70, Arts & Activities; reviewer, Audio-Visual Guide. Mailing Add: 153 W Jefferson Pl Broken Arrow OK 74012

BROADLEY, HUGH T
ART HISTORIAN, ART ADMINISTRATOR
b Sacramento, Calif, June 5, 22. Study: Park Col, AB; Yale Univ, AM; NY Univ, PhD. Teaching: Prof art hist, Bowling Green State Univ, 61-65; prof art hist, Ariz State Univ, 69- Pos: Mus cur, Nat Gallery Art, 54-61; cur art collections, Ariz State Univ, 65-67; dir, Phoenix Art Mus, 67-69; pres, Western Asn Art Mus, 68. Mem: Ariz Coun on the Humanities & Pub Policy; Col Art Asn Am; Am Asn Mus; Friends of Mex Art. Res: Flemish painting of the fifteenth and sixteenth centuries. Mailing Add: 4102 N 50th Pl Phoenix AZ 85018

BROCK, ROBERT W
SCULPTOR, EDUCATOR
b Tacoma, Ohio, June 27, 36. Study: Sch of Dayton Art Inst, 54-60, dipl, with Robert C Koepnick; Univ Dayton, BFA, 60; Ohio Univ, MFA, 62, with David Hostetler. Work: Dayton Art Inst; State Univ NY Col, Fredonia. Exhib: Artists of Southern Ohio, Dayton Art Inst, 60 & 61; Ohio Sculpture & Ceramic Show, Butler Inst Am Art, Youngstown, 62; Western NY Show, Albright-Knox Art Gallery, Buffalo, 65-67, 69 & 75 & Outdoor Sculpture Exhib, 68; Unordinary Realities, Xerox Ctr, Rochester, 75. Teaching: Prof sculpture, State Univ NY Col, Buffalo, 62- Pos: Mem adv comt, Burchfield Ctr, 70-; chmn fine arts dept, State Univ Col, Buffalo, 70-73; pres, Patteran Artists Inc, Buffalo, 77-78. Style & Technique: Semi-abstract to non-objective. Media: Polyester Resin and Formica; Mixed Media. Mailing Add: 104 Fordham Dr Buffalo NY 14216

BROD, STANFORD
PAINTER, EDUCATOR
b Cincinnati, Ohio, Sept 29, 32. Study: Col of Design, Archit & Art, Univ Cincinnati, BS(design), 55. Work: Nat Collection of Fine Arts, Washington, DC; Mus Mod Art, New York; Hebrew Union Col, Jewish Inst Relig Mus, Los Angeles; Contemp Art Ctr & Cincinnati Art Mus, Ohio. Comn: Urban Walls: Cincinnati (ten story bldg wall mural), Solway Gallery for Cincinnati Community, 72; Six Urban Banners, Contemp Art Ctr, 75. Exhib: Greetings, Mus Mod Art, New York, 66; US Info Agency Graphics USA, Australia, India, Japan, Orient, 67; Typomundus 20/2, Worldwide Int Traveling Exhib, 70; HUD Nat Community Art, Nat Collection Fine Arts, Washington, DC, 73; Print, Drawing & Watercolor, Cincinnati Art Mus, 74; Sao Paulo Biennial, USA Pavilion, Brazil, 75; Vision-Chicago 77, Ill, 77; Third Int Poster Exhib, Listowel, Ireland, 77. Teaching: Teacher exp typography, Art Acad Cincinnati, 60-75; adj assoc prof graphic design, Col Design, Archit & Art, Univ Cincinnati, 62- Pos: Designer, Rhoades Studio, Cincinnati, 55-62; designer, Lipson-Jacob Assocs, Cincinnati, 62- Awards: Communication Arts Award, Commun Arts J, 59, 64, 66 & 70; Typomundus 20/2 Int Award, 70; Int Typographic Composition Award, 70-72 & 75. Publ: Illusr, How Would You Act, 62; contribr, Graphis Ann, 67-; contribr, Mod Publicity, 69-; contribr, HUD Nat Community Art, 73; auth, Packaging Design, 73. Mailing Add: 429 W Galbraith Rd Cincinnati OH 45215

BRODERSON, MORRIS
PAINTER
b Los Angeles, Calif, Nov 4, 28. Study: Pasadena Mus, life drawing classes with De Erdeley; Univ Southern Calif, spec studies in art, four yrs. Work: Whitney Mus Am Art, New York; Mus Fine Arts, Houston; Joseph H Hirshhorn Collection & Nat Collection Fine Arts, Washington, DC; San Francisco Mus Art, Calif. Exhib: One-man shows, M H De Young Mem Mus, San Francisco, 61 & Fine Arts Gallery, San Diego, 69; Pittsburgh Invitational, Carnegie Inst Int, 66; Inaugural Exhib, Hirshhorn Mus & Sculpture Garden, Washington, DC, 74; traveling retrospective, Univ Ariz Art Mus, 75; Am Acad Arts & Lett Candidates for Awards, 76; Watercolor USA, Springfield Art Mus, Mo, 76; Nat Acad Design Ranger Fund Exhib, 77; 153rd Ann, Nat Acad Design, 78. Awards: New Talent, USA, Art in Am, 60; Excellence in Art, Art Dirs Club Philadelphia, 63; Great Ideas of Western Man, Container Corp Am, 63. Bibliog: Bruce Barton, Jr (auth), That heavy secret, Time Mag, 3/1/63; Dorothy Adlow (auth), Broderson's fantastic reach, Christian Sci Monitor, 63; John Canaday (auth), The special world of Broderson, New York Times, 11/13/71. Dealer: Staempfli Gallery 47 E 77th St New York NY 10021. Mailing Add: c/o Ankrum Gallery 657 N La Cienega Blvd Los Angeles CA 90069

BRODERSON, ROBERT
PAINTER
b West Haven, Conn, July 6, 20. Study: Duke Univ, AB, 50; State Univ Iowa, with Mauricio Lasansky, James Lechay & Stuart Edie, MFA, 52. Work: Nat Inst Arts & Lett, NY; Whitney Mus Am Art; Wadsworth Atheneum, Hartford, Conn; Colorado Springs Fine Arts Ctr; Princeton Univ Art Mus. Exhib: Four shows, Pa Acad Fine Arts, 51-67; Denver Art Mus, 63; Univ Ill, 63 & 65; Nebr Art Asn, 64; Carnegie Inst, 64; plus others. Teaching: Instr, Duke Univ, 57-64. Awards: Duke Univ Summer Res Fel, 63; Guggenheim Fel, 64; Childe Hassam Purchase Award, 68; plus others. Dealer: Terry Dintenfass Inc 18 E 67th St New York NY 10021. Mailing Add: PO Box 190 Raleigh NC 27602

BRODIE, REGIS CONRAD
ARTIST, POTTER
b Pittsburgh, Pa, Nov 19, 42. Study: Ind Univ Pa, BSc(art educ) & MEd; Temple Univ, MFA. Work: Univ Utah Art Mus, Salt Lake City; Del Art Mus, Wilmington; Everson Mus of Art, Syracuse, NY; Tyler Sch of Art, Temple Univ, Philadelphia; Schenectady Mus, NY. Exhib: Inter-D2, Int Craft Exhib, McAllen, Tex, 71; 22nd Wichita Nat Crafts Show, Wichita, Kans, 72; 10th Ann Nat Southern Tier Arts & Crafts Show, Corning Mus of Glass, NY, 73; Philadelphia Art Alliance, Nat Invitational Show, Art Alliance, 74; 18th Ann Nat Art Round-Up, Las Vegas, Nev, 75; Soup Tureens: 1976, Mus of Contemp Crafts, New York, 76; Nat Functional Ceramics: 1977, Wooster Mus, Col of Wooster, Ohio, 77; two-man show, Robineau Gallery, Everson Mus of Art, Syracuse, 76. Teaching: Assoc prof studio art, Skidmore Col, 69- Awards: Second Prize/Ceramics, Wichita Nat Crafts Show, 72; Purchase Prize, 17th Ann Exhib of Contemp Crafts, Del Art Mus, Wilmington, 73; First Prize/Ceramics, 42nd Ann Nat Art Exhib, Cooperstown, NY, 77. Mem: Nat Coun on Educ for Ceramic Arts; Am Crafts Coun; World Craft Coun; NY State Craftsmen. Style & Technique: The integration of surface decoration and structure. Media: Clay, porcelain; stoneware, Raku. Mailing Add: Skidmore Col Saratoga Springs NY 12866

BRODSKY, JUDITH KAPSTEIN
PRINTMAKER, PAINTER
b Providence, RI, July 14, 33. Study: Radcliffe Col, BA(art hist); Tyler Sch Art, Temple Univ, MFA. Work: Libr Cong, Washington, DC; Fogg Art Mus, Cambridge; NJ State Mus, Trenton; First Nat Bank, Boston; Princeton Univ, NJ. Comn: The Magic Muse, traveling art environ (with Ilse Johnson, M K Johnson & Jane Teller), Asn Arts NJ State Mus, 72; Bicentennial Portfolio, Princeton, NJ, 75. Exhib: Boston Printmakers, De Cordova Mus, 71; Soc Am Graphic Artists, Kennedy Gallery, New York, 71; Rose Art Mus, Brandeis Univ, 72; one-woman shows, Brown Univ, RI, 73; NJ State Mus, Trenton, 75. Teaching: Lectr art hist, Tyler Sch Art, 66-71; asst prof printmaking, Beaver Col, 72- Pos: Assoc dir, Princeton Graphic Workshop, Inc, 66-68. Awards: Purchase Prizes, Washington Printmakers, Libr Cong, 69, NJ State Mus, 70 & 71 & Boston Printmakers, 71. Mem: Col Art Asn Am; Philadelphia Print Club; Calif Soc Printmakers; Boston Printmakers. Style & Technique: Large intaglio prints involving intense color; fragmented real and conceptual images; mixed media with photo. Media: Intaglio. Dealer: Princeton Gallery of Fine Art 9 Spring St Princeton NJ 08540; Assoc Am Artists 663 Fifth Ave New York NY 10022. Mailing Add: 59 Castle Howard Ct Princeton NJ 08540

BRODSKY, STAN
PAINTER, EDUCATOR
b Brooklyn, NY, Mar 23, 25. Study: Univ Mo, BJour; Univ Iowa, MFA, with Jim Lechay, Byron Burford; Columbia Univ, EdD. Work: NY Univ; Port Authority, World Trade Ctr, New York; Brooklyn Mus, NY; Dr James Watson, Cold Spring Harbor Lab, NY; Heckscher Mus, Huntington, NY. Comn: Electronic Abstract Symbols (lobby mural), PRD Electronics, Syosset, NY, 70. Exhib: Art Today, NY State Fair, Syracuse, 67; 33rd Midyear Ann, Butler Inst Am Art, Youngstown, Ohio, 68; The New Landscape, Artists of Suffolk Co Exhib, Heckscher Mus, Huntington, NY, 70; Lerner Heller Gallery, New York, 75, 77-78; Heckscher Mus, Huntington, NY, 75; Bronx Mus Art, NY, 76; Parrish Mus, Southhampton, NY, 76; Mus Stony Brook, NY, 77; Benson Gallery, Bridgehampton, NY, 77. Teaching: Prof art, C W Post Col, LI Univ, 60- Awards: First Prize, Del Art Ctr, Wilmington, 58; Second Prize, Huntington Twp Art League, 68; Second Prize, N Shore Community Art Ctr, Great Neck, NY, 71. Mem: Univ Coun on Art Educ. Style & Technique: Minimal landscapes achieved through simplified planes and use of mineral spirits which allows color to blend and flow into one another. Media: Oil, Pastel, Watercolor. Dealer: Lerner-Heller Gallery 956 Madison Ave New York NY 10021. Mailing Add: 7 Glen-A-Little-Trail Huntington NY 11743

BRODY, ARTHUR WILLIAM
PRINTMAKER, PAINTER
b New York, NY, Mar 2, 43. Study: Harvey Mudd Col, BS, 65; Claremont Grad Sch & Univ Ctr, MFA, 67. Work: Southern Ill Univ, Carbondale, Ill, St Lawrence Univ, Canton, NY; Neville Mus, Green Bay, Wis. Exhib: 1st & 3rd Los Angeles Printmaking Soc Print Exhib, 64 & 67; 14th & 15th Black & White Exhib, Print Club, Philadelphia, 66 & 67; Albrecht Dürer Commemorative Competition, Univ Wis, Milwaukee, 72; Mainstreams 74, Marietta, Ohio; Potsdam Prints, State Univ NY, Potsdam, 74. Teaching: Instr printmaking, design, drawing, painting & art hist, beginning & advanced; instr, Univ Alaska, 67-69; asst prof, Ripon Col, Wis, 70-75; asst prof, Univ Alaska, 77- Awards: Achievement Award, Riverside Art Asn, Riverside, Calif, 66; Merit Award, 71 & First Prize, 74, NE Wis Ann, Green Bay. Mem: Col Art Asn. Style & Technique: Color woodcut and mezzotint; airbrush acrylic and ink; indeterminate representations of lines in a cubist/surrealist picture. Media: Woodcut, intaglio; acrylic and india ink. Publ: Auth, Communications & Intent, Communications—Tyrant or Liberator?, Ripon Col, 74. Dealer: Lawson Galleries 54 Kissling St San Francisco CA 94103. Mailing Add: 858D Yak Estates Fairbanks AK 99701

BRODY, JACOB JEROME
MUSEUM DIRECTOR, EDUCATOR
b Brooklyn, NY, Apr 24, 29. Study: Brooklyn Mus Art Sch, with Gross & Ferren, 46-50; Art Student League, with Groth, 47; Cooper Union, cert, 50; Brooklyn Col, 50-52; Univ NMex, BA, 56, MA, 64 & PhD, 71. Exhib Arranged: The Collection of George May, Everhart Mus, Scranton, Pa, 57; Oriental Spring, 58-59 & Early Masters of Modern Art, 59, Isaac Delgado Mus Art, New Orleans, La; Indigo, Mus Int Folk Art, Santa Fe, NMex, 61; The Corn Series of Joseph Imhof, 64, Hopi Kachina Dolls, 65 & Navajo Weaving, the Maxwell Collection, 63, Between Traditions, 76 & Myth, Metaphor & Mimbreno Art, 77, Maxwell Mus Anthrop, Univ NMex, Albuquerque; American Indian Art, Univ NMex Fine Arts Mus, 71. Teaching: Assoc prof museology, Univ NMex, 63-, assoc prof Am Indian art, 65- Pos: Cur art, Everhart Mus, 57-58; cur collection, Isaac Delgado Mus Art, 58-60; cur collection, Mus Int Folk Art, 61-62; dir & cur, Maxwell Mus Anthrop, NMex, 62- Awards: Nat Found Humanities Mus Internship, 68; Non-fiction Award, Border-Regional Libr Asn, 71; Tom L Popejoy Dissertation Award, Univ NMex, 72. Bibliog: John Ewers (auth), rev, In: Am West, 71. Publ: Auth, The Kiva murals of pottery mound, 70; auth, Indian painters and white patrons, 71; auth, In advance of the readymade, 74; auth, Southwest Indian art, In: Handbook of North American Indians; auth, Mimbrees Painted Pottery, 77 & The creative consumer, In: Ethnic & Tourist Arts, 77, Univ NMex Press. Mailing Add: Maxwell Mus Anthrop Univ NMex Albuquerque NM 87131

BRODY, JACQUELINE
ART EDITOR
b Utica, NY, Jan 23, 32. Study: Vassar Col, AB, 53; London Sch of Econ, 53-57. Pos: Ed, The Print Collector's Newsletter, 72- Mailing Add: c/o Print Collector's Newsletter 205 E 78th St New York NY 10021

BRODY, MYRON ROY
SCULPTOR
b New York, NY, Apr 5, 40. Study: Nat Inst Fine Arts, Mexico City, Mex; Philadelphia Col Art, BFA, 65; Grad Sch Fine Art Univ Pa, MFA, 68; Ateneum, Helsinki, Finland, 68-69; Univ Va, 70-71; Harvard Univ, 75. Work: Philadelphia Col Art; Princeton Univ Art Mus, NJ; Univ Va Art Mus, Bayly Bldg, Charlottesville. Comn: Polished bronze, N Patrol Sta, Kansas City Police Dept, Mo, 77. Exhib: One-man shows, US Info Agency, Helsinki, 69, Hollins Col, Va, 73, Va Mus Fine Arts, Richmond, 75; SW Tex Ann, San Marcos, 72; Springfield Art Mus, Mo, 76; Hudson River Mus, Yonkers, NY, 76; Nelson Gallery-Atkins Mus, Kansas City, Mo, 77; Allan Stone Gallery, New York, 77; Wichita Art Mus, Kans, 77. Teaching: Asst prof sculpture & design, Va Western Community Col, 69-76, chmn dept art, 69-72; instr ceramics, art educ & sculpture, Univ Va Sch Continuing Educ, 70-76; lectr sculpture, Hollins Col, Va, 75-76; assoc prof art, Avila Col, Kansas City, Mo, 76-, chmn art dept, 76- Pos: Grants consult, Roanoke Valley Arts Coun, Va, 75-76; art consult, Partners of Americas, Santa Catarina, Brazil & Va, 75-76. Awards: Nat Community Art Competition, HUD, Washington, DC, 73; Fulbright-Hays Fels, US Govt, 68-69 & 73-74; Va Comn Arts & Humanities Award, 75. Bibliog: F D Cossitt (auth), rev in Richmond Times Dispatch, 4/30/75; Payton Klein (auth), rev in Roanoke Times, 9/22/74; Roy Proctor (auth), rev in Richmond Leader, 4/30/75. Mem: Col Art Asn. Style & Technique: Mirror finish, polished surface on concave and convex bronze forms; polished stone, concave and convex; clay form studies painted with polymer paint. Media: Bronze, Stone, Wood, Clay. Publ: Contribr, Decorative Art in Modern Interiors, 73-74; contribr, New Designs in Ceramics, 70. Mailing Add: 1309 W 50th St Kansas City MO 64112

BRODY, MR & MRS SIDNEY F
COLLECTORS
Pos: Mr Brody, Trustee, Los Angeles Co Mus Art, 59-, pres, 66-70, chmn trustees, 70-73. Collection: Contemporary paintings and sculpture. Mailing Add: 360 S Mapleton Dr Los Angeles CA 90024

BROEKE, JAN TEN
See Ten

BROEMEL, CARL WILLIAM
PAINTER, ILLUSTRATOR
b Cleveland, Ohio, Sept 5, 91. Study: Cleveland Sch Art, 06-10; Royal Sch Appl Arts, Munich, Ger, 13-15; Art Student League & Nat Acad, 17-18. Work: Cleveland Mus Art; New Brit Mus Am Art; Brooklyn Mus Art, NY; USAF Art Mus, Washington, DC. Exhib: American Paintings & Sculpture, Art Inst Chicago, 32-33; Exhib Am Paintings, Cleveland Mus Art, 37; Am Watercolor Soc, New York, 41; Nat Watercolor Competition, Springfield Art Mus, Mo, 68; Berkshire Art Mus, Pittsfield, Mass, 69. Teaching: Instr watercolor, pvt classes, 25-28. Pos: Art studio painting & illus, Cleveland, Ohio, 19-40; archit designing & decorating, Cleveland, 22-26; art studio painting & illus, New York, 41-57; mem USAF art staff to Gaffin Island, 55; art studio painting, Sharon Co, Conn, 57- Awards: First Prizes (watercolor), May Show Cleveland Mus, 28 & 29; Third Prize (abstr), Berkshire Art Asn, Mass, 67. Mem: Life mem Am Watercolor Soc; Kent Art Soc (juror, 59-); USAF Art Prog (Arctic artist). Media: Watercolor, Oil. Publ: Auth, Specialty shops, Archit Forum, 24; auth, American watercolor (series), Am Artist, 59; auth, article, In: North Light-Fletcher, 71. Dealer: The Bonfoey Co 1710 Euclid Ave Cleveland OH 44115. Mailing Add: 805 Palm Grove Ct Daytona Beach FL 32019

BROKAW, LUCILE
PAINTER
b New York, NY, Mar 12, 15. Study: Grand Cent Sch Art, 27-29; sculpture, Paris, France, 30-32; George Grosz Art Sch, New York, 33-34. Work: Many pvt collections. Exhib: San Francisco Mus Art Ann, 59; Theatre Collects American Art, Whitney Mus Am Art, New York, 61; Craftsmen USA, Los Angeles Co Mus, 66; California Stitchery, Calif Arts Comn Traveling Exhib, 69-70; People Figures, Smithsonian Traveling Exhib, 69-70; plus others. Awards: Nat Orange Show Award, San Bernardino, 55; 8th All City Outdoor Art Festival Award, 60; First Prize, Artist-Craftsman-Westside Jewish Community Ctr, 64. Bibliog: Bentley Schaad (auth), The Realm of Contemporary Still Life Painting, Reinhold, 62; Dona Meilach (auth), Contemporary Rugs and Wall Hangings, Abelard, 70; Meilach Snow (auth), Creative Stitchery, Reilly & Lee, 70. Mem: Artists for Econ Action (adv bd); Am Crafts Coun; Los Angeles Art Asn (trustee). Media: Collage. Dealer: Silvan Simone Gallery 11579 W Olympic Blvd Los Angeles CA 90064. Mailing Add: 831 Paseo Miramar Pacific Palisades CA 90272

BROMBERG, FAITH
PAINTER
b Los Angeles, Calif, Mar 8, 19. Study: Univ Southern Calif; Otis Art Inst; also with Wayne Thiebaud & June Wayne. Exhib: Butler Inst Art, Ohio, 68; Springfield Art Mus, Mo, 69; one-man shows, Penelope Gallery, Rome, 63, Jaqueline Anhalt Gallery, Los Angeles, 71-74 & Roko Gallery, New York, 75 & 77, plus many others. Awards: Purchase Award, Am Acad Arts & Lett, 75 & 76. Mem: Womanspace; Los Angeles Inst Contemp Art; Artists for Econ Action; Artists Equity Asn. Style & Technique: Figurative and abstract in oil paintings. Media: Oil, Spray Paint, Enamel. Publ: Contribr, Los Angeles Times, 71; contribr, Artweek, 73-75; auth, Designers West, 75; contribr, Feminist Art J, 76 & Arts Mag, 77. Dealer: Roko Gallery 90 E Tenth St New ork NY 10003. Mailing Add: 4731 Conchita Way Tarzana CA 91356

BROMM, HAL
ART DEALER, LECTURER
b NJ, June 6, 47. Study: Pratt Inst, BA. Pos: Dir, Hal Bromm Gallery, New York. Mem: Nat Trust; Victorian Soc; Am Friends of Attingham. Specialty: Conceptual, minimal & post-minimal art—art of the 1970's. Mailing Add: 90 W Broadway New York NY 10007

BROMMER, GERALD F
PAINTER, WRITER
b Berkeley, Calif, Jan 8, 27. Study: Concordia Teachers Col, BSc(educ); Univ Nebr, MA; Chouinard Art Inst; Otis Art Inst, Univ Southern Calif; Univ Calif, Los Angeles. Work: Howard Ahmanson Collection, Los Angeles; Ariz Bank Collection, Phoenix; Festival of the Arts Collection, Laguna Beach, Calif; State of Calif Collection, Sacramento; Utah State Univ. Comn: Mural (duco on Masonite), Lutheran High Sch, Los Angeles, 61, mosaic mural (freeform var mat), comn by Grad Class, 67. Exhib: Am Watercolor Soc, New York, 69; Nat Acad Design, New York, 71; Watercolor USA, Springfield, Mo, 73; Nat Watercolor Soc, Los Angeles, 74; Royal Watercolor Soc, London, 75; plus over 60 one-man shows. Teaching: Chmn dept art, Lutheran High Sch, Los Angeles, 55-74. Pos: Chief designer, Daystar Designs, Inc, 63-73. Awards: Landmark Purchase Award, Watercolor USA, 69; Crescent Cardboard Co Purchase Award, Nat Watercolor Soc, 72; Utah State Purchase Award, Watercolor West Invitational, 73. Bibliog: Barclay Sheaks (auth), Painting the Natural Environment, 74, Davis; articles in SW Art Mag, 8/77 & Today's Art, 7/77. Mem: Nat Watercolor Soc (treas, 63, vpres, 65-66, pres, 67-68); WCoast Watercolor Soc; Nat Art Educ Asn; Artists for Econ Action. Style & Technique: Watercolors in traditional and innovative styles, using rice paper collage; landscapes and urban interpretations. Media: Transparent Watercolor. Publ: Auth, Relief Printmaking, 70, Drawing: Ideas, Materials and Techniques, 71, Transparent Watercolor: Ideas and Techniques, 73, Art in Your World, 77 & The Art of Collage, 78; plus many articles on art and art education for the high school and editor of a series of books on design. Dealer: Challis Galleries 1390 S Coast Hwy Laguna Beach CA 92652. Mailing Add: 11252 Valley Spring Ln North Hollywood CA 91602

BROMUND, CAL E
PAINTER
b Marinette, Wis, June 6, 03. Study: Self taught. Work: Nev State Legis Bldg Art Collection, Carson City, Nev; Nev State Hist Mus; Whitney Art Gallery, Cody, Wyo; William Harrah's Collection, Harrah's Lodge, Idaho & Casino, Reno, Nev; Stephenson Pub Libr, Marinette, Wis; also many pvt collections. Comn: Indian Attack on Stage Coach (5'x9' canvas), Vario's Dinner House, Reno, 54; desert landscape comn by Gov Grant Sawyer, Nev, 59; Pyramid Lake (landscape), Nev First Nat Bank, Reno, 65; Wild House Roundup, Security Nat Bank, Reno, 68; Western Cattle Drive (36x48 canvas), comn by George C Hillenbrand, Batesville, Ind, 74. Exhib: Kingsley Art Club, Crocker Art Gallery, Sacramento, 50; Ebell Club Los Angeles, 59; one-man show, Furnace Creek Inn, Death Valley, 58; Phoenix Little Theatre, 62; Charles M Russell Auction, Great Falls, Mont, 74. Pos: Owner, Bromund Art Gallery, Virginia City, Nev, 50-; owner, Bromund Art Gallery, Apache Junction, Ariz, 58-62. Awards: Jr League Award Watercolor, Crocker Art Gallery, 50; First Prize Oil Painting, Ebell Club, 59; First Award Ann Exhib, Nev Art Asn, 55. Mem: Am Inst Fine Arts. Style & Technique: Authentic and realistic but not photographic; bristle and sable brushes. Media: Oil. Mailing Add: 101 B St Virginia City NV 89440

BRONER, ROBERT
PRINTMAKER, PAINTER
b Detroit, Mich, Mar 10, 22. Study: Wayne State Univ, BFA, 44, MA, 46; Soc Arts & Crafts, Detroit, 42-45; painting with Stuart Davis, 49-50; Atelier 17, New York, with S W Hayter, 49-52. Work: Mus Mod Art, New York; Boston Pub Libr Collection; Los Angeles Co Mus; Art Inst of Chicago; Bibliot Nat, Paris; Brooklyn Mus; Detroit Inst of Arts; Elvehjem Art Ctr, Univ Wis, Madison; Fogg Mus, Harvard Univ; Guggenheim Mus, New York, Israel Nat Mus, Jerusalem; Metrop Mus of Art, New York; New York Pub Libr; Philadelphia Mus of Art; Nat Collections, Smithsonian Inst, Washington, DC; US Info Serv; Univ of Wis-Green Bay; Walker Art Ctr, Minneapolis, Minn; Pa Acad of Fine Arts, Philadelphia; Nat Gallery Art, Washington, DC; Cincinnati Art Mus. Comn: Ed etchings, Detroit Inst Arts, 67 & London Arts Gallery, 67-69. Exhib: Eight shows, Brooklyn Mus Prints Nat, 51-76; Print Coun Am Show, 18 mus, USA & Europe, 59-60; Brit Int Print Biennale, 68, 70 & 72; Salon de Mai, Mus Art Mod, Paris, 69 & Belgrade, 70; Soc Am Graphic Artists, 69, 71, 76 & 77. Teaching: Prof art & art hist, Wayne State Univ, 64- Awards: Print Purchase Prize, Brooklyn Mus, 64; Purchase Prize, Soc Am Graphic Artists, 69; Detroit Inst Award, 61 & 66. Mem: Brit Printmakers Coun; Soc Am Graphic Artists; Philadelphia Print Club; Drawing & Print Club, Detroit Inst Arts (bd dirs, 66-76); Mich Asn of Printmakers (pres). Mailing Add: 5440 Cass Ave Detroit MI 48202

BRONSON, A A (MICHAEL WAYNE TIMS)
POST-CONCEPTUAL ARTIST, WRITER
b Vancouver, BC, June 16, 46. Work: Art Gallery Ont, Toronto; Nat Gallery Can, Ottawa; Alan Power, Eng; Vancouver Art Gallery (all work in collab with Jorge Saia & Ron Gabe under the name General Idea). Exhib: 1971 Miss General Idea Pageant, Art Gallery Ont, 71, Videoscape, 74; Canada Trajectoires '73, Mus Mod Art, Paris, 73; Actionen der Avant-garde, Berlin, Ger, 73; Project '74, Cologne, Ger, 74; Paris Biennale, France, 77; Kunsthalle, Basel, Switz, 78; Lucio Amelio, Naples, 78. Pos: Ed, File Mag, Toronto, 72- Awards: Can Coun Arts Awards, 71, 75 & 77. Ont Arts Coun Award Art Criticism, 74. Bibliog: Willoughby Sharp (auth), Gold-Diggers of '84, Avalanche, New York, 73; John Mays (auth), General Idea, Open Letter, Toronto, summer 74; Germano Celant (auth), General Idea in Canada, Domus, Milan, Italy, 10/74. Mem: General Idea, Toronto; Video Ring, Toronto. Publ: Illusr, Is, 72 & Orgasms, 74, Coach House, Toronto; contribr, Only Paper Today, Toronto, 73-74; illusr, Hosanna, Talonbooks, 74. Dealer: Carmen Lamanna Gallery 840 Yonge St Toronto ON Can. Mailing Add: 241 Yonge St Toronto ON Can

BRONSON, CLARK EVERICE
SCULPTOR, PAINTER
b Kamas, Utah, Mar 10, 39. Study: Art Instr Inst, 56-57; Univ Utah, 59. Exhib: Game Coin, San Antonio, Tex, 72 & 74; Nat Acad Western Art, Nat Cowboy Hall Fame, 73, 74 & 75; Mo Safari Found Conf, Reno, Nev, 73 & 74; Safari Int, Las Vegas, Nev, 73 & 74. Pos: State of Utah Fish & Game Staff Artist, 60-63. Awards: First Prize, Nat Art Competition, Art Instr Inst, 57; Silver Medal (bronze sculpture), Nat Acad Western Art, 74, 75 & 77. Bibliog: Dick Kirkpatrick (auth), National Wildlife visits Clark Bronson, Nat Wildlife, 63; Don Jardine (auth), The continuing success of Clark Bronson, Illustrator, 71; Bruce Davis, Mother Nature's Son, Southwest Art Mag, 75. Mem: Nat Acad Western Art; Nat Sculpture Soc; Soc Animal Artists. Style & Technique: Wildlife Realism. Media: Bronze sculpture and painting. Publ: Illusr, Nat Wildlife Mag, 63 & Sports Afield, 64; illusr, Album of North American Animals, 66 & Album of North American Birds, 67. Mailing Add: 17 Hitching Post Rd Bozeman MT 59715

BROOK, ALEXANDER
PAINTER
b Brooklyn, NY, July 14, 98. Study: Art Students League; also with Kenneth Hayes Miller. Work: Metrop Mus Art, New York; Carnegie Inst, Pittsburgh; Art Inst Chicago; Boston Mus; Corcoran Gallery Art, Washington, DC. Exhib: Art Inst Chicago, 29; Corcoran Gallery Art, 34; City Art Mus, St Louis, 38; American Painting, Worcester Mus, Mass, 38; Carnegie Inst Int, 39. Awards: Temple Gold Medal, Philadelphia Acad Art, 29; First Prize, Los Angeles Mus, 54; First Prize, Carnegie Inst, 39. Media: Oil. Dealer: Rehn Gallery 665 Madison Ave New York NY 10021. Mailing Add: Fahys Rd North Haven NY 11101

BROOKE, DAVID STOPFORD
MUSEUM DIRECTOR
b Walton-on-Thames, Eng, Sept 18, 31. Study: Harvard Univ, AB, 58 & AM, 63. Pos: Asst cur, Fogg Art Mus, Cambridge, Mass, 60-61; asst to dir, Smith Col Mus, Northampton, 63-65; chief cur, Art Gallery Ont, Toronto, 65-68; dir, Currier Gallery Art, Manchester, NH, 68-77; dir, Clark Art Inst, 77- Mem: Asn Am Art Mus Dirs. Res: British painting of the eighteenth and nineteenth centuries. Publ: Co-auth, James Tissot (catalog), Art Gallery Ont, 68; auth, Mortimer at Eastbourne and Kenwood, Burlington Mag, 68; auth, James Tissot's amateur Circus, Boston Mus Bull, 69; co-auth, The Dunlaps of New Hampshire, Antiques, 70; auth, Raeburn's portrait of John Clerk of Eldin, Currier Gallery Bull, 71. Mailing Add: 40 Whitman St Williamstown MA 01267

BROOKINS, JACOB BODEN
CRAFTSMAN, SCULPTOR
b Princeton, Mo, Aug 28, 35. Study: Boise Jr Col, AA(painting); Univ Ore, BS(ceramics), MFA(metalsmithing), MFA(sculpture); also with Max Nixon, Jan Zach, Robert James & James Hanson. Exhib: Northwest Craftsmen, Henry Gallery, Seattle, 61; Mus Art, Eugene, Ore, 68; Ariz Comn for Arts & Humanities Touring Exhib, 72-73; Southwestern Invitational, Yuma, Ariz, 72-73; Intermountain Crafts Exhib, Flagstaff, 73. Collections Arranged: Nat Coun Educ Ceramic Arts Conf '72 Exhib, 72; Intermountain Crafts Exhib, Ariz Designer Craftsmen, Flagstaff, 73. Teaching: Instr jewelry, Univ Ore, 67-68; instr sculpture, Northern Ariz Univ, 69-75. Pos: Dir, Northern Ariz Univ Mus, 76- Mem: Nat Coun Educ Ceramic Arts; World Crafts Coun; Am Crafts Coun; Ariz Designer Craftsmen (mem bd dir, 70-, state pres, 71-72); Nat Sculptors Conf. Style & Technique: Space forms; drawn clay and metal; expressionistic use of materials. Media: Metal, Ceramic, Stone. Mailing Add: RR 1 Box 430 Flagstaff AZ 86001

BROOKS, BRUCE W
PAINTER
b New York, NY, July 10, 48. Study: Pratt Inst, BFA(art educ), 70, MFA(painting), 75. Exhib: One-man shows, T W Wood Mus, Montpelier, Vt, 72 & Lotus Gallery, 75; Fac Drawings, Pratt Inst, 74; Skowhegan Benefit Exhib, Gramercy Artists Asn, 75; 415 W Broadway, New York, 78. Teaching: Vis instr painting & drawing, Pratt Inst, 72-, asst to chmn dept, 72-74; adj lectr painting, LaGuardia Community Col. Mem: Japan Soc; Japanese Sword Soc; Col Art Asn. Style & Technique: Non-objective, large, acrylic paintings. Mailing Add: 60 Plaza St Brooklyn NY 11238

BROOKS, FRANK LEONARD
PAINTER, WRITER
b London, Eng, Nov 7, 11; Can citizen. Study: Ont Col Art, Toronto. Work: Nat Gallery Can; Art Gallery Ont; Worcester Art Mus, Mass; Mus Mod Art, Mex; Ayala & Samuel J Zacks Collection, Can. Exhib: Can Artists Abroad, Nat Gallery Can, 56; Bienal Interam, Mex, 58; New York World's Fair, 59; 4th Biennial Exhib Can Art I, 61; plus major exhibs across Can. Teaching: Instr art, Northern Voc Sch, Toronto; also guest art prof, var univs & art schs. Pos: Official war artist, Royal Can Navy, 42-45. Mem: Royal Can Acad Arts. Style & Technique: Early figurative work evolved to abstract, non-objective, free-form collage acrylics, richly textured; large tapestries being made under artist's direction transposed from his paintings by fine Mexican weavers. Publ: Auth, Watercolor...A Challenge, 57, Painting and Understanding Abstract Art, 64, Painter's Workshop, 69 & Oil Painting—Basic and New Techniques, 71, Van Nostrand Reinhold. Dealer: Roberts Gallery 641 Yonge St Toronto ON Can. Mailing Add: PO Box 84 San Miguel de Allende Gto Mexico

BROOKS, JAMES
PAINTER
b St Louis, Mo, Oct 18, 06. Study: Southern Methodist Univ, 23-25; Dallas Art Inst, 25-26, with Martha Simkins; Art Student League, with Kimon Nicolaides & Boardman Robinson; pvt study with Wallace Harrison, 45. Work: Brooklyn Mus, Solomon R Guggenheim Mus, Mus Mod Art & Metrop Mus Art, New York; Tate Gallery, London; plus many others. Comn: Murals, Woodside Libr, NY, La Guardia Airport, New York & US Post Off, Little Falls, NY. Exhib: San Francisco Mus Art, Calif, 63; retrospective, Whitney Mus Am Art, 63-64; Dunn Int, Tate Gallery, London, 64; one-man show, Philadelphia Art Alliance, Pa, 66; The New American Painting and Sculpture, Mus Mod Art, New York, 69; plus many other group & one-man exhibs. Teaching: Instr drawing, Columbia Univ, 46-48; instr lettering, Pratt Inst Art Sch, 48-59; vis critic, Yale Univ, 55-60; artist-in-residence, Am Acad Rome, 63; vis artist, New Col, Sarasota, Fla, 65-67; Miami Beach Art Ctr, Fla, 66; prof art, Queens Col, 66-67, 68-69. Awards: Norman Wait Harris Silver Medal & Prize, 61; Ford Found Purchase Award, 62; Guggenheim Found Fel, 67-68; plus others. Bibliog: George A Flanagan (auth), Understanding and enjoying modern art, Thomas Y Crowell, 62; Sam Hunter (auth), James Brooks, Whitney Mus Am Art, 63; Sam Hunter (ed), New art around the world, Abrams, 66; plus many others. Dealer: Martha Jackson Gallery 32 E 69th St New York NY 10021. Mailing Add: 128 Neck Path The Springs East Hampton NY 11937

BROOKS, (JOHN) ALAN
PAINTER, INSTRUCTOR
b Burbank, Calif, Oct 11, 31. Study: City Col San Francisco; San Jose State Col, with Eric Oback, MA; San Francisco Art Inst, with William Morehouse. Work: State of Calif, Sacramento; City of San Francisco. Exhib: Pioneer Mus & Haggan Galleries, Stockton, Calif, 62; Phelan Awards Biennial, San Francisco, 65, 67 & 69; one-man show, St Marys Col Calif, 67; John Bolles Gallery, San Francisco, 68-71; Newman Ctr, Univ Calif, Berkeley, 69. Teaching: Instr painting, City Col San Francisco, 71- Awards: Second Award, Santa Clara Co Fair, 59; Purchase Award, Calif State Fair, 60; hon mention, San Francisco Ann Art Festival, 70. Style & Technique: Realism. Media: Oil, Watercolor. Publ: Contribr, Sch Arts Mag, 71. Dealer: Van Doren Gallery 10 Gold St San Francisco CA 94133. Mailing Add: 633 Alvarado St San Francisco CA 94114

BROOKS, JOHN H
ART ADMINISTRATOR, EDUCATOR
b Cambridge, Mass, June 13, 35. Study: Princeton Univ, BA, 58; Columbia Univ, MA, 64. Teaching: Lectr Am art, North Adams State Col, Mass, 71-75. Pos: Staff lectr, Nat Gallery Art, Washington, DC, 64-68; assoc dir, Sterling & Francine Clark Art Inst, Williamstown, Mass, 68- Mem: Am Asn Mus; Col Art Asn; Int Coun Mus. Mailing Add: 43B Gale Rd Williamstown MA 01267

BROOKS, LOIS ZIFF
TEXTILE ARTIST, EDUCATOR
b Chicago, Ill, May 6, 34. Study: Art Inst Chicago, 53; Univ Calif, Los Angeles, BA, 56, MFA, 69; Ctr for the Visual Arts, Harvard Univ, 64, study with Sekler; Mass Inst Technol, 65, study with Filopowski. Comn: Textile mural, Disneyland Hotel, Anaheim, Calif, 70; wall hanging, Arco Ctr Law Off, Los Angeles, 74; ark curtain, Temple Isaiah, Los Angeles, 76. Exhib: Southwest Regional Exhib, New York Mus contemp Crafts, New York, 72; Fiber Art by Am Artists, Ball State Univ, Muncie Ind, 72; Southern Calif Designer-Crafts, Mus Art, Laguna Beach, 73; Focus on Crafts, Univ Minn, St Paul, 77; one-person shows, Dickson Art Gallery, Univ Calif, Los Angeles, 69, The Egg & The Eye Gallery, Los Angeles, 70, Gallery Batsheva de Rothchild, Tel Aviv, Israel, 73 & Southwest Craft Ctr Gallery, San Antonio, Tex, 76. Collections Arranged: The Near East in UCLA Collections (auth, catalog), Univ Calif, Los Angeles, 69; Ceramics, Form and Function (auth, catalog), Univ Calif, Los Angeles, 71. Teaching: Instr textile art/design extension div, Univ Calif, Los Angeles, 70-; instr textile art, Immaculate Heart Col, Los Angeles, 74- Pos: Res assoc, Mus Cult Hist, Univ Calif, Los Angeles, 68-; co-ordinator, Professional Designation in Textiles, Univ Calif, 75-76. Bibliog: Dona Meilach (auth), Contemp Batik & Tie-dye, Crown 73; Esther Dendel (auth), African Fabric Crafts, Taplinger Publ Co, 74; Robin Tucker (auth), Art & Artisan: Lois Ziff Brooks, Designers W Mag, 2/78. Mem: World Craft Coun (Am rep, 78); Am Craft Coun; Surface Design Asn (region rep, 78-); Southern Calif Designer Crafts (bd, 76-); Col Art Asn. Style & Technique: Wall and free standing fabric pieces; non-objective; flat and manipulated surfaces. Media: Dye, Resist Media (Batik, Plangi, Pastes), Printing. Publ: Auth, Adire Eleko, Starch Resist Method of Textile Design, Craft Horizons, 71. Mailing Add: 2351 Veteran Ave Los Angeles CA 90064

BROOKS, LOUISE CHERRY
COLLECTOR, CERAMIST
b Phoenix City, Ala, Aug 28, 06. Study: With Kelly Fitzpatrick & Charles Shannon. Pos: Mem bd trustees, Montgomery Mus Fine Arts & Montgomery Art Guild. Awards: Ala Art League & Nat Soc Arts & Lett. Collection: Early English Staffordshire figures, especially ceramic bird groups. Mailing Add: 3604 Narrow Lane Rd Montgomery AL 36106

BROOKS, ROBERT
ART DEALER, PAINTER
b Fall River, Mass, Oct 19, 22. Study: Swain Sch Design, New Bedford, Mass; Vesper George Sch Art, Boston, Mass, scholar. Work: Guild House, Barnstable, Eng; First Nat Bank, Boston; Bass River Savings Bank, Hyannis; Gen Electric Corp, Framingham. Comn: Series of int scenes, Nationwide Insurance Co, Columbus, Ohio, 67-68; mural, Am Legion of Yarmouth, Mass, 77; series of paintings, comn by Arthur A Kaplan, Inc, New York, 77; mural, Cape Cod Synagogue, Hyannis, 78. Exhib: Falmouth Art Asn, Mass, 72; Provincetown Art Asn, Mass, 73; Fuller Mem Mus, Brockton, Mass, 74; Cartmell Gallery, Plymouth, Mass, 75; Cape Cod Hosp Group Show, Hyannis, 77; one-man shows, New Bedford Pub Libr, 46, Lincoln Savings Bank, New York, 75 & Cape Cod Art Asn, Barnstable, 76. Teaching: Art instr drawing, Swain Sch Design, 46-47; tutor design, Veteran's Admin, 47-49; instr painting, Cape Cod Art Asn, 69-73. Pos: Illusr, Armed Forces, 43-46; designer, NE Stencil Engraving Co, New Bedford, 46-53; artist, Screencraft Prod, Yarmouth, 53-67; gallery dir, Robert Brooks Art Gallery, Hyannis, 69- Awards: First Prize Watercolor, Cape Cod Art Asn, 74 & 77. Mem: Assoc, Am Watercolor Soc; Cape Cod Art Asn (dir); New Bedford Art Group (charter mem); Cape Cod Painters Group. Style & Technique: Traditional. Media: Watercolor. Specialty: Traditional landscapes and seascapes. Mailing Add: Robert Brooks Art Gallery 762 Falmouth Rd Hyannis MA 02601

BROOKS, WENDELL T
PRINTMAKER, EDUCATOR
b Aliceville, Ala, Sept 10, 39. Study: Ind Univ, BS(art educ), 62, Martin Luther King, Jr fel, 68-70, scholar, 69-71, Southern fel, 70-71, MFA(printmaking), 71; Woodstock Artist's Asn, scholar, summer 61; Pratt Graphic Art Asn, scholar, 62; Univ Md, 65-66; Howard Payne Col, 66-67. Work: Libr of Cong, Washington, DC; Nasson Col; Mount Union Col; Carleton Col; Bethel Col; plus others including pvt collections. Exhib: A Return to Humanism, Burpee Art Mus, Rockford, Ill, 71; Social Comment in Recent Art, Concordia Teachers Col, Seward, Nebr, 71; The Black Experience in Prints, Pratt Graphic Ctr, New York, 72; Black Artists of America, NJ State Mus, Trenton, 72; Jew Jersey, 1972, 7th Ann Exhib, Trenton, 72; plus many other group & one-man shows. Teaching: Instr printmaking, Ala A&M Univ, 67-68; asst prof printmaking & artist in residence, Nassan Col, 70; asst prof printmaking, Trenton State Col, 71-; lectr art at var art groups, cols & univs, 69-72. Awards: Am Spirit Honor Medal, Citizens Comt for Army, Navy & Air Force, Inc, 63. Bibliog: Article in Negro Heritage, 10/68; article in Chalkboard, 11/68; article in Christian Sci Monitor, 6/22/70; plus many other newspapers. Mem: Philadelphia Print Club. Mailing Add: Dept of Art Trenton State Col Trenton NJ 08625

BROOMFIELD, ADOLPHUS GEORGE
PAINTER, DESIGNER
b Toronto, Ont, Aug 26, 06. Study: Ont Col Art, Toronto & Port Hope, Ont; addn studies with group of seven Can painters including Lismer, MacDonald & Carmichael. Work: War Collection, Nat Gallery Can, Ottawa, Ont; Imperial War Col, Ottawa; Can Wire & Cable Co Collection, Toronto. Exhib: RCAF World Wide Exhib, Can & Eng, 45; Can Traveling Show, Montreal, PQ & Vancouver, BC, 62; Royal Can Acad Arts, Nat Gallery Can, 65. Bibliog: L de Corriveau (auth), Broomfield, Can Rev, 46; G Broomfield RCA, Roundel, RCAF, 64; L Schrag (auth), Broomfield, Globe & Mail, 64. Mem: Royal Can Acad Arts (academician, 74). Media: Oil, drypoint etching and heavy textile tapestry. Mailing Add: Brackenwood 232 Isabella Ave Mississauga ON Can

BROSE, MORRIS
SCULPTOR
b Wyszkow, Poland, May 16, 14. Study: Detroit Inst Arts & Crafts; Wayne State Univ; Cranbrook Acad Art, Bloomfield Hills, Mich. Work: Detroit Inst Art; Grosse Pointe Libr, Mich; Chase Manhattan Bank Collection, New York; Zieger Osteop Hosp, Detroit; J L Hudson Eastland Ctr, Mich; plus others. Exhib: Mich Artists Ann, 54-; Mus Mod Art, 61; Spoleto Festival, Italy, 61; one-man shows, Gertrude Kasle Gallery, Detroit, 67 & 69 & Confederation Ctr, PEI, Can, 75; Westminster Sculpture Exhib, 69; Cranbrook Acad Art Alumni Exhib, 68; Retrospective, Art Gallery Windsor, Ont, 77; plus others. Teaching: Lectr contemp sculpture, Detroit Inst Art, Wayne State Univ, Montieth Col & others; instr sculpture, Cranbrook Acad Art & Soc Arts & Crafts; instr, Oakland Univ. Awards: Prize, Detroit Soc Women Painters & Sculptors, 59; Leon & Joseph Winkleman Found Prize, 59; Mich Artists Founders Prize, 62; plus others. Mailing Add: 65 McLean St Highland Park MI 48203

BROSS, ALBERT L, JR
PAINTER
b Newark, NJ, June 29, 21. Study: Art Students League, with Messrs Dumond, Bridgeman & McNulty. Work: NJ State Mus, Trenton; Am Tel & Tel, New York; Roebling Collection; Springville Mus Art, Utah; Hanover Park High Sch. Exhib: Nat Arts Club Print Show, New York, 72; Hudson Valley Art Asn Regional Show, White Plains, NY, 72; Acad Artists Asn, Springfield, Mass, 72; Springville Mus Art, 72. Awards: Oil Award, Nat Show, Springville, 70; Award, Am Asn Univ Women, 72; Lt Melvin D Brewer Mem Award, 76. Mem: Life mem

Art Students League; Hudson Valley Art Asn; Acad Artists Asn; Hunterdon Co Art Ctr, NJ; Summit Art Ctr, NJ. Media: Oil. Mailing Add: Village Rd New Vernon NJ 07976

BROTHERTON, NAOMI
PAINTER, INSTRUCTOR
b Galveston, Tex. Study: Baylor Univ, Waco, Tex, BA(fine arts); Art Students League; Art Career Sch, New York; also with Edgar A Whitney, Milford Zornes, Gerry Pierce, Robert E Wood, John Pike, Rex Brandt & John C Pellew. Work: SArk Art Ctr, Eldorado; Baylor Univ Permanent Collection; Ft Worth Pub Sch Syst; Brownsville Art Asn Gallery. Exhib: Am Watercolor Soc, New York, 67; Southwestern Watercolor Soc, 64-77; Southwestern Watercolor Soc Regional Exhib, 69; Tex Fine Arts Asn, Austin, 73; Watercolor Okla, Oklahoma City, 75-76. Teaching: Instr adult watercolor painting, Creative Arts Ctr & the Artists Courtyard, Dallas, 62-; instr many art orgn sponsored workshops, incl Ruidoso, NMex. Awards: Best of Exhib, Artist & Craftsmen Assoc, Dallas, 71; Third Prize, Watercolor Okla, 75; Best of Show, Richardson Civic Arts Asn, 75. Mem: Tex Fine Arts Asn; Tex Watercolor Soc; Southwestern Watercolor Soc (pres, 67-68); Artists & Craftsmen Assoc, Dallas; Okla Watercolor Asn. Style & Technique: Transparent watercolor; landscape, still life & figures in several techniques such as glazing, stamping, wipe-out; impressionist. Publ: Illusr, Ford Times Mag, 63, 64 & 69; article in North Light Mag, 1-2/76; Spotlight on the artist, SWS Scene, Southwestern Watercolor Soc, 3/77. Mailing Add: 4808 Oak Trail Dallas TX 75232

BROUDE, NORMA FREEDMAN
ART HISTORIAN, EDUCATOR
b New York, NY, May 1, 41. Study: Hunter Col, AB, 62; Columbia Univ, MA, 64 & PhD, 67. Teaching: Instr art hist, Conn Col, New London, 66-67; vis asst prof, Oberlin Col, Ohio, 69-70; asst prof art hist, Columbia Univ, New York, 72-73; vis asst prof, Vassar Col, Poughkeepsie, NY, 73-74; asst prof art hist, Am Univ, Washington, DC, 75-77, assoc prof art hist, 77- Awards: Woodrow Wilson Found Fel, 62-63 & Woodrow Wilson Dissertation Fel, 65-66. Mem: Col Art Asn of Am (mem, Status of Women Comt, 72-73); Women's Caucus for Art (affirmative action officer, 72-75; adv bd mem, 74-78; ed of Caucus Notes for the Col Art Asn newsletter & Art J, 78-). Res: Late 19th and early 20th century painting. Publ: Auth, The Macchiaioli: Effect and Expression in 19th century Italian Painting, Art Bull, 70 & New Light on Seurat's Dot, 74; auth, The Influence of Rembrandt Reproductions on Seurat's Drawing Style, Gazette des B-A, 76; auth, Degas' Misogyny, Art Bull, 77; ed, Seurat in Perspective, Prentice-Hall Inc, 78. Mailing Add: c/o The Dept of Art The Am Univ Mass & Nebr Ave NW Washington DC 20016

BROUDO, JOSEPH DAVID
EDUCATOR, CERAMIST
b Baltimore, Md, Sept 11, 20. Study: Alfred Univ, BFA, 46; Boston Univ, MEd, 50. Work: Int Mus Ceramics, Faenza, Italy; Prieto Collection, Mills Col, Calif. Exhib: Int Exhib, Ostend, Belg, 60; Ten Boston Area Craftsmen, New York World's Fair, 64-65. Teaching: Prof hist art, ceramics, drawing & painting, Endicott Col, 46-, chmn art dept. Awards: Grand Prize, Int Exhib, Ostend, Belg, 60; Top Honors, Eastern States Expos & De Cordova Craftsmen Exhib; plus others. Mem: Mass Asn Craftsmen (chmn, 55-56, dir, 72); Am Crafts Coun (chmn, Bennington Craft Fair, 71-72, exec coun, 71-72); Boston Soc Arts & Crafts (dir, 62-). Mailing Add: 5 Gary Ave Beverly MA 01915

BROUGH, RICHARD BURRELL
EDUCATOR, DESIGNER
b Salmon, Idaho, May 31, 20. Study: Chouinard Art Inst, Los Angeles, dipl; Witte Mem Mus, San Antonio, Tex. Work: Montgomery Mus Fine Arts, Ala; Birmingham Art Mus, Ala; Ford Motor Co, Dearborn, Mich. Comn: Mural for Serv Club, USAF, Sheppard Field, Tex, 41; 12 hist paintings, Gulf States Paper Corp, 60; 14 paintings, Vulcan Mat Corp, Birmingham, Ala. Exhib: American Painting Today, Metrop Mus Art, New York, 50; US Variety Show, US Info Agency, traveling exhib to Mid East, 60; Ford Exhib, New York World's Fair, 64; 21 paintings in Hyplar, Grumbacher US Traveling Collection, 69. Teaching: Prof graphics, Univ Ala, 48- Awards: First Award, Loveman, Joseph & Loeb, 60; First Purchase Award, Bluff Park Asn, 70-74; Purchase Award, Ala Watercolor Soc, 74. Bibliog: Meet the artist, TV spec, Birmingham, Ala, 69. Mem: Birmingham Art Asn; Ala Watercolor Soc; Tex Watercolor Soc. Style & Technique: Realism, open design (watercolor); abstract, strong color (acrylic). Publ: Illusr, 99 Fables, 65; illusr, Ford Times (220 illus), 50-74. Mailing Add: Dept Art Univ Ala University AL 35486

BROUILLETTE, AL
PAINTER, INSTRUCTOR
b Holyoke, Mass, Jan 9, 24. Study: Ft Worth Art Ctr Sch, Tex; also with John Pellew, Edgar Whitney, Don Stone, John Terelak & W C Austin. Work: Butler Inst Am Art, Youngstown, Ohio; Hermann Fine Arts Ctr, Marietta, Ohio; New York Transit Authority, Brooklyn; Steck-Warlick Printing Co, San Antonio, Tex; Hallmark, Kansas City, Mo. Exhib: Southwestern Watercolor Soc, Dallas, 69-74; Tex Watercolor Soc, San Antonio, 69-75; Watercolor USA, Springfield, Mo, 74-75 & 77; Nat Acad Design, New York, 74-75; Am Watercolor Soc, New York, 75-77. Teaching: Instr acrylics, pvt art classes & workshops, Tex. Pos: Art dir, Dallas-Ft Worth Ad Agencies, 52- Awards: Rockport Art Asn Gold Medal of Honor, Mass, 74; Payton Award, Nat Acad Design, 75; CFS Award, 75, Mary S Litt Medal, 76 & Antoinette Graves Goetz Award, 77, Am Watercolor Soc. Bibliog: Diana Bonelli (auth), article in Ft Worth Star Telegram, 75; O K Carter (auth), article in Arlington Citizen J, 75. Mem: Tex Watercolor Soc; Southwestern Watercolor Soc (prof standards, 74-75); Rockport Art Asn; Allied Artists of Am; Salmagundi Club. Style & Technique: Impressionistic. Media: Acrylic Watercolor, Canvases, Masonite Panels. Mailing Add: 1300 Sunset Ct Arlington TX 76013

BROUSSARD, JAY REMY
MUSEUM DIRECTOR, PAINTER
b New Iberia, La, Dec 20, 20. Study: La State Univ; Univ Southwestern La. Exhib: Butler Inst Am Art; Fla Int, Lakeland; Southeastern Ann, Atlanta; Denver Mus Art; New Orleans Art Asn; plus others. Teaching: Mem fine arts fac, La State Univ, 49-56. Pos: Juror selections & awards, many major regional & nat art exhibs, Tex Gen, Univ Miami, Lowe Gallery Ann, Jacksonville Mus Ann, Miss Art Asn Ann, Beaumont Art Mus & others; dir, State La Art Comn, Baton Rouge, 47- Awards: Silver Medal, 1st Nat Amateur Painters Exhib, Art News Mag, 50; Prize, Delgado Mus Art, 50, spec mention, Southeastern Ann, Atlanta, 52. Mem: Southeastern Mus Conf (past pres); Southern Art Mus Dirs Asn; Am Asn Mus; Nat Trust Hist Preservation. Mailing Add: 3640 Marigold Ave Baton Rouge LA 70808

BROUSSARD, NORMAJ
COLLECTOR, PAINTER
b Lake Providence, La, Aug 28, 31. Study: Stephen F Austin State Univ; Univ Tex Corresp Workshops; Danish Sch Design, Paris; also with Jan Maters, Prof Harry Ahysen & Prof Jerry Newman. Work: Tex Artists Mus Soc, Port Arthur; Columbia Folk Art Mus. Comn: Louisiana Sunset, comn by C Arthur French, Lake Providence; Summer Memory, Gulf States Theatres. Exhib: Beaumont Art League, Tex; Sabine Area Art Show, Beaumont; Lone Star Conservative Art Guild State Conv; Cav-Oil-Cade Art Exhib; La Art & Folk Festival, Columbia. Pos: Columnist, Art Happenings, News, Port Arthur, 72- Awards: First in Fedn, Gen Fedn Women's Clubs; Three First Place Awards, La Art & Folk Festival; Tex Artists of Year, 75. Mem: Tex Artists Mus Soc (pres, 72-75); Tex Fine Arts Asn; Southeast Tex Arts Coun (treas, 74-75); Tex Fedn Women's Clubs (fine arts chmn, Magnolia Dist); Beaumont Art Mus. Style & Technique: Impressionistic. Media: Oil, Acrylic. Interest: To promote a museum and art activities in Jefferson County to preserve works of Texas artists. Collection: Approximately 300 paintings, including those by Archile Gorky, Robert Woods, Edouard Cortes & A D Greer. Publ: Contribr, Sweet Seventies Anthology, 74. Mailing Add: 101 Dryden Pl Port Arthur TX 77640

BROWN, BO
CARTOONIST
b Philadelphia, Pa, July 2, 06. Study: Univ Pa, AB & Law Sch. Work: Var cartoon collections, 50- Pos: Free lance cartoonist, 30- Mem: Nat Cartoonists Soc; Cartoonists Guild. Media: Ink. Publ: Contribr, Best cartoons of year, 42-; contribr, Jokes wagen, 69; contribr, Sons and hair, 70; contribr, Tee party, 70; My shell was recalled, 74. Mailing Add: 218 Wyncote Rd Jenkintown PA 19046

BROWN, BRUCE ROBERT
PAINTER, SCULPTOR
b Philadelphia, Pa, July 25, 38. Study: Tyler Sch Art, Temple Univ, BFA(painting), 62, MFA(sculpture), 64. Work: Telfair Acad Arts & Sci, Savannah, Ga; Arts & Humanities Coun WVa; Festival Arts Collection, Erie, Pa. Exhib: Carnegie Inst, 55-57; Nat Show, Pa Acad Fine Arts, Philadelphia, 62; Nat Show, Butler Inst Am Art, Youngstown, Ohio, 62 & 63; Am Acad Arts & Lett, New York, 68; 21st Ann Int Exhib, Beaumont, Tex, 72; plus many others. Teaching: Instr, Adult Ceramics Prog, Dept Recreation, City of Philadelphia, 61-64; instr ceramics & art, Philadelphia Pub Sch, 65-66; instr art, West Liberty State Col, 67-68; asst prof art, Monroe Community Col, State Univ NY, 69- Awards: Award Painting, Appalachian Corridors: Exhibition I, Charleston, WVa, 68; Purchase Award, Arts & Humanities Coun WVa, 67; Purchase Award, Am Acad Arts & Lett, 68. Mem: Col Art Asn Am; Tyler Alumni Asn (mem adv bd); Southern Sculptors Asn; Rochester Print Club; Artist's Equity Asn of New York. Media: Oil. Interest: Donated sculpture to Bertrand Russel Peace Found, London, Eng. Mailing Add: 17 Sedgewick Dr Honeoye NY 14471

BROWN, BUCK
CARTOONIST
b Morrison, Tenn, Feb 3, 36. Study: Wilson Jr Col, Chicago, AA, 62; Univ Ill, BFA, 66. Pos: Cartoonist, Playboy, Esquire, True, Cavalier, Rudder, Tuesday, Rogue, 61-; founder pres, Fat Chance Prod, Ltd. Mem: Mag Cartoonists Guild. Mailing Add: c/o Playboy Mag 919 N Michigan Ave Chicago IL 60611

BROWN, CATHARINE HOMAN
POTTER
b Washington, DC, May 23, 44. Study: Mills Col, Oakland, Calif, BA, with Antonio Prieto; Univ Mass, MFA, with Lyle N Perkins; Haystack Mountain Sch of Crafts, Deer Isle, Maine, summers with Arline Fisch. Work: First & Merchant's Bank, Richmond, Va; Mills Col, Oakland; Hand Work Shop Permanent Collection, Richmond. Exhib: Syracuse Nat, Everson Mus, Syracuse, NY, 66-68; Art of Organic Forms, Smithsonian Inst, Washington, DC, 68; Crafts Biennial, Va Mus of Fine Arts, Richmond, 68-76; Ceramic & Glass Competition, Corning Mus, NY, 72; Crafts Invitational, Scope Mus, Hampton, Va, 74; Object Makers & All Creatures, 20th Century Gallery, Williamsburg, Va, 74-77; Collector's Show, NC Mus, Raleigh, 76-77; Christmas Invitational, Crafts Concepts, Ridgewood, NJ, 76-77; New Faces Invitational, Inc, New York, 76-77; Baltimore Winter Market, 78. Teaching: Instr crafts & design, Va Commonwealth Univ, Richmond, 68-69; teacher porcelain, Richmond, 70-76; instr, Bennington Col, Vt, 75. Pos: Art consult, Chesterfield Co Sch, Va, 69-70. Awards: Ceramics Award, Mills Col, Oakland, Calif, 65, Sculpture Award, 66; Merit Award, Portsmith Nat Art Show, Va, 75. Mem: Am Crafts Coun; Va Crafts Coun (regional rep, 77-78); Piedmont Craftsmen, Inc; Carolina Designer Craftsmen; Object Makers (past pres, 76-77). Style & Technique: Handbuilt functional and non-functional objects of colored porcelain; millefiori and lamination. Mailing Add: 1806 Floyd Ave Richmond VA 23220

BROWN, DANIEL QUILTER (DAN Q)
ILLUSTRATOR, CARTOONIST
b Fremont, Ohio. Exhib: Butler Art Inst, Youngstown, Ohio, 40; Mansfield Art Club, Ohio, 41; Am Soc Mag Cartoonists War Show, 43; Sandusky, Ohio, 44. Pos: Art dir, Ferrando Publicidad, Buenos Aires, Arg, 49-50. Style & Technique: Predominately realistic in style. Media: Ink, Wash, Watercolor, Pencil. Publ: Contribr, cartoons, In: Am Weekly, Sat Eve Post, Am Weekly, Wall St Jour, King Features Syndicate & many other publ in US & abroad; works publ in many books & anthologies. Mailing Add: 930 W Adams St Sandusky OH 44870

BROWN, DAVID ALAN
ART HISTORIAN, CURATOR
b Bellevue, Ohio, July 25, 42. Study: Harvard Col, BA(magna cum laude), 64; Cambridge Univ, Fulbright fel, 64-65; Yale Univ, MA, 67, PhD, 73. Teaching: Lectr art hist, Yale Univ, New Haven, Conn, 73-74 & Smithsonian Assoc Prog, Washington, DC, 75- Pos: Cur Italian Renaissance painting, Nat Gallery Art, Washington, DC, currently. Awards: Finley Fel, Nat Gallery Art, 68-71; Fel Villa I Tatti, Harvard Ctr for Renaissance Studies, Florence, 69-70. Mem: Renaissance Soc Am. Res: Italian Renaissance painting; Leonardo Da Vinci; Correggio. Publ: Auth, articles on Leonardo Da Vinci and on Correggio, Mitteilungen des Kunst Historischen Inst, Florence, 71, Mus Studies, 72, Master Drawings, 74 & 75. Mailing Add: Nat Gallery of Art Sixth St & Constitution Ave Washington DC 20565

BROWN, GARY HUGH
PAINTER, EDUCATOR
b Evansville, Ind, Dec 19, 41. Study: DePauw Univ, Greencastle, Ind, BA, 63; Acad Belli de Arti, Rome & Florence, Italy, 63-64; Univ Wis-Madison, MFA, 66. Work: Elvehjem Art Ctr, Madison, Wis; Yale Univ, New Haven, Conn; Glenbow Art Mus, Alta, Can; Utah Mus of Fine Arts, Salt Lake City; Tyler Mus of Art, Tex. Comn: Ltd ed paper suite, Source Gallery, San Francisco, publ by Twinrocker, Ind, 76. Exhib: One-man shows, Fleischer-Anhalt Gallery, Los Angeles, Calif, 68, Mayan Journey, de Saisset Art Gallery, Univ Santa Clara & Santa Barbara Mus of Art, 71-72, Comsky Gallery, Beverly Hills, Calif, 75, United Arts Club, Dublin, Ireland, 75 & Source Gallery, San Francisco, 76 & 78. Teaching: Assoc prof painting, papermaking & drawing, Univ Calif, Santa Barbara, 66- Pos: Artist-in-residence, Int Inst for Experimental Papermaking, Pajaro Dunes, Calif, 74, New Harmony, Ind, 76. Awards: Greenshields Found Grant for Europ Travel/Study, 63. Mem: Col Art Asn. Style &

Technique: Drawings and works on and of paper. Media: Perspective, papermaking, hands, labyrinths and highway design. Publ: Illusr, Tim Reynolds (auth), Catfish Goodbye, Anubis Press, 66; illusr, Hitchcock (auth), The Dolphin With the Revolver in Its Teeth, Unicorn, 67; illusr, Peter Whigham (auth), The Blue Winged Bee, Anvil, 69; illusr, John Logan (auth), Poem in Progress, Dryad, 75; illusr, Morton Marcus (auth), The Santa Cruz Mountain Poems, Capra, 75. Dealer: Source Gallery 1099 Folsom St San Francisco CA 94103 Mailing Add: Dept of Art Univ of Calif Santa Barbara CA 93106

BROWN, GWYNETH KING (MRS JOSEPH BROWN)
PAINTER
b Barry, Wales; US citizen. Study: Pa Acad Fine Arts, Philadelphia; also with Arthur B Carles & Dr R Tait McKenzie. Work: Libr Cong; Princeton Univ Graphics Collection; Calif State Libr; Smith Col; Free Libr Philadelphia. Exhib: Art Inst Chicago, 58; Carnegie Art Inst, 50; Nat Acad Design, New York, 51; Newark Mus, NJ, 51; Pa Acad Fine Arts, 64. Bibliog: Articles in Free World Mag, Free Asia Press, Manila Art News & New York Sunday Times. Mem: Fel Pa Acad Fine Arts; Philadelphia Artists Equity. Style & Technique: Realistic drawings and monoprints; dancers; landscapes, Asian subjects; social commentary. Publ: Illusr, Drawings About War. Mailing Add: 13 Vandeventer Ave Princeton NJ 08540

BROWN, HARRY JOE, JR
COLLECTOR
Study: Phillips Exeter; Stanford Univ; Yale Univ, BA(magna cum laude); Oxford Univ, Marshall fel & MA. Pos: Producer, 20th Century Fox; pres, Little Antigone Theaters. Collection: Major abstract expressionists; pop; Los Angeles school. Mailing Add: 622 N Roxbury Dr Beverly Hills CA 90210

BROWN, HILTON EDWARD
EDUCATOR, PAINTER
b Momence, Ill, Sept 22, 38. Study: Goodman Theatre & Sch Drama, Art Inst Chicago, 56-58; Skowhegan Sch Painting & Sculpture, Maine, summers 60 & 61; Art Inst Chicago, George T & Isabelle Brown foreign travel fel & dipl fine arts, 62, BFA, 63, MFA, 64; Univ Ill, Chicago, 62-63; Univ Chicago, 59. Work: Skowhegan Sch Painting & Sculpture; Ball State Univ Art Collection; Macomb Co Community Col, Detroit; Goucher Col; Mary Inst, St Louis. Comn: Exterior wall paintings, City of Baltimore, 73-75. Exhib: Chicago & Vicinity Show, Art Inst Chicago, 60; Nat Print Exhib, Brooklyn Mus, 64; Twelve Chicago Painters, Walker Art Ctr, Minneapolis, 65; 20th Mo Show, City Art Mus, St Louis, 66; Md Regional Exhib, Baltimore Mus Art, 75. Teaching: Instr color, drawing & design, Art Inst Chicago, 62-65; asst prof drawing & compos, Sch Fine Arts, Washington Univ, 65-68; chmn art dept & prof drawing, painting & printmaking, Goucher Col, 68-; vis prof artists mat & tech, Winterthur Prog Conserv Art, Univ Del, 74- Pos: Mem contemp art accession comt, Baltimore Mus Art, 68-; mem alumni coun, Skowhegan Sch Painting & Sculpture, 72-; mem art comn, Baltimore, 73-; mem mural jury, City of Baltimore, 75- Awards: Renfrow Art Award, City Art Mus, St Louis, 65; Berney Award Painting, Baltimore Mus Art, 70. Bibliog: Franz Schultz (auth), Chicago Art Inst, 3/67; John Brod Peters (auth), Art views: Hilton Brown: new directions, St Louis Globe Dem, 8/12/67; Lincoln F Johnson (auth), Paintings of Hilton Brown, Sunday Sun, Baltimore, 4/29/71. Mem: Col Art Asn Am; Am Asn Univ Prof. Style & Technique: Figurative paintings, drawings and prints. Media: Oil, Acrylic, Watercolor. Publ: Auth, Some thoughts about my work, Art Scene, 5/69. Mailing Add: 1432 Park Ave Baltimore MD 21217

BROWN, JAMES MONROE, III
MUSEUM DIRECTOR
b Brooklyn, NY, Oct 7, 17. Study: Amherst Col, BA, 39, hon MA, 54; Harvard Univ, MA, 46, Advan Mgt Prog, 58. Pos: Asst to dir, Inst Contemp Art, Boston, 41, asst dir, 46-48; asst to dir, Dumbarton Oaks Res Libr & Collection, Washington, DC, 46; dir, William A Farnsworth Art Mus, Rockland, Maine, 48-51; dir, Corning Glass Ctr, 51-63, dir pub affairs, 56-59, dir mgt develop, 59-61; pres, Corning Found, 61-63; pres, Corning Mus Glass, 61-63; dir, Oakland Mus, Calif, 64-67; dir, Norton Simon, Inc Mus Art, 68-69; dir, Va Mus Fine Arts, Richmond, 69-76; dir, Soc Four Arts, Palm Beach. Mem: Am Asn Mus (past vpres & treas, pres, 70-72); Asn Art Mus Dirs; Am Fedn Arts; Int Coun Mus (past USA chmn); Int Exhibs Found. Mailing Add: Soc of the Four Arts Four Arts Plaza Palm Beach FL 33480

BROWN, JEANETTE H
COLLECTOR, ART ADMINISTRATOR
b Brooklyn, NY, Dec 20, 11. Pos: Dir, The Tyringham Inst & Jean Brown Archive. Collection: Dada, surrealism, fluxus, happenings, concrete poetry, lettrisme, conceptual art. Mailing Add: Shaker Seed House Tyringham MA 01264

BROWN, JEFFREY ROGERS
ART DEALER, ART HISTORIAN
b Rockville Centre, NY, Feb 7, 40. Study: Dartmouth Col, AB, 61; Univ Pa, AM, 68; Univ Md. Collections Arranged: Jewish Art (collection of Mr & Mrs Jacob Schulman), 65; George Ortman, 71; Alfred Thompson Bricher (with catalog), 73; Leonard Baskin in Massachusetts, 74; Three American Purists: Mason, Miles, von Wiegand, 75. Teaching: Asst prof art, State Univ NY Cortland, 67-68. Pos: Cur educ, Munson-Williams-Proctor Inst, Utica, NY, 64-67; cur collections, Indianapolis Mus Art, 69-73; dir, Mus Fine Arts, Springfield, Mass, 73-75. Mem: Am Asn Mus; Asn Art Mus Dir. Res: American painting of 19th century; James Peale, Alfred Bricher & Dennis Bunker. Publ: Contribr, Recent Accessions-a Six Year Retrospective, Indianapolis, 72; auth, Alfred Thompson Bricher, Am Art Rev, Vol 1, 74 & Antiques, 76. Mailing Add: PO Box 537 North Amherst MA 01059

BROWN, JOHN CARTER
MUSEUM DIRECTOR
b Providence, RI, Oct 8, 34. Study: Harvard Univ, AB, 56, MBA, 58; Munich Univ, 58; with Bernard Berenson, Florence, Italy, 58-59; Neth Inst Art Hist, 60; NY Univ Inst Fine Arts, MA, 62; Brown Univ, hon LLD, 70; Mt St Mary's Col, hon LDH, 74; Georgetown Univ, hon LDH, 75. Pos: Asst to dir, Nat Gallery Art, 61-63, asst dir, 64-68, dep dir, 68-69, dir, 69- Awards: Gold Medal of Honor, Nat Arts Club, 72. Mem: Asn Art Mus Dirs; Col Art Asn Am; Am Asn Mus; Soc Archit Historians; hon Am Inst Architects. Res: Seventeenth century Dutch art. Publ: Auth & dir, American vision (film), 65. Mailing Add: Nat Gallery Art Washington DC 20565

BROWN, JOHN HALL
PAINTER, ARCHITECT
b Houston, Tex, June 6, 10. Study: Tex A&M Col, BA, 33, post-grad study, 35-36. Work: City of Richardson Pub Libr, Tex; Art Soc Permanent Collection, Sherman, Tex. Exhib: Southwest Watercolor Soc Regional; Tex Fine Arts Soc Regional; Artists & Craftsmen Regional; Richardson Civic Art Soc Regional; Jefferson Arts Festival, New Orleans, La. Awards: Third Prize, Nat Okla Watercolor, 77. Pos: Architect. Awards: Harold Michler Purchase Prize, 70; First & Second Award, watercolor, Artists & Craftsmen, 70; Best of Show, Richardson Civic Art Soc, 71. Mem: Southwest Watercolor Soc (vpres, 70); Richardson Civic Art Soc (vpres, 72); Artists & Craftsmen; Tex Fine Arts Soc. Media: Watercolor. Dealer: Curl Gallery 4843 Massachusetts Ave NW Washington DC 20016. Mailing Add: 120 Westshore Dr Richardson TX 75080

BROWN, JONATHAN
ART ADMINISTRATOR, ART HISTORIAN
b Springfield, Mass, July 15, 39. Study: Dartmouth Col, AB, 60; Princeton Univ, PhD, 64. Teaching: Asst prof art hist, Princeton Univ, 65-71, assoc prof, 71-73; assoc prof art hist, Inst Fine Arts, NY Univ, 73-77, prof art hist, 77- Pos: Actg dir, Inst Fine Arts, NY Univ, 73-78. Awards: Arthur Kingsley Porter Prize, Col Art Asn Am, 71. Mem: Metrop Mus Dept Europ Paintings, New York (adv comt, 74-); Master Drawings, New York (adv bd, 75-). Res: Spanish art 16th-19th centuries. Publ: Ed, Sources & Documents in the History of Art: Italy & Spain 1600-1750, 70; auth, Hieroglyphs of death & salvation, Art Bull, 70; auth, Prints & Drawings by Jusepe de Ribera, 73; auth, Zurbaran, 73; auth, Murillo and His Drawings, 76. Mailing Add: 1 E 78th St New York NY 10021

BROWN, JOSEPH
SCULPTOR, EDUCATOR
b Philadelphia, Pa, Mar 20, 09. Study: Temple Univ, BS(educ); apprentice & studio asst to R Tait McKenzie, 31-38. Work: Pa Acad Fine Arts, Philadelphia; RI Sch Design Mus Art, Providence; NC Art Mus, Raleigh; Univ Tex, Austin; Yale Univ, New Haven. Comn: Portraits from life, Robert Frost, 63 & John Steinbeck, 64, Univ Tex, Austin; Discus Thrower and Runner (bronzes), Johns Hopkins Univ, Baltimore, 65; Gymnasts (bronze), Temple Univ, Philadelphia, 69; four heroic athletic statues (bronze), City of Philadelphia, Vet Stadium, 70. Exhib: Pa Acad Fine Arts Ann, Philadelphia, 32-; Nat Acad Design, New York, 33-; Art Exhib, Olympic Games, Berlin, 36; Int Sculpture Exhib, Philadelphia Mus Art, 49; Expo 67, Montreal, 67. Teaching: Sculptor-in-residence, Princeton Univ, 39- Pos: Mem Philadelphia Art Comn. Awards: First Prize for sculpture, Montclair Mus Art, NJ, 40; Barnett Prize, Nat Acad Design, 44; Distinguished Serv Citation, Am Asn Health, Phys Educ & Recreation, Nat Educ Asn, 67. Bibliog: Red Smith & Norman Thomas (auth), Introd to Joe Brown, retrospective catalogue, 32-66; Harry Olesker (auth), Shaping things and vice-versa (TV film), NBC-TV, 55. Mem: Fel Nat Sculpture Soc; Pa Acad Fine Arts; Artists Equity Asn. Style & Technique: Realist. Media: Bronze. Publ: Auth, Unpredictability—margin for inspiration, Archit Rec, 9/55; auth, Dynamics of group interaction, viewpoint of an artist, Am J Psychiat, 3/66; auth, And you hear your name, Univ Mag, summer-fall 66; Movement and figurative sculpture, Quest, 1/75. Mailing Add: 185 Nassau St Princeton NJ 08540

BROWN, JUDITH GWYN
ILLUSTRATOR, PAINTER
b New York, NY, Oct 15, 33. Study: New York Univ, with Philip Guston, 52-56, BA, 56; Parsons Sch of Design, with Richard Lindner, 56-57. Work: Metrop Mus of Art, New York; Huntington Libr, San Marino, Calif; Kerlan Collection, Univ Minn, Minneapolis. Mem: Graphic Artist's Guild; Comt for the Picture Collection, New York Pub Libr (mem bd dir, 76 & officer & treas, 78). Style & Technique: Drawings based in the traditional manner of illustration combined with modern forms; figurative painting bridging reality and the dream. Media: Pen, Ink, Conté Crayon; Watercolor, Oil. Publ: Illusr, Mandy, Harper & Row, 71; illusr, Lavender Green Magic, Thomas Y Crowell, 74; illusr, Chad and the Elephant Engine, Atheneum, 75; auth & illusr, Alphabet Dreams, Prentice-Hall, 76; illusr, Jeminalee, McGraw-Hill, 77. Mailing Add: 522 E 85th St New York NY 10028

BROWN, LARRY K
PAINTER, SCULPTOR
b New Brunswick, NJ, June 1, 42. Study: Wash State Univ, BA, 67; Univ Ariz, MFA, 70. Work: Walker Art Ctr, Minneapolis. Exhib: 8th Tyler Nat, Tyler Mus Art, Tex, 71; Invitation 74, Walker Art Ctr, 74; one-man shows, RI Sch Design, Providence, 74 & Lamagna Gallery, New York, 75; New Directions in Abstraction, State Univ NY Potsdam, 75. Teaching: Instr painting, Univ Wis, Stevens Point, 70-74; asst prof painting, St Lawrence Univ, 74-75; asst prof painting, Univ Pittsburgh, 75- Awards: Milwaukee Art Ctr Award, 71. Mem: Col Art Asn Am. Style & Technique: Three-dimensional reliefs using Rhoplex and latex rubber. Media: Mixed Media. Dealer: Lamagna Gallery 380 W Broadway New York NY 10012. Mailing Add: 1225 Adon St Pittsburgh PA 15204

BROWN, MARION B
PAINTER
b Brooklyn, NY, Oct 15, 13. Study: Pratt Inst, Sch Fine & Appl Arts, cert teaching; also with Edgar A Whitney. Work: Dimes Savings Bank New York, Brooklyn; First Nat City Bank, Syosset, NY; Long Island Lighting Co. Exhib: Hudson Valley Art Asn, White Plains, NY, 61-77; Am Watercolor Soc, Nat Acad Design Galleries, New York, 62, 69, 71-74 & 76-77; Audubon Artists, Nat Acad Design Galleries, 65 & 66; Am Artists Prof League, New York, 66-76, Catharine Lorillard Wolfe Art Club, Nat Arts Club, New York, 67-77; Edward Dean Mus, Cherry Valley, Calif, 71, 73 & 77; Frye Mus, Seattle, Wash, 73, 76 & 77; Columbia Mus Art, SC, 74 & 76; Mus Fine Arts, St Petersburg, Fla, 76. Teaching: Watercolor workshops, Malverne, NY, 67-; instr watercolor, Garden City Community Club, NY, 67- Awards: Herb Olsen Award, Am Watercolor Soc, 71; Gold Medal, Hudson Valley Art Asn, 71; Gold Medal, Franklin Mint Gallery of Am Art, 73. Mem: Am Watercolor Soc; Hudson Valley Art Asn; Am Artists Prof League; Catharine Lorillard Wolfe Art Club; Nat Art League. Style & Technique: Traditional landscape, wet method. Media: Watercolor. Dealer: Garden City Galleries Ltd 923 Franklin Ave Garden City NY 11530; Piccolo Mondo 311 Worth Ave Palm Beach FL 33480. Mailing Add: 18 Nassau Ave Freeport NY 11520

BROWN, MARVIN PRENTISS
PAINTER, SCULPTOR
b New York, NY, July 2, 43. Study: Brooklyn Mus Art Sch, 61-62, with Donald Fabricant & Peter Forakis; Yale Univ Summer Sch, Yale-Norfolk fel, 64, with Leland Bell & Richard Ziemann; Philadelphia Col Art, BFA, 65, with Robert Keyser, Natalie Charkow & Jean Cohen; Ind Univ, 65-66, with Ronald Slowinski; Brooklyn Col, 67, with Carl Holty. Work: Minami Gallery, Tokyo, Japan; Eastern Mich Univ, Ypsilanti; Corp Design Ctr, Westinghouse Corp, Gateway Ctr, Pittsburgh; Health & Hosp Corp, New York; Moravian Col, Bethlehem, Pa. Comn: Wall sculpture, Howard Beach Br, Queensborough Pub Libr, Dept Gen Serv, New York, 71. Exhib: Ann Exhib Contemp Am Painting, 69 & 72, Ann Exhib Contemp Am Sculpture, 70, Whitney Mus Am Art; Afro-American Artists: New York and Boston, Mus Fine Arts, Boston, 70; Untitled I, Art Lending Serv, Mus Mod Art, New York, 71; American Drawings: The Last Decade, Katonah Gallery, NY, 71; Painting or Sculpture?, Newark Mus, NJ, 72; Hayden Gallery, Mass Inst Technol, 75. Teaching: Lectr painting, Philadelphia Col Art, Pa, 70-71; vis artist, Univ RI, summer 72; adj lectr art, Hunter Col, 71-; lectr, Calif State Univ, Hayward, 72-73; asst prof, Brown Univ, 74- Awards: Corp Yaddo Residence Award, 68; John Simon Guggenheim Mem Found Fel, 73; Fulbright Sr Scholar Grant in Fine Arts, Australia, 77. Bibliog: Barbara Rose (auth), Black art in America, Art in

Am, 9-10/70; Carter Ratcliff (auth), The Whitney annual: part I, Artforum, 4/72; Holloway (auth), Memory, Arts Melbourne, 77. Media: Industrial Material. Mailing Add: Box 39 Kingston RI 02881

BROWN, MARY RACHEL
See Marais

BROWN, MILTON WOLF
ART HISTORIAN
b Newark, NJ, July 3, 11. Study: New York Univ, BA, 32, MA, 35, PhD, 49; Courtauld Inst, summer 34; Univ of Brussels, summer 37; Harvard Univ, 38-39. Collections Arranged: Jacob Lawrence Retrospective, Whitney Mus of Am Art, New York, 74; Modern Spirit, American Painting & Photography, Arts Coun of Great Brit, 77. Teaching: From instr to prof art hist, Brooklyn Col, NY, 46-70; prof art hist & exec off, PhD Prog in Art Hist, Grad Sch, City Univ New York, 71- Awards: Sachs Fel, 38-39 & Fogg Mus Fel, 40-41, Harvard Univ; Bollingen Found Fel, 59-60. Mem: Col Art Asn of Am; Soc of Archit Hist; Archives of Am Art (adv coun, 65-); Smithsonian Inst (coun, 76-); Victorian Soc in Am. Res: American art, especially early 20th century, art nouveau. Publ: Auth, Painting of the French Revolution, Critics Group, 37; auth, American Painting from the Armory Show to the Depression, Princeton Univ Press, 55; co-auth, Encyclopedia of Painting, Crown, 55; auth, Story of the Armory Show, Hirshhorn Found, 63; auth, American Art to 1900, H N Abrams, 77. Mailing Add: 15 W 70th St New York NY 10023

BROWN, PEGGY ANN
PAINTER
b Ft Wayne, Ind, Mar 15, 34. Study: Marquette Univ, BS(jour); Ft Wayne Art Inst. Work: Ind Univ, Bloomington; Columbus Art Ctr, Ohio; Ricks Col, Rexburg, Idaho; Continental Ill Bank, Chicago; Menninger Found, Topeka, Kans. Exhib: Allied Artists Am, New York, 70-76; Mainstreams, Marietta Col, Ohio, 70-77; Watercolor USA, Springfield, Mo, 72-73, 75 & 77; Nat Watercolor Soc, Los Angeles, 72-74 & 76; Am Watercolor Soc, New York, 74 & 76; one-person shows, Ft Wayne Mus of Art, Ind & Dahl Fine Art Ctr, Rapid City, SDak. Teaching: Instr creative watercolor, Ind Univ, currently. Awards: McCarthey Watercolor, Chautauqua Nat, New York, 73; First Award, Ala Watercolor Soc Nat, 76; Purchase Award, San Diego Watercolor Soc Nat, 77. Bibliog: Mary Owen (auth), Contemporary corner, Nat Antiques Rev, 71; James Voirol (auth), Catalog, Ft Wayne Mus Art Publ, 75; Gerald Brommer (auth), Collaging With Paper, 78. Mem: Nat Watercolor Soc; Allied Artists Am; La Nat Watercolor Soc; Watercolor West; Midwest Watercolor Soc (bd dir). Style & Technique: Natural images and abstractions from nature. Media: Transparent Watercolor, Drawings. Mailing Add: 5209 Westbreeze Trail Ft Wayne IN 46804

BROWN, PETER C
PAINTER, EDUCATOR
b Port Chester, NY, Oct 10, 40. Study: Ohio Wesleyan Univ, BFA, 63; Cranbrook Acad of Art, MFA, 65. Work: Cranbrook Acad of Art, Bloomfield Hills, Mich; Miami Univ, Oxford, Ohio; Baldwin-Wallace Col, Berea, Ohio. Exhib: Butler Inst of Am Art, Youngstown, Ohio, 66 & 67; Ohio Artists, Dayton Art Inst, 66 & 67 & Cincinnati Art Mus, 67 & 68; Philadelphia Art Alliance, 72; Fac Exhib, Philadelphia Mus of Art, 73; Contemp Reflections 1976, Aldrich Mus of Contemp Art, Ridgefield, Conn, 76; one-man show, Lotus Gallery, New York, 76. Teaching: Asst prof drawing, painting & printmaking, Western Col, Oxford, Ohio, 65-70; assoc prof drawing, painting & printmaking & coordr art dept, La Guardia Community Col, City Univ of New York, 73- Awards: Purchase Awards, Drawing & Small Sculpture, Ball State Univ, 67 & Ohio Images, Baldwin-Wallace Col, 69. Style & Technique: Paintings; abstractions, geometric & linear patterns. Media: Acrylic; oil on canvas. Dealer: Don Ahn Assocs c/o Lotus Gallery 81 Spring St New York NY 10012. Mailing Add: 464 W Broadway New York NY 10012

BROWN, REYNOLD
PAINTER, ILLUSTRATOR
b Los Angeles, Calif, Oct 18, 17. Study: Otis Art Inst, Los Angeles; Chouinard Art Sch; also with Will Foster. Work: Alamo Mus, San Antonio, Tex; Home Savings & Loan Collection, Los Angeles. Comn: Portrait of VPres Eng, NAm Aviation, 45; Portrait of Col Dean Hess, US Air Force, 65; Portrait of First Pres, Sch Dentistry, Univ Calif, Los Angeles, 72, Portrait of Second Pres, 74. Exhib: Calif State Fair, 35; Laguna Beach Festival; Los Angeles All City Festival, 71; Buena Park All City Festival, 72; San Gabriel All City Festival, 72-76; Pasadena Arts Coun, Calif, 75-76; Ambassador Col, Pasadena, 77. Teaching: Prof illus, Los Angeles Art Ctr Col Design, 50- Pos: Illusr, NAm Aviation, Los Angeles, 42-49; free lance advert illusr mag story & cover, New York, 49-55; illusr & art dir advert, all major motion picture co, 50-73. Awards: Purchase Award, Los Angeles All City Festival, 72; Best of Show, Buena Park All City Festival, 72 & 75 & San Gabriel All City Festival, 72 & 75. Mem: Master & Fel Am Inst Fine Arts (adv bd); Los Angeles Soc Illusr; San Gabriel Fine Art Asn. Style & Technique: Realistic. Media: Oil, Watercolor. Dealer: Trailside Gallery Jackson WY 83001; Kachina Gallery 114 Old Santa Fe Trail Santa Fe NM 87501. Mailing Add: 4840 N Live Oak Canyon Rd LaVerne CA 91750

BROWN, RHETT DELFORD (HARRIETT GURNEY BROWN)
FIBER ARTIST, ILLUSTRATOR
b Atlanta, Ga, Nov 12, 24. Study: Duke Univ, BA; New Sch for Social Res; Sch of Visual Arts, cert; Valentine Mus, study in mixed media stitchery, study with Constance Howard & photography with Bob Hanson. Work: Smithsonian Inst; ICA, London; also in pvt collections. Exhib: One-person exhib, Great Building Crack-Up, 74; Union Carbide Invitational, 78. Teaching: Instr fabric as art medium, New Sch of Social Res, 77- Pos: Founder & dir, Cricket Theatre, New York, 59-63; dir, Great Building Crack-Up Gallery, New York, 70-76; founder & dir, Ctr for Contemp Fabric Arts, New York, 78- Bibliog: Anne Beatts (auth), Double Your Pleasure Dots Double Your Fun, Oui Mag, Vol 3, No 5, 5/74; Merridee Merzer (auth), Homespun Hardcore, Penthouse Mag, 1/75. Mem: Women's Art Caucus. Style & Technique: Comic erotica and fabric collage. Media: Fabric; Threads. Publ: Contribr & illusr, Titters, Macmillan, 76; contribr & illusr, Hardcore Crafts, Ballantine, 76. Mailing Add: c/o Great Bldg Crack-Up 251 W 13th St New York NY 10011

BROWN, RICHARD F
MUSEUM DIRECTOR
b New York, NY, Sept 20, 16. Study: Bucknell Univ, AB, 40; Inst Fine Arts, NY Univ, 40-42; Harvard Univ, MA, 48, Bacon-Rich traveling fel, 49, PhD, 52. Teaching: Teaching fel art hist, Harvard Univ, 47-49; res scholar & lectr, Frick Collection, New York, 49-54; vis prof 19th century Fr painting, Harvard Univ, 54. Pos: Chief cur, Los Angeles Co Art Mus, Calif, 55-62, dir, 62-65; dir, Kimbell Art Found, Ft Worth, Tex, 66- Awards: Phi Beta Kappa Award; Decoration Arts & Lett, Repub France, 62. Mem: Col Art Asn Am (pres); Asn Art Mus Dirs (pres); Am Asn Mus (mem coun); Nat Coun Arts. Mailing Add: Kimbell Art Mus Ft Worth TX 76107

BROWN, ROBERT DELFORD
CONCEPTUAL ARTIST
b Portland, Colo, Oct 25, 30. Study: Univ Calif, Los Angeles, BA, 52, with Howard Warshaw, 54-55, MA, 58. Work: Smithsonian Inst, Washington, DC; RCA Collection, New York; Archive, Sohm, Ger; Yale Univ; Polaroid Collection, Boston, Mass. Comn: Meat Show, Nathan Romanoff, New York, 64; London St Happening, Robert Frazier Gallery, London, 66. Exhib: Ann Exhib Painting, Los Angeles Co Art Mus, Los Angeles, 58; Graphics, Brooklyn Mus, NY, 63; Graphic Exhib, Washington Gallery Mod Art, 65; Inst Contemp Art, London, 68; Book Exhib, Kansas City Art Inst, Mo, 68; one-man shows, Drawings 1959-1971, Great Bldg Crack-Up Gallery, 71, Wall Hangings & Ceramics From 1962, 72, Tinted Photographs 1964-1972, 72, A Bear Has Fur But the Wrong Kind of Face, A Manifestation, 74 & Ikonobiles (sculpture), 76, all in New York; Bob Brown & His Friends, A Photog J, New York, 71; Artists Bks, Moore Col, Philadelphia, 73; Altered Photog, M H de Young Mem Mus, San Francisco, 75; Victory Over Dumbness Day, New York, 76; NC Mus Art, Raleigh, 77; 15 Yr Retrospective, 1963-1978, Iran-Am Ctr, Tehran, Iran, 78; plus others. Pos: Founder, First Nat Church of the Exquisite Panic, Inc, 64 & Great Bldg Crack-Up, 67. Awards: Strangest Artist in the World, Olympics of Art, Donald Collender, 72. Bibliog: Lil Picard (auth), The work of art, Das Kunstwerk, Ger, 12/64; Lette Eisenhauer (auth), Portrait Bob Delford Brown, Art & Artists, London, 7/73; Contemporary Artists, St James Press, London & St Martin's Press, New York, 77. Style & Technique: Classic iconoclasm. Media: Sight, Sound. Publ: Auth, Hanging, 67, First Class Portraits, 73, Ulysses by Robert Delford Brown, An Altered Plagiarism, 75 & Ikonobiles & Maranathas, 78, First Nat Church of the Exquisite Panic Press; contribr, A D Coleman, ed, Grotesque Photography, Ridge Press, 77. Mailing Add: c/o Great Bldg Crack-Up 251 W 13th St New York NY 10011

BROWN, ROBERT K
ART DEALER, BIBLIOGRAPHER
b Springfield, Mass, May 22, 42. Study: Boston Univ, BS; Annenberg Sch Commun, Univ Pa, MCommun Arts. Pos: Dir & co-owner, Reinhold-Brown Gallery, New York. Mem: Antiquarian Booksellers Asn Am; Int League Booksellers. Specialty: Rare posters relating to the early avant-garde including constructivism, functionalism, art nouvbau-deco, Vienna secession; rare books on 20th century art and architecture. Publ: Contribr, Art Deco Minneapolis Inst, 70; ed, Art in Design in Vienna, 72; auth, Art Deco Internationale, Quick Fox, 77. Mailing Add: 120 E 86th St New York NY 10028

BROWN, SUZANNE GOLDMAN
GALLERY OWNER, ART HISTORIAN
b New York, NY, Sept 8, 29. Study: Radcliff Col, BA(cum laude; Am hist since 1785), 51; Harvard Law Sch, 51-52; Tufts Col, grad work in hist, 52-53; Ariz State Univ, 68-69. Collections Arranged: Numerous exhibs arranged through docent prog, Phoenix Art Mus, 60-63. Pos: Gallery owner, Art Wagon Gallery, 68-; officer, Friends of Mex Art, Phoenix, 68-70; mem & docent, Phoenix Art Mus League, 69-73; pres, Main St Art Asn, 76- Bibliog: Marlan Miller (critic), articles in Phoenix Gazette, 69-77; Maggie Wilson (auth), articles in Ariz Repub, 72-77. Mem: Friends of Mex Art; Scottsdale Ctr for the Arts; Heard Mus, Phoenix; Phoenix Art Mus League & Guild; Ariz State Univ Collections League & Patron. Res: Mexican art history with emphasis on Orozoco; in-depth study of history of Southwestern art from the 1830's; Aleschinsky; graphics. Specialty: Contemporary and contemporary Southwestern art. Collection: Nineteenth and 20th century graphics; contemporary Southwestern art; Eskimo art; Oriental art. Publ: Contribr, Southwestern Art, Craig Cornelius, 76. Mailing Add: c/o Art Wagon Gallery 7156 Main St Scottsdale AZ 85251

BROWN, WILLIAM FERDINAND, II
ILLUSTRATOR, WRITER
b Jersey City, NJ, Apr 16, 28. Study: Princeton Univ, AB, 50. Mem: Nat Cartoonists Soc; Artists & Writers. Style & Technique: Line drawings, black and white and color. Publ: Auth & illusr, Beat beat beat, 59, The girl in the Freudian slip, 60, The abominable showmen, 60 & The world is my yo-yo, 63; co-auth & co-artist, Boomer, comic strip, United Feature Syndicate. Mailing Add: 44 Grahampton Lane Greenwich CT 06830

BROWNE, ROBERT M
COLLECTOR, PATRON
b Brooklyn, NY, Apr 12, 26. Exhib: (Of Collection) Oceanic Arts, Honolulu Acad Arts, Hawaii, 67; Sculpture of Polynesia, Art Inst Chicago, 67 & Mus Primitive Art, New York, 68; Arts of Oceania, Dallas Mus Fine Arts, 70; Art of the Sepik River, Art Inst Chicago, 71; Art Collections in Hawaii, Univ Hawaii Art Gallery, 76. Bibliog: Allen Wardwell (auth), The sculpture of Polynesia, 67 & The art of the Sepik River, 71, Art Inst Chicago; John Lunsford (auth), The arts of Oceania, Dallas Mus Fine Arts, 70. Mem: Cath Art Asn Hawaii (pres, 65-); Honolulu Acad Arts; Bishop Mus Asn; Anthrop Soc Hawaii. Interest: Primitive art; Japanese Mingei ceramic collection. Mailing Add: 3625 Anela Pl Honolulu HI 96822

BROWNE, SYD J
PAINTER
b Brooklyn, NY, Aug 21, 07. Study: Pratt Inst; Art Student League. Work: Libr Cong, Washington, DC; New Brit Inst, Conn; New York Pub Libr, NY; Staten Island Inst, NY; Fairleigh Dickinson Univ, NJ. Awards: Mischa Lempert Mem Purchase Prize, Salmagundi Club, 50; William Church Osborn Purchase Prize, Am Watercolor Soc, 50; Soc Am Artists Award, Salmagundi Club, 70. Mem: Nat Acad Design; Salmagundi Club. Style & Technique: Impressionistic, romantic realism. Media: Oil, Watercolor. Dealer: Grand Cent Galleries Hotel Biltmore New York NY 10017. Mailing Add: Winter Harbor ME 04693

BROWNE, TOM MARTIN
SCULPTOR, PAINTER
Study: Calif Col Arts & Crafts, BFA(sculpture) & BFA(indust design), 63, MFA(sculpture), 66. Work: Oakland Mus, Calif; Calif Col Arts & Crafts Alumni Collections, Oakland; President Kennedy's Collection Mod Art, Washington, DC. Comn: Porcelain & wood sculpture, Shell Chem Co, 69; porcelain cube sculptures, Crown Zellerbach Chem Co, San Francisco, 70; DJ (18' outdoor sculpture), comn by Herman Miller, Zeeland, Mich, 71; commemorative sculptures, Northwestern Bell Tel, Nebr, 73; Judy August (porcelain & bronze cube), Napa Community Redevelop Agency for City of Napa, 75; plus others. Exhib: Mus Contemp Crafts, New York; Calif Palace Legion of Honor, San Francisco, 65; Stanford Univ, 66; Richmond Art Ctr, 73; Urban Environ Sculpture, Oakland Mus, 74. Awards: Gold Medal Award, Calif State Fair, Sacramento, 64; Crown Zellerbach Scholar, Crown Zellerbach Chem Co, 62 & Crown Zellerbach Mem Competition, 65. Style & Technique: Sculpture, abstracted with reference to nature; bronze, wood, cor-ten, stainless & porcelain on steel and ceramic, often in combinations. Media: Bronze, Porcelain; Acrylic, Oil. Publ: Co-auth, Methods in Casting (Nine Prog), KPIX TV, 64; co-auth, Driftwood sculpture, Brit Broadcasting Co, 64. Mailing Add: Tom Martin Browne & Assoc 158 Hillcrest Rd Berkeley CA 94705

BROWNE, VIVIAN E
ART ADMINISTRATOR, PAINTER
b Laurel, Fla, Apr 26, 29. Study: Hunter Col, BS, MFA; Art Students League; Pratt Graphics Ctr; New Sch Social Res. Work: NY State Off Bldg, New York; Dana Libr, Newark Col Arts & Sci; City Chemical Bank, New York; Bronx Hosp, New York. Exhib: Mus Mod Art, New York, 68; Ill Bell Tel Traveling Exhib, 70-71; Carnegie Inst Int, Pittsburgh, Pa, 71; New York Cult Ctr, 73; Spokane World's Fair, Wash, 75. Teaching: Asst prof painting, Rutgers Univ, Newark, 71-75, assoc prof painting & chmn art dept, 75- Awards: Huntington Hartford Found Painting Fel, 64; Rutgers Univ res grants, 73 & 75. Bibliog: Archives of American Art Smithsonian Inst, 69; Grace G Alexander, Making more than one, WNYE Television Series on Printmaking, 71; Oakley N Holmes (auth), Black Artists, film, 75. Mem: Col Art Asn; Women's Caucus for Art; Nat Conf of Artists. Style & Technique: Space relationships in abstract mode; large work of mixed-media using photographic and painting techniques on silk canvas. Media: Oil, Acrylic with Mixed Media; Intaglio, Lithography. Publ: Illusr, National Holidays Around the World, Fleet Publ, 66; contribr, Eight by Ten Art Protfolio, Elohim Raman, 71-73; auth, Afro-American Art: An Annotated Bibliography, New York City Bd Educ, 72; contribr, Graphics Portfolio, Printmaking Workshop, 72; contribr, Attica Book, Benny Andrews & Rudolf Baranik, (auth), 72. Mailing Add: 451 W Broadway New York NY 10012

BROWNETT, THELMA DENYER
PAINTER
b Jacksonville, Fla, Oct 26, 24. Study: Wesleyan Conserv, BFA(magna cum laude), 46, with Emile Holzhauer; Columbia Univ, 48, with Dr Edwin Ziegfield; Univ Ga, MFA, 52, with Lamar Dodd, James Johnson Sweeny & William Zorack. Work: Ga Mus Art, Athens; Gertrude Herbert Art Mus, Augusta, Ga; Atlanta Art Mus, Ga; Ringling Mus Art, Sarasota, Fla; also pvt collections in the US & abroad. Comn: Mural, Puppet Playhouse, Augusta, Ga, 51; hundreds of portraits, 56-; Reredos, St Peter's Church, Jacksonville, Fla, 58; Triptych, St Mark's Episcopal Church, Jacksonville, 63; mural, Off Bldg, San Jose Plaza, Jacksonville, 65. Exhib: Am Artists Prof League Nat Exhib, New York, 52; Nat Asn Women Artists, Argent Gallery, New York, 54; ACA Gallery Nat, New York, 55; Arts Festival Twelve, Regional Int, Jacksonville, 71; Fla Artist Group State Exhib, St Augustine, Fla, 72 & 73; Columbia Mus Art, SC; Norton Gallery of Art, Palm Beach, Fla; Daytona Art Mus, Fla; Tampa Art Mus, Fla; Columbus Mus Art, Ga; Telfair Art Mus, Savannah, Ga; Hunter Col, New York. Teaching: Chmn dept art, Augusta Col, 52-55; chmn dept art, Jacksonville Univ, 56-58; chmn dept art, Fla Jr Col, 65-70, prof art, 70-; restorer of paintings, pvt studio, 56- Pos: Dir, Gertrude Herbert Art Inst, 51-55; art comnr, State of Ga, 54-57; chmn visual arts, Arts Festival Eleven, Jacksonville, 68-69; dir & owner, Oxford Gallery Ltd, Jacksonville, Fla, 75- Bibliog: Articles in Mademoiselle, 6/53 & La Rev Mod, Paris, 55. Mem: Asn Ga Artists (pres, 53-55); Fla Artist Group (secy-treas, 74-); Fedn Fla Artists (bd dir, 57-59); Jackson Coun Arts (mem bd dirs, 69-). Style & Technique: Portraits: traditional, direct oil paintings; exhibition paintings in indirect and direct technique with oil or acrylic; murals: oil on canvas or board. Publ: Auth, Painting, Student Handbook, 71 & 75; auth, Painting Studio Handbook, 78. Mailing Add: 4774 Apache Ave Jacksonville FL 32210

BROWNHILL, HAROLD
PAINTER, ILLUSTRATOR
b Sheffield, UK; Can citizen. Study: Abbeydale & Cent Schs; Lancasterian Sch, Ecclesall Bierlow Sch; Sheffield Col Art, scholar, 7 yrs. Exhib: NS Traveling Exhib, 18 months; A Quiet Prospect (oil painting), NS Soc Artists 50th Anniversary Golden Jubilee Exhib, Halifax, 72; plus many others. Mem: NS Soc Artists (pres, 2 yrs, treas, 6 yrs). Style & Technique: Realism. Media: Watercolor. Publ: Auth, Acadia—A Response to Some Questions, 71. Mailing Add: 6322 Norwood St Halifax NS Can

BROWNING, COLLEEN
PAINTER
b Eire; US citizen. Study: Slade Sch Art, London, Eng. Work: Calif Palace Legion of Honor, San Francisco; Detroit Art Inst; Columbia Mus, SC; Rochester Mem Art Gallery, NY; Milwaukee Art Ctr; St Louis Art Mus, Mo; Wichita Art Mus, Kans. Comn: Olympic Editions 1976 (lithograph); Kent Bicentennial Portfolio (lithograph). Exhib: Five shows, Whitney Mus Am Art Contemp Ann, New York, 51-63; Carnegie Int, Pittsburgh, 52 & 55; Art Inst Chicago, 54; ann shows, Nat Acad Design, New York, 57-78; Biennial Inter-Americana, Mexico, 61; Cleveland Mus, Ohio, 75; Indianapolis Mus, Ind, 76. Teaching: Instr painting & drawing, City Col New York, 60-76. Awards: Figure Composition Award, Stanford Univ, 56; Second Prize for oils, Butler Inst Am Art, 60 & 74; Adolph & Clara Obrig Prize, Nat Acad Design, 70. Bibliog: Articles in Newsweek, 52 & 54 & Time, 52; Norman Kent (auth), Colleen Browning, Am Artist, 57; John Canaday (auth), Art against the current, New York Times, 65; Sidney Field (auth), Daily News, 72; Jerry Tallmer (auth), NY Post, 76. Mem: Academician, Nat Acad Design (coun mem, 69-72, jury of selection, 72, corresp secy, 72-73, jury of awards, 78); Audubon Artists (jury of awards, 72). Style & Technique: Poetic realism. Media: Oil. Publ: Illusr, Portrait of a Lady, Ltd Ed Club, 67; illusr, The Poet's Eye, Prentice-Hall, 69; illusr, Every Man Heart Look Down, Crowell-Collier, 70; illusr, Downtown Is, McGraw-Hill, 72. Mailing Add: c/o Kennedy Galleries 40 W 57th St New York NY 10019

BROWNING, DIXIE BURRUS
PAINTER
b Elizabeth City, NC, Sept 9, 30. Study: Mary Washington Col; Richmond Prof Inst; and with Barclay Sheaks, Ray Prohaska & Ric Chin. Work: US Coast Guard Mus, New London, Conn; Statesville Mus Arts & Sci, NC; Munic Collection, Southport, NC; Rachel Maxwell Moore Art Found, Greenville, NC; Reynolds World Hq, Winston-Salem, NC; Christmas Card, Collectors Print, Integon, Inc, Winston-Salem, 72, also used as cover for NAm Moravian Mag, 73. Exhib: Gallery Contemp Art, Winston-Salem, 65-69; Marine Exhib, James River Juried, Mariners Mus, Newport News, Va; Southern Contemp Arts Festival, Rocky Mount, NC, 66 & High Point, NC, 67; Irene Leache Mem Biennial, Norfolk Mus Art, Va, 68; Regional Gallery Art, Boone, NC, 71 & 74; Ashville Civic Ctr Gallery, NC; Manufacturers Hanover Trust Gallery, New York, 71; Southeastern Ctr for Contemp Art, Winston-Salem, 76. Teaching: Teacher watercolor & acrylics, Arts & Crafts Asn, Inc, Winston-Salem, 67-73; watercolor lectr & demonstr in schs & art orgns, NC. Pos: Founder & co-dir, Art Gallery Originals, Winston-Salem, 68-73; co-dir, Art V Gallery, Clemmons, NC, 74-75. Awards: Three First Prizes & 1 Second Prize, Southport Art Festival, 67, 68 & 71; Best in Show, Assoc Artists NC, 71; Third Prize, Watercolor Soc NC, 76. Bibliog: Ola Mae Foushee (auth), North Carolina Artists, Univ NC; Anthony Swider (auth), Going to the Gallery, Winston-Salem & Forsyth Co Sch Syst, 69; Ward Nicholls (auth), Artists & Craftsmen in North Carolina, Wilks Art Guild, 74. Mem: Int Soc Artists; Assoc Artists Winston-Salem (vpres, 68-69); Watercolor Soc NC (co-organizer & pres, 72-73); Winston-Salem Arts Coun; Arts & Crafts Asn, Inc. Style & Technique: Impressionistic watercolors; landscapes; peoplescapes. Media: Watercolor, Chinese Ink. Publ: Illusr, North Carolina Parade, Univ NC, 66; contribr, Drawing & Painting the Natural Environment, Davis, 74. Dealer: Art Gallery Originals 120 Reynolda Village Winston-Salem NC 27106; Edward Greene Island Gallery Manteo NC 27954. Mailing Add: 5316 Robinhood Rd Winston-Salem NC 27106

BRUCKER, EDMUND
PAINTER, EDUCATOR
b Cleveland, Ohio, Nov 20, 12. Study: Cleveland Inst Art, dipl(painting), 34, postgrad study, 34-36; Wayman Adams Summer Sch, 44. Work: Cleveland Mus Art; Indianapolis Mus Art, Ind; Butler Inst Am Art, Youngstown, Ohio; Evansville Mus Arts & Sci, Ind; Dartmouth Col, Hanover, NH. Comn: Portrait of L G Balfour, L G Balfour Co, Attleboro, Mass, 63; portrait of Gov, Off of Gov, Ind State Capitol, Indianapolis, 64; portrait of Col H Weir Cook, Munic Airport, Indianapolis, 67; portrait of pres, Ind Univ, Bloomington, 75; portrait of pres, Ind State Univ, Terre Haute, 75. Exhib: Directions in American Painting, Carnegie Inst, Pittsburgh, Pa, 41; Libr Cong, Washington, DC, 45; Paintings of the Year, Pepsi-Cola 3rd Ann, New York, 46; Univ Ill, Urbana, 48; 145th Ann of Painting & Sculpture, Pa Acad Fine Arts, Philadelphia, 50; Metrop Mus Art, New York, 52; Cincinnati Mus Art, Ohio, 55; Contemporary Arts of United States, Los Angeles, Calif, 56; Herron Mus Art, Indianapolis, 63; La State Univ Int Drawing Invitational, Baton Rouge, 65; Contemp Ind Artists, Ind State Mus, Indianapolis, 75; 200 Yrs Ind Art, Indianapolis Mus Art, 76. Teaching: Instr drawing, Cleveland Inst Art, 36-38; instr drawing & painting, John Herron Art Sch, Indianapolis, 38-67; prof drawing & painting, Herron Art Sch, Ind Univ, Indianapolis, 67- Pos: Portrait cover artists, Ind Bus & Indust Mag, Culver, 60-71. Awards: First Prize in Oils, Ill State Fair 12th Prof Art Exhib, 58; William H Block Co First Prize, Hoosier Salon Patrons Asn, 62; Millikin Award for Artistic Achievement, Art Asn Indianapolis, 63. Bibliog: Jacob Getlar Smith (auth), The drawings of Edmund Brucker, Am Artist Mag, 56; Medium of the ancients, Indianapolis Star Mag, 59. Mem: Ind Artists Club (first vpres, 70); Hoosier Salon Patrons Asn; Indianapolis Mus Art. Style & Technique: Quite diversified, ranging from very representational painting for portraits to a partially semi-abstract painting for exhibition. Media: Oil. Mailing Add: 545 King Dr Indianapolis IN 46260

BRUDER, HAROLD JACOB
PAINTER, EDUCATOR
b Bronx, NY, Aug 31, 30. Study: Cooper Union, cert, 51; New Sch Social Res; Pratt Graphic Art Ctr. Work: NJ State Mus, Trenton; Palm Springs Desert Mus; Joseph H Hirshhorn Mus. Exhib: Corcoran Gallery Biennale, Washington, DC, 63; Modern Realism & Surrealism, Am Fedn Arts Traveling Show, 64, The Realist Revival, 72-73; 22 Realists, Whitney Mus Am Art, New York, 70; Painting from the Photo, Riverside Mus, New York, 70; Aspects of the Figure, Cleveland Mus Art, 74; plus many others. Teaching: Assoc prof art, Kansas City Art Inst, 63-65; vis lectr, Pratt Inst, 65-66; prof art, Queens Col, 65- Pos: Artist-in-residence, Aspen Sch Contemp Art, summer 67. Bibliog: The paintings of Harold Bruder, Ohio Rev, 6/61; Ralph Pomeroy (auth), Harold Bruder and immediate family, Art & Artists, 10/68; Alan Gussow (interviewer), A sense of place, Saturday Rev Press, 72. Style & Technique: Representational painting dealing with multiple figure composition; portraits and landscapes. Media: Oil. Mailing Add: c/o Forum Gallery 1018 Madison Ave New York NY 10021

BRULC, DENNIS
PRINTMAKER, PAINTER
b Milwaukee, Wis, Aug 30, 46. Study: Univ Wis, BFA, 69. Work: Winston Collection, Detroit, Mich; Milwaukee Art Ctr; S Johnson Collection, Racine, Wis; Akron Art Inst, Ohio; Univ Wis-Milwaukee & Univ Wis-Madison. Comn: Pneumatic Matrice (with Richard Tupper & Orrel Thompson), Akron Art Inst, 69; Pneumatic Matrice II (with John Loyd Taylor), Milwaukee Art Ctr, 70; Homage to Sharon Tate (print/sculpture), comn by Lawrence Esser, Milwaukee, 71. Exhib: Reflection Thru A Collectors Eye, Milwaukee, 71; 20 American Printmakers, Oneonta, NY, 72; Albrecht Durer Print & Drawing Show, Milwaukee, 72; Printmakers Midwest Invitational, Walker Art Ctr, Minneapolis, 73; Nat Print Invitational, Calif State Univ, 74; plus others. Awards: Wis Painters & Sculptors Award, Milwaukee Art Ctr; 37th Madison Salon Art First Prize, Univ Wis-Madison, 71; Albrecht Durer Print & Drawing Show First Prize, Goethe House, 72. Bibliog: M Kirkhorn (auth), Review of Brulc, Milwaukee J, 68; R Manglesdorff (auth), Multiple reality flow arte, Kaleidoscope, 71; C Kohlmann (auth), Directions, Midwest Art, 3/75. Mem: Arts Technol Found (pres, 68-); Wis Painters & Sculptors; Negative Movement (dir, 66-69); Artsupports, Inc (pres, 75). Publ: Contribr, Cheshire Mag & Fashions of Moving Times, 67; contribr, La Guardia, 68-71; co-auth, Pneumatic matrice (color movie), Milwaukee Art Ctr, 70; contribr, Los Angeles Staff, 71; contribr, Shore Rev, 74. Mailing Add: Caswell Bldg Suite 933 152 W Wisconsin Ave Milwaukee WI 53203

BRULC, LILLIAN G
PAINTER, SCULPTOR
b Joliet, Ill. Study: Art Inst Chicago, George D Brown Foreign Travel fel, 55, with Louis Ritman, Robert Lifvendahl & Egon Weiner, BFA, 55, MFA, 64, with Max Kahn & Joshua Taylor; also with Franz Gorse, NY. Work: Major works in permanent architectural environments, smaller works in private collections. Comn: Murals & sculpture, Cardinal's Comt for Span Speaking, Chicago, 63-64; murals, San Miguelito Ctr, Panama, 65, metal grillwork designs, in process; mural, Chapel, San Miguelito, Panama, 66; sculptures (assisted by Che Torres & Ruben Arboleda), Chapel & Garden, San Miguelito, 68-69; murls, Archdiocesan Latin Am Comt, Chicago, 71. Exhib: Prints, Drawings & Watercolors 2nd Biennial by Ill Artists, Art Inst Chicago, 64; one-man show, Drawings & Lithographs, Casa de Escultura, Panama City, 69; Murals for People (slide of Chicago works), Mus Contemp Art, Chicago, 71. Teaching: Asst instr lithography, Art Inst Chicago, 61-64; lectr theol & art, Divine Word Sem, Techny, Ill, 66-68; instr design, mat, portrait & drawing, Chicago Acad Fine Arts, 72- Pos: Artist in residence, Chicago Archdiocese Panama Mission, San Miguelito, 65-70, art adv & part-time resident, 73-; artist in residence, Archdiocesan Latin Am Comt, Chicago, 71-72. Bibliog: Charlando (TV presentation), Univ Chicago WGN-9, 68; Jorge Amado (auth), Perfiles, Cuem en Marcha, Panama City, 70. Mem: Alumni Art Inst Chicago. Style & Technique: Figurative, with emphasis on symbolic content; visible brushwork, textured surfaces; sense of architecture in both painting and sculpture. Media: Acrylic, Mixed Media, Clay to Cement or Plaster; Welding. Publ: Auth, The Bible & today's artist, 72 & auth, Birth of a sculpture, 73, Faith & Art Mag; illusr & auth, Make me a people, Bible Today Mag, 74; illusr, Thirsting For the Lord, Alba House, 76; auth, Visit with Franz Gorse in Carinthia, Austria, SRCA Bull, 78. Mailing Add: 909 Summit St Joliet IL 60435

BRUMBAUGH, THOMAS BRENDLE
ART HISTORIAN, WRITER
b Chambersburg, Pa, May 23, 21. Study: Indiana Univ Pa, BS; State Univ Iowa, MA; Ohio State Univ, PhD; Harvard Univ, fel East Asian Studies, 59; Fulbright fel, India, 60. Teaching: Instr, Ohio State Univ, 53-54; from asst prof to assoc prof, Emory Univ, 55-63; from assoc prof to prof, Vanderbilt Univ, 64- Mem: Col Art Asn Am; Archaeol Inst Am. Res: 19th century American painting, sculpture and architecture; J A D Ingres. Publ: Ed, Middle Tenn Archit, 74; auth, articles on art and artists in Art News, Art Quart, Art J, Gazette Beaux-Arts & others. Mailing Add: Box 1648 Station B Nashville TN 37235

BRUMER, MIRIAM
INSTRUCTOR, PAINTER
b New York, NY, Oct 7, 39. Study: Univ of Miami, BA(art & eng); Boston Univ, MFA(painting). Work: Chase Manhattan Bank, New York; Citibank, New York; Boston Univ, Mass. Comn: Painting for office, New York Bank for Savings, comn by Arthur J Quinn, pres, 73. Exhib: Unmanly Art, Suffolk Mus, New York, 72; Woman's Work—Am Art, Mus of the Philadelphia Civic Ctr, 74; Salon des Femmes Peintres, Mus de l'Art Mod, Paris, 75; Invitational, Nabisco World Hq, East Hanover, NJ, 77; The Animal in Art, Summit Art Ctr, Summit, NJ, 78; 20th Century Drawings, A Wauters Gallery, NY, 78; one-woman shows, Lotus Gallery, New York, 76 & 77. Collections Arranged: Unmanly Art, Suffolk Mus, New York, 72; Women in the Arts, C W Post Col, New York, 72; New York Drawings 1947-73, 73 & Abstract Watercolors 1942-75, 75, Buecker & Harpsichords Gallery, New York; Invitational, Yugoslav Cult Ctr, Paris, 75. Teaching: Asst prof studio art & art hist, NY Inst of Technol, Old Westbury, 69-75; lectr studio art & art hist, Marymount Manhattan Col, New York, 76- & Hunter Col, New York, 76. Pos: Writer & ed, Feminist Art J, New York, 72-74. Bibliog: Aline Dallier (auth), Peintures, Cahiers Theoriques 10 & 11, In: Des Plasticiennes Americaines, Paris, 75: 178-183; Cindy Nemser (auth), Towards a Feminist Sensibility, Feminist Art J, 76; Hilde Marx (auth), Unsere Zweite Generation, Aufbau, New York, 3/76; William Zimmer (auth), Miriam Brumer, Arts Mag, 9/77. Style & Technique: Abstracted views of organic forms, close-up aspects of insects, flowers and related objects, in which energy and motion is explored. Media: Acrylic painting; color pencil drawings. Dealer: Don Ahn c/o Lotus Gallery 81 Spring St New York NY 10012. Mailing Add: 250 W 94th St New York NY 10025

BRUMER, SHULAMITH
SCULPTOR, INSTRUCTOR
b Russia, July 5, 24; US citizen. Study: Art Students League, with William Zorach; Columbia Univ, with Oronzio Malderelli. Exhib: One-man shows, Sculpture Ctr, New York, 65, 68 & 73; Philbrook Mus, Tulsa, Okla; Nat Acad Design, New York; Riverside Mus, New York; Brockton Art Ctr, Mass. Teaching: Instr stone & wood carving, Sculpture Ctr Art Sch, 71- Awards: Knickerbocker Prizes, 57 & 76; Audubon Artists Awards, 58 & 63; Honorable Mention, Archit League, 66. Mem: Sculpture Ctr (trustee, 71-); Nat Asn Women Artists; New York Soc Women Artists; Allied Artists; Knickerbocker Artists. Style & Technique: Stone-direct carving; abstract bronze; lost wax casting. Media: Stone. Dealer: Sculpture Ctr 167 E 69th St New York NY 10021. Mailing Add: 473 Franklin D Roosevelt Dr New York NY 10002

BRUN, THOMAS
SCULPTOR, INSTRUCTOR
b London, Eng, Nov 1, 11; US citizen. Study: Soc Arts & Crafts, Detroit, with John Foster, Sarkis Sarkisian, Guy Palozolla, Jay Bursma & Lilly Saarimen. Work: Detroit Inst Arts; Edison Elec Co; also several pub schs in Detroit. Comn: Lansing Birdman, Forbes Cohen, Lansing, Mich, 70; Bronze Hippo & Bird Mobile (four wood figures), Kalamazoo, Mich, 71; Bronze Hippo & Bird in Flight, Jackson, Mich, 72. Exhib: Detroit Inst Arts, 50-70; regional exhibs, Ill, Mich, Minn & Wis, 53-57; Pa Acad Fine Arts, 64. Teaching: Instr clay modeling, Detroit Inst Arts, 60-65; instr clay modeling, Birmingham Art Asn, 65-67; instr wax modeling, Detroit Jewish Community Ctr, 67- Awards: Purchase Prize, Detroit Inst Arts, 59, Lawrence Fleischman Award, 53. Bibliog: Work reviewed by Broner, Detroit Times, M Driver, Detroit Free Press & H Shiff, Detroit News, 49-72. Mailing Add: 4811 Orion Rd Rochester MI 48063

BRUNEAU, KITTIE
PAINTER
b Montreal, Que, Oct 12, 29. Study: Ecole Beaux Arts Montreal, EBA. Work: Mus d'Art Contemporain, Montreal; Mus Que; Univ Montreal Libr; Univ Que Libr, Montreal; Sir George William Univ. Exhib: Peintures Dessins, Mus d'Art Contemporain, Montreal, 66; Vancouver Print Int, 67; l'Expo Centenaire l'Ont, Toronto, 67; 2nd Biennale Gravure Cracovie, Pologne, 68; Foire Int Bale, Suisse, 72; plus many other group & one-man shows. Bibliog: Guy Viau (auth), Kittie Bruneau-peintre et sculpteur, Cite Libre, Montreal, 62; J de Roussan (auth), Kittie Bruneau, Lidec, Montreal, 67. Mem: Asn Artistes Prof Que; Guild Graphique. Media: Acrylic, Graphics. Mailing Add: c/o Galerie Libre 2100 rue Crescent Montreal PQ H3G 2C1 Can

BRUNER, LOUISE KATHERINE (MRS PAUL ORR)
ART CRITIC, WRITER
b Cleveland, Ohio, June 13, 10. Study: Denison Univ, BA; Bowling Green State Univ, MA. Teaching: Instr reviews & criticism, Univ Toledo, 72- Pos: Art critic, Cleveland News, 40-56; art critic, Toledo Blade, 58-; mem, Comt of Art & Relig in Am, 71-; oral interviewer, Archives of Am Art, 73- Awards: Roy Neuberger Found Award, Am Fedn Arts Nat Coun Arts Criticism Workshop, 68; First Prize for Critical Writing, Ohio Newspaperwomen's Asn, 71; Alumni Citation, Denison Univ, 71. Mem: Toledo Artists Club (trustee, 60-); Toledo Mod Art Group (trustee, 68-71); Art Interests, Inc (trustee, 69-); Archaeol Inst Am (trustee, Toledo Chap, 55-). Publ: Ed, Blade Art Directory-Public and Private Collections, 59; contribr, Arts Mag, 64-; contribr, Craft Horizons, 71; contribr, Am Artist, Art Gallery Mag & St Louis Post-Dispatch, 72- Mailing Add: 560 E Sixth St St Perrysburg OH 43551

BRUNKUS, RICHARD ALLEN
PRINTMAKER, CURATOR
b Cleveland, Ohio, Mar 31, 50. Study: Miami Univ, Oxford, Ohio, BFA(printmaking & painting), 72 & MFA(printmaking), 74. Work: Honolulu Acad of Arts, Hawaii; Bradley Univ Art Mus, Peoria, Ill; Tex Tech Univ Art Mus, Lubbock, Tex; Minot State Col, NDak; Univ of Mich Mus, Ann Arbor. Exhib: Boston Printmakers 26th Ann Exhib, Needham, Mass, 74; Cincinnati Art Mus Print Invitational, Ohio, 74, 15th Nat Print Exhib, Bradley Univ Art Mus, 75; 17th Ann Nat Print & Drawing Exhib, Oklahoma City, Okla, 75; 3rd US Int Graphics Ann, Hollis, NH, 75; Colorprint US, Tex Tech Univ Art Mus, 76; 11th Dulin Nat Print and Drawing Competition, Knoxville, Tenn, 77; 4th Nat Hawaii Print Exhib, Honolulu Acad of Arts, 78. Collections Arranged: Japanese Book Illustrations from the 18th and 19th centuries, 12/76; An American Image 1900-1950, 11/76; Architectural Prints of the 17th, 18th and 19th Centuries, 10/76; 20th Century Master French Prints, 8/77; Georges Rouault's Miserere Et Guerre, 1/77. Teaching: Asst prof printmaking & drawing & Am art hist, Albion Col, Mich, 74. Pos: Cur of print collection, Albion Col, 75- Awards: Purchase Award, Colorprint US, Tex Tech Univ, 74, 15th Nat Bradley Print Exhib, Bradley Univ, 75 & 3rd Nat Hawaii Print Exhib, Honolulu Acad of Arts, 75. Mem: Graphics Soc, Hollis, NH. Style & Technique: Color intaglio printing from multiple plates; color modulation in serigraphs; color multiple plate lithographs. Media: Engraving, Color Intaglio, Color Lithography. Collection: Early 18th and 19th century Japanese woodblock prints of courtesans; prints by Giovanni Battista Piranesi, 18th century printmaker. Dealer: Adi Gallery 530 McAllister St San Francisco CA. Mailing Add: 28450 C-Dr N Albion MI 49224

BRUNO, PHILLIP A
ART DEALER, COLLECTOR
b Paris, France. Study: Columbia Col, hist fine arts & archit, BA; Inst Fine Arts, NY Univ. Comn: Restored 17th century house on Martha's Vineyard, Mass, 64. Collections Arranged: First one-man exhib in Europe of Jose Luis Cuevas, Paris, 55; first one-man show in the South of Elmer Livingston Macrae, Nashville, Tenn, 63; first retrospective exhib, Ralph Rosenborg, Washington, DC, 52. Pos: With Weyhe Gallery, New York, 50-51; co-founder, Grace Borgenicht Gallery & assoc dir, 51-55; dir, World House Gallery, New York, 56-60; dir, Am Exhibs for La Napoule Found, New York & France; dir, Staempfli Gallery, New York, 60- Mem: Hon life mem St Paul Art Ctr; first hon mem Tenn Fine Arts Ctr Cheekwood, Nashville; Dukes Co Hist Soc, Edgartown, Mass; Nat Trust Hist Preservation. Collection: Mainly mid-twentieth century American watercolors and drawings, ranging from Marin to Kline, including Lachaise, Demuth, Tobey, Bravo, Lopez-Garcia, Wunderlich. Part of the collection has been exhibited at the Krannert Art Museum, Tennessee Fine Arts Center, Finch College Museum of Art and Minnestoa Museum. Mailing Add: 342 E 67th St New York NY 10021

BRUNO, SANTO MICHAEL
PAINTER, LECTURER
b Reading, Pa, June 29, 47. Study: Tyler Sch Art, Temple Univ, Philadelphia, BFA, 69, grant to Italy, 69-71, MFA, 71; also with Stephen Green, Romas Viesulas & David Pease. Work: High Mus Art, Atlanta, Ga; Univ Osaka, Japan; Nat Print Collection, Rome. Exhib: Three-man show, USIS, Naples, Italy, 71; Painting & Sculpture Invitational, Loyola Univ, Rome, 71; Ga Artists I & II, High Mus, 72 & 74; Painting Invitational, Philadelphia Civic Ctr Mus, 73; Painting Invitational, Oglethorpe Univ, Atlanta, 74; Sister City Exchange, Mus of Contemp Art, Olinda, Brazil, 75; NE/SE Exchange, Raw Gallery, Hartford, Conn, 78. Teaching: Instr painting & drawing, Atlanta Col Art, 71-, head painting dept, 76- Pos: Owner, Artist in Residence Sch, Atlanta, 74-; cur, Javo Gallery, Atlanta, 77- Awards: Italian-Am Origination Grant, Italian-Am Soc, Philadelphia, 68; Nathan Margolis Mem Award, Temple Univ, 69; exhib grant, Bur of Cult Affairs, City of Atlanta, 77. Bibliog: Clyde Burnett (auth), Folds become an art form, 3/73 & Bruno's works defies art's usual borders, 9/77, Atlanta J; Louise Wiener (auth), Around the world, Leonardo's Mag, Milan, Italy, 75; John Howett (auth), Santo Bruno, Atlanta, 1/78. Mem: Atlanta Art Workers Coalition, Ltd (founding mem & first pres, 76-78). Media: Acrylic, Plastic, Wood. Dealer: AIR Gallery 1175 W Peachtree St Atlanta GA 30309. Mailing Add: Atlanta Col of Art 1280 Peachtree St Atlanta GA 30309

BRUNO, VINCENT J
ART HISTORIAN, ART ADMINISTRATOR
b New York, NY, Feb 8, 26. Study: Bard Col, painting, 46-48; Academie Julian, Paris, cert(painting), 49; Kenyon Col, Philosophy of Art, BA, 51; Columbia Univ, MA, 62 & PhD, 69. Teaching: Instr art hist, Wellesley Col, 64-65; assoc prof art hist, C W Post Col, Long Island Univ, 65-66. Pos: Chairperson of dept of art/art hist & assoc prof, art hist, SUNY Binghamton, NY, 66-76; chairperson of dept of art & prof of art hist, Univ of Tex at Arlington, 76- Awards: John Simon Guggenheim Mem Fel, 78- Mem: Col Art Asn of Am (mem, Porter prize comt, 78-); Archaeological Inst of Am; Am Inst of Nautical Archaeology. Res: Conducted excavations at Cosa under auspices of American Academy in Rome; ancient painting techniques. Publ: Auth, The Parthenon, Norton Critical Studies in the History of Art, 74 & Form and Color in Greek Painting, 77, W W Norton & Co; articles in the Am J of Archaeol, Archaeol Mag; Princeton Encyclopedia of Classical Sites, Int J of Nautical Archaeol. Mailing Add: Dept of Art Univ of Tex Arlington TX 76019

BRUSCA, JACK
PAINTER
b New York, NY, Nov 18, 39. Study: Univ NH; Sch Visual Arts, New York, with Alex Gottlieb, Alex Katz, Joe Tilson & Helen Frankenthaller. Work: Aldrich Mus Contemp Art, Ridgefield, Conn; Powers Gallery, Univ Sydney, Australia; RI Sch Design; Albright-Knox Art Gallery, Buffalo, NY; Cleveland Mus Art, Ohio. Exhib: Plastic Presence, Jewish Mus, New York, 69; Flint Invitational, Mich, 70; Toledo Mus Art, Ohio, 70; Paintings & Sculptures of Today, Indianapolis Mus Art, Ind, 70; Highlights of the Season, Aldrich Mus Contemp Art, 70. Media: Acrylic. Dealer: Bonino Gallery 7 W 57th St New York NY 10002. Mailing Add: 171 Bowery New York NY 10002

BRUSH, LEIF
SOUND SCULPTOR, INSTRUCTOR
b Bridgeport, Ill, Mar 28, 32. Study: Art Inst of Chicago, dipl, 70, MFA, 72. Work: Art Inst of Chicago; plus others. Exhib: May 26, Mus of Contemp Art, Chicago, 69; Fel 70 & Fel 72, Art Inst of Chicago; Omaha Flow Systems, Joslyn Art Mus, Omaha, Nebr, 73; Free Spectral Range, 73 & Ann Shows, 73, 74 & 76, Mus of Art, Iowa City, Iowa; Mid-Miss Ann, Davenport Art Mus, Iowa, 74; Ripoff Show, Visual Studies Workshop, Rochester, NY, 74; Iowa Ann, Des Moines Art Ctr, 74 & 75; Pictorial Hist of the World, Kemper Gallery, Kansas City Art Inst, Mo, 75; Fac Exhib, Tweed Mus, Duluth, Minn, 76; New Music from Chicago: Explorations in Sight & Sound, Goodman Theatre, Chicago, 76; one-man shows, All Occurrences are Linked, Clapp Hall, Univ Iowa, Iowa City, 75, Orchestral Concept Array, Terrain Instruments & Personal Scans, NAME Gallery, Chicago, 76, Terrain Instruments Structure Series & Voltages from Nature, Gallery, State Univ NY, Alfred, 76, Imported Sources, Performance/Midway, Univ Chicago, 77 & Imported Sources: Terrain Instruments & Tree Clusters, Gallery, Univ Md, Baltimore Co, 77; Imported Sources: Forest Compression, Minneapolis Inst of Arts, 77; Graspable Atmospheres, Wright State Univ Gallery, Dayton, Ohio, 78. Teaching: Instr audible constructs, Art Inst of Chicago, 70-72 & Univ Iowa, Iowa City, 72-76; instr sculpture, Univ Minn, Duluth, 76- Pos: Vis artist, Univ Victoria, 73, Univ Colo, 75, State Univ NY, Alfred, 76, Univ Md, Baltimore Co, 77 & Wright State Univ, Dayton, Ohio, 78. Awards: Travelling fel, Art Inst of Chicago, Fel Exhib, Anna Louise Raymond, 70 & Art Sales & Rental Gallery, 72; Nat Endowment for the Arts grant, 73; Minn State Arts Bd Artist's Grant, 77. Bibliog: Helio Costa (auth, 30-minute video segment), Globo Brazilian Television Network, 75; Oscar Brand (auth), Voices in the Wind, Nat Pub Radio, 75; Jerome Downs & Stewart Turnquist (auth, 30-minute color videotape), Leif Brush: Inside the Hidden Landscape, Minneapolis Inst of Arts, 78. Style & Technique: Sound-monitored and orchestrated outdoor sculptural structures and configurations; sound/image performances. Media: Audible sculptural structures. Publ: Contribr, Volume Two, Ctr for New Performing Arts, Iowa City, 73; contribr, 12x12, State Univ NY, Alfred, 73; auth, Yony, Generative Systems J, Art Inst of Chicago, 10/74; auth, Riverharps—A Generative Public-Use Sculpture, Iowa Transit, 74 & Numus West Mag, 75; contribr, Fifth Assembling, New York, 75. Mailing Add: 2909 Jefferson Ct Duluth MN 55812

BRUSSEL-SMITH, BERNARD
PRINTMAKER
b New York, NY, Mar 1, 14. Study: Pa Acad Fine Arts, 31-36. Work: Libr Cong; Univ Ill; Philadelphia Mus; Smithsonian Inst; J B Speed Mus; plus others. Teaching: Instr, Cooper Union, Brooklyn Mus, Philadelphia Mus Sch Art, Nat Acad Design & Col City New York.

Pos: Art dir, Geyer Publ, 39-42; head advert dept, Chance-Voight Aircraft Co, 42-44; art dir, Noyes & Sproul, 44-45; free lance wood engraver, 45- Awards: Frank Hartley Anderson Award, 48; Am Artist Group Award, 48; John Taylor Arms Mem Prize, 70. Mem: Art Dirs Club; Type Dirs Club; Nat Acad Design. Mailing Add: 328 Cherry St Bedford Hills NY 10507

BRUSTLEIN, DANIEL
PAINTER
b Mulhouse, France, Sept 11, 04; US citizen. Study: Ecole des Arts, Geneva, Switz, cert of capacity. Work: Centre Nat d'Art Contemp, Mus Pompidou, Paris, France; Ministere des Affaires Culturelles, Paris. Exhib: Stable Ann, New York, 52 & 53; Corcoran Gallery Ann, Washington, DC, 58; Ecole de Paris, Galerie Charpentier, 61 & 62; Nat Inst Arts & Lett, 67; Patricia Learmonth Gallery, New York, 77; Am Painters in the French Nat Collections, Centre Beaubourg, Paris, 77; A M Sachs Gallery, New York, 78. Awards: Premiere Selection du Prix P L Weiller, Mus Marmottan, Paris, 71. Bibliog: Jack Tworkov (auth), Religious art without God, Art News, 11/64; cover illus, Art News, 10/60. Style & Technique: Figurative. Mailing Add: 8 rue de General Bertrand Paris 75007 France

BRY, EDITH
GLASS ARTIST
b St Louis, Mo, Nov 30, 98. Study: Ethical Cult Sch, 17; Art Students League, with lithographers, Charles Locke, G P Dubois, Winold Reiss, Archipenko & Abraham Rattner. Work: Mus City of New York; NY Hist Soc; Lincoln Ctr Libr, New York; Wichita State Univ Art Mus, Kans. Comn: Carnegie Hall, Philadelphia; Metrop Mus Art, New York. Exhib: Fedn Mod Painters & Sculptors Ann; Am Soc Contemp Artists Ann; Pa Acad Fine Arts, Philadelphia; Whitney Mus Am Art, New York; Los Angeles Mus Art, Calif; Seattle Mus, Wash; Union Theological Sem; Butler Inst Am Art, Youngstown, Ohio. Awards: Nat Asn Women Artists Award; Am Soc Contemp Artists Award; Painters & Sculptors Soc NJ Award. Bibliog: American Archives, Smithsonian Inst, Washington, DC. Mem: Fedn Mod Painters & Sculptors; Am Soc Contemp Artists; Artist-Craftsmen, New York. Style & Technique: Collage: torn colored papers, cut and assembled fused glass (in kiln). Media: Oil, Fused Glass. Mailing Add: c/o 211 Central Park W New York NY 10024

BRYANT, EDWARD ALBERT
MUSEUM DIRECTOR, ART HISTORIAN
b Lenoir, NC, June 23, 28. Study: Univ NC, Chapel Hill, BA(art), 50, MA(art hist), 55; Univ Pisa, Fulbright grant, 54-55; Univ Ravenna, cert Byzantine art, 55; Brooklyn Mus Training Prog, fel, 57-58. Work: Munson-Williams-Proctor Inst, Utica, NY. Exhib: Drawings USA, St Paul Art Ctr, Minn, 64; Nat Graphic Arts & Drawing Exhib, Wichita Art Asn, 67; Drawing & Small Sculpture Ann, Ball State Univ, 67; Piedmont Graphics, Mint Mus Art, Charlotte, NC, 67; Artists of Cent NY Ann, Munson-Williams-Proctor Inst, 72, 76 & 77. Exhibitions Organized: Contemp Italian Drawings & Collage, Am Fedn Arts, 59; Masterpieces from University Collections, 67; Jack Tworkov, Whitney Mus Am Art, 64; Graphics 68: Recent American Prints, 68; Folk Arts of Cent NY, 77; plus many one-man exhibs. Teaching: Asst prof art hist & studio courses, Univ Ky, 65-68; assoc prof art hist, Colgate Univ, 68- Pos: Gen cur, Wadsworth Atheneum, Hartford, Conn, 59-61; assoc cur, Whitney Mus Am Art, New York, 61-65; dir univ gallery, Univ Ky, 65-68; dir, Picker Gallery, Colgate Univ, 68- Awards: Mus Prof Fel Grant, Nat Endowment for Arts, 74. Mem: Gallery Asn NY (treas, 73-74 & 74-77, bd dirs, 74-). Media: Watercolor, Drawing Media. Res: 20th century artists, primarily Americans; 19th century sepulchral sculpture. Publ: Contribr, Pioneers of Modern Art in America, 62, co-auth, Forty Under Forty, 62 & auth, Jack Tworkov, 64, Praeger; auth, Robert Broderson: 32 Drawings, Duke Univ, 64; contribr, Art in Educational Institutions in the United States, Scarecrow, 74; plus articles in Art News & Art in Am. Mailing Add: Box 54 Poolville NY 13432

BRYANT, LINDA GOODE
ART DEALER, ART HISTORIAN
b Columbus, Ohio, July 21, 49. Study: Spelman Col, BA, 72; City Univ New York, MA candidate. Pos: Dir, Just Above Midtown Gallery, New York, 74-; dir educ, Studio Mus in Harlem, 74-75; panelist, NY State Coun on the Arts & DCA, 77- Awards: Grad Intern, Metrop Mus, 73, Rockefeller Fel, 73-74. Bibliog: Satterwhite (auth), Black Dealer/57th St, New York Post, 11/74; USA's Linda Bryant, African Woman, 76; Essence Woman, Essence Mag, 7/77. Res: American abstract art: theory on stylistic development in the 1970s termed contextures. Specialty: New and emerging artists working in contexturalist vein; utilizing materials not heretofore used as primary in art object (smoke, hair, clothes, nylon mesh, etc). Publ: Co-auth, Contextures (American Abstract Art 1945-1978), Just Above Midtown, 78. Mailing Add: 50 W 57th St New York NY 10019

BRYANT, OLEN L
SCULPTOR, EDUCATOR
b Cookeville, Tenn, May 4, 27. Study: Murray State Col, BS; Cranbrook Acad Art, MFA; Inst Allende, San Miguel, Mex; Cleveland Inst Art; Art Students League. Work: Tenn Fine Arts Ctr Collection, Nashville; Hunter Gallery, Chattanooga, Tenn; Carroll Reece Mus, Johnson City, Tenn. Exhib: One-man shows, Tenn Fine Arts Ctr, 68, Hunter Gallery, 69, Evansville Mus, Ind, 70, Haas Gallery Bloomsburg, Pa, 71 & Morehead Univ, 71. Teaching: Instr art, Shaker Heights Schs, Ohio, 58-61; instr art, Union Univ, 62-65; assoc prof art, Austin Peay Univ, 66- Mem: Nashville Artists Guild; Am Crafts Coun; World Crafts Coun. Media: Wood, Clay. Mailing Add: Dept of Art Austin Peay Univ Clarksville TN 37040

BRYANT, TAMARA THOMPSON
See Thompson, Tamara

BRZOZOWSKI, RICHARD JOSEPH
PAINTER
b New Britain, Conn, Sept 9, 32. Study: Paier Art Sch, New Haven, Conn. Work: Grumbacher Collection, New York; Phoenix Mutual Inst, Hartford, Conn; Springfield Mus Art, Mass. Exhib: Nat Acad, New York, 68; Watercolor USA, Springfield, Mo, 68 & 71; Am Watercolor Soc, New York, 71 & 74; De Cordova Mus, Lincoln, Mass, 72 & 77; Audubon Artists, New York, 72; Rocky Mountain Nat, Golden, Colo, 76; Mainstreams, Marietta, Ohio, 77; Allied Artists, New York, 76; Copley Soc, Boston, Mass, 78. Awards: Grumbacher Purchase Award, Am Watercolor Soc, 63; Sagendorph Award, Copley Soc, 76; Spencer Stuward Award, Silvermine Guild, 76. Mem: Am Watercolor Soc; Conn Watercolor Soc (bd dirs, 69-70); Nat Soc Painters in Casein & Acrylics; Acad Artists Am; Copley Soc Boston. Style & Technique: Realistic and semi-abstract. Media: Watercolor, Acrylic. Mailing Add: 13 Fox Rd Plainville CT 06062

BUBA, JOY FLINSCH
SCULPTOR, ILLUSTRATOR
b Lloyd's Neck, NY, July 25, 04. Study: Eberle Studio, New York; Staedel Kunst Inst, Frankfurt, Ger; Art Acad, Munich, Ger; also with Theodor Kaerner & Angelo Yank. Work: David Mannes, Metrop Mus Art, New York; Florence Sabin, Statuary Hall, Capitol Bldg, Washington, DC; Norman Thomas, Henry Stimson, Margaret Sanger, Nat Portrait Gallery, Washington, DC; John D Rockefeller, Jr, Rockefeller Plaza, New York; Konrad Adenauer, Palais Schaumburg, Bonn, Ger; James V Forrestal, Princeton Univ; Karl von Frisch, Munich Univ, WGer; George Washington Corner, Am Philosophical Soc, Philadelphia; Charles Revlon Inc, New York; Wilmarth S Lewis, Yale Univ; John James Audubon & Lucy Audubon, Nat Audubon Soc & NY Hist Soc; Henry Fairfield Osborn, Am Mus, New York. Mem: Nat Sculpture Soc. Publ: Illusr, Elephants, Proboscidea Memoir; Elephants, Rabbits, Frogs & Toads, Goldfish; Written in Sand; Lyrico, the Only Horse of His Kind. Mailing Add: Villa Evelyn 22017 Menaggio Como Italy

BUBB, NANCY (JANE)
SCULPTOR, CURATOR
b Bronx, NY, Jan 3, 45. Study: State Univ NY, Farmingdale; Greenwich House Pottery, with Bob Stull & Jane Hartsook; Clay Art Ctr with Jim Howard. Exhib: Calhoun Col Ann Craft Expos & Symp, Yale Univ, 73; Fun & Fantasy, Xerox Corp Gallery, Rochester, 73; Folk Roots Contemp Crafts, Fairtree Gallery, New York, 75; one-woman show, Millersville State Col, 75; two-woman show, Clay & Fiber Gallery, Taos, NMex, 75; 100 Artists Celebrate 200 Yrs, Fairtree Gallery, New York & Xerox Sq, Rochester, NY, 76; Landscape: New Views, Herbert F Johnson Mus, Cornell Univ, Teaching: Teacher, St Mary's Sch, Peekskill, NY, Ithaca, NY. Pos: Cur, Art Now Inc, 74- Awards: Court of Honor/Ithaca, NY State Craftsmen, 73. Bibliog: A Christmas portfolio, four young artists, AD Mag, 12/74; Satirical crafts, Ceramics Monthly, 3/75; Bicentennial Bagatelle, Craft Horizons, 6/76. Mem: Am Crafts Coun; World Crafts Coun; NY State Craftsmen; Hunterdon Art Ctr. Style & Technique: Soft and clay sculpture with animals and or landscapes, using glazes and paint for color; soft bold forms, sometimes fantasy detail. Media: Clay, Fabric. Publ: Contribr, Art Now Color Slide Mag, 74- Dealer: Webb & Parsons Bedford Village NY. Mailing Add: Heavensent Farm Charleston RD 1 Box 118 Hampton NJ 08827 Pattenburg-Asbury NJ 08802

BUCHANAN, SIDNEY ARNOLD
INSTRUCTOR, SCULPTOR
b Superior, Wis, Sept 12, 32. Study: Univ Minn, Duluth, BA, 62; NMex Highlands Univ, Las Vegas, MA, 63. Work: Sheldon Mem Art Gallery, Univ of Nebr, Lincoln; Joslyn Art Mus, Omaha, Nebr; Springfield Art Mus, Mo; Jacksonville Art Mus, Fla; City Art Gallery, Manchester, Eng. Comn: Sculpture, Univ of Minn, Duluth, 67; wall sculpture, Mem Sculpture, Performing Arts Bldg, Univ of Nebr, 74; sculpture, Security Nat Bank, Omaha, Nebr, 75; Tornado (memorial), Pipal Park, Omaha, Nebr; sculpture, Med Ctr Sculpture Garden, Univ of Nebr Med Ctr, 77. Exhib: Springfield Art Mus Ann, Mo, 64-66; Midwest Biennial, 64-70 & Nebr 75, 75, Joslyn Art Mus, Omaha, Nebr; Mid-Am Exhib, William Rockhill Nelson Gallery of Art, Atkins Mus of Fine Arts, Kansas City, Mo, 65-66; Colo/Nebr Exchange Exhib, Omaha & Denver, 67; Report on the Sixties, Denver Art Mus, 69; Northwestern Biennial, SDak Mem Art Ctr, 72. Teaching: Prof sculpture, Univ of Nebr, Omaha, 64- Pos: Vis sculptor, Manchester Col of Art & Design, Eng, 69-70; artist-in-residence, Southern Ill Univ, Edwardsville, 72, Bemidji State Col, Minn, 75. Awards: Purchase Awards, Midwest Biennial, Joslyn Art Mus, Omaha, Nebr, 64-66 & Western Wash Univ State Col, 67; Nat Endowment for the Arts Grant, 75. Bibliog: Dr Judith Van Wagner (auth), Metal Paintings, Leonardo Mag, Spring 77 & Award Winning Sculpture, Margaret Harold Publ, 67. Style & Technique: Non-objective, welded steel. Media: Steel, aluminum. Dealer: Gallery 72 2709 Leavenworth Omaha NE 68105. Mailing Add: 1202 S 62nd St Omaha NE 68106

BUCHER, GEORGE ROBERT
EDUCATOR, SCULPTOR
b Sunbury, Pa, Oct 14, 31. Study: Univ Pa & Pa Acad Fine Arts, BFA, 57, MFA, 59; Barnes Found, Merion, Pa, 56-58. Work: Civic Fine Arts Ctr, Philadelphia; Sioux Falls Col; Kleinberg, Ont. Exhib: Nat Coun Jewish Women, Philadelphia, Pa, South Orange, Teaneck & Essex Co, NJ, 67-70; Binder Twine Festival, Toronto, Ont, 69-72; one-man show, New Holland Sperry Rand, Pa, 71; Art 71, William Penn Mus, Harrisburg, Pa, 71; Fellowship Show, Pa Acad Fine Arts, Philadelphia, 72; plus others. Collections Arranged: Med Exhibs, Wistar Inst Anat Mus, Philadelphia, 55; Mayan Art, Univ Pa Mus, 58, Phrygian Art, 59, Philadelphia Artists, 59, Copic Art, 60 & Ruins of Rome, 61, also designed permanent NAm Art Sect, 61. Teaching: Artist, Wistar Inst Anat, 55-56; artist & asst to mgr exhibs, Univ Pa Mus, 58-61; instr art & mech drawing, Salem High Sch, NJ, 59-60; instr & artist, Univ Pa Fine Arts Sch & Mus, 60-61; assoc prof art & chmn dept, Sioux Falls Col, 61-65; assoc prof art, Susquehanna Univ, 65- Pos: Creator, original music for five-string banjo concert workshops & exhibs with sculpture titled Stringed Instruments for Vision & music & handmade banjos as Sound Sculpture in the Round, presented at var cols, univs, pvt collections, television & galleries. Mem: Col Art Asn Am. Media: Fibers, Polyester. Collection: Twine fiber sculpture. Publ: Auth, No Island is a Man (cartoon bk), 65. Mailing Add: Freeburg PA 17827

BUCHMAN, JAMES WALLACE
SCULPTOR
b Memphis, Tenn, Dec 3, 48. Study: Dartmouth Col, BA; Skowhegan Sch Painting & Sculpture. Exhib: LoGiudice Gallery, New York, 72; Mid-South Exhib, Brooks Mus, Memphis, Tenn, 73; Vt 73, Fleming Mus, Burlington, 73; one-man show, Granite & Steel, Sculpture Now, Inc, New York, 75; Sculpture Outdoors, Nassau Co Mus Fine Arts, Roslyn, NY, 75. Teaching: Vis artist sculpture, Richard DeMarco Summer Sch, Edinburgh, Scotland, 73 & Duke Univ, 75. Bibliog: Robert Hughes (auth), Working on the rock pile, Time Mag, 4/7/75; Ingeborg Hoesteret (auth), Buchman (Sculpture Now), Art Int, 6/15/75; Donald B Kuspit (auth), James Buchman at Sculpture Now, Art in Am, 7-8/75. Style & Technique: Large scale sculpture constructed of scrap granite and steel. Dealer: Sculpture Now Inc 142 Greene St New York NY 10012. Mailing Add: Bldg 9 Gero Bros Indust Park Ft Ethan Allen Winooski VT 05404

BUCK, ROBERT TREAT, JR
ART HISTORIAN, MUSEUM DIRECTOR
b Fall River, Mass, Feb 16, 39. Study: Williams Col, BA; NY Univ, with Dr Walter Friedlaender, MA. Collections Arranged: Sam Francis: Paintings 1947-1972 (with catalog), 72; Paintings by Auguste Herbin; Here and Now: 13 Young Americans; Modernist Painting; Pollock to the Present; Master Drawings from the Art Inst Chicago & Mus Mod Art; Homage to Albers; Max Bill, 74; Bradley Walker Tomlin: A Retrospective View, 75; Richard Diebenkorn: Paintings & Drawings 1943-1976, 76-77; Antoni Tàpies: 33 Years of His Work, 77; Cleve Gray: Serial Paintings, 77. Teaching: Adj assoc prof mus training, Univ Toledo,

65-66; adj assoc prof mus training & 19th & 20th century art, Wash Univ, 66-70; adj assoc prof mus training, State Univ NY Buffalo, 72- Pos: Lectr-researcher, Toledo Mus Art, 64-65; asst cur & instr, Wash Univ, 65-67 & dir, Gallery of Art, 68-70; asst dir, Albright-Knox Art Gallery, Buffalo, 70-73, dir, 73- Awards: NY State Coun Arts Traveling Fel, summer 71; Nat Endowment for Arts Fel for Museum Professional, summer 75. Mem: NY Coun for Humanities. Res: 19th century French painting; art of the 20th century. Mailing Add: 1285 Elmwood Ave Buffalo NY 14222

BUCKLEY, MARY L (MRS JOSEPH M PARRIOTT)
PAINTER, EDUCATOR
b New Haven, Conn. Study: Yale Univ Art Sch; also with Victor Candell & Hans Hoffman. Work: Yale Art Mus; Heckscher Mus, Huntington, NY; Lake Erie Col, Painesville, Ohio; Pratt Inst, New York. Comn: Murals, Philip Johnson, Seagrams Bldg, New York, 59; Color & Design, comn by Philip Johnson, Architect, Pavillion at New York World's Fair, 64; People I (sculpture), Paragon Oil, Melville, NY; State Symbols Standards & People II (sculpture), NY State Legislature Bldg, Albany. Exhib: Nat Acad Design, 59; J Walter Thompson Gallery, New York, 60; Nat Asn Women Artists, 60 & 61; Pratt Inst, Brooklyn, 60 & 74; Heckscher Mus, Huntington, NY, 63; Waverly Gallery, New York, 65; Caravan Gallery, New York, 68; Manhattan Community Col, 70; Nassau Community Col, 71; Midtown Gallery, New York, 77; Women's Inter-art Exhib, New York, 77; Munson Gallery, New Haven, Conn, 77 & 78. Teaching: Prof art & design, Pratt Inst, Brooklyn, 58-; adj prof, Union Col, Antioch, Ohio, 75- Pos: Dir, Margaret Gate Inst, 73- Mem: Nat Asn Women Artists; Indust Designers Soc of Am; Eastern Arts Asn; Fel MacDowell Asn. Style & Technique: Figurative paintings; concept of simultaniety; sculpture silhouettes. Media: Oil; Wood, Plate Aluminum. Publ: Auth, Color Theory Bibliography, Gale Res; auth, Color Glimpses, UR Brooklyn J, 76. Dealer: Munson Gallery 33 Whitney Ave New Haven CT 06510. Mailing Add: Bay Crest Huntington NY 11743

BUCKNALL, MALCOLM RODERICK
PAINTER
b Twickenham, Eng, Feb 1, 35. Study: Univ Viswa-Bharati, West Bengal, India, 54-55; Chelsea Art Sch, London, Intermediate Nat Dipl Design, 58; Univ Tex, Austin, BFA(hon), 61; Univ Wash, Seattle, MFA, 63. Work: Butler Inst of Am Art, Youngstown, Ohio; Okla Art Ctr, Oklahoma City; Univ of Va Art Mus, Charlottesville. Exhib: Asian Acad Ann, Calcutta, India, 55; Nat Jury Show, Chautauqua Inst, NY, 65-76; Midyear Show, Butler Inst of Am Art, Youngstown, Ohio, 65-77; New Realists, Gallery of Mod Art, Taos, NMex, 70; Eight State Show, Okla Art Ctr, Oklahoma City, 71, 72, 74 & 77; Artists Biennial, New Orleans Mus, La, 71, 75 & 77; Delta Show, Ark Art Ctr, Little Rock, 73 & 74; SW Biennial, Santa Fe Mus, NMex, 74 & 76. Teaching: Instr drawing & design, Univ Wash, Seattle, 61-63. Awards: Best in Oil, Sun Carnival, El Paso Mus, Tex, 68; Nat Jury Show, Chautauqua Inst, NY, 72; Medal, Midyear Show, Butler Inst of Am Art, 72. Bibliog: Lisa Tuttle (auth), Risky Artist Wins Worthwhile Gamble, Austin Statesman, 6/76; Patricia Sharpe (auth), Different Strokes, Tex Mo, 10/76. Mem: Austin Contemp Art Asn. Style & Technique: Eclectic figures with historical art references and anthropomorphic themes. Media: Oil paintings; ink drawings, pen and wash. Mailing Add: 808 West Ave Austin TX 78701

BUCKNER, KAY LAMOREUX
PAINTER
b Seattle, Wash, Dec 26, 35. Study: Sch of Art, Univ Wash, BA(art), 58; Claremont Grad Sch, MFA(painting), 61, study with Roger Kuntz & Phil Dike. Work: Olympic Col, Bremerton, Wash; First Nat Bank Ore, Portland; Ga-Pac Co, Portland, Ore; Emanuel Hosp, Portland, Ore; Great Western Nat Bank, Portland, Ore. Exhib: Exhib of Northwest Artists, Seattle Art Mus, Wash, 56 & 64; Mayor's Invitational, Salem Civic Ctr, Ore, 72 & 76; Mainstreams Int, 74 & 76, Marietta Col, Ohio, 74 & 76; Nat Drawing Exhib, Mercyhurst Col, Pa, 66; Greater Fall River Nat Exhib, Mass, 76. Teaching: Vis instr drawing, Univ Ore, Eugene, 76-78. Awards: First Prize Drawing Exhib, 58 & First Prize Figure Exhib, 62, Woessner Gallery; First Prize Painting, 18th Nat Greater Fall River Exhib, Mass, 76. Style & Technique: Figure composition in oil; strong emphasis on drawing and unusual placement of figure. Mailing Add: 2332 Rockwood Ave Eugene OR 97405

BUCKNER, PAUL EUGENE
SCULPTOR
b Seattle, Wash, June 16, 33. Study: Univ Wash Sch of Art, BA(sculpture), 59; Claremont Grad Sch, MFA(sculpture), 61, study with Albert Stewart; Fulbright grant, Slade Sch, Univ Col, London, 61-62. Work: Olympic Col, Bremerton, Wash; Salem Civic Ctr, Ore; Leighton Pool, Univ Ore, Eugene, Ore; First Nat Bank Ore, Portland; Multnoma Athletic Club, Portland, Ore. Comn: Wood carving, Myrtle Creek Pub Libr, Ore, 67; eight 8 ft wood reliefs, Cascade Manor, Eugene, Ore, 67; concrete & bronze relief, Tigard Sch Dist, Ore, 71; Centennial Medallion, Univ Ore, Eugene, 76; woodcarving of risen Christ, St Paul's Liturgical Comt, Silverton, Ore, 77. Exhib: Northwest Artists, Seattle Art Mus, Wash, 64; one-man show, Ore Mus Art, Eugene, 64; Sculpture 67, Seattle Art Mus, Wash, 67; Ore Sculpture 68, Portland, 68; Mainstreams Int, Marietta Col, Ohio, 71, 76 & 77; Sculptors of Ore, Ore Mus Art, Eugene, 74; Works in Wood by Northwest Artists, Portland Art Mus, Ore, 76. Teaching: Prof sculpture, Univ Ore, Eugene, 62- Awards: Nat Sculpture Rev Prize, Nat Sculpture Soc, 77; Award of Distinction, Mainstreams 77, Marietta Col, Ohio, 77. Style & Technique: Human and animal form; carvings in wood and stone; cast metals. Mailing Add: 2332 Rockwood Ave Eugene OR 97405

BUCZAK, BRIAN ELLIOT
PAINTER, SCULPTOR
b Detroit, Mich, Aug 25, 54. Study: Wayne State Univ; Ctr for Creative Studies, Col Art & Design, BFA. Work: Kansas City Art Inst, Mo; Boymans-Van-Beuningen Mus, Rotterdam; Stedelijk Mus, Amsterdam; Galleria D'Arte Mod, Bologna, Italy; Sonja Henie-Neils Onstad Art Ctr, Oslo, Norway. Comn: Image Bank 1984 Mural (with Flaky Rosehips), Image Bank, Vancouver, 73; portrait in landscape, comn by Carl Heiden, Elkson, Mich, 74; 26 assemblages (with Geoffrey Hendricks), comn by Francesco Conz, Asolo, Italy, 77; collaborative performance (with Geoffrey Hendricks), Cavriago Sound & Performance Festival, Italy, 77. Exhib: Mail Art Show, Stedelijk Mus, 74; Mail Art Show, Kansas City, 74; Bologna Art Fair, Italy, 77. Awards: State Fair Mural, Mich State Fair, 71. Bibliog: Joseph Bernard (auth), Slide presentation, 75; Susan Moon (auth), Film of Rules, Buckets, Ladders, 77 & Film of Musical Wisdom Clock, 78. Style & Technique: Mixed media incorporating all available media including mail, performance, paint, construction, etc. Publ: Contribr, File Mag, Art Metropole, 74; illusr, Strange Feces Publ No 13, Strange Feces Press, 75; co-auth, Rulers, Ladders & Buckets, 77, auth Flax, 77 & co-auth, Saved, 78, Money for Food Press. Dealer: Poppy Johnson c/o $100 Gallery 319 Greenwich St New York NY 10013. Mailing Add: 486 Greenwich St New York NY 10013

BUECHNER, THOMAS SCHARMAN
MUSEUM DIRECTOR, PAINTER
b New York, NY, Sept 25, 26. Study: Princeton Univ, 44-45; Art Students League, 46-47; Ecole Beaux-Arts, Fontainebleau & Paris, France, 47-48. Comn: Portrait of Lewis Francis, Packer Col Inst, 64; portrait of Paul Sheaffer, Brooklyn Hosp, 65; portrait of David Atwater, Grace Episcopal Church, 70; portrait of Joseph Hill, State Univ NY Downstate Med Ctr, 72; portrait of Alfred Gelhorn, Univ Pa. Exhib: Ithaca Art Gallery, NY; Elmira Arnot Art Gallery, NY; Nat Acad Design. Collections Arranged: Vincent Van Gogh (arranged), Metrop Mus Art, 49; Glass 1959 (assembled), Corning Mus Glass, 59; Levine-Shikler (cataloged), Brooklyn Mus, 71. Teaching: Head dept art, Corning Community Col, 58-60; head painting & drawing, Heights Casino, Brooklyn, 65-68; prof drawing arts & social change, Salzburg Sem Am Studies, 71. Pos: Dir, Corning Mus Glass, 50-60, 75- dir, Brooklyn Mus, 60-71; pres, Corning Glassworks Found, 71; pres, Steuben Glass, 72; mem bd, Parsons Sch of Design, New York; illusr, Book World & Dubbings Electronics; mem adv bd, Nat Collection Fine Arts, 72. Awards: Brooklyn Man of Year, Brooklyn Col, 63; Forsythia Award, Brooklyn Botanic Garden, 71; Gari Melcher's Gold Medal, Artist's Fellowship, 71. Mem: Louis Comfort Tiffany Found (trustee, 71); fel Royal Soc. Style & Technique: Traditional representative painting of landscape, still life and portrait, usually emphasizing odd characteristics of subject, often through lighting. Res: American illustration, emphasis on cover artists; glass history with emphasis on art glass. Publ: Auth, Glass Vessels in Dutch Painting in the 17th Century, 52; auth, Life and Work of Frederick Carder, 52; auth, A Guide to the Corning Museum of Glass, 55; contribr, A Guide to the Brooklyn Museum, 67; auth, Norman Rockwell: Artist and Illustrator. Mailing Add: Corning Glass Works Corning NY 14830

BUECKER, ROBERT
GALLERY DIRECTOR, PAINTER
b Pittsburgh, Pa, 1935. Study: Pa State; Carnegie Tech. Exhib: Purism, Yale Univ Art Gallery, New Haven, Conn, 57; Six Artists & Serial Works, Riverside Mus, NY, 65; Other Ideas, Detroit Inst of Arts, Mich, 69; one-man shows, Mills Col, NY, 57, Grouped Panels, 59 & Diamonds, 60, Condon Riley Gallery, New York, 63, Cruciforms, 66 & Cembalos, 69, Richard Feigen Gallery, New York & Serial Paintings: Geometries 1955-1977, Zolla/Lieberman Gallery, Chicago, 77; Six Greek Crosses, Cathedral of St John the Divine Mus of Religious Art, 77; plus others. Pos: Owner, Buecker & Harpsichords, New York, 70- Bibliog: Lillian Lonngren (auth), article in Art News, 3/59; Suzy Gablic (auth), article in Art News, 1/64; Michael Andre (auth), article in Village Voice, 8/11/75. Res: Contemporary New York Art History. Specialty: Contemporary American art. Mailing Add: Buecker & Harpsichords 465 W Broadway New York NY 10012

BUENO, JOSE (JOE GOODE)
SCULPTOR, PAINTER
b Oklahoma City, Okla, Mar 23, 37. Work: Mus Mod Art, New York; Pasadena Art Mus, Calif; Los Angeles Co Mus Art; Victoria & Albert Mus, London; Ft Worth Art Mus, Tex. Awards: Cassandra Found Award; Am Fedn Arts Award. Media: Wood; Oil. Mailing Add: 1159 S Hayworth Los Angeles CA 90035

BUGBEE, JOAN SCOTT
SCULPTOR, EDUCATOR
b Oakland, Calif, Dec 17, 41. Study: Univ Mont; San Jose State Col, BA & MA; Art Students League, with R B Hale; Sch of Fine Arts, Nat Acad Design; also with M Wildenhain, EvAngelos Frudakis, Joseph Kiselewski, Granville Carter & Adolph Block. Work: Cordova Pub Libr, Alaska. Comn: Portraits, comn by D Goldsmith, New York, 71, Milton Shaw, New York, 71 & C Crawford, Forest Hills, NY, 72; Merle K Smith Medal, comn by Kenneth Van Brocklin, Cordova, 72; Bob Korn Commemorative Plaque, City of Cordova, 74; monument, Eyak Native Corp, Cordova, Alaska; wall mural, Anchorage Pioneer's Home, Alaska. Exhib: One-woman show, Springvale, Maine, 70; Nat Sculpture Soc Ann, New York, 70-73; Allied Artists Am Ann, New York, 70-72; Nat Acad Design Ann, New York, 71 & 74; Joan Bugbee, Retrospective, New York, 72. Teaching: Instr design, De Anza Col, Cupertino, Calif, 67-68; instr pottery & glaze chem, Greenwich House Pottery, New York, 69-71; instr pottery, Univ Alaska, Cordova, 72- Pos: Pres, Cordova Arts & Pageants Ltd, 75-76. Awards: Helen Foster Barnet Prize, Nat Acad Design, 71; Daniel Chester French Prize, Nat Sculpture Soc, 72 & C Percival Dietsch Prize, 73. Bibliog: Jim Seay (auth), A move for inspiration, Anchorage Daily News, 8/13/72. Mem: Greenwich House Potters & Sculptors; Nat Sculpture Soc; Catharine Lorillard Wolfe Art Club. Style & Technique: Realistic portrait and figure sculpture, traditional techniques. Media: Fired Stoneware Clay, Cast Bronze. Publ: Contribr, Nat Sculpture Review, winter 70-71 & spring 71. Dealer: Jean Shadrach c/o The Artique Ltd Gallery 314 G St Anchorage AK 99501. Mailing Add: Box 374 Cordova AK 99574

BUITRON, DIANA M
CURATOR, ART HISTORIAN
b Quito, Ecuador, Apr 17, 46; US citizen. Study: Smith Col, BA, 69; Inst of Fine Arts, New York Univ, MA, 72 & PhD, 76; Am Sch of Classical Studies, Athens, Greece, 72-73. Pos: Curatorial asst, Fogg Art Mus, Harvard Univ, 70-72; Andrew Mellon & Chester Dale Fel, Metrop Mus of Art, New York, 73-75; Cur Greek & Roman art, Walters Art Gallery, Baltimore, Md, 76- Mem: Archaeol Inst of Am. Res: Emphasis has been on Greek art, above all, Greek vase painting in Athens in the late Archaic and early Classical periods; also Greek bronzes. Publ: Auth, Attic vase painting in New England collections, 72 & A Greek bronze mirror, 73, Fogg Art Mus; auth, The Alexander Nelidow, a Renaissance Bronze, Art Bull, 73; auth, A bronze statuette of Hermes in the Metropolitan Museum, 77 & ed, Essays in honor of Dorothy Kent Hill, 77, J Walters Art Gallery. Mailing Add: c/o The Walters Art Gallery 600 N Charles St Baltimore MD 21201

BUKI, ZOLTAN
CURATOR, ART ADMINISTRATOR
b Pecs, Hungary, Oct 26, 29; US citizen. Study: Acad de Belle Arti, Rome; Art Inst Chicago, BFA; Wayne State Univ Grad Sch; Tulane Univ Grad Sch, MFA. Collections Arranged: George Rickey-James Seawright (with catalog), 69-70; Richard Anuszkiewicz & George Segal, 71; Responsive Environment, 72; For the Mind & The Eye, 77. Teaching: Instr drawing & painting, Univ Southwestern La, 61-62; instr drawing & anat, Layton Sch Art, Milwaukee, 62-63. Pos: Dir exhibs, Ark Arts Ctr, Little Rock, 63-68; chmn art dept, Humboldt State Col, 68-69; cur art, NJ State Mus, 69- Publ: Co-auth, The Trenton Monument Eakins Bronzes, 73. Mailing Add: 205 W State St Trenton NJ 08625

BULLARD, EDGAR JOHN, III
MUSEUM DIRECTOR, ART HISTORIAN
b Los Angeles, Calif, Sept 15, 42. Study: Univ Calif, Los Angeles, BA, 65, MA, 68; Samuel H Kress Found fel, Nat Gallery Art, 67-68; Harvard Univ Inst Arts Admin, 71. Exhibitions Arranged: German Expressionist Watercolors in American Collections, Nat Gallery Art, Washington, DC, 69, Mary Cassatt 1844-1926, 70 & John Sloan 1871-1951 (with catalog),

71; Richard Clague 1821-1873, New Orleans Mus of Art, 74 & Zenga & Nanga: Paintings by Japanese Monks & Scholars, 76; The Contemp South: Photog, USIA, 77. Pos: Asst cur, J Paul Getty Mus, Malibu, Calif, 67; mus cur, Nat Gallery Art, 68-70, asst to dir, 70-71, cur spec projs, 71-73; dir, New Orleans Mus Art, 73-; trustee, Ga Mus of Art, Univ of Ga. Mem: Am Asn Mus; Col Art Asn Am; Nat Endowment for the Arts (mus adv panel, 74-77); Nat Arts Club. Res: Late 19th & 20th century American and European art. Publ: Auth, John Sloan as an illustrator, Am Artist, 10/71; auth, The centennial year of artist John Sloan, Smithsonian Mag, 10/71; auth, Edgar Degas, McGraw-Hill, 71; auth, Mary Cassatt: Oils and Pastels, Watson-Guptill, 72; auth, A Panorama of American Painting (exhib catalog), 75; auth, American paintings from the John J McDonough Collection, Antiques, 11/77. Mailing Add: New Orleans Mus of Art PO Box 19123 New Orleans LA 70179

BULLEN, REESE
CERAMIST, CALLIGRAPHER
b Richmond, Utah, Mar 9, 13. Study: Utah State Univ, BS(art); Stanford Univ, MA(art); Calif Col Arts & Crafts with Dewilde, Lederer, Purdy & Coykendahl; Mills Col with Prieto; workshop with Hamada Shoji, 63. Work: Nora Eccles Treadwell Mem Ceramics Collection, Oakland Mus Art; Everson Mus, Syracuse; State Calif Collection, Sacramento; St Paul Art Ctr, Minn; Prieto Mem Collection, Mills Col. Exhib: Fibre-Metal-Clay Nat, 60; US Info Agency Europ Travel Exhib, 60-62; Ceramic Nat, Everson Mus, Syracuse, 60 & 67; Mus West of Am Crafts Coun Travel Exhib, 68-70. Teaching: Teacher ceramics, Mills Col, summer 55; prof art, Humboldt State Univ, Calif, 46-75. Awards: Phelan Purchase Award, Phelan Collection, 56; Purchase Prize, Calif State Fair, 58; Outstanding Prof Award, Humboldt State Univ, 67. Style & Technique: Ceramics executed in high-fire reduction stoneware and Raku; abstract expressionism; calligraphy with square nib pens and pointed brush. Media: Clay; Inks on Paper. Publ: Auth, Calligraphy Workbook, Cloud Marauder Press, Berkeley, 70. Mailing Add: PO Box 807 Arcata CA 95521

BULTMAN, FRITZ
SCULPTOR, PAINTER
b New Orleans, La, Apr 4, 19. Study: With Morris Graves, 31; New Bauhaus, Chicago, 37-38; Hans Hofmann Sch Fine Arts, 38-41. Work: Whitney Mus Am Art; Rockefeller Art Gallery, Seal Harbor, Maine; Mus Art, RI Sch Design; Riverside Mus; Univ Nebr; plus others. Exhib: One-man shows, Delgado Mus, New Orleans, 59, Martha Jackson Gallery, New York, 74 & 76, Drawings-1974, New Orleans Mus; Oklahoma City Art Ctr; Newport Art Asn; also exhibs in US, Paris, Cologne, Turino, Milan & Japan. Teaching: Lectr, univs, cols, art clubs & mus; instr painting, Sch Educ, Pratt Inst, 58-63; instr painting, Grad Art Sch, Hunter Col, 59-63; instr & artist-in-residence, Fine Arts Work Ctr, Provincetown, Mass, 68-70. Awards: Prize, Art Inst Chicago, 64; Fulbright Res Grant, Paris, 64-65; Guggenheim Mem Award, 75-76; plus others. Bibliog: Nathaniel Pousett-Dart (ed), included in American Painting Today, Hastings, 56. Publ: Auth, article on Hans Hofmann, Art News, 63. Mailing Add: 176 E 95th St New York NY 10028

BUMBECK, DAVID A
PRINTMAKER, EDUCATOR
b Framingham, Mass, May 1, 40. Study: RI Sch Design, BFA, 62; Syracuse Univ, with Robert Marx, MFA, 66. Work: Everson Mus, Syracuse, NY; New York Pub Libr; Rochester Mem Galleries, NY; Ithaca Mus, NY; Wiggin Collection, Boston Pub Libr. Exhib: Boston Printmakers Nat Exhib, 67-72; Graphics 69, Nat Print Exhib, NY State Fair, 69; Nat Print Exhib, Northern Ill Univ, 70; Nat Exhib, Soc Am Graphic Artists, 71; Living American Artists and the Figure, Mus Art, Pa State Univ, 74. Teaching: Instr painting & printmaking, Mass Col Art, Boston, 66-68; asst prof printmaking, Middlebury Col, 68- Pos: Dir, Christian A Johnson Gallery, 73- Awards: Purchase Award, Everson Mus, 66; David Berger Memorial Award, Boston Printmakers Nat Exhib, 68; Purchase Awards, Ga State Univ Nat Print Exhibs, 70 & 71. Mem: Boston Printmakers (mem exec bd, 68-); Silvermine Guild Artists. Style & Technique: Figurative images in diverse intaglio techniques. Media: Intaglio. Dealer: Ainsworth Gallery 42 Bromfield St Boston MA 02108. Mailing Add: Drew Lane RD 3 Middlebury VT 05753

BUMGARDNER, GEORGIA BRADY
CURATOR, ART HISTORIAN
b Mt Kisco, NY, Dec 12, 44. Study: Wellesley Col, BA(art hist), 66. Pos: Cur graphic arts, Am Antiqn Soc, Worcester, Mass, 69- Mem: Print Coun Am; Am Hist Print Collectors Soc; Archives of Am Art (mem New Eng adv comt); Colonial Soc Mass. Res: Eighteenth and 19th century American prints. Publ: Auth, American Broadsides, 1680-1800, Imprint Soc, 71; co-auth, Massachusetts Broadsides of the American Revolution, Univ Mass, 76; auth, Bibliography on American Graphic Arts, Arch Am Art, 78. Mailing Add: Am Antiqn Soc 185 Salisbury St Worcester MA 01609

BUMGARDNER, JAMES ARLISS
PAINTER, EDUCATOR
b Winston-Salem, NC, Mar 25, 35. Study: Univ NC; Salem Col, Winston-Salem; Richmond Prof Inst, BFA; also with Hans Hofmann. Work: NC Mus Fine Arts, Raleigh; First & Merchant's Bank, Richmond, Va; Philip Morris & Co, Richmond; Davidson Col, NC; Salem Col, Winston-Salem, NC. Exhib: NC Show, var times, 57-62; Art USA, New York, 59; Va Artist's Show, var times, 59-75; Southcoast Art Show, 61; Art Across America, New York, 65. Teaching: Assoc prof drawing & painting, Va Commonwealth Univ, 58- Awards: NC Mus Art Scholar, 57 & five Spec Awards for Painting, 57-62; four Cert of Distinction, Va Mus Fine Art, 59-63 & 77; Purchase Prize, Southeastern Ctr for Contemp Arts, 77. Style & Technique: Former abstract painter, now imagist. Media: Oil. Dealer: Gallery K 2032 P St NW Washington DC 20023. Mailing Add: 406 N Allen Ave Richmond VA 23220

BUNCE, FREDRICK WILLIAM
DRAFTSMAN, ART HISTORIAN
b Princeton, Wis, June 28, 35. Study: Macalester Col, St Paul, Minn, BS, 57; Cranbrook Acad of Art, Bloomfield, Mich, MFA, 59; Ohio Univ, PhD, 73. Work: Musee des Beaux Arts, St Jean D'Angely, France; Flaten Gallery, St Olaf Col, Northfield, Minn; Western Nat Bank, Sioux Falls, SDak. Comn: Six ft x 9 ft wall hanging, Pipestone Fed, Minn, 77; 4 ft x 7 ft drawing, St Augustin's, Columbia, SC, 60. Exhib: Duo Show, Columbia Mus, SC, 60; NW Biennial, SDak Mem Art Ctr, Brookings, 75; solo show, Sioux Falls Art Ctr, SDak, 76. Teaching: Fel humanities, Paracollege, St Olaf Col, 71-74; prof art survey, SDak State Univ, 74- Pos: Head art dept, SDak State Univ, 74- Awards: Painting Award, SC Artists, 61; Best of Show, 1st Religious Art Show, First Presby Church, St Paul, Minn, 64; Purchase Recommendation, SDak Biennial III, Jan K Muhlert, 77. Mem: Col Art Asn; Mid-Am Art Asn. Style & Technique: Bio-morphic drawings in graphite. Res: Sixteenth century French and Italian erotology. Mailing Add: Dept of Art SDak State Univ Brookings SD 57006

BUNCE, LOUIS DEMOTT
PAINTER
b Lander, Wyo, Aug 13, 07. Study: Mus Art Sch, Portland, Ore; Art Students League. Work: San Francisco Mus Art; Whitney Mus Am Art, New York; Portland Mus; Seattle Art Mus; Butler Inst Am Art, Youngstown, Ohio. Comn: Mural, Port of Portland, Portland Int Airport, 58; 600 serigraphs, Hilton Hotel, Portland, 63. Exhib: 3rd Biennial, Sao Paulo, Brazil, 55-56; Print Coun Am, 62-63; Univ Ill Art Mus, 67; Nat Drawing Soc, 70; Denver Mus Art, 71. Teaching: Instr painting, Mus Art Sch, Portland, 46-; vis prof painting, Univ Calif, Berkeley, 60; vis prof painting, Univ Ill, Urbana, 66-67. Awards: Ford Found Fel, Tamarind Lithographic Workshop, 61; Ford Found Purchase Award, Seattle Art Mus Ann, 65; Painting Award, Portland Art Mus Ann, 71. Bibliog: New painters, Art in Am, 55; West coast painters, Life Mag, 11/57. Media: Oil, Acrylic. Dealer: Fountain Gallery 115 S W Fourth Ave Portland OR 97204. Mailing Add: 1800 S E Harold St Portland OR 97202

BUNCH, CLARENCE
EDUCATOR, SCULPTOR
b Gray Ridge, Mo. Study: Univ Mo; Art Students League, study with Kantor; Columbia Univ. Work: Portsmouth Mus, Eng; Columbia Univ; Helen Wurlitzer Found Mus, Taos, NM; Univ Va. Exhib: Brooklyn Mus, NY; Bronx Mus, NY; Portsmouth Mus, Eng; Nat Mus Wales, Cardiff. Teaching: Supv, Univ Mo, Columbia; asst prof, Radford Col, Va; chmn & assoc prof, Appalachian State Univ, Boone, NC; chmn & assoc prof, Queens Col of the City Univ NY, 67; vis prof grad art, Pratt Inst, Brooklyn, 73. Awards: Danforth Fel; MacDowell Fel; Ossabaw Island Proj Fel. Bibliog: Carter Ratcliff (auth), article in Art Int, 69; article in Arts Rev, London, 73 & Art News, 73. Mem: Col Art Asn; Nat Art Educ Asn; Univ Coun for Art Educ (past pres & presently gov); Inst for the Study of Art in Educ (bd dirs). Publ: Auth, Acrylic for Sculpture & Design, 73 & co-auth, Working Big, 75, Van Nostrand Reinhold; auth, Art Education; A Guide to Information Sources, Gale Res, 78. Mailing Add: 539 E 78th St New York NY 10021

BUNDY, STEPHEN ALLEN
SCULPTOR, INSTRUCTOR
b Denver, Colo, Apr 10, 42. Study: Univ Colo, Boulder, BA(physics), 64, MA(physics), 67, MFA(painting & sculpture), 72. Exhib: Twelfth Midwest Biennial, Joslyn Art Mus, Omaha, Nebr, 72; Performance (with Hans Breder), Mus Art, Univ Iowa, Iowa City, 74; Midwest Fac Painters & Sculptors, Krannert Art Mus, Univ Ill, 76; one-man show, Nancy Lurie Gallery, Chicago, Ill, 77. Teaching: Asst prof sculpture & video, Univ Iowa, Iowa City, 73-; head 4-D studies, Hornsey Col Art at Middlesex Polytechnic, London, Eng, 77-78. Pos: Cur, Corroboree: Gallery of New Concepts, Univ Iowa, Iowa City, 76- Bibliog: Art ed (auth), New Sculpture, Al-Mesa, Cairo, Egypt, 6/77. Mem: Col Art Asn Am. Style & Technique: Slow moving abstract machines which make drawings on walls from their rubber tire marks; made of soft wood and common hardware. Media: Wood, metal. Dealer: Nancy Lurie Gallery 1632 N La Salle Chicago IL 60614. Mailing Add: c/o Ken Bundy 3435 S Ash St Denver CO 80222

BUNKER, GEORGE
PAINTER, PRINTMAKER
b Denver, Colo, May 27, 23. Study: Yale Univ, BA, 46; Art Students League, 46-47; Brooklyn Mus Art Sch, 47-49; also with Kuniyoshi, Reginald Marsh & Vytlacil, NY; and with Victor Candell, Brooklyn. Work: Philadelphia Mus Art; Rosenwald Collection, Nat Gallery, Washington, DC; Joseph Pennell Collection, Libr Cong; Univ NMex Art Mus; Weatherspoon Art Gallery, Univ NC, Greensboro. Comn: Lithographs, Tamarind Inst, Albuquerque, 73; color lithograph, Print Club Philadelphia, 73. Exhib: Cincinnati Mus Art, 58; Philadelphia Mus Art Festivals, 59, 61 & 62; Prints of Two Worlds, Philadelphia Mus & Rome, Italy, 67; Am Color Print Soc, 73; NY Studio Sch Sculpture & Painting, 73 & 74. Teaching: From instr to prof painting, drawing & printmaking, Philadelphia Col Art, 55-73; vis prof painting, Univ NMex, 73-74; prof painting & drawing & chmn dept art, Univ Houston, 74- Pos: Dean of fac, Philadelphia Col Art, 65-72. Awards: Lessing J Rosenwald Award, Print Club of Philadelphia, 61; Am Color Print Soc Award, 73; Mid-Western Graphics Award, 73. Mem: Am Asn Univ Prof; Cult Affairs Comt, Houston; Mus of Fine Arts, Houston; Contemp Art Mus, Houston. Style & Technique: Abstract realist and color field, from landscape motifs. Media: Oil, Lithograpy. Publ: Ed, Leon Karp Portfolio, 60; ed & contribr, Alexey Brodovitch & His Influence, 72; ed (catalogue), Melnicoff Memorial Exhib, 73; ed (catalogue), Victor Candell Memorial Exhib, 78. Dealer: Mitzi Shalit 41 Conshocken State Rd Bala Cynwyd PA 19004. Mailing Add: 2028 Quenby St Houston TX 77005

BUNN, CECINE COLE
PAINTER, LECTURER
b Springfield, Ill. Study: MacMurry Col, Jacksonville, Ill; Univ Colo; Univ Ill; also with Dan Umberger, George Post & Elliott O'Hara. Work: San Francisco Hall of Justice; Triton Mus, Santa Clara, Calif; Menlo Park Civic Ctr, Calif; Sheila Spenser Mem Fine Art Gallery, Univ Ark. Comn: Designed rug, Northern Calif Handweavers Conf, 71; designed plates for 25th Silver Anniversary, City Los Altos, Calif, 77. Exhib: San Jose Mus, Calif; De Young Mus, San Francisco, 69-71; Directors Choice Show, Triton Mus, 71; Cedar City Nat Invitational, 72; plus other nat shows in Tex, Utah, La, Ill & Miss. Teaching: Guest demonstr, Col San Mateo, 70; lectured on acrylics & watercolor in over 80 cols, univs & grade schs. Pos: Demonstr, Van Guard Acrylics, Hunt Mfg Co, 2 yrs. Awards: Second Contemporary, Cal Expo, Calif State Fair, 70; Best of Show in Watercolor, Palo Alto Art Club, Palo Alto Holiday Show, Calif, 71; Best of Show in Watercolor, Sunnyvale Coun for Arts, Calif, 73; plus many others. Mem: Soc Western Artists; Palo Alto Art Club (vpres, 71); Santa Clara Watercolor Soc; Nat League Am Pen Women (achiever in arts, Santa Clara Br, 68). Style & Technique: Landscape impressionist, watercolorist (transparent). Media: Transparent & Salt Watercolor. Publ: Illusr, Painting Warps, 74; auth technique enrichment programs for Los Altos Sch Dist, Calif & Hillbrook Sch, Los Gatos; auth technique enrichment notebook for teachers, Huff Elem Sch, Mt View, Calif. Dealer: Lescaut, Inc 220 State St Los Altos CA 94022. Mailing Add: c/o Viewpoint Art Studio 172 Hamilton Ct Los Altos CA 94022

BUNN, KENNETH RODNEY
PAINTER, SCULPTOR
b Denver, Colo, June 1, 38. Study: Univ Md; Smithsonian Inst. Inst. Work: In pvt collections. Exhib: 145th-149th Ann, Nat Acad Design; 36th-41st Ann, Nat Sculpture Soc. Awards: Bronze Medal, Nat Sculpture Soc 36th Ann; Helen Foster Barnett Prize, Nat Acad Design 146th Ann. Mem: Nat Sculpture Soc; Soc Animal Artists; assoc Nat Acad Design. Mailing Add: Elizabeth CO 80107

BUNNELL, PETER CURTIS
EDUCATOR, CURATOR
b Poughkeepsie, NY, Oct 25, 37. Study: Rochester Inst Technol, BFA, 59; Ohio Univ, MFA, 61; Yale Univ, MA, 65. Collections Arranged: Paul Caponigro, Mus Mod Art, New York, 68, Photography as Printmaking, 68, Photography into Sculpture, 70, Clarence H White, 71 & Barbara Morgan, 72; The Eads Bridge, Princeton Univ Art Mus, 74. Teaching: Vis lectr

hist photog, Dartmouth Col, 68; vis lectr hist photog, Inst Film/TV, NY Univ, 68-70; McAlpin prof hist photog & mod art, Princeton Univ, 72-; vis lectr hist photog, Yale Univ, 73. Pos: Cur photog, Mus Mod Art, New York, 66-72; cur photog, Art Mus, Princeton Univ, 72-, dir, 73-78. Mem: Soc Photog Educ (nat chmn, 72-77); Col Art Asn Am (bd dirs, 75-); Friends of Photog (bd trustees, 74-). Res: History of photography with primary emphasis on the 20th century. Publ: Ed, The Literature of Photography, 73; auth, Diane Arbus, 73; auth, Gertrude Kasebier, 75, Walker Evans, 76 & Helen Gee and the Limelight, 77. Mailing Add: Dept Art & Archaeol Princeton Univ Princeton NJ 08540

BUNSHAFT, MR & MRS GORDON
COLLECTORS
Mr Bunshaft, b Buffalo, NY, May 9, 09. Study: Mr Bunshaft, Mass Inst Technol, BArch, 33, fel & MArch, 35; Univ Buffalo, hon DFA, 62. Comn: Mr Bunshaft, design of Lever House, New York, Beinecke Rare Bk & Mss Libr, Yale Univ, Albright-Knox Art Gallery, Buffalo & Joseph H Hirshhorn Mus & Sculpture Garden, Washington, DC. Pos: Mr Bunshaft, mem, Pres Comt on Fine Arts, 63-; mem int coun, Mus Mod Art, New York, trustee, presently. Awards: Mr Bunshaft, Brunner Award, Nat Inst Arts & Lett, 55; Medal Honor, NY Chap Am Inst Architects, 61; Chancellor's Medal, Univ Buffalo, 69. Mem: Mr Bunshaft, Academician Nat Acad Design; Nat Inst Arts & Lett; Munic Art Soc New York; hon mem Buffalo Fine Arts Acad; fel Am Inst Architects. Collection: Contemporary art. Mailing Add: 200 E 66th St New York NY 10021

BUNTING, BAINBRIDGE
ART HISTORIAN
b Kansas City, Mo, Nov 23, 13. Study: Univ Ill, BS, 37; Harvard Univ, PhD, 52. Teaching: Prof art, Univ NMex, 48- Pos: Survey dir, Cambridge Hist Comn, 64-74. Mem: Col Art Asn; Soc Archit Hist. Res: 19th century American architecture, especially Boston area; Spanish colonial architecture, emphasizing New Mexico. Publ: Auth, Taos Adobes, 62; auth, Houses of Bostons Back Bay Area, 67; auth, Historic Architecture in Cambridge: Old Cambridge, 73; auth, Of Earth and Timbers Made, 73. Mailing Add: 5021 Guadalupe Trail Albuquerque NM 87107

BUNTS, FRANK
PAINTER
b Cleveland, Ohio, Mar 2, 32. Study: Yale Univ; Cleveland Inst; Western Reserve, BA & MA. Work: Philadelphia Mus Art, Pa; Larry Aldrich Mus Contemp Art, Ridgefield, Conn; Cleveland Mus Art, Ohio; Fine Arts Gallery San Diego, Calif; Libr Congress, Washington, DC. Exhib: Nat Exhib, San Francisco Mus Art, 65; traveling show, Western Asn Art Mus, Calif, 65-67; traveling exhib, Cleveland Mus Art, 66 & 68; New Aquisitions Show, Fine Arts Gallery San Diego, 70; Painting & Sculpture Today, Indianapolis Mus Art, 76; one-man shows, Comara Gallery, Los Angeles, 67 & 68, Franz Bader Gallery, Washington, DC, 69, 73 & 75, Deson-Zans Gallery, Chicago, 72 & Nat Acad Sci, Washington, DC 76. Teaching: From instr to full prof art, Univ Md, College Park, 67-77. Style & Technique: Abstract; painting, drawing. Media: Graphite; Ink; Paint; Epoxy. Dealer: Zaks Gallery 620 N Michigan Ave Chicago IL 60611; Gallery K 2032 P St NW Washington DC 20036. Mailing Add: 15 W 24th St New York NY 10010

BURANABUNPOT, PORNPILAI
DESIGNER, WEAVER
b Nakorn-Pathom, Thailand, Jan 5, 45. Study: Univ Calif, Berkeley, BA, 68; Cranbrook Acad Art, Bloomfield Hills, Mich, MFA, 70; weaving with Ed Rossbach & Lilian Elliot, Berkeley. Work: Mint Mus Art, Charlotte, NC; Art Comn Collection, State Ky; Minn Mus Art, St Paul. Exhib: One-woman show, Fabric Design, Paducah Col, 72; two-person exhib, Craft Alliance, St Louis, Mo, 77; Fabric Design Int, Univ Kans, 77; Focus on Crafts: An Exhib, Univ Minn, 77; New Directions in Surface Design, Towson State Univ, Baltimore, Md, 77. Teaching: Instr art, Murray State Univ, 70-71, asst prof art, 71-72; asst prof art, Gustavus Adolphus Col, 72- Awards: Student Design Competition Award for Textile Design, P Kaufman Co, 69 & 70; Purchase Award, Mint Mus Art, 72; Purchase Award, Minn Mus Art, 73. Mem: Surface Design Asn; Am & Minn Craftsmen Coun. Media: Textiles. Mailing Add: Dept of Art Gustavus Adolphus Col St Peter MN 56082

BURCH, CLAIRE R
PAINTER, WRITER
b New York, NY, Feb 19, 25. Study: Wash Sq Col, NY Univ, BA, 47. Work: Butler Inst Am Art, Youngstown, Ohio; Guild Hall, East Hampton, NY; Birmingham Mus, Ala; Brooklyn Mus, NY; Beth Israel Hosp, New York. Exhib: One-man shows, Ruth White Gallery, New York, 63, Galerie L'Antipoete, Paris, France, 63, Southampton Col, 64-65 & Roko Gallery, 64; Maniacal Laughter, Westbeth Gallery, New York, 71. Awards: First Prize for Representational Painting, Guild Hall, 65; First Prize for Watercolor, North Shore Community Art Ctr, 65; Third Prize for Watercolor, Brooklyn Mus, 65. Mem: New York Playwrights Coop; Schizophrenics Anonymous Int. Media: Watercolor, Collage. Publ: Auth, Ten Cents a Dance (play), 69; auth, Careers in Psychiatry, Macmillan, 68; auth, Stranger in the Family, Bobbs-Merrill, 72; auth & illusr, Notes of a Survivor, Westbeth Poets Press, 72; auth, The Secret Songs of Claire Burch & auth (music, lyrics & bk), Blues to be Called Crazy When Crazy's All There Is (play), 72; plus others. Mailing Add: 463 West St New York NY 10014

BURCHARD, PETER DUNCAN
ILLUSTRATOR, PHOTOGRAPHER
b Washington, DC, Mar 1, 21. Study: Philadelphia Mus Sch of Art, cert, 47. Awards: Christopher Award (for illus in Clyde Robert Bulla's, Pocahontas), 73. Style & Technique: Traditional, representational illustrations with an accent on drawing rather than painting. Media: Wash, Gouache, Acrylic and others, on Illustration Board treated with Gesso; Black and White Photography, used in the Illustration of Books. Interest: Book illustration, book design and photography. Publ: Auth & illusr, Rat Hell, Coward McCann & Geoghegan, 71, Whaleboat Raid, 77; auth & illusr, Ocean Race, G P Putman's Sons, 78; illusr, The Street of the Flower Boxes, Coward McCann & Geoghegen, 66, For Ma and Pa, 73; illusr, Pocahontas, T Y Crowell, 73; illusr, Night Spell, Atheneum, 77. Mailing Add: 12 Trumbull St Box 455 Stonington CT 06378

BURCHESS, ARNOLD
PAINTER, SCULPTOR
b Chicago, Ill, June 7, 12. Study: City Col New York, BSS; also with George W Eggers & Robert Garrison. Comn: Three bas reliefs (with Robert Garrison), Radio City Music Hall New York, 35; portrait in bronze of Senator Edmund S Muskie, State Capital, Augusta, Maine, 74. Exhib: Am Watercolor Soc, New York, 55-; Birmingham Mus Art, Ala, 55; one-man show, Van Dimant Gallery, Southampton, NY, 57; Mus Mod Art, New York, 59; Maine Art Gallery, Wiscasset, 75. Teaching: Lectr, Shapes in Clay, Metrop Mus Art, New York, 39; prof fine art & chmn dept, Fashion Inst Technol, New York, 59-74; vis prof figurative sculpture, Bowdoin Col, 75. Awards: Watercolor Prize, Birmingham Mus Art, 55. Bibliog: Article in La Rev Mod, 56; Arnold Burchess-watercolorist, Am Artist Mag, 59; Norman Kent (auth), 100 Watercolor Techniques, Watson-Guptill, 70. Mem: Am Watercolor Soc; Audubon Artists. Media: Watercolor, Bronze. Dealer: Aries East Art Gallery Rte 6A East Brewster MA 02640. Mailing Add: South Harpswell ME 04079

BURCHFIELD, JERRY LEE
PHOTOGRAPHER, EDUCATOR
b Chicago, Ill, July 28, 47. Study: Calif State Univ, Fullerton, BA(photo-commun), 71, MA(art, photo emphasis), 77. Work: Los Angeles Ctr for Photog Studies, Calif; San Francisco Camerawork Gallery, Calif; Calif State Univ, Fullerton; Eastern Wash Univ, Cheney, Wash. Exhib: Through Ones Eyes, Muckenthaler Ctr, Fullerton, Calif, 73; 1st All Calif Photog Show, Laguna Beach Mus, Calif, 75; Calif Invitational, Cypress Col, Calif, 75; New Photographics 76; Cent Wash State Col, Ellensburg, Wash, 76; Color Photog, Arco Ctr for Visual Art, Los Angeles, Calif, 76; Variations With No Theme, Los Angeles Co Mus Art, Los Angeles, Calif, 77; Tyler Sch Art, Philadelphia, Pa, 77; Southern Calif 100, Laguna Beach Mus Art, Calif, 77. Collections Arranged: Through Ones Eyes, Muckenthaler Ctr, Fullerton, Calif, 73; 1st All Calif Photog Show, Laguna Beach Mus, Calif, 75; New Photographics 76, Cent Wash State Col, Ellensburg, 76; Convergence—Six Directions in Photography, Orange Coast Col, Costa Mesa, Calif, 76; Southern Calif 100, Laguna Beach Mus Art, 77. Teaching: Instr photog, Univ Calif, Irvine Exten, 73-75, lectr, Photogr on Photog, Calif State Univ, Fullerton, 74 & instr photog, 78- Pos: Asst dir, Newport Gallery, Newport Sch Photog, Calif, 73-75; dir-co-owner, BC Space, Photog Gallery, Laguna Beach, Calif, 76- Bibliog: Hilary Kaye (auth), Art Lovers Seek Fine Photography, Daily Pilot & Times Mirror, 5/74; Martha Spellman (auth), Photographic Metamorphoses, Art Week, 7/76; Donald Huntsman (auth), Haddad's Fine Arts, Photo Image, 76. Mem: Soc for Photog Educ; Visual Studies Workshop; Los Angeles Ctr for Photog Studies; Friends of Photog. Style & Technique: Straight and manipulated color photography. Media: Photography. Publ: Auth, Color Solarization, 73 & Cameraless photography, 75, Peterson's Photogs; illusr/contribr, Basic Darkroom Book, Plume, 77. Mailing Add: PO Box 1502 Laguna Beach CA 92652

BURCK, JACOB
CARTOONIST, PAINTER
b Poland, Jan 10, 04. Study: Cleveland Sch Art; Art Students League; also with Albert Sterner, 24-26 & Boardman Robinson. Exhib: Cleveland Mus Art, 24; Whitney Mus Am Art; Mus Mod Art; Fine Arts Bldg, New York; Archit League, Art Inst Chicago. Pos: Creator daily ed cartoon, Chicago Sun-Times, currently. Awards: Pulitzer Prize, 41; First Prize ed cartoon, Birmingham Mus Art, 58. Mailing Add: 921 Castlewood Terr Chicago IL 60640

BURCKHARDT, RUDY
PHOTOGRAPHER, FILM MAKER
b Basel, Switz, Apr 5, 14; US citizen. Study: Ozenfant Sch, New York, 48; Brooklyn Mus Sch, 49; Acad Naples, 50 51. Work: Photo collection, Metrop Mus Art, New York & Univ New Orleans; film collection, Art Inst Chicago. Exhib: Painting exhibs, Tanager Gallery, 59 & Green Mountain Gallery, New York, 70 & 73; photo exhibs, Limelight Gallery, 58, Gotham Bookmart, 72 & Brooke Alexander Gallery, New York, 75. Teaching: Lectr filmmaking, Grad Sch Art, Univ Pa, Philadelphia, 65- Bibliog: Alex Katz (auth), feature article in Art News, 63; Lucy Lippard (auth), feature article in Art in Am, 75; Thomas B Hess (auth), feature article in New York Mag, 75. Style & Technique: Realist painting; documentary films and comedies, underground style; photos of places and people. Publ: Illusr, Mediterranean Cities, 55. Dealer: Brooke Alexander Gallery 26 E 78th St New York NY 10021 (photos); Green Mountain Gallery 135 Greene St New York NY 10012 (paintings). Mailing Add: 50 W 29th St New York NY 10001

BURCKHARDT, YVONNE HELEN
See Jacquette, Yvonne Helene

BURDEN, CARTER
COLLECTOR
b Los Angeles, Calif, Aug 25, 41. Study: Harvard Univ; Columbia Univ Law Sch. Pos: Founder & pres, The Studio Mus in Harlem. Mem: Mus Mod Art, New York (exec comt, Jr Coun & acquisitions comt, Int Coun). Collection: Works of the contemporary period, mainly American abstract paintings since 1950. Mailing Add: 1457 Lexington Ave New York NY 10028

BURDEN, CHRIS
CONCEPTUAL ARTIST, SCULPTOR
b Boston, Mass, Apr 11, 46. Study: Pomona Col, BFA, 69; Univ Calif, Irvine, MFA, 71. Work: Long Beach Arts Mus, Calif; Mus Mod Art, New York. Exhib: One-man shows, Riko Mizuno Gallery, Los Angeles, 72, 74 & 75, Ronald Feldman Fine Arts, New York, 74 & 75, Hansen Fuller Gallery, 74 & Alessandra Castelli Gallery, 75; 112 Green St, Video-Performance, New York. Teaching: Instr avant-grande art, LaVerne Col, 73-74; vis artist, Fresno State Univ, 74. Awards: New Talent Award, Los Angeles Co Mus, 73; Nat Endowment for Arts Individual Artist Grant, 74. Bibliog: Sharp & Bear (auth), Church of human energy, Avalanche, summer-fall 73; R Hughs (auth), Young Sadhu, Time Mag, 2/24/75; Jan Butterfield (auth), Through the night softly, Arts Mag, 3/75. Style & Technique: Conceptual artist often using my own personal presence or energy. Media: Live Performance, Broadcast Television. Dealer: Ronald Feldman Fine Arts 33 E 74th St New York NY 10021. Mailing Add: 823 Oceanfront Walk Venice CA 90291

BURFORD, BYRON LESLIE
PAINTER, EDUCATOR
b Jackson, Miss, July 12, 20. Study: Univ Iowa, BFA & MFA. Work: Worcester Art Mus, Mass; Walker Art Ctr, Minneapolis; Nelson/Atkins Gallery, Kansas City, Mo; Sheldon Art Mus, Lincoln, Nebr; High Mus Art, Atlanta, Ga. Exhib: Am Acad Arts Ann, New York, 66 & 72; Venice Biennale, Italy, 68; Bienal Arte Coltejer, Colombia, 70; Kunsthaus, Zurich, Switz, 72; one-man shows, Babcock Galleries, 66, 67, 69 & 75; plus many others. Teaching: Prof painting, Univ Iowa, 47-; prof painting, Univ Minn & Univ Mass, summer 67. Awards: Guggenheim Found Fel, 60 & 61; Ford Found Award, 61, 62 & 64; Nat Inst Arts & Lett Grant, 67. Media: Oil, Acrylic. Dealer: Babcock Galleries 805 Madison Ave New York NY 10021. Mailing Add: 113 S Johnson Iowa City IA 52240

BURFORD, WILLIAM E
ART DEALER, ART ADMINISTRATOR
b Lubbock, Tex, May 16, 36. Study: Tex Tech Univ, BA. Pos: Pres, Tex Art Gallery, Dallas, 76-; vchmn, Tex Comn on the Arts & Humanities, Austin, 76, chmn, 77-78; mem, Dallas City Art Comn, 77- Specialty: Predominately contemporary Western art with Americana, wildlife, landscapes, books, prints, sculpture and porcelains. Mailing Add: Tex Art Gallery 1400 Main St Dallas TX 75202

BURGART, HERBERT JOSEPH
EDUCATOR, ART ADMINISTRATOR
b St Marys, Pa, Apr 27, 32. Study: Calif State Univ, Long Beach, BA, 54; Pa State Univ, MA, 57, PhD, 61. Work: La State Univ Gallery Fine Arts, Baton Rouge; Cohen Mem Mus, Nashville; Univ Ga Fine Arts Mus; Anderson Gallery, Richmond, Va; Pa State Univ Gallery. Teaching: Prof art & chmn dept, La State Univ, 58-60; prof art & chmn dept, Univ Ga, 62-65; prof art & dean, Va Commonwealth Univ, 66-76; pres, Moore Col Art, 76- Mem: Nat Asn Schs Art (secy, 75-); Nat Coun Art Adminr (bd dirs); Southeastern Col Art Conf (pres, 71-73); Nat Art Educ Asn (pres, Southeastern Region, 70-72); La Arts Asn (pres, 58-60). Res: Creative process. Publ: Auth, Art in Higher Education, 61; auth, Creative Art: the Child & the School, 63; auth, The Development of a Visual-Verbal Measure of Creativity, 68; auth, Administration in Higher Education, 73; auth, Computer Assisted Instruction & Research, 74. Mailing Add: 1924 Race St Philadelphia PA 19103

BURGER, W CARL
EDUCATOR, PAINTER
b Baden, Ger, Dec 27, 25; US citizen. Study: New York Univ, BS, MA; Columbia Univ, prof dipl. Work: Am Tel & Tel, Bedminster, NJ; Kean Col of NJ, Union; Trenton Mus, NJ; David Yunich Collection, Bambergers, NJ. Comn: Space Mural (15ft x 30ft; with Meyers Rohowsky), Lockheed Electronics, Woodbridge, NJ, 60. Exhib: Drawings USA, Ball State Univ, 70; Nylander Mus, Caribou, Maine, 72, 74; Small Drawing Show, Philadelphia Mus, 74; Audubon Ann, Nat Acad, New York; Nabisco Galleries, Hanover, NJ, 77; Assoc Artists of NJ, Benedict Gallery, Madison, NJ, 78; Somerset Col, Tri-State Show, Somerville, NJ, 78; Watercolor Show, Holyoke Mus, Mass, 78. Teaching: Prof of design & drawing, Kean Col of NJ, Union, 60- Pos: Set designer, Capemay Playhouse, 54-55. Awards: Jocelyn Mus Award, Ball State Drawing Ann, Jocelyn Mus, 73. Mem: Federated Art Asn of NJ (vpres, 77); Univ Coun on Art Educ, New York; Hunterdon Art Ctr (trustee, 69-72); Audubon Artists (nat acad). Style & Technique: Basically expressionistic, drawings surrealistic. Media: Watercolor, Ink. Dealer: Peter Jones Gallery 57 Main St Flemington NJ 08822. Mailing Add: Beacon Hill Rd Califon NJ 07830

BURGESS, DAVID LOWRY
ENVIRONMENTAL ARTIST
b Philadelphia, Pa, Apr 27, 40. Study: Pa Acad Fine Arts, Philadelphia; Univ Pa; Inst Allende, San Miguel, Mex. Work: Houghton Libr; Harvard Univ, Cambridge, Mass; Mus Fine Arts, Boston; Smithsonian Collection, Washington, DC; Archives, Boston Pub Libr. Exhib: Earth, Air, Fire, Water, The Elements, Mus Fine Arts, Boston, 71 & Drawings of the 19th & 20th Centuries, 72; CAYAC Traveling Exhib, Spain, Peru, Arg & Chile, 72; Multiple Interaction Team, Chicago, San Francisco, Cincinnati & Philadelphia; Art Transition, Mass Inst Technol; Documenta 6, Kassel, Ger. Teaching: Prof visual fundamentals, Mass Col Art, Boston, 70- Pos: Mem, Nat Humanities Faculty, 69-; fel, Ctr Advan Visual Studies, Mass Inst Technol, 71- Awards: Prize, Am Acad Arts & Lett & Nat Inst Arts & Lett, 72; Guggenheim Fel, 73-74; Nat Endowment for the Arts Individual Artist Grant, 77. Bibliog: Baker (auth), articles in Archit Forum, 6/69 & Art Forum, 3/71; Kepes (auth), Art of the Environment, 72; Starpits Waiting for Light Planes, Leonardo, winter 75. Style & Technique: Large cosmic space-time relationships. Publ: Auth, Fragments, 69; auth, Looking and Listening, 72; auth, Memory, Environment and Utopia, 75. Mailing Add: 27 Sherman St Cambridge MA 02138

BURGESS, JOSEPH JAMES, JR
ART DEALER, ART WRITER, PAINTER
b Albany, NY, July 13, 24. Study: Hamilton Col, BA, 47; Yale Univ, MA, 48; Pratt Inst, 52-54; Cranbrook Acad of Art, MFA, 54. Exhib: Recent Drawings USA, Mus of Mod Art, New York, 56; three-man show, Flint Inst of Arts, Mich, 56; Flint Inst of Arts Ann, Mich, 56-65; Artists of the Upper Hudson Show, Albany Inst of Hist & Art, NY, 57; one-man show, Albany Inst of Hist & Art, NY, 58; Ball State Teachers Col Show, 58; Drawing Nat, Palace of the Legion of Honor, San Francisco, 59; two-person show, DeWaters Art Ctr, Flint, Mich, 64; Calif Design Ten Show, Pasadena Art Mus, 68; First Ann City of Angels Int Exhib of Photog, 74. Teaching: Asst prof fine arts & head dept, St Lawrence Univ, Canton, NY, 54-55; art instr, chmn dept & dir, DeWaters Art Ctr, Flint Community Jr Col, 56-65; asst prof design, Ariz State Univ, Tempe, 65-66. Pos: Dir, Blair Galleries, Ltd, Santa Fe, NMex, 76- Style & Technique: Painter and designer, latest work involves painted constructions in acrylic, wood and metal. Media: Acrylic, Oil; Wood. Specialty: Painting, sculpture and graphics. Publ: Auth, Three Chinese poems, translations from T'ang Dynasty poets, winter 61-62, Four Chinese poems, translations from T'ang poetry, fall 61 & Some thoughts on non-communication in the arts, spring 63, Mich Voices; auth, A random poem, translation from the T'ang Dynasty poet Wang Wei, 10/12/73, A shining legend, 9/10/74, Asia's first iron-clad warship, 5/19/75 & The making of a gentleman, 7/3/75, Christian Sci Monitor. Dealer: Blair Galleries Ltd PO Box 1931 Santa Fe NM 87501. Mailing Add: 140 Cedar St Santa Fe NM 87501

BURGGRAF, RAY LOWELL
PAINTER, EDUCATOR
b Mt Gilead, Ohio, July 26, 38. Study: Ashland Col, BS, 61; Cleveland Inst Art, BFA, 68; Univ Calif, Berkeley, MA, 69, MFA, 70. Work: Drawing, Mint Mus Art, Charlotte, NC, 71; drawing, De Kalb Col, Clarkston, Ga, 71. Exhib: Artists of the Southeast & Texas, Isaac Delgado Mus Art, New Orleans, 71; 16th Nat Sun Carnival Art Exhib, El Paso Mus Art, Tex, 71; 12th Ann Calgary Graphics Exhib, Alta Col Art, 72; 13th Dixie Ann, Montgomery Mus Fine Arts, Ala, 72; 61st Ann Exhib, Laguna Gloria Art Mus, Austin, Tex, 72. Teaching: Asst prof painting & drawing, Fla State Univ, 70- Awards: Purchase Award, Mint Mus Art, 71; First Nat Bank Award, Mobile Art Patrons League, Ala, 71; Award, Ball State Univ, Muncie, Ind, 72. Mem: Col Art Asn Am. Media: Acrylic. Mailing Add: 1507 Marion Ave Tallahassee FL 32303

BURGUES, IRVING CARL
SCULPTOR, PAINTER
b Austria, Oct 16, 06; US citizen. Study: Vienna Arts Sch, BA(fine arts), 26; Brooklyn Mus; Sch of Indust Fine Arts, Newark, NJ; sculpture apprentice to Mollet, Paris; Art Students' League; Mod Sch of Art, New York. Work: White House Mus; Vatican; Kremlin; Smithsonian Inst, Washington, DC; Brooklyn Mus. Comn: New Testament mural, Rio de Janeiro, 30; Big Horn Sheep sculpture, State of Nev, 73; Am Wild Goat, State of Mont, 76. Exhib: Brooklyn Mus, NY, 35; Indianapolis Mus, 70; Mus of Sci & Indust, Chicago, 72; NJ State Mus, 74; Smithsonian Inst, 76. Mem: Artists Equity. Style & Technique: Naturalist sculptor, known for subjects of animals, birds and flowers. Mailing Add: 183 Spruce St Lakewood NJ 08701

BURGY, (DONALD THOMAS)
CONCEPTUAL ARTIST
b New York, NY, Aug 3, 37. Study: Mass Col Art, BFA, 59; Rutgers Univ, MFA, 63. Work: Rutgers Univ Collection, New Brunswick, NJ; Addison Gallery Am Art, Andover, Mass; Salem State Col, Mass. Comn: Hello Day (city-wide art work), Salem State Col, 71; Mirror (mural), Subway Sta, City of Boston, 72. Exhib: Concept Art, Stadtisches Mus, Lever Kusen, Ger, 69; Software, Jewish Mus, New York, 70; Information, Mus Mod Art, New York, 70; Elements, Mus Fine Arts, Boston, 71; Colombia Bienal, SAm, 72. Teaching: Instr, Bradford Col, 66; Mass Col Art, 72; Nat Humanities Fac, 72. Bibliog: Schley (auth), Software (film), Jewish Mus, 69-70; Burnham (auth), Introduction to Art ideas for the year 4000, 70; Ursula Meyer (auth), article in Conceptual art. Publ: Auth, Check-up, Art in Am, 70; auth, Art ideas for the year 4000, 70; auth, Context completion ideas, Centro Communication y Arte, Buenos Aires, 71 & Schuring Galerie, Krefeld, Ger, 71. Mailing Add: 294 S Main St Bradford MA 01830

BURK, ANNA DARLENE
ART DEALER
Study: Seminar with Cal Goodman. Pos: Owner-dir, The Burk Gal'ry, Boulder City, Nev, 72- Specialty: Contemporary Western art. Mailing Add: Box 246 400 Nevada Hwy Boulder City NV 89005

BURKE, DANIEL V
PAINTER, EDUCATOR
b Erie, Pa, Apr 21, 42. Study: Columbus Col Art & Design, 60-62; Mercyhurst Col, BA(art), 69; Edinboro State Col, MEd(art), 72; MacDowell Colony, Peterborough, NH, 70 & 73. Work: Del Mar Col Art Gallery, Corpus Christi; Laguna Gloria Art Mus, Austin, Tex; Southern Utah State Col; IBM Corp, Austin; NC Nat Bank, Boone; and others. Exhib: 61st through 64th Ann Tex Fine Arts Asn Exhibs, Austin, 72-75; 4th Greater New Orleans Int, 74; Appalachian Nat Drawing Competition, Boone; 18th Nat Chautauqua Art Asn Show, NY, 75; Drawings USA, Minn Mus Art, St Paul, 75; and others. Teaching: assoc prof art, Mercyhurst Col, 69- Awards: Award of Excellence, Mainstreams, Marietta Col Ann Int, 70; Purchase Awards, 62nd & 63rd Tex Fine Arts Asn Exhib, 73-74; Best of Show, Greater New Orleans Int, 74; Purchase Award, Appalachian Nat Drawing Competition, 75; Chautauqua Art Asn Award, 18th Nat Show, 75. Mem: Northwestern Pa Artists Asn (co-exec chmn, 75-78). Style & Technique: Sharp focus non-objective paintings. Media: Acrylic. Mailing Add: 223 E Sixth St Erie PA 16507

BURKE, E AINSLIE
PAINTER, EDUCATOR
b Omaha, Nebr, Jan 26, 22. Study: Md Inst Fine Arts; McCoy Col, Johns Hopkins Univ; Inst Allende, San Miguel, Mex; Art Students League; Fulbright fel, 57-58. Work: Springfield Mus, Mass; Nat Broadcasting Corp, 76; Everson Mus, Syracuse, NY, 77; Munson-Williams-Proctor Inst, Utica, NY; Lowe Art Gallery, Syracuse Univ. Exhib: 17th Biennial Int Exhib, Brooklyn Mus, NY; one-man shows, Kraushaar Galleries, New York, 60-77, Oxford Gallery, Rochester, NY, 77 & Stonington Gallery, Maine, 77; Pa Acad Fine Arts Ann, Philadelphia, 69; Finger Lake Exhib, Rochester Mem Gallery, NY, 69 & 71-73; Munson-Williams-Proctor Inst Ann, 70-71 & 74-76. Teaching: Vis artist, Exeter Acad, 64-; vis artist, Syracuse Univ Sch Art, 62-64, prof drawing & painting, 64-77; chmn studio arts dept, Syracuse Univ Col Visual & Performing Arts, 70-77. Awards: Woodstock Found Award, 57; Paul Puzinas Mem Award, Nat Acad Design, 73; Creative Artists Pub Serv Grant in Painting, 77. Mem: Am Asn Univ Prof; life mem Art Students League; Woodstock Artists Asn (pres, 60-62); Deer Isle Artists Asn. Dealer: Kraushaar Galleries 1055 Madison Ave New York NY 10028. Mailing Add: RD 1 Eldredge Rd Manlius NY 13104

BURKE, JAMES DONALD
ART HISTORIAN, CURATOR
b Salem, Ore, Feb 22, 39. Study: Brown Univ, BA, 61; Univ Pa, MA, 67; Harvard Univ, PhD, 72. Collections Arranged: Charles Meryon, 74-75; plus others. Teaching: Mem fac, Yale Univ, 72- Pos: Cur, Allen Art Mus, Oberlin Col, 71-72; cur drawings & prints, Art Gallery, Yale Univ, 72- Awards: Fulbright-Hays Fel, Holland, 68-69; Mus Fel, Nat Endowment for Arts, 73. Mem: Am Asn Mus; Col Art Asn. Res: 17th century Dutch art. Publ: Auth, Charles Meryon: Prints & Drawings, 74; Jan Both: Paintings, Drawings & Prints, 75; plus others. Mailing Add: Yale Univ Art Gallery New Haven CT 06520

BURKERT, ROBERT RANDALL
PAINTER, PRINTMAKER
b Racine, Wis, Aug 20, 30. Study: Wustum Art Ctr, Racine; Univ Wis-Madison, with John Wilde & Alfred Sessier, 48-55; Jacques Desjobert Atelier, Paris, France, summer 70. Work: Metrop Mus Art, New York; Mus Fine Arts, Boston; Nat Collection Fine Arts, Washington, DC; Tate Gallery, London; Fogg Mus, Harvard Univ; plus others. Comn: Outdoor wall (with Derse Outdoor Advert), Mortgage Guarantee Ins Co, 72. Exhib: Recent Drawings, USA Exhib, Mus Mod Art, New York, 56; Presentation Artist, Boston Printmakers, 62; Butler Art Inst Ann, 65; New Talent Graphics Show, Assoc Am Artists, New York, 66; Univ Ill Graphics Invitational, Champaign-Urbana, 70; Okla Printmakers, 77. Teaching: Prof graphics & drawing, Univ Wis-Milwaukee, 56- Bibliog: James Schineller (auth), Art: Search and Self Discovery, Int Textbook Co, 69; Ross & Romano (auth), The Complete Printmaker, Macmillan Free Press, 72; Fritz Eichenberg (auth), Art of the Print, Abrams, 76; plus others. Style & Technique: Representational imagery drawing with illusion, atmosphere, qualities of ephemeral light. Dealer: Associated American Artists 605 Fifth Ave New York NY 10022; Bradley Galleries 2565 N Downer Ave Milwaukee WI 53211. Mailing Add: 3228 N Marietta Ave Milwaukee WI 53211

BURKHARDT, HANS GUSTAV
PAINTER, COLLECTOR
b Basel, Switz, Dec 20, 04; US citizen. Study: Cooper Union, 25-28; Grand Cent Sch Art, 28-29; Arshile Gorky Studio, 29-36. Work: Los Angeles Co Mus Art, Los Angeles; Joslyn Art Mus, Omaha, Nebr; Hirshhorn Mus, Washington, DC; Mod Mus, Stockholm, Sweden; Oakland Mus, Calif. Exhib: American Painting Today, Metrop Mus Art, New York, 50; 46th Ann, Pa Acad Fine Arts, 51; Chicago Art Inst Ann, 52; Art in the Twentieth Century, San Francisco Mus, 55; Weihnachts Ausstellung, Kunsthalle, Basel, 64; Calif State Univ, Northridge, 73; Santa Barbara Mus of Art, Calif, 76. Teaching: Prof painting & drawing, Univ Southern Calif, 59-60; asst prof painting & drawing, Univ Calif, Los Angeles, 61-63; assoc prof painting & drawing, Calif State Univ, Northridge, 63-73, emer prof, 73- Awards: Award for Oil, Jr Art Coun, Los Angeles Co Mus Art, 57; Ala Story Purchase Award for Oil, Santa Barbara Mus Art, 58; First Purchase Award for Oil, Howard Ahmanson, 61. Bibliog: Henry Seldis (auth), Abstractionist defends his sensitive craft, Los Angeles Times, 4/23/61, Artist in His Studio, 9/10/61 & Thirty-Year Retrospective, 4/21/62, KHJ-TV, Los Angeles. Mem: Phi Kappa Phi; Contemp Art Inst, Los Angeles; Long Beach Mus Art. Style & Technique: Abstract, using collage and heavy paint. Media: Oil, Pastel, Linocut. Collection: Arnoldo Pomadoro sculptures; deKooning watercolors and lithographs; numerous works of Mark Tobeys; also prints by Picasso, Kollwitz, Tamayo, Rapael Sawyer, Roualt and many others; large collection of Gorky oils and drawings. Publ: Contribr, Ray Bradbury, auth, God Dead? Then Man Is Slain, 77. Mailing Add: 1914 Jewett Dr Los Angeles CA 90046

BURKO, DIANE
PAINTER, EDUCATOR
b Brooklyn, NY, Sept 24, 45. Study: Skidmore Col, BS, 66; Univ Pa Grad Sch Fine Arts, MFA, 69; Brooklyn Mus; Fleischer Art Mem. Work: Philadelphia Mus Art; De Cordova Mus, Lincoln, Mass. Reading Pub Mus; in pvt collections of AT&T, First Pa Bank, FMC Corp, Prudential Life Assurance Co; Continental Bank & others. Exhib: One-person shows, Philadelphia Art Alliance, 73, Marian Locks Gallery, Philadelphia, 76 & Ariz State Univ, 77; Objects and..., Univ Mass, Amherst, 73; Woman's Work-1974, Philadelphia Civic Ctr Mus, 74; Year of the Woman-1975, Bronx Mus Arts, 75; Contemp Reflections, Aldrich Mus of Contemp Art, Ridgefield, Conn, 77; New Talent, Genesis Galleries, New York, 77. Teaching: Asst prof drawing, painting & design, Philadelphia Community Col, 69- Pos: Pres & founder, Philadelphia Focuses on Women in Visual Arts, 73- Awards: Allentown Art Mus Ann Award, 71 & 72; Del Valley Citizen's Coun for Clean Air Award & Scott Paper Co Award, Earth Art Exhib, Philadelphia Civic Ctr Mus, 73. Bibliog: Lenore Malen (auth), Diane Burko, Arts Mag, 76; Cindy Nemser (auth), interview with Diane Burko, Feminist Art J, 77; Gary Grissom (auth), Diane Burko at Marian Locks, Art in Am, 77. Mem: Col Art Asn Am; Philadelphia Print Club; Women's Caucus for Art (secy nat adv bd, 75-). Style & Technique: Landscapes mostly of mountains and mountain ranges, currently of the Southwest and Grand Canyon, usually large scale. Media: Oil, Acrylics. Dealer: Marian Locks 1524 Walnut St Philadelphia PA 19102; Genesis Galleries, Ltd 41 E 57th St New York NY 10022. Mailing Add: 510 S 46th St Philadelphia PA 19143

BURNETT, CALVIN
GRAPHIC ARTIST, ILLUSTRATOR
b Cambridge, Mass, July 18, 21. Study: Mass Col Art, BFA & BS(educ); Sch Boston Mus Fine Arts; Boston Univ, MFA. Work: Boston Mus Fine Arts, Mass; Oakland Mus, Calif; Fogg Art Mus, Harvard Univ; Wiggins Collection, Boston Pub Libr; Wellesley Col; plus others. Teaching: Prof art, Mass Col Art, 56- Awards: Second Award, Assoc Am Artists, 59; First Award for Printmaking, Boston Printmakers, 64; First Award for Painting, Atlanta Univ Ann, 66. Bibliog: Della Taylor (auth), Skill adds to communication, Charleston Gazette, 66; M Holsen (auth), Introducing some Boston printmakers, The Connoisseur, London, 67; V E Atkinson (auth), Black Dimensions in Contemporary American Art, New Am Libr, 71. Style & Technique: Non-objective fine art, figurative illustration, commercial art. Media: Oil. Publ: Auth-designer, Objective Drawing Techniques, Van Nostrand Reinhold, 66; also auth & illusr of children's bks. Mailing Add: 87 Fisher St Medway MA 02053

BURNETT, DAVID GRANT
ART HISTORIAN, ART CRITIC
b Lincoln, Eng, Oct 1, 40; Can citizen. Study: Birkbeck Col, Univ London, BA, 65; Courtauld Inst of Art, MA, 67, with Sir Anthony Blunt & M Kitson, PhD, 73, under M Kitson. Pos: Lectr art hist, Univ Bristol, Eng, 67-70; assoc prof art hist, Carleton Univ, 70- Mem: Fel Royal Soc of Arts; Univ Art Asn of Can. Res: The art of Paul Klee; landscape painting. Publ: Auth, The Landscapes of Aelbert Cuyp, Apollo, 69; auth, Donald Judd, 75 & Quebec 75, 76, Artscanada; auth, Paul Klee and the Romantic Landscape, Art J, 77; auth, Paul Klee as Senecio: Self Portraits 1908-22, Art Int, 12/77. Mailing Add: Dept of Art Hist Carleton Univ Ottawa ON K1S 5B6 Can

BURNETT, PATRICIA HILL
PAINTER, SCULPTOR
b Brooklyn, NY. Study: Univ Toledo; Goucher Col; Corcoran Art Sch; Soc Arts & Crafts; Inst Allende, Mex; Wayne State Univ; Truro Sch Art; also with John Carroll, Sarkis Sarkisian, Wallace Bassford, Walter Midener & Seong Moy. Work: Detroit Inst Arts, Mich; Bloomfield Art Asn, Mich; Wayne State Univ; Wooster Col; Ford Motor Co Collection, Detroit. Comn: Oil portrait, Joyce Carol Oates, Windsor, Ont, 72, Indira Ghandi, Prime Minister, New Delhi, India, 73, Roman Gribbs, Mayor Detroit, 73, Hiram Walker, Windsor, 74 & Benson Ford, Ford Motor Co, Detroit, 75; plus many pvt comn. Exhib: Michigan Artists Show, Detroit Inst Arts, 67; Show of Paintings, Palazzo Pruili Gallery, Venice, Italy, 71; Butler Mus Nat Art Show, Youngstown, Ohio, 72; Int Art Show, Windsor, Ont, 73; Ms & Masters, Midland Ctr Arts, Midland, Mich, 75; Weisbaden, Ger, 76; one-person show, Provincetown, Mass, 77; San Diego, Calif, 78. Teaching: Teacher, painting techniques, Univ Mich Exten Courses; teacher sculpture techniques, Grosse Pointe War Mem. Pos: Mem bd dirs, Scarab Club, 65-67; mem bd dirs, Founders Soc, Activities Comt, Detroit Inst Arts, 66-78. Awards: First Prize Sculpture, Scarab Club, 66, First Prize in Painting, 77; First Prize Painting, Figure Painting Show, Boston, 69; First Prize, Western Art Show, Albuquerque, NMex, 74. Bibliog: Marg Levin (auth), Taking women's word to Russia, Detroiter Mag, 73; Christine Hinz (auth), Detroit artist: feminist home-maker and painter, Daily News, Midland, Mich, 75; Have women artists been brushed aside? & Why are there no great women painters?, J Milano, Italy, 77. Mem: Mich Acad Arts; Detroit Soc Women Painters & Sculptors; Ibex Club (pres, 50-51); Sculptors Guild Birmingham. Style & Technique: Romantic realism; alla-prima method; sculpture is impressionistic realism. Media: Oil on Canvas; Wax for Casting in Bronze & Clay. Res: Lost women painters, 1400 AD to the present and reproducing their work on slides. Publ: Contribr, Painting the Female Figure, Bassford, Watson-Guptill Founders Gallery, 73; auth, Will NOW and the Junior League ever meet?, Jr League Mag, 73; auth, Have women artists been brushed aside?, Women in the Arts Mag, 75; The winds of change are blowing, Zonta Mag, Int, 75; Women today in Russia, Israel, India & Thailand, PHP Int Mag, Japan, 75. Dealer: Portraits Inc Gallery 41 E 57th St New York NY 10022; Rubiner Gallery 621 S Washington Royal Oak MI 48053. Mailing Add: 18261 Hamilton Rd Detroit MI 48203

BURNETT, W C, JR
ART CRITIC
b East Point, Ga, May 22, 28. Study: Univ Ga, BFA(painting). Pos: Art ed & art critic, Sarasota Herald Tribune, 61-69 & Atlanta Journal, 69- Mailing Add: 144 Ponce de Leon Ct Decatur GA 30030

BURNHAM, ELIZABETH LOUESE
MUSEUM REGISTRAR, ART ADMINISTRATOR
b La Jolla, Calif. Study: Scripps Col, Claremont, Calif, BA; Chouinard Art Inst, Los Angeles; Asian Conserv Lab, New York. Collections Arranged: Practical arrangements (packing, shipping, insurance, temporary storage, condition reporting, records) in the US and abroad for traveling exhibitions including, The Machine as seen at the End of the Mechanical Age, 69, Frank Stella, 70, A Salute to Alexander Calder, 70 & Charles Rennie Mackintosh, 75, Mus Mod Art, New York & The Royal Pavilion at Brighton, Cooper-Hewitt Mus, New York, 77. Teaching: Coord yearly regist training class, NJ State Coun for the Arts Mus Training Prog, Mus of Mod Art, 69-72. Pos: Sr cataloger, Mus Mod Art, New York, 53-57, assoc registr, 59-76; registr, Yale Univ Art Gallery, New Haven, Conn, 57-59; registr, Cooper-Hewitt Mus, Smithsonian Inst, New York, 76- Mem: Am Asn Mus; Col Art Asn. Publ: Co-dir with Rowlison, E, Nat Gallery of Victoria, Melbourne, Australia, Handling Works of Art (3/4in video tape & 16mm film), Mus Mod Art, 75; registr assoc, (with Hoachlander, M), Development of Materials & Methods for the Training & Education of Museum Registrars, City Univ of New York, NEA grant research proj report, (in prep), 78; contribr, Cooper-Hewitt Newsletter, Vol 1, No 2, winter 77-78; contribr, Museum Registration Methods, Dudley & Wilkinson (auths), Am Asn Mus, 3rd rev, 78. Mailing Add: 30 W 60th St Apt 4X New York NY 10023

BURNHAM, JACK WESLEY
ART CRITIC, ART ADMINISTRATOR
b New York, NY, Nov 13, 31. Study: Boston Mus Sch, 53-54 & 56-57; Wentworth Inst, Boston, AE, 56; Sch of Art & Archit, Yale Univ, BFA, 59, MFA(sculpture), 61. Teaching: Prof art & chmn art dept, Northwestern Univ, 62-; Dana prof of fine arts, Colgate Univ, Hamilton, NY, 75-76. Pos: Contrib ed, Artforum Mag, 71-72; assoc ed, Arts Mag, 72-76; contrib ed, New Art Examr, 74- Awards: Guggenheim fel, Guggenheim Found, 73; Critics Award, Chicago Art Awards, 77. Bibliog: Albert Elsen (auth), Beyond Modern Sculpture, Artforum, 5/69; Tom Conley (auth), The Radicality of Modern Art, Diacritics, Spring 73; R Blazer (auth), Blazer on Burnham—Great Western Salt Works, Criteria, 11/74. Res: Contemporary criticism, art semiotics; the writings and art of Marcel Duchamp. Publ: Auth, Beyond Modern Sculpture, Braziller, 68; auth, Art in the Marcusean Analysis (monogr), Pa State Univ Press, 69; auth, The Structure of Art, 71 & Great Western Saltworks, 74, Braziller; co-auth, Hans Haacke: Framing and Being Framed, NY Univ Press, 75. Mailing Add: 2150 Sherman Ave Apt 3C Evanston IL 60201

BURNHAM, LEE
SCULPTOR, PAINTER
b New York, NY, Feb 16. 26. Study: Cranbrook Acad Art, 43-45, sculpture with Carl Milles; Art Students League, 46-47, sculpture with W Zorach; Syracuse Univ, 47-51, sculpture with Ivan Mestrovic; Porta Romano Scuola, Firenze, Italy, 51-52; Reinhold Sch Art, Baltimore, Md, with Sidney Waugh & Cecil Howard. Work: Bronze Head of Christ, Inst Cath, Paris; bronze crucifix, Visitation Convent, St Paul, Minn; bronze head, Daytona Hist Soc, Fla; bronze statue, Dixie Plantation, Quitman, Ga. Comn: Bronze bust of Pierre Henry, comn by family & Cath Univ Louvaine; head of Marjorie Kinnen Rawlings, comn by Norton Baskin; stations, appointments & sculpture, St Joseph's Cath Church, Zephyrhills, Fla, 60; stone figure, Sch Ment Retarded, Downington, Pa, 65; ceramic tile, St Patrick-St Joseph Chapels, 66. Exhib: One-man shows, Firenze, Italy 51 & St Augustine, Fla, 58; Gallerie St Placide, Paris, 59; Bicentennial Medal Design Competition, Franklin Mint, 72. Awards: Mus Mod Art Award, 40; Watercolor Award, Fla Fedn Art, 57. Mem: Nat Sculpture Soc. Media: Bronze, Stone, Ceramics, Wood, Synthetics. Mailing Add: Box 388 Hawthorne FL 32640

BURNS, G JOAN
ART LIBRARIAN
b Belleville, NJ, Mar 6, 18. Study: Newark State Col, BA(art educ), 39; Columbia Univ, 42-44; Rutgers State Univ, MLS, 63. Pos: Draftswoman, Archit Forum, 42-45; free-lance archit illusr, Progressive Archit, Archit Forum, Holiday, plus others, 45-57; principal art librn, Newark Pub Libr, 68-; reviewer art titles, Libr J, 70-75 & Am Reference Bks Ann, 72- Mem: Art Libr Soc/NAm; Victorian Soc in Am. Interest: Twentieth century architectural history and design. Publ: Illusr, Forms & Functions of 20th Century Architecture, Columbia Univ Press, 52. Mailing Add: 5 Washington St Newark NJ 07101

BURNS, JEROME
PAINTER
b Brooklyn, NY, Mar 26, 19. Study: Art Students League, 36-39; Hans Hofmann Art Sch, New York, 42; Brooklyn Mus Art Sch, 49. Work: Okla Mus; C W Post Col Mus, Long Island Univ. Exhib: Nat Acad Exhib, New York, 63; Audubon Artists Exhib, New York, 64; Am Watercolor Soc, New York, 65; Allied Artists of Am, New York, 66; Nat Soc Painters in Casein & Acrylic, New York, 66- Teaching: Instr painting, Brooklyn Mus Art Sch, 60-61. Pos: Pres, Brownstone Gallery Inc, Brooklyn, 69- Awards: Samuel F B Morse Medal, Am Nat Acad, 63; Tesser Mem Award, Audubon Artists, 64; Dir Award, Nat Soc Painters in Casein & Acrylic, 66. Mem: Artists Equity Asn (bd dirs, 73-74); MacDowell Colony Fels; Nat Soc Painters in Casein & Acrylic; Appraisers Asn of Am. Media: Casein, Acrylic. Mailing Add: 248 Garfield Pl Brooklyn NY 11215

BURNS, JOSEPHINE
PAINTER
b Llandudno, North Wales, July 2, 17. Study: Cooper Union Art Sch, grad, 39, BFA, 76; Art Students League, 49 & 50. Work: C W Post Col Mus, Long Island Univ; Okla Mus Art, Oklahoma City. Exhib: Brooklyn & Long Island Artists, Brooklyn Mus, 58; Nat Arts Club, New York, 58, 63 & 73; Audubon Artists, New York, 61; Nat Acad Design, 64; one-woman show, Alonzo Gallery, New York, 66. Pos: Co-dir, Hicks Street Gallery, Brooklyn, 58-63; assoc-dir, Brownstone Gallery, Brooklyn, 69- Awards: Resident Fel, MacDowell Colony, 60, 62, 64, 65 & 68; Resident Fel, Yaddo, Saratoga Springs, NY, 61. Mem: Artists Equity Asn, New York; MacDowell Colony Fels. Mailing Add: 248 Garfield Pl Brooklyn NY 11215

BURNS, PAUL CALLAN
PAINTER, INSTRUCTOR
b Pittsburgh, Pa. Study: Pa Mus Sch of Art, Philadelphia; Philadelphia Acad of Fine Art; Cape Cod Sch of Art, Provincetown, Mass. Work: Clearing House, New York; Supreme Court, NJ; John R Wanamaker Collection, Philadelphia; Permanent Collection of the Wilmington Acad of Fine Arts, Del; Permanent Collection of the Bergen Community Mus, Paramus, NJ. Comn: Flower Mart-France (landscape), comn by John R Wanamaker, Philadelphia, 65; Justice Weintraub (portrait), NJ Bar Asn, Trenton, 74; Rockport Street (landscape), comn by John Jobs, Ridgewood, NJ, 74; Bishop Gibson (portrait, with Portraits Inc, New York), Diocese of Richmond, Va, 75; Dean Alvin Kernan (portrait, with Portraits Inc, New York), Princeton Col, NJ, 77. Exhib: John Herron Art Mus, Ind, 34; Carnegie Art Mus, Pittsburgh, 35; Corcoran Art Gallery, Washington, DC, 36; Acad of Fine Arts, Philadelphia, 40; Portrait Soc of Ireland, Dublin, 64; Portraits Inc, New York, 65-; Nat Acad of Design, New York, 77; one-man shows, Fairleigh Dickinson Col, Teaneck, NJ, 68, William Edwards Col, Teaneck, NJ, 69, Bergen Community Mus, Paramus, NJ, 72, Omaha Mus, Nebr, 76 & M & L Gallery of Fine Arts, New York, 76. Teaching: Prof portrait painting & life-figure drawing, Ridgewood Art Asn, NJ, 63- Awards: Gold Medal, Nat Arts Club Exhib, New York, 69; Puzinas Award, Allied Artists of America Exhib, Nat Acad of Design, New York, 72; Newington Award, Hudson Valley Art Asn Exhib, New York, 73. Bibliog: Susan Meyer (auth), Water Color Page, 73 & Joe Singer (auth), Painting Womans Portraits, 77, Watson-Guptill; Radio interview, KSIL Radio, Silver City, NMex, 77. Mem: Am Watercolor Soc (dir, 76-79); Artists Fel (trustee, 75-78); Allied Artists of Am (bd mem, 76-77); Hudson Valley Art Asn (bd mem, 76-77); Ridgewood Art Asn (bd mem, 76-77). Style & Technique: Impressionistic realism, traditional manner; free oil (direct) medium and watercolor medium. Media: Oil, Watercolor. Publ: Contribr, Painting Portraits of Men, Watson-Guptill, 77. Dealer: Grand Cent Art Galleries Biltmore Hotel 44th & Madison Ave New York NY 10017;

Portraits Inc 41 E 57th St New York NY 10022. Mailing Add: 248 Kenilworth Rd Ridgewood NJ 07450

BURNS, SHEILA
PAINTER, LECTURER
b Scotland; US citizen. Study: Detroit Soc Arts & Crafts; Wayne State Univ, BA. Work: Grand Rapids Mus, Mich; Wayne State Univ; Founders Soc Gallery Loan Collection, Detroit Inst Art. Comn: Mag cover & illusr, Detroit Free Press; Children's Hosp Mich; plus many pvt comns. Exhib: Mich Biennial Exhib Painters & Printmakers, Grand Rapids Mus; Four Winds Gallery, Kalamazoo; Mich Acad Sci, Art & Lett & Mich Regional Exhib, Univ Mich; Blue Water Int Exhib, US & Can, 74 & 75; Eastern Mich Int, 75; plus many others. Awards: Purchase Award, Mich Biennial Painters & Printmakers, Grand Rapids Mus; Awards, Scarab Club Detroit; Blue Water Int Exhib, Mich Acad Sci, Arts & Lett, 73 & Mich Watercolor Soc. Mem: Am Asn Prof Artists. Style & Technique: Realistic and semi-abstract landscapes and children; literary and historic collages. Media: Watercolor, Oil, Acrylic. Mailing Add: 23036 Ardmore Park St Clair Shores MI 48081

BURNS, SID
SCULPTOR, COLLECTOR
b Tulsa, Okla, May 10, 16. Study: Self-taught. Work: Thomas Gilcrease Inst Am Hist & Art, Tulsa; Favell Mus-Gallery, Klamath Falls, Ore. Exhib: J H Matthews Co Traveling Show of Western Bronze Sculptures, 70-73; Ann Death Valley 49ers Western Art Show, Calif, 71-77; 1st Ann George Phippen Mem Western Art Show, Prescott, Ariz, 75; Nebraskaland Days Exhib, 75 & 76; Bicentennial Sect, Freedom Train, 76. Pos: Co-chmn art div, Ann Death Valley 49ers Invitational Western Art Show, 71-77. Awards: Artist's Artist Award & First Prize, Bronze Div, Ann Death Valley 49ers Western Art Show, 71, 74 & 77; Best of Show, 1st Ann George Phippen Mem Western Art Show, 75. Mem: Laguna Beach Art Asn; Laguna Beach Festival of Arts Asn; Thomas Gilcrease Inst Am Hist & Art Found; Nat Cowboy Hall of Fame Found. Style & Technique: Realistic bronze sculptures easily recognized by their feeling of continuing motion; detailed Western subjects. Media: Bronze. Collection: Western paintings, sculptures and artifacts. Mailing Add: 101A E Palm Lane Phoenix AZ 85004

BURNS, STAN
PAINTER, SCULPTOR
b Suitersville, Pa. Study: Wayne State Univ, BA & MA; Detroit Soc Arts & Crafts, with Reginald Bennett, Sarkis & Mary Chase Stratton; Pewabic Pottery. Work: Wayne State Univ; Ford Motor Co; Founders Gallery Loan Collection, Detroit Art Inst. Comn: Numerous pvt comns. Exhib: Mich Acad Sci, Art & Lett & Mich Regional Exhib, Univ Mich; Mich Artists Exhib, Detroit Inst Art; Mich Watercolor Soc; Blue Water Int Exhib, 73 & 74; Eastern Mich Int, 75; plus many one-man shows. Awards: Best of Show Award, Scarab Club, Detroit; Board of Directors' Award, Scarab Gold Medal Show, Detroit; Blue Water Int Exhib, Port Huron Mus, Mich. Mem: Nat Asn Prof Artists; Scarab Club. Style & Technique: Romantic theme, semi-abstract to realistic land and seascapes, figures and portraits. Media: Oil, Acrylic, Silver Point; Lost Wax Bronze Sculpture. Mailing Add: 23036 Ardmore Park St Clair Shores MI 48081

BURNSIDE, KATHERINE TALBOTT
PAINTER
b Ft Worth, Tex. Study: Colorado Springs Fine Art Ctr; Claremont Col; Ohio Univ; also with Henry Lee McFee, Maurice Sterne, Josef Albers, Victor Candell & Leo Manso. Work: Arts & Humanities WVa Collection; IBM Corp Collection; Charleston Art Gallery, WVa; Huntington Gallery, WVa; WVa Univ. Exhib: Dayton Art Inst, Ohio, 62; Nine Artists of WVa Traveling Show, 63; Four Arts, Palm Beach, Fla, 65; Provincetown Art Asn, Mass, 73; WVa Univ Ctr, 74; Sci & Cult Ctr, Charleston, WVa, 77. Awards: Graphics & Drawings Award, Charleston Art Gallery, 70; Purchase Award, Allied Artists WVa, 72 & Nat Graphic & Drawing Show, Provincetown Art Asn, 76; Best in Show, WVa Invitational, 77. Mem: Allied Artists WVa; Provincetown Art Asn; The Group, Provincetown; Parkersburg Art Ctr (bd mem); Ohio Valley Arts & Lett Soc (bd mem). Media: Oil, Acrylic. Mailing Add: 922 Juliana St Parkersburg WV 26101

BURNSIDE, WESLEY M
ART HISTORIAN, PAINTER
b Mt Pleasant, Utah, Nov 6, 18. Study: Brigham Young Univ, BS, 41, MS, 49; Art Inst Chicago, 46; Art Students League, with Kenneth H Miller & Reginald Marsh, 49; Univ Utah, summers 50-54; Univ Calif, Los Angeles, 55-58; Ohio State Univ, PhD, 70. Work: Brigham Young Univ; Orem City Collection; Dixie Col Collection; Idaho State Univ Collection. Teaching: Instr art & art hist, Idaho State Col, 48-55; prof art hist, Brigham Young Univ, 58- Pos: Dir art acquisitions, Brigham Young Univ, 71- Mem: Nat Soc Lit & Arts. Style & Technique: Romantic realism. Media: Watercolor, Oil. Res: Maynard Dixon; Mormon architecture; Ebon Comins, artist of the Indians. Collection: Americana; Hudson River School & Western art. Publ: Auth, Maynard Dixon Artist of the West, Brigham Young Univ, 74. Mailing Add: 605 Sagewood Provo UT 84601

BUROS, LUELLA
PAINTER, DESIGNER
b Canby, Minn. Study: Teachers Col, Columbia Univ, 29-30 & 33-34; Rutgers Univ, 31-32; Ohio State Univ, 34-35. Work: Newark Mus, NJ; Montclair Art Mus, NJ; City of Cape May, NJ. Exhib: Five Watercolor & Print Exhibs, Pa Acad Fine Arts, Philadelphia, 37-47; Contemp Exhib Painting & Sculpture, Golden Gate Int Expos, San Francisco, Calif, 39; Corcoran Biennial Art, Corcoran Gallery Art, Washington, DC, 39, 43 & 45; Four Int Exhibs of Watercolors, Art Inst Chicago, 40-43; Contemp Am Art Exhib, Artists for Victory, Metrop Mus Art, New York, 43. Awards: Hon Mention in Watercolor, Springfield Art League, 41; First Prize in Watercolor, Contemp Va Oil & Watercolor Exhib, Norfolk Mus Arts & Sci, 44-45; Medal of Honor in Oil, Nat Asn Women Artists, Nat Acad, 53. Mem: NJ Watercolor Soc; Assoc Artists NJ (dir, 58-60); Nat Asn Women Artists; Philadelphia Watercolor Soc. Style & Technique: Realistic; wash and dry brush technique. Media: Watercolor. Mailing Add: 220 Montgomery St Highland Park NJ 08904

BURPEE, JAMES STANLEY
PAINTER, INSTRUCTOR
b Oakland, Calif, Feb 12, 38. Study: San Jose State Col, BA, 58; Calif Col Arts & Crafts, MFA, 60 with James Weeks. Comn: Painting (8ft x 20ft), F&M Savings Bank, Minneapolis, 73. Exhib: Wide Regional Ann Painting & Sculpture Exhib, Dallas Mus of Fine Arts, Tex, 65 & 66; A Sense of Place: Artists & the American Land, Sheldon Mem Art Gallery, Lincoln, Nebr, 73-74; Northwestern Biennial II, SDak Mem Art Ctr, Brookings, 74; The Am Nude, Minneapolis Inst of Arts, 75; Bicentennial Landscape Exhib, Capricorn Asunder Gallery, San Francisco Mus of Mod Art, 76; America 1976, Minneapolis Inst of Arts, 77. Collections Arranged: State of Minn (arts coun purchase), 69; State Univ NY, Albany, 69; Ellerbe Archit Assoc, Minneapolis, 73; State of Hawaii (arts coun purchase), 74; Metromedia Corp, 74; Gelco Corp, 75 & Fed Reserve Bank, 75, Minneapolis; Am Nat Bank & Trust, St Paul, 75 & 76; Minn Civil Liberties Found on Loan to Minneapolis Inst of Arts, 77. Teaching: From asst prof to assoc prof painting & drawing, Minneapolis Col of Art & Design, 67-; vis artist painting, Kansas City Art Inst, 74 & Calif Col of Arts & Crafts, 74 & 75. Awards: Indiv Artist grant, Minn State Arts Coun, 73; Nat Endowment for the Arts Artist-in-Residence, Volcanoes Nat Park, Hawaii, Hawaii State Arts Coun, 73-74; Fel, MacDowell Colony, 76. Style & Technique: Figurative; acrylic on canvas and paper. Media: Acrylic. Dealer: Sunne Savage Gallery 105 Newberry St Boston MA. Mailing Add: 3208 Aldrich Ave S Minneapolis MN 55408

BURR, HORACE
CURATOR, COLLECTOR
b New Castle, Ind, Feb 9, 12. Study: DePauw Univ, BA; Univ Southern Calif, MA; Acad Fine Arts, Florence, Italy, cert; also with Senior Berti; Alfred Van Loen; Salvatori Li Rose. Exhib: One-man shows, Ceramic Sculpture, Mark Dixon Dodd Sch Fine Arts, 50, Sculpture & Driftwood, St Augustine Gallery Fine Art, 53 & Wall Sculpture in Mexed Media, Univ Va, 75; Human Figure, Acad Fine Arts, Florence, 53; Contemp Southern Art Exhib Tour, 65. Teaching: Prof design, NY Univ, summers, 44-46; prof art hist, Jefferson Col Fine Arts, Charlottesville, Va, 54-55; prof hist Japanese art, Univ Va, 74-77; cur fine arts & art consult, James Madison Univ, Harrisburg, 77- Awards: Int Medal, Kokusai Bunka Shinkokai, Tokyo, Japan, 41; Award of Merit, Albermarle Art Asn, Charlottesville, Va, 65; Best of Show, Contemp Southern Art Exhib, 64. Bibliog: The Ancient City (doc film), St Augustine Rec, 57; Bd Dirs Albermarle Art Asn (auth), Sculpture of Horace Burr, 63 & Collection of Horace Burr, 73, Wayside Press. Mem: Kappa Pi; Albermarle Art Asn (pres, 55-65, emer pres, 65-); Albermarle Mus Art Found (dir, 63-). Style & Technique: Contemporary sculpture. Media: Mixed Media. Res: Art history and fine arts. Interest: Developing permanent collections for exhibition and study in universities, colleges, museums and foundations. Collection: Extensive collection of 14th to 20th century oil paintings; porcelain and faience; furniture, concentration on Oriental art. Publ: Auth, The Blending of Oriental and Occidental Cultures, 40; auth, Art in Albermarle, five sect, Wayside Press, 59-70; auth, The Heirloom Museum, Daughters Am Revolution, 60; Privately Owned I, Acme Visible Records, Inc, 61; auth, Privately Owned II, Allen Co, 63. Mailing Add: Carrsgrove Stribling Ave Charlottesville VA 22902

BURROUGHS, JOHN COLEMAN
PAINTER, ILLUSTRATOR
b Chicago, Ill, Feb 28, 13. Study: Otis Art Inst, Los Angeles, 26; Los Angeles Col, 27; Pomona Col, Claremont, scholar (grad magna cum laude & Phi Beta Kappa with distinction in art), with Nicolai Fechin, Elmer Schofield, Thomas Beggs, Fredrick Taubes, Burt Procter & Cyril Jurecka. Work: Los Angeles Mus Natural Hist, Calif. Comn: Bk covers & interior illus, Oakdale Affair & The Rider, 37, Tarzan & the Forbidden City, 38, Carson of Venus, 39 & Synthetic Men of Mars, 40, Edgar Rice Burroughs, Inc, Tarzana, Calif; bk cover & interior illus, John Carter of Mars Sunday Page, United Feature Syndicate, New York, 41. Exhib: Ebell Women's Ann Exhib, Los Angeles, 57; Catalina Art Festival, Avalon, Calif, 63 & 64. Teaching: Art instr, Los Angeles Pierce Col, 55-56; pvt classes, Tarzana, 57-60. Pos: Illusr & writer, Whitman Publ Co, Racine, Wis, 40-46, United Feature Syndicate, New York, 41-43; illusr & writer training manuals, Douglas Aircraft Co, Los Angeles, 44-45; motion picture studio & sketch artist, Warner Bros & Universal Studios, Los Angeles, 46-49. Awards: First Place, Ebell Women's Ann Exhib, 57, Catalina Art Festival, 63 & 64. Bibliog: Vern Coriell (auth), David Innes of Pellucidar, 68 & John Carter of Mars, 70, House of Greystoke; Russ Cochran (auth), Edgar Rice Burroughs Library of Illustrations, privately publ, 77. Style & Technique: Impressionistic, traditional, realistic, imaginative. Media: Oil; Pastel; Pen & Ink. Publ: Illusr, The Funnies, Numbers 34-56, Whitman Publ Co, 39-41; co-auth & illusr, The Bottom of the World, Startling Stories, 41; illusr, Tarzan & the Golden Lion, Whitman Publ Co, 43; auth, Thre Treasure of the Black Falcon, Ballantine Bks, 67; contribr, Erb-Dom, Camille Cazedessus, 73. Mailing Add: Tarzana Dr 18341 Tarzana CA 91356

BURROUGHS, MARGARET T G
LECTURER, PAINTER
b St Rose, La, Nov 1, 17. Study: Art Inst Chicago, BAE, 46, MAE, 48; Teacher's Col, Columbia Univ, 59-61; Lewis Univ, Hon PhD. Work: Atlanta Univ Art Collection; Howard Univ Art Collection; Ala A&M Univ Print Collection; Jackson State Col Art Collection, Miss; George Carver Mus, Tuskegee, Ala. Exhib: One-woman shows, South Side Art Ctr, Chicago, 72 & 74 & YWCA, Chicago, 73. Teaching: Teacher art, Du Sable High Sch, Chicago, 46-69; teacher art hist, Art Inst Chicago, 68-69; teacher humanities, Kennedy-King City Col, 69- Pos: Mem, Gov's Comn to Study Financing of Arts in Ill, 72-73; mayoral app mem, Chicago Coun on Fine Arts, 76. Awards: First Watercolor Award, Atlanta Univ, 55; Best in Show, Nat Conf Artists, Lincoln Univ, Jefferson City, Mo, 63; Third Place Sculpture, Atlanta Univ, 69. Mem: Nat Conf Artists. Style & Technique: Representational; social significance; silkscreen; lithography; sculpture. Media: Watercolor, Oil. Publ: Contribr, Black World & Nat Conf Artists Bull; illusr, Jasper the Drummer Boy, Crowell, 50; illusr, What Shall I Tell My Children Who are Black?, 65 & For Malcolm, 67. Mailing Add: 3806 S Michigan Ave Chicago IL 60653

BURROWS, SELIG S
COLLECTOR, PATRON
b New York, NY, 1913. Study: Fordham Univ, grad, 33; NY Univ Law Sch, grad, 36. Pos: Trustee, Aldrich Mus Contemp Art. Collection: Late 19th & 20th century American art. Mailing Add: Serena Mill Neck NY 11765

BURT, CLYDE EDWIN
CERAMIST, EDUCATOR
b Melrose, Ohio. Study: Ft Wayne Sch Fine Arts, Ind, 49-50, cert; Provincetown Sch Art, Mass, cert; Cranbrook Acad Art, Bloomfield Hills, Mich, 52-54. Work: Cranbrook Acad Art; Detroit Inst Art; Toledo Mus Art; Am Art Clay Co Collection, Indianapolis; Syracuse Mus Fine Arts. Comn: Ceramic wall reliefs, Oldsmobile Eng Bldg, Lansing, Mich, 65; wall mural, Int Res Corp Bldg, Kalamazoo, Mich, 66; sectional ceramic relief, Wolfram Corp, Lansing, 66; textural wall, Consumer's Power Co Off Bldg, Jackson, Mich, 69; wall murals, Gen Tel Corp Bldg, 76. Exhib: One-man shows, Toledo Mus Art, 54, Chicago Art Inst, 60-61 & 35 others; Designer-Craftsmen USA, Brooklyn, 53 & 55; Mich Artists-Craftsmen, Mus Art, Detroit, 54, 55 & 60; Nat Exhib Contemp Arts US, Los Angeles & Pomona, Calif, 56; Scripps Col Ceramic Exhib, Claremont, Calif, 57; Craftsmen in Changing World, Mus Contemp Crafts, New York, 57; Am Pottery, Univ Southwestern La, Lafayette, 63; Beaus-Art-Designer Craftsmen, Columbus Gallery Fine Art, Ohio, 64, 66 & 68; Arts in Embassies Prog, Wall Relief, Nigeria, Africa, 67-69; Bicentennial Crafts Exhib, Ind Univ, Bloomington, 76. Teaching: Instr, Dayton Art Inst, Ohio & Univ Wis, Madison, summer sessions, 60 & 61; instr ceramics, Ft Wayne Art Inst, Inc, 65-76; assoc prof fine arts & ceramics, Ind Univ/Purdue Univ at Ft Wayne, 76- Pos: Mem bd trustees & gov bd, Ohio Designer Craftsmen, 60-64; chmn joint meeting, Am Craftsmen Coun-NCent Region & Ohio Designer Craftsmen,

Dayton, 64; mem chmn, Nat Coun Educ for Ceramic Arts, 73. Style & Technique: Classical wheel-thrown shapes and built-up clay wall reliefs; known for hard-edge designs on pottery. Media: Stoneware: fired Clay in oxidation with heavy use of englobes. Mailing Add: Pottery Studio PO Box 26 Melrose OH 45861

BURT, DAN
PAINTER
b Owensboro, Ky, Aug 17, 30. Study: Ramon Froman Sch Art, Cloudcroft, NMex; Simon Michael Sch Art, Rockport, Tex; also with Harold Roney, Joy Carrington & William H Earle. Comn: Oil landscape selected to hang in State Capitol, Austin, Tex, 73. Exhib: One-man shows, Bee Co Col, Beeville, Tex, 69, McNamara-O'Conner Mus, Victoria, Tex, 69 & San Antonio Pub Libr, 70; Artist & Craftsmen Prize Awards Exhib, Dallas, 71-77; Am Artists Prof League Exhib, New York, 74-76; Allied Artists of Am, Nat Acad Galleries, New York, 75. Awards: Best of Show, Cent Park Invitational, San Antonio, Tex, 75; Gold Medal, Coppini Acad of Fine Arts, San Antonio, 76; Merit Award, Artists & Craftsmen Assoc Prize Awards Exhib, Dallas, Tex, 77. Bibliog: Article in Art Rev Mag, fall 68; Odene Crawford (auth), article in San Angelo Standard Times, 9/68; Harry Reed (auth), feature story in SW Art Mag, 3/78. Mem: Coppini Acad Fine Arts, San Antonio (vpres, 71-72, pres, 73-74); Artists & Craftsmen Asn, Dallas; Am Artists Prof League. Style & Technique: Direct painting and impressionistic landscapes and still life; transparent watercolor landscape. Media: Oil, Watercolor. Mem: San Antonio Watercolor Group; Southwestern Watercolor Soc, Dallas. Dealer: Yellow Bird Gallery 218 S Washington San Angelo TX 76901; Glassiers Gallery 2121 N Main Ave San Antonio TX 78212. Mailing Add: 1304 Ford Kerrville TX 78028

BURT, DAVID SILL
SCULPTOR, WRITER
b Evanston, Ill, Feb 20, 17. Study: Harvard Univ, BA, 40. Work: Fine Art Ctr, Univ Wis-Milwaukee; US Art in Embassies Prog, Stamford Mus. Comn: Suspended metal screen, Anaconda Copper Co, 66; fountain, Ital Steamship Lines, 66; two mobiles, Pavilion Apt, 67; sculptures, Am Can Co, 69, Harvey Hubbell Co, 74 & Largo Corp, 75. Exhib: Pa Acad Fine Arts Exhib, 64; New Eng Exhib, 65-67 & 69-70. Pos: Promotion writer, Archit Forum, Indust Design & Interiors; dir, Studio Workshop, Stamford, Conn. Mem: Sculptors League; Silvermine Guild Artists; Stamford Mus Art Comt. Media: Sheet Metal, Electrified Plastics. Publ: Auth, Detour to sculpture, Am Artist Mag. Dealer: The Sculpture Ctr 167 E 69th St New York NY 10021. Mailing Add: 61 Studio Rd Stamford CT 06903

BURTCHAELL, DEANN
See Jones, Claire

BURTON, GLORIA
SCULPTOR, PAINTER
b New York, NY. Study: Mt Holyoke Col, Mass; Art Students League; Univ Calif, Los Angeles. Work: Holyoke Mus Art, Mass. Comn: Aluminum-bronze sculpture, Stanley Folb Bldg, Hollywood, 68; bronze, brass & copper sculpture, Empire Savings & Loan, Santa Ana, Calif, 69; bronze sculpture, Dillingham Corp, Los Angeles, 71; bronze sculpture, Danmour & Assoc (in mall), Reseda Village Green, Reseda Village, Calif; 2 bronze sculptures, Security Pac Bank, Oxnard, Calif, 72. Exhib: Sacramento State Fair; San Francisco Mus Art; two-person shows, Machinations, Mus Sci & Indust, Los Angeles, 73 & Chicago, 75 & Of Art & Medicine, Mus Sci & Indust, Los Angeles, 75. Pos: Owner, Abby Art Gallery, Los Angeles, 73- Awards: Awards for People of the City, Southland Ann, Del Mar, Calif, 69, Decent, Westwood Art Asn & Revelation, Santa Monica Ann. Bibliog: John R Hamilton (auth), Gloria Burton, sculptress in metal, Progressive Woman, 7/71; Maxine Bartlett (auth), Machines for art's sake, Los Angeles Herald Examiner, 10/14/73; Felice Paramore (auth), Asbestos jacket's her style, Christian Sci Monitor, 12/5/74. Style & Technique: Melting and pouring metals and chemicals in a variety of ways, then cutting, welding and grinding; pouring paint. Media: Bronze; Watercolor. Mailing Add: 2019 Pontius Ave Los Angeles CA 90025

BURTON, SCOTT
SCULPTOR, CONCEPTUAL ARTIST
b Greensboro, Ala, June 23, 39. Study: Hans Hofmann Studio, Provincetown, 57-59; Columbia Univ, BA(magna cum laude), 62; NY Univ Grad Sch Eng, MA, 63. Exhib: One-Person Performance-Piece Exhibs, Whitney Mus Am Art, New York, 72, Mus Fine Arts, Boston, 73, Allen Art Mus, Oberlin, Ohio, 73, Idea Warehouse, New York, 75 & Guggenheim Mus, New York, 76; Whitney Biennial, New York, 75; Rooms, PS 1, New York, 76; Parrish Art Mus, Southampton, NY, 76; plus others. Awards: Nat Endowment for Arts Visual-Arts Grants, 73 & 75; Creative Artists Pub Serv Prog Multi-Media Grant, 75- Bibliog: Athena T Spear (auth), Thoughts on Contemporary art, Allen Art Mus Bull, spring 73; Ronald Argelander (auth), Scott Burton's behavior tableaux, Drama Rev, NY, 9/73; An article on Scott Burton, Art-Rite Mag, NY, winter 75. Style & Technique: Sculpture as furniture; narrative tableaux vivants. Media: Multi-Media, Found Objects, Live Performance. Publ: Auth, Instructions, In: Art in the Mind, Allen Mus, Oberlin, 70; auth, Street works 1969, Drama Rev, 3/72; auth, Three furniture works, Tri-Quarterly, winter 75. Mailing Add: 86 Thompson St New York NY 10012

BUSA, PETER
PAINTER, SCULPTOR
b Pittsburgh, Pa, June 23, 14. Study: Carnegie Inst Technol, with Raymond Simboli, Sam Rosenberg, Alex Kostellow & Tom Benton; Art Students League; Hans Hofmann Sch Fine Art. Work: Smithsonian Inst; Peggy Guggenheim; Smith Col Mus; Walker Art Ctr; Whitney Mus Am Art; plus others. Exhib: Art of the Century, Peggy Guggenheim, 46; Bertha Schaefer Gallery, New York, 49-51; Albright-Knox Art Gallery, Buffalo, NY, 54; Retrospective, Chrysler Art Mus, 59; Selections from Permanent Collections, Whitney Mus Am Art, 72; plus many others. Teaching: NY Univ, 45-53; Cooper Union, 45-54; prof art, State Univ NY Col Buffalo, 54-57; prof art, Univ Minn, Minneapolis, 60- Pos: Dir summer art prog, Southampton Col, 71. Awards: Spec Donor Award, Walker Art Ctr, 66; College of Liberal Arts Distinguished Teacher Award, Univ Minn, Minneapolis, 75; Guggenheim Award for Painting, US & Europe, 76-77. Bibliog: Peter Busa, Tweed Gallery, Univ Minn, 66; Sidney Simon (auth), Concerning the beginnings of the NY School, Art Int, 67. Mem: Col Art Asn Am; Artists Equity Asn (pres, Minn Chap, 62-65); life mem Art Students League. Style & Technique: Geometric abstractionist influenced by American Indian art. Media: Oil, Plaster. Publ: Auth, Creative Imagination in Science & Art, 57; auth, Art to Eat & Diet, 67. Mailing Add: 2124 Riverside Ave Minneapolis MN 55404

BUSCAGLIA, JOSE
SCULPTOR
b San Juan, PR, Sept 15, 38. Study: Harvard Univ, BA(cum laude), 60; also with Enrique Monjo, sculptor, 58-59 & 60-62. Work: Robert Frost, Nat Portrait Gallery, Washington, DC; Dean Delmar Leighton, Harvard Univ; Autobiography of an Inspiration, Ponce Mus Art; Ramos Antonini, Capitol PR; Justice, US Fed Dist Court. Comn: Monuments (bronze, 14 ft high), Rio Piedras, PR, 72 & Bar Asn Bldg, San Juan, PR, 73; Allegorical Figure (bronze, 12 ft high), Munic Sch Bd 84, New York, 73; monument of Ramos Antonini (bronze, 9 ft high), Capitol grounds, San Juan, PR, 76; five sculptural groups (bronze, 11 ft high), Park of the Americas, San Juan, PR, 77. Exhib: One-man shows, Harvard Univ, Banco Popular at Rockefeller Ctr, Lisner Auditorium, George Washington Univ, 67; several exhibs, Univ PR Mus & Inst PR Cult. Teaching: Prof art, Univ PR, Rio Piedras, 63- Awards: Gran Premio Puertorrigueno, Acad Arts & Sci of PR, 67. Bibliog: Film, Not by Bread Alone, Esso Co, 65. Mem: Acad Arts & Sci PR (bd mem, 64 & 69); Nat Sculpture Soc. Media: Bronze. Publ: Auth, Anatomia del proceso creativo, 66 & Creatiology as a new approach to the teaching of the arts, Acad Arts & Sci Bull, 67; La intuicion y la velosidad del reflejo, 71. Mailing Add: Fine Arts Dept Univ of PR Rio Piedras PR 00931

BUSCH, JULIA M
WRITER, SCULPTOR
b Teaneck, NJ, Mar 27, 40. Study: Juilliard Sch Music; Univ Miami, with Eugene Massin & Dr August Freundlich; Columbia Univ, with Dr Douglas Frasier, BA. Comn: Acrylic & light mural (with Eugene Massin), City Nat Bank of Miami, 73. Teaching: Instr art hist, Miami-Dade Community Col, 67-68; instr drawing, Univ Miami, 67-68. Pos: Assoc, Eugene Massin Studio, 70-; columnist & feature writer, Ideas Mag, 77-78. Awards: Scholar, Univ Miami, 68. Bibliog: Mark A Stuart (auth), Mingling art, science, fun in the sun, Bergen Rec, 3/75. Style & Technique: Using lost wax process, sculpts miniature portraits to be cast in gold or silver and worn as sculpture-jewelry. Res: Polester castings and acrylic; art sensitivity training for children. Publ: Auth, A painter's plastic sculpture, Art J, 70; contribr, Plastics as Design Form, 72 & contribr, Plastics as Sculpture, 74, Chilton; auth, A Decade of Sculpture, the New Media of the 1960's, Art Alliance, 74. Mailing Add: 3891 Little Ave Coconut Grove FL 33133

BUSH, BEVERLY
PAINTER, SCULPTOR
b Kelso, Wash. Study: Univ Wash, BA; Nat Acad Design Sch Fine Arts; Art Students League. Exhib: Nat Asn Women Artists, 58; City Ctr, New York, 58; Art: USA, 59; Audubon Artists, 59; Seattle Art Mus, 64; plus others. Pos: Ed, Nat News Letter, Artists Equity Asn, 58- Awards: Youth Friends Asn Scholar, Nat Acad Design, 54-55; Joseph Isador Merit Scholar, 55-57. Mem: Artists Equity Asn (exec secy, 58-). Mailing Add: 3521 E Spruce St Seattle WA 98102

BUSH, CHARLES ROBERT
See Robb, Charles

BUSH, DONALD JOHN
ART HISTORIAN, EDUCATOR
b San Francisco, Calif. Study: Ariz State Univ, BS, 59; Univ Notre Dame with Dr John Howett, MA(art), 64; Univ NMex with Dean Clinton Adams, Van Deren Coke & Dr Peter Walch, PhD(art hist), 73. Teaching: Teaching asst art, Univ Notre Dame, 63-64; chmn art dept, Univ Albuquerque, 64-75; asst prof art hist & humanities, Ariz State Univ, 75- Mem: Col Art Asn; Am Asn Univ Prof; Nat Asn Humanities Educ. Res: Development of American industrial design and architecture. Publ: auth, De Rivera's Construction No 72, Bull Univ NMex Art Mus, 73; auth, Streamlining and American industrial design, autumn 74 & reviewer, Italy—the new domestic landscape, Leonardo Mag, spring 75; auth, The Streamlined Decade, George Braziller, 75. Mailing Add: Dept of Humanities Ariz State Univ Tempe AZ 85281

BUSH, LUCILE ELIZABETH
PAINTER, EDUCATOR
b Mt Sterling, Ky, July 26, 04. Study: Univ Ky, AB; Teachers Col, Columbia Univ, MA & PhD; Art Students League; also with Leger, L'Hote & Marcoussis, Paris. Work: Skidmore Col, Saratoga Springs, NY. Comn: Portraits, pvt cols; scenery & costume design, Harwich Jr Theatre, Mass. Exhib: One-man shows, Saratoga Springs, Schenectady & Glens Falls, NY. Teaching: Lectr var aspects mediaeval iconography; instr art, Skidmore Col, 28-43; instr art & chmn dept, Wheaton Col, Mass, 47-65, prof art, 66-73, emer prof, 73- Pos: Dir, Watson Gallery, 62-66. Awards: Carnegie Scholar, 30; Elizabeth Avery Colton Fel, Am Asn Univ Women, 45-46. Mem: Col Art Asn Am; Am Asn Univ Prof; Mediaeval Acad; Renaissance Soc; Soc Archit Historians. Publ: Auth, Bartolo di Fredi, Sienese Painter of the Late 14th Century (microfilm), 50. Mailing Add: North Rd West Harwich MA 02671

BUSH, MARTIN HARRY
MUSEUM DIRECTOR, ART HISTORIAN
b Amsterdam, NY, Jan 24, 30. Study: State Univ NY Albany, BA & MA, 58; Syracuse Univ, PhD, 66. Collections Arranged: Photo Realism: Rip-Off or Reality, 75; George Grosz, 75; Wayne Thiebaud, 75; Robert Goodnough, 75; Richard Pousette-Dart, 75; Kathe Kollwitz Prints, 75; American Pop Art, 75; Richard Anuszkiewicz, 75. Teaching: Instr, Syracuse Univ, 63-65, asst dean, 65-70. Pos: Dir, E A Ulrich Mus Art, Wichita State Univ, 71-, vpres acad resources develop, 74- Mem: Am Asn Art Mus; Col Art Asn. Res: 20th century American art. Publ: Auth, Ben Shahn: The Passion of Sacco and Vanzetti, 68 & Doris Caesar, 70, Syracuse Univ; contribr, James Earle Fraser: American Sculptor, Kennedy Galleries, 69; auth, Goodnough, Ulrich Mus Art, 73; contribr, Isabel Bishop, Univ Ariz, 75; auth, Duane Hanson, 76 & Ernest Trova, 77; plus others. Mailing Add: Wichita State Univ Box 46 Wichita KS 67208

BUSH-BROWN, ALBERT
WRITER, EDUCATOR
b West Hartford, Conn, Jan 2, 26. Study: Princeton Univ, AB, 47, Woodrow Wilson fel, 47-48, MFA, 49, PhD, 58; Emerson Col, hon LLD, 65; Providence Col, hon HHD, 66; Mercy Col, hon DFA, 76. Teaching: Instr art & archaeol, Princeton Univ, 49-50; asst prof art & archit, Western Reserve Univ, 53-54; asst prof archit, Mass Inst Technol, 54-58, assoc prof & exec officer archit, 58-62; pres, RI Sch Design, 62-68; Bemis vis prof, Mass Inst Technol, 68-69; vpres, State Univ NY Buffalo, 69-71; chancellor, Long Island Univ, 71- Pos: Nat adv comt, Archives Am Art, 62-; mem, Nat Coun on The Arts, White House, 64-70; dir-at-large, Nat Coun Arts in Educ, 65-71. Awards: Howard Found fel, Brown Univ, 59-60; Ford Found fel, 68-69; fel, Harvard Univ, John F Kennedy Inst & Joint Ctr for Urban Studies, 68-69. Mem: Century Asn; hon mem Am Inst Architects. Publ: Auth, Louis Sullivan, 60; co-auth, The Architecture of America: a Social Interpretation, 61; auth, Books, Bass, Barnstable, 67; auth, numerous articles in encycl, art & archit journals, 52-65. Mailing Add: Piping Rock Rd Locust Valley NY 11560

BUSHMAN, DAVID FRANKLIN
PAINTER, EDUCATOR
b Toledo, Ohio, Aug 2, 45. Study: Univ Wis, BFA, 67; Univ Wis-Madison, MFA, 69; also with Al Leslie, Jack Beal, James Rosenquist & Richard Artschager. Work: Johnson Wax Co,

Racine, Wis; Wis State J, Madison; Univ Wis-Madison; C M Bruckner Collection, New York; St Johns Univ, Jamaica, NY; Madison Art Ctr, Wis. Comn: Mural, comn by Mr & Mrs G Lauderdale, Ft Lauderdale, Fla, 70; painting, comn by H C Westerman, Brookfield Ctr, Conn, 73; portrait, comn by Mr & Mrs S Crane, Chicago, 75; painting, comn by Mr & Mrs James Stewart, Chicago, 75. Exhib: One-man shows, Univ Wis-Madison, 69, Louisville Art Ctr, Ky, 72, Pa State Univ, University Park, 73, George Peabody Univ, Nashville, Tenn, 74 & Univ Ill, Champaign, 75; Burpee Art Ctr, Rockford, Ill, 67; Sheldon Swope Gallery, Terre Haute, Ind, 70; Mus Contemp Art, Chicago, 74; Ball State Drawing & Small Sculpture, Muncie, Ind, 75. Teaching: Instr painting & drawing, Univ Wis-Madison, 67-69; asst prof painting & drawing, Univ Ill, Urbana-Champaign, 69-; guest lectr, Louisville Art Ctr, Ky, 72; guest lectr, George Peabody Univ, 74. Awards: Cash Award, Wis Salon Art, 68; Cash Award, Nat Drawings, NY Univ, 69; Cash Award, Ill State Fair, 70. Mem: Col Art Asn; New Col Art Asn; Am Fedn Teachers. Style & Technique: Realist. Dealer: Gilman Gallery 103 E Oak St Chicago IL 60611. Mailing Add: 209 Water St Champaign IL 61820

BUSHMILLER, ERNIE PAUL
CARTOONIST
b New York, NY, Aug 23, 05. Study: Nat Acad Design. Pos: Cartoonist, syndicated comic strip, Nancy & Sun comic strip, Fritzi Ritz, United Features, 31- Mem: Soc Illusr; Nat Cartoonists Soc; Dutch Treat Club; Artists & Writers Asn. Publ: Fritzi Ritz & Nancy comic books publ monthly. Mailing Add: 552 Haviland Rd Stamford CT 06903

BUSHNELL, MARIETTA P
ART LIBRARIAN
b Vienna, Austria, July 26, 32; US citizen. Study: Wheaton Col, Norton, Mass, BA(art hist); Drexel Univ, Philadelphia, MLS. Pos: Photograph librn, Mus of Fine Arts, Boston, 56-61; asst, Slide Dept, Mus of Art, Philadelphia, 68-72; librn, Pa Acad of Fine Arts, 75- Mem: Art Librn Soc NAm. Mailing Add: Pa Acad of Fine Arts Broad & Cherry Sts Philadelphia PA 19102

BUSINO, ORLANDO FRANCIS
CARTOONIST
b Binghamton, NY, Oct 10, 26. Study: State Univ Iowa, BA, 52. Pos: Cartoonist, Sat Eve Post, McCall's, Ladies Home Jour, Sat Rev, Look, True, Argosy, Boys' Life, Family Circle & other US & foreign mags. Awards: Best Mag Cartoonist of Year, Nat Cartoonists Soc, 65, 67 & 68. Mem: Nat Cartoonists Soc; Mag Cartoonists Guild. Mailing Add: 12 Shadblow Hill Rd Ridgefield CT 06877

BUSSABARGER, ROBERT FRANKLIN
SCULPTOR, PAINTER
b Corydon, Ind, Sept 17, 22. Study: Wittenberg Univ, AB, 44, with Ralston Thompson; Mich State Univ, MA, 47, with John de Martelli, Louis Raynor, Carl Schmidt; Ohio State Univ, with Paul Bogatay & Edgar Littlefield, 49-51; res scholar to India, Fulbright Exchange Fel, 61-62 & Hays Univ SAsia Ctr Fac Fel, 68-69. Work: Air India Collection, Bombay, India; Springfield Art Mus, Mo; Mo Hist Soc, Columbia. Exhib: One-man shows, Indo-American Soc, Calcutta, India, 62 & Chemould Art Gallery, Bombay, India, 78; Corner Gallery, Louisville, Ky; Sculptors Gallery, St Louis, Mo, 66; Acad Fine Arts, Calcutta, India & Am Cult Ctr, Bombay, 69. Collections Arranged: Univ Mo Fine Arts Gallery, 55-59 & 63-67; Indian art exhib based on Bussabarger & Robins Collections, Univ Mo, Stephens Col, Westminster Col & Carleton Col. Teaching: Teacher art, Benton Harbor Jr & Sr High Sch, Mich, 48-49; asst prof art, Stephen F Austin State Univ, Nacogdoches, Tex, 51-53; prof art, Univ Mo-Columbia, 53- & chmn dept, 70-73. Awards: Awards, San Antonio Watercolor Ann, 52 & 53; Art Assoc Purchase Award, Decorative Arts Ann, Wichita, Kans, 56; Merit Award in Sculpture, 30th Springfield Ann, Mo, 60. Bibliog: L Bhattacharia (auth), Robert Bussabarger, US Info Serv, 10/62; A B Pine (auth), Bussabarger & ceramic art, Mo Alumnus, 11/60. Mem: Mo Crafts Coun (vpres in charge circulating exhib); Columbia Art League; Mid-Am Art Conf. Style & Technique: Sculpture, direct ceramic forming from pots and slabs of clay; painting, representational expressionism. Media: Ceramic, Metal; Pastel, Watercolor. Publ: Auth, Terracotta temples of India, Craft Horizons, 66; ed, John Sloans Etchings, Univ Mo, 67; co-auth & illusr, The Everyday Art of India, Dover, 68; co-auth, The Makara, Archaeology, 1/70; co-auth, Folk images of Sanjhi Devi, Atribus Asiae, 7/75. Mailing Add: 1914 Princeton Columbia MO 65201

BUSTER, JACQUELINE MARY
ART DEALER, LECTURER
b Huntington, NY, Nov 1, 26. Study: Univ WVa, Bradley Univ, BA. Pos: Gallery dir, Peoria Art Guild, Ill, 70-72; dir & owner, Tower Park Gallery, Peoria Heights, Ill, 72- Specialty: Contemporary mid-western paintings and graphics and other contemporary artists. Mailing Add: Tower Park Gallery 4709 Prospect Rd Peoria Heights IL 61614

BUTCHKES, SYDNEY
PAINTER, SCULPTOR
b Covington, Ky, Oct 13, 22. Study: Cincinnati Art Acad, Ohio; Art Students League; New Sch Social Res, New York. Work: Brooklyn Mus, NY; Cincinnati Art Mus; Wadsworth Atheneum, Hartford, Conn; Nat Collection Fine Arts, Smithsonian Inst, Washington, DC; Sheldon Mem Art Gallery, Lincoln, Nebr. Comn: Sculpture for lobby of Financial Progs Bldg, Denver, 69; hanging sculpture for bar of Ritz Carlton Hotel, Boston, 69; painting for lobby of Skidmore, Owings, Merrill, Chicago, 70; paintings, World Trade Ctr, NY & Continental Tel Co, Washington, DC. Exhib: Art for the Collector, San Francisco Mus Art, 65; Painting Without a Brush, Inst Contemp Art, Boston, 65; Painting Out from the Wall, Des Moines Art Ctr, Iowa, 67; Plastic as Plastic, Mus Contemp Crafts, New York, 69; Mus Acquisitions, Colorado Springs Art Ctr, 69. Mem: Abstr Am Artists. Style & Technique: Abstract, geometric. Media: Acrylic Paint; Acrylic Sheet. Dealer: Alonzo Gallery 30 W 57th St New York NY 10022. Mailing Add: Sagg Main St Sagaponack NY 11962

BUTLER, DOROTHY DENNISON
See Dennison, Dorothy

BUTLER, JAMES D
PRINTMAKER, PAINTER
b Ft Dodge, Iowa, Aug 30, 45. Study: Omaha Univ, Nebr, BS, 67; Univ Nebr, Lincoln, MFA, 70. Work: Brooklyn Mus, NY; Brit Mus, London, Eng; Tamarind Inst, Albuquerque, NMex; Libr of Cong, Washington, DC; Smithsonian Inst, Washington, DC. Comn: First Ill Print Comn, Ill Arts Coun, 73. Exhib: Nat Invitational Prints & Objects, Evanston Art Ctr, Ill, 72; Corp Collections Show, Minn Mus of Art, St Paul, 72; Prints: Midwest Invitational, Walker Art Ctr, Minneapolis, 73; 19th Nat Print Exhib, Brooklyn Mus, 74; Mod Printmaking Exhib of Contemp Prints, Bevier Gallery, Rochester Inst of Technol, NY, 74. Teaching: Asst prof, Southern Ill Univ, Edwardsville, 70-76; vis artist lithography, Univ Colo, Boulder, 74; vis artist lithography, Northern Ariz Univ, Flagstaff, 76; assoc prof, Ill State Univ, Normal, 76- Awards: Robert Cooke Enlow Award, 1971 Mid-States Art Exhib, Evansville Mus of Arts & Sci, Ind, 71; First Place, Fine Art of Printmaking, Lexington, Ky, Nat Soc of Arts & Lett, 71; Workshops/Alternative Spaces, Nat Endowment for the Arts, 75-76. Bibliog: Clinton Adams & Susan Ellis (auths), Drawing Color Separations on Surfaced Mylar, Tamarind Tech Papers, 74. Mem: Mid-Am Col Art Asn; Col Art Asn. Style & Technique: Multi-colored pastel drawings and lithographs; light, space and objects occupying a place in these spaces. Media: Lithography, drawing and oil on linen. Dealer: Marianne Deson Gallery 226 E Ontario Chicago IL 60611. Mailing Add: 102 Warner Bloomington IL 61701

BUTLER, JOSEPH (GREEN)
ART ADMINISTRATOR, PAINTER
b Youngstown, Ohio, Sept 5, 01. Study: Dartmouth Col; Youngstown State Univ, hon DFA, 73. Work: Dartmouth Col Collection; Kalamazoo Inst Art, Mich; Phillips Exeter Col; Butler Inst Am Art, Ohio; Massillon Mus, Ohio; plus others. Exhib: Mid-Year Shows, Butler Inst Am Art, 38-60; Oil & Watercolor Shows, Pa Acad Fine Arts, Philadelphia, 46-48; Am Watercolor Soc, New York, 47-50; Miss Art Asn, 48-49; Audubon Artists, New York, 50-52. Collections Arranged: National Annual Mid-Year Shows, 38-; Ohio Painters of the Past; David G Blythe; William T Richards & Anna Richards Brewster; Art of the Carrousel; Area Artists Annuals, 40-; Ohio Ceramic & Sculpture Shows, 49- Pos: Dir, Butler Inst Am Art, 34-, pres bd trustees, 74- Awards: Patron of Am Art Award, Chautauqua Art Asn, 62; Ohio Arts Coun Award for 35 Yrs Serv, 71. Mem: Hon mem Friends Am Art (founder, 71); Archives Am Art; Artists Equity Asn. Mailing Add: Butler Inst Am Art 524 Wick Ave Youngstown OH 44502

BUTLER, JOSEPH THOMAS
ART HISTORIAN, WRITER
b Winchester, Va, Jan 25, 32. Study: Univ Md, BS, 54; Univ Ohio, MA, 55; Univ Del, Winterthur fel & MA, 57. Teaching: Adj assoc prof archit, Columbia Univ, 71- Pos: Cur, Sleepy Hollow Restorations, Tarrytown, NY, 57-; Am ed, The Connoisseur, 68- Mem: Nat Arts Club; Furniture Hist Soc; Victorian Soc in Am. Res: American decorative arts. Publ: Auth, American Antiques, 1800-1900, 65; auth, Candleholders in America, 1650-1900, 67; auth, The Family Collections at Van Cortlandt Manor, 67; co-auth, The Arts in America, the 19th Century, 70; auth, Washington Irving's Sunnyside, 75; plus others. Mailing Add: 635 S Broadway Tarrytown NY 10591

BUTLER, MARIGENE H
CONSERVATOR
b Ann Arbor, Mich, July 20, 31. Study: Mt Holyoke Col, AB, 53; Fogg Art Mus, Harvard Univ, 53-55; Art Inst Chicago, 66-68. Pos: Asst conservator, Art Inst Chicago, 68-70, assoc conservator, 70-73; dir & head training, Intermuseum Lab (which cares for the collections of 18 mus: Albright-Knox Art Gallery, Allen Art Mus, Univ Ky Mus Art, Cleveland Mus Art, Columbus Gallery Fine Arts, Cranbrook Mus, Davenport Munic Art Gallery, Dayton Art Inst, Flint Inst Arts, Indianapolis Mus Art, Univ Iowa Art Mus, Univ Mich Mus Art, Milwaukee Art Ctr, Univ Rochester, J B Speed Art Mus, Taft Mus & Toledo Mus Art), Oberlin, 73- Mem: Fel Int Inst Conserv Hist & Artistic Works (coun mem); fel Royal Micros Soc; Am Inst Conserv Hist & Artistic Works; Quekett Micros Soc. Publ: Auth, Portrait of a lady by Frans Hals, Mus Studies 5, 70; auth, Technical note, In: Painting in Italy in the 18th Century: Rococo to Romanticism, Art Inst Chicago, 70; auth, Application of the polarizing microscopy in the conservation of painting and other works of art, IIC/AG Bull, 71; auth, Technical note, In: Paintings by Renoir, Art Inst Chicago, 73; auth, An investigation of pigments and techniques in the Cezanne painting Chestnut Trees, AIC Bull, 73. Mailing Add: Intermuseum Lab Allen Art Bldg Oberlin OH 44074

BUTTERBAUGH, ROBERT CLYDE
SCULPTOR, EDUCATOR
b Freeport, Ill, May 28, 31. Study: Univ of the Pac, BFA, 54; Claremont Grad Sch, with Paul Darrow & David Scott, MFA, 62. Work: Sunderland Col Art, Eng. Comn: Sculpture relief (copper sheet), Temple Beth El, Salinas, Calif, 64; sculpture (welded corten steel), T Merrill Hall, Hartnell Col, Salinas, 65; fountain (redwood & cast bronze), Cent Plaza Bldg, 66; sculpture (redwood & plastic), Salinas City Hall Foyer, 68; sculpture group & low relief (cast concrete), Aquatic Complex, Hartnell Col, 73. Exhib: Midland Group Gallery, Nottingham, Eng, 69; Sunderland Col Art, 69; Cerritos 70, Norwalk, Calif, 70; Form and the Inner Eye, Los Angeles, Calif, 71; Southern Ore Col Gallery, Ashland, 71. Teaching: Prof art, Hartnell Col, 62-; lectr sculpture, Sunderland Col Art, 68-69. Awards: Fulbright-Hays travel grant, 68-69. Style & Technique: Cast and fabricated sculpture for architecture and public environments. Media: Plastics, Metals, Woods. Mailing Add: 908 Riker St Salinas CA 93901

BUTTS, H DANIEL, III
MUSEUM DIRECTOR
b Pittsburgh, Pa, July 15, 39. Study: Yale Univ, BA, 60, BFA, 61; Pa State Univ, MA, 62. Teaching: Instr hist of art/painting & drawing, Shady Side Acad, Pittsburgh, 62-65. Pos: Dir, Arts & Crafts Ctr of Pittsburgh, 65-68; dir, Mansfield Art Ctr, 68- Mailing Add: 700 Marion Ave Mansfield OH 44903

BUTTS, PORTER
ART HISTORIAN, ART ADMINISTRATOR
b Pana, Ill, Feb 23, 03. Study: Univ Wis-Madison, with O F L Hagen, BA, MA(art hist). Collections Arranged: Wis Salon of Art Ann, 34-68; chmn, Wis State Territorial Centennial Art Exhib, 36; Wis Union Collection of Art (some 700 paintings, watercolors, graphics & sculptures principally by Wis artists). Pos: Dir, Wis Union Galleries, Univ Wis-Madison, 28-68; planning consult, Milwaukee Arts Ctr & many col & univ cult-social ctrs, 46-73. Awards: Creative Arts Award, given annually by Univ Wis-Madison, in recognition of Porter Butts' contribution to the arts; Distinguished Serv Award, Univ Wis Alumni Asn, 75. Mem: Madison Art Asn (secy-treas, 29-32). Res: Regional art history, especially development of art in Wisconsin in the 19th & 20th centuries. Publ: Auth, Art in Wisconsin: the Art Experience of the Middle West Frontier, 36; auth, Research in regional art, Art in Am, 10/45. Mailing Add: 2900 Hunter Hill Madison WI 53705

BUZZELLI, JOSEPH ANTHONY
PAINTER, SCULPTOR
b Old Forge, Pa, May 6, 07. Study: Art Students League; Univ Southern Calif; Beaux-Arts & Grande Chaumiere, Paris, France. Work: Philadelphia Pub Libr, Pa. Comn: Murals in churches; One Religion, Early New York City to Present & Man Striving for Peace (murals), Fed Detention House, New York, 44; The Pool, Wiltwyck Sch for Boys, 45. Exhib: Whitney Mus Am Art; Smithsonian Inst; Art USA, New York; Metrop Mus Art; Carnegie Art Inst; Anti-Pollution Exhib, Sarasota Art Asn, Fla, 78; The Future of SW Fla by Design or Default, Univ South Fla New Col, Coples House, Sarasota; plus many others. Teaching: Instr, Henry St Settlement House, Educ Alliance, Long Beach Art Ctr & Brooklyn Mus Wiltwyck Sch for

Boys & Youth House; also lectr on anti-pollution art exhibs. Awards: First Prize in Watercolor, Nat Emily Lowe 7th Ann Award Show; First Prize in Oils, New York Ctr; Spec Award for Enamels Fired on Steel, Guild Hall Galleries, East Hampton; plus others. Mem: Artists Equity. Bibliog: Reviews in Art News Int, Arts Digest, New York Herald Tribune, New York Times & others. Style & Technique: Free modern; fired enamels on steel. Media: Enamels, Oil; Metals, Woods, Plastics. Publ: Auth, The Dirty Book (on anti-air-pollution. Mailing Add: 608 N Casey Key Osprey FL 33559

BYARD, CAROLE MARIE
PAINTER, ILLUSTRATOR
b Atlantic City, NJ, July 22, 41. Study: Fleisher Art Mem, sculpture with Aurelius Renzetti; New York-Phoenix Sch Design, painting with Felix & Trini DeCosio, cert. Comn: Religious mural, House of Light, Ibadan, Nigeria, 72; panel for Kwanza celebration, Studio Mus, Harlem, NY, 73 & 74. Exhib: Kujichagulia, Studio Mus, Harlem, 73; Blacks: USA Now, New York Cult Ctr, 73; In Her Own Image, Fleisher Art Mem, Philadelphia, 74; Children of Africa, Am Mus Natural Hist, New York, 74-75; Sojourn, Carole Byard, Valerie Maynard, Gallery 1199, New York, 75; Amherst Univ, 77; Gallery 1199, New York, 78. Teaching: Instr life drawing & basic drawing, New York-Phoenix Sch Design, 68-71; instr painting, First Fruits Prog, Metrop Mus Art, New York, 74- Pos: Pres, Darshan, New York, 74-; mural artist, NJ State Coun on the Arts, 76; US artist partic, FESTAC, Lagos Nigeria, 77; artist-in-residence, NY Found for the Arts, 78. Awards: Ford Found Travel Grant, Inst Int Educ, 72; Unique New Yorker Art Award, 77; Coretta Scott King Award for Africa Dream, 78. Bibliog: Barbara Cohen (auth), Careers (filmstrip), Harcourt Brace Jovanovich, 74; Marla Hoffman (auth), Two women who paint, World Mag, Long View Publ, 74; Helen King (auth), Carole Byard speaks with her art, In: What It Is, Let's Save the Children Inc. Mem: Westbeth Graphic Artist; Black Artist Guild. Style & Technique: Imaginative realistic oil paintings, charcoal drawings, lithographs and linocuts; portrayals of humanity through Black experience. Publ: Illusr, Willy, 71, illusr, Nomi and the Magic Fish, 73 & illusr, The Sycamore Tree, African Folktales, 74, Doubleday; illusr, Under Christopher's Hat, Scribners, 72; illusr, Arthur Mitchell, Crowell, 75; auth, Africa Dream, 77 & I Can Do It By Myself, 78, Crowell. Mailing Add: 463 West St New York NY 10014

BYARS, DONNA
SCULPTOR, COLLAGE ARTIST
b Rock Island, Ill. Study: Stephens Col, Columbia, Mo; Iowa State Univ, BA; Parsons Sch of Design, New York, with John Kacere & Leo Manso. Work: Va Mus of Fine Arts, Richmond. Exhib: Filth, Hudson River Mus, Yonkers, NY, 71; US Int Artists, Berlin, 72; Works on Paper/Art by Women, Sarah Lawrence Col, Bronxville, NY, 75; Collage, Leslie Rankow Gallery, New York, 75; Soft Sculpture, Akron Art Inst, Ohio, 75-76; Contemp Reflections 1975-76 (auth, catalogue), Aldrich Mus of Contemp Art, Ridgefield, Conn, 75-76; 40 Years of Am Collage, Buecker & Harpsichords, New York/St Peter's Col Art Gallery, Jersey City, NJ, 76; Contact: Women & Nature 30 Contemp Women, Lucy Lippard, Hurlbutt Gallery, Greenwich, Conn, 77; Paper, Fabric, Glass, Just Above Midtown Gallery, New York, 77; Artists-in-Residence, Palisades Interstate Park, NY, 75-77; Women Artists 78, City Univ New York, 78; Drawing Show, Ginza Kaigakan, Tokyo, Japan, 78; Overview: An Exhib in 2 Parts by AIR Gallery, Queens, NY, 78; one-woman shows, 55 Mercer, New York, 75 & AIR Gallery, New York, 77. Teaching: Instr basic drawing, Evening Div, Parsons Sch of Design, 76-; instr collage, New Sch for Social Res, New York, 77- Awards: Artist-in-residence grant, Palisades Interstate Park, Am the Beautiful Fund, Washington, DC, 76. Bibliog: Jill Dunkar (auth), article in Villager, 5/77; Ellen Lubell (auth), article in Arts Mag, 9/77; Carolee Thea (auth), article in Womanart, Fall 77. Mem: Col Art Asn. Style & Technique: Soft sculpture/assemblage and collage. Media: Sculpture, boxes and collage. Dealer: AIR Gallery 97 Wooster St New York NY 10012. Mailing Add: 4970 Independence Ave Bronx NY 10471

BYE, RANULPH (DEBAYEUX)
PAINTER, EDUCATOR
b Princeton, NJ, June 17, 16. Study: Philadelphia Col Art; Art Students League. Work: Mus Fine Arts, Boston; Munson-Williams-Proctor Inst, Utica, NY; Reading Pub Mus, Pa; Smithsonian Inst, Washington, DC; Pa Hist & Mus Comn, Harrisburg, Pa. Comn: Mine Force (paintings of naval base), US Navy Dept, Charleston, SC, 66. Exhib: Ann Exhibs, Allied Artists Am, Am Watercolor Soc, Philadelphia Water Color Club, Salmagundi Club & Nat Arts Club New York. Teaching: Assoc prof art, Moore Col Art, Philadelphia, 48- Awards: John L Ernst Award, Am Watercolor Soc, 66, William Church Osborne Mem Prize, 71, Goldsmith Award, 73; Eastman Prize for Watercolor, Salmagundi Club, 72, Louis E Seley Cash Purchase Prize, 78. Bibliog: Wendy Buehr (auth), Station Closed, Am Heritage Press, 66. Mem: Salmagundi Club; Am Watercolor Soc; Allied Artists Am; Garden State Watercolor Soc; assoc Nat Acad Design; plus others. Style & Technique: Pictorial record in watercolor of railroad stations in eight eastern states, circa 1900. Media: Watercolor, Oil. Publ: Auth, Seascapes and Landscapes, 56 & Watercolor Technique American Artists, 66, Watson-Guptill; auth, The Vanishing Depot, Livingston, 73. Mailing Add: RD 4 Doylestown PA 18901

BYNUM, E ANDERSON (ESTHER PEARL)
LITHOGRAPHER, ART ADMINISTRATOR
b Henderson, Tex, Dec 19, 22. Study: Dallas Mus Fine Arts, 52; NTex State Univ, BA, 65; Univ Md, MA, 72, advan grad specialist cert, 73; also lithography with Tadeusz Lapinski. Work: US Civil Serv Bldg, Washington, DC; Montgomery Co Contemp Print Collection & Montgomery Co Pub Schs, Md. Exhib: New York Int Art Show, 70; Baltimore Mus, 73-74; Jersey City Mus, NJ, 74; 26th Ann Exhib Tex Watercolor Soc, McNay Art Inst, San Antonio, 75; Lowe Art Mus, Univ Miami, Fla, 75. Teaching: Teacher art, Montgomery Co Pub Schs, Rockville, Md, 65-75, elem art coordr, 75- Mem: Nat Art Educ Asn; Tex Watercolor Soc; Am Craft Coun; Graphics Soc. Style & Technique: Landscape in watercolor, plastic sculpture, geometric, photographic collage in light lithography. Media: Watercolor, Plate & Stone Lithographs. Res: Effect of how the stimuli in the environment influences the elementary child's art product. Dealer: Md Fedn of Art PO Box 1886 Annapolis MD 21404. Mailing Add: 1221 Pinecrest Circle Silver Spring MD 20910

BYRD, D GIBSON
EDUCATOR, PAINTER
b Tulsa, Okla, Feb 1, 23. Study: Univ Tulsa, with Alexandre Hogue, BA; Univ Iowa, MA. Work: Butler Inst Am Art, Youngstown, Ohio; Philbrook Art Ctr, Tulsa; Kalamazoo Art Ctr, Mich; Wright Art Ctr, Beloit Col; Madison Art Ctr, Wis. Exhib: Walker Art Ctr Biennial Exhib, Minneapolis, 58; Wisconsin Renaissance, Marine Bank, Milwaukee, 65; 2nd Nat Drawing Exhib, Univ Wis-Green Bay, 70; Arts: USA II, Northern Ill Univ, 71; Wisconsin Directions, Milwaukee Art Ctr, 75; plus others. Teaching: Prof art, Univ Wis-Madison, 55-; vis lectr, Sch Art Educ, Birmingham, Eng, 65-66. Pos: Dir, Kalamazoo Art Ctr, 52- 55. Mem: Madison Art Ctr (vpres); Inst Study Art in Educ, New York (bd mem); Col Art Asn; Nat Art Educ Asn; Wis Art Educ Asn. Style & Technique: Figurative. Media: Oil, Gouache. Publ: Auth, The artist-teacher in America, Col Art J, winter 63-64; auth, Theodore Robinson (exhib monogr), Univ Wis, 64; auth, Artist-teacher in America: John Sloan, Sch Arts Mag, 66; auth, Visiting artists: thoughts & second thoughts, Visual Arts Educ, 70; auth, Thomas Hart Benton (exhib catalog), Madison Art Ctr, 70. Dealer: Bradley Galleries 2565 N Downer Ave Milwaukee WI 53211. Mailing Add: Dept of Art Univ Wis Madison WI 53711

BYRD, ROBERT JOHN
ILLUSTRATOR, INSTRUCTOR
b Atlantic City, NJ, Jan 11, 42. Study: Philadelphia Mus Col of Art, BFA(graphic arts), 66. Work: Free Libr of Philadelphia; Philadelphia Col of Art. Exhib: Soc of Illusr, New York, 71-77; The Graphis Press, Zurich, Switz, 74-77; Philadelphia Art Alliance, 74; Bologna Worlds Children's Bk Fair, Italy, 75; Design & Illus: USA, Teheran, Iran, 78. Teaching: Portfolio sem illusr, Philadelphia Col of Art, 76-77; instr illus, Moore Col of Art, Philadelphia, 77- Awards: Citation of Merit, Soc of Illusr, 76; Jr Lit Award for The Gondolier of Venice, 76 & The Detective of London, 78. Bibliog: Diana Klemin (auth), The portfolio of Robert Byrd, Am Artist, 71; Linda Munich & Marty Jacobs (producers), For Your Information, WKBS Television, 78. Mem: Philadelphia Col Art Alumni Asn; Philadelphia Children's Reading Round Table; Illusr Guild (Graphic Arts Guild). Style & Technique: In black and white work, ink line or ink line and watercolor washes; in color work, ink line and glazes or washes of ink and watercolor and colored pencils. Publ: Illusr, Rebecca Hatpin, 73, Pinch Penny Mouse, 74, The Gondolier of Venice, 76 & The Detective of London, 78, Windmill Bks. Mailing Add: 409 Warwick Rd Haddonfield NJ 08033

BYRNE, CHARLES JOSEPH
DESIGNER
b Louisville, Ky, Oct 15, 43. Study: Univ Louisville, BS; Wayne State Univ. Work: Detroit Inst of Arts, Mich; Mus of Mod Art, New York. Comn: Wall graphics with Smith, Hinchman & Grylls Assoc, Inc, State Univ NY Col, Stony Brook, 73, John Deere Co, Waterloo, Iowa, 74, Caterpillar Tractor Corp, Peoria, Ill, 74 & Mich Bell Tel, Grand Rapids, 76; wall graphic, Interior Designers Guild, San Diego, Calif, 77. Exhib: Best Am Posters, Print Mag, New York, 74; 15th Ann, Commun Arts Mag, Palo Alto, Calif, 74; Int Poster Exhib, Dublin Arts Festival, 75; Am Inst of Graphic Arts Ann 1974-75, New York, 75. Teaching: Instr, Interior Designers Guild, San Diego, 77- Pos: Cur, Dept of Fine Arts, Univ Louisville, Ky, 63-66, asst univ designer, 66-70; chief designer graphics & signage, Smith, Hinchman & Grylls Assoc, Inc, Detroit, 70-76. Awards: Indust Design Mag, Design Rev, 73; Commun Arts Mag Award, 74; Commun Graphics Award, Am Inst of Graphic Arts, 75. Bibliog: Articles in Signs of the Times Mag, 12/73, Indust Design Mag, 11-12/76 & Print Casebooks II, Best in Environmental Graphics, 77. Style & Technique: Typography oriented in graphic work. Media: Poster. Publ: Co-auth, Computer Graphics, Mich Soc of Archit Bull, 4/75; co-auth, Downtown vs Suburban Shopping Centers: a Clear Case of Identity, Detroit Free Press Mag, 2/76. Mailing Add: 8525 Via Mallorca La Jolla CA 92037

BYRNE, JAMES RICHARD
VIDEO ARTIST
b St Paul, Minn, July 19, 50. Study: Univ of Minn, BES. Work: Walker Art Ctr, Minneapolis, Minn; Univ of Mass, Amherst. Exhib: Thirteenth Sao Paulo Biennial, Sao Paulo, Brazil, 75; The Video Show, Serpentine Gallery, London, 75; Video Art, Inst of Contemp Art, Philadelphia, 75; Biennial Exhib, Whitney Mus of Am Art, New York, 75; Moving Image Makers, Minneapolis Inst of the Arts, 76; Video: An Overview, San Francisco Mus of Mod Art, 76; 10th Biennial de Paris, Mus of Mod Art, Paris, 77. Bibliog: Lisa Lyons (auth), James Byrne, Studio Int, 5-6/76; Tim Harding (auth), James Byrne, Video Art/Hartcourt Brace, 76; Will Jones (auth), Video Art Broadcast, Minneapolis Tribune, 6/77. Style & Technique: Video tape installations & performance; printmaking. Media: Video tape, mixed; intaglio. Dealer: Hanson Cowles Gallery 331 Second Ave N Minneapolis MN 55401. Mailing Add: 649 Spring NE Minneapolis MN 55413

BYRNES, JAMES BERNARD
MUSEUM DIRECTOR, ART HISTORIAN
b New York, NY, Feb 19, 17. Study: Nat Acad Design, New York, 36-38; Am Artists Sch, New York, 38-40; Art Students League, 41-42; Ist Meschini, Univ Perugia, Rome, 51-52. Collections Arranged: Edgar Degas, His Family & Friends in New Orleans (with catalog), 65; Odyssey of an Art Collector—the Collection of Mr & Mrs Frederick S Stafford, Paris (with catalog), 66; Arts of Ancient & Modern Latin America (with catalog), 68; Rothko, 74; Artist as Collector—Ethnic Art, 75. Teaching: Vis prof hist 20th century art, Univ Fla, 60-61. Pos: Cur mod & contemp art, Los Angeles Co Mus, 46-54; dir, Colorado Springs Fine Arts Ctr, 54-56; assoc dir, NC Mus Art, 56-58, dir, 58-60; dir, New Orleans Mus Art, 61-72; dir, Newport Harbor Art Mus, Newport Beach, Calif, 72-75; consult fine arts. Awards: Knight in the Order of Leopold II, Belg Govt, 72. Mem: Asn Art Mus Dirs; Appraisers Soc Am; Appraisers Asn Am; Am Asn Mus; Int Coun Mus; hon life mem Am Inst Designers. Res: Nineteenth and twentieth century art; seventeenth century Dutch art; pre-Columbian and African art. Mailing Add: James B Byrnes & Assoc 7820 Mulholland Dr Los Angeles CA 90046

BYRON, CHARLES ANTHONY
ART DEALER
b Istanbul, Turkey, Dec 15, 19. Study: Ecole Libre Sci Polit, Paris, France; Univ Paris; Harvard Univ; BA, LLB & MA. Pos: Dir, Byron Gallery, New York. Mem: Art Dealers Asn Am, Inc. Specialty: Contemporary and surrealist art. Mailing Add: 25 E 83rd St New York NY 10028

BYRON, GENE
PAINTER, DESIGNER
b London, Ont, Can, May 20, 15; US citizen. Study: Detroit Sch Fine & Appl Arts; Art Students League; also with Fletcher Martin. Work: Gen Motors of Mex collection. Comn: Lighting fixtures (with O'Neil Ford & Assoc, San Antonio, Tex), St Mary's Hall, San Antonio, 66 & Harding L Lawrence residence, Patagonia, Ariz, 69; lighting fixtures & decorative pieces (with W M Pahlam, New York), Exten Tex A&M Col, Col Sta, 72; Balcones develop (with Lance, Larcade, Bechtol, San Antonio), San Miguel de Allende, Gto, Mex, 74. Exhib: Spring Show, Laguna Gloria Art Gallery, Tex Fine Arts Asn, Austin, 57; one-man shows, Salon de la Plastica Mex, Inst Nac Bellas Artes, Mex, 55, Witte Mus, San Antonio, Tex, 57, Arte A C Monterrey, Mex, 62 & Arte y Libros SA, Monterrey, Mex, 73. Teaching: Instr drawing & painting, Univ Nuevo Leon, Monterrey, Mex, 49-57; artist in residence, San Antonio Art Inst, Tex, 57-58. Bibliog: Thomas M Granfill (auth), Image of Mexico, Tex Quart, Univ Tex, Austin, 69; TV profile, Artist at Work, Siempre Mag, Mex, 69. Mem: Arte A C, Monterrey, Mex; Arts & Crafts Guild, San Antonio, Tex. Media: Oil, Brush; Metals, Wood. Mailing Add: Apartado 74 Guanajuato Gto Mexico

BYWATERS, JERRY
PAINTER, ART HISTORIAN
b Paris, Tex, May 21, 06. Study: Southern Methodist Univ, AB; Art Students League; spec study in Europe & Mex. Work: Mus Fine Arts, Dallas Dallas, Tex; Southern Methodist Univ, Dallas; Houston, Quanah, Farmersville & Trinity Post Off Bldgs, Tex. Exhib: Golden Gate Int Expos, San Francisco, 39; New York World's Fair, 39 & 40; City Art Mus, St Louis, Mo, 40; 53rd Ann Am Painting & Sculpture, Art Inst Chicago, 42; Am Painting & Sculpture, Metrop Mus Art, New York, 50. Collections Arranged: 200 Years of American Painting, 46; Six Southwestern States, 47; Pre-Columbian Art, 50; Lasker Collection, 53; Otis Dozier, 56; Survey of Texas Painting, 57; Andrew Dasburg, 58; Religious Art of the Western World, 58; South American Art Today, 59; Century of Art & Life in Texas, 61; The Arts of Man, 62; Indian Art, 63; Texas Painting & Sculpture, 71. Teaching: Asst prof painting, Southern Methodist Univ, 36-63, prof NAm arts, 64-71, emer prof, 71- Pos: Art critic, Dallas Morning News, 33-39; dir, Dallas Mus Fine Arts, 43-64; dir, Pollock Galleries, Southern Methodist Univ, 65-70; regional archivist, Tex Proj, Archives Am Art, Smithsonian Inst, 75- Awards: First Prize, Tex Ann, Houston Mus, 40; Dealey Purchase Prize, Dallas Mus Fine Arts, 42; Caller-Times Purchase Prize, Corpus Christi Mus, 47. Publ: Auth, Diego Rivera and Mexican popular art, Southwest Rev, 28; auth, Twelve from Texas, Southern Methodist Univ, 52; co-auth, Everett Spruce, Univ Tex, 58; auth, Andrew Dasburg, Am Fedn Arts, 59; co-auth, Texas Painting & Sculpture: the 20th Century, 71. Mailing Add: 3625 Amherst Dallas TX 75225

C

CABALLERO, EMILIO
EDUCATOR, PAINTER
b Newark, NJ, July 4, 19. Study: Amarillo Col, AA, 40; WTex State Univ, BA, 42; Columbia Univ, MA, 49, DEd, 55. Work: Col Southwest; Lovett Mem Libr, Pampa, Tex; St Anne's Cath Church, Canyon, Tex; YWCA, Amarillo, Tex; Pampa Youth Ctr. Comn: Mosaic facade, Tex Midland Pub Libr, 58; copper enamels, Amarillo Savings & Loan, 68, Amarillo Munic Bldg, 69 & Bank Southwest, Midland, 70; Marion Koogler McNay Art Inst, San Antonio, 74-75. Exhib: Tex Oil 58, Dallas Pub Libr, 58; Tex Fine Arts Circuit Show, 68; 104th Ann Am Watercolor Soc Exhib, New York, 71; 9th Ann Southwestern Exhib Prints & Drawings, Dallas; Mid-Am Ann, William Rockhill Nelson Gallery, Kansas City; plus many one-man shows. Teaching: Spec instr art, Amarillo Pub Schs, 46-49; prof art, WTex State Univ, 49- Pos: Art consult, Agnes Russell Ctr, Columbia Univ, 51-52. Awards: Kappa Pi Gold Plaque Hall of Fame, 70; Faculty Excellence Award, WTex State Univ, 72; Purchase Prizes, Tex Watercolor Soc, 74 & 75. Bibliog: Elsie Wilbanks (auth), Art on the Texas plains, Lubbock Art Asn, 59. Mem: Fel Royal Soc Gt Brit; life mem Plainview Art Asn; Llano Estacado Heritage NMex (art ed, 70). Style & Technique: Evocative wet wash watercolor method; direct application of glass enamel to copper surfaces and single firing. Media: Watercolor, Enamel. Publ: Contribr, Expression through puppetry, Tex Outlook, 47; contribr, Evocative painting, Design, 49; contribr, Watercolor Painting in Elementary Grades, Am Crayon Co, 49; contribr, Design Mag, 74-75. Mailing Add: 6317 Calumet Amarillo TX 79016

CABLE, MAXINE ROTH
SCULPTOR
b Philadelphia, Pa. Study: Tyler Sch Fine Art, Temple Univ, AA; Corcoran Sch Art, George Washington Univ, AB; Am Univ, with Hans Hofmann. Work: Allied Chem Corp Gallery, New York; Nat Acad Sci, Washington, DC; George Washington Univ. Comn: Environ sculpture, Allied Chem Corp, 69-70; sculpture, Wolf Trap Farm Performing Arts, Va, 73. Exhib: Area Exhibs, Corcoran Gallery Art, 55-67; Artists Equity Traveling Exhib, Columbia Mus, SC, 73-74; one-woman shows, Adams Morgan Gallery, Washington, DC, 64, Hodson Gallery, Hood Col, Frederick, Md, 69 & Gallery Ten, Washington, DC, 75. Teaching: Consult art, Montgomery Co, Md, 57-65 & Head Start Prog, Washington, DC, 70. Pos: Dir, Glen Echo Graphics Workshop, Md, 75. Awards: Sculpture Award, David Smith, Corcoran Gallery Art, 55; First Prize in Painting, Smithsonian Inst, 67. Bibliog: Washington Artists Today, Artists Equity Asn, 67; Art for Public Places, Dept Housing & Urban Develop, 73. Style & Technique: Environmental sculpture using water, wind, light, aluminum and Plexiglas. Media: Mixed Media, Natural and Man-Made. Dealer: Gallery Ten Ltd 1519 Connecticut Ave Washington DC 20036. Mailing Add: 7000 Buxton Terr Bethesda MD 20034

CABRERA, GELES
SCULPTOR
b Mexico, DF, Aug 2, 30. Study: Univ NAm, Mex; Acad San Carlos; Acad San Algejandro, Univ Nac de Habana, Cuba; Sch Sculpture & Painting, La Esmeralda, S E P, Mex, DF. Work: Mus Arte Mod, Mexico City; Mus Mod Art, Tel Aviv; Gallery Plastica Mexicana. Exhib: One-woman shows, Galeria Mot Orendain (sculpture), Mexico, DF, 49, Salon de Plastica Mexicana, Inst Nac Bellas Artes, 54; Casa del Arquictecto, Nat Col Archit, 59 & Pan Am Union, Washington, DC, 59; Mus de Arte Mod, Mexico, DF, 75; Galeria Mer-Kup, 77. Collections Arranged: Permanent Collection, Museo Escultorico Xicotencatl. Teaching: Teacher sculpture & drawing, Univ NAm, Mex, 55- Pos: Owner & founder, Museo Escultorico Xicotencatl, Mexico, DF. Awards: First & Second Prize, Salon de Bellas Artes, la Habana, Cuba, 49; Hon Mention, 3rd Biennal, Nac Sculpture Exhib, Inst Bellas Artes. Bibliog: Antonio Luna Arroyo (auth), Panorama de la escultura Mexicana contemporanea, I B N A, 64; Mario Montforte M (auth), Las piedras vivas, Sculpture Soc Mex, 65; Paul Westheim (auth), Geles Cabrera, Mexico, 77. Mem: Plastica Mexicana, Inst Bellas Artes; Col de Dibujo y Modelado, Univ NAm, Mex. Mailing Add: Corina 49 Colonia del Carmen Mexico 21 DF Mexico

CADDELL, FOSTER
PAINTER, INSTRUCTOR
b Pawtucket, RI, Aug 2, 21. Study: RI Sch Design; pvt study with Peter Helck, Robert Brackman & Guy Wiggins. Comn: Off portraits of Sen Thomas J Dodd of Conn, Washington, DC & Judge L P Moore, US Circuit Ct Appeals, Second Dist, New York; portrait of Dr George S Avery, Dir of Brooklyn Bot Gardens, NY; portrait of Carl Cuttler, Founder of Marine Hist Asn Mystic Seaport, Mystic, Conn; relig paintings for many denominations incl Church of Eng; portraits of many bus & civic leaders. Exhib: Acad Artists Am Nat Exhib, Springfield Mus Fine Arts, 63-77; Am Artists Prof League Grand Nat Exhib, 70-75; Am Watercolor Soc Ann, Nat Acad Galleries, 71; Slater Mus, Norwich Acad, 71-77; Nat Arts Club, New York, 73-75; one-man show, Slader Mem Mus, Norwich Free Acad. Teaching: Instr, Foster Caddell's Art Sch, currently. Pos: Lithograph artist, Providence Lithograph Co, 39-52; artist with Far East Air Force, 43-46. Awards: William W White Memorial Prize, Salmagundi Club, New York, 73; Lucien Schimpf Award, Acad Artists Am, 73; Michael Guiheen Award, 75. Bibliog: Norman Kent (auth), Foster Caddell-artist & teacher, Am Artist Mag, 12/68; Wendon Blake (auth), Creative Color, Watson-Guptil, 73; Foster Caddell—landscape painter, The Artist, London. Mem: Providence Art Club; Am Artists Prof League; Acad Artists Am; Salmagundi Club. Style & Technique: Traditional modified impressionism. Media: Oil, Pastel. Publ: Illusr, educ bks, Ginn, 53-68; illusr, series sports bks, Little, Brown & Co; auth & illusr, Keys to Successful Landscape Painting, 76 & Keys to Successful Color in Landscape Painting, (in press), Pitman & Sons, London & Watson-Guptil; also relig illusr for most Protestant denominations educ & instructional bks & mat. Mailing Add: Northlight Rte 49 Voluntown CT 06384

CADE, WALTER, III
PAINTER
b New York, NY, Jan 17, 36. Study: Inst Mod Art, New York. Exhib: C W Post Col, Long Island Univ, Brookville, NY, 68; Art Ann, Whitney Mus Am Art, New York, 69-70, Contemporary Black Artists in America, 71; Huntington Twp Art League Show, Hecksher Mus, Huntington, NY, 69 & 71; Corcoran Gallery, Washington, DC, 72; Queens Cult Ctr for the Arts, New York, 73; one-man show, Ocean Co Col, 77. Media: Acrylic, Collage. Bibliog: Jeanne Paris (auth), The ghetto sparkles, Long Island Sun Press, 5/7/72; article in Playboy Mag, 72; article in New York Amsterdam News, 5/6/72. Mailing Add: c/o Studio Gallery 172-03 119th Ave Jamaica NY 11434

CADGE, WILLIAM FLEMING
DESIGNER, PHOTOGRAPHER
b Philadelphia, Pa, May 5, 24. Study: Philadelphia Mus Sch Art, 45-49. Pos: Freelance designer, Philadelphia, 49-50; asst art dir, Eve Bull, Philadelphia, 50-52 & Woman's Home Companion, 52-56; art dir, Doyle, Dane & Bernbach, New York, 56-57; assoc art dir, McCall's Mag, 59-61; art dir, Redbook Mag, 61-76; owner, Bill Cadge Inc, 76- Awards: Numerous Gold Medals & Awards, Art Dirs Club, NY, NJ & Philadelphia; Awards Excellence, CA Mag Show, 67 & 68; Gold Medal, Soc Illusr, 71 & 72. Mem: Soc Illusr; Art Dirs Club NY (exec bd, 66-68). Mailing Add: 33 Colonial Ave Dobbs Ferry NY 10522

CADIEUX, MICHAEL EUGENE
EDUCATOR, PAINTER
b Missoula, Mont, June 15, 40. Study: Univ Mont, BA & MA. Work: Univ Mont Fine Arts Collection, Missoula; Yuma Fine Arts Asn Permanent Collection, Ariz. Exhib: Spokane-Pac NW Ann, Cheney Cowles Mus, 66; SW Yuma Fine Arts Arts, 66-68; Ariz Ann, Phoenix Art Mus, 67; Tucson Art Mus Ann, Ariz, 68; Mid-Am, Nelson-Atkins Mus, Kansas City, Mo, 72, 30 Miles, 75; Mid-Am, St Louis Art Mus, 72; Davidson Nat Drawing, Davidson Col Galleries, 75. Collections Arranged: Univ Wis Ctr Syst, 67; Univ Md, 67; Western Asn Art Mus Traveling Exhib, 69; fac shows, Spiva Art Ctr, Memphis Acad, 75-78; Mo Art Coun-Mid Am Arts Alliance Shows. Teaching: Instr painting & drawing, Ariz Western Col, Yuma, 66-69; assoc prof art hist, Kansas City Art Inst, Mo, 69- Pos: Reviewer art publ, SE Asia in Rev, 76- Awards: Third Place, 2nd Southwestern, Yuma Fine Arts, 67; Off Educ grant study in India, US Off Educ, 71. Bibliog: Donald Hoffman (art ed), Here's Art All in a Row, Kansas City Star, 72 & Michael Cadieux, Kansas City Star, 77. Style & Technique: Kaliedoscopic skeins of brightly colored decorative paintings and collage. Media: Painting collage. Res: Cross-cultural art history. Publ: Auth (review), The mural tradition in Indian painting, SE Asia in Rev, 77. Mailing Add: 5807 Locust Kansas City MO 64110

CADLE, RAY KENNETH
PAINTER, CRAFTSMAN
b Ravenswood, WVa, Aug 26, 06. Study: Dayton Art Inst; woodblock printing with Kiyoshi Saito & suiboku painting with Ryukyu Saito, Tokyo. Exhib: Hanga Group Exhib, Metrop Gallery, Ueno Park, Tokyo, 52; one-man shows, Int House Gallery, Tokyo, 54 & Centernary Col Gallery, Shreveport, La, 65; Morris Harvey Col, Charleston, WVa, 59; La State Mus, Shreveport, 75; Barnwell Art Ctr, Shreveport. Pos: Staff arts & crafts dir, Hq Fifth Air Force, Nagoya, Japan, 49-50; staff arts & crafts dir, Hq Far E Air Forces, Tokyo, 50-57; staff arts & crafts dir, Hq Pac Air Forces, Honolulu, 57-58; command arts & crafts dir, Hq Second Air Force and Eighth Air Force, Barksdale AFB, La, 61- Awards: Nat Recreation & Park Asn Fel Arts & Crafts, 64. Mem: Allied Artists, WVa; Honolulu Printmakers; Men's Art Guild, Shreveport (bd mem, 66-); Int Suiboku Soc, Japan. Style & Technique: Oriental concepts, batiks, papier mache objects. Dealer: C C Hardman 712 Texas St Shreveport LA 71101 Mailing Add: Towne House Apt 523 726 Cotton St Shreveport LA 71101

CADMUS, PAUL
PAINTER, PRINTMAKER
b New York, NY, Dec 17, 04. Study: Nat Acad Design, 16-26; Art Students League, with Joseph Pennell, 28. Work: Whitney Mus Am Art, New York; Metrop Mus Art, New York; Mus Mod Art, New York; Fogg Art Mus, Cambridge, Mass; Smithsonian Inst, Washington, DC. Comn: Costumes & scenery, Filling Station Ballet, Ballet Caravan, 38; mural, Parcel Post Bldg, Richmond, Va, 38. Pos: Vpres, Bd Control, Art Students League, 35- Awards: Flora Mayer Witkowsky Prize, Art Inst Chicago, 45; Nat Inst Arts & Lett Grant, 61; Purchase Prize, Norfolk Mus Arts & Sci, 67. Bibliog: Paul Cadmus of Navy fame has his first art show, Life Mag, 3/29/37; Harry Salpeter (auth), Paul Cadmus: enfant terrible, Esquire Mag, 7/37; Una E Johnson (auth), Paul Cadmus/prints and drawings, sw Brooklyn Mus, 68. Mem: Soc Am Graphic Artists; Nat Inst Arts & Lett. Style & Technique: Representational; straight-forward and precise. Media: Tempera. Dealer: Midtown Galleries 11 E 57th St New York NY 10022. Mailing Add: PO Box 1255 Weston CT 06883

CADY, DENNIS VERN
ART CONSERVATOR, PAINTER
b Portland, Ore, Nov 10, 44. Study: Portland State Univ; Brooklyn Mus Art Sch, printmaking & drawing with Rubin Tam; Pratt Inst Graphic Ctr; Empire State Col, BS, plus independent study of tech aspects of paper restoration; Margo Fieden Galleries, New York, apprenticeship in restoration and preserv of works on paper, 74-77. Comn: Poster, 72, costumes for dance (with Frank Garcia), 74, costumes, 77, Phillis Lamhut Dance Co; poster, Emery Hermans Dance Theatre, 75. Exhib: Max Beckman Scholar Students Paintings, Brooklyn Art Mus, 69; Ore Artists Drawings & Watercolors, Portland Art Mus, 70; Prints & Drawings, 73, Miniature Prints, 73 & Prints, 74, Terrain Graphics, New York; one-man shows, Drawings & Prints, Renshaw Gallery, Linfield Col, Ore, 71 & Margo Fieden Gallery, New York, 76. Pos: Free lance restorer, New York, 77- Awards: Nat Scholastics Award, New York, 62. Mem: Portland Art Asn. Style & Technique: Abstract-expressionism of landscape and city mass; watercolor; monotype, etching and lithographic printmaking. Media: Oil on Canvas; Silkscreen. Publ: Auth, Block Prints by Dennis Cady, Hillside Ctr, Portland, Ore, 71. Dealer: Katsko Suzuki 38 E 57th St New York NY 10022. Mailing Add: 45 Orchard St New York NY 10002

CAGLIOTI, VICTOR
PAINTER, SCULPTOR
b Inwood, NY, July 20, 35. Study: Pasadena City Col; State Univ NY Buffalo, with Peter Busa; NY Univ, BS, with Howard Conant, John Opper, Hale Woodruff & Martin Craig; Columbia Univ, with Stephen Greene. Work: NY Univ; 3M Co, St Paul, Minn; Honeywell Corp of Minn; St Louis Park Ctr, Minn; Fed Reserve Bank, Minn. Comn: Wall relief (an assemblage), comn by Dept Health, Educ & Welfare, Nassau Co, NY, 69; comn to experiment with indust process works of art, Colwell Press, 72. Exhib: Albright-Knox Regional, Buffalo, 55; six one-man shows, Buffalo, NY & Minneapolis, 56-71; Nat Inst Arts & Lett Ann, New York, 70; Collectors Exhib, Parrish Art Mus, New York, 71 & 76; Ashawagh Invitational, 75, 76 & 77; Guild Hall, East Hampton, NY, 77; Italian-Am Inst, Chicago, 77. Teaching: Assoc prof drawing & painting & asst chmn dept, Univ Minn, 70- Awards: Albright Art Sch Fel, 54; Artists-Writers Revolving Fund Award, Nat Inst Arts & Lett, 68; Nat Competition for Govt Comn, 69. Bibliog: Jack Azarch (auth), interview in Avanti, 70; Gordon Brown (auth, Editorial focus, Arts Mag, 70; Don Morrison (auth), news rev in Minneapolis Star, 71. Mem: New Art Asn (exec comt, 71-); Artists Equity Asn. Media: Acrylic, Oil, Constructions. Publ: Illusr, Opera News, 53; ed & auth, Pictures on exhibit, 69 & 70; The Artist (doc film), 75. Mailing Add: 167 Bedford St SE Minneapolis MN 55414

CAHILL, JAMES FRANCIS
ART HISTORIAN, EDUCATOR
b Fort Bragg, Calif, Aug 13, 26. Study: Univ Calif, Berkeley, BA, 50; Univ Mich, with Max Loehr, MA, 53, PhD, 58. Collections Arranged: Guest-dir, The Art of Southern Sung China (with catalog), Asia House Gallery, New York, 62, Fantastics and Eccentrics in Chinese Painting (with catalog), 67 & Scholar-Painters of Japan: the Nanga School (with catalog), 72. Teaching: Prof hist art, Univ Calif, Berkeley, 65- Pos: Cur Chinese art, Freer Gallery Art, Washington, DC, 58-65. Awards: Louise Wallace Hackney Scholar, 50-52; Fulbright Scholar, 54-55; Guggenheim Fel, 72-73. Mem: Col Art Asn Am. Res: Chinese and Japanese painting; Chinese bronzes. Publ: Auth, Chinese Painting, Skira, Geneva, Switz, 60; co-auth, The Freer Chinese Bronzes, 67; auth, Hills Beyond a River: Chinese Painting of the Yuan Dynasty, 76; auth, Parting at the Shore, Chinese Painting of the Early & Middle Ming Dynasty, 78. Mailing Add: 2422 Hillside Ave Berkeley CA 94704

CAIMITE (LYNNE RUSKIN)
PAINTER, ILLUSTRATOR
b Youngstown, Ohio, Jan 23, 22. Study: Syracuse Univ, 38-40; Cleveland Inst Art, 40-41; Western Reserve Med Sch, spec study in anat, 52-53. Work: Butler Inst Am Art, Youngstown, Ohio; Nat Gallery Guatemala; Nat Gallery Haiti; Elliott Mus, Fla. Comn: Oil portrait, comn by UN rep from Holland, Van der Heijden, Haiti, 63; oil landscape, comn by Baroness Von Bronkhurst, San Juan, PR, 64; oil portrait, Mrs Oscar L Seagle, St Croix, 77. Exhib: One-woman shows, Butler Inst Am Art, Ohio, 62, La Casa del Arte, PR, 65, Marche Hare Gallery, San Juan, 65, Lord & Taylor Art Gallery, New York, 66 & Elliott Mus, Fla, 74; Inst Francaise, Haiti, 63; Ferre Mus, PR, 64; among other one-woman shows. Pos: Med illusr, St Luke's Hosp, Cleveland & Res Dept, Western Reserve Med Sch, 52-62. Bibliog: Aubelin Jolicoeur (auth), Caimite exhibits, Haiti Sun, Port-au-Prince, 62-63; Aage Heinberg (auth), Voodo Manden, Berlingske Tidende, Denmark, 5/14/65; Emeline Paige (auth), Caribbean impressionist exhibiting..., Stuart Daily News, Fla, 11/17/74. Style & Technique: Oil painting with brush or palette knife; landscapes, ethnic groups. Media: Oil, Watercolor. Mailing Add: PO Box 2719 Christiansted St Croix VI 00820

CAIN, JAMES FREDERICK, JR
PRINTMAKER, MUSEUM CURATOR
b Philadelphia, Pa, June 24, 38. Study: Assumption Col, Mass, AB; Tyler Sch Art, Temple Univ, MFA; Laval Univ; Harvard Univ; Univ Pa. Work: Mus Mod Art; Los Angeles Co Mus; Lessing J Rosenwald Collection, Jenkintown, Pa; Art Inst Chicago; Pasadena Art Mus; Mus Fine Arts San Diego; plus others. Collections Arranged: M C Escher, Prints from the Roosevelt Collection & Alfred Stieglitz, Key-Set on deposit with the Nat Gallery of Art, 72-76; Medieval Miniatures from the Rosenwald Collection, Nat Gallery, 74-75. Teaching: Instr art hist, Smithsonian Inst, Washington, DC, 72-76. Pos: Mus cur, Dept Graphic Arts, Nat Gallery Art, Washington, DC, 66-76; cur fine arts, Charleston Art Gallery of Sunrise, WVa, 77-78. Awards: Ford Found Cur Training Grant, Tamarind Lithography Workshop, Los Angeles, 67; Eng Speaking Union Grant Study at Brit Mus, 68. Mem: Eng Speaking Union; Am Asn Mus; Col Art Asn Am; Southeastern Mus Conf (WVa rep, 78); Philobiblon Club; Philadelphia Print Club. Res: American art. Publ: Designed illus sect, Fifteenth Century Engravings of Northern Europe (catalog), Nat Gallery Art, 67; contribr, l'Incisone Europa dal XV al XX Secolo, Museo Civico, Torino, Italy, 68; auth, Rodolphe Bresdin, a drawing and a print, Print Collector's Newsletter, Vol 1, No 3, 70; contribr, Recent Acquisitions of Sculpture, Drawings, Prints, Nat Gallery of Art, Washington, DC, 74; ed, Bernie Peace: Paintings & ed, Douglas Chadwick: Photographs, Charleston Art Gallery of Sunrise, 78. Mailing Add: 910 Pine Rd Charleston WV 25314

CAIN, JOSEPH ALEXANDER
PAINTER, EDUCATOR
b Henderson, Tenn, May 27, 20. Study: Univ Calif, Berkeley, BA, 47, MA, 48. Work: Butler Inst Am Art, Youngstown, Ohio; Nat Watercolor Soc Collection; Witte Mus, San Antonio, Tex; Univ Utah Permanent Collection; Laguna Gloria Mus, Austin, Tex. Comn: Oil mural, CofC, Corpus Christi, Tex, 59; mosaic mural, comn by Freeman Martin, Spohn Hosp, 62; mosaic murals, comn by Joe Williams, Buccanneer Bowl, 65. Exhib: Philadelphia Watercolor Club Exhib, Pa Acad Fine Arts, 65; Butler Inst Am Art Mid-Year Ann, 65; Nat Soc Painters in Casein Exhib, New York, 67; Southwestern Watercolor Soc Regional Show, Dallas, 69; Nat Watercolor Soc Ann, Los Angeles, 69; Watercolor USA, Springfield Art Mus, Mo, 73; Am Painters in Paris, 75; Nat Acad of Design, New York, 77-78. Teaching: Prof art, Del Mar Col, 50-, chmn dept, 66- Pos: Chmn, Munic Arts Coun, Corpus Christi, 72-73. Mem: Fel Royal Soc Arts; Nat Watercolor Soc (spec rep, 71-72); Tex Fine Arts Asn (third vpres, 77-78); Tex Watercolor Soc (third vpres, 71-72); Nat Soc Painters in Acrylics & Casein; Tex Fine Arts Asn (regional dir, 70). Style & Technique: From semi-abstract to non-figurative treatment. Media: Acrylic, Watercolor. Publ: Auth, Art news and reviews (weekly column of art criticism), Corpus Christi Caller-Times, 56-74; auth, The Ten, Art Voices/South, 3/78. Mailing Add: 402 Troy Dr Corpus Christi TX 78412

CAISERMAN-ROTH, GHITTA
PAINTER, PRINTMAKER
b Montreal, PQ, Mar 2, 23. Study: Parsons Sch Design, BA; Am Artists Sch; Ecole Beaux-Arts, with Albert Dumouchel. Work: Montreal Mus Fine Arts; Vancouver Art Gallery, BC; Confederation Art Gallery, Charlottetown, PEI; London Pub Libr & Art Mus, Ont; Beaverbrook Art Gallery, Fredericton, NB. Comn: Hommage a Dumouchel, Univ Quebec Press, 72. Exhib: Expo '67, 67; Joint Int Exhib, Soc Can Etcher-Painters & Engravers & Can Soc Graphic Arts, 70; group show, Can Embassy, Washington, DC, 70; solo show, Waddington Galleries, Montreal, 70. Teaching: Instr art, Sir George Williams Univ, 60; instr art, Queen's Univ, 63; instr art, Saidye Bronfman Ctr, Montreal, 70. Awards: Can Coun Sr Fel, 62; Can Centennial Medal, Can Govt, 67; plus various purchase awards. Mem; Can Soc Painter Etchers; Can Soc Graphic Art; Royal Can Acad Art. Media: Acrylic, Oil, Mixed Media, Graphics. Dealer: Waddington Gallery 1452 Sherbrooke W Montreal PQ Can. Mailing Add: 5 Bellevue Ave Westmount PQ Can

CAJORI, CHARLES F
PAINTER
b Palo Alto, Calif, Mar 9, 21. Study: Colorado Springs Fine Arts Ctr; Cleveland Art Sch; Columbia Univ; Skowhegan Sch Painting & Sculpture. Work: NY Univ; Geigy Chem Corp, Ardsley, NY; Mitchner Collection, Univ Tex, Austin; Walker Art Ctr, Minneapolis; Whitney Mus Am Art, New York. Exhib: One-man shows, Howard Wise Gallery, New York, 63, Landmark Gallery, New York, 75 & Ingber Gallery, New York, 76; Decade of American Drawings, Whitney Mus Am Art, 65; three-man show, Loeb Ctr, NY Univ, 70. Teaching: Instr drawing & painting, Cooper Union Art Sch, 56-65; instr drawing & painting, New York Studio Sch, 64-69; prof drawing & painting, Queens Col, Flushing, 65- Awards: Longview Found Purchase Award, 62; Ford Found Purchase Award, 63; award in painting, Inst Arts & Lett, 70. Bibliog: L Finkelstein (auth), Cajori: figure in the scene, Art News, 63. Mem: Col Art Asn Am. Media: Oil, Pencil. Mailing Add: Litchfield Rd Watertown CT 06795

CALAPAI, LETTERIO
PRINTMAKER
b Boston, Mass. Study: Mass Sch Art; Sch Fine Arts & Crafts; Art Students League; Am Artists Sch; also with Robert Laurent, Ben Shahn & Stanley Hayter. Work: Metrop Mus Art, New York; Fogg Art Mus, Cambridge, Mass; Art Inst Chicago; Libr Cong, Washington, DC; Bibliot Nat, Paris, France; Kyobashi Mus Mod Art, Tokyo, Japan; plus many other pub & pvt collections. Exhib: Intag One, Calif, 71; 20-yr retrospective of graphic work, touring univ & cols throughout the US, 72-73; plus many others. Teaching: Chmn graphic arts dept, Albright Art Sch, Univ Buffalo, 49-55; instr graphics, New Sch Social Res, 55-62; instr graphics, NY Univ, 62-65; vis assoc prof fine arts, Brandeis Univ, 64-65; instr, Univ Ill, Chicago Circle, 65. Pos: Founder-dir, Intaglio Workshop for Advance Printmaking, New York, 60-65; adv panel, Ill Arts Coun, 71-73. Awards: Tiffany Found grant, 59; Rosenwald Found, 60; New York World's Fair, 64-65; plus others. Mem: Soc Am Graphic Artists (past vpres); Audubon Artists (former dir). Style & Technique: Semi-abstract; intaglio and woodcut and engraving. Mailing Add: PO Box 158 344 Tudor Glencoe IL 60022

CALAS, NICOLAS
WRITER
b Lausanne, Switz, 07; US citizen. Study: Univ Athens, Greece, Law Degree. Teaching: Prof art hist, Fairleigh Dickinson Univ, 63-76. Publ: Auth, Foyers d'incendie, Paris Denoel, 38; auth, Confound the Wise, Arrow Ed, New York, 42; co-auth, The Peggy Guggenheim collection of modern art, 66; auth, Art in the Age of Risk, Dutton, 68; co-auth, Icons and Images of the Sixties, Dutton, 71. Mailing Add: 210 E 68th St New York NY 10021

CALCAGNO, LAWRENCE
PAINTER
b San Francisco, Calif, Mar 23, 13. Study: Calif Sch Fine Arts, San Francisco, 47-50; Acad Grande Chaumiere, Paris, France, 50-51; Acad Delgi Belli Arte, Florence, Italy, 51-52. Work: San Francisco Mus Art; Whitney Mus Am Art, New York; Brooklyn Mus; Nat Collections, Smithsonian Inst, Washington, DC. Exhib: Albright Art Gallery, Buffalo, NY, 56; Am Pavilion, Brussels World's Fair, 58; Carnegie Inst Mus Int, 61; Mus Fine Arts, Houston, 65; Nat Collection Fine Arts, Smithsonian Inst, 68; Whitney Mus Am Art, 70; SITES, 73-75. Teaching: Vis Andrew Mellon prof painting, Carnegie-Mellon Univ, 65-68. Awards: Ford Found Grant, 65. Mailing Add: 215 Bowery New York NY 10002

CALDERON, JUAN
ARCHITECT, PAINTER
b Monclova, Coah, Mex, Apr 21, 38. Study: Instituto Tecnologico Y De Estudios Superiored De Monterrey; ITESM; Universidad De Nuevo Leon; Universidad De Mex. Work: Museo De Grabado, Buenos Aires, Argentina; Museo De Arte Contemp, Bogota, Colombia; Museo De Arte Contemp, Caracas, Venezuela; Casa De La Cultura, Monterrey, Mex; Museo Biblioteca Pape, Monclova, Mex. Exhib: Salon Bienal De Arte Grafico, Mex, 77; Salon De Agosto, Colombia, 77; New Mex Plastic Art, New Delhi, India, 77; one-man shows, Universidad De Coahuila, Mex, 76-78; Galeria Espacio, San Salvador, Republica De El Salvador, Galeria Arvil, Mex, 76-77 & many others. Teaching: Instr archit, Universidad Iberoamericana, Mexico DF, Mex, 63-75. Bibliog: Marques Rodiles (auth), La Santificacion De Los Objetos, El Sol De Mex, 76; Carol Miller (auth), Mi Cuerpo Es Un Jardin, Activa Mag, 77; De Neuvillate (auth), Juan Calderon, Novedades, 77. Style & Technique: Realistic; etching and oil painting. Mailing Add: c/o Galeria Arvil CDA Hamburgo 9 Mexico 6 DF Mexico

CALDWELL, BENJAMIN HUBBARD, JR
COLLECTOR, ART HISTORIAN
b Humboldt, Tenn, May 1, 35. Study: Vanderbilt Univ, BA, 57, MD, 60. Collections Arranged: Made in Tennessee, Tenn Fine Art Ctr, Cheekwood, 71. Res: Tennessee silver; Tennessee silversmiths. Collection: Tennessee silver; 18th century American furniture; 19th and 20th century American art. Publ: Auth, Tennessee Silver & Checklist of Tennessee Silversmiths, Antiques, 71. Mailing Add: 329 22nd Ave W Nashville TN 37203

CALDWELL, ELEANOR
EDUCATOR, JEWELER
b Kansas City, Mo, May 1, 27. Study: Southwest Mo State Univ, Springfield, BS in Educ, 48; Columbia Univ, MA, 53, EdD, 59; study with Robert von Neuman, John Leary, Dr Edwin Zeigfield, Dr Jack Arends & Arthur Young. Work: Colo Women's Col, Denver; Ft Hays Kans State Col, Hays; Denver Pub Schs; Northern Ill Univ, DeKalb; Sheldon Mem Art Gallery, Lincoln, Nebr. Comn: Presidential medallion, Northern Ill Univ, 70. Exhib: Ann Exhib, Springfield Art Mus, Mo, 52-71; Nat Decorative Arts Exhib, Wichita Art Asn, Kans, 54-70; Am Jewelry & Related Objects (first nat jewelry exhib in US), Huntington Galleries, WVa, 55; Midwest 3rd Biennial Exhib of Utilitarian Design, Joslyn Art Mus, Omaha, Nebr, 55; 3rd Nat Exhib of Contemp Jewelers, Walker Art Ctr, Minneapolis, Minn, 55; Am Jewelry, Smithsonian Inst Travelling Exhib, 55-57; Art Asn of New Orleans Ann, Issac Delgado Mus, La, 57, 59 & 60; Handweaving II, Smithsonian Inst Travelling Exhib, 58-59; Ann Own Your Own Exhib, Denver Art Mus, Colo, 61-63 & 65-67; Jewelry & Precious Objects by Eight Am Women Metalsmiths, Wichita Art Asn, 72; 7th Ann Prints, Drawings & Crafts Exhib, 74 & Toys Designed by Artists, 75, Ark Art Ctr, Little Rock; Am Metalwork 1976, Sheldon Mem Art Gallery, Lincoln, 76; The Metalsmith Int Exhib, Phoenix Art Mus, Ariz, 77. Collections Arranged: Nat Jewelry & Holoware Exhib (dir & auth, catalogue), Northern Ill Univ Art Gallery, DeKalb & Lakeview Ctr for the Arts & Sci, Peoria, Ill. Teaching: Assoc prof jewelry & graphics, Ft Hays Kans State Univ, 54-57 & 64-67; assoc prof jewelry & graphics, Edinboro

State Col, Pa, 60-62; prof jewelry & metals, Northern Ill Univ, 67-; prof jewelry & metals, Arrowmont Sch of Crafts, Univ Tenn, Gatlinburg, 74-77. Pos: Consult, Cult Heritage Ctr, Dodge City, Kans, 66-74; res grant, Grad Sch, Northern Ill Univ, 68-71. Awards: Hon Mention, Midwest 3rd Biennial Exhib of Utilitarian Design, Joslyn Art Mus, 55; Jewelry Award, 12th Nat Decorative Arts, Cent States Craftsmen's Guild, 57; Purchase Award, 5th Ann Own Your Own Exhib, Denver Pub Schs, 61. Bibliog: Meg Torbert (ed), American Jewelry, Design Quart, Walker Art Ctr, 59 & 61; Lois E Franke (auth), Handwrought Jewelry, McKnight & McKnight, 62; Jon Nelson (auth), American Metalwork 1976 (slide set), Sheldon Mem Art Gallery, Lincoln, 76. Mem: Soc of NAm Goldsmiths; Am Crafts Coun; Artists Equity. Style & Technique: Fabricated and cast jewelry and metal objects in the media of gold, silver, bronze and copper. Media: Jewelry and related objects in gold and silver. Publ: Auth, Paint a Movie, Mo Art Educ J, 54; auth, Pop Art-Culture Mirror, J Fine Arts Coun, Alta, Can, 64; ed, Art: Kindergarten Through Grade Six, Curriculum Guide, Kans State Dept of Pub Instruction, 68; ed manuscript, Philip Morton (ed), Contemporary Jewelry, Holt, Rinehart & Winston, 1st ed, 68; auth, 1970 Oakbrook Invitational Crafts Exhib, Crafts Horizons, 70. Dealer: Tapestry 2859 E Third Ave Denver CO 80206. Mailing Add: 1306 Stafford DeKalb IL 60115

CALDWELL, MARTHA BELLE
EDUCATOR, ART HISTORIAN
b Chapel Hill, NC, Dec 12, 31. Study: Cornell Univ, BA; Univ Miss, MA; Ind Univ, MA & PhD. Teaching: Instr art hist, Westhampton Col, Univ Richmond, 60-63 & Rice Univ, 66-68; from asst prof to prof art hist, James Madison Univ, 68- Mem: Southeastern Col Art Conf; Col Art Asn; Soc of Archit Historians; Am Comt for Irish Studies; Am Inst of Archaeol. Res: Nineteenth and twentieth century art and architecture. Mailing Add: 216 Governors Lane 10 Harrisonburg VA 22801

CALE, ROBERT ALLAN
PRINTMAKER
b Stonington, Conn, Jan 9, 40. Study: RI Sch Design, BFA, 64; S W Hayter's Atelier 17, Paris, France, 69-70. Work: Bibliot Nat, Paris; Dickinson Pub Libr, NDak; Trinity Col & Wadsworth Atheneum, Hartford, Conn; Libr Cong, Washington, DC; Comn: Ed of 100 black & white prints, New York Graphics Soc, Greenwich, 71; ed of 225 three-color prints from several plates (with Will Barnet, artist & Elisabeth Egbert, asst), Ferdinand Roten Galleries, Baltimore, Md, 71-72; Richard Black, artist, Lakeside Studios, 74; collector's ed, Lakeside Studios, 76; subscription ed, Lion's Gallery of the Senses, Wadsworth Atheneum, 77. Exhib: Four Young American Printmakers in Paris, Europ Tour, 69-72; 3rd Ann Print Exhib, Atlanta, Ga, 72; Silvermine 9th Nat Print Exhib, Conn, 72; Potsdam Prints 1972, NY, 72; Trinity Col, Hartford, Conn, 74; 5th Biennial Exhib, Dickinson, NDak, 75; Pratt Graphic Ctr, New York, 76; Am the Beautiful Pictorial Prints 1776-1976 (travelling exhib); Paperworks, Lions Gallery of the Senses, 77; Boston Printmakers 29th Ann, De Cordova Mus, Boston, 77; Print Club Biennial Int, Philadelphia, 77; 50th Yr Retrospective (travelling exhib), Atelier 17, New York, 77-78; Pensacola Nat Printmaking Exhib, Pensacola Jr Col, Fla, 78; Monotypes Today II, John Slade Ely House, New Haven, Conn, 78. Teaching: Instr printmaking, Printmaking Workshop, New York, 71-73; instr printmaking, Pratt Graphics Ctr, New York, 72-73; vis artist, Trinity Col, 72-75. Pos: Asst cur, Pratt Graphics Ctr, 71-72; master printer, Printmaking Workshop, 71-73; dir, Stonington Workshop, 74- Awards: Conn Comn on Arts Grant for Stonington Workshop, 74; Purchase Award, 5th Biennial Exhib, Dickinson, NDak, 75; First Prize, 20th Ann, Mystic Art Asn, Conn, 76. Mem: Mystic Art Asn; Boston Printmakers; Nature Printing Soc. Bibliog: Eight young Americans in Paris, US Embassy, Paris, 70; Ellen Zeifer (auth), The marine prints of Bob Cale, Am Artist, 7/72; feature story in Hartford Courant, 4/75. Style & Technique: Concern for new visions of reality, often printing real things, fish, flowers, people, etc; most printmaking techniques including multiple color viscosity printing. Media: All Printmaking. Publ: Auth, Description of methods involved in the prints of Robert A Cale in the Rosenwald Collection, 71. Dealer: Assoc Am Artists 663 Fifth Ave New York NY 10022. Mailing Add: 32 Gold St Stonington CT 06378

CALFEE, WILLIAM HOWARD
SCULPTOR
b Washington, DC, 09. Study: Ecole Beaux-Arts, Paris, France; Cranbrook Acad Arts. Work: Philadelphia Mus Art; Nat Collection Fine Arts, Washington, DC; Corcoran Gallery of Art, Washington, DC; Honolulu Art Acad; Phillips Gallery; Edward Bruce Mem Collection; Selden Rodman Collection; Andrew S Keck Collection; Metrop Mus Art, New York; Cranbrook Acad Arts; Philbrook Art Ctr, Tulsa, Okla; Baltimore Mus Art. Comn: Eight murals & two sculptures, Sect Fine Arts, US Treas Dept, 36-41; font, altar & candlesticks, St Augustine Chapel, Washington, DC, 69. Exhib: One-man shows, Southern Vt Art Ctr, Manchester, Baltimore Mus Art, Corcoran Gallery Art, Washington, DC, Franz Bader Gallery, Washington, DC & numerous others; Carnegie Int, Pittsburgh, Pa; Metrop Mus of Art, New York; Heritage of Am Art, Nat Archives; Loan Exhib of Washington Artists, Phillips Gallery; Nat Acad of Sci, Washington, DC; Three Sculptors, Zabriski Gallery, New York; and numerous others. Teaching: Instr drawing & painting, Phillips Gallery, Washington, DC; chmn dept painting & sculpture, Am Univ, 46-54; instr mural tech, Centre Art, Port au Prince, Haiti, 49; guest assoc prof painting, Univ Calif, Berkeley, 51; adj prof, Am Univ, presently. Publ: Collabr design & auth, introd, In: Tradition and Experiment in Modern Sculpture. Mailing Add: 7206 45th St Chevy Chase MD 20015

CALHOUN, LARRY DARRYL
CERAMIST
b Revere, Mo, Oct 9, 37. Study: Iowa Wesleyan, BA(art); Univ Iowa, MA(ceramics). Work: Bowling Green State Univ, Ohio. Comn: Outdoor sculpture, Ill Arts Coun for Decatur, Ill, 78. Exhib: May Show, Cleveland Art Mus, Ohio; Ann Crafts Exhib, Butler Mus Art, Youngstown, Ohio; Designer Craftsman Biennial, Columbus Mus Art, Ohio; Ann Crafts Exhib, J B Speed Mus, Louisville, Ky & Evansville Mus Art, Ind; Invitational, Akron Art Inst, Ohio; Marietta Crafts Regional, Ohio. Teaching: Instr art, Westmar Col, Le Mars, Iowa, 61-63; asst prof art, Millikin Univ, Decatur, Ill, 63-70; assoc prof ceramics, Akron Univ, 70-76. Pos: Ill craftsman-in-residence, Ill Arts Coun, Decatur, 77-78; owner, Village Pottery, 76- Awards: Prize, Ball State Univ Small Sculpture & Drawing Exhib. Mem: Nat Coun Educ in Ceramic Arts. Mailing Add: Village Pottery Lane IL 61750

CALIFANO, EDWARD CHRISTOPHER
ART DEALER, PUBLISHER
b Italy; US citizen. Study: City Col New York, Romance lang & art; Fine Arts Acad, Naples & Rome, Italy. Collections Arranged: Cross-Currents, Barbizon Sch, 55, World Trade Fair, NY Coliseum, 58; Gems of Expressionism, Span Pavillion, Hall of Sci & Top of the Fair, New York World's Fair, 64; I Rice Pereira Retrospective, New York, 65; Jacques Lipchitz Retrospective, Hastings, NY, 68; Bicentennial Exhib, New York, 76. Pos: Art consult, Goulart Enterprises, Rio de Janeiro, Brazil, 54-55; owner-dir, Califano Art Gallery, New York, 49-57; dir, Galerie Int, New York, 57- Awards: Italian Lit & Art Award, Friends of Italy, 48; Aspects of French Painting Award, French Teachers Asn, 50. Specialty: Contemporary art. Publ: Ed, Men at Work (official art book, New York World's Fair), Leo Oelski, 64; ed, Artists International, 74, Art Guide Int, 75 & Bicentennial Issue Art Guide, 76, Galerie Int, plus work on several filmed art documentaries. Mailing Add: 1095 Madison Ave New York NY 10028

CALIFF, MARILYN ISKIWITZ
PAINTER, DESIGNER
b Memphis, Tenn, Apr 27, 32. Study: Memphis Acad Arts, BFA. Work: Brooks Mem Art Gallery, Overton Park, Memphis. Comn: Glass mosaic murals (with Barbara Shankman), Memphis Hebrew Acad, 62, Baron Hirsch Synagogue, 66 & Memphis Jewish Community Ctr, 68. Exhib: 8th & 13th Delta Exhib, Little Rock, Ark, 65 & 70; 4th Nat Exhib, Tyler, Tex, 67; 13th Ann Mid-South Exhib, Memphis, Tenn, 68; 10th All-State Artists Exhib, Nashville, 70; Ball State Univ Drawing Exhib, 71. Awards: First in Oils, 13th Mid-South Exhib, Brooks League, 68; Three Purchase Prizes, First Tenn Artists & Craftsman Show, 72. Style & Technique: Abstract expressionistic paintings; contemporary approach to quilt design. Media: Oil, Collage. Publ: Auth, Your First Quilt, 72. Mailing Add: 5305 Denwood Ave Memphis TN 38117

CALKIN, CARLETON IVERS
PAINTER, RESTORER
b Grand Rapids, Mich, July 27, 14. Study: Univ SDak, BFA; Minneapolis Inst Art Sch; Chouinard Art Inst; Ohio Univ, MA; Univ Calif, PhD; Univ Michoacan, Mex; Inter-Am Univ, Panama. Work: SDak Hist Mus, Vermillion; Tex Christian Univ; Ohio Univ; Rio Hato AFB, Panama. Exhib: Regional exhibs, Ft Worth, Tex; local, regional & state fair shows, Ind. Teaching: Lectr pre-Columbian, Latin Am archaeol & colonial & contemp Latin Am art; instr art, Ohio Univ, Univ Calif & Tex Christian Univ; head dept art, Purdue Univ, Lafayette, 55-62, prof art hist, 62-66. Pos: Cur, Hist St Augustine Pres Bd, 66-73; operating own studio & restoring paintings for museums and collectors. Publ: Contribr, Latin Am art sect, In: Encycl Britannica, 57. Mailing Add: 265 Matanzas Blvd St Augustine FL 32084

CALKINS, KINGSLEY MARK
PAINTER, EDUCATOR
b South Lyon, Mich, May 13, 17. Study: Eastern Mich Univ, BS, 48; Univ Mich, MS, 49; Univ Mich & Detroit Soc Arts & Crafts, post grad study. Work: South Bend Mus, Ind; Dayton Mus Nat Hist; Ford Motor Co; Parke-Davis; Steelcase Corp. Comn: Watercolors, Ford Motor Co Publ, 65-75; murals, Mayflower Hotel, Plymouth, Mich; watercolor, Mich Heart Asn. Exhib: Col Art USA, Andover Acad; Audubon Artists, New York; Mich Show, South Bend, Ind; Mich Artists Ann; Mich State Fair. Teaching: From instr to prof watercolor & head dept, Eastern Mich Univ, Ypsilanti, 50- Pos: Instr adult educ, Univ Mich, 48-50. Awards: Mich Watercolor Soc; Scarab Club; South Bend Mus. Mem: Nat Asn Art Adminr; Mich Watercolor Soc (chmn, awards chmn); Mich Art Educ Asn (secy-treas); Ann Arbor Art Asn (exhib chmn). Style & Technique: Animals, swamps, meadows. Media: Watercolor, Acrylic. Publ: Illusr, The Scarlet Ibis, Lincoln Mercury Times; illusr, several restaurants, Ford Times. Dealer: Galleria Luisa 2177 Wealthy St East Grand Rapids MI 49506. Mailing Add: 1327 Collegewood Ypsilanti MI 48197

CALKINS, ROBERT G
ART HISTORIAN
b Oakland, Calif, Dec 29, 32. Study: Woodrow Wilson Sch Pub & Int Affairs, Princeton Univ, AB, 55; Harvard Univ, MA, 62, PhD, 67. Collections Arranged: A Medieval Treasury, An Exhib of Medieval Art from the Third to the Sixteenth Century, Andrew Dickson White Mus Art, Cornell Univ, Ithaca, NY & Munson-Williams Proctor Inst, Utica, NY, 68. Teaching: Assoc prof medieval art & archit, Cornell Univ, 66-, chmn dept hist of art, 76- Mem: Int Ctr Medieval Art (mem bd adv, 71-); Col Art Asn; Medieval Acad Am. Res: Fifteenth century manuscript illumination. Publ: Auth, A Medieval Treasury, Cornell Univ, 68; auth, The Brussels Hours Reevaluated, Scriptorium, 70; auth, The Master of the Franciscan Breviary, Arte Lombara, 71; auth, Medieval & Renaissance Manuscripts in the Cornell University Library, Cornell Libr J, 72. Mailing Add: Dept of Hist of Art Cornell Univ Ithaca NY 14850

CALLAHAN, HARRY
PHOTOGRAPHER
b Detroit, Mich, 12. Study: Mich State Univ, 36-38; self-taught. Work: Int Mus Photog, George Eastman House, Rochester, NY; Mus Mod Art, New York; Nat Gallery of Can, Ottawa, Ont; Victoria & Albert Mus, London, Ont; Metrop Mus Art, New York; Ctr for Creative Photog, Tucson, Ariz. Exhib: Family of Man, Mus Mod Art, New York, 55; Retrospective, Int Mus Photog, George Eastman House, 58 & Mus Mod Art, 76; Mod Mus, Stockholm, Sweden, 78; one-man shows, Mass Inst Technol, 68 & traveling exhib, George Eastman House, 71. Teaching: Instr photog, Inst of Design, Ill Inst of Design, 46. Pos: Head photog dept, Inst of Design, Ill Inst of Design, 49-61 & RI Sch of Design, 64-75. Bibliog: Hugo Weber (auth of introd), Harry Callahan: photographs, El Mochuelo Press, 64; Sherman Paul (auth), The Photography of Harry Callahan, Mus Mod Art, 67; John Szarkowski (auth), Callahan, Museum of Modern Art, Aperture, 76. Mailing Add: c/o Light Gallery 724 Fifth Ave New York NY 10019

CALLAHAN, KENNETH
PAINTER
b Spokane, Wash, Oct 30, 05. Work: Whitney Mus Am Art, New York; Mus Mod Art, New York; Metrop Mus Art, New York; Pa Acad Fine Arts, Philadelphia; Brooklyn Mus; plus many other pub & pvt collections. Comn: Murals, US PO Bldgs, Centralia & Anacortes, Wash & Rugby, NDak; murals, Wash State Libr, Olympia, 60, Seattle Civic Theater, 62, Syracuse Univ, 64 & Wash Mutual Savings Bank, 70; plus others. Exhib: Many nat & int group & one-man shows. Teaching: Vis artist, Syracuse Univ, Pa State Univ, Boston Univ, Univ Southern Calif, Skowhegan Sch Painting & Sculpture & others. Pos: Panel selection, Tamarind Lithography Workshop, 59-69. Awards: Guggenheim Fel, 54-55; Nat Inst Arts & Lett Grant, 68; Am Acad Arts & Lett Purchase Award, New Orleans Art Mus, 72; plus others. Bibliog: Sheldon Cheney (auth), Expressionism & Story of Modern Art; S H Richardson (auth), Painting in America; Henry Geldzahler (auth), 20th Century Art; plus many others. Mem: Wash State Arts Comn; assoc mem Nat Acad Design. Publ: Auth, articles in Seattle Times, Art News, Art Digest, Creative Art & Am Mag Art. Dealer: Kraushaar Galleries 1055 Madison Ave New York NY 10021. Mailing Add: Box 493 Long Beach WA 98631

CALLE, PAUL
PAINTER, WRITER
b New York, NY, Mar 3, 28. Study: Pratt Inst. Work: Phoenix Art Mus, Ariz; Pac Northwest Indian Ctr, Spokane, Wash; Nat Air & Space Mus, Washington, DC; NASA Fine Art Collection; US Dept Interior. Comn: NASA, Cape Kennedy, Jet Propulsion Lab, Star City, Moscow, USSR, 68-75; Basic History of Iron & Steel, Basic Indust, 68-70; Nat Park Serv,

Mesa Verde, Yosemite, Cape Hatterus, 70-74; Classics in Surgery, Schering Co, 71-73. Exhib: 1st Convocation Western Art, Dallas, Tex; 2nd Convocation Western Art, Arlington, Tex; NASA Eyewitness to Space, Nat Gallery Art, Washington, DC, 70; NASA Apollo-Soyuz, Moscow, 75. Awards: Contemp Achievement Medal, Pratt Inst, 70; Distinguished Western Art Gold Medal, Franklin Mint, 74; Hamilton King Award, Soc Illusr. Mem: Soc Illusr. Media: Oil, Pencil. Publ: Auth & illusr, The Pencil, Watson & Guptill, 75. Mailing Add: c/o McCulley Fine Art Gallery 2539 Cedar Springs Dallas TX 75201 Stamford CT c/o McCulley Fine Art Gallery 2539 Cedar Springs Dallas TX 75201

CALLICOTT, BURTON HARRY
PAINTER, CALLIGRAPHER
b Terre Haute, Ind, Dec 28, 07. Study: Cleveland Sch Art, cert, 31. Work: Brooks Art Gallery, Memphis, Tenn; Tenn Art Comn, Nashville; Miss Art Asn, Jackson; Ark Art Ctr, Little Rock. Comn: Three mural panels, Pub Works Admin Proj, 34-35. Exhib: New York World's Fair Exhib Am Painting, 39; Iron Horse in Art, Fort Worth Mus Art, Tex, 58; one-man shows, Brooks Art Gallery, 65, Miss Art Asn, 69 & Memphis Acad Arts, 71; Brooks Art Gallery, 74. Teaching: Prof drawing, painting & calligraphy, Memphis Acad Arts, 37-73. Awards: Purchase Award, Ark Art Ctr, 69 & Hors Concour Award, 70; Worthen Bank Award, Little Rock, 71. Bibliog: Edward Faiers (auth), catalog foreword, Memphis Acad Arts, 61. Style & Technique: Formalized or semi-abstract treatment of landscape themes in a very controlled manner, using multi-layers of transparent oil glazes. Media: Oil. Mailing Add: 3395 Douglass Ave Memphis TN 38111

CALLISEN, STERLING
ART HISTORIAN, LECTURER
b New York, NY, Mar 30, 99. Study: Princeton Univ, AB, 20; Harvard Univ, MA, 34, PhD, 36. Teaching: Asst fine arts, Harvard Univ, 34-36; asst prof, Rochester Univ, 36-41; assoc dean, Wesleyan Univ, 45-49; dean educ, Metrop Mus Art, 49-59; prof art hist, Pace Univ, 65-71; vis lectr, NY Univ, 72- Pos: Pres, Parsons Sch Design, 59-64, emer pres, 64-; dir, Col Art Asn Art Slide Proj, Ford Found, 71- Mem: Sch Art League (pres); Col Art Asn Am; Scarsdale Art Asn; Am Asn Archit Historians; Mus Asn Clubs; plus others. Mailing Add: 10 Ridgecrest W Scarsdale NY 10583

CALLNER, RICHARD
PAINTER, EDUCATOR
b Benton Harbor, Mich, May 18, 27. Study: Univ Wis, BS(art); Art Students League; Acad Julian, Paris, France, cert; Columbia Univ, MAFA. Work: Philadelphia Mus Art, Pa; Chicago Art Inst; Cincinnati Art Mus; Detroit Inst Art; Mus Painting & Sculpture, Istanbul, Turkey. Comn: Tapestries, Mambush Tapestry Workshop, Ein Hod, Israel, 75-77. Exhib: Butler Inst Am Art Mid Yr Ann, Youngstown, Ohio, 57, 59, 61 & 62; Pa Acad Fine Arts Ann, Philadelphia, 58, 59, 61 & 63; group exhib, DeCordova Mus, Lincoln, Mass, Ann Nat Print Exhib, Washington, DC; Watercolor Soc Ann, Washington, DC; Premio Int dell Arte, Sicily; one-man exhib, US Info Serv, Turkey, 73, Ger, 68 & 69 & Italy, 67; one-man exhib, Bristol Mus, RI, 73. Collections Arranged: Kalamazoo Art Ctr, Mich, 64; Tyler Sch Art, 70; US Info Serv, Turkey, 73; Bristol Mus, RI, 75; State Univ NY Albany, 76. Teaching: Dir & prof painting, Tyler Sch Art, Temple Univ, Rome, Italy, 65-70; chmn dept art & prof painting, State Univ NY Albany, 75- Pos: Founding dir, Tyler Sch Art, Rome, Italy, 65-70; Pres Coun Art Dept Chmn, State Univ NY, 77- Awards: Guggenheim Found fel painting, 59. Style & Technique: Oil painting, glaze technique, figurative, fantasy, contemporary mythology. Media: Oil; lithography. Mailing Add: 11 Davis Pl Latham NY 12110

CALROW, ROBERT F
INSTRUCTOR, PAINTER
b Lansing, Mich, Oct 20, 16. Study: Minn Sch Art, St Paul; Univ Minn, BArch; Minneapolis Sch Art. Comn: Hist montage watercolor, Kraft Foods Inc, New York, 71. Exhib: Salon of the Fifty States, Duncan Galleries, New York & Paris, 69; 13th Ann Conn Classic Arts, 70; Salmagundi Club Spring Exhib, 70; Mystic Conn Art Festival, 71; 22nd Ann Knickerbocker Artists, New York, 72; Am Watercolor Soc Annuals, Nat Acad Gallery, New York, NY, 70, 72 & 77; Acad Artists Annuals, Springfield Mus, Mass, 72 & 73; NJ Soc Painters, Jersey City Mus, 72; Ann Juried Shows, Stamford Art Asn, Stamford Mus, Conn, 74 & 76; and others. Teaching: Teacher watercolor, Stamford & Greenwich, Conn & San Juan, PR, 68-75. Pos: Dir, Caribbean Painting Tours. Awards: Prix de Paris, Salon of the Fifty States, 69; Best of Show & Gabriel Dante Luchetti Award, 13th Ann Conn Classic Arts, 70; Best of Show, Salmagundi Club Spring Exhib, 70 & Mystic Conn Art Festival, 71; Medal of Merit & Best of Show, 22nd Ann Knickerbocker Artists, 72 & Marshall Howe Medal of Hon & Best of Show Award, 74; Bainbridge Prize, NJ Soc Painters, 72; Gabriel Luchetti Award & Best of Show, Conn Classic Arts Ann Juried Show, 73; Best of Show, Old Saybrook Conn Art Festival, 75. Mem: Stamford Art Asn (pres, 71-73); Salmagundi Club; Knickerbocker Artists; Hudson Valley Art Asn; Conn Watercolor Soc; Acad Artists Inc, Springfield, Mass; assoc mem Am Watercolor Soc. Style & Technique: Watercolors, ink drawings and combinations of ink and wash; representational and often impressionistic. Media: Transparent Watercolor and Ink Drawing. Mailing Add: 30 Glenbrook Rd Stamford CT 06902

CAMARATA, MARTIN L
EDUCATOR, PRINTMAKER
b Rochester, NY, June 10, 34. Study: NY State Univ Col Buffalo, BA, 56; NY Univ, MA, 57. Work: Mus Belles Artes, Caracas, Venezuela; Univ of the Pac; Calif State Col, Stanislaus. Exhib: 22nd Painting Ann, Butler Inst Am Art, 57; Boston Printmakers Ann, 62-66; Philadelphia Print Club Ann, 65 & 66; Print-Drawing Ann, Pa Acad Fine Arts, 65, 66 & 68; Potsdam Ann Print-Drawing, NY, 74. Teaching: Prof drawing & printmaking, Calif State Col, Stanislaus, 64- Pos: Mem adv bd, Calif Graphics, 73-74. Awards: First Prize Print, William J Keller Award, 56; Best of Show, Calif State Fair Art Exhib, 65; Print Award, Haggin Gallery-Mus, Calif, 66. Bibliog: T Albright (auth), rev in San Francisco Chronicle, 72 & 75. Style & Technique: Woodcuts, drawings, figure dominates, metaphorical, subjective, symbolic. Publ: Auth, Lithography at Collectors Press, Artists Proof Mag, 72. Mailing Add: c/o Graphics Gallery Three Embarcadero Ctr San Francisco CA 94111

CAMBLIN, BOB BILYEU
PAINTER
b Ponca City, Okla, Aug 1, 28. Study: Kansas City Art Inst, BFA, 54, MFA, 55; Fulbright study grant to Italy, 56-57. Work: Nelson-Atkins Mus Art, Kansas City, Mo; Joslyn Art Mus, Omaha, Nebr; Brooklyn Mus, NY; Yale Mus, New Haven, Conn; Fogg Mus, Harvard Univ, Cambridge, Mass. Exhib: Other Coasts (8 Tex Artists), Univ Calif, Long Beach, 71; Proj South/SW, Ft Worth Art Mus, Tex, 71; Extraordinary Realities, Whitney Mus Am Art, New York, 73; La State Univ, Baton Rouge, 76. Collections Arranged: Traveling Show, St Paul Art Ctr, Minn, 66; Am Tel & Tel Traveling Show Drawings, 75; Hand Colored Prints Traveling Exhib, Brooke Alexander, NY, 75; Contemp Images in Watercolor Exhib, Akron Art Inst; Indianapolis Inst Art & Mem Art Gallery; Univ Rochester. Bibliog: N Laliberte & A Mogelon (auth), Art in Boxes, Van Nostrand, Reinhold, 74. Media: Watercolor; Pen & Ink. Mailing Add: c/o Moody Gallery 2015 J West Gray Houston TX 77019

CAMERON, BROOKE BULOVSKY
EDUCATOR, PRINTMAKER
b Madison, Wis. Study: Univ Wis, Madison, BS(art educ; honors); summer art hist tour of Europe with Prof Lorenz Eitner, Univ Minn; Univ Iowa, MA(printmaking), with Mauricio Lasansky. Work: Stephens Col, Columbia, Mo; Univ Wis Union, Madison; Mo State Hist Soc. Comn: Miss Willie, ed prints, Lakeside Studios, Mich, 77. Exhib: Mid-Am, St Louis Art Mus & Nelson-Atkins Mus, Kansas City, 68; Davidson Nat Print & Drawing Show, NC, 72; two-woman show with Nanch Bickford Bandy, US Info Agency/US Embassy, Turkey, 74-75; 3rd Ann Printmaking Competition, Tulsa City-Co Libr, Okla, 75; Women 77, Univ Mo Gallery, Kansas City, 77. Teaching: Instr art & art hist, Tex Christian Univ, Ft Worth, Tex, 66-67; from instr to assoc prof fine arts, Univ Mo, 67- Awards: Printmaking Award, Crown Ctr Exhib Halls, Kansas City, Mo, 74. Mem: Col Art Asn Am. Style & Technique: Figurative intaglio; photo-intaglio. Media: Intaglio Printmaking; Drawing. Dealer: Lakeside Studios 150 S Lakeshore Rd Lakeside MI 49116. Mailing Add: 923 College Park Columbia MO 65201

CAMERON, ELSA S
CURATOR, ART ADMINISTRATOR
b San Francisco, Calif, Nov 19, 39. Study: San Francisco State Univ, BA, 61 & MA, 65. Collections Arranged: Native American Ceramics: Contemporary Pueblo Works, 73, Works of Benemeno Serrano, 74, Food Show, 76, Foot Show, 76, Downtown Ctr & Downtown Dog Show, 78, M H de Young Mem Mus, San Francisco, Calif. Pos: Cur-in-charge, M H de Young Mem Mus Art Sch, Downtown Ctr, Fine Arts Mus of San Francisco, 66- Awards: Nat Endowment for the Arts Fels, to study mus progs for the active audience, 73 & to mus prof, urban community arts, 76-77. Res: Writer and researcher in museum education and community arts. Publ: Contribr, Museum as educator, Univ Calif, Berkeley, 78. Mailing Add: M H de Young Mem Mus Golden Gate Park San Francisco CA 94118

CAMERON, ERIC
ART ADMINISTRATOR, PAINTER
b Leicester, Eng, Apr 18, 35. Study: Kings Col, Univ Durham, Newcastle, Eng, BA, 57, study with Lawrence Gowing, Victor Pasmore & Richard Hamilton; Courtauld Inst, Univ London, Acad Dipl(hist art), 59. Work: Can Coun, Art Bank, Ottawa, Ont; Art Gallery Ont, Toronto; Owens Art Gallery, Sackville, NB; Univ East Anglia, Norwich, Eng; Univ Leeds, Eng. Exhib: Woods II, Nat Gallery Can, 71 & Woods I, Art Gallery Ont, 71; Videoscape, Art Gallery Ont, 74; Video Show, Serpentine Gallery, London, Eng, 75; Int Video Exhib, Aarhus, Denmark, 76; Paintings in Mixed Exhib, Art Gallery NS, Halifax, 77; Newspaper Paintings & Lawn, Anna Leonowens Gallery, Halifax, NS, 77; Keeping Marlene Out of the Picture—and Lawn, Vancouver Art Gallery, BC, 78. Teaching: Lectr art & art hist, Univ Leeds, Eng, 59-69; assoc prof painting & video, Univ Guelph, Ont, 69-76. Pos: Dir grad prog, NS Col Art & Design, Halifax, 76- Awards: Can Coun grant collective projs, 71; Can Coun travel grant, 74; Can Coun video grant, 75. Mem: Univs Art Asn Can (Ont rep, 72-73, secy-treas, 73-76 & 76, vpres, 76-); fel Royal Soc Artists; Col Art Asn Am. Style & Technique: Process-based work. Media: Painting, oil and acrylic; video. Publ: Auth, Lawrence Weiner: The Books, Studio Int, 74; auth, Mac Adams: The Mysteries, 76, Dan Graham: Appearing in Public, 76, Art as Art and the Oxford Dictionary, Vanguard, 77 & Bill Beckley's Lies, 77, Artforum. Dealer: Art Metropole 241 Yonge St Toronto ON Can. Mailing Add: 613 Scotia Towers 1991 Brunswick St Halifax NS B3J 2G8 Can

CAMFIELD, WILLIAM ARNETT
ART HISTORIAN
b San Angelo, Tex, Oct 29, 34. Study: Princeton Univ, AB, 57; Yale Univ, MA, 61, PhD, 64. Collections Arranged: Francis Picabia Exhib (orgn & auth, catalogue), The Solomon R Guggenheim Mus, New York, 70. Teaching: From asst prof to assoc prof mod Am & mod Europ art, Univ St Thomas, Houston, Tex, 64-69; from assoc prof to prof mod Am & mod Europ art, Rice Univ, Houston, Tex, 69- Awards: Am Philos Soc grant, 65; Am Coun Learned Socs grant-in-aid, 68, fel, 73-74. Bibliog: F Will-Levaillant (auth), Picabia et la machine: symbole et abstraction, Rev de l'Art, Paris, Number 4 (1969): 74-82; Douglas David (auth), Big Dada, Newsweek, 9/70. Mem: Col Art Asn (mem nominating bd, 72); Asn pour l'Etude de Dada et du Surrealisme (founding mem). Res: Emphasis on Dada in Paris and art in France from about 1910 to 1925. Publ: Auth, Juan Gris and the Golden Section, 65 & The Machinist Style of francis Picabia, 66, Art Bull; auth, Philip Renteria, Pelham-von Stoffler Gallery, 76; auth, Francis Picabia, Princeton Press, 78. Mailing Add: 1117 Milford Houston TX 77006

CAMINS, JACQUES JOSEPH
PAINTER, PRINTMAKER
b Odessa, Russia, Jan 1, 04; US citizen. Study: Paris, France; Art Students League; spec study with Jean Liberty & Byron Browne; Pratt Graphics Ctr, with Matsubara Naoka & Carol Summer. Work: Israel Mus, Jerusalem; Negev Mus, Bersheba, Israel; Fr Embassy Cult Inst in Israel; Copper-Hewitt Mus; Arnot Art Mus. Exhib: Veverly Gallery, New York, 64; Cript Gallery, Columbia Univ, 65; 50th Anniversary Audubon Artists at the Nat Acad Galleries, New York, 67; Artists Equity Asn Gallery, 71; Provincetown Art Asn, Mass, many years. Teaching: Instr painting, Lakewood, NJ Bd Educ, 67. Bibliog: Frank Crotty (auth), profiles in Worchester Sunday Telegram & Provincetown Advocate, 65; Barbara Sloan (auth), profile in The Observer, 67. Mem: Artists Equity Asn; Provincetown Art Asn; Art Students League; Westbeth Graphics Workshop; Am Fedn Arts. Media: Oil. Mailing Add: 847 81st St Studio 6 Stillwater Island FL 33141

CAMLIN, JAMES A
PAINTER
b Hopkinton, Mass, Jan 16, 18. Study: Sch Practical Art, Boston; also with Aldro T Hibbard. Exhib: Acad Artists, Springfield Mus Fine Arts, Mass, 69; Allied Artists Am, Nat Acad Gallery, 70, Am Artists Prof League, Lever House, 70-75, Nat Art Club Ann Watercolor, 71, New York; Grand Prix de la Cote d'Azur, Cannes, France, 74. Pos: Citizen's art comt, Gendrot Fund, Melrose, Mass, 65-70. Awards: Diplome l'Honneur, Grand Prix de la Cote d'Azur, 73; Popular Award, Ogunquit Art Ctr, 73. Mem: Am Artists Prof League, New York; North Shore Art Asn, Gloucester, Mass. Style & Technique: Seascapes and landscapes. Media: Watercolor. Mailing Add: 234 W Emerson St Melrose MA 02176

CAMPBELL, COLIN KEITH
VIDEO ARTIST
b Reston, Man, Can, June 15, 42. Study: Univ Man, Winnipeg, BFA, 66; Claremont Grad Sch, Calif, MFA, 69. Work: Art Gallery of Ont, Toronto. Exhib: Art/Video/Confortation, Musee d'Art Moderne de la Ville de Paris, 74; Kunst Bleibt Kunst: Proj 74, Wallrafrichartz-Mus, Cologne, Ger, 74; Videoscape, Art Gallery of Ont, 75; Video Art, Inst of Contemp Art, Philadelphia, 75; Video Int, Aarhus Mus of Art, Denmark, 75; Southland Video Anthology, Long Beach Art Mus, Calif, 77; Documenta 6, Kassel, Ger, 77. Bibliog:

Eric Cameron (auth), Colin Campbell—The Story of Art Star, Vie des Arts, 76; Peggy Gale (auth), Colin Campbell—Windows & Mirrors, Video by Artists, 77 & Video Art in Canada, Studio Int, 77. Style & Technique: Narrative. Media: Video Mailing Add: c/o Art Metropole 241 Yonge St Toronto ON M5M 3J1 Can

CAMPBELL, DAVID PAUL
PAINTER
b Washington, DC, Mar 31, 36. Study: Art Students League. Exhib: Smithsonian Inst, Washington, DC, 59; Concorso Donatello, Florence, 66; The Representational Spirit, State Univ NY Albany, 70; A Sense of Place, Univ Nebr & Joslyn Mus, Omaha, 73; one-man shows, Cramer Gallery, Glen Rock, NJ, 73 & 75, Spence Gallery, Manchester, Mass, 74 & Davis & Long Co, New York, 76; Del Water Gap Exhib, Corcoran Gallery, Washington, DC, 75; Kutztown State Col, Pa, 77; Artist's Choice, Soho Gallery, New York, 77; Art on Paper, Univ NC, 77. Teaching: Instr landscape painting, Garland Col, Florence, summers 68 & 69. Pos: Artist in residence, Artists for Environment Found, Del Water Gap, NJ, 75. Awards: Fourth Prize Extemporaneous Landscape, Community Casale, Italy, 66; Hallmark Purchase Award, Watercolor USA, Springfield Art Mus, Mo, 74. Style & Technique: Naturalist landscapes, rural and urban, painted entirely outdoors, mostly in watercolor. Media: Watercolor, Oil, Tempera. Mailing Add: 121 Raymond St Cambridge MA 02140

CAMPBELL, DOROTHY BOSTWICK
PAINTER, SCULPTOR
b New York, NY, Mar 26, 99. Study: Study with Eliot O'Hara, Washington, DC & Marilyn Bendell, Cortez, Fla. Work: Cooperstown Art Asn, NY; Mystic Mus, Conn; Pioneer Gallery, Cooperstown. Exhib: Cooperstown Art Asn, var group & one-man shows, 65; var shows, Sarasota Art Asn, Fla & Pioneer Gallery, Cooperstown; Cortez Art Sch, Fla, 72. Awards: First Prize for Watercolor, Collectors Corner, Washington, DC; Purchase Prize for Watercolor, Cooperstown Art Asn, 65; Merit Award for Oils, Cortez Sch Art Exhib, 72. Mem: Am Art League; Am Fedn Arts; Coopertown Art Asn (dir); Sarasota Art Asn; Longboat Art Asn, Fla. Publ: Auth & illusr, Passing Thoughts, Bks I-XII, 67-77. Mailing Add: 4315 Mangrove Pl Sarasota FL 33581

CAMPBELL, GRETNA
PAINTER, EDUCATOR
b New York, NY, Mar 23, 23. Study: Cooper Union; Art Students League, with Morris Kantor. Work: Long View Found. Exhib: Whitney Mus Am Art; Corcoran Gallery Art; Pa Acad Fine Arts; Mus Mod Art. Teaching: Lectr painting, Philadelphia Col Art, 63-71; instr painting, New York Studio Sch, 71-72; asst prof, Yale Univ, 73- Awards: Pearl Fund Grant, 47-50; Tiffany Found Grant, 52-53; Fulbright Fel, 53-54. Mem: Artists Alliance. Style & Technique: Direct landscape and figure painting; painterly, loose, coloristic. Media: Oil. Dealer: Green Mountain Gallery 135 Greene St New York NY 10012. Mailing Add: 145 W 88th St New York NY 10024

CAMPBELL, (JAMES) LAWRENCE
PAINTER, WRITER
b Paris, France, May 21, 14; US citizen. Study: London Cent Schs Arts & Crafts; Acad Grande Chaumiere, Paris; Art Students League. Work: Joseph H Hirshhorn Mus & Sculpture Garden, Washington, DC. Exhib: One-man show, Contemp Arts, New York, 51; Am Fedn Arts Traveling Exhib, 55-56; Pa Acad Fine Arts Ann, Philadelphia; Weatherspoon Gallery, Univ NC; Realist Shows, circulated through State Univ NY, 70-72; plus others. Teaching: Assoc prof studio art, Brooklyn Col, prof, 72-; vis lectr art hist, Pratt Inst, 68- Pos: Ed assoc, Art News Mag, 49-; dir publ, Art Students League, 50- Mem: Int Asn Art Critics (mem, Am Sect); Art Students League. Media: Oil, Watercolor. Res: 19th century European and American painting; also Ruskin; history of Art Students League. Publ: Auth, feature articles and reviews in Art News, 49-; contribr, The Mosaics of Jeanne Reynal; auth, Thomas Sills, 65; ed, The Elements of Drawing, Dover, 71; auth, articles in Vogue, Craft Horizons, Washington Post, J Aesthetic Criticism & others. Dealer: Green Mountain Gallery 135 Greene St New York NY 10014. Mailing Add: 215 W 98th St New York NY 10025

CAMPBELL, JEWETT
EDUCATOR, PAINTER
b Hoboken, NJ, Aug 10, 12. Study: Cooper Union; Art Students League; Skowhegan Sch Art, Maine; Hans Hofmann Sch of Art. Work: Mus Mod Art, New York; Va Mus Fine Arts, Richmond; Univ Va, Charlottesville. Comn: Mural, Va Educ Asn, Richmond, 50; mural, Chesapeake Corp, West Point, Va, 65. Exhib: One-man shows, Va Mus Fine Arts, Richmond, 43-70; Va Mus Fine Arts, Biennials, 48-70; Corcoran Biennial, Washington, DC; Art of the Armed Forces, Nat Gallery, Washington, DC, 44. Collections Arranged: Avant-Garde Exhib, Richmond Artists Asn, 58. Teaching: Instr painting, Univ Richmond, 51-57 & Exten, Univ Va, 55-60; prof painting, Va Commonwealth Univ, 48- Awards: Purchase Awards, Va Mus, 40 & 60. Style & Technique: Magic realist; neo-plastic geometric black and white paintings. Media: Oil. Dealer: Marc Moyens 2109 Paul Spring Rd Alexandria VA; Gallery K 2032 P St NW Washington DC. Mailing Add: 3715 Douglasdale Rd Richmond VA 23221

CAMPBELL, KENNETH
SCULPTOR, PAINTER
b West Medford, Mass, Apr 14, 13. Study: Mass Sch Art, with Ernest Major, Cyrus Darlin, Richard Andrews & William Porter; Nat Acad Design, with Leon Kroll & Gifford Beal; Art Students League, with Arthur Lee. Work: Kalamazoo Art Inst; Walker Art Ctr, Minneapolis, Minn; Whitney Mus Am Art. Exhib: Audubon Artists, 64 & 65; Sculptors Guild, NY, 64, 65 & 67; Univ Ill, 65; Univ NC, 66; retrospective, Univ Ky, 67; plus others. Teaching: Instr drawing, painting & sculpture, Studio Five, Boston & Provincetown, Mass, 47-51; instr, Erskine Sch, Boston, 47-48; instr, Silvermine Col Art, 62 & 63; instr, Queens Col, NY, 63-66; artist in residence, Univ Ky, 66; Univ RI, 67; lectr, Columbia Univ & Univ Md, 68-69. Awards: Ford Found Purchase Award, 63 & 64; Richard Davis Mem Award, Audubon Artists, 65; Guggenheim Fel, 65; plus others. Mem: Artists Club; Art Students League; Sculptors Guild (bd mem); Audubon Artists; Boston Soc Independent Artists (bd dirs). Mailing Add: 79 Mercer St New York NY 10012

CAMPBELL, MALCOLM
ART HISTORIAN, EDUCATOR
b Hackensack, NJ, May 12, 34. Study: Princeton Univ, AB, MFA & PhD. Teaching: Assoc prof hist art, Univ Pa, past chmn dept. Res: 16th & 17th century Italian art. Publ: Contribr, Art Bull, Burlington Mag & Revista Arte. Mailing Add: G-29 Fine Arts Bldg Univ Pa Dept Hist of Art Philadelphia PA 19104

CAMPBELL, MARJORIE DUNN
PAINTER, EDUCATOR
b Columbus, Ohio, Sept 14, 10. Study: Ohio State Univ, BS & MA; Claremont Col Grad Inst Art; Teachers Col, Columbia Univ; also with Hans Hofmann, Emil Bisttram & Millard Sheets. Teaching: Instr appl art, Univ Mo, 42-45; asst prof fine arts, Ohio State Univ, 45-49; asst prof art, Univ Northern Iowa, 49-71, assoc prof, 71- Mem: Art Educ Asn Iowa; Int Soc Educ through Art; Western Art Asn; Nat Art Educ Asn. Publ: Contribr, Sch Arts, Art Educ J & Everyday Art Mags. Mailing Add: Dept of Art Univ Northern Iowa Cedar Falls IA 50613

CAMPBELL, RICHARD HORTON
PAINTER, PRINTMAKER
b Marinette, Wis, Jan 11, 21. Study: Cleveland Sch Art; Art Ctr Sch, Los Angeles; Univ Calif, Los Angeles. Work: Theater Guild Am, New York; Hilton Hotel, Denver. Exhib: Butler Inst Am Art, Youngstown, Ohio; Denver Mus; Frye Mus, Seattle, Wash; Oakland Art Mus, Calif; Saratoga Nat, Fla. Pos: Bd dirs, Santa Monica Art Gallery. Awards: Second Prize, Los Angeles All-City Exhib, 51; First Prize, Cleveland May Show, 54; First Prize, 7th Festival of Arts, Los Angeles, 58. Mem: Nat Watercolor Soc; Los Angeles Art Asn; fel Int Inst Arts & Lett. Media: Oil. Mailing Add: 643 Baylor St Pacific Palisades CA 90272

CAMPBELL, VIVIAN (VIVIAN CAMPBELL STOLL)
COLLECTOR, WRITER
b Belmont, Mass, May 20, 19. Pos: Asst cur, Fogg Art Mus, Harvard Univ, 37-42; dir, Harry Stone Gallery, New York, 42-44; prod mgr & art ed, Woman's Press Mag, 44-47; ed art publ, UNESCO, Paris, 48-50; art reporter & ed, Life Mag, Paris & New York, 48-66; freelance writer, 60- Mem: ARC Directions (ed bd, 66-); New York Printmakers Workshop (bd dirs, 69-). Collection: Early and contemporary American painting and miniature portrait before 1830. Publ: Auth, A Christmas Anthology of Poetry & Painting, 47; contribr, Life Mag, L'Oeil, Am Scholar & others. Mailing Add: 408 W 20th St New York NY 10011

CAMPOLI, COSMO
SCULPTOR, EDUCATOR
b South Bend, Ind, Mar 21, 22. Study: Art Inst Chicago, grad, 50, Anna Louise Raymond traveling fel to Italy, France & Spain, 50-52. Work: Mus Mod Art, New York; Richmond Art Mus, Va; Unitarian Church, Chicago; City of Chicago Park Dist; Exchange Nat Bank, Chicago; plus many pvt collections. Exhib: The New Images of Man, Mus Mod Art, New York, 59; US Info Agency Show, Moscow & Petrograd; The Chicago School Exhibition, Galerie due Dragone, Paris; Festival of Two Worlds (sculpture exhib), Spoleto, Italy, 30-yr retrospective, Mus Contemp Art, Chicago, 71; plus many others. Teaching: Instr adult art group, Hull House, 47-49; instr sculpture, Contemp Art Workshop, Chicago, 52-; assoc prof sculpture, Inst Design, Ill Inst Technol, 53-, chmn dept sculpture, 55-; vis prof, Univ Chicago, summers 63-65; lectr original artist-mkt-concept, Conf World Affairs, Univ Colo, 72. Pos: Juror, var shows in Chicago area, Nelson Gallery, Atkins Mus, Columbus Art League & Walker Art Ctr. Awards: Bronze Medal, Deleg Nat Educ-Fisica, Madrid, 69; Automotive Asn Spain Award, An Expression of the Automobile Obsession, 69; appointed Knight of Mark Twain, 71; plus others. Bibliog: Harold Haydon (auth), rev in Chicago Sun-Times, 5/19/71; Franz Schulze (auth), rev in Chicago Daily News, 5/29/71; Rev of 30-yr Retrospective, Fr TV, 6/71; plus many others. Publ: Auth, Artists Market, Alumni Asn Newspaper, Sch Art Inst Chicago, 71. Mailing Add: Dept Sculpture Inst Design Ill Inst Technol 3360 S State St Chicago IL 60616

CAMPUS, PETER
VIDEO ARTIST
b New York, NY, May 19, 37. Study: Ohio State Univ, BSc(exp psychol), 60. Exhib: Re-Vision, Contemp Arts Mus, Houston, 73; one-man show, Everson Mus Art, Syracuse, NY, 74; Project 74, Kolnisher Kunstverein, Cologne, WGer, 74; Projected Images, Walker Art Ctr, Minneapolis, 74; Sao Paulo Bienal, Brazil, 75; San Francisco Mus Art, Calif, 76; Hayden Gallery, Mass Inst Technol, Cambridge, 76; Projects Gallery, Mus Mod Art, New York, 77; Documenta 6, Kassel, Ger, 77; Whitney Mus Am Art, New York, 78. Awards: Guggenheim Fel, 75. Bibliog: Bruce Kurtz (auth), Fields, Peter Campus, Arts Mag. 5/73; Roberta Smith (auth), About faces, the new work of Peter Campus, Art in Am, 3-4/77. Style & Technique: Closed circuit video installations. Media: Video Tape. Mailing Add: c/o Leo Castelli Gallery 420 W Broadway New York NY 10012

CANADAY, JOHN EDWIN
ART CRITIC
b Ft Scott, Kans, Feb 1, 07. Study: Univ Tex, BA; Yale Univ, MA; Ecole Louvre, Paris, France. Teaching: Assoc prof art hist, Univ Va, 38-50; prof art hist & head, Sch Art, Newcomb Col, Tulane Univ, 50-52. Pos: Chief, Div Educ, Philadelphia Mus Art, 51-59; art critic, New York Times, 59-76, guest writer, 76- Publ: Auth, Mainstreams of modern art, Metropolitan seminars in art, Lives of the painters, Embattled critic & Culture gulch. Mailing Add: New York Times 229 W 43rd St New York NY 10036

CANADAY, OUIDA GORNTO
PAINTER, EDUCATOR
b Lake Wales, Fla, Apr 26, 22. Study: Univ Tampa; Atlanta Art Inst; Flat Rock Sch Art; Ga State Univ. Work: Ga State Univ; Eufaula Art Mus, Ala; Emory Univ; Mus Art, Greenville, SC. Comn: Acrylic, Morris Brown Col, 68; six 6'x6' batiks, Ga Tech Univ, 69; 8'x12' stained glass, Cobb Fed Bldg, Marietta, Ga, 69; Woodrow Wilson Commemorative, First Fed Bldg, Atlanta, 71; 4'x16' acrylic, US Corps Eng 200 Anniversary Commemorative, 75. Exhib: Mus Arts & Sci, Macon, Ga, 64 & 74; Southeastern Art Exhib, High Mus, Atlanta, 67 & Ga Artists Show, 72; Hunter Ann, Chattanooga, Tenn, 69; Calloway Gardens Art Show, Pine Mountain, Ga, 71. Teaching: Teacher, Studio Group Classes, 60-; teacher, Worldwide Painting Group Tours, 65-; mem fac art, Emory Univ, 68-73; mem fac art, Reinhardt Col, 72. Awards: Purchase Award, Eufaula Arts Festival; Honorable Mention, Calloway Gardens Art Show; Spec Award, Atlanta Beautiful Comn. Bibliog: Charlotte Hale Smith (auth), Ladies paint the world, 64 & The wide world beckons, 65, 65 & Doris Lockerman (auth), Painters world, 70, Atlanta J-Constitution Mag. Mem: Arts Festival Atlanta (pres, bd dirs); Atlanta Artist Club (pres); Ga Arts Comn (vpres); Fine Arts Comn (adv comt). Style & Technique: Figures. Media: Oil & Metallic Media; Reflective Media. Dealer: Ann Jacob Gallery Peachtree Ctr Atlanta GA 30303. Mailing Add: 2722 Rovena Ct Decatur GA 33034

CANARIS, PATTI ANN
PAINTER
b Billings, Mont, Feb 27, 19. Study: Eastern Mont State; Wash State Univ; Univ Mont, BFA(with honors). Comn: Off ctr fountain design, Architect Don Miller, Spokane, Wash, 64; watercolor, Univ Mont, Missoula, 71; cover, NMex Wildlife Mag, 72. Exhib: Western Mont Art Potpourri, Missoula, 71-74; Southwest Wildflower Contest, Santa Ana, Calif, 75; El Prado Galleries, Sedona, Ariz; Gallery 85, Billings; Dos Pajaros Gallery, El Paso, Tex; Baker Gallery of Fine Art, Lubbock, Tex; Chamisa Gallery, Taos, NMex; plus others. Pos: Asst vpres, Award Pictures Calif, 57-60; dir publ, Univ Mont, 66-70, dir non-acad classes; dir, Univ Ctr Art Gallery. Awards: Montague Commercial Artist of the Year, 52; Award, Award Pictures Calif, 58. Style & Technique: Watercolor wet-on-wet washes. Mailing Add: 6453 Dawn El Paso TX 79912

CANBY, JEANNY VORYS
ART HISTORIAN, CURATOR
b Columbus, Ohio, July 14, 29. Study: Bryn Mawr Col, BA, 50, PhD, 59; Oriental Inst, Univ Chicago, MA, 54. Collections Arranged: Egyptian Collection (rearranged), Walters Art Gallery, Baltimore, 65, Ancient Near Eastern and Egyptian Collection (re-installed new wing), 74-75; special exhibits, Ancients Seals, Egyptian Sculptor's Models & Sculpture from Sumer and Akkad (with catalog), 70; In Search of Ancient Treasure, 78. Teaching: Vis lectr, Near Eastern archaeol, Johns Hopkins Univ, Baltimore, 60-64. Pos: Asst cur ancient art, Walters Art Gallery, 64-71, cur ancient Near Eastern & Egyptian art, 71- Publ: Auth, Decorated garments in Ashurnasirpalis sculpture, XXXII: 31-53, & The Stelenreihen at Assur, Tell Halaf & Massebôt, XXXVIII: 113-128, Iraq; auth, Some Hittite figurines in the Aegean, Hesperia, XXXVIII: 14-149; auth, The pedigree of a Syrian bronze in the Walters Art Gallery, Berytus, XVIII: 107-122; auth, The Ancient Near East in the Walters Art Gallery, 74; auth, Walters Gallery Cappadocian tablet and the Sphinx in Anatolia in the Second Millennium, BC, J Near Eastern Studies, Vol 34 (1975): 225-248. Mailing Add: 211 Haviland Mill Rd Brookeville MD 20729

CANDAU, EUGENIE
ART LIBRARIAN
b San Francisco, Calif, Jan 26, 38. Study: Fat City Sch Finds Art, MFA, 73; San Francisco State Univ, BA, 74; Univ Calif, Berkeley, MLS, 78. Exhibitions Arranged: Kaethe Kollwitz, San Francisco Mus Art, 70; Hand Bookbinding Today, An International Art (traveling exhib), San Francisco Mus Mod Art, 78. Pos: Librn, Louise Sloss Ackerman Fine Arts Libr, San Francisco Mus Mod Art, 68- Mem: Col Art Asn; Art Libr Soc NAm; Int Inst Conserv; Man Mus Finds Art (chmn, Chloe Footstar Award Comt, 73-). Interest: Arts of the book; modern and contemporary art. Publ: Ed (catalogue), Permanent Collection of Painting & Sculpture, San Francisco Mus Art, 70; auth, Philip Smith, artist of the book, Fine Print: Rev of Arts of the Bk, 76; auth (catalogue), Hand bookbinding today, an International Art, 78. Mailing Add: 2108 Derby St Berkeley CA 94705

CANEPA, ANNA L
VIDEO EXPERT
b Trieste, Italy, Nov 12, 40. Study: Liceo Artistico; N Barabino, Genoa, Italy, BA(art hist); grad study in art hist & archit, Univ Florence, Italy; grad study in hist of film, Sorbonne, Paris. Work: Centre Nat d'Art Contemporain, Paris; The Kitchen, New York; Art Gallery of New South Wales, Sydney, Australia; Nat Gallery of Victoria, Melbourne, Australia; Donnell Libr, New York. Exhib: Proj 74, Koln, Ger, 74; Video Art, Inst of Contemp Art, Philadelphia, 75; Camel Award, Milan, Italy, 75; Today Together, Int Art Fair, Koln, Ger, 75; Biennale di Venezia, Italy, 76; Sydney Biennale, Australia, 76; Whitney Mus of Am Art Biennale, New York, 77; Dokumenta 6, Kessel, Ger, 77. Collections Arranged: Allan Kaprow Performances in Turin, Naples, Genoa, Milan, Paris, Madrid & New York, 74-76; A Search for Clues, D Oppenheim, Framart Gallery, Naples, 4/76; Visiting Artist: Les Levine, Australia, 76; Video From Outside, 76 & The Angel of Mercy: Eleanor Antin, 77, M L d'Arc Gallery, New York. Pos: Coordr & dir, Video Distribution, Inc, 74-75; pres & dir, Anna Canepa Video Distribution, Inc, 75- Bibliog: Les Levine (producer of videotape), Portrait of Anna, 74; Deborah Perlberg (auth), Video from Out-side, Artforum, 77; Gianfranco Mantegna (auth), Videografare, Fotografare, 77. Mailing Add: 431 W Broadway New York NY 10012

CANFIELD, JANE (WHITE)
SCULPTOR
b Syracuse, NY, Apr 29, 97. Study: Art Students League; James Earle & Laura Gardin Fraser Studio; Borglum Sch; also with A Bourdelle, Paris, France. Work: Whitney Mus Am Art; Cornell Univ Mus Art. Comn: Six animals in lead for gate posts, comn by Paul Mellon, Upperville, Va, 40; animals in lead for gym entrance, Miss Porters Sch, Farmington, Conn, 60; St John Apostle in stone, Church of St John of Lattington, Locust Valley, NY, 63; herons in stone, Mem Sanctuary, Fishers Island, 69; Canada geese in bronze for pool, Long Lake, Minn, 71. Exhib: Sculpture Pavilion, New York World's Fair, 39; one-man shows, Brit-Am Art Gallery, New York, 55 & Far Gallery, New York, 61, 65 & 74; Country Art Gallery, Locust Valley, 71. Media: Stone, Bronze. Publ: Auth, The Frog Prince, Swan Cove, Harper, 70. Dealer: Far Gallery 20 E 80th St New York NY 10021. Mailing Add: Guard Hill Rd Bedford Village NY 10506

CANIFF, MILTON ARTHUR
CARTOONIST
b Hillsboro, Ohio, Feb 28, 07. Study: Ohio State Univ, with Martha Schauer, James Hopkins, Ralph Fanning, Guy Brown Wiser & Hoyt Sherman, BA; Rollins Col, hon FAD. Work: Metrop Mus Art, New York; Louvre (graphics), Paris, France; Air Force Mus, Dayton, Ohio; Nat Aviation Club, Washington, DC. Comn: Murals, Nat Aviation Club, 60, Flag Plaza, Pittsburgh, Pa, 68, Alumni House, Ohio State Univ, 71 & Conv Ctr, Dayton, 72. Exhib: One-man shows, Soc Illusr Gallery, New York, 47 & Jean Renoir Gallery, Paris, 65; Art of the Cartoon, Graphics Hall, Louvre, Paris, 66 & Lever Gallery, New York, 71; Cartoon Now, Kennedy Ctr, Washington, DC, 75. Awards: Reuben Award, Nat Cartoonists Soc, 47 & 72, Segar Award, 71; Arts & Lett Award, US Air Force Asn, 49. Bibliog: Stephen Becker (auth), Comic art in America, Simon & Schuster. Mem: Nat Cartoonists Soc (pres, 48-50, hon chmn, 70-); Soc Illustrators. Style & Technique: Illustrative adventure story in cartoon form. Media: Ink, Watercolor, Oil. Publ: Auth & illusr, Dickie Dare, 32-34; auth & illusr, Terry and the Pirates, syndicated newspaper feature, 34-46; auth & illusr, Male Call, US Serv Newspapers, 42-45; auth & illusr, Steve Canyon, syndicated newspaper feature, 47- Dealer: Toni Mendez 140 E 56th St New York NY 10022. Mailing Add: PO Box 2022 Palm Springs CA 92262

CANIN, MARTIN
PAINTER
b Brooklyn, NY, Oct 1, 27. Study: Syracuse Univ, BFA. Work: Philadelphia Mus Art; San Francisco Mus Art; St Petersburg Mus Art; Yale Univ Art Gallery; Boston Mus Fine Arts. Exhib: Pa Acad Fine Arts Ann, 54; Hard Edge Painting, Mus Mod Art, 63 & group show, 68, Mus Mod Art Penthouse; Int Drawing Show, Darmstaat, Ger, 70; Prints from Kelpra Studio, Hayward Gallery, London, 71. Teaching: Instr painting, drawing & design, Parsons Sch Design, 61-69. Media: Oil on Canvas. Dealer: Graham Gallery 1014 Madison Ave New York NY 10021. Mailing Add: 109 W Broadway New York NY 10013

CANNON, MARGARET ERICKSON
PAINTER, LECTURER
b Marquette, Mich, May 26, 23. Study: Univ of the Americas, BA(art educ); Univ Calif, Los Angeles; Long Beach City Col; Calif State Univ, Fullerton, MA(drawing & painting); Univ Barcelona. Teaching: Prof art hist, Univ of the Americas, 53-54; instr art hist & lectr community servs, Cerritos Col, 62-66; lectr art appreciation, Calif State Univ, Fullerton, 67; prof art, Escuela de Arte Activo, Ensenada, Baja California, Mex. Mem: Los Angeles Art Asn; Calif Art Educ Asn; Nat Art Educ Asn; Southern Calif Art Ther Asn; Am Asn Univ Women; Int Soc of Artists (rep). Media: Oil, Acrylic. Publ: Auth, History of the Waves, US Naval Reserve; illusr, Patriots—Female Version. Dealer: Galeria de Arte Anna A V Piveroll No 122 Ensenada Baja California Mex. Mailing Add: 1711 E Grove Pl Fullerton CA 92631

CANNON, T C (TOM WAYNE)
PAINTER, PRINTMAKER
b Lawton, Okla, Sept 27, 46. Study: Inst Am Indian Arts, Santa Fe, NMex; San Francisco Art Inst; Cent State Univ, Okla. Work: Southern Plains Mus, Anadarko, Okla; Hon Collection, Inst Am Indian Affairs; Washington Arts & Crafts Bd, Bur Indian Affairs, Washington, DC. Exhib: Young Indian Painters, Fine Arts Mus NMex, Santa Fe, 66; Scottsdale Nat, Ariz, 66; one-man shows, American Before Columbus, Dennis Larkins Gallery, 70 & Paintings & Graphics, Southern Plains Mus, 71; Two American Painters, Smithsonian Inst, Washington, DC, 72. Awards: First Prize, Southwestern Interscholastic Meet, 62, 63 & 64; Gov Trophy, Scottsdale Nat, 66. Publ: Illusr, Tales of the Kiowa Indians, 72. Dealer: Joachim Jean Aberbach 241 W 72nd St New York NY 10023. Mailing Add: Timberwick Rd Santa Fe NM 87501

CANO, MARGARITA
ART LIBRARIAN, PAINTER
b Havana, Cuba, Feb 27, 32. Study: Univ Havana, PhD(physics & chem), 56, MLibSc, 62; studies in art hist & mus conserv with Helmut Ruheman from Nat Gallery, London, Eng. Work: Mutual of Omaha Ins Co, Miami, Fla; Lowe Art Mus, Univ Miami, Coral Gables, Fla. Exhib: Mem Exhib, Ft Lauderdale Mus, Fla; Piedmont Graphics Ann, Mint Mus, Charlotte, NC; Hunterton Art Ctr, Clinton, NJ; Mem Exhib, Metrop Mus & Art Ctr, Miami, Fla; Pan-Am Exhib, Miami, Fla. Collections Arranged: A New Reality (exhib of paintings), 75, African Arts (exhib of sculptures, textiles & beads), Dept of Art, 76, A Collection of Am Patchwork Quilts, 76 & Cintas Fellows, Paintings by Cuban Artists (auth, catalogue), 77, Miami-Dade Pub Libr, Fla; Latin Am Graphics, Permanent Collection, Miami-Dade Pub Libr Syst, 76; The Face in Art (Fayum Portraits to Warhol), Hispanic Branch, Miami-Dade Pub Libr, Fla, 77. Teaching: Instr contemp Latin Am art, Miami-Dade Community Col, South Campus, 77. Pos: Registr, Julio Lobo Found, Napoleonic Art Mus, 57-58; art librn, Miami-Dade Pub Libr, 63- Awards: Cintas Found fel, 75-76. Mem: Art Libr Soc NAm. Style & Technique: Woodcuts and lines on paper and mixed media. Media: Incaustic on paper, board or canvas. Res: Contemporary Latin American art and keeping up-to-date materials on new artists. Publ: Auth, How to Bridge the Art Gap, Art Libr Soc NAm, 76; auth, Dictionary of Latin American Artists (bibliog), Cintas Found, 76. Mailing Add: 501 SW 24th Ave Miami FL 33135

CANRIGHT, SARAH ANNE
PAINTER
b Chicago, Ill, Aug 20, 41. Study: Art Inst Chicago, BFA. Work: Kresge Found, New York; Sam Koffler Found & Ill Bell Tel Co, Chicago; Gould Corp, Ill. Exhib: Nonplussed Some, Hyde Park Art Ctr, Chicago, 68-69; Famous Artists, Mus Contemp Art, Chicago, 69; Famous Artists, Another Load, San Francisco Art Inst, 70; 73rd Vicinity Show, Art Inst Chicago & Phyllisteens, Phyllis Kind Gallery, Chicago, 71. Awards: Armstrong Award, Art Inst Chicago, 71. Bibliog: W Halsted (auth), Chicago, Artforum, 68; F Schulze (auth), Chicago, Art News, 71 & var articles in Chicago Daily News. Media: Oil, Acrylic. Mailing Add: 161 Mulberry St New York NY 10013

CANTEY, SAM BENTON, III
COLLECTOR
Study: Culver Mil Acad; Washington & Lee Univ, BA. Collection: Modern prints, drawings and watercolors; School of Fontainebleau prints and drawings; work of Ft Worth and Tex artists. Publ: Auth, articles in var newspapers, catalog introductions on Tex artists and catalog for Sch of Fontainebleau Exhib. Mailing Add: 1220 Washington Terr Ft Worth TX 76107

CANTIENI, GRAHAM ALFRED
PAINTER, ART ADMINISTRATOR
b Albury, Australia, Aug 26, 38; Can citizen. Study: Royal Melbourne Teachers' Col, sec teaching cert; Royal Melbourne Inst of Technol; Univ Melbourne. Work: Swan Hill Art Gallery, Victoria, Australia; Univ Sherbrooke, Que; Centre Hospitalier Univ, Sherbrooke, Que; La Soc Teleglobe Can, Montreal; La Chambre des Notaires, Montreal, Que. Exhib: S Yarra Gallery, Melbourne, 61; New Brunswick Mus, St John, 71; Dalhousie Univ, Halifax, NS, 71; Wells Gallery, Ottawa, Ont, 72; Galerie Signal, Montreal, 75; La Serie Polyphonie, Galerie Claude Luce, Montreal, 76; Galerie de l'Anse-aux-Barques, Mus Que, Quebec, 77. Collections Arranged: Artisanat 1976, 76, Concours d'Art Graphique Quebecois, 77 & La Nouvelle Tapisserie au Que, 77, Centre Cult, Univ Sherbrooke. Teaching: Art master practice & hist of art, Wesley Col, Perth, Australia, 67-68; animateur painting & graphics, Ateliers d'Animation Cult, Sherbrooke, 69-76. Pos: Art dir, Cult Centre, Univ Sherbrooke, 76- Bibliog: Louise Provonost-Tremblay (auth), Graham Cantieni, explorateur de la matiere, Vie des Arts, 75; Denyse Gerin (auth), The Paintings of Graham Cantieni, Art Mag, 76; Jean-Claude Leblond (auth), Dessins recents de Graham Cantieni, Galerie Claude Luce, 76; Jean Tourangeau (auth), Graham Cantieni, polyphonies, Vie des Arts, Number 89, 77-78. Mem: Regroupement des Artistes des Cantons de l'est (pres, 73-75); Soc des Artistes Prof du Que (vpres, 77). Style & Technique: Gestual painting in which restructured composition creates an effect of dynamic and syncopic movement. Media: Oil, ink. Publ: Auth, Art and Marxism, Dissent, 65; auth, Art and Education, Partisan, 64; co-auth, Approche concrete de mathematique et langue seconde, HMH, Montreal, 74; auth, La ceramique de nos cantons, Option Globale, 76; auth, Tapisseries quebecoises contemporaines, Art Mag, 77. Dealer: Mitzi Bidner 400 Slater St Suite 607 Ottawa ON Can. Mailing Add: 425 Rue London Sherbrooke PQ J1H 3M8 Can

CANTINE, DAVID
PAINTER
b Jackson, Mich, June 7, 39. Study: Univ Iowa, BA, 62, MA, 64. Work: Mazur Mus, Monroe, La. Exhib: One-man shows, Univ Saskatchewan, Univ Alberta & Northern State Univ, 66, 67 & 69, Mazur Mus, 72 & Kraushaar Galleries, New York, 77. Mem: Col Art Asn Am. Style & Technique: Small scale, high key, geometric/still-life. Media: Oil, Acrylic Polymer. Dealer: Kraushaar Galleries 1055 Madison New York NY. Mailing Add: 99 St Georges Crescent Edmonton AB T5N 3M7 Can

CANTINI, VIRGIL D
PAINTER, SCULPTOR
b Italy, Feb 28, 20. Study: Carnegie Inst Technol, BFA, 46; Univ Pittsburgh, MA, 48. Work: Wichita Mus Art, Kans; Carnegie Mus Art, Pittsburgh, Pa; Westmoreland Co Mus Art, Greensburg, Pa; Hillman Libr, Univ Pittsburgh; Point Park Col. Comn: Man (sculpture), Grad Sch Pub Health, Univ Pittsburgh, 66, three sculptures & two tapestries, Hillman Libr, 69, Nat Sci Bldg, 74; Joy of Life (fountain sculpture), Urban Redevelop Authority Pittsburgh. 69; Skyscape (enamel mural), Oliver Tyrone Co, Pittsburgh, 71-; enamel murals (40 ft x 30 ft & 70 ft x 12 ft), Univ Pittsburgh, 75 & 77. Exhib: Assoc Artists Pittsburgh, 45-70; Brussels

World's Fair, 58; Pittsburgh Int, Carnegie Mus Art, 61, 64 & 67; one-man shows, Westmoreland Co Mus Art, 62 & Pittsburgh Plan for Arts, 62, 67, 71 & 75. Teaching: Prof art & chmn dept studio arts, Univ Pittsburgh, 52- Pos: Vpres, Pittsburgh Coun for Arts, 68-70. Awards: Guggenheim Fel, 58; Pope Paul VI Bishop's Medal, 64; Davinci Medal-Ital Sons & Daughters Am, Cultural Heritage Found, 68. Bibliog: Dorothy Sterling (auth), article in Am Artist, 52; Helen Knox (auth), article in Pitt Mag, 64; Lloyd Davis (auth), article in Appalachian, 67. Mem: Assoc Artists Pittsburgh (pres, 62-64); Arts & Crafts Ctr (vpres, 55-57); Pittsburgh Plan for Arts; Col Art Asn Am; Am Crafts Coun. Media: Enamel. Dealer: Pittsburgh Plan for Arts 1251 N Negley Ave Pittsburgh PA 15206. Mailing Add: Dept of Studio Arts Univ of Pittsburgh Pittsburgh PA 15260

CANTOR, B GERALD
COLLECTOR
b New York, NY, Dec 17, 16. Study: NY Univ. Pos: Chmn, Cantor, Fitzgerald, New York, Chicago, Atlanta & Beverly Hills; trustee, Los Angeles Co Mus Art; mem pres coun, Col of the Holy Cross; mem bd gov, Hebrew Univ. Mem: Am Fedn Arts; Fine Arts Soc San Diego; Brooklyn Inst Arts & Sci; fel Metrop Mus Art; fel Cleveland Mus Art. Interest: Large scale donations, scholarships to museums and universities. Collection: 19th and early 20th century sculpture and paintings; major collection of Auguste Rodin; George Kolbe. Mailing Add: Cantor Fitzgerald & Co Inc PO Box 811 Beverly Hills CA 90213

CANTOR, ROBERT LLOYD
EDUCATOR, DESIGNER
b New York, NY, Aug 14, 19. Study: NY Univ, PhD. Exhib: One-man show, Charleston Art Gallery, WVa. Teaching: Prof fine & indust arts, WVa Inst Technol; instr art, NY Univ; instr art, City Col New York; instr art, Fashion Inst Technol; instr art, Columbia Univ. Pos: Exec dir, Artists Equity Asn, New York; educ dir, Am Craftsmen Sch, New York. Mem: Eastern Artists Asn; Nat Educ Asn; Indust Art Asn; Comn Art Educ, Mus Mod Art; Soc Plastic Eng. Publ: Auth, History of Art Workbook; auth, Plastics for the Layman; also training film scenarios, manuals, textbks & contribr to art, educ & polit jour. Mailing Add: 15 Gulf Rd Lawrence Brook East Brunswick NJ 08816

CANTRELL, JEANNETTE LOUISE
See Albro, Jeannette

CANTRELL, JIM
PAINTER, CERAMIST
b Sulpher, Okla, Nov 23, 35. Study: Univ Nebr, Lincoln, BFA, 58; Pa State Univ, 59; Univ Northern Colo, Greeley, MA, 65. Work: Sheldon Mem Art Gallery, Lincoln, Nebr; Utah Mus Fine Art, Salt Lake City; Armand Hammer Bldg, Island Creek Coal Co, Lexington, Ky; FDS Corp Collection, Charlotte, NC; Lincoln-Davies Collection, Nashville, Tenn. Exhib: One-man shows, Sheldon Mem Art Gallery, 70, Hunter Mus of Art, Chattanooga, Tenn, 73 & Distelheim Galleries, Chicago, 75; Mainstream, Grover M Hermann Fine Arts Ctr, Marietta, Ohio, 74; Eight State Ann, Speed Art Mus, Louisville, Ky, 74. Teaching: Guest instr art, Univ Northern Colo, summer 66; assoc prof art, John F Kennedy Col, 66-70. Pos: Resident artist, Berea Col, 70-71. Awards: 12th Hunter Gallery Ann Award, Lincoln-Davies Ins Co, 72; J B Speed Art Mus Eight State Ann Award, WAVE TV, Louisville, Ky, 74; Bardstown Invitational Art Exhib Award, Stephen Foster Drama Asn, Ky, 74. Bibliog: Franz F Kriwanek (auth), Keramos, Kendall/Hunt, 75; Jim Cantrell: an artist not by choice but by providence, Ky Artist & Craftsmen Mag, 76; Thelma Newman (auth), The Container Book, Crown, 77. Mem: Ky Guild Artists & Craftsmen (bd trustees, 73-75); Am & World Crafts Couns; Piedmont Craftsmen, Inc; Craft Alliance, St. Louis. Style & Technique: Strong, direct brush strokes, figurative, people and still life; clay, functional and sculptural. Media: Oil, Watercolor, Clay. Publ: Auth, Cut Decoration, Ceramics Mo, 75. Dealer: Bardstown Art Gallery PO Box 437 Bardstown KY 40004; Distelheim Galleries 67 E Oak St Chicago IL 60611. Mailing Add: PO Box 437 Bardstown KY 40004

CAPA, CORNELL
PHOTOGRAPHER, MUSEUM DIRECTOR
b Budapest, Hungary, Apr 10, 18. Study: Madach Imre Gymnasium, Budapest, 28-36. Exhib: Margin of Life, Ctr of Inter-Am Relations, New York, 74; Johnson Mus, Cornell Univ, Ithaca, NY, 75. Collections Arranged: War in Focus: Robert Capa, 64 & Chim's Times: The Photographs of David Seymour, 66. Teaching: Lectr photog, NY Univ, 68-72 & Int Ctr of Photog, 74- Pos: Staff & contrib photogr, Life Mag, New York, 46-67; mem photogr, Magnum Photos, New York & Paris, 54-; guest dir, The Concerned Photographer, Riverside Mus, New York, 66, The Concerns of Roman Vishniac, Jewish Mus, New York, 73, Behind the Great Wall: China, Metrop Mus Art, New York, 72 & The Concerned Photographer Two, Israel Mus, Jerusalem, 73; ed, The Concerned Photographer One & Two, Grossman/Viking, 69-72; exec dir, Int Ctr of Photog, 74- Awards: Morris Gordon Mem Award, Photog Admin Inc, 72; Honor Roll, Am Soc Mag Photogr, 75; Joseph A Sprague Mem Award, Nat Press Photogr Asn, 76. Bibliog: Feature prof, Who Am I?, NBC Television, Channel 4, 71; Russ Arnold (auth), article in Camera 35; feature prog, Center of Concern, CBS Television, 77. Mem: Magnum Photogs (pres, 57-60); Overseas Press Club of New York (exec comn, 67-70 & 69-73); Am Soc Mag Photogr (vpres, 53-55; exec comn, 55-56, 57-61 & 67-69). Style & Technique: Photojournalist, documentary, straight photography. Publ: Co-auth (with Maya Pines), Retarded Children Can Be Helped, Channel Press, 57; co-auth (with Matthew Huxley), Farewell to Eden, Harper & Row, 64; co-auth (with J M Stycos), Margin of Life, 73 & ed, International Center of Photography Library of Photographers (first six titles), 74, Grossman Publ. Dealer: Magnum Photog Inc 15 W 46th St New York NY 10036. Mailing Add: 275 Fifth Ave New York NY 10016

CAPARN, RHYS (RHYS CAPARN STEEL)
SCULPTOR
b Onteora Park, NY, July 28, 09. Study: Bryn Mawr Col, 27-29; Ecole Artistique Animaux, with Edouard Navellier, 30; Archipenko Art Sch, New York, 31-33. Work: Morton May Collection, City Art Mus, St Louis; Riverside Mus Collection, Brandeis Univ; Fogg Mus; Whitney Mus Am Art, New York. Comn: Figures on armillary sphere (with Harold A Caparn), Brooklyn Bot Garden, 32; wall reliefs in concrete, bronze screen, drawings in ceramic tile & fountain head (with O'Conner & Kilham), Wollman Libr, Barnard Col, 58-59. Exhib: 15 Sculptors, Mus Mod Art Traveling Exhib, 41; Five Ann, Whitney Mus Am Art, 41-60; New York Six, Petit Palais, Paris, 50; Pa Acad, 51-53, 60 & 64; Unknown Political Prisoner, Tate Gallery, London, 53; Drawings, US Info Agency Exhibs, Europe & Far East, 56-57, Eight Americans, 57-58; Nat Inst Arts & Lett, 68 & 76. Teaching: Instr sculpture, Dalton High Sch, New York, 46-55 & 60-72. Pos: Mem Mayors Comt Beautification City of New York, 63-64; founding mem, Harlem Cult Coun, 64. Awards: Am Sculpture Second Prize, Metrop Mus Art, 51; Medals of Honor for Sculpture, Nat Asn Women Artists, 60 & 61. Bibliog: Robert Beverly Hale (auth), Rhys Caparn, Retrospective Press, 72. Mem: Sculptors Guild; Am Abstr Artists; Fedn Mod Painters & Sculptors; fel Int Inst Arts & Lett. Style & Technique: Abstractions from natural and architectural forms which have been acted upon by nature; builds directly in plaster, to remain as such, or to be cast in bronze or stone. Publ: Illusr, Down the Mountain, 62. Mailing Add: RD 1 Taunton Hill Rd Newtown CT 06470

CAPLAN, JERRY L
SCULPTOR, EDUCATOR
b Pittsburgh, Pa, Aug 9, 22. Study: Carnegie-Mellon Univ, BFA & MFA; Art Students League; Univ NC. Work: NC State Art Gallery, Raleigh; Pittsburgh Bd Educ; Westinghouse Corp. Comn: Terra-cotta sculptures, Friendship Fed Plaza, Pittsburgh, 68; porcelain symbols, Westinghouse Ceramic Div, Derry, Pa, 72; terra-cotta, Kossman Group, Kossman Assocs, Pittsburgh, 72; symbol, Rockwell Corp, Pittsburgh, 72; ceramic panels, Temple Emanuel, 70, wood panels, 75. Exhib: Five shows, Butler Inst Am Art, 55-75; Kent State 69; Carnegie Inst, 71; Mainstreams, Marietta, Ohio, 74 & 75; Appalachian Corridors, Charleston, WVa, 75. Teaching: Instr sculpture & ceramics, Chatham Col, 59-; instr painting, Arts & Crafts Ctr, Pittsburgh, 62-; lectr, Frick Educ Comn, Pittsburgh, 64- Awards: Purchase Award, Assoc Artists Pittsburgh, 65; Soc Sculptors Award, 70; Pittsburgh Artist of the Year, 75; plus others. Mem: Assoc Artists Pittsburgh (pres, 65); Soc Sculptors (treas); Am Crafts Coun; Pittsburgh Craftsmen's Guild. Style & Technique: Semi-abstract to figurative. Media: Terra-cotta. Publ: Auth, articles in Ceramic Mo, 9/76 & 11/76. Mailing Add: 5812 Fifth Ave Pittsburgh PA 15232

CAPLES, BARBARA BARRETT
PRINTMAKER, PAINTER
b Providence, RI, Oct 28, 14. Study: Smith Col, AB(magna cum laude), 36; Yale Univ Sch Fine Arts, 36-38; also with George Laurence Nelson & Ruth Starr Rose. Work: Smith Col Mus, Northampton, Mass; Univ Va, Charlottesville. Exhib: Am Watercolor Soc, 38; Soc Washington Printmakers, 68-; one-man shows, Smith Col & Art League, Alexandria, Va, 70; Boston Printmakers, 71. Teaching: Instr art & art hist, Rye Country Day Sch, NY, 38-40; instr art, Walter Reed Hosp, Washington, DC, 43-45; instr serigraphy, YWCA, Alexandria, 65-75. Awards: Numerous Awards, Art League, Alexandria, 65-71; Honorable Mention, Fairfax Co Cult Asn, 71; NVa Fine Arts Assoc, 71 & 72; plus others. Mem: Soc Washington Printmakers; Art League, Alexandria (mem bd, 69); NVa Fine Arts Asn. Mailing Add: 1111 Roan Lane Alexandria VA 22302

CAPONI, ANTHONY
SCULPTOR, EDUCATOR
b Pretare, Italy, May 7, 21. Study: Univ Flore, Italy; Cleveland Sch Art; Walker Art Ctr, Minn; Univ Minn, BS & MEd. Work: Minneapolis Inst Art; St Cloud State Col; Minn Mus Art. Comn: Sculpture, columns & figures, St Joseph Sch, Red Lake Falls, Minn, St Mary's Church, Warroad, Minn; St John's Church, Rochester, Minn; wax models for all bronze motifs in Eisenhower Libr, Abilene, Tex; two bronze relief sculptures, Ascoli, Italy; plus others. Exhib: Walker Art Ctr, Minneapolis, 47-58; St Paul Gallery Art, 47-58; Iowa State Teachers Col, 58; Minneapolis Art Inst Ann; Augustana Col, Sioux Falls, SDak, 71; plus other group & one-man shows. Teaching: Prof art & chmn dept, Macalester Col, 58- Pos: Co-dir, Sculpture in Minnesota (film), 50; pres, Minn Sculpture Group, 52; vpres, Minn Soc Sculptors, 58; producer, Forms that Live & Forms (film), Univ Minn, 59. Awards: Ford Found Grant & Four Prizes, Minneapolis Inst Art, 47-59; six Awards, Minn State Fair, 48-65; Awards, St Paul Gallery Art, 49 & 55. Mem: Artists Equity Asn; Soc Minn Sculptors. Media: Stone. Publ: Auth, Boulders & Pebbles of Poetry & Prose, Independence Press, 72. Mailing Add: Art Dept Macalester Col St Paul MN 55105

CAPONIGRO, PAUL
PHOTOGRAPHER
b Boston, Mass, Dec 7, 32. Study: With Benjamin Chin & Minor White. Exhib: One-man shows, In the Presence Of, George Eastman House, Rochester, NY, 58, A Photographers Place, Philadelphia, 63, Mus Mod Art, New York 68, Focus Gallery, San Francisco, 69; Princeton Univ, 70; Baldwin St Gallery, Toronto, Can, 71. Teaching: Instr creative photography, NY Univ, 67-71; instr photography, Yale Univ, 71-; workshops conducted at St Lawrence Univ, 67, 68 & 71, Calif Col Arts & Crafts, 69; Center of Eye & Kalamazoo Inst Arts, 70, Princeton Univ and many others, 71; lectr, George Eastman House, Rhode Island Sch Design, Princeton Univ and many others. Pos: Consult photo res dept, Polaroid Corp, Cambridge, 60- Awards: First Prize Photography, 10th Boston Arts Festival, 61; Guggenheim Fel to Eng, France & Ireland, Guggenheim Found, 66; Fel-Grant for Arts Photography, Nat Endowment for Arts, 71. Mem: Am Heliographers Asn, New York. Style & Technique: Large format camera, straight unmanipulated photography. Publ: Auth, An Aperture, monograph, 66; auth, Sunflower, Film Haus, Inc, New York, 74; auth, Landscape, McGraw Hill Paperbacks, 75. Mailing Add: Rte 3 Box 96D Santa Fe NM 87501

CAPP, AL
CARTOONIST
b New Haven, Conn, Sept 28, 09. Study: Pa Acad Fine Arts; Mus Fine Arts, Boston. Pos: Auth syndicated comic strip, Li'l Abner; columnist, New York Daily News; commentator, daily syndicated radio-TV prog. Mailing Add: Capp Enterprises 124 Brattle St Cambridge MA 02138

CARD, GREG S
SCULPTOR, PAINTER
b Los Angeles, Calif, Aug 28, 45. Work: Los Angeles Co Mus Art, Los Angeles; Southern Ill Univ Art Galleries, Carbondale; Minneapolis Inst Arts; Am Tel & Tel, New York; Warner Bros Corp, Los Angeles; plus many others. Comn: Act of Temporary Placement (process & environ sculpture), Univ Southern Calif, 74. Exhib: One-man shows, Mizuno Gallery, Los Angeles, 70-71 & Cirrus Gallery, Los Angeles, 71-74; Plastic Paintings & Sculpture from Los Angeles, Calif State Col, Los Angeles, 68; Nat Drawing Exhib, Southern Ill Univ, 71; Card, Carson, Hill, Trowbridge, Brooke Alexander Gallery, New York, 75; plus many others. Teaching: Guest lectr, Col Creative Studies, 72. Awards: Contemp Art Coun Award, Los Angeles Co Mus Art, 69; Purchase Award, Southern Ill Univ, Carbondale, 71; Individual Artists Fel, Nat Endowment Arts, 75. Bibliog: Fidel A Danieli (auth), Two younger Los Angeles artists, Greg Card, Mary Course, Artforum, summer 68; Jane Livingston (auth), Four Los Angeles artists, Art in Am, 9/10/70; Gerry Rosen & Andy Easson (auths), Living Artists Series: Greg S Card (video tape), Art Video Prod, 75. Style & Technique: Interaction of light with physical materials; combinations of glass, mirrors, redwood, metals, hand coloration of Xerox images. Mailing Add: Cirrus Gallery 708 N Manhattan Pl Los Angeles CA 90038

CARDINAL, DOUGLAS JOSEPH HENRY
ARCHITECT
b Calgary, Alta, Mar 7, 34. Study: Univ BC, Vancouver; Univ Tex, Austin, BArch. Work: Edmonton Art Gallery, Alta; Burnaby Art Gallery, BC. Comn: St Mary's Cath Church, comn by St Mary's Cath Church Bd, 67; Grande Prairie Regional Col, comn by Grande Prairie Regional Col Bd, 76; Ponoka Gov Servs Ctr, Govt of Alta, 77. Exhib: Spectrum Can, Royal

Can Acad of Arts, Montreal, 76; Can Archit, Dept of External Affairs, Warsaw, Poland, 77; Evolution of Mod Archit, Mus Mod Art, New York, 78. Awards: Honor Award, St Mary's Cath Church, Alta Asn of Architects, 68; Award of Excellence for Grande Prairie Regional Col, The Can Architect, 72; Achievement of Excellence Award, Field of Archit, Govt of Alta, 74. Bibliog: R Gretton (auth), Alberta Indian Education Centre, The Can Architect, 9/70; A Rogatnick & A Balkind (auth), The work of Douglas Cardinal, Arts Canada, 10/76; G Melnyk (auth), Of the Spirit, privately publ, 10/77. Style & Technique: Organic forms resulting from first resolving internal functions then wrapping a shell around them; earthy materials. Publ: Contribr, Douglas Cardinal Architect, White Pelican, 73; contribr, Art in public places, Arts Canada, 12/77; contribr, Heritage, Habitat Mag, 9/77. Mailing Add: 8830 85th St 1601 Edmonton AB T6C 3C3 Can

CARDINAL, MARCELIN
PAINTER
b Gravelbourg, Sask, Apr 26, 20. Study: Self-taught. Work: Quebec Mus, PQ; Can Coun, Ottawa; Hirshhorn Mus, Washington, DC; Musée d'Art Contemporain, Dunkerque, France; Schniewind, Wuppertal, WGer. Exhib: Boston Art Festival, Boston Mus, 53; Guggenheim Mus, New York, 54 & 58; Bertha Schaefer Gallery, New York, 54 & 56; Musée des Ponchette, Nice, France, 55; Biennial Int, Menton, France, 55; Mattheisen Gallery, London, Eng, 58; Columbus Gallery of Fine Arts, Ohio, 60; Feingarten Galleries, Chicago, 60 & New York, 61; Knox Albright Gallery, Buffalo, NY, 60; Galerie Denyse Delrue, Montreal, 62; Elvehjem Art Ctr, Univ of Wis, 70; 5th Int Art Fair, Basel, Switz, 74; Galerie Gilles Corbeil, Montreal, 75; Musée d'Art Contemporain, Dunkerque, France, 77; l'Art dans la Rue, Montreal, 77; Musée d'Art Contemporain, Montreal, 77. Awards: Creation et Recherche, Minister Cult Affairs, Quebec, 72, 73 & 75. Bibliog: Article in Art News & Rev, London, 4/12/58; Robert Ayre (auth), article in Montreal Star, 4/62; Christian Allegre (auth), Marcelin Cardinal, Vie des Arts, 72. Mem: Soc Prof Artists Quebec (vpres, 72-73); Can Conf Arts; Can Artists' Representation. Style & Technique: Abstract. Media: Oil, Acrylic. Mailing Add: 4897 Queen Mary Rd Montreal PQ H3W 1X1 Can

CARDMAN, CECILIA
PAINTER
b Soveria Mannelli, Italy; US citizen. Study: Univ Colo, BFA; Inst Belli Arte, Naples, Italy; with Giuseppe Aprea, Naples; Nat Acad, New York, with Leon Kroll, Milford Zornes & E A Whitney. Work: Mesa Col, Grand Junction, Colo; Grand Junction CofC; Cathedral Rectory, Denver, Colo; Chapel House, Denver Art Mus. Exhib: One-man show, Naples, Italy & Grist Mill Gallery, Chester Depot, Vt; Nat Arts Club, Hammond Mus; Gallery North Star, Grafton, Va; Denver Art Mus; Knickerbocker Artist, Catherine Lorillard Wolfe Art Club; plus others. Teaching: Instr, Mesa Col, Grand Junction; asst, Univ Colo; summer sch fac, Colo State Col Educ & Univ Calif. Awards: Old Man, Grand Junction CofC; Shadows & Mexican Doorway, Jackson Heights Art Club. Mem: Jackson Heights Art Club (mem bd & exhib chmn); Catherine Lorillard Wolfe Art Club (bd dirs); Nat Arts Club, New York; Am Artists Prof League; Artists' Fel Inc; Salmagundi Club. Style & Technique: Traditional impressionist. Media: Watercolor, Oil. Mailing Add: Penthouse 34-06 81st St Jackson Heights NY 11372

CARDOSO, ANTHONY
PAINTER, INSTRUCTOR
b Tampa, Fla, Sept 13, 30. Study: Univ Tampa, BS(art); Art Inst Minn, BFA; Univ SFla, MA. Work: Minn Mus Art, St Paul; Newsboy, Tampa Tribune; Del Webb Corp, Sun City, Fla. Comn: Sports Authority, Tampa Stadium Off, 71; sports theme paintings, Leto High Sch & Pierce High Sch, Tampa, 71; two murals, Sun Coast Credit Union Bldg, Tampa, Fla, 75; plus many others. Exhib: 22nd Smithsonian Biennial Traveling Show, 69-70; Prix de Paris, Raymond Duncan Galleries, Paris, France, 70; Salon of 50 States, Ligoa Duncan Gallery, New York, 70; New York Int Art Show, 70; Drawings USA, Minn Mus Art, St Paul, 71; Washington & Jefferson Col, Pa, 71; Rotunda Gallery, London, Eng, 72; Rochester Festival of Art, NY, 73; Brussell's Int, Belg, 73; Ringling Mus Archives, Sarasota, Fla, 78; Latin Quarter Gallery, Tampa, 78. Teaching: Head art dept, Jefferson High Sch, 57-65; instr fine arts & head dept, Leto High Sch, 65- Pos: Rep of high schs, Tampa Arts Coun, 70- Awards: Smithsonian 22nd Biennial Award, Norfolk Mus & Smithsonian Inst, 69-70; Prix de Paris Award, Raymond Duncan Galleries, 70; Drawings USA Purchase Award, Minn Mus Art, 71. Bibliog: Bob Martin (auth), article in Tampa-Times & Tribune, 71; Bertrand Sorlot (auth), article in La Rev Mod, 71; G Deebs (auth), rev in Tampa Tribune, 75. Mem: Fla Arts Coun (rep, 70-72); Ringling Art Mus; Tampa Realists Artists; Latin Quarter Gallery. Style & Technique: Modern-geometric; hard-edge. Media: Oil, Acrylic. Publ: Contribr, La Rev Mod, 71 & 72. Dealer: Warren Gallery 2710 MacDill Ave Tampa FL 33609. Mailing Add: 3208 Nassau St Tampa FL 33607

CAREWE, SYLVIA
PAINTER, TAPESTRY ARTIST
b New York, NY. Study: New Sch Social Res, with Kunyoshi; also with Hans Hofmann, New York & Provincetown. Work: Metrop Mus Art, New York; Whitney Mus Am Art, New York; Mus Art Mod, Paris, France; Tel-Aviv Mus, Israel; Joseph H Hirshhorn Collection; plus many other pvt & pub collections. Exhib: Tapestries, Butler Inst Am Art, Youngstown, Ohio, 60; Pastel Paintings for Tapestry, Donnell Art Libr, New York, 68; Poster Exhib, Am Embassies throughout the world, 69; Paintings, Fordham Univ, 70; 300 Years of Women's Paintings & Sculpture, NC Show of Women, 72; plus many others. Teaching: Lectr tapestry, Columbia Univ. Awards: Prize, ACA Gallery, 47. Mem: Artists Equity Asn; Am Soc Contemp Artists; Am Watercolor Soc; Philadelphia Print Club; New York Soc Women Artists; plus many others. Publ: Illusr, many covers for nat art mag. Mailing Add: 500 E 83rd St New York NY 10028

CAREY, JAMES SHELDON
EDUCATOR, CERAMIST
b Bath, NY, July 28, 11. Study: State Univ NY Col Ceramics, Alfred Univ, with Andre Billeci, BS; Teachers Col, Columbia Univ, AM; Toledo Mus Art, with Fritz Dreisbach. Work: Metrop Mus Art, New York; Everson Mus Art, Syracuse, NY; Scripps Col; Univ SFla; Joslyn Art Mus, Omaha, Nebr. Exhib: 20th Ceramic Int, Everson Mus, 58; 2nd Int Ceramic Exhib, Ostend, Belg; Int Cult Exchange, Geneva, Switz; Wichita Nat Ceramic Exhib, Wichita Art Asn, Kans. Teaching: Lectr ceramics & sculpture, Teachers Col, Columbia Univ, 40-42; instr ceramics & sculpture, RI Sch Design, 42-43; prof ceramics & glass, Univ Kans, 44-76, emer prof ceramics & glass, 76- vis prof, San Jose State Col, summers 45 & 47. Pos: Adv ed, Ceramics Mo, 53-55. Awards: Prize for Textured Urn (stoneware), Syracuse Mus Fine Arts, 58; Award for Out of Orbit (glass), First Nat Space Art Exhib, 69; Nat Endowment for the Arts Grants, 72 & 73. Bibliog: Fruit of the wheel, Time Mag, 2/16/69; Glenn Nelson (auth), Ceramics: A Potter's Book, Holt, Rinehart & Winston, 71. Mem: Fel Am Ceramic Soc; Am Crafts Coun (trustee, 67-69); Nat Coun Educ for Ceramic Arts (bd dir, 66-71). Style & Technique: Off hand glass forming; simple sculptural and functional forms. Media: Ceramics, Glass. Res: Originator of throwing on an upside-down wheel, pulling clay down to make tall pots; developer of new liquid for throwing. Mailing Add: Design Dept Univ of Kans Lawrence KS 66044

CAREY, JOHN THOMAS
EDUCATOR, ART HISTORIAN
b Wilmont, Minn, Aug 23, 17. Study: Milwaukee State Teachers Col, BA; Univ Wis, MS; Ohio State Univ, PhD; Harvard Univ. Teaching: Art instr, Univ Wis-Madison, 47-48; asst prof art, Ill State Univ, 49-51; instr art, Ohio State Univ, 53-54; asst prof art, Bowling Green State Univ, 54-56; prof art & chmn dept, Northern Ill State Univ, 56-66; vis prof, Rollins Col, 66-67; prof art, Univ West Fla, 67-, chmn art dept, 67-77; vis prof, World Campus Afloat, Chapman Col, spring 69 & spring 73; vis prof, Univ Hawaii, Manoa, fall 77. Awards: Pac Cult Found study grant, Imperial Palace Collection of Art, Taipei, Taiwan, spring 77. Mem: Col Art Asn Am; Southeastern Col Art Asn (ed, newslett & rev, 71-, pres, 75). Res: Introduction and development of lithography in America. Publ: Ed, Ill Art Educ Yearbk, 57; contribr, William Fendrick, early American lithographer (monogr), Libr Cong, 57. Mailing Add: 2320 Risen Dr Cantonment FL 32533

CAREY, TED
COLLECTOR, DESIGNER
b Chester, Pa, June 3, 32. Study: Philadelphia Mus Sch Art, BFA. Teaching: Former instr, Pratt Inst, Brooklyn, NY. Pos: Textile designer & free lance illusr. Collection: Contemporary paintings, sculpture and drawings. Mailing Add: 20 Oyster Pond Lane East Hampton NY 11937

CARIOLA, ROBERT J
PAINTER, SCULPTOR
b Brooklyn, NY, Mar 24, 27. Study: Pratt Inst Art Sch; Pratt Graphic Ctr. Work: Fordham Univ; De Pauw Univ; La Salle Col; Hofstra Col; Topeka Pub Libr, Kans. Comn: Metal mural, altar & artifacts for St Gabriel's Church, Oakridge, NJ, 70-71; murals, Walker Mem Baptist Church, Bronx, NY, 75; two chapel murals, Mt St Mary Cemetery, Queens, NY, 77. Exhib: Boston Mus Printmakers Exhib, 62; Corcoran Gallery Art, Washington, DC, 63; Pa Acad Fine Arts, Philadelphia, 63; Vatican Pavilion, New York World's Fair, 64; Nat Acad Design, New York, 70. Teaching: Instr art, La Salle Acad, Oakdale, NY, 63-65; instr art, Catholic Youth Orgn Summer Workshop; instr art, Huntington Twp Art League, 71. Pos: Art consult, Cath Youth Orgn, Rockville Ctr, NY, 67-; art coordr, St John's Cloister, Queens, NY, 72-74. Awards: Tiffany Grants, 64-67; First Prize Painting, John Kennedy Cult Ctr Bankers Trust Award, 71; Grumbacher Cash Award, Silvermine Guild Artists, New Canaan, Conn, 76. Bibliog: A V LesMez (auth), Cariola, Long Island Rev Mag, 64; Walt Carlson (auth), Vatican Pavilion gets Long Island exhibit, New York Times, 8/27/64; Jeanne Paris (auth), Cariola's works on exhibit at Merrick Gallery, Long Island Press, 5/28/67. Mem: Prof Artists Guild (pres, 69-70); hon mem Cath Fine Arts Soc. Style & Technique: Electric arc and gas welded metals into figure and abstract constructions; textural surface build up of paint impasto for figures, landscape, still life and abstractions. Media: Acrylic. Publ: Illusr, Writers's Ann, 58; illusr, Sign Mag, 71; contribr, Liturgical Arts Mag, 71-72. Dealer: Merrick Art Gallery 8 Merrick Ave Merrick NY 11566; Contemporary Christian Art Gallery 1060-A Lexington Ave New York NY 10021. Mailing Add: 1844 Gormley Ave Merrick NY 11566

CARL, JOAN
SCULPTOR, GRAPHIC ARTIST, DESIGNER
b Cleveland, Ohio, Mar 20, 26. Study: Cleveland Sch Art; Chicago Art Inst; Mills Col; with Dong Kingman, Bordman Robinson, Carl Morris & Albert Wein; New Sch Art, with Arnold Mesches & Ted Gilien. Work: NC Mus Art, Raleigh; Int Cult Ctr for Youth, Jerusalem, Israel. Comn: Carved walnut pulpit, Methodist Church, Palm Springs, Calif, 67; brazed welded steel Menorah, Eternal Light & Candlesticks, Temple Adat Ariel, Los Angeles, 69; bonded bronze relief, Capital Nat Bank, Cleveland, 72; poly bronze & welded steel relief, Repub Savings & Loan, Los Angeles, 74; mosaic wall, Mt Sinai Mem Park, Los Angeles, 75. Exhib: Am Inst Architects Design Ctr, Los Angeles, 68; one-woman show, Bakersfield Col, Calif, 67; Laguna Beach Art Mus, 69; Fresno Art Mus, 71; Linden-Kicklighter Gallery, Cleveland, Ohio, 71 & 73; Muskegon Community Col, 73; Chai (graphics), Nat & Int Traveling Show, 74-75. Pos: Teacher, Valley Ctr of Arts, Los Angeles, 59-64; lectr Title III Prog, San Bernardino, Inyo & Moro Co, Calif, 69-70. Awards: Honorable Mention, Nat Orange Show, San Bernardino, 58 & Calif State Fair, Sacramento, 70 & 72; Design Award, Ceramic Tile Inst, 75. Bibliog: Will H Tagress (auth), Valley sculptor believes in reflecting world around her, The News, 74. Mem: Artists Equity Asn (Los Angeles chap pres, 74-76); Calif Confederation of the Arts (bd mem); Los Angeles Art Asn; Artists for Economic Action. Style & Technique: Simplified forms based on human form and emotion; mostly smooth tactile surfaces and an interest in groups of figures, each completing the other. Media: Stone, Wood. Publ: Illustr, A World of Questions and Things, 50. Dealer: Art Works 812 N La Cienega Blvd Los Angeles CA 90069; American Crafts 10310 Larchmere-Woodland Cleveland OH 44120. Mailing Add: 4808 Mary Ellen Ave Sherman Oaks CA 91423

CARLBERG, NORMAN KENNETH
SCULPTOR, INSTRUCTOR
b Roseau, Minn, Nov 6, 28. Study: Brainerd Jr Col, Minn, 47-49; Minneapolis Sch Art, 50; Univ Ill, Urbana, 53-54; Yale Univ, BFA, 58, MFA, 61. Work: Addison Gallery Am Art, Phillips Acad, Andover, Mass; Whitney Mus Am Art, New York; Schenectady Mus, NY; Pa Acad Fine Arts, Philadelphia; Art & Archit Gallery, Yale Univ. Comn: Modular screen, Baltimore City Hosp, 65; four modular sculptures, Baltimore City Schs, Northern Parkway Jr High, 70-73 & for PS 39, 73-75; modular column, Harry Seidler, Trade Group Complex, Canberra, Australia, 73-75 & Black Widow (steel modular), 75- Exhib: Recent Sculpture USA, Mus Mod Art, New York, 59; Structured Sculpture, Galerie Chalette, New York, 60; one-man shows, Cath Univ, Santiago, Chile, 60 & Baltimore Mus Art, 68; Whitney Ann, Whitney Mus Am Art, 62. Teaching: Instr Sculpture, Cath Univ, Santiago, 60-61; sculptor in residence, Rinehart Sch Sculpture, Md Inst Col Art, Baltimore, 61- Awards: Fulbright Teaching Grant, Santiago, Chile, 60; Purchase Award, Ford Found, 62; Mus Prize, Baltimore Mus Art, 66. Bibliog: Josef Albers (auth), The Yale School-Structured Sculpture, Art in Am, 61; George Rickey (auth), Constructivism, George Braziller, 67; Peter Blake (auth), Architecture for the New World, the work of Harry Seidler, Wittenborn & Co, 73. Style & Technique: Modular systems and other forms based on reasoned relationships; constructivism. Mailing Add: 120 W Lanvale St Baltimore MD 21217

CARLIN, ELECTRA MARSHALL
ART DEALER
b Ft Worth, Tex. Study: George Washington Univ, BA. Pos: Dir, Carlin Galleries; mem, Art Comn Bd, Ft Worth, 63- Mem: Ft Worth Art Asn; Dallas Mus Art Asn; Am Fedn Arts. Specialty: American artists and craftsmen; Eskimo prints and carvings. Mailing Add: 710 Montgomery St Ft Worth TX 76107

CARLIN, JAMES
PAINTER
b Belfast, Ireland, June 25, 10; US citizen. Study: Belfast Munic Col, grad; London Art Schs; Newark Sch Fine & Indust Art; apprenticeship stained glass painting studios with Ger, Eng & Irish instrs. Work: Montclair Art Mus, NJ; also in pvt collections of Dore Schary, Los Angeles & many others. Comn: Design of stained glass windows (in collaboration), Londonderry Guild Hall & several prominent churches in Ireland, 26-28. Exhib: 12th Brooklyn Mus Int, NY, 41; Victory Exhib, Metrop Mus Art, New York, 42; Allied Artists Am Exhib, New York, 45; Portrait of America, Pepsi-Cola Co, New York, 45; Allied Artists Am Oils Exhib, Nat Acad Galleries, New York, 46. Teaching: Mem fac, Queen's Col; instr fine arts & head dept, Newark Sch Fine & Indust Art, 46- Awards: First Award/Watercolor, 77 & Purchase Award, 77, NJ State Show; First Award/Oil, Am Tel & Tel; First Prize in Oils, Audubon Artists. Bibliog: Norman Kent (auth), The Artist Speaks His Mind, 69 & Wendon Blake (auth), Acrylic Watercolor Painting, 71, Watson-Guptill; Michael Jenson (auth), Carlin and nature, Newark News, 71. Mem: Am Watercolor Soc; Philadelphia Watercolor Soc; NJ Watercolor Soc; Audubon Artists; Assoc Artists NJ; plus others. Style & Technique: Geometric realism. Media: Oil, Watercolor. Dealer: Grand Central Art Galleries 40 Vanderbilt Ave New York NY 10017. Mailing Add: 73 Cathedral Ave Nutley NJ 07110

CARLIN, ROBERT EUGENE
PAINTER, ART HISTORIAN
b Rockford, Ill, May 22, 24. Work: Smithsonian Inst, Washington, DC; US Nat Archives, Washington, DC; USAF Mus, Dayton, Ohio; USAF Acad, Colorado Springs, Colo; Lafayette Escadrille Mus, Luxeuil, France. Comn: Historic series, City Houston Aviation Dept, 70; print series, Printmakers, Houston, 73; mural (23ft), Superior Oil, Houston, 73; Lindbergh Mural, Lindbergh Comt, Houston, 77. Exhib: Meredith Long Galleries; SW Galleries; Sportsman's Galleries; numberous others. Collections Arranged: Collection for attending guests Baron Kur von Richthofen, Francis Gary Power & Capt O C Le Boutillier, SW Galleries, Houston. Awards: Best in Show, Leeward & Hart, Opa Locka, Fla, 69; Exhibitor's Award, Univ Tex Aviation Col, 70. Bibliog: Martin Dreyer (reporter), This week, Houston Chronicle, 10/69; William Freckleton (auth), article in SW Art, 6/75. Mem: Guild Aviation Artists, Great Britain; Cross & Cockade; Am Aviation Hist Soc; Univ Tex Aviation Collection (mem adv bd). Style & Technique: Opaque watercolors, oils of combat and civil aviation, combining technical and artistic techniques. Res: Aviation. Publ: Auth & illusr, History of Paul Redfern, 71, Air Combat Over Spain, 73 & Flying the B-24, 74, Air Classics. Dealer: Sportsman's Gallery The Galleria Houston TX 77027. Mailing Add: 10523 Eddystone Houston TX 77043

CARLOS, (JAMES) EDWARD
PAINTER, ART ADMINISTRATOR
b Kingsville, Pa, Nov 8, 37. Study: Indiana Univ Pa, BS(art educ), 59; Colo Col, with Enrique Montenegro, summer 60; Cath Univ Am, with Ken Noland, Alexander Giampietro & Bernard Leach, MFA, 63; Univ Hawaii, with Gustav Ecke; Ohio Univ, fel & PhD. Exhib: Mainstreams '72, Marietta, Ohio, 72; Italy, Sweden & Scotland, 75; one-man show, Edinburgh Int Festival, Scotland, 76. Teaching: Vis prof art, Portland State Col, summer 65; asst prof art, Western Ill Univ, 65-66; instr art, Ohio Univ, 67-69; assoc prof & chmn dept fine arts, Univ of the South, 69- Pos: Lectr various art groups & schs; dir gallery & mus, Univ of the South, Tenn. Awards: Int Snapshop, East-Kodak, 71. Style & Technique: Abstract impressionist style; technique is soft, muted-multicolor, essence oriented. Media: Oil. Mailing Add: Dept of Art Univ of the South Sewanee TN 37375

CARLSON, ALEXANDER
ART DEALER, LECTURER
b Philadelphia, Pa, Jan 22, 48. Study: Philadelphia Col of Art; Syracuse Univ, NY. Collections Arranged: Norman Bluhn (ed, catalogue), 73, Medieval Art in Upstate New York, 74 & The Everson Mus Permanent Collection, 74, Everson Mus. Teaching: Lectr museology, Grad Dept Mus Studies, Syracuse Univ, 73-74; lectr mus archit & aesthetics, Grad Dept, Kean Col, Union, NJ, 76. Pos: Asst dir, Lowe Art Ctr, Syracuse, NY, 72; lectr contemp art, Everson Mus of Art, Syracuse, 73-74, cur collections & exhibs, 73-74; dir, Martha Jackson Gallery, New York, 74-75; dir, Brooks Jackson Gallery Iolas, New York, 77- Bibliog: Peter Frank (auth), New Form, New Media, New Space, Art Gallery, 3/75. Mem: Am Asn of Mus. Specialty: Modern European masters and contemporary American and European paintings, drawings and sculptures. Publ: Auth, Communication as an Art Form—a Final Discussion of Yoko Ono at the Everson, Cent New Yorker, 71; ed, Billy Apple/Stefan Eins/Dieter Froese/Jane Greer/Philippa Quarrel, Martha Jackson W Gallery, 75. Mailing Add: 52 E 57th St New York NY 10022

CARLSON, CYNTHIA J
PAINTER, INSTRUCTOR
b Chicago, Ill, Apr 15, 42. Study: Chicago Art Inst, BFA; Pratt Inst, MFA. Work: Va Mus Fine Art, Richmond; Kemper Ins; Philadelphia Mus of Art. Exhib: Whitney Mus of Am Art Bi-Ann, 72; Pattern Painting, Proj Studios 1, New York, 77; Artpark, 77; one-woman exhibs, Marianne Deson Gallery, Chicago, 77; Hundred Acres, New York, 75 & 76; City Univ New York Grad Mall, 77; plus others. Teaching: Assoc prof art, Philadelphia Col Art, 67- Style & Technique: Rapid thick strokes, using the paint through a cake froster; abstract. Media: Oil, Acrylic. Mailing Add: 101 W 27th St New York NY 10001

CARLSON, JANE C
PAINTER
b Boston, Mass, Sept 1, 28. Study: Art Students League; Mass Col Art; study with Charles Kinghan & Robert Davis. Exhib: Hudson Valley Art Asn, 69-77; Am Artists Prof League, 70-77; Am Watercolor Soc, Nat Acad Design, New York, 71-77; Audubon Artists, 73-77. Teaching: Watercolor demonstrations. Awards: James Holton Mem Award, Audubon Artists, 73; Robert Simmons Award, Hudson Valley Art Asn, 73, Maynard Landa Mem Award, 77; Windson & Newton Award, Am Artists Prof League, 74, Gold Medal, 77. Mem: Am Watercolor Soc; Am Artists Prof League; Hudson Valley Art Asn; Westchester Arts Asn. Style & Technique: Primarily watercolor landscape in pure traditional style; oil in traditional style. Dealer: Douglas Gallery 1117 High Ridge Rd Stamford CT 06901; Grand Central Galleries Biltmore Hotel Madison Ave New York NY 10017. Mailing Add: 81 Park Ave Bronxville NY 10708

CARLYLE, JULIAN (JULIAN CARLYLE WELLS)
COLLAGE ARTIST, SCULPTOR
b Monticello, Ark, Dec 5, 42. Study: Ohio Wesleyan Univ, Del, BFA, 64; Ohio State Univ, MFA(sculpture), 67. Work: Continental Bank, Cleveland; Central Carolina Bank, Raleigh; Ohio Wesleyan Univ. Exhib: One-man shows, Chiara Galleries, Cleveland, 73, Villa Montalvo, Saratoga, Calif, 75, Kendall Gallery, Wellfleet, Cape Cod, Mass, 75; Dusseldorf Art Fair, Ger, 73; Columbus Art Gallery May Show, 75. Awards: Gerald B Fenton Award, Columbus Art League, Battelle Inst, Ohio, 74. Mem: Vt Coun Arts; Craft Prof, Vt. Style & Technique: Leather collage sculpture. Media: Leather; Cooper, Bronze. Dealer: Kirk Wilkerson c/o Kendall Art Gallery Wellfleet Cape Cod MA 02667. Mailing Add: RFD 2 St Johnsbury VT 05819

CARMEAN, E A, JR
ART HISTORIAN, CURATOR
b Springfield, Ill, Jan 25, 45. Study: MacMurray Col, BA(hist art); Univ Ill, with Allen Weller. Collections Arranged: The Collages of Robert Motherwell (with catalog); Toward Color & Field; Picasso; Friedel Dzubas (with catalog); Blast: Early Modern Art; Modernist Art 1960-1970 (with catalog); Jasper Johns; Picasso: Illustrated Books; Morris Louis: Major Themes & Variations (with catalog); American Painting of the 19th century: Three Young Am Painters. Teaching: Lectr art hist, Univ Ill, Urbana, 67-69; vis prof 20th century art, Rice Univ, 73-74; vis prof 20th century art, George Washington Univ, 75- Pos: Cur 20th century art, Mus Fine Arts, Houston, 71-74; cur 20th century art, Nat Gallery Art, 74- Mem: Col Art Asn; Am Asn Mus. Res: Picasso & cubism; abstract expressionism; color painting 1950-1970; modern sculpture. Publ: Auth, Julio Gonzalez, Mus Fine Arts Bull, 73; auth, Kenneth Noland and the compositional cut, 75, Robert Motherwell's Spanish elegies, 76, Morris Louis and the modern tradition, 76 & Juan Gris' Fantômas, 77, Arts Mag. Mailing Add: Nat Gallery Art Sixth St & Constitution Ave NW Washington DC 20565

CARMEL, HILDA ANNE
PAINTER
b New York, NY. Study: City Col New York; NY Univ; Art Students League, with Reginald Marsh. Work: Jewish Mus, New York; Evansville Mus Arts & Sci, Ind; Bat Yam Mus & Sholom Ash Mus, Israel; Long Island Univ Mus, Brooklyn, NY. Exhib: Soc Ecole Francaise Expos, Paris, 70; Yonkers Art Asn, Hudson River Mus, NY, 71; Painters & Sculptors NJ, Jersey City, 72; Lehigh Univ, Bethlehem, Pa, 72; Opening Exhib, Bronx Mus Art, 72. Pos: Gallery dir, Hilda Carmel Gallery, 59-63. Awards: First Prize, Soc Ecole Francaise Expos, Mus Mod Art, Paris, 70; Hon Mention, Bronx Coun on Arts, 70; Medal of Honor, Cent Studi e Scambi Int, Italy, 71. Mem: Artist Equity Asn New York (exhib chmn & corresp secy, 70-); League Present Day Artists (exhib chmn & pres, 71-); hon mem Gallery 84; Bronx Coun on Arts (visual art comt, 70). Mailing Add: 3210 Fairfield Ave Riverdale NY 10463

CARMICHAEL, DONALD RAY
PAINTER, EDUCATOR
b Elnora, Ind, Dec 26, 22. Study: Herron Art Inst, BFA, 51; Univ Tenn, Knoxville, MFA, 75; also with John Taylor & David Freidenthal, New York, Edwin Fulwider, Ford Times & Garo Antreasian, NMex. Work: Cheekwood Fine Arts Ctr, Nashville, Tenn; Jackson-Madison Co Pub Libr, Jackson, Tenn; Dyersburg Pub Libr, Tenn; Jackson Ment Health Ctr. Comn: Life-size minuteman statue, stoneware mounted on face of bldg (with Warren Kessler), Carl Smith Agency, Jackson, 67; official seal (engraving), Jackson State Community Col, 67; five panel mural, History of Jackson, McDonalds, Inc, 68. Exhib: Tennessee Painting Today, Cheekwood Fine Art Ctr, 67; three-man show, Lynn Kottler Galleries, New York, 71; 23rd Grand Prix Int, Deauville, France & Palace of Fine Arts, Rome, Italy, 72; Watercolor USA, Springfield Art Mus, 74-75; Southeastern Collection of Contemporary Art, Mich Artrain Tour, 74; plus others. Teaching: Instr painting, Shelbyville Art League, Ind, 51-55; instr art appreciation, Union Univ, Tenn, 64-66, instr drawing, painting & composition, 66-69, head dept art, 69-74; grad asst, Univ Tenn, Knoxville, 74-75; instr evening classes, Dyersburg State Community Col, Tenn, 76- Pos: Pres, Jackson Art Asn, 65-67; pres, Jackson Arts Coun, 68-70; chmn visual arts adv panel, Tenn Arts Comn, 72-75, field rep, 75-; juror, H O Forgy Steel Sculpture Statewide Competition, 74; juror, Southeastern Sculpture Competition, Oakridge Civic Ctr, 74. Awards: Purchase Award, Enjay Chem Nat, 66; Tennessee Painting Today Purchase Award, Tenn Arts Comn, 67. Bibliog: Newman Jones (auth), Art leagues in small communities, Delta Rev, 68; William T Alderson (auth), Tennessee lives, Historical Rec Asn, 71; article in La Rev Mod, 72. Mem: Artists Equity Asn; Tenn Col Arts Coun (chmn nominating comt, 70-); Tenn Watercolorist (dir & mem chmn, 71-); Southern Watercolor Soc; Tenn Watercolor Soc (co-founder & pres, 74). Style & Technique: From abstract to representational; wet-in-wet transparent technique. Media: Watercolor, Oil. Publ: Illusr, (cover), The Old Hickory Review, Jackson Writers Guild, 69; contribr, The Torch, Union Univ, 70-72. Dealer: Main St Studio-Gallery 204 1/2 Wilson Bldg Jackson TN 38301; Dulin Gallery of Art 3100 Kingston Pike Knoxville TN 37919. Mailing Add: 110 Carlisle Dr Jackson TN 38301

CARMICHAEL, JAE
PAINTER, ART ADMINISTRATOR
b Los Angeles, Calif, Aug 22, 25. Study: Mills Col, 42-44; Univ Southern Calif, BFA, 51, PhD(art & cinematography), 72; Claremont Grad Sch, MFA, 55. Work: Long Beach Mus Art; Mills Col; Scripps Col; Charles & Emma Frye Mus; Computer Measurements Corp; plus many others including pvt collections. Exhib: Pasadena Sister Cities Exhib, 72 & 75; two-man show, Four Oaks Gallery, Pasadena, 75; plus over 100 Int, Nat & Regional Shows since 45 & many one-man shows. Teaching: Instr drawing & painting, Pasadena Art Mus, 53-60; instr drawing & painting, Pasadena Sch Fine Arts, 54-58 & 66-72, dir, 70-72; instr children's art, Laguna Beach Art Asn, 57-62; instr drawing & painting, Rex Brandt Sch, Calif, 61-62; instr drawing & painting, Palos Verdes Community Art Asn, 66-72; lectr art hist & cinema, Pasadena City Col, 68-71; lectr Renaissance art hist, Otis Art Inst, Los Angeles, 70-; lectr, Motion Picture & TV Engr, 73-75; lectr, Nat Asn Mus, 74-75. Pos: Spec cur, Galka Scheyer Children's Art Collection, Pasadena Art Mus, 54; dir, Wooden Horse Gallery, Laguna Beach, 62-66; producer-dir multi-media productions, 68-74; cur photog arts, Pacificulture-Asia Mus, Pasadena, 71-72, dir, 72- Awards: Hors Concours Award, Pasadena Soc Artists Ann, 70; Brit Fel, 73; Diploma Merit & Medal of Honor, Leonardo da Vinci Acad, Rome; plus numerous others. Bibliog: Kim Blair (auth), Pacificulture Center becomes a reality, Los Angeles Times, 10/25/71; Ray McConnell (auth), More or less personal, 11/19/71 & Margaret Stovall (auth), Jae Carmichael fulfills dreams at Pacificulture Foundation, 12/11/71, Star News; plus others. Mem: Nat Asn Mus; Calif Watercolors Soc (mem bd, 59-60 & 70-72, historian, 75); Pasadena Soc Artists (mem bd, 58-60, 62 & 63, pres, 70-72); Women Painters West; Los Angeles Art Asn (mem bd, 65-69). Mailing Add: 985 San Pasqual St Pasadena CA 91106

CARO, FRANCIS
ART DEALER
b New York, NY, Aug 22, 38. Pos: Dir, Frank Caro Gallery, New York. Specialty: Antique arts of China, India and Southeast Asia. Mailing Add: c/o Frank Caro Gallery 41 E 57th St New York NY 10022

CARPENTER, ARTHUR ESPENET
CRAFTSMAN, LECTURER
b New York, NY, Jan 20, 20. Study: Dartmouth Col, BA. Work: City of San Francisco, Calif; San Francisco State Univ; Mus of Sci & Indust, Chicago; Oakland Mus, Calif; Johnson Wax Collection. Comn: Furniture, Stan Sobel, 70, Old St Mary's, 71, San Francisco; furniture, Mill

Valley Libr, Calif, 72. Exhib: Inst of Contemp Art, Boston, 49; Good Design Show, Mus of Mod Art, New York, 50-54; Mus of Contemp Crafts, New York, 56; Magnani Mem Craft Collection, San Francisco State Univ, 66; Mus of Contemp Crafts, New York, 66; Objects USA, Johnson Collection, 68; Wooden Works, Smithsonian Inst, Washington, DC, 72; E B Crocker Art Gallery, Sacramento, Calif, 73; Craft Multiples, Smithsonian Inst, 75; and others. Teaching: Lectr furniture, San Francisco State Univ, 72- Mem: Bolinas Craft Guild (pres, 77). Style & Technique: Sculptural wood in utilitarian forms. Media: Wood. Publ: Auth, Eames Furniture, Craft Horizons, 73. Mailing Add: Lower County Rd Bolinas CA 94924

CARPENTER, E
PAINTER
b Mianus, Conn, June 11, 17. Study: Nat Acad Design, with Mario Cooper; also with Edgar Whitney. Comn: Calendar & cards, New Eng Biol Lab, Point Judith, RI, 69; cover for calendar & watercolor pad, Aquabee, Bee Paper Co, Passaic, NJ, 69-70. Exhib: Nat Miniature Painters, Sculptors & Gravers Soc Show, Washington, DC, 69; Knickerbocker Artists, Nat Arts Club, 69-70; Nat Am Artists Prof League, Lever House, New York, 69-71; Catharine Lorillard Wolfe, Nat Gallery, NY. Awards: Salmagundi Scholar, Washington Square Art Exhib, New York, 68 & NY Phoenix Sch Design Award, 69; Minor S Jamison Award, Nat Miniature Painters, Sculptors & Gravers Soc, 69; plus others. Mem: Am Artists Prof League; Catharine Lorillard Wolfe Art Club; Int Soc of Artists; Bergen Co Artists Guild. Style & Technique: Realist, scenes of today's and yesterday's Americana; florals, seascapes. Media: Watercolor. Mailing Add: 248 Wyckoff Ave Wyckoff NJ 07481

CARPENTER, EARL L
PAINTER
b Long Beach, Calif, Nov 13, 31. Study: Chouinard Art Sch, 1 yr; Art Ctr Col Design, 4 yrs. Work: Mus Northern Ariz, Flagstaff; Ariz Bank Collection State Traveling Exhibs; Valley Nat Bank Gallery Western Art, Valley Ctr, Phoenix; also in pvt collections of Olaf Weighorst, Ray Schlicting, Sen Barry Goldwater, Walter Bimson & Adm Beardsley. Comn: Ray Schlicting, Hillsboro, Kans, 75; H Earl Hoover, Los Angeles, Calif, 75; and others. Exhib: Retrospective, Wyo State Arch & Hist Dept, 74; Gallery Western Art, Valley Nat Bank Art Dept, Phoenix, 75; Ariz State Capitol Bldg, 77; Grand Canyon Art, Northern Ariz Univ, Flagstaff, 78; Troy Gallery Ann, Scottsdale, Ariz, 78. Awards: Stacey Scholar, 67 & 69. Mem: Western Art Assocs. Style & Technique: Watercolor technique for oil painting; vibrant and rich transparent earth colors, as observed from nature. Media: Oil on Canvas & Panel. Publ: Auth, My painting technique, Am Artist Mag, 68; auth, Sandstone Creations, Ariz; illusr, paintings in Ariz Highways Mag, Phoenix, 73 & 74; auth, article in Artist of the Rockies Mag, winter/spring 76-77; illusr, cover of Ariz Living Mag, 3/78; plus others. Dealer: El Prado Sedona AZ; Troy Galleries Scottsdale AZ. Mailing Add: Earl Carpenter Studio Pinewood AZ 86017

CARPENTER, GILBERT FREDERICK (BERT)
PAINTER, MUSEUM DIRECTOR
b Billings, Mont, July 14, 20. Study: Stanford Univ, AB; Chouinard Art Inst; Ecole Beaux Arts, Paris, France; Columbia Univ. Work: Honolulu Acad Art; Sheldon Mem Mus, Lincoln, Nebr; Westherspoon Gallery, Univ NC, Greensboro; Kresge Found, Mich State Univ; Univ Mass, Amherst. Exhib: Honolulu Acad Art, 51 & 59-61; one-man shows, Calif Palace Legion of Honor, 52, Joslyn Mus, Omaha, Nebr, 52 & 54, A M Sachs Gallery, 72 & 77 & Zabriskie Gallery, 70, 72 & 74. Teaching: Instr art, Columbia Univ, 54-60; head dept art, Univ Hawaii, 60-64; prof art & head dept, Univ NC, Greensboro, 64-74; prof art, Weatherspoon Gallery, 74- Pos: Dir, Weatherspoon Gallery, 74- Mem: NC State Art Soc. Publ: Art critic, Honolulu Star Bull, 61-62. Dealer: A M Sachs Gallery 29 W 57th St New York NY 10019. Mailing Add: 2505 W Market St Greensboro NC 27403

CARPENTER, HARLOW
MUSEUM DIRECTOR
b Calif, Oct 20, 26. Study: Harvard Univ Sch Design, BArch. Pos: Dir, Bundy Art Gallery, Waitsfield, Vt. Mailing Add: c/o Bundy Art Gallery Waitsfield VT 05673

CARPENTER, JAMES MORTON
ART HISTORIAN
b Glens Falls, NY, Dec 7, 14. Study: Harvard Univ, AB & PhD. Teaching: From instr to asst prof fine arts, Harvard Univ, 43-50; from assoc prof to prof art, Colby Col, 50-, chmn dept, 55- Pos: Dir, Colby Col Art Mus, 59-66; bd gov, Skowhegan Sch Painting & Sculpture, 65-74; bd trustees, Haystack Mountain Sch Crafts, 68-73; mem, Maine State Comn Arts & Humanities, 68-73. Mem: Col Art Asn Am. Res: Aspects of art theory; history of Maine art. Publ: Co-auth, Maine & Its Role in American Art, 63; co-auth, Color in Art. Mailing Add: Dept of Fine Arts Colby Col Waterville ME 04901

CARR, SALLY SWAN
SCULPTOR
b Minong, Wis. Study: NY Univ; advan sculpture, Phoenix Sch Design; life sketch, Clay Club; also with John Hovannes, Frederick Allen Williams & wax tech with Paul Manship; Art Students League. Work: Am Numismatic Soc, New York; Basketball Hall of Fame, Springfield, Mass; Cayuga Mus Art & Hist, Auburn, NY; Florentine Craftsmen, New York. Comn: Indian Queen (woodcarving) & Eagle (reliefs), Sheraton Hotel, Philadelphia, Pa, 57; Great Seal of US (woodcarving), comn by M Ketchum, Jr, US Embassy, Rabat, Morocco, 59; Lion of St Marks (bronze relief), Marco Polo Club, Waldorf Astoria Hotel, New York, 60; Cardinal Virtues (cararra marble reliefs), Riverside Mem Park, St Joseph, Mich, 65; Dr A Schweitzer (bust), Town Hall, Kaysersburg & Gunsbach, France, 70. Exhib: Archit League New York, 55-71; Catharine Lorillard Wolfe Art Club, New York, 60-; Nat Arts Club, New York, 67-70; Nat Acad Design, Allied Artists, 69-70; Acad Artists, Springfield Mus Art, Mass, 70; Burr Artist, Metrop Mus Art, 77, Caravan Galleries, New York, 77; Goldboro Mus, NC, 77; Spec Award Winners Show, Nat Arts Club, New York, 78. Awards: A H Huntington First Prize Trophy, Catharine Lorillard Wolfe Art Club, 70; Founders Prize & Plaque, Pen & Brush Club, New York, 70; bronze & silver medals, City of Kaysersburg, 70. Mem: Archit League New York (mem exhibs comt, 60); Burr Artists (second vpres, 69-72); Catharine Lorillard Wolfe Art Club (first vpres, 66-71, pres, 71-74); Composers, auth & Artists Am (dir & historian, 69-72); hon mem Smithsonian Style & Technique: Traditional for modeled and cast work; representational for carving; impressionistic for fabricated sheet metal. Media: Stone. Mailing Add: 530 E 23rd St New York NY 10010

CARRERO, JAIME
PAINTER, INSTRUCTOR
b Mayaguez, PR, June 16, 31. Study: Polytechnic Inst, Columbia Univ, BA(art hist); Pratt Inst, MS. Work: Ponce Mus, PR; Mus Inst of of PR Art, San Juan; Univ PR, San Juan; Inter-Am Univ Collection, San German. Comn: Illus for bk, Cuentos Puertorriquenos, 73. Exhib: Univ PR, San Juan, 60 & 65; Inst Cult PR, San Juan, 62; Acad Fine Arts, Calcutta, India, 65; Ateneo Puertorriqueno, San Juan, 66; Ponce Mus, 68. Teaching: Assoc prof painting, drawing & art hist, Inter-Am Univ, 57-; assoc prof art hist, Rum, Mayaguez, PR, 74-75. Awards: Ill State Coun Poetry Award, 74. Bibliog: Josemilio Gonzalez (auth), Jaime Carrero, Pintor, El Mundo, 60; Drawings by Jaime Carrero, El Corno Emplumado, Mex, Nos 28, 26, 28 & 30, 64-66. Media: Acrylic, Watercolor, Ink Drawing, Mixed-Media. Publ: Auth, Aqui Los Angeles, 60, Tyranosauro Rey, Amen, Amen, 63 & Neorican Jetliner, 64, Inter-Am Univ. Mailing Add: A-26 Urb Interamericana San German PR 00753

CARR-HARRIS, IAN REDFORD
SCULPTOR, PHOTOGRAPHER
b Victoria, BC, Can, Aug 12, 41. Study: Queen's Univ, Kingston, Ont, BA(hon), 63; Univ Toronto, Ont, BLS, 64; Ont Col of Art, Toronto, AOCA, 71. Work: Nat Gallery of Can, Ottawa; Can Coun Art Bank, Ottawa; Art Gallery of Ont, Toronto. Exhib: Contemp Ont Art, Art Gallery of Ont, 74; Wood, London Pub Libr & Art Mus, Ont, 74; Carmen Lamanna at the Owens Gallery, Sackville, NB, 75; Carmen Lamanna at the Can Cult Centre, Paris, France, 75; 9th Biennale of Paris, Mus d'Art Mod, Paris, 75; Another Dimension, Nat Gallery of Can, 77. Pos: Chief librn, Ont Col of Art, Toronto, 71-76. Awards: Can Coun Proj Cost Grant, 72 & 75. Bibliog: Alex Mogelon (auth), Art in Boxes, Van Nostrand Reinhold, New York, 74. Style & Technique: Elegant analysis technique; window display and stage set constructions. Media: Wood; Photographs; Film; Letraset. Publ: Contribr, Image Nation, Toronto, 71; contribr, Parachute, Montreal, 75. Dealer: Carmen Lamanna 840 Yonge St Toronto ON M4W 2H1 Can. Mailing Add: 68 Broadview Ave 4th Floor Toronto ON M4M 2E6 Can

CARRINGTON, JOY HARRELL
PAINTER, ILLUMINATOR
b Jacksonville, Tex. Study: Kansas City Art Inst, three years; Am Acad Art, Chicago; Nat Acad Chicago; Chicago Art Inst, with Pougialis; Art Students League, four years; also with Frank Peyraud, Highland Park, Ill & Robert Brackman, Noank, Conn. Work: Long Barrack Mus, Alamo; First Methodist Church, Jacksonville; Alamo Libr; Coppini Acad Fine Arts; San Antonio; State Capitol Bldg, Austin. Exhib: One-man shows, Witte Mem Mus, San Antonio, 63 & St Marys Univ, 64; Ann Western Art Show, Coliseum, San Antonio, 64-72; Am Artists Prof League Grand Nat Exhib, 67-72; Meinhard Galleries, Houston, 67-72; Panhandle Plains Mus Ann, Canyon, Tex; Cent Tex Mus, Salado, Tex; McNamara O'Conner Mus, Victoria, Tex; Univ Tex, San Antonio, 76-78. Pos; Com artist for Frank Bros, San Antonio, Hartman Furniture Co & Handelan & Staff Shoe Agency, Chicago & Loesers, Brooklyn. Awards: Coppini Acad Award for Oil Painting, Witte Mus, 57; Grumbacher Award for Oil Painting, Am Artists Prof League, 69; Sculpture Award, Kansas City Art Inst; Gold Merit Award, Univ Tex, San Antonio Watercolor Group, 76-77. Bibliog: Glenn Tucker (auth), Arts Rev, San Antonio Light, 8/63; Herweck (auth), article in The Record, spring 72. Mem: Am Artists Prof League; Nat Soc Arts & Letters; Coppini Acad Fine Arts; Kerrville Art Club; San Antonio Watercolor Group; Hill Country Arts Found. Style & Technique: Post-impressionist; values toned in with actual color, using dry brush with no medium; broken color. Media: Oil. Dealer: Meinhard Galleries 1714 S Post Oak Rd Houston TX 77027. Mailing Add: T Anchor Ranch Rte 16 Box 30 Medina TX 78055

CARROLL, ROBERT JOSEPH
PAINTER, ILLUSTRATOR
b Syracuse, NY, Oct 11, 04. Study: Crouse Col Fine Arts, Syracuse Univ, 23-27; Parsons Sch Design, NY. Work: In many pvt collections. Exhib: Brooklyn Mus; Syracuse Mus Fine Arts; Albright Art Gallery, Buffalo, NY; Rochester Mus Art; NY Galleries, 68; plus others. Pos: Free lance illusr; illusr, rec covers for var co. Publ: Illusr, Vogue, Harpers Bazaar & McCall's Mags; illusr bk jackets, Doubleday. Mailing Add: 327 W 11th St New York NY 10014

CARRON, MAUDEE LILYAN
PAINTER, SCULPTOR
b Melville, La. Study: Creative Arts Sch, Houston, scholar, with McNeill Davidson; Lamar Univ; & with Dr James McMurray. Work: Univ Tex Austin. Comn: Poster & stage sets for Glass Menagerie, Who's Afraid of Virginia Woolf? & Macbeth, Univ Tex Austin Drama Dept, 70 & 72. Exhib: 16 Southeastern States & Tex Exhib, New Orleans Mus, 63; Eight State Exhib, Okla Art Ctr, Oklahoma City, 68; one-man shows, Images, Univ Tex Fine Arts Gallery, 70, Environment 71, Univ Tex Austin, 71 & Et Cetera 3, Southwestern Univ, 72; All-Media Exhib 77, Univ Houston, 77. Teaching: Instr elements of visual design, Art & Alma's Art Ctr, 63-69 & two workshops for Beaumont Art League, 72 & 73. Awards: Miller Award for Incognito, Beaumont Art Mus, 68 & two awards for A Dangerous Game in Archaic Form, 70; Award for A Temple for All Delights, Tex Fine Arts Asn, 69. Mem: Tex Watercolor Soc; Tex Prof Sculptors Soc; Tex Fine Arts Asn; Beaumont Art Mus; Graphic Soc, Lamar Univ. Style & Technique: New experimental techniques in hanging cut-out figures in fabric, printmaking and handmade paper sculpture. Media: Metal, Acrylic. Mailing Add: 2147 Ninth St Port Arthur TX 77640

CARSTENSON, CECIL C
SCULPTOR, LECTURER
b Marquette, Kans, July 23, 06. Study: Kansas City Art Inst; Univ Nebr; Art Inst Chicago; also with several sculptors in Italy. Work: Joslyn Mus, Omaha, Nebr; Phoenix Art Mus, Ariz; Univ Mo-Kansas City; Nelson Gallery Art, Kansas City; Jewish Community Ctr, Kansas City; plus others. Exhib: Mid America, Nelson Gallery Art; Joslyn Art Gallery Show; Mo Pavilion Exhib, New York World's Fair,; St Louis Mus Show; Denver Art Gallery Show. Teaching: Instr sculpture, Univ Mo-Kansas City, 51-53. Pos: Comt mem, Mo Coun on Visual Arts, 68-72. Awards: Hon Mention & Purchase Award, Mid America, Nelson Gallery Art. Style & Technique: Contemporary sculpture, carved and abstract. Media: Wood. Publ: Auth, Film, sculpture, Nelson Gallery Art, 62; Craft and Creation of Wood Sculpture, Scribner, 71. Dealer: Pucker Safrai Gallery 171 Newbury St Boston MA 02116. Mailing Add: 1018 W 38th St Kansas City MO 64111

CARSWELL, RODNEY
PAINTER, EDUCATOR
b Carmel, Calif, Dec 15, 46. Study: Univ NMex, BFA, 68; Univ Colo, MFA, 72. Work: Univ NMex, Albuquerque; Univ Colo, Boulder; Ill State Mus, Springfield; Evansville Mus Art, Ind. Exhib: Chicago & Vicinity Show, Art Inst Chicago, 73, New Horizons in Art, Chicago, 73; Ill Invitational, Springfield, Ill, 73 74; EB and Flo, Peoria, Ill, 75; Evansville Ann, Evansville Mus, Ind, 75; one-man shows, Not in New York Gallery, Cincinnati, Ohio, 76 & Roy Boyd Gallery, Chicago, 78; The Chosen Object,. Joslyn Mus, Omaha, Nebr, 77; Carl Solway Gallery, New York, 77. Teaching: Asst prof painting & drawing, Ill State Univ, Normal, 72- Awards: Viewler Award, Art Inst Chicago, 73; Purchase Awards, Ill State Mus, 73 & Evansville Mus, 74. Style & Technique: Brush and spray on canvas. Media: Acrylic. Dealer: Roy Boyd Gallery 233 E Ontario St Chicago IL 60611; Carl Solway Gallery 139 Spring St New York NY 10012. Mailing Add: Dept of Art Ill State Univ Normal IL 61701

CARTER, ALBERT JOSEPH
MUSEUM CURATOR
b Washington, DC, Apr 20, 15. Study: Howard Univ, BS; Teachers Col, Columbia Univ, MA; Teamer Schs Educ, Charlotte, NC, DHL in Educ. Collections Arranged: Ceramics, Textiles, Metals & Wood, 47-48; Japanese Wood Block Color Prints, 47-48; Contemporary Indian Paintings, 47-48; Expressionism in Graphic Arts, 48-49; Miniatures for Illuminated Books of the Middle Ages, 49-50; Contemporary American Paintings, 49-50; New Vistas in American Art, 61. Teaching: Instr commercial art, GI Sch, Letchers Art Ctr, Washington, DC, 46-59. Pos: Cur, Howard Univ Art Gallery, Washington, DC. Awards: Fel, Corning Mus Glass, NY, 57. Mem: Am Asn Mus; DC Art Asn. Mailing Add: Howard Univ Gallery of Art Washington DC 20001

CARTER, BERNARD SHIRLEY
PAINTER, INSTRUCTOR
b Boston, Mass, Oct 22, 17. Study: Art Students League, with Raphael Soyer & Arnold Blanch; Oqunquit Sch Art, Maine, with Bernard Karfiol. Work: Metrop Mus Art, New York; Boston Mus Fine Arts, Mass. Exhib: Int Watercolor Exhib, Brooklyn Mus, NY, 51; Am Watercolor Soc Ann, New York, 60 & 61; 100th Ann Exhib, Am Watercolor Soc, Metrop Mus Art, 67; Audubon Ann Exhib, Nat Acad Galleries, New York, 70. Teaching: Instr painting, Parsons Sch Design, New York, 46-65; instr painting & dir, Bedford Art Ctr, NY. Awards: Non-mem award, Am Watercolor Soc, 60; Katonah Gallery Award, 65; First Prize for watercolor, Artists Northern Westchester, NY, 65. Mem: Am Watercolor Soc; Century Asn. Media: Watercolor. Mailing Add: 350 Cherry St Bedford Hills NY 10507

CARTER, CLARENCE HOLBROOK
PAINTER, DESIGNER
b Portsmouth, Ohio, Mar 26, 04. Study: Cleveland Sch Art, 23-27; with Hans Hofmann, Capri, Italy, summer 27. Work: Metrop Mus Art; Mus Mod Art; Brooklyn Mus, NY; Corcoran Gallery Art; Philadelphia Mus, Pa; plus others. Comn: Murals, sect painting & sculpture, Treasury Dept, Portsmouth, Ohio & Ravenna, Ohio Post Off & Cleveland Pub Auditorium. Exhib: One-man shows, Mus Art, Carnegie Inst, 40, Minneapolis Inst Arts, 49 & NJ State Mus, 74; plus many Europ, SAm, Can mus & others. Teaching: Lectr art, mus, cols & art schs; asst prof painting & design, Carnegie Inst, 38-44; dir art, Chautauqua Inst, NY Univ, 43; guest instr painting, Cleveland Inst Art, summer 48; guest instr, Minneapolis Sch Art, fall 49; guest instr, Lehigh Univ, 54; guest instr, Ohio Univ, 55; guest instr, Atlanta Art Inst, 57; vis lectr, Lafayette Col, 61, artist-in-residence, 61-69; guest artist, Univ Iowa, spring 70; consult, Lafayette Col, 70-71, Kent State Univ, 75 & Iowa State Univ, 75. Pos: Dir, FAP for Northeastern Ohio, 37-38. Awards: Prizes, Cleveland Arts & Crafts, 27-39, Butler Inst Am Art, 37, 40, 43 & 46 & Carnegie Inst, 41, 43 & 44; plus others. Mem: Assoc Nat Acad Design; Del Valley Art Asn (pres, 62-63); Am Watercolor Soc (bd dirs, 61-62, vpres, 62). Publ: Auth, chap, In: Work for artists; contribr, articles in Col Art J & Am Artist. Dealer: Gimpel & Weitzenhoffer Galleries 1040 Madison at 79th St New York NY 10021. Mailing Add: Spring Mills RD 1 Milford NJ 08848

CARTER, DAVID GILES
ART CONSULTANT, MUSEUM DIRECTOR
b Nashua, NH, Nov 2, 21. Study: Princeton Univ, with C R Morey & A M Friend, AB, 44; Harvard Univ Grad Sch Arts & Sci, with P Sachs, C R Post, C Kuhn & others, MA, 49; Inst Fine Arts, NY Univ, 51, with W Cook, E Panofsky, G Schoenberger & H Bober. Collections Arranged: Turner in America (with Wilbur D Peat), 56; The Young Rembrandt and His Times, 58; The G H A Clowes Collection, 59; Dynamic Symmetry, 61; El Greco to Goya (with Curtis Coley), 63; The Weldon Collection, 64; Masterpieces from Montreal, 66; The Painter and the New World, 67; Rembrandt and His Pupils, 69; Jan Menses, 76; plus many others. Teaching: Vis lectr, Art of the Northern Renaissance, Ind Univ, Bloomington, 58-59. Pos: Curatorial asst, Metrop Mus Art, New York, 50-54; cur paintings & prints, John Herron Art Mus, 55-59; dir, Mus Art, RI Sch Design, 59-64; dir, Montreal Mus Fine Arts, 64-76. Awards: Gold Medal of Ital Cult, Ital Ministry Foreign Affairs, 63. Mem: ICOM; Mediaeval Acad; Grolier Club; Royal Soc Arts; plus others. Res: Primary focus on 15th century Netherlands; secondary interest in Mannerist and northern Baroque painting. Collection: Minor masters of 17th century Netherlands and Italianized Dutch artists. Publ: Auth, Two Romanesque frescoes from San Baudelio de Berlanga, 3/54, auth, A portrait by Rembrandt, 8/56 & auth, Christ's triumphal entry into Jerusalem, 6/58, Herron Art Inst Bull; auth, The Providence crucifixion, its place and meaning for Dutch XVth century painting, Mus Notes, 5/62; auth, Rencontre avec Valentin, l'Oeil, 70; auth, The Winnipeg flagellation and the master of the View of St Gudule, Miscellanea in Memoriam Paul Coremans (1908-1965), Bull de l'Institut royal du Patrimoine artistique, xv, 75; auth, Spanish itinerary, Apollo, 5/76; auth, Northern Baroque and the Italian connexion, Apollo, 5/76; auth, Montréal musée des beaux-arts, The Art Gallery, 4-5/76; plus others. Mailing Add: 100 Edgehill Rd New Haven CT 06511

CARTER, DEAN
SCULPTOR, EDUCATOR
b Henderson, NC, Apr 24, 22. Study: Corcoran Sch Art; Am Univ, BA; Ogunquit Sch Painting & Sculpture; Indiana Univ, MFA; Ossip Zadkine Sch Art, Paris, France. Work: Cranbrook Acad Art, Mich; Hollins Col; Washington & Lee Univ; Wichita Art Asn Galleries, Kans; Wachovia Bank & Trust Co, NAm, Winston-Salem, NC. Comn: Bronze portrait, Gropius, Col Archit, Va Polytech Inst, 65; welded bronze screen, Roanoke Mem Hosp, Va, 70; three piece bronze group, St Joseph's Preparatory Sch, Philadelphia, 70; welded bronze relief, First Colony Ins Co, Lynchburg, Va; bronze portrait, Stuart Cassell, Cassell Colesium, Va Polytech Inst, 77; plus others. Exhib: Pa Acad Fine Arts, Philadelphia, 54; Cini Found, Venice, Italy, 64; Smithsonian Circulating Exhib, 69-71; one-man show, Artists' Mart, Washington, DC, 70; Contemp Gallery Art Ann Sculpture Show, Winston-Salem, 71. Teaching: Chmn art prog, Va Polytech Inst & State Univ, 63- Pos: Mem art adv bd, Va Highlands Community Col, Abigdon, 69-71 & Mountain Empire Community Col, Wise, 71-75; consult, US Fine Arts Surv, 72; past pres, Blacksburg Regional Art Asn; state rep & bd mem, Southeastern Col Art Conf, 74-75. Awards: Cini Found Fel, 64; Honorable Mention for Sculpture, Contemp Gallery Art, Winston-Salem, 65; AIA Award for Sculpture, Roanoke Fine Arts Ctr, 73, Sidney's Award, 75; plus others. Bibliog: Ted Kliman (auth), A World of Sculpture (film), Va Polytech Inst & State Univ, 62; W M White, Jr (auth), Sculpturing by Dean Carter, Maelstrom, 66; W C Burleson (auth), On campus—Dean Carter, Context, summer 69. Mem: Soc Washington Artists; Southern Sculptors Asn (vpres, 66-68); Am Crafts Coun (state rep, 65); Col Art Asn Am; Am Fedn Art; plus others. Style & Technique: Human figure and birds in the environment; from realistic to semi-abstract. Media: Bronze, Wood. Dealer: Area Landscape 4118 Olley Lane Fairfax VA 22039. Mailing Add: 1011 Highland Circle Blacksburg VA 24060

CARTER, DUDLEY CHRISTOPHER
SCULPTOR
b New Westminster, BC, May 7, 91. Work: Seattle Art Mus; Golden Gate Park, San Francisco; Evergreen East, Bellevue, Wash. Comn: Big Horn sculpture, San Francisco City Col, 40; totem column, Northgate Shopping Ctr, Wash, 53; carved relief, Schaefer Brothers Co, Aberdeen, Wash, 54; totem column, Shell Oil Refinery, Anacortes, Wash, 55. Exhib: Golden Gate Expos, San Francisco, 39; Bellevue Art Fair, 56; Seattle World's Fair, 61; David L Vaughn Exhib, Vancouver, BC, 72; US Dept Housing & Urban Develop, Washington, DC, 73. Awards: Sculpture, Music & Art Found, Seattle, 48; Achievement Award for Sculpture, Past Pres Assembly, 62; Int Sculpture, US Dept Housing & Urban Develop, 73. Bibliog: Michael Minot (auth), BC Sculptors, F Cameron Wilkenson Co Ltd, 74. Mem: Seattle Art Mus; Can Fed Arts; Artists Equity Asn; BC Sculptors Asn. Style & Technique: Large scale architectural wood sculpture; sculpture from the great trees of the West and redwood trees from California. Media: Wood. Mailing Add: 3075 Bellevue Redmond Rd Bellevue WA 98008

CARTER, FREDERICK TIMMINS
PAINTER, ILLUSTRATOR
b Galveston, Tex, Sept 22, 25. Study: Franklin Sch Prof Art, New York, grad with hons, 45-48. Work: D D Feldman Collection Tex Artists, Dallas. Comn: Paintings, El Paso Natural Gas Co, Tex, 73, Ford Motor Co, Dearborn, Mich, 75. Exhib: Tex Ann Paintings Exhib, Dallas, Houston & San Antonio Mus, 53-58; Audubon Artists Nat Exhib, Nat Acad Galleries, New York, 55 & 70; Sun Carnival Nat Exhib, El Paso Mus Fine Art, 58-68; Nat Soc Painters in Casein, New York, 60; one-man show, Dos Pajaros Gallery, El Paso Int Airport, 75. Pos: Staff artist, Wilkinson-Schiwetz & Tips, Houston, 50-55; art dir, Mithoff Advert, El Paso, 57-65. Mem: El Paso Mus Art. Style & Technique: Southwestern colorist using sensitive line, strong sunlight and vivid color to depict life, architecture and landscapes of Southwest and Mexico. Media: Acrylic. Publ: Illusr, Frank Mangan's Bordertown, 64, El Paso, 71 & Bordertown Revisited, 73; illusr, Ford Times Mag, 75. Dealer: Dos Pajaros Gallery Int Airport El Paso TX 79925; Jean Seth Canyon Rd Gallery 710 Canyon Rd Santa Fe NM 87501. Mailing Add: 5744 Beaumont El Paso TX 79912

CARTER, GRANVILLE W
SCULPTOR, INSTRUCTOR
b Augusta, Maine, Nov 18, 20. Study: Corburn Class Inst; Portland Sch Fine & Applied Art; New York City Sch Indust Art; Nat Acad Sch Fine Arts; Grande Chaumiere, Paris, France; Scuolo Circolare Int, Rome, Italy; Am Acad Rome. Work: Smithsonian Inst, Washington, DC; Thomas Alva Edison Mus, West Orange, NJ; Hall of Fame for Great Americans, NY Univ; Morristown Hist Mus, NJ; Maine State Mus, Augusta. Comn: Bronze bust of Jane Addams, Hall of Fame for Great Americans, 68; monumental bust of Alexander Stewart, Garden City, NY, 69; West Texas Pioneer Family Monument (heroic bronze), Lubbock, Tex, 71; Brig Gen Casimir Pulaski Equestrian Monument (heroic bronze), Hartford, Conn, 76; heroic bronze bust of Charles Lindbergh, Garden City Hist Soc, 77. Exhib: Am Acad Rome Ann, 55; Archit League, New York, 56-58; Nat Sculpture Soc, Lever House, New York, several yrs; Int Expos Medals, Paris & Prague, 67 & 70; Am Artists Prof League Ann, New York, 70. Teaching: Instr sculpture, Nat Acad Design, 66-; lectr sculpture, Washington Cathedral & Hofstra Univ, 66- Pos: Deleg, Fine Arts Fedn New York, 72. Awards: Louis Comfort Tiffany Found fels, 54 & 55; Henry Hering Mem Medal, Nat Sculpture Soc, 68; Gold Medal, Am Artists Prof League, 70. Bibliog: Charles Guy (auth), editorial in Lubbock Avalanche J, 6/10/71; Ford Mitchell (auth), West Texas Pioneer Family Monument (film), KCBD TV, 71; James M Goode (auth), Outdoor Sculpture of Washington, DC. Mem: Fel Nat Sculpture Soc (coun mem, 60-72, rec secy, 63-65); fel Am Artists Prof League (bd dirs, 72-); Academician Nat Acad Design; Coun Am Artists Socs (bd dirs, 69-). Media: Wood, Stone, Metals. Publ: Contribr, Nat Sculpture Rev, spring 67; contribr, Hall of Fame for Great Americans Brochures, 63-72. Mailing Add: 625 Portland Ave Baldwin NY 11510

CARTLEDGE, ROSEANNE CATHERINE
GRAPHIC ARTIST
b Milwaukee, Wis, Mar 1, 39. Study: Alverno Col, Milwaukee, BA, 61; Okla Univ, Norman, MA(art educ), 69; Inst Allende, San Miguel de Allende, GTO, Mex, graphics & sculpture, summers 60 & 61. Comn: Five drawings for permanent display, US Forest Serv Hq, Williams, Ariz, 77. Collections Arranged: Ariz State Univ Mem Union Gallery (10-12 per yr), Tempe. Exhib: A Technical Workshop, 4/74 & Design Awareness Seminar, 2/75, Ariz State Univ; 4th Colo Ann Exhib, Denver Art Mus, 76; 17 Ways to Draw a Picture, Harlan Gallery, Tucson, Ariz, 76; 12th Southwestern Invitational, Yuma Art Ctr, Ariz, 78. Teaching: Instr art, Homestead High Sch, Mequon, Wis, 61-63; instr art, Am Sch, Tegucigalpa, 63-65; asst prof design, Sch Home Econ, Okla Univ, 65-71. Pos: Head of Exhib & Fine Arts Adv, Mem Union, Ariz State Univ, Tempe, 71-75. Mem: Asn Col Union Int (visual arts coordr region 13, 74-75). Mailing Add: 5 N Sunset Strip Williams AZ 86046

CARTMELL, HELEN
PAINTER, ART ADMINISTRATOR
b Bridgeport, Conn, Jan 6, 23. Study: Detroit Soc Arts & Crafts, scholar; Wayne State Univ. Work: Ossabaw Island Proj Found, Savannah, Ga; Wayne State Univ Collection; Chrysler Corp, Detroit; Int Nickel Co, New York; also in pvt collection of Sen Philip Hart, Washington, DC & many others. Exhib: Nine Univ Mich Regional, 63-72; Willistead Gallery, Ont, 65; six shows, Mich Acad Sci, Arts & Lett, 65-72; Grand Rapids Art Mus, Mich, 69 & 71; one-woman show, Arwin Galleries, Detroit, 70 & 75. Pos: Dir prod dept & media art dir, Ctr Instrnl Technol, Wayne State Univ, 68- Awards: Silver Medal Award, Scarab Club Detroit; Oil Award, Mich Acad Sci, Arts & Lett; Oil & Esther Longyear Mem Awards, Mich Soc Women Painters & Sculptors; plus others. Mem: Mich Acad Sci, Arts & Lett; Scarab Club Detroit; Detroit Soc Women Painters & Sculptors. Style & Technique: Uses oils transparently on a totally white, well-primed canvas; landscapes and still lifes have a soft, ethereal effect. Dealer: Arwin Galleries 222 W Grand River Detroit MI 48226. Mailing Add: 21700 Winshall Rd St Clair Shores MI 48081

CARTWRIGHT, CONSTANCE B & CARROLL L
COLLECTORS
b US citizens. Mem: Mrs Cartwright, Am Fedn Arts (trustee); Mus of Mod Art Int Coun; Mus of Mod Art (drawing comt); Mus of Fine Arts, Boston (visitor's comt Asiatic Art). Collection: Late 19th and 20th century drawings; Chinese blue and white porcelain. Mailing Add: One East End Ave New York NY 10021

CARULLA, RAMON
PAINTER
b Havana, Cuba, Dec 7, 36. Work: Havana Mus Fine Arts; Montreal Mus Fine Art, PQ; Princeton Gallery Collection; Lukacs Gallery, Montreal, Que; New York. Exhib: Ann Lawn Tennis Art Exhib, Havana, 65; Beaux Art Lowe Art Mus Ann Exhib, 67, 69 & 71; 3rd & 4th Ann Pan Am Art Exhibs, 71-72; one-man shows, Mirell Gallery, 71-73; Sala Mendozo Exhib,

Caracas, Venezula, 76; Virginia Miller Galleries, Coconut Grove, Fla, 76; Cintas Fel Exhib, Miami, Fla, 77; one-man show, Atelier Lukacs, Montreal, 77; Ridge Art Asn Fine Art Exhib, Winterhaven, Fla, 78; 15th Ann Major Fla Artists Exhib, Harmon Gallery, Naples, Fla, 78; plus others. Awards: Best Young Artist, Ann Lawn Tennis Art Exhib, 65; Honorable Mention, 4th Ann Pan Am Exhib, 71-73; Cintas Fel Grant, 73-74; plus others. Bibliog: K Flanders (auth), article in Time Guide, 70-71; Nat Coun Cult (auth), Young Artists at Work, Ministry Pub Works, Havana. Mem: Miami Art Ctr; Artists Equity Asn. Style & Technique: Oil and acrylics on canvas. Dealer: Virginia Miller Galleries 3112 Commodore Plaza Coconut Grove FL 33133 Mailing Add: 4735 NW 184th Terr Miami FL 33055

CASANOVA, ALDO JOHN
SCULPTOR, EDUCATOR
b San Francisco, Calif, Feb 8, 29. Study: San Francisco State Univ, BA, 50 & MA, 51; Ohio State Univ, PhD, 57. Work: Whitney Mus, New York; San Francisco Mus Art; Columbus Mus Fine Arts, Ohio; Sculpture Garden, Univ Calif, Los Angeles; Joseph Hirshhorn Collection, Washington, DC. Comn: Bronze sculpture, Ford Motor Co, Detroit, 63; Skidmore, Owings & Merrill, Archit, San Francisco, 66, Atlantic-Richfield Co, Los Angeles, 69, Washington Mutual Savings Bank, Seattle, 69 & Calif Inst Technol, Pasadena, 74. Exhib: One-man shows, Ester Robles Gallery, Los Angeles, 67, Santa Barbara Mus, Calif, 67 & Calif Inst Technol, 72 & many others; Pa Acad Ann, Philadelphia, 62-67; Art Dealers Asn Am, Parke-Bernet Gallery, New York, 64; The New Vein, Smithsonian Inst, SAm travel tour, 68-70; New Aquisitions, Whitney Mus Am Art, New York, 70. Teaching: Instr art, San Francisco State Univ, Calif, 51-53; asst prof sculpture, Antioch Col, Ohio, 56-58; asst prof sculpture, Temple Univ, Philadelphia, 61-64; prof sculpture, Scripps Col, Claremont, Calif, 66- & chmn art dept, 71-73; summer fac, Skowhagan Sch Painting & Sculpture, Maine, 74 & head summer fac, 75. Awards: Rome Prize Fel Sculpture, Am Acad in Rome, 58-61; Best of Show in All Media Award, Woodmere Gallery, Philadelphia, 62; Louis Comfort Tiffany Award, Tiffany Found, 69. Mem: Sculptors Guild, New York. Style & Technique: Abstract monumental; direct wax or other media. Media: Bronze, Casting; Carving, Stone or Wood. Dealer: Mitzi Landau 20th Cent Art 1725 Thayer Ave Los Angeles CA 90024. Mailing Add: 727 N College Ave Claremont CA 91711

CASARELLA, EDMOND
SCULPTOR, PRINTMAKER
b Newark, NJ, Sept 3, 20. Study: Cooper Union, BFA, 42; Brooklyn Mus Art Sch. Work: Whitney Mus Am Art, New York; Brooklyn Mus Art, NY; NJ State Mus, Trenton; Speed Mus, Louisville, Ky; Libr Cong, Washington, DC. Comn: Sculpture, Northern Valley Bank, Cresskill, NJ; sculpture, Unitarian Church, Louisville, Ky. Exhib: Corcoran Gallery, Washington, DC; Nat Print Coun Competition, Am Prints Today & others. Teaching: Artist in residence, Norfolk Summer Art Sch, Yale Univ, 58; instr graphics, Brooklyn Mus Art, 56-60; instr graphics, Columbia Univ, summers; instr graphics & sculpture, Cooper Union, 63-70; instr, Pratt Inst, Yale Univ & Rutgers Univ, 64; instr graphics & sculpture, Finch Col, 70-; instr, Manhattanville Col, Italy, summer 73 & Purchase, NY, summer 74. Awards: Fulbright Award for Graphics, Italy, 51-52; Tiffany Award for Graphics, Louis Comfort Tiffany Found, 55; Guggenheim Fel for Graphics, 59-60. Bibliog: Bernard Chaet (auth), Artists at Work: Gabor Peterdi (auth), Printmaking; Ross-Romano (auth), The Complete Printmaker, Macmillan Free Press. Media: Steel, Bronze. Dealer: Cramer Gallery 7 Main St Glen Rock NJ 07452. Mailing Add: 83 E Linden Ave Englewood NJ 07631

CASAS, FERNANDO RODRIGUEZ
PAINTER, DRAFTSMAN
b Cochabamba, Bolivia, Mar 25, 46. Study: Colo Col, BA(philos); Rice Univ, MA, PhD(philos); pvt training with Raul Prada. Work: Nat Mus Art, La Paz, Bolivia; Pinacoteca Nac, Cochabamba, Bolivia; Art of the Americas Collection (B Duncan), New York. Comn: Mural, Dominican Convent, Bolivia, 67. Exhib: One-man shows, Salon Munic de Exposiciones, Cochabamba, Bolivia, 64, Palacio de la Cult, Cochabamba, 67, Salon Munic de Exposiciones, La Paz, Bolivia, 68, Mus Mod Art, La Paz, 73 & Harriet Griffin Gallery, New York, 76; Ed La Humiere, Paris, France, 77. Awards: First Nat Award Painting & First Nat Award Drawing, Concurso Nac de Artes Plasticas, City of Cochabamba, Bolivia, 72; First Nat Award Drawing, XXI Nat Art Contest, Pedro Domingo Murillo, City of La Paz, Bolivia, 73. Bibliog: Claudia Cooper (auth), Casas (film), Rice Univ Media Ctr, 76. Media: Oil painting; pencil, ink drawings. Publ: Illusr, Poetas Bolivianos, 66 & Indios en Revelion, 68, UTO, Bolivia; contribr (with Yves Froment), Rosee Aveugle, E Canelas, 68. Dealer: Harriet Griffin Gallery 850 Madison Ave New York NY 10021. Mailing Add: 1203 Bartlett 3 Houston TX 77006

CASAS, MELESIO
PAINTER, EDUCATOR
b El Paso, Tex, Nov 24, 29. Study: Univ Tex, El Paso, BA, 56; Univ of the Americas, Mex, MFA, 58. Exhib: Artists of the Southeast & Tex, Biennial Painting & Sculpture, 71; Tex Painting & Sculptures: 20th Century, 72; Mex-Am Art Symp, Trinity Univ, 73; 12 Tex Artists, Contemp Art Mus, Houston, 74; 1975 Biennial Contemp Am Art, Whitney Mus Art, 75; Dále Gas—Chicano Art of Tex, Contemp Arts Mus, Houston, 77. Teaching: Prof art, design & painting, San Antonio Col, Tex, 61- Pos: Book reviewer, Choice Mag, Am Libr Asn, 54- Awards: Purchase Prize, El Paso Art Mus, 6th Ann Sun Carnival, 59 & Cash Award, 64; Cash Award, San Antonio Art League, 66. Bibliog: Jacinto Quiarte (auth), The Art of Mexican Americans, Univ Tex, 73; Philip D Ortega (ed), We Are Chicanos, Washington Sq Press, 73; rev in Art News, 12/77; Mimi Crossley (auth), Dale Gas at the Contemporary Art Museum, Art in Am, 1-2/78. Mem: Con Safo Painters (founder, past pres). Style & Technique: Humanscapes, dealing with and about social commentary. Media: Acrylic on Canvas. Mailing Add: 5019 Ayrshire San Antonio TX 78217

CASCIERI, ARCANGELO
SCULPTOR, EDUCATOR
b Civitaquana, Italy, Feb 22, 02; US citizen. Study: Sch Archit, Boston Archit Ctr, 22-26; Boston Univ, 32-36. Work: Boston Col; Holy Cross Col; Buffalo Courier Express Bldg; Parlin Jr High Sch, Everett, Mass; Lexington Jr High Sch, Mass. Comn: Am War Mem World War I, Belleau Woods, France & World War II, Margraten, Holland; exterior Mem Auditorium, Lynn, Mass; exterior Boys' Stadium, Franklin Field, Dorchester, Mass; sculpture on fountain, Parkman Plaza, Boston; plus sculpture statues in many cathedrals & churches in US. Exhib: Sculpture Exhib, Boston Mus Fine Arts; Sculpture Exhibs, New Eng Sculpture Asn; one-man exhib, Sch Design, Harvard Univ; Lit Arts Soc Exhib, New York. Teaching: Pvt classes, Boston, 32-37; instr design, Boston Archit Ctr, 36-, head, Sch Archit, 38-, mem bd dirs; instr, Craft Ctr Sch, Boston, 39-40; instr design, New London Jr Col, Conn, 41-43. Pos: Asst dir sculpture & wood carving, W F Ross Studio, Cambridge, 23-41; sculptor & asst dir, Schwamb Assocs Studio, Arlington, 41-46, sculptor & dir, 46-52; partner studio for sculpture & decorations, Boston, 52-; gov app mem, Post-Sec Comn on Educ, 77- Awards: Anniversary Citation, Boston Archit Ctr, 64; Citation Boston 200, 75; Silver Medal for Distinguished Pub Serv in the Arts & Educ, Boston Univ Alumni Asn, 76. Mem: Fel Am Inst Architects (chmn comt collaborative arts); hon mem Dante Alighieri Soc; hon mem Naples Asn of Inst of Architects & Engineers; New Eng Sculptors Asn; Boston Soc Architects; Mass Asn Architects. Mailing Add: 500 Concord Ave Lexington MA 02173

CASE, ELIZABETH
PAINTER, WRITER
b Long Beach, Calif, July 24, 30. Study: French Inst, New York, 46, with Mr Lee; Art Students League, 48 & 49, with Vlascov Vytlacil, Robert Hale, Reginald Marsh & Harry Sternberg; Elmira Col, 49-51; Syracuse Univ, New York, exten courses; study with Doug McClellan, 54; Scripps Col, 54, with Dr Schardt. Work: USN Combat Art Collection, Washington, DC; Elmira Col Ford Mus, NY. Comn: Murals with Walt Disney artists, Los Angeles Co Hosp, Pediatrics Wing, 56; murals, Good Shepherd, Church of the Good Shepherd, Ft Lee, NJ, 71, Reflections, Palisadeum Restaurant Banquet Facility, Cliffside Park, NJ, 74, View Through Trees, comn by Dr & Mrs S I Heller, New York, 75 & Wall of Discovery (hist of children's lit), Old Bridge Pub Libr, 77. Exhib: One-man shows, Research Libr, Walt Disney Studios, Burbank, Calif, 56 & 57, D'Alessio Gallery, 64 & Gallery 8, Henderson Place, New York, 69; Am Freedoms Caravan Mural Design Exhib, Nat Arts Club, New York, 75 & Wilmington Opera House, 76; Nat Exhib Miniature Paintings, Nutley, NJ, 75; Inaugural Exhib, Ft Lee Libr, 75 & Ridgefield Pub Libr, 77. Teaching: Instr basic drawing, Ft Lee Adult Sch, 75-78. Pos: Asst animator, Walt Disney Prod, 56-58; sr copywriter/designer spec proj, Prentice-Hall Col Advert Dept, Englewood Cliffs, 75-77; art dir, Designs for Int Artware, Twinsburg, Ohio, 77- Awards: Second Award, Wyn Rogers Gallery, Cliffside Park, NJ, 64; Honorable Mention, Leonardo da Vinci Art Soc Ann, Bergen Community Mus, NJ, 71; Award & Citation for Outstanding Achievement, Elmira Col, 76. Bibliog: Thomas Oat (auth), article in Groton News, Conn, 75; Judy Plummer (auth), article in Dolphin Newspaper, New London, Conn, 75; Roberta Roesch (auth), There's Always a Right Job for Every Woman, Berkeley, 76. Mem: Navy Art Coordination & Liaison; Nat Soc Mural Painters Inc (publicity, 73-75, secy, 75); Art Soc NJ; Ft Lee Libr Fine Arts Coun; Fine Arts Fed. Style & Technique: Realistic paintings concerning community events and scenes, interiors, portraits, Navy & Marine scenes: submarines and sailing ships. Media: Egg Tempera & Oil in Mixed Technique; Elaborate Pencil, Pen & Ink. Publ: Auth, Feature article on Michael Grando's Jewelry, 70 & Burton Silverman, 71, Am Artist Mag; auth, Nat Soc Mural Painters Brochure, 73; illusr (cover), Weidenbaum, auth, Business, Government & the Public, Prentice-Hall, 76; illusr (covers & part openings), Algren & Hackworth, auth, Programmed Algebra, Vols I & II, Prentice-Hall, 77 & Gregory R Kimble, auth, Use & Misuse of Statistics, 78. Mailing Add: Fine Arts Studio 1351 River Rd Edgewater NJ 07020

CASEY, ELIZABETH TEMPLE
CURATOR
b Providence, RI, Sept 24, 01. Study: Pembroke Col, Brown Univ. Collections Arranged: Exhibs from permanent collection of Mus Art, RI Sch Design, Providence. Pos: Mus asst, Mus Art, RI Sch Design, 26-35, cur textiles, 35-43, cur Aldrich Collection, 50-, cur Oriental art, 56- Res: English, Chinese and Japanese ceramics; Oriental costumes and textiles; Japanese color prints. Publ: Auth, The Lucy Truman Aldrich Collection of European Porcelain Figures of the Eighteenth Century, 65. Mailing Add: 89 Ingleside Ave Cranston RI 02905

CASEY, JACQUELINE SHEPARD
DESIGNER, DESIGN DIRECTOR
b Qunicy, Mass, Apr 20, 27. Study: Mass Col Art, BFA, 50; study of drawing with Hyman Bloom, 51-53. Work: Libr of Cong, Washington, DC; Mass Inst Technol Fac Club & Comt on the Visual Arts, Cambridge, Mass. Exhib: Direction 1968, Philadelphia Col Art, 68; Mass Inst Technol Graphic Design, New York Art Directors Club, 71, Plaza Dic, Tokyo, Japan, 72, London Sch Printing, Bath, Revensbourne, Eng, 72-74, Kent State Univ & Univ of Cincinnati, 75-76 & Fukuoka Am Ctr, Japan, 76; Mass Inst Technol Hayden Gallery Corridor, Cambridge, Mass, 72; Images of an Era, The American Poster, 1945-1975, Corcoran Gallery Art, Washington, DC, 76; Graphic Design for Pub Serv, Kuntzgewerbemuseum der Stadt, Zurich, Switz, 77. Collections Arranged: Ann Design for Printing and Commerce, Am Inst Graphic Arts; Typomundus 20 & 20 II; Creativity on Paper; New York Type Directors Club. Pos: Design consult, Nat Endowment for the Arts, Washington, DC, 72- Bibliog: J J de Lucio-Meyer (auth), The Design Services Office of MIT, Novum Gebrauchsgraphik, WGer, 7/73; Jean Coyne (auth), MIT Design Services Office, Commun Arts, 9-10/74; Stanley Mason (auth), Objective Graphic Design (MIT), Graphis, Zurich, Switz, 74-75. Mem: Alliance Graphique Int; Am Inst Graphic Arts. Publ: Contribr, Design Through Discovery, Holt, Rhinehart & Winston, 70; contribr, The Design of Advertising, William C Brown, 73; contribr, A Primer of Visual Literacy, MIT Press, 73; contribr, Print Casebooks, RC Publ, 1st ed, 75, 2nd ed, 76; contribr, Images of an Era, MIT Press, 76. Mailing Add: Mass Inst of Technol Design Servs Rm 5-133 77 Massachusetts Ave Cambridge MA 02139

CASEY, JOHN JOSEPH
EDUCATOR, PAINTER
b New London, Conn, June 27, 31. Study: Univ Ore, BA; Calif Col of Arts & Crafts, MFA with Nathan Oliveira. Work: Univ Ore, Eugene; State of Ore, Salem; Coos Art Mus, Ore. Exhib: NW Inst of Sculptors, Portland Art Mus, Ore, 58; 68th Western Ann, Denver Art Mus, 62; The Painted Flower, Oakland Art Mus, Calif, 63 & 64; Supplement 66, Fountain Gallery, Portland, 66; Ore Artists Ann, Portland Art Mus, 67, 71-73, 75 & 77; 22nd Spokane Ann, Cheney Cowles Mus, Wash, 70, 72, 74 & 76; 32nd Ann NW Watercolor Exhib, Seattle Art Mus Pavilion, Wash, 71. Teaching: Assoc prof drawing, painting & sculpture, Ore Col of Educ, Monmouth, 65-; vis instr design, Ore State Univ, Corvalis, summer 66. Pos: Adv & consult, Ore State Fair, Salem, summer, 67. Awards: Hon Mention, The Painted Flower, Oakland Art Mus, 63. Bibliog: G E Guilbert (auth), The Art Forms Explosion, Spokane Spokesman-Rev, 7/72. Mem: Col Art Asn; Portland Art Asn. Style & Technique: Vacuum-formed plastic wall sculptures, spray-painted with acrylic lacquers. Media: Painting, sculpture. Publ: Auth, On Black and White in Art, The Jason, Willamette Univ, 74. Mailing Add: 2615 Adams Rd Dallas OR 97338

CASSANELLI, VICTOR VI
PAINTER
b Dubrovnik, Yugoslavia, Feb 7, 20. Study: Ist Tecnico d'Arte, Fiume, 34-37; Art Students League, with Will Barnet & Julio Llort, 66-67. Work: La Coun Music & Arts, New Orleans; Palace Cong, Monaco; Butler Inst Am Art, Youngstown, Ohio; Philadelphia Mus; Herman & Ruth Goodman Found, New York. Exhib: Inst PR, New York, 68; La Watercolor Soc, New Orleans, 72; Allied Artists Am, New York, 73; Audubon Artists, New York, 73 & 74; Am Vet Soc Artists, New York, 74. Awards: M Grumbacher Award of Merit, Painters & Sculptors Soc NJ, 75; Eugenia Atwood Purchase Prize of Philadelphia Print Club, Philadelphia Mus, 77; Michael M Engel Mem Award, Nat Acad Galleries, Audubon Artists, 78. Bibliog: Pino Zanchi (auth), Alberi Personaggi di Cassanelli, Giornale di Pavia, Carlo Delfino Marusich (auth), Presentazione: Vittorio Cassanelli, Arte di Milano, Mario

Albertazzi (auth), Spiritualita Geometrica, Progresso Mem: Int Art Exchange; Artists Equity Asn; Audubon Artists; Painters & Sculptors Soc NJ (jury of selection, 74-, exhib chmn, 75). Style & Technique: Geometrical abstract collage; silkscreen. Media: Print, Oil, Collage. Dealer: Reece Galleries 39 W 32nd St New York NY 10018. Mailing Add: PO Box 144 Village Sta New York NY 10014

CASSARA, FRANK
PAINTER, PRINTMAKER
b Partinico, Sicily; US citizen. Study: Colorado Springs Sch Fine Arts, Colo; Univ Mich, MS(design); also spec study, Atelier 17, Paris, France. Work: Libr Cong, Washington, DC; Bibliot Nat, Paris, France; Stedelijk Mus, Amsterdam, Neth; Detroit Inst Arts; Free Libr Philadelphia. Comn: Murals, US Post Off, East Detroit, 39, Donald Thompson Sch (fresco), Highland Park, Mich, 39, US Post Off, Sandusky, Mich, 40 & Water Conditioning Plant, Lansing, Mich, 41. Exhib: 7th Int Exhib Lithography & Wood Engr, Art Inst Chicago, 39; Int Asn Plastic Arts, US Info Agency Tour, SAm, 59; 1st Int Calif Soc Etchers, San Francisco, 64; 1st Exhib Am Printmakers, Gallerie Nees Morphes, Athens, Greece, 65; 22nd Nat Exhib Prints, Libr Cong, 71; Atelier 17: A Retrospective, Elvehjem Art Ctr, Madison, Wis, 77. Teaching: Instr drawing, Detroit Soc Arts & Crafts, 46-47; prof printmaking, Univ Mich, 47- Awards: Over 50 in national and regional exhibitions; Rackham Res Grants, Univ Mich, 61, 68 & 74. Media: Intaglio. Publ: Contribr, Artists' Proof, A Collectors Edition, 71. Dealer: Forsythe Gallery 201 Nickels Arcade Ann Arbor MI 48104. Mailing Add: Sch of Art Univ of Mich Ann Arbor MI 48109

CASSILL, HERBERT CARROLL
PRINTMAKER, EDUCATOR
b Percival, Iowa, Dec 24, 28. Study: State Univ Iowa, BFA, 48, MFA, 50, with Mauricio Lasansky. Work: Mus Mod Art, New York; Cleveland Mus Art; Brooklyn Mus; Libr Cong, Washington, DC; Oakland Art Mus, Calif. Exhib: Libr Cong, 52, 54 & 60; six shows, Philadelphia Print Club, 53-60; Int Exhib Graphic Arts (shown in Europe), Mus Mod Art, 54, Modern Art in the USA (shown in Europe), 55; Soc of Am Graphic Artists Overseas Exhib, US State Dept, 60. Teaching: Instr printmaking, State Univ Iowa, 53-57; head dept printmaking, Cleveland Inst Art, 57- Awards: Louis Comfort Tiffany Found Fel Printmaking, 53; Purchase Prize, Philadelphia Print Club, 56; First Prize, Print Show, State Univ NY Col Potsdam, 61. Media: Intaglio, Wood. Mailing Add: 3084 Coleridge Rd Cleveland OH 44118

CASTANO, ELVIRA
ART DEALER, COLLECTOR
b Cincinnati, Ohio, July 23, 32. Study: Emerson Col, AB, Boston, Mass; Villa Schifanoia, Florence, Italy; Univ Florence, Italy. Pos: Asst historian, Castano Art Gallery, Boston, 55- Mem: Boston Mus Mass. Res: Italian Renaissance art and the Macchiaioli school of art. Specialty: Traditional and Renaissance art. Collection: American, Dutch and Italian art. Mailing Add: 245 Hunnewell St Needham Heights MA 02194

CASTANO, GIOVANNI
ART DEALER, PAINTER
b Calabria, Italy, Oct 2, 96. Study: Mus Fine Arts, Boston, grad; also with Philip L Hale, William James, Frank Mortimer Lamb, Hugo Elliot & Leslie P Thompson. Work: Brockton Pub Libr, Mass; Music Hall, Boston. Comn: Stage settings, Boston Opera House, 16-22; scenic artist & designer, Cincinnati Grand Opera, 22-27; murals, First Baptist Church, Covington, Ky; stage scenery, Town Hall, Peterborough, NH, 36; restored Albert Herter murals in Mass House Rep, comn by Gov Frank Sargent, 71. Exhib: Boston 200 Bicentennial Exhib, 75; Springfield High Sch, Utah; Pa Acad. Pos: Appraiser, Kennedy Libr. Awards: Cavalier, Ital Govt, 65; Accademico Corrispondente, Academia Tiberina, Rome, 66; Silver Plaque, Gov Frank Sargent. Mem: Boston Mus Fine Arts; fel Int Inst Arts & Lett. Style & Technique: Landscapes; portraits; scenic designer. Media: Watercolor, Oil. Mailing Add: 245 Hunnewell St Needham Heights MA 02194

CASTELLI, LEO
ART DEALER
b Trieste, Italy, Sept 4, 07. Study: Univ Milan; Columbia Univ, grad work hist. Pos: Dir, Leo Castelli Gallery. Specialty: American vanguard painting and sculpture. Mailing Add: c/o Leo Castelli Gallery 420 W Broadway New York NY 10012

CASTELLON, ROLANDO
CURATOR, PAINTER
b Managua, Nicaragua, Oct 10, 37. Work: Consejo Superior Universitario Centroamericano, San Jose, Costa Rica; San Francisco Art Comn. Exhib: Artistas de la Raza, Oakland Art Mus, Calif, 70; Primera Bienal de Pintura Centroamericana, San Jose, Costa Rica, 71; Drawings USA, Minn Mus of Art, St Paul, 73; Arte Actual de Iberoamerica, Inst de Cult Hispanica, Madrid, Spain, 77. Collections Arranged: Roots II: Asian Community, Third World Photograhic Vision, MIX Sculpture/Ceramics, MIX Graphics I: Prints, MIX Graphics II: Drawings, A Third World Painting/Sculpture Exhib, Art-Naif, Posters & Society, Contemp Icons, Carlos Gutierrez-Solana/Oliver L Jackson, People/Places, Fetishes, Rene Gelpi: Photographs, People's Murals, Americana, Michael Bradley/Ceremonies, Marie Johnson/Betye Saar & Mod Argentine Drawing, San Francisco Mus of Mod Art, 72-77. Pos: Dir, Galeria de la Raza, San Francisco, 70-71; cur, San Francisco Mus of Mod Art, 72- Awards: Nicaragua Nat Prize, 1st Biennial of Cent Am Painting, Consejo Superior Universitario Centroamericano, 71. Bibliog: Jerome Tarshis (auth), Artistas de la Raza, Artforum, 12/70; Mayra Jimenez (auth), Pintura: Rolando Castellon, Imagen, Venezuela, 4/72; Esmeralda Cardenal (auth), Artistas Nicaraguenses, La Prensa Literaria, Nicaragua, 6/77. Style & Technique: Acrylic on paper. Media: Drawing and painting. Mailing Add: San Francisco Mus of Mod Art Van Ness Ave at McAllister St San Francisco CA 94102

CASTER, BERNARD HARRY
PAINTER, ENAMELIST
b Wolcott, NY, May 27, 21. Study: Syracuse Univ, AA(fine arts), 56, BA, 60. Work: St Lawrence Univ; Newark Pub Libr, NY; Sch St Croixe de Neuilly, Paris, France. Exhib: 21st Ann Western NY Regional, Buffalo, 55; 19th Ceramic Nat, Syracuse Mus, 56; NY State Artists Exhib, NY State Fair, 58; The Kentucky Guild Train, 66; 14th Ann Rochester Festival of Religious Arts, 72. Awards: Marie Wilner Award, Cayuga Mus Hist & Art, Auburn, NY, 62, Ceramic Award, 64; Hon Mention, 8th Ann Westchester Outdoor Art Exhib, New Rochelle, NY, 67. Style & Technique: From abstract to fantasy; complex with use of bright colors. Dealer: Galerie Paula Insel 987 Third Ave New York NY 10022. Mailing Add: Box 154 South Butler NY 13154

CASTILE, RAND
GALLERY DIRECTOR
b North Carolina, July 15, 38. Study: Drew Univ, BA; Urasenke Tea Ceremony Hq, Kyoto, Japan; also study with Grand Master Sen Soshitsu, XV, diplomae. Collections Arranged: Three exhib per yr, Japan House Gallery, 71- Pos: Lectr, Japanese art & tea ceremony, US & Japanese Univs & mus; dir, Japan House Gallery, Japan Soc Inc, New York, 70-; consult-panelist, Nat Endowment Arts, 75; consult, Nat Endowment Humanities, 75-; bd adv, Japan Study Ctr, Columbia Univ. Awards: Fulbright Scholar, 66-67. Mem: Asn Art Mus Dirs; Metrop Mus Art (vis comt); Am Fedn Arts (Nat Exhib Comt); Am Asn Mus; US-Japan Educ & Cult Conf. Publ: Auth, numerous articles in Art News, Geijutsu Shincho, Bijutsu Techo & Print Collector's Newslett, 63-; auth, The Way of Tea, 72; auth, Ikeda & Ida: Two Japanese Printmakers, 74. Mailing Add: Japan House Gallery 333 E 47th St New York NY 10017

CASTLE, WENDELL KEITH
DESIGNER, SCULPTOR
b Emporia, Kans, Nov 6, 32. Study: Univ Kans, BFA & MFA. Work: Addison Gallery Am Art, Andover, Mass; Rochester Mem Art Gallery, NY; Nordenfieldske Kunstindustrimus, Norway; Mus Contemp Crafts, New York; Philadelphia Mus Art; Metrop Mus of Art, New York. Exhib: One-man shows, Mem Art Gallery, Rochester, NY, Lee Nordness Galleries, New York, The Schuman Gallery, Rochester, NY, Univ of Kans Art Mus, Lawrence, Wichita Art Mus, Kans, Ithaca Col Mus of Art, NY, Univ of NH Gallery, Durham, State Univ NY Cortland, Carl Solway Gallery, New York & Louisville Art Asn, Ky; Int Kunsthandwerk, 66; Attitudes, Brooklyn Mus, NY, 69; Objects USA Traveling Show, US & Europe, 70-; Wooden Work, Smithsonian Inst, 72; 13th Triennale, Milan, Italy. Teaching: Instr drawing, Univ Kans, 60-61; assoc prof furniture design, Rochester Inst Technol, 62-70; prof sculpture, State Univ NY Col Brockport, 70- Awards: Louis Comfort Tiffany Found & NY State Grants, 72; Nat Endowment Arts Grants, 73, 75 & 76; plus others. Bibliog: Wilson (auth), The Music Rack, produced by ACC, 66; Limber Timber, Newsweek, 5/13/68; Pierce (auth), Transitions (film), Nat Educ TV, 69. Mem: Am Craftsman Coun (NY rep). Style & Technique: Laminated wood sculpture; furniture organic in form. Media: Wood. Publ: Auth, George Sugarman, 68, Mike Nevelson, 69 & Wharton Esherick, 71, Craft Horizons. Dealer: Shop 1 127 Alexander St Rochester NY 14607. Mailing Add: 18 Maple St Scottsville NY 14546

CASTLEMAN, RIVA
CURATOR, ART HISTORIAN
b Chicago, Ill, Aug 15, 30. Study: State Univ Iowa, BA; Inst Fine Arts, New York Univ. Collections Arranged: Picasso Master Printmaker, Mus Mod 70, Technics & Creativity: Gemini G E L (with catalog), 71, Jasper Johns, Lithographs (with catalog), 70-71, The Prints of Edvard Munch, 73, Modern Prints (with catalog; int traveling exhib), 73-75, Latin American Prints from Mus Mod Art (with catalog; int traveling exhib), 74-75; Impresario-Ambroise Vollard, 77. Pos: Curatorial asst, Art Inst Chicago, 51-55; cur, Calif Hist Soc, San Francisco, 56-57; from curatorial asst to cur, Mus Mod Art, New York, 63- Mem: Print Coun Am. Res: Contemporary prints. Publ: Auth, Contemporary Prints, 73; auth, Prints of the Twentieth Century: a History, 76. Mailing Add: Mus Mod Art 11 W 53rd St New York NY 10019

CASTORO, ROSEMARIE
PAINTER, SCULPTOR
b Brooklyn, NY, Mar 1, 39. Study: Mus Mod Art, New York, scholar, 54-55; Pratt Inst, BFA(cum laude), 56-63. Work: Berkeley Mus, San Francisco; Woodward Found, Washington, DC. Comn: Procession of Strokes, NY State Coun Arts, 72. Exhib: Distillation, Tibor de Nagy Art Gallery, New York, 66 & one-man shows, 71-73, 75 & 76; The Drawn Line, 470 Parker St Gallery, Boston, 71; Highlights of the 70-71 Art Season, Aldridge Mus Contemp Art, Conn, 71; Painting & Sculpture, Storm King Mountain, NY, 72, 74 & 75; one-man show, Syracuse Univ Lubin House Gallery, 73; 67-68 Paintings, Halbromm Gallery, New York, 76; Otis Art Inst, Los Angeles, Calif, 76; Henderson Mus, Univ Colo, 77. Teaching: Lectr, Boston Mus Sch, 71, Hunter Col, NY, 72, New Sch Social Res, 73, Calif State Univ, Fresno, 73, Philadelphia Col Art, 74, Mt Berry Col Art, Ga, 74, Syracuse Univ, NY, 75 & Univ Colo, Boulder, 77. Atlanta Col Art, 74. Awards: Awards: NY State Coun Arts, 72 & 74; Nat Endowment Arts, 75; Tiffany Found, 77. Bibliog: E C Goosen (auth), Distillation, 11/66 & Lucy Lippard (auth), rev, 5/72 & 2/74, Art Forum; Carter Ratcliff (auth), rev in Art Int, 5/75. Style & Technique: Utilization of linear lengths of arcs to bridge the gap between the mind and its manifestations; troweling of pigmented epoxy impregnated Fiberglas cloth over and around steel reinforced styrofoam legs. Publ: Auth, Open hearing, Art Workers Coalition, 69; auth, The artist & politics, Art Forum, 9/70; auth, Artists transgress all boundaries, Art News, 1/72; ed, Art in the mind, 70 & Conceptual Art, 72; Tracks, 75. Dealer: Tibor de Nagy Art Gallery 29 W 57th St New York NY 10019. Mailing Add: 151 Spring St New York NY 10012

CASTRO, ALEX
PAINTER, BOOKMAKER
b Washington, DC, Feb 1, 43. Study: Yale Univ, BA; Univ Pa, MArch. Work: Corcoran Gallery of Art, Washington, DC. Exhib: Five Plus One, The Corcoran Gallery, Washington, DC, 76. Teaching: Asst prof drawing & painting, George Mason Univ, Fairfax, Va, 77- Pos: Pres, The Hollow Press, Washington, DC, 77- Awards: Yaddo fel, Trask Found, 77. Bibliog: Paul Richard (auth), Article in Washington Post, 9/76; B Forgey (auth), Catching Up with Morris Louis, Art News, 11/76; D Tannous (auth), Five Plus One at the Corcoran, Art in Am, 1-2/77. Style & Technique: Graphite notation on paper; large graphite floor drawings; glass and panel wall pieces; printed books. Media: Graphite on paper; letterpress. Publ: Auth-illusr, Uncle E's Lessons from Nursery Rhymes, 77 & co-auth, Klavierstucke, Vol I, in press, The Hollow Press. Mailing Add: 1501 N Rhodes St Apt 4 Arlington VA 22209

CASTRO (PACHECO FERNANDO)
PAINTER
b Merida, Mex, Jan 26, 18. Study: Escuela Artes Plasticas, 34. Work: Mus Arte Mod, Bosque Chapultepec, Mex; Palacio Bellas Artes, Mex; Libr of Cong, Washington, DC; Dallas Mus Fine Arts, Tex. Comn: Cosmogonia Maya (mural), Palacio Gobierno, Palacio Estado, Merida, 70-71; Jacinto (mural), Sala de Recepciones, Gobierno Estado; Canek (mural) & Yucatan en la Historia (mural), Palacio Gobierno, Merida, 72. Exhib: 3rd & 4th Expos Int de Arte, Tokyo, 55 & 57; 5th Muestra Int de Blanco y Negro, Lugano, Suiza, 58; 10th Int Biennial Watercolor Exhib, Brooklyn, NY, 59; Expos de Pintura Mexicana, Rome, Italy, 67; plus many others. Teaching: Instr art, Escuela Pintura y Escultura, La Esmeralda, Mex, 46-61, dir, 61-; instr art, Escuela Nac Artes Plasticas, Nat Univ Mex, 49- Pos: Juror, Oposiciones y Examines Profesionales, Escuela Nac Artes Plasticas, 55-; juror, Salon Plastica Mexicana, Eventos Pintura, Dibujo y Grabado. Awards: First Prize in Painting, Salon Plastica Mexicana, 54, 55 & 61. Bibliog: Antonio Mediz Bolio (auth), article in Diario del Sureste, 51; Justino Fernandez (auth), article in El Universal, 72; Raquel Tibol (auth), article in Diorama Cultura, Excelsior, 72. Mem: Soc Mex Grabadores (pres); Plastica Mex (consejero, 58, asesor, 60); Escuela Nac Artes Plasticas UNAM (consejero technico, 57); Escuela Pintura y Escultura SEP (consejero technico, 56). Publ: Illusr, Acabo su Camino con la Muerte, 52, La Nube Esteril, 52, Los Pozos Sagrados, 54, Voz y Sangra del Hijo de Yucatan, 55 & La

Flauta de la Cana, 60. Mailing Add: c/o Galeria de Arte Mexicano Milan 18 Mexico DF Mexico

CASWELL, HELEN RAYBURN
PAINTER, WRITER
b Long Beach, Calif, Mar 16, 23. Study: Univ Ore Sch Fine Arts. Comn: Murals, Federated Church, Saratoga, Calif, 65; Mem Paintings, San Jose Hosp, Calif, 67 & Emanuel Lutheran Church, Saratoga, 69. Exhib: De Young Mus Show, Soc Western Artists, 61; one-man shows, Northwest Mo State Col, 66 & Rosicrucian Mus, San Jose, 70; Montalvo Cult Ctr, Saratoga, 68. Awards: James D Phelan Award for Narrative Poetry, 58; San Francisco Browning Soc Award, 66. Mem: Soc Western Artists. Style & Technique: Alternating layers of palette knife impasto and translucent glass. Media: Oil. Publ: Auth & illusr, A Wind on the Road, 64 & A New Song for Christmas, 66, Van Nostrand Reinhold; Shadows from the Singing House, Charles Tuttle, 67; auth & illusr, Thank You for Being You, Gibson, 73; auth, Never Wed an Old Man, Doubleday, 75. Dealer: Park's Art Gallery 322 Town & Country Village San Jose CA 95128; Gallery Americana Lincoln St & Sixth Ave Carmel CA 93921. Mailing Add: 15095 Fruitvale Ave Saratoga CA 95070

CATALAN, EDGARDO OMAR
PAINTER, EDUCATOR
b Valparaiso, Chile; US citizen. Study: Sch of Fine Arts, Vina Del Mar, Chile, MA, 60, with Hans Soyka; Calif Col of Arts & Crafts, Oakland, 67; lithography with Carlos Gonzalez, Stade, Ger. Work: Museo de Bellas Artes, Vina Del Mar; Fine Arts Gallery, San Diego, Calif. Exhib: Artists From the Sch of Fine Arts of Vina Del Mar, 59 & Chilean Printmakers, 69, Mus of Art, Lima, Peru; Concurso Crav, Mus of Contemp Art, Santiago, Chile, 62; one-man shows, Oils & Lithographs, Edgardo Catalan, Fine Arts Gallery, San Diego, 68, Edgardo Catalan, Paintings, Santa Barbara Mus of Art, 75; Santa Barbara Selection, Santa Barbara Mus of Art, 74; Hist of Chilean Printmaking, Mus of Art, Valparaiso, Chile, 76; Paintings, New Media Gallery, Ventura Col, Calif, 77; Drawings, Experimental Grafisch Werkcentrum, Orvelte, Holland, 77. Teaching: Prof painting & drawing, Acad of Fine Arts, Vina Del Mar, Chile, 62-64; chmn fine arts dept, Thacher Sch, Ojai, Calif, 64-75. Awards: First Prize/Mural, Summer Salon, Dept of Cult & Fine Arts, Vina Del Mar, 60; First Prize/Painting, Autumn Salon, Mus of Art, Valparaiso, 64; First Prize/Poster, Cafe de Brasil, Brazilian Govt, 64; Calif Arts Coun grant, Artist-in-Residence Prog, Santa Barbara Pub Schs. Style & Technique: Semi-figurative paintings, with emphasis on the human figure; bright, glazed color. Media: Oil painting and watercolor. Mailing Add: 2786 Ben Lomond Dr Santa Barbara CA 93105

CATALDO, JOHN WILLIAM
EDUCATOR, CALLIGRAPHER
b Boston, Mass, Nov 28, 24. Study: Mass Col Art, BSEd; Columbia Univ, MA & EdD; Sch Am Craftsmen, Rochester, NY, with L Copeland; Univ Calif, Los Angeles, with J P Jones; Teachers Col, Univ Buffalo & Pa State Univ. Work: Wichita Art Asn, Univ Mo; Albright-Knox Art Gallery, Buffalo, NY; NY State Crafts Fair, Ithaca; Teachers Col, Columbia Univ; Munic Art Ctr, Long Beach, Calif. Comn: Films on art, Nat Educ Asn, 61; screen-divider, Sheraton-Palace Hotel, San Francisco, 62; sculpture, Lithuanian Social Ctr, DuBois, Pa, 65; 30 films, Nat Inst TV, Bloomington, Ind, 70-72; five bronze sculptures, Boston Archit Ctr, 78. Exhib: Young Americans, USA, Contemp Crafts Show, 56; Wichita Art Asn Sculpture & Jewelry Show, 56 & 61; Albright-Knox Art Gallery Show, 60; Graphic Design, Syracuse Univ, 61; Ball State Drawing & Sculpture Ann, 63-64. Teaching: Assoc prof art, Teachers Col, Columbia Univ, 60-61; assoc prof art, Pa State Univ, 61-65; dir art educ & prof art, Philadelphia Col Art, 65-70; acad dean & instr calligraphy, Mass Col Art, 70- Pos: Assoc ed, Art Educ, 60-63; ed, Sch Arts, 62-67. Awards: Lacey Print Prize, Western NY Ann, Albright-Knox Art Gallery, 56 & Ceramic Sculpture Prize, 58; Words & Calligraphy, selected for AIGA 50 Best Books Award, Van Nostrand Reinhold, 70. Mem: Nat Art Educ Asn (bd dirs, 66-70, pres, Eastern Region, 68-70); Educ Press Asn; Am Asn Univ Prof; Col Art Asn Am. Publ: Auth, Lettering—a Guide for Teachers, David Publ, 58; auth, Graphic Design & Visual Communication, Intext, 66; auth, Words & Calligraphy for Children, Van Nostrand Reinhold, 69. Mailing Add: 364 Brookline Ave Boston MA 02215

CATAN-ROSE, RICHARD
PAINTER, EDUCATOR
b Rochester, NY, Oct 1, 05. Study: Royal Acad Fine Arts, Italy, MFA; St Andrews Univ, London, LLD; Cooper Union Art Sch; also with Pippo Rizzo, Antonio Quarino, J Joseph & A Shulkin. Work: Our Lady Queen of Martyrs Church, Forest Hills, Long Island; Royal Acad Fine Arts, Italy. Exhib: Allied Artists Am, 39 & 40; Vendome Gallery, 39-41; one-man shows, Forest Hills, Long Island, 44-46 & Argent Gallery, 46; also in Europe. Pos: Pres, Catan-Rose Inst Art, Jamaica, Long Island. Mem: Am Fedn Arts. Res: How the artist-designer will play a new role as major contributor to urban living and to improve the goal of the artist for our future civilization. Mailing Add: 72-72 112th St Forest Hills Long Island NY 11375

CATCHI (CATHERINE O CHILDS)
PAINTER, SCULPTOR
b Philadelphia, Pa, Aug 27, 20. Study: Briarcliff Jr Col, 37; Commercial Illus Studios, 38-39; also with Leon Kroll, Harry Sternberg & Hans Hofmann & with Angelo Savelli, Positano, Italy. Work: Rosenberg Found; Hofstra Univ, Hempstead, NY. Exhib: One-person shows, Rayburn Hall (by Congressional invitation), Washington, DC, 68 & 76, Gallerie di Arte Spinetti, Florence, Italy, Gallery Coin d'Arte, Genoa, Italy, Galveston Art League, Tex, Galleria, Austin, Tex & Alfredo Valente Gallery, New York, 68; Lever House, New York, four times; Royal Acad Galleries, Edinburgh, Scotland; Royal Birmingham Soc Artists Galleries, Eng. Awards: Lillian Cotton Mem Award & Medal of Honor, Nat Asn Women Artists, 66; Irene Sickle Feist Mem Prize, 71; Goldie Paley Award, Nat Asn Women Artists, 77. Bibliog: Nan Ickeringill (auth), Art & at home with Catchi, New York Times, 68; Doris Herzig (auth), She has painted since she was 12, Newsday, 68; Molly Sinclair (auth), Oil brush & canvas, Atlanta Constitution, 69. Mem: Nat Asn Women Artists (second vpres, 72-73); Audubon Artists; Int Platform Asn. Style & Technique: Expressionistic as well as portraits. Media: Oil, Watercolor; Stone, Cast Metals. Publ: Illusr (cover), La Vue Art Mag, France, 7/75. Dealer: Harbor Gallery Cold Spring Harbor NY 10516; Gallery 19 2107 K St NW Washington DC 20037. Mailing Add: 2 Gristmill Lane Manhasset NY 11030

CATE, PHILLIP DENNIS
ART HISTORIAN, CURATOR
b Washington, DC, Oct 19, 44. Study: Rutgers Univ, BA(art hist), 67; Ariz State Univ, MA(art hist), 70. Collections Arranged: Meryon's Paris/Piranesi's Rome (with catalog), 71; Thomas Hart Benton, A Retrospective of His Early Years (with catalog), 72; The Ruckus World of Red Grooms (with catalog), 73; Japonisme: Japanese Influence on French Art, 1854-1910 (with catalog), 75. Pos: Asst to dir, Pa Acad Fine Art, 67-68; dir & cur, Fine Arts Collection & Univ Art Gallery, Rutgers Univ, 70- Mem: Print Coun Am; Printmaking Coun NJ (adv bd, 74-); Am Asn Mus; Col Art Asn. Res: 19th century French prints. Mailing Add: Art Gallery Rutgers Univ New Brunswick NJ 08903

CATHCART, LINDA LOUISE
CURATOR, ART HISTORIAN
b Lafayette, Ind, Oct 20, 47. Study: Calif State Univ, Fullerton, BA(fine arts), 69; Hunter Col, City Univ New York, MA(art hist), 72; Cortauld Art Inst, London, postgrad study, 73-74. Collections Arranged: Bruce Nauman (auth catalog), Martha Jackson Collection at the Albright-Knox Art Gallery (auth catalog), Gilbert & George (auth catalog), Edward Ruscha (auth catalog), Four for the Fourth (auth catalog), Paul Sharits (auth catalog), Richard Diebenkorn (auth catalog), In Western New York (auth catalog), Joel Shapiro (auth), Rafael Ferrer (auth catalog), Roger Welch (auth catalog), Charles Simonds (auth catalog), Alfred Jensen XIV San Paulo Bienal (auth catalog), Richard Diebenkorn XXXIX Venice Biennale (auth catalog), Albright-Knox Art Gallery, Buffalo, NY. Teaching: Instr art hist, Sch Visual Arts, New York, 73-75; instr color theory, Cambridge Univ, Eng, 74; adj prof mus studies, State Univ NY Buffalo, 75- Pos: Curatorial asst, Whitney Mus Am Art, New York, 71-73; coordr spec progs, Brooklyn Mus, NY, 74-75; cur, Albright-Knox Gallery, 75- Awards: Nat Endowment for the Arts & Humanities Award, 71-72; Fulbright fel, 73-74. Mailing Add: 828 Potomac Buffalo NY 14209

CATHERS, JAMES O
SCULPTOR, EDUCATOR
b St Louis, Mo, June 2, 34. Study: Univ Louisville, BS, 67; RI Sch Design, MFA, 69. Work: Univ Louisville. Comn: Commemorative gift, Ky Opera Asn, Louisville, 67. Exhib: NE Sculpture Open, Brockton Art Ctr, Mass, 75; Small Sculpture Open, Providence Art Club, RI, 76; 65th Ann Am Exhib, Art Asn of Newport, RI, 76; 58th Nat Exhib, George W V Smith Art Mus, Springfield, Mass, 77; Works by New Eng Sculptors, Copley Soc, Boston, 77. Teaching: Prof sculpture & drawing, Roger Williams Col, Bristol, 72-; sculptor-in-residence, Art Asn Newport, 74- Pos: Dir, Sch Art Asn, Newport, 74-77; three-dimensional nominator, RI State Coun on the Arts, 77. Awards: First Prize Sculpture, 61st Ann Am Exhib, 72 & Second Prize Sculpture, 65th Ann Am Exhib, Art Asn Newport, Gertrude Vanderbilt Whitney, 76; Cianfarni Award, Small Sculpture Open, Providence Art Club, 76. Mem: Art Asn Newport (mem bd dir); New Eng Sculptors Asn, Boston; Anyart Contemp Arts Ctr, Providence. Style & Technique: Realistic figurative sculpture. Media: Polyurethane, Plaster; Acrylic Plastic. Mailing Add: 23 John St Newport RI 02840

CATLETT, ELIZABETH
SCULPTOR, PRINTMAKER
b Washington, DC, Apr 15, 19. Study: Howard Univ, BS(art); Univ Iowa, MFA; also with Ossip Zadkine. Work: Mus Arte Mod, Mexico City; Mus Mod Art, New York; Nat Mus, Prague, Czech; Schomburg Collection Black Hist, New York; Libr Cong, Washington, DC. Comn: Bronze sculpture, Nat Polytech Inst, Mexico City, 66; bronze bust of Phillis Wheatley, Jackson State Col, Miss, 73; bronze of Louis Armstrong, L Armstrong Statue Comt, New Orleans, La, 75; bronze relief, Howard Univ, Washington, DC, 77. Exhib: Golden Jubilee Exhib, Chicago, 41; Sculpture Biennial, Mexico City, 64-66; Nat Print Salon, Mexico City, 69; one-woman sculpture show, Mus Arte Mod, Mexico City, 70; Intergraphic, Berlin, EGer, 71. Teaching: Prof sculpture, Sch Fine Arts, Nat Univ Mex, 58-75, head dept, 60-73. Awards: Julius Rosenwald Found Fels, 45-47; Brit Coun London Grant, 71; Elizabeth Catlett Week, City of Berkeley, Calif, Bibliog: Marc Crawford (auth), My art speaks, Ebony Mag, Raquel Tibol (auth), Experiencia Negra de E Catlett, Oposicion Mag, Mex, Elton Fax (auth), 17 Black Artists, Dodd, 71. Mem: Salon Plastica Mex. Style & Technique: Realist sculpture with emphasis on form expressing idea. Media: Wood, Stone, Bronze; Lithography, Relief Prints. Publ: Auth, The role of the Black artist, Black Scholar Mag, 75. Dealer: Contemporary Crafts 5271 W Pico Blvd Los Angeles CA 90019. Mailing Add: Apartado Postal 694 Cuernavaca mor Mexico

CATLIN, STANTON L
MUSEUM DIRECTOR, ART HISTORIAN
b Portland, Ore, Feb 19, 15. Study: Oberlin Col, AB; Acad Fine Arts, Prague, Czech; Am Sch Classical Studies, Athens; Fogg Mus, fel mod art; Inst Fine Arts, NY Univ, MA. Teaching: Prof NAm art, Fac Fine Arts, Univ Chile, 42-43; lectr hist of art, Yale Univ, 62-64; dir art of Latin Am since independence, Yale Univ-Univ Tex, 65-67; vis assoc prof art, Hunter Col, 72-73; prof art, Col Visual & Performing Arts, Syracuse Univ, 74- Pos: Asst to dir circulating exhibs, Mus Mod Art, 39; secy comt art, Coordr Inter-Am Affairs, 41-42; supvr exhib contemp Am painting sent to S & Cent Am by Mus Mod Art, 41; exec dir, Am Inst Graphic Arts, 46-50; from ed to cur Am art, Minneapolis Inst Arts, 52-58; asst dir, Yale Univ Art Gallery, New Haven, Conn, 58-67; dir art gallery, Ctr Inter-Am Rels, NY, 67-71; dir, Lowe Art Gallery & grad mus training prog, Syracuse Univ, 74- Mem: Grolier Club; Latin Am Studies Asn; Am Asn Mus; Col Art Asn Am. Res: History of modern Latin American art, foundation sponsored textbook project. Publ: Auth, La peinture Mexicaine, 52; co-auth, Art of Latin America since independence (catalog); auth, articles, In: Minneapolis Inst Art Bull, Art News, New York Times, New Yorker, Columbia Rec Legacy Album (Mexico-Grammy Award), Art in Am, Am Indigena & exhib catalogs of Ctr Inter-Am Rels. Mailing Add: Lowe Art Gallery Syracuse NY 13210

CATOK, LOTTIE MEYER
PAINTER
b Hoboken, NJ. Study: New York Sch Appl & Fine Arts; also with Guy Wiggins, W Lester Stevens & Robert Brackman. Work: Fla Southern Col, Lakeland; dorm living rms, Smith Col, Northampton, Mass; Bay Path Jr Col, Longmeadow, Mass; plus many portraits in pub bldgs. Comn: Portraits of judges of law, Law League, Superior & Probate Cts, Mass, 61, 66, 69 & 74; portrait of pres of Am Int Col, Springfield, 63; portraits of clergymen, churches & temples, Springfield, 63-77; portrait of Ted Shawn (ballet), Jacob's Pillow, Lenox, Mass, 64; portrait of med men, Med Ctr of Western Mass, 66-71. Exhib: Grand Cent Art Galleries, New York, 55-57 & 77; North Shore Art Asn, Gloucester, Mass, 63-78; Hudson Valley Art Asn, White Plains, NY, 69-78; Allied Artists Am, New York, 70; Am Artists Prof League, New York, 70-78. Awards: First for Landscape, Springfield Artist Guild; Patron's Prize, Figure Award, Acad Artists, 71, Portrait Award, 76. Bibliog: Jack Steiner (auth), I know what I like, New York World Tel, 66. Mem: Copley Soc Boston; Royal Soc Art, London, Eng; Salmagundi Club; Acad Artists (pres, 69-70 & 75-78); Am Artists Prof League (dir, 75). Style & Technique: Classical style with some impressionistic technique. Media: Oil, Watercolor. Publ: Contribr, Art News, 58; contribr, The Fifty American Artists' Book, 69; contribr, Robbins Reproductions, 69. Mailing Add: 45 May Fair Dr Longmeadow MA 01106

CATRON, PATRICIA D'ARCY
ART ADMINISTRATOR
b Memphis, Tenn. Study: Memphis Art Acad; Wittenberg Univ. Collections Arranged: Ralston Thompson—A Retrospective, 1933-74, Springfield Art Ctr & James Roy Hopkins, Ohio Artist, 1877-1969 (auth, catalogue), 77. Pos: Managing dir, Springfield Art Ctr, Ohio, 70-72, dir, 72- Mem: Am Asn Mus; Ohio Mus Asn (mem bd trustees); Int Coun Mus. Publ: Contrib ed, The New Concept, 77. Mailing Add: 107 Cliff Park Rd Springfield OH 45501

CATTELL, RAY
PAINTER, ART DIRECTOR
b Birmingham, Eng, May 5, 21; Can citizen. Study: Birmingham Col Art, Eng; Univ Toronto. Work: London Art Gallery & Sarnia Art Gallery, Ont; Saskatoon Art Gallery, Alta; mural, Windsor Pub Libr. Exhib: Royal Can Acad Art, 60-71; Ont Soc Artists, 60-71; Flint Inst Fine Arts, Mich, 65; Can Soc Painters in Watercolour, 66-72; Am Watercolor Soc, 72. Pos: Exec vpres, Royal Can Acad Art, 74-75. Awards: Watercolour Award, City of Toronto, 63; Hon Award, Can Soc Painters in Watercolour, 65, 68 & 72; Baxter Purchase Award, 66. Mem: Royal Can Acad Art; Ont Soc Artists (vpres, 67-68); Can Soc Painters in Watercolour (pres, 77); Arts & Lett Club; Art Dirs Club Toronto (pres, 64-65). Media: Acrylic, Watercolor, Oil. Publ: Auth, article on creativity, Marketing Mag, 60. Dealer: Arwin Galleries 222 Grand River W Detroit MI 48226; Gallery Moos 138 Yorkville Ave Toronto ON Can. Mailing Add: 21 Knightswood Rd Toronto ON Can

CATTI (CATHERINE JAMES)
PAINTER, ENAMELIST
b Mount Vernon, NY, Oct 8, 40. Study: Boston Univ, BFA; Columbia Univ, MA. Work: Harlem Art Collection. Comn: Acrylic for The Last Jesus (film), Sepia Theater, Toledo, Ohio, 72; costume design, Harry Belafonte Tour, 74 & Walter Nicks Dance Theater & Repertory Co, 74. Exhib: Contemporary Black Artists in America, 71 & Whitney Ann, Whitney Mus Am Art, 72; one-woman shows, Cinque Gallery, New York, 71 & VAM Gallery, 76; Projected Art: Artists at Work, & Women in the Arts, Finch Mus, 71 & 72; Images & Shapes, Clinton Co Govt Ctr, 76; New Talent Exhib, Allan Stone Gallery, New York, 77. Teaching: Art consult, Wiltwyck Sch Boys, 68-70 & Graham Sch, currently; instr anat, Col New Rochelle, 72; lectr African art & workshops on African design. Awards: Creative Artists Coun Grant in Painting, NY State Coun Arts, 71. Bibliog: Black artists in America (slides), Univ SAla & H Kress Found; Robert Doty (auth), Contemporary Black Artists in America. Mem: Am Crafts Coun. Style & Technique: Visual rhythm—the relationships or interaction of organic and geometric forms using a patchwork of painting and printing processes. Media: Acrylic, Plexiglas, Enamel, Copper. Publ: Auth, three articles in Arts & Activities Mag, 67-70; auth, A Black perspective on art, Black Enterprise Mag, 75. Dealer: Allan Stone Gallery 48 E 86th St New York NY 10028; Craftsman's Gallery 16 Chase Rd Scarsdale NY 10583. Mailing Add: 6 Fulton St Hastings-on-Hudson NY 10706

CATUSCO, LOUIS
PAINTER, SCULPTOR
b Liberty, NY. Study: Brooklyn Mus Sch of Art with John Ferren & Xavier Gonzalez, 47-50. Work: Santa Fe Mus of Fine Art, NMex; US Bank of Omaha Gallery, Nebr; Midland Bank Gallery, Denver, Colo. Exhib: Brooklyn Mus of Fine Art; Mus of Santa Fe Biennials, 64-76; Albuquerque Mus of Fine Art, 66; Dallas Mus of Fine Art, 66-70; Johnson Mus of Fine Art, Albuquerque, 67; Joslyn Mus of Fine Art, 70; El Paso Mus of Fine Art, 70-73. Collections Arranged: Two spec shows, Fine Arts Dept, Odessa Col, 69-70. Awards: Blumenschein, TAA Award Show, Helen Blumenschein, 66 & 67; Wurlitzer, TAA Award Show, Wurlitzer Found, 68; Gaspard Graphic, TAA Award Show, Dora Kaminsky Gaspard, 70-71. Bibliog: Tricia Jones (auth), The most private or lonely of men?, Southwest Arts Mag, 74 & Solitude is Catusco (objective), US Nat Bank of Omaha Art Gallery, 72. Mem: Taos Art Asn. Style & Technique: Nonobjective free style; subjective, working from within. Media: Acrylic; Oil; Construction, Wood. Dealer: Stables Art Gallery Taos NMex; Total Arts Gallery Taos NMex. Mailing Add: Box 1166 Taos NM 87571

CAVALLI, DICK
CARTOONIST
b New York, NY, Sept 28, 23. Exhib: Punch Exhib Humor, London, 53. Pos: Cartoonist, Syndicated Comic Strip Winthrop, Newspaper Enterprise Asn; mem founding fac, Famous Cartoonists Course, Famous Artists Schs. Mem: Nat Cartoonists Soc; Newspaper Comics Coun. Publ: Contribr cartoons, numerous bks, anthologies & cartoon collections; contribr cartoons in Sat Eve Post, Coller's, Look, This Week, True & many other US & foreign mags. Mailing Add: 6 Braeburn Dr New Canaan CT 06840

CAVALLON, GIORGIO
PAINTER
b Sorio, Italy, Mar 3, 04; US citizen. Study: Nat Acad Design; also with Charles Hawthorne. Work: Solomon R Guggenheim Mus, Mus Mod Art, Whitney Mus Am Art & Chase Manhattan Bank Collection, New York; Michener Collection, Univ Tex, Austin. Exhib: Yale Univ Art Gallery, New Haven, Conn, 67; Large Scale American Paintings, Jewish Mus, New York, 67; Painting as Painting, Art Mus, Univ Tex, Austin, 68; The 1930's, Painting & Sculpture in America, Whitney Mus Am Art, 68; The New American Painting & Sculpture, Mus Mod Art, New York, 69; plus many others. Teaching: Artist in residence, Univ NC, Greensboro, 64; vis critic in art, Yale Univ, 66-67; instr art, Columbia Univ, 69. Awards: Guggenheim Fel, 66; award in painting, Nat Inst Arts & Lett, 70; award in painting, New Eng Art/Painting & Sculpture Show, 71. Bibliog: Frank O'Hara (auth), Cavallon paints a picture, Art News, 12/58; John Sedgwick (auth), Discovering Modern Art, Random House, 66; Barbara Rose (auth), American Art Since 1900, Praeger, 67. Media: Oil. Dealer: Gruenebaum Gallery Ltd 38 E 57th St New York NY 10022. Mailing Add: 178 E 95th St New York NY 10028

CAVANAUGH, JOHN W
SCULPTOR
b Sycamore, Ohio, Sept 20, 21. Study: Ohio State Univ, BFA; Univ Iowa, Iowa City, grad study; Sculpture Ctr, New York. Work: Colorado Springs Gallery Fine Art; Columbus Gallery Fine Arts, Ohio. Comn: Sculptured wall, Landmark, Baltimore, Md, 63; bull fighter & life-sized standing figure, Crown Towers, New Haven, Conn, 66; cross for altar, St Thomas's Church, Washington, DC, 74; Remembrance of Things Past (seven life-size panels), Swan St NW, 77. Exhib: One-man shows, Sculpture Ctr, New York, biennially 63-, Antioch Col, Yellow Springs, Ohio, 56, Ohio State Univ, 64, Ball State Univ, Muncie, Ind, 67 & Univ Pa, 75. Awards: Ford Found Purchase Prize, Pa Acad Show; Richard Award, Nat Sculpture Soc. Mem: Sculpture Ctr, New York; Nat Sculpture Soc. Style & Technique: Hammered lead figurative sculpture. Mailing Add: 1742 Corcoran St NW Washington DC 20009

CAVANAUGH, TOM RICHARD
PAINTER, EDUCATOR
b Danville, Ill, July 19, 23. Study: Univ Ill, BFA, 47, McLellan fel & MFA, 50; Fulbright grant to Italy, 56-57. Work: William Rockhill Nelson Gallery Art, Kansas City, Mo; Mulvane Art Mus, Topeka, Kans; Joslyn Art Mus, Omaha, Nebr; Ark Art Ctr, Little Rock; Isaac Delgado Mus Art, New Orleans. Exhib: Univ of Ill Contemp Am Painting, 48; Am Painting Today, Metrop Mus Art, New York, 50; Whitney Mus Am Art Ann, 51; Ft Worth Art Mus, 51; Boston Arts Festivals, 52 & 55; Mid-Am Annuals, Nelson Gallery of Art, 52, 53, 54 & 55; Mo Annuals, St Louis Mus of Art, 52, 54 & 56; Kans State Col Biennials, 54 & 56; Colorado Springs Fine Arts Ctr, 54 & 55; New Orleans Mus, 58, 59, 60, 61 & 63; Provincetown Nat Art Festival, 58; Southeastern Annuals, High Mus, Atlanta, Ga, 58, 59, 60, 61, 62, 63 & 65; Birmingham Mus, 59; Dallas Mus, 59; Corcoran Biennial Exhibs, Washington, DC, 59 & 61; Maine: 100 Artists of the 20th Century, Colby Col, Waterville, 64; Am Painting, Va Mus Quadriennial, Richmond, 62. Teaching: Instr painting & drawing, Kansas City Art Inst, 52-55 & Wash Univ Sch Fine Arts, 55-56; prof painting & drawing, La State Univ, 57- Pos: Art & educ dir, Springfield Art Asn, Ill, 47-49; dir, Bay St Studio, Boothbay Harbor, Maine, summers 50- Awards: Painting Prize for Athletics, La State Univ Union, 69; Winner, mural competition, Govt Bldg, Baton Rouge, La, 78. Bibliog: Bartlett H Hayes (auth), Artist and advocate, Renaissance Ed, 68. Style & Technique: Realist-impressionist. Media: Oil. Publ: Auth, A city is not built in a day: the architecture of Springfield, Illinois, 1819-1949, 49; contribr, Maine Artists Calendar, 67. Mailing Add: Bay St Studio Boothbay Harbor ME 04538

CAVAT, IRMA
PAINTER, EDUCATOR
b New York, NY. Study: New Sch Social Res; Archipenko Art Sch; Acad Grande Chaumiere, Paris; also with Ozenfant, Paris & Hans Hofmann. Comn: Murals, Vodun, Port-au-Prince, Haiti, 48 & pvt hotel, Athens, Greece, 70; wall of portraits, Fac Club, Univ Calif, Santa Barbara, 68; wall piece, Los Angeles, Calif, 70. Exhib: Recent Drawings, Mus Mod Art, New York, 50; Ill Nat, Urbana, 59; Festival of Two Worlds, Spoleto, Italy, 58-59; Ten Americans, Palazzo Venezia, Rome, 60; one-man shows, Santa Barbara Mus, Calif & Phoenix Mus, Ariz, 66-67; one-man shows also in Detroit, Chicago, Los Angeles, New York, Paris, Rome & Trieste. Teaching: Prof painting & drawing, Univ Calif, Santa Barbara, 64- Awards: Yaddo Fel, Trask Found, 50; Fulbright Fels, 56-58; Creative Arts Inst Award, Univ Calif, 70. Style & Technique: Figurative. Media: Acrylic, Oil, Mixed Media. Dealer: Arwin Galleries 222 Grand River W Detroit MI 48226. Mailing Add: Dept of Art Univ of Calif Santa Barbara CA 93106

CAVE, LEONARD EDWARD
SCULPTOR, EDUCATOR
b Columbia, SC, Oct 22, 44. Study: Furman Univ, BA; Univ Md, College Park, with Kenneth Campbell, MA. Work: Banker's Trust, Columbia, SC; Baptist Village, Waycross, Ga. Comn: Sculptural menorahs, Beth Torah Synagogue, Hyattsville, Md, 72; Duame Mem, Bells Mill Sch, Potomac, Md, 75. Exhib: Sculptors Guild Ann, New York, 71-75; Southeastern Mus Tour, Corcoran Gallery Art, 73; one-man shows, Sculpture Ctr, New York, 74, Wash Co Mus Fine Arts, Hagerstown, Md, 77, Malton Gallery, Cincinnati, Ohio, 77, George Meany Ctr for Labor Studies, Silver Spring, Md, 77 & HOM Gallery, Washington, DC, 78; Wash Sculpture, Wolfe St Gallery, 77. Teaching: Asst prof art, Georgetown Univ, 70-77. Awards: Chaim Gross Sculptor's Exhib First Prize, Nat Young Sculptors Guild, 69. Bibliog: William Bradley (auth), Art, Magic Impulse & Control, Prentice-Hall, 73. Mem: Sculptors Guild, New York; Artists Equity, Washington, DC (vpres, 73-75). Style & Technique: Nonobjective form emphasizing contruction and carving. Media: Stone; Wood. Dealer: Janak Khendry Sculpture Ctr 167 E 69th St New York NY 10021. Mailing Add: 10217 Oldfield Dr Kensington MD 20795

CAVER, WILLIAM RALPH
SCULPTOR, PAINTER
b Longview, Tex, Oct 11, 32. Study: NTex State Univ, BS; Univ Guanajuanto, MFA; Univ Barcelona. Work: Houston Mus Fine Arts; NTex State Gallery, Denton; Inst Allende Gallery, San Miguel de Allende, Mex. Comn: Sculpture, Louisville Libr, 71 & Texarkana Col Libr, Tex, 72. Exhib: Dallas Ann Libr Exhib, 63 & 64; Inst Allende Ann Show, 66; Texarkana Regional Art Show, 67-69; Denton Regional Art Show, 70; Paris, Tex Regional & Four States Regional, 74. Teaching: Instr art, Dallas Pub Sch Syst, 58-67; from assoc to prof art, Texarkana Col, 67- Awards: First Prize each yr, Texarkana Regional Art Show, 67-69, Denton Regional Art Show, 70 & Paris, Tex Regional, 74-76; Second Prize, Four States Regional, 74, First Prize, 77. Mem: Tex Asn Art Schs. Style & Technique: Welded metal sculpture with emphasis on an arrangement of found objects. Dealer: Casa Del Bosque Texarkana TX 75501. Mailing Add: Rte 6 Box 453 Texarkana TX 75501

CAWEIN, KATHRIN
PRINTMAKER, ILLUMINATOR
b New London, Conn, May 9, 95. Study: Art Students League, with George Bridgman, Allen Lewis & Harry Wickey. Work: Metrop Mus Art, New York; Nat Gallery, Washington, DC; Oberlin Col, Ohio; Tampa Univ, Fla; Pa State Univ. Comn: Illuminated manuscripts, St Marks Church, Van Nuys, Calif, St Andrew Church, Sarasota, Fla, Congregational Church, Colorado Springs, Colo & St John's Church, Pleasantville, NY Exhib: Tex Centennial, 32; Century of Progress (traveling exhib, US, Eng, France, Italy & Ecuador), 34; one-man show, Co Ctr, White Plains, NY, 35; World's Fair, 39; Village Art Ctr, New York, 45; Town Hall, New York, 50; 8th St Playhouse, New York, 53; Breezeway, Sarasota, Fla, 73; Tampa Univ, Fla, 73; Oberlin Col, 74; St John's Church, Pleasantville, 75; Berea Col, Ky, 76. Teaching: Etching, Westchester Co Workshop, White Plains, 35-36; drawing for children, pvt studio, 50-55. Awards: First Prize Drypoint, Pleasantville Women's Club, 50 & Fedn Women's Club, 51; Hon Mention, Hudson Valley Women's Club, 52. Mem: Art Students League; Nat Asn Women Artists, New York. Mailing Add: 35 Mountain Rd Pleasantville NY 10570

CECERE, ADA RASARIO
PAINTER
b New York, NY. Study: Art Students League; Beaux-Arts Inst New York; Nat Acad Design. Work: Norfolk Mus Arts & Sci, Va; Ohio Univ Founder's Collection, Athens; Oklahoma City Mus; Children's Hosp Founder's Libr, Baltimore; Am Art Arch, Smithsonian Inst, Washington, DC. Comn: Sand-carved mural, US Treas Dept Nat Competition, 47; Triptych, altar for Ft Gordon, US; mural, Hyde Park Restaurant, New York; mural, Lobby of Hotel Newton, New York. Exhib: Brooklyn Mus, NY, 60; Am Watercolor Soc Traveling Exhibs, 60 & 69; Richmond Mus Traveling Exhibs, 60-72; Asn Women Artists, US, Can, France & Italy, 72; Nat Soc Painters in Casein & Acrylics, 75-76; seven one-man shows, New York, NY & Pa, 60-72. Teaching: Pvt painting classes in studio, 47- Awards: Medal of Honor for Pastel, Nat Asn Women Artists, 55; Solo Exhib Award, Fairleigh Dickinson Univ, 63; Maria Cantarella Mem Prize, Allied Artists Am, 68; plus others. Mem: Audubon Artists (dir, 60-74); Nat Asn Women Artists (adv bd, 50-72); Allied Artists Am (award jury, 61-); Knickerbocker Artists (vpres, 57-59); Pen & Brush Club (officer, Brush Sect, 60-). Media: Oil, Watercolor. Mailing Add: 240 Waverly Pl New York NY 10014

CECERE, GAETANO
SCULPTOR, LECTURER
b New York, NY, Nov 26, 94. Study: Nat Acad Design; Beaux-Arts Inst Design; Am Acad in Rome, fel, 20-23. Work: Metrop Mus Art, New York; Numismatic Mus, NY; Norfolk Mus Art. Comn: Plaques, US Capitol, Washington, DC; reliefs, Fed Reserve Bank, Jacksonville, Fla; war mem, Clifton, Plainfield & Princeton, NJ; plus others. Exhib: Nat Sculpture Soc, 24-58; Nat Acad Design, 24-69; Allied Artists Am, 62-64; Knickerbocker Artists, 62-64; Audubon Artists, 62,

64 & 65; plus others. Teaching: Lectr contemp & ecclesiastical sculpture; former dir sculpture dept, Beaux-Arts Inst Design; former mem fac, Mary Washington Col & Sch Fine Arts, Nat Acad Design. Awards: Award in Sculpture, Nat Arts Club, 68; Sculpture Award, Audubon Artists, 69; Therese Richard Mem Award, Allied Artists Am, 70; plus others. Mem: Academician Nat Acad Design; Nat Sculpture Soc; New York Archit League. Mailing Add: 240 Waverly Pl New York NY 10014

CEDERSTROM, JOHN ANDREW
PAINTER, INSTRUCTOR
b Philadelphia, Pa, Apr 26, 29. Study: Philadelphia Col Art, study of illus with Henry Pitz, painting with Gertrude Schell & watercolor with Ben Eisenstat; Pa Acad Fine Arts, study of painting with Roswell Weidner. Work: Philadelphia Mus Art, Pa; Allentown Art Mus, Pa; UN UNICEF Collection, New York; Lehigh Univ, Bethlehem, Pa; Fed Reserve Bank, Philadelphia, Pa. Comn: Poster, Tinicum Wildlife Refuge, Philadelphia, Pa, 55; Corp logo, Am Medicorp, Riverside Gen Hosp, NJ, 76, FOCUS Orgn, Wallingford, Conn, 76 & Bala Libr, Bala Cynwyd, Pa, 76; posters & logo, Nat Coun for Arts & Educ, New York, 77. Exhib: 148th Ann Int, Pa Acad Fine Arts, Pa, 51; Regional Exhib, Philadelphia Mus Art, Pa, 54; one-man shows, Woodmere Art Gallery, Philadelphia, Pa, 69 & Lehigh Univ, Bethlehem, Pa, 76; 13th Ann Nat Exhib, Allentown Art Mus, Pa, 75; 34th & 36th Ann Audubon Artists, Nat Acad Design, New York, 76-78; The Artist Views the City, Philadelphia Art Alliance, Pa, 76; Print Show, Philadelphia Art Alliance, Pa, 76. Collections Arranged: Friends Cent Collection 40th Anniversary: Ernest Lawson to Karel Appel, 71, Wildlife in Art: Benefit Philadelphia Zoo Wolf Woods, 73, A Child's World: Benefit Exhib, 74, Women in Art: 1776-1976, 76 & Surrealism, Fantasy & Sci Fiction: Dali to Miro, 77, Friends' Cent Gallery, Philadelphia, Pa. Teaching: Dir art educ, Bryn Mawr Art Ctr, Pa, 53-63; chmn art & art hist, Friends' Cent Sch, Philadelphia, Pa, 63- Pos: Mem acquisitions comt, Woodmere Gallery, Philadelphia, Pa, 72-77; art chmn, Independent Sch Teachers Asn, Philadelphia, Pa, 77. Awards: Charles K Smith Prize, 14th Ann Exhib, Woodmere Art Gallery, Philadelphia, Pa, 54; First Prize, First Ann Etchers Show, Philadelphia Sketch Club, Pa, 54 & 1975 Graphics Ann, Chester Co Art Asn, West Chester, Pa, 75. Bibliog: Dorothy Grafly (auth), Artist Has His Own Zoo, Philadelphia Sunday Bull, Pa, 60; Eleanor Cederstrom (auth), A Poetry and Painting Festival, Gloucester Daily Times, Essex Co News, 77; Charles Movalli (auth), A Conversation With John Cederstrom, Am Artist, 78. Mem: Artists Equity Asn, Philadelphia Chap (treas & vpres, 65-71; chmn ethics comt, 68-77); Am Color Print Soc, Philadelphia, Pa; Philadelphia Print Club; Philadelphia Watercolor Club; Am Artists Prof League, New York. Style & Technique: Surreal and organic form in all media; landscape and floral elements in oil and silk screen. Media: Oil, silk screen. Dealer: Hahn Gallery 8439 Germantown Ave Philadelphia PA 19118. Mailing Add: 518 Prescott Rd Merion PA 19066

CEGLIA, VINCENT
PAINTER, INSTRUCTOR
b Braintree, Mass, Mar 11, 23. Study: Brooklyn Mus Sch of Art; Pratt Inst. Work: Pa State Univ; Educ Testing Serv, Princeton, NJ; Rider Col, Trenton, NJ; Cybis Porcelains Inc, Trenton, NJ; Raccolta Arte Moderna, Florence, Italy. Exhib: Newark Mus, NJ, 70; NJ State Mus, Trenton, 70-75; Philadelphia Mus of Art, 71; Philadelphia Art Alliance, 71 & 75; Butler Inst of Am Art, Youngstown, Ohio, 72; Am Watercolor Soc, 75-77; Cedar Rapids Art Ctr, Iowa, 77; Frye Mus, Seattle, Wash, 77. Teaching: Asst prof visual arts, Trenton Jr Col, 60-68; assoc prof visual arts, Mercer Col, 68; dir painting, Gargonza Painting Workshop, Tuscany, Italy, summers, 75-78. Awards: Best of Show, 3rd Regional Exhib Bristol, Bucks Co Art Collection, 67; 1st Patron Priza, Phillips Mill Ann Exhib, 68, 70 & 75; Traveling Show 77-78; 109th Am Watercolor Soc Show, 77. Mem: Am Watercolor Soc; Philadelphia Watercolor Club; Salmagundi Club, NY; Artists Equity; Philadelphia Art Alliance. Style & Technique: Semi-abstract landscapes in very large sizes. Media: Watercolor, acrylic; collage. Publ: Illusr, A History of American Art Porcelain, Renaissance Ed, NY, 67; illusr, Vaughn Associates Architects, Vaughn Assoc, 69; auth & illusr, Watercolor Page, Am Artist Mag, 77 & Am Artist Exec Calendar, 79. Mailing Add: RD 1 Washington Crossing PA 18977

CELENDER, DONALD DENNIS
ART HISTORIAN, CONCEPTUAL ARTIST
b Pittsburgh, Pa, Nov 11, 31. Study: Carnegie-Mellon Univ, BFA, 56; Univ Pittsburgh, MEd, 59, A W Mellon scholar, 60-63, PhD, 63. Work: Centro Arte y Communicacion & Mus Arte Mod, Buenos Aires; Allen Mem Art Mus, Oberlin Col, Ohio; Latrobe Mus, Pa; Gen Mills Collection, Minneapolis. Comn: Stained glass panels, Children's Hosp, Pittsburgh, 61; moving water sculpture, Nokomis Br, stained glass mural, Main Br, & Eva Rhodes Freeman Mem (stained glass mural), Lake St Br, Minneapolis Pub Libr, 67; mem (stained glass panels), St James Lutheran Church, Minneapolis, 68. Exhib: Walker Art Ctr Biennial, 64; Art in the Mind, Allen Mem Art Mus, 70; 2,972,453, Centro Arte y Comunicacion, Buenos Aires, 70; one-man shows, O K Harris Gallery, New York, 70-75; Art Systems I & II, Mus Arte Mod, Buenos Aires, 71-72. Teaching: Edith M Kelso prof art hist, Macalester Col, 64- Pos: Cur, Nat Gallery Art, 61-63; dir educ & pub activities, Minneapolis Inst Arts, 63-64. Awards: Man of Year in Art, Pittsburgh Jaycees, 61; fac, foreign & res fels, 67-75; Ford Fel in Humanities, 70-71. Bibliog: Gareth Hiebert (auth), Grand Canyon sweet & other delicacies, St Paul Pioneer Press & Dispatch, 5/28/72; Max Kozloff (auth), article in Art J, fall 73; Marcel Jean (auth), article in La Quinzaine Litteraire, 2/15/75; among others. Mem: Col Art Asn Am; Am Mus Asn; Delta Phi Delta; Minn Arts Forum; Minneapolis Soc Fine Arts. Res: Development of conceptual art movements and ideas. Publ: Auth, articles on Bellows, Caneletto, Duccio, DeHooch, Grunewald, Manet & Turner for Nat Gallery Art, 61-63; auth, Musical Instruments in Art, 65; auth, The Dance, 72; auth, Eight Conceptual Art Movements, 72; auth, Olympics of Art, 74; auth, Observation & Scholarship Examination for Art Historians, Museum Directors, Artists, Dealers & Collectors, 75. Dealer: O K Harris Gallery 383 W Broadway New York NY 10012. Mailing Add: 15 Duck Pass Rd St Paul MN 55110

CELENTANO, FRANCIS MICHAEL
PAINTER
b New York, NY, May 25, 28. Study: NY Univ Inst Fine Arts, MA, 57; Fulbright fel, 57; Acad Fine Arts, Rome, Italy, 58. Work: Mus Mod Art, New York; Albright-Knox Art Gallery, Buffalo; Columbia Broadcasting Co, New York; Seattle Art Mus, Wash; Rose Art Gallery, Brandeis Univ, Waltham, Mass. Comn: Painting, Hwy Bldg, Wash State Hwy Dept, 70; mural, Port of Seattle, Seattle-Tacoma Airport, 71. Exhib: The Responsive Eye, Mus Mod Art, New York, 65; Kinetic & Optical Art Today, 65 & Plus by Minus: Today's Half Century, 68, Albright-Knox Art Gallery; Whitney Ann, Whitney Mus Am Art, 67; Pacific Cities, Auckland City Art Gallery, New Zealand, 71. Teaching: Prof art, Univ Wash, 66- Awards: Int Artist's Sem Award, Fairleigh Dickinson Univ, 65. Bibliog: Faulkner (auth), Art Today, Holt, Rinehart & Winston, 69; Moore (auth), Letters from 31 Artists, Albright-Knox Art Gallery, 70; Kingsbury (auth), Art, Seattle Mag, 1/70. Style & Technique: Acrylic media on polyvynl chloride; paintings are cut, reassembled and laminated to plywood; vertical strips are displaced and reversed serially. Media: Acrylic. Dealer: Foster/White Art Gallery 311 1/2 Occidental S Seattle WA 98104. Mailing Add: 1919 1/2 Second Ave Seattle WA 98101

CELLI, PAUL
PAINTER, EDUCATOR
b Boston, Mass, May 8, 35. Study: Mass Col Art, BFA, 60; RI Sch Design, MFA, 62. Exhib: Providence Art Festival, RI, 61-69; New England Contemp Artists Asn, Boston, 63; Berkshire Mus, Pittsfield, Mass, 66; one-man shows, Bennett Col, Millbrook, NY, 67 & McIvor Reddie Gallery, Boston, 68 & 70. Teaching: Asst prof 4D theory, Mass Col Art, 70- Style & Technique: A semi-figurative style that attempts to show existence of time in pictorial form; 4D theory. Media: Oil, Tempera, Watercolor. Mailing Add: Walpole St Dover MA 02030 Boston MA Walpole St Dover MA 02030

CERNUSCHI, ALBERTO C
ART DEALER, ART CRITIC
US citizen. Study: Univ Milan, PhD; Univ Lausanne, PhD. Teaching: Lectr mod art, Ecole du Louvre, Mus Cernuschi. Pos: Founder, Cernuschi & Caravan de France Galleries, Paris, France & New York; trustee, Cernuschi Mus, Paris. Specialty: Modern art. Publ: Auth, Theory of Autodeism, Philos Libr. Mailing Add: c/o Caravan de France/Cernuschi Galleries 5 E 57th St New York NY 10022

CERVANTES, PEDRO
SCULPTOR
b Mexico City, Mex, Oct 10, 33. Study: Escuela Nac Artes Plasticas, San Carlos, Mex, 51-52. Work: Banco Fomento Cooperativo, Mex; Banco Attantico, Mex; Financiera Nuevo Leon, Mex; Leona Textil Bldg, Monterrey, Mex; Entrance to Port of Alvarado, Mex. Comn: Welded iron sculpture, Jorge Gonzalez Reyna, 62; iron sculpture, Inst Nac Vivienda, 65; Incongruente, chromed steel, Hojalata & Lamina Hylsa, 71; Euridice, steel, Club Industriales, A C, 72; Septentrion, chromed steel, Nylon Mex, 72. Exhib: New Values Show, Salon Plastica Mex, 62; Exhibition Young Artists Show, 65 & one-man show, 72, Mus Mod Art, Mexico City; Contemporary Mexican Painting, La Habana, Cuba, 65; Expo 67, Montreal, Que, 67. Awards: First Prize, Solar Exhib, Mex Ministry Educ, 68; First Prize, Ann Salon Sculpture & Engraving, Salon Plastica Mex, 72. Bibliog: Alfonso de Neuvillate & Luis Cardoza y Aragon (auths), Mexico pintura actual, Artes Mex; Raquel Tibol (auth), Pedro Cervantes o/a ahbivalencia, Excelsior, 2/72; Jorge Crespo de la Serna (auth), La escultura de Pedro Cervantes, Novedades, 3/72. Media: Welded Steel. Mailing Add: c/o Galeria de Arte Misrachi S A 20 Genova Mexico City 6 Mexico

CERVENKA, BARBARA
EDUCATOR, PAINTER
b Cleveland, Sept 28, 39. Study: Siena Heights Col, Studio Angelico, Adrian, Mich, 57-64, BA, 64; Wayne State Univ, Detroit, 67-69; Univ Mich, Ann Arbor, 69-71, MFA, 71. Work: Alumni Mem Mus, Univ Mich, Ann Arbor; Eastern Mich Univ, Sill Hall Art Collection, Ypsilanti. Exhib: Watercolor USA, Springfield, Mo, 69, 73 & 75; Mid-Mich Show, Midland, 71; Mich Watercolor Soc Show, Birmingham, 71, 72 & 74; Am Watercolor Soc Show, New York, 73; Toledo Area Artists Show, Ohio, 73. Teaching: Instr drawing & watercolor, Siena Heights Col, 71- Awards: Purchase Prize, Eastern Mich Univ, 71 & Watercolor USA, 73; First Prize, Toledo Area Artists Show, 73. Mem: Mich Watercolor Soc; Midwest Col Art Asn. Style & Technique: Drawing and calligraphy in abstract watercolors. Dealer: Habatat Galleries 1260 Telegraph Dearborn MI 48228. Mailing Add: 614 Oakwood Adrian MI 49221

CESAR, GASTON GONZALEZ
SCULPTOR
b San Felipe del Progreso, Mex, Feb 6, 40. Study: Escuela Nac Artes Plasticas, Prof (artes plasticas). Work: Stone sculpture, Fine Arts Gallery San Diego, Calif. Comn: Figure of Fray Bernardino de Sahagin en Cuidad Sahagin, Hidalgo, Mex, 62; figure of Guadalupe Victoria en Gomez Palacio, Durango, Mex, 64; stone sculpture, Inst Mexicano del Seguro Social, Oaxtepec; stone sculpture, Medicos de la Colonia (Epoca). Exhib: 2nd & 3rd Vienal Escultura Mexico, 64 & 66; Seccion Arte Pabellon Mexicano, New York World's Fair, 65 & Expo '67, Montreal, Can, 67; Tendencias del Arte Abstracto en Mexico, Mus Univ Mex, 67. Teaching: Prof art, Escuela Diseno Indust, Nat Univ Mex. Mailing Add: Hidalgo 30-B Coyocan 21 DF Mexico

CHADEAYNE, ROBERT OSBORNE
PAINTER
b Cornwall, NY, Dec 13, 97. Study: Colgate Univ; Art Students League; also with C K Chatterton, Henry Martin Hoyt, George Luks & John Sloan. Work: John Lambert Collection, Pa Acad Fine Arts; Columbus Gallery Fine Arts; Butler Inst Am Art; IBM Collection Am Art; Schumacker Collection, Capital Univ. Comn: Paintings, Broad & High St 1920, Trautman Off Bldg, Columbus, Ohio, 64 & Cent Ohio, 65; cityscape, Huntington Nat Bank, Columbus, 70. Exhib: Art Inst Chicago Ann; Pa Acad Fine Arts Ann; Nat Acad Design Ann, New York; Corcoran Biennial, Washington, DC; Butler Inst Am Art Midyear Nat Exhib, Youngstown, Ohio, 65-70. Teaching: Dir drawing & painting, Columbus Art Sch, 27-42; prof fine arts, Ohio State Univ, 42-63. Awards: Norman Waite Harris Medal, Art Inst Chicago, 20; Purchase Prize, Pa Acad Fine Arts, 20; IBM Medal for contribution to world of art. Mem: Columbus Art League (vpres, pres, 29-32 & mem bd dirs); Columbus Gallery Fine Arts (bd mgrs). Style & Technique: Direct painting with oil on canvas and masonite; pastel painting on pastel paper. Dealer: Capricorn Galleries 8003 Woodmont Ave Bethesda MD 20014. Mailing Add: Riverside Dr Dublin OH 43017

CHADWICK, WHITNEY
ART HISTORIAN, EDUCATOR
b Niagara Falls, NY, July 28, 43. Study: Middlebury Col, BA, 65; San Francisco Art Inst, Calif, 66; Pa State Univ, MA, 68, PhD, 75. Teaching: Assoc prof art hist, Mass Inst Technol, 72-; vis asst prof art hist, Univ Calif, Berkeley, 77. Pos: Juror, Art in Pub Places Prog, Cambridge Arts Coun & Nat Endowment for the Arts, 77-78. Res: Surrealist painting, contemporary art. Publ: Auth, Masson's Gradiva: the metamorphosis of a surrealist myth, Art Bull, 70; auth, Eros or Thanatos: the surrealist cult of love re-examined, Artforum, 75. Mailing Add: Mass Inst Technol Rm 3-309 Cambridge MA 02139

CHAET, BERNARD
PAINTER, EDUCATOR
b Boston, Mass, Mar 7, 24. Study: Boston Mus Sch, with Karl Zerbe, 42-45; Tufts Univ, BS, 49. Work: Fogg Art Mus, Harvard Univ; Univ Calif Art Gallery, Los Angeles; Brooklyn Mus, NY; Addison Gallery Am Art, Andover, Mass, RI Sch Design Mus, Providence. Exhib: Univ Ill Biennial Am Painting, 51, 53 & 60; Golden Years of American Drawing 1900-56, Brooklyn Mus, 56; Recent Drawings USA, Mus Mod Art, New York, 56; Corcoran Biennial Am Painting, Washington, DC, 62; Pa Acad Fine Arts Ann, Philadelphia, 62. Teaching: Prof drawing & painting, Yale Univ Art Sch, 51- Awards: Grant, Nat Found Humanities Arts, 66-67. Publ: Auth preface, 20th Century Drawing (catalog), Yale Art Gallery, 55; auth, Studio talk, monthly articles in Art Mag, 56-59; auth, Artists at Work, Webb, 61; auth, The Art of Drawing, Holt, 71, 2nd ed, 77; auth, An Artist's Notebook: Techniques and Materials,

Holt, 78. Dealer: Marilyn Pearl Gallery, New York, NY; Alpha Gallery 121 Newbury St Boston MA 02116. Mailing Add: 141 Cold Spring St New Haven CT 06511

CHAFETZ, SIDNEY
PRINTMAKER, EDUCATOR
b Providence, RI, Mar 27, 22. Study: RI Sch Design, BFA, 47; Acad Julian, Paris, 47-48; L'Ecole Am Beaux Arts, Fontainebleau, 47; with Fernand Leger, Paris, 48 & S W Hayter, Atelier 17, 50-51. Work: Libr Cong, Washington, DC; Cincinnati Art Mus; Nat Woodblock Inst, Tokyo; Philadelphia Mus Art; New York Pub Libr. Comn: Dedication etching, Ohio State Univ Col Law, 64; Hawthorne Keepsake, Ohio State Univ, 64; Robert Lowell Poster, Int Poetry Forum, Pittsburgh, Pa, 67; F Scott Fitzgerald Keepsake, Fitzgerald Newslett, Ohio State Univ, 68; Poor Richards Almanacks Original Woodblock Portrait, Imprint Soc, Barre, Mass, 70. Exhib: Ten Years of American Prints, 1947-57, Brooklyn Mus, NY, 57; Young American Printmakers, Mus Mod Art, New York, 58-59; 9th Int Expos Gravure, Switz, Norway & Sweden, 66; 1st Biennial Int Gravure Sur Bois, Banska Bystrica, Czech, 70; 2nd Triennial Int Graphica Contemp, Capri, Italy, 72; 30-Year Retrospective, Antioch Col & throughout Ohio, 78-79. Teaching: Prof art, Ohio State Univ, 48-; vis prof art, Univ Ariz, spring 65, Univ Wis-Madison, summer 67 & Univ Denver, summer 71. Awards: Tiffany Found Award, 49; Fulbright Fel, 50-51; Purchase Prize & Awards, 1st Biennial Int Gravure, Banska Bystrica, Czech, 70. Mem: Soc Am Graphic Artists; Am Color Print Soc; Am Asn Univ Prof. Style & Technique: Woodcut and intaglio processes are congenial media expressing ideas concerning politics, academe, and portraits of significant people. Dealer: Assoc Am Artists 663 Fifth Ave New York NY 10022. Mailing Add: Dept of Art Ohio State Univ Columbus OH 43210

CHAFFEE, JOHN W
SCULPTOR, LECTURER
b Huntington, WVa, Jan 24, 31. Study: Univ NC, Chapel Hill, AB(anthrop), 52; Art Students League, 56. Work: City of Algonac, Mich; City of Warren, Mich; Renaissance Ctr, Detroit, Mich; Hartland Arts Coun, Mich; Hermann Fine Arts Ctr, Marietta Col, Ohio. Comn: Sculpture (8ft x 15ft x 10ft), Novi Community Sch Dist, Mich, 76-77; sculpture (22ft x 17ft x 9ft), City of Algonac, Mich, 78-79; sculpture, Schoolcraft Col, Livonia, Mich, 78. Exhib: 4th Biannual Mich Artists Exhib, Grand Rapids Art Mus, Mich, 70; 58th Exhib for Mich Artists, Detroit Inst Arts, 70; one-man show, Huntington Galleries, WVa, 74; Mainstreams, Marietta Col, 74 & 75; Detroit Art Dealers Asn, Alpena, Mich, 75-76; Cranbrook Acad Art Mus, Bloomfield Hills, Mich, 76; Drawing & Small Sculpture Show, Ball State Univ, Muncie, Ind, 76; Regional Bicentennial Art Exhib, Eastern Ill Univ, Charleston, 76. Pos: Artists-in-the-sch adv panel, Sch Coun for the Arts, 77, visual arts adv panel, 78- Awards: Second Prize, Grand Rapids Art Mus, 70; Purchase Prizes, Mainstreams 75 & Hartland Arts Coun, 77. Bibliog: Wayne Loder (auth), 14 months work ends for Novi sculptor, Novi News, 5/4/77; Louis Cook (auth), Sculptor John thinks (and works) big, Detroit Free Press, 5/9/77; Corinne Abatt (auth), Sculpture moves, Birmingham Eccentric, Mich, 5/19/77. Mem: Southeastern Asn Sculptors; Mid-Mich Working Artists Asn. Style & Technique: Abstract sculpture in forged and welded steels. Media: Metal. Dealer: Robert L Kidd Assoc 107 Townsend St Birmingham MI 48011. Mailing Add: 46010 Nine Mile Rd Northville MI 48167

CHALAT ZIEGLER, JACQUELINE
See Ziegler, Jacqueline

CHALK, MR & MRS O ROY
COLLECTORS
Collection: Contemporary Art. Mailing Add: 1010 Fifth Ave New York NY 10028

CHALKE, JOHN
CERAMIST, SCULPTOR
b Gloucestershire, Eng, Sept 28, 40; Can citizen. Study: Bath Acad of Art, Wiltshire, Eng, teacher's cert art educ, 62. Exhib: Crafts Centre of Great Brit, 63, 64 & 67; Design Centre of Great Brit, 67-68; Brit Potters 68, Qantas Gallery, London, 68; Crafts Dimensions, Toronto, 69; Can Ceramics 69 & Can Ceramics 71, 69 & 71; Int Exhib of Rakuware, Copenhagen, 69; Better Design Can Exhib, Toronto, 69, 71, 73 & 75; Int Ceramics Exhib, Faenza, Italy, 70; Int Exhib of Ceramics, Victoria & Albert Mus, London, Eng, 72; Int Ceramics Exhib, Calgary, Alta, 73; 5th Int Ceramics Exhib, Vallauris, France, 76; 35th Concorso Int Della Ceramica d'Arte, Faenza, Italy, 77. Teaching: Instr ceramics, var art schs in Southern Eng, 64-68; instr visual fundamentals, Univ Alta, Edmonton, 71-76. Awards: Avant-Garde Award, Can Crafts Exhib, Toronto, 70; Award of Excellence, Can Olympic Exhib, Montreal, 76; Dipl d'Honneur, 5th Int Ceramics Exhib, Vallauris, 76. Bibliog: E Lewenstein (auth), New Ceramics, Van Nostrand Reinhold, 75; R Fournier (auth), Illustrated Dictionary of Practical Ceramics, Van Nostrand Reinhold, 73; C Tyler (auth), Low-Fire Ceramics, 77. Mem: World Crafts Coun; Int Acad of Ceramics; Can Crafts Coun; Ont Crafts Coun. Style & Technique: Sculptural and non-sculptural (wheel) use of clay. Media: Clay. Mailing Add: 429 12th St NW Calgary AB T2N 1V9 Can

CHALLIS, RICHARD BRACEBRIDGE
ART DEALER
b London, Eng, Aug 12, 20. Study: King's Col, London, 34-37; Chelsea Col, 38-39. Pos: Dir, Challis Galleries, 50-; art dir, Los Angeles Home Show, 65-67. Mem: Laguna Beach Mus Art; Art Dealers Asn Southern Calif. Specialty: 20th century paintings and sculpture, representing Rexford Brandt, Gerald Brommer, Philip Dike, Robert Frame, John Leeper, Frank M Hamilton and Dale Peche. Mailing Add: 1390 S Coast Hwy Laguna Beach CA 92651

CHALMERS, E LAURENCE, JR
ART ADMINISTRATOR, EDUCATOR
b Wildwood, NJ, Mar 24, 28. Study: Princeton Univ, AB(psychol), 48, MA(exp psychol), 50, PhD(exp psychol), 51. Pos: Dean col arts & sci, Fla State Univ, 64-66, vpres acad affairs, 66-69; chancellor, Univ Kans, 69-72; pres, Art Inst Chicago, 72- Mailing Add: Art Inst Chicago Michigan at Adams Chicago IL 60603

CHALMERS, MARY EILLEEN
ILLUSTRATOR
b Camden, NJ, Mar 16, 27. Study: Sch Indust Art, Philadelphia, 45-48; Barnes Found, 49-50. Style & Technique: Realism. Media: Watercolor, Pen & Ink; Pencil. Publ: Auth & illusr, A Christmas Story, 56 & Throw A Kiss, Harry, 57, Harper & Bros; auth & illusr, Take a Nap, Harry, 64, Harper & Row; illusr, Letitia Rabbit's String Song, 73 & When Daisies Died, And Violets Blue, 74, Coward, McCann & Geoghegan. Mailing Add: 1644 Oak Ave Haddon Heights NJ 08035

CHAMBERLAIN, BETTY
ART ADMINISTRATOR, WRITER
b Feb 10, 08. Study: Smith Col, AB; Sorbonne, Paris, with Henri Focillon. Pos: Metrop Mus Art, 29-32; Philadelphia Mus Art, 38-40; compiler & auth weekly art sect, Time Mag, 40-42; asst to dir & ed, Mus Mod Art Bull, New York, monthly, 40-42; Off War Info Domestic Graphic Prog, 42-43; publicity dir, Mus Mod Art, New York, 48-54; managing ed, Art News, 54-56; publicity & community develop dir, Brooklyn Mus, 56-59; founder & dir, Art Info Ctr, Inc, 59-; mem adv comt, Mus Am Folk Art, New York. Mem: Am Asn Mus. Publ: Auth, Lincoln Ctr & Carnegie Hall Programs (monthly art column), Sat Rev, 69-74; auth monthly column & features, In: Am Artist Mag, 71-; auth, Artist's Guide to His Market, 2nd ed, 75. Mailing Add: Art Info Ctr 189 Lexington Ave New York NY 10016

CHAMBERLAIN, CHARLES
CERAMIST, EDUCATOR
b Brockton, Mass, Aug 7, 42. Study: Mass Col Art, BFA; Col Ceramics, Alfred Univ, MFA. Work: Smithsonian Inst, Washington, DC; Archie Bray Found, Helena, Mont; Mass Col Art, Boston; Col Ceramics, Alfred Univ, NY. Exhib: Soc Arts & Crafts, Boston, 65; Artist, Craftsmen, Inst Art, Jacksonville, Fla, 73; one-man retrospective, NC Mus Art, Raleigh, 73; 27th Ceramics Nat, Everson Mus, Syracuse, NY, 74; Craft Multiples, Smithsonian Inst, Washington, DC, 75. Teaching: Instr ceramics, Worcester Art Ctr, Mass, 65; instr ceramics, Univ NH, 66-67; chmn art dept & assoc prof ceramics, East Carolina Univ, Greenville, NC, 67- Pos: Jury chmn, Carolina Designer Craftsmen, Raleigh, NC, 69-73; jury mem, Piedmont Craftsmen, Winston-Salem, NC, 74- Awards: Best in Show, Mass Assoc Craftsmen, 65; Merit Award, Emerging Craftsmen of New Eng, 65; Hon Mention, Piedmont Craftsmen Ann, 71. Mem: Piedmont Craftsmen; Carolina Designer Craftsmen; Am Crafts Coun. Style & Technique: Stoneware and salt glaze functional ware; sculpture, wheel-thrown and hand-built. Dealer: Appalachiana Old Georgetown Plaza Bethesda MD 20014; Piedmont Craftsmen 936 W Fourth St Winston-Salem NC 27101. Mailing Add: 2307 E Third St Greenville NC 27834

CHAMBERLAIN, JOHN ANGUS
SCULPTOR
b Rochester, Ind, Apr 16, 27. Study: Art Inst Chicago, 50-52; Univ Ill; Black Mt Col, 55-56. Work: Albright-Knox Gallery, Buffalo, NY; Los Angeles Co Mus Art; Mus Mod Art, New York; Univ NC; Rome Naz; plus others. Exhib: Contemporary American Sculpture, Selection I, Whitney Mus Am Art, 66; one-man show, Cleveland Mus Art, 67; HemisFair '68, San Antonio, Tex, 68; York Univ, Toronto, Ont, 69; Guggenheim Mus, 71; plus others. Awards: Guggenheim Fel, 66. Bibliog: Sam Hunter (ed), New Art Around the World: Painting & Sculpture, Abrams, 66; Wayne Craven (auth), Sculpture in America, Crowell, 68; Gregory Battcock (ed), Minimal Art: a Critical Anthology, Dutton, 68; plus others. Dealer: Leo Castelli Inc 4 E 77th St New York NY 10021. Mailing Add: c/o Leo Castelli Gallery 420 W Broadway New York NY 10012

CHAMBERS, JOHN
PAINTER, FILM MAKER
b London, Ont, Mar 25, 31. Study: Univ Western Ont, 52-53 & Hon LLD; Royal Acad Fine Arts, Madrid, Spain, DFA, 59; H B Beal Sec Sch. Work: Nat Gallery Can, Ottawa, Ont; Vancouver Art Gallery, BC; Art Gallery Ont, Toronto; Mus Mod Art, New York; Philadelphia Mus Fine Arts. Exhib: Forum Art Gallery, New York, 65; New York World's Fair, 65; Int Exhib, Paris, Brussels & Switz, 67; Art Gallery of Ontario Retrospective, Vancouver Art Gallery, 70; Gallery Contemp Art, Chicago, 71. Awards: Can Coun Grants, 67-70; Univ Alta Nat Award, Banff Sch Fine Arts, 72. Bibliog: Chambers (film), Fraser Boa Prod, 70 & Peter Mellen Prod, 74; Pierre Berton (interviewer), Jack Chambers, 71 & Man Alive, 71, CBC-TV. Mem: Assoc Royal Can Acad Arts; Nat Asn Artists, Can Artists Representation (pres, 68); London Film Co-op, Ont (founder, pres & dir, 68-). Style & Technique: Realism and traditional technique. Media: Oil, Ink, Pencil. Publ: Contribr, Chambers, Coach House Press, 67; auth, Perceptual Realism, Arts Can, 69; auth articles, In: Art in Am & Arts Int, 70; contribr, Modern Canadian Painting, McClelland & Stewart Ltd, 72; auth article on perceptualism, Arts & Artists, London, 12/72. Mailing Add: c/o Nancy Poole's Studio Ltd 554 Waterloo St London ON N6B 2P8 Can

CHAMBERS, KAREN SUE
ART HISTORIAN, ART DEALER
b Madison, Ind, Sept 28, 48. Study: Wittenberg Univ, 66-70, BFA, 73; Case-Western Reserve Univ, study with Wolfgang Stechow; Univ Cincinnati, MA, 78. Pos: Cur asst, Dayton Art Inst, Ohio, 70-73; asst registr, Cincinnati Art Mus, 75; asst cur, Contemp Arts Ctr, Cincinnati, 75-77; asst dir, Sperone Westwater Fischer, New York, 77- Mem: Col Art Asn; Am Asn Mus. Res: Ventriloquial figures; photographic career of Jane Reece. Specialty: Contemporary. Publ: Auth, Five Terra Cotta Figures from Syria, Dayton Art Inst, 72; auth/ed, Selections from the Collection of the Vent Haven Museum, Contemp Arts Ctr, 77. Mailing Add: Sperone Westwater Fischer 142 Greene St New York NY 10012

CHANDLER, DANA C, JR (AKIN DURO)
PAINTER, EDUCATOR
Study: Mass Col, Art, Boston, BS(art educ); consult with Benny Andrews, Romare Bearden & Nelson Stevens. Work: Mus Fine Arts, Boston; Mus Nat Ctr Afro-Am Arts, Boston. Comn: Murals, Massachusetts & Columbus Aves, 68, Intervale & Blue Hill Ave, 68, Grove Hall Libr, 70 & Zeigler St, Roxbury, 73, City of Boston; Bicentennial Comn, Boston 200 Painting Comn, 75. Exhib: 12 Black Artists from Boston, guest cur, Rose Mus, Brandeis, Mass, 68 & Studio Mus, Harlem, NY, 69; Afro-Am Artists, New York & Boston, Boston Mus Fine Arts, 70; Blacks/Now, New York Cult Ctr, 73; one-man show, Mus Nat Ctr Afro-Am Artists, 74; De Cordova Mus, Lincoln, Mass, 77; Lowell Mus, Mass, 78; Mass Col of Art, Boston, 78. Teaching: Asst prof painting & Black art hist, Simmons Col, 71-77, assoc prof African-Am art hist, 77-; asst prof Black art hist & resident artist, Northeastern Univ, 74- Pos: Interim dir art dept, Model Cities Consortium Col, 68-69; dir African arts curric proj, Educ Develop Ctr, 69-71; radio announcer/critic, What's Happening in Boston, Station WILD, 75; dir, African-Am Master Artist-in-Residence Prog, Northeastern Univ, 77- Awards: Simmons Col Grant for Research, 71, 72 & 73; Painter's Award, Nat Endowment for the Arts, 74; Artist-in-Residence grant, 100 Most Influential Blacks in Boston, Mass Coun on Arts & Humanities, 77-78. Bibliog: Waddy/Lewis (auth), Black artists on art, Contemp Craft Publ, Calif, 69; Elsa Honig Fine (auth), The Afro-American Artist, Holt, Rinehart, Winston, 73. Mem: Boston Black Artists Asn; Boston Visual Artists Union; Am Asn Univ Prof; Nat Conf (Black) Artists; Nat Soc Lit & the Arts. Style & Technique: Figurative, social commentary, still life, semi-abstract African imagery; drawing, silk screen, painting, sculpture. Media: Acrylic; Wood. Res: History of African American image makers documented through slides and tapes of living Black artists' words and works. Mailing Add: c/o African Am Master Artist in Res Prog Northeastern Univ Boston MA 02115

CHANDLER, ELISABETH GORDON
SCULPTOR
b St Louis, Mo, June 10, 13. Study: Pvt study with Edmondo Quattrocchi; Art Students League, anat. Work: Columbia Univ Sch Law; Princeton Univ Sch Pub & Int Affairs & James Forrestal Res Ctr; Aircraft Carrier USS Forrestal; Gov Dummer Acad Libr; Storm King Art Ctr, Mountainville, NY. Comn: Bust of Owen R Cheatham, Founder, Georgia Pac Corp, bust of Albert A Michelson, Hall of Fame for Great Americans, NY Univ, 73; Adlai E Stevenson High Sch, 74; Messiah Col, Grantham, Pa, 75; statue of Queen Anne, Queen Anne's Co Courthouse Sq, Centerville, Md, 77. Exhib: Mattituck Mus, Waterbury Conn, 49; Nat Acad Design Ann, New York, 50-78; Nat Sculpture Soc Ann, 53-78; Acad Artists, Springfield, Mass, 61; Smithsonian Inst, Washington, DC, 63. Pos: Dir, Coun Am Artist Soc, 71-73; trustee & instr portrait & sculpture, Lyme Acad Fine Arts, 77- Awards: Gold Medal, 75 & Huntington Award, 76, Am Artists Prof League; Founder's Prize, Pen & Brush, 76; Gold Medal, 75 & Newington Award, 76, Hudson Valley Art Asn. Mem: Fel Nat Sculpture Soc (rec secy, 73-76, coun, 76-); fel Int Inst Arts & Lett; fel Am Artists Prof League (dir, 71-73); Nat Sculpture Rev (bd mem); Lyme Art Asn (vpres, pres, 75-). Style & Technique: Traditional style sculpture, primarily in bronze; portraiture, medals, monumental and garden sculpture. Media: Bronze, Marble. Mailing Add: Mill Pond Lane Old Lyme CT 06371

CHANDLER, JOHN WILLIAM
PAINTER, INSTRUCTOR
b Concord, NH, Sept 28, 10. Study: Exeter Sch Art, Boston; Manchester Inst Arts & Sci; St Anselms Col, AB; Boston Univ, scholar, 59-60, EdM; Harvard Univ; Columbia Univ; study in Europe & with Aldro T Hibbard. Work: Pvt collections only. Exhib: Represented NH in Pasadena Nat, 46; Currier Gallery Art Regional, 47; one-man show, Keene State Col, 51; De Cordova & Dana Mus, 52; Nebr Wesleyan Univ, 58. Collections Arranged: Cataloged Richard J Healey Collection, Currier Gallery Art. Teaching: Exec dir & instr design & painting, Manchester Inst Arts & Sci, 33-46; assoc prof art & head dept, Lycoming Col, 52-70; instr painting, Concord Artists, Inc, 71-72; instr, Studio Two, 72- Pos: From asst to dir to actg dir, Currier Gallery Art, 42-52. Awards: First Watercolor Award, Currier Gallery Art, 47; Danforth Found Award, 52. Mem: Concord Artists (founding mem); NH Art Asn (charter mem & former pres). Publ: Auth var articles on glass & silver. Mailing Add: 2 Coolidge Ave Concord NH 03301

CHANG, DAI-CHIEN
PAINTER
b Szechwan, China, May 19, 99. Study: Col Chinese Cult, Taipei, Hon Dr, 68. Work: The Lotuses, Jeu de Paume Mus, Paris; Mus Mod Art, New York; The Great Yangtze River, Nat Hist Mus, Taipei, 68. Exhib: One-man shows, Peking, 34, Shanghai, 37, New Deli, 50, Athens, 60, Los Angeles, 73; plus many others. Awards: Gold Medal, Int Coun Fine Arts, NY, 58. Mailing Add: PO Box 3543 Carmel CA 93921

CHANNING, SUSAN ROSE
ART ADMINISTRATOR, PHOTOGRAPHER
b Englewood, NJ, Aug 16, 43. Study: Pa State Univ, University Park, BA(fine arts) & BA(gen arts & sci), 65; George Washington Univ, Washington, DC, MFA, 67. Exhib: 18th Ann Corcoran Gallery of Art Area Show, Washington, DC, 67. Collections Arranged: Design in Transit, State Subway Station Competition, 71 & Points of View, Recent Work By Area Photographers (auth, catalog), 72, Inst of Contemp Art, Boston: Photography Fellowship Recipients, Enjay Gallery, Boston, 76; Prints & Drawings, Frank Tanzer Gallery, Boston, 77; Art of the State, Recipients & Finalists in Painting, Printmaking & Drawing, Rose Art Mus, Brandeis Univ, Waltham, Mass, 77; Photography Fellowship Recipients, Mass Inst of Technol Creative Photog Gallery, Cambridge, Mass, 78. Teaching: Instr photog & serigraphy, Wadsworth Atheneum, Hartford, Conn, 68-70. Pos: Performing arts prog coordr & art instr, Wadsworth Atheneum, Hartford, Conn, 68-70; dir urban action prog & spec proj, Inst of Contemp Art, Boston, 70-72; asst dir, Mass Coun on the Arts & Humanities, Boston, 72-73; dir artists fel prog, Mass Arts & Humanities Found, Boston, 73- Media: Black and White Photography, Photo-Serigraphy. Publ: Auth & ed, Art of the State—Massachusetts Photographers 1975-1977, Addison House, 78. Mailing Add: 8 W Hill Pl Apt 1 Boston MA 02114

CHAPIAN, GRIEG HOVSEP
PAINTER, CONSERVATOR
b Varna, Bulgaria, May 27, 13; US citizen. Study: Cooper Union, 30-31; Nat Acad Design, 31-36, with Leon Kroll, Karl Anderson, Charles C Curran, Arthur S Covey, Francis Scott Bradford, Jr, Gifford Beal, Charles S Chapman & Ivan Olinsky. Work: Univ Eastern NMex; NMex State Fair Permanent Collection, Albuquerque. Comn: Two murals for Auto Racing Syndicate, Johannesburg, SAfrica, 39. Exhib: Allied Artists Am, New York, 36; Pa Acad Fine Arts, Philadelphia, 37; 1st Nat Wartime Art Show, Camden, NJ, 44; NMex State Fair Art Exhib, Albuquerque, 71; Grand Nat Exhib, Am Artists Prof League, New York, 72; Int Art Show, Univ Eastern NMex, Portales, 75. Teaching: Dir hist art & landscape, Murray Art Schs, Scranton & Wilkes-Barre, Pa, 48-50; dean & dir figure drawing & painting, Cooper Sch Art, Cleveland, 50-55; dean fashion illus & philos of art, Pan-Am Art Sch, New York, 60-66. Pos: Mem bd dirs, NMex Art League, 69-71; founder & dir, Albuquerque Inst Art, 74- Awards: Grand Prize & First for Oils, Local One, CIO, 44; First for Oils & Best of Show for Graphics, NMex Art League, 69; Purchase Prize, NMex State Fair, 74. Bibliog: Louise Bruner (auth), Commercial shows now rival fine art, Cleveland News, 12/15/51; Flo Wilks (auth), Magic realism in noted artist's work reflects his wide range of interests, Albuquerque J, 6/14/70; Lynn B Villella (auth), Chapian work top winner, Albuquerque Tribune, 9/12/74. Mem: Am Artists Prof League; Southwest Watercolor Soc; Artists Equity Asn (pres, 73-74); Nat Art League. Style & Technique: Southwestern landscapes and figure paintings, realistic with subtle blendings of surrealism and magic-realism. Dealer: Fields Art Gallery PO Box 2053 Raton Rd Taos NM 87571. Mailing Add: 1850 Gretta St NE Albuquerque NM 87112

CHAPIN, LOUIS (LE BOURGEOIS)
WRITER, ART CRITIC
b Brooklyn, NY, Feb 6, 18. Study: Principia Col, BA; Boston Univ, AM. Teaching: Asst prof fine arts, Principia Col, 46-60; tutor & consult writing, Empire State Col, 73. Pos: Staff critic, Christian Sci Monitor, 60-66; dir, The Earl Rowland Found, New York, 67-; theater critic, Christianity & Crisis, New York, 70-; book & classical record critic, NBC Radio, 75. Interest: Audio filmstrips documenting major art exhibitions. Publ: Contribr, Fifty Masterpieces, Charles M Russell, Crown; contribr, Music at the Cross-roads, Macmillan; auth, numerous reviews & articles in nat publ. Mailing Add: 7 Dandy Dr Cos Cob CT 06807

CHAPLIN, GEORGE EDWIN
PAINTER, EDUCATOR
b Kew Gardens, NY, Aug 30, 31. Study: Yale Univ Sch Art, with Josef Albers, BFA & MFA. Work: Yale Univ Gallery; State Univ NY Col Cortland. Exhib: Feingarten Galleries, Los Angeles, 64-65 & Bednarz Galleries, 67; State Univ NY Col Cortland, 69; Carpenter Ctr, Harvard Univ, 74; Univ Conn, 74. Teaching: Head dept painting, Silvermine Col Art, 65-71; dir studio prog, Trinity Col, Hartford, Conn, 72-, acting chmn dept fine arts, 75-77, assoc prof fine arts, 77- Scaling of space through color via landscape themes. Media: Oil. Mailing Add: Box 488 ORS Oxford CT 06483

CHAPMAN, DAVE
DESIGNER
b Gilman, Ill, Jan 30, 09. Study: Armour Inst Technol, BS, 32. Teaching: Consult & vis lectr, Design & Develop Ctr, Northwestern Univ, currently. Pos: Head prod design div, Montgomery Ward & Co, 34-36; sr partner, Dave Chapman, Indust Design, 36-58; pres, Design Res, Inc, 55-; pres, Dave Chapman Design, Inc, 58- Awards: Design Award Medal, Indust Designers Inst, 54 & 60; numerous awards & citations, Am Inst Graphic Arts, Soc Typographic Arts & Art Dirs Club. Mem: Fel Am Soc Indust Designer (bd dirs & past pres); life mem Art Inst Chicago; Soc Typographic Arts; Benjamin Franklin fel Royal Soc Arts; fel Int Inst Arts & Lett. Mailing Add: 3240 N Lake Shore Dr Chicago IL 60657

CHAPMAN, MRS GILBERT W
COLLECTOR, PATRON
b Evanston, Ill. Study: Atelier Julien, Paris; Art Inst Chicago; also with Fernand Leger. Pos: Pres, Art Club Chicago, 31-40. Mem: Int Coun Mus Mod Art, New York; fel Metrop Mus Art, New York; fel Pierpont Morgan Libr; Whitney Mus Am Art; Mus Primitive Art. Collection: Modern art; Polynesian art; pre-Columbian art. Mailing Add: 1 Sutton Pl S New York NY 10022

CHAPMAN, HOWARD EUGENE
ART DIRECTOR, CARTOONIST
b Martinsburg, WVa, Dec 20, 13. Study: Corcoran Sch Art, with Richard Lahey; George Washington Univ, BS; Tiffany Found, with Hobart Nichols. Work: Corcoran Gallery Art. Pos: Art dir, Cong Quart Serv, Inc, Washington, DC; creator self-syndicated daily comic panel, Federal Fidgets; designer, publ, ed graphics, bk covers, direct mail promotion, ed cartoons & caricatures. Awards: Prize, Washington Co Mus Fine Arts, Hagerstown, Md, 39; Tiffany Found Scholar; Bronze Medal, Washington Art Club, 48. Style & Technique: Landscapes; drawings and paintings with religious themes. Media: Watercolor, Acrylic. Mailing Add: Congressional Quart Inc 1414 22nd St NW Washington DC 20037

CHAPMAN, ROBERT GORDON
JEWELER, PAINTER
b Los Angeles, Calif, 26, 41. Study: Ventura Col; San Jose Univ, with Fred Spratt & J Richard Sorby, BA(painting), with David Hatch, John Leary & Dr Robert Coleman, MA(jewelry design), Pupil Serv Credential(career coun in visual arts). Work: Metal Arts Guild, San Francisco; San Jose State Univ Gallery; San Jose Art League. Comn: Moon Pendant (commemorating first lunar landing), 68; Ring, comn by David San Jose, 69; plus pendants, rings, pins & body adornment comn by various individuals. Exhib: Art '65, Univ Santa Clara; Calif Expos of the Arts, 66-69; Crafts 10, 67; Western US Traveling Exhib, 68; Triton Mus, Santa Clara, Calif, 69. Teaching: Instr art & chmn dept, Piedmont Hills High Sch, San Jose, 64-74; instr jewelry & metalsmithing, West Valley Col, Saratoga, Calif, 66-; coun visual arts, Santa Teresa High Sch, San Jose, 74- Pos: Dir, Group 21 Gallery, Los Gatos, Calif, 72-73; mem art educ screening comt, San Jose State Univ, 73- Awards: Ellen Brucker Jewelry Award, 69; Achiever of the Year in Art, Nat Pen Women Asn, 69; San Jose Regional Art Second Award, 75. Mem: Metal Arts Guild San Francisco; Calif Art Educators Asn. Style & Technique: Interpretive, stylistic approach to the humor and pathos of symbolic family and cultural groups to the idealistic landscape; paintings employ hard-edge/mixed media; jewelry uses lost-model, fabrication and forging. Media: Aqueous Media, Organic Material, Silver, Gold. Publ: Auth, An Analysis of Photomicrography as a Design Source for Lost-Model Jewelry 69. Mailing Add: 6060 Loma Prieta Dr San Jose CA 95123

CHAPMAN, WALTER HOWARD
PAINTER, ILLUSTRATOR
b Toledo, Ohio, Dec 7, 12. Study: Cleveland Inst of Art; John Huntington Polytech, Cleveland; Art Students League; study of portraiture with Rolf Stoll, Cleveland, and of figure painting with Jon Corbino, New York. Work: Toledo Fedn of Art Collection, Toledo Mus of Art; Zanesville Art Mus, Ohio; Springfield Mus of Art, Mo; Hallmark Collection, Mo; Univ Toledo. Comn: Two portraints, comn by St Vincents Hosp, Toledo, 68; landscape, Toledo Hosp, 70; two portraits, Law & Sci Bldgs, Univ Toledo, 70 & 77; Bicentennial painting, Waterville Chamber of Commerce, Ohio, 76; three portraits, First Fed Bank, Toledo, 77. Exhib: Fedn of Art Ann, Toledo Mus of Art, 50-77; one-man shows, Toledo Mus of Art, 58 & 65, Sienna Heights Col, Adrian, Mich, 62; Art in Embassies, Katmandu, Napel, 65; Allied Artists in Am, Nat Acad of Design, New York, 70; Watercolor USA, Springfield Mus of Art, Mo, 72; Grand Prix de Deauville, France, 72; Zanesville Mus of Art, 73 & Ella Sharp Mus, Jackson, Mich, 74; Springfield Art Ctr, Ohio, 74; Ohio Watercolor Show, Capital Univ, Columbus, Ohio, 74; Mid-Yr Ann, Butler Mus of Art, Youngstown, Ohio, 75. Teaching: Instr illus, Toledo Mus Sch of Design, 50-54; instr portrait & figure, Toledo Artists Club, 55-64. Pos: Illusr, New York, 39-42; combat artist, US Army, 43-45; creative dir, Phillipps Assoc, Toledo, 46-; owner, Chapman Art Gallery, Sylvania, 70- Awards: Purchase Award, Watercolor USA, Hallmark, 71-72; First Award, Summer Show, Salmagundi Club, New York, 72; First Prize & Purchase Award, Mainstreams Ann, Marietta Col, Ohio, 73. Bibliog: Murray Kalis (auth), article in Art Rev, 68. Mem: Allied Artists of Am; Salmagundi Club of New York; Toledo Fedn of Art Soc (pres, 54-56); Art Dir Club of Toledo (pres, 62-63); NW Ohio Watercolor Soc (pres, 71-72). Style & Technique: Realistic style; impressionistic technique. Media: Watercolor, oil. Publ: Contribr (cartoons), Stars & Stripes & Railsplitte, US Army newspapers, 45; illusr, Battle of Germany, Viking Press, 46; contribr ed cartoons, Toledo Monitor, 65; contribr, Prize Winning Art, Allied Publ, 66; contribr (cover art), Exhibit Mag, 67. Dealer: Chapman Art Gallery 5151 S Main St Sylvania OH 43560. Mailing Add: 6001 Gregory Dr Sylvania OH 43560

CHAPPELL, BERKLEY WARNER
PAINTER, PRINTMAKER
b Pueblo, Colo, Mar 21, 34. Study: Univ Colo, BFA, 56, MFA, 58. Work: San Francisco Mus Art; Henry Gallery, Univ Wash, Seattle; Tacoma Mus Art, Wash; Univ BC, Vancouver; Salishan Lodge, Gleneden Beach, Ore. Exhib: Young West Coast Artists, Pasadena, Calif, 59; Abstract Expressionism Today, San Francisco, 60 & Landscape Painting Today, 61; Am Printmaking Today, Ger, Greece, France, 69; Grand Gallerie, Seattle, 75. Teaching: Asst painting, Univ Colo, 56-58; instr to asst prof painting, Univ Puget Sound, Tacoma, 58-63; asst prof to prof painting & printmaking, Ore State Univ, Corvallis, 63- Awards: Purchase Awards, San Francisco Art Inst, 61 & Henry Gallery, Univ Wash, 64 & 69. Media: Oil; Engraving. Mailing Add: Ore State Univ Corvallis OR 97331

CHAPPELL, WARREN
DRAFTSMAN, GRAPHIC ARTIST
b Richmond, Va, July 9, 04. Study: Univ Richmond, BA; Art Students League; Offenbacher Werkstatt, Ger; Colorado Springs Fine Arts Ctr; also with George Bridgman, Allen Lewis, Boardman Robinson & Rudolf Koch; Univ Richmond, Hon DFA, 68. Work: Newberry Libr, Chicago; Alderman Libr, Charlottesville, Va; New York Pub Libr. Teaching: Instr drawing & graphic arts, Art Students League, 32-35; instr drawing & graphic arts, Colorado Springs Fine Arts Ctr, 35-36. Awards: Goudy Award, Rochester Inst Technol, 70. Bibliog: Isabel Bishop (auth), foreword to Sixty-three Drawings by Warren Chappell, The Typophiles, New York, 55. Style & Technique: Figurative drawing with pen, sometimes with wash or color; calligraphic design. Publ: Illusr, The Temptation of Saint Anthony, Ltd Ed Club, 43; illusr, The History of Tom Jones, Illus Mod Libr, 43; auth, A short history of the printed word, New York Times, 70; auth, The Living Alphabet, Univ Va, 75; illusr, Moby-Dick, Norton, 75; plus others. Mailing Add: James St RR 3 Norwalk CT 06850

CHAPPELLE, JERRY LEON
EDUCATOR, SCULPTOR
b Fredericktown, Mo, Nov 14, 39. Study: Murray State Univ, BS; Univ Minn, MFA. Work: High Mus Art, Atlanta, Ga; Greenville Co Mus of Art, SC; Ga Coun of the Arts; Mus of Arts & Crafts, Columbus, Ga. Comn: Floor, wall sculpture & exterior sculpture, Kenneth Jordon Collection, Athens, Ga, 78. Exhib: Nat Ceramic Arts Exhib, Flagstaff, Ariz, 73; Fun and Fantasy, Xerox Corp Gallery, Rochester, NY, 73; Fantasy Invitational, Fairtree Gallery, New York, 74; Biggies & Buddies Nat Exhib, Macon, Ga, 74; Regional Invitational, Gallery Contemp Art, Winston-Salem, NC, 75. Teaching: Instr ceramics, Univ Minn, 69-70; asst prof ceramics, Univ Ga, 70-76. Pos: Dir, Scorpio Rising Workshops, 70-77. Awards: Two First Prizes, Atlanta Arts Comt, 75; Second Prize, Covington Arts Exhib, Covington Art Ctr, 74. Bibliog: Larry Smith (auth), Ceramic Art (movie), Univ Ga, 74; Evolution of the artist craftsman in Georgia, highlight of contemp ceramics, (movie), Ga NEA-TV, 74. Mem: Am Crafts Coun; Ga Designers; Piedmont Craftsmen Inc. Style & Technique: Fantasy and a love to develop humor as an art form; clay and color are spontaneous. Media: Clay, Glass. Mailing Add: Rte 3 Box 278 Farmington GA 30638

CHARLOT, JEAN
PAINTER, ART HISTORIAN
b Paris, France, Feb 7, 98; US citizen. Work: Metrop Mus Art & Mus Mod Art, New York; Philadelphia Mus Art; Mus Arte Mod, Mex; Acad Arts, Honolulu. Comn: Frescoes, comn by Mex Govt, Escuela Preparatoria, Mexico City, 22, Univ Ga, 44, First Nat Bank, Hawaii, 66 & Leeward Community Col, Oahu, Hawaii; ceramic tile mural, United Pub Workers Bldg, Honolulu, 70-75; plus others. Exhib: One-man shows, Calif Palace of Legion of Honor, San Francisco, 42 & US Cult Ctr, Maracaibo, Venezuela, 67; Smith Col Mus, 48; Fifty Years Retrospective, 1916-1966, Honolulu Acad Arts, 66; retrospective, Mus Arte Mod (cult event for Olympics), Mexico City, 68. Teaching: Instr painting, Art Students League, 33-42; artist in residence, Univ Ga, 42-44; vis prof painting, Smith Col, 44-45; Ryerson lectr, Yale Univ, 47; dir art sch, Colorado Springs Fine Arts Ctr, 47-49; sr prof painting & art hist, Univ Hawaii, Honolulu, 49-67, emer sr prof, 67- Awards: Guggenheim Fel, 45-47; Metrop Mus Art Fel in Perpetuity, 60; Sr Specialist, East-West Ctr, US Govt, 67; Nat Coun Arts Grant, 68. Bibliog: Charlot Murals in Georgia, Univ Ga, 45; George Tahara (producer), films, Cine-Pic, Syracuse Univ, 55, 60, 72 & 74. Mem: Benjamin Franklin fel Royal Soc Arts; Col Art Asn Am; Hawaiian Hist Soc; Hawaiian Painters & Sculptors. Res: Hawaiian historical research; archaeology of Yucatan; Mexican art both colonial and modern. Collection: Mexican pre-Hispanic; Pacific Island artifacts; modern art. Publ: Auth, Mexican Art and the Academy of San Carlos, Univ Tex, 62; auth, Mexican Mural Renaissance: 1920-1925, Yale Univ, 63; auth, Three Plays of Ancient Hawaii, 63 & An Artist on Art, 72, Univ Hawaii; auth, Picture Book II, 73. Mailing Add: 4956 Kahala Ave Honolulu HI 96816

CHARLOT, MARTIN DAY
PAINTER, ILLUSTRATOR
b Athens, Ga, Mar 6, 44. Work: Bishop Mus, Honolulu. Comn: Mural, Konawena High Gym, 75-76. Exhib: One-man shows, Gima Art Gallery, Honolulu, 64 & 69, De Mena Gallery, New York, 67 & Hawaii State Libr, Honolulu, 72. Teaching: Lectr art-film, Univ Hawaii, 62-; lectr filmmaking, St John's Univ, 69; teacher cinema, Honolulu Acad Arts, 70; artist in residence, Doe Sch Syst, Hawaii, 75. Pos: Illusr, Collins Assoc, New York, 69; art dir, Bravura Films, Mountain View, Calif, 70. Mem: Hawaii Painters & Sculptors League. Style & Technique: Real, surreal. Media: Oil, Pencil. Publ: Illusr, Mystery on the Rancho Grande, Young Scott Bks, 69; illusr & contribr, Our Hawaiian Music, 71; auth & illusr, Once Upon a Fishhook, 72 & Sunnyside Up, 72 & illusr, Felisa, 73, Island Heritage Press. Mailing Add: PO Box 979 Pahoa HI 96778

CHASE, ALICE ELIZABETH
EDUCATOR, WRITER
b Ware, Mass, Apr 13, 06. Study: Radcliffe Col, with G H Edgell & P J Sachs, AB; Yale Univ, with Henri Focillon, Sumner Crosby & G H Hamilton, MA. Teaching: Lectr iconography hist art; docent, Art Gallery, Yale Univ, 31-70, asst prof hist art, 46-70, emer prof, 70- Pos: Cur educ, Brooklyn Mus, 46-47. Awards: Citations, Wilson Col & Radcliffe Col, 69. Mem: Archaeol Inst Am; Col Art Asn Am. Publ: Auth, Famous Paintings, an Introduction to Art for Young People, 51, 61 & 62 & Famous Artists of the Past, 64, Platt; auth, Looking at Art, Crowell, 66 & 74. Mailing Add: 18 Pleasant St Ware MA 01082

CHASE, ALLAN (SEAMANS)
SCULPTOR, DESIGNER
Study: Univ Ga, BFA. Comn: Brass on steel, Sherwood Theatre, Gainesville, Ga, 66 & Oxford Chem Co, Atlanta, 67; welded steel, Woodward Acad, College Park, Atlanta, 68; five steel murals, Gi-Gi's Restaurant, Rochester, NY & 17 steel & polyester murals, Fla, 71-75. Exhib: 5th Biennial Nat Relig Art Exhib, Bloomfield, Mich, 66; Southeastern Ann Exhib, Atlanta, 66 & 68; Piedmont Park Arts Festival, Atlanta, 66-72; Mus Arts & Sci, Macon, Ga, 67; C & S Bank, Atlanta, 75. Pos: Designer, Gi-Gi's Restaurants, Fla, Atlanta, Ga & Rochester, NY, 65- Mem: High Mus Art, Atlanta. Style & Technique: Cold rolled steel, ground, welded, brazed and coated with transparent dyes. Media: Steel and other metals. Mailing Add: 5435 Peachtree Rd Atlanta GA 30341

CHASE, DORIS (TOTTEN)
SCULPTOR, FILM MAKER
b Seattle, Wash, Apr 29, 23. Study: Univ Wash; also with Mark Tobey. Work: Mus Mod Art, Kobe, Japan; Art Inst Chicago; Pa Acad Fine Arts, Philadelphia; Nat Collection Fine Arts, Washington, DC; Mus Fine Arts, Boston; plus many others. Comn: Monumental Kinetic Sculpture, Expo '70, Osaka, Japan, Atlanta Sculpture Park, Ga, Kerry Park, Seattle, Wash & four ballets, Seattle Opera Asn, Wash; Play-Ground of Tomorrow, Los Angeles. Exhib: One-man shows, Ruth White Gallery, New York, 67, 69 & 70, Formes Gallery, Tokyo, Japan, 63 & 70, Henry Gallery, Univ Wash, Seattle, 71 & Western Mus Asn Circulating Exhib, 70-72; Wadsworth Atheneum, Hartford, Conn, 73; plus many other one-man & group shows. Bibliog: Article in Geijutsh-Schincho, Tokyo, 4/70; Robert Heyer & Richard Payne (auth), Discovery Patterns, S I Paulist-Newman, 71; Louis Chapin (auth), article in Christian Sci Monitor, 2/10/71; plus many others. Publ: (Films), The Expanding Universe of Sculpture, Hartley Prod, Mantra, ABC-TV, Seattle, Doris Chase—Sculpture on the Move, William Jenson Prod, Tondo, King Screen & Circles II (computer animated), Creative Film Soc. Mailing Add: c/o Chelsey Hotel 222 W 23rd New York NY 10011

CHASE, ROBERT M
ART DEALER, COLLECTOR
b Chicago, Ill, Dec 5, 40. Study: Univ Wis, BS. Pos: Pres & ed newsletter, Merrill Chase Galleries, 64- Mem: Am Soc Appraisers; Mus Contemp Art, Chicago; Art Inst Chicago. Specialty: American, European and South American pre-17th and 20th century paintings, prints, drawings and sculptures. Collection: Mixed media, Dali, Kipniss, Rembrandt, Durer, Addison, Renoir, Likan, Chagall & Picasso. Publ: Ed, Story of Prints, 77 & Rediscovered Printmakers of the 19th Century, 78, Merrill Chase Galleries. Mailing Add: Merrill Chase Art Galleries 225 Fencl Lane Hillside IL 60162

CHASE, SAUL ALAN
PAINTER
b New York, NY, Apr 7, 45. Study: City Col New York, BFA, 65, MFA, 68. Work: Detroit Inst Art, Mich; Ga Mus Art, Univ Ga, Athens; Brooklyn Mus Art, NY; Sara Roby Found, New York; High Mus, Atlanta, Ga. Exhib: Nat Acad Design Ann, 69 & 72; Childe Hassam Purchase Award Exhib, 71; Audubon Artists Soc Ann, 72; Butler Art Inst Midyear Exhib, 72; Am Acad Arts & Lett Exhib of Works by Candidates for Art Awards, 74. Awards: S J Wallace Truman Prize, Nat Acad Design, 69 & 72 & Julius Hallgarten Award, 74; Salmagundi Club Award, Audubon Artists, 72. Media: Acrylic. Dealer: Andrew Crispo Gallery 41 E 57th St New York NY 10022. Mailing Add: 148 Greene St New York NY 10012

CHASE, WILLIAM THOMAS (W THOMAS CHASE)
ART CONSERVATOR
b Boston, Mass, May 31, 40. Study: Oberlin Col, Ohio, BA, 62; NY Univ, MA, 67, conserv cert, 67; Brit Coun Course on conserv of antiquities, 69. Pos: Wadsworth Atheneum, Hartford, Conn, 62 & 63; conservator to Nemrud Dagh Excavations, Adiyaman Villayet, Turkey, 64; Chester Dale fel in Conserv Dept, Metrop Mus Art, New York, 66; asst conservator, Freer Tech Lab, 66-68, head conserv, 68-; adv to JDR 3rd Fund for Thai Bronze Treatment Proj, 73-75. Mem: Int Inst Conserv Hist & Artistic Works (mem Am group, 63-73); Am Inst Conserv; Washington Conserv Guild (vchmn, 68-69, pres, 70). Res: Technical studies of Oriental art, particularly ancient Chinese bronzes and belt-hooks, mirrors and other objects; corrosion study and analysis. Publ: Co-auth, with Gettens & Clarke, Two Early Chinese Weapons with Meteoritic Iron Blades, Freer Occasional Papers, 71; auth, Comparative analysis of Archaeological bronzes, In: Archaeol Chem, 75; dir (movie), Art of the Hyogushi, Freer Gallery, 73; auth, Bronze Disease and Its Treatment, Dept Fine Arts, Thailand, 75; co-ed, Corrision and Metal Artifacts, Nat Bur Stand, 77. Mailing Add: c/o Freer Gallery of Art Smithsonian Inst Washington DC 20560

CHASE-RIBOUD, BARBARA DEWAYNE
SCULPTOR, DRAFTSMAN
b US, June 26, 39. Study: Temple Univ, BFA; Yale Univ, MFA. Work: Mus Mod Art, Metrop Mus Art & St John's Univ, NY; Berkeley Mus, Univ Calif; Newark Mus, NJ; Inst Contemp Arts, Centre Pompidou & Mus Mod Art, Paris. Comn: Aluminum wall relief, Pierre Simon, New York; aluminum screen fountain, Wheaton Plaza Ctr, Washington, DC; forged steel sculptures, Pierre Cardin, Paris; cast bronze sculpture, Schoenburg Collection, NY; multi-colored bronze sculpture, Lannan Found, Fla. Exhib: One-man shows, Univ Art Mus, Berkeley, 73, Detroit Art Inst, 73, Indianapolis Art Mus, 73, Mus Mod Art, Paris, 74 & Kuntsmuseum, Dusseldorf, 74. Awards: Nat Endowment Arts Individual Grant, 73; US State Dept Traveling Grant, 75; Outstanding Alumni Award, Temple Univ, 75. Bibliog: Alvin Yudkoff (auth), Five, Silvermine Films, 72; Françoise Nora (auth), Another country, Art News, 72; Waller (auth), Textile sculptures, Studio Vista, 73. Style & Technique: Cast and polished bronze or aluminum or multi-colored bronze combined with cords of wool, silk, hemp or other soft materials. Media: Cast Bronze, Cast Aluminum. Dealer: Mirrior D'Encre 159 Chaussee de Charlerol Bruxelles Belg. Mailing Add: 199 Rue de Vaugirard Paris France

CHAVEZ, EDWARD ARCENIO
PAINTER, SCULPTOR
b Wagonmound, NMex, Mar 14, 17. Study: Colorado Springs Fine Arts Ctr, Colo, with Boardman Robinson, Frank Mechau, Arnold Blanch & Peppino Mangravite; Tiffany Found painting grants, 48; Inst Int Educ, Italy, Fulbright grant, 51. Work: Libr of Cong Print Collection & Watkins Gallery, Washington, DC; Mus Mod Art, New York; Detroit Mus Art; Butler Inst Am Art, Youngstown, Ohio. Comn: Murals, Govt Art Com, Post Off, Center, Tex, 38, Post Off, Geneva, Nebr, Post Off, Glenwood Springs, Colo, West High Sch, Denver; mural, USA 200th Sta Hosp, Recife, Brazil. Exhib: Nat Inst Arts & Lett, New York; Whitney Mus Am Art, New York; Nat Acad Design, New York; Pa Acad Art Ann, Philadelphia; Am Art Exhib, Metrop Mus Art, New York. Teaching: Instr painting, Art Students League, 54-58; vis prof art, Colo Col, Colorado Springs, 59-60; prof art, Syracuse Univ Sch Art, 60-62. Awards: Childe Hassam Award for Painting, Nat Inst Arts & Lett, 53. Style & Technique: Abstract. Mem: Woodstock Art Asn (chmn, 49-); academician Nat Acad Design. Mailing Add: 370 John Joy Rd Woodstock NY 12498

CHAVEZ, JOSEPH ARNOLD
SCULPTOR, CRAFTSMAN
b Belen, NMex, Dec 25, 39. Study: Univ Albuquerque, BS(art educ), 63; Univ NMex, MA(art educ), 67, MA(art), 71; Univ Cincinnati, 74. Work: Slide Libr Collection, Univ Southern Ala; plus 40 works in pvt collections in NMex, Colo, Tex & NY. Exhib: One-man show, Jonson Gallery, Univ NMex, 71; NMex Arts & Crafts Fair Ann, Albuquerque; Southwest Arts & Crafts Fair Ann; Southwest Crafts Biennial, Santa Fe Folk Art Mus, 74; State Fair Dallas, Tex, 75. Teaching: Teacher art, Lincoln Jr High, Albuquerque, 63-70; supvr student teachers art educ, Univ NMex, 70-71; teacher art, Sandia High Sch, Albuquerque, 71-; instr art, Univ Albuquerque, summer 70; supvr student teachers art educ, Univ Cincinnati, 74. Awards: First Place, Art Show in Black & White, Stagecoach Gallery, Albuquerque, 72; Second Place, Pottery & Sculpture Expos, Rio Grande Art & Crafts Fair, 74; Spec Merit, State Fair Tex, 75. Bibliog: Dr Jacinto Quirarte (auth), Mexican-American Artists, Univ Tex, 73; The Man Who Fell to Earth, London Film Co, 75; Joseph Chavez (auth, videotape), The Art of Carving Stone. Mem: Designers & Craftsmen NMex (pres, 73). Style & Technique: Organic abstract; carving; inlaying and modelling. Media: Stone, Clay, Metal. Publ: Auth, Critique on art, Col St Joseph News, 64. Dealer: The Art Compound First Plaza Gallery Albuquerque NM 87103. Mailing Add: 4618 Sorrell Lane SW Albuquerque NM 87105

CHAVEZ-MORADO, JOSE
PAINTER, EDUCATOR
b Silao, Mex, Jan 4, 09. Study: Self-taught except for brief study at Art Sch, Mex Univ. Work: Nat Mus Mod Art, Mexico City; Varsovia Art Mus, Poland; Mus Mod Art, New York; Haifa Mus, Israel; Mus Nat de Historia, Mexico City. Comn: Glass mosaics, University City, Mexico City, 52; stone mosaics, Ministry of Pub Works, Mexico City, 54; frescoes & mixed mosaics, CIBA Labs, Mexico City, 55; oil mural & bronze pilar (with Tomas Chavez Morado in sculptural works), Mus Anthrop, Mexico City, 64; fresco & acrylic murals, Mus Alhondiga de Granaditas, Guanajuato, 55, 66 & 67. Exhib: 5th Int Art Exhib, Tokyo, Japan, 59; Biennal of Sao Paulo, Brazil, 59; Portrait of Mexico Traveling Exhib, several countries, 60-70; Mus Nac Arte Mod, Mexico City, 61; Kunst der Mexikanishen Revolution, West Berlin, 74. Collections Arranged: Designing the Museo de la Alhondiga de Granaditas, History, Arquelogia, Etnography, Guanajuato, Mex. Teaching: Prof painting, Escuela Nat Artes Plasticas, Mexico City, 42-52; dir-founder, Taller de integracion Plastica, Mexico City, 50-60; dir-founder, Escuela de Diseno y Artesanias, Mexico City, 60-66. Pos: Inspector of art teaching, Inst Nac Bellas Artes, Mexico City, 34-36, head art educ, 36-40, dir art schs, 40-66; dir, Mus Hist, Inst Nac Antropologia e Historia, Guanajuato, 70- Awards: Medalla de Prata, 10th Salao Pan Americano, Inst Bellas Artes Rio Grande, Brazil, 58; Medalla Colaboration Gran Premio, 8th Biennal Sao Paulo, Brazil, 65; Mex Nat Price of Arts, 74. Bibliog: Julio Prieto (auth), Jose Chavez Morado, Ed Mexicanas, Mex, 51; Luis Cardosa y Aragon (auth), Pintura Mexicana, Fondo de la Plastica, Mexicana, 64; Antonio Rodriguez (auth), A history of Mexican mural painting, Thames & Hudson, London, 69. Style & Technique: Eclectic. Media: Fresco, Oil, Tempera. Collection: Pre-hispanic, Mexican colonial and folk art. Publ: Illusr, Rin-Rin Renacuajo (children's book), 50. Dealer: Ines Amor Galeria Arte Mexicano Milan 18, Mexico City, Mexico; Galeria de Arte Contemporaneo de Lourdes Chumacero Estocolmo 30 Mexico. Mailing Add: Pastita 158 Torre del Arco Guanajuato Mexico

CHEA-SE-QUAH
See Hill, Joan

CHEATHAM, FRANK REAGAN
PAINTER, DESIGNER
b Beeville, Tex, Feb 20, 36. Study: Art Ctr Col Design, BPA; Chouinard Art Inst; Otis Art Inst Los Angeles Co, BFA & MFA, study with Lorser Feitelson, Louis Danziger & Arthur Ames. Work: Los Angeles Co Mus Art; NMex Mus Fine Arts, Santa Fe. Comn: Catalog, Simon Rodia's towers in Watts, Los Angeles Co Mus Art, 62. Exhib: Los Angeles Munic Art Gallery Ann, Los Angeles Co Mus, 69; Sixth Ann Art Show, La Jolla Mus Art, 69; Ann Exhib, Long Beach Mus 70; Southwest Fine Arts Biennial, Mus NMex, 74. Teaching: Assoc prof design, Tex Tech Univ, Lubbock, 73- Pos: Creative dir, Porter, Goodman & Cheatham Design, Los Angeles, 61-73. Awards: Cert of Merit, Art Dir Club New York, 60, 70 & 74; Award of Excellence, Am Inst Graphic Arts, 63, 65, 72 & 74; Purchase Award, Mus NMex Found, 74. Mem: Am Inst Arts; Am Craftsmans Coun. Style & Technique: Non-objective hard edge acrylic painting; boxed assemblages in various media, polychromed. Media: Acrylic on Canvas; Wood; Polychromed Ceramic. Dealer: Silvan Simone 11579 Olympic Blvd W Los Angeles CA 90064. Mailing Add: 2305 53rd St Lubbock TX 79412

CHEN, HILO
PAINTER
b Taiwan, Repub of China, Oct 15, 42; US citizen. Study: Chong Yen Col, BS(archit). Work: Guggenheim Mus. Exhib: Wadsworth Atheneum, Hartford, Conn, 74; Indianapolis Mus of Art, 74; Pa State Mus of Art, 74; Baltimore Mus of Art, 75; Lafayette Natural Hist Mus & Planetarium, La, 75; Edwin Ulrich Mus, Wichita State Univ, Kans, 76. Collections Arranged: New/Photo Realism, Wadsworth Atheneum, 74. Bibliog: Robert Hughes (auth), An Omniverous & Literal Dependence, Arts Mag 6/74; Andrea Mikotajuk (auth), American Realists at LKM, Arts Mag, 1/75; Dorothy Belden, (auth), Realism Exaggerated in Ulrich Art Exhibition, Wichita Eagle, 3/76. Style & Technique: Sexy, alive girls with brush & air brush. Media: Oil on canvas; colored ink on paper. Dealer: Louis K Meisel 141 Prince St New York NY 10012. Mailing Add: 302 Bowery 3rd Floor New York NY 10012

CHEN, TONY (ANTHONY YOUNG CHEN)
ILLUSTRATOR, COLLECTOR
b Kingston, Jamaica, WIndies, Jan 3, 29; US citizen. Study: Art Career Sch, 49-51; Pratt Inst, BFA with honors, study with Richard Lindner & Dong Kingman, 55. Work: Univ Southern Miss, Hattiesburg; Kerlan Collection, Cedar Rapids, Minn; Fire House Gallery, Nassau Community Col, NY; plus numerous pvt collections. Comn: Bees, Defenders of Wildlife, Washington, DC, 74; Lyre Birds, 75 & Bamboo, 76, Nat Wildlife, Washington, DC; US Wildlife, Nat Geographic Soc, Washington, DC, 76; Siamang, Bronx Zoo, NY, 77. Exhib: One-man shows, Art Dir Club New York, 70, Uptown Gallery, New York, 73 & Sixth Estate Gallery, Brooklyn, NY, 77; Nat Collection of Fine Arts, Washington, DC, 74; Va Mus Fine Arts, Richmond, 75; Del Art Mus, Wilmington, 75; Wadsworth Atheneum, Hartford, Conn, 75; 200 Years of Am Illus, New York Hist Soc, 77. Collections Arranged: Contemp Am Illustrators of Childrens Books, Soc Illus Ann, 69-77; 200 Years of Am Illustration, Am Artist Mag, 72; Children's Bk Showcase, 72 & 76. Teaching: Instr drawing, Nassau Community Col, 72-74. Pos: Art dir, Newsweek Mag, 59-70. Awards: Award of Distinction, Creativity, 71, Art Direction Mag, 71; Award for Excellence, Soc Illusr Show, 73; Award of Distinction, Washington, DC, Educ Press Asn US, 77. Bibliog: Dianna Klemin (auth), The Book Illustration of Tony Chen, Am Artist, 5/72; Anne Commire (auth), Something About the Author, Contemp Authors, 74; Hyatt Mayor (auth), Contemporary American Illustrators of Children's Books, 74. Style & Technique: Pen and ink watercolors, naturalistic and detailed, emphasis on composition and graphics. Media: Watercolor; acrylic. Collection: African art with emphasis on early tribal art forms; Americana, especially wood carvings and paintings; Islamic bronzes, miniatures and ceramics. Publ: Illusr, Hello Small Sparrow, 71 & auth-illusr, Run, Zebra, Run, 72, Lothrop, Lee & Shepard; illusr, UNICEF Cookbook, T Y Crowell, 73; illusr, Honshi, Parents Mag Press, 74; illusr, About Owls, Scholastic Mag, 76. Mailing Add: 53-31 96th St Corona NY 11368

CHEN CHI
PAINTER
b Wu-sih, China, May 2, 12. Study: Study in China. Work: Metrop Mus Art, New York; Pa Acad Fine Arts, Philadelphia; Butler Inst Am Art, Youngstown, Ohio; Fort Worth Art Mus, Tex; Charles & Emma Frye Art Mus, Seattle. Exhib: American Watercolors, Drawings & Prints, Metrop Mus Art, 52; Whitney Mus Am Art Ann, New York, 54-63; 24th Biennial, Corcoran Gallery Art, Washington, DC, 55; Contemporary American Painting & Sculpture, Univ Ill, Urbana, 57; Brooklyn Mus 22nd Int Watercolor Biennial, 63; one-man shows in museums & galleries throughout the US, 47- Teaching: Instr watercolor, St Johns Univ, Shanghai, 42-46; vis prof watercolor, Pa State Univ, 59-60; artist in residence, Ogden City Schs, Utah, 67 & Utah State Univ, 71. Awards: Watercolor of the Year Award, Am Watercolor Soc, 55; Nat Inst Arts & Lett Grant for Creative Work in Art, 60; Saltus Gold Medal of Merit, Nat Acad Design, 69. Mem: Nat Acad Design (counr, 69-71); Am Watercolor Soc (dir, 56-59); Audubon Artists (dir, 64-69 & 72-); Allied Artists Am (dir, 58-60); Nat Arts Club (gov, 72-). Style & Technique: Impressionistic with the expression of subjective brush stroke in the character of Chinese calligraphy. Media: Watercolor, Oil. Publ: Illusr, American cities: San Francisco, Collier's Mag, 52; illusr, A single pebble, In: Readers Digest Condensed Bks, 56; illusr, Pageantry of VIII Winter Olympics, Squaw Valley, Sports Illus, 60; Two or Three Lines from Sketchbooks of Chen Chi, New York, 69; China from the Sketchbooks of Chen Chi, New York, 74; plus others. Dealer: Grand Central Art Galleries 40 Vanderbilt Ave New York NY 10017. Mailing Add: 23 Washington Sq N New York NY 10011

CHENEY, SHELDON
WRITER, ART HISTORIAN
b Berkeley, Calif, June 29, 86. Study: Univ Calif, Berkeley, AB; Calif Sch Arts & Crafts; Harvard Univ. Teaching: Hon fel in art, Union Col, 37-40. Mem: Benjamin Franklin fel Royal Soc Arts; Am Fedn Arts; Authors League Am; Soc Am Historians; Univ Art Mus Coun, Univ Calif, Berkeley. Res: Theatre arts; sculpture; modern painting. Publ: Auth, A New World History of Art, 56; auth, The Story of Modern Art, 58; auth, Sculpture of the World: a History, 68; auth, The Theatre, 72; contribr to many mags, symp, encycl & others. Mailing Add: 1555 Oxford St Berkeley CA 94709

CHENG, FU-DING
FILMMAKER, PAINTER
b Palo Alto, Calif, Feb 5, 43. Study: Sch Archit, Univ Southern Calif; Alliance Francaise, Paris; Univ Calif, Berkeley, BArch. Exhib: New Am Filmmakers, Whitney Mus Am Art, New York, 70; film exhibs, Yale Film Festival, 72, Belg Int Film Festival, 73 & Media Ctr, New York, 75. Teaching: Instr art, Univ Calif, Los Angeles, 76- Awards: Second Place, Yale Film Festival, Yale Univ, 70; independent grant, Film Proj, Am Film Inst, 77; First Place, Foothill Nat Film Festival, Foothill Col. Style & Technique: Watercolor; luminous landscapes; irridescent people. Media: Filmmaking. Publ: Illusr, Solar Energy House, US Info Agency, 77; auth, Oasis Foods' Dehydrated Water, Wet Mag, 77. Dealer: Ed Lau 6015 Santa Monica Blvd Los Angeles CA 90038. Mailing Add: 209 Seventh Ave Venice CA 90291

CHEREPOV, GEORGE
PAINTER, INSTRUCTOR
b Lithuania, Mar 28, 09; US citizen. Study: With profs Konstantin Wisotzky, Riga, Latvia & Aalexis Hansen, Dubrovnic, Yugoslavia. Work: Mus, Kempten, WGer; Town Hall, Memmingen, WGer; State Bank, Munich WGer; Stamford Mus, Conn; Mus of Art, Tucson, Ariz. Exhib: Allied Artists Am, New York; Acad Artists Asn, Springfield, Mass; Southern Vt Art Ctr, Manchester; Grand Cent Art Galleries, New York; Hudson Valley Art Asn. Pos: Fac, Painting Holiday Orgn, 73- Awards: Best in Show, First Award, Allied Artists Am, 68; Gold Medal, Hudson Valley Art Asn, 69; Medal of Honor, Kent Art Asn, Conn, 71. Mem: Fel Allied Artists Am; Hudson Valley Art Asn (mem bd dirs); Acad Artists Asn; Southern Vt Art Ctr; Am Artists Prof League Inc. Media: Oil. Publ: Auth, Discovering oil painting, 71; illusr, Wendon Blake, auth, Landscape Painting in Oil, Watson-Guptill, 76. Dealer: Newman Gallery 1625 Walnut St Philadelphia PA 19103; Grand Central Art Galleries Biltmore Hotel 40 Vanderbilt Ave New York NY 10017. Mailing Add: 1050 King St Greenwich CT 06840

CHERMAYEFF, IVAN
DESIGNER, PAINTER
b London, Eng, June 6, 32; US citizen. Study: Harvard Univ, 50-52; Inst Design, Ill Inst Technol, four Moholy-Nagy scholar, 52-54; Yale Univ Sch Design, Mohawk Paper Co fel, BFA, 55. Comn: Moveable Paintings (mounted on tracks), Gen Fireproofing Co Showroom, New York, 66; Exploding Triangles (shaped canvases), IBM Data Processing Hq, Harrison, NY, 70; Dimensional Abstractions (plastic laminate wall constructions), Bartholomew Consol Sch Corp, Columbus, Ind, 71; Abstraction I (Aubusson tapestry), Westinghouse Elec Corp, Pittsburgh, 72; Metal Abstractions II & III, Philip Morris Inc, Richmond; Construction (wall with painted steel components), Am Repub Ins Co, Des Moines, Iowa. Exhib: Industry Sculpture Show, Butler Inst Am Art, Youngstown, Ohio, 71; Venice Biennale, 72; Va Mus Art, Richmond, 74; Jacksonville Art Mus, 75. Teaching: Instr design, Brooklyn Col, 56-57 & Sch Visual Arts, 59-65. Pos: Trustee & comt mem painting & sculpture, film, design, Mus Mod Art, New York, 65-; vpres, Yale Arts Asn, 68-; mem comt arts & archit, Yale Univ Coun, 71-; mem comt visual & environmental arts, Harvard Univ Bd Overseers, 72- Awards: Indust Arts Medal, Am Inst Architects, 67; Gold Medal, Philadelphia Col Art, 71. Bibliog: Douglas Davis (auth), article, In: Newsweek Mag, 71 & 200 American leaders, Time Mag, 74. Mem: Am Inst Graphic Arts (vpres, pres, bd dirs, 60-); Int Design Conf Aspen (vpres, co-chmn bd dirs, 67-); Indust Designers Soc Am; Alliance Graphique Int; Benjamin Franklin fel Royal Soc Arts. Publ: Illusr, The Thinking Book, Keep It Like a Secret, The New Nutcracker Suite & Blind Mice & Other Numbers; auth, Observations on American Architecture, Viking, 72. Dealer: Pace Editions 115 E 23rd St New York NY 10010. Mailing Add: 830 Third Ave New York NY 10022

CHERNOW, ANN
PAINTER, INSTRUCTOR
b New York, NY, Feb 1, 36. Study: Syracuse Univ, 53-55; NY Univ, BS, 57, MA, 69; with Irving Sandler, Jules Olitski, Hale Woodruff & Howard Conant. Work: Butler Inst Am Art, Youngstown, Ohio; Lyman Allyn Mus, New London, Conn; Housatonic Mus Art, Bridgeport, Conn; Neuberger Mus, Purchase, NY; Univ Ariz Art Collection, Tucson. Exhib: One-woman shows, Silvermine Guild Art, New Canaan, Conn, 69, Bel Gallery, 73, Westport Mus Art, Sci & Indust, Bridgeport, Conn & Aaron Berman Gallery, New York, 78; New Eng Ann, Silvermine Guild Art, 69 & 74. Teaching: Instr studio work, Mus Mod Art, New York, 66-70; instr painting & drawing, Silvermine Col & Silvermine Guild, 68-; instr art hist, Univ Conn, summer 69; instr art, Norwalk Community Col, 74- Awards: Edwards Watercolor Award, New Eng Ann, 73; Conn Comn Arts Grant for pub art proj, 74 & 78, Purchase Prize, Town of Fairfield, Conn, 75. Bibliog: Articles in New York Times, 6/25/74, Cosmopolitan Mag, Signs of the Times Mag, 9/74; Barbara Cavaligre (auth), review in Women Art, Fall 1976. Mem: Silvermine Guild Art; Westport Weston Arts Coun (bd dirs until 70). Style & Technique: Figurative; deals with images of women in our century; tragi-comedic and communication themes. Media: Acrylic, Oil, Silkscreen. Publ: Auth, Let's remember, 69, Reuben Nakian, sculptor, 69, Palette, Mag of Conn Art Asn; auth (catalog), Odd Man In, Krushenick Exhib, Housatonic Mus of Art, Conn, 75. Dealer: Aaron Berman Gallery 50 W 57th St New York NY 10019. Mailing Add: 2 Gorham Ave Westport CT 06880

CHERNOW, BURT
INSTRUCTOR, MUSEUM DIRECTOR
b New York, NY, July 28, 33. Study: NY Univ, BA, 58, MA, 60; with Lawrence Alloway, Jules Olitski, Irving Sandler & Hale Woodruff. Work: Jacksonville Mus, Fla; Bridgeport Mus Art, Sci & Indust, Conn; Col Art Mus, Hampton, Va; Le Mus de L'Art Contemporain, Skopje, Yugoslavia; Housatonic Mus Contemp Art, Bridgeport, Conn. Exhib: Loeb Student Ctr, NY

Univ; Bridgeport Mus; UN Pavilion, New York World's Fair, 64-65; US Info Agency Traveling Exhib; Silvermine Guild, New Canaan, Conn. Collections Arranged: 20th Century American & European Contemporary Art, Housatonic Mus Art. Teaching: Staff, Mus Mod Art, New York, 67-70; chmn art dept, Housatonic Community Col, Bridgeport, 68-; staff, Silvermine Guild Artists, 70- Pos: Mem, Nat Comt Art Educ, 61-64; mem, Inst for Study Art Educ, 68-70; consult, Col Art Asn Am, 69-70; consult & writer, Educ Directions, 68-; dir, Housatonic Mus Contemp Art, 68-; mem bd dir, Art Resources of Conn, 76-78. Awards: First Prize (sculpture), Barnum Art Festival, Bridgeport Mus, 60. Bibliog: M Bishop (auth), For arts sake, Conn Mag, 3/72. Mem: Westport-Weston Arts Coun, Conn (bd dirs, 69-); Conn Art Asn (bd dirs, 64-65); Silvermine Guild Artists. Style & Technique: Photographic montages and repetitive element constructions. Publ: Auth, The New ambiguity, Art Educ J, 1/69; auth, Paper, paint & stuff, Educ Directions, Vols I I & II, 69; auth, Milton Avery Drawings, 73; auth, Lester Johnson, Paintings: the Kaleidoscope Crowd, 75 & Contemp Graphics, 77; auth of articles on Lester Johnson, Zuniga & Lindner, Arts Mag, 77 & 78. Mailing Add: 2 Gorham Ave Westport CT 06880

CHESHIRE, CRAIG GIFFORD
PAINTER, EDUCATOR
b Portland, Ore, Dec 31, 36. Study: Univ Ore, BA, 58, with David McCosh, MFA, 61; also with Francis Chapin. Work: Mus Art, Eugene, Ore; Univ Ore; Eastern Ore Col. Exhib: Northwest Artists Ann, Seattle; Artists of Ore Ann, 58-75; Northwest Painters, Smithsonian Inst Traveling Exhib, 59; Mus Art, Eugene, 61-74; Gallery West, Portland, 72. Teaching: Assoc prof drawing & painting, Portland State Univ, 63- Awards: Ina McClung Award in Painting, Univ Ore, 61, Ore Develop Fel, 62; Purchase Award, Mus Art, Eugene & Ore Arts Comn, 74. Mem: Portland Art Mus. Style & Technique: A colorist approach to landscapes and figures. Media: Oil, Watercolor. Mailing Add: 3540 SW 108th Ave Beaverton OR 97005

CHESLEY, PAUL ALEXANDER
PHOTOGRAPHER
b Red Wing, Minn, Sept 10, 46. Study: Ariz State Univ; Univ Minn; Colo Mountain Col. Work: Bell Mus of Natural Hist, Minn; Honolulu Acad, Hawaii. Exhib: One-man shows, High Country Photography, Phoenix Art Mus, Ariz, 74, Ecuador, Colorado Springs Fine Arts Ctr, 74 & Gargoyle Gallery, Colo, 75, Nature, Nishi Ginza Galleries, Tokyo, Japan, 75, Indians of the Andes, Birmingham Mus Art, Ala & Sci Mus of Minn, 75, Retrospective, James Ford Bell Mus of Natural Hist, Minn, 75 & Nature, Honolulu Acad of Art, Hawaii, 76. Bibliog: Julia Scully (auth), Four photographers, Mod Photog, 7/77; Constance Brown (auth), It's always hot springs time in the Rockies, Smithsonian, 11/77 & Woman Alive, Quest, 11/77; plus others. Media: Color Photography. Publ: Auth, Paul Chesley's Japan, Nikon World, 2/76; auth, In his own backyard, Camera, 1/77; auth, Yellowstone abstracts, US Camera, 9/77; and others. Dealer: Gargoyle Galleries Aspen CO 81611. Mailing Add: PO Box 94 Aspen CO 81611

CHESNEY, LEE R, JR
PRINTMAKER, PAINTER
b Washington, DC, June 1, 20. Study: Univ Colo, BFA, 46; Univ Iowa, MFA, 48; Univ Michoacan, Morelia, Mex; also with James Boyle, James Lechay & Mauricio Lasansky. Work: Rosenwald Collection, Nat Gallery Art, Washington, DC; Mus Mod Art, New York; Tate Gallery Art, London; Bibliot Nat, Paris; Nat Gallery Art, Stockholm, Sweden. Comn: Spec print ed, Honolulu Print Soc, 75. Exhib: Nihon Sosaku Hanga Kyokai Exhib, Japan Print Asn Int Ann, Tokyo & Osaka, 57-75; Six Artists in Paris, Am Cult Ctr, Paris, 64; Epinal Print Biennial, France, 70-71; Int Print Biennial, Seoul, Korea, 70 & 72; 10 yr retrospective, Fisher Gallery, Univ of Southern Calif, 68. Teaching: Instr drawing, Univ Iowa, 48-50; prof painting & printmaking, Univ Ill, 50-67; assoc dean fine arts, Univ Southern Calif, 67-72; prof painting & printmaking, Univ Hawaii, 72- Awards: Francis G Logan Medal for Painting, Art Inst Chicago, 62; Univ of Ill Res Award, 63; Vera List Purchase Award, Soc Am Graphic Artists, 65. Mem: Soc Am Graphic Artists; Col Art Asn Am; Los Angeles Printmaking Soc (adv bd, 67-); Hawaii Painters & Sculptors League; Honolulu Printmaking Soc. Media: Oil. Publ: Contribr, Printmaking today, Col Art J, Vol XIX, No 2; contribr, A brief glance at Ukiyo-e and Hanga, Japan Print Quart, winter 67. Dealer: Downtown Gallery 125 Merchant St Honolulu HI 96813. Mailing Add: c/o Comsky Gallery 9489 Dayton Way Beverly Hills CA 90210

CHESNEY, LEE ROY, III
PRINTMAKER, EDUCATOR
b San Antonio, Tex, July 5, 45. Study: Univ Ill, with Dennis Rowan, Eugene Telez, BFA; Univ Calif, Los Angeles, with Ray Brown; Ind Univ, with Rudy Pazzatti, Marvin Lowe, MFA. Work: Honolulu Acad Arts; San Diego State Univ Mus; State Univ NY Potsdam; Dickinson State Col Mus, NDak; Graphic Chem & Ink Co Collection, Chicago. Exhib: Libr Cong, Nat Collection Fine Arts, Smithsonian, Washington, DC, 69, 73; USIA Exhib to Rome, Italy, US Embassy, 73; Soc Am Graphic Artists, New York, 73; 1st Int Pratt Graphics, Bath, Eng, 73-74; 3rd Int Print Biennial, Epinal, France, 75. Teaching: Assoc instr printmaking & etching, Ind Univ, Bloomington, 69-72; instr design & prints, Univ Tex, Austin, 72-75, asst prof printmaking, 75- Awards: Graphic Chem & Ink Purchase Award, Soc Am Graphic Artists, 73; Honolulu Acad Arts Purchase Award, 73; Prints from Am Univs Purchase Award, US Info Agency, 74. Mem: Col Art Asn Am; The Graphic Soc (Int), Hollis, NH. Style & Technique: Relationship of non-objective form and mechanical symbols by the full use of photo and intaglio processes. Media: Intaglio Prints, Mixed Media Drawing. Mailing Add: 3505 Bridle Path Austin TX 78703

CHESTER, CHARLOTTE WANETTA
PAINTER, PRINTMAKER
b Columbus, Ohio. Study: Ft Wright Col, Wash, BFA; Capitol Univ; Oklahoma City Univ; Pa Acad Fine Arts, with Blackburn & Sloan; Philadelphia Col Art, with Niebert; also with Eric Irmer, Frankfurt, Ger, two years; numerous teachers and workshops in US and Europe. Work: Artist and Space, Nat Air & Space Mus, Smithsonian Inst, Washington, DC; The Barn, Millville, NJ; also in collection of Soovia Janis, New York. Comn: Many paintings. Exhib: Frankfurt Ger Juried Exhib, 65; Atlantic City Art Ctr, NJ, 65-70; Cult Art Ctr of Ocean City, 68; Kerr Mus, Okla, 70; plus numerous traveling exhibs. Teaching: Instr advan oil painting, Atlantic Community Col, 68-69; pvt art classes, 65- Awards: Too numerous to mention. Mem: Am Fedn Art; League South Jersey Artist (pres, 68-70); Fed Art Asn NJ (chmn South Jersey, 71); Green Co Art Asn; Watercolor Soc London; Printmaking Coun NJ; Allied Arts, Spokane; Wash Art Asn. Style & Technique: Creative painting and printmaking. Publ: Contribr, Yearbook Ocean City, 68. Mailing Add: RT 1 Box 53 Reardan WA 99029

CHESTER, JANIE KATHLEEN
MUSEUM DIRECTOR, EDUCATOR
b Port Huron, Mich, Apr 19, 49. Study: Univ Mich, BA(Eng lit & art hist), 71, MA(mus practice), 75; Toledo Mus Art, Nettie Poe Ketcham fel Mus Educ, 72-73. Collections Arranged: Rome Through the Eyes of the Eighteenth Century, Univ Mich Mus Art, Ann Arbor, 71; Decorative Arts of New Brunswick, 76 & What's It To You? (auth, catalog for children), 77, Rutgers Univ Art Gallery; Patrick Thibert: Young Canadian Sculpture, Saginaw Art Mus, 77. Teaching: Instr mus arts & educ, Grad Sch Educ, Rutgers Univ, New Brunswick, NJ, 76. Pos: Fel coordr, Toledo Mus Art, Ohio, 73-75; cur educ, Rutgers Univ Art Gallery, 75-77; dir, Saginaw Art Mus, Mich, 77- Mem: Mich Mus Asn. Res: First interdisciplinary, professional bibliography of museum education. Collection: Art nouveau jewelry; Michigan quilts; English pottery of the 1920's and 30's. Mailing Add: 1126 N Michigan Ave Saginaw MI 48602

CHESTERTON, DAVID
EDUCATOR, GRAPHIC ARTIST
b Leicester, Eng, Sept 19, 30; Can citizen. Study: Leicester Col Art & Technol, dipl; Leicester Univ Col Educ, dipl; spec studies in ceramics (with Roy Porter) & environ design; seminars with Bernard Leach. Teaching: Chmn visual arts, Humber Col, 70- Pos: Art dir, Procter & Gamble, Toronto, Ont, 51-63; vpres, Mkt Serv, Don Mills, Ont, 65-67; pres, Dave Chesterton Graphics, Oakville, Ont, 67- Mem: Am Inst Graphic Arts; Ceramic Designers Can; Art Dirs Club Toronto; Indust Graphics Int; Royal Soc Arts. Media: Brush & Ink, Stoneware. Mailing Add: 1342 Langdale Crescent Oakville ON L6H 2K8 Can

CHESTNEY, LILLIAN
ILLUSTRATOR, PAINTER
b New Haven, Conn. Study: Pratt Inst Sch Fine & Appl Arts, study with Khosrov Ajootian, Alexander Kostello, Maitland Graves, William Gorham and others. Work: Grand Cent Galleries, New York; Bantam Bks Inc, New York. Comn: Bk covers, Theodore Driesers' An American Tragedy, The Charter House of Parma & De Maupassants' Boule De Suife; bk illus, Gullivers' Travels & Arabian Nights; plus others. Exhib: Grand Cent Galleries; Am Watercolor Soc; Soc of Illusrs; Allied Am Artists; Artists Guild of New York. Awards: Three Cert of Merit, Soc Illusrs. Mem: Allied Artists Am; Grand Cent Art Galleries. Style & Technique: Very fine detail. Media: Oil & Egg Tempera. Mailing Add: 21 Old Farm Rd Levittown NY 11756

CHETHAM, CHARLES
MUSEUM DIRECTOR
US citizen. Teaching: Prof art, Smith Col. Pos: Dir, Smith Col Mus Art. Mailing Add: Smith Col Mus of Art Northampton MA 10160

CHETHLAHE (DAVID CHETHLAHE PALADIN)
PAINTER, DESIGNER
b Chinle, Ariz, Nov 4, 26. Study: Santa Fe Indian Sch; Art Inst Chicago. Work: William Penn Mem Mus, Harrisburg, Pa; US Dept Interior, Washington, DC; US State Dept, Washington, DC; UNICEF, New York. Comn: Sand painted mural, Howard Johnson's, Detroit, 69; four tapestries, comn by City of Phoenix, Phoenix Civic Plaza, 72. Exhib: One-man shows, William Penn Mem Mus, 69 & Martin Gallery, Scottsdale, Ariz, 71-78; Scottsdale Indian Nat, 69-72; American Indians Today, Mem Mus, Santa Ana, Calif, 70; Am Indian Art Ctr, New York, 75. Teaching: Dir fine arts workshop, Prescott Col, 71-74. Pos: Dir, Renaissance Acad Creative Develop, 75- Awards: Spec Purchase Award, Scottsdale Nat, 69, First Prize, 70 & Grand Prize, 71. Bibliog: Peterson (auth), Indian Art '70 & 3 Indians, 72, KAET-TV, Phoenix; Jules Power (auth), Chethlahe, Indian Artist, Discovery '71, ABC-TV, 71. Mem: Am Craftsmen Coun; Artists Equity Asn; Am Indian Designer Craftsmen (pres, 68-69); Coun Am Indian Artists. Media: Acrylic, Sand. Mailing Add: 2206 Sandia Prescott AZ 86301

CHEW, HARRY
PAINTER, EDUCATOR
b San Francisco, Calif, Mar 16, 25. Study: Study with Bruce Mitchell, 48, Reginald Marsh, 49 & Ben Shann, 50; Kansas City Art Inst & Sch of Design, BFA & MFA, 51. Work: Springfield Art Mus, Mo; Albrecht Art Mus, St Joseph, Mo; Univ Mo Kansas City Art Mus; Mo State Hist Soc Art Mus, Columbia; Utica Col Art Mus, NY. Comn: His of Coal Mining (mural), Bituminous Coal Asn, Kansas City, Mo, 51. Exhib: Mid-Am Ann, William Rockhill Nelson Gallery of Art, Kansas City, Mo, 48-52 & 54; Young Am Painters, Addison Gallery Am Art, Andover, Mass, 49; Outstanding Am Painters, Travelling Exhib, Am Fedn Art, 51-52; one-man shows, Kansas City Art Inst, Mo, 51, Yaddo Found Gallery, Saratoga Springs, NY, 53, Kansas State Univ, 53 & 64 & Christmas Ann, Union Carbide Gallery, NY, 74; Midwest Ann, Mulvane Art Mus, Topeka, Kans, 52 & 54; Western Ann, Denver Art Mus, Colo, 53 & 54; Twelve States Ann, Springfield, Mo, 54-56; Haghfelt Gallery, Copenhagen, Denmark, 58; Joslyn Art Mus Ann, Omaha, Nebr, 62 & 64; Watercolor USA, Springfield Art Mus, Mo, 68 & 70. Teaching: Prof fine arts, Cottey Col, Nevada, Mo, 51- Pos: Dir art therapy, Nevada State Hosp, Mo, 55-; visual arts consult, Mo State Coun on the Arts, St Louis, 68-70. Awards: Yaddo Found Creative fel, Saratoga Springs, NY, 54; Am Scand Found fel, Europe, 57-58. Mem: Nat Coun Art Adminrs; Col Art Asn; Am Asn Art Therapy. Style & Technique: Colorist using a marriage of the eastern and western forms of painting. Media: Oil; watercolor. Publ: Illusr, Winston Weathers (auth), Messages from the Asylum, Joseph Nichols, 70; illusr, Nimrod, Tulsa Univ, 71; illusr, Missouri Historical Review, State Hist Soc Mo, 75; illusr, Ten Missouri Painters, Mo State Coun on the Arts, 75. Mailing Add: 178 Country Club Dr Nevada MO 64772

CHEW, PAUL ALBERT
ART ADMINISTRATOR, LECTURER
b Norristown, Pa, Apr 22, 25. Study: Univ Pittsburgh, BA, 50, Henry Clay Frick Fine Arts Dept grad asst, 50-51, MA, 52; Univ Manchester, Eng, fel, 55-57, PhD, 57. Collections Arranged: 250 Years of Art in Pennsylvania (with catalog), 59; One-Man Show: Lawrence Calcagno, 67; Recent Trends in American Art, 69; One-Man Show: Henry Koerner, 71; Art & the Kitchen, 75; David Hanna, 77. Teaching: Instr art hist, Univ Pittsburgh, Greensburg, 63- Pos: Asst to dir, Carnegie Mus, 52-53; exec to dir circulating exhibs, Mus Mod Art, New York, 53-54; dir, Westmoreland Co Mus Art, 57-; trustee, Southern Alleghenies Mus Art, Loretto, Pa; mem visual arts adv panel, Pa Coun on the Arts, Harrisburg. Mem: Col Art Asn Am; Am Asn Mus. Publ: Ed (catalogue), Permanent Collection of Westmoreland County Museum of Art, 78. Mailing Add: 208 N Maple Ave Greensburg PA 15601

CHIARA, ALAN ROBERT
PAINTER
b Cleveland, Ohio, May 5, 36. Study: Cooper Sch Art, Cleveland; Cleveland Inst Art. Work: Butler Inst Art, Youngstown, Ohio; Springfield Art Mus, Mo; Cent Nat Bank Cleveland; Bethany Col, Lindsborg, Kans; Nat Acad Design, New York. Exhib: Butler Inst Art, 68; Watercolor USA, Springfield, Mo, 68; Nat Art Exhib, Wichita, Kans, 70; Nat Acad Design, New York, 71; Am Watercolor Soc, New York, 72. Pos: Master designer, Am Greetings, Cleveland, 58-70; pres, Chiara Galleries, Cleveland, 69- Awards: Silver Medal Award, Am Watercolor Soc, 66; Adolph & Clara Obrig Prize, 67 & William A Paton Prize, 70, Nat Acad Design. Mem: Am Watercolor Soc; assoc Nat Acad Design. Media: Watercolor. Specialty:

Living American artists. Publ: Auth, Watercolor page, Am Artist Mag, 11/67. Mailing Add: 8316 Glen Oak Cleveland OH 44147

CHICAGO, JUDY
PAINTER
b Chicago, Ill, July 20, 39. Style & Technique: Univ Calif, Los Angeles, BA, 62, MA, 64. Work: Mus Mod Art, New York; Legion of Hon. Exhib: Primary Structures, Jewish Mus, New York, 66; Sculpture of the Sixties, Los Angeles Co Mus Art & Philadelphia Mus Art, 67; West Coast Now, Seattle Art Mus, Portland Mus Art & San Francisco Mus Art, 68; one-woman show, Pasadena Art Mus, 69; Color as Structure, Whitney Mus Am Art, 70; Univ Wash, Seattle, 72; de Saisset Mus, Santa Clara, Calif, 73; Univ NDak, Grand Forks, 73; Western Wash State Col, Bellingham, 74; Cerritos Col, Newark, Calif, 75; plus others. Pos: Founder, Feminist Art Educ. Bibliog: Susan Stocking (auth), Thru the feminist looking glass with Judy Chicago, Los Angeles Times Calendar, Priscilla English (auth), New Woman, Womanhouse, Lucy R Lippard talking to Judy Chicago, article in Art Forum, Style & Technique: Decorative china painting as a fine art. Interest: Porcelain painting. Publ: Auth, Through the Flower: My Struggle as a Woman Artist, Doubleday, 75. Dealer: Re/Vision 3122 Santa Monica Blvd Santa Monica CA 90404. Mailing Add: 1651 B 18th St Santa Monica CA 90404

CHICOINE, RENE
DRAFTSMAN, EDUCATOR
b Montreal, PQ, 1910. Study: Beaux-Arts, Montreal. Work: Mus Quebec; Court House, Montreal. Exhib: Regional & nat exhibs, 32-40, 48 & 73. Teaching: Instr, Design Dept, Pavillon Arts, Univ Quebec. Mailing Add: Pavillon des Arts Univ du Quebec Montreal PQ Can

CHIEFFO, CLIFFORD TOBY
PAINTER, PRINTMAKER
b New Haven, Conn, July 23, 37. Study: Southern Conn State Col, BS; Teachers Col, Columbia Univ, MA. Work: Baltimore Mus Art; Berkshire Mus Art; Georgetown Univ; US State Dept Art in Embassies Prog; Nat Collection Fine Art, Washington, DC; plus others. Exhib: Corcoran Gallery Art, 63, 65 & 67; Baltimore Mus Art, 65 & 66; Washington Gallery Mod Art, 68; Munson-Williams-Proctor Inst, Ithaca, NY, 68; Four American Printmakers, Am Embassy, Ireland, 68; plus others. Teaching: Instr painting, drawing & silk-screen, Univ Md; Corcoran Sch Art; prof fine arts & chmn dept, Georgetown Univ, presently. Awards: Artist in residence grants, Am Fedn Arts, Colo, 65 & Mo Coun Arts, 67; Distinguished Alumni Award, Southern Conn State Col, 74; Nat Mus Act Grant, 76-77. plus others. Mem: Col Art Asn Am. Style & Technique: Semi-abstract figures in silk-screen and oils. Media: Painting, Graphic. Publ: Auth, Silk-Screen as a Fine Art, Van Nostrand-Reinhold, 67; auth, Contemporary Oil Painters Handbook, Prentice-Hall, 76. Mailing Add: 7601 Glackens Dr Potomac MD 20854

CHIHULY, DALE PATRICK
GLASS ARTIST, DESIGNER
b Tacoma, Wash, Sept 20, 41. Study: Univ of Wash, Seattle, BA; Univ of Wis, Madison, MS; RI Sch of Design, MFA. Work: Metrop Mus of Art, New York; Kunstgewerbemuseum und Museum Bellerive, Zurich; Seattle Art Mus; Wadsworth Atheneum, Hartford, Conn; Philadelphia Mus of Art. Comn: Leaded glass wall, Corning Mus of Glass Libr, NY; window, Australia Coun of the Arts. Exhib: One-person shows, Yuma Mus of Fine Arts, Ariz, Mus of Contemp Crafts, New York, 72, Utah Mus of Fine Arts, Salt Lake City, 75, Inst of Am Indian Art, 75, Wadsworth Atheneum, Univ of Minn, Minneapolis, 76, Blankets/Cylinders, Bell Gallery, Brown Univ, 76, Hadler Galleries, Houston, Tex, 77; three-person show, Seattle Art Mus, Mod Art Pavillion, 77; Drutt Gallery, Philadelphia, Pa, 77 & Dale Chihuly-Glass Cylinders and New Work, Foster/White Gallery, Seattle, 77. Teaching: Chmn, Dept of Glass Blowing, RI Sch of Design, 67-, chmn, Dept of Sculpture, 76-77; educ coordr & founder, Pilchuck Glass Ctr, Stanwood, Wash, 71- Awards: Louis Tiffany Found Award, 67; Fulbright Fel, Murano, Italy, 68; Master Craftsman-Apprenticeship Grant, Nat Endowment for the Arts, 75. Bibliog: David Manzella (auth), The Fluid Breath of Glass, Craft Horizons, 71; Roni Horn (auth), Dale Chihuly and the Glass Cylinders, Studio Potter, 76; film, Hot Glass Symposium, Royal Col of Art, 76. Style & Technique: Glass working, hot and cold techniques. Media: Glass. Mailing Add: c/o RI Sch of Design 2 College St Providence RI 02903

CHILDERS, BETTY BIVINS
COLLECTOR, PATRON
b Amarillo, Tex, Sept 4, 13. Study: Randolph Macon; Univ of Tex, BA. Pos: Chmn bd of trustees, Amarillo Art Ctr, 68-76. Mem: Am Asn of Mus; Tex Asn of Mus. Interest: Welfare of Amarillo Art Ctr; education of this area and exposing area people to good art. Collection: Impressionists, abstract expressionism, living American artists. Mailing Add: 1600 S Lamar St Amarillo TX 79102

CHILDERS, MALCOLM GRAEME
PRINTMAKER, PHOTOGRAPHER
b Riverside, Calif, Feb 19, 45. Study: Humboldt State Univ, Arcata, Calif, BA, 69; Fullerton State Univ, Calif, MA, 72. Work: Springfield Art Mus, Mo; Tenn State Mus, Nashville; Meadows Mus Art, Shreveport, La; Brooks Mem Art Gallery, Memphis, Tenn; Standard Oil Co-Ind, Chicago Corp Art Collection. Comn: Photo Essay of Corp Subjects, Rocky Mountain Energy Corp, Denver, Colo, 77. Exhib: Uses of Realism, Univ Calif, Riverside, 74; Davidson Nat Print & Drawing Competition, NC, 74-76; Mid-South Biennial, Memphis, Tenn, 75; Hunter Mus Art Ann, Chattanooga, Tenn, 75; Appalachian Corridors Biennial Art Exhib 4, Charleston, SC, 75; Bradley Print Show, Peoria, Ill, 75-76; La Grange Nat Competition II, Ga, 75-76; Tenn Bicentennial Exhib, Nashville, Tenn, 76. Teaching: Instr printmaking, Loma Linda Univ, Calif, 72-74; asst prof drawing, painting & printmaking, Southern Missionary Col, Collegedale, Tenn, 74- Awards: Purchase Awards, La Grange Nat II, La Grange Art Mus, 75, Mid-South Biennial, Brooks Mem Art Gallery, 75 & Tenn Bicentennial, State of Tenn, 76. Style & Technique: New realism and experimental nonobjective expressionism using photography, printmaking, drawing and painting. Media: For high resolution realism: printmaking and paint; for expressionism: paint and constructions. Dealer: Assoc Am Artists 663 Fifth Ave New York NY 10022. Mailing Add: Dept of Art Southern Missionary Col Collegedale TN 37315

CHILDERS, RICHARD ROBIN
PAINTER
b El Paso, Tex, Nov 28, 46. Study: Dallas Mus of Fine Arts Sch; Pa Acad of Fine Arts; Northwood Inst. Work: New Orleans Mus of Art, La; Ark Art Ctr, Little Rock; Southwestern Med Ctr, Univ of Tex, Dallas; Dallas Co Community Col; Texas Bank, Houston. Comn: Energy stick (2 1/2 ton concrete sculpture), Dr & Mrs S Ainslie Shelburne, Cincinnati, 72. Exhib: Tex Painting & Sculpture Ann, Dallas Mus of Fine Art, 71; 15th Ann Delta Art Exhib, Ark Art Ctr, Little Rock, 72; 1973 Artist Biennial for the Southeast & Tex, New Orleans Mus of Art, La, 73; Eight State Exhib, Oklahoma Art Ctr, Oklahoma City, 74; First Ann Crossroads of Am Art Exhib, Chicago, Ill, 75; Dallas Art 78, Dallas City Hall, 78; one-man show, New Orleans Mus of Art, La, 74. Awards: First Place, Tex Painting and Sculpture Ann, Dallas Mus of Fine Art, 71; Grand Purchase Award, 15th Delta Art Exhib, Ark Art Ctr, 72; Purchase Prize, 1973 Artist Biennial, New Orleans Mus of Art, 73. Bibliog: Janet Kutner (auth), Richard Childers, Arts Mag, 9/77; Jim Stratton (auth), Pioneering in the Urban Wilderness, Urizen Books Inc, 77; Leellen Patchen (auth), Richard Childers, film, 78. Style & Technique: Glitter, glass and paint splattering; slipping, sliding, drips and drops on canvas. Media: Acrylic on Canvas. Publ: Ed, First Saturday Art Magazine, 76. Dealer: 500 Exposition Gallery Inc 500 Exposition Ave Dallas TX 75226. Mailing Add: 842 First Ave Dallas TX 75226

CHILDS, CATHERINE O
See Catchi

CHIN, RIC
LECTURER, PAINTER
b Hong Kong, July 16, 35; US & UK citizen. Study: State Univ NY; Art Students League; Sch Chinese Brushwork, New York; also with Barse Miller, Cheng Dai-Chien & Wang Chi-Yuan. Work: Nat Palace Mus, Taiwan; Penang Mus, Malaysia; Manhattan Savings Bank, Eastchester, NY; Houston's Ethan Allen Gallery, Greensboro, NC; Wantagh Sch Syst, NY. Exhib: Am Artists Prof League Grand Nat, Lever House, NY, 71-75; Fire House Art Gallery, Nassau Community Col, Garden City, NY, 73 & 74; Nat Palace Mus Ann, Taiwan, 74; one-man shows, Winston-Salem Hyatt House, NC, 74 & Ctr Asian Studies, St John's Univ, NY, 75. Teaching: Lectr Chinese cult & art, Long Island Univ, 70-71; instr Chinese brushwork, var workshops, Southeastern US & Nat Art League, Douglaston, NY, currently. Pos: Dir, Bertrick Assoc Artists, Inc, Seaford, NY, 65-74. Mem: Salmagundi Club (mem bd dir, 74 & 75); Am Artists Prof League; Sumi-E Soc Am; Nat Art League; Art League Nassau Co. Style & Technique: East-West style of watercolor brushwork on rice paper. Media: Watercolor; Water-Ink. Mailing Add: 3423 Carrollton Ave Wantagh NY 11793

CHINN, YUEN YUEY
PAINTER
b Kwantung, China, Dec 24, 22; US citizen. Study: Columbia Univ, Brevoort Eickmeyer fel, 52-53, BFA, 53, study with Shahan, Keliker & Mangravite, 53-54, MFA, 54; Atelier 17, Paris with W Hayter, 58-59. Work: Nat Collection Fine Arts; Wadsworth Atheneum Mus; Fogg Art Mus; Nat Mus, Stockholm. Comn: Mural comn by Mrs Joanna Gunderson, 71. Exhib: Young American Printmakers, Mus Mod Art, New York, 53-54; Abstrakt Landskap, Nat Mus, Stockholm, 60; Salone de Mai, Musee Nat d'Art Mod, Paris, 61; 9Europaische Kunstler, Haus Am Waldsee, Berlin-Zehlendorf, 63; 2e Salon Int Galeries Pilotes, Musee Cantonal Beaux Art, Lousanne, 66. Awards: Fulbright fel, 54-55; John Hay Whitney Fel, 56-57. Bibliog: C Von Wiegand (auth), The World of Abstract Art, 57; Alexander Watt (auth), In Paris the painter is at home, Studio, 60; Otto Hahn (auth), Review Art in Paris, Art Int, 5/64. Style & Technique: Abstract and used ink and gouache to form vague, blocky shapes, crisscrosses them with lines, then roughens and punctures the rice-papers base until the surfaces of drawings nearly achieve the texture of oils. Media: Oil, Gouache. Dealer: Galerie Karl Flinker 25 Rue de Tournon Paris France. Mailing Add: 283 W 11th St New York NY 10014

CHINNI, PETER ANTHONY
SCULPTOR, PAINTER
b Mount Kisco, NY, Mar 21, 28. Students League; Acad Belle Arti, Rome, Italy; also with Roberto Melli, Rome & Felice Casorati, Turin. Work: Whitney Mus Am Art, New York; New Sch Social Res, New York; St Louis Art Mus, Mo; Nat Gallery Art, Smithsonian Inst, Washington, DC; Shah of Iran. Exhib: Carnegie Int, Pittsburgh, Pa, 64-65; Whitney Mus Am Art Ann, 64-65; New Sch Social Res, 69; Biennale Roma, 69; Gallery Mod Art, Rome, 70. Mem: Sculptors Guild. Style & Technique: Abstract; cast in bronze from wax, plaster or balsa originals; fabricated in sheet metals; carved in marble. Media: Bronze, Stainless Steel; Oil. Mailing Add: Osceola Ave Irvington NY 10533

CHIPP, HERSCHEL BROWNING
EDUCATOR, CURATOR
b New Hampton, Mo, Nov 9, 13. Study: Univ Calif, Berkeley, BA & MA; Columbia Univ, PhD; Univ Paris; Fulbright fel to France, 51-52; Belg-Am Educ Found fel, 52. Teaching: Chmn art dept, Univ Calif, Berkeley, 61- Pos: Dir, Univ Art Gallery, Univ Calif, Berkeley, 61-; dir, Am Exhib, Paris Biennale, 63; mem selection comt, Fulbright-Hayes Prog & other agencies, Nat Endowment Humanities, 77-80. Mem: Col Art Asn Am (dir, 61-65); Soc Hist Art Fr. Publ: Auth, Viennese Expressionism, 63; auth, Jugendstil & Expressionism in German Posters, 65; auth, Theories of Modern Art, 68; auth, Friedrich Hundertwasser, 69; contribr articles in nat mag, newspapers & jour. Mailing Add: Dept of Hist of Art Univ of Calif Berkeley CA 94720

CHO, DAVID
SCULPTOR
b Los Angeles, Calif, Aug 13, 50. Study: Calif State Univ, Los Angeles, BA, 72. Work: Long Beach Mus Art, Calif. Exhib: Sound Show, Civic Art Gallery, Walnut Creek, Calif, 71; Long Beach Mus Art 10th Ann, 72; Small Environments, Southern Ill Univ & Wis Art Ctr, Madison, 72; The David Cho Show, Amerasia Gallery, Los Angeles, 74; Collage & Assemblage in Southern California, Los Angeles Inst Contemp Art, 75. Awards: Dr & Mrs Maurice Rosenbaum Purchase Award, 72. Bibliog: Articles in San Francisco Chronicle, Oakland Tribune & Los Angeles Herald-Examr, 71 & Los Angeles Times Calendar Mag & Art Gallery Mag, 72. Style & Technique: Visual fables manifested in forms of mixed media wall reliefs and audio-kinetic robots. Dealer: Joyce/Jeannette 11831 S Park Ave Los Angeles CA 90066. Mailing Add: 1787 Sunny Heights Dr Los Angeles CA 90065

CHODKOWSKI, HENRY, JR
PAINTER, EDUCATOR
b Hartford, Conn, Mar 20, 37. Style & Technique: Univ Hartford, with Gail Martin, Paul Zimmerman, James Van Dyke, William Wondriska & Hendrick Mayer, BFA, 61; Yale Univ, with Bernard Chaet, Gabor Peterdi & Reginald Pollack, MFA, 63. Work: J B Speed Art Mus, Louisville, Ky; Montgomery Mus Fine Arts, Ala; NJ State Mus, Trenton; Floyd Co Mus, New Albany, Ind; Philip Morris Co, Inc, New York. Exhib: One-man shows, J B Speed Art Mus, 68 & 72, Duke Univ Mus, 72 & NY, 75; Gallery Contemp Art, Winston-Salem, NC, 74; Nat Soc Painters in Casein & Acrylic 22nd Ann, Lever House, NY, 75. Teaching: From instr to prof drawing, Univ Louisville, 63-, printmaking, 63-73, advan painting, 73- Awards: Yale-Norfolk Summer Art Sch Fel, Yale Univ, 59; Polaroid Corp Grant, 68; Univ Louisville Res Grant, 67, 68 & 75. Mem: Watercolor Soc Ala; Yale Arts Asn; Nat Soc Painters in Casein & Acrylic; Nat Soc Lit & Arts; Southeastern Graphic Soc. Media: Acrylic. Dealer:

Middendorf Gallery P St Washington DC 20001. Mailing Add: 2015 Baringer Ave Louisville KY 40204

CHOMICKY, YAR GREGORY
EDUCATOR, PAINTER
b Chicago, Ill, Dec 29, 21. Study: Art Inst of Chicago, 36; Wilmington Acad of the Fine Arts, 40; Pa State Univ, BA, 49 & MS, 52; study with Frank Schoonover, Gayle Hoskins, Orville Peets, N C Wyeth, Hobson Pittman & Viktor Lowenfeld. Work: William Penn Mem Mus, Harrisburg, Pa; Pa State Univ, University Park; Mansfield State Col, Pa; Lock Haven State Col, Pa; Shippensburg State Col, Pa. Comn: Exterior stainless steel sculpture, Elks Home, Indiana, Pa, 55; stainless steel fountain, 63 & stainless steel sculpture, 64, Viktor Lowenfeld Mem, Pa State Univ. Exhib: Addison Gallery, Phillips Acad, Andover, Mass, 50; 32nd Ann, Butler Inst of Am Art, 67; Third Bucknell Ann Nat Drawing Exhib, 67; Chatauqua Am Art Ann, 67; Pa, 71, William Penn Mem Mus, Harrisburg, Pa, 71; Drawings and Paintings, Mus of Art, Pa State Univ, 73; Chico State Invitational Watercolor, Calif, 74; Pa Group Traveling Exhib, Old Bergen Art Guild, NJ, 72-78; Pa Artists, Am Wind Symphony Orchestra Bi-Centennial Odyssey, 76; one-man show, John Mariani Gallery, Univ of Northern Colo, 76. Teaching: Prof art educ, mural design, painting, sculpture & printmaking, Pa State Univ, 49-; vis prof painting, Mankato State Col, Minn, 73. Awards: Second Prize, Edinboro Watercolor Ann, 62; Christian R & Mary R Lindback Found Award for Distinguished Teaching, Penn State Univ, 70; Third Prize, Cent Pa Art Alliance, 75. Bibliog: Alice Schwartz (auth), Meaning in Art Series Painting, WPSX-TV, Pa Dept of Educ Grant, 63. Mem: Nat Art Educ Asn; Pa Art Educ Asn. Style & Technique: Watercolor media, transparent, opaque, mixed techniques; Central Pennsylvania landscape and related topics, abstract and representational styles based on washes and line. Media: Transparent Watercolor on Rice Paper, Pencil. Publ: Auth, Watercolor issue, Everyday Art Magazine, Am Crayon Co, 60; auth, Watercolor Painting: Media, Methods, Materials, Prentice-Hall, 68; co-auth, Drawing: sum and spirit, Lock Haven Rev, 75. Dealer: Old Bergen Art Guild 43 W 33rd St Bayonne NJ 07002. Mailing Add: PO Box 117 Pine Grove Mills PA 16868

CHOO, CHUNGHI
METALSMITH, FABRIC DESIGNER
b Inchon, Korea, May 23, 38; US citizen. Study: Ewha Women's Univ, Seoul, Korea, BFA; Cranbrook Acad Art, Bloomfield Hills, Mich, MFA; Penland Sch of Crafts; Tyler Sch Art. Work: Metrop Mus Art, New York. Exhib: Young Americans 1969, Mus Contemp Crafts, New York; one-woman show, Jack Lenor Larsen Show Rm, New York, 71; Fabric Vibrations, Eastern & Western Europe, Near & Far East & Pac Islands sponsored by Smithsonian Inst (under Int Art Prog), 72-75; North American Goldsmith, Renwick Gallery, Washington, DC, 74; Forms in Metal, Mus Contemp Crafts, New York, 75; Dyers Art, Mus Contemp Crafts, New York, 76; Int Fiberworks, Cleveland Mus Art, Ohio, 77. Teaching: Assoc prof metalworking & jewelry, Sch of Art & Art Hist, Univ Iowa, 68- Pos: Judge, Int Prof Fabric Designers Competition & Int Student Fabric Competition of Surface Design Conf I, Lawrence, Kans. Bibliog: Jack Lenor Larsen (auth), Dyer's Art, Reinhold; Textile surface, Craft Horizons, 4/76. Mem: Soc NAm Goldsmith; Am Crafts Coun. Style & Technique: Decorative tapestry done in abstract painterly manner by tie-dye-tritik techniques; jewelry and functional objects and small sculptural forms by traditional metalworking techniques and electroforming. Media: Metal; Fiber. Dealer: Hardler Galleries 35-37 E 20th St New York NY 10003. Mailing Add: Sch of Art & Art Hist Univ of Iowa Iowa City IA 52242

CHOW CHIAN-CHIU
PAINTER, ART HISTORIAN
b Canton, China, Dec 23, 10. Style & Technique: Nat Univ China, BA; Tsing Hwa Univ, Peking; Hopkins Ctr Art Galleries, Dartmouth Col, NH; Cernuschi Mus, Paris; St Lawrence Univ, Canton, NY; Kans State Univ, Manhattan. Exhib: 2nd Nat Art Exhib, Chinese Govt, Nanking, 35; Chinese Contemp Art, Chinese Embassy, London, 37; 5th Contemp Art, Japanese Govt, Tokyo, 58; Yugoslavia Traveling exhib, 57-60, Trans World Airlines, Galerie des Deux Mondes, New York, 68, Kansas State Univ, Univ Calif, Berkeley, Stanford Univ, Calif, Univ Pittsburgh, Pa, Univ Rochester, NY; Art Mus Seattle, Wash; Dartmouth Col, Hanover, NH. Teaching: Pres, Int Studio Chinese Art, 52-67; instr Chinese art, Grove Art Sch, Miami Art Ctr, Fla, 68-70. Awards: Respect Award, Inst Chinese Cult, New York, 70. Bibliog: Walter Foster (auth), Chinese Art, film, Wilbur T Blume, 62. Mem: Chinese Artist Asn, Nanking; Chinese Artist Asn, Hong Kong; hon mem Miami Artist Asn. Style & Technique: Chinese. Publ: Co-auth, Easy Way to do Chinese Painting, 61; co-auth, Chinese Painting No 2, 72; auth, The Biographies of Chinese Painting New School Founder in History, Libr Cong, 75-835623. Mailing Add: Suite 2406 100 Biscayne Blvd Miami FL 33132

CHOW LEUNG CHEN-YING
PAINTER
b Canton, China, Mar 20, 20. Study: Art Teacher Training Col of China. Work: Hopkins Ctr Art Galleries, Dartmouth, NH; Mus Cernuschi, Paris, St Lawrence Univ, Canton, NY. Exhib: 5th Contemp Art Exhib, Tokyo, 58; two-person shows, Yugoslavia Traveling Exhib, 57-60 & Galerie des Deux Mondes, New York, 68; Univ Calif, Berkeley, Univ Rochester, NY, Dartmouth Col, Hanover, NH, Art Mus of Seattle, Wash, Kans State Univ, Manhattan & Stanford Univ, Calif, 68. Teaching: Prof Chinese art, Int Studio Art, 52-67; instr Chinese art, Grove Art Sch, Miami Art Ctr, Fla, 69-70. Foster (auth), Chinese Art, film, Wilbur T Blume, 62. Mem: Chinese Artist Asn, Hong Kong; hon mem Miami Artist Asn. Style & Technique: Chinese. Publ: Co-auth, Easy Way to do Chinese Painting, 61; co-auth, Chinese Painting No 2, 72. Mailing Add: Suite 2406 100 Biscayne Blvd Miami FL 33132

CHOY, TERENCE TIN-HO
PAINTER, EDUCATOR
b Hong Kong, Nov 26, 41; US resident. Study: San Francisco State Univ, BA; Univ Calif, Berkeley, MA, with David Hockney, Elmer Bischoff & Earl Loren. Work: Alaska State Coun on the Arts, Anchorage; Alaska State Mus at Juneau; Univ Alaska, Anchorage; Univ Alaska, Fairbanks. Exhib: Rosicrusian Egyptian Mus & Art Galleries, San Jose, Calif, 63; Richmond Art Ctr, Calif, 68; M H de Young Mem Mus, San Francisco, 69; Alaska State Mus, Juneau, 72; Anchorage Hist & Fine Arts Mus, 74; Honolulu Acad of Art, Hawaii, 76; Woodson Art Mus, Wausau, Wis, 76; Nat Collection of Fine Arts, Washington, DC, 78. Teaching: Instr art, de Young Mus Art Sch, San Francisco, 69-70; assoc prof art, Univ Alaska, Fairbanks, 70- Pos: Photographer, Univ Calif, Berkeley, 68-70; gallery coordr, Art Galleries, Univ Alaska, Fairbanks, 71-75; Rockefeller fel, Fine Arts Mus of San Francisco, 77-78. Awards: Best of Show, 29th Ann Alaskan Arts & Crafts Exhib, Alaska State Mus, Juneau, 73; Second Prize, Alaska Prints 76, Alaska State Coun on the Arts, 76; Third Prize, Alaska Bicentennial Banner Competition, Univ Alaska, Anchorage, 76. Mem: Col Art Asn; Am Asn of Mus; Alaska Asn for the Arts; San Francisco Mus of Mod Art; Visual Art Ctr of Alaska. Style & Technique: Hard-edge, colorful and semi-abstract figurative dealing with juxtaposition of psychological settings and realities. Media: Painting; printmaking. Mailing Add: Dept of Art Univ of Alaska Fairbanks AK 99701

CHRISTENSEN, DAN
PAINTER
b Lexington, Nebr, 1942. Study: Kansas City Art Inst, BFA. Exhib: Corcoran Biennial, Washington, DC, 69; Guggenheim Mus, New York, 69; Color & Field 1890-1970, Albright-Knox Gallery, Buffalo, NY, 70; The Structure of Color, Whitney Mus, New York, 71; Abstract Painting in the 70's, Boston Mus Fine Arts, 72. Bibliog: Dan Christensen (auth), Fine Young Artists Theodoron Awards, Guggenheim Mus, 69. Bibliog: Grace Glueck (auth), Like a beginning, Art in Am, 5-6/69; Emily Wasserman (auth), New York, Artforum, 9/69. Dealer: Andre Emmerich Gallery Inc 41 E 57th St New York NY 10022. Mailing Add: 17 Leonard St New York NY 10013

CHRISTENSEN, HANS-JORGEN THORVALD
DESIGNER, CRAFTSMAN
b Copenhagen, Denmark, Jan 21, 24. Study: Sch Arts & Crafts, Copenhagen, 39-44, dipl, 50; Georg Jensen Silver, apprentice; Col Tech Soc, Copenhagen, 51-53; Sch Arts & Crafts, Oslo, Norway, 52. Work: Johnson Wax Collection, Objects USA; silver pieces in pvt collections & churches. Exhib: Expo, Universal & Int Exhib, Brussels, Belg, 58; one-man shows, Albright-Knox Art Gallery, Buffalo, NY, 60 & Security Trust Co, Rochester, NY, 69; Johnson Wax Collection, Objects USA, traveled in US & Europe, 69; Radial 80, Xerox Art Show, Rochester, NY, 72. Teaching: Instr design, Sch Arts & Crafts, Copenhagen, 52-54; instr silversmithing & design, Sch Am Craftsmen, Rochester Inst Technol, 54-59, assoc prof, 59-63, prof, 63- Pos: Head model dept, Georg Jensen Silver, Copenhagen, 52-54. Awards: Hertz Legazy, King Christian X of Denmark, 44; Damascene Plate of Leo Brom, Utrecht, Huntington Gallery, 55; Rochester Silversmith Guild Award, Mem Art Gallery, Rochester, 60. Bibliog: Herald Brennan (auth), Why handmade?, Craft Horizons, 5-6/55; Talis Bergmanis (auth), Hans Christensen & the silver pots, Democrat & Chronicle, 68; Lee Nordness (auth), Objects USA, Viking, 70. Style & Technique: Holloware and design. Media: Sterling Silver, Metals. Mailing Add: 119 Faircrest Rd Rochester NY 14623

CHRISTENSEN, LARRY R
ART DIRECTOR, PAINTER
b Manti, Utah, Jan 18, 36. Study: Utah Tech Col, cert, 2 yrs. Work: Vernal High Sch, Utah; Cliff Lodge, Snowbird, Utah. Comn: Idaho Telephone Dir Cover, Mountain Bell, 61. Exhib: Cody Country Regional Art Exhib, Wyo, 67-77; Springville Mus Art Nat, Utah, 69-77; Ala Watercolor Soc Ann, Birmingham, 71; Cedar City Nat Exhib, Utah, 72-77; two-man show, Phillips Gallery, 73, 74 & 76; Univ Utah Mus Fine Art, 76-77; plus others. Pos: Art dir, Mountain Bell, 71-; instr, Watercolor Workshop, Salt Lake City, 75 & 76; instr, Div Continuing Educ, Univ Utah, 75, Photo Blue Workshop, 77- Awards: Silver 2nd Award, Utah State Expos, 70; First Place, Cody Country Art 70; Third Place, Springville Mus Art, 74. Mem: Assoc mem Am Watercolor Soc; Utah Watercolor Soc. Style & Technique: Transparent watercolor landscapes. Publ: Contribr, Art West, 72. Dealer: Blair Galleries Ltd PO Box 2342 Santa Fe NM 87501; Phillips Gallery 444 E 2nd Salt Lake City UT 84111. Mailing Add: 3534 Dover Hill Dr Salt Lake City UT 84121

CHRISTENSEN, RONALD JULIUS
PRINTMAKER, PAINTER
b Quincy, Mass, May 1, 23. Study: Sch Boston Mus Fine Arts, 47-50. Work: Rijksmuseum, Amsterdam, Holland; Springfield Mus Fine Art, Mass; Phoenix Art Mus, Ariz; Continental Can Co, New York; Bankers Trust, New York; Smithsonian Inst, Washington, DC. Comn: Three landscape murals, Celanese Corp Am, New York, 66; Americana Series painting, H B Hamilton Co, New York, 70. Exhib: Holland Floriade, Rotterdam, 59-60; Corcoran Biennial, Washington, DC, 59-60; Inst Contemp Art, Boston, 60; De Cordova & Dana Mus, Lincoln, Mass, 60; Eileen Kuhlik Gallery, New York, 73; plus others. Bibliog: Malcolm Preston (auth), Reminders of past masters of nature, Newsday, 70. Style & Technique: Bold impressionist, semi-abstract. Media: Watercolor, Acrylic Painting; Serigraphy. Publ: Illusr, Original Print Collectors Group, Ltd, New York, 73-77; illusr, Ferdinand Roten Publ, Baltimore, Md, 74; illusr, New York, NY; Guild, Ltd, New York, 75. Dealer: Allen S Park Gallery 33940; Frank Fedele Fine Arts Inc 91 Eighth Ave Brooklyn NY 11215. Mailing Add: 1023 Third Ave New York NY 10021

CHRISTENSEN, SHARLENE
PAINTER, INSTRUCTOR
b Fountain Green, Utah, Aug 24, 39. Work: Cliff Lodge, Snowbird, Utah. Exhib: Cody Country Regional Art Exhib, Wyo, 67-77; Ann Dinosaurland Regional Competition, Vernal, Utah, 67-76; Springville Mus Art Nat, Utah, 69-77; Cedar City Nat Art Exhib, Utah, 72-76; two-man show, Phillips Gallery, 73, 74 & 76; 110th Ann Exhib, Am Watercolor Soc, Nat Acad Galleries, New York, 77; Univ Utah Mus Fine Art, Salt Lake City, 76-77; plus others. Teaching: Instr watercolor, Salt Lake Art Ctr, 72- Pos: Artists-in-schs prog, Nat Found Arts & Utah Inst Fine Arts, 73-74; instr, Watercolor Workshop, Salt Lake City, 75 & 76. Awards: First Place, 33rd Ann Cedar City Awards: Best of Show, Dinosaurland Art Competition Regional, 74 & 75. Mem: Am & Utah Watercolor Soc. Style & Technique: Wet-in-wet. Media: Transparent Watercolor. Publ: Contribr, Art West, 72. Dealer: Blair Galleries Ltd PO Box 2342 Santa Fe NM 87501; Phillips Gallery 444 E 2nd S Salt Lake City UT 84111. Mailing Add: 3534 Dover Hill Dr Salt Lake City UT 84121

CHRISTENSEN, TED
PAINTER, PRINTMAKER
b Vancouver, Wash, Mar 20, 11. Study: Art Ctr Sch, Los Angeles, with King & Feitelson; Mus Art Sch, Portland, Ore, with Givler & Bunce; Otis Art Inst, Los Angeles, with Hansen & Zornes. Work: Wurlitzer Found, Taos, NMex; City of Sausalito Collection, Calif; Harwood Found, Taos; Col of Marin, Kentfield, Calif; Vancouver High Sch Collection, Wash. Exhib: Los Angeles Co Mus Ann, Los Angeles, 45 & 46; Ore Soc of Artists, Portland Art Mus, 46 & 47; Painters & Sculptors Ann, Oakland Art Mus, Calif, 46-47 & 54; Int Ceramic Ann, Syracuse Mus of Art, NY, 49 & 50; one-man shows, Col of Marin, Kentfield, Calif, 54 & 63, Marin Mus, San Rafael, Calif, plus over 40 others. Collections Arranged: Paintings of Mendocino Area, Mendocino Hist Res Soc, Calif, 77. Teaching: Instr life drawing, Col of Marin, Kentfield, 52-60. Awards: First Prize, Ore Soc of Artists, Portland Art Mus, 46 & 47; First Prize, Marin Soc of Artists, Webb Gallery, Ross, Calif, 58. Bibliog: Hilda Pertha (auth), A Visit with Ted Christensen, West Art, 68; Mary Carrol Nelson (auth), Ted Christensen—Itinerant Painter, Am Artist, 12/76; Susan E Myer (auth), 20 Landscape Painters & How They Work, Watson-Guptil, 77. Mem: Artist Equity; Otis Art Inst; Mendocino Art Ctr; Marin Soc of Artists (dir, Artists Coun, 55 & 56). Style & Technique: Representational/impressionist; mainly landscape. Media: Acrylic, oil; clay. Publ: Auth, Mendocino Sketchbook, pvt publ, 72; illusr, Kitchen Magic with Mushrooms, San Francisco Mycological Soc, 63. Dealer: Lester Kierstead Henderson Gallery 712 Hawthorne St Monterey CA 93940. Mailing Add: 573 Third St E Sonoma CA 95476

CHRISTENSEN, VAL ALAN
PRINTMAKER, INSTRUCTOR
b Valentine, Nebr, Jan 26, 46. Study: Univ Nebr-Lincoln, BFA, 68, with Thomas P Coleman; Wichita State Univ, MFA, 70. Work: Springfield Art Mus, Mo; Sioux City Art Ctr, Iowa; Sheldon Mem Art Gallery, Lincoln, Nebr; Kearney State Col, Nebr; Hastings Col, Nebr. Exhib: 35th Nat Graphic Arts & Drawing Exhib, Wichita Art Asn, Kans, 71; 29th Nat Print Exhib, Silvermine Guild of Artists, New Canaan, Conn, 72; 3rd Ann Nat Print Exhib, Ga State Univ, Atlanta, 72; 43rd Ann Art Exhib, Springfield Art Mus, Mo, 73; Nebraska 75, Joslyn Art Mus, Omaha, 75; one-person show, Sheldon Mem Art Gallery, Lincoln, 76. Teaching: Asst prof printmaking, Univ Nebr-Lincoln, 71-72; instr printmaking/drawing, Hastings Col, Nebr, 72-75. Pos: Artist-in-sch, Grand Island Cent Cath, 75-; panel mem, Community Arts Prog, Nebr Arts Coun, Omaha, 77- Awards: Vreeland Award, Univ Nebr-Lincoln Found, 67; Purchase Awards, 40th Ann Art Exhib, Springfield Art Mus, Mo, 70 & 33rd Ann Fall Show, Sioux City Art Ctr, 71. Mem: Mid-Am Col Art Asn; Col Art Asn; Grand Island Area Arts Coun (visual arts coordr, 76-77, pres, 77-78). Style & Technique: Meta-physical images; etching, engraving. Media: Intaglio prints. Mailing Add: 3115 W 17th St Grand Island NE 68801

CHRISTIANA, EDWARD
PAINTER, INSTRUCTOR
b White Plains, NY, May 8, 12. Study: Pratt Inst, dipl; Munson-Williams-Proctor Inst Sch Art, Utica, NY, with William C Palmer. Work: Currier Gallery Art, Manchester, NH; Syracuse Mus Fine Arts, NY; Worcester Mus, Mass; Albany Inst Hist & Art, NY; Cooperstown Art Asn, NY. Exhib: 53rd & 55th Watercolor & Drawing Ann, Art Inst Chicago, 42 & 44; Am Watercolor Soc Ann, New York, four times, 45-50; Audubon Artists, New York, 50; 37th Allied Artists Am Ann, New York, 50; 146th Painting & Sculpture Ann, Pa Acad Fine Arts, Philadelphia, 51; Oils & Watercolors, Munson-Williams-Procter Inst & Mus of Art, Utica, 78. Teaching: Instr painting, drawing & design, Munson-Williams-Proctor Inst Sch Art, Utica, 42-76, instr watercolor, 71- Awards: William Church Osborn Purchase Prize, Am Watercolor Soc, 49 & 51; 27th Ann Exhib Award, Assoc Artists Syracuse, 54; 21st Ann Upper Hudson Exhib Award, Albany Inst Hist & Art, 56. Mem: Cooperstown Art Asn (bd dirs, 50-, vpres, 75). Style & Technique: Abstract to realistic. Media: Watercolor. Dealer: Sales & Rental Gallery Munson-Williams-Proctor Inst 310 Genesee St Utica NY 13502 Mailing Add: 6 Steuben St Holland Patent NY 13354

CHRISTISON, MURIEL B
MUSEUM DIRECTOR, EDUCATOR
b Minneapolis, Minn. Study: Univ Minn, BA & MA; Univ Paris Inst Art & Archaeol, dipl art hist; Univ Brussels, dipl art hist. Collections Arranged: The Impressionists & Post-Impressionists, Va Mus Fine Arts, Richmond, 51, Goya, 53, Masterpieces of Chinese Art, 55, Les Fetes Galantes, 55, Masterpieces of American Silver, 60 & Sport & the Horse, 60; Art of India & Southeast Asia, Univ Ill, 63 & For Your Home, 60 & 70; plus many others. Teaching: Instr art in civilization & Am art, Univ Minn, Minneapolis, 45-47; instr visual awareness, Univ Ill, Champaign, 71-72, instr art museology, 72- Pos: Head educ dept, Minneapolis Inst Arts, 44-47; assoc dir, Va Mus Fine Arts, Richmond, 48-61; consult, Ark Art Ctr, Ill Art Coun & Ill Off Pub Instr, 61-; assoc dir & oper dir, Krannert Art Mus, Champaign, 62-71, dir, 71 & 75- Awards: Carnegie scholar, Inst Int Educ, 36; CRB fel, Belg-Am Educ Found, 38. Mem: Asn Art Mus Dirs; Col Art Asn Am; Am Asn Mus; Midwest Mus Conf; Int Inst Conserv Hist & Artistic Works. Publ: Auth, Circular on museum education: seven titles, 51-55; auth, The artmobile, an experiment in education, Art J, 55; auth, Le Museobus de Virginia Museum of Fine Arts, Mus, 55; auth, 25th anniversary in Virginia, 60 & The design game, 71, Mus News; plus others. Mailing Add: Krannert Art Mus 500 Peabody Dr Champaign IL 61820

CHRIST-JANER, ARLAND F
PAINTER, PRINTMAKER
b Garland, Nebr, Jan 27, 22. Work: Am Repub Ins Co, Des Moines, Iowa; Bankers Trust Co, New York; Hershey Foods Corp, Pa; Montclair Art Mus, NJ; Motion Picture Asn Am, New York; plus others. Exhib: Oxford 1st Ann Nat Print Exhib on Tour, Ga State Univ, 70; Am Art at Mid-Century, West Orange, NJ, 71; Nat Print Competition, Auburn Univ, Ala; Nat Print & Drawing Exhib, Univ NMex; Painters & Sculptors NJ; Columbia Art League, Mo, 76; plus others. Style & Technique: Hard edge, metal on metal; non-objective. Media: Graphic. Dealer: (prints) Associated American Artists 663 Fifth Ave New York NY 10022 & Nielson Gallery 179 Newbury St Boston MA 02116; (paintings) Krasner Gallery 1061 Madison Ave New York NY 10028. Mailing Add: Stephens Col PO Box 2001 Columbia MO 65201

CHRISTO (JAVACHEFF)
SCULPTOR
b Gabrovo, Bulgaria, June 13, 35. Study: Fine Arts Acad, Sofia, 52-56; Burian Theatre, Prague, Czech, work-study, 56; Vienna Fine Arts Acad, Austria, 57. Work: Mus of Mod Art, New York; Whitney Mus, New York; Stedelijk Mus, Amsterdam; Tate Gallery, London, Eng; Albright-Knox Mus, Buffalo, NY; plus many others. Projects: Packed Mus, Kunsthalle Berne; Packed Fountain & Medieval Tower, Spoleto; 5600 Cubicmeter Package, Kassel, 68; Wrapped Coast, One Million Sq Ft, Little Bay, Australia, 69; Wrapped Monuments, Vittorio Emanuele, Piazza Duomo & Leonardo, Piazza Scala, Milano, 70); Valley Curtain, Rifle, Colo, 70-72; Running Fence, Sonoma & Marin Co, Calif (24 miles long), 72-76; The Wall, Wrapped Roman Wall, Rome; Ocean Front, 150,000 Sq Ft, Newport, RI, 74. Exhib: One-man shows, Walker Art Ctr, Minneapolis, Minn, 66, Mus of Mod Art, New York, 68, Mus of Contemp Art, Chicago, 69, Nat Gallery of Victoria, Melbourne, Australia, 69, New Gallery, Cleveland, Ohio, 70, Kaiser-Wilhelm-Mus Krefeld, WGer, 70, Mus of Fine Arts, Houston, Tex, 71, Joslyn Art Mus, Omaha, Nebr, 72, Stedelijk Mus, Amsterdam, Holland, 73, Louisiana Mus, Humleback, Denmark, 74 & 78, M H de Young Mem Mus, San Francisco, 75, Mus of the 20th Century, Vienna, Austria, 76, Israel Mus, Jerusalem, 77, Mus Boymans-van-Beuningen, Rotterdam, Holland, 77 & Landische Mus, Bonn, WGer, 77; plus many others. Bibliog: Lawrence Alloway (auth), Christo, 69, David Bourdon (auth), Christo, 70 & Werner Spies (auth), Christo—The Running Fence, 77, Harry N Abrams, New York. Mailing Add: 48 Howard St New York NY 10013

CHRYSLER, WALTER P, JR
COLLECTOR
b Oelwein, Iowa. Exhib: (Paintings from Walter P Chrysler, Jr Collection) Whitney Mus Am Art, New York; Metrop Mus Art, New York; Va Mus Fine Arts, Richmond; Mus Fine Arts, Dallas, Tex; Nat Gallery Can Ottawa; Portland Art Mus, Ore; Los Angeles Co Mus Art, Los Angeles, Calif; plus many others. Pos: Organizer, York Publ House, 26; pres & chmn bd, Cheshire House, 30; pres & trustee, Chrysler Mus, Provincetown, Mass, 58-71; trustee, Chrysler Mus, Norfolk, Va, 69-, pres, 71-, dir, 71-77. Interest: Every civilization and cultural effort of man; gifts from collection made to, Museum Fine Arts, Boston; Museum of Modern Art, New York, Virginia Museum of Fine Arts, Chrysler Museum at Norfolk, Detroit Institute of Arts, Michigan, Dayton Art Institute, Ohio and Portland Art Museum. Collection: Encompasses most all of the important periods of painting. Mailing Add: c/o Chrysler Mus Norfolk VA 23510

CHRYSSA, (VARDEA)
SCULPTOR
b Athens, Greece, 1933; US citizen. Study: Acad Grande Chaumiere, Paris, 53-54; Calif Sch Fine Art, 54-55. Work: Mus Mod Art, Whitney Mus Am Art & Guggenheim Mus, New York; Albright-Knox Art Gallery, Buffalo, NY; Walker Art Ctr, Minneapolis; plus others, incl major Europ mus. Exhib: One-man shows, Solomon R Guggenheim Mus, 61, Mus Mod Art, New York, 63, Pace Gallery, 66 & 67, Harvard Univ, 68, Galerie Rive Droite, Paris, 69 & Whitney Mus of Am Art, New York, 72; Documenta IV, Kassel, Ger, 68; Whitney Mus Am Art, New York, 72; Musée de l'Art Moderne de la Ville de Paris, France, 79; Kunsthaus, Zurich, 79. Bibliog: Lucy R Lippard (auth), Pop Art, Praeger, 66; Gregory Battcock (ed), Minimal Art: a Critical Anthology, Dutton, 68; Diane Waldman (auth), Chryssa: Selected Works 1955-1957, Pace Gallery, 68; Sam Hunter (auth), Chryssa, Verlag Gerd Hatje, Stuttgart, WGer, 74; Pierre Restany (auth), Chryssa, Harry Abrams, New York, 77. Mailing Add: c/o Denise Rene Gallery 6 W 57th St New York NY 10019

CHU, GENE
PRINTMAKER, LECTURER
b China, Dec 8, 36; Can citizen. Study: Ont Col Art; Art Students League, with Harry Sternberg & Edwin Dickerson; Claremont Grad Sch, MFA. Work: Tom Thomson Mem Gallery & Mus Fine Art, Owen Sound, Ont; McMaster Univ; Art Bank of Can Coun, Ottawa; Soc Can Painter-Etchers & Engravers; Univ Guelph. Exhib: Soc Can Painter-Etchers & Engravers Ann, 70-74; 25th Boston Printmakers Anniversary, 73; Calif Col Art & Craft World Print Competition, 73; 4th Brit Int Print Biennial, 74; 2nd NH Int Graphics Asn. Teaching: Instr drawing & Printmaking, Mary Washington Col, 68 & 69; asst prof drawing & printmaking, Univ Guelph, 69- Pos: Juror, Can Painter-Etcher & Engravers Ann Exhib, Toronto, Ont, 72; juror, Soc Graphic Art Ann Exhib, 74; juror, Kitchener-Waterloo Art Gallery, Ont, 75. Awards: First Prize, Tom Thomson 7 Mem Gallery & Mus Fine Art Ann Exhib, 72; Jurors Award of Merit, Second NH Int Graphics Ann, 74; Editions Award, Art Gallery of Brant, 75. Mem: Soc Can Painter-Etchers & Engravers; Graphics Soc. Style & Technique: Metaphoric or expression of being in washes and crayon work. Media: Lithography; Watercolor. Mailing Add: 9 Uplands Pl Guelph ON Canada

CHUEY, ROBERT ARNOLD
PAINTER, LECTURER
b Barberton, Ohio, Nov 15, 21. Study: Los Angeles Art Ctr Sch, 45-46; Los Angeles Co Art Inst, 47-49; Jepson Art Inst, 49-52, with Rico LeBrun. Work: Los Angeles Co Mus; City Mus St Louis. Exhib: Seven Los Angeles Co Mus Ann, 49-60; Carnegie Inst, Pittsburgh, 53; Sao Paulo Biennial, Brazil, 55; Pa Acad Fine Arts, Philadelphia, 58; Santa Barbara Mus Art, 57. Teaching: Lectr art, Los Angeles Co Art Inst, 54-56, Chouinard Art Inst, 58-63 & 67-68, Univ Calif, Los Angeles, 63-65 & 68-69, Univ Calif, Santa Barbara, 65-67 & Univ Southern Calif, 67-68. Style & Technique: Expressionist; semi-abstract. Media: Oil, Ink. Publ: Contribr, Realm of Contemporary Still-life, 63; contribr, Drawing—a Search for Form, 66; contribr, Painting Techniques, 68; contribr, The Art and Logic of Drawing, 75. Dealer: Jacqueline Anhalt Gallery 750 N La Cienega Blvd Los Angeles CA 90069. Mailing Add: 2460 Sunset Plaza Dr Los Angeles CA 90069

CHUMLEY, JOHN WESLEY
PAINTER
b Rochester, Minn, Sept 12, 28. Study: Ringling Sch Art; Posey Sch Sculpture; Amaganset Art Sch; Pa Acad Fine Art. Work: Everhard Mus, Scranton, Pa; WTex Mus, Lubbock; Norfolk Mus, Va; R W Norton Gallery, Shreveport, La; Washington Co Mus, Hagerstown, Md. Exhib: Pa Acad Biennial, Philadelphia, 58; Nat Acad Arts & Lett, New York, 59; Carnegie Inst, Pittsburgh, Pa, 64; Twentieth Century Realists, San Diego, Calif, 68; Butler Art Inst, Youngstown, Ohio, 73 & 75; plus several one-man shows. Pos: Artist in residence, Ft Worth Art Ctr, Tex, 58-61. Awards: Philadelphia Watercolor Club Prize, 57; Hallgarten Prize, Nat Acad Arts & Lett, 59; Childe Hassam Award, Am Acad Arts & Lett, 59. Mem: Am Watercolor Soc; Philadelphia Watercolor Club. Style & Technique: Realistic; controlled watercolor with infinite detail. Media: Egg Tempera; Watercolor. Dealer: Electra Carlin Galleries 710 Montgomery Ft Worth TX 76107; Lee Fitch 5121 Kingston Pike Knoxville TN 37919. Mailing Add: PO Box 152 Middletown VA 22645

CHUNG, ROGER K
ART DEALER, PAINTER
b Canton, China, Oct 24, 46; US citizen. Study: Hong Kong Int Art Sch; Nat Acad Sch Fine Arts, New York, with Raymond Breinn & Wong Siuling; Brooklyn Col, BA; Pratt Inst, MFA. Work: HwaKang Mus Fine Arts, China; Nat Mus Fine Arts, Maltas; Chinese Cult Ctr, New York; Mus Mod Art, Mexico City; China Inst, New York. Exhib: Nat Acad Design Ann, New York, 70; Am Watercolor Soc Ann, New York, 70; Nat Art League Ann, New York, 71; Glastonbury Art Guild Ann, Conn, 74; Int Arts Festival, Lincoln Ctr, 74. Teaching: Art instr, Chinese Cult Ctr, New York, 73-75; asst prof art, Pratt Inst, 74-75. Pos: Dir, Pacem in Terris Gallery, New York, 74-75; dir, Gallery Int, Hong Kong, 75- Awards: Nat Arts Club Second Prize in Watercolor, 72; Chinese Cult Ctr First Prize in Watercolor, 72; Glastonbury Art Guild First Prize in Watercolor, 74. Bibliog: Lee Yuen Ming (auth), Young Painter (film), 71; Bernard Murphy (auth), Poetic painter (article), 73; Wong Suling (auth), Oriental brush painting (article), 73. Mem: Am Watercolor Soc; Sumie Soc; Chinese Artists Asn. Style & Technique: Wet in wet, combined with oriental brush technique; very poetic. Media: Watercolor, Chinese Ink. Specialty: Contemporary art. Collection: Old Oriental Chinese paintings and calligraphy; contemporary watercolor paintings. Publ: Auth, How to paint bamboo, 73; auth, Watercolor West and the East, 73; contribr, Chinese Arts Mag, 74. Dealer: Contemp Arts Gallery 2186 Grand Concourse Bronx NY 10451. Mailing Add: 457 40th St Bayridge NY 11232

CHURCH, C HOWARD
PAINTER
b South Sioux City, Nebr, May 1, 04. Study: Art Inst Chicago, with Boris Ainsfeld, John Norton & William P Welsh, 28-32, BFA, 35; Univ Chicago, BA, 38; Ohio State Univ, MA, 39. Comn: Murals, Morgan Park Mil Acad, Chicago, 32-36. Exhib: One-man shows, Mulvane Art Mus, Thayer Mus Art, Univ Nebr, Joslyn Art Mus & Kresge Art Ctr, East Lansing, Mich; plus others. Teaching: Head art dept, Washburn Univ, 40-45; head art dept, Mich State Univ, 45-60, prof, 60-72; retired. Pos: Dir, Morgan Park Sch Art, Chicago, 33-36; dir, Mulvane Art Mus, Washburn Univ, 40-45. Awards: Fine Arts Medal, 63 & Purchase Award, mem exhib, 66, Mich Acad Sci, Arts & Lett; Print Purchase Award, Mich Artists Exhib, Mich Educ Asn, 69 & 70; plus others. Mem: Mich Acad Sci, Arts & Lett; Midwest Col Art Asn. Mailing Add: 271 Lexington Ave East Lansing MI 48823

CHURCHILL, DIANE
PAINTER
b Bronxville, NY, Jan 8, 41. Study: Wellesley Col, BA(art hist); Brooklyn Mus Art Sch; Hunter Col, MA(painting), with Ray Parker & Vicent Longo. Work: Chase Manhattan Bank Collection, New York; Wellesley Col Collection, Mass; Jay Hambridge Art Found, Rabun Gap, Ga. Exhib: Yr of the Woman, Reprise, Bronx Mus of Art, 76; Drawings/USA/77, Minn Mus Art, St Paul, 77; Contemp Issues, Works by Women on Paper, Los Angeles, 77; Women's Caucus for Art, Grad Ctr, City Univ NY, 78. Pos: Artist catalyst, Brigate-In-Action, New York, 68-73; publ & ed, Fourth St i, 71-73; adj instr, Jersey City State Col, NJ, 73-75; market developer, Printshop, New York, 74-75; field rep, Visual Arts Dept, NY State Coun on the Arts, New York, 76-77. Bibliog: Ellen Lubell (auth), Review, Arts Mag, 3/76; Marian Courtney (auth), article in NJ Herald News, 10/76. Mem: Soho 20 Gallery, Inc (secy, 75). Style & Technique: Two-dimensionally shaped canvases, exploring organic shapes. Media: Acrylic. Dealer: Soho 20 Gallery 99 Spring St New York NY 10012; Hilary Sloane 486 E 74th St New York NY 10021. Mailing Add: 57 Hudson Pl Weehawken NJ 07087

CHWAST, SEYMOUR
DESIGNER, ILLUSTRATOR
b New York, NY, Aug 18, 31. Study: Cooper Union. Work: Mus of Mod Art, New York. Exhib: The Push Pin Style, Musee Des Arts Decoratif, The Louvre, Paris, France, 71 & The Art of the NY Times, 73; A Century of Am Illus, Brooklyn Mus, 73. Teaching: Instr design & illus, Cooper Union, 75- Pos: Ed, The Push Pin Graphic Bi-Monthly Mag, 56-; dir, Push Pin Studios, New York, 57- Bibliog: T Nishio (auth), Seymour Chwast, Shinkosha Publ, Tokyo, 74. Mem: Am Inst of Graphic Arts, (vpres; dir). Style & Technique: Varied. Mailing Add: c/o Push Pin Studios 207 E 32nd St New York NY 10016

CIANFONI, EMILIO
CONSERVATOR, PAINTER
b Rome, Italy, Oct 9, 46; US citizen. Study: Studied drawing, painting & restoration with Giustino Caporali, 58-63, Manieri Art Inst, 60-63, Accad di Belle Arti, 64-66 & conserv of paintings at Inst Centrale del Restauro, 66-67, Rome; Art Students League, New York, 70-72; Baldwin Sch (glazes chemistry), New York, 73. Comn: Paintings, Lowenbrau Co, Munich, Bavaria, Ger, 67; painting & sculpture, Pacifici Family, Rome, Italy, 67; mural, Church Hosp Comples, Vilalba, Italy, 69; Bicentennial Coins Competition, Metrop Mus of Art, New York, 74. Exhib: Galeria Modigliani, 63, 20th Century Competition, City Bldg, 64 & Mus of Mod Art, 65, Rome; New Talent (2 shows), Betty Parsons Gallery, New York, 74; Primitive & Contemp Art, Tucson, Ariz, by Betty Parsons Gallery, 75; UN Group Am Exhib, New York, by Truman Gallery, 77. Pos: Design painter/conservator, Gucci Shops, Rome & New York, 68-70; sr craftsman, Alva Reproductions, New York, 70-72; restorer, Metrop Mus of Art, New York, 72-74; chief conservator, Vizcaya Mus & Gardens, 75- Awards: 1st Prize, 20th Anniversary of Italian Partisans Competition, Rome, 64; 2nd Prize, Ciac Poetry & Arts Competition, Rome, 66. Style & Technique: Works convey a personal yet universal feeling. Media: Drawing on paper, mixed media; ink, watercolor & other media. Dealer: Truman Gallery 38 E 57th St New York NY 10022. Mailing Add: 1522 SW 16th St Miami FL 33145

CIARROCHI, RAY
PAINTER
b Chicago, Ill. Study: Chicago Acad Fine Arts; Wash Univ, BFA, with Fred Conway; Boston Univ, MFA. Work: Ciba-Geigy Collection, Ardsley, NY; Citibank, New York; Owens-Corning Glass Found; Am Tel & Tel; Brooklyn Mus. Exhib: One-man shows, Tibor De Nagy Gallery, 71-72, 74, 76 & 78; Nat Inst Arts & Lett, New York, 72 & 75; 76 Maine Artists, Augusta Mus, 76; Am Watercolors, 1800 to the Present, Brooklyn Mus, NY, 76; Artist's Choice—Figurative Painting in New York, Soho Ctr for Visual Arts, 77; Works on Paper from the Ciba-Geigy Collection, Neuberger Mus, Purchase, NY, 77. Teaching: Instr painting & drawing, Parsons Sch Design, New York, 66-71; lectr drawing, Columbia Univ Sch Arts, 69-71 & 76-; instr painting, Md Inst Col Art, 71-72; instr, Brooklyn Col, 72-76. Awards: Fulbright Grant to Italy, 63-64; Tiffany Grant, 67; Ingraham Merrill Found, 77. Bibliog: John Gruen (auth), rev in New York Mag, 6/7/71; James R Mellow (auth) & Hilton Kramer (auth), rev in New York Times, 4/1/72 & 3/2/74. Media: Oil, Watercolor. Dealer: Tibor de Nagy Gallery 29 W 57th St New York NY 10019. Mailing Add: 463 West St New York NY 10014

CICANSKY, VICTOR
SCULPTOR
b Regina, Sask, Feb 12, 35. Study: Univ Sask, Saskatoon, BEd; Univ Regina, BA; Univ Calif, Davis, MFA, with Bob Arneson & Roy DeForrest. Work: Sask Govt Arts Bd; Can Coun Art Bank; Sacramento State Col; Mus of Mod Art, Tokyo, Japan; Mus of Mod Art, Montreal. Comn: Sask Grain Bin (sculpture), COJO-Olympic Comt, Montreal, 76; Settlement of the West (sculpture), Sask Govt, Saskatoon, 77. Exhib: One, Two, Three, Hansen-Fuller Gallery, San Francisco, 70; Contemp Ceramics, Mus of Fine Arts, Kyoto, Japan, 71; Int Ceramics, Victoria & Albert Mus, London, Eng, 72; Trajectories 73, Musee de Art Moderne de Ville de Paris, France, 73; Cicansky, Espace 5, Montreal, Que, 74; Fired Clay Show, Greater Victoria Art Gallery, Victoria, BC, 75; New York Clay, Monique Knowlton Gallery, New York, 75; plus others. Teaching: Assoc prof art, Univ Regina, Sask, 70-78. Awards: Can Coun grants/travel & work, 68, 69, 71 & 74; Kingsley Ann Award/Sculpture, Sacramento, 69; Royal Albert Award, Ceramic Sculpture, Toronto, 71. Media: Clay. Publ: Contribr to Arts Mag, Fall 70, Mus of Mod Art J, Amsterdam, 4/71, Arts Can, 5/73; Art & Artists, 8/73 & Time, 4/73. Mailing Add: Box 79 Craven SK S0G 0W0 Can

CICERO, CARMEN L
PAINTER
Study: Newark State Col, NJ, BS; Hunter Col, New York. Work: Guggenheim Mus, New York; Mus Mod Art, New York; Whitney Mus Am Art, New York; Newark Mus Asn, NJ; Stedlijh Mus de Lakenhal, Neth. Exhib: Whitney Mus Ann, 55-66; one-man shows, Peridot Gallery & Leslie Rankow Gallery, New York; Premiere Bienale de Paris, France. Teaching: Mem fac, Sarah Lawrence Col, 59-68; instr, Montclair State Col, 60- Awards: Guggenheim Found Fel, 57 & 63; Purchase Prize, Ford Found, 65. Media: Oil, Acrylic. Dealer: Rankow Gallery 108 E 78th St New York NY 10021. Mailing Add: 278 Bowery New York NY 10012

CIKOVSKY, NICOLAI
PAINTER, MURALIST
b Pinsk, Russia, Dec 10, 94. Study: Royal Art Sch, Vilna; Tech Inst of Arts, Moscow. Work: Brooklyn Mus, NY; Art Inst Chicago; Cleveland Mus Art, Ohio; William Rockhill Nelson Gallery of Art, Kansas City, Mo; Los Angeles Co Mus Art, Los Angeles, Calif; Mus Mod Art, New York. Comn: Murals, Interior Dept, Washington, DC & US Post Off, Towson & Silver Spring, Md. Exhib: Mus Mod Art, New York; Walker Art Ctr, Minneapolis, Minn; Carnegie Inst Int, Pittsburgh, Pa; Corcoran Gallery of Art, Washington, DC; Boston Mus Fine Art; Cleveland Mus Art, Ohio; Los Angeles Co Mus Art, Calif; one-man shows, Allied Artists of Am, 42-44 & 46 & ACA Gallery, 59, 63 & 67. Teaching: Instr, Ekaterinenburg Higher Tech Art Inst, Russia, Mus Arts & Crafts, Columbus, Ohio, St Paul Sch of Art, Art Acad of Cincinnati, Corcoran Sch of Art, Chicago Art Inst Sch & Art Students League, New York. Awards: Norman Wait Harris Bronze Medal, Art Inst Chicago, 32; Isaac N Maynard Prize, Nat Acad of Design, New York, 64; First Prize, Parrish Mus, Southampton, NY, 68. Mem: Nat Acad Design. Style & Technique: Landscape and figure painter. Media: Oil, Watercolor, Graphic. Dealer: Am Contemp Artists Gallery 23 E 73rd St New York NY 10021. Mailing Add: 500 W 58th St New York NY 10019

CIKOVSKY, NICOLAI, JR
ART HISTORIAN, EDUCATOR
b New York, NY, Feb 11, 33. Study: Harvard Col, AB; Harvard Univ, AM & PhD. Collections Arranged: Sanford Robinson Gifford, Univ Tex Art Mus, 70-71; The White Marmorean Flock; 19th Century American Women Neoclassical Sculptors, Vassar Col Art Gallery, 72. Teaching: Assoc prof art, Vassar Col, 71-74; prof & chmn dept art, Univ NMex, 74- Pos: Dir, Vassar Col Art Gallery, 71-74. Res: 19th & 20th Century American painting and sculpture. Publ: Auth, George Inness, 71 & Life & Work of George Inness, 77. Mailing Add: Dept of Art Univ NMex Albuquerque NM 87131

CIMBALO, ROBERT W
SCULPTOR, GRAPHIC ARTIST
b Tiriolo, Italy; US citizen. Study: Pratt Inst, Brooklyn; Syracuse Univ; Sorita Dante Alighari, Belle Arte & Univ Studi Roma, Rome. Work: Kirkland Art Ctr, Clinton, NY; Munson-Williams-Proctor Inst, Utica, NY; Syracuse Univ; State Univ NY Col Cortland; Pratt Inst. Style & Technique: Figurative-expressionist. Media: Graphics, Wood. Dealer: FAR Gallery 746 Madison Ave New York NY 10021. Mailing Add: 1602 Harrison Ave Utica NY 13501

CINDRIC, MICHAEL ANTHONY
SCULPTOR, EDUCATOR
b Pittsburgh, Pa, Jan 2, 47. Study: Ind State Univ, BS & MS; NY State Col Ceramics, Alfred Univ, MFA. Work: R J Reynolds World Hq, Winston Salem, NC; NC Mus of Art, Raleigh; Krannert Art Gallery, Evansville, Ind; Huntington Galleries, WVa; J Patrick Lannan Found, Palm Beach, Fla. Exhib: Nat Sculpture 75, Huntsville Mus of Art, Ala, 75; Biennial Exhib of Piedmont Crafts, Mint Mus of Art, Charlotte, NC, 76; Nat Exhib of Crafts, Scottsdale Ctr for the Arts, Ariz, 76; Exhib 280, Huntington Galleries, 76; Concepts: Clay-Nat Ceramics, Mt Pleasant, Mich, 76; NC Invitational Exhib, Southeastern Ctr for Contemp Art, Winston-Salem, 77; Ceramic Conjunction 1977, Long Beach Mus of Art, Calif, 77; Mainstreams Int Painting & Sculpture Exhib, Marietta Col, Ohio, 77. Collections Arranged: Contemp Ceramic Sculpture, Ackland Art Ctr, Chapel Hill, NC, 77. Teaching: Asst prof ceramic sculpture, Univ NC, 75- Awards: Wulfmand Purchase Award, Exhib 280, Huntington Gallery, 76, 1st Prize Purchase Award/Sculpture, 76; Carolina Designer Craftsman Purchase Award, NC Artists Exhib, NC Mus of Art, Raleigh. Mem: Am Craftsmen Coun; Nat Coun on Educ for the Ceramic Arts; Southern Asn of Sculptors. Style & Technique: Ceramic sculpture. Media: Sculpture, clay. Publ: Contribr, Portable Museum Series, Am Craftsmen Coun. Dealer: Garden Gallery Hwy 70 W Raleigh NC. Mailing Add: 116 North St Chapel Hill NC 27514

CINTRON, JOSEPH
PAINTER, INSTRUCTOR
b Ponce, PR, Aug 4, 21. Study: Univ Dayton, BA, 43; Ohio State Univ; Cleveland Inst Art, dipl, 54; with Robert Brackman, Madison, Conn; Art Students League, with Sidney Dickinson. Work: Portrait of a Young Girl, Cuyahoga Valley Art Ctr, Cuyahoga Falls, Ohio; Portrait of Dr John A Budd, Acad of Med of Cleveland; Portrait of Bishop Aponte Martinez, Bishops Residence, Ponce, PR; portrait of Dr Paul Weaver, Lake Erie Col, Painesville, Ohio. Comn: Portrait of Frank & Robert Stranahan, Champion Spark Plugs, Toledo, Ohio, 65; portrait of Eric Fromm, Case Western Reserve Univ, Cleveland, Ohio, 69; copy of Copley's Nathaniel Hurd, Edward A Hurd, Chicago, Ill, 73; portrait of Gov Luis a Ferre, La Fortaleza, San Juan, PR, 74; portrait of Capt Antoine Paulint of the Continental Army, W L L'Esperance, Columbus, Ohio, 78. Exhib: Cleveland Mus Art Regional May Show, 60; Canton Art Inst Regional, 65-69; Mid-Year Nat, Butler Inst Am Art, 70; Sch of Fine Arts, Willoughby, Ohio, 72; Cleveland Invitational, 73; Cleveland Athletic Club, 73-75; Beck Ctr for Cult Arts, Lakewood, Ohio, 76. Teaching: Secondary level, San Juan, PR & Cleveland & Cincinnati, Ohio, 43-51 & 54-63; instr painting & drawing, Cleveland Inst Art, 56- & Cooper Sch Art, 63- Pos: Art adv, Purcell High Sch Yearbk, 51-52; guest artist, Canton Art Inst Summer Sch, 66-69; guest artist, Sch of Fine Arts, Willoughby, Ohio, summer 78. Awards: Poster Award, Dem Womens Educ Coun, San Juan, 35; Painting Award, Cuyahoga Valley Art Ctr, 67 & 68. Bibliog: Marie Kirkwood (auth), Cintron trademark is realism, Sun Press, Cleveland, 8/5/71; Gloria Borras (auth), Pintar Rostros es Captar Almas, Puerto Rico Ilustrado, San Juan, 3/30/75. Style & Technique: Realistic, impressionist. Media: Oil. Dealer: Portraits Inc 41 E 57th St New York NY 10022. Mailing Add: 3853 Princeton Blvd South Euclid OH 44121

CITRON, MINNA WRIGHT
PAINTER, PRINTMAKER
b Newark, NJ, Oct 15, 96. Study: Brooklyn Inst Arts & Sci; New York Sch Appl Design; Art Students League; City Col New York; also with K Nicolaides & Kenneth Mayes Miller; Atelier 17. Work: Nat Collection Fine Arts, Smithsonian Inst; Rosenwald Collection, Nat Gallery Art; The White House & US Info Agency, Washington, DC; Mus Mod Art, Whitney Mus Am Art, Metrop Mus Art & Joseph H Hirschhorn Collection, New York; plus many others. Exhib: Dulin Gallery, Philadelphia, 66; Am Color Print Soc, Philadelphia Mus Art, 67; Calif State Col, Long Beach, 69; NJ State Mus, Trenton, 68 & 70; plus one-man shows throughout US, Europe & SAm. Teaching: Instr art, Brooklyn Mus, 40-44; lectr, US & abroad; instr art, Pratt Inst, Manhattan Ctr, 71-72. Pos: Rep, US Govt, Congres Int Educ Artistique, Paris, 47; mem, Washington Conf Women in Arts, Corcoran Gallery, 72. Awards: Soc Am Graphic Artists Award, Los Angeles Co Mus, 69; Awards, NJ State Mus, 68 & 70; Yaddo Fel, Artist in Residence, Lakeside Studio, Mich, 70; plus others. Bibliog: Herta Wecher (auth), Cimaise, Paris, 56; Adela Jaume (auth), El Diario de la Marina, Havana, Cuba, 57; Dario Suro (auth), Cuadernos Hispano-Americanos, 60; plus others. Dealer: AAA Gallery 663 Fifth Ave New York NY 10022; Ingber Gallery 3 E 78th St New York NY 10021. Mailing Add: 145 Fourth Ave New York NY 10003

CIUCA, EUGEN
SCULPTOR, PAINTER
b Miluan, Romania, Feb 27, 13. Study: Univ Cluj, Romania, 34-38; Univ Bucharest, Romania, 42-46. Work: Nat Mus of Art, Bucharest; Mod Galerija, Lublijana, Yugoslavia; Forma Viva Open Air Mus, Kostanjevica, Yugoslavia; Nat Mus of Art, Budapest, Hungary; White House, Washington, DC. Comn: Monument to the Heroes of the Rumanian Army, Piestany, Czech, 46; Festive Column (stone & concrete, 16 meters high), Herastrau Park, Bucharest, 64; Monument to the Partisans (wood & stone, 9 meters high), Munic of Kostanjevica,

Yugoslavia, 68; Dante Alighieri Monument, Town Hall Pontelongo-Padova, Italy, 67; Dante Alighieri (monumental bust), Col Mus of Art Arsenale, Venice, Italy, 77. Exhib: One-man shows, Int Joint Exhib, 33 & 35; State House of Art, Bucharest, 47, Nat Gallery of Art, Dalles, Romania, 65, Palazo Firenze, Rome, Italy, 67, Palazzo Al Valentino, Turin, Italy, 68 & Bevilaqua la Masa, Town Gallery, Venice, Italy, 70; Exhib of Rumanian Art, Budapest, Hungary, 47; Int Exhib, Bucharest, 55; Divine Comedy in Images & Sculpture, Ravenna, Italy, 76; Int Exhib of Madrid, Spain, 77; Dante Alighieri Exhib, Rome, 77; Fourth Dimension in Art (travelling exhib), Rome, 77. Teaching: Asst prof human anat drawing, Univ Bucharest, Romania, 43-50; prof arts & sculpture, Dowling Col, Oakdale, NY, 74-75. Pos: Dir monumental art sculpture, Studio of Fondul Plasric, Bucharest, 58-60. Awards: Gold Medal, Int Joint Exhib, Int Cult Ctr, Jesolo, 71; Gold Medal, one-man exhib, City of Ravenna, Italy, 76; Premio Cronaca 77 for The Fourth Dimension in Art, Int Archit TV-Art Info, Rome, 77. Bibliog: Marziano Bernardi (critic), La Stampa, Italy, 68; Carlo Giulio Argan (critic), article in Catalogo, Rome, 72; Paolo Rizzi (critic), article in Catalogo, Ravenna, Italy, 76. Mem: Accad Tiberina-Roma Arte-Lett-Sci; Accad di Cinquecento, Rome, 75; fel Int Biographical Asn, 75; hon men Mark Twain Soc; Legion d'Oro, Rome; Accad Art Sci Tetradrahma. Media: Sculptor. Dealer: Art Studio Palazzo Alesandrini 65 Via Nazionale 30034 Mira-Venezia Italy. Mailing Add: 21 Shore Lane Bay Shore NY 11706

CIVITELLO, JOHN PATRICK
PAINTER
b Paterson, NJ, Aug 17, 39. Study: William Paterson Col, BA, 61; NY Univ, MA, 62. Work: NJ State Mus, Trenton; Monterey Peninsula Mus Art, Calif; 3M Co, St Paul, Minn; Nat Broadcasting Co Television, New York; Lloyd's Bank, Calif. Exhib: Fourteen Contemporary New Jersey Artists, NJ State Mus, 67; 30th Biennial of Am Art, Corcoran Gallery Art, Washington, DC, 67; John Civitello: Paintings, Am Acad Art Gallery, Rome, 70; What's Happening in Soho, Univ Md Art Gallery, 71; one-man show, Art Club Chicago, 74; Am Acad Arts & Lett Ann, 76; Drawing Today in New York, Sewall Art Gallery, Houston, Tex & Dayton Art Inst, Ohio. Awards: Gov NJ Purchase Award, NJ State Mus, 71; Creative Artists Pub Serv Grant, Cult Coun Found, 72; Childe Hassam Purchase Award, Am Acad Arts & Lett, 76. Bibliog: E Bilardello (auth), Pittori Americani a Roma, Margutta-Periodico d'Arte Contemporanea, Rome, 70; article in Arts Mag, 7/75. Media: Acrylic. Dealer: Dubins Gallery 11948 San Vicente Blvd Los Angeles CA 90049. Mailing Add: 226 Vreeland Ave Paterson NJ 07504

CLAGUE, JOHN ROGERS
SCULPTOR
b Cleveland, Ohio, Mar 14, 28. Study: Cleveland Inst Art, BFA. Work: Cleveland Mus Art; Larry Aldrich Mus, Ridgefield, Conn; Art Gallery of Ont; Univ Mass Mus. Comn: Limestone sculpture, Cleveland Recreation Ctr, 56; Israel (bronze sculpture), Jewish Community Ctr, Cleveland, 61; limestone motif, Child Guid Ctr, Cleveland, 64; kinetic sound-making sculpture (stainless steel), Ashland Col, Ohio, 72. Exhib: Cleveland Mus Art May Show, 55-77; Whitney Mus Am Art Ann, New York, 64-65; Waddell Gallery, New York, 66; Highlights of 1966-1967 Art Season, Larry Aldrich Mus, 67; Int Monumental Sculpture Exhib, Blossom Music Ctr, 68. Teaching: Instr sculpture, Oberlin Col, 57-61 & Cleveland Inst Art, 56-71. Awards: Yale Norfolk Fel, 54; Catherwood Found Traveling Fel, 56; Nat Scholastic Mag Hall of Fame, 70. Style & Technique: Kinetic structures, geometric in form, produce music when set in motion; tig, arc, and oxy-acet welding; brazing and casting. Media: Stainless Steel, Bronze. Mailing Add: 11625 County Line Rd Gates Mills OH 44040

CLANCY, JOHN
ART DEALER
Pos: Dir, Frank Rehn Gallery. Mailing Add: 655 Madison Ave New York NY 10021

CLANCY, PATRICK
PAINTER, VIDEO ARTIST
b Hornell, NY, Oct 19, 41. Study: Pratt Inst, with Ernest Briggs & Brie Taylor, BS, 64; Yale Univ, BFA, 64 & MFA(painting), 67, with Jack Tworkov, Al Held, Helen Frankenthaler, Frank Stella & electronic music with Bulent Arel. Exhib: Spaces, Mus Mod Art, New York, 69 & 70; Works for New Spaces, Walker Art Ctr, Minneapolis, 71; Music with its Roots in Ether, Mills Col, Oakland, Calif, 71; Pulsa, Automation House, New York, 71; Critics Choice, Andrew Dickson White Mus, Cornell Univ, NY, 71. Teaching: Lectr & res assoc, Pulsa Sem, Yale Univ, 67-72; vis artist, Calif Inst Arts, 71 & 72; instr hist of cinema & environ art, Colgate Univ, NY, 73- Awards: Yale Univ Fel, 64-67; Graham Found Grant, Advan Studies in Visual Arts, 68-72. Style & Technique: Interactive real-time environment systems, the human bio-field, semiology, painting involving memory, cameras without lenses, image generation through destruction of videcon tubes over long periods of time, recto-verso hanging paintings. Publ: Co-auth, Pulsa, Eye Mag, 5/68; auth, Proposal, Spaces Catalog, Mus Mod Art, 1/70; co-auth, Pulsa, radio interview, KPFA, Berkeley, Calif, 3/71; auth, The city as an artwork, Arts of the Environ, 72. Mailing Add: RD 2 River Rd Hamilton NY 13346

CLAPSADDLE, JERRY
PAINTER
b Hastings, Nebr Dec 12, 41. Study: Drake Univ, Des Moines, Iowa, BFA, 64; Ind Univ, MFA, 66. Work: Albright-Knox Art Gallery, Buffalo, NY; Honolulu Acad of Art, Hawaii; Libr Cong, Washington, DC; Lilly Libr of Rare & Fine Bks, Ind Univ, Bloomington; Mus Mod Art, New York. Exhib: Eastern US Drawing Competition, Jacksonville, Fla, 70; Lenore Gray Gallery, Providence, 70, 73, 74 & 77; 13th Nat Exhib Prints & Drawings, Okla Art Ctr, Oklahoma City, 71; 7th Dulin Nat Print & Drawing Competition, Knoxville, Tenn, 71; 24th Northeastern Exhib of Painting & Sculpture, Silvermine Guild, New Canaan, Conn, 73; Regional, Everson Mus, Syracuse, NY, 74; Artists of Cent New York, Munson-Williams-Proctor Inst, Utica, NY, 74; Corp Collect, De Cordova Mus, Lincoln, Mass, 74; Catskill Regional, State Univ NY Col, Oneonta, 75; Susan Caldwell Gallery, New York, 77; Max Protetch Gallery, Washington, DC, 77, Protetch-McIntosh Gallery, Washington, DC, 77; Pattern Painting, PS 1, New York, 77. Teaching: From instr to asst prof studio art & printmaking, Univ RI, Kingston, 67-74; asst prof painting, Univ Md, College Park, 76- Pos: Designer exhib catalogues, Univ RI, Kingston, State Univ NY Col, Oneonta & Univ Md, College Park, 71-76; exhib organizer, Fine Arts Ctr, Univ RI, Kingston, 71-74; dir, Fine Arts Ctr Gallery, State Univ NY Col, Oneonta, 74-76. Awards: Hon Mention, Eastern US Drawing Competition, Jacksonville, Fla, 70; Aldrich Award/Painting, 24th Northeastern Exhib of Painting & Sculpture, Silvermine Guild, 73; Creative Artists Pub Serv Fel, 77. Bibliog: Jo Ann Lewis (auth), Galleries, Washington Post, 10/15/77 & 4/30/77, Mary Swift (auth), Jerry Clapsaddle: Max Protetch, Washington Rev of the Arts, Vol 3 (1977). Mem: Col Art Asn; Advocates for the Arts. Style & Technique: Interwoven, highly textured, brush strokes over grid formats on stretched and unstretched canvas and paper; nonfigurative paintings. Media: Acrylic-latex. Publ: Designer of exhib catalogues, Folk Textile From Northern India, 74, Linda Benglis: Physical & Psychological Moments in Time, 75, Michelle Stuart, 75, State Univ NY & Maurice Prendergast: Art of Impulse & Color, 76 & From Delacroix to Cezanne: French Watercolor Landscapes of the 19th Century, 77, Univ Md. Dealer: Protetch-McIntosh 2115 P St NW Washington DC 20037. Mailing Add: 5807 Taylor Rd Riverdale MD 20840

CLARE, STEWART
RESEARCH ARTIST
b Montgomery City, Mo, Jan 31, 13. Study: Univ Kans, scholar, BA, 35; Iowa State Univ, fel, MS, 37; Univ Chicago, fel, PhD, 49; Kansas City Art Inst & Univ Mo, Kansas City, 46-49. Work: Work in libr & nat libr in US, Eng, Can, Australia & other countries. Exhib: Univ Alta, 50-54; The Science of Color & Design, 62-66, Chromatology: the Science of Color, 65-66, Scientific Illustrations & Diagrams, Designs & Writings, 68-70, at univs, cols & mus, US; Brit Asn for Advan Sci, Durham Mus & Art Ctr, 70; plus others. Teaching: Lectr, Dept Fine Art, Univ Alta, 50-53, Union Col, 58-61 & State Univ NY Col Twin Valleys, 62-66. Pos: Res artist sci of color, Kansas City Art Inst, Univ Mo, Kansas City, Univ Alta, Univ Adelaide, Union Col & others, 46-66; res in chromatology, Col Emporia, 67-74; color consult & info resource, Vol for Int Tech Assistance, 62-, Nat Referral Ctr for Sci & Technol, Libr Cong, 70- Awards: Awards for Sci Illus, Univ Mo, Columbia, 29-31; Var Univ Res Grants, 46- Mem: Am Fedn Arts; Nat Art Educ Asn; Soc NAm Artists (adv bd, 71-); Int Soc Educ Through Art; Inter-Soc Color Coun. Res: Science of color and design; technology in art; physical and chemical properties of earth pigments, gums, resins, adhesives and binders. Collection: Original and reproduced art, art objects and books. Publ: Contribr, sci illus in var periodicals & textbooks, 37-72; auth, The Theory of Color & Design, plus others. Mailing Add: 405 NW Woodland Rd Indian Hills in Riverside Kansas City MO 64150

CLARK, CAROL CANDA
CURATOR
b New York, NY, July 21, 47. Study: Univ Mich, AB with distinction, 69, MA, 71; Kress Found fel, Cleveland Mus Art, 72-75. Teaching: Instr art hist & mus studies, Tex Christian Univ, Ft Worth, 75-77. Pos: Registr, Univ Mich Mus Art, Ann Arbor, 71-72; cur paintings, Amon Carter Mus Western Art, Ft Worth, Tex, 77- Mem: Am Asn Mus; Col Art Asn; Western Hist Asn; Am Asn State & Local Hist; Tex Asn Mus. Res: American nineteenth century landscape painting, particularly of the West. Publ: Auth, Jean Baptiste Simeon Chardin, Still Life with Herring, 74 & American Japonism: Contacts Between America and Japan, 1854-1910, 75, Bull Cleveland Mus Art; contribr, Three Centuries of American Art, Philadelphia Mus Art, 76; contribr, Exhibition of Masterpieces, East and West, from American Museum Collections from Ancient Egypt through Contemporary, Mus Western Art, Tokyo & Nat Mus, Kyoto, 76; co-auth, Jasper Francis Cropsey, The Narrows from Staten Island, Am Art Rev, 2/78. Mailing Add: PO Box 2365 Ft Worth TX 76101

CLARK, CHEVIS DELWIN
PAINTER, INSTRUCTOR
b Charleston, SC, Sept 5, 22. Study: High Mus Sch Art, grad, 50; also with Dong Kingman, Atlanta. Work: Gibbes Art Gallery, Charleston, SC; Beaufort Art Gallery, SC; SC Arts Comn, Columbia; C&S Bank Collections, Columbia; USN Combat Art Gallery, Washington, DC. Comn: Murals, USS Yorktown, USN, Charleston, 67-69. Exhib: New South Show, Norfolk Mus, Va, 53-54; Carolina Art Asn Shows, Charleston, 53-71; Southeastern Ann Exhibs, Atlanta, 54-57; Ala Watercolor Soc, 54-57; Spring Mills Traveling Exhib, Lancaster, SC, 70-71; Am Watercolor Soc Exhib, 76; SC Bank Bicentennial Comn Traveling Exhib, 76-77. Teaching: Pvt classes, 50-; instr acrylics & watercolors, Hastie Sch Art, 70-77; instr acrylics & watercolors, Gibbes Art Gallery, Charleston, SC, 72- Awards: First Award, Purchase Award & Third Award, Carolina Art Asn State Show, 60-70; First Award, Fripp Island 1st Ann State Show, 69; Purchase Award, Guild SC Artists State Show. Bibliog: Jack Morris (auth), Contemporary Artist of South Carolina. Mem: Carolina Art Asn; SC Artist Guild (past treas); Salmagundi Club; Charleston Artist Guild (past pres). Media: Watercolor. Mailing Add: c/o Gibbes Art Gallery 135 Meeting St Charleston SC 29401

CLARK, CLAUDE
LECTURER, PAINTER
b Rockingham, Ga, Nov 11, 15. Study: Philadelphia Mus Sch Art, dipl; Barnes Found, painting fel, 42-44; Sacramento State Col, BA; Univ Calif, Berkeley, MA. Work: Pa Mus, Philadelphia; Atlanta Univ; Oakland Mus, Calif; Fisk Univ; Nat Collection Art, Smithsonian Inst, Washington, DC. Comn: Freedom Morning (canvas interpretation), Philadelphia Orchestra Asn, 44. Exhib: Negro Artist Comes of Age, Brooklyn Mus, 45; Century of Uncle Tom's Cabin, Sorbonne, Paris, 53; Evolution of Afro-American Artists: 1800-1950, City Univ New York, 67; Amistad II: Afro-American Art (traveling), Fisk Univ, 75-76; Black American Artists 1750-1950 (traveling), Los Angeles Co Mus, 76- Teaching: Assoc prof art, Talladega Col, Ala, 48-55; instr art, Alameda Co Schs, Calif, 59-68; instr art, Merritt Col, 68- Pos: Artist, Fed Art Proj, Philadelphia, 39-42. Awards: Carnegie Found Grants in Research & Painting & Ceramic Research, 49-50 & 51. Bibliog: David Driskell (auth), Retrospective Exhib, Fisk Univ, 72. Style & Technique: Variety of palette knife techniques. Media: Oil. Res: African and African American art history; research in African art and culture in Ghana. Publ: Auth, A Black Art Perspective, 70. Mailing Add: 788 Santa Ray Ave Oakland CA 94610

CLARK, ELIOT CANDEE
PAINTER
b New York, NY, Mar 27, 83. Study: Art Students League, with John Twachtman; also study in Europe. Work: Metrop Mus Art; Baltimore Mus Art; Dayton Mus Art, Ohio; San Antonio Art Mus, Tex; Nat Acad Design, New York; plus others. Exhib: Nat Acad Design, Soc Am Artists & Am Watercolor Soc, New York; Art Inst Chicago; St Louis Art Mus; Retrospective 1905-1975, Univ Va Mus, Charlottesville; Pictures of Savannah, Telfair Mus, Ga, 77. plus many others. Teaching: Instr painting, Art Students League, Univ Va & Savanah Art Club; staff lectr arts of India, Asia Inst & hist of art, Roerich Mus. Pos: Art critic, The Studio, London. Awards: Third Hallgarten Prize & Ranger Fund Purchase Prize, Nat Acad Design; Allied Artist of Am Burton Prize. Mem: Nat Acad Design (pres, 56-59); Am Watercolor Soc (pres, 20-23); Allied Artists of Am (pres, 45-53); hon mem Nat Sculpture Soc; life mem Nat Arts Club; plus one other. Media: Oil, Watercolor, Pastel. Publ: Auth, Alexander Wyant, 16; auth, John Twachtman, 24; auth, J Francis Murphy, 26; auth, History of the National Academy of Design (1825-1951), 54; auth, Theodore Robinson (mss). Mailing Add: RD 5 Charlottesville VA 22901

CLARK, FRED, JR
MUSEUM DIRECTOR, COLLECTOR
b Philadelphia, Pa, May 31, 11. Pos: Mus owner, Fred Clark Mus, Carversville, Pa, 73- Bibliog: The Fred Clark Museum, article in Bucks Co Gazette, New Hope, Pa, 9/27/73; Frank M Dineen (auth), One man's dream...is another man's museum, Discovery, The Philadelphia Bull, 74; Joe Halperstein (auth), Scenic countryside makes Bucks ride, Bucks Co Courier Times, 9/4/75. Mem: Doylestown Art League, Pa. Collection: Consists of paintings and sculpture by artists of international, National and Regional Renown. Mailing Add: c/o Fred Clark Mus Aquetong Rd Carversville PA 18913

CLARK, G FLETCHER
SCULPTOR
b Waterville, Kans, Nov 7, 99. Study: Univ Calif, BA; Beaux-Arts Inst Design in Europe. Work: Wood Mem Gallery, Montpelier, Vt; also in pvt collections in US & abroad. Exhib: One-man shows, Calif Palace of Legion of Honor, San Francisco, 33 & Avant-Garde Gallery, New York, 59; Gilbert Gallery, San Francisco, 68 & Paris Art Gallery, 72. Style & Technique: Direct carving in wood; walnut and mahogany. Mailing Add: 550 Battery St Apt 818 San Francisco CA 94111

CLARK, JOHN DEWITT
SCULPTOR
b Kansas City, Mo. Study: Kansas City Art Inst; San Diego State Col, MA; also with Lowell Houser & Everett Jackson. Work: Palomar Col; Southwestern Col; La Jolla Mus Contemp Art. Exhib: 11 California Sculptors, Western Mus Asn, 62-64; Mex NAm Cult Inst, Mexico City, Mex, 66; Esther Robles Gallery, 72; Seven San Diego Artists, La Jolla Mus Contemp Art, 73; City is for People Exhib, San Diego Fine Arts Gallery, 74; plus numerous others. Teaching: Prof sculpture & design, Southwestern Col (Calif), 66- Awards: Southern Calif First Nat Bank Award, San Diego, 71; Med Growth Indust Award, San Diego, 71; M H Golden Construct Co Award, San Diego, 72. Bibliog: Rev in Artforum, 58. Style & Technique: Architectural, minimal; organic. Media: Black Granite, Bronze, Wood. Mailing Add: 10514 San Carlos Dr Spring Valley CA 92077

CLARK, JON FREDERIC
EDUCATOR, GLASS BLOWER
b Waterloo, Wis, Aug 13, 47. Study: Univ Wis, BSc; Royal Col of Art, London, MFA. Work: Royal Col of Art, London, Eng; Archie Bray Found, Helena, Mont; Portnoy Ltd, New York; Hadler Galleries, New York; Lannan Found, Palm Beach, Fla. Exhib: One-man show, Hadler Galleries, New York, 76; New Am Glass, Focus WVa, Huntington, 76; Contemp Art Glass, Lever House, New York, 76; Art of Craft, The Am View, Ill State Univ, Normal, 76; Nat Glass III, Univ Wis, Madison, 76; Nat Craft Exhib, Del Mus of Art, Wilmington, 76; Philadelphia Craft Show, Philadelphia Mus of Art, 77. Collections Arranged: Cup Show, Fritz Driesbach, 76 & Eisch Retrospective, Littleton Collection, 77, Tyler Sch of Art, Temple Univ, Philadelphia. Teaching: Glass technician, Calif Col of Arts & Crafts, Oakland, 73; asst prof, Tyler Sch of Art, 73- Bibliog: Judith Stein (auth), Exhibition Review, Vol 3 (1) & Richard Avidon (auth), Exhibition Review, Vol 4 (1), Glass Art Mag. Mem: Am Crafts Coun; Glass Art Soc; Nat Coun on Educ for Ceramic Arts. Style & Technique: Blown glass constructions. Media: Glass, polyester. Dealer: Warren Hadler 35 E 20th St New York NY 10010. Mailing Add: 7703 Union Ave Elkins Park PA 19117

CLARK, MARK A
CURATOR
b Dayton, Ohio, Jan 20, 31. Collections Arranged: The Lipton Collection of Antique Tea Silver, 58; Glass from Area Collections, 66; The Folger Collection of Antique Silver Coffee Pots, 67; Paul Storr Silver in American Collections (with catalog), 72; Vermeil Collection (cataloger), White House, 72. Pos: Mus registr, Dayton Art Inst, 57-61, assoc cur decorative arts, 61-68, cur decorative arts & mus registr, 68-; cur dec arts, Chrysler Mus at Norfolk, 77- Mem: Am Asn Mus; Montgomery Co Hist Soc (nat trust & adv bd). Mailing Add: 800 Graydon Ave Norfolk VA 23507

CLARK, MICHAEL VINSON
PAINTER
b Tex, Nov 20, 46. Work: Corcoran Gallery of Art, Nat Collection of Fine Art, Nat Gallery of Art & Phillips Mem Collection Washington, DC; Everson Mus, Syracuse, NY. Exhib: One-man shows, Corcoran Gallery of Art, 71 & Everson Mus of Art, 73; The Art of Organic Form, Smithsonian Inst, Washington, DC, 68; New Painting: Structure, Corcoran Gallery, 68; Nat Drawing Soc Show, Philadelphia Mus, Pa, 70; Ten Washington Artists 1950-1970, Edmonton Art Gallery, Can, 70; Washington Art: Twenty Years, Baltimore Mus of Art, 70; 75th Anniversary, Cooper-Hewitt Mus, New York, 77; Critics Choice 1977, Lowe Mus, Syracuse Univ, Syracuse, NY, 77. Collections Arranged: The 35th Corcoran Biennial Exhib of Contemp Am Painting (auth, catalogue). Awards: Purchase Award, Nat Drawing Soc, Philadelphia Mus, 70; Purchase Award, 35th Corcoran Biennial Contemp Painting, The Friends of the Corcoran, 77. Bibliog: James Harithas (auth), Michael Clark, Everson Mus of Art, 73; Gene Baro (auth), Michael Clark, Andrew Crispo Gallery, New York, 74; Harry Lunn (auth), Michael Clark—New Paintings, Harry Lunn Gallery, Washington, DC, 75. Style & Technique: Graphite on paper; acrylic and oil on linen. Publ: Illusr, The Art of Organic Form, Smithsonian Inst, 68. Dealer: Andrew Crispo Gallery 41 E 57th St New York NY. Mailing Add: 220 E 60th St Apt 64 New York NY 10022

CLARK, NANCY KISSEL
SCULPTOR
b Joplin, Mo, Jan 27, 19. Study: Mo Southern Col; Del Art Mus, with Henry Mitchell; Fleisher Art Mem, Philadelphia, with Aurelius Renzetti. Work: Woodmere Art Gallery; Univ Del, Newark; Pa Mil Col, Chester; Provident Nat Bank Gallery, Philadelphia; Spiva Art Gallery Mo Southern Col, Joplin. Comn: Bald Eagle (steel sculpture), Joplin Munic Bldg, Mo, 63; Crucifix (metal sculpture), Oblates of St Francis, Camp Brisson, Childs, Md, 64; steel sculpture, Walter Piel Mem, Corkran Gallery, Rehoboth, Del, 65; metal sculpture, Wood-Haven Kruse Sch, Wilmington, 66; Christ (5 ft), Notre Dame Brothers, St Edmon's Acad Chapel, Wilmington, 74. Exhib: Galeria Munic, Guadalajara, Mex, 66; Allied Artists Am Ann, Nat Acad Design, New York, 66; Catharine Lorillard Wolfe Art Club Ann, Nat Arts Club, NY, 67; June Week, US Naval Acad Mus, Annapolis, 69; Nat Sculpture Soc Ann, Lever House, New York, 71-73. Awards: First Binswanger Award, Philadelphia Mus at Civic Ctr, 66; First Award, Nat League Am Pen Women Biennial, Tulsa, Okla, 66; Artist of the Year Award for Christ in Christmas, Wilmington Coun Churches, 69. Bibliog: Louisa Turley (auth), Welded sculpture, Christian Sci Monitor, 68; Art in, National Competition, US Dept Housing & Urban Develop, 73; Archives, Am Art, Smithsonian Inst, 74 & Dallas Mus of Fine Arts, Tex, 78. Mem: Philadelphia Art Alliance; Artists Equity Asn, Philadelphia; Nat League Am Pen Women, Diamond State Chap. Style & Technique: Animals, whimsical children, in welded metals; religious sculpture in welded steel and stained glass. Mailing Add: 5542 Montrose Dr Dallas TX 75209

CLARK, PARASKEVA
PAINTER
b St Petersburg, Russia, Oct 28, 98. Study: Leningrad Acad Arts, 18-21; also with S Zaidenberg, V Schoukhaeff & C Petrov-Vodkin. Work: Nat Gallery Can; Art Gallery Ont; Napler Art Gallery, NZ; Dalhousie Univ. Comn: Winnipeg Art Gallery, Man; Assumption Univ, Windsor; Art Gallery Hamilton; Hart House, Univ Toronto; Victoria Col, Univ Toronto. Exhib: Two-man shows, Art Gallery Toronto, 53 & Art Asn Montreal, 55-56; one-man show, Hart House, Univ Toronto, 56; Walker Art Ctr, Minneapolis, Minn, 58; NZ, 58; plus others. Awards: Award, Hamilton, Ont, 48; Purchase Prize, Winnipeg Art Gallery, 54; Purchase Award, Art Gallery Hamilton, 64. Mem: Can Soc Painters in Water Colour; Royal Can Acad. Mailing Add: 56 Roxborough Dr Toronto ON M4W 1X1 Can

CLARK, R DANE
PAINTER, DESIGNER
b Plainview, Tex, Dec 28, 34. Study: Southern Methodist Univ; Tex Tech; McMurry Col, BS; Colo Inst Art, grad; also study in Europe, 72. Work: Am Embassy, Paris, France; WTex Mus, Lubbock; US State Dept, Washington, DC; US Treas Dept, Washington, DC. Exhib: Ars Longa Opening, Houston, Tex, 73; Dallas Art Festival, 74. Teaching: Dir design, Colo Inst Art, 61-71. Pos: Design consult, Unit I, Inc, 70-74. Awards: First Place Nat MG Poster Contest, MG Sports Cars, Inc, 59. Bibliog: John Jellico (auth), Adobe landscapes, Am Artist Mag, 4/71; Goergia Day (auth), Man of independent spirit, Southwest Art Mag, 10/74; Frank Howell (auth), gallery rev in Artists of the Rockies, 8/74. Style & Technique: Unusual effects of light and play of design in an impressionist manner; clearly visible brush strokes; heavily applied paint. Media: Acrylic, Oil. Mailing Add: Rte 3 Box 588-A Golden CO 80401

CLARK, ROBERT CHARLES
PAINTER, LECTURER
b Minneapolis, Minn, Aug 31, 20. Study: Minneapolis Sch Art; Walker Gallery Art Sch, Minneapolis. Work: Palos Verdes Estates Art Gallery, Calif; Los Angeles Co Mus Hist, Sci & Art, Los Angeles; Norton B Simon, Inc & Hunt's Foods & Industs Found, Los Angeles; Glendale Fed Collection of Calif Art. Comn: The Resurrection (mural), Forest Lawn Mem Park, Glendale, 65. Exhib: Artists of Los Angeles & Vicinity, Los Angeles Co Mus Art, 55-58; Illusion & Reality, Santa Barbara Mus Art, Calif, 56; one-man shows, Calif Palace of Legion of Honor, San Francisco, 56 & Rosicrucian Egyptian Mus, San Jose, 73; Charles & Emma Frye Mus, Seattle, Wash, 57-58. Pos: Background artist, Natural Hist Dept, Los Angeles Co Mus, 54-62. Awards: Artists of Los Angeles & Vicinity Award, Los Angeles Co Mus Art, 55; Purchase Award, Palos Verdes Estates Art Gallery, 56. Bibliog: Janice Lovoos (auth), The tempera paintings of Robert Clark, Am Artist, 12/69; William F Taylor (auth & producer), Robert Clark: An American Realist (film), 74. Mem: Am Artists Prof League; fel Am Inst Fine Arts; Int Platform Asn; Nat Soc Lit & Arts. Style & Technique: Realist of the American scene using egg tempera technique. Media: Tempera, Watercolor, Oil. Dealer: Zantman Art Galleries Ltd Sixth & Dolores Sts Carmel CA 93921. Mailing Add: PO Box 597 Cambria CA 93428

CLARK, SARAH ANN
CURATOR, LECTURER
b Lynchburg, Va, May 14, 43. Study: Randolph-Macon Woman's Col, Lynchburg, Va, BA(art hist), 65; Univ Md, College Park with Dr Alan DeLeiris & Dr Francis O'Conner, 68; Univ Wash, MA(art hist) with Dr Martha Kingsbury & Francis Celentano, 70. Exhibitions Arranged: Art of the 70's, From Collections of Contemp Art Coun of Seattle Art Mus (auth, catalogue), 72; Am Art 1948-1973 (asst to Jan Van der Marck; res on 75 artists in exhib), Seattle Art Mus, 73; Tribute to Zoe Dusanne (auth), 77 & Guy Anderson (ed, catalogue), 77, Seattle Art Mus. Teaching: Lectr art hist, S Seattle Community Col, Spring 75; lectr contemp art hist, Cornish Sch of Fine Arts, Seattle, 77-78. Pos: Assoc educ dept, Yale Univ Art Gallery, New Haven, Conn, 65-67; assoc educ dept, Albright-Knox Art Gallery, Buffalo, 67-68; curatorial asst, San Francisco Mus of Mod Art, Summer-Fall 70; assoc educ dept, Seattle Art Mus, 71-73 & 74-75; consult educ, New York Cult Ctr, 73-74; asst cur mod art, Seattle Art Mus, 75-76, assoc cur mod art, 76- Awards: Kress Found fel, Univ Wash, 70. Res: Presence of Henry Moore in contemporary British sculpture, 1945-1965 (MA thesis). Mailing Add: 933 11th Ave E Seattle WA 98102

CLARK, WILLIAM W
ART HISTORIAN
b Tampa, Fla, Jan 17, 40. Study: Pa State Univ, BA(with hons); Columbia Univ, MA & PhD. Teaching: Assoc prof medieval archit, Queens Col, City Univ NY, Flushing, 67- Mem: Col Art Asn; Société d'Archéologie Française; Int Ctr for Medieval Art; Centre des Recherches d'Archéologie Médiévale; Soc of Archit Historians. Res: Twelfth-century early Gothic architecture, sculpture and manuscripts in North France, Normandy and England. Publ: Auth, The Central Portal of Saint-Pierre at Lisieux..., 72 & The Nave of Saint-Pierre at Lisieux..., 77, Gesta; auth, The Nave Vaults of Noyon Cathedral, Soc of Archit Hist J, 77. Mailing Add: 395 Riverside Dr 12-B New York NY 10025

CLARKE, JOHN CLEM
PAINTER
b Bend, Ore, June 6, 37. Study: Ore State Univ; Mexico City Col; Univ Ore, BFA, 60. Work: Whitney Mus Fine Arts, New York; Dallas Mus Fine Arts, Tex; Va Mus Fine Arts; William Rockhill Nelson Gallery Art, Kansas City, Mo; Baltimore Mus Fine Arts, Md. Exhib: Whitney Mus, Bi-Ann, 67-73; Realism Now, New York Cult Ctr; Tokyo Biennale, Japan; Mus Mod Art, New York; USA Bicentennial, US Dept Interior. Style & Technique: Air brush and stencils. Media: Oil on Canvas. Mailing Add: c/o O K Harris 383 W Broadway New York NY 10012

CLAYBERGER, SAMUEL ROBERT
PAINTER, EDUCATOR
b Kulpmont, Pa, Mar 26, 26. Study: Chouinard Art Inst, Los Angeles; Jepson Art Inst; study with Don Graham, Rico Lebrun & Richard Haines. Work: Pasadena Art Mus, Calif. Exhib: One-man shows, Pasadena Art Mus, 60, Laguna Beach Mus Art, Calif, 67, Whittier Art Asn, Calif, 70 & Orange Coast Col, Costa Mesa, Calif, 73; Otis Art Inst Gallery, Los Angeles, 73. Teaching: Instr design, Chouinard Art Inst, 60; instr design & painting, Otis Art Inst of Los Angeles Co, 63-69, asst prof drawing & painting, 69- Pos: Designer-colorist, U P A Pictures Inc, Burbank, 53-58 & Jay Ward Prod Inc, Los Angeles, 59-64; demonstr-lectr acrylic. Awards: Nat Watercolor Soc, 56, 58, 60 & 69; Los Angeles All-City Exhib, Home Savings & Loan, 62. Bibliog: George De Groat (auth), Sam Clayberger eyes the human condition, Star News, Pasadena, 70. Mem: Nat Watercolor Soc; Artists Equity Asn. Style & Technique: Figures and landscapes using acrylic glazes and mixed media watercolor. Media: Painting; Drawing. Mailing Add: 486 Mavis Dr Los Angeles CA 90065

CLEARY, FRITZ
SCULPTOR, ART CRITIC
b New York, NY, Sept 26, 14. Study: St John's Univ; Nat Acad Design; Beaux-Arts Inst, with Alexander Finta. Comn: Presidential heads, Long Br Jr High Sch, NJ; Robert Mount Mem, Monmouth Col, NJ; World War II Mem, Point Pleasant, NJ; John F Kennedy Mem, Asbury Park, NJ; Rocco Bonforte Mem, Long Branch, NJ. Exhib: Nat Acad Design, New York; Pa Acad Fine Arts, Philadelphia; Oakland Art Mus, Calif; Nat Sculpture Soc, Allied Artists & Hudson Valley Art Asn Ann; also in col art mus & city mus in Eastern US. Pos: Art critic, Asbury Park Press, weekly 45-62, Sun, 62-72; ed adv, Nat Sculpture Rev, 74-78. Awards: NJ Soc Archit Ann Award, 72; John Spring Award, Nat Sculpture Soc, 74; Anna

Hyatt Huntington Award for Sculpture, Hudson Valley Art Asn, 75; plus others. Mem: Allied Am Artists; fel Nat Sculpture Soc (deleg, New York Fedn Arts, 71-); Asbury Park Soc Fine Arts (pres, cur mus, 66-); plus others. Media: Bronze. Publ: Auth & illusr, Sixty Days Around the World, 56; auth, editorials & articles, In: Nat Sculpture Rev, 72-75. Mailing Add: 205 Grassmere Ave Interlaken Asbury Park NJ 07712

CLEAVER, ELIZABETH
ILLUSTRATOR, PRINTMAKER
b Montreal, Que, Nov 19, 39. Study: Sir George Williams Univ; Sch Art & Design, Montreal Mus Fine Arts; Ecole des Beaux Arts, Montreal; Fac Fine Arts, Concordia Univ. Work: Osborne & Lillian H Smith Collections, Toronto; Rare Book Rm, McLennan Libr, McGill Univ; Nat Libr, Ottawa; Cent Fine Arts Libr, Toronto. Comn: Poster, Young Can Book Week, Can Libr Asn, 69; designed shadow puppets for Eskimo fables and legends, Centaur Theatre, Montreal, 71; filmstrip, Miraculous Hind, Nat Filmboard Can, 71. Exhib: Int Exhib Graphics, Montreal Mus Fine Arts, 71; Can rep, Int Book Year Commonwealth Book Fair, Commonwealth Art Gallery, London, 72; Children's Book Fair, Bologna, Italy, 72-74; Rare Book Rm, McLennan Libr, McGill Univ, 73; Bratislava Biennial Children's Books, illus, Czech, 73 & 75. Teaching: Instr printmaking, Visual Art Ctr, Montreal, 74-75 & shadow puppetry, 75- Awards: Amelia Frances Howard Gibbon Award, Can Asn Children's Librns, 71; Book of the Year Award, 74; Hans Christian Andersen Award Nominee Cert of Honor, Int Bd Books Young People, 72. Bibliog: William Toye (ed), Supplement to the Oxford Companion to Canadian History & Literature, Oxford Univ, 73; Shelia Egoff (auth), The Republic of Childhood, Oxford Univ Can Br, 75; Irma McDonough (ed), Profiles, Can Libr Asn, 75. Mem: Royal Can Acad Arts. Style & Technique: Collage and printmaking techniques; limited edition books; silkscreen; collagraph; linocut. Publ: Illusr, How Summer Came to Canada, 69; illusr & auth, The Miraculous Hind, 73; illusr, Canadian Wonder Tales, 74; illusr, The Witch of the North, Folktales from French Canada, 75; auth, Love and Kisses Heart Book, Melville Press. Dealer: Galerie & Editions Gilles Gherbrant 2130 Crescent Montreal PQ Can. Mailing Add: 257 Melville Ave Montreal PQ H3Z 2J6 Can

CLEMENS, PAUL
PAINTER, WRITER
b Superior, Wis, Oct 29, 11. Study: Univ Wis, BA(art hist), 32; Chicago Art Inst, 33. Work: Metrop Mus Art, New York; Los Angeles Co Mus, Calif; Milwaukee Art Inst, Wis; Sterling Clark Mus, Williamstown, Mass; William Rockhill Nelson Gallery, Kansas City, Mo. Comn: Portraits of Frank Sinatra, Clare Booth Luce, Robert Six, Julie Andrews, Katherine Hepburn and others. Exhib: Am Show, Chicago Art Inst, 38; World Fair Expos, 38 & 40; Carnegie Inst Int, 39-43; Show Am Artists, Metrop Mus Art, New York, 45; Nat Acad Design, New York, 44-72. Teaching: Painting, Otis Art Inst, Los Angeles & Univ Wis-Superior. Awards: American Show, Chicago Art Inst, 37; Milwaukee Art Inst Medal, 37; Alman Prize for Figure Painting, Nat Acad Design, New York, 43. Bibliog: Articles in Time Mag, Art News & Life Mag. Mem: Academician, Nat Acad Design. Style & Technique: Oil on canvas or panel. Media: Oil; Pastel. Mailing Add: Suite 3 11757 San Vicente Blvd Los Angeles CA 90049

CLEMENTS, ROBERT DONALD
EDUCATOR, SCULPTOR
b Pittsburgh, Pa, Dec 24, 37. Study: Carnegie-Mellon Univ, with Samuel Rosenburg & Roger Anliker, BFA(painting), 59; Pa State Univ, with George Zoretich & George Pappas, MA(art), 62, with Ken Biettel & Yar Chomicky, PhD(art educ), 64. Work: Nat Collection Fine Arts, Smithsonian Inst, Washington, DC; Jacksonville Mus Fine Arts. Exhib: One-man show, Totems to Southerners & the South, Hunter Mus Art, Chattanooga, Tenn; Montgomery Mus Fine Arts, Ala; Asheville Art Mus, NC; Contemporary Religious Imagery in American Art, Ringling Mus, Sarasota, Fla. Teaching: Asst prof art, Ball State Univ, 64-68; assoc prof art, Univ Ga, 69- Pos: Art consult, Arts & Humanities Prog, US Off Educ, 68-69. Mem: Nat Art Educ Asn; Ga Art Educ Asn (vpres, 74). Style & Technique: Eight-feet tall painted wood totemic sculptures commemorating persons & events. Res: Aesthetic appreciation and educational motivation. Publ: Auth, Art student-teacher questioning, Studies in Art Educ, Fall 64; auth, The junior high art teacher's guide to research, 11/69, A case for art education: Frank Lloyd Wright's kindergarten training, 3/75 & Encouragement of CBTE in the art working period, 4/76, Art Educ; auth, Instructional objectives & objectionable instructions, J Aesthetic Educ, 4/76. Dealer: Henri Gallery 1500 21st St NW Washington DC 20036. Mailing Add: 155 Bar H Ct Athens GA 30601

CLERK, PIERRE
PAINTER, SCULPTOR
b Atlanta, Ga, Apr 26, 28. Study: Loyola Col; McGill Univ; Montreal Sch Art & Design; Acad Julian, Paris; Acad Grande Chaumiere, Paris. Work: Mus Mod Art, Guggenheim Mus & Whitney Mus Am Art, New York; Nat Gallery Can, Ottawa, Ont; Mus Contemp Art, Montreal. Comn: City Walls, NY; Com Bank of Kansas City; First Wis Develop Corp, Milwaukee; Marine Midland Bank, NY; Oxford Develop Edmonton Ctr, Alta. Exhib: Venice Biennale, Italy, 56 & 58; Carnegie Inst Int, Pittsburgh, 59; Expo 67, Montreal, 67; Rosc Int, Dublin, Ireland, 71; Third Brit Int Print Biennial, 71; one-man exhibs, Pierre Clerk Tapestries, Graphics & Paintings, Hong Kong Art Ctr, 77, Everson Mus of Art, Syracuse, NY, 77, Waterside Gallery, 77, Monumental Outdoor Sculpture, NY, 77-78, Iran-Am Ctr, Tehran, Iran, 78 & Metrop Mus of Art, Manila, Philippines, 78. Awards: Can Coun Travel Grant & Quebec Govt Travel Grant, 71; US Info Serv exhib grant, 77; pub arts coun sponsoring grant, Munic Art Soc, NY, 77; Am specialist, US State Dept travel grant, 77-78. Mailing Add: 70 Grand St New York NY 10013

CLERMONT, GHISLAIN
ART HISTORIAN, ART CRITIC
b Ste-Adele, PQ, Sept 30, 40. Study: Univ Montreal, DES(hist art); Univ BC, Vancouver. Collections Arranged: Second APAC Biennial Exhib, Serigraphs of Alex Colville. Teaching: Prof hist art, Univ Moncton, 67- Pos: Dir art gallery, Univ Moncton, 67-70. Mem: Univ Art Asn Can (Atlantic rep, 73-75). Res: Contemporary Canadian art. Publ: Auth, articles in, Vie des Arts, Montreal, Rev Univ Moncton, Montreal-Medical & exhib catalogs. Mailing Add: 254 Cameron Moncton NB Can

CLEVELAND, HELEN BARTH
ART ADMINISTRATOR, INSTRUCTOR
b Alliance, Ohio. Study: Mt Union Col, with George A Gibbs & Eric Johanson; Kent State Univ, with Novotny; Syracuse Univ, with George SanderSluis & James A Smith; NY Univ; London Acad Art, Eng; Univ San Juan; Acad Arts Honolulu. Work: Art Gallery Ont, Toronto; Chautauqua Gallery Art, NY. Comn: Murals, Wildwood Gallery, Lake Orion, Mich, 67, Prendergast Libr, Jamestown, NY, 68 & Galerie 8, Erie, Pa, 69; correlate & design art ctr, Patterson Libr, Westfield, NY, 70-71; natural hist murals, Hist Ctr, Gov Gilligan's Art Exhib, Alliance, 71. Exhib: Chautauqua Gallery Art Nat & Regional, 52, 56 & 63; Albright-Knox Regional, Buffalo, NY, 65; Cleveland Art Mus, Ohio, 67; Hemingway Gallery, New York & Jamestown, 68-70; Canton Cult Ctr, Ohio, 70. Collections Arranged: Directed & assembled nat jury shows, Am Exhib Art, Chautauqua, 57-72; NY Univ Shows, 50-51; Syracuse Univ Shows arranged & assembled, 53-55 & 65-68. Teaching: Instr art, Alliance Pub Schs, 27-; instr crafts, Syracuse Univ, Chautauqua & NY Univ, 50-52 & 61-64; instr art, Sierra Leone, Africa, 63. Pos: Chmn, Masonic Cult Arts, Alliance, 45-; collabr creativity in art, Syracuse Univ, 63-65; pres & dir, Chautauqua Gallery Art, 63-; chmn, Patterson Libr Art Grant, Westfield, NY, 70-71. Awards: Chautauqua Art Asn Ribbons, Bestor Plaza Art Festival, 50, 54 & 57; Community Meritorious Award as art judge, Am Legion, Alliance, 66-67; Citation for Winning Poster, State of Ohio, 69. Bibliog: Lee Nelson (auth), Outstanding woman of today, Erie Times, Pa, 65-66; Jean Reeves (auth), The director, Chautauqua Gallery of Art, Buffalo Eve News, NY, 71. Mem: Am Fedn Art; Nat Educ Asn; life mem Ohio Educ Asn; Asn Am Univ Women; Canton Cult Art Ctr; plus others. Media: Oil, Pastel. Publ: Co-auth, Arts & Crafts, Grade Teacher, 55; co-auth, Art in Poetry, Solvay Publ Co, 59; co-auth, Creativity in Elementary Schools, 63-64; co-auth, Arts Illustrated (children's ser), Rowe-Peterson, 65; co-auth, Chautauqua Gallery of Art, Art Gallery Mag, 66. Mailing Add: 1192 Parkside Dr Alliance OH 44601

CLEVELAND, ROBERT EARL
ART ADMINISTRATOR, EDUCATOR
b Union, Miss, June 8, 36. Study: Miss Col, BA; Univ Miss, MFA; Univ Tenn, EdD. Work: Univ Miss Fine Arts Ctr, University, Miss. Comn: Redwood sculpture (4 ft x 4 ft x 10 ft), Carson-Newman Col, 76; Smokey Mountain Landscape (30 ft x 60 ft acrylic painting, in collab with William Houston), Jefferson City, Tenn, Tenn Arts Comn, 78. Exhib: The 55th Nat Oil Painting Exhib, Jackson, Miss, 65; Nat Drawing & Sculpture Exhib, Ball State Univ Art Gallery, Muncie, Ind, 67; 2nd Nat Print & Drawing Exhib, Dulin Gallery of Art, Knoxville, Tenn, 67; Tenn Watercolor Exhib, Cheekwood Mus, Nashville, Tenn, 75; Quinlan Ann Art Exhib, Gainesville, Ga, 76; Carroll Reece Mus, Johnson City, Tenn, 77; plus others. Teaching: Part-time instr art, Univ Miss, Oxford, 63-64; prof art & chmn dept, Carson-Newman Col, Jefferson City, 64- Pos: Artist-illusr, Ling-Temco-Vought, Inc, Dallas, Tex, 61-62. Awards: First Prize, Painting, Morristown Art Competition, Tenn, 66 & Macon Ann Arts Exhib, Macon Arts Coun, 73; First Prize, Drawing, Oak Ridge Relig Art Exhib, Oak Ridge Art Ctr, Tenn, 76. Mem: Nat Asn Schs of Art; Nat Coun Art Adminrs; Nat Art Educ Asn; Southeastern Col Art Conf; Tenn Watercolor Soc. Media: Oil, watercolor. Res: Major areas of research—arts administration in higher education and art and law issues. Publ: Illusr, Sexual Happiness in Marriage, 67 & illusr, Sexual Understanding Before Marriage, 71, Zondervan Publ; auth, Art and the Law, 77 & auth, The Art Department Chairperson: An Ambiguous Role, 78, Nat Coun Art Adminrs; auth, The Law: Public Aid and the Private Sector, Fac Studies, 78. Mailing Add: Box 1901 Art Dept Carson-Newman Col Jefferson City TN 37760

CLIFFORD, JUTTA
ART DEALER
b The Hague, Holland; US citizen. Study: Univ Dallas, 74 with Jurgen Strunck; Abitur Klosterscule, Hamberg, Ger, 64. Pos: Owner/dir, Clifford Gallery, 74- Specialty: Fine prints, drawings and small sculpture. Mailing Add: 6610 Snider Plaza Dallas TX 75205

CLIFTON, JACK WHITNEY
INSTRUCTOR, PAINTER
b Norfolk, Va, Feb 3, 12. Study: Art Inst of Pittsburgh, 31-32; Pa Acad of the Fine Arts, Philadelphia, 33-39. Work: Va Mus of Art, Richmond; Springfield Mus of Art, Mass; Grumbacher Collection, New York; State Capitol Bldg, Richmond; Chrysler Mus, Norfolk. Comn: Portraits, Newport News Courthouse, Newport News Bar Asn, 46-; USS Enterprise Atomic Carrier, US Navy, Washington, DC, 63; Houses of Parliament, London, Eng (4ft x 7ft hist painting), Jamestown Found, Va, 68; State Capitol Bldg, Richmond (4ft x 7ft painting), Jamestown Found, 69-74. Exhib: Chrysler Mus Ann, Norfolk, 46-70; Va Mus Ann, Richmond, 46-70; Exhib of Unification, Pentagon, Washington, DC, 57; Springfield Ann, Springfield Mus of Art, 60; Nat Biennial Exhib, Corcoran Gallery of Art, 62. Teaching: Instr basic art, Clifton Sch of Art, 34-; instr basic art, Davis & Elkins Col, Elkins, WVa, 46; art prof life class, Christopher Newport Col, Newport News, 74- Media: Acrylic Polymer. Publ: Auth, Manual of Drawing & Painting, Watson-Guptill, 57; auth, Self-expression or self-indulgence, Am Artist Mag, 10/62; auth, The Eye of the Artist, Watson-Guptill, 73. Dealer: Chase Gallery 64th at Madison Ave New York NY. Mailing Add: 1615 Chesapeake Ave Hampton VA 23661

CLIFTON, MICHELLE GAMM
SCULPTOR, PRINTMAKER
b Los Angeles, Calif, July 11, 44. Study: Yale Univ, summer scholar, 65; Univ Ill, Urbana-Champaign, BFA, 66, with Lee Chesney; Pa State Univ, University Park, MFA, 68, with Carol Summers. Work: Mus of City of New York; Los Angeles Co Mus Art, Los Angeles, Calif; Meany Ctr for Labor Studies, Silver Spring, Md; State Univ NY Col, Potsdam; US Info Agency, Washington, DC. Comn: Soft New York Times, comn by Carey Peck, A O Sulzberger at New York Times, 76. Exhib: Libr Cong, Washington, DC, 69; Artists Choice, Potsdam Prints, State Univ NY Col, Potsdam, 71; City Mus & Art Gallery, Hong Kong, 72; Sewn, Stitched & Stuffed, Mus Contemp Crafts, New York, 73; Fun & Fantasy, Xerox Ctr, Rochester, NY, 73; Renwick Gallery, Smithsonian Inst, Washington, DC, 74-75; Dayton Art Inst, Ohio, 77; two-person show, Cordy Gallery, New York, 77; Whimsy, Taft Mus & Cincinnati Inst of Fine Arts, 78; one-person shows, Gallery Rebecca Cooper, Washington, DC, 76 & Pa State Univ, 68. Teaching: Teaching asst drawing & printmaking, Pa State Univ, 66-68. Pos: Art dir, Hardtimes Movie Co, Garrison, 72-; art dir & vpres, Hudson River Film Co, Garrison, 77- Awards: First Prize in Painting, 2nd Ann Cent Pa Festival of Arts, 68; Purchase Prize, Artists Choice, State Univ NY Col, Potsdam, 71; Hon Mention as Art Dir, Emmy Winner Christina's World, 77. Bibliog: Steven Lindstedt (auth), Soft Sculpture, Family Creative Workshop, 76; Erica Brown (auth), Bunking in a barnyard, New York Times, 12/25/77; Carol Sama (auth), Michelle Gamm Clifton lives in a material world, Houston Home & Garden, 5/77. Mem: Am Crafts Coun; Nat Acad Television Arts & Sci. Style & Technique: Work with fabrics to create objects and things that look like the real thing, but actually soft & squishy; use of fabrics relatively new in past ten years. Media: Fabric & Stuffing; Waterbase Painting. Publ: Illusr (series), Gerald Ford's America, San Francisco Pub TV, 75; auth & illusr (cover), New York City couch, Art Now Gallery Guide, summer 77. Mailing Add: Avery Rd Garrison NY 10524

CLINEDINST, KATHERINE PARSONS
PAINTER, LECTURER
b Stamford, Conn, July 13, 03. Study: Pratt Inst, with Jessie Leigh; China Inst, with Prof Wang. Exhib: Smithsonian Inst, Washington, DC; Springfield Mus, Mass; Asbury Park Mus, NJ; Hammond Mus, South Salem, NY. Pos: Asst mgr, Boston Soc Arts & Crafts, New York, 23-24. Awards: Hudson Valley Art Asn Award for Dr Woodrow, White Plains, NY, 63; Meridan Art Asn Award, Conn, 67; Mt Vernon Art Asn Award, NY, 67. Mem: Ocean Co Art Guild; Asbury Fine Arts Asn; Nat League Am Pen Women (pres, Westchester Br, 59-61);

Kent Art Asn, Conn; Am Artist Prof League. Media: Watercolor, Oil. Mailing Add: 951 A Argyll Circle Lakewood NJ 08701

CLIPSHAM, JACQUELINE ANN
CERAMIST, EDUCATOR
b Welwyn Garden City, Hertfordshire, Eng, July 27, 36; US citizen. Study: Carleton Col, BA; Western Reserve Univ, MA; Cleveland Inst Art; Haystack Mountain Sch Crafts; Brooklyn Mus Art Sch; study with Toshiko Takaezu, Shoji Hamada, Peter Voulkous, William McVey. Comn: Architectural tile comn, Mr & Mrs Basil Whiting, Brooklyn, NY, 77. Exhib: May Show, Cleveland Mus Art, Ohio, 62; Butler Inst Show, Butler Inst Am Art, Youngstown, Ohio, 63-65; Northeast Regional Exhib Am Crafts Coun, Del Art Ctr, Wilmington, 66; Craftsmen USA 1966, Mus Contemp Crafts, New York, 66; Brooklyn Mus Sch, 69-78; Ceramics Show, Pratt Inst, Brooklyn, 73; one-person show, Atlantic Gallery, Brooklyn, 76 & 77. Teaching: Instr ceramics, Brooklyn Mus Art Sch, 69-; dir art workshop, CORE Community Ctr, Sumter, SC, 65-66. Awards: Award for Sculpture, Ohio Ceramic & Sculpture Show, Butler Inst Am Art, 63, Award for Ceramics, 65; Nat Merit Award, Craftsmen USA 1966 Exhib, Mus Contemp Crafts, 66. Bibliog: Ann Ockene (auth), Ceramics by J A Clipsham, Craft Horizons, Am Crafts Coun, 76. Mem: Col Art Asn; Nat Conf Educ in the Ceramic Arts; Am Crafts Coun; Women's Caucus for Art; Atlantic Ave Artist's League, Inc. Style & Technique: One of a kind stoneware and porcelain pieces; mostly slab construction; small to large non-utilitarian containers. Media: Stoneware, Porcelain Clay; Ink on Paper. Dealer: Atlantic Gallery 91 Atlantic Ave Brooklyn NY 11201. Mailing Add: PO Box 387 Califon NJ 07830

CLISBY, ROGER DAVID
CURATOR, ART HISTORIAN
b New York, NY, Feb 8, 39. Study: Pa State Univ, BA & MA. Teaching: Instr Northern Renaissance art, Univ of Calif, Davis, 73; lectr gallery admn, Calif State Univ, Sacramento, 74-75. Pos: Chief cur, E B Crocker Art Gallery, 70- Mem: Sacramento Film Festival (bd of dirs, 77-); Sacramento Regional Arts Coun (festival judge, 72-). Res: General research on Italian, German, Dutch, French painting and drawing from Renaissance to the present. Publ: Auth, Sacramento Sampler I (gallery catalog), 72, Sacramento Sampler II (exhib catalog), 73 & 19th & 20th Century Prints & Drawings from the Baltimore Mus (exhib catalog), 73, contribr, The Collecting Muse—The Weisgall Collection (exhib catalog), 75 & ed & contribr, Forty American Photographers (exhib catalog), 78, E B Crocker Art Gallery. Mailing Add: c/o E B Crocker Art Gallery 216 O St Sacramento CA 95814

CLIVE, RICHARD R
PAINTER
b New York, NY, Jan 8, 12. Study: Nat Acad Design, 30; NY Univ, BFA, 35; also with Dan Greene & Harold Wolcott. Work: US Navy Combat Art Collection, Washington, DC; Munic Collection, Ossining, NY; Arts & Sci Ctr, Nashua, NH; Munic Collection, Gloucester, Mass; Addison-Gilbert Hosp, Gloucester, Mass. Comn: WAVES at US Naval Training Ctr, Bainbridge, Md; Marines & Civilians, S Vietnam, Dept of Navy, Washington, DC. Exhib: Westchester Year of History Celebration, 59; Salmagundi Club Ann, 61-78; Am Friends of the Hebrew Univ Art Festivals, 63-65; four presentations, Naval Art Coop & Liaison Comt, 63-72; Stevens Ctr Art Exhib, Stevens Inst Technol, 68. Awards: Prize for Portrait, New Rochelle Art Asn, 67 & First for Graphic, 68; Lt Harry E Breng Award, Am Legion, 68; Purchase Award, Miniature Art Soc NJ. Mem: Salmagundi Club (mem NACAL comt); Am Artists Prof League; Acad Artists Asn; Artists Fel; Miniature Art Soc NJ. Style & Technique: Representational. Media: Oil, Pastel, Watercolor. Mailing Add: 29 Holly St Yonkers NY 10704

CLOAR, CARROLL
PAINTER
b Earle, Ark, Jan 18, 18. Study: Southwestern at Memphis, BA; Memphis Acad Arts; Art Students League, MacDowell fel, 40. Work: Metrop Mus Art, Mus Mod Art & Whitney Mus Am Art, New York; Brooks Mem Art Gallery, Memphis; Joseph H Hirshhorn Mus, Washington, DC. Exhib: Retrospective, NY Univ, Albany; Pittsburgh Int; Whitney Ann, New York; Pa Acad Fine Arts Ann, Philadelphia; Brooks Mem Art Gallery, Memphis. Pos: Bd trustees, Brooks Mem Art Gallery, 69-71. Awards: Guggenheim Fel, 46; Am Acad Arts & Lett Prize, 67. Bibliog: An Arkansas boyhood, Horizon, 11/58; Summer dies as slowly, Time Mag, 8/19/66; Growing up in the Arkansas Delta, Esquire, 6/69. Style & Technique: Acrylic on gesso (Masonite) using the tempera technique. Publ: Auth, Hostile Butterflies & Other Paintings, Memphis State Univ Press. Dealer: Forum Gallery 1018 Madison Ave New York NY 10021. Mailing Add: 235 S Greer Memphis TN 38111

CLOSE, CHUCK
PAINTER
b Monroe, Wash, July 5, 40. Study: Everett Community Col, Wash, 58-60; Yale Summer Sch Music & Art, Norfolk, Conn, 61; Univ Wash Sch Art, Seattle, BA, 62; Yale Univ Sch Art & Archit, New Haven, Conn, BFA, 63, MFA, 64; Acad Fine Arts, Vienna, Austria, Fulbright grant, 64-65. Work: Mus Mod Art & Whitney Mus Am Art, New York; Walker Art Ctr, Minneapolis; Neue Gallerie, Aachen, Ger; Art Gallery Ont, Toronto. Exhib: 22 Realists, Whitney Mus Am Art, 70; one-man shows, Los Angeles Co Mus, 71, Mus Contemp Art, Chicago, 71 & Mus Mod Art, New York, 73; Documenta V, Kassel, WGer, 72. Teaching: Instr art, Univ Mass Sch Art, Amherst, 65-67; Sch Visual Arts, New York, 67-71; NY Univ, 70-73. Awards: Nat Endowment Arts Grant, 73. Bibliog: Cindy Nemser (auth), An interview with Chuck Close, Artforum, 1/70; Robert Hughs (auth), The realist as corn god, Time Mag, 1/31/72; William Dykes (auth), The photo as subject—the paintings & drawings of Chuck Close, Arts Mag, 2/74. Style & Technique: Photo-realist. Media: Acrylic, Watercolor. Mailing Add: c/o Pace Gallery 32 E 57th St New York NY 10022

CLOSE, DEAN PURDY
ART DEALER, COLLECTOR
b Holmesville, Ohio. Study: Ohio Northern Univ; Ohio State Univ; also with Charles William Duvall. Work: Am Embassies, Japan & WGer & in many pvt collections. Exhib: Columbus Art League, Ohio, 38-50; Butler Art Inst Am, 40; Ogonquit, Maine, 40. Pos: Dir, Fifth Avenue Galleries, Columbus, Ohio, 61- Style & Technique: Bold realism. Media: Oil, Acrylic. Specialty: American art. Interest: The status of American impressionism. Collection: Works of Croft, Leslie Cope, R Wagner and other fine American realists. Dealer: Fifth Avenue Galleries Inc 1790 W Fifth Ave Columbus OH 43212. Mailing Add: 3130 Glenrich Pkwy Columbus OH 43221

CLOSE, MARJORIE (PERRY)
PAINTER, LECTURER
b Chloride, Ariz, Nov 11, 99. Study: Calif Sch Fine Arts, four yr scholar; Univ Calif, 18-20; Art Inst Chicago, 20-22; Wana Derge Studio, Berkeley, Calif; San Francisco Art Inst; with George Post, 36; San Francisco City Col, 51-57; Rudolf Schaeffer Sch, 56; also with Matteo Sandona, 52-56 & Thomas Leighton, 56-68. Comn: Portraits, Marjorie Markel & Molly Parker, 53 & Admiral John Redman, 54, San Francisco; Cinerarias (still life), Col & Mrs R F Elliott, Arlington, Va, 60; Elizabeth Stoddard Huntington, Southern Pac RR Co, San Francisco, 69. Exhib: Four shows, Nat Asn Women Artists, Nat Acad Design, New York, 61-72; one-artist shows, Rosicrucian Mus, San Jose, Calif, 67-73, Univ Club San Francisco, 70 & Charles & Emma Frye Mus, Seattle, 73; six shows, Calif State Fair, Sacramento, 67-74; Soc Western Artists, Charles & Emma Frye Mus, 71; 23rd Acad Art Asn Ann, Springfield, Mass, 72; plus many others. Teaching: Lectr & demonstr, San Francisco Pub Schs & Art Orgns. Pos: Deleg, Calif State Fair Art Adv Bd, 65- Awards: Trompe l'Oeil Still Life Award, Dan Le Gear Mem Award, San Francisco, 66, 67 & 71; Pres Award & Best Still Life Award, Am Artists Prof League, New York, 69-71; Premier Grand Prix Award (still-life painting), 23rd Int Grand Prix, Deauville, France, 72; plus many others. Bibliog: Virginia Lee (auth), Hidden Realities, San Francisco Trumpeteer, spring 59; Marjorie Close, US artist, La Rev Mod, 61; Frederic Whitaker (auth), Marjorie Close, Am Artist Mag, 1/70. Mem: Soc Western Artists (treas, 66-67, pres, 68-69, dir exhibs, 71-72); Nat Asn Women Artists; Am Artists Prof League; Catharine Lorillard Wolfe Art Club. Style & Technique: Trompe l'oeil still life painting knife landscape; portraits bristle brush technique. Media: Oil. Publ: Co-auth, Color, Form & Composition, 66. Mailing Add: 50 Beachmont Dr San Francisco CA 94132

CLOTHIER, PETER DEAN
ART ADMINISTRATOR, ART CRITIC
b Newcastle-on-Tyne, Eng, Aug 1, 36; US citizen. Study: Cambridge Univ, Eng, BA & MA; Univ Iowa, PhD. Work: Los Angeles Co Mus of Art, Los Angeles; Univ Southern Calif. Teaching: Asst prof comparative lit, Univ Southern Calif, Los Angeles, 68-76. Pos: Dean col, Otis Art Inst, 76-77, actg dir, 77- Awards: Dart Award for Acad Innovation, Univ Southern Calif, 72; Art Critics fel Grant, Nat Endowment for the Arts, 76-77. Bibliog: Joseph E Young (auth), Re-evaluating the Tradition of the Book, Art News, 75. Mem: Los Angeles Inst of Contemp Art; Los Angeles Co Mus of Art. Publ: Co-auth, Bob Went Home, A Book-Object, Ellie Blankfort Gallery, 73; auth, Parapoems, Horizon Press, 74; auth, Magic of the Possible, Artforum, 77; auth, After the Concept, Studio Int, 77. Mailing Add: 2341 Ronda Vista Dr Los Angeles CA 90027

CLOUD, JACK L
GALLERY OWNER, PUBLISHER
b Fremont, Ohio, Mar 15, 25. Pos: Owner/pres, Litho-Graphics (publ), 72-; owner/chmn bd, Odyssey Int Gallery, Livonia, 75- Mem: Rockport Art Asn; Univ of Mich Artist Guild; Int Platform Asn; Am Printing Hist Asn; Check Collector Round Table. Specialty: Contemporary American art and limited edition graphics and prints. Dealer: Odyssey Int Gallery 31177 Schoolcraft Rd Livonia MI 48150. Mailing Add: 4253 Brandywyne Dr Troy MI 48098

CLOVER, JAMES B
SCULPTOR, EDUCATOR
b Oskaloosa, Iowa, Apr 13, 38. Study: Kansas City Art Inst, BFA; Tulane Univ, MFA. Work: High Mus Art, Atlanta, Ga; Emory Univ, Atlanta; Brandeis Univ, Waltham, Mass; Univ Southern Ill; Ga Comn Arts. Comn: Playground, Atlanta League Jewish Women, 70; Miss Art Assoc for Jackson Airport, 73; The High Mus Art, Atlanta, 73; Northlake Office Park, Atlanta, 74; fountain, City Park, Atlanta, 75. Exhib: Emory Univ, 66; Georgia Artists 2, 72 & Artists in Ga, 75, High Mus, Atlanta; Galerie Simonne Stern, New Orleans, 74 & 75. Teaching: Head sculpture, Atlanta Sch Art, 64-75; asst prof sculpture & drawing, Ohio State Univ, Columbus. Awards: Southeastern Award of Merit, High Mus Art, 65; Purchase Awards, Western Mich Univ & Univ Southern Ill, 69. Style & Technique: Large-scale welded sculpture, working models for sculpture, colored-pencil and ink drawing. Dealer: Galerie Simonne Stern 516 Royal St New Orleans LA 76130. Mailing Add: c/o Div of Art 128 N Oval Dr Ohio State Univ Columbus OH 43210

CLOWES, ALLEN WHITEHILL
COLLECTOR, PATRON
b Buffalo, NY, Feb 18, 17. Study: Harvard Univ, BS(fine arts), 39; Fogg Mus, with Chanler Post, Benjamin Rowland, Leonard Opdyke, Kuhn & Paul Sachs; Harvard Univ Grad Sch Bus Admin, MBA, 42; Franklin Col, Hon DFA, 64. Pos: Dir, Clowes Fund Collection Old Masters, 58-71; cur, Clowes Fund Collection Old Masters, Indianapolis Mus Art, 71-, trustee & chmn fine arts comt. Awards: Resolution of Thanks for Clowes Pavilion housing Clowes Fund Collection, Indianapolis Mus Art. Collection: Paintings by the Old Masters from the 14th to 19th Century, including Bellini, Bosch, Bruegel, Caravaggio, Clouet, Constable, Cranach, Duccio, Durer, El Greco, Goya, Hals, Holbein, Rembrandt, Rubens and Titian; Clowes Fund Collection originally formed by the late Dr G H A Clowes and now belongs to Clowes Fund, Inc, located in Clowes Pavilion, Indianapolis Museum of Art. Mailing Add: 250 E 38th St Indianapolis IN 46205

CLURMAN, IRENE
ART CRITIC
b San Francisco, Calif, Mar 2, 47. Study: Stanford Univ, BA(art hist; Phi Beta Kappa), 69. Pos: Art ed, Rocky Mountain News, Denver, 75- Mem: Denver Int Film Festival (secy-treas, 78). Publ: Auth, Surrealism and the Painting of Matta and Magritte, Stanford Univ, 70. Mailing Add: Box 6713 Denver CO 80206

CLUTZ, WILLIAM
PAINTER
b Gettysburg, Pa, Mar 19, 33. Work: Mus Mod Art & Chase Manhattan Bank, New York; Joseph H Hirshhorn Collection, Washington, DC; Fogg Art Mus, Cambridge, Mass; Newark Mus, NJ; plus many others. Exhib: Recent Painting USA: The Figure, Mus Mod Art, New York, 62; The Figure International, Am Fedn Arts, 63; Pa Acad Fine Arts Ann, Philadelphia, 64-66; one-man shows, David Herbert Gallery, NY, 61, Bertha Schaefer Gallery, 63, 64, 66 & 69 & Graham Gallery, 72; Brooke Alexander, NY, 73; Alonzo Gallery, 77 & 78; Berlin: Kunstaunt Wedding, 78; plus many other group & one-man shows. Style & Technique: Painterly, light concerned streets; autos and people moving. Mailing Add: 370 Riverside Dr New York NY 10025

CLYMER, ALBERT ANDERSON
PAINTER
b Memphis, Tenn, Feb 16, 42. Study: Tex A&M Univ, with Joseph Donaldson. Work: Newport Mus Mod Art, Calif; Oakland Mus Mod Art, Calif; Berkeley Mus Mod Art, Calif; San Francisco Mus Mod Art, Calif; de Young Mus, San Francisco. Comn: Ten paintings for Army Recruiting, US Army Reserve, Mountain View, Calif, 77. Exhib: Dallas Mus Fine Arts, Tex, 65; Festival of Arts, Laguna Beach, Calif, 65-67; Vintage 76 Int Exhib, Yountville, Calif, 68; Newport Mus Mod Art, 69; Exhib of Am Art, Chautauqua, NY, 69-71; Santa Rosa Statewide Ann Exhib, 70-72; Univ Berkeley Mus, Calif, 71; Mus Mod Art, Roseville, Calif, 72; plus 108 one-man shows. Pos: Pres bd dir, Berkeley Arts/Crafts Coop, 71-72. Awards:

First Prize in Mod Oil, Vintage 76 Int, 68 & Santa Rosa Statewide Ann, 71 & 72. Bibliog: Stephens (auth), Albert Anderson Clymer, La Rev Mod, Paris, 66 & 74; Paul Gillette (auth), The Single Man's Indispensable Guide Handbook, Playboy Press, 73. Mem: Berkeley Arts/Crafts Coop. Style & Technique: Acrylic washes to develop a layering of visual textures rather than actual textures that you can feel. Publ: Illusr, Oakland Redevelopment Agency's Annual Report, Abby Press, 66; illusr, Bodega Bay, Nut Tree, 75; illusr (catalogue), Works by Albert Anderson Clymer, Arlene Lind Gallery, 78. Dealer: Arlene Lind Gallery 435 Jackson San Francisco CA 94111; Challis Galleries 1390 S Coast Hwy Laguna Beach CA 92652. Mailing Add: 22 St Stephens Dr Orinda CA 94563

CLYMER, JOHN F
PAINTER, ILLUSTRATOR
b Ellensburg, Wash, Jan 29, 07. Study: Vancouver Sch Art; Ont Col Art; Wilmington Acad Art; Grand Cent Art Sch, with Harvey Dunn. Work: Glen Bow Found, Calgary; Mont Hist Soc, Helena; Cowboy Hall of Fame, Oklahoma City; Whitney Gallery Western Art, Cody, Wyo. Comn: Series of three large paintings, comn by Winchester Firearms Co, Winchester Gun Display, Buffalo Bill Hist Ctr & Whitney Gallery Western Art, 69. Exhib: Soc Animal Artists, 62-72; Whitney Gallery Western Art, 69; Cowboy Artists Am, 69-77; Mont Hist Soc, Helena, 72-73; Animals in Art, Royal Ont Mus, Toronto, 75. Awards: Silver Medal, Cowboy Artists Am, 69 & 76, Gold Medals, 70 & 72-77; Prix de West Award, Nat Acad of Western Art, 76. Mem: Soc Animal Artists; Salmagundi Club; Ont Soc Artists; Cowboy Artists Am; Nat Acad Western Art; plus others. Publ: Contribr, illus in Sat Eve Post & Field & Stream, prior to 65. Mailing Add: Box 369 Teton Village WY 83025

COATES, ANN S
SLIDE CURATOR, ART HISTORIAN
b Louisville, Ky. Study: Univ of Louisville, BA & MA. Collections Arranged: Cataloged Slide Collection (circa 200,000), Univ of Louisville. Teaching: Instr mod art, mod archit & Am art, Univ Louisville, 62. Pos: Art historian, Louisville Sch Art, 62-69; art historian, Ky Southern Col; slide cur, Univ Louisville, 69- Bibliog: Betty Jo Irvine (auth), Slide Libraries, Libr Unlimited, Colo, 74. Mem: Col Art Asn (co-chmn visual resources, 74); Art Libr Soc NAm (conf panelist, 77); Soc Archit Historians. Res: Female image in 19th century art. Interest: Slide classification and cataloging systems. Mailing Add: 1819 Woodburne Louisville KY 40205

COATES, ROSS ALEXANDER
ART HISTORIAN, PAINTER
b Hamilton, Ont, Can, Nov 1, 32. Study: Univ Mich; Art Inst Chicago, BFA; NY Univ, MA & PhD. Work: Finch Col; Univ Alta; Chase Manhattan Bank, New York; NY Univ; Univ Calif, Berkeley. Exhib: One-man shows, Camino Gallery, New York, 61, Jerrold Morris Gallery, Toronto, 67, Galerie Seyfried, Munich, 67, Univ Rochester, 74 & Schenectady Mus, NY, 74. Teaching: Art tutor, Canon Lawrence Col, Uganda, EAfrica, 68-70; chmn dept fine arts, Wash State Univ, 77- Mem: Col Art Asn Am. Style & Technique: Subjective realism. Media: Oil. Res: Non-Western art, particularly Africa; occult and how it relates to contemporary art. Publ: Co-auth, Some potential values of primary art education, Educ in Eastern Africa, 71; co-auth, New cattle sculpture of Uganda, African Arts, 73. Mailing Add: Dept Fine Arts Wash State Univ Pullman WA 99164

COBB, RUTH
PAINTER
b Boston, Mass, Feb 20, 14. Study: Mass Col Art, cert. Work: Boston Mus Fine Arts; Va Mus Fine Arts, Richmond; Butler Inst Am Art, Youngstown, Ohio; Munson-Williams-Proctor Inst, Utica, NY; Brandeis Univ, Waltham, Mass. Exhib: Am Watercolor Exhib, Metrop Mus Art, New York, 52; 22nd Biennial Int Watercolor Exhib, Brooklyn Mus, NY, 63; Am Watercolor Soc Ann, 68-77; Watercolor USA, Springfield Art Mus, Miss, 69; 35 Years in Retrospect, Butler Inst Am Art, 71. Awards: Purchase Award, Nat Acad Design, 68; Emily Lowe Award, 74 & Emily Goldsmith Award, 75, Am Watercolor Soc. Bibliog: Norman Kent (auth), Ruth Cobb, Am Artist Mag, 9/61 & reprod & article, In: 100 Watercolor Techniques, Watson-Guptill, 69. Mem: Nat Acad; Am & Boston Watercolor Soc; Allied Artists Am. Style & Technique: Transparent watercolor still-life or figures; color used as translucence. Mailing Add: 38 Devon Rd Newton Center MA 02159

COBB, VIRGINIA HORTON
PAINTER, LECTURER
b Oklahoma City, Okla, Nov 23, 33. Study: Colo Univ; Community Col of Denver; additonal study with William Schimmel, Chen Chi & Edward Betts. Work: Foothills Art Ctr, Golden, Colo; Nat Acad of Design, New York; NMex Watercolor Soc, Albuquerque. Exhib: Am Watercolor Soc, Nat Acad Galleries, New York, 73-78; Nat Watercolor Soc, Los Angeles, 74-76; Midwest Biennial, Joslyn Art Mus, Omaha, 74; Butler Inst Am Art, Youngstown, Ohio, 75; Springfield Art Asn Invitational Exhib, Ill, 77; Nat Acad Design, New York, 78; plus others. Teaching: Instr watermedia painting, Foothills Art Ctr, Golden, 72-74; instr watercolor seminar, Arts Coun, Oklahoma City, 73; lectr-demonstr, Emphasis-KRDO Channel 13, Colorado Springs, Colo, 77; instr, Crafton Hills Col Master Seminars, Yucaipa, Calif, 77 & 78. Awards: Elmer Fox Purchase Award, Watercolor USA, Springfield Art Mus, 73; Century Award of Merit, Rocky Mountain Nat Watermedia Exhib, 74 & Foothills Art Ctr Award, 76; Paul B Remmey Mem Award, Am Watercolor Soc, 74 & Arches Paper Co Award, 77; Walter Biggs Mem Award & Henry Ward Ranger Fund Purchase, Nat Acad of Design, 78. Mem: Watercolor Art Soc Houston; Nat Watercolor Soc. Style & Technique: Structural abstract form taken from nature. Media: Mixed Watermedia; Graphics. Dealer: Jack Meier Gallery Houston TX. Mailing Add: 1314 W Alabama Houston TX 77006

COBURN, BETTE LEE DOBRY
PAINTER
b Chicago, Ill. Study: Grinnell Col, Iowa; Art Inst Chicago; Univ NC; Art Students League; watercolor with Eliot O'Hara. Work: US Army Air Corps, Washington, DC; SC State Art Comn Collection, Columbia; Greenville Co Mus Art, SC; Univ NC, Greensboro; Univ Ga, Athens; plus many others. Comn: Mural, Evanston Art Ctr, Ill, 54; First Fed Bank, Henderson, NC, 65; mural, Ivey's Pres Off, Greenville, 69; space murals, Astro Theatre I, 70 & Astro Theatre II, 71, Greenville. Exhib: Hunter Art Ann, Chattanooga, Tenn, 68; 23rd Southeastern Ann, High Mus Art, Atlanta, 69; 6th Piedmont Ann, Mint Mus, Charlotte, NC; Nat Asn Women Artists Nat Traveling Exhib, US, 70-75; Della Citte Etterno, Pallazzio delle Exposizioni, Rome, 73; Univ Wyo Art Mus, 77; one-person show, Greenville Co Mus of Art, SC, 77; plus many others. Teaching: Instr painting, Greenville Co Mus Art Sch, 68, 70 & 75; adult painting classes, Furman Univ, 68-70. Pos: Staff artist for publ, Keesler Field Air Corps, Biloxi, Miss, 44; art dept, The Fair, Chicago, 46 & 47; graphic designs, Southern Bleachery, Taylors, SC, 57 & 58; mem, SC State Arts Comn Comt, 76-77. Awards: First Pl Grand Prix de Abstract, 23rd Int de Peinture, Deauville, France, 72; M Grumbacher Award, Nat Acad Art, Nat Asn Women Artists, New York, 73; First Place Oils, Greenville Artists Guild, Greenville Co Mus Art, 75; plus many others. Bibliog: Charles E Thomas (auth), B L Coburn abstract artist, Sandlapper Mag, 69; Art of Bette Lee Coburn, Le Semaines Int de la Femme, France; J A Morris, Jr (auth), Contemporary artists of South Carolina, Tricentennial Comn, 70; plus many others. Style & Technique: Exploring unchartered areas of sensibility. Media: Oil, Acrylic. Publ: Cover for Am Pen Women's '64 Biennial Conv, Washington, DC; Greenville's Cultural Brochure, C of C, 64; Greenville Art's Festival Cover, 65; Human in the Future Cities Symp Cover, Furman Univ, 68. Dealer: Hampton III Gallery Ltd Gallery Centre Greenville-Taylors SC 29687. Mailing Add: 436 Henderson Rd Greenville SC 29607

COBURN, RALPH
PAINTER, DESIGNER
b Minneapolis, Minn, Aug 10, 23. Study: Mass Inst Technol, 47; pvt study with Esther Geller, Carl Nelson, John Wilson & Barbara Swan, 46-49; Acad Julian, Paris, 50. Work: Stedlijk Mus, Amsterdam, Holland; Mus of Mod Art, Caracas, Venezuela; Chase Manhattan Bank, New York; Smithsonian Inst, Washington, DC. Pos: Graphic designer, Mass Inst of Technol, Cambridge, 57- Style & Technique: Systematic constructive abstraction; figurative drawing. Media: Oil or acrylic on canvas; pen & ink; watercolor. Dealer: Alpha Gallery 121 Newbury St Boston MA 02116. Mailing Add: 1269 Washington St Gloucester MA 01930

COCHRAN, DEWEES (DEWEES COCHRAN HELBECK)
DESIGNER, PAINTER
b Dallas, Tex, Apr 12, 92. Study: Walnut Hill, Natick, Mass; Gunston Hall, Washington, DC; Sch Indust Art, Philadelphia; Acad Fine Arts, Philadelphia; spec study in Ger, Austria & France; anthrop with Prof Preuss & art hist with Oscar Fischel, Berlin. Exhib: Marie Sterner Galleries, New York, 32; Philadelphia Print Club, 32; Salzburg Festivals, Austria, 32; 17th Ann Women's Nat Expos, Grand Cent Palace, New York, 38; Women's Int Expo, 71st Armory, New York, 59. Teaching: Dir design, Sch Am Craftsmen, Educ Coun, 46-47. Pos: Chmn art, Am Women's Club, Berlin, 31-32; chmn activities & lectr Ger art, Am Church of Berlin, 31-32. Awards: Award for Excellence, United Fedn Doll Collectors USA, 62-70. Bibliog: Jerry Fairbanks (auth), 3 Paramount Shorts, USA & Worldwide, 37-50; publ by King Features Syndicate, 50-51; Mazlin (auth), Woman of Tomorrow, TV documentary. Mem: Hon mem Doll Collectors Am Inc, Boston; assoc Int Inst Arts & Lett; Montalvo Asn, Saratoga, Calif; Nat Inst Am Doll Artists (pres, 67-69, dir, 75-). Style & Technique: Impressionism into abstraction; expressionism, magic realism. Media: Graphic; Watercolor, Oil. Collection: Dolls. Publ: Auth, Toward Design, articles in Crafts Horizons, 45 & 46; many articles on dolls as art, 62-75. Mailing Add: 155 Quail Hollow Rd Felton CA 95018

COCHRAN, GEORGE MCKEE
PAINTER, WRITER
b Stilwell, Okla, Oct 5, 08. Work: Pac Western Traders Art Gallery, Folsom, Calif; Pan Am Gallery, Pan Am Highway, Albuquerque, NMex; Northern Plains Indian Mus, Browning, Mont. Comn: Series of 40 Indian life drawings, Warm Springs Indian Reservation, KahNeeTah Lodge, Ore, 64; I Am an American (oil), Starline Corp, Albuquerque, 71; portraits of Pacific NW Indians, Western Equipment Co, Eugene, Ore, 73; Black & Whites & Sepias series of caricatures (oil), Nighthorse Studio Dee's Indian Supply, Sacramento, 75; First Sight of Sacramento Valley (oil), Am River Col Libr, Sacramento, 75. Exhib: Indian Festival Arts, LeGrande, Ore, 60-61; American Indian Days, Sheridan, Wyo, 61-62; America Discovers Indian Art Show, Smithsonian Inst, Washington, DC, 67; Univ Calif Med Ctr, San Francisco, 74; NMex State Fair, Indian Village, 71 & 75. Teaching: Instr drawing in native American Studies, Univ Calif, Berkeley, 73-74. Awards: Am Eagle Feather Award, Am Indian Coun, 60, Indian Festival Arts, 60-61 & American Indian Days, Sheridan, Wyo, 61-62. Bibliog: Flo Wilks (auth), Indian Artist Seeks Understanding, Albuquerque J, 10/71; Hubert Guy (auth), George Cochran-Cherokee Artist, Indian Trader, 3/75; Mary Shearly (auth), He paints his people's history George Cochran, Southwestern Art Mag, Vol 4 No 2. Style & Technique: Oil on stretched canvas, use earth tones mostly, colors blended on canvas, smoothed into background giving pastel quality; drawings, use powdered carbon applied with brush or powder puff, dark to light, fine lines-carbon pencil. Media: Oil, Watercolor; Lampblack & Conte A Paris. Publ: Auth & illusr, ABC Book, 47; co-auth, The Celiloh Indians, 49; auth & illusr, Indian Portraits of the Pacific Northwest, 59; illusr, Who did it First?, 59; illusr cartoons, The Indian Trader, 75. Mailing Add: 6517 Burdett Way Sacramento CA 95823

COCKRILL, SHERNA
PAINTER, INSTRUCTOR
b Chicago, Ill. Study: Univ Ark, BA & MA; Malden Bridge Sch Art, 67 & 68; also study with R Y Goetz, 65-69. Work: Smithsonian Inst Archives Am Art, Washington, DC; Ozark Art Ctr, Springdale; First Nat Bank, Little Rock. Comn: Many portrait comn. Exhib: Okla Eight State Exhib, Oklahoma City, 68; Philbrook Mus Ann Exhib, Tulsa, 68 & 69; Greater New Orleans Nat Exhib, 73; Tex Fine Arts Asn Ann, Austin, 73. Teaching: Instr oil painting, Ozarks Arts Ctr, 72-75; also pvt classes. Awards: First Prize, Okla Mus Art Ann, 70; First Prize in Art, Little Rock Ten State Arts Fair, State of Ark, 73; Top Award Ark Festival Art, 73 & 74 & Top Award Ark Festival & Art Invitational, 75. Mem: Ozark Artists & Craftsmen (bd dir, 75-). Style & Technique: Realistic colorist; neo-figurative; semi-abstract. Media: Oil, Acrylic. Publ: Auth, Women artists in mid-USA, Feminist Art J, Brooklyn, 74-75. Dealer: DuBois Gallery 2950 Kirby Dr Houston TX 77098; Moulton Gallery Ft Smith AR 72701. Mailing Add: Sunrise Mt Rd Fayetteville AR 72701

CODY, JOHN (ALEXIS)
SCULPTOR
b New York, NY, Dec 15, 48. Work: Soverign Life Ins Corp, Santa Barbara, Calif; NC Mus Art, Raleigh; Wayne State Univ, Sch of Med, Detroit; Times-Mirror Corp, Los Angeles; Mary Duke Biddle Gallery for the Blind, Raleigh, NC. Comn: Posters, Huntington-Sheraton Galleries, Pasadena, Calif, 75; sculpture, NC Sch Arts, Raleigh, 77; Auction Theme-78, KCET-TV, Los Angeles, 77; sculpture, Gilliand Oil Co, Santa Maria, Calif, 77; sculpture, Ladera Ranch, Ojai, Calif, 77. Exhib: One-man shows, Copenhagen Galleries, 67-73; Cody Exhib of Sculpture for the Blind, NC Mus Art, Raleigh, NC, 70; John Cody Exhib Sculpture, Mint Mus Art, NC, 70; exhib of sculpture, Columbia Mus Art, SC, 70; Exhib of Sculpture for the Blind, Converse Col, Spartenberg, SC, 70; Cody Sculpture Exhib, Allen Hancock Col, Santa Maria, Calif, 72; Founder's Festival, Grand Cent Galleries, New York, 76; Variations of the Sculptural Idea, Oakland City, Calif, 77. Bibliog: Ray Hamilton (auth), A Natural Gift for Beauty, US Info Agency, 68; Kimmis Hendrick (auth), There's Got to be Control, McGraw-Hill, 70; Hans Sorenson & C V Aronson, Conversation with John Cody (doc color film), 72. Mem: Artist's Equity Asn; US Fine Arts Registry; Ctr for the Visual Arts. Style & Technique: Personal interpretations of human and animal forms from realistic to abstract style; direct carving in stone entirely by hand. Media: All types of stone; metal. Dealer: John Cody Gallery 2884 Grand Ave Los Olivos CA 93441; Dazell Hatfield Galleries 3400 Wilshire Blvd Los Angeles CA 90010. Mailing Add: PO Box 227 Los Olivos CA 93441

COE, MATCHETT HERRING
SCULPTOR
b Loeb, Tex, July 22, 07. Study: Cranbrook Acad Art, with Carl Milles. Work: US Navy C B Mus, Port Hueneme, Calif; Am Numismatic Soc & Metrop Mus Art, New York; Carnegie Mus, Pittsburgh; Corcoran Gallery Art, Washington, DC. Comn: Bronze statues, Dick Dowling, State of Tex, Sabine Pass, 36 & The Texan, Vicksburg Nat Mil Park, 60; entrance to zoo (stone relief), City of Houston, 52; 75th Issue, Soc Medalists, New York, 67; bas-relief, Grotto of Libby Dam, 75. Exhib: Patron Church, Mus Contemp Crafts, 57; Church Archit Guild Am, Los Angeles, 59; Nat Sculpture Soc 75th Anniversary Exhib, 68 & Medals By Mem Show, Smithsonian Inst, 68; Am Numismatic Asn Conv, San Diego, Calif, 68. Awards: First Place for Dick Dowling Monument, Nat Competition; First Place for Frieze on New London Sch Mem, State Competition; selected by noted panel of sculptors to design 75th Issue, Soc Medalists. Bibliog: Emma Lila Fundaburk (auth), Art in Public Places in the United States, 75. Mem: Nat Sculpture Soc. Style & Technique: Resurface a volume of material by modeling or carving to give substance to a concept in a form that is compatible with the material and the setting in which it will be placed. Media: Bronze, Stone. Mailing Add: 2554 Gladys St Beaumont TX 77702

COELHO, LUIZ CARLOS
PAINTER, PRINTMAKER
b Campinas, Brazil, May 16, 35; US citizen. Study: Escola Nat Belas Artes, Univ Brazil. Work: Mus & Libr of Campinas, Sao Paulo, Brazil; Mus Colonial, Quito, Ecuador; Mus Nat of Lisbon, Portugal. Comn: Agricultural Labor Scenes, Pub Market of Rio de Janeiro, comn by Bank of Rio de Janeiro, 62. Exhib: Mus Nat de Belas Artes, Rio de Janeiro, 58; Mus Colonial, Quito, Ecuador, 63; Casa de la Cult, Quayaquil, Ecuador, 63; Fairfield Pub Libr, Conn, 68; Brazilian Consulate, Toronto, Can, 69; Brazilian Ctr of New York, 69; Bergen Community Mus, NJ, 77; Mus de Arte, Ponce, PR, 77. Teaching: Prof art hist, Inst Sousa Leaõ Rio de Janeiro, Brazil, 61-63. Bibliog: Maria Heller (auth), Catalog for Exhibit, Brazilian Embassy, Ecuador, 63; Sain-Euremond (auth), Le Courrier des Arts, France Amerique, New York, 69; Betsy Polier (auth), Art and artists, Park East, New York, 72. Mem: Shelter Island Community of Artists, NY; Hunterdon County Art Ctr, Clinton, NJ. Style & Technique: Surrealistic oils. Media: Oil and Printmaking. Mailing Add: Lake Dr Shelter Island NY 11964

COEN, ARNALDO
PAINTER
b Mexico City, Mex, June 10, 40. Study: Estudios Arte Publicitario IFAP, Mexico City, 58; study with Taller Lawrence Calcagno, Mexico City, 60. Work: Mus Art Mod, Mex; Coleccion Club de Indust, Mex; Mus Art Mod, Israel. Comn: Mural, Mex Pavilion, Osaka World's Fair, 70; lithographs, Bank St Atelier, New York, 70; painted sail, vessel Acalli, Santiago Genoves, 73; mural, Palacio de Los Deportes, 74. Exhib: IV Biennial for Young Artists, Paris, 65; Mexico: The New Generation Traveling Exhib, Phoenix Art Mus, 66, 15 Mexican Painters, 73; Contemp Mex Art, Mus Mod Art, Tokyo & Kyoto, 74. Awards: Grant, Fr Govt, Paris, 67. Style & Technique: Semi-figurative within a hard edge; poetic abstraction. Media: Acrylic, Pastel. Dealer: Malu Block Galeria Juan Martin Amberes 17 Mexico 6 DF Mexico. Mailing Add: Los Juarez 3 Mexico 19 DF Mexico

COES, KENT DAY
PAINTER, DESIGNER
b Chicago, Ill, Feb 14, 10. Study: Grand Cent Sch Art, New York; Art Students League; NY Univ. Work: Frye Mus Art, Seattle; Montclair Art Mus, NJ; Holyoke Mus Fine Arts, Mass; Norfolk Mus Arts & Sci, Va; Bergen Community Mus, Paramus, NJ. Exhib: Ann exhibs, Nat Acad Design, Allied Artists Am & Am Watercolor Soc, New York, Acad Artists Asn, Springfield, Mass; exchange exhibs, London, Mexico City, Ont, Can & Sydney, Australia. Pos: Art ed for several publ, McGraw-Hill, 47-75. Awards: Gold Medal of Honor, Allied Artists Am, 59; Gerhard Miller Award, Am Watercolor Soc, 71; Silver Medal, NJ Watercolor Soc, 73. Bibliog: Kent Day Coes insists—, Am Artist Mag, 10/57; Norman Kent (auth), 100 watercolor techniques, 68 & Norman Kent & Susan Meyer (auth), Watercolorists at work, 72, Watson-Guptill. Mem: Assoc Nat Acad Design (aquarelle); Am Watercolor Soc (dir, var terms 52-); Allied Artists Am (dir, secy, vpres, 50); NJ Watercolor Soc (founder-mem & pres, 47-48); Acad Artists Asn. Media: Watercolor. Dealer: Grand Cent Galleries 40 Vanderbilt Ave New York NY 10017. Mailing Add: 463 Valley Rd Upper Montclair NJ 07043

COFFELT, BETH
ART ADMINISTRATOR, WRITER
b Benton Harbor, Mich, Mar 9, 29. Collections Arranged: Looking at Pictures with Gertrude Stein, 65 & 71; cur, travel exhib Univ Calif & Hansen Fuller Gallery, San Francisco, 71. Pos: Cur/prog dir, Univ Calif, San Francisco, 63-66; dir pub info, Los Angeles Mus Art, 67-70; consult, B G Cantor Art Found, 69-71; Fed Arts Proj, Calif Fed Savings, 70; chmn art adv bd, San Diego Redevelop Agency, 74; writer, Wine Mus, San Francisco, Swift Exhib, Mus Sci & Indust, Chicago, 75; lectr, US Info Agency, Lisbon & Madrid. Res: Chicano art, aesthetics and evolution, role of art impulse, form and metaphysics, transformism, history San Francisco art. Publ: Numerous art & rev in San Francisco Chronicle, San Francisco Sun Examr, Calif Living, San Diego Mag, Studio Int & KPFA-Pacific radio critic, 72; auth, Eleanor Dickinson (catalog essay), Corcoran Gallery, 72; auth, Bruce Conner, Walnut Creek Art Ctr, 75; auth (catalogue), Wiley, Hudson, Geis, Allan, US Info Agency; auth, Celebration of Ourselves, Hearst Corp & San Francisco Mus Mod Art. Mailing Add: 4540 Garfield La Mesa CA 92041

COFFEY, DOUGLAS ROBERT
PAINTER, EDUCATOR
b Cleveland Heights, Ohio, Dec 27, 37. Study: Cleveland Inst Art, dipl, 59; Univ Denver, BFA, 61; Western Reserve Univ, MA, 65. Work: Xerox Corp, New York; Kodak Corp, Rochester, NY; Cleveland Mus Art. Exhib: Butler Inst Am Art Exhib, Youngstown, Ohio, 63; Rochester Fingerlakes Exhib, 71; 13th Ann Rochester Festival of Relig Art, 71; 16th Nat Print Exhib, Hunterdon Art Ctr, 72; one-man show, Mem Art Gallery, 75. Teaching: Asst prof fine arts, Rochester Inst Technol, 67- Awards: Sullivan Award for Painting, Fingerlakes Exhib, 70; First Award, 13th Ann Festival of Relig Art, 71; Painting Award, Mem Art Gallery, 75. Media: Polymer, Oil. Dealer: Mem Art Gallery 490 University Ave Rochester NY 14607. Mailing Add: Parrish Rd Honeoye Falls NY 14472

COGGESHALL, CALVERT
PAINTER
b Utica, New York, 07. Study: Univ Pa, 29; study with Bradley Walker Tomlin, 49. Work: Yale Univ Art Gallery, New Haven, Conn; Boston Mus Fine Arts, Mass; NY State Collection; Albright-Knox Art Gallery, Buffalo; Chase Manhattan Collection; plus others. Exhib: Abstract painting and Sculpture in America, 54 & Young American Painters, 67, Mus Mod Art, New York; Toledo Art Mus, Ohio, 54; Whitney Mus Am Art Painters Ann, New York, 67; Pittsburgh Plan for Art, Pa, 68; Univ Colo, Boudler, 68; plus one-man shows. Bibliog: Reviews in Art News, summer 67, 2/69 & 5/70, New York Times, 5/6/67 & 12/14/68 & Arts Mag, 2/69. Media: Oil. Mailing Add: Newcastle ME 04553

COGSWELL, DOROTHY MCINTOSH
EDUCATOR, PAINTER
b Plymouth, Mass, Nov 13, 09. Study: Yale Univ, BFA & MFA. Work: Springfield Mus Fine Arts, Mass; Wisteriahurst, Holyoke Mus, Mass; Newport Art Asn; Mt Holyoke Col. Comn: Egg tempera mural, Libr, 44, acrylic mural, Buckland Hall, 61 & acrylic mural & relief, Torrey Hall, 63, Mt Holyoke Col. Exhib: New Haven Paint & Clay Club, 29-; New York Watercolor Soc, 32-; Am Watercolor Soc, 33-; Conn Acad, 37; New York World's Fair, 39; plus many others. Collections Arranged: Caroline R Hill Collection of Medieval & Renaissance Art. Teaching: Prof art hist, Mt Holyoke Col, 39-74, emer prof, 74- Pos: Dir collections, Mt Holyoke Col, 70-74. Awards: First Prize in Watercolor, Eastern States Exhib, 41; Fulbright lectr, Nat Art Sch, Sydney, Australia, 57-58; Purchase Prize, Holyoke Bicentennial, 76. Mem: Springfield Art League (pres, 42-43); New Haven Paint & Clay Club; Am Asn Mus; Mt Holyoke Friends of Art (chmn, 47-60); Col Art Asn Am. Style & Technique: Realist for watercolors; semi abstract for acrylics on raised gesso relief. Interest: Renaissance and modern art. Publ: Auth, A visitor's impressions of Australian art, Soc Artists, Sydney, 58; auth, Mt Holyoke College art collection, Col Art J, 72. Mailing Add: 3860 Ironwood Lane Apt 402 G Bradenton FL 33505

COGSWELL, MARGARET PRICE
ART ADMINISTRATOR
b Evanston, Ill, Sept 15, 25. Study: Wellesley Col, BA, 47; Pratt Inst; Art Inst Chicago; Columbia Univ; Art Students League. Collections Arranged: Communication Through Art, 64; The American Poster, 68; American Exhib, 34th & 35th Venice Biennales, 68 & 70; Explorations, 70; The Audio-Visual Magazine, 72; George Catlin's American Indians, 74; Images of an Era: the American Poster (with catalog), 75. Teaching: The Poster & The Collector (sem), Smithsonian Inst, 70. Pos: Head dept publ & assoc foreign exhib, Am Fedn Arts, 55-66; ed, The Am Artists Series, 59-63; chmn, 50 Bks of the Yr, Am Inst Graphic Arts, 64; dep chief, Off Prog Support, Nat Collection Fine Arts, Smithsonian Inst, 66-, mem, Women's Coun, 77-79. Awards: Gold Medal for Printmaking, Am Artist Mag, 53. Mem: Am Asn Mus; Ben & Abby Grey Found, St Paul (trustee, 63-). Publ: Ed, The Ideal Theater: Eight Concepts, 63; co-ed, The Cultural Resources of Boston, 64; ed, Sao Paulo 9, 67; ed, The American Poster, 68. Mailing Add: 2929 Connecticut Ave NW Washington DC 20008

COHELEACH, GUY JOSEPH
PAINTER, ILLUSTRATOR
b New York, NY. Study: Cooper Union, with Don Eckelberry, grad; Col William & Mary, Hon Dr Arts, 75. Work: Nat Wildlife Gallery, Washington, DC; Nat Audubon Soc; Am Mus Natural Hist; Dean Amadon Collection; Beware, presented to President Nixon. Comn: Snowy Egrets, Nat Audubon Soc, 68; American Eagle, US Govt, presented to Vice President Agnew, 71; Elephant, African Safari Club, Washington, DC, for President Nixon, 72; Leopard & Elephant, World Wildlife Fund, 72; Elephant & Leopard, Mzuri Safari Found, 72. Exhib: Wildlife Art of America, Frame House Gallery, Louisville, Ky, 68 & 72; Linnean Soc Exhib, Am Mus Natural Hist, New York, 69; Bird Artists of the United States, Graham Gallery, New York, 72; Bird Artists of the World, Tryon Gallery, London, 72. Awards: Blue Ribbon Awards for Peregrine, 69, Great Horned Owl, 70 & Leopard Stare, 71, Printing Indust Am; Conservationist of the Yr, African Safari Club, Washington, DC, 75. Bibliog: R B Kirkpatrick (auth), National Wildlife visits Guy Coheleach, Nat Wildlife Mag, 70; Herman Kitchen (auth), Guy Coheleach & the bald eagle, Unit One Films, 70; Roger Caras (auth), Ouest: An Artist & His Prey. Mem: Soc Animal Artists; Explorer's Club; African Safari Club; Adventurer's Club. Media: Oil, Tempera. Interest: First occidental artist to exhibit in post-WWII Pelsing. Publ: Illusr, Audubon, 65-; illusr, Sat Eve Post, 67; illusr, Nat Wildlife Mag, 67-; illusr, Readers Digest, 67-; illusr, Int Wildlife Mag, 71- Mailing Add: c/o Regency House Art Inc Box 147 Plainview NY 11803

COHEN, ADELE
SCULPTOR, PAINTER
b Buffalo, NY. Study: Art Inst Buffalo; Albright Sch Buffalo; Parsons Sch Art, New York. Work: Albright-Knox Art Gallery, Member's Gallery, Buffalo, NY; Mus Arts & Sci, Evansville, Ind; Univ Mass, Amherst; Towson Col, Baltimore, Md. Comn: Stage sets sculpted of polyester resins & fibres for the play, Fando, Buffalo Fine Arts Acad & Workshop Repertory Theater, NY State Theater, 67. Exhib: Art Across Am, Inst Contemp Art, Boston, 65; Western NY Exhib, Buffalo Fine Arts Acad, 57-71; Patteran Artists, NY State travel tour, 75-77; Unordinary Realities, Xerox Corp, Rochester, NY, 75; Michael C Rockefeller Arts Ctr Gallery, State Univ NY Col, Fredonia, NY, 75; Foreign Inst, Dortmund, WGer, 76; Burchfield Ctr, Buffalo, NY, 77; Daemon Col, 77; Essex Arts Ctr, Conn, 77; Artpark, 78. Teaching: Instr drawing, State Univ NY Col Buffalo, 74-75. Awards: Best of Show, Western NY Exhib, 64; Painting Award, Ann New England Exhib, Silvermine Guild Artists, 65 & 66; Paul Lindsay Sample Mem Award, Chautauqua Exhib Am Art, 67. Mem: Nat Asn Women Artists, Inc; Patteran Artists. Style & Technique: Polyester fibers, resins form abstract sculptures, encased in Plexiglas; graphite drawings, collages & oils. Dealer: Phoenix Gallery 30 W 57th St New York NY 10021; Rosalind Van Gelder 7 Florence Rd Harrington Park NJ 07640. Mailing Add: 66 Burbank Dr Snyder NY 14226

COHEN, ARTHUR A
COLLECTORS
Mr Cohen, b New York, NY, June 25, 28. Study: Univ Chicago, BA & MA. Pos: Organizer of opening exhib, The Hebrew Bible in Christian, Jewish & Muslim Art, Jewish Mus, 63; managing ed, The Documents of 20th Century Art, Viking Press, 68-72; founder, Ex Libris for the Documentation of 20th Century Art. Collection: Primitive and ancient arts; modern painting and rare books, Dada and Constructivism. Publ: Auth, Sonia Delaunay, Abrams, 75; auth, Motherwell, 77; auth, The New Art of Color: The Writings of Robert & Sonia Delaunay, Viking, 78. Mailing Add: 160 E 70th St New York NY 10021

COHEN, ELAINE LUSTIG
PAINTER, DESIGNER
b NJ, Mar 6, 27. Study: Tulane Univ, 45-46; Univ Southern Calif, BFA, 48. Work: Mus Mod Art, New York; Am Tel & Tel; Chase Manhattan Bank. Comn: Graphic designs for Am Fedn Arts, Philip Johnson (architect), Lincoln Ctr, Fed Aviation Agency & Meridian Bks. Exhib: Greetings Exhib, Mus Mod Art, New York, 66; Fifty Years Graphic Arts in America, Am Inst Graphic Arts, 66; Tibor de Nagy Gallery, 69 & John Bernard Myers Gallery, New York, 70 & 72; Women, NC Mus, 72; plus others. Pos: Designer (with Alvin Lustig), until 55; freelance designer, 55-67; mem adv comt art & archit, Yale Univ Sch Design, 57-62. Mailing Add: 160 E 70th St New York NY 10021

COHEN, H GEORGE
PAINTER, EDUCATOR
b Worcester, Mass, Sept 14, 13. Study: Worcester Mus Art Sch, 33-36; Inst Design, Chicago, 49; also with Herbert Barnett & Kenneth Shopen. Work: Mt Holyoke Col Mus; Univ Mass; DeCordova & Dana Mus Art; Slater Mem Mus, Norwich, Conn; Loeb Ctr, NY Univ; plus others. Exhib: Va Mus Fine Arts, Richmond, 61; Brooklyn Mus, 64; DeCordova & Dana Mus, 64 & 68; Brockton Art Mus, 68; Amherst Col, 68; plus many others. Teaching: Lectr mod painting, mod art, art of film & kinetic art; instr, Smith Col, 42-46, prof art, 46- Awards: Prizes, Springfield Art League, 45-49, 51-58 & 60; Macdowell Fel, 58; prize, Berkshire Art Asn, 59; plus others. Mem: Springfield Art League; Soc Cinematologists; Col Art Asn Am; Am Asn Univ Prof; Am Film Inst; plus others. Publ: Contribr, Lincoln Times & Ford Times. Mailing Add: Hillyer Bldg Smith Col Northampton MA 01060

COHEN, HAROLD
ARTIST-THEORIST, EDUCATOR
b London, Eng, May 1, 28. Study: Univ London, DipFA, 51. Work: Tate Gallery, London; Stedelijk Mus, Amsterdam, Holland; Victoria & Albert Mus, London; Los Angeles Co Mus Art, Los Angeles, Calif; Walker Art Ctr, Minneapolis, Minn. Comn: Wallhanging, Milan Triennale, 63; tapestry, Brit Petroleum Co, 65. Exhib: One-man shows, Ashmolean Mus, Oxford, Eng, 50, Whitechapel Gallery, London, 65, Mus d'Art Contemporain, Montreal, Que, 67, Victoria & Albert Mus, 68 & Stedelijk Mus, 77; Documenta, Kassel, WGer, 64 & 77; 33rd Venice Biennale, 66; Three Behaviors for the Partitioning of Space, Los Angeles Co Mus Art, 72; Retrospective, Scottish Arts Coun Gallery, Edinburgh, 76. Teaching: Instr art, Univ Col London, 61-65; prof art, Univ Calif, San Diego, 68- Pos: Chmn visual arts dept, Univ Calif, San Diego, 68-69; vis scholar, Artificial Intelligence Lab, Stanford Univ, 73-75; dir, Ctr for Art/Sci Study, Univ Calif, San Diego, 74- Awards: Harkness Fel of Commonwealth Fund, Harkness Found, 59-61; Purchase Award, Gulbenkran Found, 61; Nat Endowment for the Arts Workshop Grant, 76. Bibliog: Lawrence Alloway (auth), Art news from London, Art News, 56; Dore Ashton (auth), rev in Studio, 63; Jack Burnham (auth), Encycl Britanica Yearbook on Sci & the Future, 73. Style & Technique: Engineering knowledge. Media: Artificial Intelligence; Drawing. Publ: Auth, The making of a tapestry, 67, Apropos work in progress, 68 & On purpose, 74, Studio Int; auth, The material of symbols, First Ann Symposium on Symbols & Symbol Processing, Univ Nev, 76; co-auth (catalogue), Harold Cohen, Stedelijk Mus, 77. Mailing Add: 921 Eolus Ave Leucadia CA 92024

COHEN, HAROLD LARRY
DESIGNER, EDUCATOR
b Brooklyn, NY, May 24, 25. Study: Pratt Inst Art Sch, Brooklyn; Northwestern Univ; Inst Design, BA. Teaching: Lectr; prof design, chmn dept & dir design res & develop, Southern Ill Univ, Carbondale, formerly. Pos: Dir, Inst Behav Res, Silver Spring, Md, formerly; dean sch archit & environ design, State Univ NY Col Buffalo. Awards: Five Good Design Awards, with Davis Pratt; Mus Mod Art Awards, 49-53; design of chair selected by US Govt for traveling exhib of one hundred leading US products. Mailing Add: Sch of Archit & Environ Design State Univ NY Col Buffalo Buffalo NY 14214

COHEN, HY
PAINTER
b London, Eng, June 13, 01. Study: Nat Acad Design; City Col New York, BS. Work: Hirshhorn Mus. Exhib: Brooklyn Mus; Art Inst of Chicago; Metrop Mus; St Louis Mus; Los Angeles Mus; Am Watercolor Soc; Washington Univ; Pa Acad; Carnegie Inst; Walker Art Ctr. Pos: Organized & moderated, Let's talk about art, weekly radio prog, 45-46. Mem: Artists Equity Asn New York (pres, 63-70, hon pres, 70-); life mem Am Watercolor Soc. Mailing Add: 166 W 72nd St New York NY 10023

COHEN, JEAN
PAINTER, LECTURER
b New York, NY, Aug 1, 27. Study: Pratt Inst, Brooklyn, 44-45; Cooper Union Art Sch, New York, 46-49; Skowhegan Sch Painting & Sculpture, Maine, summer 50. Work: Ciba-Geigy Corp, Ardsley, NY; Hampton Inst Mus, Va; Bocour Color Collection, Garnersville, NY; Colby Col Mus, Waterville, Maine; Wright State Univ Mus. Exhib: Contemp Artists, Riverside Mus, New York, 63; Pa Acad Regional, Philadelphia, 64; Visual R&D, Univ Tex Art Mus, Austin, 73; Contemp Am Painting, Randolph-Macon Col, 74; West Bronx Art League, Bronx Mus, 75. Teaching: Instr painting & design, Cooper Union, spring & summers, 51-63; lectr painting, Philadelphia Col Art, 62-69; lectr painting, Queens Col Art Dept, 72- Pos: Consult, West Bronx Art League, 69-75; founder, Landmark Gallery, New York, currently. Awards: Landscape Painting Prize, Skowhegan Sch Painting, 50. Mem: Women in Arts; Am Abstract Artists. Style & Technique: Purely abstract; simple shapes, psychologically evocative, with emphasis on vibrant color. Media: Oil, Compressed Charcoal. Dealer: Landmark Gallery 469 Broome St New York NY 10013. Mailing Add: 96 Bowery New York NY 10002

COHEN, JOAN LEBOLD
ART HISTORIAN, PHOTOGRAPHER
b Highland Park, Ill, Aug 19, 32. Study: Smith Col, BA, 54. Work: Smith Col Mus Art. Exhib: Mus Fine Arts, Boston, 72; Harvard Trust Co, 73 & 74; Northwestern Univ Law Sch, 76; The Yr of the Dragon—Asian Images, Harvard Law Sch, 76; The Gallery, Univ City Pub Libr, Univ City, Mo, 77; Worcester Art Mus, 77; Fac Show, Sch of Mus Fine Arts, Boston, 77. Teaching: Lectr, Dept Pub Educ, Mus Fine Arts, Boston, 65-71; lectr Asian ideas & images, China, Japan & India, Sch of Mus Fine Arts, Tufts Univ, Boston, 68- Awards: Two awards for bk, China Today & Her Ancient Treasures, 74 & 75. Style & Technique: Photographer in the style of an Asian artist. Media: Photography; Cultural History. Res: Words and images of the cultural history of Asia. Publ: Contribr photog & co-auth, with Jerome Alan Cohen, China Today & Her Ancient Treasures, Harry N Abrams, 74; auth, Angkor—Monuments of the God-Kings, Abrams, 75; contribr, The Domestication of the Fourth Dimension, Abrams, 75; contribr photog & text, Japan Today & Her Ancient Treasures, Abrams, 76; auth & illusr filmstrips, Ancient Art & History in People's China & Art Today in People's China, Mass Commun, 77. Dealer: Art/Asian 20 Palmer St Cambridge MA 02138; Nancy Singer 31 Crestwood St Louis MO 63105. Mailing Add: 21 Bryant St Cambridge MA 02138

COHEN, LYNNE G
PHOTOGRAPHER, LECTURER
b Racine, Wis, July 3, 44. Study: Univ Wis, Madison, BS(art); Slade Sch Art, London, Eng; Univ Mich, Ann Arbor, grad study; Eastern Mich Univ, MA(art). Work: Int Mus Photog, George Eastman House, Rochester, NY; Art Inst Chicago; Univ NMex Art Mus; Nat Gallery of Can, Ottawa; Bibliot Nat, Paris, France. Exhib: Photog: Midwest, Walker Art Ctr, Minneapolis, 73; Nat Film Bd Can, Ottawa, 75; one-person shows, Univ NMex, Albuquerque, 75 & Int Ctr of Photog, New York, 78; Destination Europe, Optica, Montreal, Que, 76; Photogr Choice, Witkin Gallery, New York, 76; Room's, Mus Mod Art, New York, 76-77; Recent Acquisitions, Nat Gallery of Can, 77. Teaching: Lectr photog-art, Eastern Mich Univ, Ypsilanti, 69-73; lectr photog, Ottawa Univ, 74- Awards: Logan Award, 71st Chicago & Vicinity Show, Art Inst Chicago, 68; Can Coun Proj Grant, 77. Bibliog: William Jenkins (auth), Portfolio, Image, 9/74; Geoffrey James (auth), Rooms with a viewfinder, Canadian, 77; Gary M Dault (auth), Destination Europe, Artscanada, 77. Style & Technique: Black and white photographs made with a 5x7 or 8x10 view camera and contact-printed. Publ: Contribr, IO, Plainfield, Vt, 74; contribr, Image, George Eastman House, 74; contribr, The Photographer's Choice, Addison House, 75; contribr, The Female Eye, Nat Film Bd Can, 75. Dealer: Yajima Gallery 1625 Sherbrooke W Montreal PQ Can; Witkin Gallery 41 E 57th St New York NY 10019. Mailing Add: 235 Cooper 19 Ottawa ON K2P 0G2 Can

COHEN, MICHAEL S
POTTER
b Boston, Mass, Mar 7, 36. Study: Mass Col of Art, BFA, 57; Cranbrook Acad of Art, Bloomfield Hills, Mich, 61; Haystack Mountain Sch of Crafts, Deer Isle, Maine, 61. Work: Mus of Mod Art, New York; Mus of Contemp Crafts, New York; Johnson Collection of Contemp Crafts, Wis; Everson Mus, Syracuse, NY; Addison Gallery, Andover, Mass. Exhib: Syracuse Int, Everson Mus, 62, 64 & 66; Am Studio Pottery, Victoria & Albert Mus, London, Eng, 63; 10th Int Exhib of Ceramic Art, Smithsonian Inst, Washington, DC, 65; one-man shows, Bonniers, New York, 67, Kendall Gallery, Wellfleet, Mass, 69, Benson Gallery, Easthampton, New York, 71, Soc of Arts & Crafts, Lexington, Mass, 74 & Gallimaufry, Croton-on-Hudson, NY, 76; Objects USA, Mus of Contemp Crafts, New York, 70; Crafts 1970, Boston City Hall, Mass, 70; Potter's Wheel, De Cordova Mus, Lincoln, Mass, 76. Awards: Nat Endowment for the Arts grant, 74; Master Craftsman grant, Nat Endowment for the Arts, 75; 2nd Int Symposium, Tenn, 75. Bibliog: Peter Sabin (auth), Studio Production, Studio Potter, 76. Mem: Am Crafts Coun; Mass Asn of Craftsmen; Asparagus Valley Potters Guild (pres, 75-76). Style & Technique: Functional pottery. Media: Stoneware. Mailing Add: RR 2 Amherst MA 01002

COHEN, STEPHEN DONALD
ILLUSTRATOR, COURTROOM ARTIST
b Bronx, NY, July 1, 40. Study: Sch of Visual Arts; Frank Riley Sch Art; pvt study with David Levine. Exhib: Huntsville Mus Art, Ala; Little Rock Mus, Ark; Columbus Mus Arts & Crafts, Ga; Lowe Art Gallery, Syracuse Univ; Bar Asn City New York. Pos: Graphic artist & sketch artist, NBC News, 64-; mem bd dir, Sch of Visual Arts, New York, 72-73 Awards: Cert of Award, Printing Indust Am, Fed Nat Mortgage Asn, 74. Bibliog: Robert J Benson (auth), Artists in the Courtroom, Print Mag, 11/77. Style & Technique: Watercolor paintings done transparently loose of famous people. Media: Watercolor; pen and ink. Mailing Add: 6 Horizon Rd Ft Lee NJ 07024

COHEN, WILFRED P
COLLECTOR, PATRON
b New York, NY, Aug 24, 99. Study: NY Univ; City Col New York. Awards: Award, Nat Conf Christians & Jews, 64. Collection: Giacometti, Arps & California painters, exhibited collections at Country Art Gallery, Westbury, Long Island & Galerie Chassaing, Paris, France. Mailing Add: 1290 Avenue of the Americas New York NY 10019

COHN, MARJORIE B
CONSERVATOR, ART HISTORIAN
b New York, NY, Jan 10, 39. Study: Mt Holyoke Col, BA, 60; Radcliffe Col, AM, 61. Collections Arranged: Albrecht Durer, 1471-1528 (auth, catalogue), Mt Holyoke Col, 71; Wash & Gouache, Watercolor at Harvard, Fogg Art Mus, Harvard Univ, 77. Teaching: Guest lectr print hist, Boston Univ, 73; vis lectr print hist, Wellesley Col, 73; vis asst prof print hist, Brown Univ, 75; sr lectr fine arts, Harvard Univ, 77- Pos: Conservator works of art on paper, Fogg Art Mus, Harvard Univ, 76-; mem bd examr (paper), Am Inst for Conserv, 76-78, mem nominating comt, 77 & ed jour. Mem: Fel Int Inst for Conserv; fel Am Inst for Conserv. Res: Materials and techniques of traditional graphic arts. Publ: Contribr, Technical Appendix, Ingres Centennial Exhibition, Fogg Art Mus, 67; contribr, A Note on Media and Methods, Tiepolo, A Bicentenary Exhibition, Fogg Art Mus, 70; auth, Le Metier des Paysages Dessines de J A D Ingres, Bull de Musee Ingres, 72; Wash & Gouache: A Study of the Development of the Materials of Watercolor, Fogg Art Mus, 77. Mailing Add: Fogg Art Mus Harvard Univ Cambridge MA 02138

COHN, RICHARD A
ART DEALER
b New York, NY, Feb 20, 24. Study: Univ Wis. Pos: Pres, Richard A Cohn Ltd, New York, 65-; partner Kimmel/Cohn Photography Arts, New York, 74- Specialty: 20th century German Expressionism, Old Master paintings, drawings and prints. Mailing Add: One W 64th St New York NY 10023

COHOE, GREY
PRINTMAKER, WRITER
b Tocito, NMex, Sept 9, 44. Study: Inst Am Indian Arts, Santa Fe, NMex, printmaking with Seymour Tubis & writing with Terry P Allen; Haystack Mountain Sch of Crafts, Deer Isle, Maine; Univ Ariz, printmaking with Andrew Rush & Lynn Schroder, BFA. Work: Pvt collections of Robert Putsch, Parker, Colo, John Humphrey, Cleveland, Ohio, Chris Isentberg, Pasadena, Calif, John Espy, New Orleans, La & Carl F Diener, Tucson, Ariz. Comn: NMex State Parks & Recreation Emblem, State of NMex, 66; Mountain Bell Calendar, Mountain Bell Tel Co, Denver, Colo, 70. Exhib: The Am Indian Heritage Art Exhib, Nat Cowboy Fall of Fame, Oklahoma City, Okla, 66; Am Discovers Indian Art Show, Exhib, Smithsonian Inst, Washington, DC, 67; Scottsdale Nat Indian Arts Exhib, Ariz, 67; Biennial Exhib of Am Indian Arts & Crafts, Washington, DC, 67; Ariz State Mus, Tucson, 68. Awards: Vincent Price Writing Award, 66; Nat Indian Short Story Contest, 70. Bibliog: Articles, in: Interior Design, 67, Native American Arts I, 68 & Pembroke Mag, 72. Media: Intaglio, Oil. Publ: Contribr prose, In: Design for Good Reading, Harcourt, 69; contribr poem & prose, In: SDak Rev, 69-71; contribr poem & prose, American Indian Literature, Houghton Mifflin, 72; contribr poem & prose, Red Eagle & illusr, The King of Thousand Islands, Doubleday, 72. Mailing Add: PO Box 448 Shiprock NM 87420

COINER, CHARLES TOUCEY
PAINTER
b Santa Barbara, Calif, Aug 20, 97. Study: Chicago Acad Fine Arts; Art Inst Chicago. Work: Philadelphia Mus Art & Pa Acad Fine Arts; Whitney Mus Am Art, New York; Univ Wichita, Kans; Syracuse Univ. Exhib: One-man shows, Philadelphia Art Alliance, Pa Acad Fine Arts, Fleisher Mus & Midtown Galleries; also nat open shows & regional exhibs in Pa. Mem: Philadelphia Art Alliance; New York Art Dirs Club; Nat Acad Design; Pa Acad Fine Arts. Style & Technique: Landscape and still life. Media: Oil. Publ: Auth articles on painting & conserv of wildlife, In: Esquire, Can, 9/63, Ireland, 2/65 & Scotland, 2/68. Dealer: Midtown Galleries 11 E 57th St New York NY 10022. Mailing Add: Mechanicsville PA 18934

COKE, F VAN DEREN
EDUCATOR, PHOTOGRAPHER
b Lexington, Ky, July 4, 21. Study: Univ Ky, BA; Ind Univ, MFA; Harvard Univ. Work: Mus Mod Art, New York; Int Mus Photog, Rochester, NY; Nat Gallery Can, Ottawa, Ont; San Francisco Mus of Mod Art; Sheldon Mem Art Gallery, Lincoln, Nebr; Denver Art Mus. Bibliot Nat, Paris. Exhib: Focus Gallery, San Francisco, 72; Witkin Gallery, New York, 74; Oakland Mus, 75; Galerie die Brücke, Vienna, 75; Schoelkopf Gallery, New York, 76; plus many others. Teaching: Asst prof photog & art hist, Univ Fla, 58-61; assoc prof photog & art hist, Ariz State Univ, 61-62; prof & chmn dept art, Univ NMex, 63-70; lectr, St Martin's Sch Art, London, 71; prof art hist, Univ Rochester, 71-72; prof photog & art hist, Univ NMex, 72-; vis prof, Univ Calif, Berkeley, 73; distinguished vis prof, Univ Calif, Davis, 74. Pos: Dir, Univ NMex Art Mus, 72- Awards: Int Competition Awards, Mod Photog Mag, 56 & US Camera Mag, 57, 58 & 60; New Talent USA Award, Art in Am, 60. Bibliog: Henry Smith (auth), Van Deren Coke, Photog, Eng, 59; Joan Murray (auth), Two views of the West, Artweek, 1/22/72; A Frankenstein (auth), A creative photographer, San Francisco Chronicle, 1/13/72. Mem: Col Art Asn Am (bd dir, 72-76); Int Folk Art Found (bd dir, 68-76); Guadalupe Found (bd dir, 76-); Soc Photog Educ (bd dirs, 67-70). Res: The use of photographs by artists; twentieth century American painters; contemporary photographers. Publ: Auth (catalogues), The Painter & the Photographer: From Delacroix to Warhol, 72 & auth, A Hundred Years of Photographic History, 75, Univ NMex, Light & Substance, 74, 12 Contemp Artists Working in New Mexico, 76 & Charles Mattox, 78; plus many others. Dealer: Witkin Gallery 41 E 57th St New York NY 10022; Susan Spiritus Gallery 3336 Via Lido Newport Beach CA 92663. Mailing Add: Art Mus Univ NMex Albuquerque NM 87131

COKER, CARL DAVID
PAINTER, EDUCATOR
b Greensboro, NC, Feb 8, 28. Study: Art Students League with Robert Beverly Hale; Univ NC; Univ NMex with Raymond Jonson, Richard Diebenkorn & Enrique Montenegro, BFA & MA; Ill State Univ. Work: Philbrook Mus, Tulsa; Performing Arts Ctr, Tulsa; Univ Okla Mus, Norman; Jonson Gallery, Univ NMex, Albuquerque; Mus of NMex, Santa Fe. Comn: Welded steel altarpiece, Holloman Air Force Hosp Chapel, USAF, 67; 3 large-scale paintings, Hillcrest, Hosp, Tulsa, Okla, 71; painting, Farmers & Merchants Bank, Tulsa, 75; fiberglass painting, 76 & welded steel sculpture, 77, Hicks Park, City of Tulsa. Exhib: Tex Ann, Dallas Mus of Fine Arts, 60; Western Ann, Denver Mus of Fine Arts, 60; Ill Print & Drawing Show, Chicago Art Inst, 63; Nat Drawing Show, Bucknell Univ, 65; Five NMex Artists, Pronaf Mus, Juarex, Mex, 65; NMex Sculptors, 66 & NMex Painters, 67, Mus of NMex, Santa Fe. Teaching: Instr painting, ETex State Univ, Commerce, 56-61; asst prof painting-sculpture, NMex State Univ, Las Cruces, 64-68; prof painting, Univ Tulsa, 68- Pos: Mem bd dirs, Albuquerque Mod Mus, 51-53, Living Arts Ctr, Tulsa, 69-71; mem exec coun, NMex Art Educ Asn, 65-66. Awards: First Prize Painting, 19th Cent Ill Exhib, Decatur, 62; First Prize Sculpture, 14th Ann, Quincy, Ill, 63; Grand Award, Okla Ann, Philbrook Mus, Tulsa, 73. Mem: Mid-Am Col Art Asn. Style & Technique: Three-dimensional fiberglass forms spray-painted with acrylic lacquer; welded steel sculpture; semi-abstract still life easel painting. Media: Acrylic and fiberglass painting; welded steel sculpture. Dealer: Tally Richards Gallery of Contemp Art 1 Ledoux St Taos NM 87571. Mailing Add: 1135 S Gary Pl Tulsa OK 74104

COLARUSSO, CORRINE CAMILLE
PAINTER, INSTRUCTOR
b Boston, Mass, Mar 22, 52. Study: Yale Summer Sch Art & Music, 72; Univ Mass, BFA, 73; Tyler Sch Art, Temple Univ, Philadelphia, MFA, 75. Exhib: Corcoran Gallery Art, Washington, DC, 75; Young Philadelphia Artists, Vick of Fischback Gallery, 75, Works on Paper, 77; Inst Contemp Art, Recife, Brazil, 76; O'Kane Gallery, Univ Houston, Tex, 77; 30 Women Artists, Peachtree Ctr, Atlanta, Ga, 78; one-person show, Oglethorpe Univ, Atlanta, 78. Teaching: Teaching asst drawing, Univ Mass, Amherst, 72-73; grad teaching asst, Tyler Sch Art, 74-75; fac mem found design & drawing, Atlanta Col Art, 75- Awards: MacDowell Colony Fel, 77. Style & Technique: Series of paintings based on four words: fan, screen, veil and shield. Media: Oil on Canvas; Gouache on Paper; Mixed-Media Drawing. Mailing Add: 756 Clemont Dr NE Atlanta GA 30306

COLBURN, FRANCIS PEABODY
ARTIST
b Fairfax, Vt, Oct 20, 09. Study: Univ Vt, PhB, 34, hon DFA, 74; Bennington Col; Art Students League, scholar. Exhib: One-man shows, Carnegie Inst, Corcoran Gallery, Whitney Mus Am Art, Nat Acad Design & Cordova Mus, Boston; plus others. Teaching: Resident artist, Univ Vt, 42-, chmn art dept, 46-, emer prof art, 75- Awards: Awards from Springfield Mus Fine Arts, Mass & San Francisco Palace Legion Honor; Distinguished Serv to the Arts Award, Vt Coun on the Arts, 68. Mem: Vt Art Teachers Asn (pres); Vt Coun Arts; Artists Equity. Mailing Add: 118 S Willard St Burlington VT 05401

COLBY, JOY HAKANSON
ART CRITIC, ART CONSULTANT
b Detroit, Mich. Study: Detroit Soc Arts & Crafts; Wayne State Univ, BFA. Pos: Art critic, Detroit News, 50-; art consult, Kasle/Colby, 76- Mem: Mich Coun Arts (adv, 72-); Detroit Coun Arts; New Detroit Inc Arts Comt; Bloomfield Hills Arts Coun; Oakland Youth Symphony (mem bd, 75-76). Publ: Auth, Art & a City, 56; auth, Arts and Crafts in Detroit, Detroit Inst Arts, 76. Mailing Add: Detroit News 615 W Lafayette Detroit MI 48231

COLBY, VICTOR E
SCULPTOR, EDUCATOR
b Frankfort, Ind, Jan 5, 17. Study: Corcoran Sch Art; Ind Univ, AB, 48; Cornell Univ, MFA, 50. Work: Cornell Univ Mus, Ithaca, NY; Ithaca Col Mus; Munson-Williams-Proctor Inst, Utica, NY; St Lawrence Univ, Canton, NY; State Univ NY Col Cortland. Comn: Wall sculpture, Wilson Nuclear Physics Lab, Cornell Univ, 68. Exhib: One-man shows, Hewitt Gallery, 58, The Contemporaries, 66 & Hartley Gallery, 74. Teaching: Prof sculpture, Cornell Univ, 50- Style & Technique: Carved, joined, and partially painted. Media: Wood. Mailing Add: RD 1 Groton NY 13073

COLE, BRUCE
ART HISTORIAN, EDUCATOR
b Cleveland, Ohio, Aug 2, 38. Study: Western Reserve Univ, BA, 62; Oberlin Col, MA, 64; Bryn Mawr Col, PhD, 69. Teaching: Asst prof art hist, Univ Rochester, NY, 69-73; assoc prof art hist, Ind Univ, Bloomington, 73-77, prof art hist, 77- Awards: Suida Fel, Kunsthistorisches Inst, Florence, Kress Found, 65-67; Nat Endowment for Humanities Fel, 72-73; Guggenheim Fel, 75-76. Res: Painting of the 14th & 15th centuries in Florence. Publ: Auth, On an early Florentine fresco, Gazette de Beaux-Arts, LXXX, 72; contribr, Old in new in the early Trecento, Klara Steinweg-In Memoriam, Florence, 73; auth, A popular painting from the Trecento, Apollo, CI, 75; auth, Giotto & Florentine Painting 1280-1375, New York, Harper, 76; auth, Agnolo Gaddi, Oxford, The Clarendon Press: Oxford Univ Press, 77. Mailing Add: Dept of Fine Arts Ind Univ Bloomington IN 47401

COLE, DONALD
PAINTER
b New York, NY, Oct 31, 30. Study: Bucknell Univ, BS(civil eng); Univ Iowa, MFA; also apprenticeship with Bruce Mitchell, Lewisburg, Pa. Exhib: 55 Mercer Gallery, New York, 70 & 71; Nancy Hoffman Gallery, New York, 73, 75 & 78; Unstretched Paintings, Brockton Art Ctr, Mass, 74; Works on Paper, Va Mus of Fine Arts, Richmond, 74; A Collection in Progress, The Clocktower, New York, 75; 200 Selections from a Collection, Moore Col of Art, Philadelphia, 77; Adirondack Ctr Mus, Elizabethtown, NY, 77; State Univ NY, Plattsburgh, 77; Paintings on Paper, Univ Rochester, NY, 78. Awards: Creative Artists Pub Serv Grant/Painting, NY State Coun on the Arts, 75; Artist-in-residence grant, Nat Endowment for the Arts, State Univ NY, Plattsburgh, 77. Bibliog: Robert Pincus-Witten (auth), article in Artforum, 72; April Kingsley (auth), article in Artforum, 73; Ellen Lubell (auth), article in Arts Mag, 73 & 75. Media: Collage, Acrylic. Dealer: Nancy Hoffman Gallery 429 W Broadway New York NY 10012. Mailing Add: 53 Mercer St New York NY 10013

COLE, FRANCES
PAINTER
b St Louis, Mo, Sept 2, 10. Study: Antioch Col; Univ Mich; Univ Dayton; Schimmel Sch Art, Scottsdale, Ariz. Work: Ariz Bank, Yuma & Phoenix; Valley Nat Bank, Phoenix; First Nat Bank, Yuma; Thunderbird Bank, Glendale, Ariz. Exhib: Am Watercolor Soc Ann, Nat Acad Design Galleries, New York, 64 & 65; Ariz Artists Guild Traveling Exhib, St Louis, Mo, Louisville, Ky & Kansas City, Mo, 65; Southwestern Invitational Yuma Fine Arts Asn, 67-70; Fine Arts Festival Watercolor Exhib, SDak State Univ, Brookings, 69; Nat Diamond Biennial Art Exhib, Nat League Am Pen Women, Washington, DC, 72. Pos: VPres, Ariz Watercolor Asn, 69-70, pres, 71-73. Awards: Spring Nat Exhib Gold Medal, Low Ruins Gallery, Tubac, Ariz, 65; Regional Art Exhib First Award in Watercolor, Nat League Am Pen Women, 67; First Nat Bank Award, Yuma, 70. Bibliog: C Bower (ed), Artists of the Southwest, Western Rev, winter 67; Gabriel Wills (auth), Scottsdale artists busy in co-op gallery, Southwestern Art Scene, 2/68; H L Cowle (auth), The Arizona bit, West Art, 1/71. Mem: Nat League Am Pen Women (Ariz state pres, 72-74); Ariz Artists Guild (pres, 63-65); Arts Coun Gtr Phoenix (pres, 68-70); assoc Am Watercolor Soc; Nat Soc Lit & Arts. Media: Watercolor. Publ: Auth, Art over four decades, Ariz Repub, 68. Mailing Add: 1701 E Cinnabar Phoenix AZ 85020

COLE, HAROLD DAVID
ART HISTORIAN, EDUCATOR
b Tulsa, Okla, Feb 28, 40. Study: Univ Tulsa, BA, MA(art criticism), with Alexander Hogue & Harry A Broadd; Ohio State Univ, MA(art hist), PhD, with Franklin Hadden & Maurice Cope. Work: Art Gallery, Univ Tulsa, Okla; Art Gallery, Baldwin-Wallace Col, Berea, Ohio; Art Gallery, Cumberland Col, Williamsburg, Ky; Art Gallery, Nicholls State Univ, Thibodaux, La. Exhib: 32nd Ann Springfield Ann Ten-State Exhib, Springfield Art Mus, Mo, 62; 12th Ann Own Your Own Exhib, Denver Art Mus, Colo, 68; 51st Ann May Show, Cleveland Mus Art, Ohio, 69; one-man shows, Cumberland Col, 70 & 72 & Nicholls State Univ, 71. Teaching: Assoc prof art hist, Baldwin-Wallace Col, 66- Pos: Mem visual art panel, Ohio Arts Coun, 77- Mem: Col Art Asn; Midwest Art Hist Asn; Int Ctr of Medieval Art; NE Ohio Art Historians Asn; Monument Historique. Res: Thirteenth century French sculpture and architecture; 19th century French painting. Publ: Auth, Kenneth R Weedman Sculpture Exhibition, Crafts Horizons, 72; auth (catalogue), Kenneth R Weedman Exhibition, 73 & co-auth, Grant Reynard: His Life & Work, 75, Baldwin-Wallace Col. Mailing Add: 28 E Fifth Ave Berea OH 44017

COLE, JOYCE
PAINTER
b New York, NY, Sept 3, 39. Study: Syracuse Univ; NY Univ; Finch Col, BA(hist art); Art Students League; Will Barnet, Jacob Lawrence & Bob Cunningham; Sch Visual Arts. Work: Aldrich Mus Contemp Art, Ridgefield, Conn. Exhib: Andre Emmerich Gallery, NY, 72; Whitney Mus Am Art Biennial, New York, 73; Contemporary Reflections, Aldrich Mus Contemp Art, 73; Galerie Denise Rene, New York, 73; Soho Ctr Visual Arts, Aldrich Mus, New York, 74; Susan Caldwell Gallery, New York, 77; Gloria Luria Gallery, Fla, 78. Bibliog: April Kingsley (auth), New York letter, Art Int, 10/73; Lawrence Campbell (auth), Reviews & previews, Art News, 9/73; Peter Frank (auth), article in Art News, 10/77. Style & Technique: Abstract geometric forms with line grids; sprayed acrylic paint on unprimed canvas. Mailing Add: 11 W 20th St New York NY 10011

COLE, MAX
PAINTER, INSTRUCTOR
b Hodgeman Co, Kans, Feb 14, 37. Study: Univ Ariz, Tucson, MFA, 64. Exhib: Drawings, USA, St Paul Art Ctr, Minn, 65; Calif Now, Ringling Mus Contemp Art, Sarasota, Fla, 68; Contemp Painting & Sculpture, Krannert Art Mus, Univ Ill, 69; Visible/Invisible, Long Beach Art Mus, Calif, 72; Whitney Mus Am Art Biannual, 75; one-person shows, Sidney Janis Gallery, New York, 77 & Louver Gallery, Los Angeles, 78. Teaching: Asst prof painting, Pasadena City Col, Calif, 67- Awards: Purchase Award, Drawings USA, St Paul Art Ctr, 65; May Lieberman Award, Frye Mus Art, 66; Purchase Award, Laguna Beach Art Asn, Calif, 69. Style & Technique: Formalist, reductive abstraction. Media: Paint on Canvas. Mailing Add: 119 E Union St Pasadena CA 91103

COLE, SYLVAN, JR
ART DEALER, WRITER
b New York, NY, Jan 10, 18. Study: Cornell Univ, BA, 39. Pos: Pres & dir, Assoc Am Artists, New York, 58-; adv bd, Pratt Graphics Ctr, 64- Mem: Art Dealers Asn Am (vpres, 68-74); Print Coun Am (dealers adv comt, 66-); Alumni Friends of Herbert F Johnson Mus (vpres, 72-75, pres, 75-). Specialty: Original prints. Publ: Auth, Raphael Soyer: Fifty Years of Printmaking, 67; auth, The Graphic Work of Joseph Hirsch, 70; auth, Will Barnet—Prints 1932-1972, 72. Mailing Add: 663 Fifth Ave New York NY 10022

COLEMAN, MICHAEL
PAINTER, ETCHER
b Provo, Utah, June 25, 46. Study: Brigham Young Univ. Work: Buffalo Bill Hist Mus, Cody, Wyo; Kennedy Gallery, New York. Exhib: Springville Mus Nat; Nat Acad Western Art, Nat Cowboy Hall of Fame, Oklahoma City. Bibliog: Diane Cochrane (auth), Romantic Western landscapes, Am Artist, 1/75; Susan Myers (auth), Twenty American Landscape Painters; Romantic Western painter, SW Art Mag, 2/77. Style & Technique: 19th century style and tradition; historical and contemporary subjects; plains Indians, trappers, and landscapes. Media: Oil. Dealer: Kennedy Gallery 40 W 57th St New York NY 10019; Zantman Art Galleries Ltd PO Box 5818 Carmel CA 93921. Mailing Add: 2843 Marrcrest E Provo UT 84601

COLESCOTT, ROBERT H
PAINTER, INSTRUCTOR
b Oakland, Calif, Aug 26, 25. Study: Univ Calif, Berkeley, AB & MA; & with Atelier Fernand Leger, Paris. Work: Portland Art Mus, Ore; Seattle Art Mus; Univ Mass, Amherst; San Francisco Mus Art; Oakland Art Mus, Calif; Exhib: Salon de Mai, Paris, 50; Pacific Profile, Pasadena Mus & others, 61; Am Painting Today, Grand Rapids Mus, Mich, 61; Trois Americains, Am Cult Ctr, Paris, 69; Third World Exhib, San Francisco Mus Art, 74; Calif Painting & Sculpture, San Francisco Mus Art, 76 & Smithsonian Inst, Washington, DC, 77; plus others. Teaching: Assoc prof drawing & art educ, Portland State Univ, 57-66; assoc prof painting, Am Univ, Cairo, 66-67; prof art, Calif State Col, Stanislaus, 70-74; lectr, Univ Calif, Berkeley, 74- Pos: Artist in residence, Am Res Ctr, Egypt, 64-65. Awards: Wash Invitational Award, Henry Gallery, Univ Wash, 53; Northwest Artists Purchase Award, Seattle Mus, 71; Nat Endowment for the Arts Grant for Creative Painting, 76. Bibliog: J Canaday (auth), rev in New York Times, 4/7/73; J Perreault (auth), Outrageous Black pop, Soho News, 5/1/75; Alfred Frankenstein (auth), Outrageous ethnic satire, San Francisco Chronicle, 7/10/75. Style & Technique: Satirical & generally expressionist paintings. Media: Acrylic on Canvas; Mixed Media. Dealer: John Berggruen Gallery 228 Grant Ave San Francisco CA 94108; Razor Gallery 464 W Broadway New YOrk NY 10013. Mailing Add: 1803 E 14th St Oakland CA 94606

COLESCOTT, WARRINGTON W
PRINTMAKER, EDUCATOR
b Oakland, Calif, Mar 7, 21. Study: Univ Calif, Berkeley, BA & MA; Acad Grande Chaumiere, Paris; Slade Sch Art, Univ Col, London. Work: Metrop Mus Art & Mus Mod Art, New York; Milwaukee Art Ctr, Wis; Art Inst Chicago; Minneapolis Inst Arts. Comn: Death in Venice (suite of ten color etchings), Ferdinand Roten, Inc, Baltimore, 71. Exhib: Brit Print Biennial, Bradford, Eng, 74; Brooklyn Mus 19th Print Biennial, 74; 15th Nat Bradley Print Show, Peoria, Ill, 75; 9th Dulin Nat Print & Drawing Competition, 75; Libr Cong 24th Nat Exhib, 75; plus others. Teaching: Prof art, Univ Wis-Madison, 49-, chmn dept art, 63-65. Pos: Mem visual arts panel, Wis Arts Bd, 77-78; co-dir, Mantegna Press, Hollandale, Wis. Awards: Purchase Awards, Hawaii Nat Print Exhib, Honolulu Acad of Art, 77 & Miami Graphics Biennial, Fla, 77-78; Ed Award, Soc Am Graphic Artists, 77. Bibliog: John Lloyd Taylor (auth), Warrington Colescott: graphics, Madison Art Ctr, 68; Warrington Colescott, environmental artist, Arts & Soc Mag, spring-summer 72; Master printmakers of Wisconsin, Art News, 3/75. Mem: Soc Am Graphic Artists. Style & Technique: Etching and aquatint, based on satirical, figurative drawing. Publ: Illusr, Death in Venice, Aquarius Press, 71; illusr, Mariposa Poems, Tetrad Press, London, 71; illusr (covers), 30 Years of Printmaking, Brooklyn Mus, 76 & Art News Mag, 3/77. Dealer: Assoc Am Artists 663 Fifth Ave New York NY 10022; Lorenz Gallery 7023 Wisconsin Ave Chevy Chase MD 20015. Mailing Add: Rte 1 Hollandale WI 53544

COLIN, GEORGIA T
COLLECTOR, DESIGNER
b Boston, Mass. Study: Smith Col; Univ Grenoble, Sorbonne, Paris, France; Ecole de Louvre. Mem: Am Inst Interior Designers; Nat Soc Interior Designers. Collection: With husband, Ralph F Colin, have for forty years collected paintings, sculpture, drawings and graphics mainly School of Paris 1890-1970. Mailing Add: 941 Park Ave New York NY 10028

COLIN, RALPH FREDERICK
COLLECTOR
b New York, NY, Nov 18, 00. Study: City Col New York, BA, 19; Columbia Univ Law Sch, LLB, 21. Pos: Dir & gen counsel, Parke-Bernet Galleries, Inc, 59-64; founder, admin vpres & gen counsel, Art Dealers Asn Am, 62- Mem: Mus Mod Art, New York (trustee, 54-69, vpres, 60-69, vpres & dir, Int Coun, 56-69); Fogg Art Mus (vis comt, 51-); Am Fedn Arts (trustee, 45-56); Adv Comt on Arts Ctr Prog, Columbia Univ. Collection: Paintings, sculpture, drawings and graphics concentrated on School of Paris 1890-1970. Mailing Add: 941 Park Ave New York NY 10028

COLINA, ARMANDO G
ART DEALER
b Veracruz, Mex, Mar 30, 35. Study: Univ Mex, BA. Pos: Rep, Contemp Mus Bogota, Colombia, currently; art consult, Festival Cervantino, Guanajuato & Puebla Musical Festival, Mex, currently; owner, Arvil Art Gallery, currently. Specialty: Contemporary art. Publ: Illusr, Toledo/Sahagun, 74; illusr, Toledo/Chilambalam, 75. Mailing Add: Arvil Art Gallery Hamburgo 241 Mexico 6 DF Mexico

COLKER, EDWARD
PAINTER, GRAPHIC ARTIST
b Philadelphia, Pa, Jan 5, 27. Study: Philadelphia Col Art, grad; NY Univ, grad; spec study with E & J Desjobert, Paris. Work: Mus Art, Philadelphia; NJ State Mus, Trenton; New York Pub Libr Print Collection; Mus Mod Art, New York; Nat Mus, Stockholm; plus others. Comn: Lithography ed, Print Club, Philadelphia, 66, Int Graphic Art Soc, New York, 66 & 69 & Ill Arts Coun, 73. Exhib: One-man shows, Kenyon Gallery, Chicago, 75; Stampe di due Mondi, Rome & Philadelphia Mus Art, 67; American Art Today, Pa Acad Fine Arts, Philadelphia, 68; Nat Collection Fine Arts, Washington, DC, 77. Collections Arranged: Spec exhibs, Symbol & Vision, Calif Painters & Sculptors, 70 & Depth & Presence, Environmental Sculpture, Corcoran Gallery Art, Washington, DC, 71. Teaching: Assoc prof fine arts, Univ Pa Grad Sch Fine Arts, 68-70; prof & dir, Sch Art & Design, Univ Ill, Chicago Circle, 72- Awards: Noyes, Coleman Prizes, NJ State Mus, 67 & 69; Printing Indust Gold Medal, Pa, 70; Univ Ill Res Bd, 77; Graham Found, 77. Bibliog: Zigrosser (auth), The Appeal of Prints (appreciation), 70. Mem: Col Art Asn Am; Am Inst Graphic Arts. Mailing Add: Sch of Art & Design Univ Ill Chicago Circle Box 4348 Chicago IL 60680

COLLETT, FARRELL REUBEN
PAINTER, EDUCATOR
b Bennington, Idaho, Nov 13, 07. Study: Brigham Young Univ, BA & MA; Sch Fine Arts, San Francisco; Art Inst Chicago; Am Acad Art, Chicago; Art Ctr Col Design, Los Angeles; Art Students League; & with Paul Bransom. Work: Springville Mus Art, Utah; Brigham Young Univ; Grand Central Art Galleries, New York; Univ Calgary. Comn: Portrait of Pres, Weber State Col, 59; Wildlife-Cougars, Brigham Young Univ, 70; Ft Buenaventura (mural), Walker Bank, Ogden, Utah, 72; Wildlife, Va Bankshares, Richmond, 73; Wildlife-Bison, Franklin Mint, Pa, 73. Exhib: Utah State Inst Fine Arts Ann, 68-; Wildlife 71, Minneapolis, 71-72; Am Natural Hist Art Show, Univ Minn, Minneapolis, 71; Soc Animal Artists Ann, New York, 72; Dismal Swamp Art Exhib, Richmond, Va, 73. Teaching: Prof art, Weber State Col, 39-, chmn dept, 39-69; guest prof painting, Brigham Young Univ, summer 53; guest prof art hist & painting, Univ Calgary, summers 66 & 67. Pos: Chmn, Utah State Inst Fine Arts, 63-65. Awards: Best of Show for White Horse, Nat Invitational, Springville Mus Art, Utah, 63; Best of Show for Girl in the Black Hood, Ogden Outdoor & Sweepstakes Award, Prize-winning Paintings Only Exhib, Salt Lake City, 65. Bibliog: George S Dibble (auth), Collett's horses are exciting, Salt Lake Trib, 11/24/74; Donald Jardine (auth), Most unforgettable lecture, Illustrator; George Harrison (auth), Painting a bright future for Dismal Swamp, Nat Wildlife, 10-11/74. Mem: Soc Animal Artists; Salmagundi Club; Ogden Palette Club; Assoc Utah Artists; Utah Watercolor Soc. Style & Technique: Primarily representational; some work in abstract. Media: Oil, Watercolor. Publ: Illusr, Pit Pony, Knopf, 46; illusr, Conserv Series Filmstrips, Chicago, 54; illusr, Annual report, Pepsi-Cola Co, 56; illusr, Calendar posters, Browning Ann, 59; auth, Felt tip diary, Illustrator, fall 69. Dealer: Grand Central Art Galleries 40 Vanderbilt Ave New York NY 10017. Mailing Add: 876 Ben Lomond Ogden UT 84403

COLLIER, ALAN CASWELL
PAINTER
b Toronto, Ont, Mar 19, 11. Study: Ont Col Art; Art Students League, with Howard Trafton. Work: Nat Gallery Can, Ottawa, Ont; Art Gallery Ont, Toronto; Art Mus London, Ont; Hamilton Art Gallery, Ont; Frye Mus, Seattle. Comn: Murals, Ryerson Polytech Inst, Toronto, 58 & 62, Bank Can, Toronto Agency, 59 & Ont Govt Bldg, Queen's Park, Toronto, 68; many portraits for educ & bus orgns. Exhib: 1st & 4th Biennial Can Art, Nat Gallery Can, 55 & 61 & Dept Can External Affairs, 57; Faces of Canada, Stratford, Ont, 64; Canadian Artists '68, Art Gallery Ont, 68. Mem: Ont Soc Artists (pres, 58-61); Royal Can Acad Art (hon treas, 65-72). Media: Oil. Dealer: Roberts Gallery 641 Yonge St Toronto ON Can; Kensington Gallery 328 Tenth St NW Calgary Alta Can. Mailing Add: 115 Brooke Ave Toronto ON Can

COLLIER, ALBERTA
ART CRITIC
b Vicksburg, Miss, Oct 25, 11. Study: Newcomb Art Sch, 34-35 & Arts & Crafts Club Sch, New Orleans, 36-37. Pos: Fine arts writer, Times-Picayune newspaper, 46-77; consult, Hist New Orleans Collection, 77- Publ: Auth, chap on art scene, The Past as Prelude-New Orleans 1718-1968, 68. Mailing Add: Hist New Orleans Collections 533 Royal New Orleans LA 70116

COLLIER, GRAHAM (ALAN GRAHAM-COLLIER)
WRITER, PAINTER
b Manchester, Eng, Sept 12, 23; US citizen. Study: Slade Sch Fine Art, Univ London, with Randolph Schwabe, dipl(painting). Work: Walker Art Gallery, Liverpool, Eng; Usher Art Gallery, Lincoln, Eng; Volunteer Park Art Mus, Seattle. Comn: Sir John Barbirolli (portrait), Halle Concerts Soc, Manchester, Eng, 50; Sir Reginald Thatcher (portrait), Royal Acad Music, London, 52; Hugo Rignold (portrait), Liverpool Philharmonic Soc, 53. Exhib: One-man shows, Piccadilly Galleries, London, 56, Leicester Galleries, London, 57, Vancouver City Art Gallery, BC, 61. Teaching: Dir art, Lancing Col, Sussex, Eng, 54-60; assoc prof art, Univ Conn, Storrs, 63-68; prof philos & psychol art, Univ Ga, Athens, 69- Awards: National Registered Designer, Royal Register of Designers, London, 52; Best Produced Book of Year, Am Typographical Award, New York, 68. Bibliog: Art of Graham Collier (radio prog), Can Broadcasting Co, 62. Style & Technique: Painter in gouache; pioneered the use of mineral dyes in series of overlaid glazes. Res: Immediate interest in the psychological bases of inspiration and image-making; the teleology of art and the issues of sense and mind. Publ: Auth, Form, Space & Vision, 3rd ed, 71 & auth, Art and the Creative Consciousness, 72, Prentice-Hall. Mailing Add: Dept of Art Univ of Ga Athens GA 30601

COLLIER, RIC
SCULPTOR, MUSEUM DIRECTOR
b Twin Falls, Idaho, Nov 4, 47. Study: Boise State Col, BFA, 72; Wash State Univ, MFA, 74. Work: Boise Gallery Art, Idaho; Wash State Univ Permanent Collection, Pullman; Boise State Univ. Comn: Sculpture, comn by Mr & Mrs Allen Dodworth, Boise, 70; sculpture, Capital High Sch, Boise, 70; wall sculpture, Pres John Barnes, Boise State Univ, 71. Exhib: One-man show, Leather Weddings, Boise Gallery Art, 70; 25th Spokane Sculpture Ann & 1973 Crafts Invitational, Cheney Cowles Mus, Wash, 73; 27th Ann Pacific Northwest Arts & Crafts Fair, Seattle, 73; Concepts & Executions, Sculpture, Missoula Mus Arts, Mont, 75. Collections Arranged: Retrospective Show Walter Hook—1933-1975, 75. Teaching: Instr sculpture, Wash State Univ, 73, instr advanced drawing, 73-74. Pos: Dir, Missoula Mus Arts, currently. Mem: Western Asn Art Mus; Am Asn Mus; Mont Art Gallery Dir Asn. Style & Technique: Enigma's in assemblage. Media: Wood, Metals. Mailing Add: 2610 Gleason Missoula MT 59801

COLLINS, CHRISTIANE C
ART HISTORIAN, ART LIBRARIAN
Study: Carleton Col, BA; Columbia Univ, MA, MLS. Pos: Cataloguing librn, Mus Mod Art, New York, 71-72; head librn, Parsons Sch of Design, Adam L Gimbel Libr, New York, 73- Mem: Art Libr Soc NAm; Soc of Archit Historians; Col Art Asn. Res: City planning; late 19th century, contemporary, German expressionist architecture. Publ: Ed & co-auth, Architecture of Fantasy, Praeger, 62; translr, Camillo Sitte. City Planning According to Artistic Principles, 65 & co-auth, Camillo Sitte & the Birth of Modern City Planning, 65, Random House/Phaidon. Mailing Add: 448 Riverside Dr New York NY 10027

COLLINS, GEORGE R
ART HISTORIAN
b Springfield, Mass, Sept 2, 17. Study: Princeton Univ, BA, 35, MFA, 42; Univ Barcelona, Dr Hon Causa, 77. Pos: From instr to prof art hist, Columbia Univ, 46- Awards: Guggenheim Fel, 62-63; Rockefeller Humanities Fel, 76-77. Res: Modern architecture and city planning; Spanish art and architecture. Publ: Auth, Antonio Gaudi, Braziller, 60; co-auth, Architecture of fantasy (transl & rev, Phantastische Architektur), 62; co-auth, Camillo Sitte..., Random House & Phaidon, Eng, Vols I & II, 65; auth numerous articles in journals & ed of a number of books on history of architecture and planning. Mailing Add: 448 Riverside Dr New York NY 10027

COLLINS, JESS
See Jess

COLLINS, JIM
EDUCATOR, SCULPTOR
b Huntington, WVa, Sept 12, 34. Study: Marshall Univ, AB, 57; Univ Mich, Ann Arbor, MPH, 61; Ohio Univ, MFA, 66. Work: Wichita Art Asn, Kans; Univ SC, Columbia; Huntington Galleries, WVa, Am Repub Ins Co, Des Moines, Iowa; Milwaukee Art Ctr, Wis. Comn: Outdoor sculpture, St Augustine Church, Signal Mountain, Tenn, 70 & Arlen Realty, Chattanooga, 71; wall-relief, B'nai Zion Synagogue, Chattanooga, 75. Exhib: 16th Ann Delta Art Exhib, Ark Arts Ctr, Little Rock, 73; 8 State Ann: Painting, J B Speed Art Mus, Louisville; Mid-South Biennial Exhib, Brooks Mem Art Gallery, Memphis, 75; Appalachian Nat Drawing, Appalachian State Univ, Boone, NC, 75; 21st Ann Drawing & Small Sculpture Show, Ball State Univ, Muncie, Ind, 75; Nat Sculpture, 75 & 76; Southern Asn Sculptors

Traveling Exhib; Dixie Ann, Montgomery Mus Fine Arts, Ala, 75 & 76; Choo Choo Art Exhib, 77; plus others. Teaching: Prof art, Univ Tenn, Chattanooga, 66- Awards: Purchase & Achievement Awards, Appalachian Corridors, WVa, 72, Tenn Watercolor Soc, 72 & Tenn Drawings, 74, Tenn Bicentennial Art Exhib, Tenn Arts Comn, 76; plus others. Mem: Southern Asn Sculptors (pres, 70-71). Media: Wood, Metals. Publ: Auth introduction, A Handbook to British Landscape Painters, 70; auth, Women Artists in America, 18th Century to the Present, 75 & Women Artists in American II, 76. Mailing Add: 109 Louisiana Ave Signal Mountain TN 37377

COLLINS, JOHN IRELAND
PAINTER
b Atlantic City, NJ, Dec 31, 26. Study: Corcoran Sch Art, Washington, DC, grad; also with Karl Knaths, Provincetown, Mass. Exhib: Int Watercolor Show, Brooklyn Mus, NY, 66; one-man show, Farnsworth Mus, Rockland, Maine, 67; 20th Exhib of New England Artists, Silvermine Guild Artists, New Canaan, Conn, 69; Landscape I, 135 Watercolors by 45 New England Artists, De Cordova Mus, Lincoln, Mass, 70 & Landscape II, 90 Oils by 45 New England Artists, 71. Awards: Emily Lowe Award, 53; Thomas E Saxe Jr Award, Silvermine Guild Artists, 69; Guggenheim Mem Grant, 72. Bibliog: Lawrence Kent (auth), John Ireland Collins, artist in residence, Maine Digest, 66; Leo Chabot (auth), Nature artist at work, Bangor Daily News, 67; Jim Moore (auth), Cushing, mecca for art, awards, Portland Press Herald, 72. Style & Technique: Figurative; transparent watercolor; oil directly painted on canvas. Dealer: Barbara Fiedler Gallery 1621 21st St NW Washington DC 20009; Joan Peterson Gallery 561 Boylston St Boston MA 02130 Mailing Add: Pleasant Point Cushing ME 04563

COLLINS, LOWELL DAUNT
PAINTER, ART DEALER
b San Antonio, Tex, Aug 12, 24. Study: Colorado Springs Fine Art Ctr, with B Robinson; Mus Fine Arts, Houston; Art Students League; Acad Grande Chaumiere, Paris; Univ Houston, BFA & ML. Work: Mus Fine Arts, Houston; Mus Fine Arts, Dallas; US Info Agency. Comn: Painting for Nelson Found. Exhib: Provincetown Arts Festival; New York World's Fair; Hemisfair, San Antonio; Columbia Biennial, SC; NZ Exchange Exhib; plus many others. Teaching: Instr art & archit, Univ Houston, 51-58; dean art dept, Mus Fine Arts, Houston, 58-66; dir art sch, Lowell Collins Gallery, 66- Pos: Art ed, Tex Cancer Bull, 47-49; cur pre-Columbian art, Mus Nat Sci, Houston, 70-; dir, Lowell Collins Gallery, 70- Awards: First Prize, Tex Fine Arts Asn, 49; Second Prize, D D Feldman Art Exhib, 56; First Prize & Purchase Award, Motorola Corp, 60. Mem: Sr mem Houston Philos Soc; sr mem Am Soc Appraisers; hon mem Hanzen Col, Rice Univ; Archaeol Soc Am; Valuation Consortium. Style & Technique: Abstract. Media: Oil. Specialty: Pre-Columbian art; African art; Oriental art; contemporary paintings and sculpture. Publ: Illusr, Houston, Land of Big Rich, 51; illusr, Houston, The Feast Years, 61; illusr, The Galveston Era, 65; illusr, Unhappy Medium, 68. Mailing Add: 2903 Saint St Houston TX 77027

COLLINS, MARCIA REED
ART LIBRARIAN
b Passaic, NJ, June 5, 45. Study: Univ NH, BA, 68; Univ Mo, MALS, 71, MA(art hist), 78. Collections Arranged: Early Books on Art (co-auth, catalogue), 77 & The Dance of Death in Book Illustration, 78, Ellis Libr, Univ Mo-Columbia. Pos: Librn art, archaeol & music, Ellis Libr, Univ Mo-Columbia, 71- Mem: Art Libr Soc NAm. Res: Literature of art history; art library methods; art bibliography; rare books. Publ: Co-auth, Libraries For Small Museums, Univ Mo Mus Anthrop, 3rd ed, 77. Mailing Add: 4D32 Ellis Libr Univ Mo-Columbia Columbia MO 65201

COLLINS, PAUL
PAINTER
b Muskegon, Mich, Dec 11, 36. Study: Self-taught. Work: Int Afro-Am Mus, Detroit; Palace de la Presidence du Senegal, Dakar, Senegal, Africa; Du Sable Mus, Chicago; White House, Washington, DC; in pvt collections of Steve McQueen & Roger Miller. Comn: Portrait of the pres of Senegal, US Embassy, 72; Black portrait of an African journey, Eerdmens Publ Co, Grand Rapids, Mich, 73; Black Struggle, Grand Rapids Pub Mus, 73; Portrait of Dr Martin Luther King, Dr Martin Luther King Ctr, Montgomery, Ala, 74; Life of the President of US, Kent Co Airport, 75. Exhib: American Artist, Butler Inst Art, Youngstown, Ohio, 71; African Perspective, Am Cult Ctr, Dakar, Africa, 73; Am Heritage Exhib, Corcoran Gallery, Washington, DC, 73; Tribal Arts Festival, Libr & Mus Performing Arts, New York, 74; Classic Revival, Ill State Mus, Springfield, 75. Awards: Mead Award, Mead Paper Co, 73; African Cult Award, Senegalese Govt, 73; Stax Spec Art Award, Stax Rec Co, 74. Bibliog: Save the Children (film featuring African paintings), Paramount Pictures, 74; Bicentennial projects, Newsweek Mag, 75; Paul Collins painter of people, Am Artist, 75. Style & Technique: Detailed realism. Media: Dry Oil, Own Media with Dry Brush. Publ: Illusr, Africa for the Africans, 72; illusr, Black Self Determination, 72; auth, Show down at Wounded Knee, Ebony Mag, 73; contribr, Black Portrait of an African Journey, 73. Dealer: Frances Wynshaw 40 Avanti Galleries 145 E 72nd St New York NY 10021. Mailing Add: 709 Logan St Grand Rapids MI 49506

COLLINS, WILLIAM CHARLES
PAINTER, ART ADMINISTRATOR
b Cambridge, Mass, Jan 18, 25. Study: RI Sch Design, BFA; Univ Ill, Urbana, MFA; Akad Bildende Kunste, Munich. Work: Wash Univ, St Louis; Cincinnati Art Mus; Univ Ill, Urbana. Comn: Mural, St John's Unitarian Church, 62; paintings, Hunter Savings & Loan, 66, Bethesda Hosp, 71, O K Transfer Corp, 72 & Stone Corp, Cincinnati, Ohio. Exhib: Dayton Art Inst, 63, 65 & 71; American Art, Whitney Mus Am Art, New York, 64; American Landscape, Fort Worth Art Ctr, Tex, 65; Mid-Am Exhibs, Butler Inst Am Art, Youngstown, Ohio; Portland Mus Art, Maine, 73-75. Teaching: Instr drawing, Albright Art Sch, Buffalo, 51-54; instr drawing & painting, Art Acad Cincinnati, 54-67; vis prof drawing & painting, Wash Univ, 67-72; dir, Portland Sch Art, Maine, 72- Awards: Morton D May Purchase Prize, City Art Mus, St Louis, 57; Fulbright Fel, Ger, 57-58; Painting Prize, Interior Valley Exhib, Contemp Art Ctr, Cincinnati, 61. Media: Acrylic. Dealer: Carl Solway Gallery 204 W Fourth St Cincinnati OH 45202. Mailing Add: Portland Sch Art 97 Spring St Portland ME 04101

COLOMBO, CHARLES
PAINTER
b Wilmington, Del, Nov 3, 27. Study: Pa Acad Fine Arts, Philadelphia; Art Students League with Charles DeFeo; privately with Frank E Schoonover. Work: Pvt collections throughout US & abroad including The Vatican, Rome, Italy & Prince & Princess Ranier, Monaco. Comn: Hagley Powder Mills, comn by State of Del for President J F Kennedy, 62. Exhib: Del Art Mus, Wilmington, 56 & one-man show, 71; Nat Arts Club, New York, 66-75; Charles & Emma Frye Mus, Seattle, Wash, 75; Mus Arts & Sci, Daytona Beach, Fla, 75. Awards: Watercolor Award, Pa Acad Fine Arts, 49; Scholar Award, Pa Acad Fine Arts; Watercolor Award, Del Art Mus, Wilmington, 56. Bibliog: Frederick Kramer (auth), Brandywine Tradition Artists, Great Am Ed, New York, 71; Nancy Mohr (auth), Charles Colombo, a part of the Brandywine tradition, Delaware Today, Wilmington, 71. Mem: Am Watercolor Soc; Delaware Art Mus; Rehoboth Art League. Style & Technique: Landscapes and figures in watercolor, dry brush technique and frequent use of Japanese paper. Dealer: Carspecken Scott Gallery 1707 N Lincoln St Wilmington DE 19806. Mailing Add: 101 E 13th St Wilmington DE 19801

COLON-MORALES, RAFAEL
PAINTER
b Trujillo Alto, PR, Oct 28, 41. Study: Univ PR, BA, 64; Am Univ, Washington, DC, grad work, 65-66; San Fernando Acad Art, Madrid, Spain, 67-68. Work: Mus de Ponce, PR; Mus de San Juan, PR; PR Cult Inst, San Juan; Univ PR Mus, Rio Piedras; Inter-Am Univ PR, Hato Rey. Exhib: IMAN, Ctr Inter-Am Relations, New York, 76; Spirit of Independence, Cayman Gallery, New York, 76; Latin Excellence, Xerox Corp, Rochester, NY, 77; Selected Puerto Rican Artists, PR Cult Inst, 77. Teaching: Instr art hist & painting, Univ PR, 68-71; instr art of PR, New York City Community Col, 72-75; artist-in-residence, Boricua Col, Brooklyn, NY, 75. Pos: Vpres, Comt for the Third World Am Art Exhib at the Metrop Mus Art. Bibliog: Marcos Dimas (auth, film), Towards a Collective Expression, WNET Ch 13, New York, 75; Holland Cotter (auth), Galleries, NY Arts J, 11-12/77; David Hershkovitz (auth), Everything was gray, Village Voice, 2/78. Style & Technique: Acrylics on glass; pasted on canvas, hanging, molded or sculpted; figurative and abstract. Media: Acrylic. Res: Pre-Columbian art of the Caribbean; painting of Puerto Rico; contemporary Caribbean culture. Publ: Auth, Mythical genealogy of Puerto Rican art, Quimbamba Bilingual Quart, Mus del Barrio, 74; auth & ed, Coabey, Caribe Mag, Phelps Stokes Fund, 77. Dealer: Sam Lacher The Brooklyn Collector 131 Seventh Ave Brooklyn NY 11215. Mailing Add: 1124 Stratford Ave 2C Bronx NY 10472

COLORADO, CHARLOTTE
PAINTER
b Denver, Colo, Jan 18, 20. Study: Colo Woman's Col; Otis Art Inst; Jepson Art Inst; Chouinard Art Inst. Comn: Auth & dir, three theatre pieces (with Alex Haye's Los Angeles Summer Theatre Piece Lab), 67; spec proj, Covina Parks & Rec, 71-72. Exhib: Pa Acad Fine Arts; Fine Arts Gallery San Diego; Long Beach Art Mus; Jewish Community Ctr; Signs of Neon Traveling Exhib, Mod Art Gallery, Washington, DC, 69-71; plus others. Pos: Founder, Changes (theatre co), 67; dir, The Ensemble Group (exp art theatre), Los Angeles, currently. Awards: Prizes, Los Angeles Mus Art, 60, Westside Jewish Community Ctr, Los Angeles, 63 & First Methodist Church, Santa Monica, 63. Style & Technique: Main creative work is in field of performance of art, combining electronic and natural sound, film and live performers. Mailing Add: 120 Westminster Apt 6 Venice CA 90291

COLSON, CHESTER E
PAINTER, EDUCATOR
b Boston, Mass, June 17, 17. Study: Mass Sch Art, BS, 46; Teachers Col, Columbia Univ, MA, 49, with Edwin Ziegfeld; also pvt study. Work: Everhart Mus, Scranton, Pa; Wilkes Col, Wilkes-Barre, Pa; Norwich Univ, Northfield, Vt. Exhib: One-man shows, Little Gallery, Wilkes-Barre, 68 & Everhart Mus, 69; Philadelphia Drawing & Print Show, 68; Fleming Mus, Burlington, Vt, 69; Norwich Armory Show, Northfield, Vt, 72. Teaching: Chmn dept fine arts, Wilkes Col, 59-72, prof fine arts, currently. Awards: Sordoni Prize, 62; Purchase Prizes, Everhart Mus, 68 & Vt Artists, Norwich Univ, 69; plus others. Mem: Col Art Asn Am; Nat Soc Painters in Casein & Acrylic; Nat Art Educ Asn; Philadelphia Watercolor Soc. Dealer: Jeanne Fairbanks Bethany Colony PA 18701. Mailing Add: 122 Frangorma Dr Trucksville PA 18708

COLT, JOHN NICHOLSON
PAINTER, EDUCATOR
b Madison, Wis, May 15, 25. Study: Univ Wis, BS & MS. Work: Whitney Mus Am Art; Milwaukee Art Ctr; Munson-Williams-Proctor Mus, Utica, NY; Le Centre d'Art, Port au Prince, Haiti; Beloit Col, Wright Art Ctr, Wis. Comn: Murals, Marquette Univ, 59 & First Wis Ctr, 73. Exhib: Butler Inst Am Art Exhib Am Painting, Youngstown, Ohio, 55; Whitney Ann Exhib Am Painting, Whitney Mus Am Art, New York, 60; one-man shows, Milwaukee Art Ctr, Wis, 62 & 69, Minneapolis Inst of Art, 70, Bradley Gallery, Milwaukee, 73, 75 & 77 & Neil Gallery, New York, 77; Chicago Vicinity, Art Inst Chicago, 62 & 64; Walker Biennial, Walker Art Ctr, Minneapolis, 62, 64 & 66; Art Across America, Knodler Gallery, New York, 68. Teaching: Prof painting, Univ Wis-Milwaukee, 58- Awards: Medal of Honor, Milwaukee Art Ctr; Ford Found Award & Top Award, Walker Art Ctr. Media: Oil, Acrylic, Pastel. Dealer: Neill Gallery 136 Greene St New York NY 10012. Mailing Add: 2840 N Stowell Ave Milwaukee WI 53211

COLT, PRISCILLA C
MUSEUM DIRECTOR
b Kalamazoo, Mich. Study: Kalamazoo Col, AB; Western Reserve Univ, MA; Harvard Univ; Inst Fine Arts, NY Univ. Teaching: Instr hist art & art theory, Goucher Col, Kalamazoo Col & Ohio State Univ. Pos: Asst, Jr Mus, Metrop Mus Art; cur educ to cur, Va Mus Fine Arts; ed cur, Minneapolis Inst Art; res asst, Portland Art Mus, Ore; consult contemp art, Dayton Art Inst, 67-74; dir, Univ Ky Art Mus, 75- Publ: Contribr, articles in Art J, Art Int, Arts, mus bulletins & others. Mailing Add: 236 W Second St Lexington KY 40507

COLT, THOMAS C, JR
MUSEUM DIRECTOR
b Orange, NJ, Feb 20, 05. Study: Dartmouth Col, BS, 26; Columbia Univ; Cambridge Univ. Pos: Writer & critic, New York, 26-27; assoc, Rehn Galleries, New York, 27-29; trustee, Richmond Acad Arts, 33-35; secy, Va Art Alliance, 34-35; dir, Va Mus Fine Arts, Richmond, 35-42, 45-48; dir, Portland Art Mus, Ore, 48-56; adv ed, J Aesthet & Art Criticism, 51-53; dir, Dayton Art Inst, 57-76. Awards: Star of Solidarity, Ital Govt, 53. Mem: Asn Art Mus Dirs; Int Inst Conserv Mus Objects; Intermus Conserv Asn (pres, 68-70); hon mem Ore Archaeol Soc; Ohio Arts Coun (exec comt, 65-70); plus others. Publ: Ed, C S Price, 1874-1950, Prehistoric stone sculpture of the Pacific Northwest, Samuel H Kress collection of paintings of the Renaissance & Fifty treasures of the Dayton Art Institute; plus others. Mailing Add: 330 W Schantz Ave Dayton OH 45409

COLVERSON, IAN
PRINTMAKER, LECTURER
b London, Eng, June 10, 40. Study: Slade Sch of Fine Art, Univ Col, Univ London, DFA, 62; post-grad study in Rome, Italy & Paris, France, 62-63. Work: Brit Mus, Victoria & Albert Mus & Tate Gallery (print collection), London, Eng; Nat Mus in Poznan, Poland; Kunsthalle, Hamburg, Ger; Cabinet des Estampes, Geneva, Switz; Detroit Inst of Art, Mich; Chicago Mus of Art; Metrop Mus of Art, New York; Mus of Mod Art, New York. Comn: Poster, 3rd Brit Int Print Biennale, 72. Exhib: The 2nd Biennale de l'estampe, Musee d'Art Moderne, Paris, 70; 2nd-4th Brit Int Print Biennale, Eng, 70-74; 9th-11th Int Print Biennale,

Yugoslavia, 71-75; 36th Venice Biennale, Italy, 72; 3rd & 4th Int Exhib of Original Drawings, Yugoslavia, 72-74; 4th & 5th Int Print Biennale, Poland, 72-74; 2nd Ashiyagawa Int Biennale, Ashiya, Japan, 74; 4th Int Print Biennale, Frechen, Ger, 76; plus numerous others. Teaching: Head, Dept Visual Commun, Bradford Col, Eng, 70-76; lectr printmaking, Univ Calif, Los Angeles, 76- Pos: Mem adv comt, Brit Int Print Biennale, Eng, 72- Awards: Giles Bequest Prize, 2nd Brit Int Print Biennale, Eng, 70; cash award, 3rd Int Biennale of Original Drawings, Yugoslavia, 72; Purchase Prize, 5th Int Print Biennale, Poland, 74. Bibliog: Heinz Ohff (auth), Mag Kunst, Ger, 71; Pat Gilmour (auth), aritcles in Art News & Rev, London, 71-; Robert Kennedy (auth), Art Int, Switz, 72. Mem: Printmakers Coun. Style & Technique: Photographic printmaking. Media: Silkscreen; etching. Publ: Co-auth & illusr, Berlin Suite, Lothar Poll, 71. Dealer: Lothar Poll Kurfurstendamm 185 I Berlin Charlottenburg Ger. Mailing Add: c/o Dickson Art Ctr Univ Calif 405 Hilgard Ave Los Angeles CA 90024

COLVILLE, ALEXANDER
PAINTER, PRINTMAKER
b Toronto, Ont, Aug 24, 20. Study: Mt Allison Univ, with Stanley Royle, BFA. Work: Nat Gallery Can; Mus Mod Art, New York; Wallraf-Richarts Mus, Cologne, Ger; Ctr Nat Art Contemporain, Paris; Boymans-Van Beuningen Mus, Rotterdam. Exhib: Venice Bienniale, 66; Kestner Gesellschaft, Hannover, 69; Marlborough, London, Eng, 70; Gemeentmuseum Arnhem, Kunsthalle, Dusseldorf; Fischer Fine Art, London, 77. Style & Technique: Realistic. Mailing Add: PO Box 550 Wolfville NS Can

COLWAY, JAMES R
PAINTER
b Oneida, NY, Nov 12, 20. Study: Syracuse Univ Sch Art, 45-48, Univ Col, 46-48. Work: US Embassy Prog, Washington, DC; Butler Inst Am Art, Youngstown, Ohio; Lyman Allyn Mus, Univ Conn, New London; St Lawrence Univ, Canton, NY; Eisenhower Col, Geneva, NY; plus others. Exhib: Munson-Williams-Proctor Inst, Utica, NY, 52-53; Grumbacher Show, Grand Cent Art Gallery, New York, 64; one-man shows, Chase Gallery, New York, 69, St Lawrence Univ, 70, Grand Haven Art Ctr, Mich, 70 & 75 & Arvest Galleries, Boston, 76. Pos: Art dir, Oneida Silversmiths, NY, 48-53, dir advert, 64-77, vpres, 77- Bibliog: Show rev in Art News, 5/69; Foreign art, La Rev Mod, 5/70; Fred A Mohr (auth), Upstate art goes around the world, Empire Mag, Syracuse Herald-Am, 1/72. Style & Technique: Combination of color and heavy texture of oil underpainting with the light wash technique found in watercolor. Paintings are in realistic vein of New England coast, Central New York state, Pennsylvania farmland and Italy. Media: Watercolor, Acrylic. Mailing Add: 101 The Vineyard Oneida NY 13421

COMBES, WILLARD WETMORE
CARTOONIST
b Cleveland, Ohio, Dec 23, 01. Study: Cleveland Inst Art, grad, 24; Gottwalk Traveling scholar, Europe, 24; Slade Sch, Univ London, Paris & Madrid, 24-25; Belgium & Holland. Work: Libr Cong; Cleveland Mus Art. Comn: Murals for churches & stained glass art. Teaching: Head dept art, Cleveland Inst Art, 26-44; instr, Archit Sch, Western Reserve Univ, 26-36. Pos: Ed cartoonist, Cleveland Press, 34-63. Awards: Pulitzer Prize, 38; Award for Best Art, Cleveland Newspaper Guild, 55; Cleveland Builders Award Best Art Mosaic Mural, Lutheran High Sch. Mem: Cleveland Soc Artists. Mailing Add: 1266 Oakridge Dr Cleveland OH 44121

COMES, MARCELLA
PAINTER, PHOTOGRAPHER
b Pittsburgh, Pa. Study: Carnegie Sch Fine Arts, Pittsburgh; Accademia Della Belle Arte, Florence, Italy; also with A Kostellow & Knath. Work: Bryn Mawr Col; US Mil Acad, West Point; Cent Intel Agency; Naval Mus, Washington, DC; Pittsburgh Pub Schs. Comn: Mural, Homewood Libr, Pittsburgh, Pa; mural, Stone Ridge Sch, Washington, DC. Exhib: Corcoran Biennial, Washington, DC; 18 Pittsburgh Artists, Carnegie Inst, Pittsburgh, Pa; Mus de la Marine, Paris, France; one-woman show, Brooks Mus, Memphis, Tenn; Tuscan Art, Florence, Italy. Collections Arranged: Travel tour, Corcoran Mus, Washington Artists, 10 Southeastern Mus, 72. Teaching: Instr painting, Catholic Univ, Figurative, Chmn, Corcoran Benefit Art Tour, 60; juror, Nat Miniature Show, 67; Nat Ed, Artists Equity Newsletter, 75- Awards: Soc Washington Artists, Katherine Kuh, 61; Soc Washington Artists, NCFA, dir, Norfolk Mus, 62; Benedictine Art Award, Am Fedn Arts, 68. Bibliog: Ami Stewart (auth), Georgetown Artist, The Georgetowner, 57; Donnie Radcliff (auth), art in Evening Star, 70; Jourdan Houston (auth), Not a portrait painter, Carroll Co Independent, 75. Mem: Artists Equity (nat vpres, 69-74); Women's Comt, Corcoran Gallery; Arts Coun, Washington, DC, Pub Libr; Artists Guild Prof Artists (pres, 56-58). Style & Technique: Realist, semi abstract, figurative, paint in oil, photography. Inst Publ: Auth, rev of Carnegie Int, Rev of Pittsburgh Artists, Carnegie Mag; auth, front page in color, portrait of Robert Frost, Wash Post, 63; auth, DC harbors underground painters, Art Scene Mag, 71; rev, Assoc Coun Arts Convention in Washington, AEA Newsletter. Mailing Add: 3106 P St NW Washington DC 20007

COMINI, ALESSANDRA
ART HISTORIAN, LECTURER
b Winona, Minn, Nov 24, 36. Study: Barnard Col, with Julius Held, BA, 56; Univ Calif, Berkeley, with Herschel Chipp, MA, 62; Columbia Univ, PhD, 69. Teaching: Asst prof art hist, Columbia Univ, 69-74; vis prof art hist, Yale Univ, 73; prof art hist & humanities, Southern Methodist Univ, 74- Awards: Am Asn Univ Women Traveling Fel, Vienna, 67-68; Alfred Hodder Fel, Princeton Univ, 72-73. Mem: Am Soc Composers, Auth & Publ. Res: Jugendstil and expressionism; changing image of Beethoven; foreign artists in Rome 1750/1914; Gothic revival and German romanticism. Publ: Contribr, Virgins, vampires & voyeurs in Imperial Vienna, In: Woman as Sex Object, 73; auth, Schiele in prison, NY Graphic Soc, 74; auth, Egon Schiele's Portraits, Univ Calif, 74; auth, Gustav Klimt, Braziller, 75. Mailing Add: 2900 McFarlin Dallas TX 75205

COMITO, NICHOLAS U
PAINTER, ILLUSTRATOR
b Brooklyn, NY, Sept 30, 06. Study: NY Univ, BS; Nat Acad Design, New York. Work: Sch Com, NY Univ; Merck & Co, New York. Comn: Youngstown with Pen & Pencil, Kelly Printing, New York, 34; Maroon, Centennial Yearbk, Fordham Univ, New York, 41; History of Aviation Medicine, Res Bldg, Randolph Field, Tex, 45; Different Cities, Astorian Manor, NY, 58; Stations of the Cross, Church of the Most Holy Rosary, Roosevelt, NY, 64. Exhib: Art in the United States, Carnegie Inst, Pittsburgh, Pa, 43-45; one-man shows, Witte Mus, San Antonio, Tex, 44, Noonan-Kocian Galleries, St Louis, Mo 46 & Southern Vt Art Ctr, Manchester, 58. Teaching: Instr drawing & painting, Comito Art Sch, Bky Brooklyn, NY, 48-60. Awards: Julian Hallgarten Prize, Nat Acad Design, New York, 40; John Milton Jr Award, Painters & Sculptors Soc NJ, 45; First Prize (oil painting), Irvington Art & Mus Asn, NJ, 46. Mem: Audubon Soc, New York; Southern Vt Artists, Manchester; Mid-Vt-Chaffee Art Gallery, Rutland. Style & Technique: Detailed and meticulous style, romantic realism. Media: Oil, Watercolor. Mailing Add: 1747 Burnett St Brooklyn NY 11229

CONANT, HOWARD SOMERS
PAINTER, ART EDITOR
b Beloit, Wis, May 5, 21. Study: Art Students League, with Kunyiyoshi; Univ Wis, BS & MS; Univ Buffalo, EdD. Work: Andrew Dickson White Gallery, Cornell Univ Ithaca, NY; Trenton State Col, NJ; Drury Col, Springfield, Mo; Tex Technol Col, Lubbock; Milton Col, Wis. Comn: Mural painting, Molloy Col, Rockville Center, NY, 70; environmental mural, NY State Art Teachers Asn, Sperry High Sch, Henrietta, NY, 71; Art for Schools: a study of children's responses to original works of art, comn by Ctr for Appl Res in Educ. Exhib: One-man shows, Molloy Col, 70, Cape May Art League, NJ, 71, Philadelphia Art Alliance, 72, Caldwell Col, 74 & Walker Street Gallery, 75. Teaching: Prof art, State Univ NY Buffalo, 47-55; prof & chmn dept, Dept Art & Art Educ, NY Univ, 55-76; head, Dept Art, Univ Ariz, Tucson, 76- Pos: Art ed, Intellect Mag, 75- Awards: Distinguished Serv to Art Educ, Nat Gallery Art, 66; Distinguished Alumnus, Univ Wis-Milwaukee, 68. Mem: Int Soc Educ through Art; Inst Study Art in Educ; Nat Art Educ Asn; NY State Art Teachers Asn. Media: Acrylic, Ink. Publ: Co-auth, Art in Education, 63; ed, Masterpieces of the Arts, 63; auth, Art Education, 64; auth, Seminar on Elementary and Secondary School Education in the Visual Arts, 65; ed, Lincoln Library of the Arts, 73; plus others. Dealer: Cele Peterson Gallery Tucson AZ; Walker Street Gallery 46 Walker St New York NY 10013. Mailing Add: Dept of Art Univ of Ariz Tucson AZ 85721

CONAWAY, GERALD
SCULPTOR, PAINTER
b Manson, Wash, Feb 15, 33. Study: Everett Jr Col, Wash, ABA; Univ Wash, Seattle, BA(art educ) & MFA(sculpture) with George Tsutakawa & Everett Dupen. Work: Anchorage Fine Arts Mus, Alaska; Alaska Methodist Univ, Anchorage. Comn: William H Seward (marble monument), Mutual Ins Co, New York & Anchorage Centennial, Anchorage, 67; Goldstream (iron & hydrostone sculpture), Elmendorf Officers Club, Anchorage; concrete wall sculptures, Raymond Lawson, AIA, 73. Exhib: All Alaska, Anchorage, 65-70; Western Regional Craft Show, Portland, 67; Sculpture Northwest, Seattle, 68. Teaching: Teacher art, Northshore Sch Dist, Wash, 57-65; assoc prof art, Alaska Methodist Univ, 65- Pos: Sign writer-artist, Univ Wash, 54-65; graphic artist, Boeing Airplane Co, 57. Awards: All Alaska (sculpture), 65-70; jewelry, Western Regional Craft Show, 67. Mem: Nat Art Educ Asn; Alaska Artists Guild. Style & Technique: Anthropomorphic to geometric in form. Media: Wood, Stone; Steel, Plastics. Dealer: Francine Seders Gallery 6701 Greenwood Ave N Seattle WA 98103. Mailing Add: 2457 Cottonwood Anchorage AK 99504

CONAWAY, JAMES D
PAINTER, EDUCATOR
b Granite City, Ill, Oct 9, 32. Study: Southern Ill Univ, Carbondale, Ill, BA; Univ Iowa, Iowa City, MA, MFA. Work: Am Embassy Collection; Waterloo Munic Art Gallery, Iowa; Davenport Munic Art Gallery, Iowa; Gen Mills, Minneapolis, Minn; 3M Company, St Paul, Minn. Exhib: Walker Biennial, Walker Art Ctr, Minneapolis, 67; Art for the Embassies, Smithsonian Inst, Washington, DC, 67; Midwestern Ann Competition, Joslyn Art Mus, Omaha, 73, Mid Year Biennial, Butler Inst Am Art, Youngstown, Ohio, 74; Manisphere, Winnepeg Art Ctr, 74; Marietta Int Painting Exhib, Ohio, 76; Palace of Fine Arts, Santiago, Chile. Teaching: Asst prof, Univ Wis, Stevens Point; prof painting & drawing, Anoka Ramsey Col, Minneapolis, currently; prof painting, Hamline Univ, St Paul, currently. Awards: Purchase Award, Davenport Munic Art Gallery, 63, Waterloo Munic Art Galleries, 65; Donors Prize, Walker Art Ctr Biennial, 66. Mem: Mid-Am Col Art Asn (treas, 77-78); Artist Equity. Style & Technique: Mid-western landscapes with the juxtaposition of flat forms & deep space. Media: Oil. Dealer: C G Rein Galleries 7010 France Ave Minneapolis MN 55435; Gilman Gallery 103 E Oak Chicago IL 60611. Mailing Add: 2758 Benjamin St Minneapolis MN 55418

CONDESO, ORLANDO
PRINTMAKER
b Lima, Peru, Dec 31, 47. Study: Visual Arts, Lima; Pratt Graphics Ctr, New York. Work: Nat Mus Hist, Repub of China; Harlem Art Collection, New York; Orgn of Am States, Washington, DC; Braniff Int, Lima; Cult Peruvian NAm Inst, Lima. Exhib: 4th Biennial of Am Prints, Santiago, Chile, 70; 2nd Biennial of Latin Am Prints, San Juan, PR, 72; 2nd Int Print Exhib, Mus Mod Art, Sao Paulo, Brazil, 72; 18th Nat Print Exhib, Brooklyn Mus, NY, 72; Young Artists 1973, Int Play Group Inc, New York, 73; Calif Palace of the Legion of Honor, San Francisco, 73; Nat Mus Hist, Repub of China, 73; 2nd Miami Graphics Biennial, Fla, 75. Awards: First Prize, 5th Nat Print Competition, USA Embassy, Lima, 70; Award, 5th Ann Exhib, Pratt Graphics Ctr, 72; Purchase Award, 2nd Miami Graphics Biennial, 75. Style & Technique: Hard-edge, flat colors; silkscreens; abstract composition of wide lines. Media: Acrylic; Silkscreen. Dealer: Scarborough Graphics Ltd PO Box 245 Scarborough NY 10510. Mailing Add: 119 W 25th St 11 floor New York NY 10001

CONDIT, LOUISE
ART ADMINISTRATOR
b Baltimore, Md, May 7, 14. Study: Vassar Col, AB, 35; Teachers Col, Columbia Univ, MA, 41. Pos: Supvr educ, Brooklyn Children's Mus, 35-42; in charge of jr mus, Metrop Mus Art, 43-74, dep vdir educ affairs, 74-77, dep dir educ affairs, 78-; pres, Am Asn Youth Mus, 72-74; mem exec comt, NY Soc, Archaeol Inst Am, 73-77; mem bd, Inst for Study Art in Educ, 74-77. Awards: Carnegie Corp Grant for Mus Educ, 39; Metrop Mus Art Travel Grants, 61, 70 & 74. Mem: Am Asn Mus (counr, 57-63, vpres, 60-63); Int Coun Mus; Mus Coun New York (secy-treas, 60-64); Metrop Mus Employees Asn (pres, 68-70, vchmn, 77-78); New York Film Coun (secy-treas, 47-50). Publ: Auth, Paul Revere, A Metropolitan Museum Picture Book, 44; contribr, Museums & education, In: UNESCO Museums & Monuments Series, 72; contribr to prof jour. Mailing Add: Metrop Mus of Art Fifth Ave at 82nd St New York NY 10028

CONDON, LAWRENCE JAMES
PAINTER, INSTRUCTOR
b Brooklyn, NY, Dec 9, 25. Study: Self-taught. Work: Grand Galleria Am Art, Cascade Gallery, Seattle, Wash; CAGUS Gallery Incarcerated Art, Florence, SC; NY State Senate Chambers, Albany; House of Paull Mus, Florence; Columbia Mus Art, SC. Comn: Murals & paintings, State Dept Corrections Hq, Columbia, 75. Exhib: 1st & 2nd Ann Grand Galleria Competition, Seattle, Wash, 72 & 73; Spring 72 & 73, Florence, SC, 74; NAPCA, Nat Acad Galleries, New York, 73; Nat Western Art Show, San Antonio, Tex, 73-75; Arena 74, Binghamton, NY, 74. Teaching: Instr art, Cent Correctional Inst, SC Dept Corrections, 74- Awards: First Grand Prize, Grand Galleria, Seattle, 72; Best of Show & Prix de Guild, CAGUS Spring 73, Florence; First Purchase Award, Arena, 74, Binghamton, 74. Bibliog: S Wershba (auth), CBS-TV morning news presentation, 1/74; B Toombs (auth), NBC-TV Sat eve news presentation, 3/74; Cosmo tells all, Cosmopolitan Mag, 7/74. Style & Technique: Realistic & impressionistic. Media: Oil, All Media. Publ: Contribr, Am Artist, 7/74; illusr, cover, Resolution, 9/74. Dealer: Lola E Russo 243 Ruhamah Ave Syracuse NY 13205. Mailing Add: 905 Delverton Rd Columbia SC 29203

CONE, GERRIT CRAIG
ART ADMINISTRATOR
b Denver, Colo, May 23, 47. Study: Univ NMex, 65-68; Long Beach City Col, AA, 69; Calif State Univ, Long Beach, BA, 72. Pos: Gallery coordr, Tucson Art Ctr, 72-73; actg dir, Tucson Mus Art, 73-74, cur collections & asst dir, 74- Mem: Am Asn Mus; Western Regional Conf Am Asn Mus (Ariz state rep, 74-76); Western Asn Art Mus (first vpres); Arch Am Art; Art Libr Soc Ariz (chmn, 75-76); Art Libr Soc Ariz (chmn, 75-76). Publ: Ed, Western Regional Conf Am Asn Mus Newslett, 75-77. Mailing Add: 235 W Alameda Tucson AZ 85701

CONE-SKELTON, ANNETTE
PAINTER, ART EDITOR
b LaGrange, Ga, Oct 20, 42. Study: LaGrange Col, Ga; Atlanta Col of Art, Ford Found scholar, BFA. Work: High Mus of Art, Atlanta, Ga; Hunter Mus of Art, Chattanooga, Tenn; Am Tel & Tel Collection, New York & Chicago; Omni Int Hotel, Miami, Fla; Kenneth of New York & Atlanta. Exhib: Emory Univ, Atlanta, Ga, 67; Southeastern Ann Exhib, High Mus of Art, Atlanta, 67 & 68; Hunter Mus of Art Ann, Chattanooga, 67, 70 & 76; Spec Fac Exhib, Atlanta Col of Art, 68; Ga Artists Show, High Mus of Art, Atlanta, 71, 72 & 74; 8th Grand Prix de Peinture, de la cote d'Azur, Paris, France, 72; 13th Atlanta Artists, Penha Gallery, Ft Lauderdale, Fla, 73; one-person shows, Image S Gallery, 74 & 75 & Heath Gallery, 77 & 78, Atlanta; Galleries Int, Winter Park, Fla, 75; 13 Women Painters, Festival of Women in the Arts, Ga State Univ, Atlanta, 75; 35 Artists in the SE, High Mus of Art, Atlanta, 76, Birmingham Mus, Ala, 77, Greenville Co Mus, SC, 77, Hunter Mus, Chattanooga, Tenn, 78 & Southeastern Ctr for Contemp Art, Winston-Salem, NC, 78. Teaching: Instr drawing & painting, Atlanta Col of Art Spec Fac, 67-71; teacher art, First Montessori Sch of Atlanta, 74- Pos: Art consult, Arnold Gallery, Atlanta, 77-; managing ed, Contemp Art/SE, Atlanta, 77- Awards: Merit Award, Southeastern Ann, High Mus of Art, Atlanta, 67; Merit Award, Ga Inst of Technol, Atlanta, 68; Purchase Award, 15th Hunter Ann, Hunter Mus, Chattanooga, Tenn, 76. Bibliog: L'Art a l'Etranger, La Revue Mod, 71. Style & Technique: Subtle, all-over imagery; multiple rows of lines applied by paint & brush, sprayers and pencils. Media: Acrylic on canvas and paper; graphite and colored pencils on canvas and paper. Dealer: Heath Gallery 34 Lombardy Way Atlanta GA 30309. Mailing Add: 2650 Shady Valley Dr NE Atlanta GA 30324

CONFORTE, RENEE
ART DEALER
b Belgrade, Yugoslavia, US citizen. Study: Mt Holyoke Col, BA(magna cum laude); Univ Paris I, Sorbonne; Ecole du Louvre, Paris. Pos: Admin asst, Marlborough Gallery, New York, 68-72; vpres, David McKee Gallery, New York, 74- Specialty: Contemporary American art. Mailing Add: 140 E 63rd St New York NY 10021

CONGDON, WILLIAM (GROSVENOR)
PAINTER
b Providence, RI, Apr 15, 12. Study: Provincetown Sch Art, with Henry Hensche; Demetrious Sch Sculpture, Boston & Folly Cove, Mass. Work: Metrop Mus Art, Whitney Mus Am Art & Mus Mod Art, New York; Cleveland Mus, Ohio; Duncan Phillips Gallery, Washington, DC. Comn: Bronze head, Stephen O Metcalf, RI Sch Design, Providence Mus, 39. Exhib: Landmarks, American Painting—50 years, Wildenstein Gallery, New York, 50; Painters under 35, Metrop Mus Art, 50; Biennale Venezia, 52 & 58; Carnegie Inst Int, Pittsburgh, Pa, 52 & 58; New Decade, Whitney Mus Am Art, 55. Awards: Temple Gold Medal, Pa Acad Fine Arts, 51; Purchase Prize, Univ Ill, 52; Clark Award, Corcoran Gallery Art, 53. Bibliog: Dorothy Seiberling & George Hunt (auth), William Congdon, Life Mag, 4/30/51; Peggy Guggenheim (auth), Pittore di Venezia, Biennale Venezia, 2/53; Emily Genauer (auth), Congdon converted, New York Herald Tribune, 8/21/68. Media: Oil. Publ: Auth, In My Disc of Gold, Reynal, 62; auth, An Artist, His Art & the Christian Community, 72 & Esistenza-Viaggio di Pittore Americano, 75, Jaca Bk, Italy. Dealer: Betty Parsons Gallery 24 W 57th St New York NY 10019. Mailing Add: Vicolo Bovi 1 Assisi Italy

CONGER, CLEMENT E
CURATOR
b Rockingham, Va, Oct 15, 12. Pos: Cur diplomatic reception rooms, US State Dept, 61-, cur, The White House, 70- Awards: Collector of the Yr, Va Mus Fine Arts, Richmond, 72; Antique Mo Mag Award, 76; Hon DHumL, Col William & Mary, Williamsburg, Va, 77. Mem: Nat Trust for Hist Preserv. Mailing Add: 320 Mansion Dr Alexandria VA 22302

CONLEY, ZEB BRISTOL, JR
COLLECTOR, ART DEALER
b Andrews, NC, Feb 12, 36. Study: Mars Hill Col, 55-57; Col William & Mary, 57-61; NMex Highlands Univ, 63. Pos: Dir, Jamison Galleries, Santa Fe, 73-, bd mem, 74- Specialty: Traditional Southwestern art, specializing in Taos and Santa Fe masters. Mailing Add: PO Box 2534 Santa Fe NM 87501

CONLON, JAMES EDWARD
SCULPTOR, ART HISTORIAN
b Cincinnati, Ohio, Dec 9, 35. Study: Ohio State Univ, BSc(art educ), 59, MA(fine arts), 62. Exhib: Southern Asn Sculptors Traveling Exhib, Smithsonian Inst; 49th Ann Exhib, Shreveport Art Guild; Competition 75, Mobile, Ala, 75. Teaching: Instr, Ind Univ, Bloomington, 62-65; from asst prof to assoc prof, Univ S Ala, Mobile, 65-73, prof, 74- Awards: Award to Establish the Afro-American Art Slide Depository, Samuel H Kress Found, 69-71, Award to Develop the Ethnic American Art Slide Library, 72-75; Award to Produce a Research Index of Afro-American Art, Am Revolution Bicentennial Comn, 73. Mem: Southern Asn Sculptors; Southeastern Col Art Asn (vpres, 74-75). Style & Technique: Figurative sculptor working subtractively at life size scale. Media: Woods of Various Kinds, Limestone. Res: An investigation of stylistic development in Afro-American, Mexican American and Native American art from 1800 to the present. Publ: Co-auth, An Afro-American slide project, Col Art Asn J, winter 70; co-auth, A Preliminary Research Index to Afro-American Art. Mailing Add: 4359 The Cedars Mobile AL 36608

CONN, DAVID EDWARD
PRINTMAKER
b Jersey City, NJ, Apr 10, 41. Study: Newark Sch of Fine Arts, NJ; Md Inst Col of Art, Baltimore, BFA; Univ Okla, Norman, MFA with Peter Milton. Work: Ark Art Ctr, Little Rock; Ft Worth Art Mus, Tex; Richard DeMarco Gallery Ltd, Edinburgh, Scotland; Univ Okla Mus of Art, Norman. Exhib: Md Regional & Md Coun on the Arts, Baltimore Mus of Art, 67; Governor's Coun on the Arts in Md (traveling exhib), 67-68; 5th & 6th Monroe Ann, Masur Mus of Art, Monroe, La, 68-69; 6th Dulin Nat Print & Drawing Exhib, Dulin Gallery of Art, Knoxville, Tenn, 70; Artist's Biennial, New Orleans Mus of Art, La, 75; 20th Exhib of Southwestern Prints & Drawings, Dallas Mus of Art, 75; 45th Ann Exhib, Springfield Art Mus, Mo, 75; Works on Paper by Southern US Artists, US Info Agency Circulating Exhib of Cent & SAm, 75-77; Footprint, NW Int Small Format Print Exhib, Davidson Galleries, Seattle, Wash, 76; 5th Ann Nat Print, Drawing & Photog Exhib, Second St Gallery, Charlottesville, Va, 77; Kans 3rd Nat Small Painting, Drawing & Print Exhib, 78. Collections Arranged: Images of the Am Revolution, Tex Christian Univ Gallery, 75. Teaching: Asst prof art-printmaking, Tex Christian Univ, 69- Awards: Cash Award, 5th & 6th Monroe Ann, Masur Mus, 68-69; Cash Award, 29/Okla Artist Ann, Philbrook Art Ctr, Tulsa, 69; Purchase Award, Ark Print, Drawing & Crafts, Ark Art Ctr, 71. Bibliog: American Printmakers 74—Graphics Group, Arcadia, Calif, 74. Style & Technique: Intaglio. Media: Intaglio and relief and crayon drawings. Dealer: Gallery In the Square 1510 W Tenth St Ft Worth TX. Mailing Add: 2549 Walsh Ct Ft Worth TX 76109

CONNER, BRUCE
PAINTER, FILM MAKER
b McPherson, Kans, Nov 18, 33. Study: Wichita Univ, with David Bernard; Univ Nebr, BFA, with Rudy Pozzatti; Brooklyn Mus Art Sch, with Reuben Tam; Univ Colo. Work: Mus Mod Art, New York; Art Inst Chicago; Los Angeles Co Art Mus; San Francisco Mus Art; Whitney Mus Am Art, New York. Comn: Poster, New York Film Festival, Am Fedn Arts, 65; film portrait, Audrey Sabol, Pa, 68. Exhib: The Art of Assemblage, Mus Mod Art, New York, 60; Whitney Biannual, Whitney Mus Am Art; Retrospective, Inst Contemp Art, Univ Pa, 67 & de Young Mem Mus, San Francisco, 74; American Sculpture of the Sixties, Los Angeles Co Art Mus, 67; Edible Art Show, San Francisco Mus Art, 68; Belly-Button Art of the Seventies, Newport Harbor Art Gallery, 72; Tyler Mus Art, Tex, 74; Smith-Anderson Gallery, Palo Alto, Calif, 74; de Young Mem Mus, 75; plus others. Teaching: Instr film making, Calif Col Arts & Crafts, 65-66; undergrad sem, Wasted Time, San Francisco Art Inst, 66-67. Pos: Pres & founder, Rat Bastard Protective Asn, San Francisco, 58-61; dir, bd dirs, Canyon Cinema Corp, San Francisco, 69-70 & 71-72. Awards: Copley Found Award, 65; Gold Medal Award, Milan Biennale Nuovo Techniques in Arts, 67; Guggenheim Fel, 76. Bibliog: Carl Belz (auth), 3 films by Bruce Conner, Film Cult Mag, spring 67. Mem: Nat Art Workers Community. Publ: Co-auth, Book: Bruce Conner/Mike McClure, Averhahn Press, 67; auth, The Dennis Hopper One-Man Show, Crown Point Press, Vols I-III, 71-73. Dealer: Quay Gallery 2 Jerome Alley San Francisco CA 94124. Mailing Add: 45 Sussex St San Francisco CA 94131

CONNERY, RUTH M
PAINTER
b New York, NY. Study: Mills Col, AA; Art Students League, with William von Schlegell & Hans Hofmann. Work: First Nat Bank, Rye, NY; Henry Bruckner Jr High Sch, Bronx, NY. Comn: Portraits, comn by Mr & Mrs Peter Sellon, Rye, Mrs & Mrs Victor Wouk, New York, Mr & Mrs Anthony Rizzo, Jupiter Island, Fla & Mr & Mrs H Canale, Larchmont, NY. Exhib: Nat Asn Women Artists, Nat Acad Design, New York, 49-69; Jersey City Mus, 55; one-person shows, Westchester Co, 60-69 & Forley & Wren Gallery, New York, 68; Mus of Southern France, 67; Leger Bldg, Park Ave, New York, 67-68; Norton Gallery, West Palm Beach, Fla, 70-71; Scranton Mem Libr, Madison, Conn, 78. Teaching: Instr creative painting, Westchester Arts Workshop & Mamaroneck Artists Guild, 60-69; instr creative painting, Palm Beach Adult Educ Inst, 70-72; instr creative painting, Recreation Comn, Madison, 77-78. Awards: Pres Prize, New Rochelle Art Asn, 65; Group Show Award, Westchester Arts Workshop, 67; One-Man Show Award, Contemporaries, Inc, New York. Mem: Nat Asn Women Artists (secy, 65); Artists Guild Norton Gallery, Palm Beach. Media: Oil, Acrylic. Mailing Add: 58 Beach Ave Madison CT 06443

CONNETT, DEE M
EDUCATOR, PAINTER
b Mulvane, Kans, May 25, 35. Study: Kans State Teachers Col, BS(art educ), 53; Wichita State Univ, MA, 64; Am Univ, Mex, 64; art sem, Florence, Italy, 70; also with Mary Kretsinger & Dorothy MacCray. Work: Wichita Art Mus, Kans; Halstead Art Asn, Kans; Nebr Wesleyan Univ, Lincoln; Centre House, Swannanoa, NC; MacCray Gallery, Western NMex State Univ, Silver City. Comn: Cement sculpture, Sch Dist 191, Wichita, 68; paintings commissioned by Harry Litwin, Litwin Enterprises, Wichita, 70. Exhib: 18th Ann Mo Valley Exhib, Mulvane Gallery, Topeka, Kans, 65; Nebr Wesleyan Univ Show, 66; Drawing: Mid-USA, Spiva Art Ctr, Joplin, Mo, 70; Graphics '71, Nat Print & Drawing Show, MacCray Gallery, 71; Religion in Art in America, Contemp Gallery, Albuquerque, NMex, 73; Kansas Artist/Craftsman Designer Show, Lawrence, 73; Kans Women Artists, Wichita Art Mus, 74; Bicentennial Portfolio, Wichita Art Mus, 76; 27th May Competition, Spiva Art Ctr, Joplin, Mo, 77; 55th Ann Exhib, Meadows Mus, Shreveport, La. Teaching: Instr art, Wichita Pub Schs, 57-64; Asst prof Wichita Art Mus, 69-70; chmn dept art, Friends Univ, Wichita, 64- Pos: Mem, Fine Arts Coun Comt, Wichita, 66-70; bd mem, Wichita Art Mus, 66-; state & local pres, Nat League Am Pen Women, Wichita, 70-72; mem, Century II Sculpture Planning Comt, Wichita, 70-72. Awards: Outstanding Teacher of Year Award, Friends Univ, 70; Exhibitor's Award, Kans Artist/Craftsman Designer Show, Lawrence, 73; First Graphic Award, Arkansas City, Kans, 76. Bibliog: Elma Byrne (auth), Wichita Spotlight, Wichita Eagle-Beacon, 8/67; article in, Apartment Living Mag, 11/71. Mem: Artist Guild Wichita; Kappa Pi (sponsor, 69); Kans Artist-Craftsmen Asn. Style & Technique: Experimental search of the acrylic media and printmaking ranging from photo-reality to abstracted subject matter. Dealer: Sales & Rental Gallery, Wichita Art Mus Wichita KS 67203; Sign of Acorn 4816 E Douglas Wichita KS 67208. Mailing Add: 1635 N Sheridan Wichita KS 67203

CONNOLLY, JEROME PATRICK
PAINTER, MURALIST
b Minneapolis, Minn, Jan 14, 31. Study: Univ Minn, BS(art educ); also with Francis Lee Jaques. Work: Diorama backgrounds & murals in more than 20 mus, incl Carnegie Mus, Pittsburgh, James Ford Bell Mus, Minneapolis, Vanderbilt Mus, Long Island, George C Page Mus, Los Angeles, William Penn Mem Mus, Harrisburg, Pa, Ill State Mus, Springfield, The Sci Ctr, St Paul, Minn, Mid-Fairfield Co Youth Mus, Westport, Conn & Mus Hist & Technol & Mus of Natural Hist, Smithsonian Inst, Washington, DC. Exhib: Soc Animal Artists Ann, New York, 65-; Hudson Valley Art Asn, White Plains, 69-; Sportsman's Gallery of Art & Bks, New York; Crossroads of Sport, New York; Abercrombie & Fitch, New York & San Francisco; Petersen Gallery, Los Angeles; one-man show, Abercrombie & Fitch, New York, 72. Pos: Staff artist, Ill State Mus, Springfield, 58-60; staff artist, Natural Sci Youth Found, Westport, Conn, 60-65; free lance artist, 65- Mem: Soc Animal Artists. Media: Oil. Publ: Illusr, The Story of Monarch X, 66; illusr, The Cat Family, 68; illusr, Adelbert the Penguin, 69; illusr, The Deer Family, 69; illusr, Aise-ce-bon: a Raccoon, 71; illusr, 15 children's bks & contribr, Audubon Mag, Nat Wildlife (& their calendars) & Hartford Life Ins Co calendar. Mailing Add: Box 158 Tetonia ID 83452

CONNOR, LINDA STEVENS
PHOTOGRAPHER, INSTRUCTOR
b New York, NY, Nov 18, 44. Study: RI Sch of Design, BFA, with Harry Calahan; Inst of Design, Ill Inst of Technol, MS, with Aaron Siskind. Work: Boston Mus of Fine Arts, Mass; Art Inst of Chicago; Int Mus of Photography, George Eastman House, Rochester, NY; William Hayes Fogg Art Mus, Harvard Univ, Cambridge, Mass; Mus of Mod Art, New York. Exhib: Pvt Realities, Boston Mus of Fine Arts, 74; 14 Am Photogr, Baltimore Mus, Md &

Long Beach Mus, Calif, 74-75; 8x10, Ten Am Photogr, Dallas Mus of Fine Arts, Tex, 76; one-person shows, Visual Studies Gallery, Rochester, NY, 76, Ctr for Photographic Studies, Louisville, Ky, 76 & de Young Mem Mus, San Francisco, 77; Center, Univ Ariz, Tucson, 77; Eye of the West, Hayden Gallery, Mass Inst Technol, Cambridge, 77. Teaching: Instr photog, San Francisco Art Inst, 69-, co-chmn, 73-75; instr photog, San Francisco State Univ, 72 & Calif Col of Arts & Crafts, Oakland, 73. Awards: Union of Independent Col of Art fac fel, 73; Nat Endowment for the Arts individual grant, 76. Mem: Soc for Photographic Educ. Style & Technique: View camera, contact printing and sun printing. Media: Photography. Publ: Contribr, Vision and Expression, George Eastman House, 69; contribr (catalogue), Private Realities, Boston Mus of Fine Arts, 74; contribr (catalogue), 14 American Photographers, Baltimore Mus, 74; contribr, The Great West, Univ Colo, Boulder, 77; contribr, Darkroom, Lustrum, 77. Dealer: Light Gallery 724 Fifth Ave New York NY 10019. Mailing Add: 1007 Haight St San Francisco CA 94117

CONOVER, CLAUDE
SCULPTOR, CERAMIST
b Pittsburgh, Pa, Dec 15, 07. Study: Cleveland Inst Art, grad cert. Work: Cleveland Mus Art, Ohio; Everson Mus Art, Syracuse, NY; Utah Mus Fine Arts, Salt Lake City; Columbus Gallery Fine Art, Ohio; Minn Mus Art, St Paul; plus others. Exhib: Ann Exhib Works by Artists & Craftsmen of the Western Reserve, Cleveland Mus Art, 14 yrs; Ceramic Nat, Everson Mus Art, four biennials; Ann Ohio Ceramic & Sculpture Show, Butler Inst Am Art, Youngstown, Ohio, 12 shows; Beaux Arts Designer/Craftsmen Biennial Exhibs, Columbus Gallery Fine Arts, Ohio, four shows; Objects USA, traveling exhib to some 35 mus in US & Europe; The Plastic Earth, John Kohler Art Ctr; plus numerous others. Pos: Commercial designer, several art studios in Cleveland, Ohio, 30-57; sculptor, 30-57; sculptor/ceramist, pvt studio, 57- Awards: Drakenfeld Award, 23rd Ceramic Nat, Everson Mus Art, 64; Governor's Award, Exhib 68, Columbus Gallery Fine Arts, 68; Spec Jury Awards, Ann Shows, Cleveland Mus Art. Bibliog: Roger Bonham (auth), Claude Conover, Ceramics Monthly, 5/66. Mem: Am Crafts Coun. Style & Technique: Hand-built pottery forms in high fired ceramics. Mailing Add: 1860 Oakmount Rd Cleveland OH 44121

CONOVER, ROBERT FREMONT
PRINTMAKER, PAINTER
b Trenton, NJ, July 3, 20. Study: Philadelphia Mus Sch Art; Art Students League; Brooklyn Mus Sch. Work: Smithsonian Inst, Washington, DC; Brooklyn Mus; Whitney Mus Am Art, New York; New York Pub Libr; Philadelphia Mus. Comn: Print ed, 200 woodcuts, 57 & 75 woodcuts, 61, Int Graphic Art Soc; print ed, 75 woodcuts, Hilton Hotels, 62; print ed, 30 woodcuts, Assoc Am Artists Galleries, 69; print ed, 60 relief prints, Ferdinand Roten Galleries, 71. Exhib: Painter of the 20th Century, Mus Mod Art, New York, 50; Whitney Mus Am Art Ann, 50-54; Carnegie Int, Pittsburgh, 54; Pa Acad Fine Arts Painting Ann, 54; one-man show, New Sch Social Res, New York, 68 & 74; Brooklyn Mus Print Biennial, 70. Teaching: Instr painting & graphics, New Sch Social Res, 51-; instr painting, Brooklyn Mus Sch, 60-; instr graphics, Newark Sch Fine & Indust Arts, 67- Awards: Purchase Prize, Brooklyn Mus, 54; Purchase Prize, Soc Am Graphic Artists, Assoc Am Artist Gallery, 67; Purchase Prize, Philadelphia Print Club. Bibliog: Article in Art in Am, 57; Seuphor (auth), Dictionary of Abstract Painting, 58; Jules Heller (auth), Printmaking Today, Holt, 72. Mem: Soc Am Graphic Artists (mem coun); Am Abstract Artists. Style & Technique: Geometric expressionist abstract; woodcut and cardboard relief. Media: Graphics, Oil. Dealer: Assoc Am Artists Gallery 663 Fifth Ave New York NY 10022. Mailing Add: 162 E 33rd St New York NY 10016

CONRAD, GEORGE
EDUCATOR, PRINTMAKER
b Newark, NJ, Feb 10, 16. Study: Newark Sch Fine & Indust Arts; NY Univ, BS; Columbia Univ, MA & EdD. Work: Butler Inst Am Art, Ohio; La Jolla Mus Art, Calif; Univ Ga; Columbus Pub Libr, Ohio; Univ Ore; plus others. Exhib: Artists from NJ, Newark Mus; Independent, New York; NJ Art in Cols, State Mus, NJ. Teaching: Prof art educ, Ill State Univ, 49-58; prof art hist, Glassboro State Col, 58- Pos: Ed, The Arts, 62-72; mem, NJ Arts Coun, 66-71. Mem: NJ Art Educ Asn (pres, 69); Eastern Arts Asn (coun, 69); Nat Art Educ Asn (state assembly, 69). Media: Oil, Multiprint Media. Publ: Auth, Process of art educ, Prentice-Hall, 64. Mailing Add: 163 N Mansfield Blvd Cherry Hill NJ 08034

CONRAD, JOHN W
EDUCATOR, CERAMIST
b Cresson, Pa, Aug 3, 35. Study: Ind Univ of Pa, BS; Carnegie-Mellon Univ, Pittsburgh, MFA(ceramics); Univ Pittsburgh, PhD. Work: Mesa Col, San Diego, Calif. Exhib: Tiffany Invitational, New York, 65; one-man show, Sculpture Gallery, San Deigo, Calif, 76; Small Sculptures: Nat Cypress Fine Arts Gallery, Cypress, Calif, 76; Ceramics Design 76, Sculpture Gallery, San Diego, 76; Soup Tureens—1976, Campbell Mus, Camden, NJ, 76. Teaching: Instr crafts, Penn Hills Sr High Sch, Pittsburgh, Pa, 59-64; prof ceramics & sculpture, Mesa Col, San Diego, 66- Mem: Col Art Asn; Nat Coun on Educ of Ceramic Arts; Southern Asn of Sculptors; Int Guild of Craft Journalists, Authors & Photogrs. Style & Technique: Ceramics & ceramic sculpture. Publ: Auth, Ceramic Formulas: The Complete Compendium, MacMillan, 73; auth, Contemporary Ceramic Techniques, Prentice-Hall, 77; auth, Ceramic Manual, Prentice-Hall, 80. Dealer: Sculpture Gallery 3030 Fifth Ave San Diego CA 92103. Mailing Add: 3675 Syracuse Ave San Diego CA 92122

CONRAD, NANCY R
PAINTER
b Houston, Tex, Jan 29, 40. Study: Houston Mus Fine Arts; Randolph Macon Woman's Col, BA; study with Henry Gadbois, Robert Fuller, Elliot Twery & Herb Mears. Work: Randolph Macon Collection Am Women Painters, Lynchburg, Va; El Paso Mus Fine Arts, Tex; Continental Oil Co Collection & Dresser Indust Collection, Houston; Aviation Am Bldg, Love Field, Dallas. Exhib: Pacific Artists Show, Tacoma Mus Fine Arts, Wash, 65; Delta Five State Exhib, Ark Art Ctr, 72; Sun Carnival Exhib, El Paso Mus Fine Arts, 73-75; Tex Painting & Sculpture, Dallas Mus Fine Arts; 52nd Ann Nat Exhib, Shreveport, La, 74. Awards: Foley Award, Foley's of Houston, 70; First Place Jurors Choice, Assistance League of Houston, 73; Purchase Award, El Paso Mus Art, 73. Mem: Art League Houston (vpres, 74-75); Tex Fine Arts Asn; Southwestern Watercolor Soc; Artists Equity Asn. Style & Technique: Precise abstract watercolors and oils dealing with clouds and atmospheric subjects. Media: Airbrush Watercolor; Oil or Acrylic on Canvas. Dealer: Source Galleries Folsom at Seventh San Francisco CA 94107. Mailing Add: c/o Ars Longa Galleries 3133 Buffalo Speedway Houston TX 77006

CONRAD, PAUL FRANCIS
CARTOONIST
b Cedar Rapids, Iowa, June 27, 24. Pos: Ed cartoonist, Denver Post, 50-64, Los Angeles Times, 64-; cartoonist, Los Angeles Times Syndicate; lectr, Cooke-Daniels Lectr Tours, Denver Art Mus, 64. Awards: Sigma Delta Chi Award, 63, 69 & 71; Pulitzer Prize Ed Cartooning, 64 & 71; Overseas Press Club Award, 69. Mailing Add: Times Mirror Sq Los Angeles CA 90053

CONSTABLE, ROSALIND
COLLECTOR, WRITER
b England. Pos: Researcher, Fortune Mag, 38-47; cult corresp, Time, Inc, 48-67; free lance writer; trustee, Mus NMex Found; guest cur, Mus Fine Arts, Santa Fe. Collection: Contemporary art. Publ: Contribr, articles in, Life Mag, New Yorker, Bk Wk, New York & others. Mailing Add: 609 Old Taos Hwy Santa Fe NM 87501

CONSTANT, GEORGE
PAINTER
b Greece, Apr 17, 92; US citizen. Study: Washington Univ, 12-14; Art Inst Chicago, 14-18; also with Charles Hawthorne & George Bellows. Work: Metrop Mus Art; Brooklyn Mus; Detroit Inst Art; Dayton Art Inst; San Francisco Mus Art; plus others. Exhib: New York World's Fairs, 39 & 64-65; 10 Years of American Prints, 47-56, Brooklyn Mus, 56; US Info Agency, 56-57 & 60-61; Art: USA, New York, 59; Humanists of the 60's, New Sch Social Res, 63 & 65; one-man shows, Parrish Art Mus, Southampton, NY, 71 & Guild Hall Mus, 76; plus others. Awards: Award, Parrish Mus, Southampton, Long Island, 50, 51 & 66; awards, 62 & 63 & Carolyn Tyson Award, 66, Guild Hall; Emily Lowe Award, Audubon Artists, 68; plus others. Mem: Fedn Mod Painters & Sculptors; Audubon Artists. Publ: Contribr, reproductions in The Art Museum in America, The Naked Truth and Personal Vision & Twentieth Century Highlights of American Painting; auth, George Constant, Arts, Inc, 61 & George Constant, Argonaut, Athens, Greece, 68. Mailing Add: 187 E Broadway New York NY 10002

CONSTANTINE, GREG JOHN
PAINTER, EDUCATOR
b Windsor, Ont, Can, Feb 14, 38. Study: Andrews Univ, Mich, BA; Mich State Univ with Angelo Ippolito, MFA; Univ Calif, Los Los Angeles. Work: Grand Rapids Art Mus, Mich. Exhib: Arkansas Nat, 69; Chicago & Vicinity, Chicago Art Inst, 71; Michigan Artists, Detroit, 71; Philbrook Art Ctr, Tulsa, Okla, 75; LaGrange Nat, Ga, 75. Teaching: Chmn dept painting & art hist & assoc prof art, Andrews Univ, 63- Awards: W & B Clusman Prize, Chicago Vicinity Show, Chicago Art Inst, 71. Bibliog: J Heriksen (auth), Artist, Insight Mag, 70; O Young (auth), Editor, Focus Mag, 75. Mem: Mus Contemp Art, Chicago; Col Art Asn; Mid-Am Art Asn. Style & Technique: Television image realism but rendered with electronic dot style. Media: Acrylic; Photography. Publ: Auth, article in Spectrum Mag, 75. Dealer: James Yu Gallery 393 West Broadway New York NY 10012. Mailing Add: Dept of Art Andrews Univ Berrien Springs MI 49104

CONSTANTINE, MILDRED
ART HISTORIAN
b Brooklyn, NY, June 28, 14. Study: NY Univ, MA, 38. Collections Arranged: The Olivetti Company, 52, The Package, 59, The Object Transformed, 66, Word & Image, 68 & Wallhangings, 69, Mus Mod Art, New York; plus others. Teaching: Instr hist graphic design, Parsons Sch of Design, 71- Pos: Asst keeper, Archiv of Hispanic Cult, Libr of Cong, Washington, DC, 40-42; assoc cur, Dept Archit & Design, Mus Mod Art, 49-71; consult art, archit & design, 71- Mem: Col Art Asn; Latin Am Studies Asn. Res: Latin American art from pre-Columbian to modern, modern art and architecture and design. Publ: Co-ed, Art Nouveau, Mus Mod Art, 59, 2nd ed, 75; co-auth, Beyond Craft: The Art Fabric, Van Nostrand, 73; co-auth, Soviet Revolutionary Film Posters, Johns Hopkins Univ Press, 74; auth, Tina Modotti, A Fragile Life, Paddington Press, 75. Mailing Add: 41 W 71st St New York NY 10023

CONSUEGRA, HUGO
PAINTER, ARCHITECT
b Havana, Cuba, Oct 26, 29. Study: San Alejandro Acad Arts, Havana, 43-46; Univ Havana, 49-55, grad archit; Univ Madrid, 69-70. Work: Nat Mus, Havana; Issac Delgado Mus, New Orleans; New York Univ; Nat Gallery, Sofia, Bulgaria; New York Pub Libr. Comn: Mural painting, Sch Nursery, Havana, 61; ceramic mural, Ministry Transp, 62. Exhib: 3rd, 6th & 7th Bienal Sao Paulo, Brazil, 55, 61 & 63; Mus Fine Arts, Houston, Tex, 55; Pittsburgh Int, Carnegie Inst, 58; Art Inst Chicago, 59; Comparisons, Mus Mod Art, Paris, France, 59; 2nd Bienal Mex, 60; 3rd Bienal Paris, France, 63; 18th Nat Print Exhib, Brooklyn Mus, NY, 72; Bienal del Grabado Latinoamericano, PR, 72 & 74; Six Cuban Painters Working in New York, Ctr for Inter-Am Relations, New York, 75; Contemp Printmakers of the Americas (traveling exhib), Orgn of the American States, 76-77. Teaching: Prof hist art, Sch Archit, Univ Havana, 60-65. Pos: Dir, Dept Plastic Arts, Ministry Pub Works, Havana, 59-63. Awards: Hon Mention, 2nd Bienal Mex, 60; Second Prize, 2nd Ann, Barranquilla, Colombia, 60; Cintas Found Fel, 70-71 & 73-74. Bibliog: Gaston Diehl (auth), La galerie des hommes celebres, L Mazenod, Paris, 63; Rene Huyghe (auth), L'art et l'homme, Larousse, Paris & Planeta, Barcelona, 66; Chase (auth), Contemporary Latin American art, Free Press, 70. Style & Technique: Abstract. Media: Oil, Etching. Mailing Add: 141-37 84th Dr Briarwood NY 11435

COOCHSIWUKIOMA, D H (DEL HONANIE)
PAINTER, SCULPTOR
b Winslow, Ariz, Jan 7, 46. Study: Hopi Reservation & Phoenix Indian Sch, 68; Black Hills State Col, Spearfish, Am Indian Develop, Inc; Inst Am Indian Arts, NMex, 70. Work: Heard Mus, Phoenix, Ariz; also in Washington, DC, Tulsa, Okla, Scottsdale, Ariz & Red Cloud, SDak. Comn: Santa Fe Agency, NMex, 69; Acad Bldg, Inst Am Indian Art, 69; Ariz State Univ, Tempe, 71; Phoenix, 68; Scottsdale, Ariz, 68; Washington, DC, 69; Tulsa, Okla, 70; Red Cloud, SDak, 70. Teaching: Instr arts & crafts, Phoenix Indian Sch, 70-72. Awards: Inductee, Phoenix Indian Sch Hall of Fame, 77. Bibliog: Art of Indian children, Vergara Printing Co, Santa Fe, NMex, 70; Clara Lee Tonner (auth), Southwest Indian Painting, Univ Ariz, 73; Ann Dutton (auth), Arizona Living, Moyca Christy Manoil, 7/11/75. Mem: Artist Hopid; Hopi Arts-Crafts Guild. Style & Technique: Versatile number of styles; traditional. Media: Polymer, Acrylic, Oil. Interest: Designing, sculpting and painting of jewelry. Publ: Artist cover, Arizona Highways Mag, 1/78. Mailing Add: PO Box 715 Second Mesa AZ 86043

COOK, AUGUST CHARLES
PAINTER, ENGRAVER
b Philadelphia, Pa, Mar 15, 97. Study: Pa Acad Fine Arts; Harvard Univ. Work: Paintings, La Salle Col, Philadelphia; Pennell Collection Print, Libr Cong, Washington, DC; print, Butler Mus Am Art, Youngstown, Ohio; prints, Gibbs Art Gallery, Charleston, SC; print, SC Art Comn Collection. Exhib: Pa Acad Fine Arts; Soc Am Graphic Artists; Libr Cong Print Exhib; Nat Acad Design, New York; Carolina 25th Ann, Gibbs Art Gallery. Teaching: Prof fine arts & head dept, Converse Col, Spartanburg, SC, 24-66. Awards: Purchase Prize, Furman Univ, Greenville, SC. Bibliog: Jack Morris (auth), Contemporary artists of South

Carolina, 70. Mem: Guild SC Artists. Media: Oil. Mailing Add: RR 3 Box 205 Chesnee SC 29323

COOK, CHRISTOPHER CAPEN
ART ADMINISTRATOR
b Boston, Mass, May 28, 32. Study: Wesleyan Univ, BA, 54; Univ Ill, MFA, 59. Exhib: One-man shows, Colby Jr Col, New London, NH, 63, Phillips Exeter Acad, Andover, Mass, 66, Eleanor Rigelhaupt Gallery, Boston, 67, Univ NH, Durham, 69, Bradford Jr Col, 70, Jack Wendler Gallery, London, Eng, 73 & Inst Contemp Art, Boston, 73; De Cordova Mus, Lincoln, Mass, 64; Boston Fine Arts Festival, 64; Northeastern Regional Mead Corp, Smith Col Mus Art, 65; Mus Mod Art, New York, 70; Ctr Art & Commun, Buenos Aires, Arg, 70; Kyoto, Japan, 71. Teaching: Instr art, Colby Jr Col, 56; instr art, Univ NH, 59-63, asst prof, 63-64. Pos: Asst dir, Addison Gallery Am Art, Phillips Acad, Andover, Mass, 64-69, dir, 69-; mem adv bd, Archiv Am Art, 72- Mem: Coun Mus & Educ in Visual Arts; Boston Visual Artists Union. Publ: Auth, Possibles, 69; auth, Book of Instants, 70; auth, Poem System-Anytime, 71. Mailing Add: c/o Dir Addison Gallery Am Art Phillips Acad Andover MA 01810

COOK, GLADYS EMERSON
ILLUSTRATOR, PAINTER
b Haverhill, Mass. Study: Skidmore Col, BS; Univ Wis, MS. Work: Metrop Mus Art, New York; Cincinnati Mus, Ohio; Boston Mus, Mass; Libr Cong, Washington, DC; Smithsonian Inst; also in many pvt collections. Comn: Dog portfolio (8 plates in full color) & cat portfolio (8 plates in full color), 60; US Equestrian Team Portraits, 68; folio of four Lipizzaner Horses, 70; also many animal portraits, pvt comns, 50-72. Exhib: Metrop Mus Art, New York, 50; Soc Illustrators; also others. Teaching: Substitute instr art, New York City Jr High Schs, 63-70. Awards: Artist of the year, Albany Print Club, 68; Artist of Accomplishment, Skidmore Col, 72. Mem: Fel Royal Soc Arts; Asia Soc; Wildlife Fedn. Publ: Auth & illusr, Hiram & Other Cats, How to Draw Cats, How to Draw Dogs, How to Draw Horses & Circus Clowns on Parade; plus many others. Mailing Add: Hotel Wolcott 4 W 31st St New York NY 10001

COOK, HOWARD NORTON
PAINTER, LECTURER
b Springfield, Mass, July 16, 01. Study: Art Students League; and with Bridgeman, Dumond, Morgan & Pennell & abroad. Work: Metrop Mus Art, Mus Mod Art & Whitney Mus Am Art, New York; Philadelphia Mus Art, Pa; Minneapolis Art Inst, Minn. Comn: Two fresco murals, comn by Works Progress Admin, Law Libr, Springfield, Mass, 34; fresco mural, comn by Sect Fine Arts, Pittsburgh Court House, Pa, 36; sixteen mural panels, Fed Bldg, San Antonio, Tex, 37-39; two Tempera murals, Post Off Bldg, Corpus Christi, Tex, 41; mural, Mayo Clin Diag Bldg, Rochester, Minn, 52-54. Exhib: Archit League New York Ann, 37; Artists for Victory, Metrop Mus Art, 51; Corcoran Gallery Art Ann, Washington, DC, 53; Detroit Pub Libr Mural Exhib, 56; Roswell Mus & Art Ctr, NMex, 75; also all important graphic arts exhibs, US & abroad, 31-50. Teaching: Prof painting, Minneapolis Inst Art, 45 & 58; guest prof painting, Univ NMex, 47, 50 & 60; prof painting, Univ Calif, Berkeley, summer 48; prof painting, Scripps Col, summer 51; guest prof painting, Washington Univ, 54; prof painting, Highlands Univ, summer 57. Pos: Mem jury, US Govt Sect Fine Arts, Washington, DC, 37; mem jury Am art, Metrop Mus Art, 51. Awards: Logan Medal, Art Inst Chicago, 33; Gold Medal for Mural Painting, Archit League New York, 37; Samuel F B Morse Gold Medal, Nat Acad Design, 63. Bibliog: Carl Zigrosser (auth), The artist in America, 42; Carl Zigrosser (auth), Howard Cook, NMex Quart, 50. Mem: Life mem Art Students League; life mem Nat Acad Design; life mem Taos Art Asn. Media: Oil, Watercolor, Pastels, Graphics. Publ: Auth, From prints to frescoes, Am Mag Art, 1/42; auth, Sammi's Army, Doubleday, 43; auth, Making a watercolor, Am Artist Mag, 45. Dealer: Kennedy Galleries 20 E 56th St New York NY 10022. Mailing Add: c/o Mission Gallery Taos NM 87571

COOK, PETER (GEOFFREY)
PAINTER
b New York, NY, June 10, 15. Study: Princeton Univ, BA(archit), 37; Nat Acad Design, Pulitzer Traveling Scholar, 37-39; Art Students League, 37-40. Work: US Supreme Court; Wells Col. Comn: Portraits, Princeton Univ, Simmons Col, Boston, New Eng Merchants Bank, Exeter Acad & St Mark's Sch. Exhib: Nat Acad Design Ann, 43-; one-man shows, Jose Galleries, Boston & Richmond, Va, 52; Ogunquit Arts Ctr, 55-69; Boston Art Festival, 67. Awards: Governor's Prize, State of Maine, 61; Bronze Medal, Nat Arts Club, 65; Century Asn Medal, 67. Mem: Nat Acad Design; Century Asn. Style & Technique: Traditional protraits and landscapes. Media: Oil. Dealer: Portraits Inc 41 E 57th St New York NY 10022; Gallery 100 100 Nassau St Princeton NJ 08540. Mailing Add: Box 202 Heathcote Farm Kingston NJ 08528

COOK, RICHARD LEE
SCULPTOR, EDUCATOR
b Big Spring, Tex, Oct 30, 34. Study: Univ NMex, BA & MA; computer drawing & sculpture with Charles Mattox; also sculpture with Ron Grow. Work: Masur Mus Art, Monroe, La; Contemp Am Collection, Mobile Art Gallery, Ala; Univ NMex Fine Arts Ctr, Albuquerque; Nicholls State Univ Fine Arts Gallery, Thibodaux, La. Exhib: One-man shows, Glade Gallery, New Orleans, La, 69-71; Sculpture: 70, traveling exhib, Southern Asn Sculptors, 70; 13th Ann 8-State Exhib, Okla Art Ctr, Oklahoma City, 71; 6th Nat Drawing & Small Sculpture Show, Del Mar Col, Corpus Christi, Tex, 72; four-man show, Tulane Univ, 73. Teaching: Assoc prof art & chmn dept, Nicholls State Univ, 68-77. Awards: Purchase Award, Masur Mus, 69; First Award, La Art Comn, Baton Rouge, 70; Second Award, Southern Asn Sculptors, 70. Mem: Southern Asn Sculptors (pres, 71-); Col Art Asn Am; Nat Art Educ Asn; Artists Equity Asn. Media: Light, Sound, Movement, Neon, Plastic, Electronics. Dealer: Michael Ledet Fine Arts Ltd 1126 S Carrolton Ave New Orleans LA 70118. Mailing Add: Hills Gallery of Contemp Art 121 Lincoln Ave Santa Fe NM 87501

COOK, ROBERT HOWARD
SCULPTOR
b Boston, Mass, Apr 8, 21. Study: Demetrios Sch, 38-42; Beaux Arts, Paris, under Marcel Gaumont, 45. Work: Whitney Mus of Am Art, New York; Pa Acad of Fine Arts, Philadelphia; Va Mus of Fine Arts, Richmond; Hirshhorn Collection, Washington, DC; State Univ NY, Oneida. Comn: Quartet (7 ft bronze), Johnson Found, Racine, Wis, 64; Thespis (12 ft long bronze), Canberra Theatre Ctr, Australia, 65; Dinoceras (20 ft long bronze), Rudin Mgt, New York, 71; Media (30 ft long bronze), Johnson City Press Chronicle, Tenn, 73; Regatta (15 ft high bronze), Southland Bldg, Dallas, Tex, 74; Lifeline (14.5 ft high bronze), Sun Co, Radnor, Pa, 78. Exhib: One-man shows, Inst of Contemp Art, Boston, 51, Munson-Williams Proctor Inst, Utica, NY, 61, Birmingham Mus of Fine Arts, Ala, 67, Carroll Reece Mus, Johnson City, 67, Mint Mus of Art, Charlotte, NC, 68, Norfolk Mus, Va, 68, Va Mus of Fine Art, Richmond, 68, Mus of Univ of Ariz, Tucson, 69 & 70, Schenectady Mus of Art, NY, 77 & Creighton Univ, Omaha, Nebr, 78; Pa Acad of Fine Arts; Whitney Ann; Nat Acad Design; Boston Art Festival; Univ Ill; Biennale Venezia, Italy, 51. Awards: Second Prize, Prix de Rome, Am Acad of Rome, 42; Cash Award & Best-of-Show, Nat Acad of Arts & Lett, 48; Tiffany Award, Tiffany Found, 48. Bibliog: Tracy O'Kates & Arnold Eagle (auth), World of Robert Cook (27-minute doc on his work), Beechtree Productions, 77. Mem: Sculptors Guild. Style & Technique: Airy, flowing, light movement. Media: Lost wax technique with bronze; wood. Publ: Auth, Family Album in Bronze (photographs by Franco Romagnoli), Jasillo, 76. Dealer: Sculpture Ctr 167 E 69th St New York NY 10021. Mailing Add: Piazza Borghese Rome 02186 Italy

COOKE, DONALD EWIN
WRITER, DESIGNER
b Philadelphia, Pa, Aug 5, 16. Study: Philadelphia Mus Sch Art. Exhib: Pa Acad Fine Arts Watercolor Show, 37 & 38. Teaching: Instr illustration, Philadelphia Mus Sch Art, 38-40. Pos: Art dir, David McKay Co, 40-41; art dir & managing ed, John C Winston Co, 45-60; pres, Edraydo, Inc, 60- Awards: Hon Mention, Int Bookplate Exhib, 33. Mem: Philadelphia Sketch Club. Style & Technique: Traditional transparent wash style. Media: Watercolor. Publ: Auth, Color by Overprinting, 55; auth & illusr, Silver Horn of Robin Hood, 56; auth, Fathers of America's Freedom, 69; auth, America's great document-The Constitution, 70; auth & illusr, Heritage 200 (bicentennial calendar featuring 12 watercolors of historic Philadelphia), 75. Mailing Add: 106 Oakford Circle Wayne PA 19087

COOKE, EDWY FRANCIS
PAINTER, EDUCATOR
b Toronto, Ont, Mar 10, 26. Study: Univ Toronto, BA; Univ Iowa, MFA. Work: Art Gallery Toronto; London Mus Art, Ont; Beaverbrook Art Gallery, Fredericton, NB; Sir George Williams Univ, Montreal; Loyola Col, Montreal; plus others. Exhib: Royal Can Acad, 44-58; Nat Gallery Can; one-man shows, Hart House, Univ Toronto, 47 & 52, London Art Mus, Ont, 55 & Art Ctr, Univ NB, 62; plus others. Teaching: Instr drawing & painting, Art Workshop, 51-59; instr, Art Gallery Toronto, 51-59; instr, Univ Toronto, 54-59; lectr hist art, Univ Toronto, 52-59; head dept fine arts, Univ NB, 59-64; prof art hist, Sir George Williams Univ, 64-, assoc dean fine arts, 77- Pos: Cur Lee collection, Hart House, Univ Toronto, 53-59; dir, Beaverbrook Art Gallery, Fredericton, NB, 59-64; dir, Sir George Williams collection art & art galleries, 66- Awards: Can Coun Grant overseas res, 58. Mem: Can Soc Painters in Water Colour; Can Mus Asn; Univs Art Asn Can; Col Art Asn Am. Mailing Add: Dept of Fine Arts Sir George Williams Univ Montreal PQ Can

COOKE, JODY HELEN
PAINTER, EDUCATOR
b Windriver, Wyo, Oct 25, 22. Study: Univ Calif, Berkeley, BA(fine arts), with Karl Kasten, Felix Ruvulo, E Loran, Chiuru Obata & Worth Ryder; Univ Minn, Minneapolis, MA, with Walter Quirt, Edward Corbett & Reid Hastie; Calif Col Arts & Crafts, with Miasaki; Univ Ore, Eugene, PhD, with C Bryan Ryan, Robert James, June King McFee, Gordon Kensler & Vincent Lanier; Univ Calif, Hayward, with Corbin LePell; also with Haley, Coykendall & Okubu. Work: Calif State Univ, Hayward; Alaska State Mus, Juneau; plus pvt collections. Exhib: Artists of the Midwest, St Paul Gallery, Minn, 61; Northrop Gallery, Univ Minn, Minneapolis, 61; Artists of Northern Calif, E B Crocker Mus & Art Gallery, Sacramento, 63; Art of All Religions, Artists' Coop, San Francisco, 63; Redding Mus & Art Ctr, Calif, 67; one-man shows, Tolman Hall, Univ Calif, Berkeley, 67, Redding Mus Art Ctr, 67 & Olive Hyde Mus & Art Ctr, Mission San Jose, Calif, 67; three-man show, Allied Arts Gallery, Sacramento, 67; All Alaska Exhib, Alaska Hist & Fine Arts Mus, Anchorage, 76 & 77; Contemp Arts of Alaska, Smithsonian Inst, Washington, DC, 78. Teaching: Head art dept, Col Siskiyous, Wood, Calif, 64-67; asst prof design-art & educ, Univ Iowa, Iowa City, 69-70; asst prof art & educ, Ore State Univ, Corvallis, 70-73; lectr art educ, Calif State Univ, Sacramento, 73-74; assoc prof & dir exhib, Univ Alaska, 74-, chmn art dept, 76- Awards: Merit Award, Auburn Arts Festival, Calif, 66; Purchase Award, All Alaska Competition, 77. Bibliog: Reid Hastie (auth), Encounter With Art, 61. Mem: Visual Arts Ctr of Alaska; Anchorage Hist & Fine Arts Mus; Anchorage Adv on Arts Comn (comnr); Alaska Art Educ Asn; Nat Art Educ Asn (state deleg). Media: Oil, Acrylic; Various Drawing Media. Collection: Prints and paintings of contemporary artists. Mailing Add: 2802 W 30th Ave 8 Anchorage AK 99503

COOKE, SAMUEL TUCKER
PAINTER, DRAFTSMAN
b Gainesville, Fla, Dec 4, 41. Study: Stetson Univ, with Fred Messersmith, BA; Univ Ga, with Lamar Dodd & Howard Thomas, MFA. Work: Asheville Art Mus, NC; Mint Mus Art, Charlotte, NC; Univ Ga Collection; Hunter Gallery Art, Chattanooga, Tenn; Davidson Col, NC. Exhib: Dekalb Nat Print & Drawing Exhib, Ill, 69 & 69; Nat Drawing & Small Sculpture Exhib, Ball State Univ, 72-74; Davidson Col Nat Print & Drawing Exhib, 74-75; Gallery Contemp Art Realist, Winston-Salem, NC, 74-75; Six for Real, Impressions Gallery, Boston, Mass, 74. Teaching: Chmn dept art, Univ NC, Asheville, 68-74. Awards: 3rd Davidson Nat Drawing & Print Award, Knight Publ Co, 74; 39th Southeastern Painting & Drawing Award, Wachovia Bank NC, 74; Mint Mus Award for Realism in North Carolina, NC Arts Coun, 74. Mem: Greenville Co Mus Art, SC. Style & Technique: Super-fantasy realism; animal & figures juxtaposed in space. Dealer: New Morning Gallery 3 1/2 Kitchen Pl Ashville NC 28803; Impressions Gallery 27 Stanhope St Boston MA 02116. Mailing Add: Univ of NC Univ Heights Asheville NC 28804

COOLEY, ADELAIDE NATION
PAINTER, CERAMIST
b Idaho Falls, Idaho, Apr 18, 14. Study: Stephens Col for Women, Columbia, Mo, AA; Univ Wis-Madison, BS; Bradley Univ, Peoria, Ill. Work: Peoria Art Guild Collection, St Paul's Episcopal Cathedral Collection, Carson Pirie Scott & Co, Peoria, Ill. Comn: Altar paraments, Univ United Methodist Church, Peoria, Ill, 67. Exhib: Quatre Femmes, Sears Vincent Price Gallery, Chicago, 67; 20th N Miss Valley Exhib, Ill State Mus, Springfield, 67; 10th Ann Rochester Religious Art Festival, NY, 68; Collectors Finds, Davenport Munic Art Mus, Iowa, 68; 24th Ann Invitational, Ill State Mus, 71. Pos: Ed, Peoria Art Ctr News, 62-65; chmn, Pub Art Comt, Peoria, Ill, 75- Awards: First Prize for Painting, Ill Art League, 65, Second Prize for Painting, 66; First Prize for Ceramic Constructions, Pekin Art Asn, Ill, 72. Bibliog: Edward Barry (auth), Art notes, Chicago Sun Tribune, 2/25/68; Don J Anderson (auth), Four women and the circle, Chicago Am, 2/18/68; Barbara Mantz (auth), Getting to know Adelaide Nation Cooley, Peoria J Star, 1/6/74. Mem: Peoria Art Guild (pres, 61-63). Style & Technique: Non-representation paintings and collages; ceramic objects with carved or incised designs. Media: Oil, Watercolor; Earthenware. Publ: Auth, History of Art in Peoria, 1800-1975, Peoria Jaycees Mag, 75; auth, Joseph Petarde, immigrant stone carver, Ill Mag, 76; auth, The Monument Maker, Biography of Frederick Ernst Triebel, Expo Press, 78. Dealer: Lakeview Ctr Mus Shop 1125 W Lake Ave Peoria IL 61611; Peoria Art Guild 1831 N Knoxville Peoria IL 61603. Mailing Add: 3308 N Bigelow St Peoria IL 61604

COOLEY, WILLIAM, JR
COLLECTOR, PATRON
b Peoria, Ill, Aug 29, 10. Study: Northwestern Univ, BA, 32, MD, 36. Bibliog: Jerry Klein (auth), Collecting as art, Peoria Jour Star, 5/10/70. Mem: Peoria Art Guild; Lakeview Ctr for Arts & Sci; Mus of Contemp Art, Chicago; Chicago Art Inst; Smithsonian Inst. Interest: Support to Bradley University School of Art, Lakeview Center, Peoria Art Guild, individual artists; donations of art to above groups and to Peoria School of Medicine. Collection: About 300 works collected over a 30 year period, including most of the major 20th century artists, mainly drawings, sculpture and signed original prints of museum quality. Mailing Add: 3308 N Bigelow Peoria IL 61604

COOLIDGE, JOHN
ART HISTORIAN
b Cambridge, Mass, Dec 16, 13. Study: Harvard Univ, BA, 35; NY Univ, PhD, 48. Teaching: Prof fine arts, Harvard Univ, 47- Pos: Dir, Fogg Art Mus, Harvard Univ, 48-; trustee, Mus of Fine Arts, Boston, 48-77, pres bd, 76-77, emer pres bd, 77- Mem: Col Art Asn Am (vpres); Soc Archit Historians (vpres). Res: History of American architecture, Italian renaissance architecture. Publ: Auth, Mill & Mansion, 42; auth, The Villa Guilea, Art Bull, 42. Mailing Add: 24 Gray Gardens West Cambridge MA 02138

COONEY, BARBARA (MRS CHARLES TALBOT PORTER)
ILLUSTRATOR, WRITER
b Brooklyn, NY, Aug 6, 17. Study: Smith Col, BA, 38; Art Students League, 40. Pos: Illusr, bks, also var mags & anthologies. Awards: Caldecott Medal, 58; Univ Southern Miss Medal, 75; Smith Col Medal, 76. Publ: Illusr, Christmas Folk, 69 & auth & illusr, Garland of Games & Other Diversions, 69, HR & W; illusr, Dionysus & the Pirates, 70 & Hermes, Lord of Robbers, 71, Doubleday; illusr, Wynken, Blynken & Nod, Hastings, 70; plus many others. Mailing Add: c/o Doubleday & Co Inc 245 Park Ave New York NY 10017

COOPER, ANTHONY J
PAINTER, INSTRUCTOR
b Chicago, Ill, Feb 28, 07. Study: Chicago Art Inst, grad; spec study with Boris Anisfeld; summer study at Julienne Acad, Paris, France. Work: Ill State Mus, Springfield; John H Vanderpoel Collection, Beverly Art Ctr, Chicago; Balzekas Mus, Chicago; The Chicago Corp; Standard Fed Savings & Loan, Chicago. Comn: St Anthony (oil painting), Lady of Vilna Church, Chicago, 67; portrait of Mrs Switalski, comn by John Switalski, Berkeley, Calif, 69; St Sebastian (oil painting), Lithuanian-Am Jesuit Fathers, Chicago, 70; marine landscape (oil painting), comn by Dr Paul Egel, Chicago, 73; still life (oil painting), comn by Dr Leonard Lesko, Univ Calif, Berkeley, 77. Exhib: One-man shows, Beverly Art Ctr, Chicago, 72, Balzekas Mus, 73 & Ill Bell Telephone Bldg, Chicago, 74; Park Forest Art Gallery, Ill, 73; Ill State Fair, Springfield, 75; Mitchell Mus, Mt Vernon, Ill, 75; Traveling Bicentennial Show, Balzekas Mus & Ill Arts Coun, 76-77; Corcoran Gallery, Washington, DC; Nat Acad Design, New York. Teaching: Instr oil painting, portraits & still life, Marquette Art Gallery, Chicago, 70-76; instr landscape & oil painting, Chicago Art Club, 71- Awards: William B French Award, 31; Munic Art League Award, Chicago Munic Art League, 64; First Place for Landscape Oils, Am-Lithuanian Artists, Balzekas Mus, 75. Bibliog: Harold Haydon (auth), Fine exhibits over town, Chicago Sun-Times, 3/14/71. Mem: Peoria Art Guild. Style & Technique: Portraits, landscapes and still lifes in oil. Media: Oil, Watercolor. Dealer: Chicago Art Inst Art Rental/Sales Gallery Michigan & Adams Chicago IL 60603. Mailing Add: 1960 Leland Ave Chicago IL 60640

COOPER, FREDERICK ALEXANDER
ART HISTORIAN
b Sewickley, Pa, Dec 12, 36. Study: Yale Univ, AB, 59; Univ Pittsburgh, MA, 62; Univ Pa, PhD, 70. Teaching: Asst prof art hist, Temple Univ, Philadelphia, 65-68; asst prof art hist, Northwestern Univ, Evanston, Ill, 70-71; assoc prof art hist, Univ Minn, Minneapolis, 71- Awards: Distinguished Teacher Award, Univ Minn, 73; Fel, Am Coun Learned Socs, 75. Bibliog: A Hood (auth), Archaeological Reports, J Hellenic Studies, 73; J Michaud (auth), Chronique des fouilles, Bull Corr Hellinique, 73. Mem: Col Arts Asn; Archaeol Inst Am; Midwest Art Hist Soc; Am Sch Classical Studies; Asn for Field Archaeol. Publ: Auth, A Reconstruction of Duccio's Maesta, 65; auth, Temple of Apollo at Bassai: New Observations on its Plan and Orientation, 68; auth, Topographical Notes from Southwest Arkadia, 72; auth, Two New Temples in Southwest Peloponnesos, 73; auth, Jacopo Pontorma and Influences from the Renaissance Theater, 73. Mailing Add: 1213 Seventh St SE Minneapolis MN 55414

COOPER, LUCILLE BALDWIN
PAINTER, SCULPTOR
b Shanghai, China, Nov 5, 24; US citizen. Study: Univ Calif, Los Angeles; Univ Hawaii; Honolulu Acad Art. Work: Painting, Hawaii Loa Col. Comn: 48 collages, Polynesian Hotel, Honolulu, Hawaii, 60: oil painting, Fiji Hotel, 71. Exhib: 3 Plus 1 Show, Ala Moana, Honolulu; Honolulu Acad Art Ann; Easter Art Festival; Hawaii Painters & Sculptors League Ann; Honorary Retrospective, Hawaii Loa Col, 70; one-person show, Downtown Gallery, 76. Teaching: Lectr ceramic jewelry design, Univ Hawaii Curriculum Ctr, lectr painting, currently. Pos: Chmn, Comn Cult & Art, Honolulu; owner-dir, Hand & Eye Gallery of Contemp Crafts, 71-; gov appt mem, State Found of Cult & Art, 78- Awards: Best in Show for Watercolor, Watercolor & Serigraph Soc; Hon Mention for Watercolor. Mem: Hawaii Artist's League (secy); Hawaii Potters Guild (secy); Hawaii Craftsmen (pres); hon mem Windward Art Guild (pres). Media: Oil, Watercolor; Clay, Acrylic. Mailing Add: c/o Hand & Eye 2855 Kihei Pl Honolulu HI 96816

COOPER, MARIO
PAINTER, SCULPTOR
b Mexico City, Mex, Nov 26, 05. Study: Otis Art Inst, Los Angeles, 24; Chouinard Art Sch, Los Angeles, 25; Grand Cent Art Sch, New York, 27-37; and with F Tolles Chamberlin, Louis Trevisco, Pruett Carter & Harvey Dunn. Work: Metrop Mus Art; Col USAF; Butler Inst Am Art; NASA; plus others. Comn: Painting of Atlas ICBM & planes, USAF, Marianas Hall, Armed Serv Staff Col, Norfolk, Va; comn by USAF to paint the capitals of Europe, 60; invited by Nat Gallery to doc flight Apollo 10 & 11 for NASA, 69. Exhib: Shows & exhibs in Japan, Gt Brit, Europe, Can, Mex & Australia. Teaching: Instr, Art Students League, 57-; instr, Nat Acad Design Sch Fine Arts, City Col New York, 61-68. Pos: Del to US Comn, Inter-Am Press Asn, 54-; in charge team artists to Japan, Korea & Okinawa, USAF, 56 & in charge team artists to Japan, 57; art consult, USAF, 60. Awards: Audubon Artists Gold Medal of Honor, 74; Am Watercolor Soc Gold Medal of Honor, 74; Samuel F B Morse Gold Medal, Nat Acad Design. Bibliog: Incl in, US Air Force, a pictorial history, 66, History of the American Watercolor Society, 69 & History of watercolor painting in America, 66. Mem: Academician Nat Acad Design; Am Watercolor Soc (pres, 59-); Audubon Artists (pres, 54-58); fel Royal Soc Arts; Can Soc Painters in Watercolor. Style & Technique: Large watercolors (30 x 40 inches), semi-abstract in design with controlled technique. Publ: Auth, Flower Painting in Watercolor, 66; auth, Drawing & Painting the City, 67 & co-auth, Painting with Watercolor, 71, Van Nostrand-Reinhold; illusr, short stories of, P G Wodehouse, Quentin Reynolds & many others; also contribr to nat mags. Mailing Add: 1 W 67th St New York NY 10023

COOPER, MARVE H
PAINTER, ART DEALER
b Bronz, NY, Jan 1, 39. Study: Caton Rose Inst, New York, 54; Cooper Union, 59; Pratt Inst; Queens Col, NY. Exhib: Kiron Gallery, New York, 61; 10/4 Gallery, New York, 63 & 64; South Co Art Asn, 67; Sch of Fine Arts, Boston, 68; Art Asn of Newport, RI, 69 & 75; Southeastern Mass Univ Regional Exhib, 77. Collections Arranged: US Environmental Protection Agency/Art, 73 & Am Drawings—1900-1975, Art Asn of Newport, RI, 75; 24 additional exhibs of Am artist-craftsmen arranged. Teaching: Instr painting, Queens Col, NY, 67; lectr art, Sch of Fine Arts, Boston, 68. Pos: Apprentice, Universal Art Ltd Ed, Islip, NY, 59-63; free-lance artist, corp design, 65-74; dir, Cooper & French Gallery, Newport, 74- Awards: First Prize & Hon Mention, Art Asn of Newport, Drury, 68; First Prize, Prints, South Co Art Asn, 69; Hon Mention, Southeastern Mass Univ, 77. Mem: Art Asn of Newport (coun mem, 75-); RI State Coun on Arts (mem adv panel, 77-). Style & Technique: Predominately abstract. Media: Acrylic, pastels. Specialty: Crafts. Publ: Contribr, Nine Independent Artists USA, Art Int, 68; auth, Painting and Sculpture, Language of the Specialists, Funk & Wagnalls, 66. Mailing Add: 130 Thames St Newport RI 02840

COOPER, PAULA
ART DEALER
b Mass, Mar 14, 38. Study: Pierce Col, Athens, Greece; Sorbonne, Paris; Goucher Col; Inst Fine Arts, NY Univ. Pos: Asst, World House Galleries, New York, 59-61; dir, Park Place Gallery, 68-; dir, Paula Cooper Gallery, 68- Specialty: Contemporary art. Mailing Add: 155 Wooster St New York NY 10012

COOPER, PHILLIS
SCULPTOR
b Oakland, Calif, July 22, 45. Study: Univ Calif, Davis, BA. Exhib: All Girls Show, Candy Store Gallery, Folsom, Calif, 71; Deep Source of Trouble, San Francisco State Col, Calif, 72; Reno's Clay Diggings, Wenger Gallery, San Francisco, 72; The Cup Show, David Stuart Gallery, Los Angeles, Calif, 72; one-woman show, Wenger Gallery, La Jolla, Calif. Awards: Kingsley Art Club Educ Found Award, 69. Bibliog: Thomas Albright (auth), Another side of Reno, San Francisco Chronicle, 7/27/72. Style & Technique: Sculptural orientation using white earthenware. Media: Ceramics. Mailing Add: Dept of Art Univ Nevada Reno NV 89507

COOPER, REBECCA (REBECCA COOPER EISENBERG)
ART DEALER, COLLECTOR
b Philadelphia, Pa, July 11, 47. Study: New York Univ, BA, 69, MA's, 71. Teaching: Lectures given in var univs & mus groups on a regular basis. Pos: Owner & dir, Gallery Rebecca Cooper, 74- Specialty: Fantasy, Realism and Imagism, national (regional) and international; ceramic sculpture; folk art. Collection: Eclectic, concentrated on American 1970's surrealism. Mailing Add: 2130 P St NW Washington DC 20037

COOPER, RHONDA
CURATOR, INSTRUCTOR
b New York, NY, Nov 5, 50. Study: Hunter Col, BA(art hist); Univ Hawaii, MA(Far Eastern art); Cornell Univ, grad study in Far Eastern art. Collections Arranged: Ando Hiroshige: A Journey on the Tokaido Road, Spring 77 & Faces of the Buddha, Fall 77, Dayton Art Inst. Teaching: Instr Asian art survey, Univ Bridgeport, Conn, summers, 74-76. Pos: Cataloguer & asst to registrar, Mus of Mod Art, New York, 72-73; intern Far East, Metrop Mus of Art, New York, 74; asst cur Asian art & registrar, Dayton Art Inst, 76- Mem: Col Art Asn; Am Asn of Mus; Ohio Mus Asn. Mailing Add: 5277 Wood Creek Dr Dayton OH 45426

COOPER, RON
PAINTER, SCULPTOR
b Ojai, Calif, July 24, 43. Study: Happy Valley Sch, Chouinard Art Inst, Los Angeles. Work: Chicago Art Inst; Solomon R Guggenheim Mus New York; Kaiser Wilhelm Mus, Krefeld, West Ger; Stedelijk Mus, Amsterdam, Netherlands; Whitney Mus Am Art, New York. Comn: Floating Volume Atmosphere, Libr Cong Dept Copyright & Artist, 68; 28 ft drawing for proj, Large Floating Volume of Light with James Meeker, Ft Worth, Tex, 71. Exhib: Arp to Artschwager, Goldowsky Gallery, New York, 67; Prospect 69, Dusseldorf, Ger, 69; Whitney Ann Painting, 69; Theodoran Awards, Guggenheim Mus, 71; Documenta V, Kassel, West Ger, 72. Awards: Los Angeles Co Mus Art Purchase Award, 68; Nat Endowment Arts Award, 70; Theodoran Purchase Award, Guggenheim Mus, 71. Style & Technique: Answering questions using energy and perceptual techniques in all media. Mailing Add: 200 Westminster Ave Venice CA 90291

COOPER, THEODORE A
ART DEALER
b Cleveland, Ohio, Feb 20, 43. Study: Muskingum Col, BA, 65; Ind Univ, MA, 67. Teaching: Teaching asst introd art, Ind Univ, 65-67. Pos: Asst dir, IFA Galleries, 68-70; dir, Studio Gallery, 70-71; pres & dir, Adams Davidson Galleries, Inc, 71- Mem: Am Soc Appraisers. Specialty: 19th century American and European Masters; early 20th century Masters. Mailing Add: 3233 P St NW Washington DC 20007

COOPER, WAYNE
PAINTER, GRAPHIC ARTIST
b Depew, Okla, May 7, 42. Study: Valparaiso Univ; Famous Artist Sch; Gary Artist League. Work: Art Inst Gallery, Chicago; Ft Wayne Mus Gallery, Ind. Comn: Story of Flight (5 x 30 ft oil), Parkview Hosp, Ft Wayne, 65; Crucifix (oil), Assembly of God Church, Hebron, Ind, 66; Christ Descending (4 x 8 oil), Endtime Tabernacle, Tulsa, Okla, 69; Painting of Christ, Church of God, Depew, Okla, 74; four original lithograph ed, Am Express Co, New York. Exhib: Country Beautiful, Minn, 68; Nat Show, Tyler, Tex, 69; Ft Wayne Mus, 75; Univ Ky, 74; Valparaiso Univ, 75. Awards: Best of Show, Twas Bay Show, Gilcrease Mus, Tulsa, 69; First Place for Oils, Southern Shores, Gary, Ind, 70; First Place for Watercolor, Ft Wayne Mus, 75. Bibliog: Green Country, TV presentation, 74. Mem: Mid-Am Art Asn; Ind Artists & Craftsmen; Am Artists Prof League; Fla Fedn Artists; Cowboy Hall of Fame. Style & Technique: Realist-Americanism. Media: Oil, Lithography, Watercolor. Collection: Realistic sculpture & paintings. Mailing Add: 126 W 1025S Kouts IN 46347

COOPER, WENDY ANN
CURATOR
b Newark, NJ, July 28, 45. Study: Pembroke Col, Brown Univ, BA, 67; Univ Del, Winterthur Prog, MA, 71; Attinham Summer Sch, Eng, 72. Collections Arranged: Herreshoff Collection, Bristol, RI, 69-71; Paul Revere's Boston: 1735-1818 (co-auth, catalogue), 4/75-10/75 &

Copley, Stuart and West: in America and England (contribr, catalogue), 7/76-9/76, Mus Fine Arts, Boston. Teaching: Lectr Am dec arts, Boston Pub Libr, Mass, 75-76 & Shelburne Mus, Univ Vt, summer 76 & 77. Pos: Asst to dir, RI Hist Soc, Providence, 67-69; Winterthur Fel, Winterthur Mus, Del, 69-71; Mellon Fel, Brooklyn Mus, 71-72, asst cur, 72-73; spec asst, Mus Fine Arts, Boston, 73-75, asst cur, 75-77; guest cur, Whitney Mus, 77- Mem: Nat Trust; Dec Arts Chap, Soc Archit Historians; Victorian Soc of Am (treas, New Eng Chap, 77). Res: Principally in the area of 18th century American furniture and silver, especially that of New England region. Publ: Auth, The Furniture and Furnishings of John Brown of Providence, I & II, 73, Antiques; auth, American Chippendale Chairback Settees, Am Art J, 77. Mailing Add: 1175 York Ave New York NY 10021

COPE, LOUISE TODD
See Todd, Louise

COPELAND, LAWRENCE GILL
EDUCATOR, DESIGNER
b Pittsburgh, Pa, Apr 12, 22. Study: Ohio State Univ, BFA, 46; Univ Stockholm, Sweden, cert, 47; study with Baron Eric Fleming, 47-48, Emeric Gomery, 48-49; Cranbrook Acad Art, MFA, 51. Work: Nat Gallery Art, Washington, DC. Comn: Mrs Vanderbilt Webb Award, Rochester Inst Technol, NY, 55; Sterling Awards, Gannett Newspapers, Rochester, NY, 59-61; off identifications, Phillips Petroleum, Hackensack, NJ, 65. Exhib: Davidson Art Ctr, Middletown, Conn, 55; Craftsmanship in a Changing World, Mus Contemp Crafts, 56; Brussels World's Fair, 58; New York Crafts, Munson-Williams-Proctor Inst, Utica, NY, 61; Mus Contemp Crafts, New York, 66. Teaching: Asst prof metal design, Sch for Am Crafts, Rochester Inst Technol, 51-59; assoc prof design, City Col New York, 63-, chmn art dept, 67-69. Mem: Am Crafts Coun; Artist-Craftsmen New York (bd mem, 67-68, pres, 75-77); NY State Craftsmen (vpres & bd mem, 56-71); Col Art Asn Am; Metrop Mus Art. Media: Metal. Mailing Add: Dept of Art City Col New York New York NY 10031

COPELAND, LILA
PAINTER, PRINTMAKER
b New York, NY. Study: Art Students League, with George Grosz; Pratt Graphic Art Ctr. Work: Brit Mus, London, Eng; Bibliot Nat, Paris, France; Nat Collection Fine Arts, Washington, DC; Philadelphia Mus Art, Pa; Boston Mus Fine Arts, Mass. Exhib: Art Inst Chicago; De Pauw Univ; Okla Mus Art; Staten Island Mus; Wis State Univ. Awards: Norman Waite Harris Bronze Medal & Prize, Art Inst Chicago. Bibliog: Joan Hess Michel (auth), Children—the drawings of Lila Copeland, Am Artist, 12/70; Joyce Hill (auth), Sketch of Lila Copeland, Lower Cape Newspaper, 12/12/72. Mem: Provincetown Artists Asn. Style & Technique: Realistic; primarily of children and mother and child. Media: Oil, Crayon, Lithography. Dealer: Assoc Am Artists 663 Fifth Ave New York NY 10022. Mailing Add: 31 W Ninth St New York NY 10011

COPLANS, JOHN (RIVERS)
ART ADMINISTRATOR, ART EDITOR
b London, Eng, June 24, 20. Pos: Ed-at-large, Artforum Mag, 62-66, assoc ed, 66-70, ed, 71-; dir, art gallery, Univ Calif, Irvine, 65-68; cur, Pasadena Art Mus, 67-70; dir, Akron Art Inst, 78-; organizer numerous exhib & catalog essays. Awards: Guggenheim Fel, 69; Frank Jewitt Mather, 74; Nat Endowment Arts Fel, 75. Publ: Auth, Serial imagery, 68 & Andy Warhol, 71, New York Graphic; auth, Roy Lichtenstein, Praeger, 72; auth, Ellsworth Kelly, Abrams, 72; Decisions, Decisions, 75, Norton; auth, Weegee: Tater und opfer, Schirmer/Mosel, 78; contribr, Artforum, Art News, Art in Am, Art Int. Mailing Add: c/o Akron Art Inst 69 E Market St Akron OH 44308

COPLEY, CLAIRE STROHN
ART DEALER, LECTURER
b Los Angeles, Calif, Aug 14, 48. Study: Bennington Col, Vt; Calif Inst of the Arts, Valencia. Teaching: Guest instr, Fresno State Col, Calif, 75. Pos: Founder-dir, The Claire Copley Gallery, Inc, 74-; mem bd dirs, Los Angeles Inst Contemp Art, 77-; founding mem, Found Art Resources, 77- Mem: Los Angeles Artists Equity Asn. Specialty: Contemporary American and European art; conceptual art. Publ: Auth, Terry Allen: a personal evaluation, Los Angeles Co Inst Contemp Art J, 76, ed, Jour, No 13, 77. Mailing Add: 916 1/2 N La Cienega Blvd Los Angeles CA 90069

COPLEY, WILLIAM NELSON
PAINTER
b New York, NY, Jan 24, 19. Study: Self-taught; Yale Univ, 42; Phillips Acad, Andover, Mass. Work: Mus Mod Art; Whitney Mus Am Art; Chicago Art Inst; Mus Mod Art, Paris; Los Angeles Co Mus Art, Los Angeles; plus others. Comn: Murals, Gov Rm, New York Cult Ctr. Exhib: Osaka, Japan, 55; Salon de Mai, Paris, 55-67; Mus Arts Decoratifs, Louvre, 62; one-man shows, Southwestern Col, Chula Vista, Calif, 65 & Stedelijk Mus, Amsterdam, 68; plus many others, US & abroad. Bibliog: Articles by Roland Penrose, Patrick Waldberg & Robert Melville. Style & Technique: Surrealist. Media: Oil, Acrylic, Charcoal. Dealer: Alexandre Iolas 15 E 55th St New York NY 10022 & 196 Blvd St Germain Paris France. Mailing Add: 52 E 89th St New York NY 10028

COPPOLA, ANDREW
SCULPTOR, DRAFTSMAN
b Cophaigue, Long Island, NY, Jan 6, 41. Study: Hartford Art Sch & Hillyer Col, BFA, 63; study with Wolfgang Behl & James Van Dyke; Fulbright Hays Fel in Sculpture, Florence, Italy, 64-65. Work: Slater Mus, Norwich Free Acad, Conn; plus pvt collections in Conn, Ariz, Fla, Colo & Italy. Comn: Star Dancer, (7 ft cast aluminum, polished, color-anodized sculpture), Berlin Town Hall, Conn, 75; Black Odesey (commemorative bronze), Amistad Resource Ctr, Hartford, Conn, 76; granite fountain (6,000 pounds), Tower Park, Winsted, Conn, 77; plus numerous com comn & gold & silver jewelry comn. Exhib: Colona Galeria, Florence, Italy, 65; one-man shows, Verle Gallery, Hartford, Conn, 67, Stairwell Gallery, Manchester, Conn, 70 & Norwich Free Acad, 74; three-man show, New Britain Mus Am Art, Conn, 73; Lion's Gallery of the Senses, Wadsworth Atheneum Mus, 77. Teaching: Instr sculpture, Univ Hartford, Hartford Art Sch, 70-71 & Jewish Community Ctr, West Hartford, 70-78. Awards: Sculpture Portrait Prize, Dessie Greer Award, Nat Acad Design, New York, 71; Painting Prize, Northwestern Community Col, Winsted, Conn, 72; Conn Coun on Arts Individual Artist's Grant, 77. Bibliog: Dan Parker (auth), Artist at work, color film, 70; Sigfried Halus (auth), Photographic survey of artist and work, 73. Style & Technique: Structural commitment to ambiguity of image merged with elements of formal tension; synthesis. Media: Carved Wood, Hammered Sheet Metal; Assemblages. Mailing Add: 262 Hudson St Hartford CT 06106

CORBIN, GEORGE ALLEN
ART HISTORIAN, WRITER
b Detroit, Mich, Oct 23, 41. Study: Oakland Univ, Rochester, Mich, BA(art hist & psychology), 63; Bucknell Univ, Lewisburg, Pa, MA(psychology), 68; Columbia Univ, New York, MA(art hist), 71, PhD(primitive & pre-Columbian art), 76. Teaching: Asst prof non-western art, Lehman Col, New York, 69- Mem: Col Art Asn. Res: Focuses on the art of the South Pacific Islands, particularly Melanesia and Polynesia, also on African, North American Indian and pre-Columbian art. Publ: Auth, The art of Africa, North American & Oceania, Encycl of World Art Suppl Vol, McGraw-Hill, 80. Mailing Add: 41 W 96th St Apt 8D New York NY 10025

CORD, ORLANDO
PAINTER
b New Orleans, La, Nov 22, 22. Study: Univ Color, 46, under Hans Hofmann, 49, Art Students League, 51; also with Fairfield Porter, 60-63. Work: Guild Hall Mus; Heckscher Mus; Mus Mod Art, Paris; NJ State Mus; Parrish Art Mus; Emile Walter Art Found. Exhib: Long Island Univ, Parrish Art Mus & Heckscher Mus, 71 & 72; Guild Hall, London, Eng, 72; Tampa, 73; Vancouver, 74 & 75; London, Eng & Frankfurt, Ger, 75 & Vancouver & New York, 76 & 77. Style & Technique: New realist. Mailing Add: Box 355 Longboat Key FL 33548

CORDINGLEY, MARY BOWLES
PAINTER
b Des Moines, Iowa, Jan 1, 18. Study: Minneapolis Sch Art & Design; Minneapolis Art Inst; Univ Minn; Colorado Springs Fine Arts Ctr; also with Steve Rettegi, New York, Hilton Leech, Fla & Paul Olsen, Minneapolis. Work: In over 190 pvt collections. Comn: Numerous portraits. Exhib: Traveling Exhibs, 66 & 67 & Print Show, 70, Mont Inst Arts; Nat League Am Pen Women Nat Biennial, Washington, DC, 67 & 70; Jr League Print Show, Great Falls, Mont, 71; plus fourteen one-man shows incl C M Russell Mus, Great Falls, 67 & 71, Univ Mont, 70 & Univ Minn. Pos: Creator & owner, Orig Pioneer Prints Notepaper Co. Mem: Mont State Arts Coun; Mont Inst Arts; Prof Women Artists Mont. Media: Oil, Pencil. Mailing Add: 42 Prospect Dr Great Falls MT 59405

CORDY-COLLINS, ALANA (ALANA KATHLEEN CORDY-COLLINS RIESLAND)
ART HISTORIAN, INSTRUCTOR
b Los Angeles, Calif, June 5, 44. Study: Univ Calif, Los Angeles, BA(art hist), 70, MA(archaeol), 72, PhD(archaeol), 76. Teaching: Instr archaeol, Univ Calif, Los Angeles Exten, 72-74; instr art & archaeol, Univ Calif, San Diego Exten, 74- & San Diego Mesa Col, Calif, 75- Pos: Mem chmn, Archaeol Inst Am, San Diego Chap, 77-78. Awards: Altman Art Award, Univ Calif, Los Angeles, 72. Res: Iconographic study of Chavin art, Peru and Manteno art, Ecuador; shamanic art; function of art in culture. Publ: Ed, Pre-Columbian Art History—Selected Readings, 77, auth, Chavin Art: Its Shamanic/Hallucinogenic Origins, 77 & auth, The Moon is a Boat! A Study in Iconographic Methodology, 77, Peek Publ; co-auth, Pre-Columbian Art: A Handbook of Style, Prentice-Hall, in prep; auth, Cotton and the Staff God: Analysis of an Ancient Chavin Textile, Textile Mus, in press. Mailing Add: Dept of Art San Diego Mesa Col 7250 Mesa College Dr San Diego CA 92111

CORISH, JOSEPH RYAN
PAINTER
b Somerville, Mass, Apr 9, 09. Study: Boston Univ, JD, 32; Harvard Univ, Adj in Arts, 38. Work: US Naval Acad Mus; US Naval War Col; Boston Univ; also in var state capitols, foreign embassies & Brit, Ger, Span, Japanese, Portuguese & US Navies. Exhib: Royal Soc Marine Artists & Bertrand Russell Centennial, London; Jordon Exhib Contemp New Eng Artists, Boston Mus Fine Arts; Grand Nat Exhib, Am Artists Prof League, New York; Olympic Int Exhib, Kiel, Ger; Busch-Reisinger Mus, Harvard Univ; Etajima Mus, Japan; Deutches Mus, Munich, Ger; Barcelona Mus, Spain; Bergen, Norway; Birmingham Mus Art, Ala; plus several one-man exhibs in US & abroad. Teaching: Guest lectr painting, Harvard Univ, Regis Col, Univ Conn, Copley Soc & other cols, mus & art asns. Pos: Art dir, Castle Hill Found, Ipswich, Mass, 58-63; hon artist in residence, US Navy First Naval Dist. Mem: NShore Arts Asn (dir & trustee, 56-); Copley Soc (dir & trustee, 62-64); Am Artists Prof League. Media: Oil. Publ: Paintings reproduced in full color as mag covers, US Naval War Col Rev, Down East Mag & others. Mailing Add: 421 Highland Ave Somerville MA 02144

CORMIER, ROBERT JOHN
PAINTER, INSTRUCTOR
b Boston, Mass. Study: R H Ives Gammeli Studios, cert. Work: Maryhill Mus, Goldborough, Wash; Boston Col Libr, Chestnut Hill, Mass; Superior Courthouse, Cambridge, Mass; Univ Sch, Shaker Heights, Ohio. Comn: Portraits for St Michael's Church, Charleston, SC, 60, Cent Savings Bank, Lowell, Mass, 72 & Univ Sch, Hunting Valley Campus, 73-75; also pvt comns for portraits of prominent individuals. Exhib: New Eng Artists Contemp Ann, 54-69; Am Artists Prof League Grand Nat, 59-69; Guild of Boston Artists, 60-78; Boston Arts Festival, 62; Coun Am Artists Socs, New York, 66. Teaching: Instr drawing & painting, Vesper George Sch Art, 69- Awards: Grand Prize, Boston Arts Festival, 62; Gold Medal of Honor, Coun Am Artists Socs, 65; Greenshields Found Award, 70. Mem: Guild Boston Artists (secy, bd gov, 70-78; Copley Soc Boston (vpres, 70-77); Am Artists Prof League (dir, Mass Chap, 65-71). Mailing Add: 30 Ipswich St Boston MA 02115

CORNELIUS, FRANCIS DUPONT
CONSERVATOR, PAINTER
b Pittsburgh, Pa, Oct 19, 07. Study: Univ Pa, BArch; Univ Pittsburgh, MA. Exhib: Assoc Artists Pittsburgh, annually. Teaching: Lectr conserv art, Colo Col, 61-68; lectr conserv methods at var univs & cols. Pos: Res fel conserv, 44-45; fel conserv, Metrop Mus Art, New York, 45-52; tech adv, Colorado Springs Fine Arts Ctr, Colo, 52-55, restorer, 55-68; conservator, Mus NMex Art Gallery, 55-61, Univ Nebr Art Gallery, 58 & El Paso Mus Art, 60-; pvt studio for preservation of works of art, Colorado Springs, Colo, 52-68; independent lab for preservation works of art, Cincinnati, Ohio, 68-; conservator, Cincinnati Art Mus, 68-75. Mem: Am Asn Mus; Span Colonial Art Soc, Santa Fe, NMex (bd trustees, 64-); fel Int Inst Conserv Mus Objects. Res: Surface films & disintegration of canvas supports. Interest: Partic, Brit Coun course conserv, London, Eng, 56. Publ: Auth, Frick pieta panels; auth, Further developments in the treatment of fire-blistered oil paintings, 66; auth, Movement of wood & canvas for paintings in response to high & low RH cycles, 68; auth, Use of microscopes in treatment of paintings and other works of art, In: Encyclopedia of Microscopy & Microtechnique, Van Nostrand, 73. Mailing Add: 2637 Erie Ave Cincinnati OH 45208

CORNELIUS, MARTY
PAINTER, ILLUSTRATOR
b Pittsburgh, Pa, Sept 18, 13. Study: Carnegie-Mellon Univ, BA, 35; Pittsburgh Playhouse, 38-39; art therapy, VA Hosp & Menninger's, Topeka, Kans; and with Reginald Marsh, New York & Alexander Kostellow, Pittsburgh. Work: 100 Friends of Pittsburgh Art; 100 Friends

Latrobe Art; New Bethlehem High Sch; Mus Mod Art, New York; others in pub schs & hosps. Exhib: Whitney Mus Am Art, New York; Corcoran Gallery Art Biennial, Washington, DC; Palace of Legion of Honor, San Francisco; Assoc Artists Pittsburgh Ann, Carnegie Mus Art, 37-; Regional Painting & Sculpture Exhib, Westmoreland Co Mus Art, Greensburg, Pa; plus many others. Teaching: Instr art, VA Hosp, Pittsburgh; art therapist drawing, Carnegie-Mellon Univ, 59-61, prof drawing, 65-69. Pos: Designer, Aluminum Co Am, New Kensington, Pa, 50-51; rehab therapist in art, Leech Farm Neuropsychiat VA Hosp, currently. Awards: Martin Leisser Sch Design Award, 46 & 48; Butler Inst Am Art Award, 48; Assoc Artists Pittsburgh Award, 39, 45 & 53 & others. Mem: Fel Int Inst Arts & Lett; Assoc Artists Pittsburgh (mem bd dirs, 39-40); plus others. Media: Oil. Publ: Illusr, Pittsburgh, the Story of an American City, 58 & 64. Mailing Add: Phoenix Nest Ligonier PA 15658

CORNELL, DAVID E
CERAMIST, SCULPTOR
b Kalispell, Mont, Feb 24, 39. Study: Mont State Univ, BS(art); Archie Bray Found, with Kenneth Ferguson & David Shaner; Corcoran Sch Art, with Teuro Hara & Richard LaFean; Alfred Univ, MFA(ceramics), with Bob Turner, Val Cushing & Daniel Rhodes. Work: Greenville Art Mus, SC; Charles M Russell Gallery, Great Falls, Mont; Libby Dam, Treaty Tower, Vis Ctr, Libby, Mont; Archie Bray Found, Helena, Mont; Mont State Univ, Bozeman. Comn: Ceramic fountain fixtures, Mont State Univ Libr, 64; Treaty Panel (sculpture), US Army Corps 18 Engineers & Mont Hist Soc, 75. Exhib: Tenth Int Exhib Ceramic Art, Smithsonian Inst, Washington, DC, 66; Norfolk Mus Art, Va, 66; Harriman Gallery, Orange Co Community Col, Middletown, NY, 69; Handblown Glass Exhib, Corning Glass Ctr, NY, 69; Mint Mus Art, NC, 70; Appalachian Corridors: Exhib 2, Charleston, Wva, 70; NW Crafts Show, Henry Gallery, Seattle, Wash, 71; Cheney Cowles Mem Mus, Spokane, Wash, 73; Mont State Hist Soc Exhib, Poindexter Gallery, Helena, 75. Pos: Artist-in-residence, Penland Sch of Crafts, 69-70; dir, Archie Bray Found, 70-77; owner-mgr, Pear Blossom Pottery, Talent, Ore. Awards: First Prize, Univ Exhib, Mont State Univ, 64; Jury Award, 11th Biennial NW Ceramics, Ore Ceramics Studio, 65; Best of Show, 11th Ann Own Your Own, Southern Colo State Col, 74. Bibliog: Mary Lou O'Neil (auth), Archie Bray Found, Mountain Lines, Mountain Bell Tel & Tel, 11/70; David Depew (auth), Archie Bray Found, Ceramics Mo, 5/72; Jerry Metcalf (auth), Today at the Bray, Mont Arts, Mont Inst of Arts, 76. Mem: Helena Arts Coun (vpres, 73); Mont Art Gallery Dir Asn (secy, 75-76); Nat Coun Educ in Ceramic Arts; Am Crafts Coun; Glass Art Soc. Media: Ceramic. Mailing Add: 2316 S Pacific Hwy Talent OR 97540

CORNELL, THOMAS BROWNE
PAINTER, PRINTMAKER
b Cleveland, Ohio, Mar 1, 37. Study: Amherst Col, Mass, BA, 59; Yale Univ, 59-60. Work: Mus of Mod Art, New York; Princeton Univ Libr; Lessing J Rosenwald Collection, Nat Gallery of Art; Cleveland Mus of Art, Ohio; Harvard Univ, Cambridge, Mass. Comn: Mural, Bowdoin Col, Brunswick, Maine, 64; bronze plaques, Maine State Comn on Arts & Humanities, 68; Dionysus (bronze plaque), J Walter Thompson Inc, New York, 70. Exhib: One-man shows, Yale Univ Libr Art Gallery, 65, Santa Barbara Mus of Art, Calif, 65 & Princeton & Dartmouth Col, 65; Contemp Painters & Sculptors as Printmakers, Mus of Mod Art, New York, 66; Wesleyan Univ, Middletown, Conn & Fisk Univ, Nashville, Tenn, 67; Young New Eng Painters (travelling exhib), 69; Living Am Artists & the Figure, Pa State Univ, 74; 30 Yrs of Am Printmaking, Brooklyn Mus, NY, 76. Collections Arranged: Thomas Cornell Drawings & Prints, Bowdoin Col, 71. Teaching: Instr art, Univ Calif, Santa Barbara, 60-62; lectr visual arts prog, Princeton Univ, NJ, 69-71; prof present art & chmn art dept, Bowdoin Col, 63- Awards: Louis Comfort Tiffany Found grant, 61; Nat Inst Arts & Lett grant, 64; Nat Found on Arts & Humanities grant, 66-67; Ford Found grant, 70. Mem: Col Art Asn; Union of Maine Visual Artists. Style & Technique: Figurative working from direct experience as well as from rational organization of pedagogical and philosophical concerns. Media: Oil, pastel; etching and monotype. Publ: Illusr, The Monkey, privately publ, 59; illusr, The Defence of Gracchus Babeuf, Gehenna Press, 64, Univ Mass, 67 & Schocken Press, 71; illusr & ed, Frederick Douglas, 64, illusr & ed, William Lloyd Garrison, 64 & illusr, Composed for Dying, 64, Tragos Press. Dealer: Barridoff 242 Middle St Portland ME 04111; Peter Tatistcheff 35 E 35th New York NY 10016. Mailing Add: Simpson's Point Rd Brunswick ME 04011

CORNETTE, MARY ELIZABETH
ART DEALER, PAINTER
b Russellville, Ky, Sept 9, 09. Study: Bowling Green Col Com, BS; Western Ky State Univ, MS; WTex State Univ, with Dr Emilio Caballero; also with Dirk Van Driest, Taos, NMex. Pos: Dir & pres, Canyon Art Gallery, Inc, Tex, 65- Awards: WTex CofC Cult Achievement Award, 72. Bibliog: Norman Nadel (auth), Mary Elizabeth Cornette brings Tenkei Tachibana wall screens to US as gift to people of US, Scripps-Howard Publs, 10/17/72. Style & Technique: Realistic & impressionistic interpretations of landscapes of Southwestern United States. Media: Watercolor, Oil. Specialty: Representational art of Southwestern United States, especially of Texas. Mailing Add: 2710 Fourth Ave Canyon TX 79015

CORNIN, JON
PAINTER, INSTRUCTOR
b New York, NY, Mar 24, 05. Study: NY Univ; Art Students League; and with Raphael Soyer. Exhib: Palace of Legion of Honor, San Francisco; Los Angeles Co Mus; de Young Mem Mus, San Francisco; Sweat Mem Mus, Portland, Maine; J B Speed Mus, Louisville, Ky; plus others. Teaching: Instr, pvt lessons in own studio, 50- Awards: Nat Exhib Hon Mention, Terry Art Inst, Miami, Fla & Albright Mus, Buffalo, NY; Second Prize for Church Art, Grace Cathedral, San Francisco. Style & Technique: Expressionist. Media: Oil, Casein Tempera. Mailing Add: 812 Northvale Rd Oakland CA 94610

CORONEL, PEDRO
PAINTER, SCULPTOR
b Zacatecas, Mex, May 25, 23. Study: Nat Sch Painting & Sculpture La Esmeralda, 40-45; also painting with Brauner & sculpture with Bruancusi, Paris, 47-48. Work: Kroller-Muller Nat Mus, Otterlor, Neth; Mus Mod Art, New York; Marion Koogler McNay Art Inst, San Antonio, Tex; Mus Arte de Ponce, PR; Mus Mod Art, Mexico City. Comn: Mural, Syndicate Mex Inst Welfare, Mexico City, 54; sculptures, Serv Ctr, Insurgentes Sur, Mexico City, 56; mural, Int Labor Orgn, Geneva, Mex Labor Dept, 74; mural, Cult Cent Antonio Galvex Aiza, Mexico City, 75. Exhib: Palace Fine Arts, Mexico City, 60, La Point Cardinal Gallery, Paris, 61; Mitsukoshi Gallery, Tokyo, 62; Galeria Arte Mexicano, Mexico City, 64-71; Marion Koogler McNay Art Inst, San Antonio, 72. Awards: Nat Award Painting, Nat Inst Fine Arts, Mex, 59; Jose Clemente Orozco Award, 2nd Inter-Am Biennial Painting & Engraving, Mex, 60; Medal, Mex Labor Dept, 75. Bibliog: Paul Westheim (auth), Pedro Coronel, Mexico en la Cultura; Octavio Paz (auth), Presentacion de Pedro Coronel, Univ Mex XV, 61; Justino Fernandez (auth), Pedro Coronel, Pinto y Escultor, Nat Auton Univ Mex, 71. Style & Technique: Expressionist painting, bold forms, totally abstract, personal palette from brilliant color to delicate nuances. Media: Oil on Canvas; Marble, Onyx, Bronze. Publ: Illusr, cover, La Region mas Transparente, Fondo de Cult Econ, 58; illusr, covers, Eloida del Tacto, 62 & Casi al Amanecer, 64, Ed Cuadernos del Viento; illusr, cover, Dialogos, Artes/Lettras/Ciencias Humanas, Col de Mex, 72; illusr, cover, Espacio del Espacio, Ed Mendrugo, 73. Dealer: Galeria Arte Mex Milan 18 Mexico 6 DF Mexico. Mailing Add: Caalejon de las Cruces 72 San Jeronimo Lidice Mexico 20 DF Mexico

CORPRON, CARLOTTA MAE
EDUCATOR, PHOTOGRAPHER
b Blue Earth, Minn, Dec 9, 01. Study: Eastern Mich Univ, BS, 25; Teachers Col, Columbia Univ, MA, 26; Art Ctr, Los Angeles, 26; study with Gyorgy Kepes on light, 44. Work: Mus of Mod Art, New York; Art Inst of Chicago; Mus of Fine Arts, St Petersburg, Fla; New Orleans Mus of Art, La; Univ Ariz Ctr for Creative Photog, Tucson. Exhib: Design with Light, Art Alliance, Philadelphia, 45; one-person shows, Carlotta Corpron, Dallas Mus of Fine Arts, 48 & Light as a Creative Medium, Art Inst of Chicago, 53; Abstraction in Photography, Mus of Mod Art, New York, 52; Design in Nature, 52 & Women in Art, 53, Contemp Arts Asn, Houston; Women of Photography, An Hist Survey, San Francisco Mus of Art, 75. Teaching: Instr design & hist of art, Univ Cincinnati, 28-35; assoc prof design, hist of art design & photog, Tex Woman's Univ, Denton, 35-68. Style & Technique: Creative and experimental photographer; light drawings, light follows form, fluid light designs; nature; shells, eggs, and other objects from nature. Media: Photography. Publ: Contribr (photograph), Gyorgy Kepes (auth), The New Landscapes, 44; contribr (photograph), Moholy-Nagy (auth), Vision in Motion, 46; contribr (photograph), Katherine Kuh (auth), Art Has Many Faces, 51. Dealer: Marcuse Pfeifer Gallery 825 Madison Ave New York NY 10021. Mailing Add: 206 Forest Denton TX 76201

CORR, JAMES DONAT
PAINTER, GALLERY DIRECTOR
b Missoula, Mont, Feb 13, 31. Study: Western Mont Col, BS(art); Univ Mont, ME(art); also with Peter Volkous & Walter Hook. Work: Western Gallery, Dillon, Univ Collection, Missoula, Heritage Gallery, Great Falls, Fort Kalispell, Copper City Mus, Anaconda, Mont. Exhib: Electra II, Helena, Copper Camp Festival, Butte, Mont. Teaching: Asst prof art, Western Mont Col, 70. Pos: Gallery dir, Western Gallery, Dillon, Mont, 70. Mem: Int Soc Artists; Mont Inst Arts; Beaver Head Watercolor Soc. Style & Technique: Illustrative, figurative painting; eclectic style with inovative experimental techniques; contemporary. Media: Alkyd, Watercolor, Acrylic; Pen, Ink. Mailing Add: 515 South Dakota Dillon MT 59725

CORREA, FLORA HORST
PAINTER
b Seattle, Wash, Feb 16, 08. Study: Univ Wash, BA(art); also with Kenneth Callahan, Sergei Bongart, Richard Yip & Raymond Brose. Work: Erb Mem Mus, Univ Ore; Seattle First Nat Bank Collection; Craftsman Press, Seattle; Pac First Fed Savings & Loan Asn, Seattle; Rainier Bank, Seattle. Exhib: Puget Sound Area Exhib, Frye Art Mus, 64-65, 67-68 & 75; Univ Ore Invitationals, 67 & 71-72; Northwest Watercolor Ann, Seattle, 64-67 & 72-75; Watercolor Exhib, Seattle Pac Col, 75; Grand Galleria Exhib, 75. Awards: First in Oils, Penwomen's Wash State Biennial, 70 & 72 & Third Award, 77; First Award, Women Painters of Wash Ann, 74 & Second Award, 77. Bibliog: Linda Plumb (auth), Flora Correa's distinctive collage art, View Northwest, 5/75. Mem: Northwest Watercolor Soc (secy, 67); Women Painters of Wash (pres, 69-70); Nat League Am Penwomen (vpres, Artist Div, Seattle Br, 74-77); Olympic Art Asn, Seattle (pres, 74-77). Style & Technique: Visual reality, with emphasis on color and shapes, landscapes, buildings, streets, figures and flowers. Media: Acrylic, Watercolor, Oil, Collage. Mailing Add: 8253 SE 29th St Mercer Island WA 98040

CORSAW, ROGER D
EDUCATOR, CRAFTSMAN
b Ithaca, NY, Nov 27, 13. Study: NY State Col Ceramics, Alfred Univ, BS; Inst Design, Ill Inst Technol, MFA, with Gyorgy Kepes & Moholy Nagy. Work: Everson Mus Fine Arts, Syracuse, NY; Smithsonian Inst, Washington, DC; Mus Contemp Crafts, New York; Denver Art Mus, Colo; Philbrook Art Ctr, Tulsa, Okla. Exhib: 11 Nat Ceramic Exhibs, Everson Mus, Syracuse Fine Arts, 37-68; 2nd Int Exhib Ceramics, Ostend, Belg, 59; Designer-Craftsmen USA, Mus Contemp Crafts, 60; Int Cult Exchange Exhib, Geneva, Switz, 60; Forms from the Earth—1000 Years of Pottery in America, Mus Contemp Crafts, 61. Teaching: Prof ceramic art, Univ Okla, 36-76. Awards: First Prize for Pottery, 6th Nat Ceramic Exhib, 37; Purchase Award, Nat Acad Arts, Smithsonian Inst, 55; First Prize, Oklahoma Artists Ann, Tulsa, 56, 60, 61 & 62. Mem: Nat Coun Educ for Ceramic Arts (chmn mem comt, 68-72, chmn honors comt, 74-75); Am Crafts Coun; Okla Designer Craftsmen. Media: Ceramic. Mailing Add: 725 Juniper Lane Norman OK 73069

CORSE, MARY ANN
PAINTER, SCULPTOR
b Berkeley, Calif, Dec 5, 45. Study: Univ Calif, 63; Calif Inst Arts, Chouinard scholar & BFA, 68. Work: Los Angeles Co Mus Art; Solomon R Guggenheim Mus, New York; Robert Mitchner Collection, Univ Tex. Exhib: Whitney Sculpture Ann, Whitney Mus Am Art, New York, 70; Permutations, Light & Color, Mus Contemp Art, Chicago, 70; 24 Young Artists, Los Angeles Co Mus, 71; Theodoron Awards, Solomon R Guggenheim Mus, 71; 15 Los Angeles Artists, Pasadena Art Mus, 72. Awards: New Talent Award, Los Angeles Co Mus, 68; Theodoron Award, Solomon R Guggenheim Mus, 70. Bibliog: Andy Eason (producer), White Light (film), Eason Design, 69. Mailing Add: c/o Richard Bellamy 333 Park S at 25th New York NY 10013

CORSO, PATRICK
PAINTER, SCULPTOR
b New York, NY, June 1, 26. Study: Art Students League, with F Dumond; Nat Acad Design, with Leon Krolle, Robert Phillips & Abraham Belskie. Work: US Marine Corps Hq, Washington, DC; Great Lakes US Naval Sta, Chicago, Ill; Butler Inst Am Art, Youngstown, Ohio; US State Dept, Washington, DC. Comn: Trinity, Cath Church, Great Lakes US Naval Sta, 53; Our Lady of Fatima, Barstow US Marine Corps Supply Depot, 54. Exhib: Allied Artists Am, 69; Salmagundi Club, New York, 69; Nat Arts Club, 72; Am Artists Prof League, 72; Butler Inst Am Art, 72. Awards: Second Prize Oil, Salmagundi Club, 71; First Prize Oil, Am Artists Prof League, 72. Mem: Salmagundi Club; Allied Artists Am; Am Artists Prof League. Style & Technique: Dimensional realism; textured true color emphasized. Media: Oil; Clay. Dealer: Harbor Gallery 43 Main St Cold Spring Harbor NY 11724. Mailing Add: c/o Hammer Gallery 51 E 57th St New York NY 10019

CORTELLA, GLORIA CHARLENE
ART DEALER
b Salt Lake City, Utah, Apr 12, 29. Study: Univ Utah, 46-48; Salt Lake City Art Barn, 48-50; Otis Art Inst, MFA, 57. Pos: Dir, Contemp Gallery, Salt Lake City, 50-52; asst dir, Paul

Kantor Gallery, Beverly Hills, Calif, 58-62 & Everett Ellin Gallery, Los Angeles, 62-64; cur, Tamarind Lithography Workshop, Los Angeles, 64-66; registrar, coordr collections & admin asst, Los Angeles Co Mus Art, Los Angeles, 66-72; dir exhib, Art Index, Los Angeles, 70-73; dir, Symphony Graphics, New York, 73-74, Galerie Ariadne, New York, 74-76 & Gloria Cortella Inc, 76- Mem: Comt to Rescue Italian Art (exec secy, Southern Calif Chap). Specialty: Contemporary art specializing in contemporary drawing. Mailing Add: 41 E 57th St New York NY 10022

CORTESE, DON F
PRINTMAKER, INSTRUCTOR
b Chicago, Ill, Dec 30, 35. Study: Sch of the Art Inst of Chicago, BFA; Syracuse Univ, MFA. Work: Libr of Cong, Washington, DC; Art Inst of Chicago; Boston Pub Libr; Houghton Libr, Harvard Univ, Cambridge, Mass; Univ Mass, Amherst. Comn: Intaglio Print, Impressions Workshop, Boston, Mass, 71; Etching & Handset Type, Kirkland Col, Hamilton, NY, 71; etching, Masterpol Design, Inc, Syracuse, NY, 74. Exhib: The 58th Conn Acad Fine Arts Exhib, Wadsworth Atheneum, Hartford, 68; 23rd Am Drawing Biennial, Norfolk Mus Arts & Sci, Va, 69; Rochester Finger Lakes Exhib, Mem Art Gallery, Rochester, NY, 70; Nat Print & Drawing Exhib, Northern Ill Univ, 70; Int Print Competition, Seattle Art Mus, Wash, 71; Graphics 71 Nat Print Exhib, Western NMex Univ, 71; Print Exhib, State Univ NY Brockport, 72; Artists of Cent NY, Munson-Williams-Proctor Inst Mus, Utica, NY, 76. Collections Arranged: Print Invitational, Art Gallery, Univ Mass, Amherst, 74; Nat Print Competition, Minot State Col, NDak, 75. Teaching: Prof printmaking, Sch Art, Syracuse Univ, NY, 65- Awards: Purchase Prize, Nat Print Competition, Bucknell Univ, Pa, 68; One-Man Show Award, Nat Print Competition, Springfield Col, Mass, 70; Purchase Prize, Nat Print Competition, Western NMex Univ, 71. Style & Technique: Intaglio prints, figurative. Mailing Add: Syracuse Univ Col of Visual & Performing Arts Syracuse NY 13210

CORTLANDT, LYN
PAINTER
b New York, NY. Study: Chouinard Art Inst & Jepson Art Inst, Los Angeles, Calif; Art Students League; Pratt Inst Art Sch; Columbia Univ Sch Painting & Sculpture; Hans Hofmann Sch Fine Arts; China Inst Am; also pvt study. Work: Metrop Mus Art, New York; Mus Nat Art Mod, Paris, France; Stedelijk Mus, Amsterdam, Neth; Mus Fine Arts, Boston, Mass; Fogg Mus Art, Cambridge, Mass; plus many others. Exhib: Pa Acad Fine Arts, Philadelphia; Nat Acad Design, New York; Art USA, many mus, galleries & cols; Munic Mus Art, Tokyo, Japan; Kunstmus, Bern, Switz; plus many others. Bibliog: Articles in, La Rev Mod, New York Post, New York Herald Tribune, New York Times; plus others. Awards: Numerous awards incl Centro Studi e Scambi Int Medal of Hon. Mem: Fel Royal Soc Arts; fel Int Inst Arts & Lett; Allied Artists Am; Knights of Mark Twain; and others. Style & Technique: Surrealistic in effect; metaphysical, employing symbolism and creative imagination; most recently, abstract expressionism. Media: Oil, Watercolor. Mailing Add: 1070 Park Ave New York NY 10028

CORTRIGHT, STEVEN M
PRINTMAKER, PAINTER
b Detroit, Mich, Mar 18, '42. Study: Stanford Univ, BA & MA; Univ NMex, Tamarind Workshop artist-teacher fel. Work: Brooklyn Mus Art; Univ Colo; Seattle Art Mus; Achenbach Found, Calif Palace Legion of Honor, San Francisco; Calif Inst Technol. Exhib: 18th & 19th Nat Print Exhib, Brooklyn Mus Art, 72 & 74; World Print Competition, 73, San Francisco Mus Art, 73; 1st & 2nd Colo Print/Drawing Competition, Univ Colo, 74 & 75; Prints California, Oakland Mus Art, 75. Teaching: Assoc prof studio art & lithography, Univ Calif, Santa Barbara, 66- Awards: Numerous purchase awards from various exhibitions over the last ten years. Mailing Add: c/o Baum Gallery Three Embarcadero Ctr San Francisco CA 94111

CORWIN, SOPHIA M
SCULPTOR, PAINTER
b New York. Study: Nat Acad Sch Fine Arts; Art Students League; Hoffman Sch; Archipenko Sch; Phillips Gallery Art Sch, Washington, DC, with Karl Knaths, scholar, 45; NY Univ, BA & MA(creative arts). Exhib: One-person shows, Capricorn Gallery & Creative Arts Gallery, New York, Colony Galleries, Washington, DC, 68-70 & Hansen Gallery, New York, 77; Women Artists 78, City Univ New York Grad Ctr; Lehigh Univ; Fordham Univ; Union Col; Queens Art Mus; Nat Acad Fine Arts. Teaching: Grad asst related arts, NY Univ, 61-62; instr painting & drawing & dir, Studio Workshop, Bronx House, NY, 62-73; lectr art hist, Coop Col Ctr Westchester, State Univ NY Col Purchase, 71-73; art, New York City Drug Rehabilitation Ctr & Bedford Hills Women's Prison. Pos: Juror, NY State Coun Arts, 70 & Queens Coun Arts, 73. Awards: Nat Competition Award for One-Man Show, Creative Arts Gallery, 54; NH Sculpture Competition Award, US Dept Housing & Urban Develop. Mem: Nat Soc Women Artists; Am Soc Contemp Artists; Women's Caucus on Art; Sculptors League; Artists Equity Asn. Style & Technique: Contemporary. Media: Steel, Marble; Oil, Acrylic. Mailing Add: 79 Franklin Ave Yonkers NY 10705

CORZAS, FRANCISCO
PAINTER, PRINTMAKER
b Mexico City, Mex, Oct 4, 36. Study: Esmeralda Inst Nac Bellas Artes, Mexico City, 51-55; Acad San Giacomo, Rome, Italy, 56-58; French Govt scholar, 67. Work: Mus Mod Art, Mexico City; Los Angeles Co Mus Art; Vatican Mus Mod Art Relig; Club Indust Mexico City; Hotel Princess, Acapulco. Comn: Litographias, Lublin Press, New York, 69; Cerastco Ed Milan, Italy, 72; Olivetti SA, Paris, 74; Banco Agropecuario, Mexico City, 75. Exhib: 9th Sao Paulo Biennial, Brazil; Mex Pavilion, World's Fairs, 67 & 70; Young Mexican Painters, Ctr Inter-Am Relations New York, 71; Int Festival, San Salvador, 72; Contemp Mex Art, Kyoto, Japan, 74; plus others. Awards: Second Prize for Via Margutta, Rome, Italy, 58; hon mention, 62 & acquisition prize, 64, Salon de la Plastica Mexicana. Bibliog: John Canady (auth), Young Mexican painters, New York Times, 70; Roberto Sanesi (auth), F Corzas, Corriere della Sera, Milano, 71; S Elizondo (auth), Corzas Metodo y Mito, Sao Paulo Biennale, 69; plus others. Media: Oil. Dealer: Galeria de Arte Misrachi Genova 20 Mexico DF Mexico. Mailing Add: Ferrocarril del Valle 68 Col S Angel-Tizapan Mexico DF Mexico

COSGROVE, STANLEY
PAINTER
b Montreal, PQ, Dec 23, 11. Study: Beaux-Arts, Montreal; Art Asn Montreal; also with Orozco, Mex. Work: Nat Gallery Can; Vancouver Art Gallery; Mus Mod Art, New York; Winnipeg Art Gallery. Exhib: Yale Univ; UNESCO; Montreal Mus Fine Arts; Quebec Provincial Mus; Nat Gallery Can, Ottawa, Ont; plus others. Awards: Medal, Beaux-Arts, Montreal; Travel Scholar in Quebec, Fr Govt, 53. Mem: Royal Can Acad Arts. Mailing Add: PO Box 11 RR 1 Hudson PQ J0P 1M0 Can

COSSITT, FRANKLIN D
SCULPTOR, ART EDITOR
b La Grange, Ill, Oct 16, 27. Study: Univ Mich, 51; Univ Florence, Italy, cert, 50. Work: Va Mus of Fine Arts, Richmond; Chrysler Mus at Norfolk, Va. Comn: 40 ft room divider, St Mary's Hosp, Richmond, Va, 63; sculpture, Carborundium Corp, Niagara Falls, NY, 65; sculpture, Reynolds Metals Co, Richmond, Va, 70; outdoor sculpture, City of Chesapeake, Va, 75 & City of Portsmouth, Va, 77. Teaching: Lectr art, Norfolk State Col, Va, 65-76; lectr art hist, Va Wesleyan Col, Virginia Beach, 77- Pos: Art ed, Richmond Times-Dispatch, 65- & Norfolk Virginian Pilot, 65- Media: Sculpture. Dealer: Franz Bader 21st & Pennsylvania Washington DC 20001. Mailing Add: 1712 Buford Rd Richmond VA 23235

COST, JAMES PETER
PAINTER
b Philadelphia, Pa, Mar 3, 23. Study: Univ Calif, Los Angeles, BA, 50; Univ Southern Calif, MS, 59. Work: R W Norton Mus, Shreveport & pvt collections. Exhib: Artists Guild Gallery Am, Carmel, Calif, 61-63; Mus Fine Arts, Springfield, Mass, 65 & 73; Nat Arts Club, New York, 66; one-man shows, Northwood Inst, Midland, 71 & R W Norton Gallery, Shreveport, 71; plus others. Teaching: Teacher art, Los Angeles City Sch Dist, formerly; lectr art, Northwood Insts, Midland, Mich & Dallas, 71. Pos: Owner, James Peter Cost Gallery, 64- Awards: Franklin Mint, 75. Mailing Add: PO Box 3638 Carmel CA 93921

COSTA, OLGA
PAINTER, COLLECTOR
b Leipzig, Ger, August 28, 13; Mex citizen. Study: San Carlos Art Sch, Nat Univ Mex, with Carlos Merida, painter & Jose Chavez Morado, painter, muralist. Work: Mus Arte Mod, Mexico City; Mus Art, Warsaw, Poland; Mus Mod Art, New York; Banco Nac de Mex, Mexico City. Comn: Mural mosaic, Banco Hipotecario for SPA Cuautla City, Mex, 53; ballet costumes & sets, Coreographer Waldeen, Mexico City. Exhib: Mus Nat d'Art Mod, Paris, France, 52; Nat Mus Tokyo, Japan, 55; 5th Int Art Exhib, Japan, 59; Mus Nac Arte Mod, Mexico City, 61; XIX Olympic Games Cult Exhib, Galeria Arte Mod, Mexico City, 68. Bibliog: Luis Cardoza Aragon (auth), Pintura Mexicana, Fondo de Cultura Economica, Mexico City, 64; Toby Joysmith (auth), Perpetuating the Mexican Barbizon, News, Mexico City, 69; Maria Sten (auth), Olga Costa, Tyija Mag, Varsovia, 70. Media: Oil, Ink. Collection: Pre-Hispanic, colonial and folk art. Dealer: Ines Amor c/o Galeria Arte Mexicano Milan 18 Mexico City Mex; Galeria Arte Contemporaneo Estocolmo 30 Mexico City Mexico. Mailing Add: Pastita 158 Guanajuato Mexico

COSTIGAN, CONSTANCE CHRISTIAN
DESIGNER, PAINTER
b NJ, July 3, 35. Study: Boston Mus Sch Fine Arts; Simmons Col, BA; Am Univ, MA; Univ Va, postgrad work in educ; Univ Calif, Berkeley, postgrad work in ceramics; ceramics with Eric Gronberg; fiber with Ron Goodman. Work: Phillips Collection, Washington, DC; Hirshhorn Mus, Washington, DC; also pvt collections in US & Gt Brit. Exhib: 19th Area Exhib, Corcoran Gallery Art, Washington, DC, 74; Paper Works, Washington Gallery Art, DC, 74; one-person shows, Talbot Rice Art Ctr, Edinburgh, Scotland, 75 & Phillips Collection, 77; Artist Immigrants of Washington, Washington Proj for the Arts, DC, 76; Craft Art, A Washington Expo, Textile Mus, Washington, DC, 77; Purchase Exhib, Univ Iowa Mus Art, Iowa City, 78. Teaching: Instr drawing & design, Smithsonian Inst, Washington, DC, 70-76; asst prof drawing, painting, studio art & two & three-dimensional design, George Washington Univ, 76- Pos: Exhib designer, Smithsonian Inst, 57-59. Awards: Grant Award, Lester Hereward Cooke Found, Washington, DC, 78. Mem: Am Crafts Coun; fel Royal Soc Arts; fel MacDowell Colony. Style & Technique: Layered graphite on paper; gouache; fiber and mixed-media objects; semi-realistic landscape and figure drawings and paintings; fetishes. Media: Graphite & Gouache on Paper; Oil on Canvas; Wrapped Fiber & Mixed-Media Objects. Dealer: Barbara Fiedler Gallery 1621 21st St NW Washington DC 20009. Mailing Add: 603 S Carolina Ave SE Washington DC 20003

COTE, ALAN
PAINTER
b Conn, May 9, 37. Study: Mus Fine Arts Sch, Boston, 55-60, Europ fel, 61-64. Work: Whitney Mus Am Art, New York; Dallas Mus Fine Art; James A Michener Collection, Univ Tex, Austin; Ludwig Collection, Swermont Mus, Aachen, Ger; Phoenix Art Mus, Ariz. Exhib: Paintings for Museum Collections, Am Fedn Arts, 68; A Tendency in Contemporary Painting, Köln, WGer, 69; Whitney Ann, 69-72 & The Structure of Color, 71, Whitney Mus Am Art, New York; New York Painting, Univ Calif, Berkeley, 72; plus many other group & one-man exhibs. Bibliog: Willoughby Sharp (auth), Points of view, Arts Mag, 12/70-1/71; Canvases brimming with color, Life Mag, 9/24/71; Robert Pincus-Witten (auth), New York, Artforum, 3/71. Publ: Contribr, Nine Notes on Color (catalog of The Structure of Color), Whitney Mus Am Art, 71; contribr, Kunst, Praxis Heute, K Thomas-Dumont-Köln, WGer, 72. Dealer: Dunkleman Gallery 15 Bedford Rd Toronto ON Can; Ricke Gallery Linderstrasse 22 Köln Ger. Mailing Add: c/o Cuningham Ward 94 Prince St New York NY 10012

COTSWORTH, STAATS
PAINTER
b Oak Park, Ill, Feb 17, 08. Study: Philadelphia Mus Sch Indust Art; Art Students League, with Reginald Marsh; and with Thornton Oakley & Herbert Pullinger. Work: Norfolk Mus Fine Art. Comn: Murals, pvt homes & pub bldgs; actors collections. Exhib: Corcoran Gallery Art; Philadelphia Watercolor Club; Nat Arts Club; Whitney Mus Am Art, 54; Hammer Galleries, 57; plus others. Pos: Chmn & custodian, Art Collection of the Players, New York. Awards: Prizes, Conn Acad Fine Arts, 54 & Knickerbocker Artists, 55. Mem: Philadelphia Watercolor Club; Salmagundi Club; Am Soc Painters in Casein; Am Watercolor Soc; Audubon Artists. Publ: Illusr, A Bacchic pilgrimage & Deep water days, reproduced in, 100 Watercolor Techniques. Mailing Add: 360 E 55th St New York NY 10022

COTTINGHAM, ROBERT
PAINTER
b Brooklyn, NY, Sept 26, 35. Study: Pratt Inst, New York, 59-64, AA, 62. Work: Syracuse Univ, NY; Honolulu Acad of Art, Hawaii; Indianapolis Mus Art, Ind; also in pvt collections of Richard Brown Baker, New York, Ivan C Karp, New York & Sydney & Francis Lewis, Richmond, Va; plus others. Exhib: The Hwy, Inst Contemp Art, Univ Pa, 70; Radical Realism, Mus Contemp Art, Chicago, 71; New Realism, State Univ NY Col, Potsdam; Documenta 5, Kassel, WGer, 72; Realism Now, New York Cult Ctr, 72; State of Calif Painting, Govett-Brewster Gallery, New Plymouth, NZ, 72; Photo Realism, Serpentine Gallery, London, 73; Grands Maitres Hyperrealistes Americains, 73; Mit Kamera, Pisnel & Spritzpistole, 73; The Super-Realist Vision, De Cordova & Dana Mus, Lincoln, Mass; Separate Realities, Los Angeles Munic Art Gallery, Calif, 73; Opeions 73/30, Contemp Arts Ctr, Cincinnati, Ohio, 73; Hyperrealistes Americains—Realistes Europeens, Centre Nat d'Art Contemporain, Paris, France, 74; Tokyo Biennale, Japan, 74; one-man shows, Molly

Barnes Gallery, Los Angeles, 68-70, O K Harris, New York, 71 & 74 & D M Gallery, London, 75. Teaching: Instr, Art Ctr Col of Design, Los Angeles, 69-70. Pos: Art dir, Young & Rubicam Advertising, New York, 59-64 & Los Angeles, 64-68. Awards: Nat Endowment for the Arts, New York, 74-75. Bibliog: Udo Kultermann (auth), New Realism, Tubingen, Ger, 72; Peter Schjeldahl (auth), Too easy to be art, New York Times, 5/74; Toni Del Renzio (auth), Robert Cottingham—the capers of the signscape, Art & Artists, London, 2/75. Dealer: O K Harris 383 W Broadway New York NY 10013; Landfall Press 63 W Ontario St Chicago IL 60610. Mailing Add: 31 Felden St London SW 6 England

COUCH, URBAN
PAINTER, EDUCATOR
b Minneapolis, Minn, Apr 27, 27. Study: Minneapolis Sch Art, BFA, 51; Skowhegan Sch Painting & Sculpture, 51; Cranbrook Acad Art, MFA, 59; Kyoto, Japan, 64-65. Work: Minneapolis Inst Arts; Walker Art Ctr, Minneapolis; Sioux City Art Ctr, Iowa; Cranbrook Mus, Bloomfield Hills, Mich; Gray Found Collection; plus others. Exhib: Walker Art Ctr, 59; Neville Mus Invitational, Green Bay, Wis, 67; Art in the Embassies, US State Dept, Sophia, Bulgaria & Canberra, Australia, 68, extended prog, 69-71; Minneapolis Inst Arts Faculty Exhib, 68; Difference of a Decade, Lee Nordness Galleries, New York, 69; plus others. Teaching: Instr art, Minneapolis Col Art & Design, 55-70, chmn found prog, 59-62, actg dir, 62-63, asst to dir, 63-64, actg chmn fine arts div, 65-66, chmn painting dept, 68-71; instr advan painting, Walker Art Ctr, 57-61; instr art, Kingswood Sch, Bloomfield Hills, Mich & Bloomfield Hills Art Ctr, 58-59; grad workshop, Univ Minn, 59-61; instr advan painting, Minnetonka Art Ctr, Minneapolis, 59-61; artist in residence, Minn Jr Cols, summers 67-69; instr grad painting, Calif Col Arts & Crafts, summer 70; prof grad paint & chmn div art, WVa Univ, 71- Pos: Graphic designer, USN, Calif, 45; alumni dir, Minneapolis Col Art & Design, 57; design consult, Control Data Corp, 60-62; consult-examiner prog, Comn on Cols & Univs, Chicago, 62-63; consult & examiner, NCent Asn, 63- Style & Technique: Color field. Mailing Add: Creative Art Ctr WVa Univ Div Art Morgantown WV 26505

COUGHLIN, JACK
PRINTMAKER, SCULPTOR
b Greenwich, Conn, Feb 19, 32. Study: Art Students League; RI Sch Design, BFA, 54, MS, 61. Work: Metrop Mus Art & Mus Mod Art, New York; Norfolk Mus Arts & Sci, Va, Staedelsches Kunst Inst, Frankfort, Ger; Nat Collection Fine Arts, Washington, DC. Comn: Ed original prints, Assoc Am Artists, 62, 67 & 68, Int Graphic Arts Soc, 66 & 68, Silvermine Guild Artists, New Canaan, Conn, 67 & Graphic Studio, Dublin, Ireland, 71. Exhib: Am Drawing Biennials, Norfolk Mus Arts & Sci, 62, 64 & 66; Contemp Artists Eligible for Awards, Nat Inst Arts & Lett, New York, 70; 17th Biennial Am Printmaking, Brooklyn Mus Art, NY, 70; 2nd San Diego Nat Print Exhib, Fine Arts Gallery San Francisco, 71; 51st & 52nd Print Exhib, Soc Am Graphic Arts, New York, 71 & 73. Teaching: From assoc prof to prof drawing & printmaking, Univ Mass, Amherst, 60- Awards: First Prize Printmaking, 60th Ann Exhib, Conn Acad Fine Arts, Wadsworth Atheneum, Conn, 70; H P Shope Purchase Award, Soc Am Graphic Artists 51st Print Exhib, 71; Purchase Award, Davidson Col Nat Print & Drawing Competition, 73. Bibliog: Robin Skelton (auth), Imagination of Jack Coughlin, 70 & Jack Coughlin: Irish portraits, 72, Malahat Rev, Univ Victoria, BC. Mem: Assoc Nat Acad Design; Soc Am Graphic Artists; Boston Printmakers. Style & Technique: Figurative imagery in humanist tradition; intaglio, lithography and woodcut; relief sculpture; lost wax into bronze casting. Publ: Illusr, Mnemosyne Lay in Dust, 66 & Synge-Petrarch, 71, Dolmen Press, Dublin, Ireland; illusr, Grotesques, 20 Etchings by Jack Coughlin, Aquarius Press, 70; illusr, 13 Irish Writers, Etchings, Godine Press, 73. Dealer: Assoc Am Artists 663 Fifth Ave New York NY 10022; David Hendriks Gallery 119 St Stephen's Green Dublin Ireland. Mailing Add: N Leverett Rd Montague MA 01351

COUGHTRY, JOHN GRAHAM
PAINTER, SCULPTOR
b St Lambert, Que, June 8, 31. Study: Montreal Sch Art & Design; Ont Col Art. Work: Toronto Art Gallery; Winnipeg Art Gallery; Nat Gallery Can; Mus Mod Art; Albright-Knox Art Gallery; plus others. Comn: Relief, Beth David Synagogue, Toronto. Exhib: Commonwealth Exhib, London, 62; Vancouver Art Gallery, 62; Art Gallery Toronto, 63; Dunn Int Exhib, Tate Gallery, London, 63; Guggenheim Int, NY, 64. Awards: Prizes, Winnipeg Nat Exhib, 57 & 62, Vancouver Art Gallery, 62 & Art Gallery Toronto, 63; plus others. Mailing Add: Nat Gallery of Can Elgin & Slater Sts Ottawa ON Can

COUPER, CHARLES ALEXANDER
PAINTER, INSTRUCTOR
b Portsmouth, NH, Feb 19, 24. Study: Vesper George Sch Art, Boston, cert; Cape Sch Art, Provincetown, Mass, with Henry Hensche; Ernest Lee Major Studio, Boston. Work: Greenshields Mus, Montreal; Attleboro Mus, Mass. Exhib: One-man shows, Cape Cod Art Asn, 73 & Guild Boston Artists, 73; Allied Artists of Am, New York, 74; Grande Prix Int, Cannes, France, 74; Deauville Int, France, 75. Teaching: Instr life drawing & painting, Vesper George Sch Art, 55-; instr, Swain Sch Design, New Bedford, Mass, 65-68. Awards: Gloria Layton Mem Award, Allied Artists Am, 68; Elizabeth T Greenschields Found Mem Grant, Montreal, 69; Medal of Distinction, Grande Prix Int de Pientre de la Cote Azur, 75; plus others. Bibliog: Critical rev in La Rev Mod, Paris, 69. Mem: Allied Artists Am; Artist de Pientre's de La Cote Azur; Guild of Boston Artists; Cape Cod Art Asn; Provincetown Art Asn. Style & Technique: Representational style imposed on traditional, allegorical, and symbolical subject matter. Media: Oil, Pastel. Dealer: Guild of Boston Artists 162 Newbury St Boston MA 02116. Mailing Add: Race Point Rd Provincetown MA 02657

COUPER, JAMES M
PAINTER, EDUCATOR
b Atlanta, Ga, Nov 21, 37. Study: Atlanta Art Inst; Ga State Univ; Fla State Univ. Work: Fla State Univ; Miami Art Ctr; John & Mable Ringling Mus Art. Comn: Mural, 20th Century Fox, 68. Exhib: Young Americans Nat, New York, 62; Soc Four Arts Nat, Palm Beach, Fla, 65; Isaac Delgado Mus Art Nat, New Orleans, 66; Drawings '72, Ft Lauderdale, Fla, 72; Fla State Dept, 72. Collections Arranged: Art of the Asian Mountains, 69; The Artist & The Sea, 69; Art of Italy, 69; Up & Out, 69-70. Teaching: Instr painting, Miami-Dade Jr Col, 64-68; instr painting, Miami Art Ctr, 65-72; from instr to assoc prof painting, Fla Int Univ, 72-, chmn art dept, 77- Pos: Asst to dir, Miami Art Ctr, 67-70. Mailing Add: 8950 SW Red Rd Miami FL 33156

COURT, LEE WINSLOW
PAINTER
b Somerville, Mass, Dec 10, 03. Study: Mass Col Art; and with Aldro T Hibbard, Rockport, Mass & Harry Leith-Ross, Philadelphia, Pa. Work: Polar Archives, Nat Arch, Washington, DC; Farnsworth Mus, Rockland, Maine; Audubon Collection; Frye Mus, Seattle, Wash; Harvard Med Sch, Boston. Comn: Cat-Bow Farm, comn by Sinclair Weeks, Lancaster, NH, 66; Beech Aircraft Co, Wichita, Kans, 67; M S Lindblad, Explorer, comn by Lars-Eric Lindblad, Norway, 70. Exhib: Salmagundi Club, New York, 53-; Acad Artists Asn, Springfield, Mass, 55-; Am Artists Prof League, New York, 58-; Guild Boston Artists, Mass, 65-; Southern Vt Artists, Manchester, 69- Pos: Dir, Coun Am Artists Socs, New York, 56-59; producer, Int Trade Fairs, 57-62; pres, Copley Soc, Boston, 57-64, hon mem, 77-; chmn, Comn Fair Representation in Art Exhibs, Boston, 61- Awards: Legion of Honor, Govt France, 49; Am Artists Prof League Award, 74; Award, Acad Artists Asn Nat, 77. Mem: Am Artists Prof League (dir, 58-62); Guild Boston Artists; Salmagundi Club; Acad Artists Asn; NShore Art Asn, Gloucester, Mass. Style & Technique: Realistic; conventional. Media: Oil. Publ: Ed, An Appreciation, Joseph Rodover De Camp, 25. Mailing Add: Rte 30 West Townshend VT 05359

COURTNEY, KEITH TOWNSEND
CURATOR
b Oshawa, Ont, July 23, 49. Study: Waterloo Lutheran Univ, BA(painting). Pos: Cur, Art Gallery Hamilton, Ont, 74-77, dir community relations, 77- Mem: Ont Asn Art Galleries; Ont Mus Asn. Mailing Add: c/o Art Gallery Hamilton Main W at Forsythe St Hamilton ON L8S 4K9 Can

COUTURIER, MARION B
ART DEALER, COLLECTOR
b US citizen. Study: Univ Lausanne, Switz, cert de Francais et Langues; Univ Dijon; Columbia Univ. Pos: Owner, Couturier Gallery, 61- Specialty: Young, international painters, sculptors and graphic artists. Interest: Work with major private and museum collections selecting works from the modern to the contemporary. Collection: Contemporary artists in all media; Latin American artists for merit and variety of their work. Mailing Add: c/o Couturier Gallerie 1814 Newfield Ave Stamford CT 06903

COVEY, VICTOR CHARLES B
CONSERVATOR
b Morehead City, NC, Nov 11, 16. Study: Baltimore City Col, 38; jewelry design & casting with Alvin Schmidt, 38-39; Corcoran Gallery, painting conserv with Russel Quandt, 53-59; NY Univ Conserv Ctr, materials of art & archeol, 68. Work: Conservator Wurtzburger Collections Pre-Columbian, African, Oceanic & Mod Sculpture, Baltimore Mus Art; Collections of African Sculpture & Contemporary Paintings, pvt collection of Mrs Robert Meyerhoff, Baltimore; Collection Contemporary Paintings, pvt collection of Mrs Israel Rosen, Baltimore; Collection Contemporary Japanese & Italian Paintings, Roland Gibson Art Found, Potsdam, NY; Corcoran Gallery Art, Washington, DC. Exhib: Conservator, US Pavilion Biennale, Venice, Italy, 60 & US Dept State Tour Exhib Archaeol Finds of People's Repub China, US & Peking, 75; US State Dept, Conservation of Holy Crown of St Stephen & Coronation Regalin, US & Budapest, Hungary, 77-78. Pos: Master template draftsman, Glenn L Martin Aircraft Co, Baltimore, 40-49; supt bldgs & art technician, Baltimore Mus Art, 49-53; chief conservator art, Baltimore Mus Art, 55-72; chief conservator art, Nat Gallery Art, Washington, DC, 72- Mem: Fel Int Inst Conserv Hist & Artistic Works; Washington Conserv Guild (pres, 74-); Am Inst Conserv (dir bd, 75); Nat Conserv Coun (mem sub-comt educ & training); Washington Conserv Guild (vpres, 72). Mailing Add: 3717 Rexmere Rd Baltimore MD 21218

COVI, DARIO A
ART HISTORIAN
b Livingston, Ill, Dec 26, 20. Study: Eastern Ill State Col, BEd, 43; State Univ Iowa, MA, 48, with Prof William S Heckscher; NY Univ, with Prof Richard Offner, PhD, 58. Teaching: From instr to prof art hist, Univ Louisville, 56-70; prof art hist, Duke Univ, 70-75; Hite prof art hist, Univ Louisville, 75- Pos: Mem exec comt, Ky Arts Comn, 65-70. Awards: Am Coun Learned Socs fel, 64; Fulbright-Hays fel, 68-69. Mem: Col Art Asn Am; Southeastern Col Art Conf; Renaissance Soc Am. Res: Italian Renaissance art. Publ: Auth, Prints...from the Allen R Hite Art Institute Collection (exhib catalog), 63; contribr, McGraw-Hill Dict Art, Art Bull, Burlington Mag, Renaissance Quart & other nat art publ. Mailing Add: Hite Art Inst Univ of Louisville Louisville KY 40208

COVINGTON, HARRISON WALL
PAINTER, EDUCATOR
b Plant City, Fla, Apr 12, 24. Study: Univ Fla, 42-43; Hiram Col, 43; Univ Fla, BFA(hons), 49, MFA, 53. Work: Herron Mus Art, Indianapolis, Ind; Mead Corp, Atlanta, Ga; Everson Mus Art, Syracuse, NY; John & Mable Ringling Mus Art, Sarasota, Fla; Jacksonville Mus Art, Fla. Exhib: Museum Director's Choice, circulated throughout Southeastern US, 56 & 59; Nat Home Furnishings Show, New York, 59; Painting USA: The Figure, Mus Mod Art, New York, 62; New York World's Fair, 64; Florida 17, Pan-Am Union, Washington, DC, 68. Teaching: Instr art, Univ Fla, 49-61; prof art, Univ SFla, 61-, chmn visual arts prog, 61-67, dean, Div Fine Arts, 67-72, dean, Col Fine Arts, 77- Awards: Sloan Found grant, 47; Guggenheim fel, 64. Style & Technique: Figurative collages and large polyester bas reliefs. Media: Acrylic, Plastic. Mailing Add: Col Fine Arts Univ of SFla Tampa FL 33620

COWAN, THOMAS BRUCE
PAINTER
b Marion, NC, Apr 18, 47. Study: NC Sch Arts, with Jose Ferrer, William Trotman, William Ball, Dame Margaret Webster & Hugh Miller; Governors Sch NC; Ringling Sch Art, Sarasota, Fla; Art Students League, with Will Barnet & Sidney Dickinson; John Pike Sch Watercolor. Work: Hallmark Galleries, New York; NC Art Mus, Raleigh; Greenville Art Mus, SC; NC Nat Bank; NATO Hosp, Belg. Exhib: 1st Army Art Competition, Ft Meade, Md, 69; 37th & 39th Semi-Annual Painting & Sculpture Exhib, Gallery of Contemporary Art, Winston-Salem, NC, 72 & 73; The Franklin Mint Watercolor Competition, 74; 2nd Nat Ann Exhib Whiskey Painters, Denver, 74; also 21 one-man shows. Awards: Honor Prize & Ten Gold Key Awards, Hallmark Galleries, 67; 37th Semi-Ann Painting & Sculpture Exhib First Hon Mention, Gallery Contemporary Art, 73; Best in Show, NC Watercolor Soc, 74. Mem: Whiskey Painters Am; NC Watercolor Soc; Rutherford Arts & Crafts Guild, NC (bd mem, 73-). Style & Technique: Realism; transparent watercolor landscapes and figures. Media: Transparent Watercolor, Oil. Dealer: Garden Gallery Hwy 70 West Raleigh NC 27603. Mailing Add: 106 N Lionel St Goldsboro NC 27530

COWLES, CHARLES
CURATOR, COLLECTOR
b Calif, Feb 7, 41. Study: Stanford Univ. Pos: Publ, Artforum Mag, 65-; cur mod art, Seattle Art Mus, 75- Mem: Int Coun Mus Mod Art. Collection: Contemporary. Mailing Add: PO Box 21228 Seattle WA 98111

COWLES, FLEUR
PAINTER, WRITER
Study: Pratt Inst, New York. Work: Seattle Art Mus, Wash; Museu Arte Mod, Sao Paulo, Brazil; Fisher Found, Iowa; Dart Indust, Orlando, Fla. Comn: Murals, Hotel Hilton, London, Eng & Athens, Greece. Exhib: VIII Biennale, Sao Paulo, Brazil, 65; Grosvenor Gallery,

London, 66; Seattle Mus Art, Wash, 70; Hammer Gallery, New York, 73; Cranbrook Mus, Bloomfield Hills, Mich, 74. Pos: Ed-in-chief, Flair Mag, 50-52; assoc ed, Look Mag, 48-55. Awards: LLD, Elmira Univ, NY. Mem: Royal Soc Arts; Univ Art Mus Coun, Berkeley, Calif. Style & Technique: Magic realism fantasy of jungle beasts and flowers. Media: Acrylic; Masonite, Hardboard. Publ: Auth, Bloody Precedent, 52; auth, The Case of Salvador Dali, 59; auth, The Hidden World of the Hadhramoutt, 63; illusr, Tiger Flower, 68; illusr, Lion and Blue, 74; auth, Friends and Memories, 76 & Romany Free, 77. Mailing Add: A5 Albany Piccadilly London England

COWLES, MR & MRS GARDNER
COLLECTORS
Mr Cowles, b Algona, Iowa, Jan 31, 03; Mrs Cowles, b Berkeley, Calif, Apr 14, 18. Pos: Mr Cowles, trustee, Mus Mod Art, New York; Mrs Cowles, mem bd, Mus City of New York & New York Botanical Garden. Collection: Contemporary paintings. Mailing Add: Cowles Communications Inc Suite 1612 630 Fifth Ave New York NY 10020

COWLES, RUSSELL
PAINTER
b Algona, Iowa, Oct 7, 87. Study: Dartmouth Col, AB, 09; Nat Acad Design; Art Students League; Am Acad in Rome; Century Asn; Grinnell Col, Hon DFA, 45; Dartmouth Col, DHL, 51; Cornell Univ, Hon DFA, 58; mural painting with Douglas Volk & Barry Faulker. Work: Denver Art Mus; Terre Haute Mus; Encycl Britannica Collection; Murdock Col, Univ Wichita; Dartmouth Col; plus others. Exhib: Carnegie Inst Int; Pa Acad Fine Arts; Whitney Mus Am Art; Los Angeles Co Mus Art; Calif Palace of Legion of Honor; plus many other group & one-man shows. Awards: Medal, Art Inst Chicago; Prizes, Denver Art Mus & Santa Barbara Mus Art. Bibliog: Monroe Wheeler (auth), Painters & Sculptors of Modern Art, Crowell, 42; Ernest W Watson (auth), Twenty Painters & How They Work, Watson-Guptill, 50; Ralph M Pearson (auth), The Modern Renaissance in American Art, Harper & Row, 54; plus others. Dealer: Kraushaar Galleries 1055 Madison Ave New York NY 10028. Mailing Add: 179 E 70th St New York NY 10021

COWLEY, EDWARD P
PAINTER, EDUCATOR
b Buffalo, NY, May 29, 25. Study: Albright Art Sch; Buffalo State Col, BS, 48; Columbia Univ, MA, 49; Nat Col Art, Dublin, Ireland, Ford Found fel, 55. Work: Albany Inst Hist & Art, NY; Schenectady Mus, NY; Smith Col, Northhampton, Mass; Colgate Univ, Hamilton, NY; Berkshire Mus, Pittsfield, Mass. Teaching: Prof art & chmn dept, State Univ NY Albany, 56-75, prof art, 76- Awards: State Univ NY Res Grant, 66 & 74. Style & Technique: Landscape painter with emphasis on architectural images. Media: Oil; Pastels; Stained Glass. Mailing Add: Box 198 Altamont NY 12009

COX, ALLYN
PAINTER
b New York, NY, June 5, 96. Study: Nat Acad Design; Art Students League; Am Acad Rome fel, 16-21. Work: Butler Inst Am Art, Youngstown, Ohio; Princeton Univ Mus, NJ; Nat Collection, Washington, DC. Comn: Ceilings & others, W A Clark Mem Libr, Univ Calif, Los Angeles, 24-28; six mural panels & others, Law Bldg, Univ Va, 31-33; murals & stained glass, George Washington Masonic Nat Mem, 52-75; frescos & others, US Capitol, Washington, DC, 62-; mosaics, U S Grant Mem, New York, 64-66. Exhib: Drawings & Paintings, Southampton Mus, NY, 53. Pos: Art comnr, New York City, 52-58. Awards: Rome Prize, Am Acad Rome, 16; Gold Medal of Honor, Archit League New York, 53; Gold Medal for Serv to Arts, Royal Arch Masons, 62. Mem: Academician Nat Acad Design; Nat Soc Mural Painters (pres, 7 yrs); Am Artists Prof League (pres, 50-52); Archit League New York (past vpres). Style & Technique: Traditional. Media: All Media. Mailing Add: 165 E 60th St New York NY 10022

COX, E MORRIS
COLLECTOR
b Santa Rosa, Calif, Feb 5, 03. Study: Univ Calif, AB; Harvard Univ Grad Sch Bus, MBA. Pos: Pres, San Francisco Mus Art, 55-60, trustee, currently; treas, Calif Acad Sci, 63-67, chmn bd trustees, currently; dir, Bay Area Educ TV Asn. Collection: Contemporary sculpture and painting. Mailing Add: 2361 Broadway San Francisco CA 94115

COX, ERNEST LEE
SCULPTOR, EDUCATOR
b Wilmington, NC, June 1, 37. Study: Col of William & Mary, BA(fine arts); Cranbrook Acad of Art, Bloomfield Hills, Mich, MFA(sculpture); Mich State Univ, Oakland. Work: St Petersburg Pub Libr, Fla; Eckerd Col, St Petersburg; Univ SFla, Tampa; 1st Nat Bank of Atlanta, Ga; 1st Nat Bank of Tampa, Fla. Comn: Steel sculptures, Wesley Manor Retirement Village, Jacksonville, Fla, 64, Fed Deposit Ins Corp, Washington, DC, 65 & Gulf Life Ins Co, Jacksonville, 67. Exhib: The 17th Va Artists Exhib, Va Mus of Fine Arts, Richmond, 58; 24th Ann NC Artists Exhib, NC Mus of Fine Arts, Raleigh, 61; Fla Sculptors & Printmakers Show, Norton Gallery, West Palm Beach, Fla, 62; 20th-22nd Southeastern Ann Exhibs, High Mus of Art, Atlanta, Ga, 65-67; Invitational Southeastern Sculpture Exhib, Atlanta Chamber of Commerce, 68 & 69; Fla 17, Pan Am Union, Washington, DC, 68; 15 Fla Artists Sculpture Exhib, Gallery of Contemp Art, Winston-Salem, NC, 70; one-man show, Jacksonville Mus of Art, Fla, 73. Teaching: From instr to prof sculpture, Univ SFla, Tampa, 62-, chmn art dept, 71-73. Awards: Second Prize, Fla Sculptors 7th Ann Exhib, 63; First Prize, Fla State Fair Fine Arts Exhib, 65; Purchase Prize, Southeastern Sculpture Exhib, Atlanta Chamber of Commerce, 69. Style & Technique: Abstract/symbolist. Media: Welded, forged steel; mixed-media. Dealer: J Camp 380 W Broadway New York NY. Mailing Add: Rt 2 Box 1604 Lutz FL 33549

COX, GARDNER
PAINTER
b Holyoke, Mass, Jan 22, 06. Study: Art Students League, 24; Harvard Univ, 24-27; Boston Mus Sch, 28-30; Mass Inst Technol, 29-31. Work: Nat Gallery Art & Nat Portrait Gallery, Washington, DC; Boston Mus Fine Arts; Fogg Art Mus, Harvard Univ, Cambridge, Mass; Addison Gallery Am Art, Andover, Mass. Comn: Portraits, Lessing Rosenwald, Nat Gallery Art, Hon Dean Acheson, State Dept, Washington, DC, 50, Robert Frost, Frost Libr, Amherst Col, Mass, 57, Justice Felix Frankfurter, Harvard Univ Law Sch, 60 & Robert F Kennedy, Nat Portrait Gallery, 68. Exhib: Carnegie Int, Pittsburgh, 41; Va Mus Fine Arts, Richmond, 46; Art Inst Chicago, 48, 49 & 51; Metrop Mus Art, New York, 50; Corcoran Gallery Art, Washington, DC, 75. Teaching: Head dept painting, Boston Mus Sch, 54-56. Pos: Exec comt, Boston Arts Festival, 55-65; exec comt, Mass Art Comn, 65- Awards: M V Kohnstamm Prize, Am Exhib Watercolors, Art Inst Chicago, 49 & Norman Wait Harris Bronze Medal, 60th Am Exhib, 51; Popular Prize, Boston Arts Festival, 60. Bibliog: Portrait painters, Life Mag, 2/3/41; Experiments in New England, Time Mag, 7/21/52; Portraits by Cox, Newsweek Mag, 6/15/53. Mem: Nat Inst Arts & Lett; Nat Acad Design; Am Acad Arts & Sci; Am Acad in Rome (trustee, 63); Cambridge Art Asn. Media: Oil, Watercolor, Tempera. Dealer: Portraits Inc 41 E 57th St New York NY 10022. Mailing Add: c/o Fenway Studios 30 Ipswich St Boston MA 02215

COX, J W S
PAINTER, INSTRUCTOR
b Yonkers, NY, May 18, 11. Study: Pratt Inst Art Sch; Acad Colorossi, Paris, France, with Othon Friesz; Boston Univ; Eliot O'Hara Sch Art. Work: Boston Mus Fine Arts; Ford Publ. Exhib: Audubon Artists; Am Watercolor Soc; Ala Watercolor Soc; Miss Watercolor Soc; Springfield Art League; plus others. Pos: Pres, New Eng Sch Art & Design, 61- Awards: Prizes, Rockport, Mass, 51 & 60 & Washington Watercolor Club, 57. Publ: Contribr, articles & illus to Christian Sci Monitor. Mailing Add: 28 Newbury St Boston MA 02116

COX, JOHN ROGERS
PAINTER
b Terre Haute, Ind, Mar 24, 15. Study: Univ Pa, BFA; Pa Acad Fine Arts, 38. Work: Cleveland Mus; Butler Inst; Springfield Mus, Mass & pvt collections. Exhib: Carnegie Inst; Pa Acad Fine Arts; Metrop Mus, New York; Boston Inst Art; Cleveland Mus; plus others. Teaching: Instr figure drawing & painting, Art Inst Chicago, 48-60, asst prof figure drawing & painting, 60-65. Pos: Dir, Swope Gallery, 41-43. Awards: Prizes, Metrop Mus, 42 & Carnegie Inst, 43 & 44. Mailing Add: Rte 1 Chelan WA 98816

COX, MARION AVERAL
PAINTER, INSTRUCTOR
b Washingtonville, Ohio. Study: With H Gauguin, W Goodrich, H Radio, B I Payne, C Wallace, J M Jehu, N Bel Geddes, Max Reinhardt (Ger), and many others. Exhib: Sixty Text Books, Am Inst Graphic Arts, Grand Cent Palace, 44 & 54; 13th Ann Ohio Artists & Craftsmen, Massillon Mus, 48; 14th New Years Show, Butler Art Inst, 49; American Painting Today, Metrop Mus Art. Teaching: Teacher art theory & practice, Art-O-Technix Inst, Carefree, Ariz, 75- Pos: Art dir, Universal Studios, Universal City, Calif, 28-30; tech illusr, My Own Studio & gallery, Salem, Ohio, 38-52; architect, Translux Construct, 50-; author, Readex Book Exchange, Cave Creek, Ariz, 68- Mem: Am Asn Advan Sci. Style & Technique: Integrated-TOTALL-that which reaches out for the social nexus contemp. Media: Pen, Ink; Watercolor, Oil. Publ: Illusr, E T Smith (auth), Exploring Biology, 38. Mailing Add: Box 325 Cave Creek AZ 85331

COX, RICHARD WILLIAM
ART HISTORIAN, WRITER
b Los Angeles, Calif, July 13, 42. Study: Univ Calif, Los Angeles, BA(hist), 64, MA(hist), 66; Univ Wis, Madison, MA(art hist), 70, PhD(art hist), 73. Teaching: Instr Am art, Univ Wis, River Falls, 71-74; from asst prof to assoc prof Am art & hist of prints, La State Univ, 74- Awards: Solon Buck Award for Best Article, Minn Hist, 75; Nat Endowment for the Humanities Fel, 75. Bibliog: Matthew Baigell (auth), The American Scene: American Painting of the 1930s, Praeger, 74; James Dennis (auth), Grant Wood, A Study in Art & Culture, Viking, 75. Mem: Col Art Asn; Art Educ Asn; La Hist Soc. Res: American painting, graphic arts in 1900-1945 period; contemporary art. Publ: Auth, Coney Island: urban symbol in American art, NY Hist Soc Quart, 75; auth, Wanda Gag and the bite of the picture book, Minn Hist, 75; auth, Art Young: cartoonist from the middle border, Wis Mag Hist, 77; auth, Caroline Durieux: the lithographs of the 1930s and 1940s, La State Univ Press, 77; auth, Adolf Dehn—jazz age satirist, Arch Am Art J, 78. Mailing Add: Dept of Fine Arts La State Univ Baton Rouge LA 70803

CRABLE, JAMES HARBOUR
MULTI-MEDIA ARTIST, INSTRUCTOR
b Bronx, NY, Aug 30, 39. Study: State Univ NY Col Buffalo, BS, 62; Rochester Inst Technol, NY, MFA, 66; Chelsea Sch Art, London, Eng, HDA, 70. Work: Mem Art Gallery, Rochester, NY; Everson Mus Art, Syracuse, NY; Univ NMex, Albuquerque; State Univ NY Art Collection, Albany. Exhib: Invitational Exhib, Mus Mod Art, Oxford, Eng, 72; Gibbes Gallery, Charleston, SC, 74; one-man show, Va Mus Fine Arts, Richmond, 76; 35 Artists in the Southwest, High Mus Art, Atlanta, Ga, 76-77; Realists, Southeastern Ctr Contemp Art, Winston-Salem, NC, 76; La Grange Nat, La Grange Col, Ga, 77. Teaching: Asst prof art survey, drawing & art educ, State Univ Col Brockport, NY, 66-69; lectr found studies, Croydon Col Art, Surrey, Eng, 70-71; asst prof drawing, art educ & art survey, James Madison Univ, Harrisonburg, Va, 73- Awards: Cert of Distinction, Va Artists 1975, F&M Bank, Richmond, Va, 75; Spec Commendation Award, 44th Southeastern Artists Competition, Southeastern Ctr for Contemp Art, Winston-Salem, NC, 76; Helen B Bonnie Mem Award (first place), Galaxy I, Norfolk, Va, Jewish Community Ctr, Tidewater, Va, 76. Mem: Col Art Asn Am; Va Art Educ Asn. Style & Technique: Photo collage techniques. Media: Photo-collage; drawing. Mailing Add: 925 College Ave Harrisonburg VA 22801

CRAFT, DOUGLAS D
PAINTER, EDUCATOR
b Greene, NY, Oct 20, 24. Study: Univ Iowa; Univ Chicago; Art Inst Chicago, BFA; Syracuse Univ; Univ NMex, MA. Work: Mus Mod Art & Whitney Mus Am Art, New York; Art Inst Chicago; Univ Ky, Lexington; Univ NMex, Albuquerque. Comn: Paintings, comn by Mr & Mrs Daniel Weinstein for Edward Weinstein Ctr for Performing Arts, Nat Col Educ, Evanston, Ill, 72. Exhib: One-man shows, Royal Col Art Galleries, London, Eng, 64, Univ Ky Art Galleries, 64, Mus Art, Carnegie Inst, Pittsburgh, Pa, 68, XXth Century West Galleries, Ltd, New York, 68 & Fischbach Galleries, New York, 73. Teaching: Assoc prof painting, Art Inst Chicago, 55-66; assoc prof painting, Carnegie Inst Technol, 66-69; vis artist, Cooper Union, 69-71; prof painting, Col New Rochelle, 71- Pos: Vis artist in residence, Univ Ky, 64; Am artist in residence, Royal Col Art, 64-65; vis artist-critic, Sunderland Col Art, Eng, 65; vis critic-artist, Gloucestershire Col Art, Cheltenham, 65. Awards: Harry Allison Logan Mem Award, Chautauqua Inst, NY, 63; Logan Bronze Medal & Prize, Art Inst Chicago, 66; Jury Award/Distinction in Painting, Mus of Art, Carnegie Inst Int, 68. Bibliog: R B Freeman (auth), D Craft, Univ Ky, 64; Max Wykes-Joyce (auth), Douglas Craft, Arts Rev, London, 64; Cordelia Oliver (auth), Exhibitions at Edinburgh, Guardian, 65. Style & Technique: Abstract. Dealer: Fischbach Gallery 29 W 57th St New York NY 10019. Mailing Add: 240 Ogden Ave Jersey City NJ 07307

CRAFT, JOHN RICHARD
MUSEUM DIRECTOR
b Uniontown, Pa, June 15, 09. Study: Phillips Acad, Andover, Mass; Yale Univ; Art Students League; Univ Paris, 36-38; Acad Julien; and with Andre l'Hote; Am Sch Classical Studies, Athens, Greece, 37-39; Johns Hopkins Univ, MA & PhD. Pos: Dir, Washington Co Mus Fine Arts, Hagerstown, Md, 40-49; dir, Columbia Mus Art, SC, 50-77, dir emer, 77- Mem: Am Asn Mus; Southeastern Mus Conf (pres, 52-55); SC Fedn Mus (pres, 70-71); Am Inst Designers. Mailing Add: Columbia Mus of Art Senate & Bull Sts Columbia SC 29201

CRAIG, EUGENE
EDITORIAL CARTOONIST
b Ft Wayne, Ind, Sept 5, 16. Comn: Designer US Postage Stamp Battle of Brooklyn, 51. Pos: Cartoonist, Ft Wayne News-Sentinel, 34-51; cartoonist, Brooklyn Eagle, 51-55; cartoonist, Columbus Dispatch, 55- Awards: Freedoms Found Top Award, three times. Mem: Am Asn Ed Cartoonists. Mailing Add: 73 E Kramer St Canal Winchester OH 43110

CRAIG, MARTIN
SCULPTOR, RESTORER
b Paterson, NJ, Nov 2, 06. Study: City Col New York, BS. Work: Nelson A Rockefeller Collection; Kalamazoo Art Inst, Mich; Montreal Star, PQ. Comn: Eternal light & three candelabra, Temple Mishkan Tefila, Newton, Mass; ark & two candelabra, Fifth Ave Synagogue, New York; ten commandments sculpture, Temple Beth El, Providence, RI; candelabrum, ten commandments sculpture & eternal light, Temple Israel, New Rochelle, NY. Exhib: Salon Jeune Sculpture Ann, Paris, 50-54; Salon Mai, Paris, 52-54; Galerie Colette Allendy, Paris, 54; New Talent Exhib, Mus Mod Art, New York, 55; Guild Hall, East Hampton, NY Garden Exhib, 74. Teaching: Lectr sculpture, Cooper Union Art Sch, 55-57; lectr sculpture, New York Univ, 56-68; asst prof sculpture & drawing, Sarah Lawrence Col, 57-58. Pos: Welder & chaser, Sculptors Workshop & Foundry, Yonkers, 67-68. Awards: First Prize, Organic Design Competition, Mus Mod Art, 40; Purchase Award, Longview Found, 62; Mark Rothko Award, 71. Media: Welded Metals; Plastics. Mailing Add: 795 Accabonac Hwy East Hampton NY 11937

CRAIG, NANCY ELLEN
PAINTER
b Bronxville, NY. Study: Acad Julien, Paris, France; Art Students League, New York; Hans Hofmann Sch, Provincetown, Mass. Work: Metrop Mus Art, New York; Baltimore Mus; New Britain Art Inst. Comn: Portraits comn by Assoc Justice Stanley Reed, Supreme Ct Bldg, Washington, DC, Gov & Mrs Herbert Lehman, New York, Mrs Franklin D Roosevelt, Jr, New York, Duke of Argyll, 69 & Princess Marie Luise of Prussia, 74. Exhib: Nat Acad Design, New York; Audubon Artists, New York; Allied Artists Am, New York; one-woman shows, Graham Gallery, New York & Galeria Betica, Madrid, Spain. Awards: First Benjamin Altman Figure Prize, Nat Acad Design, 57; Gold Medal of Honor, Allied Artists Am; Patron's Prize, Audubon Artists. Bibliog: Nardi Campion (auth), Nancy Ellen Craig & her portraits, Am Artist. Style & Technique: Portraits and large figure paintings, often mythological subjects. Media: Oil on Canvas. Publ: Auth, Portrait painting in oil, 60. Dealer: Grand Central Galleries Hotel Biltmore Madison Ave & 43rd St New York NY 10017; Galeria Betica General Goded 12 Madrid Spain. Mailing Add: Box 57 Truro MA 02666

CRAMER, ABRAHAM
PAINTER, CARTOONIST
b Kiev, Russia; US citizen. Study: Kiev Sch Fine Arts, Russia; Acad Fine Arts, Mexico City, Mex. Comn: Portraits & landscapes. Exhib: Paintings, Mexico City, 30. Media: Oil, Watercolor, Pastel. Publ: Contribr, cartoons in, Sat Eve Post, New Yorker, Ladies Home J, Redbook, King Features Syndicate, Esquire, True & var other mag. Mailing Add: 1909 Quentin Rd Brooklyn NY 11229

CRAMER, RICHARD CHARLES
PAINTER, EDUCATOR
b Appleton, Wis, Aug 14, 32. Study: Layton Sch Art, BFA; Univ Wis-Milwaukee, BS, Univ Wis-Madison, MS, 61, MFA, 62. Work: Pa Acad Fine Arts; Everhart Mus, Scranton, Pa; Everson Mus, Syracuse, NY; Univ Wis; Southern Univ, New Orleans; plus others. Exhib: Syracuse Regional, 63-65; Drawing Biennial, Norfolk Mus Art, 65; Drawings, Smithsonian Inst Traveling Exhib, 65; Philadelphia Art Festival, 67; Bertha Schaefer Gallery, 71; one-man shows, Gloria Cortella Gallery, New York, 77-78, Barbara Fiedler Gallery, Washington, DC, 77 & Pa Acad Fine Arts, Philadelphia, 78; plus others. Teaching: Instr drawing & design, Univ Wis, 60-62; instr painting & drawing, Elmira Col, 62-66; instr painting & drawing, Tyler Sch Art, Temple Univ, 66-70, assoc prof, 70- Awards: Prizes, Milwaukee Art Inst, 54, Syracuse Allied Artists, 64 & Munson-Williams-Proctor Inst, Utica, NY, 65; plus others. Mem: Col Art Asn Am; Am Asn Univ Prof. Style & Technique: Abstract color field; precise color notation; all over lyrical style. Media: Acrylic. Mailing Add: 723 Chestnut St Philadelphia PA 19106

CRANE, BARBARA BACHMANN
PHOTOGRAPHER, EDUCATOR
b Chicago, Ill, Mar 19, 28. Study: Mills Col, with Alfred Neumeyer, 45-48; NY Univ, BA(art hist), 50; Inst of Design, Ill Inst Technol, MS(photog), 66, with Aaron Siskind. Work: Libr of Cong, Washington, DC; Int Mus of Photog, George Eastman House, Rochester, NY; Art Inst of Chicago; Pasadena Mus of Art, Calif. Comn: 26 photomurals (film collage, sequential imagry; 8 ft x 8 ft & 7 ft x 9 ft), Corp Hq in Employee Canteen Areas, Baxter Travenol Labs, Deerfield, Ill, 76; Chicago Epic (photomural, 4 ft x 26 ft), Chicago Bank of Commerce, Standard Oil Bldg, Chicago. Exhib: One-woman shows, Friends of Photog, Carmel, Calif, 69 & 75, Limited Image Gallery, Chicago, 71, People of North Portal, Mus of Sci & Indust, Chicago, 72 & Univ Iowa Mus, Iowa City, 73 & 75; group shows, New Acquisitions, Pasadena Mus of Art, 70, Being Without Clothes, Hayden Gallery, Mass Inst of Technol, Cambridge, Mass, 70, Bibliot Nat du Que, Can, 74 & The City, Mus of Contemp Art, Chicago, 77. Collections Arranged: Ill Landmark Buildings, Chicago Comn Hist & Archit Landmarks, continually exhibited. Teaching: Assoc prof photog, Sch of Art Inst of Chicago, 67-; artist-in-residence, Oxbow Summer Art Sch, 76; vis prof photog, Philadelphia Col of Art, 77. Pos: Office photogr, Chicago Comn Hist & Archit Landmarks, 73- Awards: Nat Endowment for Arts grant, 75. Mem: Soc Photog Educ (mem bd, 72-76); Friends of Photog (trustee, 75-78). Style & Technique: Abstract, sequential and social documentary photography. Publ: Illusr, Fragments (4 Nudes), New York, 68-69; auth, Portfolios, Popular Photog, 67 & 74; auth, Portfolio, Creative Camera, 74; auth, Portfolio, Lightwork, 74; auth (catalogue), The Photographer and the City, Mus of Contemp Art, Chicago, 76. Mailing Add: 3164 N Hudson Chicago IL 60657

CRANE, FRANCES ANN
See Sherwood, A

CRANE, JAMES
PAINTER, CARTOONIST
b Hartshorne, Okla, May 21, 27. Study: Albion Col, BA; State Univ Iowa, MA; Mich State Univ, MFA. Teaching: Prof art, Eckerd Col, currently. Awards: Awards, Fla State Fair, 65, Fla Art Group, 65 & Soc Four Arts, Palm Beach, Fla, 67; plus others. Media: Acrylic Collage, Plexiglas. Publ: Auth, On Edge, 65, Great Teaching Machine, 66 & Parables, 71, John Knox; auth, Inside Out, 67; illusr, A Funny Thing Happened on the Way to Heaven, 69; plus others. Mailing Add: Dept of Art Eckerd Col St Petersburg FL 33733

CRANE, MICHAEL PATRICK
PHOTOGRAPHER, PERFORMANCE ARTIST
b St Louis, Mo, Dec 24, 48. Study: Sch of Art Inst Chicago, MFA(design & commun), 76. Work: Fluxus W Arch, San Diego, Calif; Jean Brown Arch, Tyringham Inst, Mass; Arch Sohm, Markgroningen, WGer; Mus Contemp Art, Univ Sao Paulo, Brazil; Mod Mus, Stockholm, Sweden. Exhib: Mus Contemp Art, Univ Sao Paulo, 74 & 77; 25-2000, Name Gallery, Chicago, 75; Mus Contemp Art, Chicago, 75; one-man show, Galerie s:t Petri, Lund, Sweden, 76; Art in the Mail (toured NZ), Manawatu Gallery, NZ, 76; 03-23-03, Mus Contemp Art, Montreal, Que & Nat Gallery Can, Ottawa, Ont, 77; Artwords & Bookworks (contribr, catalogue), Los Angeles Inst Contemp Art, Los Angeles, Calif, 78. Collections Arranged: Chicago (co-arranger), Name Gallery, 73. Teaching: Vis artist performance, Univ Chicago, 77 & Calif State Univ Univ, Sacramento, 77; vis lectr mail art, San Diego State Univ, 78. Pos: Original mem & co-dir, Name Gallery, Chicago, 73-74; ed, Running Dog Press, San Diego, 74-; adminr, All the Chicago Fog Performance Gallery, Chicago, 75-76; res fel, Inst Advan Studies in Contemp Art, San Diego, Calif, 77- Mem: Assoc Art Publ (adv bd mem, 77-). Style & Technique: Structural, serial and conceptual works incorporating photographs, language and/or kinesthetics. Media: Books, Posters, Live Performances. Res: Mail Art. Publ: Contribr, Anti-Object Art, Northwestern Univ Press, 74; auth, Fill in This Space, 75 & Landscapes I'd Love to Perform/Do, 76, Running Dog Press. Mailing Add: 7720 Missy Ct St Louis MO 63123

CRANE, ROY (CAMPBELL)
CARTOONIST, WRITER
b Abilene, Tex, Nov 22, 01. Study: Hardin-Simmons Univ, 18-19; Univ Tex, 19-22; Chicago Acad Fine Arts, 20; asst to H T Webster, 23-24; Rollins Col, Hon LHD, 57. Work: Carnegie Libr, Syracuse Univ, NY; Univ Tex Libr, Austin. Exhib: Mus Arts Decoratifs, Palais Louvre, Paris, 68; Smithsonian Inst, 69; var exhibs with Nat Cartoonists Soc & Newspaper Comics Coun Collections. Pos: Staff mem, Art Dept, New York World, 22-24. Awards: Billy De Beck Mem Award, Nat Cartoonists Soc, 50; USN Distinguished Pub Serv Award, 57; Best Story Strip Cartoonist, Nat Cartoonists Soc, 65. Mem: Nat Cartoonists Soc; Newspaper Comics Coun. Media: Ink. Publ: Auth-cartoonist, Wash Tubbs & Captain Easy (comic strips), Newspaper Enterprise Asn Serv, Cleveland, 24-43; auth-cartoonist, Buz Sawyer (comic strip), King Features Serv, New York, 43- Mailing Add: 5585 Jessamine Lane Orlando FL 32809

CRANER, ROBERT ROGERS
PAINTER, EDUCATOR
b New York, NY, Aug 13, 35. Study: New York Univ, BS, 68; Columbia Univ, anat; Art Students League, anat with Robert Beverly Hale, 68-71; City Col, New York, MA, 70, with Robert Borgatta; also study with Niever Billmyer & Frank Mason. Work: Permanent Collection, Providence Col, RI; Cent Soya Co, Ft Wayne, Ind. Exhib: One-man shows, Cerberus Gallery, New York, 69, Providence Col, 70 & Italiaander Gallery, New York, 74; MacDowell Colony Artist 1970, Thorne Art Gallery, Keene State Col, NH, 70; Fac Exhib, Fashion Inst Technol, State Univ New York, 72. Teaching: Instr radical anatomy & unconventional representationalism, Sch Visual Arts, New York, 68-75; vis instr drawing & figure, Pratt Inst, 72; instr basic drawing & advanced anat, Parsons Sch Design, 73-75. Awards: Fel-in-residence, Huntington Hartford Found, Pacific Palisades, Calif, 64, MacDowell Colony, 70 & Va Ctr for Creative Arts, Charlottesville, 73 & 75. Bibliog: Victor A Acconci (auth), Reviews & Previews, Art News, 11/69; Bradford J Swan (auth), Four Exhibitions, All of them good, Providence Sunday J, 3/8/70; Lawrence Campbell (auth), review in Art News, 4/74. Mem: Art Students League; Col Art Asn. Style & Technique: Two- and three-dimensional problem solving; painterly realism involving simultaneity, different eye levels of subject viewed. Media: Oil, Watercolor. Dealer: James Caradine 301 E 64th St New York NY 10021. Mailing Add: Univ Calif Exten Div Santa Barbara City Col Santa Barbara CA 93106

CRAVEN, ROY CURTIS, JR
GALLERY DIRECTOR, EDUCATOR
b Cherokee Bluffs, Ala, July 29, 24. Study: Univ Chattanooga, BA, 49; Art Students League, 49-50, with George Grosz, Yasuo Kuniyoshi & Byron Browne; Univ Fla, MFA, 56. Work: Va Mus Art, Richmond; Mus Arqueolgia y Etnologia Guatemala, Guatemala City; Esso Standard Oil Collection, New York; New Col, Sarasota, Fla; Chattanooga Art Asn, Tenn. Comn: Sculptural relief, Civic Auditorium, Jacksonville, Fla, 62; sculptural relief, Duval Fed Savings & Loan Asn, Jacksonville, 62; archit relief, facade of Med Bldg, Wesley Manor Retirement Village, St Johns Co, Fla, 63; archit relief, facade of Music & Fine Arts Bldg, Jacksonville Univ, Fla, 64. Exhib: American Prints & Watercolors, Metrop Mus Art, New York, 50; Forecast, 57-58 & Painting of the Year, 61-62, Am Fedn Arts touring exhibs, US; also exhibs at Delgado Mus, New Orleans, La & Four Arts Club, Palm Beach, Fla, several yrs. Collections Arranged: Miniatures & Small Sculptures from India, 66; Spec loan retrospective exhib of works by Yasuo Kuniyoshi, 69; The Maya, a spec exhib of photog & artifacts, 70. Teaching: Prof art, Univ Fla, 54-, head advert design, 55-65. Pos: Dir univ gallery, Univ Fla, 66-, dir, Ctr Latin Am & Tropical Arts, 72- Awards: Fulbright sr res scholar to India, 62-63; four Ctr Latin Am Studies travel grants to Cent Am, 68-75; Am Philos Soc Res Travel Grant, India, 76. Mem: Am Asn Mus; Southeastern Mus Conf (bd mem, ed jour, 67-); Asia Soc; Asn Asian Studies; fel Royal Soc Arts. Res: Publications in ancient and contemporary art of India; pre-Columbian art. Publ: Auth, Ten Contemporary Painters from India (catalog), 63; auth, Miniatures and small sculptures from India (catalog), 66; contribr, A short report on contemporary painting in India, Art J, spring 65; Ceremonial Centers of the Maya, 74; auth, A Concise History of Indian Art, London, 76. Mailing Add: 6818 NW 65th Ave Gainesville FL 32601

CRAVEN, WAYNE
ART HISTORIAN, WRITER
b Pontiac, Ill, Dec 7, 30. Study: John Herron Art Sch, Indianapolis, Ind; Ind Univ, BA, 55, MA, 57; Columbia Univ, PhD, 63. Collections Arranged: Co-cur, Exhib Celebrating the Creative American (sculpture sect), White House, Washington, DC, 65; guest cur, 200 Years of American Sculpture, Whitney Mus Am Art, New York, 76. Teaching: Instr art hist, Wheaton Col, Norton, Mass, 58-60; prof art hist, Univ Del, Newark, 60- Pos: Mem bd ed, Am Art Rev, Los Angeles, 73- & The Am Art J, New York, 74-; mem adv bd, Daniel Chester French Papers, Nat Trust, Washington, DC, 75- Mem: Col Art Asn; Victorian Soc in Am (mem adv comt, 72). Res: Eighteenth and nineteenth century American painting and sculpture. Publ: Auth, Sculpture in America, T Y Crowell, Co, New York, 68; co-auth, Britannica Encycl Am Art, Chanticlair Press, 74; plus many jour articles on Am art. Mailing Add: 300 Dove Dr Newark DE 19713

CRAWFORD, CATHERINE BETTY
PAINTER
b Ingersoll, Ont, Feb 5, 10. Study: Univ Toronto, BA; summer study with Eliot O'Hara, & at Doon Sch & Queen's Univ; also study with Gordon Payne, E H Varley & Carl Schaeffer.

Work: London Art Gallery, Ont; Arch Can Painter-Etchers, Hamilton, Ont; Woodstock Art Gallery, Ont. Exhib: Western Art League Shows, London, Ont & Soc of Can Painter-Etchers, various yrs; one-man shows, London, Burlington & Woodstock, 48-67 & London, 73; Brantford, 73. Pos: Mem bd, Ingersoll Creative Arts Centre. Awards: Purchase Award, London Women's Comt at Gallery, 53; First Prize for Watercolor, Western Fair, London, 64. Gallery, 74. Mem: Mem: Print & Drawing Coun of Can. Style & Technique: Direct, on the spot painting of natural forms and atmosphere. Media: Watercolor. Mailing Add: 1 Duke Lane Ingersoll ON Can

CRAWFORD, JOHN MCALLISTER, JR
COLLECTOR, PATRON
b Parkersburg, WVa, Aug 6, 13. Study: Brown Univ, AB, 37, LittD, 64; Harvard Univ Sch Educ; Syracuse Univ, LHD, 67. Exhib: William Morris Collection shown at Brown Univ, 59 & Grolier Club, New York, 64; Chinese Calligraphy & Painting Collection shown at Morgan Libr, New York, 62, Fogg Art Mus, Harvard Univ, 63, William Rockhill Nelson Gallery Art, Kansas City, Mo, 63; Victoria & Albert Mus, London, Eng, 65; Nat Mus, Stockholm, Sweden, 65; Mus Cernuschi, Paris, France, 66. Pos: Trustee, Asheville Sch, NC, 50-74; libr comt, Brown Univ, 58-73; vis comt, Fogg Art Mus, Harvard Univ, 61-66; mem coun friends, Columbia Univ Librs, 67-; mem art adv comt, Brown Univ, 74- Mem: China Inst Am (chmn art comt, 67-77, trustee, 71-; Friends of the Asia House Gallery (treas, 64-69); fel Morgan Libr (music comt, 63-); Century Asn; Grolier Club (coun, 58-76, chmn exhib comt, 65-70). Interest: Chinese art in calligraphy, painting, also early bronzes, gilt bronzes, sculpture, jade & ceramics. Collection: Chinese calligraphy & painting; William Morris & the Kelmscott Press; Medieval manuscripts; early printed books; other printed masterpieces & modern painting. Publ: Chinese calligraphy, Philadelphia Mus, 71; Friends of Wen Cheng-Ming, China Inst, 74; auth, William Morris and the Art of the Book, Morgan Libr, 76; contribr, Wango Weng, auth, Chinese Calligraphy & Painting—Crawford Collection, Dover, 78. Mailing Add: 46 E 82nd St New York NY 10028

CRAWFORD, MEL
PAINTER, ILLUSTRATOR
b Toronto, Ont, Sept 10, 25. Study: Royal Ontario Col Art, Toronto; also watercolor with John Pike. Work: Anchorage Mus, Alaska; Mattatuck Mus, Waterbury, Conn; Stamford Mus, Conn. Exhib: Conn Watercolor Soc, Hartford; Hudson Valley Art Asn, White Plains, NY; Allied Artists Am, Am Watercolor Soc, New York; Franklin Mint Gallery Am Art, Franklin Center, Pa, 74. Awards: Salmagundi Award, Am Watercolor Soc, 69; Thora M Eriksen Award, Hudson Valley Art Asn, 71; Franklin Mint Gold Medal Award for Distinguished Watercolor Art, Franklin Mint Gallery Am Art, 73. Mem: Allied Artists Am; Hudson Valley Art Asn; Kent Art Asn; Housatonic Art League (vpres, 72-74). Style & Technique: Marines and landscapes. Media: Watercolor, Acrylic. Publ: Illusr of 300 children's books, magazines & calendars. Mailing Add: 21 Mountain View Ave New Milford CT 06776

CRAWFORD, RALSTON
PAINTER, LITHOGRAPHER
b St Catharines, Ont, Sept 25, 06; US citizen. Study: Otis Art Inst, Los Angeles, 27; Pa Acad Fine Arts, with Henry Breckenridge & Henry McCarter, 27-30; Barnes Found, 28-30; Acad Colarossi & Acad Scandinave, Paris, 32-33; Columbia Univ, 33. Work: Metrop Mus Art; Whitney Mus Am Art; Sheldon Mem Art Gallery; Libr Cong; Mus Fine Arts, Houston; plus others. Exhib: Corcoran Gallery Art; Metrop Mus Art; Whitney Mus Am Art; retrospective exhibs, Univ Ill, 66 & Creighton Univ, 68; plus others. Teaching: Lectr mod art & instr, Cincinnati Art Acad, 40; instr, Buffalo Sch Fine Arts, 41-42; guest dir, Honolulu Sch Art; instr, Art Sch Brooklyn Mus, 48; instr, Cincinnati Art Acad, 49, Univ Minn, 49, La State Univ, 50, Univ Colo, 52, New Sch Social Res, 52-57, Univ Colo, 58, Univ Southern Calif, 60, Univ Ky High Sch Wk, 60, Hofstra Col, 60-62 & Univ Minn, 61; Ford Found & Am Fedn Arts vis artist, Sheldon Art Gallery, Univ Nebr, 65; vis artist, Univ Ill, 66. Pos: Res consult, New Orleans Jazz Arch, Tulane Univ, 45; art observer, Bikini Atom Bomb Test, 46. Awards: Tiffany Found Award, 31; Purchase Prize, Metrop Mus Art, 42; plus others. Bibliog: Richard B Freeman (auth), Lithographs of Ralston Crawford, Univ Ky, 62; Lee Nordness (ed), incl in, Art USA: now, C J Bucher, 62; Barbara Rose (auth), incl in, American Art Since 1900, a Critical Essay, Praeger, 67; plus others. Publ: Illusr, Stars: Their Facts & Legends, 40; illusr, covers & articles, In: Fortune Mag, 44-46; contribr, Le Figaro, Brit Jazz J, Le Jazz Hot & others. Dealer: Middendorf-Lane Gallery Washington DC; Corcoran Greenberg Gallery 800 Douglas Entrance Coral Gables FL 33134. Mailing Add: 60 Gramercy Park New York NY 10010

CRAWFORD, WILLIAM H
CARTOONIST, SCULPTOR
b Hammond, Ind, Mar 18, 13. Study: Chicago Acad Fine Arts; Ohio State Univ, BA, 35; Grande Chaumiere, Paris. Work: Syracuse Univ; Libr of Cong; cartoons, Can Pavilion, Montreal. Exhib: Italy, Paris & Israel. Teaching: Instr, Newark Sch Fine & Appl Arts & Rutgers Univ. Pos: Ed cartoonist, Newark Eve News, NJ, 38-61; chief ed cartoonist, Newspaper Enterprise Asn, New York, 62- Awards: Prize, Cleveland Mus Art, 34; Best Ed Page Cartoonist, Nat Cartoonists Soc, 56-58 & 66. Mem: Nat Cartoonists Soc (pres, 60-61); Asn Am Ed Cartoonists. Publ: Contribr, nat mags; illusr, Barefoot Boy with Cheek, 43, Zebra Derby, 46 & others. Mailing Add: 128 E 28th St New York NY 10016

CRAWLEY, WESLEY V
SCULPTOR, EDUCATOR
b Akron, Ohio, Mar 1, 22. Study: Chicago Art Inst, 37; Univ Ariz, 47-48; Univ Ore, AB, 52, MS, 59. Work: Dream & Mass, Space & Motion, Univ SC; Requiem, Greenville Art Ctr, NC; Study for Tomorrow, ECarolina Univ, Greenville; Superstition, Pembroke State Univ, NC. Comn: Cascades (stone carving), Bethel Sch Dist, Ore, 58; Tomorrow (life size bronze), People's Bank & Trust Co, 65; Garden Figure (cast lead), Wright Chem Corp, Acme, NC, 66; Portrait of W E Debnam, comn by family, Greenville, 67; portrait, Anthony Brannock, II, Raleigh, NC, 74; plus many other garden sculptures & portraits. Exhib: Pac Northwest Inst Sculpture, Portland Art Mus, Ore, 56 & Vancouver Art Mus, BC, 58; NC Artists Traveling Show, Raleigh Art Mus & through state, 64; Southern Asn Sculptors Traveling Show, galleries of the South & Southwest, 67; Art & Academia, NC Nat Bank Traveling Exhib, 73 & 74. Teaching: Prof drawing & sculpture, ECarolina Univ, 59-, coordr I found, 72- Awards: Contemp Southern Sculpture Purchase Award, Univ SC, 68; Small Southern Sculpture Purchase Award, Southern Asn Sculptors, 67; Purchase Award, NC Nat Bank Show, 74. Bibliog: J Hall (auth), Hall Marks (interview), Raleigh News & Observer, 8/4/63; L Holmes (auth), article in, Rocky Mount News & Observer, NC, 56; L Siegel (auth), rev in, Art Rev, summer 66. Mem: Southern Asn Sculptors (former bd mem). Style & Technique: Romantic realist with a love of subtle surface enrichment. Mailing Add: 104 Dogwood Dr Greenville NC 27834

CREAMER, PAUL LYLE
ART DEALER
b Chicago, Ill, Sept 3, 28. Study: Albion Col, BA; NY Univ, grad study. Pos: Dir, New Bertha Schaefer Gallery, Inc. Specialty: Contemporary American and European paintings, sculpture and graphics. Mailing Add: 983 Park Ave New York NY 10022

CREATORE, MARY-ALICE
SUMIE ARTIST, PAINTER
b New York, NY, Aug 11, 20. Study: Nat Acad Design; Art Students League, Nippon Club, New York; also studies in Japan. Comn: Japanese wall murals, KiKu Restaurant, 74. Exhib: Sumie Soc Am, 64 & 73; Nippon Club, 68 & 69. Awards: Cup of Japanese Consulate (First Prize), 64; Silver Cup, Charles Gracie Award (First Prize), 68; Silver Cup, Nippon Club Award (First Prize), 69. Mem: Sumie Soc Am (treas, 74, bd dir). Style & Technique: Sumie artist, Japanese. Media: Brush on Rice Paper; Watercolor, Oil. Mailing Add: 255 Mohegan Way Ft Lee NJ 07024

CREECH, FRANKLIN UNDERWOOD
PAINTER, PRINTMAKER
b Smithfield, NC, Oct 14, 41. Study: Univ NC, Chapel Hill, summers 63 & 64; Duke Univ, BA, 64; Fla State Univ, MS, 66; Det Danske Selskab, Holbaëk, Denmark, printing with Hugo Arne Bock. Work: Duke Univ Art Mus; NC Nat Bank; Appalachian State Univ; Atlantic Christian Col; Mint Mus, Charlotte, NC. Exhib: 33rd & 34th NC Artist Exhib, 71 & 72; 1971 Crafts Exhib, Gallery Contemp Art, Winston-Salem, NC, 71; 8th Int Grand Prix du Cote d'Azur, Cannes, France, 72; 1972 Regional Painting Exhib, Lauren Roger Mus, Laurel, Miss, 72. Teaching: Instr pottery, design & graphics, Gaston Col, Dallas, NC, 66-, chmn dept, 69- Awards: Purchase Award, Piedmont Drawing & Graphic Show; First Place, Appalachian Nat Drawing Competition, 77; Second Place, First Sofa Exchange, 77. Bibliog: Artist in the 33rd North Carolina Artists exhibition, La Rev Mod, 10/71. Mem: Am Crafts Coun; World Crafts Coun; Nat Art Educ Asn. Style & Technique: Figurative, fantasy abstract. Media: Conte, Charcoal, Aluminum, Bronze, Silkscreen, Lithography. Publ: The development of art departments in the community college, Art Teacher Mag, 1/76. Mailing Add: 111 W Parker St Smithfield NC 27577

CREECY, HERBERT LEE, JR
PAINTER, SCULPTOR
b Norfolk, Va, Aug 14, 39. Study: Univ Ala, 58-60; Atlanta Sch Art, BFA, 64; Atelier 17, Fr Govt Scholar, with Stanley Hayter. Work: Whitney Mus Am Art, New York; High Mus Art, Atlanta, Ga; Indianapolis Mus Art, Ind; Akron Mus Art, Ohio; Norton Gallery of Art, West Palm Beach, Fla. Exhib: Mead 9th Ann Painting of the Yr Exhib, Atlanta, 66; Art in the Embassies Prog Touring Exhib, US Dept of State, Washington, DC, 67; Drawing Soc Nat Touring Exhib, Am Fedn of Arts, New York, 70; one-man shows, High Mus Art, 71, O K Harris Gallery, New York, 72 & Univ Tenn, Knoxville, 75; Ga Artists Exhib, High Mus Art, 72-74; New Am Abstract Painting, Vassar Col, Poughkeepsie, NY, 72; Italia 2000, Naples, Italy, 74; 35th Biennial Exhib, Corcoran Gallery Art, Washington, DC, 77; Thirty-five Artists in the SE Traveling Exhib, 77; plus others. Style & Technique: Surrealistic abstract expressionist landscapes. Media: Acrylic on Canvas. Mailing Add: c/o Dick Jemison Gallery 929 1/2 S 22nd St Birmingham AL 35205

CREESE, WALTER LITTLEFIELD
EDUCATOR
b Danvers, Mass, Dec 19, 19. Study: Brown Univ, AB; Harvard Univ, MA & PhD; Columbia Univ. Teaching: Instr & teaching fel, Harvard Univ, 44-45; instr, Wellesley Col, 45; instr, Univ Louisville, 46-47, asst prof, 47-52, assoc prof, 52-55, prof, 56-58; prof, Univ Ill, Urbana, 58-63; vis prof, summer sch, Harvard Univ, 61-63; dean sch archit & allied arts, Univ Ore, 63-68; chmn archit hist & prof archit, Univ Ill, Urbana, 68- Pos: Ed, jour, Soc Archit Historians, 50-53; chmn, Louisville & Jefferson Co Planning & Zoning Comt, 54-55; ed adv, Col Art J. Awards: Rehmann fel, Am Inst Architects, 60; Smithsonian fel, 69; Rockefeller Found Fel in Humanities, 76-77; plus others. Mem: Soc Archit Historians (pres, 58-59); hon mem Am Inst Architects; Col Art Asn Am. Mailing Add: Dept of Architecture Univ of Ill Urbana IL 61801

CREIGHTON, GWEN LUX
See Lux, Gwen

CREMEAN, ROBERT
SCULPTOR
b Toledo, Ohio, Sept 28, 32. Study: Alfred Univ, 50-52; Cranbrook Acad Art, BA, 54, MFA, 56. Work: City Art Mus St Louis; Detroit Inst Art; Santa Barbara Mus Art; Univ Nebr; Univ Miami; plus others. Exhib: Univ Iowa, 64; Newport Harbor, 64; Denver Mus Art, 64; Venice Biennale, 68; Smithsonian Traveling Exhib, Europe & SAm, 68-69; plus many others. Teaching: Instr, Detroit Inst Arts; instr, Univ Calif, Los Angeles, 56-57; instr, Art Ctr La Jolla, Calif, 57-58. Awards: Fulbright Scholar to Italy, 54-55; Tamarind Lithography Workshop Grant, 66-67. Mailing Add: c/o Esther Robles Gallery 1218 Glenncross Ct Los Angeles CA 90023

CRESPO, MICHAEL LOWE
PAINTER, EDUCATOR
b New Orleans, La, Jan 3, 47. Study: La State Univ, BA; Queens Col, MFA, with James Brooks, John Ferren, Paul Georges, Louis Finklestein, Charles Cajori. Comn: Mural, Diversified Indust, Baton Rouge, La, 74; mural, Brown-Eagle Corp, Baton Rouge, 76; large painted floor covering, pvt residence, Baton Rouge, 77. Exhib: Representational Spirit, State Univ NY, Albany, 70; Painterly Realism, Am Fedn of Art Travelling Exhib, Queens Mus, New York, 71; La Bicentennial Exhib, Masur Mus, Monroe, La, 73; Exhib of Drawings, Del Mar State Col, Corpus Christi, Tex, 73; 20th Exhib Southwestern Prints & Drawings, Dallas Mus of Fine Arts, Tex, 75; Artist's Choice: Figurative Art in New York, var Manhattan galleries, 77; one-man shows, Bowery Gallery, Manhattan, 70, Purdue Univ Art Gallery, 74, Southern Mo State Univ, 76 & La State Univ Union Art Gallery, 77. Teaching: Instr painting, Univ Southwestern La, 71; asst prof painting, La State Univ, 71-; vis artist painting, Purdue Univ, 74. Mem: Col Art Asn; Am Asn of Univ Prof. Style & Technique: Figurative & abstract. Media: Oil on canvas, gouache. Dealer: Dixon Smith Lobdell Ave Baton Rouge LA 70808. Mailing Add: 535 Cornell Ave Baton Rouge LA 70808

CRESS, GEORGE AYERS
PAINTER, EDUCATOR
b Anniston, Ala, Apr 7, 21. Study: Emory Univ; Univ Ga, BFA, MFA. Work: Tenn Fine Arts Ctr; Mead Corp; Ford Motor Co; Birmingham Mus, Ala; Mint Mus, Charlotte, NC; plus many others. Exhib: Pa Acad Fine Arts; Springfield Watercolor Ann; Grand Cent Moderns, NY; one-man shows, Addison Gallery Am Art 20 Yr Retrospective, Hunter Gallery & var southeastern mus; Bampton Arts Centre, Oxon, Eng; plus many other group & one-man

shows. Teaching: Instr art, Judson Col, Marion, Ala, 45-46, Mary Baldwin Col, Staunton, Va, 46-47, Univ Md, 47-48, Univ Ga, 49, 65 & 69, Univ Tenn, 49-51, Ont Dept Educ, 63 & Univ SC, 67; prof art & head dept, Univ Tenn, Chattanooga, 51- Pos: Chmn, Tenn Col Arts Coun, 66-68. Awards: Southeastern Ann, Birmingham Mus Ann & Atlanta Arts Festival; plus many others. Mem: Southeastern Col Conf (pres, 65-66); Col Art Asn Am. Mailing Add: Dept of Art Univ of Tenn Chattanooga TN 37404

CRETARA, DOMENIC ANTHONY
PAINTER, EDUCATOR
b Chelsea, Mass, Mar 29, 46. Study: Boston Univ Sch Fine Arts, BFA(magna cum laude), 68, MFA, 70, Tanglewood Inst, summer 68. Exhib: Group Exhib of Past & Present Instrs, Fitchburg Mus Art, 73; Fulbright-Hayes Grantee Exhib, US Info Serv Gallery, Rome, Italy, 75; one-man show, McIvor Reddie Gallery, Art Inst Boston, 76 & George Sherman Union Gallery, Boston Univ, 77. Teaching: Instr painting & design, DeCordova Mus Art, Lincoln, Mass, 71-74; chmn dept fine arts, Art Inst Boston, 73- Awards: Fulbright-Hayes grant, Italian & US govts, 74-75. Mem: Boston Visual Artist's Union. Style & Technique: Figure paintings and landscapes in oil; drawings in various media. Media: Oil on canvas or masonite; pencil and mixed media drawings. Publ: Contribr, Figure Drawing, 76, The Art of Responsive Drawing, rev ed, 77 & Painting: Perceptual and Technical Fundamentals, 79, Prentice Hall. Mailing Add: 27 Shirley Ave Revere MA 02151

CRILE, SUSAN
PAINTER
b Cleveland, Ohio, 42. Study: Bennington Col, Vt, 61-62 & 64-65; NY Univ, 62-64; Hunter Col, 71-72. Work: Phillips Collection, Washington, DC; Hirshhorn Mus, Washington, DC; Brooklyn Mus, NY. Exhib: Whitney Ann Exhib Am Paintings, Whitney Mus Am Art, New York; Art Inst Chicago Ann, 72; group show, 72, The Way of Color, 33rd Corcoran Biennial, 73, Corcoran Gallery Art, Washington, DC; one-person shows, Kornblee Gallery, New York, 71-73, Fischbach Gallery, New York, 74-75 & 77, Brooke Alexander Inc, New York, 75, Phillips Collection, Washington, DC, 75 & The New Gallery, Cleveland, Ohio, 77; Works on Paper, Va Mus Fine Arts, Richmond, 75; MacDowell Colony Artists, James Yu Gallery, New York, 76. Teaching: Instr painting, Princeton Univ, 74-76, Sch Visual Arts, New York, 76- & Sarah Lawrence Col, 76- Bibliog: Kenneth Baker (auth), Susan Crile: abstraction's the image, Arts Mag, 12/75; Judith Goldman (auth), Catalogue: The Phillips Collection, Washington, DC, 75; Judith Lopes Cardozo (auth), Review, Artforum, 4/77. Style & Technique: Oil and gesso on canvas; charcoal, graphite, gesso on paper. Mailing Add: c/o Droll/Kolbert 724 Fifth Ave New York NY 10019

CRIMI, ALFRED D
PAINTER, INSTRUCTOR
b San Fratello, Italy, Nov 21, 24; US citizen. Study: Nat Acad Design; life drawing with Ivan Olinsky, Beaux Arts Inst; Preparatory Sch Ornamental Arts; fresco painting & Pompeian encaustic with Prof Venturini Paperi, Rome, Italy. Work: Norfolk Mus Arts & Sci, Va; Butler Inst Am Art, Youngstown, Ohio; Columbia Mus, SC; Libr Cong, Washington, DC; Smithsonian Inst, Washington, DC. Comn: Fresco, Rutgers Presby Church, New York, 35-37; fresco, sect painting & sculpture, Post Off Dept, Washington, DC, 37-38; oil mural, sect painting & sculpture, Northampton, Mass, 38-39; mosaic, comn by New York Bd Educ, Einstein Jr High Sch, 66-67 & Adlai Stevenson High Sch, 68-69. Exhib: Mus Mod Art, New York, 36; Art Inst Chicago, 36; Whitney Mus Am Art, 46 & Metrop Mus Art, New York, 52-53; First Int Exhib Liturgical Art, Trieste, Italy, 61. Teaching: Instr drawing & painting, City Col New York, 47-53; instr advan drawing, Pratt Inst, 48-51; instr painting, Pa State Univ, 63; also instr, lectr & critic, cols & univs, 44- Pos: Mural decorator, Barnett Philip, New York, 28-32; consult, Meyer & Frank Dept Store, Portland, Ore, 31-32; field artist, Sperry Gyroscope Co, Lake Success, NY, 42-45; art consult, Nippon Mus. Awards: Mainstream Int, Marietta Col, Ohio, 69 & 70; top purchase award, Butler Inst Am Art, 69; gold medal of honor, Audubon Artists, 71; plus others. Bibliog: Ernest Watson (auth), Making of fresco, Am Artist, 10/41; Mechanical brains (artist's drawings of war machinery), Life Mag, 1/21/44; Carrie Timpano (photographer & collabr), The making & fascination of fresco painting (color film), 57-59. Mem: Audubon Artists (pres, 51-52, chmn admis comt, 69-72); Allied Artists Am (bd dir, 47-72); Art Comn City New York; Am Watercolor Soc; Fedn Mod Painters & Sculptors. Style & Technique: Multi-dimensional principle of color animation, dealing with color related overlapping planes, working from the picture plane, receding ad infinitum; pure form to abstract hard-edge geometric technique; representational. Media: Oil, Watercolor. Publ: Auth, articles in, Am Artist Mag, 1/57 & 2/62; auth, Art of Abstract Dimensional Painting, Grumbacher Libr, 77. Mailing Add: 186 W Fourth St New York NY 10014

CRIMP, DOUGLAS
ART CRITIC, ART HISTORIAN
b Coeur d'Alene, Idaho, Aug 19, 44. Study: Tulane Univ, BA(art hist); City Univ New York, PhD candidate. Teaching: Instr art hist, Sch Visual Arts, New York, 70-76. Pos: Curatorial staff, Solomon R Guggenheim Mus, 68-71; ed assoc, Art News, 71-76; ed assoc, Oct Mag, 77- Awards: Art Critics Fel, Nat Endowment for the Arts, 73. Publ: Auth, Quartered and drawn (on Jack Tworkov), Art News, 71; auth, Agnes Martin: Numero, Misura, Rapporto, Data, 73; auth, Daniel Buren's New York Work, Van Abbemuseum, Eindhoven, Holland, 76; auth, Joan Jonas' performance works, Studio Int, 76; auth, Positive/negative: a note on Degas' photographs, Oct Mag, 78. Mailing Add: 93 Nassau St New York NY 10038

CRIQUETTE (RUTH DUBARRY MONTAGUE)
PAINTER, WRITER
b Paris, France; US citizen. Study: Ecole Beaux Arts, Paris; Univ Nev, MFA; seminars at Metrop Mus Art; Lumis Art Acad; also with Roland Pierson Prickett. Work: Many in pvt collections. Exhib: Da Vinci Exhib Artes, Rome, Italy, 69; Repertorium Artis Exhib, Monaco, 70; Int Exhib Artes, Rome, 71; 14th & 15th Int Exhib, Gallerie Int, New York, 72; Int Inst Arts & Lett Perpetual Exhib, Switz. Teaching: Dir & instr oil painting, Prickett Sch Color, 48-60; dir & instr oil painting, Montague Sch Painting, Washington, DC, 61-68; instr oil painting, Ecole Marsan, Vernon, Normandy, France, 69-70. Pos: Dir, Montague Studio-Gallery, Orlando, Fla, 71-73. Mem: Int Arts Guild, Monte Carlo, Monaco; Centro Studi E Scambi Int, Rome (hon rep); Acad Int Leonardo Da Vinci, Rome (hon rep); life fel Int Inst Artes et Lett, Switz; Metrop Mus Art, New York. Style & Technique: Free rhythm interpretive realism; brush and knife techniques. Media: Oil. Publ: Contribr, New Yorker, 53; co-auth, 5 Home study courses in oil painting, 60; contribr, Let's live, 60-61; auth & illusr, Bahamian ah-h-h, 69; auth & illusr over 100 monogrs in oil painting field, 71-72. Dealer: Gallerie Int 1095 Madison Ave New York NY 10028. Mailing Add: Blue Ridge Studio PO Box 344 Sterling VA 22170

CRISPO, ANDREW JOHN
ART DEALER, COLLECTOR
b Philadelphia, Pa, Apr 21, 45. Study: St Joseph's Col (Pa). Collections Arranged: Pioneers of American Abstraction (with catalog); Richard Pousette Dart: Paintings (with catalog); Ten Americans: Masters of Watercolor (with catalog); Edward Hicks: A Gentle Spirit (with catalog); Twelve Americans: Masters of Collage; Lowell Nesbitt: An Autobiography; Matta: A Totemic World. Pos: Assoc dir, ACA Gallery, 69-72; owner & dir, Andrew Crispo Gallery, 73- Bibliog: Rev in, New York Times, New York Post, Time Mag, Arts Mag & Art Gallery Mag. Specialty: American and European art of the 19th and 20th century. Collection: Morris Louis, John Marin, Georgia O'Keeffe, Helen Frankenthaler, Edward Hicks, Horace Pippin, Robert Motherwell & William de Kooning. Mailing Add: 126 E 79th St New York NY 10021

CRISPO, DICK
PAINTER, PRINTMAKER
b Brooklyn, NY, Jan 13, 45. Study: Ariz Sch Art; Carmel Art Inst; Monterey Peninsula Col; Hartnell Col; St Sophia Divinity Sch; also with Victor DiGesu, Sam Colburn, Jan Hannah, Alexander Napote, Kay Rodgers & others. Work: Libr Cong, Washington, DC; Bibliot Nat, Paris, France; Inst Nac de Bellas Artes, Mexico City, Mex; Mus Western Art, Tokyo, Japan; Nat Libr Ireland, Dublin; plus others. Comn: Ecology (mural), Monterey High Sch, Calif, 72; Ecology, Robert Louis Stevenson Sch, Pebble Beach, Calif, 72; Spirit of Youth, Carmel Youth Ctr, Calif, 73; History of the Migrant Worker (mural), Opportunity Indust Ctr, Salinas, Calif, 74; Twelve Master Teachers of the World (mural), Church of Antioch, Pacific Grove, Calif, 75. Exhib: Calif State Fair, Sacramento, 64; Small Painting Biennial, Purdue Univ, 68; Univ Calif, Berkeley, 72; Pan-Am Graphics, Mexico City, 72; Western Graphics, Tokyo, 73. Teaching: Instr arts & Crafts, York Sch, Monterey, 71-73; instr folk & ethnic arts, Monterey Peninsula Col, 74-75; instr folk & ethnic arts & art hist, St Sophia Divinity Sch, Pacific Grove, 75- Pos: Chmn, Fine Arts Div, Monterey county Fair, 72-74; co-founder, Mus on Wheels, Monterey, 74-; exhib dir, Pacific Grove Art Ctr, 74-; art counr, Monterey Co Probation Dept, 75- Awards: Calif State Fair First Prize, State of Calif, 64; All Calif Watercolor Competition Third Prize, Pacific Grove, 67; San Juan Bautista Invitational Second Prize, Calif, 68; plus others. Bibliog: Pat Griffith (auth), An artist with a sense of humor, Carmel Valley Outlook, Carmel, Calif, 72; Robert Miskimon (auth), Social consciousness of art, Pine Cone, Carmel, 73. Mem: Artists Equity; Carmel Art Asn; Pacific Grove Art Ctr; Pac Art Asn (chmn); Art Workers United. Style & Technique: Social commentary. Res: Eclectic study of world folk art. Collection: Folk and eccentric art from over 40 countries. Publ: Auth, Contemporary Print Making Renaissance in Japan, 69. Mailing Add: c/o Fireside Gallery Dolores St Carmel CA 93921

CRIST, WILLIAM GARY
SCULPTOR, EDUCATOR
b Pocatello, Idaho, Jan 17, 37. Study: Univ Wash, Seattle, BAArt(educ), 66; Cranbrook Acad Art, Detroit, MFA(sculpture), 71; study with Michael Hall, Julius Schmidt, Everett DuPenn & George Tsutakawa. Work: Cameron Univ, Lawton, Okla; Univ Mo, Kansas City. Exhib: 58th Exhib for Mich Artists, Detroit Inst Arts, 70; Blossom-Kent Sculpture, Kent State Univ, Ohio, 70; Ga Artists, High Mus Art, Atlanta, 72; Nat Sculpture Traveling Exhib, Chapel Hill, NC, 73; Great Plains Sculpture Exhib, Sheldon Mem Art Gallery, Lincoln, Nebr, 76; 19th Ann Delta Exhib, Ark Arts Ctr, Little Rock, 76; 23 at 10, Soho, New York, 77; one-man exhib, Organic Pneumatics, Cranbrook Art Galleries, Bloomfield Hills, 71, Umbilical, Contemp Arts Found, Oklahoma City, Okla, 74 & 7E7 Gallery, Lawrence, Kans, 78. Teaching: Asst prof art, Wesleyan Col, Macon, Ga, 71-72; instr art, Cameron Univ, Lawton, Okla, 72-74; asst prof sculpture, Univ Mo, Kansas City, 74- Awards: Awards for ceramic shell casting & aluminum sculpture, Univ Mo Res Coun, 76 & 77. Mem: Southern Asn Sculptors; Col Art Asn; Am Asn Univ Prof. Style & Technique: Large abstract constructions and fabrications in metal; inflatable environments with blowers, timers and lights. Media: Aluminum; Steel; Vinyl, Polyethelene. Dealer: Noho Gallery Inc 542 LaGuardia Pl New York NY 10012. Mailing Add: Dept of Art & Art Hist Univ Mo-Kansas City Kansas City MO 64110

CRITE, ALLAN ROHAN
PAINTER, ILLUSTRATOR
b Plainfield, NJ, Mar 20, 10. Study: Boston Mus Fine Arts Sch; Mass Sch Art; Boston Univ, CBA; Harvard Univ, BA. Work: Boston Mus Fine Arts; Spelman Col, Atlanta, Ga; Addison Gallery Am Art, Andover, Mass; Marine Hosp, Carville, La; Villanova Col, Pa; plus others. Comn: Insignia, USS Wilson; mural, Grace Church, Martha's Vineyard, Mass; stations of the cross, Holy Cross Church, Morrisville, Vt, 57; Allan Crite Wing, Blackstone Sq Community Sch, Boston; plus many others. Exhib: One-man shows, Boston Mus Fine Arts, Fogg Mus Art & Farnsworth Mus Art; Religious Art Festival, Brandon, Vt, 61; Festival Arts, Ecumenical Youth Assembly NAm, Ann Arbor, Mich, 61; plus many other group & one-man shows. Teaching: Lectr Christian art, Oberlin Col, 58; past lectr, Regis Col. Pos: Artist-historian, Semitic Mus, Harvard Univ. Awards: Boston Mus Fine Arts Sch & Seabury Western Theol Sem Award, 52; Fourth Prize, Franklin Mint Bicentennial Medal Design. Mem: Harvard Club Boston; Nat Geog Soc; Faculty Club Harvard Univ; Boston Mus Fine Arts Sch. Publ: Auth & illusr, Cultural heritage of the United States, 68 & Were you there when they crucified my Lord, McGrath, 69; contribr, mags & bulls; auth & illusr, many relig bks & articles. Mailing Add: 410 Columbus Ave Boston MA 02116

CRITTENDEN, JOHN WILLIAM NEIL
PAINTER, PRINTMAKER
b Brandon, Man, Feb 10, 39. Work: Nat Gallery of Can, Ottawa; Metrop Toronto Cent Libr, Ont; Glenbow Art Gallery, Calgary, Alta. Comn: Mag cover painting, Golden West, 70 & 72 & Can Rides, 72; Ltd, ed painting, Coast Paper Ltd, Vancouver, BC, 74; calendar painting, Alta Wheatpool, 71-73. Exhib: One-man show, Calgary Exhib & Stampede Art Salon, 71; Alta Art Festival, Edmonton, 71. Bibliog: Ruth Gorman (auth), John Crittenden—Artist, Golden West Mag. Style & Technique: Realism: big game animals and Western paintings, rural Canadiana and portraits; romanticism coupled with poetry. Media: Oil, acrylic and egg tempera; limited edition serigraphs. Dealer: Canadiana House 509 2nd St SW Calgary AB Can. Mailing Add: RR 1 Chase BC V0E 1M0 Can

CROCKETT, GIBSON M
CARTOONIST, PAINTER
b Washington, DC, Sept 18, 12. Study: Studied watercolor under several nationally known artists; illustration with Harry Anderson. Work: Represented in many pvt collections. Exhib: Landscape painting in local & nat exhibs. Pos: Mem staff, Washington Eve Star, 33-, ed cartoonist, 47-75, sport cartoonist, 40-46; free lance illusr, 43-; art dir, Am Publ Co, Washington, 45- Awards: Cartoon Awards from Headliner Asn & Freedoms Found. Mem: Washington Landscape Club; Olney Art Asn; Ed Cartoonists Asn. Style & Technique: Portrait painting. Mailing Add: c/o Olney Art Asn 16501 Norwood Rd Sandy Spring MD 20860

CROFT, LEWIS SCOTT
PAINTER
b Chester Basin, NS, Mar 25, 11. Study: Study with M Denton-Burgess, Vancouver, BC & William S Schwartz, Chicago, Ill. Work: Swope Art Gallery, Terre Haute, Ind; Parrish Art

Mus, Southampton, NY; Art Bank of NS; Maritime Art Asn; NC Mus Art, Raleigh; Elliott Mus, Stuart, Fla; Philbrook Art Ctr, Tulsa, Okla; plus 40 others. Exhib: Am Artists Prof League, New York, 57-58; Fla State Fair, Tampa, 58-59; Southeastern Ann, Delgado Mus, New Orleans, La, 60; Allied Artists Am, New York, 61, 63 & 65; Audubon Artists Ann, New York, 62. Awards: Best of Show, Sunshine Art Festival, Fla, 58; Best Oil, Mystic, Conn, 62-64; Grand Prize Gold Medal, Washington Sq Outdoor Art Show, 65. Mem: Allied Artists Am; Int Platform Asn; Nat Soc of Lit & the Arts; Int Inst Arts & Lett. Style & Technique: Slightly abstract versions of landscapes; oils painted with knife. Media: Oil, Watercolor. Publ: Auth, article in, Am Artist Mag, 3/68. Mailing Add: RR 1 Chester Basin NS Can

CROFT, MICHAEL FLYNT
GOLDSMITH, EDUCATOR
b Minneapolis, Minn, Oct 11, 41. Study: Univ NMex, Albuquerque, BFA; Southern Ill Univ, Carbondale, MFA. Work: Southern Ill Univ Art Mus, Carbondale; Renwick Gallery, Smithsonian Inst, Washington, DC; Tucson Art Mus, Ariz. Comn: Offertory basin, All Saints Episcopal Cathedral, Indianapolis, 65. Exhib: Am Jewelry Today, Everhart Mus, Scranton, Pa, 65; Art of Personal Adornment 69 & Young Americans, 69, Mus Contemp Crafts, New York; 10th & 11th Ann Southern Tier Crafts Exhib, Corning Mus Glass, NY, 73 & 74; Marietta Col Crafts Nat, Ohio, 75; Craft Multiples, Renwick Gallery, Smithsonian Inst, Washington, DC, 75; Contemp Enamel Work, Huntsville Mus Art, Ala, 76; The Metalsmith, Soc NAm Goldsmiths Exhib, Phoenix Art Mus, 77; Nat Invitational Metalwork Exhib, Pittsburgh Ctr for Arts & Crafts, Pittsburgh, Pa. Teaching: Asst prof jewelry & metalsmithing, Univ Wis-Milwaukee, 65-72; assoc prof jewelry & metalsmithing, Univ Ariz, Tucson, 72- Pos: Dir, Copper, Brass & Bronze Competition, Univ Ariz Art Mus, Tucson, 77- Awards: Endicott Award, First Hon Mention, 12th Ann Kans Designer Craftsmen, 65; Jury Award, 10th Ann Southern Tier, 73; State Award, Marietta Col Crafts Nat, Ariz Comn Arts & Humanities, 75. Bibliog: Art of Personal Adornment (film strip), Mus Contemp Art, 65; James Schineller (auth), Art: Search & Self Discovery, Int Textbook Co, 2nd ed, 68. Mem: Soc NAm Goldsmiths; Am Crafts Coun. Style & Technique: Jewelry and small objects. Media: Silver, gold and enamel. Mailing Add: 1441 N Day Rd Tucson AZ 85715

CRONBACH, ROBERT M
SCULPTOR
b St Louis, Mo, Feb 10, 08. Study: St Louis Sch Fine Arts, with Victor Holm, 25-26; Pa Acad Fine Arts, with Charles Grafly & Albert Laessle, 27-30; Cresson scholar to Europe, 29-30. Work: Nat Collection of Smithsonian Inst, Washington, DC; St Louis Art Mus; Springfield Art Mus, Mo; Walker Art Ctr, Minneapolis; Mus Fine Arts, Skopje, Yugoslavia; plus others. Comn: Bronze screen, Dorr Oliver Bldg, Stamford, Conn, 60; bronze & steel wall sculpture, UN Gen Assembly Bldg, New York, 60; fountain, Fed Off Bldg, St Louis, 63 fountain, Kanawha Co Pub Libr, Charleston, WVa, 66; Tribute to Leroy Grumman (stainless steel sculpture), Long Island Asn Hall of Fame, 72; fountain, Libr of Cong, Washington, DC, 74. Exhib: Whitney Mus; HemisFair, San Antonio, Tex; Pa Acad Fine Arts; Houston Mus Fine Arts; Brooklyn Mus; plus many other group & one-man shows. Teaching: Instr, Adelphi Univ, 48-62, vis assoc prof, 74 & 75; instr, N Shore Community Arts Ctr, 50-55; instr, Skowhegan Sch Painting & Sculpture, 59, 60, 64, 65 & 72. Pos: Chmn bd gov, Skowhegan Sch Painting & Sculpture; mem, Nassau Co Fine Arts Comn; mem, Mayor's Comt Beautification of New York. Awards: Nat competition for sculpture for Social Security Bldg, Washington, DC, 39; competition for sculpture for UN Bldg, New York, 60; Reynolds Metals Sculpture Trophy, 61; plus others. Bibliog: John I H Baur (auth), Revolution and Tradition in Modern American Art, Harvard Univ Press, 59; Minor L Bishop (auth), Fountains in contemporary architecture, Am Fedn Arts, 65; Louis G Redstone (auth), Art in Architecture, McGraw-Hill, 68. Mem: Sculptors Guild; Munic Art Soc; Archit League New York; Fedn Mod Painters & Sculptors; Artist-Craftsmen New York. Style & Technique: Work principally, but not entirely, with hammered and welded metal; present style might be called organic abstractions. Publ: Auth, New new deal art projects, an anthology of memoirs, Smithsonian Inst Press, 72. Mailing Add: c/o New Bertha Schaefer Gallery 983 Park Ave New York NY 10022

CRONIN, ROBERT (LAWRENCE)
PAINTER
b Lexington, Mass, Aug 10, 36. Study: RI Sch Design, BFA, 59; Cornell Univ, MFA, 62. Work: Worcester Art Mus, Mass; Boston Mus Fine Arts, Mass. Exhib: ICA, Boston, 71; Sculpture in Copley Square, Boston, winter 72-73; Worcester Art Mus, 74; Zabriskie Gallery, New York, 74; Bennington Col, Vt, 74; plus others. Teaching: Instr painting, Bennington Col, 66-68; instr art, Sch Worcester Art Mus, 68- Awards: First Prize in Painting, Boston Fine Arts Festival, 63; Mass Arts & Humanities Grant, 75. Bibliog: Hilton Kramer (auth), New talent, New York Times, 6/17/73; Hilton Kramer (auth), rev in, New York Times, 9/21/74. Style & Technique: Simple but aware. Mailing Add: 55 Salisbury St Worcester MA 01608

CROOKS, W SPENCER
PAINTER, LECTURER
b Ireland, July 26, 17; US citizen. Study: RI Sch Design, cert, Shrivenham Am Univ, Eng, cert; summer sem with Edgar Whitney; RCA Scholar (scenic design), Berkshire Music Ctr. Work: RI Sch Design Fine Art Mus; Boston Symphony Hall, Mass; Pawtucket Boys Club, RI. Comn: Watercolor, covers for RI Providence J, 61-65; watercolor, Old Colony Banks, RI, 71-73; watercolor, Indust Leasing Corp, Indust Nat Bank, Providence, RI, 72. Exhib: Royal Acad, London, Eng, 44; Watercolor, USA, Springfield, Mo, 64; Am Watercolor Soc Ann, Nat Acad Art Gallery, 67, 72 & 75; Springfield Mus Fine Arts, 75; one-man show, Rockport Art Asn, 75. Teaching: Instr Watercolor, Brown Univ Exten Sch, 68-74; instr watercolor, Cranston East High Sch (adult educ), 65-68; teacher graphic art, RI Col, 72- & instr watercolor, 74-75. Pos: Creative artist, Hallady, Inc, Providence, RI, 52-58; creative artist, Hassenfeld Inc, Central Falls, 59-60; art dir, Cardono Inc, Pawtucket, 60-61; demonstr, watercolor, Grumbacher's Palette Talk, 75. Awards: Spec Serv Award, All-Southern New Eng Open, US Army, 44; Travel Award, Washington Sq Show, New York, Forbes Mag, 67; James G Geddes Mem Award, Rockport Art Asn, 71. Mem: Providence Art Club; Providence Watercolor Club, Rockport Art Asn, Mass; Salmagundi Club, New York; Philadelphia Watercolor Club. Style & Technique: Impressionist, dry brush and wet-in-wet technique. Media: Watercolor; Pen, Ink. Publ: Illusr, Providence J Mag Sect, 61-65; ed, DeCordova Mus Gallery (catalog), 62; RI Sch Design Alumni Bull, 75; illusr, Palette Talk, Grumbacher Artist Material, NY, 75. Dealer: Art Shanty Inc 7 Main St Wickford RI 02852. Mailing Add: 84 Davis Ave Cranston RI 02910

CROSBIE, HELEN BLAIR
See Blair, Helen

CROSBY, RANICE W
MEDICAL ILLUSTRATOR, EDUCATOR
b Regina, Sask, Apr 26, 15. Study: Conn Col, AB; Johns Hopkins Med Sch, under Max Broedel; also under Robert Brackman; Johns Hopkins Univ, MLA. Teaching: Illusr for N J Eastman, Johns Hopkins Hosp; assoc prof art as appl to med & dir dept, Johns Hopkins Med Sch, 44- Mem: Asn Med Illusr; Am Asn Univ Prof. Publ: Illusr, med textbks & contribr illus, med jours. Mailing Add: 3926 Cloverhill Rd Baltimore MD 21218

CROSBY, SUMNER MCKNIGHT
ART HISTORIAN
b Minneapolis, Minn, July 29, 09. Study: Yale Univ, BA, 32, PhD, 37; Minneapolis Col Art, hon DFA. Teaching: Prof medieval art, Yale Univ, 36- Awards: Chevalier, Legion of Honor, 50. Mem: Am Acad Arts & Sci; Col Art Asn Am (pres, 44-45); Am Fedn Art (trustee, 41-44, 47-); Int Ctr Medieval Art (chmn, 70-); Archeol Inst Am (trustee, 65-69). Res: Excavations in the Abbey Church of St-Denis. Publ: Auth, Abby of St-Denis, 42; auth, L'Abbaye Royale de St-Denis, 53; ed, Art through the Ages, 4th ed, 59; auth, Apostle Bas-Relief at St-Denis, 72. Mailing Add: 29 Fairgrounds Rd Woodbridge CT 06525

CROSS, MARIA CONCETTA
PAINTER, COLLECTOR
b Ft Worth, Tex, Jan 25, 11. Study: Tex Christian Univ; Tex Woman's Univ; also study in Europe, Italy, Mex & Taos, NMex. Work: Dr M E Houtzager, Dir, Cent Mus Art, Utrecht, Neth; Dr Orsla Sarzana, Pres, Inst Learning, Palermo, Italy; Tex Wesleyan Col; Jon Starnes, Houston, Tex. Exhib: Ft Worth Art Ctr; Beaumont Art Mus; Dallas Mus Fine Arts; Witte Mem Mus, San Antonio; Springfield Mo Art Gallery; plus many others. Awards: Awards for Old House, Tex Wesleyan Col, Old Ruins, Tex Art Guild & Melons, Beaumont Art Mus, Tex. Media: Oil, Watercolor. Specialty: Western Americana art and bronzes; contemporary American art. Collection: Western paintings and bronzes. Mailing Add: 3629 W Seventh St Ft Worth TX 76107

CROSS, WATSON, JR
PAINTER, INSTRUCTOR
b Long Beach, Calif, Oct 10, 18. Study: Chouinard Art Inst, scholar, 38-42. Comn: Illustrations of Air Bases, USAF, Alaska, 63. Exhib: San Francisco Mus Art Ann, 47-48; Calif Watercolor Soc Traveling Exhib, Riverside Mus, New York, 48; John Herron Art Inst, 48; Los Angeles Co Mus Art Ann, 53-54. Teaching: Prof drawing & painting, Chouinard Art Inst, 44-71; assoc prof, Calif State Univ, Northridge, 75-78; instr drawing, Art Ctr Col of Design, Pasadena, Calif, 75-78. Pos: Secy, Calif Watercolor Soc, 51-53, pres, 53-54; judge, Princeton Univ's Creativity Testing, 65. Style & Technique: Expressionistic; semi-abstract. Media: Watercolor, Oil. Publ: Contribr, Content of Watercolor, Van Nostrand Reinhold, 69; illusr (cover), Westways Mag, 8/78. Mailing Add: 1238 E Workman Ave West Covina CA 91790

CROSSGROVE, ROGER LYNN
PAINTER, EDUCATOR
b Farnam, Nebr, Nov 17, 21. Study: Kearney State Col; Univ Nebr, BFA; Univ Ill, MFA; Univ Michoacan. Work: Butler Inst Am Art, Youngstown, Ohio; Montclair Art Mus, NJ; Des Moines Art Ctr, Iowa; New Britain Mus Am Art; Inst Mex-Norteamericano Relac Cult, Mexico City. Exhib: Whitney Mus Am Art, New York, NY, 56; Pa Acad Fine Arts, Philadelphia, 64; Audubon Artists, New York, 68; Conn Watercolor Soc, Wadsworth Atheneum, Hartford, Conn, 70; Monotypes, Pratt Graphics Ctr, New York, 72; New Am Monotypes, SITES, 78. Teaching: Prof art & assoc chmn dept graphic arts, Pratt Inst, 52-68; prof art, Univ Conn, 68- Awards: Emily Lowe Award, 51; Gold Medal, Nat Arts Club, 67; Am Watercolor Soc Award, 67. Bibliog: Henry N Rasmusen (auth), Printmaking with monotype, Chilton, 60. Mem: Col Art Asn Am; Am Watercolor Soc; Conn Acad Arts; Conn Watercolor Soc; Am Asn Univ Prof. Style & Technique: Lyrical, abstract, figurative, aquamedia on paper, especially monotypes. Media: Pastel, Watercolor. Publ: Contribr, Paperbound Books in Print, 63; contribr & ed, Artists Proof, 67- Mailing Add: One Minnesota Rd Storrs CT 06268

CROTTO, PAUL
PAINTER, SCULPTOR
b New York, NY, Oct 24, 22. Study: Art Students League; Beaux-Arts, Florence, Italy; also with Fernand Leger, Paris. Work: Villeneuve-sur-Lot Mus, France; Mus Art Int, San Francisco; Galerie Grave, Munich, Ger. Comn: Portraits, L E Kaplan, New York & Robert Aries, Paris. Exhib: Mostra Artisti Am, Florence, 51; Mostra Int, Bordighera, Italy, 53; Am Painters in France, Galerie Craven, Paris, 53; Salon Automne, Paris, 56; Salon Comparaisons, Mus Mod Art, Paris, 68. Awards: Prix Int de Peinture, Villeneuve-sur-Lot, 63. Bibliog: T Ehrenmark (auth), American Artist in Sweden, Dagens Nyheter, 63; A Blasco Ibanez (auth), American artist in Paris, Los Angeles Herald Examr, 68; Betty Werther (auth), Art, Time-Life, Paris, 69. Mem: Soc Coop Entre Aide Artistes. Media: Oil. Mailing Add: 19 Rue Cauchois Paris France

CROUCH, NED PHILBRICK
SCULPTOR, CURATOR
b Nashville, Tenn, Mar 14, 48. Study: Austin Peay State Univ, Clarksville, Tenn, BS(art), 72; Cranbrook Acad Art, Bloomfield Hills, Mich, MFA(sculpture), 74. Work: Tenn Fine Arts Comn, Nashville; Cheekwood Fine Arts Ctr, Nashville; Ark Arts Ctr, Little Rock; Montgomery Bell Acad, Nashville; Austin Peay State Univ, Clarksville. Exhib: Michigan II, Flint Inst Arts, Flint, Mich, 74; Mid-South Biennial, Brooks Mem Art Gallery, Memphis, Tenn, 75; Artists Biennial, New Orleans Mus Art, La, 75; Nat Sculpture USA, Huntsville Mus Art, Ala, 75; 18th Ann Delta Exhib, Ark Arts Ctr, Little Rock, 75; Tenn Bicentennial, Brooks Mem Art Gallery, Memphis, 76; Invitational, Southeastern Ctr for Contemp Art, Winston-Salem, NC, 77. Teaching: Instr sculpture, Austin Peay State Univ, Clarksville, 74-75. Pos: Guest cur, Am Folk-Exhib of 20th Century Quilts, Drawings & Sculpture, Vanderbilt Univ, Nashville, 76-; consult spec proj, Cheekwood Fine Arts Ctr, Nashville, 77- Awards: Hon Mention, Delta Exhib & Purchase Award, Toys by Artists, 75, Ark Arts Ctr, Little Rock; Purchase Award, Tenn Bicentennial, Tenn Fine Arts Comn, 76. Mem: Col Art Asn Am; Southern Asn Sculptors. Style & Technique: Linear fabricated steel constructions. Media: Welded steel; wood. Dealer: Martin/Wiley Gallery 2122 Acklin Ave Nashville TN 37214. Mailing Add: 1834 Madison St B-11 Clarksville TN 37040

CROUSE, JOHN L (JAY)
ART DEALER, PHOTOGRAPHER
b Lima, Ohio, Apr 13, 49. Study: Denison Univ, BA(economics), 71; George Washington Univ, MBA, 75; Maine Photog Workshop, 75-76. Pos: Dir, Atlanta Gallery of Photog, Ga. Mem: Soc Photog Educ; Nexus Coop Photog Gallery, Atlanta. Specialty: Nineteenth and twentieth century photographers; southeastern photographers. Mailing Add: c/o Atlanta Gallery of Photog 3077 E Shadowlawn Ave NE Atlanta GA 30305

CROUTON, FRANCOIS (FRANCOIS LAFORTUNE)
ART ADMINISTRATOR, PHOTOGRAPHER
b Montreal, PQ, Mar 9, 21. Study: Col Montreal, BA & DLibrarianship. Work: Municipal Libr Montreal; Libr Can Inst, Quebec; Pub Libr Serv, Quebec; Quebec Mus. Exhib: Toronto Univ, 49; Laval Univ; Municipal Libr Montreal, 50; All Art Ctr, PQ. Pos: Librn, Municipal

Libr Montreal, 48-52; chief librn, Libr Can Inst, Quebec, 53-60; asst dir, Pub Libr Serv, Quebec, 60-75; conservator, Quebec Mus, 75- Publ: Auth, Ou La Lumiere Chante, Laval Univ with Toronto Univ, 66; Les Photographes—Photographiés, Crouton. Mailing Add: 809 Ave Levis Quebec PQ Can

CROVELLO, WILLIAM GEORGE
PAINTER, SCULPTOR
b New York, NY, Sept 1, 29. Study: RI Sch Design, BFA, 51; also Japanese calligraphy with Taiun Yanagida, Tokyo, 57-61. Work: Time-Life Bldg, New York; Greenway Plaza, Houston; Registry, Dallas; Franklin Nat Bank, New York. Exhib: Carnegie Inst Int, Pittsburgh, 61; one-man shows, Grosvenor Gallery, London, 70, A M Sachs Gallery, New York, 71, Agra Gallery, Washington, DC, 73, Galerie Suzanne Egloff, Basel, 74, Galerie Anita Rutz, Dusseldorf, 75 & Alexandra Monett, Brussels, 75; plus many others. Bibliog: Jose de Castro Arines (auth), Dinamica de Crovello, Informaciones, 4/68; James Burr (auth), Review of Grosvenor Exhibitions, Apollo Mag, 10/70; Frank Getlein (auth), Two art exhibitions expressing a single image, Washington Star, 3/70; plus others. Style & Technique: Nonfigurative. Media: Marble, Steel; Acrylic. Mailing Add: c/o Galeria Bonino 48 Great Jones St New York NY 10019

CROWELL, LUCIUS
PAINTER, SCULPTOR
b Chicago, Ill, Jan 22, 11. Study: Williams Col; Chicago Acad Art; Pa Acad Fine Arts; Barnes Found, Acad De la Grande Chaumiere, with Arthur B Carles & Franklin Watkins; Philadelphia Col Art; Tyler Sch, Temple Univ. Work: Boston Mus Fine Art; Philadelphia Mus Art; Pa Acad Fine Arts, Philadelphia; Columbus Mus; Univ Pa. Comn: Fresco secco mural, comn by Oskar Stondrov, Hopkinson House & mosaic mural, Venice Island, Philadelphia; oil mural, Overbrook Golf Club, Philadelphia; lobby paintings, Parker Pen Co, Janesville, Wis; portrait, Univ Pa Law Sch. Exhib: Art Inst Chicago; Whitney Mus Art; Philadelphia Mus Art; Boston Mus Art; Worcester Mus; Pa Acad Fine Arts; Nat Acad Art; Calif Palace of the Legion of Honor, San Francisco; one-man shows, Boston, Philadelphia, Chicago, Milwaukee, New York, Wilmington, Beloit & Lawrenceville, NJ. Teaching: Instr oil painting, Stuido Group, Wilmington, Del, 50-63; instr painting, Chester Co Art Asn, 63-78. Pos: Vpres educ & exhib, Chester Co Art Asn, 69-75. Awards: Medal of Honor, Concord Mus, Mass; Popular Prize, Worcester Mus, Mass; Christian Brinton Award, Chester Co Art Asn. Mem: Philadelphia Art Alliance; Col Art Asn; fel Pa Acad Fine Arts; Artists Equity Asn; Philadelphia Watercolor Club. Style & Technique: Representational, chiefly in oil, bronze and ceramic sculpture. Media: Oil; Fresco Secco, Ceramic. Dealer: Coe Kerr Gallery 49 E 82nd St New York NY 10028. Mailing Add: Charlestown Rd Phoenixville PA 19460

CROWN, KEITH ALLEN
PAINTER, EDUCATOR
b Keokuk, Iowa, May 27, 18. Study: Art Inst Chicago, 36-40, 45-46, BFA, 46. Work: Ackland Mus, Chapel Hill, NC; Long Beach Mus Art, Calif; Springfield Mus, Mo. Exhib: Important California Artists, Witte Mus Art, San Antonio, Tex, 65; Crown, Long Beach Mus, Calif, 66; Painting as Painting, Univ Tex, Austin, 68; retrospective, Idea Painter, Occidental Col, 69; Lyric View, Lang Gallery, Scripps Col, 74; one-man shows, Loyola Univ, Chicago, 78, Ariz State Univ Mus Art, Tempe, 78 & Univ Utah Mus Art, Salt Lake City, 78. Teaching: Prof painting & drawing, Univ Southern Calif, 46-; prof painting, Univ NC, summer 68; prof painting, Univ Ill, 70-71 & 77-78. Awards: Purchase Awards, Nat Watercolor Soc, 60, 63 & 71; Purchase Award, Rio Hondo Col, 71; Purchase Award; Watercolor USA, Springfield Mus, Mo, 74. Bibliog: Article in Am Artist Mag, Fall 1978. Mem: Taos Art Asn Inc, NMex. Nat Watercolor Soc (vpres, 58, pres, 59); Col Art Asn Am. Style & Technique: Personal, symbolic, poetic abstraction derived directly from subject matter in synthesis with the medium. Media: Watercolor, Oil. Publ: Contribr, Introduction to Arts of Southern California XVII: watercolor (catalog), Long Beach Mus Art, 66; contribr, Content of Watercolor, Van Nostrand Reinhold, 69; contribr, Transparent Watercolor, Davis Publ, 73; plus others. Dealer: Hall Gallery 4719 Camp Bowie Ft Worth TX 76107. Mailing Add: Fine Arts Dept Univ of Southern Calif Los Angeles CA 90007

CROZIER, WILLIAM K, JR
CRAFTSMAN, DESIGNER
b Stanwood, Wash, Mar 23, 26. Study: Wash State Univ, BFA; Univ Wash, MFA(silversmithing, design). Work: Slides in The Henry Gallery, Univ Wash, Am Crafts Coun, Res Div, New York & Cheney Cowles Mem Mus, Spokane, Wash. Exhib: Contemp Craftsmen of the Far West Mus Contemp Crafts, 61 & Craftsmen USA 66, 66; Northwest Craftsmen's Exhib, Henry Gallery, Seattle, 61, 65, 67, 71 & 77; The Kentucky Guild Train, State Ky, 67; Calif Crafts VI Pac Dimensions, E B Crocker Art Gallery, Sacramento, 69; Am Crafts Coun Northwest Metal Exhib, traveling six NW states plus Colo, Alaska & Wyo, 73-75. Teaching: Asst prof design, jewelry, Ore Col Educ, 61-66; assoc prof art educ &dir art educ prog, Ore State Univ, 66-69, prof jewelry & metalsmithing, 66- Pos: Cur slides & visuals, Sch Art, Univ Wash, 59-61; chmn dept art, Ore State Univ, 72-75. Awards: Nat Merit Award, Am Crafts Coun, 66; Ore State Univ Grad Sch Res Grant, 70, Gen Res Grant, 77; Spec Recognition Award, Ore Summer Festival Arts, 74. Bibliog: Paul Soldner (auth), Craftsmen USA '66/pt 2, Crafts Horizons, 66; R Phillips (ed), Faculty Section, Ore State Univ Summer Bull, 72. Mem: Northwest Designer Craftsmen; Am Crafts Coun; World Crafts Coun; Nat Coun Art Adminr. Style & Technique: Contemporary design in fabricated jewelry, raised hollow ware & forged flatware. Media: Sterling Silver; Gold, Pewter. Mailing Add: 1906 NW 29th Pl Corvallis OR 97330

CRUM, JASON ROGER
PAINTER, MURALIST
b La Harpe, Ill, Oct 9, 35. Study: Chouinard Art Inst, with Richards Ruben & Donald Graham; studied murals of Jose C Oroszco, Guadalajara, Mex. Work: Mus Mod Art, New York; Los Angeles Co Mus, Los Angeles; NY Univ; Bradley Univ; Westinghouse Corp, Norman, Okla. Comn: Tammuz (mural), Bernhard Found, New York, 69; Peace (mural), City Walls, Inc, New York, 69; facade mural hanging, Jewish Mus, New York, 70; Libre (mural), comn by Garry Moore, Bronx, 71; Haven (mural), Buttenweiser Found, New York. Exhib: Ann Exhib, Los Angeles Co Mus, 59; City Walls, Mus Mod Art, New York, 69; Using Walls, Jewish Mus, 70. Teaching: Instr drawing & painting, Bradley Univ, 72-73; instr drawing & painting, Windham Col, 73-74. Pos: Founder & mem bd dirs, City Walls, Inc, 68, pres, 70-71, chmn bd dirs, 71- Bibliog: Juliette Boisriveaud (auth), Et les rues deviendrot des chefs - d'oeuvre pour tous, Elle Mag, 5/4/70; Painting the Town, Life Mag, 7/17/70; Hughs Rudd (auth), Public art, CBS News, 70. Mailing Add: c/o L'Affiche Galerie Ltd 145 Spring St New York NY 10012

CRUMBO, MINISA
PAINTER, GRAPHIC ARTIST
b Tulsa, Okla, Sept 2, 42. Study: Wasatch Acad; Tex Western Col, El Paso; Univ Colo; Taos Acad Fine Art, NMex, with Ray Vinella; Sch Visual Arts, New York, with Harvey Dinnerstein; Soc of Illusrs, with Daniel Schwartz. Work: Heard Mus, Phoenix, Ariz; Gilcrease Inst Am Hist & Art, Tulsa; Philbrook Art Ctr, Tulsa; Univ Tulsa. Exhib: Gallery A, Taos; Tribal Arts Gallery, Oklahoma City; 29th Am Indian Exhib, Philbrook Art Ctr, 74; Am Indian Art Traveling Show, Univ Ore, 76; two-person show, with Woody Crumbo, Pottawatomi Agency & Cult Ctr, Shawnee, Okla; Gov's Spec Showing, Tulsa, 76; Roy Clark Ranch Party-Television Spec, Tulsa, 76; Adobe Gallery, Las Vegas, Nev, 77; one-person shows, Tulsey Town Gallery, Tulsa, Gilcrease Inst Am Hist & Art, 77 & traveling show, Moscow, Leningrad & Kiev, USSR, 78. Teaching: Vis instr art, Taos Pueblo Day Sch Ctr. Awards: Oil Award & Graphics Award, 29th Am Indian Exhib, Philbrook Art Ctr, 74. Bibliog: Tricia Hurst (auth), Minisa Crumbo, Taos, New Mexico, SW Art Art, 1/75; Hardy Price (auth), Miss Crumbo dabbles no longer, Ariz Repub, 1/75; Ann DeFrange (auth), Spirit flows through brush, Sunday Oklahoman, Oklahoma City, 6/19/77. Style & Technique: Portraits of Indians in mixed-media, charcoal, watercolor or oil. Mailing Add: c/o Jim Halsey Co Inc 3225 S Norwood Tulsa OK 74135

CRUMBO, WOODY
PAINTER, PRINTMAKER
b Lexington, Okla, Jan 31, 12. Study: Am Indian Inst, Wichita, Kans; Wichita Univ, 33-36; Univ Kans, Lawrence; Univ Okla, 36-38, with Oscar Jacobson. Work: San Francisco Mus Art; Metrop Mus Art, New York; Smithsonian Inst, Washington, DC; Gilcrease Inst Am Hist & Art, Tulsa, Okla; Philbrook Art Ctr, Tulsa. Comn: Stained glass windows, Rose Chapel, Bacone Col, Muskogee, Okla, 36-38; Buffalo Hunt, Peyote Birds & Symbols, Flute Player & Wild Horses (murals), US Dept of Interior, Washington, DC, 39-41; Rainbow Trail (mural), Post Office, Nowata, Okla, 43. Exhib: Two-person exhib, with Minisa Crumbo, Pottawatomi Agency & Cult Ctr, Shawnee, Okla; over 1200 one-man shows, including, Gilcrease Inst Am Hist & Art. Pos: Dir art, Bacone Col, Muskogee, 38-41; cur & assembler, Am Indian art Collection, Gilcrease Inst Am Hist & Art, 45-48; asst dir, El Paso Mus Art, Tex, 60-68, dir & chief cur, 68-74; state chmn, Okla Indian Bicentennial Comn, 76. Awards: Julius Rosenwald Fel, 45; Okla Hall of Fame, 78. Style & Technique: Traditional Indian art. Media: Painting; Silkscreen; Etching. Mailing Add: c/o Jim Halsey Co Inc 3225 S Norwood Tulsa OK 74135

CRUME, GREGG
SCULPTOR, MOSAIC ARTIST
b Dayton, Ohio, Nov 8, 31. Study: Alfred Univ, BA; also sculpture with Frederick Allen Williams; Columbia Univ; Nat Defense & Educ Art Media Inst, Boston Univ; State Univ NY Buffalo, grad prog. Exhib: Nat Arts Club Ann Art Show, New York, 74; Burr Artists Inc 8th Ann, Caravan House Galleries, New York, 75; Composers, Authors & Artists of Am, Nat Conv for All Arts, New York, 75. Teaching: Instr mosaics, Niagara Wheatfield Cent Sch Syst Adult Educ, 63-65; teacher sculpture, Buffalo Bd Educ Plus Prog, 64-65. Awards: Award for Forgotten (sculpture), Composers, Authors & Artists Am, 75. Bibliog: Work featured on front & back covers of Composers, Authors & Artists Am Mag, winter-spring 75. Mem: Burr Artists; Composers, Authors & Artists Am, Inc; Eleanor Gaylee Gallery Found, New York; Nat Arts Club, New York; Salmagundi Club, New York. Style & Technique: Realistic, utilizing old world techniques; sculpture is incorporated into mosaics. Media: Wood, Clay; Semi-Precious Stone, Venetian Glass Tile. Mailing Add: 10880 Keller Rd Clarence NY 14031

CRUMP, WALTER MOORE
PRINTMAKER, PAINTER
b Winston-Salem, NC, Mar 18, 41. Study: Gilford Col, NC, 61-64; Harvard Univ Exten, 64-66; Boston Univ, BFA, 70; additional study with Walter Murch, David Aronson & Susan Smiley. Work: DeCordova Mus, Lincoln, Mass; R J Reynolds World Corp, Winston-Salem; Davidson Galleries, Seattle, Wash; NC Mus of Art, Raleigh; Southeastern Ctr for Contemp Art, Winston-Salem. Exhib: Davidson Nat Drawing & Print Exhib, NC, 73; Color Print USA, Tex Tech Univ, Lubbock, 75; Artists Under 36, DeCordova Mus, 76; Nat Print & Drawing Exhib, Miami Univ, Ohio, 77; Int Miniature Print Exhib, Pratt Graphics Ctr, New York, 77; Boston Printmakers Nat Exhib, Mus of Fine Arts, Boston, 75, Boston Ctr for the Arts, 76 & DeCordova Mus, 77. Teaching: Chmn art dept & instr printmaking, Commonwealth Sch, Boston, 72- Awards: Purchase Prize & Juror's Award, Southeastern Ctr for Contemp Art, Winston-Salem, 75; Purchase Prizes, Footprint Int Exhib, Davidson Galleries, Seattle, Wash, 76; Minot Drawing & Print Exhib, Minot State Col, NDak, 77. Mem: Boston Visual Artists Union (mem by-laws comt, 75, housing comt, 76 & printmakers comt, 76 & 77); Boston Printmakers (mem exec bd, 76-). Style & Technique: Landscape and figurative images. Media: Prints—collagraph & intaglio; oil on board & oil on free form cast shapes. Mailing Add: 59 Delle Ave Roxbury MA 02120

CRUTCHFIELD, WILLIAM RICHARD
PAINTER, PRINTMAKER
b Indianapolis, Ind, Jan 21, 32. Study: Herron Sch Art, Ind Univ, Indianapolis, BFA, 56; Tulane Univ, La, MFA, 60. Work: Mus Mod Art, New York; Art Inst Chicago; Cleveland Mus Art; Philadelphia Mus Art; Libr of Cong, Washington, DC. Comn: Countdown II (watercolor), Skylab II, NASA, 73; Alphabet Spire VI (laminated wood sculpture), Westfarms, West Hartford, Conn, 74. Exhib: Minneapolis Inst Art, 67; Ft Lauderdale Mus Arts, 71; NJ State Mus, Trenton, 71 & 72; California Prints 1972, Mus Mod Art, New York, 72; Dorsky Gallery, New York, 72, 73 & 75. 72. Awards: Mary Milliken Award for Travel in Europe, Herron Sch Art, Ind Univ, Indianapolis, 56; Fulbright Scholar, State Art Acad, Hamburg, Ger, 61. Bibliog: Jane Livingston (auth), Crutchfield phenomena, Art in Am, 1-2/71; article in Horizon, winter 72; Howard E Wooden (auth), Sage of machine wit, Studio Int, 74. Style & Technique: Satirical watercolors and prints of ships, trains & airplanes; sculpture of letter forms. Media: Watercolor; Lithography Screenprints. Publ: Illusr, Americana, 67, Owl Feathers, 70, Air, Land, Sea, 70, Six Rainbow Trains, 71 & A Report on the Art & Technology Program of the Los Angeles County Museum of Art 1967-1971, 71. Mailing Add: 1933 S Mesa St San Pedro CA 90731

CRUZ, EMILIO
PAINTER, INSTRUCTOR
b New York, NY, Mar, 1938. Study: John Hay Whitney fel, 64-65; Cintas Found fel, 65-66. Work: Mus Mod Art; World Trade Ctr; Ciba-Geigy Collection; plus many others in pvt collections. Exhib: Nat Collection Fine Arts, Smithsonian Inst, Washington, DC, 68; San Francisco Mus Art, Calif, 69; Univ Tex Mus, Austin, 69; Spanish Pavillion, St Louis, Mo, 70; one-man show, Loretto-Hilton Gallery, Webster Col, Mo, 69; plus many other group & one-man shows. Teaching: Ramblerny Sch Performing Arts, Bucks Co, Pa, 67; mem bd educ, South Bronx Multi-Purpose Educ Serv, New York, 67-68; artist in residence team, Rockefeller Danforth grant, Metrop Educ Coun Arts, St Louis Mo, 69; asst prof painting, Art Inst Chicago, 70- Pos: Chmn events & exhibs comt & dir, Wabash Transit Gallery, 72- Awards: Walter Gutman Found, 62; Nat Endowment Arts, 70-71. Mailing Add: 541 W North Ave Chicago IL 60610

CRUZ, HECTOR
PAINTER
b Chimalhuacan, Mex, July 2, 33. Study: La Esmeralda Sch Painting & Sculpture, grad, 51; Taller de Integracion Plastica; Inst Bellas Artes, 55. Work: Mus Arte Mod, Mus Bellas Artes, Salon Plastica Mex Belles Artes, Misrachi Gallery Mod Art & Gallery Plastica de Mex, Mexico City. Exhib: Collective Exhib Contemp Mex Art, Moscow, Russia, 57; Salon de Plastica Mexicana, Mexico City, 57 & 69; Art Mexicain Contemporain, France, 58; New Masters of San Carlos, Mexican Art Gallery, San Antonio, Tex, 62; New Vision of Landscape, Misrachi Gallery Mod Art, Mexico City, 71. Awards: Gold Medal, Collective Exhib Contemp Mex Art, Moscow, 57; New Year's Prize & First Place, Salon Plastica Mex, 57 & 69. Media: Oil. Mailing Add: Sierra Gorda 225 Mexico 10 DF Mexico

CRYSTAL, BORIS
PAINTER
b Poland, Dec 25, 31; US citizen. Study: Plocer's Sch Fine Arts, 62-63; Acad Fine Arts, Israel, 63-64. Work: Israel Mus, Tel-Aviv; Journalist House Art Gallery, Tel-Aviv; Herzl Inst Collection, New York; Nicholas Roerich Mus, New York; Mus Mod Art, New York; plus numerous other museums. Exhib: Israel Mus, Tel-Aviv, 64; Katz Art Gallery, Tel-Aviv, 64; Journalist House Art Gallery, Tel-Aviv, 66; Herzl Inst Art Gallery, New York, 68; Nicholas Roerich Mus, New York, 70; Mus Mod Art, New York, 72; Lerner Art Gallery, New York, 75; La Galerie Mouffe, Paris, France, 77; plus numerous others. Collections Arranged: Zionist Orgn Int Exhib USA, 65; Human Relations Coun in Coop with Art League USA, 68; Int Group Exhib of Paintings, Sculpture & Graphics, New Haven, Conn, 71. Awards: Int Award, Crown Art Gallery, 71; Vallombreuse Prize, Biarritz, France, 76. Bibliog: Max Founry (auth), Boris Crystal, Art News, 69. Mem: Artists Equity Asn; Art League New York. Style & Technique: Oil, watercolor; palette knife technique. Media: Oil on canvas. Dealer: Ella Lerner 241 E 76th St New York NY 10021. Mailing Add: 65-10 108th St Forest Hills NY 11375

CSOKA, STEPHEN
PAINTER, ETCHER
b Gardony, Hungary, Jan 2, 97; US citizen. Study: Budapest Royal Acad Art, 22-27. Work: Budapest Mus Art; Libr Cong; Brit Mus Art; Metrop Mus Art; Norfolk Mus Art; plus others. Exhib: Nat Acad Design, 40-45; one-man shows, Philadelphia Art Alliance, 43, Minn State Fair, 43, Galerie Paula Insel, New York, 67; I Biennial New Delhi, India, 68; Biennial Venize, Italy, 72. Teaching: Resident artist, Philadelphia Mus Sch Art, 57; lectr art, San Jose State Col, 70, Fullerton Col, 75 & Wash State Univ, 75. Awards: First Int Prize for Drawing, V Biennial of Sao Paulo, Brazil, 59; First Int Award, Mostra Bianco e Nero, 62; First Prize for Engraving, I Biennial of New Delhi, India, 68. Bibliog: Carlos Fuentes (auth), Los mundos de Jose Luis Cuevas, Misrachi Gallery, Mexico City, 70. Publ: Illusr, Recollections of Childhood, Kanthos Press, 62; illusr, Cuevas Charenton, Tamarind Workshop, 65; auth, Cuevas by Cuevas, Era, Mexico City, 65; illusr, Crime by Cuevas, Lublin Ed, 68; illusr, Homage to Quevedo, 69 & Cuevas Comedies, 71, Collectors Press; plus others. Dealer: Grace Borgenicht Gallery 1018 Madison Ave New York NY 10021; Misrachi Gallery Genova 20 Mexico City Mexico. Mailing Add: Galeana 109 San Angel Mexico City DF Mexico

CUFFARI, RICHARD J
ILLUSTRATOR, INSTRUCTOR
b Brooklyn, NY, Mar 2, 25. Study: Pratt Inst, Brooklyn, NY. Work: Kerlan Collection, Univ Minn; de Grummond Collection, Univ Southern Miss; plus others. Exhib: Soc Illustr Ann Show, New York, 69 & 70; Children's Bk Show, 73, 74 & Bk Show, 77, Am Inst Graphic Arts, New York; Children's Bk Showcase, Children's Bk Coun, New York, 74 & 75; Art of Children's Lit, Contemp Art Mus, Houston, Tex, 75. Teaching: Instr bk illus, Parsons Sch Design, New York, 76- Awards: Citation of Merit, Illusr Show, New York Soc Illusr, 69 & 70; Citation, Children's Bks Show, Am Inst Graphic Arts, 73 & 74; Christopher's Medal, Christopher Award, New York, 73. Bibliog: Commire (auth), Something about the author, Gale Res, Detroit, Vol 6 (1974); rev in Libr J, Sch Libr J, New York Times & Publ Weekly. Style & Technique: Book illustrations, mixed-media, black and white and color. Media: Pen & Ink; Watercolor. Publ: Illusr, The Wind in the Willows, Grosset & Dunlap, 66; illusr, The Endless Pavement, Seabury Press, 73; illusr, The Perilous Gard, Houghton Mifflin, 74; illusr, Two That Were Tough, Viking, 76; illusr, The Melodeon, Doubleday & Co, 77. Mailing Add: 1320 E 27th St Brooklyn NY 11210

CULBERTSON, JANET LYNN (MRS DOUGLAS KAFTEN)
PAINTER, INSTRUCTOR
b Greensburg, Pa, Mar 15, 32. Study: Carnegie Inst Technol, BFA, 53; Art Students League, 54; graphics, Atelier 17, New York, 55; NY Univ, MA, 63; Pratt Graphic Arts Inst, 64-65. Work: Univ Mass, Amherst Mus Collection; AT&T, Chicago; Westinghouse Corp, Pittsburgh; Delta Corp, NY. Exhib: One-woman shows, Molly Barnes Gallery, Los Angeles, 70, Midtown Gallery, Atlanta, Ga, 71 & Lerner-Heller Gallery, New York, 71, 73, 75 & 77; Philadelphia Mus Art, 74; Heckscher Mus, New York, 75; Brooklyn Mus, 75; Am Acad Arts & Lett, 75; Bronx Mus, New York, 76; Benson Gallery, Bridgehampton, 78; plus others. Teaching: Instr art, Pace Col, 64-68; adj prof, Pratt Art Inst, 73-74 & Southampton Col, NY, 76. Awards: Award, Palos Verdes Mus Ann, 70; Bibliog: Mary Vaughn (auth), article in Arts Mag, 4/77. Mem: Women in Arts; Heresies; Women's Caucus for Art. Style & Technique: Realist, surrealist. Media: Acrylic, Silver Point. Dealer: Lerner-Heller Gallery 956 Madison Ave New York NY 10021. Mailing Add: 525 E 82nd St New York NY 10028

CULKIN, JOHN MICHAEL
ART ADMINISTRATOR, EDUCATOR
b Brooklyn, NY, June 21, 28. Study: Woodstock Col, STL, 61; Harvard Univ, EdD, 64. Teaching: Asst prof commun, Fordham Univ, New York, 63-69; lectr media studies, New Sch for Social Res, New York, 74- Pos: Dir, Ctr for Commun, Fordham Univ, 63-69; dir & founder, Ctr for Understanding Media, New York, 69- & Media Studies Prog, New Sch for Social Res, 74- Mem: Am Film Inst (trustee, 68-73); Media Educators Asn (founder, 70); Art, Educ & Americans (media adv). Publ: Auth, A Schoolman's Guide to Marshall McLuhan, Saturday Rev, 67; ed, Trilogy—An Experiment in Multi-Media, Macmillan, 68; contribr, Summerhill—For and Against, Hart, 68; co-auth, Films Deliver, Citation, 69; auth, The New Literacy: From the Alphabet to Television, Media & Methods, 77. Mailing Add: 69 Horatio St New York NY 10014

CUMMENS, LINDA TALABA
See Talaba, L

CUMMING, GLEN EDWARD
MUSEUM DIRECTOR
b Calgary, Alta, July 2, 36. Study: Alberta Col Art, 4 yr dipl. Collections Arranged: Sakatchwan, Saskatoon & Regina, 1970; Nine Out of Ten, A Survey of Contemporary Canadian Art 1974-75; Ontario Now: A Survey of Contemporary Art 1976; Karel Appel, The Complete Graphic Collection (1957-1977), 77. Pos: Cur, Regina Pub Libr Art Gallery, Sask, 67-69; dir, Kitchener-Waterloo Art Gallery, Kitchener, Ont, 69-72; dir, Robert McLaughlin Gallery, Oshawa, Ont, 72-73; dir, Art Gallery Hamilton, Ont, 73- Awards: Queen Elizabeth Prize, Govt Alberta, 60. Mem: Ontario Asn Art Galleries (pres, 74-75); Asn Art Mus Dir; Can Art Mus Dirs Orgn; Can Mus Asn; Am Mus Asn; Int Coun Mus. Mailing Add: 222 Jackson St W 1502 Hamilton ON Can

CUMMING, ROBERT H
CONCEPTUAL ARTIST
b Worcester, Mass, Oct 7, 43. Study: Mass Col Art, Boston, BA, 65; Univ Ill, Champaign, MFA, 67. Work: Univ NMex, Albuquerque; San Diego State Col, Calif. Comn: Outdoor sculpture, Walker Art Ctr, Minneapolis, Minn, 70; Nation's Capitol Documentation, Corcoran Gallery, Washington, DC. Exhib: Art by Telephone, Mus Contemp Art, Chicago, 69; 9 Artists/9 Spaces, Walker Art Ctr, Minneapolis, Minn, 70; 24 Young Los Angeles Artists, Los Angeles Co Mus, 71; Narrative Art, Palais des Beaux Arts, Brussels, Belg, 75; one-man shows, John Gibson Gallery, New York, 73 & 75; Whitney Biennial, New York, 77; Paris Biennale, Mus d'Art Mod, France, 77. Teaching: Instr painting & drawing, Univ Wis, Milwaukee, 67-70; lectr photography, Univ Calif, Los Angeles, 74- Awards: Frank Logan Prize, Chicago Art Inst, 69; Nat Endowment for Arts Awards, Washington, DC, 72 & 74. Bibliog: D Zack (auth), The Phenomenon of Mail Art, Art In Am, New York, 2/73; M Jochimsen (auth), Story Art, Mag Kunst, Mainz, Ger, 2/74; P Foschi (auth), Robert Cumming's Eccentric Illusions, Artforum, New York, 6/75. Style & Technique: Sculptural props exhibited in photo form; books as long-range works; currently, fictional stories & photos. Media: Conceptual Art. Publ: Auth, Picture Fictions, Anaheim, Calif, 71; auth, The Weight of Franchise Meat, Anaheim, Calif, 71; auth, A Training in the Arts, Toronto, Can, 73; auth, A Discourse on Domestic Disorder, Irvine, Calif, 75 & Interruptions in Landscape & Logic, 77. Dealer: John Gibson Gallery 392 W Broadway New York NY 10012. Mailing Add: 227 S Shaffer Orange CA 92666

CUMMINGS, DAVID WILLIAM
PAINTER
b Okmulgee, Okla, July 15, 37. Study: Kansas City Art Inst, Mo, BFA, 63; Univ Nebr, Lincoln, MFA, 67. Work: Whitney Mus Am Art, New York; Los Angeles Co Mus Art, Los Angeles, Calif; Phoenix Art Mus, Ariz; Les Ateliers Du Grand Hornu, Mons, Belg; Aldrich Mus Contemp Art, Ridgefield, Conn. Exhib: One-man shows, Henri Gallery, Washington, DC, 69, Katz Galleries, New York, 70, Gallery Alexandra Monett, 75-77 & Allan Stone Gallery, New York, 75-77; Lyrical Abstraction, Philadelphia Mus, Pa, 70 & Whitney Mus Am Art, 71; New Work, New York (traveling show), Am Fedn Arts, 70-72; 20th Century Am Artists, Corcoran Gallery Art, Washington, DC, 71; Columbus Mus Fine Arts, Ohio, 71; Contemp Reflections, Aldrich Mus Contemp Art, 71-72; Dix Jeunes Americains Jeugd en Plastische Kunst, Gent, Belg, 76; USA Les Ateliers Du Grand Hornu, Mons, Belg. Pos: Vis artist, Ohio State Univ, Columbus, 74 & Univ Iowa, Iowa City, 76; coordr painting symposium, Colo Mountain Col, Vail, 76-78. Awards: Purchase Award, Nelson Gallery, Kansas City, Mo, Ford Found, 63; John Lehmann Award, St Louis Mus Art, Mo, 65; Woods Found Fel, Univ Nebr, 66-67. Bibliog: David Shirey (auth), Lyrical abstraction, New York Times, 71; George Clary (auth), Current Gotham art, Athens Banner-Herald, Ga, 71; Dix Jeunes Americains, La Libre Belgique, 76. Style & Technique: Non-objective color paintings. Media: Alkyd & Oil on Panel; Pastel. Dealer: Allan Stone Gallery 48 E 86th St New York NY 10028. Mailing Add: 458 Broome St New York NY 10013

CUMMINGS, FREDERICK JAMES
ART ADMINISTRATOR, ART HISTORIAN
b Floydada, Tex, Aug 19, 33. Study: Willamette Univ, BA, 54; Harvard Univ, MA, 56; Univ Chicago, PhD(hons), 66; Courtauld Inst Art, Univ London, 60-61. Collections Arranged: American Decorative Arts from the Pilgrims to the Revolution, 67; Art in Italy, 1600-1700, 65; Romantic Art in Britain: Paintings & Drawings, 1760-1860; Painting in France, 1774-1830. Teaching: Instr art hist, Univ Mo, 61-64; adj prof art hist, Wayne State Univ, 65- Pos: Actg dir, Mus Art & Archaeol, Univ Mo, 63-64; asst dir & cur European art, Detroit Inst Arts, 64-73, dir, 73-; ed, Art Quart, 66-69. Awards: Hon Fine Arts Silver Medal Award, Mich Acad Sci, Arts & Lett, 72. Mem: Col Art Asn Am (bd dirs, 71-); Am Asn Mus; Am Soc 18th Century Studies. Res: Romantic painting in Western Europe. Publ: Co-auth, Romantic art in Britain: painting & drawings, 1760-1860; auth, Charles Bell & anatomy of expression, Art Bull, 64; auth, Wright's Boothby, Rousseau, & the romantic malady, Burlington Mag, 68; auth, Folly & mutability in Joseph Wright's alchemist & democritus, Art Quart, 70; contribr, Proc, Am Soc 18th Century Studies, 72. Mailing Add: Detroit Inst of Arts 5200 Woodward Ave Detroit MI 48202

CUMMINGS, NATHAN
COLLECTOR
b St John, NB. Collection: Impressionists; post-impressionists; Fauves; cubists. Mailing Add: Waldorf Towers 100 E 50th St New York NY 10022

CUMMINS, KAREN GASCO
ART ADMINISTRATOR
b Trenton, NJ, Jan 30, 45. Study: Goucher Col, BA; Temple Univ, MEd; NY Univ, course work completed for doctorate. Collections Arranged: NJ traveling art exhibs, Intaglio Printmaking, Planographic Printmaking, Relief Printmaking, Merci (prints & posters by Ben Shahn), For the Sake of a Single Verse (by Ben Shahn), Olympic Games Posters, The Dreigroschen Film, Eleven Pop Artists, also two portfolios by John Randolph Carter. Pos: Sr mus technician, NJ State Mus, Trenton, 67-68, coordr traveling exhib & pub info officer, 68-73, asst to dir, 73- Mem: Mus Coun NJ (chmn, 73-75); Northeast Mus Conf; Am Asn Mus. Mailing Add: NJ State Mus 205 W State St Trenton NJ 08625

CUNINGHAM, ELIZABETH BAYARD (MRS E W R TEMPLETON)
ART DEALER
b New York, NY. Study: Bronxville Sch, NY; Vassar Col, Poughkeepsie, NY; Finch Col, NY, BA; Hunter Col, New York, MA(art hist). Pos: Exec secy, Olana Preserv Inc, New York, 65-66; dir publicity, Comt to Rescue Italian Art, New York, 66-67; asst to pres, Nat Trust for Hist Preserv, 68-70; asst dir, Reese Palley Art Gallery, New York, 70-72; pres, Cuningham Ward Inc, 72- Mem: Drawing Soc Inc (exec comt, 70-). Specialty: Contemporary painting. Mailing Add: Cuningham Ward Inc 94 Prince St New York NY 10012

CUNNINGHAM, (CHARLES) BRUCE
PAINTER
b Bayonne, NJ, Mar 30, 43. Study: Baylor Univ, BFA; Univ Tex, Austin; Univ Calif, Berkeley, MA & MFA; also with Erle Loran, Elmer Bischoff & David Simpson. Work: Baylor Univ; Am Tel & Tel Co, NJ; Univ Tex, Arlington; Dallas Mus Fine Art, Tex; McLennan Community Col, Waco, Tex. Exhib: 16th Ann Eight State Exhib Painting & Sculpture, Okla Art Ctr, 74; Univ Tex Nat Bicentennial Art Exhib, Arlington, 75; SW/Tarrant Co Ann, Ft Worth Art Mus, Tex, 75 & 76; 112 Green St Gallery, New York, 75; Paperworks, Watson de Nagy Gallery, Houston, Tex, 76; Tex-Can Painters Exchange Show, David Mirvish Gallery, Toronto, Ont, 77; New in the Seventies, Univ Art Mus, Austin, Tex, 77; one-man shows, Paintings & Drawings, Tyler Mus Art, Tex, 75, Projects II, Dallas Mus Fine Arts, 75, Christian Univ, Ft Worth, Richland Col, Dallas, Univ Okla, Norman, 75-76, Amarillo Art Ctr, 77, Longview Mus & Art Ctr, Tex, 77 & Watson de Nagy Gallery, Houston, 77; plus others. Teaching: Instr painting & drawing, Baylor Univ, 72-74; asst prof painting & drawing, Univ Tex, Arlington, 75-77. Pos: Artist-in-residence, Tex Comn Arts & Humanities, Longview Mus & Arts Ctr, 74-75. Awards: Nat Endowment for the Arts Fel, 75; Amarillo Two-Dimensional Three State Exhib Cash Award, Amarillo Art Mus, 75; First Award in Painting, SW/Tarrant Co Ann, Ft Worth Art Mus, 76. Style & Technique: Abstract paintings; large scale drawings. Media: Acrylic, Charcoal. Mailing Add: 40 Great Jones St New York NY 10012

CUNNINGHAM, CHARLES C, JR
ART ADMINISTRATOR
b Boston, Mass, May 25, 34. Study: Harvard Univ, AB, 56 & MBA, 60. Pos: Chmn, Overseers Comt to Visit Harvard Univ Art Mus, 71-; trustee, Mus Fine Arts, Boston, 72-; participant, 46th Am Assembly, 74. Mem: Fel Pierpont Morgan Libr, New York. Mailing Add: 100 Charles River Plaza Boston MA 02114

CUNNINGHAM, CHARLES CREHORE
CURATOR, LECTURER
b Mamaroneck, NY, Mar 7, 10. Study: Harvard Univ, AB, 32; Courtauld Inst, Univ London, BA, 33; Harvard Grad Sch, 34; Univ Hartford, hon DFA, 59; DePaul Univ, LittD, 70. Collections Arranged: Fifty Painters of Architecture, 47, Life in 17th Century Holland, 51, Romantic Circle, 52, Harvest of Plenty-De Gustibus, 63, all Wadsworth Atheneum, Hartford; Rembrandt After Three Hundred Years (with catalog), Art Inst Chicago, 69; Elegant Academics, Clark Art Inst, 74 & Jongkind and the Pre-Impressionists, 77. Teaching: Lectr, Williams Col, 73-77. Pos: Asst cur, Mus Fine Arts, Boston, 34-41; dir, Wadsworth Atheneum, 46-66; dir, Art Inst Chicago, 66-72; chief cur, Sterling & Francine Clark Art Inst, Williamstown, Mass, 73-77; pres, ICOM Found, 77- Awards: Univ Club Chicago Distinguished Serv to Arts Award, 72; Order of Merit, Repub of Italy. Mem: Asn Art Mus Dirs (pres, 58); Benjamin Franklin fel Royal Soc Arts; Conn Comn on Arts (chmn, 64-66). Res: Dutch school; Rembrandt and Rembrandt school; 19th century French painting. Collection: French, Dutch and American paintings. Publ: Medicine Man, 54, Pierpont Morgan Treasures, 64; Modern French Painting & Drawing in The Art Institute of Chicago, Japanese ed, Kodansha Press, 70; Jongkind and the Pre-Impressionists, Painters of the École Saint-Siméon, 77. Mailing Add: 218 South St Williamstown MA 01267

CUNNINGHAM, FRANCIS
PAINTER
b New York, NY, Jan 18, 31. Study: Art Students League, with Edwin Dickinson & Robert Beverly Hale. Work: Berkshire Mus, Pittsfield, Mass. Exhib: One-man shows, Hirschl & Adler Galleries, New York, 67, 70 & 75; Butler Inst Am Art, Youngstown, Ohio, 67, 72 & 74; Nat Acad Design, New York, 67, 69, 71-73 & 76-77; one-man shows, Berkshire Mus, Pittsfield, Mass, 69, Distelheim Galleries, Chicago, 70, Mickelson Gallery, Washington, DC, 71 & Welles Gallery, Lenox Libr, Mass, 71; Contemporary Figure, Suffolk Mus, Stony Brook, NY, 71; A Sense of Place, Lincoln, Nebr, 73; Contemp Portraits, Lowe Art Mus, Tampa, Fla, 74. Teaching: Lectr art hist, painting & drawing, City Col New York, 62-65; instr painting & drawing, Brooklyn Mus Art Sch, 62- Awards: Peebles Award, Berkshire Mus, 65; Berkshire Art Asn Purchase Award, Berkshire Mus, 68; Louis Comfort Tiffany Found Grant, 73. Style & Technique: Realistic. Media: Oil. Publ: Co-auth, Polykleitos' Diadoumenos: measurement & animation, Art Quart, summer 62; illusr, Fundamentals of roentgenology, 64. Dealer: Hirschl & Adler Galleries 21 E 67th St New York NY 10021. Mailing Add: 789 West End Ave New York NY 10025

CUNNINGHAM, J
SCULPTOR
b Greenwich, Conn, Sept 18, 40. Study: Kenyon Col, BA, 62; Yale Sch Art & Archit, BFA, 63 & MFA, 65. Work: Hirshhorn Mus; plus others and many pvt collections. Exhib: One-man shows, Hathorn Gallery, Skidmore Col, 69, Takumi Gallery, Saratoga Springs, 71, Atelier Chapman Kelley, 71 & 73, Hurlbutt Gallery, Greenwich, Conn, 72 & Okla Art Ctr, 74; Structured Sculpture, Galerie Chalette, New York, 68; Baltimore Mus, 70; Lenox Hill Show, Gimbel's East & Denis Rene Gallery, 72, New York & others. Teaching: Vis critic design, Williams Col, spring 68 & Union Col, spring 71; instr sculpture, Inst Arts & Sci, Williamstown, Mass, summer 68 & Skidmore Col, summer 69; vis lectr, Saratoga Performing Arts Ctr, 71; asst prof art, Skidmore Col, Saratoga Springs, 75- Awards: Fel in Sculpture, Univ Pa, 66. Style & Technique: A synthesis of contour, mass, interior and exterior reflections and refraction brought about by lens-like modulations of thickness and curvature of Plexiglas. Mailing Add: Dept of Art Skidmore Col Saratoga Springs NY 12866

CUNNINGHAM, J
PAINTER, EDUCATOR
b Madison Twp, NJ, Apr 5, 06. Study: Univ Calif, Berkeley, AB, 27, MA(art), 28, hon traveling fel to Munich, Ger, with Hans Hofmann; anat, Univ Munich & Andre L'Hote, Paris; Cagnes-Sur-Mer, with Beniamino Bufano, AM; Carmel Art Inst, with Fernand Leger, 41 & Alexander Archipenko, 51. Exhib: One-man shows, M H De Young Mem Mus, San Francisco, 32 & Carmel Art Asn Galleries, 64 & 70; Calif Palace of Legion of Honor, 33; Cranbrook Mus Art & Detroit Art Inst, 33. Teaching: Head dept art, Cranbrook Sch, Bloomfield Hills, Mich, 31-33, resident artist painting, Cranbrook Acad Art, 31-33, dir summer sch, 33; vis prof art in indust, Mills Col, Calif, 35; dir painting & pres, Carmel Art Inst, Calif, 39- Pos: Chief designer exhibs, US Resettlement Admin, Washington, DC, 73; staff artist, Gov Comn, Univ Calif Hall of Sci, 38; mural painter, exhib designer & articulator, Palace of Fine & Decorative Arts, Golden Gate Int Expos, San Francisco, 38. Awards: First Hon Mention, San Francisco Art Asn, 70th Ann. Bibliog: Bob Kaller (auth), John Cunningham, painter, Carmel Pine Cone, 11/55; Steve Hauk (auth), Close up John Cunningham, Carmel Valley Outlook, 68; Bonnie Gartshore (auth), Europe with camper & canvas, Monterey Peninsula Herald Weekend Mag, 12/73. Mem: Carmel Art Asn (pres, 65). Style & Technique: Contemporary; all subject matter; palette knife and brush. Media: Oil. Dealer: Howard Terhune's The Gallery 168 N Palm Canyon Dr Palm Springs CA 92262; Carmel Art Asn Galleries Carmel CA 93921. Mailing Add: 43 El Potrero Carmel Valley CA 93924

CURRAN, DARRYL JOSEPH
PHOTOGRAPHER, PRINTMAKER
b Santa Barbara, Calif, Oct 19, 35. Study: Ventura Col, AA, 58; Univ Calif, Los Angeles, BA, 60 & MA, 64. Work: Fogg Art Mus, Harvard Univ, Cambridge, Mass; Univ Art Mus, Univ NMex, Albuquerque; Nat Gallery Can, Ottawa; Int Mus Photog, George Eastman House, Rochester, NY; Art Inst Chicago. Exhib: Vision & Expression, George Eastman House, 68; Photog into Sculpture, Mus Mod Art, New York, 70; Photog into Art, Brit Arts Coun, 73; Photog Unlimited, Fogg Art Mus, 74; one-man shows, Focus Gallery, San Francisco, Calif, 74, Midway Studios, Univ Chicago, 75 & Univ RI, Kingston, 75; Photo/Synthesis, Johnson Mus Art, Cornell Univ, Ithaca, NY, 76. Collections Arranged: Graphic/Photographic (auth, catalogue), Art Gallery, Calif State Univ, Fullerton, 71; 24 From LA (auth, catalogue), San Francisco Mus Mod Art, 73; Photo Visionaries, Floating Wall Gallery, Santa Ana, Calif, 76; Los Angeles Perspectives, Secession Gallery, Victoria, BC, 76; Premeditated Fantasy, Univ Colo, Boulder, 76. Teaching: Assoc prof creative photog, Calif State Univ, Fullerton, 67-; vis artist creative photog, Sch of Art Inst Chicago, spring 75. Awards: Phelen Award in Photog, James Phelan Trust, Oakland Mus, 71; First Place in Photog, 76 Calif Art Expo, Calif State Fair, 76. Bibliog: Robert Stuart (auth), Light & Substance, Univ NMex, Coke/Barrow, 74. Mem: Soc Photog Educ (bd dir, 75-79); Los Angeles Ctr for Photog Studies (bd dir, 73-77); Los Angeles Inst Conte Art. Style & Technique: Photography and graphic media; cyanotype, brown print, print; photolitho and photo-silkscreen; limited edition books; offset. Publ: Contribr, Revolution in a Box, Univ Calif, Riverside, 7 contribr, Untitled 11, Emerging Lo Angeles Photographers, Friends of Photog, Carmel, Calif Dealer: G Ray Hawkins Gallery 9002 Melrose Ave Los Angeles C Mailing Add: 10537 Dunleer Dr Los Angeles CA 90064

CURRIE, BRUCE
PAINTER
b Sac City, Iowa, Nov 27, 11. Work: Nat Acad Design, New York; State Univ NY Albany; Butler Inst Am Art, Youngstown, Ohio; Dwight Art Mem, Mt Holyoke Col; Kalamazoo Inst Arts, Mich. Exhib: Butler Inst Am Art, 13 Ann Exhib, 53-74; Nat Acad Design, 69-78; Conn Acad Fine Arts, Hartford, 70; Colorado Springs Fine Arts Ctr, Colo, 71; Albany Inst Hist & Art, 75; plus many others incl one-man shows. Awards: Thomas B Clarke Prize, Nat Acad Design, 66; Charles Noel Flagg Mem Prize, Conn Acad Fine Arts, 68; The Ralph Fabri Award, Audubon Artists, 76. Mem: Nat Acad Design; Conn Acad Fine Arts; Am Watercolor Soc; Audubon Artists; Woodstock Artists Asn. Media: Oil. Mailing Add: RFD Box 284 Woodstock NY 12498

CURRY, NOBLE WILBUR
PAINTER, PRINTMAKER
b Findlay, Ohio, Jan 22, 94. Study: Under Julius Galz, Columbus Sch Art, Ohio. Work: Cleveland Pub Libr; Ernest Bohn Collection, Case Western Reserve Univ; Wilmington Col, Ohio. Comn: Oil painting of St Michael, Fed Art in Cleveland, 39, plus many others. Exhib: Art Asn of Newport, 44; 13th Ann, Oakland Art Gallery, Calif, 45; 19th NW Printmakers, Seattle Art Mus, 47; Wilmington Col, 51; Creative Gallery, New York, 53; Cleveland Mus Art. Awards: Second Prize, Ohio State Fair, 20; Hon Mention, Cleveland Art Mus, 30. Bibliog: Stan Feinstein (auth), Review of show at Creative Gallery, Art Digest, 3/53; Betty Holliday (auth), Reivew of show at Creative Gallery, Art News, 3/53; Jane Scott (auth), Federal Art Show 1974, Cleveland Plain Dealer. Style & Technique: Brush, pallet knife, collage, dry paint and regular etching. Media: Oil. Publ: Auth, History of Battery C, 324th FA(H), 83rd Division, USA, 19 & auth, Frank L Zimpfer, 19, Heer Printing Co. Mailing Add: 4625 Porter Rd North Olmsted OH 44070

CURTIS, MARY CRANFILL
PRINTMAKER, PAINTER
b Ft Worth, Tex, Aug 6, 25. Study: Columbia Univ, BS; Southern Methodist Univ, MFA; grad print workshop, ETex State Univ; also workshops in NMex & San Miguel de Allende, Mexico. Dallas Mus Fine Arts, Tex; Okla Art Ctr, Oklahoma City; Southern Methodist Univ; Mobil Oil Collection; Heard Mus Natural Hist, McKinney, Tex; plus others. Comn: Portraits, Austin Col, 57; designed 25 ft rug woven in Hong Kong showing Texas history, Grayson Co State Bank, Sherman, Tex, 63 & designed glass murals, 65. Exhib: SW Print & Drawing, Dallas Mus Fine Arts, 66; NH Int Graphics Ann, Rivier, 73; Boston Printmakers, Mass, 73-76; Davidson Nat Print & Drawing, NC, 74; Int Miami Graphics Biennial, Fla, 75 & 77; Libr of Cong & Nat Collection Fine Arts Nat Exhib Prints, Washington, DC, 75; Los Angeles Printmaking Nat, 75; three-person show, Masur Mus Art, Monroe, La, 76. Teaching: Instr art, Austin Col, 55-57 & 65-67; instr art, Sch Continuing Educ, Southern Methodist Univ, 68-75 & Artists Courtyard, Dallas, 75- Pos: Bd mem & prog chmn, Sherman Art League, 63-67 & Richardson Civic Art Soc, Tex, 72- Awards: First Graphics Prize, Univ Tex, Arlington, 73; Midwestern Graphics Purchase Award, Tulsa City-County Libr, Okla, 75; Juror's Commendation, Boston Printmakers, 75. Mem: Boston Printmakers; Graphics Soc, Hollis, NH; Artists Equity; Dallas Print & Drawing Soc; Tex Fine Arts Asn (first vpres, Dallas Chap, 74-). Style & Technique: New realist in printmaking; semi-realist in painting. Dealer: Assoc Am Artists 663 Fifth Ave New York NY 10022. Mailing Add: 328 Sutton Pl Richardson TX 75080

CURTIS, PHILIP CAMPBELL
PAINTER
b Jackson, Mich, May 26, 07. Study: Albion Col, BA, 30; Univ Mich Law Sch; Yale Univ Sch Fine Arts, cert, 35; Harvard Univ, 41; Albion Col, hon DFA, 71. Exhib: 20 yr retrospective exhib, Northern Ariz Univ, 67; one-man shows, Palm Springs Desert Mus, Calif, 71, Dickson Art Ctr, Univ Calif, Los Angeles, 72, Univ Nev, Las Vegas, 72, Utah Mus Fine Arts, Salt Lake City, 72, Galerie Ariadne, Vienna, 74, Scottsdale Ctr for the Arts, Ariz, 78 & Phillips Gallery, Washington, DC, 78, Ariz Invitational 75, Phoenix Art Mus, 75; plus 15 other one-man shows. Pos: Supvr mural painting, Works Progress Admin Proj, New York, 35; founder & first dir, Phoenix Art Ctr & Phoenix Art Mus, Ariz, 36-39; designer, WPA Art Proj Exhib, de Young Mus, San Francisco, Calif, 38; mem staff, Des Moines Art Ctr, 39-41. Bibliog: Jose Bermudez (auth, film), The Time Freeze, 74. Mem: Benjamin Franklin fel Royal Soc Arts. Style & Technique: Surreal. Media: Oil. Dealer: Coe Kerr Gallery 49 E 82nd St New York NY 10028; Jan Krugier Gallery Geneva Switz. Mailing Add: 109 Cattle Track Scottsdale AZ 85253

CURTIS, PHILLIP HOUSTON
CURATOR, LECTURER
b Little Rock, Ark, July 25, 45. Study: Univ Ark, BA(hist); Univ Del, Henry Francis du Pont Winterthur Mus, MA(early Am cult); Attingham Park Summer Sch, Eng. Collections Arranged: NJ Craftsmen, 72, Am Folk Quilts (auth, catalogue), 73, Whaling Days in NJ, 74, Silk, Tea & Procelain: Trade Goods from the Orient, 75, The Art of the Fan, 76, The Ballantine House (auth, catalogue), 76, In the Latest Style—Costumes, 76, Am Coverlets, 77 & Chinese Ceramics (contribr, catalogue), 77, Newark Mus. Pos: Cur decorative arts, Newark Mus, 72- Res: Tucker porcelain, 1828-1838; New Jersey furniture and ceramics. Publ: Contribr, Ian M Quimby, ed, Ceramics in America: Winterthur Conference Report 1972, Winterthur Mus, 73; contribr, Encyclopedia of Victoriana, Rainbird Press, London, 74. Mailing Add: Newark Mus 43-49 Washington St Newark NJ 07101

CURTIS, ROGER WILLIAM
PAINTER, ART DEALER
b Gloucester, Mass, Dec 20, 10. Study: Exten courses, Boston Univ, Harvard Univ, Mus Sch Boston; pvt study with Aldro T Hibbard; Burdett Col. Work: Concord Art Asn Permanent Collection; plus pvt & indust collections. Exhib: Jordan Marsh Exhib, 45-75; Arts Atlantic Exhib, NShore Arts Asn, Gloucester, 47-75; Sheldon-Swope Mus, Terre Haute, Ind; Symphony Hall Exhib, Boston, 65-70; Acad Artist Asn, Springfield, Mass, 72-75. Teaching: Instr painting, pvt classes, 53- Pos: Pres, Burlington Art Asn, Mass, 60-64; adminr, Ledgendsea Gallery & Riverview Gallery, currently. Awards: Waters of the World, Gorton Corp, 71 & 74; First Prize Mem Award, Acad Artists Asn, 73; First Prize, Conn Art Asn, Meriden, 73. Mem: Guild Boston Artists (treas, 68-, bd mgrs); NShore Arts Asn (pres, 52-58, treas, 65-); Am Artists Prof League (past vpres, treas, Mass Chap, 72-); Cape Ann Festival Arts (treas, presently). Style & Technique: Traditional painting of the sea; brush and/or pallette knife. Media: Oil. Specialty: Aldro T Hibbard; landscapes, marine, still life, portraits in traditional manner. Collection: Aldro T Hibbard, William Paxton, Frank Rehn, Edmund Tarbell, Gordon Grant, Frank Benson, Frederick Mulhaupt; plus others. Publ: Auth & illusr, How to Paint Successful Seascapes, 75 & Color in Outdoor Painting, 77, Watson-Guptill. Mailing Add: c/o New England Artists 30 Riverview Rd Gloucester MA 01930

CURTISS, GEORGE CURT
PAINTER, ILLUSTRATOR
b Rasnov, Romania, Feb 15, 11. Study: Acad Art, Milan, Italy, BFA; Acad Fine Arts, Berlin, Ger, BFA; also with Prof Holst & Erik Richter. Work: Mus Mod Art, Munich; Mus Art, Vienna; Mus Sci & Natural Hist, Miami; Galeria del Sagrato, Milan; Artist's Arch, Thieme-Becker Int Artist's Lexicon, Heilbronn, WGer; plus others. Comn: Murals, Galeria del Sagrato, Milan, Italy, 50, murals, Am Red Cross, Salzburg, Austria, 51; posters, Teatro Lirico, Milan, Italy, 57; exhibits, backgrounds & murals, Mus Sci & Natural Hist, Miami, 57-64; scenery designs, Cinetron Film Co, Miami, 68. Exhib: Mus Sci & Natural Hist, 57-68; El Centro Gallery Art, Coral Gables-Miami, 59; Loft Gallery Arts, Hollywood, 63; Montmartre Art Galleries, Palm Beach, 67; exhib in most of Europe. Collections Arranged: As cur of exhib of the Mus of Sci & Natural Hist, planned, designed & executed over one hundred exhibits, including painting the backgrounds in oil in various sizes. Teaching: Art teacher portrait, Channel 4, WTVJ, Miami, 52-57; instr drawing, Mus Sci & Natural Hist, 57-64. Pos: Scenery & costume designer, Ballett-Revue Carise, Vienna-Milan, 48-51; cur, Mus Sci & Natural Hist, 57-64; dir, Loft Gallery Art, Hollywood, 64-67; dir, R Gallery Art, Miami, 52-75. Awards: Medal, Acad Fine Arts, Munich, 51; Medal, Galeria Del Sagrato, Milan, Cert Honor, Mus Sci & Natural Hist, 61. Bibliog: Artist's Archives, Heilbronn, 70; Thieme-Becker (auth), International Artists, Bonn, 71; May H Edmonds (auth), Local Authors & the Florida Scene, 71; plus others. Mem: Am Fedn Arts; Artists Equity. Style & Technique: Portraits, landscapes, contemporary, modern, stylized realism. Media: Oil, Graphics. Specialty: Promotion of local American artists. Publ: Illusr, Who Smiles with Us, 49; illusr, The Illustration, 52; contribr, Artist's See Themselves, 59; auth & illusr, Li'l Piccolo's Adventures with Music & Instruments, Univ Miami, 71. Mailing Add: 832 NE 124th St North Miami FL 33161

CUSICK, NANCY TAYLOR
PAINTER
b Washington, DC. Study: Am Univ, BA, 59, MA, 61, Elizabeth Van Swinderin scholar & with Gates, Calfee, D'Arista & Summerford; Corcoran Art Sch, 68; Univ Calif, 71, with Lindgren. Exhib: Washington Artists Ann, Smithsonian Inst, Washington, DC, 60-69; three-man show, Art Asn Newport, RI, 65; Corcoran Gallery Art Area Exhib, Washington, 67; area show, Washington Co Mus, Hagerstown, Md, 67; Univ Va, Charlotte, 68; Washington Artists Today, Massillon Mus, Ohio, 69; Seven Women Artists, Dunbarton Col, Washington, DC, 72; Southeastern Mus Tour, Artists Equity, 73; Washington Women Artists, George Washington Univ, 75; Wash Proj for the Arts Drawing Show, 75; 1st Ann Alumnae Artists Show, Am Univ, 76; St Johns Col, Annapolis, Md, 76. Teaching: Instr advanced painting & art hist, Dunbarton Col Holy Cross, 66-72, instr painting, design, art hist & drawing, Prince George's Col, 72-77. Awards: First Prize for Painting, Soc Washington Artists, 66; Best in Show, Hagerstown Mus, Pangborn Corp, 67. Bibliog: Article in Washington Artists Today, Acropolis, 67. Mem: Artists Equity Asn (mem chmn, 71-73); Col Art Asn; Women's Caucus for Art; Studio Gallery Artist's Coop; Soc Washington Artists (ann exhib chmn, 64 & 68). Media: Collage, Oil, Mixed Media, Acrylic. Dealer: The Studio Gallery 802 F St NW Washington DC 20004. Mailing Add: 1609 Mt Airy Ct Crofton MD 21114

CUTHBERT, VIRGINIA
PAINTER
b West Newton, Pa, Aug 27, 08. Study: Syracuse Univ, BFA, 30; Acad Grande Chaumiere, Acad Colarossi, Paris, France & Chelsea Polytech Inst, Eng, Augusta-Hazard fel, 30-31; study with George Luks, 32; Univ Pittsburgh, 33-34; Carnegie Inst Technol, 34-35. Work: Albright-Knox Art Gallery, Buffalo, NY; Princeton Univ Art Mus, NJ; Rutgers Univ Libr Collection, NJ; also in collections of Seymour H Knox, Buffalo & Vincent Price, Los Angeles, Calif. Comn: Mural, comn by Works Progress Admin, Munic Bldg, Mt Lebanon, Pa, 34; Fortune Mag covers, 51 & 56; Southwestern Rev cover, 52; painting comn by Nat Gypsum Co, Buffalo. Exhib: 8 Pa Acad Fine Arts Ann, Philadelphia, 35-53; 10 Carnegie Int & Am Ann, Carnegie Inst, Pittsburgh, Pa, 37-52; Metrop Mus Art, New York, 43, 44 & 50; 7 Whitney Mus Am Art Ann, New York, 44-53; Good Will Exhib to Brazil, 60; Retrospective, Burchfield Ctr, Buffalo, NY, 71; In Western NY, Albright-Knox Art Gallery, Buffalo. Teaching: Instr painting, Albright Art Sch, 42-54; instr painting, Univ Buffalo, 42-54; instr painting, State Univ NY Buffalo, 54-66. Pos: Art columnist, Buffalo Courier Express, 54-55. Awards: First Prize, Western NY Exhib, Albright-Knox Art Gallery, 46-52; Nat Inst Arts & Lett Grant for Painting, 54; Prize, Chautauqua Nat Exhib, NY, 55. Mem: Patteran Artists, Buffalo. Media: Oil. Publ: Auth, spec art rev in, Buffalo Eve News, 54-56. Dealer: Frank Rehn Gallery 655 Madison Ave New York NY 10021. Mailing Add: 147 Bryant St Buffalo NY 14222

CUTLER, ETHEL ROSE
PAINTER, DESIGNER
b New York, NY, Mar 13, 15. Study: Hunter Col, BA; Columbia Univ, MA; Sch Prof Arts, cert advert & interior design; NY Univ; Univ Mo; Inst Design, Ill Inst Technol; Am Artist Sch, grant; New Sch Social Res, with Yasua Kunyioshi & Alexei Brodovitch. Exhib: New York City Ctr Gallery; Design Derby, Hialeah, Fla; Young American Artist Group, New York; Lynn Kottler Galleries, New York; Sch Home Econ, Univ Mo-Columbia; Artist Equity Exhib, New York; East Galleries, NY Univ; plus others. Teaching: Instr fine arts, Women's Col, Univ NC, Greensboro, 43-47; instr, Adelphi Col, 47-50; asst prof interior design & related arts, Univ Mo-Columbia, 50-55; asst prof surface design, RI Sch Design, 55-59. Pos: Design consult, artist & designer, Cutler Designs, 50- Awards: Award for Boats, New York City Ctr Gallery, 59; Award for Brothers, Macy's Gallery; Grant, Metrop Mus Art, New York, 68. Mem: Col Art Asn Am; Artists Equity Asn; Allied Bd Trade; Am Soc Interior Designers; Advertising Dir Club. Media: All media. Res: Techniques of William Morris and the arts and crafts movement of the Beaux Arts, the Bauhaus and other influences of the 19th century. Publ: Illusr, New York City: Its parks, institutional & historic buildings; Miami Beach, Fla & Floral studies. Mailing Add: 230 E 88th St New York NY 10028

CUTLER, GRAYCE E
PAINTER, WRITER
b Salt Lake City, Utah. Study: Univ Utah; Art Students League, with Kuniyoshi & Morris Kantor; New York Sch Design, cert; Hans Hofmann Sch Art, Provincetown, Mass; also with Eliot O'Hara. Work: Granite Schs Admin Art Collection, Salt Lake City; Pollard Collection, Greater Victoria Art Gallery, BC; Alice Merrill Horne Collection, Utah; also Royal Family of Saudi Arabia & numerous other pvt collections. Exhib: Springville Art Mus Ann Exhib, 64-; Burr Artists, New York World's Fair, 65; Soc Western Artists Ann, De Young Mus, San Francisco, 66, 68 & 69; San Francisco Women Artists Exhib, Kaiser Ctr, Oakland, 68; one-woman show, Rosicrucian Egyptian Mus & Gallery, San Jose, 68 & 71; Watercolor W, Utah State Univ, Logan, 73; plus others. Teaching: Instr art. Pos: Western regional dir, Am Art Month promoting Am art & artists, Am Artists Prof League, 55-65; pres & organizer, traveling exhibs in Western States for Utah artists, Utah Creative Artists, 56-58; mem judiciary comt, Utah High Schs Ann, 62. Awards: First Prize for watercolor, Utah State Fair, 69; Watercolor Award of Honor, Intermountain States Traveling Exhib, Utah Inst Fine Arts, 70; Watercolor First Award, Nat League Am Pen Women Biennial, Washington, DC, 72; plus one other. Bibliog: Articles in Rosicrucian Digest, 68 & 71 & Relief Soc Mag, 69. Mem: Soc Western Artists; Am Soc Interior Designers (pres, Utah Chap, 73-74); Am Watercolor Soc (vpres, 75); Burr Artists, NY; San Francisco Women Artists. Media: Watercolor, Acrylic, Oil. Res: Early writings and drawings as an art form. Mailing Add: 10-D Bonneville Towers 777 E South Temple St Salt Lake City UT 84102

CUTTLER, CHARLES DAVID
ART HISTORIAN
b Cleveland, Ohio, Apr 8, 13. Study: Ohio State Univ, BFA & MA; Inst Art & Archeol, Paris, France; Univ Bruxelles; Inst Fine Arts, NY Univ, PhD. Exhib: Cleveland May Show, Ohio, 35-36; Philadelphia Watercolor Ann, Pa, 37. Teaching: Asst instr art hist, Ohio State Univ, 35-37; from instr to asst prof art hist, Mich State Univ, 47-57; from assoc prof to prof art hist, Univ Iowa, 57-, res prof, 65-75; guest lectr, Sem Europ Art & Civilisation Belg, Ghent, summer 69. Awards: Ann Watercolor Competition Award, Ohio State Univ, 35; CRB fel, Brussels, 53-54; Fulbright-Hays Sr Fel, 65-66. Mem: Col Art Asn Am; Midwest Art Hist Soc (founding pres); Renaissance Soc Am; Medieval Acad Am; Int Ctr Medieval Art. Res: Netherlandish and German art of the 14th to 16th centuries; art of Hieronymus Bosch. Publ: Auth, Some Grünewald sources, Art Quart, 56; auth, Lisbon Temptation of St Anthony by Jerome Bosch, Art Bull, 57; auth, Northern painting, from Pucelle to Bruegel, XIVth, XVth & XVIth centuries, 68; auth, Bosch & the Narrenschiff: a problem in relationships, Art Bull, 69; auth, Two aspects of Bosch's Hell imagery, Miscellanea F Lyna (Scriptorium, 23), 69. Mailing Add: 1691 Ridge Rd Iowa City IA 52240

CYRIL, R
PAINTER, DESIGNER
b New York, NY. Study: Art Students League; New Sch Social Res; NY Univ; Sorbonne, Inst Art & Archeol, Paris, Fulbright fel; and with Jacques Villos & S W Hayter. Work: Metrop Mus, New York; Smithsonian Inst, Washington, DC; Corning Glass Mus; Nat Gallery Art; Libr Cong; plus others. Exhib: Circle & Square Gallery, New York; von Drejcin Gallery, New York; Peter Deitsch Gallery, New York; Redfern Gallery, London; Schneider Gallery, Rome; plus 100 one-man shows, US & Europe; many group shows. Teaching: Instr painting, graphics, design & crafts, Adelphi Univ, 63-66. Awards: First Prize Purchase Award, Dallas Mus Art, Tex; First Prize, Philadelphia Mus; First Prize, Delgado Mus, New Orleans. Style & Technique: Ecological impressions, atmospheric, abstract, lyrical and poetic; 3 dimensional sculptured surfaces in abstract. Media: Oil, Watercolor, Acrylic. Mailing Add: 800 West End Ave New York NY 10025

CZACH, MARIE
MUSEUM DIRECTOR, CURATOR
b Chicago, Ill, Sept 9, 45. Study: Univ Chicago, 63-67; Art Inst of Chicago, BAE, 67; Columbia Univ, MA, 68. Pos: Res assoc, Int Mus of Photog & Cinematography, George Eastman House, Rochester, NY, 68-70; asst cur photog, Art Inst of Chicago, 70-72; dir studies, hist & criticism photog, Columbia Col, Chicago, 72-74; dir mus/gallery, Western Ill Univ, Macomb, 74-; guest cur, St Louis Art Mus, 75- Mailing Add: 11 Heat Ct Macomb IL 61455

CZESTOCHOWSKI, JOSEPH STEPHEN
GALLERY DIRECTOR
b Brooklyn, NY, Aug 8, 50. Study: Univ Ill, Champaign-Urbana, 71; Jagellonian Univ, Cracow, Poland, dipl, 71; Univ Ill, MA, 73. Collections Arranged: A Question of Regionalism, American Collections & Armin Landeck Graphics, Brooks Mem Art Gallery, Memphis, Tenn, 75; Arthur B Davies Retrospective (with catalog), M Knoedler & Co, Inc, New York, 75; Polish Graphic Art & Design, Baltimore, 78; Charles Burchfield - Charles Rand Penney Collection, Mem Art Gallery, Rochester, 78. Pos: Student asst, Krannert Art Mus, Univ Ill, 72; art ed, Perspectives, Inc, Washington, DC, 72-; cur collections, Brooks Mem Art Gallery, Memphis, Tenn, 73-; dir, Decker Gallery, Md Inst, Col of Art. Awards: US-Poland Exchange Grantee, Kosciuszko Found, NY, 71 & Jurykowski Scholar, 72; Smithsonian Inst Foreign Currency Prog Res Award, 76-78. Mem: Am Asn Mus, Washington, DC; Col Art Asn, NY; Polish Inst Arts & Sci in Am, New York. Res: 19th & early 20th century American paintings, drawings and prints; contemporary American painters and printmakers; Polish art. Publ: Auth, 20th Century American Prints, Brooks Mem Art Gallery, 74; Carl Gutherz (1844-1907), 5/76, Published prints of Charles Burchfield, 76 & John Stewart Curry's Lithographs, Am Art J; auth, The Pioneers, Phaidon Press, London, 77; auth, Childe Hassam, 78 & Arthur B Davies, 78, Am Art Rev. Mailing Add: Md Inst Col of Art 1300 Mt Royal Ave Baltimore MD 21217

CZIMBALMOS, MAGDOLNA PAAL
PAINTER
b Esztergom, Hungary. Study: Art Schs, Hungary & Ger. Work: Staten Island Mus, NY; Mus Int Inst, Detroit; Carnegie Inst Int Centennial, NY; Bergstron Art Centennial, Ill; City Mus, Esztergom, Hungary. Comn: Portraits, Most Rev Daniel Ivancho, Nicholas Telko, Msgr Ernest Dunda, Mrs Jacqueline Kennedy & family of Congressman John M Murphy, NY. Exhib: One-man shows & group exhib in US, France, Ger, Monaco & Can. Teaching: Czimbalmos Pvt Art Sch, 65- Pos: Founder & dir, Hungarian Doll & Handicraft Factory, Reichenbach. Awards: Staten Island Mus Gold Medal, 58, 62, 63, 66 & 69; Italian Cult Award, 67; Szinnyei Merse Gold Medal, New York, 71. Mem: World Orgn Hungarian Artists (dir); Staten Island Mus (dir exec bd). Style & Technique: Oil painting; palette knife technique. Mailing Add: Czimbalmos Art Studio 31 Bayview Pl Ward Hill Staten Island NY 10304

CZIMBALMOS, SZABO KALMAN
PAINTER, EDUCATOR
b Esztergom, Hungary, 1914. Study: Royal Hungarian Acad Fine Arts, Budapest, grad, 36; also with prof J Haranghy & E Domanowsky Vienna, Prague, Munich, Paris, London & Rome. Work: Nat Gallery Budapest; City Mus Esztergom, Hungary; Staten Island Mus, NY; Staten Island Community Col. Comn: Murals 32 churches US; Hungarian Govt & pvt owners. Exhib: Pulitzer Art Gallery, NY; Int Inst, Detroit; Cornet Gallery, NY; Staten Island Mus; one-man shows & group exhib in Hungary, Germany, France & Monaco. Pos: Owner, Czimbalmos Art Studio, Esztergom, 37-38, studio, Reichenbach, Ger, 45-49 & Staten Island, NY, 50-; art dir & partner, Hungarian Doll & Handcraft Factory, Reichenbach; art dir, Hungarian Relief, New York, 50; dir, Czimbalmos Pvt Art Sch, 55- Awards: Hungarian Art Award, Budapest, 34; Staten Island Mus Prize, 62, 64, 67 & 71; St Stephan Gold Medal, Pannonia Exhib, 71. Mem: Bavaryan Fine Art Soc; Staten Island Mus Art (vpres, art sect, 61-62, pres, 63-64, exec bd, 63-); Pannonia World Orgn Hungarian Artists (chmn bd dirs, 67). Style & Technique: Figurative abstraction. Media: Oil, Tempera. Mailing Add: Czimbalmos Art Studio 31 Bayview Pl Ward Hill Staten Island NY 10304

CZUMA, STANISLAW J
ART HISTORIAN, CURATOR
b Warsaw, Poland, Oct 26, 35; US citizen. Study: Jagiellonian Univ, BA & MA; Paderewski Found scholar studies in India, 58-60; Nat Defense Foreign Lang fel studies in India, 65-67; Banares Hindu Univ, with Vasudeva S Agrawala; Univ Calcutta, with S K Saraswati; Sorbonne, with Louis Renou; Univ Mich, PhD, 68, with Walter Spink. Collections Arranged: Cambodian Art (with catalog), Asian House Gallery, New York, 69; Permanent Indian Gallery, Brooklyn Mus; Indian Art from the George P Bickford Collection (with catalog), Cleveland Mus, 75. Teaching: Res asst Oriental art, Univ Mich, Ann Arbor, 62-64; adj prof, Case Western Reserve Univ. Pos: Ford Found curatorial trainee, Cleveland Mus, 68-70; cur Oriental art, Brooklyn Mus, 70-72; cur Indian art, Cleveland Mus, 72- Mem: Asn Asian Studies, Asia Soc; Int Coun Mus, Paris. Res: Art of India and Southeast Asia, especially Gupta and Medieval India. Publ: Auth, Gupta style bronze Buddha, 2/70, A masterpiece of early Cambodian sculpture, 4/74 & Mathura sculpture in the Cleveland Mus Collection, 3/77, Bull Cleveland Mus. Mailing Add: Oriental Dept Cleveland Mus East Blvd Cleveland OH 44106

D

DA CUNHA, JULIO
EDUCATOR, PAINTER
b Colombia, SAm, Mar 18, 29; US citizen. Study: Nat Univ of Bogota, Colombia; Univ Fla, Gainesville, BArch, 52; Cranbrook Acad of Art, Bloomfield Hills, Mich, MFA, 54. Work: Univ Del; Del Mus, Wilmington; Bloomsburg State Col, Pa. Exhib: Ann Regional Exhib, Del Art Mus, Wilmington, 56-77 & Univ Del, 61-77; Four Del Artists, 64, 20 Yr Retrospective, 77, Del Mus; Am Painters in Paris Bicentennial Exhib, France, 76; 5 Yr Retrospective of Self Works, Haas Gallery, Bloomsburg State Col, Pa, 76. Teaching: Prof art, Univ Del, 56- Awards: Purchase Award, Univ Del, 63 & Del Art Mus, 62. Bibliog: A Profile: J Da Cunha, 71 & Clint Collins (auth), Paradoxes of J Da Cunha, 77, Del Today Mag; John S Crawford (auth), J Da Cunha: 20 Years of His Work, Del Art Mus, 77. Style & Technique: Abstract and figurative. Media: Acrylic, charcoal. Dealer: Pleiades Gallery 152 Wooster St New York NY 10012. Mailing Add: PO Box 893 Newark DE 19711

D'AGOSTINO, VINCENT
PAINTER
b Chicago, Ill, Apr 7, 98. Study: Art Inst Chicago, grad(cum laude); and with George Bellows & Charles Hawthorne. Work: Whitney Mus Am Art, New York; Logan Collection, Art Inst Chicago. Comn: Mural, Mexican Village, Chicago World's Fair, 33; mural for Gloucester Post Off, NJ, US Treas Dept, 35; mural for college, Mt Loretto, NY, comn by Patrick Cardinal O'Boyle, 41; mural, Riccardo's Studio Restaurant, Chicago, 48. Exhib: Metrop Mus Art, New York, 39; New York World's Fair Fine Art Exhib, 40; 100 Years of American Art, Los Angeles Co Fair, Calif, 53; Los Angeles Co Mus Art, 54; Graham Gallery Nat Show, New York, 66; plus many others. Teaching: Artist in residence, Mt Loretto, NY, 41-42; prof art, Woodbury Col, Calif, 49-54. Awards: Tiffany Found Award, 31 & 32. Bibliog: Whitney Museum of Art, Macmillan, 31; Ben Hecht (auth), Wistfully yours, Theatre Arts Mag, 7/51; Arthur Millier (auth), Painting in the USA: 1721 to 1953, Los Angeles Co Fair Asn, 53. Mem: Nat Soc Mural Painters; Artists Equity; United Scenic Artists. Media: Oil, Watercolor. Mailing Add: 11006 Klina No 2 North Hollywood CA 91602

DAGYS, JACOB
SCULPTOR
b Lithuania, Dec 16, 05; Can citizen. Study: Kaunas Art Sch, Lithuania. Work: Balzekas Mus, Chicago, Ill; Ciurlionis Gallery, Chicago. Comn: Crucifix, sacre coeur & others, St Monicas Church, Toronto, Ont, 58; St Anthony & others, Church Resurrection, Toronto, 67; Chicago, 73 & Cleveland, 77. Teaching: Instr art, Raseiniai High Sch, Lithuania, 32-44. Bibliog: Album, Dagy's - Sculptures & Paintings, Am Lithuanian Art Asn, 67. Mem: Sculptor Soc Can. Style & Technique: Between realism, primitivism and deformism. Media: Wood, Bronze. Publ: Articles about art for Lithuanian Press. Mailing Add: 78 Chelsea Ave Toronto ON Can

DAHILL, THOMAS HENRY, JR
PAINTER, EDUCATOR
b Cambridge, Mass, June 22, 25. Study: Tufts Col, BS, 49; Harvard Univ, summer 53; Sch Mus Fine Arts, Boston, dipl, 53, cert, 54; Skowhegan Sch Painting & Sculpture; Am Acad in Rome, fel, 55-57; Max Beckmann Gesellschaft, Murnau, Ger, resident, 56; Emerson Col, AM, 67. Comn: Mural, Unitarian Church, Brockton, Mass, 58; film strips, ser of paintings on Old & New Testaments, 61-62; film strip, life of George Washington Carver, 61; portrait, Dr Richard D Pierce, 74. Exhib. Boston Art Festival, 55, 56 & 63; Archit League, NY, 58; Int Bienale Relig Art, Salzburg, Austria, 58-59; Emerson Col, 64 & 67; Drawings of NAfrica exhibited through Mus Fine Arts Boston to galleries of New Eng Prep Schs, 67-69; plus others. Teaching: Lectr gen art hist & contemp use of art in churches; instr hist art, Tufts Univ, 54-55 & 60-65; instr dept drawing, Sch Mus Fine Arts, Boston, 58-65; prof fine arts & chmn dept, Emerson Col, 67-, summer sch abroad, Europe & Africa, 67- Awards: Abbey Mem Fel to Am Acad in Rome, 55-57. Mem: MacDowell Colonists; Alumni Asn, Sch Mus Fine Arts, Boston; Gibson House Victorian Mus (bd mem, 73). Style & Technique: Paintings strongly figurative, subject matter subjective with expressionistic qualities; loose color; shaped panels derived from development of painting non-geometric. Media: Acrylic on Canvas. Mailing Add: 223 Broadway Arlington MA 02174

DAHLBERG, EDWIN LENNART
PAINTER
b Beloit, Wis, Sept 20, 01. Study: Art Inst Chicago, grad, John Quincy Adams fel. Work: Charles & Emma Frye Mus, Seattle, Wash; Wesleyan Univ. Exhib: Am Watercolor Soc Ann, 54-; Nat Acad Design; Pa Acad Fine Arts, 54-61; Art Inst Chicago, 54-61; Royal Soc Watercolor Painters, London, Eng, 66. Awards: Medal of Merit for Best in Show for All Media, Knickerbocker Artists, 70; Gold Medal of Hon, Am Watercolor Soc, 72; Gold Medal of Hon for Watercolor, Hudson Valley Art Asn, 74. Bibliog: Edwin L Dahlberg seeks mood in a motif, Am Artist, 2/65; Norman Kent (auth), 100 Watercolor Techniques, Watson-Guptill, 68; Edwin L Dahlberg Paints a Watercolor on Location (film), Electrographic Corp Am, 71. Mem: Am Watercolor Soc (bd dirs, 65-68); Allied Artists Am (bd dirs, 67-71); Hudson Valley Art Asn; Knickerbocker Artists; assoc Nat Acad Design. Style & Technique: Impressionistic, realistic. Media: Transparent Watercolors. Mailing Add: 6 South Boulevard Nyack NY 10960

DAILEY, CHARLES ANDREW (CHUCK)
MUSEUM DIRECTOR, PAINTER
b Golden, Colo, May 25, 35. Study: Univ Colo, BA(art), 61; study in Western Europe, 62-63. Work: Mus NMex Permanent Collection, Santa Fe; Vincent Price Collection, Hollywood, Calif. Exhib: Fiesta Biennial, 64 & 65 & Southwest Biennial, 68, Mus NMex; NMex State Fair, Albuquerque, 68; one-man show, Gallery 5, Santa Fe, 64. Collections Arranged: Afro-Arabic World, 66-67, New Mexican Santero, 70-71 & World of Folk Costume, 71-72, Museum International Folk Art, Three Culture-Sculpture Exhibition & Rain Cloud Callers (Indian art), Fine Arts Mus & Spanish Endure (Spanish hist in Southwest), Palace of Governors, Mus NMex. Teaching: Mus training dir, Inst Am Indian Arts, Santa Fe, 71- Pos: Mus preparator, Univ Colo Mus, Boulder, 59-61; exhibs tech, Mus Northern Ariz, Flagstaff, 62-63; cur-in-charge exhib div, Mus NMex, 64-71. Bibliog: Catherine Wenzell (auth), Artists of Santa Fe, privately publ, 68. Mem: NMex Asn Mus (mem chmn, currently); Am Asn Mus; Midwest Mus Asn; Far West Mus Asn. Style & Technique: Magic realism or trompe l'oeil. Media: Acrylic. Publ: Auth, Creating a Crowd (maniken development & how to), NMex Asn Mus, 72. Dealer: Jamison Gallery 111 E San Francisco Santa Fe NM 87501. Mailing Add: 412 Sosaya Lane Santa Fe NM 87501

DAILEY, DANIEL OWEN
SCULPTOR, DESIGNER
b Philadelphia, Pa, Feb 4, 47. Study: Philadelphia Col Art, BFA(glass); RI Sch Design, MFA(glass), with Dale Chihuly. Work: Corning Mus of Glass, NY; New Indian Mus, Flagstaff, Ariz. Comn: Glass window (8ft x 8ft), Lovett & Linder Co, Providence, RI, 72; glass window (4ft x 8ft), comn by Ms Jane Mayerson, Providence, 74; illum family portraits & glass & bronze sculptures, comn by the Otto Piene family, Cambridge, Mass, 78. Exhib: One-man shows, Philadelphia Art Alliance, Pa, 72, Ctr for Advan Visual Studies, Mass Inst Technol Gallery, 75 & 77 & Theo Portnoy Gallery, New York, 77; Am Glass Now, Toledo Mus Art, Ohio, 72-74; Three Am Artists, US Info Serv, Rome, Italy, 73; Pilchuck Glass Invitational, Seattle Art Mus, Wash, 76; New Am Glass-Focus, WVa, Huntington Galleries, 76; Twelve Glass Artists, Hadler Galleries, New York, 78. Teaching: Teaching fel glass, RI Sch Design, Providence, 70-72; asst prof glass, Mass Col Art, Boston, 73-; res fel sculpture & glass, Mass Inst Technol, 75- Pos: Guest designer, Fabrica Venini, Murano, Venice, Italy, 72-73; chmn three-dimensional fine arts dept, Mass Col Art, Boston, 74-; designer & free lance artist, Cristallerie Daum, Nancy, France, 77- Awards: Fulbright-Hays Grant as Designer, Fabrica Venini, Murano, Italy, 72-73. Bibliog: Otto Piene (auth), Glas, Gas und Electrizitat, Du Mag, Zurich, Switz, 5/77; Richard Avidon (auth), Correspondent's Correspondence, Glass Mag, 5/77; Un American Faccone le Cristal Chez Daum, L'Est Republicain, Paris-Nancy, France, 7/77. Mem: Glass Art Soc (bd dir nominee). Style & Technique: Sculpture, abstract genere, illuminated electronically, blown, cut, polished, fabricated glass, bronze, cast glass and cast bronze. Media: Glass, Metal. Dealer: Theo Portnoy Gallery 56 W 57th St New York NY 10019. Mailing Add: 122 Market St Amesbury MA 01913

DAILEY, JOSEPH CHARLES
See Jocda

DAILEY, MICHAEL DENNIS
PAINTER, EDUCATOR
b Des Moines, Iowa, Aug 2, 38. Study: Univ Iowa, BA & MFA. Work: Smithsonian Inst, Washington, DC; Munic Gallery Mod Art, Dublin, Ireland; Seattle Art Mus, Wash; Mercyhurst Col, Erie, Pa; Mus of Mod Art, New York. Exhib: Art Across Am, San Francisco Mus Art, 65; Ultimate Concerns Drawing Exhib, Ohio Univ, Athens, 65; one-man shows, Tacoma Art Mus, Wash, 66 & 75, Univ Wis, Madison, 67, Francine Seders Gallery, Seattle, 71, 73 & 76, William Sawyer Gallery, San Francisco, 72, 74 & 76 & Univ Idaho, Moscow, 74; Drawings USA, St Paul Art Ctr, Minn, 66 & 68; 73rd Western Ann, Denver Art Mus, Colo, 71; Art of the Pacific Northwest, Smithsonian Inst, 74. Teaching: Prof drawing & painting, Univ Wash, 63- Awards: Purchase Award, Mercyhurst Nat Graphics Exhib, Erie, Pa, 65; First Pl Award in Painting, Wash State Ann Art Exhib, 67; Northwest Watercolor Soc Award, 30th Ann Northwest Watercolor Exhib, Seattle Art Mus, 70. Style & Technique: Abstractions based upon the landscape image. Media: Oil, Watercolor. Mailing Add: 5805 17th Ave NE Seattle WA 98105

DAILY, EVELYNNE B
PAINTER, PRINTMAKER
b Indianapolis, Ind, Jan 8, 03. Study: Herron Sch Art, Ind Univ; Art Inst Chicago; Butler Univ; Ecole Beaux Arts, Fontainebleau, France, dipl; Wayman Adams Sch Portrait Painting, New York; also Bauhaus with Moholy-Nagy, Chicago. Work: Indianapolis Mus Art; Ft Wayne Mus; Richmond Art Asn; Libr Cong, Washington, DC; Philadelphia Mus Art. Exhib: Nat Acad Design, New York; Pa Acad Fine Arts; Brooklyn Mus, NY; Libr Cong Exhib Prints; Los Angeles Mus. Teaching: Instr drawing & painting, pub & pvt schs, Indianapolis,

40-60; instr painting & printmaking, Oxbow Acres Summer Art Sch, Brown Co, Ind, 64- Pos: pres, Ind Fedn Art Club, 67-69. Awards: Allen Clowes Prize for Painting, Ind Artists Club; P R Mallory Co Prize for Lithograph, 75; United Farm Bur Insurance Co Prize for Painting, 77. Mem: Nat Soc Arts & Lett; Ind Artists Club; Ind Artist-Craftsmen; Hoosier Salon; Brown Co Art Gallery Asn. Mailing Add: 6237 Central Ave Indianapolis IN 46220

DAISY (DAISY BLACK LANGHAUSER)
PAINTER, ART DEALER
b Long Island, NY. Study: NY Univ; Suffolk Community Col; Art Students League; Adelphi Col; and with W Hoier, R Fabre & M Anderson. Work: Parrish Art Mus, Southampton, NY; Museo de Arte de Ponce, PR; Winter Haven Cult Art Ctr, Fla. Comn: Friendship Tree (oil), Pequot House, Moriches, NY, 60; Sunburst (oil), Freedom House, Southampton, 70. Exhib: Parrish Art Mus, 66-75; Am Artists Prof League Grand Nat, 72-74; Catharine Lorillard Wolfe, Lever House, New York, 72-74; Nat Arts Club, 72-75; Museo de Arte de Ponce, 74. Teaching: Teacher painting, pvt lessons, 69- Pos: Vpres, Studio Gallery, Greenport, NY, 74- Awards: Best in Show, Suffolk Art League, 69; First Prize, Fla Coun Arts, 71; First Prize, Suffolk Co Coun Arts, 71. Mem: Am Artists Prof League; Catharine Lorillard Wolfe Art Club; Nat Arts Club; Parrish Art Mus; Lauderdale by the Sea Art Guild, Fla. Style & Technique: Realistic and impressionistic oil and watercolor; brush and knife. Media: Oil, Water Base Paint. Mailing Add: 105 Front St Greenport NY 11944

DALE, WILLIAM SCOTT ABELL
ART HISTORIAN
b Toronto, Ont, Sept 18, 21. Study: Univ Toronto, BA & MA; Harvard Univ, PhD. Teaching: Prof art hist, Univ Western Ont, 67- Pos: Res cur, Nat Gallery Can, Ottawa, Ont, 51-57; cur, Art Gallery Toronto, 57-59; dir, Vancouver Art Gallery, BC, 59-61; asst dir, Nat Gallery Can, 61-66, dep dir, 66-67. Mem: Col Art Asn Am; Mediaeval Acad Am. Res: Romanesque ivories; Bulwer Collection; Canadian art. Publ: Contribr, Arts in Canada, 58; contribr, Oxford companion to art, 70. Mailing Add: Univ of Western Ontario London ON Can

D'ALESSIO, GREGORY
CARTOONIST, ILLUSTRATOR
b New York, NY, Sept 25, 04. Study: Art Students League, New York, with Walter Jack Duncan, Kimon Nikolaides & George Bridgman. Work: Syracuse Univ, NY. Exhib: Metrop Mus of Art, New York; Gallery of Mod Art, New York; Mus of the City of New York. Teaching: Instr drawing, anat & compos, Art Students League, New York, 62- Pos: Vpres, Art Students League, New York, 37-44; cartoonist, These Women, 40-62. Awards: Am Soc Graphic Arts Award, 51; Reuben Award, Nat Cartoonists Soc, 61. Mem: Life mem Art Students League New York; life mem Soc Illusr New York; Nat Cartoonists Soc, New York (secy, 46-48); Soc Classic Guitar (vpres, co-ed & illusr, Guitar Rev, 15 yrs). Style & Technique: Use of the techniques of the cartoonist, the illustrator and the painter. Media: Acrylics. Publ: Illusr, New Yorker, Esquire, Saturday Evening Post, Colliers, Look, Holiday, New York Times, American Ladies Home Journal, House & Garden, American Home & numerous others. Mailing Add: Art Students League 215 W 57th St New York NY 10019

D'ALESSIO, HILDA TERRY
See Terry, Hilda

DALEY, WILLIAM P
CERAMIST, SCULPTOR
b Hastings-on-Hudson, NY, Mar 7, 25. Study: Mass Col Art, BS; Columbia Univ Teachers Col, MA. Work: Philadelphia Mus Art; Campbell Mus, Camden, NJ; Cent Iowa Art Mus, Marshaltown; St Lawrence Univ Mus, Camden, NY; plus pvt collection of Robert Pfannebecker, Holtwood, Pa. Comn: Ceramic screen abacus (10ft x 7ft), comn by Int Bus Machines Corp, Seattle World's Fair, 61; ceramic & copper modular wall (10ft x 12ft), SAfrican Airlines, New York, 70; ceramic wall (10ft x 6ft), Fairfield Maxwell Corp, New York, 72; circular bronz form (5ft), Germantown Friends Sch, Philadelphia, 72; ceramic sculpture (10ft x 20ft), Ritz Theatre, Philadelphia, 78. Exhib: One-man shows, Pace Gallery, Boston, 59, Drutt Gallery, Philadelphia, 74 & 76; Nat Ceramic Exhib, Everson Mus, Syracuse, NY, 62 & 68; Philadelphia: Three Centuries of Am Art, Philadelphia Mus Art, 76; Soup Toureens 1976, Mus Contemp Crafts, New York & Campbell Mus, Camden, NJ, 76; 41st Int Eucharistic Cong Exhib of Liturgical Art, Civic Art Mus, Philadelphia, 76; Contemp Clay: Ten Approaches, Hopkins Ctr, Dartmouth Col, 76; Am Crafts, Philadelphia Mus Art, 77; Clay USA, Fendrick Gallery, Washington, DC, 76; Vessel as Metaphore, Evanston Mus, Ill, 77; plus others. Teaching: Prof ceramics & design, Philadelphia Col Art, 57-, chmn crafts dept, 66-69; guest prof ceramics, Univ NMex, 72. Pos: Mem bd dir, Philadelphia Coun Prof Craftsmen, 67-73 & Nat Coun Educ for Ceramic Arts, 69-70. Awards: Purchase Awards, Am Wing, Philadelphia Mus Art, 76 & Soup Toureen 1976, Campbell Mus, 76; Nat Endowment for the Arts Grant, 77. Mem: Artists Equity; Am Craftsmens Coun; Philadelphia Crafts Group. Style & Technique: Large vessels, fountains and walls with clay; occasionally metal. Dealer: Drutt Gallery 1625 Spruce St Philadelphia PA 19103. Mailing Add: 307 Ashbourne Rd Elkins Park PA 19117

DAL FABBRO, MARIO
SCULPTOR, WRITER
b Cappella Maggiore, Italy, Oct 6, 13; US citizen. Study: Inst Indust Art, Venice, Italy; Magistero Art, Venice. Work: Kemerer Mus, Bethlehem, Pa; Mus Art, Sci & Indust, Bridgeport, Conn; Allentown Art Mus, Pa. Exhib: Nat Art Exhib, Vittorio Veneto, 69; Allentown Art Mus Exhibs, 69-76; one-man shows, Allentown Art Mus, Pa, 72 & Mus Art, Sci & Indust, Bridgeport, 78; Cheltenham Art Ctr, Philadelphia, 71; Phillips Mill Art Gallery, New Hope, Pa, 71; Mus Philadelphia Civic Ctr, Pa, 71-73; Ctr Artistico Ital Belle Arti, Trieste, Italy, 72-75; New Eng Exhib, Silvermine Art Ctr, 77; Stamford Mus & Nature Ctr, 77; Mus Art Sci & Indust, 77. Awards: First Prize/Sculpture, Lehigh Art Alliance, 70, 72 & 73; First Prize, Woodmere Art Gallery, Philadelphia, 74; First Prize/Sculpture, Green Farms Acad Westport, Conn, 77. Mem: Int Acad Tommaso Campanella, Rome, Italy; Silvermine Guild of Artists. Media: Wood. Publ: Auth, Costruzione e funzionalita' del mobile moderno, Hoepli, Italy, 50; auth, Furniture for Modern Interiors, Van Nostrand Reinhold, 52; auth, How to Make Built-in Furniture, McGraw-Hill & Ceac, Spain, 55; auth, How to Build Modern Furniture, 57 & auth, Upholstered Furniture, Its Design & Construction, 69, McGraw-Hill & Hoepli & Ceac. Mailing Add: 67 Sherman Ct Fairfield CT 06430

DALI, SALVADOR
DESIGNER, PAINTER
b Figueras, Spain, May 11, 04. Study: Sch Fine Arts, Madrid, 21-26. Comn: Decorated residence, Edward James London, 36; designed, Dali's Dream House, New York World's Fair, 39; scenery & costumes for Metrop Opera, 39 & 41. Exhib: Julien Levy Gallery, New York, 33; Arts Club, Chicago, 41; Dalzell Hatfield Galleries, Los Angeles; Mus Mod Art, New York; Knoedler Gallery, New York; plus others. Awards: Huntington Hartford Found Award, 57. Publ: Auth, Secret Life of Salvador Dali, 42; Diary of a Genius, 65. Dealer: Knoedler & Co 21 E 70th St New York NY 10021. Mailing Add: Hotel St Regis New York NY 10022

D'ALMEIDA, GEORGE
PAINTER
b Paris, France, June 30, 34; US citizen. Exhib: Fairweather Hardin Gallery, Chicago, 70, 72 & 74; Meredith Long & Co, Houston, 71 & 74; Ankrum Gallery, Los Angeles, 72; Gloria Luria Gallery, Miami, 75; Drian Galleries, London, 75; plus others. Style & Technique: Nonfigurative; alla prima. Media: Acrylic, Watercolor. Dealer: M Knoedler & Co 21 E 70th St New York NY 10021; Fairweather Hardin Gallery 101 E Ontario Chicago IL 60611. Mailing Add: Casina di Selvole 53017 Radda in Chianti Siena Italy

DALTON, HARRY L
COLLECTOR, PATRON
b Winston-Salem, NC, June 13, 98. Study: Duke Univ, AB & Hon LHD; Brit Univ; NY Univ. Mem: NC Art Soc; Mint Mus; NC Mus; NC Arts Coun; Weatherspoon Gallery. Collection: Various schools of European and American art; collection has been loaned to various galleries. Mailing Add: 322 East Over Rd Charlotte NC 28207

DALY, KATHLEEN (KATHLEEN DALY PEPPER)
PAINTER
b Napanee, Ont, May 28, 98. Study: Ont Col Art, assoc, with Arthur Lismer, J E H MacDonald & J W Beatty; Acad Grande Chaumiere, Paris; Ont Col Art; also woodcuts with Rene Poitier, Paris. Work: Nat Gallery Can, Ottawa, Ont; Art Gallery Ont, Toronto; London Libr & Art Gallery, Ont; McMichael Mus, Kleinburg, Ont; Dept Nat Affairs, Ottawa. Comn: Portraits, Dr Thomas Cullen, Baltimore, 41, Premier Herbert Greenfield, 46 & Senor Hach, Tangiers, Morocco. Exhib: Group of Seven, 31; Brit Empire Exhib, 37-38; Great Lakes Exhib, 38-39; New York World's Fair, 39; Ann, Ont Soc Arts, Royal Can Acad & Can Group Painters. Bibliog: Life in Eskimoland, London Press, 62. Mem: Royal Can Acad; Ont Soc Artists; Toronto Helicomian Club; Zonta Club Toronto. Style & Technique: On the spot painting and drawing. Media: Oil, Crayon. Publ: Co-illusr, Kingdom of Saguenay, 36; illusr, North, Dept Northern Affairs, 62; auth, Morrice, Clarke, Irwin, Toronto, 66. Mailing Add: 561 Avenue Rd Apt 1101 Toronto ON Canada

DALY, NORMAN
PAINTER, SCULPTOR
b Pittsburgh, Pa, Aug 9, 11. Study: Univ Colo, BFA; Ohio State Univ, MA; grad study, Paris, Inst Fine Arts & NY Univ. Work: Rochester Mem Art Gallery, NY; Herbert F Johnson Mus Art, Ithaca, NY; Everson Mus Art, Syracuse; Univ Wash, Seattle; St Paul Mus Art, Minn. Major Work: The civilization of Llhuros—a mythical culture complete with paintings, sculpture, music, rituals, poetry, architectural fragments, murals, stained glass windows, mosaics, bas-reliefs, scientific instruments, fames, maps, jewelry, crafts and a full annotated illustrated catalog. Comn: Stained glass windows, Mt Savior Monastery, Pine City, NY; bas-relief, Meditation Rm, Student Union, NY State Univ Col Cortland; text and explanatory step by step processes, Ten Techniques Demonstrated in Pictorial Art Exhib & Ancient Origins of Modern Art, comn by Roberson Art Ctr. Exhib: One-man shows, Akron Mus Art, 72, Indianapolis Mus Art, 73, Univ Pa Mus, 74, Int Projekt 74, Römisch-Germanischen, 74, Llhuros-Eine Entdeckte Kultur-1974, Mus, Cologne, Ger, 74 & State Mus, Bocum, Ger, 75; Andrew White Art Mus, Cornell Univ, 72; Rochester Mem Art Gallery, 72; Roberson Art Ctr, 73; Univ Art Mus, State Univ NY Albany, 73. Teaching: Prof art, Cornell Univ, 42- Awards: Fel, Yaddo, 67-71; NY State Coun Arts fel, 71; Nat Endowment Arts fel, 74. Bibliog: Charles Michener (auth), The fabulous Llhuroscians, Newsweek, 2/28/72; Kenneth Evett (auth), Llhuros, New Repub, 1/12/72; David Galloway (auth), The Civilization of Llhuros, Cleveland, 9/72. Publ: Illusr, Epoch, 71; contribr, Abrazas Press, 72; auth, The Civilization of Llhuros, 72; auth, Llhuros-Eine Entdeckte Kiltur-1974. Mailing Add: 110 N Quarry St Ithaca NY 14850

D'AMATO, JANET POTTER
ILLUSTRATOR, CRAFTSMAN
b Rochester, NY. Study: Pratt Inst; Harriet FeBland Workshop. Bibliog: Anne Commire (auth), Something About the Author, Gale Publ, 75; Carmel Marchionni (auth), Lifestyles, Westchester Gannett Publ, 75 & 77. Style & Technique: Collage; crafts. Media: Woodcut; Acrylic. Res: Primitive and folk art and crafts, American Indian and African. Publ: Auth & illusr, African Crafts for You to Make, Messner, 68; auth & illusr, Gifts to Make for Love or Money, Golden, 73; auth & illusr, Colonial Crafts for You to Make, Messner, 75; auth & illusr, Quillwork, Craft of Paper Filigree, 75 & Italian Crafts, 77, Evans. Mailing Add: 32 Bayberry St Bronxville NY 10708

DAMAZ, PAUL F
WRITER, COLLECTOR
b Portugal, Nov 8, 17; US citizen. Study: Ecole Speciale Archit, Paris, France, BA(arch); Inst Urbanisme, Sorbonne, Paris, MA(town planning). Teaching: Design critic archit, Columbia Univ, 52-53. Pos: Coun mem, Arts Acquisition Comt, State Univ NY Stony Brook, 70; dir, Fine Arts Fedn New York, 72-75. Awards: Arnold Brunner fel, Archit League New York, 58. Bibliog: Anne Le Crenier (auth), Names, Archit & Eng News, 67. Mem: Am Inst Architects (collab arts comt, 67-70); Am Inst Planners; Ordre Architectes, France; Archit League New York (vpres, 63); Munic Arts Soc. Res: Integration of art in modern architecture; art in public spaces. Collection: Contemporary art, mostly North and Latin American. Publ: Auth, Art in European architecture, 56 & Art in Latin American Architecture, 62, Van Nostrand Reinhold. Mailing Add: 302 E 88th St New York NY 10028

DAME, LAWRENCE
ART CRITIC, WRITER
b Portland, Maine, July 2, 98. Study: Harvard Univ; Univ Paris; Univ Grenoble, France; Inst de Burgos, Spain. Teaching: Lectr on art & ruins & relics of Yucatan; rev of art bks & other publ. Pos: Art ed, Boston Herald, 50-60; art ed, Sarasota Herald-Tribune, Fla, 60-65; with Social Pictorial, Palm Beach, Fla, 61-; art ed, Post, Palm Beach, 69-73; pres, Palm Beach Art Council, 74- Res: World's leading museums. Publ: Auth, Yucatan, Random House, 40; auth, Maya Mission, Doubleday, 69; auth, Der Dschungel Missionar, Reinhardt, Basel, Switz, 70; contribr, Sat Eve Post, Reader's Dig, Am Mercury, Mag Dig, Arts Mag, New York Times & others. Mailing Add: 424 Brazilian St Palm Beach FL 33480

D'AMICO, AUGUSTINE A
COLLECTOR, PATRON
b Lawrence, Mass, May 15, 05. Study: Colby Col, BS, MA & hon DFA. Exhib: Paintings & graphics, 61 & contemp ceramics, 63, Univ Maine, Orono; paintings & graphics, Colby Col Art Mus, Waterville, Maine, 63 & 78; contemp ceramics, Lincoln Co Mus, Wiscasset, Maine, 65; selected graphics from collection, tour sponsored by Maine Comn Arts & Humanities, 71. Pos: Trustee, Haystack Mountain Sch Crafts, Deer Isle, Maine; mem art adv coun, fel

& former trustee, Colby Col, Waterville; chmn, patron fine arts, Univ Maine; mem, Maine State Comn Arts & Humanities; mem adv bd, Maine Coast Artists. Awards: Distinguished Art Patron Award, Skowhegan Sch Painting & Sculpture, 74. Mem: Am Fedn Arts; Mus Mod Art; Am Craftsmen Coun; World Craft Coun. Interest: Advancement of art and craft programs in teaching institutions. Collection: 20th century paintings, graphics and ceramics. Mailing Add: 201 Broadway Bangor ME 04401

DAMRON, JOHN CLARENCE
PAINTER, ILLUSTRATOR
b Brooklyn, NY. Study: Pratt Inst, NY; Grand Cent Sch Art, with Harvey Dunn; and with Edmund Oppenheim & Henry Gasser. Comn: Portraits, chmn bd US Banknote Corp, 66, pres Bloomfield Col, NJ, 69 & pres Barrington Col, RI, 71; plus many others. Exhib: Six Exhib: Am Artists Prof League Grand Nat, Lever House, NY, 68-77; Am Watercolor Soc 104th & 109th Ann, Nat Acad Design Galleries, New York, 71 & 76; Hudson Valley Art Asn 43rd Ann, White Plains, NY, 71; NJ Watercolor Soc, Brookdale Col, Lindcroft, 73, 75 & Morris Mus, Morristown, 74 & 77; Daughters of the Am Revolution Bicentennial, New York, 76. Teaching: Instr portraiture, Art Ctr Sch, East Orange, NJ, 65-; instr portraiture & landscape, Summit Art Ctr, NJ. Awards: Am Artists Prof League Grand Nat First Award for Oil, 71 & 73; Art Ctr of NJ First Award for Watercolor, 72; Am Artists Prof League NJ State Show First Award for Watercolor, 71. Mem: Fel Am Artists Prof League (dir nat bd, 70-); Grand Cent Art Galleries; Art Ctr of NJ (pres, 66, hon dir, 71-); NJ Watercolor Soc; plus others. Style & Technique: Traditional. Media: Oil, Watercolor. Publ: Illusr, covers for Colliers & Liberty Mag, 43 & Capper's Farmer Mag, 46; illusr, Toronto Star Weekly, 46; illusr, New York Life Insurance Co calendars, 74 & 75. Dealer: Grand Central Art Galleries 40 Vanderbilt Ave New York NY 10017. Mailing Add: 742 Sterling Dr Orange NJ 07050

DANBY, KEN
PAINTER, PRINTMAKER
b Sault Ste Marie, Ont, 1940. Study: Ont Col Art, Toronto, 58-60. Work: Nat Gallery Can, Ottawa, Ont; Mus Mod Art, New York; Montreal Mus Art, PQ; Art Inst Chicago; Univ Calif Art Gallery, Berkeley. Comn: Designer Series III Can Olympic Coins 1976 Olympics, Montreal. Exhib: Man & His World Exhib, Montreal, 71; American Realists Exhib, Paris, France, 72, 2nd Am Biennial Graphic Arts, Cali, Colombia, 73; 6th Int Triennial Coloured Graphic Prints, Grenchen, Switz, 73; touring exhib, Can Cult Ctr, Paris, Can Embassy, Brussels, Canada House Gallery, London & Can Consulate, New York, 74; Living Am Artists & the Figure, Pa State Univ, 74; 3rd Bienal Americana de Artes Graphicas, Colombia, 76; Aspects of Realism, Rothman's Touring Can Exhib, 76-78; Can Sport Art Collection, 76 Olympics, Montreal; 1st Bienniel of Am Graphics, Maracibo, Venezula, 77. Awards: First Recipient of R Tait McKenzie Chair for Sport 1975, Nat Sport & Recreation Ctr, Ottawa; Ont Arts Coun Editions Award, 76; Queen's Can Silver Jubilee Medal, 77. Bibliog: Rex Bromfield (producer), Ken Danby (film), 71; Paul Duval (auth), High Realism in Canadian Art, Clarke-Irwin, 74; Paul Duval (auth), Ken Danby, Clarke-Irwin, 76. Mem: Royal Can Acad Arts. Media: Egg Tempera. Mailing Add: c/o Gallery Moos Ltd 136 Yorkville Ave Toronto ON Can

DANCE, ROBERT BARTLETT
PAINTER, PRINTMAKER
b Tokyo, Japan, May 31, 34; US citizen. Study: Philadelphia Col of Art, with Henry C Pitz & W Emerton Heitland. Work: NC Mus of Fine Art, Raleigh; R J Reynolds Indust, Winston-Salem, NC; Hanes Dye & Finishing, Winston-Salem; Integon Ins Corp, Winston-Salem; Wachovia Bank & Trust, Winston-Salem. Exhib: NC Artists Ann, 58-62 & NC Printmakers (travelling show), 60, NC Mus of Fine Arts, Raleigh; one-man show, Roanoke Fine Arts Ctr, Va, 62; Realist Invitational, Southeastern Ctr for Contemp Art, Winston-Salem, NC, 71-77; Northwestern Open Carolina Art Competition, Winston-Salem, NC, 74; two-man show, Southeastern Ctr for Contemp Art, Winston-Salem, 76; NC Watercolor Soc Exhib, Asheville Art Mus, NC, 76; R J Reynolds Indust NC Collection, Winston-Salem, 77; Critz Exhib, Reynolda House Am Art, 77. Awards: First Place, NC Watercolor Soc, 73, 74 & 77, Assoc Artists of Winston-Salem, 72, 73 & 74 & Northwestern Open Carolina Art Competition, Northwestern Bank, 74. Bibliog: Susan E Meyer (auth), R B Dance—The Watercolor Page, Am Artist Mag, 2/76, 40 Watercolorists and How They Work, Watson-Guptill, 76 & Sir Isaac Pitman & Sons Ltd, Great Brit, 76. Mem: NC Watercolor Soc; Assoc Artists of Winston-Salem; NC Mus of Fine Art (mem NC Artists Exhib Comt, 78). Style & Technique: Realist; landscape & seascape. Media: Watercolor, acrylic, alkyd; woodcut. Publ: Illusr (cover), The World of the Racoon, 64 & The World of the Coyote, 64, Lippincott. Dealer: Remarque Inc 1412 Wiltshire High Point NC 27760; Southeastern Ctr for Contemp Art 750 Marguerite Dr Winston-Salem NC 27106. Mailing Add: 320 Anita Dr Winston-Salem NC 27104

D'ANDREA, ALBERT PHILIP
EDUCATOR, SCULPTOR
b Benevento, Italy, Oct 27, 97; US citizen. Study: Nat Acad Design; Pratt Inst; Univ Rome; City Col New York, BA, 18. Work: Nat Portrait Gallery, Smithsonian Inst, Washington, DC; Libr Cong, Washington, DC; City Col New York; Biblioteca Apostolica Vatican, Vatican City, Italy; Jewish Mus, NY. Comn: Bernard M Baruch Medal, Baruch Col, City Univ New York, 54; Thomas A Edison Medal, Edison Elec Inst, New York, 59; Grover Cleveland Medal, NY Univ Hall Fame, New York, 66; Lincoln Medal, Lincoln Mem Univ, Cumberland Gap, Tenn, 71; Series of sculptured medals depicting Heroes of the Bible, comn by Cath Dig, 74-77. Exhib: Nat Acad Design Graphics Ann, 44; Portrait Sculpture Exhib, 71 & Nat Sculpture Soc 39th Ann Exhib, 72, Nat Sculpture Soc Gallery, New York; Audubon Artists 30th Ann Exhib, New York, 72; Am Artists Prof League Grand Nat Exhib, New York, 72. Teaching: Mem faculty art, City Col New York, 18-48, prof art & chmn dept, 48-68, emer prof, 68- Pos: Dir planning & design, City Col New York, 48-67. Awards: Pennel Award, Libr Cong, Nat Acad Design, 44; Townsend Harris Medal, City Col New York Alumni Asn, 55; Lindsey Morris Mem Prize for bas-relief sculpture, Nat Sculpture Soc, 63; Semifinalist, Nat Bicentennial Coin Competition, 76. Bibliog: I E Levine (auth), Portrait of an artist, City Col New York Alumnus, 56. Mem: Nat Sculpture Soc; Audubon Artists; Am Artists Prof League; Fedn Int Medaille; Royal Soc Arts. Style & Technique: Figurative. Media: Bronze, Terra Cotta. Publ: Contribr, Nat Sculpture Rev, 63, 67 & 72. Mailing Add: 2121 Bay Ave Brooklyn NY 11210

D'ANDREA, JEANNE
ART ADMINISTRATOR, DESIGNER
b Chicago, Ill, Dec 9, 25. Study: Art Inst Chicago; Colo Col, with Rico Lebrun; Univ Chicago, with Joshua Taylor, Ulrich Middledorf & Carlos Castillo, PhB, MA. Exhibitions Arranged: Gericault, Los Angeles Co Mus Art, 71, The American West, 72 & A Decade of Collection, 75; plus others. Pos: Designer sets, costumes, Turnau Opera Co, NY & Arlington Opera Theatre, Arlington, Va, 59-72; head educ dept, Ringling Mus Art, Sarasota, Fla, 60-62; coordr exhib & publ, Los Angeles Co Mus Art, 69- Mem: Am Asn Mus; Col Art Asn Am. Mailing Add: Los Angeles Co Mus Art 5905 Wilshire Blvd Los Angeles CA 90036

DANE, WILLIAM JERALD
ART LIBRARIAN
b Concord, NH, May 8, 25. Study: Drexel Inst Technol, MLS; NY Univ Inst Fine Arts; Sorbonne, Paris, France; Attingham Park Summer Sch, Eng. Collections Arranged: Fine Print Collection, Newark Pub Libr; 150 Years of Graphic Art in New Jersey; Silkscreen, a Survey Show of Serigraphs & Screenprints for the NJ State Coun on Arts. Pos: Supvr art & music libr, Newark Pub Libr, 67- Mem: Grolier Club; Victorian Soc Am (nat bd mem, 74-, chmn NY chap, 72-74); Comt for Preserv of Archit Records (NJ chap secy). Publ: Auth, Picture Collection Subject Headings, 69; auth, rev art publ in, Libr J, Ref Bks Ann; contribr, A Bibliography of the Arts in America from Colonial to Modern Times, Smithsonian Inst. Mailing Add: 5 Washington St Newark NJ 07101

DANENBERG, BERNARD
ART DEALER
Pos: Owner & dir, Danenberg Beilin, Inc. Specialty: 19th and 20th century American art. Mailing Add: 129 E 81st St New York NY 10028

DANES, GIBSON ANDREW
EDUCATOR
b Starbuck, Wash, Dec 13, 10. Study: Univ Ore; Art Inst Chicago, BFA; Northwestern Univ, BS & MA; Yale Univ, univ fel, 46, PhD; Lake Erie Col, hon DFA. Teaching: Prof art, Univ Tex, Austin, 40-43; prof art, Ohio State Univ, 48-52; chmn dept art, Univ Calif, Los Angeles, 52-58; dean, Sch Art & Archit, Yale Univ, 58-68; dean visual arts, State Univ NY Col Purchase, 68-75. Awards: Rockefeller Post-War Fel, 46; Ford Found Fel, 51. Mem: Col Art Asn Am; hon mem Conn Chap Am Inst Architects. Publ: Auth, Looking at Modern Painting, 67; contribr, nat art mag & col jour. Mailing Add: Sch of Visual Arts State Univ NY Col at Purchase Purchase NY 10577

DANHAUSEN, ELDON
SCULPTOR
US citizen. Study: Art Inst Chicago, BFA, James Nelson Raymond foreign traveling fel, 47. Work: Hackley Art Gallery, Muskegon, Mich; Civic Ctr, New Orleans, La; Standard Club Chicago; Roosevelt Univ, Chicago. Comn: Sculpture, Int Minerals & Chem Corp, Skokie, Ill, 60; sculpture, Home Mutual Appleton, Wis, 63; sculpture, WOC TV, Davenport, Iowa, 64; sculpture, Civic Ctr, New Orleans, 67; sculpture, 150 N Wacker Dr Bldg, Chicago, 71. Exhib: Downtown Gallery, New York; Chicago Ann Show, Art Inst Chicago, 45-60; Rivinia Festival Art Exhib, 57, 59 & 60; American Business & the Arts, San Francisco Mus Art, 61; Sculpture 70, Art Inst Chicago, 70. Teaching: Assoc prof sculpture, Art Inst Chicago, 48- Awards: Linde Co Prize, Chicago Ann Show, Art Inst Chicago, 60; Citation for Art in Architecture, Am Inst Archit Iowa Chap, 63. Bibliog: Something to talk about in Chicago, Mademoiselle Mag, 1/54; Art in Chicago, CBS TV, 67; Meilach & Seiden (auth), Direct Metal Sculpture, Crown. Publ: Auth, Art in the market place, sculptor's viewpoint, Chicago Mkt Scene, 3/70; contribr, Contemporary Stone Sculpture, Crown. Mailing Add: 1418 N LaSalle St Chicago IL 60610

DANIEL, SUZANNE GARRIGUES
ART HISTORIAN
b New York, NY, May 15, 45. Study: Lindenwood Col, St Charles, Mo, BA(art), 67; Univ de las Am, Mex, MA(Latin Am art hist), 70; Johns Hopkins Univ, MA(art hist), 75, with Phoebe Stanton; Univ Md, ABD(art hist), with James B Lynch. Teaching: Asst prof art hist, Morgan State Univ, 70- Pos: Mem archaeol team, Las Pilas, Morelos, Mex, 73 & Xochicalco, Morelos, 78. Awards: Fac grant-in-aid res, Morgan State Univ, 71, 72 & 75. Mem: Col Art Asn Am; Latin Am Studies Asn; Soc Am Archaeol; Baltimore Mus Art; Res Ctr Arts, Univ Tex, San Antonio. Res: Iconography of highland Olmec and lowland Izapa monumental art. Mailing Add: 1216 N Calvert St Baltimore MD 21202

DANIELI, FIDEL ANGELO
PAINTER, ART CRITIC
b Ironwood, Mich, June 15, 38. Study: Pasadena City Col, with Leonard Edmondson, AA; Univ Calif, Los Angeles, with Jan Stussy & William Brice, BA & MA. Exhib: One-man shows, Orlando Gallery, Encino, Calif, 69-75 & Suburban Sections, Los Angeles Valley Col, 73; Magic Machine Traveling Exhib, Univ Calif, Berkeley, 74; Munic Gallery, Barnsdall Park, Los Angeles, 75. Collections Arranged: Inaugural Exhib, Brand Art Ctr, Glendale, Calif, 69; Nine Senior Southern California Painters, Los Angeles Inst Contemp Art, Century City, 74-75. Teaching: Assoc prof art, Los Angeles Valley Col, 61-, chmn dept, currently. Pos: Ed, Los Angeles Artists' Publ, 72-73; Southern Calif adv bd mem, West Coast Div, Arch Am Art, 75. Awards: Nat Endowment Humanities Grant for Jr Col Teachers, 74. Mem: Los Angeles Inst Contemp Art (guest cur, 74, ed jour, 74, mem jour comt, 75). Style & Technique: Latex and acrylic on canvas and constructions; symbolic geometric abstractions. Publ: Art in Artforum, 63-68 & Artweek, 74- Dealer: Orlando Gallery 17037 Ventura Blvd Encino CA 91316. Mailing Add: 7858 Goodland Ave North Hollywood CA 91605

DANIELS, DAVID M
COLLECTOR, PATRON
b Evanston, Ill, Apr 10, 27. Study: Yale Univ; Curtis Inst Music. Pos: Trustee & accessions comt, Minneapolis Inst Fine Arts, 65-; trustee, Skowhegan Art Sch, 69-; pres, Drawing Soc, 71- Collection: Drawings and sculpture of all periods; medals and paintings. Publ: Contribr, Drawings of Morris Graves, New York Graphics, 73. Mailing Add: 4 Sutton Pl New York NY 10022

DANIELSON, PHYLLIS I
ART ADMINISTRATOR, FIBER ARTIST
b Marion, Ind. Study: Ball State Univ, BA(art), 53; Mich State Univ, MA, 60, EdS, 66; Ind Univ, EdD, 68. Work: Mint Mus Art, Charlotte, NC. Exhib: Weatherspoon Gallery, Greensboro, NC, 69 & 70; Stitchery, Pa, 71 & Iowa, 75; Matrix Gallery, Bloomington, Ind, 72; one-person shows, Jewish Community Ctr, Indianapolis, Ind, 72 & Eye-Opener Gallery, Cincinnati, Ohio, 72; Mint Mus Art, 74; Herron Art Gallery, Indianapolis, 74; Sloane O'Stickey Gallery, Cleveland, Ohio, 74; Women in Art, West Bend, Wis, 76. Teaching: Asst prof art, Ball State Univ, Muncie, Ind, 66-67; asst prof art educ, Univ NC, Greensboro, 68-70; assoc prof educ & art, Herron Sch Art, Indianapolis, 70-76. Pos: Chmn art studies dept, Herron Sch Art, 70-76; pres, Kendall Sch Design, Grand Rapids, 76- Bibliog: Kathleen Fisher (auth), Women in Action, Asn Art Hist Educ Bull, 75. Mem: Nat Art Educ Asn; Nat Coun Art Adminr; Nat Asn Sch Art; Col Art Asn. Style & Technique: Stitchery wallhangings; surface decoration and three-dimensional forms. Media: Fabric, Fiber. Publ: Auth, Art for the Second & Third Grades, Kimball/Hunt, 66; auth, Paper mache and the elementary teacher, Arts & Activities, 12/70; auth, Selected teacher characteristics of art student teachers, Studies Art Educ, winter, 71; auth, Art education: an international survey, Educ Studies, 72; auth, The woman administrator in art, Col Art J, 76; plus others. Mailing Add: 6137 Chamonix Ct SE Grand Rapids MI 49506

DANIKIAN, CARON LE BRUN
WRITER, ART CRITIC
b Rochester, NY, May 2, 42. Study: Marymount Manhattan Col, BA, 64. Pos: Art ed & critic, Boston Herald Traveler, Mass, 66-72; art ed & critic, Boston Herald Am, 72-73, art critic, Christian Sci Monitor, 73-; vpres, Arvest Galleries, Inc, Boston. Res: Turn of the century American impressionists and Boston artists. Publ: Contribr, Sunday Herald Traveler Mag, Boston Arts Mag, Nat Antiques Rev, Sunday Herald Advertiser Mag & Christian Sci Monitor. Mailing Add: 790 Boylston St 19B Boston MA 02199

DANK, LEONARD DEWEY
MEDICAL ILLUSTRATOR, AUDIO-VISUAL CONSULTANT
b Birmingham, Ala, Dec 21, 29. Study: Cornell Univ, BA, 52; Sch of Med Illus, Mass Gen Hosp, Boston, cert, 55; Art Students League; Jules Laurents Studio, New York. Work: McGraw-Hill Publ Co, New York; Stravon Educ Press, Inc, New York; H S Stuttman Co, Inc, New York; Proj-in-Health, New York; Doubleday & Co Inc, New York. Comn: Diabetes (animated film), Synapse Inc, Greenwich, Conn, 74; plus many career comns. Pos: Staff artist, Plastic Surgery Clin, Manhattan Eye & Ear Hosp, New York, 55-57 & Eye Bank for Sight Restoration, New York, 57-59; owner, Leonard Dank Studio, New York, 59-61; owner, Medical Illus Co, New York & Cutchogue, NY, 61-; consult med illusr, St Luke's Hosp & Woman's Hosp, New York. Awards: First Prize (motion picture), Am Col of Surgery, 59 & 62; Better Teller Award, Asn Indust Advertisers, 73. Mem: Asn Med Illusr; Guild of Natural Sci Illusr. Style & Technique: Anatomical renderings for medical books, journals, animated movies, encyclopedias, etc. Media: Wash, Airbrush; Pen & Ink. Publ: Illusr, Encyclopedia Int, Grolier, 63; illusr, Medical Aid Encylopedia, Stravon Educ Press, New York, 65; illusr, Cells: The Basic Structure of Life, Franklin Watts, 70; contribr, Clinical Obstetrics & Gynecology, Harper & Row, 73-76; co-auth, Gynecologic Operations, Harper & Row, 78. Mailing Add: 113th St & Amsterdam Ave New York NY 10025

DANOFF, I MICHAEL
CURATOR, ART HISTORIAN
b Chicago, Ill, Oct 22, 40. Study: Univ Mich, BA; Univ NC, Chapel Hill, MA; Syracuse Univ, PhD. Exhibitions Arranged: Mauricio Lasansky, 73; Mel Ramos, 73; Roger Welch, 74; Kazys Marnelis, 74; Wisconsin Directions, 75; Foreign Born Artists, 76. Teaching: Asst prof 19th & 20th century & contemp art, Dickson Col, 70-73, Univ Tex, Austin, 73 & Univ Wis-Milwaukee, 75- Pos: Cur collections, Dickinson Col, 70-73; cur Michener Collection, Univ Tex, 73-74; cur collections & exhibs, Milwaukee Art Ctr, 74- Awards: Nat Endowment Arts mus prof fel, 73. Mem: Col Art Asn Am; Midwest Art Hist Soc; Am Asn Mus. Res: 20th century American art, especially contemporary. Publ: Auth, Gallery Guides to Collections, Milwaukee Art Ctr, 74-75; auth, Mary Nohl: sophisticated naive, Midwest Art, 75; auth, Europe in the Seventies, Art in Am, 1/78. Mailing Add: 750 N Lincoln Mem Dr Milwaukee WI 53202

DANSEREAU, MIREILLE
FILM MAKER
b Montreal, PQ, Dec 19, 43. Study: Univ Paris, BA, 61; Univ Montreal, Lic es Lett, 65; Royal Col Art, London, MA, 69. Exhib: Montreal Film Festival, 67; Student Film Festival, London, 69; Can Film Awards, 72; San Francisco Film Festival, 73; Toulon Film Festival, 73; Francophone Film Festival, 73- Awards: First Prize for Compromise (30mm-b/w film), Student Film Festival, London, 69; Wendy Mitchener Award, Can Film Awards, 72; Best Young Film Maker Award, San Francisco & Prix Spec de Jury, Toulon, France, 73, for La Vie Revee (80 min, 35mm color film). Mailing Add: 5922 Jeanne Mance Montreal PQ Can

DAOUST, SYLVIA
SCULPTOR
b Montreal, PQ, May 24, 02. Study: Ecole Beaux-Arts, Montreal. Work: Mus PQ; Col St Laurent; Monastere St Benoit-du-lac, Montreal; Univ Montreal; plus others. Comn: IBM Corp; portraits, Can Bar Asn; Govt PQ. Exhib: Nat Gallery Can; Mus PQ; Art Gallery Toronto; Royal Can Acad Ann, 30-; Expos Relig Art, Rome, 50; plus others. Teaching: Instr, Ecoles Beaux-Arts, Montreal. Awards: Award, Royal Can Acad, 51; Can Govt Scholar, France, 55-56; Medal, Royal Archit Inst Can, 61; plus others. Mem: Royal Can Acad Art; Sculptors Soc Can. Mailing Add: 2105 Bord du Lac Dorval PQ H9S 2G4 Can

DAPHNIS, NASSOS
PAINTER, SCULPTOR
b Krokeai, Greece, July 23, 14; US citizen. Work: Mus Mod Art, New York; Whitney Mus Am Art, New York; Albright-Knox Gallery Art, Buffalo; Carnegie Inst, Pittsburgh; Larry Aldrich Mus, Ridgefield, Conn. Comn: Wall paintings, City Walls, Inc, 70 & Nat Endowment Arts, 71; art environment, Arlen Realty Develop Corp, 71. Exhib: One-man exhibs, Mint Mus, Charlotte, NC, 49, Work Since 1951, Albright-Knox Mus, Buffalo, NY, 69, Everson Mus, Syracuse, NY, 69, Andre Zarre Gallery, New York, NY, 74 & 76 & numerous others; 26th Biennial Exhib, Corcoran Gallery, Washington, DC, 59, 28th Biennial, 63 & 31st Biennial, 69; Ann Exhib—Painting, Whitney Mus of Am Art, New York, NY, 59, 61, 64, 65 & 67 & Ann Exhib—Sculpture & Drawing, 62; Purist Painting, Walker Art Ctr, Minneapolis, Minn, 61 & Geometric Abstraction in Am, 62; Am Abstract Expressionists & Imagists, Guggenheim Mus, New York, NY, 61; Highlights of the 68-69 Season, Aldrich Mus, Ridgefield, Conn, 69; Pittsburgh Int, Carnegie Inst, Pa, 70; Birmingham Festival of Art, Birmingham Mus of Art, Ala, 76; Provincetown Painters 1890s-1970s, Everson Mus of Art, Syracuse, NY, 77; plus others. Awards: Nat Found Arts & Humanities Award, 66; Nat Endowment Arts Grant, 71; Guggenheim Mem Found Fel, 77. Bibliog: Robert M Murdock (auth), Nassos Daphnis: Work Since 1951, Albright-Knox Art Gallery, 69; Hilton Kramer (auth), The Corcoran Biennial, 2/23/69 & 12 artists join in an uncommon show, 3/18/71, New York Times. Mem: Am Abstract Artists. Style & Technique: Geometric; spraying. Media: Epoxy, Plexiglas. Dealer: Leo Castelli Gallery 420 W Broadway New York NY 10013. Mailing Add: 362 W Broadway New York NY 10013

DAPHNIS-AVLON, HELEN
PAINTER, SCULPTOR
b Manhattan, NY, June 18, 32. Study: Brooklyn Mus, 50-53; Colorado Springs Fine Arts Mus, 53; Hunter Col, BFA, 53 & MA, 57. Work: Chrysler Mus; Sonnabend Art Collection, NY. Comn: Painting, 59. Exhib: Bertha Schaeffer Gallery, New York, 59-62; Provincetown Art Asn, Mass, 60-72; Wadell Gallery, New York, 69; Peace Exhib, Mus Mod Art, New York, 70; Westbeth Gallery, New York, 70; Warde-Nesse Gallery, New York; Landmark Now Show, 78; plus others. Teaching: Art instr graphics, Brooklyn Mus, 53-62; instr art, pub & pvt schs, NY & Mass, 60-; adult instr art, Brooklyn Col, 68-69. Pos: Dir, Avlon's Art Co-op Gallery, Provincetown, Mass, 69-72; chmn window display & multi-media films, Westbeth Graphic Arts Workshop, 70-72. Awards: Ten yr outstanding achievement award, Hunter Col, 63. Mem: Westbeth Tenants (grants & health, 70); Provincetown Art Asn; Mus Mod Art, New York; Village Community Sch (class rep, 72). Media: Acrylic, Ceramics, Metal, Graphics, Photo-silk Screen. Mailing Add: 463 West St New York NY 10014

DARBOVEN, HANNE
CONCEPTUAL ARTIST, GRAPHIC ARTIST
b Munich, Ger, Apr 29, 41. Study: Hochscule for Bildende Kunst, Hamburg. Work: Stedelijk Mus, Amsterdam, Holland; Kaiser Wilhelm Mus, Krefeld, WGer. Exhib: Normal Art, Lannis Mus of Normal Art, New York, 67; When Attitudes Become Form (traveling exhib), Kunsthalle Bern, Switz, 69; 955,000, Vancouver Art Gallery, BC, 70; Conceptual Art/Arte Povera/Land Art, Galleria Civica d'Arte Mod, Turin, 70; Guggenheim Int, New York, 71; 7th Biennale, Paris, France, 71; Documenta 5, Kassel, WGer, 72; 7th Biennale, Sao Paulo, Brazil, 73; Projekt 74, Kunsthalle, Cologne, 74; Eight Contemp Artists, Mus Mod Art, New York, 74; one-person shows, Stadtisches Mus, Monchengladbach, WGer, 69, Art & Proj, Amsterdam, 70, Mus fur Kunst und Gewerb, Hamburg, 72, Leo Castelli Gallery, New York, 73-75, Palais des Beaux-Arts, Brussels, Belg, 74, Mus Mod Art, Oxford, Eng, 74, Kabinett fur Akutelle Kunst, Bremerhaven, WGer, 74, Kunstmuseum, Basel, Switz, 74-75, Sonnabend Gallery, New York, 74-75, Stedelijk Mus, 75 & Kunstmuseum Lucerne, Switz, 75. Bibliog: J Collins (auth), Reviews: Hanne Darboven, Castelli Downtown, 9/73, Lucy R Lippard (auth), Hanne Darboven: deep in numbers, 10/73 & Max Kosloff (auth), Transversing the field: eight contemporary artists at Museum of Modern Art, 12/74, Artforum. Style & Technique: Drawings using non-representation numbers as texts. Publ: Contribr, 6 Manuskripte 69, Kunstzeltung, Dusseldorf, 69; auth, Ein Jahrhundert, Amsterdam, 71; auth, Words, Avalanche, New York, spring 72. Dealer: Leo Castelli Gallery 420 W Broadway New York NY 10012. Mailing Add: c/o Sonnabend Gallery 420 W Broadway New York NY 10012

D'ARCANGELO, ALLAN M
PAINTER
b Buffalo, NY, June 16, 30. Study: Univ Buffalo, AB(hist); City Col New York; Mexico City Col. Work: Whitney Mus Am Art, Mus Mod Art, New York; Albright-Knox Mus, Buffalo; Gemeente Mus, The Hague; Joseph H Hirshhorn Mus, Washington, DC. Exhib: Am Landscape Painting, Mus Mod Art Traveling Exhib, USA & Spoleto, Italy, 64; Two Decades of Am Painting, Japan, India & Australia, 66; New Forms, Stedelijk Mus, Amsterdam, Holland, 66; Environ USA, Biennial of Sao Paulo, Brazil, 67; L'art Vivant Am, Found Maeght, St Paul de Vence, France, 69. Teaching: Instr painting, Sch Visual Arts, New York, 63-68, Cornell Univ, 68, Syracuse Univ, 71 & Univ Wis, 72; prof art, Brooklyn Col, 73- Awards: Artist in residence, Aspen Inst Humanistic Studies, 65 & 67; Nat Inst Arts & Lett Ann Award, 70. Bibliog: N Calas (auth), Art in the Age of Risk, 68 & N Calas (auth), Icons & Images of the Sixties, 71, Dutton; Dore Ashton (auth), A Reading in Modern Art, Case Western Reserve Univ, 69. Mem: Soc Am Graphic Artists; City Walls Inc. Mailing Add: PO Box 33 Kenoza Lake NY 12750

D'ARISTA, ROBERT
PAINTER, EDUCATOR
b New York, NY, 1929. Study: Washington Sq Col, NY Univ; Columbia Univ; Acad Grande Chaumiere, Paris, France; Fulbright scholar, Florence, 55. Work: Yale Univ Art Gallery, New Haven, Conn; Toledo Mus Art, Ohio; Hirshhorn Collection, Washington, DC; Neuberger Collection; Nat Collection Fine Arts, Washington, DC. Exhib: Carnegie Inst, Pittsburgh; Solomon R Guggenheim Mus, New York; Whitney Mus Am Art, New York; four one-man shows, Nordness Gallery, New York, 64-72. Teaching: Prof art, Am Univ, 61-; distinguished vis artist, Boston Univ, spring 73. Awards: Rosenthal Found Award, Inst Arts & Lett, 67. Style & Technique: Figurative. Media: Oil on Canvas. Publ: Auth, Reflections on painting, In: Painters on Painting, Grosset & Dunlap. Mailing Add: 3125 Quebec Pl NW Washington DC 20008

DARLING, SHARON SANDLING
CURATOR, ART HISTORIAN
b Mitchell, SDak, Feb 28, 43. Study: NC State Univ, BA; Duke Univ, MAT; Uinterthur Summer Inst, Am Dec Arts. Collections Arranged: Chicago Metalsmiths, Chicago Hist Soc, 77. Pos: Cur dec arts, Chicago Hist Soc, 75- Res: Decorative arts and architecture of Chicago and the Midwest. Publ: Contribr, Silver Mag, 75 & 77; co-auth (with Gail Farr Casterline), Chicago Metalsmiths, 77 & auth, Arts & crafts shops in the fine arts building, Chicago Hist, 77, Chicago Hist Soc; auth (rev), Chicago Metalsmiths, Am Art Rev, 78. Mailing Add: c/o Chicago Hist Soc N Clark & W North Chicago IL 60614

DARR, WILLIAM HUMISTON
ART HISTORIAN, PAINTER
b New York, NY, June 20, 20. Study: Pomona Col, 38-40; Pa Acad Fine Arts, 40-42; Wesleyan Univ, BA, 51; Yale Univ, 57-58, MFA, 62; also with Millard Sheets, Joseph Albers, James Brooks, Neil Welliver & Russell Limbach. Work: Smith Col, Northampton, Mass; Williams Col Mus, Williamstown, Mass; Cedar Rapids Art Ctr, Iowa; Drake Univ, Des Moines, Iowa; Earlham Col, Richmond, Ind. Exhib: Calif Watercolor Ann, Los Angeles Co Mus Art, Los Angeles, 39-41; Nat Watercolor Soc, Riverside Mus, New York, 41-42; Traveling Exhib of Paintings in State Dept, Metrop Mus Art, New York, 46; Audubon Soc Nat, Nat Acad Design, New York, 54; Drake Univ Artists, Des Moines Art Ctr, 71. Teaching: Asst prof painting & printmaking, Amherst Col, Mass, 51-61; instr printmaking, Hartford Art Sch, Conn, 53-55; vis artist design, Smith Col, 55-57; assoc prof art, Earlham Col, 62-68; prof art & chmn dept, Drake Univ, Des Moines, 68- Pos: Co-dir, Studio Art Ctr Int, Florence, Italy, 76- Awards: Duncan Vaile Award, Calif Watercolor Ann, 41; Peabody Award, Audubon Soc Ann, 56; Design Award, Nat Soc Graphic Designers, 56. Style & Technique: Metaphysical realist. Media: Watercolor, Acrylic; Woodblock. Res: The last half of the 19th century; Paul Gauguin's development. Publ: Illusr, The Goolibah Tree, Nat Coop, 44; illusr & auth, La Corrida, privately publ, 51; auth, Eros & Thanatos in Picasso's Guernica, Art J, 67. Mailing Add: 20 Commonwealth Ave Boston MA 02116

DARRAH, ANN CLARKE
LECTURER, PAINTER
b Norwich, Eng, Aug 27, 44; Can citizen. Study: Slade Sch Fine Art, Univ Col, London, dipl fine art & design. Work: Ministry of Pub Bldg & Works, Great Brit; Alta Art Found, Can; Hill Trust Fund Collection, Calgary, Alta; Prov Courthouse Collection, Edmonton, Can; Queensland Art Gallery, Brisbane, Australia. Exhib: Prairies, Saidye Bronfman Cult Centre, Montreal, Que & Ottawa, Ont & Edmonton Art Gallery, 74; Norman Mackenzie Art Gallery, Regina & Alta Col Art, Calgary, 75; Black Expo, Mem Univ Art Gallery, St Johns, Nfld, 76; Abstraction West: Emma Lake and After, Nat Gallery, Ottawa, Ont & Mendel Art Gallery, Saskatoon, Sask, 76; Beaverbrook Art Gallery, Frederickton, NB, 76; NS Mus Fine Art, Halifax, 76; Mus d'Art Contemporain, Montreal, Que, 76; Art Gallery of Windsor, Ont, 76; Collector's Choice, 76 & Acrylic on Canvas & New Abstract Art, 77, Edmonton Art Gallery; Contemp Can Drawings, Mackenzie Art Gallery, Univ Regina, Sask, 77; one-person shows, Latitude 53 Gallery, Edmonton & Edmonton Art Gallery, 77. Teaching: Asst prof art, NS Col Art & Design, Halifax, 75-76; lectr art, Univ Alta, Edmonton, 76- Awards: Can Coun Art Bank Award, 73 & 76; Govt Alta Cult Award, 74. Style & Technique: Painterly; abstract

and non-representational. Media: Acrylic on Canvas. Mailing Add: 8107 149th St Edmonton AB T5R 1B1 Can

DARRICARRERE, ROGER DOMINIQUE
SCULPTOR, STAINED GLASS ARTIST
b Bayonne, France, Dec 15, 12; US citizen. Study: Ecole des Beaux-Arts, Bayonne, 30-35; Ecole Nat Super Decoratifs Paris, dipl, 38; Inst Metiers, Paris, 45. Comn: Spatial kaleidoscope, Lytton Ctr, Los Angeles, 59; revolving steel & glass sculpture depicting moving picture indust; leaded glass window wall, World's Fair Contest, St Stephen's Lutheran Church, Granada Hills, Calif; Columbia Savings & Loan Asn, Los Angeles, 66; massive bronze sculpture, Atlantis, Lytton Savings & Loan Asn Northern Calif, Oakland, 67; plus others. Exhib: Pasadena Art Mus, 59-63; Otis Art Inst, Los Angeles, 61-65; New York World's Fair, 64-65; Mus Contemp Crafts, New York, 66; Craftsman USA, Los Angeles Co Mus, Los Angeles, 66; plus others. Teaching: Instr, interior design & painting, Coe Col, 48-51; workshop prof glass in archit, Calif State Col, Long Beach, 68-69; lectr stained glass & sculpture, Mt St Mary's Col, spring 69. Awards: Fine Arts & Craftsmanship Awards, Am Inst Architects, 58, 59, 61 & 63; First Prize, Nat Competition stained glass panel, New York World's Fair, 64-65; Nat Merit Award, Craftsman USA, 66; plus others. Mem: Southern Calif Designer-craftsmen; Guild Relig Archit. Media: Steel, Glass. Mailing Add: 1204 San Fernando Rd Los Angeles CA 90065

DARROW, PAUL GARDNER
PAINTER, EDUCATOR
b Pasadena, Calif. Study: Colorado Springs Fine Art Ctr; Claremont Grad Sch & Univ Ctr. Work: Pasadena Art Mus, Calif; Times-Mirror Collection, Los Angeles; US Navy, Washington, DC; Lytton Savings & Loan Collection, Los Angeles; Long Beach Mus Art, Calif. Comn: Murals, Air France, Los Angeles, 61, Balboa Yacht Club, 63 & Newport Bank, Calif, 71. Exhib: Mus Mod Art, Sao Paulo, Brazil, 55; Pasadena Art Mus, 55; Downtown Gallery, New York, 57; San Francisco Mus Art, 59; Calif Inst Technol, Pasadena, 70. Teaching: Prof art & chmn dept, Scripps Col, 60-; prof art, Claremont Grad Sch, 70- Pos: Vpres, Calif Watercolor Soc, 60-62; founder, Los Angeles Printmaking Soc, 62; artist-corresp, US Navy 7th Fleet, Viet Nam & Japan, 63. Awards: Purchase Awards, Los Angeles Mus Art, 55; Purchase Award, Pasadena Art Mus, 58; Res Grant, Ford Found, 69. Bibliog: Bently Schaad (auth), The Realm of Contemporary Still Life Painting, 62 & Edmondson (auth), Printmaking, 72, Van Nostrand Reinhold. Style & Technique: Collage; mixed media; experimental & documentary film. Media: Graphic. Publ: Illusr, Aldous Huxley, Paris Rev, 62; illusr, The Concrete Wilderness, Meredith, 67; illusr, The Guide for the Married Man, Price Stern, 68; illusr, Psychological Perspectives, C G Jung Inst, 70. Dealer: Comara Gallery La Cienega Los Angeles CA 90034. Mailing Add: 690 Cuprien Way Laguna Beach CA 92651

DARROW, WHITNEY, JR
CARTOONIST
b Princeton, NJ, Aug 22, 09. Study: Princeton Univ; Art Students League. Pos: Cartoonist, New York Mag, 33- Media: Pencil, Charcoal, Watercolor. Publ: Auth, You're Sitting On My Eyelashes, 43, Please Pass the Hostess, 49 & Stop Miss, 57, Random House; auth, Give Up, Simon & Schuster, 66; illusr, Nutty Riddles, Doubleday, 76; plus others. Mailing Add: 331 Newtown Tpk Wilton CT 06897

DARTON, CHRISTOPHER
PAINTER
b New York, NY, Dec 9, 45. Study: New York Inst Technol, BFA, 69; Pratt Inst Grad Sch, MFA, 71. Exhib: Daniel Weinberg, San Francisco, Calif, 76; Mary Berne Gallery, 78. Publ: Auth, Matter as subject, Arts Mag, 11/77. Style & Technique: Acrylic extruded on Dacron mesh from back of stretcher; transparent; side; composition-linear format. Media: Acrylic Paint. Mailing Add: 9 E 16th St 4th Floor New York NY 10003

DASBURG, ANDREW MICHAEL
PAINTER
b Paris, France, May 4, 87. Study: Art Students League with Kenyon Cox & Frank V DuMond; also with Birge Harrison & Robert Henri; Univ NMex, Hon DFA, 58. Work: Whitney Mus Am Art; Denver Art Mus; Los Angeles Mus Art; Calif Palace of Legion of Honor; Dallas Mus Fine Arts; plus others. Exhib: Whitney Mus Am Art; San Francisco Mus Art; Mus Mod Art; one-man show, Dallas Mus Fine Arts, 57; retrospective, Am Fedn Arts-Ford Found, 59; plus others. Awards: Guggenheim Fel, 32; Ford Found Grant; Nat Found Arts Award, 67; plus others. Bibliog: Lloyd Goodrich & John I H Baur (auth), Included in, American Art of Our Century, Whitney Mus Am Art, 61; Van Deren Coke (auth), included in, Taos and Santa Fe The Artistic Environment, 1882-1942, Univ NMex, 63; Barbara Rose (auth), included in, American Art Since 1900, A Critical Essay, Praeger, 67; plus others. Mailing Add: PO Box 36 Taos NM 87571

DASH, HARVEY DWIGHT
ART ADMINISTRATOR, PAINTER
b Brooklyn, NY, June 28, 24. Study: Pratt Inst; Tyler Sch Fine Arts, Temple Univ, BFA, BSEd & MFA; Rutgers Univ; Columbia Univ; Montclair State Col. Exhib: Pa Acad Fine Arts, Philadelphia; Temple Univ; one-man shows, Fairleigh Dickinson Univ & Brighton Gallery, New York. Teaching: Instr fine art, Temple Univ, 46-47; chmn dept art, Tenafly High Sch, 51-57 & Paramus High Sch, NJ, 57-63. Pos: Supvr art, Bound Brook Bd Educ, 48-51; dir creative arts, Paramus Sch Syst, 63-67; dir Lighthouse Art Gallery, Nyack, NY, 67-69; dir, Dash Sch of Art (formerly Lighthouse Sch Art), Grandview, NY, 67- Awards: Paramus Bd Educ grants, 65 & 66. Mem: NY State Art Teachers Asn; Nat Art Educ Asn. Style & Technique: Abstract: hard edge acrylic, silk screen; semi-abstract-romantic. Media: Oils, watercolor. Mailing Add: 654 Rte 9W Upper Grandview NY 10960

DASH, ROBERT (WARREN)
PAINTER
b New York, NY, June 8, 34. Work: Brooklyn Mus, NY; Mod Art Mus of Munich, WGer; NY Univ; Chase Manhattan Bank Collection; Philadelphia Mus Art; plus others. Comn: Stage set for Port, 64; Garden (lithographs with lines by James Schuyler), 72; var covers for vols of poetry. Exhib: The New York Season, 60-61; Yale Univ Exhib, 61; Landscapes by Five Americans, Festival of Two Worlds, Mus Mod Art Traveling Exhib, 66; Inform & Interpret, Am Fedn Arts Traveling Exhib, 68; A Sense of Place, Guild Hall, East Hampton, NY, 72. Teaching: Adj prof advan painting, Southampton Col, spring 70 & 75. Bibliog: Article In: Art Now, Vol 9, No 2; Gerrit Henry (auth), The making of the new Utopia, Art Int, spring 73; article, In: Am Artist, spring 74. Style & Technique: Painterly realist. Media: Acrylics, Pastels. Dealer: Fischbach Gallery 29 W 57th St New York NY 10019. Mailing Add: Sagg Main Sagaponack NY 11962

DASKALOFF, GYORGY
PAINTER
b Sofia, Bulgaria, May 15, 23; US citizen. Study: Acad Fine Arts, Sofia, grad. Work: Metrop Mus Art, New York; Nat Mus, Sofia; Royal Libr, Brussels, Belg; Butler Inst Am Art, Youngstown, Ohio. Comn: Mural, comn by ARA, Ann Arbor, Mich; portrait of Judge Theodor Levin, Detroit Bar Asn, 71; An American Family (mural), comn by Amos Cahan, New York, 73. Exhib: Bulgarian Art in Berlin, 58, Moscow, 59 & Prague, 59; Int Biennial Graphic Arts, Ljubliana, 59; Int Exhib Graphics, Leipzig, 60; Comparisons, Paris, 65-67. Awards: First Prize for Graphics, Bulgaria, 54 & 59. Bibliog: Pierre Rouve (auth), article in Arts Rev, London, 6/3/61; L L Sosset (auth), article in Les Beaux Arts, Brussels, 5/6/65; Pierre Lubecker (auth), article in Politiken, Copenhagen, 5/25/67. Style & Technique: Neo-figurative. Media: Oil; Lithography. Mailing Add: 46 Great Jones St New York NY 10012

DAUGHERTY, MARSHALL HARRISON
SCULPTOR, ART ADMINISTRATOR
b Macon, Ga, Sept 6, 15. Study: Ringling Art Sch; Mercer Univ, Macon, Ga; Yale Sch Fine Arts & Cranbrook Acad Art, with Carl Milles et al, 31-38. Work: Solomon R Guggenheim Mus, film, New York; Hay House Mus & Washington Libr, Macon, Ga; Middle Ga Col, Cochran. Comn: Numerous portrait busts and small sculptures, comn by orgns & individuals, 30-77; Royal Monument, Royal Singing Convention, Mystic, Ga, 55; John Wesley Monument (heroic size, bronze & granite), United Methodists, Savannah, Ga, 69; The Praying World, Macon Bicentennial Comn, Macon Coliseum, 76; spec grant for distribution of bronze medals to leading mus & collections, Yin-Yang, 75, Apollonian-Dionysian, 76 & Winterset, 77. Exhib: Grand Cent Galleries, New York, 37; Detroit Art Mus, Mich, 40; Houston Mus Art, Tex, 50; Mint Mus Art, Charlotte, NC, 61. Teaching: Instr sculpture, Wesleyan Sch Fine Arts, Macon, Ga, 40-45; prof art, Mercer Univ, Macon, Ga, 45- Pos: Pres, Ga Art Teachers Asn, 44 & Asn Ga Artists, 44; chmn dept art, Mercer Univ, Macon, Ga, 45-; pres, Macon Art Asn, 48; vpres, Southern Asn Sculptors, 64-67. Awards: Yaddo fel, Saratoga Springs, NY, 39; Carnegie grants, 46 & 47. Style & Technique: Figurative sculpture; originator of cineform—abstract animated sculpture on film. Mailing Add: 1831 Upper River Rd Macon GA 31211

DAUGHERTY, MICHAEL F
EDUCATOR, SCULPTOR
b Seattle, Wash, Sept 30, 42. Study: Univ Wash, Seattle, 60-62; Barcelona, Spain, 65; Univ Wash, Seattle, BA(sculpture), 69; Univ Tenn, Knoxville, MFA(sculpture), 71. Comn: Outdoor fountains, Walter H Stevens, Knoxville, 70, Genevieve Stoughton, Oak Ridge, Tenn, 71, Alvin Rotenberg, 73, Janice Sachse, 74 & Derwood Facundus, 76, Baton Rouge, La. Exhib: The 7th Ann Small Sculpture & Drawing Exhib, Bellingham, Wash, 70; Southern Sculpture: 6th Touring Sculpture Exhib, 70; Tenn Sculpture 1970, Tenn Arts Comn, 70; 5th Ann Nat Drawing & Sculpture Exhib, Corpus Christi, Tex, 71; Dulin Gallery of Art, Knoxville, 71; Artists of the SE & Tex Biennial, New Orleans Mus of Art, La, 71; 14th Ann Delta Art Exhib, Little Rock, Ark, 71; 6th Ann Nat Drawing & Sculpture Exhib, Corpus Christi, 72; Nat Community Art Competition, US Dept Housing & Urban Develop, Washington, DC; 8th Ann Nat Drawing & Sculpture Exhib, Corpus Christi, 74; 3rd Biennial Five-State Art Exhib, Port Arthur, Tex, 75; Piedmont Biennial, Mint Mus of Art, Charlotte, NC, 75; SPAR Nat Art Exhib, Shreveport, La, 76; Sculpture of the SE Exhib, Univ New Orleans, 76; Small Sculptures: Nat Invitational, Cypress, Calif, 76; 4th Biennial Five-State Exhib, Port Arthur, 77; 11th Ann Nat Drawing & Sculpture Show, Corpus Christi, 77; Univ Ga Fine Arts Gallery, 77; Nat Ann Art Exhib, Edison Col, Cape Coral, Fla, 77. Teaching: Teaching asst, Univ Tenn, 69-71; instr, Art Ctr, Oak Ridge, Tenn, 70; assoc prof sculpture & course adv, La State Univ, 71- Awards: First Place, Southern Sculpture: 6th Touring Sculpture Exhib, 70; Purchase Award, Tenn Sculpture 1970, Tenn Arts Comn, 71; Purchase Award, 7th Ann Mobile Art Exhib, Mobile, Ala, 72. Mem: Southern Asn of Sculptors; Col Art Asn. Dealer: Adelle M Taylor Gallery 3317 McKinney Ave Dallas TX 75204. Mailing Add: 5246 N Chalet Ct Baton Rouge LA 70808

D'AULAIRE, EDGAR PARIN
ILLUSTRATOR, LITHOGRAPHER
b Munich, Ger, Sept 30, 98; US citizen. Study: Kunstgewerbeschule (Sch Appl Arts); Hans Hofmann Sch; Ecole Andre Lhote; Ecole Pola Gaugin, Paris. Comn: Fresco in church, Drammen, Norway; Hopkin Ctr, Hanover, NH; pub libr & cols in USA & Europe. Exhib: Salon d'Automne, Paris; Galerie Wang, Oslo, Norway; Awards: Caldecott Medal, Am Libr Asn, 40; Regina Award, Cath Libr Asn, 70. Bibliog: Esther Averill (auth), Caldecott Medal Books, Vol II, Horn, 57; B Hürlimann (auth), Die Welt im Bilderbuch, Atlantis Verlag, Zurich, 65; L B Hopkins (auth), Books Are by People, Citation, 69. Mem: Artists Guild. Media: Mixed Media. Publ: Co-auth & illusr, Ola, 32, Greek Myths, 62, Norse Gods & Giants, 67, Trolls, 72, Terrible Troll Bird, 76, Doubleday; co-auth & illusr, Children of the Northlights, Viking, 36; plus many others. Mailing Add: 74 Mather Rd Georgetown CT 06829

D'AULAIRE, INGRI (MORTENSON) PARIN
WRITER, ILLUSTRATOR
b Kongsberg, Norway, Dec 27, 04; US citizen. Study: Kunstindustriskolen, Oslo, 23-24; Hans Hofmann Sch Art, Munich, Ger, 24-25; Acad l'Hote; also with Pola Gaugin & Scandinaie, Paris, 25-29. Work: Hopkin Ctr, Hanover, NH; pub libr & col collections both in USA & Europe. Exhib: Salon d'Automne, 27-29. Awards: Caldecott Medal, Am Libr Asn, 40; Regina Medal, Cath Libr Asn, 70. Bibliog: B Hürliman (auth), Die Welt im Bilderbuch, Atlantis Verlag, Zurich, 65; L B Hopkins (auth), Books Are by People, Citation, 69. Mem: Authors Guild Am. Media: Oils, Pastels, Lithographs. Publ: Co-auth & co-illusr, Ola, 32, Abraham Lincoln, 39, Greek Myths, 62, Trolls, 72, & Terrible Troll Bird, 76, Doubleday; Children of the Northlights, Viking, 35; plus others. Mailing Add: Lia Farm 74 Mather Georgetown CT 06829

DAUTERMAN, CARL CHRISTIAN
ART HISTORIAN, LECTURER
b Newark, NJ. Study: Newark Sch Fine & Indust Art; Newark Mus Apprentice Training Course; NY Univ, BA; Columbia Univ, MA(art hist). Collections Arranged: Numerous exhibs in decorative arts, especially ceramics. Teaching: From lectr to adj prof Europ & Am decorative arts, Columbia Univ, 51- Pos: Mgr spec exhibs, Cooper Union Mus Arts of Decoration, 38-42; catalogue writer, Parke-Bernet Galleries, 46-53; spec admin consult, Metrop Mus Art, 53-55, from assoc cur to cur Western Europ arts, 55-73, emer cur, 73- Awards: Guest archaeologist, Mex Govt Field Exped, Monte Alban, Oaxaca, 36; trustee, Campbell Mus, Camden, NJ, 74-; Award for Distinguished Teaching, Sch Gen Studies, Columbia Univ, 75. Mem: Am Friends Attingham Summer Sch (dir, 70-72); Am Ceramic Circle (pres, 70-72, trustee, 70-); Wedgwood Int Sem (dir & hon dir, 64-); Nat Trust Hist Preserv; Am Soc 18th Century Studies. Res: Analyzing 18th century archives of Manufacture Nationale de Sevres. Publ: Auth, Checklist of American silversmiths' work in the

Metropolitan Museum of Art, 68; auth, Sevres, 69; co-auth, Catalogue of the Wrightsman Collection III: furniture, snuffboxes, silver, 70; auth, Catalogue of the Wrightsman Collection IV: porcelains, 70; auth, 18th Century Sevres Porcelain: Makers & Marks, Metrop Mus Art, 78. Mailing Add: 1326 Madison Ave New York NY 10028

DAVEY, RONALD A
ART HISTORIAN, EDUCATOR
b United Kingdom. Study: Wallasey Sch Art; Courtauld Inst, Univ London; Ecole Hautes Etudes, Univ Paris. Teaching: Asst lectr art, Slade Sch Fine Art, Univ London, 54-58; lectr art, Univ Newcastle upon Tyne, 58-64; prin, West Sussex Col Art, 64-67; prof art & design, Univ Alta, 67-, chmn, 67-76. Mem: Fel Royal Soc Arts. Mailing Add: Dept Art & Design Univ Alta Edmonton AB T6G 2J9 Can

DAVID, DIANNE
ART DEALER, COLLECTOR
b Corpus Christi, Tex, Nov 9, 39. Study: Univ Ariz; Mt Vernon Jr Col, Washington, DC; Parsons Sch Design, New York. Collections Arranged: The Tattoo Show, 70 & The Document Show, 71, David Gallery, Houston. Pos: Owner & dir, David Gallery, Houston, 65-74; owner & dir, Gorrilla Gallery, Houston, 75- Bibliog: Roy Fridge (auth), Dianne David Lives (film), 75. Specialty: Bizarre realism, box sculptures, toys and fetish type objects. Collection: Boxes and oils; nostalgistic ecclecticism. Publ: Auth of articles in Art in Am, 69, Look Mag, 69, Art Gallery Mag, 70 & Holiday Mag, 71. Mailing Add: 1807 Wroxton Houston TX 77005

DAVID, DON RAYMOND
PAINTER, INSTRUCTOR
b Springbrook, Ore, May 2, 10. Study: Art Ctr Sch Los Angeles; Chouinard's, Los Angeles; Hans Hoffman Sch, New York. Work: Ciba Geigy Corp; IBM Corp. Exhib: One-man shows, Webb Gallery, Los Angeles, 47, Camino Gallery, New York, 56, 58 & 60, New Sch Social Res, New York, 65, Baruch Col, 72 & Alonzo Gallery, New York, 69, 70 & 72. Teaching: Instr drawing, Art Ctr Sch Los Angeles, 46-48; instr hist pictorial art & illus, Newark Sch Fine & Indust Art, NJ, 68- Style & Technique: Paintings in neo-plastic abstract tradition; drawings and watercolors in a modern naturalistic mode. Media: Acrylics, Watercolors. Dealer: Alonzo Gallery 26 E 63rd St New York NY 10012. Mailing Add: 32 E 22nd St New York NY 10010

DAVID, HONORE SALMI
EDUCATOR
b Parral, Chihuahua, Mex, Aug 3, 31; US citizen. Study: Our Lady of the Lake Col, San Antonio, Tex, BA, 52; Univ Tex, Austin, MA(art hist), 76. Teaching: Art teacher, San Antonio & Pasadena, Tex, 54-57, Muskogee, Okla, 57-58 & New Martinsville, WVa, 58-63; chmn art dept, Dayton Art Inst, Ohio, 75- Pos: Cur community serv, Dayton Art Inst, Ohio, 73-75. Mem: Am Asn Mus; Midwest Mus Asn (Ohio rep educators); Col Art Asn. Publ: Auth (catalogue), Laguna Gloria Mus, Austin, 71; contribr, Dayton Art Inst Bull, 74 & 75; auth, Oriental Action Pack, 76 & African Action Pack, 77, Dayton Art Inst. Mailing Add: 1875 Highland Meadows Dr Centerville OH 45459

DAVIDEK, STEFAN
PAINTER
b Flint, Mich, May 15, 24. Study: Flint Inst Arts, with Jaroslav Brozik; Art Students League, with Morris Kantor; Cranbrook Acad, with Fred Mitchell. Work: Detroit Inst Arts, Mich; Flint Inst Arts, Mich; Muskegon Community Col & Hackley Art Mus, Mich; Albion Col. Comn: Dioramas, Carol Churchill Pierson Children's Gallery, Sloan Mus, Flint, 65-72 & 77-mosaic, St Luke Cath Church, Flint, 69; sanctuary wall, Luke M Powers Sch, Flint, 70. Exhib: Mich Artists Show, 46-61; Flint Ann, 46-75; Butler Midyear Show, 59; Pa Acad Fine Art 9; Flint Invitational, 70. Awards: Founder's Prize, 61 & Lou R Maxon Prize, Detroit Inst Art. Style & Technique: Representational expressional colorist. Media: Oil, Watercolor. Dealer: Forsythe Galleries 201 Nickels Arcade Ann Arbor MI 48108. Mailing Add: 5391 W Coldwater Rd Flint MI 48504

DAVIDOVITCH, JAIME
PAINTER
b Buenos Aires, Arg, Sept 27, 36; US citizen. Study: Univ of the Republic, Uruguay, scholar, 59; Sch Visual Arts, New York, 63. Work: Mus Arte Mod, Buenos Aires; Mus Belas Artes, Rio de Janiero, Brazil. Comn: Carroll Wall Proj, John Carroll Univ, Cleveland, Ohio, 71. Exhib: One-man show, Retrospective 1962-1972, Drake Univ, Des Moines, Iowa, 71; Exp in Art & Technol Show, Lake Erie Col, Ohio, 71; Five Artists, New Gallery, Cleveland, Ohio, 72; Arte de Sistemas, Mus Mod Art, Buenos Aires & Mus Fine Arts, Santiago, Chile, 72; Akron Art Inst, Ohio, 72. Teaching: Prof painting, Sch Visual Arts, Bahia Blanca, Arg, 61-62. Pos: Off rep to US, Di Tella Found, 63-64; coun mem, Int Soc Educ Through Art, 63- Awards: Di Tella Found grant to rep Arg at Int Cong Educ Through Art, Montreal, 63; Creative Artists Pub Serv grant, video, 75. Bibliog: R Squirru (auth), International art exhibit, Mus Art Mod, Buenos Aires, 60; R Welchans (auth), Carroll project 1971, Fine Arts Mag, 71. Mailing Add: 152 Wooster New York NY 10012

DAVIDSON, ABRAHAM A
EDUCATOR, WRITER
b Dorchester, Mass, June 27, 35. Study: Harvard Univ, AB, 57; Hebrew Teachers Col, Boston, BJEd, 60; Boston Univ, AM(art hist), 60; Columbia Univ, PhD(art hist), 65. Teaching: Instr art hist, Wayne State Univ, 64-65; asst prof art hist, Oakland Univ, 65-68; from asst prof art hist to prof, Tyler Sch Art, Temple Univ, 68- Pos: Ed bd, J Mediterranean Archaeol. Res: History and 19th and 20th century American painting and sculpture. Publ: Auth, John Marin: dynamism codified, Art Forum, 71; auth, The Story of American Painting, Abrams, 74; auth, John Storrs, early sculptor of the machine age, Artforum, 11/74; auth, Two from the second decade: Manierrc Dawson & John Covert, Art in Am, 9-10/75; auth, The Eccentrics & Other American Visionary Painters, Dutton, 78. Mailing Add: Tyler Sch Art Temple Univ Beech & Penrose Ave Elkins Park PA 19126

DAVIDSON, ALLAN ALBERT
PAINTER, SCULPTOR
b Springfield, Mass, Feb 24, 13. Study: Sch Mus Fine Art, Boston; Ecole Beaux Arts, Paris; Fogg Mus, BA; Maitre Arts. Exhib: Boston Watercolor Soc; NShore Art Asn; Provincetown Art Asn; Berkshire Mus; Fitchburg Mus; among others. Pos: Pres, Cape Ann Soc Mod Art; set designer, S Shore Playhouse, Cohasset, Mass, 41; corresp, Stars & Stripes, World War II; mem, Commonwealth Mass Art Comn, 61-65. Awards: Joseph H de Vicq Mem; Benson-Hayes-Stuart Award; Charles Francis Adams Prize for Bronze Sculpture, Raytheon Co; plus many others. Mem: Am Watercolor Soc; Boston Watercolor Soc; Am Artists Prof League; Rockport Art Asn; NShore Art Asn. Style & Technique: Post impressionism in painting and sculpture. Media: Watercolor, Oil; Marble, Bronze. Mailing Add: 8 Dean Rd Rockport MA 01966

DAVIDSON, HERBERT LAURENCE
PAINTER
b Green Bay, Wis, Sept 6, 30. Study: Art Inst Chicago, Anna Raymond Foreign Traveling fel, 56. Exhib: Butler Mus, Youngstown, Ohio, 65; Rotond Della Besana, Milan, Italy, 71; Royal Col Art, London, Eng, 71; Koninlijk Mus Schone Kunsten, Belg, 72; Kunstverein, Hanover, Ger, 72; Gemeentemuseum, Arnham, The Netherlands, 72; Mus des Arts Decoratifs, Lausanne, Switz, 72; Lowe Mus, Univ Miami, Coral Gables, Fla, 73; New York Cult Ctr, 74; Los Angeles Munic Mus, Calif, 74; Philadelphia Art Alliance, Pa, 74; Alta Col of Art, Calgary, 76; Mendel Art Gallery, Saskatchewan, Can, 77; Harmon Gallery, Naples, Fla, 78. Style & Technique: Representational figurative. Media: Oil; Lithography. Dealer: Oehlschlaeger Galleries 107 E Oak St Chicago IL 60611. Mailing Add: 406 W Webster Ave Chicago IL 60614

DAVIDSON, IAN J
COLLECTOR, PATRON
b Toronto, Ont, July 21, 25. Study: Univ BC, BA; FRAIC. Teaching: Archit at Univ Toronto, Univ BC, Carleton Univ & Bezalel Acad, Jerusalem, Israel. Pos: Dir, Vancouver Art Gallery, 70-74; mem adv art comt, Can Coun, 75-; dir, Community Arts Coun, Vancouver. Awards: Awards in architecture in every major design award program. Mem: Assoc Royal Can Acad Art. Interest: Commissioning original works by major artists in the non-objective and conceptual fields. Mailing Add: 4488 Ross Crescent West Vancouver BC V7W 1B2 Can

DAVIDSON, J LEROY
ART HISTORIAN
b Cambridge, Mass, Mar 16, 08. Study: Harvard Univ, AB; Inst Fine Arts, NY Univ, MA; Yale Univ, PhD. Teaching: Asst prof Asian art, Yale Univ, 47-55; prof Asian art, Claremont Grad Sch, 56-61; prof Asian art, Univ Calif, Los Angeles, 61-76, emer prof, 76- Res: Oriental art. Publ: Numerous articles and books on Asian art. Mailing Add: Art Dept Univ Calif Los Angeles Los Angeles CA 90024

DAVIDSON, MARSHALL BOWMAN
ART CRITIC, WRITER
b New York, NY, Apr 26, 07. Study: Princeton Univ, BS, 28. Teaching: Lectr Am decorative graphic & fine arts. Pos: Asst cur, Am Wing, Metrop Mus Art, New York, 35-41, assoc cur, 41-47, ed publ, 47-60; ed, Horizon Bks, 61-64; ed, Horizon Mag, Am Heritage Publ Co, New York, 64-66, sr ed, 66- Awards: Carey-Thomas Award creative publ, 51. Publ: The Writers' America & The Artists' America, 73; Great Historic Places of Europe, 74; The World in 1776 & Fifty Early American Tools, 75. Mailing Add: 140 E 83rd St New York NY 10028

DAVIDSON, MAXWELL, III
ART DEALER
b New York, NY, Feb 8, 39. Study: Williams Col, BA(art hist). Pos: Owner, Maxwell Davidson Gallery, 76- Mem: Art Dealers Asn Am. Specialty: Surrealist and modern masters. Mailing Add: Maxwell Davidson Gallery 970 Park Ave New York NY 10028

DAVIDSON, MORRIS
PAINTER
b Rochester, NY, Dec 16, 98. Study: Md Inst Design, dipl, 16; Art Inst Chicago, with Harry Walcott, 17-18; with George Elmer Browne, 20; Acad Grande Chaumiere, Paris, 25. Work: Baltimore Mus Art; Univ NC; Gallery Living Art, NY Univ; Sarah Lawrence Col; Jerusalem Mus, Israel. Exhib: Whitney Mus Am Art, New York, 34, American Modern Artists, Riverside Mus, 50 & New Sch Social Res, 53; Detroit Inst Arts, 60; Pa Acad Fine Arts, Philadelphia, 60; one-man shows, Schenectady Mus, NY, 71 & Berkshire Mus, Pittsfield, Mass, 71, plus over 40 others. Teaching: Instr drawing, Art Inst Chicago, 17-18; instr painting, Minneapolis Sch Art, 22-23 & Master Inst New York, 31. Mem: Provincetown Art Asn (vpres, 50-60); Am Artists Cong (NY exec bd, 39); Fedn Mod Painters & Sculptors (pres, 50-). Style & Technique: Abstraction based upon fourth dimensional space relations and personal color concepts. Media: Oil, Watercolor, Acrylic. Publ: Auth, Understanding Modern Art, 31 & auth, An Approach to Modern Painting, 48, Coward; auth, Painting for Pleasure, Hale, Cushman & Flint, 38; auth, Painting with Purpose, Prentice-Hall, 64. Mailing Add: 7 Orchard Terr Piermont NY 10968

DAVIDSON, ROBERT WILLIAM
SCULPTOR, EDUCATOR
b Indianapolis, Ind, Mar 13, 04. Study: John Herron Art Inst; Chicago Art Inst; State Acad Fine Arts, Munich, Ger; apprentice to O L Davidson, R A Baillie, Anton Bauer & Ernst Melaun. Work: Indianapolis Mus Art; Munson-Williams-Proctor Inst, Utica, NY; IBM Collection, Art of the Western Hemisphere; Skidmore Col, Saratoga, NY; Univ NC, Greensboro. Comn: Two exterior reliefs, Shortridge High Sch, Indianapolis, 30; bronze life-size figure, Ind Univ, Indianapolis, 32; bronze portrait head, Community Silversmiths, Oneida, NY, 40; portrait head, Simpson Methodist Church, Rock City Falls, NY, 50; bronze figure, NY State Legis Bldg, Albany. Exhib: Glas Palast Int, Munich, Ger, 32; Nat Acad, New York, 33; Whitney Mus, 37; New York World's Fair, 39. Teaching: Resident sculptor, Skidmore Col, Saratoga Springs, NY, 33-72, prof art, sculpture & drawing, 40-72. Awards: Art Asn Prize, Herron Art Inst, 25 & Indianapolis Art Asn, 28; Hoosier Salon Prize, Hoosier Salon Art Asn, 37. Style & Technique: Direct forming wax to bronze; wood, direct carving; stone carving; style, romantic-modern. Media: Bronze, Lost Wax & Preformed; Print Making & Drawing. Mailing Add: Highlands Rock City Falls NY 12863

DAVIDSON, SUZETTE MORTON
DESIGNER, COLLECTOR
b Chicago, Ill, Aug 24, 11. Study: Vassar Col, AB, 34; Art Inst Chicago, 36-40. Exhib: Printing Design by Suzette Morton Zurcher (former name), Chicago Pub Libr, Albion Col, Mich & Univ Calif, Santa Barbara. Pos: Trustee, Art Inst Chicago; trustee, Newberry Libr; trustee, Morton Arboretum, Lisle, Ill; owner, The Pocahontas Press, 37- Awards: Five Selections, 50 Bks of the Year Award, Am Inst Graphic Arts, 42-67. Mem: Am Fedn Arts; Am Inst Graphic Arts; Soc Typographic Arts. Collection: From classical antiquity to Picasso, with emphasis on seventeenth century Italian painting, pre-Raphaelite paintings and drawings; pre-Columbian gold; old and rare books pertaining to gardens and botany. Publ: Designer numerous exhib catalogs, Art Inst Chicago. Mailing Add: 1301 Astor St Chicago IL 60610

DAVIEE, JERRY MICHAEL
CURATOR, WRITER
b Oklahoma City, Okla, Mar 29, 47. Study: San Francisco Art Inst, 65-66; Oklahoma City Univ, BA, 69; Univ Tex, Austin, MA, 76. Collections Arranged: Human Form in Modern Latin American Art, 75, Recent Argentine Painting & Drawing, 75 & Lyrical Tradition in

American Painting 1900-1945, 76, Univ Tex Art Mus, Austin; Young Texas Artists Series (contribr, catalogue), 77-78 & Remington & Russell, The Sid Richardson Collection, 78, Amarillo Art Ctr, Tex. Teaching: Instr art hist survey & art appreciation, Amarillo Art Ctr Sch, 77- Mem: Am Asn Mus; Col Art Asn. Res: Contemporary art. Publ: Contribr, Alejandro Otero: A Retrospective Exhibition, Univ Tex Press, 75; contribr, ARTSPACE: Southwestern Contemp Arts Quart, 77-78 & Austin Am Statesman, 75-76. Mailing Add: PO Box 447 Amarillo TX 79178

DAVIES, HUGH MARLAIS
ART HISTORIAN, GALLERY DIRECTOR
b Grahamstown, SAfrica, Feb 12, 48; Brit citizen. Study: Princeton Univ, AB, MFA & PhD cand. Collections Arranged: Artist & Fabricator, Univ Mass, 75- Pos: Asst dir, Monumenta Int Sculpture Exhib, Newport, RI, 74; dir, Fine Arts Ctr Gallery, Univ Mass, Amherst, 75-77. Res: 20th century American and European painting, sculpture and photography. Publ: Contribr, Josef Albers: Painting and Graphics, 1917-70, 71; auth, Pop prints: New Acquisitions, Rec Art Mus, Princeton Univ, 72 & contribr, 19th & 20th Century French Drawings, 72, Princeton Univ; co-auth, Scale in Contemporary Sculpture, Monumenta, 74; auth, Bacon's Black triptychs, Art in Am, 75. Mailing Add: 513 Main St Amherst MA 01002

DAVIES, KENNETH SOUTHWORTH
PAINTER, INSTRUCTOR
b New Bedford, Mass, Dec 20, 25. Study: Mass Sch Art, Boston; Yale Sch Fine Arts, BFA, 50. Work: Wadsworth Atheneum, Hartford, Conn; New Britain Mus Am Art, Conn; Detroit Inst Arts; Springfield Mus Fine Arts, Mass; Univ Nebr, Lincoln. Comn: US Postage Stamp commemorative for pharmacy, US Postal Serv, 72, chemistry, 76. Exhib: American Symbolic Realism, London, Eng, 50; Carnegie Inst Int, 52; Whitney Mus Am Art Ann, 52; Univ Ill Ann, 52; 25 yr retrospective exhib, New Britain Mus Am Art, 71. Teaching: Dean drawing, painting & perspective, Paier Sch Art, Hamden, Conn, 53- Awards: Louis Comfort Tiffany scholar, 50; Purchase Award, Berkshire Mus, Pittsfield & Springfield Mus, Mass, 50. Mem: Silvermine Guild Artists; New Haven Paint & Clay Club (vpres, 69); Conn Acad Fine Arts (coun mem, 70, pres, 74-76). Media: Oil. Publ: Auth, Painting Sharp Focus Still Lifes, Watson-Guptill, 75. Mailing Add: 40 Walnut Hill Rd Madison CT 06443

DAVIES, THEODORE PETER
PRINTMAKER, PAINTER
b Brooklyn, NY, Oct 9, 28. Study: Sch Mod Photog, New York, 52; Art Students League, with George Grosz & Harry Sternberg, 57-60, John Sloan merit scholar, 58. Work: Photograms, Mus Mod Art, New York; woodcuts, Nat Gallery Art, Washington, DC & Philadelphia Mus Art; Art Students League; Queens Mus, NY. Comn: Six woodcuts on process of papermaking, Scott Paper Co, 60; three ed, woodcuts of New York financial dist, Picture Decorator, 68. Exhib: Print Club Philadelphia Ann; Silvermine Guild Ann; Boston Printmakers Ann, 59; The Sense of Abstraction, Mus Mod Art, New York, 59; Big Prints, State Univ NY Albany, 68; plus others. Awards: First Prize Graphics, Atlantic City Ann Art Exhib, 59; Hon Mention, Boston Printmakers, 59; Creative Artists Pub Serv Fel in Graphics, 73-74. Bibliog: Laurence Campbell (auth), article, In: Art Stud League News, 12/61; Gene Paris (auth), article, In: Long Island Press, 4/23/67; plus others. Mem: Life mem Art Students League (mem bd control, 61-63, recording secy, 63-64); Print Coun Am; Print Club Philadelphia; Queens Coun Arts (show coordr, 72); Jamaica Art Mobilization. Style & Technique: Use of photography in serigraphy, use of mixed media in painting. Media: Woodcut, Serigraphy. Publ: Contribr, Woodcuts, 60; contribr, Realistic abstract drawing, 60; illusr, Picture framing, 60. Dealer: Harbor Gallery 43 Main St Cold Spring Harbor NY 11724. Mailing Add: 87-38 Santiago St Hollis NY 11423

DAVILA, CARLOS
PAINTER, PRINTMAKER
b Lima, Peru, Feb 1, 35. Study: Nat Sch Fine Art, Lima. Work: Pan Am Union, Washington, DC; Mus Mod Art, Miami; Univ San Marcos, Lima; Ctr Inter-Am Rels, New York; Mus Arte, Lima. Comn: Restoration pre-Colombian archaeol monuments (collabr), Chan-Chan, Peru, 63-65. Exhib: 5th Biennale, Mus Mod Art, Paris, 65; Miami Mus Mod Art, Fla, 66; Mus Arte, Lima, 68; Painting in the Richard Brown Baker Collection, Univ Tampa, Fla, 69; Young Artists from Around the World, Int Play Group, New York, 71. Awards: First Award, Soc Hebraica Nat Competition, 64; First Award, Jovenes Artistas, Univ San Marcos, 67; First Award, Adela Investment, Mus Arte, 68. Publ: Auth, articles in Artes Visuales Mag, Washington, DC, 66-67. Dealer: Nabis Fine Art Inc 276 Park Ave S New York NY 10010. Mailing Add: 200 E 33rd St New York NY 10016

DAVIS, ALONZO JOSEPH
VISUAL ARTIST, ART ADMINISTRATOR
b Tuskegee, Ala, Feb 2, 42. Study: Pepperdine Univ, BA, 64; Otis Art Inst, Los Angeles, BFA, 71, MFA, 73, with Charles White. Work: Afro-Am Studies Ctr, Univ Calif, Los Angeles; Libr Collection, Calif Polytechnic Inst, Pomona. Comn: Group mural, 50th & Crenshaw, Los Angeles, Calif, 73-75; sculpture, Rogers Recreational Ctr, Los Angeles, 74; mural-retainer wall, Santa Monica Freeway underpass at La Brea, Los Angeles, 75. Exhib: One-man shows, Bowers Mus, Santa Ana, Calif, 75, Just Above Midtown Gallery, New York, 75 & Transition Gallery, Idaho State Univ, 76; Mural & Graffiti Exhib, Fisher Gallery, Univ Southern Calif, 76; Festival in Black, Otis Art Inst, Los Angeles, 77; Charles White & Selected Ex-Students, Los Angeles Munic Arts Gallery, 77; Calif Black Artists, Studio Mus in Harlem, New York, 77; Festival of the Mask, Craft & Folk Art Mus, Los Angeles, 77. Collections Arranged: Brockman Gallery, Los Angeles, ten mo installations, 67-73. Teaching: Instr African art, Calif State Univ, Northridge, 76-78; instr, Otis Art Inst, 78- Pos: Exec dir, Brockman Gallery Productions, Los Angeles, 73- Bibliog: J Edward Atkinson (auth), Black Dimensions in Contemp Am Art, 71; Lewis & Waddy (auth), Black Artists on Art, Vol II, Pub Contemp Crafts Inc, 71; Elton Fax (auth), Black Artists of the New Generation, Dodd Mead, 77. Mem: Artists for Econ Action; Calif Confedn of the Arts (bd mem); Nat Conf of Artists; Am Mus Asn; Smithsonian Assoc. Style & Technique: Visual statements on canvas, paper and various mixed media; abstract images that relate to the human condition. Media: Mixed-Media; Collagraph; Printmaking. Publ: Auth (catalogue introd), Varying Directions of Contemporary Black Artists, State of Calif, 75. Dealer: Sol Del Rio Gallery 1020 Townsend Ave San Antonio TX 78209. Mailing Add: c/o Brockman Gallery 4334 Degnan Blvd Los Angeles CA 90008

DAVIS, ANN
CURATOR, ART HISTORIAN
b Ottawa, Ont, Oct 31, 46. Study: Bishop's Univ, BA with Hons(hist, polit sci), 68; Univ Toronto, MA, 69; York Univ, with G Ramsay Cook & T A Heinrich, PhD(hist), 73. Collections Arranged: Master Paintings from the Heritage & State Russian Mus & Gold for the Gods, Winnipeg Art Gallery. Teaching: Teacher Can survey, York Univ, Toronto, 70-71, teacher Can cult hist, 72-73. Pos: Res historian, Nat Hist Sites Serv, 69-70; cur, Winnipeg Art Gallery, 73- Awards: York Univ Grad Fel, 70; Can Coun Grad Fel, 71 & 72. Mem: Can Conf of Arts (bd gov, 74-); Can Mus Asn; Can Hist Asn. Publ: Auth, The Wembley Controversy in Canadian art, 3/73; auth, Christiane Pflug, 74; auth, Canvas, Quill, Brush & Hide, 75. Mailing Add: 300 Memorial Blvd Winnipeg MB Can

DAVIS, BEN H
PAINTER, VIDEO ARTIST
b Syracuse, NY, June 5, 47. Study: Stetson Univ, Fla, ABA; Univ Fla, BS(commun), with John Lindstrom & Jerry Ulesmann; Fla State Univ, MFA, with Robert Fichter & Jim Roche. Work: Ctr Creative Photog, Univ Ariz, Tucson; Atlanta Col Art Video Archive, Ga; Fla State Univ & Fla State Archive & Mus, Tallahassee; Senoj Archive, Atlanta, Ga. Comn: Marianas Islands (doc film), Am Bicentennial Comn, 75. Exhib: Masters, Fla State Mus, Tallahassee, 75; Exchange, Mus Contemp Art, Recife, Brazil, 75; Magnetic Image, Gallery 413, Mem Arts Ctr, Atlanta, Ga, 75-76; Surface Appearances, Midtown Gallery, New York, 76; Exercise in Parameters, Okla Mus Art, Norman, 77; Southern Fried, Tyler Sch Art, Temple Univ, Philadelphia, Pa, 77; Summer Light, Light Gallery, New York, 77. Collections Arranged: Producer, Magnetic Images, Ann Exhib of Video Pieces, 75-77, In the Omni, Omni Int Trade Ctr Exhib, 76 & Optional Narrative, Gallery 413, Atlanta Col Art, 76, Atlanta, Ga; Heliography & Collage, Chicago Art Inst, Ill, 77. Teaching: Head dept video & instr photog, Atlanta Col Art, 75-; instr, Douglas Davis Video Workshop, Atlanta, 77-78. Pos: Illusr, Fla State Archives & Mus, 74-75; producer-dir, Children's Art Festival, High Mus Art, Atlanta, 76-77; dir, Senoj, Inc, Atlanta, Ga, 76- Bibliog: Sarah Daniels (auth), Alternative Publications, Contemp Arts Southeast, 77. Mem: Independent Media Artists of Ga Etcetera (IMAGE); Senoj, Inc (dir, 76-); Big Bend Photog Club, Fla (pres, 73-75). Style & Technique: Constructions using paint, video, photography; mass media publishing; correspondence art. Media: Electronic media, video-audio; photography and paint. Publ: Auth, Bend Magazine, Big Bend Photog Club, Fla, 73-75; auth, A History of Photography, pvt publ, Fla, 73; contribr, Quiver, Tyler Sch Art, Philadelphia, Pa, 77; co-auth, BEO, Senoj, Atlanta, 77; illusr, Contemporary Arts of the Southeast, Atlanta, 77. Dealer: V A Schrager 140 Greene St New York NY 10012. Mailing Add: 1197 Virginia Ave NE Atlanta GA 30306

DAVIS, BRADLEY DARIUS
PAINTER
b Duluth, Minn, Apr 24, 42. Study: Univ Minn, BA; Hunter Col. Work: Univ Minn, Minneapolis; Walker Art Ctr, Minneapolis; Whitney Mus Am Art, New York. Exhib: Whitney Mus Am Art Painting Ann, New York, 72; Am Drawings, 1963-1973, Whitney Mus, 73; Fantastics & Eccentrics, State Univ Albany, 74; Artist's Toys, Clocktower, New York, NY, 75; two-man shows (with Ned Smythe), Holly Solomon Gallery, New York, 76 & 77; Contemp Am Art from New York, Artworks Gallery, Milwaukee, Wis, 76; Painting 75-77, Sarah Lawrence Col, Bronxville, NY, 77; Decoration, Basel Art Fair, Basel, Switz, 77; A Painting Show, PS 1, Queens, NY, 77; and others; one-man shows, Holly Solomon Gallery, New York, 72, 75 & 77 & White House Gallery, El Paso, Tex, 77. Awards: First Prize & Spec Jury Award, Minneapolis Inst Art Biennial, 65; Second Prize & Purchase Prize, Walker Art Ctr, 66. Style & Technique: Semi abstract fantasy landscapes; oil pastel, graphite, acrylic on canvas and paper mounted on various fabrics. Media: Mixed Media. Mailing Add: c/o Holly Solomon Gallery 392 W Broadway New York NY 10012

DAVIS, D JACK
EDUCATOR, ART ADMINISTRATOR
b Canton, Tex, May 17, 38. Study: Baylor Univ, BA, 59, MA, 61; Univ Minn, PhD, 66, studies with Reid Hastie, Paul Torrance & Malcolm Myers. Teaching: Prof art, Tex Tech Univ, 65-69; prof & chmn dept, NTex State Univ, Denton, 71- Pos: Assoc dir & dir evaluation, Aesthetic Educ Prog, Arts in Gen Educ Proj, Cemrel, Inc, St Louis, Mo, 69-71; ed, Studies in Art Educ, Nat Art Educ Asn, 75- Mem: Life mem Nat Art Educ Asn (chmn higher educ div, 73-75); Tex Art Educ Asn; Nat Coun Art Adminrs. Publ: Co-auth, The Artist in the School, Cemrel, Inc, 70; auth, Research in Art Education, Art Educ, 71; ed, Behavioral Emphasis in Art Education, Nat Art Educ Asn, 75; contribr, Arts & Aesthetics: An Agenda for the Future, Cemrel, Inc, 77. Mailing Add: 2007 Locksley Lane Denton TX 76201

DAVIS, DAVID ENSOS
SCULPTOR
b Rona de Jos, Romania, Aug 27, 20; US citizen. Study: Beaux Arts, Paris, France, 45; Cleveland Inst Art, scholar & BFA, 48; Case Western Reserve Univ, MA, 61. Work: James Michener Collection; Cleveland Mus Art, Ohio; John Carroll Univ, University Heights, Ohio; Kent State Univ; Akron Art Inst. Comn: David-Berger Monument, Jewish Community Ctr, Cleveland, 73; Gornik Monument, John Carroll Univ, 74; sculpture award, Ohio Arts Coun; outdoor sculpture (22 ft tall), Progressive Insurance Co; outdoor sculpture (8 ft tall), Beck Cult Ctr, Lakewood, Ohio. Exhib: Ohio Sculptors Invitational, Blossom Music Ctr, Cleveland, 72; one-man shows, Akron Art Inst, 72 & Mather Gallery, Case Western Reserve Univ, 75; May Show Ann, Cleveland Mus Art, 72-75; Ohio Painting & Sculpture, Dayton Art Inst, 74; plus others. Pos: Staff artist, Am Greetings Corp, Cleveland, 48-49, dir creative dept, 49-54, asst to vpres creative dept, 54-58, vpres creative dept, 58-61. Awards: Major Sculpture Cash Prize, May Show, Cleveland Mus Art, 77. Bibliog: Terry Breen (auth), Profile of a sculptor, New Rev, Vol 2 (Jan, 1976); Gerry O Patno (auth), Portrait of a welder as an artist, Welding Design & Fabrication, 4/76; review, Art News, 78. Mem: Cleveland Inst Art (bd trustees & alumni asn); Nova (bd trustees). Media: Steel, Aluminum, Bronze, Wood. Mailing Add: 26611 Fairmount Blvd Beachwood OH 44122

DAVIS, DONALD JACK
EDUCATOR
b Canton, Tex, May 17, 38. Study: Baylor Univ, Waco, Tex, BA, 59 & MA, 61; Univ Minn, PhD, 66, with W Reid Hastie & E Paul Torrance. Teaching: Instr art, Wayland Col, Plainview, Tex, 61-63; prof art, Tex Technol Univ, Lubbock, 65-69; prof art, N Tex State Univ, Denton, 71-, chmn art dept, 76- Pos: Assoc dir aesthetic educ prog, CEMREL Inc, St Louis, Mo, 69-71. Mem: Nat Art Educ Asn (chmn higher educ div, 72-74); Int Soc for the Study of Educ Through Art; Tex Art Educ Asn; Nat Coun Art Adminr; Nat Soc for the Study Educ. Publ: Auth, Research trends in art education, 67 & Human behavior: its implications for curriculum development in art, 71, Art Educ; co-auth, The artist in the school, 70 & contribr, Arts & aesthetics: an agenda for the future, 77, CEMREL, Inc; ed, Behavioral emphasis in art education, Nat Art Educ Asn, 75. Mailing Add: 2007 Locksley Lane Denton TX 76201

DAVIS, DONALD ROBERT
PAINTER, ART DEALER
b Toronto, Ont, July 30, 09; US citizen. Study: Syracuse Univ; Art Students League. Work: Berkshire Mus, Pittsfield, Mass; also in many pvt collections. Comn: Prehistoric Lascaux cave fresco, Bandag, Inc, Jamaica, WI. Exhib: Berkshire Art Asn Ann Exhib, 67 & 68; one-man shows, Berkshire Mus, 67 & Tyringham Gallery, Mass, 69; Albany Inst Art Regional Exhib, NY, 68. Pos: Owner & dir, Tyringham Gallery. Mem: Am Asn Mus; Berkshire Art Asn. Specialty: Paintings, sculpture, prints and objets d'art. Media: Mixed Media, Oil, Acrylic.

Collection: Prints by American and European contemporaries; pre-Colombian; ivories. Publ: Auth, article in Am Artist Mag. Mailing Add: Tyringham Art Gallery Tyringham MA 01264

DAVIS, DOUGLAS MATTHEW
ARTIST, CRITIC
b Washington, DC, Apr 11, 33. Study: Abbott Art Sch, Washington, DC: Am Univ, BA, 56; Rutgers Univ, New Brunswick, MA, 58. Exhib: Ten Videotape Performances, Finch Col Mus Art, 71; retrospective, Everson Mus, Syracuse, 72; Projekt 74, Kunstverein & Kunsthalle, Cologne, Ger, 74; San Francisco Mus Art, 75; Projected Video, Whitney Mus Am Art, New York & San Paulo Biennale, 75. Collections Arranged: Wallraf-Richartz Mus, Cologne; Finch Col Mus; De Saisset Art Gallery; Everson Mus Art; Panza di Biuma, Milan. Teaching: Vis artist, Corcoran Sch Art, 70 & 71; State Univ NY Buffalo, 73; art critic in residence, NY Univ, 75; regents lectr, Univ Calif, San Diego, 76. Pos: Contribr ed, Am Art, 68-70; art critic, Newsweek Mag, 70-; artist in residence, TV Lab, WNET-TV, New York; res fel, Mass Inst Technol Ctr Advan Visual Studies, 74-75. Awards: Nat Endowment for Arts Grants, 70 & 75; NY State Coun Arts Grant for Creative Work in Mixed Media, 70. Media: Videotape, Printmaking. Publ: Auth, Media/art/media, Arts Mag, 9/71; auth, Video obscura, 4/72 & What is content, 10/73, Artforum; auth, Art and the Future, Praeger, 73; auth, Fragments for a New Art of the Future, 75. Mailing Add: 80 Wooster St New York NY 10012

DAVIS, ELLEN N
ART HISTORIAN
b Hackensack, NJ, July 20, 37. Study: Inst Fine Arts, NY Univ, PhD, 73, with Peter H Von Blanckenhagen. Teaching: Asst prof ancient art hist, Queens Col, City Univ New York, 66- Mem: Archaeol Inst Am (fel comt, 74-77; New York Soc, prog comt, 76- & govt comt, 77). Res: Aegean metalworking. Publ: Auth, The Vapheio cups: one Minoan & one Mycenean?, Art Bull LVI, 74; ed, Symposium on the Dark Ages, Archaeol Inst Am, 74; auth, The classic ideal sculpture, Newsweek, 75; auth, The Vapheio Cups and Aegean Metalware, Garland Press, 76. Mailing Add: 225 E 76th St New York NY 10021

DAVIS, GENE
PAINTER
b Washington, DC, Aug 22, 20. Study: Univ Md; Wilson Teachers Col. Work: Mus Mod Art, New York; Whitney Mus Am Art; Tate Gallery, London, Eng; San Francisco Mus Art; Corcoran Gallery Art, Washington, DC; plus many others. Comn: Mural, South Mall Proj, NY State Capitol Bldg, Albany, 69; mural, Neiman-Marcus, Bal Harbour, Fla, 70; official poster comn by List Found, Lincoln Ctr Concert Ser, New York. Exhib: One-man shows, Corcoran Gallery Art, 64 & 68, San Francisco Mus, 68, Jewish Mus, New York, 68 & Univ Utah Art Mus, Salt Lake City, 72; Whitney Ann Exhib Am Painting, Whitney Mus Am Art, 67 & 68; plus many other one-man and group shows. Teaching: Instr painting, Corcoran Gallery Sch Art, 67-68, 70-; instr painting, Am Univ, 68-70; artist in residence, Skidmore Col, summer 69 & Univ Va, spring 72. Awards: Bronze Medal for Painting & Award, Am Painting Biennial, Corcoran Gallery Art, 65; Nat Coun Arts grant, 67; Guggenheim fel, 74-75. Bibliog: Donald Wall (auth), The micro-paintings of Gene Davis, Artforum, 12/68; Barbara Rose (auth), Coversation with Gene Davis, Artforum, 3/71; Donald Wall, ed, Gene Davis, Praeger, 75; plus others. Style & Technique: Acrylic on unprimed canvas. Publ: Auth, Statement by the artist, Art Now, 2/70; auth, Random thought on art, StuJio Int, 11/70. Mailing Add: 4120 Harrison St NW Washington DC 20015

DAVIS, GEORGE
CARTOONIST, ILLUSTRATOR
b Newark, NJ, Feb 6, 14. Study: Cartoonist's & Illustrator's Sch; Art Stud League. Work: New York Pub Libr. Pos: Med illusr, Vet Admin, 50-54. Media: Ink. Publ: Contribr, Sat Eve Post, Look Mag, True Mag, King Features Syndicate & other nat publ, 50- Mailing Add: 108 Charles St New York NY 10014

DAVIS, GERALD VIVIAN
PAINTER
b Brooklyn, NY, Sept 8, 99. Study: Ecole des Beaux Arts, Paris, France; Julian Acad, cert; Acad Grande Chaumiere, Paris; also with Dechenaud & Royer. Work: Many works in private collections around the world. Comn: President of Danish England (portrait), Soc Danish Eng, Copenhagen, 38; Rev Dr Clayton Williams (portrait), Am Church in Paris, France, 40; Dr Knutson (portrait), Dir Watkins Hosp, Univ Kans, Lawrence, 51; Father Leopold Bruekberger (portrait), Paris, 69; Sir Ove Arup (portrait), Arup & Partners, London, 70; plus others. Exhib: Nat Acad Design, 40; Kansas City Nelson Art Mus, 51; Trenton Art Mus & Newark Mus, NJ, 68; Galt's Gallery, Chatham, NJ, 74; Hait Gallery, Maplewood, NJ, 74-; plus many other group & one-man shows. Teaching: Instr art, Univ Ill, Champaign, 25-28; asst prof art, Univ Kans, 47-51. Awards: Contemp NJ Artists, 60; NJ State Show, East Orange Art Ctr, 68 & Summit Art Ctr, 69. Mem: Assoc Soc Nat Beaux Arts. Media: Oil, Gouache, Charcoal, Pastel, Ink. Mailing Add: 86 Elm St Summit NJ 07901

DAVIS, HARRY ALLEN
PAINTER, EDUCATOR
b Hillsboro, Ind, May 21, 14. Study: Herron Sch Art, Ind Univ-Purdue Univ, Indianapolis, BFA, 38; Am Acad Rome, FAAR, 41. Work: Butler Inst Am Art, Youngstown, Ohio; Springfield Art Mus, Mo; Evansville Mus Arts & Sci, Ind; Grover M Hermann Fine Arts Ctr, Marietta Col, Ohio; Carroll Reece Mus, Johnson City, Tenn; plus others. Comn: Panorama of Indianapolis (acrylics), Am Fletcher Nat Bank (now owned by Indianapolis Mus Art), 66; 1 Virginia Avenue, Ind Nat Bank, 69; Union Station, Am Fletcher Nat Bank, 73; Pathology Building, Surgeons' College, Ind Mus Med Hist, Indianapolis, 74; Monument Circle, Am Fletcher Nat Bank in Luxemburg, 74. Exhib: Six Butler Midyear Exhibs, Youngstown, 61-76; Watercolor USA, Nat Watercolor Exhib, Springfield, Mo, 65-76; Governors' Nat Art Tour, representing Ind throughout the USA, 66; Mainstreams Int Exhibs, Marietta, Ohio, 68-77; 24th Am Drawing Biennial, Norfolk, Va, 71; Bicentennial Traveling Show, Ind State Mus, Indianapolis Mus Art, plus others, 76-77; Hassam Fund Purchase Exhib, Am Acad & Inst Arts & Lett, New York, 77. Teaching: Artist in residence, Beloit Col, 41-42; prof painting & drawing, Herron Sch Art, Ind Univ-Purdue Univ, Indianapolis, 46- Awards: Prix de Rome, Am Acad Rome, 38; Award of Distinction, Mainstreams, Marietta Col, 71 & 74; Mo Sesquicentennial Award, State of Mo, 71. Bibliog: Clifford (auth), Hoosier artists: Harry A Davis, 6/13/65 & Lennis (auth), The Davises: two for the show, 10/8/72, Indianapolis Star Mag; Mendelowitz (auth), Drawing: Guide to Drawing, Holt, 66. Mem: Fel Am Acad Rome; Ind Artists Club (pres, 55-56, dir, 72); Assoc Prof Artists (vpres, 69-70); Ind Acad. Style & Technique: Textural quality combined with strong light/dark patterns to convey sense of volume, especially in series of richly realistic decaying buildings. Media: Acrylic, Watercolor, Ink. Mailing Add: 6315 Washington Blvd Indianapolis IN 46220

DAVIS, J RAY
PAINTER, PRINTMAKER
Study: Cent State Univ (Okla), BA; Univ Okla, MFA(painting & printmaking). Work: State of Okla Collection & Traveling Exhib. Exhib: Kans State Univ Exhib to Grad Midwestern Univs, 69; one-man shows, Painting Prints & Vacuum Forms, Contemp Arts Found, Oklahoma City, 70 & Graphic Retrospective, Emporia, Kans, 70; 31st Ann Exhib Okla Artists, Philbrook Art Ctr, Tulsa, 71; Okla Featured Artist of Month, Okla Art Ctr, 4/72. Teaching: Instr art, Okla Sci & Arts Found, 67-70; asst prof art, Oklahoma City Univ, 69-; instr art, state supported art classes for all fifth graders in Oklahoma City Pub Sch Syst, 71-72. Awards: Graphics Awards, 30th & 31st Ann Exhib Okla Artists, Tulsa, 70 & 71 & 57th Ann Tulsa Regional Exhib, 71. Mailing Add: 4436 NW 19th St Oklahoma City OK 73107

DAVIS, JAMES WESLEY
PAINTER, WRITER
b Los Angeles, Calif, Oct 9, 40. Study: Calif Col Arts & Crafts, BA(educ) & BFA; Univ Colo, Inst Arts & Humanities fel, 67, MA & MFA. Work: Minn Mus Art; Ill State Mus; Alberta Col Art; Mulvane Art Mus; Laguna Gloria Mus; plus others. Exhib: Mid-America 4, St Louis Art Mus & Nelson/Atkins Mus, 72; Smithsonian Inst Traveling Show, 73-74; Calgary Int Biennial, Alta Col Art Gallery, 74; Mid-Year Ann, Butler Inst Am Art, 74 & 75; 19th Mid-South Biennial, Brooks Mem Gallery, 75. Teaching: Instr painting & art hist, Univ Ark, 67-69; assoc prof painting & drawing, Western Ill Univ, 69- Awards: Sworovski Int Award, Sworovski of Belg, 67; James D Phelan Award, 73. Bibliog: S W Semaj (auth), Memories, Structure, Vol 2, No 3; Alfred Frankenstein (auth), Visual, surreal acrobatics, San Francisco Chronicle, 1/74; Sylvia Brown (auth), Editorial highlights, City Mag, 2/16/74. Mem: Col Art Asn Am. Style & Technique: Air-brushed procion dyes; stencil technique; images drawn from memories and imagination. Media: Dyes and Liquid Watercolor on Raw Canvas or Paper. Publ: Auth, Self-actualized sculpture, Sculpture Int, Vol 3, No 2; auth, Unified drawing by means of hybrids and grids, Leonardo, Vol 5, No 1; auth, Some perceptual considerations on vermeer and Op art, Studies in the 20th Century, 73; auth, Revival in the slumbering cornfield, Art J, fall 74; auth, On mounds, Studio Int, 4/74. Dealer: James Willis Gallery 109 Geary St at Grant San Francisco CA 94109. Mailing Add: 216 N Normal St Macomb IL 61455

DAVIS, JERROLD
PAINTER
b Chico, Calif, Nov 2, 26. Study: Univ Calif, Berkeley, BA, 53, MA. Work: Carnegie Inst Int, Pittsburgh; Santa Barbara Mus Art, Calif; Los Angeles Mus Art; San Francisco Mus Art; Oakland Mus Art; plus others. Exhib: One-man shows, Calif Palace of Legion of Honor, 60-64, Flint Art Inst, 64 & Newport Harbor Art Mus, Newport Beach, Calif, 73; Especially for Children, Los Angeles Co Mus, 65; Art in the Embassies Prog; Univ Ariz, 67; Lytton Ctr, Los Angeles, 67 & 68; A Sense of Place, 74; plus others. Teaching: Instr, Univ Calif, summer 67. Awards: Guggenheim Fel, 58-59; Am Fedn Arts-Ford Found artist in residence grant, Flint, Mich, 64; Prizes, Calif Palace of Legion of Honor, 60 & 62; plus others. Dealer: Jacqueline Anhalt Gallery 750 N La Cienega Blvd Los Angeles CA 90069. Mailing Add: 66 Twain Ave Berkeley CA 94708

DAVIS, JOHN HAROLD
GALLERY DIRECTOR, ILLUSTRATOR
b Milwaukee, Wis, Feb 8, 23. Study: Layton Art Inst, Milwaukee; Art Inst Chicago. Comn: Stations of the Cross, Mt St Frances, Iowa, 49; new altar & reconstruct of church, Monsefu, Peru, 64-66; Veracruz (tapestry applique), Chimbote, Peru, 68; mural of cast concrete, San Antonio de Padua, Lima, Peru, 69; decoration of interior, Church of San Juan de Miraflores, 70. Exhib: Am Printmakers, Philadelphia, 45-55; Art Ctr, Lima, 56, 58 & 70; Charles Allis Art Libr, Milwaukee, 71; Inst Cult Peruano Norteamericano, Lima; Munson-Williams-Procter Inst, Utica, NY; plus many others. Collections Arranged: 15 Impressionists, 50; Spanish painting included in prog exhibs, Iowa Art Ctr & Syracuse Univ, 52; Folk Art of Peru, Los Angeles Co Fair, 68; Peruvian Crafts Exhibition, Fardoms & Masions, London, Eng; First Biennial Crafts of Peru (Artesania del Peru), Museo Arte Lima, 68; plus others. Teaching: Instr painting & drawing, Syracuse Univ, 48-55. Pos: Dir painting & drawing, Inst Art Ctr Gallery & Shop, Miraflores, 55- Bibliog: Petterson (auth), Folk Art of Peru, Scripps Col; Serven Rodman (auth), South American of the Poets & The Peru Traveler, Meredith. Mem: World Crafts Coun (dir for Latin Am, 68-); Asociacion Nacional de Artesanos del Peru (founder, 68-); Inst Art Ctr; Fundacion Peruana Pro-Arte y Educacion (pres, 65-). Collection: Peruvian folk art; 20th century drawings. Publ: Illusr, Mis Antepasados, 54; illusr, Manuel Pardo Rivadeneyra, 55; illusr, Conquest of Peru, New Am Libr Ed, 58; illusr, The New Testament in Quechua, 72-73; auth & illusr, Slice of Life. Mailing Add: Inst Centro de Arte Alameda Ricardo Palma 246 Miraflores Lima Peru

DAVIS, JOHN SHERWOOD
POTTER, ART ADMINISTRATOR
b Kingstree, SC, Jan 24, 42. Study: Univ SC, BFA(art), 71, grad work dept art, 73; Harvard Inst Art Admin, 76. Work: Mint Mus, Charlotte, NC. Exhib: The 22nd Ann Exhib, Guild of SC Artists, Greenville Co Mus Art, SC, 72; Artists Guild of Columbia, Columbia Mus Art, SC, 73; Piedmont Crafts Exhib, Mint Mus Art, Charlotte, NC, 74; Southeastern Ctr for Contemp Art, Winston-Salem, NC, 74; Am Crafts Coun Regional Exhib, Am Crafts Coun Mus, New York, 74; Marietta Col Crafts Nat, Ohio, 75; 26th Ann Exhib, Guild SC Artists, Greenville Mus Art, SC, 76. Collections Arranged: Alan Davis Drawing Exhib, 76, Mike French Jewelry Exhib, 76, Depression Glass, 77, An Artist Collects (Jasper Johns Collection), 77 & Guild of SC Artists Exhib, 77, Columbia Mus of Art, SC. Teaching: Instr painting, Richland Art Sch, 69-70, instr ceramics, 71-72; teaching asst ceramics, Univ SC, 72-74. Awards: Merit Award, Guild SC Artists, Greenville Co Mus Art, SC, 72; Purchase Awards, Artist Guild Columbia, 74 & Piedmont Crafts Exhib, Mint Mus, Charlotte, NC, 74. Mem: Guild of SC Artists (pres, 76-77); SC Fedn Mus (vpres, 76-78); Am Asn Mus; Artists of Columbia. Style & Technique: Potter, functional ware and ceramic sculpture; painting. Media: Clay; acrylic. Dealer: Objects Gallery 410 Meeting St W Columbia SC 29169. Mailing Add: 1015 Laurens St Columbia SC 29201

DAVIS, L CLARICE
ART BOOK DEALER, ART HISTORIAN
b Akron, Ohio, Jan 30, 29. Study: Univ Akron, BA(fine arts), 55; Univ Calif, Los Angeles, MLS, 61, MA(art hist), 68, PhD candidate. Teaching: Asst prof mod art hist, Calif State Univ, Northridge, 61-63 & 68-69; lectr mod art hist, Otis Art Inst, Los Angeles, 69-70. Pos: Chief mus librn, Art Libr, Los Angeles Co Mus Art, 63-68; owner-mgr, Davis Art Book Store & Gallery, Los Angeles, 71-; actg unit head, Art Libr, Univ Calif, Los Angeles, 73-75. Mem: Col Art Asn Am; Art Libr Soc NAm; Antiquarian Booksellers Asn Am. Specialty: Out of print books and exhibition catalogues; original prints, drawings and paintings; agent for fine art. Publ: Contribr (bibliog; catalogue), R B Kitaj, 65 & Peter Voulkos, Sculpture, 65, Los Angeles Co Mus Art; contribr introd, Pornography in Fine Art From Ancient Times, Los

Angeles Elysium, 69; auth, Annuals of auction sales, Am Libr Soc NAm Newsletter, Vol 5 (Dec, 76). Mailing Add: 1547 Westwood Blvd Los Angeles CA 90024

DAVIS, LEROY
ART DEALER
Pos: Dir, Davis & Long Galleries. Specialty: Contemporary art. Mailing Add: 746 Madison Ave New York NY 10021

DAVIS, LEW E
PAINTER
b Jerome, Ariz, Nov 2, 10. Study: Nat Acad Design, New York. Work: Newark Mus, NJ; Coe Col, Cedar Rapids, Iowa; Ariz State Collection Am Art, Tempe; Univ Ariz Art Gallery, Tucson; Phoenix Art Mus. Comn: US Post Off, Los Banos, Calif, 38 & Marlow, Okla, 41. Exhib: 107th Ann, Nat Acad Design, 32; Corcoran Gallery, Washington, DC, 37; Whitney Mus Am Art, New York, 37-41; Los Angeles Mus, 38; San Francisco Mus, 38-40. Bibliog: Harry Wood (auth), 25 year Retrospective, Ariz State Univ, 40; Jon Hopkins (auth), The Art of Lew Davis, Northland, 70. Media: Oil. Mailing Add: Pinnacle Peak Scottsdale AZ 85255

DAVIS, MARIAN B
ART HISTORIAN, CURATOR
b St Louis Co, Mo, Sept 24, 11. Study: Wash Univ, BA, 32, MA, 35; Radcliffe Col, MA, 39, PhD, 48. Collections Arranged: Sch of Fontainebleau, 65; plus many others. Teaching: Instr art hist, Worcester Art Mus, 41-44; from instr to assoc prof art hist, Univ Tex, Austin, 44-50, prof art hist, 50- Pos: Chief cur & actg dir, Art Teaching Gallery, Univ Tex, Austin, 63- Mem: Col Art Asn (dir, 51-55); Soc Archit Historians; Archaeol Inst Am; Renaissance Soc; Nat Trust Hist Preserv. Res: Italian Renaissance; United States architecture. Publ: Auth, Two eighteenth century paintings, Worcester Art Mus Ann V, 46; auth, Summer travel for students, Col Art J, 54; auth, Some first impressions of Sicily, Tex Trends in Art Educ, autumn, 59; auth, Art history—contribution to understanding, Western Arts Asn Bull, 61. Mailing Add: 2701 Wooldridge Dr Austin TX 78703

DAVIS, PHIL DOUGLAS
PAINTER, INSTRUCTOR
b Los Angeles, Calif, Aug 12, 47. Study: Univ Calif, Los Angeles, BA; Univ Calif, San Diego, MFA. Exhib: One-man show, Ellie Blankfort Gallery, Los Angeles, 74; Southern Calif Drawing Show, Santa Monica City Col, 74; Faculty Show, Pasadena City Col Gallery, Calif, 74; 1975 Whitney Biennial of Contemp Am Art, Whitney Mus, New York, 75; Galerie Krebs Bern, Basel Art Fair, Switz, 75. Teaching: Instr art, La Jolla Mus Contemp Art, Calif, summer 74; instr art, Pasadena City Col, 74-75. Awards: Res Grant, State of Calif, 71-72; Individual Artist Grant, Nat Endowment Arts, 74-75 & 75-76. Media: Acrylic on Paper. Mailing Add: 931 Tenth St Apt C Santa Monica CA 90403

DAVIS, PHILIP CHARLES
PHOTOGRAPHER, EDUCATOR
b Spokane, Wash, Oct 15, 21. Study: Albright Art Sch, Buffalo, NY, cert. Work: Mus Art Inst Chicago; Int Mus Photog, Rochester, NY; Detroit Art Inst; Mus Mod Art, New York. Comn: Outdoor exhib photos, Univ Mich Sesquicentennial Comt, 66. Exhib: One-man show photographs, Kalamazoo Art Ctr, Mich, 62; The University, Univ Mich, Ann Arbor, 66; three-man show photographs, 831 Gallery, Birmingham, Mich, 71; Group Invitational, Kresge Art Ctr, Mich State Univ, 72; Midwest Invitational, Walker Art Ctr, Minneapolis, Minn, 73-74. Teaching: From instr to prof art, Univ Mich, Ann Arbor, 48- Pos: Photogr, var photo-illus studios, Detroit, 52- Awards: Gold Medal, 59, Silver Medal, 60 & Bravo Gold Medal, 61, Art Dirs Club Detroit. Bibliog: Irving Desfor (auth), Camera angles, Assoc Press Newsfeatures, 72. Mem: Soc Photog Educ. Style & Technique: Documentary style; major interest in historic-obsolete processes and mixed media. Publ: Auth & illusr, The university, 67, Take photography step by step, 70, Photography, 72 & The Dexter portfolio (50 set ed), 72. Dealer: 831 Gallery 831 E Maple Rd Birmingham MI 48011. Mailing Add: 7385 Webster Church Rd Whitmore Lake MI 48189

DAVIS, ROBERT TYLER
ART ADMINISTRATOR, ART HISTORIAN
b Los Angeles, Calif, Aug 11, 04. Study: Harvard Univ, BA & MA; Fogg Mus, with Paul J Sachs & also painting & design with Arthur Pope & Martin Mower. Teaching: Prof art, McGill Univ, 47-52; coordr humanities, Univ Miami, 57-59. Pos: Dir, Portland Art Mus, Ore, 39-47, Mus Fine Arts, Montreal, Can, 47-52 & Vizcaya-Dade Co Art Mus, Miami, Fla, 52-57; asst dir, Nat Collection Fine Arts, Smithsonian Inst, 69-72, spec asst for collections, 72-75. Res: The American Renaissance, paintings and patrons, late 19th to early 20th centuries. Mailing Add: Lily Dale NY 14752

DAVIS, RONALD WENDEL
PAINTER, PRINTMAKER
b Santa Monica, Calif, June 29, 37. Study: San Francisco Art Inst, 60-64. Work: Los Angeles Co Mus; Mus Mod Art, New York; Tate Gallery, London; Albright-Knox Art Gallery, Buffalo; San Francisco Mus Art. Exhib: A News Aesthetic, Washington Gallery Mod Art, DC, 67; Documenta 4, Kassel, Ger, 67; Whitney Mus Am Art Ann, New York, 67; Color, Univ Calif, Los Angeles Art Galleries, 69; Venice Biennial, Italy, 72. Awards: Nat Endowment Arts, 68. Bibliog: M Fried (auth), Ronald Davis: surface and illusion, Artforum, 4/67; R Hughes (auth), Ron Davis at Kasmin, Studio Int, 176, 12/68; B Rose (auth), American painting, Vol 2, 70. Style & Technique: Abstract illusionism; paint on canvas. Media: Polyester Resin, Fiberglas. Collection: Contemporary art. Dealer: Nicholas Wilder Gallery 8225 1/2 Santa Monica Los Angeles CA 90046. Mailing Add: 6950 Grasswood Ave Malibu CA 90265

DAVIS, STEPHEN A
PAINTER
b Ft Worth, Tex, Apr 24, 45. Study: Univ Madrid, 66; Claremont Men's Col, BA(polit sci), 67; Univ Tex, 67-68; Claremont Grad Sch, MFA, 71. Exhib: Fullerton Col Painting Show, 71; two-man show, Pomona Col, 71; Off the Stretcher, Oakland Mus, 72; Bay Area Underground, Univ Calif Art Mus, Berkeley, 72; one-man shows, Hansen Fuller Gallery, 72, 74 & 76, Reed Col, Portland, Ore, 72 & Cirrus Gallery, Los Angeles, 74; Whitney Biennial, New York, 73 & 77; Hardware, Walnut Creek Art Ctr, 73; Biennial of Painting & Sculpture, Krannert Art Mus, Champagne, Ill, 74; three-man show, Univ Calif, Berkeley, 75; Exchange, Ft Worth Art Mus, Tex & San Francisco Mus Mod Art, Calif, 75-76. Collections Arranged: Conceptual Show 11 Young Bay Area Artists & Collectors & Four Young Berkeley Artists, Hansen Fuller Gallery. Pos: Mus asst, Univ Tex, 67-68; gallery asst, Pomona Col, 68-69; asst, Hansen Fuller Gallery, 70. Mailing Add: c/o Hansen Fuller Gallery 228 Grant Ave San Francisco CA 94108

DAVIS, MR & MRS WALTER
COLLECTORS, PATRONS
Mr Davis, b New Orleans, La; Mrs Davis, b Natchez, Miss. Study: Mr Davis, Tulane Univ Law Sch; Mrs Davis, Newcomb Art Sch. Pos: Mr Davis, Bd New Orleans Opera. Mrs Davis, trustee & women's bd, New Orleans Mus Art; women's bd, New Orleans Symphony & New Orleans Opera; trustee comt, Am Asn Mus; bd, New Orleans Ctr Creative Arts; bd, Mayor's New Orleans Cult Resources Comt; bd, Los Angeles Co Mus, Los Angeles. Collection: Drawings by Mary Cassatt, Louis Valtat, Chagall & Krebs; gouaches by Tamayo, Raoul Dufy, Cuevas; sculpture by Henry Moore, L Nierman & L Wercollier; watercolors by John Marin, Raoul Dufy, David Smith, Jean Dufy, Merida & Montenegro; oils by Modigliani, R Dufy, de Chirico, Vasarely, Roualt, Utrillo, Harold Carney, Merida, Montenegro & Guayasamin. Awards: Mr Davis, La Coun Award. Mailing Add: 1819 Octavia St New Orleans LA 70115

DAVIS, WALTER LEWIS
PAINTER
b Americus, Ga, Jan 12, 37. Study: NY Community Col; Abracheff Sch Art, New York. Work: Detroit Bd Educ, Mich; NY State Brookdale Hosp, Brooklyn; NY State Lincoln Hosp, Bronx. Exhib: One-man shows, Arts Extended Gallery, Detroit, Mich, 66-67 & 71 & Mt Vernon Coop Col Ctr, NY, 74; Childe Hassam Found Purchase Exhib, Am Acad Arts & Lett, New York, 69; Contemp Black Artists Am, Whitney Mus, 71. Awards: Purchase Award Painting, Okinawa Art Ctr, 57. Bibliog: William Tall (auth), Walter Davis' Totems for Charlie Parker, Detroit Free Press, 71. Style & Technique: Shaped canvas in oils, collage with black & white photos and water base paints. Media: Oil, Collage. Mailing Add: 801-12 Tilden St Bronx NY 10467

DAVIS, WAYNE LAMBERT
PAINTER, ILLUSTRATOR
b Oak Park, Ill, Jan 3, 04. Study: Art Students League, with Joseph Pennell; Columbia Univ; NY Univ, State NY cert art teacher. Work: Smithsonian Inst, Washington, DC; First Nat City Bank New York; Newman Galleries, Philadelphia; plus others. Comn: Mural of skiing, Vail, Colo, comn by Vernon Taylor, Denver, 68; Stairway murals of Brooklyn Bridge area, 53rd St Br, First Nat City Bank New York, 69. Exhib: One-man shows, Kennedy Galleries, 67, Country Art Galleries, 69 & Hunter Gallery, Aspen, Colo, 69; 69. Teaching: Instr art, Hit Sch Art, Locust Valley, NY, 53-63; instr watercolor, Great Neck High Sch, NY, 54- Pos: Art dir & staff artist, Grumman Aircraft Eng Corp, Bethpage, NY, 41-53. Awards: First in watercolor for The Lobster Weir, Stony Brook Mus, NY, 68; First in oil for The Salmon Run, Oper Democracy, Locust Valley, 71. Mem: Nassau Art League. Style & Technique: Realistic, egg tempera on panels; transparent watercolors. Media: Tempera, Watercolor; Etching. Publ: Illusr, Fortune & Liberty, 43, Vanity Fair, 44 & Sportman Pilot, 45; auth, Pathway to expression (color film), privately publ, 66. Dealer: Country Art Gallery The Plaza Locust Valley NY 11560. Mailing Add: RFD 1 Five Mile River Rd Putnam CT 06260

DAVIS, WILLIS BING
PAINTER, CERAMIST
b Spartanburg, SC, June 30, 37. Study: DePauw Univ, Greencastle, Ind, BA, 59; Dayton Art Inst, Ohio, 64-65; Miami Univ, Oxford, Ohio, MEd, 67; Ind State Univ, Terre Haute, MFA, 76. Work: Dayton New Vision Mus, Ohio; Columbus Gallery Fine Arts, Ohio; Hallmark Mus, Kansas City, Mo; Earlham Col, Richmond, Ind; Purdue Univ Afro-Am Art Collection. Exhib: Mid-States Art Exhib, Evansville Mus Arts & Sci, Ind, 72; one-man shows, Univ Dayton, 75, Vincennes Univ, Ind, 75, Turman Gallery, Ind State Univ, 75; Skin Show, 77 & All-Ohio Painting & Print Exhib, 77, Dayton Art Inst, Black Artists Together, Columbus Inst Contemp Arts, 78; AFROHIO Art 78, Cleveland State Univ, 78; John F Kennedy Gallery, Univ Dayton, 78; plus many others. Teaching: Instr art, Wright State Univ, Dayton, 69-71; coordr Black studies, DePauw Univ, 71-72, asst prof art, 71-76; assoc prof art & asst dean grad sch, Miami Univ, 76- Pos: Art dir, Living Arts Ctr, Dayton, 67-71. Awards: Purchase Awards, Discovery 70, Hallmark Mus, 70, Wabash Valley Exhib, Ind State Univ, 73 & 74. Bibliog: Lewis & Waddy (auth), Black artists on art, Contemp Crafts, 72; P Rothenberg (auth), Ceramics, Horizon, 73; Samella Lewis (auth), African-American Art, Harcourt Brace, 78. Mem: Nat Conf Artists (vpres, 73-); Ohio Arts Coun (visual arts panel, 77-); Ind Comn for Arts & Humanities in Educ; Mixed-Media Inc, Cincinnati; Ind Comt for Humanities (consult, 75-76). Style & Technique: Expressionistic-symbolism. Media: Painting, Ceramic. Dealer: Gallatin Gallery 337 S Main St Ann Arbor MI 48104. Mailing Add: 110 N University Oxford OH 45056

DAVISON, ROBERT
PAINTER, DESIGNER
b Long Beach, Calif, July 17, 22. Study: Los Angeles City Col. Work: James Philip Gray Collection, Springfield Mus Fine Arts, Mass. Comn: Designer scenery & costumes, Cirque de Beaux, Ballet Russe de Monte Carlo, 48, Constanzia, Ballet Theatre, 51, La Barca di Venetia per Padova, Festivo Due Mondi, Spoleto, Italy, 63 & Natalia Petrovna, 65 & La Boheme, 70, Opera Soc Washington; plus others. Exhib: Am Watercolor Soc, 59; Boston Art Festival, 59; Eastern States Exhib, Springfield, Mass, 59; Allied Artists Am, 59; The Life of Christ Exhib, Birmingham, Mich, 60; plus others. Pos: Archit designer, Valerian S Rybar, Paris & New York, 67- Mailing Add: 21-18 45th Ave Long Island City NY 11101 Paris France 21-18 45th Ave Long Island City NY 11101

DAVISSON, DARRELL
ART HISTORIAN, LECTURER
b Long Beach, Calif, July 27, 37. Study: Univ Calif, San Diego, BA, 60; Univ Calif, Los Angeles, MA, 65, with Prof Karl M Birkmeyer; Johns Hopkins Univ, Baltimore, Md, PhD, 71, with Prof John White. Teaching: Asst prof hist art, Colo Col, Colorado Springs, 65-68, Univ Sask, 70-71, Univ Ariz, Tucson, 71-74 & Univ Tex, Austin, 75-76; asst prof Medieval & Renaissance studies, Univ Calif San Diego, La Jolla, 76- Awards: Kress Found Travel Fel, 70. Mem: Renaissance Soc Am; Col Art Asn Am. Res: Sacred art of the 14th and 15th centuries in Italy with emphasis on religious, social and historical interrelationships; Renaissance religious and social traditions as they pertain to art. Publ: English Brass Rubbings (catalog), Colorado Springs, 66; co-auth, Benvenuto di Giovanni (catalog), J Paul Getty Mus, Malibu, Calif, 66; contribr, Optical & Historical Distance, Colo Col Studies, No 9, 67; auth, Iconology of the S Trinita Sacristy 1418-1435, Art Bull, No 57, 75. Mailing Add: 6747 Radcliffe Ct San Diego CA 92122

DAWDY, DORIS OSTRANDER
WRITER, ART HISTORIAN
b Minn. Study: MacPhail Sch Music, Minneapolis; Colo State Univ; Los Angeles City Col. Res: American Indian paintings; artists of the American West born prior to 1900. Publ: Auth, Annoted Bibliography of American Indian Painting, 68; auth, Artists of the American West, Swallow, Vol I, 74 & Vol II, 78. Mailing Add: 8520 Hazelwood Dr Bethesda MD 20014

DAWLEY, JOSEPH WILLIAM
PAINTER, ART DEALER
b Nashville, Ark, June 19, 36. Study: With Raymond Froman, 58-61; Southern Methodist Univ, BFA, 59; Dallas Mus Fine Arts, 60; Art Students League, 61. Work: Mus Arts & Crafts, Columbus, Ga; Davenport Mus Art, Iowa; Henderson Arts Coun, Tex; Southern Methodist Univ, Dallas, Tex; plus others. Comn: Two portraits, St Elizabeth Ann Seton for canonization ceremonies, Rome, 75; Exhib: Allied Artists Show, New York, 69 & 70; Acad Artists Show, Springfield, Mass, 69 & 70; Hudson Valley Art Show, White Plains, NY, 69 & 70; Am Artists Prof League, New York, 69-71; Salmagundi Club Show, New York, 70 & 72. Pos: Creator comic strip, Chief, 64-67; owner, Joseph Dawley Gallery. Awards: Figure or Portrait Anonymous Award, Acad Artists, 69; William Collins Award, Hudson Valley Art Asn, 69; Jane Peterson Portrait Award, Allied Artists, New York, 70. Bibliog: Kolbe (auth), Dawley reasserts realism, Am Artist Mag, 70; Singer (auth), Meet the artist—Joseph Dawley, Suburban Life Mag, 70; Calaway (auth), Bringing sanity back to art, Southwest Scene Mag, 70. Mem: Allied Artists Asn; Hudson Valley Art Asn; Am Artists Prof League; Acad Artists; Salmagundi Club. Style & Technique: Traditional style of the old masters, primarily in oils. Publ: Auth, Character Studies in Oil, 72, The Painters' Problem Book, 73, Painting Western Characters, 75, Painters' Problem Book II, 78, Watson-Guptill. Dealer: Grand Central Gallery 40 Vanderbilt Ave New York NY 10017. Mailing Add: 13 W Holly St Cranford NJ 07016

DAWSON, BESS PHIPPS
PAINTER, ART DEALER
b Tchula, Miss. Study: Belhaven Col; Southwest Miss Jr Col; workshops, Allisons Art Colony, Way, Miss & Miss Art Colony, Laurel. Work: Art in Embassy Prog, Taiwan; Old Capitol Hist Mus, Jackson, Miss; Miss Art Asn Gallery, Jackson; Miss State Col Women, Columbus; First Nat Bank Miss Collection, Jackson. Comn: Murals, (with Ruth A Holmes), Church of God, McComb, Miss, 58, (with Halcyone Barnes & Ruth A Holmes), Delta Elec Co, Greenwood, Miss, 58, First Nat Bank, McComb, 59 & Hankins Container Corp, Magnolia, Miss, 59; painting, Order Eastern Star, Jackson, 69. Exhib: High Art Mus, Atlanta, Ga, 65; Delgado Mus Art, New Orleans, La, 67; Brooks Mem Gallery, Memphis, Tenn, 69; Ark Arts Ctr, Little Rock, 70; Art Asn Gallery, Jackson, 70. Teaching: Supvr art, McComb Pub Schs, 68-71. Pos: Co-owner & dir, Gulf South Galleries, 71-; dir, Miss Art Colony, 77- Awards: First Purchase Prize, S Cent Bell, 69; Award of Merit, 71 & First Award of Merit, 74, Miss Art Colony. Mem: Southwest Miss Art Asn (secy, 66-); Miss Art Colony (bd dirs, 62-); Allisons Art Colony (bd dirs); Miss Art Asn (coordr State bd, 68-69). Style & Technique: Large semi-abstract paintings in oil and acrylic; small flower and landscape paintings in acrylic. Specialty: Continuous showing of invited Mississippi artists in all media. Publ: Co-auth, Manual for classroom teachers, 69 & illusr, Elementary art (TV doc), 69, McComb Pub Schs. Dealer: Gulf South Galleries 211 Llewellyn Ave McComb MS 39648 & Mainstream Mall Greenville MS 38701. Mailing Add: PO Box 32 Summit MS 39666

DAWSON, EVE
PAINTER
b Somersetshire, Eng; US citizen. Study: Art Students League. Work: In pvt collections in US, Eng, Malta & Australia. Exhib: 34 one-man shows in New York & Vt; Nat Acad Design; Nat Arts Club; Metrop Mus Art; plus two- and three-man shows. Awards: First Award, Nat Pen Women Am; four First Awards, Pen & Brush Club; two Hon Mentions, Nat Arts Club. Mem: Knickerbocker Art Club; Catharine Lorillard Wolfe Art Asn; Burr Artists; Salmagundi Club; Southern Vt Art Ctr; plus others. Dealer: Lord & Taylor Gallery Fifth & 39th New York NY 10016. Mailing Add: National Arts Club 15 Gramercy Park New York NY 10003

DAWSON, JOHN ALLAN
PAINTER
b Joliet, Ill, Sept 12, 46. Study: Northern Ill Univ, BFA, 69; Univ NMex; Ariz State Univ, MFA, 74. Work: El Paso Mus Art, Tex; Phoenix Art Mus, Ariz; Ariz State Univ, Tempe; Western NMex Univ; Del Mar Col. Exhib: 8th Dulin Nat Exhib, Dulin Gallery, Knoxville, Tenn, 72; 16th Ann NDak Drawing Exhib, Univ NDak, 73; 18th Ann Art Exhib, El Paso Mus Art, 74; 17th Ann Nat Exhib, Okla Art Ctr, Oklahoma City, 75; Ariz Invitational 75, Phoenix Art Mus, 75. Pos: Artist in residence, Mesa Pub Schs, Ariz Comn Art, 74. Awards: Purchase Award, Del Mar Col, 73 & El Paso Mus Art, 75. Bibliog: B Cortwright (auth), Fear and terror human and animal, Art Week, 1/75 & Ariz Invitational, 75, Current Art Mag, 8/75; H Broadly (auth), Portraits Paraphrasis, Art News, 4/75. Style & Technique: Figurative; expressive; distorted figures. Media: Oil. Dealer: Elaine Horwitch Gallery 4200 N Marshall Way Scottsdale AZ 85251. Mailing Add: 226 E Colgate Tempe AZ 85283

DAY, CHON (CHAUNCEY ADDISON)
CARTOONIST
b Chatham, NJ, Apr 6, 07. Study: Art Students League, with Boardman Robinson & John Sloan. Exhib: Metrop Mus Art, 42; Pa Acad Fine Arts. Awards: Best Gag Cartoonist, Nat Cartoonists Soc, 56 & 61. Mem: Mag Cartoonists Guild; Nat Cartoonists Soc. Publ: Auth & illusr, I Could Be Dreaming, 45, What Price Dory, 55, Brother Sebastian, 57, Brother Sebastian Carries On, 59 & Brother Sebastian at Large, 61; contribr cartoons, New Yorker, Good Housekeeping, Ladies Home J & others. Mailing Add: 22 Cross St Westerly RI 02891

DAY, HORACE TALMAGE
PAINTER, ART DIRECTOR
b Amoy, China, July 3, 09; US citizen. Study: Art Students League, 28-32; with Kimon Nicolaides & Kenneth H Miller; Tiffany Found, Oyster Bay, 30-35. Work: Va Mus Fine Arts, Richmond; Norfolk Mus, Va; Philip Morris Collection; Randolph-Macon Woman's Col Collection, Lynchberg, Va; Fleming Mus, Burlington, Vt. Comn: Mural, Tenn Treas Dept, 38; three paintings, Dept Reclamation, US Dept Interior, Washington, DC, 69. Exhib: Whitney Mus Am Art Ann, New York, 39-41 & 44; one-man shows, Va Mus Fine Arts, 48 & Bodley Gallery, New York, 58; Biennial Am Painting, Va Mus Fine Arts, 58; Biennial Am Drawing, Norfolk Mus, 70; Bicentennial of Vt Painting Exhib, 76. Teaching: Prof art, Mary Baldwin Col, Staunton, Va, 42-63; instr painting, Kansas City Art Inst, 47-48. Pos: Dir painting, Herbert Inst Art, Augusta, Ga, 36-41; dir, Northern Va Fine Arts Ctr, Alexandria, 72- Mem: Southern Vt Art Asn. Media: Oil, Watercolor. Publ: Contribr, Art in the armed forces, Hyperion, 45; illusr, Staunton in the Valley of Virginia (folio), McClure, 47. Dealer: Liros Gallery 628 N Washington St Alexandria VA 2231; Capricorn Gallery 8004 Norfolk Ave Washington DC 20014. Mailing Add: 113 N Fairfax St Alexandria VA 22314

DAY, JOHN
PAINTER, EDUCATOR
b Malden, Mass, May 27, 32. Study: Yale Univ, BFA(design), 54, MFA, 56; study with Josef Albers, Burgoyne Diller & James Brooks. Work: Mus Mod Art, New York; Whitney Mus Am Art, New York; Mus Cantini, Marseilles, France; Flint Inst Arts, Mich; Mus Pompidou, Centre Nat de l'Art Contemporain, Paris. Exhib: Painting Exhib, Lyman Allyn Mus, New London, Conn, 61; Recent Acquisitions, Whitney Mus Am Art, New York, 67; l'Art Vivant 1965-1968, Found Maeght, St Paul De Vence, France, 68; Director's Choice, Brooklyn Mus Community Gallery, 72; Acquisitions Recentes, Mus Cantini, Marseilles, France, 72; l'Art de Trois Villes, Mus Pompidou, Paris, 77; 1st Biennial, NJ Artists, Newark Mus, NJ, 77. Teaching: Assoc prof painting, Univ Bridgeport, Conn, 58-70; prof painting, William Paterson Col, NJ, 70- Awards: Artists Award, 50 States of Art, Burpee Mus Art, Rockford, Ill, 65; First Prize, 20th New Eng Exhib, Silvermine Guild Artists, Conn, 69; First Prize, Members Exhib Abstract Painting, Guild Hall, East Hampton, Conn, 77. Bibliog: Daniel Abadie (auth), John Day, l'Americano deo luogi immaginari, le Arti, Milan, Italy, 9/71; Henry Galy-Carles (auth), Clefs pour John Day, Lettres Francaise, Paris, 3/71; Karl Lunde (auth), John Day, Arts Mag, 3/77. Style & Technique: An investigation of color through variables and constants, sometimes with added collage elements. Media: Oil; collage. Publ: Auth, Art, Student Art Asn, William Paterson Col, 75; auth, The Artery, William Paterson Col, 77. Dealer: Alonzo Gallery 30 W 57th St New York NY 10019. Mailing Add: 22 E 89th St New York NY 10028

DAY, LARRY (LAWRENCE JAMES DAY)
PAINTER, INSTRUCTOR
b Philadelphia, Pa, Oct 29, 21. Study: Tyler Sch Fine Arts, Temple Univ, BFA & BS(educ). Work: Philadelphia Mus Art, Pa; Miami-Dade Col, Fla; Philadelphia Col Art, Pa; Fleischer Art Mem, Philadelphia; Corcoran Gallery Art, Washington, DC. Exhib: Realism Now, Vassar Col; The Figure in Recent Am Painting (travelling show; co-auth, catalog), Westminster Col, Pa, 74; The Realist Revival, Am Fedn Arts Travelling Show; Bicentennial Exhib, Philadelphia Mus Art, 76. Teaching: Prof painting, drawing & theory, Philadelphia Col Art, Pa, 53- Style & Technique: Representational painter of figures and places; large format; refined forms. Media: Oil, watercolor. Publ: Co-auth, American Figure Drawing (catalog), Victorian Col Art, Melbourne, Australia, 76. Dealer: Gross-McCleaf Gallery 1713 Walnut St Philadelphia PA 19103. Mailing Add: 310 Myrtle Ave Cheltenham PA 19012

DAY, LUCIEN B
PAINTER, ART DEALER
b Hartford, Conn. Study: Yale Univ. Work: Chase Manhattan Bank; Prudential Life Ins Co; Am Tel & Tel. Exhib: One-man shows, Green Mountain Gallery, 69, 72 & 75; Painterly Realism, Am Fedn Arts, 70-72; New Image in American Figurative Painting, Queens Mus & Squibb Gallery, 75. Pos: Owner, Green Mountain Gallery, currently. Bibliog: Lawrence Campbell (auth), rev, Art News, 69 & 72; Laura Schwartz (auth), rev, Arts Mag, 2/73. Style & Technique: Perceptual painter working on experimentation in watercolor medium by combining the photograph as source material and painterly realism as a sensibility. Mailing Add: Green Mountain Gallery 135 Greene St New York NY 10012

DAY, MARTHA B WILLSON
PAINTER, COLLECTOR
b Providence, RI, Aug 16, 85. Study: RI Sch Design; Julian Acad, Paris, France; also with Lucia F Fuller. Work: Philadelphia Mus Art; Smithsonian Inst. Exhib: Am Soc Miniature Painters Ann; Pa Miniature Painters Soc Ann. Teaching: Lectr miniatures. Awards: Prize, Pa Acad Fine Arts, 32; McCarty Medal, Pa Miniature Painters Soc. Mem: Providence Art Club; Am Soc Miniature Painters; Pa Miniature Painters Soc. Mailing Add: 88 Congdon St Providence RI 02906

DAY, ROBERT JAMES
CARTOONIST
b San Bernardino, Calif, Sept 25, 00. Study: Otis Art Inst, 18-27. Exhib: Many cartoon exhibs throughout US & Europe. Interest: Line & wash drawings. Publ: Illusr, Seen any good movies lately?, The mad world of bridge, 60, Over the fence is out, 61, What every bachelor knows, 61 & Rome wasn't burned in a day, 72; plus many others & contribr to New Yorker & other nat mags. Mailing Add: c/o The New Yorker Magazine 25 W 43rd St New York NY 10036

DAY, WÖRDEN
SCULPTOR, PRINTMAKER
b Columbus, Ohio, June 11, 16. Study: Randolph-Macon Womans Col, BA; NY Univ, MA; also with Jean Charlot, Emilio Amero, Maurice Sterne, Vaclav Vylacil, Hans Hofmann & Stanley William Hayter. Work: Nat Gallery Art & Libr Cong, Washington, DC; Philadelphia Mus Art; Metrop Mus Art & Whitney Mus Am Art, New York; State Mus, NJ; plus others. Exhib: Nat Print Exhibs, Libr Cong, Brooklyn Mus & Philadelphia Mus Art, 48-62; Int Print Exhibs, Europe, Asia & Mex, 50-62; Abstract Painting and Sculpture in Am, Mus Mod Art, New York, 51; Third Carnegie Inst Int, Pittsburgh, 53; Int Watercolor Exhib, Brooklyn Mus, NY, 62. Teaching: Instr design, Pratt Inst, 55-56; vis artist, Iowa State Univ, 61; instr woodcut & watercolor, New Sch Social Res, 61-66; instr multimedia, Art Students League, 66-69. Awards: Va Mus Fine Arts grant, 40-42; J Rosenwald Awards, 42-44; Guggenheim fel, 51-52 & 61-62. Bibliog: Una Johnson (auth), Solo prints - paintings (catalog), Montclair Art Mus, 59; Printmakers USA (film), US Info Serv, 61; Three Mid-Atlantic artists, Kalamazoo Art Ctr, 63. Mem: Fedn Mod Painters & Sculptors; Montclair Art Mus; MacDowell Colony; Art Students League; Sculptors Guild. Dealer: Sculpture Center of New York 167 E 69th St New York NY 10021. Mailing Add: Studios 21/28 427 Bloomfield Ave Montclair NJ 07042

DEADERICK, JOSEPH
PAINTER, EDUCATOR
b Memphis, Tenn, Jan 17, 30. Study: Univ Ga, BFA, 52; Cranbrook Acad Art, MFA, 54; Ind Univ, 58-59. Work: Kalamazoo Col, Mich. Comn: Ceramic tile mural, Univ Wyo, Laramie, 68; faceted glass window, Lutheran Campus Ctr, Laramie, 68. Exhib: 6th Midwest Biennial, Joslyn Art Mus, Omaha, Nebr, 60; Brooklyn Mus Biennial Print Show, 64; Drawing USA traveling show, St Paul, Minn, 66-68; one-man show, Colorado Springs Fine Arts Ctr, 67; Fedn Rocky Mountain States Traveling Show, 72. Teaching: Instr design, Ind Univ, Bloomington, 56-59; prof art, Univ Wyo, Laramie, 59- Awards: Two grants, Univ Wyo Grad Res Coord Comt, 64 & 69; hon mention, Survey '69, Univ Mont, 69; First Place award for design of medal commemorating Bicentennial Celebration of the US, Franklin Mint, 72; Nat Award for excellence in design, Printing Indust Am Graphic Arts Competition, 72; plus others. Media: Oil, Acrylic, Watercolor. Mailing Add: Art Dept Univ Wyo Laramie WY 82070

DEAK, EDIT
ART CRITIC, CURATOR
b Albania, Sept 16, 48; US citizen. Study: Columbia Univ, BA(art hist). Exhib & Events Arranged: Mus, 73; Coenties Slip & Frank O'Hara, 74, Person-a, 74, Not Photography (photography), 75; Secret of Rented Island, 76; Artists Books, Santa Barbara Mus Art, Calif, 77. Pos: Mus intern, Whitney Mus, 73-74; co-publr & ed, Art-rite Mag, 73-; asst dir, Comt Visual Arts, 74-75; critic, lectr, cur & organizer, 74- Awards: Helena Rubinstein Fel, 73 & 74; NY State Coun Arts Grant, 74-75; AZDA Int Grant, Paris, 75. Bibliog: Gary Wright (dir), Edit, (film), NY Univ Inst of Film, 69; Lawrence Alloway (auth), Museum, show at Whitney, Nation, 73; Anette Kuhn (auth), Culturesock, Village Voice, 75. Mem: Int Art Critics Asn;

Col Art Asn (panelist, 75-76). Res: Public art registry assembled with Irving Sandler; artists' books. Interest: Surfacing nascent ideas and work of young avant-garde artists. Publ: Contribr, Art in Am, 73- & Data, Italy, 74- Mailing Add: 149 Wooster St New York NY 10012

DEAL, JOE
PHOTOGRAPHER
b Topeka, Kans, Aug 12, 47. Study: Kansas City Art Inst, BFA, 70; Univ NMex, MA, 74, study with Van Deren Coke. Work: Mus Mod Art, New York; Mus Fine Arts, Boston; Int Mus Photog at George Eastman House, Rochester, NY; Univ Louisville, Ky; Seagram's Collection, NY. Exhib: Group Show, Yale Univ Art Gallery, New Haven, Conn, 73; Ten Am Photogrs, The Photogrs Gallery, London, 74; New Topographics: Photographs of a Man-Altered Landscape, Int Mus Photog at George Eastman House, Rochester, Princeton Univ & Otis Art Gallery, Los Angeles, 75-76; Contemp Am Photographs, Mus Fine Arts, Houston, 77; The Great West: The Real & The Ideal, Univ Colo, Boulder, 77. Teaching: Lectr photog, San Francisco Art Inst, summer, 76; asst prof photog, Univ Calif, Riverside, 76- Awards: Nat Endowment for the Arts photographer's fel, 77. Bibliog: Carter Ratcliff (auth), Route 66 Revisited: The New Landscape Photography, Art in Am, 1-2/76; Ariz State Univ (auth), Joe Deal: New Topographics, Northlight Five, 77. Mem: Soc Photog Educators. Style & Technique: Black and white photog, landscape and man-made environment. Media: Photography. Dealer: Light Gallery 724 Fifth Ave New York NY 10019. Mailing Add: 4006 Fifth St Riverside CA 92501

DEAN, ABNER
ILLUSTRATOR, WRITER
b New York, NY. Study: Nat Acad Design; Dartmouth Col, BA. Mem: Soc Illusrs. Interest: Patents for multi-level folding table and building system assembly. Publ: Auth (bks of drawings), It's a Long Way to Heaven, 45, What am I doing here?, 47, And on the Eighth Day, 49, Cave Drawings for the Future, 54 & Abner Dean's Naked People, 63; also two bks verse & drawings plus illusr other bks & mags & for indust. Mailing Add: 166 E 61st St New York NY 10021

DEAN, JAMES
ART ADMINISTRATOR, PAINTER
b Fall River, Mass, Oct 14, 31. Study: Swain Sch Design, New Bedford, Mass. Work: Nat Aeronaut & Space Admin, Dept of Interior, Washington, DC. Exhib: American Artists & Water Reclamation, Nat Gallery Art, Washington, DC, 72; Smithsonian Inst Traveling Exhib, 72-73; Corcoran Gallery Art, Washingon, DC, 74; 107th Ann, Am Watercolor Soc, New York, 74; Washington Area Art, US Info Agency Worldwide Tour, 75-76. Collections Arranged: Nat Air & Space Mus, Smithsonian Inst Art Collection. Pos: Dir fine arts prog, Nat Aeronaut & Space Admin, 61-74; cur art, Nat Air & Space Mus, 74- Awards: Cert Merit, Nat Acad Design, NY, Award of Excellence, Com Arts Mag, 76 & 77; Citation of Excellence, Am Inst Graphic Arts, 76-77. Bibliog: R J Williams (auth), James Dean painting the spirit of the past, Am Artist Mag, 3/71; R J Williams (auth), James Dean painter of the past, Southern Living Mag, 6/73; Alice Laurich (auth), James Dean, Focus Mag, 9-10/75. Mem: Washington Landscape Club; Hereward Lester Cooke Found (vchmn bd trustees, 73-). Style & Technique: Watercolor landscapes, realistic. Media: Dry Brush Watercolor. Publ: Co-auth, Eyewitness to Space, Abrams, 72. Dealer: Franz Bader Gallery 2124 Pennsylvania Ave Washington DC 20037. Mailing Add: Nat Air & Space Mus Washington DC 20560

DEAN, NICHOLAS BRICE
PRINTMAKER, PHOTOGRAPHER
b Huntington, NJ, July 20, 33. Study: Dartmouth Col; Harvard Col, with Ansel Adams & Minor White. Work: Int Mus Photog, George Eastman House, Rochester, NY; Mus Mod Art, New York; Univ Calif, Los Angeles; Portland Mus Art, Maine; Lessing J Rosenwald Col, Jenkintown, Pa; plus others. Comn: Poster, Maine State Comn on the Arts & Humanities, 70; poster & T-shirt, NC Folklife Festival, Durham, 75; poster, Maine Film Alliance, Augusta, 77. Exhib: Photog at Mid-Century, 59, Photog, 63 & Three Photogr, 63, George Eastman House; The Sense of Abstraction, Mus Mod Art, New York, 60; Sixth Minn Biennial, Minn Art Inst, 67; Photo in the 20th Century, Nat Gallery Can, Ottawa, Ont, 67; Into the Seventies, Ohio Art Inst, Akron, 70; Realists Invitational, SE Ctr for Contemp Art, Winston-Salem, NC, 73; one-man show, Univ Ga, Athens, 75. Collections Arranged: West Coast Photographers, Boston Arts Festival, 58; Traditional Piedmont Potters, US/USSR Track Meet, Durham, NC, 74; As Others See Us, Photographs of Maine, Maine Art Gallery, Wiscasset, 76; Directions in Maine Living, Portland, 76. Teaching: Head photog dept, Portland Sch Art, Maine, 68-72; instr photog, Penland Sch Crafts, NC, summers 69, 71, 72 & 78; instr graphics, Haystack Sch Crafts, Deer Isle, Maine, summer 72 & 78. Pos: Res craftsman, Penland Sch Crafts, 72-73; artist-in-residence, Sandhills Community Col, Southern Pines, NC; mem, Visual NC, 73-74; mem, Visual Arts & Archit Adv Panel, Maine State Comn Arts & Humanities, 75- Mem: Maine Art Educ Asn. Style & Technique: Silver prints and photo-silkscreens dealing with landscape and vernacular architecture, including highways. Media: Silver Print for Photography; Silkscreen & Intaglio for Printmaking. Publ: Illusr, Bulfinch's Boston, Oxford Univ Press, 64; auth, Lubec, Identity, Cambridge, Mass, 67; co-auth (with Jonathan Williams), Blues & Roots/Rue & Bluets, Grossman, New York, 71; illusr, A Social History of the Boston Private Clubs, Barre, 71; illusr, Portland, Greater Portland Landmarks, 72. Dealer: Carl Siembab Gallery 172 Newbury St Boston MA; Frost Gully Gallery 92 Exchange St Portland ME. Mailing Add: RFD 1 Box 242 River Rd North Edgecomb ME 04556

DEAN, PETER
PAINTER
b Berlin, Mont, July 9, 39. Study: Cornell Univ; Univ Wis, BA; Pratt Graphic Art Ctr; also with Andre Girard. Work: Delgado Mus Art, New Orleans; Mus Mod Art, New York; Brooklyn Mus, New York; Los Angeles Co Mus, Los Angeles. Exhib: 2nd Bienal Int, Madrid, Spain, 69; one-man shows, Bienville Gallery, New Orleans, 70, 73, 75 & 77, Allan Stone Gallery, New York, 70, 73 & 78, New Orleans Mus Art, 72, Heath Gallery, Atlanta, Ga, 75 & Alexandre Monett Gallery, Bruxelles, 76 & 78; 32nd Corcoran Biennial Am Painting, Washington, DC, 71; plus others. Pos: Artist in residence, La State Univ, 74. Style & Technique: Fantastic, magic, figurative paintings of reality in controlled expressionistic style. Media: Oil. Dealer: Allan Stone Gallery 48 E 86th St New York NY 10028; Bienville Gallery 228 Decatur St New Orleans LA 70130. Mailing Add: 686 Academy St New York NY 10034

DEANDREA, JOHN LOUIS
SCULPTOR
b Denver, Colo, Nov 24, 41. Study: Univ Colo, BFA; Univ NMex. Work: Sammuel Ludwig Collection, Neue Mus, Aachen, Ger; Everson Mus, Syracuse, NY; Rudolf Zwirner Gallery, Cologne, Ger; Fey & Northelfer Gallery, Berlin, Ger. Comn: Nude female figure, William Kaufman Bldg, New York, 71; seated negro youth, Countess Susanna Ratazzi, New York. Exhib: Whitney Mus Am Art Ann, New York, 70; Sharp Focus Realism, Sidney Janis Gallery, New York, 71; New Realism, Old Realism-Oanenburg & Roman Contemporaries, New York, 71; Paris Biennale, France, 71; Documenta 5, Kassel, Ger, 72; plus other group & one-man shows. Teaching: Asst art, Univ NMex. Bibliog: Bodies for sale, Village Voice, 71; The new corn god, Time Mag, 72; Udo Kulterman (auth), Radical Realism, 72. Media: Fiberglas. Dealer: O K Harris Gallery 465 W Broadway New York NY 10013. Mailing Add: 1235 Pierce St Lakewood CO 80214

DE ARMOND, DALE B
PRINTMAKER
b Bismark, NDak. Study: Study with Dannie Pierce, Carol Summers & Jules Heller. Work: Alaska State Mus; Anchorage Hist & Fine Arts Mus, Alaska Methodist Univ, Anchorage. Exhib: Charles & Emma Frye Art Mus, Seattle, Wash, 70; Alaska State Mus, Juneau, 75; Anchorage Hist & Fine Arts Mus, 77. Awards: Purchase Award, Alaska Centennial, 67; First Prize, Woodblock, All-Alaska Show, Exxon Corp, 75. Bibliog: Pat McCullough (auth), Alaskan Artist, Alaska J Hist & Art, 76. Style & Technique: Printmaking, mostly woodblock. Media: Woodblock and etching. Publ: Auth, Juneau—a Book of Woodcuts, 73 & Raven, 75, Alaska Northwest Publ. Dealer: Alaska Northwest Publ Co 130 Second Ave S Edmonds WA 98020. Mailing Add: 422 Calhoun Ave Juneau AK 99801

DEATON, CHARLES
SCULPTOR, ARCHITECT
b Clayton, NMex, Jan 1, 21. Comn: Designs for sculptured bank, Key Savings & Loan, Littleton, Colo, 67 & sculptured stadia (with Kivett & Meyers, Architects), Jackson Co Sports Complex Authority, 72. Teaching: Instr design, Franklin Sch Prof Art, 45-48; also lectr var art & archit depts, 60- Bibliog: Len Leddington (auth), Architecture as sculpture, Today Show, NBC TV, 66; Hermine Mariaux (auth), Freedom in space, Town & Country, 67; Mary Roblee Henry (auth), Live-in sculpture, Vogue, 70. Media: Concrete, Mixed Media. Publ: Auth, The sculptured house, Art Am, 66. Mailing Add: Genesee Mountain Golden CO 80401

DEATS, MARGARET (MARGARET DEATS BOTT)
ART DEALER, ART WRITER
b Houston, Tex, May 27, 42. Study: Univ Houston; Univ St Thomas, Houston. Exhibitions Arranged: Gulf Coast Invitational Sculpture Exhib, 6-8/76. Pos: Fine Arts writer, Galveston Daily News, 71-75; owner-pres, Loft on Strand Gallery, 71- Bibliog: Gay McFarland (auth), Living on The Strand, Sculptor & Wife Preserve Old Building, Houston Post, 5/73; Patrice McCullen (auth), Loft-on-Strand Features Eleven, Tex City Sun, 8/75; Dancie Perugini (auth), Loft-on-Strand, Houston Town & Country Mag, 4/76. Mem: Galveston Art League (vpres, 76-77); Galveston County Cultural Arts Coun (bd mem, 73-74); Young Women for the Arts of Houston. Res: Art movements and exhibitions for areas away from major art centers. Specialty: Contemporary paintings, sculpture, conceptual art and process installations. Publ: Auth, Sheila Hicks Searches World for Material & Fabrics, Galveston News, 73; auth, Nancy Hanks, The Gentle Persuader Brings Art to All People, United Press Int, 73; auth, Art World Competitiveness Disliked by Jane Freilicher, 73 & Piled Sugar, Sacrificed Painting are Michael Tracy's Statements, 74, Galveston Daily News; auth, The Arts of Galveston, Galveston Mag, 75. Mailing Add: 2118 1/2 Strand Galveston TX 77550

DEBASSIGE, BLAKE R
ILLUSTRATOR, PAINTER
b West Bay, Ont, June 22, 56. Work: McMichael Can Collection; Royal Ont Mus; New Col Univ Toronto; Indian Affairs Collection; Art Gallery of London, Ont. Comn: Panels (two 4ft x 6ft), West Bay Sports Centre, Ont, 72; eight bas-relief carvings, Chincousy Park, Bramalea, Ont, 72; six posters, Ojibwe Cult Found, Educ Dept, 76. Exhib: One-man shows, Samuel J Zacks Gallery, York Univ, Toronto, 73, Ont Inst for Studies in Educ, Toronto, 73 & Gallery 103, Toronto, 74; Can Indian Art, Royal Ont Mus, Toronto, 74; McMichael Can Collection, 75; Indian Art, Woodland Indian Cult Educ Centre, Brantford, 75-77; Contemp Native Art of Can (traveling exhib to London, Eng & Ger), 76; New Col, Univ Toronto, 76; two-man show, Walter Engel Gallery, Toronto, 76. Awards: Cult Grant, Ont Inst Studies in Educ, Dept Indian & Northern Affairs, 73; Third Prize, Aviva Art Show, Auction, 77. Bibliog: Michael Greenwood (auth), The Canadian canvas, Artscanada, 3/75; Shaking tents—medicine snakes, Arts Mag, 76; James Purdie (auth), Woodland Art, Globe & Mail, 3/76. Style & Technique: Representational. Media: Acrylic on Canvas & Watercolor Paper. Mailing Add: Excelsior PO West Bay ON P0P 1G0 Can

DE BELLIS, HANNIBAL
SCULPTOR, MEDALIST
b Accadia, Italy, Sept 22, 94; US citizen. Study: Univ Ala, MD, 20; also with Gaetano Cecere, Jean De Marco & George Lober. Work: Navy Art Mus, Navy Combat Mus, Pentagon & Smithsonian Inst, Washington, DC; Numismatic Soc; Bronze medallions, Rudolph Matas, Tulane Univ Libr, La & R Tagore, Consulate India, New York. Comn: Portrait medallions of Adm King, Burke & Richets & Navaquila, Navy eagle, US Navy; Groedal Medal, Am Col Cardiol, 49; bronze plaques for St Vincent's Hosp & Med Ctr, New York; Adm Arleigh Burke Fleet Trophy, Navy Mus, Washington, DC; Salmagundi Club Honor Award Medal, 72. Awards: Salmagundi Sculpture Prizes, 60 & 71; Adm A Burke Sculpture Award, 62; Am Artists Prof League Award, 64. Mem: Medalist Soc; Nat Sculpture Soc; Am Artists Prof League; Salmagundi Club (art cur, 60-). Media: Bronze. Mailing Add: 10 Holder Pl Forest Hills NY 11375

DE BLASI, ANTHONY ARMANDO
PAINTER
b Alcamo, Italy, Jan 1, 33; US citizen. Study: Pan Am Sch Art, New York; Art Students League, with Sidney Dickenson & Will Barnet; Univ RI, BA; Ind Univ, Bloomington, with William Bailey, James McGarrell, Henry Hope & Albert Elsen, MFA. Work: Riverside Mus Collection, Rose Art Mus, Brandeis Univ; Wichita State Univ Mus Fine Arts, Kans; Detroit Art Inst; Ind Univ, Bloomington; Bethany Col, WVA. Exhib: Midyear Show Contemp Am Art, Butler Inst, Youngstown, Ohio, 67; Mus Mod Art, New York, 68; one-man shows, Spectrum Gallery, New York, 68, 69, 71 & 73, Kresge Art Ctr, Mich State Univ, East Lansing, 69, 72 & 76, Detroit Art Inst, 72 & Razor Gallery, New York, 75 & 77; 33rd Corcoran Biennial Contemp Am Painting, Corcoran Gallery, Washington, DC, 73; plus others. Teaching: Chmn & artist in residence, Washington & Jefferson Col, 63-66; assoc prof painting & drawing, Mich State Univ, 66- Awards: Louis Comfort Tiffany Found grant, 66-67; First Prize, Exhib Am Art, Chatauqua Art Asn, 67, Founders Purchase Prize, Detroit Art Inst, 70. Bibliog: Emily Wasserman (auth), rev, In: Artforum, 4/68; Atirnomis (auth), rev, In: Arts Mag, 12-1/70; Gene Baro (auth), The 33rd Corcoran Biennial (catalog), 73; plus others. Mem: Col Art Asn Am; Midwest Col Art Asn; Art Students League. Style & Technique: Subject to change depending on the ideas being advanced. Media: Acrylic. Dealer: Razor Gallery 464 W Broadway New York NY 10012. Mailing Add: Dept of Art Mich State Univ East Lansing MI 48824

DE BORHEGYI, SUZANNE SIMS
ART ADMINISTRATOR
b Pittsburgh, Pa. Study: Milwaukee-Downer Col; Ohio State Univ, BA; Univ Ariz, grad study anthrop; Univ Okla, cert sec educ; Univ Wis-Milwaukee, MA. Pos: Dir, Albuquerque Mus, 74- Mailing Add: Albuquerque Mus PO Box 1293 Albuquerque NM 87103

DE BOTTON, JEAN PHILIPPE
PAINTER, SCULPTOR
French & US citizen. Study: Ecole Beaux-Arts, Paris, France; Sorbonne, Paris; Rollins Col, PhB; also with Antoine Bourdelle, Georges Braque & Jules Romains. Work: Metrop Mus Art, New York; Mus Mod Art, Paris; Albertina Mus, Vienna, Austria; Dallas Mus Art, Tex; Wallraff-Richards, Cologne, Ger; plus others. Comn: Paris Int Expos (painting), Fr Govt, 25; Seine River Bridge (painting), Int Paris Colonial Exhib, 37; HM King George VI, Coronation at Westminster Abbey (painting), HM King George VI, Eng, 38; San Francisco War Mem Poster, City of San Francisco, 42; America at War with H J Kaiser, City of San Francisco for Marine Mus, 45. Exhib: Carnegie Inst Int, Pittsburgh, Pa, 32 & 38; Brit Empire Bldg, New York, 37; Knoedler & Wildenstein Galleries, New York & Paris, 39 & 56; Calif Palace of Legion of Honor, San Francisco, 45. Teaching: Prof fresco, Ecole Beaux-Arts, Paris, 32-37; prof painting, Acad Montmartre, Paris, 32-38; prof fine arts, Acad Montmartre, New York, 57-59. Awards: Grand Prix, Salon Honneur Beaux-Arts, Fr Govt, 25 & Grand Prix, Expos Int, Paris, Fr Govt, 37; City Honor, Scranton, Pa, 70. Bibliog: A Frankenstein (auth), Jean de Botton, Calif Palace Legion of Honor Publ, 45; Frank Elgar (auth), Jean de Botton, Georges Fall, Paris, 68; Eric Newton (auth), Jean de Botton, Parrish Art Mus, 70. Mem: Salon Automne Paris (jury mem, 28-); Salon Mod Paris (vpres, 37-); Salon France Nouvelle (pres, 38); Nat Soc Mural Painters (bd dirs, 68-69); Am Fedn Arts. Style & Technique: Humanized abstraction. Media: Oil. Res: Chiaroscuro killed painting, Cezanne revived it; modern conception and the approach to contemporary art; French art through the ages; the art of the fresco through the ages. Publ: Auth, Fou-Fou Discovers America, San Francisco, 45; auth, Triumph of Hope (ballet), San Francisco Opera, 45. Dealer: Randall Galleries 823 Madison Ave New York NY 10021; Dalzell-Hatfield Galleries Ambassador Box K Los Angeles CA 90070. Mailing Add: 930 Fifth Ave New York NY 10021

DE BRETTEVILLE, SHEILA LEVRANT
DESIGNER, INSTRUCTOR
b Brooklyn, NY, Nov 4, 40. Study: Barnard Col, Columbia Univ, BA(art hist); Yale Sch Art & Archit, MFA(graphic design). Work: Am Inst Graphic Arts, New York; Design Collection, Mus Mod Art, New York; Woman's Bldg, Community Gallery, Los Angeles. Comn: 40 under 40 show, Archit League, New York, 65; catalog of the Art of Latin America since Independance (with Alvin Eisenman), Yale Art Gallery, 66; book design, Canavese, Olivetti, Milan, Italy, 68; poster design, Calif Inst Arts, Valencia, 70; spec issue design, Art Soc Wis, 70. Exhib: Communications Graphics, Am Inst Graphics Art, 72; 5e Biennale des Arts Graphiques, Brno Czech, 72; Color, Am Inst Graphic Arts, Whitney Mus, 74; Poster from the Vietnam Years, New York, 75; Women and the Printing Arts, Woman's Bldg, Community Gallery, 75. Teaching: Dir inst & graphic design dept, Calif Inst Arts, 70-74; pres feminist educ, Woman's Bldg Community Gallery, 73-; lectr at var cols & univs. Pos: Typographer, Yale Univ Press, New Haven, Conn, 65-68; designer, Olivetti, Milan, Italy, 68-69; designer, Calif Inst Arts, 69-74; co-founder & pres, Woman's Bldg Community Gallery, 73-; judge, Nat Endowment Arts-Civil Serv Comn, 75; co-founder, ed & designer, Chrysalis Mag, 77- Awards: Grand Award Excellence, Soc Publ Designers, 71; Communication Graphics Awards, Am Inst Graphic Arts, 72; IBM Fel, Int Design Conf Aspen, 74. Bibliog: Gilles de Bure (auth), Right on Sheila, Creations Recherches Esthetiques Europeenes, 73. Mem: Am Inst Graphic Arts. Publ: Ed, Calif Institute of the Arts: prologue to a community, Vol 7 No 2 & A reexamination of some aspects of the design arts from the perspective of the women designer, Arts Soc, 74; auth, A reevaluation of design, Icographic 6, 73; auth, Habitability, In: Proc of the Calif Chap Am Inst Archit, 74. Mailing Add: 8067 Willow Glenn Rd Los Angeles CA 90046

DE BRUN, ELSA
See Nuala

DECAPRIO, ALICE
PAINTER, INSTRUCTOR
b Marshall, Mich, Feb 10, 19. Study: Mich State Univ, AB; Northwestern Univ, MA; also watercolor with Arthur Barbour & Nicholas Reale; Hilton Leech Sch, Sarasota, Fla, with Valfred Thëlin. Work: Ocean Co Col, NJ; US Navy; RCA Corp Hq, New York; Rheem Mfg Co, NJ; Ringling's Circus World, Sarasota, Fla. Comn: Three collages relating to textile & sewing, Mary Ann Silks & Woolens, Evanston, Ill, 71; eight drawings of hist bldgs, Chatham Twp Bicentennial Comt, 76; Carousel Horse (drawing), Ringling Mus, Sarasota, 78. Exhib: Open Show, NJ Watercolor Soc, 66, 69, 73, 76 & 77; Watercolor Shows, Nat Arts Club, New York, 70-75; Ann Traveling Exhib, Nat Soc Painters in Casein & Acrylic, 70-76; Audubon Artists, 74-76, & Nat Soc Painters in Casein & Acrylic, 74, Nat Acad Gallery; one-person shows, Nat Arts Club, 77, SVt Art Ctr, 77, Short Hills Mall, Nat Carousel Asn Conf, Atlantic City, NJ, 77 & Benedict Gallery, NJ, 78; Nat Arts Club Anniversary Show, 78. Teaching: Instr watercolor, Madison-Chatham Adult Sch, 68-76, instr outdoor sketching, 70- Awards: Exhib Comn Award, Nat Arts Club Open Watercolor Show, 75; Grumbacher Award, NJ Watercolor Soc, 77; Louis E Seley NACAL Award for Achievement in Watercolor, Salmagundi Club, 77. Mem: Salmagundi Club; NACAL; Soc Marine Painters; Fla Watercolor Soc; Am Artists Prof League. Style & Technique: Strong black and white ink landscapes in realistic and impressionistic styles; drawings of carousel animals. Media: Watercolor, Charcoal, Pastel, Ink. Mailing Add: 27 Dogwood Dr Chatham NJ 07928

DE CHAMPLAIN, VERA CHOPAK
PAINTER
b Ger; US citizen. Study: Art Students League; spec studies with Edwin Dickinson. Work: Permanent Collection of Fusco Galleries, New York & in Collections abroad. Exhib: Interlaken, Switz, 66; Rudolph Gallery, Woodstock, NY, 67; Seamen's Bank for Savings, New York, 69; Artists Equity Gallery, New York, 70, 72 & 75-77. Fontainebleau Gallery, New York, 72 & 74; Lincoln Ctr, New York, 77. Teaching: Art dir & instr oil painting, Emanu-El Ctr, New York, 68- Pos: Art chmn, Nat Soc Arts & Lett, Empire State, 69- Awards: Award, Twilight & Onteora Club, Haines Falls, NY, 65; US Investor, 69. Bibliog: Samuel M La Corte (auth), Creative images, Clifton Leader, 70. Mem: Fel Royal Soc Arts; Artists Equity Asn New York; Kappa Pi; Int Platform Asn; Art Students League. Media: Oil, Watercolor. Mailing Add: 230 Riverside Dr New York NY 10025

DECHAR, PETER
PAINTER
b New York, NY, Apr 19, 42. Work: Mus Mod Art, New York; Whitney Mus Am Art, New York; Larry Aldrich Mus, Conn; Walker Art Ctr, Chicago; Fiberglas Tower Art Collection. Exhib: Highlights from the 1967 Season, Larry Aldrich Mus, Conn, 67; Contemp Painting & Sculpture, Krannert Art Mus, 67; Whitney Mus Am Art Ann, New York, 67 & 69; one-man show, Cordier & Ekstrom Gallery, New York, 67, 69 & 75; Twentieth Century Art from the Rockefeller Collection, Mus Mod Art, New York, 69. Media: Oil. Mailing Add: c/o Cordier & Ekstrom Gallery 980 Madison Ave New York NY 10021

DECKER, LINDSEY
SCULPTOR
b Lincoln, Nebr, 1923. Study: Am Acad Art, Chicago, 42-43; State Univ Iowa, BFA & MFA, 46-50. Work: Albion Col; Cranbrook Acad of Art, Bloomfield Hills, Mich; Detroit Inst of Arts, Mich. Comn: Eastland Ctr, Detroit, 57; Atomic Energy Comn, Oak Ridge, Tenn. Exhib: Exhib Momentum, Art Inst Chicago, 50-54; Whitney Mus Am Art Ann, New York, 56 & 60; Irons in the Fire, Houston Mus Fine Arts, Tex, 57; Recent Sculpture USA, Mus Mod Art, New York, 59; Pa Acad Fine Arts, 60; Midwest Sculpture, Cincinnati Art Mus, Ohio, 60; one-man shows, Mich State Univ, Kalamazoo Inst of Art, Mich, Zabriskie Gallery, 59-60 & 131 Prince St Gallery, 69, New York. Teaching: Instr, Mich State Univ, 50-62, Queens Col, 62-64, Cooper Union, 62-65 & Univ Wis, 65. Awards: Purchase Prize & Cantor Prize, Detroit Inst Arts, Mich, 56; Italian Govt Fel (work in creative sculpture), 57; Fulbright Fel, Italy, 57. Bibliog: The World of Lindsey Decker (film, drawings & sculpture). Mailing Add: 78 Greene St New York NY 10012

DE COURSEY, JOHN EDWARD
COLLECTOR, ART DEALER
b Kansas City, Kans, Nov 21, 30. Pos: Owner, Mary Livingston's Gallery 2, 74- Mem: Art Dealers Asn of Southern Calif. Specialty: Contemporary art on all subjects and in all media; abstracts; Western and American art; land and seascapes; Indian traditional and modern art; sculpture. Collection: Modern contemporary art: Western, Indian, land and seascapes, abstracts, sculptures. Mailing Add: c/o Mary Livingston's Gallery 2 1211 N Broadway Santa Ana CA 92701

DE COUX, JANET
SCULPTOR
b Niles, Mich. Study: Carnegie Inst Technol, two yrs; NY Sch Indust Design; RI Sch Design; Art Inst Chicago; asst to C Paul Jennewein, A B Cianfarani, Gozo Kawamura, Alvin Meyer & James Earl Fraser. Work: Many in pvt collections. Comn: William Penn, William Penn Mem Mus, Harrisburg, Pa; Madonna (black granite), Manhasset, Long Island, NY; St Benedict, St Vincent's Archabbey, Latrobe, Pa; St Benedict sculpture proj, Liturgical Art Soc; five pieces sculpture, St Scholastica's Church, Aspinwall, Pa; plus many others. Exhib: One-man show, Carnegie Inst; Artist of Year Show, Arts & Crafts Ctr, Univ Pittsburgh; plus many other group shows. Teaching: Resident instr art, Cranbrook Acad Art, 42-45. Awards: Guggenheim Fel; Widener Gold Medal, Pa Acad Fine Arts; Lindsay Mem Prize, Nat Sculpture Soc; plus many others. Mem: Nat Acad Design; Nat Sculpture Soc; Pittsburgh Assoc Artists. Media: Stone, Wood. Mailing Add: Gibsonia PA 15044

DE CREEFT, JOSE
SCULPTOR, EDUCATOR
b Guadalajara, Spain, Nov 27, 84; US citizen. Study: Acad Julien, Paris, France, 06; Maison Greber, Paris, 11-14. Work: Mus Mod Art, New York; Whitney Mus Am Art, New York; Philadelphia Mus Art; Smithsonian Inst, Washington, DC; Metrop Mus Art, New York; plus others. Comn: Soldier War Mem (granite), Saugues, Puy de Dome, France, 18; 200 sculptures in stone, Forteleza de Ramonje, Mallorca, Spain, 27-29; Alice in Wonderland (bronze group), Delacorte Found, Central Park, New York, 59; Nurses (mosaic mural), Bronx Munic Hosp, NY, 62; The Gift of Health to Mankind (bronze relief), Pub Health Lab, Bellevue Hosp, New York, 67. Exhib: US Contemporary Art, Moscow, USSR, 59; Ford Found Retrospective Traveling Show, US, 59-60; Festival of the Arts, Rose Garden, White House, Washington, DC, 65; New Sch Art Ctr, 74; Sculptors Guild 37th Ann Exhib, Lever House, 74; plus others. Teaching: Instr sculpture, New Sch Social Res, 32-39 & 57-65; instr sculpture, Art Students League. Awards: First Prize for Maternity, Artist for Victory, Metrop Mus Art, 42; G D Widener Mem Gold Medal for Portrait of Rachmaninoff, Pa Acad Fine Arts, 45; Brevoort-Eyckemeyer Prize, Columbia Univ, 75. Bibliog: Robert Hanson (auth), Jose de Creeft (film), CBS Camera 3, 67; Alfredo Gomez-Gil (auth), Cerebros Espanoles en USA, 71; Jules Campos (auth), Jose de Creeft, 72. Mem: Fel Nat Sculptor Soc; Audubon Artists (vpres, 58); fel Nat Inst Arts & Lett; academician Nat Acad Design (vpres, 72); founding mem Sculptors Guild (exec bd, 40, vpres, 58); plus others. Style & Technique: Direct carving. Media: Stone, Marble. Mailing Add: c/o Kennedy Galleries 40 W 57th St New York NY 10019

DE CREEFT, LORRIE J
See Goulet, Lorrie

DE DIEGO, JULIO
PAINTER, ILLUSTRATOR
b Madrid, Spain, May 9, 00; US citizen. Study: Study in Madrid, Paris & Rome. Work: Metrop Mus Art, New York; Wash Univ, St Louis, Mo; Montclair Art Mus, NJ; Encycl Britannica, New York; Santa Barbara Mus Art; plus others. Comn: Murals & chapel doors, St Gregory Church, Chicago, 29; Bullfight (mural), Hotel Sherman, Chicago, 33; Ft Sheridan (mural), Ft Sheridan, Chicago, 36; Story of Wine (mural), Hotels Ambassador & Sherman, Chicago, 37; metal sculptures & murals, Ling Nang Restaurant, New York, 59; also many others. Exhib: One-man show, Art Inst Chicago, 35; Surrealist Exhib, Paris, France & London, Eng, 47; Int Cult Affairs Exhib, Dept of State, Paris, London & Rome, 48; Pa Acad Fine Arts, Philadelphia & Carnegie Inst, Pittsburgh, several yrs; plus others. Teaching: Prof painting, Art Inst Chicago, 39-40; prof painting, Univ Denver, 48-52; prof painting, Artist Equity Workshop, 55-57; plus others. Awards: Men & Steel Show First Prize, Birmingham Mus, Ala, 54, Cotton Exhib First Prize, 56; First Prize for the Figure, Arvida Corp, Sarasota, Fla, 71; plus others. Bibliog: Bruce Henderson (auth), He paints weird war & peace, Life Mag, 46; Ralph M Pearson (auth), Julio de Diego workshop, Desingne, 50; Bruce Barton (auth), 38 views of the Armada, Time Mag, 62; plus others. Mem: Artists Equity Asn New York (pres); Sarasota Artist Asn. Media: Oil, Watercolor, Tempera. Collection: African, Mexican, Indian toys and artifacts; imaginative junk. Publ: Auth, Comentaries: Europe 1952, Col Art J, 52; illusr, Have You Seen Birds...?, 68; illusr, A Stranger in the Spanish Village, 64; auth, The Book of Ah!, 70; auth, Cuckoo Heads, 71. Dealer: Frank J Oehlscchlaeger 107 E Oak St Chicago IL 60611; 28 Blvd of the Presidents St Armands Key Sarasota FL 33578. Mailing Add: 2235 Alameda Ave Sarasota FL 33580

DEDINI, ELDON LAWRENCE
CARTOONIST
b King City, Calif, June 29, 21. Study: Hartnell Col, AA; Chouinard Art Inst, Los Angeles. Work: Achenbach Collection, Legion of Honor, San Francisco; Libr of Cong, Washington, DC; NY Univ. Exhib: Nat Cartoonists Soc Group Exhib, New York; Int Cartoonale, Heist-Duinbergen, Belg, 64-66; Three Cartoonists Show, Richmond Art Mus, Calif, 68. Pos:

Cartoonist, Salinas-Index-Jour, Calif, 40-42; story cartoonist, Disney Studios, Burbank, Calif, 44-46; cartoonist-gagman, Esquire, Inc, Chicago, 46-50; cartoonist, New Yorker Mag, 50-; cartoonist, Playboy, Inc, Chicago, 60- Awards: Best Mag Cartoonist, Nat Cartoonists Soc, 58, 61 & 64. Mem: Nat Cartoonists Soc; Mag Cartoonists Guild (2nd vpres, 71). Style & Technique: Black and white wash, charcoal drawings and full color watercolor cartoons on social and political topics, preferably very funny. Publ: Contribr, Esquire, 43-50, New Yorker, 50-78 & Playboy Mag, 60-78; auth, The Dedini Gallery, 61 & illusr, La Clef, 70, Holt. Mailing Add: PO Box 1630 Monterey CA 93940

DEE, ELAINE EVANS
ART HISTORIAN
b Cleveland, Ohio, Jan 11, 24. Study: Oberlin Col, BA, 45, with Wolfgang Stechow; Radcliffe Col, MA, 51, with Jakob Rosenberg. Collections Arranged: Old Master Drawings (contribr, catalogue), 19th Century Master Drawings (collabr), 61, Newark Mus, NJ; 19th & 20th Century European Drawings (auth, catalogue), Am Fedn of Arts, 65; Views of Florence & Tuscany, Washington, DC, 68; Master Printmakers from the Cooper-Hewitt Mus (auth, catalogue), New York, 70; Winslow Homer, A Selection from the Cooper-Hewitt Mus (auth, catalogue), Washington, DC, 72; An American Museum of Decorative Art & Design (contribr, catalogue), Victoria & Albert Mus, London, Eng, 73; Etchings of the Tiepolos, Ottawa, Ont, 75. Pos: Asst cur drawings, Fogg Art Mus, Harvard Univ, 45-51 & 52-53; asst cur drawings & prints, Cleveland Mus Art, Ohio, 51-52 & Pierpont Morgan Libr, New York, 61-68; cur drawings & prints, Cooper-Hewitt Mus Design, New York, 68- Awards: Samuel H Kress Found Traveling Fel, 73; Nat Endowment for the Arts Mus Prof Fel, 76. Mem: Int Comt of Cur of Pub Collections of Graphic Arts; Am Fedn of Arts (nat exhib comt); Print Coun of Am; Am Mus Asn. Res: Specialist in 18th century French and Italian drawings, particularly the artists Gilles-Marie Oppenord and Guiseppe Zocchi. Publ: Contribr, One Hundred Master Drawings, Harvard Univ Press, 49. Mailing Add: c/o Cooper-Hewitt Mus Design 2 E 91st St New York NY 10028

DEE, LEO JOSEPH
PAINTER
b Newark, NJ, July 8, 31. Study: Newark Sch Fine & Indust Art, dipl, with Hans Weingartner, Benjamin Cunningham, James Rosati & Ruben Nakian. Work: Newark Mus Art; Springfield Mus Art, Mass; Cooper-Hewitt Mus, New York; NJ State Mus, Trenton; Yale Univ Art Gallery. Exhib: Drawing Soc Regional, Philadelphia Mus, circulated by Am Fedn Arts, 65-66; Meticulous Realism, Tawes Art Ctr, Univ Md, 66; NJ State Mus, Trenton, 66-70; 4th Invitational Painting & Sculpture, Van Deusen Gallery, Kent State Univ, 70; one-man show, Coe Kerr Gallery, 75. Teaching: Instr drawing & painting, Newark Sch Fine & Indust Art, 58- Bibliog: William H Gerdts (auth), Painting and sculpture in New Jersey, Vol 24, In: New Jersey Historical Series, Van Nostrand Reinhold, 64, 150 Years of American Still Life Painting, 70 & Art of Leo Dee, 75, Coe Kerr Gallery. Media: Oil. Dealer: Coe Kerr Gallery 49 E 82nd St New York NY 10028. Mailing Add: 38 Ridgewood Terr Maplewood NJ 07040

DEEM, GEORGE
PAINTER
b Vincennes, Ind, Aug 18, 32. Study: Sch of the Art Inst of Chicago, BFA, 58 with Paul Wieghardt & Boris Margo. Work: Indianapolis Mus Art, Ind; Ludwig Collection, Neue Galerie, Aachen, WGer; Evansville Mus Arts & Sci, Ind; Albright-Knox Art Gallery, Buffalo, NY; Allen Mem Art Mus, Oberlin Col, Ohio. Exhib: Contemp Am Painting & Sculpture, Krannert Art Mus, Univ Ill, Urbana-Champaign, 65, 69 & 74; Aspects of a New Realism, Milwaukee Art Ctr, Wis, 69; Paintings & Drawings by George Deem, Indianapolis Mus Art, 74-75 & Witte Mem Mus, San Antonio, Tex, 75; Artists Look at Art, Spencer Mus Art, Univ Kans, Lawrence, 78; Art About Art, Whitney Mus Am Art, New York, 78. Teaching: Instr, Sch Visual Arts, New York, 65-66; instr painting, Leicester Polytechnic, Eng, 66-67; instr painting, Univ Pa, Philadelphia, 68-69. Bibliog: Ronald Vance (auth), Painting Lists, Art & Artists, London, Eng, 2/68; Udo Kultermann (auth), George Deem, Arts Mag, New York, 11/77; Edgar Buonagurio (auth), Modern Vermeers, Am Art Rev, Los Angeles, 3/78. Style & Technique: Quotations from art of the past incorporated in work. Media: Oil on canvas; drawing, various media. Dealer: Allan Stone Gallery 48 E 86th St New York NY 10028. Mailing Add: c/o Artservices 463 West St New York NY 10014

DEFENBACHER, DANIEL S
DESIGNER, LECTURER
b Dover, Ohio, May 22, 06. Study: Carnegie Inst; Ind Univ; Lawrence Col, hon DFA, 50. Teaching: Lectr mod art & mus admin. Pos: Asst to nat dir, Fed Art Proj, Works Proj Admin, 36-39; dir, Walker Art Ctr, Minneapolis, Minn, 39-51; dir, Fort Worth Art Ctr, Tex, 51-54; mem exec comt, Int Design Conf, 51-62; pres, Calif Col Arts & Crafts, Oakland, 54-57; mgt consult design & assoc, Victor Gruen Assoc, Architects, Beverly Hills, Calif, 57-59; dir design & commun, Raychem Corp, Menlo Park, Calif, 59-73; mgt consult design & painter, 73- Awards: Carnegie fel, 29-30. Publ: Ed, Jades, 44 & American Watercolor and Winslow Homer, 45; auth, Watercolor—USA; contribr, Sch Arts, Better Design & others. Mailing Add: 2178 54th Ave St Petersburg FL 33712

DEFEO, JAY
PAINTER, PHOTOGRAPHER
b Hanover, NH, Mar 31, 29. Study: Univ Calif, Berkeley, BA, MA. Work: Oakland Mus Art, Calif; San Francisco Mus Art; Pasadena Mus Art, Calif. Exhib: Sixteen Americans, Mus Mod Art, New York, 58; Pasadena Mus Art, 67; San Francisco Mus Art, 68; Oakland Mus Art, 70; Poets of the Cities, Dallas Mus Fine Arts & San Francisco Mus Art, 75; Calif Painting & Sculpture, San Francisco Mus Art, 76 & Nat Gallery, Washington, DC, 77; Perceptions of the Spirit—20th Century Am Art, Indianapolis Mus Art, Ind, 77; Mod Era, Bay Area Update, Huntsville Mus Art, Ala, 77. Teaching: Instr drawing & painting, San Francisco Art Inst, 62-70 & Sonoma State Col. Awards: Sigmund Martin Heller Fel, 51; Nat Endowment for the Arts, 73. Bibliog: Bruce Conner (auth, film), The Rose, 64. Style & Technique: Abstract/symbolic imagery; expressionistic and traditional styles combined. Media: Acrylic, Mixed-Media. Mailing Add: 29 Millard Rd Larkspur CA 94939

DE FOIX-CRENASCOL, LOUIS
ART HISTORIAN, EDUCATOR
b Italy, June 2, 21; US citizen. Study: Maffeo Vegio State Col, Italy, MA; Pontif Univ St Anselm, Rome, LLD; Inst Archaeol & Art Hist, Univ Rome, with Cesare Brandi, dipl. Collections Arranged: Joseph Stella Retrospective, 64, Haitian Artists, 65, Religion in the Art of Haiti, 68, Imperial China, 77 & Shapes & Techniques of Oriental Pottery, 78, Seton Hall Univ. Teaching: Prof art hist, Seton Hall Univ, 61-, chmn dept art, 68-77. Pos: Inspector antiq & fine art, Ital Govt, 53-57; dir art gallery, Seton Hall Univ, 63-68, dir art ctr, 74-77; founder & cur, Wang Fang-yu Collection of Oriental Art, 77- Awards: Fulbright scholar, 65; Knight Comdr SS Mauritius & Lazarus (Italy), Knight of Malta. Mem: Asn Int Archeol Classique; Nat Trust Hist Preserv; Col Art Asn Am; Soc Archit Historians. Res: Italian Renaissance painting and architecture; Indian and Far Eastern art. Publ: Co-auth, Franchino Gaffurio (1451-1522), 51; auth, The Pallavicino chorals and the Lombard miniature of the 15th century, 55; auth, The incoronata of Lodi, 56; also contribr to many Europ & Am art jour & mag. Mailing Add: Dept of Art Seton Hall Univ South Orange NJ 07079

DE FOREST, ROY DEAN
PAINTER, SCULPTOR
b North Platte, Nebr, Feb 11, 30. Study: Yakima Jr Col, 48-50; Calif Sch Fine Arts, 50-52; San Francisco State Col, BA, MA. Work: San Francisco Mus Art; Art Inst Chicago; Joslyn Art Mus, Omaha, Nebr; Crocker Art Mus, Sacramento, Calif; Whitney Mus Am Art, New York; plus others. Exhib: West Coast Now, group exhibs at Portland, Ore, San Francisco, Los Angeles, New York & Paris 68; retrospective exhib, Whitney Mus Am Art, San Francisco Mus Art, Utah Art Ctr, Denver Art Mus & Fort Worth Art Ctr, 68-74; Biennial Painting & Sculpture, Univ Ill, 69 & 73; The Spirit of the Comics, Am Fedn Arts, Philadelphia, 70-71; one-man shows, Hansen-Fuller Gallery, San Francisco & Allan Frumkin Gallery, New York & Chicago; Galerie Darthea Speyer, Paris; Benton Gallery, Santa Fe, NMex; plus many other group & one-man shows. Teaching: Calif, 63-65; prof painting & drawing, Univ Calif, Davis, 65- Pos: Dir, Larsen Gallery, Yakima Jr Col, 58-60. Awards: Neallie Sullivan Award, San Francisco Art Asn, 64; Purchase Prize, La Jolla Art Mus, 65; Nat Endowment for Arts, 72. Bibliog: Article, In: Art Int, Vol 12; Thomas Albright (auth), Wildest of funk art, San Francisco Chronicle, 2/6/69; Charles Johnson (auth), The new symbolism, Sacramento Bee, 4/13/69. Mem: San Francisco Art Asn (chmn artists coun, 64). Style & Technique: Dogmatic rustics. Dealer: Hansen-Fuller Gallery 228 Grant Ave San Francisco CA 94108; Allan Frumkin Gallery 41 E 57th St New York NY 10022. Mailing Add: PO Box 47 Port Costa CA 94569

DE GARTHE, WILLIAM EDWARD
PAINTER, SCULPTOR
b Finland, Apr 14, 07; Can citizen. Study: Studied art in Montreal. Work: Mt Allison Univ, Sackville, NB; Art Students League; Acad Belle Art, Rome, Italy; Acad Grande Chaumiere, Paris, France; Acad Julian, Paris; plus others in pvt collections. Exhib: One-man shows, Montreal, Toronto, Rothesay, Fla, West Indies & others; group shows, Royal Soc Marine Painters, London, Eng, also in Europe, West Indies, Can & US. Mem: Int Platform Asn; fel Int Inst Art & Lett; Nova Scotia Mus Fine Arts (past pres); Am Artist Prof League; Royal Soc Marine Painters. Media: Oil. Publ: Auth, Painting the Sea; auth, This is Peggy's Cove. Mailing Add: Ocean Gallery Peggy's Cove NS B0J 2N0 Can

DEGEN, PAUL
ILLUSTRATOR
b Basel, Switz, Mar 24, 41. Study: Basel Kunstgewerbeschule, 56-60; also with Herbert Leupin, 64. Pos: Art dir, Theo Ballmer Studios, Paris, 60-62; art dir, Stand Art Publicidade, Rio De Janeiro, 70-71. Style & Technique: Pastel, watercolor, pen-ink; collage sculptor. Publ: Illustrations in New Yorker, NY Times, Esquire, Harpers & Ms Mag, plus others. Mailing Add: 106 Bedford St 4E New York NY 10014

DE GERENDAY, LACI ANTHONY
SCULPTOR
b Budapest, Hungary, Aug 17, 11. Study: SDak Sch Mines & Technol; Ursinus Col; Nat Acad Design; Beaux Arts Inst, New York. Work: Salle d'Honneur, Mus Africa, Algiers; Adm Farragut Medal, NY Univ Hall of Fame Mus. Comn: Wood reliefs, Fed Govt, Tell City, Ind, 39 & Aberdeen, SDak, 41; gold medal, Soc Elec Engrs, 60; bronze relief, St Francis of Assisi Sch, Torrington, Conn, 65; bronze medal, NY Univ Hall of Fame, 70. Exhib: Pa Mus, Philadelphia; Acad Arts & Lett, New York; Nat Acad Design, New York; Smithsonian Inst, Washington, DC; Gold Medal Exhib, Archit League, New York. Awards: Lindsey Morris Mem Awards, Allied Artists Am, 69 & 76, Silver Medal of Honor, 77; Coun Am Artists Soc Award, Nat Sculpture Soc, 77. Mem: Hudson Valley Art Asn; Nat Soc Lit & the Arts; Acad Artists Asn; Fel Nat Sculpture Soc; Allied Artists Am. Style & Technique: Based on nature, but abstracted in the sense that forms and planes are utilized for expression. Media: Wood, Bronze. Mailing Add: 22-27 76th St Jackson Heights NY 11370

DEGOOYER, KIRK ALAN
GALLERY DIRECTOR, ART ADMINISTRATOR
b Houston, Tex. Study: Univ Calif, BA; Inst Arts Admin, Harvard Univ, cert; also with James Strombotne & Connor Everts. Collections Arranged: Photographic Process (auth, catalogue), 74, Impressionists & the Salon 1874-1886, 74, Fong Chung Ray, 75, Joseph Beuys (ed, catalogue), 75, F W Billing & the 19th Century Landscape in America, 76, Joe Deal, 77, Myrna Shiras, 78, Käthe Kollwitz, (ed, catalogue), 78 & Eleanore Lazarof (co-auth, catalogue), 78, Univ Calif Art Galleries, Riverside. Teaching: Intern coordr mus studies, Univ Calif, Riverside, 75- Pos: Exec vpres, Art Spies Inc, 72-; gallery dir, Inland Empire Gallery, Riverside, 75-76; dir art galleries, Univ Calif, Riverside, 74- Bibliog: Alan Horowitz (auth), Profile: Kirk deGooyer, Inland Empire Mag, 76; Pat Eickman (auth), Kirk deGooyer: the artful battle against apathy, Riverside Press-Enterprise, 78; Jan van der Marck (auth), Inside Europe outside Europe, Artforum, 78. Res: American and European art post 1900 as well as 19th century American landscape. Publ: Auth, Peter Liashkow/Stephen Zaima, Art Galleries, Univ Calif, Riverside, 76. Mailing Add: PO Box 5014 Riverside CA 92517

DE GRAAFF, MR & MRS JAN
COLLECTORS, PATRONS
Collection: Structurist, Barbizon paintings and sculpture. Mailing Add: 14 Sutton Pl S New York NY 10022

DE GRAZIA, ETTORE TED
PAINTER
b Morenci, Ariz, June 14, 09. Study: Univ Ariz, BA, 44, BS & MA, 45. Work: Way of the Cross (paintings depicting 15 stas of the cross); Kino Collection (scenes from life of Jesuit priest Father Eusebio Kino). Comn: Los Ninos (painting), reproduced as UNICEF greeting card, 60. Exhib: Numerous one-man shows, 32- Awards: Achievement Award, Univ Ariz, 68. Style & Technique: Palette knife. Publ: Auth, De Grazia and his Mountain the Superstition, 72 & auth, De Grazia Paints Cabeza De Vaca, 73, Univ Ariz; auth, De Grazia Moods in Gold, Silver, Precious Gems and Cookies, 74; auth, De Grazia Paints the Papago Indian Legends, 75; plus others. Mailing Add: 6300 N Swan Tucson AZ 85718

DEGROAT, DIANE L
ILLUSTRATOR, DESIGNER
b Newton, NJ, May 24, 47. Study: New York Phoenix Sch of Design, summer 64; Pratt Inst, 65-69, BFA. Comn: Ann Report, Robert Wood Johnson Found. Exhib: Soc Illusr Ann Nat Exhib, New York, 73 & 75; Insides, 74 & Ann Bk Show, 78, Am Inst Graphic Arts, New York; Poster USA/74, Art Dir Club, 74; 15th Ann Exhib, Art Dir Club, NJ, 77. Pos: Designer & art dir, Holt, Rinehart & Winston, New York, 69-72. Bibliog: Upcoming illustrator, Art Dir Mag, 74. Style & Technique: Picture books in pencil, charcoal & watercolor; for older

children stylized realism in charcoal or watercolor. Publ: Illusr, Luke Was There, Holt, Rinehart & Winston, 73; illusr, Little Rabbit's Loose Tooth, Crown, 75; illusr, A Book for Jodan, Atheneum, 75; illusr, Antrim's Orange, Scribner's, 76; auth & illusr, Alligator's Toothache, Crown, 77. Mailing Add: 20 Sherman Ave Yonkers NY 10705

DE GROAT, GEORGE HUGH
PAINTER, PRINTMAKER
b Newark, NJ, Jan 7, 17. Study: Newark Sch Fine Arts, 34-38; Newark Prep Col, BA, 40; Art Sch Detroit Soc Arts, 54-56. Work: Monterey Penninsula Mus Art, Calif; Downey Mus Art, Calif. Exhib: Santa Barbara Mus Art, 69; one-man shows, Univ Southern Calif, 70, Monterey Penninsula Mus Art, 72 & Loyola Marymount Univ, 74; Faculty Exhib, Otis Art Inst, Los Angeles Co, 72. Teaching: Instr painting, Calif State Col, San Diego, 66-67; instr painting, Art Ctr Col Design, Los Angeles, 68-71; instr life drawing & painting, Otis Art Inst, Los Angeles Co, 68- Pos: Lectr various cols and mus and similar orgns, 60-; art critic, Pasadena Star-News, 68-70; artist-in-residence, Monterey Peninsula Mus of Art, 77- Awards: First Prize, 4th Ann Southern Calif Exhib, Long Beach Mus Art, 66; McBride Award, Pasadena Art Mus, 69; Ford Found Grant/Color Field Painting, 77. Bibliog: Mugnaini (auth), Drawing-A Search for Form & Oil Painting Techniques, Van Nostrand-Reinhold; Haddad (auth), Reproductions-1974, Haddad's Fine Arts Publ, 74. Mem: Am Asn Univ Prof; Los Angeles Art Asn (bd gov, 70-). Style & Technique: Expressionistic combination of abstraction with recognizable imagery. Media: Oil on Canvas, Intaglio Etching on Copper Plates. Publ: Auth, article in Am Artist Mag, 73. Dealer: Laky Gallery Carmel CA 93921; Assoc Am Artists 663 Fifth Ave New York NY 10022. Mailing Add: 148 Manzanita Way Salinas CA 93908

DEHN, VIRGINIA
PAINTER
b Nevada, Mo. Study: Stephens Col, Columbia, Mo; Traphagen Sch of Design, New York; Art Students League, with George Grosz, Julian Levi & John Hovannes; additional study with Adolf Dehn. Work: Columbus Gallery of Fine Arts, Ohio; Univ Calif, Berkeley; Columbia Univ, New York; New York Pub Libr. Exhib: Butler Inst of Am Art, Youngstown, Ohio; Mus of Fine Arts, Springfield, Mass; Jewish Mus, New York; Am Acad & Inst of Arts & Lett, Nat Acad of Design; Pratt Inst & Graphic Art Ctr Travelling Exhib; Ten Artists Foreign & Am, Lafayette Col, Pa. Awards: Oil Painting Award, Nat Acad of Design, Salmagundi Club, 68. Bibliog: Mary Carroll Nelson (auth), Virginia Dehn Paints Inscapes, Am Artist Mag, 77. Mem: Artists Equity. Style & Technique: Landscape abstracted into color, light and movement. Media: Oil on canvas. Mailing Add: 443 W 21st St New York NY 10011

DEHNER, DOROTHY
SCULPTOR, PRINTMAKER
b Cleveland, Ohio. Study: Univ Calif, Los Angeles; Skidmore Col, BS; Art Students League, with Nicolaides, K H Miller & Jan Matulka; Atelier 17, New York. Work: Metrop Mus Art & Mus Mod Art, New York; Seattle Art Mus, Wash; Minn Art Mus, Minneapolis; Cleveland Mus Art, Ohio. Comn: Aluminum grill, 59 & bronze room divider, 61, James Marston Fitch, Stony Point, NY; plexiglas relief, NY Med Col, Valhalla, 72; bronze sculpture, Union Camp Corp, Wayne, NJ, 72; bronze wall sculpture, Rockefeller Ctr, New York; bronze sculpture, Am Tel & Tel, Basking Ridge, NJ. Exhib: Whitney Mus Am Art, New York, 49-63; Recent Sculpture, Mus Mod Art, New York, 60; Hirshhorn Collection, Guggenheim Mus, New York, 61; Carnegie Inst Ann, 63; one-man retrospective, Jewish Mus, New York, 65; Boston Mus Fine Arts; Baltimore Mus Art; Dallas Mus Contemp Art; San Francisco Mus Art; Los Angeles Co Mus, Los Angeles; plus others. Awards: First Prize for Sculpture, Kane Mem Exhib, Providence, 65; Tamarind Lithography Inst Artist in Residence, 70-71; Yaddo Found fel, 71. Mem: Sculptor's Guild (bd mem, 60-62); Fedn Mod Painters & Sculptors; Artists Equity Asn. Style & Technique: Abstract sculpture in cast bronze (lost wax method) or wood. Media: Bronze. Publ: Auth, Buying art, 47 & Review of exhibition of oceanic art, Mus Mod Art, 48, Archit Forum; auth, Making & fabricating plexiglas sculpture, 68 & John Graham, 69, Leonardo; auth, Foreword for John Graham's System & Dialectrics of Art, Johns Hopkins Press, 71. Publ: Auth poems, Tracks, Fall 1977; auth, David Smith's medallions, Art J, 1/78. Dealer: Associated American Artists 663 Fifth Ave New York NY 10022. Mailing Add: 33 Fifth Ave New York NY 10003

DE HOYOS, LUIS
COLLECTOR
b New York, NY, Mar 6, 21. Study: Colgate Univ, BA, 43. Collection: Contemporary Latin American paintings; lithographs of Orozco, Rivera, Siqueiros; paintings and drawings of Covarrubias of primitive art objects, exhibited at the Museum of Primitive Art, New York; Guerrero stone sculpture, circulated by the American Federation of Arts. Mailing Add: 30 Lake St Monticello NY 12701

DE JONG, GERRIT, JR
LECTURER, WRITER
b Amsterdam, Netherlands, Mar 20, 92. Study: Univ Utah, AB, 20, MA, 25; Nat Univ Mex, 21; Stanford Univ, PhD, 33; Univ Munich. Pos: Pub lectr art appreciation, Brigham Young Univ, 25-, dean Col Fine Arts, 25-59, lectr aesthetics, 40-; dir, Centro Cult Brasil-Estados Unidos, Santos, 47-48. Awards: Distinguished Serv Arts & Lett, Utah Acad Sci, Arts & Lett, 53; David O McKay Humanities Award, Brigham Young Univ, 72. Mem: Fel Utah Acad Sci, Arts & Lett (pres, 48); Coun Latin Am Studies. Res: Art appreciation. Publ: Auth, An approach to modernity in art, 50; auth, Art in Brazil, Brazil, portrait of half a continent, 50; auth, The quest for beauty, Instr, 5/63; auth, Evolution of art in Brazil, 72 & auth, Brazilian architecture, 72, Mod Brazil. Mailing Add: 640 N University Ave Provo UT 84601

DEKAY, JOHN
PAINTER
b Ithaca, NY, Apr 8, 32. Study: Ithaca Col, BS, 55. Comn: Portraits, John F Kennedy, Nat Arch, Washington, DC; painting, President Johnson's Inauguration, Johnson pvt collection; portrait, Gen Eisenhower, President's Mus, Abilene, Kans; portrait, Pope Paul VI, Vatican City; portrait, Martin Luther King, Mrs King; murals, Sterling Forest Conf Ctr. Exhib: Athens, Greece; Paris, France; Madrid, Spain; Spoleto, Italy & Palm Beach, Fla; paintings of animals and birds publ worldwide. Awards: Maurice Fromkes Scholar to Segovia, Spain, 61. Mailing Add: 251 E 51st St New York NY 10022

DE KERGOMMEAUX, DUNCAN
PAINTER, EDUCATOR
b Premier, BC, July 15, 27. Study: Banff Sch Fine Art; Inst Allende, Mex; Hans Hofmann Sch Fine Art. Work: Nat Gallery Can; London Pub Art Gallery; Confederation Ctr, PEI: Hart House, Univ Toronto; Can Coun Art Bank. Comn: Exterior wall mural, Vanier Post Off, Dept Pub Works, Can, 70; Man Centennial Caravan, Dept Secy State & Man Govt, 70; shaped banners, Schoeler, Heaton Archit, Univ Ottawa, 71; art wall, Benson & Hedges, Ottawa, Ont, 71; mall environment, Schoele, Heaton Archit, Garneau Sch, Orleans, Ont, 71. Exhib: 3rd & 6th Biennials Can Art, Nat Gallery Can, Can Painting, Albright Knox Gallery, 66; Contemporary Prints & Drawings, Australia, 67; DeKergommeaux-DeNiverville Touring Exhib, Nat Gallery Can, 67-68; London Pub Art Gallery, 71. Teaching: Assoc prof drawing & painting, Univ Western Ont, 70-75; vis prof drawing & painting, Banff Sch Fine Arts, summer 74-75. Pos: Dir, Can Pavilion Art Gallery, Expo 67, Montreal, 66-67. Awards: Monsanto Can Art Competition, 57; Purchase Award, Minneapolis Biennial, Boutels, 58; Art Wall Competition, Benson & Hedges, 71. Bibliog: Groves (auth), DeKergommeaux at the Blue Barn, Can Art, 63. Mem: Univ Art Asn Can. Style & Technique: Large environments, nonobjective conceptual paintings. Mailing Add: 68 King St London ON N6A 1C2 Can

DE KNIGHT, AVEL
PAINTER
b New York, NY, 33. Study: Ecole Beaux-Arts, Acad Grande Chaumiere & Acad Julien, Paris. Work: Metrop Mus Art, New York; Walker Art Inst, Minneapolis, Minn; Norfolk Mus Arts & Sci, Va; Springfield Art Mus, Mo; Massillon Art Mus, Ohio. Exhib: Afro-American Artists, Boston Mus Fine Arts, 70; Black American Artists, Ill Arts Coun, 71; Projected Art/Artists at Work, Finch Col Mus, New York, 71; Nat Acad Design, 72 & Mus Mod Art, 72, New York. Teaching: Instr painting, Brooklyn Mus Art Sch, 69. Pos: Art critic, France-Amerique, 58-68. Awards: Childe Hassam Purchase Awards, Am Acad Arts & Lett, 60 & 70; Gold Medal Grand Award, Am Watercolor Soc Centennial, 67; William A Paton Prize, Nat Acad Design, 67-71. Mem: Academician Nat Acad Design; Am Watercolor Soc. Media: Gouache, Oil. Dealer: Babcock Galleries 805 Madison Ave New York NY 10021. Mailing Add: 81 Perry St New York NY 10014

DE KOLB, ERIC
COLLECTOR, WRITER
b Vienna, Austria, Mar 10, 16; US citizen. Study: Acad Art, Vienna, Austria; Graphic Inst, Vienna; Archit Acad, Vienna. Work: Art Mus, Toronto, Can. Exhib: Kleeman Galleries, 50 & 63; Bodley Gallery, 78. Awards: Welsh Award for Best Graphic Package, Package Designer Coun, 53 & 55, Prizes, 54 & 55. Mem: Art Dir Club; Package Design Coun. Interest: Sculpture in gold. Collection: Romanesque, Greek, Etruscan & African art; Romanesque Madonnas. Publ: Auth, Primitive Negro Art, 43; auth, African Collection, Eric de Kolb, 44; auth, Romanesque Madonnas, 62; auth, Ashanti Goldweights, 70; auth, Senufo Soothsayer Bronzes, 71. Mailing Add: 1175 Park Ave New York NY 10028

DE KOONING, ELAINE MARIE CATHERINE
PAINTER, WRITER
b New York, NY, Mar 12, 20. Study: With Willem de Kooning & Arshile Gorky; Moore Col Art, Philadelphia, Pa, DFA; Western Col Women, DFA. Work: Mus Mod Art, New York; NY Univ; Elmira Col, NY; Greenville Mus, SC; Drew Univ, Madison, NJ. Comn: Portrait of Casey Stengel & Eddie Robinson, Baltimore, Md, 58; portrait of Joseph Hirshhorn, comn by Mr Hirshhorn, 62; portrait of John F Kennedy, Truman Libr, Independence, Mo, 62-63; two portraits of John F Kennedy, John F Kennedy Libr, 62-63; portrait of Allen Ginsberg, Channel 13, NET-TV, 71. Exhib: 4th Int Exhib, Tokyo, Japan, 54; Sixty American Painters, Walker Art Ctr, 60; Carnegie Inst Int, 60; Whitney Mus Am Art Ann, New York, 62; Figure Painting, Mus Mod Art, New York, 63. Teaching: Prof painting, Yale Univ Grad Sch, 67-68; Mellon chair painting, Carnegie-Mellon Univ, 69-70; prof painting, Univ Pa Grad Sch. Awards: Hallmark Award. Bibliog: In quest of a famous likeness, Life Mag, 64; Lawrence Campbell (auth), Elaine de Kooning paints a picture, Art News. Mem: Artists Equity. Media: Oil. Dealer: Graham Gallery 1014 Madison Ave New York NY 10021. Mailing Add: 51 Raynor St Freeport NY 11520

DE KOONING, WILLEM
PAINTER
b Rotterdam, Holland, Apr 24, 04. Study: Acad Beeldende Kunsten ed Technische Wetenschappen, Amsterdam, 16-24. Work: Art Inst Chicago; Metrop Mus Art; Mus Mod Art; Whitney Mus Am Art; Walker Art Ctr, Minneapolis, Minn; plus others. Comn: Murals, New York World's Fair, 39 & French Line Pier (with Fernand Leger), New York. Exhib: Two Decades of American Painting, Melbourne Nat, 67; Frankfurter Kunstverein, Kimpass New York, 68; retrospective, Stedelijk Mus, Amsterdam, 68; retrospective, 68 & The New American Painting and Sculpture, 69, Mus Mod Art; Whitney Mus Am Art Ann, 69 & 70; plus many other group & one-man shows. Teaching: Instr, Black Mt Col, 48; instr, Yale Univ, 50-51. Awards: Silver Medal, Acad Plastic Arts, Rotterdam; Mr & Mrs Frank G Logan Medal, Art Inst Chicago, 51; President's Medal, 63; plus others. Bibliog: Dore Ashton (auth), included in The Unknown Shore, Little, 62; Oto Bihalji-Merin (auth), included in Adventures of Modern Art, Abrams, 66; Gregory Battcock (ed), included in Minimal Art: a Critical Anthology, Dutton, 68; plus others. Mem: Nat Inst Arts & Lett. Publ: Auth, articles in popular and prof publ. Dealer: Fourcade Droll Inc 36 E 75th St New York NY 10021. Mailing Add: Woodbine Dr The Springs East Hampton NY 11973

DE KUPER, MERLE PORTNOY
GALLERY DIRECTOR
b Polonia, Janowa, Pinsk, July 10, 10. Pos: Directress & pres, Mer-Kup Gallery, Mexico DF. Specialty: Contemporary art, including Goeritz, Rivera, Tamayo, Moreno, Siqueiros, Cuevas, Messeguer, Bejar, Nierman, Marysole, Baschet, Gutmann, Castaneda and others. Mailing Add: Moliere 328-C Mexico DF Mexico

DE LAMA, ALBERTO
PAINTER
b Havana, Cuba. Study: De La Salle Sch, Havana; Univ Havana; Am Acad Art, Chicago, with William Mosby & Joseph Vanden Broucke. Work: Pullman Bank Art Collection, Chicago; Home Fed Savings Art Collection, Chicago; Stop Publicidad, Caracas, Venezuela. Exhib: Ill State Fair Prof Art Exhib, 67 & 70; Munic Art League Chicago, 66 & 70; Galeria Sans Souci, Caracas, 73 & 76; Wildlife Gallery, Minocqua, Wis, 73-77; Talisman Gallery, 76; plus others. Teaching: Instr painting & drawing, Am Acad Art, 69-74. Awards: Diamond Awards 70 & 71 & Gold Medal, 70 & 75, Palette & Chisel Acad Fine Arts. Mem: Palette & Chisel Acad Fine Arts (bd dirs, 70-). Style & Technique: Realist. Media: Oil. Dealer: Talisman Gallery 115 E 12th St Bartlesville OK 74003. Mailing Add: PO Box 17 Chicago IL 60690

DELAMONICA, ROBERTO
PRINTMAKER, EDUCATOR
b Ponta Pora, State of Mato Grosso, Brazil, 33. Study: Sao Paulo & Rio de Janeiro. Work: Mus Mod Art, Rio de Janeiro & New York; Nat Mus of La Paz, Bolivia; Stedelijk Mus, Amsteram, Holland; Metrop Mus Art, New York; Smithsonian Inst & Libr of Cong, Washington, DC. Exhib: Brazilian Art Today, Royal Col Art, London, Eng, 64; New Talent in Printmaking, Assoc Am Artists Gallery, New York, 67; one-man shows, Pan Am Union, Washington, DC, Walker Art Ctr, Minneapolis, Minn & Columbia Mus, SC. Teaching: Instr graphics, Mus Mod Art, Rio de Janeiro, Nat Sch of Fine Arts, Lima, Peru, Univ Santiago, Chile, Cath Univ, Santiago, Sch of Fine Arts, Valparaiso, Chile, Minneapolis, Pratt Graphic

Arts Ctr, New York; instr, Art Students League, currently. Awards: Best Brazilian Printmaker, 7th Sao Paulo Biennale; Grand Prize, 2nd Biennale of Santiago, Chile, 65; Guggenheim Fel, 65. Mailing Add: c/o Art Students League 215 W 57th St New York NY 10019

DELANEY, JOSEPH
PAINTER, WRITER
b Knoxville, Tenn, Sept 13, 04. Study: Art Students League, with Thomas Hart Benton & Alexander Brook, 29-35 & continuing educ; NY Univ, writing with Horace Coohn; also with George Bridgeman. Work: Nat Gallery, Smithsonian Inst, Washington, DC; Univ Ariz, Tucson; Truman Libr, Independence, Mo; Huntington Hartford Collection, New York; New York City Mus; plus others. Comn: Environment, mural of 126th St & 7th Ave, Harlem Mus, New York, 71. Exhib: Contemp Am Painters, Whitney Mus Am Art, New York, 50; Univ Tenn, Knoxville, 70; Berkshire Mus, Pittsfield, Mass, 70; Studio Mus, Harlem, 71; US Embassy, Lusaka, Zambia, 75; plus others. Teaching: Art instr anat, Vt Acad, summer 68. Pos: Art instr & researcher, Works Progess Admin Fed Art Proj, 34-40; researcher, Am Wing, Metrop Mus Art, 36-38 & 38-39. Awards: Rosenwald fel, 42. Bibliog: Evelyn Brown (auth), Artist at work, Horman Found, 42; Hilton Kramer (auth), article, In: New York Times, 70; Roamin' fever, New York Mag, 5/26/75. Mem: Life mem Art Students League; Old Independent Art Soc; Bumshell Art Group; Artists Equity Asn. Media: Oil. Publ: Auth, Dralen Locke, Negro in art, 44; auth, Robert Dincus-Witten, Artforum, 70; auth, Circuit preacher on religion, Story of Am Bicentennial, Reader's Dig; also articles in Ebony 68 & New York Post, 71. Mailing Add: PO Box 383 New York NY 10010

DE LANGLEY, HELEN HAAS
See Haas, Helen

DELANO, JACK
ILLUSTRATOR, PHOTOGRAPHER
b Kiev, USSR, Aug 1, 14; US citizen. Study: Pa Acad of Fine Arts, Philadelphia. Work: Libr of Cong, Washington, DC; New York Pub Libr; George Eastman House, Rochester, NY; Univ Ky Photog Arch, Louisville. Exhib: Family of Man, 55 & The Bitter Years, 62, Mus of Mod Art, New York; A Vision Shared, Witkin Gallery, New York, 76; Masters of the Camera, Int Ctr Photog, New York, 76; Spoleto Festival, Charleston, SC, 77. Pos: Artist-photographer, Farm Security Admin, 40-43; photographer, Govt of PR, 46-47, dir films, 47-52, dir educ TV, 57-69. Awards: Guggenheim fel, 46; Cresson Travelling Scholar, Pa Acad of Fine Arts, 36. Bibliog: F Jack Hurley (auth), Portrait of a Decade, La State Univ Press, 72; Roy E Stryke (auth), In This Proud Land, New York Graphic Soc, 73; Hank O'Neal (auth), A Vision Shared, St Martin's Press, 76. Dealer: Sonnabend Gallery 420 W Broadway New York NY 10012. Mailing Add: RD 2 Box 8BB Rio Piedras PR 00928

DELAP, TONY
SCULPTOR
b Oakland, Calif, Nov 4, 27. Study: Menlo Jr Col, Calif; Calif Col Arts & Crafts, Oakland; Claremont Grad Sch, Calif. Work: Whitney Mus Am Art, New York; Walker Art Inst, Minneapolis; San Francisco Mus Art; Mus Mod Art, New York; Tate Gallery, London, Eng. Comn: 13 sculptures, Carborundum Abrasive Mkt Awards, Niagara Falls, NY, 69; sculpture-fountain complex, C C H Bldg, San Rafael, Calif, 70. Exhib: Whitney Mus Am Art Sculpture Ann, 64 & 66; The Responsive Eye, Mus Mod Art, New York, 65; Primary Structures, Jewish Mus, New York, 66; Sculpture of the 60s, Los Angeles Co Mus Art, 67; West Coast 1945-69, Pasadena Art Mus, 69; one-man shows, Calif State Univ, Laguna Beach, 74 & Calif Inst Technol, Pasadena, 75; La Jolla Mus Art, Calif, 73; Newport Harbor Mus Art, Newport Beach, Calif, 74; plus others. Teaching: Lectr fine arts, Univ Calif, Davis, 63-64; assoc prof fine arts, Univ Calif, Irvine, 65- Pos: Mem, San Francisco Art Comn, 64-65. Awards: Am Fedn Arts & Ford Found Grants, Mus in Residence Prog, Haverford, Pa; Nealie Sullivan Award, San Francisco Art Inst, 64. Bibliog: John Coplans (auth), DeLap, space and illustion, Artforum, 64; Alan Solomon (auth), Tony DeLap: the Last Five Years, Univ Calif, Irvine, 68; Lawrence Alloway (auth), Trio (catalog), Owens-Corning Fiberglas, 70. Dealer: Nicholas Wilder Gallery 8225 Santa Monica Blvd Los Angeles CA 90046; Robert Elkon Gallery 1063 Madison Ave New York NY 10028. Mailing Add: 225 Jasmine St Corona del Mar CA 92625

DE LARIOS, DORA
SCULPTOR, POTTER
b Los Angeles, Calif, Oct 13, 33. Study: Univ Southern Calif, BFA, 57. Work: Oakland Art Mus, Calif; Craft & Folk Art Mus, Los Angeles. Comn: Ceramic mural (8ft x 40ft), Compton Co Libr, Calif, 73; cement mural (8ft x 10ft), Security First Nat Bank, 76; ceramic mural (8ft x 16ft), Norwood Co Libr, Calif, 77; ceramic mural (2ft x 173ft), Lynwood Co Libr, Calif, 77; two sculptural wall panels, Camarillo City Hall, Calif, 77. Exhib: Scripps Nat Exhib, Claremont Cols, Calif, 66; 25 Yrs of Am Art in Clay, Scripps Col, 69; Am Crafts at the White House, Renwick Gallery, Smithsonian Inst, Washington, DC, 77 & Contemp Craft Mus, New York, 77; Craft & Folk Art Mus, Los Angeles, 77; Kohler Art Ctr, Wis, 77; Everson Mus, Syracuse, NY, 77; Indianapolis Mus Art, Ind, 78. Teaching: Vis instr ceramics, Univ Southern Calif, Los Angeles, 58. Awards: Purchase Award for Ceramic Sculpture, Calif State Fair, 61. Style & Technique: Cast bronze & cement, thrown ceramic sculpture, slab built clay, tiles & dinnerware. Mailing Add: 4023 Irving Pl Culver City CA 90230

DELAURO, JOSEPH NICOLA
SCULPTOR, EDUCATOR
b New Haven, Conn, Mar 10, 16. Study: Yale Univ, BFA, 41; Univ Iowa, MFA, 47; also in Italy, 53, 62, 66 & 71. Work: In private collections of Dr D Corradini, Quito, Ecuador, Dr B Clemente, Akron, Ohio, Rev Ralph Kowalski, Detroit & Bishop Ernest Primeau, Manchester, NH. Comn: Mankato stone sculpture, St Columba Cathedral, Youngstown, Ohio, 59; glass & plastic mural, Windsor Bd Educ, Ont, 64; bronze sculpture, Hiram Walker & Sons, Ltd, Ont, 67; bronze sculpture, Detroit Pub Libr, Mich, 67; bronze sculpture, Jewish Community Centre, Windsor, Ont, 70. Exhib: Walker Gallery, Minneapolis, 47; Mich Regional Exhib, Detroit, 48; Ecclestical Art Guild, Detroit, 50; Fine Arts Dept Fac Exhib, Art Gallery Windsor, Ont, 70-72; Biannale de Fiorino, Florence, Italy, 71. Teaching: Prof sculpture & drawing, Marygrove Col, Detroit, 47-59; prof sculpture & drawing, Univ Windsor, 60-, head fine arts dept, 60-73, head sculpture area, Fine Arts Dept, 73- Awards: Alice Kimball Fel, 40, Tiffany Fel, 41 & Elizabeth Pardee Scholar, 41, Yale Univ. Mem: Fel Royal Soc Arts; Nat Sculpture Soc; Col Art Asn Am; Mid Am Col Art Asn; Univ Art Asn Can. Media: Bronze, Marble. Mailing Add: 7560 Bircklan Dr Plymouth MI 48170

DE LA VEGA, ANTONIO
PAINTER, DESIGNER
b El Paso, Tex, July 13, 27. Study: NY Univ; Art Students League; also study in Mex, Spain, France, Italy & Port. Exhib: Pintores Nuevos, Galeria Ciga, Buenos Aires, Arg, 60; Antonio de la Vega, Galeria Fuentes, Mexico City, Mex, 61; Spanish Impressions, Galeria Gran Via, Madrid, Spain, 62; Portugal Viejo, Galeria Sesimbra, Lisbon, 66; de la Vega, Galeria Botto, Rome, Italy, 68. Pos: Art dir & designer, Cushing & Nevell, Inc, New York, 51-62; art dir & designer, Persons Advertising Inc, New York, 63-74; free-lance art dir, designer & illusr advert, 74- Mem: Nat Asn of Portrait Painters; Am Artists Prof League; Am Inst Graphic Arts; Artists Guild New York (vpres, 64-65). Media: Oil, Acrylic. Mailing Add: 2500 Johnson Ave Riverdale NY 10463

DE LA VEGA, ENRIQUE MIGUEL
SCULPTOR, DESIGNER
b Los Angeles, Calif, June 13, 35. Study: Los Angeles City Col, AA, 60; Los Angeles Co Art Inst, MFA, 64; study of sculpture with Renzo Fenci and of drawing & design with Joe Magnani. Comn: Two monumental symbolic forms, South West Produce Ctr, Nogales, Ariz, 65; Ressurrection (22 ft monument), Nat Shrine of the Millenium, Doylestown, Pa, 67; bronze equestrian monument, Robert Atkinson Mem Park, Cascade, Mont, 68; Birds in Flight (bronze forms), Air Force Village, San Antonio, Tex, 72; 15 ft sculpture/mosaic design, St Francis of Assisi Church, South Windsor, Conn, 75. Exhib: Group Exhib, Simon Patrich Gallery, Los Angeles, 67; one-man show, Galeria Teatro Casa de la Paz, Mexico City, Mex, 69; Valyermo Ann Art Festival (relig art), St Andrew's Priory, Valyermo, Calif. Pos: Art ed, Larchmont Chronicle, Hancock Park, Los Angeles, Calif, 65-70. Awards: Harriman Jones Portrait Award, Harriman Jones Clinic, Long Beach, Calif, 65; Nat Design Award, St Francis of Assisi Church, South Windsor, Conn, 75. Bibliog: Obras del la Vega, Am Embassy Mag, Mexico City, 68; Enrique de la Vega, Designers West Mag, 69; The Siesta Is Over (sculptures by de la Vega), KNX-TV Interview, Los Angeles, Calif, 72. Mem: Artists Equity. Style & Technique: Figurative, abstract, architectural, monumental; religious, secular and symbolic. Media: Bronze; epoxy/polyester resins; slate, stone and wood carvings. Mailing Add: 4507 Atoll Ave Sherman Oaks CA 91403

DE LA VERRIERE, JEAN-JACQUES
JEWELER, ENAMELIST
b Paris, France, Mar 8, 32; US citizen. Study: Escuela de Artes Suntuarias, Barcelona, Spain, 51; London Cent Sch, Eng, with Prof Edward Woodward, 57; Pratt Inst, with Prof Albert, MFA, 75. Work: Cooper Mus, New York; Nat Mus Design; Contemp Crafts Mus; Metrop Mus, New York. Comn: Processional Cross, Notre Dame Cathedral, Montreal, 59; Monstrance, Eglise du Gesu, Montreal, 59; Masonic Jewelry, 68, ritual pieces, 70 & commemoration medals, 75, var Masonic Lodges, New York. Exhib: Jewelry as an Art, Cooper Union Mus, 60; Americans 62 & Fiber, Clay, Metal, 62, Am Contemp Crafts Mus; American Jewelry Today, Everhart Mus, Pa, 63; Jewelry Int, Plattsburg, NY, 63. Teaching: Instr enameling, Haystack Sch Art, 68; asst prof sculpture & electroforming, Pratt Inst, 72-75. Awards: Hon Mention Enameling, Cooper Mus, 60; First Prize Jewelry, Greenwich Village Outdoor Show, 61 & New York Craftsmen, 63. Mem: New York Craftsmen; Am Crafts Coun; Am Electroplating Asn. Style & Technique: Enameling, traditional and modern techniques; ancient techniques of metallurgy. Media: Gold, Precious & Semi-precious Stones, Precious Woods, Ivory, Turtle Shell & Coral. Publ: Auth, Electroforming for Jewelry & Sculpture, 70. Mailing Add: 99 MacDougall St No 18 New York NY 10012

DE LEEUW, LEON
PAINTER, SCULPTOR
b Paris, France, May 5, 31; US citizen. Study: Art Students League; NY Univ, with Philip Guston; also with Hans Hofmann. Exhib: NJ Artists, NJ State Mus, 69; Montclair Artists, Montclair Mus, 70; one-man shows, Montclair Libr, 71, Highgate Gallery, 71, Fairlong Libr, 71, Rivercel Gallery, 75 & NJ Inst Technol, Newark, 76; plus others. Teaching: Instr painting & sculpture, Wilson Col, 59-60; asst prof painting, sculpture & drawing, Montclair State Col, 63- Bibliog: Russel Woody (auth), Painting in Polymer Media (two reproductions of paintings), Van Nostrand Reinhold, 71. Dealer: Discovery Gallery Valley Rd Clifton NJ 07013. Mailing Add: 317 N Fullerton Ave Montclair NJ 07042

DELEHANTY, SUZANNE E
ART ADMINISTRATOR
b Southbridge, Mass. Study: Skidmore Col, BA(hist of art); Univ Pa, with Richard Brilliant. Collections Arranged: Grids, 72; Nancy Graves: Sculpture & Drawing 1970-72, 72; Agnes Martin (with catalog), 73; Six Visions (with catalog), 73; Robert Morris/Projects, 74; Cy Twombly: Paintings, Drawings, Constructions 1951-1974 (with catalog), 75; Video Art (with catalog), 75; George Segal: Environments, 76; Pieces & Performances, 76; Improbable Furniture, 77; Paul Thek/Processions, 77. Pos: Curatorial asst, Inst Contemp Art, Univ Pa, 68-71, dir, 71- Mem: Am Asn Mus Dir; Greater Philadelphia Cultural Alliance (vpres, 77-); Am Fedn Arts (mem exhib comt, 75-). Mailing Add: Inst Contemp Art Univ Pa Philadelphia PA 19104

DE LESSEPS, TAUNI
SCULPTOR, PAINTER
b Paris, France, Mar 10, 20; US citizen. Work: Three bronzes, The White House; Lausanne Mus, Switz; Hirshhorn Mus, Washington, DC; also works in pvt collections of Princesa Jose de Baviera y Borbon, Madrid, Spain, Mr & Mrs Nicholas du Pont; plus others. Comn: Headless Horseman (metal), Sleepy Hollow Country Club, Scarborough, NY; Scenic View of London (mural), Cumberland Ct, London, Eng; entire collection in solid 18-karat gold & silver, F J Cooper, Philadelphia, Pa; sculptures, Baccarat Crystal of France; three fountains, Spastic Children's Hosp, Kuwait. Exhib: Cooper's Int Gallery, Amsterdam, Holland, 69; Palm Beach Galleries, Fla, 71; Agra Gallery, Washington, DC, 71; Incurable Collector, New York, 74; Osawa Gallery, Tokyo, Japan, 75; one-person shows, Bruce Mus & Bell Gallery, Greenwich, Conn, 77; plus others. Mem: Soc Illusr; Nat Art Mus of Sports (consult). Style & Technique: Sculptures depict tremendous movement and power with spatial quality; paintings are flowed lacquer in mystic realism style. Media: Bronze, Burnished Aluminum, Lacquer. Mailing Add: 535 E 86th St New York NY 10028

DELFORD BROWN, ROBERT
SCULPTOR, ENVIRONMENTAL ARTIST
b Portland, Colo, Oct 25, 30. Study: Long Beach City Col, Calif, AA, 50; Univ Calif, Los Angeles, BA, 52, MA, 58; also drawing with Howard Warshaw, Los Angeles, 53-54. Work: Involved in pvt collections of Walter C Hopps, Washington, John Coplans, New York, Edwin Janss, Los Angeles, H C Westerman, Conn, A D Coleman, New York, Arch Sohm, Margroningen, Ger & Arch Jean Brown, Tyringham, Mass. Exhib: Originale (happening, directed by Allan Kapro), Judson Hall, New York, 64; Environment Meat Show, New York, 64; Natural Hist (happening, directed by Jim Dine), Art & Technol, New York, 65; Book, Kansas City Art Inst, Mo, 71; Artists' Books (traveling exhib), Moore Col Art, Philadelphia, 73; Polaroid Photographis (traveling US & Can), Neikrug Gallery, New York, 73; New Photography, de Young Mus, San Francisco, Calif & Corcoran Gallery Art, Washington, DC, 74; one-man shows, Drawings 1959-1971, 71, Bob Brown & His Friends, Photographic Journal 1965-1969, 71, Turd Forest, 72, Tinted Photographs 1964-1972, 72 & A Bear Has Fur But the Wrong Kind of Face, a Manifestation, 74, Great Bldg Crack-Up, New York, in

asn with NY Univ, New Sch for Social Res & City Col of New York, 72- Pos: Pres, Robert Delford Brown Enterprises, Ltd, New York, 64; founder & pres, First Nat Church of the Exquisite Panic, Inc, New York, 64-; dir, The Great Bldg Crack-Up Gallery, New York, 64- Bibliog: Howard Smith (auth), Scenes, Village Voice, New York, 3/72; A D Coleman (auth), Two shows off the beaten track, New York Times, 1/72; Ernest Leogrande (auth), Neo-Dada in Cerise Hair, New York Daily News, 3/72. Style & Technique: Graphic, sculptural and work. Publ: Auth, First Protraits, A D Coleman, New York, 73; auth, Ulysses by Robert Delford Brown, New York, 75. Mailing Add: c/o Bldg Crack-Up 251 W 13th St New York NY 10011

DELGADO-GUITART, JOSE
PAINTER, SERIGRAPHER
b Tanger, Spain, Sept 24, 47. Study: Univ Madrid; Univ Cincinnati; Pratt Graphics Ctr, New York. Work: McDowell Colony Collection, NH; Galeria Circulo 2, Madrid, Spain; also many works in pvt collections. Exhib: Galeria Circulo 2, Madrid, 70; Galeria Panorama, Port, 70; Nommo Gallery, Uganda, 71; IV Expos Internationale de Dessins, Yugoslavia, 74; Philadelphia Art Alliance, Pa, 75; plus others. Awards: Pratt Graphics Ctr fel, 73; Edward McDowell fel, 73-74. Bibliog: Manuel Moreno (auth), Talking about painting, Sol de Espana, 7/70; Art & politics do mix, The Drummer, 4/75. Mem: Artists Equity Asn; Print Club of Philadelphia; Found for Community Artists. Style & Technique: Social abstraction (art with a political base); mixed media. Mailing Add: 94A Bartlett Pl Charlestown MA 02113

DELHOM, MARY MELLANAY
CURATOR, ART HISTORIAN
b Ft Worth, Tex, Feb 9, 08. Study: Brantley-Draughen Bus Sch; Tex Christian Univ; DePaul Univ; Queens Col, Hon PhD. Collections Arranged: 18th Century Wedgwood, Paine Art Ctr, Oshkosh, Wis, 65; Vignettes of Unusual Works of Glass (with catalog), 71, Japanese & Chinese Exhib, 72, Exhibition of William Littler, 74 & Exhibition of Bristol & Plymouth Porcelains, 75 & Carolina's Last Royalty, 76-77, Mint Mus of Art, Charlotte, NC, 71; chmn, Herculaneum Pavilion, Bicentennial Exhib of Wedgwood Int Sem, 76. Pos: Cur, Delhom Gallery & Inst Res & Study Ceramics, Mint Mus Art, 68-; organized Eng pottery & porcelain forums & seminars, Pennsbury Manor, 73-75 & 77; organized Sept seminar, Mint Mus & Eng Ceramic Study Tours for Joseph Stanley, Ltd, 74, 75 & 77 & overseas travel concept of The Roving Classroom; lectr hist Eng pottery & porcelain, Brit Studies Series, Univ NC, Charlotte, 77- Awards: Ruth Coltrane Cannon Cup, State NC, 72; Illustrious Moderns Award, Wedgwood Soc Chicago, 73. Bibliog: J K des Fontaines (auth), The Bastille Medallion-second thoughts, In: Proc Wedgwood Soc London, 66; Jane Roehrs (auth), Delhom asked to ceramics symposium, Charlotte News, 6/4/70; Janet Green (auth), Delhom Gallery is collection for study, Antique Monthly, 12/71. Mem: Am Ceramic Circle (founder & trustee, 70-); Mus Asn Gt Brit; Wedgwood Soc London; fel Royal Soc Encouragement Arts, London; Wedgwood Int Seminar (chmn & pres, 73-76, mem bd gov); plus others. Res: Tin-glaze, stonewares and porcelain at archaeological sites. Collection: Historical pottery and porcelain, including Oriental, Mid Eastern, Continental and English. Publ: Auth, James Tassie & Josiah Wedgwood: a study in parallels, Seventh Wedgwood Int Seminar, Art Inst Chicago, 62; auth, Two trial plates for the Catherine service, Ninth Wedgwood Int Sem, Metrop Mus, New York, 64; co-auth, Wedgwood from Midwestern collections, 6/65 & auth, A new center of documentary ceramics at the Mint Museum of Art, 4/68, Antiques; auth (catalogue), Encaustic Vases by Josiah Wedgwood, Wedgwood Int Sem, 76. Mailing Add: Mint Mus Art 501 Hempstead Pl Charlotte NC 28207

DELIHAS, NEVA C
SCULPTOR
b New Haven, Conn, Dec 29, 40. Study: Univ Conn; Southern Conn State Col; Empire State Col, BA. Work: Assoc Univs, Brookhaven Nat Lab, Upton, NY. Exhib: 23rd Ann New Eng Exhib, Silvermine Guild Artists, New Canaan, Conn, 72; The Heckscher Mus, Long Island, NY, 73 & 74; NJ Painters & Sculptors Soc, 73 & 75; Artists Equity Asn, New York, 75; 32nd & 34th Ann Nat Exhibs, Nat Arts Club, New York; Aldrich Mus, Ridgefield, Conn, 76; Norman Kramer Gallery, Danbury, Conn, 76; Cent Hall Gallery, Long Island, NY, 76; plus many others. Awards: Silvermine Guild Artists 50th Ann Award, 72; Sculpture House Award, West Chester Art Soc, 73; Award of Excellence, Huntington Art League, 74. Mem: Artists Equity Asn; Long Island Artists Alliance. Style & Technique: Studies of sculptural transparencies and the creation of illusions using sheet acrylic and cast plastic along with a laser beam and motors to produce kinetic light studies. Dealer: Hansen Gallery 80 Wooster St New York NY 10013. Mailing Add: 25 Locust Rd Brookhaven NY 11719

DE LISIO, MICHAEL
SCULPTOR
b New York, NY. Work: Joseph H Hirshhorn Collection; Minneapolis Inst Arts; Wichita Mus, Kans; Christ Church Col, Oxford Univ. Exhib: One-man shows, Minneapolis Inst Arts, 71 & Brooke Alexander Gallery, New York, 78; Addison Gallery Am Art, Andover, Mass, 73; Princeton Univ Libr, 73; Smith Col Mus Art, Northampton, Mass, 74; plus others. Bibliog: Ralph Pomeroy (auth), Literary figures, Art & Artists, 7/70; Anthony Clark (auth), Michael de Lisio, Minneapolis Inst Arts Catalogue, 1/71; Robert Phelps (auth), Portraits by a knowing naïf, Life Mag, 1/29/71. Media: Terra Cotta, Bronze. Mailing Add: 32 E 64th At New York NY 10021

DELLA-VOLPE, RALPH EUGENE
PAINTER, EDUCATOR
b NJ, May 10, 23. Study: Nat Acad Design; Art Students League. Work: Chase Manhattan Bank Collection, New York; Treas Bldg, Washington, DC; Slater Mus, Norwich, Conn; Pennell Collection, Libr of Cong, Washington, DC; Wichita Art Asn, Kans. Exhib: Pa Acad Fine Arts, Philadelphia, 52; Butler Inst Am Art, Ohio, 63; Final, Nat Inst Arts & Lett, New York, 63 & 64; Columbia Mus, SC, 76; Seattle Art Mus, Wash; Berkshire Mus, Pittsfield, Mass; plus many one-man shows. Teaching: Prof drawing & painting & artist in residence, Bennett Col, 49-77; prof drawing & painting, Marist Col, Poughkeepsie, 77- Awards: Wichita Art Asn Purchase Award, 50; Libr of Cong Purchase Award, 52; Berkshire Mus Drawing Prize, 54. Bibliog: Reviews of shows in NY Times, Art News & Arts Mag, 60-63; Arts 7: New York art world, Art Dig, 64. Style & Technique: Oil painting, beach paintings & figurative paintings; simplified forms. Mailing Add: Box 828 Millbrook NY 12545

DELLIS, ARLENE B
ART ADMINISTRATOR
b Brooklyn, NY, Apr 12, 27. Study: Antioch Col; Univ NC, Greensboro, BA. Pos: Head lending serv, Brooklyn Mus, NY, 49-55; head traveling exhibs & registr, Solomon R Guggenheim Mus, New York, 55-63; registr, Gallery Mod Art, New York, 64; registr, Marlborough-Gerson Gallery, New York, 64-67; registr, ed-designer & dir circulating exhibs, Bernard Danenberg Galleries, New York, 69-72; asst to dir, La Boetie Gallery, New York, 72-77; assoc dir, Helios Gallery, 78-; designer-craftsman fine leather. Publ: Ed, Max Weber drawings, 72; ed, Kurt Seligmann: His Graphic Work, 73; ed, inventory catalogues, 73 & 74; ed & designer, Hans Bellmer: Graphic Work, 74; auth, Essay on Kurt Seligmann graphics for exhib catalogue, Mus Fine Arts, Springfield, Mass, 74. Mailing Add: 320 Central Park West New York NY 10025

DELONEY, JACK CLOUSE
PAINTER, ILLUSTRATOR
b Enterprise, Ala, Nov 2, 40. Study: Auburn Univ, BFA, 64. Work: First Nat Bank, Montgomery, Ala; People's Bank & Trust Co, Tupelo, Miss; First Ala Bank, Birmingham; Coca Cola Co, Montgomery, Ala; Pope & Quint Co, Mobile, Ala; Fla Gas Corp, Winter Park, Fla. Exhib: La Watercolor Soc Exhib, New Orleans, 71-72; Ala Watercolor Soc Exhib, Birmingham Mus of Art, 71-72; 7th Juried Art Exhib, Mobile Art Mus, 72; Mainstreams 73 & 76; Hudson Valley 46th Nat, 74; WTex Watercolor Asn Nat, 75; Rocky Mountain Nat Watermedia, Colo, 76; Okla Nat Watercolor Exhib, Okla Mus of Art, 76; plus one-man shows. Pos: Book designer, Methodist Publ House, Nashville, Tenn, 64-65; illusr & painter, Ft Rucker, Ala. Awards: Purchase Award, People's Bank & Trust, Tupelo, 72; Second Prize, Washington, DC, Miniature Art Soc Nat, 72; Best Landscape, NJ Miniature Art Soc, 73; Purchase Award, Bluff Park Show, Birmingham, Ala, 77. Mem: Ala Watercolor Soc; La Watercolor Soc; Southern Watercolor Soc; assoc mem Am Watercolor Soc; assoc mem Allied Artists of Am. Publ: North Light, 4/78. Mailing Add: Rte 4 Box 560 Ozark AL 36360

DELONGA, LEONARD ANTHONY
SCULPTOR, EDUCATOR
b Cannonsburg, Pa, Dec 18, 25. Study: Univ Miami, BA, 50; Univ Ga, MFA, 52. Work: Del Art Mus, Wilmington; Lowe Art Gallery, Univ Miami, Coral Gables, Fla; Montclair Mus, NJ; Ga Mus Art, Athens; Nat Collection Fine Arts, Smithsonian Inst, Washington, DC. Comn: Marshalltown Iowa Community Ctr. Exhib: One-man exhibs, Allentown Art Mus, Pa, 65, Univ Mass, Amherst, 65 & Univ NH, Durham, 67; Nat Inst Arts & Lett, New York, 61; Humanism in Sculpture, DeCordova & Dana Mus, Lincoln, Mass, 70. Teaching: Head dept art, Tex Wesleyan Col, Fort Worth, 54-56; instr art, Univ Ga, 56-62, asst prof art, 62-64; prof art, Mt Holyoke Col, 65- Bibliog: Leonard DeLonga (catalogues of one-man exhibs), Kraushaar Galleries, 61, 64, 67, 70 & 76. Style & Technique: Figurative. Media: Steel, Stone, Wood, Bronze. Dealer: Kraushaar Galleries 1055 Madison Ave New York NY 10028. Mailing Add: 23 Woodbridge St South Hadley MA 01075

DE LOOPER, WILLEM
PAINTER, ART ADMINISTRATOR
b The Hague, Neth, Oct 30, 32. Study: Am Univ, BA, 57. Work: Hirshhorn Collection & Sculpture Garden, Washington, DC; Fed Reserve Bank, Richmond, Va; Nat Sci Found; Phillips Collection, Washington, DC; Art in Embassies. Exhib: One-man shows, Jefferson Place Gallery var times, 66-74, Phillips Collection, 75, Washington, DC & Jean Marie Antone Gallery, Annapolis, 78; retrospective, 60-75, Northern Va Community Col, 75; Group Seven, Washington Gallery Mod Art, 68; Washington 20 Years, Baltimore Mus Art, 70; Art Now '74, Kennedy Ctr, Washington, DC, 74; The Golden Door—Artist Immigrants of Am, 1876-1976, Hirshhorn Mus & Sculpture Garden & Nat Acad, 77; Nat Acad Sci, 77; retrospective, Fed Reserve Bd, Washington, DC, 78. Pos: Assoc cur, Phillips Collection, Washington, DC, 73- Bibliog: Rev in Arts, 65, Artforum, 67, Art in Am, 1/72 & summer 74, Art News, summer 74; An interview with Willem de Looper, Art Int, 12/77. Style & Technique: Non-objective paintings, much concerned with color. Media: Acrylic Emulsion on Canvas. Dealer: Protetch-McIntosh Gallery 2151 P St NW Washington DC 20009. Mailing Add: 2219 California St NW Washington DC 20008

DELORY, PETER
PHOTOGRAPHER, INSTRUCTOR
b Cape Cod, Mass, Oct 2, 48. Study: San Francisco Art Inst, BFA(photog), 71; Univ Colo, MFA(photog), 74. Work: Minneapolis Inst Art, Minn; William Hayes Fogg Art Mus, Harvard Univ, Cambridge, Mass; Mass Inst Technol, Cambridge; Nat Gallery of Can, Ottawa, Ont; Addison Gallery Am Art, Andover, Mass. Exhib: On Being Without Clothes, Minor White Workshop, Aperture Publ Exhib, 70; Ctr of the Eye Gallery, Aspen, Colo, 71; Mass Inst Technol, 72; Boise Mus Fine Art, Idaho, 72; two-man show, Addison Gallery Am Art, 74; Carl Siembab Gallery Photog, Boston, Mass, 76; Sheldon Mus Art, Lincoln, Nebr, 77; The West: Real & Ideal, Univ Colo, 77. Teaching: Instr photog, Ctr of the Eye Sch, Aspen, 69-71; asst photog, Minor White Workshop, Hochkiss, Conn, 72-73; instr advan photog, Sun Valley Ctr for Arts & Humanities, Idaho, 74- Pos: Dir photog dept, Sun Valley Ctr for Arts & Humanities, 75- Awards: Western States Art Found Fel, Boise Art Gallery, 76-77. Bibliog: Alex Sweetman (auth), Peter deLory Photographs, A Afterimage, Visual Studies Workshop, Rochester, NY, 11/76. Mem: Soc Photog Educ. Style & Technique: Hand-colored black and white photographs, 16x20 & 30x40. Publ: Contribr, Aperture, Inc, 73; contribr, Creative Camera, English, 12/73. Mailing Add: Box 276 Orleans MA 02653

DELSON, ELIZABETH
PAINTER, PRINTMAKER
b New York, NY, Aug 15, 32. Study: Pa Acad Fine Arts; Smith Col, BA, 54; Hunter Col, MA, 72. Work: New York Pub Libr; Boston Pub Libr; Univ Southern Ill; Columbia Univ; Brooklyn Mus. Comn: Etchings comn and distributed by Assoc Am Artists, Collector's Guild Ltd, Landmarks Collection & Framemakers, Ltd. Exhib: 100 Artists Honor the Prospect Park Centennial, 66; one-man shows, Hicks Street Gallery, 64, Paerdegat Libr, 72 & 74, Park Gallery, 73, Brownstone Gallery, 74 & Long Island Univ, 74; Brooklyn Mus Nat Print Biennials. Teaching: Instr printmaking, Pratt Inst, 62-66. Awards: Audubon Artists Medal of Honor for Graphics, 61. Mem: Soc Am Graphic Artists; League Present Day Artists (secy, 61-64); Contemp Artists (vpres, 71-75). Style & Technique: Oil painting on three dimensional surfaces; etchings combining intaglio and relief techniques. Media: Oil Reliefs, Etchings. Mailing Add: 625 Third St Brooklyn NY 11215

DE LUE, DONALD
SCULPTOR
b Boston, Mass, Oct 5, 97. Study: Boston Mus Fine Arts Sch. Comn: Two heroic figures (22 ft golden bronze), State of La Mem, 71 & two-figure group (16 ft bronze), State of Miss Mem, Gettysburg, Pa; four 8 ft bronze figures for The Alamo, San Antonio, Tex; Thomas Jefferson (8 1/2 ft bronze figure), Jefferson Parish, La, Bicentennial; Firestone Mem Exedra (100-ft diameter granite), Akron, Ohio; plus many others. Pos: Chmn Art comt, Hall of Fame for Great Am, NY Univ; adv ed, Am Artist Mag. Awards: Am Artists Prof League Gold Medal; Medal of Honor, Nat Sculpture Soc; Acad Achievement Gold Plate Award; plus others. Mem: Academician Nat Acad Design; Nat Sculpture Soc (past pres); Nat Inst Arts & Lett; Am Artists Prof League; plus others. Media: Bronze, Marble, Granite. Mailing Add: 82 highland Ave Leonardo NJ 07737

DELUIGI, JANICE CECILIA
SCULPTOR, PAINTER
b Indianapolis, Ind, Nov 27, 15; Italian & Am citizen. Work: Ill Bell Tel Co, Chicago; Art Inst Chicago; Civic Mus Revltella, Trieste, Italy. Comn: Sculpture in memory of John F Kennedy & Robert F Kennedy, Community of Milano, Italy, 69; stained glass windows, San Giorgio Maggiore, Benedictine Monastery, 73 & painting of St John Morocini, 77; stained glass windows, Cini Found & Benedictine M Nuovalese, 73; artistic glass sculpture of Murano for the best film presented at the VII Festival Int Film of Sch & Fiction, Trieste, 69. Exhib: Gallery Art, Muova Spazio, Tolgaria, Italy, 75; Gallery Art, San Marco, Venice, 75; La Cappella, Art Ctr, Trieste, 75; The Women of Today, Italian Inst Cult, Vienna, 75; Engravings, Int Ctr Grafics, Venice, 75. Collections Arranged: Exhibition of the Nude, Art Inst Venice, 75; 34th, 35th & 36th Biennales, Int Art Exhib, Venice, 68, 70 & 72. Teaching: Prof painting, Mercyhurst Col, Erie, Pa, in Venice, 66-; prof glass sculpture, mosaics & art hist Venetian painters, NY Univ, in Venice, 66- Awards: First Prize Int Painting & Sculpture, Fruili-Venezia Guilia, 71; Silver Medal for Painting, Pope Paul VI, 73. Mem: Arts Club Chicago; Renaissance Soc Univ Chicago; Artists Equity; Alumni Asn Sch Art Inst Chicago. Style & Technique: Drawing; engraving; silk screen; mosaics; lithographs; collage. Media: Glass; Oil, Watercolor. Mailing Add: Piscina San Moise 2053 San Mardo 30124 Venice Italy

DEL VALLE, JOSEPH BOURKE
DESIGN CONSULTANT
b New York, NY, Feb 6, 19. Study: Cooper Union Art Sch, Cert; Fulbright grant in painting-graphic design, Paris; Inst Fine Arts, NY Univ. Pos: Sr publ designer, Mus Mod Art, New York, 60-68; sr designer, Orgn Comt, XIX Olympic Games, Mexico, 69; publ design-prod consult, Whitney Mus Am Art, 70- Awards: 50 Best Bks (two awards), Am Inst Graphic Arts, 67; My Best Work, Mead Libr Ideas, 71; Cert Award, Printing Indust Am, 74. Publ: Designer, Sculpture of Picasso, 67, Treasures of the Philadelphia Museum of Art, 73, Great American Nude, 74, In Praise of Hands, 74 & Catalogue of the Collection Whitney Museum of American Art, 75. Mailing Add: 41 Union Square W New York NY 10003

DE MARCO, JEAN ANTOINE
SCULPTOR
b Paris, France, May 2, 98; US citizen. Study: Ecole Nat Arts Decoratif, Paris. Work: Sculpture, Brooklyn Mus, NY, engraving print, Metrop Mus Art, New York; sculpture, Norfolk Mus Art & Sci, Va; sculpture, Nat Art Collection, Smithsonian Inst, Washington, DC; prints, Joslyn Art Mus, Omaha, Nebr. Comn: Twelve stone high reliefs, Cathedral of the BVM, Baltimore, Md; sculpture for two chapels and three heroic size statues (with Magginis Walsh & Kennedy), Nat Shrine Immaculate Conception, Washington, DC; two heroic size marble portrait medallions (with J George Stewart, Architect), House of Cong, Washington, DC; sculpture for West Coast War Mem Second World War (with Clark & Beutler Architects), comn by Am Comn Battles Monuments, Presidio, San Francisco; two marble statues for House of Theology (with Brother Cajetan, Architect), Centerville, Ohio; twelve reliefs relative to St Benedict, Abbey of Monte Cassino Libr, Italy; plus others. Exhib: Nat and regional exhibs and in mus in US. Teaching: Instr sculpture, Columbia Univ, Boston Mus Fine Arts Sch, Nat Acad Design & Bennett Jr Col; instr bronze casting & drawing, Iowa State Univ. Pos: Mem joint comt artists and writers revolving funds, Nat Inst Arts & Lett-Am Acad Arts & Lett, 60. Awards: Nat Inst Arts & Lett Grant, 50; Medal of Merit, Am Acad Arts & Lett, 59; Saltus Gold Medal & Elizabeth Watrous Gold Medal, Nat Acad Design; plus others. Mem: Nat Inst Arts & Lett; Nat Acad Design; Nat Sculpture Soc. Mailing Add: c/o Nat Acad Design 1083 Fifth Ave New York NY 10028

DEMAREE, ELIZABETH ANN (BETTY)
PAINTER, COLLECTOR
b Denver, Colo, Oct 19, 18. Study: Cooper Union Sch Art; with Robert E Wood, Calif; with Edgar A Whitney, Herb Olsen & Mario Cooper, New York; also with Milford Zornes, Utah & Charles Reid, Conn. Work: Kissinger Oil Bldg, Denver; Van Schack, Littleton, Colo; Marathon Oil Bldg, Littleton; Cheyenne Pub Libr, Wyo; Rocky Mountain Energy Co, Denver. Comn: Ceramic plaque of oil scene, Indust of Lowell Williamson, Calgary, Can, 62; ceramic, Off Gov of Colo, 62; watercolor scenes of Denver bldgs, Cassidy Paint, Hilb & Co & J Signs, Denver, 69-72; Old Main (painting), Colo State Univ, Ft Collins, 70; watercolor portraits of children, James F Kuhns, Dallas, Tex, 71-72. Exhib: Denver OYO, Denver Art Mus, 68; Gilpin Co Arts Asn, Central City, Colo, 68-72; Southwestern Watercolor Soc, Dallas, 69-75 & Albuquerque, NMex, 72; Cheyenne Artist Guild Ann Exhib, 70-75; Am Watercolor Soc Traveling Exhib, 76; Watercolor West Traveling Exhib, Utah State Univ, 77-78. Teaching: Instr pvt classes, 68-; demonstr & lectr, art asns of Colo, Wyo & SDak, 68- Awards: Top Merit Awards, Southwestern Watercolor Soc, Dallas, 74, 75 & 76; Emily Lowe Mem Award, Am Watercolor Soc, New York, 76; John Young-Hunter Award, Allied Artists Am, 77. Mem: Denver Artists Guild; Cheyenne Artists Guild; Southwestern Watercolor Soc; Assoc Am Watercolor Soc; Artists Equity Asn. Style & Technique: Impressionistic, loose, covering many techniques and subjects; exploratory, experimental and forever changing. Media: Watercolor. Dealer: Austin Gallery 7103 Main St Scottsdale AZ 85251; De Colores Gallery 2817 E Third Ave Denver CO 80206. Mailing Add: 4989 E Iliff Ave Denver CO 80222

DE MARIA, WALTER
SCULPTOR
b Oct 1, 35; US citizen. Study: Univ Calif, Berkeley, MA, 59. Work: Mus Mod Art & Whitney Mus Am Art, New York; Basel Kunstmuseum, Basel, Switz. Exhib: Primary Structures, Jewish Mus, New York, 66; Sculpture of the 60's, Los Angeles Co Mus, 67; Whitney Mus Am Art Sculpture Ann, 68; When Activities Become Form, Bern, Switz, 69; Information, Mus Mod Art, New York, 70. Awards: Guggenheim Fel, 69-70. Bibliog: O Bourdon (auth), Walter De Maria, the singular experience, Art Int, 12/68. Media: Earth. Publ: Contribr, Hard core (land film ed 100), 69. Dealer: Noah Goldowsky Gallery 1078 Madison Ave New York NY 10021. Mailing Add: 27 Howard St New York NY 10013

DE MARTELLY, JOHN STOCKTON
PAINTER, PRINTMAKER
b Philadelphia, Pa, Sept 10, 03. Study: Pa Acad of Fine Arts; Carnegie Inst Int; Acad delle Belle Arte, Florence, Italy; London Royal Col of Design, Eng; additional study with prominant painters of the 1920's, including Henry McCarter, Daniel Garbel, George Luks & Tom Hart Benton. Work: Pa Acad of Fine Arts; Whitney Mus of Am Art, New York; Metrop Mus of Art, New York; Cranbrook Acad of Art Mus, Bloomfield Hills, Mich; Tel Aviv, Israel. Comn: Portraits of pres & fac, Mich State Univ, 43-51; over-mantel painting, Mich State Univ, 45; Mich on Canvas, Life Mag, 45-46; Niagara Falls, Niagara Alkilico, Buffalo, NY, 46. Exhib: Carnegie Inst Int Nat Exhib, Pittsburgh; Midwestern Exhib, Kansas City Art Inst, Kans; Pa Acad Fine Arts; Cranbrook Acad of Art Mus, Bloomfield Hills; Mich Acad of Sci, Arts & Lett (travelling exhib); Retrospective, Kresge Art Gallery, Mich State Univ; Youngstown Art Mus, Ohio; and others. Teaching: Artist-in-residence, Mich State Univ, East Lansing, 43- Awards: Gold Medal, Art Dir Club, 55; Distinguished Prof, Mich State Univ, 73; Artist of Yr, Mich Acad of Sci, Arts & Lett, 75. Media: Drawing, painting in oils, printmaking. Mailing Add: 5088 Powell Rd Okemos MI 48864

DE MARTINI, JOSEPH
PAINTER
b Mobile, Ala, July 20, 96. Study: Nat Acad Design, with Leon Krill & Ivan Olinsky. Work: Addison Gallery Am Art, Andover, Mass; City Art Mus St Louis; Boston Mus Fine Arts; Mus Mod Art; Metrop Mus Art; plus many others. Exhib: City Art Mus St Louis, 38, 41, 42 & 46; Corcoran Gallery Art, 41, 43 & 45; Va Mus Fine Arts, Richmond, 42, 44 & 46; John Herron Art Inst, 45; Nebr Art Asn, 45 & 46; plus many others. Teaching: Artist in residence, Univ Ga, 52-53. Awards: Prize, Nat Acad Design, 50; Guggenheim Fel, 51; Gold Medal, Pa Acad Fine Arts, 52; plus others. Bibliog: Rosamond Frost (auth), included in Contemporary Art: the March of Art from Cezanne until Now, Crown, 42; Emily Genauer (auth), included in Best of Art, Doubleday, 48; John I H Baur (auth), included in Revolution and Tradition in Modern American Art, Harvard Univ Press, 59; plus others. Mem: Assoc Nat Acad Design; Audubon Artists. Mailing Add: 103 W 27th St New York NY 10001

DEMARTIS, JAMES J
PAINTER
b Corona, NY, Mar 30, 26. Study: Acad Fine Arts, Florence, Italy, 50-54. Work: Pvt collections in Europe & US. Exhib: One-man shows, Ward Eggleston Gallery, Ruko Gallery, Marcaleo Gallery, Artemis East Gallery, Hicks St Gallery & Brownstone Gallery. Awards: Emily Lowe Award Painting, 61. Mem: Artists Equity. Dealer: Brownstone Gallery 76 Seventh Ave Brooklyn NY 11217. Mailing Add: 161 Berkeley Pl Brooklyn NY 11217

DEMATTIES, NICK FRANK
PRINTMAKER
b Honolulu, Hawaii, Oct 19, 39. Study: Long Beach State Col, BA, 64; Inst Design, Chicago, with Misch Kohn, MS, 67. Work: Cabinet Estampes, Bibliot Nat Paris; Libr Cong; Sheldon Mem Art Gallery; San Francisco Mus Mod Art; Columbia Univ. Exhib: One-man shows, Smithsonian Inst, Washington, DC, 76, Scottsdale Ctr for the Arts, Ariz, 78, Davidson Galleries, Seattle, Wash, 78, The Workshop Gallery of Letterio Calapai, Glencoe, Ill, 78; Biennial 77, Phoenix Art Mus, Ariz, 77; 2nd Ariz Print Exhib, Matthews Ctr, Ariz State Univ, Tempe, 77; 7th Ann Colorprint USA, Tex Tech Univ, Lubbock, 76. plus others. Teaching: Instr printmaking & drawing, San Diego State Col, 67-69; asst prof printmaking & drawing, Mt St Mary's Col, Calif, 69-70; vis prof printmaking, Univ Ore, 72; printmaking, Albion Col, Mich, 73-74; asst prof printmaking & drawing, Ariz State Univ, Tempe, 74-76, assoc prof printmaking & drawing, 77- Pos: Founder & dir, Pac Northwest Graphics Workshop, 70- Awards: Purchase 70-75. Awards: Purchase Awards, 16th Bradley Nat Print & Drawing Exhib, Peoria, Ill, 77 & 19th Ann Nat Exhib of Prints & Drawings, Okla Art Ctr, Oklahoma City, 77; Juror's Award, Biennial 77, Phoenix Art Mus, 77; Cash Award, Scottsdale Fine Arts Festival, Ariz, 77. Bibliog: Article, In: Vol 11, Artists Proof, Pratt Graphics Ctr & NY Graphic Soc Ltd. Mem: Los Angeles Printmaking Soc. Style & Technique: Strongly influenced by color processes related to printing of intaglio plates, viscosity and lately some photographic influence; somewhat visionary, surreal, poetic style. Mailing Add: c/oDept Art Ariz State Univ Tempe AZ 85281

DEMETRION, JAMES THOMAS
ART ADMINISTRATOR
b Middletown, Ohio, July 10, 30. Pos: Cur, Pasadena Art Mus, Calif, 64-66, dir, 66-69; dir, Des Moines Art Ctr, Iowa, 69- Mailing Add: Des Moines Art Ctr Greenwood Park Des Moines IA 50312

DE MILLE, LESLIE BENJAMIN
PAINTER
b Hamilton, Ont, Apr 24, 27; US citizen. Study: Hamilton Tech Inst; Art Students League; also with Leon Franks, Laguna Beach, Calif. Work: Portraits, President Nixon & others, Whittier Col Collection, Calif; Death Valley 49ers Collection. Comn: Portrait, Gov Ronald Reagan, Gov Mansion, Calif, 67; oil painting, Princess Lorayne Kamienski, Rynn-Berry, London, Eng, 71; oil paintings & sketches, US Sixth Fleet, Mediter (naval combat artist), 72 & Pearl Harbor, Hawaii painting, 73, Off Naval Art Collection. Exhib: Laguna Beach Festival Arts, 65-74; Death Valley 49ers Exhib, Calif, 69-; Lahaina Art Soc, Maui, Hawaii, 70; Grand Nat Ann Exhib, Am Artists Prof League, New York, 71-; San Gabriel Fine Arts Asn Ann, Calif, 72-74. Teaching: Organizer, dir & instr, sem for art orgn in US, 66- Awards: Best of Show, Am Artists Prof League, 71; Best of Show, Catalina Festival Arts, 72-74; Best of Show & Gold Medal, 72 & City of San Gabriel Award & Gold Medal, 75, San Gabriel Fine Arts Asn; plus others. Mem: Fel Am Inst Fine Arts (past dir); fel Am Artists Prof League; Coun Traditional Artists Soc (past pres); Death Valley 49ers (dir); Soc Western Artists; plus others. Style & Technique: Free style (traditional), representational; brush, palette knife or pastel; portrait, figure and still life. Media: Oil, Pastel. Mailing Add: 1432 S Coast Hwy Laguna Beach CA 92651

DEMING, DAVID LAWSON
SCULPTOR, EDUCATOR
b Cleveland, Ohio, May 26, 43. Study: Cleveland Inst Art, with William McVey & John Clague, BFA; Cranbrook Acad Art, with Julius Schmidt, MFA. Work: Ft Worth Nat Bank, Tex; State Nat Bank El Paso; Cameron Col, Lawton, Okla. Comn: Portrait bust of Euclid, Euclid Nat Bank Cleveland, 68; portrait bust of Charles Patterson, Cleveland Engine Plant, Ford Motor Co, 68; portrait plaque of Alvan & Estelle Macauley, comn by Alvan Macauley, Jr, 70; portraits of Mitchell, Sophia & Eric Kafarsky, comn by Karfarsky Family, 70; portrait of Marvin & Hue Prestwood, comn by Prestwood Family, 72. Exhib: 13th Ann Eight State Exhib Painting & Small Sculpture, Oklahoma City, 71; Nat Sculpture 74, 10th Ann Exhib, South Asn Sculptors Traveling Exhib, 74; 20th Ann Drawing & Small Sculpture Show, Ball State Univ, 74; 3rd Hawaii Nat Print Exhib, Honolulu Acad Arts, 75; Mainstreams, 75. Teaching: Instr sculpture, Sch Fine & Appl Arts, Boston Univ, 67-68; instr sculpture & drawing design, Univ Tex, El Paso, 70-72; asst prof sculpture & drawing, Univ Tex, Austin, 72- Awards: First Award in Sculpture, Int Designer Craftsman El Paso, 71; Best Sculpture of Show Award, Barnwell Art Ctr, Shreveport, La, 74; Ford Found Grant, 75. Bibliog: Kenneth Weedman (auth), National Sculpture '74, Sculpture Quart, Vol 2, No 2. Mem: Southern Asn Sculptors. Media: Steel, Bronze. Mailing Add: 2504 Baxter Dr Austin TX 78745

DE MISKEY, JULIAN
SCULPTOR, PRINTMAKER
b Hungary; US citizen. Study: Art Students League; Cleveland Art Inst; Acad Grande Chaumiere, Paris. Work: Mus City of New York; Nat Collection Fine Arts, Washington, DC; Mus Mod Art & Metrop Mus Art, New York. Comn: 100 cover paintings, New Yorker Mag, 25-59. Exhib: One-man shows, Paris, 32-34 & Sculpture, Westbeth Galleries, 72; Artists for Victory Exhibs. Awards: Purchase Award for War Painting, Am Red Cross. Bibliog: D Z

Meilach, Box Art, Crown, 75. Mem: Provincetown Art Asn. Style & Technique: Polychrome figurative sculpture with painted background in Lucite boxes; satirical. Media: Ceramics, Papier Mache, Oil, Lithographs. Publ: Illusr, What? no pie charts, New Yorker Mag, 27; illusr, Tim's Mountain, World, 59; auth & illusr, Piccole (children's bk), Random House, 67; illusr, Chucaro, Harcourt, Brace; among others. Mailing Add: c/o Westbeth Studio D719 463 West St New York NY 10014

DE MONTE, CLAUDIA
EDUCATOR, CONCEPTUAL VIDEO ARTIST
b Astoria, NY, Aug 25, 47. Study: Col Notre Dame, Md, BA; Cath Univ Am, MFA. Work: Mus Mod Art, New York; Franklin Furnace Arch, New York. Comn: Mural, in conjunction with Park Dept, Astoria Park, Queens, NY, 70; mural, Prince George's Community Col, Largo, Md, 72; process parkway, Philadelphia Mus of Art, Pa, 72. Exhib: Liberation: 14 Am Artists (int travelling exhib); Md Ann, Baltimore Mus of Art, 72; Queen's Talent, Queens Mus of Art, Flushing Meadows, NY, 73; 19th Area Exhib, Corcoran Gallery of Art, Washington, DC, 74; Int Women's Exhib, Olympia Int Art Ctr, Kingston, Jamaica, 75; Plus One, Corcoran Gallery of Art, Washington, DC, 76; 6th Int Encounter on Video, Caracas Mus of Fine Arts, Venezuela, 76; 7th Int Encounter on Video, Centre d'Estudio d'Art Contemporani, Barcelona, Spain, 77; Time, Philadelphia Col of Art, Pa, 77; Am Narrative/Story Art, Contemp Art Mus of Houston, 77; Art Words/Bookworks, Los Angeles Inst of Contemp Art, Calif, 78; Contemp Arts Ctr, New Orleans, La, 78. Teaching: Instr drawing, design & painting, Bowie State Col, Md, 71-72; instr art survey, Prince George's Community Col, Largo, Md, 72; asst prof design, Univ Md, College Park, 72- Pos: US rep sculpture, Int Women's Exhib, Olympia Art Ctr, Kingston, Jamaica, 75. Awards: Creative award, Univ Md, summer grant, 74 & 77. Bibliog: Artist Gives City Thanks in Very Big Way, New York Daily News, 11/70; Paul Richard (auth), Showy T-shirt Trade-in, Washington Post, 4/76; David Tannous (auth), Five Plus One at Corcoran, Art in Am, 1-2/77. Mem: Am Asn of Univ Prof; Washington Women's Art Ctr. Style & Technique: Narrative, documentary; concept, process, video. Media: Photographs, written material. Publ: Contribr, Damozel, Col Notre Dame, 69; contribr, Women in the Arts: American Women and Social Change: Visual Arts, US Info Agency, 75; auth, Public Poet: Tom Jones, Andy Warhol's Interview, 1/77. Mailing Add: 460 Broome St New York NY 10013

DE MONTEBELLO, GUY-PHILIPPE LANNES
ART ADMINISTRATOR
b Paris, France, May 16, 39. Study: Harvard Col, BA, 61; NY Univ Inst Fine Arts, 61-63. Collections Arranged: The Spingold Collection Exhibition, Brandeis Univ, 65, 67 & 68; Summer Loan Exhibition, Metrop Mus Art. Teaching: Lectr Fr art, romanticism & 18th century women painters. Pos: Assoc cur Europ paintings, Metrop Mus Art, 63-69; dir, Mus Fine Arts, Houston, Tex, 69-73; vdir curatorial & educ affairs, Metrop Mus Art, 74-77, actg dir mus, 77- Awards: Woodrow Wilson Fel, 61-62. Mem: Col Art Asn Am; Am Asn Mus; Am Asn Mus Dirs. Publ: Auth, Peter Paul Rubens, McGraw, 69; contribr, Metrop Mus Art Bull & others. Mailing Add: Metrop Mus Art Fifth Ave at 82nd St New York NY 10028

DEMPSEY, BRUCE HARVEY
MUSEUM DIRECTOR
b Camden, NJ, July 4, 41. Study: Fla State Univ, BA, MFA & study exten sch, Florence, Italy; Mozarabic manuscripts with Dr Gulnar Bosch. Exhibitions Arranged: Photons-Phonons (elec sculpture), 71; Lewis Comfort Tiffany, 72; Realizations & Figurizations, 72; Karl Zerbe Mem Exhibition, 73; Photo Phantisists, 73; Colors (photog exhib), 74; Talent USA, 76; Elizabethan Portraiture, Nat Portrait Gallery, London, 76; New Realism, 77; New Floridians No 1, 77; The Fla Connection: Jim Rosenquist & Robert Rauschenberg, 77; Helen Frankenthaler, 77. Teaching: Instr fundamental art & art hist, Fla State Univ, 66-74. Pos: Dir art gallery, Fla State Univ, 68-74; dir, Jacksonville Art Mus, 75- Mem: Am Asn Mus; Am Fedn Arts. Publ: Lewis C Tiffany—Beauty in Many Mediums, 72. Mailing Add: 2415 Mandarin River Lane Mandarin FL 32223

DE NAGY, EVA
PAINTER
b Hungary. Study: Acad Royal Beaux-Arts, Brussels, Belg. Work: Color slides, Guild Libr, Church Archit Guild Am, Washington, DC. Exhib: Provincetown Art Asn, 60 & 61; Ecclesiastical Crafts Exhib, Pittsburgh, 61 & 62; Painters & Sculptors Soc NJ, 61 & 62; Am-Hungarian Art Asn, New York, 62 & 63; Catharine Lorillard Wolfe Art Club, 62 & 64; plus many others. Pos: Owner-dir, Eva de Nagy Gallery, Provincetown, Mass; state art chmn, NJ Fedn Women's Clubs, 60 & 62; mem art comn, Trenton State Mus, 60 & 62; chmn, Roebling-Boehm art scholar, 62 & 64. Awards: Prizes, NJ State Fedn Women's Club, 54 & 59; Bronze Medal, Seton Hall Univ, 56; Prize, NJ State Med Asn Convention Art Exhib, 58 & 60; plus others. Mem: Provincetown Art Asn; Cape Cod Art Asn; Am Artists Prof League (publicity chmn, NJ Chap); Painters & Sculptors Soc NJ (treas). Mailing Add: 427 Commercial St Provincetown MA 02657

DE NAGY, TIBOR (J)
ART DEALER, COLLECTOR
b Debrecen, Hungary, Apr 25, 10; US citizen. Study: DEcon & PhD; Univ Frankfurt; Kings Col, Cambridge, Eng & Owens Col, Manchester; Univ Basel, Switz. Pos: Pres & dir, Tibor de Nagy Gallery, Inc, New York, 50- & Tibor de Nagy Gallery Texas, Houston, 73- Mem: Art Dealers Asn Am; Mus Mod Art. Specialty: Pioneer work to start out and promote contemporary talents, most of whom are Americans. Collection: 17th and 19th century Flemish and Italian art collection was destroyed in Budapest during the war; present collection is of contemporary Americans. Mailing Add: Tibor de Nagy Gallery 29 W 57th St New York NY 10019

DENBY, JILLIAN
PAINTER
b New York, NY. Study: Pratt Inst, BFA; Brooklyn Col, MFA. Exhib: Phases of New Realism, Lowe Art Mus, Univ Miami, 72; The Male Nude, Emily Lowe Gallery, Hofstra Univ, 73; Living American Artists & the Figure, Pa State Univ Mus Art, 74; one-man shows, A M Sachs Gallery, New York, 74, 75 & 77; The Nude in American Art, New York Cult Ctr, 75; Am Artists 76, Marion Koogler McNary Art Inst, 76; Am Figure Drawing 200 Yrs Later, Lehigh Univ, Melbourne, Australia, 76. Pos; Artist in residence, Roswell Mus, 73-74. Awards: Nat Endowment for the Arts Fel, 76-77. Media: Oil. Mailing Add: 87 Franklin St New York NY 10013

DENES, AGNES C
MULTIMEDIA ARTIST, CONCEPTUAL ARTIST
b Budapest, Hungary, May, 38; US citizen. Study: Col City of New York; New Sch for Social Res, New York; Columbia Univ, M L Robinson Scholar, 64-65. Work: Mus Mod Art, New York; Whitney Mus Am Art, New York; Nat Collection Fine Arts, Washington, DC; Allen Mem Art Mus, Oberlin, Ohio; Chase Manhattan Bank Art Collection, New York; plus others. Exhib: Software, Jewish Mus, New York, 70; Mus Mod Art, Buenos Aires, Arg, 71; New Acquisitions, 71 & Am Drawings 1963-73, 73, Whitney Mus Am Art; Allen Mem Art Mus, Oberlin, 72; Brooklyn Mus, NY, 72, 76 & 77; Mus Fine Arts, Santiago, Chile, 72; Inst Contemp Art, Lima, Peru, 72; Mus Emilio A Caraffa, Cordoba, Spain, 73; Kunsthause, Hamburg, Ger, 73; Neuer Berliner Kunstverein, Ger, 73; New Acquisitions, Mus Mod Art, New York, 73; San Francisco Mus Art, Calif, 74; Painting & Sculpture Today, Indianapolis Mus Art, 74; Projekt 74, Kunsthalle, Cologne, Ger, 74; Mus Philadelphia Civic Ctr, Pa, 74; Inst Contemp Art, Philadelphia, 75; Drawing USA, Stadtisches Mus Leverkusen, Ger, 75; Basel Art Fair, Switz, 75; Biennale of Sydney, Australia, 76; J & E Lowe Art Gallery, Syracuse Univ, NY, 77; New Gallery Contemp Art, Cleveland State Univ, Ohio, 77; Documenta 6, Kassel, WGer, 77; Maps, Mus Mod Art, New York, 77; Numerals (traveling to Yale Univ & Dartmouth Col, et al), Leo Castelli Gallery, New York, 78; Venice Biennale, Italy; one-person shows, Corcoran Gallery of Art, Washington, DC, 74, Ohio State Univ, Columbus, 74, Douglass Col, Rutgers Univ, New Brunswick, NJ, 76, Newport Harbor Art Mus, Newport Beach, Calif, 76, Tyler Sch of Art, Temple Univ, Philadelphia, 77, Centre Cult Americain, Paris, France, 78 & Amerika Haus, US Cult Ctr, Berlin, 78; plus many others. Awards: Creative Artists Pub Serv Grant, 72 & 74; Nat Endowment for the Arts, 74 & 75; DAAD Fel, Berliner Kunstlerprogramm, 78. Bibliog: Lucy Lippard (auth), Six Years, Praeger, 73; Philip Smith (auth), Dynamic Visual Systems in Process: the work of Agnes Denes, Arts Mag, 12/75; Peter Selz (auth), Agnes Denes: the visual presentation of meaning, Art In Am, 3-4/77. Style & Technique: Mixed-media, graphics, pringmaking in all media and environmental artist. Publ: Auth, Sculptures of the Mind, Univ Akron Press, 76; auth, Paradox & Essence, Tau/Ma Publ, Rome, Italy, 77. Mailing Add: 93 Crosby St New York NY 10012

DE NIKE, MICHAEL NICHOLAS
SCULPTOR
b Regina, Sask, Sept 14, 23; US citizen. Study: Nat Acad Fine Arts; also with Jean de Marco & Carl Schmitz. Comn: Albert Payson Terhune Mem, Collie Fanciers Am, Paramus, NJ, 71; Medallion, Int Chef's Asn, New York, 72; Stations of the Cross, Christ Church, Pompton Lakes, NJ, 75; Bicentennial Mural, Twp Wayne, NJ, 75; Young St Francis (bronze), St David's in Kinnelon, NJ; plus others. Exhib: Nat Acad Design, New York, 64; Audubon Artists, 65; Knickerbocker Artists, 65; Nat Sculpture Soc Ann, 66; Am Artists Prof League, 74; plus others. Teaching: Instr woodcarving, Fair Lawn Adult Educ, 68-74; adj fac, Essex Co Col, Newark, NJ, 74-75. Pos: Vpres, Paterson Art League, NJ, 67-68; co-chmn, Mayor's Coun Cult Develop, 68-69; dir, Am Carving Sch, Wayne, NJ, 74-75; sr judge, Can Nat Carving Exhib, 77. Awards: Dr Ralph Weiler Award, Nat Acad Design, 64; Herald-News Award, Passaic-Clifton, NJ, 69; Allied Artists Am Award. Style & Technique: Classic and impressionistic; hand carved, textured and polished. Media: Media: Wood, Stone. Mailing Add: 2343 Hamburg Turnpike Wayne NJ 07470

DE NIRO, ROBERT
SCULPTOR, PAINTER
b Syracuse, NY, May 3, 22. Study: Black Mountain Col; also with Hans Hofmann. Work: Brandeis Univ; Houston Mus Fine Arts; Longview Found; Univ NC. Exhib: Whitney Mus Am Art Ann, New York; Jewish Mus, New York; Inst Contemp Art, Boston; Ball State Univ, Muncie, Ind; Colorado Springs Fine Arts Ctr; plus others. Teaching: Instr, Sch Visual Arts, New Sch Social Res & State Univ NY Buffalo. Awards: V Hallmark Int Competition; Longview Found Grant; Guggenheim Found Fel, 68. Dealer: Zabriskie Gallery 29 W 57th St New York NY 10019. Mailing Add: 465 W Broadway New York NY 10012

DENIS, PAUL ANDRE S
PAINTER, INSTRUCTOR
b Chicago, Ill, Nov 16, 38. Study: Cleveland Inst of Art, BFA; Kent State Univ, MA; additional study with Julian Stanczak & Louis Bosa. Work: Tweed Mus, Duluth, Minn; Massillon Mus, Ohio; Utah State Univ, Logan; Bertha Eccles Art Ctr, Ogden, Utah. Exhib: Nat Soc of Painters in Casein, New York, 67; Cleveland Mus of Art Travelling Exhib, Ohio, 68; Butler Inst of Am Art, Youngstown, Ohio, 68; one-man show, Massillon Mus, Ohio, 69; Akron Art Inst, Ohio, 71; Am Watercolor Soc, Nat Acad Galleries, New York, 71-73, 75 & 77; Canton Art Inst, Ohio, 73; Aqueous Open, Pittsburgh Watercolor Soc, 74 & 75; Watercolor West, Utah State Univ, 76 & 77; Nat Watercolor Soc, Laguna Beach Mus of Art, Calif, 77. Teaching: Instr painting, Kent State Univ, Ohio, 68-70, Cooper Sch of Art, Cleveland, 70-77, Cleveland Inst of Art, 73- Pos: Chmn art dept, Interlochen Ctr for the Arts, Mich, summers, 69- Awards: Award, Am Watercolor Soc, Nat Acad Galleries, New York, 73; Purchase Prize, Nat Watercolor Soc, Laguna Beach Mus of Art, Calif, 77; First Prize & Purchase Prize, Aqueous Open, Pittsburgh Watercolor Soc, 74. Mem: Nat Watercolor Soc. Style & Technique: Abstract acrylic wash; landscape and floral in watercolor. Media: Watercolor and acrylic. Mailing Add: 30601 Ashton Lane Bay Village OH 44140

DENNIS, CHARLES HOUSTON
CARTOONIST
b Springfield, Mo, Nov 11, 21. Study: Art League Calif, San Francisco; Acad Art, San Francisco. Pos: Staff artist, Springfield Leader & Press, 39-42; free lance mag cartoonist, 50- Style & Technique: Mag gag cartoons Publ: Contribr, numerous mags, 50-; auth, Cartoon gag writing principles and techniques, 55. Mailing Add: 1831 Magnolia Way Walnut Creek CA 94597

DENNIS, CHERRE NIXON
PAINTER, ETCHER
b Raton, NMex. Study: Univ Tulsa, with Adah M Robinson; Univ NMex, with Emil Bisttram; Okla State Univ, with Doel Reed; also with Rexford E Brandt & Phillip L Dike. Exhib: Watercolor & Print Ann, Oakland Art Gallery, Calif, 42; Philbrook Art Ctr, Tulsa, Okla, 56; Nat Representational Art Ann, Thomas Gilcrease Inst, Tulsa, 58; Southwestern Biennial, Mus NMex, Santa Fe, 62; Artist of the Month (one-man show), Four Hills Gallery, Albuquerque, 74; plus others. Teaching: Art instr etching & drawing, Philbrook Art Ctr, 40-41. Pos: Pres & chmn bd, Adah M Robinson Mem Fund, Tulsa, 67-69. Awards: First Award for graphics, Tulsa Art Ann, 35 & 36; Second Award for watercolor, Philbrook Art Ctr, 50; Graphic Awards, NMex Art League, 72. Mem: NMex Art League; Lake Region Arts & Crafts Colony. Style & Technique: Varies with media, for watercolor, wet into wet and drybrush; in etching, linear outline with aquatint tonal values. Media: Watercolor. Dealer: 3000 Monterey Dr SE Albuquerque NM 87106. Mailing Add: Lakeview on Gibson Rte 1 Box 304B Wagoner OK 74467

DENNIS, ROGER WILSON
PAINTER
b Norwich, Conn, Mar 11, 02. Study: Art Students League. Exhib: Lyme Art Asn; Conn Acad; Copley Soc, Boston. Pos: Conservator painting, Lyman Allyn Mus, New London, Conn, 45-78. Mem: Lyme Art Asn; Copley Soc. Media: Oil, Watercolor. Dealer: Foot of Main Gallery Essex CT 06426. Mailing Add: 9 Columbus Ave Niantic CT 06357

DENNISON, DOROTHY (DOROTHY DENNISON BUTLER)
PAINTER, LITHOGRAPHER
b Beaver, Pa, Feb 13, 08. Study: Pa Acad Fine Arts, Cresson traveling scholar, 29. Work: Columbus Gallery, Ohio; Canton Art Inst, Ohio; Pa Acad Fine Arts, Philadelphia; Butler Inst Am Art, Ohio. Exhib: Pa Acad Fine Arts; Butler Inst Am Art; Newport Art Asn, RI; Portland Mus, Maine; Northwest Territory Exhib, Ill. Teaching: Head art dept, Knox Sch, Cooperstown, NY, 40-41; instr drawing, Syracuse Univ, 41-43; Russell Sage Col, 43-44. Awards: Purchase Prize, Butler Inst Am Art, 50; First Prize, Ohio State Fair, 69. Mem: Fel Pa Acad Fine Arts. Media: Oil. Dealer: Kennedy Galleries 20 E 56th ST New York NY 10022. Mailing Add: 1915 Walker Mill Rd Poland OH 44514

DENNISON, KEITH ELKINS
MUSEUM DIRECTOR, ART HISTORIAN
b Oakland, Calif, Sept 20, 39. Study: San Francisco State Univ, BA, with Dr Ernest Mundt, spec training, M H de Young Mem Mus, San Francisco. Collections Arranged: Horizons, A Century of California Landscape Painting. Teaching: Instr museology, Univ of the Pac, 74- Pos: Asst cur educ, M H de Young Mem Mus, 68-70; visual arts adv, Calif Arts Comn, Sacramento, Calif, 70-71; dir, Pioneer Mus & Haggin Galleries, Stockton, Calif, 71- Publ: Auth, Horizons, a century of California landscape painting, 70. Mailing Add: Pioneer Mus & Haggin Galleries 1201 N Pershing Stockton CA 95203

DENNISTON, DOUGLAS
PAINTER, EDUCATOR
b Cornwall-on-Hudson, NY, Nov 19, 21. Study: Col William & Mary, cert, 42; Univ NMex, BFA, 45, MA, 48. Work: Va Mus Fine Arts, Richmond; Denver Art Mus; Tucson Mus Art & Yuma Art Ctr, Ariz; Jonson Gallery, Albuquerque, NMex. Exhib: Am Watercolors, Prints & Drawings, Metrop Mus Art, New York, 52; Young Am Printmakers, Mus Mod Art, New York, 53; 18th Ann Watercolor Exhib, San Francisco Art Mus, 54; 67th & 73rd Western Ann, Denver Art Mus, 61 & 71; Southwestern Prints & Drawings, Dallas Mus Fine Arts, 52-62; Southwest Fine Arts Biennial, Mus Fine Arts, Santa Fe, NMex, 76. Teaching: Prof art, Univ Ariz, 59- Awards: Purchase Awards, Denver Artists Ann, Denver Art Mus, 53, Fifth & Seventh Southwestern, Yuma Art Ctr, Ariz, 70 & 72. Style & Technique: Traditional. Media: Watercolor, oil. Publ: Illusr, Calendar, Balcen Press, 72. Dealer: Cob-Web Hall PO Box 2035 Prescott AZ 86301. Mailing Add: 1844 N Vine Ave Tucson AZ 85719

DE NORONHA, MARIA M (MRS DAVID GALLMAN)
PAINTER, LECTURER
b Cascais, Port; US citizen. Study: Jr Col Sagrado Coracao, Port; Hunter Col, BA; Montclair Col; Art Students League; Am Ctr Students & Artists, Paris, France; also with Doug Kingman, New York & Roger Barr, Paris. Work: Grumbacher Co, New York; Oglethorpe Univ, Atlanta, Ga; George Washington Carver Mus; White House Collection, Washington, DC; Col Charleston; Am Ctr Students & Artists, Paris. Exhib: US Embassy, Saigon, Vietnam, 70; Nat Acad Design, New York, 71; State Dept, Washington, DC, 71; Washington Mus, Md, 71; Southeastern Art Exhib, 72; Metrop Mus of Art, New York, NY, 77; plus others. Teaching: Instr art & chmn dept, Lyndhurst High Sch, NY, 58-60; instr art, Oglethorpe Univ, 64-67; asst prof art, Atlanta Univ, 68-70; lectr, Altanta Univ Grad Sch & Alice Lloyd Col, Ky. Pos: Owner, Art Studio, Charleston, 60-62; mem art comt, off & lectr, Int Platform Asn, 68-72; dir, Noronha Art Studio, Atlanta, 69- Awards: M Grumbacher Award as Painter of the Year, 62; Southeastern Art Exhib Award for Seas, 65; Oglethorpe Univ Res Grant, 66; Lauro Accademico, Paris, 74. Bibliog: Armando Troni (auth), Int Contemp Art Mag, 71. Mem: Life fel, Royal Soc Arts; Altrusa Int; Am Asn Univ Prof; Southeastern Art Conf. Style & Technique: Expressionism and neo-impressionism in any media. Mailing Add: PO Box 9606 Atlanta GA 30319

DENTON, PAT
PAINTER, INSTRUCTOR
b Scottsbluff, Nebr, July 20, 43. Study: Art Student Tour, Europe, 60; Univ Kans, 61; Univ Denver, cert painting, 62; also with Virginia Cobb, John Pellew, Charles Reid, Lee Weiss & Asterio. Work: Greeley Nat Bank, Colo; Lunnon Haus, Golden, Colo; Mus Tex Tech Univ; Lutheran Med Clin, Wheatridge, Colo; United Banks Colo, Denver; plus many in pvt collections. Exhib: Miniature Painters, Sculptors & Gravers Soc, Washington, DC, 72 & 74; Nat Small Paintings Exhib, NMex Art League, Albuquerque, 72-78; Catharine Lorillard Wolfe Art Club, Inc, New York, 74; WTex Watercolor Asn Exhib, Mus Tex Tech Univ, 74; Cody Country Western Nat, 75; plus many other nat group & one-man shows. Teaching: Pvt lessons, Golden, Colo, 71-72; instr drawing, Foothills Art Ctr, Golden, 72, instr watercolor, 73; instr workshop, Parma Tyson Studio, 75. Awards: First Prize in Graphics, NMex Art League, 72; First Prize in Watercolor, Nat Fete, Scottsbluff, 73-77; Ida Becker Mem Award, Catharine Lorillard Wolfe Club, 74. Bibliog: B Hosicowa (auth), Art of Pat Denton, Empire Mag, Denver Post, 11/12/72; J Mills (auth), Dimensions, Denver Post; Con Marshall (auth), New York Award, Chadron Rec, Nebr & Scottsbluff Star Herald. Mem: Foothills Art Ctr; NJ Miniature Art Soc. Style & Technique: Tight traditional, transitional and contemporary. Media: Graphics, Watercolor & Acrylic. Mailing Add: 2948 Pierson Way Lakewood CO 80215

DENTZEL, CARL SCHAEFER
MUSEUM DIRECTOR, WRITER
b Philadelphia, Pa, Mar 20, 13. Study: Univ Calif, Los Angeles; Univ Berlin; Univ Mex. Teaching: Lectr, Pomona Col, formerly. Pos: Pres, Los Angeles Co Mus Asn; mem bd, Univ Calif Art Coun, Los Angeles; pres, Western Mus Conf, 57-58; dir, Southwest Mus, Los Angeles, currently; pres, Cult Heritage Bd, City Los Angeles, 63-64. Mem: Los Angeles Mus Art (exec comt). Publ: Auth, introd & bibliog, In: Diary of Titian Ramsay Peale: Oregon to California, Overland Journey September and October, 1841, 57; auth, Cinco de Mayo—an Appraisal, 60; auth, The Universality of Local History, 60; auth, The art of Leon Gaspard (introd), In: A Memorial Exhibition of Paintings and Sketches by Leon Gaspard (catalog), 64; auth, introd, In: Edward H Davis and the Indians of the Southwest United States and Northwest Mexico, 65; plus many others. Mailing Add: Southwest Museum Museum Dr Highland Park Los Angeles CA 90065

DE PAOLA, TOMIE
ILLUSTRATOR, DESIGNER
b Meriden, Conn, Sept 15, 34. Study: Pratt Inst, BFA, 56; Calif Col Arts & Crafts, MFA, 69; Lone Mountain Col, 70; also with Ben Shahn & Richard Lindner. Work: Kerlan Collection, Minneapolis, Minn; Worcester Art Mus, Mass. Comn: Mural, Dominican Sisters Retreat House Chapel, Schnectady, NY, 58; two murals, Conception Abbey Retreat House, Mo, 59; renovation, design & murals, St Sylvester's Church, Graniteville, Vt, 61; murals, Glastonbury Monastery, Hingham, Mass, 62; altar painting, Newman Cult Ctr, Rensselear Polytech Inst, Troy, NY, 68. Exhib: Outstanding Children's Bks, Am Inst Graphic Artists, New York, 70; Children's Bk Coun Showcase, New York, 73; Children's Bk Illusr, Everson Mus, Syracuse, NY, 77; 1978 Illusr Exhib, Bologna, Italy, 78. Collections Arranged: Kerland Collection, Univ Minn, Minneapolis. Teaching: Asst prof design & painting, Newton Col of Sacred Heart, Mass, 63-66; asst prof design, Lone Mountain Col, San Francisco, 67-70; assoc prof design, illus & graphic design, New Eng Col, Henniker, 76- Awards: Art Bks for Children Award, Brooklyn Mus & Brooklyn Pub Libr, 75, 77 & 78; Caldecott Honor Bk Award, Am Libr Asn, 76; Second Place Owl Prize, Shiko-sha Co, Tokyo, Japan, 77. Bibliog: Z Sutherland (auth), Children & Books, Scott Foresman, 5th ed, 77. Mem: Authors Guild; Soc Children's Bk Writers. Media: Watercolor, Pencil, Colored Ink, Tempera. Publ: Auth & illusr, Charlie Needs a Cloak, 73 & Strega Nona, 75, Prentice-Hall; auth & illusr, The Quicksand Book, Holiday House, 77; auth & illusr, Helga's Dowry, 77 & The Clown of God, 78, Harcourt Brace. Dealer: Florence Alexander 50 E 42nd St New York NY 10017; Botolph Gallery 44 Brattle St Cambridge MA 02138. Mailing Add: Whitebird Village Rd Wilmot Flat NH 03287

DE PEDERY-HUNT, DORA
SCULPTOR, DESIGNER
b Budapest, Hungary, Nov 16, 13. Study: Royal Sch Appl Art, Budapest, MA. Work: Nat Gallery Can; Art Gallery, Toronto, Ont; Art Gallery Ont; Dept External Affairs, Ottawa; Mus Contemp Crafts, Charlottetown, PEI; plus others. Exhib: Canadian Religious Art Today, Regis Col, Toronto, 63 & 66; Int Exhib Contemp Medals, The Hague & Rome, 63, Athens, 66, Paris, 67 & Prague, 69; Biennial Christian Art, Salzburg, 64; Can Pavillion, Expo '67; plus others. Pos: Can rep, Fedn Int Medaille, Paris. Awards: Purchase Prizes, Uno-a-Erre, Arezzo, Italy, 64-66; Nat Coun Jewish Women Award, 66; Can Govt Centennial Medal, 67; plus others. Mem: Royal Can Acad; Sculptors' Soc Can (past pres); Ont Soc Artists. Mailing Add: 65 Glen Rd Toronto ON M4W 2V3 Can

DEPILLARS, MURRY N
ART ADMINISTRATOR, ILLUSTRATOR
b Chicago, Ill, Dec 21, 38. Study: Kennedy-King Community Col, AA(fine arts); Roosevelt Univ, BA(art educ) & MA(urban studies); Pa State Univ, University Park, PhD cand. Work: Paul Roberson Cult Ctr, Pa State Univ, University Park. Comn: Mural, African & African-Am Studies Ctr, Univ Mich, Ann Arbor, 71; illus, J Negro Educ, Howard Univ, 74; Destruction of Black Civilizations (illus), 74 & Steps to Break the Circle (illus), 75, Third World Press; Story of Kwanza (illus), Inst of Positive Educ, Chicago, 75. Exhib: Mus Sci & Indust, Chicago, 70; The Indignant Eye, Whitney Mus Am Art, New York, 71; Am Greeting Card Gallery, New York, 72; Rainbow Sign Gallery, Los Angeles, 74; World Expo '74, African-Am Pavilion, Spokane, 74. Teaching: Instr, Chicago Comt of Urban Opportunity, 68; asst prof art & asst dean sch arts, Va Commonwealth Univ, 71-, asst prof fundamentals of drawing, 72-73. Pos: Asst dir, Educ Asst Prog, Univ Ill, Chicago, 68-71. Awards: Danforth Found Assoc, 73; Outstanding Serv Award, Nat Conf Artists, 75. Bibliog: F D Cossitt (auth), DePillars is Artist with Message, Richmond Times Dispatch Newspaper, 6/15/70; Semella Lewis & Ruth Waddy (auth), Black Artists on Art, Contemp Crafts, Inc, Vol II; Robert Doty (auth), Contemporary Black Artists in America, Whitney Mus Am Art, 72. Mem: Nat Conf Artists (pres, 73-); Second World Black & African Festival Arts & Cult (bd dirs, NAm Zone, 73-74); Nat Art Educr Asn; Pan African Artists Alliance; Kuumba Workshop (art dir, 69-). Style & Technique: Social commentary in various art media. Media: Acrylic, Oil & Graphics. Publ: Illusr, Aunt Jemima, 69 & Black Family, 69; illusr, Children at Play, Blackman & Haynes, 70; illusr, A People of the Sun, 73; auth, The Emerging Voice of the Black Visual Artists, Nat Conf Artists, 75. Dealer: Third World Press 7524 S Cottage Grove Chicago IL 60619. Mailing Add: 901 W Franklin St Richmond VA 23284

DE POL, JOHN
ENGRAVER, DESIGNER
b New York, NY, Sept 16, 13. Study: Art Students League; Sch Technol, Belfast, Northern Ireland. Work: Libr Cong; New York Pub Libr; Metrop Mus Art; Syracuse Univ Libr; Bucknell Univ Libr. Comn: Presentation prints, Woodcut Soc, 52, Miniature Print Soc, 53 & Albany Print Club, NY, 58-59. Exhib: One-man exhibs, Albany Print Club, Bucknell Univ, Syracuse Univ & Lycoming Col; Nat Acad Design Ann, 72. Pos: Free lance art dir & design consult for var corp; illusr, Franklin Keepsake Ann Ser. Awards: Albany Print Club Purchase Prize, 68; John Taylor Arms Mem Prize, Nat Acad Design, 68; Nat Arts Club Purchase Prize, 68. Bibliog: P K Thomajan (auth), John De Pol, wood engraver, Print Mag, 8/54; Norman Kent (auth), The wood engravings of John De Pol, 3/56 & William Caxton, Jr (auth), A new chiaroscuro wood engraving by John De Pol, 2/68, Am Artist. Mem: Soc Am Graphic Artists; Albany Print Club; life mem Art Students League; assoc Nat Acad Design. Media: Wood. Mailing Add: 280 Spring Valley Rd Park Ridge NJ 07656

DERGALIS, GEORGE
PAINTER, SCULPTOR
b Athens, Greece, Aug 31, 28; US citizen. Study: Sculpture with Ambrose, 48-50; Accad Belle Arti, Rome, MA, 51; Sch Mus Fine Arts, Boston, dipl, 58. Work: Brockton Mus, Mass; Inst Sarro, Barcelona, Spain; Sch Mus Fine Arts, Boston; St Matthew Church, Fitchburg, Mass; Advert Inst Assocs, Newton Centre, Mass; plus others. Exhib: Prima Mostra Int, Rome, 50; Quadrienale, Mus Mod Art, Rome, 51; Kurhaus Wiesbaden, Ger, 53; De Cordova Mus, Lincoln, Mass, 62; Brockton Mus, 72; Nashua Art & Sci Mus, NH, 74. Teaching: Instr painting, De Cordova Mus, 61-78; art instr, Sch Mus Fine Arts, Boston, 51-70; instr art, YMHA, Boston, 62-64; pvt art classes, Wayland, Mass, 78- Awards: Prix Rome, Accad Belle Arti, 51; Paige scholar, 59; Gold Medal, Concord Art Asn, 69. Bibliog: Art and Antiques, Melrose Press, London, 72. Mem: Copley Soc of Boston (vpres & art chmn); Int Soc Arts & Lett; Sch Mus Fine Arts Alumni, Boston (vpres, 64-65, pres, 66-68); Cambridge Art Asn. Style & Technique: Bold, some abstract, subtle rich color, textural and at times dimensional, with symbolism. Dealer: Miss P Patton 2 Oxbow Rd Wayland MA 01778. Mailing Add: 72 Oxbow Rd Wayland MA 01778

DE RIVERA, JOSE
SCULPTOR
b West Baton Rouge, La, Sept 18, 04. Study: With John W Norton, Chicago; Washington Univ, St Louis, Mo, hon doctorate, 74; also study in Spain, Italy, France, Greece & Egypt. Work: Mus Mod Art, New York; Art Inst Chicago; San Francisco Mus Art; Smithsonian Inst, Washington, DC; Tate Gallery, London, Eng; plus many others. Comn: Steel Century Two (sculpture), Am Iron & Steel Inst, 65. Exhib: Whitney Mus Am Art Ann, New York, 34-68; Grace Borgenicht Gallery, New York, 52-72; White House, Washington, DC, 66; Sculpture of the '60's, Los Angeles Co Mus Art, Los Angeles & Philadelphia Mus Art, 67; Retrospective 72, La Jolla Mus Contemp Art, Calif & Whitney Mus Am Art, 72; plus many other group & one-man shows. Teaching: Instr sculpture, Brooklyn Col, 53; critic in sculpture, Yale Univ, 53-55; instr sculpture, Sch Design, NC State Col, 57-60. Awards: Watson F Blair Prize, Art Inst Chicago, 57; Nat Inst Arts & Lett grant, 59; Creative Awards Medal, Brandeis Univ, 69; plus others. Mailing Add: c/o Grace Borgenicht Gallery 1018 Madison Ave New York NY 10003

DERN, F CARL
SCULPTOR
b Salt Lake City, Utah, Apr 24, 36. Study: San Francisco Art Inst, 69, with Richard Shaw, Fletcher Benton; Univ Calif, Berkeley, 71-72, with Robert Hudson & James Melchert. Work: In many pvt collections. Exhib: San Francisco Art Inst, Calif, 70; San Francisco Art Inst Centennial Exhib, de Young Mus, 70; Sculpture 72, Stanford Univ Art Mus, Calif, 72; Univ Art Mus, Berkeley, 72 & 75; San Francisco Ann Art Festival, 71 & 73; New Mus Mod Art, Oakland, 70-73; 1st Ann Soap Box Derby, San Francisco Mus Mod Art, 75; San Jose Mus Art, 78. Awards: Anne Bremer Prize in Art, Univ Calif, Berkeley, 69 & 72; First Prize, 1st Int Contemp, Jon Morehead Gallery, Chico, Calif, 71. Mem: Artists Equity. Dealer: Lester Gallery PO Box 485 Inverness CA 94937. Mailing Add: 47 Oak Rd Fairfax CA 94930

DE RUTH, JAN
PAINTER, WRITER
b Karlovy Vary, Czech, July 31, 22; US citizen. Study: Rotter Art Sch, Prague, Czech; Ruskin Sch Drawing, Oxford Univ, Eng; Art Students League; New Sch Social Res, New York; also with Frederic Taubes. Exhib: 45 nat juried exhibs, 14 mus one-man shows & 71 gallery one-man exhibs. Awards: Gold Medal, Allied Artists of Am & Nat Arts Club; Purchase Award, Butler Inst Am Art; Purchase Award, Audubon Artists. Mem: Allied Artists Am (vpres); Audubon Artists; Am Artists Prof League; artists fel Royal Soc Art, London. Style & Technique: Representational expressionism. Media: Oil. Publ: Auth Portrait painting, 64; auth, Painting the nude, 68. Mailing Add: 1 W 67th St New York NY 10023

DESHAIES, ARTHUR
PRINTMAKER
b Providence, RI, July 6, 20. Study: Cooper Union Art Sch, 39-42; RI Sch Design, BFA, 48; Ind Univ, MFA, 50. Work: Bradley Univ; Brooklyn Mus; in many mus US & Europe & in univ & pvt collections. Exhib: American Prints Today, Print Coun Am Traveling Exhib, 59-62; Brooklyn Mus; 3rd Int Biennial Exhib Prints, Tokyo, 62; Otis Art Inst, Los Angeles; Whitney Mus Am Art; 20th Nat Print Exhib, 77. Awards: Fulbright Fel to France, 52; Tiffany Found Grant, 60; Guggenheim Fel creative printmaking, 61; plus others. Bibliog: Gabor Peterdi (auth), included in Printmaking: Methods Old and New, Macmillan, 59; S W Hayter (auth), included in About Prints, Oxford Univ Press, 62. Media: Graphics. Publ: Contribr, Am Prints Today (catalog), 62. Mailing Add: 1314 Dillard St Tallahassee FL 32303

DESHAZO, EDITH KIND
ART CRITIC, ART HISTORIAN
b Philadelphia, Pa, Feb 2, 20. Study: With Emlen McConnell. Pos: Consult, Del Art Mus & Munson-Williams-Proctor Inst, Utica, NY; art critic, Courier Post, Camden, NJ, 66-; free lance & cult writer, News Jour, Wilmington, Del & other papers, 77- Mem: Artists Equity. Res: Collecting primary material including letters, photographs, sketches on Everett Shinn. Publ: Everett Shinn—a figure in his time, Clarkson Potter, 74; auth, Everett Shinn, Am Art Rev, 74. Mailing Add, Box 40 Woodstown NJ 08098

DESMIDT, THOMAS H
PAINTER, EDUCATOR
b Sheboygan, Wis, Sept 6, 44. Study: Lincoln Col, AA; Layton Sch Art, BFA; Syracuse Univ, MFA. Work: Milwaukee Art Inst, Wis; Francis & Sidney Lewis Collection Contemp Art; F&M Corp, Richmond, Va; Miller Brewing Co, Milwaukee, Wis; Everson Mus Art, Syracuse; Rochester Mem Art Mus, NY; Va Mus, Richmond. Exhib: Rochester Mem Art Gallery, NY, 71; OK Harris Works of Art, New York, 71 & 72; Max Protetch Gallery, Washington, DC, 72 & 74; James Yu Gallery, New York, 73 & 74; 19th Corcoran Biennial, Washington, DC, 74; Va Artists, Va Mus, Richmond, 77; one-man shows, Mem Art Gallery, Univ of Rochester, NY, 72, Everson Mus, Syracuse, NY, 73 & Va Mus, Richmond, 78. Teaching: Instr painting, Va Commonwealth Univ, 70-73, dir, Art Found, 73-76, asst prof art, 73-, asst dean, 76- Awards: One-Man Exhib Award, Rochester Mem Gallery, 70; Fac Res Grant, Va Commonwealth Univ, 73; plus many regional awards in juried exhibitions. Style & Technique: Contemporary paintings; geometric abstraction. Media: Canvas, Acrylic. Dealer: OK Harris Works of Art 383 W Broadway New York NY 10013; James Yu Gallery 393 W Broadway New York NY 10012. Mailing Add: 7711 Woodman Rd Richmond VA 23226

DESOTO, RAFAEL M
PAINTER, ILLUSTRATOR
b Auadilla, PR. Study: Columbia Univ, 25; Pratt Inst, 33; Art Students League, 35-37; also with G Bridgeman, E Dickerson & I Soyer. Work: Bishop Mus, Bradenton, Fla; State Capitol Fla, Tallahassee; Mus Fine Arts, San Juan; State Univ NY, Greenly Mem Gallery, Farmingdale. Comn: Mural (fresco painted), Lens of Life, Westchester Med Ctr, NY, 38; mural (oil on canvas), New World, Knights of Columbus Hall, Patchogue, NY, 66; monument (sculpture design), Lady of the Island (with Rock of Ages, Barry, Vt), comn by, Montfort Fathers, Manorville, NY, 75. Exhib: One-man shows, Bishop Mus, Bradenton, Fla, 70, Brookwood Hall Art Gallery, East Islip, NY, 73, Ponce Mus Art, PR & San Juan Inst Cult, Mus Fine Arts, PR, 74; group shows, Nat Soc Painters in Casein & Acrylic, Nat Arts Club, Gramercy Park, NY, 72; Am Artists Prof League, Lever House Bldg, New York, 72-74. Teaching: Pvt instr, 58-; assoc prof art & design, State Univ NY Col Farmingdale, 62- Pos: Illusr, various mag, pocket books, 33-60; asst art dir, Pop Publ Inc, 37. Awards: Nat Poster Art Alliance Award, NY State Armory, 25; Great Seal State Fla, Former Gov Haydon Burns, 65; Emily Griffin Award, Nat Arts Club, 72. Bibliog: El Show de Tommy, TV interview, Channel 47, 74. Mem: Am Artists Prof League; Nat Arts Club; Parrish Art Mus; South Bay Art Asn. Style & Technique: Realism in figures, portraiture & landscapes. Media: Acrylic, Oil, Watercolor, Tempera, Casein. Mailing Add: 23 Roosevelt Blvd East Patchogue NY 11772

DESPORTES, ULYSSE GANDVIER
PAINTER, ART HISTORIAN
b Winnsboro, SC, Apr 12, 20. Study: Richmond Prof Inst, Col William & Mary, with Julien Binford, Marion Junkin & Theresa Pollack, BFA; Ecole Normale Super Beaux-Arts, Paris, France, with Maurice Brianchon; Inst Art & Archeol, Univ Paris, with Pierre Lavedan & Andre Chastel. Work: Va Mus Fine Arts, Richmond; Washington & Lee Univ, Lexington, Va; Va Commonwealth Univ, Richmond. Exhib: Va Artists 1961 & Va Artists 1963, Va Mus Fine Arts; SC Artists, Gibbs Art Mus, Charleston, 62. Teaching: Asst prof art hist & painting, Hollins Col, 57-62; prof art & chmn dept, Mary Baldwin Col, 62- Pos: Dir catalogues, Kende Galleries, New York, 46-48; dir, Florence Mus, SC, 57. Awards: Second Prize, SC Artists Asn, 62; Cert of Merit, Va Mus Fine Arts, 63. Style & Technique: Naturalistic painting using traditional techniques to interpret relation of spatial forces and colors. Media: Oil. Res: Neoclassic art; sculptor Guiseppe Ceracchi; painter Louis David. Publ: Contribr, Bull Mus Bernadotte, 62; contribr, Princeton Libr Chronicle, 62; contribr, Art Quart, 63 & 64; contribr, Antiques Mag, 69. Mailing Add: 322 N New St Staunton VA 24401

DES RIOUX, DEENA (VICTORIA COTY)
PAINTER, DESIGNER
b Cambridge, Mass, Dec 7, 41; Fr & US citizen. Study: RI Sch Design, 59-62; Brown Univ, 60-62; Ecole de la Grande Chaumiere, Paris, 61; Univ Paris I at Sorbonne, 61 & 63. Work: Am Contemp Arts & Crafts Slide Libr, Palm Beach, Fla; Women's Mus at Women's Interart Ctr, New York; plus many pvt collections in US & Fr. Comn: Seven at Large (inaugural poster), Art Inst Boston for MacIvor Reddie Gallery, 75; Organic Visions (poster), Boston's Mus Sci, 77. Exhib: 16th Ann Nat Exhib, Fall River Art Asn, Mass, 73; 62nd Ann Nat Exhib, Art Asn Newport, RI, 73; 45th Ann New Eng Painting Exhib, Jordan Marsh, Boston, Mass, 74; guest exhibitor, Danvers Art Asn & Hist Soc, Mass, 74; Attleboro Mus, Mass, 74; Berkshire Mus Ann Exhib, Pittsfield, Mass, 74; Nashua Arts & Sci Ctr, NH, 74; Organic Visions, Design Around US Gallery, Boston's Mus Sci, 77-78; one-person shows, Ward-Nasse Gallery, New York, 78. Pos: Designer package & corp image, free lance illus & design, Boston, 62- & Fed Distillers Inc, Cambridge, 65-69; juror, Cambridge Art Asn, 74 & 77; lectr, Lesley Col, Mass Col Art & Harvard Grad Sch Design, 75-78; founder & dir, Seven at Large, NE Women Artists' Collab, 75- Awards: RI Sch Design Scholar, 59-61; Painting Award, New Mem Show, Cambridge Art Asn, 73; Full Funding, Organic Visions, Boston's Mus Sci, 77. Bibliog: Garry Armstrong (auth), Boston Women Artists, WNAC-TV Channel 7 Spec Feature, Boston, 75; Mary Lou Kelley (auth), Organic visions, Christian Sci Monitor, 78; Lisa Taylor (producer), Woman 78, WBZ-TV Channel 4 Interview, Boston, 78. Mem: RI Sch Design Alumni Coun (area rep, Boston, 76-); Asn Artist Run Galleries, New York (assoc group dir, 75-); Boston Visual Artists Union Inc (exhib coordr, Am Citifair, 74); Women Exhibiting in Boston Inc (exhib coordr, Boston Chap, 73-75). Style & Technique: Figurative, human-like subjects: metamorphic human forms emerging from or existing within suspended organic masses. Media: Acrylic on Smooth Ragboard or Textured and Stretched Canvas. Dealer: Ward-Nasse Gallery 178 Prince St New York NY 10012. Mailing Add: 6 Exeter Park Cambridge MA 02140

DESSNER, MURRAY
PAINTER
b Philadelphia, Pa, Nov 11, 34. Study: Pa Acad Fine Arts, William Emlen Cresson traveling scholar, 65 & J Henry Schiedt traveling scholar, 66; also with Franklin C Watkins & Hobson Pittman. Work: Painting & Print Collection, Philadelphia Mus Art; Pittman Collection, Bryn Mawr Col, Pa; Penn Fed Collection. Exhib: Int Arts Festival PR, 69; two-man show, East Hampton Gallery, New York, 69; Cheltenham Ann, 69-72; one-man shows, Peale Galleries, Pa Acad Fine Arts, 70 & Marion Locks Gallery, Philadelphia, 72. Teaching: Instr painting, Pa Acad Fine Arts. Awards: Philadelphia Mus Art Purchase Prize, Cheltenham Art Ctr, 69. Bibliog: Two Philadelphians, Time Mag, 69; work reviewed in Art News, 69. Dealer: Marion Locks Gallery 1530 Walnut St Philadelphia PA 19102. Mailing Add: 802 Sansom St Philadelphia PA 19107

DE TOLNAY, CHARLES
ART HISTORIAN, WRITER
b Budapest, Hungary, May 27, 99; US citizen. Study: Univ Berlin, 20-21; Univ Frankfurt, 22; Univ Vienna, PhD, 25; Inst Advan Study, 39-48; Univ Rome, hon DLitt, 64; Univ Budapest, hon DPl, 70. Teaching: Vis prof, Columbia Univ, 53-64; emer prof, Univ Hamburg. Pos: Dir, Casa Buonarroti, Florence, Italy. Awards: Laureat Acad Inscriptions & Belles-Lett, Inst France, 37; Guggenheim & Bollingen fels. Mem: Col Art Asn Am; hon mem Accad Disegno, Florence; Accad Naz dei Lincei, Rome; Accad San Luca, Rome. Publ: Auth, The Youth of Michelangelo, Vol 1, 43 & 69, The Sistine Chapel, Vol 2, 45 & 69, The Medici Chapel, Vol 3, 48 & 70, The Tomb of Julius II, Vol 4, 54 & 70, The Final Period, Vol 5, 60 & 70 & Michelangelo, Architect, Vol 6, (in prep), In: Michelangelo, Princeton Univ; plus others. Mailing Add: Casa Buonarroti Via Ghibellina 70 Florence Italy

DE TONNANCOUR, JACQUES G
PAINTER, INSTRUCTOR
b Montreal, PQ, Jan 3, 17. Study: Col Brebeuf; Ecole Beaux-Arts, Montreal; Art Asn Montreal, with G Roberts. Work: Nat Gallery Can; Art Gallery Toronto. Comn: Murals, Dow Planetarium, Montreal, 67 & Univ Montreal, 68. Exhib: Yale Univ, 44; Rio de Janeiro, 44 & 46; UNESCO; retrospective exhib, Vancouver Art Gallery, 66; Mus Art Contemporain, 67; plus others. Teaching: Lectr Can art; instr, Ecole Beaux-Arts, Montreal. Awards: Brazilian Govt Scholar to Rio de Janeiro, 45-46; Can Coun Fel, 58 & Medal, 68; Second Prize, Quebec Ann Art Competition, 64. Mem: Royal Can Acad Art. Publ: Auth, Roberts. Mailing Add: 117 Lesperance St Lambert PQ G0S 2W0 Can

DE TURCZYNOWICZ, WANDA (MRS ELIOT HERMANN)
DESIGNER, PAINTER
b Krakow, Poland, June 16, 08; US citizen. Study: Study with Earl of Tankerville, Northumberland, Britain; with Hetherington, La Jolla, Calif; Ont Col Art, Toronto, with Beach. Work: Art Mus Juarez; Vancouver Mus Art; Victoria, BC. Comn: Costume designs & sets for operas, San Diego Community Chest, Calif, 25-26, Gilbert & Sullivan, La Jolla, 25-26, Toronto Univ Opera, 27-29 & Victoria Opera, 30-34. Exhib: Vancouver Mus Art, 30-35; Sun Carnival Shows, El Paso Mus Art, 40-60; El Paso Mus Art, 60's; Santa Fe Bicentennial, NMex, 60's; El Paso Mus Art Asn Show, 71-75. Teaching: Pvt lessons all media, 30-; instr painting, drawing & sculpture, Boy Scouts Am, 61-74. Pos: Prog chmn, El Paso Art Asn, 45 & 64, vpres, 55 & 57, pres, 56; chmn, 6th Ann Sun Carnival, El Paso Mus Art, 62. Awards: Three Best of Show, 14 Firsts, 5 Seconds & many Hon Mentions, El Paso Mus Art. Bibliog: Hudson Bay Co news coverage, Winnipeg, Can, 33; article in Hermosa Beach Women's Club Mag, Calif, 37; rev in Western Rev, Western NMex Univ, 67. Mem: Artists Equity Asn. Style & Technique: Palette knife and brush in traditional manner; collage and abstract. Media: Oil, Polymer, Watercolor. Mailing Add: 4215 Santa Rita El Paso TX 79902

DEUTSCH, PETER ANDREW
PAINTER
b Truava, Czech, July 31, 26; Can citizen. Study: Univ St Andrews, BSc(with hon). Work: Nat Gallery Can, Ottawa, Ont; Art Gallery Ont, Toronto; Agnes Etherington Art Gallery, Queen's Univ (Ont); Rothmans Art Gallery, Stratford, Ont. Exhib: 6th Can Biennial Exhib, Nat Gallery Can, Ottawa, 65; Ont Centennial Exhib Can Art, Art Gallery Ont, 67; Royal Can Acad Ann, 67, 68, 70 & 71; Ont Soc Artists Exhibs, 67 & 69; Art Gallery Hamilton Ann, 69 & 70. Media: Acrylic. Mailing Add: c/o Gallery Moos 138 Yorkville Ave Toronto ON M4W 1L2 Can

DEVINE, WILLIAM CHARLES
ART DEALER, COLLECTOR
b Brooklyn, NY, Aug 22, 32. Study: Union Col, Cranford, NJ. Pos: Owner, D Fine Arts Inc, Westfield, NJ. Specialty: Eighteenth and nineteenth century paintings and bronzes; east coast agent for contemporary artists; Alois LeCoque; Harry Devlin. Collection: Work by Alois LeCoque, Thomas Gainsborough, J R Grabach, H Gasser, Eugene Gauss, Grant Wood, Louis

Lozowick, Ben Sahn, Waldo Pierce & William Palmer. Mailing Add: D Fine Arts Inc 133 Harrison Ave Westfield NJ 07090

DEVLIN, HARRY
ILLUSTRATOR, PAINTER
b Jersey City, NJ, Mar 22, 18. Study: Syracuse Univ, BFA, 39; studied briefly with Hans Hoffman, New York. Comn: Themes of Am Domestic Archit (44 paintings), Corp Hq, City Fed Savings, Hillsboro, NJ, 77. Exhib: Am Cartoonists, Metrop Mus Art, New York, 54; Am Children's Bk Illusr, Voorhees Gallery, Rutgers Univ, 76. Teaching: Instr hist fine arts, Union Col, Cranford, NJ, 70-74, instr hist Am domestic archit, 76- Pos: Pres, Nat Cartoonists Soc, 56-57; chmn grants comt, NJ State Coun on the Arts, 76-, vchmn, 77- Awards: Best in Advert Cartooning, Nat Cartoonists Soc, 56 & 62; Arents Medal for Art & Lit, Syracuse Univ, 77. Mem: Soc Illusrs; Artists Equity; Nat Cartoonists Soc; Dutch Treat Club. Media: Oil. Publ: Co-auth & illusr, Old Black Witch, 63, auth & illusr, To Grandfather's House We Go: A Roadside Tour of American Homes, 67, auth & illusr, What Kind of House Is That?, 69, co-auth & illusr, Cranberry Thanksgiving, 71 & auth & illusr, Tales of Thunder & Lightning, 75, Parents Press. Mailing Add: 443 Hillside Ave Mountainside NJ 07092

DEW, JAMES EDWARD
EDUCATOR, PAINTER
b Barnesville, Ohio, Sept 15, 22. Study: Univ Ala, 43-44; Oberlin Col, AB, 46, AM, 47. Teaching: Prof painting, Univ Mont, 47- Style & Technique: Simplified realism. Media: Acrylic, Watercolor, Oil. Mailing Add: 531 E Sussex Ave Missoula MT 59801

DE WAAL, RONALD BURT
COLLECTOR
b Salt Lake City, Utah, Oct 23, 32. Study: Univ Utah, BS, 55; Mexico City Col, summer 55 & 58; Univ Denver, MA, 58. Exhib: Beethoven in the Arts, Univ Utah, 65 & Colo State Univ, 66, 67 & 70. Pos: Humanities librn & exhibs chmn, Colo State Univ, Ft Collins, 66- Mem: Col Art Asn Am; Nat Sculpture Soc. Collection: Beethoven statuary and paintings; pewter, porcelain, and wood figure sculptures. Publ: Auth, The World Bibliography of Sherlock Holmes and Dr Watson, New York Graphic Soc, 74; auth, Beethoven in the Fine Arts, (in prep). Mailing Add: Univ Libraries Colo State Univ Ft Collins CO 80521

DE WELDON, FELIX GEORGE WEIHS
SCULPTOR, ARCHITECT
b Vienna, Austria; US citizen. Study: Univ Vienna Sch Archit, BA, MA, MS & PhD; Oxford Univ; also study in Italy, Spain & France. Work: Bronze statue of John Glenn, Air & Space Mus, Washington, DC; Truman Libr, Independence, Mo; Kennedy Libr, Boston. Comn: Flag raising on Iwo Jima, Marine Corps War Mem Found, Washington, DC, 54; Simon Bolivar (equestrian statue), Washington, DC, 58; Red Cross Monument, Washington, DC, 59; Truman Monument, Athens, Greece, 63; Nat Monument, Govt Malaysia, Kuala Lampur, 66. Exhib: Royal Acad, London, 36; Salon, Paris, 38; Archit League New York, 39; Mus Montreal, Can, 40; Art Asn, Newport, RI, 46. Teaching: Dir, Newport Acad Fine Arts, 52-60. Pos: Comnr, Comn Fine Arts, 50-63; chmn, Comn Arts & Sci for President Eisenhower, 52-60; chmn, Arts & Sci Comt Taft Inst Govt, 71. Awards: Medal of Honor for Arts & Sci, Austria, 62; Award for Outstanding Serv, Daughters Am Revolution, 72; Knight, Order of Malaysia Brit Commonwealth. Bibliog: Uncommon Valour (film), USN, 52; US Marines, Nat Geog Mag, 52; Tribute in transit, Life Mag, 54. Mem: Art Asn Newport, RI. Mailing Add: 2818 McGill Terr NW Washington DC 20008

DEWEY, KENNETH FRANCIS
PAINTER, ILLUSTRATOR
b New York, NY, Oct 5, 40. Study: Sch Visual Arts, New York; also with B Hogarth & Philip Hayes. Exhib: One-man shows, Dal Bohrer's Design Gallery, 69 & Yares Gallery, 72; Firebird Festival Fine Arts, 70; Strathmore Paper Int, 70; Southwest Graphics Int, 72. Awards: Strathmore Paper Award, 70; Mod Publicity Int Award, 70; Bronze Medal, Two Awards, Communigraphics, 71. Media: Watercolor, Oil; Pen & Ink. Publ: Illusr, Rip Van Winkle, Simon & Schuster, 70; auth & illusr, Don's trek, Ariz Repub & Gazette, 70; illusr, Spirit of Cochise, Scribner, 72; auth & illusr, Onyamarks, The Studio, 72. Dealer: Yares Gallery PO Box 1662 Scottsdale AZ 85252. Mailing Add: 5222 W Banff Ln Glendale AZ 85306

DEWIT, FLOYD TENNISON
SCULPTOR, PAINTER
b Wolf Point, Mont, Aug 25, 34. Study: Minneapolis Sch Art, Minn, scholar, 57, with Paul Granlund; Rijksakademie Van Beeldende Kunsten, Amsterdam, Netherland, scholar, 61-66, sculpture with V P S Esser. Work: Rijksakademie Collection, Amsterdam; City Collection, Utrecht; Royal Collection, Princess Benedicte, Denmark; Nat Medallion Soc, Hague, Netherlands; Rijks Collection, Amsterdam. Comn: Seven welded reliefs, Michaels Supper Club, Rochester, Minn, 60; Eleanor Roosevelt Medallion, Royal Begeer, Vorschaten, Netherlands, 64; Inheritor (bronze equestrian monument), City of Amsterdam, 67; bronze donkeys, Utrecht, Netherlands, 67; Pegasus (cast bronze), Utrecht, 72. Exhib: 20th Century Sculpture, Walker Art Ctr, Minneapolis, 58; Interacademial Exhib Sculpture, Hague, 63; Het Paard, Paardenburg on Amstel, Netherlands, 64; Mod Dutch Sculpture, Singer Mus, Harlem, Netherlands, 69; Ann Salons Arti Et Amicitiae, Amsterdam, 70-72. Awards: Purchase Awards, Rijksacademie, 61-66 & Denmark, 63. Mem: Arti & Amicitiae Amsterdam (mem jury, 68-); Int Asn Art, Paris; Amsterdam Soc Medallion Art. Media: Bronze, Iron; Oil. Mailing Add: Gijsbrecht van Aemstelstraat 29 Amsterdam Netherlands

DEY, KRIS
SCULPTOR, DESIGNER
b Buffalo, NY, Oct 17, 49. Study: Univ Calif, Los Angeles, BA, 72, MA, 74, MFA, 76; also with Vasa & Bernard Kester. Comn: Hanging partition in fiber, ABC Entertainment Off, Century City, Calif, 74; wall relief, Ackerman Union, Univ Calif, Los Angeles, 74; two wall reliefs, Security Pac Bank, Receda, 75; wall relief, San Antonio Hosp, Upland; wall relief, Valley Bank Nev, Las Vegas, 75. Exhib: Fiberworks, Lang Art Gallery, Scripps Col, Claremont, 73; tapestry & other fiber forms, Calif State Univ, Northridge, 74; Artist's Choice, Los Angeles Co Mus Art, 75; New Talents in Fiber, Wenger-Casat Galleries, La Jolla, 75; Calif Design, 76, Pac Design Ctr, 76. Teaching: Teaching asst design, Univ Calif, Los Angeles, 73-74, teaching assoc textile design, 74- Bibliog: Bernard Kester (auth), A letter from LA, Craft Horizons, 4/75, 8/75 & 10/75 & A new forum for fiber art, Artweek, 1/75. Style & Technique: Abstract composition exploring visual illusions in color; planes assembled from a series of hard and soft tubing, individually wrapped with fiber. Media: Yarns, Torn Fabric. Mailing Add: 1856 1/2 Pandora Ave Westwood CA 96137

DHAEMERS, ROBERT AUGUST
PRINTMAKER, EDUCATOR
b Luverne, Minn, Nov 24, 26. Study: Calif Col Arts & Crafts, BFA, 52, MFA, 54. Work: City San Francisco Art Comn, Calif; First Christ Lutheran Church, Burlingame, Calif; San Jose State Col; Mills Col; St Catherine Indian Sch, Santa Fe, NMex. Comn: Wrought iron wall mural, Jerrys Restaurant, San Leandro, Calif, 60; sculpture crucifix, First Christ Lutheran Church, 61; fountain, Frank Hunt Archit, Oakland, Calif, 63; Sundial Cor-Ten (steel 2 ton), Sci Complex, Mills Col, 70; bronze tabernacle, Holy Cross Hosp, San Fernando, Calif, 77. Exhib: Am Fedn Arts New Talent USA Traveling Exhib, 57-59; Mus NMex, 59; San Francisco Art Comn, Palace Legion Honor, 61; de Young Mus, San Francisco, 62; Univ Calif, 62; Univ Minn, 63; Univ Iowa, 64; Univ Columbia, 64; Mus Contemp Crafts, Creative Casting, NY, 64; Bertrand Russell Centenary Int, Nottingham, Eng, 73; Commissioned Arts in Archit, Civic Art Gallery San Jose, 74; Brigham Young Univ, Utah, 76. Teaching: Asst prof art, Calif Col Arts & Crafts, 51-56; assoc prof art, Mills Col, 57-75, prof, 75-, actg head dept art, 63-64, head dept, 73- Awards: Fist Award Sculpture Gold Medal, Oakland Mus Art, 52; First Award Metal Work, Calif State Fair, 62; Mills Col Fac Res Grant, 75. Bibliog: Rose Slivca (auth), First congress of world craftsmen, Crafts Horizon, 65; Lunar suite, environmental sculpture, Look, 69; New talent, Art Am, 66. Mem: Western Col Asn (accreditation comt, 69-); Western Asn Schs & Cols; Accrediting Comn Sr Cols & Univs. Style & Technique: Work in all metal techniques, currently working in stainless steel and galvanized painted steel; graphics includes etching, litho and silk screen. Publ: Co-auth, Simple Jewelry Making for the Classroom, 58; contribr, Metal Techniques for Craftsmen, 68; contribr, Craftsmen of the SW, 65 & The Crafts of the Modern World, 68; co-auth, article in Mills Mag, 70. Mailing Add: Mills Col Box 9924 Oakland CA 94613

D'HARNONCOURT, ANNE (J)
ART HISTORIAN, CURATOR
b Washington, DC, Sept 7, 43. Study: Radcliffe Col, BA, 65; Courtauld Inst Art, Univ London, MA, 67. Collections Arranged: Marcel Duchamp, Philadelphia Mus Art (with catalog), 73. Pos: Cur asst, Philadelphia Mus Art, 67-69; asst cur 20th century art, Art Inst Chicago, 69-71; cur dept 20th century art, Philadelphia Mus Art, 71- Mem: Arch Am Art; Col Art Asn Am; Smithsonian Coun; Am Asn Mus; Int Coun Mus. Publ: Co-auth, Etant Donnes: Reflections on a New Work by Marcel Duchamp, 69; auth, A W Gallatin & the Arensbergs, pioneer collectors of 20th century art, Apollo, 7/74. Mailing Add: Philadelphia Mus Art PO Box 7646 Philadelphia PA 19101

DIAMOND, ABEL JOSEPH
DESIGNER, ARCHITECT
b Piet Retief Transvaal, SAfrica, Nov 8, 32; Can citizen. Study: Univ Capetown, BArch(with distinction), 56; Oxford Univ, MA(politics, philos, econ), 58; Univ Pa, MArch, 61. Teaching: From instr archit to asst prof archit, Univ Pa, 62-64; assoc prof postgrad archit, Univ Toronto, 64-69; from assoc prof to prof, Fac Environ Studies, York Univ, 70-75. Awards: Eedee Award, First Prize in Design, Can Fed Govt, 67; Award for Residential Design & Hon Mention, Can Housing Design Coun, 74; Design Award for Neighborhood Develop, Urban Design Mag, New York, 76. Mem: Royal Inst Brit Architects; Royal Archit Inst Can (registration bd, 74-77); cert, NCARB, US; Am Inst Planners; Can Inst Planners. Mailing Add: 322 King St W Toronto ON M5V 1J5 Can

DIAMOND, PAUL
PHOTOGRAPHER
b Brooklyn, NY, June 20, 42. Study: Pratt Inst, BFA, 65. Work: Int Mus Photog, George Eastman House, Rochester, NY; Nat Gallery Can, Ottawa, Ont; Fogg Art Mus, Cambridge, Mass; Boston Mus Fine Arts. Exhib: 60s Continuum, George Eastman House, 72; one-man shows, Sq Bromides, Gallery Optica, Montreal, Que, 73 & Floating Found of Photog, New York, 74; Peculiar to Photog, Univ NMex, 76; Five, St Charles on the Wazee, Denver, Colo, 77; Contemp Photog, Fogg Art Mus, 77. Teaching: Instr photog, Calif Col Arts & Crafts, Oakland, 77-78; guest lectr photog, Univ Colo, Boulder, 77. Awards: Guggenheim Found Fel, 75-76; Nat Endowment for the Arts Grant, 78. Mem: Soc Photog Educ. Style & Technique: Photographic penetration. Publ: Contribr, Photographer's Choice, Addison House, 75, Ctr for Creative Photog, Vol 4, Univ Ariz, 77 & Grotesque in Photography, Ridge Press, 77. Dealer: Witkin Gallery 41 E 57th St New York NY 10022. Mailing Add: 21 St James Pl Brooklyn NY 11205

DIAO, DAVID
PAINTER
b Szechuan, China, Aug 7, 43; US citizen. Study: Kenyon Col, AB, 64. Work: Whitney Mus Am Art, New York; San Francisco Mus; Art Gallery Ont, Toronto; Va Mus, Richmond. Exhib: Beaux Arts 25th Anniversary Exhib, Columbus Gallery Fine Arts, Ohio, 71; Paintings & Sculpture Today, Indianapolis Mus Art, Ind, 72; Ten Painters from New York, Mus Art, Univ Calif, Berkeley, 72; Painting & Sculpture Today, Indianapolis Mus, 74; New York Sch, State of Art, Albany, NY, 77; plus others. Teaching: Instr independent study prog, Whitney Mus, New York, 70- Awards: Guggenheim Fel, 73-74; Creative Artists Pub Serv Award, 78. Bibliog: James Harithas (auth), David Diao, Arts Mag, 4/70; Carter Ratcliff (auth), Painted vs painterly, Art News Ann, 71; Peter Schjeldahl (auth), Two on the move, New York Times, 3/19/72. Mailing Add: 72 Franklin New York NY 10013

DIBBETS, JAN
ARTIST
b Weert, Amsterdam, May 9, 41. Exhib: Kunst und Fotographie, Kunsthalle Hamburg, Ger, 73; Contemporanea, Rome, Italy, 73; Art in Space, Detroit Inst Art, Mich, 73; Proj 74, Walraf Richard Mus, Cologne, Ger, 75; Eight Contemporary Artists, Mus Mod Art, New York, 74; plus many other group & one-man shows. Mailing Add: c/o Leo Castelli Gallery 420 W Broadway New York NY 10012

DIBBLE, CHARLES RYDER
EDUCATOR, PAINTER
b Richmondville, NY, Apr 14, 20. Study: Syracuse Univ, BFA(fabric design), 41, MA(clothing & textiles), 50, PhD(polit sci), 61; also with F Montague Charman. Work: Univ Col, Syracuse Univ & Col Human Develop; Syracuse Univ Permanent Collection; Everson Mus, Syracuse; Rochester Mem Gallery, NY. Exhib: Am Watercolor Soc; Munson-Williams Proctor Inst, Utica, NY; Rochester Mem Art Gallery; Everson Mus. Collections Arranged: Ruth H Randall Contemporary Japanese Ceramics, Syracuse Univ, 63, African Sculpture (with M Peter Piening), 64, John R Fox Korean Ceramics, 65 & Romantic Painting in the University Collection, 66. Teaching: Prof fashion design, Syracuse Univ, 46-, asst dean acad affairs, Col Visual & Performing Arts, 70-, prof Japanese & other Oriental art, 61- Pos: Designer, Etchcraft, Herkimer, NY, 41-42. Awards: Sanctuary (watercolor), Rochester Mem Art Gallery, 66 & Ghosts (watercolor), 68; Florence Disaster (watercolor), Asn Artists Syracuse, 69. Mem: Ukioye Soc; Oriental Ceramic Soc; Am Ceramic Soc (exec comt, design div, 67-69, chmn, 68-70); Asn Asian Studies; Nat Trust Hist Preservation. Style & Technique: Watercolor semi-abstract; action painting based on natural forms. Media: Watercolor, Pencil. Res: Oriental ceramics, mainly Japanese and Korean, especially the influence of Korean on Japanese. Publ: Auth, Contemporary Japanese Ceramics, 61; auth, The John R Fox

Collection of Korean Ceramics, 66; contribr, Seventeen Prints, 68; contribr, Printmaking, 70. Mailing Add: 848 Livingston Ave Syracuse NY 13210

DIBBLE, GEORGE
PAINTER, ART WRITER
b Laie, Hawaii, Mar 29, 04; US citizen. Study: Art Students League with George Bridgman, Ivan Olinski & Howard Giles; Columbia Univ with Charles Martin, Arthur Young & Sallie Tannahill, BS & MFA. Work: Utah State Div of Fine Arts, Salt Lake City; Univ Utah Mus of Fine Arts; Utah State Univ, Logan; Southern Utah State Col, Cedar City; Granite Dist Sch & Davis Dist Sch, Utah. Comn: Watercolor collections of Hawaii, United Airlines, San Francisco Airport, Calif. Exhib: Ann Exhib, Utah State Fair, 38-65; Utah Biennial, Salt Lake Art Ctr, 50; Utah State Inst of Fine Arts Ann, 52-60; Ben Franklin Hotel, San Mateo, Calif, 56; one-man show, Ogden Eccles Art Ctr, 67; Watercolor W, Utah State Univ, 74-76; Centennial Exhib, Utah Artists, Salt Lake City Art Ctr, 76; two-man show, Art Gallery, Univ Utah, 76; Eight-State Regional—Watercolor, Utah State Inst of Fine Arts. Teaching: Assoc prof watercolor, Univ Utah, 47-57, prof watercolor, 57-72, emer prof, 72- Pos: Vis fac mem, Southern Utah State Col, Cedar City, summer sessions, Wash State Col, 52, San Jose State Col, 55 & Brigham Young Univ, 55; auth, weekly column, Art Scene, Salt Lake Tribune, 57- Awards: First Purchase Awards, Utah State Fair Asn, 35 & 38 & Utah State Inst of Fine Arts Watercolor, 52. Bibliog: 100 Yrs of Utah Painting, James Haseltine Salt Lake Art Ctr, 65. Mem: Fel Utah Acad of Sci, Arts & Lett. Media: Transparent and opaque watercolor and oil. Publ: Auth, Art and the Unadjusted School Child, Art Educ Today, Columbia Univ, 36; auth, Watercolor, Materials and Techniques, Holt, Rinehart & Winston, 66. Mailing Add: 2049 Wilmington Ave Salt Lake City UT 84109

DIBNER, MARTIN
MUSEUM DIRECTOR
b New York, NY, Oct 5, 11. Study: Univ Pa, BS(econ); Art Students League. Pos: Art dir, Miami Daily News, Fla, 48-50; exec dir, Calif Arts Comn, 64-66; dir, Joan Whitney Payson Gallery of Art, Westbrook Col, Portland, 76- Publ: Auth, Seacoast Maine, Doubleday. Mailing Add: Mayberry Hill Casco Village ME 04015

DICE, ELIZABETH JANE
CRAFTSMAN, EDUCATOR
b Urbana, Ill, Apr 3, 19. Study: Univ Mich, BDesign, 41, MDesign, 42; Ind Univ, MA, 66; Int Sch Art, Mex; Inst Allenda, Mex; Columbia Univ Teachers Col; Norfolk Art Sch; painting with Jerry Farnsworth. Exhib: Miss Art Asn, 48-51, 67 & 68; Nat Crafts Exhib, Wichita, Kans, 50; Nat Watercolor Show, Jackson, Miss, 51; Starkville Craft Exhib, Miss, 54; New Orleans Art Asn, 55; plus many others. Teaching: Assoc prof art, Miss State Col Women, 45- Awards: Prizes, Jackson, Miss, 46 & 51; Miss River Craft Exhib Award, 63. Mem: Col Art Asn Am; Handweavers Guild Am (state rep, 72-77); Miss Art Asn; Southeastern Col Art Conf; Columbus Art Asn. Style & Technique: Design, the important thing, leans heavily on art nouveau; technique depends upon the media being used. Mailing Add: 134 King St Columbus MS 39701

DICKERSON, BETTY
PAINTER, LECTURER
b Nashville, Kans, Feb 11, 08. Study: Univ Kans, AB; Wichita Art Asn; and with Albert Bloch, Karl Mattern, B J O Nordfeldt & William Dickerson. Work: Wichita Art Mus; Wichita Art Asn; Kans State Univ; also pvt collections. Exhib: Kans State Univ; Kans Watercolor Soc, 70-74; Sandzen Mem Gallery, 74; Wichita Art Asn Exhib, 77-78; Kans State Fedn Art, 78. Teaching: Instr drawing & painting, Wichita Art Asn Sch, 31-78; instr, Hutchinson Recreation Ctr, Kans, 65-78; lectr, univs, clubs & art mus throughout Midwest. Pos: Created KARD-TV daily art-fashion prog, 56; co-dir, Wichita Art Asn, 63-64, asst dir, 65-67; assembled inivational Nat Decorative Arts Exhibs, Wichita, 64, 68 & 70. Media: Oil, Watercolor. Mailing Add: 509 N Martinson Wichita KS 67203

DICKERSON, DANIEL JAY
PAINTER, EDUCATOR
b Jersey City, NJ, Dec 22, 22. Study: Cooper Union Art Sch, 41-43 & 45-46; Cranbrook Acad Art, BFA, 47, MFA, 49. Work: Joseph H Hirshhorn Collection; Adelphi Univ Mus; Ill Wesleyan Mus; Cranbrook Mus; Weatherspoon Gallery, Univ NC. Exhib: Whitney Mus Am Art Ann, 47; Pa Acad Fine Arts, 53; Audubon Artists Exhib, 64; Nat Inst Arts & Lett, 68; Nat Acad Design, 74; plus others. Teaching: Lectr art, Manhattanville Col, 65-69; chmn dept art, Finch Col, 69-78; instr, Fairleigh Dickinson Univ, 78- Awards: First Prize, Springfield Art Mus, 54; Emily Lowe Award for Painting, Audubon Artists, 64; Henry Ward Ranger Purchase Award, Nat Acad Design, 74; plus others. Style & Technique: Cityscapes and figures in motion, depicted in semi-abstract style. Media: Acrylic, Oil. Mailing Add: 104 High St Leonia NJ 07605

DICKERSON, TOM
PAINTER, CERAMIST
Study: Univ NMex, BA, 55; Wichita State Univ, MA, 63. Exhib: Hill's Galleries, Santa Fe, NMex. Teaching: Lectr, Col Santa Fe. Pos: Cur traveling exhib, Mus NMex, Mus Int Folk Art, Santa Fe, 67-73; potter, La Cueva Mountain Pottery, Glorieta, NMex; consult, Pecos Nat Monument Living Hist Pottery Proj, 75- Mailing Add: Box 4581 Santa Fe NM 87501

DICKEY, HELEN PAULINE
PAINTER
b Cleveland, Ohio. Study: Mus Sch, Toledo Univ; Western Reserve Univ; Tampa Univ, with Harold Nosti; Cleveland Sch Art, with Carl Gaertner. Work: Loew's Hotels, New York; Fla Presby Col, St Petersburg; Merritt-Phinney-Southard, Cleveland; Fla Power Co, St Petersburg; Clearwater Fed, Fla; plus others. Exhib: Hunter Ann, Chattanooga, Tenn, 67; 22nd Southeastern Ann Exhib, High Mus, Atlanta, Ga, 67; Juried Arts 6th Nat Exhib, Tyler, Tex, 69; Chautauqua Nat Exhib Am Art, 69-70; Gulf Coast Art Exhib, Mobile, Ala; one-person show, Weir Gallery, Vero Beach, Fla, 78. Teaching: Instr, Studio Four, 64-69; instr, Arts Ctr, St Petersburg, 71-72 & 75; instr, Art Club St Petersburg, 72. Pos: Dir Art Gallery, Main Pub Libr, St Petersburg, 68-78; dir, Arts Ctr Gallery, St Petersburg, 71-73. Awards: Many state awards, 62- Bibliog: Mariane Kelsey (auth), Artist says, I paint for myself, 67; Charles Benbow (auth), reviews, In: St Petersburg Times, 67-; Jeanette Crane (auth), interview, 74 & rev, 75, In: Times Independent, St Petersburg. Mem: Fla Artist Group; Fla League Arts; Arts Ctr Asn St Petersburg (vpres, 71-72); Fine Arts Mus. Media: Polymers, Oil. Specialty: Original paintings, sculpture and crafts. Publ: Contribr & illusr, A brighter dawn awaits the human day, Churchman Mag, 12/68. Mailing Add: 1723 Lakewood Dr S St Petersburg FL 33712

DICKINSON, DAVID CHARLES
PRINTMAKER, LECTURER
b Hendon, Middlesex, Eng, Jan 3, 40. Study: Chelsea Sch Art, London, 56-61; Statens-Kunst-og-Handverks Industrie Skoolen, Oslo, Norway, 61-62; Rochester Inst Technol, MFA, 72. Work: Southampton Civic Ctr, Eng; Comn of Arts, Atlanta, Ga; Rochester Inst Technol; Rochester Print Club, NY; Lake Erie Col, Painesville, Ohio. Comn: Portfolio of Prints, Cold Cream Alley, Rochester, 73; 20 prints, EGR Commun, Rochester, 73 & 35 prints, 74. Exhib: Royal Acad Summer Exhib, London, 67; Big Bend Nat Exhib, Tallahassee, Fla, 68; 2nd Nat Print Exhib, Atlanta, 71; Finger Lakes Regional, Rochester, 71 & 73; Epinal Biennial, France, 75; two-man show, Univ Mo, Columbus, 76; Printmaker's Invitational, Rochester Inst Technol, NY, 78. Teaching: Instr printmaking & drawing, Rochester Inst Technol, 72- Pos: Mem Art Gallery visiting artist in NY high schs, 73-; artist in residence, Fairport High Sch, NY, 75. Awards: Best in Show, Big Bend Nat Exhib, 68; Purchase Award, Comn Arts, 71; Purchase Award, Finger Lakes Regional Exhib, 73. Style & Technique: Photoetching and gravure techniques; interaction of organic and inorganic forms. Media: Intaglio & Non-Silver Photographic Processes. Mailing Add: 6825 Rte 408 Mt Morris NY 14510

DICKINSON, EDWIN
PAINTER
b Seneca Falls, NY, Oct 11, 91. Study: Pratt Inst Art Sch, 10-11; Art Students League, 11-12; Paris, France, 19-20; also with William M Chase & C W Hawthorne. Work: Metrop Mus Art; Albright-Knox Art Gallery; Mus Mod Art; Whitney Mus Am Art; Art Inst Chicago; plus others. Exhib: Fifteen Americans, 52, Mus Mod Art, 59 & Traveling Exhib, 61; retrospectives, Boston Univ, 58 & Whitney Mus Am Art, 65; Brooklyn Mus; Boston Mus Fine Arts; Venice Biennale, 68; plus others. Teaching: Lectr, Hartford, Boston & Columbia Univs; instr art, Art Students League, 22-23 & 45-65; instr art, Cooper Union Art Sch, 45-50; instr art, Brooklyn Mus, 49-53. Awards: Creative Arts Medal, Brandeis Univ, 59; Ford Found Grant, 59; Brevoort-Eickenmeyer Prize, Columbia Univ, 65; plus others. Bibliog: Werner Haftman (auth), Painting in the Twentieth Century, Praeger, 60; Lloyd Goodrich (auth), The Drawings of Edwin Dickinson, Yale Univ, 63; plus others. Mem: Fedn Mod Painters & Sculptors; Nat Acad Design; Patteran Soc, Buffalo; Am Acad Arts & Lett; Nat Inst Arts & Lett; plus others. Mailing Add: PO Box 793 Wellfleet MA 02667

DICKINSON, ELEANOR CREEKMORE
PAINTER, GRAPHIC & VIDEO ARTIST
b Knoxville, Tenn, Feb 7, 31. Study: Univ Tenn, with C Kermit Ewing, BA, 52; San Francisco Art Inst, with James Weeks, 61-63. Work: Corcoran Gallery Art, Washington, DC; San Francisco Mus Art; Butler Inst Am Art, Youngstown, Ohio; Libr Cong Collection, Washington, DC; Nat Collection Fine Arts, Washington, DC; plus others. Exhib: One-artist shows, McClung Mus, Univ Tenn, Knoxville, 64, San Francisco Mus Art, 65, Santa Barbara Mus Art, Calif, 66, Fine Arts Mus, San Francisco, 68 & 75, Dulin Gallery, 70, Corcoran Gallery Art, 70 & 74, Poindexter Gallery, New York, 72 & 74, J B Speed Art Mus, Louisville, Ky, 72, Wash State Mus, 75, Cheney Cowles Mus, Spokane, Wash, 75, Triton Mus of Art, Santa Clara, Calif, 75 & 77 & Smithsonian Inst Travelling Exhib, 75-79; Montgomery Mus of Fine Arts, 75; Huntsville Mus, 75; plus others. Teaching: Lectr drawing & painting, Univ Calif, 69-71; assoc prof life drawing, Calif Col Arts & Crafts, Oakland, 71- Pos: Trustee, San Francisco Art Inst, 63-66; dir galleries, Calif Col Arts & Crafts, Oakland, 71- Awards: San Francisco Women Artists Pres Prize, San Francisco Mus, 59; Purchase Award, Butler Inst Am Art, 60; Graphics Prize, City of San Francisco, 74; plus others. Bibliog: Aline Saarinen (auth), Revival!, NBC Today Show, 70; James R Mellow (auth), Eleanor Dickinson, New York Times, 72; Walter Hopps (auth), Introd to Revival!, Harper, 74; plus others. Mem: Artists Equity Asn Northern Calif (mem bd dirs); Ctr for Visual Arts (bd dir); Col Art Asn. Style & Technique: Life-size contour drawings of figures, felt pen on paper; small works of dreams in mixed media on paper. Media: Mixed media; black velvet; video tapes; bronze; graphics. Publ: Auth, Tennessee revival services, Libr Cong Arch Folk Song, 71; illusr, Complete Fruit Cookbook, Scribner, 72; auth, Revival!, 74 & illusr, That Old Time Religion, 75, Harper; plus others. Dealer: Poindexter Gallery 24 E 84th St New York NY 10028; William Sawyer Gallery 3045 Clay St San Francisco CA 94115. Mailing Add: 2125 Broderick St San Francisco CA 94115

DICKINSON, WILLIAM STIRLING
LECTURER, ART ADMINISTRATOR
b Chicago, Ill, Dec 22, 09. Study: Princeton Univ, BA(cum laude); Art Inst Chicago; Fontainebleau Ecole des Beaux Arts, France. Teaching: Lectr surv of Mex, Inst Allende, San Miguel de Allende, Mex, 45-, lectr Mex writers viewpoints, 71- Pos: Dir, Escuela Univ Bellas Artes, San Miguel de Allende, 38-51; dir & pres, Inst Allende, 51- Publ: Co-auth & illusr, Mexican odyssey, 35; co-auth & illusr, Westward from Rio, 36; co-auth & illusr, Death is accidental, 37; co-auth, San Miguel de Allende, 71; translr, Imperial Cuzco, 71. Mailing Add: Santo Domingo 38 Guanajuato San Miguel de Allende Mexico

DICKSON, JENNIFER JOAN
PHOTOGRAPHER, PRINTMAKER
b Piet Retief, Repub of S Africa, Sept 17, 36; Can citizen. Study: Goldsmith's Sch for Art, Univ London, 54-59; Atelier 17, Paris, with S W Hayter, 61-65. Work: Victoria & Albert Mus, London, Eng; Nat Gallery Can, Ottawa; The Hermitage, Leningrad, USSR; Bibliot Nat, Paris, France; Smithsonian Inst, Washington, DC. Comn: The Secret Garden (collabr: Henry J Kahanek & Ray Van Dusen), Still Photog Div, Nat Film Bd Can, 76. Exhib: Biennale de Paris, Mus Mod Art, France, 63; Mod Prints, Victoria & Albert Mus, London, 65; Contemp Brit Prints, Mus Mod Art, Tokyo, Japan, 70; Camerart, Optica Gallery, Montreal & Europe, 75; Exposure (touring Can), Art Gallery of Ont, 76. Collections Arranged: Imprint 76, a survey of current Canadian graphic art in conjunction with the Ontario Arts Coun. Teaching: Vis prof fine Arts, Univ Wis, Madison, 72; vis artist fine arts, Queen's Univ, Kingston, Ont, 77- Awards: Prix des Jeunes Artistes pour Gravures, Paris Biennale, Mus Mod Art, Paris, 63; James A Reid Award, Can Painters-Etchers & Engravers, 73; Special Purchase Award, World Print Competition, San Francisco Mus Art, 73. Bibliog: John Brunsdon (auth), The Technique of Etching & Engraving, Batsford & Reinhold, 67; Michael Rothstein (auth), Frontiers of Printmaking, Studio Vista, 70; Anthony Gross (auth), Etching, Engraving & Intaglio Printing, Oxford Univ Press, 72. Mem: Academician Royal Acad Arts; Print & Drawing Coun Can; Can Artists Representation. Style & Technique: Romantic symbolism with erotic content; photo etchings. Media: Etching. Dealer: Galerie Dresdnere 130 Bloor St W Toronto ON M5S 1N5 Can. Mailing Add: 508 Gilmour St Ottawa ON K1R 5L4 Can

DIEBENKORN, RICHARD
PAINTER
b Portland, Ore, Apr 22, 22. Study: Stanford Univ, 40-43; Univ Calif, 43-44; Calif Sch Fine Arts, 46; Univ NMex, MA, 52. Work: Toronto Mus; Phoenix Mus; Albright-Knox Gallery, Buffalo; Oberlin Col Gallery; San Francisco Mus Art; plus others. Exhib: Five shows, Whitney Mus Am Art Ann, 55-70; one-man shows, DeYoung Mem Mus, San Francisco, 63,

Jewish Mus, 65 & Los Angeles Co Mus, Los Angeles, 69 & 72; Venice Biennale, 68; 20th Nat Print Exhib, 77; plus many other group & one-man shows. Teaching: Prof art, Univ Calif, Los Angeles, 66-73. Awards: Albert M Bender fel, 46; Purchase Prize, Olivet Col; Gold Medal, Pa Acad Fine Arts, 68. Bibliog: David M Mendelowitz (auth), included in: A History of American Art, Holt, 61; Lee Nordness (ed), included in: Art: USA, now C J Bucher, 62; Alfred Neumeyer (auth), included in: The Search for Meaning in Modern Art, Prentice-Hall, 64; plus others. Mem: Am Acad Arts & Lett. Publ: Auth, Drawing, 65. Dealer: Marlborough Gallery 41 E 57th St New York NY 10022. Mailing Add: 334 Amalfi Dr Santa Monica CA 90402

DIEHL, SEVILLA S
PAINTER
b Philadelphia, Pa, May 15, 17. Study: Fleisher Art Mem, Philadelphia, 35-37; Philadelphia Mus Sch, 66-67; Barnes Found, 66-68; pvt studies with Hobson Pitman, Chinese brush painting with Pheobe Shih, mixed media with Ithzak Sankowsky & watercolor with Edgar Whitney. Work: Thomas Jefferson Univ; Widener Col; RCA Radio Corp, Washington, DC. Exhib: Woodmere Art Gallery 31st Ann Exhib, Chestnut Hill, Pa, 71; Catharine Lorillard Wolfe Art Club 66th Ann Show, Gramercy Sq, New York, 72 & Nat Soc Painters in Casein & Acrylic 18th Ann, 72; three-woman show, Philadelphia Art Alliance, Pa, 73 & Regional Oil & Acrylic Show, 75; plus numerous others. Awards: Shiva Artists Colors Award, Catharine Lorillard Wolfe Art Club, New York, 72; Best of Show, Maine Line Ctr of the Arts, Haverford, 74 & Jury Selection Award, 74; plus numerous awards in local competitions. Bibliog: Marion Guthrie (auth), article in Montgomery Post, Norristown, Pa, 6/10/70; Dorothy Grafly (auth), articles in Philadelphia Sunday Bull, 8/2/70 & Art-in-Focus, Philadelphia, 1/75. Mem: Artists Equity, Philadelphia Chap; Philadelphia Art Alliance; Philadelphia Watercolor Club; Woodmere Art Gallery, Chestnut Hill, Pa; Nat League Pen Women, Philadelphia Chap. Style & Technique: Impressionistic to abstract, the feeling rather than the actuality, using both brush and knife on a variety of surfaces, rice paper, canvas and board. Media: Acrylic. Dealer: Sidney Rothman c/o The Gallery Barnegat Light NJ 08006. Mailing Add: 227 Swedeland Rd Gulph Mills King of Prussia PA 19406

DIENES, SARI
SCULPTOR, PRINTMAKER
b Debrecen, Hungary, Oct 8, 98; US citizen. Study: With Fernand Leger & Andre Lhote, Paris, France; Ozenfant Sch Art, London, Eng; also with Henry Moore. Work: Brooklyn Mus, NY; Mus Mod Art Print Collection, New York; also in many pvt collections. Comn: Stage set & costume designs for Fire, Univ Ill Art Festival, 52; 400 rubbings of prehistoric Indian carvings on stones bordering Columbia River, comn by Archaeol Dept, Univ Wash, 55-58; figures & masks for Questions from the Floor, Buffalo Art Festival, 68; Electric Circus, 68; two screens, Hearing Rooms, Legis Bldg, Albany, NY, 72. Exhib: One-artist shows, Recent Work, AIR Galleries, New York, 73, 75 & 77, Andre Zarre Gallery, New York, 74, Petroglyph Rubbings, Byrd Hoffman Found, Inc, 74, Ceramics, Andrew Crispo Gallery, New York, 77 & Color Xerox, Rockland Ctr for the Arts, 77; Games, Reflection and Divination, 74, Works in Progress Art Exhib, 74 & Sketch Bks, 78, Women's Interart Ctr, New York; Group Show, AIR Galleries, 74-75, 77 & 78, US, Tokyo & Kyoto; New York Prof Women Artists, New Sch Social Res, New York, 75; Year of the Women, Bronx Mus Art, 75; Artist's Choice, Women in the Arts, New York, 77 & Bethlehem, Pa, 77; Art in Pub Spaces, Orgn Independent Artists, US Ct House, Brooklyn, NY, 77; plus others. Teaching: Asst dir, Ozenfant Sch Art, London; instr art, Parsons Sch Design & Brooklyn Mus Art Sch, New York; artist in residence, Stout State Univ, 66. Awards: Am Fedn Art grant, 71; Mark Rothko Found grant, 71; Int Women's Yr Award, 76; plus others. Bibliog: Articles, In: Life Mag, 11/15/55, Craft Horizons, 10/57 & 10/62 & Domus, 7/63; plus others. Mailing Add: Gate Hill Stony Point NY 10980

DIERINGER, ERNEST A
PAINTER
b Chicago, Ill, July 6, 32. Study: Art Inst Chicago. Work: Dayton Art Inst, Ohio; Cleveland Mus Art, Ohio; Pet Milk Collection; Chase Manhattan Collection; Guggenheim Mus, New York; plus others. Exhib: One-man shows, Poindexter Gallery, 62-75, Hurlbutt Gallery, Greenwich, Conn, 73 & William Sawyer Gallery, San Francisco, 74; Post Painterly Abstraction Traveling Show, 64; Chicago Expatriates, 72; plus others. Awards: New Eng Ann Awards, Edwin C Andrews, 71 & Am Tobacco Co, 72. Media: Acrylic. Mailing Add: RD 1 Sport Hill Rd West Redding CT 06896

DIETRICH, BRUCE LEINBACH
MUSEUM DIRECTOR, ART ADMINISTRATOR
b Reading, Pa, Oct 10, 37. Study: Kutztown State Col, BS, 60; State Univ NY, MS, 69. Collections Arranged: The Sea, 76, Reading & Berks Collects, 77, Winter Winds, 78, Master Prints, 78 & Director's Choice, 78, Reading Pub Mus & Art Gallery. Pos: Dir, Reading Planitarium, 69-; dir, Reading Pub Mus & Art Gallery, 76- Mailing Add: 500 Mus Rd Reading PA 19611

DI GIOIA, FRANK
PAINTER
b Naples, Italy, Dec 18, 00; US citizen. Study: Cooper Union; Art Students League, with John Sloan, painting with Walt Kuhn; studied in Paris, Rome & Madrid. Work: Univ Ariz, Tucson; Art Inst Chicago; Albright Art Gallery, Buffalo; Hirshhorn Collection, Washington, DC; New Britain Art Mus, Conn. Exhib: Phillips Gallery, 38; New York World's Fair, 39; Whitney Mus, 39, 45 & 51 & Metrop Mus, 42-43, New York; Painting in USA, Carnegie Inst, Pittsburgh, 47-48. Teaching: Pvt classes. Bibliog: A D Gruskin (auth), Painting in the USA, Doubleday, 46; Arizona art collection, Life Mag, 46; European sketches of Frank di Gioia, Am Artist, 4/66. Style & Technique: Modern but not abstract paintings, drawings and murals. Media: Oil, Watercolor. Publ: Illusr, Baroque architecture masterpieces, 1/61, Chateaux of France, 6/65 & Moorish masterpieces, 2/67, M D Mag. Dealer: Milch Gallery 1014 Madison Ave New York NY 10021. Mailing Add: 77 Washington Pl New York NY 10011

DIGIUSTO, GERALD N
SCULPTOR
b New York, NY, June 30, 29. Study: Mass Col Art, 49-50; Boston Mus Sch, dipl, 57; Yale Univ Sch of Art, BFA, 58; Univ Florence, Italy, 59-60. Work: Munson-Williams-Proctor Inst Mus, Utica, NY; Schenectady Mus, NY; State Univ NY Collection, Albany. Comn: Bronze screen, Honors Col, Univ Ore, Eugene, 62; Great Am Eagle, Everson Mus, Syracuse, NY, 69; 24 ft laminated wood sculpture, Marine Midland Computer Ctr, Syracuse, NY, 69; 40 ft x 20 ft wood relief, State Off Bldg, Watertown, NY, 71-72; 40 ft x 9 ft steel relief, Pub Sch 116, Bronx, NY, 74. Exhib: Inst Contemp Art, Boston, Mass, 57; Seattle Art Mus, Wash, 60; San Francisco Mus Art, 61; Munson, Williams, Proctor Inst Mus, Utica, NY, 63-64; Everson Mus, Syracuse, NY, 67; Carpenter Ctr, Harvard Univ, Cambridge, Mass, 74; Mus Fine Arts, Boston, Mass, 77; De Cordova Mus, Lincoln, Mass, 77; one-man exhibs, Munson, Williams, Proctor Inst Mus, 66 & State Univ NY Albany, 75. Teaching: Assoc prof sculpture & drawing, Syracuse Univ, NY, 62-66; prof sculpture & drawing, State Univ NY Cortland, 66- Awards: Mrs David Hunt Scholar for study abroad, Boston Mus Sch, Mass, 58-60; State Univ NY Res Award, 77. Style & Technique: Geometric sculptures of welded steel. Media: Steel. Mailing Add: 10 Hill St Cortland NY 13045

DIGNAC, GENY (EUGENIA M BERMUDEZ)
SCULPTOR, PAINTER
b Buenos Aires, Arg, June 8, 32. Work: Mus Mod Art, Cali, Colombia; Galeria Banco Cent, Quito, Ecuador; Latin Am Art Found, San Juan, PR. Exhib: Some More Beginnings, Exp in Art & Technol, Brooklyn Mus, NY, 68; IX Festival of Art, Cali, Colombia, 69; Earth, Air, Fire, Water Elements of Art, Boston Mus Fine Arts, 71; Arte de Sistema, Centro de Arte y Communicacion, Mus Art Mod, Buenos Aires, 71; III Biennial of Art Coltejer, Medellin, Colombia, 72; plus many one-woman shows, 67-71. Awards: Uranus II (light & plastic sculpture), IX Festival of Art, Mus Mod Art, Cali, 69. Bibliog: J Bermudez (producer), Dignac, 67-68 & Three fire gestures (films), 70-71; R Osuna (producer), D Dig Dignac (film), 68. Media: Plastics. Publ: Auth, Three Fire Gestures (film), limited ed, 70. Dealer: Pyramid Gallery 2121 P St NW Washington DC 20037. Mailing Add: 4109 E Via Estrella Phoenix AZ 85028

DIKE, PHILIP LATIMER
PAINTER, DESIGNER
b Redlands, Calif, Apr 6, 06. Study: Chouinard Art Inst; Art Students League; Am Acad, Fontainebleau, France; also with Clarence Hinkle, F Tolles Chamberlin, George Luks & M St Hubert. Work: Hearne Collection, Metrop Mus Art, New York; Butler Inst Am Art, Youngstown, Ohio; Pennell Collection, Libr Cong, Washington, DC; Springfield Mus; Pasadena Art Inst, Calif. Comn: Painted altar piece, First ME Church, Redlands, Calif, 46; ceramic tile, Gladding McBean, Los Angeles, 51; ceramic tile entrance, San Antonio Col Fine Arts Ctr, 52; ceramic tile pool area, Scripps Col, 52; mosaic, chapel, Claremont Community Congregational Church, 62. Exhib: Calif Watercolor Soc Nat, 26-71; Am Watercolor Soc, New York, 29-72; one-man & juried exhibs, Los Angeles Co Mus, Los Angeles, 31-55; Carnegie Inst Int, Pittsburgh, Pa, 36-58; Nat Acad Design Exhib, 51. Teaching: Instr painting, Chouinard Art Inst, 30-49; prof painting, Scripps Col & Claremont Grad Sch, 49-69, emer prof painting, 70- Pos: Color coordr, Walt Disney Prod, 34-44. Awards: First Prize for oil, Los Angeles Co Mus, 31; First Prize for watercolor, Butler Inst Am Art, 59; Purchase Prizes, Nat Watercolor Exhibs, Springfield, 67-72. Mem: Nat Acad Design; Am Watercolor Soc (hon vpres, 57); Nat Watercolor Soc (Calif pres, 38-39); West Coast Watercolor Soc (hon vpres, 64). Media: Watercolor, Oil. Publ: Auth, Watercolors, Am Artist Mag, 11/40. Dealer: Richard Challis Gallery 9390 S Coast Hwy Laguna Beach CA 92652. Mailing Add: 2310 N Forbes Ave Claremont CA 91711

DILL, GUY GIRARD
SCULPTOR
b Duval Co, Fla, May 30, 46. Study: Chouinard Sch Art, Los Angeles, BFA. Work: Guggenheim Mus, New York; Staedelijk Mus, Amsterdam, Neth; Mus of Mod Art, New York; Roy R Neuberger Mus, Purchase, NY; Newport Harbor Art Mus, Newport Beach, Calif; Wright State Univ, Dayton, Ohio; Calif State Univ, Long Beach; Pasadena Mus, Los Angeles; Whitney Mus Am Art, New York; Long Beach Mus Art, Calif. Comn: In Irons, Mr & Mrs Frederic Wiseman, Malibu, Calif, 74; Hume Ranch, Mr & Mrs Albert List, Conn, 74; untitled, Mr & Mrs Burton Tremaine, Conn, 74; Pit Bull Bitch No 3, ABC Entertainment Ctr, Los Angeles, 74; untitled, Mr & Mrs Frank Salacuse, New York, 76; untitled, Prudential Ins Co, Canoga Park, Calif, 77. Exhib: Guggenheim Mus, 71; Ace Gallery, Los Angeles, 71, 73 & 77; Felicity Samuel Gallery, London, Eng, 72; Pace Gallery, New York, 74 & 76; Biennial Show, Whitney Mus Am Art, 74; Sculpture Made in Place, Walker Art Ctr, Minneapolis, Minn, 76; Arco Ctr for Visual Arts, Los Angeles, Calif, 77; plus others. Awards: Theodoron Award, Guggenheim Mus, 71; Nat Endowment Arts, 74; First Prize, Am Show, Chicago Inst Art, 74. Bibliog: D Waldman (auth), Theodoron (catalogue), Guggenheim Mus, 71; Bill Packer (auth), Interview with Guy Dill, Art & Artists, London, 72. Style & Technique: Element manipulation. Media: Mixed Media. Dealer: Pace Gallery 32 E 57th St New York NY 10022. Mailing Add: 200 Mildred Ave Venice CA 90291

DILL, LADDIE JOHN
PAINTER, SCULPTOR
b Long Beach, Calif, Sept 14, 43. Study: Chouinard Art Inst, BFA, 68. Work: Los Angeles Co Mus Art, Los Angeles, Calif; Norton Simon Mus, Pasadena, Calif; San Francisco Mus Mod Art, Calif; William Rockhill Nelson Gallery, Kansas City, Mo; Smithsonian Inst, Washington, DC. Exhib: One-man shows, Pasadena Mus Mod Art, Calif, 71, Portland Univ Gallery, Ore, 71 & Sonnabend Gallery, New York, 72; 24 artists, Los Angeles Co Mus Art, Los Angeles, 71; Recent Acquisitions, Pasadena Mus Mod Art, 71; New Works for New Spaces, Walker Art Ctr, Minneapolis, Minn, 71; 15 Abstract Artists, Santa Barbara Mus Art, Calif, 74; Three Calif Painters, Rose Art Mus, Brandeis Univ, 75; Current Concerns, Los Angeles Inst Contemp Art, 75; The Mod Era, San Francisco Mus Mod Art, 76 & Smithsonian Inst, Washington, DC, 77; Calif Painting & Sculpture, San Francisco Mus Mod Art, 77. Teaching: Lectr painting, Univ Calif, Los Angeles, 75- Awards: Nat Endowment for the Arts, 75. Bibliog: Kasha Linville (auth), New York rev, Artforum, 71; Robert Hughes (auth), Los Angeles, Time Mag, 71; Judy Goodman (auth), Laddie Dill new work, Arts Mag, 75. Style & Technique: Multimedia. Media: Cement, Polymer, Glass. Dealer: James Corcoran Gallery 8221 Santa Monica Blvd Los Angeles CA 90046. Mailing Add: 9 Wavecrest Ave Venice CA 90291

DILLINGHAM, DOROTHY HOYT
See Hoyt, Dorothy

DILLINGHAM, RICK (JAMES RICHARD II)
CERAMIST, ART DEALER
b Lake Forest, Ill, Nov 13, 52. Study: Calif Col Arts & Crafts, 1 yr; Univ NMex, BFA; Scripps Col, MFA. Work: Sheldon Mem Art Mus, Lincoln, Nebr; Scripps Cols Art Collection, Claremont, Calif; Univ Art Collections, Ariz State Univ, Tempe; Utah Mus Fine Arts, Salt Lake City; Mus Albuquerque. Exhib: The 29th Ann Scripps Col Ceramics, Lang Art Gallery, Claremont, 73; Pottery III, IV, V & VI, Calif Polytech State Univ, San Luis Obispo, 73-76; Brand IV, V & Ceramic Conjunction, Long Beach Mus Art, Calif, 76-77 & Glendale, Calif, 73-75; Rex W Wignal Mus/Gallery, Alta Loma, Calif, 76; Univ Mont Mus, Bozeman, 76; Moreau Gallery, St Mary's Col, Notre Dame, Ind, 77; Francis McCray Gallery, Silver City, NMex, 77; David Stuart Gallery, Los Angeles, Calif, 76; Marietta Col Crafts Nat, Ohio, 77. Collections Arranged: Pueblo Pottery & Demonstration, Dewey-Kofron Gallery, Santa Fe, NMex, 77; Seven Families in Pueblo Pottery (auth, catalogue), Maxwell Mus Anthrop, Univ NMex, 74. Teaching: Asst prof ceramics, Calif Col Arts & Crafts, 76; ceramics workshop, Tucson Mus Art, Ariz, 76; plus numerous other national workshops and lectures. Awards: Best of Show & Purchase Award, Craft 5, Mus Albuquerque, 75; Purchase Award, Pottery 5, Calif Polytech State Univ, San Luis Obispo, 75. Bibliog: Hal Riegger (auth), Primitive

Pottery, Van Nostrand Reinhold, 72. Mem: Am Crafts Coun. Style & Technique: Contemporary primitive, simple form and construction with little use of technological aids. Media: Ceramics. Specialty: American Indian art. Collection: American Indian art, contemporary ceramics and lithography. Publ: Nine Pueblo potters, Studio Potter, 77; auth, The Pottery of Acoma Pueblo, Am Indian Art, 77. Dealer: Hand & Spirit Gallery 4200 N Marshall Way Scottsdale AZ 85251; Clarke-Benton Gallery 149 E Alameda Santa Fe NM 87501. Mailing Add: Box 2601 Santa Fe NM 87501

DILLON, C DOUGLAS
ART ADMINISTRATOR, COLLECTOR
b Geneva, Switz, Aug 21, 09. Study: Harvard Univ, AB. Pos: Trustee, Metrop Mus Art, 51-, pres, 70- Collection: French impressionist painting; 18th century continental and British porcelain; 18th century French furniture and decorative objects. Mailing Add: 767 Fifth Ave New York NY 10022

DILLON, MILDRED (MURPHY)
PAINTER, PRINTMAKER
b Philadelphia, Pa, Oct 12, 07. Study: Philadelphia Col Art, 25-28; Pa Acad Fine Arts, 28-29; Barnes Found, with Henry McCarter & Earle Horter, 29-31. Work: Philadelphia Mus Art; Barnes Found, Merion, Pa; Free Libr Philadelphia; Arch Can Painters & Etchers; Am Colorprint Soc Collection, Philadelphia. Exhib: Four-man show, Print Club Philadelphia, 59; Libr Cong Nat, 57; Contemp Graphics Overseas, Mus Bellas Artes, Caracas, Venezuela, 60; Color Prints of the Americas, NJ State Mus, 70; one-man show, Philadelphia Art Alliance, 75; plus others. Pos: Vpres, Am Color Print Soc, Philadelphia, 55-; chmn, Rittenhouse Sq Outdoor Exhib, 58-70; demonstr, Print Club Philadelphia, 61-70. Awards: Harrison Morris Prize, Pa Acad Fine Arts, 53; George Lear Mem Prize, Woodmere Art Gallery, 58; Klein Prize, Print Club Philadelphia, 67. Mem: Artists Equity Asn; Philadelphia Art Alliance (mem bd dirs, 60-73); fel Pa Acad Fine Arts; Woodmere Art Gallery (mem adv comt); Alumnae Philadelphia Col Art. Media: Serigraphy, Woodcut. Mailing Add: 627 E Wadsworth Ave Philadelphia PA 19119

DILLON, PAUL SANFORD
PAINTER
b Newport, Vt, Aug 5, 43. Work: Los Angeles Co Mus Art, Los Angeles, Calif; La Jolla Mus Art, Calif; Cheney Cowles Mus, Spokane, Wash; Security Pac Bank Collection, Los Angeles; Prudential Insurance Co Collection, Los Angeles. Exhib: Los Angeles Six, Los Angeles Co Mus Art, 74; Biennial of Am Painting, Whitney Mus Am Art, New York, 75 & Corcoran Gallery Art Washington, DC, 77; Los Angeles Painting, Mus Mod Art, New York, 77; Collector's Choice, Los Angeles Inst Contemp Art, 77; one-man shows, Jack Glenn Gallery, Newport Beach, Calif, 75, Tortue Gallery, Los Angeles, 77 & Iolas Gallery, New York, 78. Awards: New Talent Award, Los Angeles Co Mus Art, 74; Purchase Award, Contemporary Painting, Cheney Cowles Mus, 77. Mem: Los Angeles Inst Contemp Art. Style & Technique: Multiple images collaged on canvas and painted. Media: Acrylic & Collage on Canvas. Dealer: Brooks Jackson c/o Iolas Gallery 52 E 57th St New York NY 10022. Mailing Add: 3660 W Pico Blvd Los Angeles CA 90019

DILLOW, NANCY E (NANCY ELIZABETH ROBERTSON)
ART ADMINISTRATOR, ART HISTORIAN
b Toronto, Ont, June 26, 28. Study: Univ Toronto, BA. Collections Arranged: J E H MacDonald, R C A, 1873-1932 (with catalog), 65; Piet Mondrian and the Hague Sch of Landscape Painting (with catalog), 69; A Selection of Italian Drawings from North American Collections, 70; Saskatchewan: Art and Artists (with catalog), 71; Nugent-Godwin (with catalog), 72; Marilyn Levine-Donovan Chester, 74. Teaching: Prof hist Can art, Univ Regina, 72- Pos: From asst cur to cur exten & educ, Art Gallery Ont, 56-67; dir, Norman Mackenzie Art Gallery, 67- Mem: Can Art Mus Dir Orgn (secy, 71-75, vpres, 75); Can Mus Asn (coun, 67-70, training comt, 68-71, pres, 77-); Sask Mus Asn (chmn training, 74-76, vpres, 75, pres, 76-78); Western Art Asn (exec, 70-72); Col Art Asn. Res: Canadian art history. Publ: Auth, Jack Cowin-Reta Cowley, 74. Mailing Add: c/o Norman Mackenzie Art Gallery Univ of Regina Regina SK S4S 0A2 Can

DI MEO, DOMINICK
PAINTER, SCULPTOR
b Niagara Falls, NY, Feb 1, 27. Study: Art Inst Chicago, four year dipl, 50, BFA, 52; Univ Iowa, MFA, 53. Work: Art Inst Chicago; Whitney Mus Am Art, New York; Ill Bell Tel Co, Chicago; Univ Mass, Amherst. Exhib: 12th Exhib Contemp Am Painting & Sculpture, Krannert Art Mus, Champaign-Urbana, Ill, 65; Ann Exhib Contemp Am Painting, Whitney Mus Am Art, 67-68; Fantasy & Figure, Am Fedn Arts, New York & Traveling Show, 68-69; Violence in Recent American Art, Mus Contemp Art, Chicago, 68-69; The Crowd: Exhibit of Sculpture, Paintings & Graphics, Arts Club Chicago, 69; Visions/Painting & Sculpture: Distinguished Alumni 1945-Present, Art Inst Chicago, 76; 16th Joan Miró Int Drawing Prize Competition, Barcelona, Spain & Sala de Cult de la Caja de Ahorros de Navarra, Pamplona, 77. Awards: Guggenheim Mem Found Fel Graphics, 72-73. Bibliog: Whitney Halstead (auth), Introduction, In: Di Meo, Work: 1959-1966, Galaxie, 67. Style & Technique: Monochromatic, usually white with one other color to emphasize relief; relief assemblages in acrylic. Media: Mixed Media. Mailing Add: 429 Broome St New York NY 10013

DIMONDSTEIN, MORTON
SCULPTOR, PAINTER
b New York, NY, Nov 5, 20. Study: Am Artists Sch, New York, 37-39; Art Students League, 39-41; Otis Art Inst, Los Angeles, 45-48; Inst Nac, Mexico City, Mex, 50-51. Work: World Bank, Washington, DC; Libr Congr, Washington, DC; Pushkin Art Mus, Moscow, USSR; Seattle Art Mus, Wash; Portland Art Mus, Ore. Exhib: One-man shows, ACA Gallery, New York, 53, Galleria Penelope, Rome, Italy, 61, Jacqueline Anhalt Gallery, Los Angeles, 67-72, James Willis Gallery, San Francisco, 75-76, Roko Gallery, New York, 77; Third Int Biennial of Sculpture, Carrara, Italy, 62; Int Biennial Art, Palermo, Italy, 64. Teaching: Instr all media, Sch Fine Art, Los Angeles, 63-72; instr drawing & sculpture, Univ Southern Calif, 64-68. Pos: Staff artist, Patzcuaro, Mex, 52-53. Mem: Soc Am Graphic Artists. Media: Wood, Bronze. Publ: Mexico (portfolio of woodcuts), Posada Graphics, 54. Dealer: James Willis Gallery 109 Geary San Francisco CA 94108; Roko Gallery 90 E Tenth St New York NY 10003. Mailing Add: 749 Longwood Ave Los Angeles CA 90005

DIMSON, THEO AENEAS
DESIGNER
b London, Ont, Apr 8, 30. Study: Ont Col Art, Toronto. Work: Typomundus 20, France. Exhib: Art Dirs Club New York; Am Inst Graphic Arts, New York; Graphica Club Toronto; Graphica Club Montreal; Int Poster Art, Bulgaria. Pos: Vpres creative design, Art Assocs Ltd, Toronto, 59-65; pres & creative dir, Dimson & Smith Ltd, Toronto, 65- Awards: Medal Awards, Graphica Club Toronto, 66 & Graphica Club Montreal, 71; Award of Excellence, Am Inst Graphic Arts, 71. Bibliog: Hara (auth), Designers, Graphic Design Mag, 62; Republic of Childhood, Oxford Univ, 67. Mem: Graphica Club Toronto; Am Inst Graphic Arts; assoc Royal Can Acad Arts. Media: Graphic. Publ: Illusr, The Sunken City, 60 & The Double Knights, 63, Oxford; illusr, Rubaboo Five, Sage, 65. Mailing Add: Dimson & Smith Ltd 172 Davenport Rd Toronto ON M5R 1J1 Can

DINE, JAMES
PAINTER, SCULPTOR
b Cincinnati, Ohio, June 16, 35. Study: Univ Cincinnati; Boston Mus Sch. Work: Mus Mod Art, New York; Tate Gallery, London, Eng; Stedelijk Mus, Amsterdam, Holland; Whitney Mus Am Art, New York; Albright-Knox Art Gallery, Buffalo. Exhib: Six Painters & the Object, Guggenheim Mus, New York, 63; 23rd Int Venice Biennial, Italy, 64; Art of USA, 1670-1966, Whitney Mus Am Art, New York, 66; Dokumenta IV, Kassel, Ger, 67. Teaching: Vis prof, Oberlin Col, 65 & Cornell Univ, 67. Awards: Norman Harris Silver Medal & Prize, Art Inst Chicago, 64. Bibliog: John Gordon (auth), Jim Dine, Whitney Mus Am Art, 70; Christopher Finch (auth), Jim Dine, Abrams. Publ: Illusr, The Poet Assassinated, 68; auth & illusr, Welcome Home Lovebirds, 69; co-auth, Work from the Same House, 69; co-auth & illusr, The Adventures of Mr & Mrs Jim & Ron, 70. Mailing Add: The Pace Gallery 32 E 57th St New York NY 10022

DINNERSTEIN, SIMON A
PAINTER
b Brooklyn, NY, Feb 16, 43. Study: City Col New York, BA, 65; Brooklyn Mus Art Sch, with David Levine & Louis Grebenak, 64-67; Hochschule für Bildende Kunst, Kassel, Ger, Fulbright fel, 70-71. Work: Minn Mus Art, St Paul; Albrecht Mus, St Joseph, Mo. Exhib: New American Landscapes, Vassar Col Art Ctr, 73; Living American Artists & the Figure, Pa State Univ, 74; Childe Hassam Mem Exhib, Am Acad Arts & Lett, 75; Drawings USA 7th Biennial, Minn Mus Art, 75; one-man show, Staempfli Gallery, 75. Teaching: Instr painting, Brooklyn Mus Art Sch, 71-72; instr painting, The New Sch, New York, 75-77. Awards: MacDowell Colony Fel, 69; Hon Mention, Edwin Austin Abbey Fel Mural Painting, Nat Acad, 75; Prix de Roma, Italy, 76 & 77. Bibliog: John Gruen (auth), On art, Freilicher, Fish, Dinnerstein, Petersen, Baber, Soho News, 2/6/75; John Russell (auth), In Dinnerstein's painting, an echo chamber, NY Times, 2/8/75; Michael Andre (auth), Simon Dinnerstein (Staempfli), Art News, 3/75. Style & Technique: Charcoal drawings; oil on wood panel. Mailing Add: c/o Staempfli Gallery 47 E 77th St New York NY 10021

DINTENFASS, TERRY
ART DEALER
US citizen. Pos: Dir, Terry Dintenfass, Inc. Specialty: Contemporary American Art. Mailing Add: 50 W 57th St New York NY 10019

DIODA, ADOLPH T
SCULPTOR, INSTRUCTOR
b Aliquippa, Pa, Sept 10, 15. Study: Carnegie Inst Technol; Cleveland Sch Art; Art Students League; also with John B Flannagan, New York. Work: Carnegie Mellon Mus, Pittsburgh, Pa; Pa Acad Fine Arts, Philadelphia; Philadelphia Mus Art; Ogunquit Mus Art, Maine; Westmoreland Mus Art, Greensburg, Pa. Comn: Figure, comn by Dahlen K Ritchey, Pittsburgh, 51; crucifix & stations of the cross for chapel, St Joseph's Prep Sch, Philadelphia, 72. Exhib: Whitney Mus Am Art Ann, New York, 40; Sculpture Int, Philadelphia Mus Art, 40-49; Carved in Stone, Bucholtz Gallery, New York, 45; Pa Acad Fine Arts Ann, 46, 47 & 69; 60th Ann Exhib Am Paintings & Sculpture, Art Inst Chicago, 51. Teaching: Instr sculpture, Tyler Sch, Temple Univ, 59-69; instr sculpture, Haverford Col, 62-69; instr wood & stone carving, Pa Acad Fine Arts, 62- Awards: Guggenheim Found grant, 45; George D Widener Medal, Pa Acad Fine Arts, 47; Eben Demarest Fund grant, Carnegie Inst Technol, 48. Mem: Artists Equity Asn, Philadelphia Chap. Style & Technique: Direct carving in wood and stone combining simple organic and geometric forms. Mailing Add: c/o 411 Healy St Jenkintown PA 19046

DIODATO, BALDO
PAINTER, SCULPTOR
b Naples, Italy, Feb 16, 38. Study: Liceo Artistico, Naples, Italy; Accad Belle Arti, Naples; Accad Albertina, Turin. Work: Melton Bruten Collection, Philadelphia. Comn: Mural, Mil Hosp, Turin, Italy, 62; Front facade, Church San Martino Valle Caudina, Benevento, Italy, 63-64. Exhib: One-man show, Mod Art Agency, Naples, Italy, 66-67; Light as Art, Newark Col Eng, 68; Artists Equity Exhib, Philadelphia Civic Ctr, 74; RI Univ, 74; NJ State Mus, Trenton, 75. Teaching: Prof Sculpture, Mattia Preti, Liceo Artistico, Reggio Calabria, 67-68; prof sculpture, Cheltenham Art Ctr, Philadelphia, 75- Awards: Mostra d'Autunno, City of Naples, Italy, 64; Best Int Exhib, State NJ, 69-71. Bibliog: Lea Vergine (auth), Intervista Sulla Cultura a Napoli, Marcatre Ed, Lerici, 65 & 66 & Dieci Anni di Cultura, Almanaco Letterario, Bompiani, 68; Achille Bonita Oliva (auth), Scultura a Palazzo Reale, Ente Turismo, Naples, 68. Mem: Artists Equity Asn. Style & Technique: Environmental sculpture; conceptual art; mixed media. Mailing Add: 359 Hamilton Ave Trenton NJ 08609

DIPASQUALE, DOMINIC THEODORE
SILVERSMITH, EDUCATOR
b Buffalo, NY, Feb 21, 32. Study: State Univ NY Col Buffalo, BS(art educ), Sch Am Craftsmen, Rochester Inst Technol, MFA(metal design), Work: In over 500 pvt collections. Comn: Inaugural medallion, State Univ NY Col Oswego, 66; inaugural medallion, Worcester State Col, Mass, 75; Coat of Arms, comn by Bishop J F Cunningham, Syracuse Diocese, NY, 75. Exhib: Profiles in Jewelry, Lubbock, Tex, 72; Munson-Williams-Proctor Mus Crafts, Utica, 73; Silversmiths of NY, Univ Mex, 75; 2nd Biennial Int Exhib, Tweed Mus, Duluth, 75; Nat Art Slide Competition, Fla, 75. Teaching: Prof jewelry & metals, State Univ NY Col Oswego, 63-, chmn dept art, 74- Awards: First Prize, Westchester Nat Competition, NY, 68; First Prize, Las Vegas Nat Art Round-Up, Nev, 69; First Prize, NY State Fair, Syracuse, 73. Bibliog: Robert Steinen (auth), Introduction to Design, Prentice-Hall, (in press). Mem: Soc NAm Goldsmiths; York State Crafts Asn; Buffalo Craftsmen; Am Crafts Coun; Col Art Asn Am. Media: Gold & Silver with Gems. Publ: Auth, Jewelry Making: an Illustrated Guide to Technique, 75. Dealer: Art Ctr Williamsville NY 14221. Mailing Add: 24 W Fifth St Oswego NY 13126

DIPERNA, FRANK PAUL
PHOTOGRAPHER, INSTRUCTOR
b Pittsburgh, Pa, Feb 4, 47. Study: Ctr of the Eye, Aspen, Colo, 71, with Gary Winogrand; Visual Studies Workshop, Rochester, NY, 71-72, with Ralph Gibson, Syl Labrot, Nathan Lyons & Alice Wells; Goddard Col, MA(photog), 77. Work: Polaroid (Europa), Amsterdam, The Netherlands; Smithsonian Inst, Washington, DC; Va Mus Fine Arts, Richmond; Corcoran Gallery of Art, Washington, DC. Exhib: Va Photogr, Va Mus Fine Arts, 73 & 75; Eye of the West: Camera Vision & Cult Concensus, Hayden Gallery, Mass Inst Technol, Cambridge, 77; one-man shows, Bushes, 74 & Color Photographs, 77, Corcoran Gallery of Art, Photographs, Diane Brown Gallery, Washington, DC, 77 & Color Photographs,

Sebastian Moore Gallery, Denver, Colo, 78. Teaching: Instr photog, NVa Community Col, Alexandria, 73- & Corcoran Sch of Art, 74- Awards: Cert of Distinction, Va Photog, 73. Bibliog: Tom Zito (auth), Washington Photography: Art, Potomac, The Washington Post, 5/23/76; Mack Power (auth), Washington, Photographers and the Contact Print, Washington Rev of the Arts, winter 76; David Taunous (auth), Frank DiPerna at the Corcoran, Mark Power at Diane Brown, Art in Am, 1-2/78. Style & Technique: Large format palladium prints; 35mm silver prints; Polaroid SX-70 color prints; urban and natural landscapes. Publ: Auth, Color photographs, Corcoran Gallery of Art, 77. Dealer: Diane Brown Gallery 2028 P St NW Washington DC 22036. Mailing Add: 1744 Lamont St NW Washington DC 20010

DIRUBE, ROLANDO LOPEZ
PAINTER, SCULPTOR
b Havana, Cuba, Aug 14, 28; US citizen. Study: Univ Havana Col Archit & Eng, 48; Art Students League, with George Grosz & Kuniyoshi, 49; Brooklyn Mus Art Sch, with Gabor F Peterdi & Max Beckman, 50; Escuela Nac Artes Graficas, Madrid, Spain, 51-52. Work: Metrop Mus Art, New York; Philadelphia Univ, Pa; Nat Mus, Havana, Cuba; Mus Mod Art, Madrid, Spain; Ponce Mus, PR. Comn: Nat Asn Architects, 56; Nat Theatre & Nat Sport Coliseum, Cuban Govt, Havana, 58; Int Theatres, GHG Enterprises, San Juan, PR, 70; One Biscayne Tower, GHG Enterprises, Miami, Fla, 72. Exhib: I Bienal Hispanoamericana Arte, Madrid, 51; Lateinamerikanische Kunst Gegenwart, Ger, 51; II Bienal Sao Paulo, Brazil, 53; Int Colour Woodcut Exhib, Victoria & Albert Mus, London, 54-55; IX Biennale Int Art Menton, France, 72. Teaching: Prof design anal, Inter-Am Univ PR Sch Archit, 64-65; lectr design, Sch Archit, Univ PR, San Juan, 67; prof painting, Art Students League, San Juan, 68- Awards: First Prize Woodcut, I Bienal Hispanoamericana Arte, 51; Gold Medal in Painting & Gold Medal in Woodcut, Univ Tampa, 51. Bibliog: E S Santovenia (auth), Historia de la Nacion Cubana, Ed Hist Nacion Cubana, SA, 52; R Guastela (auth), Dirube painter & sculpture (film), Viguie Guastela, 68; J Gomez Sicre (auth), San Juan muralists, Pan Am Union Rev Am, 71. Style & Technique: Large indoor and outdoor murals; reinforced concrete sculptures in parks and buildings. Publ: Illusr, En la Habana ha muerto un turista, 63; illusr, Los combatientes, 68. Mailing Add: PO Box 929 Catano PR 00632

DISKA
SCULPTOR
b New York, NY. Study: Vassar Col, BA; Acad Jullian, Paris. Work: Finch Mus, New York; Cornell Art Mus, Ithaca, NY; Musee d'Art et d'Industria St Etienne, France; Int Sculpture Parks, Austria, Israel, Czech, Yugoslavia & France. Comn: Fountain in secondary sch, Aix-en-Provence, France, 75; monumental sculpture for secondary sch, Valence (Drome), France, 76; fountain sculpture, planters & others (stone & wood), Salon-de-Provence, France, 76-78; fountain for tech sch, Valréas, 77; group of play sculptures for nursery sch, Avignon, France, 77. Exhib: One-man shows, Galerie Colette Allendy, Paris, 61, Am Cult Ctr, Paris, 61, Galleria 22 Marzo, Venice, Italy, 61, Galerie Suzanne de Coninck, Paris, 65, Galerie Les Contards, Lacoste, 65, Southern Methodist Univ, Dallas, Tex, 65, Galerie Jacques Casanova, Paris, 66, Ruth White Gallery, New York, 69. Teaching: Instr sculpture, Sarah Lawrence Summer Sch, Lacoste, France, 74 & 75. Awards: Competition for nursery sch sculpture, Cavaillon, France, 72 & Apt, France, 73. Bibliog: Marjorie Hichisson (auth), article in Archit Asn J, London, 65; Dona Meilach (auth), Contemporary Stone Sculpture, Crown Publ, 70; article in Archit d'Aujourd'hui, Paris, 73. Mem: Sculptor's Guild; French Syndicate of Sculptors. Style & Technique: Monumental work; abstract, organic. Media: Stone, wood, cast iron. Mailing Add: 305 W 28th St New York NY 10001

DI SUVERO, MARK
PAINTER, SCULPTOR
b Shanghai, China. Study: Univ Calif, BA. Work: Wadsworth Atheneum, Hartford, Conn; NY Univ. Exhib: Art Inst Chicago, 63; Peace Tower, Los Angeles, 66; American Sculpture of the Sixties, Los Angeles Co Mus Art, 67; Whitney Mus Am Art, New York, 67 & 75; San Francisco Mus Art, 69; 20th Nat Print Exhib, 77; plus others. Awards: Longview Found Grant; Walter K Gutman Found Grant; Art Inst Chicago Award, 63. Mailing Add: 195 Front St New York NY 10038

DIVOLA, JOHN MANFORD, JR
PHOTOGRAPHER
b Santa Monica, Calif, June 6, 49. Study: Calif State Univ, Northridge, BA; Univ Calif, Los Angeles, MA, 73, MFA, 74. Work: Mus Mod Art, New York; Int Mus Photog, George Eastman House, Rochester; New Orleans Mus Art; Univ Calif, Los Angeles. Comn: 11 photographs, US Info Agency, 74. Exhib: 24 from Los Angeles, San Francisco Mus Art, 73; Three Photographers, Calif State Univ, Northridge, 73; Dimensional Light, Calif State Univ, Fullerton, 75; Photography II, Jack Glenn Gallery, Newport Beach, Calif, 75; Summer Light, Light Gallery, New York, 75. Awards: Endowment Arts Photography Fel, 72. Mailing Add: 245 Ruth Ave Venice CA 90291

DIXON, ALBERT GEORGE, III
MUSEUM DIRECTOR, EDUCATOR
b San Francisco, Calif, Dec 17, 35. Study: Univ Calif, Riverside; San Francisco Art Inst, BFA; Mills Col, MFA. Collections Arranged: Mills Col Print Collection (with catalog), 71; Black Craftsmen of California (with catalog), 71; Mills Col Watercolor Collection (with catalog), 72. Teaching: Prof hist mod art, San Jose State Univ, 74- Pos: Asst dir, Mills Col Art Gallery, 68-71, dir, 71-72; dir, San Jose Mus Art, 73- Mem: Am Asn Art Mus; Western Asn Art Mus. Publ: Auth, Cinco de Mayo, 74; auth, Intertices, 75. Mailing Add: 110 S Market St San Jose CA 95113

DIXON, KENNETH RAY
PAINTER, GALLERY DIRECTOR
b St Clair, Mo, May 30, 43. Study: Drury Col, Springfield, Mo, BA, 65; SW Mo State Univ, Springfield, 66; Univ Ark, Fayetteville, MFA, 68, with David Durst & Howard Whitlach. Work: Drury Col Art Gallery; Baldwin-Wallace Col Art Gallery, Berea, Ohio; Kalamazoo Inst Arts, Mich; Mus Mod Art, Miami, Fla; Ky State Univ, Frankfort; plus others. Exhib: 36th Ann Southern Utah State Nat, Cedar City, 77; Miami Graphics Biennial, Mus Mod Art, Fla, 77; 12th Coos Art Mus Nat, Coos Bay, Ore, 77; 8th Nat Print & Drawing, Minot State Col, NDak, 78; Appalachian Nat Drawing Competition, Boone, NC, 78; Scottsdale Nat Watercolor Biennial, Ariz, 78; one-man shows, Camden Inst, London, Eng, 73, Kalamazoo Inst Arts, 75 & Ky State Univ Gallery, 78. Collections Arranged: Ann Print & Drawing Regional (auth, catalogue), Baldwin-Wallace Col, 69, 70 & 71; Instructors & Their Students (auth, catalogue), Nat Prints & Drawings, Tex Tech Univ, 78, Nat Drawing Invitational Exhibition, 78, Color Print USA (auth, catalogue), 78. Teaching: Instr painting, Kalamazoo Col, 66-69 & Baldwin-Wallace Col, 69-72; asst prof painting, Tex Tech Univ, 75- Pos: Gallery dir, Baldwin-Wallace Col, 69-72 & Tex Tech Univ, 77- Awards: Purchase Award, 19th Ann Exhib, Newman Ctr, Case-Western Reserve, Cleveland, 71; First Award in Watercolor, 36th Nat Southern Utah State Univ, 77; Purchase Award, Miami Graphics Int, Mus Mod Art, Miami, 77. Style & Technique: Landscape and figure in watercolor and gum bichromate technique. Media: Watercolor; Pencil. Mailing Add: 2007 31st St Lubbock TX 79411

DIXON, SALLY FOY
FILM CURATOR, LECTURER
b Seattle, Wash. Study: Carnegie-Mellon Univ; Chatham Col. Pos: Cur film sect, Carnegie Inst Mus Art, 70-; weekly film commentator, Sta WQED-FM, 74-; chmn, Regional Film Coun, Pittsburgh, 74; adv panel pub media prog, Nat Endowment Arts, 74-77; chmn Comt Film & TV Resources & Serv, 74-75; consult, Pa Coun Arts Bicentennial Film Proj; film consult, Western Psychiat Inst. Bibliog: Robert Gangenihl (auth), Interview, Carnegie Mag, 2/73. Mem: Pittsburgh Film-Makers Asn (bd dirs, 71); Pittsburgh Plan for Art (bd gov, 72-); Nat Soc Lit & Arts. Media: Film. Res: First two decades of Film in Pittsburgh. Publ: Contribr, Carnegie Mag, 70-72; contribr, QED Renaissance, 12/71; contribr, Pittsburgh Opens Up to Film-makers, Am Film Inst Report, 2/73. Mailing Add: Film Sect Carnegie Inst Mus Art 4400 Forbes Ave Pittsburgh PA 15213

DMYTRUK, IHOR
PAINTER,
b Ukraine, Feb 11, 38; Can citizen. Study: Univ Alta; Vancouver Sch Art. Work: Alta Art Found; Univ Calgary, Alta; Ukranian Inst Mod Art, Chicago; Art Gallery, Windsor, Ont; Art Bank, Can Coun; plus others. Exhib: Winnipeg Show, 64, 66 & 68; All Alta Show, 64-67, 69 & one-man show, 71; Alta Contemp Drawings, Edmonton Art Gallery, 73; 9 out of 10 & Surv Contemp Art, Hamilton Art Gallery, Ont, 74; Landscape Abbreviations, Art Gallery Greater Victoria, 74-75; one-man show, Latitude 53 Gallery, 75 & 77; plus others. Teaching: Instr drawing & painting, Fac Exten, Dept of Art, Univ Alta. Awards: All Alberta 1966 Award, Reeves & Sons Ltd; Can Coun travel grant, 66 & art Bursary, 72 & 74. Bibliog: E N Yates (auth), Four Edmonton artists, 10/69 & Myra Davies (auth), Recent work by Ihor Dmytruk, 10-11/71, Arts Can; Karen Wilkin (auth), A report on the West, Art Am, 5/72. Mem: Alta Art Found (rev comt); Can Artists Representation. Style & Technique: Semi-abstract, at times heavily symbolic, at other times resembling terrestrial images having microscopic or landscape reference. Media: Acrylic, Pencil, Watercolor. Mailing Add: 11139-110 A Ave Edmonton AB Can

DOBBINS, JAMES JOSEPH
CARTOONIST
b Woburn, Mass, Aug 12, 24. Study: Cornell Col, 45; Mass Col Art, BS, 51; Boston Univ, 51-52. Teaching: Teacher, Boston Pub Schs, 52. Pos: Ed cartoonist, Lowell Sun, Mass, 52-53, New York Daily News, 53, Boston Post, 53-55, Boston Herald Traveler, 56-72 & Boston Herald Am, 72- Awards: Christopher Lit Award, 58; Grand Prize, Int Competition, Wayne State Univ, 60; Cert of Merit, Syracuse Univ, 69. Mem: Nat Cartoonist Soc; Asn Am Ed Cartoonists. Publ: Auth, Dobbins Diary of the New Frontier, 64. Mailing Add: 96 Church St Winchester MA 01890

DOBBS, JOHN BARNES
PAINTER
b Passaic, NJ, Aug 2, 31. Study: RI Sch Design; Brooklyn Mus Art Sch, with Gregorio Prestopino; Skowhegan Sch Painting & Sculpture, with Jack Levine. Work: Syracuse Mus Art, NY; Fairleigh Dickinson Univ; Butler Inst Am Art, Youngstown, Ohio; Univ Mass; Springfield Mus Art, Mass. Exhib: One-man shows, ACA Gallery, New York, 64-75, Long Island Univ, 71 & Wesleyan Univ, 71; Nat Acad Design, New York, 67, 68 & 71; Nat Inst Arts & Lett, New York, 68-71. Teaching: Instr, Brooklyn Mus Art Sch, 56-59; instr, New Sch Social Res, 65-; instr, City Col New York, 70-71; asst prof, John Jay Col Criminal Justice, 72- Awards: Louis Comfort Tiffany Found Grant, 67; Childe Hassam Purchase Prize, Nat Inst Arts & Lett, 71; Ranger Fund Purchase Prize, Nat Acad Design, 74; plus others. Mem: Assoc Nat Acad Design. Media: Oil. Publ: Auth & illusr, Drawings of a Draftee, 59; illusr, Death and Justice Frescoes, 70; illusr, Fortune Mag, 70; illusr, Liberation Mag, 4/72. Dealer: ACA Gallery 25 E 73rd St New York NY 10014. Mailing Add: 463 West St New York NY 10014

DOBIE, JEANNE
PAINTER, INSTRUCTOR
b Philadelphia, Pa. Study: Philadelphia Col Art; Rangemark Masterclass, Maine, with Barse Miller, Edward Betts & Chen Chi. Work: Lewis Univ, Lockport, Ill; NC Nat Bank; City Hall of N Wildwood, NJ; First Pa Bank, Philadelphia; Celanese Corp, Charlotte, NC. Exhib: Am Watercolor Soc, New York, 69-75; Nat Watercolor Soc, Los Angeles, 70; Audubon Artists, New York, 71, 74 & 77; Watercolor USA, Springfield Mus, Mo, 72, 74 & 75; Schink/Dobie Watercolors, Columbia Mus Art, NC, 77; Nat Arts Club Show of Past NAC Prize Winners & Jurors, New York, 78. Teaching: Instr/staff watercolor, Rangemark, summers 74-77; instr watercolor clinic throughout US, Hawaii & Europe, 76-78. Awards: Nat Painters & Sculptors Award, Nat Painters & Sculptors Soc, NJ, 71; Sydney Taylor Mem Award, Knickerbocker Artists, New York, 71; Charles Taylor Pres Award, Philadelphia Watercolor Club, 76. Mem: Am Watercolor Soc; Nat Watercolor Soc; Philadelphia Watercolor Club; Knickerbocker Artists; NJ Watercolor Soc. Style & Technique: Pure transparent watercolor using glazing technique; landscapes and people. Mailing Add: 597 Weadley Rd Wayne PA 19087

DOBKIN, JOHN HOWARD
ART ADMINISTRATOR
b Hartford, Conn, Feb 19, 42. Study: Yale Univ, BA, 64; Inst d'Etudes Politiques, Paris, France, 65; NY Univ, JD, 68. Pos: Exec asst to secy, Smithsonian Inst, Washington, DC, 68-71; adminr, Cooper-Hewitt Mus Design, 71-78; dir, Nat Acad Design, New York, 78- Awards: Exceptional Serv Award, Smithsonian Inst, 71. Mailing Add: c/o Nat Acad of Design 1083 Fifth Ave New York NY 10028

DOBRIN, ARNOLD JACK
ILLUSTRATOR
b Omaha, Nebr, June 6, 28. Study: Chouinard Art Inst, Los Angeles; Acad de la Grande Chaumiere, Paris. Exhib: Los Angeles Co Mus Art Exhib, Los Angeles, 57; Pa Acad Fine Arts, Philadelphia, 59. Awards: Evansville Mus First Prize in Watercolor, Ind, 54; Best Illus Bks of the Yr, Inst Children's Bk Comt, 67; Outstanding Bks of the Yr, New York Times, 69. Style & Technique: Quick spontaneous use of the media often combined with india ink. Media: Watercolor; Tempera. Publ: Auth & illusr, Taro & The Sea Turtles, Coward-McCann, 67; auth & illusr, Josephine's 'Magination, Four Winds, 73; auth & illusr, Gilly Gilhooley, Crown Publ, 76. Mailing Add: 8 Cross Hwy Westport CT 06880

DOCKSTADER, FREDERICK J
ART CONSULTANT, SILVERSMITH
b Los Angeles. Calif, Feb 3, 19. Study: Ariz State Univ, AB & MA; Western Reserve Univ, PhD. Work: Cleveland Mus Art, Ohio. Exhib: Cranbrook Acad Art, Bloomfield Hills, Mich, 48; Cleveland Mus Art, 49-51. Collections Arranged: Specialized in exhib installation & reorganization at Cranbrook Inst Sci, Dartmouth Col Mus & Mus Am Indian. Teaching: Instr silversmithing, Cranbrook Acad Art; instr silversmithing, NH League Arts & Crafts, 52-55;

prof art & archaeol, Columbia Univ, 61-64, mem adv coun, 61-; lectr silversmithing, American Indian art & arts & crafts. Pos: Staff ethnologist, Cranbrook Inst Sci, 46-53; cur anthrop, Dartmouth Col Mus, 53-56; asst dir, Mus Am Indian, 56-59, dir, 59-75; comnr, US Indian Arts & Crafts Bd, 56-68, chmn, 61-68. Awards: Second Prize in Silversmithing, Cleveland Mus Art, 50, First Prize in Silversmithing, 51; Lotos Award, Lotos Club, New York, 72. Mem: Cosmos Club, Washington, DC; Century Club, New York. Publ: Auth & illusr, The Kachina and the White Man, 54; auth & illusr, Indian Art in America, 61, Indian Art in Middle America, 64, Indian Art in South America, 67, Indian Art of the Americas, 73 & North American Indian Weaving, 78; contribr, articles on arts & crafts to various nat publ. Mailing Add: 165 W 66th St New York NY 10023

DODD, ED (EDWARD BENTON)
CARTOONIST
b La Fayette, Ga, Nov 7, 02. Study: Ga Inst Technol, 21-22; Art Students League, 23-24; also with Daniel Beard. Teaching: Instr & dir, Dan Beard Camp for Boys, 20-38; instr outdoor activities, NY Mil Acad, Cornwall, NY, 26-27. Pos: Commercial artist, New York, 29-30; drew humor panel, Back Home Again, United Feature Syndicate, 30-45; cartoonist, Mark Trail, Field Syndicate, 46- Awards: Awards from Nat Forestry Asn, Wis Humane Soc, Detroit Sportsman's Conf & Nat Wildlife Fedn. Mem: Outdoor Writers Asn. Publ: Mark Trail's Fishing Tips; Mark Trail's Hunting Tips; Mark Trail's Camping Tips. Mailing Add: Lost Forest Atlanta GA 30328

DODD, ERIC M
GALLERY DIRECTOR, EDUCATOR
Can citizen. Study: Univ Durham, BA, 49, dipl(educ), 50; Ohio State Univ, MA, 51. Teaching: Prof art, Univ Calgary, 67-, head dept, 68-76. Pos: Dir, Univ Calgary Art Gallery, 67-76. Mailing Add: Univ Calgary Dept Art 2920 24th Ave NW Calgary AB T2N 1N4 Can

DODD, LAMAR
PAINTER, EDUCATOR
b Fairburn, Ga, Sept 22, 09. Study: Ga Inst Technol, 26-27; Art Students League, with George Luks, Boardman Robinson, John Steuart Curry, Jean Charlot & George Bridgeman, 29-33; LaGrange Col, LHD, 47; Univ Chattanooga, DFA, 59; Fla State Univ, DFA, 68. Work: Atlanta Art Inst; Art Inst Chicago; Metrop Mus Art; Montclair Art Mus; Pa Acad Fine Arts; plus others. Exhib: Am Acad Arts & Lett; Am Fedn Arts; Art Inst Chicago; Am Watercolor Soc; Brooklyn Mus; plus others. Teaching: Lectr, US, Denmark, Ger, Turkey, Italy, Austria & Greece; assoc prof art, Univ Ga, 37-29, head dept art, 38-73, regent's prof art, 48-76, chmn fine arts div, 60-76, Lamar Dodd prof art, 70-76, Regent's Prof Emer art, chmn emer fine arts div & Lamar Dodd prof emer, 76- lectr, United Chap Phi Beta Kappa, 67-68. Pos: Pres, Col Art Asn Am, 54-56; mem, US Dept State Comt Arts Tour, India, Thailand, Belg, Japan, Korea, Manila & others, 58; NASA artist, Apollo 7 & 10, 68-69. Awards: Award, Nat Arts Club, 54; Purchase Prizes, Pa Acad Fine Arts & Whitney Mus Am Art, 58; plus others. Bibliog: Monroe Wheeler (auth), Painters and sculptors of modern America, Crowell, 42; Ray Bethers (auth), How paintings happen, Norton, 51; John I H Baur (auth), Revolution and tradition in American art, Harvard Univ, 59; plus others. Mem: Assoc Nat Acad Design; Col Art Asn Am; Southeastern Art Asn; Asn Ga Artists; Athens Art Asn; plus others. Publ: Illusr, The Savannah and the Santee, Rivers of Am Series; contribr, Col Art J, Bk Knowledge & others. Mailing Add: Dept of Art Univ of Ga Athens GA 30602

DODD, LOIS
PAINTER, EDUCATOR
b Montclair, NJ, Apr 22, 27. Study: Cooper Union, with Byron Thomas & Peter Busa. Work: Cooper Union Mus, New York; First Nat City Bank, New York; Kalamazoo Art Ctr, Mich; Ciba-Geigy Chem Corp, Ardsley, NY; Chase Manhattan Bank Collection, New York. Exhib: One-man shows, Tanager Gallery, New York, 54-62 & Green Mt Gallery, New York, 69-76; Colby Col, Waterville, Maine, 77; Washington Art Asn, Conn, 77; Fischbach Gallery, New York, 78. Teaching: Instr, Philadelphia Col Art, 63 & 65; instr Wagner Col. 63-64; instr, Brooklyn Col, 65-72, assoc prof, 75- Pos: Co-founder, Tanager Gallery. Awards: Ital Govt Study Grant, 59-60; Longview Found Purchase Award, 62; Ingraham, Merrill Found Grant, 71. Dealer: Fischbach Gallery 29 W 57th St New York NY 10019. Mailing Add: 30 E Second St New York NY 10003

DODGE, JOSEPH JEFFERS
PAINTER
b Detroit, Mich, Aug 9, 17. Study: Sch Fine Arts, Harvard Col, BS(hons), 40; also study with Yasuo Kuniyoshi, Woodstock, NY, 44. Exhib: Artists of the Upper Hudson, Albany Inst Hist & Art, NY, 42-61; 64th Am Art Exhib, Art Inst Chicago, 61; Realist Invitational, Gallery Contemp Art, Winston-Salem, NC, 69; Florida Creates, var mus, 71-72; Joseph Jeffers Dodge—A Ten Year View, Cummer Gallery Art, 75. Exhibitions Arranged: French Art of the Sixteenth Century, Cummer Gallery Art, 64, Artists of Victoria's England, 65; Age of Louis XIII, Cummer Gallery Art & Mus Fine Arts, St Petersburg, Fla, 69-70; plus others. Teaching: Instr drawing & painting, Hyde Collection, 41-62; substitute prof art hist, Hamilton Col, 47; instr art hist, Adirondack Community Col, 61-62. Pos: Cur, The Hyde Collection, 41-62; dir, Cummer Gallery Art, 61-72; treas, Art Celebration I and II, 73-74. Style & Technique: Poetic images of landscapes and figures in a classical-realist style. Media: Oil, Pencil. Collection: 19th century realists and academic; drawings. Dealer: Art Sources Inc Gulf Life Bldg Jacksonville FL 32207. Mailing Add: 6910 Silver Lake Terr Jacksonville FL 32216

DODWORTH, ALLEN STEVENS
MUSEUM DIRECTOR, PRINTMAKER
b Long Beach, Calif, Nov 19, 38. Study: Stanford Univ, BA(fine arts & design); Portland State Univ. Collections Arranged: 34th-39th Ann Exhibs for Artists of Idaho, Boise Gallery Art, 69-75, Painters of the Idaho Scene, 72 & American Masters in the West, 74. Pos: Chmn, White Gallery, Portland State Univ, 67-69; dir, Boise Gallery Art, Boise Art Asn, 69-76; dir, Salt Lake Art Ctr, 76- Awards: Museum Professionals Fel, Nat Endowment Arts, 73. Mem: Western Asn Art Mus (regional rep, 71-73, trustee, 74-); Western Regional Conf, Am Asn Mus; Salt Lake Coun for the Arts (dir, 77-); Utah Mus Asn; Friends of the Wagnerian Opera. Mailing Add: 54 Finch Lane Salt Lake City UT 84102

DOGANCAY, BURHAN CAHIT
PAINTER
b Istanbul, Turkey, Apr 24, 25. Study: Ankara Halk Evi; Acad Grande Chaumiere, Paris, France. Work: Guggenheim Mus, New York; Ga Mus Art; Brooklyn Mus; Mus Mod Art, New York; Los Angeles Co Mus Art. Exhib: Devlet Resim Heykel Sergisi, Ankara, 60; About New York 1915-1965, Huntington Hartford Mus, New York, 65; Contemporary Turkish Paintings, USA, 71; Artist's at Work, Finch Col Mus, New York, 71; Printmakers at Pace, New York, 72. Awards: City New York Cert Appreciation, 64; Tamarind Lithography Workshop Fel, 69. Bibliog: Jay Jacobs (auth), Back to the walls, Gallery Mag, 70; Louise Schultz (auth), Dogancay and His Work, 71; E G Bowles & Tonny Russell (auth), This Book is a Movie, 71. Mailing Add: 220 E 54th St New York NY 10022

DOHANOS, STEVAN
ILLUSTRATOR, PAINTER
b Lorain, Ohio, May 18, 07. Study: Cleveland Sch Art. Work: Whitney Mus Am Art, New York; Cleveland Print Club; Avery Mem, Hartford, Conn; New Britain Inst; Dartmouth Col. Comn: Murals, Charlotte Amalie, St Thomas, VI, Forest Serv Bldg, Elkins, WVa & US Post Off, West Palm Beach, Fla. Exhib: New Britain Mus Am Art, Conn, 72. Teaching: Founding fac mem, Famous Artists Sch, Westport, Conn. Awards: Medal, Philadelphia Watercolor Club; Art Dirs Club; Prize, Cleveland Printmakers. Mem: Soc Illustrators (pres, 61-63); Am Watercolor Soc. Mailing Add: 279 Sturges Hwy Westport CT 06880

DOHERTY, ROBERT J
MUSEUM DIRECTOR, EDUCATOR
b Everett, Mass, Jan 16, 24. Study: RI Sch Design, BFA, 51; Yale Univ, MFA, 54; Fulbright travel grant to Ger, 65-66. Comn: Design & supvr construction, Rice River House, Louisville, Ky, 62. Exhib: Photographs & Graphic Design, Louisville Art Ctr, Asn Sch, 55 & 58; Photographs, Arts-Club Louisville, 56; Photographs, Allen R Hite Art Inst, Univ Louisville, 64. Collections Arranged: Circulated throughout France, Visual Arts in Louisville, US Info Serv, 57; Graphic Design, Allen R Hite Art Inst, 61; USA-FSA Photo Exhib, Univ Louisville, 61, 19th Century Photographs, 64; traveling exhib, The Art of Typeface, Ky Arts Comn, 67, 19th Century Coal Hole Covers, 69. Teaching: Assoc prof fine arts, Univ Louisville, 59-65, prof, 65-72, chmn dept, 67-72; instr, Free Univ, 70-71 & 71-72; prof, Univ Rochester, 73-; prof, Rochester Inst Technol, 73- Pos: Consult, AEC, Visual Commun Ctr, Washington, DC. 52; dir graphic design, Reynolds Metals Co, 53-57; dir develop, RI Sch Design, 57-59; art ed, Landscape Archit, 60-62; cur photog collection, Allen R Hite Art Inst, 62-68, actg dir, 64-65, dir, 67-72; graphic designer, Firma Dorland GmbH, Munich, Ger, 65-66; dir, Int Mus Photog, George Eastman House, Rochester, NY, 73- Awards: Am Inst Architects Design Award, 56; Am Inst Graphic Arts Design Award, 57; Lithographers & Printers Nat Asn Award for Aluminum Foil Design, 60. Mem: Royal Photog Soc; Asn Art Mus Dir; Deutches Gesellschaft fÜ Photographie; Louisville Jr Art Gallery (dir, 60-65, vpres, 63-65); Louisville Art Ctr Asn (trustee, 67-70). Res: Photographic collections as sources of historic information. Publ: Auth, Aluminum Foil Design, 59; auth, USA-FSA Camera, 10/62 & Foto, 64; picture ed, Documenting a Decade, 72; auth, Preservation, 73; auth, Social Documentary Photography, 74. Mailing Add: Int Mus Photog at Eastman House 900 East Ave Rochester NY 14907

DOLAN, MARGO
ART DEALER, COLLECTOR
b Philadelphia, Pa, Mar 19, 46. Study: Conn Col, BA(art hist). Pos: Docent, Univ Mus, Philadelphia, Pa, 68-70; asst dir, Print Club, 70-73, dir, 73-77; dir, Assoc Am Artists, Philadelphia, 78- Mem: Advocates Arts. Specialty: Original prints and photographs. Collection: Original prints and photographs of the 20th century. Publ: Contribr, Jerome Kaplan prints, 73; contribr, Home is where the art is, 74; contribr, Folio 76, 75. Mailing Add: 1614 Latimer St Philadelphia PA 19103

DOLE, WILLIAM
PAINTER, EDUCATOR
b Angola, Ind, Sept 2, 17. Study: Olivet Col, AB, 38; Univ Calif, Berkeley, MA, 47. Work: Fogg Art Mus, Boston; Joseph H Hirshhorn Mus, Washington, DC; Pa Acad Fine Arts, Philadelphia; Santa Barbara Mus Art; Walker Art Ctr, Minneapolis; plus others. Exhib: One-man shows, Santa Barbara Mus Art, 51-77, Galerie Springer, Berlin, 56 & 64, Jodi Scully Gallery, Los Angeles, 71, 74 & 77 & William Sawyer Gallery, San Francisco, 77; M H de Young Mem Mus, San Francisco, 51; Graham Gallery, New York, 58 & 60; McRoberts & Tunnard, London, 66; Staempfli Gallery, New York, 74 & 76; Los Angeles Munic Art Gallery, 76; Fine Arts Gallery of San Diego, Calif, 76; Hirshhorn Mus, 77; plus many others. Teaching: Lectr, Univ Calif, 47-49; instr art, Univ Calif, Santa Barbara, 49-51, asst prof, 51-58, assoc prof, 58-63, chmn dept, 58-63 & 71-74, prof, 63- Pos: Artist-in-residence, Tamarind Inst, Albuquerque, NMex, 71. Bibliog: Gerald Nordland (auth), William Dole Retrospective 1960-1975 (exhib catalog), Munic Art Gallery, Los Angeles, 76; John Russell (auth), New Collage by William Dole, New York Times, 11/12/76; Henry Seldis (auth), William Dole, Arts Mag, 12/76. Style & Technique: Collage; drawing. Publ: Auth, The Wu Wei to Collage, Art Spectrum, 2/75; co-auth, The Collage of William Dole, Visible Language, IX, 75. Dealer: Staempfli Gallery 47 E 77th St New York NY 10021; Mekler Gallery 651 N La Cienega Los Angeles CA 90060. Mailing Add: Dept of Art Univ Calif Santa Barbara CA 93106

DOLL, DONALD ARTHUR
EDUCATOR, PHOTOGRAPHER
b Milwaukee, Wis, July 15, 37. Study: St Louis Univ, BA(philos), MA(psychology). Work: Sheldon Art Gallery, Lincoln, Nebr; Mid-Am Arts Alliance, Kansas City, Mo; Rochester Inst Technol, NY. Exhib: Crying for a Vision, A Rosebud Sioux Trilogy (traveling exhib), Nat Endowment for the Arts, 76-78. Teaching: Assoc prof photog, Creighton Univ, 69-, chmn fine & performing arts dept, 76- Awards: World Understanding Through Photog, Univ Mo Sch of Journalism, Nat Press Photog Asn & Nikon, 76. Mem: Soc Photog Educ; Nat Press Photog Asn. Style & Technique: Documentary. Media: Straight Photography. Publ: Co-auth & ed, Crying for a Vision, Morgan & Morgan, 76; contribr, Photojournalism, Nat Geographic & Nikon, 76. Mailing Add: Dept of Fine Arts Creighton Univ Omaha NE 68178

DOLLOFF, FRANK WESLEY
CONSERVATOR
b Whitman, Mass, Jan 27, 08. Study: Mass State Col; Boston Univ. Work: Peabody Mus, Salem, Mass; Essex Inst, Salem; Mystic Mus, Conn; Mass Audubon Soc, Lincoln; Cleveland Art Mus, Ohio. Comn: Monuments Dept, Dept of State, Washington, DC, 60; plus many others. Exhib: Nat Art Gallery, Washington, DC, 39; plus many others. Pos: Training & talks on conserv, Mus Fine Arts, Boston. Bibliog: Perkinson (auth), How to care for works of art on paper, Mus Fine Arts Boston Bull, 51. Mem: Int Inst Conservators; Am Int Conservators. Mailing Add: Mus Fine Arts 465 Huntington Ave Boston MA 02115

DOMANSKA, JANINA
ILLUSTRATOR
b Warsaw, Poland; US citizen. Study: Acad Fine Arts, Warsaw. Work: Mus Mod Art, Warsaw & pvt galleries, Rome. Exhib: Roman Found Fine Arts, 51; Int Exposition Biennale, Genoa, Italy, 51; Studio 3, Kew Gardens, NY, 59; three one-man exhib, Lyn Kottler Galleries, New York. Pos: Illusr books, publs & mag, 59- Awards: Award Mischievous Meg Ann Book Jacket Competition, 63; First Class Cert, The Golden Seed, Printing Indust Meeting, 63; Herald Tribune Children's Spring Book Festival Award, The Coconut Thieves, 64. Publ: Illusr, The Golden Seed, 63, The Coconut Thieves, 64 & The Trumpeter of Krakow, 66; auth & illusr,

Why so Much Noise?, 65; auth, Palmiero & the Ogre, 67. Mailing Add: 3 Sweetcake Mountain Rd New Fairfield CT 06810

DOMAREKI, JOSEPH THEODORE
PAINTER, SCULPTOR
b Newark, NJ, May 17, 14. Study: Newark State Col, BS, 37; Univ Iowa, MA, 47; NY Univ, 48-50. Work: Norfolk Mus Arts & Sci, Va; Navy Dept, Pentagon Bldg, Washington, DC; Montclair Mus, NJ; Columbia Mus Art, SC; Broad Nat Bank, Newark; Monmouth Col, West Long Branch, NJ. Comn: Bronze & stone wall mural, Sinclair Res Ctr, Tulsa, Okla, 63; hammered lead relief sculpture (exterior side), St Luke's Episcopal Church, Haworth, NJ, 65; oil painting, Newark Brush Co, Kenilworth, NJ; Corten free-standing sculpture (exterior), Clean-Way Laundry, South Orange, NJ; multi-media painting, Secord Mem, Columbia High Sch, Maplewood, NJ. Exhib: Newark Mus Biannual, 54-73; Newark Mus Triennial State Exhib, 62-71; Art Gallery 64, Hall of Educ, New York World's Fair, 64-65, American Art Today, Pavilion Fine Arts, 64; Silvermine Ann Exhib, Conn, 65; NJ Artists Ann, Trenton State Mus, 66, 68 & 70. Teaching: Head dept art, Sch Dist South Orange & Maplewood, NJ, 64-74. Pos: World War II combat artist, US Navy; vis artist, Chatauqua Arts Festival, 67. Awards: Medal of Hon/Sculpture, Knickerbocker Artists Ann, 55 & 64; John J Newman Mem Medal, Nat Soc Painters in Casein, 62; Medal of Honor for Painting, Audubon Artists Ann, 64, Medal of Honor for Sculpture, 75; plus others. Mem: Audubon Artists (pres, 64-68); hon mem Salmagundi Club, New York; Assoc Artists NJ (vpres, 58-60); Nat Soc Painters & Sculptors (vpres, 56-58); NJ Watercolor Soc; Knickerbocker Artists. Style & Technique: Contemporary; semi-abstract. Media: Oil; Steel, Bronze. Dealer: Gallery Madison/90 1248 Madison Ave New York NY 10028. Mailing Add: 11 Sunset Lane Monmouth Beach NJ 07750

DOMBEK, BLANCHE M
SCULPTOR
b New York, NY. Study: With Alexandre Zeitlin & Leo Amino. Work: Brooklyn Mus, NY; Currier Gallery Art, Manchester, NH; Randolph-Macon Woman's Col; Broese Collection, Ger. Comn: Portrait of Melissa, comn by Mrs R Tompkins, Rolling Hills, Calif, 65; The Accuser (welded iron & steel), comn by Mrs T Ortner, Palos Verdes Peninsula, Calif, 66; Capricornus (bronze), comn by Isabella Gardner, New York, 69; Gemini (sculptured fountain), comn by Bess Harris, Worcester, Eng, 72; Portrait of Felicity, comn by Patricia Joudry, Glos, Eng, 72. Exhib: Colette Allendy Gallery, Paris, 54; Peridot Gallery, 54; Pasadena Mus, Calif, 60; Thorne Gallery, Keene, NH, 69; Currier Gallery Art, Manchester, 71-72; Exhib, St Paul's Sch, Concord, NH, 77. Bibliog: Evelyn Eaton (auth), Progression (film), Draco Found, 65; American visitor's sculpture helps launch new play, Stroud Daily, Glos, Eng, 12/8/71; Kate Kendall (auth), Sculptor's range to mark Dombek show, Peterborough Transcript, 1/23/69. Media: Wood, Metal, Clay. Mailing Add: RFD Hancock NH 03449

DOMINIQUE, JOHN AUGUST
PAINTER
b Virserum, Sweden, Oct 1, 93; US citizen. Study: Portland Art Asn Sch, 13; San Francisco Inst Art, 15-16; Van Sloan Sch Painting, 17; Santa Barbara Sch Arts, 21 & 27-29; also with Colin Campbell Cooper, Armin Hanson & Carl Oscar Borg. Work: Univ Va Art Gallery. Exhib: Portland Art Mus, Ore, 36; Oakland Art Mus, Calif, 41; Los Angeles Art Mus, Calif, 44; Calif Watercolor Soc, Pasadena Art Mus, 61; Charles & Emma Frye Art Mus, Seattle, Wash, 62. Awards: Painting Award for Covered Bridge, Ore State Fair, 40, Painting Award for Oregon Landscape, 41; Painting Award for Peach Tree in Bloom, Glendale Art Asn, 50. Bibliog: Arthur Millier (auth), article in Los Angeles Times, 10/8/33; Maxine Buren (auth), article in Ore Statesman, 10/9/38; Melba Meredith (auth), article in Ojai Valley News, 7/5/62. Mem: Nat Watercolor Soc. Media: Oil, Watercolor. Mailing Add: 216 N Pueblo Ave Ojai CA 93023

DOMIT, MOUSSA M
MUSEUM DIRECTOR, ART HISTORIAN
b Lebanon, May 24, 32; nat US. Study: Ohio State Univ, BA(art hist); Southern Conn State Col, MS(art educ); Yale Univ. Collections Arranged: Sculpture of Thomas Eakins, Corcoran Gallery Art (with catalog), 69; Art of Wilhelm Lehmbruck, Nat Gallery Art, Washington, DC, 72. Teaching: Instr hist art, Columbus Col Art & Design, Ohio, 62-64; lectr art appreciation, Corcoran Sch Art, Washington, DC, 68-70; lectr art hist, Hood Col, 71-72, adj prof art, Univ NC, Chapel Hill, 76-77. Pos: Cur intra-univ loan collection & registrar collections, Yale Univ Art Gallery, 66-68; assoc dir, Corcoran Gallery Art, 68-70; mus cur, Nat Gallery Art, 70-72; assoc dir, NC Mus Art, Raleigh, 72-74, dir, 74-; bd adv, Univ Ga Mus Art, Athens, 77- Mem: Asn Art Mus Dir; Am Asn Mus; Nat Soc Lit & Arts. Res: American impressionist painting. Publ: Auth, George Lee: Recent Color Photography, Corcoran Gallery Art, 69; auth, American Impressionist Painting, Nat Gallery Art, 73; plus many intro to exhib catalog. Mailing Add: NC Mus of Art Raleigh NC 27611

DOMJAN, JOSEPH (ALSO SPIRI)
PAINTER, GRAPHIC ARTIST
b Budapest, Hungary, Mar 15, 07. Study: Hungarian Royal Acad Fine Arts, BFA & MA; also study in Italy, Ger & France. Work: Metrop Mus Art, New York; Nat Mus Mod Art, Paris; Brit Mus, London; Smithsonian Inst & Libr of Cong, Washington, DC; Domjan Mus, Sarospatak, Hungary; plus others. Comn: Cards & calendar, UNICEF, 60-63; Fifteen Battles (bd & album of originals), Limited Ed Club, 69 & 70; silver snowflake & gold star, Metrop Mus Art, 71-75, silver & gold heart, 78. Exhib: One-man show, Cincinnati Art Mus, 58 & 74; Telfair Acad, Savannah, Ga; New York World's Fair, 64; Columbia Mus Art, 64 & 77; retrospective, NJ State Mus, Trenton, 66 & 73; Triennale Int Xilografia, Carpi, Italy, 69 & 72; Print Club, Albany, NY, 68; US Capitol; Int Exhib Exlibris, Marlboro, 75; Mint Mus Art, Charlotte, NC, 78; plus many others. Teaching: Vis lectr, coast to coast, 56- Awards: Master of Color Woodcuts, Chinese Govt, 55; Kossuth Prize, Hungarian Govt, 56; Rockefeller Found Grant, 58; plus others. Bibliog: Magic of Wood (film), Haverland Film Prod, 61; K W Prescott (auth), Domjan the Woodcutter, NJ State Mus, 65; Pierre Mornand (auth), Domjan in the Forest of the Golden Dragon, Opus, 73. Mem: Fel Metrop Mus Art; Soc Illusr; Soc Am Graphic Arts; Soc Encouragement Progress, Paris; Nat Acad Design. Style & Technique: Three-dimensional color woodcuts printed by hand, limited editions, 15 prints per subject. Media: Woodcut; Tapestry. Publ: Illusr, Domjan, 32 Color Woodcuts, Corvina, Budapest, 56; illusr, Little Princess Goodnight, 66 & illusr, Faraway Folk Tales, 72, Holt, Rinehart & Winston; illusr, Bellringer, 74 & auth & illusr, Artist & the Legend, 75, auth & illusr, Wing Beat, A Collection of Eagle Woodcuts, Domjan, 76. Dealer: Arwin Gallery 222 Grand River W Detroit MI 48226. Mailing Add: West Lake Rd Tuxedo Park NY 10987

DONAHUE, KENNETH
MUSEUM DIRECTOR, ART HISTORIAN
b Louisville, Ky, Jan 31, 15. Study: Univ Louisville; Inst Fine Arts, NY Univ. Pos: Asst art dept & art librarian, Univ Louisville, 36-38; staff lectr, Mus Mod Art, New York, 38-43; res fel, Am Coun Learned Soc, Rome, Italy, 47-49; lectr & cur asst, Frick Collection, New York, 49-53; cur, Ringling Mus Art, Sarasota, Fla, 53-57, dir, 57-64; dep dir, Los Angeles Co Mus Art, 64-66, dir, 66-; mem, Internal Revenue Commissioner's Art Adv Panel, Washington, DC, 70-74. Mem: Col Art Asn (bd dirs, 67-71); Asn Art Mus Dirs (vpres, 71-72); Am Asn Mus (coun, 68-78, vpres, 70-72). Publ: Auth, articles in professional journals and exhibition catalogs; contribr, Enciclopedia degli Italiani. Mailing Add: Los Angeles Co Mus of Art 5905 Wilshire Blvd Los Angeles CA 90036

DONALDSON, JEFF R
PAINTER, ART ADMINISTRATOR
b Pine Bluff, Ark, Dec 15, 32. Study: Univ Ark, Pine Bluff, BA(studio art); Ill Inst of Technol, MS(art educ); Northwestern Univ, PhD(art hist). Work: Studio Mus in Harlem, New York; Corcoran Gallery of Art, Washington, DC; Fisk Univ, Nashville, Tenn; Univ Ark, Pine Bluff; Johnson Publ Co, Chicago. Comn: P B S Pinchaback portrait, State of Ill Hist Soc, 63; Wall of Respect, Miles Col, Birmingham, Ala, 69. Exhib: Mus la Tertulia, Cali, Colombia, 71; Studio Mus in Harlem, New York, 75; Nat Ctr for Afro-Am Art, Boston, Mass, 75; Southside Art Ctr, Chicago, 75; Herbert Johnson Mus, Cornell Univ, Ithaca, NY, 76; Howard Univ, Washington, DC, 76; Afro-Am Hist/Cult Mus, Philadelphia, Pa, 77. Collections Arranged: Directions in Afro-Am Art, Johnson Mus, Cornell Univ, 75. Teaching: Lectr art hist, Northwestern Univ, Evanston, Ill, 68-70; chmn art dept, Howard Univ, Washington, DC, 70-76. Pos: Bd dir, Nat Ctr for Afro-Am Artists, 70-; vpres USA/Can zone, FESTAC 77, Lagos, Nigeria, 75- Awards: First Place/Painting, Art & Soul Exhib, Westside Gallery, 68; First Place/Painting, Black Expressions, Southside Art Ctr, Chicago, 69; E Catlett-Mora Award, Nat Conf of Artists Ann, 77. Bibliog: Harold Hayden (auth), Right On Art Lovers, Chicago Sun-Times, 9/70; Edward S Spriggs (auth), Africobra; Pro/Position, Studio Mus in Harlem, New York, 11/71; Paul Richard (auth), A Bright New School, Washington Post, 3/76. Mem: Nat Conf of Artists; Africobra-Farafindugu (founder-spokesman, 68-). Style & Technique: Pan-Africanist compositional and color principles; figurative, narrative political awareness. Media: Opaque and transparent watercolor. Publ: Auth, Civil Rights Yearbook, Henry Regenry, 63; illusr, Riot, Broadside Press, 68; ed, Directions 69, Ill Art Educ Asn, 69; illusr, Book of Life, Broadside Press, 74. Mailing Add: 3900 16th St NW Washington DC 20011

DONALDSON, MARJORY (ROGERS)
CURATOR, PAINTER
b Woodstock, NB, Apr 22, 26. Study: Univ NB Summer Sch, 45, with Pegi Nicol MacLeod; Mt Allison Univ, BFA, 51; City & Guilds of London Sch, Eng, 63-64. Work: Prov NB Art Bank, Fredericton; NB Mus, St John; Mt Allison Univ, Sackville, NB; City Hall, St John, NB. Comn: Forty portraits, NB Sports Hall of Fame, 69-77; official portraits, Univ NB, 71-77; official portrait of ex-pres, St Thomas Univ, 77 & Acadia Univ, 77. Exhib: One-person shows, Univ NB, Fredericton & NB Mus, St John, 64-76, Mem Univ Nfld Art Gallery, 71, Atlantic Prov Art Galleries Asn (traveling exhib), 71-72 & Art Gallery of NS (traveling exhib of prov), 76; Can Soc Painter-Etchers & Engravers; Calgary Graphics. Teaching: Printmaking, Univ NB, Fredericton, 65- Pos: Art mistress, Edgehill Sch for Girls, Windsor, NS, 48-50; actg dir, Univ NB Art Centre, Fredericton, 54-55, asst to dir, 64-70, cur, 70-; art ed, The Fiddlehead, Fiddlehead Soc, 69- Awards: O'Keefe Brewery Award, Toronto, 50. Mem: Can Mus Asn; Atlantic Prov Art Galleries Asn (secy & treas); Asn of Mus of NB. Style & Technique: Expressionistic realism. Media: Oil, Intaglio. Publ: Illusr, Atlantic Advocate, 50-60; illusr (four cover designs; used 2 yrs each), Fiddlehead, 60-70; auth (catalogues), Univ NB Art Centre, 64-77. Dealer: Morrison Art Gallery 221 Union St St John NB Can. Mailing Add: 435 Mansfield St Fredericton NB E3B 3A1 Can

DONATI, ENRICO
PAINTER, SCULPTOR
b Milan, Italy, Feb 19, 09; US citizen. Study: Univ Pavia, Italy, Dr(soc & econ sci), 29; Art Students League, 40; New Sch Social Res, New York, 41. Work: Albright-Knox Art Gallery, Buffalo, NY; Univ Art Mus, Univ Calif, Berkeley; Mus Mod Art, New York; Whitney Mus Am Art, New York; Baltimore Mus Art. Exhib: Eight Carnegie Int Exhibs, 45-61; Embellished Surfaces, Mus Mod Art, New York, 53-54; Younger American Painters, Solomon R Guggenheim Mus, 54-55; Palais des Beaux-Arts, Brussels, Belg, 61; Friends Collection, Whitney Mus Am Art, 64. Teaching: Vis lectr & critic, Yale Univ, 60-62. Pos: Mem adv bd, Brandeis Univ, Waltham, Mass, 56-72; mem adv bd, Parsons Sch Design, New York, 59; mem pres coun arts & archit, Yale Univ, 62-72; chmn nat comn, Univ Art Mus, Univ Calif, Los Angeles, 70-72; mem exec bd, Art Ctr Col Design, Calif, 70-72. Bibliog: Peter Selz (auth), Enrico Donati, Mus de Poche, 65. Dealer: Staempfli Gallery 47 E 77th St New York NY 10021. Mailing Add: 222 Central Park S New York NY 10019

DONDE, OLGA
PAINTER
b Mexico City, Mex, May 23, 35. Work: Mus San Antonio, Tex; Mus Contemp Art, Bogota, Colombia; Mus of Dallas, Tex; Mus Mod Art, Mexico City. Exhib: Fine Arts Palace, Mexico City, 68; Latinamerican Painters, ETenn State Univ, 69; Arvil Gallery, 71; Serra Gallery, Caracas, Venezuela, 75; Salon de la Plastica, 77. Awards: Gran Mencion, Mus Mod Art, Sogamoso, Colombia, 73. Style & Technique: Surrealismo. Media: Oil and Acrylic on Canvas. Mailing Add: Angel Urraza 523-1019 Col del Valle Mexico DF Mexico

DONHAUSER, PAUL STEFAN
SCULPTOR
b Berlin, Ger, May 6, 36; US citizen. Study: Univ Wis-Milwaukee, BS(art); Univ Wis-Madison, MS(art); Ill State Univ, PhD(art). Work: Int Mus Ceramics, Faenza, Italy; Nat Mus Art, Gdansk, Poland; Maison des Metiers d'Art Francais, Paris; Everson Mus Art, Syracuse, NY. Comn: Relief mural (6ft x 15ft), Student Union, Wis State Col, Oshkosh, 71; series of five free standing outdoor sculptures, Univ Wis Campus, 78. Exhib: 23rd Ceramic Nat Exhib, 64 & Ceramic Nat, 71, Everson Mus; Ceramics Int, Alta Col of Art, Can, 73; Ceramics in Contemp Art, Nat Mus, Gdansk, Poland, 75; 35th Int Exhib of Ceramic Arts, Int Mus Ceramics, Faenza, Itlay, 76; Wis Directions, Milwaukee Art Ctr, 76; 4th Chunichi Int Exhib, Nat Mus, Nagoya & Tokyo, Japan, 77; Contemp Ceramics: The Artist's Viewpoint, Kalamazoo Inst of Art, 77; Landscape: New Views, Johnson Mus, Cornell Univ, Ithaca, NY, 78; Int Biennial Exhib of Ceramic Sculpture, Ballauris, France, 78; Clay & Fiber, Wustum Fine Arts Mus, Racine, Wis, 78; Donhauser Retrospective: 1957-1977, Paine Art Ctr, Oshkosh, 77; one-man show, Bergstrom Art Ctr, Neenah, Wis, 77. Teaching: Instr ceramic sculpture, Madison Area Tech Col, Wis, 60-63; instr drawing & ceramics, Ill State Univ, Normal, 63-65; prof ceramic sculpture, Univ Wis, Oshkosh, 65- Awards: Nat Award for Ceramic Sculpture, 8th Miami Ceramic Nat Exhib, Coral Gables Art Asn, Fla, 72; Grand Prize of Faenza, 35th Int Exhib of Ceramics, Int Mus of Ceramics, 76; Scandoli Mem Prize, Nat Exhib, Burpee Art Mus, Rockford, Ill, 77. Bibliog: Sergio Cavina (auth), Emilia Romagna, Regione, Bologna, Italy, 9/76; Linda Witt (auth), Donhauser wins Italy's top ceramic prize, People Weekly, 10/11/76; James Auer (auth), Uncommon clay, Milwaukee J, 9/77. Mem: Int Acad of Ceramics, Geneva, Switz; Am Crafts Coun; Wis Designer

Craftsmen. Style & Technique: Fantasy/surreal ceramic sculpture combined with mixed-media, such as plastics, concrete and neon. Publ: Co-auth, New Ceramics, St Martins, London, 74; auth, History of American ceramics, The Studio Potter, Kendall/Hunt, 78. Dealer: Gilman Galleries 201 E Ohio St Chicago IL 60611. Mailing Add: Dept of Art Univ of Wis Oshkosh WI 54901

DONNELLY, MARIAN CARD
ART HISTORIAN
b Evanston, Ill, Sept 12, 23. Study: Oberlin Col, AB, 46, MA, 48; Yale Univ, PhD, 56. Teaching: Instr art hist, Upsala Col, 48-50; from asst prof to prof art hist, Univ Ore, 66- Pos: Art librn, Univ Rochester, 51-53; res assoc, Art Inst Chicago, 56-57. Mem: Archaeol Inst Am; Nat Trust Hist Preserv; Royal Soc Arts, London; Soc Archit Historians (dir, 64-67, second vpres, 72-74, first vpres, 74-76, pres, 76-). Res: Vernacular and technological architecture in North Europe and America, particularly during the sixteenth, seventeenth and eighteenth centuries. Publ: Auth, Astronomical Observations in New England, Old Time New Eng, 60; auth, New England Pyramids, J Soc Archit Historians, 60; auth, New England Meeting Houses of the Seventeenth Century, Wesleyan Univ Press, 68; auth, Materials in Early New England, Old Time New England, 71; auth, A Short History of Observatories, Univ Ore Bks, 73. Mailing Add: 2175 Olive St Eugene OR 97405

DONNESON, SEENA
PRINTMAKER, SCULPTOR
b New York, NY. Study: Pratt Inst; Art Students League, with Morris Kantor; Pratt Graphic Arts Ctr, with Michael Ponce de Leon; New Sch Social Res. Work: Mus Mod Art, New York; Brooklyn Mus; Los Angeles Co Mus Art; Smithsonian Mus, Washington, DC; NJ State Mus, Trenton. Comn: Ed of prints, Touchstone Press; tapestry design, Equitable Life & Insurance Co, New York, 76; ed prints, Ft Lauderdale Mus Fine Arts, Fla, 77. Exhib: 4th Int Triennale of Original Colored Graphics, Grentchen, Switz, 65; 15th & 19th Biennale, Brooklyn Mus, 65 & 75; 2nd, 3rd & 4th Int Miniature Prints, Pratt Inst & NY State Coun Fine Arts, 66-72; Projected Art: Artists at Work, Finch Col, 71; San Diego Mus, Calif, 75; Reflections/Refractions, Ft Lauderdale Mus Fine Art & Marymount Col, New York, 77-78. plus others. Teaching: Lectr hist mod art, NY Univ, 61-63; in-sch-artist, Nassau Co Cult Coun, 71-; lectr, New Sch Social Res, 74- Pos: Guest Artist, Tamarind Lithography Workshop, 68; app mem, Nassau Co Fine Arts Comn, 70-; exhib coordr, Dept Parks, Recreation & Cult Affairs, New York, 72-74. Awards: Res fel, MacDowell Colony, 63 & 64; Purchase Award, Western Wash State Col, 70. Bibliog: Gordon Brown (auth), Young artists rebel against rectangular format, winter 63 & article, 66, Art Voices; Emily Genauer (auth), article in New York Herald Tribune, 10/63; Sidney Tillim (auth), article in Arts Mag, 12/63. Mem: Artists Equity Asn NY; Print Club Philadelphia; Nat Asn Women Artists; Prof Artists Guild; Women in Art. Style & Technique: Non-figurative sculpture; heavily embossed collographs, etchings. Dealer: Associated American Artists 663 Fifth Ave New York NY 10022. Mailing Add: 319 Greenwich St New York NY 10013

DONOHOE, VICTORIA
ART CRITIC, WRITER
b Philadelphia, Pa. Study: Rosemont Col, BA; Univ Pa Grad Sch Fine Arts, MFA; Pius XII Inst Fine Arts Advan Study, Florence, Italy, scholar, 52-53, cert; Am Fedn Arts Workshop Art Criticism, scholar, 68. Collections Arranged: Relig & Liturgical Art From the Eastern US, Philadelphia Civic Ctr, 63. Teaching: Lab asst studio art & art hist, Rosemont Col, 50-52, lectr, 54-55. Pos: Art critic, Standard & Times, Philadelphia, 59-62; art critic, Philadelphia Inquirer, 62-; guest cur, Into Storage Exhib, Univ Mus, Univ Pa, 74; corresp, Art News, 75-; dir for selection, Exhib Liturgical Art, 41st Int Eucharistic Cong, Philadelphia, 76; adv, Philadelphia Craft Show, 77. Mem: Philadelphia Mus Art; Mus Mod Art; Soc Archit Historians; Metrop Mus of Art, New York; Irish Georgian Soc, Dublin; Philadelphia Art Alliance; Mediaeval Acad of Am; Am-Italy Soc; Univ Mus, Univ Pa; Pa Acad Fine Arts. Res: Late 19th & early 20th century American sculpture. Publ: Contribr, Sculpture of a City: Philadelphia's Treasures in Bronze and Stone, 74; contribr, Knight-Ridder Newswire, 73-; also contribr to anthologies, mags & Sunday supplements. Mailing Add: 34 Narbrook Park Narberth PA 19072

DONSON, JEROME ALLAN
GALLERY DIRECTOR, ART DEALER
b New York, NY, Mar 20, 24. Study: Univ Southern Calif, BA, 49, MSEd, 50, with Prof DeErdely & Prof Don Goodall; Am Grad Sch, Denmark, Jean Hershholt Fund scholar, 50; Univ Copenhagen, 51, with Johannes Brøndsted & Dr Vagn Poulsen; New Sch Social Res, with Seymour-Lipton & Camillo Egas; Univ Calif, Berkeley, MA(art), 57, with Prof Herschel Chipp & Clark Winter. Exhib: Guild SC Artists, Florence, 55, Thor Gallery, Louisville, 75. Collections Arranged: Arts of Southern California, 55-61; The Exodus Group, 60; Landscape Past & Present, 61. Teaching: Lectr art hist, Long Beach City Col Exten, 57; lectr mod art hist, Univ Calif, Los Angeles, 58-60; dir art & assoc prof art hist, Fairleigh-Dickinson Univ & appreciation chmn art depts, Rutherford, Madison & Teaneck, 62-63; prof & art consult, Long Island Univ, 65; vis prof visual hist, Inst Design, Ill Inst Technol & Chicago Bd Educ, 70-72; prof, Louisville Sch Art, 72- Pos: Dir, Florence Mus, SC, 54-56; munic art dir, Long Beach, Calif, 56-61; Am art spec, US State Dept, US Info Agency, Washington, DC & Europe, 61-62; exec dir, Off Cult Affairs, New York, 63-64; ed, Col Art News Art J, 64-70; exec dir, Fine Arts Ctr, Anderson, Ind, 66-68; dir, Louisville Sch Art & Art Ctr Asn, Louisville, 72-; dir, Collectors' Showroom, Chicago, 77- Awards: First Prize in Sculpture, Guild SC Artists, 55; Cult Award of Yr, Long Beach CofC, 61; Award of Merit, Prof Photog Calif, 62. Mem: Col Art Asn Am; Am Coun Educ (pres, 72-; Am Asn Higher Educ; Western Mus League (regional vpres, 61); Western Asn Art Mus Dirs (stand chmn, 60); plus others. Style & Technique: Carving and construction, images and abstract sculpture; hard-edge and diaphanous, images and exploratory painting. Media: Wood; Acrylic. Res: Scandinavian arts, modern and contemporary, primitive. Collection: Living artists of Southern California, the Midwest, New York, and internationally known artists. Publ: Auth, University & College Courses for Potential Art Museum Professionals, 60; auth, Light & shadow, ceramic exploration, Design, fall 60; auth, American vanguard exhibitions in Europe, Art J, summer 63; auth, New Bauhaus Approach, New Art Asn, 71; auth, Eight by Eight, 73; auth, Community resource directory, Jefferson Co Bd of Educ, 77. Mailing Add: 3150 N Sheridan Rd Chicago IL 60657

DOOLEY, HELEN BERTHA
PAINTER, ART DEALER
b San Jose, Calif, July 27, 07. Study: San Jose State Col, AB; Claremont Grad Sch, MA; Douglas Donaldson Sch Design; Calif Sch Fine Arts, San Francisco; Chouinard Art Inst, Los Angeles; Univ Calif, Berkeley; Teachers Col, Columbia Univ. Work: Univ Pac; Shimizu Mus, Japan. Comn: Portrait of Dr D Elton Trueblood (oil), 55-56; portrait of Mrs Lloyd Bertholf (oil), Stockton, 56; portrait of Dr Irving Goleman (oil), comn by Mrs Irving Goleman, Stockton, 62; Floral (oil), G Douglas Burck, Pres, Am Inst Foreign Studies, 69. Exhib: Pa Acad Fine Arts, Philadelphia, 41; Soc Western Artists, De Young Mus, San Francisco, 51 & 66; Am Watercolor Soc, Nat Acad Galleries, New York, 63; Lord & Taylor Galleries, New York, 69; Los Angeles Co Art Exhib & West Coast Watercolor Soc, Sacramento, Calif, 71 & 75; plus others. Teaching: Instr art, Oakland City Schs, 28-30; com artist, Hale Bros, San Jose, 31-32; adult educ instr art, San Jose City Schs, 33-37; instr art, Scripps Col, 37-39; supvr art, Kern Co Schs, Bakersfield, Calif, 39-47; prof art, Univ Pac, 48-68. Pos: Owner, Dooley Gallery, Carmel, Calif, 64- Awards: Award for Mist on the Bay (watercolor), Soc Western Artists, 51; Award for How Green the Valley (oil), Calif State Fair, 65; Award for Festival (oil), Monterey Peninsula Mus Art, 67. Mem: Carmel Art Asn (bd dirs, 70-71, 73-74 & 78); West Coast Watercolor Soc. Style & Technique: Contemporary realism, abstract symbolism; palette knife work in broad areas of flat tones of brilliant color. Media: Oil, Watercolor. Publ: Auth, Figure Drawing Teaching Charts, 48-49; auth, Elementary Grade Crafts in a Nutshell, 63. Mailing Add: Dooley Gallery Box 5577 Carmel CA 93921

DOOLIN, JAMES LAWRENCE
PAINTER, INSTRUCTOR
b Hartford, Conn, June 28, 32. Study: Philadelphia COl of Art, BFA, 54, with Henry Pitz; Univ Calif, Los Angeles, MFA, 71, with Richard Diebenkorn. Work: Long Beach Mus of Art, Calif; Univ Vt, Burlington; Nat Gallery of Victoria, Melbourne, Australia; Gallery of NSW, Sydney; Australian Nat Gallery, Canberra. Exhib: One-man shows, Gallery A, Melbourne, Australia, 66, Cent St Gallery, Sydney, 67-70, Boise State Univ, Idaho, 74, Barnsdall Munic Gallery, Los Angeles, 77; The Field, Victorian Nat Gallery, Melbourne, 68; two-man show, Palos Verdes Art Mus, Calif, 72; De Young Mus Downtown Ctr, San Francisco, 77; plus others. Teaching: Instr drawing & painting, Prahran Tech Col, Melbourne, Australia, 65-66; instr drawing & painting, Univ Calif, Los Angeles, 72-; instr drawing, Otis Art Inst, Los Angeles, 77. Awards: Purchase Prize, 9th Ann Southern Calif Exhib, Long Beach Mus of Art, 70. Style & Technique: Realist pictures, cityscapes and all subjects. Media: Oil and acrylic. Mailing Add: 840 Basin Dr Topanga CA 90290

DOOLIN, MARY N
ART DEALER, COLLECTOR
b Manila, Philippines, Jan 24, 26. Study: Goucher Col in affiliation with Corcoran Gallery of Art, Washington, DC; also with Iouthe Jefferson, Ralph de Burges, Retda Sedel, Fran Jenks & Joy Luke. Pos: Owner, Prince Royal Gallery Inc. Mem: Art League Alexandria. Style & Technique: Realism to impressionism. Media: Oil, Acrylic. Specialty: Original art in watercolor, oil, acrylic, pastel, collage drawings and sculpture. Collection: Various periods and techniques in lithographs, oils, etchings, watercolors, etc. Mailing Add: c/o Prince Royal Gallery Inc 204 S Royal St Alexandria VA 22314

DOOLITTLE, WARREN FORD, JR
PAINTER, EDUCATOR
b New Haven, Conn, Apr 3, 11. Study: Yale Univ, BFA; Syracuse Univ, MFA. Work: Evansville Mus Art, Ind; Eastern Ill Univ; Univ Fla, Gainesville; Seattle Art Mus, Wash; New Haven Pub Sch Syst. Comn: Many pvt & pub portraits. Exhib: Pepsi Cola's Paintings of the Year, New York, 46; Art Inst Chicago Ann Drawing Exhib, 63; 1st Spring Ann, Calif Palace Legion of Hon, San Francisco; Corcoran Gallery Art 20th Biennial, Washington, DC; retrospective one-man show, Fla Gulf Coast Art Ctr, Belleair, 73; plus others. Teaching: Asst drawing, Yale Univ, 34-35; instr painting, Univ Fla, 35-38; prof painting, Univ Ill, Urbana, 38-41, prof-in-charge undergrad & grad painting, 48-68, chmn grad progs art, 56-71, emer prof art, 71- Pos: Asst to Eugene Savage, New York World's Fair, 38. Awards: Scholarships, Yale Univ, 33-35; Faculty Fel, Ford Found, 54; Nat Watercolor Soc First Prize, Washington Ann Nat Exhib, 60. Mailing Add: PO Box 1225 Crystal River FL 32629

DORFMAN, BRUCE
PAINTER, INSTRUCTOR
b New York, NY, Aug 15, 36. Study: Art Students League, with Yasuo Kuniyoshi & Arnold Blanch; Univ Iowa, BA. Work: Butler Inst Am Art, Youngstown, Ohio; Syracuse Univ, NY; Collection Mourlot, Paris; Com Trust Co Found; plus others. Exhib: Fla Art, New York World's Fair, 64; Modern American Paintings, Mus Art, Univ Kans, 67; Professional Who Teach, New York Cult Ctr, 69; Litografias Coleccion Mourlot, Mus of Univ PR, 71; Butler Inst Am Art Ann, 71, 72 & 75; Kennedy Galleries, New York, 72; Images Gallery, Toledo, Ohio, 75; Nassau Community Col, New York, 76-77; Barrett House Gallery, Poughkeepsie, NY, 77; Nobe Gallery, New York, 78. Teaching: Guest artist, Norton Mus, W Palm Beach, Fla, 62-64; instr painting & drawing, Art Students League, Woodstock, NY, 64-72, coordr & moderator Friday Noon Forum, 68-71; resident artist, Syracuse Univ, 71; instr, Art Students League, New York, 69 & Barrett House Sch of Art, Poughkeepsie, 76- Awards: Julius Hallgarten Award, Nat Acad Design, 62; New York World's Fair Exhib Award, State of Fla, 64; Friends of Am Art Purchase Award, Butler Inst Am Art Ann, 72; plus others. Bibliog: John Canaday (auth), article in New York Times, 10/67; Joseph Morgenstern (auth), Bruce Dorfman, Kennedy Galleries, 1/72; David L Shirey (auth), article in New York Times, 1/77. Mem: Life mem Art Students League. Publ: Auth, Color Mixing, Grosset & Dunlap, 67. Dealer: Nobe Gallery 250 W 57th St New York NY 10019; Kennedy Galleries 40 W 57th St New York NY 10022. Mailing Add: Art Students League 215 W 57th St New York NY 10019

DORN, PETER KLAUS
DESIGNER
b Berlin, Ger, June 30, 32; Can citizen. Study: Journeyman compositor, Berlin; Ont Col Art, Toronto; Hochschule für Grafik & Buch Kunst, Leipzig. Work: Toronto Pub Libr Fine Arts Sect. Exhib: Don Mills Pub Libr, Toronto, 67; Royal Can Acad, 70; Agnes Etherinton Art Ctr, Kingston, 71; Look of Books, 74, 76 & 77; Design Can, 75; Spectrum Can, 76. Pos: Proprietor, Heinrich Heine Press, Toronto, 63; typographer, Univ Toronto Press, 66-71; dir, Graphic Design Unit, Queen's Univ, 71. Awards: Spec Recognition, Am Asn Univ Prof, 75; Award of Excellence, Am Inst Graphic Arts, 75; Hon Mention, Int Book Art Exhib, Leipzig, 77. Mem: Royal Can Acad; Guild Hand Printers (dir); Graphic Designers Can (nat past pres, Kingston pres). Style & Technique: Book design and communication design. Mailing Add: 72 Queen's Crescent Kingston ON Can

DORN, RUTH (RUTH DORNBUSH)
PAINTER
b Leipzig, Ger, Feb 16, 25; US citizen. Study: Studied in Ger & Bolivia; Brooklyn Mus; Brooklyn Col; Nat Acad Fine Arts, with Philip. Exhib: Brooklyn Mus, 69 & 77; Artists League of Brooklyn, Metrop Mus Art, New York, 77; Brooklyn Come to the Met, Hudson Valley Art Asn, 77; Nat Arts Club, New York; Allied Artists of Am, 78; Cork Gallery, Lincoln Ctr, New York, 78; Union Carbide Corp, New York, 78. Awards: First Prize, Composers, Authors & Artists of Am, 74, Nell Van Hook Mem Prize, 75. Mem: Composers Authors & Artists of Am; Am Artists Prof League; Burr Artists; Artists League at Brooklyn; Artists Equity. Style & Technique: Impressionistic; impasto, palette knife technique. Media: Oil. Mailing Add: 6316 Strickland Ave Brooklyn NY 11234

DORR, GOLDTHWAITE HIGGINSON, III
ART DEALER
b New York, NY, Jan 11, 32. Study: Harvard Univ, BA, 56; Univ Minn, 61-62. Collections Arranged: David Park: A Retrospective Exhibition, 69; Robert McCall: Space Artist, 72; plus numerous others. Pos: Cur & chief preparator, Minneapolis Inst Arts, 61-68; dir, Santa Barbara Mus Art, 68-70; dir, Phoenix Art Mus, 70-74; dir, Portland Mus Art, Maine, 75-76; rep, Steven Straw Co, Newberry Port, Mass. Mem: Am Asn Mus. Publ: Auth, Minneapolis Inst Arts Bull, 12/61; contribr, Minneapolis Inst Arts Bull, 3/62, 65, 67 & 68. Mailing Add: 7230 E Vista Dr Scottsdale AZ 85253

DORRA, HENRI
ART HISTORIAN, EDUCATOR
b Alexandria, Egypt, Jan 17, 24; US citizen. Study: Univ London, BSc, 44; Harvard Univ, MS & MA, 50, PhD, 53. Collections Arranged: Visionaries and Dreamers & Ryder, Corcoran Gallery Art, San Francisco Mus Art & Cleveland Mus Art, 55-60; Years of Ferment, Univ Calif, Los Angeles, 65. Teaching: Lectr art hist; mem fac, Univ Calif, Los Angeles, 63-65; prof art, Univ Calif, Santa Barbara, 65- Pos: Asst dir, Corcoran Gallery Art, 54-61; asst dir, Philadelphia Mus Art, 61-62; exec vpres, Indianapolis Art Asn, 62-63; trustee, Santa Barbara Mus Art. Awards: Bowdoin Prize, Harvard Univ, 49; Student Fel, Metrop Mus Art, 51-52; Nat Endowment Humanities Fel, summer 75. Mem: Col Art Asn Am. Publ: Auth, Gauguin, Metrop Mus Art, 53; auth, Seurat, Beaux-Arts, Paris, 60; auth, The American Muse, 61; auth, Art in Perspective, 73; contribr, Gazette Beaux-Arts, Metrop Mus Art Bull & others. Mailing Add: Dept of Art Univ of Calif Santa Barbara CA 93106

DORSKY, MORRIS
ART HISTORIAN, EDUCATOR
b New York, NY, July 8, 18. Study: Brooklyn Col, BA, 40; NY Univ, MA, 66. Teaching: Prof art hist, Brooklyn Col, City Univ New York, 48-, chmn dept art, 70- Res: Ben Shahn. Mailing Add: 120 W 70th St New York NY 10023

DORST, CLAIRE V
PAINTER, EDUCATOR
b Plymouth, Wis, June 4, 22. Study: Beloit Col, BA, 49; Univ Iowa, MA, 53; Univ Wis-Madison, United Lutheran Church Am scholar, 62-63, MFA, 63. Work: Univ Iowa Collection; Univ Wis Collection; also in pvt collections. Exhib: Wisconsin at Work, Mem Mus, Milwaukee, 50 & Wisconsin Painters & Sculptors Ann, 64; Fla State Fair Show, Tampa, 65; Nat Exhib Contemp Painting, Soc Four Arts, Palm Beach, Fla, 66 & 70; Hortt Mem Exhib, Mus Arts, Ft Lauderdale, Fla, 68 & 70. Teaching: Asst prof studio art, Wayne State Col, 53-59; prof art & art hist & chmn dept art, Carthage Col, 59-64; prof studio art, Fla Atlantic Univ, 64-, chmn dept art, 68- Awards: Tellus Madden Award, Wis Spring Show, 63; First Prize in Painting, Winter Park Art Fair, 65; Atwater Kent Award, Soc Four Arts Nat Exhib, 66. Mem: Fla League Arts (mem bd dirs, 71-); Fla Craftsmen; Am Crafts Coun; Col Art Asn Am. Dealer: Tahir Gallery 823 Chartres St New Orleans LA 70116. Mailing Add: Dept of Art Fla Atlantic Univ Boca Raton FL 33432

DORST, MARY CROWE
INSTRUCTOR, ARTIST
b Wis. Study: Beloit Col, BA(art); Northern Ill Univ, MA(drawing), thesis subject: Paper for the Artist; grad work, Univ Wis. Exhib: Fla Craftsmen Ann Exhib, 65, 72 & 74; Nat Exhib, Soc of the Four Arts, Palm Beach, Fla, 68; Hortt Mem Exhib, Ft Lauderdale Mus Arts, 69; Piedmont Crafts Exhib, Mint Mus, Charlotte, NC, 71-75. Collections Arranged: The Other Side of the Generation Gap, Constructions in Flexible Materials, Printmakers of the Americas, Edward S Curtis: Indians of North America, Fla Atlantic Univ, 73-77. Teaching: Instr art, Marymount Col, Fla, 65-67, Fla Atlantic Univ, 67-68 & 77-, Broward Community Col, Fla, 73-75 & Palm Beach Jr Col, 75-; gallery dir, Fla Atlantic Univ, 73-77; art reviewer, Boca Raton News, Fla, 75-76. Awards: First in Drawing, Quincy Ann, 61; Jewelry Purchase Prize, Univ Wis Student Exhib, 63; First in Show, Ann Open, Ctr for the Arts, 71. Mem: Fla Craftsmen (area dir, 75-78); Am Crafts Coun; Arts Alliance of Boca Raton (pres, 77); Morikami Mus Japanese Cult (mem adv bd). Media: Drawing; crafts. Res: Papermaking. Publ: Auth, A Day in Mino, Crafts Horizons, 6/71; auth, Kozo Futura: Living National Treasure, Innovations in Paper. Mailing Add: 618 NW High St Boca Raton FL 33432

DOTY, ROBERT MCINTYRE
ART ADMINISTRATOR
b Rochester, . Dec 23, 33. Study: Harvard Univ, AB; Univ Rochester, MA. Collections Arranged: Photo-Secession, 1960; Photography America, 65 & 74; Whitney Ann, 66-71; Adolph Gottlieb, 68; Human Concern/Personal Torment, 69; Contemporary Black Artists of America, 71; Lucas Samaras, 72; American Folk Art in Ohio Collections, 76. Pos: Dir, Currier Gallery Art, currently. Mailing Add: Currier Gallery of Art 192 Orange St Manchester NH 03104

DOUAIHY, SALIBA
PAINTER
b Lebanon, Sept 14, 15; US citizen. Study: Ecole Nat Superieure et Spec des Beaux de Arts, Paris. Work: Mus Mod Art, New York; Albright-Knox Mus, Buffalo, NY; Guggenheim Mus, New York; Butler Inst Am Art, Youngstown, Ohio; Akron Art Inst, Ohio. Comn: Eight panels on Plexiglas, Xerox Co, Stanford, Conn, 70; ten religious subjects in glass, Church of Annaya, Lebanon, 73; created subject in oil and one copy in glass, Our Lady of Lebanon Church, Brooklyn, NY, 75; ten paintings, comn by Dr Elias Saadi, Youngstown, Ohio, 77; 65 abstract panels, Cedars of Lebanon Church, Jamaica Plain, Mass, 78. Exhib: Salon des Artistes Francais, 34; Sch Fine Arts, Paris, 43; Philaldelphia Mus Art, 53; Retrospective, NC Mus Art, Raleigh, 78; one-man shows, Contemporaries Gallery, New York, 64, Gallery One, Beirut, 71 & Lermouth Gallery, New York, 76. Teaching: Prof art, Col de la Sagesse, Beirut, 46-48. Awards: Hon Mention, Pa Acad Fine Arts, 68. Bibliog: Victor Hakim (auth), Une Osmose Par Le Style, L'Imprimerie Catholique, 49; Arturo Garcia Formenti (auth), Destellos, El Universal, Mex, 11/22/54; Charlotte Willard (auth), The Language of Color, New York Post, 3/20/66. Mem: Artists Equity. Style & Technique: Hard edge abstract. Media: Oil, Acrylic, Encaustic. Mailing Add: c/o Fenway Studios 30 Ipswich St Boston MA 02215

DOUDERA, GERARD
EDUCATOR, PAINTER
b Sharon, Conn, Dec 29, 32. Study: Hartford Art Sch, BFA; Univ Ill. Work: Wadsworth Atheneum, Hartford; Butler Inst Am Art, Youngstown, Ohio; New Britan Mus, Conn. Exhib: One-man shows, DeCordova & Dana Mus, Lincoln, Mass, 59; New Britain Mus Am Art, Conn, 61; Univ Hartford, 71. Teaching: Prof painting, Univ Conn, 62-, head art dept, 74-77. Awards: Grant, Tiffany Found, 58; First Hallgarten Award, Nat Acad Design, 58; Painting Award, Conn Acad Fine Arts, 75. Mem: Conn Acad Fine Arts. Style & Technique: Representational paintings, impressionistic. Media: Oil, Watercolor. Mailing Add: 312 Babcock Rd Tolland CT 06084

DOUGLAS, EDWIN PERRY
PAINTER, INSTRUCTOR
b Lynn, Mass, June 18, 35. Study: RI Sch Design, BFA; San Francisco Art Inst, MFA. Work: Montreal Mus Fine Arts, Can; San Francisco Art Inst Art Bank; Dayton Art Mus, Ohio; Cincinnati Art Mus; Lincoln Land Community Col Art Mus, Springfield, Ill. Exhib: San Francisco Art Inst Nat Painting & Sculpture Tour, 63; 81st Ann Spring Exhib, Montreal Mus Fine Arts, 64; 31st Ann Can Soc Graphic Art, Kingston, Ont, 64; Cincinnati Biennial, Cincinnati Art Mus, 69; Portland Mus Art, Maine, 74; plus others. Teaching: Instr painting, Univ Man Sch Art, 63-64; asst prof drawing, Cincinnati Art Acad, Ohio, 64-68; asst prof drawing, Wash Univ Sch Fine Arts, 69-72; vis lectr painting, Univ Cincinnati, 72-73; instr painting & drawing, Portland Sch Art, 73- Bibliog: Dialogue on painting, Miami Univ TV, 67. Mailing Add: 993 Highland Ave South Portland ME 04107

DOUKE, DANIEL W
PAINTER, EDUCATOR
b Los Angeles, Calif, Sept 18, 43. Study: Pasadena City Col, AA, 66; Calif State Univ, Los Angeles, BA, 70, MA, 71. Work: Avco Savings & Loan, Newport Beach, Calif; Nicholas Treadwell Galleries, London, Eng; Gallerie des Quatre Mouvements, Paris, France. Exhib: Oakland Mus Art, Calif, 73; State Univ NY Col, Potsdam, 74; one-man shows, Jack Glenn Gallery, Newport Beach, 75, Warren Benedek Gallery, New York, 75 & Dobrick Gallery, Chicago, 76; Mus Mod Art, New York, 76; Los Angeles Inst Contemp Art, 77. Collections Arranged: Douglas Bond: Twelve Year Survey (auth, catalogue), Calif State Univ, 78. Teaching: Instr painting, Calif State Univ, Los Angeles, 75- Pos: Visual arts specialist, Cult Arts, Co of Los Angeles, 73-75; gallery dir, Calif State Univ, Los Angeles, 75- Awards: James D Phelan Award in Painting, Oakland Mus, San Francisco Found, 73. Mem: Los Angeles Inst Contemp Art; Newport Harbor Art Mus; Col Art Asn. Style & Technique: Super realist paintings in airbrushed acrylic paints of common objects. Publ: Auth, Project Outreach, Nat Endowment for the Arts, 74; co-auth, Ceramic Conjunction, Co of Los Angeles, 74-75; contribr, Bradley Smith, auth, Erotic Art of the Masters, Lyle Stuart, 75; contribr, Gregory Battcock, auth, Super Realism, Dutton, 75; contribr, Udo Kultermann, auth, New Painting 2nd Edition, Wasmuth, 76. Dealer: Jan Baum & Iris Silverman Gallery 8225 Santa Monica Blvd Los Angeles CA 90046; Dobrick Gallery Ltd 161 E Erie Chicago IL 60611. Mailing Add: 5151 State Univ Dr Los Angeles CA 90032

DOUMATO, LAMIA
ART LIBRARIAN, RESEARCHER
b Aug 26, 47; US citizen. Study: RI Col, BA; Pa State Univ, MA(art hist); Simmons Col, Boston, MLS; Boston Univ; Columbia Univ. Collections Arranged: Rhode Island Architecture, Providence Pub Libr. Teaching: Teaching asst art hist, Pa State Univ, 70. Pos: Art librn, Providence Pub Libr, 70-71; ref librn, Boston Univ Libr, 71-74; ref librn, Mus Mod Art Libr, New York, 74- Mem: Int Ctr Medieval Art; Art Librn Soc NAm; Art Librn Soc New York. Interest: All periods of art including Modern and Ancient. Publ: Auth, Understanding Modern Art, Providence Pub Libr, 70; contribr, articles to Microform Rev, 78 & Col & Res Libr, 78; auth, American Drawings, Gale Publ, 79. Mailing Add: 382 Central Park W New York NY 10025

DOWDEN, ANNE OPHELIA TODD
PAINTER, ILLUSTRATOR
b Denver, Colo, Sept 17, 07. Study: Univ Colo; Carnegie Inst Technol; Art Students League. Work: Hunt Bot Libr, Pittsburgh, Pa. Comn: Paintings for reproduction as facsimile prints, Frame House Gallery, Louisville, Ky, 69-72 & 78; painting of three azaleas. Callaway Gardens, Pine Mountain, Ga, 71; painting of tulip tree flowers, New York Bot Garden, 72; painting of rhododendron, Holden Arboretum, Cleveland. Exhib: American Textiles, Metrop Mus Art, New York, 48; Decorative Arts Today, Newark Mus, 48; Int Group Shows, Hunt Bot Libr, 64, 68 & 72, one-man show, 65. Teaching: Instr drawing, Pratt Inst, 30-32; head dept art, Manhattanville Col, 32-53. Awards: Tiffany Found Fel, 29-31. Style & Technique: Accurate botanical paintings in the classical manner. Media: Watercolor. Publ: Auth & illusr, Look at a Flower, 63, illusr. Shakespeare's Flowers, 69, auth & illusr, Wild Green Things in the City, 72, The Blossom on the Bough, 75, The Golden Circle, 77 & State Flowers, 78, Crowell; auth & illusr, The Secret Life of the Flowers, Western, 64; Wildflowers and the Stories Behind Their Names, Scribner, 77. Mailing Add: 205 W 15th St New York NY 10011

DOWLING, DANIEL BLAIR
EDITORIAL CARTOONIST
b O'Neil, Nebr, Nov 16, 06. Study: Univ Calif, Berkeley; Chicago Acad Fine Arts. Pos: Ed cartoonist, Omaha World Herald, 40-48; ed cartoonist, New York Herald Tribune, 48-65; ed cartoonist, Kansas City Star, 67-73; retired. Awards: Awards, Sigma Delta Chi & Freedoms Found; Christopher Award. Mem: Assoc Am Ed Cartoonist (pres, 58-60). Mailing Add: 26335 Rio Ave Carmel CA 93923

DOWNEY, JAMES
See Egleson, Jim

DOWNEY, JUAN
SCULPTOR, EDUCATOR
b Santiago, Chile, May 11, 40. Study: Sch Archit, Cath Univ Chile, BArch, 61; Atelier 17, Paris, 63-65, printmaking with S W Hayter; Pratt Inst, 67-69. Work: Mus Mod Art, New York; Casa Americas, Havana, Cuba; Tel Aviv Mus, Israel; Bibliot Nat, Paris; Nat Collection Fine Arts, Washington, DC; plus others. Exhib: Galeries Pilotes, Mus Cantonale Beaux Arts, Lausanne, Switz, 70; Lucht-Kunst, Stedelijk Mus, Amsterdam, 71; Art & Science, Tel Aviv Mus, 71; Long Beach Mus, Calif, 76; Contemp Art Mus, Houston, Tex, 76; Whitney Mus of Am Art, New York, 76; Everson Mus of Art, Syracuse, NY, 77; Documenta 6, Kassel, Ger, 77; Anthology Films Archive, New York, 77; Mus Arte Contemporaneo, Caracas, Venezuela, 77; plus many others. Teaching: Asst prof archit, Pratt Inst, New York, 70-; instr art, Hunter Col, New York, 70- Awards: First Prize, Casa Americas, Havana, 64; Orgn Am States Fel, 70, Guggenheim Found Fel, 71 & 76 & Mass Inst Technol Fel, 73. Bibliog: Howard Wise (auth), Pollution Robot (film), 70. Style & Technique: Videotape and drawing. Dealer: Howard Wise 84 Fifth Ave New York NY 10011; Castelli Sonnabend Video 420 West Broadway New York NY 10012. Mailing Add: 39 White St New York NY 10013

DOWNING, THOMAS
PAINTER
b Suffolk, Va, June 13, 28. Study: Randolph-Macon Col, BA, 48; Pratt Inst, 48-50; Cath Univ Am. Work: Corcoran Gallery of Art, Washington, DC; Wadsworth Atheneum, Hartford, Conn; La Jolla Mus Art, Calif; Norfolk Mus Arts & Sci, Va; Philadelphia Mus Art, Pa. Exhib: New Experiments in Art, De Cordova & Dana Mus, Lincoln, Mass; Corcoran Gallery of Art

Biennial, Washington, DC, 63 & 67; Post Painterly Abstraction, Los Angeles Co Mus Art, Los Angeles, Calif, 64; The Colorists, San Francisco Mus Art, Calif, 65; The Responsive Eye, Mus Mod Art, New York, 65; Washington Gallery of Mod Art, 65; Corcoran Gallery of Art, 66; Systemic Painting, Guggenheim Mus, New York, 66; Pa Acad of Fine Arts Ann, Philadelphia, 66; one-man shows, Corcoran Gallery of Art, 66 & 69; A M Sachs Gallery, 68 & Pyramid Art Galleries Ltd, 70, New York. Teaching: Instr, Va pub sch & Corcoran Sch of Art. Awards: Travel Study Grant, Va Mus Fine Arts, Richmond, 50. Mailing Add: c/o Pyramid Art Galleries Ltd 2121 P St NW Washington DC 20037

DOWNS, LINDA ANNE
CURATOR, ART ADMINISTRATOR
b Detroit, Mich, May 30, 45. Study: Monteith Col, Wayne State Univ, PhB, 59; Univ Mich, MA(hist of art), 73. Collections Arranged: Student Art Exhibs, 69-77, Barbara Chase Ribaud Sculpture, 72, Diaghilev & Russian Stage Design, 72, Caravaggio's Conversion of the Magdalene: An Analysis of the Painting, 73 & African Art of the Dogon, 74, Detroit Inst of Arts. Teaching: Adj asst prof art hist, Wayne State Univ, Detroit, Mich, 76- Pos: Spec asst, Proj Outreach, Detroit Inst Arts, Mich, 68-69, jr cur educ, 69-73, asst cur educ, 73-76, cur educ, 76- Awards: Best Cult Film Award for Only Then Regale My Eyes, Midwest Pub Broadcasting Serv, 76. Mem: Am Asn Mus; Col Art Asn; Mich Mus Asn; Midwest Mus Asn; Midwest Art Hist Asn. Publ: Auth, Claes Oldenburg's Giant Three-Way Plub and Chrysler Airflow, Bull Detroit Inst Arts, 71; producer, Only Then Regale My Eyes (60 minute color film produced for the exhib, French Painting 1774-1830: The Age of Revolution), WTVS, Detroit, 75. Mailing Add: Detroit Inst of Arts 5200 Woodward Ave Detroit MI 48202

DOYLE, JOHN LAWRENCE
PRINTMAKER, PAINTER
b Chicago, Ill, Mar 14, 39. Study: Sch of Art Inst Chicago, BAE, 62; Northern Ill Univ, MA, 68. Work: Libr of Cong, Washington, DC; Smithsonian Inst Collection Traveling Exhib, Washington, DC; Norfolk Mus Arts & Sci, Va; Miss Art Mus, Jackson; Art Inst Chicago. Exhib: Int Printmakers, Seattle, Wash, 69 & 71; 22nd Boston Printmakers Exhib, De Cordova Mus, Lincoln, Mass, 70; Images on Paper, Miss Art Mus, Jackson, 70; Colorprints USA, Tex Tech Univ, Lubbock, 72; 73rd Chicago Show, Art INst Chicago, 72; 24th Am Drawings Biennial, Norfolk Mus, 72; Prints & Drawings, Los Angeles Co Mus Art, Los Angeles, Calif, 73. Awards: Eisendrath Prize, 73rd Chicago Show, Art Inst Chicago, 72; Purchase Prizes, 24th Am Drawings Biennial, Norfolk Mus Arts & Sci, 72 & Images on Paper, Miss Art Mus, 72. Bibliog: Ill Printmakers, Ill Arts Coun, 71; Mendelowitz (auth), Drawings (Illustration), Univ Iowa, 76; Ben Dallas (auth), Mysticism through visual metaphor, SW Arts Mag, 77. Style & Technique: Intense fascination for figures and their relationship with functional objects, costumes and ritualistic apparatus. Media: Lithograph; Drawing; Watercolor. Dealer: Judy Black c/o Carlson/Black Gallery Box 1117 Taos NM 87571. Mailing Add: 3116 Thompson Rd Wonderlake IL 60097

DOYLE, THOMAS J
SCULPTOR, INSTRUCTOR
b Jerry City, Ohio, May 23, 28. Study: Ohio State Univ, BFA, 52, MA, 53, with Roy Lichtenstien & Stanley Twardewicz. Work: Brooklyn Mus; Carnegie Inst, Pittsburgh; Kley Collection, Ger. Comn: Fiberglas sculpture, Pub Arts Coun, City of New York, 72. Exhib: Kunsthalle, Bern, Switz, 64; Kunsthalle, Dusseldorf, Ger, 65; Dwan Gallery, New York, 66 & 67; Sculpture of the Sixties, Los Angeles Co Art Mus, Calif, 67; Primary Structures, Jewish Mus Mus, New York, 67. Teaching: Instr sculpture, Brooklyn Mus Art Sch, 60-68; instr sculpture, New Sch Social Res, 61-68; lectr sculpture, Queens Col, 70- Bibliog: Lucy R Lippard (auth), Tom Doyle, Kunsthalle, Dusseldorf, 65 & Space embraced: Tom Doyle's recent sculpture, Arts, 4/66; Irving Sandler (auth), Gesture & non-gesture in recent sculpture, Los Angeles Co Mus Art, 67. Mailing Add: 55 Mercer Gallery 55 Mercer St New York NY 10013

DOYON, GERARD MAURICE
GALLERY DIRECTOR, ART HISTORIAN
b Manchester, NH, Apr 6, 23. Study: Manchester Inst Arts, dipl fine arts, 49; St Anselm's Col, AB, 51; Fulbright scholar to Paris, 51-52; Ecole Beaux-Arts, Paris, 52; Ecole Mus du Louvre, AE, 52; Boston Univ, MA, 54, PhD, 64. Teaching: Chmn dept art, St Anselm's Col, 52-61 & Miami-Dade Jr Col, 61-64; assoc prof art hist & chmn art dept, Fla Atlantic Univ, 64-68; prof art hist & chmn dept art, Washington & Lee Univ, 68- Awards: Danforth Scholar, 60-61 & 62-63. Res: French art of the 18th and 19th centuries, especially painting. Publ: Auth, The mural paintings of Theodore Chasseriau, Gazette Beaux-Arts, Paris, 69. Mailing Add: Dept of Art Washington & Lee Univ Lexington VA 24450

DOZIER, OTIS
PAINTER, PRINTMAKER
b Forney, Tex, Mar 27, 04. Study: Dallas Mus Fine Arts; Fine Arts Ctr, Colorado Springs, Colo, with Boardman Robinson; Denver Art Mus; Metrop Mus Art; Wadsworth Atheneum; plus others. Comn: Murals, US Post Off, Arlington, Giddings & Fredericksburg, Tex. Exhib: Whitney Mus Am Art, 45; Carnegie Inst, 46; Dallas Allied Artists, 46; one-man shows, Witte Mem Mus, 48 & Dallas Mus Fine Arts, 56. Teaching: Instr, Dallas Mus Fine Arts, 45-69. Awards: Award, Dallas Allied Artist, 32 & 46; Award, Southwestern Art Asn, 48; Award, New Orleans Arts & Crafts, 48; plus others. Media: Graphic. Mailing Add: 7019 Dellrose Dr Dallas TX 75214

DRAGUL, SANDRA KAPLAN
PAINTER, PRINTMAKER
b Cincinnati, Ohio, May 23, 43. Study: Art Acad Cincinnati with Julian Stanczak, 60-61; Pratt Inst, Deans scholar, 62-65, BFA(with hons), 65; City Univ New York, with Richard Linduer, Stephen Greene, Jacob Landau, 68-70. Work: PTI Restaurant, Houston, Tex; John Mansville Corp, Chicago; Midland Fed Savings Bank, Denver, Colo; Ideal Basic Industries Denver; US Plywood Corp, New York; plus numerous pvt collections. Exhib: First Colo Biennial, Denver Art Mus, 71 & Denver Metrop, 72 & 74; one-woman shows, William Kastan Gallery, Denver, 74, Pavilion Gallery, Scottsdale, Ariz, 74 & 75 & Attitudes Gallery, 75; Rocky Mountain Nat Watermedia Exhib, Golden, Colo, 74. Teaching: Instr painting, design, Arapahoe Community Col, 74-75; instr oil painting, Emily Griffith Opportunity Sch, 74- Awards: Deans Medal in Graphic Arts, Pratt Inst, 75; Best of Show, Jefferson Unitarian Church, Golden, Colo, 75. Bibliog: Marlan Miller (auth), Nonobjective Dragul art is inventive, Phoenix Gazette, 3/30/74; James Mills (auth), Artistic trio...natural forms, Denver Post, 12/15/74; Duncan Pollock (auth), Three for the price of one, Rocky Mountain News, 12/22/74. Style & Technique: Hard-edge; coloristic abstractions of natural forms in acrylic and watercolor; unique plaster block printing process utilizing modular units of color. Media: Acrylic, Watercolor, Plaster Relief, Silk Screen. Publ: Illusr, Rationale, 65; contrib, Art Work, No Commercial Value, Grossman, 71. Mailing Add: c/o Attitudes Gallery Contemp Art 1333 18th St Denver CO 80202

DRAKE, JAMES
PRINTMAKER, SCULPTOR
b Lubbock, Tex, Sept 12, 46. Study: Art Ctr Col of Design, fel, BFA with Hons, 69, MFA, 70; Work: El Paso Mus Art, Tex; Phoenix Art Mus, Ariz; Univ NMex Art Mus, Albuquerque; Univ Tex, El Paso; Mathews Art Ctr, Ariz State Univ, Tempe. Exhib: Art Competition, Long Beach Mus Art, Calif, 71; Tex Fine Arts Asn 63rd Ann Exhib, Austin Art Mus, 74; 2nd NH Int Graphics Ann, Hollis, 74; 18th Nat Art Round-Up, Las Vegas Art Mus, Nev, 75; Int Biennial of Graphic Art, Mus of Mod Art, Yugoslavia, 75; 16th Bradley Nat Print & Drawing Exhib, Peoria, Ill; Lakeview Ctr of the Arts & Sci, Peoria; Premio Int Biella Per L, Incisione, Cassadi Risparmio di Biella, Italy, 76; Art Exhib Peace 75—30 UNO, Slovenj Gradec, Yugoslavia, 76. Teaching: Instr life drawing, Art Ctr Col of Design, Los Angeles, 69-70 & Univ Tex, El Paso. Awards: Third Place Painting, El Paso Mus Art, 67; Jurors Award of Merit, 2nd NH Int Graphics Ann, Graphics Soc, 75; Purchase Award, Lakeview Ctr of Arts & Sci, 77. Bibliog: Barbara Cortright (auth), Sculpture & graphics, Art Week, 2/76. Style & Technique: Contemporary sculpture and graphics. Dealer: Gallery Rose 9025 Santa Monica Blvd Los Angeles CA 90069. Mailing Add: 5330 Gateway E El Paso TX 79905

DRAPER, JOSIAH EVERETT
PAINTER
b East Orange, NJ, Oct 17, 15. Study: Pratt Inst, Brooklyn, advert design & illus; Grand Cent Sch Art, New York, with Harvey Dunn; also with Edgar Whitney, Paul Strisik & John Pike. Work: Cummer Gallery Art, Jacksonville, Fla; Jacksonville Univ; Merritt Island Pub Libr, Fla; City of Bahia Blanca, Arg; Jacksonville Mus of Arts & Sci. Comn: Painting, Jacksonville Area CofC, 72; ten paintings, Sea Pines Co, Amelia Island, Fla, 73. Exhib: Am Watercolor Soc Ann, New York, 62-74; Soc Four Arts, Palm Beach, Fla, 63; Nat Arts Club 71st Ann Watercolor Exhib, 69; one-man shows, Fla Gulf Coast Art Ctr, Clearwater, 73 & Jacksonville Art Mus, 74; plus many others. Teaching: Instr watercolor technique, Jacksonville Art Mus, 70-75; spec watercolor workshops in Fla & WIndies. Pos: Artist, Prudential Ins Co Am, 35-50, art dir, 51-72; retired. Awards: Ann Traveling Exhib, Am Watercolor Soc, 66 & 69 & Carolyn Stern Award, 69. Mem: Am Watercolor Soc; Fla Watercolor Soc (bd dirs, 72-77, pres, 77-78); St Augustine Art Asn (pres, 72-74, bd dirs, 75-78); Sarasota Art Asn; Art League of Daytona Beach (bd trustees, 72-75). Style & Technique: Landscape and marine. Media: Transparent Watercolor. Dealer: Brush & Palette 11 Aviles St St Augustine FL 32084; Four Winds Gallery 415 W Lovell Kalamazoo MI 49001. Mailing Add: 20 Ponte Vedra Circle Ponte Vedra Beach FL 32082

DRAPER, WILLIAM FRANKLIN
PAINTER
b Hopedale, Mass, Dec 24, 12. Study: Harvard Univ, 31-32; Nat Acad Design, 31-34; Grande Chaumiere, Paris, France, 35; Art Students League, 37; also with Jon Corbino, Leon Kroll & Henry Hensche. Work: Nat Portrait Gallery; Pavilion, Music Ctr, Los Angeles; Off Housing & Urban Develop; CIA; NASA. Comn: Portraits, President John F Kennedy, 62, Shah of Iran, 67, Terrence Cardinal Cooke, 71, Gen Lauris Norsted, 72 & Ambassador Walter Annenberg; plus others. Exhib: Nat Gallery, London, Eng, 44; Metrop Mus Art, 45; Cent Asn Ann; Graham Gallery, New York, 69 & 71; Palm Beach Gallery, Fla, 72. Teaching: Instr, Art Students League, 65- Mem: Boston Allied Artists; Century Asn. Media: Oil. Dealer: Portraits Inc 41 E 57th St New York NY 10022; Grand Central Art Galleries Madison Ave at 43rd St New York NY 10017. Mailing Add: 535 Park Ave New York NY 10021

DREAPER, RICHARD EDWARD
ART DEALER, ART HISTORIAN
b Mobile, Ala, Aug 24, 35. Study: St Bernard Col; La State Univ; Univ Ariz; Univ Calif, BA. Teaching: Lectr Chinese art hist, Univ Calif, Irvine, 76- Pos: Asst to dir, Univ Ariz Gallery, Tucson, 59-62; assoc, Ancient Art, Laguna Beach, Calif, 63- Specialty: Chinese and Southeast Asian art; classical antiquities; pre-Columbian and ethnographic. Mailing Add: 31691 Wildwood South Laguna CA 92677

DREIBAND, LAURENCE
PAINTER
b New York, NY, Nov 8, 44. Study: Chouinard Art Inst, Los Angeles, 61; Art Ctr Col Design, Los Angeles, BFA(with distinction), 67, fel & MFA, 68. Work: Home Savings & Loan Collection; Container Corp Am Collection. Comn: Great Ideas of Western Man, Container Corp Am, 70. Exhib: West Coast 70, E B Crocker Art Gallery, Sacramento, Calif, 70; Beyond the Actual, Pioneer Mus, Stockton, Calif, 70; one-man shows, David Stuart Galleries, 70-72; California Artists, Long Beach Mus Art, 71; L A-14 Painters, Art Galleries, Univ Calif, Santa Barbara, 72. Teaching: Instr painting & photog, Art Ctr Col Design, 70-, chmn dept fine arts, 72-; instr painting, Calif State Col, Los Angeles, 71. Awards: First Prize, Fine Arts Gallery San Diego, 70; Great Ideas of Western Man Purchase Award, Container Corp Am, 70; 19th All City Festival Purchase Award, Munic Art Gallery, Los Angeles, 71. Bibliog: Joseph Young (auth), Los Angeles artist—Laurence Dreiband, Art Int, 70; Barbara Witus (auth), Paintings of Laurence Dreiband, Los Angeles Free Press, 3/31/72; Dr Udo Kulterman (auth), New realism, New York Graphic Soc, 72. Media: Oil, Acrylic. Publ: Auth, Laurence Dreiband, Paintings and Drawings, David Stuart Galleries, 72. Dealer: David Stuart Galleries 807 N La Cienega Blvd Los Angeles CA 90069. Mailing Add: 2450 Yosemite Dr Los Angeles CA 90041

DREITZER, ALBERT J
COLLECTOR, PATRON
b Sept 6, 02; US citizen. Collection: French impressionists and post impressionists. Mailing Add: 45 Sutton Pl S New York NY 10022

DRESKIN, JEANET STECKLER
PAINTER, INSTRUCTOR
b New Orleans, La, Sept 29, 21. Study: Newcomb Col, Tulane Univ, with Xanvier Gonzales, BFA, 42; Johns Hopkins Univ, med art cert, 43; John McCrady Sch, New Orleans; Clemson Univ, MFA. 73. Work: SC State Art Collection, Columbia Mus Art; Ga Mus Art, Athens; Greenville Co Mus Art, SC; Guild Hall Mus, East Hampton, NY; Nat Parks Collection, Great Smoky Mountains, Tenn. Comn: Seals, painting & plaque, SC State Bd Health, Columbia, 57; painting, Fiber Industs, Imp Chem, Dorchester, Eng, 66; mixed media mural, Piedmont Industs, New York, 67; wood block print, SC Tricentennial Comn, Greenville, 70. Exhib: Hunter Ann, George Thomas Hunter Gallery Art, Chattanooga, Tenn, 67 & 74; Dixie Ann, Montgomery Mus of Art, Ala, 68-72; Piedmont Ann, Mint Mus Art, Charlotte, NC, 69-72 & Greenville Co Mus of Art, SC, 75-77; Chautaugua Exhib of Am Art, New York, 70; Nat Asn Women Artists, Nat Acad, New York, 70-77 & USA Traveling Exhib, 70-77; 4th Int La Watercolor Exhib, 72; Int Grand Prix, Deauville, France, 73; 38th Ann Mid-Year Show, Butler Inst Am Art, Youngstown, Ohio, 74; Mainstreams Int, Marietta Col, Ohio, 75; Expressions of Art in Nature Bicentennial Exhib, Gibbes Art Gallery, Charleston, SC, 76; plus many others. Teaching: Painting & graphics, Greenville Co Mus Sch Art, 50-52 & 62-, head sch, 68-74; adj prof art, Univ SC, 73-75. Pos: Staff artist, Am Mus Nat Hist, New York,

43-45; staff artist, Univ Chicago Med Sch, 45-50; juror, SC Scholastic Art Awards, 66 & 71. Awards: Owen H Kenan Mem Award of Merit, Am Contemp Exhib, Soc Four Arts, Fla, 68; Merit Award, Int Grand Prix, Cannes, France, 73; Tex Fine Arts Asn Purchase Award, 63rd Nat Exhib, Austin, 74; plus others. Bibliog: Lucien Felli (auth), Jeanet Steckler Dreskin, 67 & National Association of Women Artists, 72, La Rev Mod, Paris, France; Jack A Morris, Jr (auth), Contemporary Artists of South Carolina, Tricentennial Comn, 70; Lucille Green (auth), Jeanet S Dreskin, artist-educator, Sandlapper, 3/70; plus many others. Mem: Guild SC Artists (mem bd, 55-, treas. 68, vpres, 71, pres, 72); Nat Asn Women Artists (mem comt, 71-); Nat League Am Pen Women (SC pres, 59-60, 65-66); Nat Asn Med Illusr; SEastern Graphics Coun (secy-treas, 74-76); plus others. Style & Technique: Subtly modulated colors that join or resist; fluid transparencies of growth patterns in transition; graphic imagery has levels of focus and areas of detailed delineation. Media: Polymers. Publ: Illusr, Anatomy of the Gorilla, for Am Mus Nat Hist, Columbia Univ, 43-46; illusr, What's New, Abbot Labs (& Latin Am ed), 46, 47 & 49; illusr, Surgery of Repair, Lippincott, 50; illusr, Williams Obstetrics, Stander-Appleton, 50; paintings reproduced as covers for Pen Women, 64 & 66; plus many others. Dealer: Hampton III Gallery Ltd 11 Hampton Ctr Taylors SC 29687. Mailing Add: 60 Lake Forest Dr Greenville SC 29609

DRESKIN-HAIG, JEANET ELIZABETH
PAINTER, PRINTMAKER
b Greenville, SC, June 8, 52. Study: Smith Col, BA; Univ Mich, MFA. Work: SC State Art Collection, Columbia; Chrysler Mus Art, Norfolk; Nat Parks Collection, Gatlinburg, Tenn; Greenville Co Mus Art. Comn: Ed of 60 lithographs, First Piedmont Mortgage Co, SC, 74. Exhib: Appalachian Corridors, Charleston, 72 & 75; Dixie Ann, Montgomery Mus Art, Ala, 73; Mt Holyoke Nat Print & Drawing Exhib, 74; Southeastern Graphics, Piedmont Graphics, 75; Tidewater Regional, Norfolk, 75; 5th Nat Print Competition, Ga State Univ, 76; Davidson Nat Print & Drawing Competition, 76; 25th Nat Exhib Prints, Libr Cong & Nat Gallery, 77; 20th NDak Ann, Univ NDak, 77; one-person show, Florence Mus, SC, 77. Teaching: Instr printmaking, Greenville Co Mus Sch Art, summer 74; teaching fel, Univ Mich, 75; instr, Tarrant Co Jr Col NE & Richland Col, 76- Awards: Purchase Award, SC State Invitational, Clemson, 74; Mich Artists Print Competition Award, 74; Purchase Award, Appalachian Corridor Exhib, 75. Media: Lithography, Etching, Drawing. Mailing Add: 608 Hyde Park Richardson TX 75080

DRESSER, LOUISA
ART ADMINISTRATOR, ART HISTORIAN
b Worcester, Mass, Oct 25, 07. Study: Vassar Col, BA; Fogg Art Mus, Harvard Univ; Courtauld Inst, Univ London. Collections Arranged: New England Painting, 1700-1775, Worcester Art Mus, 43, Christian Gullager, 49, Edward Savage, 51, The Dial and The Dial Collection, 59. Pos: Assoc in decorative arts & cur decorative arts, Worcester Art Mus, 32-49, actg dir, 43-46, cur of collection, 49-72, trustee, 72-77, hon trustee, 77- Mem: Mass Hist Soc; Am Antiqn Soc; Soc Arts & Crafts, Boston; Salisbury Mansion Assocs (pres, 71-); Worcester Craft Ctr (corporator, 64-); Am Asn Mus. Res: American painting of the 17th & 18th centuries, primarily New England. Publ: Co-auth, Seventeenth Century Painting in New England, 35; auth, Early New England Printmakers, 39; co-auth, Maine and Its Role in American Art, 63; auth, Portraits in Boston, 1630-1720, J Archives Am Art, 66; auth, The Background of Colonial American Portraiture, 66; ed, European paintings in the collection of the Worcester Art Mus, 74. Mailing Add: 17 Beechmont St Worcester MA 01609

DREW, JOAN
PRINTMAKER, SCULPTOR
b Indianapolis, Ind, Dec 21, 16. Study: Mass Col Art; Art Students League; graphics with Sternberg. Work: Rochester Mem Art Gallery; Philadelphia Mus Art; Lyman Allyn Mus Art; New York Pub Libr; Princeton Univ; plus others. Exhib: Mus Mod Art, 57, 58 & 60; Boston Printmakers, Boston Mus Fine Arts, 57-68; one-man shows, Lyman-Allyn Mus, 59; Albright-Knox Art Gallery, 64; Art in Embassies, 64-65; plus many others. Teaching: Lectr serigraph-collage. Mem: Boston Printmakers. Media: Graphic. Publ: Contribr, children's bk sect cover, New York Times, 60. Mailing Add: 19 Elmwood Ave Rye NY 10580

DREWAL, HENRY JOHN
ART HISTORIAN, EDUCATOR
b Brooklyn, NY, Mar 11, 43. Study: Hamilton Col, BA; Inst African Studies, Columbia Univ, cert, MA, PhD. Collections Arranged: Contemporary Art of the Ori Olokun Workshop, Ife, Nigeria, Columbia Univ, 72; Dimensions in Black Art, African, Afro-American & Afro-Brazilian Art at CSU, Cleveland State Univ, 75; Visions of Africa: an Exhibition of Prints & Textiles by Nigerian Artists, 75 & African Fabrics: Tradition and Change, 76, Cleveland State Univ; Traditional Art of the Nigerian Peoples: the Rattner Collection (auth, catalogue), Mus African Art, 77. Teaching: Asst prof African, Oceanic, Am Indian & Afro-Am art, Cleveland State Univ, 73-77, assoc prof, 77- Awards: Res grant, Inst Intercult Studies, 70-75; Inst African Studies Dissertation Grant, Columbia Univ, 70-71; Nat Endowment for the Humanities Fel, 77-78. Mem: Col Art Asn; Triennial Symp Traditonal African Art. Res: History of art among the Yoruba, Fon and Ewe of West Africa and the African Diaspora of Brazil and Cuba; principles of performance structure and aesthetics; iconology. Publ: Auth, Gelede Masquerade: Imagery & Motif, African Arts, 74; auth, Masked Theatre in Africa, Mime J, 75, transl, Dialog, Poland, 76; contribr, The Fabric of Cultures: The Anthropology of Clothing, Mouton, (in press); auth, Art & the Perception of Women in Yoruba Culture, Cahiers d'Etudes Africaines, (in press). Mailing Add: Dept of Art Cleveland State Univ Cleveland OH 44115

DREWELOWE, EVE
PAINTER, SCULPTOR
b New Hampton, Iowa. Study: Univ Iowa, BA, 23, MA, 24; Univ Colo, 54. Work: Univ Iowa Mus; Univ Colo, Boulder; Harkness House, London, Eng; Utah State Univ; Wartburg Col. Comn: Two oil paintings, First Nat Bank Fort Collins, 61. Exhib: 18th Int Watercolor Exhib, Art Inst Chicago, 39; New York World's Fair, 39-40; Nat Acad Galleries, New York, 46; UNESCO Travel Exhib, Eng, 48-49; Midwestern Show, Nelson Gallery & Atkins Mus, Kansas City, Mo, 60; Colorado Springs Fine Art Ctr, Colo, 60; Denver Art Mus, 64-65, 67 & 69; The West—80 Contemporaries, Univ Ariz, Tucson, 67; Founders of the Boulder Art Scene, Boulder Art Ctr, Colo, 76. Pos: Mem art adv comt, Boulder Pub Libr, 63-69. Awards: Honorable Mention, Springfield Art Mus, Mo, 44; Award, Tri-State Exhib, Cheyenne, Wyo, 56; First Prize in Oil, Boulder Art Asn Regional, 63; plus others. Mem: Hon life mem, Artists Equity Asn; Colo Chap Artists Equity (pres, Boulder Chap, 63-68, actg pres, 69); Boulder Artists Guild (pres). Style & Technique: Contemporary. Media: Mixed Media. Publ: Illusr, In Denim and Broadcloth, 53. Mailing Add: 2025 Balsam Dr Boulder CO 80302

DREWES, WERNER
PAINTER, PRINTMAKER
b Canig, Ger, July 27, 99; US citizen. Study: Charlottenburg Technische-Hochschule, Berlin, Ger; Stuttgart Sch Archit, Ger; Stuttgart Sch Arts & Crafts; Weimar Staatliches Bauhaus, with Itten & Klee; Dessau Staatliches Bauhaus, with Kandinsky & Feininger. Work: Represented in more than 60 public collection in USA and abroad. Exhib: Carnegie Int, Pittsburgh, 45-47; one-man shows, Prints, Drawings & Painting, Cleveland Mus Art, Ohio, 61, Prints, Achenbach Found, Calif Palace of Legion of Honor, San Francisco, 62, Paintings, Prints, Retrospective, Wash Univ, St Louis, 65 & Prints, Retrospective, Nat Collection Fine Arts, Washington, DC, 69. Teaching: Instr painting, drawing & printmaking, Columbia Univ, 37-40; instr design, Inst Design, Chicago, 45; dir design & first yr prog, Wash Univ Sch Fine Arts, 46-65. Pos: Founding mem, Am Abstract Artists, New York, 37-46. Awards: Plexiglas Sculpture Competition, Mus Mod Art, 39; Award for Autumn Harvest (painting), St Louis City Art Mus, 59. Bibliog: R Frost (auth), Werner Drewes, nature & abstract, Art News, 2/15/49; Germain Bazin (auth), History of modern painting, Hyperion, 51; Caril Dreyfuss (auth), Werner Drewes, woodcuts, Smithsonian Inst, 69. Mem: Washington Soc Printmakers. Media: Oil, Watercolor, Woodcut. Dealer: Assoc Am Artists 653 Fifth Ave New York NY 10022; Princeton Gallery Fine Art 9 Spring St Princeton NJ 08540. Mailing Add: 11526 Links Dr Reston VA 22090

DREXLER, LYNNE
PAINTER
b Newport News, Va. Study: Richmond Prof Inst, BFA; Hunter Col; Col William & Mary; Hans Hoffman Sch Fine Arts, scholar. Work: Prentice Hall Collection, Englewood Cliffs, NJ; Ciba-Geigy Collection, Hudson River Mus; Tamarind Print Collection, Mus Mod Art, New York; Univ Mass, Amherst. Exhib: One-man show, Tanager Gallery, 59; Norfolk Mus Regional Show, 60; Galleria, San Miguel de Allende, Mex, 62; Tetra-Centennial, Va Mus Fine Arts, Richmond, 66; Traveling Show, mus in West & South, 66; plus others. Style & Technique: Abstractions based on landscape composed of circles, squares of individual brush strokes, curved or straight in oil or crayon. Dealer: Alonzo Gallery 26 E 63rd St New York NY 10021. Mailing Add: 495 Broome St New York NY 10013

DREXLER, PAUL EUGENE
ART DEALER
b New York, NY, Oct 18, 40. Study: Queens Col, BA, 61; NY Univ, LLB, 65, LLM, 70. Pos: Drexler Gallery, New York, 67- Specialty: Contemporary international graphics, drawings and paintings. Mailing Add: 1062 Madison Ave New York NY 10028

DREYER, MARGARET WEBB
PAINTER, ART DEALER
US citizen. Study: Westmoreland Col, San Antonio, Tex; Univ Tex Sch Archit & Fine Arts; Mus Fine Arts, Houston, Tex; Inst Allende, San Miguel de Allende, Mex. Work: Witte Mus, San Antonio; Elizabeth Ney Mus; Thomas P Creaven Estate; Inst Int Educ; Abe Issa Interests, Kingston, Jamaica. Comn: Mosaic murals (Plexiglas), comn by Buffington, McAllister for Mading Pub Sch, Houston, 66, face of Cavallini Mosaic Co Bldg, San Antonio, 66 & face of Crawford Bldg, Joseph Holland, 67; mosaic mural & fountain for home, comn by Rudy Dean, 67. Exhib: Midwest Biennial, Joslyn Art Mus, Omaha, Nebr, 70 & 74; 15th Ann Sun Carnival Exhib, El Paso Mus, Tex, 71; Tex Watercolor Soc 21st Ann, San Antonio, 71; 60th Ann Exhib Tex Fine Arts Asn, Austin, 71; also circuit selections & invitations for all major Tex mus. Teaching: Dir fine arts, Tex Recreation Dept, City of Houston, 50-60. Pos: Owner & dir, Mural Originals, Houston; owner & dir, Dreyer Galleries, Houston. Awards: First Purchase Award for Blueprint for Survival II, Tex Watercolor Soc, 70; Sibley Mem Purchase Award for Pendulum, 22nd Tex Watercolor Soc Nat, 71; King Award for Blueprint for Survival V, 60th Ann Tex Fine Arts Asn, 71. Bibliog: David Dolin (auth), Fine arts feature Margaret Webb Dreyer, artist, 70 & Ann Holmes (ed), Feature Margaret Webb Dreyer, 72, Houston Chronicle; plus other articles in Houston Chronicle & Houston Post. Mem: Tex Watercolor Soc; Tex Fine Arts Asn; Art League Houston; Mus Fine Arts, Houston; Nat Soc Lit & Arts. Style & Technique: Abstract in acrylic; wet watercolor on unsized canvas and watercolor board; drawings in oil pastels, watercolor and ink. Media: Acrylic, Watercolor. Res: Pre-Columbian works; African works; contemporary painting and sculpture; murals; antique art objects. Mailing Add: 4713 San Jacinto Houston TX 77004

DRIESBACH, DAVID FRAISER
PRINTMAKER, EDUCATOR
b Wausau, Wis, Oct 7, 22. Study: Univ Ill, Beloit Col; Univ Wis; Pa Acad Fine Arts; Iowa State Univ, Atelier 17, with S W Hayter, 69. Work: Seattle Mus, Wash; Dayton Art Inst, Ohio; Columbus Gallery Fine Arts, Ohio; Bibliot Nat, Paris, France, Univ Windsor. Comn: Fiscal Flight (ed 150 color etchings), Sears Roebuck Co, 67; series of bronze reliefs, Assoc Am Artists, NY, 68; color intaglio ed, Checker Cab Co, Kalamazoo, Mich, 74. Exhib: Contemporary Art in USA, Worcester Mus, Mass, 51; Young Printmakers of America, Mus Mod Art, New York, 53; Ten Printmakers of USA, Purdue Univ, 66; 162nd Ann Am Watercolors, Prints & Drawings, Pa Acad Fine Arts, 67; American Graphics 1969, Col of the Pac, 69. Teaching: Prof printmaking, Northern Ill Univ, 64- Awards: Ford Found Purchase Prize for Intaglio, 60; Carlton Col Prize for Intaglio, 66; Uris Bros Prize for Intaglio, 66. Bibliog: Bob White (auth), David Driesbach, Chicago Art Scene, 1/68; The complex world of David Driesbach, Northern Alumnus, 3/68. Mem: Midwest Col Art Asn; Assoc Am Artists, New York. Style & Technique: Color viscosity and engraving; subject matter often humorous social satire. Media: Intaglio, Bronze. Dealer: Van Straaten Gallery 646 N Michigan Ave Chicago IL 60611. Mailing Add: PO Box 32 Kingston IL 60145

DRIESBACH, WALTER CLARK, JR
SCULPTOR, INSTRUCTOR
b Cincinnati, Ohio, July 3, 29. Study: Sch Dayton Art Inst, 47-52, with Robert Koepnick; studio asst to Joseph Kiselewski, New York, 54-55; Art Acad Cincinnati, 55-56, with Charles Cutler. Comn: St Anthony of Padua (limestone relief), St Anthony of Padua Church, Cincinnati, 59; Life of St Teresa (limestone entablature), St Teresa Church, Cincinnati, 62; The Lord's Supper (walnut relief), Mt St Mary Seminary, Norwood, Ohio, 64; limestone relief & incised designs of Apostles, Immaculate Conception Church, Dayton, Ohio, 65; Fireman Monument (granite fiture), Cincinnati, Ohio, 68. Exhib: Ohio Sculptors, Akron & Canton Art Insts, 60; Northwest Territory Sculpture Show, Cincinnati Art Mus & John Herron Inst Art, Indianapolis, Ind, 61; one-man shows, Wilmington Col, Ohio, 63 & 70, Univ Dayton, 69 & Hanover Col, 75; Cincinnati Exhib, Cincinnati Art Mus, Ohio, 72; plus others. Teaching: Instr sculpture & drawing, Memphis Acad Arts, 56-58; instr sculpture, Dayton Art Inst Eve Sch, 58-60; instr sculpture & drawing, Wilmington Col, 63-66; instr sculpture, drawing & 3-D design, Univ Dayton, 66-72; instr drawing, Thomas More Col Eve Sch, 70-71; instr sculpture & 3-D design, Art Acad Cincinnati, 70-; instr sculpture, Col Mt St Joseph, 72. Awards: Fleischmann Purchase Prize, Zoo Arts Festival, Cincinnati, 64; First Prize, Prof Sculpture Div, Ohio State Fair Fine Arts Exhib, 66, Second Prize, 68. Mem: Cincinnati MacDowell Soc; Prof Artists Cincinnati. Style & Technique: Moderate abstract interpretation of natural forms; clay sketches and drawings are used in process of carving. Media: Stone, Wood. Publ: Contribr, Contemporary Stone Sculpture, 70 & Creating Small Wood Objects as Functional Sculpture, 76, Crown. Dealer: Herbert E Feist 1125 Madison Ave New York NY 10028. Mailing Add: 2541 Erie Ave Cincinnati OH 45208

DRIGGS, ELSIE
PAINTER,
b Hartford, Conn, Aug 5, 98. Study: Art Students League; also with Maurice Sterne, Rome. Work: Whitney Mus Am Art; Baltimore Mus Art; Yale Univ Mus; Phillips Gallery, Washington, DC; Sheldon Mem Gallery, Lincoln, Nebr. Comn: Animal cartoons & WAfrican gold weights, Works Prog Admin, Harlem House, New York, 34; La Salle, Post Off, Huntsville, La, 35; Indian Village, pvt comn, New York, 38. Exhib: 35 Under 35, Mus Mod Art Opening Show, 30; A Mile of Art, Munic Art Exhib RCA Bldg, 34; Edward J Gallagher, III Collection, Baltimore Mus Art, 53; Root Collection, Metrop Mus Art, 54; The Precisionists, Whitney Mus Am Art, 63. Teaching: Instr, 45-48. Pos: Asst, Metrop Mus Art, 23. Bibliog: Samuel M Kootz (auth), Modern American Painters, Brewer & Warren, 30; Sheldon Cheney (auth), The Story of Modern Art, Viking, 41. Mem: Nat Soc Lit & Arts. Style & Technique: Oils are washed and buffed down to the canvas; watercolor collages are sometimes free standing. Media: Oil. Dealer: Coe Kerr Gallery Inc 20 E 56th New York NY 10022. Mailing Add: 31 Grove St New York NY 10014

DRISCOLL, EDGAR JOSEPH, JR
ART CRITIC
b Boston, Mass, Sept 1, 20. Study: Cambridge Sch Weston; Univ Iowa, with Grant Wood; Yale Univ Sch Fine Arts. Teaching: Lectr art, var groups. Pos: Juror, many art shows & panels; art critic, Boston Globe, 46-73; Boston corresp, Art News, 73- Mem: St Botolph Club; Yale Club; Harvard Club. Mailing Add: 75 Hancock St Boston MA 02114

DRISKELL, DAVID CLYDE
PAINTER, EDUCATOR
b Eatonton, Ga, June 7, 31. Study: Skowhegan Sch Painting & Sculpture, scholarship, 53, with Jack Levine & Henry V Poor; Howard Univ, with James A Porter & Morris Louis, BA, 55; Cath Univ Am, with Nell Sonnemann & Ken Noland, MFA, 62; Riksbureau voor Kunsthistorisches Documentatie, The Hague, Neth, cert, 64. Work: Smithsonian Inst, Washington, DC; Birmingham Mus Art; Corcoran Gallery Art, Washington, DC; Carl Van Vechten Gallery Fine Arts, Fisk Univ, Nashville, Tenn; Ark Fine Arts Ctr, Little Rock; plus others. Comn: Mountain and Tile Suite (10 woodcuts-color), Tenn Arts Comn, 72. Exhib: Baltimore Mus Area Exhib, 65; Corcoran Area Exhib, 66; Birmingham Festival Exhib, 72; Cent South Ann, Nashville, 72; Mid-South Exhib, Memphis, 75; plus others. Collections Arranged: Modern Masters from the Solomon R Guggenheim Museum (catalog-Modern Masters, Klee, Kandinsky and Picasso), Talladega Col, 56; The Afro-American Series, 12 exhibs each with 16 page catalog of the work of 12 black artists, Fisk Univ, Univ Miami & others; Amistad Exhib Afro-Am Art. Teaching: Prof painting & art hist, Talladega Col, 55-62; prof painting & art hist, Howard Univ, 62-66; prof art & chmn dept, Fisk Univ, 66-76; vis prof, Univ Ife, Nigeria, 70; vis prof, Bowdoin Col, 73; vis prof, Bates Col, 73; prof art, Univ Md, College Park, 76- Pos: Mem bd adv, Mus African Art, 67-; mem visual arts adv panel, Tenn Arts Comn, 69-, mus adv bd, 73-; guest curator, Smithsonian Inst, 72; guest curator, Los Angeles Co Mus Art, 74-76; mus adv panel, Nat Endowment Arts, 74-77; bd gov, Skowhegan Sch Painting & Sculpture, 75- Awards: John Hope Award in Art, Atlanta Univ, 59; Museum Donor Award, Am Fedn Art, 62; Graphics Art Award, Corcoran Gallery Art, 65. Bibliog: Afro-American Series: 12 monographs & Moss (auth), Missing pages (film), 71, Fisk Univ. Mem: Col Art Asn Am; Nat Conf Artists; Am Mus Asn; Am Fedn Art (trustee, 69-); Tenn Col Art Coun (co-chmn, 68-71). Style & Technique: Semi-abstract, basic compositions influenced by nature. Media: Oil, Tempera, Watercolor. Res: Role of the black artist in American society and traditional African art, its impact on Afro-American art. Dealer: Franz Bader Gallery 2124 Pennsylvania Ave Washington DC 20037; Frost Gully Gallery Freeport ME 04032. Mailing Add: 4206 Decatur St Hyattsville MD 20781

DRIVER, MORLEY-BROOKE LISTER
ART CRITIC, COLLECTOR
b London, Eng, Jan 13, 13. Study: Slade Sch, London; Univ Calif, BA & MA; also with Roger Fry & Bernard Berenson. Pos: Writer & art critic, Detroit Free Press & Ward's Quart. Collection: All media—impressionists, Braque to Giacometti, Shahn, Baskin, Piper, Moore, Robert Parker, Picasso, Matisse and others. Mailing Add: c/o Detroit Free Press 321 W Lafayette Blvd Detroit MI 48231

DROEGE, ANTHONY JOSEPH, II
EDUCATOR, PAINTER
b Philadelphia, Pa, Sept 22, 43. Study: Pa State Univ, BA, 65; Univ Iowa, MA, 67, MFA, 68. Work: Kemper Ins Co Collection, Long Grove, Ill; Clara Eagle Gallery, Murray State Univ, Ky; Art in the Embassy Prog, US State Dept. Comn: Numerous pub & pvt portrait comns. Exhib: Mid-Year Show, Butler Inst Am Art, Youngstown, Ohio, 70; Mainstreams, 5th Ann Marietta Col Int Competitive Exhib, Ohio, 72; The Emerging Real, Storm King Art Ctr, Mountainville, NY, 73; New Realism Re-Visited, Brainerd Hall Art Gallery, State Univ NY Col Potsdam, 74; Living American Artists & the Figure, Pa State Univ Mus Art, 74; The Big Show, J B Speed Art Mus, Louisville, Ky, 75; Am Painters in Paris, 76; Ind-Ill Bicentennial Painting Exhib, 76. Teaching: Instr painting & drawing, Murray State Univ, Ky, 68-71; assoc prof painting & drawing, Ind Univ, South Bend, 71- Awards: Commendation from Elmer Bishoff, Mid-Am Show, Joslyn Art Mus, Omaha, 68; First Place Painting, 7th Biennial Michiana Regional Art Competition, South Bend Art Ctr, 72; Best of Show at 8th Biennial Michiana Regional Art Competition, First Bank & Trust Co, 74. Bibliog: Byron Burford (auth), View from the Midwest, Readers & Writers, summer 68; Gene Porter (auth), Mirrors repeated in Droege paintings, Ft Wayne News-Sentinel, 4/73; Dennis Shapiro (auth), rev in New Art Examr, Chicago, 4/75. Style & Technique: Figures and landscapes; underpainting, glazing and alla prima; drawing on toned French paper. Media: Oil, Conte Crayon, Pastel & Oil Pastel. Mailing Add: 202 S Filbert St New Carlisle IN 46552

DROLL, DONALD E
ART DEALER
b Chicago, Ill. Pos: Dir, Fischbach Gallery, 64-69; assoc dir, M Knoedler Inc, 67-72; partner-owner, Fourcade-Droll Inc, 72-76; partner, Droll/Kolbert Gallery Inc, 76- Mailing Add: Droll/Kolbert Gallery 724 Fifth Ave New York NY 10019

DROWER, SARA RUTH
PAINTER, ILLUSTRATOR
b Chicago, Ill, Oct 15, 38. Study: Roosevelt Univ, BS, 59; Univ Ill, Chicago, MS, 61; Art Inst Chicago. Work: Ill State Mus, Springfield; Minn Mus Art, Minneapolis; Borg-Warner Corp, DePaul Univ & Standard Oil, Chicago. Exhib: One-person exhib, Ill Art Coun, Chicago, 73; Ill State Mus, Springfield, 71-73; Nat Print & Drawing Exhib, Western Ill Univ, Macomb, 72-74; Drawings USA '73, Minneapolis, 73; Mid-Western Graphics, Tulsa, Okla, 75; Marietta Col Crafts Nat, Ohio, 76; Lake Superior 77, Int Crafts Exhib, Duluth, Minn, 77; Craft Show Wearables Exhib, Philadelphia Mus Art, Pa, 77; 4th Ann Fibers & Fabric Exhib, Springfield, Ill, 78; plus many others. Pos: Sci illusr, Turtox-Biol Supply, 62-64; free lance illusr, 64- Awards: First Prize Watercolors, Union League Club, Chicago, 72; Purchase Award Drawing, Field Enterprises, Chicago, 72; Best of Show, Fine Art Exhib, Artists Guild Chicago, 74. Mem: Surface Design; Am Crafts Coun; Nat Asn Handcraftsmen. Style & Technique: Surface design techniques and dyes on fabric; organic quality, linear detailed work, semi-abstract. Media: Drawing & Watercolor. Mailing Add: 127 Laurel Wilmette IL 60091

DR SEUSS
See Geisel, Theodor Seuss

DRUMM, DON
SCULPTOR, CRAFTSMAN
b Warren, Ohio, Apr 11, 35. Study: Hiram Col; Kent State Univ, BFA & MA. Work: Akron Art Inst; Cleveland Mus Art; Bowling Green State Univ; Columbus Gallery Fine Arts; Massillon Mus; plus others. Comn: Reliefs, walls, aluminum & steel sculpture & fountains, Alcoa Co, Pittsburgh, Episcopal Diocese, Sao Paulo, Brazil, Richard Gossar Mem Sculpture, Toledo, Ohio, Curtain Bluff Hotel, Antigua BWI & City of Akron, Ohio; plus others. Exhib: Group shows, Mus Contemp Crafts, New York, 64 & 65, Traveling Exhib circulated by Am Fedn Arts, 65-67 & 72; Cleveland Mus Art, 64-68; Columbus Gallery Fine Arts, 66 & 67; plus others. Teaching: Instr sculpture, Akron Art Inst; artist in residence, Bowling Green State Univ, 66-71; instr, Penland Sch Crafts, 66-72. Awards: Purchase Prize, Cleveland Mus Art, 64; Prize, Nat Soc Interior Design, 65; Prize, Columbus Gallery Fine Arts. Bibliog: Oppi Untracht (auth), Metal Techniques for the Craftsman; Louis G Redstone (auth), Art and Architecture; Meilach & Seiden (auth), Direct Metal Sculpture. Mem: Ohio Designer Craftsmen; Am Craftsmen's Coun. Res: Investigation into the use of contemporary materials and construction techniques to create urban sculpture specializing in the use of cast aluminum and concrete. Mailing Add: 110 Corson Ave Akron OH 44302

DRUMMOND, (I G)
PAINTER, SCULPTOR
b Edmonton, Alta, Apr 11, 23; US citizen. Study: Pa Acad Fine Arts & Univ Pa, BFA, 51, MFA, 52; also, murals with George Harding. Comn: New York World's Fair Trade Ctr, 63-64; colored concrete murals, Aeromatic Travel Corp, 69, A C Camera, Grand Cent Sta, New York, 70, Ahi Ezer Synagogue, Brooklyn, NY, 71 & Blake Equip Corp, Englewood, NJ, 72; plus pvt comn, 72- Exhib: Pa Acad Fine Arts, Philadelphia, 50; Silvermine Guild, Conn, 64; East Hampton Gallery, NY, 68-69; Art Image, Manhattan, 69-70. Style & Technique: Abstract colored concrete design is trowelled over an abstract design of wire lathe forms to form a mix of painting and bas-relief sculpture. Mailing Add: 18-44 21 Rd Astoria NY 11105

DRUMMOND, SALLY HAZELET
PAINTER
b Evanston, Ill, June 4, 24. Study: Rollins Col, 42-44; Columbia Univ, BS, 48; Inst Design, Chicago, 49-50; Univ Louisville, MA, 52. Work: Mus Mod Art, New York; Whitney Mus Am Art; Speed Mus Art, Louisville; Univ Iowa Mus, Iowa City; Joseph Hirshhorn Collection, Greenwich, Conn. Exhib: Am Artists Ann, Whitney Mus Am Art, New York, 60; Lyric Abstraction in America, Am Fedn Arts Traveling Exhib, 62-63; Americans 63, Mus Mod Art, New York, 63; Focus on Light, NJ State Mus, Trenton, 67; 21st New Eng Painting & Sculpture Ann, Silvermine, Conn, 70; Retrospective, Corcoran Gallery Art, Washington, DC, 72; plus others. Awards: Fulbright Grant, Venice, 52; Guggenheim Grant, France, 67. Bibliog: Lawrence Campbell (auth), Dotted light, Art News Mag, 4/72. Media: Oil. Dealer: Fishbach Gallery 29 W 57th St New York NY 10019. Mailing Add: One Wilton Rd E Ridgefield CT 06877

DRUTT, HELEN WILLIAMS
GALLERY DIRECTOR, ART HISTORIAN
b Winthrop, Mass, Nov 19, 30. Study: Tyler Sch Art, Temple Univ, BFA; Barnes Found. Exhib: (Helen Drutt Collection) The Collector, Mus Contemp Crafts, New York, 74. Collections Arranged: Making It, Benjamin Franklin Inst Sci Mus, 71; Ten Potters, Cheltenham Art Ctr, 71; Philadelphia Craftsmen & Philadelphia Collects, Mus of Philadelphia Civic Ctr, 71; Another Cup Show, 73; Stanley Lechtzen, Goldsmith's Hall, London, 73; Two British Goldsmiths, Ramshaw & Watkins, Am Inst of Architects Gallery, Philadelphia, 73; UICA: Craft Faculty, Philadelphia Col Art, 74; Soup Tureens: 1976, Campbell Mus, Mus of Contemp Crafts, New York & Cranbrook Acad of Art, Mich, 76; Olak Skoogfors Retrospective, Philadelphia Col of Art, 78-79. Teaching: Lectr mod craft hist, Philadelphia Col of Art, 72-; assoc prof mod craft hist, Moore Col Art, Philadelphia, 74- & Tyler Sch Art, Temple Univ, 78- Pos: Curatorial consult, Mus of Philadelphia Civic Ctr, 67, 70 & 73; exec dir, Philadelphia Coun of Prof Craftsmen, 67-73; dir, Helen Drutt Gallery, 74-; galley consult, Moore Col of Art, 78. Awards: Award of Merit for Dedicated Serv to the Crafts, Philadelphia Col Art, 72. Bibliog: Carol Saline (auth), Crafty Lady, Philadelphia Mag, 75; doc film, Professional Women, Channel 6 Television, Philadelphia, 76. Mem: Collab 20th Century, Philadelphia Mus Art; Am Crafts Coun (Pa state rep, 75-); Pa State Coun on the Arts (crafts panel, 75-). Res: Developed the first course in the history of modern crafts in the United States, 1860-to present; forumlated curriculum & developed supportive slide library. Specialty: Twentieth century work in fiber, ceramics & metal; contemporary crafts. Interest: All aspects of contemporary crafts. Publ: Contribr, Craft Horizons, Am Crafts Coun, 70; ed, Soup Tureens: 1976, Philadelphia Col Art, Campbell Mus, 76; contribr, Philadelphia Craft Show, Philadelphia Mus Art, 77. Mailing Add: c/o Helen Drutt Gallery 1625 Spruce St Philadelphia PA 19103

DRUTZ, JUNE
PAINTER, EDUCATOR
b Toronto, Ont, Feb 14, 20. Study: Cent Tech Sch; Ont Col Art, hon grad, 65. Work: McMaster Univ, Hamilton, Ont; Univ Waterloo, Ont; Royal Can Art Collection, Nat Gallery, Ottawa; Univ Guelph, Ont; London Trust Co, Ont. Comn: Seeds of Spring Returning (serigraph ann print), Glenhyrst Art Asn, Brantford, Ont, 68-69. Exhib: Soc Graphic Artists, Ottawa, 67; Can Soc Painters & Etchers, Toronto, 69; Can Soc Graphic Artists, Ottawa, 69; Int Print Show, Montreal, Que, 71; one-person shows, Merton Gallery, Toronto, 73, Erindale Col, Mississauga, Ont, 74, McMaster Univ Med Centre, Hamilton, Ont, 76 & Sisler Gallery, Toronto, 77; Graphex-3, Brantford, Ont, 75; Can Soc Painters in Watercolor, 75-77; 103rd Ann Ont Soc Artists Exhib, O'Keefe Centre, Toronto, 75; Paper to Handle, Chelsea Sch of Art, London, Eng, 75; Four Women Printmakers Traveling Exhib, 76; 100 Yrs, Ont Col of Art Traveling Exhib, 76; Imprint 76 (traveling show), Sadye Bronfman Centre, Montreal & Art Gallery of Ont, 76; On View (traveling exhib), Visual Arts Ont Show, Toronto Dominion Centre, 76; Ontario Now, Art Gallery of Hamilton, 76; Japan-Can Print Show, Japanese Cult Centre, Don Mills, Ont, 77; two-man show, Art Gallery of Brantford, Ont, 77. Teaching: Instr hist res, watercolour & life drawing, Ont Col Art, Toronto, 67-71; instr costume drawing, life drawing & watercolour, Ont Dept Educ, summers 68-72; instr life drawing, printmaking & hist res, Ryerson Polytech Inst, Toronto, 72-73; instr painting, compos & figure drawing, Ont Col of Art & Toronto Art Sch. Pos: Exec officer, Can Soc Graphic Artists, Toronto, 72- Awards: Metrop Award, Soc Graphic Artists, 69; A G Reid Award, Soc Painters & Etchers,

69; Purchase Award, Graphex-3, Brantford, Ont, 75. Mem: Royal Can Acad; Ont Soc Artists; Can Soc Painter's in Watercolor; Print & Drawing Coun Can. Bibliog: Robert Myers (auth), The youth cult maidens of June Drutz, Art Mag, Vol 6, No 22, 75. Style & Technique: Dry pigments combined with egg yolk or acrylic medium. Media: Tempera, Watercolor. Dealer: Nancy Poole Studios Ltd 16 Hazelton Ave Toronto ON Can & 554 Waterloo St London ON Can; Wells Gallery Sussex Dr Ottawa ON Can. Mailing Add: 352 Spadina Rd Toronto ON Can

DRYFOOS, NANCY
SCULPTOR
b New Rochelle, NY. Study: Sarah Lawrence Col, sculpture with Oronzio Maldarelli & painting with Curt Roesch, dipl; Columbia Univ Sch Archit, with Oronzio Maldarelli, also sculpture with Jose de Creeft. Work: Brandeis Univ; Columbia Univ; Sarah Lawrence Col; Evanston Mus Fine Arts; NY Univ. Comn: Am Jewish Tercentenary, 54; reliefs for Kingsbridge House Synagogue, Home for Aged Hebrews, 57; Edel Award for Fine Arts, Wedgwood-Dickenson Col, 59; Naomi Lehman Mem Award, 62; Jos M Proskauer Bar Asn Award, NY, 62. Exhib: Allied Artists Am Ann, Nat Acad Design Gallery, 48-72; Pa Acad Fine Arts Biennale; Syracuse Mus Ann, NY, 54; Brooklyn Mus Ann, NY, 56; Nat Sculpture Soc Ann, New York, 65-72; eight solo shows, Washington, DC, Silvermine, Conn & New York, NY. Awards: Gold Medal of Honor, Allied Artists Am, 58; Second Prize, Knickerbocker Artists, 60; Constance K Livingston Award, Am Soc Contemp Artists, 70. Mem: Fel Nat Sculpture Soc (secy, 72-, former rec secy & exhib chmn); NY Soc Women Artists (vpres, 71-73, pres, 77-79); Nat Asn Women Artists (mem jury, 71-73, chmn nominating comt); Allied Artists Am (juror, 72); Am Soc Contemp Artists (dir, 70-72). Style & Technique: Semi-realistic; carving and modeling in marble and terra cotta. Publ: Contribr, Nat Sculpture Rev, 70-71. Mailing Add: 45 E 89th St New York NY 10028

DUANE, TANYA
PAINTER, COLLAGE ARTIST
b New York, NY. Study: Washington Sq Col, BA & MA. Exhib: One-woman show, Ahda Artzt Gallery, 62; Contemp Art Gallery, 65; Caravan House, 74, New York; Arts in the Embassies Prog, Nairobi, Kenya & Kuala Lampur, Malaysia, 67-69; Brooklyn Mus, 75; Butler Inst Am Art, Youngstown, Ohio, 76; plus many others. Mem: Artists Equity Asn (bd mem); Women in the Arts (coordr in-gallery, 74 & 75); Contemp Circle (pres, 75). Style & Technique: Collage, retranslating material into new forms using scissors as if it were a paint brush; oils whose imagery is sensed. Mailing Add: 50 Commerce St New York NY 10014

DUBACK, CHARLES S
PAINTER, PRINTMAKER
b Fairfield, Conn, Mar 10, 26. Study: Whitney Sch of Fine Arts, New Haven, Conn; Newark Sch of Fine & Indust Arts, NJ; Skowhegan Sch of Painting & Sculpture, Maine; Brooklyn Mus Art Sch. Work: Corcoran Gallery of Art, Washington, DC. Exhib: Prints & Drawings, 53, Trends in Watercolor Today, 57, 20th Biennial Int Watercolor Exhib, 59 & Print Show, 70, Brooklyn Mus, NY; Whitney Ann Exhib of Contemp Am Painting, New York, 59-60; Mus Mod Art, New York, 62; Hassam Purchase Fund Exhib, Am Acad of Arts & Lett, New York, 73; Landmark Gallery, New York, 73, 76 & 77; 63rd Ann Exhib Contemp Am Painting, Randolph-Macon Woman's Col, Lynchburg, Va, 74; 20th Ann Exhib Contemp Am Painting, Lehigh Univ, Bethlehem, Pa, 74; Works on Paper, Weatherspoon Art Gallery, Greensboro, NC, 75; Ft Wayne Mus of Art, Ind, 76. Collections Arranged: Ten Painters of Maine, Landmark Gallery, New York, 77. Bibliog: Connie Smith (auth), A sentimental journey, Village Voice, 4/76; Laura Pipune (auth), Window exhibit at museum, Ft Wayne Jour-Gazette, 10/76; Holland Cotter (auth), Charles DuBack, Arts Mag, 11/77. Style & Technique: Sculpture, drawing, etching & silkscreen. Media: Oil on Canvas, Pastel, Watercolor; Wood, Stone. Mailing Add: c/o Landmark Gallery 469 Broome St New York NY 10013

DUBANIEWICZ, PETER PAUL
PAINTER
b Cleveland, Ohio, Nov 17, 13. Study: Cleveland Inst Art, scholar, 31, grad, 35; Agnes Gund traveling scholar, 35; Mus Sch Fine Arts, Boston, Mass; Albert Whitin traveling fel, France, Ger & Italy, 38. Work: Ohio Bell Tel Co; Cleveland Mus Art; Ford Motor Co; St Paul's Episcopal Church; Butler Inst; plus many other pub & pvt collections. Exhib: Metrop Mus Art, New York; Ten-Thirty Art Gallery, Cleveland; Corcoran Gallery, Washington, DC; Springfield Mus, Mass; 39th Ann Mid Year Show, Butler Inst Am Art; plus many others. Teaching: Instr, Boston Mus Sch Fine Art, 38-41; instr, Cleveland Inst Art, 45-; lectr, Skowhegan Sch Painting & Sculpture; instr, Oberlin Col, winter 72. Pos: Pres, Cleveland Soc Artists, 49-51; pres, Poloniase Arts Cleveland, 49-50; mem adv bd, Cleveland Inst Art, 75- Awards: Buffalo Art Club Prize, 63; Second Prize, Int Platform Asn Show, 66; H M Newman Relig Art Show, Cleveland, Ohio, 70. Publ: Illusr, color cover, Cleveland Plain Dealer. Mailing Add: 3289 Fairmount Blvd Cleveland Heights OH 44118

DUBIN, RALPH
PAINTER, SCULPTOR
b New York, NY, Sept 2, 18. Study: Am Artist Sch, with Moses Soyer & James Lechay; New Sch Social Res, with Robert Gwathmey & Stuart Davis; Brooklyn Mus Art Sch, with Gabor Ptererdi & Ben Shahn; Brooklyn Col, BA; Hunter Col, New York, MA(art), 76; also with Hans Hofmann. Work: Pa Acad Fine Art, Philadelphia; Smithsonian Inst, Washington, DC. Exhib: Nat Inst Arts & Lett, New York, 68; Pa Acad Fine Arts; Cornell Univ; Whitney Mus Am Art; 8 one-man shows, Kraushaar Gallery, New York; plus others. Teaching: Lectr art, Queen's Col, 61-68; instr art, New York Community Col, 65-68. Style & Technique: Based on natural forms and human anatomy; flat plus mixed surfaces. Media: Oil. Mailing Add: 463 West St New York NY 10014

DUBOIS, MACY
ARCHITECT, ART CRITIC
b Baltimore, Md, Dec 20, 29; Can citizen. Study: Md Inst; Tufts Univ, BSE; Harvard Univ, MArch. Comn: Ont Pavilion, Expo 67, Ont Govt, 66; Lakehead Sci Bldg, Lakehead Univ, 66; Albert Campbell Libr, Scarborough Pub Libr Bd, 73; George Brown Col Applied Arts & Technol, Toronto, 73; Govt Can Bldg, North York, Ont, 78. Exhib: Toronto City Hall Competition, 58; Sao Paolo Exhib, 62; Massey Medals for Archit, 64 & 67; Amsterdam City Hall Competition, 69. Pos: Archit critic, Can Architect, 63-; chmn, Toronto Chap Ont, 68-69. Mem: Ont Asn Architects; fel Royal Archit Inst Can, academician Royal Can Acad Arts Mailing Add: 76 Richmond St E Toronto ON Can

DUCA, ALFRED MILTON
SCULPTOR, PAINTER
b Milton, Mass, July 9, 20. Study: Pratt Inst, 38-41; Boston Mus Fine Arts, 43-44. Work: Addison Gallery Am Art, Andover, Mass; Fogg Mus & Divinity Sch, Cambridge; Worcester Art Mus, Mass; Munson Procter Inst, Utica, NY; Boston Univ Sch Basic Studies. Comn: Sculptures, Prudential Ins Co, Boston, 68-69, Standard Oil Co Ind Res Ctr, 71-72 & Computer Sphere, J F Kennedy Post Off, Boston, 71-72; steel screen, Proj 57, Boston, 71-72; sculpture, bronze screen, John McCormack Bldg, Boston, 75-76. Exhib: Local, regional & nat exhibs, 58-72. Teaching: Proj dir youth aid, Gloucester Community Develop Corp. Pos: Beaux art dir, Brandeis Univ, 52-53; vis lectr, Boston Univ, 57-58; res assoc, Mass Inst Technol, 58-65; consult, White House Conf Children & Youth, 70-71; auth-dir dissemination network syst, Channel One. Awards: Grants, Rockefeller Found, 58 & Ford Found, 60; New Eng Res Ctr Educ Award, 72. Mem: Mass Coun Arts & Humanities. Media: Polymer; Metal. Res: Development of polymer processes for painters and sculptors; development of the foam vaporization process for casting metal for sculpture. Publ: Auth, Polymer Tempera, A Handbook for Artists, 52; auth, Polymer Tempera, Significant Teaching Aid, 54; auth, Art casting, Mass Inst Technol J, 62; co-auth, Plastics as Art Form, Newman, 64; co-auth, Synthetic Pating Media, Jensen, 64. Mailing Add: Annisquam Gloucester MA 01930

DUCKWORTH, RUTH
SCULPTOR, CERAMIST
b Hamburg, Ger, Apr 10, 19. British citizen. Study: Liverpool Sch Art; Cent Sch Art & Crafts, London. Work: Victoria & Albert Mus, Eng; Stedelijk Mus, Holland; Mus Mod Art, Kyoto, Japan; Art Inst Chicago; Smart Gallery, Univ Chicago. Comn: Menorah, Solel Synagogue, Highland Park, Ill, 65; entrance mural, Geophysical Sci Bldg, Univ Chicago, 67-68; mural (24 ft x 10 ft), Dredner Bank, Chicago; mural (painted background, collage & stoneware), Hodag, Skokie, Ill. Exhib: Craft Ctr Gt Brit, 64; Primavera, London, 67; Jaques Baruch Gallery, Chicago, 72; Kunstkammer Ludger Koster Monchengladbach, 73; Exhibit A Gallery, Evanston, 74. Teaching: Instr ceramics, Cent Sch Art & Design, 60-64; asst prof ceramics, Midway Studio, Univ Chicago, 64-76. Awards: Third Prize, Int Handicrafts Exhib, Stuttgart, Ger, 62; Third Prize, Int Crafts, Istanbul, Turkey, 67; First Prize for Foreign Craftsmen, Nippon Gendai Kohgei Bijutsuka, Kyokai, Japan, 68. Bibliog: Tony Birks (auth), The Art of the Modern Potter, Country Life, 67. Mem: Arts Club Chicago; Am & World Crafts Couns. Style & Technique: Delicate porcelain, small, heavy, sometimes chunky stoneware in large, organic forms. Media: Stoneware, Porcelain. Dealer: Alice Westphal Exhibita 1708 Central St Evanston IL 60201. Mailing Add: 1835 S Halsted St Chicago IL 60608

DUFF, ANN MACINTOSH
PAINTER, PRINTMAKER
b Toronto, Ont. Study: Cent Tech Sch; Queen's Univ Summer Sch Fine Arts. Work: Nat Gallery Can, Ottawa; Art Gallery Ont, Toronto, Agnes Etherington Gallery, Queen's Univ; Huron Col, Univ Western Ont; Art Gallery Brant, Brantford, Ont. Comn: Watercolor painting, Reader's Digest for Expo 67, Montreal. Exhib: Five Toronto Painters, Montreal Mus Fine Art; Six Ways with Watercolor, London Art Gallery, Ont; Can Soc Painters in Watercolour & Am Watercolor Soc Joint Exhib, 72; eight one-man shows in Toronto. Awards: J Grant Glassco Purchase Award, Can Soc Painters Watercolor, 68 & John Labatt Award, 73; Loomis & Toles Award, Ont Soc Artists, 69. Bibliog: Frances Duncan Barwick (auth), Pictures from the Douglas M Duncan Collection, Univ Toronto, 75. Mem: Royal Can Acad Arts; Can Soc Painters Watercolour (exec, 70-75); Can Soc Graphic Art (treas, 67-69); Ont Soc Artists (exec coun, 72). Style & Technique: Watercolour-wet. Dealer: Merton Gallery 68 Merton St Toronto ON Can. Mailing Add: 133 Imperial St Toronto ON M5P 1C7 Can

DUFF, JAMES H
MUSEUM DIRECTOR, ART ADMINISTRATOR
b Pittsburgh, Pa, Oct 11, 43. Study: Washington & Jefferson Col, BA, 65; Univ Mass, MA, 70. Collections Arranged: Wildlife in Art, Brandywine River Mus, Chadds Ford, Pa, 73, Maxfield Parrish: Master of Make-Believe, 74, Harvey Dunn, 74, & Peter Hurd, 77. Pos: Dir, Mus Hudson Highlands, 66-73; consult, NY State Coun Arts, 70-72; dir, Brandywine River Mus, 73-; panel mem, Pa Coun Arts, 76- Mem: Asn Art Mus Dirs; Am Asn Mus; NE Mus Conf (Pa gov, 76-). Mailing Add: RD Chadds Ford PA 19317

DUFF, JOHN EWING
SCULPTOR
b Lafayette, Ind, Dec 2, 43. Study: San Francisco Art Inst, BFA, 67; with Manuel Neri, Paul Harris & Ron Nagle. Work: Kaiser Wilhelm Mus, Aachen, Ger; Mus Mod Art, New York. Exhib: Anti-Illusion, Procedures & Materials Show, Whitney Mus, 69, David Whitney Gallery, 70 & 71, John Meyers Gallery, 72 & 73 & Willard Gallery, 75, New York; Irving Blum Gallery, Los Angeles, 72. Bibliog: Barbara Rose (auth), Where we are & what we like, New York Mag, 4/72 & 4/75; John Russell (auth), current shows in New York Times, 3/75; J Tannenbaum (auth), rev in Arts Mag, 6/75. Style & Technique: Non-figurative, construction. Media: Fiberglas, Wood. Publ: Contribr, Art Now: New York, 72. Dealer: Miani Johnson c/o Willard Gallery 29 E 72nd St New York NY 10021. Mailing Add: 7 Doyers St New York NY 10013

DUFFY, BETTY MINOR
ART DEALER
Pos: Dir, Bethesda Art Gallery. Specialty: American Fine Prints from the first half of the 20th century. Mailing Add: c/o Bethesda Art Gallery 7950 Norfolk Ave Bethesda MD 20014

DUFOUR, PAUL ARTHUR
PAINTER, DESIGNER
b Manchester, NY, Aug 31, 22. Study: Univ NH, BA, 50; Yale Univ, BFA, 52; also with Takahiko Fujita & Ikuo Hirayama, Japan, 64. Work: Masur Mus Art, Monroe, La; Springfield Art Mus, Mo; La State Collection, Baton Rouge; La Bicentennial Collection. Comn: Stained glass, sculpture & mosaic (with Desmond-Miremont, Architects), St Joseph Prep Sch, Baton Rouge, La, 68; stained glass windows (with Desmond-Miremont, Architects), Holy Ghost Church, Hammond, La, 74; stained glass windows & bronze sculpture (with Desmond-Miremont, Architects), Our Lady of Mercy, Baton Rouge, 74; stained glass (with Glankler & Broadwell, Architects), St Patrick Church, Lake Providence, La; plus many others. Exhib: St Paul Biennial, Minn, 62; Tokyo and Kyoto Invitational, 64; 4th & 5th Int Watercolor, 72 & 74; American Revolution Bicentennial, 73; plus others. Teaching: Asst prof painting, St John's Univ, 55-58; vis prof design, Sienna Heights Col, 57; prof design & stained glass, La State Univ, Baton Rouge, 58- Pos: Supvr educ, Currier Gallery Art, Manchester, NH, 52-55; artist in residence, Viterbo Col, 68. Awards: Top Award & Purchase Prize, Masur Mus Art, 67; Top Award, La Int Watercolor Exhib, 69; First Purchase Award, 4th Int Watercolor, 72; plus others. Bibliog: This is their South, Southern Living, 69. Mem: Am Asn Univ Prof; Col Art Asn; Am Craft Coun; La Watercolor Soc. Media: Sumi, Stained Glass. Dealer: Baton Rouge Gallery 205 N Fourth St Baton Rouge LA 70801. Mailing Add: Dept of Art La State Univ Baton Rouge LA 70803

DUGMORE, EDWARD
PAINTER
b Hartford, Conn, Feb 20, 15. Study: Hartford Art Sch, scholarship, 4 years; Calif Sch Fine Arts; Univ Guadalajara, Mex, MA. Work: Albright-Knox Art Gallery, Buffalo; Ciba-Geigy Corp, Ardsley, NY; Walker Art Inst, Minneapolis; Des Moines Art Ctr, Iowa; Mus Purchase Fund, New York. Exhib: Solomon R Guggenheim Mus, New York, 61; San Francisco Mus Art, Calif, 63; Painting as Painting, Univ Tex, Austin, 68; Albright-Knox Permanent Collection Show, 72; A Period of Exploration, San Francisco 1945-50, Oakland Mus, 73; one-man shows, Stable Gallery, 53, 54 & 56, Howard Wise Gallery, 61, 62 & 63 & Green Mountain Gallery, 71 & 73; plus others. Teaching: Vis artist, Mont Inst, Great Falls, 65; vis artist, Univ Minn, Minneapolis, spring 70; vis artist, Des Moines Art Ctr & Drake Univ, 72. Awards: Kohnstamm Award, Art Inst Chicago, 62; Guggenheim fel, 66-67; Nat Endowment Arts fel, 76-77. Bibliog: Harold Rosenberg (auth), The art world, New Yorker, 3/6/71; Mary Fuller McChesney (auth), A Period of Exploration San Francisco 1945-1950; Peter Plagens (auth), Sunshine Muse, Praeger, 74; plus others. Style & Technique: Abstract expressionist. Media: Oil. Mailing Add: 118 W 27th St New York NY 10001

DUHME, H RICHARD, JR
SCULPTOR, EDUCATOR
b St Louis, Mo, May 31, 14. Study: Pa Acad Fine Arts, 32-38; Univ Pa, 34; Barnes Found, Marion, Pa, 40-41; Am Sch Classical Studies, Athens, Greece, summer 51; Wash Univ, BFA, 53. Comn: Girl with Dog (bronze), Nat Humane Educ Ctr, Waterford, Va, 68; Lion Club Fountain (bronze), Mycenaean Found, Mycenae, Greece, 69; Mo Sesquicentennial Medallions (silver & bronze), Sesquicentennial Comt, 71; St Martin & the Beggar (monumental bronze group), Bishop of Erie, Pa, 71; Chautaqua New York Centennial Medallions (silver & bronze), 74. Exhib: Pa Acad Fine Arts Ann, Philadelphia, 38-41 & 50; Metrop Mus Art Summer Sculpture Show, New York,42; St Louis City Art Mus Group Show, 49-50 & 52; Cincinnati Art Mus, Ohio, 61; Expos Int Medaile Contemporaine, Nat Mus, Athens, Greece, 66. Teaching: Prof sculpture, Wash Univ, 47-; head dept sculpture, Chautauqua Inst Summer Schs, 53-; head dept sculpture, Syracuse Univ Chautauqua Ctr, 53-69. Awards: Cresson Foreign Travel Award, 35, Lewis S Ware Foreign Fel, 38 & May Audubon Post Prize Fel, 41, Pa Acad Fine Arts; First Hon Mention, Prix de Rome, Am Acad Rome, 39. Mem: Fel Nat Sculpture Soc; Allied Artists Am. Style & Technique: Mainly human and animal subjects in simplified traditional style. Media: Bronze, Stone, Terra Cotta. Mailing Add: 8 Edgewood Rd St Louis MO 63124

DUIS, RITA (RITA DUIS ASTLEY-BELL)
PAINTER
b New York, NY. Study: Nat Acad Design; Art Students League; Banff Sch Fine Arts, Univ Alta; China Inst; also with Rex Brandt, Edgar Whitney, George Post, Robert Wood, Mario Cooper, Carl Molno, Louis Bouche & Edwin Dickenson. Exhib: American Art Week, Nat Collection Fine Arts, Smithsonian Inst, Washington, DC, 63; Am Watercolor Soc, Nat Acad Design, New York, 70, 71, 73 & 76; Painters & Sculptors Soc NJ, Jersey City Mus, 71; Watercolor USA Nat Ann, Springfield Art Mus, Mo, 72; Arts Atlantic, Gloucester, Mass, 72; Women in Art, 18th Century to Present, Hammond Mus, North Salem, NY, 74; Am Fortnight, Am CofC, Hong Kong, 75; Nat Acad Design, New York, 76; Midwest Watercolor Soc, Tween Mus, Duluth, Minn & St Paul Mus, Minn, 77. Awards: Bronze Medal of Honor for Watercolor, Nat Arts Club Ånn, NY, 71; Anna Hyatt Huntington Medal for Watercolor, 72; Award of Merit, Midwest Watercolor Soc, Tweed Mus, 77. Mem: Salmagundi Club (jury awards, 77, dir-at-large, 77-78); Nat Arts Club (artist mem; exhib comt, 69-71); Am Watercolor Soc; Nat Asn Watercolor Artists; Am Artists Prof League. Style & Technique: Representational, also impressionistic and abstract style, using mostly wet into wet technique with watercolor. Media: Watercolor, Oil. Mailing Add: 207 E 74th St New York NY 10021

DU JARDIN, GUSSIE
PAINTER, PRINTMAKER
b San Francisco, Calif, Feb 19, 18. Study: Univ Colo, BA; Univ Iowa, MA. Work: NMex Mus Art, Santa Fe; NMex Highlands Univ; Univ Iowa; Roswell Mus, NMex; Univ Colo Mus. Exhib: Butler Inst Am Art 26th Ann, 61; Tucson Festival Art Exhib, 64; NMex Biennial, 71, 73 & 75; Mus NMex Southwest Biennial Exhib, 72, 74 & 76, Invitational, 78. Pos: Artist-in-Residence Prog, Roswell Mus, 77- Awards: First Purchase Award, Mus NMex, 61. Media: Acrylic. Mailing Add: RT 1 Box 244 Roswell NM 88201

DULAC, MARGARITA WALKER
PAINTER, ART CRITIC
b Asheville, NC. Study: Art Inst Chicago, summer 38, 40, 54 & 55; Acad Andre Lhote, Paris, France, Woolley fel, 38-39, cert, 39; Northwestern Univ, scholar & BS(cum laude), 42; Univ Chicago, fel & MA, 44; Univ Iowa, fel; also with F Leger, Paris, 52. Work: New Trier Twp High Sch, Winnetka, Ill; Deering Libr & Patten Gym, Northwestern Univ, Evansville; Wilmette Pub Libr, Ill; Poetry Soc Am, New York, NY; Ministere Affaires Etrangeres, Paris. Comn: Portraits, Hans Lange, dir, Chicago Symphony Orch, 37, Andre Gerard (Pertinax), 44, Gen de Gaulle, Paris, 44, Andres Segovia, New York, 47 & Candy Bergen, 72; plus others. Exhib: Chicago Artists Exhib, Art Inst Chicago, 35, 36 & 38; Salon Tuileries, Paris, 39 & 50; Int Exhib Drawings, Bodley Gallery, New York, 58; Jersey Painters & Sculptors Nat Exhib, Jersey City Mus, 69 & 70; Nat Arts Club, 74; plus many others. Teaching: Head dept art, De Kalb High Sch, Ill, 37-38; instr painting, Heidelberg Univ, 44-46; instr painting, Acad Leger, Paris, 47-51; pvt lessons, 51-65. Pos: Art critic, Arts Mag, summer 66; art critic, Jersey Jour, 67-70; art critic, The Herald, New York, 70-; plus others. Awards: First Prize Painting, Univ Chicago, 42; First Prize Pastel, Univ Guild, Evanston, 42. Bibliog: Winning honors easy for artists, Chicago Am, 7/13/38; Andre Lhote (auth), Un peintre Americain, Nouvelle Rev Francaise, 6/1/60; Artistic talent-one family, Jersey J, 1/21/74; plus others. Mem: Hudson Valley Artists Asn; Composers, Authors & Artists Am (chmn publicity); Salmagundi Club. Style & Technique: Broad realism, leaning toward impressionism; paints directly on linen, from tube. Media: Oil. Publ: Auth, Cyclorama, Univ Chicago, 42; auth, Ivan Albright—mystic-realist, 1/66, Raymond Katz, master of mixed media, 1/69 & Werner Goshans, realism and fantasy, 6/70, Am Artist; plus many other articles in various newspapers. Mailing Add: Box 334 Murray Hill Sta PO New York NY 10016

DUNBAR, JILL H
ART WRITER, ART CRITIC
b New Haven, Conn, Feb 10, 49. Pos: Mem staff, Betty Parsons Gallery, New York, 75-76; mem staff, Truman Drawing Inc, 76-; art critic, The Villager, Byron Publ, 76-; contrib ed, ArtWorld, 76-78; contrib ed, 57th St Rev, 76-77; contribr, Womanart, Mag, 77-; contribr, Phoenix, 77- Mailing Add: 290 W 11th St New York NY 10014

DUNCAN, (ELEANORE) KLARI
PAINTER, INSTRUCTOR
b Hungary; US citizen. Study: Pratt Graphic Ctr; Acad Grande Chaumiere, Paris, France, 5 yrs with Prof Jean Aujame; New York Phoenix Sch Design, NY State scholar. Work: Ulmann Collection, Paris; Ecole de France, Paris; Cornell Club, New York. Comn: Pen & ink drawings of Paris, Pariscope, 63-65; Hon & Mrs Robert F Wagner (oil portraits), comn by Barbara Wagner, 67, 68 & 75; Juanita Lake, Kirkland, Wash (oil painting), comn by Mr E Smalley, Roseburg, Ore, 72; oil painting, comn by Brian T Myers, Yorkville's E 86th St, New York, 77. Exhib: Galerie Andre Weil, Paris, 64; Mus Art Mod, Paris, 64-65; Expos Intercontinentale de Monaco, 68; Maitland Art Ctr, Fla, 72-73; Metrop Mus Art, New York, 77; one-woman show, Cornell Club, New York, 75. Teaching: Instr painting classes, SHAPE, Paris & Cape Cod, Mass, 73- Awards: Cert of Appreciation of Recognition of Outstanding Serv to US Navy Recruiting Serv, New York Recruiting Serv, 66. Mem: Nat Arts Club; Burr Artists, New York. Style & Technique: Figurative-realistic. Media: Oil, Woodcut, Etching, Watercolor. Publ: Illusr, Stories of Jesus, Baby Finger Games, Big Story Book & other children's books, 60-67. Mailing Add: 342 E 81st St New York NY 10028

DUNCAN, RICHARD HURLEY
PRINTMAKER, EDUCATOR
b Daytona Beach, Fla, Feb 11, 44. Study: Southern Ill Univ, BA, 66, MFA, 73. Work: Ill State Univ; Springfield Civic Collection, Ill; Aukland City Art Gallery, New Zealand; Cooperstown Art Asn, NY; SE Ctr for Contemp Art, Winston-Salem, NC. Comn: Two lithographs, Verein fur Originalgraphik, Zurich & Baden, Switz, 74. Exhib: Boston Printmakers 24th Ann Exhib, Waltham, Mass, 72; 1st Davidson Nat Print & Drawing Exhib, NC, 72; Los Angeles Print Soc Nat Print Show, 73; 11th Nat Print Exhib, Silvermine, Conn, 76; Footprint, NW Int Small Format Print Exhib, Seattle, Wash, 76; 35 Artists in the SE, High Mus, Atlanta, Ga & SE Ctr for Contemp Art, Winston-Salem, 76-78; World Print 77, Mus of Mod Art, San Francisco, 77; one-man shows, Vanderbilt Univ Art Gallery, 77 & Paperworks, Hunter Mus of Art, Chattanooga, 77; 25th Nat Print Exhib (travelling exhib), Nat Collection of Fine Arts, 77 & Libr of Cong, Washington, DC, 77-78; 100 World Prints, Smithsonian Inst Travelling Exhib, 77-79. plus others. Teaching: Instr printmaking, Univ of the South, 73- Awards: Third Place Award Graphics, New Horizons, Chicago, 72; First Place Merit Award, Okla Nat Print & Drawing Show, Oklahoma City, 76; Ford Found Grants, 74 & 76; plus others. Mem: Col Art Asn; Am Asn Univ Prof. Style & Technique: Figurative and formal line work and rendering; currently geometric abstraction. Media: Intaglio; Litho Relief-Printed Construction; Pencil. Mailing Add: SPO 1251 Sewanee TN 37375

DUNCAN, RUTH
PAINTER
b Greeley, Colo, Feb 19, 08. Study: Stephens Col, AA; Univ Okla, BFA; and with Harold A Roney, Simon G Michael & Warren Hunter. Work: Stephens Col, Columbia, Mo; San Antonio Jr Col Libr, Tex; Royal Bldg, Dallas; Bexar Co Court House & Bexar Co Nat Bank, San Antonio. Comn: Many. Exhib: 36 one-man shows; Exposition Intercontinentale, Congres des Palais, Monaco; Stephens Col, 68; Witte Mem Mus, San Antonio; Univ Tex, Austin; San Antonio Main Libr, 68 & 75; among others. Awards: Wonderland Gallery Award, 71 & Coppini Acad Fine Arts Award for Best Conserv Painting, 72, River Art Group; Order of the Rose Award for Achievement & Success in Chosen Field with nat & int acclaim, Delta Gamma Sorority, 73. Mem: Fel Am Artists Prof League; Coppini Acad Fine Arts (rec secy, 60-67, bd dirs, 75-); River Art Group; Soc Western Artists, San Francisco. Style & Technique: Oil painter of landscapes, landmarks and marines. Media: Oil, Watercolor. Mailing Add: 1511 Fulton Ave San Antonio TX 78201

DUNKELMAN, LORETTA
PAINTER
b Paterson, NJ, June 29, 37. Study: Douglass Col, BA, 58; Accad delle Belle Arti, Florence, Italy, 60-61; Hunter Col, with Tony Smith & Ralph Humphrey, MA, 66. Work: City Univ Grad Ctr, New York; Dana Art Ctr, Colgate Univ; Univ Cincinnati; Univ Kans Art Mus. Exhib: Whitney Biennial Contemp Art, 73 & Am Drawings 1963-73, Whitney Mus Am Art, New York; Of Paper, Newark Mus, NJ, 73; Women Choose Women, New York Cult Ctr, 73; one-artist shows, AIR Gallery, NY, 73, 74 & 78 & Univ RI, 75; Waves: An Artist Selects, Cranbrook Acad Art, Bloomfield & Grant Rapids Art Mus, Mich, 74; Cornell Artists/Past & Present, Johnson Mus, 77; AIR: An Overview, PS 1, Queens, NY, 78; plus many others. Teaching: Vis artist, Univ Cincinnati, 74; asst prof art, Univ RI, 74-75; asst prof art, Cornell Univ, 77- Awards: Nat Endowment for the Arts Fel-Grant, 75; Creative Artists Pub Serv Fel, 75-76; Am Asn Univ Women Fel, 76-77. Bibliog: April Kingsley (auth), Women choose women, Artforum, 3/73; Paul Stitelman (auth), Reviews, 4/73 & Ellen Lubell (auth), Reviews, 5/74, Arts Mag; Lawrence Alloway (auth), Art in Am, 5/76. Style & Technique: Classical and personal layered surfaces in an encaustic process. Media: Oil & Wax Chalks on Paper. Dealer: AIR Gallery 97 Wooster St New York NY 10012. Mailing Add: 151 Canal St New York NY 10002

DUNLAP, LOREN EDWARD
PAINTER, INSTRUCTOR
b Anderson, Ind, Feb 2, 32. Study: Herron Art Sch, BFA; Ogunquit Sch of Painting & Sculpture; Tulane Univ, MFA. Work: Addison Gallery of Am Art, Andover, Mass; Santa Barbara Mus, Calif; Univ Calif Collection; Flint Art Mus, Mich; Fine Arts Ctr, Anderson, Ind. Comn: Mural, comn by Jane Blaffer Owen, for Blaffer Trust, New Harmony, Ind, 65; 3 panel paintings, Jane Arneberg, New York, 70; painting, Pfizer Chemical Co, New York, 74. Exhib: Ind Artist, John Herron Mus, Indianapolis, 56-60; Mich Regional Exhib, South Bend, Ind, 59; one-man show, Purdue Univ, West Lafayette, Ind, 59, Santa Barbara Mus of Art, Calif, 63; Drawing Ann, Norfolk Mus, Va, 60; Albright-Knox Art Gallery, Buffalo, NY, 60; Boston Mus of Contemp Arts, Mass, 60; Univ Calif Fac Show, 63. Teaching: Instr studio & art hist, Herron Sch, Indianapolis, 58-62; lectr studio & art hist, Univ Calif, Santa Barbara, 63-65. Awards: Louis Comfort Tiffany grant, 55 & 65. Style & Technique: Still life and landscapes. Media: All media, but primarily oil. Publ: Auth, Traditions of the East, Revolutions of the West, Herron J, 60. Dealer: Wally Findlay Int 814 N Michigan Ave Chicago IL 60611. Mailing Add: Box 332 Sagg Rd Sagaponack NY 11962

DUNN, CAL
PAINTER, FILM MAKER
b Georgetown, Ohio, Aug 31, 15. Study: Cincinnati Art Acad, 27; Cent Acad Commercial Art, 32-34. Work: Ford Motor Co, Detroit; Allstate Ins Co, Chicago; Am Artists Group, New York; Tavern Club Chicago. Exhib: Am Watercolor Soc Exhibs, New York, 55-56 & Traveling Exhib, 63; Chicago & Vicinity Exhib, Art Inst Chicago, 57; 100 American Watercolorists, Royal Gallery, London, 63. Pos: Animation art dir, USAAF, Wright Field, Dayton, Ohio, 43-44; art dir, Sarra, Inc, 44-47; pres, Cal Dunn Studios, Chicago, 47-; illusr watercolor story assignments, Ford Times—Lincoln Mercury Times, Ford Motor Co, 50-62. Awards: Awards for Edge of Town, Am Artists Mag, 56; Emmy Award for TV Art Direction; plus many major film awards. Mem: Am Watercolor Soc; Artist Guild Chicago (pres, 55-57); hon mem Artists Guild Chicago (pres, 55-57); Dir Guild Am. Media: Oil, Watercolor. Publ: Auth, article in Am Artists Mag, 56. Mailing Add: 141 W Ohio St Chicago IL 60610

DUNN, NATE
PAINTER, INSTRUCTOR
b Pittsburgh, Pa, July 4, 96. Study: Carnegie Inst Technol, with Arthur Sparks, Alfred Taylor & Geo Sotter. Work: Butler Inst Am Art; Thiel Col; Pa State Univ. Exhib: Butler Inst Am Art, Youngstown, Ohio; Mansfield Col; Playhouse, Pittsburgh, Pa; Canton Art Gallery, Ohio; Trumbull Art Guild, Warren, Ohio; plus others. Teaching: Instr painting & drawing, Girls Buhl Club, 58- Pos: Mem, Sharon Mayor's Comt Arts. Awards: Purchase Prizes, Butler Inst Am Art Area Shows, 64 & Steubenville Art Asn, 72 & 74-75; St John's Episcopal Church Award, 66. Mem: Friends Am Art, Youngstown; Steubenville Art Asn; Canton Gallery; fel Royal Soc Arts. Style & Technique: Impressionistic; semi-abstract; abstract; landscape and figure. Media: Oil, Acrylic. Dealer: Queen's Gallery Cleveland OH 44101; Bogarad Fine Art Gallery 326 Penco Rd Wierton WV 26062. Mailing Add: 490 Carley Ave Sharon PA 16146

DUNN, O COLEMAN
COLLECTOR
b Raymond, Alta, Mar 27, 02; US citizen. Collections Arranged: British and American paintings and drawings; European old masters. Mailing Add: 917 Kearns Bldg 136 S Main St Salt Lake City UT 84101

DUNN, ROGER TERRY
ART DEALER, LECTURER
b Bethesda, Md, Feb 24, 46. Study: Am Univ, Washington, DC; Pa State Univ, BA(art hist & painting); Pratt Inst, MFA(painting), 70; Northwestern Univ. Collections Arranged: Quilts from the Plymouth Antiquarian Soc, 74; John J Enneking: American Impressionist (with catalog), 75; The Painting Invitational, 75, Bridgewater State Col, Mass; American Pastimes (ed, catalogue), 77. Teaching: Vis lectr art, Bridgewater State Col, Mass, 75-76. Pos: Cur, Brockton Art Ctr, Mass, 74-77; dir, Gallery at OUI, Boston, 76- Res: Monet and his symbolist circle; exhibition research on 19th century American art. Publ: Auth, Lawrence Kupferman: A Retrospective Exhibition, 74; ed, Landscape and Life in 19th Century America, 74. Mailing Add: c/o Gallery at OUI 54 Canal St Boston MA 02114

DUNNIGAN, MARY CATHERINE
ART LIBRARIAN
b Shawvers Mill, Va, May 7, 22. Study: Mary Washington Col, BA; Columbia Univ, MLS. Pos: Librn, Col of Archit, Va Polytech Inst, Blacksburg, 66-73; librn, Fiske Kimball Fine Arts Libr, Univ Va, Charlottesville, 73- Mem: Soc Archit Historians; Art Libr Soc NAm; Spec Libr Asn Arts & Humanities Div (chmn mus, 73-74). Interest: Development of research library for support of art, architecture and drama curriculum. Mailing Add: Fiske Kimball Fine Arts Libr Bayly Dr Univ of Va Charlottesville VA 22903

DUNNINGTON, MRS WALTER GREY
COLLECTOR, PATRON
b Long Branch, NJ, Aug 17, 10. Study: Smith Col, BA; Bryn Mawr Col. Pos: Treas, women's comt, Philadelphia Mus Art, 38-41; former pres bd trustees, Parrish Art Mus, Southampton, NY, 64-70; former dir, NY Hort Soc. Collection: Furniture, porcelain, paintings, drawings. Mailing Add: 3 E 77th St New York NY 10021

DUNWIDDIE, CHARLOTTE
SCULPTOR
b Strasbourg, France. Study: Acad Arts, Berlin, Ger, with Wilhelm Otto; also with Mariano Benlliure y Gil, Madrid, Spain & Alberto Lagos, Buenos Aires, Arg. Work: Cardinal's Palace, Buenos Aires; Church of Good Shepherd, Lima, Peru; Marine Corps Mus, Washington, DC; Aquaduct Racecourse, New York; Mt St Alfonsus, Suffield, Conn. Exhib: Salon Bellas Artes, Buenos Aires, 40-45; Allied Artists Am, 56-72; Nat Sculpture Soc, 58-72; Am Artists Prof League, 59-70; Nat Acad Design, 59-72. Pos: Pres, Pen & Brush Club, 66-70; mem ed bd, Nat Sculpture Rev, 70-75, secy, 73-75. Awards: Speyer Award, Nat Acad Design, 69, Artists Fund Prize for Best in Show, 72 & 74; Lindsey Mem Prize, Nat Sculpture Soc, 70; plus others. Mem: Nat Acad Design (secy, 66-69); Nat Sculpture Soc; Royal Soc Arts; Am Artists Prof League (dir, 60-); Salmagundi Club. Mailing Add: New York NY

DU PEN, EVERETT GEORGE
SCULPTOR, EDUCATOR
b San Francisco, Calif, June 12, 12. Study: Univ Southern Calif, with Merril Gage; Yale Univ Sch Fine Arts, Clara Kimball English traveling fel, 37, BFA, with George Eberhard, George Snowden & Alexander Archipenko. Work: Seattle Art Mus; Washington Mutual Savings Bank, Seattle; Univ Wash Faculty Club; Aberdeen City Hall, Wash. Comn: Three limestone carvings, Elec Eng Bldg, Univ Wash, 48; bronze sculptures for fountains, State of Wash, Olympia Libr, 60 & Seattle World's Fair, 62; crucifix & wall carving, St John Episcopal Church, Seattle, 63; carved walnut screens, Munic Bldg, City of Seattle, 63; heroic bronze portrait, pres Univ Wash, 73. Exhib: Nat Acad Design, New York, 50, 59, 72 & 76-77; Seattle Art Mus Northwest Ann, 47-63; Pa Acad Fine Art, 50, 54 & 58; Nat Sculpture Soc, 50, 59, 72, 75 & 77; Mainstreams 72, Marietta Col, 72. Teaching: Asst sculpture, Carnegie Inst Technol Art Sch, 39-40; asst sculpture, Wash Univ Art Sch, 40-42; from instr to prof sculpture, Univ Wash Sch Art, 45- Pos: Sculpture mem, Munic Art Comn, Seattle; sculpture adv, Art Adv Bd Seattle World's Fair, 60-62. Awards: Saltus Gold Medal, Nat Acad Design. Bibliog: Minor L Bishop (auth), Fountains in contemporary architecture, Am Fedn Arts, 65; Louis G Redstone (auth), articles in Art Archit, 68 & Nat Sculpture Rev. Mem: Fel Nat Sculpture Soc; academician Nat Acad Design. Style & Technique: Traditional and contemporary. Media: Wood, Bronze. Mailing Add: 1231 20th Ave E Seattle WA 98112

DU PRÉ, GRACE ANNETTE
PAINTER
b Spartanburg, SC. Study: Converse Col; Grand Cent Sch Art, with Greacen, Wolfe, Karl Anderson, Hildebrandt, Wayman Adams & Frank V Dumond. Work: Charleston City Hall Collection of Portraits, SC; US Supreme Court, Washington, DC; New York Main Post Off Collection; State House, Columbia, SC; Church of the Ascension Collection of Rectors' Portraits, New York. Comn: 14 paintings of judges from life, US Court Appeals, 7th Circuit, Chicago, 54-61; double portrait of Pres Truman & his mother, now in Truman Mus Collection; Dr Hu Shih (portrait from life), Columbia Univ Low Libr; plus many others, including four portraits of James F Byrnes, now in pub collections. Exhib: Allied Artists Am Ann, New York, NY, 42-63; Nat Arts Club Ann, 42-63; Am Artists Prof League Ann, 43-62; Nat Exhib Am Paintings, Ogunquit, Maine, 51 & 58; one man show, Wofford Col, 75; plus others. Teaching: Pvt classes, Spartanburg, SC, 32-42. Awards: Second Prize for Portrait, Mint Mus Regional Exhib, 43; Award, 31st Nat Exhib Am Painting, 51; Prize for Portrait, Catharine Lorillard Wolfe Art Club Ann, 55. Bibliog: Art in South Carolina 1670-1970, SC Tricentennial Comn; articles in State Mag, SC Mag & many newspapers. Mem: Allied Artists Am; Grand Cent Art Galleries; Nat Arts Club; Catharine Lorillard Wolfe Art Club; Am Artists Prof League (nat exec bd, 50-55). Media: Oil. Dealer: Grand Central Art Galleries Vanderbilt Ave New York NY 10017. Mailing Add: 361 Mills Ave Spartanburg SC 29302

DUPUY, JEAN
MULTIMEDIA ARTIST
b Moulins, Allier, France, Nov 22, 25. Study: Ecole des Beaux-Arts, Paris, 45-46. Work: Phoenix Mus Art, Ariz; Mus d'Art Mod & Centre Pompidou, Paris, France; Galleria Toselli, Milan, Italy; Los Angeles Co Mus Art, Los Angeles, Calif. Exhib: The Machine, Mus Mod Art, New York, 68; Art & Technol, Los Angeles Co Mus Art, 71; 72/72, Grand Palais, Paris; About 405 E 13th St, 405 E 13th St Gallery, New York, 73-75; Soup & Tart, The Kitchen (with Phil Glass, Yvonne Rainer, Richard Serra, et al), New York, 74; Sculpture's Drawings, Scale 1 to 1, Yu Gallery, New York, 75; Three Evenings on a Revolving Stage, Judson Church, New York, 76; Sunday Afternoon on a Revolving Stage, Whitney Mus Am Art, New York, 76; 112 Greene St, New York, 77; Grommets, PS 1, New York, 76 & Grommets Art Theatre, New York, 76 & 77; A Tower, PS 1, 78; one-man shows, The Visual Energy of Sound, Judson Church, 68, Heart Beats Dust (traveling exhib of US, France & Italy), Mus Mod Art, New York, 68; 15-16-Chorus for Six Hearts (traveling France & Italy), Mus Mod Art, New York, 69, Sonnabend Gallery, Paris & New York, 69-72, Paris-Bordeaux, Mus d'Art Mod, Paris & Whitney Mus Am Art, 70, Scragow Gallery, 77 & Multiples Gallery, 78, New York; Teaching: Instr, Sch Visual Arts, New York, 70-72. Awards: First Prize for Heart Beats Dust, Mus Mod Art, New York, 68; Nat Endowment for the Arts Grant, Washington, DC, 77 & 78. Bibliog: Jean Prather (auth), Heart beat art fascinates onlooker, Republic, Columbus, Ind, 4/70; Union of art, technology may promote appreciation, Republic, Columbus, Ind, 5/70; Maurice Tuchman (auth), A Report on the Art & Technology Program of the Los Angeles Co Mus of Art 1967-1971, Los Angeles, 71. Publ: Auth, Conversation a Trois, Opus Int, Paris, 4/70; auth, De Los Angeles a Bordeaux, Plaisir de Fr, Paris, 10/71; letter in Opus Int, Paris, 9/74 & Tracks, New York, winter 76. Mailing Add: 537 Broadway New York NY 10012

DURAN, ROBERT
PAINTER
b Salinas, Calif, 1938. Study: Richard Stockton State Col, 58-60; San Francisco Sch of Fine Arts, Calif, 60-61. Work: Columbus Gallery of Fine Arts, Ohio; Nat Gallery, Washington, DC; Port Authority of NY & NJ; J Henry Schroder Banking Corp. Exhib: Rejective Art, Am Fedn of Arts, New York, 67; Between Object & Environment, Univ Pa, 69; Whitney Mus Am Art, New York, 69 & 73; Beaux-Arts 25th Anniversary Exhib, Columbus Gallery of Fine Arts, 71; Corcoran Gallery of Art Biennial, Washington, DC, 71; Indianapolis Mus Art, Ind, 72; Storm King Art Ctr, Mountainville, NY, 72; two-man shows, Bykert Gallery, 68 & 70-73; Tex Gallery, 73. Dealer: Bykert Gallery 24 E 81st St New York NY 10028. Mailing Add: 431 Broome St New York NY 10013

DURHAM, WILLIAM
PAINTER, PRINTMAKER
b Flint, Mich, Mar 14, 37. Study: Mich State Univ, BA, 61; painting with Morris Kantor, Boris Margo & Abraham Rattner. Work: Guild Hall, East Hampton, NY; Warnaco Inc, Park Ave, New York; Mich State Univ, East Lansing; Woodside Church, Flint, Mich. Comn: Painting, New York World's Fair, 64. Exhib: One-man shows, Benson Gallery, Bridgehampton, NY, 67, 71, 72 & 74; Am Acad Arts & Lett, New York, 74; Hecksher Mus, Huntington, NY, 74; Artist of the Hamptons, Guild Hall, Easthampton, NY, 75; Chicago Art Inst. Bibliog: Article in New York Herald Tribune, 64 & New York Times, 64-75. Style & Technique: Large acrylic paintings dealing with various scientific phenomena relating to the sea. Media: Acrylic; Serigraphy. Mailing Add: Main St Amagansett NY 11930

DURIEUX, CAROLINE WOGAN
PRINTMAKER
b New Orleans, La, Jan 22, 96. Study: Newcomb Col, BA(art educ), 17; Pa Acad Fine Arts, fel, 18-20; La State Univ, MA, 49. Work: Rosenwald Collection, Nat Gallery Art, Washington, DC; Mus Mod Art, New York, NY; Philadelphia Mus Fine Arts, Pa; Bibliot Nat, Paris, France. Exhib: Libr of Cong Print Ann, Washington, DC, 46; Cincinnati Mus Fine Arts Int Biennial, Ohio, 56; Print Coun Am, Europe & Far East, 62; 2nd Nat Lithography Exhib, Fla State Univ, 66; one-person shows, Baton Rouge Gallery, La, 76, New Orleans Hist Collection, La, 76 & Loyola Univ, 77. Teaching: Instr life class painting, Newcomb Col, 20-21 & 38-43; from asst prof to prof graphics, La State Univ, Baton Rouge, 43-65, emer prof, 65- Pos: Consult, Fed Art Proj, Works Proj Admin, 38-43. Awards: Res grants for develop of electron prints & Cliches Verres, La State Univ Coun Res, 51-60 & 72-73. Bibliog: Salpeter (auth), About Caroline Durieux, Coronet, 37; Caroline Durieux, La State Univ, 49 & 78; Zigrosser (auth), The appeal of prints, NY Graphics, 70. Mem: Audubon Artists; Baton Rouge Gallery. Style & Technique: Realistic satirist; electron prints from radioactive drawings; Cliches-Verres by means of light. Publ: Illusr, Gumbo Yaya, Houghton, 38; illusr, New Orleans City Guide, Works Proj Admin, 38; co-auth, Mardigras Day, Holt, 48. Dealer: Taylor Clark Prints 2623 Government St Baton Rouge LA 70806; Tahir Gallery 823 Chartres St New Orleans LA 70116. Mailing Add: 772 W Chimes Baton Rouge LA 70802

DUTTON, PAULINE MAE
ART LIBRARIAN
b Detroit, Mich. Study: Calif State Univ, Fullerton, BA(art), with Jerry Samuelson; Univ Southern Calif, MLS; Univ Calif, Los Angeles, with Joel Schecter. Pos: Fine arts librn, Pasadena Pub Libr, 71- Mem: Art Libr Soc NAm. Interest: Antiques, painting, picture file. Mailing Add: 285 E Walnut St Pasadena CA 91101

DUVOISIN, ROGER
WRITER, ILLUSTRATOR
b Geneva, Switz, Aug 28, 04; US citizen. Study: Col Mod, Geneva; Ecole Arts Decoratifs, Geneva. Work: Univ Libr Collection, Minneapolis; Rutgers Univ Libr Collection; Univ Southern Miss Libr Collection. Exhib: Am Fedn Arts Traveling Exhib US Mus, 44-45; Mus Mod Art Touring Exhib, 46-49; Philadelphia Mus Sch Art, 52; US Graphic Art Touring Exhib, Russia & E Europe, 63-66; Univ Minn, 67. Teaching: Vis prof illus, Parsons Sch Design, New York, 43-51. Awards: Rutgers Univ Bicentennial Award, Ger Govt Award, Bonn, 56; NY Acad Sci Award, 75; plus others. Bibliog: Henry Pitz (auth), article in Am Artists, 12/49; John Hutchins (auth), article in Herald Tribune Bk Rev Mag, 11/16/52; Hashel Frankel (auth), article in Sat Rev, 8/22/64. Style & Technique: Collages with gouache and tempera; casein or tempera painting; lithographic hand-separation of color on acetate. Media: Gouache, Collage; Ink. Publ: Auth & illusr, Petunia Books, 50-66; illusr, Happy Lion Books, 54-70; illusr, The Three Cornered Hat, 60; auth & illusr, Veronica Books, 60-71; co-auth & illusr, Marc & Pixie, 75; plus others. Mailing Add: Box 116 Gladstone NJ 07934

DWIGHT, EDWARD HAROLD
MUSEUM DIRECTOR
b Cincinnati, Ohio, Aug 2, 19. Study: St Louis Sch Fine Arts; Yale Univ; Art Acad Cincinnati. Collections Arranged: Juan Gris, 48; Paintings by the Peale Family, 54; Rediscoveries in American Painting, 55; Still Life Painting since 1470, 56; El Greco, Rembrandt, Goya, Cezanne, Van Gogh, Picasso, 57; Ralston Crawford, 58; American Painting, 1760, 60;

Masters of Landscape: East and West, 63; Audubon Watercolors and Drawings (with catalog), 65; John Quidor (with catalog), 65-66; Worthington Whittredge Retrospective (with catalog), 69. Pos: Cur Am art, Cincinnati Art Mus, 54-55; dir, Milwaukee Art Ctr & cur, Layton Col, 55-62; dir, Mus Art, Munson-Williams-Proctor Inst, 62- Awards: Ford Found Humanities & the Arts Prog fel for res on J J Audubon, 61; Nat Endowment Arts fel; Mus Prof fel for res on J J Audubon, 75. Mem: Asn Art Mus Dirs. Publ: Auth, Raphaelle Peale, The Peale Collection of the Maryland Hist Soc, Baltimore, 75. Mailing Add: Munson-Williams-Proctor Inst 310 Genesee St Utica NY 13502

DWORZAN, GEORGE R
PAINTER, SCULPTOR
b New York, NY, Mar 28, 24. Study: Cooper Union, with Morris Cantor; Art Students League, with Harry Sternberg; Acad Grande Chaumiere, Paris, France; Acad Leger, Paris, with Fernand Leger. Work: NY Univ; Chase Manhattan Bank, New York; Univ Mass, Amherst; Ohio State Univ; Herron Mus Art, Indianapolis, Ind. Exhib: Salon Realities Nouvelles, Mus Art Mod, Paris, 48-49; Art USA, Coliseum, NY, 59; Nat Print Competition, AAA Gallery, New York, 60; Contemp Arts Soc Ann, Herron Mus, 64 & 68; Univ NC Ann, Chapel Hill, 68. Teaching: Instr painting & drawing, NY Univ. Media: Oils on Canvas, Wood. Dealer: East Hampton Gallery 305 W 28th St New York NY 10025. Mailing Add: 17 Bleecker St New York NY 10012

DWYER, EUGENE JOSEPH
ART HISTORIAN
b Buffalo, NY, Sept 14, 43. Study: Harvard Univ, BA(classics cum laude); NY Univ Inst Fine Arts, MA, 67, PhD, 74. Teaching: Asst prof art hist & chmn art dept, Kenyon Col, Gambier, Ohio, 73- Awards: Tatiana Warsher Award for the Archaeol of Pompeii, Herculaneum & Stabia, Am Acad Rome, 73-74. Mem: Col Art Asn Am; Archaeol Inst Am; Am Numismatic Soc; Pompeiana Inc (acad adv bd); Amici di Pompei. Res: Greek and Roman art and classical tradition. Publ: An Alexander-Macedonia Contorniate, Am Numismatic Soc Mus Notes, 68; The Subject of Durer's Four Witches, Art Quart, 71; A Note on Mantegna's Virtus Combusta, Marsyas, 72; Augustus & the Capricorn, Roemische Mitteilungen, 73; Narrative & Allegory in a Coptic Tapestry, Am J Archaeol, 74. Mailing Add: Art Dept Kenyon Col Gambier OH 43022

DWYER, JAMES EUGENE
PAINTER, EDUCATOR
b Tulsa, Okla, Oct 24, 21. Study: Art Inst Chicago, BFA, 47; Acad Grande Chaumiere, Paris, 47-48; Syracuse Univ, MFA, 50; Univ Chicago; De Paul Univ; study with Boris Anisfeld. Work: Everson Mus, Syracuse, NY; Munson, Williams, Proctor Inst, Utica, NY: State Univ NY; Syracuse Univ, NY; Ashland Col, Ohio. Comn: 3100 sq ft mural decoration, Onondaga Co Civic Ctr, Syracuse, NY, 76. Exhib: Art Inst Chicago, 47; Up-State Regional Shows, Binghamton, Rochester, Syracuse & Utica, NY, 50-70; Metrop Mus Art, New York, 51; City Ctr Gallery, New York, 55; Silvermine Guild Artists Conn, 56; Univ Maine, Portland-Gorham, 74; Lubin House, New York, 77. Teaching: Prof painting & drawing, Syracuse Univ, NY, 49- Style & Technique: Abstract acrylic. Mailing Add: 223 DeForest Rd Syracuse NY 13214

DWYER, MELVA JEAN
ART LIBRARIAN, ART HISTORIAN
b Kamloops, BC, Oct 29, 19. Study: Univ BC, BA, 42, MA, 61; Univ Toronto, BLS, 53. Teaching: Hon lectr fine arts bibliog & res methods, Univ BC, Vancouver, 67- Pos: Head librn fine arts div, Univ BC, Vancouver, 53- Mem: Can Art Libr Sect Can (chairperson, 70-78); Univ Art Asn Can; Art Libr Soc NAm. Res: A study of the enclosed choir in Norfolk churches. Interest: Medieval architecture and art; art bibliography and acquisitions. Mailing Add: 603-2233 Allison Rd Vancouver BC V6T 1T7 Can

DYCK, PAUL
PAINTER, ART DIRECTOR
b Chicago, Ill, Aug 17, 17. Study: With Johann Von Skramlik, Florence, Italy, Prague, Czech, Rome, Italy & Paris, France, 26-33. Work: Phoenix Art Mus, Ariz; Mus Northern Ariz, Flagstaff; Franklin Inst, Philadelphia; Whitney Gallery of Western Art, Cody, Wyo; plus pvt collections in US, Can & Europe. Comn: Indians of the Overland Trail (painting), sponsored by pub mus, 56; Flame of Man (painting), F O Hess, Franklin Inst, Philadelphia, 70. Exhib: One-man exhibs, Southwest Mus, Los Angeles, Calif, Mont Hist Soc, Helena, Chicago Mus Nat Hist, Phoenix Art Mus & Ariz State Univ Mus, plus others, 54- Teaching: Lectr, Am Indian cult. Pos: Dir, Paul Dyck Res Found Am Indian Cult. Awards: Artist Commendation, US Navy, 45. Mem: Life mem Buffalo Bill Hist Ctr, Cody, Wyo; Manuscript Soc; Appraisers Asn Am. Style & Technique: 14th century Florentine technique; egg tempera and oil glaze. Media: Oil. Publ: Auth, Brule, Sioux People of the Rosebud, 69; contribr, articles in Montana, Mag of Western Hist, 72; contribr, articles in Buffalo Bill Hist Ctr, 72. Mailing Add: PO Box 217 Rimrock AZ 86335

DYER, CAROLYN PRICE
ART CRITIC, TAPESTRY ARTIST
b Seattle, Wash, Dec 19, 31. Study: Univ Wash, Seattle; Mills Col, Oakland, Calif, BA, 53, MA, 55, with Alfred Neumeyer, Ilse Schultz Hiller. Comn: Tapestries, Magic Garden, Intermountain Gas Co, Boise, Idaho, 65, The Fullness Thereof..., comn by Daniel Healy, Pasadena, Calif, 75, The Quiet..., comn by Edward Sowers, Beverly Hills, 75, Noon Meadow, Weatherite, Los Angeles, 75 & Moon Clearing, comn by Mary Blaylock, Pasadena, 78. Exhib: NW Craftsmen's Exhib, Henry Gallery, Univ Wash, Seattle, 58-64; Media 68, Walnut Creek, 68; Tapestry West, Laguna Beach Mus Art, Calif, 72; Southern Calif Designer Crafts, Galeria del Sol, Santa Barbara, Calif, 76; two-person show, Craft & Folk Art Mus, Los Angeles, 68. Collections Arranged: Fiber Expressions (curated), Jewish Community Ctr, Long Beach, Calif, 76. Teaching: Instr art hist, Los Angeles Trade/Tech Col, 69-76. Pos: Critic, Artweek, Oakland, Calif, 76- & Fiberarts, Albuquerque, NMex, 77-; columnist critic, Visual Dialog, Los Altos, Calif, 77- & Follies, Pasadena, 77- Awards: Textiles/Tapestries Awards, NW Craftsmen's Exhib, Seattle, 64 & Pac NW Arts & Crafts Exhib, Bellevue, Wash, 68. Bibliog: Judy Haddad (auth), Carolyn Dyer, Tapestries (videotape), Pasadena City Col, 76; Maria Bishop (auth), Fiber workspaces: in a room of your own, Fiberarts, 77. Mem: Southern Calif Designer-Crafts Inc; Am Crafts Coun; World Crafts Coun; Pasadena Arts Coun (trustee, 77-78); Int Guild of Craft Journalists, Authors & Photogr. Style & Technique: Wall hung tapestry, designed and handwoven on loom in wool and silk; subjects are abstract landscapes or non-objective forms. Media: Handspun Natural Colored or Artist-Dyed Wools & Silks. Res: Contemporary American fiber artists, historical and ethnic textiles. Publ: Illusr, The road to good health, Yakima Valley Home Economists, 64; contribr, Craft Horizons, NW Crafts Exhib & Am Crafts, 6/65; contribr, Wall Hangings, Davis, 71; contribr, The Goodfellow Catalogue of Wonderful Things, Berkeley Windhover, 77. Mailing Add: 28 N Marengo Pasadena CA 91101

DYSON, JOHN HOLROYD
PAINTER
b Folkestone Co, Kent, Eng, Jan 10, 10; Can citizen. Study: Heatherley Sch Art, London, Eng; Vancouver Sch Art, BC, Can; study under Algernon Newton in London & Jack Shadbolt in Vancouver. Work: Numerous pvt collections. Comn: Bethlehem Copper Mine, Bethlehem Copper Corp, Ashcroft, BC, 67 & 68; two Western Mines, Western Mines Ltd, Vancouver, BC, Can, 69. Exhib: Summer Exhibs, Royal Cambrian Acad, Caernarvon, NWales, 55, Royal Acad, London, Eng, 55 & Royal Birmingham Soc Artists, Eng, 55; group exhibs, Cariboo Art Soc, Williams Lake, BC, Can, 58-68 & Vancouver Art Gallery, 60-69; one-man shows, in Vancouver at Danish Art Gallery, Alexander G Harrison Galleries & Alex Fraser Galleries, 60-70 & Pub Libr, Kelowna, BC, Can, 64; Prince George Art Gallery, BC, Can, 70-77. Bibliog: Art critic (auth), Salon Birmingham, La Revue Mod, Paris, 10/55; Eric Green (auth), Valemount Artist Has Ties With Chilcotin, Williams Lake Tribune, BC, 8/76. Mem: Cariboo Art Soc, Williams Lake, BC; Fedn Can Artists. Style & Technique: Landscapes in oil; still life oil paintings; brush and palette knife technique. Media: Oil. Dealer: Peder Bertelsen The Danish Art Gallery 3757 W Tenth Ave Vancouver BC Can. Mailing Add: Box 21 Valemount BC V0E 2Z0 Can

DZIGURSKI, ALEX
PAINTER
b Stari Becej, Vojvodlina, Yugoslavia, May 15, 11; US citizen. Study: Sch of Art, Belgrade, Yugoslavia; Acad Art, Munich, Ger. Work: Boston Mus of Fine Arts; Norton Gallery, Shreveport, La; Franklin Mint Am Art, Pa; Okla Art Ctr, Oklahoma City; Belgrade Art Mus, Yugoslavia. Comn: Altars in Serbian churches, Cleveland, Ohio, 52, Aliquippa, Pa, 55 & Canton, Ohio, 56; interior church & altar, St Sava Serbian Church, Milwaukee, Wis, 58; altar in Serbian church, Kansas City, Kans, 59. Exhib: Rome, Italy, 49; Soc Western Artists Exhib, De Young Mus, San Francisco, 72 & 73; Findlay Galleries, Chicago, Ill, 74. Teaching: Prof art, Padova, Italy, 47-48. Awards: Gold Medal, Biennale Venice, Italy, 48; First Prize, Popular, Soc Western Artists, De Young Mus, San Francisco, 65; Gold Medal, Franklin Mint Bicentennial, Pa, 73. Mem: Prof League Am Artists; Soc Western Artists; fel Fine Art Inst, Los Angeles. Style & Technique: Oil seascapes and landscapes; brush and palette knife. Media: Oil. Dealer: Findlay Galleries 814 N Michigan Chicago IL 60611. Mailing Add: PO Box 4119 Blossom Valley Sta Mountain View CA 94040

DZUBAS, FRIEDEL
PAINTER
b Berlin, Ger, Apr 20, 15; US citizen. Work: Solomon R Guggenheim Mus, New York; Boston Mus Fine Arts, Mass; Metrop Mus Art; Mus Fine Arts, Houston; Hirschhorn Mus. Comn: Nat Shawmut Bank, Boston, 75. Exhib: Color and Field, Albright-Knox Gallery, Cleveland Mus & Dayton Art Inst, 70-71; Abstract Painting in the 70's, Boston Mus Fine Arts, 72; one-man shows, Mus Fine Arts, Houston, 74 & Boston Mus Fine Arts, 75; 34th Biennial, Corcoran Gallery, Washington, DC, 75; plus others. Teaching: Artist in residence, Dartmouth Col, 62; vis artist critic, Inst Humanistic Studies, 65-66; vis artist critic, Univ Pa, 68-69; vis artist critic, Cornell Univ, 69- Awards: Guggenheim Fel, 66 & 68; Nat Coun on Arts Award, 68. Bibliog: John Elderfield (auth), Abstraction in the 70's, summer 72 & Kenworth Moffett (auth), Recent paintings by Friedel Dzubas, 5/75, Art Int; Roald Nasgaard (auth), Friedel Dzubas, Arts Mag, 5/75; plus others. Media: Acrylic; Oil. Publ: Auth, Statement & color plate, Art in Am, 67 & Art Now, 72. Dealer: Knoedler Contemporary Art 19 E 70th New York NY 10021; David Mirvish Gallery 596 Markham St Toronto ON Can. Mailing Add: Lakeville CT 06039

E

EADES, LUIS ERIC
PAINTER, EDUCATOR
b Madrid, Spain, June 25, 23; US citizen. Study: Bath Sch Art, Eng; Slade Sch, Univ London; Inst Polytech Nac, Mexico City, Mex; Univ Ky, Lexington, BA. Work: Whitney Mus Am Art, New York; Mus Fine Arts, Houston; Dallas Mus Fine Arts; Ft Worth Art Ctr; Mus Fine Arts, Holyoke, Mass. Comn: Airport mural, Govt Honduras, Toncontin, Tegucigalpa, 48. Exhib: Recent Painting USA: The Figure, Mus Mod Art, New York, 62; Forty Artists Under Forty, Whitney Mus Am Art, 62; State of Man, New Sch Social Res, New York, 64; 2nd Intermountain Biennial Exhib, Salt Lake Art Ctr, Utah, 65; Colorado Springs Fine Arts Ctr, 69. Teaching: Prof painting & drawing, Univ Tex, 54-60; prof painting & drawing, Univ Colo, 61- Media: Oil, Acrylic. Publ: Illusr, The Precipice, Univ Tex, 69. Dealer: Carlin Galleries 710 Montgomery Fort Worth TX 76107. Mailing Add: 1627 Fifth St Boulder CO 80302

EAGERTON, MARI M
See Mari

EAGERTON, ROBERT PIERCE
PRINTMAKER, PAINTER
b Florence, SC, Mar 17, 40. Study: Atlanta Sch Art, BFA; Acad Fine Arts, Vienna, Austria; Cranbrook Acad Art, Bloomfield Hills, Mich. Work: Nat Collection Fine Art, Smithsonian Inst, Washington, DC; Art Inst Chicago Mus; Lessing J Rosenwald Collection, Jenkintown, Pa; Sheldon Swope Gallery Art; Norman McKenzie Mus Art, Regina, Sask. Exhib: Biennale Int l'Estampe, Paris, France, 70; Contemporary American Prints, Krannert Mus, Univ Ill, 71; Lithographs de la Collection Mourlot, PR, 71; one-man show, Norman McKenzie Mus Art; Prints: USA 1974, Univ Pittsburgh; plus others. Teaching: Assoc prof lithography, Herron Sch Art, Ind Univ-Purdue Univ, Indianapolis, 66-, head dept printmaking, 69-; guest artist printmaking, Univ Ill, Champaign, 70; vis prof printmaking, Tyler Sch Art, summer 72; guest artist, Emma Lake Workshop, Regina. Pos: Co-founder, Transfigurations Press, Sarasota, Fla, 64-66; owner, Cloud Race Press. Awards: Southeastern Arts Grant, Atlanta Arts Comn, 65; First Prize, 59th Ann Ind Print Exhib, Indianapolis Mus, 68; Res Grant, Ind Univ, 70. Dealer: Associated American Artists Gallery 663 Fifth Ave New York NY 10022. Mailing Add: 4004 Arthington Blvd Indianapolis IN 46226

EAGLEBOY, WAYNE
PAINTER, CRAFTSMAN
b Feb 22, 46; US citizen. Study: Fine Arts Prog, Univ NMex, with sculptor Charles Mattox; extensively self-educated. Work: Red Cloud Permanent Collection, Holy Rosary Mission, Pine Ridge, SDak; Heard Mus, Phoenix, Ariz; US Dept of Interior Collection, Sioux Mus, Rapid City, SDak. Exhib: New Worlds in Indian Art, Bowers Mus, Santa Ana, Calif, 71; Scottsdale Indian Arts & Crafts Nat, Ariz, 71; Red Cloud Indian Art Show, Holy Rosary Mission, Pine Ridge, SDak, 71-73; Invitational 74, Heard Mus, Phoenix, Ariz, 74; The Am

Indian-The Am Flag, Mus Contemp Crafts, Flint Inst Arts, Milwaukee Art Ctr, Wis, 76, Houston Mus Natural Sci, 77 & Heard Mus, 77. Awards: Second Place Acrylics & Water-base Media, Red Cloud Indian Art Show, 71 & First Place Acrylics & Water-base Media, 72. Bibliog: Lloyd E Oxendine (auth), 23 Contemp Indian Artists, Art in Am, 72; Ann Patterson (auth), Heard Museum: Invitational 74, Ariz Living, 73; Richard A Pohrt (auth), Observations on the Flag Motif in Indian Art, The Am Indian-The Am Flag, 75. Style & Technique: Acrylic glaze transparency in combination with canvas and stretched rawhide, such as that from buffalo, elk and deer. Media: Acrylic; pencil; feather work (fans, dance bustles and similar items). Mailing Add: 355 Lakeview Sandia Park NM 87047

EAMES, JOHN HEAGAN
ETCHER, PAINTER
b Lowell, Mass, July 19, 00. Study: Harvard Univ, AB, 22; Royal Col Art, with Malcolm Osborne & Robert Austin, 33, 35 & 37. Work: Metrop Mus Art, New York; Libr of Cong, Washington, DC; Albany Inst Hist & Art, NY. Exhib: Royal Acad, London, Eng, 35, 37 & 40; New York World's Fair, 39; Int Print Exhib, Art Inst Chicago, 39; Biennial Exhib, Venice, Italy, 40; Contemp Am Drawings, Metrop Mus Art, New York, 42 & 52. Awards: Kate W Arms Mem Prize, Soc Am Graphic Artists, 52, 54 & 57, John Taylor Arms Prize, 53, Henry B Shope Prize, 57. Mem: Soc Am Graphic Artists; Nat Acad Design; Royal Soc Painters-Etchers, London, Eng. Style & Technique: Representational. Mailing Add: Boothbay Harbor ME 04538

EARL, JACK EUGENE
SCULPTOR
b Uniapolis, Ohio, Aug 2, 34. Study: Bluffton Col, BA; Ohio State Univ, MA. Work: Butler Mus Art, Youngstown, Ohio; Columbus Gallery Fine Arts, Ohio; Butler Mus of Art, Youngstown, Ohio; Everson Mus of Art, Syracuse, NY; Mus of Contemp Crafts, New York, NY; Emerson Art Ctr, Syracuse, NY. Comn: Mural, Kohler Co, Kohler, Wis, 76. Exhib: Toledo Mus Art, Ohio, 68; Objects USA, Smithsonian Inst, Washington, DC, 69; Mus Contemp Crafts, New York, 71, 72 & Clay Works by 20 Americans, 72; Ft Wayne Mus Art, Ind, 71; Int Exhib Ceramics, Victoria & Albert Mus Art, London, Eng, 72; First World Crafts Exhib, Toronto, Ont, 74; Clay Things, Whitney Mus of Am Art, New York, 74; The Object as Poet, Renwick Gallery, Washington, DC, 76. Collections Arranged: Ojbects USA, 68; The Plastic Earth, John Michael Kohler Arts Ctr, Sheboygan, Wis; Decade of Ceramic Art, San Francisco Mus of Art, Calif, 73. Teaching: Instr ceramics, Toledo Mus Art, 63-72; from asst prof to assoc prof ceramics, Va Commonwealth Univ, 72-77. Awards: Nat Coun Educ Ceramic Arts Prize, Emerson Art Ctr, 68; Merit Award, Louisville Art Ctr, 68-70; Purchase Award, Columbus Gallery Fine Arts, 72. Bibliog: Down Home, Arts in Va, 74; Art in industry, Crafts Horizon, 74. Mem: Nat Coun Educ Ceramic Arts. Style & Technique: Porcelain sculpture. Media: Ceramic. Dealer: Theo Portnoy Gallery New York NY. Mailing Add: Lakeview OH 43331

EASLEY, LOYCE ROGERS
PAINTER, CERAMIST
b Weatherford, Okla, June 28, 18. Study: Univ Okla, BFA; Eastern NMex Univ; Art Students League; also with Frederic Taubes. Work: US Air Force Acad, Colorado Springs; Mus NMex, Santa Fe; WTex Mus, Tex Tech Univ; Roswell Mus Art, NMex; Southwest Tex State Col. Comn: Many portrait & easel painting commissions. Exhib: Bon Marche Gallery, Seattle, Wash, 64; Nat Exhib, The Gallery, Ft Lauderdale, Fla, 64; 51st Allied Artists Am Ann Exhib, 65; Brigham Young Univ, 70; NMex Mus Painting Show, 71; plus others. Awards: First Award, 48th Fiesta Exhib, Mus NMex, 61; Distinguished Former Student, Univ Okla, 63; Llano Estacado Art Asn Ann First Prize in Painting, 72; plus others. Bibliog: Montez (auth), New Mexico artist, NMex Mag, 63; Wendes (auth), article in New Mexican, 71; Margaret Harold (auth), Prize Winning Paintings. Mem: Hon mem NMex Art League. Style & Technique: Semi-abstract with emphasis on structure, paint quality and color. Media: Oil. Dealer: Ojo de Sol 612 N Oregon El Paso TX 79901. Mailing Add: 812 N Dal Paso Hobbs NM 88240

EAST, N S, JR
DESIGNER, SCULPTOR
b Delaware Co, Pa, Mar 21, 36. Study: Philadelphia Col Art, 62-65; also with Herman Cohen. Work: Glassboro Col, NJ; Univ City Arts League, Philadelphia; Philadelphia Bd Educ, Tilden Jr High Sch; Bell Tel Co, Philadelphia. Exhib: One-man shows, Color 65, Allentown, Pa, 65 & Antonio Souza Gallery, Mexico City, Mex, 69; Sculpture 68, Grabar Gallery, Philadelphia, 68; Nat Forum Prof Artists, Philadelphia, 68-72; two-man show, Wood-Type Workshop, 72; Oh-Ho, Franklin Inst Symmetry Exhib, 75. Teaching: Instr AV art, Philadelphia Sch Syst, 65-67; instr lang of art, Bell Tel Co & Univ City Arts League, 67-70; instr welding, Univ City Arts League, 70-73; prof art, Glassboro State Col, 75- Pos: Pres, NE:Design Consults, 70-; owner ornamental iron studio, The Iron Men; partner, Apollo Light Labs; founder, 5000 Willows Design Ctr, 77- Mem: Univ City Arts League (vpres, 65-66); Nat Forum Prof Artists (bd mem); Philadelphia Mus Art; Smithsonian Mus; New York Mus Nat Hist; plus others. Style & Technique: Assemblage of pre-used metal objects into an aesthetic order; organization of somatic elements of art using design principles to form new, dynamic, multi-dimensional concepts; exploring symmetry via design. Publ: Auth, The Language of Art/Toward Another Bauhaus, 67; auth, Beachhead of the stars, Apollo Mission, 69; auth, Design and the Social Dimension, 69; auth, The Combined Graphics Department, 70; auth, The City of '76, Philadelphia Bicentennial. Mailing Add: 4820 Chester Ave Philadelphia PA 19143

EASTERWOOD, HENRY LEWIS
EDUCATOR, TAPESTRY ARTIST
b Villa Rica, Ga, Oct 29, 34. Study: West Ga Col, 53-55; Memphis Acad Arts, BFA, 58, spec studies in Europe & Scandinavia, 65. Work: Brooks Mem Gallery Art, Memphis; Miss Art Asn, Jackson; State of Tenn Collection of Crafts, Nashville; Fall Creek Falls State Park, Tenn. Comn: Seven tapestries, Virgin Gorda, Virgin Islands, 66; three panel triptych, Mayo Clin, Rochester, Minn, 70; two tapestries, Tupperware Int, Orlando, Fla, 71; tapestry, Vanderbilt Univ, 74; four tapestries, Memphis Mem Gardens, 74. Exhib: Fiber, Clay & Metal, St Paul Mus, Minn, 59, 61 & 63; Craftsmen USA, Mus Contemp Crafts, New York, 66; Miss Art Asn, 72. Teaching: Assoc prof textiles & chmn dept, Memphis Acad Arts, 59- Pos: Craft adv, Tenn Arts Comn, 70. Awards: Textile Award, Miss River Crafts Award, 65, 67 & 69; Nat Merit Award, Am Craftsmen's Coun, 66; Am Inst Archit Gold Medal, 69. Mem: Am Craftsmen's Coun (Tenn rep, 63-65); Tenn Craftsmen's Asn; hon mem Memphis Weavers Guild. Style & Technique: Woven tapestries, abstract expressionistic in style using varied techniques. Dealer: Fairweather Hardin Gallery 101 E Ontario St Chicago IL 60611. Mailing Add: 694 N Trezevant Memphis TN 38112

EASTMAN, GENE M
PAINTER, ART ADMINISTRATOR
b Council Grove, Kans, Jan 1, 26. Study: Univ Kans, BFA; Art Inst Chicago; Univ Iowa, MFA with Stuart Edie. Exhib: Houston Mus Fine Arts, Tex, 58 & 61; Dallas Mus Fine Arts Ann, 59, 63 & 66; Seven States Artists Ann, Delgado Mus, New Orleans, 61; Watercolor USA, Springfield, Mo, 64; 24-64 Nat Exhib Small Paintings, Purdue Univ, 64. Teaching: Prof drawing & painting, Sam Houston State Univ, 58-, chmn art dept, 72-; guest instr drawing & painting, Mus Fine Arts Sch, Houston Mus Fine Arts, Tex, 68-70. Awards: First Prize, Painting, Tex Fine Arts Asn, 58; Purchase Award, Okla Printmaker Soc, 64; First Prize, Painting, Tri-State Exhib, Beaumont Mus, Tex, 67. Style & Technique: Figurative. Media: Oil; watercolor. Mailing Add: Rte 6 Box 468 Huntsville TX 77340

EASTMAN, JOHN, JR
ART ADMINISTRATOR
b Wellesley Hills, Mass, Jan 10, 16. Study: Univ DiJon. Pos: Exec vpres, Skowhegan Sch Painting & Sculpture, Maine & New York City, 63- Mailing Add: 329 E 68th St New York NY 10021

EATON, THOMAS NEWTON
CARTOONIST, ILLUSTRATOR
b Wichita, Kans, Mar 2, 40. Study: Univ Denver, 58; Univ Kans, BFA, 62. Comn: Mag covers, Jr Scholastic, 3/20/75 & Jack & Jill, 5/78; posters, Scholastic Mag Inc, 74-76; plus others. Pos: Artist/writer contemp cards dept, Hallmark Cards, Inc, Kansas City, Mo, 62-66; art ed, Scholastic Mag Inc, New York, 66-68; free lance cartoonist/writer, 68- Awards: Cert of Excellence for Cover, Catch the Eye, 75, Am Inst Graphics Arts. Bibliog: Eleanor Van Zandt (auth), A cartoonist looks at the comics, Practical Eng Mag, 68. Style & Technique: Cartoon illustration in line work; black and white, some color. Media: Pen & Ink. Publ: Auth & illusr, Chicken-Fried Fudge & Other Cartoon Delights, 70, Captain Ecology, Pollution Fighter, 73, Otis G Firefly's Phantasmagoric Almanac, 74 & Tom Eaton's Book of Marvels, 76, Scholastic Bk Serv; auth & illusr, Flap, Delacorte Press, 72; plus numerous others. Mailing Add: 911 W 100th St Kansas City MO 64114

EBERMAN, EDWIN
ART ADMINISTRATOR, EDUCATOR
b Black Mountain, NC, Feb 20, 05. Study: Carnegie-Mellon Col Fine Arts, BA. Teaching: Dir educ, painting, illustrating & cartooning, Famous Artists Schs, 48-65. Pos: Art dir, Arts & Decorative Mag, 33-35; art dir, McCalls Mag, 36-38; art dir, Look Mag, 41-46; dir & co-founder, Famous Artists Schs, 47-65. Publ: Co-auth, Techniques of the Picture Story, 45; auth, Nantucket Sketchbook, 46; co-auth, numerous textbooks for Famous Artists Sch, 48-65. Mailing Add: 370 Wahackme Rd New Canaan CT 06840

EBIE, WILLIAM DENNIS
ART ADMINISTRATOR, PAINTER
b Akron, Ohio, Feb 7, 42. Study: Akron Art Inst Sch Design, scholar, 60, Univ Akron & Akron Art Inst Sch Design, BFA, 64; Calif Col Arts & Crafts, scholarships, 67-68, MFA, 68. Work: Calif Col Arts & Crafts Gallery. Exhib: Two-man show, Fla A&M Univ Art Gallery, 70; Five States Art Exhib, Port Arthur, Tex, 71; Four Corner States Biennial, Phoenix, Ariz, 71; Roswell Mus/Juarez Mus Exchange Exhib, Mus de Arte y Historia de Cuidad Juarez, Mex, 73; Arts From Roswell, NMex Arts Comn Gallery, Santa Fe, 74. Teaching: Instr painting, Fla A&M Univ, 69-70; instr painting, Roswell Mus Adult Educ, NMex, 71- Pos: Ceramic specialist, Peace Corps, Cuzco, Peru, 64-66; graphic artist, Alameda Co Health Dept, Oakland, Calif, 67-68; asst dir, Roswell Mus & Art Ctr & managing dir, Roswell Mus Artist in Residence Prog, 71- Style & Technique: Figurative approach to the female form with oils and charcoal, applied with knife and brush. Mailing Add: Rte 1 Box 244 A Roswell NM 88201

EBSEN, ALF K
DESIGNER
b Berlin, Ger, July 29, 08; Can citizen. Study: Kunstgewerbeschule, Hamburg, Ger, 2 yrs. Comn: Honour scrolls, IBM Can, 72-78; honour scrolls, STELCO, 72 & 74; design of advert, Volkswagen AG, Ger; Mem Plaque, Windsor Libr, Ont; handwritten menus for restaurants; Medieval Studies Advertising, Univ Toronto. Exhib: Continual exhibs in Toronto Librs, 69- Teaching: Instr design with handwriting, High Schs, 68- Pos: Dir graphic arts, Eddy Match Co, Ontario, 55-63. Mem: Handwriters Guild of Toronto (founder, 76); Royal Can Acad Arts. Style & Technique: Handwriting with hard-nibbed tool in all historical styles, designing of new alphabets. Media: Paper, Vellum. Mailing Add: 60 Logandale Rd Willowdale ON Can

ECKE, BETTY TSENG YU-HO
PAINTER, ART HISTORIAN
b Peking, China, Nov 29, 23; US citizen. Study: Fu-jen Univ, Peking, BA, 42; Univ Hawaii, MA, 66; Inst Fine Arts, NY Univ, PhD, 72. Work: Honolulu Acad Arts, Hawaii; Walker Art Ctr, Minneapolis; Nat Mus Mod Art, Stockholm, Sweden; Mus Cernuschi, Paris, France; Stanford Art Gallery, Calif. Comn: Mural, St Katherine's Church, Kaui, Hawaii, 57; mural, Manoa Chinese Pavilion, Honolulu, 68; mural, Golden West Savings & Loan, San Francisco, Calif, 64; wall painting, Castle & Cooke Co, Ltd, Honolulu, 68; wall painting, Honolulu Int Airport, 72. Exhib: Contemporary American Painting & Sculpture, Univ Ill, Urbana, 58, 61 & 65; Carnegie Inst Painting & Sculpture Int, Pittsburgh, Pa, 61 & 65; Kunstverein, Munich & Frankfurt, Ger; Walker Art Ctr; San Francisco Mus Art, Calif; plus others. Teaching: Instr studio art, Honolulu Acad Art, 50-63, consult Chinese art, 53-; assoc prof Chinese art hist, Univ Hawaii, 63-66; Fulbright visitor Chinese art hist, Acad Bildenden Künste & Univ, 66-67; prog chmn art hist, Univ Hawaii, 71-, prof art, 73- Awards: Am Artists of the Western States Award, Stanford Art Gallery; NY Univ Founders Day Award for Outstanding Scholarship, 72. Bibliog: Rev of exhib at Downtown Gallery, New York, in Time Mag, 1/19/62; Seldis (auth), Pacific heritage, Art in Am, 65; plus others. Mem: Honolulu Acad Art; Am Col Art Asn; Asian Soc; Asian & Pacific Art Asn Hawaii (organizer, 72). Media: Watercolor, Collage, Plexiglas. Res: Chinese art; some contemporary elements in Chinese classic pictorial art; Chinese calligraphy; folk art. Publ: Contribr, four articles, Studies of 16th Century Chinese Artists, 54-63; contribr, Encyclopedia World Art, Rome, 64; auth, Some Contemporary Elements on Chinese Classic Pictorial Art, 65 & 71; illusr, The Analects of Confucious, 70; auth, Chinese Calligraphy. Mailing Add: 3460 Kaohinani Dr Honolulu HI 96817

ECKELBERRY, DON RICHARD
PAINTER
b Sebring, Ohio, July 6, 21. Study: Cleveland Inst Art. Comn: Bird postage stamp, British Honduras, 62; murals, Adirondack Mus, 60. Exhib: One-man shows, New York, 43, 46 & 56 & Louisville, Ky, 70; Cleveland Inst Art, 70. Pos: Staff artist, Nat Audubon Soc, 43-45; free lance artist, 45-; art dir, Frame House Gallery; patron, Asa Wright Nature Ctr, Trinidad. Mem: Fel Am Ornithol Union; Audubon Soc; Cooper Ornithol Soc; Soc Animal Artists;

Wilson Ornithol Soc. Publ: Illusr 14 books, 46- Mailing Add: 180 Woodsome Rd Babylon NY 11702

ECKERSLEY, THOMAS CYRIL
PHOTOGRAPHER, EDUCATOR
b Detroit, Mich, Nov 23, 41. Study: Ohio Univ, with Clarence White, Jr, BFA, 66, MFA, 69. Work: Erie Art Ctr, Pa; Creative Eye Photo Gallery, Calif. Exhib: FocusErie Nat Photog Exhib, Pa, 73; 15th 16th & 19th, Sidney Int Exhib Photog, Australia; New Photographics/74, Washington; Des Moines Int Salon Photog, Iowa, 74; one-man show, Cayuga Mus Hist & Art, NY, 74, Rome Art Ctr, New York, 75; Everson Mus of Art, New York, 76; Americana Photo Postcard, Calif, 75 & 76; Lander Col, SC, 75; Cent Pa Festival of the Arts, 76; 2nd St Gallery Nat, Va, 76; NW Community Col, Wyo, 76; Refocus, Iowa, 77; Button-Button (travelling exhib), New York, 77; 10th Biennial Nat, 2nd Crossing Gallery, NDak, 77; Green Mountain Col, Vt, 77; Calvin Col, Mich, 77; plus others. Teaching: Instr photog, Columbus Col Art & Design, 69-70; assoc prof art & chmn art dept, State Univ NY Col Oswego, 70- Pos: Studio mgr & admin asst, Josten's Am Photog, 67-68; photogr, WOSU-TV, Ohio State Univ, 68-69. Awards: Hon Mention, Des Moines Int, 74; First Prize, Oswego Art Guild, 75. Mem: Soc Photog Educ. Style & Technique: Exploration and arrangement of photographic images into reliefs so spacial relationships are achieved physically as well as through illusion. Publ: Co-auth, Jewelry Making: an Illustrated Guide to Technique, 75. Mailing Add: Box 44 Hannibal NY 13074

ECKERT, LOU
ART DEALER, PAINTER
b Lancaster, Pa, Jan 27, 28. Study: Univ Rochester, with John Mennihan, BA; workshops under Jan Horton, Univ Nebr, Ida Kohlmeyer, Univ New Orleans, Richard Brough, Univ Ala & Stuart Purser, Univ Fla; also with Marie Hull, Jackson, Miss, Andrew Bucci, Washington, DC & other. Work: Miss Art Asn Munic Gallery, Jackson; First Nat Bank (Miss Collection), Jackson; Gtr Gulf Coast Art Asn Collection, Biloxi, Miss. Exhib: Mid-South Ann, Brooks Mem Art Gallery, Memphis, Tenn, 65 & 69; Miss Art Asn Ann Shows, Jackson, 67-70; Gulf Coast Art Exhib, Mobile, Ala, 68; Second Greater New Orleans Nat Exhib, 72; five-man show, Gulf South Galleries, Macomb, Miss, 78; one-man shows, Percy H Whiting Art Ctr, Fairhope, Ala, 69 & New Orleans Theatre for Performing Arts, 77; plus others. Pos: Owner & operator, 22, Ltd Gallery, New Orleans, 73- Awards: First Nat Bank Award (Miss Collection), 67; Grand Hotel Purchase Award, Biloxi, 75. Bibliog: Jan Horton (auth), Art for the Day (film), ETV Ctr, Jackson, 70. Mem: Miss Art Asn, Jackson; New Orleans Art Asn; La Watercolor Soc, New Orleans. Style & Technique: Abstract; minimal landscapes and studies; detailed drawings. Media: Oil, Watercolor. Specialty: Original oils, watercolors, and mixed media; gallery handles; original prints, weavings and pottery; original sculpture and three dimensional work; all works by contemporary, regional artists. Mailing Add: 3631 Post Oak Ave New Orleans LA 70114

ECKERT, WILLIAM DEAN
PAINTER, ART HISTORIAN
b Coshocton, Ohio, Oct 10, 27. Study: Ohio State Univ, BA(with distinction), BFA(cum laude) & MA; Univ Iowa, PhD. Work: Butler Inst Am Art, Youngstown, Ohio; State Hist Soc Mus, Columbia, Mo. Exhib: Mid-Am Regional, Nelson Gallery, Kansas City, 52; Midwest Regional, Joslyn Mus, Omaha, Nebr, 52; Upper Hudson Valley Regional, Albany Art Inst, NY, 66; Quincy Art Ctr Regional, Ill, 74; Mid-South Biennial, Brooks Gallery, Memphis, 75. Teaching: Assoc prof art hist, Western Ill Univ, Macomb, 59-65; assoc prof art hist, Union Col, Schenectady, NY, 65-68; assoc prof art hist, Lindenwood Cols, 68-, chmn art dept, 75- Awards: Award in Painting & Graphics, Akron May Show, 54; First Prize in Graphics, Ohio State Fair Exhib, 56; Third Award in Painting, Quincy Art Ctr Regional, Ill, 71. Mem: Col Art Asn Am; Soc Archit Historians; Midwest Col Art Conf; Mo Col Art Asn. Style & Technique: Hard-edge paintings in an abstract-surrealistic style. Media: Acrylic. Res: Renaissance stage in Italy; evolution of the perspective scene. Publ: Contribr, The college gallery & the liberal arts, Symposium, summer 67. Mailing Add: 620 Yale Blvd St Charles MO 63301

ECKHARDT, FERDINAND
ART HISTORIAN, MUSEUM DIRECTOR
b Vienna, Austria; Can citizen. Study: Univ Vienna; Univ Man, hon LLD, 71. Pos: Dir educ, State Mus, Vienna; dir, Winnipeg Art Gallery, 53-74. Awards: Austrian Cross of Honor for Sci & Art, 72. Mem: Can Mus Asn; Can Art Mus Dirs Asn (past pres); Int Coun Mus, Can; Am Asn Art Mus Dirs. Mailing Add: 54 Harrow St Winnipeg MB R3M 2Y7 Can

ECKMAIR, FRANK C
PRINTMAKER
b Norwich, NY, June 21, 30. Study: Whitney Sch Art, New Haven, Conn, 48; State Univ NY Col Oneonta, 50; State Univ Iowa, with M Lasansky & Warshaw, 50-53, BA, 53; Ohio Univ, MFA, 62; State Univ NY Col Buffalo, fac fels, 68, 71 & 72. Work: Metrop Mus Art, New York; Libr Cong, Washington, DC; Smithsonian Inst, Washington, DC; Philadelphia Mus Art, Pa; New York Pub Libr. Comn: Editions of woodcuts, Roten Galleries, Baltimore, 63-73 & Assoc Am Artists, New York, 64-72. Exhib: Northwest Printmakers Int, Seattle, Wash, 61; Philadelphia Print Club Invitational Int, Philadelphia, 62; Five American Printmakers, Ball State Univ Invitational, Ind, 66; Libr Cong Nat Print Exhib, 67; Big Prints, State Univ NY Albany, 68. Teaching: Prof printmaking, State Univ NY Col Buffalo. Pos: Dir gallery, State Univ NY Col Buffalo, 63-65; pres, TAROT Designing & Printing, Buffalo, 69- Awards: First Prize for Graphics, 180 Exhib, Huntington, WVa, 61; Hon Mention, Silvermine Print Exhib, Conn, 63; First Prize for Graphics, Cooperstown Art Asn, NY, 66; three NY fac res fels & NY State Bicentennial grant for portfolio of prints. Mem: Patteran, Buffalo, NY; Cooperstown Art Asn (exhib chmn, 72); Col Art Asn. Style & Technique: Relief printmaking and papermaking. Publ: Auth, Relief Printmaking-An Outline, 69; contribr, A Pride of Rabbis (portfolio), 71; ed, Centennial 1971 (portfolio), State Univ NY Col Buffalo, 71; contribr, Witches of Salem (portfolio), 72; auth, Printmakers 73 (portfolio), State Univ Col at Buffalo, 73; auth, Options for Printmaking, Gallery Asn of NY. Dealer: Associated American Artists 663 Fifth Ave New York NY 10022. Mailing Add: 2 Green St Gilbertsville NY 13776

ECKSTEIN, JOANNA
COLLECTOR, PATRON
b Seattle, Wash, July 28, 03. Study: Goucher Col, BA. Pos: Cur, USIA Exhib Am Paintings & Sculpture, Eng & France, 57-58; trustee & docent, Seattle Art Mus. Collection: Contemporary paintings. Mailing Add: 802 33rd St E Seattle WA 98112

ECKSTEIN, RUTH
PRINTMAKER, PAINTER
b Nuremberg, WGer, May 11, 16; US citizen. Study: New Sch Social Res, New York, with Stuart Davis; Art Students League, with Harry Sternberg, Julian Levy & V Vitlacyl; Pratt Graphic Ctr, New York, with Seong Moy & Roberto Delamonica. Work: Philadelphia Mus Art; Brooklyn Mus; Israel Mus, Jerusalem; Univ Mass, Amherst; US Info Agency, Graphic Arts Proj. Exhib: Prints & Watercolors, Pa Acad Fine Arts, Philadelphia, 59, 64 & 65; Nat Print Exhib, Libr Cong, Washington, DC, 60; Triennial of Original Colored Graphics, Grenchen, Switz, 64; Carroll Reece Mus, Johnson City, Tenn, 68; one-woman shows, Alonzo Gallery, New York, 68, 70, 72, 75 & 77, Kunsthalle, Nuremberg, 74-75, Nassau Co Ctr Fine Arts, 75, Cherry Stone, Wellfleet, Mass, 74 & 77. Awards: Purchase Award, Hofstra Univ, 56; Village Art Ctr Award, New York, 63; Audubon Artists Award, 77 & 78. Mem: Am Abstr Artists (secy, 70-); Soc Am Graphic Artists; Audubon Artists. Dealer: Alonzo Gallery 26 E 63rd St New York NY 10021. Mailing Add: 5 Cricket Lane Great Neck NY 11024

EDDY, DON
PAINTER
b Long Beach, Calif, Nov 4, 44. Study: Univ Calif, Santa Barbara, 69-70; Univ Hawaii, Honolulu, BFA, 67, MFA, 69. Work: Cleveland Mus Art, Ohio; Toledo Mus Art, Ohio, St Etienne Mus, France; Neue Galerie, Aachen, Ger; Williams Col Mus Art, Williamstown, Mass. Exhib: Documenta, Kassel, WGer, 72 & 77; Fogg Art Mus, Harvard Univ, Cambridge, Mass, 73; Storm King Art Ctr, Mountainville, NY, 73; New York Avant-Garde, Saidye Bronfman Centre, Montreal, Que, 73; Hyper-realisme Americaine, Realism Europ, Centre Nat d'Art Contemporain, Paris, 74; Wadsworth Atheneum, Hartford, Conn, 74; Tokyo Biennial, Japan, 74; Baltimore Mus Art, Md, 76; Realist & Illusionist Art (six city tour, Australia), 77; plus others. Bibliog: Udo Kulterman (auth), New realism, NY Graphic Soc, 72; Peter Sager (auth), Realismus, Verlag M DuMont Schauberg; H W Janson (auth), History of Art, Abrams, 77. Style & Technique: Contemporary representational painting. Media: Acrylic on Canvas. Dealer: Nancy Hoffman Gallery 429 W Broadway New York NY 10012. Mailing Add: 30 Christopher St Apt 3F New York NY 10014

EDELHEIT, MARTHA
PAINTER, FILMMAKER
b New York, NY. Study: Columbia Univ Teachers Col, BS, 56; Univ Chicago. Exhib: (Paintings) Figure Show, Wadsworth Atheneum, Hartford, Conn, 64; Eleven From the Reuben, Guggenheim Mus, New York, 65; Humor, Satire, Irony, 72 & Erotica Show, 73, New Sch Art Ctr; Women Choose Women, New York Cult Ctr, 73; Sons & Others, Queens Mus, New York, 75; Three Centuries of the Am Nude, New York Cult Ctr, 75 & Minneapolis Mus for the Arts, Minn, 75; Works on Paper, Brooklyn Mus, NY, 75; (Films) Graz Mus, Austria, 74; Mus of the 20th Century, Vienna, Austria, 74; Portland Mus, Ore, 76; Brooklyn Mus, 77; Mus Mod Art, New York, 77. Teaching: Vis artist, Feminist Art Prog, Calif Inst of the Arts, 73; artist-in-residence painting, Wilson Col, Chambersburg, Pa, 75; artist-in-residence film, Univ Cincinnati, Ohio, 76; artist-in-residence painting & drawing, Sch of Art Inst Chicago, 76; guest lectr film, New Sch Social Res, New York, 77. Pos: Ed bd fourth issue, Heresies Mag, 77-78. Bibliog: Tiiu Lukk (auth), Super-8 filmmaker, Profile, 10/75; Daryl Chin (auth), Female films, Soho News, 6/9/77; Carrie Rickey (auth), Women shoot women: films about women artists, Womanart, spring 78. Mem: Women/Artist Filmmakers Inc (vpres, 74; pres, 75-77); Women in the Arts (coord bd, 74); Women's Caucus for Art, Col Art Asn (adv bd, 75-76). Style & Technique: Nudes, objects in land/cityscapes; acrylic, smooth brush technique; fantasy watercolors; pencil drawings. Media: Acrylic; Pen & Ink, Watercolor on Rice Paper; Pencil on Smooth Rag Paper. Publ: Contribr, Women in the Year 2000, Arbor House, 74; contribr, Anonymous Was a Woman, 74 & Art: A Woman's Sensibility, 75, Calif Inst of the Arts; auth, The Invention of the Albino Queen, ANIMA, Conococheague Assoc, 75; auth, Georgia O'Keefe: a reminiscence, Women Artists Newsletter, 12/77. Mailing Add: 1140 Fifth Ave New York NY 10028

EDELSON, ELIHU
ART CRITIC, INSTRUCTOR
b New York, NY, Mar 30, 25. Study: Ringling Sch Art, Sarasota, Fla; Univ Fla, BAE, MEd; NY Univ, with Victor d'Amico. Comn: Relief inscription in sculptured Hebrew letters, Temple Beth Sholom, Jacksonville, Fla, 70. Exhib: Artists of Metropolitan Denver, Denver Art Mus; Southeastern Ann, High Mus, Atlanta, Ga; Sarasota Art Asn Nat, Ringling Mus Art; Jacksonville Art Festival, Fla. Teaching: Instr art hist & educ, Manatee Jr Col, Bradenton, Fla, 62-65; art resource teacher, Duval Co Pub Sch, Jacksonville, 65-74; instr art educ, Edward Waters Col, 66-67; lectr humanities, Jacksonville Univ, 66-68, lectr art hist & criticism, 75-77; lectr art appreciation & criticism, Jacksonville Art Mus, 75-77, calligraphy instr, 77- Pos: Art critic, The Sarasota News, 57-63, Sarasota Citizen, 64-65, St Petersburg Times, 65, Jacksonville J, 67-77, Fla Times-Union & Jacksonville J, 78- Mem: Arcande Order, Renaissance Artists & Writers Asn; Soc for Italic Handwriting; Hon mem Crown Craftsmen. Res: New Age directions in contemporary culture. Publ: Auth, Florida: supra-regional regionalism, Arts Mag, 4/65; articles in Art for Humanities & Both Sides Now. plus exhib catalog notes for Sarasota Art Asn, Fla State Fair Fine Arts Exhib & Jacksonville Art Mus. Mailing Add: 1232 Laura St Jacksonville FL 32206

EDELSON, MARY BETH
LECTURER, CONCEPTUAL ARTIST
b US. Study: Art Inst of Chicago; DePauw Univ, BA; NY Univ, MA. Exhib: One-person shows, Sheldon Swope Mus, Terre Haute, Ind, 65, Indianapolis Mus of Art, Ind, 68, Passage Environment, Corcoran Gallery of Art, 73, Your 5000 Yrs Are Up, Mandeville Art Gallery, Univ Calif San Diego, La Jolla, 77, Energy Rituals in Nature, Douglas Libr, Rutgers Univ, 78 & Story Gathering Boxes, Franklin Furnace, New York, 78; Contemp Work, Nat Collection of Fine Art, Smithsonian Inst, Washington, DC, 72; Six From Washington, Corcoran Gallery of Art, 72; Artists Making Art, Baltimore Mus, Md, 72; Contemp Reflections 3rd Ann, Larry Aldrich Mus, Ridgefield, Conn, 74; Painting & Sculpture Today, Indianapolis Mus of Art, Ind, 74; Paperworks, Washington Gallery of Art, DC, 74; Nothing But Nudes, Whitney Downtown, New York, 77; Primitivism: Contemp Women's Work, Univ Art Gallery, Rutgers Univ, New Brunswick, NJ, 77; Contemp Women: Consciousness & Content, Brooklyn Mus Sch in conjunction with the museum's exhib, Women Artists 1550-1950, 77. Teaching: Instr, Corcoran Sch of Art, 71-76. Bibliog: Jack Burnham (auth), Mary Beth Edelson's Great Goddess, 11/75; Karen Peterson & J J Wilson (co-auths), Women Artists, Harper & Row, 76; Lucy Lippard (auth), From the Center, E P Dutton & Co Bks, NY, 76. Style & Technique: Conceptual works; sculpture; photographs; drawings; books; posters. Mailing Add: 110 Mercer St New York NY 10012

EDEN, F BROWN
PAINTER, PRINTMAKER
b Jericho Center, Vt, Oct 10, 16. Study: Univ Fla, 54-55; Univ Mich, 62-63; Jacksonville Art Mus, seminars with Gabor Peterdi, Arthur Deshaies & Willian Parker. Work: Ga Inst Technol; Jacksonville Art Mus; Tupperware Co, Orlando, Fla; Trust Co Ga, Atlanta; Columbia Rec Co, Atlanta. Exhib: Southeastern States Exhibs, Jacksonville, Fla, 60-68; Mead Ann Painting of the Year Exhib & Nat Traveling Show, Atlanta, 62-63; Philadelphia Print Fair, 62; Nat Print Fair, Burr Galleries, New York, 62; Fla Artists Show, Norton Gallery Art, West Palm Beach, 75; Am Painters in Paris, 75; Contemp Am Paintings, Soc of Four Arts, Palm Beach, 77; Gulf Coast Juried Exdib, 78; plus others, incl 33 one-man shows. Pos:

Teacher, Jacksonville Art Mus, 63-68. Awards: Painting of Distinction Award, Mead Painting of the Year Exhib, 62; First in Painting Award, Art '69, Invitational Fla Artists, 69; First Award, Fla Artist Group Ann Exhib, 71; plus 25 other first awards. Bibliog: Elihu Edelson (auth), One-person exhibition, 9/22/73 & 3 For The Show, 1/12/74, Jacksonville J; Juliette deMarcellus (auth), Juror's choices at Norton, The Times, Palm Beach, 5/20/75. Mem: Le Moyne Art Found, Tallahassee; Jacksonville Art Mus; Fla Artist Group, Inc (area chmn, 74-); Artists Assoc, Inc; Artists Equity Asn, Washington, DC. Style & Technique: Large, poetric and semi-abstract paintings, evocative of nature; some heavily textured and three-dimensional, in golden earth-tones. Dealer: Art Sources Inc Gulf Life Bldg Jacksonville FL 32301; Artists Assoc Gallery 3261 Roswell Rd NE Atlanta GA 30305. Mailing Add: 5375 Sanders Rd Jacksonville FL 32211

EDENS, LETTYE P
ART DEALER, PAINTER
b La Luz, NMex, Jan 25, 20. Study: Col Desert; also with Frederic Taubes, Joyce Pike, Claud Parsons, Keith Ward, Mona Mills, Marshall Merritt, John Hilton & J Wellington Smith. Exhib: Women Artists American West, Saddleback Inn, Santa Ana, Calif, 73-75; Western Art Gallery, Albuquerque, NMex, 74; Nat Date Festival, Indio, Calif, 74; The Gallery, Palm Springs, Calif, 74; George Phippen Mem, Prescott, Ariz, 75. Teaching: Instr & owner, Edens Art Ctr, 75- Awards: First Award, Nat Date Festival, 75, Palette Club, 75 & Women Artists Am West, 75. Bibliog: Article in, Desert Sun, 73; Artists on the Desert, Indio Daily News, 73; art in Western Horseman, 74. Mem: Des-Arts Inc (pres, 73-75); Women Artists Am West (publicity dir, 73-75); Shadow Mountain Palette Club; Nat League Am Pen Women; Desert Art Ctr (publicity dir, 73-74, secy, 75-). Style & Technique: Western painting, portraits, Landscapes using oils, pastels, pencil, acrylic with palette knife and brush, occasionally use the rub-out method. Mailing Add: 81-447 Fuchsia Indio CA 92201

EDER, EARL
PAINTER
b Poplar, Mont, Nov 17, 44. Study: Inst Am Insian Arts, Santa Fe, NMex, 62-65; San Francisco Art Inst, 65-70; Univ Mont, MA, 71. Exhib: Edenbourgh Art Festival, 65; Alaska Centennial, 66; Riverside Mus Biennial Exhib, 68; 7 Plus 3, Am Indian Hist Soc Show, 68; Univ San Francisco, 69. Awards: First Place in Biennial Exhib, Am Indian Arts & Crafts, 67; Second Place, Scottsdale Nat Indian Arts Exhib, 70; First Place, Heard Mus, 70. Bibliog: The Dance in Contemporary American Indian Art, Harkness House, 67; Alfred Frankenstein (auth), 7 Plus 3, San Francisco Chronicle, 68; Return of red man, Life Mag, 68. Mailing Add: 1914 42nd Ave Missoula MT 59801

EDGE, DOUGLAS BENJAMIN
SCULPTOR, PHOTOGRAPHER
b Fennimore, Wis, Aug 4, 42. Study: San Fernando Valley State Col, BA. Work: Mus Mod Art, New York; Patrick Lannon Mus, Fla. Comn: Threshold staircase doorway, comn by Mr & Mrs Fred Tackett, Topanga, Calif, 75. Exhib: West Coast Now, Seattle Art Mus, 68; Violence in Am Art, Mus Contemp Art, Chicago, 69; Continuing Surrealism, La Jolla Mus Art, 71; Calif Prints, Mus Mod Art, New York, 72; Separate Realities, Los Angeles Munic Art Gallery, 73. Teaching: Instr sculpture, Calif Inst Art, Valencia, 70-72; instr painting workshop, Art Ctr Sch Design, Los Angeles, 73-74; lectr sculpture & drawing, Univ Calif, Santa Barbara, 75-76. Awards: Cassandra Found Grant, 70. Bibliog: Thomas Garver (auth), rev, 10/69 & Peter Plagens (auth), rev, 11/73, Artforum; Milinda Terbell (auth), Art News, 10/73. Style & Technique: Mystical imagery embracing illusive space infused with energy. Mailing Add: c/o Jean Milant 708 N Manhattan Pl Los Angeles CA 90038

EDIE, STUART
PAINTER
b Wichita Falls, Tex, Nov 10, 08. Study: Kansas City Art Inst; Art Students League. Work: Whitney Mus Am Art, New York; Toledo Art Mus, Ohio; Newark Mus, NJ; Brooklyn Mus, NY; Metrop Mus Art, New York. Comn: Mural, comn by Treas Dept, Honeoye Falls, NY, 42. Exhib: Carnegie Inst Int, Pittsburgh, 48; many exhibs, Whitney Mus Am Art Ann, Art Inst Chicago Ann, Pa Acad Fine Arts Ann, Philadelphia & Corcoran Biennial, Washington, DC. Teaching: Instr painting, Am Artists Sch, 40-51; instr painting, Univ Iowa, 44-70. Awards: Artists of the Midwest Award, Kansas City Art Inst, 55; Artists of the Miss Valley Award, Davenport Mus, 58; Walker Biennial Award, 60. Media: Oil, Acrylic. Mailing Add: Apartado 129 Guanajuato Gto Mexico

EDMISTON, SARA JOANNE
EDUCATOR, DESIGNER
b Independence, Mo, June 21, 35. Study: Univ Kans, BAE; ECarolina Univ, MA. Work: NC Mus Art, Raleigh; Mint Mus of Art, Charlotte, NC; NC Nat Banks, several cities in NC; Wachovia Banks, several cities in NC; Duke Univ. Comn: Door frontal piece & handles, Mr & Mrs Phillip Michelove, Advance, NC, 73; door knocker, NC Nat Bank, Charlotte, 74; door frontal piece, handles & knocker, Mr & Mrs Tom King, Raleigh, NC, 77. Exhib: NC Artists Ann, NC Mus Art, Raleigh, 65-67 & 76; Nat Graphic Arts Drawing Exhib, Wichita Art Mus, Kans, 67; Enamels 70 Nat, Crafts Alliance, St Louis, Mo & William Rockhill Nelson Gallery of Art, Kansas City, Mo, 70; Piedmont Crafts, Mint Mus of Art, Charlotte, 70-73; NC Crafts, NC Mus Art, Raleigh, 71 & 73; Crafts Invitational, Jacksonville Mus, Fla, 72; Southeastern Crafts Exhib, Greenville Co Mus, SC, 74; New Directions in Fabric Design, Fine Arts Gallery, Towson State Univ, 76. Teaching: Assoc prof textiles & design & chmn dept design, ECarolina Univ, 66- Awards: Purchase Award, 5th Ann Piedmont Graphics Exhib, Mint Mus Art, 69; Hon Mention, NC Crafts Exhib, NC Mus Art, 73; Purchase Award, 39th Ann NC Artists Exhib, NC Art Soc, 76. Mem: Surface Design Asn (treas & nat mem chmn, 76-); Am Crafts Coun; Piedmont Craftsmen, Inc (mem standards comt, 73-77); Carolina Designer-Craftsmen (mem standards comt, 70-72); NC Crafts Asn (mem bd dirs, 76-). Style & Technique: Fabric design in batik and other dye techniques; enamels; bronze functional and decorative works. Media: Dye, enamel, cast bronze. Dealer: Piedmont Craftsmen Inc Sales Gallery 936 W Fourth St Winston-Salem NC 27101. Mailing Add: 406 W Fourth St Greenville NC 27834

EDMONDSON, LEONARD
ETCHER
b Sacramento, Calif, June 12, 16. Study: Univ Calif, Berkeley, AB, 40, MA, 42. Work: Metrop Mus Art, New York; Bibliot Nat, Paris, France; New York Pub Libr; San Francisco Mus Art; Pasadena Art Mus. Comn: Edition of etchings, Int Graphic Arts Soc, NY, 60, Hilton Hotel, NY, 62, Ferdinand Roten Galleries, Inc, NY, 66 & US Info Agency, Washington, DC, 67. Exhib: American Watercolors, Drawings & Prints, Metrop Mus Art, 52; Younger American Painters, Guggenheim Mus, 54; American Prints Today, Print Coun Am, 62; Int Triennial of Original Colored Graphics, Switz, 64; Graphics '71 West Coast USA, Univ Ky, 71. Teaching: Prof art, Calif State Univ, Los Angeles, 64-74; chmn dept printmaking, Otis Art Inst, Los Angeles, 74- Awards: Purchase Prize for Oil, Univ Ill, 55; Purchase Prize for Etching, Brooklyn Mus, 56; Purchase Prize for Etching, Pasadena Art Mus, 58. Bibliog: Mugnaini (auth), Oil Painting, Techniques & Materials, 69 & Reep (auth), The Content of Watercolor, 69, Van Nostrand; Heller (auth), Printmaking Today, Holt, 71. Publ: Auth, Etching, Van Nostrand, 73. Mailing Add: 714 Prospect Blvd Pasadena CA 91103

EDMONSTON, PAUL
EDUCATOR, ART EDITOR
b Newton, Mass, Nov 15, 22. Study: Mass Sch of Art, with Ernest L Major & Cyrus Dallin; Boston Univ, AB(Eng lang & lit), with William Jewell, Edgar Brightman, Gerald Brace & Peter Bertocci; Fla State Univ, MA(art), with Karl Zerbe; Ohio State Univ, PhD(fine art), with Hoyt Sherman, Manuel Barkan, Jerome Hausman & Ross L Mooney; Univ Pa, SAsian studies, 72-73. Teaching: Instr art, Ohio State Univ, 56-60; from assoc prof to prof art appreciation, printmaking & art ed, Pa State Univ, 60-77; prof art appreciation, drawing & painting & art ed, Univ Ga, 77- Pos: Int Platform Asn, Washington, DC, 77- Mem: Int Soc for Educ Through Art (World Coun, 78-); Nat Art Educ Asn (res sem, 70-); Asn for Asian Studies; Sri Aurobindo Soc, Int Centre for Educ, Pondicherry, India; Smithsonian Assoc. Style & Technique: Semi-abstract designed landscapes. Media: Watercolor; Brush & Ink on Rice Paper. Res: Studio way of learning in art, model of creative, visual intelligence, nature of the creative process in art, nature of creative teaching act in art. Publ: Assoc ed, Sch Arts, 62-67; ed, PSPAE: Pa State Papers in Art Education (seven monographs), Pa State Univ, 68-74; auth, Photography taken as a creative act, Art Ed, 75; auth, A conceptual model of creative visual intelligence, J Creative Behavior, 75; auth, Myth and symbol in Indian art, Proceedings: Int Art Sem 76, Franklin Perkins Sch, Mass, 76; contribr & ed, An Anthology of Faculty Papers: 1976-77, Pa State Univ, 77. Mailing Add: Dept of Art Univ Ga Athens GA 30602

EDMUNDS, ALLAN LOGAN
PRINTMAKER, ART ADMINISTRATOR
b Philadelphia, Pa, June 7, 49. Study: St Joseph's Col; Tyler Sch Art, Philadelphia & Rome; also with Romas Viesulas & John Dowell, BFA & MFA. Work: Philadelphia Mus Art; Temple Univ; First Pa Bank. Comn: Photosilkscreen ed, Philadelphia Mus Art, 71-72. Exhib: Silkscreen: History of a Medium, Philadelphia Mus Art, 71-72; Expanded Photograph, Philadelphia Civic Ctr Mus, 72; one-man show, Univ Md, Baltimore Co, 72; Second World Black & African Festival Art & Cult, Univ Pa Mus, 74; Nat Invited Print Exhib, Cent Wash State Univ, 75. Teaching: Workshop adminr, Print Club Workshops, Philadelphia, 71-72; instr graphics, Haystack Mountain Sch Crafts, Maine, 74; lectr printmaking, Philadelphia Col Art, 75; art coordr, Parkway Prog Sch Dist Philadelphia, 72- Pos: Mem adv bd, Our Thing Art & Commun Ctr, Philadelphia, 72-; founder dir & treas, Brandywine Graphic Workshop, Inc, 72-; artist comt, Prints in Progress, 73-; mem artist comt, Print Club Philadelphia, 74-; bd mem, Visual Arts Collective, Inc, 75. Awards: Philadelphia Civic Ctr Award Painting, 67; Temple Univ Scholar Study in Rome, 60. Bibliog: Baltimore Sun, 11/12/72; Philadelphia Inquirer, 11/15/72; Philly Talk Mag, 3/74. Mem: Artists Equity Asn; Philadelphia Print Club; Brandywine Graphic Workshop Assocs (treas, dir). Style & Technique: Figurative, social commentary using photographic imagery as the dominant reference. Res: Continuous research project on the history of the Black graphic artist; collection of slides, manuscripts and original works as well as developing own papers for publication. Dealer: Mitzi Shalit 5114 Bond Ave Drexel Hill PA 19026. Mailing Add: 5533 W Master St Philadelphia PA 19131

EDVI ILLES, EMMA
DESIGNER, TAPESTRY ARTIST
b Budapest, Hungary; US citizen. Study: NY Sch Interior Design, 58; Int Asn Color Consults, dipl, 59; Sogetsu Sch Flower Design Tokyo, prof degree, 62. Pos: Owner & founder, Academia de Decoration, Caracas, Venezuela, 56-67; lectr & consult, Channel 2 & 4 TV, Caracas, 58-66. Awards: Dipl de Honor, Ministerio de Educ, Caracas, 66. Publ: Auth, Teoria de Color, 2 vols, 59; auth, Commercial Flower Design, 2 vols, 61. Mailing Add: 436 Londonberry Rd NW Atlanta GA 30327

EDVI ILLES, GEORGE
PAINTER, SCULPTOR
b Budapest, Hungary, Apr 29, 11. Study: Acad Fine Arts Budapest, also with Oscar Glatz, Stephan Bosznay & Ede Telcs. Work: Still Life (oil), High Mus Art; 20 medallions, Hungarian Nat Mus. Comn: Portrait (oil), Marcos Perez Jimenez, 55; portrait (oil), Andres Eloy Blanco, Capitolium Caracas, 63; portrait (oil), Otto Habsburg Crownprince; life size portrait (oil), Sen Russell & his mother's family; cast gold medallion of Mrs Jacquelyn Kennedy. Exhib: Nat Mus Caracas, Venezuela; one-man show, Budapest, Hungary, 26; competition of posters, Hungarian Thermal Resort, Hajduszoboszlo, 39; competition for poster, Nepszava Newspaper, 46. Awards: First Prize, Thermal Resort Hajduszoboszlo, 39; First Prize, Nepszava Newspaper, 46; First Prize sport medallion competition, Basketball Asn Budapest, 46. Style & Technique: Impressionistic with personal and modern feeling. Media: Oil, Pastel. Mailing Add: 436 Londonberry Rd NW Atlanta GA 30327

EDWARDS, ALLAN W
COLLECTOR, ILLUSTRATOR
b Edmonton, Alta, Can, Jan 15, 15. Study: John Russell Acad Art, Toronto, Can. Work: Art Gallery Greater Victoria, Can. Comn: Murals, Skyline Hotel, Ottawa, Heathrow Hotel, London, Eng, Plaza Hotel, New York & Royal Hawaiian Hotel, Honolulu. Exhib: One-man shows, Toronto, 36, Detroit, 38, Victoria, 64 & Vancouver, 76; Art Gallery Detroit, Mich, 38; group exhib, Toronto Art Gallery, 41; De Young Mus, San Francisco, 50; Palace of the Legion of Honor, San Francisco, 50. Teaching: Instr painting, Meinzinger Found, Detroit, 38-40; instr illus, Art League Calif, San Francisco, 50-52. Pos: Advert mgr, W & J Sloane, Beverly Hills, Calif, 52-54; art dir, City of Paris, San Francisco, 49-51; owner-dir, Gallery 22, West Vancouver, BC, 73-76; archit illusr & interior renderings, presently. Awards: Second Award Watercolor, De Young Mus, 50. Mem: Fedn Can Artists (pres, 76-). Style & Technique: Representational transparent watercolor. Media: Watercolor. Collection: British artists, 19th and 20th century. Dealer: Exposition Art Gallery 313 Water St Vancouver BC V6B 1B8 Can. Mailing Add: 2228 Marine Dr West Vancouver BC V7V 1K4 Can

EDWARDS, ELLENDER MORGAN
PRINTMAKER, PHOTOGRAPHER
b Hagerstown, Md. Study: Tyler Sch Art; pvt study art hist in Europe; Md Inst Col Art, BFA, 58; Art Students League, with Jean Liberte; Hunter Col, grad study; Corcoran Art Sch, George Washington Univ; also with Reuben Kramer & Victor D'Amico. Exhib: 29th & 30th Cumberland Valley Artists, Washington Co Mus Art, Hagerstown, Md, 61 & 62; Md Regional, Baltimore Mus Art, 61 & 76; 21st Ann Life in Baltimore, Peale Mus, Md, 61; Denim Art, Mus Contemp Crafts, New York, 74; Focus 76 Photo Competition, Amarillo Civic Ctr, Tex, 76; Bicentennial Competition, Goldman Fine Arts Gallery, 76. Pos: Secy, Montgomery Co Art Educators Asn, Rockville, Md, 70-73, treas, 73-75; treas, Glen Echo Graphics, 73- Awards: Second Prize Serigraphy, Waterford Found, Inc, Va, 60; First Prize Graphics, Shepherd Col, 71; Honorable Mention, Int Platform Asn, 73 & 74 & Goldman Fine Arts Gallery, 76; plus others. Mem: Nat League Am Penwomen; Nat Art Educ Asn; Int

Platform Asn. Style & Technique: Abstract and realistic. Mailing Add: Box 106 Rockville MD 20850

EDWARDS, ETHEL (MRS XAVIER GONZALEZ)
PAINTER
b New Orleans, La. Study: Newcomb Col Art Sch; also with Xavier Gonzalez. Work: IBM Collection; Chase Manhattan Bank, NY; Commerce Trust Bank, Kansas City, Mo; Boston Mus Fine Arts; Springfield Mus Fine Art; plus others. Exhib: Butler Inst Am Art, Youngstown, Ohio, 64-69; Whitney Mus Am Art, 64 & 65; Hartford Atheneum, 67 & 68; Watercolor: USA, Springfield, Ill, 67-69; Cape Cod Art Asn, 69. Awards: Larry Aldrich Prize, Silvermine Guild Artists; Prizes, Watercolor: USA, Springfield, Ill, 67 & Ball State Univ, Muncie, Ind, 67. Mem: McDowell Colony Alumni. Mailing Add: 222 Central Park S New York NY 10019

EDWARDS, GWENDOLYN TYNER
ART DEALER, GALLERY DIRECTOR
b Madison, Wis, Aug 20, 33. Study: Univ Ill, Urbana. Pos: Co-owner & co-show mgr, House of Art, Champaign, Ill. Mem: Krannert Art Mus Asn. Specialty: Contemporary midwestern American artists; painting; sculpture and ceramics. Mailing Add: 805 W University Ave Champaign IL 61820

EDWARDS, JAMES F
VIDEO ARTIST, PHOTOGRAPHER
b New York, NY, July 25, 48. Study: Univ Calif, Santa Barbara, BA, MFA. Work: Everson Mus Art, Syracuse, NY; SC Arts Comn, Columbia; Univ Calif, Santa Barbara; Univ SC, Columbia. Exhib: Santa Barbara Mus Art, 74; Mus Mod Art, Ferrara, Italy, 75; one-man shows, Columbia Mus Art, SC, 75, La Mamelle Art Ctr, San Francisco, 76, Greenville Co Mus Art, Greenville, SC, 76 & Everson Mus Art, Syracuse, NY, 77; Int Cult Ctr, Antwerp, Belg, 76; Ctr for the Study of Contemp Art, Barcelona, Spain, 77; Heath Gallery, Atlanta, Ga, 77. Teaching: Asst prof drawing & video, Univ SC, 72- Pos: Cur video gallery, Univ SC, 77- Awards: Nat Endowment for the Arts Fel, 74-75; First Place, Ithaca Video Festival, NY Coun for the Arts, 75, 77 & 78; Proj Grant, SC Arts Comn, 76-77. Style & Technique: Photomontage, documents and video, conceptual orientation. Media: Video, Photography; Drawing. Publ: Auth, Getting into video, Contemp Art/SE, 77. Dealer: David Heath 34 Lombardy Way Atlanta GA 30309. Mailing Add: Dept of Art Univ SC Columbia SC 29208

EDWARDS, JOY M
ART DEALER
b Newbury, Berkshire, Eng, Aug 5, 19. Study: Sorbonne Univ, with Prof Guinebert; Reading Univ. Pos: Gallery dir, David B Findlay Gallery, New York, 60-69; gallery dir, Gimpel & Weitzenhoffer Ltd, New York, 69-76; gallery dir, Comsky Gallery, Los Angeles, 76- Mem: Mus Mod Art; Metrop Mus; Mus Contemp Crafts; Art Dealers Asn. Specialty: Contemporary 20th century paintings and sculpture. Mailing Add: 317 S Doheny Dr Los Angeles CA 90048

EDWARDS, PAUL BURGESS
See Pablo

EDWARDS, STANLEY DEAN
PAINTER, ILLUSTRATOR
b Joliet, Ill, Dec 5, 41. Study: Art Inst Chicago; Univ Chicago; BFA; Saugatuck Summer Sch. Work: Corcoran Gallery Art, Washington, DC; Ball State Univ Art Gallery. Exhib: 12 Chicago Painters, Walker Art Ctr, 65; Corcoran Biannual, Washington, DC, 65; Protest & Hope Group Show, New Sch Social Res, 67; Butler Ann, Youngstown, Ohio, 68; Violence in Art, Mus Contemp Art, Chicago, 69; plus others. Teaching: Instr art, Trinity Sch, New York, 69-70; instr, Chicago Acad Fine Arts, 72. Awards: Hon Mention & Purchase Prize, Corcoran Gallery, 65; Vanderbilt Purchase Fund, 69. Bibliog: Whitney Halsted (auth), article in Artforum, 66; Franz Schultz (auth), article in Panorama Mag, Chicago Daily News, 65-69. Mailing Add: c/o Fairweather-Hardin Gallery 101 E Ontario Chicago IL 60611

EFRAT, BENNI
SCULPTOR
b Lebanon, Aug 13, 36; Israeli citizen. Work: Mus Mod Art, New York; Guggenheim Mus, New York; Albright-Knox Art Gallery, Buffalo, NY; Stedelijk Mus, Amsterdam, Holland; Israel Mus, Jerusalem. Comn: Prism (sculpture), Lee Turner, Kans, 69; Energy (sculpture), Steven Shalom, New York, 70; Information (sculpture), John Murchison, Dallas, Tex, 72; Barbara (sculpture), Nelson Rockefeller, Albany, NY, 72; sculpture, Haifa Auditorium, Israel, 73. Exhib: Paris Biennale, France, 65-69; one-man shows, Concrete, Israel Mus, 72, On Paper, Stedelijk Mus, 74, Palais des Beaux Arts, Brussels, Belg, 76, Whitney Mus Am Art, New York, 77; Dokumenta 6, Kassel, WGer, 77 & Wadsworth Atheneum, Hartford, Conn, 78. Awards: Sandberg Found Prize, 71. Bibliog: Barbara Reise (auth), article in Studio Int, 69; R Pincus-Witten (auth), article in Arts Mag, 77. Media: Sculpture. Publ: Auth of own exhib catalogues, Stedelijk Mus, 74, Palais des Beaux Arts, 76 & Whitney Mus Am Art, 77. Mailing Add: 280-290 Lafayette St New York NY 10012

EGELI, PETER EVEN
PAINTER, ILLUSTRATOR
b Miami, Fla, Apr 19, 34. Study: Corcoran Sch Art; Md Inst, BFA; Art Students League; George Washington Univ; 3 yrs study with Jacques Maroger. Comn: Portrait of Dr T Mendenhall, Smith Col, 74; print, Swallow/Reprisal Action, 76; portraits of Rev Charles Martin, St Alban's Sch, Washington, DC, 77, Eugene Casey for Red Hill Shrine, 77 & Dr T E Powell, Jr, Carolina Biological, Burlington, NC, 77. Exhib: Two-man show, Md Fedn Arts, Annapolis, 70; one-man show, Bendann Art Galleries, Baltimore, 74; Franklin Mint Distinguished Am Marine Painting, Media, Pa, 74. Teaching: Instr painting, St Mary's Col of Md, 61-67. Pos: Illusr, Marine Corps Inst, Washington, DC, 53-56. Awards: Gold Medal for Distinguished Am Marine Painting, Franklin Mint, 75. Bibliog: Bonnie Ayres (auth), Portrait of Peter Egeli, Md Mag, 71. Style & Technique: Classical, portraits in oils, pastels, marines in oil, watercolor. Media: Oil, Pastel, Watercolor. Res: 17th century English ships, 19th and early 20th century Chesapeake Bay craft. Dealer: Bendann Art Galleries 105 E Baltimore St Baltimore MD 21202. Mailing Add: Westbank Drayden MD 20630

EGLESON, JIM (JAMES DOWNEY)
PRINTMAKER-ETCHER, PAINTER
b Capelton, PQ, Mar 12, 07; US citizen. Study: Swarthmore Col, BS, 29; Mass Inst Technol, 29-30; apprenticeship with Jose Clemente Orozco, Mex, 35-36. Work: Metrop Mus Art, New York; New York Pub Libr Print Collection; Addison Gallery Am Art, Mass; Fairfield Univ; Springfield Col. Comn: 12 panel frescoes, Swarthmore Col, 38; fresco lobby, US Post Off, Marysville, Ohio, US Treas Dept, 39-40. Exhib: Nat Acad Design Ann, New York, 68-71, 73 & 76; Silvermine Nat Print Exhib, 68 & 70; Soc Am Graphic Artists, Kennedy & Assoc Am Artists Galleries, 71 & 73; one-man shows, Silvermine Guild Artists, New Canaan, 73, Swarthmore Col, Pa, 74 & Lyman Allyn Mus, New London, Conn, 75, New Brit Mus of Am Art, Conn, 76 & Mattatuck Mus, Waterbury, Conn, 76; Connecticut Printmakers-100 Years, Bridgeport, 75; Slater Mus, Norwich, Conn, 77; Metrop Mus & Art Ctr, Miami, Fla, 77. Teaching: Instr intaglio, Silvermine Guild Artists, 72- Pos: News artist, CBS-TV, 48-50; free lance sci illusr, Sci Am Mag, McGraw-Hill & others, 50- Awards: Prize, New Haven Festival of Arts, 68; Purchase Prize, Springfield Col, 69; Anonymous Prize, Nat Acad Design Ann, 71. Mem: Soc Am Graphic Artists; Conn Acad Fine Arts; Silvermine Guild Artists. Style & Technique: Humanistic and representational; surrealist overtones; highly selective details; overall mood predominant. Dealer: Assoc Am Artists 663 Fifth Ave New York NY 10022. Mailing Add: 22 Dock Rd Norwalk CT 06854

EGRI, TED
SCULPTOR
b New York, NY May 22, 13. Study: Master Inst Roerich Mus, dipl, 31-34; Duncan Phillips Mem Gallery Art Sch, 42; Hans Hofmann Sch Art, New York & Provincetown, Mass, 48. Work: William Rockhill Nelson Mus, Kansas City, Mo; Mus NMex, Santa Fe; Millicent A Rogers Mem Mus, Taos, NMex; Harwood Found Collection, Univ NMex; Northern Iowa Univ. Comn: Sculpture (welded Cor-ten steel), Northern Iowa Univ, 65; ark doors & eternal light, Mt Sinai Temple, El Paso, Tex, 65; fountain (welded brass), Exec Life Bldg, Beverly Hills, Calif, 66; monument on pedestal (welded of Kaiseloy steel), City Albuquerque, NMex, 69; menorah & eternal light (welded & stained glass), Temple Shalom, Dallas, Tex, 72. Exhib: Denver Art Mus Regional Ann, Colo, 49, 53 & 54; Colorado Springs Fine Arts Ctr, Colo, 50 & 52; Four Shows, Contemporary American Painting & Sculpture, Univ Ill, Champaign, 52-61; Pa Acad Fine Arts Ann, Philadelphia, 53; Art: USA 58, Madison Sq Garden, New York, 58; Religious Art Western World, 58 & Southwestern Art Show, 60, Dallas Mus Fine Arts, Tex; Roswell Mus, NMex, 58 & 72. Teaching: Instr oil painting & life drawing, Kansas City Art Inst, 48-50; lectr art sculpture, life drawing & painting, Univ Wyo, 59-60; vis lectr art, Univ Ill, 60-61; Nat Endowment Arts & US Off Educ artist in residence, Taos Co Schs, 72-74. Pos: Mem art adv comt, Mus NMex, 58 & 62-63; mem art adv comt, NMex Arts Comn, 69-70. Awards: A I Friedman Award, Audubon Artists Ann, 47; Top Award for Sculpture & Honorable Mention for Drawing, Mus NMex Fiesta Biennial, 65; Top Award for Sculpture, Mus NMex Five-State Regional, 69. Bibliog: Louis G Redstone (auth), Art in Architecture; John Baldwin (auth), Contemporary Sculpture Techniques; John Rood (auth), Sculpture with a Torch; plus others. Mem: Artists Equity Asn (nat vpres, 67-68 & 71-72); Taos Art Asn (art comt, 71-72 & 75). Style & Technique: Expressionist, semi-abstract; polyester resin, fiberglass carved urethane foam; bronze casts. Media: Metal, Wood. Dealer: Stables Gallery Taos NM 87571; Carlson-Black Gallery Taos NM 87571. Mailing Add: Taos NM 87571

EGUCHI, YASU
PAINTER
b Japan, Nov 30, 38. Study: Horie Art Acad, Japan, 58-65. Work: Frye Art Mus, Seattle. Comn: Paintings & relief, Sandpiper Golf Course, Santa Barbara, Calif, 72. Exhib: Tokyo Mus Art, 63 & 66; one-man shows, Austin Gallery, Calif, 68, 71 & 73, Copenhagen Gallery, Calif, 74 & Frye Art Mus, 75; Santa Barbara Mus Art, 72-74; Hammer Galleries, New York, 77; plus many others. Bibliog: Article in Southwest Art, 1/75. Media: Watercolor, Oil. Mailing Add: Santa Barbara CA

EHRESMANN, DONALD LOUIS
ART HISTORIAN, EDUCATOR
b Newark, NJ, Oct 11, 37. Study: Rutgers Univ, BA, 59; NY Univ, MA, 63, PhD, 66; study with Willibald Sauerlander & Wolfgang Lotz. Teaching: Asst prof & chmn dept art hist, Bloomfield Col, NJ, 64-69; assoc prof art hist, State Univ NY Col Brockport, 69-71; assoc prof art hist, Univ Ill, Chicago Circle, 71-, chmn dept art hist, 73- Awards: Fritz Thyssen Found Res Fel, Ger Nat Mus, Nurenberg, WGer, 63-64; Alexander von Humboldt Found Res fel, Ger Nat Mus, Nurenberg, WGer, 67-68. Mem: Col Art Asn Am; Mid-West Art Hist Soc. Res: Medieval art and architecture; fine arts bibliography. Publ: Auth, articles & rev, Art Bull, Art J & Art Quart, 68-; auth, Fine Arts—A Bibliographic Guide to Basic Reference Works, Histories and Handbooks, 75 & auth, Applied and Decorative Arts—A Bibliographic Guide to Basic Reference Works, Histories and Handbooks, 77, Libr Unltd. Mailing Add: 217 N Third St Geneva IL 60134

EHRESMANN, JULIA MOORE
ART WRITER, INSTRUCTOR
b New Orleans, La, Apr 12, 39. Study: Pomona Col, BA, 61; NY Univ, MA, 67; Rutgers Univ, MLS, 66. Teaching: Instr humanities, William Rainey Harper Col, Palatine, 72- Mem: Col Art Asn; Midwest Art Hist Soc; Art Libr Soc NAm. Res: Art bibliography; women in the fine arts; regional architectural history. Publ: Ed, Pocket Dictionary of Art Terms, New York Graphic Soc, 71; contribr, Donald L Ehresmann (auth), Applied and Decorative Arts—A Bibliographic Guide to Basic Reference Works, Histories and Handbooks, 75 & contribr, Donald L Ehresmann (auth), Applied and Decorative Arts—A Bibliographic Guide to Basic Reference Works, Histories and Handbooks, 77, Libr Unlimited; ed, Geneva, Illinois: A History of Its Times and Places, Graphic Arts Production, 77. Mailing Add: 217 N Third St Geneva IL 60134

EHRIG, WILLIAM COLUMBUS
PAINTER
b Brooklyn, NY, Oct 12, 92. Study: Brooklyn Acad Fine Arts; also with Michael Falanga & Constantin Westchiloff of Imperial Acad. Work: Grand Cent Galleries, Inc, New York; Brooklyn Mus Arts; Ft Lauderdale Mus Arts, Fla; Ogunquit Art Ctr, Maine. Comn: Marines, Our Navy Mag & New York Life Ins Co. Exhib: One-man shows, Grand Cent Galleries, Inc; Univ NH; Syracuse Univ; Nasson Col; Ogunquit Art Ctr. Teaching: Instr marines, Brooklyn & Ogunquit, 25 yrs. Awards: Maine Coast First Prize; plus numerous awards in pub exhibs. Mem: Am Artists Prof League; Nat Arts Club; Salmagundi Club; Ogunquit Art Asn; Art Guild of Boca Raton. Style & Technique: Special technique and formula applied to marine painting; known for transparency and wave action. Media: Oil. Mailing Add: 101 Shore Rd Ogunquit ME 03907

EHRLICH, GEORGE
ART HISTORIAN
b Chicago, Ill, Jan 28, 25. Study: Univ Ill-Urbana, BS, 49, MFA, 51, PhD, 60. Teaching: Prof art hist, Univ Mo-Kansas City, 54- Pos: Chmn dept art & art hist, Univ Mo-Kansas City, 64-75. Mem: Mid-Am Col Art Asn (pres, 75); Col Art Asn Am; Soc Archit Historians (pres, Mo Valley chap, 71 & 72). Res: Architectural history of Kansas City, Missouri; interrelationship of art and science to technology. Publ: Auth, Chautauqua 1880-1900: Education in Art History and Appreciation, Art Bull, 56; auth, Jean Baptiste Bossier by John James Audubon, Nelson Gallery, Atkins Mus Bull, 60; auth, The Magic Theatre Exhibition: An Appraisal, Art J, 69; auth, Afro-American Art and Art in America, Am Studies, 70; auth,

Robert Henri and Sissy, Ga Mus Art Bull, 76. Mailing Add: 5505 Holmes Kansas City MO 64110

EICHENBERG, FRITZ
ILLUSTRATOR, PRINTMAKER
b Cologne, Ger, Oct 24, 01; US citizen. Study: State Acad Graphic Arts, Leipzig, MFA, 23; Southeastern Mass Univ, hon degree, 72; Univ RI, hon degree, 74; Pratt Inst, hon degree, 76. Work: Metrop Mus Art, New York; Vatican Art Collection, Rome; Rosenwald Collection, Nat Gallery Art, Washington, DC; Bibliot Nat, Paris, France; Hermitage Mus, Leningrad, USSR. Comn: Illustrations of more than one hundred classics, children's bks, comn by publ in the US & abroad. Exhib: Soc Am Graphic Artists Ann; Xylon Int Exhibs in Geneva, Switz, Yugoslavia & elsewhere; US Info Agency Traveling Exhibs; one-man show, Pratt Manhattan Ctr, New York, 72; Klingspor Mus, Offenbach, Ger, 75; Boston Pub Libr, Mass, 76; Assoc Am Artists, New York, 77; plus others. Teaching: Prof art & chmn dept, Pratt Inst, 56-63; chmn dept art, Univ RI, 66-69, mem fac art, 69-72; mem fac art, Albertus Magnus Col, 72. Pos: Dir emer, Pratt Graphic Arts Ctr, 56-; mem, Pennell Comt, Libr Cong, 59-65; ed, Artist's Proof Ann, Pratt Inst, 60-72; sr adv, US Graphics Exhib, US Info Agency, USSR, 63; graphic survey Southeast Asia, J D Rockefeller, III Fund, 68. Awards: Joseph Pennell Medal, Pa Acad Fine Arts, 44; Distinguished Serv Medal, Ltd Ed Club; S F B Morse Medal, Nat Acad, 73. Bibliog: An artist's career, Idea Mag, Tokyo, Japan, 74; Kay Cassill (auth), Fritz Eichenberg, the gentle touch of humanity, Am Artists, 75; Emily Chewning (auth), Eichenberg's confessions, Print Mag, 76. Mem: Soc Am Graphic Artists; Nat Acad Design; Royal Soc Arts; Xylon Int. Style & Technique: Prefers lithographs and wood engravings as graphic media for single prints and illustrations for books. Media: Graphics. Res: Graphic arts, printmaking, art education, art history. Publ: Illusr, Wuthering Heights & Jane Eyre, Random, 43; illusr, Erasmus in Praise of Folly, Aquarius, 72; auth, The Print: Masterpieces, History & Technique, Abrams, 75; auth & illusr, The Wood and the Graver, Clarkson N Potter, 77; auth & illusr, Fables with a Twist, privately publ, 77; auth & illusr, Yours in Peace, FOR, 77. Dealer: Associated American Artists 663 Fifth Ave New York NY 10022. Mailing Add: 142 Oakwood Dr Peace Dale RI 02883

EIDE, JOHN
PHOTOGRAPHER, INSTRUCTOR
b Minneapolis, Minn, Jan 28, 43. Study: Lawrence Univ, BA; Univ Minn, MFA; also with Jerome Liebling, Elaine Mayes & Allan Downs. Exhib: 6th Minn Biennial, Minneapolis Art Inst, 70; Photovision '72 & '75, Boston Ctr Arts, 72 & 75; one-man shows, Portland Mus Art, 73, Lawrence Univ, 75 & Westbrook Col, Portland, Maine, 78; Cyanotypes—Boston Visual Artists Union; Thayer Acad, Braintree, Mass; Images of Woman, Portland Mus Art; Eros in Photog, Camerawork Gallery, San Francisco. Teaching: Area head photog, Portland Sch Art, 70- Pos: Hon cur photog, Portland Mus Art. Mem: Soc Photog Educ. Style & Technique: Straight photography, black and white and color. Publ: Contribr, Io Mag (Earth Geog Issue, No 2), 72. Mailing Add: 97 Spring St Portland ME 04101

EIDE, PALMER
SCULPTOR, DESIGNER
b Sioux Falls, SD, July 5, 06. Study: Augustana Col, BA; Art Inst Chicago; Harvard Univ; Yale Univ; Cranbrook Acad Art; St Olaf Col, DFA, 68. Work: Civic Fine Arts Ctr, Sioux Falls. Comn: Mosaic, First Presby Church, Sioux Falls, 54; sculpture, First Lutheran Church, Sioux Falls, 62; sculpture, Jehovah Lutheran Church, St Paul, Minn, 64; sculpture, St Philips Lutheran Church, Minneapolis, 66; Augustana Col, 75; plus others. Exhib: Sioux City Art Ctr, 61, 62 & 66; Fine Arts in Serv of Church, Seattle, Wash, 63; 6th Ann Ecclesiastical Arts Exhib of the Church Archit Conf, Dallas, Tex, 64; Lutheran Art USA Traveling Exhib, 67; Cult Opportunities Resource Ctr Traveling Exhib, Minn, 69; Palmer Eide Retrospective Exhib, SDak Mem Art Ctr, Brookings, 77; Dakota Prairie Mus, 77; Civic Fine Arts Ctr, Sioux Falls, SDak, 77; Lee Fine Arts Ctr, Univ SDak, Vermillion, 77; Dahl Fine Arts Ctr, Rapid City, SDak, 77. Teaching: Prof painting, Augustana Col, 31-71, emer prof, 71-; Fulbright prof art, Nat Col Art, Lahore, WPakistan, 64-65. Awards: Award in Sculpture, Fine Arts in Serv Church, Seattle, 63; Award in Painting, 29th Ann Fall Show, Sioux City Art Ctr, 66; Governor's Award in Arts for Creative Achievement, SDak, 76. Bibliog: Mary Roche (auth), New ideas & inventions, New York Times, 3/14/48; Louis G Redstone (auth), Art in Architecture, McGraw, 68. Mem: Col Art Asn; Midwest Col Art Asn. Media: Oil, Acrylic; Wood, Stone. Mailing Add: 2025 Austin Dr Sioux Falls SD 57105

EIKERMAN, ALMA
JEWELER, DESIGNER
b Pratt, Kans. Study: Kans State Col; Kans Univ; Columbia Univ, MA; spec study with Karl Gustav Hansen (silversmith), Baron Eric Fleming (metalsmith), Ossip Zadkine (sculptor) & Michael Wilm (goldsmith). Work: Smithsonian Inst, Washington, DC; Mus Contemp Crafts, New York; Sheldon Gallery Art, Univ Nebr, Lincoln; Hans Hansen Solvemedie, Kolding, Denmark; Home Galleries, Toulouse, France. Comn: Sterling silver plaque honoring Dean Wilfred Bain's yrs of serv to Ind Univ Music Sch, Bloomington; plus pvt comns. Exhib: Midwestern Crafts Exhib, Art Inst Chicago, 58; Soc NAm Goldsmiths Show, Minn Mus of Art, St Paul, 70, Renwick Gallery, Washington, DC, 74 & Henry Gallery, Univ Wash, Seattle, 77; 4th Int DeBijoux d'Art Contemporain, Toulouse, France, 73-74; Forms in Metal, 275 Yrs of Metalsmithing, Mus Contemp Crafts, New York, 75; Outstanding Jewelry Sch in USA, Nat Goldsmiths Show, Melbourne, Australia, 76; Objects USA, Smithsonian Traveling Exhib, Europe, 68-72. Collections Arranged: Creative Silversmithing Workshop I & II, summer 55 & 56 & Carnegie Grant for Graduate Student Experimental Silversmithing Project (with booklet & film), 68, Fine Arts Ctr, Ind Univ, Bloomington. Teaching: Asst prof design & jewelry, Kans State Univ, Wichita, 41-43, 45-46; head jewelry dept, Ind Univ, 47-; prof, Univ Wis, Madison, summer 63. Awards: First Place Cash Award, Nat Silversmithing, 51; Nat Endowment for the Arts Craft Award, 75; numerous travel grants for res. Bibliog: Lee Nordness (auth), Objects USA, Viking, 70; Phillip Morton (auth), Contemp Jewelry, Holt Rinehart & Winston, 76; Oppi Untracht (auth), Contemporary Craftsman, 78. Mem: Nat Soc Am Goldsmiths; Am Asn Univ Prof; Nat Soc Arts & Lett; Col Art Asn; Ind Craftsmen. Style & Technique: Bold, structural forms; pieces assume compositional tensions usually associated with contemporary abstract sculpture. Media: Gold, Silver; Copper, Brass, Silver. Res: Mixtec Jewelry in Oaxaca, Mexico; Etruscan jewelry in the major collections in Italy & France; Scythian and Sarmatian gold objects in the museums in Leningrad, Kiev & and Moscow; Medieval objects in France & Southern Ger; jewlery and metal objects in the Far & Near East and especially the jewelry of Indian and Tibet and the metal object Hittite in the Ankara and Istanbul, Turkey museums; Hallstatt, LaTene and Celtic metal objects in Switzerland, Germany, England and Scotland. Collection: African sculpture, small Oriental and contemporary bronzes, enamel, ceramics, contemporary glass, paintings and prints. Mailing Add: Dept of Fine Arts Room 405 Ind Univ Bloomington IN 47401

EILERS, FRED (ANTON FREDERICK),
PAINTER, DESIGNER
b Wilmington, NC. Study: William & Mary Col, BS; Richmond Prof Inst, with Theresa Pollack. Work: Evansville Mus, Ind; St Marys Hosp, Evansville; First Lutheran Church, Richmond, Va; Univ Evansville; Ind State Univ; plus others. Comn: Mural, Colonial Nat Bank, 69. Exhib: Hoosier Salon, Indianapolis, Ind; Ohio Valley Watercolor, Athens; Mid States Exhib, Evansville; one-man shows, Gallery R, Evansville Mus Gallery, Univ Evansville, Old Gallery, Evansville, Hoosier Gallery, Indianapolis & Thor Gallery, Louisville. Teaching: Instr portrait painting, Univ Evansville, 46-, instr figure drawing, 50- Pos: Bd dirs, Evansville Mus, 58-60; consult art purchases, Old Nat Bank, 69- Awards: Bronstein Purchase Award, Evansville Mus, 60, Graphics Purchase Award, 68; Hoosier Salon Merit Award, 65. Style & Technique: Traditional portrait painter & restorer. Media: Oil. Dealer: Risley Evansville IN 47708; Thor Gallery 734 S First St Louisville KY 40202. Mailing Add: 2140 E Chandler Ave Evansville IN 47714

EINO (EINO ANTTI ROMPPANEN)
SCULPTOR
b Mynamaki, Finland, Feb 6, 40; US citizen. Comn: Portrait of Sibelius (marble), Finlandia Found, Los Angeles, 64; 15' Christ, Ga Marble Co, Tate, 66; Portrait of Chairman of Board (bronze), Imperial Oil & Grease Co, Los Angeles, 68; memorial portrait, Univ Southern Calif, Los Angeles, 73; freeform marble, Sculpture Garden, Church of Perfect Liberty, Japan, 73. Exhib: One-man shows, Int Design Ctr, Los Angeles, 65, Pepperdine Univ, Malibu, Calif, 73; Calif Expos, Sacramento, 71; Gallerie Juarez, Los Angeles & Palm Springs, 70; Opening Exhib, Palm Springs Desert Mus, Calif, 76. Teaching: Teacher sculpture, Pepperdine Univ, 69, instr TV credit course, Theta Cable, 71. Bibliog: Ulla Kakonen (auth), Eino, Eva Mag, Finland, 72; NBC-TV Show, Ray Duncan, 72; Stan Pantovic (auth), The earth is shaking (Eino), The Geijutsu Seikatsu, Japan, 75; plus many others. Style & Technique: Modern nonfigurative large negative spaces that interrelate the environment to the sculpture. Media: Marble. Mailing Add: 32926 Mulholland Hwy Malibu CA 90265

EINSTEIN, GILBERT W
ART DEALER
b New York, NY, June 27, 42. Study: Columbia Univ, AB, 63, MBA, 68. Pos: Pres, G W Einstein Co, Inc, New York, 70- Specialty: Twentieth century American art; publisher of fine prints. Mailing Add: G W Einstein Co Inc 243 E 82nd St New York NY 10028

EISENBERG, MARVIN
ART HISTORIAN, EDUCATOR
b Philadelphia, Pa. Study: Univ Pa, BA, 43; Princeton Univ, MFA, 49, PhD, 54. Teaching: Instr art hist, Univ Mich, 49-53, asst prof, 54-58, assoc prof, 58-61, prof, 61-, chmn dept, 61-69; vis prof, Stanford Univ, 73. Pos: Mem, Inst for Advan Study, winter 70. Awards: Guggenheim Fel, 59; Star of Solidarity, Ital Govt, 61. Mem: Col Art Asn Am (pres, 68-69); Benjamin Franklin Fel Royal Soc Arts. Res: Italian late mediaeval painting. Publ: Auth, articles on early Italian painting in journals and museum bulletins. Mailing Add: Dept of Hist of Art Univ of Mich Ann Arbor MI 48109

EISENBERG, REBECCA
See Cooper, Rebecca

EISENBERG, SONJA MIRIAM
PAINTER, PHOTOGRAPHER
b Berlin, Ger; US citizen. Study: NY Univ, BA, 54; Nat Acad Sch Fine Arts, with Leon Kroll, 61; also with Daniel Dickerson, 62-68 & Sidney Delevante, in 60's. Work: Palm Spring Desert Mus; Fordham Univ Mus; Huntsville Mus Art, Ala; Anglo-Am Art Bus, Baton Rouge, La. Comn: Designer, WF UNA Cachet, UN Water Conf, 77. Exhib: One-man shows, Galerie Art Du Monde, Paris, 72, Mus Fine Arts, St Petersburg, Fla, 73, Galerie de Sfinx, Amsterdam, 74 & Palm Spring Desert Mus, 75; Am Watercolor Soc 108th Ann Exhib, New York, 75. Bibliog: Reva Remy (auth), Galerie art du monde, Le Monde, 9/72; Jan deCarpentier (auth), Kijk's kunst, De Typhoon, 6/74; Gordon Brown (auth), Sonja Eisenberg, Art Mag, 4/75. Style & Technique: Intuitive abstracts. Media: Oil, Watercolor; Color Prints. Dealer: Bodley Gallery 1063 Madison Ave New York NY 10028. Mailing Add: 1020 Park Ave New York NY 10028

EISENSTAT, BENJAMIN
PAINTER, ILLUSTRATOR
b Philadelphia, Pa, June 4, 15. Study: Fleisher Art Mem; Pa Acad Fine Arts; Albert Barnes Found. Work: Philadelphia Mus Art; Fleisher Art Mem, Philadelphia; Springfield Art Mus, Mo; Woodmere Gallery, Philadelphia; Jefferson Hosp, Philadelphia. Comn: Official painting of nuclear ship Savannah, US Maritime & NY Ship Comn, Washington, DC, 59; three panel historical mural, First Bank NJ, Philadelphia, 60; three panel historical mural, Provident Mutual Life Ins Co, Philadelphia, 62; two panel historical mural, Burlington Co Trust Co, Moorestown, NJ, 63; two panel historical mural, Oreland Episcopal Church, Pa, 70. Exhib: Artists for Victory, Metrop Mus Art, New York, 45, Nat Drawing Show, 55; Norfolk Mus Art Nat Drawing Show, 71; Watercolor USA, Springfield, Mo; Nat Acad Design Ann, New York; Am Watercolor Soc Ann, New York; Rutgers Nat Drawing Show, Rutgers Univ, Camden, NJ, 77. Teaching: Assoc prof painting & drawing, Philadelphia Col Art, 46-69, prof painting & drawing & chmn illustrating dept, 69-; instr watercolor, Philadelphia Mus Art, 62-66; instr illus, Cambridge Col Arts & Technol, Eng, 76; lectr Am illus, Royal Col Art, London, Eng, 76; lectr hist Am illus, Parsons Sch Design, NY, 76, 77 & 78. Awards: Ann Medal Achievement, Philadelphia Watercolor Club, 62; Harrison Morris Prize, Fellowship, Pa Acad Fine Arts; Watercolor USA Prize, 72. Bibliog: Hugh Scott (auth), Mural on Market Street, Today Mag, 6/12/60; Henry Pitz (auth), Documentary drawings of Benjamin Eisenstat, Am Artists, 12/65. Mem: Am Watercolor Soc; Philadelphia Watercolor Club (bd dirs); Philadelphia Art Alliance (bd dirs, 62-68); Artists Equity (bd dirs, 67-71); Fellowship, Pa Acad Fine Arts (bd dirs, 55-60). Style & Technique: Expressionistic, with a greater degree of realism in illustrations and murals. Collection: Original illustrations. Publ: Auth & illusr, articles in Today Mag, 54-71; auth & illusr, articles in Ford Times, 54-72; auth & illusr, articles in travel sect, New York Sunday Times, 55-61; auth & illusr, Coming Events in Britain, 61. Dealer: Newman Gallery 1625 Walnut St Philadelphia PA 19103; Mangel Gallery Bala Cynwyd PA. Mailing Add: 438 Camden Ave Moorestown NJ 08057

EISENSTEIN, MR & MRS JULIAN
COLLECTORS
Mr Eisenstein, b Warrenton, Mo, Apr 3, 21. Study: Mr Eisenstein, Harvard Univ, BS, 41, MA, 42, PhD, 48. Pos: Mr Eisenstein, pres & trustee, Washington Gallery Mod Art, 61-65. Collection: Contemporary art. Mailing Add: 82 Kalorama Circle NW Washington DC 20008

EISENTRAGER, JAMES A
PAINTER
b Alvord, Iowa, Sept 3, 29. Study: Augustana Col, Sioux Falls, SDak, BA, 51; Univ Md in Weisbaden, Ger, 52-53; Univ Northern Iowa, 55; Univ Iowa, Iowa City, MFA, 61; studies with Stewart Edie, Byron Burford & Mauricio Lasansky. Work: Sioux City Art Ctr, Iowa; Springfield Art Mus, Mo; Univ Iowa, Iowa City; Sheldon Mem Art Gallery, Lincoln, Nebr; Millersville State Univ, Pa. Exhib: Ann Exhib, Springfield Art Mus, Mo, 64-72; one-man shows, Sheldon Mem Art Gallery, 66, Univ Del, Newark, 75 & Northern Ariz Univ Art Gallery, Flagstaff, 77; 31st Mid-Yr Show, Butler Inst Am Art, Youngstown, Ohio, 66; Mid-Am Exhib, William Rockhill Nelson Gallery of Art, Kansas City, Mo, 66 & 70; Mid-W Biennial, Joslyn Art Mus, Omaha, Nebr, 66 & 70; Ten Artists W of the Mississippi, Colorado Springs Fine Art Ctr, 67. Teaching: Prof painting, Univ Nebr-Lincoln, 61-; prof & lectr, Vail Summer Workshop, Colo, 71-76; vis prof art, Univ Colo, Boulder, summer 68. Awards: Purchase Award, May Show, Sioux City Art Ctr, Iowa, 63; Best Painting Purchase Award, Images on Paper Nat Competition, Springfield Art Asn, Ill, 73; Jesse Loomis Award, Waterloo Ann, Waterloo Munic Gallery, Iowa, 73. Mem: Mid-Am Col Art Asn (prog off, 76). Style & Technique: Since 68, geometric abstract; previously, figurative-representational. Media: Polymer, oil. Mailing Add: 5114 M St Lincoln NE 68510

EISINGER, HARRY
PAINTER
b Berlin, Ger, Apr 23, 32; US citizen. Study: Calif Sch Fine Arts, San Francisco, 57-59; also with Ralph Putzker, Nathan Oliveira & Wayne Thiebaud. Work: Slides, Whitney Mus, New York. Comn: Drawings, Territorial Gazette, San Francisco, 59; posters, Marin Co Art Ctr, Calif, 60. Exhib: One-man shows, Panoras Gallery, New York, 73 & Gallery 84, 77; 32nd & 33rd Nat Audubon Exhibs, Nat Acad Galleries, 74 & 75 & Allied Artists Am Exhib, 75; Gallery 84, New York, 75. Awards: Spinaker Award, Sausalito Mayor, Calif, 60; Hon Mention for Oil Painting, Allied Artists Am, 74. Bibliog: Herb Caen (auth), article in San Francisco Chronicle, 60. Mem: Allied Artists Am; Audubon Artists. Style & Technique: Abstract, using knife and brush. Media: Oil. Dealer: Gallery 84 1046 Madison Ave New York NY 10021. Mailing Add: 330 E 19th St New York NY 10003

EISNER, ELLIOT WAYNE
EDUCATOR
b Chicago, Ill, Mar 10, 33. Study: Roosevelt Univ, BA; Ill Inst Technol, MS; Univ Chicago, MA & PhD. Teaching: Instr art educ, Ohio State Univ, 60-61; asst prof educ, Univ Chicago, 61-65; prof educ & art, Stanford Univ, 65- Awards: Palmer Johnson Award, Am Educ res Asn, 67; Guggenheim Fel, 70. Mem: Nat Art Educ Asn (chmn res, 64; pres, 77-79); Am Educ Res Asn. Publ: Co-auth, Readings in Art Education, Ginn, 66; auth, Confronting Curriculum Reform, Little, 71; auth, Educating Vision, Macmillan, 72. Mailing Add: Dept of Art Stanford Univ Stanford CA 94305

EITEL, CLIFFE DEAN
PAINTER, DESIGNER
b Salt Lake City, Utah, June 18, 09. Study: Nat Acad Art; Art Inst Chicago; Inst Design; also with Roy C Eitel, Joseph Binder, Gyorgy Kepes, Hubert Ropp & Charles Wilimovsky. Work: Seattle Art Mus, Wash. Comn: Four ceramic tile murals, Mercy Hosp, Canton, Ohio, 56; two ceramic tile murals, Tampa Munic Hosp, Fla, 57; mural (oil). Flavorama Prods, Northfield, Ill, 59; ceramic tile mural, Augustinian Seminary, Olympia Fields, Ill, 59; two mosaic tile murals, St Marys Hosp, Kankakee, Ill, 60. Exhib: Libr Cong, Washington, DC, 46; Art Inst Chicago, 50; Brooklyn Mus, NY, 50; State Dept Exhib, Ger, 51; Benjamin Galleries, Chicago, 56. Teaching: Instr abstract & mod art, Chicago Prof Sch Art, 41-43; demonstr printmaking, Northbrook Pub & Jr High Sch, 71-72. Pos: Art dir, Swan Studios, Chicago, 37-39; art dir, Hanks & Assoc, Chicago, 39-41; free lance designer & artist, Chicago, 41- Awards: Landscape in Motion, Artists Guild Chicago, 45. Bibliog: Alex Weaver (auth), Evolution of a Cliffe Eitel design, Am Artist Mag, 50; Kunst des Gestaltens, Der Polygraph, Frankfurt, Ger, 50; Clyde Walton (auth), Historical records, Ill Lives, 69. Mem: Northbrook Art League (design dir, 70-74; pres, 74-76); Northshore Art League; Renaissance Soc, Univ Chicago; Nat Soc Lit & Arts. Style & Technique: Abstract and experimental. Mailing Add: 1819 Oakwood Rd Northbrook IL 60062

EITELJORG, HARRISON
COLLECTOR, PATRON
b Indianapolis, Ind, Oct 1, 04. Study: Ind Univ Law Sch. Mem: Indianapolis Mus Art (chmn bd trustees, gov, ex-officio mem comts); Contemp Art Soc; Decorative Arts Soc; Am Asn Mus; Nat Acad Western Art (trustee). Interest: Sponsor of museum of western artifacts. Collection: Abstract and modern American art; School of Paris; Western painting and sculptor; African art. Mailing Add: 4567 Cold Spring Rd Indianapolis IN 46208

EITINGON, BRIGITTE
ART DEALER
b Paris, France, Sept 12, 27. Study: NY Univ, BA, 46; Sorbonne, Paris, Lic Lett, 48; Ecol du Louvre, Paris, dipl hist art, 48. Pos: Owner, Brigitte Eitingon Fine Arts Ltd, New York. Specialty: Twentieth century masters, as well as young up-coming artists, both American and European in all media. Mailing Add: c/o Brigitte Eitingon Fine Arts Ltd 245 E 63rd St New York NY 10021

EITNER, LORENZ E A
ART HISTORIAN, MUSEUM DIRECTOR
b Brünn, Czech, Aug 27, 19; US citizen. Study: Duke Univ, AB, 40; Princeton Univ, MFA, 48, PhD, 52. Collections Arranged: Masterdrawings, Guggenheim Mus, New York & Univ Gallery, Univ Minn, 60; Gericault, Los Angeles Co Mus, Detroit Inst Art & Philadelphia Mus Art, 71-72; numerous art exhibs at Stanford Mus. Teaching: Prof art, Univ Minn, 49-63; prof art & chmn dept, Stanford Univ, 63- Pos: Dir, Stanford Mus, 63- Mem: Col Art Asn Am (vpres, dir, 56-71 & 76-); Res: European painting of the latter half of the eighteenth century and the beginning of the nineteenth century. Publ: Auth, The Flabellum of Tournus, Col Art Asn, 44; auth, Introduction to Art, Burgess, 60; auth, Gericault, Univ Chicago, 60; auth, Neoclassicism and Romanticism, Prentice-Hall, 69; auth, Gericault's Raft of the Medusa, Phaidon, 72. Mailing Add: Dept of Art Stanford Univ Stanford CA 94305

EKSTROM, ARNE H
ART DEALER
Pos: Dir, Cordier & Ekstrom Inc. Specialty: Contemporary American art. Mailing Add: 980 Madison Ave New York NY 10021

ELAM, CHARLES HENRY
ART ADMINISTRATOR, ART HISTORIAN
b Ashland, Ky, Feb 13, 15. Study: Univ Cincinnati, AB, 38; Inst Fine Arts, NY Univ, AM, 52; Courtauld Inst, Univ London, 53. Collections Arranged: Catalogued & asst assembler, Rendezvous for Taste, Peale Mus, 56, French Paintings 1789-1929 from the Collection of Walter P Chrysler, Jr, Dayton Art Inst, 60 & The Peale Family, Detroit Inst Arts, 67. Pos: Archivist, Peale Mus, 54-59; chief cur, Dayton Art Inst, 59-64; cur Am art, Detroit Inst Arts, 64-67; ed, Wayne State Univ Press, 67-70; mus registr, Detroit Inst Arts, 70- Publ: Auth, The Peale Family, 67; co-ed, The Detroit Institute of Arts Illustrated Handbook, 71. Mailing Add: 25 E Palmer Ave Detroit MI 48202

ELDER, DAVID MORTON
SCULPTOR, ART ADMINISTRATOR
b Windsor, Ont, July 3, 36; US citizen. Study: Wittenberg Univ, BA, 57; Ohio State Univ Grad Sch, MA, 61. Work: Denver Art Mus, Colo; Long Beach Art Mus, Calif. Comn: Sculpture (metal), Gloria Christi Chapel, Valparaiso Univ, 62, St Paul Lutheran Church, Glenn Bermie, Md, 63, Coconut Grove Ambassador Hotel, Los Angeles, 69 & Barnsdall Park, Los Angeles, 74; sculpture (resin), Pac Home Burbank, 74. Exhib: Long Beach Mus Art, 66, 70 & 71; Calif Sky Scape Show, Calif Col Arts & Crafts, Oakland, 69; Calif Landscape Show, La Jolla Mus Art, 69; San Francisco Centennial Show, De Young Mus, 71; Last Plastics Show, Calif Inst Arts, Valencia, 72. Teaching: Asst prof sculpture, Calif State Univ, Los Angeles, 68-71; prof sculpture, Calif State Univ, Northridge, 71-, chmn dept 3-D art, 72-, assoc dean, Sch Arts, 74- Awards: 4th Ann Long Beach Mus First Prize, 66; Purchase Award Comn, Southwestern Col, 67; Artist of the Year, Pasadena Arts Coun, 71. Style & Technique: Organic Forms. Media: Bronze, Polyester Resin. Dealer: Orlando Gallery 17037 Ventura Blvd Encino CA 91316. Mailing Add: 22441 Lassen Chatsworth CA 91311

ELDER, MULDOON
PAINTER, SCULPTOR
b Los Angeles, Calif, June 24, 35. Work: Long Beach Mus Art; Downey Mus Art; Pentagon Collection; Syntex Collection. Exhib: Long Beach Mus Art, 57; Houston Mus, 58; Dallas Mus Art, 58; Downey Mus Art, 60; San Francisco Mus Art, 69. Awards: Purchase Awards, Long Beach Mus Art, Pentagon Collection & Downey Mus Art. Bibliog: R Ellsworth (auth), Muldoon Elder (catalog), Vorpal Gallery. Media: Oil. Mailing Add: c/o Vorpal Gallery 1168 Battery St San Francisco CA 94111

ELDERFIELD, JOHN
ART HISTORIAN, CURATOR
b Yorkshire, Eng, Apr 25, 43. Study: Univ Leeds, BA & MPhil; Courtauld Inst Art, Univ London, PhD. Collections Arranged: Morris Louis (auth, catalogue), London Arts Coun of Gt Brit, 74; The Wild Beasts: Fauvism and Its Affinities (auth, catalogue), 76 & European Paintings from Swiss Collections: Post-Impressionism to World War II (auth, catalogue), 76, Mus Mod Art, New York. Teaching: Lectr hist art, Winchester Sch of Art, Eng, 66-70; lectr hist art, Univ Leeds, Eng, 73-75. Pos: Harkness fel, Yale Univ, New Haven, Conn, 70-72; Guggenheim Found fel, 72-73; contrib ed, Artforum, 72-74 & Studio Int Mag, 73-75; cur painting & sculpture, Mus Mod Art, New York, 75- Mem: Fel Royal Soc Arts. Res: Twentieth century art. Publ: Ed, Hugo Ball (auth), The Flight from Time—A Dada Diary, Viking, 75. Mailing Add: c/o Mus of Mod Art 11 W 53rd St New York NY 10019

ELDREDGE, CHARLES CHILD, III
MUSEUM DIRECTOR, ART HISTORIAN
b Boston, Mass, Apr 12, 44. Study: Amherst Col, BA, 66; Univ Minn, PhD, 71. Collections Arranged: The Arcadian Landscape: Nineteenth Century Am Painters in Italy (co-auth & ed, catalogue), 72, Marsden Hartley Lithographs and Related Works (auth, catalogue), 72, Gene Swenson: Retrospective for a Critic (contribr & ed, catalogue), 71 & John Ward Lockwood, 1894-1963 (auth, catalogue), 74, Helen Foresman Spencer Mus of Art, Univ Kans, Lawrence. Pos: Cur of collections, Univ Kans Mus of Art, Lawrence, 70-71, dir & chief cur, Helen Foresman Spencer Mus of Art (formerly Univ Kans Mus of Art), 71- Mem: Am Asn of Mus; Asn of Art Mus Dirs; Col Art Asn; Midwest Art Hist Soc; Mid-Continent Am Studies Asn (mem ed bd, 73-77). Res: American and 19th-20th century European art; museum management techniques. Publ: Contribr, Works by John Rood: A Memorial Exhibition, Univ Minn, 74. Mailing Add: Helen Foresman Spencer Mus of Art Univ of Kans Lawrence KS 66045

ELDREDGE, MARY AGNES
SCULPTOR
b Hartford, Conn, Jan 21, 42. Study: Vassar Col, with Concetta Scaravaglione & Juan Nickford, BA; Pius XII Inst, Florence, Italy, with Josef Gudics, MFA. Work: Dartmouth Col Collection. Comn: Madonna & Child, St Gabriel Episcopal Church, Milton-Oak Ridge, NJ, 75; Crêche, Corpus Christi Church, New York, 75; Stations of the Cross, Rising Christ, Church of Sts Joachim & Ann, Staten Island, NY, 76; Madonna & Child, Sanctuary Lamp, Mercy Hosp Chapel, Springfield, Mass, 76-77; Mary Immaculate, St Patrick, Cathedral of the Immaculate Conception, Burlington, Vt, 77; plus others. Exhib: Mostra dell 'Arte Religiosa per Pasqua, Florence, 65; Nat Arts Club Religious Art Exhib, New York, 66; Acad Artists Asn Nat Exhib, Springfield, Mass, 67; Modern Art and the Religious Experience, Fifth Ave Presby Church, New York, 68; 6th Biennial Nat Religious Art Exhib, Cranbrook Acad Art, 69. Awards: Therese Richard Mem Prize, Nat Arts Club, 66; Acad Artists Asn Award, 67; Staten Island Chamber of Com Award, 77. Mem: Southern Vt Artists, Inc; Vt Coun on the Arts. Style & Technique: Contemporary traditional. Media: Copper, Stone, Wood. Dealer: Contemp Christian Art, Inc 1060 A Lexington Ave New York NY 10021. Mailing Add: RFD 1 Box 472 Springfield VT 05156

ELDREDGE, STUART EDSON
PAINTER
b South Bend, Ind, July 1, 02. Study: Dartmouth Col, AB; Art Students League, with Kimon Nicolaides; Beaux Arts Inst, New York. Work: Butler Inst Am Art, Youngstown, Ohio; Springfield Art Mus, Mass; Southern Vt Artists, Inc, Manchester; Dartmouth Col, Hanover, NH; Robert Hull Fleming Mus, Burlington, Vt. Comn: Murals, First Nat Bank, Springfield; mural, Springfield Hosp; Stations of Cross, St Joseph's Church, Chester, Vt; murals in textile bldg, World's Fair, New York, 39. Exhib: 9th Ann Print Exhib, Libr Cong, Washington, DC, 51; Philadelphia Watercolor Club, 52 & 53; Ind Artists 50th Ann Invitational, 57; Am Watercolor Soc, 61 & 63; plus others. Teaching: Instr drawing & painting, Cooper Union, 32-40; instr drawing & painting, Art Students League Summer Sch, 34 & 35; prof drawing, Pius XII Inst, Florence, Italy, summer 64. Awards: Tiffany Fel, 32. Mem: Nat Soc Mural Painters; Southern Vt Artists (trustee, 50-78); Springfield Art & Hist Soc (trustee, 59-74). Media: Watercolor, Tempera, Oil. Dealer: Gallery 2 Woodstock VT 05091. Mailing Add: Parker Hill Rd Springfield VT 05156

ELIAS, HAROLD JOHN
PAINTER, LECTURER
b Cleveland, Ohio, Mar 12, 20. Study: Art Inst Chicago; De Paul Univ; Mich State Univ, BFA & MFA; also with John Rogers Cox & Katherine Blackshear. Work: Art Inst Chicago; Upjohn Collection, Kalamazoo, Mich; Ill State Mus, Springfield; Massillon Mus, Ohio; Univ Idaho.

Comn: Mich scenes, Fraternal Order Eagles, Muskegon Heights, Mich, 56; Mich scenes, Round Lake Lodge, Watervliet, Mich, 64; mobile, Mercy Hosp, Benton Harbor, Mich, 66; Triligy (mobile), Cath Church, Muskegon Heights, 67; aluminum & plastic mural, Letourneau Col, 72. Exhib: American Art Today 1950, Metrop Mus Art, New York, 50; Pa Acad Fine Art, 51; Detroit Inst Art, 52, 53 & 55; Int Sculpture Competition, Brussels, Belg, 53; Baltimore Mus Art, 53; plus many others. Teaching: Instr art hist & oil painting, Muskegon Community Col Eve Div, 52-57; instr drawing & oil painting, Lake Mich Col Eve Div, 60-66; instr drawing & oil painting, Kilgore Col Eve Div, 69-; instr drawing & painting, Ambassador Col, Tex, 73- Pos: Asst dir, Hackley Art Gallery, Muskegon, 52-56, actg dir, 56-57. Awards: Awarded One-Man Show, Chicago Esquire Theatre Exhib, 50; Hollis S Baker Best of Show, Western Mich Artists Exhib, 52; Schiller Award for Watercolor, Mich Exhib, 65. Bibliog: Review of show, Art News, 50; New talent, Art in Am, 57. Mem: Mich Acad Sci, Arts & Lett; Centro Studi E Scambi Internazionali; Mich State Coun Arts; Tex Comn Arts & Humanities. Media: Oil, Watercolor, Wire. Publ: Auth, Why not beauty, Longview Daily News; plus others. Mailing Add: 1800 McCann Rd Longview TX 75601

ELIASON, SHIRLEY (SHIRLEY ELIASON HAUPT)
MIXED-MEDIA ARTIST, INSTRUCTOR
b Kanawha, Iowa. Study: Art Inst of Chicago, BAE; Univ Iowa, MFA with Mauricio Lasansky & James Lechay; Fulbright Scholar, Courtauld Inst of Art, Univ London, 2 yrs. Work: Des Moines Art Ctr, Iowa; Grinnell Col, Iowa; Yale Univ Art Gallery; Libr of Cong, Washington, DC; KWWL Collection, Waterloo, Iowa. Comn: Pvt comns. Exhib: Pratt Int Miniature Print Exhib, New York; Young Am Printmakers, Mus of Mod Art, New York; Nat Black & White Exhib, Erie, Pa; Joslyn Art Mus Biennial, Omaha, Nebr; Int Print Exhib, Libr of Cong; plus numerous others. Collections Arranged: Am Prints 1950-1960 (auth, catalogue), Yale Univ Art Gallery, 60; and others. Teaching: Instr, Univ Iowa, 54-55; assoc prof drawing, painting & printmaking, Univ Northern Iowa, 66- Pos: Docent, Yale Univ Art Gallery, 58-59, asst cur of prints, 59-61. Awards: Purchase Award, Iowa Artists, Des Moines Art Ctr, 54 & 56; Best-in-Show, All-Iowa, KWWL, 68. Mem: Midwest Col Art Asn; Col Art Asn. Style & Technique: Combined techniques, gessoed panel, paper or canvas (pencil, watercolor, acrylic); woodcut variables; selected collage elements. Publ: Contribr (poems, intaglios), To a Veteran, A Painter, Dead at Twenty-Four & The Game of Chess, Western Rev, 56; auth, What Makes a Good Studio Teacher?, Col Art J, 56; illusr (cover), The Burden of Memory, 69 & Iowa, Black Field, Bernini, 74, NAm Rev. Mailing Add: 803 Iowa Cedar Falls IA 50613

ELIOT, LUCY CARTER
PAINTER
b New York, NY. Study: Vassar Col, BA; Art Students League with Bridgman, Brackman, Raphael Soyer, William Von Schlegell & Kantor; Columbia Univ, with Ralph Mayer. Work: Rochester Mem Art Gallery, NY; Munson-Williams-Proctor Inst, Utica, NY. Exhib: Pa Acad Fine Arts, Philadelphia, 46, 48-50, 52 & 54; Va Biennial, 48; Corcoran Biennial, Washington, DC, 47 & 51; Ringling Bros Mus, Sarasota, Fla, 58; Nat Acad Design, New York, 71; Butler Inst, Youngstown, Ohio, 65-; Upland Idyll, Everson Mus, Syracuse Mus, NY, 76. Teaching: Instr painting & drawing, Occup Ther Dept, Bronx Vet Hosp, New York, 50-52. Pos: Mem bd, Artists' Tech Res Inst, 75- Awards: Award, Rochester Mem Art Gallery, 46; Purchase Prize, Munson-Williams-Proctor Inst, 49; Painting of Indust Award, Silvermine Guild, 57. Mem: NY Soc Women Artists (corresp secy, 70-73, pres, 73-75, mem, mem comt & chmn painting jury, 77-); Audubon Artists; Artists Equity Asn. Style & Technique: Recognizable subject matter; semi-abstract; brush and painting knife. Media: Oil, Pencil & Casein. Mailing Add: 131 E 66th St New York NY 10021

ELISCU, FRANK
SCULPTOR
b New York, NY, July 13, 12. Comn: War mem, Cornell Med Col; heroic horses in slate, Bankers Trust Bldg, NY; Presidential Eagle, Oval Off, White House; inaugural medal, Pres Ford; inaugural medal, VPres Rockefeller, plus others. Exhib: Pa Acad Fine Arts; Conn Acad Fine Arts; Cleveland Mus Art; Springfield Mus Art; Detroit Inst Art; plus others. Awards: Bennet Prize Sculpture, Nat Sculpture Soc, 53; Prize, Archit League New York, 55, Silver Medal, 58; Henry Hering Award, 60; plus others. Mem: Fel Nat Sculpture Soc (pres, 67-70); Nat Acad Design (academician); Archit League New York. Publ: Auth, Sculpture: Three Techniques—Wax, Slate, Clay; auth, Direct Wax Sculpture. Mailing Add: 4707 Ocean Blvd Sarasota FL 33587

ELKIN, BEVERLY DAWN
ART DEALER
b Chicago, Ill, Apr 23, 33. Study: Univ Ill, BA, 55, MA, 65. Pos: Co-owner & co-show mgr, House of Art, Champaign, Ill. Mem: Prof Picture Framers Asn. Specialty: Contemporary midwestern American artist; painting, sculpture and ceramics. Mailing Add: 1103 W Green Champaign IL 61820

ELKINS, (E) LANE
EDUCATOR, POTTER
b McDonald Co, Mo, Mar 26, 25. Study: Southwest Mo State Col, BSEd(with honors), 49; Columbia Univ, MAFA & FAEd, 50; with Marquerite Wildenhain, 56 & 63; Cranbrook Acad Art, MFA, 62. Work: Contentment (granite), Covered Jar (stoneware) & Handbuilt Globe on Pedestal (stoneware), Springfield Art Mus, Mo. Comn: Several jewelry comns for individuals. Exhib: Springfield Art Mus Ann Regional Show, 53-72; Wichita Art Asn Galleries 15th & 17th Decorative Arts & Ceramics Exhib, 60 & 62; Ann Drawing & Sculpture Show, Ball State Univ Art Gallery, 63; American Jewelry Today, Ala Mus Fine Arts, 64; Am Craftsmen Show, Smithsonian Inst, 70. Teaching: Prof ceramics, Southwest Mo State Univ, 50- Pos: Pres, Alpha Theta Chap, Delta Phi Delta, 48-49, regional dir, 52-60; pres, Teachers Col Art Club, Columbia Univ, 49-50. Awards: Covered Jar (stoneware) Award, 57 & Handbuilt Globe on Pedestal (stoneware) Award, 70, Springfield Art Mus; Protective Image (cast bronze) Award, Edmund F Ball, Nat Sculpture Show, 63. Mem: Am Craftsman Coun; Mo Craftsman Coun. Style & Technique: Thrown stoneware; earthy glazes, also hand built and thrown sculptural pots; jewelry lost wax cast sterling, occasional use of found stones or tropical woods with silver. Media: Stoneware, Wood, Sterling. Publ: Contribr, Walker Art Quart, spec issue, 59. Mailing Add: Rte 3 Box 198 Rogersville MO 65742

ELKON, ROBERT
ART DEALER, COLLECTOR
b Belg, 1928. Study: Univ Wis-Madison, BA; Harvard Univ Law Sch; Columbia Univ; NY Univ Inst Fine Arts. Pos: Owner-dir, Robert Elkon Gallery. Mem: Art Dealers Asn; Harvard Club. Specialty: 20th century masters; contemporary painters and sculptors. Publ: Auth, literary revs in New York Times & Art News. Mailing Add: 1063 Madison Ave New York NY 10028

ELLINGER, ILONA E
PAINTER, EDUCATOR
b Budapest, Hungary, June 12, 13. Study: Royal Hungarian Univ Sch Art, MFA; Royal Swedish Art Acad; Johns Hopkins Univ, with David M Robinson & W F Albright, PhD; Univ Freiburg; Univ Wis. Exhib: Soc Washington Artists; one-man show, Am-Brit Art Ctr, George Washington Univ, 50; Silver Spring Art Gallery, 51; Corcoran Gallery Art, 58; Batiks, Gallery N, Setauket, 77; plus others. Teaching: Prof art & head dept, Trinity Col, Washington, DC, 43-; Fulbright prof hist art & archit, Nat Col Arts, Lahore, W Pakistan, 63-64; lectr Am art, US Info Serv, Lahore, Rawalpindi, Dacca; vis prof, State Univ NY Stony Brook, 69-77. Mem: Soc Washington Artists; Archaeol Inst Am. Mailing Add: 67 Quaker Path Stony Brook NY 11790

ELLINGSON, WILLIAM JOHN
EDUCATOR, PRINTMAKER
b Forrestburg, SDak, Mar 29, 33. Study: Minneapolis Sch Art & Design, Minn, BFA, 60; Skowhegan Sch Sculpture & Painting, Maine; State Univ Iowa, Iowa City, MFA, 63; postgrad work, Univ Minn, Minneapolis. Work: Nelson Gallery, Kansas City, Mo; Springfield Art Ctr, Mass; Col S Idaho, Twin Falls; Permanent Collection, Hamline Univ, Minneapolis; plus numerous pvt collections in Denmark, Japan, Can, Ger & Eng. Comn: Ltd ed etching, Minn State Arts Coun, Minneapolis, 67 & New Eng Life Insurance Co, Wichita, Kans, 75-77; ltd ed silkscreen, Denmark Prog, St Cloud State Univ, 76. Exhib: Art in the Embassies, US State Dept; Pasadena Art Mus Print Exhib, Calif, 62; Silvermine Guild Artists Inc, New Canaan, Conn, 62; Ultimate Concerns Nat Print Exhib, Athens, Ohio, 65 & 68; Springfield Art Ctr, Mass, 65; Hunterdon Co Art Ctr, Clinton, NJ, 66 & 67; Am Drawing Biennial, Norfolk, Va, 66; Audubon Artists Inc, New York, 67; Pa Acad Fine Arts; 142nd Ann Exhib, Nat Acad Design, New York; Conn Acad Fine Arts, Hartford; Boston Printmakers 19th Ann, Boston, Mass; Nat Drawing Exhib, Okla Mus Arts; plus many others. Teaching: Prof print media, St Cloud State Univ, Minn, 63-; vis artist, Univ Saskatoon, Sask, 77. Awards: Edna Stauffer Award, Audubon Artists, Inc, 67. Mem: Nat Graphic Soc. Style & Technique: Combination lithography and etching media for multi-colored graphic images; life-size silkscreens. Media: Etching; Lithography; Woodcut; Silkscreen. Dealer: Fairweather Hardin Gallery 101 E Ontario Ave Chicago IL 60611. Mailing Add: 1723 Seventh Ave S St Cloud MN 56301

ELLIOTT, B CHARLES, JR
ART CONSULTANT, ART HISTORIAN
b Grove City, Pa, Apr 9, 24. Study: Allegheny Col, BA, 47; Syracuse Univ, scholar, 52, 53 & 55, MA, 55; Univ Pittsburgh, travel grants, 53 & 56. Collections Arranged: Valfred Thelin (with catalog), 69; Joseph Domjan (with catalog), 70; George Papashvily (with catalog), 70; Gloria Vanderbilt (with catalog), 71; Carol Dudley Pritchett (with catalog), 73. Pos: Dir, Cult Exchange Prog, Univ Pittsburgh, 56-58; dir, Cheekwood Fine Arts Ctr, 59; dir, Reading Pub Mus & Art Gallery, 67-73; consult, 73- Awards: Eben Demarst Award, 63. Mem: Archeol Soc Lorraine, France; Am Asn Mus; Nat Hist Trust. Res: History of the fetes of Lorraine. Mailing Add: 855 N Park Rd Wyomissing PA 19610

ELLIOTT, BRUCE ROGER
PRINTMAKER, EDUCATOR
b New York, NY, Aug 3, 38. Study: Silvermine Artists Guild; State Univ NY Buffalo, BS; State Univ NY Col Oswego; Univ Md, MA. Exhib: Graphics 68, Ultimate Concerns, Ohio Univ, 68; Graphics USA 1970, Clarke Col, 70; 13th Nat NDak Print & Drawing Exhib, Univ NDak, 70; 9th Ann Nat Print & Drawing Exhib, Olivet, Mich, 70; Nat Print & Drawing Exhib, Minot State Col, 70. Teaching: Asst prof drawing & printmaking, Holy Cross Col, 71-77, sponsor spec studies, 71-; artist (illusr) & photogr, Old Sturbridge Village, Archaeol Field Sch, 77- Pos: Chmn dept art, Kings Park High Sch, NY, 65-67; co-chmn Grad Art Asn, Univ Md, College Park, 68-69. Awards: Lewisboro Fine Arts Comn Fine Arts Scholar, NY, 56; Fine Arts Award, State Univ NY Buffalo, 59; Graphics Award, 41st Nat Print & Drawing Exhib, Springfield, Mass, 70. Mem: Springfield Art League; Worcester Art Mus; Artists Equity Asn; Copley Soc Boston, Inc; Boston Visual Artists Union. Style & Technique: Formal and classical manner, using letters and collage techniques in balanced figure and landscape compositions; imagery includes floating grid like shapes surrounded by soft but rich colors. Dealer: Franz Bader Galleries 2124 Pennsylvania Ave Washington DC 20037; The Galleries 464 Washington St Wellesley MA 02181. Mailing Add: RFD 152 Pleasant St Spencer MA 01562

ELLIOTT, JAMES HEYER
MUSEUM DIRECTOR
b Medford, Ore, Feb 19, 24. Study: Willamette Univ, AB, 47; Univ de Paris, 47-48; l'Ecole du Louvre, 48; Harvard Univ, MA(hist art), 49; Fulbright scholar to Europe, 52-53. Teaching: Teaching fel art hist, Harvard Univ, 50-51; assoc prof hist of art mus, Hunter Col, 66-67; adj prof art, Univ Calif, Berkeley, 76- Pos: Chief cur & actg dir, Walker Art Ctr, 53-56; cur mod art & asst chief cur, Los Angeles Co Mus, 56-63, chief cur, 63-66; dir, Wadsworth Atheneum, Conn, 66-76; dir, Univ Art Mus, Univ Calif, Berkeley, 76-; mem adv panel, Nat Endowment for the Arts. Mem: Am Asn Mus (mem coun, pres, New Eng Conf, 71, Int Comn Art Mus); Asn Art Mus Dirs; Conn Comn on the Arts (comnr & vpres); Col Art Asn; Int Comt Mus. Publ: Auth, title essay for catalog, Pierre Bonnard Exhibition, 65. Mailing Add: Wadsworth Atheneum 600 Main St Hartford CT 06103

ELLIOTT, LILLIAN
WEAVER, DESIGNER
b Detroit, Mich. Study: Wayne Univ, BA; Cranbrook Acad Art, Bloomfield Hills, Mich, MFA. Work: Mus Contemp Crafts, New York; Detroit Inst Arts; San Francisco City Art Collection; Objects, USA—Johnson's Wax Collection of Contemp Crafts, Smithsonian Inst Traveling Exhib; Univ Art Collections, Ariz State Univ, Tempe. Exhib: Calif Design Exhibs, Pasadena Art Mus, 62-71; Fabric Collage Invitational, Mus Contemp Crafts, New York, 65; Collagen—Collage Invitational Exhib, Kunstgewerbe Mus, Zurich, Switz, 68; Objects, USA—Johnson's Wax Collection, Smithsonian Inst Traveling Exhib, 70-72, Tapestry, Tradition & Technique Invitational, Los Angeles Co Mus Art, 71. Teaching: Instr art, Univ Mich Col Archit & Design, Ann Arbor, 59-60; lectr textiles, Univ Calif, Berkeley, 66-76; past mem fac art, Laney Col, Oakland, Calif. Pos: Fabric designer, Ford Motor Co Styling Div, Dearborn, Mich, 56-59. Awards: Tiffany Found Grant in Weaving, 64; San Francisco Art Festival Purchase Award, 65 & 69; Founder's Soc Purchase Award, Mich Craftsmen's Show, Detroit Inst Arts, 69. Media: Textile. Publ: Auth, Chap, In: The New American Tapestry, Van Nostrand Reinhold, 68. Mailing Add: c/o Anneberg Gallery 2721 Hyde St San Francisco CA 94109

ELLIOTT, PHILIP CLARKSON
PAINTER, EDUCATOR
b Minneapolis, Minn, Dec 5, 03. Study: Univ Minn, 21-23; Yale Univ, BFA, 26. Work: Univ Pittsburgh; Albright-Knox Art Gallery; Burchfield Ctr, State Col of NY at Buffalo; Charles R Penney Found, Lockport, NY; Chaloner Found, New York, NY; also in pvt collections.

Exhib: Carnegie Inst, 43 & 45; Mus Mod Art, 52; NY State Fair, 62; Albright-Knox Art Gallery, 62-68; Western NY Exhib, 62-68; Retrospective, Burchfield Ctr, Buffalo, NY, 71; Patteran traveling exhib, Gallery Asn of NY; plus others. Teaching: Lectr techniques of painting; asst prof fine arts, Univ Pittsburgh, 34-40; chmn dept art, State Univ NY Buffalo, 54-71, prof painting & drawing, 54-74, emer prof, 74- Pos: Dir, Albright Art Sch, Buffalo, 41-54. Awards: Prizes, Albright Art Gallery, 49 & 52; Prize, Springville, NY, 62; Prize, Western NY Exhib, 65; plus others. Mem: Patteran. Mailing Add: 147 Bryant St Buffalo NY 14222

ELLIOTT, RONNIE
PAINTER
b New York, NY, Dec 16, 16. Study: Hunter Col; NY Univ; Art Students League. Work: Mus Mod Art, New York; Whitney Mus Am Art, New York; Carnegie Inst, Pittsburgh; Andrew Dickson White Mus, Cornell Univ; Jewett Arts Ctr & Farnsworth Mus, Wellesley Col; plus others. Exhib: Col Int Exhib, Mus Mod Art, New York, 48; one-man shows, Paintings, Galerie Colette Allendy, Paris, France, 52 & Rose Fried Gallery, New York, 58 & 67; Collage Retrospective, 1943-1963, 63. Awards: Wellesley Col Purchase Award, Jewett Arts Ctr, 70. Bibliog: Michel Seuphor (auth), Dictionaire de la Peinture Abstraite, Paris, 57; Harriet Janis & Rudi Blesh (auth), Collage, 1961, Chilton, 61; Herta Wescher (auth), Die Collage, Harry N Abrams, NY; plus others. Style & Technique: Figures of people in every day scene and celebrities. Media: Oil, Collage, Gouache. Mailing Add: 68 E Seventh St New York NY 10003

ELLIOTT, SCOTT CAMERON
ART DEALER, COLLECTOR
b Chicago, Ill, Aug 6, 41. Study: Art Inst Chicago; Yale Drama Sch. Pos: Assoc dir, La Boetie Gallery, 69-72; dir, Scott Elliott Gallery, 73-75; dir, Helios Gallery, 76- Specialty: German and Austrian expressionism; the Bauhaus; surrealism; 19th and early 20th century English and German posters; English and American arts and crafts; furniture of William Morris, Gustave Stickley and others. Mailing Add: 18 E 67th St New York NY 10021

ELLIS, EDWIN CHARLES
EDUCATOR
b Iowa City, Iowa, May 29, 17. Study: State Univ Iowa, BFA, MA & MFA; also with Grant Wood, Fletcher Martin, Philip Guston & Maurico Lasanky. Teaching: Prof art hist & drawing & head dept, Cent Mo State Univ, 49- Style & Technique: Drawing with felt tip pens; watercolor, etching, engrav ing. Mailing Add: 207 Broad St Warrensburg MO 64093

ELLIS, FREMONT F
PAINTER
b Virginia City, Mont, Oct 2, 97. Study: Art Students League. Work: El Paso Mus, Tex; Mus NMex, Santa Fe; Thomas Gilcrease Inst Am Hist, Tulsa, Okla; Art Inst, Lubbock, Tex; Univ Calif, Los Angeles. Comn: S S America (mural). Awards: Navajo Girls Purchase Prize, Springville Utah Mus; Henry E Huntington Award for When Evening Comes, Los Angeles Co Mus Art, 24; Adele Hyde Morrison Prize & Bronze Medal, Oakland Mus, Calif, 50. Mailing Add: 553 Canyon Rd Santa Fe NM 87501

ELLIS, GEORGE RICHARD
MUSEUM DIRECTOR
b Birmingham, Ala, Dec 9, 37. Study: Univ Chicago, BA & MFA. Pos: Art supvr, Jefferson Co Schs, 62-64; former cur, Birmingham Mus Art; dir of develop & asst dir, Mus Cult Hist, Univ Calif, Los Angeles, presently; consult ed, African Arts Mag. Mem: Los Angeles Ethnic Art Coun; Am Mus Asn. Mailing Add: Mus Cult Hist Rm 55A Univ Calif Haines Hall Los Angeles CA 90024

ELLIS, RICHARD
PAINTER, ILLUSTRATOR
b New York, NY, Apr 2, 38. Study: Univ Pa, BA. Work: New Bedford Whaling Mus; Philadelphia Zoological Garden; Denver Zoological Garden; Kendall Whaling Mus; Sea Life Park, Hawaii. Comn: Mural of whales (18 1/2ft), pvt collection in Buffalo, NY, 77; mural of whales (60ft), Denver Mus Natural History, 78. Exhib: Whale paintings, S Street Seaport Mus, 75; whale paintings, New Bedford Whaling Mus, 75, Mystic Seaport, 75 & Am Mus Natural Hist, 76; drawings, Mansfield Art Ctr, Ohio, 76; Animal Art Show, Los Angeles Co Mus, Los Angeles, 77; shark paintings, Am Mus Natural Hist, 78. Pos: Exhib designer, Am Mus Natural Hist, 65-68. Bibliog: T Walker Lloyd (auth), Richard Ellis, Am Artist; Steve Blount (auth), Richard Ellis, Sport Diver Mag. Mem: Soc Animal Artists. Style & Technique: Realistic paintings of animals, primarily marine species. Media: Acrylic; Pen & Ink; Watercolor. Publ: Illusr, New York Mag, 74; illusr, The Great Whales, Audubon Mag, 75; illusr, Sci Am, 75; auth & illusr, Why I Became an Ex-Shell Painter, Audubon Mag, 76; auth & illusr, The Book of Sharks, Grosset & Dunlap, 76. Dealer: Sportsman's Edge Ltd 136 E 74th St New York NY 10021. Mailing Add: 1185 Park Ave New York NY 10028

ELLIS, ROBERT CARROLL
PAINTER, PRINTMAKER
b Jacksboro, Tex, Feb 3, 23. Study: Univ NMex, Albuquerque, BFA(art); New Sch for Social Res, NY, with Abraham Rattner, Seymour Lipton & Adja Yunkers. Work: Libr of Cong, Washington, DC; Roswell Mus, NMex; Univ Art Mus, Univ NMex, Albuquerque; Univ Art Mus, Univ Kans, Lawrence; Inst Mexicano Norte Americano de Relaciones Culturales, Mexico City. Exhib: The 23rd & 24th Ann Northwest Printmakers Int, Seattle Mus, Wash, 51 & 52; Artists of the USA in Latin Am, Pan Am Union, Washington, DC, 55; 20th Biennial Int Watercolor Exhib, Brooklyn Mus, NY, 59; Museo Nac de Arte Mod, Mex, 64; State Dept Exhib at Am Embassy, Tokyo, Japan, 65; NMex Invitational, Mus of NMex, Santa Fe, 69; NMex Fiesta Biennial, Mus of NMex, Santa Fe, 69; SW Drawing Biennial, Tucson Art Ctr, Ariz, 69. Awards: Theodora Shaskin Award, 16th Ann New Eng, Theodora Shaskin Estate, 65. Bibliog: Luis Quintanilla (auth), Pintura Moderna, Orgn Ed Novard, Mex, 68; Ronald L Nelson (auth), R C Ellis—An Abstract Classicist, Southwest Art, 75. Style & Technique: Abstract, minimal. Media: Painting in oil and various printing techniques. Dealer: Venable-Neslage Galleries 1742 Connecticut Ave NW Washington DC 20009; Kirby Gallery 2800 Kirby Dr Houston TX 77098 Mailing Add: PO Box 1011 Taos NM 87571

ELLISON, NANCY
PAINTER, PHOTOGRAPHER
b Los Angeles, Calif, May 12, 36. Study: Finch Col, BS(fine art), with Leon Kroll. Work: Allen Mem Art Mus, Oberlin, Ohio; pvt collections of William de Kooning, Donald Sutherland, Mr & Mrs Joel Grey, Robert Goodnough, Athena Spear & Virginia Zabriskie. Exhib: Wadsworth Atheneum, Hartford, Conn; Visual Arts Gallery, New York; 10th St Invitationals, Aegis Gallery, New York; Zabriskie Gallery, New York, 66; Finch Col Mus, New York, 69; New York Cult Ctr, 73; New Sch Art Ctr, New York, 73; In Praise of Women Artists, 77. Pos: Free lance photojournalist. Awards: Leon Kroll Award, Finch Col, 56. Style & Technique: Concerned with literary role of female metaphores in addition to the geometry of forms, painted large scale post pop art realism, always involved with paint. Media: Oil. Mailing Add: 68 Malibu Colony Malibu CA 90265

ELLOIAN, CAROLYN AUTRY
See Autry, Carolyn

ELLOIAN, PETER
PRINTMAKER, INSTRUCTOR
b Cleveland, Ohio, Apr 20, 36. Study: Cleveland Inst Art, BFA; Univ Iowa, MFA, study with Mauricio Lasansky; Pratt Graphic Ctr. Work: Dayton Art Inst, Ohio; Libr Cong, Washington, DC; Philadelphia Mus of Art; Okla Art Ctr, Oklahoma City; Albrecht Art Mus, St Joseph, Mo. Exhib: Nat Exhib Prints, Libr Cong, 71 & 73 & 77; Soc Am Graphic Artists Nat Print Exhib, New York & Chicago, 73 & 77; Calif Col Arts & Crafts World Print Competition '73, Chicago & San Francisco, 73; Engraving Am 1974, St Joseph, 74; Int Biennial Exhib Graphic Art & Multiples, Segovia, Spain, 74. Teaching: Instr printmaking, Toledo Mus Art Sch, 66- Awards: Purchase Award Drawings USA, Minn Mus Art, 68, Potsdam Nat Print Exhib, State Univ New York, 72 & Nat Print Show, Bradley Univ, Peoria, Ill, 75. Mem: Soc of Am Graphic Artists; Philadelphia Print Club; Boston Printmakers. Media: Engraving, Drypoint, Pen & Ink. Mailing Add: 3348 Indian Rd Toledo OH 43606

ELMAN, EMILY
PAINTER, EDUCATOR
Study: Syracuse Univ, BFA; Hunter Col, MA. Exhib: Chicago Art Inst; Joselyn Art Mus, Omaha, Nebr; Sheldon Mem Art Gallery, Lincoln, Nebr; Nat Acad of Design, New York; San Francisco Mus; Pa Acad of Art, Philadelphia; one-person show, Kornblee Gallery, New York. Teaching: Instr painting & drawing, Brooklyn Mus Art Sch, NY. Awards: Ossabow Island Proj Grant; Yaddow Residency, Saratoga Springs, NY; MacDowell Colony Fel, Peterborough, NY. Mailing Add: c/o Kornblee Gallery 20 W 57th St New York NY 10019

ELMO, JAMES
PAINTER, SCULPTOR
b Athens, Tex. Study: Los Angeles Art Ctr, with Lorser Feitelson & Robert Frame. Work: Norfolk Mus, Va. Exhib: Smithsonian Inst, Washington, DC; Frye Art Mus, Seattle, Wash; Bradley Mus, Columbus, Ga; Grand Rapids Art Gallery, Minn; Everhard Mus, Scranton, Pa; Rensselaer Art Gallery, Cornell Univ, Ithaca, NY; Univ Art Gallery, Univ Southern Calif, Los Angeles; Samuel Bookharz Gallery Art, Alexandria, Va. Style & Technique: Expressionistic. Media: Wax Cast in Bronze; Oil, Watercolor. Dealer: Collector's Gallery 2401 Abbott Martin Nashville TN 32715. Mailing Add: c/o S/R Gallery 337 S Robertson Blvd Beverly Hills CA 90211

ELOUL, KOSSO
SCULPTOR
b Jan 22, 20; US citizen. Study: Art Inst Chicago, 39-43; sculptor symposiums, Austria, 60, Yugoslavia, 61, Italy & Israel, 62, Berlin, Ger, 63, Montreal, 64 & Long Beach, Calif, 65. Work: Shalom 7 (painted steel), Rose Mus, Brandeis Univ; Art Gallery Ont, Toronto; Mus d'Art Contemp, Montreal; Mus Tel Aviv, Israel; Bezalel Mus, Jerusalem, Israel. Comn: Hardfact (concrete & stainless steel), Calif State Univ, Long Beach, 65; Silent Thunder (painted steel), J Patrick Lannan Found, Palm Beach, Fla, 67; Morning Night (gunite fountain), Beverly Woods, Los Angeles, 68; Double You (stainless steel), Greenwin Housing Porj, Davisville, Toronto, 69; Now (environ sculpture), Fanshawe Col, London, Ont, 71. Exhib: 29th Venice Biennial, 59; Middlheim Park Int, Antwerpen, 59; 5th Festival Spoleto, Italy, 62; Carnegie Inst Int, 64 & 67; Calif Artists in US Mus, Lytton Art Ctr, Los Angeles, 67. Teaching: Artist in residence sculpture, Calif State Univ, Long Beach, 65-66; artist in residence form & space, Univ Toronto Sch Archit, 69-70. Bibliog: T H Heinrich (auth), The razor's edge, Vol 156/157 & Gilles Hemault (auth), Kosso Eloul, Artscanada; Fernande St Martin (auth), Lettre de Montreal, Art Int, 11/64; Curt Oplinger (auth), article in Artforum, 1/66. Mem: L'Accademia Tiberina, Rome, Italy; Royal Can Acad Arts. Media: Stainless Steel, Concrete. Dealer: Arras Gallery 29 W 57th St New York NY 10019; Marlborough-Godard Gallery 22 Hazelton Toronto ON Can. Mailing Add: No 2-C 61 W 74th St New York NY 10023

ELOWITCH, ANNETTE
ART DEALER, ANTIQUE DEALER
b Portland, Maine, Dec 24, 42. Study: Boston Univ, 61; Westbrook Col, Portland, Maine, AA, 63; Univ Maine. Collections Arranged: Assembled numerous exhibs of renowned printmakers (including Jim Dine, Josef Albers & Motherwell) on a monthly basis, Barridoff Galleries. Pos: Co-owner, Barridoff Galleries, 75- Specialty: Fine American antiques and accessories; 19th century oils; limited-edition contemporary graphics, oils and watercolors. Collection: Fine works of art of all periods. Mailing Add: 242 Middle St Portland ME 04101

ELOWITCH, ROBERT JASON
ART DEALER, PATRON
b Portland, Maine, Apr 8, 43. Study: Amherst Col, BA. Pos: Drama/film critic, Portland Press Herald & Eve Express, 67-69; drama/film critic, Maine Times, 70-75; owner, Barridoff Galleries, 75- Mem: Maine State Comn Arts & Humanities (comnr, 73-75); Skowhegan Sch Painting & Sculpture (dir, 68-, chmn, Maine Comt, 67-); Portland Sch Art (sch comt mem, 74-75); United Portland Regional Orgn of Arts Resources (vchmn, 74). Specialty: 19th century American oils and contemporary American graphics. Interest: Creation, promotion and support of the arts in the state of Maine. Mailing Add: 87 Carroll St Portland ME 04102

ELPHICK, JEAN
See Hanson, Jean

ELSE, ROBERT JOHN
EDUCATOR, PAINTER
b Wayne, Pa, Nov 26, 18. Study: Columbia Univ, BS & MA. Work: Cincinnati Mus of Art; Crocker Art Gallery, Sacramento; Univ of Calif-Los Angeles Libr; Calif State Libr Prints Rm. Exhib: The 1st Biennial Exhib of Contemp Color Lithography, Cincinnati Mus of Art, 50; 4th Print Ann Exhib, Brooklyn Mus, 50; Kingsley Ann Exhib for Northern Calif Artists, Crocker Art Gallery, 50-64; Oakland Art Gallery's Ann Exhib, 51; Survey of Pac Coast Painting, Walnut Creek, Calif, 51; 17th Ann Watercolor Exhib, San Francisco Mus of Art, 53; Retrospective, Crocker Art Gallery, 77. Teaching: Prof art pract, painting & drawing, Calif State Univ, Sacramento, 50- Pos: Coun mem, Comt on Art Educ, Mus of Mod Art, 49-52; mem joint bd trustees, Crocker Art Gallery, 73-75. Awards: Purchase Award, 1st Int Biennial of Contemp Color Lithography, Cincinnati Mus of Art, 50; First Prize Oil Painting, Kingsley Ann, Kingsley Club, 64. Media: Acrylic on canvas; drawing. Mailing Add: 5871 Shepard Ave Sacramento CA 95819

ELSEN, ALBERT EDWARD
ART HISTORIAN
b New York, NY, Oct 11, 27. Study: Columbia Col, AB; Columbia Univ, MA & PhD. Teaching: Asst prof art hist, Carleton Col, 52-58; prof art hist, Ind Univ, Bloomington, 58-68; prof art hist, Stanford Univ, 68-75, Haas prof art hist, 75- Awards: Fulbright Fel, 49-50; Guggenheim Fel, 66-67; Nat Endowment Humanities Sr Fel, 73-74. Mem: Col Art Asn Am (bd dirs, 66-70, secy, 70-72, vpres, 72-74, pres, 74-76). Res: Modern art, principally modern sculpture. Publ: Auth, Seymour Lipton, 70; auth, The Sculpture of Henri Matisse, 72; auth, Paul Jenkins, Abrams, 73; auth, Origins of Modern Sculpture: Pioneers and Premises, 74; co-auth, with John Merryman, Law, Ethics & the Visual Arts, 78; plus others. Mailing Add: 723 Alvarado Row Stanford CA 94305

ELSKY, HERB
SCULPTOR
b 1942. Study: Univ Calif, Los Angeles, MA. Work: US Information Serv World Tour Collection; Bank of Am Collection, Los Angeles. Exhib: San Fernando Valley State Col; one-man shows, Esther-Robles Gallery, 71, Collabarative Gallery, Zephyr Gallery, Luis Roeha Gallery, Los Angeles, 75 & Richard Mann Gallery, Los Angeles, 76; Washington Int Art Fair, Washington, DC, 77. Teaching: Mem fac, Art Ctr Col of Design, Los Angeles. Mailing Add: 145 S Kingsley Dr Los Angeles CA 90004

ELSNER, LARRY EDWARD
SCULPTOR, EDUCATOR
b Gooding, Idaho, 1930. Study: Utah State Univ, BS; Columbia Univ, MFA. Work: Ariz State Univ; Salt Lake City Art Ctr, Utah; Archie Bray Found, Helena, Mont; Utah State Univ. Comn: Wood relief, Edith Bowen Sch, Logan, 68; metal relief, Col Family Life, Utah State Univ, 69. Exhib: Intermountain Painting & Sculpture, Salt Lake Art Ctr, 63; 23rd Ceramic Nat, Everson Mus, Syracuse, NY, 64; Southern Sculpture, Columbia, SC, 67; Smithsonian Inst Show Sculpture, Washington, DC, 69; one-man shows, 100 Pieces of Pottery, Tokyo, Japan, 71 & 74. Teaching: Assoc prof sculpture, Utah State Univ, 60- Awards: Ford Found Sculpture Purchase Award, 63; Honorable Mention, Southern Sculpture 67, 67. Mem: Am Craftsmen Coun; Col Art Asn. Style & Technique: Purity and clarity of organic form. Media: Wood. Mailing Add: 1229 Thrushwood Dr Logan UT 84321

ELWELL, CHIP
MASTER PRINTER, PRINTMAKER
b Kansas City, Mo, Dec 5, 40. Study: Columbia Col, 58-64; Columbia Univ, 64-65; Cooper Union, 65-70. Comn: Untitled pochoir prints, comn by Larry Zox, 75, 76 & 78; Al Held (stencil print), comn by Alex Katz, 76; Trillium (linocut), comn by Jack Beal, 77; Picasso Goes to Heaven (stencil print & etching), comn by Red Grooms, 77; Blue Crab (linocut), comn by Jack Beal, 78. Exhib: Prints, Ten Yrs of Publ, Boston Univ. Pos: Cur, Bank St Atelier, 71-72. Media: Linocut, Pochoir Print. Mailing Add: One Union Sq 905 New York NY 10003

ELZEA, ROWLAND PROCTER
MUSEUM CURATOR, PAINTER
b Columbia, Mo, Sept 19, 31. Study: Univ Mo, BA & MA; Hunter Col, MSEd; also with Esteban Vicente, New York. Work: Del Art Mus, Wilmington. Collections Arranged: American Painting Since World War II, 71; American Painting 1840-1940, 72; Golden Age of American Illustration: 1880-1914 (with catalog), 72; Howard Pyle: Diversity in Depth (with catalog), 73; Jean Dubuffet, 74; Avant-Garde Painting and Sculpture in America, 1910-1925, 75-; The Pre-Raphaelite Era: 1848-1914, 76. Teaching: Instr art hist & painting, Sch Art & Design, Philadelphia, 69-71, pres, 69-70. Pos: Cur collections, Del Art Mus, 58- Mem: Am Asn Mus. Publ: Auth, Samuel and Mary R Bancroft English Pre-Raphaelite Collection, 78; auth, Howard Pyle Collection, 71. Mailing Add: 2013 Baynard Blvd Wilmington DE 19802

EMBRY, NORRIS
PAINTER
b Louisville, Ky, Jan 14, 21. Study: Acad Fine Arts, Florence, Italy. Work: Guggenheim Mus, New York; also in pvt collections. Exhib: Inst Contemp Art, Boston, 57; Rochester Mem Art Gallery, NY; one-man shows, Robert Elkon Gallery, New York, 63 & 65; 100 American Drawings, Mus Mod Art, New York, 65; Baltimore Mus; plus others. Media: Mixed Media. Dealer: Gruenebaum Gallery Ltd 25 E 77th St New York NY 10021. Mailing Add: 1216 St Paul St Baltimore MD 21202

EMERSON, EDITH
PAINTER, CURATOR
b Oxford, Ohio. Study: Art Inst Chicago; travel in Japan & Mex; Pa Acad Fine Arts; two Cresson scholarships to Europe; travel to Europe & India. Work: Plays & Players Theatre, Philadelphia, Pa; Philadelphia Mus Art; Woodmere Art Gallery, Philadelphia; Bryn Mawr Col; Haverford Col; plus others. Comn: Stained glass window in memory of Theodore Roosevelt, Temple Keneseth Israel, 19; two panels, The Sacred Heart & St Joseph with the Christ Child, Lower Church of the Nativity of the Blessed Virgin Mary; five triptych altarpieces for Army & Navy, 42-43; four panels, The Life of St Joseph & chancel decorations, Nativity Convent, Sisters of St Joseph, 46; plus others. Exhib: Nat Acad Design, New York; Archit League, New York; Pa Acad Fine Arts, Philadelphia; Corcoran Gallery Art, Washington, DC; Woodmere Art Gallery, Philadelphia; plus many others. Teaching: Instr hist art, Agnes Irwin Sch, 16-27; lectr art appreciation, Philadelphia Mus Sch Indust Art, 29-36; instr hist art, Chestnut Hill Col, 48-56; plus lectr at var cols & clubs. Pos: Libr asst, Art Inst Chicago, 08-11; exhib chmn, Woodmere Art Gallery, 42-72, pres, 45, cur, 46-; chmn, Regional Coun Community Art Ctrs, Philadelphia, 50-; pres & cur, Violet Oakley Mem Found, 61- Awards: Granger Prizes, Pa Acad Fine Arts; Medal of Honor, Philadelphia Watercolor Club. 69; Medal Community Service, Chestnut Hill College, 74. Bibliog: L Mechlin (ed), Mural decorations for Little Theatre, Philadelphia, Am Mag Art, 5/18; H Eberbein (auth), Mooorestown Trust Co, Archit Forum, 4/27; M A Barney (auth), E Emerson's bookplate designs, Am Soc Bookplates Designers & Collectors, 33. Mem: Nat Soc Mural Painters; fel Pa Acad Fine Arts (jury, 45); Philadelphia Watercolor Club (dir jury, 44); Art Inst Chicago Alumni Asn; Philadelphia Mus Art; plus others. Style & Technique: Italian and Oriental influences; decorative design is of primary importance in mural painting. Media: Oil, Watercolor. Publ: Auth, Splendid Spain, 3/24, Age of innocence, 6/25 & Opening book of the law, 1/27, Am Mag Art; auth, The Madonna in East Christian art, Asia Mag, 12/30; illusr, Song of Roland, 38 & Pageant of India's History, 48, Longmans; illusr, Asia Mag. Mailing Add: 627 St George's Rd Philadelphia PA 19119

EMERSON, ROBERTA SHINN
MUSEUM DIRECTOR
b Indianapolis, Ind, Feb 14, 22. Study: Northwestern Univ; Univ Chicago; Marshall Univ. Collections Arranged: WVa Artists on the Move (traveling exhib), 67; A Room Full of Ropes (participatory exhib), 72; Ancient Art of Middle America, 74; New Am Glass: Focus WVa, 76. Teaching: Asst prof art appreciation, Marshall Univ, 68-69. Pos: Interim dir, Huntington Galleries, 67, dir, 71- Mailing Add: Huntington Galleries Huntington WV 25701

EMERSON, WALTER CARUTH
EDUCATOR, WRITER
b Dallas, Tex, Jan 24, 12. Study: Aunspaugh Sch Art; with Olin Travis; Southwestern Sch Theatre; with John Knott; Southern Methodist Univ, BA. Work: Tex State Mus, Washington-on-the-Brazos, Tex; also in pvt collections. Comn: Life size full figure of Indian Chief Quanah Parker, Metrop Fed Savings, Dallas, 69; portraits of presidents, Repub Tex & portrait of Gen Santa Anna, Tex State Mus, 72. Exhib: Rainbowman Gallery, Santa Fe, NMex, 69; one-man show, Quadrangle Galleries, Dallas, 70 & 72 & Tex State Mus, 73; Cushing Gallery, Dallas, 71. Teaching: Creator & instr courses in art & art hist, eve div, Southern Methodist Univ, 40-63; conception, production & illustration of Pencil Personalities (TV series), 58; instr art, Christian Col of Southwest, 69-70; instr art hist & art appreciation, Dallas Co Community Col Dist, 72-74; founder & dir, Art Acad Dallas, 74- Pos: Art dir, Pollock Paper Corp, Dallas, 37-52; officer in chg, Art Dept, USN, Washington, DC, 41-45; art dir, Food & Drug Div, Hunt Oil Co, Dallas, 63-69. Awards: Best in Class, Cherokee Nat Mus, 76. Bibliog: Keith Kathan (auth), Walter Emerson Portraitist, Dallas Times Herald, 70; William Payne (auth), Portraits by Walter Caruth Emerson, Dallas Morning News, 73; Lorraine Haacke (auth), A guide to Dallas art galleries, Parade Mag, 74. Mem: Artists Coalition of Tex; Dallas Mus Fine Arts. Style & Technique: Portraits, figures, birds, impressionist and stylized techniques. Media: Oil, acrylic & gouache from wash to impasto. Publ: Editorial cartoons, Nationally Distributed, 37-56, Dallas Morning News, 41, NY Daily Mirror, 56-58; auth, American tragedy at Brussels, Am Mercury Mag, 10/58; auth & illusr, The Truth About Santa Anna, 73 & 75 & column, Art Alive, Dallas Morning News, 77- Dealer: S S Eisenberg Galleries 2800 Routh St Dallas TX 75201. Mailing Add: 3637 Haynie Ave Dallas TX 75205

EMERY, CHARLES ANTHONY
GALLERY DIRECTOR
b Farnborough, Eng, Apr 30, 19; Can citizen. Study: Oxford Univ, BA, 48, MA, 53. Teaching: Assoc prof art hist, Univ Victoria, BC, 56-67; instr art hist, Selkirk Col, David Thompson Univ Centre, Nelson, BC, 76. Pos: Dir, Vancouver Art Gallery, 67-74. Mailing Add: RR 1 Nelson BC V1L 5P4 Can

EMERY, LIN (LIN EMERY BRASELMAN)
SCULPTOR
b New York, NY. Study: Ossip Zadkine Studio, Paris; Sculpture Ctr, New York. Work: Nat Collection of Art, Washington, DC; New Orleans Mus of Art; Norton Art Galleries, West Palm Beach, Fla; Huntington Mus Art, WVa; Walter P Chrysler Mus, Provincetown, Mass. Comn: Monument & aquamobile, State of La, Civic Ctr, New Orleans, 68-71; aquamobile, Univ SC, Columbia, 70-72; aquamobile, Fidelity Nat Bank, Oklahoma City, 71; magnetmobile, SCent Bell, Birmingham, Ala, 72; aquamobile, Helmerich Park, Tulsa, Okla, 77. Exhib: One-man show, Southern Art Mus Dirs Asn, six-mus tour, 55-56; Pa Acad Fine Arts Ann, Philadelphia, 60 & 64; Far East Tour, Int House & US Info Serv, three countries, 62; New Directions, Am Fedn Arts Tour, 62-63; Sculpture: 1900-1965, DeWaters Art Mus, 65. Pos: Vis critic, Tulane Univ Sch Archit, 67-68; chmn, 9th Int Sculpture Conf, New Orleans, 76. Bibliog: Lansford (auth), New talent, Art in Am, 55; Moore & Allen (auth), Metal that moves, La Mag, 67; Pierce (auth), Lin Emery's aquamobiles, Art Int, 69. Mem: Sculptors Guild New York; Contemp Arts Ctr, New Orleans (mem bd); Nat Sculpture Ctr, Univ Kans (mem bd). Media: Kinetics, Metals. Mailing Add: 7520 Dominican St New Orleans LA 70118

EMIL, ARTHUR D
COLLECTOR
b New York, NY, Dec 29, 24. Study: Yale Univ; Columbia Law Sch. Mem: Int Coun Mus Mod Art (mem exec comt); Am Fedn Arts (vpres & mem exec comt); Brooklyn Acad Music (chmn bd trustees). Collection: Modern painting; ancient sculpture. Mailing Add: 540 Madison Ave New York NY 10022

EMMERICH, ANDRE
ART DEALER, WRITER
b Frankfort, Ger, Oct 11, 24. Study: Amsterdam Lyceum, Neth; Kew Forest Sch, New York; Oberlin Col, BA, 44. Mem: Art Dealers Asn Am (pres, 72-74). Specialty: Contemporary art; pre-Columbian art. Publ: Auth, Art before Columbus, Simon & Schuster, 63; auth, Sweat of the sun and tears of the moon—gold and silver in pre-Columbian art, Univ Wash Press, 65. Mailing Add: 41 E 57th St New York NY 10022

EMORI, EIKO
GRAPHIC DESIGNER
b Japan. Study: LCC Cent Sch of Arts & Crafts; Yale Univ. Pos: Pres, Eiko Emori Inc. Mem: Royal Can Acad Arts. Media: Typography, Printed Media. Mailing Add: 2036 Cabot St Ottawa ON K1H 6J8 Can

ENDO, ROBERT AKIRA
ART DEALER
b Los Angeles, Calif, Feb 12, 48. Study: Yale Univ, BA. Pos: Trainee, Sotheby & Co, London, 71-72; dir, Gimpel & Weitzenhoffer Ltd, 73- Mem: Col Art Asn of Am. Specialty: Twentieth century American and European paintings and sculpture. Mailing Add: c/o Gimpel & Weitzenhoffer Ltd 1040 Madison Ave New York NY 10021

ENDSLEY, FRED STARR
PHOTOGRAPHER, VIDEO ARTIST
b Houston, Tex, Oct 13, 49. Study: Univ Calif, Los Angeles, BA & MS; Fla State Univ, with Nathan Lyons, MFA. Work: High Mus Art, Atlanta; Gallery of the Univ Osaka, Japan; Raindance Corp Video Collection, New York. Comn: Video Documentary, 8th Ann Atlanta Int Film Festival (with Danny Talley, Kaye Wakefield), 74. Exhib: 10th Anniversary Print Exhib, Univ Osaka, 73; Magnetic Image, Nat Video Showing, High Mus Art, 75; Jurors' Selection Nat Photog Exhib, Ohio Silver Gallery, Los Angeles, 75; Macho Intelligencia, Gallery Atlanta Col Art, 75; Rochester Inst Technol, 75; Int Festival of Video, Aarhus Mus Art, Copenhagen, Denmark, 76; Columbia Univ, New York, 76; Rose Art Mus, Brandeis Univ, 76; Purdue Univ, 76; Murray State Univ, Ky, 76; plus others. Teaching: Instr photog, Atlanta Col Art, 73-75, head dept video, 74-75; vis instr photog, Art Inst Chicago, 75- Bibliog: Robert Mantrer (auth), The jurors' selection, Art Week, 5/75. Mem: Soc Photog Educ; Big Bend Photo Club; Nexus Photog Gallery & Cooperative. Style & Technique: Large multiple photographs; gum-bichromate and other hand applied emulsions, sabattier, hand colored; experimental video; hand made photography. Dealer: Light Gallery Madison Ave New York NY 10021. Mailing Add: 1153 Greenbriar Lane Northbrook IL 60062

ENGEL, MICHAEL MARTIN, II
PAINTER, ILLUSTRATOR
b New York, NY, Mar 20, 19. Study: With A Katchemakoff; Art Students League, with Kimon Nicolaides & George Picken; Am Sch Design, with Cherkasoff. Work: Parrish Art Mus, Southampton, NY; St Lawrence Univ, Canton, NY; US Navy Combat Art Collection; Antioch Col, Yellow Springs, Ohio; Clayton-Liberatore Gallery, Bridgehampton, NY. Exhib: Hofstra Col Invitational, 59; Audubon Artists Ann; Salmagundi Club; Suburban Art League, NY; Wall St Art Asn, NY. Awards: First Prize for watercolor, Suburban Art League, 64; Prof Award, Wall St Art Asn; Prize, Nat Arts Club, 77. Mem: Audubon Artists (historian, 45-, pres, 62-63); Int Asn Arts (vpres, 70-73); Salmagundi Club; Artists Fellowship (trustee, 63-, pres, 77-); Nat Arts Club; life fel Royal Soc Arts. Style & Technique: Representationally based, atmospherically oriented. Media: Watercolor. Mailing Add: 22 Lee St Huntington NY 11743

ENGEL, WALTER F
ART CRITIC, ART DEALER
b Vienna, Austria, June 11, 08; Can citizen. Study: Art & art hist with Oscar Lichtenstern, Vienna, 25-27; Joseph Floch, Paris, 28; Ludwig H Jungnickel, Vienna, 29-30. Pos: Art critic, Revista de las Indias, 41-51, El Tiempo, 44-55, Art Mag Plastica, 56-60 & El Espectador, 60-65, Bogota, Colombia, SAm; co-founder, critic & adv bd, Art Mag, Toronto, 69- Mem: Int Asn Art Critics; hon Soc Can Artists. Res: 20th century Latin American art, Canadian art, surrealism and fantastic art. Specialty: Contemporary art, with preference for Canadian, European and Latin American art, surrealism and figurative expressionism. Publ: Auth, Social Problems in the Visual Arts, 46; auth, The Painter Fernando Botero, 52; auth, Contemporary Colombian Paintresses, 59; auth, Wiedemann (Colombian painter), 59. Mailing Add: 2100 Bathurst St Suite 113 Toronto ON Can

ENGELHARD, MR & MRS CHARLES
COLLECTORS
Collection: Paintings. Mailing Add: Waldorf Towers 50th St & Park Ave New York NY 10022

ENGELHARDT, THOMAS ALEXANDER
EDITORIAL CARTOONIST
b St Louis, Mo, Dec 29, 30. Study: Denver Univ, 50-51; Ruskin Sch Fine Arts, Oxford Univ, 54-56; Sch Visual Arts, New York, 57. Work: State Hist Soc Mo, Columbia. Comn: Mural (humorous animals), Pediat Assoc, Mo, 73. Exhib: One-man show, Fontbonne Col, Mo, 72; Sch Visual Arts Alumni Exhib, Hansen Gallery, New York, 75; plus numerous group shows. Pos: Free-lance cartoonist, New York, 57-60; editorial cartoonist, Newspaper Enterprise Asn, Cleveland, Ohio, 60-61; editorial cartoonist, St Louis Post-Dispatch, 62- Style & Technique: Pen and ink with lithographic crayon. Publ: Auth, Cartoonist Profiles, 69; auth, Dateline 1976, Overseas Press Club, 76. Mailing Add: 900 N 12th Blvd St Louis MO 63101

ENGELSON, CAROL
PAINTER
b Seymour, Ind, Apr 19, 44. Study: Carnegie-Mellon Univ, BFA. Work: Aldrich Mus Contemp Art, Ridgefield, Conn; Chase Manhattan Bank, New York. Exhib: Women Choose Women, New York Cult Ctr, 73; one-woman exhibs, Recent Paintings by Carol Engelson, Pace Univ, 73 & Ruth S Schaffner Gallery, Los Angeles, Calif, 78; 3rd Ann Contemp Reflections, 1973-1974, Aldrich Mus Contemp Art, 74; Soho Ctr Visual Artists, 74; Contemp Reflections 1971-1974, Selections from Aldrich Mus, Am Fedn Arts Nat Touring Exhib, 75-77; Collegiate Sch, New York, NY, 77; Gen Servs Admin, Washington, DC, 77-78. Teaching: Vis artist painting, Pace Univ, 73; guest instr painting & drawing, Keene State Col, 73; vis artist, State Univ NY, Binghamton, 76; guest lectr painting, Carnegie-Mellon Univ, 76 & vis artist, 78-; vis artist, Richmond Col, Staten Island, NY, 77 & 78. Awards: MacDowell Colony Residence Fel, 67, 71, 72, 74 & 75; Comt Visual Arts Grant, 74; Change, Inc Grant, 74; Nat Endowment Arts grant, 77-78. Bibliog: Emily Genaver (auth), Art and the artist, NY Post, 4/20/74; Bill Marvel (auth), Aching feet, dingy doorways...and good art, Nat Observer, 5/4/74; Grace Glueck (auth), They create a new art scene, New York Times, 5/5/74. Style & Technique: Non-figurative, seascape and landscape as a statement of human emotions; physical manipulation of paint, pouring, scraping and brushing; washes and thick pigment. Media: Acrylic & Oil on Canvas, Pastel. Publ: Auth, Carnegie-Mellon University, 77. Mailing Add: 164 Bowery New York NY 10012

ENGERAN, WHITNEY JOHN, JR
ART ADMINISTRATOR, PAINTER
b New Orleans, La, Feb 1, 34. Study: Spring Hill Col, BA & MA; St Louis Univ, STL. Work: Cunningham Mem Libr, Terre Haute, Ind; Vincennes Univ. Comn: Fire ritual mural, St Marys Col, 62; suffering servant mural, Martin Army Hosp, Columbus, Ga, 66. Exhib: Creole Belles, Rockhurst Col, 62; Winter Polarities, Topeka Savings Asn Gallery, Kans, 64; Red, White, Blue & Black, Orleans Gallery, New Orleans, 67; Confractio, Shircliff Gallery, Vincennes, Ind, 74; Atmospheric Drawings, Barnwell Art Ctr, Shreveport, La, 75; Hands On—Hands Off (Review of 20 Yrs of Paintings & Drawings), Art Gallery, St Mary of the Woods Col, Terre Haute, Ind, 77. Collections Arranged: Ida Kohlmeyer Retrospective, Turman Gallery, Terre Haute, 72, Images of Our Time, 73 & American 6 Pak: Six Bicentennial Exhibits, 74-75. Teaching: Asst prof aesthet & chmn dept art, Loyola Univ, 66-68; assoc prof aesthet, Stephens Col, 68-71; prof art theory & chmn dept art, Ind State Univ Terre Haute, 71- Pos: Cur permanent collection & dir, Turman Gallery, 71-75. Awards: First Prize Watercolor, Kans Artists' Exhib, 62 & 65. Mem: Col Art Asn Am; Nat Coun Art Adminr; Mid-Am Col Art Asn. Style & Technique: Atmospheric drawings. Media: Water media and enamels sprayed on Arches Reeves paper and canvas. Publ: Auth, Humanitics today, Choice Mag, 11/68; auth, Ida Kohlmeyer: a Retrospective Exhibition (catalog), High Mus, Atlanta, 12/71. Mailing Add: 1509 S Center St Terre Haute IN 47802

ENGGASS, ROBERT
ART HISTORIAN
b Detroit, Mich, Dec 20, 21. Study: Harvard Univ, AB, 46; Univ Mich, MA, 50, PhD, 55. Teaching: Assoc prof art hist, Pa State Univ, 58-65, prof art hist, 66-71; prof art hist, Univ Kans, 71- Awards: Grants-in-Aid, Am Coun Learned Socs, 58 & 70; Fulbright Res Scholar, Univ Rome, 63-64; six Res Grants, Univ Kans, 66-70. Publ: Auth, Tiepolo & the concept of the barocchetto, Atti del Congresso Int sul Tiepolo, Udine, 72; co-ed, Hortus Imaginum, 74; auth, Early Eighteenth Century Sculpture in Rome (illus catalog raisonne, 2 vols), Pa State Univ, 76; auth, Un problème du baroque romain tardif, Revue de l'Art, 76; co-ed, Nicola Pio, le vite de Pittori Scultori et Architetti, Vatican Libr, 78. Mailing Add: Spencer Mus of Art Univ of Kans Lawrence KS 66044

ENGLAND, PAUL GRADY
PAINTER, EDUCATOR
b Hugo, Okla, Jan 12, 18. Study: Carnegie Inst Technol, BA, 40; Univ Tulsa, MA, 59; Art Students League, 43-46; Zadkine Studio, Paris, 48 & 49. Work: Philbrook Art Ctr, Tulsa, Okla; permanent print collection, NY Pub Libr, NY; Joslyn Mus Art, Omaha, Nebr; State Collection, Oklahoma City, Okla; Bank of Okla, Tulsa; Fitzwilliam Mus, Cambridge, Eng; Williams Col Mus, Mass; Staten Island Mus, NY. Exhib: One-man shows, Creuze Gallery, Paris, 49, Iolas Gallery, New York, 51, Grand Cent Moderns, New York, 55, Philbrook Art Ctr, Tulsa, 71 & St Mary's Col Md, 72. Teaching: Assoc prof painting, Hofstra Univ, 59- Awards: Graphics Award, Joslyn Mus Art, 57; Grand Awards, Philbrook Art Ctr, 57 & 63. Mem: Art Student League. Style & Technique: Abstract, expressionist; experimental techniques. Media: Oil. Publ: Auth, Dust to dust, New Yorker Mag, 9/14/41; auth, Art critiques, France-Amerique, 55-57. Mailing Add: 359 Soundview Dr Rocky Point NY 11778

ENGLANDER, GERTRUD
CERAMIST
b Ger, Jan 29, 04; US citizen. Study: Kunstgewerbeschule Cologne; Craft Students League, YWCA, New York; NY Univ. Exhib: Designer-Craftsmen USA 1960, Mus Contemp Crafts, 60, Am Craftsmen's Coun Touring Exhib, 61; Craftsmen of Northeastern States, Worcester Art Mus, 63; Artist Craftsmen New York Ann, Lever House, 71. Teaching: Instr ceramics, Craft Students League YWCA, New York; instr ceramics, Little Art Workshop, New York, 53-55. Awards: Award of Merit for Outstanding Craftsmanship, Artist Craftsmen New York, 71; Award of Merit, Invitation Pen & Brush Club Show, 77. Mem: Artist Craftsmen New York; Am Craftsmens Coun; Craft Students League YWCA. Mailing Add: 345 E 52nd St New York NY 10022

ENGLE, BARBARA JEAN
PAINTER, PRINTMAKER
b Grandin, NDak. Study: Honolulu Acad Arts, Hawaii; Chouinard Art Inst & Otis Art Inst, Los Angeles. Work: Amfac, Honolulu; Castle & Cooke Inc, Honolulu; Honolulu Acad Arts; State Found Cult & Arts; Dept of Educ, Honolulu. Comn: Three wall panels, Kauai High Sch, 73; gift print, Honolulu Printmakers, 74. Exhib: Nat Print Exhib, Honolulu Acad Arts, 71-77; one-woman shows, Silk Screen Prints, Honolulu Acad Arts, 71, Barbara Engle, Serigraphs, Santa Fe, NMex, 72 & Barbara Engle, Jewelry, Santa Barbara, Calif, 72 & Kauai Mus, 73; plus others. Teaching: Instr drawing, silkscreen painting & painting, Honolulu Acad Arts, 64- Bibliog: Helen Hutton (auth), Technique of collage, Batsford, Eng & Watson-Guptill, New York, 68; Lee Nordness (auth), Objects USA, Viking Press, 70; Ramona Solberg (auth), Inventive jewelry, Van Nostrand Reinhold Co, 73. Mem: Hawaii Artists League; Hawaii Craftsmen; Honolulu Printmakers. Style & Technique: Abstract painter, silk screen printer, primitive use of bones and found objects with sterling silver necklaces and earrings in jewelry. Media: Oil. Dealer: Downtown Gallery 125 Merchant St Honolulu HI 96813. Mailing Add: 2231 Noah St Honolulu HI 96816

ENGLE, CHET
PAINTER, SCULPTOR
b Danville, Ill, June 25, 18. Study: Am Acad Art, Chicago; Art Ctr Sch Design, Los Angeles. Work: Calif State Collection Art, Sacramento; Air Mus, Smithsonian Inst, Washington, DC. Exhib: Paintings in the United States, Carnegie Inst Fine Arts, Pittsburgh, 49; Los Angeles Co Mus, 47, 50 & 55; one-man shows, Cowie Gallery, Los Angeles, 58, Manhattan Gallery, Pasadena, 59 & 60 & Maxwell Galleries, San Francisco, 63. Pos: Instnl advert artist, Lockheed Aircraft Corp, Burbank, Calif, 50-73. Awards: First Prize, Servicemans Show, Butler Inst Art, Youngstown, Ohio, 43; First Prize, Calif State Exhib, Sacramento, 49. Style & Technique: Full range of subject matter, real and fantasy; oil painting technique determined by subject. Media: Oil, Tempera. Publ: Illusr, Lockheed Horizons, 65-70. Dealer: Green Dragon Colony La Jolla CA 92037; O'Brien's Art Emporium 7122 Stetson Dr Scottsdale AZ 85251. Mailing Add: 3639 Weslin Ave Sherman Oaks CA 91423

ENGLE, GEORGE RICHARD
PRINTMAKER
b New Albany, Ind, Nov 14, 32. Study: Ind Univ, BS, 55; Univ Louisville, MA, 66. Work: J B Speed Mus, Louisville, Ky; Carroll Reese Mus, ETenn State Univ, Johnson City; Univ Dayton, Ohio; Ind Cent Univ, Indianapolis; Univ Louisville, Ky. Exhib: Hunter Mus Art Ann, Chattanooga, Tenn, 64; Mid-S Ann, The Parthenon, Nashville, Tenn, 67 & 69; Ind Artists Exhib, Herron Mus, Indianapolis, 68; one-man shows, Cincinnati Mus Art, 69 & Carroll Reese Mus, Johnson City, Tenn, 73; Evansville Mus Arts & Sci, 71; Ind Artists, Ind State Mus, Indianapolis, 75; Printmakers Exhib, J B Speed Mus, Louisville, Ky, 75. Awards: Best in Combined Media, Art Ctr Ann, Louisville, Ky, 66; Merit Award, Nashville Mid-S Ann, 67; Exhib Award, Cincinnati Mus Art Biennial, 69. Mem: Ky Guild Artists & Craftsmen; Ind Guild Artists & Craftsmen. Style & Technique: Realistic images in etching and aquatint; semiabstract form of painting and collage. Media: Etching; aquatint. Mailing Add: RR 2 466A New Albany IN 47150

ENGLISH, JOHN ARBOGAST
PAINTER
b Trenton, NJ, Nov 7, 13. Study: Trenton Sch Indust Art; Trenton State Col, BS. Comn: Numerous marine paintings & yacht portraits comn by pvt individuals. Exhib: Yardley Pa Art Guild Ann Show, 72-74; Am Artists Prof League, NJ Chap Ann Exhib, 73-74; Ocean Co Artists Guild Ann Show, 73-75; Franklin Mint Nat Marine Art Competition, 74; Miami Int Boat Show Marine Exhib, 74-75. Pos: Publ lithographic reproductions marine subj, Riverside Studio, Island Heights, NJ. Awards: Gold Medal, Franklin Mint; First Award Oil Painting, Ocean Co Artist Guild; Second in Show, Miami Int Boat Show Exhib. Mem: Ocean Co Artist Guild; Grove House, Miami. Style & Technique: Representational style marine subjects. Media: Oil. Dealer: Newman Galleries 1625 Walnut St Philadelphia PA 19103. Mailing Add: 236 Ocean Ave Island Heights NJ 08732

ENMAN, TOM KENNETH
PAINTER, MUSEUM DIRECTOR
b Salt Lake City, Utah, Feb 22, 28. Study: Univ Wash, Exten, 48-49; Chicago Acad Fine Arts, cert, 52; Cape Sch Art, Provincetown, Mass, scholar, 52; Calif Col Arts & Crafts, Oakland, 53-54; Univ Calif, Los Angeles, Exten, 58-61; Laguna Beach Sch Art, Calif, 69; also with Alex Villumsion & Playa Del Ray, Calif, 62. Exhib: 19th Newport Ann, Newport Beach, Calif, 64; Laguna Beach Art Gallery Ann Fall Mem, 64; All Calif Exhib, Laguna Beach, 65; 7th Nat Ann Art Round Up, Las Vegas, 66; Laguna Beach Art Asn Graphic & Drawing Exhib, 67. Pos: Dir, Artist Guild Laguna Beach, 64-65; dir, Laguna Beach Mus Art, 65- Awards: First in Graphic (pen & ink), 64 & hon mention in oil, 65, Laguna Beach Art Asn. Mem: Laguna Beach Art Asn (dir). Media: Oil, Watercolor. Mailing Add: 2160 S Coast Hwy Laguna Beach CA 92651

ENOS, CHRIS
PHOTOGRAPHER, ART ADMINISTRATOR
b Calif, Aug 21, 44. Study: San Francisco State Univ, BA(sculpture); San Francisco Art Inst, MFA(photog). Work: Fogg Art Mus, Cambridge, Mass; Mus Fine Arts, Boston; San Francisco Mus Art; Wellesley Col, Mass; Portland Mus Art, Maine. Exhib: Fogg Art Mus, 74 & 76; Recent Acquisitions, Boston Mus Fine Arts, 76; Portland Mus Art, 77; one-person shows, Bibliot Nat, Paris, France, 75, Carl Siembab Gallery, Boston, 75, Univ Calif, San Francisco, 76, Univ Rochester, NY, 77 & Camerawork Gallery, San Francisco, 77. Teaching: Prof photog, Hampshire Col, Amherst, Mass, 75-76; prof photog, New Eng Sch Photog, 77- Pos: Dir, Photog Resource Ctr, Boston, 76- Awards: Mass Arts & Humanities Found Grant, 75; Cutler Delong West Found Grant, 77. Mem: Soc Photog Educ (exec comt); Boston Visual Artists Union; Visual Studies Workshop, New York. Media: Photography. Publ: Contribr, Octave of prayer, Aperture, 72; contribr, Camera 35 Mag, New York, 73; contribr, Camera Mag, Bucher/Switz, 75; contribr, Horticulture Mag, Boston, 77; contribr, Women See Women, Crowell, 77. Mailing Add: PO Box 507 Boston MA 02102

ENRIQUEZ, GASPAR
DESIGNER, INSTRUCTOR
b El Paso, Tex, July 18, 42. Study: Univ Tex, El Paso, BA; printmaking with Loren Janzen & jewelry with Walt Harrison. Work: State Nat Bank; Univ Tex, El Paso. Exhib: Int Designers Craftsman, El Paso Mus Art, 70 & 75; Calif Int Artist of Year, Huntington Beach, Calif, 74; NMex State Univ, 76 & 77. Teaching: Instr art, El Paso Pub Schs, 70- Mem: El Paso Art Asn; Int Designers Craftsman. Style & Technique: Contemporary Mexican-American artist, working from both cultures. Dealer: Mikasa Gallery San Elizario TX 79849. Mailing Add: Box 17112 El Paso TX 79917

ENTE, LILY
SCULPTOR, PRINTMAKER
b Ukrania, Russia, May 20, 05. Work: Hirshhorn Mus, Washington, DC; Mass Mus, Amherst; Phoenix Art Mus, Ariz; Safad Mus, Israel; Rose Art Mus, Waltham, Mass. Exhib: Claude Bernard Gallerie, Paris, France; Great Burlington Gallery, London, Eng; Whitney Mus Am Art, New York; Int Exhib 84 Artists, Bundy Art Gallery, Waitsfield, Vt; plus numerous one-person shows. Style & Technique: No reference to the human form; undulating scalloped edges, light-filled slits in the stone and lean slabs that seem like miniature models of architecture. Mailing Add: 400 Riverside Dr New York NY 10025

ENYEART, JAMES LYLE
ART HISTORIAN, MUSEUM DIRECTOR
b Auburn, Wash, Jan 13, 43. Study: Kansas City Art Inst, BFA, 65; Univ Santiago, Chile, cert, 66-67; Univ Kans, MFA, 72. Work: Inst Mus Photog, George Eastman House, Rochester, NY; Bibliot Nat, Paris, France; Sheldon Mem Gallery, Univ Nebr, Lincoln; Albrecht Mus Art, St Joseph, Mo; Mus Art, Univ Kans, Lawrence. Comn: Nineteenth Century archit of St Joseph, 74 & stained glass windows of St Joseph, 75, Albrecht Mus Art, St Joseph, Mo. Collections Arranged: Invisible in America: Photographs of Marion Palfi (auth, catalogue), 73; Francis Brugviere: A Retrospective, 77. Teaching: Assoc prof hist photog, Univ Kans, 69-76. Pos: Cur photog, Helen Foresman Spencer Mus Art, Univ Kans, Lawrence; exec dir, Friends of Photog. Awards: Prof Mus Fel, Nat Endowment for the Arts, 75; Orgn Am States Fel, 66. Bibliog: Jacob Deschin (auth), Daguerreotype Restoration, Popular Photog, 11/70; Linda Troeller (auth), Current museum attitudes in the collection of color photographs, Exposure, Vol 14 (Feb, 76) & Caring for photographs, Life Libr of Photog, 72. Mem: Nat Soc Photog Educ (conf chmn, 76). Res: Research and publication on conservation and restoration of photographs; same on individual 19th and 20th century photographers. Publ: Auth, Saving a daguerreotype, J Royal Photog Soc, 70; auth, Francis Brugviere: His Life & His Photographs, Alfred A Knopf, 77; auth, Untitled No 12: The Photographs of Albert Renger-Patasch, Friends of Photog, 77; ed, Kansas Album: Nine Photographers, Kans Banker's Asn, 77. Mailing Add: Friends of Photog Box 239 Carmel CA 93921

EPLER, VENETIA
PAINTER, MURALIST
b Linwood, WVa. Study: Ecole de Louvre; London Sch Arts & Crafts, Eng; Slades, London. Work: DeSaisset Gallery, Santa Clara Mus, Calif; Am Embassy, London, Eng; San Bernardino Co Mus, Redlands, Calif; Chapel St Francis, Episcopal Church, Glendale, Calif; Occidental Col Libr. Comn: Portrait of Pres Dwight D Eisenhower, Western White House, San Clemente, Calif, 69; portrait of founding pres, Dean Atherton, Phiffer Hall, Claremont Col, 70; portrait of Peter J Velez de Silva, Ambassador from Malta to Guatemala Embassy, Guatemala City, 71; 12 stained glass altar windows, Church of Relig Sci, Beverly Hills, 74; Life of Christ mural, facade of Christian Heritage Mausoleum, Forest Lawn Mem Park, West Covina, Calif, 75; plus others. Exhib: Am Inst Fine Arts Competition, Los Angeles, 69; Grand Nat Competition, Am Artists Prof League, 71; Los Angeles Co Mus, 72; All California Art Competition, Nat League Am Pen Women, 74. Pos: Illusr, layout & bakcground artist, Motion Picture Indust, 60- Awards: Emmy & Nat Award for Art Work, Motion Picture Coun, Los Angeles, 66; Am Inst Fine Arts Fel & Gold Medal, 69; Am Artists Prof League Fel, New York, 71. Bibliog: Maria Antonieta Somoza (auth), En honor de distinguidas pintoras Norteamericanas, Grafico, Guatemala City, 8/71; Jackie Dashiel (auth), Artists of the forest lawn mosaic, 10/74 & Al Bine (auth), The birth, life, & works of Jesus Christ, 3/75, Los Angeles Herald Examr. Mem: Am Artists Prof League; Am Inst Fine Arts; Nat League Am Pen Women; Artists of Southwest; San Gabriel Fine Arts Asn. Style & Technique: Various styles, traditional, stylized impressionistic. Media: Oil, Watercolor. Res: Ten years of research on Biblical customs, costumes, types, architecture and history; two years research on Leonardo da Vinci and on Christian art. Mailing Add: 1835 Outpost Dr Los Angeles CA 90068

EPPINK, HELEN BRENAN
PAINTER
b Springfield, Ohio, Aug 19, 10. Study: Cleveland Art Inst; John Huntington Polytech Inst, Cleveland, Ohio; Colorado Springs Fine Art Ctr. Work: Wichita Art Mus, Kans; Kans State Univ, Manhattan; Kans Fedn Womens Clubs Collection. Exhib: Cleveland May Show, Ohio, 34; 3rd Air Capitol Show, Wichita Art Mus, 56; Midwest Biennial, Joslyn Art Mus, Omaha, Nebr, 56; 8th Biennial Regional Exhib, Kans State Univ, 65; 22nd Ann Exhib Oils by Kans Artists, Manhattan, 70; two-man show, Topeka Pub Libr, 77. Teaching: Instr art, Col Emporia, 44-53; instr art, Ottawa Univ, Kans, 48-51; instr art, Kans State Teachers Col, 51-52, 60-61; head dept art, Col Emporia, 61-74. Awards: Second Prize for watercolor, Midwestern Show, Kansas City Art Inst, 39; Purchase Prize for watercolor, Wichita Art Mus, 56; Purchase Prize for oil, 8th Biennial Exhib, Kans State Univ, 65. Mem: Kans Fedn Art; Kans State Art Teachers Asn. Media: Acrylic, Oil. Mailing Add: 2101 Canterbury Rd Emporia KS 66801

EPPINK, NORMAN R
PRINTMAKER, PAINTER
b Cleveland, Ohio, July 29, 06. Study: Cleveland Art Inst, BEA; Western Reserve Univ, MA. Work: Brit Mus, London; Metrop Mus Art, New York; Art Inst Chicago; Nat Gallery Art, Washington, DC; Cleveland Mus Art. Comn: Court of Romance (mural), comn by Lakewood Bd Educ for Harding Jr High Sch, Ohio, 30; indust mural, Mansfield Pub Libr, Ohio, 35. Exhib: 3rd Int Color Lithography, Cincinnati Art Mus, Ohio, 54; Pratt Inst Int Print Show, 64 & 68; one-man show, 101 Prints, Linda Hall Libr, Kansas City, Mo & circulating exhib, Nat Gallery Art, Washington, DC, 68; two-man show, Topeka Pub Libr, 77. Teaching: Instr art, Lakewood Pub Schs, 28-30; instr art, Cleveland Pub Schs, 35-37; instr art, Kans State Teachers Col, 37-75, head dept art, 47-68, lectr (prof) art hist, 68-75. Pos: Med illusr, Cleveland Clin Found, 30-33; mem, Kans Cult Arts Comn, 66-67. Awards: Second Prize Lithography, 53, First Prize, 54 & First Prize Color Lithography, 55, Cleveland Mus Art. Bibliog: Norman Eppink, printmaker, The Rotarian, 12/68. Mem: Kans Fedn Art (trustee, 72); Kans State Art Teachers Asn. Media: Oil, Watercolor. Res: Printmaking processes. Publ: Auth & illusr, 101 prints, ltd ed, pvt press, 67, trade ed, Univ Okla Press, 71. Mailing Add: 2101 Canterbury Rd Emporia KS 66801

EPSTEIN, ANNABEL WHARTON
ART HISTORIAN
b New Rochelle, NY. Study: Univ Wis, Madison, BSc, 66; Univ Chicago, MA, 69; Courtauld Inst, London Univ, PhD, 75. Teaching: Res fel Byzantine art, Barber Inst, Univ Birmingham, Eng, 71-75; asst prof Medieval art, Oberlin Col, 75- Awards: Sr fel, Dumbarton Oaks, Harvard Univ, 78-79. Mem: Inst Archit & Urban Studies, New York (bd mem); Col Art Asn; Soc Archit Historians. Res: Reevaluation of the aesthetic value of provincial art through a study of its function. Publ: Auth, Rock-cut Chapels in Cappadocia: Column Churches & the Yilanli Group, Cahiers Archaeol, 75; auth, Iconoclast Churches in Cappadocia, Iconoclasm, Univ Birmingham, 76. Mailing Add: Dept of Art Oberlin Col Oberlin OH 44074

EPTING, MARION AUSTIN
PRINTMAKER, EDUCATOR
b Forrest, Miss, Jan 28, 40. Study: Los Angeles City Col, AA; Los Angeles Co Art Inst, Otis, MFA, 69; also with Ernest Freed, Lee Chesney, Shiro Ikegawa & Charles White. Work: Oakland Mus, Calif, Seattle Art Mus; Libr of Cong, Washington, DC; Auchebach Found, DeYoung Mus, San Francisco; Whitney Mus, New York. Comn: Intaglio prints comn by John Wilson, Lakeside Studios, Mich, 72-74. Exhib: 1st Nat Print Exhib, San Diego Fine Arts Soc, 69; Northwest Printmakers, Seattle Art Mus, 69; Oakland Art Mus, 73; traveling exhib, Western Asn Art Mus, 73-75. Collections Arranged: Black Untitled III, Western Asn Art Mus; Chico Group, Old Bergen Art Guild, NJ. Teaching: Assoc prof art, Calif State Univ, Chico, 69- Pos: Resident artist, Lakeside Studios, Mich, 70-; art dir, J-Squared B-Squared Consult, Los Angeles, 71- Awards: Calif South 7 Best of Show, San Diego Fine Arts Guild, 69; Northwest Printmakers Purchase Award, Seattle Art Mus, 69; First Place for Graphics, Cal Expo, Del Mar, Calif, 69. Bibliog: Wady Lewis (auth), Black Artists on Art, Contemp Crafts, Los Angeles, Vol 1, 70; J Edward Atkinson (auth), Black Dimensions in Contemporary American Art, Times Mirror, 71; Theresa Dickason Cederholm (auth), Afro American Artists, Boston Pub Libr, 73. Style & Technique: Symbolism; pedestaled rectangel with a simultaneous symmetrical and asymmetrical division of that space. Media: Intaglio. Dealer: Patrick Reilley c/o Marquoit Galleries 40 Gold St San Francisco CA 94133. Mailing Add: 1224 Bidwell Ave Chico CA 95926

ERBE, JOAN (MRS JOAN ERBE UDEL)
PAINTER
b Baltimore, Md, Nov 1, 26. Work: Munic Court, Washington, DC; Peale Mus, Baltimore; Baltimore Mus Art; Morgan Col. Exhib: Peale Mus, 51-61; seven shows, Baltimore Mus Art, 54-65; Smithsonian Inst, 56; Corcoran Gallery Art, 57-60; 16 one-person shows, IFA Galleries, Washington, DC, 58-77; Butler Inst Am Art, 60 & 61; Am Acad of Arts, 76; plus others. Awards: Prizes, Artists Equity Asn, 60 & 61; Prizes, Corcoran Gallery Art, 60 & 62; Prizes, Baltimore Mus Art, 63, 64 & 66; plus others. Mem: Artists Equity Asn. Mailing Add: 5603 Wexford Rd Baltimore MD 21209

ERBES, ROSLYN MARIA
See Rensch, Roslyn

ERDELAC, JOSEPH MARK
COLLECTOR, PATRON
b Cleveland, Ohio. Mem: Life mem Cleveland Mus Art, Butler Inst Am Art, Youngstown, Ohio & Royal Photographic Soc of Brit. Interest: Donor of art works to local and national museums, universities, schools and educational television; trustee of art institutions; lecturer on art and collecting. Collection: Oils, watercolors and graphics by local and national Washington Project for the Arts artists; oils, watercolors, drawings and graphics by Rockwell Kent; watercolors, drawings and collages by Stephen Longstreet; also work by Henry Miller, Charles Bukowski, Kenneth Patchen and Udinotti. Mailing Add: 16515 Lorain Ave Cleveland OH 44111

ERDLE, ROB
PAINTER, EDUCATOR
b Selma, Calif, Aug 17, 49. Study: Reedley Col, Calif, AA; Calif State Univ, Fresno, BA; Bowling Green Univ, Ohio, MFA. Exhib: Two-man shows, St Francis Col, Ft Wayne, Ind & NTex State Univ, 76; Fresno State Univ, Calif, 72; Nat Watercolor Soc Exhib, Los Angeles-Otis Art Inst, Palm Springs Art Mus, 74; Watercolor USA, Springfield Art Mus, Mo, 74 & 77; Ala Nat Watercolor Exhib, Birmingham Art Mus, 75-76; Toledo May Show, Toledo Mus of Art, Ohio, 75-76; Southern Watercolorist Nat Exhib, Cheekwood Arts Ctr, Nashville, Tenn, 77; Rocky Mountain Nat Watercolor Exhib, Foothills Arts Ctr, Golden, Colo, 77; one-man show, Del Mar Col, Corpus Christi, Tex, 77; Tex Fine Arts Nat Exhib, Laguna Gloria Art Mus, Austin, 77. Teaching: Asst prof watercolor works on paper, NTex State Univ, 76- Pos: Dir, Chautauqua Nat Exhib of Am Art, Chautauqua Art Asn, 78-; dir, Chautauqua Inst Art Gallery, Chautauqua, NY, currently. Awards: Outstanding Painting Award, Toledo May Show, Toledo Mus of Art, 75 & 76; First Prize, Purchase, Ala Nat Watercolor Exhib, Birmingham Art Mus, 76; Mus Cash Award, Watercolor USA, Springfield Art Mus, 77. Mem: Nat Watercolor Soc, Los Angeles; Tex Watercolor Soc, San Antonio; Watercolor Soc Ala, Birmingham; Southern Watercolor Soc, Memphis; Southwestern Watercolor Soc, Dallas. Style & Technique: Fantasy landscapes achieved through transparent layering of paint. Media: Watercolor and drawing-ink, pencil. Mailing Add: 1701 Greenwood Dr Denton TX 76201

ERDMAN, R H DONNELLEY
ART DEALER
b Pasadena, Calif, Jan 19, 38. Study: Princeton Univ, BA(arch), MFA(arch) & PhD(arch); Univ Calif, BArch. Teaching: Asst prof archit, Rice Univ Sch Archit. Pos: Dir, Tex Gallery.

Mem: Contemp Art Mus, Houston (trustee). Publ: Auth, Christmas in Houston, Architex, 71; auth, The Museums of Fine Arts, Rice Univ Sch Archit, 72. Mailing Add: Texas Gallery 2439 Bissonnet Houston TX 77005

ERES, EUGENIA
PAINTER
b Winiza, Ucrania, Apr 28, 28; US citizen. Study: Fine Art Sch, Sao Paulo, Brazil, with Prof Murillo; Famous Artists Sch, Westport, Conn, with Norman Rockwell, Fletcher Martin & Doug Kingman; Nat Acad Fine Arts, New York, with Hugh Cumpel. Work: Galleria de Artes IV Centenario, Sao Paulo; Russian Am Historical Mus, Lakewood, NJ. Exhib: Hudson Valley Art Asn, 66-67; Hammond Mus, North Salem, NY, 68; Grand Nat, Am Artists Prof League, 68-76; Expo Int, Monaco, 69; Allied Artists Am, Nat Acad Gallery, 71; Nat Art League, New York, 74-77; Knickerbocker Artists, 74-77; Pen & Brush, 77-78; Salmagundi Club, 77-78. Awards: First Prize, Russian Am Soc, 75-77; First Prize, Pen & Brush, 77; Gold Medal of Honor, Nat Art League, 77; plus others. Mem: Fel Am Artists Prof League; Knickerbocker Artists; Catharine Lorillard Wolfe Art Club; Pen & Brush; Salmagundi Club. Style & Technique: Landscapes and seascapes; realism and impressionism with individual technique. Media: Oil. Mailing Add: 84-21 108th St Richmond Hill NY 11418

ERICSON, BEATRICE
PAINTER
b Paris, France; US citizen. Study: With Morris Davidson & Boris Margo, Provincetown, Mass; also with Max Schnitzler, New York. Work: NY Univ Fine Arts; Marist Col, Poughkeepsie, NY; Miami Mus Mod Art; also Gov Nelson A Rockefeller Collection. Exhib: Silvermine Guild Artists, New Canaan, Conn; Norfolk Mus Arts & Sci; one-man shows, Angeleski Gallery, 60, Letters to the Unknown, Brata Gallery, 67 & Archaic Past, Caravan House, 72 & 77, New York. Bibliog: Reviews, In: Art News & Arts Mag, 57-72; Leo Soretsky (auth), article, In: FM Guide, 4/72. Style & Technique: Acrylics with stripes and raised calligraphic invented letters. Dealer: Caravan House Gallery 132 E 65th St New York NY 10021. Mailing Add: 14 Watkins Ave Middletown NY 10940

ERICSON, DICK
CARTOONIST, ILLUSTRATOR
b New York, NY, Apr 12, 16. Work: Nat Cartoonists Soc Collection; Libr Cong. Teaching: Lectr cartooning & advert, schs, serv clubs, bus conventions & others. Pos: Advert & pub rels consult, writer & illusr; creator syndicated newspaper features, Citizen Sibley & Trixie the Trader, Al Smith Features, Imagene, publ by Banking & Stewart the Steward. Awards: Spec Award Outstanding Pub Rels Achievements, Nat Automobile Dealers Pub Rels Comt, 54; ENIT Trophy, Cartoon Category, 13th Int Humor Festival, Bordighera, Italy, 60. Mem: Nat Cartoonists Soc (vpres, bd gov, chmn ACE awards comt, pub rels comt, slide shows & overseas tours). Publ: Contribr, Best Cartoons of the Year; contribr, Sat Eve Post, True, Playboy, Ladies Home J & many others. Mailing Add: Roxbury CT 06783

ERICSON, ERNEST
ILLUSTRATOR, INSTRUCTOR
b Boston, Mass. Study: Boston Mus Fine Arts Sch; Art Inst Chicago; Art Students League; Acad Grande Chaumiere, Paris. Exhib: Detroit Inst Art; New York Watercolor Soc; Pa Acad Fine Arts, Philadelphia; Soc Illustrators, New York. Teaching: Instr advan design, Sch Visual Arts, 56- Pos: Illusr, Kenyon & Eckhardt, New York, 55- Mem: Soc Illustrators. Style & Technique: Decorative, stylized, impressionistic; realistic: pen and ink; figures: portraits, landscapes and still life. Mailing Add: 305 E 86th St New York NY 10028

ERIQUEZZO, LEE M
PAINTER
b Danbury, Conn. Study: Md Inst Art; Mus Mod Art; Art Students League; Cooper Union, scholar; Rome Acad Belle Arts, Ital Cult Soc travel scholar; also with Edwin Dickensen, Joseph Hirsch, Zolton Hecht & Frank Mason, Foster & E Mayan. Work: Slater Mus, Norwich, Conn; Brooklyn Mus, NY; Art Students League Collection, New York; Nat Acad Design, New York. Comn: Paintings for film John & Mary. Exhib: Nat Arts Club, New York; Nat Acad Design; Audubon Soc, New York; Slater Mus; La Galerie Mouffe, Paris, France. Pos: Bd dirs, Art Students League; exhib chairlady, Nat Arts Club. Awards: Benedictine Award; Nat Art Club & Cooper Union Awards. Mem: Greenwich Art Soc; Cooper Union Alumni Soc. Style & Technique: Impressionistic realism. Media: Oil, Lithograph. Publ: Illusr, Rachael Karr book on Yoga, 74. Mailing Add: c/o I L Sell 245 E 21st St New York NY 10010

ERNST, JAMES ARNOLD
PAINTER, INSTRUCTOR
b New York, NY, Aug 5, 16. Study: Pratt Inst Sch Art, 37-39; Grand Cent Art Sch, 40. Work: Acad Arts, Easton, Md. Exhib: One-man shows, Barzansky Galleries, New York, 51, 53, 54, 56 & 58, Galerie Tedesco, Paris, 52 & 55, Cosmos Club, Washington, DC, 70, Phoenix-Chase Galleries, Baltimore, 70, Lyford Cay Gallery, Nassau, Bahamas, 74, Veerhoff Galleries, Washington, DC, 76 & Inst Cult Dominico-Americano, Santo Domingo, Dominican Repub, 76. Teaching: Instr drawing, beginning & advan watercolor, City Col New York, 51-62. Pos: Specialist in design & line drawing, Batten, Barton, Durstine & Osborne, Inc, New York, 51-62. Awards: Best Watercolor, Md State Fedn Arts, Annapolis, 67; First Prize & Purchase Award, Land of Pleasant Living Exhib, 69; Best in Show, Lee Lawrie Award, Acad Arts, Easton, 75. Mem: Joint Ethics Comt; Artists Guild, New York (vpres, mem bd, 56-75); Baltimore Watercolor Club; Acad Arts, Easton. Style & Technique: Lyric, romantic style with a free flowing technique. Media: Watercolor, Oil. Dealer: Phoenix-Chase Galleries 5 W Chase St Baltimore MD 21201; Veerhoff Galleries 1512 Connecticut Ave Washington DC 20036. Mailing Add: Crescent Coves Bozman MD 21612

ERNST, JIMMY
PAINTER, EDUCATOR
b Cologne, Ger, June 24, 20; US citizen. Study: Altona Arts & Crafts Sch, 38. Work: Metrop Mus Art; Whitney Mus Am Art; Brooklyn Mus; Wadsworth Atheneum; Art Inst Chicago; plus many others. Comn: Sculpture, NBC Producer's Showcase, 54; paintings, Abbott Labs, 55 & Fortune Mag, 55 & 61; murals, USS Adams, 56 & Continental Bank, Lincoln, Nebr, 58-59. Exhib: Pa Acad Fine Arts, 53, 55, 57 & 65; Bielefeld Mus, Ger, 64; Berlin, 65; one-man show, Grand Rapids Mus Art, 68; Whitney Mus Am Art Ann, 69 & 70; Guggenheim Mus Paris show, 72-78; Lucie Weil Gallery, Spiegel Gallery, Cologne, Ger, Yares Gallery, Scottsdale, Ariz, 77-78; plus many others. Teaching: Lectr contemp art, art asns & mus in US; prof art, Brooklyn Col, 51-; vis artist, Univ Colo, 54 & 56; vis artist, Mus Fine Arts, Houston, 56; lectr, US Info Serv, USSR & Ger, 61 & 63. Awards: Norman Wait Harris Award, Art Inst Chicago, 54; Creative Arts Award, Brandeis Univ, 57; Guggenheim Grant, 61. Dealer: Borgenicht Gallery 1018 Madison Ave New York NY 10021. Mailing Add: Lee Ave East Hampton NY 11937

ERTMAN, EARL LESLIE
ART HISTORIAN, EDUCATOR
b Parma, Ohio, Nov 13, 32. Study: Univ Southern Miss, BS, 65; Case Western Reserve Univ, MA, 67; Egyptian art with John D Cooney, Cleveland Mus, 67-71; classics with T T Duke, Univ Akron, 67-70. Teaching: Instr Western art, Dept of Art Hist & Educ, Cleveland Mus of Art, Ohio, 65-67; assoc prof art hist, teaching Western, primitive & Egyptian art, Univ Akron, 67- Pos: Art dept rep, Visual Arts Comt of the Greater Akron Arts Fedn, 71-72; art historian & field photogr, Johns Hopkins Exped to pyramid area, Giza, Egypt, summer 72 & 74. Bibliog: Edward K Werner (auth), The Amarna Period of 18th Dynasty Egypt, A Bibliography: 1965-1974, Am Res Ctr in Egypt Newsletter No 95, 76; Edward K Werner (auth), The Amarna Period of 18th Dynasty Egypt, Bibliography Supplement, 76, Am Res Ctr in Egypt Newsletter, Numbers 101-102, 77; Pauline Albenda (auth), Landscape Bas-reliefs in the Bit-Hilani of Ashurbanipal, Am Schs of Oriental Res Bull, 77. Mem: Northeastern Ohio Art Hist Asn; Midwest Art Asn; Archaeol Inst of Am; Am Res Ctr in Egypt. Res: Iconographic and stylistic analysis of ancient Egyptian art and documentation of Egyptian objects in minor collections in the United States. Publ: Ed, African Sculpture: Selections from the Gussman Collection, Philbrook Art Ctr, Tulsa, Okla (catalogue), Neighborhood Arts, Akron, 71; auth, The Oldest Known Three-Dimensional Representation of the God Ptah, J Near Eastern Studies, 72; auth, A Manuscript Fragment by the Parisian Miniaturist Honoré in Cleveland, Ohio, Scriptorium, Paris-Brussels, 73; auth, The Cap-Crown of Nefertiti: Its Function and Probable Origin, J Am Res Ctr in Egypt, 76; contribr, Recording and Documentation of Minor Collections in the United States, 1st Int Cong of Egyptology, Inst for Hist & Archaeol, Berlin (in press). Mailing Add: 3150 Eighth St Cuyahoga Falls OH 44221

ESCOBEDO, AUGUSTO ORTEGA
SCULPTOR, PAINTER
b Mexico City, Mex, Nov 22, 14. Work: Eisenhower Mus, Abilene, Kans; Mus Mod Art, Mexico City; Gallery Int Airport, Mexico City. Comn: Fountain & 11 bronze figures, Ministry of Educ, Mexico City, 57; bronze equestrian group, Govt Tabasco, Villahermosa City, 61; 9 bronze figures, Nat Inst Children's Welfare, Mexico City, 61; 3 figures, polyester, Palace Versailles Shopping Ctr, Montreal, Can, 66; fountain & 16 bronze figures, Universal Studios, Universal City, Calif, 69. Exhib: Mex Art Show, Tokyo, Japan, 55; Int Telecommun Union Sculpture Contest, Geneva, Switz, 65; Mex Art Show, Denver Mus Fine Arts, 67; Mex Art, Waddington Galleries, Montreal, 68; Contemp Mex Artists, HemisFair Plaza, San Antonio, Tex, 72. Teaching: Prof sculpture, Univ Morelia, Michoacan, Mex, 56. Awards: Man of Vision Award, Vision Mag, 56; Contemp Sculpture Show Award, Univ Chihuahua, 64 & 65. Bibliog: A Luna Arroyo (auth), Panorama de la Escultura Mexicana, Ed Inst Nac Bellas Artes, 64; Raquel Tibol (auth), Historia del Arte Mexicano, Ed Hermes, 64; M Monteforte Toledo (auth), Las Piedras Vivas, Univ State Mex, 65. Media: Bronze, Marble. Mailing Add: Callejon de las Flores 4 San Francisco Coyoacan Mexico DF Mexico

ESCOBEDO, HELEN
ENVIRONMENTAL SCULPTOR
b Mexico City, Mex, July 28, 36. Study: Univ Motolinia, BA(humanities); ARCA, 3 yr scholar; also with Frank Dobson, John Skeaping & Leon Underwood. Work: Mus Mod Art, Mex; Prague Nat Gallery, Czech; Palacio de Bellas Artes, Mexico City; also in pvt collection of Stanley Marcus, US. Comn: Mercury (bronze), Banco de Comercio, Mexico City, 66; Movement (bronze), Hotel Aristos, Mexico City, 67; Gateway to the Wind (concrete), Mex Olympic Games, Friendship Rte, 68; Signals (aluminum), City of Aukland Golden Jubilee, NZ, 71; Total House (environment), pvt comn, Mexico City, 72. Exhib: One-man shows, Prague Nat Gallery, 69, Park Lazienkowsky, Stara Kordegarda, Warsaw, Poland, 70 & Mus Mod Art, Mexico City, 75; Kunstindustri Mus, Oslo, Norway, 70; Middelheim Sculpture Bienale, Antwerp, Belg, 71. Pos: Dir, Dept Mus & Galleries, Nat Univ Mex, 61-77 & res fel, Fac Humanities, Centre for Sculptural Space, Univ Mex, 78. Bibliog: 4 Shapes 4 Spaces, Nat Film Bd, NZ, 74; Alfredo Gurrola (auth), Helen Escobedo, Cent Univ de Estudios Cinematog, 75. Mem: Nat Sculpture Ctr, Lawrence, Kans (mem bd, 71-); Int Comn Mus (mem bd, 75-). Style & Technique: Environmental sculpture; habitats. Building Materials: Aluminum, Concrete, Wood, Brick. Dealer: Galeria de Arte Mexicano Milan 18 Mexico DF 6 Mexico. Mailing Add: AV San Jeronimo 162 Mexico DF Mexico

ESHOO, ROBERT
PAINTER
b New Britain, Conn, Apr 27, 26. Study: Boston Mus Fine Arts Sch Mass, cert & dipl; Vesper George Sch Art, Boston; Syracuse Univ, BFA & MFA. Work: Boston Mus Fine Arts; Wadsworth Atheneum, Hartford, Conn; Currier Gallery Art, Manchester, NH; Munson-Williams-Proctor Inst, Utica, NY; Addison Gallery Am Art, Andover, Mass; St Anselm's Col; Dartmouth Col; Portland Mus, Maine; Brandeis Univ. Exhib: Chicago Art Inst Ann, 57; Young America, Whitney Mus Am Art, New York, 57; Quadrennial, Am Painting 1962, Va Mus Fine Arts, Richmond, 62; 28th Biennial Exhib, Corcoran Gallery, Washington, DC, 63; retrospective, Currier Gallery Art, 67. Teaching: Supvr painting & graphics, Currier Art Ctr, 58-; instr studio art, Derryfield Sch, Manchester, 65- Media: Oil, Watercolor. Mailing Add: 83 Hanover St Manchester NH 03101

ESHRAW, RA
PAINTER, ILLUSTRATOR
b 1926; US citizen. Study: Ecole des Beaux Arts, Paris, Fr Govt scholar; Acad de la Grande Chaumiere, Paris; Acad Ranson, Paris. Work: Pvt collections of Pierre Mueller, Mane Katzt & Bruno Bassano, Paris; collection being held for future space-age museum. Exhib: One-woman show, Galerie Bruno Bassano, Paris, 55; Salon des Poetes-Peintres, Galeries Raymond Duncan, Paris, 58; La Creation du Genre Humain, Mus Mod Art, Paris, 59; Minifest: Painting of Future, Galerie des 4 Vents, Paris, 63 & 67; Homo Cosmicus, Women's Interart Gallery, New York, 72. Bibliog: Ra Eshraw: La Creation du Genre Humain (eurovision-movie), Mus Mod Art, Paris, 59; Painting Homo Cosmicus, TV, Channel 5, 72. Style & Technique: Monumental, symbolic-expressionistic, spiritual, cosmic, past and future visions (fine layer). Media: Acrylic, Watercolor, Oil. Res: Telepathic messages, received with pineal gland; remembrance of past lives through insight in Akashic record. Publ: Auth, Vox Humana (poetry), 67; auth & illusr, Homo Cosmicus (poetry), 70 & 72; auth & illusr, Ad Astra, Story About My Ten Past Lives, 73; auth & illusr, Intergalactic Revelations, 75; auth & illusr, Bermuda Triangle-Teleportation Chamber of the Gods, 75. Mailing Add: PO Box 1097 Southampton NY 11968

ESLER, JOHN KENNETH
PRINTMAKER
b Pilot Mound, Man, Jan 11, 33. Study: Univ Man, BEd, Univ Man Sch Art, BFA. Work: Mus Mod Art, New York; Victoria & Albert Mus, London; Albright-Knox Gallery, Buffalo; Nat Gallery Can, Ottawa; Montreal Mus Fine Arts. Exhib: 3rd Biennal Am Grababo, Santiago, Chile, 68; 3rd Int Gravure, Krakow, Poland, 70; 2nd Int Print Biennale, Bradford, Eng, 70; Premio Int Biella, Italy, 71; Int Buchkunst-Ausstellung, Leipzig, 71. Teaching: Assoc

prof printmaking, Alta Col Art, Calgary, 64-68; assoc prof printmaking, Univ Calgary, 68- Awards: C W Jefferies Award, Can Soc Graphic Arts, 68; First Purchase Award, Burnaby Biennial Print Exhib, 69; First Purchase Award, Graphic Exhib, Art Alliance Cent Pa, 70. Mem: Can Soc Graphic Art (Western rep, 68-); Royal Can Acad Arts. Soc Can Etchers & Engravers. Style & Technique: Colored etching and collograph. Mailing Add: Box 2 Site 7 SS 1 Calgary AB T2M 4N3 Can

ESMAN, ROSA M
ART DEALER, COLLECTOR
b New York, NY, Nov 29, 27. Study: Smith Col, BA. Work: (Limited Editions) New York 10 & 7 Objects in a Box, Mus Mod Art, New York Int, Whitney Mus Am Art & Metropolitan Scene, Metrop Mus Art, New York; 7 Objects 69, Brit Arts Coun, London; Whitney Mus Am Art, New York. Pos: Pres & dir, Tanglewood Press, New York, 64-69 & 72-; dir, Abrams Original Editions, 69-72; pres & dir, Rosa Esman Gallery, 72- Specialty: Contemporary American paintings, drawings and sculpture; Russian avant-garde material, 1911-1923. Collection: (With Aaron H Esman, MD) Contemporary drawings, prints and paintings, with emphasis on New York artists of the 60's and 70's; also African and pre-Columbian art. Publ: Ed, Seven objects in a box, 66; ed, New York 10/69, 69; ed, Six drawing tables by Saul Steinberg, 71; ed, Four Pochoirs by Helen Frankenthaler, 71; ed, No gas by Red Grooms, 72; plus others. Mailing Add: 29 W 57th St New York NY 10019

ESSERMAN, RUTH
PAINTER
b Chicago, Ill, May 21, 27. Study: Univ Ill, BA & MA; Univ Mex; Art Inst Chicago. Exhib: Roosevelt Univ-Pan-Am Exhib, 57; New Horizons, 58; Denver Art Mus, 59 & 60; Chicago Sun-Times Competition, 60-62; Minneapolis Inst Art, 64; plus others. Teaching: Instr art, Highland Park High Sch, Ill, 57-, chmn fine arts dept, 60- Pos: Adv, US Off Educ, 67-68. Awards: Recipient of numerous prizes & awards. Mem: Ill Art Educ Asn (pres, 65-66); Nat Art Educ Asn (nat chmn sec art teachers, 76-77). Mailing Add: 433 Vine St Highland Park IL 60035

ESTABROOK, REED
PHOTOGRAPHER, EDUCATOR
b Boston, Mass, May 31, 44. Study: RI Sch of Design, BFA, 69; Art Inst of Chicago, MFA, 71. Work: Mus of Mod Art, New York; Art Inst of Chicago; Int Mus of Photog, Rochester, NY; RI Sch of Design, Providence; Humboldt State Univ, Arcata, Calif. Exhib: Photo Media, Mus of Contemp Crafts, New York, 71; Ctr of the Eye, Aspen, Colo, 71; Am Photographics, Andromeda Gallery, Buffalo, 76; Photo Synthesis, H F Johnson Mus, Cornell Univ, 76; Light II (nat competitive), Arcata, 77; Great W/Real: Ideal (travelling exhib), Univ Colo Mus of Art, Boulder, 77; one-men shows, Tyler Sch of Art, Philadelphia 75 & Midway Studios, Univ Chicago, 76. Teaching: Instr photog, Univ Ill, Urbana-Champaign, 71-74; asst prof photog, Univ Northern Iowa, 74- Awards: W R French fel Competition, Art Inst of Chicago, 71; First Place, Am Photographics, Andromeda Gallery, Buffalo, 76, Photog fel, Nat Endowment for the Arts, 76. Mem: Soc for Photog Educ. Style & Technique: Hand colored silver prints and multiple negative images. Media: Photography, wood. Publ: Contribr, Art of Photography, Time/Life Libr of Photog, 71; contribr, New Horizons, US Info, 76; contribr, Aura, Vol 1 (76) & Vol 2 (77), Andromeda Gallery; contribr, Creative Camera, Coos Press, Vol 153 (77). Mailing Add: 703 Iowa St Cedar Falls IA 50613

ESTERN, NEIL
SCULPTOR
b New York, NY, Apr 18, 26. Study: Temple Univ, BFA & BS(educ), 47. Work: Brooklyn Mus. Comn: Portraits of LaGuardia, J Robert Taft, Danny Kaye, John F Kennedy, J Edgar Hoover; portrait bust of John F Kennedy, Kennedy Mem, Grand Army Plaza, Brooklyn, 65; Franklin D Roosevelt memorial, Washington, DC, in preparation. Exhib: Numerous one-man and group shows in Conn, New York, Philadelphia, NH & Italy. Awards: John Gregory Award, 66; Samuel F B Morse Gold Medal, 70. Mailing Add: 82 Remsen St Brooklyn NY 11201

ESTEROW, MILTON
ART EDITOR, PUBLISHER
b New York, NY, July 28, 28. Study: Brooklyn Col, NY. Teaching: Lectr art, museums, colleges & universities. Pos: Asst cult news dir, New York Times, 63-68; ed & publ, Art News, 72-; ed & publ, ART Newsletter, 75-; publ, Antiques World, 78- Publ: Auth, The Art Stealers; contribr, Art News, New York Times Mag & Atlantic Mag. Mailing Add: 750 Third Ave New York NY 10017

ESTES, RICHARD
PAINTER
b Ill, 1936. Study: Chicago Art Inst, 52-56. Work: Whitney Mus Am Art, New York; Rockhill Nelson Mus, Kansas City, Mo; Toledo Mus, Ohio; Chicago Art Inst, Des Moines Art Ctr, Iowa. Exhib: Documenta V, Kassel, Ger, summer 72; Venice Biennale, Italy, summer 72; Whitney Mus Ann, 72; Twelve American Painters, Va Mus Fine Arts, Richmond, 74; Trends in Contemp Realist Painting, Boston Mus Fine Arts, 75. Bibliog: Peter Schjeldahl (auth), Flowering of the super-real, 3/2/69 & John Canaday (auth), Realism-waxing or waning, 7/13/69, New York Times; Mary Lou Kelly (auth), Popart inspired objective realism, Christian Sci Monitor, 4/1/74. Style & Technique: Realistic urban landscapes. Media: Oil on Canvas. Mailing Add: c/o Allan Stone Gallery 48 E 86th St New York NY 10028

ETCHISON, BRUCE
ART CONSERVATOR, PAINTER
b Washington, DC, Dec 19, 18. Study: Am Univ, BA; Yale Univ Sch Fine Arts, BFA & MFA. Pos: Dir, Washington Co Mus Fine Arts, 50-64; dir, Abby Aldrich Rockefeller Folk Art Collection, 64-66; conservator for pvt collectors mus, univs, cols, hist soc & the State of Pa, which included cleaning & repairing ten murals in the Senate Chambers at the State Capitol. Mem: Int & Am Insts Conserv Hist & Artistic Works; Washington Conserv Guild (mem exec coun, 72-); Nat Conserv Adv Coun. Publ: Co-auth, Roentgen Examination of Painting, 60; auth, Radiant Heat for Vacuum Tables, 69. Mailing Add: Bear Pond Studio Rte 2 Box 57 Clear Spring MD 21722

ETNIER, STEPHEN MORGAN
PAINTER
b York, Pa, Sept 11, 03. Study: Yale Art Sch; Pa Acad Fine Arts; also with Rockwell Kent & John Carroll; hon degrees from Bowdoin Col & Bates Col. Work: Metrop Mus Art; Boston Mus; Yale Univ; Toledo Mus; Duncan Phillips, Washington, DC. Comn: Many private collections. Exhib: Carnegie Inst; Corcoran Gallery Art; Pa Acad Fine Arts; Nat Acad Fine Arts; Milch Gallery, 31-64; Midtown Galleries, New York, 76; plus others. Awards: Samuel F B Morse Gold Medal, Altman Prize & Saltus Gold Medal, Nat Acad Design. Bibliog: Harry Saltpeter (auth), Stephen Etnier, bad boy artist, Esquire, 39; Howard Deoree & Ernest Watson (auths), Stephen Etnier, 56 & Betty Chamberlain (auth), Stephen Etnier, a long voyage home, 72, Am Artist. Media: Oil. Dealer: Midtown Gallery 11 E 57th St New York NY 10022. Mailing Add: Old Cove South Harpswell ME 04079

ETROG, SOREL
SCULPTOR, PAINTER
b Jassy, Romania, Aug 29, 33. Study: Inst Painting & Sculpture, Tel Aviv, Israel; Brooklyn Mus Sch Art. Work: Art Gallery Toronto; Montreal Mus Fine Arts; Mus Art Contemp, Montreal; Nat Gallery Can; Boymans Mus, Rotterdam, Holland; plus many others, US & Can. Exhib: Venice Biennial, 66; Legnano, Italy, 66; Expo '67; one-man retrospective, Palazzo Strozzi, Florence, Italy, 68; Ont Cols Traveling Exhib, Art Gallery Toronto, 68-69; Fine Arts Mus, Montreal, 68; Winnipeg Art Gallery, Man, 71; 4th Int Exhib Contemp Sculpture, Mus Rodin, Paris, 71; plus many others. Mem: Royal Can Acad Arts. Mailing Add: PO Box 5943 Terminal 4 Toronto ON M5W 1P3 Can

ETS, MARIE HALL
ILLUSTRATOR, WRITER
b North Greenfield, Wis, Dec 16, 95. Study: NY Sch Fine & Appl Art, 16-17; Univ Chicago, PhB, 24; Art Inst Chicago; also with Frederick V Poole. Work: Kerlan Collection, Univ Minn Libr; Iowa City Pub Libr; Milwaukee Pub Libr. Comn: Set of illus, Childcraft & How & Why Libr. Exhib: 1st Ann Exhib Selected Bks for Children, Am Fedn Arts, 45; one-woman show, original drawings, Libr Exhib Gallery, Teachers Col, Columbia Univ, 63; Albright-Knox Gallery Art, 64. Awards: Hans Christian Andersen Award, Stockholm, Sweden, 56; Am Inst Graphic Arts Award, 58-60; Caldecott Award, 60. Publ: Auth & illusr, In the forest, 44, Gilberto and the wind 63, Just Me, 65, Talking without words, 68 & Elephant in a well, 72, Viking Press (total: 21 picture bks & 1 adult biog). Mailing Add: c/o Viking Press Inc 625 Madison Ave New York NY 10022

ETTENBERG, FRANKLIN JOSEPH
PAINTER, DRAFTSMAN
b Brooklyn, NY, May 7, 45. Study: Univ Mich, BS(design), 66, with Milton Cohen, Fred Bauer & John Stephenson; Univ NMex, MA, 71, with John Kacere. Work: Detroit Inst Art, Mich; Univ NMex Fine Arts Mus, Albuquerque; Roswell Mus & Art Ctr, NMex; Fine Arts Mus, Santa Fe. Comn: Paired paintings, NMex Arts Comn, 77. Exhib: Mich Artists Ann, Detroit Inst Arts, 65; Mus NMex Biennials, 72, 74, 75 & 76; 19th Exhib Southwestern Prints & Drawings, Dallas Mus Fine Arts, 72; Roswell Mus Exhib, NMex, 74; Hill's Gallery, 75; Tomlinson Gallery, 73-77. Awards: Artist in residence grant, Roswell Mus & Art Ctr, 72, Purchase Award, Drawings/USA 77, Minn Mus of Art, St Paul, 77. Style & Technique: Drawing: abstract, serial compositions executed in varied handlings; painting: wide-ranging abstractions involving serial compositions, with Southwest landscape and interior references. Media: Pen & Ink, Oil. Dealer: Elaine Horwitch Gallery Palace Ave Santa Fe NM 87501. Mailing Add: 215 W San Francisco St Santa Fe NM 87501

ETTER, HOWARD LEE
PAINTER, LECTURER
b Moberly, Mo, Jan 22, 31. Study: Art League Calif, San Francisco; Acad Art, San Francisco. Work: Butler Inst Am Art, Youngstown, Ohio. Exhib: 37th & 39th Midyear Show, Butler Inst Am Art, 73 & 75; Nat Painting Show, Washington & Jefferson Col, 74; 17th Ann Delta Art Exhib, 74. Teaching: Lectr drawing, painting & watercolor, Lawrence Inst Technol, 68-77. Awards: Spec Jurors Award, Washington & Jefferson Col Painting Show, 74; 39th Butler Inst Midyear Show Purchase Award, Friends of Am Art, 75. Mem: Mich Watercolor Soc; Artist Equity Asn; NMex Watercolor Soc; Midwest Watercolor Soc. Style & Technique: Traditional realism; magic realism. Media: Watercolor & Egg Tempera, Acrylic. Dealer: Xochipilli Inc 115 E Fourth St Rochester MI 48063; Collectors' Showroom Inc 325 N Wells St Chicago IL 60610. Mailing Add: 1643 Valley Rd SW Albuquerque NM 87105

ETTING, EMLEN
PAINTER, ILLUSTRATOR
b Philadelphia, Pa, Aug 24, 05. Study: Harvard Univ, BS, 28; Grande Chaumiere & Andre Lhote, Paris. Work: Whitney Mus Am Art, New York; Pa Acad Fine Arts, Philadelphia; Addison Gallery Am Art, Andover, Mass; Philadelphia Mus Art; Atwater Kent Mus, Philadelphia. Comn: Philadelphia Industries (oil on canvas), Market St Nat Bank, 47; oil on canvas, Italian Consulate, Philadelphia, 55. Exhib: Whitney Mus; Carnegie Inst, Pittsburgh; Corcoran Gallery Art, Washington, DC; Pa Acad Fine Arts; San Francisco World's Fair; Retrospectives, Fla Southern Col, Lakeland, 73 & Allentown Art Mus, Pa, 74. Teaching: Instr painting & drawing, Sch Indust Art, Philadelphia Mus Art; Philadelphia Col Art & Tyler Sch Art, Temple Univ. Pos: US artist-deleg, Second Int Cong Plastic Arts, Dubrovnik, 57. Awards: Chevalier, Legion d'Honneur, Fr Govt; Star Solidarity, Italian Govt. Bibliog: Mary Rupert (auth), Emlen Etting, Paintings of an American Romantic, London Studio, 39. Mem: Artists Equity Asn (nat pres, 55-58, hon pres & pres, Philadelphia Chap, 50-53, hon pres); Nat Soc Mural Painters; Century Asn; Philadelphia Art Alliance; Alliance Francaise (hon pres); plus others. Media: Oil, Acrylic. Publ: Illusr & translr, Valery, Le Cimetiere Marin, Centaur Press, 32; illusr, Amerika & Ecclesiastes, New Directions, 40; illusr, Born in a Crowd, Crowell-Collier; auth & illusr, Drawing the Ballet, Studio Bks, 44. Dealer: Midtown Galleries 11 E 57th St New York NY 10022. Mailing Add: 1927 Panama St Philadelphia PA 19103

ETTINGER, SUSI STEINITZ
PAINTER, LECTURER
b Berlin, Ger, July 29, 22; US citizen. Study: Univ Louisville, BFA(cum laude in art hist), 43; with Dr Justus Bier. Work: Springfield Art Mus, Mo; State Hist Soc Mo, Columbia; Sch of the Ozarks, Point Lookout, Mo; Greenwood Lab Sch, Springfield. Exhib: Ann Ten State Regional Competition, Springfield Art Mus, 61-72 & 74 & Watercolor USA, 66-67; Ann Delta Art Exhib, Little Rock, Ark, 68 & 70; Midsouth Ann Exhib, Brooks Mem Gallery, Memphis, Tenn, 69; Mid-West Bi-Ann, Joslyn Art Ctr, Omaha, Nebr, 70; 7 Missouri Painters, Mo State Coun of Arts Touring Show, 73-74; Ann Regional Art Exhib, Spiva Art Ctr, Joplin, Mo, 75; Women Artists 77 Exhib, Kansas City, Mo Univ, 77; one-artist show, Springfield Art Mus, 76. Teaching: Dir children's art classes, Springfield Art Mus, 60-66; lectr art, Southwest Mo State Univ, 64- Awards: Regional Ten State Competition Purchase Award, Springfield Art Mus, 69; First Prize Painting, Mo Col Fac Show, 70; Juror's Selection & Purchase Award, Sch of the Ozarks Ann Regional, 74. Style & Technique: Experiential realist, using synchronistic imagery; mainly acrylic painting, glazing techniques, occasionally collage. Media: Acrylic, Charcoal. Mailing Add: 2020 S Ventura Ave Springfield MO 65804

ETTINGHAUSEN, RICHARD
ART ADMINISTRATOR, EDUCATOR
b Frankfort am Main, Ger, Feb 5, 06; US citizen. Study: Univ Frankfort, PhD, 31. Comn: Paintings of emperors & sultans of India, Lalit Kala, Bombay, 61. Teaching: Lectr fine arts, Inst Fine Arts, NY Univ, 37-38, adj prof fine arts, 60-67, prof fine arts, 67-; assoc prof Islamic art, Univ Mich, 38-44, res prof, 49- Pos: Mem staff, Islamic Dept, Staatliche Museen, Berlin,

31-33; res assoc, Am Inst Iranian Art & Archael, 34-37; mem staff, Inst Advan Studies, 37-38; ed, Ars Islamica, 38-54 & Near Eastern ed, Ars Orientalis, 54-57; assoc, Near Eastern Art, Freer Gallery Art, Smithsonian Inst, 44-58, cur, 58-61, head cur, 61-67; adj cur Near Eastern art, Los Angeles Co Mus Art, Calif, 67-72. Mem: Col Art Asn; Am Orient Soc. Res: Iranian & Islamic art; pottery; Persian miniatures. Publ: Auth, Studies in Muslin Iconography, the Unicorn, Freer Gallery Art; auth, Arab paintings, 62 & co-auth, Treasures of Turkey, 66, Skira, Geneva; auth, Turkish Miniatures, New Am Libr, 65. Mailing Add: Inst Fine Arts NY Univ 1 E 78th St New York NY 10021

ETTLING, RUTH (DROITCOUR)
PRINTMAKER, PAINTER
b Pittsburgh, Pa, Mar 30, 10. Study: RI Sch Design; Marshall Univ, BA; spec study with Charles Burchfield, Arnold Blanch, William Thon, Fletcher Martin, Victor Candell & Walter Murch. Work: Charleston Gallery Sunrise, WVa; Dayton Art Inst, Ohio; Hunterdon Co Art Ctr, Clinton, NJ; Huntington Galleries, WVa; WVa Arts & Humanities Collection, Charleston. Exhib: Hunterdon Co Nat Print Show, Clinton, 62; Ohio Printmakers, Dayton, 62; Exhib 180, Huntington, 70; Ruth Ettling's Recent Prints, Huntington Galleries, 71; Allied Artists WVa, Charleston, 72. Teaching: Instr drawing & painting, Huntington Galleries, 52-66, summer dir, print workshop, 72. Awards: Charleston Gallery Sunrise First Graphics Award, 71; WVa Coun Arts & Humanities Award, 72; First Prize/Graphics, Cardinal Valley Show, Ashland, Ky, 77. Mem: Tri-State Arts Asn (pres, 72); Nat Art Educ Asn. Style & Technique: Semi-abstract, based mainly on nature forms. Publ: Illusr, Dear Bob, love mother, 67. Mailing Add: 1475 Spring Valley Circle Huntington WV 25704

ETTLINGER, LEOPOLD DAVID
ART HISTORIAN
b Konigsberg, Ger, Apr 20, 13; Brit citizen. Study: Univs of Halle & Marburg, PhD, 37. Teaching: Durning-Lawrence prof hist art, Univ London, Eng, 59-70; prof hist art, Univ Calif, Berkeley, 70- Pos: Cur photog collection, Warburg Inst, Univ London, Eng, 48-56, lectr, 56-64. Mem: Fel Soc Antiquaries, London. Publ: Auth, The Sistine Chapel Before Michelangelo, Oxford Univ Press, 64; co-auth, Botticelli, Thames & Hudson/Oxford Univ Press, 76; auth, Antonio & Piero Pollaiuolo, Phaidon Press, 78. Mailing Add: Dept of Art Hist Univ Calif Berkeley CA 94720

EVANS, BRUCE HASELTON
MUSEUM DIRECTOR, ART HISTORIAN
b Rome, NY, Nov 13, 39. Study: Amherst Col, BA; NY Univ Inst Fine Arts, MA. Collections Arranged: The Paintings of Edward Edmondson, 72; Jean-Léon Gérôme—The Paintings (with catalog), 72. Pos: Cur asst to dir, Dayton Art Inst, 65-67, chief cur, 68-72, asst dir, 72-74, dir, 75- Mem: Am Asn Mus; Asn Art Mus Dirs; Ohio Mus Asn (trustee). Publ: Auth, Fifty treasures of the Dayton Art Institute, 69; auth, Edward Edmondson—a biography and critical study of his paintings, 72; plus numerous articles in mus bulletins and exhib catalogues. Mailing Add: PO Box 941 Dayton OH 45401

EVANS, BURFORD ELONZO
PAINTER, LECTURER
b Golinda, Tex, July 20, 31. Study: Sorbonne Univ, cert 55. Work: Mus Fine Arts, Lubbock, Tex; Black Arts Ctr, Waco, Tex; Northwood Inst, Midland, Mich; Bishop Col, Dallas, Tex. Comn: Josephite Black Arts Calendar, Josephite Pastoral Ctr, Washington, DC, 74. Exhib: Mobile Arts Festival, Ala, 70; Discovery 70, Nat Black Arts Festival, Cincinnati, Ohio, 70; Nat Black Arts Festival, Normal, Ill, 73; one-man show, State Capitol, Austin, Tex, 73; Tex Fine Arts Festival, Houston, 74. Awards: Second Award, Dimension IV Houston Art League, Humble Oil Co, 68; Betty McGowan Award, Mobil Arts Festival, 70; Distinguished Artist Award, Nat Coun Negro Women, 72. Bibliog: James Kennedy (auth), Ethnic American Art, Slide Libr, Univ Ala, 70-75; Charolette Phelen (auth), Evans remembers June tenth, Houston Chronicle, 71; Theresa Dickason Cederholm (auth), Afro American Artist, Boston Pub Libr, 73. Mem: Art League Houston; Tex Fine Arts Asn; Contemp Arts Asn. Style & Technique: Contemporary realism depicting ethnic lifestyle of the young and old in the rural and ghetto. Media: Oil, Acrylic, Oil Wash, Graphite Pencil. Mailing Add: 5327 Knottyoaks Houston TX 77045

EVANS, GROSE
ART HISTORIAN
b Columbus, Ohio, Dec 14, 16. Study: Ohio State Univ, BFA, 39, MA, 40; Inst Fine Arts, NY Univ, 41-43 & 45-46; Johns Hopkins Univ, PhD, 53. Teaching: Prof lectr Baroque-mod art, George Washington Univ, 53-61, adj assoc prof art hist, 73-; prof lectr Am painting, Johns Hopkins Univ, 65; curric dir art teachers' training, George Washington Univ & Nat Gallery Art, 66 & 67. Pos: From lectr to assoc cur, dept educ, Nat Gallery Art, 46-60, cur exten serv, decorative arts & index Am design, 60-70, cur exhibs & loans, 70-73, cur decorative arts, 73. Mem: Col Art Asn Am. Res: Anglo-American art of the eighteenth century. Publ: Auth, Benjamin West and the taste of his time, Southern Ill Univ Press, 59; auth, Vincent Van Gogh, McGraw, 68. Mailing Add: 2308 Glasgow Rd Alexandria VA 22307

EVANS, HENRY
PRINTMAKER
b Superior, Wis, May 16, 18. Work: Albertina, Vienna; Libr Cong, Washington, DC; Hunt Bot Inst, Pittsburgh; Clark Libr, Calif, Los Angeles; Oakland Mus, Calif. Exhib: One-man shows, Royal Hort Soc, London, 65, Hunt Bot Inst, 66, Biomed Libr, Univ Calif, Los Angeles, 68, Calif Acad Sci, San Francisco, 70 & Oakland Mus, 71; plus many others. Bibliog: A Frankenstein (auth), Evans' botanical portfolios, San Francisco Chronicle, 8/25/68; staff (auth), Henry Evans, printmaker (doc film), KQED, 69; Johan Kooy (auth), Henry Evans, printmaker, Pac Discovery, 12/70. Style & Technique: Linocuts; subjects drawn from life; life-size, editions limited and numbered, all handprinted. Publ: Illusr, Champagne and shoes, Peregrine Press, 62; illusr, Hortulus, 66; illusr, Flower pot gardens, Crowell Collier, 67; auth, illusr & printer, State flowers, Vol 1-5, hand printed at Peregrine Press, 68-72; auth, Botanical Prints with Excerpts from the Artist's Notebooks, Freeman & Co, 77. Mailing Add: 555 Sutter Rm 306 San Francisco CA 94102

EVANS, JOHN
PAINTER, COLLAGE ARTIST
b Sioux Falls, SDak, Aug 24, 32. Study: Art Inst Chicago, BFA, 61, MFA, 63. Exhib: Pa Acad Fine Art Ann, 64; Newport Harbor Art Mus, Newport Beach, Calif, 74; Davidson Nat, NC, 76; Works on Paper, Kornblee Gallery, New York, 76; Mandeville Gallery, Univ Calif, San Diego, La Jolla, 77; Gruenebaum Gallery, New York, 77; Franklin Furnace Arch, New York, 78. Bibliog: Hilton Kramer (auth), Works on paper, New York Times, 76. Style & Technique: Acrylic on canvas; collage and watercolor in chronological books; surreal and mail art. Publ: Auth, Collection of 38 Collage Books, privately publ, 76. Dealer: Gruenebaum Gallery 38 E 57th St New York NY 10022. Mailing Add: PO Box 1004 New York NY 10009

EVANS, MINNIE
PAINTER
b Long Creek, NC, Dec 12, 92. Work: Newark Mus, NJ; Ill Bell Tel, Chicago; L'Institut de L'Art Brut, Paris; Nat Collection Fine Arts; Whitney Mus Am Art. Exhib: One-man shows, Davison Art Ctr, Wesleyan Univ, 69 & 70, Portal Gallery, London, Eng, 70, St John's Art Gallery, Wilmington, 70; Deson Zaks Gallery, Chicago, 75; Whitney Mus Am Art, 75. Bibliog: Nina Howell Starr (auth), The lost world of Minnie Evans, Bennington Rev, summer 69; Diana Loercher (auth), Regaining a world lost to moderns, Christian Sci Monitor, 7/21/75. Media: Crayon, Oil. Dealer: Ms Nina Howell Starr 333 E 68th St New York NY 10021. Mailing Add: Rte 3 Box 377 Wilmington NC 28401

EVANS, NANCY
PAINTER
b New York, NY. Study: Cult Ctr, Naha, Okinawa, with Prof Yasutaro Kinjo, cert, 64; Ikebana, cert, 64; Ikenobo Art Ctr, New York, cert (floral art), 70. Exhib: Two-man exhib paintings, Naha, Okinawa, 64; paintings, Enid Pub Libr, Enid Artist League, 65; paintings, Mat Gallery, New York, 69; paintings & floral art, Japan House Gallery, 70; paintings & floral art, Bd Trade, New York, 70; Floral Art, World Trade Ctr, New York, 77. Awards: Hon Mention, Bryant Park Flower Show, New York, 69; Hon Mention, Sumie Soc Am, Inc, 71-72; Second Prize, Horticultural Soc NY, 73. Bibliog: US Forces (ed), An interested American, Shurei n Hikari Mag, 10/64; Gwen Hendrickson (auth), Oriental Art, Orbit, Sunday Oklahoman, 8/66; contestant, To Tell the Truth, Goodson-Todman Prod, 10/66. Mem: Sumi Soc Am (trustee, 70, treas, 71-73, pres, 74); Ikebana Int; Ikenobo Soc Floral Art; Japan Soc Inc. Style & Technique: Landscapes; birds; flowers; bamboo handle conical shaped brush; black ink-water; brush technique; Sumie. Publ: Ed, Ikebana Int, Newslett Floral Art, 62; contribr, Ikebana, 71, Ink-stick-Sumi, 72, Aesthetics at the Japan House, 73 & On Japanese art, 73, Sumie Soc Notes. Mailing Add: 144 Farragut Rd North Babylon NY 11704

EVANS, PAUL FREDRIC
ART HISTORIAN, WRITER/CONSULTANT
b Elizabeth, NJ, June 3, 37. Study: Drew Univ; Univ Buffalo, AB; Berkeley Divinity Sch, STB. Collections Arranged: California Design, 1910: Pottery 1974 (with catalog). Pos: Ed, Western Collector, 67-69; ed, Western Div, Spinning Wheel, 69- Bibliog: J J Miller, II (auth), rev in Spinning Wheel, 3/75; F Danieli (auth), article in Art Libr Soc NAm Newslett, 4/75. Mem: Arch Am Art; Calif Hist Soc. Res: Art pottery of the United States from 1870 to 1920. Publ: Contribr, The Dedham Pottery, Dedham Hist Soc, Mass, 68; contribr, Complete Book of Antiques, Grosset & Dunlap, 72; auth, Art Pottery of the United States: An Encyclopedia of Producers & Their Marks, Scribners, 74. Mailing Add: 34 Octavia St San Rafael CA 94901

EVANS, RICHARD
PAINTER, EDUCATOR
b Chicago, Ill, Oct 1, 23. Study: Otis Art Inst, dipl; Calif Col Arts & Crafts; Studio of George Miller, New York; Univ Wyo, MA; Stacey Found fel, 47; Tiffany Found fels, 48 & 50. Work: San Francisco Fine Arts Comn; Univ Wyo; Col Southern Utah. Comn: Tile mural, Univ Wyo, 68; portrait of Sam S Knight, Univ Wyo Geol Mus; twenty sculptures of prominent personages for private comns. Exhib: Northwest Printmakers Int, 65; Gov Nat Touring Art Exhib, 66-67; Otis Art Inst 50th Anniversary Exhib, 68; Denver Mus Inaugural Exhib, 72; Joslyn Mem Mus Midwest Biennial, 72. Teaching: Instr drawing, Calif Col Arts & Crafts, Oakland, 50-52; instr drawing & painting, Miami Univ, Oxford, Ohio, 56-57; prof printmaking, drawing & painting, Univ Wyo, 57- Awards: San Francisco Art Festival Purchase Award for Drawing, 50; 26th Cedar City Invitational Purchase Award, 66; Anonymous Donor Award, Otis Art Inst 50th Anniversary Exhib, 68. Bibliog: Victor Flach (auth), The Making of Ikon 13 (film & TV tape), Univ Wyo, 70; Bruce Cady (auth), American Printmaking Today, NY Graphics Soc. Media: Oil, Acrylic; Intaglio. Publ: Auth, On large scale prints, Am Artist, 11/62. Mailing Add: Dept of Art Univ of Wyo Laramie WY 82070

EVANS, ROBERT GRAVES
SCULPTOR, EDUCATOR
b Rawlins, Wyo, Nov 19, 44. Study: Atlanta Sch Art, BFA; Paris, France, French Govt fel, 69, also with Stanley Hayter; Tulane Univ, with Julius Struppeck, MFA. Comn: Sculpture, Man of Year Award, Atlanta, Ga, 69; sculpture, Film Festival Award, Atlanta, Ga, 69; sculpture (bronze bust), Portrait of Rankin, President, Ind State Univ, 75; outdoor sculpture, Cent Mich Univ, 75. Exhib: Galerie Ilien, Atlanta, 69 & 70; Simonne Stern Galerie, New Orleans, 71; La Crafts Coun Spring Fiesta, New Orleans, 71; one-man show, Bienville Gallery, New Orleans, 72; Indianapolis Mus Art, Artery Gallery, 75. Teaching: Asst prof sculpture, Ind State Univ, Terre Haute, 72- Mem: Southern Sculpture Asn. Style & Technique: Sculpture using casting and welding, figurative. Media: Bronze, Aluminum. Mailing Add: 1500 S Sixth St Terre Haute IN 47802

EVANS, ROBERT JAMES
PAINTER, MUSEUM CURATOR
b Chicago, Ill, May 2, 44. Study: Parsons Col; Univ Iowa; Northeast Mo State Univ, BSEd; Drake Univ; Southern Ill Univ, Carbondale, MFA. Work: Southern Ill Univ, Carbondale; Western Ill Univ, Macomb; Ill State Univ, Normal; MacMurray Col, Ill; Northeast Mo State Univ. Exhib: Mid-States Ann, Evansville Mus Art & Sci, Ind, 69-70; Ark Nat Exhib, Ark State Univ Gallery, Jonesboro, 70; one-man shows, Ill Bell Tel Gallery, Chicago, 72 & South Bend Art Ctr, Ind, 73; Illinois Painters II, Ill Arts Coun Circulating Exhib, 71-73; Northeast Mo State Univ, 76. Teaching: Instr drawing & painting, Springfield Art Asn, Ill, 71-76; adj asst prof arts mgt, Sangamon State Univ, 73- Pos: Res asst, Univ Galleries, Southern Ill Univ, Carbondale, 69-70; cur art, Ill State Mus, Springfield, 70- Awards: First Prize, Quincy Art Club Ann Exhib, Ill, 71 & Best in Show Award, 72; Resident Award, Va Ctr Creative Arts, Charlotteville, summer 72; Second Award in watercolor, Prof Art Exhib, Ill State Fair, 74. Mem: Am Crafts Coun; Am Asn Mus; Ill Arts Coun (visual art adv panel, 74-76). Style & Technique: Non-objective, abstract, work described as concerned with lush color and detailed formal complexity. Publ: Auth, articles in Living Mus, 70-; auth, rev in Craft Horizons; contrib auth, article in Mus News; auth, numerous exhibit catalogs. Mailing Add: 2516 Churchill Rd Springfield IL 62702

EVEN, ROBERT LAWRENCE
EDUCATOR
b Breckenridge, Minn, June 7, 29. Study: Valley City State Col, BS; Univ Minn, MA & PhD; Art Inst Chicago; Minneapolis Col Art & Design. Teaching: Instr art, Univ Minn, 52-54; prof art, Northern Ill Univ, 63-, chmn dept, 74- Awards: Res Grant, State Ill, 64 & Dean's Fund, Northern Ill Univ, 65 & 73. Mem: Col Art Asn Am; Mid-Am Col Art Asn; Nat Coun Art Adminr. Mailing Add: 413 Fairmont DeKalb IL 60115

EVERETT, LEN G
PAINTER
b Burlington, Iowa. Study: State Univ Iowa, BFA & MFA; Art Students League, with Robert Brackman, Joseph Hirsch & Robert Hale; Nat Acad Design, New York, with Robert Philipp; also with Henry Hensche, Provincetown, Mass. Work: Washington & Jefferson Col, Washington, Pa. Exhib: One-man show, Mus Conserv Art, Oklahoma City, 63; Butler Inst Am Art Midyear Ann, Youngstown, Ohio, 69, 72 & 77; Mainstreams 71, Marietta, Ohio, 71; Nat Art Round-Up, Las Vegas, Nev, 71; 32nd Ann Cedar City Nat Art Exhib, Utah, 72; plus others. Awards: Hon Mention, Allied Artists of Am, 76; Cornelia & Phillip Cummings Award, Hudson Valley Art Asn, White Plains, NY, 76; Best Still Life in Show Award, Am Artists Prof League, New York, NY, 77; plus 18 others. Bibliog: Ralph Fabri (auth), Medal of merit in Allied Artists Annual, Today's Art, 70. Mem: Allied Artists Am (exhib chmn, 76-77); Am Artists Prof League; Hudson Valley Art Asn; Audubon Artists (mem bd, 76-); Silvermine Guild of Artists, New Canaan, Conn. Style & Technique: Colorful, realistic, bird's eye view still life arrangements, emphasizing geometric, abstract-like design; also portraits and nudes. Media: Oil, Pastel. Dealer: Talisman Gallery 115 E 12th St Bartlesville OK 74003; FAR Gallery 22 E 80th St New York NY 10021. Mailing Add: 150 E 27th St New York NY 10016

EVERSLEY, FREDERICK JOHN
SCULPTOR
b Brooklyn, NY, Aug 28, 41. Study: Carnegie Inst Technol, BSEE, 63; Inst Allende, San Miguel de Allende, Mex. Work: Smithsonian Inst, Washington, DC; Whitney Mus Am Art, New York; Milwaukee Art Ctr, Wis; Oakland Art Mus, Calif; Hayden Gallery, Mass Inst Technol, Cambridge; plus others. Comn: Plastic sculpture, Bayshore Properties, San Francisco, 70 & Lenox Sq Ctr, Atlanta, Ga; plastic sculpture fountain, Dallas Hyatt-Regency Hotel; kinetic stainless steel sculpture, Miami Int Airport, Fla; laser beam sculpture, Detroit Gen Hosp. Exhib: One-man shows, 70 & Sculpture Ann, 71 & 73, Whitney Mus Am Art, Los Angeles Inst of Contemp Art, Calif, 76, Nat Acad of Sci, Washington, DC, 76, Santa Barbara Mus of Art, Calif, 76, Newport Harbor Art Mus, Newport Beach, Calif, 76 & Oakland Mus of Art, Calif, 77; Permutations—Light and Color, Mus Contemp Art, Chicago, 70; Art and Technology, Los Angeles Co Mus Art, Calif, 71; American Kunst 1950-1970, La Mus Contemp Art, Denmark, 71; Andrew Crispo Gallery, NY. Pos: Tech consult, Art & Technol Exhib, Los Angeles Co Mus Art, 71; first artist-in-residence, Nat Air & Space Mus, Smithsonian Inst, Washington, DC, 77-78. Awards: First Purchase Prize, 4th Ann Calif Small Images Exhib, Calif State Col, Los Angeles, 70; Nat Endowment Arts Fel, 72; Purchase Prize, 10th Ann Southern Calif Exhib, Long Beach Mus, 72. Bibliog: Henry Seldis (auth), Eversley show in New York, Los Angeles Times, 6/8/70; John Canaday (auth), rev of Whitney Sculpture Ann, New York Times, 4/7/71; Paul Richard, The Space Museum's latest craft, Washington Post, 12/8/77. Style & Technique: Cast and polished polyester resin, circular and parabolic shapes, transparent and opaque; kinetic metal sculpture and solar energy actuated fountains. Media: Multicolored Cast Transparent Plastic; Stainless Steel; Laser Light. Mailing Add: c/o Engineered Aesthetics 1110 W Washington Blvd Venice CA 90291

EVERTS, CONNOR
PAINTER, PRINTMAKER
b Bellingham, Wash, Jan 24, 26. Study: Chouinard Art Inst, Los Angeles; El Camino Col, Calif, AA; Univ Wash; Mexico City Col, BA; Courtauld Inst, Univ London. Work: Mus of Mod Art, San Francisco; Mus of Mod Art, New York; Mus of Mod Art, Tokyo, Japan; Pushkin Mus, Moscow, Soviet Union; Chicago Art Inst. Comn: Collage mural, El Camino Col, 58; mural, Goldwater Bldg, Calif, 63. Exhib: Long Beach Mus of Art, Calif, 58; Pasadena Art Mus, Calif, 60; Nat Drawing Exhib, 64; 4th Int Young Artists Exhib, Japan, 67; Int Print Exhib, Calif, 70; 1st Czech Biennial, 72; Univ Calif, 72; Brand Art Ctr, Calif, 73; Univ Southern Calif, 75; Los Angeles Munic Gallery. Teaching: Chmn graphic dept, Calif Inst of Art, 60-64; guest artist painting, San Francisco Art Inst, 64-65; head, Dept of Printmaking, Cranbrook Acad of Art, 75- Awards: Painting Award, Los Angeles Artists & Vicinity, Los Angeles Co Mus, Los Angeles, 55; Prize, 4th Int Young Artists Exhib, Tokyo, 67; Purchase Award, Southern Calif, Muzkenthalor Found, 74. Bibliog: G Nordland (auth), Drawings of Connor Everts, Pasadena Art Mus, 60 & Self-Portraits 1949-1969, Western Asn of Art Mus, 69; D Brewer (auth), The Studies of Connor Everts, Brand Art Ctr, 73. Mem: Nat Adv Bd on Print (secy, presently); Los Angeles Printmaking Soc (pres, 63-64); Nat Asn of Univ Prof. Style & Technique: Symbolic realist—use of water-based color in fugitive application to a gesso ground. Media: Aqua paint; collage. Dealer: Adam Meckler Gallery 651 N La Cieniga Los Angeles CA 90069. Mailing Add: 45 Valley Way Bloomfield Hills MI 48013

EVETT, KENNETH WARNOCK
PAINTER
b Loveland, Colo, Dec 1, 13. Study: Colo State Col, AB; Colo Col, MA; also with Boardman Robinson, George Biddle & Henry V Poor. Work: Montclair Mus, NJ; Colorado Springs Fine Arts Ctr, Colo; Munson-Williams-Proctor Inst, Utica, NY; Andrew Dickson White Mus, Cornell Univ, NY; Univ Ariz. Comn: Three murals for rotunda of Nebr State Capitol, 54. Exhib: Pa Acad Fine Arts, 52; Whitney Mus Am Art Ann, 52-54; Metrop Mus Art, 53; Corcoran Gallery Art Biennial, 54; Art Inst Chicago Biennial, 54. Teaching: Prof art, Cornell Univ, 48-, chmn dept, currently. Pos: Art critic, New Republic. Awards: Drawing Prize, Norfolk Mus, 66; Drawing Prize, Rochester Mus, 68; Purchase Prize, Munson-Williams-Proctor Inst, 68. Media: Watercolor, Oil. Publ: Auth, The civilization of Liboros, 72 & auth, The new realism, 72, New Republic. Dealer: Antoinette Kraushaar Galleries 1055 Madison Ave New York NY 10028. Mailing Add: 402 Oak Ave Ithaca NY 14850

EVJEN, RUDOLPH BERNDT
SCULPTOR, PAINTER
b San Francisco, Calif, Sept 26, 30. Study: Oberamergau, Bavaria, Ger, with Albert Sieg & Joseph Mayr; Mendocino Art Ctr, Calif; Richmond Art Ctr, Calif; Contra Costa Col, San Pablo, Calif; Royal Acad of Sculpture, London, Eng. Work: San Pablo Libr, Calif; Russian Consulate, San Francisco; Point Richmond Ctr, Calif. Exhib: Brit Int, Cartwright Hall, West Yorkshire, Eng, 60; Paris Int, France, 61; Mendocino Art Ctr, Calif, 67; Ft Bragg Art, Ft Bragg Ctr Bldg, Calif, 69; Richmond Art Ctr, 70. Teaching: Instr sculpture, Point Richmond Rec Ctr, 70-72; instr wood carving, San Pablo Parks & Rec Dept, 72-74; instr wood carving & painting, Dias Rec Ctr, San Pablo, 74- Bibliog: Joan Palm (auth), Birdman of Richmond, 73 & John McKenney (auth), Evjen sculptor, Oakland Tribune; Vicky Godbey (auth), Evjen shares with others, Tri City News, Pinole, Calif, 5/29/74. Mem: Artists Equity; Richmond Art Ctr; Mendocino Art Ctr; Sacramento Art Guild; Norwegian Folk Art League (founder, pres). Style & Technique: Medieval and Gothic sculpture in wood, bronze, stone; palette knife paintings and brush in oils, some acrylic. Dealer: Katherine Glenn Gallery 11461 San Pablo El Cerrito CA 94530. Mailing Add: 530 22nd St Richmond CA 94801

EWALD, ELIN LAKE
ART DEALER, ART WRITER
b Raleigh, NC. Study: Students League with Edwin Dickinson; Am Acad of Art; Art Inst of Chicago, 65. Pos: Assoc, Gallery Mayer, New York; free-lance art writer, 70-72; art ed, Pageant Mag, 72-74; exec vpres, O'Toole Assoc, 74- Mem: Nat Asn of Rev Appraisers; assoc Am Soc of Appraisers. Specialty: Consultants and fine art appraisers of all periods, including decorative arts. Interest: For over 60 years, firm has arranged artists' exhibitions and assembled private collections for individuals, corporations and museums; additionally, it has arranged donations of collections to museums. Publ: Auth, Hester Bateman and English Women Silversmiths of the 18th Century, Ms Mag, 76. Mailing Add: 667 Madison Ave New York NY 10021

EWALD, LOUIS
PAINTER, DESIGNER
b Minneapolis, Minn, Dec 19, 91. Study: Pa Mus & Sch Indust Art. Comn: Altar paintings, murals, gilding & color on walls, ceilings & entrance doors in 85 churches, 16-72. Mem: Church Archit Guild Am; Nat Soc Mural Painters; Alumni Asn Philadelphia Col Art. Mailing Add: PO Box 954 Poulsbo WA 98370

EWEN, PATERSON
PAINTER, EDUCATOR
b Montreal, Que, Can, Apr 7, 25. Study: Montreal Mus Sch Fine Art & Design, Can, dipl with high standing in painting, drawing & the teaching of child art. Work: Nat Gallery Can & Can Coun Art Bank, Ottawa, Ont; Brandeis Univ, Waltham, Mass; Art Gallery Vancouver, BC; Mus de la Province de Que. Exhib: A Response to the Environ, Rutgers Univ, NJ, 75; Forum 76, Montreal Mus Fine Arts, Que, 76; Retrospective, London Pub Art Gallery, Ont, 77; Three Generations of Que Painting, Mus d'Art Contemporaine, Montreal, Que, 77; one-man shows, The Art Gallery of Vancouver, BC, 77 & Nat Gallery Can travelling show, Montreal, Que, Windsor, Ont, Lethbridge, Alta & Halifax, NS, 77-; Seven Can Painters, Can Coun Art Bank travelling show, NZ, Australia, Japan, Western Europe & US, 77-; Changing Visions, Toronto, Windsor, Montreal, Lincoln, Mass, Edmonton, Winnipeg, Calgary, Burnaby & London, Ont, BC. Teaching: Asst prof painting & drawing, Univ Western Ont, London, 72- Awards: Second Prize Painting, Concour de la Province de Que, 57; Purchase Award, Montreal Spring Exhib, Montreal Mus Fine Arts, 61; Sr Can Coun Award, Can Coun, 71. Mem: Royal Can Acad; Can Artists' Rep. Style & Technique: Mixed media on plywood. Mailing Add: Carmen Lamanna Gallery 840 Yonge St Toronto ON M4W 2H1 Can

EWING, BAYARD
ART ADMINISTRATOR, COLLECTOR
b Sorrento, Maine, Aug 19, 16. Pos: Trustee, RI Sch Design, 55-, chmn bd, 67-, actg pres, 75-77; pres & dir, Am Fedn of Arts, 77- Collection: Twentieth century painting and sculpture, chiefly American. Mailing Add: 2000 Hosp Trust Tower Providence RI 02903

EWING, EDGAR LOUIS
PAINTER
b Hartington, Nebr, Jan 17, 13. Study: Art Inst Chicago, grad, 35, Edward L Ryerson fel, 35-37 & also with Boris Anisfeld; two years European travel and study. Work: Richmond Mus Fine Arts, Va; Los Angeles Co Mus Art; Santa Barbara Mus; De Young Mem Mus, San Francisco; Nat Gallery, Athens, Greece. Exhib: Sao Paulo Mus Art Int, Brazil; Carnegie Mus Int, Pittsburgh; Art Inst Chicago; Metrop Mus Art, New York; Pa Acad Fine Arts, Philadelphia; one-man shows, Green Nat Gallery, 73, Munic Gallery Los Angeles, 74, 30 Yrs Retrospective, Palm Springs Desert Mus, 76-77 & Fisher Gallery, Univ Southern Calif, 78. Teaching: Instr painting, Art Inst Chicago, 37-43; prof fine arts, Univ Southern Calif, 46-78, emer prof, 78-; Mellon prof painting, Carnegie Mellon Univ, 68-69. Awards: Louis Comfort Tiffany Grant, 49; Samuel Goldwyn Award, Los Angeles Co Mus Art, 57; Los Angeles Libr Asn Award, 76; Floresheim Award, Art Inst Chicago. Bibliog: Schaad (auth), The realm of contemporary still life painting, 62 & Mugraini (auth), Oil painting—techniques and materials, 69, Van Nostrand. Mem: Am Asn Univ Prof; Nat Watercolor Soc (pres); Col Art Asn; Los Angeles Mus Asn. Style & Technique: Paints in series without regard to style or emphasis on technique or recent trends. Media: Oil. Publ: Auth, Syllabus for drawing and painting, Univ Southern Calif Press, 66. Dealer: Esther Bear Gallery 1125 High Rd Santa Barbara CA 93108. Mailing Add: 4226 Sea View Lane Los Angeles CA 90065

EWING, THOMAS R
PAINTER, INSTRUCTOR
b Pittsburgh, Pa, Nov 5, 35. Study: Corcoran Sch Art, 58; Pa Acad Fine Arts, 60-63. Work: Pa Acad Fine Arts, Philadelphia; Phoenix Art Mus, Ariz. Exhib: 159th, 161st & 163rd Ann Exhib Am Painting & Sculpture, Pa Acad Fine Arts, 64-68; Atlier Chapman Kelly Galleries, Dallas, 66; one-man show, Makler Gallery, Philadelphia, 69; Drawings, Univ Bordeux, France. Teaching: Instr painting, Pa Acad Fine Arts, 70-; instr painting & life drawing, Philadelphia Mus Art, 72- Awards: Emily Lowe Competition Award, 66; Louis Comfort Tiffany Grant, 72. Style & Technique: Trash and glass paintings in acrylic and oil. Mailing Add: 1811 Chestnut St Philadelphia PA 19103

EYEN, RICHARD J
ART DEALER, DESIGNER
b Lincoln, Nebr, Mar 24, 30. Study: Univ Calif, Los Angeles, Univ Cincinnati, BS(design). Pos: Owner & dir, Environment Gallery, New York, 63- Mem: Artist-Craftsmen Soc New York; Nat Soc Lit & Arts. Specialty: Contemporary American artists, especially sculptors. Mailing Add: 205 E 60th St New York NY 10022

EYRE, IVAN
PAINTER, SCULPTOR
b Sask, Apr 15, 35. Work: Nat Gallery Can, Ottawa; Montreal Mus Fine Arts, PQ; Winnipeg Art Gallery, Man; Vancouver Art Gallery, BC; London Pub Libr & Art Gallery, Ont. Exhib: One-man show, Gallery XII, Montreal Mus Fine Arts, 64, Frankfurter Kunstkabinett, Ger, 73, Winnipeg Art Gallery, 74 & Siemenswerk, Erlangen, Ger, 74; Realisms '70, Montreal Mus Fine Arts & Art Gallery Ont, 70. Teaching: Prof drawing & painting, Univ Man, Winnipeg, 59-; prof painting & drawing, Banff Sch Fine Arts, Alta, summer 73. Awards: Sr Fel, Can Coun, 66 & 78 & Travel Grant to Ger, 73. Bibliog: Barry Lord (auth), Sundogs in the sky, 2-3/71 & Terrence Heath (auth), A response to Ivan Eyre's new paintings, 5/73, Artscanada; C V H (auth), Ein Maler aus der Kanadischen Prarie, Frankfurter Allgemeine Zeitung, 8/73. Mem: Royal Can Acad Arts. Style & Technique: All subject matter with varying techniques in his own style. Media: Acrylic, Oil; Wood, Terra Cotta. Mailing Add: Dept of Art Univ of Man Winnipeg MB Can

F

FABE, ROBERT
PAINTER, EDUCATOR
b Chicago, Ill, May 24, 17. Study: Art Acad Cincinnati, cert fine art, 38; Art Students League, Out of Town scholar & with George Grosz, Arnold Blanch & Raphael Soyer, 38-39. Work: Cincinnati Art Mus, Dayton Art Inst, Univ Cincinnati, Miami Univ & Procter & Gamble, Cincinnati, Ohio; plus other pub & pvt collections. Comn: Murals, Shrimp Boat Restaurant, Dayton, Otter Bein Press, Dayton & Highland Towers, Marvin Warner Corp, Cincinnati. Exhib: Butler Inst Am Art, Youngstown, Ohio, 40-68; Cincinnati Ann, 40-70 & Laser Art Exhib, 71, Cincinnati Art Mus; one-man shows, Mt St Joseph Col, Cincinnati, 70 & Ohio State Capitol, 71; plus many other group & one-man shows. Teaching: Assoc prof art, Univ Cincinnati, 58- Awards: Dayton Art Inst Purchase Award; Butler Inst Am Art Purchase Award; Ohio Univ Show Award. Mem: MacDowell Soc (pres, 70-72); Cincinnati Prof Artists (pres, 70-72). Media: Tempera, Watercolor. Mailing Add: 4235 Rose Hill Ave Cincinnati OH 45229

FABION, JOHN
SCULPTOR, EDUCATOR
b Vienna, Austria, Oct 31, 05; US citizen. Study: Art Inst Chicago, 26-30 & 33-34, grad 34; Royal Acad Florence, 31; Arts & Crafts Sch, 32; Ryerson travel fel, 34; Nat Acad of Krakow, Poland, 34-37. Work: Krakow, Poland; Polish Nat Mus, Chicago. Comn: Sculpture relief, Cong Rm, Statler Hotel, Los Angeles, 40 & Hotel, 50; Cath Hosp, Anderson, Ind; PO Decoration, Bedford, Ind; portrait of Secy Forrestal, Naval Mus, Annapolis, Md. Exhib: First Nat Exhib of Sculpture, Warsaw, Poland, 36; Int Watercolor, Chicago; Am Artist Exhib, Chicago; Golden Gate Exposition, San Francisco; Pa Acad, Philadelphia; plus others. Teaching: Prof art, Art Inst Chicago, 46-70, prof emer, 70- Awards: Clausman Prize, Art Inst Chicago, 33, Carr Prize, 37 & Palmer Prize, 60. Mem: Alumni Asn, Art Inst Chicago; Chicago Arts Club; Polish Am Soc of Arts & Lett; Artist Equity Asn; Artist Union. Style & Technique: Conventional; semi-abstract. Media: Oil; Watercolor; Stone, Wood, Bronze. Mailing Add: 920 Castlewood Terr Chicago IL 60640

FACCI, DOMENICO (AURELIO)
SCULPTOR, INSTRUCTOR
b Hooversville, Pa, Feb 2, 16. Study: Roerich Acad Arts, 36. Work: Norfolk Mus Arts & Sci, Va; Fla Southern Col, Lakeland. Comn: St Rita (bronze sculpture), comn by Rambusch, St Rita's Church, Long Island City, NY, 66; St Paul (aluminum sculpture), comn by Rambusch, Fredericksburg, Va, 67; St Vincent de Paul (aluminum sculpture), comn by Rambusch, Guam, 68; St Ann & St Mary (stone sculptures), comn by Rambusch, St Ann's Church, Hagerstown, Md, 69; figures of Martin Luther King, Abraham Lincoln, Mary McLeod Bethune & W Wilberforce plus 16 corbels carved in situ on facade, comn by Episcopalian Diocese, St Thomas' Church, New York, 71; Neptune (15ft figure), Williamsburg, Va, 78; Pablo Casals (bust), Pub Sch 181, New York, NY, 78; cartouche for lobby (7ft), Am Express Bldg, New York, NY, 78; cartouche for bronze doors (3ft x 4ft), St Peter's Cathedral, Philadelphia, Pa, 78; Rudy Vallee (bust), 78; and numerous others. Exhib: 20th Century Sculpture, Silvermine Guild, New Canaan, Conn; Art: USA, Coliseum, New York, 59; First Int Art Exhib, Fla Southern Col; Artists Equity Exhib, Whitney Mus Am Art; Butler Inst Am Art; Nat Acad, 78; Painters & Sculptors Soc, 78; Knickerbocker Artists, 78; Audubon Artists, 78; and numerous others. Teaching: Vis prof sculpture & stone carving, Fla Southern Col, 52-; instr sculpture & stone carving, Ridgewood Art Sch, NJ, 61-65; instr sculpture & stone carving, Craft Student League, New York, 66-72. Awards: Louisa Robins Award, Silvermine Guild, 54; Medal of Hon, Sculptors & Painters Soc NJ, 56; Albert Dorne Prize, Audubon Artists, 56-61 & Cash Award, 78; Cash Award, Nat Acad, 78; Gold Medal, Knickerbocker Artists, 78; and numerous others. Bibliog: Domenico Facci, sculptor (film), WEDO-TV, Tampa, Fla, 70. Mem: Audubon Artists (pres); Am Soc Contemp Artists (dir); Sculptors League (treas, 71-); League of Present Day Artists (treas, 65); fel Nat Sculpture Soc; Artists Equity NY (vpres). Style & Technique: Representational style which takes liberties with realism so as to capture the feel or impression of the subject. Mailing Add: 248 W 14th St New York NY 10011

FADEN, LAWRENCE STEVEN
PAINTER, SCULPTOR
b Brooklyn, NY, Oct 21, 42. Study: Brooklyn Mus student scholar; Sch Visual Arts; NY Studio Sch; and with Nicholas Carone. Work: Chase Manhattan Bank, New York. Exhib: The Representational Spirit, Univ Art Gallery, State Univ NY Albany, 70; Painterly realism, Smith Col Mus Art, 70-72; New Images, Figuration in Am Painting, Queens Mus, 74. Bibliog: Alfred Frankenstein & Ann Van Devanter (co-auth), The American Self Portrait?, Praeger, 75. Mem: Alliance Figurative Artists (prog dir, 75). Style & Technique: Realism. Media: Windsor Newton Oil; Terra Cotta Clay. Dealer: Rose Walsh 544 E 83rd St New York NY 10028. Mailing Add: 184 E Seventh St New York NY 10003

FAFARD, JOE (JOSEPH YVON)
SCULPTOR
b Ste Marthe, Sask, Sept 2, 42. Study: Univ Man, BFA; Pa State Univ, MFA. Work: Winnipeg Art Gallery, Man; Glenbow Mus, Calgary, Alta; Brock Collection, Vancouver; Montreal Mus Fine Arts; Can Coun. Exhib: Realism 70, Montreal, 70; Realism, Emulsion, Omission, Kingston, Ont, 72; Ceramic Objects, Toronto, New York, 73; Trajectories 73, Paris, 73; Joe Fafard's Pensee, Winnipeg, Calgary, Vancouver, Regina, 73. Awards: Sr Arts Grant, Can Coun, 74. Bibliog: Mike McKinnery (auth), I Don't Have to Work that Big, Nat Film Bd, 73. Style & Technique: Highly detailed, small ceramic statues of acquaintances. Media: Low Fire Clay; Glazes; Acrylic. Dealer: Marta Landsman 1115 Ouest Ruc Shcrbrooke Montrcal PQ Can. Mailing Add: Box 121 Pense SK S0G 3W0 Can

FAGER, CHARLES J
EDUCATOR, CERAMIST
b Osage City, Kans, Feb 3, 36. Study: Kans State Univ, Manhattan, BArch, 59; Univ Kans, Lawrence, MA(ceramics), 63. Exhib: Craftsman USA, Smithsonian, Washington, DC, 66; Wichita Nat Decorative Arts & Ceramics Exhib, Kans, 66; 20th Wichita Nat Invitational Ceramics Exhib, 68; Int Crafts Exhib, World Coun of Craftsman, Lima, Peru, 68; Ann Craft Exhib, Ringling Mus Art, Sarasota, Fla, 72; Artists Biennial, New Orleans Mus Art, La, 73; Ann Craft Exhib, Ringling Mus Art, Sarasota, 73; Southeastern Am Crafts Coun Exhib, Greenville Co Art Mus, SC, 74; Univ S Fla Fac Exhib, Ringling Mus Art, Sarasota, 74; Piedmont Craftsman, Mint Mus, Charlotte, NC, 76; Ceramic Conjunction, Long Beach Mus Art, Calif, 77; Nat Cone Box Show, Edward Orton, Jr Ceramic Found traveling exhib, Univ Kans, Lawrence & Univ Northern Colo, Greeley, 77; one-man shows, Univ Southern Fla, Tampa, 63-76, Stetson Univ, Deland, Fla, 63, Colo State Col, Greeley, 63, Pensacola Jr Col, Fla, 63, Fla Ctr Mod Art, Micapony, 70 & Univ N Fla, Jacksonville, 76. Comn: Wichita Art Asn, Kans; First Financial Corp, Tampa, Fla; Tampa Pub Libr; Trend Publ, Tampa; Gulf Life Ins Co, Jacksonville, Fla. Teaching: Art instr, Kans State Univ, Manhattan, 60-61; grad asst instr, Univ Kans, Lawrence, 61-63; prof ceramics, Univ S Fla, Tampa, 63-; instr, Tampa Bay Art Ctr, 75. Pos: Consult archit, Rowe Holmes Assoc Archits Inc, Tampa, Fla, 73-74. Awards: Irving Hill First Award for Ceramics, Ninth Ann Kans Designer-Craftsman Exhib, Lawrence, 62; Ceramics Purchase Award, Wichita Nat Decorative Arts & Ceramics Exhib, Wichita, 62; Award of Excellence, cash prize, Ann State Fla Craftsmen Exhib, 76. Bibliog: Angelo Garzio (auth), Portfolio: Raku, Ceramics Monthly, 6/67; photograph of sculpture in Am Crafts Coun Newsletter, 1/70 & Art Week, 77. Mem: Col Art Asn; Southeastern Col Art Conf; Am Crafts Coun (Fla state rep); World Crafts Coun; Nat Coun on Educ for Ceramic Arts. Res: Application of industrial clay form processes to art; slip casting ceramic figures from life; photoceramics. Mailing Add: Dept of Art Univ S Fla Tampa FL 33620

FAGG, KENNETH (STANLEY)
ILLUSTRATOR, SCULPTOR
b Chicago, Ill, May 29, 01. Study: Univ Wis, BA; Art Inst Chicago; Art Students League; Pa Acad Fine Arts; Otis Art Inst, Los Angeles; also with Harvey Dunn & Joseph Pennell. Work: Art Inst Chicago; US Mil Acad, West Point; US Naval Acad, Annapolis; Smithsonian Inst, Washington, DC; Nat Mus Can, Ottawa. Exhib: Am Watercolor Soc, New York, 52-60. Teaching: Instr illus, Workshop Sch, New York, 48-49; instr drawing & painting, Chappaqua Adult Sch, 51-54. Pos: Art dir, advert dept, Fox Films, New York, 30-35; free lance illusr, 36-60; creative dir geophys dept, Rand McNally & Co, 61- Mem: Life mem Art Students League; life mem Soc Illustrators. Style & Technique: Realistic. Media: Tempera, Oil; Plastic. Res: Creator of geo-physical relief globes of the earth, ocean floors and moon. Publ: Illusr, Holiday, 46, Sat Eve Post, 53, Look & Cavalier, 54-58, Life, 54-70 & Mechanix Illustrated, 55-58. Mailing Add: Box 76 Chappaqua NY 10514

FAHLEN, CHARLES
SCULPTOR
b San Francisco, Calif, 1939. Study: San Francisco State Col, BA, 62; Otis Art Inst, Los Angeles, Calif, MFA, 65; Slade Sch, London Univ Col, Eng, 66. Work: Mus Mod Art, New York; Philadelphia Mus Art, Pa; NJ State Mus, Trenton; Pa Acad of Fine Arts, Philadelphia; Oakland Mus, Calif. Exhib: 17th Nat Print Biennial, Brooklyn Mus, NY, 70; Ray Johnson's Corresp Sch, Whitney Mus Am Art, New York, 70; Recent Acquisitions, Mus Mod Art, New York, 71; Portfolio & Ser, Oakland Mus, Calif, 72; Biennial of Contemp Am Painting & Sculpture, Whitney Mus Am Art, 73; 71st Am Exhib, Art Inst of Chicago, 74; Made in Philadelphia, Inst Contemp Art, 74; Recent Acquisitions, Philadelphia Mus Art, 74; Philadelphia: Three Centuries of Am Art, Philadelphia Mus Art, 76; Philadelphia-Houston Exchange, Inst Contemp Art, Univ Pa, Philadelphia, 76; Artists' Sketchbooks, Philadelphia Col of Art, 76; one-man shows, Gallerie Passepartout, Copenhagen, Denmark, 66, Richard Feigen Gallery, New York, 71, Peale House Galleries of Pa Acad of Fine Arts, 73, Steffanotti Gallery, New York, 75, Marian Locks Gallery, Philadelphia, 76 & 78, J H Duffy & Sons, New York, 76 & Droll Kolbert Gallery, New York, 78. Mailing Add: c/o Droll/Kolbert Gallery Inc 724 Fifth Ave New York NY 10019

FAIERS, EDWARD SPENCER (TED)
PAINTER, PRINTMAKER
b Newquay, Eng, Oct 26, 08; Can citizen. Study: Univ Alta, with H G Glyde; Banff Sch Fine Arts; Arts Students League, with Will Barnet. Work: Willistead Gallery Art, Windsor, Ont; Glenbow Found, Calgary, Alta; Brooks Mem Art Gallery, Memphis, Tenn; Ark Art Ctr, Little Rock; Tenn Arts Comn, Nashville. Exhib: Western Can Painters, 51; Mid-South Exhib Painting Awards, Memphis, 56 & 60; Delta Annual Awards, Little Rock, 61, 65 & 70; Six Americans, Ark Arts Ctr, Little Rock, 70; Retrospective, Memphis Acad Arts & Southwestern at Memphis, 72. Teaching: Prof painting & printmaking & chmn painting dept, Memphis Acad Arts, 52- Pos: Advert mgr, Western Can Hardware, Lethbridge, Alta, 40-50; chmn, Fedn Can Artists, Southern Alta Br, 48-50; mem, Cult Activities Bd, Prov Alta, 49-50; artist in residence, Univ Miss, summer 68. Style & Technique: Figurative, three dimensional. Media: Oil, Acrylic; Woodcut, Lithograph. Publ: An approach to painting in oils, Cult Activities Br, Prov Alta, 51. Dealer: Van Straatan Gallery 646 N Michigan Chicago IL 60611. Mailing Add: 3710 Friar Tuck Rd Memphis TN 38111

FAINTER, ROBERT A
EDUCATOR, PAINTER
b Austin, Tex, Aug 18, 42. Study: Univ Tex, Austin, with Prof Everett Spruce, BFA, 64 & MFA, 67. Work: Laguna Gloria Art Mus, Austin, Tex; WTex Art Mus, Lubbock; Tex Fine Arts Asn, Austin; Univ Tex Art Mus, Austin; Del Mar Col Collection, Corpus Christi. Exhib: 15th, 16th & 18th Ann Nat Drawing & Sculpture Exhib, Ball State Univ, 69, 70 & 72; 3rd, 5th & 6th Ann Nat Drawing & Sculpture Exhib, Del Mar Col, 69, 71 & 72; 12th Ann Eight State Exhib Painting & Drawing, Oklahoma City, 70; Mainstreams '70, Int Exhib Painting & Sculpture, Marietta, Ohio, 70; Am Drawing Biennial XXIV, Norfolk Mus, Va, 71. Teaching: Instr art, Univ Tex, Austin, 67-68; asst prof art, Tex Tech Univ, 68-72; vis instr art, San Antonio Col, Tex, 72- Pos: Tech staff asst, Design/Installation Dept, Univ Tex Art Mus, Austin, 64-67, assoc educ cur, 67-68. Awards: Award for drawing, 18th Ann Nat Exhib, Ball State Univ, 72; Purchase Award, 6th Ann Nat Exhib, Del Mar Col, 72; Jurors Award, Southwest Graphics, San Antonio, Tex, 72. Mem: Tex Fine Arts Asn. Style & Technique: Figure in spacial environment, using naturalistic style to establish image relationships and concepts. Media: Acrylic on Canvas/Board; Mixed Media on Paper. Dealer: Odyssey Galleries 2222 Breezewood San Antonio TX 78209. Mailing Add: 9507 Wahada St San Antonio TX 78217

FAIRBANKS, AVARD
SCULPTOR
b Provo, Utah, Mar 2, 97. Study: Art Students League, 10-12; study in Paris, 13-14, Ecole Nat des Beaux Arts, La Frande Chaumiere Acad Colarrossi; Leo Fairbanks, James E Fraser, Charles R Knight, Jean Antoine Ingalbert, F Rossi, A E Zardo, Dante Sodini; Yale Univ, BFA, 25; Univ Wash, MFA, 29; Univ Mich, MA, 33, PhD, 36; Lincoln Col, hon DFA; Lincoln Mem Univ, hon Lincoln dipl. Comn: The Doughboy of Idaho (hist marker); portrait busts & relief portraits, Pony Express, Utah Centennial; Marcus Whitman, Statuary Hall, Washington; bust Lincoln, New Salem, Ill; series of portrait busts for Western Hall Fame; plus many others. Teaching: Asst prof art, Univ Ore, 20-27; assoc prof sculpture, Univ Mich, 27-47; prof sculpture & dean col fine arts, Univ Utah, 47-65, emer prof, 65- sculptor in residence & spec consult, Univ NDak, 65- Awards: Medal of Knights of Themopylae, King of Greece; Medal of Lycurgus, Mayor, Sparta, Greece. Mem: Archit League New York; Nat Sculpture Soc; Mich Acad (chmn fine arts sect). Mailing Add: 1489 Michigan Ave Salt Lake City UT 84105

FAIRBANKS, JONATHAN LEO
CURATOR
b Ann Arbor, Mich, Feb 19, 33. Study: Brigham Young Univ & Univ Utah, BFA, 53; Univ Pa & Acad Fine Arts, MFA, 57; Univ Del, MA, 61. Teaching: Teaching fel, Pa Acad Fine Arts, 55-57; adj prof, Boston Univ; lectr, many univs. Pos: Cur asst, Winterthur Mus, 61-62, asst cur, 62-67, assoc cur, 67-; cur Am decorative arts, Mus Fine Arts, Boston, 71- Awards: Winterthur Fel, 59-61; Mural Award, Acad Natural Sci. Mem: Int Inst Conserv Hist & Artistic Works; Am Asn Mus; Soc Archit Historians; Washington Region Conserv Guild (adv coun); Victorian Soc Am (vpres, 69-71); plus others. Publ: Auth, Benjamin Ferris: A Friend of Many Talents (catalog), Del Antiques Show, 66; auth, American antiques in the collection of Mr and Mrs Charles L Bybee, Antiques, 12/67 & 1/69; auth, Address to the Friends of Wilmington for the 150th Anniversary Celebration of the Building of the Meetinghouse at 4th and West Streets, Wilmington, privately publ, 68; auth, Friends of Wilmington, Quaker Hist, spring 69; auth, The craftsman in early America, Role of Crafts in Educ, Dept Health Educ & Welfare, 6/69; plus others. Mailing Add: Mus of Fine Arts Boston MA 02115

FAIRWEATHER, SALLY H
ART DEALER
b Chicago, Ill, Sept 29, 17. Study: Art Students League, 36; Art Inst Chicago, BA, 39. Teaching: Instr life drawing, Katherine Lord Sch, Evanston, Ill, 39-43. Pos: Dir, Fairweather-Hardin Gallery, Chicago, 47-; dir, Art Dealers Asn Am, 62-63; dir, Found for Arts Scholarships, Chicago, 64-; co-founder, Chicago Art Dealers Asn, 66. Specialty: Modern paintings, graphics and sculpture. Mailing Add: 101 E Ontario St Chicago IL 60611

FAISON, SAMSON LANE, JR
MUSEUM DIRECTOR, EDUCATOR
b Washington, DC, Nov 16, 07. Study: Williams Col, BA, 29; Harvard Univ, MA, 30; Princeton Univ, MFA, 32; Williams Col, hon LittD, 71. Collections Arranged: Permanent collections & temporary exhibs, Williams Col Mus Art. Teaching: From instr to asst prof art, Yale Univ, 32-36; from asst prof to prof art, Williams Col, 36-77, chmn dept, 40-69; vis prof, Univ Pa, NY Univ, Columbia Univ, Univ Calif, Berkeley & Harvard Univ, summers; vis res prof, Univ Ga, spring 68. Pos: Exec secy, Comt on Visual Arts, Harvard Univ, 54-55; dir, Williams Col Mus Art, 48-77. Awards: Chevalier, Legion of Honor, Fr Govt, 47; Guggenheim Fel, 60-61. Mem: Col Art Asn Am; Asn Art Mus Dirs; Int Asn Art Critics; Mass Coun Arts & Humanities. Res: German 18th century architecture; 19th and 20th century French and American painting. Publ: Auth, Barna and Bartolo di Fredi, Art Bull, 36; auth, Dominikus Zimmermann, Mag Art, 52; auth, Manet, Abrams, 53; auth, Guide to art museums of New England, Harcourt Brace Jovanovich, 58; auth, Art tours and detours in New York State, Random, 64. Mailing Add: Scott Hill Rd Williamstown MA 01267

FALCONIERI, VIRGINIA
PAINTER, INSTRUCTOR
b Paterson, NJ, Mar 18, 43. Study: Entwistle Sch Art, Ridgewood, NJ, one year, Ridgewood Art Sch, three years. Work: Solar Syst, Bergen Community Mus, 76. Comn: Mural of the universe, Paterson Mus, 64. Exhib: Catharine Lorillard Wolfe Art Club, 75; Salmagundi Club, 75; Am Artist Prof League, 75; Composers, Authors & Artists Am, New York Chap, 75; Nat Arts Club Washington DC, 75. Teaching: Pvt classes in oil painting, 66- Pos: Assoc cur art, Paterson Mus, 64- Awards: Am Artist Prof League Award, 73; Catharine Lorillard Wolfe Art Club Merit, 73; Burr Artist of New York Award, 74. Mem: Assoc mem Allied Artist Am; Nat Soc Lit & Arts; Am Artist Prof League; Catharine Lorillard Wolfe Art Club; Salmagundi Club. Style & Technique: Realistic still life and landscape. Media: Oil. Mailing Add: 228 Lafayette Ave Hawthorne NJ 07506

FALK, GATHIE
SCULPTOR, PAINTER
b Alexander, Man, Jan 31, 28. Study: Univ BC, art educ. Work: Vancouver Art Gallery, BC; Dept External Affairs Collection, Can; Toronto Dominion Bank Collection; Nat Gallery of Can; Art Bank, Ottawa; Rothman's Art Gallery, Stratford, Ont; Victoria Art Gallery, BC; Govt of BC Collection; Art Gallery of Ont, Toronto; CBC Bldg, Vancouver, BC. Comn: Two ceramic and paint wall murals, Dept External Affairs Bldg, 72. Exhib: One-man shows, Douglas Gallery, Vancouver, 68, Single Right Men's Boots, Can Cult Ctr, Paris, 74, 39 Drawings, Bau Xi Gallery, Vancouver, 76, Can Nat Gallery Tour, 76-77, Herd I at Forest City Gallery, London, Ont, 77 & Edmonton Art Gallery, 78; New Vancouver Art, Newport Harbor Art Mus, Univ Calif, Santa Barbara, 69; Works Mostly on Paper, Inst Contemp Art, Boston, 70; two-man show, 29 Pieces, Vancouver Art Gallery, 70; 4 Places at Vancouver Art Gallery, 77; Some Can Women, Nat Gallery, Ottawa, Ont, 75. Awards: Arts bursary, Can Coun, 68, 69 & 71. Bibliog: Elfleda Wilkinson (auth), Artists of Pacific, Can, Nat Film Bd, 71; Doris Shodball (auth), Gathie Falk, Arts Can, 6-7/72; Alex Mugelan & Norman Laliberte (auths), Art in boxes, Van Nostrand Reinhold Co, 74. Style & Technique: Mixed bag technique; personal realistic style. Media: Clay, Wood; Canvas, Oil Paint. Publ: Articles in Capilanu Rev, Fall 74 & Spring 76, Time Canada, 12/75, Art Mag, 76 & 6/77, Arts Can, Winter 75/76, 12/76 & 6/77, Vancouver Mag, Spring 76 & Vanguard, 10/76, 3/77 & 2/78. Mailing Add: 2861 W Third Ave Vancouver BC V6K 1N8 Can

FALKENSTEIN, CLAIRE
SCULPTOR
b Coos Bay, Ore. Study: Univ Calif, Berkeley. Work: Addison Gallery Am Art, Andover, Mass; Baltimore Mus Art; Boston Mus Fine Arts; Solomon R Guggenheim Mus, New York; Los Angeles Mus Art; plus many others. Comn: Floor to ceiling stair railing for Gallery Sapzio, Milan, Italy & for Gallery Stadler, Paris, France; fire-screen for Baron de Rothschild's chateau; fountain, Wilshire Blvd, Los Angeles; stained glass windows, rectory screen & doors, St Basil's Cath Church, Los Angeles; copper & fused glass fountain, Calif Fed Savings Bldg, Los Angeles; plus other fountains, gates & murals for pvt homes, US & abroad. Exhib: Il Segno Gallery, Rome, Italy, 58; Inst Contemp Art, Boston, 59; Art for Use, Louvre, Paris, 62; Carnegie Inst, Pittsburgh, 64; Whitney Mus Am Art, New York, 64; plus many others. Media: Glass. Dealer: Martha Jackson Gallery 32 E 69th St New York NY 10021. Mailing Add: 719 Ocean Front Walk Venice CA 90291

FALLER, MARION
PHOTOGRAPHER, EDUCATOR
b Passaic, NJ, Nov 5, 41. Study: Hunter Col, City Univ New York, BA(art educ); additional study at William Paterson Col, NJ, NY Univ, New York & The Visual Studies Workshop, Rochester, NY. Work: Carnegie Mus Art, Pittsburgh, Pa; Int Mus Photog, George Eastman House, Rochester, NY; Ctr for Photog Studies, Louisville, Ky; Light Work, Inc, Syracuse, NY; Visual Studies Workshop Res Ctr, Rochester, NY. Exhib: One-person shows, SohoPhoto Found, New York, 72 & 73, Midtown Y Gallery, New York, 74 & Gertrude Thomas Chapman Art Ctr, Cazenovia Col, NY, 77; Vegetable Locomotion (with Hollis Frampton), Visual Studies Workshop Gallery, Rochester, NY, 75; Surface Appearances: An Exhib in Flux, Midtown Y Gallery, New York, 76; Photo-Images, Dayton Art Inst, Ohio, 77; Locations in Time, Int Mus Photog, George Eastman House, Rochester, NY, 77. Exhibitions Arranged: Autobiography: Painting, Photography, Film, 75 & Two Turn-of-the-Century Hamilton Photographers: Joseph F McGregory & Edward H Stone, 76, Picker Gallery, Dana Art Ctr, Colgate Univ; Edward S Curtis: Photogravures—Volumes I & III from The North American Indian, 76 & Upstate Color: Photographs by Bishop, Block, Pfahl, 77, Everson Mus Art, Syracuse, NY. Teaching: Lectr photog, Dept Art, Hunter Col, City Univ New York, 71-74; lectr photog, Dept Art, Marymount Manhattan Col, New York, 73-74; instr photog & hist photog, Dept Fine Arts, Colgate Univ, Hamilton, NY, 74- Pos: Photogr, Monkmeyer Press Photo Serv Photo Agency, New York; mem photog adv comt, Everson Mus Art, Syracuse, NY; artist/photogr, Visual Arts Referral Serv, Creative Artists Pub Serv Prog New York. Awards: Humanities Develop Awards, Colgate Univ, Hamilton, NY, 75, 76 & 77; Photogr's Grant, Light Work Visual Studies, Inc, Syracuse, NY, 76; Creative Artists Pub Serv Prog (CAPS) fel, NY, 77. Bibliog: Marion Faller, Gallery 35, 35-mm Photog Mag, New York, Summer 73; Marion Faller, A Portfolio of Photographs, Creative Camera Mag, London, 7/74; Portfolio: Marion Faller, Ms Mag, 4/75. Mem: Soc for Photog Educ; Photog Hist Soc NY. Style & Technique: Black and white and color photography, occasionally manipulated with hand work, collage, type, and other techniques. Publ: Auth & illusr, Images & Explorations, Set Two—Marion Faller, Paulist Press, New York, 72; contribr, Messages/a Portfolio of Found Images, Rye Press, Chicago, 76; co-auth, 5x5, Visual Studies Workshop Press, Rochester, NY, 77; auth & illusr, A Resurrection of the Exquisite Corpse, Visual Studies Workshop Press, Rochester, 78. Dealer: Visual Studies Workshop Gallery 31 Prince St Rochester NY 14607. Mailing Add: Box 42 River Rd Eaton NY 13334

FALTER, JOHN
ILLUSTRATOR
b Plattsmouth, Nebr, Feb 28, 10. Study: Kansas City Art Inst; Art Students League; Grand Cent Sch Art. Mem: Soc Illusrs; Artists & Writers Club. Publ: Illusr, A ribbon and a star, 46; illusr, The horse of another color, 46; contrib, covers to Sat Eve Post. Mailing Add: 21 Summit St Philadelphia PA 19118

FANARA, CONTESSA ANTONIO MASTROCRISTINO
See Sirena

FANGOR, VOY
PAINTER
b Warsaw, Poland, Nov 15, 22; US citizen. Study: Warsaw Acad Fine Arts, MFA. Work: Guggenheim Mus, New York; Mus Mod Art, New York; Univ Calif Art Mus, Berkeley; Muzeum Sztuki, Lodz, Poland; Stedelijk Mus, Amsterdam, Holland. Exhib: The Responsive Eye, Mus Mod Art, 65; 34th Biennale Venezia, Padiglione Centrale, 68; Guggenheim Mus, 70. Teaching: Asst prof painting, Warsaw Acad Fine Arts, 53-61; prof painting, Fairleigh Dickinson Univ, 65. Bibliog: R C Kennedy (auth), Notes on Fangor, Art Int, 66; Jay Jacobs (auth), Pertinent and impertinent: illusionist, Art Gallery Mag, 69; John Canaday (auth), Fangors romantic op, New York Times, 2/15/70. Media. Oil. Mailing Add: 96 Grand St New York NY 10013

FANNING, ROBBIE
ART WRITER, LECTURER
b West Lafayette, Ind, Jan 30, 47. Study: Knox Col, two yrs; State Univ NY, BS (in progress); spec study with Constance Howard. Teaching: Instr machine embroidery for artists & photog for textiles, Nat Standards Coun Convention, New Orleans, La, Fall 76; lectr self-publ for artists, Stanford Univ Pub Conf, Fall 77. Pos: Consult fiber art, 73-; fiber ed, Westart, Auburn, Calif, 73-76; ed/publ, Open Chain, 75-; mem adv coun, Ctr for Hist Am Needlework, Pittsburgh, Pa, 77- Mem: Am Crafts Coun; Nat Standards Coun Am Embroiderers; Embroiderers Guild Am; Peninsula Stitchery Guild (chmn, 74-75); Int Guild Craft Auth, Journalists & Photogr (conf workshop leader, 78). Res: The roots in traditional needlework that give rise to contemporary fiber and fabric art and craft. Publ: Auth, Stitches (weekly column). Country Almanac, Woodside, Calif, 73-; auth, West Coast Fiber Calendar (monthly), Westart, 73-76; auth, Decorative Machine Stitchery, 76 & co-auth, Here and Now Stitchery: Ethnic Embroidery & Applique, 78, Butterick Publ Co. Mailing Add: 632 Bay Rd Menlo Park CA 94025

FARAGASSO, JACK
ILLUSTRATOR, PAINTER
b Brooklyn, NY, Jan 23, 29. Study: Art Students League, 48-52, with Frank J Reilly. Work: George Washington Carver Mus, Tuskegee Inst, Ala. Exhib: Gallery Mod Art, New York, 69; Am Artists Prof League, 69-71 & 73-75. Teaching: Instr drawing, painting & illus & dir, treas & trustee, Frank Reilly Sch Art, New York, 67-68; instr drawing, painting & illus, Art Students League, 68- Mem: Art Students League; fel Am Artists Prof League. Media: Oil. Interest: Realistic school of painting, ranging from illustrative to Surrealistic to Malerische. Publ: Paperback illustrations for Ballantine, Paperback Lib, Popular Lib & Curtis Publ, 57-; also many covers & book illus for Pocket Bks, Macfadden, Berkeley Bks, Belmont Bks, Lancer, Pinnacle Bks, Harcourt, Brace Jovanovich & Signet Bks. Mailing Add: 340 E 55th St New York NY 10022

FARBER, MRS GEORGE W
COLLECTOR
Collection: Graphics. Mailing Add: 138 Newton Ave N Worcester MA 01609

FARBER, MAYA M
PAINTER
b Timisoara, Rumania, Jan 24, 36; US citizen. Study: Pratt Inst, with Edwin Oppler; Hunter Col; Hans Hoffman Sch; Art Students League, with Reginald Marsh. Work: Butler Inst Am Art, Youngstown, Ohio; Int Tel & Tel, New York; Columbia Mus Art, SC; Ga Mus Art, Athens; Jacksonville Art Mus, Fla. Exhib: One-man shows, Chase Gallery, 68 & 74, Telfair Acad Art, Savannah, Ga, 69 & Sheldon Swope Art Gallery, Terre Haute, Ind, 70; NY State Fair, 70; Rochester Festival Relig Art, 72. Awards: Second Prize, Jamaica Festival Art, 67. Media: Oil, Acrylic, Collage. Dealer: Chase Gallery Inc 31 E 64th St New York NY 10021. Mailing Add: 435 E 52nd St New York NY 10022

FARES, WILLIAM O
PAINTER
b Compton, Calif, July 16, 42. Study: San Francisco Art Inst, BA & MFA. Work: Chase Manhattan Bank; Va Mus Fine Arts; State Univ NY Col Purchase. Exhib: Painting & Sculpture Today, Indianapolis Mus Art, 74; Collage Drawings, Vassar Col Mus, 74; Biennial, Whitney Mus, New York, 75; Biennial, Whitney Mus of Am Art, New York, 75; Albright-Knox Art Gallery, Buffalo, NY, 75; Freedom in Art, Lehigh Univ, Bethlehem, Pa, 76; The Handmade Paper Object, Santa Barbara Mus of Art, Calif, traveling exhib, 76; New Work/New York, Univ Calif Los Angeles, Calif, 76; Drawings & Collage, Grey Art Gallery, NY Univ, 76; Paperworks, Mus of Mod Art, New York, 76; Art of the 60s & 70s, Ctr for

the Arts, Muhlenberg Col, Allentown, Pa, 77; Am Drawing 1927-1977, Minn Mus of Art, St Paul, 77; New Ways with Paper, Nat Collection Fine Arts, Smithsonian Inst, Washington, DC, 77 Skin, Dayton Art Inst, Ohio, 77; New Work/New York, Univ NDak, 77; one-man exhibs, John Doyle Gallery, Chicago, 74, Rosa Esman Gallery, New York, 75(twice) & 76 & Zolla/Lieberman Gallery, Chicago, 77. Media: Acrylic. Dealer: Kathren Markel 50 W 57th St New York NY 10019; Zolla/Lieberman 368 W Huron Chicago IL 60610. Mailing Add: 110 W 26th St New York NY 10001

FARIAN, BABETTE S
PAINTER, DESIGNER
b New York, NY, June 6, 16. Study: New York Sch Fine & Appl Art, two years; Cooper Union, three years; Art Students League, three months, with Bridgman; Mus Mod Art, three years; additional study with Donald Stacy, Addison Lamar, Joseph Margulies & Morris Kantor. Work: First Unitarian Church, Flushing, NY; Tamassee DAR Sch Gallery; Women's Fine Arts Mus; also in many pvt collections. Exhib: Am Artists Prof League; Nat Art League; Burr Artists; US Fine Arts Registry; Westchester Art League; Northwestern Conn Art Asn; Wall St Art Asn; Metrop Mus Art & Antique Coun (Gallery 81); one-person shows, Walter Reade Theatres & elsewhere. Teaching: Instr color & design, Cooper Union Art Sch, 40-41; pvt classes, 73-74. Pos: Color consult, Addison Lamar, 37-40; textile designer-artist, Krasom Co, New York, 55-57; free-lance designer, 58-59; asst head studio, Manhattan Shirt Co, New York, 60-65; designer, Hanscom Fabrics. Awards: Blue Ribbon for oils, watercolors & graphics, Martha's Vineyard Fair, 67 & Blue Ribbon for graphics, 68; Grumbacher Award, Composers, Authors & Artists Am, 74; Marion & Jeff Paol Award/Oil; First Prize/Acrylics, Wall St Artists, 76. Bibliog: Photos of work in Artist Mag, 66; article in Vineyard Gazette & Queens Tribune, 74. Mem: Artist's Equity Asn; Burr Artists (catalogue chmn); Composers, Authors & Artists Am (head nat membership comt); Jackson Heights Art Club (chmn publicity & state chmn Am pen women & Gotham Painters). Style & Technique: Semi-abstract to academic in acrylic; line detail drawing in ink. Media: Acrylic, Watercolor, Ink. Publ: Auth, The pendulum of time and the arts, 68; auth, article in Artist's Equity Mag, 75. Dealer: Roads/Lewis Horwin 400 E 57th St New York NY 10022. Mailing Add: 34-48 81st St Jackson Heights NY 11372

FARIS, BRUNEL DE BOST
PAINTER, INSTRUCTOR
b Oklahoma City, Okla, Aug 9, 37. Study: Univ Okla, BFA & MFA. Work: Univ Okla Art Mus, Norman; State of Okla Collection; Philbrook Art Ctr, Tulsa, Okla; Barkouras Found, Oklahoma City; Performing Arts Ctr, Tulsa, Okla; Privatklinik-Diabetiker, Bad Lauterberg, WGer. Exhib: Mid-Am Ann, Nelson Gallery Art, Kansas City, Mo, 65; 35th Ann Exhib, Springfield Art Mus, 65; 8 State Exhib Southwestern Art, Okla Art Ctr, Oklahoma City, 68 & 71; Okla Ann, Philbrook Art Ctr, Tulsa, 69 & 75; one-man shows, Univ Okla Art Mus, 74 & Barkouras Found, Okla, 77. Teaching: Instr art, Tulsa Pub Schs, 61-64; instr art, Oklahoma City Pub Schs, 65-66; asst prof art & chmn dept, Oklahoma City Univ, 69- Pos: Art dir, Okla Sci & Arts Found, 66-69. Mem: Col Art Asn. Style & Technique: Variable abstract compositions, low contrast drawings and studies of human figure. Media: Collage. Mailing Add: 1012 N W 39th St Oklahoma City OK 73118

FARM, GERALD E
PAINTER
b Grand Island, Nebr, Mar 8, 35. Study: Famous Artist Sch, Westport, Conn; Nebr State Col, BS. Work: Deming Fed Savings, NMex; Citizens Bank, Farmington, NMex; Bank of Beaver City, Okla; NMex State Univ; plus many pvt collections. Exhib: First Nat Bank, Albuquerque, 73; Nat Rodeo Asn, Tulsa, 73; Western Artist Show, Reno, 73; C M Russell Auction, Int Rodeo Finals, Great Falls, Mont, 73 & 75; NMex State Capital Bldg, Santa Fe, 74. Bibliog: Helen Lally (auth), Gerald Farm—Guardian of our western heritage, Southwest Art, 74. Style & Technique: Realistic western. Media: Oil. Mailing Add: 5609 Foothills Dr Farmington NM 87401

FARMER, JOHN DAVID
ART HISTORIAN, ART ADMINISTRATOR
b Washington, Ga, Jan 25, 39. Study: Columbia Univ, BA, 60; Univ NC, Chapel Hill, MA, 63; Princeton Univ, MFA, 65. Collections Arranged: Virtuouso Craftsman (with catalog), 69; Concepts of the Bauhaus (with catalog), 72; German Master Drawings of the 19th Century (with catalog), 72-73. Teaching: Instr art hist, Clark Univ, 68-69; lectr art hist, Harvard Univ, 71. Pos: Curatorial asst, Worcester Art Mus, Mass, 67-69; curator, Busch-Reisinger Mus, Harvard Univ, 69-72; curator earlier painting, Art Inst Chicago, 72-75; dir, Birmingham Mus Art, 75- Mem: Col Art Asn; Am Asn Mus; Asn Art Mus Dir; Southeast Mus Conf. Res: Art of the Northern Renaissance, especially painting and decorative arts of early 16th century Low Countries. Publ: Co-auth, Catalogue of European Paintings, Worcester Art Mus, 74; auth, Gerard David's lamentation and an anonymous St Jerome, Mus Studies, 75; auth, Ensor, Braziller, 77. Mailing Add: Birmingham Mus Art 2000 Eighth Ave N Birmingham AL 35203

FARNHAM, ALEXANDER
PAINTER, WRITER
b Orange, NJ, May 5, 26. Study: Art Students League, with George Bridgeman, W C McNulty & Frank Vincent DuMond; also with Van Dearing Perrine & Anne Steel Marsh. Work: Newark Mus, NJ; Nat Arts Club, New York; Monmouth Col; James A Michener Collection; Morgan Guaranty Trust Co, New York. Comn: Murals, Naval subjects, Naval Repair Base, New Orleans, 45; portrait of dir, Am Found for Blind, 50; painting of off bldg, NJ Mfrs Ins Co, Trenton, 69; Washington Crosses the Del (pewter plate design), Franklin Mint, 76. Exhib: Methods and Materials of the Painter, Montclair Art Mus, circulated in Can, 54; Nat Acad Design 135th Ann Exhib, New York, 60; Eastern States Art Exhib, Springfield, Mass, 65-67; NJ Award Artists Exhib, Montclair Art Mus, 66; NJ Artists, Newark Mus Invitational, 68. Pos: Artist, US Navy, 45-46. Awards: Agnes B Noyes Award, Montclair Art Mus, 50; Second Award, NJ Tercentenary, State of NJ, 63; Purchase Award, Newark Mus, 68. Bibliog: Diana Bainbridge (auth), art review and commentaries, NJ Mus & Arts, 6/69. Mem: Assoc Artists NJ (pres, 72-77; Hunterdon Art Ctr. Style & Technique: Realistic painting built on abstract design usually of architectural subjects. Media: Oil. Publ: Auth & illusr, Tool collectors handbook, 70; auth, Architectural patterns, subjects for the artists brush, 74. Dealer: Benedict Gallery 254 Main St Madison NJ 07940. Mailing Add: RD 2 Box 365 Stockton NJ 08559

FARNHAM, EMILY
PAINTER, WRITER
b Kent, Ohio, May 27, 12. Study: Kent State Univ, BSc(educ); Art Students League; Cleveland Sch Art; Hans Hofmann Sch Fine Arts; Ohio State Univ, MA & PhD. Comn: Murals, Cine Sonora, Hermosillo, Sonora, Mex, 47. Exhib: Works in Competition for World's Fair, Rocky Mountain Region, Denver Art Mus, 39; one-man shows, Art Ctr, Salt Lake City, 40 & Univ Va, Charlottesville, 58; 6th Nat Exhib, Okla Printmakers Soc, Oklahoma City, 64; Traveling Show, Assoc Artists NC, 68. Teaching: Asst & instr design, Ohio State Univ, Columbus, 34-37; instr painting, Mich State Univ, East Lansing, 37; instr painting & drawing, Utah State Univ, Logan, 38-41; head dept design, Stout State Col, Menomonie, Wis, 42-45; asst prof painting & drawing, Southern Ill Univ, Carbondale, 47-53; asst prof watercolor painting, Ohio State Univ, Columbus, 54-55; prof painting & art hist, Mary Baldwin Col, Staunton, Va, 56-62; prof painting & art hist, E Carolina Univ, Greenville, NC, 62-77, chmn art hist dept, 68-73. Pos: Mem art comn, NC Mus Art, Raleigh, 73- Awards: Biography, Charles Demuth: Behind a Laughing Mask, nominated for Nat Bk Award, 72. Mem: PEN; Southeast Col Art Conf; NC Art Soc; Assoc Artists NC; E Carolina Art Soc. Style & Technique: Watercolors of cloud forms; watercolor collages; abstract oils. Res: Current research being done in the area of abstract form resident in the great paintings of the past. Publ: Auth, Charles Demuth's Bermuda landscapes, Art J, New York, 65; auth, Charles Demuth: Behind a Laughing Mask, Univ Okla, Norman, 71. Dealer: Rental/Sales Gallery NC Mus Art 107 E Morgan St Raleigh NC 27601. Mailing Add: 1108 S Overlook Dr Greenville NC 27834

FARNSWORTH, HELEN SAWYER
See Sawyer, Helen

FARNSWORTH, JERRY
PAINTER, WRITER
b Dalton, Ga, Dec 31, 95. Study: Corcoran Art Sch, Washington, DC; also with C W Hawthorne. Work: Metrop Mus Art & Whitney Mus Am Art, New York; Pa Acad Fine Arts, Philadelphia; Houston Mus Art, Tex; Toledo Art, Ohio. Exhib: Carnegie Inst Nat & Int Exhibs; American Painting Today, Metrop Mus Art; San Francisco World's Fair; Century of Progress, Chicago; retrospective, Univ Ill, Champaign; plus others. Teaching: Carnegie resident painter, Univ Ill; instr figure & portrait painting, Farnsworth Sch Art. Awards: Altman Prize, Thomas Proctor Prize & Maynard Portrait Prize, Nat Acad Design. Bibliog: Articles in Am Artist Mag. Mem: Nat Acad Design (coun mem); Nat Arts Club. Style & Technique: Simplicity of line, beauty of surface quality, depth of feeling. Media: Oil. Interest: Preparation of archives of American art at Syracuse University and archives of American art, Smithsonian. Publ: Auth, Painting with Jerry Farnsworth, Learning to paint in oil & Portrait and figure painting. Dealer: Frank Oehlschlaeger Galleries 107 E Oak St Chicago IL 60611 & 28 S Blvd of Presidents Sarasota FL 33578. Mailing Add: 3482 Flamingo Sarasota FL 33581

FARRELL, PATRIC
MUSEUM DIRECTOR, WRITER
b New York, NY, July 22, 07. Study: Private and independent study. Collections Arranged: Jack B Yeats Show, Wild Earth, 31; Robert Flaherty, Man of Aran, 34; Sir William Orpen Mem, 34; Power O'Malley, 35; Irish Painting, New York World's Fair, 39; Nuala (Elsa de Brun), Carstairs Gallery, 47; James Joyce/Finnegans Wake (with catalog), Lyman Allyn Mus; Either/Or, Bymuseum, Copenhagen, Denmark, 73 (TV spec with Malcolm Muggeridge). Pos: Dir, Irish Theatre, New York, 27-30; dir, Mus Irish Art, New York, 30-; artist in residence, Pocono Environ Educ Ctr, 74. Res: Visual arts and theatre; Irish art from pre-Christian to present; illuminated manuscripts. Publ: Auth, Jack B Yeats, 30; auth, Power O'Malley, 34; ed, Images and illuminations, 60; ed, Kierkegaard's either/or exhibition, 71. Mailing Add: 161 E 81st St New York NY 10028

FARRELL, STEPHANIE KRAUSS
CURATOR
b Jackson Heights, NY, Sept 28, 40. Study: Univ Chicago, BA. Collections Arranged: The Art of George R M Heppenstall (with catalog), 72; Selections from the Collection, 75-76 & Craft of the Artist: An Investigation into the Working Methods of William Sidney Mount, 76, Mus at Stony Brook. Pos: Registr, Carnegie Inst Mus Art, 66-70, asst cur painting & sculpture, 70-73; consult, Art Collection, Mus at Stony Brook, 75- Awards: Spec honors in art, Univ Chicago, 62. Mem: Life mem Art Students League. Publ: Contrib numerous articles on the collection, Carnegie Mag, 66-72. Mailing Add: 26 Bramar Rd East Setauket NY 11733

FARRIS, JOSEPH
CARTOONIST, PAINTER
b Newark, NJ, May 30, 24. Study: Art Students League; Biarritz Univ; Whitney Sch Art. Work: Paintings in private collections. Exhib: One-man show, Ward Eggleston Gallery, New York. Pos: Contract artist, New Yorker. Awards: Emily Lowe Award. Mem: Mag Cartoonists Guild. Publ: Contribr cartoons to Sat Eve Post, True, Ladies Home J, Playboy, Penthouse, Sat Rev, New Woman, Punch & other nat mag; illusr, Slave boy in Judea; illusr bk jackets for others; auth & illusr, UFO ho ho; auth & illusr, Phobias & Therapies (cartoon bk), Grosset & Dunlap. Mailing Add: Long Meadow Lane Bethel CT 06801

FARRUGGIO, REMO MICHAEL
PAINTER
b Palermo, Sicily, Mar 29, 06; US citizen. Study: Nat Acad Design, Beaux Arts Inst, Educ Alliance & Indust Art Sch, New York. Work: Metrop Mus Art, New York; Butler Inst Am Art, Youngstown, Ohio; Portland Mus Art, Ore; Santa Fe Art Mus, NMex; Mus St Paul, Minn. Exhib: Blues and other paintings, Julien Levy Gallery, New York, 39; Galleria Art Mod, Mexico City, 50; John Heller Gallery, New York, 55, 56 & 58; Schneider Gallery, Rome, Italy, 57; Nuovo Sagitario Gallery, Milano, Italy, 73-74. Teaching: Instr painting, Fedn Artists, Detroit, Mich, 40; teacher painting, Portland Mus Art Sch, 54-55. Awards: Award for Dear Old Southland, Detroit Art Inst, 43; Butler Inst Am Art Award, 57; Award for Rocks, Hyannis Art Asn, Mass, 70. Mem: Artists Equity; Am Fedn Arts & Lett. Style & Technique: Romantic abstractionist. Media: Oils, Mixed Media. Mailing Add: 47 W 28th St New York NY 10001

FARWELL, BEATRICE
ART HISTORIAN
b Santa Barbara, Calif. Study: Knox Col, BA(art); NY Univ, MA(art hist); Univ Calif, Los Angeles, PhD(art hist). Teaching: Lectr & sr lectr, Metrop Mus Art, New York, 43-66; vis lectr art hist, Univ Calif, Santa Barbara, 66-67, lectr art hist, 67-74, assoc prof art hist, 74-77, prof, 77- Pos: Mem bd trustees, Santa Barbara Mus of Art, 71-76. Mem: Col Art Asn (bd dir); Southern Calif Art Historians. Res: Manet; modern western art; 19th century popular media, French, chiefly lithography. Publ: Auth, Sources for Delacroix's Death of Sardanapalus, Art Bull, Vol 40 (1958); auth, A Manet masterpiece reconsidered, Apollo, 7/63; auth, Manet's Espada & Marcantonio, Metrop Mus J, Vol 2 (1969); auth, Courbet's Baigneuses & the rhetorical feminine image, Art News Ann, 72; auth, Manet's Nymphe Surprise, Burlington Mag, 4/75. Mailing Add: 4523 Auhay Dr Santa Barbara CA 93110

FASANO, CLARA
SCULPTOR
b Castellaneta, Italy; US citizen. Study: Cooper Union Art Sch; Art Students League; also with Prof Arturo Dazzi, Rome, Italy; Acad Julien & Colarossi Acad, Paris, France. Work: Metrop Mus Art, New York; Nat Collection Fine Arts, Smithsonian Inst, Washington, DC; Norfolk Mus Arts & Sci, Va. Comn: Sculpture for Middleport Post Off, Ohio, Richmond High Sch, Staten Island, NY & Tech High Sch, Brooklyn, NY; many portraits for pvt comns. Exhib: Whitney Mus Am Art, New York; Metrop Mus Art; Nat Acad Design, New York; Pa Acad Fine Arts, Philadelphia; Salon Automne in Paris, London, Rome & others. Teaching: Instr sculpture, Indust & Fine Arts Sch of New York & Adult Educ, Bd Educ, New York, 46-56; instr sculpture, Manhattanville Col, 56-66. Awards: Nat Inst Arts & Lett Grant, 52; Medal of Honor for Sculpture, Nat Asn Women Artists, 55; Daniel Chester French Medal, Nat Acad Design, 65, Dessie Greer Prize, 68. Bibliog: Fred Whitaker (auth), Clara Fasano and her terra cotta, Am Artist Mag, 2/57. Mem: Academician Nat Acad Design; fel Nat Sculpture Soc (coun, 52, 60-63); Sculptors Guild; Audubon Artists (bd dirs); Nat Asn Women Artists (adv bd). Media: Terra-Cotta, Bronze. Mailing Add: c/o Nat Acad of Design 1083 Fifth Ave New York NY 10028

FASSETT, KAFFE HAVRAH
PAINTER, TEXTILE CONSTRUCTOR
b San Francisco, Calif, Dec 7, 37. Study: Boston Mus of Fine Arts Sch, Mass; yrs study with Alba Heywood, Calif. Work: Royal Scotish Mus, Edinboro, Leeds Mus, Eng. Comn: Dining room ceiling, David Bagler, London, Eng, 75; landscaped halls & ceiling, Westwell Manor, Westwell, Eng, 76. Exhib: One-man Calif Palace of the Legion of Honor, San Francisco, 63; Nat Acad of Design, New York, 76; two-man show, Textiles, Royal Scotish Mus, Edinboro, Leeds Mus, Eng & Aberdeen Mus, Scotland, 77. Awards: Salmagundi Award, Nat Acad of Design, 76. Style & Technique: Figurative painting; textiles. Media: Acrylic on canvas; canvas work and knitting in multi-fibers. Publ: Illusr, Rinzler (ed), The New York Spy, Blond Trav, 66. Mailing Add: 62 Fordwych Rd London NW2 England

FASTOVE, AARON (AARON FASTOVSKY)
PAINTER
b Kiev, Russia, Aug 20, 98; US citizen. Work: Nat Gallery Art, Washington, DC. Exhib: Nat Acad Design, 63; Univ Notre Dame, 64; Expos Intercontinental, Monaco, 66 & 68; Prix de Paris, Raymond Dun Duncan Gallery, Paris, France, 67; Parson Sch Design Gallery, 77; Art Students League, 78; one-man show, Woodstock, NY, 76; two one-man shows, New York; plus many other group exhibs. Awards: Award, Munic Art Gallery, 39; Spec Mention for Contribution to First Index of American Design, Metrop Mus Art, 42. Mem: Am Fedn Arts. Media: Oil. Publ: Contribr, Art Digest, 50. Mailing Add: 2720 Bronx Park E Bronx NY 10467

FAUL, ROBERTA HELLER
CONSULTANT, WRITER
b York, Pa, Dec 11, 46. Study: Wilson Col, 65-67; George Washington Univ, BA(hons), 69. Pos: Ed, Mus News, 71-76; mem bd, Mus Educ Roundtable, 73-74; film juror, Coun Int Nontheatrical Events, 75-; ed publ, Am Asn Mus, 76; sem fac mem, Cult Resources Mgt Prog, Banff Ctr, 76; consult, 76-; ed, Hist Preserv & Environ Rev Handbk, 77; mem bd & finance comt chmn, Don't Tear It Down, 77-; ed/writer, Reusing Hist Pub Bldgs, 78. Publ: Articles in House & Garden, Nov 76 & Cult Post, Mar/Apr 77. Mailing Add: 1346 Connecticut Ave Suite 219 Washington DC 20036

FAULCONER, MARY (FULLERTON)
PAINTER, DESIGNER
b Pittsburgh, Pa. Study: Pa Mus Sch Art; also with Alexey Brodovitch. Work: Mr & Mrs Paul Mellon; Mrs Gilbert Miller; Mr & Mrs Richard Rheem; Mr & Mrs John Hay Whitney; Duchess of Windsor; plus many others. Comn: Designed stamp, US Postal Serv, Philatelic Affairs Div, Washington, DC, 72; two paintings for UNICEF, 72; paintings for Steubin Glass; designed six stamps, US Postal Serv, 74. Exhib: Alex Iolas Gallery, New York, 55, 58 & 61; Philadelphia Art Alliance, 62; Bodley Gallery, New York, 64, 66, 69 & 72; Tenn Fine Arts Ctr, Nashville, 67; De Mers Gallery, Hilton Head, SC, 71-72. Teaching: Instr advert, Philadelphia Mus Sch Art, 36-40. Pos: Art dir, Harper's Bazaar Mag, 40; art dir, Mademoiselle Mag, 45. Awards: Distinctive Merit Award, 54, 57 & 61, Silver Medal, 58 & 59, Art Dir Club. Media: Gouache. Dealer: Bodley Gallery 1063 Madison Ave New York NY 10028. Mailing Add: 20 Beekman Pl New York NY 10022

FAULKNER, FRANK
PAINTER
b Sumter, SC, July 27, 46. Study: Univ NC, Chapel Hill, BFA, 68, MFA, 72. Work: Hirshhorn Mus, Washington, DC; Nat Collection of Fine Arts, Washington, DC; Albright-Knox Art Gallery, Buffalo, NY; Smith Col, Northampton, Mass; Chase Manhattan Bank, New York. Comn: Urban wall proj, SECCA-Nat Endowment for the Arts, Winston-Salem, NC, 74. Exhib: Whitney Mus of Am Art Biennial, New York, 75; Material Dominant, Univ Pa, Philadelphia, 77; Southeast 7, Southeastern Ctr for Contemp Art, Winston-Salem, NC, 77; Painters & Sculptors of the SE, High Mus of Art, Atlanta, Ga, 77; Slocumb Gallery, Univ Tenn, 76. Awards: Individual Artist Grant, Nat Endowment for the Arts, 75; Regional Artist Grant, SECCA-Nat Endowment for the Arts, 76; NC Architects Award, 76. Bibliog: William Zimmer (auth), Frank Faulkner, Arts Mag, 10/76. Style & Technique: Paintings of unstretched collages combined with acrylic. Media: Acrylic; mixed-media. Dealer: Monique Knowlton Gallery 19 E 71st St New York NY 10021. Mailing Add: 37 W Tenth St New York NY 10011

FAUNCE, SARAH CUSHING
MUSEUM CURATOR
b Tulsa, Okla, Aug 19, 29. Study: Wellesley Col, BA; Washington Univ, MA; Columbia Univ. Collections Arranged: New Black Artists, 69; Peruvian Colonial Painting, 71; Pearlman Collection of Post-Impressionist Painting, 74; Anne Ryan Collages (with catalog), 74; Folk Sculpture USA (with catalogue interview), 76. Teaching: Lectr art theory & criticism, Barnard Col, 64. Pos: Cur art collections, Columbia Univ, 65-69; exhib consult, Jewish Mus, 68-70; cur painting & sculpture, Brooklyn Mus, 69- Mem: Col Art Asn Am; Victorian Soc; Nat Trust for Hist Preserv. Publ: Auth, criticisms and articles in Art News, 62-71; Kurt Kranz Bauhaus and Today, Art in Am, 74. Mailing Add: c/o Brooklyn Museum Eastern Pkwy Brooklyn NY 11238

FAURER, LOUIS
PHOTOGRAPHER
b Philadelphia, Pa, Aug 28, 16. Work: Mus Mod Art, New York; New Orleans Mus. Exhib: In and Out of Focus, Mus Mod Art, New York, 48; Newly Purchased Work by 51 Am Photographers, Mus Mod Art, 50; Photography, Mid Century, Los Angeles Co Mus, 50; Christmas Show, Mus Mod Art, New York, 51-52; Family of Man, Mus Mod Art, 54; Then and Now, Mus Mod Art, 54; Photographs from the Mod Museums Collection, Mus Mod Art, 59; Limelight, solo exhib, Helen Gee, New York, 60; Ben Schultz Mem Exhib, Mus Mod Art, 68; Portals, 76, Appearances, 77, Solo Exhib, 77 & Summer Exhib, 77, Marlborough Gallery, New York; New York New York, Light Gallery, 78; New Standpoints, Mus Mod Art, New York, 78. Teaching: Instr photog sem, Parsons Sch Design, New York, 75-77. Awards: Nat Endowment Arts grant, 75; Creative Artists Pub Serv grant, New York, 78. Style & Technique: Through art, to penetrate communication barriers and transform adversities into victories of life and love. Publ: Contribr, Art News, 50. Dealer: c/o Harry Lunn Jr Graphics Int Ltd 3243 P St NW Washington DC 20007; Light Gallery 724 Fifth Ave New York NY 10019. Mailing Add: c/o Westbeth Group Suite 520-H 464 West St New York NY 10014

FAUSETT, (WILLIAM) DEAN
PAINTER, ETCHER
b Price, Utah, July 4, 13. Study: Brigham Young Univ; Art Students League; Nat Inst Archit Educ; Colorado Springs Fine Arts Ctr. Work: Metrop Mus Art; Mus Mod Art; Whitney Mus Am Art; Whitney Gallery of Western Art, Cody, Wyo; Toledo Mus Art; New Brit Mus; plus many others. Comn: Murals, US Post Off, Augusta, Ga, Grant's Tomb, NY, Bldg for Brotherhood, New York, US Air Acad, Colorado Springs, Colo, Global Power, USAF, Armed Forces Comn Rm, US Capitol, Washington, DC, Buffalo Bill Hist Ctr, Cody, Wyo, 4-H Nat Ctr, Washington, DC & State House Complex, Trenton, NJ (mural on pub educ); plus many others. Exhib: Seven shows, Whitney Mus Am Art Ann, 32-46; Carnegie Inst, 41-46; Univ Utah, 60, 68 & 70; one-man shows, Southern Vt Art Asn, 40-42, 54-55 & 69-77, Springville Art Mus, Utah, 68, B F Larsen Art Ctr, Brigham Young Univ, Provo, Utah, 69-70, Northern Ariz Univ, Flagstaff, 70, Ariz State Univ, Tempe, 70, Palm Springs Desert Mus, Calif, 70 & 71, Colorado Springs Fine Art Ctr, Colo, 70, Univ of Ariz, Tucson, 71, Utah State Univ, Logan, 71, Miller Art Ctr, Springfield, Vt, 75 & Norwich Univ, Northfield, Vt, 77; plus numerous others. Awards: Guggenheim Found fel, 43-45; Prize, Nat Soc Mural Painters, 45; Prize, Salmagundi Club, 46; Distinguished Serv in Art Award, Brigham Young Univ, 69; Gold Medal & Cash Award, Franklin Mint, 76; plus others. Mem: Nat Soc Mural Painters (vpres); Southern Vt Art Asn. Mailing Add: 1 W 67th St New York NY 10023

FAVRO, MURRAY
MIXED-MEDIA ARTIST, PAINTER
b Huntsville, Ont, Dec 24, 40. Study: Beal Tech Sch, London, Ont, 58-64. Work: Art Gallery of Ont, Toronto; Nat Gallery of Can, Ottawa, Ont. Comn: Sculpture, Ministry of Transport Bldg, Cornwall, Ont, 78. Exhib: The Heart of London (traveling exhib), Nat Gallery of Can, 68; Slides & Projections, 38 Weston St, London, Ont, 70; Can Nat Exhib, Toronto, 71; Realism: Emulsion & Omission, Agnes Etherington Art Centre, Kingston, Ont, 72; Mus d'Art Mod, Paris, France, 73; New Media Art, Pub Libr & Art Mus, London, Ont, 73; Nat Gallery of Can, Ottawa, 73, 74, 77 & 78; Projekt 74, Kunsthalle, Cologne, 74; Contemp Ont Art, Art Gallery of Ont, Toronto, 74; Rutgers Univ Art Gallery, New Brunswick, NJ, 75; Changing Visions: The Can Landscapes (traveling exhib), 76; London Art Gallery, Ont, 76; Dalhousie Univ, Halifax, NS, 78; one-man shows, 20/20 Gallery, London, Ont, 68, Carmen Lamanna Gallery, Toronto, 68, 71-72 & 76-78; plus others. Bibliog: Ross Woodman (auth), A New Regionalism, 8/67, Gary Michael Dault (auth), Murray Favro, Carmen Lamanna Gallery, November 1968, 2/69 & K Dewdney (auth), Form-image replicas: Murray Favro, Carmen Lamanna Gallery, 8/71, Artscanada. Publ: Auth, Notes, Region, London, Ont, summer 66; auth, Ron Martin's conclusions & transfers at 20/20 GAllery, 20 Cents Mag, London, Ont, 9/67; auth text, Heart of London (catalogue), Ottawa, 68; auth, Murray Favro's journal, 20 Cents Mag, 12/69. Mailing Add: c/o Carmen Lamanna Gallery 840 Yonge St Toronto ON M4W 2H1 Can

FAX, ELTON CLAY
PAINTER, WRITER
b Baltimore, Md, Oct 9, 09. Study: Syracuse Univ Col Fine Arts. Work: US Navy & Marine Corps Exhib Ctr, Washington, DC. Awards: Louis E Seley Naval Art Coop & Liaison Comt Award, 72; Coretta Scott King Award, 72; Areana Players Award, 72. Bibliog: Brawley (auth), The Negro genius, 36; Locke (auth), The Negro in art, 37; Dover (auth), American Negro art, 61. Mem: Salmagundi Club (Naval Art Coop & Liaison Comt); Author's Guild Am; Poets, Essayists & Novelists. Publ: Auth, West Africa vignettes, 61; auth, Seventeen black artists, 71; auth, Garvey, 72; auth, Through Black eyes, Dodd Mead & Co, 74; auth, Black Artists of the New Generation, Dodd Mead & Co, 77. Mailing Add: 51-28 30th Ave Woodside NY 11377

FAY, JOE
PAINTER, PRINTMAKER
b Newport, RI, Oct 26, 50. Study: RI Sch Design, 70; Southwestern Col, 71-72, AA(painting); San Diego State Univ, 72-74, BFA(painting & printmaking). Work: Univ Calif San Diego, La Jolla; La Jolla Mus, Calif; Newport Harbor Art Mus, Newport Beach, Calif; Oakland Mus, Calif. Comn: Mural painting, City of Los Angeles, 78. Exhib: Whitney Mus Ann, New York, 73; Am Painters, Mexico City Mod Art Mus, Mex, 75; Seven Los Angeles Artists, Southwestern Col, Chula Vista, Calif, 77; Paintings, Dobrick Gallery, Chicago, 77; Jewish Mus, San Diego, Calif, 77; one-man show, Paintings, Seder-Creigh Gallery, Coronado, Calif, 76. Mem: Los Angeles Inst Contemp Art. Style & Technique: Large color abstract expressionistic landscapes using brush and hands. Media: Acrylic and Mixed Media on Canvas and Paper. Dealer: Timothea Stewart Gallery 669 N La Cienega Blvd Los Angeles CA 90069. Mailing Add: 5 Wavecrest Venice CA 90291

FEARING, KELLY
PAINTER, EDUCATOR
b Fordyce, Ark, Oct 18, 18. Study: La Tech Univ, BA; Columbia Univ, MA. Work: Dallas Mus Fine Arts; Ft Worth Art Ctr; Tex Fine Arts Asn; Mus Fine Arts Houston; Inst Contemp Arts, Boston; Milwaukee Art Ctr. Exhib: Contemporary Painting & Sculpture, Univ Ill, Urbana, 55, 57 & 63; Carnegie Inst Int, Pittsburgh, Pa, 56; Museum Director's Choice, Colorado Springs Fine Arts Ctr, 61; The Bird in Art (with catalog), Univ Ariz & Ark Art Ctr, 66; Texas Painting & Sculpture: 20th Century, 71-72; 17th Ann Nat Invitational Exhib Painting & Sculpture, Longview Mus of Art, Tex, 75; Drawings USA 1978, Tex Tech Univ Mus of Art, 78; one-man shows, Witte Mem Mus, San Antonio, Tex, 69; Mary Moffett Gallery, La Tech Univ, 76; Du Bose Gallery, Houston, Tex, 77; L&L Gallery, Longview, Tex, 78. Teaching: Prof art, Univ Tex, Austin, 47- Bibliog: Allen S Weller (auth), The new romanticism, Art in Am, 60; New talent USA, Art in Am, 62. Res: Comparative arts: relationship between music and the visual arts. Style & Technique: Style: imaginative, figurative, surrealistic & romantic; technique: underpainting with glazes; drawing: frottage, silverpoint, pencil & crayon. Publ: Co-auth, Our expanding vision, Benson, 60; illusr, Confabulario & other inventions, Univ Tex Press, 64; co-auth, The creative eye, Benson, Vols I & II, 69; co-auth, Art and the creative teacher, Benson, 71; ed, Creativity and the human spirit, Tex Quart, spring 73 & spec issue, 75. Dealer: Du Bose Gallery 2950 Kirby Dr Houston TX 77098; L&L Gallery 1107 N Fourth St Longview TX 75601. Mailing Add: 914 Calethea Austin TX 78746

FEBLAND, HARRIET
PAINTER, SCULPTOR
b New York, NY. Study: Pratt Inst; NY Univ; Art Students League; Am Artists Sch. Work: New Sch Art Ctr, New York; Westchester Co Court House, White Plains Civic Plaza; Cincinnati Art Mus; Emily Lowe Mus, Coral Gables, Fla; Metromedia, Los Angeles, Calif; Hempstead Bank of Long Island Collection of Am Art; plus others. Exhib: Retrospects, Hudson River Mus, NY, 63 & Silvermine Guild, Conn, 73; Mus Mod Art, Paris, 70; Alwin Gallery, London, 70; Women Choose Women, New York Cult Ctr, 73; Potsdam Plastics, State Univ NY, 74; plus many others. Teaching: Instr-lectr, NY Univ, 60-62; instr & dir, Harriet FeBland's Advan Painters Workshop, New Rochelle, 62-; instr, Westchester Art Workshop, White Plains, 65-72. Bibliog: Harriet FeBland, Encycl Polymer Sci & Technol, 67; Newman (auth), Plastics as sculpture, Chilton, 74; Dona Meilach (auth), Collage and assemblage, Doubleday, 75; plus many others. Mem: Artists Equity Asn (vpres, 70-76, prog dir, 69-75); League of Present Day Artists (adv bd, 71-72); Col Art Asn Am; Silvermine Guild of Artists; Nat Asn of Women Artists; Sculptors League. Style & Technique: Constructivist; geometric abstractions in relief and free standing; constructions, with color on wood, canvas and plexiglas; also aluminum and steel. Media: Acrylic; Sculpture in Steel, Welded Metal, Plastics, Plexiglas, Stone, Marble & Wood. Mailing Add: Premium Point New Rochelle NY 10801

FEDELE, FRANK D
ART DEALER, PUBLISHER
b New York, NY, May 23, 36. Study: Sch Art & Design/Indust Arts, serigraphy with Biegeleison and sculpture with Eliscu. Pos: Pres, Frank Fedele Fine Arts Inc, 73- Specialty: Exclusive agent and publisher of graphic works by Ronald J Christensen; agent and publisher of works by Bob Pardo and Hank Laventhol; distributor of many American and European editions. Mailing Add: 91 Eighth Ave Park Slope Brooklyn NY 11215

FEDELLE, ESTELLE
PAINTER, LECTURER
b Chicago, Ill. Study: Art Inst Chicago; Northwestern Univ; Inst Design; Am Acad Fine Arts; Colo State Christian Col, hon PhD, 73. Exhib: Am Artists Prof League; Grand Cent Galleries, New York; Barron Galleries, Chicago & Las Vegas; Kenosha Pub Mus, Wis; Chicago Pub Libr. Teaching: Art instr, Fedelle Art Studio, Chicago, Ill; lectr, eastern & midwestern US on style & techniques in oil painting and demonstration of procedures. Mem: Life fel Royal Soc Arts London; Am Artists Prof League; Artists Guild Chicago; Regent Art League (hon dir); Munic Art League. Publ: How to Begin Painting for Fun, 65; weekly column, The Leader Newspapers. Mailing Add: 1500 S Cumberland Park Ridge IL 60068

FEDER, BEN
DESIGNER, PAINTER
b New York, NY, Feb 1, 23. Study: Parsons Sch Design; Vet Ctr, Mus Mod Art, with Prestopino. Exhib: Stamford Mus Art, Conn, 60; Bodley Gallery, NY, 64; Inst Allende, San Miguel Allende, Mexico City. Teaching: Lectr design & typography. Pos: Designer, major bk publ, US & abroad; designer, bks & bk jackets; designer & graphic arts consult, New Bk Knowledge, Grolier, Inc; pres, Ben Feder, Inc, New York. Mem: Int Ctr Typographic Arts. Style & Technique: Representational. Mailing Add: One Rockefeller Plaza New York NY 10021

FEDERE, MARION
PAINTER, GRAPHIC ARTIST
b Vienna, Austria; US citizen. Study: Early art educ in Vienna with Frances Haendel; Brooklyn Col; Brooklyn Mus Beckman scholar, two yrs; Charles Seiden's Workshop, two yrs; Pratt Graphics Ctr. Work: Butler Inst Am Art, Youngstown, Ohio; Philathia Col Mus Mod Art, London, Ont; Union Steel Chest Co; New York Hilton Gallery; pvt collections of Dr & Mrs Herbert Drobes, Dr Gerald Rosen, NY, Dr N Braunstein, Mex & Edward Moles, Jr. Exhib: Allied Artists Am, Nat Acad Galleries, New York, 58; Colo-Rama Galleries, New York Worlds Fair, 64-65; Artists Equity Asn Show at Westchester Art Soc, NY, 67; Brooklyn Mus Gallery, NY, 69, 72, 74, 75 & 76; United Nations Gallery, 75-77; Lincoln Ctr, 75-78. Awards: 19th Ann Drawing Award, Village Art Ctr, 64; Floyd Bennett Field First Prize, First Place Prof Award, 69; Kashka Mem Award, 77. Bibliog: Gordon Brown (auth), article in Arts Mag, 3/72; H G L (auth), Federe at Skylight, Park East, 3/16/72; Marion Federe, France-Amerique: Le Courier des Etats Unis, 3/23/72; plus others. Mem: Artists Equity Asn New York; Am Soc Contemp Artists; Contemp Circle NY (treas); Contemp Artists Guild (treas); Womens Int Art Club, Eng. Mailing Add: 2277 E 17th St Brooklyn NY 11229

FEHER, JOSEPH
DESIGNER, PAINTER
b Hungary, Apr 23, 08; US citizen. Study: Royal Hungarian Acad Fine Arts, Budapest; Acad Bella Arti, Firenze, Italy; Art Inst Chicago. Work: Abbott Labs, Chicago; Nemes Collection, Budapest; Honolulu Acad Arts; United Air Lines Collection, Chicago; Eli Lilly Collection, Indianapolis. Comn: Across the US (mural), United Air Lines, 46; The Navy in Micronesia-Documentation (watercolor drawings), US Navy, 50-51; Hawaii Statehood commemorative postage stamp, US Govt, 59. Exhib: Int Watercolor Exhib, Chicago Art Inst, 28; one-man show, Univ Ill, Urbana, 45; Hawaii Painters & Sculptors, 48, The Navy in Micronesia, 51 & three-man show, 68, Honolulu Acad Arts. Teaching: Instr graphic design, Inst Design, Chicago, 45-46; instr painting, drawing & design, Honolulu Acad Arts, currently. Pos: Artist-historian, Bishop Mus, Honolulu, 55-69; designer publ, Honolulu Acad Arts, 47-, dir art sch, 62-, cur prints & drawings, 66. Awards: Distinctive Merit Award, 20th Ann New York Art Dirs Show, 41; six Medal Awards, Chicago Art Dirs Ann, 42-48; Award Cert, Soc Typographic Arts, Chicago, 46. Media: Oil. Publ: Auth, Tale bearing winds (portfolio), Bishop Mus, 58; illusr, The voyage of the flying bird, Dodd, 65; illusr, Claus Spreckels, Univ Hawaii Press, 67; auth, Hawaii; a pictorial history, Bishop Mus, 69. Dealer: Downtown Gallery Ltd 125 Merchant St Honolulu HI 96813. Mailing Add: Honolulu Acad Arts Honolulu HI 96814

FEHL, PHILIPP P
PAINTER, ART HISTORIAN
b Vienna, Austria, May 9, 20; US citizen. Study: Art Inst Chicago; Stanford Univ, BA & MA; Univ Chicago, PhD. Work: Neue Galerie Joanneum, Graz, Austria. Exhib: One-man shows, Chapel Hill Art Gallery, NC, 69 & 70, Neue Galerie Joanneum, Graz, 71, Krannert Art Mus, Univ Ill, 71, Folger Shakespeare Libr, 75 & Col William & Mary, 77. Teaching: Prof hist art, Univ NC, Chapel Hill, 63-69; prof hist art, Univ Ill, Urbana-Champaign, 69- Pos: Art historian in residence, Am Acad Rome, 66-67; assoc, Ctr Advan Study, Univ Ill, 70-71. Awards: Res Fel, Warburg Inst, Univ London, 57-58; Nat Endowment Humanities fel, 77-78. Bibliog: Wilfried Skreiner (auth), Capricci by Philipp Fehl, Neue Galerie, Graz, 71. Mem: Col Art Asn Am (bd dirs, 68-71); Renaissance Soc Am; Am Soc Aesthetics & Art Criticism; Southeastern Renaissance Conf; Midwestern Renaissance Conf. Style & Technique: Pictorial poems, wash drawings. Media: Watercolor. Res: Renaissance art; history of the classical tradition in art; history of art criticism. Collection: Prints, Renaissance to modern. Publ: Ed, A course in drawing, Univ Chicago Press, 54; illusr, The bird: a series of capricci, Final Press, 70; auth, The classical monument, NY Univ Press, 72; ed, Franciscus Junius, Literature of Classical Art, Univ Calif Press, 78; auth, articles in Art Bull, Burlington Mag, J Warburg & Courtauld Inst, Gazette Beaux Arts & others; illusr, Voyager, Lillabulero & other mags. Mailing Add: Dept of Art Univ Ill at Urbana-Champaign Champaign IL 61820

FEIFFER, JULES
CARTOONIST, WRITER
b New York, NY, Jan 26, 29. Study: Art Students League, 46; Pratt Inst, 47-51. Pos: Asst to syndicated cartoonist, Will Eisner, 46-51; cartoonist, Village Voice, 56-; cartoons publ weekly, London Observer, Eng, 58-66 & 72- & Playboy Mag, 59-; syndicated nationally, 59- Awards: Acad Award Animated Cartoon, Munro, 61; George Polk Mem Award, 62; Outer Circle Drama Critics Award, 69 & 70. Mem: Authors Guild. Publ: Auth, nine collections cartoons including Sick Sick Sick, 58, Feiffer on Civil Rights, 67, Feiffer's Marriage Manual, 67 & Feiffer on Nixon, 67; auth, plays & novels. Mailing Add: c/o Field Newspaper Syndicate 401 N Wabash Ave Chicago IL 60611

FEIGEN, RICHARD L
ART DEALER, COLLECTOR
b Chicago, Ill, Aug 8, 30. Study: Yale Univ, BA, 52; Harvard Univ, MBA, 54. Pos: Pres, Richard L Feigen & Co, Inc, 57-; vpres & trustee, John Jay Homestead, Katonah, NY. Mem: Life fel Metrop Mus Art; life fel Minneapolis Soc Fine Arts; Art Dealers Asn Am (dir); Cooper-Hewitt Mus (Friends Comt); Collectors Inst New Sch Art Ctr (adv comt). Specialty: Paintings, drawings and sculpture, 1400 to the present. Collection: Old Master paintings; Beckmann, Grosz, Kandinsky, Cornell, Dubuffet. Publ: Contribr, Arts Mag, 67; auth, Dubuffet and the anticulture, 69; contribr, Office design, 70; auth, George Grosz: dada drawings, 72. Mailing Add: 900 Park Ave New York NY 10021

FEIGENBAUM, HARRIET (MRS NEIL CHAMBERLAIN)
SCULPTOR
b New York, NY, May 25, 39. Study: Art Students League; Nat Acad Sch Fine Arts; Columbia Univ. Work: Andrew Dickson White Mus, Cornell Univ; Colgate Univ Mus. Exhib: Hundred Acres First Sculpture Ann, New York, 71; one-person shows, Warren Benedek Gallery, 72 & 74 & Tuscan Valley Configurations of Hay and Wood, City Univ Grad Ctr Mall, NY, 76; New York Artists on Tour-3, Sculpture, 1973, Dept Cult Affairs; New York Today—Works on Paper, Univ Mo, St Louis, 73; Cinquantenaire De La Parution Du Manifeste Surrealiste, Services Culturels Français, New York, 73; Sculpture Sited, Nassau Co Mus of Fine Arts, Roslyn, NY, 76; Artpark, Lewiston, NY, 77; Women in Am Archit: A Hist & Contemp Perspective, Brooklyn Mus, NY & Hayden Gallery, Mass Inst of Technol, 77-78. Awards: Hallgarten Traveling Fel, 61; Creative Artists Pub Serv Prog, 77. Style & Technique: Site sculpture, notably Cycle Series—A sequence of site-specific projects that deal with a juxtaposition of unrelated cultures via forms of landscape architecture. Publ: Auth, Bernini and Galileo, Art Bull, 3/77. Mailing Add: 39 Claremont Ave New York NY 10027

FEIGIN, MARSHA
PRINTMAKER, PAINTER
b New York, NY, June 17, 46. Study: Univ Hawaii, MFA; City Col New York, BA; Cooper Union; Syracuse Univ. Work: Minn Mus Art; Indianapolis Mus Art; State Found Cult & Arts, Hawaii; De Cordova Mus, Mass; Nat Mus, Poland; US Info Agency; Del Mus of Art; IBM Corp; Charles Rand Penney Found, New York; Minneapolis Inst Arts. Comn: Etching, Creative Artists Pub Serv Prog, New York, 75. Exhib: 22nd Nat Exhib Prints, Libr of Cong, 71; Graphikbiennale, Vienna, Austria, 72 & 75; 18th Nat Exhib Prints, Brooklyn Mus, 72; 10th & 11th Biennial Graphic Art, Ljubljana, Yugoslavia, 73 & 75; 5th Int Biennial Graphic Art, Crakow, Poland, 74; 20th Nat Exhib of Prints, Brooklyn Mus, 76; 6th Int Biennial Graphic Art, Crakow, Poland, 76; Printmaking: New Forms, Whitney Mus Am Art, 76; Am Graphics in Venice, Galleria Bevilacqua La Masa, Venice, Italy, 77; Art Today: USA, Iran-Am Soc, Teheran, Iran, 77. Teaching: Teaching asst printmaking, Univ Hawaii, 69-71; instr life drawing & painting, Bishop Mus, 71; guest lectr printmaking, Rutgers Univ, 73; guest lectr & juror, Fla Technol Univ, 77. Pos: Master-printer, Printmaking Workshop, New York, 71-72. Awards: NY State Coun Arts CAPS Prog Grant Printmaking, 73 & 75; Nat Endowment Arts Grant Printmaking & Drawing, 75. Mem: Artists Equity Asn; Women's Caucus for Art; Col Art Asn; Graphic Arts Coun of NY; Philadelphia Print Club; Printmaking Workshop, New York. Style & Technique: Figurative, large-scale airbrushed and sandblasted etchings; line drawings; wash paintings. Media: Intaglio; Watercolor, Acrylic. Dealer: Assoc Am Artists 663 Fifth Ave New York NY 10022. Mailing Add: 228 E 81st St New York NY 10028

FEIGL, DORIS LOUISE
PAINTER
b Bayonne, NJ, Aug 19, 16. Study: Portrait study with Emily Nichols Hatch, 35-37; Grand Cent Sch Art, 38-40, with Edmund Graecon & Jerry Farnsworth; Art Students League, 5 yrs, with Joseph Hirsch, Bruce Dorfman & Sidney Dickenson. Exhib: Tri-State Ann, 76; Bergen Co Artist Guild Ann, Paramus, 66-72; Catharine Lorillard Wolfe Club Ann, Nat Arts Club, New York, 66-77; Allied Artists Show, 77, Nat Acad Design, New York, 67; An Artists Prof League Grand Nat, Lever House, New York, 68-76; plus others. Teaching: Instr painting, Englewood Women's Club, NJ, 68-72. Awards: Best in Show, Bergen Co Artists Guild, 66, First Prize for Oil, 69; Award for Oil, Catharine Lorillard Wolfe Art Club, 70; Best in State, Fedn of Woman's Clubs, 76, Second in State, 77. Mem: Bergen Co Artists Guild (secy, 66-68); Am Artists Prof League; Catharine Lorillard Wolfe Art Asn. Media: Oil. Mailing Add: 728 Catalpa Ave Teaneck NJ 07666

FEIN, B R
PAINTER, LECTURER
b Brooklyn, NY, Dec 11, 41. Study: Brooklyn Col, 58-62, BA, 62; City Univ New York, 62-67, MA, 67; Univ Md, 64-66; Univ NH, 70-74. Work: New York Pub Libr; Seacoast Regional Coun Ctr, Portsmouth, NH; York Co Coun Ctr, Sanford, Maine; Deaconess Hosp, Boston; Kittery Art Asn, Maine. Comn: Mural, Child at a Circus, Capt R Fisichella, USN Hosp, Portsmouth, 71. Exhib: Seacoast Artists, Walt Kuhn Mem-Norton Hall Gallery, Cape Neddick, Maine, 69-72; Drawings '71, Minn Mus Art, Minneapolis, 71; 6th Ann Drawing & Small Sculpture Exhib, Del Mar Col, Corpus Christi, Tex, 72; Wadsworth Atheneum, Conn Acad Fine Arts, Hartford, 72; 33rd & 34th Ann Nat Art Exhib, Southern Utah State Col, Cedar City, 73 & 74. Teaching: Guest lectr abstract painting, Univ Maine, Orono, 71; vis lectr drawing & oil painting, Univ NH, Durham, 73- Pos: Gallery exhib dir, Portsmouth-Seacoast YWCA, 68-73; bd dir, Seacoast Area Artists, Kittery Pt, 68-72. Awards: Third Place Prof, Manchester Art Asn, NH, 70; First Place Oil-Acrylic & Hon Mixed Media, Newbury Port Art Asn, Mass, 71; Hon Mention Graphics, York Art Asn, Maine, 71 & 73. Mem: Maine State Art Asn (bd dir, 73-74); Copley Soc; WEB; Sharon Art Ctr; Boston Visual Artists Union. Style & Technique: Realistic; impressionistic to abstract detail; loose washes; wet and

dry brush; landscapes and studies. Media: Watercolor; Pencil. Publ: Illusr, Dora Young's Tatting Manuals, 74 & 75; illusr, Single's Circle, 74. Dealer: 1623 Gallery Sagamore Rd Portsmouth NH 03801. Mailing Add: 4 Trefethen Ave Kittery ME 03904

FEIN, STANLEY
PAINTER, ILLUSTRATOR
b Brooklyn, NY, Dec 21, 19. Study: Parsons Sch Design; NY Univ. Work: NY Univ Collection. Comn: Paintings of New York State history, 71 & paintings of the cities of New York State, 72, Bank of New York. Teaching: Instr design & color, Pratt Inst, 56-58. Awards: Art Dirs Club NY, 56-65; Wall Street Art Asn, 60; Soc Illusrs, 70 & 71. Style & Technique: Work with emphasis on color and drawing; color is often crystal clear. Media: Oil, Ink, Watercolor. Dealer: Phoenix Gallery 939 Madison Ave New York NY 10022. Mailing Add: 313 DeGraw St Brooklyn NY 11231

FEINBLATT, EBRIA
ART HISTORIAN
b Hedera, Palestine; US citizen. Study: NY Univ; Inst Fine Arts; Univ Calif, Los Angeles, MA. Exhibitions Arranged: Jacques Callot: Prints & Drawings, 57; Honoré Daumier: Prints, Drawings, Paintings & Sculpture, 58; Pieter Bruegel the Elder: Prints & Drawings, 61; Georges Rouault Prints, 62; Agostino Mitelli Drawings, 65; Picasso Prints, 65; Munch Prints, 69; Old Master Drawings, 76. Pos: Sr cur prints & drawings, Los Angeles Co Mus Art, currently. Mem: Print Coun Am. Res: Prints and drawings; XVII century Bolognese ceiling decoration. Publ: Exhib catalogs; articles in Art Quarterly, Burlington Mag & Master Drawings. Mailing Add: Los Angeles Co Mus Art 5905 Wilshire Blvd Los Angeles CA 90036

FEININGER, T LUX
PAINTER, WRITER
b Berlin, Ger, June 11, 10; US citizen. Study: Bauhaus, Dessau, Ger, 26-32; stage design with Oskar Schlemmer; also with Paul Klee, W Kandinsky & Josef Albers, dipl, 29; Inst Fine Arts, NY Univ, 46-47, with Salmony, Lopez-Rey, Cook & Friedlaender. Work: Mus Mod Art, New York; Busch-Reisinger Mus & Fogg Art Mus, Harvard Univ; Altonaer Mus, Hamburg, Ger. Exhib: American Realists and Magic Realists, Mus Mod Art, New York, 43; Revolution and Tradition in Modern American Art, Brooklyn Mus, 51; Whitney Mus Am Art Ann, New York, 51; Four American Painters, Mass Inst Technol, 54; Retrospective, Busch-Reisinger Mus, 62; Wheaton Col, 73; Wamsutta Club, New Bedford, Mass, 74. Teaching: Instr design, Sarah Lawrence Col, 50-52; lectr drawing & painting, Harvard Univ, 53-62; instr drawing & painting, Boston Fine Arts Mus Sch, 62-75; retired. Awards: Hon mention, Arts & Crafts Club, New Orleans, 48; hon mention, Cambridge Art Asn, 63. Bibliog: Thomas B Hess (auth), Profile, Art News, 2/47; Feininger family, Life Mag, 11/51; E Bitterman (auth), Art in modern architecture, Van Nostrand Reinhold, 52. Mem: Cambridge Art Asn; Westport Art Group. Style & Technique: Style: magic realism and cubist form; technique: oil on canvas or panel. Media: Pen and ink, watercolor. Publ. Auth, The Bauhaus: evolution of an idea, Criticism, summer 60; auth, Lyonel Feininger: city at the edge of the world, Praeger, 65; auth, Address on modern art, Harvard Art Rev, 66; auth, The heritage of Lyonel Feininger, Am-Ger Rev, 66. Mailing Add: 22 Arlington St Cambridge MA 02140

FEINMAN, STEPHEN E
ART DEALER
b New York, NY, Sept 29, 32. Pos: Pres, Gary Arts Ltd, 65-72; pres, Multiple Impressions Ltd, 72- Specialty: Twentieth Century European and American prints; Haitian paintings. Mailing Add: 17 Greenwich Ave New York NY 10014

FEINSTEIN, ANITA ASKILD
See Askild, Anita

FEIST, WARNER DAVID
GRAPHIC ARTIST, PAINTER
b Augsburg, Ger, Dec 3, 09; Can citizen. Study: Bauhaus, Dessau, Ger, with Joseph Albers, Paul Klee, Oscar Schlemmer, Josef Schmidt & photog with Walter Peterhaus. Work: Concordia Univ, Montreal, Que; Montreal Mus Fine Arts. Exhib: One-man shows, Mansfield Art Gallery, Montreal, 64 & 69, Picture Loan Gallery, Toronto, Ont, 74 & Goethe Inst, Montreal, 74; O'Keefe Ctr, Toronto, 75. Teaching: Lectr basic principles of art, Sir George Williams Univ, 63-68. Pos: Art dir, Harold F Stanfield Ltd, Montreal, 51-58 & Vickers & Benson Ltd, Montreal, 58-66; pres, Art Dir Club, Montreal, 58-60; design consult, ICAO Bull, Int Air Transport Asn, 68- Mem: Societe des Graphistes du Que. Style & Technique: Hardedge, sometimes combined with collage and areas of free painting. Media: Acrylics. Mailing Add: 592 Luck Ave Montreal PQ H4X 1S4 Can

FEITELSON, HELEN LUNDEBERG
See Lundeberg, Helen

FEITELSON, LORSER
PAINTER
b Savannah, Ga, Feb 11, 98. Work: Mus Mod Art, New York; Nat Gallery of Art, Washington, DC; San Francisco Mus; Los Angeles Co Mus Art; Joseph F Hirshhorn Collection. Exhib: Dada, Surrealism & Fantastic Art, Mus Mod Art, 36-37; Am Drawing, Metrop Mus of Art, New York, 53; Abstract Classicism, Los Angeles Co Mus Art & Inst Contemp Art, London, 59; Geometric Abstraction in America, Whitney Mus Am Art, New York, 62; Whitney Mus Am Art Ann, 65; Westcoast Invitational, E B Crocker Art Gallery, Sacramento, Calif, 67 & 68; West Coast 1945-1969, Pasadena Art Mus, Calif, 69; Am Painting 1970, Va Mus of Art, Richmond; Retrospective Exhib, Munic Art Gallery, Los Angeles, 72; Los Angeles Painters of the 1920s, Pomona Col Gallery, Claremont, Calif, 72; Avant-Garde Painting & Sculpture in Am 1910-25, Del Art Mus, Wilmington, 75; Calif Painting & Sculpture: The Mod Era, San Francisco Mus of Mod Art & Nat Collection of Fine Arts, Washington, DC, 76; Surrealism & Am Art, Rutgers Univ Art Gallery, New Brunswick, NJ, 77; plus others. Bibliog: Jules Langsner (auth), Permanence and change in the art of Lorser Feitelson, 9/25/63, Henry Seldis (auth), Lorser Feitelson, 5/20/70 & Diane Moran (auth), On Lorser Feitelson, 10-11/77. Art Int. Mem: Los Angeles Art Asn (chmn bd trustees). Mailing Add: 8307 W Third St Los Angeles CA 90048

FELD, AUGUSTA
PAINTER, PRINTMAKER
b Philadelphia, Pa, Apr 18, 19. Study: Fleisher Art Mem & Music Settlement Sch, Philadelphia; Philadelphia Col Art, BA; Tyler Sch Fine Arts, Temple Univ; Pa Acad Fine Arts, MA. Work: Woodmere Art Gallery, Philadelphia; Marple-New Town Libr, Broomall, Pa; Acad Fine Arts, Philadelphia; permanent collection of Philadelphia Sch Dist; Hahnemann Hosp, Philadelphia. Comn: Tree of Life (mural of wood inlays, gold paint and vinyl, with Joseph Brahim), Del Co Community Ctr, Springfield, Pa, 64; dance mural (oil painting), Melita Dance Studio, Philadelphia, 68. Exhib: Woodmere Art Gallery, 61-; Wilmington Soc Fine Arts, Del, 71; Earth Show, Philadelphia Civic Ctr, 74; Artist Equity Asn, Philadelphia, 74; Philadelphia Art Alliance, 74-75. Teaching: Instr art, Philadelphia, 54-65; instr art, Wallingford Art Ctr, Pa, 63-64; instr art, Haverford, Pa, 63-65. Pos: Dir art, Hillview-Trout Nursery Sch, Broomall, Pa, 61- Awards: Van Sciver Award, Woodmere Art Gallery, 62; First Prize for oils, Atlantic City CofC, 68; First Prize, print exhib, Cheltenham Art Ctr, 71. Bibliog: Article in La Rev Mod, 64. Mem: Artists Equity Asn; Pa Acad Fine Arts; Philadelphia Art Alliance; Community Art Ctr Wallingford; Woodmere Art Gallery. Style & Technique: Versatile and emotional paintings, very free and expressive in all art medias, ink, acrylic, oils, etchings, collagraphs, woodcuts, collage and bas-reliefs. Mailing Add: c/o Daniel Feld 2835 Century Lane Apts A54 Cornwell Heights PA 19020

FELD, MARIAN PARRY
See Parry, Marian

FELD, STUART PAUL
CURATOR
b Passaic, NJ, Aug 10, 35. Study: Princeton Univ, AB, 57; Harvard Univ, AM, 58. Work: Addison Gallery of Am Art, Andover, Mass; Metrop Mus Art, New York. Collections Arranged: Three Centuries of American Painting, Metrop Mus Art, 65; plus many others. Pos: Var curatorial positions leading to assoc cur-in-charge, Dept Am Paintings, Metrop Mus Art, 61- Interest: American and European paintings of 18th and 20th century. Publ: Co-auth (with Albert Ten Eyck Gardner), American Paintings: Painters Born by 1815 (Catalogue of the Permanent Collection of the Metropolitan Mus of Art), Vol 1, NY Graphic Soc, 65. Mailing Add: c/o Hirschl & Adler Galleries Inc 21 E 70th St New York NY 10021

FELDENHEIMER, EDITH
COLLECTOR
b New York, NY, Aug 29, 1900. Study: Smith Col, Northampton, Mass. Pos: Founder & chmn, Arts Assoc of Reed Col, 61- Collection: Grande Rue, Argenteuil, painting by Utrillo, Western Town by Mark Tobey; drawings by Modigliani and Toulouse-Lautrec; drawings by Picasso, Rembrandt, Timothy Cole, et al. Mailing Add: 4125 SW Bertha Portland OR 97201

FELDHAUS, PAUL A
EDUCATOR, PRINTMAKER
b Cincinnati, Ohio, July 19, 26. Study: Cincinnati Art Mus; Miami Univ, Oxford, Ohio, BFA, 50; Bradley Univ, Peoria, Ill, MA, 52; study with Edwin Fulwider & Ernest Freed, printmakers. Work: Calif Col Arts & Crafts, Oakland; Carroll Reece Mus, ETenn State Univ; Friends Meeting House, Boston, Mass; Montomgery Mus Fine Arts, Ala; Mobile Pub Lbir, Ala. Comn: Mural, Mastin Sch Nursing, Mobile, Ala, 66; mural, Woman's Clinic, Mobile, Ala, 67. Exhib: The 8th Libr of Cong Print Exhib, Washington, DC, 50; Carnegie Inst Int Print Exhib, Pittsburgh, Pa, 52; Brooklyn Mus Print Show, NY, 53; 3rd Festival Contemp Southern Art, Brooks Mem Art Gallery, Memphis, Tenn, 67; Old Bergen Art Guild Nat Tours of Outstanding Artists of Calif in Cols, Univ & Libr, 75-78; invitational travelling exhib of 40 prints in Turkey, US Embassy, 75; Int Biennial Graphic Art, Mus Mod Art, Ljubljana, Yugoslavia, 75; Int Exhib Graphic Art, Frechen, WGer, 76; Seventh Premio Int Biella of Printmaking, Italy, 76. Teaching: Assoc prof art, Spring Hill Col, Mobile, Ala, 52-71; prof printmaking & drawing & coordr printmaking dept, Calif State Univ, Chico, 71- Pos: Pres, Ala Art League, 69-70; trustee, Montgomery Mus Art, Ala, 69-70. Awards: First Place Purchase Award, Dauphin Island Nat Competition, 65, 66, 68 & 70; Flack Purchase Prize, 7th Dixie Print Ann, Montgomery Mus of Art, 66; First Place Graphics, Mobile Watercolor & Graphic Arts Show, 69. Bibliog: Messenger From Hell, 65, 26th Ann Watercolor Exhib, Jackson, Miss, 66, La Revue Mod, Paris. Mem: Col Art Asn; Graphics Soc. Style & Technique: Photolithographic and photoengraving techniques emphasizing strong linear motifs. Media: Lithography, engraving. Mailing Add: 310 W Legion Ave Chico CA 95926

FELDMAN, ARTHUR MITCHELL
MUSEUM DIRECTOR
b Philadelphia, Pa, Dec 22, 42. Study: Villanova Univ, BS; Univ Pa with George Tatum; Univ Mo, MA(art hist & archaeol). Pos: Vis cur, Victoria & Albert Mus, London, Eng, 70-71; assoc cur & asst adminr, Renwick Gallery, Smithsonian Inst, Washington, DC, 71-73; dir, Spertus Mus of Judaica, 73- Mem: Am Asn of Mus; Soc of Archit Historians; Ethnic Preserv Coun (vpres). Publ: Auth, Magic & Superstition in the Jewish Tradition, 74, Jewish Artists of the 20th Century, 75, The Hill Page Collection, 75, The Jews of Yemen, 76 & Faith and Farm: Synagog Architecture of Illinois, 76, Spertus Col Press. Mailing Add: 618 S Michigan Ave Chicago IL 60605

FELDMAN, BELLA TABAK
SCULPTOR
b New York, NY. Study: Queens Col, City Univ New York, BA; Calif Col Arts & Crafts; Calif State Univ, San Jose, MA. Work: Oakland Mus, Calif; Berkeley Art Mus, Univ Calif. Comn: Sculptures, Marshal Tulin, Hydronautics Inc, Silver Spring, Md, 64, Sasaki-Walker Landscape Architects, Newport Shopping Ctr, Newport Beach, Calif, 65 & Royston Hanamoto Landscape Architects, Potrero Park, Richmond, Calif, 66. Exhib: Palace of the Legion of Honor, San Francisco, 61; Summer Series, San Francisco Mus, 64; Berkeley Art Ctr, 74; San Francisco Art Inst, 75; Univ Calif, Santa Barbara, 75. Teaching: Asst prof sculpture, Calif Col Arts & Crafts, 64-; lectr art, Makerere Univ Col, Fine Art Sch, Uganda, 68-70. Awards: Calif Mus Trustees Award, 67; First Prize, San Francisco Women Artists, 67. Mem: Women's Caucus Col Art Asn; Committee-West, East Bag. Style & Technique: Surreal; cast materials. Media: Metal, Paper, Resin. Dealer: Grapestake Gallery 2876 California St San Francisco CA 94115. Mailing Add: 12 Summit Lane Berkeley CA 94708

FELDMAN, EDMUND BURKE
EDUCATOR, ART CRITIC
b Bayonne, NJ, May 6, 24. Study: Newark Sch Fine & Indust Arts, with John R Grabach & Emile Alexay, dipl, 41; Syracuse Univ, BFA, 49; Univ Calif, Los Angeles, with Karl With, Stanton MacDonald Wright & Abraham Kaplan, MA(art hist), 51; Columbia Univ, with Lyman Bryson & George Counts, EdD, 53. Teaching: Assoc prof art, Livingston State Col, 53-56; assoc prof painting, sculpture & design, Carnegie-Mellon Univ, 56-60; chmn art div, State Univ NY Col New Paltz, 60-66; prof art, Ohio State Univ, summer 66; prof art, Univ Ga, 66-; vis prof, Univ Calif, Berkeley, winter 74. Pos: Cur paintings & sculpture, Newark Mus, 53. Awards: Named Alumni Found Distinguished Prof Art, Univ Ga, 73. Mem: Kappa Pi; Col Art Asn Am; Nat Art Educ Asn. Res: Theory of art criticism. Publ: Auth, Engaging art in dialogue, Sat Rev, 7/15/67; auth, The critical act, J Aesthetic Educ, 2/67 & Rivista di Estetica, 67; auth, Art as image and idea, 67 & Becoming human through art, 70, Prentice-Hall; auth, Varieties of visual experience, Prentice-Hall & Abrams, 72. Mailing Add: 140 Chinquapin Pl Athens GA 30605

FELDMAN, HILDA (MRS NEVILLE S DICKINSON)
PAINTER, EDUCATOR
b Newark, NJ, Nov 22, 99. Study: Newark Sch Fine & Indust Art, grad; Pratt Inst, alumni class, 5 yrs. Work: Reading Mus & Art Gallery; Marine Hist Asn, Mystic Seaport, Conn; Ford Motor Co, Detroit; Seton Hall Univ, South Orange, NJ; many in pvt collections. Exhib: Am Watercolor Soc & Nat Asn Women Artists, New York; Audubon Soc, New York & NJ Galleries; one-woman show, Springfield, NJ, 77; plus traveling shows in Can, Holland, Belg, Japan & Switz. Teaching: Instr design & watercolor, Newark Sch Fine & Indust Art, 23-72; instr painting, Millburn Adult Sch, NJ, 46-63; teacher, Springfield Recreation Classes, NJ. Awards: Winsor Newton Prize, 55 & B W Hamm Prize, 68; Nat Asn Women Artists; plus others from several NJ exhibs. Mem: Nat Asn Women Artists (chmn watercolor jury & traveling watercolor jury); Am Watercolor Soc; NJ Watercolor Soc; Maplewood & South Orange Gallery. Media: Watercolor. Mailing Add: 507 Richmond Ave Maplewood NJ 07040

FELDMAN, RONALD
ART DEALER
Pos: Owner & dir, Ronald Feldman Gallery, New York. Specialty: Contemporary artists; Modern European and American masters, painting, sculpture and prints. Mailing Add: 33 E 74th St New York NY 10021

FELDMAN, WALTER (SIDNEY)
PAINTER, EDUCATOR
b Lynn, Mass, Mar 23, 25. Study: Yale Univ Sch Fine Arts, BFA, 50, Sch Design, MFA, 51; also with W de Kooning, Stuart Davis & Josef Albers. Work: Addison Gallery Am Art, Andover, Mass; Metrop Mus Art, New York; Fogg Art Mus, Cambridge, Mass; Israel Mus, Jerusalem; Mus Mod Art, New York. Comn: Mosaic pavements, Temple Beth-El, Providence, RI, 57; stained glass windows, Sugarman Mem Chapel, Providence, RI, 61; World's Fair poster, IBM Corp, 63; Quezalcoatl (mural), Pembroke Col, Brown Univ, 66; 32 panel mural, Temple Emanu-El, Providence, RI, 68. Exhib: American Watercolors, Drawings and Prints, Metrop Mus Art, 52; Recent Drawings USA, Mus Mod Art, New York, 55; Mostra Int, Milan, Italy, 57; 26th Biennial, Corcoran Gallery, Washington, DC, 59; Nat Inst Arts & Lett, New York, 61; one-man show, Hopkins Ctr, Dartmouth Col, 78. Teaching: Instr painting & design, Yale Univ Sch Design, 50-53; prof painting & printmaking, Brown Univ, 53-; vis prof drawing, Harvard Univ, 68; artist in residence, Hopkins Ctr, Dartmouth Col, 78. Awards: Metrop Mus Art Award, 52; Gold Medal, Mostra Int, Milan, Italy, 57; First Painting Award, Boston Arts Festival, Mass, 64. Bibliog: G Y Loveridge (auth), Providence practitioner of ancient art, The Rhode Islander, 4/25/54; Michael Forster (auth), The color of Mexico is black, Nivel 41, German P Garcia (Mexico City), 5/25/62; Jane Shelton (auth), Walter Feldman, Harvard Art Rev, spring 66. Mem: Am Color Print Soc. Mailing Add: 224 Bowan St Providence RI 02906

FELDSTEIN, MARY
COLLECTOR, ART LIBRARIAN
b Berlin, WGer, Dec 17, 51; US citizen. Study: City Col New York; Univ Mich; New Sch Social Res. Work: Univ Mich Undergrad Libr; New York Pub Libr. Collections Arranged: New York Public Library Permanent Video Collection; 1st Ann Video Art & Video Documentary Festival, Goddard Col, Plainfield, Vt, 77; Meet the Makers (video & film series), Donnell Libr Ctr, New York, 77 & 78. Teaching: Fac mem contemp trends in video art & doc, New Sch Social Res, 78- Pos: Media specialist & info asst, Bronx Bookmobiles, New York, 74-75; film/video historian, New York Pub Libr, 76- Bibliog: Carol Anshiem (auth), Video in New York State Libraries, Videoscope, Vol 2 (1976); Marianne Cocchini (auth), Cataloging video art, Film Libr Quart, Vol 10 (1977); Victor Ancona (auth), Doings at Donnell, Videography, 10/77. Mem: Asn Independent Video & Filmmakers. Res: Original cataloging of video art, public access to films and video tapes; circulating video tapes in library context. Interest: Conceptual, minimal, architecture, video, film, holograms, multi-media, inter-media. Mailing Add: Video/Film Study Ctr Donnell Libr Ctr 20 W 53rd St New York NY 10019

FELGUEREZ, MANUEL
PAINTER, SCULPTOR
b Zacatecas, Mex, Dec, 1928. Study: With Ossip Zadkine, Paris. Work: Mus Arte Mod, Mex, Israel, Tokyo, New Delhi & Bogota. Comn: Spec murals, Seattle Worlds Fair, Mex Govt, 62; mural, Concamin, Mexico City, 64; mural, Montreal Worlds Fair, Mex Govt, 67; mural, Hemisfair San Antonio, Mex Govt, 68; sculpture, Olympic Games, Mex Govt, 68. Exhib: II Salon Anual de Pintura, Barranquilla, Colombia, 60; VI Bienal Tokyo, 61; VI Bienal Sao Paulo, 61; I Trienal India, New Delhi, 68; Mus Mod Art, Japan; plus others. Teaching: Prof sculpture, Iberoamerican Univ, Mex, 56-62; vis prof sculpture, Cornell Univ, 66; prof format design, Nat Univ Mex, 69-70, dean cols visual invest, 71. Awards: Segundo Premio, II Salon Anual, Barranquilla, 60; Segundo Premio Int, I Trienal India, 68; Guggenheim Fel, 75-76. Bibliog: L Cardoza (auth), Mexico: pintura activa, Era, Mex, 61; Pintura actual: Mexico 1966, Artes Mex y Mundo, 66; J Garcia Ponce (auth), Nueve pintores Mexicanos, Era, Mex, 68. Style & Technique: Lacquer on canvas in painting; metal polychromed in sculpture. Media: Oil, Acrylic, Plastic. Dealer: Galeria Juan Martin Amberes 17 Mexico City 6 Mexico. Mailing Add: Galeana 37 bis Mexico City 20 Mexico

FELLER, ROBERT L
CONSERVATION SCIENTIST
b Newark, NJ, Dec 27, 19. Study: Dartmouth Col, AB, 41; Rutgers Univ, MS, 43 & PhD, 50. Teaching: Vis sci, Conserv Ctr, NY Univ Inst Fine Arts, spring 61. Pos: Head, Nat Gallery Art Res Proj, Carnegie-Mellon Inst Res, Pittsburgh, 50-76, dir, Ctr on the Materials of the Artist & Conservator, 76-; ed, Int Inst Conserv Hist & Artistic Works, Am Group Bull, 60-74. Awards: Fel, Illum Eng Soc, 75. Mem: Fel Int Inst Conserv Hist & Artistic Works (pres, Am Group, 64-66); Int Coun Mus, Comt Conserv (pres, 69-); Nat Conserv Adv Coun (pres, 76-); Inter Soc Color Coun; Fedn Soc Paint Technol. Res: Picture varnishes; effects of light on museum objects; analysis of pigments in works of art. Publ: Co-auth, On Picture Varnishes and Their Solvents, 59, rev ed, 71. Mailing Add: Carnegie-Mellon Inst Res 4400 Fifth Ave Pittsburgh PA 15213

FELLOWS, FRED
PAINTER, SCULPTOR
b Ponca City, Okla, Aug 15, 34. Comn: Portfolio of prints, Winchester on the Frontier, Winchester Firearms; painting, Armco Steel Corp. Exhib: Cowboy Artists Am Show, Phoenix & Okla, 68-; Cowboy Hall of Fame; Whitney Gallery; C M Russell Mus; Mont Hist Soc; Los Angeles Co Mus Art; Long Beach Mus Art. Pos: Commercial artist & art dir. Awards: Gold Medal, Phippen Award, Cowboy Artists Am Exhib, 75; painting selected for int advert by Marlboro; Award for Contrib to Fine Art in Am, Grumbacher; Ann Exhib Award, Printing Inst NY, 76. Bibliog: E Ainsworth (auth), Cowboy in Art; Jim Serven (auth), Conquering the Frontier; Royal B Hassrick (auth), Western Painting Today. Mem: Cowboy Artists Asn (secy-treas & vpres, 74-75, pres, currently). Publ: Auth, Saddles of the early west, Mont Hist Soc Mag, 68. Mailing Add: Box 464 Bigfork MT 59911

FELS, C P
PAINTER, WRITER
b Kirksville, Mo, Aug 29, 12. Study: Univ Calif, Berkeley, with Margaret Petersen, 38; Univ Southern Calif, with Francis deErdely, BFA(painting), 49, with Jules Heller, MFA(graphics), 50. Work: Everett Gallery, Univ Wash; San Francisco Mus Art. Exhib: San Francisco Art Asn Ann, 54; Los Angeles Co Mus Ann, 56; Brooklyn Mus Print Exhib, 58; Hawthorne Art Ann, 67; Southbay Art Ann, 72; plus others. Teaching: Lectr painting & drawing, Univ Calif, Los Angeles, 50-54; asst prof art, Univ Southern Calif, 54-67; assoc prof art, Calif State Univ, Los Angeles, 68- Pos: Exhib dir, Southbay Art Asn, Redondo Beach, Calif, 52-58; mem bd dirs, Southbay Coop Gallery, 58-61; mem bd dirs, Downey Mus Art, 75- Awards: First Prize Watercolor, Hawthorne Art Asn, 67; Wurlitzer Fel, 70; plus many others. Bibliog: Erwin O Christensen (auth), Pictorial Western Art, Mentor, 64. Mem: Artists Equity Asn Inc (secy-treas, 74-75, pres, Los Angeles Chap, 76-78); Artists Econ Action; Am Soc Aesthetics. Style & Technique: Disciplined and organized realism in gouache, watercolor and oil; landscape and architectural subjects. Media: Oil, Woodcut. Res: Byzantine and Islamic art and architecture. Publ: Ed, The Graphic Work of Louis Monze, Plantin, 73; auth, Kieth Crown, 73, Presence of absence: Leonard Heath sculpture, 74 & Influences on Chicano art, 75, ASAAC; auth, Aesthetic reaction and autonomus choice, FWEPS, 74. Dealer: Numasters 1408 S Raymond Ave Alhambra CA 91803. Mailing Add: Dept Art Calif State Univ Los Angeles CA 90032

FELT, MR & MRS IRVING MITCHELL
COLLECTORS
Collection: Contemporary painting and sculpture. Mailing Add: Plaza Hotel Fifth Ave at W 59th New York NY 10019

FELTER, JAMES WARREN
PAINTER, CURATOR
b Bainbridge, NY, Aug 25, 43; Can citizen. Study: Univ S Fla, Tampa, BFA(painting), 64; Univ Wash, studies in art & Pre-Columbian archaeol. Work: Univ S Fla Centre Collection, Tampa; Selkirk Col, Castlegar, BC; Simon Fraser Univ Collection; City of Vancouver, BC; BC Prov Collection, Can; Manawatu Art Gallery, NZ; Mildura Arts Centre, Australia; Cabinet des Estampes, Musee d'Art et d'Histoire, Geneva, Switz. Comn: Trademark, OCEPA-Ecuadorian Handcrafts, Quito, 65; posters, Seattle Opera Asn, Wash, 67; Simon Fraser Univ Arts Centre, Burnaby, BC, 70 & 72. Exhib: 138th Ann Exhib, Nat Acad Design, New York; Mariano Aguilera Ann Exhib, Quito, Ecuador, 65; Mystic Circle, Burnaby Art Gallery, BC (circulated 1974-75), 73 & 7th Burnaby Biennial Print Show, 73; 1st New York City Postcard Show, NY Univ, 75; Timbers et Tampons d'Artistes, Cabinet des Estampes, Musee d'Art et d'Histoire, Geneva, Switz, 76; The Seventies, Mus of Mod Art, Sao Paulo, Brazil, 76; 37th Venice Biennale (ECART Invitational), Italy, 76; Four Can Artists, Moderna Galerija, Liubljana, 76 (toured Yugoslavia, 76-77); Sixth Int Miniature Print Competition, Pratt Graphics Ctr, New York, NY (toured US, 77-78). Collections Arranged: Simon Fraser Collection, Simon Fraser Univ; The British Columbia Craft Exhibition (with catalog), Vancouver, BC, 72; Artist's Stamps and Stamp Images (circulated 1975-76), 74. Teaching: Vis artist, Escuela de Bellas Artes, Univ Cent Ecuador, 66; resident visual arts, Simon Fraser Univ, 69. Pos: Dir, Galeria de Ocepa, Quito, Ecuador, 65-66; cur-dir exhib, Simon Fraser Univ, 70- Awards: Finalist-Major Work of Art Competition, Univ Calgary, Alta, 74; Winner, Trademark Competition, Craftsmen's Asn BC, 75. Bibliog: James Warren Felter, La Rev Mod, Paris, 8/63; Mario Leon Meneses (auth), James W Felter en la Galeria Siglo XX, El Comercio, Quito, 2/24/66; Francoise Le Gris (auth), James Warren Felter, Vie des Arts 69, Montreal, 73. Mem: Community Arts Coun Vancouver (bd dirs); Western Can Art Asn (chmn, 75); Univs Art Asn Can; Can Mus Asn; Int Coun Mus (Can comt). Style & Technique: Non-objective with mathematical formulas; hard and soft edge technique. Media: Ink, Acrylic, Oil. Res: Pre-Columbian and native arts. Publ: Auth, 450 Desinos Del 500 DC, publ in Span, Quito, 66; ed, Paul Rand 1896-1970, Vancouver, BC, 72; contribr, Contemporaries of Emily Carr in British Columbia, Vancouver, 74; contribr, Vehicule Art: in Transit, Montreal, PQ, 75. Dealer: Five/Cinq Aesthet Ltd PO Box 91519 West Vancouver BC Can. Mailing Add: 2707 Rosebery Ave West Vancouver BC Can

FENCI, RENZO
SCULPTOR
b Florence, Italy, Nov 18, 14; US citizen. Study: Royal Inst Art, Florence; Work: Permanent Gallery Mod Art, Florence; Santa Barbara Mus Art, Calif. Comn: Nine banks in Los Angeles area, Home Savings & Loan Asn; Dr Charles Leroy Loman Mem, Orthopedic Hosp, Los Angeles, 68; George C Page Bldg, Children's Hosp, Los Angeles, Calif, 76; portrait of Edwin Lester, Music Ctr, Los Angeles, 77; Hughes Space & Commun Bldg, El Segundo, Calif, 77. Exhib: Art Inst Chicago, 41; Calif State Fair, 50; Los Angeles Co Mus Art, 55; Nat Exhib Contemp Arts US, Pomona, Calif, 56; one-man show, Santa Barbara Mus Art, 68. Teaching: Instr sculpture, Univ Wash, Pullman, 42; asst prof sculpture, Univ Calif, Santa Barbara, 46-54; prof sculpture & head dept, Otis Art Inst, 54-77. Awards: Calif State Fair, 47, 49 & 50; Los Angeles Co Mus Art, 55; Santa Barbara Mus Biennial Show. Bibliog: Bette Howell (auth), Twelve California sculptors, Am Artist Mag, 68; Dialogues in art, produced by ABC-TV in Los Angeles, in cooperation with Univ Calif, Los Angeles Exten Serv & Los Angeles Co Mus Art, 69. Media: Bronze. Mailing Add: 3206 Deronda Dr Los Angeles CA 90068

FENDELL, JONAS J
EDUCATOR, PAINTER
b Brooklyn, NY. Study: New Sch Social Res; Brooklyn Mus Art Sch; Syracuse Univ, BFA & MFA. Work: Print collection, Mus Mod Art, New York; painting, Baltimore Mus Art; print, Syracuse Univ; print, Univ Maine; IBM Collection. Exhib: Butler Inst Am Art; Brooklyn Mus Print Show; Baltimore Mus Art; Whitney Mus Am Art; Mus Mod Art. Teaching: Instr design & materials, Md Inst Col Art, 58-; prof design, printing & painting, Essex Col, 68- Pos: Designer, Hurdell/Designs, 56-57; asst dir, Syracuse Mus, 57-58. Awards: Purchase Award, Mus Mod Art, New York; Purchase Prize, Baltimore Mus Art. Mem: Col Art Asn Am. Style & Technique: Semi-abstractions of figure and landscape using water base resins on foam and non-woven material. Dealer: Ifa Gallery 2623 Connecticut Ave NW Washington DC 20008. Mailing Add: 1905 Dixon Rd Baltimore MD 21209

FENDER, TOM MAC
SCULPTOR
b Tyler, Tex, Oct 12, 46. Study: Baylor Univ, BFA, 69; Univ Calif, Los Angeles, MA, 75; also with Bernard Kester & Vasa Mihich. Work: Nat Mus of Mod Art, Kyoto, Japan; Kilpatrick Life Insurance Co, Shreveport, La; AISIN, USA(div of Toyota Indust), Torrance, Calif. Comn: Wrapped & woven sculptures, Aramco Oil Corp, Houston, Tex, 75, Am Med Asn Hq, Chicago, 76 & Shaklee Corp, Oakland, Calif, 77. Exhib: One-man show, Rhythms, Chips & Packages, Allrich Gallery, San Francisco, 76; Texas Artists Show, Dallas Mus of Art,

Tex, 72; Calif Design 76, Pac Design Ctr, Los Angeles, 76; Fiber Works: Am & Japan, Nat Mus of Mod Art, Kyoto & Tokyo, Japan, 77; Fiber/Metal, Boehm Gallery, Palomar Col, San Marcos, Calif, 77; Packages, Kaplan-Baumann Gallery, Los Angeles, 77; California, Riverside Art Ctr, Calif, 77. Teaching: Teaching asst fiber structures, Univ Calif, Los Angeles, 73-75. Bibliog: Bernard Kester (auth), Tom Fender's fiber forms, Artweek, 11/76; Alfred Frankenstein (auth), Winning unique Packages by Tom Fender, San Francisco Chronicle, 11/19/76; Suzanne Muchnic (auth), article in Artweek, 11/77. Style & Technique: Woven sculptures in large scale; miniature package forms in homemade paper and wool. Media: Fiber materials and homemade paper. Dealer: Tamara B Thomas c/o Fine Arts Serv Inc 1075 Irving Blvd Los Angeles CA 90004. Mailing Add: 4802 W Adams Blvd Los Angeles CA 90016

FENDRICK, BARBARA COOPER
ART DEALER
US citizen. Pos: Dir, Fendrick Gallery Specialty: Graphics, works on paper. Mailing Add: 3059 M St NW Washington DC 20007

FENICAL, MARLIN E
PAINTER, PHOTOGRAPHER
b Harrisburg, Pa, July 22, 07. Study: Wellfleet Sch Art; also with Xavier Gonzales & Ben Wolff. Work: Univ Detroit; Rehoboth Art League, Del; Munic Ct & Nat Archives, Washington, DC. Exhib: Washington Watercolor Asn, 53-71; Rehoboth Art League, 58-74; Southeastern Exhib, Atlanta, 60; Va Biennial, Va Mus Fine Arts, 65; Finch Col Mus Art, NY, 74. Pos: Chief art dir, US Army Publs, 47-73; retired. Awards: Washington Watercolor Asn Award, 53; Rehoboth Art League Award, 59, 61 & 70; Am Art League Award, 59 & 63. Bibliog: Beryl Dill Kneen (auth), Artist prepares booklet, Northern Va Sun, 63; Sara Wright (auth), The army's art dir, Fed Times, 67. Mem: Washington Arts Club; Arts Club Washington (chmn pictorial photo comn, 72); Soc Washington Artists; Rehoboth Art League & Artists Equity; Washington Watercolor Asn. Media: Watercolor, Oil. Publ: Auth & illusr, A picture tour of historic Harpers Ferry, privately publ, 61; Collecting nostalgia 1974, Antiques J, 9/72. Mailing Add: 3192 Key Blvd Arlington VA 22201

FENTON, ALAN
PAINTER, INSTRUCTOR
b Cleveland, Ohio, July 29, 27. Study: Pratt Inst, BFA; Art Students League; New Sch Social Res; also pvt study with Adolph Gottlieb & Jack Tworkov; Cleveland Sch Art. Work: Corcoran Gallery Art, Washington, DC; Pace Gallery, New York; Baltimore Mus Art; Ivan Karp Collection & Vincent Melzac Collection. Exhib: Pace Gallery, New York, 65-66; Larry Aldrich Mus, Ridgefield, Conn, 68; Corcoran Gallery Art, 71-72; Bridgeport Mus Art, Conn, 73; NY Cult Ctr Mus, 74; one-man shows, Ft Wayne Mus of Contemp Art, Ind, 77, NC Mus of Art, 77, Houston Mus of Contemp Art, Tex, 77, Univ Iowa Mus of Art, 77 & Phillips Collection, Washington, DC, 77. Teaching: Instr drawing, Pratt Inst, 69-; instr drawing, Housatonic State Col, 71-73; spec asst, Cleveland Inst Art, Ohio, 77-78. Awards: Jury mention, Cleveland Mus Art, 59; jury mention, City Ctr, New York, 59; First Prize, Cleveland Mus Art, 60-61. Mailing Add: 333 Park Ave S New York NY 10010

FENTON, BEATRICE
SCULPTOR
b Philadelphia, Pa, July 12, 87. Study: Philadelphia Mus Sch Indust Art, Pa, 03-04; Pa Acad Fine Arts, 04-11; Cresson scholars to Europe, 09-10; Moore Inst Art, Sci & Indust, hon DFA, 54. Comn: Fountain figure, Brookgreen Gardens, SC; mem tablet, Pratt Libr, Baltimore; mem sun-dial, Rittenhouse Sq, Philadelphia; two fish fountains & seaweed fountain, Fairmount Park, Philadelphia; Comn: Statuettes of dancers & bronze portrait-bust of painter, Marjorie D Martinet, Philadelphia Mus Art, 77; plus many others. Exhib: Pa Acad Fine Arts, 20-68; Philadelphia Art Alliance, 24-65; Nat Sculpture Soc; DaVinci Alliance, 57; Woodmere Art Gallery, 58-68. Teaching: Instr sculpture, Moore Inst Art, Sci & Indust, Philadelphia, 42-53. Awards: Percy M Owens Mem Award, 67; Gold Medal, Pa Acad Fine Arts; Bronze Medal, Sesqui-Centennial Int Expo, Philadelphia. Mem: Philadelphia Art Alliance; fel Nat Sculpture Soc. Media: Bronze. Mailing Add: 621 Westview St Philadelphia PA 19119

FENTON, HOWARD CARTER
PAINTER, EDUCATOR
b Toledo, Ohio, July 2, 10. Study: Chouinard Art Inst; Univ Calif, Los Angeles, BA & MA; also with S McDonald Wright. Work: Santa Barbara Mus Art Calif; Univ Calif, Santa Barbara; Galleria Piazza di Spagna, Rome. Exhib: One-man shows, Santa Barbara Mus Art, 64, Esther Bear Gallery, 66 & 75, Univ Calif Art Galleries, 67, Galleria Piazza di Spagna, 67 & Alwin Gallery, London, 68. Teaching: Prof art, Univ Calif, Santa Barbara, 48- Bibliog: David Gebhard (auth), Howard Fenton, Haagen Press, 68. Mem: Santa Barbara Mus Art; Col Art Asn Am. Style & Technique: Landscape paintings in acrylic and oils. Collection: Contemporary American artists. Dealer: Esther Bear Gallery 1125 High Rd Santa Barbara CA 93103. Mailing Add: 1000 Ladera Lane Santa Barbara CA 93108

FENTON, JULIA ANN
MULTI-MEDIA ARTIST, ART ADMINISTRATOR
b Tupelo, Miss, Feb 11, 37. Study: Millsaps Col, Jackson, Miss, BA(relig), 58; Pa State Univ, grad study in philos & visual arts, 62-65; Atlanta Col of Art, 70-74. Exhib: Exhib Women's Int Yr, 75 & Without Words, 76, Atlanta Bur of Cult Affairs, Ga; Magnetic Image (video show), Atlanta Col of Art, 76; Encuentro Int de Video 1977, Museo de Arte Contemporaneo de Caracas, Venezuela, 77. Pos: Ed & vpres ed affairs & mem bd dirs, Contemp Art/Southwest, 76-77. Mem: Atlanta Artworkers Coalition, Ltd (dir activities & prog coordr, 77-); Atlanta Women's Art Collective. Style & Technique: Post-conceptual, narrative and autobiographical installations. Media: Video and multi-media installations. Publ: Contribr, John Y Fenton (ed), Theology and Body, Westminster, 74; contribr, Contemporary Art/Southeast, 77. Mailing Add: 397 Emory Dr NE Atlanta GA 30307

FERBER, ELISE VAN HOOK
ART ADMINISTRATOR, CURATOR
b New York, NY. Study: Smith Col, BA; NY Univ Grad Sch. Pos: Asst to cur, Mus Mod Art, New York, 37-45; res asst, Am Inst Architects, Washington, DC, 54-56; mus cur, Nat Gallery Art, 56-70 & cur in charge of art info serv, 72-; asst to dir, Dumbarton Oaks Res Libr & Col, 70-72. Mailing Add: Nat Gallery of Art Washington DC 20565

FERBER, HERBERT
SCULPTOR, PAINTER
b New York, NY, Apr 30, 06. Study: Beaux-Arts Inst Design; City Col New York; Columbia Univ. Work: Metrop Mus Art, Whitney Mus Am Art & Mus Mod Art, New York; Albright-Knox Art Gallery, Buffalo; Detroit Inst Art; plus others. Comn: Copper sculpture, John F Kennedy Off Bldg, Boston; copper & environ sculpture, Rutgers Univ; steel sculpture, Am Dental Asn Bldg, Chicago; steel sculpture, Ottumur, Iowa; plus others. Exhib: Whitney Mus Am Art; Mus Mod Art, New York; Pa Acad Fine Arts; Boston Mus Fine Arts; Documenta 5, Kassel, Ger; plus others. Teaching: Vis prof sculpture, Univ Pa, Rutgers Univ. Bibliog: Many articles in nat art periodicals. Mailing Add: 44 MacDougal St New York NY 10012

FERGUSON, CHARLES
PAINTER, ART HISTORIAN
b Fishers Island, NY, June 30, 18. Study: Williams Col, AB; Art Students League, painting with Frank Dumond & graphics with Harry Sternberg; Trinity Col, MA. Work: New Britain Mus Am Art, Conn; Mattatuck Mus, Waterbury, Conn. Comn: Stained glass window, Fishers Island, 71; murals, Williston Acad, Easthampton, Mass, Renbrook Sch, West Hartford, Conn & private home, Fishers Island. Exhib: Conn Acad Fine Arts; Conn Watercolor Soc; Greater Hartford Civic Arts Festival. Collections Arranged: Aaron Draper Shattuck, 70; Robert B Brandegee, 71; William T Richards, 73; Dennis Miller Buwiler, 78. Teaching: Instr hist art & studio painting, Trinity Col; instr hist art & studio painting, Loomis Sch. Pos: Dir, New Britain Mus Am Art, 65-; chmn, New Britain Design Rev Comt. Awards: Sage Allan Prize, 69; New Britain Herald Prize, 70; Sanford Low Prize, Conn Acad Fine Arts, 71. Mem: Conn Acad Fine Arts (pres); Henry L Ferguson Mus, Fishers Island (vpres). Mailing Add: 56 Lexington St New Britain CT 06052

FERGUSON, EDWARD ROBERT
PAINTER, PRINTMAKER
b Pueblo, Colo, Mar 21, 14. Study: Flint Inst Arts, 33-37. Work: Flint Inst Arts, Mich; Detroit Inst Arts; Carter Mus Western Art, Ft Worth, Tex; Hunterdon Co Art Ctr, Clinton, NJ; Panama Art Asn, Panama City Auditorium, Fla. Comn: Portrait murals, Genessee Co Court House, Flint, Mich, 39-68. Exhib: 18th Nat Exhib Prints, Libr Cong, Washington, DC, 60; Contemp Graphic Arts Overseas Exhib Exhib, Soc Am Graphic Artists, 61; Print Fair, Burr Galleries, New York & Free Libr Philadelphia, 62; Northwest Printmakers 35th Int Exhib, Seattle Art Mus & Portland Art Mus, 64; First Ann Exhib Lithography, Fla State Univ, 64. Awards: Dr Herbert Schiller Purchase Award, South Bend Art Asn, Ind, 62; Seventh Nat Print Exhib Purchase Award, Hunterdon Co Art Ctr, 63; 11th Bay Ann Art Show Purchase Award, Panama Art Asn, 72. Media: Oil, Acrylic. Mailing Add: 1618 Carolina Ave Lynn Haven FL 32444

FERGUSON, FRANK WAYNE
INTERMEDIA ARTIST
b Grenada, Miss, Jan 31, 47. Study: Mont State Univ, BS, 70, MFA, 76; Eastern Mont Col, BA, 73, with Whibon (Peter W Warren). Work: Mont State Univ, Bozeman; Oxo Found, Butte, Mont; Kansas City Art Inst, Mo. Comn: Landscape, (15ft x 23ft), Billings Mont Youth Ctr, 73; graphic, (10ft x 50ft), Watson Furniture Systs, Seattle, Wash, 74. Exhib: Calif Inst Arts, Valencia, 74; Schwarz Gallery, Milan, Italy, 74; Contemp Arts Gallery, New York, 75; Venice Biennale, Venice, Italy, 76; Nat Gallery, Wellington, NZ, 76; Los Angeles Inst Contemp Art, Calif, 77; Galerie Marika Malacorda, Geneva, Switz, 77. Collections Arranged: Postfolk 1978 show of 150 artists, Mont State Univ, Bozeman. Pos: Nat chmn, Nat Acad Conceptualists, Bozeman, Mont, 74-75; pres, Buffalo Energy Co, Bozeman, 74-77; founder, Postfolk Movement, Bozeman, 77- Bibliog: Neil Megson (auth), Critic, Arts & Artists Mag, 75; Tom Cassidy (auth), Critic, Portland Scribe, 77. Mem: Int Artists Coop; United SLUJ Workers (treas); Contart, E Berlin Hq. Style & Technique: Postfolk: cooperative intermedia using sculpture, graphics, mails and contextual situations. Media: Mail; Intermedia. Publ: Contribr, Vile San Francisco, California, Banada Prods, 75-77; contribr, The SLUJ Book, SLUJ Press, Billings, Mont, 76; contribr, One and Done, Running Dog Press, Chicago, 76; contribr, Spatial Poem, Mieko Shiomi, Osaka, Japan, 76; contribr, Assembling Press, New York, 78. Mailing Add: 403 N Broadway Bozeman MT 59715

FERGUSON, GARTH MICHELE
ART HISTORIAN, EDUCATOR
b Anderson, SC, Sept 14, 42. Study: Univ of NC, Chapel Hill, BA(art ed), 65; Va Commonwealth Univ, MA(art hist), 70. Collections Arranged: The Floating World of Japanese Prints (auth, catalog), Mint Mus Art, Charlotte, NC, 71. Teaching: Prof art, Wingate Col, NC, 66-; exchange prof art, Osaka Seikei Gakuen, Osaka, Japan, 67-68. Awards: Teacher of the Yr at Wingate Col, 72. Mem: Southeastern Col Art Conf; Am Asn Univ Profs; Art League of Union Co. Res: Authority on Fernand Lèger, compiling comprehensive bibliography on Lèger and researching his four visits to the United States. Mailing Add: PO Box 171 Wingate NC 28174

FERGUSON, KATHLEEN ELIZABETH
SCULPTOR
b Chicago, Ill, Jan 31, 45. Study: Stephens Col, Columbia, Mo, 63-64; Layton Sch of Art, Milwaukee, Wis, BFA, 69; RI Sch of Design, Providence, MFA. Exhib: The 1st Ann Sculpture Exhib, Hundred Acres Gallery, New York, 71; one-person shows, Smithsonian Inst, Washington, DC, 72, Conn Col, New London, 74 & Univ RI, Kingston, 75; Va Mus of Fine Arts, Richmond, 73; Drawing Invitational, Rutgers Univ, NJ, 75; Biennial of Contemp Am Art, Whitney Mus of Am Art, New York, 75; Ginza Nissan Gallery, Tokyo, Japan, 76. Collections Arranged: Artist Space, New York, 75; Am Narrative/Story Art: 1967-1977, Contemp Arts Mus, Houston, Tex, 77; Pvt Myths, Queens Mus, Flushing, NY, 78. Teaching: Teacher children's art, Wis Comn for Educ, 68-69; asst prof ceramics, Long Island Univ, Greenvale, NY, 73-75; asst prof sculpture, Nassau Community Col, Garden City, NY, 75-76. Bibliog: Phil Casey (auth), Why Teeth, Washington Post, 72; William Zimmer (auth), This is Not a Pipe, Soho Weekly News, 77; Peter Frank (auth), Small is Beautiful, Village Voice, 77. Style & Technique: Fabric reliefs constructed over wire mesh; complex forms; blend of elegance and macabre expressionism. Media: White plaster-fabric and ceramic. Publ: Auth & illusr, A Romance, pvt publ, 72; contribr, Milton Klonsky (auth), Speaking Pictures, Crown, 74; auth & illusr, Natti's Navigations, pvt publ, 78. Dealer: Nobe Gallery 250 W 57th St New York NY 10019. Mailing Add: 23-25 Warren St New York NY 10007

FERIOLA, JAMES PHILIP
PAINTER, ART ADMINISTRATOR
b Great Notch, NJ, July 4, 25. Study: Phoenix Sch Design, New York, grad. Work: Nassau Co Mus, Syosset, NY; R Peerman Corp & H Butt Corp, Corpus Christi, Tex; Country Art Gallery, Locust Valley, NY. Exhib: Smithsonian Inst, Washington, DC; Nat Acad Design, New York; New York World's Fair Fine Arts Pavilion; Hammond Mus; Prince Rainier III Palace, Monaco. Teaching: Instr watercolor, Baldwin Art Ctr, NY. Pos: Supvr art & exhib dept, Nassau Co Mus, presently. Awards: Gold Medal of Honor, Smithsonian Inst; Travel Grant to Europe, Greenwich Village Art Show; Silver Medal Honor, Am Vet Soc Artists. Bibliog: Famous People of Hempstead, NY (film). Mem: Am Watercolor Soc; Hudson Valley Artists; Am Artists Prof League; Am Vet Soc Artists; Art League of Nassau Co. Media: Watercolor. Publ: Illusr, Of plates and purlins; illusr, A rural heritage for today. Mailing Add: 226 Perry St Hempstead NY 11550

FERN, ALAN MAXWELL
ART HISTORIAN, ART ADMINISTRATOR
b Detroit, Mich, Oct 19, 30. Study: Univ Chicago, AB, 50, MA, 54 & PhD, 60; Courtauld Inst, Univ London, res scholar. Collections Arranged: Diverse print, poster & photo shows, Libr Cong, 62-; Leonard Baskin, Nat Collection Fine Arts, Smithsonian Inst, 70. Teaching: From asst to instr to asst prof, The Col, Univ Chicago, 52-61. Pos: From asst cur to cur, asst chief to chief, Prints & Photographs Div, Libr Cong, 61-76, dir, Res Dept, 76- Awards: Fulbright Fel, 54-55. Mem: Print Coun Am (dir, 63-, pres, 69-71); Col Art Asn Am; Am Inst Graphic Arts (dir, 68-71); Spec Libr Asn; Grolier Club. Res: History of prints, posters, book design, 19th and 20th century art. Publ: Auth, A note on the Eragny Press, Cambridge Univ Press, 57; co-auth, Art nouveau, 60 & auth, Word and image, 69, Mus Mod Art, New York; auth, Leonard Baskin, Smithsonian Press, 70; co-auth, Revolutionary Soviet film posters, Johns Hopkins Press, 74. Mailing Add: Res Dept Libr of Congress Washington DC 20540

FERNANDES, MICHAEL ADRIAN
PAINTER, INSTRUCTOR
b Port-of-Spain, Trinidad & Tobago, WI, Mar 5, 44; Can citizen. Study: Montreal Mus Sch Fine Arts. Work: Mt Allison Univ, NB, Can. Exhib: Group show, Montreal Mus Art, Can, 66; Expo 67, Trinidad & Tobago Pavillion, 67; West Indian Artist Aborad, Saidye Bronfman Centre, Montreal, Que, 67; Black Show, Meldura Centre, Australia, 75; one-man shows, Eye Level Gallery, Halifax, NS, Can, 75, 76 & 77, Dalhousie Univ, Halifax, NS, Can, 75 & Mt Allison Univ, Sackville, NB, 77; Atlantic Coast Journal (circulated to five centres in Can & Can Cult Centre & Paris, France), 76; 03-23-03 Projects/Performances, Nat Gallery Can, Ottawa, Ont, 77. Teaching: Instr drawing, NS Col Arts & Design, presently. Pos: Mem bd, Eye Level Gallery, 75-76. Style & Technique: Mixed media. Mailing Add: 2146 Brunswick St Halifax NS B3K 2Y8 Can

FERNANDO, PACHECO
See Castro

FERNIE, JOHN CHIPMAN
SCULPTOR, INSTRUCTOR
b Hutchinson, Kans, Oct 22, 45. Study: Colo Col, 63-65; Kansas City Art Inst, BFA, 68; Univ Calif, Davis, grant, 69, teaching fel & MFA, 70. Exhib: One-man shows, Reese Palley Gallery, 70 & 72, Sacramento State Col, 72, Nova Scotia Col Art, 74 & John Gibson Gallery, 77; group shows, Documenta 5, Kasel, Ger, 72; 8th & 9th Biennale de Paris; Israel Mus, 76; Houston Mus of Contemp Art, 77; plus others. Teaching: Asst, Univ Calif, Davis, 69; instr sculpture, Calif Col Arts & Crafts, 70-72; instr sculpture, Stephens Col, 72-75, instr sculpture, Nova Scotia Col Art & Design, 75- Bibliog: Richardson (auth), article in Arts Mag, 2/71; Albright (auth), Exciting, compelling show, San Francisco Chronicle, 7/1/71; Jochimsen (auth), Magazin Kunst, 7/74. Style & Technique: Technique involves looking around a lot and thinking about it; materials used are frequently very weighty. Media: Wood, Cardboard, Photo, Plaster. Publ: Auth, Petit trianon, twikkel, I worship you, God bless your symmetry, 70; auth, Masters survey, 70. Dealer: John Gibson 392 W Broadway New York NY 10012. Mailing Add: PO Box 1057 Nederland CO 80466

FERRARI, VIRGINIO LUIG
SCULPTOR, EDUCATOR
b Verona, Italy, Apr 11, 37. Study: Scuola d'Arte & Acad Cignaroli, Verona. Work: Biennale Nazionale di Verona; High Mus Art, Atlanta, Ga; Fondazione Pagani, Legnano, Famiglia Meneguzzo, Malo, Vicenza & Univ di Parma Museo, Italy. Comn: Bronzes, Doctor's Hosp, Philadelphia, 63, Wyler Children's Hosp, 66 & Pick Hall for Int Studies, Univ Chicago, 70, Northwestern Univ, Evanston, Ill, 73 & Univ Miami, 75; bronze fountain, Loyola Univ Med Ctr, Hines, Ill, 66. Exhib: Inst Contemp Art, Philadelphia, 66; Art Inst Chicago, 68; Mus Contemp Art, Chicago, 68; Brooklyn Mus, 68; traveling exhibs, State Ill Arts Coun, 69 & Ill Bronzetto Italiano, 71. Teaching: Asst prof sculpture, Univ Chicago, 67- Pos: Sculptor in residence, Univ Chicago, 66- Awards: Cinisello Balsamo Milano, Italy, 63; Nostra Ministero Publica, Istruzione Roma, Italy, 64; Biennale Nazionale di Verona, 65. Bibliog: Arturo Quitavalle, Ferrari Gocce d'Amor Pop, Univ di Parma, 70. Mem: Sindacato Artisti; Arts Club Chicago. Style & Technique: Lyrical abstract. Media: Bronze; Electronic; Stainless Steel. Mailing Add: 5429 East View Park Chicago IL 60615

FERREIRA, (ARMANDO) THOMAS
EDUCATOR, SCULPTOR
b Charleston, WVa, Jan 8, 32. Study: Chouinard Inst; Long Beach City Col; Univ Calif, Los Angeles, BA & MA. Work: Wichita Art Asn Galleries; State Calif Collection; Univ Utah Art Mus. Exhib: One-man shows, Pasadena Mus, 59, Long Beach Mus, 59 & 69 & Ariz State Univ, 62; Mus of Contemp Crafts, 58; Los Angeles Co Mus, 58, 60 & 66; Wichita Art Mus, Kans, 59, 60, 61, 66, 68 & 70; Smithsonian Inst, 61; Fine Arts Gallery, San Diego, 61, 69 & 73; Art Mus, Oakland, Calif, 63; Otis Art Inst Galleries, 65; Pasadena Mus of Art, 68; Univ of Calif, Santa Barbara, 73. Teaching: Prof ceramic sculpture, Calif State Univ Long Beach, 57- Awards: Purchase Award, Calif Expos, 61 & Wichita Art Asn, 66. Mem: Nat Asn Schs Art (bd dirs, 74-). Style & Technique: Sculpture abstract monolithic. Media: Stoneware. Mailing Add: 7871 Cramer St Long Beach CA 90808

FERRER, RAFAEL
PAINTER, SCULPTOR
b Santurce, PR, 1933. Study: Saunton Military Acad, Va, 48-51; Syracuse Univ, NY, 51-52; Univ PR, Mayaquez, 52-54, with E Granell. Exhib: Art of Latin Am, Pa Acad of Fine Arts, Philadelphia, 67; Outdoor Sculpture, Univ PR, Mayaquez, 68; When Attitudes Become Form, Kunsthalle Bern, Switz, 69; Op Losse Schroven, Stedelijk Mus, Amsterdam, 69; Univ PR, Mayaquez, 69; Info, Mus Mod Art, New York, 70; Whitney Mus Am Art Ann, New York, 70; Depth & Presence, Corcoran Gallery Art, Washington, DC, 71; Biennial of Medellin, Colombia, SAm, 72; Whitney Biennial, 73; one-man shows, Univ PR Mus, 64, Leo Castelli Gallery, New York, 68 & 70, Philadelphia Mus Art, Pa, 70, Univ Pa, Philadelphia, 71, Whitney Mus, 71, Pasadena Mus Art, Calif, 72, Contemp Art Ctr, Cincinnati, Ohio, 73, Nancy Hoffman Gallery, New York, 74 & 75 & Mus Mod Art, New York, 74. Bibliog: Stephen Prokopff (auth), Rafael Ferrer, an interview, Art & Artists, London, 4/72; Kenneth Baker (auth), New York: Rafael Ferrer, Whitney Museum, Artforum, 3/72; J L Dunham (auth), Rafael Ferrer, Artweek, Oakland, Calif, 11/74. Dealer: Nancy Hoffman Gallery 429 W Broadway New York NY 10012. Mailing Add: 511 Mt Pleasant Ave Philadelphia PA 19199

FERRIS, (CARLISLE) KEITH
ILLUSTRATOR, PAINTER
b Honolulu, Hawaii, May 14, 29. Study: Tex A&M Col; George Washington Univ; Corcoran Sch Art. Comn: Ser of paintings, Pratt & Whitney Aircraft, Chandler Evans Div, Colt Industs, Fairchild Republic, Grumman, Gen Dynamics, Aviation Week, Space Tech & many others. Exhib: USAF Exhib, New York Soc Illusr, 61-78; USAF Hq, The Pentagon, Washington, DC; mural (25 ft x 75 ft, or 1875 sq ft), Nat Air & Space Mus, Smithsonian Inst, Washington, DC, 76; one-man shows, Aerospace Hall, Nat Air & Space Mus, Smithsonian Inst, Washington, DC, 69-70 & New York Soc Illusr, 70. Pos: Art dir/prod mgr, Cassell Watkins Paul Art Studio, St Louis, 52-56; chmn, Air Force Art Comt, Soc Illusr, 68-70. Awards: Citation of Merit, Soc Illusr, 66. Mem: NY Soc Illusr. Style & Technique: Realistic oil paintings; aviation/aerospace art. Mailing Add: 50 Moraine Rd Morris Plains NJ 07950

FERRIS, EDYTHE
PAINTER, GRAPHIC ARTIST
b Riverton, NJ, June 21, 97. Study: Philadelphia Sch Design for Women, dipl. Work: Free Libr Philadelphia; Philadelphia Mus Art; Archive Collection, Can Painters & Etchers, Toronto Mus; Randolph-Macon Woman's Col; Philadelphia Art Alliance. Exhib: Norfolk Drawing Biennial, Va, 64; Artists Equity Asn Mem, Civic Ctr, Philadelphia, 68 & 71; Fibonocci Exhib, Art Alliance, Philadelphia, 72; Am Color Print Soc Ann, Philadelphia Art Alliance, 72; retrospective, Univ City Arts League, Philadelphia, 74. Collections Arranged: 78 exhibs of living artists of German origin or ancestry in Old Customs House for Carl Schurz Asn, 53-64; 20 traveling exhibs of original prints, German Expressionists, with notes & catalogue, 57-67. Teaching: Dir crafts, adult educ, Cent YWCA, Philadelphia, 34-38; dir crafts, Fletcher Farm, Proctorsville, Vt, summers 34-36; instr crafts, Montgomery Co Day Sch, Wynnewood, Pa, 42-49; lectr art appreciation, Junto, Philadelphia, 50-54. Pos: Art adv, Nat Carl Schurz Asn, 53-67; founder neighborhood rehabilitation proj, Friends of Clark Park, 75. Awards: J Lessing Rosenwald Prize for woodcut, Print Club, 55; hon mention, Am Automobile Asn, 70. Bibliog: Bet Jones (auth, Two bird pictures, Randolph Macon Woman's Col, 68; Janet Mowery (auth), The birds of Edythe Ferris and Morris Graves, 69. Mem: Am Color Print Soc; Artists Equity Asn; Moore Col Art Alumnae; Univ City Arts League (founder, 65). Media: Oil. Publ: Contrib, American German Review, various years during 50's. Dealer: Sidney Rothman—The Gallery Barnegat Light NJ 08006. Mailing Add: 240 S 45th St Philadelphia PA 19104

FERRITER, CLARE
PAINTER, COLLAGE ARTIST
b Dickinson, NDak, June 18, 13. Study: Mass Col Art, Boston; Yale Univ, BFA; Stanford Univ, MA. Work: Butler Inst Am Art, Youngstown, Ohio; Harcourt, Brace, Jovanovich, Inc, New York; George Washington Univ; Massillon Mus, Ohio; Addison Gallery Am Art, Andover, Mass. Comn: Portrait of Miss H D Lamont, comn by Class of 1909 for Westover Sch, Middlebury, Conn, 59. Exhib: One-man shows, Univ PR Mus, 62, Corcoran Gallery Art, Washington, DC, 63, Franz Bader Gallery, Washington, DC, 64 & 76 & Int Monetary Fund, Washington, DC, 73; regional exhibs, Del Art Ctr, Wilmington, 66, Baltimore Mus, 68 & Univ Del, 71. Teaching: Instr art, MacMurray Col, 36-38; instr art, Westover Sch, 40-42; lectr painting, Cath Univ Am, 66- Awards: Nat Asn Women Artists, 63 & 66; Baltimore Mus, 66; Soc Washington Artists, 64, 66 & 72. Mem: Nat Asn Women Artists; Washington Watercolor Asn; Soc Washington Artists; Artists Equity Asn. Style & Technique: The art of improvisation, abstractions based on nature; use of gold, metal & aluminum leaf. Media: Oil, Acrylic, Metallic. Publ: Illusr, Manila lights and shadows (weekly page), Manila Sun Tribune Mag, 10/4/31-8/32; illusr, covers in Philippine Mag, 9/32-2/33. Dealer: Franz Bader Gallery 2124 Pennsylvania Ave Washington DC 20037. Mailing Add: 4722 Rodman St NW Washington DC 20016

FERRO, WALTER
PRINTMAKER
b Brooklyn, NY. Study: Art Students League, 46-48; Brooklyn Mus Art Sch, color theory with John Ferren, 48-52. Work: Permanent print collection, Metrop Mus Art, New York. Exhib: Audubon Artists, 53; Am Inst Graphic Artists, 56 & Soc Am Graphic Artists, New York, 59; United Nations Traveling Exhib, 66; one-man show, Kings Col, 67. Awards: Kenneth Hays Miller Mem Prize, Audubon Artists, 53; Kate W Arms Mem Award, Soc Am Graphic Artists, 59; Guggenheim Fel, 72. Bibliog: Norman Kent (auth), The woodcuts of Walter Ferro, Am Artist Mag, 1/62. Style & Technique: Cutting and printing of multi-color woodblocks utilizing transparent colors to create infinite color effects. Media: Woodcuts. Publ: Illusr, The best of two worlds, Morrow, 53; illusr, Beowulf, Random, 62; illusr, Hold April, McGraw, 62; illusr, UN calendar, UN, 66; illusr, The invisible pyramid, Scribner, 70; illusr, Another Kind of Autumn, Scribners, 77. Mailing Add: RD 2 Hoyt Rd Pound Ridge NY 10576

FERRON, MARCELLE
GLASS ARTIST
Study: Prof-Aggregee. Work: Stedelick, Amsterdam; Mus Sao Paulo; Mus of British Arts, Montreal; Mus Quebec; Nat Gallery Can. Comn: Metro; Gouv of Quebec, 67; metro-vendome, City of Montreal, 78; murals, La Portage, Can Govt, 74; sculpture, Int Aviation, 76; stained glass, church, Quebec. Exhib: Antagnismes, Le Louvre, Paris, 59; Les Automatistes J Borduas, Grand Palais, Paris, 72; Peintres Canadians, Tate Gallery, Londreu, 66; Silver medals Biennial, Sao Paulo, 61; one-woman shows, Paris, 57, 60, 72 & Bruxelles & Munich, 58, 62 & 66. Dealer: Galerie Gilles Corbeil 2165 Crescent Montreal PQ H3G 2C1 Can Mailing Add: 218 Bloomfield Outremont PQ H2V 3R4 Can

FESSLER, MARY THOMASITA
See Sister Thomasita

FETT, WILLIAM F
INSTRUCTOR, PAINTER
b Ann Arbor, Mich, Sept 22, 18. Study: Sch Art Inst, Chicago. Work: Mus Mod Art, New York; Mus Mod Art, Rome, Italy; Chicago Art Inst; Mus Mod Art, Mexico City; Weatherspoon Art Gallery, Univ NC, Greensboro. Exhib: Romantic Paintings in America, Mus Mod Art, New York, 43; one-man shows, Int Watercolor Show, Art Inst Chicago, 44, De Young Mus, San Francisco, 54 & Weatherspoon Art Gallery, Univ NC, Greensboro, 71; Seattle Art Mus, Wash, 45; Santa Barbara Mus Art, Calif, 45; Mex-Am Cult Inst, Mexico City, 65; Watercolor USA, Springfield Art Mus, Mo, 71. Teaching: Prof drawing & painting, Art Sch, Washington Univ, St Louis, Mo, 46- Awards: Anna Louise Raymond Grad Student Award, Art Inst Chicago, 41-43; Fulbright Scholar to Italy, US Govt, 50-51. Style & Technique: Abstract Surrealism, using wet paper technique in watercolor and later in oils, drawing in charcoal, ink, pencil, etc. Media: Watercolor; Oil; Charcoal. Publ: Articles in View Mag, View Inc, New York, 43, Dyn Mag, Wolfgang Paalen, Mex, 45 & Romantic Paintings in America, Mus Mod Art, New York, 44. Dealer: Martin Schweig Gallery 4647 Maryland Ave St Louis MO 63108. Mailing Add: Art Sch Washington Univ St Louis MO 63130

FEUERHERM, KURT K
PAINTER
b Berlin, Ger, Mar 3, 25. Study: Albright Art Sch; Univ Rochester, BFA; Cranbrook Acad Art, MFA; Yale Summer Sch, Norfolk, Conn, with Naumgabo, Peter Blume & Ben Shawn; Yale Univ, with Josef Albers, Stuart Davis & Abraham Rattner. Work: Cranbrook Art Mus,

Bloomfield Hills, Mich; Mem Art Gallery, Rochester, NY; Albright-Knox Art Gallery, Buffalo, NY; Henry Gallery, Univ Wash, Seattle; Am Fedn Art. Comn: Ceramic abstract mural, Midtown Plaza, Rochester, NY, 64; Stations on the Cross, Our Lady of Mercy Church, Rochester, 64; St John's the Evangelist Church, Rochester, 65; Liberty Pole (consult designer), City of Rochester, 66. Exhib: American Painting Today, Metrop Mus Art, New York, 50; Cranbrook Painting Exhib, Bloomfield Hills, Mich, 52; Finger Lakes Exhib, Rochester, NY, 53-76; Recent Acquisitions, Contemp Art Ctr, Cincinnati, Ohio, 55; 25th Graphic Arts & Drawing Exhib, Wichita, Kans, 56; Columbia Mus of Art Painting Biennial, SC, 57; Everson Mus Art, Syracuse, NY, 57-70; one-man shows, Univ Rochester Gallery, NY, 57 & Henry Gallery, Univ Wash, Seattle, 69; New York Crafts, Munson-Williams-Proctor Inst, Utica, NY, 61; four-man show, Mem Art Gallery, Univ Rochester Fac Show, 70. Teaching: Asst prof painting, Univ Rochester, NY, 60-71; mentor studio arts, Empire State Col, Rochester, 73- Pos: Conservator, Intermuseum Lab, Oberlin, Ohio, 71-72. Awards: Purchase Awards (painting & watercolor), Cortland Art Mus, 53; Award of Merit, Columbia Painting Biennial, 57; Henri Projansky Award, Rochester Finger Lakes Exhib, 69. Style & Technique: Abstract langscape done in collage, stain and gravity painting. Media: Collage; Acrylic. Dealer: Oxford Gallery 267 Oxford St Rochester NY 14607; Malton Gallery 2709 Observatory Ave Cincinnati OH 45208. Mailing Add: 70 Harper St Rochester NY 14607

FEUERSTEIN, ROBERTA
ART DEALER
b Los Angeles, Calif, Apr 16, 50. Pos: Dir-owner, Bird's Eye View Gallery. Specialty: Contemporary prints, paintings and sculpture. Mailing Add: c/o Bird's Eye View Gallery 3420 Via Oporto 3 Newport Beach CA 92663

FICHTER, HERBERT FRANCIS
PRINTMAKER, PAINTER
b Jamaica, Long Island, NY, Dec 25, 20. Study: Sch Art League Scholar, New York Sch Fine & Applied Arts, 39; Corcoran Sch Art, Washington, DC; spec instr with Hal Reed, 75-76. Work: Pennell Collection, Libr Cong, Washington, DC; J F Kennedy Libr, Mass; MGM Grand Hotel, Las Vegas, Nev; Life/Time Mag Collection, New York; Parker Farms Collection, El Centro, Calif. Comn: Portrait of B De Klyn, comn by Dr Ward De Klyn, Danbury, Conn, 57; Oil-Scotch motif, Vince Dundee, Scotch Mist Restaurant, LaCanada, Calif, 65; portrait of Kathy Woodhouse, comn by R Woodhouse, Sunland, Calif, 65; Oil figure, Stockton Elec Co, Montrose, Calif, 66; three paintings for pub rels, comn by William Freelove for McDonalds, New Bern & Greenville, NC, 74-75. Exhib: Pennell Show, Libr Cong, Washington, DC, 50-52; Traveling exhib, Carnegie Inst, Pittsburgh, Pa, 51; Soc Am Etchers, Kennedy Gallery, New York, 52; Bi-Ann, Corcoran Gallery Art, Washington, DC, 53; Bi-Ann, Laguna Mus Art, Calif, 76; Nat Exhib, Fla Miniature Soc, Clearwater, 77; Nat Exhib, Soc Miniature Soc, Clinton, 78; two-man show, Burbank Creative Arts Ctr, Calif, 51; one-man show, Intalgio Graphics, Smithsonian Inst, Washington, DC, 51. Teaching: Instr in banknote engraving, Vignette Engraving, Jefferies Banknote Co, Los Angeles, 62- Pos: Banknote Engraver, Bur of Engraving & Printing, Washington, DC, 41-54. Awards: Purchase, Ann Pennell, Libr Cong, 51; Kate W Arms Mem, Kennedy Gallery, Soc Am Etchers, 52; First Graphics, Nat Exhib, Miniature Art Soc NJ, 78. Bibliog: Man of Steel, article in Ticor Mag, 74; Staff auth of Bank of Am, Traveler's Checques, Banking Bus, 72; David Kuczynski (auth), Techniques on Engraving, Artists Market, 77. Mem: Coun of Traditional Artists, Pasadena, Calif (bd mem); Calif Art Club, Los Angeles; Los Angeles Art Asn; Laguna Art-A-Fair Festival, Calif. Style & Technique: Traditional banknote engraving, semi-surrealistic and traditional; intaglio, copper and steel; oils traditional and surrealism. Media: Intaglio Mediums, Engraving thru Mezzotint; Oils on Canvas & Panels. Mailing Add: c/o Jeffries Banknote Co 1330 W Pico Blvd Los Angeles CA 90015

FICHTER, ROBERT
PHOTOGRAPHER
Study: Univ Fla, MFA(printmaking & painting), 63; Ind Univ, MFA, 66. Work: Int Mus Photog, George Eastman House, Rochester, NY; Pasadena Art Mus, Calif; Nat Gallery of Can, Ottawa; Mus Fine Arts, Boston, Mass; Princeton Univ, NJ. Exhib: Thirteen Contemp Photogr, Tex Tech Univ Gallery, Lubbock, 73; Photog into Art, Camden Art Ctr, Eng, 73; Recent Acquisitions, Int Mus Photog, George Eastman House, 73; Lens & Light, Hudson River Mus, Yonkers, NY, 73; Shaping of Vision, Santa Rosa Jr Col, Calif, 74; Photog Dir, State Univ Col, New Paltz, NY, 74; Contemp Photog from the Collections, Boston Mus Fine Arts, 74; Photog Unlimited, Fogg Mus, Harvard Univ, Cambridge, Mass, 74; Hist of Photog as Subject Matter, Orange Coast Jr Col, Costa Mesa, Calif & Friends of Photog, Carmel, Calif, 75; New Am Graphics, Madison Art Ctr, Wis, 75; VSW Ripoff Show, Visual Studies Workshop, Rochester, NY, 75; one-man shows, Recent Photo-Drawings, Univ Calif, Davis, 70, Robert Fichter, Ctr of the Eye Gallery, Aspen, Colo, 72 & Sch of Dayton Art Inst, Ohio, 73, The Black Winged Heart, Light Gallery, New York, 74, Robert Fichter/Photogr/Filmmaker, Sch of Art Inst Chicago, 74 & Univ NMex Art Gallery, 75. Mailing Add: c/o Dept of Art Univ Calif 405 Hilgard Ave Los Angeles CA 90024

FICKLEN, JACK HOWELLS
CARTOONIST
b Waco, Tex, Apr 18, 11. Study: Southern Methodist Univ, 30-32; Dallas Creative Ctr, 64- Work: Asn Am Ed Cartoonists. Exhib: Archiv Am Art; Detroit Univ; Mo Sch Journalism; Wayne State Univ. Pos: Sports cartoonist, Dallas News, 37-40, ed cartoonist, 37-40 & 46-; syndicated cartoonist, Register & Tribune Syndicate, Des Moines, 40-45; owner & mgr, Avalon Features Syndicate, Dallas, 60- Mem: Am Ed Cartoonists Asn; Artists & Craftsmen Asn, Dallas (pres, 75-76); Asn of Traditional Artists, Dallas. Publ: Illusr, Fundamental Principles of Driving, 45; illusr, Self Government by Texans, 50. Mailing Add: 6657 Avalon Ave Dallas TX 75214

FIELD, LYMAN
ART ADMINISTRATOR, COLLECTOR
b Kansas City, Mo, Oct 6, 14. Study: Univ Kans, AB, 36; Harvard Law Sch, LLB, 39. Pos: Founding mem, Mo State Coun on Arts, 65-75, chmn, 66-74; founding mem & 1st chmn, NAm Assembly of State & Prov Arts Agencies, 68-70; trustee & bd dir, Kansas City Art Inst, 69-74; mem bd dir, Findlay Galleries, Chicago, New York, Palm Beach, Fla & Paris, France, 72-76; participant, 46th Am Assembly on Art Mus, Arden House, Harriman, NY, 75; chmn, Thomas Hart Benton Homestead Mem Adv Comn of Mo, 75-, trustee Benton Testamentary Trusts. Mem: Kress Found, New York (trustee, 65-); Mid-Am Arts Alliance, Mo (mem bd dir, 71-); Kansas City Soc of Western Art (mem bd dir, 75-); Soc Fellows Atkins-Nelson Gallery of Art, Kansas City, Mo. Collection: Thomas Hart Benton paintings & lithographs; Jansem, Kluge, Michel Henry & Ardissone paintings. Mailing Add: 600 E 11th St Kansas City MO 64106

FIELD, PHILIP SIDNEY
PAINTER, PRINTMAKER
b Brooklyn, NY, Sept 17, 42. Study: Art Students League with Arnold Blanch; Syracuse Univ, BFA, 63; Yale Norfolk Summer Sch of Music & Art, 62; RI Sch of Design with Michael Mazur, MFA, 65; Fulbright grant, Vienna Acad of Fine Arts, 65-67. Work: Ark Arts Ctr, Little Rock; Hunterdon Art Ctr, Clinton, NJ; Syracuse Univ; Univ Dallas; Tulsa City-Co Libr, Okla. Exhib: One-man shows, Terrain Graphics Gallery, New York, 73 & Art Mus of STex, Corpus Christi, 76; Colorprint USA, Nat Exhib, Lubbock, Tex, 73, 74 & 77; Prints, Drawings & Crafts Ann, Ark Arts Ctr, 74 & 76; Fantastic Images & Imaginary Worlds, Ark Arts Ctr, 75; Boston Printmakers Ann, Boston Mus of Fine Arts, 75; Nat Print Show, Hunterdon Art Ctr, 75; Southwestern Prints & Drawings, Dallas Mus of Fine Arts, 75; Miami Graphics Biennale, Fla, 75; 3rd Print Invitational, Univ Dallas, 76; Dulin Nat Print & Drawing Competition, Dulin Gallery of Art, Knoxville, Tenn, 76 & 77; Nat Print & Drawing Competition, Okla Art Ctr, Oklahoma City, 76 & 77. Teaching: Instr art studio, Juniata Col, Huntingdon, Pa, 69-70; from instr to asst prof, Pan Am Univ, 71- Awards: Augusta Hazard Award, Lowe Art Ctr, Syracuse Univ, 63; Merchants Prize, Corpus Christi Art Found Ann, 72; Purchase Award, Prints, Drawings & Crafts Ann, Ark Arts Ctr, 74. Bibliog: Al Brunelle (auth), Rev Sect, Art News Mag 5/73; Maurice Schmidt (auth), Reflections on Art (rev), 1/76 & Art, Light and History (rev), 6/76, Corpus Christi Caller. Mem: Col Art Asn. Style & Technique: Figurative with fantasy, emphasizing religious, Philosophical and autobiographical themes. Media: Intaglio prints; oil painting. Mailing Add: 1123 S Closner Blvd Edinburg TX 78539

FIELD, RICHARD SAMPSON
CURATOR, ART HISTORIAN
b New York, NY, Aug 26, 31. Study: Harvard Univ, AB, AM & PhD. Collections Arranged: 15th Century Woodcuts & Metalcuts from the National Gallery of Art (with catalog), 65; Jasper Johns: Prints 1960-1970, Philadelphia Mus Art (with catalog), 70 & Silkscreen: History of a Medium (with catalog), 71; The Fable of the Sick Lion: a Fifteenth Century Blockbook, Wesleyan (with catalog), 74 & Gabriel de Sanit-Aubin (with catalog), 75. Teaching: Assoc prof art, Wesleyan Univ, 72- Pos: Asst to dir, Fogg Art Mus, Cambridge, Mass, 61-62; asst cur of prints, Alverthorpe Gallery-Nat Gallery Art, 62-68 & Philadelphia Mus Art, 69-72; cur, Davison Art Ctr, Wesleyan Univ, Middletown, Conn, 72- Awards: Fulbright Grant, France, 59-60; Finley Fel, Nat Gallery Art, 65-67. Mem: Print Coun Am (dir, 70-72). Res: 15th century woodcuts; Gauguin; contemporary prints. Publ: Auth, Gauguin's Noa Noa suite, Burlington Mag, 68; auth, Woodcuts from Altomünster, Gutenberg-Jahrbuch, 69; auth, Gauguin's Monotypes, 73; auth, The Prints of Richard Hamilton, 73. Mailing Add: Cedar Swamp Rd Deep River CT 06417

FIELD, ROBERT JAMES
See Fish, Robert

FIELDS, FREDRICA H
STAINED GLASS ARTIST, GLASS ENGRAVER
b Haverford, Pa, Jan 10, 12. Study: Landscape painting with Frank Morley Fletcher, 30 & Frank Logan, 31; Wellesley Col, 30-32; Art Students League, with Nicolaides, 33; stained glass with Mrs Orin Skinner, 38-39 & with George Sotter, 51. Work: Washington Cathedral, Washington, DC; Marie Cole Auditorium, Greenwich Libr, Conn; YWCA, Greenwich. Exhib: 4th & 6th Int Exhib of Ceramic Arts, Nat Collection of Fine Arts, Washington, DC, 53 & 57 & 3rd Biennial Creative Crafts Exhib, 58; 9th & 11th Ann Area Exhibs, Corcoran Gallery of Art, Washington, DC, 55 & 56; Nat Conf on Relig Arch, New York, 67; Danbury Pub Libr, Conn, 74; one-woman exhibs, Artist's Mart, Washington, DC, 55; First Presbyterian Church, Stamford, Conn, 76. Teaching: Instr stained glass, YWCA, Greenwich, 66-67 & pvt studio, 68-71. Awards: For stained glass, 4th & 6th Int Exhib of Ceramic Arts, Nat Collection of Fine Arts, 53 & 57; 9th & 11th Ann Area Exhib, Corcoran Gallery of Art, 55 & 56; work included in US Info Agency Traveling Exhib, 57. Mem: Stained Glass Asn Am; Greenwich Art Soc; affil Soc for Relig Art & Archit. Style & Technique: Specializing in a unique 3-dimensional abstract stained glass construction for buildings and exhibition. Publ: Contribr, Stained Glass Asn Am Quart, 58-75; contribr, The Complete Book of Creative Glass Art, 74; contribr, Step by Step Stained Glass, 74; contribr, Decorating Glass, 76. Mailing Add: 561 Lake Ave Greenwich CT 06830

FIFE, MARY (MRS EDWARD LANING)
PAINTER
b Canton, Ohio Study: Carnegie Inst Technol, BA; Cooper Union; Acad Russe, Paris, France; Art Students League. Exhib: Metrop Mus Art, New York; Whitney Mus Am Art, New York; Art Inst Chicago; one-man shows, Pen & Brush Inc, New York & Brooklyn Art Gallery, NY; plus others. Teaching: Instr drawing, Kansas City Art Inst, Mo, 45-50; head dept art, Birch-Wathem Sch, New York, 61-70. Awards: Figure Prize, Nat Acad Design, 67; Pen & Brush Prize, 69; Elizabeth McGenius Award, 70. Mem: Pen & Brush Inc (mem bd); Nat Asn Women Artists (mem bd). Media: Oil. Dealer: Brooklyn Arts Gallery 1358 Flatbush Ave Brooklyn NY 11210. Mailing Add: 82 State St Brooklyn NY 11201

FIFIELD, MARY
ADMINISTRATOR, WRITER
b Chicago, Ill, Apr 10, 46. Study: Clarke Col, AB; Univ Madrid; Art Inst Chicago; Pratt Inst, fel, 70-71, with Elaine de Kooning, Irving Sandler, Walter Rogalski & Ralph Wickiser, MFA. Work: Clarke Col Exhib; Pratt Manhattan Ctr, New York, 70; 26th Ill Exhib, Ill State Mus, 73; 37th Ann Midyear Show, Butler Inst Am Art, Ohio, 73; Small Paintings USA traveling exhib, Gallery North, 74; Mid-South Biennial, Brooks Mem Art Gallery, Memphis, Tenn, 75; Contemporary Issues: Works on Paper by Women, Womens Bldg, Los Angeles, 77. Teaching: Asst prof design, color, drawing & printmaking, St Louis Community Col, 72-77, chmn dept, 77- Pos: Guest artist, SC Arts Comn, 74; design workshop dir, Lindenwood Cols, 74-75; speaker-panelist, Nat Art Educ Asn Women's Caucus Art, 76 & Midwest Women's Art Conf, 77; moderator, Nat Women's Caucus for Art Conf Panel, 78. Awards: Positano Art Workshop Fel, Italy, 70; Ford Found Grant, 71; Brooks Mem Art Gallery League Merit Award, 75. Bibliog: George Constable (auth), Show offers wide range of talent, Mansfield News J, 71; Mary Stuart (auth), Portrait: A new woman, Peoples Press, 74; Mary King (auth), Painting, photographs by Forest Park Faculty, St Louis Post Dispatch, 74. Mem: Col Art Asn Am; Nat Women's Caucus Art (affirmative action officer, 76-78, vpres, 78-); Mid Am Col Art Asn; Community Women Artists, St Louis; Nat Art Workers Community. Style & Technique: Colorist. Media: Acrylic, Intaglio, Serigraphy. Publ: Co-auth, Contemporary Women Artists, Forest Park Community Col, 74; ed, Women and the EEOC, Feminist Art J, 75; auth, Affirmative action in academia: An unfulfilled promise, Visual Dialog, 77; ed, Anger to action: A sex discrimination guidebook. Mailing Add: St Louis Community Col St Louis MO 63110

FIGERT, SAM A
ART DEALER, WRITER
b Ft Wayne, Ind, May 23, 35. Pos: Owner & dir, Humboldt Galleries, San Francisco, 68-75 & owner & dir, Humboldt Galleries, New York, 75- Mem: San Francisco Art Dealers Asn (secy-treas, 73-74). Specialty: Modern master drawings and contemporary paintings and drawings with emphasis on Northwest coast artists. Mailing Add: c/o Humboldt Galleries 1641 Third Ave 7K New York NY 10028

FIGURES, ALFRED
PAINTER, EDUCATOR
b Mobile, Ala, Oct 8, 34. Study: Ala State Univ with Hayward L Oubre, BA; Univ Minn with Reid Hastie, MA. Work: Atlanta Univ; Slide Collection, NY Pub Libr, Cleveland State Univ, Upper Iowa Col & Ky State Univ; Ethnic Am Art Slide Libr, Univ SAla; plus numerous pvt collections. Exhib: 19th Ann Nat Exhib, Atlanta Univ, 69; Gulf Coast Regional Exhib, 75; plus numerous one-man shows. Teaching: Chmn dept art, Bishop State Jr Col, 64-71. Awards: First Purchase Prize Watercolor & Hon Mention, Oil, Atlanta Univ, 69; plus numerous hon mentions. Mem: Nat Conf Artists. Style & Technique: Abstract expressionist. Media: Oil, Pencil. Mailing Add: 6200 Moffat Rd Mobile AL 36618

FILIPOVIC, AUGUSTIN
SCULPTOR, PAINTER
b Davor, Yugoslavia, Jan 8, 31; Can citizen. Work: Art Gallery Ont, Toronto; Ft William Libr, Ont; Palazzo Braschi, Rome, Italy; The Inn on the Park, Toronto, Ont. Comn: Cardinal Stepinac (bronze bust), Our Lady of Croatia Church, Toronto, 60, Fiberglas Crucifixion, 66; Spirit of the Dance (cement), Colonial Tavern, Toronto, 60; reclining figure (bronze), Parkin & Assocs for Don Mills Post Off, 69. Exhib: Mostra Arte Lazio, Rome, Italy, 55; Nat Gallery Art, Ottawa, Ont, 62; Gallery Moos, Toronto, 67; Gallery Agnes Lefort, Montreal, PQ, 68; Bertha Schaefer Gallery, New York, 71. Teaching: Resident sculptor, Univ Toronto Sch Archit, 62. Awards: Second Prize, Mostra Arte Lazio, Rome, 52; Prize of the Mayor of Rome, via Margutta, Rome, 58; Prize in Centennial Competition, Niagara Falls, 66. Mem: Sculpture Soc Can. Media: Bronze. Mailing Add: c/o Gallery Moos 138 Yorkville Toronto ON Can

FILIPOWSKI, RICHARD E
SCULPTOR, EDUCATOR
b Poland, May 29, 23; US citizen. Study: Inst Design, Ill Inst Technol, BA, with L Moholy-Nagy. Work: Addison Gallery Am Art, Andover, Mass; State St Bank & Trust Co & First Nat Bank, Boston; Boston Safe Deposit & Trust Co; Chase Manhattan Bank, New York. Comn: Sculptural ark, Temple B'rith Kodesh, Rochester, 62; sculptural cross, Trinity Lutheran, Chelmsford, Mass, 63; sculpture, Atlantic, Sheraton Corp, Prudential Ctr, Boston, 64; sculptural cross, Trinity Evangel Lutheran, Philadelphia, 65; sculpture, Echo, Revere Copper & Brass Corp, New York, 65. Exhib: Art for US Embassies, Inst Contemp Art, Boston, 66; Nat Exhib Art, Ogunquit, Maine, 67; one-man shows, Fitchburg Art Mus, Mass, 68 & State Univ NY Col Oneonta, 69; Outdoor Sculpture Exhib, De Cordova Mus, Lincoln, Mass, 72. Teaching: Assoc prof visual design, Mass Inst Technol, 53- Awards: First Prize for sculpture, Boston Arts Festival, 58; Aleck & Ruth McLean Award, Nat Exhib Art, Ogunquit, 67. Bibliog: Katherine Kuh (auth), Abstract and surrealist American art, Art Inst Chicago, 48; Patricia Boyd Wilson (auth), The home forum, Christian Sci Monitor, 65; Phoebe Cutler (auth), Richard Filipowski's sculpture, Harvard Art Rev, 67. Media: Bronze, Brass, Silver, Steel, Aluminum. Dealer: Joan Peterson Gallery 561 Boylston St Boston MA 02130. Mailing Add: 10 Round Hill Rd Lexington MA 02173

FILKOSKY, JOSEFA
SCULPTOR, EDUCATOR
b Westmoreland City, Pa, June 15, 33. Study: Seton Hill Col, BA, 55; Carnegie-Mellon Univ, BFA, 63; Cranbrook Acad Art, MFA, 68; Art Inst Chicago, summer sculpture sem, 68. Work: Pipe Dream IV, Gateway Ctr, City of Pittsburgh; Pipe Dream V, Hudson River Mus, Yonkers, NY; Red-Winged, Alcoa Merwin Tech Ctr, Pittsburgh; Pipe Dream VIII, Harlan Corp, Southfield, Mich. Comn: Pipe Dream IX, Taubman Corp, Southfield. Exhib: Young Americans, 1962, Mus Contemp Art, NY, 63, plus two yrs travel exhib; one-man show, The Art Image In All Media, NY, 70, Ind Univ, 72 & Bertha Schaefer Gallery, New York, 73; two-man show, Pittsburgh Plan for Art, 71, 73 & 75; Sculpture in the Fields, Storm King Art Ctr, 74-76. Teaching: Assoc prof art, Seton Hill Col, 56- Awards: Three Rivers Purchase Award, 72. Bibliog: Suzanne Vlamis (auth), Pipe Dream Nun, M D Mag, 5/72; Suzanne Benton (auth), Metal Sculpture, 75; Sandak Slide Set, Am Woman's Art, 74. Mem: Assoc Artists Pittsburgh; Pittsburgh Plan for Art. Media: Aluminum, Plexiglas. Dealer: Dorothea Silverman 500 E 83rd St New York NY 10028; RM Gallery 563 Eglington Ave W Toronto ON Can. Mailing Add: Seton Hill Col Greensburg PA 15601

FILLERUP, MEL
PAINTER
b Lovell, Wyo, Jan 28, 24. Study: Art Students League; study with Paul Bransom, Serge Bongart, Wiliam Reese, Conrad Schwiering & Robert Meyers. Comn: Husky dogs, Husky Oil Co. Exhib: Western States Show, Cody Country Art League, 65-75; Springville Art Mus Show, 70-75; C M Russell Auction, Great Falls, Mont; Wind River Artists Asn; New York Life Ann Calendar Competition. Teaching: Oil painting, North West Community Col, 74-75. Awards: Purchase Award, Cheyenne Artists Guild, 65; First Place, Cody Country Art League, 68 & 76; Purchase Award, First Nat Bank, Cody, 74. Mem: Yellowstone Artists Guild; Cody Country Artist Asn (pres, 68-70). Style & Technique: Impressionistic. Media: Oil, Watercolor. Mailing Add: PO Box 929 Cody WY 82414

FILLMAN, JESSE R
COLLECTOR
b Pittsburgh, Pa, May 5, 05. Study: Amherst Col, BA; Columbia Univ, LLB. Collection: Mostly American paintings and sculpture. Mailing Add: 28 State St Boston MA 02109

FILMUS, TULLY
PAINTER, LECTURER
b Otaki, Russia, Aug 29, 08; US citizen. Study: Pa Acad Fine Arts, Philadelphia; NY Univ; Barnes Found, Philadelphia; Art Students League; Crisson traveling scholar for study in Paris & Rome. Work: Metrop Mus Art & Whitney Mus Am Art, New York; Joslyn Art Mus, Omaha; Butler Inst of Art, Youngstown, Ohio; Univ of NC Permanent Collection; St Lawrence Univ Permanent Collection, Canton, NY; Syracuse Univ Mus; Canton Art Inst, Ohio. Exhib: Whitney Mus Am Art, 40-46; Art Inst Chicago, 41; Carnegie Inst Int, Pittsburgh, 41-46; Pa Acad Fine Arts, Philadelphia, 41-46; Corcoran Gallery Art, Washington, DC, 42; Yeshiva Univ Mus, NY, 77; one-man shows, ACA Gallery, New York, 71, The Berkshire Mus, Pittsfield, Mass, 73 & ACA Gallery, Rome, Italy, 74. Teaching: Instr painting & drawing, Am Artists Sch, New York, 36-38 & Cooper Union Art Sch, New York, 38-50. Awards: Pa Acad Fine Arts Fel, 48; Salmagundi Prize, Audubon Artists, 69. Bibliog: Dr Alfred Werner (auth), The painter Tully Filmus, World Publs, 63; Tully Filmus—selected drawings, Jewish Publ, 71. Mem: Artist Equity NY; Audubon Artists; Art Comn Nassau Co, NY. Media: Oil. Dealer: A C A Gallery 25 E 73rd St New York NY 10021. Mailing Add: 17 Stuart St Great Neck NY 11023

FINCH, KEITH BRUCE
PAINTER
Work: Calif Dept Agr; Los Angeles Co Mus Art; Whitney Mus Am Art; Home Savings & Loan Asn; Denver Art Mus; plus others. Exhib: Santa Barbara Mus Art; Corcoran Gallery Art; Pa Acad Fine Art; Am Watercolor Soc; Art Inst Chicago; plus others. Teaching: Instr, Kann Art Inst, Finch-Warshaw Studio, Univ Calif, Los Angeles, Long Beach Mus Art & Serisawa Studio. Awards: Awards, Nat Orange Show, Nat Acad Design & Soc Illusr; plus others. Mailing Add: 2401 Wilshire Blvd Los Angeles CA 90057

FINCH, RUTH WOODWARD
PATRON, PHOTOGRAPHER
b Rochester, NY, Feb 27, 16. Study: Bryn Mawr Col, BA(art hist), 37; Le Louvre, Paris, France; Photographic Workshop, New Canaan, Conn. Exhib: Indians of the SW, Silvermine Guild Artists Gallery, Norwalk, Conn, 76. Pos: Chmn, Photographic Exhibits, New Canaan Libr, 76- Awards: Albert Jacobson Patron's Award, Silvermine Guild Artists, 72. Mem: Silvermine Guild of Artists; Ridgefield Guild of Artists, Conn; Friends of Photog, Carmel, Calif; New Canaan Soc for the Arts, Conn. Style & Technique: Black and white and color photography; travel, landscapes, people and seascapes. Interest: American sculpture and prints by American artists; give a sculpture prize yearly at Silvermine Guild of Artists, New England Show. Mailing Add: 1081 Ponus Ridge Rd New Canaan CT 06840

FINCHER, JOHN H
PAINTER, EDUCATOR
b Hamilton, Tex, Aug 4, 41. Study: Hardin-Simmons Univ, 60-61; Tex Tech Col, BA, 64; Univ Okla, teaching fel, 64-66, MFA, 66. Work: Dallas Mus Fine Arts; Univ Okla Mus Fine Arts; Wichita Mus Art; Honolulu Acad. Exhib: Southwestern Biennial, Mus NMex, Santa Fe, 63; 15th Exhib Southwestern Prints & Drawings, Dallas Mus Fine Arts, 65; Ball State Univ Ann Exhib Drawings & Small Sculptures, Ind, 68-70; The Drawing Society, Mus Fine Arts, Houston, 70; Long Beach Mus Art, 72. Teaching: Assoc prof art, Wichita State Univ, 66-77. Awards: Wurlitzer Found Grant, Taos, NMex, 72. Media: Oil, Ink. Mailing Add: 905 Camino Santander Santa Fe NM 87501

FINCK, FURMAN J
PAINTER, INSTRUCTOR
b Chester, Pa, Oct 10, 00. Study: Pa Acad Fine Arts, dipl; Ecole des Beaux Arts & Acad Julian, Paris; Am Acad, Rome; Muhlenberg Col, DFA. Work: Mass Gen Hosp; Temple Univ Health Sci Ctr; Nat Portrait Gallery; Toledo Mus; Dartmouth House, London. Comn: Med faculty (ser of portraits), Temple Univ, 44-; med clinics (ser), Med Schs US, 45-; portrait of President Truman, Nat Dem Club, New York, 50; portrait of President Eisenhower, Union League, Philadelphia, 54; deans schs pharm US (ser), Wyeth Labs, 60-64. Exhib: Pa Acad Fine Arts Ann; Carnegie Inst Int; Nat Acad Design Ann; Corcoran Gallery Art Biennial; Portraits Inc Ann. Teaching: Instr drawing & painting, Cheltenham Art Ctr, Pa, 67-; mem staff painting, Philadelphia Mus Art, 69-; dean, du Cret Sch of Arts, Plainfield, NJ, 70- Awards: Cresson European Traveling Scholar, Pa Acad Fine Arts, 24; First Altman Prize, Nat Acad Design, 55; Krindler Prize, Salmagundi Club Ann, 64. Bibliog: Henry Pitz (auth), Furman Finck, Am Artist Mag, 3/56; Martin Zipin (auth), Finck paints a portrait (film), produced by WFIL-TV. Mem: Salmagundi Club (chmn pub rels, 50-); Twenty Five Year Club of Temple Univ (art comt, 51-); Players (vchmn art comt, 70-); Saint George's Soc New York; Artists' Fellowship, Inc (pres, 73-77). Media: Oil. Publ: Auth, The meaning of art in education, Columbia Univ Publ, 38; co-auth, The artist as teacher, Appleton, 50; auth, The artist and the architect, Am Inst Architects J, 59; auth, Complete guide to portrait painting, Watson-Guptill, 70. Mailing Add: 285 Central Park W New York NY 10024

FINDLAY, DAVID B
ART DEALER
Pos: Co-dir, David Findlay Galleries. Mailing Add: 984 Madison Ave New York NY 10021

FINDLAY, HELEN T
ART DEALER
b Kansas City, Mo, July 21, 09. Study: Vassar Col, AB, 30. Pos: Pres, Jr League Kansas City, 35-36; art secy, Asn Jr Leagues Am, 36-39; fund raising, Nat Recreation Asn, 39-43; secy & mgr, Wally Findlay Galleries, Chicago, 62- & secy & dir, Wally Findlay Galleries, Int, Inc; bd mem, Chicago Vassar Club. Awards: Named One of Nine Women of the Year, Chicago Munic Art League, 59. Specialty: Contemporary art. Mailing Add: Wally Findlay Galleries 814 N Michigan Ave Chicago IL 60611

FINDSEN, OWEN KENNETH
ART CRITIC
b Cincinnati, Ohio, Nov 19, 35. Study: Univ Cincinnati, BSD(graphic design), 68. Pos: Art critic, Cincinnati Enquirer, 68- Mailing Add: 3417 Mooney Ave Cincinnati OH 45208

FINE, JUD
SCULPTOR
b Los Angeles, Calif, Nov 20, 44. Study: Univ Calif, Santa Barbara, BA; Cornell Univ, MFA. Work: Minneapolis Inst Art; Los Angeles Co Art Mus; Pasadena Mus Mod Art; Art Inst Chicago; Yale Univ Art Mus. Exhib: 8th & 9th Biennale de Paris, 73 & 75; 71st Am Exhib, Art Inst Chicago, 74; Gallery Alexandra Monett, Brussels, Belg, 75; one-man shows, Dayton's Gallery 12, Minneapolis, 73 & 74 & Ron Feldman Gallery, New York, 72, 73 & 75. Awards: Contemp Art Coun New Talent Grant, Los Angeles Co Art Mus, 72; Laura Slobe Mem Award, Art Inst Chicago, 74. Bibliog: Articles in Art Forum, 10/72, 11/73 & 4/75; Arts Mag, 5/72, 10/73, 9/74 & 3/75; J J Kelly (auth), Living materials, Holt, Rinehart & Winston, 72. Media: Mixed Media. Publ: Auth, Or: an Introduction, 74 & Walk, 75, privately publ. Mailing Add: 329 Holly Ave Carpinteria CA 93013

FINE, PERLE
PAINTER, EDUCATOR
b Boston, Mass, May 1, 08. Study: Atelier 17; also with Hans Hofmann & William Hayter. Work: Whitney Mus Am Art, New York; Brandeis Univ, Waltham, Mass; Mus of Mod Art, New York; Solomon R Guggenheim Mus, New York; Brooklyn Mus, NY; plus others. Exhib: One-person shows, Betty Parsons Gallery (ten yrs), Marian Willard Gallery, Graham Gallery, Tanager Gallery & Cornell Univ; Carnegie Int, Pittsburgh; Art of this Century, Guggenheim Gallery, New York; Geometric Abstraction in Am & Nature in Abstraction, Whitney Mus of Am Art, New York; Mex Biennial, Palacio Bellas Artes, Mexico City; Art of Assemblage, Mus of Mod Art, New York; Bykert Zarre Gallery, 77 & 78; plus others. Teaching: Vis prof fine arts, Cornell Univ; assoc prof fine arts, Hofstra Univ. Awards: First Prize for collage,

Silvermine Guild, Conn; Purchase Award for Wood-Collage, Brooklyn Mus; Am Acad Arts & Lett Grant for Painting, 74. Bibliog: Lyricism in Abstract Art. Mem: Am Abstract Artists; Fedn Mod Painters & Sculptors; Guild Hall, East Hampton. Media: Oil, Acrylic, Wood-Collage & Collage. Mailing Add: 538 Old Stone Hwy The Springs NY 11937

FINE, RUTH EILEEN
CURATOR, PRINTMAKER
b Philadelphia, Pa, 1941. Study: Philadelphia Col Art, 58-62, BFA; Univ Pa, 62-64, MFA; Skowhegan Sch Painting & Sculpture. Work: Philadelphia Mus Art; Bd Educ, Philadelphia; Mobile Oil Corp; Lessing J Rosenwald Collection; Fidelity Banks. Exhib: Univ Pa; Philadelphia Mus Art; Univ Notre Dame Art Gallery, 77-; Contemporary Issues: Works on Paper by Women, traveling exhib organized by Women's Caucus for Art. Collections Arranged: Contemp Printmaking (with video tape), Miami Dade Community Col, 77. Teaching: Lectr printmaking, Philadelphia Col Art, 65-69; lectr prints & printmaking, Univ Vt, Burlington, 76 & 77. Pos: Mus cur for Alverthorpe Gallery, Jenkintown, Pa, Nat Gallery Art, Washington, DC, 72- Mem: Print Club of Philadelphia (bd govs, vpres, 77-); Print Coun Am; Grolier Club; Col Art Asn Am; Women's Caucus for Art (adv bd, 76-78). Media: Printmaking; Painting. Res: Nineteenth and twentieth English and American prints. Publ: Contribr, Jerome Kaplan Prints, Print Club, Philadelphia, 73; auth, The Janus Press: 1955-1975, Univ Vt, 75; auth, A Checklist of Blake material in the Lessing J Rosenwald Collection, Blake Newsletter 35, 75-76; contribr, Philadelphia: Three centuries of American art, Philadelphia Mus Art, 76; auth, Ernest Haskell: 1876-1925, Bowdoin Col Mus Art, 76. Mailing Add: PO Box 26756 Elkins Park PA 19117

FINGESTEN, PETER
GRAPHIC ARTIST, EDUCATOR
b Berlin, Ger, Mar 20, 16; US citizen. Study: Hochschule fuer Bildende Kuenste, Berlin, prof dipl; Pa Acad Fine Arts; Asia Inst, New York, cert. Comn: Archit relief, Villa Mantero, Como, Italy, 38; sculpture of Christ (bust), First Presby Church, Washington, DC, 48; portrait, Glycerine Corp Am, New York, 54; Mem plaque, Pace Univ, New York, 68. Exhib: Int Exhib Black & White, Milan, Italy, 38; Art of Democratic Living, Am Fedn Arts Nat Traveling Show, 46. Teaching: Instr art hist, Manhattan Col, New York, 46-50; lectr Asian art, Asia Inst, 50-51; prof art hist, Pace Univ, 50-, chmn dept art, 68- Awards: First Sculpture Award, Int Exhib Black & White, 38; Louis Comfort Tiffany Grant, 48. Bibliog: Fortunate Fingesten, Time Mag, 3/4/40; J K Reed (auth), Fingesten's 30th, Art Digest, 3/1/47. Mem: Am Soc Aesthetics (secy eastern region, 71-); Col Art Asn Am. Style & Technique: Graphics, presently as more flexible medium for surrealism. Media: Watercolor. Res: Symbolism of art. Publ: Auth, East is East, Muehlenberg Press, 56; auth, The Eclipse of Symbolism, Univ SC Press, 70; auth, Symbolism and Reality, J Psycholinguistic Res, 71; auth, Surrealism and the Symbolic Paradox, Humanitas, spring 72. Mailing Add: Pace Univ 41 Park Row New York NY 10038

FINK, ALAN
ART DEALER
b Chicago, Ill, July 17, 25. Study: Univ Ill, BA. Pos: Dir, Alpha Gallery Inc. Mem: Asn Boston Art Dealers (pres). Specialty: Contemporary American painting, sculpture and graphics; modern master prints. Mailing Add: c/o Alpha Gallery 121 Newbury St Boston MA 02116

FINK, HERBERT LEWIS
PAINTER, EDUCATOR
b Providence, RI, Sept 8, 21. Study: Carnegie Inst Technol, 41; RI Sch Design, BFA, 49; Yale Univ, MFA, 56; Art Students League; also with John Frazier, Gabor Peterdi, Arshile Gorky & Rico Lebrun. Work: Univ Mich; Univ Iowa; Baltimore Mus Art; Md Inst; Brown Univ; plus others. Comn: Mural, RI Post Off Lobby, Providence, 59; metal sculpture, Sen Green Airport, 60; archit screen, Hartford Bank & Trust Bldg. Exhib: Am Color Print Soc, 59; Soc Am Graphic Artists, 59; Art Dirs Ann, 59; Libr Cong, 59; Philadelphia Mus Art, 59; plus others. Teaching: Instr painting & drawing, RI Sch Design, 51-61; instr, Yale Univ, 56-61; prof art & chmn dept, Southern Ill Univ, Carbondale, 61- Pos: Print ed, Int Graphic Arts Soc; trustee, Tiffany Found. Awards: Purchase Prize, Soc Am Graphic Artists, 59; Purchase Prize, Libr Cong, 59; Guggenheim Fel, 65-66; plus others. Mailing Add: 1003 W Hillcrest Dr Carbondale IL 62901

FINK, LAURENCE B
EDUCATOR, PHOTOGRAPHER
b Brooklyn, NY, Mar 11, 41. Study: With Lissette Model, 59. Work: Mus Mod Art, New York; Corcoran Gallery Art, Washington, DC. Exhib: Harkis Krakow Gallery, Boston, 75, Broxton Gallery, Los Angeles, 76 & Case Solway Gallery, Cincinnati, 77; one-man shows, Light Gallery, New York, 77, Lehigh Univ, Bethlehem, Pa, 78 & Sander Gallery, Washington, DC, 78. Teaching: Parsons Sch Design; Inst Contemp Photog, Lehigh Univ; Kingsborough Community Col, City Univ New York; prof photog, Yale Sch Fine Arts, 77- Awards: Creative Artists Pub Serv Fel, 71-72 & 73-74; John Simon Guggenheim Fel, 76-77. Dealer: Sander Gallery Inc 2604 Connecticut Ave NW Washington DC 20008 Mailing Add: PO Box 295 Martins Creek PA 18063

FINK, LOUIS R
PAINTER, PHOTOGRAPHER
b Jersey City, NJ, Jan 7, 25. Study: Art Students League, 3 yrs. Work: Staten Island Mus. Comn: Sewn canvas painting, comn by Robert Lindgren, Water Mill, NY, 73. Exhib: Mus Mod Art, New York; Art Inst Chicago; Nat Acad Design; Pa Acad Fine Arts; Audubon Artists. Style & Technique: Construct sewn canvas paintings and heavily textured acrylic paintings. Dealer: Richard J Eyen Environment Gallery 205 E 60th St New York NY 10022. Mailing Add: 14 Concord St Sag Harbor NY 11963

FINK, RAY (RAYMOND RUSSELL)
SCULPTOR, EDUCATOR
b Long Beach, Calif, July 8, 22. Study: Art Inst Chicago, BAE, 52; Ill Inst Technol, Chicago, MSAE, 55. Work: Nev Southern Univ, Las Vegas. Comn: Steel sculpture & six woodcuts, 50 & steel sculpture, 51, US War Bonds, US State Dept; relief painting, Pittman & Moore, Chicago, 54; sculptural mural (in collab with Rip Woods), Nat Housing Indust, Phoenix, Ariz, 73 & Greyhoud Inc, Phoenix, 75. Exhib: US Steel's Iron in the Fire, Birmingham Mus Art, Ala, 54; one-man show, Am Univ, Washington, DC, 56; Int Sculpture, Contemp Art Mus, Houston, Tex, 57; Am Exhib, Art Inst of Chicago, 57; Art USA 58, Madison Sq Garden, NY, 58; Seven State Regional Contemp Art Traveling Exhib, Fedn Rocky Mountain States Coun on the Arts & Humanities, 75. Teaching: Instr metal sculpture, Sch of Art Inst of Chicago, 53-55; instr sculpture, Inst of Design, Chicago, 53-58; prof art, Ariz State Univ, Tempe, 58- Awards: First Prize, Momentum Mid-Continental, Momentum, 53; Walter M Campana Award, Chicago & Vicinity, Art Inst of Chicago, 56; George Bright Mem Prize, Phoenix Art Mus, Ariz, 67. Bibliog: Watercolor Painting (videotape), KAET-TV, Ariz State Univ, 68. Style & Technique: Expressionistic-sculpture, relief painting and drawing. Media: Wood, Metal, Mixed-Media. Dealer: Yares Gallery 3625 Bishop Lane Scottsdale AZ 85251. Mailing Add: 7036 N 22nd St Phoenix AZ 85020

FINKE, LEONDA FROELICH
SCULPTOR, DRAFTSMAN
b Brooklyn, NY, Jan 23, 22. Study: Art Students League; Educ Alliance; Brooklyn Mus Art Sch. Work: Norfolk Mus Arts & Sci, Va; Nassau Community Col. Exhib: Norfolk Mus Drawing Biennial, 65 & 67; Pa Acad Fine Arts Painting & Sculpture Ann, 66; one-woman shows, Port Washington Libr, Nassau Community Col, 69 & Nassau Co Mus, 73; Nat Sculpture Soc, Lever House, 69-75; Suffolk Mus, 74; Sculpture Ctr Gallery, 76; Harbor Gallery, 72 & 75; Dallas Mus Fine Arts; Hecksher Mus; Images of Am, US Info Agency traveling exhib (bronze figure sculpture selected). Teaching: Adj assoc prof sculpture & drawing, Nassau Community Col, 70- Awards: Medal for Creative Sculpture, Audubon Artists, 72; Audubon Artist Medal of Merit, 73; Bronze Medal, Nat Sculpture Soc, 74; Tallix Foundry Prize, Nat Sculpture Soc, 77; Jeffrey Childs Willis Mem Prize, Nat Asn Women Artists, 77. Mem: Nat Asn Women Artists (sculpture jury, 70-71 & 77-78, recording secy, 71-72); Audubon Artists (sculpture selection jury, 72 & 78); New York Soc Women Artists (exhib comt, 70); Nat Sculpture Soc. Style & Technique: Work with the human figure, usually women, using the forms to express feeling or human condition; work in direct plaster for cast bronze; also portraits of people whose life or work I can relate to. Media: Bronze, Wood; Ink, Silverpoint. Dealer: Harbor Gallery 43 Main St Cold Spring Harbor NY 11724; Sculpture Ctr Gallery 167 E 69th St New York NY 10021. Mailing Add: 623 Garden Lane East Meadow NY 11554

FINKELSTEIN, LOUIS
EDUCATOR, PAINTER
b New York, NY, Mar 24, 23. Study: Cooper Union; Art Students League; New Sch, Brooklyn Mus Art Sch. Exhib: Whitney Mus Ann; Pa Acad; Corcoran Biennial; Stable Ann; plus var others. Teaching: Prof art, Philadelphia Col Art, 58-62; prof art, Yale Univ, 62-64; chmn dept art, Queens Col, City Univ New York, 64-69, prof, 64- Awards: Fulbright Fel, Italy, 56-58. Mem: Col Art Asn Am (mem bd dir, 68-70); Int Asn Art Critics. Style & Technique: Nature. Media: Oil. Res: Abstract expressionism; impressionism; art theory. Publ: Auth, Gotham News, 69 & Thoughts about Painterly, 70, Art News; auth, Seeing Stella, Artforum, 73; auth, Al Held, Art in Am, 74. Dealer: Ingber Gallery 3 E 78th St New York NY 10028. Mailing Add: 457 W Broadway New York NY 10012

FINKELSTEIN, MAX
SCULPTOR, INSTRUCTOR
b New York, NY, June 15, 15. Study: Los Angeles City Col; Sculpture Ctr, New York; Calif Sch Art, Los Angeles; Univ Calif, Los Angeles. Work: Krannert Art Mus, Univ Ill, Champaign; Hirshhorn Mus, Washington, DC; Univ Calif Mus, Berkeley; Santa Barbara Mus Art, Calif; Los Angeles Co Mus Mod Art; Michener Found Collection, Univ Tex, Austin. Exhib: Krannert Art Mus Biennial, Univ Ill, Champaign, 67; Highlights of the 1967-1968 Art Season, Larry Aldrich Mus, Ridgefield, Conn, 68; one-man shows, La Jolla Mus Art, Calif, 68 & Esther Robles Gallery, 70; Microcosm, Long Beach Mus Art, 69; Painting & Sculpture Today, Indianapolis Mus Art, Ind, 70; plus many others. Teaching: Instr sculpture, Univ Judaism. Awards: Los Angeles Munic Gallery, 65; Long Beach Mus, 65 & 67; Krannert Mus, Univ Ill, Champaign, 67. Bibliog: Ray Faulkner & Edwin Ziegfield (auths), Art Today, Holt, 69. Media: Metal. Mailing Add: 621 N Curson Ave Los Angeles CA 90036

FINKLER, ROBERT ALLAN
EDUCATOR, PAINTER
b Chicago, Ill, Nov 22, 36. Study: Ill Wesleyan Univ, BFA, 59, with Rupert Rilgorex & Fred Brian; State Univ Iowa, MFA, 62, with Byron Burford & Robert Knipschild. Work: St Cloud State Col, Minn; Waldorf Col, Iowa; Wis State Univ, Oshkosh; Mankato State Univ; Hubbard Milling Co, Minn. Exhib: Mid-Am Exhib, Nelson Gallery, Kansas City, Mo, 61; Iowa Artists Ann, Des Moines Art Ctr, 61; Drawings & Small Sculpture Show, Ball State Univ, Ind, 61 & 66; Ultimate Concerns, Athens, Ohio, 65; NDak Ann, Grand Forks, 66; Drawings USA, St Paul Art Ctr, Minn, 66; Minn Artists Biennial, Minneapolis Art Inst, 67 & 70; Akron Art Inst, Ohio, 70; Rochester Art Ctr, Minn, 77. Teaching: Prof art, Mankato State Univ, 61- Awards: Pres lectureship, Winter Holidays, Presidents Fund, Mankato State Univ, 77. Mem: Mid-Am Art Conf. Style & Technique: Semi-figurative polymer paintings and drawings in various media. Mailing Add: Dept of Art Mankato State Univ Mankato MN 56001

FINLEY, GERALD ERIC
ART HISTORIAN
b Munich, Ger, July 17, 31; Can citizen. Study: Univ Toronto, BA, MA; Johns Hopkins Univ, PhD. Teaching: Lectr art & archaeol, Univ Toronto, 59-60; lectr art, Univ Sask, Regina, 62-63, actg dir, Norman Mackenzie Art Gallery, 62-63; from asst prof to prof art hist, Queen's Univ, 63- Awards: Banting Award, Hart House, Univ Toronto, 57; Gustav Bissing Rotating Fel, Johns Hopkins Univ, 61. Mem: Royal Can Acad Art; Ont Soc Artists; Arts & Lett Club. Res: British late 18th and early 19th centuries painting; landscape, especially J M W Turner; history of ideas. Publ: Auth, Turner and Scott's poetry: new evidence, 10/73 & J M W Turner's proposal for a royal progress, 75, Burlington Mag; auth, J M W Turner's colour and optics, 73 & Turner's illustrations to Napoleon, 73, J Warburg & Courtauld Inst. Mailing Add: 53 Earl St Kingston ON K7L 2G5 Can

FINN, DAVID
ILLUSTRATOR, PHOTOGRAPHER
b New York, NY, Aug 30, 21. Study: City Col of Univ New York, BA. Exhib: Oceanic Sculptures, Metrop Mus of Art, New York, 74; Henry Moore Photographs, l'Orangerie, Paris, France, 77. Collections Arranged: Exploring Sculpture, Andrew Crispo Gallery, New York, 77; Henry Moore Sculpture and Environment (photographs), Fischer Fine Art Ltd, London, Eng, 77. Mem: Am Inst of Graphic Arts; Am Soc of Mag Photographers; Int ctr of Photog (mem bd dir & trustees); Am Crafts Coun (mem bd dir); Parsons Sch of Design (mem bd overseers). Publ: Illusr, Embrace of Life: The Sculpture of Gustav Vigeland, Hale (ed), 69, As the Eye Moves, 71, Frederick Hartt (auth), Donatello, Prophet of Modern Vision, 73 & Michelangelo's Three Pieta's, 76, co-auth & illusr, Henry Moore, co-auth, Henry Moore Sculpture & Environment, 77, Harry Abrams. Mailing Add: 110 E 59th St New York NY 10022

FINNEGAN, SHARYN MARIE
GALLERY DIRECTOR, PAINTER
b New York, NY, Aug 16, 46. Study: Art Students League, New York; Acad de Belli Arti, Rome, Italy, one yr; Marymount Col, Tarrytown, NY, BFA; NY Univ, New York, MA, studied with Esteban Vicente. Exhib: Report from Soho, Grey Art Gallery, New York, 75; Artists' Choice: Figurative Art in New York, Bowery Gallery, plus four others, New York, 76; one-woman exhib, Roswell Mus & Fine Arts Ctr, NMex, 77. Teaching: Artist-in-residence, Roswell Mus & Fine Arts Ctr, 76. Pos: Gallery coordr, Prince St Gallery,

New York, 74-75 & 77- Bibliog: J Mellow (auth), Rev, New York Times, 1/74; P Frank (auth), Rev, Soho Weekly News, 1/74; J Dreiss (auth), Rev, Arts Mag, 4/74. Mem: Women in the Arts, New York; Col Art Asn. Style & Technique: Realist, landscapes, portraits, including self-portraits and cityscapes. Media: Oil and Gouche. Dealer: Prince St Gallery 106 Prince St New York NY 10012 Mailing Add: 515 W 11th St New York NY 10025

FINSON, HILDRED A
CHILDREN'S BOOK ILLUSTRATOR
b Warner, Okla, June 3, 10. Study: Univ Northern Iowa, Cedar Falls, AA, 30-32; Drake Univ, BS(elem art educ), 56; Ariz State Univ, Tempe, post-grad work, summers 65, 66, 69-70. Work: J C Clegg Pub Libr, Central City, Iowa. Comn: Equestrian, Clyde Slininger, Jefferson, Iowa, 43; five large animal paintings, Patrick Cudahy, Jefferson, 44; painting of home, Max & Bebe Pett, Jefferson, 63. Exhib: One-person shows, Gallery West, Jefferson, 73, Jefferson State Bank, 77 & Carroll Pub Libr, Iowa, 77; 1-40 Expo Realistic Art Competition, Winslow, Ariz, 75. Teaching: Elem art teacher, Jefferson Community Schs, 39-62, art dir, 63-75. Mem: Nat Art Educ Asn. Style & Technique: Realistic, modern and abstract. Media: Oil, Watercolor; Pen & Ink. Publ: Auth & illusr, Klipspringer Twins, Carlton Press, 75; auth & illusr, Dik-Dik and Shrew, Dorrance, 77. Mailing Add: 304 S Wilson Jefferson IA 50129

FIORE, JOSEPH A
PAINTER, EDUCATOR
b Cleveland, Ohio, Feb 3, 25. Study: Black Mountain Col, with Josef Albers, Ilya Bolotowsky & William De Kooning, 46-48; Calif Sch Fine Arts, 48-49. Work: Whitney Mus Am Art; Corcoran Gallery, Washington, DC; Chase Manhattan Collection, New York; Colby Mus, Waterville, Maine; Weatherspoon Art Gallery, Greenboro, NC. Exhib: One-man shows, Staempfli Gallery, 60, Robert Schoelkopf Gallery, New York, 65 & 69 & Fischbach Gallery, 77; Whitney Ann, 59; Krannert Mus, Univ of Ill Biennial, 61; Maine: 100 Artists of the 20th Century, Colby Mus, 65; 50 Artists from 50 States, Burpee Art Mus, Rockford, Ill, 65; Painterly Realism, Smith Col Mus, 70; Green Mountain Gallery, New York, 73 & John Bernard Myers Gallery, 74; The Delaware Water Gap, Corcoran Gallery, 75; 76 Maine Artists, State Mus, Augusta, 76. Teaching: Instr painting & drawing, Black Mountain Col, 49-56, chmn dept art, 51-56; instr painting, Philadelphia Col Art, 62-70; instr painting, Md Inst Col Art, 70-75; artist in residence, Artists Environ Found, Del Water Gap, Columbia, NJ, 76. Awards: Prize for Painting, San Francisco Mus Art Ann Show, 49; First Prize, Metrop Young Artists First Ann, Nat Arts Club, 58. Media: Oil, Watercolor. Publ: Illusr, The Dutiful Son, Jargon Bks, 56. Mailing Add: 178 W 82nd St New York NY 10024

FIORE, ROSARIO RUSSELL
SCULPTOR
b New York, NY, Jan 5, 08. Study: Nat Acad Design; Beaux Arts Inst Fine Arts; Mech Inst. Work: Ft Dobbins, Ga; Home of Pres Suharto. Comn: Bronze sculptures, Interior Dept, Washington, DC, US Air Force, Ft Dobbins, Ga, Freeport Minerals Co, New York, White House, Washington, DC & Cornell Univ. Exhib: Grand Central Art Gallery & Archit League, New York; Montclair Exhib, NJ; Westchester Art Gallery, NY; Corcoran Art Gallery, Washington, DC. Teaching: Instr sculpture, Jekyll Island Art Ctr, Ga, 69-70; instr sculpture, Glynn Art Ctr, St Simons, Ga, 70-72. Pos: Visual info officer, US Army Exhibs, 42-47. Awards: Nat Acad Prize, 30; Anna V Huntington Award, Nat Acad, 31. Mem: Jekyll Art Ctr (vpres, 75); Ga Coun for Arts Panel; Nat Sculpture Soc. Style & Technique: Classical. Publ: Auth, Fundamentals of Clay Modeling, House of Little Books, 46. Mailing Add: 5 Nelson Lane Jekyll Island GA 31520

FIORI, DENNIS ANDREW
ART ADMINISTRATOR, MUSEUM DIRECTOR
b Brunswick, Maine, Jan 29, 49. Study: Wis State Univ, Eau Claire; St Michael's Col, Winooski, Vt, BA(Am studies); Univ Vt, grad study with Webb fel. Pos: Cur, Nat Heritage Ltd, Toronto, Ont, 73-75; ed calendar & newsletter & assoc mus/visual arts/archit, Maine State Comn on the Arts & Humanities, 75-; comn mem, Maine Hist Preserv Comn, 75-; pres, Design & Landmarks, Inc, Brunswick, 76-; mem prog comt, New Eng Conf Am Asn Mus, 77- Mem: Am Asn Mus; New Eng Conf Am Asn Mus; Asn for Preserv Technol; Soc for Preserv of New Eng Antiq; Nat Trust for Hist Preserv. Mailing Add: 7 Lincoln St Brunswick ME 04011

FIRFIRES, NICHOLAS SAMUEL
PAINTER
b Santa Barbara, Calif, Nov 10, 17. Study: Los Angeles Art Ctr; Otis Art Inst, Los Angeles. Work: Riveredge Found Mus, Calgary, Can; Santa Barbara Hist Mus, Calif; Southwest Mus, Los Angeles; Univ Wyo Mus, Laramie. Exhib: C M Russell Gallery, Helena, Mont, 64; Cowboy Artists Am, Cowboy Hall of Fame & Ariz Mus Art, 66-77; Western Art Show, San Antonio, Tex, 68-77; O S Ranch Art Exhib, Post, Tex, 74-77; Stamford Art Found Exhib, Tex, 74-77; Trailside Galleries, Scottsdale, Ariz, 77; De Silva Gallery, Santa Barbara, Calif, 77. Bibliog: Ed Ainsworth (auth), The Cowboy in Art, World Publ Co, 68; Dorothy Harmsen (auth), Harmsen's Western Americana, Northland Press, 71; Royal B Hassrick (auth), Western Painting Today, Watson-Guptill, 75. Mem: Cowboy Artists of Am. Style & Technique: Realistic impressionist, direct painting. Media: Oil, Watercolor. Publ: Illusr, The Vaquero, 64 & Conquering the Frontiers, 74. Mailing Add: 1330 Pepper Lane Santa Barbara CA 93108

FISCH, ARLINE MARIE
GOLDSMITH, EDUCATOR
b Brooklyn, NY. Study: Skidmore Col, BS(art); Univ Ill, Urbana, MA(art); Fulbright student grant to Denmark, Inst Int Educ, 56-57; Fulbright res grant to Denmark, Bd for Scholars, 66-67; Sch Arts & Crafts, Copenhagen, Denmark; also with Bernhard Hertz Guldvaerefabrik, Copenhagen. Work: Objects: USA, Johnson Wax Collection; Worshipful Company of Goldsmiths, London; Minn Mus Art, St Paul; Western Ill Univ, Macomb; Mus Contemp Crafts, New York. Exhib: California Design, Pasadena Art Mus Triennial, 65, 68, 71 & 76; Form and Quality, Int Handicraft Fair, Munich, Ger, 68-78; Schmuck-Objekte, Mus Bellerive, Zurich, Switz, 71; First World Crafts Exhib, Toronto, 74; Goldsmith, 74 & 76; plus many solo exhibs. Teaching: Instr design & weaving, Skidmore Col, 58-61; prof jewelry & weaving, San Diego State Univ, 61-; guest lectr design, Guldsmedshøjskole, Copenhagen, Denmark, 67 & 71; vis lectr, Crafts Coun of Australia, 75; vis prof, Boston Univ, 75-76. Pos: Mem, US Nat Comn to UNESCO, 77- Awards: Gold Medal, Int Handicraft Fair, Munich, 71; Nat Endowment Arts craftsman's fel, 74-75 & craftsman's apprenticeship grant, 77-78. Bibliog: R Radakovich (auth), The expanding wonderland of Arline Fisch, Craft Horizons, 9/68; Arline Fisch, creadora de joyas extraordinarias, Temas, 2/69; Lee Nordness (auth), Objects: USA, Viking, 70; J Coyne (auth), The Penland Book of Jewelry, 75; O Emery (auth), Craftsman Lifestyle, The Gentle Revolution, 77. Mem: World Crafts Coun (dir, 74-, vpres for NAm, 76-80); Soc NAm Goldsmiths (founder, 70); Am Crafts Coun (Calif rep, southwest regional assembly, 69-72, craftsman-trustee, 72-75); Allied Craftsmen San Diego. Style & Technique: Large scale jewelry in silver using fabrication techniques (chasing, repoussé, textile techniques); combinations with other materials (feathers, leather, glass). Media: Precious Metals. Publ: Auth, Textile Techniques in Metal, Van Nostrand Reinhold, 75. Mailing Add: 4316 Arcadia Dr San Diego CA 92103

FISCHBACH, MARILYN COLE
ART DEALER, COLLECTOR
b New York, NY. Study: NY Univ; New York Sch Interior Design; painting with Nicolas Takis, Victor D'Amico & Peggy Bacon. Pos: Owner, Fischbach Gallery, New York. Specialty: Contemporary American art. Collection: Contemporary. Mailing Add: c/o Fischbach Gallery 29 W 57th St New York NY 10019

FISCHER, JO
CARTOONIST
b Chicago, Ill, Dec 18, 04. Study: Chicago Acad Arts, 20-21; Art Inst Chicago, 21-22. Pos: Staff artist, sports cartoonist, Chicago Hearst Newspapers, 22-42; asst to cartoonist Jimmy Hatlo, King Features Syndicate, 42-49; nat syndicated cartoonist, From 9 to 5, Publ-Hall Syndicate, 44-; judge, ann cartoon contest, 60-61 & Art Proj Nat Hospitalized Vets. Awards: Citation, Dept Defense, 53 & 54. Mem: Nat Cartoonists Soc; Chicago Press Vets Asn. Mailing Add: 1082 Lincoln Ave S Highland Park IL 60035

FISCHER, JOHN J
PAINTER, SCULPTOR
b Antwerp, Belg, Aug 11, 30; US citizen. Study: Educ Alliance Art Sch. Work: Carnegie Inst, Pittsburgh; Univ Ky, Lexington. Comn: Wall piece, Keebler Co, Elmhurst, 68. Exhib: All Fur Show, Alan Stone Gallery, New York, 65; Jewelry by Contemp Painters & Sculptors, Mus Mod Art, New York, 67; Critics, Curators, Collectors Choice, A M Sachs, New York, 68; Everson Mus, Syracuse, 72; NY Cult Ctr, 73; plus others. Teaching: Lectr & instr sculpture, NY Univ Sch Continuing Educ. Pos: Dir, Environ Community Arts Corp. Bibliog: Grace Glueck (auth), Vie de Bohemia in a project, NY Times, 64; Howard Smith (auth), article in Village Voice, 68. Publ: Contribr, Cookies and breads—the bakers art, Am Craftsman Coun, 66; Recordings: LP Stereo Albums CC721 & CC722. Mailing Add: c/o Lerner-Heller Gallery 956 Madison Ave New York NY 10021

FISCHER, MILDRED (GERTRUDE)
DESIGNER, TAPESTRY ARTIST
b Berkeley, Calif, Sept 15, 07. Study: Mt Holyoke Col, AB; Wiener Kunstgewerbe Schule; Art Inst Chicago; Cranbrook Acad Art; Wetterhoff Inst, Finland, cert in tapestry; tapestry with Martta Taipale, Finland & Else Halling, Oslo, Norway; papermaking with Eishiro Abe, Japan. Work: Mus Contemp Crafts, New York; Grand Rapids Art Mus, Mich; Witherspoon Gallery, Univ NC Woman's Col, Greensboro; Davis Gallery, Stephens Col, Columbia, Mo; Univ Cincinnati Art Collection. Exhib: Designer-Craftsmen USA, circulated by Am Fedn Arts, 60-61; Woven Wall Hangings by Eleven Americans, circulated by Victoria & Albert Mus, London, 62-63; Ohio State Univ, Columbus, Ohio, 69; Magic of Fibers, Grand Rapids Art Mus, 70; Exhibition '72, circulated by Columbus Art Gallery, 72; Miami Univ, Oxford, Ohio, 77; Louisville Sch of Art, Anchorage, Ky, 78. Teaching: Asst prof art & head dept, Knox Col, 46-49; assoc prof art & head dept, Lindenwood Col, 52-55; assoc prof design, Univ Cincinnati Col Design, Archit & Art, 55-72. Awards: First Prize for tapestry, Nat Decorative Arts Exhib, 53; Centennial Award in Fine Arts, Mt Holyoke Col Alumnae Asn, 72; Award, Cincinnati Art Mus Invitational Awards Exhib, 75. Mem: Ohio Designers/Craftsmen; Am Crafts Coun. Style & Technique: Abstract woven wall hangings and handmade papermold compositions. Media: Fiber. Dealer: Miller Gallery 2722 Erie Ave Cincinnati OH 45208; Jacques Baruch Gallery 900 N Michigan Ave Chicago IL 60611. Mailing Add: 3610 Pape Ave Cincinnati OH 45208

FISCHETTI, JOHN
CARTOONIST
b Brooklyn, NY, Sept 27, 16. Study: Pratt Inst, 37-40; Colby Col, Hon DFA, 69. Pos: Worked on animated films for Walt Disney; illusr for Coronet, Esquire, Sat Eve Post, Collier's, New York Times; syndicated cartoonist, Newspaper Enterprise Asn, 50; staff cartoonist, NY Herald Tribune, 62; cartoonist, Publ Newspaper Syndicate; chief ed cartoonist, Chicago Daily News; with Publ-Hall Syndicate. Awards: Pulitzer Prize, 69; Best Editorial Cartoonist, Nat Cartoonists Soc. Am Civil Liberties Award, 72. Mailing Add: 401 N Wabash Ave Chicago IL 60611

FISH, ALICE GROSS
See Gross, Alice

FISH, GEORGE A
PAINTER
b Cornwall, Eng; US citizen. Study: Nat Acad Design; Art Students League; Grand Cent Sch Art. Comn: Calendar Art for Provident Mutual Ins Co, Philadelphia, 72 & NY Life Ins Co, 73. Exhib: Audubon Artists, Allied Artists Am & Am Watercolor Soc Shows, Nat Acad Galleries, New York; Nat Arts Club & Salmagundi Club, New York; plus many others. Awards: Nell Broadman Scholar, Washington Sq Outdoor Art Exhib, 66; Purchase Award, Salmagundi Club, 67; Best in Show, Hudson Artists, 68; plus many others. Mem: Salmagundi Club; Am Watercolor Soc; Allied Artists Am; NJ Watercolor Soc; Am Artists Prof League; plus others. Media: Watercolor. Mailing Add: 281 Oak Ave River Edge NJ 07661

FISH, JANET I
PAINTER
b Boston, Mass, May 18, 38. Study: Smith Col, BA, with Leonard Baskin; Yale Sch Art & Archit, with Alex Katz & Phillip Pearlstein; Skowhegan Summer Sch. Work: Whitney Mus Am Art, New York; Dallas Mus Art, Tex; Minn Mus Art, Minneapolis; Cleveland Mus Art, Ohio; Nat Gallery Victoria, Melbourne, Australia. Exhib: One-person shows, Kornblee Gallery, 71-75, Pace Col, New York, 72, Russell Sage Col, 72, Galerie Alexandra Monett, Brussels, Belg, 74; Galerie Kostiner-Silvers, Montreal, 74, Tolarno Gallery, Melbourne, 75 & 76 & Hogarth Gallery, Paddington, Australia, 75; Am Fedn Art Traveling Exhib, 71, Realist Revival, 72; Nat Inst Arts & Lett, 72; Art Inst Chicago, 72 & 74; Painting & Sculpture Today, Indianapolis Mus Art, Ind, 72; American Women: 20th Century, Lakeview Ctr for Arts & Sci, Peoria, Ill, 72; Paintings by some Contemp Am Women, Randolph-Macon Col, 72; 32 Realists, Cleveland Mus Art, 72; Am Drawings 1963-1973, Whitney Mus Am Art, 73; Focus, Philadelphia Mus Art & Mus Philadelphia Civic Ctr, 74; Art Inst Chicago, 74; Tokyo Biennial, Mus Mod Art, 74; Yr of the Women, Bronx Mus, NY, 75; The Liberation, Corcoran Gallery, Washington, DC & US Info Agency Traveling Exhib, Europe, 76-77; Am 76 (traveling exhib), Brooklyn Mus, NY & US Dept Interior, 76-78; Eight Contemp Am Realists, Pa Acad Fine Arts & NC Mus Art, 77. Teaching: Vis artist, Univ Chicago, 76. Awards: MacDowell Fel, 68, 69 & 72; Harris Award, Chicago Biennale, 74; Australia Coun Arts Grant, 75. Bibliog: David Shiney (auth), Through a glass brightly, 2/74 & Allen Ellensweig, Janet Fish, 10/76, Arts Mag. Mem: Artists Equity. Style & Technique: Realist.

Media: Oil on Canvas; Pastel. Dealer: Robert Miller 724 Fifth Ave New York NY 10019. Mailing Add: 101 Prince St New York NY 10012

FISH, RICHARD G
PAINTER, DESIGNER
b Philadelphia, Pa, Apr 7, 25. Study: Univ Pa, BAppArts; Philadelphia Mus Sch of Art, advert design dipl, with Azio Martinelli; Haverford Col. Comn: Paintings, Dravo Corp, Pittsburgh, Pa, 69. Exhib: One-man shows, Arts Coun Galleries, YMHA, Philadelphia, 65, Kenmore Galleries, Philadelphia, 66-74, Munson Gallery, Chatham, Mass, 68, 72, 74 & 75 & Gross-McCleaf Gallery, Philadelphia, 75 & 78; Del Art Mus, Wilmington, 68-70; Butler Inst of Am Art, Youngstown, Ohio, 68, 70 & 74; Norfolk Mus of Art, Va, 69; Philadelphia Mus of Art, 69; Cummer Gallery of Art, Jacksonville, Fla, 69. Pos: Freelance designer/owner, Richard Fish Assoc, Ardmore, 52- Awards: Gold Medal, Philadelphia Graphic Arts, 62-65 & 76; Gold Medal, Philadelphia Art Dirs, 65; Silver Medal, Pennational Arts Ann, State of Pa, 67. Mem: Print Club, Philadelphia. Style & Technique: Realism; landscape, figure and still life. Media: Drybrush, pen & ink; watercolor, egg and acrylic tempera. Publ: Co-auth & illusr, Exploring Old Cape Cod, Chatham Press, 68; illusr, Life & Death of the Salt Marsh, Atlantic Little Brown, 69; illusr, One Day in Summer, Random House, 69; auth, The Artist in Scotland, Small World/Volkswagen of Am, 72; illusr, Pathways to Independence, Chatham Press, 75; illusr, Haym Salomon, Liberty's Son, Jewish Publ, 75. Dealer: Gross-McCleaf Gallery 1713 Walnut St Philadelphia PA 19103. Mailing Add: 1733 Academy Lane Havertown PA 19083

FISH, ROBERT (ROBERT JAMES FIELD)
SCULPTOR, EDUCATOR
b Kelowna, BC, July 24, 48. Study: Univ BC, BEd, with G Smith & J Macdonald; Vancouver Sch Art; also apprenticeship with Michael Morris & Gary Lee Nova. Work: Nat Gallery Can, Ottawa. Teaching: Instr painting, Banff Sch Fine Arts, 72. Awards: Coutts-Hallmark Scholar, 66; Eagle Pencil Scholar, 66; BC Art Teachers Asn Scholar, 66. Mem: Intermedia Soc; Image Bank (mgr off br, 71-72); Citizens of Sea. Media: Rubber. Mailing Add: 1956 Graveley St Vancouver BC V5L 3B5 Can

FISHER, CAROLE GORNEY
PAINTER, SCULPTOR
b Minneapolis, Minn. Study: Minneapolis Col Art & Design, BFA, 64; Pa State Univ, MFA, 66. Work: Roanoke Fine Arts Ctr, Va. Comn: Print ed, Minn State Arts Coun, 70; sculpture, Univ Minn, Morris, 73. Exhib: Pa State Univ, 72; Two Nations, Six Artists, Minn-Can, 74; Walker Art Ctr, Minneapolis, 74; Whitney Biennial Contemp Am Art, New York, 75; Woman as Viewer Exhib, Winnipeg Art Gallery, 75. Teaching: Instr printmaking & drawing, Minneapolis Col Art & Design, 68-69; artist in residence printmaking, Bemidji State Univ, 69-70; instr drawing, Col St Catherine, 73- Pos: Comnr, Minneapolis Art Comn, 75- Bibliog: Cindy Nemser (auth), Whitney Biennial, Changes, New York, 75; Amy Goldin (auth), The New Whitney Biennial, Art in Am, 5-6/75; Chris Kohlmann (auth), 1975 Whitney Biennial, Mid West Art, 5/75. Mem: Col Art Asn Am (mem women's caucus, 74-); WARM. Style & Technique: Constructions; paper and glass; two and three dimensional permanent and temporary pieces executed for specific locations. Media: Paper, Found & Manufactured Materials. Dealer: One Hundred Eighteen: An Art Gallery 1007 Harmon Minneapolis MN 55401. Mailing Add: 2524 Stevens Ave S Apt 2 Minneapolis MN 55404

FISHER, ELAINE
PHOTOGRAPHER, EDUCATOR
b Newark, NJ, July 17, 39. Study: Carnegie Mellon Univ, Pa, BFA, 61; study with Minor White, Cambridge, Mass, 66, 68 & 75. Work: Mass Inst of Technol; Still Photog Div, Nat Film Bd Can. Exhib: New Group, 67, Light 7 (traveling show), 68 & Exhib Two, 69, Mass Inst of Technol; Exhib Commun Graphics, Am Inst Graphic Arts, Boston, 70; Photovision of New Eng Photogrs (traveling show), Boston Ctr for the Arts, 72 & 75; one-artist shows, Light Gallery, New York, 73 & Image Gallery, Stockbridge, Mass, 75. Collections Arranged: Images by Women, Southeastern Mass Univ, North Dartmouth, 74. Teaching: Instr photog, Sch Fashion Design, Boston, Mass, 69-70; instr photog, pvt group workshops, NY, Va & Mass, 70-72; asst prof advan photog & grad design conception, Southeastern Mass Univ, North Dartmouth, 73-76, assoc prof, 76- Pos: Artist, Art Dept, Houghton Mifflin Publ, Boston, Mass, 63-66, advert artist, Ad dept, 66-67; free-lance photogr, many Boston book publ & Penguin Ltd, London, 66-73; visual dir & photogr, Info Syst for Vocational Decisions, Harvard Univ, 68-69. Awards: Cert of Excellence, Exhib Commun Graphics, Am Inst Graphic Arts, Boston, Mass, 70; First Prize, Photovision 72 of New Eng Photogrs, Boston Ctr for the Arts, 72; Nat Endowment for the Arts Fel Photog, 72-73. Bibliog: Sophie Rivera (auth), Eight women's statements for the eye, Majority Report Newspaper, NY, 10/74. Mem: Northeast Region Soc for Photog Educ (first pres, 76-78); Nat Soc Photog Educ (leader conf workshop, 74). Style & Technique: Black and white still photography using multiple-negative printing techniques. Media: Black and White Still Photography. Publ: Contribr, Light 7 Issue, Aperture Mag, 68; contribr, Fox Photog Mag (12 print portfolio), 72; contribr, Women See Women, Thomas Crowell Co, 76; contribr, Contemporary Female Self-Portraits, Godine Publ, 78. Mailing Add: Dept of Visual Design Southeastern Mass Univ North Dartmouth MA 02747

FISHER, ELIZABETH
ART DEALER
b Los Angeles, Calif, July 4, 45. Study: Univ Calif, Los Angeles; Univ Mich. Pos: Owner, Tempe Gallery of Art, 76- Specialty: Contemporary American paintings. Mailing Add: 1925 W Second Pl Mesa AZ 85201

FISHER, JAMES DONALD
SCULPTOR, MUSEUM DIRECTOR
b Houghton, Mich, July 24, 38. Study: Corcoran Sch Art, with Richard Lahey, 56-61; George Washington Univ, 68-73, with H Irving Gates, BA, 71, MFA, 73. Exhib: Washington Area Exhib, Corcoran Gallery Art, Washington, DC, 67; two-man show, Prince Georges Community Col, Largo, Md, 68. Collections Arranged: Dual Retrospective-Peter Hurd/Millard Sheets, Amarillo Art Ctr, 74, When You Say Cowboy-Survey of Western Art in Texas (with catalog), 74 & A Little World of the Saints-Larry Frank Collection of New Mexican Santos (with catalog), 74. Teaching: Grad teaching asst & asst prof lectr design & drawing, George Washington Univ, 71-73. Pos: Technician Mus Hist & Technol, Smithsonian Inst, 60-68; dir, Amarillo Art Ctr, 73-77; dir, Elizabeth Ney Mus & O Henry Mus, 77- Mem: Col Art Asn; Soc Indust Archeol; Am Asn Mus. Style & Technique: Non-objective large-scale sculpture; realistic drawings and graphics. Media: Welded Steel, Vacuum-Formed Plastics. Res: 19th century industrial design and 20th century non-objective sculpture. Publ: Illusr, Conjectural Reconstruction, The Engines of Capt John Ericsson's Ship Caloric, 61; auth, The history of railroad station architecture, Smithsonian Inst, 68; auth, Two centuries of American quilts and coverlets, Amarillo Art Ctr, 76. Mailing Add: 1311 Westover Rd Austin TX 78703

FISHER JOEL A
PAINTER, WRITER
b Salem, Ohio, June 6, 47. Study: Kenyon Col, AB. Work: Butler Art Inst, Youngstown, Ohio; Va Mus Fine Arts; Victoria & Albert Mus, London, Eng; Städtisches Mus of Mönchengladbach, Ger; Muzeum Sztuki, Lodz, Poland. Exhib: One-man mus shows, Whitney Mus of Am Art Resources Ctr, New York, 70; Victoria & Albert Mus, London, 71; Neue Gallerie, Aachen, Ger, 74; Stadt Mus Mönchengladbach, 75; Palais des Beaux Arts, Brussels, Belg, 77; Mus Mod Art, Oxford, Eng, 77; Stedleijk Mus, Amsterdam, 78. Bibliog: Simon Field (auth), Joel Fisher on Paper, Art & Artists, 1/72; Lisa Bear (auth), Strong as a Spider's Web, Avalanche, 12/74. Style & Technique: Papermaking as art, drawing, assorted media, grounded in a personal ideological position. Publ: Auth, Hazard, Pot Hanger Press, 69; auth, Double Camouflage, Mansfield Fine Arts Ctr, 70; auth, The Berliner Book, Berlin Kunstler Prog des DAAd, 73; auth, Instances of Change, Bonomo Diffusione, Bari, Italy, 75; auth, Dissolution, Stadt Mus Mönchengladbach, 75; auth, An Image in Blankness, Mus Mod Art, Oxford, 77. Dealer: Max Protetch Gallery 29 W 57th St New York NY. Mailing Add: 31 Crosby St New York NY 10013

FISHER, LEONARD EVERETT
PAINTER, ILLUSTRATOR
b New York, NY, June 24, 24. Study: With Moses Soyer, New York, 39; Art Students League, with Reginald Marsh, 41; Brooklyn Col, with Serge Chermayeff, 41-42; Yale Univ Sch Fine Arts, BFA, 49, MFA, 50. Work: Butler Inst Am Art, Youngstown, Ohio; Libr of Cong, Washington, DC; Univ Ore, Eugene; Mt Holyoke Col, South Hadley, Mass; New Brit Mus Am Art, Conn. Comn: Three panels (silk screen) for wall montage in main elevator lobby, Washington Monument, Washington, DC, comn by US Dept Interior, 64; 14 stations of cross (painted wall decoration), St Patricks Church, Armonk, NY, 70; Am Bicentennial (four block eight cent commemorative postage stamps), 72, Legend of Sleepy Hollow (ten cent commemorative postage stamp), 74, Liberty Tree (thirteen cent embossed envelope), 75 & Skilled Hands for Independence (four block thirteen cent commemorative stamps), 77, US Postal Serv, Washington, DC. Exhib: 12th Ann Spring Exhib, Springfield Mus, Mass, 53; Painters Panorama, Am Fedn Arts Sponsored Tour, 54-56; New Eng Painting Ann, Silvermine Guild Artists, 68, 69 & 71; Butler Inst Am Art, Youngstown, Ohio, 72; retrospect, New Brit Mus Am Art, Conn, 73. Teaching: Asst design theory, Yale Univ Sch Fine Arts, 49-50; dean studies, Whitney Sch Art, 51-53; instr art hist, painting & bk illus, Paier Sch Art, 66- Pos: Illusr children's books for major publ, 54- Awards: William Wirt Winchester Traveling Fel, Yale Univ, 49; Pulitzer Fel Art, 50; Premio Grafico, 5th Int Book Fair, Bologna, Italy, 68. Bibliog: G Alan Turner (auth), Leonard Everett Fisher, Pulitzer prize winner, Design, 6-9/52; Joan Hess Michel (auth), Leonard Everett Fisher, illustrator and painter, Am Artist, 9/66. Mem: Soc of Illusr; New Haven Paint & Clay Club; Authors Guild/Authors League Am; Silvermine Guild Artists (bd dir, 70-74); Audubon Artists. Style & Technique: Painting: symbolic realism (acrylic, egg-tempera); bk illus: conceptual realism and design (scratchboard, line separations). Publ: Auth & illusr, The Colonial Americans, Watts, Vols 1-18, 64-76; auth & illusr, Two if by Sea, Random, 70; auth & illusr, The Death of Evening Star, Doubleday, 72; auth & illusr, The Art Experience: Oil Painting 15-19 C, Watts, 73; auth & illusr, Across the Sea from Galway, Four Winds, 75. Dealer: Capricorn Galleries 8003 Woodmont Ave Bethesda MD 20014. Mailing Add: 7 Twin Bridge Acres Rd Westport CT 06880

FISHER, SARAH LISBETH
ART CONSERVATOR
b Washington, DC, Nov 1, 45. Study: Wellesley Col, BA(art hist), 67; Florence, Italy, with pvt painting conservator, 67-68; Inst for Technol of Paintings, Stuttgart, Ger, directed by Dr R Straub, 69-70; Swiss Inst Art Res, Zurich, Switz, conserv of paintings & polychrome sculpture, with Dr T Brachert, 70-72, cert in conserv; fresco restoration with T Hermanes, pvt conservator, Canton of Vaud, Switz, 69 & 70; Cent Inst Art Res, Amsterdam, Holland, study analytical tech under Dr J Mosk, 73; Inst Royal du Patrimoine Artistique, Brussels, Belg, supervised by N Gortghebeur, 74-75, cert in conserv. Teaching: Instr painting conserv, Intermuseum Conserv Asn, Oberlin, Ohio, 75-77. Pos: Conservator & asst to the dir, Swiss Inst for Art Res, Zurich, Switz, 72-74; conservator, Intermuseum Lab, Oberlin, 75-77 & Balboa Art Conserv Ctr, San Diego, Calif, 77- Mem: Am Inst Conserv Hist & Artist Works; Int Inst Conserv Hist & Artistic Works; Western Asn Art Conserv. Mailing Add: c/o Balboa Art Conserv Ctr Box 2107 San Diego CA 92112

FISHER, VERNON
PAINTER, EDUCATOR
b Tex, Feb 19, 43. Study: Univ Ill, MFA. Work: Ft Worth Art Mus, Tex; Purdue Univ, West Lafayette, Ind; Skidmore, Owens & Merrill, Houston, Tex; El Paso Mus Fine Arts, Tex; Sheldon Swope Gallery, Terre Haute, Ind. Exhib: Proj South/Southwest, Ft Worth Contemp Art Mus, 70; Southern Ill Univ Drawing Show, Carbondale, Ill, 70; Ten Tex Painters, Skidmore, Owens & Merrill, 71; Tex Drawing Exhib, Smith Gallery, Dallas, 73; Exchange/DFW/SFO, San Francisco Mus/Ft Worth Contemp Art Mus, 75. Teaching: Assoc prof art, Austin Col, 69- Awards: Purchase Awards, El Paso Mus, 68 & Purdue Univ, 69 & 72; Individual Artists Fel, Nat Endowment for Arts, 74-75. Bibliog: Henry Hopkins (auth), Contemporary art in Texas: on the road to maturity, Art News, 73; Janet Kutner (auth), Vernon Fisher, Dallas Morning News, 73; Charlotte Moser (auth), Termagant Texans, Currant, 75. Media: Acrylic, Stitched Vinyl. Dealer: Delahunty Gallery 1611 Cedar Springs Dallas TX 75202. Mailing Add: 611 N Lee Sherman TX 75090

FISHKO, BELLA
ART DEALER
b Russia; US citizen. Study: Hunter Col. Pos: Dir, Forum Gallery. Mem: Art Dealers Asn Am; Friends of Whitney Mus Am Art. Specialty: American art of the 20th century, painting and sculpture. Publ: Contribr to var nat art mags. Mailing Add: 1018 Madison Ave New York NY 10021

FISK, EVI ESTER
PAINTER
b Helsinki, Finland; US citizen. Study: Art Students League; Mus Mod Art; also with Theodoros Stamos, Byron Brown, Steven Green & Julian Levi. Work: Riverside Mus, New York; Norfolk Mus Art, Va; Fleisher Art Mem, Philadelphia; plus pvt collections. Exhib: Nat Acad Gallery, New York, 73; Award Winner Show, Eastside Gallery, 68; Festival d'art deaville, Trouville, France, 69; Riverside Mus, 70; Albany Art Mus, NY; Little Gallery, New York, NY; Nev Art Gallery, Las Vegas; one-man show, Jersey City Art Mus, NJ, 73. Awards: Award Winner Selection Show, Allied Arts Guild, 63; Samuel Fleisher Art Mem Prize, 69; Purchase Prize, Norfolk Mus, 72. Bibliog: Eli Levin (auth), Art News (column), Philadelphia Inquirer; John Canaday (auth), rev, New York Times; Anith Ventura (auth), rev, Arts Mag. Mem: Pa Acad Fine Arts; Print Club; Am Abstract Artist. Style & Technique: Non-objective mystical quality. Media: Oil, Watercolor. Dealer: Eastside Gallery 307 E 37th St New York NY 10016. Mailing Add: 310 Riverside Dr New York NY 10025

FITCH, GEORGE HOPPER
COLLECTOR, PATRON
b New York, NY, Nov 29, 09. Study: Yale Univ, BA, 32. Pos: Gov bd, Yale Univ Art Gallery; vpres & trustee, Fine Arts Museums of San Francisco; comnr, Asian Art Mus, San Francisco. Mem: Mus Soc, De Young Mus & Calif Palace of Legion of Honor (chmn, 71-72); Art Comn City New York (vpres, 67-68); founder Art Collectors Club Am; Fel Pierpont Morgan Libr (coun, 66-69); Royal Oak Found (trustee); Munic Art Soc of New York, NY (div pres, 58-60). Interest: Increasing art appreciation. Collection: Twentieth century American watercolors; East Indian miniatures; Melanesian dagger handles; African Bobbins. Publ: Auth, So You're Going to Heaven, 71. Mailing Add: 1960 Broadway San Francisco CA 94109

FITZGERALD, EDMOND JAMES
PAINTER, LECTURER
b Seattle, Wash, Aug 19, 12. Study: Calif Sch Fine Arts; study with Eustace Zeigler & Mark Tobey. Work: Nat Acad Design, New York; Seattle Art Mus; New Brit Mus, Conn; George Washington Univ & USN Combat Art Collection, Washington, DC. Comn: Battle of Bear River, US Post Off, Preston, Idaho, 40; Man and the land, Am Mus Natural Hist, New York, 50; Pasteur, White Lab, Kenilworth, NJ, 51; Long Island History, Jamaica Savings Bank, NY, 63; Normandy Invasion, Nat Maritime Union's Curran Plaza Bldg, New York, 70. Exhib: Am Watercolor Soc, New York, 39; one-man show, Seattle Art Mus, 41; Nat Acad Design, 53; Art USA, Madison Sq Garden, New York, 58; Metrop Mus Art, New York, 66. Teaching: Lectr watercolor, Parsons Sch Design, New York, 47-49; lectr anat & drawing, Nat Acad Sch Fine Arts, New York, 69- Awards: First Prize, Nat Soc Mural Painters, 46; Grand Prize, Art USA, 58; Winsor & Newton Prize, Am Watercolor Soc, 72. Mem: Am Watercolor Soc (hon pres, 71-); Nat Acad Design; Allied Artists Am (pres, 60-63); Nat Soc Mural Painters (vpres, dir); Artists Fel (vpres, dir), Style & Technique: Representational. Media: Watercolor, Oil. Publ: Auth, Painting and Drawing in Charcoal and Oil, 59; auth, Marine Painting in Watercolor, 72. Mailing Add: 2094 Boston Post Rd Larchmont NY 10538

FITZPATRICK, ROBERT JOHN
ART ADMINISTRATOR
b Toronto, Ont, May 18, 40; US citizen. Study: Spring Hill Col, BA & MA; Woodrow Wilson Fel, Johns Hopkins Univ, 64-65. Pos: Pres, Calif Inst Arts, 75- Mailing Add: 24700 McBean Pkwy Valencia CA 91355

FIX, JOHN ROBERT
SCULPTOR, SILVERSMITH
b Pittsburgh, Pa, Oct 31, 34. Study: Rochester Inst Technol, Sch Am Craftsmen, BFA; Conn Col, MAT; study with Lawrence G Copeland, Hans Christianson, William A McCloy & Frances Felten. Comn: Host box, Glenwood Lutheran Church, Minn, 57; chalice, St Andrew's Episcopal Church, New Kensington, Pa, 62; chalice, 68 & menorah, 71, Harkness Chapel, Conn Col, New London; plus many pvt comn in sculpture & metalsmithing. Exhib: Assoc Artists Pittsburgh Ann, Carnegie Mus, 57-74; New England Invitational, DeCordova Mus, Lincoln, Mass, 62; RI Arts Festival, Providence, 64; Soc Conn Craftsmen Traveling Show, 66; Three Rivers Arts Festival, Pittsburgh, 71, 73 & 74. Teaching: Teacher metalsmithing, Norwich Art Sch, Conn, 60-; instr sculpture & hist art, Upward Bound, Conn Col, 69; dir young peoples prog, Lyman Allyn Mus, New London, 74-; jewelry workshops, Guilford Handcraft Ctr, Conn. Awards: First Prize in Crafts, 58, Mrs Roy A Hunt Award, 61 & Jury Award for Distinction in Crafts, 68, Assoc Artists Pittsburgh Ann. Bibliog: Murray Bovin (auth), Jewelry Making, Forest Hills, NY, 67; John D Morris (auth), Creative Metal Sculpture, Bruce Pub Co, NY, 71; Shirley Charron (auth), Modern Pewter, Van Nostrand Reinhold Co, 73. Mem: Mystic Art Asn Inc (pres, 74); Assoc Artists Pittsburgh; Soc Conn Craftsmen (scholar comt). Style & Technique: Jewelry; silver and pewter smithing; sculpture in pewter using surface casting and others. Media: Silver, Gold, Pewter. Mailing Add: Box 167 Groton Long Point CT 06340

FLACH, VICTOR H
DESIGNER, WRITER
b Portland, Ore, May 31, 29. Study: Univ Ore, Sch Archit & Allied Arts, with Jack Wilkinson, BS & MFA; Univ Pittsburgh, Henry Clay Frick Fine Arts Dept, with Walter Read Hovey; also with R Buckminster Fuller. Comn: Three-wall collage mural, with John Otto, Erb Mem Union, Univ 52; Ore, 52; three-wall mural, Clearlake Sch, Eugene, Ore, 56; The Heritage Series Interview with American Painter Ben Shahn, PBS-TV, 66; two-wall, three-story mosaic tile mural, Sci Ctr, Univ Wyo, 67-68; The Arts in Practice, TV prog, with Richard Evans, UW-TV, 71. Exhib: One-man show, Henry Kaiser Skyroom, Vanport, Ore, 51; Oregon Painters, Portland Art Mus, 52; 1st Ann 5-State Exhib, Univ Wyo, 65; six-state traveling shows, Paintings 4 By 4 & Photographs Counter-Encounters, 70-73; 73rd Western Ann Inaugural, New Denver Art Mus, 71; 12 experimental films variously exhibited, 70-74; macrographic drawings in group shows, Interaction & praxis, UW Art Mus, 74 & 76; plus others. Teaching: Prof design, painting & iconography, Univ Wyo, 65- Pos: Ed, In/sert: Active Anthology for the Creative, 55-62. Style & Technique: Perceptual-structural ideographic imagery. Res: Toward a comprehensive tetradic typologic systems programming as model for archetypal-prototypal iconographic and colorfielding structural morphology. Publ: Auth, IJHTBIW20: Early Poems, 49; co-auth (with Vernon Witham), 12 New Painters: Serigraph Folio, 53; auth, Gloss of the four universal forms and their six combinations & The eye's mind: ideographic structures, Ideas & Figures, 59-64; auth, Anatomy of the Canvas: Paintings by Richard Wells, Frick Gallery-Univ Pittsburgh Publ, 61; auth, Prologue to the Stage: A Series of Drawings by Joseph Deaderick, UW Publ, 78; plus many poems and essays in various magazines. Mailing Add: Dept Art Univ Wyo Laramie WY 82071

FLACK, AUDREY L
PAINTER, INSTRUCTOR
b New York, NY, May 30, 31. Study: Cooper Union, grad, 51; Cranbrook Acad Art; Yale Univ, scholar & study with Josef Albers. Work: Whitney Mus Am Art, New York; Rose Art Mus, Brandeis Univ; NY Univ Art Collection; Riverside Mus & Mus Mod Art, New York. Comn: Family portrait comn by Oriole Farb, Dir, Riverside Mus & Stuart M Speiser Collection. Exhib: 22 Realists, Whitney Mus Am Art, 70; Painter & the Photograph, Riverside Mus, 70; Whitney Mus Am Art Ann, 72; Tokyo Metrop Art Mus, 74; Toledo Mus Art, 75; Lowe Art Mus, Fla, 76; Rothman's of Pall Mall Can Traveling Exhib, Can, 76; Jacksonville Mus, Fla, 77; Australia Coun Traveling Exhib, through 78. Teaching: Instr drawing, Pratt Inst, Brooklyn, NY, 65-71; instr anat, NY Univ, 68-71; instr drawing, Sch Visual Arts, NY, 71-74. Awards: Albert Dorne Prof, Univ Bridgeport, 75; Nat Exhib Paintings Second Prize, Butler Inst Am Art, 74; The Cooper Union Citation, 77. Bibliog: Van Deren Coke (auth), Painter & the Photograph, Univ NMex, 72; Udo Kulterman (auth), Radical Realism, Praeger, 72; Cindy Nemser (auth), Art Talk, Scribner, 75; Man of the Year, cover illus, Time Mag, 77; articles in New York Times, 4/76, Art News, 11/77 & Arts Mag, 12/77. Style & Technique: Photorealism. Media: Oil. Publ: Illusr & contribr, 22 Realists (catalog), Whitney Mus, 70; illusr, Close up vision, Arts Mag, 5/72; illusr, Whitney Ann (catalog), 72; illusr, Tokyo Biennale (catalog), 74; illusr, Art in Am, 74. Mailing Add: c/o Louis K Meisel Gallery 141 Prince St New York NY 10012

FLAGG, MR & MRS RICHARD B
COLLECTORS
Mr Flagg, b Frankfurt am Main, Ger, Feb 8, 06. Study: Mr Flagg, Acad Arts, Vienna, Austria; sculpture with Joseph Heu, Vienna. Collection: European wood sculpture of the 15th, 16th and 17th century; European furniture—Gothic, Renaissance and Baroque; silver and metalcraft of the same periods; important private collection of European clocks with emphasis on the early 16th and 17th centuries. Mailing Add: 7170 N River Rd Milwaukee WI 53217

FLAKEY ROSE HIP (GLENN ALUN LEWIS)
DESIGNER, SCULPTOR
b Chemainus, BC, Oct 26, 35. Study: Vancouver Sch Art, Univ BC; and with Bernard Leach, Eng. Work: Winnipeg Art Gallery, Man; Vancouver Art Gallery, BC; Can Govt, Ottawa; Can Coun Art Bank, Ottawa; Nat Gallery, Ottawa. Comn: Ceramic wall mural, Can Govt Expo 70, Ottawa, 70; bronze dog, City Vancouver, 72; mural plastic boxes, Nat Sci Libr, Ottawa, 73. Exhib: One-man shows, Douglas Gallery, Vancouver, 68; Wall Graphs, Ace Gallery, 69 & 8 Closets, Vancouver Art Gallery, 70; Realisms, Montreal Mus Fine Art & Art Gallery Ont, 70; Can Trajectoires 73, Musee Mod Ville Paris, France, 73. Teaching: Instr ceramics, Univ BC, 64-67; vis prof ceramics, NY State Col Ceramics, Alfred Univ, 70-71; instr ceramics & sculpture, Univ BC, 71-74. Pos: Proj coordr, Intermedia Soc, 71-72; trustee, Vancouver Art Gallery, 73 & 75-76; pres & trustee, Western Front Soc, 75. Awards: Can Coun Art Bursary, travel to Japan, 67, study sculpture 68 & 70. Bibliog: Joan Lowndes (auth), Forest industry, Vancouver Sun Newspaper, 7/3/70; John B Mays (auth), Ottawa notebook, Proof Only, 2/22/74; Alex Mogelin & Normand Laliberte (co-auths), Art in Boxes, Reinholt, Van Nostrand, 75. Style & Technique: Ceramics; porcelain, Plexiglas and found sculpture; 16mm movies; collage; postal art; performance; photographs. Publ: Illusr & contribr, BC Almanac, Nat Film Bd Can, 70; illusr & contribr, Is 13, 72 & Topiary & Artists Recipes (microfische cards), 73, Coach House; co-auth, Mondo Artie, episode 1681 Art's birthday and Hollywood decca dance, 74; illusr & contribr, Mondo Artie episode 1625, Source, 74. Dealer: Gallery Allen 3025 Granville St Vancouver BC Can. Mailing Add: 358 Powell St Vancouver BC V6A 1G5 Can

FLANNERY, THOMAS
CARTOONIST
b Carbondale, Pa, Dec 16, 19. Study: Pratt Inst, 39-40; Univ Scranton, 46-47. Pos: Staff cartoonist, Yank Mag, 43-45; polit cartoonist, Lowell Sun, Mass, 47-57, Baltimore Eve Sun, 57-73 & Baltimore Sun, 73- Mem: Am Soc Ed Cartoonists. Mailing Add: 518 Orkney Rd Baltimore MD 21212

FLAVIN, DAN
ARTIST, WRITER
b New York, NY, Apr 1, 33. Study: Self-educated as artist; studied art hist, Univ Md, Repub Korea; New Sch Social Res & Columbia Univ. Work: Metrop Mus Art, New York; Mus Mod Art, New York; Nat Gallery Can, Ottawa; Tate Gallery, London; Stedelijk Mus, Amsterdam, Neth. Comn: Courtyard & inner arcade, Kunstmuseum Basel, 75; several platforms of Grand Cent Station, New York, 76. Exhib: Alternating Pink & Gold, Mus Contemp Art, Chicago, 67-68; Fluorescent Light, Etc, Nat Gallery Can, Ottawa, Ont, Vancouver Art Gallery, BC & Jewish Mus, New York, 69-70; drawings & diagrams, 63-72 & corners, barriers & corridors in fluorescent light (dual exhib), St Louis Art Mus, 73; five installations fluorescent light, Kunsthalle, Basel, Switz, 72-75; drawings, diagrams, prints & posters, 72-75; cornered installations in fluorescent light, Albright-Knox Art Gallery, Buffalo, 72; cornered fluorescent light, Inst Arts, Rice Univ, 72; three installations in fluorescent light, Wallraf-Richartz Museums in Kunsthalle Cologne, 73; fluorescent light, Ft Worth Art Museum, 75; Mus Boymans-van Beuningen, Rotterdam, 75; cornered installations ultra-violet & red fluorescent light, Portland Art Ctr, 76; fluorescent light, Ft Worth Art Mus, 76; three installations in coloured fluorescent light, Charlotte Sq Gallery of Scottish Arts Coun, Edinburgh, 76; artists and friends: Dan Flavin & Michael Venezia, Contemp Arts Ctr, Cincinnati, 77; installations fluorescent light, Art Inst Chicago, 77 & Univ Art Mus, Berkeley, 78. Teaching: Lectr grad fac, Univ NC, Greensboro, spring 67; Albert Dorne vis prof, Univ Bridgeport, 73. Awards: William & Noma Copley Found Award, 64; Nat Found Arts & Humanities Award, 66; Skowhegan Medal for Sculpture, 76. Mem: Scenic Hudson Preserv Conf; Nat Trust Hist Preserv; Nat Audubon Soc. Publ: Auth, ...in daylight or cool white, 12/65, auth, Some remarks..., 12/66 & auth, ...on an American artist's education, 3/68, Artforum; auth, Several more remarks..., Studio Int, 4/69. Dealer: Leo Castelli Gallery 420 W Broadway New York NY 10012; Heiner Friedrich Inc 393 W Broadway New York NY 10012 Mailing Add: PO Box 21 Garrison NY 10524

FLAX, SERENE
PAINTER
b Chicago, Ill, May 25, 25. Study: Northwestern Univ; Chicago Acad Fine Arts, degree; Art Inst Chicago; Inst Design. Work: Caravan Gallery, Tulsa, Okla; Deerfield High Sch, Ill; Art Inst Chicago. Exhib: Calif Watercolor Soc, Los Angeles, 64-67; Am Watercolor Soc, Nat Acad Design, New York, 64-69; Watercolor USA, Springfield Art Mus, Ill, 66-68; Ill State Mus, Springfield, 68 & 72; one-person shows, Ill Arts Coun, Chicago, 73, Ill State Mus, 74, TWO Ill Ctr, 76 & Lake Forest Col, 78. Teaching: Instr painting & techniques, Highland Park High Sch, Ill, spring 68 & 70; lectr, local cols. Pos: Chmn, Old Orchard Art Festival, 65. Awards: Award for Transparent Watercolor, Brugger's Fine Arts Serv, 64; Purchase Award, Caravan Gallery, 66; Municic Art Award, Art Inst Chicago, 69; plus var local awards. Bibliog: Dr Ralph Fabri (auth), article in, Today's Art, 1/75. Mem: Arts Club Chicago; Nat & Am Watercolor Socs. Media: Watercolor. Publ: Auth, article in, Am Artist Mag, 1/67; contribr, Women's Art Caucus Newsletter & Art League News. Mailing Add: 400 Park Ave Highland Park IL 60035

FLECK, IRMA L
ART ADMINISTRATOR
b Vienna, Austria, Oct 28, 19; US citizen. Study: Queens Col, BA; NY Univ, MA(human rels). Pos: Exec dir & founder, Bronx Coun Arts, 67-75, consult develop, 75; develop dir & founder, Bronx Mus Arts, 68-71; consult arts mgt, NY State Coun Arts, 75 & comt appointment, 75. Awards: Community Arts Award, Arts & Bus Coun NY, 71; Arts Adminr Year Award, Arts Mgt Publ, 72. Mem: Bronx Mus Arts (vpres, 71-75); Alliance NY State Community Arts Coun; Metrop Mus Art (mem visiting comt, 71-); Arts & Bus Coun NY; Asn Coun Arts (panelist, mem task force arts adminr accreditation, 72-). Mailing Add: 1777 Grand Concourse New York NY 10453

FLECKENSTEIN, OPAL R
PAINTER, EDUCATOR
b Macksville, Kans, Nov 19, 11. Study: Eastern Wash State Col, BA & MA(educ); Univ Wash; Study with Guy Anderson, James Fitzgerald & Mark Tobey. Exhib: Seattle Art Mus; Cheney Cowles Mus, Spokane, Wash; one-man show, Watercolors & Oils, Seattle Art Mus; one-man retrospectives, Cheney Cowles Mus & Eastern Wash Univ, Cheney. Teaching: Assoc prof painting & humanities, Eastern Wash Univ, 49-75; guest instr art educ, Univ Sask, 57, 58 & 60; emer prof art, Int Prog, Guadalajara, Mex, 77- Awards: Watercolor Purchase Prize, Seattle Art Mus, 50. Mem: Wash Art Asn. Style & Technique: Modern, abstract and expressionist. Media: Oil, Watercolor, Mosaic. Mailing Add: S 3118 Ultra Spokane WA 99204

FLECKER, MAURICE NATHAN
PAINTER, EDUCATOR
b Brooklyn, NY, Feb 27, 40. Study: State Univ NY Col, New Paltz, BS, with Ilya Bolotowsky, Gabriel Laderman, George Wexler & George Wardlaw; Brooklyn Col, MFA, with Philip Pearlstein, Ad Reinhardt, Carl Holty & R J Wolff; Art Students League; New Sch for Social Res; Brooklyn Mus; Pratt Inst. Work: State Univ NY Col, New Paltz; Brooklyn Mus; Fed Savings Bank of New Paltz. Exhib: One-man shows, Aegis Gallery, New York, 62, Icarus Gallery, New York, 66, Bank Gallery, New York, 69 & 1st Street Gallery, New York, 77; Wadsworth Atheneum, Hartford, Conn, 65; W V Smith Art Mus, Springfield, Mass, 65; Brooklyn Mus, New York, 68-75. Teaching: Instr, Brooklyn Mus Art Sch, New York, 68-75; asst prof life drawing & sculpture, Suffolk Co Community Col, asst head art, music & philos, 72- Awards: Painting Scholar, Art Students League & Brooklyn Mus. Bibliog: Reviews, Art News, 3/62 & 12/66; Amei Wallach (auth), One Road to Realism, Newsday, 77; Maria Latona (auth), Inspiration From Life, Long Island Press, 77. Mem: Soho Ctr for Visual Arts; Col Art Asn. Style & Technique: Nudes, landscapes; oil Venetian method. Media: Oil painting, watercolor. Dealer: First Street Gallery 118 Prince St New York NY 10012. Mailing Add: 101 Cooper Ct Port Jefferson NY 11777

FLEISCHMAN, LAWRENCE
ART DEALER, COLLECTOR
b Detroit, Mich, Feb 14, 25. Study: Western Mil Acad, Alton, Ill; Purdue Univ; Univ Detroit, BS. Pos: Comn mem, Fine Arts Comt, US Info Agency, 57-59; pres, Arch Am Art, 59-66; pres, Detroit Inst Arts, 62-66; White House Comt Fine Arts, 62-66; pres, Detroit Arts Comn; dir, Kennedy Galleries; trustee, Skowhegan Sch Art, 68-; fel, Morgan Libr, New York, 68-; ed, Am Art J, 69-; dir, Kennedy Galleries. Awards: Spec award, City Detroit, 66; Lotus Club Art Award, 67. Mem: Arch Am Art (trustee); life mem Pa Acad Fine Arts; life mem Pa Hist Soc; Art Dealers Asn New York; Soc Arts & Crafts (treas art sch, 55-66, hon trustee). Specialty: 18th, 19th and 20th century American art. Collection: American art and Roman and Greek antiquities. Publ: Auth (catalogues), Edward Hopper, 77, Charles E Burchfield—Early Years, 77 & City as a Source, 77, Kennedy Galleries. Mailing Add: 40 W 57th St New York NY 10019

FLEISHER, PAT
ART CRITIC, ARTIST
b Toronto, Ont. Study: Univ Toronto, BA; painting, Skowhegan, Maine with Henry Varnum Poor; Ontario Col Art with Jock MacDonald; St Adele, Quebec with Agnes Lefort; printmaking, York Univ with Eugene Tellez, 72. Exhib: Colour & Form Soc, Toronto, 66; Rodman Hall Show, St Catherines, 67; Soc Canadian Artists, Toronto, 67-69. Teaching: Teacher art, North York Bd Educ, Rec Dept, 60-64; Toronto Bd Educ; lectr & art guide, Toronto & New York galleries & studios, 71-78; founder/ed, Art Mag, 69- Pos: Pres, Artmagazine, Inc, 74- Awards: Award of Merit to Art Mag, Soc Publ Designers New York, 75; Can Silver Jubilee Medal, awarded by Jules Léger, Gov Gen of Can, 78. Mem: Int Asn Art Critics (mem, Can Br). Style & Technique: Surrealist expressionist. Media: Collage; Etching, Lithography, Photography. Publ: Auth, Catalog introd, John Gould Exhib, 74; auth, catalog introd, Almuth Cutken haus, 74; auth, Atlantic Provinces Journal, Artmagazine, 76; auth, A Western Pilgrimage, Artmagazine, 77. Mailing Add: 299 Roehampton Ave Apt 423 Toronto ON M4P 1L6 Can

FLEMING, ALLAN ROBB
DESIGNER, CALLIGRAPHER
b Toronto, Ont, May 7, 29. Study: Western Tech Sch. Work: Mus Mod Art, New York. Comn: 19th Century Signage, Upper Can Village, comn by Anthony Adamson, Toronto, 58; Can Nat Railways symbol, comn by James Valkus, New York, 59; interior calligraphy, Massey Col, 62; Ont Hydro symbol, Ont Hydro-Elec Power Comn, 65; Hall of Memory, Toronto City Hall, 65. Exhib: Several exhibs at Art Dir Club New York & Type Dir Club New York; Twenty Five Books of the Year, Am Asn Univ Press, 68-72; Am Inst Graphic Arts Covers, 71; Fifty Books of the Year, Am Inst Graphic Arts. Teaching: Instr typographic design, Ont Col Art, 58-61. Pos: Vpres & dir creative serv, Cooper & Beatty Ltd Typographers, Toronto, 57-62; vpres & dir creative serv, Maclaren Advert Co Ltd, 63-68; chief designer, Univ Toronto Press, 68- Awards: Gold Medal for Distinguished Contrib to Art of Typographic Design, Royal Can Acad Arts, 65; Centennial Medal, Can Govt, 67; Gold Medal for Design of Econ Atlas of Ontario, Int Bk Fair, Leipzig, 70. Bibliog: Robert Fulford (auth), Allan Fleming, Can Art, 60; Arnold Rockman (auth), Visual communication in Canada, Idea, Japan, 61. Mem: Fel Graphic Designers Can; Royal Can Acad Arts; Nat Design Coun; fel Ont Col Art. Mailing Add: Univ Toronto Press Toronto ON M5S 1A1 Can

FLEMING, BETTY CORCORAN
ART DEALER
b Miami Beach, Fla, Feb 12, 47. Study: Syracuse Univ, BA. Pos: Vpres, Art Dealer's Asn SFla, 77-; owner, Betty C Fleming Fine Art Inc, Miami, Fla. Mem: Art Dealer's Asn SFla. Specialty: Contemp Am art. Mailing Add: PO Box 013838 Flagle Sta Miami FL 33101

FLEXNER, JAMES THOMAS
WRITER, ART HISTORIAN
b New York, NY, Jan 13, 08. Study: Lincoln Sch, Teacher's Col; Harvard Col, grad (magna cum laude), 25. Awards: Guggenheim Fel, 53; Parkman Prize, 62; Nat Bk Award, 74; Pulitzer Prize, 74. Mem: Century Asn; Soc Am Historians (pres, 75-78); PEN Am Ctr (pres, 54-55). Res: American painting as an expression of American life. Publ: Auth, America's Old Masters, 39, rev ed, 67; auth, Amer- ican Painting, first flowers of our wilderness, 47 & 69; auth, Pocket History of American Painting, 50; American Painting, the Light of Distant Skies, 54 & 69; auth, American Painting, that Wilder Image, 62 & 70; plus others. Mailing Add: 530 E 86th St New York NY 10028

FLICK, PAUL JOHN
PAINTER, COLLECTOR
b Rock Island, Ill, Feb 5, 43. Study: Univ Minn, BA & MFA(printing & printmaking); studied with Herman Cherry & Mario Valpe. Teaching: Instr drawing & color, Bureau of Engraving, 72- Mem: Twin Cities Metrop Arts Alliance. Media: Encaustic, Assemblages. Collection: Primitive art, American Indian and African. Dealer: Brittany Box 30031 St Paul MN 55165. Mailing Add: 4032 Lyndale Ave S Minneapolis MN 55409

FLICK, ROBERT
PHOTOGRAPHER, EDUCATOR
b Amersfoort, Holland, Nov 15, 39; Can citizen. Study: Univ BC, BA, 67; Univ Calif, Los Angeles, MA, 70, MFA, 71, with Robert Heinecken & Robert Fichter. Work: Visual Studies Workshop, Rochester, NY; Nat Gallery of Can, Ottawa; Art Inst of Chicago; Madison Art Ctr, Wis; Ctr for Creative Photog, Univ Ariz, Tucson. Exhib: Extensions (travelling exhib), Univ BC, 68-70; Calif Photographers (travelling exhib), Univ Calif, Davis, 70; New Photographs of Ill, Chicago Art Inst, 74; The Photographer's Choice (travelling exhib), 75; Midwest Diary, LIGHT Gallery, New York, 76. Teaching: Instr photog, Univ Calif, Los Angeles Exten, 69-71; asst prof photog, Univ Ill, Champaign, 71-76; asst prof photog, Univ Southern Calif, Los Angeles, 76- Awards: Can Coun Bursary in the Arts, 67 & 69; fel, Ctr for Advan Studies, Univ Ill, 73. Mem: Soc for Photog Educ; Col Art Asn. Style & Technique: Highly manipulated montage; straight silverprint. Media: Silverprint. Publ: Contribr, Photographer's Choice, Addison House, 75. Dealer: Light Gallery 724 Fifth Ave New York NY 10019. Mailing Add: 126 1/2 S Market Inglewood CA 90301

FLINN, ELIZABETH HAIGHT
EDUCATOR
b Ann Arbor, Mich. Study: Wellesley Col, BA; Inst Fine Arts, MA. Pos: Assoc mus educr, Jr Mus, Metrop Mus Art, 74- Mem: Am Asn Youth Mus. Res: Medieval manuscript, preparation of educational materials on the museum's collection for students and teachers. Publ: Auth, Medieval towns and guilds (sch picture set), auth, America: 1750-1789 (sch picture set) & auth, A magnificent manuscript—a historical mystery, the hour of Jeanne d'Evreux, Metrop Mus Art Bull, 71. Mailing Add: Jr Mus Metrop Mus Art 82nd St & Fifth Ave New York NY 10028

FLINT, JANET ALTIC
CURATOR, ART HISTORIAN
b Louisville, Ky, Aug 24, 35. Study: Louisville Art Ctr; Univ Louisville, BS(painting & art hist); Univ Minn, MA(art hist). Collections Arranged: Prints: 1800-1945, 66; Watercolors of William Henry Holmes, 70; Boris Anisfeldt: 20 Years of Designs for the Theatre, 71; Drawings by William Glackens, 72; J Alden Weir, An American Printmaker, 72. Pos: Assoc cur, Minneapolis Inst Arts, 59-66; asst cur & cur prints & drawings, Nat Collection Fine Arts, Smithsonian Inst, 69- Mem: Print Coun Am. Res: American prints and drawings. Publ: Catalogs, Way of Good & Evil Popular Religious Lithographs of 19th Century America, 72, Johann Herman Carmiencke: Drawings & Watercolors, 73, Modern American Woodcuts, 74, Two Decades of American Prints, 1920-1940, 74 & Chamim Gross: Sculpture & Drawings, 74. Mailing Add: c/o Nat Collection of Fine Arts Eighth & G Sts NW Washington DC 20560

FLINT, LEROY W
PAINTER, EDUCATOR
b Ashtabula, Ohio, Jan 29, 09. Study: Univ Minn; Cleveland Inst Art; Western Reserve Univ; Cleveland Col. Work: Cleveland Mus Art; Akron Art Inst; Libr of Cong; Butler Mus Am Art. Comn: Relief & painted mural, Cleveland Metrop Housing Authority, 38; mobile, Akron Pub Libr, Northfield Br, 70; mobile & mobile sculpture in pvt collections. Exhib: Cleveland Mus Art May Shows, 37-50; Akron Art Inst Spring Shows, 50-55; Few Are Chosen, Columbus Gallery Fine Arts & Houston, Tex, 53; Butler Inst Am Art, Youngstown, Ohio, 71; one-man shows, 50-54, 56, 65, 66 & 75-77. Collections Arranged: A Bourdelle, Akron Art Inst, Ann Collection Show, 60-65, Ann Spring Show, 56-65; Kent State Univ Ann, 67-72. Teaching: Assoc prof painting & gallery docent, Cleveland Mus Art, 49-50; assoc prof painting, drawing & art hist, Akron Art Inst, 56-65; prof painting & drawing, Kent State Univ, 65- Pos: Cur educ, Akron Art Inst, 53-56, dir, 56-65; gallery dir, Kent State Univ, 65-73. Awards: Awards & Mentions, Cleveland May Show, 38-41 & 46-50. Mem: Am Asn Mus; Int Inst Conserv; Col Art Asn Am; Am Soc Aesthet. Media: Tempera, Acrylic, Aluminum. Publ: Auth, The volunteer & museum education, Curator, winter 59. Mailing Add: Div of Painting & Sculpture Kent State Univ Kent OH 44242

FLOETER, KENT
SCULPTOR
b Saginaw, Mich, Oct 22, 37. Study: Boston Univ, BFA; Yale Univ, MFA. Work: Pangborn Found Collection, Hagerstown, Md; Etzold Collection, Stadtisches Mus, Monchengladbach, Ger. Exhib: One-man shows, Bykert Gallery, New York, 73, Ricke Gallery, Cologne, Ger, 76 & Bernier Gallery, Athens, Greece, 78; Biennial Exhib Contemp Am Art, Whitney Mus Am Art, New York, 75; Drawings Series Number 3, Painters-Sculptors USA, Stadtisches Mus, Schlob Morsbroich, Levenkusen, Ger, 75; Soho Downtown Manhattan, Akad der Kunst, Berlin, Ger, 76; Selections, La Mus Mod Art, Humlebaeck, Denmark, 76. Bibliog: Carl Baldwin (auth), Kent Floeter, 6/75 & Robert Pincus-Witten (auth), Entries, 3/76, Arts Mag. Mailing Add: c/o Mary Boone 42 Bone St New York NY 10012

FLOETHE, RICHARD
ILLUSTRATOR, DESIGNER
b Essen, Ger, Sept 2, 01; US citizen. Study: Acad Appl Arts, Dortmund, Ger; Acad Appl Arts, Munich, Ger, with Willy Geiger & Edward Ege; Bauhaus Weimar, Ger, with Moholy-Nagy & Paul Klee. Work: Metrop Mus Art, New York; Libr Cong, Washington, DC; Philadelphia Mus Art, Pa; Kerlan Collection, Univ Minn; Spencer Collection, Fifth Ave Libr, New York. Comn: Hist mural, Pressa, Cologne, Ger, 28. Teaching: Instr com design, Cooper Union, 41-42; instr illus, Ringling Sch Art, 55-67. Pos: Art dir, Fed Art Proj, 36-39; art dir, New York City War Serv, 42-43. Awards: Int Contest for Best Illus Bks award for Tyl Ulenspiegl, 35 & award for Pinocchio, 38, Limited Ed Club; Am Inst Graphic Arts Award for English is our Language, 50. Bibliog: Ronald K Floethe (auth), Kid Stuff, Gordon Kerckhoff Prod, 70. Media: Woodcut, Serigraphy. Publ: Illusr, If I were Captain, 56, Blueberry Pie, 62, Jungle People, 71 & Fishing Around the World, 72, Scribner's; illusr, A Thousand & One Buddhas, Ariel, 67; plus many other titles, 32-73. Mailing Add: 1391 Harbor Dr Sarasota FL 33579

FLORA, JAMES ROYER
ILLUSTRATOR, PAINTER
b Bellefontaine, Ohio, Jan 25, 14. Study: Urbana Univ, Ohio, 31-33; Art Acad Cincinnati, 34-39; also study & asst to Carl Zimmerman (muralist) & Stanley William Hayter at Atelier 17. Pos, Art dir, Columbia Records, Bridgeport, Conn, 42-50, Park East Mag, New York, 51-53 & Computer Design Mag, Littleton, Mass, 62- Style & Technique: Magazine and record album illustrations range from humorous pen, ink and watercolor to abstract computer designs in all media. Media: Ink; Watercolor; Acrylic. Publ: Auth & illusr, The Fabulous Firework Family, 55, The Day the Cow Sneezed, 57 & Leopold, the See-Through Crumbpicker, 61, Harcourt Brace; auth & illusr, The Great Green Turkey Creek Monster,

76 & Grandpa's Ghost Stories, 78, Atheneum. Dealer: Frank Lavaty 45 E 51st St New York NY 10022 Mailing Add: St James Pl Rowayton CT 06853

FLORIO, SAL ERSENY
SCULPTOR
b San Piezo Patti, Messina, Italy, Dec 17, 1899; US citizen. Study: Nat Acad Design; also with Herman MacNeil & A Sterling Calder. Comn: Created models as chief sculptor assoc of Rene Chiambellan Firm, New York, 28-33 & during this period created: group of 20 figures, symbols of Am Democracy for facade of News Bldg, New York, 29-30; models for Yale Sterling Mem Libr & Sterling Quadrangle, Law Sch & Divinity Col (with Gamble-Rogers, archit) for Yale Univ, New Haven, Conn, 32; clay models for figure sculpture work, Charity Crucifix Tower, Royal Oak, Mich (Henry J McGill, archit), 33; co-designed American Culture Moving West (sculpture figure panels, high relief, north facade, with Herman A MacNeil), Mo State Capitol, Jefferson City, 34. Exhib: Queen of Atlantis, Nat Sculpture Soc, New York, 25; American Venus, New York Main Pub Libr, 25; Hudson Valley Virgin, Nat Sculpture Soc, 70. Awards: First Prize for Sculpture Figure, Silver Medal & Hon Mention, Group Compos, Nat Acad Design; Bronze Medal for Sculpture, Int Expos, San Francisco, 15; Hon Mention for Medallion of Rear Adm Christian Joy Peoples, Philadelphia Exhib, 21. Mem: Emer mem Nat Sculpture Soc; Ital Hist Soc Am. Media: Bronze, Marble. Mailing Add: 52 Clifford Pl Bronx NY 10453

FLORSHEIM, RICHARD A
PAINTER, PRINTMAKER
b Chicago, Ill, Oct 25, 16. Study: Univ Chicago. Work: Mus Mod Art & Metrop Mus Art, New York; Art Inst Chicago; Libr Cong, Washington, DC; Musee Nationale d'Art Moderne, Paris, France; plus many others. Exhib: Inst Nac de Bellas Artes, Mexico, 52; Rijksakademie, Amsterdam, 68; Art Inst Chicago, 46, 58 & 70; Am Acad Arts & Lett, New York, 71; Ill State Mus, Springfield, 71; Nat Acad Design, New York, 71-78; plus many other group & one-man exhibs. Teaching: Instr painting, Layton Sch Art, Milwaukee, 49-50; Contemp Art Workshop, Chicago, 52-63; artist in residence, Atlanta Mus, Ga, 64. Pos: Asst dir, Arts Ctr Asn, Chicago, 51-52; bd mem, Ill Arts Coun, Chicago, 65-73. Awards: Chicago Newspaper Guild Award, Art Inst Chicago, 54; Pennell Fund Award, Libr Cong, 56; Silvermine Guild Artists, 59. Bibliog: N Kent (auth), Color lithographs of Richard Florsheim, Am Artist, 66; E Barry (auth), Artist is busy, Chicago Tribune Mag, 70; August L Freundlich (auth), Richard Florsheim—The Artist & His Art, Barnes & Co, New York, 76 & Thomas Yoseloff, Ltd, London; plus many others. Mem: Nat Acad Design; Soc Am Graphic Artists; Audubon Soc Artists; Provincetown Art Asn (trustee & vpres, 62-71); Artists Equity Asn (pres, 53-54; now hon pres). Media: Oil, Lithography. Publ: Articles in Col Art J, Art League News, Motive, Chicago Sun-Times, Cape Cod Standard Times, plus others. Dealer: Assoc Am Artists 663 Fifth Ave New York NY 10022; Oehlschlaeger Galleries 107 E Oak Chicago IL 60611. Mailing Add: 5 E Ontario St Chicago IL 60611

FLOWERS, THOMAS EARL
PAINTER, EDUCATOR
b Washington, DC, Feb 17, 28. Study: Furman Univ, BA; Univ Iowa, MFA. Work: Greenville Co Mus Art, SC; Columbia Mus Art, SC; Chase Manhattan Bank, New York; SC Arts Comn, Columbia; Vincent Price Enterprises, Chicago. Comn: Mural, Vince Perome, Greenville, SC, 62; mural, Saad Rug Co, Greenville, 63; mace & medallion, Furman Univ, Greenville, 65. Exhib: 18th Ann Guild SC Artists Exhib, 68; 11th Ann Southern Contemp Art Exhib, Mobile, Ala, 69; 12th Ann Springs Art Exhib, Lancaster, SC, 70; Atlanta Artists Club, Nat 1, Ga, 70; Southeastern Painter's Choice Exhib, Ga Col, Milledgeville, Ga, 71. Teaching: Asst prof art & chmn dept, Ottawa Univ, 56-58; instr sculpture, E Carolina Col, 58-59; assoc prof art & chmn dept, Furman Univ, 59- Pos: State rep, Am Craftsman's Coun, 62-64. Awards: First Purchase Award, Southeastern Painter's Choice Exhib, 71; Purchase Award, SC Arts Comn, 71; Second Award, Franklin Mint, 72; Art in Archit Award, SC Chap, Am Inst of Architects, 77. Bibliog: Jack A Morris (auth), Contemporary artists of South Carolina, Greenville Co Mus Art, 70; R Smeltzer (auth), article in Southern Living Mag, 12/70; M Hays (auth), article in Furman Univ Mag, spring 72. Mem: Guild SC Artists (pres, 61-62, bd dirs, 71-72); Greenville Artists Guild (pres, 72-73); Southeastern Col Art Asn. Media: Acrylic, Oil, Mixed Media. Publ: Illusr, Furman Univ Mag covers, winter 67, summer 68 & 5/69; illusr, Springs Cotton Mill Ann Report cover, 69; illusr, Images, Univ NC, Asheville, summer 69. Dealer: Hampton III Gallery Ltd 14 Hampton Corners Greenville SC 29601. Mailing Add: Box 28606 Furman Univ Greenville SC 29613

FLUDD, REGINALD JOSEPH
PAINTER, INSTRUCTOR
b New York, NY, June 10, 38. Study: Ind Univ, BS(art); Queens Col, MS(art); study with Barse Miller; Art Inst Chicago. Work: Alcoa Aluminum Corp, New York; Norton Mus, Palm Beach, Fla; Nassau Community Col, Garden City, NY; Ocean City Cult Arts Ctr, NJ. Exhib: Am Drawing Biennial, Norfolk Mus, 71; Okla Art Ctr, Oklahoma City, 72; Aldrich Mus, Ridgefield, Conn, 74; New Britian Mus Contemp Art, Conn, 74; one-man show, Hecksher Mus, Huntington, NY, 75. Teaching: Teacher drawing, painting & sculpture, Syosset High Sch, NY, 64-; asst prof painting, Suffolk Community Col, 74- Pos: Instr painting, Huntington Art League, 68-69. Awards: Best in Show, Bayshore CofC, 68 & Patchoque CofC, 70; Grand Prix, Locust Valley Art Show, Operation Democracy, 73. Bibliog: Laurie Anderson (auth), article in Art News, 1/72; Malcom Preston (auth), article in Newsday, 3/12/75; Jean Paris (auth), article in Long Island Press, 7/6/75. Mem: NEA; Nat Art Educ Asn; Huntington Art League (bd mem); Huntington Group. Style & Technique: Abstract, poured paint. Media: Acrylic, Mixed Media, African Influenced Collage. Dealer: Lotus Gallery 81 Spring St New York NY 10012. Mailing Add: 27 Lantern St Huntington NY 11743

FLUEK, TOBY
PAINTER, GRAPHIC ARTIST
b Czernica, Poland, Feb 20, 26; US citizen. Study: Art Students League, with Robert Beverly Hale; also with Joe Hing Lowe & Irving Koenig. Exhib: Bronx Mus Arts Ann, NY, 72, 74, 75 & 76; Am Artists Prof League Grand Nat Exhib at Lever House, NY, 72-75; Hudson Valley Art Asn Ann, White Plains, NY, 73, 75, 76 & 77; Knickerbocker Artists Exhib, Nat Arts Club, New York, 74; Catharine Lorillard Wolfe Art Club, Nat Arts Club Gallery, 74, 75 & 76; plus many other group & one-woman shows. Teaching: Instr oil painting, Woodside Jewish Ctr, NY, 72. Awards: First Prize, Brush & Palette Soc, 71, 73 & 75; Best in Show, Fellowship Art Gallery, 72; Hon Mention, Hudson Valley Art Asn, 73; plus others. Bibliog: Bibliog: Jeanne Paris (auth), Art, Long Island Press, 10/8/72; Jack Besterman (auth), Big Six Art League is on the go, 4/74 & Rubia Olf (auth), Art & graphoanalysis, 6/75, Towers Reporter. Mem: Am Artists Prof League; Art League of Nassau Co; Brush & Palette Soc; Catharine Lorillard Wolfe Art Club; Big Six Art League. Style & Technique: Realistic technique used to depict the primitive life in an Eastern Poland village. Media: Oil, Pastels, Graphics. Mailing Add: 60-10 47th Ave Woodside NY 11377

FOGEL, SEYMOUR
PAINTER, SCULPTOR
b New York, NY, Aug 25, 11. Study: Art Students League, 29, with George Bridgeman; Nat Acad Design, 29-32. Work: Whitney Mus Am Art, New York; Joseph H Hirshhorn Collection, Washington, DC; Dallas Mus Art, Tex; Nat Archives of Am Art; City of St Louis Art Mus, Mo. Comn: Sand sculpture wall, Hoffmann-La Roche Res Tower, Nutley, NJ, 64; mosaic mural, US Customs Courts Bldg, New York, 68; mosaic mural, Intermediate Sch 29, New York, 71; stained glass screen, Bellevue Hosp, New York, 72; four mosaic murals, New Park West High Sch, New York, 75-76. Exhib: Houston Mus of Fine Arts, Tex, 51; Metrop Mus Art, New York, 51; one-man shows, Ft Worth Art Mus, Tex, 55, Santa Barbara Art Mus, Calif, 57, MacNey Inst, San Antonio, Tex, 58, Archit League of New York, 60, Mich State Univ, 61 & Springfield Mo Art Mus, 64; Carnegie Int, Pittsburgh, Pa, 58-59; many shows, Archit League New York, Whitney Mus Am Art & Nat Gallery Art, Washington, DC. Teaching: Asst prof painting, design & mural, Univ Tex, Austin, 46-54; guest prof life drawing & grad painting, Mich State Univ, 61. Pos: Vpres, Archit League & Int Fine Arts Coun. Awards: First Prize, Gulf Carribean Int, Houston, 56; First Prize, Tex Gen, Dallas, 56; First Prize in Design, Archit League New York, 58. Bibliog: Zeigfield et al (auth), Art Today, Henry Holt; Ralph Pearson (auth), Modern renaissance in American art, Harper & Row, 54; Redstone (auth), Art & architecture, McGraw, 70. Mem: Archit League New York; Int Platform Asn; Nat Soc Lit & Arts. Publ: Auth, Ethyl silicate & architecture, Archit & Engr News, 60; auth, Painter & architect, Am Inst Architects J, 60; auth, Art & the church, Liturgical Arts, 60; auth, Architect discovers painting & sculpture, Mich Am Inst Architects J, 61; auth, Painting & sculpture as architecture, Art in Am, 62. Mailing Add: Torandor 68 Georgetown Rd Weston CT 06883

FOHR, JENNY
SCULPTOR, INSTRUCTOR
b New York, NY. Study: Hunter Col, BA; Alfred Univ; Univ Colo, MA; City Col. Work: Norfolk Mus, Va; Long Beach Island Found Arts & Sci, NJ; Dr Wardell Pomeroy, New York; Oakland Mus, Calif; Charles Suter, Ciba-Geigy, New York. Exhib: One-man show, Chautauqua Art Asn Galleries, NY, 60 & Brooklyn Mus, 61; Nat Asn Women Artists, Chauteau de la Napoule, France, 65; Nat Asn Women Artists Traveling Show, India, 66; NJ State Mus, Trenton, 68; Am Color Print Soc Traveling Show, 72. Teaching: Asst instr sculpture, Brooklyn Mus, 49-51; instr art, Beekman Hill Sch, 69- Awards: First Prize, Pen & Brush Soc, 61; Andrew Nelson Award, 62; Medal of Honor, Painters & Sculptors Soc, NJ, 63; Paige Electric Award, 65; Windsor Newton Award, 66; Andrew Nelson Whitehead Award, 67; Fabian Zaccone Award, 68; Samuel Mann Award, Am Soc Contemp Artists, 71; May Granick Award, Nat Asn Women Artists, 75. Bibliog: Article, New York News, 76. Mem: Am Soc Contemp Artists (pres, secy, bd dir); Nat Asn Women Artists (secy, jury chmn, dir); Painters & Sculptors Soc NJ (selection jury, bd); Am Color Print Soc; New York Soc Women Artists (dir, cat chmn). Style & Technique: Abstract sculpture, collage watercolors, graphics, etching and woodcuts; interested in color, shapes and movement. Mailing Add: 165 E 32 St New York NY 10016

FOLDA, JAROSLAV (THAYER, III)
ART HISTORIAN
b Baltimore, Md, July 25, 40. Study: Princeton Univ, AB, 62; Johns Hopkins Univ, PhD, 68. Teaching: Asst prof medieval art, Univ NC, Chapel Hill, 68-72, assoc prof, 72- Pos: Fulbright Award, res in Paris, Inst Int Educ-Fulbright Comn, 66-67; jr fel, Dumbarton Oaks Ctr for Byzantine Studies, 67-68; Jr Humanist Award, res in Jerusalem, Nat Endowment for the Humanities, 74-75. Mem: Medieval Acad Am; US Nat Comt Byzantine Studies; Int Ctr Medieval Art; Am Schs Oriental Res; Soc Francaise d'Archeol. Res: Medieval art of the High and Late Middle Ages, especially Crusader art, 1099-1291. Publ: Auth, Kreuzzuge, Lexikon der christlichen Ikonographie, Verlag Herder, 70; co-auth, A Medieval Treasury from Southeastern Collections, Ackland Mus, 71; auth, Manuscripts of the History of Outremer, Scriptorium Vol 27, 73; auth, Crusader Manuscript Illumination at St Jean d'Acre, Princeton Univ Press, 76; contribr, K M Setton (ed), A History of the Crusades, Vol 4, Univ Wis Press, 77. Mailing Add: Dept of Art Ackland Art Ctr Univ of NC Chapel Hill NC 27514

FOLDS, THOMAS MCKEY
ART CONSULTANT, EDUCATOR
b Connellsville, Pa, Aug 8, 08. Study: Yale Col, BA, 30; Yale Univ Sch Fine Arts, BFA, 34. Comn: Mural, US Govt, Pub Works Admin, 34. Exhib: Painting a Mural & Art in Advertising, traveling exhibs for Am Fedn Arts. Teaching: Art dir, Phillips Exeter Acad, 35-46; prof art hist & chmn dept art, Northwestern Univ, 46-60; dean educ, Metrop Mus Art, 60-73, guest lectr, 73- Mem: Col Art Asn Am; Sch Art League New York (pres, 68-75). Publ: Auth, A critique of color reproductions, Col Art J, 48-49; co-auth, Masterpieces of painting in the Metropolitan Museum of Art, 70; auth, Abstract painting (exhib), Macmillan, 70. Mailing Add: 909-B Heritage Village Southbury CT 06488

FOLEY, KATHY KELSEY
CURATOR, ART HISTORIAN
b Perth Amboy, NJ, Aug 24, 52. Study: Trinity Col, Hartford, Fall semester in Rome, 72-73; Vassar Col, AB(hist art), 74; Nat Gallery Art, Washington, DC, internship cert, Summer 74; Johns Hopkins Univ, MA(hist art), 75. Collections Arranged: Reinstallation of the American Collection, Pre-Columbian-Mid 20th Century, 76; Mezzotints from the Collection of Edward Miller, spec exhib, 76 & Edward Weston's Gifts to His Sister, spec exhib of 125 Photographs Given by Weston to His Sister, 78, Dayton Art Inst. Pos: Instr, Brooklyn Mus, NY Dept Educ, Summer 73; intern dept prints & drawings, Nat Gallery Art, Washington, DC, Summer 74; asst cur, Dayton Art Inst, Ohio, 75-76, cur, 76- Mem: Am Asn Mus; Col Art Asn; Ohio Mus Asn; Int Coun Mus. Publ: Co-auth, Selected Checklist of the Collection of the Dayton Art Inst, 76 & auth, Handbook of the American Collection of the Dayton Art Inst, 76 & auth, Joseph Stella-Enigmatic Painter, Bull of Dayton Art Inst, 77, Dayton Art Inst; contribr, Promised Gifts, Berdie in Blue Tea Towel, Larry Rivers (catalogue entry), Vassar Col, 77; auth, Edward Weston's Gifts to His Sister (ehixb (exhib catalogue), Dayton Art Inst, 78. Mailing Add: Dayton Art Inst PO Box 941 Dayton OH 45401

FOLEY, KYOKO Y
INSTRUCTOR, PAINTER
b Tokyo, Japan, Dec 23, 33; US citizen. Study: Mt San Antonio Col, 67-69, AA, 69; Calif State Univ; Fullerton, 69-71, BA/MA, 72; Claremont Grad Sch, 75-77, MFA, 77. Work: Mt San Antonio Col Gallery; Home Savings & Loan Asn, Calif; Press Bldg Art Gallery, El Monte, Calif. Comn: Flower Garden 'n Forest, Amar Nursing Sch, Valinda, Calif, 74. Exhib: Southern Calif Exhib, Long Beach, 71 & 72; Nat Orange Show, San Bernardino, Calif, 72-75; All Calif Exhib, Laguna Beach, 73-75; Art Unlimited, Downey Mus Exhib, Calif, 74; All Calif Exhib, Mt San Antonio Col Biannual, Walnut, 74. Teaching: Instr drawing & painting, Hacienda-LaPuente United Sch Dist, 72- & gifted children's art prog, 72- Awards: First Award, Downey Mus Art, 72; Purchase Awards, Mt San Antonio Col, 74 & Home Savings & Loan, 75. Mem: Orange Co Prof Art Asn; 58F. Style & Technique: Multiple color passages

of small brush strokes, describing depth and flatness simultaneously. Media: Acrylic on Canvas. Mailing Add: 5700 Carbon Canyon Rd Sp 132 Brea CA 92621

FOLLETT, JEAN FRANCES
SCULPTOR, PAINTER
b St Paul, Minn, June 5, 17. Study: Univ Minn, AA; Hans Hofmann Sch Art, New York; Sch of Fernand Leger, Paris, France, 46-51. Work: Mus Mod Art, New York; Whitney Mus Am Art, New York; Univ Mass; Univ Calif; Univ Tex. Exhib: Group shows & four one-man shows, Hansa Gallery, New York, 51-59; Guggenheim Mus, 54; Leo Castelli Gallery, New York, 60; Soho Gallery, New York, 77; Landmark Gallery, New York, 77. Awards: Cash Award, Nat Found Arts & Humanities, 66. Bibliog: Fred W McDarrah (auth), The Artists World, E P Dutton & Co, 61; Alan Kaprow (auth), Assemblage, Environments & Happenings, Harry N Abrams, Inc, 62; Tom Hess (auth), Art and Sexual Politics, Macmillan, 73. Style & Technique: Found objects applied to wood using oil paint, wire and glue. Res: A celebration of death; exploratory in dealing with subconscious and conscious worlds. Mailing Add: 1510 English St St Paul MN 55106

FOLSOM, KARL LEROY
PRINTMAKER, PHOTOGRAPHER
b Seattle, Wash, Oct 18, 38. Study: Diablo Valley Col, Pleasant Hill, Calif, AA, 71, study with John Spence Weir; San Francisco State Univ, BA, 73, study with Jack Welpott & Don Worth, MA, 77, study with Dennis Beall & John Ihle. Work: Erie Cult Ctr, Pa; Univ Calif, Los Angeles; Palo Alto Cult Ctr, Calif. Exhib: Photography into Sculpture, Mus Mod Art, New York, 70; Visual Dialogue, Musee Reattu, Arles, France, 71; Erie Festival of the Arts, 74; 2nd NH Int Graphica Ann, 75; Bradley Print Show, Bradley Univ, Peoria, Ill, 75; Calif Invitational, Golden West Col, Huntington Beach, Calif, 75 & 76; 3rd & 4th Hawaii Nat Print Exhibs, 75 & 76; 30 Yrs of Am Printmaking, Brooklyn Mus, 76 & 77. Pos: Guest lectr, San Francisco State Univ, 74; instr photo-etching, Univ Calif Laguna Ext, San Francisco, 75-78; instr silk screen, Adult Educ, Tiburon, Calif & San Francisco Community Col District, 77- Awards: Purchase Award, Refocus 74, Univ Iowa, 74. Mem: Calif Soc Printmakers (coun mem, 74-); Assoc Visual Dialogue Found. Style & Technique: Use of a fusion of photo-etching and printmaking techniques to produce an image that goes beyond the limitations of other media; use of linear and spatial elements which re-enact and continue the elements of the photo-etching in an abstract manner, thereby reducing the actual objects to non-specific forms; subtle collagraphic repetitions of the elements which appear within the actual photo-etching results in the stretching of the boundaries of the photo-etching into infinite space. Dealer: Source Gallery 1099 Folsom St San Francisco CA 94103; van Straaten Gallery 646 N Michigan Ave Chicago IL 60611. Mailing Add: 3380 22nd St San Francisco CA 94110

FON, JADE
PAINTER, INSTRUCTOR
b San Jose, Calif, Sept 7, 11. Study: Northern Ariz Univ; Art Students League. Work: Trans-Am Corp, Los Angeles; Mus Sci & Art, Los Angeles; Lepersarium, Carlinville, Ill. Exhib: Soc Western Artists Ann, De Young Mus, San Francisco, 62; Am Watercolor Soc, New York, 69; Haggin-Pioneer Mus, Stockton, Calif, 72; Calif State Fair, Sacramento, 73; Franklin Mint Gallery Am Art, Pa, 74. Teaching: Art teacher, Diablo Valley Col, 54; art teacher, Alameda Adult Sch, 54. Pos: Founder & dir, Asilomar Watercolor Workshop, 64. Awards: Ford Times Award, Am Watercolor Soc, 69; Gold Medals, Calif State Fair, 73 & Franklin Mint Gallery Am Art, 74; Foothills Ctr Cash Award, Golden, Colo, 77. Mem: Am & West Coast Watercolor Socs; Soc Western Artists. Style & Technique: Representative; oriental; seascape; landscape; portrait. Media: Watercolor, Pastel. Mailing Add: 1237 Raymond Dr Pacheco CA 94553

FONDREN, HAROLD M
ART DEALER
b Canton, Ohio, Feb 5, 22. Study: Harvard Col, AB. Pos: Asst dir, Stable Gallery, 54-55; asst dir, Poindexter Gallery, 55- Specialty: Contemporary painting and sculpture. Mailing Add: Poindexter Gallery 24 E 84th St New York NY 10028

FONTANEZ, CARMELO
PAINTER, EDUCATOR
b Rio Piedras, PR, July 16, 45. Study: Univ PR, BA(art educ); NY Univ, MA(art educ). Exhib: Univ PR Mus; Ateneo Puertorriqueno, 68; Ponce Art Mus, 68; Galeria Santiago, San Juan, 68, 69, 70 & 72; Inst Cult Puertorriqueno, 69. Teaching: Instr art, Univ PR, 67- Awards: First Prize for Watercolors, 67-69 & First Prize for Drawing, 69, IBEC Contest; First Prize for Watercolor, Ateneo Puertorriqueno, 69. Media: Watercolor. Dealer: Galeria Santiago Calle Cristo 207 San Juan PR 00901. Mailing Add: Calle Pedro Diaz Correa 412 Urb del Carmen Rio Piedras PR 00923

FONTANINI, CLARE
EDUCATOR, SCULPTOR
b Rutland, Vt. Study: Col St Catherine, AB; Columbia Univ, with Josef Albers & Oronzio Maldarelli, MA. Work: Lamentations of Jerimiah (marble), Barnett-Aden Gallery, Washington, DC; Seat of Wisdom (walnut), Col St Catherine, St Paul, Minn; Copper Crucifix, Trinity Col Libr, Washington, DC. Comn: St Michael Archangel (aluminum), church in Annandale, Va, 60; Rood Figures (walnut), All Saints Episcopal Church, Chevy Chase, Md, 66; Madonna & Child (cherry wood), St Agnes & Ascension Episcopal Church, Washington, DC, 69 & Rood Figures (walnut); Emily Reeder Mem, 72; Four Stations of the Cross, St Ann's Church, Manlius, NY; plus others. Exhib: Mint Mus Art, Charlotte, NC; Walker Art Gallery, Minneapolis; Va Mus Fine Arts, Richmond; Corcoran Gallery Art, Washington, DC; Nat Collection Fine Arts, Smithsonian Inst, Washington, DC; plus many others. Teaching: Instr design, Phillips Mem Gallery, Am Univ, Washington, DC, 46-47; asst prof sculpture, Cath Univ Am, 47-58, head dept art, 47-68, prof sculpture, 58-73, emer prof art, 73- Pos: Pres, Washington Sculptor's Group, 50; pres, Washington Artists Guild, 55. Awards: First Prize Medal for Sculpture, Nat Christian Arts Festival, Univ Wis, 55; Frank E Jellef Award for Sculpture, Washington, DC, 57; First Prize for Sculpture, Corcoran Gallery Art Ann Area Show, 59. Mem: Artists Equity Asn; Soc Washington Artists (secy, 43-45, vpres, 47). Style & Technique: Direct carving; welding carving and repousse; semi-abstract; figurative. Media: Stone, Wood, Metals. Mailing Add: 1029 Perry St NE Washington DC 20017

FOOSANER, JUDITH ANN
PAINTER
b Sacramento, Calif, Aug 10, 40. Study: Univ Calif, Berkeley, BA(Eng), 64, dean's award, 61, univ grant & MA(art), 68. Exhib: San Diego Fine Arts Gallery, Calif, 70; one-woman show, Wenger Gallery, 71. Teaching: Instr painting & drawing, Calif Col Arts & Crafts, 70- Media: Acrylic, Oil. Publ: Auth articles in Art Week, 11/71 & Art Gallery Mag, 1/72. Dealer: Wenger Gallery 855 Montgomery St San Francisco CA 94133. Mailing Add: 5326 James Ave Oakland CA 94618

FOOSE, ROBERT JAMES
PAINTER, DESIGNER
b York, Pa, Oct 17, 38. Study: Univ Ky, AB, 63. Work: J B Speed Art Mus, Louisville, Ky; Springfield Art Mus, Mo; Ind Cent Col, Indianapolis; New York Pub Libr; Libr of Cong, Washington, DC. Comn: Bks & bk jackets, Univ Ky Press, 60-75 & bk illus, 75; posters & catalogs, Univ Ky Art Gallery, 65-77; portrait, Biol Sci Dept, Univ Ky, 69. Exhib: Nat Polymer Exhib, Ypsilanti, Mich, 68; Cult Exchange Prog, US Embassy, Quito, Ecuador, 70; 8 State Painting Exhib, J B Speed Art Mus, Louisville, 74; Mainstreams 77, Marietta Col, 77; Watercolor USA, Springfield Art Mus, Mo, 77. Teaching: Workshop instr painting, Ky Art Comn, Frankfort, 70-75; guest lectr watercolor, Western Ky Univ, 75. Pos: Art dir-sr graphic artist, Univ Ky, currently; founder & proprietor, Buttonwood Press, Lexington, Ky, 68-72. Awards: Grand Prize & First Place, Ky State Fair, Louisville, 73 & 74; Purchase Prize, Watercolor USA, Springfield Art Mus, Mo, 75. Mem: Ky Guild Artists & Craftsmen (pres, 69-73); Lexington Art League (pres, 68-69); Ky Arts Comn (consult, currently); Ind Artists & Craftsmen. Style & Technique: Realistic landscapes. Media: Watercolor; all Print Media. Publ: Ed, Eight Fables of Aesop, 68 & auth & illusr, Amish Portfolio, 68 & Shaker Landscapes, 77, Buttonwood Press; illusr, Gold Rush Diary, 68, Uncle Will of Wildwood, 74 & Bestiary, 75, Univ Ky. Dealer: Guild Gallery 811 Euclid Ave Lexington KY 40503. Mailing Add: 203 Tahoma Rd Lexington KY 40503

FOOTE, HOWARD REED
ARTIST, PRINTMAKER
b Richmond, Ind, Dec 15, 36. Study: Toledo Mus Art, Ohio, 54-55; Sch of Mus Fine Arts, Boston, 55-57; San Francisco Art Inst, BFA, 60; Stanford Univ, MA, 70; additional study with Nathan Oliveira. Work: Achenbach Found, Palace of the Legion of Honor, San Francisco; City of Leeds, Eng; City of San Francisco; Stanford Univ. Exhib: Bay Area Printmakers Soc Fourth Nat Exhib, Oakland Mus, Calif, 58; 1970 Peace Exhib, Philadelphia Mus Art, 70; San Francisco Art Inst Centennial Exhib, Palace of the Legion of Honor, San Francisco, 71; Four Printmakers, San Francisco Mus Art, 71; 18th Nat Print Exhib, Brooklyn Mus, NY, 72; San Francisco Area Printmakers, Cincinnati Art Mus, Ohio, 73; Interstices, San Jose Art Mus, Calif & Cranbrook Acad Art Mus, Bloomfield Hills, Mich, 75. Teaching: Instr printmaking, Acad Art, San Francisco, 70-75 & Calif State Univ, Hayward, 71-72; instr printmaking, drawing & 3-D design, Col Notre Dame, Belmont, Calif, 75-77. Style & Technique: Intaglio; lithography; painting; three-dimensional design; computer graphics; wood sculpture. Publ: Contribr, Ramparts Mag, 6/70. Mailing Add: Box 462 Inverness CA 94937

FOOTE, NANCY
ART EDITOR, ART CRITIC
b Bennington, Vt. Pos: Managing ed, Artforum Mag, New York, 75- Mailing Add: c/o Artforum 667 Madison Ave New York NY 10021

FORAKIS, PETER
SCULPTOR
b Hanna, Wyo, Oct 2, 27. Study: Calif Sch Fine Arts, BFA, 57. Comn: Tower of the Lakotas (steel tubing sculpture), Williams Col, Williams, Mass, 66; Gateway (cast iron tubing sculpture), Great Southwest Corp, Atlanta, Ga, 66-67; Earth Handle (wood sculpture), Denver City Park, Colo, 68; Tower of the Cheyenne (corten steel tubing sculpture), Univ Houston, Tex, 72. Exhib: New Forms New Media, Martha Jackson Gallery, New York; one-man show, Tibor de Nagy, New York, 63-64; American Artists Drawings, Guggenheim Mus, New York, 64; Primary Structures, Jewish Mus, New York, 65; Sculpture of the 60's, Los Angeles Co Mus, Los Angeles, 66. Publ: Auth & illusr, Grope Comics, Vol I & II, 63 & 66. Mailing Add: RFD 1 Putney VT 05346

FORBES, DONNA MARIE
MUSEUM DIRECTOR
b Albion, Nebr, Mar 19, 29. Study: Mont State Univ; Pratt Inst; Eastern Mont Col, BS(art educ); Harvard Summer Inst in Arts Admin. Collections Arranged: Art and Illustration of 19th Century Montana, 76 & Montana Sculptors, 76, Yellowstone Art Ctr, Billings, Mont. Teaching: Instr design & art educ, Eastern Mont Col, 52-53. Pos: Dir, Yellowstone Art Ctr, Billings, Mont, 74- Mem: Western Asn of Art Mus; Am Asn of Mus; Mont Art Gallery Dirs Asn. Mailing Add: 1116 Eighth St W Billings MT 59102

FORD, CHARLES HENRI
PAINTER, PHOTOGRAPHER
b Mississippi. Work: Univ Southern Ill, Carbondale (complete run of poem posters); Univ Tex Arch, Austin. Exhib: Photographs, Inst Contemp Art, London, Eng, 54 & Carleton Gallery, New York, 75; Drawings & Paintings, Galerie Marforen, 56, Galerie du Dragon, 57 & 58, Paris, France; Photographs & Lithographs, Cordier & Eckstrom, New York, 65; sculptures & tapestries, New York Cult Ctr, 75. Bibliog: Parker Tyler (auth), article in, Screening the Sexes, Holt, Rinehart & Winston, 72. Publ: Auth, Overturned Lake, 41, Sleep in a Nest of Flames, 49, Spare Parts, 66, Silver Flower Coo, 68 & Flag of Ecstasy, 72. Mailing Add: c/o Minotaur Films Inc Zambeliou 73 Xania Greece

FORD, HARRY XAVIER
EDUCATOR, ART ADMINISTRATOR
b Seymour, Ind, Jan 12, 21. Study: John Herron Art Inst; Univ Calif Los Angeles, BA; Sacramento State Col, MA; Univ Calif Berkeley, grad study. Teaching: Teacher art, Placer Union High Sch, 51-53 & Stuttgart Am High Sch, Ger, 53-58. Pos: Chmn dept teacher educ, Calif Col Arts & Crafts, 58-60, pres, 60- Mem: Nat Asn Schs Art (treas, 76-); Union Independent Cols Art (chmn, 72-74). Style & Technique: Abstract expressionist. Media: Oil. Mailing Add: 21 Humphrey Pl Oakland CA 94610

FORD, JOHN CHARLES
PAINTER
b Choudrant, La, Sept 29, 29. Study: La Polytech Inst, BFA, 50; Univ Tex; Austin Presby Theol Sem, BD, 53; Art Students League, 57; Univ Ore, MFA, 60. Work: Seattle Art Mus, Wash; Victoria Art Mus, BC; NY Univ; Neuberger Mus, Purchase, NY; Ark Art Ctr, Little Rock; Hirschhorn Mus, Washington, DC; Corcoran Mus, Washington, DC. Comn: Altarpiece, Chapel La Grande, Ore, 65; outdoor painted screen construction, Lady Peter Norton, London, 69. Exhib: San Francisco Art Mus, 59 & 60; Seattle Art Mus, 63; Contemp Am Drawings, Smithsonian Inst, Washington, 63; Cambridge Sch Archit, Eng, 69; one-man shows, Guild Hall Mus, East Hampton, NY, 74, Neuberger Mus, Purchase, NY, 77 & Sid Deutsch Gallery, New York, NY, 77; plus many others. Awards: Second Prize, Art Students League Universal Int Drawings & Painting Competition, New York, 57; Prize Winning Drawing, Little Rock Art Mus, Ark, 57; Award, Boise Art Mus, 60; First Place/Painting, Long Island Painters Exhib, Guild Hall Mus, East Hampton, NY, 74. Bibliog: David Shirey (auth), Paintings that prod, New York Times, 2/6/77. Dealer: Sid Deutsch Gallery 43 E 80th St New York NY 10021. Mailing Add: 121 Mercer St New York NY 10012

FORD, JOHN GILMORE
COLLECTOR
b Baltimore, Md. Study: Baltimore City Col, degree; Johns Hopkins Univ; Loyola Col; Md Inst Col Art, BFA. Exhib: Collection Indo-Asian art, Walters Art Gallery, Baltimore, 71. Pos: Nat vpres, Am Inst Interior Designers, 70- Awards: Citation of merit, Md Inst Col Art, 60. Bibliog: P Pal (auth), Indo-Asian art, 71, Walters Art Gallery, Apollo Mag & Connoisseur Mag. Mem: Am Fedn Arts; Asia Soc. Collection: Indian, Nepalese, Tibetan, Javanese, Chinese & Japanese bronzes, stone sculptures and paintings. Mailing Add: 2601 N Charles St Baltimore MD 21218

FORD, RUTH VANSICKLE
PAINTER, EDUCATOR
b Aurora, Ill, Aug 8, 98. Study: Chicago Acad Fine Arts, cert; Art Students League; summers with John Carlson and spec classes with George Bellows, Guy Wiggins, Jonas Lie & Bruce Crane. Work: Aurora Col, Ill; Lafayette Col, Ind; Aurora Pub Libr; Northern Ill Gas Co; Aurora YMCA. Comn: Portrait of Freeman for Freeman Room, Aurora YMCA, 68; portrait of head dept drama, Aurora Col, comn by sr class for gift to col, 69. Exhib: One-man show, Chicago Art Inst, 34; Grand Cent Galleries, New York, 47; Watercolor USA, Springfield, 62-63; Nat Acad Design; Am Artists, Chicago Art Inst; plus many others. Teaching: Prof life class, Chicago Acad Fine Arts, 30-60; prof painting, Aurora Col, 64- Pos: Pres-dir, Chicago Acad Fine Arts, 37-60. Awards: Fine Arts Bldg Prize, Chicago Art Inst, 30, Chicago Woman's Aid Prize, 31; Gold Medal Award for Oil Painting, Palette & Chisel Acad, 63; plus many others. Mem: Am Watercolor Soc; hon mem Artist Guild Chicago; Am Artists Prof League; Palette & Chisel Acad; Rockport Art Asn, Mass. Style & Technique: Portraits, landscapes and still lifes. Media: Watercolor, Oil. Dealer: Schramm Galleries 215 SW Second St Ft Lauderdale FL 28315. Mailing Add: 69 Central Ave Aurora IL 60506

FORESTER, RUSSELL
PAINTER
b Salmon, Idaho, May 21, 20. Study: Inst of Design, Chicago, 50. Work: Guggenheim Mus, New York; La Jolla Mus Contemp Art, Calif; Sheldon Mem Art Gallery, Lincoln, Nebr; Fine Arts Gallery of San Diego, Calif. Exhib: Houston Mus Fine Art, Tex, 62; Nat Drawing Exhib, San Francisco Mus Art, 70; La Jolla Mus Contemp Art, 72; Santa Barbara Mus Art, Calif, 74; Phoenix Art Mus, Ariz, 75; Sheldon Mem Art Gallery, 76; Fine Arts Gallery of San Diego, 76 & Drawing Show, 77; Everson Mus Art, Syracuse, NY, 77; New Acquisitions, Guggenheim Mus, 77; La Galerie, Paris, France, 77. Bibliog: Roland Anrig (auth), Russell Froester, Art Int, 1/73; Henry J Seldis (auth), The Art of Russell Forester, San Diego Mag, 5/77. Style & Technique: Acrylic washes over hundreds of painted squares, then washed off and repainted, which gives a depth to the surface. Media: Acrylic. Mailing Add: 2025 Soledad Ave La Jolla CA 92037

FORGE, ANDREW MURRAY
ART WRITER, PAINTER
b Hastingleigh, Kent, Eng, Nov 10, 23. Study: Camberwell Sch Art, London, 57-59, with William Coldstream & Kenneth Martin. Work: Tate Gallery, London; Arts Coun Gt Brit. Exhib: Retrospective, Bristol Mus, Eng, 64; Inst Contemp Arts, Boston, Mass, 75. Collections Arranged: Wilson Steer Centenary, Tate Gallery, 61, David Bomberg, 69; Painting and Perception, Stirling Univ, 70; British Painting 1974, Hayward Gallery, 74. Teaching: Lectr painting, Slade Sch, London, 50-64; prof painting, Yale Sch Art, 75- Pos: Trustee, Tate Gallery, London, 64-72 & Nat Gallery, London, 66-70. Media: Oil. Res: 19th and 20th century art. Publ: Auth, Soutine, 65; auth, Rauschenberg, Abrams, 69; auth, Monet at Giverny, Miller, Mathews, 74; auth, Painting and the Whole Self, Artforum, 75. Mailing Add: 684 Whitney Ave New Haven CT 06511

FORMAN, ALICE
PAINTER, DESIGNER
b New York, NY, June 1, 31. Study: Cornell Univ, with Kenneth Evett & Norman Daly, BA; Art Students League, with Morris Kantor. Exhib: Whitney Mus Am Art, 60; White Mus Art, Cornell Univ, 61; Phoenix Gallery, NY, 66, 68, 71, 74 & 75; Marist Col, 68 & 71; Butler Inst Exhib, 72; Kornblee Gallery, 77; plus others. Teaching: Lectr, Marist Col, 77. Awards: Nat Student Asn Regional Awards; Daniel Schnackenberg Merit Scholar, Art Students League. Style & Technique: Painterly realism. Media: Oil. Dealer: Kornblee Gallery 20 W 57th St New York NY 10019. Mailing Add: 8 Croft Rd Poughkeepsie NY 12603

FORMAN, KENNETH WARNER
PAINTER, EDUCATOR
b Landour, India, June 5, 25; US citizen. Study: Wittenberg Col, AB, BFA; Ohio State Univ, MA. Work: Wittenberg Col, Springfield, Ohio; Univ RI, Kingston; Hartford CofC Festival Collection, Conn; Univ Conn Hon Ctr, Storrs. Exhib: Nat Drawing Exhib, Ball State Teachers Col, Muncie, Ind, 65; 12th Biennial Exhib Contemp Am Prints, Brooklyn Mus, 65; 23rd Int Exhib Soc Printmakers, US Nat Mus, 66; Contemp Am Painting, Mem Art Mus, Rochester, NY, 67; Nat Watercolor Exhib, Peoria Art Ctr, Ill, 67. Teaching: Instr media & techniques, painting, Am Archit & art hist, Univ Conn, 57-, prof art, 68- Awards: First Painting Award, Silvermine Guild Artists, 57; First Painting Award, Mystic Art Asn, Conn, 63; Hartford Art Festival Purchase Award, Hartford CofC, 72. Mem: Conn Watercolor Soc; Mystic Art Asn; Victorian Soc Am; Victorian Soc Eng; Am Fedn Arts. Media: Oil, Watercolor, Serigraphy. Res: Victorian architecture in England and New England; traditional media with synthetic media in painting. Publ: Auth, Understanding in the Arts, 59 & illusr, 61, Fine Arts Mag; illusr, spec ed, Penny Paper, 64; auth, Salvador Dali's moustache, Floating Opera, 67; auth, Connecticut Architecture During the Growth of the Nation, William Benton Mus of Art, Univ Conn, 76. Mailing Add: RFD 1 Mansfield Center CT 06250

FORMAN, NESSA RUTH
ART EDITOR
b Atlantic City, NJ, Aug 22, 43. Study: Univ Pa, MA(art hist). Pos: Art ed, Philadelphia Bulletin. Mailing Add: Philadelphia Bulletin 30th & Market Sts Philadelphia PA 19101

FORMIGONI, MAURIE MONIHON
PAINTER, SCULPTOR
b Louisville, Ky, Nov 6, 41. Study: Kalamazoo Col, Mich, BA; Bell Studios, Chicago, with Arnold Zweerts; Art Inst Chicago; Sangamon State Univ, Springfield, Ill, MA; Contemp Art Workshop, Chicago, with Cosmo Campoli. Work: Sangamon State Univ; Sangamo Club, Springfield; Boromeo Collection, Pavia, Italy; plus many pvt collections. Comn: Mural painted with children, McFarland Zone Ctr, Dept Mental Health, Springfield, 74; painted costumes, dancers & set designs, Mid-Mo Dance Theatre, Columbia, 75; designed playground, Enos Pub Sch, Springfield, 75. Exhib: Ill State Fair Prof Art Exhib, Springfield, 71, 72 & 74; one-woman shows, Jane Shair Gallery, Quincy, Ill, 72 & Sangamon State Univ, Springfield, 74; Ill State Mus 27th Invitational, Springfield, 74; Appalachian Nat Drawing Competition, Boone, NC, 75. Teaching: Instr figure drawing & children's art, Springfield Art Asn, 70-74 & Lincoln Land Community Col, Springfield, 71-75; adj asst prof creative arts, Sangamon State Univ, 75- Pos: Res asst for Bruno Bettelheim, Univ Chicago, 63-66; courtroom artist, ABC-TV, Chicago, 71. Bibliog: Sensory Wall (video tape of tactile experiments with young children), Sangamon State Univ, 72; John Ratliff (auth), Pyrex (film on techniques for teaching color and light to children), 72. Style & Technique: Large figurative acrylic paintings; soft painted sculpture; multi-media work. Publ: Illusr, cover jacket, Brainchild, 73. Mailing Add: 1317 N Third St Springfield IL 62702

FORNAS, LEANDER
PRINTMAKER, INSTRUCTOR
b Gardner, Mass, June 18, 25. Study: Pratt Inst, cert, 50; Kunstgewerbeschule, Zurich, 51; Ateneum, Helsinki, 51-53; Univ Mass, MFA, 73. Work: Mus Mod Art, New York; Ateneum, Helsinki; Libr Cong; Rockefeller Collection; New York Pub Libr. Comn: Developed new glass engraving methods, Steuben Glass, New York, 55; graphic indust illus, portrait comns & misc design, Finland, 59-65; designed & instituted graphics facilities, Pratt Inst, NY, 58, Fine Arts Ctr, Univ RI, 66 & Holyoke Community Col (entire art dept), 72-75. Exhib: One-man shows, New Talent, Mus Mod Art, 55 & Sao Paulo Biennial Prints, 59; Curator's Choice, Print Club, Philadelphia, 56; Printmakers Soc Finland (throughout Europe, US & Far E), 59-66. Teaching: Instr printmaking & drawing, Holyoke Community Col, 70- Pos: Dir, Design & Graphics Studio, Helsinki, 58-66; chmn art dept, Holyoke Community Col, 70-74. Mem: Soc Printmakers Finland (bd dir, 59-61, juror exhib, 59-65). Style & Technique: Impressionistic; surrealistic; personal statements. Media: All printmaking methods, traditional drawing media. Mailing Add: Moores Corner Leverett MA 01054

FORREST, JAMES TAYLOR
MUSEUM DIRECTOR, ART HISTORIAN
b New Castle, Ind, Sept 22, 21. Study: Hanover Col, Ind; Ind Univ, Indianapolis; Univ Wis, BS, 48 & MS, 49. Comn: Art and artifacts for interior trapper room, Grand Teton Lodge, Jackson Lake, Wyo, 55. Collections Arranged: National Painting Exhibition, Gilcrease Inst, Tulsa, Okla, 59; Collector's Choice-European Art, Fine Arts Mus, Santa Fe, NMex, 61; Art of the American West, Fine Arts Mus, Santa Fe; plus several retrospectives and others. Teaching: Instr Am hist, Tulsa Univ, 58-60; instr Am art, Sheridan Col, Wyo, 66-67; instr, Am art hist, Univ Wyo, Laramie, 68- Pos: Cur mus, Colo State Mus, Denver, 53-55; dir, Gilcrease Inst, 55-61; dir, Mus NMex, Santa Fe, 61-64; dir, Univ Wyo Art Mus, 68- Mem: Am Asn Mus (state rep, 72-74, coun mem, 77-78); Western Asn Art Mus (regional coun, 74-); Mountain-Plains Mus Conf (coun, 72-); Colo-Wyo Asn Mus (chmn, 73-); Wyo Coun Arts (coun, 67-; chmn, 71-73). Res: Art and artists of the American 19th century. Publ: Contribr, Keepers of the Past, Clifford Lord, Chapel Hill, 65; auth, Hans Kleiber-Artist of the Big Horns, 67 & Bill Gollings-Ranahan Artist, 69, Bradford Brinton Mem Ranch Mus, Big Horn, Wyo; auth, History of New Mexico, Teachers Press, Columbia, 72. Mailing Add: Box 3138 Univ Station Laramie WY 82071

FORRESTALL, THOMAS DE VANY
SCULPTOR, PAINTER
b Middleton, NS, Mar 11, 36. Study: Mt Allison Univ, 54-58; Can Coun grant to travel & study in Europe, 58-59, sculpture grant, 67. Work: Can Coun; Winnipeg Art Gallery; Art Gallery Windsor; Confederation Mem Gallery; New Brunswick Mus. Comn: Kennedy & Churchill Mem, Prov NB, 64; steel sculpture, Atlantic Pavilion, Expo 67; welded relief mural, Centennial Bldg Fredericton, 68; two large welded steel sculptures, Can Govt, Fed Bldg, Antigonish, NS, 70; mural abstract for playhouse, Beaverbrook Can Found, Fredericton, 72. Exhib: 26 paintings exhibited at Dartmouth Col, 66; 54 paintings organized by Beaverbrook Art Gallery for travel across Can, 71-72; Canada Visits Boston, 31 paintings exhibited at City Hall Art Gallery, Boston, 72; Centre Cult, Paris, 72; Thirteen Artists from Marlborough Godard, Marlborough Gallery, New York, 74; plus others. Pos: Asst cur, Beaverbrook Art Gallery, 59-60. Awards: Citation of Art Merit, Secy State, Commonwealth Mass, 72. Bibliog: Alex Mogelon (auth), Art profile, Montrealer, 68; D S Richardson (auth), Tom Forrestall Exhibition, Beaverbrook Art Gallery, 71; Berry Lord (auth), Shaped by This Land. Mem: Royal Can Acad Arts. Media: Tempera, Steel, Iron, Bronze. Publ: Co-auth, Shapes, 72. Dealer: Roberts Gallery Ltd 641 Yonge St Toronto ON Can. Mailing Add: c/o Three Oaks Corp 3 Albert St Dartmouth NS B2Y 3M1 Can

FORRESTER, CHARLES HOWARD
SCULPTOR, EDUCATOR
b Jersey City, NJ, Sept 30, 28. Study: Univ Wash, BFA, 58; Univ Ore, MFA, 60. Work: Bundy Art Gallery, Waitsfield, Vt; Shakespeare Mem Theatre, Ashland, Ore; Medford Pub Parks, Ore; Western Ky Univ, Bowling Green. Comn: Abstract sculpture in cast stone, Red Cross Bldg, Medford, Ore, 62; Five Sisters, Broughton Sch, Salford, Eng, 65; Two Figures, Mathews Co, Little Rock, Ark, 67; 2 sculptures in cast aluminum & cor-ten steel, PCA Bldg, Glasgow, Ky, 74; Family Group, Bowling Green Hosp, Ky. Exhib: Festival of Sculpture, First Nat Bank of Atlanta, Ga, 68; Art in the Embassies 1968, US Dept State, 68; Southern Sculpture, Smithsonian Inst Travelling Exhib, 69; Blossom-Kent State Art Festival, Kent State Univ, Ohio, 70; Eight-State Sculpture Exhib, J B Speed Mus, Louisville, Ky, 75; Mid-States Art Exhib, Evansville Mus of Art, Ind, 76; Southeastern Sculpture Exhib, Univ New Orleans, La, 76; Saenger Nat Small Sculpture Exhib, Saenger Mus, Hattiesburg, Miss, 76. Teaching: Lectr sculpture, Salford Tech Col, Eng, 63-65; assoc prof sculpture, Western Ky Univ, Bowling Green, 65- Bibliog: Anon (auth), Some Younger Northwest Sculptors, NW Rev, 61; M Harold (ed), Prize-Winning Sculptures, Allid Publ Inc, 67. Mem: Southern Asn of Sculptors (vpres, 66-70). Style & Technique: Abstract figurative sculpture in cast metal and cast stone; large scale fabricated sculptures in metal. Media: Cast metal; fabricated metal. Mailing Add: PO Box 102 Col Heights PO Bowling Green KY 42101

FORSBERG, JIM
PAINTER, PRINTMAKER
b Sauk Center, Minn, Nov 21, 19. Study: Minneapolis Art Sch; St Paul Sch Art; Art Students League; Hans Hofmann Sch Fine Art. Work: Mus Mod Art, New York; Smith Col, Mass; Cincinnati Art Mus, Ohio; Philadelphia Mus, Pa; Chrysler Mus, Norfolk, Va. Exhib: Print Show & Drawing Show, Mus Mod Art, New York; nat & int print shows, 50-63. Teaching: Pvt instr, Mass, 69-70 & 72- Media: Oil. Mailing Add: 441 Commercial St Provincetown MA 02657

FORSMAN, CHUCK (CHARLES STANLEY FORSMAN)
PAINTER, EDUCATOR
b Nampa, Idaho, May 5, 44. Study: Univ Calif, Davis, BA, 67, MFA, 71, study with Wayne Theibaud & William Wiley; Skowhegan Sch Painting & Sculpture, study with Gabriel Laderman. Work: Phoenix Art Mus, Ariz; Marion Koogler McNay Art Inst, San Antonio, Tex; Grinnel Col, Iowa; Univ Calif, Davis; US Army, Pentagon, Washington, DC. Exhib: One-man shows, Tibor De Nagy Gallery, New York & six others, 73, 75 & 77; Four Corners Biennial, Ariz, NMex, Utah & Colo, Phoenix Art Mus, Ariz, 73; Nat Acad Art Exhib for Award Candidates, New York, 74; Third Colo Ann, Denver Art Mus, 75; 20/20 Show, Colo

& NMex Artists, Colorado Springs Fine Arts Ctr, 75; group show, Marion Koogler McNay Art Inst, San Antonio, Tex, 75; Painting & Sculpture Today, Indianapolis Mus of Art, 76; Art and the Automobile, Flint Inst of the Arts, Mich, 77. Teaching: Asst painting & sculpture, Univ Calif, Davis, 70-71; asst prof drawing & painting, Univ Colo, Boulder, 71- Awards: Purchase Award, Four Corners Biennial, Phoenix Art Mus, 73; Best in Category, Ann Show, Aspen Found for the Arts, 76; fac grant-in-aid, Billboard 4 Doc, Univ Colo, 76. Style & Technique: Realist painting tradition; interiors, landscapes, cityscapes, figures, often roadside or travel related. Media: Oil on masonite. Dealer: Tibor De Nagy Inc 29 W 57th St New York NY 10019. Mailing Add: 511 Pleasant St Boulder CO 80302

FORST, MILES
PAINTER
b Brooklyn, NY, Aug 18, 23. Study: Mus Mod Art Vet Ctr; Art Students League, with Morris Kantor; Esquela Obrera, Mexico City; Hans Hofmann Sch Fine Arts. Work: Mus Mod Art, New York; Newark Mus, NJ; Mass Inst Technol, Cambridge; Chrysler Mus, Provincetown, Mass; Bowdin Col Mus. Exhib: Green Gallery, New York, 64 & 66; Goldowsky-Bellamy Gallery, New York, 69; Univ NC, 70; Sch Visual Arts, New York, 70; Otis Art Inst, Los Angeles, 74; 112 Green St, New York, 76. Teaching: Instr painting & drawing, Sch Visual Arts, 63-71; assoc prof painting, San Francisco State Univ, 71-72; head, Intermedia Dept, Otis Art Inst, 71- Pos: Charter mem, Hansa Gallery, New York, 53-58; organizer, Radiance Prod, 72-73. Awards: Working artist award, Walter K Gutman Found, 60, 62 & 65; working artist award, Longview Found, 61 & 62; artist in residence, Ford Found, 65. Bibliog: Article in Art Collectors Ann, 67; Kaprow (auth), Happenings, 68; Drs P & E Kronhausen (auth), Erotic art, Grove, 69. Mem: Los Angeles Inst Contemp Art. Style & Technique: Intermedia. Dealer: Richard Bellamy 333 Park Ave S New York NY. Mailing Add: 14 Westminster Ave Venice CA 90291

FORSYTH, CONSTANCE
PAINTER, PRINTMAKER
b Indianapolis, Ind, Aug 18, 03. Study: Butler Univ, BA; John Herron Art Sch, dipl & study with W Forsyth & Clifton Wheeler; Pa Acad Fine Arts, with Henry McCarter & George Harding; Broadmoor Art Acad, Colorado Springs, Colo, with Ward Lockwood & Boardman Robinson. Work: Indianapolis Art Mus, Ind; Tex Fine Arts Asn; Ball State Teachers Col, Muncie, Ind; Joslyn Mem Mus, Omaha, Nebr; Dlas Mus Fine Arts, Tex; plus others. Exhib: Watercolor, Bern, Switz, 57, Tokyo, Japan, 60, traveling print show to India, 65 & foreign exhib, Florence, Italy, 72, Nat Asn Women Artists; 16th Libr Cong Print Exhib, Esslingen on the Necker, Ger, 59. Teaching: Instr art, John Herron Art Sch, Indianapolis, 31-33; interim instr art, Western Col, Oxford, Ohio, spring 39; prof art, Univ Tex, Austin, 40-73, emer prof, 73- Awards: Naomi Goldman Prize for Surf (aquatint), Nat Asn Women Artists, 61; Maco Press Prize for Deluge (aquatint), John Herron Art Mus, 61; Purchase Prize for Up Close (watercolor), Tex Fine Arts Asn, 72. Style & Technique: Mainly personal, usually free, varying with intent of expression of mood or subject undertaken. Media: Watercolor, Aquatint. Publ: Illusr, Friends, Steck Co, 51. Mailing Add: 7102 Kenosha Pass Austin TX 78749

FORSYTH, ROBERT JOSEPH
ART HISTORIAN, COLLECTOR
b Neligh, Nebr, Sept 4, 21. Study: Univ Ore, BA, 43, MA, 47; Univ Minn, PhD, 65. Teaching: Tex Christain Univ, 47-49; Univ Minn, 49-51; Hamline Univ, 57; Univ Minn, St Paul, 58-68; prof art hist, Colo State Univ, 68-; Univ Notre Dame, summer 71. Pos: Educ cur, Minneapolis Inst Arts, Minn, 51-55. Mem: Col Art Asn; Am Fedn Arts; Nat Trust for Hist Preservation. Res: American art with emphasis on sculpture; Romanesque art. Collection: 20th century American drawings, sculpture and prints. Publ: Auth, Sculpture & Drawings: John B Flannagan, Univ Notre Dame, 63; auth, Early Flannagan & carved furniture, Col Art J, fall 67; auth, Colorado collects & Thomas Moran in Yellowstone (catalogs), Colo State Univ, 72; auth, John B Flannagan: Sculpture/Drawings 1924-1938, Minn Mus Art, 73; auth, Contemporary Crafts of the Americas, Regnery, 75. Mailing Add: Dept of Art Colo State Univ Ft Collins CO 80521

FORTESS, KARL E
PAINTER, PRINTMAKER
b Antwerp, Belgium, Oct 13, 07; US citizen. Study: Art Inst Chicago; Art Students League; Woodstock Sch Painting, with Yasuo Kuniyoshi. Work: De Cordova Mus; Mus Mod Art, New York; Brooklyn Mus; Nat Collection Fine Arts, Smithsonian Inst; Butler Inst Am Art; plus many others incl pvt collections. Exhib: Art Inst Chicago; Mus Mod Art, New York; Whitney Mus Am Art; Nat Inst Arts & Letters; Nat Acad Design; plus many other group & one-man shows. Teaching: Instr art, Art Students League, Brooklyn Mus Art Sch, La State Univ & Am Art Sch; vis artist, Ft Wright Col; from prof art to emer prof, Boston Univ Sch Fine & Appl Arts. Pos: Artist fed art projects, Works Proj Admin; contract with US Dept Health, Educ & Welfare for tape-recorded interviews with contemp Am artists (over 350 tapes). Awards: First hon mention, Carnegie Inst, 41; Guggenheim Fel, 46; Childe Hassam Fund Purchase Award, 52; Nat Endowment Arts Grant. Bibliog: Holger Cahill (auth), New Horizons in American Art; Ralph Pearson (auth), Modern Renaissance in American Art; Arthur Zaidenberg (auth), Prints & How to Make Them; plus many others. Mem: Artists Equity Asn; Soc Am Graphic Artists; Art Students League; Am Asn Univ Prof; Brit Film Inst. Style & Technique: Romantic landscapes. Media: Oil. Res: Participated in making a pictorial record of the Territory of Alaska for the US Dept of Interior. Publ: Auth, On the nature of things or the things of nature, In: Art of the Artist, Crown, 52; auth, Comics as non-art, In: Funnies: an American Idiom, Free Press, 63. Mailing Add: 311 Plochmann Rd Woodstock NY 12498

FOSBURGH, JAMES WHITNEY
PAINTER, WRITER
b New York, NY, Aug 1, 10. Study: Yale Univ, BA, 33; Univ Rome, lauria degree, 33-34; Yale Univ, MA, 35. Work: Metrop Mus Art; Boston Mus Fine Arts; Pa Acad Fine Arts; Toledo Mus Fine Arts; Hirshhorn Collection, Smithsonian Inst, Washington, DC; also in pvt collections. Exhib: Corcoran Gallery Art; Pa Acad Fine Arts; one-man shows, Durlacher Bros, 50-63, Calif Palace of Legion of Honor, 55, Los Angeles Mus Art, 55, Mus of Legion of Honor, San Francisco & Los Angeles Co Art Mus. Teaching: Lectr painting & art hist, Frick Collection, Nat Gallery Art, Yale Univ & Metrop Mus Art, 34-60. Pos: Chmn, Comt Paintings for the White House, 61-63; mem, Landmarks Preservation Comn, New York, 62-; mem, Comt Preservation of the White House, 64-; trustee, assoc in fine arts & mem comt, Garvin Collection, Yale Univ, currently. Awards: Hallmark Award, 60. Media: Oil, Watercolor. Publ: Auth, Winslow Homer in the Adirondacks (catalog), Adirondacks Mus, 59; contribr, Art News, Harper's Bazaar & Art in Am, 55-65. Dealer: Coe Kerr Gallery 49 E 82nd St New York NY 10028. Mailing Add: 32 E 64th St New York NY 10021

FOSDICK, SINA G
ART ADMINISTRATOR, COLLECTOR
b Odessa, Russia. Study: Berlin, Vienna, Paris & Leipzig. Pos: Dir, Master Inst of United Arts, New York, 25-35; co-dir, Roerich Acad of Arts, New York, 45-50; exec vpres, Nicholas Roerich Mus, 58- Collection: Ancient Buddhist art. Publ: Auth, Nicholas Roerich, Roerich Mus, 64. Mailing Add: 319 W 107th St New York NY 10025

FOSHAG, MERLE
PAINTER
b Spokane, Wash. Study: Corcoran Sch Art; Am Univ, Diego Revera; also with Eliot O'Hara & others. Work: Smithsonian Inst, Washington, DC; also in pvt collection of Robert Woods Bliss. Exhib: Am Watercolor Soc, New York; Corcoran Gallery, Washington, DC, Fla, West Coast & Mex; Smithsonian Inst; Washington Watercolor Asn; Nat Arts Club, New York. Awards: First Watercolor Award, Corcoran Gallery, 65, Smithsonian Inst, 65 & Washington Arts Club, 70. Mem: Washington Watercolor Asn (corresp secy); Miniature Soc; Miniature Art Soc NJ; Miniature Art Soc Fla. Style & Technique: Impressionism; abstract; collage. Media: Watercolor. Dealer: W P Woodring US Nat Mus Washington DC 20008. Mailing Add: 5202 Westwood Dr Washington DC 20016

FOSTER, APRIL
PRINTMAKER, INSTRUCTOR
b Berwyn, Ill, Oct 9, 47. Study: Univ Ill, Champaign-Urbana, BFA, 70, fel, 70-71, MA(art educ), 71; Temple Univ, fel, 72-73; Tyler Sch Art, Philadelphia, MFA(printmaking), 73. Exhib: Color Print USA, Tex Tech Univ, Lubbock, 73; Mem Exhib, Print Club, Philadelphia, 74; Cincinnati Exhib: Drawings & Prints, Cincinnati Art Mus, 74; All Ohio Graphics & Photography 1975, Dayton Art Inst; Works on Paper by Six Artists From the Midwest, San Diego Univ, 75. Teaching: Asst printmaking, Temple Univ, 71-72, instr printmaking, summer 73; instr printmaking & drawing, Art Acad Cincinnati, 73- Mem: Col Art Asn; Print Club, Philadelphia. Style & Technique: Directness of drawing with emphasis on line, value and shapes; naturalistic elements and spatial figurations. Media: Lithography, Intaglio. Mailing Add: Art Acad Cincinnati Eden Park Cincinnati OH 45202

FOSTER, BARBARA LYNN
PRINTMAKER, INSTRUCTOR
b Glendale, Calif, July 27, 47. Study: Univ Calif, Santa Barbara, BA(art); San Francisco State Univ, MA(printmaking). Work: Oakland Mus, Calif; Mills Col. Exhib: Davidson Nat Print & Drawing Competition, NC, 75; Prints California, Oakland Mus, 75; Appalachian State Univ Nat Drawing Exhib, Boone, NC, 75. Teaching: Instr lithography & drawing, Calif State Col, Stanislaus, 72-73; instr lithography, Acad Art Col, San Francisco, 75-; instr lithography, San Francisco State Univ, 77- Pos: Co-owner & printer, Wellspring Press, San Francisco, 71-75; asst printer, Editions Press Atelier, San Francisco, 72-73. Bibliog: Spec (15 min), KQED TV, San Francisco, 78. Mem: Calif Soc Printmakers (coun mem, 72, pres, 78). Style & Technique: Representational. Media: Watercolor, Lithography. Mailing Add: c/o The Graphics Gallery Three Embarcadero Ctr San Francisco CA 94111

FOSTER, DONALD ISLE
ART DEALER
b Seattle, Wash, July 9, 25. Study: Stanford Univ, BA, 47, MBA, 49. Pos: Owner, Foster/White Gallery, Seattle, 72- Specialty: Contemporary Northwest art. Mailing Add: 311 1/2 Occidental Ave S Seattle WA 98104

FOSTER, HAL
CARTOONIST, PAINTER
b Halifax, NS, Aug 16, 92. Pos: Creator & artist, Prince Valiant. Awards: Banshees' Silver Lady; Nat Soc Cartoonists Reuben & inductee, Hall of Fame. Bibliog: Prince Valiant movie, 20th Century Fox, 53. Publ: Auth & illusr, Prince Valiant & the Three Challenges, 60, Prince Valiant on the Island Sea, 68, Prince Valiant in the New World, 68, Prince Valiant & the Golden Princess, 68 & Prince Valiant in the Days of King Arthur, 69, Hastings; Prince Valiant, Vols 1 & 2, Nostalgia Press. Mailing Add: 336 Sun Bird Lane Spring Hill FL 33512

FOSTER, HOLLAND
PAINTER, SCULPTOR
b Caledonia, Iowa, Feb 15, 06. Study: Nat Acad Design; State Univ Iowa, BA & MA; Columbia Univ, also with John F Carlson, Sidney Dickinson, Alice Murphy & Wayman Adams; study in Eng, France, Spain & Holland. Work: Ames Col; Woodstock Guild Craftsmen, NY; Univ Iowa, also in many pvt collections. Comn: Portraits of family members, comn by Mrs Charlotte S McLean, Kingston, NY, 63, Mrs Nathan Katatsky, 69 & Dr David S Gerberg, 73; Grand Tetons (landscape), comn by Dr Norman Foster, Denver, Colo, 74; Mont Blanc (landscape), comn by Mr Robert Foster, Foncenex, France, 75. Exhib: One-man show, Savings & Loan Asn, Kingston, 71; Woodstock Guild Craftsman Exhib, Kleinart Gallery, 78- Mem: Woodstock Guild Craftsmen. Style & Technique: Brush and palette knife technique. Media: Oil, Clay. Publ: Co-auth, Art in Kingston schools, 56; auth, The Ghost Town of Caledonia, 78. Mailing Add: 75 Country Club Lane Woodstock NY 12498

FOSTER, JAMES W, JR
ART ADMINISTRATOR
b Baltimore, Md, Jan 4, 20. Study: Johns Hopkins Univ, 38-41; George Washington Univ; Corcoran Sch Art, 45-46; Am Univ, BA, 47. Pos: Exec asst, Baltimore Mus Art, 47-52, asst dir, 52-57; dir, Santa Barbara Mus Art, 57-63; dir, Honolulu Acad Arts, 63- Mem: Asn Art Mus Dirs; Am Asn Mus; Western Asn Art Mus; Hawaii Mus Asn. Mailing Add: 900 S Beretania St Honolulu HI 96814

FOSTER, STEPHEN C
ART HISTORIAN, ART WRITER
b Princeton, Ill, Dec 3, 41. Study: Northern Ill Univ, BA; Univ Ill, MA; Univ Pa, PhD. Teaching: Asst prof art hist, Bowdoin Col, Brunswick, Mass, 72-74, mem fac, Am Painting Summer Inst, 74 & 76; asst prof art hist & criticism, Univ Iowa, Iowa City, 74-; mem fac, Dublin Seminars, Boston Univ, Dublin, NH, summer 76. Pos: Co-dir, Corroboree, Gallery of New Concepts, Univ Iowa, Iowa City, 76- Mem: Col Art Asn Am; Mid-W Art Hist Soc. Res: Sociology of modern art with research emphasis in the areas of Dada and Abstract Expressionism; folk art. Publ: Auth, Greenberg: Formalism in the 40's and 50's, Art J, 75; auth, The Avant-Garde and the Privacy of Mind, 75 & auth, Making a Movement Modern: The Role of the Avant-Garde Critic, 76, Art Int: The Art Spectrum; auth, Turning Points in Pollock's Early Imagery, Univ Iowa Mus Bull, 76; auth, From Significant Incompetence, Proceedings of the Dublin Seminars, Boston Univ, 77. Mailing Add: 212 Sixth St Apt A-1 Coralville IA 52241

FOULGER, RICHARD F
SERIGRAPHER, PAINTER
b Kamloops, BC, Apr 30, 49. Study: Cult Develop Visual Arts & Crafts scholarships, Edmonton, Alta, 69-70; Alta Col Art, with Harold Fiest, 70; Vancouver Sch Art, with Don Jarvis, dipl fine art, 71; Notre Dame Univ, BFA, 74; Simon Fraser Univ, with Bob Crumlin, 75. Work: Alta Col Art; Soc Can Painter-Etchers & Engravers; Vancouver Art Gallery. Exhib: Int Can Soc Graphic Art Print Exhib, Montreal, 71; touring exhibs, 6th Nat Print Show, Burnaby Art Gallery, 73 & Graphics Can, Ont Art Gallery, 73-74; Survey of Can Art Now Exhib, Vancouver Art Gallery, 74; Int Print Club Exhib, Philadelphia, 75; Kootenay Exhib Visual & Performing Arts, Nelson, BC, 77; 24th Galerie Int Exhib, New York, NY, 77; Valley Visions Touring Exhib, Vallican Whole Community Centre, Vallican, BC & Langhorn Cult Centre, Kaslo, BC, 77; Exhib of BC Artists, Civic Centre, Nelson, BC, 77; one-artist show, Cobble Hill Loft Studio, Winlaw, BC, 78. Bibliog: Article in Canadian Artists in Exhibition, Roundstone Press, Toronto, 74-75; article in Performance, Promotion Arts Enterprises, Vancouver, 75. Mem: Soc Can Painter-Etchers & Engravers; Malaspina Printmakers Soc; Can Artists Representation (area rep). Style & Technique: Serigraphic abstracted; landscape visions. Publ: Contribr, Waves, York Univ, 74; contribr, Playboard Mag, Archway Publ, 74; contribr, Three Hours Later, New Era Social Club, Vancouver, 74. Dealer: Bau-Xi Gallery 3003 Granville St Vancouver BC Can; Nancy Poole's Studio 16 Hazelton Ave Toronto ON Can. Mailing Add: Cobble Hill Loft Studio RR 1 Winlaw BC V0G 2J0 Can

FOULKES, LLYN
PAINTER
b Yakima, Wash, Nov 17, 34. Study: Cent Wash Col Educ; Univ Wash; Chouinard Art Inst. Work: Whitney Mus Am Art, New York; Guggenheim Mus, New York; Beaubourg Mus, Paris, France; Art Inst Chicago; Los Angeles Co Mus Art; Mus Mod Art, New York; Mus des 20 Jahrhunderts, Vienna, Austria. Exhib: 7th & 9th Sao Paulo Biennial, Mus Mod Art, Sao Paulo, 63 & 67; New York World's Fair, 65; 5th Paris Biennial, Mus Mod Art, Paris, 67; Whitney Ann Am Painting, 67, 69 & 74 & American Art of Our Century, 71, Whitney Mus Am Art, New York; 71st Am Exhib, Chicago Art Inst, 74; Los Angeles, Mus of Mod Art, New York, NY, 76; 30 Yrs of Am Art, Whitney Mus, New York, 77; one-man shows, Pasadena Art Mus, Calif, 62, Oakland Mus Art, Calif, 64 & Galerie Darthea Speyer, Paris, 70 & 75, Retrospective, Newport Mus, Los Angeles, Calif, 74, Willard Gallery, New York, 75 & Gruenebaum Gallery, New York, 77. Collections Arranged: Cur, Imagination, Los Angeles Inst of Contemp Art, Calif. Teaching: Prof painting & drawing & artist in residence, Univ Calif, Los Angeles, 65-71; resident painter, Painting Workshop, Art Ctr Sch, Los Angeles, 71-75. Awards: First Award for Painting, San Francisco 82nd Ann, San Francisco Mus Art, 63; New Talent Purchase Grant, Los Angeles Co Mus Art, 64; Medal of France (first award for painting), 5th Paris Bienniale, Mus Mod Art, Paris, 67; Guggenheim Found fel, 77-78. Bibliog: Demetrion (auth), USA, fifth Paris biennale, Pasadena Art Mus, 67; Michael Compton (auth), Pop art, Movements Mod Art, 68; Henry Seldis (auth), Hollywood collects, Otis Art Inst, 70. Mem: Hon mem Pasadena Mus Art; hon mem Whitney Mus Am Art. Media: Oil, Acrylic. Mailing Add: c/o Gruenebaum Gallery 25 E 77th St New York NY 10021

FOURCADE, XAVIER
ART DEALER
b Paris, France, Sept 20, 26. Study: Politic Sci Sch, Paris; Univ Paris Law Sch; Sch Oriental Languages, Paris; Univ Paris Sch Advan Studies; Oxford Univ. Pos: Vpres & dir, M Knoedler & Co, Inc, New York, 66-72; pres, Fourcade, Droll, Inc, New York, 72-76; pres, Xavier Fourcade, Inc, New York, 76- Specialty: 20th century art and contemporary artists such as De Kooning, Gorky, Newman, Tony Smith, Moore, Joan Mitchell, Catherine Murphy Heizer and others. Mailing Add: Xavier Fourcade Inc 36 E 75th St New York NY 10021

FOURNIER, ALEXANDER PAUL
PAINTER, PRINTMAKER
b Simcoe, Ont, Oct 11, 39. Study: McMaster Univ, with Prof George Wallace. Work: Art Gallery Ont, Toronto; Nat Gallery Can, Ottawa; Can Coun Collection, Ottawa; Art Gallery of Hamilton, Ont; Winnipeg Art Gallery, Man. Comn: Acrylic painting for lobby of apt bldg, Greenwin Construction Co, Toronto, 72. Exhib: Ont Centennial Art Exhib, Art Gallery Ont, 67; 3rd Int Miniature Print Exhib, IBM Gallery, New York, 68; Five Lyrical Painters, Art Gallery Ont, 71; 3rd Int Exhib of Original Drawings, Mus Mod Art, Yugoslavia, 72; Graphic Art Today, 36th Int Venice Biennale, Italy, 72; plus many others. Pos: Artist in residence, Waterloo-Lutheran Univ, 69-70. Awards: First Prize, Hadassah Art Auction, 64 & Second Prize, 66; C W Jeffery's Award, Can Soc Graphic Art, 67. Bibliog: George Wallace (auth), Paul Fournier at the Westdale Gallery, Hamilton, 7-8/62 & Alan Jarvis (auth), Canadian art to-day, 7/66, Can Art. Media: Acrylic. Mailing Add: c/o Pollock Gallery 122 Scollard St W Toronto ON M5R 1G2 Can

FOUSEK, FRANK DANIEL
PRINTMAKER, PAINTER
b Cleveland, Ohio, Dec 8, 13. Study: John Huntington Polytechnic Inst & Cleveland Inst Art, Cleveland, Ohio. Work: Cleveland Mus Art, Ohio; Nat Collection Fine Arts, Washington, DC; US Marine Hosp, Ft Stanton, NMex; Cleveland Pub Libr, Main Br, Ohio; Am Art Clay Co, Indianapolis, Ind. Exhib: Paintings & Prints by Cleveland Artists, Whitney Mus Am Art, 37; San Francisco Art Asn Exhib Drawings & Prints, San Francisco Mus Art, 38; 43rd Ann Exhib of the Washington Water Color Club, Corcoran Gallery Art, Washington, DC, 38-39; 5th Int Exhib Etching & Engraving, 38-39 & 7th Int Exhib Lithography & Wood Engraving, 39-40, Art Inst Chicago, Ill; 3rd Nat Print Show, Buffalo Print Club, Albright-Knox Art Gallery, Buffalo, NY, 40; Artists for Victory Exhib of Contemp Am Art, Metrop Mus Art, New York, 42-43; Ann Exhib Ceramic Art, Kiln Club of Washington, Nat Collection Fine Arts, Washington, DC, 51 & 52; WPA/FAP Graphics (Works Progress Admin/Fed Art Proj), Smithsonian Inst Travelling Exhib Serv, 76. Pos: Artist-in-charge graphic dept, Fed Art Proj, Cleveland, Ohio, 39-41. Awards: Second Prize Etching, 21st Ann May Show, Cleveland Mus Art, Ohio, 39; Second Prize Metal Plate, First Ann Color Print Exhib, Philbrook Art Mus, 40; First Prize Etching, 23rd Ann May Show, Cleveland Mus Art, Ohio, 41. Media: Etching, lithography; oil painting, watercolor. Mailing Add: 2121 Central Pkwy Florissant MO 63031

FOWLER, MEL
PAINTER, PRINTMAKER
b Chicago, Ill, July 29, 22. Study: Minneapolis Inst Art, scholarships, 39-40; Calif Sch Fine Art, with Ralph Stackpole. Work: Brit Mus, London; Klingspor Mus, Offenbach, Ger; Walker Mus, Minneapolis; Clark Libr, Univ Calif, Los Angeles; New York Pub Libr. Comn: Porcelain steel sculpture, comn by M Mogenson, Burlingame, Calif, 58; porcelain steel sculpture, Kaiser Hosp, Oakland, Calif, 59; hammered bronze sculpture, comn by F Rosenthal, San Francisco, 59; porcelain steel mural, comn by M Wornum, San Francisco, 59; aluminum sculpture, comn by Cris Caras, Los Angeles, 65. Exhib: San Francisco Annual, 42 & 43; Mondrianna, Ann Arbor Film Festival & Mus Mod Art, 70; Museo de Ponce, PR, 73; Westbeth Graphic Arts Workshop, Belles Artes, Mexico City, Mex, 73-74 & traveling exhib sponsored by NY State Coun Arts, 74-75; plus ten one-man shows. Pos: Pres, Westbeth Painters, New York, 72-73. Mem: Fedn Mod Painters & Sculptors, New York. Style & Technique: Oil paintings in prismatist manner; etchings and wood block prints in illustrative style. Publ: Illusr, Home for the Night, 64; illusr, Lyric Poems, Franklin Watts Co Inc, 68 & Psychiatry: What It Is, 69; illusr, Row With Your Hair, 69; illusr, The King of Numbers (childrens' bk), Jarrow, 71; plus many others. Dealer: Brentano's The Roten Collection 9645 Gerwig Lane Columbia MD 21064; Multiple Impressions Gallery 17 Greenwich Ave New York NY. Mailing Add: Studio G-224 Westbeth 463 West St New York NY 10014

FOX, CHARLES HAROLD
CRAFTSMAN
b Clarks Harbour, NS, Jan 15, 05. Comn: Jewelry, as gift to Princess Elizabeth & Duke of Edinburgh, by Govt NS, 51. Exhib: Crafts Exhib, Nat Gallery, Can, 57; Brussels World's Fair, 58; Int Exhib, Dept External Affairs, Ottawa, Ont, 66 & 68; Expo '67; Okinawa World's Fair, 76. Awards: Prizes, Can Nat Exhib, Toronto, 51, 53 & 55, Nat Exhib St John, NB, 57 & Montreal, 61. Mailing Add: 18 Caldwell Ave Kentville NS B4N 2C6 Can

FOX, JOHN
PAINTER
b Montreal, PQ, July 26, 27. Study: Montreal Mus Fine Arts; Slade Sch, London, Eng. Work: Nat Gallery Can, Ottawa; Montreal Mus Fine Arts; Mus Que, PQ; Beaverbrook Art Gallery, Frederickton, NB; Art Gallery Greater Victoria, BC. Media: Acrylic. Mailing Add: c/o Marlborough-Godard Ltd 1490 Sherbrooke W Montreal PQ H3G 1L3 Can

FOX, TERRY ALAN
SCULPTOR
b Seattle, Wash, May 10, 43. Study: Acad Belli Arti, Rome, Italy, 62-63. Work: Sternum, Univ Calif Med Ctr, San Francisco. Exhib: Arte de Sistemas, Mus Mod Art, Buenos Aires, Arg, 71; Prospect 71, Kunsthalle, Dusseldorf, Ger, 71; Projektion, Louisiana Mus, Denmark, 72; Dokumenta 5, Kassel, Ger, 72; Venice Biennale, Italy, 72; plus many others. Teaching: Instr art I levitation & art II singing, Mus Conceptual Art, San Francisco, 69- Pos: Curator, Mus Conceptual Art, 69-71; West Coast Ed, Art Info, Dusseldorf, 69- Bibliog: Sharp (auth), I want my mood to affect their looks, Avalanche, 71; Plagens (auth), Terry Fox: the impartial nightmare, Artforum, 72; Lippard (auth), Excerpts, Praeger, 72. Mem: Fluxus West. Media: Mixed Media. Publ: Contribr, Bevys and fox, Interfunktionen 6, 71; contribr, Pisces, Interfunktionen 7, 71; contribr, Environmental surfaces, Interfunktionen 8, 72; plus films & video tapes. Dealer: Sonnabend Gallery 420 W Broadway New York NY 10012 & 12 Rue Mazarine Paris France. Mailing Add: 16 Rose St San Francisco CA 94102

FOX, WINIFRED GRACE
CRAFTSMAN, PAINTER
b Avondale, NS, Nov 26, 09. Study: Sch Fine Arts, Mt Allison Univ; Art Students League, with George Bridgman. Work: St John Mus, NB; Centennial Permanent Collection, NS; Mt St Vincent Univ, Halifax. Comn: Jewelry, as gift to Princess Elizabeth & Duke of Edinburgh, by Govt NS. Exhib: NS Soc Artists Ann; Nat Gallery Can, 57; Brussels World's Fair, 58; Int Exhib, Dept External Affairs, Ottawa, Ont, 66 & 68; Expo '67; Okinawa World's Fair, 76; plus others. Pos: Designer, dept handcrafts, NS Prov Govt, 45-60. Awards: Prizes, Can Nat Exhib, Toronto, 51, 53 & 55, Nat Exhib, St John, NB, 57 & Montreal, 61; plus others. Mem: NS Soc Artists. Media: Oil, Watercolor. Publ: Illusr, We Keep a Light & Flowing Summer. Mailing Add: 18 Caldwell Ave Kentville NS B4N 2C6 Can

FRACE, CHARLES LEWIS
ILLUSTRATOR, PAINTER
b Mauch Chunk, Pa, Feb 18, 26. Study: Philadelphia Col of Art, Pa. Work: Nat Wildlife Fedn, Washington, DC. Comn: Official portrait of Morris the Cat, 9-Lives Cat Food, 76; paintings, Frame House Gallery, for the reprod of limited ed prints, 73- Exhib: Soc of Animal Artists, NY; Mus of Sci & Space Transit Planetarium, Miami, Fla, 75-76; Mzuri Safari Found Conf, San Francisco, Calif, 76; Leigh Yawkey Woodson Art Mus, Wausau, Wis, 77; one-man show, Wedel, Ger, 77 & Cumberland Mus & Sci Ctr, Nashville, 78. Awards: Christopher Award for Paintings, The Wolf, 74. Mem: Soc of Animal Artists, New York. Style & Technique: Wildlife in natural habitat, mostly large mammals, hawks and eagles; oil on canvas or acrylic on canvas, palette knife technique is often used on backgrounds, paintings are very realistic. Media: Oil & Acrylic. Publ: Illusr, Last Chance on Earth, Chilton 5096, 66; illusr, The Life of the Jungle, McGraw-Hill, 70; illusr, Wonders of Island Life & Animals in Action, Readers Digest, 72; illusr, The Wolf, Coward, McCann, 73. Dealer: Frame House Gallery 110 E Market St Louisville KY 40202. Mailing Add: 28 Bryan Pl Brentwood TN 37027

FRACKMAN, NOEL
ART CRITIC, LECTURER
b New York, NY, May 27, 30. Study: Mt Holyoke Col, 48-50, Sarah Williston Scholar, 50; Sarah Lawrence Col, BA, 52, MA(Eng lit), 53; Columbia Univ, 64-67; Inst Fine Arts, NY Univ, MA, 76. Pos: Lectr, Aldrich Mus Contemp Art, Ridgefield, Conn, 67-75; partic, Art Critics Workshop, Am Fedn Arts, 68; lectr, Gallery Passport Ltd, New York, 68-; contrib ed, Arts Mag, New York, 68-; cur educ, Storm King Art Ctr, Mountainville, NY, 73-75. Awards: Mademoiselle First Prize, Col Publ Contest, 61. Publ: Auth, Super-chair, Art Voices, fall 66; auth, The Stein family and the era of avant-garde collecting, 2/71 & The enticement of watercolor, 6/74, Arts Mag; auth, Jump into the New York art world, Harper's Bazaar, 2/72; plus art rev in Scarsdale Inquirer, 62-67, Patent Trader, 62-71 & Arts Mag, current issues. Mailing Add: 3 Hadden Rd Scarsdale NY 10583

FRADON, DANA
CARTOONIST
b Chicago, Ill, Apr 14, 22. Study: Art Inst Chicago; Art Students League. Work: Libr Cong. Publ: Contribr cartoons, New Yorker, Look, Sat Rev, Sat Eve Post; auth, Breaking the Laugh Barrier, 61; auth, My son the medicine man, 64. Mailing Add: RFD 2 Brushy Hill Rd Newtown CT 06470

FRAME, ROBERT (AARON)
PAINTER
b San Fernando, Calif, July 31, 24. Study: With Henry Lee McFee, 47-50; Pomona Col, BA, 48; Claremont Col, MFA, 51. Work: Pasadena Art Mus, Calif; State Calif, Sacramento; Nat Acad Design, New York; Munic Art Dept, City Los Angeles; Santa Barbara Art Mus, Calif. Exhib: Ill Biennial, Urbana, 61-65; American Painting, Richmond, Va, 65; De Young Mus, San Francisco; Los Angeles Co Mus; plus 26 one-man exhibs. Awards: Purchase Prize, Pasadena Art Mus, 52; Guggenheim Fel, 57-58; First Prize, James D Phelan Awards, 65. Bibliog: Schaad (auth), Realm of Contemporary Still Life, Reinhold, 61; Mugniani (auth), Oil Painting, Van Nostrand, 69. Style & Technique: Underpainting and overpainting with some

glazing searching for color richness and expression in painterly freedom of subject. Media: Oil. Dealer: David Findlay Galleries 984 Madison Ave New York NY 10021; Richard Challis Gallery 1390 South Coast Hwy Laguna Beach CA 92651. Mailing Add: 2102 Edgewater Way Santa Barbara CA 93109

FRAMPTON, HOLLIS
FILMMAKER
b Wooster, Ohio, 1935. Study: Phillips Acad, Andover, Mass, 51-54; Western Reserve Univ, Cleveland, Ohio, 54-57. Exhib: Filmmakers Cinematheque, New York, 66; Toronto Cimethon, Ont, 67; 3rd Independent Filmmakers Festival, St Lawrence Univ, Canton, NY, 68; 15th Westdeutsche Kurzfilmtage, Oberhausen, Ger, 69; Info, Mus Mod Art, New York, 70; Prospekt, Kunsthalle, Dusseldorf, Ger, 71; New Forms in Film, Guggenheim Mus, New York, 72; Retrospective, Walker Art Ctr, Minneapolis, Minn, 72 & Mus Mod Art, New York, 72; one-man shows, Am Int Sch, New Delhi, India, 69, Seattle Art Mus, Wash, 69, Sch Visual Arts, New York, 70, Yale Univ, New Haven, Conn, 70 & 71, Art Inst Chicago, 70, Carnegie Inst Int, Pittsburgh, 71, Mus Contemp Art, Chicago, 72 & Visual Studies Workshop, Rochester, NY, 72. Collections Arranged: Museum of Modern Art & Anthology Film Archives, New York; Univ Harvard, Conn; Carnegie Inst Int, Pittsburgh; Ger Film Arch, Berlin. Teaching: Instr, Hunter Col & Cooper Union, New York, 69-71. Bibliog: Simon Field (auth), Alphabet as Ideogram, Arts & Artists, London, 8/72; Simon Field & Peter Sainsbury (auths), Interview with Hollis Frampton, Afterimage, London, autumn 72; Mark Segal (auth), Hollis Frampton/Zorns Lemma, Film Cult, New York, 72. Mem: NY State Coun on the Arts (mem vis artists prog, 71-). Publ: Auth, Meditations around Paul Strand, Artforum, Vol 10 (1972); auth, Nostalgia: voice-over narrations for a film of that same name, dated 1/8/71 & Notes on nostalgia, Film Cult, New York, Nos 53-55 (1972); auth, A pentagram for conjuring the narrative, In: Form & Structure in Recent Film, Vancouver, 72; auth, Stan & Jane Brakhage talking, Artforum, Vol 11 (1973). Mailing Add: c/o Anthology Film Arch 80 Wooster St New York NY 10012

FRANCES, HARRIETTE ANTON
PAINTER, PRINTMAKER
b San Francisco, Calif. Study: Jean Turner Sch Fashion Design, San Francisco, scholar, 41; San Francisco Sch Fine Arts, 42-45; Univ Pac, 55-57; San Francisco Art Inst, 63, 65-66; also with James Weeks, William H Brown & Richard Graf. Work: Fresno Art Ctr, Calif; Charles D Clark Collection, McAllen, Tex; Achenbach Found Graphic Arts; San Francisco Legion of Honor. Exhib: James D Phelan Award Exhib, De Young Mus, San Francisco, 63 & Palace Legion of Honor, 65; Fifth Winter Show, Palace Legion of Honor, 64 & Calif Printmakers, 71; one-person shows, Calif Palace Legion of Honor, San Francisco, 68 & Western Asn Art Mus traveling one-man shows at mus & univ galleries throughout US, 68-70; New Sch Art Ctr, New York, 73; San Francisco Women Artists, Bicentennial Exhib, Mus of Mod Art, San Francisco, 76. Teaching: Instr life drawing & lithography, Exten, Univ Pac. Awards: Calif State Fair Award, 64; James D Phelan Award in Art, 65; First Pl, San Francisco Women Artists, 74. Bibliog: George Christy (auth), Are you with it, Town & Country Mag, 67; Martin Fox (ed), A graphic artist depicts her LSD trip, Print Mag, 67; Joan Lisetor (auth), Reviving an ancient art, Independent J, 75. Mem: San Francisco Women Artists; Calif Soc of Printmakers; Marin Soc Artists (juror, calendar chmn & receiving chmn, 68-75); Graphics Soc. Style & Technique: Realism; work deals with figures in political/satirical statement. Media: Lithography, Acrylic. Publ: Contribr, Ramparts Mag, 66; contribr, USA & Espanol issue, MD Mag, 66; contribr, Print Mag & Psychedelic Art, 67; Erotic Art of the Masters, 18th, 19th & 20th Centuries, Lyle Stewart Publ. Dealer: Contemporary Gallery 2425 Cedar Springs Dallas TX 75201. Mailing Add: 105 Rice Lane Larkspur CA 94939

FRANCIS, BILL DEAN
DESIGNER, EDUCATOR
b Salem, Ill, Oct 14, 29. Study: Ill State Univ, BS(art educ), 51; Univ Wis, MS(appl art), 52; Ind Univ, 56-63. Comn: Tapestry, Phillips Petrol Co, Phillips, Okla, 64 & Bank South Austin, Tex, 75. Exhib: Midwest Landscape Art Exhib, Ill State Fair, Springfield, 52; Exhib Momentum, Inst Design, Chicago, 53; 29th Ann Am Graphic Arts & Drawing Exhib, Wichita, Kans, 60; Tex Designer-Craftsman Exhib, Wichita Falls, 72; one-man exhib, Longview Mus, Tex, 73. Teaching: Asst prof sec & elem art methods, Drake Univ, 58-60; assoc prof sec & elem art methods, Univ Tex, Austin, 64-74, prof art & educ & assoc dean, Col Fine Arts, 74- Pos: Conv mgr, Western Arts Asn, 62-67. Mem: Nat Art Educ Asn (co-chmn bldg promotion, 72-75); Tex Art Educ Asn (pres, 71-73, chmn bicentennial exhib, 75-). Style & Technique: Rya and punch needle tapestries using cotton & rayon with mixed media; abstractions from nature dealing with color and texture. Publ: Auth, Getting to Know Art (TV ser), KLRN, Tex, 70; auth, The Humanities in Retrospect, Kendall/Hunt, 74. Mailing Add: 1100 Yaupon Valley Rd Austin TX 78746

FRANCIS, JEAN THICKENS
PAINTER, SCULPTOR
b Laurel, Miss, Mar 15, 43. Study: Millsaps Col, Memphis Art Acad, BFA(sculpture), 66. Work: Southern Bell Tel & Tel Collection, Fulton, Miss; Bank Miss, Tupelo. Comn: Wall relief sculpture, Canton Libr, Miss, 76. Exhib: Mid-South Exhib, Brooks Mem Art Mus, Memphis, Tenn, 66; two-person shows, Lauren-Rodgers Mus Art, Laurel, Miss, 67 & Meridian Mus Art, Miss, 77; Miss Artist Competitive Exhib, Miss Art Asn, 76 & 77; Greater New Orleans Int Art Exhib, 76 & 77; Ann Bi-State, Meridian Mus, 76-78; Miss River Crafts Exhib, Brooks Mem Art Mus, 77; guest artist, Miss Arts Festival, Jackson, Miss, 77; four-man show, Art on Small Scale, Southeastern Ctr for Contemp Art, Winston-Salem, NC, 78; 50 Miss Artists, Miss Mus Art, Jackson, 78. Teaching: Sculpture, Memphis Acad Arts, summer 74; vis artist ceramic sculpture, Artists in the Sch Prog, Jackson City Sch, 76. Awards: Grand Prize, Miss Artist Competitive Exhib, Miss Art Asn, 76, Second Prize-Merit Award, 77; Merit Award, Greater New Orleans Int Art Exhib, 76-77. Bibliog: Dick Knowles (auth), Artists outside the system, Untitled, 76; Annette Cone-Skelton, Southeastern artists today: A cross section, Contemp Art/SE, 78. Mem: Miss Art Asn; Southern Independent Artists Asn. Style & Technique: Porcelain; handmade and poured paper; watercolor collages. Mailing Add: 512 Magnolia Dr Tupelo MS 38801

FRANCIS, MADISON KE, JR
SCULPTOR, PRINTMAKER
b Memphis, Tenn, Aug 19, 45. Study: Miss State Univ, Starkville; Memphis State Univ, Tenn; Memphis Acad Art, Tenn; Cleveland Inst Art, Ohio, BFA(sculpture), 69; Cape Sch Art, Provincetown, Mass, study of painting with Henry Hensche. Work: Southeastern Ctr Contemp Art, Winston-Salem, NC; Meridian Mus Art, Miss; Cleveland Inst Art, Print Collection, Ohio; Unifirst Nat Bank Permanent Collection & Miss Art Asn Travelling Exhib, Jackson, Miss. Comn: Bronze fountain, Reed's Dept Store, Tupelo, Miss, 71; 10 ft x 4 ft steel sculpture, People's Bank, Tupelo, Miss, 73; sculpture, Prouine High Sch, NEA Vis Artist Workshop, 74; Tombigbee State Park, Artist in the Park, vis artist, 75; and numerous pvt comn. Exhib: Mid-S Exhib, Brooks Mem Mus, Memphis, Tenn, 72; Drawings USA, Minn Art Ctr, St Paul, 74; Hunter Nat Painting Exhib, Hunter Mus, Chattanooga, Tenn, 74; Sixth Ann New Orleans Int Art Show, New Orleans Art Asn, La, 75; Mainstreams of Am Art, Marietta Col, Ohio, 77; Del Mar Nat Drawing Exhib, Del Mar Col, Corpus Christi, Tex, 77. Collections Arranged: One-man show, Southwestern at Memphis, Tenn, Miss Art Asn Gallery, Jackson, Miss & Delta State Univ, Cleveland, Miss; two-person show with wife, Jean Thickens Francis, Meridian Mus, Miss; two-person show, 2 Plus 2 Gallery, New Orleans, La. Teaching: Tech instr dept sculpture, Cleveland Inst Art, Ohio, 69-71; instr sculpture, Memphis Acad Art, summer 73. Awards: Gallery Contemp Art Purchase Award, 40th Semi-Ann Show, Secca, Southeastern Ctr for Contemp Arts, Winston-Salem, 73; Second Prize Painting, New Orleans Int Art Show, New Orleans Art Asn, 75; Best in Show, Fourth Miss-Ala Bi-State, Meridian Mus, Miss, 77. Bibliog: NEA Artist in the Schools Program, Miss ETV (Skip Allen, Miss Arts Comn), 75. Mem: Southern Sculpture Soc; Guerilla Supermarket (independent artist asn). Style & Technique: Abstract sculpture, based primarily on industrial fabrication techniques; cast metal pieces. Media: Steel, cor-ten and stainless; bronze; intaglio; silkscreen prints. Dealer: Sol Del Rio Gallery (Dorothy Katz) 1020 Townsend San Antonio TX 78209; Southeastern Ctr for Contemp Arts Winston-Salem NC. Mailing Add: 512 Magnolia Dr Tupelo MS 38801

FRANCIS, SAM
PAINTER
b San Mateo, Calif, June 25, 23. Study: Univ Calif, Berkeley, BA, 49, MA, 50; Atelier Fernand Leger, Paris; Univ Calif, Berkeley, Hon DFA, 69. Work: Guggenheim Mus, NY; Mus Mod Art; Albright Art Gallery; Kunsthaus, Zurich, Switz; Dayton Art Inst; plus others. Comn: Murals, Kunsthalle, Berne, Switz, 57, Sofu Sch Flower Arrangement, Tokyo, Japan, 57 & Chase Manhattan Bank, New York, 59. Exhib: One-man shows, Seattle Art Mus, 59, Pasadena Mus Art, 59, San Francisco Mus Art, 59 & 67 & Mus Fine Arts Houston, 67; retrospective, Stedelijk Mus, Amsterdam, 68 & Albright-Knox Art Gallery, Buffalo, NY, 72; The Fifties, Robert Elkon Gallery, New York, 75; 20th Nat Print Exhib, 77; plus many other group & one-man shows, US & abroad. Awards: First Prize, 3rd Int Biennial Exhib Prints, Tokyo, 62; Dunn Int Prize, Tate Gallery, London, 63; Tamarind Fel, 63; plus others. Bibliog: Werner Haftman (auth), Paintings in the Twentieth Century, Praeger, 60; Sam Hunter (ed), New Art Around the World: Painting & Sculpture, Abrams, 66; plus many others. Dealer: Galerie Smith-Anderson 200 Homer St Palo Alto CA 94301. Mailing Add: 345 W Channel Dr Santa Monica Canyon Los Angeles CA 90402

FRANCIS, SHERRON
PAINTER
b Oct 28, 40; US citizen. Study: Univ Okla, 58-60; Kansas City Art Inst, BFA, 63; Ind Univ, MFA, 66. Exhib: Speed Mus, Louisville, Ky, 64; Ind Artists Exhib, John Herron Mus, Indianapolis, 66; Galleria II Fante Di Space, Rome, 72; Whitney Biennial Exhib, Whitney Mus, New York, 73; Three Young American Painters, Mus Fine Arts, Houston, 74; Modern Painting: 1900 to Present, Mus of Fine Arts, Houston, 75; New Abstract Art, Edmonton Art Gallery, Alta, 77; Am Acad & Inst of Arts & Lett, New York, 78; one-person shows, Andre Emmerich Gallery, New York, 73 & 77, Jonie C Lee Gallery, Houston, 74, Barbara Kornblatt Gallery, Baltimore, 77 & Tibor de Nagy Gallery, New York, 78. Bibliog: Peter Schjeldahl (auth), Abstract painting-the crisis of success, New York Times, 2/4/73; Ann Holmes (auth), Two young Americans follow gallery's stars, Houston Chronicle, 10/3/74; New York letter, Art Int, 11/15/74; Kim Whee, A personal definition of pictorial space, Arts Mag, 11/74. Dealer: Tibor de Nagy Gallery 29 W 57th St New York NY 10019. Mailing Add: 16 Waverly Pl New York NY 10003

FRANCK, FREDERICK S
PAINTER, WRITER
b Maastricht, Holland, Apr 12, 09; US citizen. Study: Belg, Eng & US; Univ Pittsburgh, hon DFA, 63. Work: Whitney Mus Am Art & Mus Mod Art, New York; San Francisco Mus Art, Calif; Stedelijk Mus, Holland; Far Gallery, New York, NY; Mus Nat France, Paris; Tokyo Nat Mus, Japan; plus many others. Comn: Murals, Temple Beth-El, Elizabeth, NJ, Albert Schweitzer Pub Sch, Levittown, NJ & Nat Mus Tokyo; stage designs for off-Broadway shows; drawings for New Yorker; build a chapel with own sculpture, stained glass & mosaics, Warwick, NY, 65-68; Pacem in Terris. Exhib: Group shows in Whitney Mus Am Art & Metrop Mus Art, New York, Corcoran Gallery Art, Washington, DC, Butler Inst Am Art, Youngstown, Ohio, Calif Palace Legion of Honor, San Francisco & shows in Paris, Amsterdam, Geneva, London, Brussels, Rome & Japan; Foster/White Gallery exhib, Seattle, Wash, 77; Puget Sound Univ exhib, Tacoma, Wash, 78; plus many other group & one-man shows. Awards: Purchase Prizes, Carnegie Inst, Am Acad Arts & Lett & others; Living Arts Found Award, Maastricht Mus, Holland, 58; Medal of the Pontificate, Pope John, 63; plus others. Mem: Fel Int Inst Arts & Lett; Found for Arts, Relig & Cult; Artists Equity Asn (hon dir, New York). Style & Technique: Representational drawing; Dutch tradition painting with Oriental influences. Publ: Auth, My Eye is in Love, 63; auth, Le Paris de Simenon, 69 & Simenon's Paris, 70; Zen of Seeing, Seeing Drawing as Meditation, 73; Pilgrimage to Now/Here, 73; auth, The Book of Angelus Silesius, 76; auth, Zen and Zen Classics, New York & London, 78; auth, EveryOne, the Timeless Myth of Everyman Reborn, Doubleday, 78; plus many other bks & articles in leading nat mag. Mailing Add: Rte 1 Covered Bridge Rd Warwick NY 10990

FRANCO, BARBARA
CURATOR
b New York, NY, Mar 16, 45. Study: Bryn Mawr Col, BA; Cooperstown Grad Progs, MA. Collections Arranged: White's Utica Pottery (with catalog), 69-70 & Shaker Arts & Crafts (with catalog), 70-71, Munson-Williams-Proctor Inst, Utica, NY; Masonic Symbols in American Decorative Arts, Mus of Our Nat Heritage, 75-76. Pos: Cur decorative arts, Munson-Williams-Proctor Inst, 66-73; cur, Mus of Our Nat Heritage, 73- Publ: Auth, Stoneware made by the White Family in Utica, NY, 71 & auth, New York City furniture bought for Fountain Elms, 73, Antiques. Mailing Add: PO Box 519 Lexington MA 02173

FRANCO, ROBERT JOHN
SCULPTOR, EDUCATOR
b Yonkers, NY, Apr 12, 32. Study: Art Students League, 52; Franklin Sch Prof Art, NY, cert com art, 53; Silvermine Col Art, cert fine art, 60; Inst de Allende, San Miguel de Allende, Mex, 59. Exhib: New Eng Exhib Painting & Sculpture, 58-61, 68, 71, 75 & 76; Conn Watercolor Soc, The Atheneum, Hartford, Conn, 59, 60, 61, 76 & 77; New Haven Festival of Art, 58 & 59; one-man show, Silvermine Guild Artists, 59, 64, 68 & 72; Boston Arts Festival, 65; Eastern States Exhib, 68. Teaching: Instr painting, drawing, watercolor & design, Silvermine Col Art, New Canaan, Conn, 58-71 & Silvermine Guild Sch of the Arts, Norwalk, Conn, 71- Pos: Exhib dir, Silvermine Guild of Artists, 69-71, dir, Sch of the Arts, 71- Awards: The 1st Sculpture Award, New Eng Exhib, Olivetti Co, 68 & 76; Sculpture Award, New Eng Exhib, Pitney Bowes Co, 75; Purchase Award, Conn Watercolor Soc, J M Ney Co, 77. Mem: Conn Watercolor Soc Inc. Style & Technique: Sculpture, wood, organic, abstract; watercolor, realism, landscape, concentration on light, mainly blacklight. Media: Sculpture; watercolor.

Dealer: Silvermine Guild of Artists Inc 1037 Silvermine Rd New Canaan CT 06840. Mailing Add: 557 Danbury Rd Wilton CT 06897

FRANK, CHARLES WILLIAM
WOOD CARVER, ART WRITER
b New Orleans, La, June 8, 22. Study: BChemEng. Exhib: New Orleans Mus Art, 75; Hills Borough Co Mus, Tampa, Fla, 76; Univ New Orleans Fine Arts Mus, 76; Huntsville Mus Art, Ala, 76-77; West Baton Rouge Hist Asn, 76; Nat Crafts Coun, Winston-Salem, NC, 77. Pos: Auth & contribr, NAm Decoys, 72-77; auth, La Duck Decoys, 75-78; master craftsman, La Crafts Coun, 77; auth & contribr, La Out of Doors, 77-78; chmn, La Wildfowl Carvers Festival, 78. Awards: Best of Show, Catahoula Lake Wildfowl Festival, 75 & 76; First Place, La Wildfowl Carvers Exhib, 76. Bibliog: Article in La Conservationist, State of La, 73 & 75; Phillips Petroleum Co (auth), Louisiana's Wetland Heritage, The Decoy, 76. Mem: La Crafts Coun; La Wildfowl Carvers & Collectors (dir guild); Int Wildlife Carvers (dir); Nat Wood Carvers Asn. Style & Technique: Wood carving of Louisiana ducks and shorebirds. Media: Wood painted with oils. Collection: Definitive collection of several thousand Louisiana and world wide duck decoys. Publ: Auth/contribr, Am Shotgunner, 76; auth/contribr, Southern Outdoors, 77. Mailing Add: 3112 Octavia New Orleans LA 70125

FRANK, DAVID
POTTER, EDUCATOR
b St Paul, Minn, Sept 13, 40. Study: Univ Minn, Duluth, with Glenn C Nelson & BS(art); Tulane Univ La, MFA. Work: Tweed Gallery, Duluth; Newcomb Art Sch Collection; Mid Tenn State Univ Collection, Murfreesboro; Miss Univ for Women, Columbus; Miss Dept Archives & Hist. Comn: Pohl Gym, Miss Univ for Women, Columbus & St Ignatius Catholic Church, Mobile, Ala. Exhib: Wichita Craft Exhib, Kans; 7th Miami Ceramic Nat, Fla; Southeast Craftsmen 66, NC; Mid South Ceramics & Crafts Exhib, Tenn; 14th Ann Delta Art Exhib, Ark; Crafts Invitational, Univ of Ala; Invitational Exhib, Nat Endowment for the Arts; Miss River Crafts Exhib, Brooks Gallery, Memphis, Tenn. Teaching: Assoc prof art, Miss Univ for Women, 65- Mem: Craftsmen's Guild of Miss (state rep); Am Craftsman's Coun. Media: Clay. Mailing Add: Dept of Art Miss Univ for Women Columbus MS 39701

FRANK, MARY
SCULPTOR
b London, Eng, Feb 4, 33. Study: With Max Beckmann, 50 & Hans Hofmann, 51. Work: Art Inst Chicago; Kalamazoo Inst Art; Mus Mod Art; Southern Ill Univ; Worcester Mus Art, Mass; plus others. Exhib: Yale Univ; Brandeis Univ; Mus Mod Art; Hans Hofmann & His Students Traveling Exhib, 63-64; Whitney Mus Am Art Ann, New York, 72 & 73; Philadelphia Mus Art & Mus Philadelphia Civic Ctr, 74; plus others. Awards: Ingram Merril Found Grant, 61; Longview Found Grant, 62-64; Nat Coun Arts Award, 68. Dealer: Zabriskie Gallery 29 W 57th St New York NY 10019. Mailing Add: 463 West St New York NY 10014

FRANK, PETER SOLOMON
ART CRITIC, CURATOR
b New York, NY, July 3, 50. Study: Columbia Col, New York, BA(art hist), 72; Columbia Univ, New York, MA(art hist), 74. Collections Arranged: Artists' books section of Documenta 6, Kassel, WGer, summer 77; Artists' Books USA (traveling exhib), Independent Curators Inc, 78-80. Teaching: Vis asst prof contemp arts sem, Pratt Inst, Brooklyn, NY, 75-76; adj assoc prof MFA contemp arts sem, Sch of Arts, Columbia Univ, 78. Pos: Art critic, SoHo News, 73-75 & Village Voice, 77-; curatorial assoc, Independent Curators Inc, 74- Awards: Nat Endowment for the Arts Critics Travel Grant, 78. Bibliog: Jacqueline Brody (auth), Peter Frank: a case for marginal collectors, Print Collectors Newsletter, 5-6/78; Diane Spodarek (auth), interview in Detroit Artists Mo, 6/78. Mem: Int Asn of Art Critics (Am sect). Mailing Add: 80 N Moore St 12C New York NY 10013 •

FRANKEL, DEXTRA
EDUCATOR GALLERY DIRECTOR
b Los Angeles, Calif, Nov 28, 24. Study: Long Beach State Col. Work: Philadelphia Free Libr; La Jolla Art Mus, Calif; St Paul Art Ctr, Minn; Pac View Mem Park, Corona Del Mar, Calif; Kennecott Copper Co, Salt Lake City, Utah; also in pvt collections. Exhib: Los Angeles Co Mus Art, 59, 62 & 66; five shows, Pasadena Art Mus, Calif, 59-68; Tucson Art Ctr, Ariz, 64 & 66; Mus Contemp Crafts, NY, 66 & 68; Los Angeles State Col, 69; Wichita Art Mus Kans; Everson Mus Syracuse, NY; Crocker Art Gallery, Sacramento; Cincinnati Art Mus; Newport Harbor Art Newport Beach, Mus, Calif; Butler Inst Am Art, Youngstown, Ohio; Calif Palace of Legion of Honor, San Francisco; Denver Art Mus; Seattle Art Mus, Wash; Portland Art Mus, Ore; San Francisco Mus Art; H M deYoung Mus, San Francisco; Smithsonian Inst. Collections Arranged: Recorded Images/Dimensional Media, 67, Intersection of Line, 67, Frazer/Lipofsky/Richardson, 68, Transparency/Reflection, 68 & others, Art Gallery, Calif State Univ, Fullerton. Teaching: Asst prof art, Calif State Univ, Fullerton, 64-68, assoc prof art, 69- Pos: Dir art gallery, cur & designer exhib, Calif State Univ, Fullerton, 67-; Southwest Region trustee, Am Crafts Coun, New York, 75-78; US deleg, World Craft Coun Conf, Mex, 76; partner, LA.X Studios. Awards: Nat Endowment for Arts grants, 75 & 77 & fel, 78. Mem: Calif Soc Printmakers; Am Color Print Soc; Am Craftsmen's Coun. Publ: Auth, Text for Pasadena Mus, 65 & 68 & Crafts Horizons Mag, 73. Mailing Add: Dept of Art Calif State Univ Fullerton CA 92634

FRANKENBERG, ROBERT CLINTON
ILLUSTRATOR, INSTRUCTOR
b Mt Vernon, NY, Mar 19, 11. Study: Art Students League, New York, 28-29; study with William McNulty. Work: War Mus, Washington, DC; St Patrick's Cath Collection, New York; Kerlan Collection of Children's Lit, Univ Minn. Comn: Murals, Pa State Bldg & NC Bldg, stage sets & dioramas, Chase Brass & Copper Exhib, New York Worlds Fair, 39. Exhib: Six one-man shows in New York, 53-70. Teaching: Instr figure drawing, Sch Visual Arts, New York, 47-, head drawing dept, 58-67. Pos: Artist, Jenter Exhib, NY & NJ, 33-40; artist, US Army Signal Corps, 40-45. Awards: Jews in Am, 54 & Einstein, 56, Nat Filmstrip Award, Nat Jewish Coun for Audio Visual Aids; First Merit Award for Teaching, Alumni Asn, Sch Visual Arts, 76. Bibliog: Nick Maglin (auth), On The Spot Drawing, Animals in Motion, Watson-Guptill Publ, 69. Style & Technique: Modern realism with loose flowing forms, accent on space, movement, landscape and figure. Media: Watercolor & Oil, Mixed Media. Publ: Illusr, Two Years Before the Mast, Doubleday, 49; illusr, The Christmas Book, 52 & The Easter Book, 54, Harcourt-Brace; illusr, Boston, Seabury, 67; illusr, Indians, Parents Mag Press, 68. Dealer: Hans Fybel Assoc 648 Kelton Ave Los Angeles CA 90024. Mailing Add: 601 E 20th St New York NY 10010

FRANKENSTEIN, ALFRED VICTOR
ART CRITIC, ART HISTORIAN
b Chicago, Ill, Oct 5, 06. Study: Univ Chicago, PhB, 32; Yale Univ; Columbia Univ. Collections Arranged: William Sidney Mount, Nat Gallery and other mus, 68; Our Land, Our Sky, Our Water, survey of American landscape painting, Spokane World's Fair, 74. Teaching: Lectr Am art, Univ Calif, Berkeley, 40-74, Mills Col, Oakland, Calif, 45-70 & Stanford Univ, 73- Pos: Art critic, San Francisco Chronicle, 34; vpres, San Francisco Art Comn, 75- Awards: Guggenheim Fel, 48; Frank Jewett Mather Prize, Col Art Asn, 70. Mem: Col Art Asn; Dunlap Soc; Newspaper Guild; Am Studies Asn. Res: American painting, mostly 19th century. Publ: Auth, After the Hunt, Univ Calif, three ed, 53, 69 & 75; auth, Angels Over the Altar, Univ Hawaii, 67; auth, The World of Copley, Time-Life Bks, 70; auth, The Reality of Appearance, New York Graphic Soc, 71; auth, William Sidney Mount, a documentary biography, Harry N Abrams, 75. Mailing Add: 24 Sixth Ave San Francisco CA 94118

FRANKENTHALER, HELEN
PAINTER
b New York, NY, Dec 12, 28 Study: Horace Mann, Brearley & Dalton Schs; Bennington Col, BA, 49; Skidmore Col, DHL, 69; Smith Col, DFA, 73; Moore Col of Art, DFA, 74; Bard Col, DFA, 76; also with Rufino Tamayo, Wallace Harrison, Paul Feeley & Hans Hofmann. Work: Brooklyn Mus, Cooper Hewitt Mus, New York Univ Art Collection, Solomon R Guggenheim Mus, Whitney Mus of Am Art, Metrop Mus Art & Mus Mod Art, New York; Art Inst Chicago; Cleveland Mus Art; Pasadena Art Mus, Calif; plus many others. Exhib: Nature in Abstraction, Whitney Mus Am Art, New York, 58; American Abstract Expressionists & Imagists, Guggenheim Mus, New York, 61; Post Painterly Abstraction, Los Angeles Co Mus Art, Calif, Walker Art Ctr, Minn & Art Gallery Ont, Toronto, 64; New York Painting & Sculpture: 1940-1970, Metrop Mus Art, New York, 69-70; Two Generations of Color Painting, Inst of Contemp Art, Univ Pa, 70; one-person shows, Portland Art Mus, Ore, 72, Metrop Mus Art, New York, 73, Guggenheim Mus, New York, 75 & Helen Frankenthaler; A Selection of Small Scale Paintings 1949-1977, US Info Agency Worldwide Traveling Exhib, 78-79; Retrospective, Whitney Mus Am Art, New York, 69 & Berggruen Gallery, San Francisco, Calif, 72; Albright-Knox Art Gallery, Buffalo, NY, 70; Abstract Painting in the 70's, Mus Fine Arts, Boston, 72; The Great Decade of Am Abstraction: Modernist Art 1960-1970, Mus Fine Arts, Houston, Tex, 74; plus many others. Teaching: Instr contemp painting sem, Yale Univ, spring 70; instr contemp painting sem, Princeton Univ & Hunter Col, 70; plus many other lectures & seminars. Pos: Trustee, Bennington Col, 67-; fel, Calhoun Col, Yale Univ, 68- Awards: Mem Nat Inst of Arts & Lett, 74; Ann Creative Artist Laureate Award of Am Jewish Cong, Women's Div, 74; Art & Humanities Award, Yale Women's Forum, 76. Biennial Int Grafica d'Arte, 72; Garrett Award, 70th Am Exhib, Art Inst Bibliog: Eugene C Goossen (auth), Helen Frankenthaler, Praeger, 69; Barbara Rose (auth), Frankenthaler, Abrams, 72. Dealer: Andre Emmerich Gallery 41 E 57th St New York NY 10022. Mailing Add: 173 E 94th St New York NY 10028

FRANKLIN, CHARLOTTE WHITE
PAINTER, SCULPTOR
b Philadelphia, Pa. Study: Tyler Art Sch, Temple Univ, BA, 45, BS(educ), 46, MFA, 47; Inst San Miguel Allende, Univ Guanajuato, 57; Mexico City Col, 58; Escuela Nat de Bellas Artes, Buenos Aires, Arg, 60; Goldsmith Col, Univ London, 62; Inst Cult Mex-NAm, Mex, 64; Tyler, Rome, Italy, 67; Univ Madrid, 68. Comn: Altar panel, St Augustine Church, Philadelphia; portrait, Cardinal Dougherty, Archdiocese of Philadelphia; plus numerous portraits & paintings in pvt collections. Exhib: Pro Show, Philadelphia Art Festival, 67; one-man shows, US Embassy, Madrid, Spain, 68, Community Col of Philadelphia, 69, Drexel Univ, 69, La Salle Col, 71, Friends Select Sch, Philadelphia, 74, Lincoln Univ Exhib, 74, Univ Pa, 74, Safari in Ancient Africa, Mus of Univ Pa, 75 & Nat Educ Conf, Capital Hilton Hotel, Washington, DC, 77; Int Art Exhib, Int Fedn Univ Women, 71; NJ Glassboro State Teachers Col, 75; Bicentennial Women's Exhib, Penwalt Galleries, Philadelphia, 76. Teaching: Instr, Philadelphia Mus Art, 43-47; chmn sec educ art, Philadelphia Pub Schs, 51-; instr, Soc Brit Artists, Buenos Aires, 60; Fulbright fel art teacher, Grammar Sch Girls, Cheam, Eng, 61-62. Pos: Pres, Les Beaux Arts, Philadelphia, 40's & 50's; lectr, Speakers' Bur Art, US Embassy, London, 61-62; mem bd, Nat Forum Prof Artists, 69-; chmn fine arts comt & mem bd, Am Asn Univ Women, 70-73; mem bd, Philadelphia North Arts Coun Inc; mem adv bd, Women's Cult Ctr Mid-City Young Women's Christian Asn, 74-75; lectr, Sch Dist of Philadelphia & Univ Pa. Awards: Bessie Calhoun Bird Award, Les Beaux Arts, 40's; Am Asn Univ Women name grant to Nat Educ Found, Women's Univ Club, 77. Mem: Philadelphia Mus Art; Philadelphia Art Alliance; Provincetown Art Asn, Mass; Hispano-NAm Asn Cult, Madrid; Soc Brit Artists. Style & Technique: People and places around the world; mosaicism and romantic cubism of African-Mexican heritage. Media: Oil. Publ: Auth, article in Philly Talk Mag, 71. Mailing Add: 24th & Franklin Pkwy Philadelphia PA 19130

FRANKLIN, ERNEST WASHINGTON, JR
COLLECTOR
b Apex, NC, Apr 13, 05. Study: Univ NC, BS; Univ Pa, MD. Collection: Contemporary art. Mailing Add: 1141 Linganore Pl Charlotte NC 28203

FRANSIOLI, THOMAS ADRIAN
PAINTER, PRINTMAKER
b Seattle, Wash, Sept 15, 06. Study: Univ Pa, BArch; Art Students League. Work: Mus Fine Arts, Boston, Mass; Whitney Mus Am Art, New York; Seattle Art Mus, Wash; Dallas Mus Fine Arts, Tex; Farnsworth Mus, Rockland, Maine. Comn: Murals in dining rm, Aetna Life Bldg, Hartford, Conn, 62; four paintings of old New York, Univ Club, New York, 64; mural in stair hall, Princeton Club, New York, 66; mural in lobby, Brevoort East Hotel, New York, 67; painting of Brit Embassy, Washington, DC, comn by the Brit Ambassador to US, 75. Exhib: Boston Art Festival, 48-49; Whitney Mus Ann, New York, 48-52 & 58; Carnegie Inst, Pittsburgh, Pa, 49 & 52; Am Art Today, Metrop Mus Art, New York, 50; Maine & Its Role in American Art, Colby Col, Waterville, Maine & Whitney Mus Am Art, New York, 63. Awards: Purchase Prize, Boston Arts Festival, 52; hon citizen, State of Maine, 54. Style & Technique: Realistic representation of individual buildings, cityscapes or landscapes. Media: Oil, Acrylic, Gouache, Pencil. Mailing Add: 55 Dodges Row Wenham MA 01984

FRANZEN, JOAN C
ART ADMINISTRATOR
b Boston, Mass. Study: Bennington Col. Pos: Asst, J B Neumann, New York, 60-63; dir, Skowhegan Sch Painting & Sculpture, Maine & New York City, 64- Mailing Add: 329 E 68th St New York NY 10021

FRASCONI, ANTONIO
ILLUSTRATOR, PAINTER
b Buenos Aires, Arg, Apr 28, 19. Study: Art Students League; New Sch Social Res. Work: Metrop Mus Art & Mus Mod Art, New York; Mus Nac Bellas Artes, Montevideo, Uruguay; Bibliot Nat, Paris, France; Arts Coun Gt Brit, London. Exhib: Casa Americas, Havana, Cuba, 65-68; Venice Biennale, Italy, 68; Art of the Americas, Yale Univ; Smithsonian Inst, Washington, DC; var ann, Pa Acad Fine Arts, Philadelphia. Teaching: Mem art faculty, State Univ NY Col Purchase, currently. Awards: Joseph Pennell Mem Medal, Pa Acad Fine Arts, 53; Grand Prix, Venice Film Festival, 60; Premio La Habana, Casa Americas, 68. Bibliog:

Manuel Gasser (auth), A Frasconi, Graphis Press (Switz), 67; Frasconi—Against the Grain, Macmillan; Pablo Frasconi (auth), Antonio Frasconi—graphic artist (film), York Univ. Publ: Illusr, Twelve Fables of Aesop, 54; illusr, Bestiary, 65; illusr, Overhead the Sun, 69; illusr, Unstill Life, 69; illusr, On the Slain Collegians, 71. Dealer: Weyhe Gallery 794 Lexington Ave New York NY 10021; Terry Dintenfass Inc 50 W 57th St New York NY 10021. Mailing Add: 26 Dock Rd Norwalk CT 06854

FRASER, CAROL HOORN
PAINTER
b Superior, Wis, Sept 5, 30. Study: Gustavus Adolphus Col, St Peter, Minn, BS; Univ Minn, MFA & seminar with Jack Tworkov; study of painting with Yasuo Kuniyoshi. Work: Walker Art Ctr; Nat Gallery Can; Sir George Williams Art Galleries; Confederation Ctr Art Gallery; Beaverbrook Art Gallery. Exhib: Sixteen Minn Artists, Walker Art Ctr, 60; Montreal Mus Fine Art Spring Show, 62-63; Nat Gallery Can Biennials, 62-63 & 64; Acquisition Exhib, Univ NB Art Ctr, 72; New Talent Festival, Midtown Galleries, New York, 74; Painting Now, 76-77, Agnes Etherington Art Ctr, 76; one-person show, Atlantic Provinces Art Circuit, travelling to five major inst, 65-67; one-person travelling show, eight provinces & inst, 77-78. Collections Arranged: Drawing USA, St Paul Art Gallery, 63; Expo 67, Atlantic Pavilion, 67; Seven Artists Travelling Show, Dalhousie Univ Art Ctr, 69-70; Artists Media, Mt St Vincent Univ Art Ctr, 74; Montreal Olympics, Atlantic Gallery, 76. Teaching: Instr drawing, Sch Archit, NS Tech Col, 62-69. Awards: First Prize & Purchase Award, Walker Art Ctr Biennial, 58; First Prize, Minn Inst Art, 59; Arts Award, Can Coun, 67. Bibliog: Mary E McLachlan (auth), Catalogue Introduction, Dalhousie Art Gallery, 77; Felicity Redgrave (auth), Homage to Carol Fraser, Art Mag, Toronto, 77. Mem: Can Artists Representation; Royal Can Acad Arts. Style & Technique: Expressionist, Surrealist; colorful, figurative, organic forms; smooth surface, modeled 3-D forms. Media: Oil on linen canvas; black india & colored ink. Dealer: Zwickers Art Gallery 5415 Doyle St Halifax NS Can. Mailing Add: 6070 Oakland Rd Halifax NS B3H 1N8 Can

FRASER, DOUGLAS (FERRAR)
ART HISTORIAN, EDUCATOR
b Hornell, NY, Sept 3, 29. Study: Columbia Col, AB; Columbia Univ, AM & PhD. Teaching: Prof art hist & archaeol, Columbia Univ. Res: Primitive and pre-Columbian art. Mailing Add: 445 Riverside Dr New York NY 10027

FRATER, HAL
PAINTER
b New York, NY, Mar 3, 09. Exhib: Nat Acad Design; Audubon Artists, Cult Ctr, New York, NY; Riverside Mus, New York; Grippi Gallery, New York; Hudson Guild Gallery, New York; Harbor Gallery, Long Island, NY; Chrysler Mus, Provincetown, Mass; Brooklyn Mus; Seton Hall Univ; Allied Artists Am; plus others. Teaching: Instr, Sch of Art & Design, New York & Educ Alliance, New York. Mem: Painters & Sculptors Soc NJ; Allied Artists Am; Soc Illusr; Artists Equity Asn. Mailing Add: 215 Park Row New York NY 10038

FRAUGHTON, EDWARD JAMES
SCULPTOR
b Park City, Utah, Mar 22, 39. Study: Univ Utah, BFA, 62; spec studies from Dr Avard T Fairbanks & Justin Fairbanks. Work: Riveredge Found, Calgary, Can; Leanin' Tree Mus Western Art, Boulder, Colo; Church of Jesus Christ of Latter-day Saints, Salt Lake City, Utah; Nat Cowboy Hall of Fame & Western Heritage Ctr, Oklahoma City, Okla; Favell Mus Western Art, Klamath Falls, Ore. Comn: Mormon Battalion Monument, Sons of Utah Pioneers, Prisidio Park, San Diego, Calif, 69; Thomas E Ricks Portrait, Ricks Family Orgn, Ricks Col, Rexberg, Idaho, 69; Ben H Bohac (relief portrait), Talman Savings & Loan, Chicago, 70; All is Well, Family Monument, Sons of Utah Pioneers, Brigham Young Cemetery, Salt Lake City, 74; Truman O Angell Portrait, Church of Jesus Christ of Latter-day Saints, Salt Lake City, Utah, 77. Exhib: Nat Acad Western Art, Oklahoma City, 73-77; Kansas City Soc Western Art, Mo, 74; Nat Sculpture Soc, New York, 75-78; Whitney Mus Western Art, Cody, Wyo, 75; Bohemian Club, Bohemian Grove, Monte Rio, Calif, 75-77. Awards: Gold Medals-Sculpture, Nat Acad Western Art, 73, 75 & 77. Bibliog: Pat Broder (auth), Bronzes of the American West, Abrams, 74; articles in Nat Sculpture Rev, fall 76 & winter 76-77 & Persimmon Hill Mag, Vol 7, No 4. Mem: Nat Acad Western Art; Soc Animal Artists; San Francisco Bohemian Club; Nat Sculpture Soc. Style & Technique: Figures and animals in clay and cast in bronze—monumental, museum size, miniature, in round and relief—American classical style. Media: Bronze & Stone Carving. Dealer: Trailside II Box 1194 Jackson WY 83001; Husberg Fine Arts Gallery PO Drawer D Sedona AZ 86336. Mailing Add: 10353 S 1300 West South Jordan UT 84065

FRAUWIRTH, SIDNEY
COLLECTOR
b Smerekowjec, Poland, Nov 2, 08; US citizen. Collection: American paintings, drawings, and sculpture. Mailing Add: 82 Reed St New Bedford MA 02740

FRAZE, DENNY T
ARTIST, ART ADMINISTRATOR
b Weatherford, Tex, May 28, 40. Study: Univ Tex, Austin, BFA(studio, art hist), 62; Univ Colo, MFA(painting), 64, study with Luis Eades & Roland Reiss. Work: Univ Tex, Austin; Univ Colo, Boulder; Amarillo Col Collection, Tex. Exhib: XIV Mid-Am Ann Exhib, Nelson-Atkins Mus, Kansas City, Mo, 64; Mat Black & White Print Exhib, Manhattan, Kans, 66; 15th Ann Delta Art Exhib, Ark Art Ctr, Little Rock, 72; one-man shows, Univ Alaska, 67, Wichita State Univ, 67, Cent Mo State Univ, 69, Ga Southern Col, 71 & E Tex State Univ, 77. Teaching: Prof studio art & chmn dept, Amarillo Col, Tex, 65- Pos: Pres, Tex Asn of Schs of Art, 70-72; bd mem, Tex Coun on the Arts in Educ, 70-72; Tex state chmn for community col sect, Higher Educ Div, Nat Art Educ Asn, 71-72; bd mem, Tex Asn Schs of Art, 72-74. Mem: Tex Fine Arts Asn (hon mem); Col Art Asn of Am; Amarillo Fine Arts Asn (hon mem). Style & Technique: Collage artist, realistic compositions; oil painting, non-objective style. Media: Collage; Oil Painting; Printmaking. Collection: 20th century prints. Mailing Add: 2213 S Hayden Amarillo TX 79109

FRAZER, JAMES NISBET, JR
PHOTOGRAPHER
b Atlanta, Ga, Oct 6, 49. Study: Amherst Col, BA(dum laude), 71; Ga State Univ, MVA, 73; also with Fairfield Porter. Work: High Mus Art, Atlanta; Ga Art Bus; City of Atlanta, Ga; Ga State Univ. Comn: Photomurals, Metro Atlanta Rapid Transit Authority, Inman Park, Reynoldstown Station, 78. Exhib: New Photographics/73, Cent Wash State Gallery, Ellensburg, 73; Artists Biennalle, New Orleans Mus Art, La, 75; Nat Photog Exhib, Ohio Silver Gallery, Los Angeles, 75; The Southern Ethic, Nexus Gallery, Atlanta, 75; Arte EUA: El Sur (SAm traveling exhib), US Info Agency, 76-77; 35 Artists in the SE, High Mus Art, 76-78; Graphics, Southeastern Ctr for Contemp Art, Winston-Salem, NC, 77. Teaching: Instr photog, Atlanta Col Art, Ga State Univ, 72-76 & Mercer Univ & Art Inst Atlanta, 77- Pos: Photog coordr, Arts Festival of Atlanta, 73; pres, Nexus Inc, Atlanta, 73-74, mem bd dir, 73- Bibliog: John David Farmer (auth), 35 Artists of the Southeast, Vol I (1977) & Southeastern artists today: A cross section, Vol 2 (1978), Contemp Art/SE. Style & Technique: Landscapes: photographs hand-colored in oil. Interest: Nexus, Inc: non-profit corporation for advancement of photographic arts, supported by National Endowment for the Arts and Georgia Council for the Arts. Publ: Contribr, The Southern Ethic, Inst for Southern Studies, 75. Dealer: Heath Gallery 34 Lombardy Way Atlanta GA 30309. Mailing Add: 1295 Lanier Pl NE Atlanta GA 30306

FRAZER, JOHN THATCHER
FILM MAKER, PAINTER
b Akron, Ohio, Apr 2, 32. Study: Univ Tex, BFA; Yale Univ, MFA, also with Joseph Albers. Work: Davison Art Ctr, Wesleyan Univ, Middletown, Conn; Libr of Cong, Washington, DC; Cullinan Collection, Houston Mus Fine Arts; Nicholson Mem Libr, Longview, Tex. Exhib: Tex Ann, Dallas Mus Fine Arts, 58; New Haven Arts Festival, Conn, 60; Boston Arts Festival, Mass, 61; Flaherty Film Festival, Lakeville, Conn, 66; Am Film Festival, New York, 68. Teaching: Prof art, motion pictures & drawing, Wesleyan Univ, 59- Bibliog: New talent, USA, Art in Am, 62; Bernard Chaet (auth), The Art of Drawing, Holt, 70. Mem: Am Asn Univ Prof; Col Art Asn Am; Univ Film Study Ctr (vpres, 70-72). Interest: Motion pictures. Publ: Auth, Documentary films & books on documentary films, Choice Mag, 69; auth, Artificially Arranged Scenes, The Films of George Méliès. Mailing Add: Art Ctr Wesleyan Univ Middletown CT 06457

FRAZIER, LE ROY DYYON
PAINTER, SCULPTOR
b Ft Meyers, Fla, May 2, 46. Work: Mus Mod Art & Whitney Mus Am Art, New York; Larry Aldrich Mus, Conn. Exhib: Cleveland Top Artists, In Town Club, Cleveland, Ohio, 69; Int Exhib Art, Cleveland, 70; Whitney Mus Am Art Ann, New York, 72; Reflections, Larry Aldrich Mus, 72-73. Mailing Add: 155 W 73rd St New York NY 10023

FRAZIER, PAUL D
SCULPTOR
b Pickaway Co, Ohio, May 6, 22. Study: Ohio State Univ, BFA; Cranbrook Acad Art, MFA; Skowhegan Sch Painting & Sculpture, with Jose de Creeft; Acad Grande Chaumiere, with Ossip Zadkine. Work: Cranbrook Mus; Skowhegan Sch Painting & Sculpture Collection; Munson-Williams-Proctor Inst; Rochester Mus Arts & Sci. Exhib: Primary Structures, Solomon R Guggenheim Mus, New York, 67; plus many other group & one-man shows. Teaching: Instr sculpture, ceramics & design, Univ Minn, 50-53; instr sculpture, Munson-Williams-Proctor Inst, 53-58; assoc prof 3-D area & drawing, Queens Col, 64- Awards: Gov Award, State of Ohio, 47; Cranbrook Found Medal for Sculpture, 49; First Prize for Sculpture, Cooperstown Mus, 57. Bibliog: Americans with a future, Art in Am, winter 54; Robert Coates (auth), Young & old, New Yorker, 3/9/57; Ralph Pomeroy (auth), Confirmed out-of-towner, Art Int, 10/28/68. Style & Technique: Geometric figuration. Media: Plaster. Mailing Add: Box 33 Washington Depot CT 06794

FREDERICKS, MARSHALL MAYNARD
SCULPTOR
b Rock Island, Ill, Jan 31, 08. Study: John Huntington Polytech Inst, Cleveland, Ohio; Cleveland Sch Art, grad, 30; Heimann Schule, Munich, Ger; Schwegerie Schule, Munich; Acad Scandinav, Paris, France; pvt studies in Copenhagen, Rome & London; Carl Milles Studio; Cranbrook Acad Art; Gund fel; Matzen Traveling fel & Cranbrook fel. Work: Detroit Inst Arts, Mich; Cranbrook Mus Art, Bloomfield Hills, Mich; Milwaukee Pub Mus, Wis; City of New York; US Govt. Comn: Spirit of Detroit, City of Detroit, 59; Christ on the Cross, Cath Church, Indian River, Mich, 59; Cleveland War Mem Fountain, City of Cleveland, 64; State Dept Fountain, Washington, DC, 64; Freedom of the Human Spirit, Flushing Meadow, NY, 64. Exhib: Carnegie Inst Nat, Pittsburgh, Pa; Philadelphia Int; Art Inst Chicago Nat; Detroit Art Inst; Whitney Mus Am Art Nat. Teaching: Instr sculpture, Cranbrook Sch, 32-38; instr sculpture, Kingswood Sch, 32-42; instr sculpture, Cranbrook Acad Art, 32-42. Pos: Trustee, Am-Scand Found; bd trustees, People-to-People Prog, Inc; vpres, Rebild Nat Park Soc; trustee, Brookgreen Gardens. Awards: Fine Arts Gold Medal, Am Inst Architects, 52; Gold Medal of Hon, Mich Acad Sci, Arts & Lett, 53; Gold Medal of Hon, Archit League New York, 56. Mem: Academician Nat Acad Design; fel Nat Sculpture Soc; hon mem Mich Soc Architects; fel Royal Soc Arts; fel Int Inst Arts & Lett. Mailing Add: 440 Lake Park Dr Birmingham MI 48009

FREDERICKSEN, BURTON BAUM
CURATOR, ART HISTORIAN
b Mitchell, SDak, Aug 6, 34. Study: Univ Calif, Los Angeles, BA & MA. Exhib: One-man show, CeeJe Gallery, Los Angeles, 64; two-man show, Long Beach Munic Art Gallery, 65; two-man show, Orange Coast Col, Costa Mesa, Calif, 69. Collections Arranged: Catalog of the Pre-Nineteenth-Century Paintings in the Los Angeles Co Mus. Pos: Cur, J Paul Getty Mus, 65-72, chief cur, 72-73 & cur of paintings, 73-; adj cur Renaissance & Baroque art, Los Angeles Co Mus Art, 69-73. Style & Technique: Figurative. Media: Oil. Res: Authorship and provenance of pre-nineteenth century Western European paintings. Publ: Auth, Census of Pre-Nineteenth Century Italian Paintings in North America, 72; auth, Giovanni de Francesco and the Master of Pratovecchio, 74. Mailing Add: 17985 Pac Coast Hwy Malibu CA 90265

FREDMAN, FAIYA R
SCULPTOR, PAINTER
b Columbus, Ohio, Sept 8, 25. Study: Calif State Univ, San Diego; Univ Calif, Los Angeles. Work: Boehm Gallery Collection, Palomar Col, San Marcos, Calif; Univ Calif, San Diego; Ariz State Univ; La Jolla Mus Contemp Art, Calif. Exhib: Invisible-Visible, Long Beach Mus, Calif, 72; Six San Diegans, La Jolla Mus, Calif, 72; Small Images, Calif State Univ, Los Angeles, 72; one-man shows, Skin '68, La Jolla Mus Contemp Art, 68 & 74, Ariz State Univ, 71, Orlando Gallery, Encino, Calif, 75, Galeria Chapultepec, Mexico City, 76, Palomar Col, 76 & Casat Gallery, La Jolla, Calif, 77; Floating Wall Gallery, Santa Ana, Calif, 76. Teaching: Instr, Exten, Univ Calif, San Diego, 77- Awards: US Dept Housing & Urban Develop Nat Community Art Competition Award, 73. Bibliog: Lucy Lippard (auth), Body, Nature & Ritual in Women's Art, Chrysalis Mag, 77; Jean Luc Bordeaux (auth), Unstretched surfaces Southern Calif, Los Angeles Inst of Contemp Art J, 11/77. Style & Technique: Sand covered canvas draped shown in conjunction with fleece, twine and beach objects. Media: Pencil. Mailing Add: 121 27th St Del Mar CA 92014

FREDRICK, EUGENE WALLACE
PRINTMAKER, EDUCATOR
b Washington, DC, Oct 29, 27. Study: Art Students League, New York; Corcoran Sch of Art & Howard Univ, Washington, DC. Work: Norfolk Mus Arts & Sci, Va. Exhib: Soc of Washington Artists, Smithsonian Inst, Washington, DC, 58; Ann Area Show, Corcoran Gallery of Art, Washington, DC, 59 & 75; 156th & 158th Ann Exhib, Pa Acad of Fine Arts,

Philadelphia, 61 & 63; Va Printmakers, Univ Va, Charlottesville, 73; Va Artists, Va Mus, Richmond, 63 & 65; Am Drawing Biennial, Mus of Arts & Sci, Norfolk, 71; Invitational Exhib, Tatum Arts Ctr, Hood Col, Fredrick, Md, 74; Smithsonian Inst, traveling exhib ser, 75; US Info Agency, Mid East traveling exhib, 77; one-man show, Va Mus, Richmond, 66. Teaching: Instr drawing, Montgomery Jr Col, Tacoma Park, Md, 70-74; asst prof printmaking, Corcoran Sch Art, Washington, DC, 65- Awards: Watercolor Prize, Ann Area Show, Corcoran Gallery of Art, 59; Awards of Distinction, Va Artists, Va Mus, Richmond, 65; Purchase Prize, Am Drawing Biennial, Norfolk Mus Arts & Sci, 71. Bibliog: Gil Golden (auth), Poor Mans America, Jerusalem Post, Israel, 75; Jack Perlmutter (auth), Eugene Fredrick, Washington, DC, Art Voices South, 78. Style & Technique: Human figure rendered in graphic techniques. Media: Etching, Engraving and Relief Methods. Mailing Add: 6137 Leesburg Pike Falls Church VA 22041

FREE, JOHN D
PAINTER, SCULPTOR
b Pawhuska, Okla, Apr 7, 29. Study: ECent State Col; Southeastern State Col; Okla State Col; also with Thomas L Lewis. Work: Gilcrease Mus, Tulsa, Okla; Nat Cowboy Hall Fame, Oklahoma City, Okla; Diamond M Foundation, Snyder, Tex; Osage Indian Mus, Pawhuska, Okla. Exhib: One-man show, Nat Cowboy Hall Fame, 71 & Nat Acad Western Art, 73; O S Ranch Art Exhib, Post, Tex, 72; A Salute to the Old West, Grand Cent Galleries, New York, 73; Cowboy Artists Am Exhib, Phoenix, 73. Awards: Second Award Sculpture & Honorable Mention, Philbrook Art Ctr, 66. Bibliog: Ed Ainsworth (auth), The Cowboy in Art, World, 68; Dean Krakel (auth), Western art of John Free, Okla Today, 68; Rich Muno (auth), Cowboys by John D Free, Nat Cowboy Hall Fame, 71. Mem: Nat Acad Western Art; Cowboy Artists Am. Style & Technique: Western naturalist; western bronzes, pastels, watercolors and oils of animals and men in a traditional manner. Media: Bronze, Pastel. Publ: Contribr, Bronzes of the American West, 75. Mailing Add: Red Eagle Rte Box 78A Pawhuska OK 74056

FREED, DAVID
PRINTMAKER, PAINTER
b Toledo, Ohio, May 23, 36. Study: Miami Univ; Univ Iowa; Royal Col Art, London. Work: Art Inst Chicago, Ill; Nat Collection Fine Arts, Washington, DC; Va Mus Fine Arts, Richmond; Mus Boymans van Beuningen, Rotterdam, Holland; Mus Mod Art, New York. Exhib: Photography in Printmaking, AAA Gallery, New York, 68-70; one-man shows, Franz Bader Gallery, Washington, DC, 68, 70, 73 & 76 & Va Mus Fine Arts, Richmond; Albright-Knox Art Gallery, Buffalo, NY; Biennial Graphic Art, Moderna Galerija, Ljubljana, Yugoslavia; among others. Teaching: Assoc prof printmaking, Va Commonwealth Univ, 66-; guest lectr etching, Cent Sch Art, London, 69. Awards: Fulbright grant, 63-64; Spec Eds Award, World Print Competition, San Francisco Mus of Arts, 77. Mailing Add: 1825 W Grace Richmond VA 23220

FREED, HERMINE
VIDEO ARTISTS, WRITER
b New York, NY, May 29, 40. Study: Cornell Univ, BA, 61; NY Univ, with Irving Sandler & Lawrence Alloway, MA, 67. Work: Univ NC, Gainsborough; Smith Col, Northampton, Mass; Sch of Chicago Art Inst; Donnell Libr, NY; Univ Ga; and numerous others. Comn: Videotape, Guild Hall, East Hampton, NY, 73; video portrait of pres Jill Ker Conway, Smith Col, Northampton, Mass. Exhib: Circuit: a Video Invitational, Everson Mus, Syracuse, NY, Cranbrook Mus, Bloomfield Hills, Mich, Henri Gallery, Univ of Wash, Los Angeles Co Mus, Boston Mus of Fine Arts & Kuntshalle, Cologne, WGer, 72-73; US-Art Now, Kennedy Ctr, Washington, DC, 74; Collector's Choice, Los Angeles Co Mus Art, 74; Experimental 5 Festival, Knokke-Heist, Belg, 74-75; Video Art 1975, Corcoran Gallery, Washington, DC, 75; Projections, Whitney Mus Am Art, 75; Biennale de Paris, Mus Mod Art, Paris, 75; Video as an Art Form II, Smith Col, 76; Galerie Magers, Bonn, WGer, 76; Changing Channels, Boston Mus of Fine Arts, 76; Open to New Ideas—A Collection for Jimmy Carter, Univ Ga Traveling Exhib, 77; Int Film Expos, LA Filmex, 77; Documenta, Kassel, WGer, 77; one-woman exhibs, De Saisset Art Mus, Univ Santa Clara, Calif, 75, Herbert Johnson Mus of Art, Cornell Univ, Ithaca, NY, 75 & Everson Mus, Syracuse, NY, 78. Teaching: Ideas in contemp art, NY Univ, 68-72; video art workshop, Sch Visual Arts, New York, 74-75. Pos: Art rental cur, Inst Contemp Art, Boston, 63-65; asst cur, NY Univ Art Collection, 65-67. Awards: Nat Endowment on the Arts Grant, 74; Grant, NYS Coun Arts for WNET-TV Lab Proj, 74 & Creative Artists Pub Serv Grant, NYS Coun Arts, 78. Bibliog: Grace Glueck (auth), Video is replacing canvas, New York Times, 75; Margot Jefferson (auth), Veni, vedi, video, Newsweek Mag, 75. Style & Technique: Use of videotape to make works of art, as the pieces exist in time, the time element is as important as spatial considerations. Media: Videotape, Photography. Publ: Auth, Video and abstract expressionism, 12/74 & auth, In time-of time, 6/75, Arts Mag; auth, Where Did We Come From, Where Are We, Where Are We Going?, Harcourt, Brace, Jovanovich, 76; auth, Collecting video, Print Collector's Newsletter, 77. Mailing Add: c/o Leo Castelli Gallery 420 W Broadway New York NY 10013

FREED, WILLIAM
PAINTER
b Poland, July 28, 02; US citizen. Study: Art Students League, with Homer Boas & Richard Lahey; Hans Hofmann Sch Fine Arts. Work: Whitney Mus; Chrysler Mus, Norfolk, Va; Jewish Mus, New York; NY Univ; Univ Tex, Dallas. Exhib: One-man shows, James Gallery, New York, 52-62; Corcoran Art Gallery, Washington, DC, 60; traveling show, Hans Hofmann and His Students, Mus Mod Art, 62-65; 1st Major New Eng Show of the Seventies, Provincetown & Boston, 70; Free Abstract Form of the Fifties, Whitney Mus, 72; Provincetown, a Painter's Place, Everson Mus, Syracuse, NY & Provincetown Mus & Art Asn, Mass, 77. Teaching: Instr painting & drawing, Bronx House, 24-25; instr art, Works Prog Admin, 37-41; lending libr, Mus Mod Art, 59-62. Pos: Assisted Hans Hofmann in mural, 60- Awards: First Prize, Cape Cod Art Asn, Hyannis, Mass, 59; Longview Found Award, 60; Chapelbrook Found Grant, 61-62; Best in Show, Goddard Col, Vt, 76. Bibliog: Dorothy Sedclev (interviewer), taped interview, 76. Mem: Artist Equity Asn New York. Media: Oil, Gouache. Mailing Add: 530 W 113th St New York NY 10025

FREEDBERG, SYDNEY JOSEPH
ART HISTORIAN, EDUCATOR
b Boston, Mass, Nov 11, 14. Study: Harvard Col, AB(summa cum laude), 36, Sachs res fel fine arts, 36-37; Harvard Univ, AM, 39, PhD, 40. Teaching: Asst & tutor fine arts, Harvard Univ, 38-40; asst prof art, Wellesley Col, 46-49, assoc prof art, 50-54; vis lectr fine arts, Inst Mod Art, Boston, 47; assoc prof fine arts, Harvard Univ, 54-60, prof, 60-, chmn dept, 59-63. Pos: Bd dirs, Col Art Asn Am, 62-66; nat vchmn, Comt to Rescue Italian Art, 66-71; dir, Save Venice, Inc, 71-; chmn, Univ Mus Coun, 77- Awards: Hon Mem, Order of the Brit Empire; Grand Officer, Order of Solidarity, Ital Repub. Mem: Fel Am Acad of Arts & Sci. Publ: Auth, Parmigianino: His Works in Painting, 50, auth, Painting of the High Renaissance in Rome & Florence, Vols I & II, 61, auth, Andrea del Sarto, Vols I & II, 63, Harvard Univ; auth, Painting in Italy, 1500-1600, Penguin Bks, London & Baltimore, 71. Mailing Add: Fogg Art Mus Harvard Univ Cambridge MA 02138

FREEDMAN, DORIS C
ART ADMINISTRATOR
b New York, NY, Apr 25, 28. Study: Albright Col, BS; Columbia Univ Sch Social Work, MSW. Pos: Dir, New York City Dept Cult Affairs, 67-70; producer-moderator weekly radio show, Artists in the City, WNYC-FM, 69-; chmn, Pub Arts Coun of the Munic Art Soc, New York, 71-; chmn, Citizens for Artists Housing, 70-; pres, City Walls, Inc, 70-; spec consult, Whitney Mus Am Art, NY State Coun on Arts, NJ Councils on Arts & Nat Endowment for Arts; trustee, Pratt Inst & Albright Col; mem bd overseers, Parsons Sch Design; mem dean's adv coun, Columbia Sch of Social Work; mem bd dirs, Eliot Feld Ballett Co, Fine Arts Fedn, Munic Art Soc, Parks Coun & Community Planning Bd No 7; pres, Pub Art Fund, Inc, 77- Awards: Jean Dale Katz Award, Queens Coun on Arts, 69; Louise Waterman Wise Laureate Award, Women's Div Am Jewish Cong, 72; Arts Mgt Award, 76. Mem: Metrop Mus Art (vis comt community rels, 71-); Parks Coun New York City (pub art chmn, 72); Munic Arts Soc (bd dirs, 71-, dir pub arts coun, currently). Publ: Auth, Can government get with it in the arts?, A Further Mag of Arts, 68; auth, City Walls, New York, 75; auth, Public Art New York, 76; auth, Mark DiSuvero, 76; auth, Walking Tour Guide to Public Art in Lower Manhattan, 77. Mailing Add: Pub Arts Coun Apt 25-R 25 Central Park W New York NY 10023

FREEDMAN, MAURICE
PAINTER
b Boston, Mass, Nov 14, 04. Study: Boston Mus Fine Arts, scholarship class, 19-21; Mass Normal Art Sch, with Andrew, Sharman & Porter, 21-25; Boston Mus Sch, 30; Acad Lhote, Paris, France, 30. Work: Nat Collection Fine Arts, Smithsonian Inst, Washington, DC; Carnegie Inst, Pittsburgh, Pa; City Art Mus, St Louis, Mo; Brooklyn Mus, NY; Los Angeles Co Mus, Calif. Exhib: Carnegie Int, 50; American Painting Today & American Watercolors, Metrop Mus Art, New York, 50-52; Am Acad Arts & Lett, New York, 70; Maurice Freedman Retrospective, Washington Univ Gallery Art, St Louis, 72; Contemp Am Oil Painting 23rd Biennial, Corcoran Gallery Art, Washington, DC. Awards: Jane Peterson Medal, Audubon Artists, 72. Bibliog: Sheldon Cheney (auth), A primer of modern art, 45; A O Gruskin (auth), Painting in USA, 46. Media: Oil, Gouache. Dealer: Midtown Galleries 11 E 57th St New York NY 11203. Mailing Add: 121 Edgars Lane Hastings-on-Hudson NY 10706

FREELAND, WILLIAM LEE
PAINTER, SCULPTOR
b Pittsburgh, Pa, June 16, 29. Study: Philadelphia Mus Sch Art; Hans Hofmann Sch, Provincetown, Mass. Work: Wilmington Mus & Soc Fine Arts, Del; Univ Del, Newark; Chester Co Fed Savings & Loan, West Chester, Pa. Exhib: One-man shows, Philadelphia Art Alliance, 56 & Touchstone Gallery, New York, NY, 78; 25th Corcoran Biennial Exhib, Washington, DC, 57; Color Show, Birmingham Mus, Ala, 63; Artists Tribute to J F K, Swarthmore Col, 64; Nat Watercolor Show, Pa Acad Fine Arts, Philadelphia, 69; Ark Art Ctr, McArthur Park, Ark, 76; Drawing Show, Montclair Mus, Montclair, NJ, 78. Teaching: Assoc prof fine arts, Moore Col Art, 69- Awards: Copeland Purchase Award, Wilmington Mus; Purchase Award, Univ Del, 71. Media: Gouache, Oil Wood, Canvas. Mailing Add: Moore Col Art 20th & Race Sts Philadelphia PA 19103

FREEMAN, DAVID L
PAINTER, EDUCATOR
b Columbia, Mo, Nov 10, 37. Study: Univ Mo, BA & MA; State Univ Iowa, MFA; Penland Sch Crafts & Penland Weavers. Work: Mint Mus Art, Charlotte, NC; Minn Mus Art, St Paul; SC Nat Bank, Columbia; SC State Art Collection; NCNB Corp, Charlotte, NC. Exhib: One-man shows, Columbia Mus Art, SC, 71, 501 Gallery, Mint Mus Art, 72 & Francis Marion Col, Florence, SC, 76; four-man show, Gallery Contemp Art, Winston-Salem, 71; 11th Piedmont Painting & Sculpture Show, Mint Mus Art, 71; 18th Drawing & Small Sculpture Show, Ball State Univ, 72; three-man show, Mint Mus of Art, Charlotte, NC, 78. Teaching: Asst prof studio art, Univ Wis, Madison, 63-70; assoc prof studio art, Winthrop Col, 70- Awards: Purchase Awards, Drawings USA, Minn Mus Art, St Paul & 8th Ann Piedmont Graphics Exhib, Mint Mus Art, 71; Spring Mills Exhib & Traveling Show, New York, 78. Mem: Nat Col Art Asn. Media: Acrylic. Dealer: Southeastern Ctr for Contemp Art, Winston-Salem NC 27102. Mailing Add: 630 University Dr Rock Hill SC 29730

FREEMAN, GERTRUDE
CONSULTANT, COLLECTOR
b Newark, NJ. Study: Newark Sch of Fine & Indust Arts, NJ; Univ Miami, Fla, BA(art hist). Pos: Artist representative for sculptor Enzo Gallo & multi-media artist Leon Gordon Miller; investment arts consult for corps & individuals; collector of contemp int art. Mailing Add: 6959 Sunrise Dr Coral Gables FL 33133

FREEMAN, MARGARET B
MUSEUM CURATOR, WRITER
b West Orange, NJ. Study: Wellesley Col, BA; Columbia Univ, MA; Sorbonne, Summer Sch. Teaching: Instr, Dana Hall Sch, 25-27; instr, Metrop Mus Art, New York. Pos: Res asst, Newark Mus, 24-25; secy, Art Mus, Wellesley Col, 27-28; asst cur, Metrop Mus Art, 40-43, assoc cur, 43-55, cur Cloisters, 55-77. Awards: Phi Beta Kappa Award. Mem: Medieval Acad Am; Am Asn Mus; Medieval Club, New York; Mus Coun New York; Int Ctr Romanesque Art. Publ: Auth, Herbs for the Medieval Household & The Story of the Three Kings; co-auth, The Belles Heures of Jean, Duke of Berry; contribr articles in Bull Metrop Mus Art. Mailing Add: 16 E 84th St New York NY 10028

FREEMAN, MARK
PAINTER, PRINTMAKER
b Austria, Sept 27, 09. Study: Columbia Col, BA; Columbia Univ, MArch; Int Inst Educ fel, Sorbonne, Paris, France, 30. Work: Libr Cong, Washington, DC; Philadelphia Mus Art, Pa; Norfolk Art Mus, Va; Hengelose Kunstzaal, Holland; Butler Art Inst, Ohio. Exhib: Int Biennial Color Lithography, Cincinnati Mus, 52-53; 80 Prints USA, State Dept Traveling Exhib, Europe & Africa, 54; Artists of the Region, Easthampton Guild Hall Mus, 56 & 66; Major Am Artists, Southampton Col, 68; Nat Inst Arts & Sci, 68 & 69. Pos: Ed-in-chief newsletter, Artist's Equity. Awards: Gold Medal, Nat Soc Artists in Casein, 64; Medal, Audubon Artists, 69; Today's Art Medal, 73. Mem: Audubon Artists (exhib chmn, 72, sr vpres, pres, 77-); Nat Soc Artists in Casein & Acrylic (pres, 74-); League Present Day Artists (pres, 75); Am Soc Contemp Artists (exhib comt, 72, pres, 75-77); Artists Equity (bd dir, vpres, 76-). Media: Oil, Acrylic. Mailing Add: 307 E 37th St New York NY 10016

FREEMAN, PHYLLIS (THERESE)
MIXED MEDIA, LECTURER
b Hammond, Ind, Dec 14, 28. Study: Monticello Col, 46-47; St Joseph's Col, 52-72; Oxbow Summer Sch Painting, 60-67; Penland Sch Arts & Crafts, 69; Haystack Mountain Sch Arts & Crafts, 72-73; Immaculate Heart Col, Hollywood, Calif, 74-75; Calumet Col, Hammond, Ind, BA(fine arts), 75. Exhib: One-person shows, Riverview Is, Ill Inst Technol, Chicago, 71 & Harbor Col, Willminton, Calif, 74; Women 71, Northern Ill Univ, DeKalb, Ill, 71; Small Environments, Southern Ill Univ, Carbondale, 72; In a Bottle, Calif State Univ, Fullerton, 73; three-person show, Palos Verdes Mus, Calif, 74; Mus Contemp Art, Chicago, Ill, 75; Los Angeles Inst Contemp Art, Calif, 76-78. Teaching: Artist-in-residence banners, Haystack Mountain Sch Arts & Crafts, Deer Isle, Maine, 74. Awards: First Prize Banners, Mid-West Banner Show, Christian Art Asn, 66; First Prize Mixed Media, Ind Art Mus, Hammon, 66, 70, 71 & 73. Bibliog: Mark Freeman (auth), View Riverview (film), 71; Claudia Chapline (auth), Fairy Tales and Other Side Shows, Art News, 77. Mem: Woman's Caucus for the Arts, Los Angeles, Calif; Los Angeles Inst Contemp Art. Style & Technique: Mixed media; box construction, assemblage, collage, found objects and paint. Media: Mixed media. Publ: Contribr, Banners, Banners, Etc, 67; contribr, Collage and Assemblage, 73, Box Art, 75 & Thelma Newmann (auth), The Mirror Book, 78, Crown. Dealer: Orlando Gallery 17037 Ventura Blvd Encino CA 91316. Mailing Add: 121 Downey San Francisco CA 94117

FREEMAN, RICHARD BORDEN
ART HISTORIAN, EDUCATOR
b Philadelphia, Pa, Oct 7, 08. Study: Yale Univ, AB, 32; Harvard Univ, AM, 34; Univ Paris, summer 35. Collections Arranged: Picasso-Gris-Miro, San Francisco Mus Art, Calif, 48; Graphics Ann, 58-75, Lithographs Ralston Crawford, 61, Niles Spencer (retrospective), 65, Lithographs by William Walmsley, 71, Univ Ky, Ralston Crawford Drawings & Watercolors, 73, Spain, 74 & Watergate (ed cartoons), 75. Teaching: Prof art & head dept, Univ Ala, Tuscaloosa, 50-56; vis prof art, Hamilton Col, 57; prof art, Univ Ky, 58-74, head dept, 58-66; retired. Pos: Asst, Nelson Gallery, Kansas City, Mo, 34-36; registrar, Fogg Mus Art, Cambridge, Mass, 36-38; asst cur, Cincinnati Art Mus, 38-41; dir, Flint Inst Art, Mich, 41-47; dir-in-charge, San Francisco Mus Art, 47-50; dir, Hartford Art Sch, 56-57. Mem: Southeastern Col Art Conf (vpres, 51-52, pres, 52-53); Mid Western Col Art Conf (vpres, 65-66, pres, 66-67); Col Art Asn Am. Res: Work of Ralston Crawford and the paintings of Niles Spencer. Publ: Auth, Ralston Crawford, Univ Ala Press, 52; auth, Lithographs of Ralston Crawford, Univ Ky, 63; auth, Niles Spencer (monogr), 65; plus many articles in Am J Archaeol, Col Art J & Art J. Mailing Add: Dept of Art Univ of Ky Lexington KY 40506

FREEMAN, ROBERT LEE
PAINTER, SCULPTOR
b Rincon Indian Reservation, Calif, Jan 14, 39. Work: Sioux Mus, Rapid City, SDak; Gonzaga Univ, Spokane, Wash; Valley Nat Bank, Phoenix, Ariz; US Dept Interior, Washington, DC; Heard Mus, Phoenix, Ariz; Palomar Col, San Marcos, Calif; William Walton Collection & numerous other pvt collections. Exhib: Nat Indian Art Exhib, Scottsdale, Ariz, 63-75; US Dept Interior Nat, 63; Heard Mus Ann Indian Art Exhib, 68-74; All-Am Indian Art Nat Exhib, Sheridan, Wyo; Red Cloud Indian Art Nat Show, Pine Ridge, SDak; one-man shows, Schiver Gallery, Kansas City, Mo, Vagabond House, Sedona, Ariz, Fifth Ave Gallery, San Diego, Calif, Sioux Mus, Rapid City, SDak, Turtle Mountain Gallery, Philadelphia, Pa, Gallery Am Indian, Sedona, Ariz & Gallery Wall, Phoenix, Ariz. Awards: Over 37 awards, incl First Watercolor & First Graphics, Red Cloud Indian Art Nat, 74; First Graphics, Heard Mus, 74; Spec Award Misc, First Graphics & Second Prints, Nat Indian Exhib, Scottsdale, 75; plus others. Bibliog: Contemporary Sioux Painting, article by US Dept Interior. Media: Pen & Ink; Oil. Publ: Illusr, The Layman's Typology Handbook; illusr, The Luiseno People; auth, For Indians Only; auth, War Whoops and All That Jazz. Mailing Add: 1697 Curry Comb Dr San Marcos CA 92069

FREIFELD, ERIC
PAINTER, EDUCATOR
b Saratov, Russia, Mar 13, 19; Can citizen. Study: St Martin's Sch Art, London, Eng; Art Students League. Work: Montreal Mus Art, Can; Vancouver Gallery Art; Univ Alta, Edmonton; St Michaels Col & Hart House, Univ Toronto; Art Gallery Ont. Exhib: Can Soc Painters in Watercolor, 48-62; Royal Can Acad Exhibs, 51-71; Can Soc Graphic Art, 55-62; Brooklyn Mus Int Biennial, 59; Allied Artists Am, 60; plus many one-man, group & nat shows in Can, Eng & USA. Teaching: Prof watercolor painting, figure drawing & artistic anat, Ont Col Art, 46- Pos: Chmn welfare comt, Ont Col Art Faculty Asn, 65-70, mem exec comt, 65-70, mem governing coun, Ont Col Art, 72-, chmn dept fine art, 75- Awards: Carnegie Trust Fund scholar, 37; C W Jeffries Award, 57; Can Coun Sr Arts Fel, 61 & 71; plus many others. Bibliog: Essay on Eric Freifeld, Arts Can Mag, 69; Nancy Beckett (auth), articles in, Can Press, Nat Release & Can Newspapers, 70; Paul Duval (auth), High Realism in Canada, 74 & Eric Freifeld, Yaneff Gallery, 77; articles on Eric Freifeld in Toronto Star, 77, Globe & Mail, 78, Art Mag, 78 & Can Forum, 78. Mem: Can Soc Graphic Art (past pres); Can Soc Painters in Watercolour; Royal Can Acad Arts (assoc rep on coun, 68-69). Style & Technique: Human, urban and rural subjects painted in two technical approaches of broad watercolor and sustained, highly detailed watercolor over complex carbon drawing. Dealer: Jerrold Morris Gallery Prince Arthur St Toronto ON Can. Mailing Add: 48 Eccleston Dr Toronto ON Can

FREILICH, ANN
PAINTER
b Czestochowa, Poland; US citizen. Study: Educ Alliance Art Sch. Work: Brooklyn Mus, New York; Peabody Mus, Nashville, Tenn; Univ of Wyo Art Mus, Laramie; Art Lending Collections, Philadelphia Mus Art & Mus Mod Art; Syracuse Univ. Exhib: Ten one-man shows, Roko Gallery, 54-78; Riverside Mus, 64; Bucknell Univ Drawing Exhib, 65; Gallery Mod Art, Huntington Hartford Mus, 67; Am Acad Arts & Lett, 70-72. Teaching: Santa Agata Art Workshop, Italy, 67; pvt art classes. Awards: Childe Hassam Purchase Award, Am Acad Arts & Lett, 72. Media: Oil, Watercolor. Publ: Contribr, Art from Found Objects, Lothorp, Lee & Shepard, Publ, 74. Dealer: Roko Gallery 90 E Tenth St New York NY 10003. Mailing Add: 250 W 94th St New York NY 10025

FREILICHER, JANE
PAINTER
b New York, NY, Nov 29, 24. Study: Brooklyn Col, AB; Columbia Univ, AM; Hans Hofmann Sch; art hist with Meyer Schapiro. Work: Brooklyn Mus, NY; Mus Mod Art, New York; Brandeis Art Mus, Mass; RI Mus Fine Arts; NY Univ. Exhib: Fourteen one-man shows, Tibor de Nagy Gallery, New York, 52- & one-man shows, John Bernard Myers Gallery, New York, 71 & Fischbach Gallery, New York, 75 & 77; Whitney Mus Am Art Ann, 55-; Figurative Painting, Vassar Col, 68; Painterly Realism, Am Fedn Arts, 70; 30 Yrs of Am Printmaking, Brooklyn Mus, 76; Am 1976, Dept of Interior Traveling Show, 76. Teaching: Vis critic & lectr, Univ Pa Grad Sch Fine Arts, Skowhegan Sch Art, Carnegie-Mellon Inst, Sch of Mus of Fine Arts, Boston & Col of Creative Studies, Univ of Calif, Santa Barbara. Awards: Hallmark Int Art Award, 60; award, Am Asn Univ Women, 74; grant, Nat Endowment for the Arts, 76. Bibliog: Fairfield Porter (auth), Jane Freilicher paints a picture, 9/55 & Peter Schjeldahl (auth), Urban pastorals, 2/71, Art News; James Schuyler (auth), The painting of Jane Freilicher, Art & Lit, autumn 66. Media: Oil. Publ: Illusr, Turandot & Other Poems, 53; illusr, Paris Review (portfolio of drawings), 65. Mailing Add: 51 Fifth Ave New York NY 10003

FREIMARK, ROBERT (MATTHEW)
PRINTMAKER, PAINTER
b Doster, Mich, Jan 27, 22. Study: Univ Toledo, BEd; Cranbrook Acad Art, MFA; independent study, Mex. Work: Nat Gallery, Prague, Czech; Libr Cong, Washington, DC; US Info Agency; Brit Mus; Smithsonian Inst, Washington, DC. Comn: Mem print, Des Moines Art Ctr, Iowa, 61; Brenton Banks, Des Moines, 74; Kundalini Found, New York, 74; Impressions Workshop, Boston, 74-75; Am Micro Systs, Inc, Santa Clara, Calif, 75. Exhib: Drawings of 12 Countries, Art Inst Chicago, 52; Pa Acad Fine Art Painting Ann, 52-53; Brooklyn Mus Biennial Watercolor Exhib, 64; one-man shows, Northamerica Cult Inst, Mexico City, 63 & Moravske Mus, Brno, Czech, 70; Official US Bicentennial Show, Amerika Haus, Munich, Ger, 76. Teaching: Instr drawing, Toledo Mus Art, 52-55; instr painting, Ohio Univ, 56-59; resident artist, Des Moines Art Ctr, 59-63; prof graphics, San Jose State Col, 64- Pos: Guest artist, Joslyn Mem Mus, Omaha, Nebr, 61; guest artist, Huntington Galleries, WVa, 63; guest artist & lectr, Columbia Univ, 63; guest artist, Riverside Art Ctr, Calif, 64; vis prof, Harvard Univ, 72-73. Awards: New Talent in USA Award, Art in Am, 57; Ford Found Grant, WVa, 65; Spec Creative Leave, Calif State Col Syst, 67. Bibliog: Eva Gatling (auth), Robert Freimark, Motive, 4/63; Yar Chomicky (auth), Watercolor Painting, Univ Pa, 68. Media: Tapestry, Lithography, Res: Mexican popular culture; rehabilitation through art; environmental planning for contemporary living. Interest: Graphics, film and environmental art. Mailing Add: Rte 2 Box 539A Morgan Hill CA 95037

FREITAG, WOLFGANG MARTIN
ART LIBRARIAN, ART HISTORIAN
b Berlin, Ger, Oct 27, 24; US citizen. Study: Univ Freiburg, Ger, PhD; Simmons Col, Boston, MS(libr sci). Teaching: Lectr bibliog & art historiography, Harvard Univ, 67-75, sr lectr bibliog & art historiography, 75- Pos: Chief librn, Fine Arts Libr, Harvard Col Libr, Fogg Art Mus, 64- Prof Travel Grant, 51 & Res Fel, 68; Coun Libr Resources Res Fel, 75. Mem: Col Art Asn (chmn art bibliog session, 75); charter mem Art Libr Soc NAm; Asn Col & Res Libr (chmn art libr subsection, 69-70; chmn subj specialists sect, 71-72). Publ: Auth, Art libraries and collections, Encycl Libr & Info Sci, 68; auth, Wanted: a new index to exhibition catalogs, Col & Res Libr, 69; auth, The proper study of librarians, Harvard Librn, 74; auth, Slides for individual use in the college library, 75 & ed, Music and art in the general library, 75, Libr Trends; auth, Tapping a serviceable reservoir: the selection of periodicals for art libraries, Art Libr J, 76. Mailing Add: Fogg Art Mus Cambridge MA 02138

FREL, JIRI
ART HISTORIAN, CURATOR
b Czech. Study: Charles Univ, Prague, PhD; École Normale Supérieure, Sorbonne. Teaching: Prof hist of Greek & Roman art, Charles Univ, Prague, 48-68 & Univ Southern Calif, 74- Pos: Assoc cur Greek & Roman art, Metrop Mus of Art, New York, 70-72; cur antiq, J Paul Getty Mus, 73- Mem: German Archaeol Inst. Res: Greek and Roman sculpture and art. Publ: Auth, Choix de Vases Attiques en Tchécoslovaquie, Nat Mus, Prague, 59; auth, Contributions à l'Iconographie Grecque, Acc Prague, 69; auth, Les Sculpteurs Attiques Anonymes, Univ Prague, 69; auth, Panathenaic Prize Amphoras, German Archael Inst, Athens, Greece, 73; ed, J Paul Getty Mus J, Vols 1, 2 & 4. Mailing Add: J Paul Getty Mus Malibu CA 90265

FRELINGHUYSEN, MR & MRS PETER H B, JR
COLLECTORS
Collection: Paintings. Mailing Add: Morristown NJ 07960

FRENCH, JARED
PAINTER, SCULPTOR
b Ossining, NY, Feb 4, 05. Study: Amherst Col, BA; Art Students League. Work: Whitney Mus Am Art, New York; Baltimore Mus Art, Md; Baseball Mus, Cooperstown, NY; Art Collection of Dartmouth Col. Comn: Cavalry Fording Stream (mural), Parcel Post Off, Richmond, Va; food murals, Coxsachie, New York; mural, Plymouth Post Off, Pa. Exhib: Carnegie Inst Int, Pittsburgh, Pa & Realism Show, Rochester Mus, NY, 64; one-man shows, Banfer Gallery, New York, 68-69; Magic Realism Show & 20th Century Portraits Show, Mus Mod Art, New York; Whitney Mus Am Art Ann, New York; Four Anonymous Collectors, New York Cult Ctr, 72. Awards: Nat Inst Arts & Lett Award, 67. Style & Technique: Precise and smooth. Media: Tempera, Cast Metals, Stone. Mailing Add: Piazza Cucchi 3 Rome Italy

FRENCH, RAY H
PRINTMAKER, SCULPTOR
b Terre Haute, Ind, May 16, 19. Study: John Herron Art Sch; Ind State Univ; Univ of Colo; Univ of Iowa, BFA & MFA; Accademia di Belle Arte, Florence, Italy; Hobart Sch of Welding Technol, Troy, Ohio; also study with Mauricio Lansansky & James Lechay. Work: Mus of Mod Art, New York; Pennell Collections, Libr of Cong, Washington, DC; Victoria & Albert Mus, London, Eng; Brooklyn Mus, NY; Bibliotique Nationale, Paris, France. Exhib: Libr of Cong; Brooklyn Mus; Chicago Art Inst; Seattle Art Mus; Boston Mus; Smithsonian Inst; San Francisco Mus; Baltimore Mus; Nat Gallery of Can; Soc of Am Graphic Artists Ann Exhib, Nat Acad, 47; A New Direction in Intaglio, the Work of Lasansky and His Students, Walker Art Ctr, Milwaukee, 49-53; Young Am Printmakers, Mus of Mod Art, New York, 53; Ray H French, 25 Yrs of Printmaking, Sheldon Swope Art Gallery, Terre Haute, Ind, 70; Forerunners of the Am Print Renaissance, Pratt Graphics Ctr, New York, 77. Teaching: Prof of printmaking, DePauw Univ, Greencastle, Ind, 48-, head dept art, 70- Pos: Pres, Ind Artists Club, Indianapolis, 62-63; pres, Ind Soc of Printmakers, 53-54. Awards: Art Asn First Prize, Indianapolis Mus Art, 56; Joseph Pennell Purchase Award for Etching, Philadelphia Free Libr, 60; Mus Purchase Award, Pasadena Mus, 70. Bibliog: Corbin Patrick (auth), Each Print A Work of Art, Indianapolis Star Mag, 59; Howard Wooden (auth), Graphic Constructions by Ray French, 67 & Ray French, Recent Sculptures, 70, Sheldon Swope Art Gallery; Karen F Beall (auth), American Prints in the Library of Congress, Johns Hopkins Press, 70. Mem: Soc of Am Graphic Artists; The Print & Drawing Soc, Indianapolis Mus of Art. Style & Technique: Engraver, etcher utilizing sculptural graphic techniques in a realistic mode; occasional abstract interpretations within a surrealistic concept. Media: Printmaking; Welded Sculpture. Dealer: Weintraub Gallery 992 Madison Ave New York NY 10021. Mailing Add: 106 E Seminary St Greencastle IN 46135

FRERICHS, RUTH COLCORD
PAINTER
b White Plains, NY. Study: Conn Col, BA(fine arts); Art Students League, lithography with Armin Landeck; watercolor with William B Schimmel & F Douglas Greenbowe. Work: Thunderbird Bank, Phoenix, Ariz; Valley Nat Bank, Ariz; First Nat Bank of Ariz; Empire

Machinery Co, Mesa, Ariz. Exhib: Southwest Watercolor Soc Regional Exhib, Dallas, Tex, 69; Wichita Nat Centennial Watercolor Exhib, Kans, 70; Am Watercolor Soc Ann, New York, 70; Watercolor USA, Springfield, Mo, 72; Watercolor West, Nat Exhib, Riverside, Calif, 72. Awards: Gold Medal, Low Ruins Nat Exhib, Tubac, 65; Award, Southwest Watercolor Soc Regional, 69; Ariz Dimensions '73 Exhib Spec Award. Mem: Ariz Artists Guild (pres, 69-71); Ariz Watercolor Asn (corresp secy, 68-69). Style & Technique: Transparent watercolor technique, generally bold brushstrokes and loosely painted; some use of mixed media for special effects. Dealer: Thompson Gallery 2020 N Central Ave Phoenix AZ 85004. Mailing Add: 321 E Pomona Rd Phoenix AZ 85020

FREUDENHEIM, TOM LIPPMANN
MUSEUM DIRECTOR
b Stuttgart, Ger, July 3, 37; US citizen. Study: Harvard Col, AB; NY Univ, MA. Collections Arranged: Pascin (with catalog), 66 & Arnaldo Pomodoro (with catalog), 70, Univ Art Mus, Berkeley, Calif. Pos: Cur, Jewish Mus, New York, 62-65; asst dir, Univ Art Mus, Berkeley, 66-71; dir, Baltimore Mus Art, 71- Mem: Col Art Asn Am; Asn Art Mus Dirs; Am Asn Mus; hon mem Artists Equity Asn; hon mem Am Inst Interior Designers. Publ: Auth, Myer Myers, American Silversmith, 65; auth, Illuminated Hebrew Manuscripts, 65; auth, Persian Faience Mosaic Wall, Kunst Orients, 68. Mailing Add: Baltimore Mus of Art Art Mus Dr Baltimore MD 21218

FREUND, HARRY LOUIS
PAINTER, ILLUSTRATOR
b Clinton, Mo, Sept 16, 05. Study: Univ Mo, 23-25; St Louis Sch Fine Arts, Washington Univ, 25-29; D H Wuerpel travel scholar, 29; Colarossi Acad, Paris, 29-30; Carnegie fel, 40; Princeton Univ, 40-41; Colorado Springs Fine Arts Ctr, 46-47; Carnegie-Stetson grant, Mex, 53; Stetson Univ grant, Cent Am, 59. Work: IBM Corp; Libr Cong, Washington, DC; Seattle Art Mus, Wash; St Louis Sch Fine Arts. Comn: Mural, Deland Mem Hosp, Fla; libr murals, Bishop Col & Shaw Univ; plus many others in pub & pvt collections. Exhib: Contemp Am Art Exhib, New York World's Fair; Nat Acad Design; Pa Acad Design; Carnegie Inst; Corcoran Gallery Art; plus many others in mus, schs & libraries in US & abroad. Teaching: Resident artist, Hendrix Col, 39-41, head dept art, 41-46; founder dept art, Little Rock Jr Col, 40; founder & dir, Art Sch Ozarks, 7 yrs; lectr & faculty artist vis, Asn Am Cols, 5 seasons; head dept art, Stetson Univ, 49-59, resident artist, 59-67. Pos: Free lance illusr, Crowell Publ & Ford Motor Co Publs; mural designer, State of Mo at Chicago World's Fair, 33; mural artist, sect fine arts, US Treas Dept, 34-40; visual aids dir, Eighth Serv Command, US Army, 45-46. Mem: Fla Artist Group (past pres); Nat Soc Mural Painters; Eureka Springs, Ark Guild of Artists & Craftspeople; Fla Craftsmen (past pres). Media: Oil, Acrylic. Mailing Add: 31 Steel St Eureka Springs AR 72632

FREUND, TIBOR
PAINTER, MURALIST
b Budapest, Hungary, Dec 29, 10; US citizen. Study: Fed Tech Univ, Zurich, dipl archit, 32; Vilmos Aba-Novak Art Sch, Budapest, 34; studies Oriental techniques of mosaics, Meshed, Iran, 40. Work: Mus Fine Arts, Budapest; James A Michener Collection, Univ Tex, Austin; Goucher Col, Md; Ravinia Art Festival Asn, Chicago, Ill; Ball State Univ, Muncie, Ind. Comn: First moving mural on ridged surface, Bd Educ, Pub Sch 111, New York, 63; first moving mural on flat surface, Bd Educ Sch 162, New York, 70. Exhib: Seven one-man shows, New York, 60-76; Am Fedn Arts Traveling Exhibs, 63-65, 66-67 & 71-72; Abstract Art, Riverside Mus, New York, 65; An American Report on the Sixties, Denver Art Mus, Colo, 69; Painting & Sculpture Today, Indianapolis Mus Art, Ind, 70. Awards: Silvermine Guild Award, First Prize at 19th Ann New Eng Exhib, 68. Bibliog: John Canaday (auth), Tibor Freund, New York Times, 10/4/69; Peter Schjeldahl (auth), Fourth show in New York, 69 & Phyllis Derfner (auth), Sixth show in New York, 74, Art Int; plus others. Mem: Fel Royal Soc Arts; Am Fedn Arts; Nat Soc Mural Painters. Style & Technique: Geometrical; space perspective. Media: Acrylic. Res: Developed motion painting from a crude 19th century invention called three-sided picture. Publ: Auth, Motion in painting—a new art form, Am Artist Mag, 11/64. Mailing Add: 34-57 82nd St Jackson Heights NY 11372

FREUND, WILL FREDERICK
PAINTER, EDUCATOR
b Madison, Wis, Jan 20, 16. Study: Univ Wis, BS, MS; Univ Mo; Tiffany Found fel, 49. Work: William Rockhill Nelson Gallery Art, Kansas City, Mo; Joslyn Mus Art, Omaha, Nebr; Okla Art Ctr, Oklahoma City; Mulvane Mus Art, Topeka, Kans; Univ Nebr Art Galleries, Lincoln; Evansville Mus Art & Sci, Ind. Exhib: Mo Pavilion, New York World's Fair, 64; New Talent USA, Art in Am Mag, 65; Watercolor USA, Springfield Art Mus, Mo, 70 & 72. Teaching: Instr art, Stephens Col, 46-64; prof fine art, Southern Ill Univ, Edwardsville, 64- Awards: First Award for Oil Painting, Wis Painters & Sculptors, 46; First Prize for Oil Painting, Mulvane Mus Art, 56; Ruth Renfro Award (First Prize for Watercolor), St Louis City Art Mus, 63. Bibliog: Prize winners, Life Mag, 9/12/55; A B Louchheim (auth), Prize $, Art News, 10/56; Will Freund, painter, potter, woodworker, boombass player, Wis Alumnus, 1/61. Mem: Ala Watercolor Soc. Style & Technique: Aesthetic potential of the equeous emulsion technique. Media: Oil, Watercolor. Mailing Add: 301 Prospect St Alton IL 62002

FREUNDLICH, AUGUST L
EDUCATOR
b Frankfurt, Ger, May 9, 24; US citizen. Study: Antioch Col, BA, Antioch Col & Teachers Col, Columbia Univ, MA; NY Univ, PhD. Exhib: Competitive exhibs in Ohio, Ark, Tenn, NC, Ga, Ky, NJ, Mich & NMex; also exhibs in com galleries. Teaching: Art educ spec, Antioch Lab Sch, 49-50; instr art educ, Univ Ark, 40-53; vis prof, State Univ NY Col New Paltz, 53-54; head art dept, Eastern Mich Univ, 54-58; chmn arts div, George Peabody Col, 58-64; chmn art dept & dir, Lowe Art Mus, Univ Miami, 64-70; dean sch art, Syracuse Univ, 70, dean col visual & performing arts, 71- Mem: Nat Art Educ Asn; Am Asn Mus; Int Coun Fine Arts Deans; Nat Coun Art Adminrs; NY Arts Deans. Res: Contemporary painting in East and West Germany. Publ: Auth, William Cropper, retrospective, 68; auth, Frank Kleinholz—the outsider, 69; Karl Schrag, Richard Florsheim; auth, numerous brochures, monogr & catalogs. Mailing Add: Col of Visual & Performing Arts Syracuse Univ Syracuse NY 13210

FREY, VIOLA
SCULPTOR, PAINTER
b Lodi, Calif, Aug 15, 37. Study: Delta Col, Stockton, Calif, AA; Calif Col Arts & Crafts, BFA; Tulane Univ, MFA. Work: Leslie Ceramic Collection, Berkeley, Calif; Oakland Mus, Calif. Exhib: One-man shows, Art Inst Chicago, 60's & Haggin Mus, Stockton, 71; Oakland Myths, Wenger Gallery, 73 & Seat of Civilization, 74; Sculpture Exhib, Hank Baum Gallery, San Francisco, 75. Teaching: Assoc prof ceramics, Calif Col Arts & Crafts, 65- Bibliog: Wenger (auth), Currant, Art Mag, 8/75. Style & Technique: Sculpture, color, drawing surfaces, large pieces, current subject and biographical. Mailing Add: c/o Hank Baum Gallery One Embarcadero Ctr San Francisco CA 94111

FRIBERG, ARNOLD
ILLUSTRATOR, PAINTER
b Winnetka, Ill, Dec 21, 13. Study: Art Instr Schs; Chicago Acad Fine Arts; Am Acad Art, Chicago. Work: Work in pvt collections. Comn: The Ten Commandments (series 15 monumental paintings), Cecil B De Mille, 56; The Book of Mormon (series 12 paintings), Church of Jesus Christ of Latter-Day Saints, 60; 100 Years of Football (series of paintings), Chevrolet Sports Asn Collection, 68; The Northwest Mounted Police (series over 100 paintings), Northwest Paper Co, 69; American West (series hist paintings), Sharp Rifle Co, 69. Exhib: Ten Commandments Series, toured every continent, 57-58; Motion Picture Indust Exhib, New York World's Fair, 64-65. Teaching: Lectr vitality in relig painting, art as serv & Russell & Remington. Pos: Chief artist-designer, Cecil B De Mille, 54-57. Mem: Life mem Royal Soc Arts, London; Art Instr Schs, Minneapolis (mem nat adv bd). Publ: Auth & illusr, The Ten Commandments, 57 & Arnold Friberg's Little Christmas Books, 58. Mailing Add: 5867 Tolcate Lane Salt Lake City UT 84121

FRICANO, TOM S
PAINTER, PRINTMAKER
b Chicago, Ill, Oct 28, 30. Study: Bradley Univ, BFA, 53; Univ Ill, Urbana, MFA, 56; Fulbright grant, Florence, Italy, 60-61; Louis Comfort Tiffany res grant, 65. Work: Libr Cong, Washington, DC; Philadelphia Mus; Art Inst Chicago; Los Angeles Co Mus Art; Detroit Inst Arts. Exhib: Art Inst Chicago, 67; Dong-A-Ilbo Int Print Show, Seoul, Korea, 70; Utah Mus Fine Art, Salt Lake City, 71; 3rd Brit Int Print Biennial, Bradford, Eng, 72; Am Colorprint Soc, Philadelphia, 74-76. Teaching: Instr painting & printmaking, Bradley Univ, Peoria, Ill, 58-63; prof painting & printmaking, Calif State Univ, Northridge, 63-; vis artist, Ohio State Univ, Columbus, 69, Univ Utah, 71, Univ Mont, Bozeman, 72 & Art Inst Chicago, 75. Awards: Calif State Univ Found Res Grant, 66, 68, 69 & 74; John Simon Guggenheim Found Mem Fel, 69 & 70; plus many prizes and awards in shows. Bibliog: Leonard Edmondson (auth), Etching, Van Nostrand Reinhold, 73. Mem: Hon mem Los Angeles Printmaking Soc (vpres, 64-65). Style & Technique: Non-objective; acrylic painting and collages; experimental intaglio prints (invented assemble graphic print process). Mailing Add: 9820 Aldea Ave Northridge CA 91324

FRICK, HELEN CLAY
ART LIBRARY DIRECTOR
Pos: Dir, Frick Art Ref Libr. Mailing Add: 10 E 71st St New York NY 10021

FRICK, ROBERT OLIVER
PAINTER, INSTRUCTOR
b Philadelphia, Pa, Feb 19, 20. Study: Pa Acad Fine Arts; also with Frank Benton Ashley Linton, Philadelphia; Daniel Garber, New Hope, Pa; Stanley Woodward, Rockport, Mass. Exhib: One-man shows, Chaffe Art Gallery, Chester Art Guild, Blue Hill Art Guild & Southern Vt Art Asn, 77; Salmagundi Club, 72-74; Acad Artists Am, Springfield, Mass, 72-74; Concord Art Asn, Mass, 73-74. Teaching: Instr oil & watercolor, Rutland Jr High, Vt, 68-; instr oil & watercolor, Chester Art Guild, Vt, 68-; instr oil & watercolor, Southern Vt Art Ctr, 71- Pos: Trustee, Chaffee Art Gallery, Rutland, Vt, 71-74. Awards: First of Show, City of Rutland, 69; First Prize, Chaffee Art Gallery Fall Show, 70 & 72; Kenneth Fitch Award, Salmagundi Club of New York, 77 & Salmagundi Award for Painting, 77. Mem: Southern Vt Artists (trustee, 72-, art chmn, 73-74); Salmagundi Club; Allied Artists Am; Am Artists Prof League; Acad Artists Am. Style & Technique: Realistic-impressionism. Media: Oil, Watercolor. Mailing Add: Elm St Pittsford VT 05763

FRIED, ALEXANDER
ART CRITIC
b New York, NY, May 21, 02. Study: Columbia Col, AB, 23; Columbia Univ, MA, 24. Pos: Art ed, San Francisco Chronicle, 30-34; art ed, San Francisco Examr, 34- Mailing Add: 22 Crown Terr San Francisco CA 94114

FRIED, HOWARD LEE
SCULPTOR
b Cleveland, Ohio, June 14, 46. Study: Syracuse Univ, 64-67; San Francisco Art Inst, BFA, 68; Univ Calif, Davis, MFA, 70. Work: Cleveland Mus Art, Ohio; Syracuse Univ, NY; Univ Calif, Davis. Comn: Mural, Syracuse Univ, 66. Exhib: Looking West, Joslyn Art Mus, Omaha, Nebr, 70; The 80's, Univ Art Mus, Univ Calif, Berkeley, 70; Prospect 71; Projection, Kunsthalle, Dusseldorf, Ger, 71 & Louisiana Mus, Denmark, 72; Documenta 5, Kassel, Ger, 72; plus many others. Teaching: Instr sculpture, San Francisco Art Inst, 68- Awards: Augusta Hazard Award, Syracuse Univ, 66; Adeline Kent Award, San Francisco Artist's Comt, 71-72; Nat Endowment for Arts Grant, 75. Bibliog: Grace Glueck (auth), New York: big thump on the bass drum, Art in Am, 5-6/71; Brenda Richardson (auth), Howard Fried; paradox of approach-avoidance, Arts Mag, 6/71; Steve Davis (auth), Howard Fried installation piece, Art Week, 3/25/72. Mem: San Francisco Artist Comt (vchmn, 71-74, chmn, 75-). Publ: Auth, Inside the harlequin, Flash Art, 71; auth, Studio relocation, Breakthroughs in Fiction, 72; auth, Cheshire cat 4, Avalanche; plus films & video tapes. Mailing Add: 16 Rose St San Francisco CA 94102

FRIED, MICHAEL
ART CRITIC
Pos: Art critic, Artforum Mag. Publ: Auth, Morris Louis, In: Contemporary Art & Artists, Abrams. Mailing Add: 430 Broadway Cambridge MA 02139

FRIED, THEODORE
PAINTER, ETCHER
b Budapest, Hungary, May 19, 02; US citizen. Study: Acad Fine Arts, Budapest, 20-23; additional study with Julius Rudnay. Work: Mus Nat Art Mod, Paris; Albertina & Osterreichische Galerie, Vienna; Butler Inst Am Art, Youngstown, Ohio; Walker Art Ctr, Minneapolis, Minn; Mem Art Gallery, Rochester, NY; Mount Holyoke Mus, Mass; E A Ulrich Mus, Wichita, Kans; Brit Imperial War Mus, London; Victoria & Albert Mus, London. Exhib: November-Gruppe, Berlin, 29; Carnegie Shows, Pittsburgh, 43 & 49; Roy & Mary Neuberger Collection, Whitney Mus Am Art, New York, 54; Contemporary Trends, Am Fed Arts traveling show, 55-57; Westbeth Printmakers, Palacio de Belles Artes, Mexico City, 72; Fedn of Mod Painters & Sculptors Traveling Show, 76-78; one-man exhib, Denver, Colo, 77; plus others. Bibliog: F Grossmann (auth), Theodore Fried, Forum, 33; L Campbell (auth), Theodore Fried, Art News, 61; C O Ennen (auth), Malerei Lexicon, Kindler, 65. Mem: Fedn Mod Painters & Sculptors (treas, 69-72, vpres, 73-75); Westbeth Graphic Artists. Publ: Illusr, Jimmy the Jeep, Lothrop, 45; illusr, Tune of the Calliope, 58. Dealer: Tyringham Gallery Tyringham MA 01264. Mailing Add: 463 West St New York NY 10014

FRIEDBERG, RAY E
PAINTER, INSTRUCTOR
b Brooklyn, NY, Jan 9, 29. Study: Art Students League, with Reginald Marsh; also with Leon Goldin & George Picken. Exhib: One-person show, Gloria Cortella Gallery, New York, 77; New Eng Exhib, Conn, 67, 70 & 72; Art from New Jersey, Trenton Mus, 71; Women in the Arts, Brooklyn Mus, 75; Aldrich Mus, Ridgefield, Conn, 75-76; plus others. Teaching: Instr art, art hist & cult arts, Saturday Col, Fairleigh Dickinson Univ, 71- Pos: Art dir, Young Men's Hebrew Asn, 70-71; artist in residence, Edward Williams Col, Fairleigh Dickinson Univ, 73- Awards: Northshore Competition First Prize, Mus Mod Art, 71. Bibliog: John Russell (auth), article in New York Times, 75; Rughann Williams (auth), New Jersey Music and Art, Music & Art Publ, Chatham, NJ, 76 & 77; Dona Z Meilach (auth), Box Art, Assemblage and Construction, Crown, 75. Mem: Women in Arts. Style & Technique: Mixed media on stainless steel; exploration of realities introduced by surrealism. Media: Constructed, Highly Polished Stainless Steel, Sculptured Acrylic and Photographic Images. Mailing Add: 821 Summit Ave River Edge NJ 07661

FRIEDEBERG, PEDRO
PAINTER, SCULPTOR
b Florence, Italy, Jan 11, 37; US citizen. Study: Iberoamerican Univ, Mex; sculpture with Mathias Goeritz. Work: Isaac Delgado Mus, New Orleans, La; Rose Art Mus, Brandeis Univ, Mass; Mus Arte Mod, Mexico City; Israel Mus, Jerusalem; Museums Mod Art, New York & Paris; plus others. Comn: Sculptures, garden of Andre Bloc, Paris, France, 63; mural, Hotel Camino Real, Mexico City, 68; several murals, pvt homes, Mexico City, 70-72. Exhib: 20th Biennale Sao Paulo, Brazil, 69; Bienal Coltejer, Medellin, Colombia, 72; Bienal San Juan PR, 74; Bienal, Montevideo, Uruguay, 74; Three Mexican Artists, touring 7 mus Can, 73-74; plus others. Pos: Art ed, Mexico this Month, 60-64. Awards: Premio Antrax, Biennale Cordoba, 66; Second Prize, Expos Solar, 68. Bibliog: Ida Rodriguez (auth), Pedro Friedeberg, Programa Cult 19th Olimpiada, Mex, 68; Ida Rodriguez (auth), Pedro Freideberg, Univ Mex, 72. Mem: Salon Plastica Mex; founding mem Los Hartos. Style & Technique: Surrealism op art and occultism in mixed media. Publ: Auth, Autobiography, Archit J, Archit Fantastique, Paris, 62; auth, Autobiography 2, Motive 62; auth, Dialogos Mag, 71. Dealer: Galeria Misrachi Genova 20 Mexico City 6 Mex; Grace Hokin Gallery 200 E Ontario Chicago IL 60611. Mailing Add: Paseo de la Reforma 334-4 Mexico City DF Mexico

FRIEDENSOHN, ELIAS
PAINTER, SCULPTOR
b New York, NY, Dec 12, 24. Study: Tyler Sch Fine Arts, Temple Univ, 42; with Gabriel Zendel, Paris, France, 46; Queens Col, BA, 48; NY Univ Inst Fine Arts, 49-51. Work: Whitney Mus Am Art; Kalamazoo Inst of Arts; Ark Art Mus; Art Inst Chicago; Minneapolis Mus Art; Walker Art Ctr; Sarah Roby Found Collection, Krannert Mus Art, Univ Ill; plus others. Exhib: Young American Painters, 59 & Whitney Mus Ann, 61-64, Whitney Mus Am Art; Art Inst Chicago Ann, 59 & 61; Corcoran Gallery Art Ann, Washington, DC, 62; Minneapolis Mus Art Drawing Ann, 71; plus 21 one-man shows. Teaching: Prof art, Queens Col, 59-; prof art & chmn arts div, Kirkland Col, 70-71. Pos: Chmn, Nat Screening Comt for Painting, Fulbright Prog, Inst Int Educ New York, 66-69, mem Cintas awards comt, 75. Awards: Fulbright Grant, Italy, 57; Guggenheim Fel, 60; Purchase Awards, Minneapolis Mus Art, 71, Univ Mass, 72 & Am Acad Arts & Lett, 73. Media: Oil. Dealer: Terry Dintenfass 18 E 67th St New York NY 11210. Mailing Add: 209 Hillcrest Ave Leonia NJ 07605

FRIEDLAND, RUTH VOLID
ART DEALER
b Chicago, Ill. Study: Art Inst of Chicago; Chouninard Art Sch, Los Angeles; Otis Art Inst; Univ of Chicago. Pos: Pres, Collectors Showroom, Inc, 70- Bibliog: Barbara Varro (auth), A New Start at Midlife, Sun Times, 10/77. Mem: Mus of Contemp Art, Chicago (bd affil, 76-); Arch of Am Art; Print & Drawing Club, Art Inst of Chicago; N Shore Art League, Am Craft Coun. Specialty: Art source for designers, architects and corporate collectors; art consultant to industry. Mailing Add: 325 N Wells St Chicago IL 60610

FRIEDMAN, ALAN
SCULPTOR, DESIGNER
b Philadelphia, Pa, Sept 9, 44. Study: Rochester Inst Technol Sch Am Craftsman, BFA, 67; Univ Wis, Madison, MFA(sculpture), 69. Work: Univ Wis, Union Galleries, Madison, 69; Ind State Univ, Terre Haute, 72; Indianapolis Mus of Art, 77. Comn: Entrance doors (wood), St Paul's Univ Cath Church, Madison, 68; sculpture (plywood), Cunningham Mem Libr, Ind State Univ, Terre Haute, 73. Exhib: 55th Ann Wis Designer-Craftsman, Milwaukee Art Ctr, 69; Art in Other Media, Rockford Ill Art Asn, 70; Objects & Crafts 75, Indianapolis Mus Art, 75; retrospective, Wis Directions, Milwaukee Art Ctr, 75; Indianapolis Mus Art Traveling Exhib & Mus Gallery Exhib, 75-76. Teaching: Vis asst prof art, Univ Wis, Madison, 69-70; assoc prof furniture design & sculpture, art dept, Ind State Univ, Terre Haute, 72- Pos: Designer furniture, E A Roffman Co, New York, 72. Awards: Grand Prize, Milwaukee Art Ctr, 69; Award, Indianapolis Mus Art, 75; Jurors Award, Marietta Col Crafts Nat Exhib, 75; Nat Endowment for the Arts, individual fel grant, 76-77. Bibliog: Thelma Newman (auth), Master Works in Wood, Chilton Bks (in prep). Mem: Am Crafts Coun. Style & Technique: Rectilinear and curvilinear forms creating a metamorphosis in positive and negative; carved lamination in plywood and solid lumber. Mailing Add: 1319 S Sixth St Terre Haute IN 47802

FRIEDMAN, B H
WRITER
b New York, NY, July 27, 26. Study: Cornell Univ, BA, 48. Teaching: Lectr Eng, Cornell Univ, 66-67. Pos: Adv coun mem, Cornell Univ Arts Col & Herbert F Johnson Mus; trustee, Am Fedn Arts, 58-64; trustee, Whitney Mus Am Art, currently; dir, Fine Arts Work Ctr, Provincetown, Mass. Publ: Auth, Whispers, 72; auth, Jackson Pollock: Energy Made Visible (biog), 72; auth, Alfonso Ossorio (monogr), 73; auth, Museum, 74; auth, Almost a Life, 75; auth, Gertrude Vanderbilt Whitney (biog), 78; plus many others. Mailing Add: 435 E 52nd St New York NY 10022

FRIEDMAN, BENNO
PHOTOGRAPHER
b New York, NY, Mar 28, 45. Study: Brandeis Univ, BA. Work: Mus Mod Art, New York; Boston Mus Fine Arts; Fogg Mus, Cambridge, Mass; George Eastman House, Rochester, NY; Vassar Col Mus, Poughkeepsie, NY. Exhib: 60's Continuum, George Eastman House, 72; Octave of Prayer, Mass Inst Technol, 72; Light & Lens, Hudson River Mus, 73; one-man show, Light Gallery, 73 & 75; Private Realities, Boston Mus Fine Arts, 74. Publ: Contribr, Art in Am, 70 & Aspen Mag; Idea, NY Photogr, 74; plus others. Dealer: Light Gallery 1018 Madison Ave New York NY 10021. Mailing Add: Kellogg Rd Sheffield MA 01257

FRIEDMAN, JOAN MARCY
CURATOR, ART LIBRARIAN
b New York, NY, Nov 30, 49. Study: Harvard Univ, AB(fine arts; magna cum laude), 71; Courtauld Inst of Art, London Univ, MA, 73; Columbia Univ, MS(honors), 74. Collections Arranged: Color Printing in Eng, Yale Ctr for Brit Art, 4-6/78. Pos: Summer intern, Metrop Mus of Art, New York, 70; asst res librn, Beinecke Libr, Yale Univ, 74-76; cur rare books, Yale Ctr for Brit Art, 76- Mem: Asn of Col & Res Libr Rare Bks & Manuscripts Sect (prog chmn, 78). Res: English drawing manuals, 1600-1850; color printing in England. Interest: English illustrated books and books related to the visual arts in England. Publ: Auth, Every Lady Her Own Drawing Master, Apollo, 77; contribr, Selected Paintings, Drawings & Books, Yale Ctr for Brit Art, 77; contribr, Book Collecting: A Modern Guide, Bowker, 77; auth, Color Printing in England 1486-1870, Yale Ctr for Brit Art, 78. Mailing Add: Yale Ctr for Brit Art Box 2120 Yale Sta New Haven CT 06520

FRIEDMAN, KENNETH SCOTT
SCULPTOR, EDUCATOR
b New London, Conn. Study: Calif Western Univ; Shimer Col; San Francisco State Univ, BA & MA; Starr King Sch, Grad Theology Union, Berkeley; Grad Sch Human Behavior, US Int Univ, PhD(sociology of art). Work: Mus d'Art Contemporain Montreal, Que; Mus am Ostwall, Dortmund; La Jolla Mus Contemp Art, Calif; Arch Am Art, Smithsonian Inst, Washington, DC; Oakland Mus, Calif. Comn: Eingepacktes, Vice Versand, Remscheid, Ger, 71; Found Course in Arts, Newport Harbor Art Mus, Newport Beach, Calif, 75-77; The Mastery of Passage, Podio del Mondo per L'Arte, Middleburg, Neth, 78-79; plus others in Can, Europe & US. Exhib: Whitney Mus Am Art, New York; Mus Mod Art, Paris, France; Nat Gallery of Can, Ottawa, Ont; Venice Biennial, Italy; Neuer Berliner Kunstverein, Berlin, WGer; Biennal of Paris, France; touring solo exhib, Western Asn of Art Mus, 73-76; one-man shows, Oakland Mus, 72, Vancouver Art Gallery, BC, 72, Sheldon Mem Art Galleries, Univ Nebr, Lincoln, 73, Joslyn Art Mus, Omaha, Nebr, 73, Daner Galeriet, Copenhagen, Denmark, 73, Nelson I C Gallery, Univ Calif, Davis, 73, Ecart Gallery, Geneva, Switz, 74, Fine Arts Gallery, Univ Colo, Boulder, 74, Alta Col of Art, Calgary, 75, Galerie St Petri, Lund, Sweden, 75, Fiatal Muveszek, Budapest, 75 & Galerie Waalkens, Finsterwold, Neth, 77. Teaching: Vis prof, vis artist or vis critic in numerous col & univ, including, Univ Sask, Regina, 72, Claremont Grad Sch, Calif, 73, Otis Art Inst, 73, Univ Calif, Davis, 73, Creighton Univ, 73, Eastern Wash State Col, 74, Vancouver Sch of Art, 74, Western Wash State Col, 74, Univ Mont, 74, Univ Colo, 74, Berry Col, 75, ETenn State Univ, 75, Univ Tenn, 75, Univ Nev, Reno, 75, Univ SC, 75, Emory Univ, 75, Atlanta Col of Art, Ga, 75, Univ Calif, Riverside, 75, Univ Nebr, Omaha, 76, Starr King Sch for the Ministry, Grad Theology Union, Berkeley, Calif, 77, Calif Col of Art & Design, 77, Univ Mich, 77, Univ Windsor, 77 & Univ Iowa, 78. Pos: Dir, Fluxus W, San Francisco, San Diego & Exeter, 66-75; gen mgr, Something Else Press, New York & Valencia, Calif, 71; consult, Who's Who in Am Art & Am Art Dir, Jaques Cattell Press, Tempe, Ariz, 73- & San Diego Dance Theatre Inc, Calif, 74-; speaker, Western Asn of Art Mus, Western Regional Conf of the Am Asn Mus Ann Conf (joint), Salt Lake City, Utah, 75; consult, Visual Arts Adv Comn, Tenn Arts Comn Conf, Jackson, 75; co-founder & mem bd dirs, Contemp Arts/SE, Atlanta, 75-; exec dir, Inst for Advan Studies in Contemp Art, San Diego, 75-; mem nat adv bd, Nat Coun for the Arts & Educ, New York, 76-; chmn, Assoc Art Publ, San Francisco & New York, 77-; deleg, Coalition of Women's Art Orgn, Exeter, 66-75; vis critic, Conf on Dada, Sch of Art & t Art Hist & Univ Art Mus, Univ Iowa, 78; consult, First Mich Cong on the Arts, Mich Coun for the Arts, 78; panelist, New Art Spaces Conf, Los Angeles Inst Contemp Art, 78. Bibliog: Marilyn Ekdahl Ravicz (auth), Aesthetic Anthropology: Theory & Analysis of Pop & Conceptual Art in America, Dept of Anthrop, Univ Calif, Los Angeles, 74; Georg M Gugelberger (auth), Ein Interview mit Ken Friedman, Kunstforum Int, 2-4/75; Diane Spodarek (auth), Ken Friedman, Detroit Artists Mo, 1/78. Awards: Gov's Award for Idaho Proj at Boise Gallery of Art, State of Idaho, 75; Vis Artists & Critics Grant for Berry Col, Nat Endowment for the Arts, 75; Tenn Arts Comn & ETenn State Univ Found Grant to support work as vis prof in art & art hist, 75. Mem: Col Art Asn (mem, Placement Standards Comn, 77-); fel Am Anthrop Asn; Soc for Anthrop & Sociology of Art (vpres, 76-); Am Asn Mus; fel Western Asn Art Mus. Publ: Auth, The Aesthetics, Beau Geste Press, Devon, Eng, 73; auth, International Sources, Composer/Performer Eds, Sacramento, Calif, 74; auth, A Conversation with Arman, Henry Art Gallery, Univ Wash, Seattle, 74; auth, James Edwards, Grossmont Col, El Cajon & Everson Mus, Syracuse, NY, 76; auth, June Wayne: Energy, Order, Humanism (catalogue for touring exhib, in prep); auth, articles in Lightworks, Art & Artists, Umbrella, La Mamelle, Flashart, Contemp Art/SE, plus others. Mailing Add: Inst for Advan Studies in Contemp Art 6361 Elmhurst Dr San Diego CA 92120

FRIEDMAN, MARTIN
MUSEUM DIRECTOR
b Pittsburgh, Pa, Sept 23, 25. Study: Univ Pa; Univ Wash, BA, 47; Univ Calif, Los Angeles, MA, 49; Columbia Univ, 56-57; Belg-Am Educ Found grant, Brussels, 57-58; Univ Minn, Am art fel, 58-60. Exhib Organized: Jean Dubuffet: Monuments, Simulacres, Praticubles, 73; Nevelson: Wood Sculpture, 73; Naives & Visionaries, 74; Projected Images, 74; Oldenburg: Six Themes, 75; among others. Pos: Fel, Brooklyn Mus, 56-57; sr cur, Walker Art Ctr, 58-60, dir, 61-; trustee, Spring Hill Found. Awards: Ford Found Fel, 61-62. Mem: Am Fedn Arts (trustee); Nat Collection Fine Arts Comn; Asn Art Mus Dirs; Int Comt Mus & Collections Mod Art; Century Asn. Publ: Auth, Charles Sheeler, Watson-Guptill; contribr, Arts, Art News, Art Int, Quadrum & Art & Artists. Mailing Add: Vineland Pl Minneapolis MN 55403

FRIEDMAN, MARVIN
ILLUSTRATOR, COLLECTOR
b Chester, Pa, Sept 26, 30. Study: Philadelphia Graphic Sketch Club; Philadelphia Mus Sch Art, Pa. Work: Playboy Collection, Chicago & Ford Motor Co, Dearborn, Ill; Boy Scouts of Am Collection, New Brunswick, NJ; Nat Broadcasting Co Collection, New York; Am Legion Collection, NJ. Exhib: Illusr, Philadelphia Art Alliance, 71; traveling exhibs, Playboy Art, Soc of Illusr & Ford Motor Co; Princeton Art Asn; NJ Artists; Pa Representational Artists; Nat Broadcasting Co Commun Art. Teaching: Lectr illus, RI Sch of Design, Pratt Inst & Philadelphia Col of Art. Awards: Soc of Illus Ann Award. Style & Technique: Graphic post impressionist, influenced by Bonnard and Vuillard. Media: Gouache, Acrylic. Collection: Large collection of Impressionist drawings and prints; large collection of American illustrators. Publ: Illusr, Chewing Gum, Prentice Hall, 76; illusr, Pinch, Little Brown, 76. Mailing Add: 35 E Broad St Hopewell NJ 08525

FRIEND, DAVID
PAINTER, EDUCATOR
b Glasgow, Scotland, Sept 6, 99; US citizen. Study: With Walter Farndon; self-taught, museums of Italy, France & US. Work: La Salle Col, Philadelphia. Exhib: One-man show, M H de Young Mem Mus, San Francisco, 54 & Hern Gallery, Palo Alto, Calif, 75; Nat Acad Design, New York, 42; Nat Exhib of Small Paintings, Albuquerque, NMex, 69; Nat Soc Painters in Casein & Acrylic & Allied Artists Am, 78, New York. Pos: Artist/instr in residence, Montalvo Found, Saratoga, Calif, 52-54; dir, Torremolinos Art Workshop, Spain,

54-58; dir, Sch Art, Seven Arts Ctr, New York, 58-59; dir, David Friend Art Group, New York, 59-72. Bibliog: Saburo Kurata (auth), Art and art education in Japan, J Art Educ, 65; Joseph E Bogen (auth), Some educational aspects of hemispheric specialization, Univ Calif Los Angeles Educr, 75. Mem: Allied Artists Am; Nat Soc Painters in Casein & Acrylic; Nat Art Educ Asn; Int Soc Educ Through Art; Creative Educ Found. Style & Technique: Abstract expressionism, non-objective. Media: Acrylic, Mixed Media. Publ: Auth, The Creative Way to Paint, Watson-Guptill, 65 & 75; contribr, Advanced training simplified for amateur painters, Leonardo Mag, 71; contribr, Art Book Reviews, Leonardo Mag, 72-78; auth, Composition: A Painter's Guide to Basic Problems and Solutions, Watson-Guptill, 75. Dealer: Hern Gallery 542 Ramona St Palo Alto CA 94301. Mailing Add: Box 405 Menlo Park CA 94025

FRINTA, MOJMIR SVATOPLUK
ART HISTORIAN, WRITER
b Prague, Czech, July 28, 22; US citizen. Study: Col Fine & Appl Arts, Prague; Karlova Univ, Prague, BA; Ecole des Beaux Arts, Paris, France; Ecole du Louvre, Paris; Univ Mich, MA, 53, PhD(hist art), 60. Teaching: Prof art hist, State Univ NY Albany, 63- Pos: Sr restorer, Metrop Mus Art, New York, 55-63. Mem: Col Art Asn; Int Inst Conserv Art; Int Ctr Medieval Art; Archaeol Soc Am. Res: Late medieval painting & sculpture; art technology. Publ: Auth, A portrait bust by the master of beautiful madonnas, 60 & auth, Authorship of the Merode altarpiece, 68; Art Quart; auth, Master of the Gerona martyrology & Bohemian illumination, 64 & auth, Investigation of the punched decoration of medieval Italian & non-Italian panel paintings, 65, Art Bull; auth, Genius of Robert Campin, Mouton, 66. Mailing Add: Dept of Art State Univ NY Albany Albany NY 12222

FRISBIE, AMY JONES
See Jones, Amy

FRISCIA, ALBERT JOSEPH
PAINTER, SCULPTOR
b New York, NY, July 22, 11. Study: Nat Acad Design, with Ivan Olinsky, 33-36; Black Mountain Col, with Ilya Bolotowsky; Escuela Univ des Bellas Artes, with Alfaro Siqueiros. Comn: Doors in bronze & nave gate in bronze (with Int Inst Liturgical Art), Cathedral Holy Name, Chicago, 68 & 69; monument in bronze, Cathedral Potenza, Italy, 75; altar in bronze, Basilica St Mary, Montesanto, Rome, 75; bronze sculpture, Ministry of Post & Telecommunications Bldg, EUR, Rome, Italy, 77. Exhib: Light, Int Show Kinetic Art, Galleria Dell Obelisco, Rome, 67; 6th & 7th Int Biennial Sculpture, Carrara, Italy, 69 & 73; Seven Americans in Rome, Kinetic Projections, Gallery Mod Art, Rome, 70; one-man show, 50th Anniversary Turkish Repub, Istanbul, Izmir, Ankara, 73. Pos: Art dir, Pan Am Airways, 54-68; air dir, Case-Shepperd-Mann, 46-47. Awards: Gold Medal of Merit, Mass of the Artists, Rome, 72. Bibliog: Frank Popper (auth), L'art Cinetique, Gauthier-Villars, Paris, 70; Trecanni (ed), Lessico Universale Della Enciclopedia Italiana, Rome, 70; Corrado Maltese (auth), Contemporary Art in Italy, Presenza, Rome, 71. Style & Technique: Sculpture abstract figurative approach; painting both abstract informal and formal approach. Media: Wax, Transparent Plastics. Mailing Add: Via Margutta 54 Rome 00187 Italy

FRISHMUTH, HARRIET WHITNEY
SCULPTOR
b Philadelphia, Pa, Sept 17, 80. Study: With Rodin & Injalbert, Paris; also with Cuno Von Enchtritz, Berlin, Ger; Art Students League, with Borglum & McNeil. Work: Slavonic Dance, also Vine, Metrop Mus Art, New York; Play Days, Dallas Mus Fine Arts. Comn: Fountain, Joy of the Waters, Mus Fine Arts, Dayton, Ohio; Mem Sundial, Englewood, NJ; Morton Mem, Windsorville, Conn; Marble Portrait Bust of Woodrow Wilson, Capitol, Richmond, Va; Crest of the Wave (fountain), Bot Gardens, St Paul; plus others. Exhib: Nat Acad Design; Archit League; Nat Asn Women Painters & Sculptors; Acad Fine Arts, Philadelphia; San Francisco Expos. Awards: Joan of Arc Silver Medal, Nat Asn Women Painters & Sculptors, 24; Gold Medal, Catharine Lorillard Wolfe Art Club; First Recipient Award, Coun Am Artists Soc; plus others. Mem: Fel Nat Acad Design; Nat Sculpture Soc; Nat Asn Women Painters & Sculptors; Allied Artists Am; League of Am Artists; plus others. Mailing Add: Heritage Village Box 168 Southbury CT 06488

FROMAN, RAMON MITCHELL
PAINTER
b Louise, Tex, Oct 13, 08. Study: Am Acad Art, Chicago; and with E F Van Amburg, Charles Schroeder, Glen Sheffer, Gerry Peirce, Rex Brandt, Ed Whitney & John Pike. Work: Univ Tex, Austin; Southern Methodist Univ; Koshare Indian Mus, LaJuanta, Colo; St Paul Hosp, Dallas; Okla Hall Fame, Heritage House, Oklahoma City. Comn: Oil portraits, Disabled Am Vets, Dallas, Lions Club, Kerrville, Tex, Dallas Crippled Children's Hosp & Southwestern Med Ctr, Grand Prairie, Tex. Exhib: All Ill Soc Fine Arts, Chicago; Joseph Sartor Gallery, Dallas; Am Artists Prof League, New York; Artists & Craftsmen Assoc, Dallas; Koshare Indian Mus; WTex Mus, Wichita Falls. Teaching: Pvt art classes, summers 58- Awards: Miriam Y Burrill Gold Medal; First Place in Portraiture, Am Artist Prof League Grand Nat Exhib, Am Coun Arts, Best of Show; First Place in Portrait, Artists & Craftsmen Exhibs, Dallas. Mem: Am Artists Prof League; Artists & Craftsmen Assoc; Coppini Acad Fine Arts, San Antonio. Style & Technique: Direct; impressionistic. Media: Oil, Watercolor. Dealer: Taos Art Gallery Taos NM 87571; Grand Cent Galleries, New York, NY. Mailing Add: 8483 Stults Rd Dallas TX 75243

FROMBERG, LAVERNE RAY
ART ADMINISTRATOR, PAINTER
b Duvall, Wash, May 6, 30. Study: Univ Wash, 47-53, BFA, 51 & MFA, 53; Univ NMex, 49-50; Art Students League, 51-52 & 63-64; Bradley Univ, 69-70, study with Alexander Archipenko & Sherman E Lee. Work: Libr Cong, Washington, DC; New Orleans Art Mus, La; Lakeview Ctr Arts & Sci, Peoria, Ill; Bradley Univ, Peoria; Employers Reinsurance Corp, Kansas City, Mo. Comn: Adoration of Shepherds and Wise Men (Triptych oil), Dillard Univ, New Orleans, 55. Exhib: New Orleans Art Mus Ann, 56; one-person shows, Fulton Gallery, New York, 64-66 & 69; Six Ill Painters Traveling Show, Ill Arts Coun, Ill & Mo, 67-69; Mus Mod Art Mem Floor, New York, 69; Butler Inst Am Art 25th. Collections Arranged: Holiday Art Ann Elem Art Exhib, 73 & 74 & Impressions of a Teenage Art Exhib, Lakeview Ctr Arts & Sci, 74 & 75. Teaching: Actg instr drawing, Bradley Univ, 54-57; lectr drawing, Ill State Univ, Normal, 69-71. Pos: Dir educ & exten, Lakeview Ctr Arts & Sci, 73- Awards: Prize for Painting, Three Times One, Am Painting & Sculpture Festival, Macon, Ga; Best in Show Purchase Prize Painting, Icon, New Orleans Art Asn; Carnegie Hall Art Award Painting, Art Students League. Mem: Midwest Mus Asn. Style & Technique: Translucent ground, engraved line & wash, semi-abstract images style, tactile surface. Media: Encaustic Watercolor. Publ: Contribr, Art Let's Try It, TV series, Lakeview Ctr Art & Sci & Bradley Univ. Dealer: Peoria Art Guild 1831 N Knoxville Peoria IL 61606; Stanley Crantson Fulton Gallery Lexington at 62nd St New York NY 10021. Mailing Add: 1205 N Glenwood Ave Peoria IL 61606

FROMBOLUTI, SIDEO
PAINTER
b Hershey, Pa, Oct 3, 20. Work: Cincinnati Art Mus, Ohio; Univ Mus, Southern Ill Univ, Carbondale; Mus Art, Providence, RI; Univ Ill Mus, Urbana; Ciba-Geigy Corp. Exhib: Speyer Gallery, Paris; Zabriskie Gallery, New York; Great Jones Gallery; Artist Gallery; Landmark Gallery. Bibliog: Sandler (auth), article in Aujourd'hui; Oeri (auth), article in Quadrum; Kingsley (auth), article in Art Int. Style & Technique: Post abstract expressionism, figurative direction. Media: Oil on Canvas. Dealer: Landmark Gallery 469 Broome St New York NY 10013. Mailing Add: 178 Prince St New York NY 10012

FROMER, MRS LEON
COLLECTOR
Collection: French impressionist paintings. Mailing Add: 1035 Fifth Ave New York NY 10028

FROST, STUART HOMER
EDUCATOR, PAINTER
b Arendtsville, Pa, Nov 22, 25. Study: Pa State Univ, BA; Brooklyn Mus Sch; Skowhegan Sch Painting & Sculpture. Work: Pa Acad Fine Arts, Philadelphia; Butler Art Inst, Youngstown, Ohio; Dulin Gallery Art, Knoxville, Tenn; Mus Art, Pa State Univ, University Park; Mansfield State Col Permanent Collection, Pa. Exhib: Am Watercolors, Drawings & Prints, Metrop Mus Art, 62; Recent Drawings USA, Mus Mod Art, 64; Watercolor USA, 66; Butler Art Inst Mid-Yr Show, 75; 9th Dulin Nat Print & Drawing Competition, 75. Teaching: Prof art, Pa State Univ, University Park, 62- Style & Technique: Realism; black and white drawing in pen and ink. Mailing Add: 139 E Hubler Rd State College PA 16801

FRUDAKIS, EVANGELOS WILLIAM
SCULPTOR
b Rains, Utah, May 13, 21. Study: Greenwich Workshop, New York, with Merli & Albino Cavalitto, 35-39; Beaux Arts Inst Design, New York, 40-41; Pa Acad Fine Arts, with W Hancock, P Manship, E J Ferris, J F Harbeson, D M Robb & W M Campbell; asst to sculptors P Manship & J Davidson: Cresson traveling scholar, 47; Henry Scheidt Mem scholar, 49; Louis Comfort Tiffany scholar, 49; Am Acad Rome, Italy, Priz de Rome fel, 50-52. Work: Pa Acad Fine Arts, Philadelphia; Lehigh Valley Art Alliance; Woodmere Art Gallery; Nat Acad Fine Arts, New York; Dupont Co Collection; plus many others. Exhib: Pa Acad Fine Arts Ann, 41-62; Nat Acad Design Ann, 48-63; Woodmere Art Gallery, Chestnut Hill, Pa, 55-59; Philadelphia Mus Art, 59 & 62 & 23 Sculptors Exhib, 72; one-man shows, Atlantic City Art Ctr, 56 & 61, Woodmere Art Gallery, 57 & 62, Philadelphia Art Alliance, 58, Pa Acad of Fine Arts, 62 & Briarcliff Col Mus of Art, 74; plus numerous other group and one-man shows. Teaching: Instr, var art centers, NY, NJ & Pa, 41-63; instr, Nat Acad Fine Art, New York, 70-; sr instr, Pa Acad Fine Arts, Philadelphia, 72-; instr, Old Church Cult Ctr, Demarest, NJ, 75-; instr, Frudakis Acad Fine Arts, Philadelphia, 76- Awards: Winner, Nat Fountain Competition, Little Rock, Ark, 65; Elizabeth N Watrous Gold Medal, 68, Dessie Greer Prize, 70 & Artists Fund Prize, 75, Nat Acad Design; Gold Medal & Therese-Edwin H Richards Prize, 72 & Herbert Adams Award, 76, Nat Sculpture Soc; plus others. Mem: Fel Pa Acad Fine Arts (bd mgrs); fel Am Acad Rome; fel Nat Sculpture Soc (mem coun); academician Nat Acad Design; Allied Artists Am. Res: Collaborated research on reconstruction of statues of Roman Forum; viewings of Michelangelo's Rondanini Pieta. Mailing Add: Frudakis Gallery 1820 Chestnut St Philadelphia PA 19103

FRUHAUF, ALINE
PAINTER, PRINTMAKER
b New York, NY, Jan 31, 07. Study: Parsons; Art Students League; and with Boardman Robinson, Kenneth Hayes Miller & Charles Locke. Work: Phillips Gallery, Libr Cong, Nat Collection Fine Arts & Smithsonian Inst, Washington, DC; Baltimore Mus Fine Art, Md. Exhib: Corcoran Gallery, Washington, DC; one-woman shows, Univ Nebr, 41, Caricatures of American Artists, 44, Caricatures of Washington Artists, 50 & Face of Music in Washington, Baltimore Mus & Making Faces, Smithsonian Inst, 65-66; Caricatures, Corcoran Gallery of Art, 77. Mem: Soc Washington Printmakers; Washington Watercolor Club; Artists Equity Asn. Media: Oil, Watercolor, Lithography, Woodcut. Publ: Contribr, America Today, Equinox, 36; contribr, Libr Cong Catalog, 70; contribr, New Deal Art Projects, Smithsonian, 72; contribr, Art for the Millions, New York Graphic Soc. Dealer: E Weyhe Inc 794 Lexington Ave New York NY 10021; Bethesda Art Gallery 7950 Norfolk Ave Bethesda MD 20014. Mailing Add: 7202 44th St Chevy Chase MD 20015

FRUMKIN, ALLAN
ART DEALER
b Chicago, Ill, July 5, 26. Study: Univ Chicago. Pos: Dir, Allan Frumkin Gallery, New York. Specialty: Contemporary American artists; 19th and 20th century drawings. Mailing Add: 50 W 57th St New York NY 10019

FRY, EDWARD FORT
ART HISTORIAN, ART CRITIC
b Philadelphia, Pa, May 6, 35. Study: Princeton Univ, 53-57; Harvard Univ, 57-61; Univ Paris, Sorbonne, Inst Art & Archeol, 61-63. Collections Arranged: 5th & 6th Guggenheim Int Exhibs, 67 & 71; David Smith (with catalog), 69; Jean Arp, 69; Japanese Art, 70. Teaching: Chmn dept art, York Univ, Toronto, 73-74; vis lectr, Yale Univ, 74-75; Kenan Prof Fine Arts, Colgate Univ, 76-78. Pos: Cur, Guggenheim Mus, New York, 67-71. Awards: Fulbright Fel, 61-63; Guggenheim Fel, 72-73. Mem: Int Coun of Mus; Col Art Asn (dir, 71-75); Asn Internationale des Critiqes d'Art. Res: Modern art, history and theory; Cubism; contemporary art; history and theory of sculpture. Publ: Auth, Cubism, 66; ed, On the Future of Art, 70; auth, Hans Haacke, 72; co-auth, The Functions of Painting, Collected Writings of Fernand Leger, 73. Mailing Add: 7 W 43rd St New York NY 10036

FRY, GUY
PAINTER
b Milton, Pa, Aug 5, 03. Study: Philadelphia Col Art, 22-26. Exhib: One-man show, Philadelphia Art Alliance; Pa Acad Fine Arts; Philadelphia Acad Alliance, Nat Acad Design; Am Watercolor Soc. Pos: Past chmn bd, Philadelphia Col Art; past trustee, Philadelphia Mus Art. Awards: Albert Dorne Award, Nat Acad Design, 70; Silver Medal, Art Dirs Club Philadelphia, 71; Antoinette Graves Goetz Award, Am Watercolor Soc. Mem: Philadelphia Art Dirs Club (past pres); Nat Soc Art Dirs (past pres). Mailing Add: 750 Old Lancaster Rd Berwyn PA 19312

FUCHS, MARY THARSILLA
EDUCATOR
b Westphalia, Tex, Apr 19, 12. Study: Our Lady of the Lake Col, BA, 38; Columbia Univ, MA, 42; Univ Sch Handicrafts, 42; Art Inst Chicago, 45; Univ Tex, 49-51; with Buckley McGurrin, 50-54; NY Univ, 52; Pratt Graphics Ctr, 69. Comn: Twelve faceted glass windows,

St Timothy Church, San Antonio, Tex, 71. Exhib: 7th & 8th Tex Gen, Witte Mus, San Antonio, 45 & 46; First Ann Tex Watercolor Soc, San Antonio, 50; San Antonio Press Club, 65. Teaching: Elem sch instr, St Joseph Acad, 32-37, high sch instr eng, hist, Ger & sci, 38-41; instr art, Our Lady of the Lake Col, 42-54, asst prof, 54-58, assoc prof, 58-68, prof, 68-, chmn dept, 42-72. Mem: Col Art Asn; Nat Art Educ Asn; Western Arts Asn; Tex Art Educ Asn; Tex Watercolor Soc; San Antonio Art League. Style & Technique: Simplified realism achieved through a free and spontaneous handing of the medium. Media: Watercolor. Publ: Designer, Toddler's rosary, 54; auth, Rocky personalities, Sch Arts Mag, 3/57; auth, Religion worksheets for beginners, Confraternity of Christian Doctrine, 62. Mailing Add: 411 SW 24th St San Antonio TX 78285

FUERST, SHIRLEY MILLER
SCULPTOR, PAINTER
b Brooklyn, NY, June 3, 28. Study: Brooklyn Mus Art Sch, with Reuben Tam; Pratt Ctr Contemp Printmaking; Art Students League, with Roberto DeLamonica; Hunter Col, MFA, 71. Work: James A Michener Found Collection of Twentieth Century Am Art, Univ Tex, Austin; Exxon Corp, NJ; Allentown Art Mus, Pa. Exhib: Five New York Artists, Mickelson Gallery, Washington, DC, 67; 32nd Mid-Yr Show, Butler Inst of Am Art, Ohio, 68; Contemp Artists, Brooklyn Mus, 71; 4th Int Miniature Print Exhib, Asn Am Artists Gallery, New York, 71; Unmanly Art, Suffolk Mus, 72; Sculpture for the Dance, Hudson River Mus, 73; Private I: An Inside Look at Art, McGraw Hill Gallery, 77; Masks & Boxes, 77; Group Indiscriminate, 112 Greene St Gallery, 78; seven one-person shows, 76; plus others. Awards: Oil Competition First Prize, Village Art Ctr, New York, 63; Merit Award with Distinction, Enjay Chem Co, NJ, 66; Eric Schwartz Graphics Award, Nat Asn Women Artists, 70. Bibliog: Sculpture for the Dance (videotape), Hudson River Mus, 73; Shirley Fuerst (videotape), Women on Women, Artdoc, New York, 75; Conversation with an artist, Shirley Fuerst, Channel 31, 77. Mem: Women in Arts; Floating Gallery; Women's Caucus for Art; Nat Asn Women Artists; Contemp Artists. Style & Technique: Mylar environmental hangings, translucent sculptural forms, precisely balanced, floating in space; oil paintings, fusion of imaginary geometric forms or human with an abstract landscape space. Publ: Auth, A method of printing or painting using heat responsive inks, 71; auth, Health hazards in art, Art Workers News, 75; auth, videotape documentaries of women artists, 70 & Women Artists Newslett, 76. Mailing Add: 266 Marlborough Rd Brooklyn NY 11226

FUGATE-WILCOX, TERRY
SCULPTOR
b Kalamazoo, Mich, Nov 20, 44. Study: Ferris Inst. Work: Western Mich Univ, Kalamazoo; Guggenheim Mus, New York; Nat Gallery of Australia, Canberra; Dept of Parks, New York. Comn: Eight ft copper & aluminum sculpture, comn by J Patrick Lannon, West Palm Beach, Fla, 73; 40 ft aluminum & magnesium sculpture, J Hood Wright Park, New York, 74; 300 copper & silver sculptures, Commodities Exchange Mkt, New York, 74; 14ft copper & aluminum sculpture, comn by Alan Stillman. Exhib: Detroit Inst Art, Mich, 68; Language IV, Dwan Gallery, New York, 69; 1st Battery Park Sculpture Show, New York, 71; Art in Evolution, Xerox Corp, Rochester, NY, 73; Fire Air Earth Water, Univ Wis-Milwaukee, 74. Awards: CAPS grant, 76; Nat Endowment for the Arts, 76-77. Bibliog: Diane B Chichura & Thelma K Stevens (auths), Super Sculpture, Van Nostrand Reinhold, 74; Lawrence Alloway (auth), The Public Sculpture Problem, Studio Int, 10/72; Ellen Lubell (auth), Terry Fugate-Wilcox, Arts Mag, 1/74. Style & Technique: Sculpture that changes with time or environment. Media: All Materials. Mailing Add: c/o Louis K Meisel Gallery 141 Prince St New York NY 10012

FUGE, PAUL H
SCULPTOR
b Plainfield, NJ, June 9, 46. Study: Yale Univ, BA, 68. Exhib: Outdoor Environments, sponsored by Housing & Urban Develop, Boston Pub Gardens, 68; Spaces, Mus Mod Art, New York, 70; Work for New Spaces, Walker Art Mus, Minneapolis, 71; Pulsa & Television Sensoriums, Automation House, 71; Pulsa, Philadelphia Mus Fine Arts, 71. Teaching: Instr art, Yale Univ Sch Art & Archit, 68-72; vis artist, Calif Inst Arts, 71-73. Pos: Mem, Pulsa Group Environ Art. Media: Electronic Environments, Video Communication. Interest: Environmental art. Mailing Add: 161 Bowers Hill Rd Oxford CT 06483

FUHRMAN, ESTHER
SCULPTOR
b Pittsburgh, Pa, Feb 25, 39. Study: Pa State Univ, 56-57; Frick Dept Fine Arts, Univ Pittsburgh, BA, 60; also with Sabastiano Mineo & Hana Geber, New York. Work: Port of New York Authority; World Trade Ctr, New York; Am Crafts Coun, New York; UAHC Architects Adv, New York; Deere & Co, Moline, Ill. Comn: Marble lobby piece, Int Educ & Training, Inc, NY, 70; bronze & acrylic wall sculptures, comn by Hon & Mrs I D Davidson, New York, 71 & 72 & Mr & Mrs G Strichman, 74. Exhib: Nat Asn Women Artists, Nat Acad Art, New York; Six Contemp Artists, Montclair Mus Art NJ; Sculptors League, Columbia Univ Club, New York; Citicorps, New York, ann; Three Contemp Sculptors, Queens Coun Arts, Queens Co Supreme Ct Bldg; Am Soc Contemp Arts, Lever House, New York. Teaching: Lectr sculpture today, Sands Point Acad, Long Island, 71 & Kimberley Sch, NJ, 72; lectr studio secrets, Montclair Mus Art; building a half ton wall sculpture, Nat Acad Art. Awards: Ann Exhib Award, Nat Asn Women Artists, 72 & 74. Bibliog: Marilyn Goldstein (auth), Massive sculpture shapes her life, Newsday, 3/69; Esther Fuhrman, La Rev Mod, 3/72. Mem: Nat Asn Women Artists; New York Soc Women Artists; Am Soc Contemp Artists; Artists Equity of New York; Philadelphia Art Alliance; Sculptors League; Artists-Craftsmen New York. Media: Bronze with Acrylics and Gemstone Materials. Dealer: Gallery Worth Ave 155 Worth Ave Palm Beach FL; H Stern Fifth Ave New York NY. Mailing Add: 428 Newbold Rd Jenkintown PA 19046

FUKUI, NOBU
PAINTER, PRINTMAKER
b Tokyo, Japan, June 2, 42. Work: Mus Mod Art, New York; Indianapolis Mus Art, Ind; Larry Aldrich Mus, Conn; Nat Mus Mod Art, Tokyo & Kyoto; Dartmouth Col, NH. Exhib: One-man shows, Daniels Gallery, New York, 65, Max Hutchinson Gallery, 70, 72, 73 & 75, Gallery Con- Contemp Art, Pittsburgh, Pa, 71 & Watari Gallery, Tokyo, Japan, 77. Japanese Artists in Europe & America, Nat Mus Mod Art, Tokyo, 65; Painting & Sculpture Today, Indianapolis Mus Art, 70, 72 & 74. Style & Technique: Pure abstraction. Media: Acrylic, Serigraphy. Dealer: Max Hutchinson Gallery 138 Greene St New York NY 10012. Mailing Add: 140 Greene St New York NY 10012

FULLER, ADELAIDE P & WILLIAM MARSHALL
COLLECTORS
Collection: American impressionists. Mailing Add: 27 Valley Ridge Rd Ft Worth TX 76107

FULLER, DIANA
ART DEALER
b New York, NY, Jan 14, 31. Study: Sorbonne, two yrs study in art hist. Pos: Co-owner, Hansen-Fuller Gallery. Specialty: Contemporary art. Mailing Add: c/o Hansen-Fuller Gallery 228 Grant Ave San Francisco CA 94108

FULLER, EMILY (EMILY FULLER KINGSTON)
PAINTER, SCULPTOR
b New York, NY, Aug 9, 41. Study: Garland Jr Col, Boston, Mass, Assoc BD, 62; Mus Sch Fine Arts, Boston, Mass, 62-66; Tufts Univ, BS(art educ), 66; Art Students League, New York, study with Richard Mayhew, 68-69. Work: Chase Manhattan Bank, New York; Aldrich Mus Contemp Art, Ridgefield, Conn; Prudential Ins Corp Am; Owens-Corning Fiberglass Corp, Ill; Berlinger, Handels Gesellschaft, Frankfurter Bank, New York; plus others. Exhib: Contemp Reflections, Aldrich Mus, Ridgefield, Conn, 72; one-person shows, 55 Mercer, New York, 72, 75 & 78, Webb & Parsons, Bedford Village, NY, 77 & Soho 20, New York, 77; Soft Sculpture, Living Arts Ctr Gallery, Dayton, Ohio & Akron Arts Inst, Ohio, 75-76; Feminie-Dialogue, de la Couture à la Peinture, UNESCO, Paris, France, 77; Art in Transition: A Century of The Mus Sch, Mus Fine Arts, Boston, Mass, 77; Paper as Medium, Smithsonian Inst Travelling Exhib Serv, 78-79. Bibliog: Andrea Mikotajuk (auth), Reviews, Arts Mag, summer 72; Susan Heinemann (auth), Reviews, Artforum, 4/75; Barbara Schwartz (auth), Exhibition of New York Sculpture, Craft Horizons, 4/75. Style & Technique: Abstract based on building structure and landscape with emphasis on patterns, using sewing and media. Media: Painting: acrylic paint on sewn canvas, paint powders on sewn paper; sculpture: sewn plastic sheeting with paint powders, metallic powders, cut glass. Publ: Contribr, Emily Fuller Poineers in Art, Garland Mag, Garland Jr Col, 74. Dealer: 55 Mercer 55 Mercer St New York NY 10013. Mailing Add: 93 Mercer St New York NY 10012

FULLER, JOHN CHARLES
ART HISTORIAN, PHOTOGRAPHER
b Laconia, NH, Oct 7, 37. Study: Rochester Inst Technol, AAS, hon; Syracuse Univ, AB & MA; Ohio Univ, PhD; postdoctoral study with J H Matthews. Work: Eastman Kodak Co; Ohio Univ; State Univ NY, Oswego. Exhib: Photo Maxima Int, New York, 59; one-man show, Student Photographer, Kodak Exhib Ctr, New York, 59; Photomedia USA Nat, San Diego State Univ, Calif, 71; Contemp Photog Nat, Univ Nebr, Lincoln, 72; Invitational, Univ of the S, Sewanee, Tenn, 72; Two Photographers, Eckerd Col, St Petersburg, Fla, 73; Two Photographers, Johnson State Col, Vt, 73; NY State Super Fair, Syracuse, 74. Teaching: Teaching fel fine arts, Ohio Univ, Athens, 64-67; asst prof art hist, State Univ NY Col Oswego, 67-69, assoc prof, 70- Awards: Develop grant photo criticism, State Univ NY, 68 & res fel Victorian Photog, 70; Nat Endowment Arts & Humanities Awards, Col Teacher Seminar, 76. Bibliog: Irving Desfor (auth), Camera News, AP Newsfeatures, 1/58; Jacob Deschin (auth), Ex-Navy Photographer, Army-Navy-Air Force Times 6/59; Ralph Miller (auth), Camera Column, NY World Telegram-Sun, 1/60. Mem: Col Art Asn Am; Soc Photog Educ; George Eastman House Assoc; Visual Studies Workshop. Style & Technique: Black and white silver prints; landscape and architecture as form and symbol. Media: Photography. Res: History and criticism of photography and interrelationships of photography and painting. Publ: Auth, An Un-Victorian Photograph, 70 & Atget and Man Ray in the Context of Surrealism, 76-77, Art J; auth, A View Through a Window, Royal Photog Soc J, 70; auth, Frederick H Evans as Late Victorian, Afterimage, 76; auth, O G Rejlander: From Philistine to Forerunner, Exposure, 76. Mailing Add: Box 373 Fancher Ave Fair Haven NY 13064

FULLER, MARY (MARY FULLER MCCHESNEY)
SCULPTOR, WRITER
b Wichita, Kans, Oct 20, 22. Study: Univ Calif, Berkeley, AA, 43. Work: San Francisco Gen Hosp; Andrew Hill High Sch, San Jose, Calif; Children's Sculpture Garden, Community Ctr, Salinas, Calif; Univ Calif Med Ctr, San Francisco. Comn: Sun, Moon, Stars, Rain, comn by Anshen-Mays, Sausalito, Calif, 71; Temko Lion, comn by Becky & Allan Temko, Berkeley, 71; Kneibler Totem, comn by B Kneibler, San Francisco, 72; Dos Liones, San Francisco Art Comn, 74; Star Tail Lion, comn by Nancy Davidson Short, Sunset Mag. Exhib: San Francisco Mus Art, 47-50 & 60; Bolles Gallery, 61 & Gump's Gallery, San Francisco, 65; Calif State Univ, Sonoma, Cotati, 71; Santa Rosa City Hall, Calif, 74. Collections Arranged: Period of Exploration (with catalog), Oakland Mus, 73. Pos: Researcher, Arch Am Art, 64-65; Ford Found fel, 65-66; writer, Currant Mag, San Francisco, 75-; Nat Endowment Arts art critic grant, 75. Awards: First Prize Ceramic Sculpture, Pac Coast Ceramic Ann, 47 & 49; Merit Award, San Francisco Art Festival, 71. Style & Technique: Carved concrete; direct method; work influenced by pre-Columbian. Publ: Auth, Ad Reinhardt, 10/70 & Was there a San Francisco school?, 1/71, Artforum; auth, A conversation with Louis Ribak, Southwest Art Gallery Mag, 5/72; auth, Porcelain by Richard Shaw & Robert Hudson, 10/73 & Michael Frimkess and the cultured pot, 12/73, Craft Horizons; auth, What's in the package? Is Christo Javacheff all wrapped up?, 4/75 & A conversation with Harold Paris, 6/75, Currant; plus many others. Mailing Add: 2955 Mountain Rd Petaluma CA 94952

FULLER, R BUCKMINSTER
DESIGN SCIENTIST
b Milton, Mass, July 12, 1895. Study: Harvard Univ, 13-15; US Naval Acad, 17; 39 hon doctorates. Work: Mus Mod Art, NY; Mus Sci & Indust, Chicago; Metromedia, NY; Con-Air Corp, NJ. Comn: Geodesic DEW Line Radome, Octe-truss & Tensegrity Mast, Mus Mod Art, New York, comn by US, 54; US Pavilion, Moscow, USSR, comn by US, 59; Climatron, St Louis, Mo, 60; US Geodesic Pavilion for Expo 67, Montreal World's Fair, Can, comn by US, 67; Radome Mt Fuji, Japan, 73. Exhib: Dymaxion House, Harvard Soc Contemp Art, Harvard Univ, Cambridge, Mass, 29; Dymaxion House, Am Inst Archit, Washington, DC, 30; Dymaxion Automobile, Chicago World's Fair, Ill, 33; Dymaxion Bathroom, Mus Mod Art, New York, 37, Dymaxion Deployment Unit, 40, Dymaxion World Map, 43, Dymaxion Car No 2 of 1934, 68 & Tetrascroll, 76; Comprehensive Exhibition of Work, Spoleto Festival, Italy, 67; traveling exhib covering three periods of R Buckminster Fuller's life, Dymaxion Period, 1927-1944, Energetic-Synergetic Geometry Period, 1944-1964 & World Resources Management Period, 1964-, Mus Sci & Indust, 73; Minneapolis Inst Art, Minn, Ont Sci Ctr, Don Mills, Can, Franklin Inst Sci Mus, Philadelphia, Pa, Saidye Bronfman Ctr, Montreal, Que & Calif Mus Sci & Indust, Los Angeles, 74; Des Moines Ctr Sci & Indust, Iowa, 75; Synergetics, Cooper-Hewitt Mus Design, 76; Fifty Years of Buckminster Fuller, Feldman Gallery, New York, 77-78. Teaching: Emer prof, Southern Ill Univ, 59- & Univ Pa, 73- Awards: 1957 Gran Premio, Triennale de Milan, Italy, 58; Gold Medal, Nat Inst Arts & Letters, 68; Gold Medal, Am Inst Archit, 70. Bibliog: Cover story, The Dymaxion American, Time Mag, Vol 83, No 2; Donald Hugh Kenner (auth), Bucky—A Guided Tour of B F, William Morrow & Co, Inc, New York, 73; Donald Robertson (auth), Mind's Eye of Buckminster Fuller, Vantage Press Inc, New York, 74. Mem: Hon fel, Royal Acad Fine Art, The Hague, Neth; hon fel, Royal Inst Brit Archit; fel, Am Inst Archit; Mex Col & Inst of Archit; hon mem, Soc Venezuelan Archit. Publ: Auth, Operating Manual for Space Ship Earth, E P Dutton & Co, Inc, New York, 77; auth, Synergetics: Explorations in the Geometry of Thinking, Macmillan Co, New York, 75, auth, And It Came to Pass Not to Stay, 76.

Dealer: Ronald Feldman Gallery 33 E 74th St New York NY 10021. Mailing Add: 3500 Market St Philadelphia PA 19104

FULLER, SUE
SCULPTOR
b Pittsburgh, Pa. Study: Carnegie Inst Technol, BA, 36; Columbia Univ Teachers Col, MA, 39; and with Hans Hofmann, S W Hayter & Josef Albers. Work: Metrop Mus Art & Whitney Mus Am Art, New York; Nat Collection Fine Arts, Smithsonian Inst, Washington, DC; Tate Gallery, London; Guggenheim Mus, New York; plus others. Comn: String Composition 52, comn by M Greef for bd rm, Com Investment Trust, New York, 53; String Composition 200, comn by Mr & Mrs Ed Forst, San Diego, Calif, 60; String Composition 900, comn by Ruth Walker, Brookline, Mass, 69; String Composition 901, comn by Martha Lou Schove, Pittsburgh, Pa, 70; String Composition T-250, Emerson Crocker Mem for Gail Borden Pub Libr, Elgin, Ill, 72. Exhib: First Biennial Sao Paulo, Brazil, 50; Abstract Art in America, Mus Mod Art, New York, 51; Edward Root Collection, Metrop Mus Art, New York, 53; Plastics USA, US Info Agency traveling exhib, USSR, 61; Responsive Eye, Mus Mod Art, New York, 65. Teaching: Instr mobile design, Mus Mod Art, New York, 45-47; guest artist, Univ Ga, 51-52; instr art, Columbia Univ Teachers Col, 52 & 58; instr two-dimensional design, Pratt Inst, 65-66. Pos: Artist for indust design firm, 55-57. Awards: Guggenheim fel, 48; Tiffany fel, 49; Nat Inst Arts & Lett Grant, 50. Bibliog: Ruth Lester (auth), String patterns, artist works with colorful twine, Life Mag, 8/31/49; Stacy Jones (auth), Artist devises a three dimensional effect, New York Times, 6/21/69; Rosalind Browne (auth), Sue Fuller: threading transparency, Art Int, 1/20/72. Mem: Soc Am Graphic Artists (vpres, Soc Am Etchers, 46-51); Comt Art Educ, Mus Mod Art (coun mem, 49-52); Artists Equity Asn New York (vpres, 52-53). Style & Technique: Constructivist. Media: Plastic, String. Publ: Auth, Mary Cassatt's use of soft-ground etching, Mag Art, 2/50; auth, 20th century cat's cradle, Craft Horizons, 4/54; auth, String composition (movie), NY State Coun Arts, 70; auth (with film maker Maurice Amar), String Composition (video cassette), 74. Dealer: Chalette Int 9 E 88th St New York NY 10028. Mailing Add: PO Box 1580 Southampton NY 11968

FULTON, FRED FRANKLIN
PAINTER
b Leslie, Idaho, Sept 27, 20. Study: Univ Fla; Mt San Antonio Col; spec study with Manuelito Leal, Guanajuato, Mex. Work: State Capitol & Cult Inst, Chihuahua, Mex; City Hall, Juarez, Mex. Exhib: Cult Inst, Chihuahua, 72 & Mexicali, Mex, 74; Univ Guanajuato, 73. Mem: Carlsbad NMex Art Asn; El Paso Tex Art Asn; CEDAM Int. Style & Technique: Modernistic, primitive, real life. Media: Oil, Acrylic. Mailing Add: 5121 Harlan Dr El Paso TX 79924

FULTON, W JOSEPH
CONSULTANT, LECTURER
b Longmont, Colo, Apr 8, 23. Study: Univ Colo, joint-hon scholar, 40-44, BFA, 44; Harvard Univ, James Rogers Rich & Townsend scholars, 45-46, AM, 46, grad fel, 46-47; Belg-Am Educ Found fel, 51; Fulbright fel to France, 53-54. Collections Arranged: Pioneer American Moderns, Norfolk Mus, Va, 53; The Blue Four, 55 & California Design, 57, Pasadena Art Mus, Calif; Marsden Hartley, Univ Southern Calif & Univ Tex, 68-69. Teaching: Lectr, The Museum & the Community, 19th & 20th Century Art, American Decorative Arts, clubs & civic groups & other lect to cols & univs; asst prof art hist, Mass Col Art, 60-63; vis prof, Univ Tex, 68-69; lectr, 69- Pos: Asst dir, Norfolk Mus, 51-53; dir, Pasadena Art Mus, 53-57; assoc, Maury A Bromsen Assocs, 58-63, vpres, 63-; asst dir, Okla Art Ctr, summer 63; cur collections, La State Mus, 66-68; actg chief cur, Univ Art Mus, Univ Tex, 68-69; mus consult, 69- Mem: Col Art Asn Am; Am Asn Mus; Soc Archit Historians; Am Asn Univ Prof. Mailing Add: 1331 E 14th Ave 7 Denver CO 80218

FUMAGALLI, BARBARA MERRILL
PRINTMAKER, ILLUSTRATOR
b Kirkwood, Mo, Mar 15, 26. Study: Univ Iowa, Iowa City, BFA, 48, MFA, 50, with Mauricio Lasansky. Work: Mus of Mod Art, New York; Nelson A Rockefeller Collection, New York; Univ Ill, Urbana; Univ Iowa, Iowa City; Hamline Univ, St Paul, Minn. Exhib: Walker Art Ctr, Minneapolis, Minn, 49, 56 & 63; Am Artists in Florence, Davanzati Palace, Florence, Italy, 51; Young Am Printmakers, Mus of Mod Art, New York, 53; Philadelphia Print Club, 46, 47, 48, 49 & 54; Graphic Arts—USA, Univ Ill, Urbana, 54; Libr of Cong, Washington, DC, 54 & 66; one-person shows, Tweed Gallery, Univ Minn, Duluth, 55, Univ Minn, St Paul, 64, Univ Minn, Minneapolis, 65, Concordia Col, Moorhead, Minn, 65, Suzanne Kohn Gallery, St Paul, 67, Hamline Univ, St Paul, 69, Paine Art Ctr & Arboretum, Oshkosh, Wis, 73; Smithsonian Inst Travelling Exhib, 66-68; NW Printmakers, Seattle Art Mus, Wash, 66-69. Awards: Post Facto Prize, City Art Mus, St Louis, Mo, 47; Purchase Prize, Univ Ill, 54; Best in Show, Arrowhead Art Exhib, 63. Bibliog: Donald M Anderson (auth), Elements of Design, Holt, Rinehart & Winston, 61. Style & Technique: Engravings on copper ranging from small to large; linear; lines vary from delicate to black; naturalistic to optical. Media: Engravings: copper; illustrations in pen and ink. Publ: Illusr, Swing Around the Sun, Lerner Publ, 65. Mailing Add: Rte 4 Box 282A Menomonie WI 54751

FUMAGALLI, ORAZIO
EDUCATOR
b Taranto, Italy, Feb 21, 21; US citizen. Study: Univ Iowa, BA, 48, MFA, 50, PhD, 61. Exhib: Wis Sculptors, Madison Art Ctr, 65; Madison Art Salon, Univ Wis, 65; Biennial Painting & Sculpture, Walker Art Ctr, Minneapolis, 66; Computer Art, Tweed Mus, Univ Minn, Duluth, 71. Teaching: Assoc prof art hist, Univ Minn, Duluth, 60-64; prof art, chmn dept, Univ Wis-Stout, 64- Pos: Educ cur, Tweed Gallery, Univ Minn, Duluth, 54-57, cur, 57-60, assoc dir, 60-64; dir univ gallery, Univ Wis-Stout, 64- Awards: Fulbright Grant study in Italy, 50; Belg-Am Found Fel, 56. Mem: Col Art Asn; Mid-Am Col Art Asn; Wis Art Educ Asn; Am Asn Mus; Midwest Mus Conf. Publ: Auth & producer, A House Divided (film), Lincoln-Douglas Debates, 74; auth, Exhibition monographs on contemporary American artists and on thematic exhibitions, 74- Mailing Add: Dept Art Univ Wis-Stout Menomonie WI 54751

FUNK, CHARLOTTE M
WEAVER
b Milwaukee, Wis, Sept 27, 34. Study: Univ Wis-Whitewater, BS, 71; Ill State Univ, Normal, MS, 75, MFA, 76. Comn: Planar Exchange (8ft x 14ft), comn by Borg-Warner Corp, Chicago, Ill, 76. Exhib: Technology and the Artist, Craftsman, Iowa, 73; 7th Int Biennial Tapestry, Lausanne, Switz, 75; Contemporary Crafts of the Americas, Colo, 75; Wisconsin Directions, Milwaukee Art Ctr, 75; Convergence, Carnegie Inst Int, Pittsburgh, 76; Clay, Fiber, Metal—Women Artists, Bronx Mus of Arts, New York, 78. Teaching: Instr textiles, Tex Tech Univ, Lubbock, 78. Awards: Wis Designer/Craftsmen Award, 57; Judges Choice Award, Contemp Crafts Americas, Handweavers Guild Am, 75. Mem: Am Craftsmens Coun; Handweavers Guild Am. Style & Technique: Twill-tapestry which presents the illusion of form on a flat surface (of weaving). Media: Weaving in Wools. Dealer: Jacques Baruch Gallery 900 N Michigan Chicago IL 60611. Mailing Add: 2312 58th St Lubbock TX 79412

FUNK, VERNE J
CERAMIST, EDUCATOR
b Milwaukee, Wis, July 19, 32. Study: Univ Wis-Milwaukee, BS, MS & MFA. Work: Milwaukee Art Ctr; Johnson Found, Racine, Wis; Lannon Found, Palm Beach, Fla; Kenosha Mus, Wis; Kohler Art Ctr, Sheboygan, Wis; Objects: USA. Comn: Trophy, Gov Awards for the Arts, Wis, 69. Exhib: Objects: USA; Clayworks, 20 Americans, Mus Contemp Crafts, New York, 71; Chicago & Vicinity Show, Chicago Art Inst, 71 & 73; Plastic Earth, Kohler Art Ctr, Wis, 73; Ceramics Int, Calgary, Can, 73. Teaching: Guest artist ceramics, Calif State Univ, Fresno, 72-73; prof ceramics & dir art sch, Bradley Univ, Peoria, Ill, 73-77; assoc prof ceramics, Tex Tech Univ, Lubbock, 77- Pos: Chmn, Visual Arts II, Wis Arts Found & Coun, 67; pres, Wis Designer-Craftsmen, 64-66. Awards: Beloit & Vicinity Show, 70; Wisconsin Designer-Crafts Award, Milwaukee Art Ctr, 70 & 72. Bibliog: Donald Key (auth), Prominent Wisconsin potters, Milwaukee J, 72. Mem: Am Craftsmen's Coun (state rep to NCent region, 68). Style & Technique: Ceramic objects in clay, usually using ceramic decals or drawing with underglaze pencil. Publ: Contribr, Objects: USA (catalog), 69; contribr, Complete Book of Ceramic Art, 72; contribr, New Ceramics, 74. Dealer: Collectors Gallery Milwaukee Art Ctr on the Lakefront Milwaukee WI 53201. Mailing Add: 2312 58th St Lubbock TX 79412

FURMAN, AARON & JOYCE
ART DEALERS, COLLECTORS
b New York, NY, Apr 25, 26 (Mr Furman) & June 9, 30 (Mrs Furman). Pos: Co-owners, Furman Gallery. Specialty: Primitive and archaeological arts. Collection: Mother and child subject in primitive art; twentieth century paintings, drawings and sculpture; primitive art. Mailing Add: Furman Gallery Inc 26 E 80th St New York NY 10021

FURMAN, DAVID STEPHEN
SCULPTOR, EDUCATOR
b Seattle, Wash, Aug 15, 45. Study: Univ Ore, BA(ceramics), 69; Univ Wash, MFA(ceramics & glassblowing), 72. Work: Univ Puget Sound Mus Art; Marietta Col Art Mus; Brand Art Mus, Glendale, Calif. Exhib: 45 Sculptors, US Info Serv World Tour, 73; Clay (ceramic sculpture), Whitney Mus, 74; one-man shows, David Stuart Galleries, 74-75; Small Scale in Contemporary Art, Chicago Art Inst, 75; Hard and Clear, Los Angeles Co Art Mus, 75; plus many others. Teaching: Prof sculpture, Claremont Grad Sch, Pitzer Col, 73-; instr clay sculpture, Otis Art Inst, 75- Awards: Juror's & Purchase Award, Marietta Col Art Mus, 74; Brand Art Ctr Purchase Award, Glendale, Calif, 75; Nat Endowment for Arts Fel, 75. Bibliog: C H Hertel (auth), David Furman-Biographical Narrative Sculpture, 74; W C Hunt (auth), David Furman-miniature environments, Ceramics Monthly, 1/75; plus others. Mem: World Crafts Coun; Am Crafts Coun; Nat Coun Educ Ceramic Arts; Artists Equity. Style & Technique: Environments and landscapes (miniature) in clay and sculpture with handbuilt techniques. Media: Clay, Paint & Glaze. Dealer: David Stuart Galleries 807 N La Cienega Blvd Los Angeles CA 90069. Mailing Add: Pitzer Col Art Dept 1150 Mills Ave Claremont CA 91711

FURR, JIM
PAINTER, PRINTMAKER
b Camden, Tenn, Aug 14, 39. Study: Univ of Tenn, BFA; Tulane Univ, MFA; Tamarind Inst of Lithography. Work: Montgomery Mus Fine Arts, Ala; Laguna Gloria Art Mus, Austin, Tex; Kans State Univ, Lawrence; Ill State Univ, Normal; Omni Int Hotel, Miami, Fla. Exhib: 8th Dulin Nat Print & Drawing, Knoxville, Tenn, 72; 2nd Hawaii Nat Print Exhib, Univ Hawaii, Honolulu, 73; Colorprint USA, Lubbock, Tex, 73; 2nd Miami Graphics Int Biennial, Fla, 75; Drawings USA 75, traveling, Minn Mus Art, St Paul, 75; 35 Artists in the Southeast, traveling, High Mus Art, Atlanta, Ga, 76; Drawing by Southeastern Artists, Southeastern Ctr for Contemp Art, Winston-Salem, 77; one-person show, Tex A&I Univ, Kingsville, 74. Teaching: Sabbatical replacement printmaking, Tulane Univ, New Orleans, La, 73-74; vis artist printmaking, Tex A&I Univ, Kingsville, 74-75; asst prof lithography & drawing, Auburn Univ, Ala, 77- Awards: Best in Show & Mus Purchase, 14th Dixie Ann, Montgomery Mus of Fine Arts, 73; Best in Show & Purchase Award, Mid-Western Graphics Ann, Tulsa, Okla, 73; Best Graphics Award, 14 Mid-East Biennial, Joslyn Art Mus, Omaha, Nebr, 76. Mem: Southeastern Graphics Coun; Philadelphia Print Club; Graphics Soc. Style & Technique: Nonobjective color paintings, abstract charcoal/colage drawings; acid-tint lithographs. Media: Mixed Acrylics (Painting); Lithography, Etching (Printmaking). Dealer: Heath Gallery 34 Lombardy Way Atlanta GA 30309; Gallerie Simonne Stern 516 Royal St New Orleans LA 70130. Mailing Add: 1014 Auburn St Opelika AL 36801

FUSSINER, HOWARD
PAINTER
b New York, NY, May 25, 23. Study: Am Peoples Sch, 38-42, with C G Nelson & John Heliker; Art Students League, 46-47; Cooper Union, 47-49, with Robert Gwathmey & John Ferren; Hans Hofmann Sch, 48; NY Univ, 49-52, with Hale Woodruff. Work: Everhart Mus, Scranton, Pa; Staten Island Inst Mus, New York; Slater Mus, Norwich, Conn; Mattatuck Mus, Waterbury, Conn; Colby Jr Col, New London, NH. Comn: Mural, NY Univ, 51-52. Exhib: Pa Acad Fine Arts Biennial, Philadelphia, 62; Silvermine Guild Artists Ann, 62; Boston Arts Festival, 63; Hartford Plaza 7, 64; New Haven Arts Festival, 64; plus many one-man shows. Teaching: Instr humanities, Morehouse Col, 51-55; instr art, Colby Jr Col, 57-60; assoc prof art, Southern Conn State Col, 60- Awards: Best in Show, New Haven Arts Festival & Hartford Plaza 7, 64 & Waterbury Arts Festival, 68. Mem: Col Art Asn Am; Conn Acad Fine Arts. Style & Technique: Neo-fauve; figurative. Media: Oil, Watercolor. Publ: Auth, Organic integration in Cezanne's painting, summer 56, Van Gogh (poem), spring 58 & Use of subject matter in recent art, spring 61, Art J; auth, Uccello's Battle of San Romano (poem), summer 60 & Giotto (poem), winter 61-62, Art J. Dealer: Munson Gallery 33 Whitney Ave New Haven CT 06510. Mailing Add: 1 Everit St New Haven CT 06511

G

GABIN, GEORGE JOSEPH
PAINTER, INSTRUCTOR
b Brooklyn, NY, Apr 16, 31. Study: Brooklyn Mus Art Sch; Art Students League, with Reginald Marsh, Ivan Olinsky & Will Barnett. Work: Repub Savings & Loan, Washington, DC. Exhib: Nat Acad Design, Allied Artists Am & Audubon Artists, 60-77; one-man shows, Carl Seimbab Gallery, 63 & 67, Gallery 7, 65, Guild Boston Artists, 72 & Doll & Richards Gallery, 75; Am Fedn Arts Nat Traveling Show, 64-65. Teaching: Instr illus & drawing, New

Eng Sch Art, Boston, 64-70; instr illus, drawing & painting, Montserrat Sch Visual Arts, 70- Awards: Jane Peterson Prize for Landscape, Allied Artists Am, 71 & Paul Puzinas Prize, 77; Eric Hudson Prize/Lithography, Rockport Art Asn, 77. Mem: Allied Artists Am; Guild Boston Artists; Rockport Art Asn (chmn arts comt, 65-69). Media: Oil. Mailing Add: 18 Antrim St Cambridge MA 02139

GABLIK, SUZI
WRITER, PAINTER
b New York, NY, Sept 26, 34. Study: Black Mountain Col, NC, summer 51; Hunter Col, BA, 55, with Robert Motherwell. Work: Hirshhorn Collection; Sarah Robbie Found. Exhib: Terry Dintenfass, Inc, New York, 72. Bibliog: L Alloway (auth), rev in, Nation, 5/8/72; H Rose (auth), New York letter, Studio Int, 5/72. Mem: Int Asn Art Critics. Style & Technique: Works in collage combining photographs and oil paint on canvas. Publ: Co-auth, Pop art redefined, 69 & auth, Magritte, 70, New York Graphic Soc; auth, Progress in Art, Rizzoli, 77. Dealer: Terry Dintenfass Inc 50 W 57th St New York NY 10022. Mailing Add: 5 Westmoreland St London W 1 England

GABRIEL, HANNELORE
GOLDSMITH
Study: Apprentice under Master Goldsmith-Essen, Ger, 4 yrs; Gewerblicke Unterrichtsanstalt, Essen, Ger. Work: Ft Lauderdale Mus of Fine Arts, Fla. Comn: Presentation piece, Cleveland Area Arts Coun, Ohio, 76. Exhib: Sculpture to Wear, Fifth Ave, New York, 75 & 76; Ann Arbor Art Festival, 75-77; Old Town Art Festival, Chicago, 76 & 77; Plaza Art Festival, Kansas City, 77; Mid Tenn State Univ Craft Exhib, 77; Ariz Nat, Scottsdale, 77; Goldsmiths 77, Phoenix Art Mus, Ariz, 77; May Show, Cleveland Mus of Art, Ohio; Beaux Arts Designer-Craftsmen, Columbus Gallery of Fine Arts, 77. Teaching: Pvt classes, 74-75; teacher, Oberlin Col, 75 & Penland Sch of Crafts, 78- Awards: Winter Park Art Festival Award, 75-77; Miami Beach Festival Arts, 75 & 76; Best of Show/Metals, Las Olas Art Festival, 76. Mem: Am Crafts Coun; Soc NAm Goldsmiths; Ohio Designer-Craftsmen. Mailing Add: 1469 Rosena Ave North Madison OH 44057

GABRIEL, ROBERT A
SCULPTOR
b Cleveland, Ohio, July 21, 31. Study: Cleveland Inst Art; Skowhegan Sch Painting & Sculpture. Comn: Design, Pittsburgh Hilton Hotel; sculpture, Allegheny Ludlum Steel Co; design for Peter Muller-Munk, Gov Proj in Ankara, Turkey, 57-58. Exhib: Cleveland Mus Art Exhib, Pittsburgh, 53-55; Western Pa Sculpture Exhib, 55 & 56; one-man shows, Carnegie Inst, Pittsburgh, 62 & Carnegie-Mellon Univ, Pittsburgh, 68; Mainstreams 69, Marietta, Ohio; plus many others. Teaching: Assoc prof design, Carnegie Inst Technol; instr art, Allegheny Col, 54. Pos: Dir educ, Arts & Crafts Ctr Pittsburgh, 71- Awards: Prize, Wichita, Kans, 53; Mary Page Traveling Scholar, Cleveland Inst Art, 54. Mem: Assoc Artists Pittsburgh (pres, 66-67); Pittsburgh Soc Sculptors (pres, 59-61). Mailing Add: 6307 Hampton St Pittsburgh PA 15206

GACH, GEORGE
PAINTER, SCULPTOR
b Budapest, Hungary, Jan 27, 09; US citizen. Study: Hungarian Acad Fine Art, grad. Work: Hungarian Nat Gallery, Budapest; Suffolk Mus, NY. Comn: Bas reliefs, Methodist Church, Dallas, Tex, 69-70; bronze bas reliefs of Okla hist, Liberty Bank Okla, 72. Exhib: Audubon Artists, Allied Artists, Nat Sculpture Soc; 24 one-man shows, Hammer Galleries, New York, 75-77. Teaching: Instr sculpture, Acad Beirut Lebanon, 48-52. Awards: Scholar, Rome, Italy, 42; Gold Medals, Hudson Valley Art Asn, NY, 59, Nat Sculpture Soc, New York, NY, 70, Art League of Long Island, NY, 77 & Nat Art League, New York, NY, 77; plus others. Mem: Allied Artists Am; Nat Sculpture Soc; Nat Art League; Hudson Valley Art Asn; Nassau Art League. Style & Technique: Classical; impressionistic. Media: Bronze, Wood, Oil, Plastic. Dealer: Hammer Galleries 51 E 57th St New York NY 10022; Country Art Gallery Birth Hill Rd Locust Valley NY 11560. Mailing Add: 212 Willow Roslyn Heights NY 11577

GAGE, FRANCES M
SCULPTOR
b Windsor, Ont, Aug 22, 24. Study: Ont Col Art; Art Students League; Ecole Beaux-Arts, Paris, Royal Soc Can scholar. Work: Rothmans of Can; Univ Western Ont Med Sch; Med Sci Bldg, Toronto; Univ Guelph; marble, Womens Col Hosp, Toronto; bronzes, Univ of Ottawa, McMaster Univ, Hamilton, Ont & Queens Univ, Kingston, Ont; Bronze of Prince Arthur, Toronto. Comn: Crest, Ont Hydro Seaway, Cornwall; Metro Rd Bridges; fountain head, Cancer Hostel, Toronto; fountain, Albright Gardens, London, Ont; figure & reliefs, Prov Inst Trades Bldg, London, Ont; plus many portraits & other sculpture. Exhib: Royal Can Acad Art; Sculptors Soc Can; Ont Soc Art. Mem: Royal Can Acad of Art. Mailing Add: 60 Birch Ave Toronto ON Can

GAGE, HARRY (LAWRENCE)
PAINTER, DESIGNER
b Battle Creek, Mich, Nov 20, 87. Study: Art Inst Chicago, foreign travel scholar; Tucson Watercolor Guild, Ariz. Exhib: Am Artists Prof League; Rockport Art Asn; NShore Arts Asn, Gloucester; Concord Art Asn; Ogunquit Art Asn. Teaching: Prof graphic arts, Carnegie Inst Technol, 12-19; lectr graphic arts, Pratt Inst, 25-30; co-founder & chmn, Annisquam Art Gallery, 54- Awards: Am Inst Graphic Arts Gold Medal, 42; First New Eng Benjamin Franklin Award, Indust Asns New Eng, 59. Mem: Am Inst Graphic Artists (founding chmn bk clin, 30-36, pres, NY chap, 32-35); Am Artists Prof League; NShore Arts Asn; Rockport Art Asn. Style & Technique: Traditional. Media: Watercolor, Typographic Design. Publ: Auth, Applied Design for Printers, United Typothetae Am, 20; co-auth, Composition Manual, Printing Indust Am, 53. Mailing Add: 16 River Rd Annisquam Gloucester MA 01930

GAGLIANI, OLIVER
PHOTOGRAPHER
b 1917. Study: Calif Col Arts & Crafts, MFA, 72. Work: Mus Mod Art, New York; George Eastman House; San Francisco Mus Art; Nat Libr France; plus others. Exhib: 22 one-man shows throughout the US and numerous group shows. Teaching: Instr photog, Univ Calif Exten, San Francisco, 69-; instr photog, Image Circle, Berkeley, 70-; instr photog, Calif Col Arts & Crafts, 72-; grad instr photog, Univ Calif, San Francisco, 74- Pos: Conducted numerous workshops in creative photography. Awards: Nat Endowment for the Arts grant, 76. Publ: Articles in Aperture, Vision & Expression & The Face of California. Mailing Add: 605 Rocca Ave San Francisco CA 94080

GAGNON, CHARLES EUGENE
SCULPTOR
b Minneapolis, Minn, Feb 24, 34. Study: Univ Minn, AA, 56, BS, 58 & MEd, 60; Minneapolis Sch Art, 59; with Berthold Schiwetz, Florence, Italy, 64-65 & with Jacques Lipchitz, 68. Work: Mayo Clin, Rochester, Minn; Rochester Art Ctr; many pvt collections throughout US, Europe, Can & UK. Comn: St Francis and The Birds (ten ft), St Mary's Hosp, Rochester, Minn, 69; Crucifixion (nine ft), Zumbro Lutheran Church, Rochester, 69; Renaissance Man and Woman (ten ft), Kenyon Col, Ohio, 73; Conrad N Hilton (seven ft sculpture), Mayo Clin, Rochester, 74; Creation, Temple Jeremiah, Chicago, 75; plus many others. Exhib: Nat Acad Galleries, New York, 62; Nat Arts Club, New York, 62; Walker Art Ctr Biennial, Minneapolis, 62; Minneapolis Art Inst, 63; one-man show, Defiance Col, 72. Teaching: Instr sculpture, Univ Minn, Rochester, 72; vis artist sculpture, Defiance Col, 72. Awards: One of ten students from US chosen to teach art in Europe, Univ Minn, 57-58; Purchase Award & Two-Man Show Award, Madison Ave Art Gallery, New York, 62. Bibliog: Montoya (auth), American artists, La Rev Mod, Paris, 63; Kling (auth), The Sculpture of Charles E Gagnon, Preview, Collegeville, Minn, 68; Hardie (auth), Charles E Gagnon, Mohave, Kingman, Ariz, 73. Style & Technique: Figurative bronze sculpture; working predominately in the field of large architectural commissions. Media: Bronze. Publ: Contribr, An artist fulfilled, 71; contribr, Progeny, 73; contribr, Kenyon College, Its Third Half Century, 75; contribr, An Art Tour of Saint Mary's, 75; contribr, Voice of a New Age, 76. Mailing Add: PO Box 4 Rochester MN 55901

GAHMAN, FLOYD
PAINTER
b Elida, Ohio. Study: Valparaiso Univ; Columbia Univ; also with Hobart Nichols & Henry Varnum Poor. Work: Pa State Univ; Ind Univ. Exhib: Allied Artists Am Ann, New York, 30; Nat Acad Design Ann, New York, 32-; New York World's Fair, 39; Hudson Valley Art Asn Ann, NY, 50-; Acad Artists, Springfield, Mass, 59. Teaching: Lectr painting, Pa State Univ, Ogontz Ctr, 46-59. Awards: Tiffany Found fel, 33-36; Landscape Prize, Allied Artists Am, 42 & Acad Artists, 59. Mem: Nat Acad Design; Salmagundi Club; Acad Artists; Allied Artists Am; Hudson Valley Art Asn. Style & Technique: Realistic. Media: Oil, Watercolor. Mailing Add: 90 La Salle St New York NY 10027

GAINES, ALAN JAY
PAINTER, PRINTMAKER
b New York, NY, Aug 23, 42. Study: NY Univ, BS, 65; New School/Parsons Sch of Design, with John Ross, 72-74. Work: South Street Seaport Mus, Mus Gallery, New York; Ainsworth Gallery, Boston; Impressions Workshop, Boston. Comn: Historic Ships of America (series of four etchings), The Franklin Mint, Franklin Center, Pa, 74 & Famous American Ships (series of two etchings), 75; Nantucket Whalers & New Bedford Whalers, comn by Collector's Guild, New York, NY, 77 & Develop of Am Transportation, 78; Gloucester Schooners (etching), comn by Bk of the Month Club & 260 Club, 77; marine etchings (incl Sloop Providence at Newport), comn by Graphics Guild, Div of Doubleday, New York, 77 & two railroad etchings, 78; spec series five important & hist Am ships, comn by Am Express, 78. Exhib: One-man shows, South Street Seaport Mus, 74, Oestreicher Gallery, New York, 74, Gallerie DeNautique, Newport, RI, 76 & Wiseman Gallery, Newport, RI, 76. Bibliog: Joseph Patrick Henry (auth), Artist of the sea, The Franklin Mint Almanac, 7/75. Style & Technique: Marine, railroad & Western artist—sailing ships, steamships, port scenes, railroad & Western scenes, & archit. Media: Etchings, Aquatints. Mailing Add: 45 Ayrault St Newport RI 02840

GAINES, WILLIAM ROBERT
ART HISTORIAN, PAINTER
b Madison, Va, Aug 12, 27. Study: Pa Mil Col; Va Commonwealth Univ, BFA; Columbia Univ, MFA; and with Renato Guttuso. Work: Univ Va, Charlottesville; Va Polytech Inst & State Univ, Blacksburg; Retreat for the Sick, Richmond; Philip Morris Inc; First & Merchants Nat Bank. Exhib: Five Va Artists Biennials, 49-63; Abingdon Sq Painters, New York, 53; Va Beach Boardwalk Exhib, 58; Va Commonwealth Univ, 64; one-man exhib, Tappahannock, Va, 72. Collections Arranged: Art Nouveau (with catalog); Francisco Goya: Portraits in Paintings, Prints & Drawings (with catalog), 72; Sculpture by Willi Gutmann, 72; 12 American Painters (with catalog), 74. Teaching: Instr painting, drawing & art hist, Va Mus, Richmond, 54-56, 57 & 62; dir, Gov Sch Gifted, Mus Ctr, 73. Pos: Registr, Va Mus, 51-53, artmobile cur, 53-54, supvr educ, 54-56, 57-62, head progs div, 62- Awards: Best in Show Awards, Va Beach Boardwalk Exhib, 58 & Thalhimers Invitational, 63. Mem: Am Asn Mus (chmn accreditation comt); Assoc Couns of Arts. Style & Technique: Extreme foreshortened figure and landscape treated in fairly realistic manner; formal emphasis is on placement of subject, often above eye level, and on light. Media: Oil, Acrylic. Publ: Auth, Art kits, Arts Va, Vol VI, No I; auth, Virginia Museum: two pioneer programs, Mus News, Vol 50, No 2; TV progs produced, 12 American Painters, 74 & Style, Form & Expression: Encounter I, 75. Mailing Add: 206 N Meadow St Richmond VA 23220

GAINS, JACOB
PAINTER
b Vilna, Poland; US citizen. Study: Nat Acad Design; New York Sch Fine & Appl Art; Educ Alliance; also with Adja Yunkers & William Baziotes. Work: Montclair Art Mus, NJ. Exhib: Knickerbocker Artists, Riverside Mus, New York, 57; Newark Mus, NJ, 59; Nat Acad Design Ann, New York, 61; Painters & Sculptors Soc Exhib, Jersey City Mus, NJ, 63; Montclair Art Mus, 66. Awards: Jersey City Mus Tercentenary Award, 60; First Prize & Medal of Honor, Painters & Sculptors Soc, 63; Permanent Collection Purchase Award, Montclair Art Mus, 66. Mem: Painters & Sculptors Soc; Miami Art League. Style & Technique: Semi-abstract. Media: Oil, Woodcut. Dealer: Freda Kruse 1007 Kane Concourse Bay Harbor Island Miami Beach FL 33154. Mailing Add: 400 Kings Point Dr Miami Beach FL 33160

GAITHER, EDMUND B
MUSEUM DIRECTOR, ART HISTORIAN
b Great Falls, SC, Oct 6, 44. Study: Morehouse Col, BA, 66; Ga State Col; Brown Univ, MA, 68. Collections Arranged: Afro-Am Artists: New York & Boston (with catalogue), Jamaica Art Since the Thirties, Henry O Tanner, A Romantic Realist, Home Folks Africa, For Us, Abdias Do Nascimento: A Brazilian Brother, African Gods in Brazil, Our Elders, Crite & Dames, Ah Haiti, Glimpses of Voudou, Haiti-Haiti, Bannister & Duncanson, Twentieth Century Afro-Am Artists, Mus Fine Arts, Boston. Teaching: Asst prof art hist, Boston Univ, 70-78; lectr art hist, Wellesley Col & Harvard Col, 71-76. Pos: Dir & cur, Mus Nat Ctr Afro-Am Artists, Boston, 69-; dir visual arts prog, Elma Lewis Sch Fine Arts, Boston, 69-; spec consult, Mus Fine Arts, Boston, 69- Bibliog: An American Collector, Mus Art, RI Sch Design, Providence, 68; Robert H Glauber (auth), Black American Artists, Ill Bell Tel Co, 71; Leo Twiggs (auth), Opinion, Mus News, 5/72. Mem: Nat Conf Artists; Col Art Asn; Pan-African Conf of Artists; Boston Negro Artists Asn. Res: Historical and critical discussion of Afro-American art. Publ: Contribr, A new criticism needed, New York Times, 5/70; ed, Affairs of Black Artists, 71; contribr, Artists Proofs, The Annual of Prints and Printmaking, NY Graphic Soc, 72; contribr, Afro-American Art, in: Negro Reference Book, Phelps-Stokes Found, New York, NY, 73; and numerous others. Mailing Add: 598 Walk Hill St Mattapan MA 02126

GALANIN, IGOR IVANOVICH
PAINTER, ILLUSTRATOR
b Moscow, USSR, June 19, 37; immigrated to US, 72. Study: With G Shchetinin & B Chernyshev. Comn: Set designs for Moscow Art Theatre, 68, Moscow Operetta Theatre, 69 & Bolshoi Theatre, Moscow, 71. Exhib: Paesi Nuovi Gallery, Rome, 72; Fishers Island, NY, 73-74; Village Gallery, Croton-on-Hudson, NY, 74 & 77; Young Artists 75, New York, 75; Brandeis Univ, Mass, 75; Pucker-Safrai Gallery, Boston, Mass, 75 & 76; Andre Emmerich Gallery, New York, 76; London Gallery, Montreal, 77; Aberbach Fine Arts Gallery, New York, 78. Style & Technique: Fantasy realism. Media: Acrylic on canvas. Dealer: Aberbach Fine Arts 988 Madison Ave New York NY. Mailing Add: 792 Pines Bridge Rd PO Box 430 Millwood NY 10546

GALE, PEGGY
ART WRITER
b Mackenzie, Guyana, May 18, 44; Can citizen. Study: Univ Toronto, 63-67; Univ degli Studi, Florence, Italy, 65-66; Univ Toronto, BA, 67. Teaching: Instr, Nova Scotia Col Art & Design; instr, Vancouver Art Gallery; lectr video, 77- Pos: Educ officer, Art Gallery of Ont, Toronto, 67-74; asst film & video officer, Can Coun, Ottawa, 74-75; video dir, Art Metropole, Toronto, 75- Publ: Ed & contribr, Video by Artists, Art Metropole, 76; auth, Video art in Canada: Four worlds, Studio Int, 5-6/76; auth, Video, regard introspectif, Vie Des Arts, 3/77; auth, Video has captured our imagination, Parachute, summer 77; ed, Performance by Artists, Art Metropole, (in press). Mailing Add: c/o Art Metropole 241 Yonge St Toronto ON M5B 1N8 Can

GALE, WILLIAM HENRY
PAINTER, DESIGNER
b Yonkers, NY, May 3, 15. Study: Columbia Univ; Art Students League; Nat Acad Design; Cooper Union; spec study with John Pike & Charles Kinghan. Work: Springfield Fine Arts Mus, Mass; Jasper Rand Mus, Westfield, Mass; Vt Art Ctr, Manchester; Manhattan Savings Bank, New York. Comn: New Eng Landmarks, comn by Anthony Jutt, Housatonic, NY, 70; Old Vt Landmarks, New York Life Ins Co, 72; varied subj, comn by Milton Bradley, East Longmeadow, Mass, 73; paintings of hist bldgs, comn by Dr Messner, Starksboro, Vt, 74 & Springfield hist campanile, comn by Dr Allan Peck, Springfield, 75. Exhib: Nat Acad Design, 67-70; Am Watercolor Soc, New York, 68-73; Smithsonian Inst, 69; Mus Fine Arts, Springfield, Mass, 69-75; Worcester Mus Fine Arts, Mass, 74-75. Pos: Artist-designer, Ruth Ruthrauff & Ryan, New York, 35-40; art dir-designer, Batten Barton Durstine, Osborn, New York, 40-68. Awards: Quimby Award, Smithsonian Inst, 69; Schults Award, Mus Fine Arts Acad Artists, 74; First Awards Mass Bicentennial, Springfield Fine Arts Mus, 75; plus many others. Bibliog: Lee Sheridan (auth), New England painter, Springfield News, Mass, 63; Watercolorists, Festival of the Arts, Vt Art Ctr, 69. Mem: Am Watercolor Soc; Salmagundi Club; Rockport Art Asn; Acad Artists (vpres, 73-75); Hudson Valley Art Asn (bd mem). Style & Technique: Landscape, still life and portrait in realistic and semi-realistic manner and design. Media: Watercolor, Oil. Dealer: Grand Central Art Gallery 40 Vanderbilt Ave New York NY 10017. Mailing Add: 14 Hunting Lane Box 156 Wilbraham MA 01095

GALEN, ELAINE
PAINTER, SCULPTOR
b New York, NY, July 12, 28. Study: Philadelphia Mus Sch Art, dipl, 50; Univ Pa, BA, 51; Art Students League, 55-59; NY Univ, MA, 63; major study with Morris Kantor. Work: Philadelphia Mus Art; Mus Rigaud, France; Rey Collection, Perpignan, France; Atelier 45; numerous pub & pvt collections, including Governor's State Univ & Univ Houston. Comn: Images from the Wind (portfolio, also co-auth), NY, 62 & Mythic Encounters (litho suite), Chicago, 74, Ed Du Grenier. Exhib: Whitney Mus Am Art Ann, New York, 61; Brooklyn Mus Int, 63; NJ State Arts Coun, 70; one-man show, Pa Acad Fine Arts, Peale House, 72; State Mus Ill, 74; numerous one-man shows and others. Teaching: Lectr hist of art, painting & drawing, NY Univ, 70-73 & Prairie State Col, Chicago Heights, Ill, 74- Pos: Teacher studio arts, Princeton & Hunterdon Ctrs, NJ, 67-72; consult & lectr-teacher, Developing Art Progs, NJ Schs, 68-72. Awards: Chautauqua Inst First Prize for Painting, 63; Nat Print Award, Hunterdon Ctr, NJ, 70; Am Iron & Steel Inst Award for Design Excellence, 72; plus others. Bibliog: In New York (TV presentation), Metro Media TV, 69; The dominant thing, East Village Other, 69. Mem: Print Club, Philadelphia (artist mem); Chicago Artists Coalition; Col Art Asn Am. Style & Technique: Abstract-Surreal; sculpture relates painterly technique in painting medium. Media: Oil, Pencil-Ink; Stainless Steel. Publ: Auth, In Forms (litho suite), Paris, 68. Dealer: Douglas Kenyon Gallery 230 E Ohio St Chicago IL 60657. Mailing Add: 3100 N Sheridan Rd Chicago IL 60657

GALLANDER, CATHLEEN S
MUSEUM DIRECTOR
b San Antonio, Tex, Feb 4, 31. Study: Univ Tex, Austin, BA(sociol); Harvard Univ, scholar art hist; Harvard Bus Sch, Inst Arts Admin. Pos: Dir, Art Mus of S Tex, Corpus Christi. Mem: Col Art Asn Am; Am Asn Mus; Am Fedn Arts; Western Asn Art Mus; Asn Art Mus Dir. Mailing Add: Art Mus of South Texas 1902 N Shoreline Corpus Christi TX 78402

GALLENKAMP, PATRICIA
ART DEALER
Pos: Owner & dir, Janus Gallery. Specialty: Contemporary art of the Southwest; painting, sculpture and graphics. Mailing Add: c/o Janus Gallery 116 1/2 E Palace Ave Santa Fe NM 87501

GALLES, ARIE ALEXANDER
EDUCATOR, ART ADMINISTRATOR
b Tashkent, Russia, Oct 29, 44; US citizen. Study: Temple Univ, BFA, 68; Univ Wis, MFA, 71. Teaching: Chmn fine arts dept, Fairleigh Dickinson Univ, Madison, 72- Pos: Dir, Madison Acad of Art & Morris Gallery, 77- Dealer: O K Harris Works of Art 383 W Broadway New York NY 10012. Mailing Add: 60 Main St Madison NJ 07940

GALLI, STANLEY WALTER
ILLUSTRATOR, PAINTER
b San Francisco, Calif. Study: Calif Sch Fine Arts, San Francisco; Art Ctr Sch, Los Angeles. Work: Air Force Mus, Colo; Baseball Hall of Fame Mus, Cooperstown, NY. Comn: Tree & wildlife conserv series for nat advert, Weyerhaeuser Co, Tacoma, Wash, 52-68; wildlife paintings, Calif Casualty Group Collection, San Mateo, 73-78. Exhib: One-man shows, Foremost McKesson Corp Hq Gallery, 74 & Nut Tree Gallery, Calif, 76; NY Hist Soc, 77; Oakland Mus, Calif, 78; two-man show, Palm Springs Desert Mus, Calif, 78. Teaching: Instr advert art, San Francisco City Col, 68-76. Pos: Illusr, Saturday Evening Post, 50-68, Reader's Digest Mag, Reader's Digest Condensed Bks, 60-78, McCall's Mag, 60-67 & US Postal Serv Stamp Design, 68-78. Awards: Gold Medal & Silver Medal, Detroit Art Dir Club, 56-58; Silver Medal, Dillon Lauritzen Award, Los Angeles Art Dir Club, 58; Best US Postage Stamp of Yr, Postal Commemorative Soc, 68, 72 & 78. Mem: Soc Animal Artists; Soc Illusr. Style & Technique: Wildlife and paintings of the Spanish Colonial Period in the West and Southwest. Media: Oil and Acrylic on Canvas. Mailing Add: PO Box 66 Kentfield CA 94904

GALLO, ENZO D
SCULPTOR
b Italy, Oct 25, 27. Study: San Alejandro Univ/Fine Arts, Havana, Cuba, MFA; Hollywood Fla Univ, BA; study with Jose Sicri, sculptor & Augusto Valderoma, painter, in Havana. Work: Pagani Mus, Milan, Italy; Young Circle, Hollywood, Fla; Town of Padua, Italy. Comn: Sculpture & mosaic murals, Hollywood Mem Gardens, Fla; mosaic murals, Am Savings & Loan, Miami Beach & Presidential Towers Lobby, Hollywood, Fla; sculpture, Doral Beach Club, Miami Beach. Exhib: Biannual Art Exhib, Mus Bella Arts, Havana, Cuba, 57, 58 & 59; Hollywood Mus, Fla; Bacardi Gallery, Miami, 71; New Orleans Mus Art, La, 73; Mus Pagani, Milan, Italy; Metrop Mus, Miami, 75; one-man shows, Heller Bldg, Miami, 77 & Hollywood Art & Cult Ctr, Hollywood, Fla. Teaching: Prof sculpture, San Alejandro Inst Fine Arts, Havana, Cuba & Broward Adult Educ, 62-65. Awards: Award of Merit, Am Inst Architects; First Prize Sculpture, Seven Lively Arts, Hollywood, Fla. Mem: Fla Sculpture Asn; Artist Equity Asn Fla (pres, 75-78). Style & Technique: Semi-abstract. Media: Marble, Bronze. Dealer: Gertrude Freeman (artist rep) 6959 Sunrise Dr Coral Gables FL 33133. Mailing Add: 500 N Ansin Blvd Hallandale FL 33009

GALLO, FRANK
SCULPTOR, EDUCATOR
b Toledo, Ohio, Jan 13, 33. Study: Toledo Mus Sch Art, BFA, 54; Cranbrook Acad Art, 55; Univ Iowa, MFA, 59. Work: Mus Mod Art, New York; Whitney Mus Am Art, New York; Art Inst Chicago; Los Angeles Mus Art; Cleveland Mus Art; plus others. Comn: Commemorative Medal for Civil Eng, Univ Ill. Exhib: Ann, Whitney Mus Am Art, 64-67, Young America, 65; Butler Inst Am Art, Youngstown, Ohio, 65; Toronto Int Sculpture Symposium, 67; Kennedy Mem Exhib; Venice Biennale, 68; Twelve Erotic Fantasies, Circle Gallery, Ltd, 74; plus others. Teaching: Prof sculpture, Univ Ill, 60- Awards: First Prize, Des Moines, 58; Prize, Interior Valley Competition, Cincinnati, 61; Guggenheim Found Fel, 66. Mailing Add: Dept of Art Univ Ill Urbana IL 61801

GALLO, WILLIAM VICTOR
CARTOONIST
b New York, NY, Dec 28, 22. Study: Columbia Exten Cartoonists & Illusr. Work: Baseball Hall Fame, Cooperstown, NY. Pos: With NY Daily News, 41-, sports cartoonist, 60- Awards: Page One Awards, NY Newspaper Guild, 65, 68, 69, 70, 72, 73 & 75; Best Sports Cartoonist, Nat Cartoonist Soc, 68, 69, 70, 72 & 73; Outstanding Achievement, Alumni Soc Sch Visual Arts, 75. Mem: Nat Cartoonists Soc; Soc Silurians. Mailing Add: 1 Mayflower Dr Yonkers NY 10710

GAMBLE, KATHRYN ELIZABETH
MUSEUM DIRECTOR
b Van Wert, Ohio, Aug 19, 15. Study: Oberlin Col, AB, 37; Atelier year of study, Dayton Art Inst, 38; Newark Mus, cert, 41; New York Univ Grad Sch Fine Arts, MA, 48. Collections Arranged: Montclair in Manhattan, exhib of permanent collection, 61; American Painting Collection (with catalog), Montclair Art Mus; Asher B Durand Retrospective, 71; A B Durand (with catalog). Teaching: Supvr art, Covington Pub Schs, Ohio, 38-40. Pos: Dir, Montclair Art Mus, 52- Mem: Am Asn Mus; NJ Mus Coun.; Coun; Int Coun Mus (secy, Northeast Mus Conf). Mailing Add: Montclair Art Mus 3 S Mountain Ave Montclair NJ 07042

GAMMON, JUANITA-LA VERNE
PAINTER, EDUCATOR
b McLeansboro, Ill. Study: Univ Ill, BFA & MFA. Work: Work in many pvt collections. Comn: Many pvt comns. Exhib: Dream Mus, Champaign, Ill, 70; McKinley Found, Urbana, Ill, 70; Nat Acad Design, New York, 70-71; Illini Union Gallery, Univ Ill, 71. Teaching: Head dept art, Parkland Col, Champaign, 67- Pos: Judge, local & regional art exhibs, 67-; art lectr & critic, Classroom Serv Clubs, 67-; supvr, Champaign Co Art Show, 69- Mem: Ad Club Champaign-Urbana (treas, mem bd, 71-); Col Art Asn Am; Am Asn Jr Cols; Nat Art Educ Asn; Ill Art Educ Asn. Media: Acrylic, Oil, Watercolor. Mailing Add: 711 W Healey Champaign IL 61820

GAMMON, REGINALD ADOLPHUS
EDUCATOR, PAINTER
b Philadelphia, Pa, Mar 31, 21. Study: Philadelphia Mus Col Art, cert; Tyler Sch Fine Art, Temple Univ, one yr. Work: Chase Manhattan Bank, Fine Arts Div, New York; Denison Col, Ohio; Endicott Bd Educ, NY; plus numerous pvt collections. Exhib: New Voices—15 New York Artists, Am Greetings Gallery, New York, 68; Afro-Am Artists Since 1950, Brooklyn Col, 68; 30 Contemp Black Artists, Minneapolis Inst Art, Minn (travel), 68-70; Afro-Am Artists, New York & Boston, Mus Fine Arts, Boston, 70; Blacks: USA: 1973, New York Cult Ctr, 73. Teaching: Assoc prof humanities, painting & drawing, Western Mich Univ, 70- Pos: Artist, Lifton, Gold & Asher Advert, New York, 55-64; artist in residence, New York Bd Educ, 67-69. Awards: Fac Res Fel & Grant, Western Mich Univ, 75. Bibliog: Eugene Redden (auth), Reggie (film), prod by Western Mich Univ, 71; Judith Wragge Chase (auth), Afro-American Art & Crafts, Van Nostrand Reinhold, 72; Barry Schwartz (auth), Humanism in 20th Century Art, Praeger, 74. Mem: Col Art Asn; fel MacDowell Colony. Style & Technique: Figurative, social commentary. Media: Oil, Acrylic, Mixed Media. Mailing Add: 2123 Amherst Ave Kalamazoo MI 49008

GANTHIERS, LOUISE MARIE
PAINTER
b New York, NY, Oct 16, 07. Study: Art Students League, with Vaclav Vytlacil, 39-40; Am Artists Studio, New York, with Moses Soyer, 41; Brooklyn Mus, with Rufino Tamayo, fall 44. Work: Mus NMex, Santa Fe; Roswell Mus, NMex; Helene Worlitzer Found, Taos, NMex; Univ Calif Los Alamos Labs, NMex; Aspen Inst, Colo. Exhib: Southwest American Art, Okla Art Ctr, Oklahoma City, 59; 7th Int Exhib Women Artists, Mus Mod Art, Paris, 62; one-man shows, Mus NMex, 63, Roswell Mus, 63 & Palace of Legion of Honor, San Francisco, 66. Awards: Nonobjective Group Third Prize, NMex State Fair, 53; Purchase Award, Mus NMex, 56; Purchase Award, Dr William Oakes, Los Alamos, 58. Mem: Taos Art Asn (vchmn art comt). Style & Technique: Abstract expressionist; nonobjective hard-edge; abstract landscapes. Media: Oil, Watercolor. Dealer: Blanch Gallery of Contemp Art Woodstock NY 12498; Stables Gallery Taos NM 87571. Mailing Add: Box 1791 Taos NM 87571

GANTZ, ANN CUSHING
ART DEALER, PAINTER
b Dallas, Tex, Aug 27, 35. Study: Memphis Acad of Art; Southwestern Univ, Memphis; Newcomb Col Tulane Univ, New Orleans, La, BFA, 55. Work: Dallas Mus Fine Arts, Tex;

Denver Mus, Colo; Smithsonian Inst, Washington, DC; Boston Mus, Mass; Laguna Gloria Gallery of Tex Fine Arts Asn, Austin. Exhib: Ann Exhib, Springfield Mus, Mass, 56 & 57; Painting Ann, Portland Mus, 56, 59 & 60; Oklahoma City Art Ctr, 56-58; Painting & Sculpture Ann, Nat Acad of Design, New York, 57, 60; Norfolk Mus, Va, 58, 59; Printmaking Today, Brooklyn Mus, NY, 59; Ann Shows, Ark Art Ctr, Little Rock, 59, 60 & 61. Teaching: Instr printmaking & painting, Dallas Mus of Fine Arts Sch, 56-62; instr painting, printmaking & drawing, Cushing Galleries Sch of Studio Art, 62- Pos: Pres, Cushing Galleries Inc, 68- Awards: Felix Harris Award, Dallas Co Exhib, Dallas Mus Fine Arts, 56; 2nd Award, Joseph Pennell Found, Smithsonian Inst, 60. Mem, Dallas Print & Drawing Soc (pres, 58-60, adv, 60-74); Tex Fine Arts Asn; YWCA Art Comt (adv, 62-67); Tex Printmakers (pres, 57-60). Style & Technique: Figurative abstraction involved with texture, portrait commissions. Media: Oil and Acrylic Painting; Woodcut, Intaglio Printmaking. Res: American and Asian 20th century paintings, prints, drawings and sculpture. Dealer: Cushing Galleries Inc 2723 Fairmount Dallas TX 75201. Mailing Add: 4654 Edmondson Dallas TX 75209

GANTZ, JEANNE A
PRINTMAKER, ART ADMINISTRATOR
b Canton, Ohio, Nov 22, 29. Study: Goucher Col; Univ Calif, Berkeley; Crown Pt Press, apprenticed intaglio printing with Kathan Brown. Comn: Intaglio ed, comn by Marvin Spohn, 69-75, Arthur Okamura, 68-75, Beth Van Hoesen, 69-71 & Robert Fried, San Francisco, 74-75, Fritz Scholder, Scottsdale, Ariz, 75. Teaching: Instr intaglio printing, Univ Calif Exten, Berkeley, 69-71. Pos: Gallery dir, Artifactrie, Berkeley, 68-70; asst printer, Crown Pt Press, Berkeley, 69-71; dir/owner, El Dorado Press, Berkeley, 71- Mem: Calif Soc Printmakers (coun mem, 70). Mailing Add: 1972 El Dorado Ave Berkeley CA 94707

GARBATY, MARIE LOUISE
COLLECTOR, PATRON
b Berlin, Ger, Mar 9, 10; US citizen. Study: Univ Berlin. Pos: Fel Perpetuity, Metrop Mus Art; life fel & int centennial patron, Mus Fine Arts, Boston; benefactor & life mem, Chrysler Mus; patron, Wadsworth Atheneum; hon mem, Allentown Mus Art; assoc, Solomon R Guggenheim Mus; Friend NY Pub Libr. Mem: Am Fedn Arts; Renaissance Soc Am; China Inst Am; Carnegie Inst Int: Mus Mod Art, New York. Interest: Substantial gifts were made to: Metrop Mus of Art; Art Mus Palm Beach; Dudley Peter Allen Mem, Oberlin Col; Lawrence Art Mus, Williams Col; Dept Textiles, Univ Wash; Art Mus, RI Sch Design; Worcester Art Mus; Princeton Art Mus; Joslyn Mem Art Mus; J B Speed Mus; Fine Arts Soc Mus, San Diego; Cooper Union Mus; Albany Inst Hist & Art; Rose Art Mus, Brandeis Univ; Boston Univ Libr; Am Mus Natural Hist; Am Numis Soc; Art Mus, Univ Vt; Mus Mus of Art, Carnegie Inst, Pittsburgh; Libr, Calif State Col, Fullerton; Libr, Yale Univ; Hoover Libr, Stanford Univ; Libr Cong & Ryerson Libr; Art Inst Chicago and others. Collection: 15th and 17th century Dutch and Flemish paintings; decorative art of the Renaissance; antique Syrian glass; 15th and 18th century blue white China; antique oriental textiles; old English silver; antique English furniture; Egyptian antiquities. Mailing Add: 923 Fifth Ave New York NY 10021

GARBER, SUSAN R
ART ADMINISTRATOR, LECTURER
b Boston, Mass, Apr 13, 50. Study: Smith Col, BA; Univ Toronto, third-year exchange prog; Boston Univ, MA. Collections Arranged: Works in Progress 1974 and 1975, Inst Contemp Art, Boston. Pos: Prog staff, Children's Mus, Boston, 70; adminr, Mayor's Off Cult Affairs, Boston, 71; dir pub art, Inst Contemp Art, 72-76 & Comn of Mass, 76-77; lectr, Boston's pub art, Harvard Grad Sch Design, Cambridge, 3/75, Mass Inst Technol, Ctr Advan Visual Studies, Cambridge, 5/75 & Spec Workshop on Pub Celebrations, 6/75; dir, Main St Proj, Nat Inst for Hist Preservation, 78. Mem: Boston Visual Artists Union; City Conserv League. Res: Boston's public art; national public art. Publ: Auth, Color Comes to Boston, Artworkers News, 10/73; auth, An Historical Summary of Public Art in Boston & Boston's Murals, Art in the Environment in the US, 75; Public Art in Boston (map), publ by Inst Contemp Art & Boston 200, 75. Mailing Add: 30 Lantern Lane Newton MA 02159

GARBISCH, EDGAR WILLIAM & BERNICE CHRYSLER
COLLECTORS
Col Garbisch, b LaPorte, Ind, Apr 7, 99; Mrs Garbisch, b Oelwein, Iowa. Style Col Technique: Col Garbisch, Washington & Jefferson Col, BA, 21; US Military Acad, BS, 25. Collection: American furniture and paintings; American and European brass and wrought iron fixtures; European and Chinese porcelains of the 17th, 18th and early 19th centuries; French furniture and French paintings of the 19th and early 20th centuries; parts of collection donated to National Gallery of Art, Metropolitan Museum of Art, Philadelphia Museum of Art, Baltimore Museum of Art and other museums; selections from collection exhibited in museums in the United States, Canada, Europe and Japan. Mailing Add: Pokety Castle Haven Rd Cambridge MD 21613

GARCHIK, MORTON LLOYD
PAINTER, PRINTMAKER
b Brooklyn, NY, June 25, 29. Study: Brooklyn Mus, painting with Max Beckmann & printmaking with Gabor Peterdi; Sch Visual Art, New York. Work: Minn Mus Art. Comn: Book cover for Gimpel the Fool, Avon Paperback, 63. Exhib: One-man show, Union of Am Hebrew Congregations, 63; DePauw Univ 7th Ann Contemp Am Printmakers Exhib, 65; Ohio Univ 7th Ann, 66; Seattle Art Mus Int Exhibs, 66 & 67; two-man show, Art Corner, Milburn, NJ, 75; Artists Equity, New York, 78. Pos: Art dir, Commun Channels, Inc, New York, 72-77. Awards: First Prize, Drawing, Sch Visual Arts, 55; Purchase Award, Olivet Col 5th Nat Print Exhib, 65. Mem: Artists Equity of New York. Style & Technique: Figurative, phantasy, realistic and semi-abstract. Media: Woodcut, etching, serigraph, lithograph; acrylic; wood, clay. Publ: Auth, Art Fundamentals: Basics of Drawing, Painting, Sculpture & Printmaking, Stravon Educ Press, in press; illusr, articles in Harpers, Avon paperback, Farrar, Straus & Cudahy, Parents Mag Press. Dealer: Assoc Am Artists 663 Fifth Ave New York NY 10022. Mailing Add: 32-15 41st St Long Island City NY 11103

GARCIA, DANNY
PAINTER
b Monterey, Calif, Apr 23, 29. Study: Monterey Peninsula Col. Work: Masur Mus Art, Monroe, La; Mus Natural Hist & Art, Holyoke, Mass; Holiday Inn, Carmel; represented in pvt collections in the US, Europe, Can, SAm, Asia & Australia. Comn: 14 Stations of the Cross, Monsr Edward Varni, 65; Cypress tree painting, Stuyvesant Fish for Princess Margaret, 65; 11 paintings for publ, Donald Art Co, New York, 66; The Crucifixion, Father Jeremiah O'Sullivan, 67; mural painting, Holiday Inn, Monterey, 69. Exhib: Continuous one-man show, Garcia Gallery, Carmel, 55- Teaching: Instr & dir art, Carmel Sch Art, 65-70. Bibliog: Articles in This Month Mag; article in House & Garden, 68; Set decoration, Universal Studios; plus others. Style & Technique: American impressionist. Media: Acrylic, Oil. Specialty: Garcia paintings and prints—reproductions textured by the artist. Mailing Add: PO Box 623 Carmel CA 93921

GARCIA, JOSE
See Ocejo

GARCIA, OFELIA
ART ADMINISTRATOR, PRINTMAKER
b Havana, Cuba, Feb 12, 41; US citizen. Study: Escuela Nacional de Bellas Artes, Havana, Cuba, 58-60; Manhattanville Col, BA, 69; Tufts Univ & Boston Mus Sch, MFA(printmaking), 72; Duke Univ, PhD. Work: Museo Grafico; Inst de Cult Puertorriquena, San Juan, PR; Col Latin Am Prints, Benson & Hedges Gallery, Buenos Aires, Arg; FDS Collection, Winston-Salem, NC. Exhib: Biennials of Latin Am Printmakers, San Juan, PR, 70, 72, 74 & 76; 34 Estampadores Latinoamericanos group traveling show, Venezuela & Arg, 71; Third Miami Graphics Biennial, Metrop Mus & Art Ctr, Fla, 77; 53rd Ann Juried Show, The Print Club, Philadelphia, 77; McCarter Theatre, Princeton Univ, NJ, 78; solo shows at Colegio Universitario, Santurce, PR, 70, Cohen Arts Ctr, Tufts Univ, 72 & Duke Univ Gallery, 74. Collections Arranged: Putnam Art Ctr, Newton Col, 71-73; Boston Col Gallery, 75-76. Teaching: Asst prof printmaking & drawing, Newton Col, Mass, 69-73 & Boston Col, 75-76. Pos: Chmn art dept & dir, Div Humanities & Fine Arts, Newton Col, 70-73; dir, Studio Art Prog, Boston Col, 75-76; dir, The Print Club, Philadelphia, 78- Awards: First Prize, All-Sch Competition, Escuela de Bellas Artes, Havana, Cuba, 59; Am Bk Builders Prize, Boston Mus Sch, 69; Kent Fel, Danforth Found, 75-78. Mem: Col Art Asn Am; Women's Caucus for Art. Style & Technique: Intaglio, particularly collagraphs; emphasis on line, cut shapes; large images, usually figurative. Dealer: The Print Club 1614 Latimer St Philadelphia PA 19103. Mailing Add: 1704 Pine St Philadelphia PA 19103

GARCIA PONCE, FERNANDO
PAINTER
b Merida, Mex, 1933. Study: Nat Univ Mex (archit). Work: Mus Mod Art, Mex; Collection Club de Industriales, Mex; Banco de Cedulas Hipotecarias, SA, Mex. Comn: Mural, Mex Pavilion, Osaka World's Fair, 70. Exhib: Salon Esso, Mus Art Mod, Mex, 65; US Traveling Exhib, Mexico: The New Generation, 66; I Trienal of India, New Delhi, 68; Bienal de Sao Paulo, Brazil, 73; Contemp Mex Painting, Mus Mod Art, Tokyo, 74. Awards: Hon Mention, Salon de la Plastica Mexicana, 60; Second Prize, Festival Pictorico de Acapulco, Mex, 64; First Prize, Salon Esso, Mex, 65. Bibliog: Juan Garcia Ponce (auth), Nueve Pintores, 68 & Cardoza Y Aragon (auth), Pintura Actual, 75, Era; Damian Bayon (auth), Aventura en Hispanoamerica, Siglo XXI, 75. Style & Technique: Abstract, incorporating relief in painting. Media: Oil, Acrylic. Dealer: Galeria Juan Martin Amberes 17 Mexico 6 DF Mexico. Mailing Add: Alberto Zamora 66 Mexico 21 DF Mexico

GARDINER, HENRY GILBERT
ART ADMINISTRATOR, ART HISTORIAN.
b Boston, Mass, Aug 27, 27. Study: Harvard Col, BA(arch), 50; Harvard Univ, MA(fine arts), 59. Collections Arranged: Color & Form 1909-1914 (with catalog), Fine Arts Gallery San Diego, 71-72, Oakland Mus, 72, Seattle Art Mus (pavilion), 72. Pos: Asst cur painting, Philadelphia Mus Art, 60-69; dir, Fine Arts Gallery San Diego, 69- Mem: Asn Art Mus Dirs; Am Asn Mus; Col Art Asn Am. Publ: Auth, Checklist of paintings in the Philadelphia Museum of Art, 65; auth, Collection of Mrs John Wintersteen, Calif Palace of Legion of Honor, 66; auth, Samuel S White, III & Vera White Collection, Philadelphia Mus Art, 68; auth, Arthur Carles: a critical & biographical study, Philadelphia Mus Art, 70; plus others. Mailing Add: Fine Arts Gallery Balboa Park San Diego CA 92101

GARDINER, ROBERT DAVID LION
COLLECTOR
b New York, NY. Study: Columbia Col; Cornell Univ; Princeton Univ; Long Island Univ, Hon LHD. Collection: Paintings, silver, furniture, sculpture, porcelain, textiles. Mailing Add: 230 Park Ave New York NY 10017

GARDNER, ANDREW BRADFORD
PRINTMAKER, PAINTER
b Chicago, Ill, Nov 17, 37. Study: Antioch Col, BA, 61; Ohio State Univ, MA, 66; Escuela Cent Bellas Artes San Fernando, Madrid, Spain, 64. Work: Metrop Mus Art, New York; Johnson Wax Collection, Atlantic Richfield. Exhib: Door, Mus Contemp Crafts, New York, 68; 16th & 18th Nat Print Exhibs, Brooklyn Mus, NY, 68 & 72; New Talent in Printmaking-1969, Asn Am Artists Gallery, New York, 69; 2nd Biennale Int Estampe, Paris, France, 70; 4th Am Print Biennial, Santiago, Chile, 70. Teaching: Instr art & design, Rochester Inst Technol, 66-67; asst prof fine arts, Rutgers Univ, Newark, 67-76. Publ: Auth & illusr, The Artist's Silkscreen Manual, Grosset & Dunlap, New York, 76. Media: Silkscreen, Photographic & Knife Cut Stencils, Spray Paint. Mailing Add: 108 Wyckoff St Brooklyn NY 11201

GARDNER, JOAN A
PAINTER, FILM MAKER
b Joliet, Ill, May 3, 33. Study: Univ Ill, Kate Neal Kinley Mem fel, 55, BFA & MFA; Norfolk Summer Art Sch, Yale Univ, fel, 56, with Rico Lebrun & Gabor Peterdi. Work: Univ Ill; Am Fedn Art; Art Inst Chicago. Exhib: Conn Acad Fine Arts, 69; John Slade Elyhouse, New Haven, Conn, 70; Yale Univ, 70; New Britain Mus Art, Conn, New York, 73, 55 Mercer Gallery, 74-75; Slater Mem Mus, Norwich, Conn, 77. traveling show, 74-75. Teaching: Instr art, Southern Conn State Col, 65-77; asst prof, Univ New Haven, 78- Awards: Conn Acad Fine Arts Award, New Britain Mus, 69; Fulbright-Hays Award, 74-75. Mem: Conn Acad Fine Arts. Style & Technique: Fantasies, sometimes whimsical. Media: Canvas collage. Publ: Co-auth, Robot (film), Crowell Collier & Macmillan, 72. Dealer: Mercer Gallery 55 Mercer St New York NY 10013. Mailing Add: 10 Silver Sands Rd East Haven CT 06512

GARDNER, ROBERT EARL
PRINTMAKER, EDUCATOR
b Indianapolis, Ind, June 29, 19. Study: John Herron Art Sch, BFA, 48; Atelier 17, New York, 48-49; Cranbrook Acad Art, MFA, 52. Work: Carnegie Mus, Pittsburgh; Univ Okla Mus, Norman; Wichita Mus Art, Kans; Ohio Univ, Athens; Ga Comn Arts. Exhib: Pa Acad Fine Arts Exhibs; Brooklyn Mus Print Biennials; Libr Cong Print Exhibs; Northwest Printmakers Exhibs; Philadelphia Print Club Exhibs. Teaching: Assoc prof printmaking, Carnegie-Mellon Univ, 53- Pos: Artisan-printer, Tamarind Lithography Workshop, Los Angeles, Calif, summer 62 & 63-64. Style & Technique: Expressionistic. Media: Intaglio, Lithography. Mailing Add: Dept of Art Carnegie Mellon Univ Pittsburgh PA 15213

GARDNER, SUSAN ROSS
PAINTER, PRINTMAKER
b New York, NY, Oct 25, 41. Study: Brooklyn Mus, 59; Antioch Col, BA, 63; Ohio State Univ, MA, 66. Work: Metrop Mus Art, New York; Southern Ill Univ; Northern Ill Univ; Atlantic Richfield Corp; Richard Grey Gallery, Chicago; Woman's Interart Ctr. Exhib: Boston Printmakers 21st, 22nd & 23rd Ann, 69-71; 100 Acres, Soho 20, New York, 71 &

72; Allan Frumkin Gallery, Chicago, 72; 18th Nat Print Exhib, Brooklyn Mus, 72; one-woman show, Terrain Graphics, Soho, 74. Teaching: Asst prof studio & art hist, Manhattan Community Col, New York, 66-70; asst prof studio & art hist, Yeshiva Univ, 75-, Laguardia Community Col, 78 & Fordham Univ, 77-78. Awards: Purchase Award, Northern Ill Univ, 71. Bibliog: Wendy Schuman (interview), New York Times, 5/27/73; photo & article, Long Island Press, 4/27/73 & East Hampton Star, 5/73. Mem: Col Art Asn Am. Style & Technique: Combining photographs and hand drawn naive stencil technique; combining naive and sophisticated dream imagery. Media: Silkscreen, Acrylic. Mailing Add: 108 Wyckoff St Brooklyn NY 11201

GAREL, LEO
PAINTER
b New York, NY, Oct 8, 17. Study: Parsons Sch Art, NY; Art Students League, with George Grosz & Vaclav Vytlacil. Work: Norfolk Mus Arts & Sci; Chase Manhattan Bank Collection. Exhib: Santa Fe Mus, NMex; Albany Inst Hist & Art, NY, 61; one-man show, Berkshire Mus, Pittsfield, Mass, 67; Pa Acad Fine Arts, Philadelphia, 69; Montclair Art Mus, NJ, 75. Teaching: Instr painting, Austen Riggs Ctr, Stockbridge, Mass, 59-75. Awards: First Prize in Watercolor, Albany Inst Hist & Art, 61. Style & Technique: Landscapes pertaining to specific time and place, but expressionistically and abstractly rendered. Media: Watercolors, Gouache. Mailing Add: c/o Image Gallery Stockbridge MA 01262

GAREY, PAT
DRAFTSMAN, PAINTER
b State College, Miss, Nov 11, 32. Study: Tex Woman's Univ, BS(costume design & fashion illus); Tex Tech Univ, Lubbock, MFA, with Jim Howze, Terry Morrow, Lynwood Kreneck, Hugh Gibbons; Art Students League, New York, 77. Exhib: Tex Fine Arts Asn 13th Ann, Lubbock, 68; Southeastern NMex Small Painting, Roswell Mus & Art Ctr, 69; Southwestern Area Art, 1972, Midland, Tex, 72; Southwest Print & Drawing, NMex State Univ, 75; 17th Ann Nat Exhib Prints & Drawings, Okla Art Ctr, 75; Southwest Fine Arts Biennial, Mus Fine Arts, Santa Fe, NMex, 76; Alumni Art Exhib, Tex Tech Univ, Lubbock, 77; Teaching: Instr drawing & painting, Col of the Southwest, Hobbs, NMex, 67-70, instr art hist, 74. Pos: Artist in sch prog, HEW Emergency Sch Aid Proj, Hobbs, 74- Awards: Tex Fine Arts Asn Citation, Laguna Gloria Mus, Austin, 69; First Premium for Watercolor, NMex State Fair, 69; Cash Award, Figure Study No 1, 72; First Prize Ceramics, Llano Estacado Art Asn, 74 & First Prize Graphics, 75. Style & Technique: Pen and ink drawings; watercolor and ink; combines surrealism with abstraction. Mailing Add: 315 E Alto Hobbs NM 88240

GARHART, MARTIN J
PRINTMAKER
b Deadwood, SDak, July 2, 46. Study: SDak State Univ, BA, 69; WVa Univ, MA, 70; Southern Ill Univ, Edwardsville, MFA, 72. Work: Libr Cong, Washington, DC; Smithsonian Inst, Washington, DC; Cleveland Mus Art; Brit Mus, London; Calif Palace Legion of Honor, San Francisco. Exhib: Drawings USA, 72; Colorprint USA, 73; Bradley Print Show 15th Nat, 74; 2nd NH Int Print Competition, 74; Davidson Nat Print & Drawing Competition, 74. Teaching: Asst prof art, Kenyon Col, 72- Awards: Spec Purchase Award, Davidson Print & Drawing Competition, 74; Purchase Award, Bradley Print Show 15th Nat, 74; Jurors Award of Merit, 2nd NH Int. Mem: Col Art Asn Am; NH Graphic Soc. Media: Lithography. Mailing Add: 100 Woodside Gambier OH 43022

GARMAN, ED
PAINTER, WRITER
b Bridgeport, Conn, July 4, 14. Study: Self-taught. Work: Sheldon Mem Art Gallery, Univ Nebr, Lincoln; Mus NMex, Santa Fe; La Jolla Mus Art, Calif; Salt Lake Art Ctr, Utah; Ariz State Univ Art Collection, Tempe. Exhib: Painters & Sculptures of the Southwest Ann, Mus NMex, 41-44; Solomon Guggenheim Found 5th Ann, New York, 43; Lure of the West, Salt Lake Art Ctr, 70; Masterpieces from the Mus of NMex, Marion Koogler McNay Art Inst, San Antonio, Tex, 70. Bibliog: Marilyn Hagberg (auth), Hot Geometry of Ed Garman, San Diego Mag, 9/68. Style & Technique: Lyric, geometric, color abstractions. Media: Oil, Acrylic. Publ: Auth, Art of Raymond Jonson, Painter, 75. Mailing Add: PO Box 1013 Imperial Beach CA 92032

GARNETT, WILLIAM ASHFORD
PHOTOGRAPHER, EDUCATOR
b Chicago, Ill, Dec 27, 16. Work: Smithsonian Inst, Washington, DC; Mus Mod Art, New York; George Eastman House, Rochester; plus others. Comn: One of ten photographic murals, Mus Mod Art & State Dept, US Pavillion, Osaka World's Fair; The Searching Eye (film), Saul Bass & Eastman Kodak & From Here to There (film), Saul Bass & United Airlines, NY World's Fair, 64-65; America Begins in New England (aerial essay), Life Mag, 67 & Splendors Where the Eagles Soar (aerial essay), 68. Exhib: William Garnett, Aerial Photography, Eastman House, Rochester; The Family of Man & Diogenes IV, Mus Mod Art; Photographer & the American Landscape & photography from mus collection, Mus Mod Art. Teaching: Prof design & photography, Univ Calif, Berkeley, 68- Awards: Ctr Advan Visual Studies Fel, Kepes, Mass Inst Technol, 67-68; Guggenheim Fel, 53, 56 & 75. Bibliog: Beaumont Newhall (auth), The History of Photography, Mus Mod Art; Peter Pollack (auth), The Pictorial History of Photography, Mus Mod Art; Peter Pollack (auth), The Pictorial History of Photography, Abrams; Walker Evans (auth), Over California, Fortune, 3/54. Style & Technique: Abstractions of earth and landscapes made from the air. Collection: Aerial photography from US, Can, Mex, Japan, Hong Kong, Manila and Australia. Dealer: Marlborough Gallery 40 W 57th St New York NY 10019. Mailing Add: 1286 Congress Valley Rd Napa CA 94558

GARNSEY, CLARKE HENDERSON
ART HISTORIAN, EDUCATOR
b Joliet, Ill, Sept 22, 13. Study: Cleveland Inst Art, dipl, 47; Western Reserve Univ, BS(art educ), 47, MA(art hist), 48 & PhD(art hist), 62. Comn: Fourteen murals, Volusia Co Schs, Fla, 34-38 & series of etchings of historic locations, eastern Fla, WPA Fed Art Proj; watercolors, Amarillo Col, Tex. Exhib: Daytona Beach Art League Ann Exhib, 34-42; Southern States Art League Ann Exhib, 35-38; Wichita Art Asn Exhib, Kans, 37-38; May Show, Cleveland Mus Art, 49 & 58; Nat Exhib Relig Art, Rochester, NY, 69. Teaching: Chmn studio work, Amarillo Col, 49-63; chmn art hist, Wichita State Univ, 63-66 & Univ Tex, El Paso, 66- Pos: Lectr, Cleveland Mus Art & Cleveland Inst, 57-59. Mem: Col Art Asn Am; Soc Archit Hist; Tex Fine Arts Asn; Int Designer Craftsmen El Paso; Rocky Mountain Coun Latin Am Studies. Style & Technique: Semi-abstract oil and watercolor; abstract to semi-abstract enamels from nature subjects. Res: Latin American colonial architecture with emphasis on Neo-Classicism. Mailing Add: 221 Carnival Dr El Paso TX 79912

GARRARD, MARY DUBOSE
ART HISTORIAN, LECTURER
b Greenwood, Miss, July 25, 37. Study: Newcomb Col, BA, 58; Radcliffe Col, MA, 60; Johns Hopkins Univ, PhD, 70. Teaching: From asst prof to prof art hist (Ital Renaissance, 20th Century Am, Women's Art), Am Univ, Washington, DC, 64- Mem: Women's Caucus for Art (pres, 74-76); Col Art Asn Am (mem bd dirs, 77-81); Am Asn Univ Prof. Res: Sculpture of Jacopo Sansovino; painting of Artemisia Gentileschi; other aspects of 16th century and 17th century Italian art; women artists, 16th-20th century. Publ: Contribr, numerous articles, Women's Caucus for Art Newsletter, 74-75; ed, Slides of Works by Women Artists—A Sourcebook, 74; auth, Jacopo Sansovino's Madonna in S Agostino, Rome—an antique source rediscovered, J of Warburg & Courtauld Insts, London, 75; auth, Of men, women and art: some historical reflections, Art J, 76. Mailing Add: 4907 Upton St NW Washington DC 20016

GARRETT, ALAN THOMAS
MUSEUM DIRECTOR, SCULPTOR
b New Kensington, Pa, May 11, 41. Study: Otis Art Inst Los Angeles Co, BFA & MFA, 66. Work: Art Gallery, Otis Art Inst Los Angeles Co; Permanent Collection, Riverside Art Ctr & Mus. Comn: Bas relief (welded copper), comn by Norman Shanks, Irvine, Calif, 68; bas relief (mixed media), Condominiums, Whitefish, Mont, 72. Exhib: Bognar Gallery, Los Angeles, 66; Ankrum Gallery, Los Angeles, 66-67; Flathead Int Art Exhib, Kalispell, Mont, 71; Utah State Univ Print Exhib, 72. Collections Arranged: Over 100 art exhibs arranged in the past five years. Teaching: Instr drawing & printmaking, Flathead Valley City Col, summers 71 & 72; instr design & sculpture, Riverside City Col, 75- Pos: Dir, Flathead Valley Art Asn, Hockaday Art Ctr, Kalispell, Mont, 70-73; dir, Riverside Art Ctr & Mus, 73- Awards: First Prize Drawing, Flathead Valley Art Asn, 71. Style & Technique: Welded and cast metals, mixed media drawings, figurative and nonobjective style; hard-edge and curve-alinear; structure and value; black and white drawing. Publ: Contribr, Techniques in Modern Mosaics, 64 & The Hidden Elements of Drawing, 75. Mailing Add: Riverside Art Ctr & Mus 3425 Seventh St Riverside CA 92501

GARRETT, STEPHEN
MUSEUM DIRECTOR
b Ashtead, Surrey, Eng. Study: Cambridge Univ, Eng, MA. Teaching: Lectr design, Cent Sch Arts & Crafts, London, 54-64; sr lectr archit, Polytech Cent, London, 64-72. Pos: Chartered architect, pvt pract, 52-73; dir, J Paul Getty Mus, 74- Mem: Assoc Royal Inst Brit Architects; Asn Art Mus Dirs. Mailing Add: The J Paul Getty Mus 17985 Pacific Coast Hwy Malibu CA 90265

GARRETT, STUART GRAYSON, JR
PAINTER, EDUCATOR
b Oklahoma City, Okla. Study: Cooper Union; Art Students League. Work: USN Hist Collection; Norfolk Mus Art, Va; NY Univ; Johns Hopkins Univ; Univ Md. Exhib: Nat Acad Design, New York; Am Watercolor Soc, New York; Am Artists Prof League, New York; Audubon Artists, New York; Mus Marine, Paris; plus others. Teaching: Assoc prof art, City Col New York, currently. Awards: Gold Medal, Am Artists Prof League, 59; Am Watercolor Soc Prizes, 61, 65, 67 & 72; Salmagundi Club Awards, 62, 63, 65 & 67; plus others. Mem: Am Watercolor Soc (dir); Allied Artists Am (past pres); Southern Vt Artists; Salmagundi Club; Artists Fel. Mailing Add: RD 2 Salem NY 12865

GARRIS, KATHLEEN (KATHLEEN WEIL-GARRIS)
EDUCATOR, ART HISTORIAN
b Cheam, Surrey, Eng. Study: Vassar Col, AB, 56; Univ Bonn, 57; Harvard Univ, AM, 58, PhD, 65. Teaching: Prof Rennaissance art, New York Univ, 65- Mem: Col Art Asn (mem bd, 78-). Res: Art of the 15th and 16th century in Italy. Publ: Auth, Notes on S Maria dell' Anima, Storia dell Arte, 70; auth, Comments on the Medici Chapel Etc, Burlington Mag, 73; auth, Cloister, Court and City Square, Gesta, 74; auth, Leonardo and Central Italian Art, NY Univ Press, 74; auth, The Santa Casa di Loreto, Garland Press, 77. Mailing Add: One E 78th St New York NY 10021

GARRISON, EVE
PAINTER
b Boston, Mass, Apr 22, 08. Study: Art Inst Chicago, grad, 31; Wayne Univ; Lawrence Inst Technol; Lewis Inst Chicago. Work: Miami Mus Mod Art, Fla; Union League Club Chicago; Drian Gallery, London, Eng; Mt Sinai, Michael Reese & Presby Hosps, Chicago; Roosevelt Univ Rehab Hosp, Chicago. Exhib: One-man shows, Drian Gallery, London, 70, Galerie Vallombreuse, Biarritz, France, 72, Maharaj Gallery, Boston, 72 & retrospectives, Ill Inst Technol, Chicago, 72 & Miami Mus Mod Art, 72; one-person show, Spertus Mus, Chicago, 76. Awards: Awards for Old Colored Maid, Corcoran Mus, 34 & Bride & Groom, Union League Club Chicago, 61. Bibliog: Dona Meilach (auth), Collage & found art, 65; Creating with plaster; Creating art from anything. Style & Technique: From realistic to poetic landscapes and figures. Media: Oil, Casein. Dealer: Drian Gallery London Eng; Galerie Vallombreuse Biarritz France. Mailing Add: 407 S Dearborn Chicago IL 60605

GARSON, INEZ
CURATOR
b Long Island, NY, July 23, 15. Study: Hunter Col, New York, BA; Inst Art et Archeol, Paris; Inst Fine Arts, NY Univ, MA. Pos: Docent & lectr, Mus Mod Art, NY, 39-46, assoc dir, Circulating Exhib, 66-70; from asst to actg dir, A D White Mus, Cornell Univ, 57-66; cur, Hirshhorn Mus & Sculpture Garden, Smithsonian Inst, Washington, DC, 71- Res: Nineteenth and twentieth century European and American painting and sculpture. Publ: Auth, exhib catalogues, Whistler, 61, Piranesi, 62 & Canaletto, 62, Cornell Univ; contribr, Hirshhorn Mus & Sculpture Garden, Abrams, NY, 74. Mailing Add: Hirshhorn Mus Smithsonian Inst Washington DC 20560

GARSTON, GERALD DREXLER
PAINTER
b Waterbury, Conn, May 3, 25. Study: Johns Hopkins Univ, BA, 51; Art Students League, 52, painting with Louis Bouche & printmaking with Harry Sternberg. Work: Rose Mus, Brandeis Univ; Los Angeles Co Mus; William Rockhill Nelson Gallery Art, Kansas City, Mo; Philadelphia Mus Art, Pa; Wadsworth Atheneum, Hartford, Conn. Exhib: Poindexter Gallery, New York, 62; A M Sachs Gallery, New York, 65; Susan Morse Hilles Collection, Mus Fine Arts, Boston, Mass, 66; Graham Gallery, New York, 67; Pucker-Safrai Gallery, Boston, 71, 74 & 76; Freedman Gallery, Albright Col, Reading, Pa, 77. Media: Oil. Dealer: Pucker-Safrai Gallery 171 Newbury St Boston MA 02116. Mailing Add: 131 Oliver Rd New Haven CT 06515

GARVAN, BEATRICE BRONSON
CURATOR, ART HISTORIAN
b New York, NY, Mar 9, 29. Study: Vassar Col, BA(hist art), 50; Barnes Found, 53-55; Univ Pa, MA(Am civilization), 65. Teaching: Lectr Am arts, Germantown Acad, Ft Washington, Pa, 65-71. Pos: Asst, Ed Dept, Art News Mag, 49; secy & asst, Van Diemen-Lilienfeld Gallery, 50-52; assoc cur, Philadelphia Mus Art, 66- Mem: Cliveden Coun, Nat Trust Hist Hist Preservation (mem bd); Victorian Soc; Hist Soc Pa (mem bd, 64-); Soc Archit Historians & Decorative Arts; Am Crafts Coun. Res: American decorative arts of the 18th and 19th century; 18th century American architecture. Publ: Auth, A Craftsman's Handbook, Tinicum Press & Philadelphia Mus, 75; auth, Mathew Clark's Charts, Philadelphia Printmaking, Tinicum Press, 76; contribr, Philadelphia—300 Years of American Art, Philadelphia Mus Art, 76. Mailing Add: Box 304 Penllyn Pike Springhouse PA 19477

GARVER, JACK
PAINTER, DRAFTSMAN
b Larned, Kans, June 11, 21. Study: Univ NMex, BFA, 49; Highlands Univ, MA, 64. Work: NMex State Art Mus, Santa Fe; Jonson Gallery, Univ NMex; Univ Maine, Orono; Highlands Univ. Comn: Mural, Eaton W Tarbell, Architects, Bangor, Maine, 47; cloth sculpture, Cooper Milliken Architect, Orono, 48; mural (4 x 16 ft), Black Place Coffee Shop, Las Vegas, NMex, 63; drawings & paintings, LaVerne Hanners, Pine Bluff, Ark, 66-75. Exhib: 1st Pasadena Ann, 46; San Francisco Ann, 60; NMex Artists, Highlands Univ, 62; NMex State Mus Biennial. Teaching: Art teacher, Albuquerque Pub Schs, NMex, 50-60; art teacher, Corcoran High Sch, Calif, 63-66; instr drawing & painting design, Univ Nev, Las Vegas, 69-70. Pos: Model builder, Eaton W Tarbell, Architects, Bangor, 47-48. Awards: First Prize, NMex State Fair, 52; First Prize, Albuquerque Art League, 54-56; Drawing Award, Santa Fe State Art Mus, 57. Bibliog: E DeKooning (auth), article in Art in Am. Style & Technique: Abstract; surrealism. Media: Pencil, Ink, Acrylic; Clay Sculpture. Publ: Auth & illusr, Prints in the Desert, 51. Mailing Add: 502 Tahoe Pl NE Albuquerque NM 87107

GARVER, THOMAS H
CURATOR, WRITER
b Duluth, Minn, Jan 23, 34. Study: Barnes Found, Merion, Pa; Haverford Col, BA; Univ Minn, MA. Collections Arranged: Rose Art Mus, Brandeis Univ; Bruce Conner; Assemblages, Drawings & Films; 12 Photographers of the American Social Landscape, Newport Harbor Art Mus; Just Before the War: Urban America From 1935-1941 as seen by Photographers of the Farm Security Administration; Robert Rauschenberg in Black and White; Tom Wesselman: Early Still Lifes, 1962-64; Wood, Sculpture of Gabriel Kohn; Edward Hopper: 15 Paintings; Don Potts: My First Car; New Art of Vancouver; Reginald Marsh Retrospective; George Tooker Retrospective, Fine Arts Mus San Francisco, 74; New Photography: San Francisco and Bay Area, 74; Representations of America (co-organized with Henry Geldzabler; co-auth, catalogue), traveling USSR, 77-78; Joseph Raffael, The California Years, 1969-78 (auth, catalogue), San Francisco Mus Mod Art, 78. Pos: Asst dir, Krannert Art Mus, Univ Ill, 60-62; asst dir, Seattle World's Fair, 62; asst dir, Rose Art Mus, 62-68; dir, Newport Harbor Art Mus, Newport Beach, Calif, 68-72, 77- consult art gallery design, Univ Chicago & Calif Inst Arts, 69; cur exhibs, Fine Arts Mus San Francisco, 72-77. Mem: Western Asn Art Mus (bd mem, 70-71, pres, 71-72); assoc Int Inst Conserv Hist & Artistic Works. Res: Contemporary American art. Publ: Contribr, Artforum & Los Angeles Reviewer, 68-70; contribr, Handbook of College and University Administration, 69; contribr, An interview with George Sawchuck, Artscan, 69; contribr, Balboa & the fun zone, Art Am, 71; George Tooker, Am Art Rev, 74; contribr, Eros & photography: an exploration of sexual imagery and photographic practice, Camerawork/NSF Press, San Francisco, 78. Mailing Add: c/o Newport Harbor Art Mus 850 San Clemente Dr Newport Beach CA 92660

GARVER, WALTER RAYMOND
PAINTER, INSTRUCTOR
b Medina, NY, Aug 29, 27. Study: State Univ NY Buffalo, BFA, 55; also with Charles Burchfield, 50. Work: Butler Inst, Youngstown, Ohio; Minn Mus, St Paul; Cincinnati Univ; Charles R Penney Found, Lockport, NY. Exhib: Nat Acad Design Ann, New York, 56, 60, 70, 71 & 75; Chautauqua Nat Jury Show, NY, 58-74; Mainstreams, 69-77; one-man show, Albright-Knox Art Gallery, 72; Cooperstown Art Asn Am Nat Art Exhib, 73, 75 & 76. Teaching: Teacher art hist, drawing, painting & photog, Amherst Sr High Sch, Snyder, NY, 58- Awards: Award of Distinction, Mainstreams, 69; Award Traditional Style Painting, E J Bellinger, Chautauqua Nat, 70-73; Grand Prize, Cooperstown Art Asn, 73 & 75; plus others. Mem: Buffalo Soc Artists (pres, 64); Pattern Soc Artists. Style & Technique: City scenes, landscapes, portraits, realism with strong emphasis on composition. Media: Oil on Masonite. Publ: Auth, I search for an idea, Am Artists Mag, 68; contribr, Creative Color (essay & reproductions), 72. Dealer: More-Rubin Gallery 460 Franklin St Buffalo NY 14202. Mailing Add: 4230 Tonawanda Creek Rd East Amherst NY 14051

GARVEY, ELEANOR
ART ADMINISTRATOR
Pos: Assoc cur printing & graphic arts, Harvard Col Libr. Mailing Add: 60 Brattle St Cambridge MA 02138

GARWOOD, AUDREY
PAINTER, PRINTMAKER
b Toronto, Ont, July 7, 27. Study: Ont Col Art; Rijksacad, Amsterdam, scholar; Le Chaumiere, Paris. Work: London Gallery & Art Mus, Ont; McLaughlin Art Gallery, Oshawa, Ont; Burnaby Art Gallery, BC; Hamilton Art Gallery, Ont; Ont Art Gallery, Toronto. Exhib: Royal Can Acad; Ont Soc Artists; Can Graphic Art Soc; Can Painters & Etchers; Nat Gallery Showcase. Awards: Can Graphic Art Soc Award; Sterling Trust Award, Can Painters & Etchers; J Forester Award, Ont Soc Artists. Mem: Royal Can Acad Art; Ont Soc Art; Can Graphic Art Soc; Can Painters & Etchers; Calif Soc Printmakers. Style & Technique: Oil glazes, rhythmic lines moving over sculptural forms; interpretations of rock faces. Media: Oil; Silkscreen. Mailing Add: 6452 Regent St Oakland CA 94618

GARY, DOROTHY HALES
COLLECTOR, WRITER
b San Francisco, Calif, Nov 21, 17. Study: Stanford Col. Pos: Owner, pvt gallery. Specialty: Abstract, contemporary art. Collection: Abstract art. Publ: Auth, Sun, Stones & Silence, Simon & Shuster, 63; co-auth, Splendors of Asia, 65 & co-auth, Splendors of Byzantium, 67, Viking Press. Mailing Add: 730 Park Ave New York NY 10021

GARY, JAN (MRS WILLIAM D GORMAN)
PAINTER, PRINTMAKER
b Ft Worth, Tex, Feb 13, 25. Study: Art Ctr Sch, Los Angeles; San Antonio Art Inst, Tex; Art Students League. Work: Butler Inst Am Art, Youngstown, Ohio; Pensacola Art Ctr, Fla; Wis State Univ, Eau Claire; Brandeis Univ, Waltham, Mass; Rosenberg Libr, Galveston, Tex. Exhib: One-man shows, Centenary Col Women, Hackettstown, NJ, 67, Ringwood Manor State Mus, NJ, 68 & Caldwell Col, NJ, 78; Am Acad Arts & Lett, 67-68; Four NJ Artists, Canton Art Inst, Ohio, 71; Cent Wyo Mus Art, Casper, 75; Charles & Emma Frye Mus of Art, Seattle, Wash, 77. Pos: Assoc dir, Old Bergen Art Guild, Bayonne, NJ, 62- Awards: M Grumbacher Purchase Award, Audubon Artists Ann, 66; Childe Hassam Fund Purchase Award, Am Acad Arts & Lett, 68; Dorothy F Seligson Mem Prize, Nat Asn Women Artists Ann, 75. Bibliog: Henry Gasser (auth), article in, Am Artist, 10/70. Mem: Nat Soc Painters Casein & Acrylic; Audubon Artists; Assoc Artists NJ. Style & Technique: Stylized realism. Media: Acrylic, Casein, Woodcut. Mailing Add: 43 W 33rd St Bayonne NJ 07002

GARZON-BLANCO, ARMANDO
DESIGNER, PAINTER
b Havana, Cuba, Feb 1, 41. Study: La State Univ, BA, 66, MA(design), 68, MA(art hist), 69, PhD(theatre-art), 76; Fulbright-Hays Res Grant, Spain, 72-73, La State Univ Coun on Res & Rodríguez-Acosta Fund Grants, Spain, 74. Work: Centroplex, Baton Rouge Govt Bldg, La; La State Univ Libr, Baton Rouge; Cath Student Ctr, Baton Rouge. Comn: Baptistry murals, St Paul Cath Church, Baton Rouge, 70; sanctuary & chapel, Christ the King Chapel, Baton Rouge, 73-75; altarpiece, St James Lutheran Church, Gonzalez, La, 77. Exhib: Jay Broussard Mem Gallery, State La Dept Art, Hist & Cult Preserv, 72; US Cult Ctr of Am Embassy, Madrid, Spain, 73; Fundación Rodríguez-Acosta Banco de Granada Gallery, Spain, 73. Teaching: From instr to asst prof design, painting & art hist, La State Univ, Baton Rouge, 68-77; assoc prof design, painting & art hist & head art dept, Nicholls State Univ, Thibodaux, 77- Awards: Purchase Award, 2nd Ann Int La Watercolor Soc, 71. Bibliog: Miguel Rodríguez-Acosta Carlström (auth), Los artistas por el sureste español, Banco de Granada & Fundación Rodríguez-Acosta, Spain, 73. Mem: La Watercolor Soc; SCent Renaissance Asn; Col Art Asn Am; Southeastern Col Art Conf; Nat Coun Art Adminr. Style & Technique: Symbolist and realist-impressionist. Media: Watercolor, Mixed Media. Res: Interrelation of the theatre arts and visual arts; Spanish Jesuit theatrical practice in the 16th and 17th century. Publ: Auth, Note on the authorship of the Spanish Jesuit play of San Hermenegildo, Theatre Survey, 74; auth, The Tragedia de San Hermenegildo, Seville, 1590, Explorations in Renaissance Culture, 78. Dealer: Baton Rouge Gallery Inc 205 N Fourth St Baton Rouge LA 70801. Mailing Add: Dept of Art Nicholls State Univ Thibodaux LA 70301

GASPARIAN, ARMEN TIGRAN
INSTRUCTOR, PAINTER
b Abadan, Iran, Nov 25, 33; US citizen. Study: Calcutta Art Inst, India; Swain Sch Art, New Bedford, Mass; Univ Kans. Work: Univ Kans; Laguna Beach Mus, Calif; Denver Fine Arts Gallery, Colo. Exhib: All Calif Ann, 67-69, 71-73; Hawaii-Calif Regional, San Diego Mus, 71; one-man shows, Martin Gallery, Scottsdale, Ariz, 68-72, 74, Saks Gallery, Denver, 69, 71, 73 & Laguna Beach Mus, 72. Teaching: Instr beginning & advan painting, Laguna Beach Sch Art, 73- Awards: First Prize, Inland V, 72 & Catalina Ann, 74; Purchase Award, All Calif Ann, 73. Mem: Laguna Beach Mus. Media: Oil. Mailing Add: 215 High Dr Laguna Beach CA 92651

GASPARRO, FRANK
SCULPTOR, INSTRUCTOR
b Philadelphia, Pa, Aug 26, 09. Study: Pa Acad Fine Arts; also with Charles Grafly. Comn: Designed reverse of Kennedy Half-Dollar, Am Numismatic Asn Medal, 69, obverse & reverse of President Richard M Nixon Medal, 69, obverse & reverse of Eisenhower Dollar & reverse of Lincoln Mem US One Cent; also many medals for US mint. Exhib: Philadelphia Mus Art Sculpture Exhib, 40; Pa Acad Fine Arts, Philadelphia, 46; Medals at French Mint, Paris, 50; Spanish Int Medallic Art Exhib, Madrid, 52 & 68; Woman on the Medal, Int Medallic Exhib. Teaching: Instr, Fleisher Art Sch, Philadelphia, 46- Pos: Engraver, US Mint, Philadelphia, 42-65, chief engraver, 65- Awards: Braverman Sculpture Prize, 59 & 62-65; Am Numismatic Soc Gold Medal as Outstanding Numismatic Sculptor of Year, 68; Gold Medal, Numismatic Expos at Pistoia Montecatini, 72; Order of Merit, Ital Repub (Cavaliere Ufficiale), 73; United Veterans of Am Distinguished Citizen Award of Philadelphia, 75; Citation for Super Performance of the US Treasury, 77. plus others. Mem: Soc Medalists; Pa Acad Fine Arts Fel (bd dirs, 56-); Fr Soc of the Medal; Artists Equity Asn. Mailing Add: 216 Westwood Park Dr Havertown PA 19083

GASSER, HENRY MARTIN
PAINTER, WRITER
b Newark, NJ, Oct 31, 09. Study: Newark Sch Fine & Indust Art, cert; Grand Cent Sch Art; Art Students League, with Robert Brackman & John R Grabach. Work: Metrop Mus Art, New York; Philadelphia Mus Art, Pa; Newark Mus, NJ; Hist Properties Sect, Dept War, Washington, DC; Boston Mus Art. Exhib: American Traditional Artists of the 20th Century, Columbus Mus, Ga, 63; 20th Century Realists, Fine Arts Gallery San Diego, 66; Nat Acad Design, 71 & 75; Am Watercolor Soc, 71 & 75. Teaching: Instr painting & compos, Art Students League, 64-70; instr painting workshop, Heritage Arts, South Orange, NJ, 70- Pos: Dir, Newark Sch Fine & Indust Art, 46-54. Awards: Julius Hallgarten Prize, Nat Acad Design, 43; Philadelphia Watercolor Club Prize, 45; Am Watercolor Soc Award, 69. Bibliog: Exploring casein (film), M Grumbacher, 60; Albert Teh Eyeck Gardner (auth), History of Watercolor in America, Van Nostrand Reinhold, 66; Norman Kent (auth), Paintings of Newark, Am Artist Mag, 66. Mem: Nat Acad Design (rec secy, 60-67); Am Watercolor Soc (vpres, 53); Philadelphia Watercolor Club; Audubon Artists; Allied Artists Am. Media: Watercolor. Publ: Auth, Oil Painting Methods & Demonstrations, 53, How to Draw & Paint, 55, Techniques of Painting, 58, Picture Making, 62 & Guide to Painting, 64. Dealer: Grand Central Art Galleries 40 Vanderbilt Ave New York NY 10017. Mailing Add: 654 Varsity Rd South Orange NJ 07079

GAST, CAROLYN BARTLETT (CAROLYN B LUTZ)
ILLUSTRATOR, ILLUMINATOR
b Cambridge, Mass, Apr 30, 29. Study: Col Practical Arts & Lett, Boston Univ, BS(bk illus), 50. Work: Depts of Zool, Nat Mus of Natural Hist, Smithsonian Inst & Paleont & Stratig Br, US Geol Surv, US Dept Interior, Washington, DC. Exhib: 17th Area Exhib of Corcoran Gallery Art, Washington, DC, 65; Scientific Illus, Nat Mus of Natural Hist, Smithsonian Inst, 68; solo exhib & demonstration, 1st Int Symp on Biol of the Sipuncula, Kotor, Yugoslavia, 70; Ann Exhibs of Asn of Med Illusr, 69-78. Pos: Scientific illusr, US Geol Surv, Dept of Interior, 52-56; scientific illusr, Nat Mus of Natural Hist, Smithsonian Inst, 59- Awards: Hon Mention for Sculpture, 17th Area Exhib of the Corcoran Gallery Art, 65. Mem: Founding mem Guild of Natural Sci Illusr (vpres, 71-73, pres, 73-75). Style & Technique: Scientifically explicit conceptual representation and precision rendering for line-cut and half-tone reproduction, stereographic miniature illuminations. Media: Damp Wash on Scratchboard, Carbon Dust & Graphite Dust on Cronaflex, other Mixed Media, Pen & Ink, Gouache, Gold Leaf. Publ: Illusr, Proceedings of the US Nat Mus, 60-67; illusr, Proceedings of the Bio Soc of Washington, DC, 61-78; illusr, Smithsonian Contributions to Zoology, 67-78; illusr, Mary S Gardiner's The Biology of the Invertebrates, McGraw-Hill, 72; illusr, numerous scientific publications and journals, 59-78. Mailing Add: 5730 First St S Arlington VA 22204

GAST, MICHAEL CARL
PAINTER
b Chicago, Ill, June 11, 30. Study: Sch Art Inst Chicago, BFA, 52; Univ of the Americas, Mex, MFA(cum laude), 60. Exhib: Washington Watercolor Asn 66th Ann Nat Exhib, Smithsonian Inst, 63 & Metrop Area Exhib, Howard Univ, Washington, DC, 70; Soc Washington Artists 70th & 71st Ann Exhib, Smithsonian Inst, 63 & 64; four-man show, Mickelson Gallery, Washington, DC, 66. Teaching: Asst prof painting, George Washington Univ, 71. Pos: Mus technician, div ceramics & glass, Nat Mus Hist & Technol, 61-64 & mus specialist, Nat Collection Fine Arts, 69-71, Smithsonian Inst. Bibliog: Andrea O Cohen (auth), Mike Gast, DC Gazette, 4/19/72. Mem: Artists Equity Asn (chap vpres, 73-77, nat secy-treas, 75-79); Col Art Asn Am; Nat Art Workers Community. Style & Technique: Expressive form in figurative modes. Media: Polymer, Oil. Publ: Contribr, Artists Equity Asn Nat Newsletter, 77, Fed Art Patronage News, 77 & Ceramics Monthly, 78. Mailing Add: 5730 First St S Arlington VA 22204

GATES, HARRY IRVING
SCULPTOR, PAINTER
b Elgin, Ill, Dec 8, 34. Study: Univ Ill, BFA, 58, MFA, 60. Work: Wadsworth Atheneum, Hartford, Conn; Chase Manhattan Bank, New York; Corcoran Gallery Art, Washington, DC; Int Art Prog Div, Nat Collection Fine Art, Washington, DC; Washington Co Mus Fine Arts, Hagerstown, Md. Exhib: 53 Painters of Chicago, circulated in France & Ger, 58-59; 24th Ann Butler Inst Show, Youngstown, Ohio, 59; 25th Drawing, Print & Sculpture Exhib, San Francisco Mus Art, 61; one-man show, Baltimore Mus Fine Art, 64; Small Sculpture Purchases for Int Art Prog, Nat Collection Fine Art, 69. Teaching: Asst prof sculpture, George Washington Univ, 64- Awards: First Prize, 21st Ann Contemp Art, Palm Beach, Fla, 59; Artists Coun Award, 25th Ann Exhib for Sculpture, 61; Gov Prize, Md Ann, 70. Mailing Add: PO Box 766 Frederick MD 21701

GATEWOOD, MAUD FLORANCE
PAINTER
b Yanceyville, NC, Jan 8, 34. Study: Univ NC, Greensboro, AB; Ohio State Univ, MA; Univ Vienna; Fulbright grant, 62-63; Acad Appl Arts, Vienna; Harvard Summer Sch. Work: Mint Mus Art, Charlotte, NC; Nat Collection of Fine Arts, Washington, DC; NC Mus Art, Raleigh; pvt collections. Exhib: NC Artists Ann, NC Mus Art, 61-71; Peidmont Painting & Sculpture Ann, Charlotte, 65-71; Art on Paper, Greensboro, 65 & 67; Am Acad Arts & Lett & Nat Inst Arts & Lett, 72. Teaching: Prof, Averett Col, Danville, Va. Awards: Am Acad Arts & Lett Award, 72. Media: Acrylic. Dealer: Heath Gallery 34 Lombardy Way NE Atlanta GA 30309. Mailing Add: Rt 1 Box 9-A Milton NC 27305

GATLING, EVA INGERSOLL
MUSEUM CONSULTANT, ART HISTORIAN.
b Mobile, Ala, Dec 28, 12. Study: Richmond Prof Inst, Col William & Mary, cert art, 35; Univ Ala, BA, 41; Yale Univ, MA, 44. Collections Arranged: Eliel Saarinsen Mem Exhib (with catalog), Cranbrook Acad Art, 51; Whence Pop, 65, Moran Family, 65 & Salute to Small Museums, 70 (with catalogs), Heckscher Mus; collections of Helen Torr, 72, Ibram Lassaw, 73, Stanley Twardowicz, 74 & Fairfield Porter, 74-75; George Grosz Works in Oil, Heckscher Mus, 77. Pos: Dir exhib & supvr art equip, Duke Univ, 45-49; cur, Mus Cranbrook Acad Art, 49-54; asst dir, Des Moines Art Ctr, 59-61; dir, Heckscher Mus, 62- Mem: Am Asn Mus; Soc Archit Historians; Col Art Asn Am. Res: American art, particularly after 1900; American architecture of the 19th and 20th centuries; Buddhist art. Collection: 20th century American painting, drawing and sculpture. Publ: Contribr, Soc Art Historians J, 51; contribr, Art J, 55; contribr, Artibus Asiae, 57. Mailing Add: 206 Perdido St Fairhope AL 36532

GATRELL, MARION THOMPSON
EDUCATOR, PAINTER
b Columbus, Ohio, Nov 13, 09. Study: Ohio State Univ, BSEd, 31, MA, 32. Work: Butler Inst Am Art, Youngstown, Ohio; Columbus Gallery Fine Arts; Massillon Mus Art, Ohio; Otterbein Col, Westerville, Ohio; Schumacher Gallery, Capital Univ Colo. Exhib: Audubon Artists Nat, 45; Butler Art Inst Regional Ann, 50 & 57; Nat Asn Women Artists, Scotland, Eng & India, 64-65; Int Womens Competition, Cannes, France, 69; Florence & Naples, Italy, 72; plus traveling shows in US. Teaching: From instr to assoc prof drawing & painting, Ohio State Univ, 43-76, emer prof, 76- Awards: Purchase Award, Butler Art Inst, 57; Baldwin Purchase Award, Massillon Mus, 64; Pace Gallery Award, Schumacher Gallery, Capitol Univ, 68 & 74. Bibliog: Frances Piper (auth), Hurd & Gatrell featured, Columbus Dispatch, 1/8/67; Mrs Jerry Baughman (auth), Keystones at Ohio State, Ohio State Univ Monthly, 3/72; cover article, 6/72 & article, 2/75, La Revue Moderne, Paris. Mem: Nat Asn Women Artists; Columbus Art League. Style & Technique: Abstracting from visual experiences into calligraphic shapes with humor and fantasy. Media: Graphics, Watercolor. Mailing Add: 2690 Berwyn Rd Columbus OH 43221

GATRELL, ROBERT MORRIS
EDUCATOR, PAINTER
b Marietta, Ohio, May 18, 06. Study: Ohio State Univ, BSEd, 29, MA, 33. Work: Libr Cong, Washington, DC; Stanley Grumbacher Collection Contemp Am Art, New York; E B Crocker Art Gallery, Sacramento, Calif; Columbus Gallery Fine Arts, Ohio; Canton Mus, Ohio; plus many others. Comn: Portraits, of Paul L Dunbar, Ohio State Archeol Mus, 38, Dean C Dye, 38 & George Rightmire, 42, Ohio State Univ, A A Shaw, Denison Univ, 38 & Dean F J Smull, Ohio Northern Univ, 43. Exhib: Am Watercolor Soc Ann, New York, 42-66; Pa Acad Watercolor & Print Show, 49-50 & 59; Watercolor USA, Springfield, Mo, 62 & 65; Am Drawing Ann, Norfolk, Va, 63; Hunterdon Art Ctr Nat Print Exhib, 64-73. Teaching: From instr to prof drawing & graphics, Ohio State Univ, 29-76, emer prof, 76- Awards: Gov Award for Ceres, Ohio State Fair, 52; Purchase Prize for Magic Dreamer, Butler Art Inst, 56; M Grumbacher Purchase Award, Am Watercolor Soc, 60; plus one other. Bibliog: Bram Dijkstra (auth), Award winning artist, Ohio State Lantern, 60; F Piper (auth), Winter showcase of the arts, 66 & Hurd & Gatrell featured, 67, Columbus Dispatch. Mem: Am Watercolor Soc; Hunterdon Co Art Asn; Columbus Art League (pres, 42-43, bd gov, 48-52, 57-59). Style & Technique: Range from naturalism to abract and combination of same. Mailing Add: 2690 Berwyn Rd Columbus OH 43221

GAUCHER, YVES
PRINTMAKER, PAINTER
b Montreal, Que, 34. Study: Ecole des Beaux Arts, Montreal, 54-56. Work: Mus Mod Art, New York; Libr of Cong, Washington, DC; Victoria & Albert Mus, London, Ont; Mus d'Art Contemp, Montreal; Nat Gallery of Can, Ottawa, Ont. Exhib: Biennale de Paris, 61; VIIe Expo Int de Gravures, Ljubljana, Yugoslavia, 61-63; 1st Am Biennial of Prints, Santiago, Chile, 63; Contemp Painters as Printmakers, Mus Mod Art, New York, 64; Venice Biennial, Italy, 66; Can 67, Inst Contemp Art, Boston, 67; Can—Art d'Aujourd' Hui, Palais des Beaux Arts, Brussels, Belg, 68; Expo 70, Japan, 70; Aspects of Can Art, Members Gallery, Albright-Knox Art Gallery, Buffalo, NY, 74; Thirteen Artists from Marlborough Gallery, New York, 74; one-man shows, Winnipeg Art Gallery, Man, 66, Vancouver Art Gallery, BC, 69, Edmonton Art Gallery, Alta, 69, Sir George Williams Univ, Montreal, 70, Univ Man, Winnipeg, 71 & New York Cult Ctr, 75. Teaching: Asst prof fine arts, Sir George Williams Univ, Montreal, 63-69, assoc prof, 70- Awards: First Prize, Nat Print Competition, Burnaby, BC, 61; Second Prize, Int Triennale of Colored Prints, Grenchen, Switz, 64; Grand Prize, Sandage 68, Montreal Mus Fine Arts, 68. Bibliog: William Withrow (auth), Contemp Can Painting, Toronto, 72; Michel Ragon (auth), Reveire de l'Absolu, Vie des Arts, Montreal, Que, spring 73; Dore Ashton (auth), Can Art in Review, Artscanada, 12/74. Mailing Add: c/o Marlborough Godard Gallery 1490 rue Sherbrooke-Ouest Montreal PQ H3G 1L3 Can

GAUDIERI, ALEXANDER V J
MUSEUM DIRECTOR
b Columbus, Ohio, Apr 23, 40. Study: Ohio State Univ; Univ Paris, Sorbonne; Colgate Univ; Barton Kyle Yount Scholar, Am Grad Sch of Int Com; Int of Fine Arts, NY Univ, with Robert Rosenblum & Francis Watson. Pos: Dir, Telfair Acad of Arts & Sci, 76- Mem: Am Asn of Mus; Appraisers Asn of Am; Savannah Art Asn; Hilton Head Art League; Harlem Sch of the Arts (chmn jr comt, 71-); Young Concert Artists Inc (vchmn bd). Res: European decorative arts—wood marquetry: development of geometric forms into curvilinear and floral motifs from circa 1715 to mid-century; French romantic painting—the horse paintings of Alfred de Dreux and the influence of Gericault on his oeuvre. Collection: Decorative arts including Georges II & III furniture, silver and porcelain. Mailing Add: 117 W Gaston Savannah GA 31401

GAUL, ARRAH LEE
PAINTER
b Philadelphia, Pa. Study: BFA; Moore Col Art, scholar, 5 years; Calla-Rousi Sch, Paris; also study in Europe, MidE, China, Japan, India & Can. Work: Reading Mus; Pa Acad Fine Arts; Rochester Mem Art Gallery. Comn: Official artist of US Sesquicentennial. Exhib: One-man shows, Philadelphia Art Club, Beaux Arts Gallery, London & US Embassy, Tokyo; Grand Palais Champs Elysees, Paris; Neno Gallery Ann & Women Artists Asn Exhib, Neno Gallery, Tokyo; Acad Music, Philadelphia; plus others. Style & Technique: French School. Mailing Add: 1530 Locust St Philadelphia PA 19102

GAUTHIER, JOACHIM GEORGE
PAINTER
b North Bay, Ont, Aug 20, 97. Study: Study under Frank Carmichael, Toronto. Work: Work in pvt collections only. Mem: Can Soc Painters Watercolour; Ont Soc Arts; sr assoc Royal Can Acad Arts. Mailing Add: 184 Ranleigh Ave Toronto ON Can

GAWARECKI, CAROLYN ANN
See Grosse

GAWBOY, CARL
PAINTER, ART HISTORIAN
b Cloquet, Minn, May 21, 42. Study: Univ Minn, Duluth, with Henry Pearson, BS; Wis State Univ-Superior, with Len Petersen; Univ Mont, with Don Bunse & Rudy Autio. Work: Minn Chippewa Tribe, Minn Hist Soc; Bemidji State Col. Comn: Murals, Ely Chamber Commerce, Minn, 60; murals, Minn Hist Soc, St Paul, 72; murals, Bemidji State Univ, Minn, 77. Exhib: Arrowhead Art Exhib, Duluth, 66; Scottsdale Nat Indian Art Exhib, Ariz, 72-74; Rainy River Jr Col, 72; Theatre in the Round, Minneapolis, 72; Minn Hist Soc, St Paul, 75; Coffman Gallery, Univ of Minn, 78. Awards: Best in Show, Arrowhead Art Exhib, 66, Third Prize, 74; Third Prize in Watercolor, Scottsdale Nat Indian Art Exhib, 74; First Purchase Prize, Ann Ojibwa Tribal Art Exhib, 74 & 75; plus others. Style & Technique: Modern regional realism; Indians and white ethnics in northern Minnesota. Media: Watercolor. Publ: Co-auth & illusr, Everything You Ever Wanted to Ask About Indians But Were Afraid to Find Out, 71; illusr, David Martinson (auth), Shemay: The Bird in the Sugarbush. Mailing Add: 2644 15th Ave S Minneapolis MN 55404

GAYLORD, FRANK CHALFANT
SCULPTOR, DESIGNER
b Clarksburg, WVa, Mar 9, 25. Study: Carnegie Inst Technol Col Fine Arts; Tyler Sch Fine Arts, Temple Univ, BFA. Comn: Firemen Mem, Mamaroneck Fire Dept, NY, 62; series of religious monuments, Archdiocese of Chicago, 62, Archdiocese of Detroit, 63 & New Haven, Conn, 64; Faith, Hope, Love (relief), New Britain, Conn, 67; 9ft Madonna & cent figure for shrine, Mt Hope Cemetery, Chicago, 74; 7 & 1/2 ft marble St Peter & St Paul, All Saints Mausoleum, Des Plaines, Ill, 76; cent figure Resurrected Christ (relief), Resurrection Cemetery, Argo, Ill, 77; portrait of Martin Luther (sculpture), New Britain, Conn, 77; animal sculpture composition, Playboy Mag, 78. Exhib: Nat Sculpture Soc Ann Exhib, 65. Teaching: Lectr advan of progressive philos on art, Am Inst Commemorative Arts, 65. Mem: Assoc Nat Sculpture Soc; assoc Vt Coun Arts. Media: Granite. Publ: Auth, Why Christ? & auth, A portrait of Hector, 68, Monumental News Rev. Mailing Add: 25 Delmont Ave Barre VT 05641

GEAR, JOSEPHINE
ART HISTORIAN, ART WRITER
b London, Eng, Nov 24, 38. Study: The English equivalent of a degree in museology: the dipl of Mus Asn Gt Brit, 65; Woodrow Wilson Dissertation fel, 73-74, Inst Fine Arts, NY Univ, scholar award, 75-76, PhD, 76; study with Bob Rosenblum & Gert Schiff. Teaching: Asst prof art hist, Briarcliff Col, NY, 75-77; adj prof art hist, Parsons Sch Design, New York, 76- & State Univ NY Col Purchase, 77- Mem: Mus Asn Gt Brit; Col Art Asn Am (co-chmn Marxist caucus, 78); Artists Meeting for Cult Change, New York. Res: Books in progress. Publ: Contirbr, Catalogue of the Oil Paintings in the London Museum, HMSO, 70; auth, Master or Servant?, A Study of Selected English Painters and Their Patrons of the Late 18th and Early 19th century, Garland, 77; co-auth, The 70's Alternative View of Design: Danger from the Drawing Boards?, Contemp Art/SE, 77; auth, Trapped Women: The Work of Two Sister Designers, Margaret and Frances Macdonald, Heresies, 78. Mailing Add: 181 E 93rd St Apt 2A New York NY 10028

GEBER, HANA
SCULPTOR, INSTRUCTOR
b Praha, Czech, Feb 14, 10; US citizen. Study: Teachers Col, Prague; Art Students League; Sculpture Ctr, New York. Work: Yeshiva Univ Mus; Jewish Mus, New York; Rose Art Mus, Brandeis Univ; Mus Ethnography & Folklore, Ramat-Aviv, Israel; Lowe Art Mus, Univ Miami. Comn: Wedding altar, Temple Emanuel, Yonkers, NY; memorial, Verona High Sch, NJ; statue, Riverdale Temple, Bronx; statue, Temple Sinai of Long Island, NY; silver wallpiece, Free Westchester Synagogue; plus others. Exhib: One-man shows, Montclair Art Mus, Union Am Hebrew Congregations, New York, Sculpture Ctr, New York, Am Jewish Hist Soc, Waltham & Boston, Mass & Pa Acad Fine Arts, Philadelphia; plus others. Teaching: Mem fac, Sculpture Ctr; also pvt instr. Awards: Mem Found Jewish Cult Fel, 69; Gold Medal,

Nat Asn Women Artists; First Prize, Am Soc Contemp Artists; plus others. Media: Silver, Bronze. Dealer: Sculpture Ctr 167 E 69th St New York NY 10021; Rudolph Gallery 338 Sevilla Ave Coral Gables FL 33134. Mailing Add: 168 W 225th St New York NY 10463

GEBHARD, DAVID
GALLERY DIRECTOR, ART HISTORIAN
b Cannon Falls, Minn, July 21, 27. Study: Univ Minn, BA, MA & PhD. Collections Arranged: Walker Art Ctr, 53; Purcell & Elmslie, Architects, 69; The Enigma of Ralph A Blakelock 1847-1919, 69, Art Galleries, Univ Calif, Santa Barbara, Charles Demuth, 71; Indian Art of the Northern Plains, 74. Teaching: Instr art hist, Univ NMex, 53-55; prof art hist, Univ Calif, Santa Barbara, 61- Pos: Dir, Roswell Mus & Art Ctr, 55-60; dir, Univ Calif Santa Barbara Art Mus, 61- Mem: Soc Archit Historians (2nd vpres). Res: 19th and 20th century architecture; architecture of California; rock art of North America. Publ: Auth, Lloyd Wright, 71; auth, Schindler, 72; co-auth, A Guide to Architecture in San Francisco and Northern California, 73; co-auth, Los Angeles in the Thirties, 1931-41, 75; co-auth, A Guide to Architecture in Los Angeles and Southern California, 75; co-auth, Two Hundred Years of American Architectural Drawings, 76 & A Guide to Architecture in Minnesota, 77. plus others. Mailing Add: 895 E Mountain Dr Santa Barbara CA 93108

GEBHARDT, ANN STELLHORN
PAINTER, EDUCATOR
b Leavenworth, Kans, Mar 13, 16. Study: Lake Erie Col; Ohio State Univ, BFA & MA, with Carolyn G Bradley, James R Hopkins & Alice Schille. Exhib: Two-man show, Mint Mus Art. Teaching: Asst prof art, Queens Col, NC, currently, admin dean of students, 58-71. Mem: Charlotte Art Guild. Mailing Add: 2500 Sherwood Ave Charlotte NC 28207

GEBHARDT, HAROLD
SCULPTOR, EDUCATOR
b Milwaukee, Wis, Aug 21, 07. Study: Layton Sch Art. Work: Milwaukee Pub Libr; Univ Wis-Milwaukee; Los Angeles Mus Art; also in pvt collections. Exhib: Whitney Mus of Am Art, New York; Smithsonian Inst, Washington, DC; Los Angeles Co Art Mus (six occasions); Chicago Art Inst; San Francisco Mus of Art; Denver Art Mus; Portland Art Mus; Museu de Arte Moderna, Sao Paulo, Brazil; DeYoung Mem Mus, San Francisco; and numerous others; one-man shows, Occidental Col, Trinity Univ Gallery, Santa Barbara Mus, San Bernardino Col & numerous others. Teaching: Prof sculpture, Univ Southern Calif, formerly, emer prof, presently. Awards: Milwaukee Art Inst Award, 37; Los Angeles Mus Art, 46 & 50; City of Los Angeles, 48. Mem: Los Angeles Mus Art. Style & Technique: The human figure, from small representational terra cottas to large wood carvings which are abstracted figure forms. Media: Acrylic; Stone, Wood. Mailing Add: 13186 Glenoaks Blvd Sylmar CA 91342

GEBHARDT, PETER MARTIN
SCULPTOR
b Los Angeles, Calif, Dec 10, 43. Study: Univ Southern Calif, 61-65; San Fernando State Col, 62-66. Exhib: Scripps Col Gallery Group Show, 55; one-man shows, Quinn Gallery, Univ Southern Calif, 58-68, The Egg & the Eye, Los Angeles, 67 & Seattle Pac Col, 69; Southwest Craft Ctr, San Antonio, Tex, 73; Elements Gallery, Greenwich, Conn, 74; Studio Gallery, West Covina, Calif, 76; Philip Morris Gallery, Los Angeles, 77; Crafts & Folk Art Mus, Los Angeles, 77; plus others. Mailing Add: 13186 Glenoaks Blvd Sylmar CA 91342

GEBHARDT, ROLAND
SCULPTOR, DESIGNER
b Paramaribo, Surinam, Sept 24, 39; US citizen. Study: Art Acad Hamburg, Ger, with Theo Ortner; Kuntsgewerbeschule, Zurich, Switz; also apprenticeship in stained glass, Marburg, Ger. Work: Art Acad, Hamburg; Brandeis Univ; Storm King Art Ctr. Mountainville, NY; City of Ludwigshafen, Ger; Neuberger Mus, Purchase, NY. Exhib: One-man sculpture & painting exhib, Hudson River Mus, 71; 20th Century Sculpture in Westchester Collection, Yonkers, NY, 72; one-man show, Gallery 84, New York, 73; Carlton Gallery, New York, 74 & 77; Storm King Art Ctr, 75 & 76. Awards: Annual Prize, Art Acad Hamburg, 62. Bibliog: Fred Salaff (auth), Roland Gebhardt—Sculptor (film), 72; Arlene Krebs (auth), Liniar Void (video), 78. Media: Metal, Stone, Fiberglass, Concrete. Mailing Add: 67 Vestry St New York NY 10013

GECHTOFF, SONIA
PAINTER
b Philadelphia, Pa, Sept 25, 26. Study: Philadelphia Mus Col Art, BFA, 50. Work: San Francisco Mus Art; Oakland Art Mus, Calif; Mus of Mod Art, New York; Baltimore Mus of Art; Univ of Iowa Art Mus; plus others. Exhib: Am Painters, US Pavilion, Brussels Fair, Belg, 58; Carnegie Inst, Pittsburgh, 58; First Paris Bienale, France, 59; Sao Paulo Bienale, Brazil, 61; Women Choose Women, New York Cult Ctr, 73; Calif Painting: Mod Era, San Francisco Mus of Art, 76 & Nat Collection of Fine Arts, Washington, DC, 76-77; Drawing Acquisition Shows, Mus of Mod Art, New York, 77 & Extraordinary Women & Am Drawn & Matched, 76-77; plus others. Teaching: Instr painting & drawing, Calif Sch Fine Arts, 57-58; adj asst prof art, NY Univ, 61-71; lectr art, Queens Col, 70-74; assoc prof art, Univ NMex, 74-75. Awards: Purchase Award, San Francisco Mus Art, 57; Ford Found Fel, Tamarind Lithography Workshop, 63; Drawing Prize, Four Corners States Bienale, Phoenix Art Mus, 75; plus others. Bibliog: Hilton Kramer (auth), Her own way, New York Times, 12/10/76. Style & Technique: Paintings and drawings conbining pencil and acrylic; contained and organic forms; non-representational. Mailing Add: 463 West St New York NY 10014

GECK, FRANCIS JOSEPH
PAINTER, DESIGNER
b Detroit, Mich, Dec 20, 00. Study: New York Sch Fine & Apl Art & Paris Atelier, France, dipl; Syracuse Univ, MFA, 46. Exhib: Washington Watercolor Club 54th Ann, Smithsonian Inst, Washington. DC, 50; Pavilion of American Interiors, New York World's Fair, 65; Boulder Nat Bank, Colo, 66; Village Theatre Lobby, Boulder, 67-74; Manufacturers Hanover Trust Gallery, New York, 71; plus many others. Teaching: Instr interior design, New York Sch Fine & Appl Art, Paris Atelier, France, 24-27; prof interior design, Univ Colo, Boulder, 30-69, prof emer, 69- Pos: Interior architect & designer, William Wright Co, Detroit, 27-30; interior architect & consult, T Eaton Co, Toronto, 30; dir, Sherwood Art Gallery, Boulder, 37-40; dir exhib, Boulder Hist Soc, 44-58; cur exhib, Univ Colo, 47-57; dir exhib, Pioneer Mus, Boulder, 58-; design consult, Mullins Plastics, 69-72. Awards: Gold Medal Winner, Grand Nat Show, Am Artists Prof League, 53; Tommaso Campanella Silver Medal, Acad Int Lettre-Arti-Scienze, 70; Benedictine Art Award for Honorable Mention, 71; plus many others. Mem: Boulder Artists Guild (secy-treas, 30-37, 51-52, pres, 44-46 & 71); Boulder Hist Soc (chmn, 37-44, trustee, 44-78, first vpres, 44-46, 56 & 69, pres, 48-50, 52-53 & 70); hon fel Am Inst Interior Designers (educ assoc, 54-72, chmn Rocky Mountain chap comt educ, 57-58); hon fel Interior Design Educ Coun (exec comt, 63-66); hon fel Am Soc Interior Designers. Publ: Auth, Art: the Period Styles, 45; auth, Exercises in Perspective, 48; auth, Introduction to Interior Decoration, 55; auth, Dial-a-Style: English Period Furniture, 66; auth, Interior Design & Decoration, 74; plus others. Mailing Add: 407 16th St Boulder CO 80302

GECSE, HELENE
PAINTER, ETCHER
b Astoria, NY. Study: Glendale Col, Calif, with Jean Abel; Otis Art Inst, Los Angeles, with Joseph Mugnaini, Shiro Ikegawa & Guy Maccoy. Work: Brand Libr Art Ctr, Glendale. Exhib: One-man show, Huntington Galleries, WVa, 65; 11th Ann Drawing & Sculpture Show, Ball State Univ, Muncie, Ind, 65; 6th Nat Prints & Drawings, Ultimate Concerns, Ohio Univ, 65; 32nd Nat Graphics Arts Exhib, Wichita Art Asn, Kans, 65; Arts Southern Calif, Long Beach Mus, 66-67. Media: Paint. Dealer: Robinson's Gallery 2848 Main St Morro Bay CA 93442. Mailing Add: 2400 Pacific Ave San Francisco CA 94115

GEE, HELEN
ART CONSULTANT
US citizen. Collections Arranged: Guest cur, Stieglitz & the Photo-Secession, NJ State Mus, 78. Interest: 19th and 20th century painting, sculpture and photography. Mailing Add: 263 W 11th St New York NY 10014

GEERLINGS, GERALD KENNETH
GRAPHIC ARTIST, ARCHITECT
b Milwaukee, Wis, Apr 18, 97. Study: Univ Pa, BA, 21, MA(archit), 22; Royal Col Art, London, two yrs. Work: Victoria & Albert Mus, London; Metrop Mus Art, New York; Libr Cong & Nat Collection Fine Arts, Washington, DC; Chicago Art Inst; plus others. Exhib: Royal Acad, London; Paris Int Exhib; New York Worlds Fair, 39; Nat Acad Design, New York; Philadelphia Acad Fine Arts; plus others. Awards: Gold Medal for Best Black & White, Philadelphia Acad Fine Arts, 31; First Prize for Best Etching, Chicago Worlds Fair, 33; Nat Arts Club Award, New York. Mem: Soc Am Graphic Artists; Am Inst Architects. Style & Technique: Cityscapes and landscapes in color & black and white. Media: Pencil, Pastels, Watercolor. Publ: Auth & illusr, Metal Crafts in Architecture, 29 & 72, auth & illusr, Wrought Iron in Architecture, 29 & 72 & auth & illusr, Color Schemes of Adam Ceilings, 28, Scribners. Dealer: Uptown Gallery 1194 Madison Ave New York NY 10028. Mailing Add: 26 Gower Rd New Canaan CT 06840

GEESLIN, LEE GADDIS
PAINTER, EDUCATOR
b Goldthwaite, Tex, June 28, 20. Study: Univ Tex; New Orleans Art & Crafts; Art Inst Chicago, BFA & MFA. Exhib: Annually with local & regional shows of the Southwest; one-man shows, Brownsville, San Angelo, Houston, Corpus Christi, Brady, Lufkin, Dallas & Texarkana, Tex, also Shreveport, La, 63- Teaching: Prof art, Sch Art, Sam Houston State Univ, past dean col fine arts. Mem: Tex Watercolor Soc; Tex Fine Arts Soc; Tex Art Educ Asn; Am Asn Univ Prof; Col Art Asn Am. Mailing Add: Sch of Art Sam Houston State Univ Huntsville TX 77340

GEFTER, JUDITH MICHELMAN
PHOTOGRAPHER
b Gloversville, NY. Study: Pratt Inst, cert; NY Univ; Univ Fla; Fla State Univ; also with William E Parker & Wilson Hicks Conf, Univ Miami. Work: Mint Mus, Charlotte, NC; Jacksonville Art Mus, Fla; Tampa Art Inst, Fla. Exhib: ASMP Traveling Show, 62-63; one-woman shows, Pratt Inst, 66 & 67, Retrospect, Jacksonville Art Mus, 70, Breast & Face, Steiglitz Gallery, New York, 75 & Jacksonville Univ-Phillips Gallery, Fla, 77; There is no Female Camera, traveling show, Neikrug Gallery, New York, 75. Pos: Mem exhib comt, ASMP, New York, 61-64; charter mem, Mayor's Adv Comn Arts, 68-74; adv, Jacksonville Arts Assembly, 74-75. Bibliog: Jim Hughes (auth), Women in photography, Camera 35 Mag, 69; Dan Kossoff (producer), Day in Life of a Photographer, PBS Film, Jacksonville, 73; Elizabeth Kaufman (auth), My life & my art, Arts Assembler, 11/75. Mem: ASMP Soc Photogr in Commun (pres, NFla Chap, 65-70); Nat Soc Lit & Arts. Style & Technique: Black & White & color photography from exploratory experimentation through pure photojournalism. Publ: Illusr, Jacksonville Calendar Diary Bicentennial Ed, 76; illusr & ed, St Augustine, 76. Dealer: Neikrug Gallery 224 E 68th St New York NY 10021. Mailing Add: 1725 Clemson Rd Jacksonville FL 32217

GEHR, MARY (MARY RAY)
PRINTMAKER, PAINTER
b Chicago, Ill. Study: Smith Col; Art Inst Chicago, with Paul Wieghardt; Inst Design of Ill Inst Technol, with Misch Kohn. Work: Art Inst Chicago; Philadelphia Mus; Libr Cong, Washington, DC; Nelson Rockefeller Collection; Free Libr, Philadelphia. Comn: Golden Santorini (intaglio-edition of 210 etchings printed by Leterio Calapai), Int Graphic Arts Soc, 67. Exhib: Chicago & Vicinity Exhibs & Soc Contemp Am Art, Art Inst Chicago; Brooklyn Mus Nat Print Exhib; Boston Printmakers, Mass; Print Club. Philadelphia. Awards: Print Fair Award, Philadelphia; First Purchase Award, Artist Guild Chicago; Award for Graphics, Old Orchard Festival, Chicago. Bibliog: John Fink (auth), The Greece of Mary Gehr, Chicago Tribune Mag, 67; T J Carbol (ed), The printmaker in Illinois, Ill Art Educ Asn, 71-72; plus many articles in local papers. Mem: Arts Club Chicago; Print Club Philadelphia; Alumnae of Art Inst Chicago; Soc Typographic Arts; Archaeological Inst Am (Chicago br). Style & Technique: Deeply embossed; multiple inking techniques. Media: Intaglio, Batik. Publ: Illusr, designer & art ed, Exploring the World of Archaeology, 65; illusr, designer & art ed, Exploring the World of Pottery, 67. Dealer: Jacques Baruch Gallery 900 N Michigan Ave Chicago IL 60611 Mailing Add: 1829 N Orleans Chicago IL 60614

GEIGER, EDITH ROGERS
PAINTER
b New Haven, Conn, July 13, 12. Study: Smith Col, BA, 34; Art Students League, 34-35; Yale Univ, with Joseph Albers. Work: Wadsworth Atheneum, Hartford; Tryon Art Mus, Smith Col; Springfield Art Mus, Mass; Art Mus, Ann Arbor, Mich; Bridgeport Univ Art Collection. Exhib: Brooklyn Mus 21st Int Watercolor Biennial; Detroit Nat Watercolor Exhib; Boston Art Festival; Providence Festival, RI; solo exhibs, Bodley Gallery, New York, 56, Ruth White Gallery, New York, 59 & 62, Naples Art Gallery, Fla, 69 & 70. Awards: Best in Show Awards, New Haven Festival Arts, 57 & 62; Woman's Award, Am Watercolor Soc, 62; Nat Asn Women Artists Award, 63. Mem: Nat Asn Women Artists; Am Watercolor Soc; Conn Watercolor Soc. Media: Mixed Media. Dealer: Naples Art Gallery Third St Naples FL 33940. Mailing Add: 2750 Gulf Shore Blvd N Naples FL 33940

GEIS, MILTON ARTHUR
PAINTER, DESIGNER
b Milwaukee, Wis, Jan 31, 26. Study: Univ Florence, Italy; Columbia Univ; Layton Sch of Art, dipl. Exhib: Vicinity Ann, Art Inst of Chicago, 54; Wis Ann, Milwaukee Art Inst, 55 & 56; St Louis Art Mus, Mo, 60; Regional Ann, St Louis Artists Guild, Mo, 74-77; WTex Watercolor Soc Nat Ann, Tex Tech Univ, Lubbock, 74; Rocky Mountain Nat Watermedia

Ann, Foothills Art Ctr, Golden, Colo, 75; Ala Nat Watercolor Soc Ann, Birmingham Mus of Art, 76; 54th Ann Shreveport Nat, Meadows Mus, Centenary Col, La, 76; Southern Watercolor Soc Ann, Nashville, Tenn, 76; 2nd Ann Nat Watercolor, Springfield Art Asn, Ill, 77. Pos: Art dir, WBAY-TV, Green Bay, Wis, 52-56, WXIX-TV, Milwaukee, Wis, 56-60; dir design, KMOX-TV, St Louis, Mo, 60- Awards: Jean Despujols Award & Meadows Mus Purchase Award, 54th Ann Shreveport Nat, Friends of the Mus & Meadows Mus Guild, 76; Arthur Stockstrom Award, St Louis Artist Guild Ann, Strockstrom Mem Fund, 76; Purchase Award, WTex Watercolor Soc Nat Ann, Tex Tech Univ Mus, 74. Mem: Ala Nat Watercolor Soc; Southern Watercolor Soc; Midwest Watercolor Soc; St Louis Artists Guild: Peninsula Arts Asn. Style & Technique: Landscapes/cityscapes. Media: Transparent watercolor, watercolor/drybrush & mixed-watermedia. Dealer: William Engel Gallery 114 E Lockwood St Louis MO 63119. Mailing Add: 8978 Lindenhurst Dr Crestwood MO 63126

GEISEL, THEODOR SEUSS (DR SEUSS)
ILLUSTRATOR, WRITER
b Springfield, Mass, Mar 2, 04. Study: Dartmouth Col, AB, 25, Hon LHD, 56; Lincoln Col, Oxford Univ, 25-26; Am Int Col, 68. Work: All Dr Seuss bk illus & mss in Libr of Univ Calif, Los Angeles. Exhib: One-man show, Fine Arts Gallery, San Diego, 58; 50th Anniversary Retrospective, Dartmouth Col, 75; Toledo Mus of Art, 75-76; La Jolla Mus of Contemp Art, Calif, 76-77. Teaching: Lect on illustrating & writing children's bks. Pos: Advert illusr for indust firms; ed cartoonist, PM (newspaper), New York; publ, Bright & Early Bks; pres, Beginner Bk Div, Random House, Inc; designer children's furniture, Sears Roebuck; producer animated cartoons for TV. Awards: Legion of Merit for Educ & Info Films, World War II; Acad Awards for Best Doc Short, 46, for Best Doc Feature, 51 & for Best Animated Cartoon, 51. Publ: Auth & illusr, The Foot Book, 68, I Can Lick 30 Tigers Today & Other Stories, 69, My Book About Me, 69, I Can Draw It Myself, 70, Mr Brown Can Moo! Can You?, 70, The Lorax, 71 & Marvin K Mooney, Will You Please Go Now!, 72; plus many others. Mailing Add: c/o Random House 201 E 50th St New York NY 10022

GEISSBUHLER, ARNOLD
SCULPTOR
b Delémont, Switz, Aug 9, 97; US citizen. Study: Apprentice with Otto Münch, Zurich, Switz, 14-19; Acad Julian, Paris, France, 19-20; Acad Grande Chaumière, with Bourdelle, 20-25. Work: Art Mus, Bern, Switz, Mus Jurassien, Delémont; Fogg Art Mus, Harvard Univ; Fansworth Mus, Wellesley Col; Chester Dale Collection, Nat Gallery Art, Washington, DC. Comn: Somloire (stone war mem), Town of Somloire, Maine-Loire, France, 24; plaques & reliefs in wood, Foxboro Post Off, Mass, 40; plus many pvt comn. Exhib: One-man show, Delémont, 24; Philadelphia Sculpture Int Show, Pa, 40; Sculpture in US, Metrop Mus, New York, 51; Art in USA, Madison Garden, New York, 58; New Eng Painting & Sculpture Show, Boston, 71; plus many others. Teaching: Instr drawing & sculpture techniques, New York Sch Design, 29-30; instr drawing & sculpture techniques, Stuart Sch Design, Boston, 36-42; instr drawing & sculpture techniques, Wellesley Col, 37-58. Awards: Bronze Medal for Figure, Acad Julian, Paris, 19; Outstanding Award, Art USA, 1958, 58; Cambridge Centennial Award, Cambridge Art Asn. Mem: Sculptor's Guild, New York. Media: Bronze. Mailing Add: Scargo Pines Box 202 Dennis MA 02638

GEISSMAN, ROBERT GLENN
ILLUSTRATOR, DESIGNER
b New Washington, Ohio, Aug 18, 10. Study: Ohio State Univ; study with Joseph Bimder. Work: USAF Art Collection; US Dept Interior, Nat Parks Serv. Exhib: Wildenstein Galleries, 55; Am Watercolor Soc, 56; Nat Soc Painters in Casein, 58; Soc Illusr, 60-74. Teaching: Vis lectr graphic design, Parsons Sch Art & Design, 64-70. Pos: Head dept art, USAF Combat Film Unit, 40-45. Awards: Exceptional Serv Award for Establishing Art Prog, USAF, 55; Dir Award, Nat Soc Painters in Casein, 60; Gold Medal, Soc Illusr, 61. Bibliog: Arthur Watson (ed), article in Am Artist Mag, 58. Mem: Soc Illusr (vpres, 51-52; pres, 53-55); Graphic Artists Guild (pres, 70-76). Style & Technique: Tromp l'oeil; realistic symbolism. Media: Casein, Acrylic. Publ: Designer, Soc Illusr Ann, 64 & 72; contribr, North Light Mag, 70; contribr, North Light Collection, 72. Mailing Add: 225 E 46th St New York NY 10017

GEIST, SIDNEY
SCULPTOR, ART CRITIC
b Paterson, NJ, Apr 11, 14. Study: St Stephen's Col; Art Students League; Acad Grande Chaumiere, Paris. Work: Bard Col, Annandale-on-Hudson, NY. Exhib: Salon Jeune Sculpture, Paris, 50; one-man shows, Paris, 50, New York, 51, 57, 60, Bard Col, 69 & New York, 74 & 76; Pittsburgh Int, 58; Am Artists Ann, Chicago, 62. Teaching: Instr sculpture, Pratt Inst, 61-65; instr sculpture, New York Studio Sch, 64-; instr sculpture, Vassar Col, 67-75. Pos: Dir, New York Studio Sch, 64-66; guest cur, Brancusi Retrospective, Guggenheim Mus, 69. Awards: Olivetti Award, Silvermine Guild, Conn, 60; Guggenheim Fel, 75-76. Bibliog: Thomas B Hess (auth), US sculpture: some recent directions, Portfolio, 59. Mem: Col Art Asn Am. Media: Wood, Stone. Publ: Auth, Brancusi: a Study of the Sculpture, Grossman, 68; auth, Constantin Brancusi: a Retrospective Exhibition, Guggenheim Mus, 69; Brancusi: Sculpture and Drawings, Abrams, 75. Mailing Add: 11 Bleecker St New York NY 10012

GEKIERE, MADELEINE
PAINTER, FILM MAKER
b Zurich, Switz, May 15, 19; US citizen. Study: Art Students League, with Kantor; Brooklyn Mus Art Sch, with Tamayo; NY Univ, with Sam Adler. Work: Worcester Art Mus, Mass; Fogg Mus Art, Cambridge, Mass; NY Univ Collection; Brooklyn Mus, NY; Currier Gallery of Art, Manchester, NH; plus others. Exhib: Univ Ga, 67; Western Carolina Univ, 72; Audubon Artists, New York; NY Univ Loeb Ctr; also many one-man shows in New York; film showings, Millenium & Artists Space, NY & 2nd Int Women's Film Festival, New York Film Forum. Teaching: Asst prof painting, NY Univ, 58-67; assoc prof painting, City Col New York, 67-; vis prof painting, Univ Ga, 67. Awards: Best Illustrated Book of Year, New York Times, 57, 59 & 63; Audubon Medal of Honor, 69; Childe Hassam Purchase Prize, Soc Art & Lett, 73. Mem: Artists Equity Asn. Publ: Auth & illusr, Who Gave Us, 53; illusr, Switch on the Night, 57; auth & illusr, The Princess & the Frilly Lilly, 60; illusr, The Reason for the Pelican, 60; illusr, John J Plenty and Fiddler Dan, 63. Media: Ink, Oil. Dealer: Aaron Berman Galleries 50 W 57th St New York NY 10022. Mailing Add: 427 W 21st St New York NY 10011

GELB, JAN
PAINTER, PRINTMAKER
b New York, NY, July 18, 06. Study: Yale Univ Sch Fine Arts, 24-27; Brittany, with Sigurd Skou, 28-29; Art Students League, 29-32. Work: Whitney Mus Am Art, New York; Metrop Mus Art, New York; Mus Mod Art, New York; Rosenwald Collection, Nat Gallery, Washington, DC; Libr Cong, Washington, DC; and other important collections. Exhib: American Watercolors, Metrop Mus Art, 51; 14 Painter-Printmakers, Brooklyn Mus, 56; Nature in Abstraction, Whitney Mus Am Art, 58; Contemp Am Painting, Birmingham Mus, Ala, 62; Alan R Hite Art Inst, Louisville, Ky, 71; plus others. Awards: Purchase Award, Dulin Gallery, Knoxville, 68; Vera List Purchase Award, Soc Am Graphic Artists, 68; Purchase Awards, State Univ NY Potsdam, 66 & 67; plus others. Bibliog: August I Freundlich (auth), Catalogue of Graphic Works 1929-1972. Mem: Soc Am Graphic Artists (vpres, 66-78); Provincetown Art Asn; fel MacDowell Colony; Printmaking Workshop, NY (bd dirs). Style & Technique: Abstract automatism-flow of color, form and texture. Dealer: Ruth White 845 Byron Lane Sarasota FL 33580; Associated Am Artists 663 Fifth Ave New York NY 10017. Mailing Add: 749 West End Ave New York NY 10025

GELBER, SAMUEL
PAINTER, EDUCATOR
b Brooklyn, NY, Mar 14, 29. Study: Brooklyn Col, BA; NY Univ, MA. Exhib: Brooklyn Mus Biennial, 56; Newark Mus, 58; Berkshire Mus, Pittsfield, Mass, 66; one-man shows, Harry Salpeter Gallery, New York, 67 & Green Mountain Gallery, New York, 72, 74 & 76, A Sense of Place, Wichita Art Mus, Kans, 73, Springfield Art Mus, Mo, 74 & Joslyn Art Mus, Mo, 74; Artist's Choice—Figurative Art in New York, 76. Teaching: Instr drawing, Pratt Inst, Brooklyn, 62-65; prof painting & drawing, Brooklyn Col, 62- Awards: Crane & Co Award for Painting, Berkshire Mus, 66. Bibliog: Gabriel Laderman (auth), Unconventional realists, Artforum, 11/67; Lee Wallin (auth), New Realism 70, St Cloud State Col, 70; Alan Gussow (auth), A Sense of Place—the Artist and the American Land, Friends of Earth, 72. Mem: Artists Equity Asn. Style & Technique: Representational. Media: Oil, Watercolor. Dealer: Green Mountain Gallery 135 Greene St New York NY 10012. Mailing Add: 215 W 98th St New York NY 10025

GELDZAHLER, HENRY
CURATOR
b Antwerp, Belg, July 9, 35; US citizen. Study: Yale Univ, BA; Harvard Univ. Pos: Curatorial asst, Dept Am Paintings & Sculpture, Metrop Mus Art, 60-62, asst cur, 62-63, assoc cur, 63-67, cur, Dept 20th Century Art, 67-; comnr, Dept of Cult Affairs, City of New York, 78- Publ: Auth, American Painting in the Twentieth Century, Metrop Mus Art; New York Painting and Sculpture 1940-1970, Dutton, 69. Mailing Add: Dept of Cult Affairs 830 Fifth Ave Rm 100 New York NY 10021

GELINAS, ROBERT WILLIAM
PAINTER, EDUCATOR
b Springfield, Mass, Mar 1, 31. Study: Univ Conn; Univ Ala, BFA & MFA; also with Lawrence Calgagno & Tatsuiko Heima. Work: Kelley Fitzpatrick Mus, Montgomery, Ala; Mead Corp Collection, Atlanta, Ga; Brooks Mem Gallery, Memphis, Tenn; Carroll Reese Mus, Johnson City, Tenn; Mus Fine Arts, Little Rock, Ark. Comn: Chapel sculpture, Wesley Found Student Ctr, Memphis, 60. Exhib: Art USA, 58, New York, 58; 26th & 27th Corcoran Biennials, Washington, DC, 59 & 61; Painting of the Yr Ann, Mead Corp, Atlanta, 61; Bon Marche Nat Gallery Exhib, Seattle, Wash, 63; Fla Showcase, Rockefeller Ctr, New York, 64. Teaching: Guest artist instr, Allisons Wells Art Colony Workshops, Canton, Miss, 58-62; asst prof art, Memphis State Univ, 58-63; assoc prof art, Univ S Fla, 63- Pos: Art dir, Tuscaloosa News, Ala, 55-57; artist in residence, Maitland Res Ctr, 65; artist in residence, Upham Studio, Naples, 66-69. Awards: Painting of the Year Award, Mead Corp, Atlanta, 61; First Purchase Prize, Mid South Ann, 61; 18th Ann Purchase Exhib Prize, Carrol Reese Mus, 67. Bibliog: Benbow (auth), All out war, St Petersburg Times, 8/65; Gelinas the modern master, Tampa Tribune, 66. Media: Acrylic. Dealer: Trend House Gallery 3629 Henderson Blvd Tampa FL 33609. Mailing Add: Rte 2 Box 1253 Odessa FL 33556

GELLER, ESTHER (ESTHER GELLER SHAPERO)
PAINTER, PRINTMAKER
b Boston, Mass, Oct 26, 21. Study: Mus Fine Arts Sch, Boston, dipl; also with Karl Zerbe. Work: Mus Fine Arts, Boston; Addison Gallery Am Art, Andover, Mass; Brandeis Univ; Walters Gallery, Regis Col; St Mark's Sch Gallery, Southboro, Mass. Exhib: Art Inst Chicago Ann; Univ Ill Ann, Urbana; Boston Art Festivals; US Info Serv Circulating Exhibs in the US & Far East; one-man show, Am Acad Art Gallery, Rome, 71. Teaching: Instr painting & drawing, Sch Mus Fine Arts, Boston, 43; instr painting & drawing, Boris Mirski Art Sch, 46-48; instr painting & drawing, Natick Art Asn Sch, 55-61. Awards: Pepsi-Cola Prize; Cabot Fel, 49; Fels, MacDowell Colony, Yaddo & Am Acad, 50-71. Bibliog: Pratt & Fizell (auth), Encaustic, Lear Publ, 49; Bern Chaet (auth), Artists at Work, Webb, 60; B Hayes (auth), The Layman's Guide to Modern Art. Media: Encaustic, Watercolors. Dealer: Boris Mirski Art Gallery 166 Newbury St Boston MA 02116. Mailing Add: 9 Russell Circle Natick MA 01760

GELLIS, SANDY L
SCULPTOR
b New York, NY, May 20, 40. Study: Sch of Visual Arts, study with Jack Sonenberg; City Col of New York; New Sch for Social Res, FTT (AAS). Exhib: AIR Gallery, New York, 72; Gevind, Charlottenborg, Denmark, 74; 55 Mercer Gallery, New York, 77 & 78; Condensed Space, Nassau Co Mus of Fine Arts, 77 & traveling with NY State Gallery Asn, 78-79. Awards: Creative Artists Pub Serv Prog Grant, 78. Bibliog: David Shirey (auth), Miniature but Monumental, New York Times, 77; Deborah Perlberg (auth), review in Art Forum, 77; Jean Feinberg (auth), Condensed Space (catalog), Nassau Co Mus, 77. Mem: 35 Bond Street Artists Corp; Women's Slide Registry. Style & Technique: Floor and/or earth pieces; models of enclosed environments where organic reactions are taking place. Media: Sand; Cement; Powdered Iron; Wax. Dealer: 55 Mercer Street Gallery 55 Mercer St New York NY 10013. Mailing Add: 39 Bond St New York NY 10012

GELLMAN, BEAH (MRS WILLIAM C MCNULTY)
PAINTER, SCULPTOR
b Philadelphia, Pa, Nov 20, 04. Study: Univ Pa, BS(educ), 25; Art Students League, with Kenneth Hayes Miller, Morris Kantor, Robert Beverly Hale & William C McNulty, 43-46. Work: In many pvt collections. Exhib: One-man & group shows, Rockport Art Asn; one-man shows, Granite Shore Hotel Gallery, Rockport, 65, Gallery Seven, Boston, 66 & Plaza Fifth Ave Gallery, St Petersburg, Fla, 73; three-man show, Lobby Gallery, Rockport, 69. Teaching: Lectr, styling & design principles in the works of masters of painting. Mem: Rockport Art Asn; life mem Art Students League. Style & Technique: Sylized, imaginative. Mailing Add: 441 33rd St N St Petersburg FL 33713

GELMAN, MILTON
COLLECTOR
b Newark, NJ, Nov 3, 14. Study: Art appreciation under John R Grabach & Henry Gasser. Collection: Extensive collection of major works of: H Gasser, Robert Philipp, J Grabach, J Dawley, G Cimiotti and others. Mailing Add: 210 Crestwood Dr South Orange NJ 07079

GENAUER, EMILY
ART CRITIC, WRITER
b New York, NY. Study: Hunter Col, grad; Sch Jour, Columbia Univ, BLit. Teaching: Lectr Am Art Today, Functions of Art Criticism & others. Pos: Staff writer & art feature writer, New York World, 29-31; art critic & ed, New York World-Tel, 32-49; art critic, New York Herald Tribune, 49-66; art critic & ed, New York World Jour Tribune, 66-67; art commentator, Educ TV, New York, 67-; art critic-columnist, Newsday Syndicate, 67-; adv bd, Sch Jour, Columbia Univ. Awards: New York Newspaper Women's Club Award for Outstanding Writing in Spec Field, 37 & for Outstanding Column in Any Field, 49, 56, 58, 60 & 69; Columbia Univ Jour Alumni Award, 60. Mem: Nat Coun Humanities; Int Asn Art Critics; New York Newspaper Women's Club. Publ: Auth, Toulouse-Lautrec (monogr), Metrop Mus Art, 53, Biography of Chagall, 57, Hommage a l'Ecole de Paris, 62, Biography of Tamayo & Chagall at the Met, 71; plus others. Mailing Add: 243 E 49th St New York NY 10017

GENDERS, RICHARD ATHERSTONE
PAINTER, DESIGNER
b London, Eng, Aug 3, 19. US citizen. Study: Herron Sch Art, Ind Univ-Purdue Univ, Indianapolis, with Edwin Fulwider, John Williams Taylor & Donald M Mattison, grad, 50. Work: US Navy Combat Art Collection, Washington, DC. Comn: Mural, Naval Sta, Dam Neck, Va, 55; many landscapes in pvt collections, 50-72. Exhib: Operation Palette Worldwide Traveling Exhib, 50-72; John Herron Art Inst, Indianapolis, 55; Norfolk Mus Arts, Va, 58; Royal Scottish Mus, Edinburgh, 60; Mus Marine, Paris, France, 63. Teaching: Instr fine arts, Indianapolis Art Inst, 48-51; instr com art, Atherstone's Studio, Indianapolis, 50-53; instr fine arts, Rappahannock Community Col, 77-78. Pos: Art dir, US Navy, Norfolk, Va & Washington, DC, 52-65; art dir, NASA, 65-66; art dir, Blair, Inc, Baileys Crossroads, Va, 66-67; dir prod div, Naval Facilities Eng Comd, Washington, DC, 69-75. Awards: First for Watercolor, Ind Artist Club, 50; Postage Stamp Design, US Post Off, Washington, DC, 58; First for Watercolor, Waukegan Art League, 65. Bibliog: Artist with a mission, Indianapolis Star Mag, 55; Operation palette, Chicago Tribune Mag, 64; Lois De Nauw (auth), Variety is the key, Alexandria Gazette, 68. Mem: New Castle Art Asn; Indianapolis Art Asn; Tidewater Art Asn (pres, 55); Waukegan Art Asn (pres, 65); Northern Va Art League (vpres, 69). Media: Casein, Oil, Watercolor. Interest: Motion picture producing and directing. Publ: Contribr, Aviation Safety Rev, 52-58; contribr, US Naval Acad Inst Proc, 59; contribr, Historic Buildings in Middlesex County, Virginia, 77. Mailing Add: Atherstone Hall Urbanna VA 23175

GENIUS, JEANNETTE (JEANNETTE M MCKEAN)
PAINTER, DESIGNER
b Chicago, Ill. Work: Ga Mus Art, Univ Ga; Columbus Mus Art, Ga; Winter Park City Hall, Fla; Jacksonville Art Mus, Fla; Univ Club, Orlando, Fla; Fla Technol Univ. Exhib: Currier Art Gallery, Manchester, NH; Nat Arts Club, New York; Nat Asn Women Artists, New York; Soc Four Arts, Palm Beach, Fla; Stetson Univ. Pos: Dir exhibs, Morse Gallery Art. Awards: First Prize, Fla Fedn Art, 48; Second Prize, Soc Four Arts, 50; First Prize, Pen & Brush Club, 58. Mem: Nat Asn Women Artists; Nat Arts Club; Artists Equity Asn; Soc Four Arts; NH Art Asn. Style & Technique: Non-representational; abstract landscapes and flower portraits. Media: Oil, Pastel. Mailing Add: PO Box 40 Winter Park FL 32790

GENN, NANCY
PAINTER
b San Francisco, Calif. Study: San Francisco Art Inst, Calif; Univ Calif, Berkeley. Work: Albright-Knox Art Gallery, Buffalo, NY; San Francisco Mus Mod Art; Aldrich Mus, Ridgefield, Conn; Cincinnati Art Mus, Ohio; Oakland Art Mus, Calif; NY Univ Art Collection, New York. Comn: Bronze lectern & five bronze sculptures for chancel table, First Unitarian Church, Berkeley, Calif, 61 & 64; bronze fountain, Cowell Col, Univ Calif, Santa Cruz, 66; bronze menorah, Temple Beth Am, Los Altos Hills, Calif, 68; 17 murals in ceramic glazed tile & two bronze fountain sculptures, Sterling Vineyards, Caligosta, Calif, 72 & 73; bronze fountain sculpture, Expo 74, Spokane, Wash, 74. Exhib: Solo shows, M H De Young Mem Mus, San Francisco, 55 & 63, San Francisco Mus Art, Calif, 61, New Worlds, Oakland Art Mus, Calif, 71 & four solo exhibs, Los Angeles Inst Contemp Art, 76; Twentieth Century Drawings, Stanford Univ, Palo Alto, Calif, 55; Winter Invitational, Calif Palace of Legion of Honor, San Francisco, 60-63; Contemp Reflections, 72-73, Aldrich Mus, Ridgefield, Conn, 72-73; Pioneer Printmakers, Contemp Graphics Ctr, Santa Barbara Mus, 74; Works on Paper, Mus Mod Art, New York, 76; The Handmade Paper Object, Santa Barbara Mus Art, 76; New Ways with Paper, Nat Collection Fine Arts, Washington, DC, 77; Paper as Medium, Smithsonian Inst Traveling Exhib, 78-80. Awards: Artists Coun Prize, San Francisco Mus Mod Art, San Francisco Art Asn, 52; Purchase Award Painting, State of Calif, 57; Honor Award for Design Excellence (fountain at Univ Calif, Santa Cruz Campus), US Dept Housing & Urban Develop, 68. Bibliog: Sandy Ballatore (auth), Four Solo Exhibs, Los Angeles Inst Contemp Art, 76. Style & Technique: Non-objective, constructivist; handmade paper, incorporating contrasting colored pulp and fibers in distinctive registers; oil/acrylic paintings on paper and on canvas; sculpture, bronze; investment casting. Media: Working in handformed and embossed paper in multiple layers. Mailing Add: c/o Susan Caldwell Gallery 383 W Broadway New York NY 10012

GENTILE, GLORIA IRENE
DESIGNER, SCULPTOR
b New York, NY. Study: Cooper Union, New York, 47-50; Yale Univ, 51-54, BFA & MFA; study with Josef Albers, Will Barnet, Abraham Rattner, Marscicano, Stuart Davis, Buckminster Fuller, Philip Johnson, Frederick Kiesler, Louis Kahn, Frank Lloyd Wright & Alvin Lustig. Exhib: One-person shows, Harbrace Gallery, 67, Aleksandra Kierekieska Gallery, 68, Art Dir Club Gallery, 68, Young & Rubican Gallery, New York, 68 & Ogilvy & Mather Inc Gallery, 68. Collections Arranged: Sculpture Happening, Mus Mod Art, 72. Teaching: Instr concepts & promotion, Sch Visual Arts, New York, 68-74 & Parsons Sch Design, 72-; instr promotional design, Cooper Union, 74- Pos: Founder & dir, Gentile Studio Graphics, 75- Bibliog: Article in New Worlds of Reading, Harcourt Brace Jovanovich, 69. Style & Technique: Sculpture is articulated with ball joints like mannekins, box sculpture assemblages. Media: Bronze with Ball Joints. Interest: Working on jointed moveable figures with singing or talking installed within to be enlarged for street, building installments. Mailing Add: 333 E 46th St New York NY 10017

GENTRY, HERBERT
PAINTER
b Pittsburgh, Pa, July 17, 19. Study: NY Univ, 38-42; Acad Grande Chaumiere, 46-49. Work: Stedlijk Mus, Amsterdam, Neth; Moderna Museet, Stockholm, Sweden; Metrop Mus of Art, New York; Butler Inst of Art, Youngstown, Ohio; Museo Espanol de Arte Contemporaneo, Madrid, Spain. Exhib: Haus des Kunst, Munich, WGer, 62; Prix Suisse, Lausanne, Switz, 62; Louisiana Mus, Humblebaeck, Denmark, 62; Moderna Museet, Stockholm, Sweden, 63; Kunstnerns Hus, Oslo, Norway, 63; Am Art Ctr, Paris, France, 64; Hallands Mus, Halmstad, Sweden, 68; Univ of Tex Art Mus, 70; Int Art Fair, Basel, Switz, 75-77; one-man shows, Galerie Pinx, Helsinki, Finland, 74, Galerie Andre Zarre, New York, 74, Royal Art Acad, Stockholm, Sweden, 75, Amos Anderson Mus, Helsinki, Finland, 76, Gallery Fabian Carlsson, Gothenburg, Sweden, 76 & Gallery de Grote Ster, Damme, Belg, 77. Mailing Add: c/o Selma Burke Art Ctr 6118 Penn Circle S Pittsburgh PA 15206

GENTRY, WARREN MILLER
INSTRUCTOR, PAINTER
b Manville, Wyo, Oct 3, 21. Study: Ariz State Univ, BA, 50, MA, 55; Univ Calif, Berkeley, 64, with Frank Lobdell. Work: Munic Collection, Orange, France. Exhib: Ariz State Fair Fine Arts Exhib, 49-63; 1st Ariz Ann, Phoenix, 59; Fresh Paint Show, M H De Young Mus, 59; Old Phoenix Art Mus. Teaching: Prof art hist & painting, Glendale Community Col, 63-, founding dir art exhibs & col collection, 67- Awards: Valley Bank Purchase Award, 1st Ariz Ann, 59. Mailing Add: PO Box 4082 Scottsdale AZ 85258

GENTRY (AUGUSTUS CALAHAN, JR)
PAINTER
b Tyler, Tex, Feb 5, 27. Study: Tyler Jr Col, AA, 48; Univ Tex, with Boyer Gonzales, Ralph White & Seymour Fogel, BFA, 52. Work: Am Nat Life Collection, Galveston, Tex. Comn: McKittrick Canyon (16 piece), Donors of McKittrick Canyon Nat Park, Houston, 70. Exhib: New York Int, 70; Southwest Watercolor Soc 100 Best Ann, 73 & 74; Midwest Wildlife Art Show, Kansas City, Mo, 74-75. Teaching: Grad asst sculpture, Univ Tex, 52-53; instr art, Tyler Independent Sch Dist, 53-59; instr watercolor, Tyler Jr Col, 70-73. Awards: Signature Mem Award, Southwest Watercolor Soc, 74; Texas Artist of Year Alt, 74. Bibliog: Wilkins (auth), The local Gentry, Chronicles, Smith Co Hist Soc, 70. Mem: Tex Fine Arts Asn; Southwest Watercolor Soc; Graphics Soc. Style & Technique: Working outside the influence of other artists. Media: Watercolor. Publ: Illusr, Chronicles of Smith Co, Tex, 70 & 71. Dealer: Bryant Galleries 826 Lakeland Dr Jackson MS 39216. Mailing Add: 623 S Chilton Tyler TX 75701

GEOFFREY, SYED IQBAL (JAFREE)
ART ADMINISTRATOR
b Chiniot, Pakistan, Jan 1, 39. Study: Govt Col, Lahore, Pakistan, BA; Sangamon State Univ, MA; Read Col, PhD. Work: Boston Mus Fine Arts; Pasadena Mus Art; Tate Gallery; Arts Coun Gt Britain; Cornell Univ Mus Art. Exhib: Conceptual Occurrences, Hyde Park, London, 60; one-man shows, Arts Coun Pakistan, 64, Cent Wash State Col, 71, Cornell Univ, 72 & Everson Mus, Syracuse, NY, 74. Teaching: Prof fine arts, St Mary's Col, Ind, 67-68; prof fine arts, Cent Wash State Col, 70-71; vis prof fine arts, Cleveland State Univ, 71-72. Awards: John D Rockefeller III Award Creative Painting, 64 & 65; Hon Mention, Paris Biennial, 65; Arts Coun Gt Brit Award, 69. Bibliog: Dr H W Janson (auth), Art of Iqbal Geoffrey, Abrams, 77. Style & Technique: Abstract, supra conceptual. Res: Modern art; aesthetics. Publ: Grad ed, Harvard Art Rev, 65-66. Mailing Add: 149 Strawberry Lane Manchester CT 06040

GEORGE, RAYMOND ELLIS
PRINTMAKER, EDUCATOR
b Cedar Falls, Iowa, Sept 13, 33. Study: Univ Northern Iowa, BA, 55 & MA, 62. Work: Smithsonian Inst, Washington, DC; Calif Palace of Legion of Honor, San Francisco; Victoria & Albert Mus, London, Eng; Libr Cong, Washington, DC; New York Pub Libr. Comn: Ceramic mural, Dubuque Pub Schs, Iowa, 60. Exhib: Contemporary American Prints, State Univ NY Col Oneonta, 69; 50th Nat Graphic Arts Ann, Wichita Art Mus, Kans, 71; Nat Drawing Exhib, Southern Ill Univ, Carbondale, 75; Biennial Int Open Competition, Print Club, Philadelphia, 75; Drawings USA 75, Minn Mus Art, St Paul, 75. Teaching: Assoc prof art, Ill State Univ, Normal, 71- Awards: Purchase Awards, Eight-State Print Exhib, J B Speed Art Mus, 74 & Nat Drawing Exhib, Southern Ill Univ, Carbondale, 75; Fay Carter Drawing Purchase Award, Univ Colo, 74. Mem: Boston Printmakers; Print Club. Style & Technique: Primarily nonfigurative. Media: Intaglio, Lithography; Graphite. Dealer: Dobrick Gallery Ltd 161 E Erie St Chicago IL 60611. Mailing Add: 1907 Garling Dr Bloomington IL 61701

GEORGE, RICHARD ALLAN
PAINTER
b Chicago, Ill, Nov 28, 35. Study: State Univ NY Buffalo, with Larry Calcagno, BFA; Art Students League, with Frank Reilly; Miami Univ, Ohio, with Edwin Fulwider, MFA. Work: Massillon Mus, Ohio; Washington & Jefferson Col, Washington, Pa; Del Mar Col, Corpus Christi, Tex; Arts Club Louisville, Ky. Comn: Painting, Ohio State Off Tower, Columbus, 74; 3 paintings, First Nat Bank, Hamilton, Ohio, 77. Exhib: Ann Mid-Year Show, Butler Inst Am Art, Youngstown, Ohio, 72; one-man shows, Not in New York Gallery, Cincinnati, Ohio, 73, 75 & Ohio State Univ, Columbus, 74; Biennial Show, Cincinnati Art Mus, Ohio, 75; Biennial Contemp Art, Whitney Mus Am Art, New York, 75; Kohler Arts Ctr, Sheboygan, Wis, 77; Contemp Figure Painting in Midwest, Contemp Arts Ctr, Madison, Wis, 77. Teaching: Instr drawing & painting, Middletown Fine Arts Ctr, Ohio, 71- Awards: Award for Painting, Chautauqua Art Asn, 73; Best of Show Award, Ohio State Fair, 73. Mem: Art Students League. Style & Technique: Realistic, contemporary figurative surrealism. Media: Acrylic, Oil. Dealer: Carl Solway Gallery 314 W Fourth St Cincinnati OH 45202; Gallery 200 200 W Mound Columbus OH. Mailing Add: 4440 W Elkton Rd Hamilton OH 45011

GEORGE, THOMAS
PAINTER, PRINTMAKER
b New York, NY, July 1, 18. Study: Dartmouth Col, BA, 40; Art Students League; Acad Grand Chaumiere, Paris; Ist Statale Arte, Florence, Italy. Work: Mus Mod Art, New York; Whitney Mus Am Art, New York; Nat Collection Fine Arts, Washington, DC; Tate Gallery, London, Eng; Guggenheim Mus, New York; plus many others. Comn: Tapestry, Slatkin Art Gallery, New York, 68; poster/print, US Olympic Comt & Kennedy Galleries, New York, 74. Exhib: Carnegie Inst Int, 58 & 61; Whitney Mus Am Art Ann, 60-62 & 65; Japan Int Biennial Art, Tokyo, Japan, 63; Ill Univ Ann, 65; Retrospective Hopkins Ctr, Dartmouth, 65; Nat Collection Fine Arts Inaugural Exhib, 68; Del Mus, 71 & 76; Henie Onstad Art Mus, Oslo, Norway, 71; Princeton Univ Art Mus, 75; Nat Collection Fine Arts, 77; Betty Parsons Gallery, 68, 70, 72, 74 & 76; NJ State Mus, 73; Okla Art Ctr, 74; plus many others. Awards: Purchase Award for Painting, Whitney Mus Ann, 61, Purchase Award for Drawing, 62; Salon Int Galeries Pilote, Lausanne, Switz, 66; Award, NJ State Mus, 72. Bibliog: Gordon Washburn (auth), Forward, Ten Year Retrospective (catalog), Dartmouth Col, 65; Martica Sawin (auth), The nature of symbols of Thomas George, Art Int, 65; J Jacobs (auth), Norway series drawings, Art Gallery Mag, 72; Thomas George (auth), Ink paintings of China, Art Int, 77. Mem: Fel Edward MacDowell Colony. Media: Oil, Gouche; Woodcut. Publ: Illusr, A Line of Poetry, a Row of Trees, Jargon, 65; illusr, Kweilin (auth), An American artist in China, 76. Dealer: Betty Parsons Gallery 24 W 57th St New York NY 10019. Mailing Add: 20 Greenhouse Dr Princeton NJ 08540

GEORGE, WALTER EUGENE, JR
ARCHITECT, DESIGNER
b Wichita Falls, Tex, Oct 28, 22. Study: Univ Tex, BArch, 49; Harvard Univ, with Walter Gropius, MArch, 50. Comn: Many archit comn, 52-77. Teaching: From asst to assoc prof archit, Univ Tex, 56-62; prof archit & chmn dept, Univ Kans, 62-67; dean, Col Archit, Univ Houston, 67-69. Pos: With archit firms, 48-57 & 69-; resident architect, Colonial Williamsburg, Va, 71-73. Awards: First Ann Southwestern Furniture Competition Award, Dallas Mus Fine Arts; Mont San Michele & Chartres Award, Am Inst Architects, 49. Mem: Soc Archit Historians; Am Inst Architects; Archaeol Inst Am. Res: History of architecture of southwest United States; proportional systems. Mailing Add: 1224 American Bank Tower Austin TX 78701

GEORGES, PAUL
PAINTER
b Portland, Ore, 1923. Study: Univ Ore; Hans Hofmann Sch Art; Atelier Fernand Leger, Paris, 49-52. Work: Longview Found; Newark Mus Art, NJ; Mass Inst Technol Collection; Reed Col, Portland; Mus Mod Art & Whitney Mus Am Art, New York; plus others. Exhib: Pa Acad Fine Arts, Philadelphia, 64; Mus Mod Art, New York, 64; Boston Univ, 64; Sch Visual Arts, 65; New Sch Social Res, 65; plus many other group & one-man shows. Teaching: Instr painting, Univ Colo, 60; artist in residence, Dartmouth Col, 64; head sem in art, Yale Univ, 64, mem staff, Sch Art, 64- Awards: Longview Fel; Hallmark Purchase Award, 61; Carol Beck Gold Medal, Pa Acad Fine Arts, 64; plus others. Publ: Contribr, Art News. Mailing Add: Sagaponack NY 11962

GERALD, ELIZABETH BART
See Bart, Elizabeth

GERAN, JOSEPH, JR
SCULPTOR, PAINTER
b 1945. Study: San Francisco City Col, AA, 66; Calif State Univ, San Francisco, BA, 70; Calif Col Arts & Crafts, MFA, 73. Comn: Prints of movie stars, Oakland Mus, 74. Exhib: Los Angeles Co Mus, Los Angeles, 74; RI Sch Design, 75; Southeastern Mass Univ, 75; Bryant Col, 75; Univ Vt, 75; plus numerous group & one-man shows. Teaching: Instr, EOC Summer Youth Prog, 69; lectr, Calif State Univ, San Francisco, 69-71; art consult & sch aide, Galileo High Sch, San Francisco, 70; instr, Booker T Washington Community Ctr, San Francisco, 71; asst prof painting, drawing & sculpture & co-dir ethnic studies div, Calif Col Arts & Crafts, 70-74; adj fac mem, Antioch Col West, 74; dean third world prog, RI Sch Design, 74- Pos: Corp vpres, Col Inc, 70-71; processing chmn, FESTAC 74, 73-74; freelance jewelry designer. Awards: Guy F Atkinson Found Award, 69-71; Ill State Univ Sculpture Award, 73; Distinguished Serv Award, Congressman Ron Dellums, 75. Mem: Nat Conf Artists; San Francisco Art Comn Screening Comt. Publ: Cover design, Black Art, Black Cult, issue, J Black Poetry, 72; photog of art work, Yardbird Reader, 73; cover design, Blacks on Paper, Brown Univ, fall 75. Mailing Add: 19 Academy Ave Providence RI 02908

GERARD, PAULA (MRS HERBERT RENISON)
PRINTMAKER, PAINTER
b Brighton, Eng; US citizen. Study: Pvt study in Florence & Venice, Italy; Univ Florence, with Toesca; Inst Français, Florence, with Soulier; lithography & etching in Paris & Brussels; Art Inst Chicago; painting with Boris Anisfeld. Work: Libr Cong, Washington, DC; Univ Chicago; George F Harding Mus, Chicago; Ringling Mus, Sarasota, Fla; Standard Oil, Chicago; plus others. Exhib: One-man show prints & drawings, Art Inst Chicago, 47, Montgomery Mus Fine Arts, Ala, 71 & Auburn Univ, 75; 1st Biennial Prints, Drawings & Watercolors, Art Inst Chicago, 61; Images on Paper 70, Miss Art Asn, Jackson, 70; Artists of Chicago & Vicinity, Art Inst of Chicago, 77; plus others. Teaching: Instr figure drawing & anat, Layton Sch Art, Milwaukee, 45-62; vis instr graphics & printmaking, Midway Studios, Univ Chicago, 58-65; prof figure drawing & anat, Art Inst Chicago Sch, 62-75, emer prof, 75- Pos: Juror, 11th Dixie Ann Exhib, Montgomery, Ala, 70. Bibliog: Margaret Fish (auth), rev, 6/25/72 & James Auer (auth), rev, 10/13/74, Milwaukee J; Harold Haydon (auth), rev in Chicago Sun-Times, 6/7/74. Mem: Alumni Asn Art Inst Chicago Schs; Renaissance Soc, Univ Chicago (mem bd, 64-75, hon bd mem, 75-); Artists Equity (dir, Chicago Chap, 72-77); Chicago Soc Artists; Arts Club, Chicago. Style & Technique: Linear analysis of form and movement; nudes, landscapes and abstractions of nature elements; silverpoint on casein-coated paper, over watercolor. Media: Silverpoint, Ink, Watercolor. Publ: Illusr, Is Your Contemporary Painting More Temporary Than You Think, 62; illusr, The Great Speckled Bird, Regnery, 64. Dealer: Fairweather Hardin Gallery 101 E Ontario St Chicago IL 60611. Mailing Add: 2043 N Mohawk St Chicago IL 60614

GERARDIA, HELEN
PAINTER, PRINTMAKER
b Russia; US citizen. Study: New York Training Sch; Art Students League; Brooklyn Mus Art Sch; Hans Hofmann Sch. Work: Metrop Mus Art, New York; Brooklyn Mus, NY; Philadelphia Mus; Libr Cong, Washington, DC; Tokyo Artists Ctr, Japan. Exhib: Whitney Mus Am Art, New York; Corcoran Gallery Art Bienniel; Brooklyn Mus Print Ann; Norfolk Mus Drawing Ann; San Francisco Mus Painting Ann; Smithsonian Art Inst, Washington, DC, 59 & 64; Cent Wyo Mus, Casper, 75; Hermitage Mus, Norfolk, Va, 77; Mint Mus, Charleston, NC, 78; one-artist exhibs, Albany Inst of Hist & Art, NY, 55, Evansville Mus, Ind, 61, Miami Mus of Mod Art, Fla, 62 & 67, Asheville Art Mus, NC, 70 & Abilene Fine Arts Mus, Tex, 71. Awards: Medal of Honor in Graphics, Nat Asn Women Artists, 61 & 64, Harry N Abrams Prize for Serigraphy, 76; Medal of Merit, Nat Soc Painters Casein & Acrylic, 70; plus others. Mem: Nat Asn Women Artists (mem permanent adv bd, 74-). Bibliog: Gordon Brown (auth), The new look in art, Art Voices Quart, spring 65. Mem: Nat Asn Women Artists (pres, 72-74); Int Asn Artists (deleg US Comn, 66-78, deleg Int Cong, 68-72); Audubon Artists (dir in oil, 74-76); Soc Am Graphic Artists (treas, 74-78). Style & Technique: Hard edge; abstract; space themes. Dealer: Rudolph Galleries Woodstock NY & Coral Gables FL. Mailing Add: 490 West End Ave 4C New York NY 10024

GERDTS, ABIGAIL BOOTH
ART ADMINISTRATOR, ART HISTORIAN
b New Milford, Conn, June 20, 37. Study: Radcliff Col, AB(fine arts), 60; Syracuse Univ, Sch Art, 62-63. Collections Arranged: Spec exhib, Charles Sheeler (with catalog), Nat Collection of Fine Arts, Smithsonian Inst, 68. Pos: Mem secy, Corcoran Gallery Art, Washington, DC, 59-61; res asst painting dept, Mus Fine Arts, Boston, 61-62; asst cur exhib, Nat Collection of Fine Arts, 64-70, coordr Bicentennial inventory of Am paintings, 70-77, coordr, 19th century exhibs index, 77- Mem: Am Asn Mus. Publ: Contribr, Directory to the Bicentennial Inventory of American Paintings Executed Before 1914, Arno Press, NY, 76. Mailing Add: Nat Collection of Fine Arts Smithsonian Inst Washington DC 20560

GERDTS, WILLIAM H
ART HISTORIAN, EDUCATOR
b Jersey City, NJ, Jan 18, 29. Study: Amherst Col, BA; Harvard Univ, MA. Exhibitions Arranged: New Jersey Artists, 57; Nature's Bounty and Man's Delight, 59; Old Master Drawings, 60, Nineteenth Century Master Drawings, 61; A Survey of American Sculpture, 62; Classical America 1815-1845, 63; The Golden Age of Spanish Still Life, 64; Women Artists of America (1707-1964), 65. Teaching: Assoc prof, Univ Md, 66-69; assoc prof art, Brooklyn Col, 71-74, prof, 74-; lectr American art, collecting art & conservation & restoration, in cols, univs & adult schs. Pos: Dir, Myers House, Norfolk, Va, 53-54; cur painting & sculpture, Newark Mus, NJ, 54-66; dir gallery, Univ Md, 66-69; assoc with Coe Kerr Gallery, New York, 69-71. Publ: Ed, Drawings of Joseph Stella, 62; auth, Painting and Sculpture in New Jersey, Rutgers Univ, 65; contribr, Antiques, Art Quart & NJ Hist Soc Proc. Mailing Add: 150 E 27th St New York NY 10016

GERHOLD, WILLIAM HENRY
PAINTER, EDUCATOR
b Ashtabula, Ohio, Mar 30, 29. Study: Oberlin Col, BA, with Jeanne Miles; Ohio State Univ, MA. Work: Army-Navy Club, Charleston, WVa; Marietta Col, Ohio; Marshall Univ, WVa; WVa Univ, Morgantown. Comn: Oil paintings, comn by Mr & Mrs William Gann, Chicago, Dr & Mrs Albert Kishler, McConnelsville, Ohio, 72, Mr & Mrs W W Watson, Granville, Ohio, Dr & Mrs James Mills, Marietta, Ohio & Dr & Mrs Bernard Wattiker, Rumson, NY. Exhib: Butler Midyear, Youngstown, Ohio; Appalachian Corridors II, Charleston; Perspectives, Cincinnati, Ohio, 70; Forest Festival, Elkins, WVa; Ohio State Fairs. Teaching: Assoc prof educ, Antioch Col, 57-58; assoc prof art hist & painting, Marietta Col, 62-, dir, Mainstreams Exhib, 68- Awards: First Prize for watercolor, Appalachian Arts & Crafts Fair, 70; Best Prof & Best WVa Landscape, Forest Festival, 71-75. Mem: Cent Ohio Watercolor Soc; Am Artists Prof League; WVa Artists & Craftsmen Guild; Allied Artists; Am Watercolor Soc. Style & Technique: Both oil and watercolors are classified as romanticism with emphasis on the landscape and figure rendered in impressionistic techniques, often surrealistic elements. Publ: Auth & illusr, Trinity Rev, 58; WVa Mag, 73 & 74. Dealer: Bonfoeys 1710 Euclid Ave Cleveland OH 44115. Mailing Add: 510 Caroline Ave Williamstown WV 26187

GERIN-LAJOIE, GUY
ARCHITECT
b Montreal, PQ, Can, May 6, 28. Study: McGill Univ, Montreal, BArch; fel, Royal Archit Inst Can; Academician, Royal Can Acad Arts. Exhib: Ital, Monaco & Que Pavilions, Expo 67, Montreal, Que; Peel & Radisson Subway Stas, Montreal, Que; Physical Educ & Univ Ctr, Univ Ottawa, Ont; Sci Res Lab, Igloolik, NW Territories; New Montreal Int Air Terminal Bldg; Girls' Residence, Univ Montreal, Que; Off Bldg, Phase IV, Govt Can, Quebec; plus many others. Awards: Award Nat Housing Design Coun, 62; Massey Medals, Quebec Pavilion, Expo 67, Montreal, 70; Ann Award, Can Archit Yearbk, Povungnituk Sch & Housing Proj, 73. Mem: Ont Asn Archit; Royal Acad Arts; Nat Design Coun; Can-Soviet Mixed Comn Sci & Tech Coop; Arctic Inst NAm. Mailing Add: 2001 University Suite 1100 Montreal PQ H3A 2A6 Can

GERNHARDT, HENRY KENDALL
SCULPTOR, CERAMIST
b Salem, Conn, Aug 3, 32. Study: Norwich Art Sch, Conn; Sch Am Craftsmen, Rochester Inst Technol, NY, with Frans Wildenhain; Sch Art, Syracuse Univ, NY, BA & MFA; Fulbright scholar, Sch Appl Arts, Helsinki, Finland, study with Kyllikki Salmenhaara. Work: Everson Mus Art, Syracuse, NY; Syracuse Univ; DePauw Univ, Greencastle, Ind; Chrysler Mus, Providencetown, Mass; Univ SDak, Vermillion. Comn: Pottery, Imperial House, New York, 60; 24 ft tile mosaic, Syracuse Univ, 63; vase, State Univ NY, Cortland, 67; baptismal font, Lynnwood Reformed Church, Guilderland, NY, 69; sculpture, comn by Alexander E Holstein, Syracuse, 72. Exhib: Ceramic Nat, Everson Mus Art, 54-72; Int Trade Fair, Posen, Poland, 58; Contemp Crafts Exhib, Skidmore Col, Saratoga Springs, NY, 62, 71 & 75; Int Ceramic Exhib, Silvermine Guild Artists, New Canaan, Conn, 64; 22nd Ceramic Ann, Scripps Col, Claremont, Calif, 66; plus 26 one-man shows, 54-75. Teaching: Prof ceramics, Sch Visual & Performing Arts, Syracuse Univ, 60- & Sch Am Craftsmen, summer 71. Awards: Merle Alling Sculpture Award, Rochester Finger Lakes Exhib, Mem Art Gallery, 63 & 71; O Hommel Prize for Pottery, Ceramic Nat, Everson Mus, 68; 1st, 2nd & 3rd Awards, NY State Expos, Syracuse, 71. Bibliog: Reviews and photos of work, Craft Horizons Mag, 64-66, 70 & 75; Lewenstein & Cooper (auth), New Ceramics, Van Nostrand Reinhold, 74; Rick Hirsch (auth), Raku, Watson Guptill, 75. Mem: Nat Coun Advan Ceramic Arts (lectr, 69); Am Crafts Coun; New York Craftsmen (educ chmn, 68-69, bd dir, 70-71). Style & Technique: Abstract, varied. Media: Clay, Glaze. Publ: Auth, Description and cataloging of 22nd & 23rd Ceramic National, Everson Mus Art, 62 & 64; auth, 22nd Ceramic National, article & photographs, Craft Horizons Mag, 63; co-auth, Get Some Clay-Raku, Gallery Asn NY, Brochure for two yr traveling show, 75. Mailing Add: 2581 Webb Rd La Fayette NY 13084

GERSOVITZ, SARAH VALERIE
PRINTMAKER, PAINTER
b Montreal, PQ. Study: MacDonald Col; commun arts grad studies, Concordia Univ; Montreal Mus Fine Arts, drawing with de Tonnancour & design with Gordon Webber; l'Ecole des Arts Appliques; seminars with Gabor Peterdi; Toshi Yoshida & Michael Rothenstein. Work: Am Embassy, Ottawa; Libr Cong, Washington, DC; Art Gallery Australia, Adelaide; Nat Gallery Can, Ottawa, Ont; l'Instituto Cultural Peruano, Lima. Exhib: Bienal Int de Arte de Ibiza, Espana, 72 & 74; 1st Bienal Int de Obra Grafica, Segovia, Spain, 74; 2nd & 3rd Norwegian Int Print Biennale, 74 & 76; 3rd & 4th Int Grafik Biennale, Frechen, Ger, 74 & 76; 11th Int Biennial Graphic Art, Ljubljana, Yugoslavia, 75; 3rd Bienal of Graphic Arts, Cali, Colombia, 76; 11th Biennale Int d'Art, Menton, France, 76; Primera Bienal del Grabado de Am, Maracaibo, Venezuela, 77; plus others. Teaching: Instr silkscreen & printmaking, Sadye Bronfman Ctr, Montreal, 72- Awards: Purchase Awards, Mus du Que, 66, Nat Gallery S Australia, 67, Dawson Col, 74 & Thomas More Inst, 77; First Prize, Concours Graphique, Univ Sherbrooke, 77. Bibliog: Robert Ayre (auth), Silkscreen finesse, Montreal Star, 70; John Graham (auth), Gersovitz serigraphs, Winnipeg Free Press, 72; Guy Robert (auth), L'Art au Quebec depuis 1940; plus others. Mem: Royal Can Acad Arts; Can Soc Graphic Art (mem jury); Can Soc Painter-Etchers & Engravers (mem jury); Soc Artistes Prof Que (mem jury, mem exec). Media: Silkscreen. Publ: Illusr, cover, Figures in a Landscape, Oberon, 67. Dealer: Galerio Martal Sherbrooke St W Montreal PQ Can. Mailing Add: 5173 Mayfair Ave Montreal PQ Can

GERST, HILDE W
ART DEALER
US citizen. Study: Ploner Acad, Italy. Pos: Owner, Hilde Gerst Gallery, New York & Palm Beach, Fla. Mem: Am Asn Mus; Nat Soc Lit & Arts. Specialty: French painting from Impressionist to contemporary; sculpture. Mailing Add: c/o Hilde Gerst Gallery 681 Madison Ave New York NY 10021

GERVASI, FRANK
PAINTER
b Palermo, Italy, Oct 5, 95; US citizen. Study: New York Sch Indust Arts; Art Students League. Work: Brueckner Mus, Albion, Mich; Lubbock Mus, Tex; Okla Mus Art, Tulsa, Comn: Paintings, comn by George T Abell, Oil & Gas Mus, Midland, Tex. Exhib: Nat Acad Design, Allied Artists Am, Am Watercolor Soc & Audubon Artists, New York; Baker Fine Arts Gallery, Tex. Awards: Medal of Honor, Allied Artists Am, 57; First Prize Oil Painting, Salmagundi Club. Mem: Nat Acad Design; Allied Artists Am (pres, 55-57); Am Watercolor Soc; Audubon Artists (treas); Salmagundi Club (vpres, 57-58). Style & Technique: Impressionist. Media: Oil, Watercolor. Mailing Add: PO Box 415 Marfa TX 79843

GERZSO, GUNTHER
PAINTER
b Mexico City, Mex, June 17, 15. Study: German Sch, Mexico City, 34; self-taught. Work: Alvar Carrillo Gil Collection, Mus Mod Art, Mexico City. Comn: Stained glass window, Hotel Aristos, Mexico City, 69. Exhib: One-man retrospectives, Palacio Bellas Artes, Mexico City, 63, Phoenix Art Mus, Ariz, 70 & Univ Tex Art Mus, Austin, 76. Sao Paulo Biennial, Brazil, 65; Galeria de Exposiciones Temporales, Mus Mod Art, Mexico City, 70 & 77. Bibliog: John Canaday (auth), Mexican modernism, New York Times, 4/65; L Cardoza y Aragon (auth), Gunther Gerzso, Nat Univ Mex, 72; Octavio Paz (auth), Gerzso: Centella Glacial, Visual Arts, Mus Mod Art, Mexico City, spring 74. Style & Technique: Abstract surrealist. Media: Oil, Acrylic. Mailing Add: Fresnos 21 San Angel Inn Mexico 20 DF Mexico

GESKE, NORMAN ALBERT
MUSEUM DIRECTOR, EDUCATOR
b Sioux City, Iowa, Oct 31, 15. Study: Univ Minn, BA; NY Univ Inst Fine Arts, MA; Doane Col, hon DFA, 69. Exhibitions Arranged: Ernst Barlach (first Am mus exhib), 55; American Participation, 34th Venice Biennale, 68; American Sculpture, 70; Ralph Albert Blakelock (with catalog), 75. Teaching: Prof, Univ Nebr-Lincoln. Pos: Asst dir, Univ Nebr Art Galleries, 50-53, actg dir, 53-56, dir, 56- Mem: Col Art Asn Am; Am Asn Mus; Asn Art Mus Dirs. Res: Nebraska Blakelock inventory. Publ: Auth, The Figurative Tradition in Recent American Art, 68; contribr, Int Art Exhibs, Arts Mag Yearbk No 10, 69; auth, Rudy Pozzatti, American Printmaker, 71. Mailing Add: 2628 High St Lincoln NE 68502

GETTINGER, EDMOND WALTER
EDUCATOR, PAINTER
b Geneva, Ill, July 9, 41. Study: Mo Valley Col, BS; Wichita State Univ, with David Bernard, MFA. Work: Wichita State Permanent Collection, Kans; Univ SDak, Springfield. Exhib: SDak Art Fac Exhib, Mitchell, 70; one-man shows, Mo Valley Col, Marshall, 71, Dickenson State Col, NDak, 72, Mt Marty Col, Yankton, SDak, 73 & Univ SDak, Vermillion, 74. Teaching: Asst prof multi-media, Univ SDak, 70-; guest artist painting, Mt Marty Col, 72. Mem: Nat Woodcarvers Asn. Style & Technique: Landscapes in oil, expressive. Media: Oil, Intaglio. Mailing Add: 1011 Pine Springfield SD 57062

GETTY, NILDA FERNANDEZ
EDUCATOR, METALSMITH
b Buenos Aires, Arg, June 2, 36; US citizen. Study: Archit at Buenos Aires Univ, Univ NC, Raleigh & Univ Pa; Stetson Univ, Deland, Fla, BFA(art); Univ South Fla, Tampa; Univ Ga, MFA(metalsmithing & printmaking). Work: Deland Mus, Fla; Univ South Fla; Denver Art Mus; Minn Mus of Art, St Paul; Colo State Univ. Comn: St Luke's Chalice, St Luke's Episcopal Church; eleven 3ft diameter copper emblems, Larimer Co High Sch. Exhib: One-person shows, Law Libr Gallery, Univ Ga, Athens, 70, Galeria Martinez, Buenos Aires, Arg, 72, Kruger Gallery, New York, 77, Minn Mus of Art, St Paul, 77; Metalsmiths Invitational, De Cordova Mus, Lincoln, Mass, 74; McGuire Gallery, Rexdale, Ont, 74; US Metalsmiths, Renwick Gallery, Smithsonian Inst, Washington, DC, 74; Goldsmiths Invitational (travelling exhib), Minn Mus Art, St Paul, 74; Lowe Art Mus, Univ Miami, Coral Gables, Fla, 75; Five Artists in Metals, Denver Art Mus, 75; Metals Invitational, Fullerton Gallery, Calif, 75; two-person show, Gryphon Gallery, Denver, 75 & 77; Sheldon Mem Art Gallery, Lincoln, Nebr, 76; NAm Goldsmith Invitational, Phoenix Mus, Ariz, 76-77; Metals Invitational, Henry Gallery, Seattle, Wash, 77. Teaching: From instr to assoc prof metalsmithing, Colo State Univ, Ft Collins, 70- Pos: Independent artist, 66- Bibliog: Donald Willcox (auth), Body Jewelry: International Perspectives, Regnery Publ, 73; Philip Morton (auth), Contemporary Jewelry, Holt, Rinehart & Winston, 2nd ed, 76. Mem: Soc NAm Goldsmiths (mem, Int Exhib Comt, 77-80); Am Crafts Coun; World Crafts Coun. Style & Technique: Silver and goldsmith; designer; fabric designs; printmaker. Publ: Auth, Contemporary crafts, Ceramics Mo, 75; auth, Crafts in the Americas, Crafts Horizons, 74. Mailing Add: 1912 Mohawk Ft Collins CO 80521

GETZ, DOROTHY
SCULPTOR
b Grand Junction, Iowa, Sept 7, 01. Study: Ohio State Univ, BA, 23, MA, 32; Acad Belle Arti, Perugia, Italy, summers 62, 63 & 65. Work: Columbus Gallery Fine Arts, Ohio; Akron Inst Am Art, Ohio; Sassaferato, Italy. Exhib: Ceramic Nat, Syracuse, NY, 52 & 54; Five Ohio Ceramic & Sculpture Shows, Akron, 55-64; Drawing & Small Sculpture Ann, Ball State Univ Art Gallery, 56, 58 & 59. Teaching: Prof art hist, drawing & interior design, Ohio Wesleyan Univ, 45-72. Pos: Fashion illusr, Fashion Co, Columbus, Ohio, 32-38; fashion illusr, The Union Co, Columbus, 38-45. Awards: Salvi Prize, 4th Piccolo Europa, Sassaferato, Italy, 63; Purchase Prize, Ohio Ceramic & Sculpture Show, Akron Inst Am Art, 64; Purchase Prize, Columbus Gallery Fine Arts, 66. Style & Technique: Semi-abstract human figures. Mailing Add: 64 W Winter St Delaware OH 43015

GETZ, ILSE
PAINTER, COLLAGE & ASSEMBLAGE ARTIST
b Nuremberg, Ger, Oct 24, 17; US citizen. Study: Art Students League, with Morris Kantor & George Grosz. Work: Carnegie Inst, Pittsburgh; Tel-Aviv Mus, Israel; Aldrich Mus, Ridgefield, Conn; Neuberger Mus, Purchase, NY; Hirshhorn Mus, Washington, DC; plus others. Comn: Designed set for Ionesco's The Killer, New York, 60. Exhib: Phoenix Art Mus, Ariz, 64; Davis Art Ctr, Wesleyan Univ, 67; Hopkins Ctr, Dartmouth Col, 67; Lawrence Art Mus, Williamstown, Mass, 73; Allentown Art Mus, Pa, 73; Kostiner-Silvers Gallery, Montreal, 75; Retrospective, Neuberger Mus, Purchase, NY & Kunsthalle, Nuremberg, Ger, 78; one-man shows, Gimpel-Weitzenhoffer Gallery, New York, Sid Deutsch Gallery, New York & Benson Gallery, Bridgehampton, NY, 78; plus others. Teaching: Instr art, Positano, Italy, summers 56 & 58. Awards: Yaddo Fel, 59. Dealer: Gimpel & Weitzenhoffer, 1040 Madison Ave New York NY 10021. Mailing Add: Saw Mill Rd Newtown CT 06470

GEYER, LUISE MARGOT
COLLECTOR
b Wilhelmshaven, Ger, Jan 24, 23. Study: Philipps Univ, Marburg/Lahn, Ger, MD; Univ WBerlin, lic specialist(psychiatry & neurology); Univ Tenn, Memphis, three yrs residency(psychiatry); Ill Univ, Chicago, lic(physician & surgeon). Collection: Antique jewelry, art objects, rugs, large collection paintings, drawings, graphics by contemporary American artists, strong in self portraits by artists; graphics and drawings of Kenneth H Verzyl; works by Twardowicz, Christopher, Swayhoover, Kim Greer Verzyl, Benda, Aebi, Naomi Hilton and many others. Mailing Add: Vet Admin Hosp Northport NY 11768

GHENT, HENRI
CRITIC, WRITER
b Birmingham, Ala, June 23, 26. Study: US Armed Forces Inst, Honolulu, Hawaii, 45-46; New Eng Conservatory, Boston, 47-51; Marian Anderson scholar, 51 & 52; Georges Longy Sch, Cambridge, 51-53; Martha Baird Rockefeller grant, 57; Univ Paris, 58-60; also pvt study in Ger & Eng. Collections Arranged: The Invisible Americans: Black Artists of the 1930s, 69; 10 Afro-American Artists, Mt Holyoke Col, 69; 15 International Artists, Community Gallery, Brooklyn Mus, 69, Allusions, 2nd Anniversary Exhib, 70 & Native North American Art: Mixed Media Works by Contemporary American Indian Artists, 72; Afro-American Artists: Since 1950, Brooklyn Col, 69; 8 Afro-American Artists, Rath Mus, Geneva, Switz, 71; 1972 All-Ohio Painting & Sculpture Biennial, Art Inst, Dayton, 72. Teaching: Vis lectr, Col Finger Lakes Series, 70-71 & Dayton Art Inst, Ohio; Queens Col, NY, 74. Pos: Consult, Minn Mus Art, St Paul, Dayton Art Inst, Mt Holyoke Col, Rath Mus, Geneva & Mus d'Art Haitien, Port-au-Prince, Haiti; with Allen Univ; dir, Community Gallery, Brooklyn Mus, 68-72. Awards: Samuel H Kress Found Res Fel, 72-73; Art Critic's Fel, Nat Endowment Arts, 73; Ford Found Res-Travel Grant, 74-75. Bibliog: Articles in Boston Sunday Globe, 12/7/75, Village Voice, 7/19/76 & Los Angeles Times, 10/10/76; plus others. Mem: Smithsonian Assocs; Int Soc Educ Through Art; African-American Inst; Nat Art Educ Asn; Nat Soc Lit & Arts. Interest: Eclectic art with emphasis on contemporary painting, sculpture and graphics. Collection: Contemporary painting, sculpture & graphics. Publ: Auth, White is not superior, New York Times, 12/8/68; auth, Black creativity in quest of an audience, Art in Am, 5-6/70; contribr, Eight Afro-American Artists (catalog), Rath Mus, 6/71; The second generation, Art Gallery Mag, 6/74; auth, Spanish art in transition, Art Int, 10/15/75. plus others. Mailing Add: 310 E 75th St Apt 1-F New York NY 10021

GHIKAS, PANOS GEORGE
PAINTER, EDUCATOR
b Malden, Mass. Study: Yale Univ Sch Fine Arts, BFA, 43, MFA, 47; Akad der Bildenden Kunste, Stuttgart, Ger, with Willi Baumeister, 53-54. Work: Wadsworth Atheneum, Hartford, Conn; Walker Art Mus, Bowdoin Col; New Britain Mus Am Art, Conn; Colby Col; Art Mus, Waterville, Maine; plus others. Exhib: Abstract & Surrealist Show, Chicago Art Inst, 47; 2nd Int Salon des Realites Nouvelles, Paris, France, 48; Annual of American Painting, Whitney Mus Am Art, 49; American Painting Annual, Univ Ill, 50; Worcester Mus Biennial Contemp Am Painting, 52. Teaching: Vis artist design, Carpenter Ctr, Harvard Univ, 64-66; vis prof drawing, Bowdoin Col, 70-71; prof painting, RI Sch Design, Providence, 71- Pos: Asst conservator, Yale Univ Art Gallery, 57-59. Awards: Fulbright Fel, 53; MacDowell Colony Fel, 67; Blanche E Colman Found Grant, 69. Bibliog: Chaet (auth), Artists at Artists at Work, Webb, 61. Style & Technique: Flat sculptural shapes in equilibrium using color contrast and the egg tempera medium to create a sense of space and form. Media: Egg Tempera. Publ: Illusr, Tales of Christophilos, 54; illusr, Again Christophilos, 56; illusr, The Golden Bird, 57; illusr, The Golden Sword, 60. Mailing Add: 30 Ipswich St Boston MA 02215

GIACOMANTONIO, ARCHIMEDES ARISTIDES
See Manton, Jock

GIAMBERTONE, PAUL
SCULPTOR
b Italy; US citizen. Study: Beaux Arts Inst Design, New York, with Gaetano Cecere; Educ Alliance, New York, with Chaim Gross. Work: Safad Mus, Israel; Philothea Mus, London, Ont. Exhib: Nat Arts Club, New York, 57; Silvermine Guild Artists, New Canaan, Conn, 58; NJ Soc Painters & Sculptors, Jersey City Mus, 59 & 60; Am Soc of Contemp Artists, Nat Arts Club, New York, 76. Awards: Ivan R Laskins Award for Sculpture, 70. Bibliog: M Eder (auth), In the art galleries, East, 6/6/57; E Pollet (auth), In the galleries, 6/57 & Margaret Breuning (auth), Margaret Breuning writes, 7/59, Arts Mag; Dorothy Hale (auth), Parkeast, 11/77. Mem: Artists Equity Asn New York; League Present Day Artists (dir, 60-); Am Soc Contemp Artists (dir, 73-); Sculptors League, Contemp Artists Guild. Style & Technique: Precast and precut metal shapes are welded together to build abstract forms expressing centrifugal and centripetal elements in nature. Media: Welded and Cast Bronze. Dealer: Brownstone Gallery 76 Seventh Ave Brooklyn NY 11217. Mailing Add: 121 E 23rd St New York NY 10010

GIAMPAOLI, JAMES FRANCIS
PAINTER, PRINTMAKER
b Baltimore, Md, Mar 11, 37. Study: Univ of Md, BA & MA; San Carlos Acad, Mexico City, Mex. Work: San Carlos Acad; Univ of Md; King's Palace, Marrakesh, Morocco; Treas Dept, Washington, DC. Exhib: Dept of Labor, 61, Smithsonian Inst, 62, Corcoran Mus, 65, Franz Bader, 65 & Nat Inst of Sciences, 77, Washington, DC; Inst Nac de Bellas Artes, San Miguel Allende, Guanajuato, Mex, 73; one-man shows, King's Palace, Marrakesh, Morocco, 66 & Wolfe Street Gallery, Washington, DC, 77. Teaching: Instr drawing, Corcoran Sch of Art, Washington, DC, 67-71; instr lithography, Inst Allende, San Miguel Allende, Guanajuato, 75- Awards: Artist-in-Residence, King's Palace, Marrakesh Moroccan Cul, Dept of Parks & Monuments, Rabat, Morocco, 66. Style & Technique: Expressionistic oil paint on canvas; figure, landscape, nudes and social-political themes. Media: Oil Paint on Canvas; Stone Lithography in Black and White and Color. Dealer: Louie Andre c/o Wolfe Street Gallery M St NW Washington DC Mailing Add: 56 Mesones San Miguel Allende Guanajuato Mexico

GIANAKOS, CRISTOS
SCULPTOR
b New York NY, Jan 4, 34. Study: Sch Visual Arts, grad cert. Work: Mus Mod Art, New York; US Info Agency; Nat Bank of Boston; Brutten & Herrick Artworks. Exhib: Whitney Mus Am Art, New York, 69; A Plastic Presence, Jewish Mus, New York, Milwaukee Art Ctr, Wis & San Francisco Mus Art, Calif, 70; Mus Mod Art, New York, 71; one-man shows, Hundred Acres, New York, 71 & 73 & 55 Mercer, New York, 75 & 77; New York Cult Ctr, 72; PS 1, Queens, NY, 78. Teaching: Instr Sch Visual Arts, 65- Awards: Creative Artists Pub Serv Grant, 76-77. Bibliog: Images of an Era: The American Poster 1945-75, Smithsonian Inst, 75; R Pincus-Witten (auth), A plastic presence, Artforum, 1/70. Style & Technique: Indoor and outdoor installation environments; series of Ramp works. Media: Mixed-Media Construction Material. Mailing Add: 93 Mercer St New York NY 10012

GIANAKOS, STEVE
SCULPTOR, PAINTER
b New York, NY, 1938. Study: Pratt Inst, Brooklyn, NY. Exhib: Plastics as Plastic, Inst Contemp Art, Univ Pa, Philadelphia, 69; Works on Paper, Mus Mod Art, Art Lending Serv, New York, 74; Chairs, Art Gallery Ont, Toronto, 75; Rooms, Proj Studio 1, Inst for Art & Urban Resources, Long Island, NY, 76; Improbable Furniture, Inst of Contemp Art, Univ Pa, 77; Theodoron Awards Exhib, Guggenheim Mus, New York, 77; Contemp Greek-Am Artists, Brooklyn Mus, NY, 77; one-man shows, Fischbach Gallery, New York, 68, The Clocktower, Inst for Art & Urban Resources, 74, Alessandra Gallery, New York, 76 & Droll-Kolbert Gallery, New York, 78. Mailing Add: c/o Droll/Kolbert Gallery Inc 724 Fifth Ave New York NY 10019

GIANNOTTI, JOHN J
SCULPTOR, EDUCATOR
b New York City, NY, Dec 28, 45. Study: State Univ New York, Buffalo, BFA(cum laude); Rutgers Univ, MFA. Work: Charles Rand Penney Collection, Lockport, NY; Rutgers Univ, Camden, NJ. Comn: Playground park, Atlantic City Housing Authority, 74; interior graphics, Philadelphia Mus of Art, 76; graphics, Philadelphia Bicentennial, 76. Exhib: Earth Art 73, Philadelphia Civic Ctr, 73; 13th Ann, Univ Del, 74; NJ Nine, NJ State Mus, Trenton, 74; Appalachian Nat Drawing Show, NC 75; From the Cast, Philadelphia Art Alliance, 77; 29th Ann, Albright-Knox Art Gallery, Buffalo, NY, 67; one-person show, Philadelphia Art Alliance, 77. Teaching: Asst prof dept art, Rutgers Univ, Camden Col 70-76 & assoc prof art, 76- Awards: Research Grant Playground Design, Rutgers Univ, 72; Logo Design, Camden Cult Comm, 74; Award of Distinction, NJ Seven, Somerset Assoc, 77. Mem: Southern Assoc of Sculptors. Style & Technique: Construction and carving. Media: Wood, Acrylic Lacquer, Traditional Casting. Mailing Add: 611 Price Dr Mt Holly NJ 08060

GIBBONS, HUGH (JAMES)
PAINTER, EDUCATOR,
b Scranton, Pa, Oct 26, 37. Study: Pa State Univ, with Elaine de Kooning & Robert Mallary, BA(painting), 59, MA(painting), 61. Work: WTex Mus, Lubbock; Bucknell Univ Collection. Exhib: One-man shows, St Peter's Gallery, New York, 72, Pan-Am Health Orgn, Washington, DC, 74 & NMex Jr Col, Hobbs, 77; New Orleans Biennial, 73; 12th Del Mar Ann, Corpus Christi, Tex, 77; The Amarillo Competition, Tex, 77; two-man show, Tex Tech Art Gallery, Lubbock, 76; plus others. Teaching: Assoc prof painting & drawing & MFA coordr, Tex Tech Univ, 63- Awards: Award for drawing, Mus NMex, 64 & 66; First Prize in Graphics, Midland, Tex, 71. Media: Oil, Pastel. Mailing Add: 3312 20th St Lubbock TX 79410

GIBBS, CRAIG STEVENS
SCULPTOR, EDUCATOR
b Summit, NJ, July 5, 48. Study: Miami-Dade Jr Col, AA; Univ Fla, with Jeff Naylor & Hiram Williams, BFA, 70; Univ Mich, Ann Arbor, with Thomas McClure, MFA, 72. Work: Marion Sr High Sch, Ind; Syracuse Univ, Col Visual & Performing Arts; Univ Fla Permanent Drawing Collection; Blackford High Sch, Ind; also in pvt collection of Jane & Ray Greenawalts, Detroit. Exhib: 1st All Mich Exhib, Flint Inst Arts, 71; 7th Biennial Michiana, South Bend, Ind, 72; Southeastern Asn Sculptors Nat Competition (traveling), 74-75; Radial 80, Xerox Corp, Rochester, NY, 74; CAST Collective Show, NY State Endowment for Arts, Everson Mus, 75. Teaching: Grad asst 3-D design & teaching fel, Univ Mich, Ann Arbor, 70-72, guest lectr, summer 72; instr sculpture, Syracuse Univ, 73- Pos: Artist in residence, Impact Prog, Nat Endowment for Arts, Marion High Sch, Ind, 72-73. Awards: Most Outstanding Sculpture in Undergrad Study, Univ SFla, 70; Ned Dybig Mem Grad Award, Univ Mich, 71; NY State Grant, Endowment for Arts, 74-75. Bibliog: Edward Breen (auth), Resident artist, Marion Newspaper Sun Mag, Ind, 1/73. Style & Technique: Industrial processes of the 70's; imagery is that of the future, plantlike, science-fiction oriented; primarily outdoor lifesize or larger sculpture. Media: Aluminum, Bronze. Res: Innovation of process and idea; paralleling and reflecting industrial processes of the times. Mailing Add: 108 Ruth Ave Syracuse NY 13210

GIBBS, TOM
SCULPTOR
b Dubuque, Iowa, Sept 17, 42. Study: Loras Col, BA(art); Univ Iowa, with Olivier Strabelle, MA(sculpture) & MFA; also with Walter Arno, Ger. Comn: Mo-Mac (exterior steel sculpture), comn by Sol Greenstein, San Francisco, 72; Winged Victory (steel), Cent Col, Pella, Iowa, 75; Untitled (steel), comn by John Tauke, Bath, Pa, 75; four large scale steel sculptures, City of Dubuque, Iowa, 75-76; Broken From Whole (steel), Franklin Pub Libr, Des Moines, Iowa, 77. Exhib: Painting & Sculpture Biennial, Walker Art Ctr, Minneapolis, 68; Mus Art, Univ Iowa, 69; Four Sculptors, Univ Ky, Moorehead & Richmond, 69; Young Sculptor's Competition, Sculptor's Guild, New York, 70; Three Large Scale Sculptures, Paducah, Ky, 76; Iowa Arts Coun Touring Exhib of Monumental Sculpture, 77. Teaching: Instr art, Clarke Col, 68-69; asst prof sculpture, Ariz State Univ, 70-72. Awards: Ariz State Univ Fac Grant, 71; Nat Community Art Competition Award, US Dept Housing & Urban Develop, 73; Sculptor-in-Residence, City of Dubuque, 75-76. Mem: Nat Art Workers Community. Style & Technique: Monumental sculpture. Media: Steel, Wood and Bronze. Dealer: Zaks Gallery 620 N Michigan Ave Chicago IL 60611. Mailing Add: 1333 Kaufman Dubuque IA 52001

GIBRAN, KAHLIL GEORGE
SCULPTOR
b Boston, Mass, Nov 29, 22. Study: Boston Mus Sch, 40-43, painting with Karl Zerbe. Work: Chrysler Collection, Va Mus, Norfolk; Pa Acad Fine Art, Philadelphia; Cheekwood Art Ctr, Nashville, Tenn; Elmira Col, NY. Comn: Bronze wall mural, Forsythe Dental, Boston, 71; bronze plaque of Judge Francis Ford, Fed Ct House, Boston, 77; bronze plaque of poet Kahlil Gibran, Copley Sq, Boston, 77. Exhib: Whitney Mus Am Art Ann, 56; Art USA, 58; Art Festival, Boston, 64; Int, Trieste, Italy, 66; New Eng Artists, Provincetown Art Asn & Cyclorama, Boston, 71; one-man show of bronze sculpture, Cambridge Art Asn, 77. Awards: George Wiedner Medal, Pa Acad Fine Arts, 58; John S Guggenheim Fel, 59-61; Nat Inst Arts & Lett Award & Fel, 61. Bibliog: Gregory MacDonald (auth), Kahlil Gibran a Boston sculptor, Boston Globe Mag, 67; Nathan Hale (auth), Welded Sculpture, Watson-Guptill, 68; Donald Irving (auth), Sculpture Material and Process, Van Nostrand Reinhold, 70. Mem: Nat Sculpture Soc; New Eng Sculpture Soc; Cambridge Art Asn (vpres, 68-); Provincetown Art Asn. Style & Technique: Welded iron wire and hammered iron sheet in humanistic and figurative form. Media: Steel. Publ: Auth, Sculpture in process, Nat Sculpture Rev, 70; auth, Sculpture Kahlil Gibran, 72; co-auth, Kahlil Gibran His Life and World, New York Graphic Soc, 74. Mailing Add: 160 W Canton St Boston MA 02118

GIBSON, GEORGE
PAINTER, ART ADMINISTRATOR
b Edinburgh, Scotland, Oct 16, 04; US citizen. Study: Edinburgh Col Art; Glasgow Sch Art, Scotland; W E Glover Scenic Studios, Glasgow; Chouinard Sch Art, Los Angeles; also with F Tolles Chamberlain, Pasadena, Calif. Work: Calif Nat Watercolor Soc Collection, Los Angeles Co Mus Art; Home Savings & Loan, Los Angeles; Laguna Beach Mus Art, Calif; Santa Barbara Mus Art, Calif; Santa Paula CofC, Calif. Exhib: Calif Nat Watercolor Soc Ann, 47-71; Am Watercolor Soc Ann, 49-72; Nat Acad Design, New York, 54-58; Phoenix Art Mus, Ariz, 72. Pos: Supvr scenic art prod, MGM Studios, Culver City, Calif, 34-69. Awards: Calif Nat Watercolor Soc 32nd Ann Award, 51; Nat Acad Design 134th Ann Watercolor Award, 59; Verda Karen McCracken Young Award, Am Watercolor Soc 105th Ann, 72. Bibliog: V Hewtschy (auth), From any angle, 10/54 & Ron Ross (auth), Cameraman's comments, 12/54, Int Photogr; G Gibson (auth), Scenic art in motion picture industry, Soc Motion Picture & TV Eng J, 10/62. Mem: Assoc Nat Acad Design; Am Watercolor Soc; Calif Nat Watercolor Soc (secy, 47, first vpres, 49, pres, 51); West Coast Watercolor Soc; Acad Motion Picture Arts & Sci. Media: Watercolor. Publ: Contribr, Am Artist, 5/68 & 9/69. Dealer: Emerson Galleries 17230 Ventura Blvd Encino CA 91316. Mailing Add: 12157 Leven Lane Los Angeles CA 90049

GIBSON, JAMES D
ART ADMINISTRATOR, PAINTER
b Milbank, SDak, Dec 13, 38. Study: Ill Wesleyan Univ, BFA; Ohio Univ, BFA. Work: SDak Mem Art Ctr, Brookings; State Univ New York Col at Fredonia; Emporia Kansas State Col. Comn: Mural, hist panorama (with Vic Runnels), First Nat Bank, Aberdeen, SDak, 76. Exhib: Artists of Montana, Senate Off Bldg, Washington, DC, 65; Hawaiian Nat Print Competition, 71; Nat Environ Print Show, Univ Wis, Green Bay, 71; 12th Midwest Biennial, Joslyn Art Mus, Omaha, Nebr, 72; Nat Print Show, Minot, NDak, 73. Teaching: Instr art, Eastern Mont Col, 65-67; assoc prof art, Northern State Col, SDak, 67- Pos: Chmn dept art, Northern State Col, SDak, 67-78; mem bd of dir, Nat Asn of Sch of Art, 71-72. Awards: Purchase Award, Paintings, 68 & SDak Works on Paper, 71-72, SDak Mem Art Ctr. Style & Technique: Expressionist. Media: Acrylic, Intaglio; Pen, Ink. Publ: Illusr, Motive Mag, Methodist Church, 68-70; auth, Campus Call, Catholic Church, 68; illusr, Sunday Clothes, Arts Coun SDak, 73. Mailing Add: RR 1 Box 60 Westport SD 57481

GIBSON, RALPH H
PHOTOGRAPHER
b Jan 16, 39. Study: US Navy, studied photog, 56-60; San Francisco Art Inst, 60-61. Work: Mus Mod Art & Metrop Mus Art, New York; Int Mus Photog, George Eastman House, Rochester, NY; Fogg Art Mus, Cambridge, Mass; Ctr for Creative Photog, Univ Ariz, Tucson; Nat Gallery of Can, Ottawa, Ont; plus many others. Exhib: Basel Art Fair, Switz, 75; Four Am Photogrs, Stadisches Mus, Leverkusen, Ger, 75; 6th Rencoutres Int d'Arles, France, 75; Photog for Collectors, 76, Rooms, 77 & Mirrors & Windows, 78, Mus Mod Art, New York; Recent Acquisitions, Stedelijk Mus, Amsterdam, Neth, 76; Baltimore Mus, Md, 76; Contemp Am Photog, Mus Fine Arts, Houston, Tex, 77; Friends of Photog, San Francisco Mus Art, Calif, 77; The Great Am Foot, Mus Contemp Crafts, New York, 78; Additonal Info, Univ Md, 78; Bologna Art Fair, Italy, 78; Walter Art Ctr, Liverpool, Eng, 78; one-man shows, Hoesch Mus, Duren, Ger, 75, Madison Art Ctr, Wis, 75, Univ Guelph, Can, 76, Baltimore Mus Art, Md, 76, Swedish Mus Photog, Stockholm, 76, Tex Ctr for Photog Studies, Dallas, 76, Fotografiska Museet, Stockholm, 77, Mus Mod Art, Oxford, Eng, 77, Camera Obscursa, Stockholm, 78 & Castelli Uptown, New York, 78. Teaching: Lectr at var places including Ont Col of Art, Toronto, Sun Valley Ctr for the Arts, Idaho, Int Festival at Arles, France, Ansel Adams Gallery, Yosemite Valley, Calif & Tyler Sch of Art, Temple Univ, Philadelphia, Pa, 75 & Cranbrook Acad, Detroit, Mich, Inst of Contemp Art, London, Eng, Sydney Acad of Art Australia, Mus Fine Art, Houston, Tex & Frei Univ, Amsterdam, Neth, 77. Awards: Nat Endowment for the Arts Grant, 73 & 75; Creative Artists Pub Serv Grant, NY State Coun of the Arts, 77. Bibliog: Julia Scully (auth), article in Mod Photog, 6/75; Allan Porter (auth), article in Camera, Switz, 4/77; Ralph Gibson (auth), How he creates his fractional images, Popular Photog, 4/77. Style & Technique: Black and white photographs of a surrealistic minimal nature. Publ: Auth, The Strip, Roger Kennedy Inc, 66; auth, The Hawk, Bobbs-Merrill Inc, 68; auth, The American Civil Liberties Union Calendar, 69; auth, The Somnambulist, 70, Deja-vu, 73 & Days at Sea, 75, Lustrum Press Inc. Dealer: Castelli Uptown 4 E 77th St New York NY 10021. Mailing Add: 331 W Broadway New York NY 10013

GIBSON, ROLAND
COLLECTOR, CURATOR
b Potsdam, NY, Feb 4, 02. Study: Dartmouth Col, AB, 35; Columbia Univ, MA, 40, PhD(econ), 47. Exhib: Exhibs circulated by Roland Gibson Art Found, at col & univ art galleries throughout US, 64-74. Pos: Pres & treas, Roland Gibson Art Found, Inc, Potsdam, 65-75; dir, Roland Gibson Mus Art, Dunbarton, NH, 67-70; cur art, State Univ NY Col Potsdam, 70- Collection: 300 works of contemporary abstract painting, prints and sculpture; Japanese and Italian abstract art. Publ: Auth, Japanese Abstract Art Colleced in Japan in 1963 (catalog), 64; auth, Italian Abstract Art Collected on a Visit to Italy in 1966 (catalog), 67; auth, A Retrospective of the Paintings of Mary Sloane (catalog), 69; auth, New New England Sculpture (catalog), 73; auth, Japanese Art of the Sixties (catalog), 73. Mailing Add: 9 Garden St Potsdam NY 13676

GIBSON, WALTER SAMUEL
ART HISTORIAN, ART WRITER
b Columbus, Ohio, Mar 31, 32. Study: Ohio State Univ, BFA, 57, MA, 60; res at Kunsthistorisch Inst Rijksuniversiteit, Utrecht, 60-61 & 64-66; Harvard Univ, PhD, 69. Teaching: Asst prof art, Case Western Reserve Univ, Cleveland, 66-71, chmn dept & assoc prof, 71- Mem: Col Art Asn Am; Int Ctr Medieval Art; Midwest Art Hist Soc. Res: Dutch and Flemish art of the 15th and 16th century; iconography. Publ: Auth, Hieronymus Bosch, Praeger, 73; auth, Bruegel, Oxford Univ Press, 77; auth, The Paintings of Cornelis Engebrechtsz, Garland, 77; auth, numerous articles in Am & Europ journals. Mailing Add: Dept of Art Case Western Reserve Univ Cleveland OH 44106

GIFFORD, J NEBRASKA
PAINTER
b Omaha, Nebr, Nov 25, 39. Study: Bennington Col, BA; Atelier 17, Paris, with S W Hayter. Work: Owens-Corning Fiberglas Collection, Toledo, Ohio; NY Univ; Joslyn Art Mus, Omaha, Nebr. Comn: Acrylic painting, indoor wall, Omaha Community Playhouse, 61; oil & enamel painting, outdoor wall, Old Market, Omaha, 69. Exhib: Contemporary Reflections (1971-72), Aldrich Mus, Ridgefield, Conn, 72; Whitney Mus Am Art Ann, New York, 72; Painting in America, 73; New Abstract Drawings, New York, 74; AFA Traveling Show, 75-76; one-person shows, Louis K Meisel Gallery, 74 & 55 Mercer Gallery, 76, New York & Univ Nebr, Omaha, 77; plus others. Media: Acrylic, Latex. Mailing Add: 4 Great Jones St New York NY 10012

GIKAS, CHRISTOPHER
EDUCATOR, SCULPTOR
b Lincoln, Nebr, Jan 26, 26. Study: Okla State Univ, BFA; Univ NMex, MA, stained glass with Hans Tatschl. Work: Okla State Univ Collection; Univ NMex Collection; WTex State Univ. Comn: Granite & stainless steel Vietnam monument, Cannon AFB, Clovis, NMex, 74; lava stone & copper monument to Eastern NMex Univ veterans, 77. Teaching: Instr art, WTex State Univ, 55-62; assoc prof art, Eastern NMex Univ, 62-, dir, Div Art, Theatre & Dance. Pos: Mem, NMex Arts Comn, 73, secy, 74-78. Awards: Eastern NMex Univ Pres Faculty Award, 69. Style & Technique: Realist. Media: Stained Glass. Publ: Co-auth, Tole' Painting for the Decorative Artists, Vols I & II, 70 & 72; illusr, Journey Through the History of New Mexico (pub sch text), 72. Mailing Add: PO Box 600 Portales NM 88130

GIKOW, RUTH (RUTH GIKOW LEVINE)
PAINTER
b Ukraine; US citizen. Study: Cooper Union; also with John Stuart Curry & Raphael Soyer. Work: Springfield Mus, Mo; Whitney Mus Am Art, New York; Smithsonian Inst, Washington, DC; prints, Metrop Mus Art & Mus Mod Art, New York. Comn: Mural for Bronx Hosp, NY, comn by Works Proj Admin, 39. Exhib: Carnegie Inst Mus Art, Pittsburgh; Corcoran Gallery Art, Washington, DC; Whitney Mus Am Art, New York; traveling shows to Japan, Ger & Eng. Teaching: Instr painting, New Sch Social Res, 65-69. Awards: Grant, Nat Inst Arts & Lett. Bibliog: Mathew Josephson (auth), Ruth Gikow, Random, 70. Style & Technique: Drawing and printmaking. Media: Oil. Dealer: Kennedy Galleries 40 W 57th St New York NY 10019. Mailing Add: 68 Morton St New York NY 10014

GILBERT, ALBERT EARL
PAINTER, ILLUSTRATOR
b Chicago, Ill, Aug 22, 39. Work: Am Mus Natural Hist, New York; Carnegie Mus, Pittsburgh; Ill State Mus, Springfield; Nat Audubon Soc, New York; du Pont Collection, Del Mus Natural Hist, Wilmington. Comn: Paintings of Am wildlife & plants, Nat Wildlife Fedn, Washington, DC, 67-74; Audubon bird proj-20 color plates of Am birds, Franklin Mint, Franklin Center, Pa, 75. Exhib: Soc Animals Artists Ann Shows, Grand Cent Galleries, New York, 65-75; Wildlife in Art, Brandywine River Mus, Chadds Ford, Pa, 73; SAm Birds, Am Mus Natural Hist, New York, 73; one-man show, Wildlife Portraits, Incurable Collector Gallery, New York, 74; Animals in Art, Royal Ont Mus, Toronto, 75; Bird Art Exhib, Leigh Yawkey Woodson Art Mus, Wausau, Wis, 77. Awards: Winner, Fed Duck Stamp Competition, 78-79. Bibliog: R H Stewart (auth), The art of Albert Earl Gilbert, Fla Naturalist Mag, 73; B J Lancaster (auth), Gilbert's birds, Cornell Univ Lab of Ornithol Bull, 75. Mem: Soc Animal Artists (1st vpres & mem juror, 73-); Ridgefield Guild Artists; USCG Art Prog. Style & Technique: Realistic, specializing in wildlife, birds and animals. Media: Opaque Watercolors, Acrylics. Publ: Illusr, Eagles, Hawks and Falcons of the World, 67; illusr, The Audubon Illustrated Handbook of American Birds, 68; illusr, The Red Book-Wildlife in Danger, 68; illusr, Curassows and Related Birds, 73; illusr, Birds of New York State, 74; auth, My studio is the jungle, Int Wildlife Mag, 9-10/76. Dealer: Sportsman's Edge Ltd 136 E 74th St New York NY 10021; Steep Rock Wildlife Art Box 107 Bridgewater CT 06752. Mailing Add: PO Box 197 Washington CT 06793

GILBERT, ALMA MAGDALENA
ART DEALER, MUSEUM DIRECTOR
b Mexico City, Mex, Apr 6, 37. Study: Univ of Mex, BA(art hist); Univ of Tex, art hist; Univ of San Francisco, art hist. Pos: Owner & dir, La Galeria Art Gallery, San Mateo, Calif, 72-78 & The Oaks Parrish Museum, Windsor, Vt, 78- Bibliog: Coy Ludwig (auth), Maxfield Parrish, Am Art Rev Mag, 5/76; Phyllis Barton (auth), The Wyeths in the West Coast, Southwest Art Mag, 5/77; Ann Gold (auth), Closing out a spectacular Wyeth exhib, 7/77 & Yet another dimension in Wyeth art, 11/77, San Francisco Mag. Mem: Calif Art Dealers for Responsible Equity (dir, 76-77). Specialty: American art, Wyeths, Maxfield Parrish, Cecil C Bell & James Bama. Interest: Have the largest collection of Parrish oils in the world housed in the Parrish home, The Oaks, now the Maxfield Parrish Museum. Collection: Maxfield Parrish, Andrew Wyeth and James Bama. Publ: Auth, Maxfield Parrish: Master of Make Believe (catalog), pvt publ, 75 & 76; auth, The Wyeths, 77 & Maxfield Parrish, 78, pvt publ. Mailing Add: c/o La Galeria 30 E Third Ave San Mateo CA 94010

GILBERT, ARNOLD MARTIN
COLLECTOR
b New York, NY, Mar 28, 21. Study: Univ of Chicago. Teaching: Prof photography, Governors State Univ, Park Forest S, Ill, 74- Pos: Adv trustee, Friends of Photography, 76- Mem: Friends of Photography. Collection: Modern 20th century photography. Mailing Add: 1610 Butterfield Flossmoor IL 60422

GILBERT, ARTHUR
COLLECTOR, PATRON
b Eng, May 16, 13. Bibliog: Anthony C Sherman (auth), The Gilbert Mosaic Collection, Pendulum, 71; Alvar Gonzalez-Palacios (auth), The Art of Mosaics Selected from the Gilbert Collection, 77 & William Ezelle Jones (auth), Monumental Silver: Selected from the Gilbert Collection, 77, Mus Asn of Los Angeles Co Mus of Art, Los Angeles, Calif. Collection: Georgian silver, primarily Paul Storr and Paul de Lamerie; Florentine mosaics and Roman micro-mosaics. Mailing Add: 1888 Century Park E Suite 1410 Los Angeles CA 90067

GILBERT, CLYDE LINGLE
PAINTER
b Medora, Ind, Oct 15, 98. Study: Sch Appl Art, Battle Creek, Mich; Nat Acad Com Art, Chicago; Studio Fine Arts, Brazil, Ind. Exhib: Wawasee Art Gallery, Syracuse, Ind, 49; Howe Mil Sch, Ind, 49; one-man show, Weddleville Sch, Ind, 66; Battle Creek Sanatorium, Mich, 66; State-Wide Show, French Lick Hotel, Ind, 66. Awards: Gold Medal for Highest Packaging Honors, 38. Mem: Ind Fedn Art Clubs. Style & Technique: Realism; brush and palette knife. Media: Oil, Watercolor. Mailing Add: 139 Riverview Ave Elkhart IN 46514

GILBERT, CREIGHTON EDDY
ART HISTORIAN
b Durham, NC, June 6, 24. Study: NY Univ, with Walter Friedlaender, Richard Offner, Lionello Venturi, Erwin Panofsky, Meyer Schapiro & Richard Krautheimer, BA, 42, PhD, 55. Collections Arranged: Baroque Painters of Naples, Ringling Mus, 61; Major Masters of the Renaissance, Rose Art Mus, Brandeis Univ, 63, 17th Century Paintings from the Low Countries, 66. Teaching: Instr hist art, Emory Univ, 46-47; from instr to asst prof hist art, Univ Louisville, 47-56; asst prof hist art, Ind Univ, Bloomington, 56-58; from assoc prof to Sidney & Ellen Wien prof hist art, Brandeis Univ, 61-69; prof hist art, Queens Col, 69-, chmn dept, 69-72; vis prof, Univ Leiden, Netherlands, 74-75; Robert Sterling Clark vis prof, Williams Col, 76; Jacob Gould Schurman prof hist of art, Cornell Univ, 77- Pos: Cur, Ringling Mus, Sarasota, Fla, 59-61. Awards: Fulbright Sr Lectr, Univ Rome, 51-52; Mather Award for Best Art Criticism of Year, Col Art Asn Am, 64; Fel, Netherlands Inst Advan Study, 72-73. Bibliog: Interview, Amerikaanse Kunsthistoricus Creighton Gilbert, Rotterdam Courant-Handelsblad, 2/75. Mem: Fel Am Acad Arts & Sci; Col Art Asn Am (mem ed bd, Art Bull, 78-); Alumni Asn Inst Fine Arts, NY Univ (chmn bd dirs, 70-74). Res: Italian Renaissance. Publ: Transl, Complete Poems & Selected Letters of Michelangelo, 63, Mod Libr Ed, 65, Vintage, 70; auth, Michelangelo, McGraw, 67; auth, Change in Piero della Francesca, Augustin, 68; ed, Renaissance Art, Harper, 70; auth, History of Renaissance Art, Abrams, 72. Mailing Add: Goldwin Smith 35 Cornell Univ Ithaca NY 14853

GILBERT, HERB
PAINTER, GRAPHIC ARTIST
b Brooklyn, NY, Oct 30, 29. Study: Art Career Sch, 48-51; Brooklyn Mus Art Sch, with Reuben Tam, 55-58; Pratt Inst with Walter Murch, Reuben Nakian & George McNiel, 56-57; Univ Calif with Aaron Hillman, 73. Work: Mus NMex, Santa Fe. Exhib: City Ctr Art Competition, New York, 57, Brooklyn Mus Alumni Sch, 58; Western Ann, Denver Art Mus, 60 & 62; Own Your Own Regional, Denver Art Mus, 64; Southwest Fine Arts Biennial, Mus NMex, 74. Teaching: Instr graphics, Inst Am Indian Arts, Santa Fe, 71-75. Pos: Art dir, Campbell Mithun Advert Agency, Denver, 64-65; art dir & graphic designer, Herb's Place, Denver, 65-71. Awards: Three Distinctive Merit Awards, Two Gold Medals & Eight Honor Awards, Art Dirs Club Denver, 59-69. Style & Technique: Abstract Neo-expressionist; lyrical and lineal. Media: Collage; Acrylic and Oil on Canvas; Drawing Mixed Media. Mailing Add: PO Box 1294 Bisbee AZ 85603

GILBERT, LIONEL
PAINTER, INSTRUCTOR
b Newark, NJ, May 29, 12. Study: Newark Sch Fine & Indust Art, grad, 29; Acad Grande Chaumiere, Paris, 33; with Suzanne Valadon, Paris, 34; Chicago Sch Design, with Maholy-Nagy, 41; NY Univ, with Sam Adler, 55. Work: Chase Manhattan Bank, New York; Joslyn Mus Art, Omaha, Nebr; Slater Mus, Conn; Eureka Col Collection; Silver Springs Acad, Colo; also in many pvt & corp collections. Exhib: One-man shows, Gallery Contemp Art, Toronto, 58, New Sch Social Res, New York, 66 & Alonzo Gallery, New York, 68, 70, 71, 73, 75 & 76; Childe Hassom Fund Exhib, Acad Arts & Lett, 69; Nat Acad Design; plus others. Teaching. Instr drawing & painting, YMHA, New York, 67-; instr drawing & painting, NY Univ, 68-69; instr painting, Summit Art Ctr, NJ, 75- Media: Oil. Mailing Add: c/o Alonzo Gallery 30 W 57th St New York NY 10019

GILBERTSON, CHARLOTTE
PAINTER
b Boston, Mass. Study: Boston Univ, BA; Art Students League; Pratt Inst, New York; also with Fernand Leger, Paris. Exhib: Iolas Gallery, New York, 62-76; Invitational Show, Flint Col, 67; Destructivist Show, Finch Col, 68; E A T Show, Brooklyn Mus, New York, 68-69; Erik Nord Gallery, Nantucket, 75; Bodley Gallery, 75 & 77; Irving Galleries, Palm Beach, Fla, 77-; plus many others. Mem: Mus Mod Art; Am Fedn Arts. Media: Oil, Acrylic. Dealer: Iolas Gallery 15 E 55th St New York NY 10022. Mailing Add: Old Sch House Rd Harwich Port MA 02646

GILCHRIEST, LORENZO
CONSTRUCTIONIST, EDUCATOR
b Thomasville, Ga, Mar 21, 38. Study: Newark Sch Fine & Indust Arts, 57-58; Newark State Col, BA, 62; Pratt Inst, MS, 67; Md Inst, MFA, 75. Work: Newark State Col; Fairleigh Dickinson Univ. Exhib: Some Negro Artists, Fairleigh Dickinson Univ, 65; one-man show, Univ Md, 70; Md Regional, Baltimore Mus Art, 71; Black Art, Towson State Col, 75; three solo & many group shows, Argus Gallery. Teaching: Asst prof art, Towson State Col, 67-; guest prof sculpture, Cornell Univ, summers 72 & 73; teacher constructions, painting & drawing, Baltimore Mus Art, 73-74; guest prof print workshop, Morgan State Univ, summer 77. Pos: Assoc art dir, Sen Robert Kennedy Proj, Bedford Stuyvesant Youth in Action, Brooklyn, NY, 65-67. Awards: Afro American Slide Depository for Afro Americans, Samuel Kress Found, 71; Fel Int Arts Sem, Fairleigh Dickinson Univ, 62. Bibliog: Barbara Gold (auth), Blackmarks, Black art, Sun Paper Art Sect, 6/75. Style & Technique: Combination of paint, wood in mixed media fashion, wood usually raw as opposed to being finished smoothly. Mailing Add: 1013 Woodbourne Ave Baltimore MD 21212

GILCHRIST, ELIZABETH BRENDA
ART EDITOR
b Coulsdon, Eng; US citizen. Study: Smith Col, BA(art hist); Art Students League. Pos: Asst, Durlacher Brothers Art Gallery, New York, 54-57; art admin asst, Brussels World's Fair, Belg & New York, 57-58; fund raiser, Mus of Mod Art, New York, 59-62; reporter, Show Mag, New York, NY, 62-64; staff writer, Am Heritage Publ Co, 64; sr art ed, Praeger Publ, New York, 65-75; ed publ, Cooper-Hewitt Mus, Nat Mus of Design, Smithsonian Inst, New York, 76-; mem adv coun for continuing educ prog, Mus Collaborative Inc, 77-78. Mem: Drawing Soc (mem bd dirs, 60-; mem exec comt); Soc Archit Historians; Col Art Asn; Am Asn of Mus; Victorian Soc of Am. Publ: Translr, Jacques Lassaigne (auth), Marc Chagall: The Ceiling of the Paris Opera, 66; ed, American Art & Artists series, Praeger, 71-75; gen ed, Smithsonian Illustrated Library of Antiques, Cooper-Hewitt Mus, 76- Mailing Add: 175 W 93rd St New York NY 10025

GILDEN, MIRIAM ANN
See Bransky, Miriam

GILES, NEWELL WALTON, JR
PAINTER
b Flushing, NY, June 20, 28. Study: Wesleyan Univ, BA(art hist); New York-Phoenix Sch Design; also studied watercolor with Herb Olsen, Westport, Conn. Comn: Watercolor renderings, Stanwich Presby Church, Greenwich, Conn, 69, main lobby, Innis Arden Golf Club, Old Greenwich, Conn, 71; Pan Ocean Oil Corp, New York, 72; plus var pvt comns. Exhib: Greenwich Art Soc Ann Show, Greenwich Libr, 66-70; Hudson Valley Art Asn Ann Show, White Plains, NY, 66-77; Am Watercolor Soc Ann Show, New York, 68; Hammond Mus Exhib Contemp Am Art, North Salem, NY, 68; Am Artists Prof League Regional Show, New York, 72-77. Teaching: Pvt instr watercolor, 70-71. Pos: Art dir, J M Mathes Inc, New York, 55-63; art & prod dir, J J Lane Inc, Advert, New York, 63- Awards: Puck Award for Newspaper Advert, New York Jour-Am, 60; First Prize for Watercolors, Greenwich Art Soc, 68 & Old Greenwich Art Soc, 70, 72, 75 & 77. Bibliog: Article in La Rev Mod, 69. Mem: Assoc Am Watercolor Soc; Am Artists Prof League; Hudson Valley Art Asn; Greenwich Art Soc; Old Greenwich Art Soc (mem bd dirs). Style & Technique: Basic traditional academic approach to rendering in watercolor and oils of landscapes and seascapes. Media: Watercolor, Oil. Mailing Add: 3 Old Wagon Rd Old Greenwich CT 06870

GILHOOLY, DAVID JAMES, III
SCULPTOR
b Auburn, Calif, Apr 15, 43. Study: Univ Calif, Davis, BA, 65, MA, 67. Work: Art Gallery of Greater Victoria, BC; Oakland Mus, Calif; Bronfman Collection Can Art, Nat Gallery, Ottawa, Ont; Stedelijk Mus, Amsterdam; San Antonio Mus of Art, Tex; San Francisco Mus Art; plus many other pub & pvt collections. Exhib: Funk Show, Univ Calif, Berkeley & Inst Contemp Art, Boston, Mass, 67; Realisms '70, Montreal Mus Art & Art Gallery Ont, 70; Whitney Mus Am Art Sculpture Ann, New York, 70; Clay, Whitney Mus, 74; Matrix Gallery, Wadsworth Atheneum, Hartford, Conn, 76; Mus of Contemp Art, Chicago, 76; Vancouver Art Gallery, BC, 76; Helen Drutt Gallery, Philadelphia, 77; ARCO Ctr for Visual Arts, Los Angeles, 77; Painting & Sculpture: the Mod Era, San Francisco Mus of Art, Nat Collection of Fine Art, Washington, DC, 77; Candy Store Gallery, Folsom, Calif, 77; Mus of Contemp Craft, New York, 78; plus many others. Teaching: Instr drawings & watercolor, San Jose State Col, 67-69; instr ceramics & sculpture, Univ Sask, Regina, 69-71; instr ceramic sculpture, York Univ, 71-75 & 76-77; instr ceramics & drawing, Univ Calif, Davis, 75-76. Bibliog: Jeannette Arneson (auth), David Gilhooly, Crafts Horizon, 8/71; Gary Dault (auth), With David Gilhooly in the frogworld, spring 72 & Dale Conathy (auth), David Gilhooly's Mythanthropy, 6/75, Arts Can; plus others. Style & Technique: Narrative expressionistically modelled and carved clay. Dealer: Hansen-Fuller Gallery 228 Grant Ave San Francisco CA 94108; Allan Frumkin Gallery 50 W 57th St New York 10022. Mailing Add: 804 Thorneycroft Dr NW Calgary AB T2K 3K4 Can

GILKEY, GORDON WAVERLY
CURATOR, EDUCATOR
b Linn Co, Ore, Mar 10, 12. Study: Albany Col, BA, 33; Univ Ore, MFA, 36; Lewis & Clark Col, hon Arts D, 57. Work: Metrop Mus Art, New York; Libr Cong, Washington, DC; Brit Mus, London; Bibliot Nat, Paris; San Francisco Art Mus. Comn: Etchings, Univ Ore Libr Construction, 36; etchings, New York World's Fair, 1939, New York World's Fair & Charles Scribner's Sons, 38-39. Exhib: Northwest Printmakers Int, 50-72; Soc Am Graphic Artists, New York, 52-72; Expos Int Gravure, Ljubljana, Yugoslavia, 65-73; Biennale Int Gravure, Cracow, Poland, 68-70 & 74; Expos in Dessins Originaux, Rijeka, Yugoslavia. Collections Arranged: Dir, Int Exchange Print Exhibs, US Prints in Europe & Africa, 56 & 65; imported & circulated Contemp Prints France, 56, 61 & 66; Contemp Prints Italy, 57; Contemp Prints Gt Brit, 58 & 65; Contemp Prints Norway, 58, 63 & 71; Contemp Prints Yugoslavia, 59, 64, 69 & 72; Contemp Prints Holland, 59; Contemp Prints Ger, 60, 63 & 70; Contemp Prints Japan, 61, 65 & 69 & Contemp Japanese Sumi Paintings, 63; Contemp Prints Denmark, 62; Contemp Prints Greece, 62; Contemp Prints Czech, 69; Contemp Prints Sweden—Woodcuts, 69; Contemp Prints from Can, 75. Teaching: Instr art & studio, Stephens Col, 39-42; prof art hist & studio & head dept, Ore State Univ, 47-64, dean, Sch Humanities & Social Sci, 63-73, dean, Col Liberal Arts, 73-77; cur prints & drawings, Portland Art Mus, Ore, 78- & mem art fac, Sch of the Art Mus, 78. Pos: Chief, US War Dept Spec Staff Art Proj Europe, 45-47; trustee & chmn art comt, Portland Art Mus, 61-67; chmn, Gov Planning Coun Arts & Humanities Ore, 65-67. Awards: Comdr, Order of Merit, Italy, 67 & Fed Ger Repub, 68; Off Order of Palms Acad, Repub France, 69; King Carl XVI Gustaf's Gold Medal-Art, Sweden, 77. Mem: Am Asn Mus; Soc Am Graphic Artists; Col Art Asn Am; Calif Soc Printmakers. Res: History of printmaking. Collection: Historical and contemporary prints. Publ: Auth, Etching Showing Construction Progress of the University of Oregon Library, 36; auth, Etchings: New York World's Fair, 1939, 39; auth, numerous articles on printmaking. Mailing Add: Portland Art Mus SW Park & Madison Portland OR 97205

GILL, GENE
PAINTER, PRINTMAKER
b Memphis, Tenn, June 18, 33. Study: Memphis State Univ; Chicago Art Inst, Ill; Chouinard Art Inst, Los Angeles, BFA. Work: Los Angeles Co Mus, Los Angeles; Palm Springs Desert Mus, Calif; Atlantic Richfield Corp, Los Angeles; Home Savings, Los Angeles; Northrop Corp, Los Angeles. Exhib: 2nd Los Angeles Ann, Munic Art Mus, 69; All Calif Print Exhibs, Los Angeles, 69-71; 9th Ann Southern Calif Exhib, Long Beach Mus Art, 71; Laguna Beach Art Mus Exhib Ten, Calif, 71; Dimensional Prints, Los Angeles Co Mus Art, 73; Laguna Beach Art Mus, 77; plus others; one-man shows, Comara Gallery, 70, 71 & 74. Awards: Purchase Award, Home Savings, 69; Purchase Award, Westside Jewish Community Ctr, 70; Jurors Award, Laguna Beach Art Mus, 70. Bibliog: Joseph E Young (auth), articles in Art Int, 70 & 71. Style & Technique: Hard-edge geometric illusions of criss-crossing lines on layers of plastic against aluminum. Mailing Add: 2430 Cascadia Dr Glendale CA 91206

GILL, JAMES (FRANCIS)
PAINTER, SCULPTOR
b Tahoka, Tex, Dec 10, 34. Study: San Angelo Jr Col; Univ Tex, fel, 60. Work: Mus Mod Art & Whitney Mus Am Art, New York; Art Inst Chicago; Univ Calif Mus Art, Berkeley; Mead Corp, Dayton, Ohio; Container Corp Am; plus one other. Comn: Cover painting, Time, Inc. Exhib: Art Inst Chicago, 64; Mus Mod Art, 65; San Francisco Art Inst, 65; Whitney Mus Am Art, 66-68; Sao Paulo, Brazil, 67; Nat Collection Fine Art Traveling Exhib, Europe, 68-69. Teaching: Instr painting & lectr, Univ Idaho, Univ Ore & Univ Calif, Irvine. Awards: Purchase Prize, Art Inst Chicago, 64. Publ: Auth, Metamage, 69. Mailing Add: Whale Gulch Whitethorn CA 95489

GILL, SUE MAY
PAINTER, SCULPTOR
b Sabinal, Tex. Study: Pa Acad Fine Arts, 20-26; Acad Colorosi, Paris, 23-24; Art Inst Chicago. Comn: Sculpture, West Point Mil Acad; numerous fountain sculptures in pvt gardens; portraits of many prominent persons in pvt collections in US. Exhib: Philadelphia Country Club, 66 & 68; Philadelphia Sketch Club, 66; Auburn Mus, NY, 67; Plastics Club, 69; Pa Acad Fine Arts, Nat Acad Design & many others. Teaching: Instr painting, Syracuse Univ, summer sessions; lectr painting, Pa Acad Fine Arts & pvt clubs. Awards: Medal, 42 & Prize, 43, Philadelphia Sketch Club; Philadelphia Plastic Club Prizes, 42-44; Wayne Art Ctr, Pa, 66; plus others. Mem: Philadelphia Artists Alliance; Philadelphia Plastic Club; Nat Asn Women Artists; Fel Pa Acad Fine Arts; Philadelphia Mus Art. Mailing Add: 639 Love's Lane English Village Wynnewood PA 19096

GILLESPIE, DOROTHY MERLE
PAINTER, ART ADMINISTRATOR
b Roanoke, Va, June 29, 20. Study: Md Inst Col Art, Baltimore; Art Students League; Clay Club, New York; Atelier 17, New York, with Stanley William Hayter. Work: State Collection, Kessel Mus, Ger; Helena Rubenstein Pavilion, Tel Aviv Mus, Israel; San Marcos Univ, Lima, Peru; Univ Miami, Fla; Fordham Univ, New York. Exhib: Va Mus Fine Arts, Richmond; Norton Gallery, Palm Beach, Fla; New York Cult Ctr; San Francisco Mus; NY Univ. Pos: Co-coordr, Women's Interart Ctr, 73- Dealer: Gertrude Stein Gallery 998 Madison Ave New York NY 10021; City Wall Mercer & Houston St New York NY. Mailing Add: 135 MacDougal St New York NY 10012

GILLESPIE, GREGORY JOSEPH
PAINTER
b Elizabeth, NJ, Nov 29, 36. Study: Cooper Union Art Sch; San Francisco Art Inst, MFA. Work: Whitney Mus Am Art; NJ State Mus, Trenton; Hirshhorn Collection. Exhib: Whitney Ann, 66, 68 & 72 & Whitney Biennial, 73; Personal Concern—Human Torment, New Sch Social Res, 69; Smith Col Mus Art, 71; Univ Ga, 71; Nat Acad Design, 72; Forum Gallery, New York, 75; Retrospective Exhib, Hirshhorn Mus, Washington, DC & Ga Mus of Art, Univ of Ga, Athens, 78; Nat Acad of Design, New York, 78. Awards: Am Acad Rome Award, 65-68; Fulbright Fel, 67; Nat Inst Arts & Lett Award, 69. Bibliog: Gregory Gillespie (paintings Italy, 1962-70), Forum Gallery, 71. Mem: Nat Acad Design. Media: Oil, Acrylic. Mailing Add: c/o Forum Gallery 1018 Madison Ave New York NY 10021

GILLETTE, W DEAN
PAINTER, ART DEALER
b Parsons, Kans. Study: Kansas City Art Inst, Kansas City, Mo; Univ Kans, Lawrence, BFA, 52; Univ London; Yale Univ, BFA, 55, MFA, 57 & study with Josef Alber, Conrad Marca-Relli, James Brooks & Burgoine Diller. Work: William Rockhill Nelson Gallery Art, Kansas City, Mo; New Orleans Mus Art; High Mus Art, Atlanta, Ga; Ga Mus Art, Athens; Am Tel & Tel Collection, New York; Sheldon Mem Mus of Art, Lincoln, Nebr; and numerous pvt collections. Exhib: Gardens Art Festival 8, Pine Mountain, Ga, 72 & Mus of Arts & Sci, Macon, 71 & 72; Ga Artists Show, High Mus, Atlanta, 71 & 72 & Mus of Arts & Sci, Macon, 72; New Orleans Mus of Art, La, 73; Haslem Gallery, Washington, DC, 73 & 74; Expo 74, Spokane, Wash, 74; William Rockhill Nelson Gallery of Art, Kansas City, Mo, 74; one-man shows, Bodley Gallery, New York, 66 & 68, Heath Gallery, Atlanta, Ga, 70, Galleria 88, Rome, Italy, 70, Bienville Gallery, New Orleans, La, 72, Montgomery Mus of Art, Ala, 74, Haslem Gallery, Washington, DC, 75, Mint Mus of Art, Charlotte, NC, 75, Hunter Mus of Art, Chattanooga, Tenn, 76, Sheldon Mus, Lincoln, Nebr, 76, ADI Gallery, Inc, San Francisco, Calif, 77 & numerous others. Pos: Owner-partner, Image South Gallery, Atlanta, 70- Mem: Pa Acad Art. Style & Technique: Acrylic stained & thrown on unprimed canvas; abstract expressionist. Specialty: Images of the current styles. Dealer: ADI Gallery Inc San Francisco CA; Image S Gallery Atlanta GA. Mailing Add: Image South Gallery 1931 Peachtree Rd Atlanta GA 30309

GILLIAM, SAM
PAINTER
b Tupelo, Miss, 1933. Study: Univ Louisville, MA. Work: Mus African Art, Phillips Collection, Nat Collection Fine Arts, Corcoran Gallery Art & Howard Univ, Washington, DC; plus many others. Exhib: Works for New Spaces, Walker Art Ctr, Minneapolis, 71; Washington Art, Madison Art Ctr, Wis, 71 & State Univ NY Albany, 71; Am Exhib, Indian Triennale, New Delhi, 71; Mus Mod Art, New York, 71; Venice Biennale, Italy, 72; plus many other group & one-man shows. Pos: Mem panel of jurors, Nat Coun Arts Fels, 75. Awards: Norman Walt Harris Prize, Art Inst Chicago, 70; Longview Found Purchase Award, 70; Guggenheim Mem Found Fel, 71; plus others. Bibliog: LeGrace Benson (auth), Sam Gilliam: certain attitudes, Artforum, 9/70; Elsie Carper (auth), Gilliam's giants in a Paris show, Washington Post, 11/6/70; Douglas Davis (auth), Washington letter, Arts, 12-1/70; plus many others. Mailing Add: 1752 Lamont St NW Washington DC 20010

GILLIES, JEAN
ART CRITIC, ART HISTORIAN
b Evanston, Ill, May 6, 29. Study: Denison Univ, BA, 51; Northwestern Univ, PhD, 70. Teaching: Assoc prof art hist, Northeastern Ill Univ, Chicago, 70- Pos: Vpres, Women's Caucus for Art, 76-78, adv bd, 78-; juror Chicago Art Awards, 78; reviewer grant proposals, Nat Endowment for the Humanities, Washington, DC, 77- Awards: L Schwartz Mem Award for Excellence in Art Hist, Northwestern Univ, 69; Grant for film project, Nat Endowment for the Arts, 76. Mem: Women's Caucus for Art (nat vpres, 76-78, mem Chicago chap); Col Art Asn; Midwest Art Hist Soc; Mid-Am Col Art Asn. Res: The iconography of images of women in art, especially American art and advertising; a reinterpertation of Botticelli's Primavera based on a new identification of the central figure. Publ: Auth, The Timeless Space of Edward Hopper, Art J, 9/72; auth, Feminist Success Raises Questions, New Art Examiner, 6/77 & auth, Sexual Imagery in Chicago Art, 12/77; auth, Images of Women in the Visual Arts, 78; auth, American Women: Daughters of a Dream (16mm film), Nat Endowment for the Arts Grant. Mailing Add: 808 Judson Ave Evanston IL 60202

GILLING, LUCILLE
PRINTMAKER
b Hamilton, Mo. Study: Kansas City Art Inst; New York Sch Fine & Appl Arts in Paris, France, Eng & Italy, dipl; Queens Univ. Work: Nat Libr Can, Ottawa; Montreal Mus Fine Art; Victoria & Albert Mus, London, Eng; Ohio State Univ; Wayne State Univ. Exhib: Soc Can Painters, Etchers & Engravers, Toronto, Ont, 56-; one-man shows, Pascall Gallery, Toronto, 66, Sobot Gallery, Toronto, 69 & Marjorie Kauffmann Graphics, 72; Can Fine Art Gallery, Toronto, 74; plus others. Awards: Sterling Trust Award, 59; Anaconda Award of Merit, 68. Mem: Print & Drawing Coun Can; Prof Artists Can (secy- treas, 68-); Toronto Heliconian Club (exec coun, 71-75). Style & Technique: Etching; aquatint on copper, multicolor one plate pull; figures stand alone without background. Publ: Portfolios of etchings, The Canterbury Tales, 66 & Don Quixote, 69, original signed etchings Ed 100. Dealer: Marjorie Kauffmann Graphics 5015 Westheimer Houston TX 77027. Mailing Add: 178 Alfred Ave Willowdale ON Can

GILLINGWATER, DENIS CLAUDE
PAINTER, SCULPTOR
b Glendale, Calif, Feb 15, 46. Study: Univ Cincinnati, BFA, 68, MFA, 70. Outlook '74, Tucson Mus Art, 74; 22nd Ann Nat Drawing & Print Exhib, Mt Holyoke Col, 74; 8th West Biennial, Western Colo Ctr Arts, 74; Southwest & Rocky Mountain States Exhib, Scottsdale Fine Arts Comn, 75; solo exhib, Scottsdale Ctr Arts, 78. Teaching: Asst prof, Ariz State Univ, 73- Awards: Nat Endowment Arts Artist in Residence, Mesa, Ariz, 73; Acquisitions, Phoenix Art Mus, 77 & Scottsdale Ctr Arts, 75; plus others. Mailing Add: 316 E 14th St Tempe AZ 85281

GILMARTIN, F THOMAS
ART DIRECTOR, INSTRUCTOR
b Palmer, Mass, Aug 6, 40. Study: Worcester Art Mus Sch, grad; Goddard Col, BA; Penland Sch Crafts, NC. Teaching: Instr exhib design & printmaking, Asheville Art Mus, NC, 73-77. Pos: Dir, Arts & Crafts Ctr, Ft Knox, Ky, 63-65; prog supvr, Arts & Crafts Ctr, Ft Eustis, Va, 68-70; civilian supvr, US Army Artist Team, Thailand, 70-71; dir, Asheville Art Mus, NC, 73-77; dir, Ga Coun Arts & Humanities, Appalachian Crafts Prog, 77- Mem: Southeastern Mus Coun; NC Mus Coun; Am Crafts Coun; Am Asn Mus. Res: Researched and authored, Contemporary Art History of the Eastern Cherokee Indians. Mailing Add: 9 College St Weaverville NC 28787

GILMARTIN, GARRY M
ILLUSTRATOR
b Palmer, Mass, Nov 14, 49. Study: Paier Sch Art, 4 yrs, spec advan study with Ken Davies, one yr. Work: Asheville Art Mus, NC. Exhib: Asheville Art Mus, 75; New Haven Paint & Clay Club, Conn, 75-76; 1st Conn Illusr Exhib, 77; Best of the Quest, Conn Art Dir Club, 77. Awards: Gold Medal Finalists, Scholastic Mag, 68; Finalists, Best of the Quest, 77. Mem: Asheville Art Mus; Conn Art Dir Club. Media: Oil. Publ: Illusr, The Crystal Ball, Ballantine, 76; illusr, Nightmare Chase, 77, The Devil's Horseman, 77, A Star in the Family, 77 & The Santaana Wind, 77, Doubleday. Mailing Add: 230 Boylston St Boston MA 02116

GILMORE, ROGER
ART ADMINISTRATOR, EDUCATOR
b Philadelphia, Pa, Oct 11, 32. Study: Dartmouth Col, AB; Univ Chicago Divinity Sch, grad study. Teaching: Dean, Sch Art Inst Chicago, 65- Mem: Soc Archit Historians, Cliff Dwellers. Mailing Add: 4371 Central Ave Western Springs IL 60558

GILPIN, LAURA
PHOTOGRAPHER, WRITER
b Colorado Springs, Colo, Apr 22, 91. Study: Clarence H White Sch Photog, 16-17, dipl; Univ NMex, hon DLitt, 70. Work: Libr Cong, Washington, DC; Art Mus, Univ NMex, Albuquerque; Mus NMex, Santa Fe; Yale Univ Art Mus; New Orleans Art Mus, La; plus pvt collections. Exhib: One-man shows, San Francisco Mus Art; Mus Natural Hist, New York; Colorado Springs Fine Arts Ctr; Amon Carter Mus Western Art, Ft Worth, Tex; Fine Arts Retrospective, Mus NMex, 74 & Traveling Exhib, 75. Pos: Photogr, Central City Theater, Robert Edmond Jones Prod, Colo, 32-36; pub relations photogr, Boeing Airplane Co, Wichita, Kans, 42-45. Awards: US Indian Arts & Crafts Bd Cert; First Ann Gov's Award, NMex Arts Comn, 74. Mem: Soc Woman Geographers; Indust Photogrs of Southwest. Style & Technique: Ultimate goal, the production of the finest prints possible; archivally produced; platinum prints are specialty. Publ: Auth & illusr, The Pueblos, A Camera Chronical, 41 & Temples in Yucatan, 48, Hastings House; auth & illusr, The Rio Grande, Duell, Sloan & Pearce, New York, 49; auth & illusr, The Enduring Navaho, Univ Tex, 68. Dealer: Lee Witkin Gallery 243 E 60th St New York NY 10022; Quivira Book Shop & Gallery 11 Cornell St SE Albuquerque NM 87106. Mailing Add: 409 Camino del Monte Sol Santa Fe NM 87501

GILVARRY, JAMES
COLLECTOR
Collection: Modern art. Mailing Add: 210 E 47th St New York NY 10017

GIMBEL, MRS BERNARD F
COLLECTOR, PATRON
Collection: Paintings. Mailing Add: Upper King St Greenwich CT 06830

GINNEVER, CHARLES
SCULPTOR
b San Mateo, Calif, Aug 28, 31. Study: With Zadkine & Hayter, Europe, 53-55; Calif Sch Fine Arts, San Francisco, BFA, 57; Cornell Univ, MFA, 59. Work: Wadsworth Atheneum, Hartford, Conn; Chrysler Mus, Provincetown, Mass. Comn: Aluminum sculpture, Vt Coun Arts, Southern Vt Art Ctr, 71-72. Exhib: Art in Environment Show, New York, 67; Paula Cooper Gallery, New York, 70-72; Dag Hammarskjold Plaza, New York, 73; plus others. Teaching: Chmn dept art, Windham Col, Putney, Vt, 67- Media: Steel. Dealer: Paula Cooper Gallery 100 Prince St New York NY 10012. Mailing Add: PO Box 411 Putney VT 05346

GINSBURG, ESTELLE
PAINTER, SCULPTOR
b St Louis, Mo, Mar 27, 24. Study: Univ Mo; Brooklyn Mus Art Sch; Cornell Univ. Work: C W Post Col, NY; Univ Mass, Amherst. Exhib: Northern Ill Univ, 69; paintings, sculpture & drawings, C W Post Col, 69; Heckscher Mus, NY, 70; drawings, Norfolk Mus Art, 72; Ball State Univ, Muncie, Ind, 73; Nat Acad, NY, 74; Audubon Soc, NY, 75; paintings, sculpture & drawings, Nassau Libr Syst, NY, 76; solo show, Fine Arts Mus Nassau Co, NY, 77; invitational, York Col, Pa, 77. Teaching: Art lectr mus collections, North Shore Community Arts Ctr, New York, NY, 70-73. Pos: Art teacher, 5 Towns Music & Art Found, Woodmere, NY, 73- & Nassau Off Cult Develop, 75-76; dir, Aida Dornbrand Brentano's Gallery, Manhassett, NY, currently. Awards: Mixed Media Award, Heckscher Mus, NY, 72; Sculpture Award, North Shore Art Exhib, 74; Painting Award, Port Washington Libr, 75. Bibliog: A Heyman (auth), About the Artist, South Shore Record, 75; Malcum Preston (auth), Review of Work, Newsday, NY, 76 & 77; Jeanne Paris (auth), Review of Work, Long Island Press, 77 & 78. Mem: Cent Hall Artists, NY; Prof Artists Asn NY (mem chmn, 74-76). Style & Technique: Mixed media on wood; painted wood and lucite; collage; Watercolors. Media: Wood, Paint; Mixed Media. Dealer: Aida Dornbrand Brentano's Gallery 20-72 Northern Blvd Manhasset NY 11030. Mailing Add: 370 Longacre Ave Woodmere NY 11598

GINSBURG, MAX
PAINTER, ILLUSTRATOR
b Paris, France, Aug 7, 31. Study: Syracuse Univ, BFA; Nat Acad Design; City Col New York, MA. Work: New York Cult Ctr. Exhib: Allied Artists Am, 56-72; Am Vet Soc Artists, 61-72; Audubon Artists, 62-72; Harbor Gallery, Cold Spring Harbor, 66, 68, 69, 71 & 72. Teaching: Instr art, High Sch Art & Design, New York. Awards: Prize, 61 & Gold Medal, 62 & 65, Am Vet Soc Artists; Allied Artists Am, 61 & 72; Nat Art Club, 63. Mem: Allied Artists Am; Audubon Artists; Am Vet Soc Artists; Artists Equity Asn. Mailing Add: c/o Harbor Gallery 43 Main St Cold Spring Harbor NY 11724

GINZEL, ROLAND
PAINTER, PRINTMAKER
b Lincoln, Ill, 1921. Study: Art Inst Chicago, BFA; State Univ Iowa, MFA; Slade Sch, London. Work: Univ Southern Calif; Univ Mich; Ill Bell Tel Co; Art Inst Chicago; US Embassy, Warsaw, Poland; plus others. Exhib: Art Inst Chicago, 69; Madison, Wis, 69; Notre Dame Univ, 69; one-man show, Phyllis Kind Gallery, 69; Whitney Mus Am Art Biennial, New York, 75. Teaching: Prof printmaking, Univ Chicago, 57-58; prof prints & painting, Univ Ill, Chicago Circle, 58-69; instr painting, Univ Wis, 60; instr art, Saugatuck Summer Sch, 61-62. Awards: Oppenheim Prize, 55, Purchase Prize, 56, Print & Drawing Prize, 67 & Campana Prize, 69, Art Inst Chicago; Fulbright Fel to Rome, 62. Dealer: Phyllis Kind Gallery 226 E Ontario St Chicago IL 60611. Mailing Add: 412 N Clark St Chicago IL 60610

GIOBBI, EDWARD GIOACHINO
PAINTER
b Waterbury, Conn, July 18, 26. Work: Tate Gallery Art, London, Eng; Boston Mus Fine Arts; Whitney Mus Am Art, New York; Hirshhorn Mus; Art Inst Chicago; Brooklyn Mus, NY; plus others. Exhib: One-man exhibs, Neuberger Mus, 77 & Gruenebaum Gallery, New York, 78; Young America, Whitney Mus Am Art, 60; Recent Figure USA, Mus Mod Art, New York, 60; 40 Painters under 40, Whitney Mus Am Art, 62; plus others. Teaching: Artist in residence, Memphis Acad, Tenn, 59-60; artist in residence, Dartmouth Col, 72. Awards: Emily Lowe Award, 49; Ford Found Artist in Residence Prog, 66; Guggenheim Fel, 72. Media: Oil, Mixed Media. Mailing Add: 161 Croton Lake Rd Katonah NY 10536

GIORGI, VITA
PRINTMAKER, PAINTER
b Mazara, Italy; US citizen. Study: Wash Univ; La Ciudadela, Mexico City, Mex. Work: New York Pub Libr; Manchester Inst Arts & Sci, NH; Potsdam Col, NY; Mus Arte Contemp, Bogota, Colombia; Mus Mod Art, Santiago, Chile. Exhib: New Eng Art & Prints, De Cordova Mus, Lincoln, Mass, 65; Int Print Show, Manchester Inst Arts & Sci, 68; Salon Independente, Mexico City, 69; 1st Pan-Am Graphics Biennal, Mus Latertulia, Cali, Colombia, 71; 3rd Brit Int Print Biennale, Bradford Mus, Eng, 72. Bibliog: Toby Joy Smith (auth), Two painter poets, The News, Mexico City, 68; Thomas M Cranfill (auth), Image of Mexico, I, Tex Quart, 69; R Brown (auth), Ten downtown, New York, Arts Mag, 71. Publ: Contribr, 66 & 68 & illusr, 66 & 68, Rev Manana, Mexico City; illusr, El Mendrugo, New York, 72. Dealer: Lerner-Heller Gallery 956 Madison Ave New York NY 10021. Mailing Add: 359 Canal St New York NY 10013

GIRAUDIER, ANTONIO
PAINTER, WRITER
b Havana, Cuba, 1926; US citizen. Work: Univ Palm Beach; Am Poets Fel Soc, Charleston, Ill; Greenville Mus Art, SC; Maryhill Mus Fine Arts, Wash; Trinity Episcopal Church, Boston; also in pvt Am & foreign collections. Exhib: New Masters Gallery, New York, 65-68; Duncan Gallery, Paris, 66; Winchester Gallery, London, 67 & 68; Wellfleet Gallery, Cape Cod & Palm Beach, 67 & 68; Long Beach Ann, New York, 68; Avanti Gallery, New York, 68-75; Univ Palm Beach; one-man shows, Eastern Ill Univ, 75 & Sr Adv Ctr, Charleston, Ill, 77; plus others in US & abroad. Awards: Premier Prix de Printemps, Paris, 59; Laureat Marguerite d'Or, Paris, 60; Prix de Paris, 66; plus others. Bibliog: Reviews in Arts Mag, 12/71-1/72 & The Inner Loom, 72; art work reproduced in many publ, US & abroad. Style & Technique: Iconlike and semi-abstract; calligraphic. Media: Acrylic, Mixed Media. Publ: Auth, many definitive works in Eng & Span; contribr, many bks & periodicals, US & abroad. Mailing Add: 215 E 68th St New York NY 10021

GIRONA, JULIO
PAINTER
b Manzanillo, Cuba, Dec 29, 14. Study: Escuela San Alejandro, Havana, 30-34; Acad Ranson, Paris, 35-36; Art Students League, 50-56, with Morris Kantor. Work: Mus Nacional de Bellas Arts, Buenos Aires, Arg; Mus Nacional, Havana; Newark Mus, NJ; Stadische Kunsthalle, Recklinghausen, Ger; NJ State Mus, Trenton. Comn: Five murals, Colegio Medicos, Havana. Exhib: Venice Biennial, Italy; Baltimore Mus Art, Md, 56, 59 & 60; Art Inst Chicago, 57; Am Painting, Minneapolis Inst of Arts, Minn, 45-57; Ball State Teachers Col, 58 & 60; Mus Mod Art, New York, 58 & 60; Brooklyn Mus, NY, 59; Albright-Knox Art Gallery, Buffalo, NY, 59 & 60; Metrop Mus of Art, New York; Mus Fine Arts, Houston, Tex; San Francisco Mus Art, Calif; Denver Art Mus, Colo; one-man shows, Colegio de Arquitectos, Havana, 34, Mus Nacional, Havana, 47, Stadische Kunsthalle, Recklinghausen, Ger, 59 & Werkkunstschule, Krefeld, Ger, 63; Retrospective, Galeria de la Habana, 75. Teaching: Instr, Werkkunstschule, Krefeld, Ger, 63-64. Awards: First Prize, Newark Mus; Mus Nacional Award, Havana. Dealer: New Bertha Schaefer Gallery 41 E 57th St New York NY 10022. Mailing Add: 53 Genesee Ave Teaneck NJ 07666

GIRONDA, R
PAINTER, SCULPTOR
b Brooklyn, NY, Dec 3, 36. Study: Pratt Inst, BFA; Nat Acad Design; Metropolitan Col, BS, 72; Art Students League. Comn: Sculptures, stainless steel, comn by Kenneth Richardson, 69, stainless steel, Selma Wallace Assoc, 72, bronze, comn by Selma Wallace, 72; plus others. Exhib: Silvermine Guild, New Canaan, Conn, 63; Nat Acad Design Galleries, 72-75; Brooklyn Mus Show, 73-75; Caravan House, New York, 74; Eric Galleries, New York, 75-78; Naples Gallery, 78. Awards: First Prize, Brooklyn Mus, 73 & 75. Mem: Nat Acad Design; Am Inst Archit. Style & Technique: Contemporary carved brass and welded stainless steel. Mailing Add: 305 Degraw St Brooklyn NY 11231

GIRONELLA, ALBERTO
PAINTER, ILLUSTRATOR
b Mexico City, Mex, Sept 26, 29. Work: Mod Art Mus, Kamakua, Japan; Tel Aviv Mus; Mus Arte Mod, Mex; Pan-Am Union, Washington, DC. Comn: Mural, The Burial of Zapata, Fine Arts Inst, Mex. Exhib: Inst Torcuato Tella, Buenos Aires, 64; 19th & 20th Salon Mai, Paris, 64-65; 50 Years of Collage, Mus Decorative Arts, Paris, 65; Alternative Attuli 12 L'Aquila, Cartello Spagoli, Italy, 65; Int Surrealistic Expos L'Oeil Gallery, Paris, 65. Awards: Jouth Bienal, Paris, Govt France. Bibliog: E Jaguer (auth), Gironella, Ed Era, 64; A Breton (auth), Le surrealisme et la pinture, Ed Gallimard, Paris, 65; J Pierre (auth), Le surrealisme, Et Rencontre, Lausanne, 66. Dealer: Arvil Gallery of Art Hamburgo 241 Mexico DF Mexico. Mailing Add: San Jose 201 Valle de Bravo Mexico

GIUSTI, GEORGE
DESIGNER, SCULPTOR
b Milan, Italy; US citizen. Study: Acad Brera, Milan. Work: Graphic Sect, Mus Mod Art, New York; also in several art cols, US & abroad. Exhib: New York, Philadelphia, Boston, Chicago, Los Angeles, Louvre in Paris, London, Milan, Vienna, Latin Am, Japan & the Orient. Teaching: Instr, Cooper Union, New York. Awards: Art Dir of Year, 58; also many major awards & gold & silver medals. Bibliog: Articles in Graphis, Switz, Communication Art, US & Daily Tel Mag, London. Mem: Alliance Graphique Int; Am Inst Graphic Arts; Int Ctr Typographic Arts. Media: Metals. Publ: Auth & illusr, The Human Heart, 61; portfolios, Graphis, Switz, Idea & FAS, Japan, Pagina, Milan, Gebrauchsgrafik, Ger, Communication Art, US & Daily Tel Mag, London; auth articles in Fortune, Sat Eve Post, Time, Holiday, US Info Agency Publ & others. Mailing Add: Chalburn Rd West Redding CT 06896

GLADSTONE, M J
ART ADMINISTRATOR, WRITER
b New York, NY, May 4, 23. Study: Harvard Univ, SB(anthrop), 44, MA(fine arts), 46. Pos: Ed, Print & Print Collector's Quart, 50-53; ed, Merriam-Webster Dictionary, 53-55; ed, Collector's Quart Report, 62-63; assoc dir publ, Mus Mod Art, New York, 63-64; consult, NY State Coun on the Arts, 67-73; dir, Mus Am Folk Art, New York, 69-70; dir, Publ Ctr for Cult Resources, New York, 73- Publ: Contribr, Britannica Encycl Am Art, 73; auth, A Carrot for a Nose, Scribner, 74; contribr, Ruth Andrews, auth, How to Know American Folk Art, Dutton, 77. Mailing Add: 310 E 75th St New York NY 10021

GLAESER, LUDWIG
CURATOR
b Berlin, Ger, Jan 15, 30. Study: Tech Univ Berlin, 48-52; Free Univ Berlin, PhD, 58. Collections Arranged: Structures for Sound, 65, The Architecture of Louis Kahn, 66, The Architecture of Museums, 78, Theo van Doesburg—The Development of an Architect, 70, The Work of Frei Otto, 71 & Mies van der Rohe-Furniture and Drawings from the Collection (auth, catalog), 77, Mus of Mod Art, New York. Teaching: Instr archit theory, Sch of Archit, The Cooper Union, New York, 72- Pos: From assoc cur to cur archit, Mus Mod Art, New York, 64-72, cur, Mies van der Rohe Archive, 72- Mem: Soc Archit Historians; Archit League New York; Am Inst Architects. Res: Nineteenth and twentieth century architecture. Publ: Auth, Mies van der Rohe-Drawings in the Collection of the Museum, 68 & The Work of Frei Otto, 72, Mus of Mod Art, New York. Mailing Add: 11 W 53rd St New York NY 10019

GLANZ, ANDREA ELISE
MUSEUM DIRECTOR, EDUCATOR
b New York, NY, Oct 14, 52. Study: Cornell Univ, BS(human develop & expressive arts); Stanford Univ, MA(art educ); Calif sec teaching credential for art, anthrop, psychol & sociol. Collections Arranged: Two Hundred Years of Santa Clara Valley Archit (co-auth, catalogue), 76, Santa Clara Unified Sch Dist Student Art Exhib, 77, Triton Mus Art. Teaching: Instr understanding the visual arts: an intro to art appreciation, West Valley Community Col, Saratoga, Calif, 76. Pos: Grad asst, Stanford Univ Mus Art, Calif, 74-75; cur educ, Triton Mus Art, Santa Clara, Calif, 75-77, dir, 77- Mem: Am Asn Mus; Mus Educators Roundtable; Am Asn Mus, Western Regional Conf. Publ: Co-auth, A Catalog of the Paintings by Theodore Wores in the Collection of the Triton Museum of Art, Triton Mus of Art, 76. Mailing Add: 3898 A Magnolia Dr Palo Alto CA 94306

GLASCO, JOSEPH M
PAINTER, SCULPTOR
b Pauls Valley, Okla, Jan 19, 25. Study: Univ Tex, 41-42; study with Rico Lebrun, 46; study in Mexico City, 47; Art Students League, New York, 48. Work: Metrop Mus Art & Mus Mod Art, New York; Hirshhorn Mus & Sculpture Garden, Washington, DC; Whitney Mus Am Art, New York; Princeton Univ Mus, NJ. Exhib: One-man shows, Perls Gallery, New York, 51 & Catherine Viviano Gallery, New York, 52, 55, 58, 60, 63, 67 & 70; 15 Americans, Mus Mod Art, New York; The New Decade, Whitney Mus Am Art, New York; Metrop Mus Art, New York; Solomon R Guggenheim Mus, New York; Art Inst Chicago, Ill; Corcoran Gallery Art, Washington, DC; Dallas Mus Fine Arts, Tex; Los Angeles Co Mus Fine Arts, Los Angeles, Calif. Collections Arranged: 15 Americans, Mus Mod Art, New York; The New Decade, Thirty-five American Painters & Sculptors, Whitney Mus Am Art, New York. Bibliog: Joseph Glasco, Art Digest; 15 Americans, Mus Mod Art, New York; The New Decade, Whitney Mus Art, New York. Mem: Nat Soc Lit & the Arts. Mailing Add: 2116 1/2 Strand Ave Galveston TX 77550

GLASER, BRUCE
ART HISTORIAN, EDUCATOR
b Brooklyn, NY, Sept 25, 33. Study: Columbia Col, BA; Columbia Univ, MA. Teaching: Instr art hist, Pratt Inst, 61-62; instr art hist, Hunter Col, 62-65; prof art hist & chmn dept, Univ Bridgeport, 70-, dean, Col Fine Arts, 77- Pos: Dir, Howard Wise Gallery, New York, 60-61; dir, Gallery of Israeli Art, Am-Israel Cult Found, New York, 65-68; exec dir, Art Ctr Northern NJ, Tenafly, 68-70. Awards: Mem Found for Jewish Cult Fel, 70-72. Mem: Col Art Asn Am; Nat Coun Art Adminr; Int Coun Mus; Am Asn Mus. Res: Modern and contemporary art; Israeli art. Publ: Ed & co-auth, Oldenburg, Lichtenstein, Warhol: a discussion, Artforum, 2/66; co-auth, Questions to Stella & Judd, Art News, 9/66; ed & co-auth, An Interview with Ad Reinhardt, Art Int, 12/66; ed & co-auth, Changing role of the modern museum, Arts Yearbk, 67; ed & co-auth, Modern art and the critics, Art J, winter 70-71. Mailing Add: 211 Buena Vista Rd Fairfield CT 06432

GLASER, DAVID
PAINTER
b Brooklyn, NY, Sept 29, 19. Study: Art Students League, scholarship; New York Sch Indust Art; New York Sch Contemp Art, with Philip Evergood; Brooklyn Mus Art Sch, with Moses Soyer, Xavier Gonzales & Edwin Dickinson. Comn: Poster series for US Army, 43-44. Exhib: Hofstra Univ, 52-58; Nat Arts Club, 59; Art Directions, 59; City Ctr, New York, 60; Allied Artists Am, 60-71. Pos: Art dir & designer, 46-48; art dir, 54-60; dir & designer, Studio Concepts, 60- Awards: Best House Redesign, Levitt & Sons, Am Home, 68; Printing Indust Metrop New York Award, 73 & 77; Monadnock Mills Graphic Excellence Award, 75; plus others. Mem: Allied Artists Am; Vet Soc Am Artists; Nat Soc Lit & Arts. Style & Technique: Realistic; abstract. Media: Oil, Mixed Media. Res: Experimental silk screen production for industry; developed process for reproducing mosaics; new approaches in advertising and media including all communication skills; developed new architectural sculpture combining oxidized copper, plastics and light; originator of Giggy F Useless, Army publications cartoon character; creator of Bicentennial map of the American Revolution. Publ: Illusr for Popular Sci, Popular Mechanix & Electronics Illustrated, 61-65; auth & illusr, Emme. Mailing Add: 33 Downhill Lane Wantagh NY 11793

GLASER, MILTON
DESIGNER, ILLUSTRATOR
b New York, NY, June 26, 29. Study: Cooper Union Art Sch, 51; Acad Fine Arts, Bologna, Italy, Fulbright scholar, with Giorgio Morandi, 52-53; Hon DFA, Minneapolis Inst Art. Work: Mus Mod Art, New York. Comn: Mural, Fed Off Bldg, Indianapolis, 74; permanent exhib, Port Authority NY, World Trade Ctr, 75. Exhib: Push Pin Decorative Arts Show, The Louvre, Paris, 70; Push Pin Style, Castello Sforzesco, Milan, Italy, 71; one-man show, Portland Visual Arts Ctr, Maine, 75, Mus Mod Art, New York, 75 & Wichita State Univ, 75; Pompidou Cult Ctr, Beaubourg, Paris, 77. Teaching: Instr design prog, Sch Visual Arts, New York; instr design prog, Cooper Union Art Sch. Pos: Pres, Push Pin Studios, New York, 54-74; chmn bd & design dir, NY Mag, 68-77; pres, Milton Glaser Inc, Design Studio, 74-; vpres & design dir, Village C Voice, 75-77 & Esquire Mag, 77- Awards: Gold Medal, Am Inst Graphics Arts, 72; St Gaudens Medal, Cooper Union. Bibliog: Arts in, Graphis, 7/62 & Art News, 9/75; John Russell (auth), art in, New York Times, 8/30/75. Mem: Int Graphic Alliance; Am Inst Graphic Arts, Aspen Design Conf (co-chmn, 73); Art Dir Club. Publ: Illusr, If Apples Had Teeth, 60, Cats and Bats and Things With Wings, 65, Fish in the Sky, 71, Don Juan (by Asimov), 72, Graphic Design, 73 & Milton Glaser Poster Book, 77. Dealer: Posters Originals 924 Madison Ave New York NY 10021. Mailing Add: 207 E 32nd St New York NY 10016

GLASER, SAMUEL
COLLECTOR
b Riga, Latvia, Jan 21, 02. Study: Mass Inst Technol, BS & MA. Collection: Late nineteenth and twentieth century drawings, paintings, sculpture and rare illustrated books. Mailing Add: 381 Dudley Rd Newton Center MA 02159

GLASGOW, LUKMAN
GALLERY DIRECTOR, SCULPTOR
b Richfield, Utah, Aug 27, 35. Study: Brigham Young Univ, BS(psychol of aesthetics), 61; Univ Calif, Santa Barbara, 69; Calif State Univ, Los Angeles, MA, 76. Work: E B Crocker Mus, Sacramento, Calif; Downey Mus of Art, Calif; Brand Art Ctr, Glendale, Calif; Riverside Art Ctr, Calif; Laguna Beach Mus of Art, Calif. Exhib: Calif Ceramic & Glass, Oakland Mus of Art, Calif, 74; Surrealism in Clay, Utah Mus of Fine Arts, Salt Lake City, 74; Impossible Skyscapes & Improbable Shadows, E B Crocker Mus, 75; 100 Artists Commemorate 200 Yrs, Xerox Exhib Ctr, Rochester, NY, 76; Calif Design 1976, Pac Design Ctr, Los Angeles, 76; Contemp Crafts of the Americas, Smithsonian Inst Travelling Exhib, 76-77; Illusionistic-Realism, Laguna Beach Mus of Art, 77. Teaching: Guest fac ceramics, Rocky Mountain Col Summer Vail, Colo, 77. Pos: Visual arts specialist, Los Angeles Co, Calif, 69-76; dir, Los Angeles Co Cult Arts Ctr, Calif, 76-77; exec dir, Contemp Crafts Gallery, Portland, Ore, 78- Bibliog: Diane Simmons (auth), Lukman Glasgow—the Sum of the Parts, Designers West, 7/73; Judith Samuel (auth), Interviews with Lukman Glasgow, Currants, 76. Mem: Am Craftsman Coun. Style & Technique: Surreal ceramic sculptures. Media: Clay and photography. Publ: Auth, Use of the Hollow Ring, Ceramic Monthly, 74; auth, Inner City Mural Program, Los Angeles Inst of Contemp Art J, 74; auth, Three Neon Sculptors, Art Week, 75; auth (catalogue), Illusionistic-Realism, Laguna Beach Mus of Art & Nat Endowment for the Arts, 77. Dealer: Jaqueline Anhalt Gallery 750 N La Cienega Blvd Los Angeles CA 90069. Mailing Add: 5479 Dahlia Dr Los Angeles CA 90041

GLASGOW, VAUGHN LESLIE
CURATOR, ART HISTORIAN
b Apr 23, 44; US citizen. Study: La State Univ, Baton Rouge, BA; Borso di Studii, Centro Int Studii Archit A Palladio, Vicenza, Italy, cert, 68; Pa State Univ, University Park, Pa, MA, 70 & ABD, 77. Collections Arranged: Permanent Collection, Anglo-Am Art Mus, La State Univ, 66-67; G P A Healy: Famous Figures and La Patrons (co-auth, catalogue), 76; Savoir Faire: The French Taste in La, 77. Teaching: Instr art hist & admin asst, Pa State Univ, University Park, 70-71; asst prof art hist, Middle Tenn State Univ, 72-73; lectr art hist, Tulane Univ, 74- Pos: Reader youth grants, Nat Endowment for the Humanities, Washington, DC, 71-76; arts mgr, State Arts Coun, New Orleans, La, 73-75; chief cur, La State Univ, New Orleans, 75- Awards: Nat Defense Educ Act Title IV grad study, Pa State Univ-US Govt, 68-72; Nat Sci Found grant, Proj SoHo (archit), 71. Res: European post-Renaissance period; Louisiana studies; architectural history; post-revolutionary French painting. Publ: Auth, Series of mus-related feature stories, var newspapers, 75-77; auth, G P A Healy and His Louisiana Portraits, Antiques Mag, 77. Mailing Add: La State Mus 751 Chartres St New Orleans LA 70116

GLASIER, ALICE GENEVA
See Kloss, Gene

GLASS, HENRY P
DESIGNER
b Vienna, Austria, Sept 24, 11. Study: Tech Univ, Vienna; Master Sch Archit, with Theiss. Comn: Design of furniture, products, com interiors display & archit. Teaching: Prof indust design, Art Inst Chicago, 46-67, retired. Pos: Design ed, Hitchcock's Woodworking Digest; chief designer, Morris B Sanders, New York, 40-41; head archit design dept, W L Stensgaard, Chicago, 42-45; owner, Henry P Glass Assocs, 46-; chmn Chicago chap, Indust Designers Inst, 57-59. Awards: Gold Medal, Indust Designers Inst, 52; Fine Hardwoods Asn Award, 55. Mem: Fel Indust Designers Soc Am. Publ: Auth, articles in Interiors, Plastics and other trade mag. Mailing Add: 245 Dickens Rd Northfield IL 60093

GLASS, WENDY D
ART DEALER, COLLECTOR
b New York, NY, Aug 28, 25. Study: Bard Col, study of art hist with Stefan Hirsch. Collections Arranged: Temple Shaaray Tefila, New York; Temple Israel, New Rochelle, NY; Temple Soc Advan of Judaism, White Plains, NY; Waldamar Cancer Res Found, Hilton Hotel, New York, 65. Pos: Dir & owner, Glass Gallery, 60- Specialty: Figurative art; American paintings and graphics; 20th Century Japanese Ukiyo-e prints. Interest: Impressionistic graphics; South American graphics. Collection: Max Weber; Matisse, Picasso, Pascin, Benny Andrews; contemporary 20th century painters. Mailing Add: c/o Glass Gallery 315 Central Park W Apt 8W New York NY 10025

GLASSMAN, JOEL A
VIDEO ARTIST, PHOTOGRAPHER
b New York, NY, Apr 10, 46. Study: Parsons Sch Design; Univ NMex, BFA; Hunter Col. Work: Ft Worth Art Mus, Tex; San Francisco Mus of Contemp Art; Everson Mus Art, Syracuse, NY; de Ssaiset Mus, Univ Santa Clara. Exhib: Kölnischer Kunstverein, Köln, Ger, 74; La Jolla Mus Contemp Art, Calif, 74; Everson Mus Art Circuit Show, 74; Malmö Konsthall, Malmö, Sweden, 75; Whitney Mus Am Art Biennial, 75. Awards: Nat Endowment Arts Award Video Work, 75 & 77-78. Bibliog: Brenda Richardson (auth), New talent, Arts Mag, 70. Publ: Auth, Contemporary Video, Harcourt Brace, Janovich, 76. Dealer: Electronic Art Intermix 84 Fifth Ave New York NY 10011. Mailing Add: 863 Florida St San Francisco CA 94110

GLASSON, LLOYD
SCULPTOR, EDUCATOR
b Chicago, Ill, Jan 31, 31. Study: Art Inst of Chicago, BFA, 57; Tulane Univ, MFA, 59. Work: New Brit Mus of Am Art, Conn; George Walter Vincent Smith Mus, Springfield, Mass; Univ NH, Durham; Forma Viva Sculpture Garden, Slovenija, Yugoslavia. Comn: DeVane Mem, comn by Fred Naumburg, Yale Univ, 68; Shapiro Mem & Herbert Portraits, Karen Horney Clin, New York, 67. Exhib: Fall Ann, 57 & 58 & Art Asn Regionals, 58 & 59, Delgado Mus of Art, New Orleans, La; Nine Conn Sculptors, Slater Mem Mus, Norwich, 65; one-man shows, Dorsky Gallery, New York, 66 & 74 & Trinity Col, Hartford, Conn, 77; John Slade Ely House, New Haven, Conn, 75; Univ NH, Durham, 76. Teaching: Assoc prof sculpture & drawing, Univ Hartford, West Hartford, Conn, 64- Pos: Manikin sculptor, Greneker Corp, New York, 59-60; exhib designer, Newark Mus, NJ, 60-61; sculptor, New York, 61-64. Awards: Third Prize, La State Ann, Baton Rouge, La State Arts Comn, 57; First Prizes, Art Asn Regional, Delgado Mus, New Orleans, 59 & Religious Art Exhib, New Orleans, 59. Bibliog: Jolene Goldenthal (auth), Adventurous Revivalist, Hartford Courant, 4/77. Mem: Sculptors Guild. Style & Technique: Figurative, polychromed sculptures; primarily female nudes or bathers. Media: Bronze and ceramic. Dealer: Dorsky Gallery 4 W 57th St New York NY 10019. Mailing Add: Wilcox Hill Rd Portland CT 06480

GLAUBER, ROBERT H
WRITER, CURATOR
b New York, NY, July 28, 20. Study: Harvard Univ. Collections Arranged: Violence in Recent American Art (with catalog), Mus Contemp Art, Chicago, 68; Decade of Accomplishment (with catalog), Chicago, 70; Black American Artists (with catalog), Univ Iowa, 71; Search for an American Image, Brooks Mem Gallery, Memphis, 74; Classic Revival, Realism in Recent American Drawings (with catalog), Chicago, 75. Pos: Cur, Ill Bell Tel, Chicago, 66-; art critic, Skyline, Chicago, 67-; cur, Am Tel & Tel Co, New York, 72- Mem: Arts Club, Chicago. Res: American prints and drawings of the 20th century. Publ: Auth, Arts & language of China & Japan, Encycl Britannica Jr, 65; auth, Two centuries of US painting, Comptons Encycl, 75. Mailing Add: 2017 N Cleveland Chicago IL 60614

GLENN, CONSTANCE WHITE
ART ADMINISTRATOR, ART HISTORIAN
b Topeka, Kans, Oct 4, 33. Study: Univ Kans, BFA; Univ Mo, Kansas City; Calif State Univ, Long Beach, MA. Exhibitions Arranged: Tom Wesselmann: The Early Years, Collages, 1959-1962 (with catalog), 74; Lucas Samaras: Photo-Transformations (with catalog), 75; Roy Lichtenstein: Ceramic Sculpture (with catalog), 77; George Segal: Pastels 1957-1965 (with catalog), 78. Pos: Mem, Gov Comn Estab Kans State Arts Coun; co-dir, Jack Glenn Gallery, 70-73; assoc prof & dir, Mus Studies Cert Prog & dir, Fine Arts Galleries, Calif State Univ, Long Beach, 73- Mem: Am Asn Mus; Western Asn Art Mus; Col Art Asn. Res: American art since 1945. Collection: (Mr & Mrs Jack W Glenn); contemporary American art & American photography. Publ: Ed & contribr, Lucas Samaras: Photo-Transformation, 75; auth, Roy Lichtenstein: Ceramic Sculpture, 77; George Segal: Pastels, 77. Mailing Add: Calif State Univ 1250 Bellflower Blvd Long Beach CA 90804

GLEZER, NECHEMIA
ART DEALER, ART HISTORIAN
b Vilno, Lithuania, 1910; US citizen. Study: Acad Fine Arts, Vilno; Stefana Batorego Univ, Vilno; Brera Acad Fine Arts, Milan, with Aldo Carpi. Collections Arranged: Fourteen Italian Artists, sponsored by Italian Ambassador to USA, Veerhoff Gallery, Washington, DC, 60; French Artists, C W Post Col, Long Island Univ, NY, 61; I Pailes, Maison Francaise, NY Univ, sponsored by French Cult Attache to USA, 63; Ferruccio Steffanutti, Vatican Pavilion, New York World's Fair, 64-65; Trento Longaretti, Casa Italiana, Columbia Univ, New York, 67; I Pailes, Maison Francaise, Columbia Univ, 72 & I Pailes Exhib, Yeshiva Univ Mus, New York, NY, 75. Pos: Pres, Nechemia Glezer Gallery, New York, 53- Awards: Award for Cult Enrichment, Fr Cult Attache, 63; Award for Introducing Italian Artists to USA, Ital Consul Gen, 69; Academician, Accad Tiberina di Rome, 72; plus one other. Bibliog: Elspeth Flynn (auth), Southeby at Glezer Gallery, Brit Info Serv, 2/5/63; Mr Glezer from NY visits Museum at Casteleone, La Notte, Milan, 5/24/64; Mario Pescara (auth), Collection of Nechemia Glezer, Am Rev Art & Sci, 4/69. Res: Macchiaioli; Italian nineteenth century artists. Specialty: School of Paris artists; contemporary Italian artists. Interest: Bringing contemporary French and Italian art to the attention of the American public. Collection: Daumier, Chagall, Pailes, Kikoine, Kremegne, Bai, Brindisi, Carpi, Carena, Quidi, Gino Moro & Longaretti. Publ: Introductions to catalogs. Mailing Add: 870 Madison Ave New York NY 10021

GLICK, PAULA FLORENCE
ART DEALER, COLLECTOR
b Baltimore, Md, Jan 8, 36. Study: Am Univ; George Washington Univ, BA. Pos: Assoc dir, Capricorn Galleries, 64- Mem: Col Art Asn Am. Specialty: American contemporary realists; Medieval-Byzantine art. Collection: Contemporary realists. Mailing Add: 9536 Lawnsberry Terr Silver Spring MD 20901

GLICKMAN, MAURICE
SCULPTOR, WRITER
b Jassy, Romania, Jan 6, 06; US citizen. Study: Educ Alliance Art Sch, New York, 21-26; Art Students League, 27 & 29-30. Work: Yvonne (bronze head), Roberson Mem Art Ctr, Binghamton, NY; Girl with Braids (bronze head), Albany Inst Hist & Art, NY; Siesta (alabaster), Hirshhorn Mus & Sculpture Garden, Washington, DC; Football Players (marble), Queens Col Collection, NY. Comn: Negro Mother & Child (bronze), Dept Interior, Washington, DC, 34; Construction (Philippine mahogany bas-relief), US Treas Dept, South River, NJ, 38; Mailmen (stone composition bas-relief), US Post Off, Northampton, Pa, 40. Exhib: One-man show, Morton Galleries, New York, 31; Govt in Art, Mus Mod Art, New York, 35; Carnegie Sculpture Invitational, Philadelphia Mus, 38; Whitney Mus Am Art Ann, New York, 38-61; Woman's Col of Univ of NC, 40; Artists for Victory, Metrop Mus Art, New York, 41; Florence Lewison Gallery, New York, 61, 65, 68 & 72; Sculpture by Maurice Glickman—A Selected Retrospective 1933-1963, Albany Inst of Hist & Art, 63; Heritage of American Art, Nat Archives Bldg Rotunda, Washington, DC, 71; plus others. Pos: Founder-dir, Sch Art Studies, New York, 45-55. Awards: Guggenheim Fel, 34. Bibliog: Karl Schwartz (auth), Jewish Sculptors, Newman Publ; Merwyn Eaton (auth), The sculpture of Maurice Glickman, Design Mag, 10/48; Oliver Larkin (auth), Art & Life in America, Rinehart, 49; Donald Johnson (auth), A visit with Maurice Glickman, Today's Art, 5/53; Janet McFarlane (auth), Selected Retrospective (exhib catalogue), Albany Inst of Hist & Art, 63; Cecil Roth (auth), Jewish Art, NY Graphic Soc, 71. Mem: Nat Sculpture Soc; Sculptors Guild (founding mem, 38-, exec secy, 54-55). Style & Technique: Realist-expressionist. Media: Bronze, Wood, Stone. Res: Inter-relation of the arts with emphasis on the relation of sculpture and architecture, stressing the master sculptors' contributions. Publ: Auth, A lesson from history on sculpture and architecture, Archit Rec, 5/40; auth, The sculptor and his market, Mag Art, 41; auth, On wood carving, 43 & Techniques in sculpture, 60, Am Artists; auth, The tools of the sculptor, Design Mag, 49; plus others. Dealer: Florence Lewison Gallery 30 E 60th St New York NY 10022. Mailing Add: 165 E 66th St New York NY 10021

GLICKSMAN, HAL
GALLERY DIRECTOR, EDUCATOR
b Los Angeles, Calif, Aug 26, 37. Study: Univ Calif, Los Angeles, BA(art hist), 59. Exhibitions Arranged: Spec installations of Environmental Art for Michael Asher, Tom Eatherton, Bruce Nauman, Larry Bell, Maria Nordman (with catalog), Eric Orr, Dan Flavin, Carl Andre & Alice Aycock. Teaching: Instr mus training, George Washington Univ, 70-72; instr contemp art, Univ Calif, Irvine, 72-75. Pos: Gallery dir, Pomona Col, Claremont, Calif, 69-70; assoc dir, Corcoran Gallery Art, Washington, DC, 70-71; gallery dir, Univ Calif, Irvine, 72-75; gallery dir, Otis Art Inst, Los Angeles, 75- Awards: Nat Endowment for Arts Grant, 72. Mem: Los Angeles Inst Contemp Art (chmn exhib comt, 75-76). Publ: Auth, Peter Alexander, Sunsets, 75; ed, John Baldessari, Throwing a Ball Once to Get Three Melodies & Fifteen Chords, 75. Mailing Add: 2401 Wilshire Blvd Los Angeles CA 90057

GLIKO, CARL ALBERT
PAINTER
b Great Falls, Mont, Apr 14, 41. Study: San Francisco Art Inst, BFA, 64; also with Richard Diebenkorn & Frank Lobdell. Work: Whitney Mus Am Art, New York; McGraw Hill Publ Hq Bldg, New York; Decort Price & Rhodes, Philadelphia. Exhib: Inst Contemp Art, Univ Pa, 70; Lyrical Abstraction, Whitney Mus Am Art, 71 & Whitney Annuals, 72 & 73; Two Generations of Color Painting, Inst Contemp Art; one-man show, Andre Emmerich Gallery, New York, 73 & Tibor de Nagy, Houston, 74. Bibliog: Jane Bell (auth), rev, Arts Mag, 11/73. Style & Technique: Multi-layer stains and gels on unsized canvas. Mailing Add: 17 Leonard St New York NY 10013

GLIMCHER, ARNOLD B
ART DEALER, WRITER
b Mar 12, 38; US citizen. Pos: Pres, Pace Gallery, New York, 63- Specialty: 20th century art. Publ: Auth, Jean Dubuffet—Simulacres (catalog), 70 & auth, Ernest Trova—Recent Sculpture (catalog), 71, Pace Ed; auth, Louise Nevelson, Praeger, 72; auth, Louise Nevelson, E P Dutton & Co, Inc, 76. Mailing Add: Pace Gallery 32 E 57th St New York NY 10022

GLOBUS, DOROTHY TWINING
GALLERY DIRECTOR, CURATOR
Study: Swarthmore Col, Pa, BA(art hist; magna cum laude). Collections Arranged: Immovable Objects Exhibition: Lower Manhattan From Battery Park to Bridge (res & design; auth, catalogue), New York, 74; MAN transFORMS (res & cur for four portions), 76, The Royal Pavilion at Brighton, Drawings, Prints & Furnishings From the Pavilion (coordr), 77, Andrea Palladio, Models & Photographs of the Work of Palladio (design & coordr), 77 & 200 Years of American Architectural Drawing (coordr), 77, Cooper-Hewitt Mus of Dec Arts & Crafts. Pos: Asst to dir, Wilcox Gallery, Swarthmore Col, Pa, 67-69; apprentice design & prod, Off of Exhib, Smithsonian Inst, Washington, DC, summer 68, exhib specialist res, design & coordr for spec exhib, DRUGS, 70-72, exhib specialist res & design on assignment to James S Ward Inc, New York, Smithsonain Inst, 72-73; coordr of exhib, Cooper-Hewitt Mus of Dec Arts & Crafts, New York, 73- Mailing Add: 889 Broadway New York NY 10003

GLORIG, OSTOR
PAINTER
b New York, NY, Feb 14, 19. Study: Am Art Sch, New York, with Robert Brackman, Raphael Soyer & Gordon Samstag, four yr cert. Work: Mark Twain Portrait, Mark Twain Libr & Mem, Hartford, Conn. Exhib: One-man shows, Lynn Kottler Galleries, Clarksville Gallery, 65 & Col Mt St Vincent, 67; Nat Soc Arts & Lett Empire State Chap Showing, 69. Awards: Interior Design Cover Award, 51; Grumbacher Merit Award, 61. Bibliog: Elaine Israel (auth), From diamond to canvas, Long Island Star-J, 5/9/67. Mem: Life fel Royal Soc Arts Eng; life mem Nat Soc Arts & Lett; hon mem Kappa Pi. Style & Technique: Realistic; palette knife and brush. Media: Oil. Dealer: Lynn Kottler Galleries 3 E 65th St New York NY 10021. Mailing Add: 21-56 47th St Long Island City NY 11105

GLOVER, ROBERT LEON
SCULPTOR, PAINTER
b Upland, Calif, May 20, 36. Study: Chouinard Art Inst, 57; Otis Art Inst, MFA, 60. Work: Otis Art Inst Gallery, Los Angeles. Comn: Sculptural screen comn by, K D Childs, Brentwood, Calif, 62; Mosaic mural, First Fed Savings, South Pasadena, 62; sculpture group comn by, Southern Calif Container Corp, Gardena, 70; stained glass murals, comn by, Cathryn Price, Santa Monica, 73-74. Exhib: San Francisco Mus Fine Arts, 57; Los Angeles Co Mus, 59; Everson Mus Fine Arts, 60; Pasadena Mus Mod Art, 71. Teaching: Asst prof design & intermedia ceramic, Otis Art Inst, 64-74, actg chmn dept sculpture, 63-76, asst prof intermedia & ceramics, 76- Pos: Art dir, Clokey Film Prod, Hollywood, 60-61; art dir design, Interpace, Los Angeles, 69. Style & Technique: Abstract including geometric pattern and color overalls on canvas with graphite, raw pigment, wax and pastel; sculptures are of ceramics and mixed media, air brush and spray techniques. Media: Raw Oxides & Pigments with Polymer Media; Clay with Low-Fire Bright Colors. Dealer: Janus Gallery 303 N Sweetzer Los Angeles CA 90048. Mailing Add: 9830 Portola Dr Beverly Hills CA 90210

GLUCKMAN, MORRIS
PAINTER
b Kiev, Russia, Aug 7, 94. Study: Odessa Art Sch; Nat Acad Design; Brooklyn Mus Sch Art; Davidson Sch Mod Art. Work: Norfolk Mus, Va; Cambridge Gallery, Roslyn, NY. Exhib: Nat Acad Design; Nordness Gallery; City Ctr; Art: USA; Contemp Arts; plus many others. Awards: Windsor Award, Brooklyn Mus; Albert Dorn Award, Am Watercolor Soc; Shannon Award, Brooklyn Soc Artists; plus many others. Mem: Artists Equity Asn; Am Watercolor Soc; Brooklyn Soc Artists; League Present Day Artists. Mailing Add: 463 West St Apt 1019 H New York NY 10014

GLUECK, GRACE (HELEN)
WRITER
b New York, NY. Study: Washington Sq Col, NY Univ, BA; Columbia Univ. Pos: Cult news reporter & art columnist, New York Times, 63- Publ: Contribr, Museums in Crisis, Braziller, 72. Mailing Add: c/o New York Times 229 W 43rd St New York NY 10036

GLYDE, HENRY GEORGE
PAINTER, EDUCATOR
b Luton, Eng, June 18, 06. Study: Hastings Sch Art & Sci; Royal Col Art, London, hons; Can Arts Coun, sr fel, 58-59. Work: Edmonton Art Gallery; Nat Gallery Can; Glenbow Found, Calgary; Alta Col Art; Univ Alta; plus others. Exhib: Royal Brit Artists; Royal Acad, London; Can Group Painters; Can Soc Graphic Art; Royal Can Acad; plus others. Teaching: Instr, Borough Polytech, London; instr, Croydon Sch Art; instr, High Wycombe Sch Art; head art dept, Prov Inst Technol & Art, Alta; emer prof fine arts, Univ Alta & Banff Sch Fine Arts. Awards: Univ Alta Nat Award, 66. Mem: Royal Can Acad Arts. Style & Technique: Figure drawing and composition; landscape; realism, direct technique. Mailing Add: RR 1 Mackinnon Rd Port Washington BC V0N 2T0 Can

G'MIGLIO (GLORIA MIGLIONICO)
PHOTOGRAPHER
b Newark, NJ, Apr 1, 49. Study: Drexel Univ, BS, 70; Int Mkt, with Prof Mercia Grassi. Work: Am Archives Art, Smithsonian Inst, Washington, DC; Lincoln Ctr Mus & Libr; Inst PR Cult, San Juan; Int Ctr Photog, New York. Comn: Magician Randi and artist Hari working, 75; photo-sculpture, comn by Donald Delue, NJ, 75; sport & ballet subjects, comn by George Preston Frazer, Va, 75; K A Porter & Hari, comn by H Sosnowitz, 75, Artist Kenneth Hari, 75. Exhib: H S Graphics Gallery, NJ, 75; Am Archives Art, 75; Photojournalism Today Travel Exhib, 75. Pos: Photo consult, H S Graphics, Ltd; photo consult, Advan Printing. Awards: McRory Scholar Award, 70. Bibliog: Lew Head (auth), Portraits of Notables, New York Times, 6/73; Leora Potter (producer), Future Vision TV,

74. Style & Technique: Photojournalism. Publ: Auth, Life of Kenneth Hari as an Artist, 73; auth, Writers (James Michener, Auden & Vonnegut, Jr), 74; auth, The Making of a Lithograph, 75; Dealer: H S Graphics Ltd Box 243 Keasbey NJ 08832. Mailing Add: 462 Ford Ave Fords NJ 08863

GOBIN, HENRY (DELANO)
PAINTER
b Tulalip Indian Reservation, May 29, 41. Study: San Francisco Art Inst, BFA, 70; Sacramento State Col, MA, 71. Work: Am Embassy, Kenya, Africa; Am Embassy, Madrid, Spain. Exhib: Am Indian Hist Soc Mus, San Francisco, 68; Mus Nac Bellas Artes, Buenos Aires, Arg, 68; San Francisco Art Inst, 70; Civic Art Gallery, San Jose, Calif, 71; Jamison Gallery, Santa Fe, NMex, 71. Teaching: Asst prof native Am Art, Sacramento State Col, 70-71; training instr humanities, Inst Am Indian Arts, 71- Awards: First Prize, NMex Wildlife Mag, 62; First Prize, 17th Ann Navajo Fair, Gallup, NMex, 63; First Prize, Scottsdale Nat Indian Art Exhib, Ariz, 64. Bibliog: Articles in Crafts Horizon, 64, Am Indian Hist Soc Mus, 68 & Artforum, 70. Media: Watercolor. Mailing Add: Inst Am Indian Arts Cerrillos Rd Santa Fe NM 87501

GODDARD, DONALD
ART EDITOR, ART WRITER
b Cortland, NY, Apr 16, 34. Pos: Writer & ed, McGraw-Hill Book Co, New York, 66-69; managing ed, ARTnews Mag, New York, 74- Publ: Auth, Tschacbasov, Am Arch of World Art, 64; ed, McGraw-Hill Dictionary of Art, 69; ed, Encyclopedia of Painting, Crown, 70; ed, Mark di Suvero: an epic reach, ARTnews, 76. Mailing Add: 425 W Broadway New York NY 10012

GODDARD, VIVIAN
PAINTER
b San Francisco, Calif. Study: Calif Sch Fine Art; Art Students League; Stanford Univ, with Ed Farmer & Dan Mendelowitz; Art League San Francisco; Robert Brackman Summer Sch, Noank & Madison, Conn; Otis Art Sch, Los Angeles; Acad Grande Chaumiere, Paris; Simi Studio, Florence, Italy. Work: Pioneer Mus & Hagan Gallery, Stockton, Calif; Hall Justice, San Francisco; City Sacramento, Calif; Stanislaus State Col. Comn: Portraits, Richard Cragin, Alexander Capurso, Otto Kruger, Mrs Bernard McFadyen, Hubert Latimer, plus many others. Exhib: One-man shows, Windblad Gallery, San Francisco, 68, Pioneer Mus & Hagan Gallery, 69, Stanislaus State Col, 69 & Rosecrucian Mus, San Jose, Calif, 69 & 72; Soc Western Artists, De Young Mus, 68-70; plus others. Teaching: Head art dept, Miss Harker's Sch, Palo Alto, Calif, 38-48; instr pvt studio, 69-71. Pos: Demonstrations, Soc Western Artists, Calif, Burlingame Art Asn, Calif, Fresno Art Asn, Calif & Am Fine Arts Asn, Los Angeles; juror. Awards: First Award for Graphics & Award for Oil Portrait, Soc Western Artists, 67; Award for Portrait, Mother Lode Nat, 70; plus others. Mem: Soc Western Artists; life mem Art Students League; Am Artists Prof League; life mem Am Inst Fine Arts; San Francisco Soc Women Artists. Media: Oil. Dealer: Portraits Inc 41 E 57th St New York NY 10022; Avatar Gallery 2226 Union St San Francisco CA. Mailing Add: c/o J P Mahoney Co 600 Montgomery St San Francisco CA 94123

GODSEY, GLENN
EDUCATOR, PAINTER
b Amarillo, Tex, June 1, 37. Study: Okla State Univ; Univ Tulsa, BA & MA; and with Alexandre Hogue. Work: Springfield Art Mus, Mo; Okla State Art Collection, Okla Arts & Humanities Coun, Oklahoma City; Magic Castle, Hollywood, Calif. Comn: Portrait, Univ Tulsa; The Petroleum Club, Tulsa; portrait, Oral Roberts Univ. Exhib: One-man show, Philbrook Art Ctr, Tulsa, 71; Watercolor, USA, Springfield, Mo, 72-75; Okla Artists Ann, Tulsa, 75; Traveling Exhib of Okla Art, Washington, DC, 76; Saltillo, Mex, 77; two-man show, Univ of Tulsa, 78. Teaching: Asst prof painting & art hist, Univ Tulsa, 67- Awards: Watercolor USA Purchase Award, SMo Mus Asn, 74; Okla Artist Ann Award, 72 & 74. Bibliog: Rev Blakey (auth), Delineating the mysterious, Univ Tulsa Mag; Maurice DeVinna (auth), Music & the arts, Tulsa World Mag, 71; Bill Donaldson (auth), Showcase, Tulsa Tribune, 71. Style & Technique: Magic realist painting, predominately still life. Media: Acrylic, Watercolor. Publ: Auth, Hip generation, Univ Tulsa Mag, 68; illusr, Okla State Univ Lit Quart, Nimrod, Tulsa Mag & Univ Tulsa Mag. Mailing Add: 2672 E 38th St Tulsa OK 74105

GODWIN, JUDITH WHITNEY
PAINTER, DESIGNER
b Suffolk, Va, Feb 15, 30. Study: Mary Baldwin Col, Staunton, Va; Va Commonwealth Univ, BFA; Art Students League, with Vaclav Vytlacil, Will Barnet & Harry Sternberg; Hans Hofmann Sch, Provincetown, Mass & New York. Work: NC Mus of Art, Raleigh; San Francisco Mus of Art, Calif; Va Mus, Richmond; Edwin A Ulrich Mus of Art, Wichita, Kans; Chase Manhattan Collection, New York. Comn: Historical restoration for pvt individuals, 68 & 72; Bicentennial Portfolio of Drawings, City of Suffolk, Va, 75; Painter's Themes (fabric design), Bloomcraft Inc, New York, 76. Exhib: Irene Leache Mem Show, Norfolk Mus of Arts & Sci, Va, 51; Valentine Mus, Richmond, Va, 52; An Environment of Expression, Theater-Go-Round, Va, 54; Va Intermont Col, Bristol, Va, 54; St Lawrence Univ, Canton, NY, 59; Univ Colo, Boulder, 60; Weatherspoon Art Gallery, Greensboro, NC, 76; Sheldon Mem Art Gallery, Univ Nebr, Lincoln, 76; Spring Recent Accessions, Vassar Col Collection, Poughkeepsie, NY, 76; Recent Acquisitions, Ulrich Mus, Wichita, Kans, 77 & NC Mus of Art, Raleigh, 77; Danforth Mus, Framingham, Mass, 77. Awards: Popular Prize, Leache Mem Exhib, Norfolk, 51. Mem: Am Fedn of the Arts; Col Art Asn; Am Soc of Interior Designers. Style & Technique: Abstractions in oil and acrylic, gouache, tempera, realistic sketches. Dealer: Ingber Gallery 3 E 78th St New York NY 10021. Mailing Add: c/o 247 W 13th St New York NY 10011

GODWIN, ROBERT KIMBALL
PAINTER
b Binghamton, NY, Aug 4, 24. Exhib: Soc Washington Artists 70th Ann, Smithsonian Inst, Washington, DC, 63; Yutenji Gallery, Tokyo, Japan, 67; one-man show, Potter's House Gallery, Washington, DC, 70; Fairfax Co Cult Asn & N Va Community Col Area Exhib, Annandale, Va, 72; N Va Fine Arts Asn 3rd Ann, Alexandria, Va, 72 & 77. Media: Oil. Mailing Add: 2402 Elba Ct Alexandria VA 22306

GOEDICKE, JEAN
PAINTER, INSTRUCTOR
b DePass, Wyo, Sept 24, 08. Study: Taos Sch Art, NMex, with Emil Bisttram; Casper Col, with Ed Gothberg, AA; Univ Wyo, with James M Boyle & Richard Evans, BA & MA(with hon); also with Robert E Wood, Calif, Mario Cooper & Dale Meyers, NY & Milford Zornes, Utah; workshops with Richard Proctor, Univ Wash & Bud Shackelford, Calif. Work: Wyo State Art Gallery, Cheyenne; Wyo State Capitol, Cheyenne. Exhib: Nat Art Exhib, Springville, Utah, 53-63; Wyo Traveling Art Exhib, 57-74; Gov First & Second Exhibs, 68-69; Univ Fed de Goias, Brazil, 69; eight state regional watercolor exhib, Fedn Rocky Mountain States, Inc, 69-71. Teaching: Instr, lectr, painter & demonstrator watercolor & drawing, Mobile Art Symp, Wyo Coun Arts, 67-, instr, Friends of Beginning Artists, summer 75; instr, Beginners in Art, West Wind Gallery, Casper, Wyo, 74-75. Awards: Ivan de Lorraine Albright Prize for Abstract IV, Wind River Nat Art Exhib, 65. Bibliog: Peggy Simson Curry (auth), A tool box & a talent, In Wyoming, summer 70. Mem: Wyo Artists Asn (pres, 66-67); Casper Artists Guild (pres, 65); Wyo State Gallery Adv Bd (chmn, 73-). Style & Technique: Traditional and experimental paintings, mainly landscapes. Media: Transparent Watercolor. Dealer: Sheridan Inn Gallery of the Arts Box 781 Sheridan WY 82801. Mailing Add: 2125 S Coffman Casper WY 82601

GOEDIKE, SHIRL
PAINTER
b Los Angeles, Calif, 1923. Study: Univ Calif, Los Angeles; Art Ctr Sch, Los Angeles. Work: Los Angeles Co Mus Art; Pasadena Mus Art; Palm Springs Mus; Home Savings & Loan, Los Angeles; Hirshhorn Mus, Washington, DC; plus others. Exhib: Los Angeles Co Mus, 55-56; Stanford Univ, 56; one-man show, Palace Legion of Honor, San Francisco, Calif, 59; Santa Barbara Biennial, Santa Barbara Mus & Nat Tour, 59; 26th Biennial, Corcoran Gallery Art, Washington, DC. Awards: Los Angeles Co Art Mus Purchase Prize, 55; All-City Art Festival Honorable Mention, Home Savings & Loan Los Angeles, 56 & 57; First Honorable Mention, James D Phelan Award, 57. Bibliog: Alfred Frankenstein (auth), article in San Francisco Chronicle, 60; Arthur Millier (auth), article in Los Angeles Herald Exam, 66; Henry Seldis (auth), article in Los Angeles Times, 72. Media: Oil. Mailing Add: c/o Ankrum Gallery 657 N La Cienega Blvd Los Angeles CA 90069

GOELL, ABBY JANE
PAINTER, PRINTMAKER
b New York, NY. Study: Art Students League, with Harry Sternberg & Charles Alston; Syracuse Univ, BA; NY Sch Interior Design, cert; Columbia Univ, with Robert Motherwell, Stephen Greene & John Heliker, MFA(painting). Work: Mus Mod Art, New York; Yale Univ Art Gallery; Chase Manhattan Bank Collection, New York; Kresge Art Ctr, Mich; Grafisches Kabinet, Munich, WGer; Sloane-Kettering Mem Ctr, New York; Univ Iowa Mus; Univ Wis Art Ctr; Atlantic Richfield Oil Co, Calif; plus others. Comn: Original print, Pratt Graphics Ctr, 75. Exhib: South London Art Gallery, 67; Brooklyn Mus Print Biennial, 70; Hudson River Mus, Yonkers, NY, 71; Childe Hassam Purchase Exhib, 77; Orgn of Independent Artists, 77; Am Acad & Inst of Arts & Lett grant show, 77; Grey Gallery & Study Ctr, NY Univ, 77; one-man show, Automation House, New York, 73; plus others. Teaching: Instr art hist, Hunter Col, 67; lectr hist of design, Lab Inst of Merchandising, 67-70. Awards: Yaddo Fel, Saratoga Springs, NY, 68. Mem: Artists' Equity Asn; Women's Caucus for Art; Am Soc of Appraisers; Victorian Soc in Am. Style & Technique: Romantic abstract; large scale. Media: Oil; Serigraph, Lithograph, Collage. Mailing Add: 37 Washington Sq W New York NY 10011

GOERITZ, MATHIAS
SCULPTOR, DESIGNER
b Danzig, Ger, Apr 4, 15. Study: Friedrich-Wilhelms Univ, PhD; Kunstgewerbeschule, Berlin-Charlottenburg. Work: Mus Arte Mod, Mexico City, Mex; Kunsthalle, Hamburg, Ger; Mus Mod Art, New York; Israel Mus, Jerusalem, Israel; Univ Ariz Art Gallery. Comn: El Eco (total environ), comn by Daniel Mont, Exp Mus, Mexico City, 52-53; environ sculpture, Towers of Satellite City, comn by L Barragan & M Pani, 57, Towers of Automex, comn by R Legorreta, Toluca, Mex, 63-64 & Pyramid of Mixcoac, Mexico City, 70-72; Route of Friendship (hwy environ), Mex Olympic Comt, Mexico City, 68. Exhib: Art of Assemblage, Mus Mod Art, New York, 61; Pittsburgh Int Exhib, Carnegie Inst, 61; Concrete Poetry, Stedelijk Mus, Amsterdam, Holland, 70-71; Art and Science, Tel Aviv Mus, Israel, 71; 11th Biennial, Open-Air Mus Sculpture, Middelheim, Belg, 71. Teaching: Prof design, Nat Univ Mex, 54- Pos: Dir Sch Fine Arts & Indust Design, Iberoamericano Univ, Mex, 57-60; ed art sect, Arquitectura-Mex, 59-; artist in residence, Aspen Inst Humanistic Studies, Aspen, Colo, 70-72. Bibliog: Olivia Zuniga (auth), Mathias Goeritz, Ed Intercontinental, Mexico City, 63; Clive B Smith (auth), Builders in the sun, Architectural, New York, 67; H Harvard Arnason (auth), History of Modern Art, Abrams, 68. Publ: Illusr, Los amantes y la noche, ed Eco, Mex, 53; auth & illusr, bks & articles. Mailing Add: Apartado 20-390 Mexico DF Mexico

GOERTZ, AUGUSTUS FREDERICK
PAINTER
b Greenwich Village, New York, NY, Aug 15, 48. Study: High Sch of Music & Art, New York; Carnegie-Mellon Univ, Pittsburgh, Pa; San Francisco Art Inst, BFA; also with Tom Akawie, Jay Defeo, Augustus Goertz, Wally Hedrick, Bruce Nauman & Jim Rienekin. Work: San Francisco Art Inst; Chicago Art Inst; Aldrich Mus of Contemp Art, Ridgefield, Conn; New York Law Sch; Hosp for Joint Diseases, New York. Exhib: San Francisco Art Inst, 70; Contemporary Reflections, Aldrich Mus of Contemp Art, Ridgefield, Conn, 73; Warren Benedek Gallery, New York, 73; New Britian Mus, Conn, 74; Soho Ctr for Visual Artists, New York, 75; United States Tour, Am Fed of Arts, 76; 112 Greene St Gallery, New York, 77; United States Courthouse, Brooklyn, NY, 77; Mail Art Show, Hiart Gallery, Cleveland, Ohio, 78; Selections from The Collection, Aldrich Mus of Contemp Art, 78; Arte Fiera, Bologna, Italy, 78; one-man shows, New York Law Sch, 77 & Sarah Rentschler Gallery, 78. Collections Arranged: Contemporary Reflections, Aldrich Mus of Contemp Art, Ridgefield, Conn, 73; Encounter, Warren Benedek Gallery, New York, 73; United States Tour, 76; Selections from the Collection, Aldrich Mus of Contemp Art, 78. Awards: Spec Acheivement Award, New York Taxi Drivers, Robert Scull, 65; Honor Student Award, San Francisco Art Inst, 67. Mem: Orgn of Independent Artists; New York WPA Artists Inc; San Francisco Art Inst Alumni Asn. Style & Technique: Hypermodern real abstractations; acrylic painting, brush and spray technique. Dealer: Sarah Y Rentschler 450 W 24th St New York NY 10013. Mailing Add: 319 Greenwich St New York NY 10013

GOETZ, EDITH JEAN
PAINTER, INSTRUCTOR
b Media, Pa, Oct 28, 18. Study: St Margaret's Sch, Waterbury, Conn, with Frederic Sexton; Cape Sch, Provincetown, Mass, with Henry Hensche; Art Students League with George Bridgeman, Arnold Blanch & Charles Chapman; Nat Acad, New York, with Charles Curran; Grand Cent Art Sch, with Mario Cooper. Work: Women's Col, Chickasha, Okla; Great Plains Mus, Lawton, Okla. Exhib: Okla Ann, Philbrook Mus, Tulsa, 65; one-man show, Okla Art Ctr, 70; Goetz/Goetz, Jamison Gallery, Santa Fe, NMex, 72; Am Artists Prof League, New York, 75; Three State Show at Lawton, Great Plains Mus, 75. Teaching: Portrait & figure drawing & painting, Goetz Art Sch, Oklahoma City, 65-75 & Santa Fe, summers 70-73. Awards: Several First Awards for Pastel. Mem: Am Artists Prof League; Grand Cent Galleries; Portraits Inc. Style & Technique: Impressionistic in color and realistic in drawing, based on the French school of impressionism. Media: Oil, Pastel. Dealer: Blair Galleries Ltd Box 2342 Santa Fe NM 87501; Shriver Gallery Taos NM 87571. Mailing Add: 800 NE 21st St Oklahoma City OK 73105

GOETZ, PETER HENRY
PAINTER, LECTURER
b Slavgorod, Russia, Sept 8, 17; Can citizen. Study: Waterloo Col, 45; Doon Sch Fine Art, with F H Varley; study watercolor in Japan. Work: London Pub Libr & Art Mus, Ont; Sarnia Pub Libr & Art Mus, Ont; Kitchener Waterloo Art Gallery; Univ Waterloo, Ont; Univ Guelph, Ont. Comn: Series of twelve paintings from around the world, Waterloo Co Health Bldg, 65; painting of Parliament bldgs, Nat Club, Toronto, 67; Peace Tower, comn by Sen John B Aird, Toronto, 69; painting of Budapest, CFTO-TV, Toronto, 69; View of Prague, Toronto Stock Exchange, 69. Exhib: Royal Can Acad; Ont Soc Artists; Can Soc Painters Watercolour; Nat Gallery Ottawa; Am Watercolor Soc, New York, 72. Teaching: Lectured and demonstrated adult education classes throughout Ont for Dept Educ. Awards: Grand Prize, Que Nat Exhib; Watercolor Prize, Western Ont Exhib; First Prize, Brampton Ann Exhib; Purchase Award Image 77, Ont Soc Artists, 77. Mem: Ont Soc Artists; Can Soc Painters Watercolour; Soc Can Artists; Centro Studi & Scambi Int, Rome; fel Int Inst Arts & Lett; Am Fedn Art. Style & Technique: Impressionistic with progressive approach. Media: Watercolor. Dealer: Shaw-Rimmington Gallery 20 Birch Ave Toronto ON Can. Mailing Add: 784 Avondale Ave Kitchener ON N2M 2W8 Can

GOETZ, RICHARD VERNON
PAINTER, INSTRUCTOR
b Lawrenceburg, Tenn, Apr 6, 15. Study: Oklahoma City Univ; Univ Okla; Cape Sch Art; Nat Acad Design; Art Students League; with Robert Brackman, Henry Henche, George Bridgman, Sidney Dickenson & Jonas Lee. Work: Butler Inst Am Art, Youngstown, Ohio; Okla Art Ctr, Oklahoma City; Okla Hist Soc, Oklahoma City; Ft Smith Art Ctr, Ark. Exhib: Butler Inst Am Art, 68; Allied Artists Am, 68; Okla Mus Art, 68; Am Artists Prof League, 71; Okla-Tex Spring Ann, 72. Teaching: Dir, Goetz Art Sch Oklahoma City, 46- & Goetz Art Sch Santa Fe, 71-; co-dir, Malden Bridge Art Sch, New York, 64-71. Awards: Best in Show, Tex-Okla Spring Show, 68; Best in Show, Am Artists Prof League, 69; McDonnough Award, Butler Inst Am Art, 68. Mem: Am Artists Prof League. Style & Technique: Traditional; realistic. Media: Oil. Publ: Auth, Painting a still life, Am Artist. 68. Dealer: Grand Central Art Galleries Vanderbilt & 44th St New York NY 10017. Mailing Add: 800 NE 21st St Oklahoma City OK 73105

GOETZL, THOMAS MAXWELL
ART WRITER, LAWYER, EDUCATOR
b Chicago, Ill, May 31, 43. Study: Univ Calif, Berkeley, AB(psychology), 65 & Boalt Hall Sch of Law, JD, 69. Teaching: Prof art and the law, Golden Gate Univ, Sch of Law, San Francisco, Calif, 75- Pos: Mem bd dirs, Artists Equity Asn, Inc, N Calif Chap, 76- Res: Active participant in drafting of and lobbying for legislation advancing the property rights (both moral and economic) of visual artists. Publ: Auth, Recent Arts Legislation-An Overview, Artweek & Glass Studio, 78. Mailing Add: 1019 Keith Ave Berkeley CA 94708

GOFF, LLOYD LOZES
PAINTER, ILLUSTRATOR
b Dallas, Tex, Mar 29, 19. Study: Art Students League, Louis Comfort Tiffany Found fel, Daniel Schnakenberg scholar, with Nicolaides; Univ NMex. Work: Whitney Mus Am Art, New York; Wadsworth Atheneum, Hartford, Conn; West Point Mus, NY; Dallas Mus Fine Arts, Dallas; Museo Nacionale de Bellas Artes, Mexico City, Mex. Comn: Mural (with Paul Cadmus), US Embassy, Ottawa, Can, 38; South American Beauty (oil panel), Helena Rubinstein, New York, 39; Delta C Before Fencing (oil on canvas), US Treas, Post Off, Cooper, Tex, 40; Planning the Route (oil on canvas), US Treas, Post Off, Hollis, Okla, 42; home mural (duco on wall), Sailtops Farm, Rudgwick, Sussex, Eng, 70. Exhib: Whitney Mus Ann, New York, 38-43; San Francisco Art Asn Exhibs, 41, 42 & 43; Carnegie Inst Int, Pittsburgh, 43; Acad Art Gallery, New York, 54 & 55; Am Artists & Water Conserv, Nat Gallery, Washington, DC, 72. Teaching: Assoc prof art, painting & drawing, Univ NMex, 44-47. Awards: Childe Hassam Purchase Awards, Am Acad Arts & Lett, 73 & 74. Bibliog: Ten Eyk Gardner (auth), History of Watercolor Painting in America, Reinhold, 66. Mem: Life mem Art Students League; Artists Equity Asn New York; Nat Soc Mural Painters. Style & Technique: Expressionist; Turneresque. Media: Mixed Media. Publ: Auth & illusr, Run Sandpiper Run, Lothrop, 57; auth & illusr, Fly Redwing Fly, 59. Mailing Add: 136 W 75th St New York NY 10023

GOFF, THOMAS JEFFERSON
SCULPTOR, MEDALIST
b Bristol, RI, Dec 22, 07. Study: RI Sch Design, grad, 30, grad work, 33-34, study under Louise A Atkins, Hugo O E Carlborg & William A Heath. Work: US Naval Mus, Washington, DC; Smithsonian Inst, Washington, DC; Newport News Mus, Va; US Naval War Col Mus, Newport, RI; RI Hist Soc Mus, Providence. Comn: Armed servs insignia, Craven & Whitaker Co, Providence, 40-45; Bryant Col bronze seal, pres Bryant Col, Providence & Smithfield, RI, 62; Gordon Col bronze seal, Seal Comt, Wrentham, Mass, 71; Univ RI bronze podium seal, Foundry-Auburn Brass Foundry, Crauston, RI, 69; Jackson State Col bronze seal, Herff-Jones Co, Indianapolis, Ind, 70. Exhib: Nat Sculpture Soc Exhib, 49 & 62; Bristol Art Mus, 65; Int Exhib by Uno A Erre, Arezzo, Italy, 69; Int Exhib, Arezzo, 70. Awards: Steel Engraving, RI Sch Design, New Eng Jewelers & Silversmiths Asn, 34; Lunar 1969 Landing Award, Uno A Erre, Arezzo, Italy, 70. Bibliog: Wayne Worchester (auth), Designs Ship's Insignia, Providence J Co, 66; K Nelson (auth), Ship's Insignia, an Art, The Newport Navalog, 67; Rose Derosiers (auth), Heraldic Art, Bull RI Sch Design, 12/73. Mem: Soc Medalists, Danbury, Conn; Orders & Medals Soc Am; Bristol Art Mus, RI; RI Hist Soc, Providence; US Naval Inst, Anapolis; Int Soc Artists, Marion, Ohio. Media: Wax, Modeling Clay, Plaster, Bronze, Die Steel. Dealer: Block Artists' Material Co 129 Dyer St Providence RI 02901. Mailing Add: 1227 Hope St Bristol RI 02809

GOHEEN ELLEN ROZANNE
CURATOR, ART HISTORIAN
b New York, NY, Mar 30, 44. Study: Univ Kans, Lawrence, BA & MA. Collections Arranged: Masters of 20th Century Photography, 73, American Impressionism, 74, Friends of Art Retrospective, 76, Joseph Cornell, 77 & Jasper Johns in Kansas City 1967-1977, 78, Nelson Gallery-Atkins Mus, Kansas City, Mo. Pos: From asst cur to assoc cur Europ painting & sculpture, Nelson Gallery-Atkins Mus, 70-75, 20th century art, 75- Awards: Sir George Trevelyan Scholar, Attingham Park Summer Sch, Shropshire, Eng, 73. Mem: Archaeol Inst Am (pres, Kans Chap, 74-77); Nat Trust for Hist Preserv; Victorian Soc in Am. Res: Twentieth century American and European art, European and American architecture. Publ: Auth, From romanticism to pop, Apollo, 12/72; contribr, European Painting & Sculpture, American 20th Century, Handbook, Nelson Gallery, 73. Mailing Add: 3681 Madison Kansas City MO 64111

GOINGS, RALPH
PAINTER
b Corning, Calif, May 9, 28. Study: Calif Col of Arts & Crafts, Oakland, BFA, 53; Calif State Univ, Sacramento, MA, 66. Work: Mus Mod Art, New York; Mus Contemp Art, Chicago; Neue Galerie, Essen, Ger; Kunstverein in Hamburg, Ger; Inst of Contemp Art, Univ Pa. Exhib: Directions 2: Aspects of a New Realism, Milwaukee Art Ctr, Wis, 69; The Hwy (traveling exhib), Univ Pa, Philadelphia, 70; Directly Seen: New Realism in Calif, Newport Harbor Mus, Newport Beach, Calif, 70; New Realsim, Mus, State Univ NY Col, Potsdam, 71; Directions 3: Eight Artists, Milwaukee Art Ctr, 71; Documenta 5, Kassel, Ger, 72; The Realist Revival, New York Cult Ctr, 72; USA West Coast, Kunstverein in Hamburg, 72; Amerikanischer Fotorealismus, Wurttembergischer Kunstverein, Stuttgart, Ger, 72; Hyperrealists Americans, Galerie Arditti, Paris, 73; Amerikanske Realister, Randers Kunstmuseum, Sweden, 73; Options 73/30, Contemp Arts Ctr, Cincinnati, Ohio, 73; Tokyo Biennale, Japan, 74; Selections in Contemp Realism, Akron Art Inst, Ohio, 74. Teaching: Instr, Del Norte High Sch, Crescent City, Calif, 55-59, Calif State Univ, Sacramento, 71 & Univ Calif, Davis, 72. Pos: Chmn art dept, La Sierra High Sch, Carmichael, Calif, 59-70. Bibliog: Udo Kulterman (auth), New Realism, Tubingen, 72; Yusuke Nakahara (auth), Man Made Nature, Vol 5, Tokyo, 72; Linda Chase (auth), The connotation of denotation, Arts Mag, 2/74. Style & Technique: Realism concerned with subject matter. Media: Oil, Watercolor. Mailing Add: c/o O K Harris Works of Art 383 W Broadway New York NY 10012

GOLBIN, ANDRÉE
PAINTER, ILLUSTRATOR
b Leipzig, Ger, June 4, 23; US citizen. Study: Art Students League; Parsons Sch Design; Hans Hofmann Sch Art. Work: Indust Bank Japan; Wako Securities Co, Tokyo, Japan; Eastman Kodak; New York Port Authority, Klopman Mills. Exhib: Los Angeles Co Mus Ann, 49-50; Recent Am Paintings, Riverside Mus, 60; Gimpel & Weitzenhoffer Gallery, 73; Women Choose Women, New York Cult Ctr, 73; Works on Paper, Brooklyn Mus, 75; Noah Goldowsky Gallery, 76; solo exhibs, Camino Gallery, 56 & 58, Grand Cent Moderns Gallery, 64 & 65 & Contemp Arts Gallery, NY Univ, 71. Teaching: Instr design, Newark Sch Fine & Indust Art, 71. Pos: Prom art dir, Mademoiselle Mag, 50-52. Awards: Grumbacher Prize, Nat Asn Women Artists, 49-50. Bibliog: Reviews in Art News, Arts Dig, New York Times, Art Forum, 3/73, Nation, 6/25/73. Mem: Artists Equity; Women in the Arts. Style & Technique: Paintings are abstract, combining loose and hard-edge technique; illustrations are realistic, specializing in nature, botanicals and some animals. Media: Acrylic, Oil, Watercolor; Pen & Ink. Publ: Illusr, New York Sunday Times gardening section, 74-75 & children's books publ by Lothrop, Lee & Shepard Co, 74, Rand McNally, Grossett & Dunlap. Mailing Add: 32 E 22nd St New York NY 10010

GOLD, ALBERT
PAINTER, EDUCATOR
b Philadelphia, Pa, Oct 31, 16. Study: Philadelphia Mus Sch Art, 35-39, dipl. Work: Pechter Collection, Bala Cynwyd, Pa; Squibb Collection; Ford Motor Co; Standard Oil, NJ; Atwater Kent Mus; plus others. Comn: Twelve paintings of Pa, Gimbel Brothers, 47-48; murals, Bur Agr; plus many others. Exhib: Nat Acad Design, New York, 40-68; Pa Acad Fine Arts Ann, 40-68; Venice Biennial, 41; Artists for Victory, Metrop Mus Art, New York, 42; Mus Galliera, Paris, 44. Teaching: Prof illus & materials of artist, Philadelphia Col Art, 46-, dir illus dept, 59- Awards: Tiffany Found Grant, 47-48; Sesnan Gold Medal for Landscape, Pa Acad Fine Arts, 50; Smith Grant, Woodmere, Chestnut Hill, Pa, 73; plus others. Bibliog: Henry C Pitz (auth), Albert Gold, painter, - draftsman, Am Artists, 11/56. Mem: Philadelphia Watercolor Club; Philadelphia Art Alliance (past chmn, 46-72, chmn watercolor, 49-65); Artists Equity; Am Watercolor Soc. Style & Technique: Representational, people and urban aspects in art. Media: Oil, Watercolor. Res: History of American illustration. Publ: Illusr, Our Philadelphia, 50; illusr, The Commodore, 54; illusr, This Was Our War, 63; illusr, The Captive Rabbi, 65. Dealer: 252 Gallery 252 S 16th St Philadelphia PA 19103. Mailing Add: 6814 McCallum St Philadelphia PA 19119

GOLD, BETTY
ART DEALER
b San Francisco, Calif, July 17, 32. Study: Univ Calif, Berkeley & Los Angeles. Pos: Cur, Ford Found Fel, Tamarind Lithog Workshop, Los Angeles, 65; exhib comt, Newport Harbor Art Mus, Newport Beach, Calif, 65-70; owner, Betty Gold Gallery, Los Angeles, 70-77; dir, ARCO Ctr for Visual Arts. Specialty: Contemporary prints and drawings; 19th and 20th century photographs. Mailing Add: 505 S Flower Los Angeles CA 90071

GOLD, DEBRA LYNN
METALSMITH, INSTRUCTOR
b Chicago, Ill, May 14, 51. Study: Ind Univ, MFA, 75. Work: Ind Univ Fine Arts Mus. Exhib: Goldsmiths 74, Renwick Gallery, Smithsonian Inst, Washington, DC, 74; Forms in Metal, Mus of Contemp Crafts, New York, 75; The Metalsmith, Phoenix Art Mus, Ariz, 77; Copper, Brass & Bronze, Univ Ariz, Tucson, 77; 3rd Profile of US Jewelry, Tex Tech Univ, Lubbock, 77. Teaching: Instr metals, E Tenn State Univ, Johnson City, 75; instr jewelry, Penland Sch of Crafts, NC, summer 1977. Mem: Soc NAm Goldsmiths; Am Craft Coun; Col Art Asn. Style & Technique: Smithed and constructed forms and objects for body adornment. Media: Metal. Mailing Add: 1315 Seminole Dr Johnson City TN 37601

GOLD, LEAH
PAINTER, PRINTMAKER
b New York, NY. Study: With Ruth Reeves & Hans Hofmann. Work: Birmingham Mus Art, Ala; Slater Mem Mus, Norwich, Conn. Exhib: Stedelijk Mus of Amsterdam, 57; Jersey City Mus, 57-75; Am Fedn of Arts, 58-60; Soc of Am Graphic Artists, 62; NJ State Mus, 73-75; Montclair Mus, NJ, 73-75; Tirca Karlis Gallery, Provincetown, Mass, 75-; Fordham Univ at Lincoln Ctr, New York, 75; Nat Art Mus of Sports, New York, 75; Cork Gallery, Lincoln Ctr, New York, 76-; Butler Inst of Am Art, Youngstown, Ohio, 77. Awards: Mrs John T Pratt Prize for Woodcut, Nat Asn Women Artists, 57; Prize for Casein Painting, Painters & Sculptors Soc NJ 18th Ann, 59; Award for Stained Glass Sculpture, Brooklyn Soc Artists, 59. Bibliog: Archives of Am Art, Smithsonian Inst, Washington, DC. Mem: Artists Equity Asn New York (bd dirs, 65-); Am Soc Contemp Artists (bd dir & co-chmn exhib comt, 77-); Contemp Cir, New York (exhib comt, 74-); Metrop Painters & Sculptors, New York (publicity & exhib comt, 72-); Nat Painters & Sculptors Soc; League Present Day Artists (chmn mem comt, 70-). Style & Technique: Abstract casein paintings with sand. Media: Casein, Graphics, Stained Glass. Mailing Add: Apt 5-A 330 W 28th St New York NY 10001

GOLD, SHARON CECILE
PAINTER
b Bronx, NY, Feb 23, 49. Study: Hunter Col, City Univ of NY, 68-69; Columbia Univ, 60-70; Pratt Inst, 74-76, BFA. Exhib: One-person shows, Judson Gallery, New York, 71 & O K Harris, 77, plus others; two-person show, O K Harris, New York, 76; Drawings & Prints-New

York, Rush Rhees Gallery, Univ Rochester, 77; Five New York Artists, Youngstown State Univ, Ohio, 77; Bertha Urdang Gallery, New York, 77; Seven Fed Bldgs, New York, 77 & US Commerce Bldg, Washington, DC, 77-78, Orgn of Independent Artists. Pos: Assoc ed, Re-View Mag, New York, 77-; field evaluator, Dept of Cult Affairs, New York, 77- Awards: MacDowell Colony Fel, 72. Bibliog: Tiffany Bell (auth), rev in Arts Mag, 12/77; Judith Lapes Cardozo (auth), rev in Artforum, 12/77; Joseph Masheck (auth), Hard-Core Painting, Artforum, 4/78. Mem: Performance Workshop (assoc dir, 75-). Style & Technique: Hard-flat surfaced acrylic on canvas on wood paintings which have evolved from 20th century reductive investigations; paintings deal with underlying/overlying relationships of color and geometric form; use of color is maximal—creating a cumlative perception of non-describable color. Publ: Auth, The cognitive create object: intuition and the creative process, Re-View Mag, 77; contribr, reviews in Artforum, 77. Dealer: Ivan Karp c/o O K Harris 383 W Broadway New York NY 10012. Mailing Add: 10 Leonard St New York NY 10013

GOLDBERG, ARNOLD HERBERT
PAINTER
b Brooklyn, NY, May 16, 33. Study: Univ Wis, BS(appl arts), 55; Pratt Inst, BArch, 59; Univ Houston, painting, 70-72. Exhib: The 12th Midwest Biennial, Joselyn Mus, Omaha, Nebr, 72; 17th Ann Delta Art Exhib, Ark Art Ctr, 74; 16th Ann Eight State Exhib, Okla Art Ctr, 74; 52nd Exhib, Shreveport Art Guild, 74; Corpus Christi Art Found Ann Exhib, Art Mus STex, 75; Univ Tex at Arlington Nat Exhib, 75; Corpus Christi Art Found Ann Exhib, Art Mus STex, 77. Awards: Dimension VI, Art League of Houston, 71; 8th Jury Award Art Exhib, Jewish Community Ctr, Houston, 72; Corpus Christi Art Found, Art Mus STex, 75 & 77. Style & Technique: Hard edge geometric abstraction; investigation of color. Media: Acrylic. Mailing Add: 425 Whitewing Houston TX 77079

GOLDBERG, CHAIM
PAINTER, PRINTMAKER
b Kazimierz, Poland, Mar 20, 17. Study: Art High Sch-Krakow, with Zbigniew Pronashko; Acad Fine Arts, Warsaw, with Tadeusz Pruszkowski; Govt Poland fel study in Paris, 47. Work: Metrop Mus Art, New York; Nat Collection Fine Art, Washington, DC; Mus Mod Art, New York; Mus Petit Palais, Geneva, Switz; Mus Fine Art, Boston, Mass; plus others. Comn: Monument, Polanica Zdroj, Govt Poland, 54; mosaic fountain, Hotel Ramat Aviv, Tel Aviv, Israel, 56, embossed copper door, 57; engravings, Govt Israel, 59-64. Exhib: Mus Fine Art, Moscow, USSR, 43; Nat Mus Fine Art, Warsaw, 50-52; one-man shows, Mus Yad Labanim, Israel, 66, Lys Gallery, New York, 67 & St John's Univ (NY), 71; Am Cong, Washington, DC, 72; Smithsonian Inst, Washington, DC; plus others. Awards: Silver Medal, Artists Guild-Novosibirsk, 44. Bibliog: I Luden (auth), articles in Art Mag, Israel, 66; D Shirey (auth), rev in New York Times, 71; Paul Scott (auth), Chaim Goldberg an artist reborn, Southwest Art Mag, 7-8/75; plus others. Style & Technique: Defying, colorful forms in surrealistic impressionism. Media: Oil, Watercolor. Mailing Add: 11007 Crestmore Houston TX 77096

GOLDBERG, JOSEPH WALLACE
PAINTER
b Seattle, Wash, Apr 27, 47. Work: Art Gallery Greater Victoria, BC; Whatcom Mus Hist & Art, Bellingham, Wash; Municipal Gallery Mod Art, Dublin, Ireland; Wichita Art Mus; Brooklyn Mus Fine Art; Seattle Art Mus Collection; plus others. Exhib: Gov Invitational, State Capitol Mus, Olympia, Wash, 70; Northwest Ann, Seattle Art Mus, 70 & group shows, 72, 74 & 78; San Francisco Centennial Exhib, 71; Northwest Drawings, Henry Art Gallery, 72. Media: Oil on Paper and Linen. Mailing Add: c/o Francine Seders Gallery 6701 Greenwood N Seattle WA 98103

GOLDBERG, KENNETH PAUL
ART HISTORIAN, ART LIBRARIAN
b Rochester, NY, Jan 13, 49. Study: Syracuse Univ, 66-70, study with William Fleming, BA(cum laude), 70 & 72-73, study with Antje Lemke, MSLS, 73; State Univ NY Binghamton, 70-72, study with Kenneth Lindsay, MA, 72. Teaching: Lectr use of art libr resources, Cleveland Inst Art, 73- Pos: Asst librn, Cleveland Inst Art, 73-; Cleveland area pvt tour guide, 77- Mem: Cleveland Archit Historians; Art Libr Soc NAm, Ohio Chap. Res: American art and architecture; special interest in architecture; paintings of Grant Wood; specialist on new copyright laws. Interest: Book reviews for local news media; special interests in galleries, antiques and decorative arts, culture and geography, urban planning and renewal, architectural restoration, communities, designing and motion pictures. Collection: American art of the 19th and 20th century. Mailing Add: 3592 Blanche Ave Cleveland Heights OH 44118

GOLDBERG, MICHAEL
PAINTER
b New York, NY, Dec 24, 24. Study: Art Students League, 38-42; City Col New York, 40-42; Hans Hofmann Sch Art, 41-42 & 48-50; Art Students League, 46, with Jose de Creeft; City Col New York, 46-47. Work: Mus Mod Art, Israel; Art Inst Chicago; Dayton Art Inst, Ohio; Nat Gallery Art, Washington, DC; Mus Western Art, Tokyo, Japan; plus many others. Exhib: Am Fedn Arts, 65; Am Art Gallery, Copenhagen, Denmark, 65; Smithsonian Inst, 66; Mus Mod Art, New York, 68; Corcoran Bienale, 69; plus many other group & one-man shows. Teaching: Instr art, Univ Calif, Berkeley, 61-62; Yale Univ, 67; Univ Minn, 68. Dealer: Paley & Lowe Inc 59 Wooster St New York NY 10012. Mailing Add: 222 Bowery New York NY 10012

GOLDBERG, NORMAN LEWIS
WRITER, LECTURER
b Nashville, Tenn, Feb 10, 06. Study: Univ Toledo, BS; Vanderbilt Univ, MD. Collections Arranged: Landscapes of the Norwich School (with catalog), Cummer Gallery Art, Jacksonville, Fla, 67; Tenn Fine Arts Ctr, Nashville, Tenn, 67; Isaac Delgado Mus of Art, New Orleans, La, 67. Teaching: Lectr, Victoria & Albert Mus, London, Eng, Castle Mus, Norwich, Eng, Fine Arts Ctr, Nashville, Tenn, Vanderbilt Univ, Isaac Delgado Mus Art, Cummer Gallery Art & Metrop Mus Art, 61-69. Mem: Col Art Asn Am. Res: Norwich School of Painting, specializing in John Crome, the Elder and John Sell Cotman. Publ: Auth, On John Crome & connoisseurship: the present day problem, 63 & auth, America honors the Norwich School, 67, Connoisseur; auth, Crome and some Cromesque mimicries, Times Literary Suppl, 69; auth, The Romantic Engraver of England's Past, Artnews, 76; auth, John Crome the Elder, NY Univ, 78; plus others. Mailing Add: 721 Brightwaters Blvd NE St Petersburg FL 33704

GOLDBERGER, MR & MRS EDWARD
COLLECTORS, PATRONS
Collection: Modern sculpture; abstract and modern art. Mailing Add: 1367 Flagler Dr Mamaroneck NY 10543

GOLDEEN, DOROTHY A
ART DEALER
b San Francisco, Calif, Nov 12, 48. Study: Univ Calif, Berkeley, BA. Teaching: Instr, Contemp Art Gallery, Col Marin, 75. Pos: Assoc, Dancer-Fitzgerald-Sample, San Francisco, 72-73; dir, Hansen Fuller Gallery, 72- Mem: San Francisco Art Dealers Asn (prog dir assoc). Specialty: Contemporary West Coast painting and sculpture. Mailing Add: 228 Grant Ave San Francisco CA 94108

GOLDEN, EUNICE
PAINTER, FILM MAKER
b New York, NY. Study: Univ Wis; Brooklyn Col; New Sch Social Res; Art Students League; Empire State Col, BFA, 77. Comn: Portrait of Poet Leon Herald, comn by Leon Herald, 71. Exhib: One-woman show, Hudson River Mus, 69; Palacio de las Bellas Artes, Mexico City, 72; Women in Art, Stamford Mus, Conn, 72; 148th Nat Acad Design Ann, New York, 73; Painting & Sculpture Today, Indianapolis Mus & Taft Mus, Cincinnati, 74; Works on Paper, Brooklyn Mus, NY, 75; Nothing But Nudes, Downtown Whitney, 77; plus others. Teaching: Lectr erotic art, New Sch Social Res, 73; instr mural painting, Guggenheim Mus Prog, New York, summer 75. Pos: Dir, Walk-On Community Art Proj, Dobbs Ferry, NY, 68; MacDowell Colony fel, Peterborough, NH, 69-; mem bd dirs, Soho 20 Gallery, New York, 73-; artist in residence, Univ SDak, spring 76. Awards: Hudson River Mus Purchase Award, 63; One of Outstanding Women, NY State Women's Univ, Albany, 68; MacDowell Colony Fel, 69 & 71. Bibliog: Hilton Kramer (auth), rev in NY Sunday Times, 6/5/71; Dorothy Seiberling (auth), Female view of erotica, New York Mag, 2/74; Lucy Lippard (auth), From the Center, Feminist Essays on Women's Art, Dutton, 76; plus others. Mem: Artists Equity; fel MacDowell Colony; Col Art Asn Am; Women in the Arts. Style & Technique: Figurative; body landscapes; geology and anatomy are made metaphors for one another by using large bold forms and color, free free, energetic line. Media: Oil, Acrylic; Photography, Cinematography. Publ: Illusr, Ararat, spring 74; illusr, MS Mag, 75; illus, A New Eros, 75; auth, article in Art Workers News, New York, 76; co-auth, article in An Anti-Catalog, The Catalog Comt, New York, 77; plus others. Mailing Add: 463 West St Apt 332 New York NY 10014

GOLDEN, LIBBY
PRINTMAKER, PAINTER
b New York, NY, Nov 18, 13. Study: Cooper Union Art Sch, dipl, 34; Hunter Col, NY Univ & Art Students League, 34-42; Pratt Graphic Arts Inst, 58-60. Work: Philadelphia Mus Art, Pa; Detroit Inst Arts, Mich; Grand Rapids Mus Art, Mich; Colby Col Mus Art, Mass; US State Dept. Exhib: Silvermine Guild, Conn, 66-68; Boston Printmakers, Boston Mus Fine Arts, Mass, 66-69; Northwest Printmakers, Seattle Mus Art & Portland Mus Art, 68 & 69; Audubon Artists, New York, 70 & 71; Colorprint, USA, Lubbock, Tex, 71; plus five one-man shows. Awards: Print Prizes, Mich State Fair, 65-69 & Nat Acad Design, New York, 69; Purchase Prize, Mich Painters & Printmakers. Dealer: Arwin Galleries 222 W Grand River Detroit MI 48226. Mailing Add: 6567 Kingsbridge Dr Sylvania OH 43560

GOLDEN, ROLLAND HARVE
PAINTER
b New Orleans, La, Nov 8, 31. Study: John McCrady Art Sch, study with John McCrady. Work: Wichita Falls Mus, Tex; Springfield Mus Art, Mo; New Orleans Art Asn; Baton Rouge Art Asn, La; Int House, New Orleans. Comn: 50 watercolors, La State Hwy Dept, Baton Rouge, 59-60; four watercolors, comn by Gov John McKeithen, La, 65. Exhib: Six Am Watercolor Soc Exhibs, New York, 65-75; Watercolor USA, Springfield, 66-75; Butler Inst Am Art, Youngstown, Ohio, 67-74; Nat Arts Club, New York, 68, 72 & 74; Nat Soc Painters in Casein & Acrylics, New York, 72-75; one-man shows, Moscow, Leningrad & Kiev, USSR, 76-77. Awards: Thomas Hart Benton Purchase Award, Watercolor USA, 66 & 69; Grumbacher Cash & Purchase Awards, Nat Watercolor Soc, 66 & 73; Barney Paisner Cash Award, Nat Soc Painters in Casein & Acrylics, 74. Bibliog: Don Lee Keith (auth), Golden Boy of watercolor, Delta Rev Mag, 68 & World of Rolland Golden, Royal Publ Co, 70; Jim Keyser (auth), Rolland Golden's Southland, WDSU TV, 73. Mem: Am Watercolor Soc; Nat Watercolor Soc (regional rep); Nat Soc Painters in Casein & Acrylics (regional rep); Nat Acad Artists Asn. Style & Technique: Precise and controlled abstract realism. Media: Watercolor, Acrylic. Publ: Auth, Watercolor Page, Am Artist Mag, 71; contribr, Transparent Watercolor-Ideas and Techniques, 73. Mailing Add: 6039 Laurel St New Orleans LA 70118

GOLDFARB, ROZ
ART ADMINISTRATOR, SCULPTOR
b New York, NY, Feb 16, 36. Study: Hunter Col, BA; Pratt Inst, BFA. Teaching: Instr fashion design & textiles, Pratt Inst Sch Art & Design, 72-74; instr hist, drawing & textiles, Pratt-NY Phoenix Sch Design, 74- Pos: Asst dir design div, Pratt Inst Sch Art & Design, 72-74, asst to dean, 74; assoc dir, Pratt-NY Phoenix Sch Design, 74-77, dir, Pratt-Phoenix Sch Design, 77- Style & Technique: Expressionistic, figurative, disections of anatomical sections. Media: Wax, Epoxy & Acrylic Sheet, Welded Steel. Dealer: Townhouse Gallery Ltd 316 E 69th St New York NY 10016. Mailing Add: 160 Lexington Ave New York NY 10016

GOLDHAMER, CHARLES
PAINTER
b Philadelphia, Pa, Aug 21, 03. Study: Ont Col Art. Work: Art Gallery Toronto; Hart House, Univ Toronto; War Records, Nat Gallery Art. Exhib: Coronation, 37; Tate Gallery Art, London, 38; Gloucester, 39; Can Soc Painters in Watercolour, 39; War Art, Nat Gallery Can, 46; plus others. Teaching: Dir art, Cent Tech Sch, Toronto, 23-69. Pos: Official war artist, RCAF, 43-46. Awards: Adamson Prize for Life Drawing, Ont Col Art. Mem: Ont Soc Artists; Can Soc Graphic Art; Can Soc Painters in Watercolour (past pres); Arts & Lett Club Toronto. Mailing Add: 1 Brule Gardens Toronto ON M6S 4J1 Can

GOLDIN, LEON
PAINTER, EDUCATOR
b Chicago, Ill, Jan 16, 23. Study: Art Inst Chicago, BFA, 48; Univ Iowa, MFA, 50. Work: Brooklyn Mus, NY; Va Mus Fine Arts, Richmond; City Mus St Louis, Mo; Pa Acad Fine Arts, Philadelphia; Munson-Williams-Proctor Inst, Utica, NY. Exhib: American Painting at Mid-Century, Metrop Mus Art, New York, 51; American Drawings, Mus Mod Art, New York, 56; Corcoran Gallery Art Biennial, Washington, DC, 62; Carnegie Inst Int, Pittsburgh, Pa, 64; Pa Acad Fine Arts Ann, 66. Teaching: Instr painting & drawing, Calif Col Arts & Crafts, 50-55; instr painting & drawing, Cooper Union, 61-64; assoc prof painting & drawing, Columbia Univ, 64- Awards: Prix de Rome, Am Acad Rome, 55; Guggenheim Fel, 59; Award in Painting, Nat Inst Arts & Lett, 68. Media: Oil, gouache. Mailing Add: 438 W 116th St New York NY 10027

GOLDMAN, LESTER
PAINTER
b Philadelphia, Pa, Aug 15, 42. Study: Philadelphia Col of Art, BFA; Skowhegan Sch; Aspen Sch; Ind Univ, MFA, with Leland Bell, William Bailey & Larry Day. Work: Nelson-Atkins Mus, Kansas City, Mo; Albrecht Mem Mus, St Joseph, Mo; Univ Maine; Ind Univ, Bloomington; Kemper Ins Co, Ill. Exhib: Mid-Am Ann, St Louis, Mo; Am Realist Painters, Galleria Il Fante di Spade, Rome, Italy, 71; From Life, Univ RI, Providence, 71; Sense of Place, Sheldon Mem Art Gallery, Lincoln, Nebr, 73; New Talent, Forum Gallery, New York, 73; one-man show, Walter Kelly Gallery, Chicago, 75; Invitational, Nelson-Atkins, Kansas City, Mo, 76 & 77; Six Painters, Springfield Art Mus, Mo, 77. Teaching: Assoc prof painting & drawing, Kansas City Art Inst, Mo, 66- Awards: Aid to Individual Artists, Six Painters, Mo Arts Coun, 77. Bibliog: James McGarrell (auth), American Realist Painters, Galleria Il Fante di Spade, Rome, 71; John Fernie (auth, film), 73; P Kase (auth, film), Genre Paintings of Lester Goldman, Johnson Co Community Col Educ Ctr, 76. Mem: Col Art Asn. Style & Technique: Figurative paintings. Media: Oil on canvas. Mailing Add: 37 W 57th St Kansas City MO 64113

GOLDMAN, LOUIS & SONDRA
ART DEALERS
b New York, NY, Mr Goldman, Nov 16, 28. Study: Mr Goldman, Univ Mich, BA, Columbia Univ, MA, with Irwin Edman & Meyer Shapiro; Mrs Goldman, Columbia Univ. Collections Arranged: Mr Goldman, Am Impressionism, 77 & The New Realists, 78, Gallery G Fine Arts Ltd; Mrs Goldman, Three Faces of Mex, Whitford Carter, Melesio Galvan & Alfredo Zalce, 69-70 & Craig McPherson, 76, Gallery G Fine Arts Ltd. Pos: Mr Goldman, pres, Gallery G Fine Arts, Ltd, 65- & Galaxy Graphics, 77; Mrs Goldman, asst dir, Davis Galleries, New York, 59-61, dir, Gallery G Fine Arts, Ltd, 65-, panelist, Washington Art Fair, 77 & contribr monthly, Decor, 78. Mem: Am Fedn of Arts. Specialty: Graphics, American painting of the 19th and 20th centuries. Publ: Mr Goldman, auth, Art as an Investment, Propeller, 70. Mailing Add: Gallery G Fine Arts Ltd 6611 E Central Wichita KS 67206

GOLDOWSKY, NOAH
ART DEALER
b Minsk, Russia, Jan 16, 09; US citizen. Pos: Dir, Noah Goldowsky Gallery. Specialty: 20th century American art. Mailing Add: 1078 Madison Ave New York NY 10028

GOLDRING, NANCY DEBORAH
GRAPHIC ARTIST, EDUCATOR
b Oak Ridge, Tenn, Jan 25, 45. Study: Smith Col, BA(art hist), with Mervin Jules; Univ Florence, two yrs with Nina Gregor; NY Univ, MFA(graphics). Exhib: One-person exhib, Politecnico, Rome, Italy, 78; group exhib, orgn at Stoney Brook, Long Island by Lawrence Alloway, 78; exhib, Inst for Archit & Urban Studies, New York, NY & Nassau Co Mus, NY, 78. Collections Arranged: Photographs, Mus of Natural Hist, Nat Park Serv, 73; Celebrations II (photographs), Mass Inst of Technol, Cambridge, 76; one-person shows, Haverford Col, Pa, 76 & Knowlton Gallery, New York, 77. Teaching: Prof drawing, Montclair State Col, NJ, 71-; vis prof contemp art, RI Sch of Design, Providence, 74-75; vis prof, Haverford Col, Pa, 78. Pos: Co-founding dir, SITE, New York, 69-72 & Chamber, New York, 76- Awards: Grant, NY State Coun on the Arts, 77. Bibliog: Jeff Nuttall (auth), SITE, Archit Design, 72; Bruno Zevi (auth), SITE, Architettura, 73; Hayden Herrerra (auth), rev in Art in Am, 77. Style & Technique: Development of photograph and graphic technique for representational purposes. Media: Drawings which eventually become photo-drawings (pen, ink, gesso, pencil). Publ: Co-auth, Peekskill Melt, Art Gallery Mag, 72; auth, Shopping Center Art, On Site, 73; auth, A Monument for the Living, Art & Artists, 73; auth, Grant National Memorial: A Monument to the Living, Art News, 74; auth, Celebrations II, The Speaking Monument, Mass Inst of Technol, 76. Dealer: Monique Knowlton 19 E 71st St New York NY 10021. Mailing Add: 463 West St H659 New York NY 10014

GOLDSCHMIDT, LUCIEN
ART DEALER
b Brussels, Belg, Mar 3, 12. Pos: Dir, Lucien Goldschmidt, Inc; vpres, Art Dealers Asn Am, Inc. Specialty: Continental European art, circa 1500-1950, mainly prints and drawings. Publ: Co-auth, Unpublished Correspondence of Henri de Toulouse-Lautrec, 69. Mailing Add: 1117 Madison Ave New York NY 10028

GOLDSMITH, BARBARA
WRITER, ART CRITIC
b New York, NY, May 18, 31. Study: Wellesley Col, BA, 53; Columbia Univ, MA, 55. Pos: Ed, Town & Country Mag & New York Mag, 66-71; sr ed, Harper's Bazaar, 70-74. Awards: New York Times Reporting Award, 68; Penny-Mo Award, 70. Mem: Whitney Mus Am Art; Mus Mod Art (jr coun, 51-73); Mus City New York (pres coun, 70-); Parks Coun City New York. Publ: Auth, articles in New York Mag, Esquire, Harpers Bazaar, McCalls & New York Times; auth, The Straw Man, 75; plus others. Mailing Add: c/o Lynn Nesbit ICM 40 W 57th St New York NY 10019

GOLDSMITH, BENEDICT ISAAC
GALLERY DIRECTOR, EDUCATOR
b New York, NY, Aug 1, 16. Study: NY Univ, BS, 40; Art Students League & Woodstock, NY, with Arnold Blanch; Teachers Col, Columbia Univ, MA, 50; Inst Del'Arte, Florence, Italy, 64. Collections Arranged: (With catalog) Potsdam Prints, 63-74; Robert Mallary, 68; Sculpture, NY Six, 69; New Realism, 71; Women in Art, 72, New Realism, Revisited, 74; Potsdam Plastics, 75; African Sculpture Selections, Anspach Collection, 75. Teaching: Prof art, State Univ NY Col Potsdam, 50- Pos: Gallery dir, State Univ NY Col Potsdam, 65- Mem: Gallery Asn NY (exec comt, 75); Asn Exhib & Gallery Dirs (pres, 68-69). Mailing Add: 4 Castle Dr Potsdam NY 13676

GOLDSMITH, C GERALD
COLLECTOR, PATRON
b Orlando, Fla, Aug 2, 28. Study: Univ Mich; Harvard Univ Bus Sch. Mem: Friends of Whitney Mus Am Art; Am Fedn Arts. Collection: Contemporary American art. Mailing Add: 540 Madison Ave New York NY 10022

GOLDSMITH, ELSA M
PAINTER
b New York, NY, Jan 26, 20. Study: Parsons Sch Fine & Appl Art, scholar award, prof cert; NY Univ; Pratt Inst (lithography); etching with Ruth Leaf; painting with Betty Holiday. Exhib: One-man show, Art Image Gallery, New York, 69; Salon Int de la Femme, Cannes, France, 69; Am Drawing Biennial, Norfolk Mus, Va, 71; Palazzo Vechio, Florence, Italy, 72; Brooklyn Mus, NY, 75. Teaching: Teacher, Elsa Goldsmith's Studio, 50-74 & North Shore Commun Ctr, 71-73, Great Neck, NY; teacher painting, Adult Educ, Sewanhake High Sch, Floral Manor, NY, 72-74. Pos: Advert artist, Newsweek Mag, New York, 40-41; indust designer, Belle Kogan Assoc, New York, 41-48; freelance artist, Book & Magazine Illustrating, New York, 42- Awards: Int Gold Medal of Honor, City of Cannes, France, 69; First Prize-Award Exhib, Guild Hall Mus, East Hampton, NY, 69; Susan Kahn Award, Nat Asn Women Artists, New York, 74. Mem: Nat Asn Women Artists (foreign chmn, 72-74; mem chmn, 75-; int rep, 76-); Int Art Asn (US deleg int cong, 74-76); Women in the Arts, Inc (bd mem & bicentennial chmn, 74-76); North Shore Community Art Ctr (bd dir & art coordr, 73-); Int Womens Year Arts Festival (bd mem, 75-76). Style & Technique: Humanistic approach; strong use of line drawing; low key color. Media: Painting, Etching. Mailing Add: 52 Ruxton Rd Great Neck NY 11023

GOLDSTEIN, DANIEL JOSHUA
PRINTMAKER, SCULPTOR
b Mt Vernon, NY, June 19, 50. Study: Brandeis Univ; Univ Calif, Santa Cruz, BA; St Martin's Col, London, Eng, post-grad study. Work: Brooklyn Mus, NY; Plains Art Mus, Morehead, Minn; Achenbach Found, San Francisco, Calif; Oakland Mus of Art, Calif; De Cordova Mus, Lincoln, Mass. Exhib: Prints Calif, Oakland Mus of Art, 75; 20th Nat Print Exhib, Brooklyn Mus, NY, 76; one-man shows, Gettler-Pall Gallery, New York, 77 & ADI Gallery, San Francisco, 77; New Talent in Printmaking, AAA Gallery, New York, 77; Calif Palace of the Legion of Honor, San Francisco; US Info Serv Travelling Exhib, Japan; 12th Nat Print Exhib, Silvermine Guild of Artists, New Canaan, Conn, 78. Awards: Purchase Prize, Palo Alto Cult Ctr, 73. Style & Technique: Multi-color woodblock prints; indoor and outdoor kinetic sculpture using cloth and metal, motivated by wind. Dealer: ADI Gallery 530 McAllister St San Francisco CA 94102. Mailing Add: 1089 Valencia St San Francisco CA 94110

GOLDSTEIN, GLADYS HACK
PAINTER
b Newark, Ohio. Study: Md Inst Art; Art Students League; Columbia Univ, New York; Pa State Univ, University Park; study with Hobson Pittman. Work: Baltimore Mus Art, Md; Pa State Univ; Univ Ariz; Goucher Col, Baltimore. Exhib: One-man shows, Baltimore Mus Art, Goucher Col, Duveen-Graham Gallery, New York, Galerie Philadelphie, Paris, IFA Gallery, Washington, DC, Western Md Col, Newark Gallery, Del, Studio North, Towson, Md, Richter Gallery, Weisbaden, Ger, 65-75. Teaching: Instr painting, Md Inst Col Art, 60-65; instr art, Col Notre Dame, Md, 65- Pos: Co-chmn art festival, City Baltimore, 71-74; art comt, Mayor's Ball, 73-74; exec comt, Mayor's Adv Comt for Arts & Cult, 74- Awards: Third Award, Md Art Today, H K & Co, 72; First Award, 25th Ann of Israel, JCC, 74; Awards, Baltimore Mus Art & Pa State Univ. Media: Acrylic, Oil, Watercolor. Dealer: IFA Gallery 2623 Connecticut Ave NW Washington DC 20008. Mailing Add: 2002 South Rd Baltimore MD 21209

GOLDSTEIN, HOWARD
PAINTER, EDUCATOR
b New York, NY, Feb 10, 33. Study: Albright Art Sch, cert; State Univ NY, Col Buffalo, BS; NY Univ, MA; Columbia Univ, EdD. Work: NJ State Mus, Trenton; Morris Mus Arts & Sci, Morristown, NJ; YMCA, New York; Univ Frankfurt, WGer; Imperial Chem Industs, US, Wilmington, Del. Exhib: Western NY Exhib, Albright-Knox Gallery, Buffalo, 53 & 54; Art USA 58, Madison Sq Garden, New York, 58; 154th Ann Nat Exhib, Pa Acad Fine Arts, Philadelphia, 59 & 65; Ann NJ State Exhib, Newark Mus, 61, 64, 66, 68 & 77; Art from NJ, NJ State Mus, Trenton, 66-73; 32nd Ann Nat Painting Exhib, Butler Inst Am Art, Youngstown, Ohio, 67; Nat Show, Chautauqua Exhib Am Art, NY, 68 & 69; Ann New Eng Exhib, Silvermine Guild Artists, New Canaan, Conn, 70, 72 & 73. Collections Arranged: Geometric Art: An Exhib of Paintings & Constructions by 14 Contemp NJ Artists, NJ State Mus, 67; Westbroadway Gallery Group, Rundetarn Mus, Copenhagen, Denmark, 73; one-man exhib, NJ State Mus, 74; Viewpoint 76, Morris Mus Arts & Sci, Morristown, NJ, 76. Teaching: Prof painting, Trenton State Col, NJ, 60- Pos: Exec dir, Comn Study Arts NJ, 64-67; chmn, Mercer Co Cult & Heritage Comn, Trenton, NJ, 70- Awards: Emily Lowe Award, Emily Lowe Found Competition, 60; Videorecord Corp Am Award, 23rd New Eng Exhib, 72; Purchase Award, Art from NJ, State of NJ, 73. Style & Technique: Geometric abstractions using modules of color with horizontal and vertical bands interweaving throughout and creating illusionistic spaces of different depths; paint densities vary from wash-thin to thick relief. Media: Acrylic on canvas and on paper. Dealer: Westbroadway Gallery 431 W Broadway New York NY 10012. Mailing Add: 49 Rockleigh Dr Trenton NJ 08628

GOLDSTEIN, JACK
MIXED-MEDIA ARTIST
b Montreal, Que, Sept 27, 45. Study: Chouinard Art Sch, Los Angeles, BFA, 70; Calif Inst of the Arts, MFA, 72. Work: Mus of Mod Art, Geneva, Switz. Exhib: Twenty-four Young Los Angeles Artists, Los Angeles Co Mus of Art, Calif, 70; Artists Films Series, Kunstmuseum, Basle, Switz, 74; Soho-Downtown Manhattan, Acad of Fine Arts, Berlin, Ger, 76; 16 Pagen, Groninger Mus voor stad en Lawde, Holland, 77; one-man shows, Nigel Greenwood Gallery, London, Eng, 71, Francoise Lambert Gallery, Milan, Italy, 74, Kabinette für Aktuelle Kunst Bremerhan, Ger, 76, Centre d'Art Contemporain, Cite Univ, Geneva, 77 & The Kitchen Ctr for Video & Music, New York, NY, 78. Awards: Can Coun Arts grant, 73-74; production grant, NY State Coun on the Arts, 77. Bibliog: Douglas Crimp (auth), Pictures, Artists Space, New York, 77; Germano Celant (auth), The Record as Artwork, Rome, Italy, 77; Morgan Fisher (interviewer), Talking with Jack Goldstein, Los Angeles Inst of Contemp Art J, 77. Style & Technique: Produce phonograph records, 45's, LPs & 16mm films. Mailing Add: 183 Duane St New York NY 10013

GOLDSTEIN, JULIUS
PAINTER, INSTRUCTOR
b New York, NY, Mar 17, 18. Study: Brooklyn Mus Art Sch, with Rufino Tamayo & John Ferren, 46-47; Art Students League; travel & study in Europe, 48, 54, 66 & 67; England, 75. Exhib: Speed Art Mus Ann, Louisville, Ky, 57; Brooklyn Mus Int Watercolor Show, 61 & 63; Butler Inst Am Art Ann, Youngstown, Ohio, 66; Nat Inst Arts & Lett Contemp Painting & Sculpture, 70; Childe Hassam Fund Exhib, Am Acad Arts & Lett, 70. Teaching: Asst prof drawing & painting, Hunter Col, 61- Awards: Yaddo Found Fel, Saratoga Springs, NY, 64-66. Style & Technique: Abstract, realistic. Media: Oil, Watercolor. Dealer: Babcock Galleries 805 Madison Ave New York NY 10021. Mailing Add: 26 W Tenth St New York NY 10011

GOLDSTEIN, MILTON
PRINTMAKER, EDUCATOR
b Holyoke, Mass, Nov 14, 14. Study: Art Students League, 46-49; also with Harry Sternberg, Morris Kantor & Will Barnet. Work: Philadelphia Mus Art; Metrop Mus Art, New York; Mus Mod Art, New York; Smithsonian Nat Mus Washington, DC; Brooklyn Mus, NY. Comn: Collection of etchings for Europe & US (200 ed), Int Graphic Arts Soc, New York, 52; collection of etchings (150 ed), 54. Exhib: Libr Cong, Washington, DC, 48; Smithsonian Inst, Washington, DC, 55; Outstanding Prints Produced in America, Brooks Mem Mus, Memphis, Tenn, 59; Am Printmakers in Italy, sponsored by Boston Pub Libr, 60; Masters Engraving

Show, Queens Col (NY), 64; 30 Yrs of Am Printmaking, Brooklyn Mus, 77. Teaching: Prof printmaking, Adelphi Univ, 53- Awards: Guggenheim Fel, 50; First Prize & Purchase Award, Philadelphia Mus, 52; First Prize & Purchase Award, Nat Print Show, Western NMex Univ, 71. Bibliog: Carl Zigrosser (auth), Fine Prints, Crown, 60; Jules Heller (auth), Printmaking Today, Holt, 60. Mem: Soc Am Graphic Artists (coun, 72); fel Royal Soc Arts, London; Am Color Print Soc; Kappa Pi (sponsor, Adelphi Univ, 60); Print Club. Publ: Auth, How to Make an Etching (film), Almanac Films, 51; auth, A new color etching process, Everyday Art; auth, Reprint, Design Mag, 55. Mailing Add: 56-16 219th St Bayside NY 11364

GOLDSTEIN, NATHAN
ART WRITER, PAINTER
b Chicago, Ill, Mar 26, 27. Study: Art Inst of Chicago, BFA, MFA, with Louis Ritman; Art Students League, with Julian Levi. Pos: Chmn, Found Prog of Study, Art Inst of Boston, 73- Style & Technique: Figurative imagery, small-scale works mainly, often single figures in interiors. Media: Oil, Pen and Ink. Publ: Auth, The Art of Responsive Drawing, 73, Figure Drawing: The Structure, Anatomy and Expressive Design of Human Form, 76, The Art of Responsive Drawing, 2 ed, 77 & Painting: Perceptual and Technical Fundamentals, 79, Prentice-Hall. Mailing Add: 350 Quinobequin Rd Waban MA 02168

GOLDSTONE, MR & MRS HERBERT
COLLECTORS
Collection: Contemporary art. Mailing Add: 25 Sutton Pl S New York NY 10022

GOLDSZER, BATH-SHEBA
PAINTER, GRAPHIC ARTIST
b Warsaw, Poland; US citizen. Study: Art Students League, with Gustav Rehberger; also with Joe Hing Lowe & Ludmila Morosova. Exhib: Two-man show, Fellowship Gallery, 72; Am Artists Prof League Grand Nat Exhib, Lever House Gallery, 74-77; Hudson Valley Art Asn, Westchester Co Ctr, 73-77; Catherine Lorillard Wolfe Arts Club, Nat Arts Club Gallery, 73-77; Nat Art League, Union Carbide Gallery 73 & Douglaston Gallery, 74-77; plus others. Awards: Group Show Award, Fellowship Gallery, 72; First Prize in Oil, Nat Art League, 74 & Queensboro Soc Arts, 74-77; and numerous others. Bibliog: Jack Besterman (auth), Big Six Art League, Chapel & Pension News, 2/72, An accomplished artist, 2/73 & Coop art scene, 4/74, Towers Reporter. Mem: Am Artists Prof League; Hudson Valley Art Asn; Catherine Lorillard Wolfe Arts Club; Nat Art League; Big Six Art League (chmn & treas, 69-). Style & Technique: Still life and character studies executed in traditional realism. Media: Oil, Pastel, Pen & Ink, Charcoal. Mailing Add: 46-10 61st St Woodside NY 11377

GOLINKIN, JOSEPH WEBSTER
PAINTER, PRINTMAKER
b Chicago, Ill, Sept 10, 96. Study: Art Inst Chicago; Art Students League. Exhib: Carnegie Int; Art Inst Chicago; Nat Acad Design; Pa Acad; Corcoran Mus; plus many others. Awards: First Gold Medal, Int Exhib Art in Relation to Sport Olympiad, 32, Medal, 36. Mem: Fel Int Inst Arts & Lett. Publ: Contribr, NY Times, Vanity Fair, Fortune, Coronet, Country Life; plus other mag & anthologies. Mailing Add: 210 E 68th St New York NY 10021

GOLLIN, MR & MRS JOSHUA A
COLLECTORS, PATRONS
Mr Gollin, b New York NY, Aug 16, 05. Study: Mr Gollin, Wash Univ. Mem: Sustaining mem Metrop Mus Art, Mus Mod Art, Guggenheim Mus & Am Fedn Arts. Interest: Donated two prizes at 1964 Biennale in Venice for a painter and a sculptor under 40 years of age. Collection: Sculpture of the past fifty years and African primitive carvings. Mailing Add: 1025 Fifth Ave New York NY 10028

GOLUB, LEON ALBERT
PAINTER
b Chicago, Ill, Jan 23, 22. Study: Univ Chicago, BA(hist art), 42; Art Inst Chicago Sch, BFA, 49, MFA, 50. Work: Mus Mod Art, New York; Art Inst Chicago; Nat Collection Fine Arts, Smithsonian Inst, Washington, DC; Univ Calif, Berkeley; Nat Gallery Victoria, Melbourne. Exhib: Carnegie Inst Int, Pittsburgh, 54, 64 & 67; one-man shows, Pasadena Mus of Art, Calif, 56, Inst of Contemp Art, London, 57, Hayden Gallery, Mass Inst of Technol, 70, Nat Gallery of Victoria, Melbourne, Australia, 70-71, Mus of Contemp Art, Chicago, 74, New York Cult Ctr, 75, San Francisco Art Inst, 76 & State Univ NY Col, Stony Brook, 78; New Images of Man, Mus Mod Art, New York, 59; Sao Paulo Biennial, 62; 2nd Biennial Int Deporte Bellas Artes, Madrid, Spain, 69; Chicago Imagist Art, Mus Contemp Art, 72; Paris-New York, Centre Beaubourg, Paris, 77; plus many others. Teaching: Prof art, Livingston Col, Rutgers Univ, 70- Awards: Ford Found Grant, 60; Cassandra Found Grant, 67; Guggenheim Found Grant, 68. Bibliog: Franz Schulze (auth), Fantastic Images: Chicago Art since 1945, Follett, 72; Lawrence Alloway (auth), Leon Golub: art & politics, Artforum, 11/74; Donald Kuspit (auth), Golub's assasins: an anatomy of violence, Art in Am, 5-6/75; plus others. Style & Technique: Scenes of violence and stress. Media: Acrylic. Publ: Auth, Bombs & helicopters, the art of Nancy Spero, Caterpillar I, 67; auth, Utopia/antiutopia, 5/72, auth, 2D/3D, 3/73 & auth, 16 Whitney Museum Annuals of American Paintings, percentages 1950-52, 3/73, Artforum. Mailing Add: 530 La Guardia Pl New York NY 10012

GOLUBIC, THEODORE
SCULPTOR, DESIGNER
b Lorain, Ohio, Dec 9, 28. Study: Miami Univ, BFA; Art Students League, with Jon Corbino; Univ Notre Dame, MFA, asst to Ivan Mestrovic. Comn: Corpus (bronze), for main altar, Little Flower Church, South Bend, Ind, 58; Angels in Mourning (limestone), St Joseph the Worker Church, Gary, Ind, 60; Circe (bronze bas relief panel), comn by Mrs H Fredrick Willkie, Elwood, Ind, 62; Crypt Relief Series, Rock of Ages Corp, Barre, Vt, 65-67; St John the Baptist (bronze), St John's Church, Lorain, Ohio, 67; Nativity (limestone heroic relief), Church of Nativity, Dubuque, Iowa, 68. Exhib: Art USA, Madison Sq Garden, New York, 58; 134th Ann Exhib, Nat Acad Design, New York, 59; 2nd Biennial Am Painting & Sculpture, Detroit Inst Arts, 60; 155th Ann Exhib, Pa Acad Fine Arts, Philadelphia, 61; 13th Ann Drawing & Small Sculpture Show, Ball State Univ, Muncie, Ind, 63; 34th Ann Exhib, Nat Sculpture Soc, New York, 67; Art for 1970, Southern Calif Expo, Del Mar, 70; one-man show, Roswell Mus in conjunction with Sunspot Observatory, NMex, 72. Teaching: Guest instr sculpture, Univ Notre Dame, summer 59; guest instr, Art Sch Air of Educ TV & ABC-TV, Elkhart, Ind, 62-63; invited artist/lectr, 28th Ann Conf Workshop, Am Soc Aesthetics, 70. Pos: Sculpture consult, Rock of Ages Corp, 65-67; artist in residence, Roswell Mus & Art Ctr, NMex, 71-72; invitation to Int Sculpture Symposium, Yugoslavia, 73. Mem: Am Soc Aesthet; Col Art Asn Am; Croatian Acad Am. Style & Technique: Two dimensional, three dimensional and time-color-dimensional design; figurative to sun environmental, projective-geometric. Media: All Media. Publ: Guest ed, 3/67, contribr cover & auth, In art there is victory, 4/67, Am Art Stone. Mailing Add: 8626 N 37th Ave Phoenix AZ 85021

GOMEZ, SITA
PAINTER
Cuban, b Paris, France, Apr 5, 32; US citizen. Study: Parsons Sch Design, New York. Exhib: One-man shows, Van Bovenkamp Gallery, Windows of Bonwit Teller & J Walter Thompson, New York, 64, Albert White Gallery, Toronto, 65, Cisneros Gallery, New York, 65 & Studio Gallery, Alexandria, Va, 66; Am Fedn Arts (traveling), 65-67; Neikrug Gallery, New York, 68; Ctr for Inter-Am Rels, New York, 75; St Peter's Col, NJ, 75; Mus of Albuquerque, NMex, 77-78; El Paso Mus of Art, Tex, 78; Los Angeles Munic Art Gallery, Calif, 78; Everson Mus, Syracuse, NY, 78-79. Awards: Casper Rittenberg Award, Artist-Craftsmen New York, 66; First Prize in Oils, Koscuisko Found, New York, 66; Cintas Found Grant, 74-75 & 75-76. Media: Acrylic, Oil. Mailing Add: 427 E Ninth St New York NY 10009

GOMEZ-QUIROZ, JUAN MANUEL
PAINTER, PRINTMAKER
b Santiago, Chile, Feb 20, 39. Study: RI Sch Design, Fulbright fel, 62-63; Yale Univ, Fulbright fel, 63-64; invited by Gabor Peterdi; Pratt Graphic Art Ctr, Pan Am Union fel, 64-66. Work: Cincinnati Art Mus; Metrop Mus Art, New York; Libr Cong, Washington, DC; Boston Mus Fine Arts; Brooklyn Mus; Everson Mus of Art, Syracuse, NY; Museo de Bellas Artes, Santiago, Chile; Museo de Arte Contemporano, Santiago; Guggenheim Mus of Art, New York, NY; New York Pub Libr; DeMenil Found; plus many others. Exhib: 200 Yrs of Latin Am Art, Yale Univ Art Gallery, 66; Int Print Exhib, Montreal Mus Fine Art, 71; 2nd Biennal de San Juan; 3rd Ann Print Exhib, Atlanta, Ga, 73; Prints from NY Univ Arts Collection, Hudson River Mus, 74; Printmaking Workshop of New York, Museo d'Arte Italiano, Lima, Peru, 75; Looking Inside: Latin Am Presence in New York, Latin Am Mus of Arts Proj, 76; Without Canvas, New York, NY, 76; Prints & Techniques, Grey Art Gallery, NY Univ, New York, 76; Galleria Balcon les Images, Montreal, Que, 76; Drawings, Gloria Cortella Gallery, New York, 77; Ten Downtown, PS 1, New York, 77; Int Drawing Show, Bronx Mus, New York, 77; plus numerous others; one-man shows, Sals Decor, Santiago, Chile, 61, Ledesma Gallery, New York, 64, Kie Kor Gallery, New Haven, Conn, 64, Alonzo Gallery, New York, 68, 70 & 72, Ars Concentra Gallery, Lima, Peru, 75, Galleria Pecanins, Mexico City, Mex, 76, Galleria Balcon les Images, Montreal, Que, 76, Schubert Gallery, Marbella, Spain, 77, Kornblee Gallery, New York, 78 & others. Teaching: Lectr studio art, Univ Calif, Santa Barbara, 67-68; lectr studio art, New York Community Col, 69-70; adj prof studio art, NY Univ, 69-; lectr, Summit Art Ctr, Summit, NJ, 72-77. Pos: Dir, NY Univ photo-etching workshop, 72-73. Awards: Fulbright Fel, RI Sch Design, 62, Fel, Sch of Art & Archit, Yale Univ, 63 & Grant, 75-76; Pan-Am Union Fel, Pratt Graphic Art Ctr, 64; Guggenheim Found Fel Painting, 66; Nat Endowment Arts Grant, 74; plus others. Bibliog: Cleve Gray (auth), Experiment grows in Brooklyn, Arts in Am, 66; Mary Stewart (auth), reviews in Arts Mag, 6/68 & 3/69; Gabor Peterdi (auth), Printmaking, Macmillan, rev ed, 71; Gordon Brown (auth), article in Arts Mag, 4/71. Media: Oil, Acrylic, Intaglio. Mailing Add: 44 Grand St New York NY 10013

GOMEZ-SICRE, JOSE
ART ADMINISTRATOR, ART CRITIC
b Matanzas, Cuba, 1916. Study: Univ Havana, dipl law, 40 & 41; Columbia Univ, 44; NY Univ, 44. Comn: (Direction of films), Easter Island; Chancay, the Forgotten Culture; Vicus; Art of Central America and Panama; Nine Artists of Puerto Rico; plus others. Collections Arranged: Permanent Collection of Latin American Contemporary Art & Exhib Prog, Orgn Am States, 46-; assisted or directed assembling of collections for numerous mus & corp, incl Esso Standard Oil Collection, now property of Lowe Mus Art, Miami Univ. Teaching: Lectr art hist & Latin Am art, cols, univs & mus throughout US, Latin Am & Europe, 50- Pos: Art critic, El Mundo, Norte, Havana & New York, 42-50; organized exhibs Cuban art for mus abroad & assisted in direction foreign & nat exhibs, Havana, 42-45; dir, Mus of Mod Art of Latin Am, Washington, DC, 46- Res: Contemporary Latin American art. Publ: Auth, Four Artists of the Americas, 57; auth, Cuevas, Art Int, 11/71; auth, Leonardo Nierman, Mexico, 73; auth, The true El Dorado: Colombian gold, Connoisseur, 5/75; auth, Torres-Garcia y la America arcaica, Mundo Hispanico, Madrid, 5/75; plus others. Mailing Add: Orgn Am States 17th St & Constitution Ave NW Washington DC 20006

GONGORA, LEONEL
PAINTER, EDUCATOR
b Cartago, Colombia. Study: Wash Univ. Work: Mus Mod Art, New York; New York Pub Libr; Wash Univ Permanent Collection, St Louis, Mo; Staatsgalerie Mus, Stuttgart, Ger; Mus Mod Art, Bogota, Colombia. Comn: Paintings, comn by Fernando Gamboa for Mex Pavilion, Expo 67, Montreal, PQ & Expo 70, Osaka, Japan; lithographs, Lublin, Inc, New York, 69, Bank St Atelier, New York, 70 & Aquarius Press, New York, 71. Exhib: Confrontacion 66, Mus Bellas Artes, Mexico City, 66; Am Acad Arts & Lett, New York, 69; 1st Pan-Am Graphics Biennial, Mus Latertulia, Cali, Colombia, 71; 4th Int Miniature Print Exhib, AAA Gallery, New York, 71; 3rd Brit Int Print Biennale, Bradform Mus, Eng, 72. Teaching: Instr painting & drawing, People's Art Ctr, St Louis, Mo, 56-59; prof painting & drawing, Iberoamericano Univ, Mex, 60-61; prof painting & drawing, Univ Mass, Amherst, 63-74. Awards: First Prize in Drawing, Nat Mus, Bogota, 64; Nat Acad Arts & Lett Award in Painting, New York, 68; Tenth Nat Arte Prize in Lithography, Mus Latertulia, 70. Bibliog: Toby Joysmith (auth), Two painter poets, The News, Mexico City, 8/69; Roberto Paramo (auth), Gongora, el erotismo en persona, El, Mexico City, 10/71; Anna Mayo (auth), Never on Good Friday, Village Voice, New York, 11/71. Publ: Illusr, Mass Rev, 67; illusr, Minn Rev, 69; illusr, The intricate land, New Rivers Press, 70; illusr, Poemas podridos, Villa Miseria Press, 72; contribr, Requirements of yesterday and today, Spectrum, 72. Mailing Add: c/o Lerner-Heller Gallery 956 Madison Ave New York NY 10021

GONZALES, BOYER
PAINTER, EDUCATOR
b Galveston, Tex, Feb 11, 09. Study: Univ Va, BS(archit); also with Henry Lee McFee & Yasuo Kuniyoshi. Work: Rochester Mem Gallery, NY; Witte Mem Mus, San Antonio, Tex; Dallas Mus Fine Arts; Seattle Art Mus. Exhib: New York World's Fair, 39; Pa Acad Fine Arts Ann, 52; Corcoran Gallery Art Biennial, 52; Pac Coast Invitational, 62-63; Artists West of the Mississippi, Colorado Springs Fine Arts Ctr, Colo, 65. Teaching: Instr painting, Univ Tex, Austin, 39-42, from asst to assoc prof painting, 46-54, chmn dept art, 46-48; prof painting, Univ Wash, 54-, dir, Sch Art, 54-66. Pos: Dir, Nat Asn Schs Art, 60-62, vpres, 62-63. Awards: Tex Exhib Painting & Sculpture, 53; Northwest Ann Exhib Painting, Seattle Art Mus, 56; Governor's Award of Special Commendation, State of Wash, 75; plus others. Media: Oil. Mailing Add: Sch of Art Univ of Wash Seattle WA 98195

GONZALES, CARLOTTA (MRS RICHARD LAHEY)
PAINTER, SCULPTOR
b Wilmington, NC, Apr 3, 10. Study: Pa Acad Fine Arts; Nat Acad Design; Art Students League; Corcoran Sch Art; Ogunquit Sch Art. Work: Am Battle Monuments Mem, Honolulu; Francis Bangs Collection, Ogunquit Mus Art, Maine; Print Collection, Corcoran Gallery Art, Washington, DC; plus many in pvt collections. Comn: The Heavens Above (star charts), 41,

state seals, 45 & flags of America, 47, Nat Geog Soc, Washington, DC; mural (battle maps), Am Battle Monuments Comns, 60; plus many portraits in pvt collections. Exhib: Nat Acad Design, New York, 30; Corcoran Gallery Art Biennial, Washington, DC, 36-38; Goucher Col, Towson, Md, 43; Montclair Art Mus, NJ, 46; Baltimore Mus, Md, 56. Teaching: Instr sculpture, Goucher Col, 35-37; instr sculpture, Corcoran Sch Art, 35-45; instr pvt classes, 55-71. Pos: Staff artist, Nat Geog Soc, 41-47. Awards: Sculpture, Nat Acad Design, 30. Mem: Ogunquit Mus Art. Media: Oil, Stone. Publ: Co-auth, Life of Rembrandt & co-auth, Life of Picasso, Stravon. Mailing Add: 9530 Clark Crossing Rd Vienna VA 22180

GONZALES, SHIRLEY
ART CRITIC, WRITER
b New Haven, Conn, Apr 19, 35. Study: Hartford Art Sch, one yr; Yale Univ, BFA(painting), 58. Teaching: Pvt classes in painting. Pos: Art critic & feature story writer on the arts, New Haven Regist, 68- Mailing Add: 1949 Durham Rd Guilford CT 06437

GONZALEZ, JOSE GAMALIEL
ART ADMINISTRATOR, DESIGNER
b Iturbide, Nuevo Leon, Mex, Apr 20, 33. Study: Chicago Acad of Fine Arts; Univ of Chicago; Am Acad of Art, Chicago, dipl; Sch of the Art Inst of Chicago, BFA; Instituto Allende, San Miguel, Mex, study with Jaime Pinto; Univ of Notre Dame, MFA candidate. Collections Arranged: Hispanic Festival of the Arts, Mus of Sci & Indust, Chicago, 74-78; Mexposicion I-25 Paintings from Bellas Artes in Mexico, 76 & Mexposicion II-Agustin Casasola-1910 Mexican Revolution (photog), 77, Univ of Ill, Chicago Circle; Anisinabe Waki Aztlan, Truman Col, Chicago, 77; La Mujer-Mexican Women of Mexico plus Midwest Latinas, Cult Ctr of Chicago Pub Libr, 78. Teaching: Instr mural painting, Ind Univ NW, Gary, 74; instr Mex crafts, Columbia Col, Chicago, 78- Pos: Art dir, Revista Chicano Riquena, Ind Univ NW, 73-78; art dir, Foxlady Mag, Chicago, 75-76; visual consult, Ill Arts Coun, 76- & Nat Endowment for the Arts, Washington, DC, 78-; nominator, Chicago Art Awards, 78- Mem: Chicago Artists Coalition; Movimiento Artistico Chicano (founder & chairperson; dir, 75-76 & 78-). Style & Technique: Expressive surrealism. Media: Acrylic, Mixed Media. Publ: Contribr, 450 Years of Chicago History, Albuquerque, NMex, 76; contribr, We Americans, 75 & Gallery, 76, Scott Foresman; art dir, Abrazo, March Inc, 76. Dealer: Guerbois Gallery 1133 W Webster Chicago IL 60614. Mailing Add: c/o March Inc PO Box 2890 Chicago IL 60690

GONZALEZ, JOSE LUIS
ART ADMINISTRATOR, RESTORER
b Aguas Calientes, Mexico, Aug 18, 39; US citizen. Study: East Los Angeles Col; also with Orlinto Marcucci Ramirez & Rudolf Vargas; painting with Aldana. Comn: Religious monument, Utter McKinley Mortuary, Sanctuary Our Lady of Guadalupe, 68; baked tile mural, Bob Kemp, First St Store, 74; authentication of art work, San Fernando Mission, Archdiocese Los Angeles, 74; Univ Southern Calif (mural with Robert Arenivar), Chicano Student Ctr, 75; mural (with Eddie Marti nez, Jacob Gutierrez, John Gonzalez, David Botello & Robert Arenivar), Smithsonian Inst, Washington, DC, 75. Exhib: Nosotros Show, Hollywood Bowl, Los Angeles, 72; Hancock Art Asn, Mus Sci & Indust, Los Angeles, 73; Ann Ebell Theater Art Show, Wilshire Blvd, Los Angeles, 73; World Cong for Peace Exhib, Russia, 74; Am Folklife Festival, Smithsonian Inst Mall, Washington, DC, 75. Teaching: Instr restoration, painting & sculp ture, East Los Angeles Sch Mex-Am Fine Arts, 71. Pos: Art supvr, Fuseks Art Studio, Los Angeles, 58-70; pres, Goez Art Studio, Los Angeles, 69-; exec dir, East Los Angeles Sch Mex-Am Fine Arts, 71-; chmn Los Angeles mural proj, Hispanic Bicentennial Cult Comt, 74. Bibliog: Jose Luis Ruiz (auth), Action Chicano, TV film spec, 74; Ralph P Davidson (auth), The Mural Message, Time Mag, 4/7/75; Dewar's Profile, numerous nat mag & newspapers, 75. Style & Technique: Extremely versatile; restoration. Media: Oil; Marble. Interest: To see that the artists have the best facilities to work and display their work and the supplies needed to expand. Collection: Chicano art. Mailing Add: c/o Goez Art Gallery 3757 E First St Los Angeles CA 90063

GONZALEZ, XAVIER
PAINTER, SCULPTOR
b Almeria, Spain, Feb 15, 98; US citizen. Study: Art Inst Chicago, 21-23. Work: Whitney Mus Am Art & Metrop Mus Art, New York; New Orleans Mus Art; Witte Mus, San Antonio, Tex; Mus Fine Arts, Seattle; plus others. Exhib: Grand Central Moderns, New York, 51-53; Pa Acad Fine Arts, Philadelphia; Carnegie Inst, Pittsburgh; Brooklyn Mus, NY; retrospective, Witte Mus, San Antonio, 68; plus many others. Teaching: Instr art, San Antonio, 24; prof art, Newcomb Col, Tulane Univ, 30; instr art, Brooklyn Mus, 45; lectr, Nat Col Asn, 46; Western Reserve Univ, 53-54; Summer Sch Art, Wellfleet, Mass; lectr, Metrop Mus Art, New York. Awards: Am Acad Arts & Lett Grant; Guggenheim Fel, 47; Ford Found Grant, 65; Gold Medal & the 79 Artist Ann Award, Nat Art Club of New York, 78; plus others. Mem: Am Watercolor Soc; Am Nat Acad; Nat Asn Mural Painters (pres, 68). Publ: Auth, Notes About Painting, 55. Mailing Add: 222 Central Park S New York NY 10019

GONZALEZ-TORNERO, SERGIO
PAINTER, PRINTMAKER
b Santiago, Chile. Study: Univ Santiago; Atelier 17, Paris, with S W Hayter. Work: Metrop Mus of Art, New York; Mus of Mod Art, New York; Libr of Cong, Washington, DC; Minneapolis Inst of Art, Minn; Smithsonian Inst, Washington, DC. Exhib: Int Trienal of Graphics, Grenchen, Switz, 64; 3rd Bienale of Prints from the Americas, Santiago, Chile, 64; Int Bienale of Prints, Krakow, Poland, 66; Couturier Galerie, Stamford, Conn, 67; Stamford Mus, Conn, 67; Int Bienal of Prints, Epinal, France, 71; Gruenebaum Gallery, New York, 75; Soc of Am Graphic Artist, New York. Awards: Exhib of Latin Am Prints, Havana, Cuba, 68; Exhib of Painting & Sculpture, Silvermine, Conn, 73; Silver Nat Print Exhib, 71. Mem: Soc of Am Graphic Artists. Style & Technique: Intaglio etching; observations of life with humor; abstract paintings of the human condition. Media: Oil Painting, chiefly Black and White. Mailing Add: c/o Couturier Galerie 1814 Newfield Ave Stamford CT 06903

GOO, BENJAMIN
SCULPTOR, PAINTER
b Honolulu, Hawaii, July 12, 22. Study: State Univ Iowa, BFA, 53; Cranbrook Acad Art, MFA, 54; Brera Acad Fine Art, Sch of Marino Marini, Milan, Italy, 54-55. Work: Roswell Mus & Art Ctr, NMex; Phoenix Art Mus, Ariz; Tucson Art Ctr, Ariz; Yuma Art Ctr, Ariz; Ariz State Univ Art Collection, Tempe; plus others. Comn: Two non-objective white marble sculptures, Phoenix Civic Plaza, 71. Exhib: 10th Anniversary Exhib of Living American Painters & Sculptors, Silvermine Guild Artists, New Canaan, Conn, 59; 155th Ann Exhib Am Painting & Sculpture, Pa Acad Fine Arts & Detroit Inst Art, 60; 24th Ann Drawing, Print & Sculpture Exhib, San Francisco Mus Art, Calif, 61; Creative Casting: Exhibit of Art in Bronze, Mus Contemp Crafts, New York, 63; 73rd Western Ann, Denver Art Mus, 71. Teaching: Prof art, Ariz State Univ, 55-; Nat Endowment for the Arts artist in residence, Mesa, Ariz, 72-73; artist in residence, Roswell Mus & Art Ctr, NMex, 75-76. Awards: First Ann Southwestern States Purchase Award, Roswell Mus & Art Ctr, 62; 4th Southwestern Invitational Purchase Award, Yuma Art Ctr, 69; 21st Ann Tucson Festival Art Exhib Award, Tucson Art Ctr, 71. Style & Technique: Non objective. Media: Metals, Stone, Wood. Publ: Auth, Education and the craftsman, 1-2/62 & auth, Dick Seeger: artist craftsman in plastics, 7-8/62, Creative Crafts Mag. Dealer: Elaine Horwitch Gallery 4200 N Marshall Way Scottsdale AZ 85251. Mailing Add: 5312 Wilkinson Rd Scottsdale AZ 85253

GOOCH, DONALD BURNETTE
PAINTER
b Bloomingdale, Mich, Oct 17, 07. Study: Univ Mich Col Archit & Design, BS(educ), with J P Slusser, 32-39, MA(design), 39; Detroit Art Acad, with C F Lopez, 33-36; Fontainebleau Sch Fine Arts, France, 37. Work: Detroit Inst Arts; Ford Motor Co, Dearborn, Mich. Comn: Seven educ film strips, McGraw Hill, New York, 49-55; seven illus, Ford Times, Dearborn, 50-60; oil mural, Mich Consolidated Gas Co, Detroit, 51; oil painting, Mich Union, Ann Arbor, 56; literary map of Mich, Mich Coun Teachers Eng, 64. Exhib: San Francisco Watercolor Show, 40; Am Fedn Arts Traveling Show Selected Watercolors, 41; Pepsi Cola's Painting of the Year, 46; Pa Acad Fine Art, 47; Terry Nat Exhib, Miami, Fla, 52. Teaching: Instr design, Detroit Art Acad, 33-36; prof design, Univ Mich Col Archit & Design, Ann Arbor, 36-73, emer prof, 73- Awards: Alumni Prize, Collaborative Competition, Am Acad Rome, 35; Detroit Inst Arts Founders Prize, 47; Faculty Res Grants, Horace H Rackham Sch Grad Studies, Univ Mich, 60-65. Mem: Ann Arbor Art Asn (pres, 47-48); Mich Watercolor Soc (dir, 46-50; Mich Acad Sci, Arts & Lett (vchmn fine arts, 51-52); fel Int Acad Arts & Lett; Nat Soc Lit & Arts; plus others. Style & Technique: Realism and surrealism. Media: Watercolor, Tempera, Oil, Acrylic. Res: Pictographic techniques for communication with non-literates, Nepal, 1961 and 1965. Publ: Ed, Advertising to the American Taste, 56, ed, Search for Certainty in Advertising, 59 & ed & illusr, Theatre & Main Street, 64, Univ Mich; illusr, The Third Crusade (film strip), McGraw, 58; contribr, Picture talk in Kathmandu, Mich Acad Sci, Arts & Lett, 63. Mailing Add: 1633 Leaird St Ann Arbor MI 48105

GOOCH, GERALD
PAINTER
b Mainington, WVa, 1933. Study: Calif Col Arts & Crafts, BFA, 65; San Jose State Col, MA, 67. Work: Time, Inc, New York; Achenbach Found, Palace Legion of Honor, San Francisco; Stanford Univ, Palo Alto, Calif; Johnson Wax Co; Mus Mod Art, New York; plus others including many in pvt collections. Exhib: Achenbach Found, Calif Palace of Legion of Honor, 67; Ill Biennial Exhib Contemp Painting, 67; Int Exhib Tokyo, Japan, 67; A Decade in the West, Collection of Harry W Anderson, Santa Barbara Mus Art, 71; West Coast '72, Painters & Sculptors, Crocker Gallery, Sacramento, 72. Teaching: Instr art, San Francisco Art Inst, 66-71; instr art, Laney Col, Oakland, 69- Awards: Calif State Fair, 65; Western Mich Univ Print Show, 66; Okla Art Ctr Print Show, Oklahoma City, 66; plus others. Mailing Add: c/o Hansen Fuller Gallery 228 Grant Ave San Francisco CA 94108

GOOD, LEONARD
PAINTER, EDUCATOR
b Chickasha, Okla, June 25, 07. Study: Univ Okla, BFA, 27; Art Students League, with Nicolaides, 30; Univ Iowa, with Jean Charlot, 40. Work: Des Moines Art Ctr, Iowa; Milwaukee Art Ctr, Wis; Oklahoma City Art Ctr; Kans State Fedn Art, Manhattan; City Hall, Kofu, Japan. Comn: Portrait, Okla Hist Mus, Oklahoma City, 49; two portraits, Univ Okla, Norman, 49-50; three portraits, Drake Univ, 54-60; portrait, Iowa Hist Mus, Des Moines, 62; series of Iowa scenes for Sun features, Des Moines Register, 65. Exhib: 1st & 2nd Nat Exhibs Am Art, Metrop Mus Art, New York, 36 & 37; Gallery of States Touring Exhib, Am Fedn Arts, Washington, DC, 45; Mid America Annual, Joslyn Mus Art, Omaha, 55; Judged Juried Arts Ann, Tyler, Tex, 69; Am Painters in Paris Exhib, Palais des Congrés, France, 75-76. Collections Arranged: Assembled permanent collection of paintings for Preferred Risk Life Ins Co Home Off Bldg, Des Moines, 69. Teaching: Prof painting & drawing, Univ Okla, 30-50; prof drawing & painting, Univ Wis, 50-52; prof art hist, Drake Univ, 52-77, head dept art, 52-68, emer prof art hist, 77- Pos: Vis artist in residence, Iowa State Univ, 60-61; artist in residence, Nat Endowment Arts & Iowa Arts Coun, Shenandoah, Iowa, 70-71. Awards: Purchase Prize for New Mexico Town (painting), Springville Mus Art, Utah, 74; 4th Ann Nat Exhib Small Paintings First Prize for NMex Art League, First Prize for Have a Nice Day (painting), Iowa State Fair, 74; plus others. Mem: Delta Phi Delta (nat vpres, 54-58, nat pres, 58-60). Style & Technique: Realistic and expressive, traditional technique. Media: Oil, Acrylic, Watercolor. Publ: Illusr, A Certain Young Widow, Univ Okla, 30; illusr, instructional manuals for US Air Force, Tinker Field, Okla, 43-44. Mailing Add: 1320 Oregon Ave Chickasha OK 73018

GOODACRE, GLENNA
PAINTER, SCULPTOR
b Lubbock, Tex, Aug 28, 39. Study: Colo Col, BA; Art Students League. Work: Tex Tech Mus, Lubbock; Presby Hosp, Denver, Colo; Diamond M Found Mus, Snyder, Tex. Comn: Bronze bust of Dr W C Holden, Tex Tech Univ, 72; bronze of Dan Blocker, City Ctr, Odonnell, Tex, 73; bronze of J Evetts Haley, Haley Libr, Midland, Tex, 73; bronze of C T McLaughlin, Diamond M Found, 73; bronze relief of Dr Kenneth Allen, Presby Hosp, Denver, Colo, 75. Exhib: Catharine Lorillard Wolfe Art Club, New York, 72; Tex Fine Arts Nat Show, Austin, 73; West Tex Nat Watercolor Show, Mus Tex Tech Univ, 73; Allied Artists Am, New York, 74; Nat Acad Design, New York, 75. Awards: Silver Medal, Nat Cowboy Hall of Fame, 75; Youth Award, Nat Sculpture Soc, 77; Gold Medal for Sculpture, Nat Acad Design, 78. Mem: Allied Artists of Am; Nat Sculpture Soc. Style & Technique: Realistic interpretation of the figure and head studies. Media: Oil, Pastel, Watercolor; Bronze. Publ: Illusr, bronze relief for jacket, The Flamboyant Judge, 73 & Trank Tenny Johnson, 75; illusr, silver relief for jacket, Robbing Banks was my Business, 74. Mailing Add: 503 Northstar Boulder CO 80302

GOODALL, DONALD BANNARD
ART ADMINISTRATOR
b Los Angeles, Calif, Oct 8, 12. Study: Univ Ore, BA; Art Inst Chicago; Univ Chicago, MA; Harvard Univ, PhD. Teaching: Chmn dept art, Univ Southern Calif, 49-59; chmn dept art, Univ Tex, Austin, 59-, dir, Univ Art Mus, 63-, actg dean fine arts, 71-72, dir, Univ Art Collections, 72- Mem: Col Art Asn Am; Nat Schs Art. Mailing Add: Dept of Art Univ of Tex at Austin Austin TX 78712

GOODBRED, RAY EDW
PAINTER, INSTRUCTOR
b Brooklyn, NY, Dec 7, 29. Study: Art Students League, with Robert Brackman, 48-51; Nat Acad Sch Fine Art, with Ogden Pleissner, 51; NY Univ Sch Educ, 53-56. Work: Gibbes Art Gallery, Charleston, SC; The Citadel; Med Univ SC; The Pentagon, Washington, DC; Univ NC; plus many others. Comn: Portraits of ten mem bd, Home Fed Savings & Loan Asn, 71; plus other portrait comns throughout the southeast. Exhib: Knickerbocker Artists, Riverside Mus, New York, 56; SC Artists Ann, 58-; one-man show, Gibbes Art Gallery, 68; Tricentennial SC Contemp Artists Invitational, 70; Allied Artists Am, Nat Acad Design,

70-73. Teaching: Instr, Hastie Sch Art, Gibbes Art Gallery, 69-74; instr painting & drawing, Art Students League, 75- Awards: First Prize & Purchase Award, SC Artists Ann, 67, Saul Alexander Award, 67 & 72; Yasotuma Award, Nat Arts Club, 74; Graphics Award, Beaufort Art Asn Ann, 74; plus others. Bibliog: Jack A Morris, Jr & Robert Smeltzer (auth), Contemporary artists of South Carolina, Greenville Co Mus Art, 70. Mem: Salmagundi Club; life mem Art Students League; Guild SC Artists; Charleston Artist Guild; Grand Cent Art Galleries. Media: Oil, Pastel. Dealer: Grand Central Art Galleries Hotel Biltmore 40 Vanderbilt Ave New York NY 10017; Portraits Inc 41 E 57th St New York NY 10022. Mailing Add: c/o Art Students League 215 W 57th St New York NY 10019

GOODE, JOE
See Bueno, Jose

GOODELMAN, AARON J
SCULPTOR
b Ataki, Arabia, Apr 1, 90; US citizen. Study: Odessa Art Sch, Russia; Trud Trade Sch, Odessa; Cooper Union Art Sch, New York; Nat Acad of Art, New York; Acad des Beaux Arts, Paris; Beaux Arts Architects, New York; also with G T Brewster, J Injalbert, Outzon Borglum & Joe Davidson. Work: Libr of Jewish Theological Seminary, New York; Eastern Mus, Russia; Tel Aviv Mus, Israel Project House, Washington, DC; Hebrew Union Col, Skirball Mus, Los Angeles, Calif. Comn: Victory Bldg, Toronto, Can, 29; Memorial monuments of Ye Hoash, H Spector, Dr Kursak & Dr Chaim Zhitlowsky, comn by Jacob Adler, Bloomgarden, 30-40; Portrait Medal, Dr Chaim Zhitlowsky Found, New York, 64; scenic designs, comn by Morris Schwarz, Jewish Art Theatre, New York. Exhib: One-man shows, Dorothy Paris Gallery, New York, 35, Univ of Judaism, Los Angeles, Calif, 67, Judas C Magnus Mem Mus, Jewish Mus of the West, Berkeley, Calif, 67; Retrospective, ACA Galleries, New York, 42, 46 & 63; Mus of Mod Art, New York; Brooklyn Mus, New York; Carnegie Inst Int, Pittsburgh; Whitney Mus of Am Art, New York; Metrop Mus of Art, New York; Art Inst of Chicago; Philadelphia Mus, Pa; Travelling Work Progress Admin Exhib, John Jay Col of Criminal Justice, New York, 77. Teaching: Instr sculpture, New Sch for Social Res, New York, 37, City Col of New York, 39-40; pvt instr sculpture, New York, 50-63. Awards: Outstanding Contribr to the Arts, Dr Chaim Zhitlowsky Found, New York, 64; artist-of-the-month, First Unitarian Church, Los Angeles, 67. Bibliog: Articles in The Citizen News, Los Angeles, 4/67, Calif Jewish Voice, 4/67 & The Tribune, Hollywood, Calif, 4/67; Francis V O'Connor, ed, Art for the Millions, Graphic Soc Ltd, Conn, 74. Style & Technique: Naturalistic, abstract and semi-abstract. Media: Marble, Granite; Terra Cotta; Hammered Copper; Sheet Steel, Wood Carving and Epoxy. Mailing Add: 68 W 238th St Bronx NY 10463

GOODMAN, BENJAMIN
PATRON
b Memphis, Tenn, Jan 18, 04. Study: Princeton Univ, AB, 24; Harvard Univ, LLB, 27. Pos: Patron of regional art (mid-south); trustee & former pres, Memphis Acad Arts; chmn, Memphis Munic Art Comn, 60-76. Mailing Add: 115 S Rose Rd Memphis TN 38117

GOODMAN, BERTRAM
PAINTER
b New York, NY, Sept 21, 04. Study: Sch Am Sculpture, 23-24; Art Students League, 25. Work: Brooklyn Mus; Libr Cong; Abbott Labs, Chicago; Butler Art Inst, Youngstown, Ohio; Metrop Mus Art; plus others. Exhib: Mus Mod Art; Whitney Mus Am Art; Carnegie Art Inst; Metrop Mus Art; Nat Acad Fine Arts. Awards: First Prize Watercolor, Screen Publicists Guild, 46; Purchase Prize, Abraham Lincoln Gallery, 47; Jo & Emily Lowe Prize, 56. Mem: Artists Equity Asn (dir, 55-56); Brooklyn Soc Artists; Am Soc Graphic Artists (gov coun). Mailing Add: 299 W 12th St New York NY 10014

GOODMAN, BRENDA JOYCE
PAINTER, INSTRUCTOR
b Detroit, Mich, July 21, 43. Study: Ctr for Creative Studies, BFA. Work: Detroit Inst Arts, Mich. Exhib: One-woman shows, Willis Gallery, 73 & Gertrude Kasle Gallery, 74, Detroit; Michigan Focus, Detroit Inst Arts, 74-75; 4th Mich Biennial, Kresge Art Ctr Gallery, Mich State Univ, 75; Mich Surv Exhib, Cranbrook Acad Art & Mus & San Diego Mus Art, 75-76. Teaching: Instr drawing & painting, Ctr Creative Studies, 66-69; instr painting, Art Gallery, Windsor, Ont, 67-68 & 72; instr drawing & painting, Wayne Co Community Col, Detroit, 72-73. Awards: Drawing Prize, 15th Ann Mid-Mich Exhib, 74; First Prize, Founders Soc, Detroit Inst Arts, 74-75. Bibliog: Dee Durkee (auth), Moving out (interview), Feminist Lit & Art J, 75; John Askins (auth), One woman's struggle to find herself, Detroit Free Press, 4/27/75. Style & Technique: Somewhere between symbolism and surrealism, from thick to thin, loose to rendered. Media: Oil, Mixed Media. Mailing Add: c/o Gertrude Kasle Gallery 310 Fisher Bldg Detroit MI 48202

GOODMAN, CALVIN JEROME
ART CONSULTANT, LECTURER
b Chicago, Ill, Mar 1, 22. Study: Harvard Univ, AB(hon), 49. Teaching: Instr bus methods for artists, Tamarind Lithography Workshop, 61-71; instr prof practices, Calif Inst Arts, 67-71; instr prof practices, Otis Art Inst, 68-71; also lectr seminar & workshops in marketing art for San Francisco Art Inst, Scripps Grad Sch of Art, Pratt Inst, among others. Pos: Mgt consult in art, 60-; vpres, Tamarind Lithography Workshop, 59-74; vpres, Orgn Arts Sponsors, Los Angeles, 70-74; nat consult, Artists Equity Asn, 74- Bibliog: Antreasian & Adams (auth), The Tamarind Book of Lithography, Abrams, 71. Res: The art market and specialized schools of art and music. Publ: Auth, A Management Study of an Art Gallery, 66, Gallery Facility Planning, 67 & Business Methods for a Lithography Workshop, 68, Tamarind; auth, Marketing Art, A Handbook for Artists and Art Dealers, 72; auth, Art Marketing Handbook, GeeTeeBee, 78. Mailing Add: 11901 Sunset Blvd Suite 102 Los Angeles CA 90049

GOODMAN, JAMES NEIL
ART DEALER, COLLECTOR
b Rochester, NY, Apr 11, 29. Pos: Dir, James Goodman Gallery. Specialty: Modern American and European masters, including Calder, Cornell, de Kooning, Klee, Leger, Matisse, Moore, Picasso & Tanguy. Mailing Add: 55 E 86th St New York NY 10028

GOODMAN, MARIAN
ART DEALER, ART PUBLISHER
b New York, NY, June 15, 28. Study: Columbia Univ Grad Sch Art Hist, BA. Pos: Dir publ, Multiples Inc, 65-, pres, 74-; dir, Marian Goodman Gallery, exhibiting works by Arakawa, Larry Bell, Marcel Broodthaers, James Lee Byars, Ger Ven Elic & others. Mem: Art Dealers Asn. Specialty: Publishing limited editions and sometimes books, records, etc by prominent contemporary artists such as Arakawa, Lichtenstein, Rauchenburg, Rosenquist, Oldenburg, Warhol and many others. Mailing Add: Multiples Inc Marian Goodman Gallery 38 E 57th St New York NY 10022

GOODMAN, SIDNEY
PAINTER
b Philadelphia, Pa, Jan 19, 36. Study: Philadelphia Col Art, 58. Work: Art Inst Chicago; Libr Cong, Washington, DC; Mus Mod Art, New York; Whitney Mus Am Art, New York; Hirshhorn Collection; plus others. Exhib: A Sense of Place, The Artist & the American Land Traveling Show, 73-74; Living American Artists & the Figure, Pa State Univ Art Mus, 74; Works on Paper, Va Mus, 74; Contemporary American Paintings from the Lewis Collection, Del Art Mus, 74; The Figure in Recent American Painting Traveling Exhib, 74-75; Three Centuries of Am Art, Philadelphia Mus of Art, 76; Am 1976 Bicentennial Exhib, US Dept of Interior, Washington, DC, 76; Eight Contemp Am Realists, Pa Acad of the Fine Arts, 77; plus others. Teaching: Instr drawing & painting, Philadelphia Col Art, presently. Awards: Guggenheim Fel, 64; Philadelphia Print Club Purchase Award, 65; Nat Endowment of Arts Grant, 74; plus others. Dealer: Terry Dintenfass Inc 18 E 67th St New York NY 10021. Mailing Add: 323 Harrison Ave Elkins Park PA 19117

GOODNOUGH, ROBERT
PAINTER
b Cortland, NY, Oct 23, 17. Study: Syracuse Univ, Hiram Gell fel, 40, BFA; NY Univ, MA; New Sch Social Res; Ozenfant Sch Art; Hans Hofmann Sch Fine Arts. Work: Albright-Knox Art Gallery, Buffalo, NY; Solomon R Guggenheim Mus, Mus Mod Art & Metrop Mus Art, New York; Wadsworth Atheneum, Hartford, Conn; plus others. Exhib: One-man shows, Univ Minn, Univ Notre Dame & Arts Club Chicago, 64; Cayuga Mus Hist & Art, Auburn, NY, 69, Albright-Knox Art Gallery, Buffalo, NY, 69 & Syracuse Univ, 72; Nat Inst Arts & Lett, 64; New American Painting & Sculpture, Mus Mod Art, 69; Univ Ill, 69; Indianapolis Mus Art, 69; Venice Biennial, 70; Am Acad Arts & Lett, 71; plus many other group & one-man shows. Teaching: Instr painting, Cornell Univ, NY Univ & Fieldston Sch, New York. Pos: Art critic, Art News, 50-57; secy, Documents of Mod Art, 51. Awards: Ada Garrett Award, Art Inst Chicago, 61; Ford Found Purchase Prize, 63. Mailing Add: 15 Barrow St New York NY 10014

GOODNOW, FRANK A
PAINTER, EDUCATOR
b Evanston, Ill, Dec 14, 23. Study: Northwestern Univ, Evanston; Art Inst Chicago, BFA; Anna L Raymond traveling fel, 48; also with Boris Anisfeld. Work: Philadelphia Mus Art; NY State Univ; Univ Rochester; Everson Mus Art, Syracuse; Syracuse Univ. Exhib: Salon des Jeunes Peintres, Paris, France, 49; Pa Acad Fine Arts, 53, 57 & 65; Whitney Mus Am Art, 55; Everson Mus Art, 60, 67, 74 & 75; one-man shows, Schuman Gallery, Rochester, 65, 69, 71 & 72; Oxford Gallery, Rochester, NY, 75 & 77; Lubin House Gallery, New York, 76. Teaching: Prof painting, Syracuse Univ, 50- Awards: Helen Everson Mem Purchase Prize, Everson Mus Art, 67; B Forman Award, Rochester Mem Gallery, 69; First Prize, Cooperstown Nat Show, 71; grant, Ford Found, 77. Style & Technique: Chromatic abstraction. Dealer: Oxford Gallery 267 Oxford St Rochester NY 14607. Mailing Add: 214 Dawley Rd Fayetteville NY 13066

GOODRICH, LLOYD
MUSEUM OFFICER, WRITER
b Nutley, NJ, July 10, 97. Study: Art Students League, with Kenneth Hayes Miller; Nat Acad Design; Cornell Col, Hon DFA, 63; Colby Col, Hon DFA, 64; RI Sch of Design, Hon DFA, 77. Pos: Res cur, Whitney Mus Am Art, 35-47, assoc cur, 47-48, assoc dir, 48-58, dir, 58-68, adv dir, 68-71, consult, 71-, mem bd trustees; chmn ed bd, Mag of Art, 42-50; founder & dir, Am Art Res Coun, 42-; mem ed bd, Art in Am, 46-70 & Am Art J, 72; chmn comt on govt & art, NY Regional Bd Arch of Am Art, 48-; mem, Nat Coun Arts & Govt, 54-, vchmn, 62-; secy, Sara Roby Found, 56-; dir, trustee & hon vpres, Am Fedn Arts; mem, Nat Collection of Fine Arts Comn; co-chmn, Joint Artists-Mus Comt; mem coun, Sci Int Enciclopedia Arte; assoc, Sem Am Civilization, Columbia Univ; mem adv comt, Art for the White House, 60-63; bd dirs, Edward MacDowell Asn; plus many other prior art positions. Awards: Art in Am Award, 59; Nat Art Materials Trade Asn Award, 64; Award of Merit, Philadelphia Mus Col Art, 64; Art Dealers of Am Award, 77. Mem: Asn Art Mus Dirs; Art Students League; hon mem Int Art Critics Asn; Drawing Soc; hon mem Am Inst Interior Designers; fel Am Acad Arts & Sci. Res: American art and artists. Publ: Auth, Thomas Eakins, 33 & 70 & co-auth, Georgia O'Keeffe, Praeger; auth, Winslow Homer, 44 & 59 & Albert P Ryder, 59; auth, Edward Hopper, 71, Raphael Soyer, 72 & Reginald Marsh, 72, Abrams; plus many other bks & articles in nat art mag. Mailing Add: Whitney Mus Am Art 945 Madison Ave New York NY 10021

GOODRICH, SUSAN
PAINTER
b La Crosse, Wis, Aug 23, 33. Study: Univ Wis, Madison, with Robert Grilley & John Wilde. Exhib: Art Across Am (traveling exhib), Mead Corp, 63-65; Mid-Yr Show, Butler Inst Am Art, Youngstown, Ohio, 65, 66 & 76; Wis Painters & Sculptors, Milwaukee Art Ctr, Wis, 67; Art in the Embassies, State Dept, 67; one-person shows, Jewish Community Ctr, Milwaukee, 69, Milwaukee Art Ctr, 73 & Allan Stone Gallery, New York, 75; Nat Acad Design, New York, 72; Contemp Figurative Painting in the Mid-West, Univ Wis, Madison, 77. Awards: Painting of the Yr, Art Across Am, Mead Paper Corp, 63; Major Award, Wis Painters & Sculptors, Milwaukee Art Ctr, 67 & Top Award, 73. Bibliog: Article in La Rev Mod, Paris, 65; Susan Braudy (auth), article in MS Mag, 8/73; feature prog, Wis Directions, Pub Broadcasting Station, Television film, Channel 10, Milwaukee, 75. Style & Technique: Small, funny, personal; sufferable romanticism; 19th century. Media: Oil. Dealer: Allan Stone Gallery 48 E 86th St New York NY 10029. Mailing Add: 3240 N Oakland Ave Milwaukee WI 53211

GOODRIDGE, LAWRENCE WAYNE
PAINTER, SCULPTOR
b Cincinnati, Ohio, Mar 18, 41. Study: Univ Cincinnati, BFA(with hon), 63; Univ Cincinnati & Art Acad Cincinnati, MFA, 67. Exhib: All-Ohio Painting & Sculpture Exhib, Dayton Art Inst, 67; Mid-States Art Exhib, Evansville Mus Arts & Sci, Ind, 70; one-man show & Louisville Biennial, J B Speed Art Mus, Ky, 71; 17th Ann Drawing & Sculpture Show, Ball State Univ, Muncie, Ind, 71. Teaching: Instr found design & color theory, Art Acad Cincinnati, 69-, co-dean, 72- Pos: Toy designer, Kenner Prod Co, 63-65. Awards: Second Prize, Eastern Fine Paper Graphic Design, 65. Publ: Auth & illusr, European diary, 70 & Truck stop, 71, Cincinnati Mag. Dealer: Richard Feigen Gallery 226 E Ontario St Chicago IL 60611. Mailing Add: Art Acad Cincinnati Eden Park Cincinnati OH 45202

GOODWIN, LOUIS PAYNE
CARTOONIST
b Flintville, Tenn, Oct 9, 22. Study: Ark Polytech Col, 41-42; Univ Chattanooga, BA, 48. Pos: Advert & ed cartoonist, Dispatch Printing Co, Columbus, 52-62; ed cartoonist, Columbus Eve Dispatch, 62- Awards: Cartoon Award, Freedoms Found, 62-69, 71 & 72; Cartoonists Award, Hwy Safety Found, 66. Mem: Asn Am Ed Cartoonists. Mailing Add: 34 S Third St Columbus OH 43216

GOODYEAR, FRANK H, JR
ART HISTORIAN, CURATOR
b New York, NY, Jan 5, 44. Study: Yale Univ, BA, 66; Univ Del, Winterthur Prog, MA, 69. Collections Arranged: Pa Academicians (with catalogue), Pa Acad of Fine Arts, 73, The Beneficent Connoisseurs—Carey, Gibson, Harrison (with catalogue), 74 & In This Acad: The Pa Acad of the Fine Arts, 1805-1976 (with catalogue), 76; Thomas Doughty: An Am Pioneer in Landscape Painting, 1793-1856 (with catalogue), Pa Acad, Corcoran Gallery of Art & Albany Inst, 73-74; Am Paintings in the RI Hist Soc, 74; Cecilia Beaux (1855-1942): Portrait of an Artist (with catalogue), Pa Acad & Indianapolis Mus of Art, 74-75; Am Art: 1750-1800 Towards Independence, Yale Univ Art Gallery, 76; Eight Contemp Am Realists: Philip Pearlstein, Alfred Leslie, Stephen Posen, Janet Fish, Duane Hanson, Joseph Raffael, Neil Welliver & Sidney Goodman, 77. Pos: Cur, Pa Acad Fine Arts, 72-, ed exhib & catalogue, var exhibs. Mailing Add: Pa Acad Fine Arts Broad & Cherry Sts Philadelphia PA 19102

GOODYEAR, JOHN L
PAINTER, ART ADMINISTRATOR
b Los Angeles, Calif, Oct 22, 30. Study: Univ Mich, BD, 52, MD, 54. Work: Corcoran Gallery Art, Washington, DC; Mus Mod Art, New York; NJ State Cult Ctr; Whitney Mus Am Art, New York; Princeton Univ Mus Art. Exhib: Responsive Eye, Mus Mod Art, New York, 65; Whitney Mus Am Art Ann, New York, 66 & 68; Radius 5 (two yr tour US mus), Smithsonian Inst, Washington, DC, 67; Albright-Knox Art Gallery, Buffalo, NY, 68; Boston Mus Fine Arts, 71; Mus Mod Art, New York, 72; Drawing exhib, Univ Tex Mus, Austin, 77; one-man shows, Inst Contemp Art, Boston, 71, Mus du Que, Can, 71, Everson Mus, Syracuse Univ, NY, 72, Addison Gallery Am Art, Andover, Mass, 76 & Mass Inst Technol Ctr Advan Visual Studies, Cambridge, 76; plus many others. Teaching: Instr, Univ Mich, Grand Rapids, 56-62 & Univ Mass, Amherst, 62-64; prof design, art fundamentals, art & media, Douglass Col, Rutgers Univ, 64-, chmn dept, 76- Awards: Graham Found Fel, 62 & 70; Ctr Advan Visual Studies Fel, Mass Inst Technol, 70-71. Media: Mixed-Media. Mailing Add: Dept of Art Walters Hall Douglass Col New Brunswick NJ 08903

GOOSSEN, EUGENE COONS
WRITER, EDUCATOR
b Gloversville, NY, Aug 6, 20. Study: Hamilton Col; Corcoran Sch Fine Arts; Sorbonne, Paris, cert; New Sch Social Res, BA. Collections Arranged: Kenneth Noland, Morris Louis & First Barnett Newman Retrospective, Bennington Col, Vt, 58-61; 8 Young Artists, Hudson River Mus, NY, 64; The Art of the Real, Mus Mod Art, New York, Grand Palais, Paris, Kunsthalle, Zurich, Switz & Tate Gallery, London, Eng, 68-69; Helen Frankenthaler, Whitney Mus Am Art, New York, Whitechapel Gallery, London, Herrenhausen, Hanover & Kongresshalle, Berlin, Ger, 69; Ellsworth Kelly, Mus Mod Art, New York, 73. Teaching: Prof art, Bennington Col, 58-61, mem visual arts comt, 61-; prof art & chmn dept, Hunter Col, 61- Pos: Art critic, Monterey Peninsula Herald, 48-58; dir exhibs, Bennington Col, 58-61; adv comt, Arch Am Art, 67-; mem, New York City Cult Coun, 70- Awards: Frank Jewett Mather Citation for Excellence in Art Criticism, 58; Guggenheim Fel, 70; City Univ New York Res Grant, 72. Bibliog: Article in Time Mag, 4/7/67; Michael Murphy (auth), The Art of the Real (film), US Info Agency, 68. Mem: Int Art Critics Asn; Am Asn Univ Prof; Col Art Asn Am. Publ: Auth, Ellsworth Kelly, 58; auth, Stuart Davis, 59; auth, The Art of the Real, Eng, Fr & Ger ed, 68-69; auth, Helen Frankenthaler, 69; co-auth, Encyclopaedia of American Art, Chanticleer Press, 72. Mailing Add: RFD 1 Buskirk NY 12028

GORAY, JOHN C
PAINTER, INSTRUCTOR
b Marinette, Wis, Aug 29, 12. Study: Minneapolis Art Inst, Minn; Art Inst of Chicago; Walt Disney Studios, Los Angeles, Calif. Work: Kenosha Mus, Wis; Wustum Mus of Fine Arts, Racine, Wis. Comn: Relief mural, Kenosha Nat Bank, Wis, 70. Exhib: Int Watercolor, New York, NY, 42; Chicago & Vicinity, Art Inst of Chicago, 41; Madison & Vicinity, Madison, Wis, 50; Beloit & Vicinity, Beloit, Wis, 71 & 77; Wis Watercolor, Racine, Wis, 75 & 77. Teaching: Instr painting, Carthage Col, Kenosha, Wis, 70-71; instr two-dimensional, Univ Wis, Parkside, 72-78; instr painting, Univ Wis, Kenosha, 75-76. Awards: Eisendrath Award, Chicago & Vicinity, Chicago, 41; Purchase Award, Wis Watercolor, Racine, 75 & 77. Style & Technique: Semi-abstractions. Media: Acrylic, watercolor. Mailing Add: 6803 Third Ave Kenosha WI 53140

GORCHOV, RON
PAINTER
b Chicago, Ill, Apr 5, 30. Study: Art Inst Chicago, 47-50; Univ Ill, 50-51. Work: Whitney Mus Am Art, New York; Hartford Atheneum, Conn; Metrop Mus of Art, New York; Everson Mus Art, Syracuse, NY. Teaching: Asst prof art, Hunter Col, presently. Media: Oil on Canvas. Mailing Add: Canal St Sta Box 337 New York NY 10013

GORDER, CLAYTON J
PAINTER, EDUCATOR
b Fargo, NDak, Mar 20, 36. Study: Concordia Col (Moorhead, Minn), BA; Univ Iowa, MFA. Work: San Francisco Mus Art; Container Corp Am, Rock Island, Ill; Des Moines Art Ctr, Iowa. Exhib: One-man shows, Davenport Munic Art Gallery, 68, William Sawyer Gallery, 70 & 72, Des Moines Art Ctr, 72 & Arras Gallery, New York, 77; two-man show, Richard Feigen Gallery, 71; Col of Marin Painting Exhib, Kentfield, Calif, 72; Striped & Shaped Canvases, Bronx Mus Arts, 74; Nine Artists at Work, Bronx Mus of Arts, New York, 75; Brunnier Gallery, Iowa State Univ, Ames, 76. Teaching: Assoc prof painting & drawing, Augustana Col (Ill), 63- Awards: First Prize Purchase Award, Container Corp Am, 63; Edmundson Award for Best Work in Show, Any Medium, Ann Iowa Artists Exhib, 69, Esther & Edith Younker Award in Painting, 72. Style & Technique: Non-figurative linear constructions using transparent acrylic stains. Dealer: William Sawyer Gallery 3045 Clay St San Francisco CA 94115; Arras Gallery 29 W 57th St New York NY 10019. Mailing Add: 910 S Dodge St Iowa City IA 52240

GORDIN, SIDNEY
SCULPTURE, EDUCATOR
b Cheliabinsk, Russia, Oct 24, 18. Study: Cooper Union, 37-41, with Morris Kantor, Carol Harrison & Leo Katz. Work: Art Inst Chicago; Newark Mus, NJ; Walter T Chrysler Mus Art at Norfolk, Va; Southern Ill Univ; Whitney Mus Am Art, New York. Comn: Sculpture, Temple Israel, Tulsa, Okla, 59 & Envoy Towers, New York, 60. Exhib: Metrop Mus Art, New York, 51; Whitney Ann, 52-57; Mus Mod Art, New York; Art Inst Chicago; Pa Acad Fine Arts, 54 & 55; Brooklyn Mus, NY; Newark Mus; San Francisco Mus Art, Calif; Oakland Art Mus, Calif; Philbrook Art Ctr, Tulsa, Okla, 60; one-man shows, New Sch for Social Res, 57, de Young Mem Mus, San Francisco & Los Angeles Co Mus Art, Los Angeles, Calif. Teaching: Instr, Pratt Inst, 53-58, Brooklyn Col, 55-58, New Sch for Social Res, 56-58, Sarah Lawrence Col, 57-58 & Univ Calif, Berkeley, 58- Mailing Add: 903 Camilia St Berkeley CA 94710

GORDLEY, MARILYN F M
PAINTER, EDUCATOR
b St Louis, Mo, Aug 4, 29. Study: Washington Univ, BFA; Univ Okla, MFA; Ohio State Univ, doctoral study. Work: Greenville Art Ctr, NC; Spring Mills, Lancaster, SC; Univ Okla; NC Nat Bank, Greenville. Comn: Portraits of Gov Kerr Scott, Arthur Tyler, Henry Belk, Elmer Browning & Weldell Smiley, ECarolina Univ, 64-74. Exhib: Nat Acad Design, New York, 64 & 68; 18th Irene Leache Mem Exhib, Norfolk, Va, 66; XXII Am Drawing Biennial, Norfolk (Smithsonian traveling exhib), 67; Cent South Exhib, Nashville, Tenn, 69; Nat Drawing Exhib, Southern Ill Univ, Carbondale, 75; two-man shows, High Point Art Exhib Ctr, NC, 77, Kinston Art Ctr, NC, 78 & Mark Twain S Co Bank, St Louis, Mo, 78. Teaching: Assoc prof drawing & painting, ECarolina Univ, 64- Awards: 18th Irene Leache Award, Norfolk Mus, 66; Spring Mills First Prize, 67; Cent South Exhib Award, 69. Mem: Am Asn Univ Women; Col Art Asn Am; NC Artists Asn. Style & Technique: Dimensional realism. Media: Oil. Mailing Add: 105 Dalebrook Circle Greenville NC 27834

GORDLEY, METZ TRANBARGER
PAINTER
b Cedar Rapids, Iowa, May 24, 32. Study: Wash Univ, BFA; Univ Okla, MFA; Ohio State Univ; Univ NC, Chapel Hill. Work: Greenville Art Ctr, NC; NC Nat Bank Collection, Charlotte; NC State Soc Print & Drawings, Raleigh. Comn: Aycock portrait for E Carolina Univ. Exhib: Watercolor USA, Springfield, Mo, 66, Traveling Show, 66-67; one-man shows, Kate Lewis Gallery, ECarolina Univ, 74 & Mint Mus, Charlotte, NC, 78; two-person shows, High Point Exhib Ctr, High Point, NC, 77 & Mark Twain S Co Bank, St Louis, Mo, 78; 11th Ann Piedmont Graphics Exhib, Greenville Co Mus Art, SC, 74; 21st Ann Drawing & Small Sculpture Show, Ball State Univ Art Gallery, 75; 1975 Biennial Exhib Piedmont Painting & Sculpture, Mint Mus, Charlotte, NC, 75; plus others. Teaching: Prof painting, ECarolina Univ, 59-, actg dean, Sch of Art, 77. Awards: First Prize, NC Print & Drawing Soc, 66; Second Prize for Watercolor & Second Prize for Oil, Kinston Art Show, 68. Bibliog: Book review in Southeastern Art Rev, 72; Emily Farnham (auth), Behind a Laughing Mask, Charles Demuth. Mem: Assoc Artists NC (bd mem, 66-67); Col Art Asn. Style & Technique: Structured realist. Media: Oil. Mailing Add: 105 Dalebrook Greenville NC 27834

GORDON, ALBERT F
ART DEALER
b Antwerp, Belg, June 18, 34; US citizen. Study: City Col of New York, BA, 55; Columbia Univ, MA, 60. Pos: Pres, Tribal Arts Galleries, Inc, New York, 69- Specialty: African art. Mailing Add: 35 E Ninth St New York NY 10003

GORDON, ANNE W
ART LIBRARIAN
b New York, NY, Jan 3, 33. Study: Swarthmore, BA; Radcliffe, MA(art hist); Univ Pittsburgh, MLS. Pos: Librn in Charge, Art Division, Carnegie Libr, Pittsburgh, Pa, 70- Mem: Art Libr Soc NAm (chmn Pittsburgh chap, 78). Mailing Add: 2208 Shady Ave Pittsburgh PA 15217

GORDON, JOHN
ART DEALER, COLLECTOR
b Philadelphia, Pa, June 30, 21. Study: Philadelphia Mus Sch; Pa Acad; NY Univ; Art Students League; Barnes Found. Work: Philadelphia Mus; Monmouth Mus, Lincroft, NJ. Exhib: New Talent Painting Exhib, New York, 48. Collections Arranged: American Pottery, IBM Gallery, New York, 69; 200 Years of American Pottery, Wilton Hist Soc, Conn, 70; Masterpieces of American Folk Art, 75. Pos: Curatorial assoc, Philadelphia Mus, 48-51; dir, John Gordon Gallery, 65-; folk art prof consult, Educreative Systs, New York, 64; guest cur, Monmouth Mus, NJ, 75. Awards: First Prize for Paintings, Philadelphia Sketch Club, 45, Second Prize, 46; First Prize, Best Design of Our Century, Albright Inst, Buffalo, 45. Bibliog: Whitney Balliett (auth), Profile, New Yorker Mag, 73. Mem: Art Students League; Arch Am Art. Specialty: American folk art; nonacademic paintings. Collection: American pottery, folk art and paintings. Mailing Add: 37 W 57th St New York NY 10019

GORDON, JOHN
ART ADMINISTRATOR, ART HISTORIAN
b Brooklyn, NY, Jan 20, 12. Study: Dartmouth Col, AB, 34. Pos: Admin asst circulating exhibs, Mus Mod Art, New York, 44-46; secy, Brooklyn Mus, 46-52, cur paintings & sculpture, 52-59; cur, Whitney Mus Am Art, 59-69; dir, Soc Four Arts, Palm Beach, Fla, 69-77; retired. Mem: Corp mem MacDowell Colony; Drawing Soc (adv bd); Am Fedn Arts; Arch Am Art; Nat Trust Hist Preserv. Res: Nineteenth and twentieth century American paintings and sculpture. Publ: Auth, Geometric Abstraction in America, 62; auth, Louise Nevelson, 67; auth, Isamu Noguchi, 68; auth, Franz Kline, 69; auth, Jim Dine, 70. Mailing Add: 596 N County Rd Palm Beach FL 33480

GORDON, JOHN S
SCULPTOR, EDUCATOR
b Milwaukee, Wis, Nov 16, 46. Study: Antioch Col, BA, 70; Claremont Grad Sch, MFA, 73. Exhib: Whitney Mus Am Art, Biennial Contemp Am Art, New York, 75; Southland Video Anthology, Long Beach Mus Art, Calif, 75; Collage & Assemblage in Southern Calif, Los Angeles Inst Contemp Art, 75; 100 plus Current Concerns, Los Angeles Inst Contemp Art, 77; Los Angeles Show, San Francisco Art Inst Gallery, 78; one-man show, Los Angeles Louver Gallery, Venice, Calif, 77. Teaching: Instr ceramics, Mt St Mary's Col, Los Angeles, 73; asst prof sculpture & ceramics, Univ Southern Calif, 73- Awards: Cash Award, Calif-Hawaii Regional, San Diego, 72; individual artist's grant, Nat Endowment for the Arts, 76; res & publ grant, Univ of Southern Calif, 77. Bibliog: Article in, Artweek, 5/13/72; Ted Forhead (auth), Clay sampler, Artweek, 4/23/74; NEA Artist's Grants, Art in Am, 11-12/76; Susan C Larsen, John S Gordon, Arts Mag, 3/77. Mem: Col Art Asn of Am; Los Angeles Inst Contemp Art. Style & Technique: Situational sculpture, with additive environmental elements. Media: Wood, Glass, Assemblage. Mailing Add: 23 Market St Venice CA 90291

GORDON, JONI
ART DEALER, COLLECTOR
b Cleveland, Ohio, Sept 24, 36. Study: Univ Calif, Los Angeles, BS, 58, cert(eng, anthrop). Exhibitions Arranged: Martha Alf, Barnsdall Municipal Gallery, Los Angeles, 77; Tom

Holste, Mus of Mod Art, New York, 76; Christopher Georgesco, La Jolla Mus of Contemp Art, Calif & Los Angeles Co Mus of Art, 76; Jean St Pierre, Grossmont Col, San Diego, 77, Claremont Col Gallery, Calif & Newport Harbor Art Mus, 78; Wade Saunders, Bob Bates, Tom Holste, Lauren Rothstein, Sidney Gordin, Robert Walker and Astrid Preston, 77, Jean St Pierre, Christopher Georgesco, Denise Gale, Jon Peterson, Martha Alf, Louie Lunetta, Brian Miller, San Diego Artists, Jeff Price, David Amico, Jonathan Thomas & Rudi Gernrich, 78, Newspace, Los Angeles. Teaching: Lectr contemp painting & sculpture, Univ Southern Calif, Univ Calif Los Angeles Extension, 78. Pos: Dir Newspace Gallery, Los Angeles. Mem: Contemp Art Coun; Ethnic Art Coun; Univ Calif Los Angeles Art Coun. Specialty: Contemporary Los Angeles painting and sculpture; 20th century Masterworks (DeKooning, Kline, Motherwell, Rothko, Calder); Books by artists. Collection: Twentieth century American; emphasis on contemp painting and sculpture; Southwest American Indian. Publ: Auth, Mongraphs, Robert Irwin, Edward Keinholz, Vija Celmins & Allan Kaprow, 73; auth, Art From, Los Angeles Inst of Contemp Art, J no 1, 74; auth, Remember Her, Los Angeles Inst Contemp Art, J no 3, 75; auth, Private Words, Cunningham Press, 76. Mailing Add: c/o Newspace Gallery 5015 Melrose Ave Los Angeles CA 90038

GORDON, JOSEPHINE
PAINTER
b Walla-Walla, Wash. Study: Univ Guadalajara, with Maria Medina; Ariz State Univ, with Dr Harry Wood; Sedona Art Ctr, Ariz, with Nassan Abiskhairoun; also with A E Park, William Kimura & Wassily Sommer, Anchorage, Alaska; and with Perry Acher, Seattle, Wash. Work: Bank of North Anchorage; Art Timm, CPA, Anchorage; Miller Construction Co, Anchorage; Walter Camp, LaCrosse, Wash; Alaska Seafood Corp, Homer. Exhib: All Alaska Exhib, 70 & 71; Artists of Alaska Traveling Show, 73-75; one-woman show, Artique, Ltd, 73-75. Bibliog: Lael Morgan (auth), Jo Gordon, Painter, Alaska J, fall 75. Mem: Alaska Artist Guild. Style & Technique: Impressionistic. Media: Acrylic, Watercolor Dealer: Artique Ltd 314 G St Anchorage AK 99501. Mailing Add: 1521 McHugh Lane Anchorage AK 99501

GORDON, JOY L
MUSEUM DIRECTOR, EDUCATOR
b New York, NY, Jan 31, 33. Study: NY Univ, BA & MA. Collections Arranged: Contemporary Latino Americano Art, 72; Prints from the NYU Art Collection, Hudson River Mus, Yonkers, 73; Paintings & Sculpture from the NYU Art Collection, Art Gallery, Univ Notre Dame, 73; William Benton Mus Art, Univ Conn, 73; Contemporary Asian & Middle Eastern Art from the Grey Foundation Collection, 75; Report from Soho, 75; Aspects of Am Realism, 76; Prints & Techniques (with catalogue), 76; Drawing & Collage (with catalogue), 76; Contemp Israeli Crafts, 77; Am Impressionist Painting, 77; Gallery of Living Art Revisited, 78. Pos: Asst cur educ, cur & researcher pvt collections, NY Univ Art Collection, 72-74; cur, Grey Art Gallery & Study Ctr, NY Univ, 74-77; dir, Danforth Mus, Framingham, Mass, 77- Mem: Col Art Asn; Am Asn Mus (steering comt univ mus); Northeast Mus Conf; Educ Forum Mus Collab (steering comt). Publ: Auth, Introduction, Inaugural Catalog, Grey Art Gallery & Study Ctr, 75. Mailing Add: 1500 Worcester Rd Framingham MA 01701

GORDON, LEAH SHANKS
WRITER
b Sharon, Pa, May 16, 34. Study: Bryn Mawr Col, BA, 56. Pos: Art reporter & researcher, Time Mag, 64-69, asst chief reporter & researcher, 69- Res: American folk art. Publ: Auth, articles in New York Times, Sunday Art Sect, 70-74; auth, Unschooled artists, deft craftsmen in a dazzling show, Smithsonian Mag, 2/74; auth, Vanes of the wind, Natural Hist; auth, Chalk-poor man's porcelain, Americana, 1/76. Mailing Add: 313 W 57th St New York NY 10019

GORDON, MARTIN
ART DEALER, COLLECTOR
b New York, NY, Aug 15, 39. Study: Rochester Inst Technol, BS. Pos: Owner & publ (Gordon's Print Price Ann & BuHot Catalog), Martin Gordon Gallery, currently. Mem: Print Dealers Asn of Am; Art Dealers Asn. Specialty: Mid-19th through mid-20th century original prints. Mailing Add: Martin Gordon Inc 25 E 83rd St New York NY 10028

GORDON, MAXWELL
PAINTER
b Chicago, Ill, Sept 4, 10. Study: Cleveland Sch Art; John Huntington Polytech Inst, Cleveland. Work: Brandeis Univ; Ein Harod Mus, Israel; Hirshhorn Mus, Washington, DC; Palacio Bellas Artes, Mexico City, Mex. Exhib: Mus Mod Art, New York, 43 & 61; Pa Acad Fine Arts Nat Ann, 45-59; Corcoran Mus Art, Washington, DC, 47; Whitney Mus Am Art, New York, 48; one-man shows, Rose Fried Gallery, New York, 44, ACA Gallery, New York, 48-62, CDI Gallery, Mexico City, 62, Turok Wasserman Gallery, Mexico City, 64, Nios Gallery, Mexico City, 64, Sala Int, Palacio Bellas Artes, 65 & 70, Jose Maria Velasco Gallery, Mexico City, 66, Gagitario Gallery, Mexico City, 68, Misrachi Gallery, Mexico City, 75 & San Miguel Gallery, San Miguel de Allende, Mex, 66. Awards: Hon Mention/Oils, Cleveland, Ohio, 31; First Prize for Oils, Butler Inst Am Art, Youngstown, Ohio, 47; Second Honorable Mention, Corcoran Biennial, 47; Second Prize/Oils, First Exhib of Old Northwest, Springfield, Ill, 47; Third Prize, Second Exhib of Old Northwest, 49; Minnie R Stern Medal, 54; Yaddo Fels, 57 & 60. Mailing Add: Apartado Postal 5-503 Mexico City DF Mexico

GORDON, VIOLET
ILLUSTRATOR, WRITER
b Buffalo, NY, May 22, 07. Study: Albright Fine Arts Acad, with Urqhart Wilcox, Harry Jacobs, Mildred Green & Franc Root McCreery, grad (with hons); Univ Buffalo, with Dr Charles LeClair, Dorothy Shay, Ha.vey Beverman & Catherine Koenig. Work: Grosvenour Libr, Buffalo, NY; State Univ NY Buffalo. Exhib: San Francisco Worlds Fair, 35; Buffalo Soc Artists, Albright Knox Art Gallery, 63; one-man shows, Roycroft-Elbert Hubbard Mus, East Aurora, NY, 66 & Lincoln Room, Wilcox Mansion, 75. Teaching: Instr art & critic teacher, var grade schs, high schs & univs, 30-68; instr art, Fosdick Masten Sr High Sch, 55-68; assoc teacher art, Univ Buffalo, 65. Pos: Fashion illusr, Buffalo Eve Times & News, 29-33; designer, Ed Muth Co, 30-35. Awards: Outstanding Achievement Award, Assoc Arts Orgn, 73. Bibliog: Betty Ott (auth), About V Gordon, Courier-Express Newspaper, 73; Natalie Fiedler (auth), And who thought up Peter Rabbit?, Ariz Repub, 74. Mem: Nat League Am Pen Women (bd dirs); Buffalo Soc Artists. Style & Technique: From realistic to lyrical abstract expressionism; generally impressionistic style. Media: Oil, Conte Crayon. Publ: Contribr & illusr, Col Humor Mag, 29-32; contribr, Sch Arts Mag & Arts & Activities Mag; yearbk ed, Herald, 64-67; auth & illusr, Who's Who at the Zoo, 72; recorded, Libr Cong, 75. Dealer: Bonnie Flickinger 31 Nottingham Terr Buffalo NY 14216. Mailing Add: 891 Amherst Buffalo NY 14216

GORDY, ROBERT P
PAINTER
b Jefferson Island, La, Oct 14, 33. Study: La State Univ, Baton Rouge, BA & MA; State Univ Iowa; Yale Univ, Yale-Norfolk fel, 53, with Hans Hofmann. Work: Whitney Mus Am Art, New York; Corcoran Gallery, Washington, DC; Dallas Mus Fine Arts; Ft Worth Art Ctr, Tex; New Orleans Mus Art. Exhib: Am Art Exhib, 67, New Acquisitions, 68 & Biennial Exhib, 73, Whitney Mus Am Art; Winners of Exhib Artists of Southeast & Tex, New Orleans Mus Art, 68 & 72; 14 Artist Award Winners in Southeast & Southwest, Selected by Nat Coun Arts, Witte Mem Mus, San Antonio, 68; Spirit of the Comics, Inst Contemp Art, Philadelphia. Awards: Purchase Prizes, New Orleans Mus Art, 58, 67 & 71 & Dallas Mus Fine Arts, 69; Nat Coun Arts Grant, 67. Bibliog: Joseph Mashek (auth), Interview with R Gordy, Studio Int, 12/69; The character of collecting-modern, Peoria Art Mus, 70; Ted Calas (auth), The art gallery guide, 5/72. Media: Acrylic, Ink. Dealer: Galerie Simonne Stern 516 Royal St New Orleans LA 70130. Mailing Add: 2630 Bell St New Orleans LA 70119

GORE, SAMUEL MARSHALL
PAINTER, SCULPTOR
b Coolidge, Tex, Nov 24, 27. Study: Atlanta Sch Art, BFA; Miss Col, BA; Univ Ala, MA; Ill State Univ, EdD. Work: Hull Gallery, Hinds Jr Col, Raymond, Miss; Ill State Univ; Miss Univ Women; Aven Galleries, Miss Col. Comn: Mural, Van Winkle Methodist Church, Jackson, Miss, 74; portrait bust (bronze), US Sen John Stennis, Miss Wing, Civil Air Patrol, 74 & William Faulkner, Sta WJTV, Howard Lett, Jackson, Miss, 74. Exhib: One-man shows, Miss Art Asn, 57 & House Admin Comt Suite, US Capitol Bldg, 75; Nat Oils Show, 58 & Mem Show, 58, Miss Art Asn, Jackson; Sears Traveling Show, 63. Teaching: Prof drawing, painting & sculpture & head art dept, Miss Col, 52- Bibliog: Ruth Campbell (producer), Conversation with Sam Gore (video tape), Miss Educ TV, 11/75. Mem: Miss Art Asn (secy, 61, vpres, 62, pres & exhib & jury chmn, 63); Nat Art Educ Asn; Southeastern Art Educ Asn (prof mat comt). Style & Technique: Impressionism with realistic and abstract variations. Media: Oil, Watercolor, Terra Cotta, Bronze. Publ: Illusr, Mississippi Game and Fish, 58-59; illusr, Freshwater species of Mississippi, 59. Mailing Add: Art Dept Miss Col Clinton MS 39058

GORE, TOM
CURATOR, PHOTOGRAPHER
b Victoria, BC, Aug 7, 46. Study: Univ Victoria. Work: Prov Collection, Parliament Bldgs, Victoria; Vancouver Art Gallery, BC; Univ Victoria, BC. Comn: Illusr, Earth Meditations, Mike Doyle, 70 & Vancouver Island Poetry Soft Press, 74. Exhib: BC Photographers Show, Simon Fraser Univ, Vancouver, 72; Can Printmakers Showcase, Carlton Univ, Ont, 73; Vancouver Island Jury Show, Art Gallery of Greater Victoria, 73, 74 & 76; Vancouver Island Photog Exhib, Open Space Gallery, 74; Victoria Kenisis, Art Gallery of Greater Victoria, 75; one-man show, Strange Ambiance, Open Space Gallery, Victoria, BC, 76. Collections Arranged: The Grice Collection, Secession Gallery, Victoria & Victoria Five, Secession Gallery. Teaching: Instr bio-illus, Univ Victoria, 71-, lectr photog, 77-; instr photog, Camosun Col, Victoria, BC, 73- Pos: Ed art mag, Tryste, 66-68; com photogr, 69-71; cur, Secession Gallery of Photog, Victoria, 75- Awards: Hon Mention, BC Photogr Show, Simon Fraser Art Gallery, 73; First Prize, Vancouver Island Juried Show, Art Gallery of Greater Victoria, 74. Bibliog: Glen Howarth (auth), Bio-article, Victoria Press, 70; Carolyn Leier (auth), Bio-article, Arts W, 76. Mem: Open Space Arts Soc (pres, 78-); Soc for Photog Educ; Photog Hist Soc of Can. Style & Technique: Colored collages of realistic nature; unmanipulated straight photographs with minimal content. Media: Collage and photography. Res: Early Canadian photography; criticism of the literature of photography; John Thomson biography. Publ: Auth, Our Trip 1974, Hyperfocal Press, 74; bibliogr, Secession Bibliography of Photographic Literature, Secession Gallery, 76; auth, Into the Silent Land, 76 & article on Herbert Siebner & Karl Spreitz, 77, Arts W; auth, Photography in Western Canada, Print Letter 11, 77. Mailing Add: 1338 Thurlow Rd Victoria BC V8S 1L6 Can

GORELEIGH, REX
PAINTER, PRINTMAKER
b Penllyn, Pa, Sept 2, 02. Study: Pvt study with Xavier J Barile, New York; Art Inst Chicago, with Francis Chapin; Andre L'Hote Acad, Paris; sculpture with Leo Z Moll, Berlin, Ger; Art Dept, Univ Chicago. Exhib: One-man show, Strindberg Gallery, Helsinki, Finland, 35; Am Artist Gallery, Chicago, 43; Watercolor Exhib NJ Artist, Trenton Mus, 50; NJ Artist, Montclair Art Mus, 53; Realities Expanded, Nat Ctr Afro-Am Artists, 73. Pos: Assoc dir, Community Ctr, Greensboro, NC, 38-39; dir, Southside Community Art Ctr, Chicago, 42-44; dir, Princeton Group Arts, NJ, 47-53; dir & owner, Studio-on-the-Canal, Princeton, 55- Awards: Certificate Award, NJ Coun Arts, 70; Award-Grant for Mural Design, NJ State Coun Arts, 73. Bibliog: Alain L Locke (auth), The Negro in Art, Hacker Co, 40; Cedric Dover (auth), American Negro Art, New York Graphic Soc, 60; Elton C Fax (auth), 17 Black Artists, Dodd, Mead & Co, 72. Mem: Artists Equity NJ; Woodmere Art Gallery; Alain L Locke Soc Princeton Univ. Mailing Add: Studio-on-the-Canal Canal Rd Princeton NJ 08540

GORELICK, SHIRLEY
PAINTER, PRINTMAKER
b Brooklyn, NY, Jan 24, 24. Study: Brooklyn Col, BA; Teachers Col, Columbia Univ, MA. Work: Norfolk Mus, Va; Phoenix Mus, Ariz; Post Col; Nassau Community Col, NY; Aldrich Mus, Ridgefield, Conn. Exhib: 2nd Int Young Artists Pan Pac Exhib, Japan, 62; Contemp Figure: A New Realism, Suffolk Mus, Long Island, NY, 71; Women Choose Women, New York Cult Ctr, 73; 3rd Ann Contemporary Reflections, Aldrich Mus, Ridgefield, Conn, 74; 19th Nat Print Exhib, Brooklyn Mus, NY, 74; 74; one-man show, Angelski Gallery, New York, 61, Cent Hall Gallery, Port Washington, NY, 74, 76 & 78 & Soho 20 Gallery, New York, 75 & 77; Sons & Others, Queens Mus, New York, 75; Women Artists see Men, Queens Mus, New York, 75; Nothing but Nudes, Whitney Mus of Am Art, New York, 77; Ranger Fund Exhib, Nat Acad, New York, 77. Teaching: Instr painting, NShore Community Arts Ctr, Great Neck, NY, 61-; instr drawing, Nassau Co Off Cult Develop, 73-74. Pos: Head oil jury, Nat Asn Women Artists, New York, 68-69. Awards: RI Arts Festival Award, 64; Purchase Award, Nassau Community Col, 72; Creative Artists Pub Serv Fel/Painting, NY State Coun on the Arts, 75 & 76. Bibliog: Ellen Lubell (auth), rev in Arts Mag, 6/75. Mem: Women's Interart Ctr, New York ;Women in the Arts; Prof Artist Guild (vpres, 71-75); Central Hall Artists (treas, 74-78); Soho 20 Gallery (treas, 76-78). Style & Technique: Large, oversize figurative paintings involved with psychological portraiture. Media: Acrylic. Dealer: Soho 20 Gallery 99 Spring St New York NY 10012. Mailing Add: 3 Mirrielees Circle Great Neck NY 11021

GORMAN, CARL NELSON (KIN-YA-ONNY BEYEH)
PAINTER, LECTURER
b Chinle, Ariz, Oct 5, 07. Study: Los Angeles Co Art Inst, cert, fine arts night courses, 47-51, with Ejnar Hansen & Joseph Mugnaini; also illus with Norman Rockwell; blueprint reading, Santa Monica Tech Sch, 54. Work: Southwest Mus, Los Angeles, Calif; Heard Mus, Phoenix, Ariz; Navajo Tribal Mus, Window Rock, Ariz; Indian Arts & Crafts Bd, Dept Interior,

Washington, DC; Col Ganado, Ariz. Comn: Watercolor for cover illus, 56 & mosaic for cover illus, 62, Westways Mag; cover illus for Vital Issues, 72. Exhib: American Indian Painting Competition, M H De Young Mem Mus, San Francisco, 54; Seven Douglas Aircraft Art Ann, Santa Monica & El Segundo, Calif, 54-60; Inter-Tribal Indian Ceremonial, Gallup, NMex, 62 & 65; Scottsdale Indian Arts Nat, Ariz, 62, 63 & 65; 1st Ann Am Indian Paintings, US Dept Interior, Washington, DC, 64; Father & Son (with R C Gorman), Philbrook Art Ctr, Tulsa, Okla, 64; Heard Mus, Phoenix, Ariz, 65. Teaching: Instr sketching, Tuller Col, Window Rock, Ariz, 68-70; lectr art, Native Am Art Workshop, Univ Calif, Davis, 70- Pos: Tech illusr, Douglas Aircraft Co, Los Angeles, Santa Monica, Lawndale, El Segundo & Torrance, 55-63; partner, Desert Designs (silk screening), Window Rock, 63-64; mgr, Navajo Arts & Crafts Guild, Window Rock, 64-66. Awards: First Prize for Mosaic Sculpture, 9th Art Ann, Douglas El Segundo Mgt Club, 61; First Award for Paintings with New Vistas, Scottsdale Indian Arts Nat, 63; First Award for Oils, Inter-Tribal Indian Ceremonial, 65. Bibliog: Fred E Huff (prog dir), Vet Day Spec, KPHO-TV, Phoenix, 69; Carl Gorman, Navajo artist, Smoke Signals, Reno, fall 70; Art Slide Libr Catalog, Univ S Ala, 75. Media: Oil, Watercolor. Dealer: Navajo Gallery PO Box 1756 Taos NM 87571. Mailing Add: PO Box 431 Window Rock AZ 86515

GORMAN, R C
PAINTER, ART DEALER
b Chinle, Ariz, July 26, 33. Study: Northern Ariz Univ, with Jack Salter & Ellery Gibson; Mexico City Col. Work: Heard Mus, Phoenix, Ariz; Philbrook Art Ctr, Tulsa, Okla; Northern Ariz Univ, Flagstaff; Gonzaga Univ, Spokane, Wash; Santa Fe Fine Arts Mus, NMex. Comn: Dance of the Hohokam Masked Figures, St Luke's Hosp, Phoenix, 71. Exhib: Am Indian Art Exhib, Kaiser Ctr, Oakland, Calif, 66; Scottsdale Nat Indian Exhib, Ariz, 69; Santa Fe Ann Biennial Exhib, NMex, 69; Philbrook Art Ctr, Tulsa, 69; Heard Mus Guild Exhib, Phoenix, 70. Collections Arranged: US Indian Arts & Crafts Bd, Washington, DC, 68. Pos: Owner, Navajo Gallery, Taos. Awards: Grand Award, Am Indian Art Exhib, Oakland, 66; First Award, Scottsdale Nat Indian Exhib, 67; First Award, Heard Mus Guild Exhib, Phoenix, 68. Bibliog: Ronald Leal (auth), R C Gorman-the two worlds of a Navajo artist, Mankind Mag, 70; John Milton (auth), R C Gorman-interview-the American Indian speaks, SDak Rev, 70; Robert A Ewing (auth), An Indian artist & hist art-this is Gorman, NMex Mag, 71. Mem: Taos Art Asn. Media: Acrylic, Oil, Pastel. Specialty: Southwest art; Indian painters. Interest: Modern Indian painters. Collection: F Scholder, Tavlos, Pletka, C Counter, C Bissell, C Lovato, C Cannon, Kin-ya-onny Beyeh & Bob Hoasous. Publ: Contribr, 23 contemporary Indian artists, Art in Am, 72; contribr, American deserts, Nat Geog Mag, 72. Dealer: Jamison Galleries 111 E San Francisco Santa Fe NM 87501; Mary Livingston c/o Gallery II 1211 N Broadway Santa Ana CA 92701. Mailing Add: c/o Navajo Gallery PO Box 1756 Taos NM 87571

GORMAN, WILLIAM D
PAINTER, GRAPHIC ARTIST
b Jersey City, NJ, June 27, 25. Study: Newark Sch Fine & Indust Arts, NJ. Work: Newark Mus; Butler Inst Am Art, Youngstown, Ohio; Springfield Art Mus, Mo; Colorado Springs Fine Art Ctr, Colo; US Dept State, Washington, DC. Exhib: One-man show, Philadelphia Art Alliance, 65; US Dept State Art in Embassies Prog, Europe, Africa & Orient, 67-75; NJ Artists, Newark Mus, 68; US Watercolor Invitational; Seven American Watercolorists, Davenport Mus, Iowa, 73; plus others. Pos: Dir, Old Bergen Art Guild, Bayonne, NJ, 62- Awards: Henry Ward Ranger Fund Purchase Prizes, Nat Acad Design, 65 & 71; Gold Medal of Honor, Allied Artists of Am, 73; Grand Prize, Am Artists Prof League, 74; plus others. Bibliog: Henry Gasser (auth), article in Am Artist, 10/70. Mem: Assoc Nat Acad Design; Audubon Artists; Am Watercolor Soc; Allied Artists Am (pres); Nat Soc Painters Casein & Acrylic; Assoc Artists NJ. Media: Casein tempera, pen & ink drawing. Publ: Auth, articles in Today's Art Mag & Am Artist. Mailing Add: 43 W 33rd St Bayonne NJ 07002

GORNEY, JAY PHILIP
ART DEALER
b Brooklyn, NY, Sept 26, 52. Study: Oberlin Col, with Ellen H Johnson, BA(art hist), 73; Whitney Mus Independent Study Prog, fall 72. Collections Arranged: City as a Source, Whitney Mus Am Art, 72-73; Matta: Totemic World (with Patricia Hamilton), Andrew Crispo Gallery, 75. Pos: Assoc dir, Hamilton Gallery of Contemp Art, New York, currently. Res: Contemporary painting, drawing and sculpture. Publ: Auth, Oberlin's tribute to Ellen Johnson, Art News, 4/75; auth, Cynthia Carlson, Arts Mag, 10/76; auth, Barbara Zucker, Arts Mag, 1/77; auth, Review of drawing today in New York, Col Art J, winter 76/77. Mailing Add: 302 W 12th St New York NY 10019

GORSKI, DANIEL ALEXANDER
SCULPTOR, PAINTER
b Cleveland, Ohio, Oct 26, 39. Study: Cleveland Inst Art, dipl, 61; Yale Univ Sch Art & Archit, with Jack Tworkow & Al Held, BFA, 62 & MFA, 64. Work: Yale Univ. Exhib: Primary Structures, Jewish Mus, New York, 66; Cool Art, Larry Aldrich Mus, Ridgefield, Conn, 68; Yale Norfolk Summer Sch, Conn, 69; Hanging and Leaning, Emily Lowe Gallery, Hofstra Univ, 70; 26 x 26, Vassar Col Art Gallery, 71; Md Biennial Exhib, Baltimore Mus of Art, 76; Sculpture Outdoors, Temple Univ, Ambler, Pa, 77. Teaching: Instr design, painting, color & drawing, Md Inst Col Art, 71-; vis lectr art hist & fashion design, Drexel Univ, 72. Awards: Mr & Mrs Jules Horelick Award, Baltimore Mus of Art, 76. Bibliog: W Berkson (auth), In the galleries, Arts Mag, 1/66; L Lippard (auth), Recent sculpture as escape, 2/66 & Escalation in Washington, 1/68, Art Int. Mailing Add: RD 2 Box 297 Seven Valleys PA 17360

GORSKI, RICHARD KENNY
EDUCATOR, GRAPHIC ARTIST
b Green Bay, Wis, Apr 20, 23. Study: Northern Ill Univ, De Kalb, 62-65; Univ Wis, Milwaukee & Madison, MS(art educ), 46-50, study with Robert Von Nueman Sr, Dean Meeker, Donald Anderson & Fredrick Logan. Work: Milwaukee Pub Schs collection of Wis Artists. Exhib: Wis Union Gallery's Fall Salon for Wis Painters & Sculptors, Madison, 39 & 49; Wis State Centennial Salon, 48; Six State Biennial, Walker Art Inst, Minneapolis Art Inst, Minn, 47-49; Wis Painters & Sculptors Ann Spring Salon, Milwaukee Art Ctr, 60. Teaching: Instr art educ, Nat Col of Educ, Evanston, Ill, 57-60; assoc prof art educ, Northeastern Ill Univ, Chicago, 61-65; prof graphic design, Northern Mich Univ, Marquette, 65- Pos: Cur & dir, Rahr Civic Ctr & Mus, Manitowoc, Wis, 50-53; illusr & designer, John Higgs Studios, Milwaukee, Wis, 56-57; art dir, United Educators Publ Inc, Lake Bluff, Ill, 60-61; dept head, art & design, Northern Mich Univ, Marquette, 65-75. Awards: Journal Purchase Award, Wis Painters Ann, Milwaukee J Pub Schs Collection, 57; Special Merit Award, Wis Gimbels Salon, Gimbels Inc, 50. Mem: Nat Art Asn; Mich Art Educ Asn; Upper Penninsula Art Teachers Asn (sec, 66-75). Style & Technique: Mixed media, from extreme super-real plastique information to syntactical inventions in color & pattern; solutions in graphic design problems. Res: The construction of a taxonomy of human response to the physical character of light and its distribution in the optical array. Publ: Auth, Color; an article in United Educators Encycl & auth, Painting; an article in The Wonderland of Knowledge Encycl, United Educ Publ, 60. Mailing Add: 1502 N Garfield Ave Marquette MI 49855

GORSLINE, DOUGLAS WARNER
PAINTER, ILLUSTRATOR
b Rochester, NY, May 24, 13. Study: Yale Univ Sch Fine Arts; Art Students League. Work: Butler Inst Am Art, Pa; Harvard Univ Houghton Libr; Libr Cong, Washington, DC; Lehigh Univ; St Paul Gallery Art, Minn. Comn: Oil painting on basketball, Sports Illustrated, New York; oil painting on sports, Westvaco, New York. Exhib: Pa Acad Fine Arts, 63; Am Acad Arts & Lett, 64; 20th Century Am Art, San Diego, 65-66; Mainstreams, 68 & 70; Butler Inst Am Art, 72; plus many one-man shows. Teaching: Instr art, Nat Acad Sch Fine Arts. Awards: Childe Hassam Fund Purchase Award, Am Acad Arts & Lett, 62; Henry Ward Ranger Fund Purchase Award, Nat Acad Design, 63; Tiffany Found Grant, 63. Mem: Nat Acad Design. Style & Technique: Cubist realism. Media: Oil, Watercolor. Mailing Add: c/o Ted Riley 252 E 49th St New York NY 10017

GOTO, JOSEPH
SCULPTOR
b Hilo, Hawaii, Jan 7, 20. Study: Art Inst Chicago; Roosevelt Univ. Work: Art Inst Chicago; Ind Univ; Mus Mod Art, New York; Univ Mich; Union Carbide Corp. Exhib: Art Inst Chicago; Carnegie Inst; Univ Ill; J B Speed Art Mus, Louisville, Ky; Whitney Mus Am Art, New York; Retrospective, RI Sch Design, 72; plus others. Awards: Graham Found Fel, 57; John Hay Whitney Fel; Guggenheim Fel, 69; plus others. Bibliog: William S Rubin (auth), Dada, Surrealism, & Their Heritage (catalog), Mus Mod Art, 68. Mailing Add: 17 Sixth St Providence RI 02906

GOTTLIEB, ABE
COLLECTOR, PATRON
b Poland, Apr 17, 08. Study: New Sch Social Res. Pos: Chmn bd, Fedn Jewish Philanthropies & United Jewish Appeal. Collection: From Renoir to Vlaminck; School of Paris; German expressionism; paintings, sculpture from Daumier to Moore. Mailing Add: 387 Grand Ave New York NY 10002

GOTTSCHALK, FRITZ
DESIGNER, LECTURER
b Zurich, Switz, Dec 30, 37. Study: Kunstgewerbeschule, Zurich, Switz, dipl; Art Inst Orell Fussli, Zurich, dipl; Allgemeine Gewerbeschule, Basel, Switz, post-grad dipl, with E Ruder & A Hofman. Exhib: The Visual Image of the Montreal Mus, Montreal Mus Fine Arts, Que, Can, 68; Swiss Design, Mus du Louvre, Paris, France, 71; Alliance Graphique Internationale: 107 Int Designers, Milan, Italy, 74; The Work of Gottschalk & Ash Ltd, Ryder Gallery, sponsored by Container Corp of Am, Chicago, 76. Pos: Designer, art dir & design dir, Gottschalk & Ash Ltd, Montreal, Que, 66-; dir design & quality control off, Organizing Comt of 1976 Olympic Games, 74-76. Awards: Award of Excellence, Swiss Contemp Design, Dept of Interior, Swiss Govt, 62; two Awards of Excellence, Soc Publ Designers, New York, 70; Bronze Medal, Foire Int du Livre, Leipzig, EGer, 77. Bibliog: Adrian Gatrail (auth), The Image Makers, The Gazette (daily newspaper), 70; Bill Bantey (auth), Gottschalk & Ash Ltd, Graphis, Switz, Vol 148 (1972); Midori Imatake (auth), Gottschalk & Ash Ltd, Idea (Japan), Vol 115 (1973). Mem: Que Soc Graphic Artists; Royal Can Acad; Asn of Swiss Graphic Artists; Alliance Graphique Internationale; Graphic Designers of Can. Style & Technique: Contemporary graphic and industrial design. Media: Graphic Design, Books and Corporate Images. Publ: Auth & illusr for an article in Idea, Seibundo Shinkosha Publ Co, Japan, Vol 115 (1972); ed for an article in Revue Suisse de l'Imprimerie, Zollikofer AG, Switz, 74; illusr & contribr for an article in Communication Arts, Coyne & Blanchard, Inc, 75; ed for an article in Graphis, Vol 185 (1977). Mailing Add: 2050 Manfield Suite 900 Montreal PQ H3A 1Z3 Can

GOTTSCHALK, MAX JULES
DESIGNER, INSTRUCTOR
b St Louis, Mo, Dec 14, 09. Study: Painting, drawing & design with father, Max Gottschalk, Edmond Wurpel, Charles Guest, Fred Conway, E Ludwig, Goetsh, Hudson & Mylonas; Wash Univ, BA. Work: Agnese Udinotti, Scottsdale, Ariz; Robert Graham, New York. Comn: Nat indigenous product form, Newfoundland Comn Govt, 39-42; new modular chassis systs, Hughes Aircraft, Tucson, Ariz, 52-60; Scott Paper Towel holder, Gerald C Johnson Assocs, New York, 44-48; first open frozen food refrigeration, Hussmann Ligonier Co, St Louis; work on lunar escape vehicle, Bell Aerosysts, Niagara Falls, NY. Exhib: St Louis Artist Guild, 35 & St Louis Art Mus, 36; St John's, Nfld, 40-42; Mus Mod Art, New York, 48-50; Int Canvas Exhib, Tokyo, 75; plus others. Teaching: Instr design, drawing & perception & chmn art & design dept, Pima Community Col, Tucson, 70-75, instr functional design, interior decoration & graphics & chmn design, decorating & drafting dept, 75-76. Style & Technique: Contemporary and functional. Dealer: Stan Schuman 545 S Russell Ave Tucson AZ; The Contemp Craftsman 112 Don Gaspar Santa Fe NM. Mailing Add: 5620 N Campbell Tucson AZ 85718

GOUGH, ROBERT ALAN
PAINTER
b Quebec, PQ, Aug 13, 31; US citizen. Study: Am Acad Art, Chicago, with William H Mosby & J Allen St John. Work: Am Fedn Arts; Butler Inst Am Art; Univ Nebr; Sheldon Swope Art Gallery; Marietta Col. Exhib: Painting & Sculpture Today, Herron Mus Art, 66; one-man shows, Gilman Galleries, Chicago, 67 & 69 & Univ of the South, 75; 35 Years in Retrospect, Butler Inst Am Art, 71; Mainstreams, Marietta Col, 74, 75 & 77; plus others. Awards: Henry Ward Ranger Purchase Prize, Nat Acad Design, 62; Friends of Am Art Purchase Prize, Butler Inst Am Art, 62; Mainstreams Purchase Prize, 74. Bibliog: Documentary, WBNS-TV, Columbus, Ohio, 70. Style & Technique: Southern Ohio landscape realism with emphasis on compositional design, texture and light. Media: Oil, Pencil. Dealer: Everett Oehlschlaeger Galleries Inc 107 E Oak St Chicago IL 60611; Harmon Gallery 1258 Third St S Naples FL 33940. Mailing Add: 220 Brookside Dr Chillicothe OH 45601

GOULD, CHESTER
CARTOONIST
b Pawnee, Okla, Nov 20, 00. Study: Okla A&M Univ, 19-21; Northwestern Univ, grad, 23. Pos: Cartoonist, Hearst Publ, 24-29, Chicago Tribune, 31-, creator cartoon Dick Tracy, 31. Mem: Nat Cartoonists Soc. Mailing Add: PO Box 191 Woodstock IL 60098

GOULD, JOHN HOWARD
PAINTER, FILM MAKER
b Toronto, Ont, Aug 14, 29. Study: Ont Col Art, AOCA, 52; Acad Julian, Paris, 52. Work: Nat Gallery Can; Montreal Mus Fine Arts; Beaverbrook Mus, Fredericton, NB; plus others in pvt collections. Comn: Portrait of Alan Jarvis, Head of Nat Gallery Can, Ottawa, 62; Pikangikum (drawn film of Indians), Nat Film Bd Can, 67; performance drawings of Marcel

Marceau, City Ctr, New York, 71; drawm drawn film of Marceau, Paris. 71. Exhib: Canadian Surrealism Today, touring exhib, 64; Focus on Drawing, Int Drawing Survey, Art Gallery Toronto, 65; Retrospective, Univ Toronto, 65; Can rep, Films on Art Category, Venice Biennale, 66; Flint Inst Arts Survey Exhib, 66. Awards: Greenshield Award for Figurative Painting, Spain, 60; Can Coun Grants, Drawn Film of Peru, 67 & Drawn Film of Japan, 70. Bibliog: Alan Jarvis (auth), John Gould, Can Art Mag, 61; John Griffin (dir), John Gould on Drawing (film), Gesture Productions, 72; included in The Nude in Canadian Painting, New Press, Can, 72. Mem: Royal Can Acad. Style & Technique: Figurative painter and draughtsman working in films employing drawing, music, and narration. Dealer: Arwin Galleries 222 Grand River W Detroit MI 48226. Mailing Add: Cedar St Waubaushene ON Can

GOULD, STEPHEN
SCULPTOR, COLLECTOR
b New York, NY, Dec 25, 09. Study: New Sch Social Res, with Manola Pascal. Work: Newark Mus, NJ; Morris Mus Fine Art, NJ; Miami Mus Mod Art, Fla; Washington Co Mus Fine Arts, Hagerstown, Md; Allen R Hite Art Inst, Univ Louisville. Exhib: Nat Exhib Prof Artists, New York, 65; New Sch Social Res, 67; Nat Soc Arts & Lett, Seamans Bank, NY, 69; Nat Coun Jewish Women, South Orange, NJ, 71; Salmagundi Club, 75. Pos: Art lectr, Bermuda Club, Tamarac, Fla, 74- Awards: Award of Month for Heart of Humanity, Washington Co Mus Art, 70; First Prize for I Protest (bronze sculpture), Soc l'Ecole Francais, 71-72; First Prize for We are the Clay & Thou Lord our Potter, De Bellis, Salmagundi Club, 75. Bibliog: M Pescara (auth), Sculptor-Stephen Gould, Am Rev Art & Sci, 69. Mem: Royal Soc Arts; Nat Soc Arts & Lett; Artists Equity Asn; Salmagundi Club. Style & Technique: Depicting human events rather than art objects. Media: Clay. Collection: Oils, French impressionist and post impressionist; prints, lithographs, watercolors, numismatics, glass; violin collection. Mailing Add: 4905 Bayberry Lane Tamarac FL 33319

GOULDS, PETER J
ART DEALER, DESIGNER
b London, Eng, Oct 5, 48. Teaching: Lectr commun design, Leeds Polytechnic, Yorkshire, Eng, 72; vis lectr video workshop & design, Univ Calif, Los Angeles, 72-75. Pos: Owner, LA Louver Gallery, Venice, Calif, 76- Awards: Leverhulme Award, Uni-Lever Trust, 71; Shell fel, Manchester Polytechnic, 71-72; univ res grants, Univ Calif, 72, 73 & 74. Specialty: Contemporary American, English painting, sculpture and video; 19th century European literature and art, 1910-1930. Mailing Add: c/o LA Louver Gallery 55 S Venice Blvd Venice CA 90291

GOULET, CLAUDE
EDUCATOR, PAINTER
b Montreal, Que, June 5, 25. Study: Univ Montreal, LScBioChem. Work: Mus of Montreal, Que; Mus of Que, Montreal; Nat Gallery Can, Ottawa; Cult Art Ctr of Can, Paris; Yoseido Gallery, Tokyo, Japan. Comn: Mural (30 ft x 10 ft), Univ Montreal, 67; mural, Negresco Nice, France, 66; mural, Radio Can, Montreal, 70; mural (9 ft x 8 ft), Toronto Dominion Ctr, Ont, 71; mobile sculpture, Thetford Mines, Asbestos Ctr, Que, 75. Exhib: Que Mus, Quebec, 69; Negresco, Nice, France, 70; 3rd Int Exhib, Cagnes-sur-Mer, France, 71; Can Cult Ctr, Paris, 71; Zwarte Panter Gallery, Anvers, Belg, 72; Neuilly-sur-Seine, Paris, 74; Galerie G Wolf, Deauville, France, 75. Teaching: Instr art environment, Univ Que, Quebec, 75- Awards: Can Art Coun grant, 70; Min of Cult Affairs grant, Prov Que, 71; Nat Prize, 3rd Int Festival, Cagnes-sur-Mer, France, 71. Bibliog: Articles in Vie Des Arts, 77. Mem: Royal Can Acad; Asn of Prof Artists, Que (vpres, 65-69); Can Soc of Artists. Media: Oil, acrylic and sand. Mailing Add: 101 Pl Charles LeMoyne Apt 1820 Longueuil PQ J4K 4Y9 Can

GOULET, LORRIE (LORRIE J DE CREEFT)
SCULPTOR, INSTRUCTOR
b Riverdale, NY, Aug 17, 25. Study: Inwood Potteries Studios, New York, 32-36, with Amiee Voorhees; Black Mountain Col, with Josef Albers; sculpture with Jose de Creeft, 43-44. Work: Sarah Roby Found; Joseph H Hirshhorn Collection; NJ State Mus; Sen William Benton; Ball State Univ Art Gallery. Comn: Ceramic relief, New York Pub Libr, Grand Concourse, Bronx, 58; ceramic relief, Nurses' Residence & Sch, Bronx Munic Hosp, 61; stainless steel relief, 48th Precinct Police & Fire Sta, Bronx, 71. Exhib: Mother & Child in Modern Art, Am Fedn Arts, 63; World Trade Fairs, Algiers, Barcelona & Zagreb, 64; Collectors Choice, Philbrook Art Ctr, 64; Dimensions 69, Temple Emein, NJ, 69; Outdoor Sculpture Show, Van Saun Park, NJ, 71; one-artist shows, Clay Club Sculpture Ctr, New York, 48 & 55 Cheney Libr, Hoosick Falls, NY, 51, Contemporaries Gallery, New York, 59, 62, 66 & 68, Rye Art Ctr, NY, 66, New Sch Assocs, New York, 68, Temple Emeth, Teaneck, NJ, 69 & Kennedy Galleries, New York, 71 & 73-75; plus many other group & one-man shows. Teaching: Instr sculpture-var media & staff mem, Mus Mod Art, New York, 57-64; sculpture staff mem, Scarsdale Studio Workshop, 59-61 & New Sch Social Res, 61-75. Pos: Guest demonstr, Around the Corner, New York Dept Educ, CBS-TV, 64-65. Awards: First Sculpture Prize, Norton Gallery, 49 & 50 & Westchester Art Soc, 64; Soltan Engel Mem Award, Audubon Artists, 67. Mem: Sculptors Guild; Audubon Artists; founding mem Visual Artists & Galleries Asn; Nat Comt Art Educ; Rye Art Ctr (bd dirs); Westchester Art Soc. Style & Technique: Direct carving; semi-abstract; representational figures. Media: Stone, Wood, Ceramics. Publ: Contribr, 20th century sculptors look at their work, The Palette; auth article on greenstone, In: Slate & Soft Stones, 71. Dealer: Kennedy Galleries 40 W 57th St New York NY 10022. Mailing Add: 241 W 20th St New York NY 10011

GOUMA-PETERSON, THALIA
ART HISTORIAN
b Athens, Greece, Nov 21, 33; US citizen. Study: Mills Col, BA(art), 54, MA(art hist), 57; Univ Wis, PhD(art hist), 63. Teaching: Inst art hist, Univ Wis, 58; inst art hist, Oberlin Col, 60-61; asst prof art hist, Col of Wooster 68-76 & prof art hist 76- Mem: Nat Comt for Byzantine Studies; Col Art Asn; Medieval Acad of Am; Int Ctr of Medieval Art; Women's Caucus for Art (adv bd). Publ: Auth, The dating of Creto-Venetian icons: a reconsideration in light of new evidence, Allen Mem Art Mus Bull, fall 72; auth, A Palaeologan Icon of St Nicholas, Byzantine, Greek and Russian Icons, Univ Col, Cardiff, Wales, 73; auth, The Parecclesion of St Euthymios in Thessalonika: art and monastic policy under Andronicos II, Art Bull, Vol 3 (1976): 168-183; auth, Piero della Francesca's Flagellation: An Historical Interpretation, Storia dell' Arte, Vol 28 (1976): 219-233; auth Christ as Ministrant and the Priest as Ministrant Christ in a Palaeologan Program of 1303, Dumbarton Oaks Papers, 78. Mailing Add: Art Ctr Col of Wooster Wooster OH 44691

GOUREVITCH, JACQUELINE
PAINTER
b Paris, France, Oct 28, 33; US citizen. Study: Black Mountain Col, NC, 50; Art Students League, 52; Univ Chicago, BA, 54; Art Inst Chicago, 54-55. Work: Chase Manhattan Bank; Am Acad of Arts & Lett, New York; Skidmore, Owings & Merrill, New York; Ball State Univ Mus, Muncie, Ind; Univ Art Mus, Berkeley, Calif. Exhib: One-woman shows, Tibor de Nagy Gallery, New York, 71, 72 & 73, Wadsworth Atheneum Mus, Hartford, Conn, 75, Wesleyan Univ, Conn, 77 & Fischbach Gallery, New York, 78. Painting & Sculpture Today, Indianapolis Mus Art, 72; Whitney Mus Am Art Ann, 73; MacNay Art Inst, San Antonio, Tex, 74; plus others. Teaching: Vis artist drawing & painting, Wesleyan Univ, 67-71; Hartford Art Sch, Univ Hartford, 73-; vis artist, Univ Calif, Berkeley, 74, Vassar Col, 77 & Univ of Houston, 78. Awards: Artist in Residence, Tamarind Inst, Albuquerque, NMex, 73; Purchase Award, Am Acad Arts & Lett, New York, 73; grants, Nat Endowment for the Arts, 76 & Conn Comn for the Arts, 76. Bibliog: Articles in Artforum, 66, 71 & 74 & New York Times, var times, 66-73. Media: Oil, Drawing. Publ: Auth article & contribr reprod, In: Art Now: New York, fall 71. Dealer: Fischbach Gallery 29 W 57th St New York NY 10019. Mailing Add: 13 Red Orange Rd Middletown CT 06457

GOVAN, FRANCIS HAWKS
EDUCATOR, PAINTER
b Marianna, Ark, Dec 19, 16. Study: Hendrix Col, BA; Art Inst South, Memphis; Univ Wis; Layton Sch Art; Columbia Univ, MA; San Miguel, Mex. Exhib: Am Watercolor Exhib, France, 53-55; one-man shows, Feigl Gallery, New York, 54, 55 & 56; retrospective, Brooks Mem Art Gallery, Memphis, 57 & 66; Kunst Am, 57-58; Art in the Embassies & Smithsonian Inst, 67-68. Teaching: Instr art & creative dramatics, Milwaukee Univ Sch, 43-45; assoc prof art, Hendrix Col, 45-52; prof art, Memphis State Univ, 56- Pos: Instr & occup therapist, Rockland State Hosp, Orangeburg, NY, 52-54; freelance artist, New York, 54-55; educ dir, Brooks Mem Art Gallery, 55-56; cur exhibs, Memphis State Univ, 57-67. Awards: First Prize in Watercolor, Memphis Biennial, 46; Carnegie Found Grants Res Ark Pottery Clays, 49 & Mus Fine Art, 50. Media: Oil, Watercolor. Publ: Illusr, Arkansas pioneer days, Ark Gazette Sun Suppl, 48-49; auth, Art—what is it?, 59 & My last duchess, 65, Educ Quest. Mailing Add: 540 Hawthorne Memphis TN 38112

GRABACH, JOHN R
PAINTER, INSTRUCTOR
b Greenfield, Mass. Study: Art Students League, with George B Bridgeman, Frank V DuMond, Kenyen Cox & H August Schwabe. Work: Philadelphia Art Alliance; Art Inst Chicago; Vanderpoel Art Asn, Chicago; John Herron Art Inst, Indianapolis; Corcoran Gallery Art, Washington, DC; plus many pvt collections. Exhib: Springfield Art Mus, Mass; Audubon Artists, Nat Acad Galleries; Pa Acad Fine Arts, Philadelphia; Nat Acad Design, New York; Detroit Inst Arts; plus many other group & one-man shows. Teaching: Heritage, South Orange, NJ; instr, Newark Sch Fine & Indust Art. Awards: Peabody Prize, Art Inst Chicago; Sesnan Gold Medal, Pa Acad Fine Arts; Preston Harrison Prize, Los Angeles Co Mus Art; plus many others. Mem: Philadelphia Watercolor Club; Audubon Artists; Salmagundi Club; Nat Acad Design. Publ: Auth, How to Draw the Human Figure. Mailing Add: 915 Sanford Ave Irvington NJ 07111

GRADO, ANGELO JOHN
PAINTER, ILLUSTRATOR
b New York, NY, Feb 17, 22. Study: Art Students League, with Robert Brackman; Nat Acad Design, with Robert Philipp & Frank Reilly. Exhib: Am Watercolor Soc Exhibs, var times, 58-71; Allied Artists Am Exhibs, 61-75; Nat Acad Design, New York, 63; Am Artists Prof League, New York, 63-77; Hudson Valley Art Asn, 69-77. Pos: Freelance art dir, 55-72; deleg, Fine Arts Fedn New York, 73-77. Awards: Salmagundi Club Prize, 69; Am Artists Prof League Awards, 69, 70 & 73; Hudson Valley Art Asn Awards, 69, 70 & 72. Bibliog: Billi Boros (auth), New talent, Art Times Mag, 64. Mem: Am Watercolor Soc; Am Artists Prof League (vpres, 72-); Hudson Valley Art Asn. Style & Technique: Realistic, based on the knowledge and standards of the Old Masters. Media: Oil, Watercolor, Pastel. Dealer: Portraits Inc 41 E 57th St New York NY 10022. Mailing Add: 641 46th St Brooklyn NY 11220

GRADY, RUBY MCLAIN
PAINTER, SCULPTOR
b Bedford Co, Va, Jan 11, 34. Study: Corcoran Sch Art, Washington, DC, with Richard Lahey; Md Univ, with Pietro Lazzari. Work: Am Fine Art Exhibs, Washington, DC; NASA Gemini Collection, Washington, DC; Imprimerie Arte Galerie Maeght, Paris, France. Exhib: Md Artist Today, Md Travel Exhib, Peale Mus, Baltimore, 68; Washington Artist Exhib, Columbia Mus Art, SC, 72; Artist Equity Tour Exhib, Macon Mus Arts & Sci, Ga, 73; Washington Artist Exhib, Birmingham Mus Art, Ala, 73; Nat Exhib, Hanover Gallery, New York, 74. Pos: Art illusr, FBI, Washington, DC, 52-55. Awards: Audubon Nat Soc Best in Show, 71; Art in Govt Bldg Int Competition Award, US Dept Housing & Urban Develop, 72; Annapolis Fine Arts Exhib Award for Metal Sculpture, 74; Md Biennial Exhib, Baltimore Mus of Art, 76; Washington Artist Photog Exhib, Corcoran Gallery, Washington, DC, 77. Bibliog: Frank Getlein (auth), Work of Ruby Grady, Brooks/Johnson, 71; Allen Smith (auth), Solo Exhibit in Washington, WTTG-TV 5 presentation, 72; Ruth Dean (auth), Profile of artist Ruby Grady, Washington Star News, 72. Mem: Artist Equity; Group 74, Washington, DC. Style & Technique: Art practice begun by Marcel Duchamp in which exploration is carried on. Media: Steel, Acrylic. Publ: Illusr, Investigator, 54-55; illusr, Virginia Beach Exhib Catalog, 60; contribr, Nat Community Arts Prog Publ, Govt Printing Off, 70; contribr, Washington Artists Directory, 71 & 78; contribr, Am Inst Archit Yearbk, 73. Dealer: A M Sachs Sachs Gallery 29 W 57th St New York NY 10019; J M Yeatts Yeatts Gallery 364 Walnut Ave SW Roanoke VA 24016. Mailing Add: Potowmack Bay Studio 431 Broadcreek Dr Ft Washington MD 20022 Washington DC Potowmack Bay Studio 431 Broadcreek Dr Ft Washington MD 20022

GRAESE, JUDY (JUDITH ANN)
PYROGRAPHY, ILLUSTRATOR
b Loveland, Colo, Nov 8, 40. Study: Augustana Col, 58-59; Univ Colo, Boulder, 65-67. Work: Nat City Bank, Denver, Colo. Exhib: One-man show, Two-Twenty Two Gallery, El Paso, Tex, 71-72 & 73, The Artisan, Princeton, NJ, 72 & 74 & Bishop's Antiques & Gallery, Scottsdale, Ariz, 73-78; De Colores, Denver, 73-78; Reflections Gallery, St Louis, Mo, 73-74. Pos: Designer, display dept, May D&F, 67-69. Bibliog: Rena Andrews (auth), The fine arts, 11/25/73 & Robert Downing (auth), Ad Lib, 2/2/75, Denver Post Roundup Sect; Betty Harvey (auth), Judy Graese, Artists of the Rockies, 5/75. Style & Technique: Vaguely pre-raphaelite, medieval thematic material in clear flowing movement of line. Media: Wood of great sculptural or colored qualities for basis of design burned into wood. Publ: Illusr, The Song of Francis, Northland Press, 73; illusr, The Treasure is the Rose, Pantheon Press, 73. Mailing Add: 2055 S Franklin Denver CO 80210

GRAHAM, BILL (WILLIAM KARR)
CARTOONIST
b Coshocton, Ohio, Dec 14, 20. Study: Centenary Col, BS(social sci), 42. Work: Syracuse Univ; Univ Mo; Univ Kans; Univ Cincinnati; Va Mil Inst. Exhib: Pavilion D'Humor, Montreal, 71; Nat Cartoonists Soc Traveling Exhib; Asn Am Ed Cartoonists Traveling Exhib. Mem: Nat Cartoonists Soc; Asn Am Ed Cartoonists. Publ: Ed cartoonist, Ark Gazette, 48- Mailing Add: Arkansas Gazette Little Rock AR 72203

GRAHAM, DANIEL H
CONCEPTUAL ARTIST
b Urbana, Ill, Mar 31, 42. Work: Tate Gallery, London; Stadisches Mus, Monchengladbach, Ger; Allen Art Mus, Oberlin, Ohio. Exhib: Konzeption-Conception, Stadisches Mus, Leverkusen, Ger, 69; Information, Mus Mod Art, New York, 70; Sonsbeck '71, Arheim, Holland, 71; Documenta V, Kassel, Ger, 72; Kunst Gleit Kunst, Projekt '74, Cologne, Ger, 74. Awards: Creative Artists Pub Serv Multi Media Grant, New York State Coun Arts, 73-74; Artists-in-Berlin, Ger Acad Serv, 76. Style & Technique: Video, film, performance and architectural projects. Publ: Auth, End Moments, 69; auth, 1966, 70; auth, Performance, 70; auth, Selected works, 1965-72, For Publication, 76 & Films, 77. Dealer: Lisson Gallery 66-68 Bell St London NW1 Eng; Sperone Westwater Fischer 142 Greene St New York NY 10012. Mailing Add: Box 380 Knickerbocker Sta New York NY 10002

GRAHAM, F LANIER
ART ADMINISTRATOR, EDUCATOR
b Shawnee, Okla, Mar 6, 40. Study: Kenyon Col, 58-60; Am Univ, 61-63; Columbia Univ, 63-66, MA, 66; NY Univ Inst Fine Arts, 66-67. Work: Chess set, Mus Mod Art, New York & Mus Arts Decoratifs, Paris. Teaching: Adj mem grad fac, Univ Calif Berkeley & Lone Mountain Col, 74- Pos: Mus asst, Phillips Collection, Washington, DC, 62-63; assoc cur, Mus Mod Art, New York, 65-70; deputy dir, Exhib & Publ & chief cur, Fine Arts Museums of San Francisco, 70-76; ed, The Libr of Sacred Art, 75-; pres, Inst for Aesthetic Develop, 75-; exec dir, Ctr for Advan Study of Cultural Planning, 75-; dir, Calif Inst of Asian Studies, 77- Mem: Col Art Asn Am (local chmn nat conv, 72); Soc Archit Historians. Publ: Auth, A History of Chess Sets, Walker, 68; auth, Hector Guimard, Mus Mod Art, 70; auth, Three Centuries of American Painting, 71 & auth, Masterpieces of French Art from the Norton Simon Collections, 73, San Francisco Mus; ed, The Rainbow Book, 75. Mailing Add: M H De Young Mem Mus Golden Gate Park San Francisco CA 94118

GRAHAM, JAMES
ART DEALER
Pos, Owner, Graham Gallery. Mailing Add: 1014 Madison Ave New York NY 10021

GRAHAM, JOHN MEREDITH, II
ART ADMINISTRATOR
b Floyd Co, Ga, Dec 23, 05. Study: Lehigh Univ, 27-28; study in Paris, 29-31; New York Sch Fine & Appl Arts, grad, 31; study in Rome, 35-36. Teaching: Lectr fine arts; frequent radio & TV speaker. Pos: Cur decorative arts, Brooklyn Mus, 39-60; dir & cur collections, Colonial Williamsburg, 50-70, vpres, 61-70; circulated Wedgwood Exhib throughout mus in US & Can, 48; completed restoration & furnishings interior, Van Cortlandt Manor House for Sleepy Hollow Restoration, 58; adv, White House Fine Arts Comt; mem hon bd gov, Wedgwood Int Sem; trustee & consult, Campbell Mus. Mem: Soc Archit Historians; Eng Ceramic Circle; Pewter Collectors Club New York (past vpres). Publ: Auth, Popular art in America, 39; ed, Old Pottery & Porcelain Marks, 47; co-auth, Wedgwood, a Living Tradition, 48; auth, American Pewter, 49; contribr, Antiques & Am Collector. Mailing Add: Libby House Mentone AL 35984

GRAHAM, K M
PAINTER
b Hamilton, Ont, Can, Sept 9, 13. Study: Univ Toronto, BA. Work: Art Gallery Ont; Art Bank Can, Ottawa; Edmonton Art Gallery, Alta; Art Gallery, Univ Guelph, Ont; Toronto Dom Bank, Toronto, Ont & Montreal, Que; plus others. Exhib: Art Gallery of Ont, Toronto, 74; Art Gallery of Windsor, Ont, 75; Stratford Art Gallery, Ont, 76; David Mirvish Gallery, Toronto, Ont, 76 & 77; Montreal Mus of Fine Arts, Que, 76; Hirshhorn Mus, Washington, DC, 77; Art Gallery of Hamilton, Ont, 77; Beaverbrook Art Gallery, Fredericton, NB, 77; Norman MacKenzie Art Gallery, Regina, Sask, 77; two shows, Edmonton Art Gallery, Alta, 77; Watson de Nagy Gallery, Houston, Tex, 77; Galerie Wentzel, Hamburg, WGer, 77; Diane Brown Gallery, Washington, DC, 77; Art Gallery of Cobourg, 77. Awards: Can Coun Travel Award, 74. Bibliog: Andrew Hudson (auth), Notes on eight Toronto painters, Art Int, 10/75; Juliana Borsa (auth), Kay Graham (rev), Arts Mag, 12/76-1/77 & Washington: 14 Canadians: a critic's choice, 5-6/77; Theodore Heinrich (auth), Canada at the Hirshhorn Museum, two responses, Arts Can, 5-6/77; Karen Wilkin (auth), Fourteen Canadians: one critic's choice, Art Int, 7-8/77; Mimi Crossley (auth), Six from Toronto, Arts Mag, 11/77; and others. Mem: Royal Can Acad of Arts. Style & Technique: Acrylic on canvas; chalk, conte and tusche drawings; lithographs. Mailing Add: c/o David Mirvish Gallery 596 Markham St Toronto ON M6G 2L7 Can

GRAHAM, MARGARET BLOY
CHILDREN'S BOOK ILLUSTRATOR
b Toronto, Can, Nov 2, 20, US citizen. Study: Univ of Toronto, BA(fine arts); New Sch for Soc Res, New York, study with Alexey Brodovitch; New York Univ, grad courses, study with Stuart Davis. Work: Illus for Harry the Dirty Dog, Lilian Smith Collection, Toronto Pub Libr, Can. Publ: Auth & illusr, Be Nice to Spiders, 67, Benjy and the Barking Bird, 71, Benjy's Dog House, 73, Harper & Row; illusr, The Pack Rat's Day, Macmillan, 74; auth & illusr, Benjy's Boat Trip, Harper & Row, 77. Mailing Add: c/o Harper & Row 10 E 53rd St New York NY 10022

GRAHAM, RICHARD MARSTON
SCULPTOR, EDUCATOR
b Lynn, Mass, July 29, 39. Study: Boston Univ, with Hugh Townley & Walter Murch, BFA, 62; RI Sch Design, with Gilbert Franklin, MFA, 64. Work: Ithaca Col Mus Art, NY; Ft Wright Col, Spokane, Wash; First Nat Bank, Atlanta, Ga; Ark Art Ctr, Little Rock; St Norbert Col, De Pere, Wis; Minn Mus of Art, St Paul; Carleton Col, Northfield, Minn. Comn: Playground sculpture, Minneapolis Parks & Recreation Bd & Minn State Arts Coun, Fair Oaks Park, Minneapolis, summer 72. Exhib: One-man shows, Albany Inst Hist & Art, NY, 67 & Paul Schuster Gallery, Cambridge, Mass, 71; 37th Ann Exhib, Sculptors Guild, Lever House, New York, 74; three-person show Environ Works, Foster Gallery, Univ Wis-Eau Claire, 74; Toys designed by Artists, Ark Art Ctr, Little Rock, 75; J Hunt Gallery, Minneapolis, Minn, 77; St Norbert Col, De Pere, Wis, 77; Coffman Gallery, Univ Minn, Minneapolis, 78. Teaching: Asst prof art, Minneapolis Col Art & Design, 70- Awards: Blanche E Colman Found Grant, 70; MacDowell Colony Fel, Peterborough, NH, 71; Union Independent Cols Art Fac Res Grant, summer 72; fac res grant, Minneapolis Col Art & Design, summer 77. Bibliog: Duane Bradley (auth), Part art, part park, Minneapolis Tribune Picture, 12/12/71; Paul Hogan (auth), Playgrounds for Free, Mass Inst Technol, 74. Mem: Artists Equity Asn; Southern Asn Sculptors; Sculptors Guild. Style & Technique: Wood carving; expressionistic. Media: Laminated Wood. Mailing Add: 200 E 25th St Minneapolis MN 55404

GRAHAM, ROBERT
SCULPTOR
b Mexico City, Mex, Aug, 38. US citizen. Study: San Jose State Col, 61-63; San Francisco Art Inst, 63-64. Work: Wallraf-Richartz Mus, Cologne, Ger; Pasadena Art Mus, Calif; Whitney Mus Am Art, New York. Exhib: Ann Exhib, Whitney Mus Am Art, 66, 68, 69 & 71; Here & Now, Washington Univ Gallery of Art, Steinberg Hall, St Louis, Mo, 69; Three Americans, Victoria & Albert Mus, London, 71; West Coast USA, Kunstverein, Hamburg, Ger, 72; one-man shows, Kunstverein, Hamburg, 71, Galerie Herbert Meyer-Ellingen, Frankfurt, Ger, 72, Dallas Mus Fine Arts, Tex, 72, Galerie Neuendorf, Hamburg, 74 & Galerie Gimpel & Hanover, Zurich, Switz, 75. Bibliog: Grace Gleuck (auth), In the Galleries, Art in Am, New York, 3/69; Cindy Nemser (auth), Review, Arts Mag, New York, 5/69; Helene Winer (auth), Robert Graham Boxes, Studio Int, London, 5/70. Publ: Auth, Robert Graham: Works 1963-69, Cologne, 70. Dealer: Nicholas Wilder Gallery 814 N La Cienega Blvd Los Angeles CA 90069. Mailing Add: 69 Windward Ave Venice CA 90291

GRAHAM, ROBERT CLAVERHOUSE
ART DEALER, COLLECTOR
b New York, NY, Apr 28, 13. Study: Yale Univ, BFA, 36; NY Univ, 38-39. Pos: Dir, Graham Gallery. Specialty: Nineteenth and twentieth century American art. Collection: American and Oriental art. Mailing Add: 1014 Madison Ave New York NY 10021

GRAHAM, WALTER
PAINTER, SCULPTOR
b Toledo, Ill, Nov 17, 03. Study: Chicago Acad Fine Arts; Chicago Art Inst; plus pvt instruction. Work: Cent Wash Mus, Wenatchee; Douglas Co Mus, Waterville, Wash; Favell Mus, Klamath Falls, Ore. Comn: Murals & wildlife paintings for ocean-going ships, State of Alaska, 69-72; murals & paintings, Rocky Reach Dam, Wenatchee, 60; fountain sculpture, Lincoln Savings, Spokane, Wash, 70. Exhib: Rendezvous of Western Art, Montana State Hist Soc, Helena, Mont, 72; Ann Western Art Exhib, Russell Mus, Great Falls, Mont, 73-74; NW Indian & Western Art Show, Ridpath Hotel, Spokane, 74-75; Artists of the Old West, Oldfield Gallery-Tacoma Inn, Wash, 75; Soc Animal Artists Exhib, Columbus Gallery of Fine Art, Ohio, 76; Mem Show, Palette & Chisel Acad, Chicago & Art Inst of Chicago. Pos: Owner, Nugent Graham Studios, Chicago, 39-50; mem, Wash State Art Comn, 60 62; pres, Cent Wash Mus, 60-65. Awards: First Prizes, Chicago Galleries, 37, 38 & 42; Gold Medal, Palette & Chisel Acad, Chicago, 40; Hon Mention, Seattle Art Dir Club, Wash, 60. Bibliog: Royal B Hassick (auth), Western Painting Today, Watson-Guptill, 75. Mem: Soc Animal Artists. Style & Technique: Realistic. Media: Oil, Watercolor; Bronze. Mailing Add: 201 S Eliott Wenatchee WA 98801

GRAHAM-COLLIER, ALAN
See Collier, Graham

GRAMATKY, HARDIE
PAINTER, WRITER
b Dallas, Tex, Apr 12, 07. Study: Stanford Univ, 26-28; Chouinard Art Sch, Los Angeles, 28-30. Work: Art Inst Chicago; Brooklyn Mus, NY; Mus Fine Arts, Springfield, Mass; Toledo Mus Art, Ohio; Marietta Col, Ohio; Univ Ore, Eugene. Exhib: Am Watercolor Soc, Nat Acad Design Galleries, New York, 38-72; Nat Acad Design, 40-72; Chicago Int Exhib, Art Inst Chicago, 42; America Observed, Soc Illusr, New York, 70; Mainstreams, Marietta Col, 72-75. Awards: For Calhoun Street, Art Inst Chicago, 42, Memphis Levee, Soc Illusr, 70 & Tiptonville Ferry, Marietta Col, 72; Barse Miller Mem Nat Acad Award, 76. Bibliog: Montgomery (auth), Story Behind Modern Books, Dodd, 49; Helen Painter (auth), Little toot-hero, Elem Eng Mag, 10/60; article in North Light Mag NAm, 75. Mem: Nat Acad Design (juror, 75); Am Watercolor Soc (dir, 69-); Soc Illusr; Author's Guild. Style & Technique: Loose, colorful watercolor; drawing from nature; strong design. Media: Watercolor, Acrylic. Publ: Auth, Little Toot, 39, Hercules, 40, Nikos & the Sea God, 63, Little Toot on the Thames, 66, Happy's Christmas, 70, Little Toot on the Mississippi, 73 & Little Toot Through the Golden Gate, 75, Putnam; co-auth & illusr, Six Artists Paint a Landscape, Watson-Guptill & North Light, 75. Mailing Add: 60 Roseville Rd Westport CT 06880

GRAMBERG, LILIANA
PAINTER, PRINTMAKER
b Treviso, Italy; US citizen. Study: Univ Rome, with Laurea; Escuela Nac Bellas Artes, Madrid; Ecole Nat Super Beaux Arts, Paris, Atelier Gravure, with Bersier; Atelier 17, Paris, with Hayter; Calif Col Arts & Crafts, MFA. Work: Mus Art Mod Ville Paris; Brit Mus, London; Nat Collection Fine Arts, Washington, DC; Albertina Graphische Sammlung, Vienna; Rosenwald Collection, Jenkintown, Pa; plus others. Exhib: Northwestern Printmakers; Silvermine Guild; Pa Acad Fine Arts; Alvarez Penteado Found, Sao Paulo, Brazil; one-man shows, Smithsonian Inst, Univ Chile, Kunstnerforbundet, Oslo, Salon Plastica Mexicana, Mexico, Galeria de Arte Mod, Lisbon & Retrospective, Folkwang Mus, Essen, Ger. Teaching: Prof fine arts, Trinity Col (DC), 67. Awards: Treadwell Award, Nat Asn Women Artists, 63; Silver Medal, Asn Incisori Italia, 64. Bibliog: Margarita Nelken (auth), El patetico grabado de Liliana Gramberg, Arte (Mex), 3/59; Cajide (auth), Tecnica y poesia de los grabados de Liliana Gramberg, Artes (Spain), 2/61. Mailing Add: 6322 32nd St NW Washington DC 20015

GRANDEE, JOE RUIZ
PAINTER, GALLERY DIRECTOR
b Dallas, Tex, Nov 19, 29. Study: Aunspaugh Art Sch, Dallas. Work: White House, Washington, DC; Xavier Univ Mus, Cincinnati, Ohio; Mont State Hist Soc Mus, Great Falls; Marine Corps Mus, Quantico, Va; Univ Tex, Arlington. Comn: Twenty Mules of Death Valley, US Borax Co, Hollywood, Calif, 65; Linda Bird & Chuck Robb Off Portrait, Pres Family & Friends, 67; portrait of Johnny Carson, comn by Rudy Tellez, Assoc Producer NBC, New York, 67; portrait of Robert Taylor, US Borax Co for Robert Taylor, Hollywood, 68; Leander H McNelly, Texas Ranger, Tex Rangers, East Wing of White House, Washington, DC, 72. Exhib: Custer Exhib, Amon Carter Mus Western Art, Ft Worth, Tex, 68; one-man shows, Norton Art Gallery Mus, Shreveport, La, 71, El Paso Mus Fine Arts, Tex, 72 & Tex Ranger Mus Show, Waco, Tex, 72 & US Capitol, 74; plus many others. Pos: Owner, Joe Grandee Gallery & Mus of Old West. Awards: Grandee Day in Arlington, City of Arlington & Mayor, 69; First Official Artist of Texas, Tex Legis & Gov, 71; Franklin Mint Gold Medal Western Art for Pursuit and Attack, 74; plus others. Bibliog: Wayne Gard (auth), Joe Grandee—painter of the old west, Am Artist Mag, 67; Grandee Paintings (TV film), US Borax Co, 68; Joy Schultz (auth), The West Still Lives: Grandee, Heritage, 70. Style & Technique: Western art. Media: Oil, Ink. Res: Ruizeem water medium. Specialty: Paintings, drawings and sculpture works of Joe Ruiz Grandee and displays of historical artifacts. Publ: Illusr, Indian Wars of Texas, 65; illusr, Pictorial History of the Texas Rangers, 69; illusr, The Grand Duke Alexis in the USA, 72; illusr, The Life of Jim Baker (mountain man) 1818-1898, 72; contribr, Cowboy Series, In: Time-Life Bks, 72. Dealer: Gene McDaniel PO Box 433

Midland TX 79701; Bob Hoff PO Box 231 Houston TX 77001. Mailing Add: Joe Grandee Gallery & Mus Old West 606 S Center St Arlington TX 76010

GRANLUND, PAUL THEODORE
SCULPTOR, INSTRUCTOR
b Minneapolis, Minn, Oct 6, 25. Study: Gustavus Adolphus Col, BA, 52; Univ Minn; Cranbrook Acad Art, George A Booth scholar, 53, MFA, 54. Work: Am Swedish Inst; Cranbrook Acad Art; Walker Art Ctr; Va Mus Fine Arts; Sheldon Mem Mus Art Gallery, Lincoln, Nebr; plus others. Comn: Sculpture, Gustavus Adolphus Col & Lutheran Church of the Good Shepherd, Minneapolis. Exhib: One-man shows, Calif Palace of Legion of Honor, 62, Univ Nebr, 64 & Washington Univ, 65; La State Univ, 64; Art ot Two Cities, Minneapolis Sch Art, 65; plus others. Teaching: Cranbrook Acad Art, 54; Minneapolis Inst Sch, 55-68; Gustavus Adolphus Col, 68- Awards: Fulbright Fel, 54; Guggenheim Fels, 57 & 58. Mem: Am Asn Univ Prof. Dealer: Allan Frumkin Gallery 41 E 57th St New York NY 10022 & 620 N Michigan Ave Chicago IL 60611. Mailing Add: c/o Dept of Art Gustavus Adolphus Col St Peter MN 56082

GRANSTAFF, WILLIAM BOYD
PAINTER, ILLUSTRATOR
b Paducah, Ky, May 17, 25. Study: Kansas City Art Inst, with Ross Braught & Ed Lanning, grad; Am Acad Art, with William Mosby & Bill Fleming. Comn: Mural, Cadet Club, Garden City, Kans, 45; Old Homeplace, B J Farless, Princeton, Ky, 70; Vietnam (painting), comn by Nat Am Legion, 75. Exhib: Mid-S, Nashville, Tenn, 53; one-man show, Planters Bank, Hopkinsville, Ky, 72. Teaching: Instr illus, Famous Artist Sch, 59-61. Pos: Mem, Art Dirs Club, Nashville, 55-58. Awards: Brackman Blue Ribbon, Nashville, 53. Bibliog: Meet your instructors, Famous Artist Mag, 61. Mem: Audubon Soc. Style & Technique: Realistic still life, warm and cool muted color; wet in wet, loose washes. Media: Oil, Watercolor. Publ: Illusr, What's in a Word, Abingdon, 65; illusr, The Way Out, Moody, 70; illusr, Golden Treasury of Bible Stories, Southern, 71; illusr, Man-US & Americas, 72 & illusr, Americans All, 72, Benefic. Dealer: Heritage Gallery Rosemont Gardens Lexington KY 40503. Mailing Add: Old Eddyville Rd Princeton KY 42445

GRANT, JAMES
SCULPTOR
b Los Angeles, Calif, 1924. Study: Univ of Southern Calif, BEd, 45, MFA, 50; Jepson Art Inst, Los Angeles, 47-49. Work: San Francisco Mus of Art; Univ of the Pacific, Stockton, Calif; Pasadena Art Mus, Calif; Mary Washington Col, Fredericksburg, Va. Exhib: Art Across Am, M Knoedler & Co, New York, 65-67; E B Crocker Art Gallery, Sacramento, Calif, 66; San Francisco Art Asn, 66; Univ of Ill, 67 & 69; Mus of Art, La Jolla, Calif; Cornell Univ; Los Angeles Co Mus of Art, Los Angeles; Mus of Mod Art, New York; retrospective, Mills Col, Calif, 70; one-man shows, Pasadena Art Mus, 52, Univ of Calif, 58, Humboldt State Col, 59, Pomona Col, 59, Pogliani Gallery, Rome, 62, M H de Young Mem Mus, San Francisco, Calif, 63 & Hansen Gallery, San Francisco, 64-66. Teaching: Instr, Pomona Col, 50-59. Mailing Add: c/o Hansen-Fuller Gallery 228 Grant Ave San Francisco CA 94108

GRASS, PATTY PATTERSON
PAINTER
b Oklahoma City, Okla. Study: Univ Okla, BFA; Ecole Beaux-Arts, Fontainebleau, France; Taos Sch Art; Art Students League; Okla State Univ; additional study with Emil Bisttram, Robert E Woods, Milford Zarnes, George Post, Edgar Whitney & Millard Sheets. Exhib: One-woman show, Univ Okla Health Sci Ctr, 76; Mass Inst Technol; Oklahoma City Art Ctr; Art Students League; Okla Mus Art. Teaching: Instr art, Oklahoma City Schs & Oklahoma City Univ, 34- Awards: Medals, McDowell Club of Allied Arts, 40, 42 & 44; Okla Art League Prize, 42; First Prize, Watercolor Okla, 75; Spec Award, Okla Art Guild, 75; Cert of Award for 100 Best Painters 76, Southwestern Watercolor Soc, Dallas, Tex, 76. Mem: Okla Art Asn (vpres & secy); Okla Watercolor Asn (vpres); Watercolor Okla; Southwestern Watercolor Soc; assoc mem Am Watercolor Soc; life mem Okla Mus Art; life mem Nat Cowboy Hall of Fame. Style & Technique: Conservative modern. Mailing Add: 2506 NW 66th St Oklahoma City OK 73116

GRASSO, DORIS (TEN-EYCK)
PAINTER, SCULPTOR
b Fremont, NY, May 3, 14. Study: Educ Alliance, New York, with Moses Soyer, Alex Dobkin & John Hovannes; N Hudson Arts Sch, with Fabian Zaccone; Rutherford Art Sch, with Lucille Hobbie. Work: Paul Whitener Mem Collection, NC Mus Art; George B Burr Collection, New York; Jersey City Mus Art; Staten Island Pub Schs Collection, NY; Women's Club Collection, Lynhurst, NJ. Exhib: Knickerbocker Artists Int, New York, 63-65; Painters & Sculptors Soc NJ Nat, 65-72; Nat Casein Soc, New York, 68; Acad Artists Regional, NJ, 68-71; Am Artists Prof League Nat, New York, 69-70. Teaching: Instr art, YWCA, Bayonne, NJ, 50-55, Doris Grasso Sch Fine Arts, 52-62 & Bayonne's Woman's Club Eve Dept, 65-68; instr, Doris Teneyck Grasso Gallery & Studio, Gloucester, Mass, currently. Awards: Jersey Gold Medallion Award, NJ Women of Achievement (Art), 63; Patrons Award for Oils, Nat Painters & Sculptors Soc, 67; Pauline Wick Award for Oils, Am Artists Prof League, 68; Golden Lady Award, Nat Women of Achievement (Art), Amita, Inc, 69; First Award for Sculpture, State Fedn Women's Clubs, 70. Mem: Fel Am Artists Prof League (pres, NJ Chap; nat dir, 60-62); Painters & Sculptors Soc NJ (bd dirs & secy, 62-65); Burr Artists (pub rels, 66-68); assoc Rockport Artists; fel Int Arts & Lett, Ger & Switz; Gotham Painters Soc; Hunterdon Art Asn. Style & Technique: Impressionistic. Media: Oil, Watercolor, Terra-cotta. Mailing Add: 15 Langsford St Lanesville Cape Ann Gloucester MA 01930

GRAUBARD, ANN WOLFE
See Wolfe, Ann

GRAUER, MELANIE KAHANE
See Kahane, Melanie

GRAUPE-PILLARD, GRACE
PAINTER
b New York, NY, Sept 28, 41. Study: City Univ NY, BA, 63; Art Students League, George Bridgman Scholar, with Marshal Glasier and Julien Levi, 64-68. Work: Roland Gibson Found, Potsdam, NY, Edward & Vivian Merrin Collection, New York; Malcolm Forbes Collection, New York. Exhib: Roswell Mus, NMex, 73; Aldrich Museum, Ridgefield, Conn, 76; Monmouth Museum, Lincroft, NJ, 76; Glassboro State College, NJ, 77; Women Artists 1978; CUNY Graduate Ctr, New York, 78; one-woman shows, Razor Gallery, New York, 74, 75 & 77 and Douglass Col, 74. Teaching: Instr painting and Life drawing, Monmouth Adult Educ Comm, 74-, and Monmouth County Parks, 76- Awards: NMex Biennial Juror's Award, 73; Women in the Arts Honorarium, Rutgers Univ, 74. Bibliog: Carol Jacobson (auth), Artforum, Daily Register, Red Bank, NJ, 3/19/75 and 2/23/76; article in Arts Mag, 4/76; Voice Choice, Village Voice, New York, 1/2/78. Style & Technique: Large, explicit paintings of nudes. Media: Oil Dealer: Razor Gallery 464 W Broadway New York NY 10012. Mailing Add: PO Box 379 Red Bank NJ 07701

GRAUSMAN, PHILIP
SCULPTOR
b New York, NY, July 16, 35. Study: Syracuse Univ, BA(cum laude), 57; Skowhegan Sch Painting & Sculpture, summers 56 & 57; Cranbrook Acad Art, MFA, 59; Art Students League, with Jose de Creeft, 59. Work: Brooklyn Mus; Pa State Univ; Wadsworth Atheneum, Hartford; Univ Mich; Univ Conn, Storrs; Univ Mass, Amherst; Akron Art Inst, Ohio; Cornell Univ; Baltimore Mus Art, Md; Munson-Williams-Proctor Inst, Utica, NY; Jewish Mus, New York; Worcester Mus, Brandeis Univ; Univ NH; Nat Portrait Gallery. Exhib: One-man shows, Alpha Gallery, Boston, Mass, 60 & 62, Grace Borgenicht Gallery, New York, 66 & 74, Dartmouth Col, 72, Univ Conn, 75, Pa State Univ & Univ NH, Durham, 77; Pa Acad Fine Arts Ann, 60 & 62; Whitney Mus Am Art, 62, 64 & 66; Contemp Sculptors' Drawings, Ohio State Univ, 66; Univ Nebr, 69; Am Drawing 1970-73, Yale Univ Art Gallery, 73; Hartford Arts Festival, Wadsworth Atheneum, 74; Portrait Exhib, Chicago Arts Club, 75; A Mus Menagerie, Mus of Mod Art, New York, 76; Invitational Am Drawing Exhib, Fine Arts Mus San Diego, Calif, 77. Grace Borgenicht Gallery, New York, 66 & 74, Dartmouth Col, 72 & Univ Conn, 75. Teaching: Instr design, Cooper Union, 65-67; instr design & drawing, Pratt Inst, 65-69; vis asst prof, Yale Univ, 73-76, vis critic archit, Grad Sch Archit, 77-79. Pos: Artist in residence, Dartmouth Col, 72. Awards: Gold Medal Sculpture, Audubon Artists, 58; Louis Comfort Tiffany Found grant, 59; Nat Inst Arts & Lett Grant, 61; Ford Found purchase Grant, 61; Alfred G A Steel Mem Prize, Pa Acad, 62; Prix de Rome Fel, 62-65. Media: Metal, Stone. Dealer: Alpha Gallery 121 Newbury St Boston MA 02116. Mailing Add: c/o Grace Borgenicht Gallery 1018 Madison Ave New York NY 10021

GRAVES, BRADFORD
SCULPTOR, EDUCATOR
b Dallas, Tex, July 26, 39. Study: Sch of Visual Arts; New Sch for Social Res, with Seymour Lipton; Goddart Col, BA & MA. Work: NJ State Mus, Trenton; Corcoran Gallery, Washington, DC; Weatherspoon Art Gallery, Univ NC, Greensboro; Sheldon Mem Art Gallery, Lincoln, Nebr. Comn: Hwy sculpture, Adirondak Northway-Interstate 87, NY, 71, Vt Sculptor's Symposium, Interstate 89, 71 & Interstate 80, Nebr, 76; stone sculpture, Chase Manhattan Bank, New York, 73. Exhib: Vt Hwy Sculpture, Fleming Mus, Burlington, 71; About John Coltrane, New York Jazz Mus, 74; Sculpture in the Park, NJ Cult Coun, Paramus, 74; Sculpture in the Fields, Storm King Art Ctr, Mountainville, NY, 74; First West Side Sculpture Exhib, New York, 76; one-man show, NJ State Mus, Trenton, 76; Whitney Counterweight, New York, 77; Forms in Focus, Co-op City, 77. Teaching: Asst prof sculpture, Fairleigh Dickinson Univ, Madison, NJ, 69-; instr sculpture, Parsons Sch of Design, New York, 74- Pos: Vpres, Am Int Sculptors Symposium, 72. Awards: Creative Artists Pub Serv Award, Hwy Sculpture, Vt, 71. Bibliog: Josh Cohn (auth), Between School and Castelli, Art in Am, 73; Anna Mayo (auth), Against Mother Wellism, Village Voice, 74; Barbara Rose (auth), Nebraska Highway Sculpture, Vogue, 76. Style & Technique: Public art and its problems, as subject matter for sculpture. Media: Stone sculpture and stone earthworks. Publ: Auth, John Coltrane, Doubleday & Co, New York, 73; auth, William Bronk—Poet, Occurrence Number 7, Philadelphia, 77. Mailing Add: c/o Patricia Hamilton Hamilton Gallery of Contemp Art 20 W 57th St New York NY 10019

GRAVES, MR & MRS JOHN W
COLLECTORS
US citizens. Collection: Late 19th and early 20th century American paintings. Mailing Add: 67 Via Verde Wichita KS 67230

GRAVES, MORRIS
PAINTER
b Fox Valley, Ore, Aug 28, 10. Work: Seattle Art Mus; Phillips Mem Gallery, Mus Mod Art, Whitney Mus Am Art & Metrop Mus Art, New York. Exhib: One-man shows, Seattle Art Mus, 36, Willard Art Gallery, 42-71, Detroit Art Inst, 43, Los Angeles Co Mus, 48 & Art Inst Chicago, 48; Univ Mich, 65; Mus Mod Art, New York, 66; Minn Mus Art, 71; Albrecht Art Mus, St Joseph, Mo, 73; Nat Acad Design, 74; plus others. Awards: Guggenheim Found fel, 46; Blair Prize, Art Inst Chicago, 48; Windsor Award, Duke & Duchess of Windsor, 57. Bibliog: Duncan Phillips (auth), article in Mag Art, 12/47; Frederick Wight (auth), Morris Graves, Univ Calif, 56; Katherine Kuh (auth), The Artist's Voice, Harper & Rowe, 60. Mem: Hon mem Am Watercolor Soc. Media: Tempera, Oil. Mailing Add: Box 90 Loleta CA 95551

GRAVES, NANCY STEVENSON
PAINTER, SCULPTOR
b Pittsfield, Mass, 40. Study: Vassar Col, BA, 61, fel, 71; Yale Univ Sch Art & Archit, BFA & MFA, 64. Work: Whitney Mus Am Art; Nat Gallery Ottawa; Wallraf-Richartz Mus, Koln, Ger; Chicago Art Inst; Mus Fine Arts, Houston. Exhib: Individual exhibs, Whitney Mus Am Art, New York, 69, Nat Gallery Can, Ottawa, 70, 71 & 73, Neue Galerie Alten Kurhaus, Aachen, WGer, 71, Mus Mod Art, New York, 71, Inst Contemp Art, Philadelphia, 72, New Gallery, Cleveland, 72, La Jolla Mus of Art, Calif, 73, Art Mus of STex, Corpus Christi, 73, Andre Emmerich Galleries, New York, 74 & 77 & Zurich, 77, Albright-Knox Art Gallery, Buffalo, 74 & M Knoedler & Co, New York, 78; 200 Yrs of Am Sculpture, Whitney Mus Am Art, New York, 76; Documenta VI, Kassel, WGer, 77; Strata, Vancouver Art Gallery, BC, 77. Awards: Fulbright-Hays Grant painting, Paris, 64-68; Paris Biennale Grant, 71; Nat Endowment for Arts Grant, 72. Bibliog: R Arn (auth), article in Artscanada, spring 74; R Channin (auth), article in Art Int, 11/74; L Lippard (auth), article in Art in Am, 11/75. Mailing Add: c/o M Knoedler & Co 19 E 70th St New York NY 10021

GRAY, CLEVE
PAINTER, SCULPTOR
b New York, NY, Sept 22, 18. Study: Princeton Univ, BA, 40. Work: Guggenheim Mus & Whitney Mus Am Art, New York; Phillips Collection, Washington, DC; Addison Gallery Am Art, Andover, Mass; Univ Art Gallery, Berkeley, Calif. Exhib: Albright-Knox Art Gallery, 77; Columbus Gallery of Fine Art, Ohio, 77; Mus Art, RI Sch Design, Providence, 78. Awards: Univ Ill Purchase Award, 51; Ford Found Award, 61; Neuberger Mus Mural Paintings, 73. Bibliog: Daniel Robbins (auth), Cleve Gray, Art Int, 3/64; 11/67; Emily Genauer (auth), article in New York Post, 5/18/74; Thomas Hess (auth), Cleve Gray 1967-1977, Albright Knox Art Gallery, 77. Style & Technique: Abstract. Publ: Ed, David Smith, 68; ed, John Marin, 70; ed, Hans Richter, 71. Dealer: Betty Parsons Gallery 24 W 57th St New York NY 10019. Mailing Add: Cornwall Bridge CT 06754

GRAY, DON
PAINTER, ART CRITIC
b San Francisco, Calif, June 16, 35. Study: Ariz State Univ, Tempe, BA, 57; Univ Iowa, Iowa City, MA, 62. Work: State Univ NY Potsdam; Dickinson State Col, NDak. Exhib: Drawings

USA, St Paul, Minn, 63; Nat Small Paintings Exhib, Purdue Univ, W Lafayette, Ind, 64; 32nd Nat Print & Drawing Show, Wichita, Kans, 65; 12th Nat Drawing Show, Ball State Univ, Ind, 65; The Art of Three Painters, Eastern Mich Univ, Ypsilanti, 66; plus 13 one-man shows and many group exhibs in galleries & univs across the country. Teaching: Art teacher, St Francis Col, Brooklyn, NY, 67-70; asst prof art, Ladycliff Col, Highland Falls, NY, 71- Pos: Art critic for var newspapers, mags & TV in New York, NY; mem Street Painters group (independent, avant-garde group), New York, NY, 77- Bibliog: Barry Schwartz (auth), The New Humanism, 74; article (in prep), Am Artist Mag, fall/winter 75. Style & Technique: Realist painter of the figure & still life using black backgrounds for symbolic & aesthetic effect to set off rich foreground colors. Media: Acrylic, Oil, Pastel, Watercolor. Publ: Contribr, New York Arts J, 75-; producer & moderator, Artist and Critic, Manhattan Cable TV Show, 75- Dealer: Allan Stone Gallery 48 E 86th St New York NY 10028. Mailing Add: Box 573 Union Corners Rd Florida NY 10921

GRAY, GLADYS
PAINTER, MURALIST
b Truckee, Calif. Study: Fresno State Univ, Calif, AB; Univ Calif, Berkeley, grad study; Claremont Col, Calif; study with Eliot O'Hara, Phil Paradise, Rex Brandt, Jean Ames & others. Work: Long Beach Mus Art, Calif; Laguna Beach Mus Art, Calif; Utah State Univ; Calif State Polytech Univ; Art Ctr, San Luis Obispo, Calif. Comn: Murals depicting history of the area, comn by Morgan Flagg, Convalescent Hosp, Hacienda, San Luis Obispo, 63, Hacienda, Livermore, Calif, 66, Hacienda, Petaluma, Calif, 69, Hacienda, Roseville, Calif, 69, Hacienda, Porterville, Calif, 69 & Hacienda, Woodland, Calif, 69. Exhib: Three Women Painters, Crocker Art Gallery, Sacramento, Calif, 59; one-woman show, Laguna Beach Mus Art, 61 & 71; 21 Paint in Polymer, M Grumbacher Co Exhib, Grand Cent, NY, 65; Grand Prix de Peinture de la Cote d'Azur, 71; Watercolor West, Utah State Univ Gallery, 72. Pos: Vol, San Luis Obispo Art Ctr, 52- Awards: Purchase Award for Triptych, Los Angeles Madonna Festival, 61; Spec Mention for Top Till, Grand Prix Int, Rome, Italy, 72; Award for Cycle Shapes, Grand Prix Int de Peinture de Deauville, 72. Bibliog: Myrtle Kerr (ed), Sketchbook of Kappa Pi, Int Art Fraternity, spring 66; Sandy Smith (auth), Mrs Gray, The Artist, Sociol of Arts, 68. Mem: Nat Watercolor Soc; fel Royal Soc Arts; hon life mem San Luis Obispo Art Asn; life mem Laguna Beach Mus Art, San Luis Obispo Art Ctr (bd trustees, secy, 6 yrs). Style & Technique: Abstract as well as traditional; broad and flowing; brilliant color, especially warm tones. Media: Transparent Watercolor, Acrylic. Dealer: Robinson's Red Door Gallery 2848 Main St N Morro Bay CA 83442. Mailing Add: 133 Orange Dr San Luis Obispo CA 93401

GRAY, JIM
PAINTER, SCULPTOR
b Middleton, Tenn, June 4, 32. Work: Carnegie Libr, Regar Mus, Anniston, Ala; Int Trade Ctr & First Fed Collection, Mobile, Ala; Loyal Am Life Ins Co, Mobile, Ala; Hibernia Nat Bank, New Orleans, La; City of Malaga, Spain; Mariners Mus, Newport News, Va. Comn: Design & sculpture for Bicentennial Medal, Sevier Co, Tenn. Exhib: One-man shows, Frame House Gallery, Louisville, Ky, 69 & Percy Whiting Mus, Fairhope, Ala, 70, 73 & 75; three-man show, Long Boat Key Art Ctr, Sarasota, Fla, 70; Watercolor USA, Springfield, Mo, 70; Realist Invitational, Gallery Contemp Art, Winston-Salem, NC, 71. Teaching: Instr painting, Buckhorn Art Workshop Ann, Gatlinburg, Tenn; instr watercolor, Atlanta Artist Club, Ga, 69-; lectr art & humanities, Univ Tenn, Knoxville, 70-71. Pos: Gov appointee, Ala State Comn Arts, 63-68. Awards: Best in Show & Permanent Trophy, Azalea Trail Arts Festival, 57, 58 & 59; Best of Show, Hammel-Adams Glass, Mobile, 62 & 63. Bibliog: Gordon Young (auth), article in Nat Geog Mag, 10/68; K Lingo (auth), Southern personalities, Southern Living Mag, 11/72; Wilma Dykeman (auth), Painter sees with different eyes, Am Artist Mag, 7-8/75. Mem: Tenn Watercolorists; Atlanta Artist Club; Knoxville Watercolor Soc; Cincinnati Art Club; Salmagundi Club. Style & Technique: Realism with spontaneous and abstract qualities. Media: Watercolor, Oil; Clay, Bronze. Publ: Illusr covers, Port Mobile, 62-66. Dealer: Jim Gray Gallery Parkway Gatlinburg TN 37738; Jim Gray Gallery S Star Rte 585 Gulf Shores AL 36542. Mailing Add: Rte 3 Buckhorn Rd Gatlinburg TN 37738

GRAY, MARIE ELISE
PAINTER
b Bremanger, Norway; US citizen. Study: Derbyshire Sch Fine Art, 64-65; Cornish Sch Allied Art, 66-70; Olympic Col, 71; and with Rex Brandt, Sergei Bongart, Warren Brandon & Raymond Brose. Work: Frye Art Mus, Seattle, Wash; Univ Ore; Boeing Airplane Co, Seattle; US Steel Co, Seattle; AMFAC, Inc, San Francisco. Comn: Four paintings (acrylic), Washington Mortgage Co, Seattle, 74. Exhib: Northwest Watercolor Exhibs, Seattle Art Mus, 61-75, Northwest Ann, 63 & 65 & 42nd Ann Int Print Exhib, 71; Am Watercolor Exhib, New York, 69; Capitol Mus, Olympia, Wash, 74. Teaching: Instr art, YWCA, Seattle, 68; instr art, Washington Athletic Club, Seattle, 73; instr art, Women's Univ Club, Seattle, 73. Pos: Pres, Quad A Art Club, Seattle, 61-62; art exhib juror, Northwest Marine Indust Marine Show, Washington, DC, 69, 71 & 74. Awards: Pac Northwest Art Ann Purchase Award, Univ Ore, 66; Edward Manet Award, Frye Art Mus, 67, Eugene Boudin Award, 68. Mem: Northwest Watercolor Soc (exhib chmn, 70-72); Nat League Am Pen Women (state art chmn, 75-76); Women Painters of Washington; Olympic Art Asn. Style & Technique: Impressionistic landscapes. Media: Watercolor; Collagraph. Dealer: Good Years Gallery 201 Fifth Ave S Edmonds WA 98020. Mailing Add: 7723 30th Ave NE Seattle WA 98115

GRAY, RICHARD
ART DEALER
b Chicago, Ill, Dec 30, 28. Pos: Owner & dir, Richard Gray Gallery. Mem: Art Dealers Asn Am (dir); Chicago Art Dealers Asn (pres); Col Art Asn Am. Specialty: Paintings, sculpture, drawings and prints by established European and American artists and the avante garde; pre-Columbian and classical antiquities, African, Oceanic and American Indian art. Mailing Add: Richard Gray Gallery 620 N Michigan Ave Chicago IL 60611

GRAY, ROBERT HUGH
EDUCATOR
b Dallas, Tex, Sept 22, 31. Study: Yale Univ, BFA(painting), 59 & MFA(painting, 61. Teaching: Instr design & visual commun, Cooper Union, New York, 60-66; instr drawing, painting & design, Silvermine Col Art, Conn, 66-71; prof painting & head dept art, Pa State Univ, State Col, 72-75. Pos: Dean, Silvermine Col Art, 66-71; dean, Visual Arts Div, State Univ NY Col Purchase, 75-; mem bd trustees, AC-BAW, Westchester Co; mem bd dirs, Clayworks, New York, NY; mem exec comt, Bd Dirs, Neuberger Mus; mem exec comt, Sch Art Campaign, Yale Univ; mem nat coun art adminr. Awards: Outstanding Educator Award, 73. Mem: Nat Coun Art Adminrs; Col Art Asn; Am Asn Higher Educ. Mailing Add: Visual Arts Div State Univ NY Col Purchase NY 10577

GRAY, ROBERT WARD
ART ADMINISTRATOR
b Tallahassee, Fla, June 26, 16. Study: Univ Fla; Tri-State Col; Grad Sch Am Craftsmen, with Herbert H Sanders. Collections Arranged: Co-dir, New Eng Craft Exhib, 55. Pos: In charge pottery shop & coordr craft prog, Old Sturbridge Village, 49-51; dir, Worchester Craft Ctr, 51-61; dir, Southern Highland Handicraft Guild, 61- Mailing Add: South Highlands Handicraft Guild 15 Reddick Rd Asheville NC 28805

GRAY, THOMAS ALEXANDER
MUSEUM DIRECTOR
b Winston-Salem, NC, Feb 7, 48. Study: Duke Univ, BA(hist art), 70; Univ Del, Am Cult Winterthur Prog & MA, 74; Summer Inst Arts Admin, Harvard Univ, 74. Pos: Develop dir, Old Salem, Inc, Winston-Salem, NC, 74-76; dir, Mus Early Southern Decorative Arts, Winston-Salem, 76- Mem: Hist Preservation Soc NC, Inc (pres, 76-); Hist Preservation Fund NC, Inc (mem bd, 76-); Stagville Preservation Ctr, Durham, NC (mem bd, 77-); Piedmont Craftsmen, Inc (mem bd, 77-). Mailing Add: Salem Sta Winston-Salem NC 27108

GRAYSMITH, ROBERT
EDITORIAL CARTOONIST
b Pensacola, Fla, Sept 17, 42. Study: Calif Col Arts & Crafts, BFA, 65. Pos: Staff artist, Stockton Rec, Calif, 65-68; ed cartoonist, San Francisco Chronicle, 68- Mailing Add: San Francisco Chronicle Fifth & Mission Sts San Francisco CA 94119

GRAYSON, VAUGHAN
See Mann, Vaughan

GRAZIANI, SANTE
PAINTER, MURALIST
b Cleveland, Ohio, Mar 11, 20. Study: Cleveland Sch Art, 38-41; Sch Fine Arts, Yale Univ, BFA, 43, MFA, 48. Comn: Murals, Bluffton Post Off, Ohio, 41, Columbus Junction Post Off, Iowa, 42, Holyoke Pub Libr, Mass, 49-51, Am Battle Monument, Henri-Chapelle, Belg, 55-58 & Mayo Clin, Rochester, Minn, 69; plus others. Exhib: One-man shows, Babcock Galleries, New York, six times, 62-71, Kanegis Gallery, Boston, 64-70, Univ Conn, Storrs, 70, Fairweather-Hardin Gallery, Chicago, 70 & Allentown Art Mus, 70; plus others. Teaching: Instr drawing & painting, Sch Fine Arts, Yale Univ, 46-51; dean, Whitney Sch Art, 50-51; head, Worcester Art Mus Sch, 51-72, dean, 72- Pos: Officer in charge arts & crafts, USA, Pac Theatre, 45-46. Awards: Pulitzer Scholar, 42; Boston Art Dirs Club Award, 54; Spec Drawing Award, Norfolk Mus, 61; plus others. Mem: Nat Soc Mural Painters. Dealer: Babcock Galleries 805 Madison Ave New York NY 10021; Fairweather-Hardin Gallery 101 E Ontario St Chicago IL 60611. Mailing Add: Worcester Art Mus 55 Salisbury St Worcester MA 01545

GRAZIANO, FLORENCE V MERCOLINO
PAINTER, SCULPTOR
b Plainfield, NJ. Study: Columbus Col Art & Design; Art Students League, with Robert Brackman, R B Hale, R de Lamonica & John Hovannes; Cape Sch Art; John Pike Watercolor Sch. Work: Washington Co Mus Fine Arts, Hagerstown, Md; Sheldon Swope Mus Art, Terre Haute, Ind; Univ Maine, Orono; Rutgers Univ, NJ; Eisenhower Col, Seneca Falls, NY. Comn: Portrait of Henri Nosco, conductor of NBC Symphony Orchestra, 58; portrait & brochure, comn by Hildegarde, New York, 65 & 70; portrait comn by Mrs Jimmy Durante, Beverly Hills, Calif, 71; portrait comn by Claude Philippe, New York, 72; prog & brochure, Plainfield Symphony, NJ, 72-73. Exhib: Jersey City Mus, NJ; Bergen Co Mus, Paramus, NJ; Hudson Valley Art Asn Ann, New York, 70-71; Salon Soc l'Ecole Francaise, Paris, 71; Biennale Int Officielle d'Art Contemporain de Vichy, France, 72; Allied Artists Am, NY, 72-73; Am Watercolor Soc, 72-73. Teaching: Dir & instr art, Graziano Sch Arts, Marion, Ohio, 59-68, dir & instr art, Graziano Studio Fine Arts, Plainfield, NJ, 69-; lectr & demonstr for var art orgns, 59-; dir-instr summer art workshop, Graziano Studios, Flemington, NJ. Pos: Dir first art show & sales, Marion Co Fair, 67; asst chmn & publ dir, Plainfield Festival Arts, 70; dir, G & G Gallery, Plainfield. Awards: First Prize for Sculpture & Second Prize for Painting, Conv Hall Art Exhib, Las Vegas, Nev, 68; First Prize Oils, Washington, DC, 69; First Prize Oils, Bergen Co Mus, Paramus, NJ, 72; Gold Medal for Oil, Int Festival Art of Saint Germain des Pres, Brussels, 73; Brush Fund Award for Oil, Pen & Brush, NY, 74; First in Oils, Circolo Dell 'Arte, Italy, 77; plus others. Bibliog: R Clermont (auth), La Rev Mod, Paris, 4/72; Lee Leary (auth), article in Spotlight Mag, 7/72; Leo Soretsky (auth), Opus artis, FM Guide, 8/72. Mem: Catharine Lorillard Wolfe Art Club, NY; Salmagundi Club, NY; Am Artists Prof League (pres, NJ Chap, 74-75); Nat Arts Club, New York; Nat Painters & Sculptors Soc NJ. Style & Technique: Impressionistic realism. Media: Oil, Watercolor; Clay. Mailing Add: 1413 Highland Ave Plainfield NJ 07060

GREACEN, RUTH NICKERSON
See Nickerson, Ruth

GREAR, JAMES MALCOLM
DESIGNER, EDUCATOR
b Mill Springs, Ky, June 12, 31. Study: Art Acad Cincinnati, Ohio, 58, cert. Comn: Graphics for The New American Painting & Sculpture: The First Generation Exhibition (designer), Mus Mod Art, New York, 69; Henri Matisse Catalogue, Detroit Inst Art, Mich, 77. Exhib: New Eng Designers, Addison Gallery of Contemp Art, Andover, Mass, 64; Commun by Design, Inst Contemp Art, Boston, 64; Int Ctr for Typographic Arts, Can Int Exhib, 66; Hon Recipient of RI Gov's Arts Award Exhib, Mus Art, RI Sch Design, 69; Malcolm Grear Designers Exhib, RI Sch of Design, 72, Worcester Art Mus, Mass, 73, List Art Bldg, Brown Univ, 73, Am Inst Graphic Arts, New York, 74 & Jorgensen Gallery, Univ Conn, 75; Biennale of Graphic Design Brno 74, Czech; New Eng Bk Show, Boston, 76; Environmental Desgin: Signing & Graphics, Am Inst Graphic Arts, 77. Teaching: Assoc prof graphic design, RI Sch Design, 61- Pos: Designer/consult publ, RI Sch Design, 63- & Guggenheim Mus, New York, 69-; design consult, Comt to Rescue Italian Art, 67-68; nat design chmn, Nat Asn Partners of the Americas, 70-; designer/consult publ, Fogg Art Mus, Cambridge, Mass, 71-76; panelist to evaluate fed graphics, Nat Endowment for Arts, 73-; design consult, RI Tall Ships 76, 75-76. Awards: Am Inst Graphic Arts Ann Award, 50 Best Bks Publ in US, 68, 70, 71, 74 & 77; Gov's Arts Award, RI Sate Coun on the Arts, 69; Art Libr Soc NAm Award, Henri Matisse: Paper Cut-Outs, 77. Bibliog: Charles R Anderson (auth), Lettering, Van Nostrand Reinhold, 69; Walter Diethelm (auth), Signet/Signal/Symbol, ABC Ed, Zurich, 70; Midori Imatake (auth), article in Idea Mag, Shigeo Ogawa, Tokyo, Japan, 75. Mem: Am Inst Graphics, New York; Providence Art Club. Style & Technique: Didactic murals, typography, environmental design, signage systems, posters, books, catalogues, symbol design and sculpture. Publ: Designer, Bibology: Helena Curtis, Worth Publ, 68, Joseph Goto, RI Sch Design Mus Art, 71, Jean Dubuffet: A Retrospective, Guggenheim Mus, 73, Jacques Villon, Fogg Art Mus, 76 & Aaron Siskind, Photographer, Light Gallery, 77. Mailing Add: 391 Eddy St Providence RI 02903

GREAVER, HANNE
PRINTMAKER
b Copenhagen, Denmark, Aug 1, 33. Study: Kunsthaandvaerkerskolen, Copenhagen. Work: Beloit Col, Wis; Univ Ga; Univ Maine, Orono; Mich State Univ; Univ Nebr. Exhib: Two-man show, Univ Ga, 64, Left Bank Gallery, Flint, Mich, 68, Univ Maine, Orono, 70 & Brick Store Mus, Kennebunk, Maine, 71; Five Women Printmakers, Kalamazoo Inst Arts, Mich, 69. Style & Technique: Representational. Mailing Add: 314 S Park St Kalamazoo MI 49006

GREAVER, HARRY
ART ADMINISTRATOR, PAINTER
b Los Angeles, Calif, Oct 30, 29. Study: Univ Kans, BFA & MFA. Work: Amherst Col, Mass; Univ Maine, Orono; New York Pub Libr; Norfolk Mus Arts & Sci, Va; Univ Utah Mus Fine Arts. Exhib: Drawings USA, St Paul, Minn, 63; Drawing & Small Sculpture Show, Ball State Univ, Ind, 68; 2nd Nat Print Show, San Diego, Calif, 71; Watercolor Invitational, Chico State Col, Calif, 72; Drawings by Living American Artists, Univ Utah Mus Fine Arts, 72-73. Collections Arranged: Paintings by American Masters, Kalamazoo Inst Arts, Mich, 66, Western Art, 67, The Surrealist, 71 & Reginald Marsh, 74. Teaching: Assoc prof art, Univ Maine, Orono, 55-66. Pos: Dir, Kalamazoo Inst Arts, 66- Awards: Purchase Awards, Norfolk Mus, 63 & 64. Style & Technique: Representational landscapes. Media: Watercolor. Mailing Add: 314 S Park St Kalamazoo MI 49006

GREAVES, FIELDING LEWIS
WRITER, PHOTOGRAPHER
b Norfolk, Va, Jan 27, 23. Study: Va Mil Inst; US Mil Acad, BS, 44; Yale Univ; Army Command & Gen Staff Col. Pos: Ed assoc, Ariz Living Mag, Phoenix, 71-72; contrib ed, Southwest Art Mag, Houston, Tex, 73-75. Mem: Nat Acad TV Arts & Sci (newslett ed, 75-). Res: Photo collection of works of Kemeys, Heikka and Phippen (all deceased); interviews with a number of living artists. Publ: Auth, Master of light: Art of Robert Rishell, 73, Conspiracy of silence, 73, Reflections of a sensitive man: Visit with Guillermo Acevedo, 75, Day of the Black Phoebe, 74 & Old West in miniature: Art of Don Polland, 75, Southwest Art Mag. Mailing Add: PO Box 3273 San Rafael CA 94901

GREAVES, JAMES L
CONSERVATOR
b Middletown, Conn, Jan 25, 43. Study: Col William & Mary, with Dr Thomas Thorne, BS; Inst of Fine Arts, NY Univ, MA(art hist), 70 & dipl art conserv, 70. Pos: Conserv intern, Los Angeles Co Mus Art, 68-70, conservator, 70; chief conservator, Detroit Inst Arts, 70-76; conservator, Los Angeles Co Mus Art, 77- Mem: Fel Int Inst Conserv Hist & Artistic Works; Am Inst Conserv; Am Asn Mus; Western Asn Art Conservators. Res: Painting conservation. Publ: Co-auth, New findings on Caravaggio's technique in the Detroit Magdalen, Burlington Mag, 74. Mailing Add: Los Angeles Co Mus of Art 5905 Wilshire Blvd Los Angeles CA 90036

GRECO, ANTHONY JOSEPH
PAINTER, SCULPTOR
b Cleveland, Ohio, Apr 24, 37. Study: Cleveland Inst Art, with Louis Bosa, BFA, 60; Kent State Univ, with Joseph O'Sickey, MFA, 66. Work: Butler Inst Am Art, Youngstown, Ohio; Kent State Univ; Ga State Art Comn; Mint Mus Art, Charlotte, NC. Comn: Urban Walls Atlanta, one of six inner-city walls. Exhib: Butler Inst Am Art Ann; Akron Art Inst Spring Exhibs, Ohio; Cleveland Mus Art May Shows; Alumni from Twenty Years, 1949-1969, Cleveland Inst Art, 70; Mint Mus Art Biennial Exhib, 75. Teaching: Chmn drawing dept, Atlanta Sch Art, 66-; vis instr drawing & painting, Univ Wis-Madison, summer 69. Awards: Hon Mention & Purchase Award, Butler Inst Am Art Midyear, 61; B F Goodrich Mem Award, Akron Art Inst Ann, 70; NC Bank Purchase Award, Mint Mus Art Biennial Exhib, 75. Style & Technique: Abstract oil paintings; plastic laminates, vinyl and wood combinations constructions. Mailing Add: 839 Crestridge Dr NE Atlanta GA 30306

GRECO, FRANK
PAINTER
b Trenton, NJ, Mar 14, 03. Study: Sch of Indust Art, Trenton, 22-27, with Henry R McGuiness, George Bradshaw & Harry Rosin; Indust Art Sch, New York; Am Artist Sch, New York, with Sol Wilson & the Soyer Brothers; Ozenfant Gl Sch of Fine Arts, New York. Work: Mus of Mod Art, New York; Nat Gallery, Washington, DC; NJ State Mus, Trenton; Mercer Co Community Col, Trenton, NJ. Exhib: One-man shows, Studio Gallery, New York, 47, New Gallery, New York, 55, Jewish Community Ctr, Trenton, 74 & Mercer Co Community Col, Trenton, 73 & 77; 1st New York City Madison Square Garden Outdoor Show; Golden Door Gallery, New Hope, Pa, 72; Charles Mann Gallery, New York, 72; Continental Gallery, Forrest Hills, NY, 72; State Show, Ringwood, NJ, 73; Italian-Am Bicentennial, Philadelphia, 76; Then & Now—WPA Exhib of 200 Artists, New York, 77. Collections Arranged: Hist of Modern Posters, Mus of Mod Art, New York, 41; Direction Gallery, Darien, Conn & New York, 41; Artists for Victory, Mus of Mod Art, New York, 42; Armenian War Relief, New York, 43. Awards: Fourth Prize, United Against Aggression, 41-42 & Hon Mention, United Hemisphere, 41-42, Mus of Mod Art, New York; Fourth Prize, Artist for Victory, Inc, 42. Bibliog: Carlyle Burroughs (auth), Greco Work Sure, Herald Tribune, 55; Linda Holt (auth), Are You the Greco Who Worked with Jackson Pollock?, Trentonian, NJ, 74; Elisabeth Stevens (auth), Still-Growing Artist—60 Years Later, Trenton Times, NJ, 77; Barbara Murphy (auth), Greco Returns to Trenton After 42 Years for Inspiration, The Trentonian, 77. Mem: Artist Equity, Philadelphia Chapter; New York Works Progress Admin. Style & Technique: Free-hand geometric; expressionistic. Media: Oil; acrylic and watercolor. Mailing Add: 461 Chestnut Ave Trenton NJ 08611

GREELEY, CHARLES MATTHEW
PAINTER, INSTRUCTOR
b Teaneck, NJ, Sept 11, 41. Study: New York Sch Visual Arts, with George Ortman. Work: NMex Mus Fine Arts, Santa Fe; Mus Contemp Art, Houston, Tex; Longview Mus, Tex; Mus of San Francisco, Calif; Ahmanson Collection, Home Savings & Loan Asn, Los Angeles. Comn: Ten Banners, comn by Dr Norman Lehman, Musto Plaza Bldg, San Francisco, 72. Exhib: Acid Painters of San Francisco, Richmond Art Ctr, Calif, 70; Visions of Elsewhere, San Francisco Art Inst, 71; Seven Year Retrospective, Capricorn Asunder Gallery, San Francisco, 71; Southwest Fine Arts Bienniel, Fine Arts Mus, Santa Fe, NMex, 74 & NMex Fine Arts Bienniel, 75. Teaching: Instr painting, Glorieta Pass Inst, Glorieta, NMex, 73- Pos: Screening judge, San Francisco Art Festival, 71. Awards: Scholarshop, New York Sch Visual Arts, 59-63; Purchase Prize Award, Home Savings & Loan Asn, Los Angeles, 71; Cash Award, Weatherhead Found, NY, 74; Purchase Prize, Longview Mus Competition, Tex, 75; First Prize Cash Award, Southwest Biennial Weatherhead Found, NY, 76. Bibliog: Tom Albright (auth), The Visionaries, Rolling Stones Mag, 71; Dr Roland Fischer (auth), The art of madness & the madness of art: an altered state experience, Md Psychiat Res Ctr, 72. Style & Technique: Painter of fantastic realities and archtypes using bright, luminescent colors and complex patterns. Media: Acrylic on Canvas, Watercolor. Publ: Contribr, Visions of Elsewhere, San Francisco Art Inst, 71. Mailing Add: PO Box 42 Glorieta NM 87535

GREEN, ART
PAINTER
b Frankfort, Ind, May 13, 41; Can citizen. Study: Art Inst Chicago, BFA, 65. Work: Art Inst Chicago; Nat Gallery Can, Ottawa; New Orleans Art Mus; BC Govt Collection, Victoria, Can; Can Coun Art Bank Collection, Ottawa, Ont. Exhib: Five-man group, The Hairy Who, Chicago, 66-68; Personal Torment-Human Response, Whitney Mus Am Art, New York, 69 & Extraordinary Realities, 73; three-man show, Darthea Speyer Gallery, Paris, France, 70; two-man show, Pa Acad Fine Arts, Philadelphia, 74; Can Canvas, Time Mag Travel Show, 75-76; Ann, San Francisco Art Inst, 77; one-man shows, Phyllis Kind Gallery, Chicago, 74, 75 & 78. Teaching: Asst prof painting, NS Col Art, Halifax, 69-71 & Univ Waterloo, Ont, 77-78. Awards: Cassandra Award, Cassandra Found, Chicago, 70; Can Coun Arts Bursary, 71-72, 72-73 & 76-77. Bibliog: A Adrian (auth), rev in Art in Am, 7-8/74; C Scher (auth), Arts Can, 3/75; T Gruber (auth), Arts Mag, 5/77. Style & Technique: Ambiguous images flatly rendered. Media: Oil. Dealer: Phyllis Kind Gallery 226 E Ontario St Chicago IL 60611; Bau-XI Gallery 340 Dundas St W Toronto ON Can. Mailing Add: 51 Avon St Stratford ON N5A 5N5 Can

GREEN, DAVID OLIVER
SCULPTOR, EDUCATOR
b Enid, Okla, June 29, 08. Study: Am Acad Art; Nat Acad Art. Work: Los Angeles Co Mus Natural Hist, Calif. Comn: Dragonfly Fountain, Welton Beckett Asn, Hillsdale Shopping Ctr, San Mateo, Calif, 55; five figure group, Lytton Savings & Loan Asn, Hollywood, 60; children's sculpture, Women's Club for Bruggemeyer Mem Libr, Monterey Park, Calif, 68; Owl Tree (wall relief), dedicated to daughters of Maurice Fletcher & Tree of Life (fountain), Guyer Mem, Altadena Libr, Calif, 69. Exhib: Los Angeles Co Mus Art Ann, 61; Tucson Art Ctr, Ariz, 63; Southern Calif Expos, San Diego Fair, Del Mar, 66; Citrus Col Invitational, Glendora, Calif, 68; 17th Ann All Calif Exhib, Laguna Beach Art Gallery, Calif, 71. Teaching: Asst prof sculpture, Otis Art Inst, 47-73; instr sculpture, Pasadena Art Mus, Calif, 56-59; asst prof sculpture, Scripps Col, Claremont, Calif, 66. Awards: First Prize for Sculpture, Laguna Beach Art Asn, 62 & 67 & Pasadena Soc Artists, 71 & 75. Bibliog: Jarvis Barlow (auth), David Green, Pasadena Independent, 7/13/47; Bev Johnson (auth), Owls, cats & bats, Los Angeles Times Sun Sect, 3/13/60; Peg Powell (auth), A way with animals, Independent Star-News, 12/15/63. Mem: Int Inst Arts & Lett; Pasadena Soc Artists; Soc Italic Handwriting (Western Am Br); Soc Calligraphy, Los Angeles. Style & Technique: Direct work in all materials; direct metal casting from styrofoam models in sand, lost wax casting; non-objective and abstracted animal forms. Media: Stone, Wood, Metals. Mailing Add: 176 W Jaxine Dr Altadena CA 91001

GREEN, DENISE G
PAINTER
b Melbourne, Australia, Apr 7, 46; US citizenship. Study: Ecole Nat Superiere des Beaux Arts; Sorbonne Univ, Paris, BA, 69; Hunter Col, New York, MFA, 76. Exhib: Contemp Reflections, Larry Aldridge Mus, Ridgefield, Conn, 74; Recent Acquisitions of the Power Bequest, Art Gallery of New South Wales, Sydney, Australia, 75; The Painting Show, PS1, Inst for Art & Urban Resources, New York, 77; Works and Projects of The Seventies, PS1, Inst for Art & Urban Resources, 77; Young Am Talent: The Exxon Nat, Soloman R Guggenheim Mus, New York, 73; one-woman shows, Whitney Mus of Am Art, Art Resources Ctr, New York, 75 & Royal Melbourne Inst of Tech, Sch of Art Gallery, Australia, 77 & Inst of Mod Art, Brisbane, Australia, 77. Teaching: Instr painting, Roger Willams Col, Bristol, RI, 72; instr studio & art hist, Fairleigh Dickinson Univ, Rutherford, NJ, 72-74; instr, Pratt Inst, Brooklyn, NY, 74; artist-in-residence, Ill State Univ, Normal, 76 & Art Inst of Chicago, Ill, 77; instr, summer program in the Art, State Univ NY, Fredonia, 77. Pos: Reviewer, Arts Mag, 70-72. Awards: Ingram Merrill Found Grant, 72 & 73; Visual Arts Bd Grant, 74 & Traveling grant for a show, 77, Australian Coun for the Arts. Bibliog: Peter Frank (auth), article in Art News, 12/73; Ann Lauterbach (auth), article in Art in Am, 12/75; Mona da Vinci (auth), article in Art News, 1/77. Publ: Ed, 2nd issue, Heresies, a feminist mag on art & politics, 77. Dealer: Protetch-McIntosh Gallery 2151 P St NW Washington DC 20057. Mailing Add: c/o Max Protetch Gallery 21 W 58th St New York NY 10019

GREEN, EDWARD ANTHONY
ART DIRECTOR, DESIGNER
b Milwaukee, Wis, Apr 20, 22. Study: Univ Wis-Madison, BS & MS, with Edward Boerner, Helmut Summ, Misch Kohn, Al Sessler, Dean Meeker & Warrington Colescott; Layton Sch Art, Milwaukee, 52; Univ Wis-Milwaukee, MFA, 66. Work: Alverno Col, Marine Bank & Manpower, Milwaukee; Cherokee Art Mus, Iowa; Univ Wis-Madison. Comn: Church for Baptist Mission, Bamenda, Brit Cameroons, 62; outdoor fountains, Conrad Mem, 66. Exhib: Wis State Fair, 49-72; Wis Painters & Sculptors, 50-72; Wis Printmakers, 54-72; Beloit & Vicinity, Wis, 58-72; Wis Watercolors, 67-72. Collections Arranged: Streets of Old Milwaukee; Hanseatic League; Hopi Pueblo; Kwakiutl Plank House; Guatemala Market; Japanese House & Garden; Mexican Courtyard; plus many others. Teaching: Instr watercolor & life drawing, Univ Wis-Milwaukee, 55-70; instr outdoor sketching, Whitnall Park, Milwaukee, 68-; instr watercolor, Cardinal Stritch Col, Milwaukee, 73- Pos: Archit designer, Off Martin White, 40-42; archit model maker, Off Allen Wadsworth, 47-48; art dir, Milwaukee Pub Mus, 51-; art & landmarks comnr, City of Milwaukee, 67- Awards: First Award for Watercolor, Grumbacher, 62; First Award for Serigraph, Wis Printmakers, 64; First Award for Watercolor, Wis State Fair, 67. Bibliog: Frank Getlein (auth), article in Milwaukee J, 55; Margaret Rahill (auth), article in Milwaukee Sentinel, 56; Jane Farley (auth), article in Milwaukee J, 63. Mem: Milwaukee Art Comn (chmn, 67-); Mus Artisans Guild (pres, 68-); Midwest Mus Asn; Am Asn Mus; Milwaukee Art Ctr. Style & Technique: Realistic landscapes and architectural statements using transparent and acrylic watercolors. Media: Watercolor; Lithographs. Dealer: Bradley Gallery 2565 N Downer Ave Milwaukee WI 53211. Mailing Add: 3173 S 31st St Milwaukee WI 53215

GREEN, ELEANOR BROOME
GALLERY DIRECTOR, ART HISTORIAN
b Covina, Calif. Study: Vassar Col, AB; George Washington Univ, MA & PhD. Collections Arranged: Edward Weston (with catalog), 67; Picasso since 1945, 67; Scale as Content (Tony Smith, Barnet Newman, Ronald Bladen, with catalog), 67; Al Held (with catalog), 68; Augustus Vincent Track (with catalog), 72; Photography Here and Now, 72; Masterpieces from the Musee de Grenoble, 73; The Apocalypse, 73; Tony Smith (with catalog), 74; Rockne Krebs, 75; Maurice Prendergast for Univ Md; Univ Mus, Austin, Tex; Des Moines Fine Arts Ctr; Columbus Gallery of Fine Arts; Johnson Mus, Ithaca, NY; Davis & Long Gallery (auth, catalog); French Watercolor Landscapes of the Nineteenth Century: From Delacroix to Cezanne at Univ Md, Speed Mus, Louisville; Univ Mich (auth, catalog). Teaching: Prof Am art, Univ Md, College Park, 72- Pos: Cur, Washington Gallery Mod Art, DC, 64-66; cur contemp art, Corcoran Gallery, Washington, DC, 66-69; dir, Art Gallery, Univ Md, 72-

Mem: Col Art Asn; Am Asn Mus. Res: Contemporary American artists; work in progress on 1916 Forum Exhibition of Modern American Painters. Publ: Auth, articles in Artforum & Am Art Rev. Mailing Add: 5140 Westpath Way Washington DC 20016

GREEN, GEORGE D
PAINTER
b Portland, Ore, June 24, 43. Work: Portland Mus of Art, Ore; Univ of Tex, Mus of Art, Austin; Everson Mus of Art, Syracuse, NY; Ft Worth Art Ctr Mus, Tex; Brainard Gallery, State Univ of New York, Potsdam. Exhib: Abstract Illusanism, Paul Mellon Art Ctr, Conn, 76; 3rd Invitational Contemp Art Fair, Paris, France, 76; 7 New York Artists Abstract Illusionism, Rice Univ, Houston, Tex, 77; Abstract Illusionism, Shore Gallery, Boston, Mass, 77; Photo Illusionism Abstract Illusionism, Tomasulo Gallery, NJ, 77; one-man shows, Witte Mus of Art, San Antonio, Tex, 70, Musela Mus of Art, Mont, 74, Triangle Gallery, San Francisco, 77, Louis K Meisel Gallery, New York, 78 & Everson Mus of Art, Syracuse, NY, 78. Pos: Artist-in-residence, Artist Space Inc, New York State Coun on the Arts, 74. Awards: Purchase Award for painting, Portland Art Mus, Ore, 77; Res Found Grant & Fel for Abstract Illusionistic Paintings, 75-76 & 78-79. Style & Technique: Large acrylic illusanitic abstract paintings. Dealer: Jack Van Hiele 251 Post San Francisco CA 94108. Mailing Add: c/o Louis K Meisel Gallery 141 Prince St New York NY 10012

GREEN, GEORGE THURMAN
SCULPTOR, PAINTER
b Paris, Tex, May 10, 42. Study: Tex Tech Univ, BFA; Univ Dallas, MA. Work: Okla Art Ctr Mus, Oklahoma City; Dallas Mus Fine Art; Ft Worth Art Mus, Tex. Comn: Sculptured doors, comn by Betty Blake, Dallas, 70; theater set design, Dallas Theater Ctr, Nat Endowment for the Arts, 74; painted mural, Painted Spaces Comt, Ft Worth, 75; projected slide drawings, Exp Rock Opera, Ft Worth Art Mus, 75; rm environment, Great Am Rodeo Bicentennial Proj, Ft Worth Art Mus, 76. Exhib: Interchange, Dallas Mus Fine Art & Art Ctr, Minn, 72; one-man show, Henri Gallery, Washington, DC, 74; Whitney Painting & Sculpture Biannual, Whitney Mus, New York, 75; North, East, West, South Ann Exhib Contemp Am Drawing, Philadelphia, 75; East, Gulf Coast, West, Contemp Arts Mus, Houston, 75. Teaching: Instr art, Univ Dallas, 68-69, Southern Methodist Univ, Dallas, 69-70 & East Field Col, Dallas, 70-74. Awards: Tex Ann Painting & Sculpture Cash Award, James & Lillian Clark Found, 71; Endowment for Theater Art, Nat Endowment for the Arts, 74; Nat Endowment for the Arts Grant, 77. Bibliog: Martha Utterback (auth), Texas, Art Forum, 1/71; Kent Biffle (auth), Art in Big D, Newsweek, 8/7/72; Janet Kutner (auth), Houston-Dallas Axis, Art in Am, 10/72. Style & Technique: Life size environments made of wood plus synthetic linoleums, vinyls and other materials; graphite and colored pencil drawings. Publ: Illusr, Visions of Dallas, D Mag, 10/75. Dealer: Murray Smither Delahunty Gallery 2611 Cedar Springs Dallas TX 75201 Mailing Add: 2701 Canton St Dallas TX 75211

GREEN, MARTIN LEONARD
PAINTER, PRINTMAKER
b Monterey Park, Calif, Oct 4, 36. Study: Brandt-Dike Sch of Painting, 53-54; Pomona Col, Calif, 54-58; Mexico City Col, 57; Orange Coast Col, Calif, 75-76, Mission: Renaissance, 76. Work: Los Angeles Co Mus of Art, Los Angeles; Gruenwald Ctr for the Graphic Arts, Univ Calif, Los Angeles; Carnegie-Mellon Univ, Pittsburgh; Standard Oil of Ind Arts Collections, Chicago; ITEL Japan Corp Arts Collection, Tokyo. Comn: Murals (oil on panels), Dr Armand Auger, Los Angeles, 76, Mr & Mrs Ed Myer, Rancho La Costa, Calif, 77 & Rockresorts/Kapulau Bay Hotel, Maui, Hawaii, 77-78. Exhib: All-Calif Show, Laguna Beach Mus of Art, 75; Contemp Monotypes, Santa Barbara Mus of Art, Calif, 76; Brand V, Brand Libr Art Gallery, Glendale, Calif, 76; 52nd Nat Art Exhib, Springville Mus, Utah, 76; New Am Monotypes, Smithsonian Inst Travelling Exhib, 78-80. Pos: Lectr monotype hist & demonstr technique, Los Angeles Co Mus of Art, Santa Barbara Mus of Art & Glendale Col. Bibliog: Mel Knoepp (auth), Sunup Show, KFMB-TV, San Diego, Calif, 2/76; Florence Goodman (auth), A Blending of Eastern & Western Philosophies and Art, SW Art, 4/76. Mem: Los Angeles Printmaking Soc; Artists Equity. Style & Technique: Nature-oriented oil paintings, prints and monotypes in color glazes and monochrome with metallic pigments. Media: Oil painting on wood and Masonite panels; multi-colored hand lithographs and monotypes. Dealer: Louis Newman 404 S Figueroa St Los Angeles CA 90071. Mailing Add: 1961 Santa Ana Ave Costa Mesa CA 92627

GREEN, MORRIS BALDWIN
PAINTER, INSTRUCTOR
b Baltimore, Md, Nov 27, 28. Study: Loyola Col, Md Inst Col Art, BFA; Md Inst Col Art, MFA; study with Edgar Whitney; St Peter's Col Acad, DFA. Work: Md Fedn Art Gallery, Annapolis; Rehoboth Art League, Rehoboth Beach, Del; Offices of Thomason, McKinnon, Auchincloss & Kohlmeyer, Baltimore. Exhib: Univ Del Regional Exhib, Newark, 71; Del Mus Fine Arts, Wilmington, 71; Mariner's Mus, Newport News, Va, 71; Cottage Tour, Rehoboth Art League, 72; Salon des Paques, Paris, 72. Teaching: Art coordr & instr, Fine Arts Com Art Studio, Co Sch System, 53-; instr pvt watercolor classes. Awards: Grumbacher Award, Baltimore Watercolor Soc, 70; Cannon & McClelland Awards, Rehoboth Art League, 70, 71 & 72; Best Maritime Painting Award, Fells Pt Festival, 70. Bibliog: Ed, Univ Del Regional Exhib, Wilmington Newspaper, 2/71. Mem: Fel Royal Soc Arts; fel Md Fedn Art; Baltimore Watercolor Soc (corresp secy, 70-72; bd mem, 72-); Artists Equity; Art Guild (co-dir, 71-72). Style & Technique: Very bold approach to watercolor where design and wet quality are prevailing features. Publ: Auth, Tin can arc welding, 11/67, contribr, Showcase of student art, 6/68 & auth, Extra fine papier mache mix-in minutes, Sch Arts Mag, 11/71; auth, Santa and the summer rotisserie, Design Mag, winter 71. Dealer: Rehoboth Art League Rehoboth Beach DE 19971; MFA Gallery 18 State Circle Annapolis MD 21401. Mailing Add: 1821 Wycliffe Rd Baltimore MD 21234

GREEN, SAMUEL MAGEE
ART HISTORIAN, PAINTER
b Oconomowoc, Wis, May 22, 09. Study: Harvard Univ, BA & PhD(cum laude); Pa Acad Fine Arts. Work: Fogg Mus Art; Smith Col Mus; Dartmouth Col; Libr of Cong. Exhib: Lyman Allyn Mus, New London, Conn, Speed Mem Mus, Louisville, Ky, 50, one-man shows, Doll & Richards Gallery, New York, 52 & 56; Acad Arts & Lett, New York, 53. Teaching: Prof art hist & chmn dept, Wesleyan Univ, 48-; spec lectr art hist, Salzburg Sem Am Studies, Austria, 53, 54 & 58; vis prof art hist, Yale Univ, 60-61; lectr, US Info Serv, US Dept State, Ecuador, Paraguay, Bolivia & Venezuela, 68-69 & Egypt, India, Iran, Indonesia & Singapore, 74-75; prof art hist, Bowdoin Col, Brunswick, Maine, 73. Awards: First Prize, Conn Watercolor Soc, 55; Hon Mention, Springfield Art League, 77. Media: Watercolor, prints. Publ: Auth, American Art: an Historical Survey, Ronald Press, 66. Mailing Add: Davison Art Ctr Wesleyan Univ Middletown CT 06457

GREEN, TOM
INSTRUCTOR, SCULPTOR
b Newark, NJ, May 27, 42. Study: Univ Md, BA, 67, MA(painting), 69. Exhib: New Sculpture: Baltimore-Washington-Richmond, Corcoran Gallery Art, Washington, DC, 70; Washington Sculpture, Philadelphia Art Alliance, 73; one-man show, Corcoran Gallery Art, 73; Whitney Biennial, Whitney Mus Art, New York, 75; North, East, West, South & Middle, Traveling Drawing Show, 75. Teaching: Asst prof sculpture & drawing, Corcoran Sch Art, 69- Bibliog: Susan Sollins (auth), Washington report, Arts Mag, 9/73; David Tannous (auth), Tom Green: words and images, Woodwind Mag, 12/11/73; Ben Forgey (auth), Washington: pyramid shapes, Grenoble and theatrics, Art News, 1/74. Style & Technique: Tableaus; half environments; mixed media. Mailing Add: 7716 Tomlinson Ave Cabin John MD 20731

GREEN, WILDER
ART ADMINISTRATOR, ARCHITECT
b Paris, France, Apr 17, 27; US citizen. Study: Yale Col, 45-47; Ill Inst Technol & Design Inst, Chicago, 47-48; Yale Univ Sch Archit, BArch, 52. Teaching: Asst prof, Yale Sch Archit, 56-57; Hunter Col, 67-68. Pos: Asst dir (cur), Dept Archit & Design, Mus Mod Art, New York, 57-61, coordr planning for bldg prog, 61-63, coordr prog, 63-67, dir exhib prog, 67-69, dep to actg dir, 69-70, dir exhib prog, 70-71; pres, Cunningham Dance Found, 69-; dir, Am Fedn Arts, 71- Mem: Munic Art Soc New York; Archit League New York; Arch Am Art; Am Asn Mus; Drawing Soc (mem exec comt, 62-). Mailing Add: Am Fedn Arts 41 E 65th St New York NY 10021

GREENAMYER, GEORGE MOSSMAN
SCULPTOR, EDUCATOR
b Cleveland, Ohio, July 13, 39. Study: Philadelphia Col Art, BFA; Univ Kans, MFA. Comn: Bronze relief, Exhib Serv Int, New York, 65 & ceramic fountain, Collaborative Workshop, 66; steel column, comn by Malcolm Wells, Cherry Hill, NJ, 68; bell tower, Haystack Mountain Sch Arts & Crafts, Deer Isle, Maine, 70; steel mountain, Basteille-Neilly Architects, Boston, 72; steel sculpture (18ft long by 9ft 4in high, by 18in deep), Mass Bay Transportation Authority, comn by Earl Flansburgh Assocs, Architects, Essex St Station. Exhib: Bakers Art, Mus of Contemp Crafts, New York, 65; Earthworks Company Presents, Boston Mus Sch, Mass, 70; Sculpture Festival, Inst of Contemp Art, Boston, 70; New Work of Natalie Alper, George Greenamyer, Ernest Silva and Dean Nimmer-Inst of Contemp Art, Boston, 72; Outdoor Sculpture Exhib, DeCordova Mus, Lincoln, Mass, 72; Boston Visual Artist Union Exhib, Hayden Gallery, Mass Inst of Technol, Cambridge, 73; Sculpture Garden Invitational, Portland Sch of Art, Maine, 73; Outdoor Sculpture, DeCordova Mus, Lincoln, 75; Northeast Sculpture, a Selection, Danforth Mus, Framingham, Mass, 75; 3-D Fine Arts Division Faculty Show, Mass Col of Art, Boston, 76; two-man show, Neill Gallery, New York, 78; Boston Architectural Ctr, Boston, 78; Boston Invitational, Brockton Art Ctr, Mass, 78; Outdoor Sculpture, DeCordova Mus, 78; New England Sculptors Asn Exhib, Boston City Hall Exhib Galleries; and many others. Teaching: Chmn dept sculpture, Mass Col Art, 71 77, assoc prof sculpture. 77- Awards: Louis Comfort Tiffany Found Grant, 77; Recipient Artist Fel, 77; Mass Arts & Humanities Found, NC, 77; First Award, South Shore Show, Brockton Art Ctr, 76. Bibliog: Picture in Crafts Horizon, 2/75; Picture in The Boston Globe, 7/10/76 & 11/11/76; an article & pictures in Patriot Ledger, 2/2/77. Mem: Boston Visual Artists Union; New Eng Sculptors Asn. Style & Technique: Welded steel with large steel wheels; early industrial revolution look; construction with many bolts. Media: Steel, Aluminum. Dealer: Neill Gallery 136 Greene St New York NY 10012. Mailing Add: 994 Careswell St Marshfield MA 02050

GREENBAUM, DOROTHEA SCHWARCZ
SCULPTOR, GRAPHIC ARTIST
b New York, NY, June 17, 93. Study: New York Sch Fine & Appl Art; Art Students League. Work: Whitney Mus Am Art; Philadelphia Mus; NJ State Mus; Smithsonian Inst; Univ Tex. Comn: Princeton Pub Libr, NJ; Mus Art, Ogunquit. Exhib: Many one-man shows, Whitney Mus Am Art, Art Inst Chicago, Pa Acad Design & others. Awards: George Widener Mem Medal, 41; Gold Medal for Sculpture, Pa Acad Design, 47; Ford Found Grant, Asn Women Artists, 56. Mem: Nat Inst Arts & Lett. Style & Technique: Representational; hammered lead. Media: Lead, Stone, Bronze. Dealer: Princeton Gallery Fine Arts 9 Spring St Princeton NJ 08540. Mailing Add: 104 Mercer St Princeton NJ 08540

GREENBAUM, MARTY
PAINTER, SCULPTOR
b New York, NY, Mar 3, 34. Study: Univ Ariz, Tucson, BA, 56. Work: Picker Art Gallery, Colgate Univ, Hamilton, NY; Chrysler Mus at Norfolk, Va; Citibank, New York; The Print Club, Philadelphia. Comn: Unique bk, Lannan Found, Palm Beach, Fla, 67; Sept Calendar (centerfold), Changes Mag, New York, 71; eds of prints, Shenanigan Press at Jones Rd Print Shop, Barneveld, Wis, 74; graphics portfolio, Creative Artists Pub Serv Prog, New York, 75. Exhib: Personal Torment & Human Concern, Whitney Mus Am Art, New York, 69; 4th Ann Contemp Reflections, Aldrich Mus Contemp Art, Ridgefield, Conn, 75; 20th Nat Print Exhib, Brooklyn Mus, NY, 76; The Object as Poet, Renwick Gallery, Smithsonian Inst, Washington, DC, 76-77; New Ways with Paper, Nat Collection of Fine Arts, Smithsonian Inst, 77; Metamorphosis of the Bk, Documenta 6, Kassel, WGer, 77; Marty Greenbaum, Picker Art Gallery, Colgate Univ, 77; Paper as Medium, Smithsonian Inst Traveling Exhib, 78-80. Awards: Creative Artists Pub Serv Prog grants, 73 & 76; Nat Endowment for the Arts grant, 74. Bibliog: Dorothea Baer (producer), Marty & Lulu's Playground, Independent Film, 65; David Bourdon (auth), Marty Greenbaum, Village Voice, 65; Edward Bryant (auth), Marty Greenbaum (catalogue), Colgate Univ, 77. Mem: Ctr for Bk Arts; Found for Community of Artists. Style & Technique: Unique books altering the shape, surface, and space; drawings and paintings of expressionistic and gestural imagery. Dealer: Ellen Sragow Ltd 43 Fifth Ave New York NY 10003; Fendrick Gallery 3059 M St NW Washington DC 20007. Mailing Add: 99 Maiden Lane New York NY 10038

GREENBERG, CLEMENT
WRITER, ART CRITIC
b Bronx, NY, Jan 16, 09. Study: Art Students League, 24-25; Syracuse Univ, AB, 30. Publ: Auth, Joan Miro, 48; auth, Matisse, 53; auth, Art and Culture, 61; auth, Hofmann, 61. Mailing Add: 275 Central Park W New York NY 10024

GREENBERG, GLORIA
PAINTER, DESIGNER
b New York, NY, Mar 4, 32. Study: Cooper Union Art Sch, cert, 52; Yale-Norfolk Art Sch, scholar, 52, painting with Nicholas Marsicano; Brooklyn Mus Art Sch, scholar, 53, printmaking with Gabor Peterdi. Work: 4 Squares (acrylic panels), Kennedy Airport, 72. Exhib: Brooklyn Mus Print Ann, 53; Soc Beaux Arts Dordogne, France, 59; 14th Ann New Eng Exhib, Silvermine Guild Artists, 63; seven one-woman shows, Mercer Gallery, New York, 71-78; New Drawings, Women's Inter-Art Ctr, New York, 74. Pos: Art consult & bk designer, Jr Bks Div, Harper & Row, 65-77; Women: Self-Image, Women's Interart Ctr, 73

& 74; Art on Paper, Weatherspoon Art Gallery, New York, 74; Report from Soho, Grey Art Gallery, New York, 75; Women in the Arts: Artists Choice (traveling show), 77; What is Feminist Art, Los Angeles, Calif, 77; Women invite Women, Warm, Minneapolis, Minn, 77. Awards: Medal of Honor, Soc Beaux Arts Dordogne, 59. Mem: Mus Mod Art. Style & Technique: Environmental units using loosely arranged shapes on canvas. Media: Acrylic; Paper Works with Ink. Publ: Co-auth & illusr, Away We Go, 63 & Strange Plants & Animals, 64, Harvey. Dealer: 55 Mercer Gallery 55 Mercer St New York NY 10013. Mailing Add: 118 E 17th St New York NY 11003

GREENBERG, IRWIN
PAINTER, INSTRUCTOR
b Brooklyn, NY, Apr 5, 22. Study: Art Students League; NY Univ, BS in Art Educ; study with Yasuo Kuniyoshi, Will Barnet, Hale Woodruff & Paul Gerchik. Exhib: Soldier Art, Nat Gallery, Washington, DC, 45; Mus Fine Arts, Boston, 45; Brooklyn Mus, 48; Am Watercolor Soc, 59-68; Springfield Mus, Mass, 60; Heckscher Mus, New York, 62; Birmingham Mus, Ala, 70-71; Allied Artists, 70; Nat Arts Club, 70-78; Le Nid Gallerie, Long Island, NY, 72, 73, 74 & 77; Audubon Artists, 75-77. Teaching: Instr life drawing, Baruch Col, City Col New York, 53-54; teacher painting & illus, High Sch of Art & Design, New York, NY 68- Awards: Mario Cooper Award, Am Watercolor Soc, 68; Award for Watercolor, Allied Artists, 70; President's Award for Oil Painting, Nat Arts Club, 76. Mem: Am Watercolor Soc. Style & Technique: Realistic style in landscapes, interiors and still lifes. Media: Oil, Watercolor. Publ: Contribr, Soldier Art, Infantry J, 45; illusr, Reader's Digest Fun and Laughter, Reader's Digest, 67; auth, Much Depends on Attitude, Am Artist Mag, 69; auth, Max Ginsburg-Above Ground & Underground, Am Artist Mag, 70; contribr, Arts and Man, Scholastic Pub & Nat Gallery Art, 75-76. Dealer: Bobbie Law Le Nid Gallerie 72 Main St Northport Long Island NY 11768. Mailing Add: 17 W 67th St New York NY 10023

GREENBOWE, F DOUGLAS
PAINTER
b Bayonne, NJ, Sept 19, 21. Study: Art Students League, with Frank DuMond. Work: Butler Inst Am Art, Youngstown, Ohio; Dayton Art Inst, Ohio; Phoenix Mus Art, Ariz; Art Inst Chicago; Seattle Art Mus, Wash; plus others. Comn: Paintings, Bank of Douglas, Tucson & Ariz Bank of Tucson. Exhib: Am Watercolor Soc Ann; Brooklyn Mus, NY; Pa Acad Fine Arts, Philadelphia; NJ Watercolor Soc; Am Acad Arts & Lett; plus others. Awards: Medal, Nat Arts Club, 53; Two Medals, Ariz State Fair, 63. Mem: Am Watercolor Soc; Ariz Watercolor Asn. Media: Watercolor. Mailing Add: 7610 E McDonald Scottsdale AZ 85253

GREENE, BALCOMB
PAINTER
b Niagara Falls, NY, May 22, 04. Study: Syracuse Univ, AB, 26; NY Univ, AM, 40; Univ Vienna, 26-28. Work: Mus Mod Art, Whitney Mus Am Art, Metrop Mus Art & Guggenheim Mus, New York; Carnegie Inst, Pittsburgh; plus many others. Exhib: Art Ctr Los Angeles, 64; Tampa Art Inst, Fla, 66; Santa Barbara Mus Art, Calif, 66; Phoenix Art Mus, Ariz, 66; Fairweather-Hardin Gallery, Chicago, 69; plus many others. Teaching: Instr art, Dartmouth Col, 28-31; assoc prof, Carnegie Inst Technol, 42-59. Pos: Ed, Art Front, 35-36. Awards: Carol H Beck Medal; Critic's Choice, Art News, four times. Mem: Am Fedn Arts; fel Int Inst Arts & Lett; Am Abstract Artists (first chmn, 36-37 & 38-41); Century Club. Dealer: Forum Gallery 1018 Madison Ave New York NY 10021; Bednarz Gallery 902 N La Cienega Blvd Los Angeles CA 90069. Mailing Add: 2 Sutton Pl S New York NY 10022

GREENE, DANIEL E
PAINTER
b Cincinnati, Ohio, Feb 26, 34. Study: Art Acad Cincinnati; Art Students League, Thelka M Bernays scholar, 54-55, with Robert Brackman; Nat Acad Design, with Robert Philipp. Work: Norfolk Mus; Greenshields Mus, Montreal; Shelburne Mus; Yale Univ; US Senate; plus many others. Comn: Portraits of Keith Funston, New York Stock Exchange, George Romney, State of Mich, Elmer Bobst, Warner Lambert Pharmaceut Co, George D Aiken, State of Vt & Archibald Davis & John Watlington, Wachovia Nat Bank; plus many others. Awards: Hilldebrand Portrait Prize, Hudson Valley Art Asn, 66; Coun Am Artists Award, Hudson Valley, 66; Pauline Law Award, Nat Art Club, 67; plus many others. Mem: Assoc Nat Acad Design; Am Watercolor Soc; Allied Artists Am; Audubon Artists; Nat Arts Club; plus others. Mailing Add: 33 W 67th St New York NY 10023

GREENE, ETHEL MAUD
PAINTER
b Malden, Mass, Nov 11, 12. Study: Boston Univ Sch Art; Sch Boston Mus; Mass Sch Art. Work: Calif Western Univ, Fine Arts Gallery & Fine Arts Collectors, Inc, San Diego; Southwestern Col, Chula Vista, Calif; La Salle Col, Philadelphia. Exhib: Artists of Los Angeles & Vicinity, Los Angeles Co Mus, 50, 52 & 55; one-man shows, La Jolla Mus, Calif, 56, Feingarten Gallery, Los Angeles, 70 & Ariz State Univ, Tempe, Ariz, 72; two-man show, Fine Arts Gallery, San Diego, 61. Awards: San Diego Co Expos Awards, 48, 54, 63 & 72; La Jolla Mus Ann Award, 58; Two Californias Award, Calif Western Univ, 63. Bibliog: Marilyn Hagberg (auth), The visual puns of Ethel Greene, San Diego Mag, 7/70. Mem: San Diego Art Guild (pres, 56). Style & Technique: Surrealism. Media: Acrylic. Publ: Illusr, A Dog Called Bum, 60. Mailing Add: 2940 Helix St Spring Valley CA 92077

GREENE, LOIS D
ART DEALER
b Cleveland, Ohio, Dec 11, 24. Study: Case Western Reserve Univ, MEduc. Collections Arranged: Ethiopian Folk Art, American Folk Art. Pos: Dir, The Piedmont Art Gallery, Augusta, Ky, 77- Mem: Bracken County Arts Coun (chmn). Specialty: Ohio and Kentucky artists and craftspersons; contemporary art. Mailing Add: The Piedmont Art Gallery 111 Riverside Dr Augusta KY 41002

GREENE, STEPHEN
PAINTER
b New York, NY, Sept 19, 18. Study: Art Students League; State Univ Iowa, BFA, 42, MA, 45; also with Philip Guston. Work: Whitney Mus Am Art, Guggenheim Mus & Metrop Mus Art, New York; Tate Gallery, London; Corcoran Gallery Art, Washington, DC. Exhib: The New Decade, Whitney Mus Am Art, 55; Abstract Expressionists & Imagists, Guggenheim Mus, 61; VI Sao Paulo Bienal, Brazil, 61; Internatinale Der Zeichnung, Darmstadt, Ger, 64; L'Art Vivant aux Etats-Unis, Fondation Maeght, France, 71. Teaching: Artist in residence, Princeton Univ, 56-59; instr painting & drawing, Art Students League, 59-65; from asst prof to prof painting & drawing, Tyler Sch Art, Temple Univ, 68- Awards: Prix de Rome, Am Acad Rome, 49; Coun Arts & Lett Grant, 66; Inst Arts & Lett Award, 67. Bibliog: H W Janson (auth), Stephen Greene, Mag Art, 48; Michael Fried (auth), The goals of Stephen Greene, Arts Mag, 4-5/63; Barbara Rose (auth), Stephen Greene, Art Int, 4/63. Media: Oil. Dealer: Marilyn Pearl Gallery 29 W 57th St New York NY 10019. Mailing Add: 408A Storms Rd Valley Cottage NY 10989

GREENE, THEODORE R
ART DEALER
b New Rochelle, NY, Dec 3, 19. Pos: Owner & dir, Greene Gallery. Mailing Add: Greene Gallery 368 North Ave New Rochelle NY 10801

GREENE-MERCIER, MARIE ZOE
SCULPTOR, DRAFTSMAN
b Madison, Wis, Mar 31, 11. Study: Radcliffe Col, Harvard Univ, AB(fine arts), 33; New Bauhaus, Chicago, with Moholy-Nagy, Archipenko & Gyorgy Kepes, 37-38. Work: Mus des Sables, Barcares, France; Ca Pesaro, Mus Mod Art, Venice, Italy; Hilles Libr, Radcliffe Col, Cambridge, Mass; Bauhaus-Archiv, West Berlin. Comn: Portrait in bronze of Rudolph Ganz, Ganz Hall, Roosevelt Univ, Chicago, 52; monumental chancel cross, First Baptist Church, Chicago, 67; monumental steel sculpture, French Govt, Barcares, 71 & Arras, 74; monumental steel sculpture, Homburg, WGer, 74. Exhib: Salon d'Automne, Paris, 61, 71 & 72; Salon de la Jeune Sculpture, Rodin Mus, Paris, 65; Mus Contemp Art, Chicago, 68; 20th Premio del Fiorino, Palazzo Strozzi, US Sect, Florence, Italy, 71; Salon de Mai, Paris, 73-78; 39 solo shows, including 40 Yr Retrospective, Amerika Haus, W Berlin, 77 & Musée de Poche Gallery, Paris, 78. Awards: Silver Medal for First Prize Compos, Semaines Int de la Femme, Cannes, France, 68 & Gold Medal for First Prize in Mod Sculpture, 69; First Prize Sculpture & Gold Medal, Festival S Germain des Pres, Paris, 75. Bibliog: Italo Mussa (auth), Marie Zoe Greene-Mercier, Sifra Editrice, 68; Guido Perocco (auth), Greene-Mercier, Le Arti, 6/70; C L Formals (auth), La femme dans l'art contemporain, Ed Christian Hals, 72; Frank Elgar (auth), Greene-Mercier, Musée de Poche, Paris, 78; Lloyd Engelbrecht (auth), Art Int, spring 78. Mem: Artists Equity Asn (pres, Chicago Chap, 59-62, first nat vpres, 62-64); Arts Club Chicago; Renaissance Soc of Univ Chicago; Amis du Louvre, Paris; Amis de Bourdelle, Paris. Style & Technique: Non figurative monumental sculpture processes by fabrication with supervision. Media: Bronze, Steel. Publ: Auth, Trieste, 101 Disegni, 69, Salzburg, 101 Zeichnungen, 70 & Venezia, 101 Disegni, 70, Ed Libr, Italo Svevo, Trieste. Dealer: Galleria Artivisive 60 V A Brunetti Rome Italy. Mailing Add: 1232 E 57th St Chicago IL 60637

GREENLEAF, ESTHER (HARGRAVE)
PAINTER, POTTER
b Ripon, Wis. Study: Univ Minn, BS(archit); Andre L'Hote, Paris; Minneapolis Sch Art; Art Students League; also with Rudolf Rey, New York. Work: Recreation House Collection in Taylor Park, Millburn, NJ; Millburn High Sch Collection. Comn: Painting, Bd Room, Tex Distribr, Inc, Dallas, 74. Exhib: Work by New Jersey Artists, 5th Statewide Triennial, Newark Mus, 64; Nat Asn Women Artists Int Traveling Oil Show, 65; Cambridge Art Asn-Symphony Hall Show in Boston, 69; NH Art Asn 25th Ann Show, Currier Gallery, Manchester, 71; solo-show of paintings, serigraphs & stoneware ceramics, Sharon Arts Ctr, 73. Teaching: Instr design & art hist, Minneapolis Sch Art, 27-30; instr hist furniture & decoration, Univ Minn Sch Archit, 28-30; instr art hist, Cooper Union Sch Art, 32-34. Awards: Zuita Gerstenzang Award for Oils, Nat Asn Women Artists, 62; First Award for Oils & Alice Standish Buell Mem Prize for Graphics, Pen & Brush, 68. Mem: Nat Asn Women Artists; Chester Co Art Asn; Artist-Craftsmen NY; Pen & Brush Soc. Style & Technique: Non-objective; acrylic applied transparently over brilliant white gessoed surface enriching and accentuating the texture. Media: Stoneware ceramics; acrylic on gessoed linen with sand; serigraphy. Mailing Add: Crosslands Apt 190 Kennett Square PA 19348

GREENLEAF, KENNETH LEE
SCULPTOR
b Damariscotta, Maine, Aug 10, 45. Work: Whitney Mus Am Art, New York; Houston Mus Fine Arts, Tex; New Sch Social Res, New York. Exhib: Painting & Sculpture, Indianapolis Mus Art, 72 & 74; Contemporary American Art, Whitney Mus Biennial, 73; one-man shows, LoGiudice Gallery, New York, 73, Tibor de Nagy Galleries, New York, 73, 74, 76 & 78 & Houston, 74 & B R Konblatt Gallery, Baltimore, Md, 77. Style & Technique: Abstract sculpture. Media: Various. Dealer: Tibor de Nagy Gallery 29 W 57th St New York NY 10019. Mailing Add: 149 Franklin St New York NY 10013

GREENLY, COLIN
INTANGIBLE ART, SCULPTOR
b London, Eng, Jan 21, 28; US citizen. Study: Harvard Univ, AB, 48; Columbia Univ Sch Painting & Sculpture, with Oronzio Maldarelli & Peppino Mangravite; Am Univ Grad Sch Fine Arts. Work: Mus Mod Art, New York; Corcoran Gallery Art, Washington, DC; Herbert F Johnson Mus, Ithaca, NY; Philadelphia Mus Art; Rosenwald Collection, Nat Gallery Art, Washington, DC. Comn: Sculpture relief, Exp Int Living, Putney, Vt, 61; wall painting, Everson Mus, Syracuse, NY, 71; participatory murals, NY State Off Bldg, Utica, 73 & Creative Artists Pub Serv Prog, 75. Exhib: One-man show, Corcoran Gallery Art, 68; Contemporary American Painting & Sculpture, Krannert Art Mus, Champaign, Ill, 69 & 75; Images, Penthouse Gallery, Mus Mod Art, 73; John Weber Galley, New York, 77; one-man show, Intangible Sculpture, Andrew Dickson White Mus, Cornell Univ, 72 & Finch Col Mus, New York, 74. Teaching: Dir art, Madeira Sch, Greenway, Va, 55-68; Dana prof art, Colgate Univ, 72-73. Pos: Vis artist, Cent Mich Univ, 72; artist in residence, Everson Mus, Syracuse, NY, 72 & Cazenovia Col, 72; Nat Endowment Arts & Humanities artist in residence, Finch Col, 74. Awards: Winning Sculpture, Nat Competition for Playground Sculpture, Corcoran Sch Art, 67; Nat Endowment Arts & Humanities Grant for Sculpture, 67; Creative Artists Pub Serv Prog Grant for Intangible Sculpture, New York, 72 & Creative Artists Pub Serv Fel, 78. Style & Technique: Intangible art; unspecified medium and dimensions; photo emulsion. Mailing Add: RD1 Box 118 Campbell NY 10916

GREENSPAN, MR & MRS GEORGE
COLLECTORS
Mr Greenspan, b New York, NY, May 17, 00. Collection: Comprehensive collection of impressionist and post-impressionist drawings; contemporary American paintings. Mailing Add: 885 Park Ave New York NY 10021

GREENSTEIN, RONNI BOGAEV
See Bogaev, Ronni

GREENWALD, ALICE (ALICE MARIAN GREENWALD-WARD)
CURATOR, LECTURER
b Oceanside, NY, Jan 2, 52. Study: Univ Exeter, Devon, Eng, with Theo Brown, 71-72; Sarah Lawrence Col, Bronxville, NY, BA(anthrop & Lit), 73; Univ Chicago Divinity Sch, Ill, AM(hist of relig), 75. Collections Arranged: Ludwig Wolpert: A Retrospective, 77, Maranora: A Graphic Interpretation of Kafka's The Trial, 77, The Jews of Yemen, 77-78, Beverly-Fairfax: Portrait of a Neighborhood by Kathrya Jacobi, 77-78 & Two Perspectives of Abraham Rattner, 78, Huc Skirball Mus, Hebrew Union Col, Los Angeles, Calif. Teaching: Mus educator Jewish art, Hebrew Union Col, Los Angeles, Calif, 75- Pos: Asst to the cur, Spertus Mus of Judaica, Chicago, Ill, 74-75; cur, Huc Skirball Mus, Hebrew Union Col, Los Angeles, 75- Mem: Am Asn of Mus; Int Coun of Mus; Coun of Am Jewish Mus. Res: All

areas of Jewish art, emphasis on late Medieval European ritual art and near eastern archaelogy. Publ: Ed, A Centennial Sampler: 100 Years of Collecting at Hebrew Union College, Huc Skirball Mus, Hebrew Union Col, 76. Mailing Add: 3077 University Mall Los Angeles CA 90007

GREENWALD, CHARLES D
COLLECTOR, PATRON
b New York, NY. Study: NY Univ. Collection: American paintings, drawings and etchings after 1900. Mailing Add: 120 E 81st St New York NY 10028

GREENWALD, DOROTHY KIRSTEIN
COLLECTOR
b New York, NY. Study: NY Sch Interior Design; Craft Students League. Collection: 20th century contemporary and modern American art. Mailing Add: 120 E 81st St New York NY 10028

GREENWALD, SHEILA ELLEN
ILLUSTRATOR
b New York, NY, May 26, 34. Study: High Sch of Music & Art; Sarah Lawrence Col, BA, 56. Style & Technique: Pen and ink line drawings, humorous and satiric illustrations for childrens books and humorous articles. Media: Pen, Ink. Publ: Auth & illusr, The Hot Day, Bobbs-Merrill, 72; auth & illusr, The Museum of the Forgotten Dolls, Lippincott, 74; illusr, Story in pictures, Cricket Mag, 75; auth & illusr, The Secret In Mirandas Closet, 76 & The Mariah Delany Lending Library Disaster, 77, Houghton Mifflin. Dealer: Harriet Wasserman c/o Russell & Volkening 551 Fifth Ave New York NY 10017. Mailing Add: 175 Riverside Dr New York NY 10024

GREENWOOD, PAUL ANTHONY
SCULPTOR, INSTRUCTOR
b Philadelphia, Pa, Sept 13, 21. Study: Pa Acad Fine Arts, Philadelphia; Barnes Found, Merion, Pa, Acad Julien, Paris; Temple Univ Sch Fine Arts; also with Jo Davidson. Work: Philadelphia Art Mus; NJ State Mus, Trenton; Phoenix Art Mus, Ariz. Comn: Bronze lion relief, Sons of Italy, Philadelphia, 55; fountains, comn by Mrs William Almy, Malvern, 66 & by Adolph Rosengarten, 70. Exhib: One-man shows, Beryl Lusch Gallery, 54, Pa Acad Fine Arts, 57 & Peale House, Philadelphia, 65 & 75; Pa Acad Fine Arts; Philadelphia Art Mus; Philadelphia Art Alliance; Contemp Club, Trenton. Teaching: Instr sculpture, Philadelphia Art Mus, 46 & Moore Inst Art & Sci, 47-49; instr sculpture & drawing, Pa Acad Fine Arts, 53- Awards: Louis Comfort Tiffany Grant, 52 & 71; May Audubon Post Prize, 53 & 54; Acad Fel Gold Medal, 55. Mem: Life mem Philadelphia Print Club; Peale Club. Media: Bronze, Plastic. Mailing Add: c/o Peale House 1811 Chestnut St Philadelphia PA 19103

GREENWOOD, WILLIAM JAMES
PAINTER, CONSERVATOR
b Syracuse, NY, Apr 26, 44. Study: Hussian Sch Art, Philadelphia, 4 yr dipl; Pa Acad Fine Arts, 2 yrs; pvt study with Morris Blackburn; conserv with Franklin Shores, 67-75; conserv of art on paper, asst to Marilyn Kemp Weidner, 75. Exhib: Fel Pa Acad Fine Arts Ann, 71 & 75; Philadelphia Watercolor Club Ann, 68-75; Best of Year Show, Woodmere Art Gallery, 71; Philadelphia Watercolor Club Mem, Philadelphia Sketch Club, 74 & 75. Collections Arranged: Ann Traveling Exhib, Philadelphia Watercolor Club, 70-; Conservation of Art on Paper in Rare Book and Other Departments, Free Libr Philadelphia, 71- Teaching: Pvt lessons in painting, 70- Mem: Fel Pa Acad Fine Arts; Philadelphia Watercolor Club (bd dir, 69-; chmn traveling exhib, 70-; hon vpres, 73-); Int Inst Conserv Hist & Artistic Works. Style & Technique: Naturalist; experimental and academic. Media: Oil, Aqueous Media. Mailing Add: 726 Sussex Rd Wynnewood PA 19096

GREER, JOHN SYDNEY
SCULPTOR
b Amherst, NS, Can, June 28, 44. Study: NS Col of Art, 62-64, bursary, dipl, 64; Montreal Mus Sch of Art and Design, 65-66, scholar, dipl(hon in sculpture), 66; Vancouver Sch of Art, dipl, 67. Work: Nat Gallery, Ottawa; Can Coun Art Bank; Art Gallery of Ontario; Owens Art Gallery, Mt Allision Univ, Sackville NB; Art Gallery of NS. Comn: Y D Klein (lithorgaph), NS Col of Art & Design, 74; Olympic poster proposal, Artist's Athletics Coalition, 75; & 75 & John Greer-His Art (videotape), 76, Mt St Vincent Art Gallery, Halifax; Silkscreen ed, Can Coun Art Bank, Grand Western Screen Shop, Winnipeg, 77. Exhib: One-man shows, Issacs Gallery, Toronto, Ontario, 70-73, 75-76 & 78, A-Space Gallery, Toronto, 71, Anna Leonowens Art Gallery, Halifax, NS, 72, Owens Art Gallery, Sackville, NB, 74, Dalhousie Art Gallery, Halifax, 74 & 76, Mt St Vincent Art Gallery, Halifax, 75, Eye Level Gallery, Halifax, 76-77, Forest City Gallery, London, Ontario, 77. Collections Arranged: The Isaacs Gallery (with catalogue) & Investigations (with catalogue), Owens Art Gallery, 74; Sceptical Spectacles (with catalogue), Dalhousie Art Gallery, 74. Bibliog: Victor Coleman (auth), John Greer-Eye Ear, Open Letter, CoachHouse Press, 72; Gary Dault (auth), Review, Arts Can, spring, 75. Mem: Eye Level Gallery, Halifax (vchmn, 75-); Can Artist Representation, Provincial, Nat. Media: Sculpture; Prints. Dealer: Isaacs Gallery 832 Yonge St Toronto ON Can. Mailing Add: R R 2 Mill Village NS BOJ 2HO Can

GREER, WALTER MARION
PAINTER
b Ware Shoals, SC, Aug 11, 20. Study: The Citadel, BS, 42; Clemson Univ, BS, 47; Atlanta Sch Art, 60; Nat Acad Design, New York, with Robert Phillipp; also with Ben Shute, Atlanta, 62 & study abroad. Work: Telfair Acad Arts & Sci, Savannah, Ga; SC State Collection, Columbia Mus Art; paintings, Sea Pines Plantation Co, Hilton Head Island, SC; Home Fed Collection, Charleston, SC; C & S Collection, Atlanta & Greenville, SC. Comn: Oil landscape, Gov Mansion, Columbia, 67; three paintings, Phipps Land Co, Hilton Head Island & New York, 70; portrait of pres, Emory Univ, 71; triptych, Simmons Collection, Atlanta, Ga. Exhib: Mead Paper Show, Atlanta, Ga, 60; Hunter Ann, Chattanooga, Tenn, 62; SC Invitational, Columbia, 69; one-man shows, Columbia Mus Art, 73 & Telfair Acad Arts & Sci, 74. Teaching: Instr pvt classes, 63-66; instr spec art classes, USMC, Parris Island, SC, 64-65 & Savannah Art Asn Sch, 66. Awards: Savannah Arts Festival Award for Rivers, 66; SC Arts Coun Purchase Award for Pond, 69; SC Archit Award for Pond (Grey Phase), 71. Bibliog: Virginia Ball (auth), The man that got away, Atlanta Mag, 65; Don Deaton (auth), Island for an artist, Atlanta J, 65; Jack Morris & Robert Smeltz (auth), Contemporary artists of South Carolina, 70. Mem: Guild SC Artists (mem bd); hon life mem Beaufort Art Asn. Style & Technique: Abstract impressionism, severely modified realism using brush, stencils and sprayed paint. Media: Oil. Dealer: Joe De Mers Gallery Ltd Harbourtown Hilton Head Island SC 29928. Mailing Add: Firethorn Hilton Head Island SC 29928

GREGG, RICHARD NELSON
MUSEUM DIRECTOR, WRITER
b Kalamazoo, Mich, Sept 4, 26. Study: Western Mich Univ; Cranbrook Acad Art, BFA & MFA. Collections Arranged: Inness, 63; Daubigny, 64; Wedgwood, 65; Remington, 67; Dutch Art of the 1600's, 68; Costigan, for the Smithsonian Inst, 68; Contemporary California Art, 70; American Art of the 1930's, 71; The City in American Painting, 72; German Expressionism, 74; Pennsylvania Folk Art, 74. Teaching: Instr, Cranbrook Sch for Boys & Worcester Mus Art. Pos: Dir, Kalamazoo Inst Art; curatorial asst, Toledo Mus Art; head mus educ, Art Inst Chicago; dir, Paine Ctr & Arboretum; dir, Joslyn Art Mus; dir, Allentown Art Mus, Pa, 72- Publ: Contribr, Curator, Antiques, Hobbies, Mus News, Midwest Mus Quart & Connoisseur. Mailing Add: Box 117 Allentown Art Mus Allentown PA 18105

GREGOR, HAROLD LAURENCE
PAINTER, EDUCATOR
b Detroit, Mi Mich, Sept 10, 29. Study: Wayne State Univ, BSEd, 51; Mich State Univ, MS(ceramics, painting), 53; Detroit Soc Arts & Crafts, 55-57, with John Foster; Ohio State Univ, PhD(painting, art hist), 60; and with Hoyt Sherman. Work: Filipacci Collection, Paris, France; Kemper Ins Co, Long Grove, Ill; Calif Col Arts & Crafts, Oakland; Fine Arts Gallery San Diego; Govett-Brewster Gallery, New Plymouth, NZ. Exhib: One-man shows, Va Commonwealth Univ, Richmond, 73, Metrop State Col, Denver, 73 & Nancy Lurie Art Gallery, Chicago, 74, 77 & 78; Norton Gallery Imagist Realism Exhib, West Palm Beach, Fla, 74; Land, Sky, Water, Spokane World's Fair, 74; Chicago Connection Show, Crocker Gallery, Sacramento, Calif, 76-77; Tibor de Nagy Gallery, New York, NY, 77 & 78. Teaching: Asst prof painting & art hist, San Diego State Univ, 60-63; asst prof painting, Purdue Univ, Lafayette, 63-66; assoc prof painting & art hist, Chapman Col, 66-70; prof painting & art hist, Ill State Univ, Normal, 70- Awards: Evansville Mus Arts & Sci Purchase Award, 72; Nat Endowment Arts Grant, 73; New Horizons Ann Exhib Award of Excellence, 75. Bibliog: F D Cossitt (auth), rev in Richmond-Times Dispatch, 4/1/73; D Pollock (auth), rev in Art in Am, 1/74; E Edwards (auth), Gregor's midwest landscapes, Reader Mag, 10/74. Mem: San Diego Art Guild. Style & Technique: Realistic agricultural imagery on oil and acrylic coupled with environmental sculpture; floor pieces. Dealer: Nancy Lurie Art 1632 N La Salle St Chicago IL 60614; Tibor de Nagy Gallery 29 W 57th St New York NY 10019. Mailing Add: 1116 E Jefferson Bloomington IL 61701

GREGOR, HELEN FRANCES
DESIGNER, EDUCATOR
b Prague, Czech, June 28, 21; Can citizen. Study: Birmingham Col Art, Eng; Royal Col Art, assoc, London. Work: Nat Gallery, Ottawa; Queens Univ, Kingston, Ont; Benson & Hedges; First Off Can Tapestry Collection, Dept External Affairs, Ottawa; Imperial Bank Com; Can Guild Crafts. Comn: Toronto Music Libr, 69; Univ Toronto, 70; Hamilton Auditorium, 73; Hydro Bldg, Toronto, 75. Exhib: One-man shows, Architect Asn Toronto, 67, Royal Ont Mus, Toronto, 76 & Can Cult Centre, Paris, 77; Queens Univ, 69; 4th Int Biennial Tapestry, Lausanne, Switz, 69 & 8th Int Biennial, Lausanne & Lisbon, Port, 78; Mus Gobelin, Paris, 4th Int Craft Show, Stuttgart, Ger, 69; plus others. Teaching: Head textiles & tapestry, Ont Col Art, 52-75. Awards: Can Coun Award for Spec Studies, 64 & 69. Bibliog: Video publ, Tapestry Today, Can Art, Gt Brit, 74; Madeleine Jarry (auth), La Tapisserie, Art du XXeme Siecle, 74. Mem: Royal Can Acad Arts; Ont Soc Artists (exec, 72-73); Centennial Comt Ont Col Art. Style & Technique: Tapestry, bas lisse. Media: Natural Fibers, Metal. Mailing Add: 218 Glen Rd Toronto ON M4W 2X3 Can

GREGOROPOULOS, JOHN
PAINTER
b Athens, Greece, Dec 16, 21; US citizen. Study: In Athens; Univ Conn, BA. Work: Minn Mus Art, St Paul; Ball State Found, Muncie, Ind; Slater Mus, Norwich, Conn; De Cordova Mus, Lincoln, Mass. Exhib: Whitney Mus Am Art Ann, 54 & Art USA, New York, 58; 1st Biennale Christlicher Kunst Gegenwart, Salzburg, 58; Drawings USA, Minn Mus Art, 71. Teaching: Prof art, Univ Conn, 53- Pos: Pres, Mystic Art Asn, 60-62. Awards: Small Drawings & Sculpture Purchase Award, Ball State Teachers Col, 55; Grumbacher Award, Chautauqua Art Asn 2nd Nat, 59; Drawings USA, St Paul Art Ctr, 63. Bibliog: F Walkey (auth), John Gregoropoulos, Art in Am, 2/55; John Gregoropoulos, Zygos, Athens, 57; Art & the new patron, WEDN-TV, 68. Style & Technique: Subjective landscapes; repeat images; enclosed in geometric form; traditional technique. Publ: Auth, Change in art, Nea Estia, Athens, 57. Mailing Add: 644 Wormwood Hill Rd Storrs CT 06268

GREGORY, ANGELA
SCULPTOR, EDUCATOR
b New Orleans, La, Oct 18, 03. Study: Art Sch, Newcomb Col, BDesign, Tulane Univ La, MA(archit); Parsons Sch, Paris & Italy, Newcomb Col scholar, 25, cert; Acad Grande Chaumiere, Paris; NY State Col Ceramics; also with Charles Keck, New York & Antoine Bourdelle, Paris. Work: Sculpture of the Western Hemisphere, IBM Collection. Comn: John McDonogh Monument, Work Progress Admin, Civic Ctr, New Orleans, 38; Bienville Monument, New Orleans, 55; Gen Hy Watkins Allen, State of La, Port Allen, 61; St Louis, Archdiocesan Bldg, New Orleans, 61; aluminum relief panels on walnut, John XXIII Libr, St Mary's Dominican Col, New Orleans, 67. Exhib: Salon Tuileries, Paris, 28 & 32; Nat Sculpture Soc Show, Calif Palace of Legion of Honor, San Francisco, 29, Nat Mus, Washington, DC, 32 & Whitney Mus Am Art, New York, 40; Salon d'Antomme, Paris, 30; one-man show, New Orleans Mus Art, 33-34; Int Exhib Contemp Medals, Numismatic Mus, Athens, Greece, 66. Teaching: Artist in residence, Newcomb Col, Tulane Univ La, 40-41; sculptor in residence & prof art appreciation, St Mary's Dominican Col, 62-, partial grant through Dominican Col, Shell Co Found grant, 72. Pos: State supvr, Work Proj Admin, New Orleans, 41-42; asst engr camouflage, Corps Engrs, New Orleans Dist, 42-43. Awards: Mary L S Neill Medal, Art Sch, Newcomb Col, 24. Bibliog: Walter Agard (auth), The new architectural sculpture, 47; Hilda P Hammond & Betsy Peterson (auth), Lady at Dominican, a tribute to a pope, Dixie-Roto, Times-Picayune, 67; Jas Cohen (auth), The birth of a medal, Numismatist, 72. Mem: Fel Nat Sculpture Soc; New Orleans Mus Art. Media: Stone, Bronze, Aluminum. Mailing Add: 630 Pine St New Orleans LA 70118

GREGORY, BRUCE
PAINTER, INSTRUCTOR
b Anadarko, Okla, June 27, 17. Study: Art Students League; Colo Springs Art Ctr; and with Fernand Leger. Comn: Murals, UN, New York, 52 & Franklin D Roosevelt Sch, New York, 56; map murals, Civil Defense Hq, New York, 57. Exhib: Terry Art Inst, Miami, Fla, 51; Pa Acad Art, Philadelphia, 52; Art USA, New York, 58; Butler Art Inst Ann, 66; Fla State Fair, 66. Teaching: Instr painting, Union Col, 56-57; instr painting, John Herron Art Inst, Ind, 60-61; instr painting, color & design, Ringling Sch Art, Sarasota, Fla, 61- Pos: Color & design consult, Harrison & Abramovitz, New York, 52-56; prof serv contractor, Fine Arts Evan, Gen Serv Admin, 73. Awards: Prix de l'Anee, Fernand Leger, 51; New York Award Show, ACA Gallery, 53; Kleinert Award, Woodstock Asn, 60. Bibliog: Aline Louchhien (auth), UN murals, 9/7/52 & Kathleen Teltsch (auth), US painter does UN Coats-of-Arms, 4/30/53,

New York Times; Gorden Brown (auth), Bruce Gregory, Arts Mag, 66. Mem: Sarasota Art Asn; Fla Artists Group. Style & Technique: Modern figure and abstract murals. Media: Oil, Acrylic. Publ: Auth, Leger's atelier & auth, UN murals, Col Art J, 62; contribr, New International Encyclopedia of Art, 67. Dealer: Ward-Nasse Gallery 178 Prince St New York NY 10012. Mailing Add: PO Box 1624 Sarasota FL 33578

GREGORY, JOAN
EDUCATOR, PAINTER
b Montgomery, Ala, Apr 1, 30. Study: Univ Montevallo, AB, 52; Peabody Col, MA, 53, EdD, 66; Inst Allende, San Miguel Allende, Mex. Work: Dillard Collection, Weatherspoon Gallery, Univ NC, Greensboro; NC Nat Bank Collection; La State Art Comn Collection; Springs Mills, Lancaster, SC; US Park Serv, Gatlinburg, Tenn. Exhib: Exhibs 80 & 180, Huntington Galleries, 56-61; one-woman show, 63 & 13th Dixie Art Ann, Montgomery Mus Fine Arts; Southeastern Painting Show, Gallery Contemp Art, Winston-Salem, NC, 71; Ann NC Artists Exhib & Traveling Show, 71-72. Teaching: Instr art, Marshall Univ, 55-61; chmn dept art, Bloomsburg State Col, 63-64; prof art & head dept, Univ NC, Greensboro, 64- Awards: Purchase Awards, Dillard Collection, 66 & Springs Art Show, Lancaster, SC, 72; Merit Award, NC/Va Art Educators, Southeast Ctr Contemp Art, 75. Mem: Nat Art Educ Asn (mem states assembly, 71-73); NC Art Educ Asn (pres, 71-75); Southeastern Col Art Conf (bd dirs, 74-76); Assoc Artists NC (bd dirs, 69-71). Media: Collage. Mailing Add: Dept of Art Univ of NC Greensboro NC 27412

GRESSEL, MICHAEL L
SCULPTOR
b Wurzburg, Ger, Sept 20, 02; US citizen. Study: Art Sch, Bavaria, with Arthur Schleglmünig; Beaux Art Inst Design, New York. Work: Bruckner Mus, Albion, Mich; Metrop Mus Art & Nat Theater & Acad, New York; Nat Theater, Washington, DC; County Trust Co, Mount Kisco, NY. Comn: Eagle, Int Motel, Kennedy Airport, New York, 58; two figures, Stepinac High Sch, White Plains, NY, 60; ivory relief portrait for Gen Eisenhower, 62; City Crest, Town Hall, Greenwich, Conn, 67; bust of Gen V Steuben, 69. Exhib: Hudson Valley Art Asn Ann, White Plains, 46-72; Valhalla High Sch, NY, 49; Allied Artists Am, Nat Acad Design, 71; Nat Sculpture Soc, New York, 72; Armonk Libr, NY. Awards: Dr Morris Woodrow Award, Hudson Valley Art Asn, 51, Mrs John Newington Award for Madonna, 63 & Gold Medal, 65; Gold Medal, Hudson Valley Art Exhib, 72. Mem: Hudson Valley Art Asn (dir, 52-); Nat Sculpture Soc. Mailing Add: Gressel Pl Armonk NY 10504

GREY, MRS BENJAMIN EDWARDS
COLLECTOR, PATRON
b St Paul, Minn. Study: Vassar Col, BA, 24. Pos: Mem sch comt, Minneapolis Sch Art, 64-; trustee, Minneapolis Soc Fine Arts, 67-; pres, Ben & Abby Grey Found, 60- Interest: Assembled Minnesota Art Portfolio exhibited in Iran & Mediterranean countries; Iranian contemporary art exhibited in the United States; commissioned American Federation of Arts to assemble sixty contemporary American works and under United States Information Service, opened three shows in Turkey, Iran and Pakistan; originated cultural exchange program, Communication Through Art; assembled Turkish Art Today, traveling with American print show in Tehran; exhibited Contemporary Art of India and Iran traveling in eastern United States; sponsor of American Section First India Triennial of Contemporary World Art. Collection: Contemporary art from various countries, specializing in Middle East and South-Asian countries. Mailing Add: 497 Otis Ave St Paul MN 55104

GREY, ESTELLE (ESTELLE ASHBY)
PAINTER, SCULPTOR
b Scranton, Pa, Dec 8, 17. Study: Traphagan Sch Fashion; Art Students League. Work: Randolph Macon Woman's Col; Butler Inst Am Art. Exhib: Fisk Univ; Riverside Mus, 60; Kaymar Gallery, 68-72; Tirca Karlis Gallery, 70-74. Mem: Art Students League. Style & Technique: Expressionistic. Media: Oil; Terra Cotta; Metal. Dealer: Tirca Karlis Commercial St Provincetown MA 02657. Mailing Add: 18 Cornelia St New York NY 10014

GRIEDER, TERENCE
ART HISTORIAN
b Cedar Rapids, Iowa, Sept 2, 31. Study: Univ Colo, BA, 53; Univ Wis, MS(appl art), 56; Univ Pa, MA(art hist), 60, PhD(art hist), 62. Teaching: Instr art, Univ Wis-Milwaukee, 56-57; instr art, Conn Col, New London, 60-61; from asst prof to prof art, Univ Tex, Austin, 61- Awards: US Govt Smith-Mundt Fel to Guatemala, 59-60; Am Coun Learned Socs Foreign Area Fel, 65-67. Mem: Col Art Asn; Soc Am Archaeol. Res: Archaeological study of the history of pre-Colombian art, emphasizing the Andean highlands of Peru. Publ: Auth, Representation of space and form in Maya painting, Am Antiq, 64; co-auth, Art of Latin America since independence, with S L Catlin, 66; auth, Rotary tools in ancient Peru, Archaeology, 74; auth, The interpretation of ancient symbols, Am Anthropologist, 75; auth, Art & Archaeology of Pashash, 78. Mailing Add: 2603 Maria Anna Rd Austin TX 78703

GRIEGER, (WALTER) SCOTT
SCULPTOR
b Biloxi, Miss, Aug 27, 46. Study: Chouinard Art Inst; Otis Art Inst; San Fernando Valley State Col, BA. Work: Whitney Mus Am Art, New York. Exhib: Information, Mus Mod Art, New York, 70; Sculpture Ann, Whitney Mus Am Art, New York, 70; one-man show, Los Angeles Co Mus Art, Calif & Reese Palley Gallery, New York, 71; Los Angeles '72, Sidney Janis Gallery, New York, 72. Teaching: Artist in residence, Univ Fla, 71; instr, Art Ctr, Col Design, 72. Bibliog: Robert Hughes (auth), Four L A Artists, Time Mag, 2/71; Jane Livingston (auth), 3 L A Artists, Art in Am, 5-6/71. Publ: Auth, Impersonations, 70; auth, Mainstream Art, 72. Mailing Add: 4360 1/2 Melrose Blvd Los Angeles CA 90029

GRIFFIN, RACHAEL S
ART ADMINISTRATOR, WRITER
US citizen. Study: Univ Ore; Portland Mus Art Sch, Ore; Reed Col. Collections Arranged: Paintings & Sculptures of the Pacific Northwest, 59; German Expressionist Painting from the Collection of Morton D May, 67; Selections from the Collection of Sterling Holloway, 66; West Coast Now (major regional), 68; also Retrospective Exhibitions of Jack McLarty, 63, Michele Russo, 66 & Charles Voorhies, 72; ed and/or wrote catalogs for these exhibs. Pos: Dir educ, Portland Art Mus, 57-60, cur, 60-76; art comt, Gifted Child Proj, Ford Found. Mem: Am Asn Mus; Nat Comn Humanities in Schs; Contemp Crafts Asn Bd; Catlin Gabel Sch Bd; Northwest Film Study Ctr Bd. Publ: Auth, Oregon art: distinctive & distinguished, Bookman, 7/54; co-auth, A Course in Understanding Art for Secondary Schools, Portland Art Mus, 62; auth, Ernst Josephson, Artforum, 12/64; auth, The understanding of art, Mus News, 3/64; auth, Ken Shores, Craft Horizons, 8/70. Mailing Add: 2327 SW Market St Dr Portland OR 97201

GRIGGS, MAITLAND LEE
COLLECTOR
b New York, NY, Sept 13, 02. Study: Christ Church, Oxford Univ. Collection: Hudson River School of painting (confined to view of and on the Hudson River); old Staffordshire china with Hudson River views; modern paintings; Oriental, African and pre-Columbian artifacts. Mailing Add: Ardsley-on-Hudson NY 10503

GRIGOR, MARGARET CHRISTIAN
SCULPTOR
b Forres, Scotland, Mar 2, 12; US citizen. Study: Mt Holyoke Col, BA; Pa Acad Fine Arts. Work: Mt Holyoke Col, South Hadley, Mass; Smithsonian Inst, Washington, DC; Medallic Art Co, Danbury, Conn. Comn: Am Med Asn Medal, 48; Alaska-Hawaii Medal, Soc Medalists, 65; Alexander Hamilton Medal, Hall of Fame Great Am, NY Univ, 71; designed Am Revolution Bicentennial Medal for 1975, 74. Exhib: Nat Sculpture Soc Ann, 69, 72 & 74 & Nat Acad Design, New York, 73. Awards: Lindsay Morris Mem Prize, Nat Sculpture Soc, 69; Semi-finalist, Bicentennial Coin Competition, 74. Mem: Nat Sculpture Soc; Nat Soc Women Artists; Am Artists Prof League. Media: Plasteline, Plaster. Mailing Add: PO Box 326 Steilacoom WA 98388

GRIGORIADIS, MARY
PAINTER
b Jersey City, NJ, June 23, 42. Study: Barnard Col, BA, 63; Columbia Univ, MA, 65. Work: Chase Manhattan Bank, Athens & Piraeus, Greece; First Nat Bank Chicago; Lincoln Hosp, New York. Exhib: One-woman show, A I R Gallery, New York, 72 & 75; Biennial Contemp Am Art, Whitney Mus Am Art, 73; Am Acad Arts & Lett Award Exhib, 74; Women's Work-Am Art 1974, Mus of Philadelphia Civic Ctr, 74; The Year of the Woman, Bronx Mus Arts, 75; Small Works, Albright-Knox Mus Art, 76-77; A I R Gallery, NY, 76-77; Noemata, Brooklyn Mus, 77; Critic's Choice, Munson-Williams-Proctor Inst, Utica, NY, 77; Pattern Painting, PS I, New York, 77; Gallery K, Washington, DC, 78. Bibliog: Max Kozloff (auth), rev in Art Forum, 75; Carter Ratcliff (auth), New York, Art Spectrum, 75; Hayden Herrera, reviews, Art in Am, 3-4/77. Mem: A I R Gallery, New York. Style & Technique: Oil paint on raw linen, richly painted, highly varnished secular icons containing geometric forms placed around a central arc. Dealer: A I R Gallery 97 Wooster St New York NY 10012. Mailing Add: 382 Central Park W New York NY 10025

GRIGSBY, JEFFERSON EUGENE, JR
EDUCATOR, PAINTER
b Greensboro, NC, Oct 17, 18. Study: Morehouse Col, with Hale Woodruff & Nancy Prophet, BA, 38; Am Artists Sch, 39, with M Hebald, H Harrari & J Groth; Ohio State Univ, with Prof Hopkins & R Fanning, MA, 40; Ecole des Beaux Arts, Marseilles, 45; NY Univ, PhD, 63; Philadelphia Col Art, DFA, 65. Work: Tex Southern Univ, Houston; Mint Mus, Charlotte, NC; Nat Mus Ghana, Cape Castle. Exhib: Am Negro Expos, Tanner Art Galleries, Chicago, 40; Baltimore Mus, 40; Ariz Ann, Phoenix Mus, 64; one-man show, Centennial Celebration, Morehouse Col, 67; Dimensions in Black, La Jolla Mus, Calif, 70. Teaching: Instr drawing & painting, Johnson C Smith Univ, 40-41; prof art ed & drawing, Ariz State Univ, 66- Pos: Head dept art, Carver High Sch, 46-54 & Phoenix Union High Sch, Ariz, 54-66. Awards: Medallion of Merit, Nat Gallery Art, 66. Mem: Nat Art Educ Asn (vpres, 72-74); Pac Arts Asn (treas, 58-60); Ariz Artists Guild; Col Art Asn Am; Nat Conf Artists. Style & Technique: Abstract. Media: Acrylic, Serigraph. Res: African art, its history, materials used and style. Publ: Co-auth, Partners with art, Sch Arts Mag, 55; auth, Ba Kuba art, In: Africa Seen by American Negroes, 58; auth, African art, exhib catalog, Heard Mus, Phoenix, 64; auth, Encounters, exhib catalog, J C Smith Univ Exhib, 68; auth, Art & Ethnics, William C Brown Co. Mailing Add: 1117 N Ninth St Phoenix AZ 85006

GRILLO, JOHN
PAINTER
b Lawrence, Mass, July 4, 17. Study: Hartford Art Sch, 35-38; Calif Sch Fine Arts, 46, Albert M Bender fel, 47; Hofmann Sch, 49-50. Work: Los Angeles Co Mus Art, Calif; Newark Mus, NJ; Solomon R Guggenheim Mus, New York; Butler Inst Am Art, Youngstown, Ohio; Wadsworth Atheneum, Hartford, Conn; plus others. Exhib: One-man shows, New Sch Social Res, 67, State Univ Iowa, 67, Simmons Col, 68; Eleanor Rigelhaupt Gallery, Boston, 68 & Benedict Art Ctr, St Joseph, Minn, 69; plus many others. Teaching: Instr, Southern Ill Univ, 60; instr, Sch Visual Arts, 61; instr, Univ Calif, Berkeley, 62-63; instr, New Sch Social Res, 64-66; instr, Pratt Inst, 64-66; instr, Univ Iowa, 67; artist in residence, Univ Mass, 68-69. Awards: Prizes, Sacramento State Fair; Ford Found Fel to Tamarind Lithography Workshop & Butler Inst Am Art, 64. Mailing Add: 111 Chestnut St Amherst MA 01002

GRIMLEY, OLIVER FETTEROLF
PAINTER, SCULPTOR
b Norristown, Pa, June 30, 20. Study: Pa Acad Fine Arts, Henry J Scheidt traveling scholar, 50; Univ Pa, BFA & MFA. Work: Pa Acad Fine Arts; Philadelphia Mus; Libr Cong, Washington, DC; Woodmere Art Galleries, Philadelphia. Comn: Murals, Commonwealth Fed Savings & Loan, Norristown, 63, Continental Bank & Trust, 65 & Am Bank, Lafayette Hills, Pa, 72; papier-mache eagle, comn by Leonard Tose, Vet Stadium, Philadelphia, 71. Exhib: Whitney Mus Am Art, Libr Cong & Metrop Mus, 52-57; Pa Acad Fine Arts Watercolor Shows, 58-63; Philadelphia Mus. Teaching: Instr drawing, Hussian Sch Art, 60-; instr drawing, Pa Acad Fine Arts, 65- Awards: Joseph Pennell Award, Philadelphia Watercolor Club, 66, 68 & 70; Bruce S Marks Prize for Drawing, Woodmere Art Galleries, 71. Bibliog: Henry Pitz (auth), Oliver Grimley, Am Artist, 71. Media: Pen & Ink, Watercolor, Papier-Mache; Bronze, Wood, Stone. Publ: Auth, article in Am Artist, 50. Mailing Add: 16 W Township Line Norristown PA 19403

GRINER, NED H
EDUCATOR, CRAFTSMAN
b Tipton, Ind, Dec 14, 28. Study: Ball State Teachers Col, BS; State Univ Iowa, MA; Ind Univ, MFA; Pa State Univ, DEd. Work: Evansville Mus Art & Ball State Univ Art Gallery, Muncie, Ind. Exhib: Craftsmen USA, Milwaukee Art Ctr, Wis, 66; Wichita Decorative Arts Exhib, Kans, 66; Jewelry 66, State Univ NY Col Plattsburgh, NY, 66; Midstates Craft Exhib, 66-67; Jewelry Exhib, Purdue Univ, 67; Indianapolis Mus of Art, 75; Ind Univ Mus of Art, Bloomington, 76; Ind State Mus, Indianapolis, 77; Ft Wayne Art Mus, Ind, 78. Teaching: Asst prof art, Ark State Col, 54-60; asst, Pa State Univ, 60-61; prof art, Ball State Univ, 61-, head dept, 70- Mem: Nat & Ind Art Educ Asns; Col Art Asn Am; Ind Artist Craftsmen (pres, 66-68); Nat Coun Art Adminr. Media: Silver, Bronze, Brass. Publ: Auth, Jewelry is sculpture, Palette Mag, spring 62; co-auth, Ned Griner: artist teacher, Sch Arts, 9/63; auth, Individuality in the arts & crafts, Asn Am Women, 12/63; auth article in Quartet Mag, Vol 2, No 10; contribr, Art—search & self discovery, 68. Mailing Add: Dept of Art Ball State Univ Muncie IN 47306

GRIPPE, FLORENCE (BERG)
PAINTER, POTTER
b New York, NY, Jan 6, 12. Study: Educ Alliance, 32-34; Works Proj Admin Art Courses, 34-38; pottery with William Soini, 39-41. Comn: Portraits comn by Doris Brewer Cohen, Lexington, Mass, 69, Signora Attilio Roveda, Locarno, Switz, 70, Dr Luis Martinez & Julio Farinos Castillo, Valencia, Spain, 70 & Jose Marina Galvao Telles, Lisbon, Portugal, 71. Exhib: Avant Garde Artists Ninth St Exhib, 51, Brooklyn Mus Art Sch, 51 & Contemporary American Art, New Sch Social Res, New York, 57; Lower East Side Independent Artists 3rd Ann Exhib, 58; Guild Hall, Southampton, Long Island, 75. Teaching: Instr drawing, painting, sculpture & puppetry, United Art Workshops, Brooklyn Neighborhood Houses, NY, 47-54; instr design & pottery, Brooklyn Mus Art Sch, 51-57. Pos: Mem screening comt, Inst Int Educ, New York, 77. Awards: Fulbright-Hayes, 78-79. Bibliog: Mr & Mrs, Inc, Glamour Mag, 4/42; P O Reilly (auth), Brooklyn Museum ideal place in which to study, Brooklyn Eagle, 11/11/51; S Sheridan (auth), Native handicrafts, New York Times Mag, 7/52. Style & Technique: Representational with particular attention to form and content; classical overtones. Publ: Auth, With the brush, Ceramic Age, 3/56; co-auth, Art news from Boston, Art News, 61-63. Mailing Add: 1190 Boylston St Newton MA 02164

GRIPPE, PETER J
SCULPTOR, PRINTMAKER
b Buffalo, NY, Aug 8, 12. Study: Albright-Knox Art Sch, 23-25; Art Inst Buffalo, 29-35, with Edwin Dickinson; Atelier 17, New York, 44-48, with William Stanley Hayter. Work: Mus Mod Art, Whitney Mus Am Art & Metrop Mus Art, New York; Newark Mus, NJ; Addison Gallery Am Art, Andover, Mass. Comn: Four Freedoms, Nat Coun US Art, 55; two sculpture murals, comn by James B Bell & Assoc, PR Info Ctr, New York, 58; sculpture, Theodore Shapiro Forum, Brandeis Univ, 63; portrait of Composer Irving Fine, Brandeis Univ, 64; Sculpture, Sci Bldg lobby, Simmons Col, Boston, 69; plus others. Exhib: Painting, Drawing & Sculpture, Am Acad Rome, Italy, 65; Sculptors Guild, New York, 67; The New American Painting & Sculpture: The First Generation, Mus Mod Art, New York, 69; Boston Now (commemorating opening of New City Hall), Inst Contemp Art, Boston, 69; Whitney Mus Am Art Ann. Teaching: Instr design, Pratt Inst, 49-50; dir printmaking, Atelier 17, New York, 51-54; prof fine arts, Brandeis Univ, 53- Awards: Contemp Watercolors, Drawings & Prints Award, Metrop Mus Art, 52; Boston Arts Festival Award, Art Comn Boston, 55; Guggenheim Fel for Sculpture, 64. Bibliog: Clement Greenberg (auth), Art chronicles, Partisan Rev, 6/49; On sculpture, It Is, autumn 65; W V Anderson (auth), The city of Peter Grippe, Connection, 66. Style & Technique: Concepts of space and movement of the 30's have achieved a new synthesis and meaning. Publ: Contribr, Credo (Iconograph), 46; producer, ed & contribr, Twenty-one etchings & poems, Morris Gallery, New York, 58; contribr, Enter Mephistopheles with images, Art News, Vol 59, No 6; contribr, Contemporary American Painting & Sculpture, Univ Ill, 61; auth, Mots Trouvees (collage-poems), Nordness Gallery, New York, 63. Mailing Add: 1190 Boylston St Newton MA 02164

GRIPPI, SALVATORE WILLIAM
PAINTER, EDUCATOR
b Buffalo, NY, Sept 30, 21. Study: Mus Mod Art Sch, 44-45; Art Students League, 45-48; Atelier 17, 51-53; Inst Statale Arte, Florence, Italy, Fulbright scholar, 53-55. Work: Whitney Mus Am Art, Metrop Mus Art & New York Pub Libr, New York; Joseph Hirshhorn Collection, Washington, DC; Milwaukee-Downer Col, Wis. Exhib: Am Drawings, Watercolors, Prints, Metrop Mus of Art, New York, 52; 50th Ann Int, Pa Acad of Fine Arts, Philadelphia, 52; Stable Gallery Annuals, New York, 52 & 56; Smithsonian Inst, Washington, DC & Whitney Mus Am Art, traveling exhib, 58-59; Pittsburgh Int, Carnegie Inst, Pa, 58; 26th & 28th Biennials, Corcoran Gallery Art, Washington, DC, 59 & 63; Whitney Mus Am Art Ann, 60; Walker Art Ctr, Minneapolis, Minn, 60; Recent Painting USA, The Figure, Mus Mod Art, New York & throughout US, 62; Calif Palace of the Legion of Honor, 65; La Jolla Mus of Art, Calif, 65; 19th Drawing Invitational, Long Beach Mus, Calif, 66 & traveling exhib, Western Asn of Mus, 66-68; Selected American Painters, Phoenix Art Mus, Ariz, 67; Elvehjem Art Ctr, Univ Wis, 77 & traveling exhib to other mus; Brooklyn Mus, New York, 78; Zabriskie Gallery, New York, 56 & 59, NY Univ, New York, 58, Feingarten Galleries, Los Angeles, 67 & 70, Everson Mus, Syracuse, NY, 78 & others in New York, Los Angeles & Milwaukee. Teaching: Instr painting, drawing & 2-D design, Cooper Union Art Sch, 56-59; instr, Sch Visual Arts, 61-62; assoc prof art, Pomona Col & Claremont Grad Sch, 62-68; prof art, Ithaca Col, 68- Pos: Partic, Ford Found Conf Visual Artists, 61. Bibliog: Brian O'Dougherty (auth), Variety of exhibitions, New York Times, 3/22/62; Larry Campbell (auth), rev in Art News, 10/64; Henry J Seldis (auth), Art walk: a critical guide to the galleries, Los Angeles Times, 5/29/70; plus many others. Mem: Life mem Art Students League (treas, 61-62, bd control, 61-64); Col Art Asn Am; Am Asn Univ Prof. Publ: Auth, Visual impressions of Italy, Inst Int Educ Bull, 56; auth, Turntable kaleidoscope, Mus Mod Art, 56, 57 & 59; contribr, Twenty-one etchings & poems, 58. Dealer: Feingarten Gallery 718 N La Cienega Blvd Los Angeles CA 90069. Mailing Add: 423 E Seneca St Ithaca NY 14850

GRISSOM, EUGENE EDWARD
EDUCATOR, PRINTMAKER
b Melvern, Kans, May 15, 22. Study: Philippine Univ, 45; Kans State Teachers Col, BS(music), 48; State Univ Iowa, with M Lasansky, MFA, 51. Teaching: Instr art educ, Kans State Teachers Col, summer 51; instr art, Univ Ky, 51-53; asst prof art, Univ Fla, 53-62, assoc prof art & head dept, 62-65, prof art & chmn dept, 65- Mem: Nat Coun Art Adminr; Col Art Asn Am; Southeastern Col Art Conf. Mailing Add: 4607 Clear Lake Dr Gainesville FL 32607

GRISSOM, FREDA GILL
PAINTER, SILVERSMITH
b Groom, Tex. Study: WTex State Univ, Canyon, BS; Univ Tex, Austin; also watercolor workshop with Millard Sheets. Work: Mongomery Mus Fine Arts, Ala. Exhib: Ann Dixie Exhib, Montgomery Mus Fine Arts, 68; Nat Art Roundup, Las Vegas, Nev, 68; Greater New Orleans Nat, 71; 9th Grand Prix Int, Cannes, France, 73; Galerie Rene Borel, Deauville, France, 73. Pos: Co-chmn, Nat Sun Carnival Art Exhib, El Paso, Tex, 65-71. Awards: Purchase Award, Montgomery Mus Fine Arts, 68; Second Prize, Greater New Orleans Nat Exhib, 71; Medaille de la Ville de Cannes, First Prize, Watercolor, 9th Grand Prix Int, Cote D'Azur, 73. Mem: El Paso Art Asn, Inc (dir, 64-65); El Paso Mus Art; Black Range Art Asn; Tex Watercolor Soc. Style & Technique: Landscape and non-objective watercolor. Media: Transparent Watercolor, Acrylic, Oil; Gold, Silver. Mailing Add: 2411 Arizona Ave El Paso TX 79930

GRISSOM, KENNETH RYLAND, II
PAINTER
b Jackson, Tenn, June 15, 44. Study: Art Inst Pittsburgh; Harris Advert Art Sch. Work: Cheekwood Fine Arts Ctr, Nashville; US Army Art Collection, Washington, DC; US Army Hall of Fame, Ft Leavenworth, Kans. Exhib: US Army Combat Art Collection, Bangkok, Thailand, 71; Cent South Exhib, 72-75; Tenn Watercolor Soc Ann Exhib (traveling), 74 & 75; Rocky Mountain Nat Watermedia Expos, Foothills Art Ctr, 75; Watercolor USA, Springfield Art Mus, Mo, 75; plus other one-man shows. Pos: Art dir, US Army Publ, Vietnam, 67; combat artist, US Army, Vietnam & Thailand, 69-70; freelance mag illusr, 70-72. Awards: Silver Medal for Experimental Illus, Art Dirs Club, Nashville, 72; Hon Mention, Bluff Park Ann, Birmingham, Ala, 74; Purchase Award, Tenn Watercolor Soc, 75. Mem: Tenn Watercolor Soc (treas, 75); Memphis Watercolor Group; Southern Watercolor Soc; Tenn Art League; Jackson Art Asn. Style & Technique: Realism. Media: Watercolor. Publ: Illusr, Pvt Pilot Mag & Face to Face Mag, 72. Mailing Add: PO Box 3539 Jackson TN 38301

GROAT, HALL PIERCE
PAINTER
b Syracuse, NY, Dec 31, 32. Study: Syracuse Univ, BFA, also Grad Sch Painting; spec summer session with Josef Albers. Work: Berkshire Mus, Pittsfield, Mass; Philatelic Mus, Geneva, Switz; Syracuse Univ, NY; State Univ NY, Morrisville; First Nat Bank Boston. Comn: Mural, Repub of Korea, Third Div, US Army, 55; hist murals, Lemoyne Manor Restaurant, Liverpool, NY, 60; auditorium murals, Johnstown, NY, 63; mural, New Brunswick Savings Bank, NJ; hist mural, Merrill Trust Co, Bangor, Maine, 75; hist mural (five panels), Syracuse Savings Bank, 77. Exhib: Rochester Finger Lakes Exhib, Rochester Mem Art Gallery, NY, 59 & 63; Springfield Nat, Mass, 62; Everson Mus Regional, Syracuse, 64 & 70; Cooperstown Nat, NY, 67-70; Butler Inst Am Art, Youngstown, Ohio, 68. Awards: Pittsfield Art League First Prize, Mass, 61; Berkshire Mus Purchase Award, Berkshire Art Asn, Pittsfield, 62; Gordon Steele Mem Medal, Assoc Artists of Syracuse, 74. Bibliog: 32nd annual midyear show—Butler, La Rev Mod, 2/68; Review of selected artist, Art Rev, fall 68. Mem: Assoc Artists Syracuse (exhib chmn); Sarasota Art Asn. Media: Acrylic. Dealer: Wellfleet Art Gallery Wellfleet on Cape Cod MA 02667. Mailing Add: 8364 Vassar Dr Manlius NY 13104

GROELL, THEOPHIL
PAINTER, INSTRUCTOR
b Pittsburgh, Pa, Feb 11, 32. Study: Carnegie Inst Technol, BFA, 53. Exhib: One-man shows, Green Mountain Gallery, New York, 70, 73 & 74; The Contemporary Figure, Suffolk Mus, Stony Brook, NY, 71; Paintings Eligible for Childe Hassam Fund Purchase, Am Acad Arts & Lett, 73 & 74; Three Centuries of the Nude in American Art, New York Cult Ctr, 75 & traveling, 76; The Classic Revival, Ill Bell Tel Traveling Show, 75-76; plus others. Teaching: Adj lectr painting, Queensboro Community Col, 67- Bibliog: Cindy Nemser (auth), Representational painting in 1971, Arts Mag, 12-1/72. Style & Technique: Realistic interpretation of the female nude, direct from life, in muted tones eliminating brush strokes as part of the look. Media: Oil. Dealer: Green Mountain Gallery 135 Greene St New York NY 10012. Mailing Add: 41 Union Sq W New York NY 10003

GRÖNBECK, JEAN
PAINTER
b Long Beach, Calif, Mar 22, 26. Study: Univ Mex, Mexico City, 43; also with Arden Von Dewitz, 61. Work: Nat Archives Am Art, Smithsonian Inst, Washington, DC; San Luis Obispo Co Collection, Calif; Bank of Am, Santa Barbara; many in pvt & pub collections. Exhib: Statler-Hilton Hotel, Beverly Hills, Calif, 62; 14th Ann Greek Theatre, Los Angeles, Calif, 62; Wilshire-Ebell Exhib, Los Angeles, 70; Santa Barbara Mus, Calif, 71-72; Fresno Art Ctr, Calif, 71-78. Pos: Gallery dir, Grönbeck Gallery, 72-78. Awards: Best of Show & Hon Mention, El Camino Art Asn, 63; 7th Ann Hawthorne, Hawthorne Art & Cult Soc, 66; Non-Purchase Award, Lompoc Art Asn, 74. Bibliog: Nonie Higgins (auth), Jean Grönbeck gives show, Los Angeles Times; Morris Cecil (auth), Prominent artist featured, Sun Newspaper, 6/65; Jim Hayes (auth), A bright airy look, Telegram-Tribune, 71. Mem: Am Inst Fine Arts; Nat Artists Equity Asn; Mendocino Art Ctr; Fresno Art Ctr. Style & Technique: Contemporary impressionism and into abstract, with emphasis on strong design and color; heavy brush and knife work. Media: Oil, Acrylic, Watercolor. Specialty: Contemporary impressionism in oil and watercolor. Mailing Add: 32004 Coburg Bottom Loop Rd Eugene OR 97401

GROOMS, RED
PAINTER
b Nashville, Tenn, June 10, 37. Study: Peabody Col; pvt study with J Van Sickle; New Sch Social Res; Art Inst Chicago; Hans Hofmann Sch, Provincetown, Mass; study in Europe & Near East. Work: Mint Mus Art, Charlotte, NC; Art Inst Chicago; Mus Mod Art, New York; NC Mus Art, Raleigh; Chrysler Mus, Provincetown; plus others. Comn: Sets & costumes, Guinevere (play), 64; mural (with Mimi Gross), Ctr for Mod Cult, Florence, Italy. Exhib: Worcester Art Mus, Mass, 65; Am Fedn Arts, 65-66; Twenty Americans, Art Inst Chicago, 66; Mus Mod Art, New York, 66; Venice Biennale, 68; Tibor de Nagy Gallery, New York, 69; Walker Art Ctr, Minneapolis, 70; Guggenheim Mus, New York, 72; one-man shows, Rutgers Gallery of Art, New Brunswick, NJ, New York Cult Ctr & Mus de Arte Contemporaneo, Caracas, Venezuela, 73, Brooke Alexander Gallery, New York, 75 & Ft Worth Art Mus, Tex, 76; Whitney Mus Am Art, 73; Stanford Mus, Calif, 76; plus many others. Bibliog: Allan Kaprow (auth), Assemblage, Environments and Happenings, Abrams, 65; Lucy R Lippard (auth), Pop Art, Praeger, 66; Susan Sontag (auth), Against Interpretation, Dell, 66; plus others. Mailing Add: 186 Grand St New York NY 10013

GROSCH, LAURA
PAINTER, PRINTMAKER
b Worcester, Mass, Apr 1, 45. Study: Wellesley Col, Mass, BA(art hist), 63-67; Univ Pa, Philadelphia, BFA(painting), 68; study with Gertrude Whiting, James Rayen, Neil Welliver & Piero Dorazio. Work: Libr Cong & Smithsonian Inst, Washington, DC; Mint Mus Art, Charlotte, NC; Brit Mus, London; Hunt Inst Botanical Documentation, Carnegie-Mellon Univ, Pittsburgh. Comn: Mural, Litchfield Plantation, Pawley's Island, SC, 69. Exhib: Color Print USA, Tex Tech Univ, Lubbock, 73-74; 36th Ann NC Artists Exhib, NC Mus Art, Raleigh, 73; Rose Mus, Glenbow-Alberta Gallery, Calgary, Alta, 74; 27th Ann Exhib Boston Printmakers, Boston Mus Fine Arts, 75; 11th Int Exhib Graphic Art, Mod Galer'ja, Ljubljana, Yugoslavia, 75; 20th Nat Print Exhib, Brooklyn Mus, NY, 77. Awards: Purchase AWard, 11th Ann Piedmont Graphics Exhib, Greenville Co Mus Art, Greenville, SC, 74; First Nat Bank of Boston Purchase Award, Boston Printmakers, 75; Purchase Award, Western Ill Univ Ann, Macomb, 75. Style & Technique: Cross hatching emphasizing the texture of natural things with either acrylic paint in a striper or pencil. Media: Acrylic; Litho Pencil. Dealer: Impressions Gallery 27 Stanhope St Boston MA 02116. Mailing Add: 506 N Main St Davidson NC 28036

GROSHANS, WERNER (EMIL)
PAINTER
b Eutingen, Ger, July 6, 13; US citizen. Study: Newark Sch Fine & Indust Art, grad; also with Bernar Gussow. Work: Newark Mus, NJ; Davenport Munic Art Gallery, Iowa; Canton Art

Inst, Ohio; New Britain Mus Am Art, Conn; William Benton Mus, Univ Conn, Storrs. Exhib: Exhibitions of Contemp Am Painting, 48-53 & Ann Exhib of Contemp Am Sculpture, Watercolors and Prints, 53, Whitney Mus of Am Art, New York; Am Painting Today, 50 & Am Watercolors, Drawings and Prints, 52, Metrop Mus of Art, New York; Selections From the 1952 Metrop Mus Exhib, Am Federation of Arts Nat Traveling Exhib, 53; Midyear Annuals, Butler Inst, Ohio, 59 & 65; Continuing Tradition of Realism In American Art, Hirschl-Adler Galleries, New York, 62; Mus of Fine Arts, Springfield, Mass, 63, 67 & 69; Meticulous Realism, Tawes Mus, Univ of Maryland, 66-67; Nat Invitational Drawing Exhib, Oklahoma Mus of Art, 69; Wadsworth Atheneum, Hartford, Conn, 65-67, 70 & 72; Retrospective, New Britain Mus of Am Art, New Britain, Conn, 73; one-man show, Babcock Galleries, New York, 73; Awards Candidates Exhib, Am Acad of Arts & Letters and Nat Inst of Arts and Letters, 75; 80th Anniversary Invitational Exhib of Prize-Winners and Jurors, Nat Arts Club, New York, 78. Pos: Chmn dept fine arts, Jersey City Mus, NJ, 66-69; mem adv bd trustees, du Cret Sch Arts, NJ, 71. Awards: Thomas B Clarke Prize, Nat Acad Design, 60 & Henry Ward Ranger Fund Purchase, 74; Margaret Cooper Mem Prize, Allied Artists Am, 66. Bibliog: Margarita Dulac (auth), Werner Groshans, painter of realism & fantasy, Am Artist Mag, 6/70; John Angelini (auth), Werner Groshans, the man without an ism, NJ Mus & Arts Mag, 5/73; M Victor Alper (auth), Werner Groshans: The Man and His Work (catalogue), Montclair Art Mus Retrospective, 2-4/76. Mem: Nat Acad Design (mem coun, 70-73); Audubon Artists; Allied Artists Am; Assoc Artists NJ (dir, 65-67); Conn Acad Fine Arts. Style & Technique: Contemporary realism. Media: Oil, Pastel. Dealer: Babcock Galleries 20 East 67th St New York NY 10021. Mailing Add: 941 Boulevard E Weehawken NJ 07087

GROSS, ALICE (ALICE GROSS FISH)
SCULPTOR
b New York, NY. Study: With Ruth Yates. Work: Berkshire Mus, Pittsfield, Mass. Exhib: Eastern States Exhib, Springfield, Mass, 64; Audubon Artists, Nat Acad Design, New York, 68 & Allied Artists Am, 69; Knickerbocker Artists, Nat Arts Club, New York, 71; New Rochelle Art Asn, Col New Rochelle, 71. Awards: Award for Duo, Allied Artists Am, 69; Award for Rhythm, Knickerbocker Artists, 70; Award for Who's the Fairest of Them All, Beaux Arts of Westchester, 71. Mem: Silvermine Guild Artists; Audubon Artists; Conn Acad Fine Arts; Allied Artists Am; Knickerbocker Artists. Style & Technique: Simplified realism. Media: Terra-Cotta, Wood, Bronze. Mailing Add: 16 Sutton Pl New York NY 10022

GROSS, CHAIM
SCULPTOR, INSTRUCTOR
b Kolomea, Austria, Mar 17, 04; US citizen. Study: Kunstgewerbe Schulle; Educ Alliance, New York; Beaux-Arts Inst Design, with Elie Nadelman; Art Students League, with Robert Laurent. Work: Metrop Mus Art, New York; Whitney Mus Am Art, New York; Mus Mod Art, New York; Newark Mus, NJ; Worcester Art Mus, Mass; plus many others. Comn: Main Post Off, Washington, DC, 36; Fed Trade Comn Bldg, Washington, DC, 38; Reiss-Davis Child Guidance Clinic, Beverly Hills, Calif, 61; Hadassah Hosp, Jerusalem, 64; Temple Shaaray Tefila, New York, 64; plus others. Exhib: American Painting & Sculpture, Moscow, USSR, 59; The Making of Sculpture, Mus Mod Art, New York, 61-62; Drawings by Sculptors, Smithsonian Inst, 61-63; New York World's Fair, 64-65; one-man shows, Medici II Gallery, Miami Beach, Fla, 71, New Sch Social Res, New York, 71, Nat Collection Fine Arts, Washington, DC, 74 & Leonard Hutton Gallery, New York, 74; plus many others. Teaching: Instr sculpture, Educ Alliance Art Sch, 27-; instr sculpture, New Sch Social Res, 48-; instr, Mus Mod Art, 52-57. Awards: Nat Inst Arts & Lett Grant, 56; First Prize, Boston Arts Festival, 63; Award of Merit Medal, Nat Inst Arts & Lett, 63; plus others. Bibliog: George A Flanagan (auth), Understanding and Enjoying Modern Art, 62 & Wayne Craven (auth), Sculpture in America, 68, Crowell; John I H Baur (auth), Revolution and Tradition in Modern American Art, Harvard Univ, 65; plus others. Mem: Sculptors Guild (mem bd); Educ Alliance Alumni Asn; Fedn Mod Painters & Sculptors; Nat Inst Arts & Lett; Artists Equity Asn. Publ: Auth, Fantasy Drawings, Beechhurst, 56; co-auth, Tree Trunk to Head & A Sculptor Speaks (art films), 56; auth, TV prog, Educ Alliance Sch Art, 64; contribr, var art mag. Mailing Add: 526 W Broadway New York NY 10012

GROSS, CHARLES MERRILL
EDUCATOR, SCULPTOR
b Cullman, Ala, Sept 18, 35. Study: Atlanta Col Art, BFA; Allende Inst, Univ Guanajuato, Mex, MFA. Work: Jackson State Univ, Miss; Demopolis Civic Ctr, Ala. Exhib: Mid-South Exhib, Brooks Mem Art Gallery, Memphis, Tenn, 69, 70 & 72; Nat Arts & Crafts Exhib, Jackson, Miss, 69 & 71; Delta Art Exhib, Ark Arts Ctr, Little Rock, 69-71 & 74; Regional Sculpture Exhib, Carroll Reece Mus, Jackson City, Tenn, 72; Monroe Nat Ann Art Exhib, Masur Mus Art, La, 73; plus others. Teaching: Instr drawing, painting & sculpture, Miss Col, 68-69; asst prof sculpture, Univ Miss, 69-73, assoc prof sculpture, 73- Awards: Merit Awards, Mid-South Exhib, Holiday Art Festival, McComb, Miss & Nat Arts & Crafts Exhib, Jackson. Mem: Nat Art Educ Asn; Southern Asn Sculptors (regional vpres, 73-75); Miss Art Asn. Style & Technique: Surrealism; metal casting using the lost wax method. Media: Aluminum. Mailing Add: 300 Longest Rd Oxford MS 38655

GROSS, EARL
PAINTER, LECTURER
b Sept 11, 99; US citizen. Study: Westminster Col; Carnegie-Mellon Univ. Work: New Britain Mus Am Art; Atlanta Art Inst, Ga; Reading Mus, Pa; Ill State Mus; Art Inst Chicago; plus others. Comn: Off combat artist, US Air Force, Far East. Exhib: Two-man show, Art Inst Chicago, 50; Paintings of Past Decade, Metrop Mus, 52; one-man show, Butler Art Mus, 52; Am Watercolor Soc, New York, 58; Frank Oehlschlaeger Galleries, Chicago & Sarasota, Fla. Teaching: Prof painting, Longboat Key Art Ctr, Fla; prof painting, New Orleans Acad Art; prof painting, Highland Park Art Ctr; instr, Chicago Acad Fine Art, Ill; instr, Am Acad, Chicago. Pos: Pres, Stevens-Gross Studios, Chicago, 26-62. Awards: Second Prize, Denver Mus, Colo & Cosmopolitan Mag Competition; First Prize, Chicago Artists Guild. Bibliog: Norman Kent (auth), Sea scapes & landscapes & Wendell Blake (auth), Acrylic watercolor painting, Watson Guptill. Mem: Am, Philadelphia & Washington Watercolor Socs; Arts Club Chicago; Artist Guild Chicago. Style & Technique: Realistic traditional paintings of sea & landscapes. Media: Watercolor, Oil. Publ: Auth, Watercolor Series, 47, Illustrators Page, 51, Robert Addison, 58 & Polymer colors in depth, 67, Am Artist Mag; also articles in Art News & Chicago Tribune. Dealer: Oehlschlaeger Galleries 107 E Oak St Chicago IL 60611; Frank Oehlschlaeger Gallery 28 Blvd of the Presidents St Armands Key Sarasota FL 33578. Mailing Add: 1810 Calle de Sebastian A 4 Santa Fe NM 87501

GROSS, ESTELLE SHANE
ART DEALER
b New York, NY. Study: Pa State Univ, BA; Temple Univ, MA; Philadelphia Mus of Art, studied with Hobson Pittman eight yrs; Parsons Inst of Design. Collections Arranged: Rockwell Kent Graphics Exhib; Fairfield Porter Exhib; Adja Yonkers Graphics Exhib; Neil Welliver Exhib; Paul Hogarth Exhib of Bk Illustrations; Hobson Pittman. Pos: Fashion model, 50-55; mgr pub rels, Bell Savings & Loan Asn, 60-63; res asst, Univ Pa Dept Psychiatry, 63-66; pres, Gross-McCleaf Gallery, Philadelphia, 66- Mem: Philadelphia Print Club; Philadelphia Art Alliance. Specialty: The best Philadelphia painters; International Graphics, Inc; expertise in Japanese prints; 19th and 20th centuries posters. Mailing Add: Gross-McCleaf Gallery 1713 Walnut St Philadelphia PA 19103

GROSS, IRENE (IRENE GROSS BERZON)
PAINTER, SCULPTOR
US citizen. Study: Parson's Sch Design; Am Art Sch. Work: Springfield Mus Fine Art, Mass; St Vincent's Col, Latrobe, Pa. Exhib: Eastern States, 58-60; Fr Exhib, Nat Asn Women Artists, Florence, Naples, 66 & Ital Exhib, 72; Silvermine Guild New Eng Exhib, New Canaan, Conn. Awards: Bocour Award, Nat Asn Women Artists, 61, Goldie Paley Award, 69. Mem: Silvermine Guild Artists; Nat Asn Women Artists; Knickerbocker Artists; New Rochelle Art Asn (treas, 69-). Media: Oil. Mailing Add: 87 Disbrow Ln New Rochelle NY 10804

GROSS, MR & MRS MERRILL JAY
COLLECTORS, PATRONS
Study: Mr Gross, Univ Pittsburgh, BA, BS, Xavier Univ, MBA; Mrs Gross, Mills Col, BA, Xavier Univ, MEd. Exhib: Paintings by Edward Potthast, Cincinnati Art Mus, 65, Butler Inst Am Art, 65, Taft Mus, 68 & Corcoran Gallery Art, 73. Collection: Nineteenth and twentieth century American art; Western, genre and impressionist. Mailing Add: 241 Springfield Pike Wyoming OH 45215

GROSS, SANDRA LERNER
PAINTER, LECTURER
b New York, NY. Study: Brooklyn Col; Pratt Graphic Inst; Artists in Am Art Sch; also with Harry Sternberg & Leo Manso; C W Post Col, with Jerry Okimoto. Work: Twp of Wantagh, NY; Aldrich Mus. Exhib: Nat Acad Design, New York, 66 & 73; Audubon Artists, Nat Acad Galleries, 65, 68, 74 & 75; Silvermine Guild of Artists, New Canaan, Conn, 70; Nat Asn Women Artists, Nat Acad Galleries, 73-75; Works on Paper, Women in Arts, Brooklyn Mus, 75; Contemp Reflections, Aldrich Mus, 76 & New Acquisitions & Loans, 78; Five Yr Retrospective, Nassau Co Mus Fine Arts, 76; Soho Ctr for Visual Arts, Aldrich Mus & Mobil Found, 76; Womens Caucus for Art, Grad Ctr, City Univ New York, 77 & 78- Teaching: Lectr-demonstr, Nassau Co Pub Sch, NY, 73-75 & Nassau Co Art Mus, 74-75; art lectr, Brandeis Univ Womens Group, 73-75; art teacher, Children's Shelter, Mineola, NY, 74. Pos: Artist in residence, Nassau Co Bd Coop Educ, 75; art coordr, Friends Sch, Old Westbury, NY, 75-; art consult, NY State Sen Minority, 75; consult on the arts, Spec Senate Comt on the Culture Indust, 78. Awards: Purchase Prize, Nassau Community Col, 70 & 74; Benjamin Altman Landscape Prize, Nat Acad Design, 73; Anne Eisner Award, Nat Asn Women Artists, 73. Bibliog: Ruth Lembeck (auth), Job ideas for today's woman, Arts Mag, 10/75; John Canaday, New York Times, 5/9/76 & David Shirey, 9/76; Art in Am, 5/77. Mem: Prof Artists Guild; Experiments in Art & Technol; Cent Hall Gallery; Womens Interart Ctr; Nat Asn Women Artists. Style & Technique: Textural and collage paintings. Media: Oil, Acrylic, Mixed Media. Dealer: Cent Hall Gallery 52 Main St Port Washington NY 10050; Pleiades/Cloud Gallery 152 Wooster St New York NY 10012. Mailing Add: 58 Birchwood Park Dr Jericho NY 11753

GROSSE (CAROLYN ANN GAWARECKI)
PAINTER, INSTRUCTOR
b Rahway, NJ, Oct 30, 31. Study: Douglass Col, scholar, 51-53, BA; Univ Calif, Berkeley; Univ Colo; Art League Alexandria; also with Lester Stevens. Work: City of Falls Church, Va; Indust Col of Armed Forces, Ft McNair, Washington, DC; First Va Bank; Holiday Inn Corp, Falls Church. Exhib: 26th & 27th Ann Metrop Exhib, Smithsonian Inst, Washington, DC, 65 & 66; Nat League Am Pen Women, Nat Exhib, Salt Lake City, Utah, 70 & State Exhib, Richmond, Va, 74; NVa Community Col Exhib, Metrop Area, Annandale, Va, 71 & 73; Watercolor USA, Springfield, Mo, 75; 43rd Ann Exhib of Miniature Painters Soc of Washington, DC, 76; First Ann Southern Watercolor Soc, Nashville, Tenn, 77 & Second Ann, Ga, 78; one-artist show, Atlantic Gallery, Washington, DC, 78. Teaching: Instr art, Highland Park High Sch, NJ, 53-55; instr watercolor, City Falls Church, 66- Pos: Exhibits artist, Mus Nat Hist, Smithsonian Inst, 56-57; partic, Art in the Embassies Prog, US State Dept. Awards: Best in Show State, Nat League Am Pen Women, 72, First Prize State, 74; Best in Show Area, Metrop Area Show, Springfield Guild, 74; Hon Mention, 43rd Ann Exhib of Miniature Painters Soc of Washington, DC, 76. Mem: Art League (secy, 66-67); Washington Watercolor Soc; Southern Watercolor Soc (prog chmn, 70-71); Potomac Valley Watercolorists (pres, 74-77). Style & Technique: Landscapes in watercolor and casein, palette knife. Dealer: Atlantic Gallery Washington DC; Art League Gallery VA. Mailing Add: 7018 Vagabond Dr Falls Church VA 22042

GROSSEN, FRANCOISE
INSTRUCTOR, SCULPTOR
b Neuchatel, Switz, Aug 19, 43. Study: Sch Archit, Polytech Univ, Lausanne, Switz; Sch Arts & Crafts, Basel, Switz, grad; Univ Calif, Los Angeles, MA, with B Kester. Work: Dreyfuss Found, GM Bldg, New York; Bank Tex, San Antonio; Mus Bellerive, Zurich, Switz; Am Dist Tel Co, New York. Comn: Thirty-eight elements in lobby-bar, O'Hare Regency Hyatt House, Chicago, 70; two lobby pieces (36ft x 15ft), One Embarcardero Ctr, San Francisco, 72; two ballroom pieces (11ft x 15ft; 15ft sq), Embarcardero Regency Hyatt, San Francisco, 73; Tensile-Ten (38ft x 18ft), NTex State Univ, Denton, 75. Exhib: Biennale Int de la Tapisserie, Lausanne, 69, 71, 73, 75 & 77; Deliberate Entanglements, Univ Calif Los Angeles Art Galleries, 71-72; Three Dimensional Fiber, New Plymouth, NZ, 74-75; Wall Hangings, Mus Mod Art, New York, 68; one-person shows, Hadler Galleries, New York, 76 & Mus Bellerive, Zurich, 76; Fiberworks, Cleveland Mus Arts, Ohio, 77; Fiberworks-The Americas & Japan, Nat Mus Mod Art, Tokyo & Kyoto, Japan, 77. Teaching: Instr macrame, New Sch Social Res, New York; instr fiber art, Kansas City Art Inst, summer 74 & Univ Calif, Los Angeles, summer 75. Pos: Designer, Larsen Design Studio, 68-71; juror, Columbus Gallery of Fine Arts, Ohio, 75. Bibliog: Jean-Luc Daval, article in Art Int, Vol 15 (1971); Andre Uenzi (auth), La Nouvelle Tapisserie, Bonvent, 73; Constantine & Larsen (auth), Beyond Craft, Van Nostrand Reinhold, 73. Media: Fiber. Mailing Add: 135 Greene St New York NY 10012

GROSSER, MAURICE
ART WRITER, PAINTER
b Huntsville, Ala, Oct 23, 03. Study: Harvard Univ, BA, 24. Work: American Collection; Smithsonian Inst, Washington DC; Brooklyn Mus; Fogg Art Mus, Cambridge, Mass; Mus Mod Art, New York. Style & Technique: Pre-impressionist. Media: Oil. Publ: Auth, Painting in Public, Knopf, 48, reprint, 64, Bobbs-Merrill; auth, The Painter's Eye, Reinhart, 51; auth, Critic's Eye, Bobbs-Merrill, 62; auth, Painter's Professions, Clarkston Potter, 71. Dealer: Fishback Gallery 29 W 57th St New York NY 10019; Capricorn Gallery 8004 Norfolk Ave Bethesda MD 20014. Mailing Add: 219 W 14th St New York NY 10011

GROSSMAN, GRACE COHEN
CURATOR, ART HISTORIAN
b New York, NY, Nov 30, 47. Study: Univ Mich, BA, 69; Hebrew Univ, jr yr study; Columbia Univ, MA, 70. Work: Am Jewish Hist Soc; Maurice Spertus Mus Judaica. Collections Arranged: Photograph Collection, Am Jewish Hist Soc, 70; Maurice Spertus Mus Judaica Permanent Collection, 73-74, Hill Page Collection, Spertus Mus Judaica. Pos: Cur collections, Maurice Spertus Mus Judaica, 70- Mem: Col Art Asn. Publ: Auth, The Maurice Spertus Museum of Judaica, 74, ed, The Jews of Yemen, 75, contribr, Faith and Form: Synagogue Architecture in Illinois, 76, contribr, The Hill Page Collection, 76 & auth, Israeli Art in Chicago Collections, Maurice Spertus Mus Judaica; auth, Miron Sima (exhib catalogue), 77. Mailing Add: Maurice Spertus Mus 618 S Michigan Chicago IL 60605

GROSSMAN, MAURIZIA M
ART DEALER, GALLERY DIRECTOR
b Udine, Italy, Aug 9, 43; US citizen. Study: Univ Florence, Italy, MA. Collections Arranged: The Native Traditions—19th Century Decorative Arts, 74-75; several photog exhibs by maj 19th & 20th century photographers, Lunn Gallery, 75- Pos: Asst ed, Collector's Ed Ltd, New York, NY, 70-72; asst dir, Lunn Gallery/Graphics Int Ltd, Washington, DC, 72- Specialty: Photography of the 19th and 20th century; 20th century graphics. Publ: Auth, Catalogue 3—19th and 20th Century Prints and Photographs, Graphics Int Ltd, 73 & Catalogue 4—19th and 20th Century Prints and Photographs, 74. Mailing Add: 2312 Tunlaw Rd NW Washington DC 20007

GROSSMAN, MORTON
PAINTER, EDUCATOR
b 1926. Study: Art Students League, scholar, 44-47; Queens Col (NY), BA(hons), 48; Louis Comfort Tiffany Found fel, 49-50. Work: Cleveland Mus Art; Norfolk Mus Art, Va; Ball State Univ, Ind; Birmingham Mus Art, Ala; SS United States; plus many pvt collections. Exhib: Whitney Mus Am Art; Cincinnati Art Mus; Dallas Mus Fine Arts; Baltimore Mus Art; Walker Art Ctr; Carnegie Inst; Philadelphia Mus of Art; Seattle Art Mus; Boston Mus Fine Art; San Francisco Mus of Art; Oakland Art Gallery; Corcoran Gallery of Art; Okla Art Ctr; Dayton Art Inst; Portland Mus Art; Inst Contemp Art, Boston; Roko Gallery, New York, NY; one-man shows, Albright-Knox Art Gallery, Farnsworth Art Mus, Maine, Kansas City Art Inst, Pub Archit Gallery, Wellington, NZ, Miami Beach Art Ctr, Akron Art Inst, Adelphia Univ, NY, Canton Art Inst, Ohio, San Joaquin Mus, Calif, Grand Central Moderns Gallery, New York & Isaac Delgado Mus Art, New Orleans; plus many others. Teaching: At Queens Col, NY, 55-56, State Univ NY Col Buffalo, 56-60, Cleveland Inst Art, 61-64, Univ Md, 64-69 & Tyler Sch Art, Temple Univ, summers 67 & 68; prof painting, Kent State Univ, 69- Awards: Grand Award & Gold Medal, Am Watercolor Soc, 60; Audubon Artists Medal for Creative Aquarelle, 62; Arches Award, Watercolor USA, Springfield Art Mus, 69. Style & Technique: Acrylic stain on raw canvas; watercolors completely transparent. Mailing Add: 217 Crain Ave Kent OH 44240

GROSSMAN, NANCY
SCULPTOR, PAINTER
b New York, NY, Apr 28, 40. Study: Pratt Inst. Work: Whitney Mus Am Art, New York; Princeton Univ Art Mus; Univ Mus, Berkeley, Calif; Dallas Mus Fine Arts; Israel Mus, Jerusalem. Exhib: Corcoran Gallery Art Biennial Exhib, Washington, DC, 63; Whitney Mus Am Art Sculpture Ann, 68 & Whitney Biennial, 73; Städtische Kunsthalle Recklinghausen, Ruhrfestspiele, 70; Recent Figure Sculpture, Fogg Art Mus, Harvard Univ, 72. Awards: Ida C Haskell Found Scholar for Foreign Travel, 62; Guggenheim Mem Found Fel, 65; Am Acad Arts & Lett/Nat Inst Arts & Lett Award, 74. Bibliog: Von Thomas Schröder & Guido Mangold (auth), Nancy Grossman Ledermonstren, Twen Mag, 5/71; Corinne Robins (auth), Man is anonymous: the art of Nancy Grossman, Art Spectrum Mag, 2/75; Cindy Nemser (auth), Art Talk, Conversations with 12 Women Artists, Scribners, 75. Dealer: Cordier & Ekstrom 980 Madison Ave New York NY 10021. Mailing Add: 105 Eldridge St New York NY 10002

GROSSMAN, SHELDON
MUSEUM CURATOR, ART HISTORIAN
b New York, NY, Aug 30, 40. Study: Hunter Col, BA, 62; NY Univ Inst Fine Arts, MA, 66. Pos: Cur, Northern & Later Ital Paintings, Nat Gallery Art, Washington, DC, 71- Awards: Fulbright-Hays Travel Grant, 66; Ital Govt Study Grant, 66; Chester Dale Fel, Nat Gallery Art, 67-69. Res: Problems in Florentine painting in the late 15th and early 16th century; analysis of problems of style; archival research. Publ: Ed, Marsyfas, 65; auth, National Gallery of Art report and studies in the history of art, 68; auth, Mitteilungen des kunst-historischen institutes in Florenz, 69; auth, Master drawings, 72; auth, National Gallery of Art, Studies in the History of Art, 74. Mailing Add: 2312 Tunlaw Rd NW Washington DC 20007

GROSVENOR, ROBERT
SCULPTOR
b New York, NY, 1937. Study: Ecole des Beaux Arts, Dijon, France, 56; Ecole Superieure des Arts Decoratifs, Paris, 57-58; Univ Perugia, 58. Work: Whitney Mus, New York; Storm King Art Ctr, Mountainville, NY; Mus Mod Art, New York; Hirshorn Mus, Washington, DC; Walker Art Ctr, Minneapolis. Exhib: Primary Structures, Jewish Mus, New York, 66; Sculpture for the 60's, Los Angeles Co Mus & Philadelphia Mus, 67; Sonsbeek 1971, Arnheim, Holland, 71; Eight, Contemp Arts Mus, Houston, 72; Monumenta, Newport, RI, 74; plus many others. Awards: Guggenheim Fel, 69; Nat Endowment Arts & Humanities Grant, 70; Nat Acad Arts & Lett Grant, 72. Bibliog: Thomas B Hess (auth), Robert Grosvenor, Shivering timbers, New York Mag, 2/4/74; Joseph Masheck (auth), Robert Grosvenor's fractured beams, Artforum, 5/74; Bruce Kurtz (auth), Robert Grosvenor's sculpture 1965-1975, Arts Mag, 10/75. Mailing Add: c/o Paula Cooper Gallery 155 Wooster New York NY 10012

GROSZ, FRANZ JOSEPH
PAINTER, DESIGNER
b New York, NY, Oct 7, 09. Study: Nat Acad Design, with Kroll, Olinsky & Nielson; Art Stud League New York, with Boardman Robinson & Brackman; also with Hans Hofmann, New York. Work: Oils, Carnegie Mus, Nat Acad Design, Currier Mus Art, Pa Acad Fine Arts & Corcoran Gallery Art. Comn: Glass murals (mixed media), Joseph's Sch Auditorium, Astoria, NY & Manhasset Congregational Church, Nassau Co, NY, 60; glass murals, Salem Lutheran Church, Bridgeport, Conn, 61, US Coast Guard Acad, New London, Conn, 63 & St Anthony Shrine, Boston, Mass, 65; over 350 murals, 41-60. Exhib: Whitney Mus Am Art, New York, 48; one-man show, Galerie Visconti, Paris, France, 71; Oil Paintings, US Info Serv, currently shown in all maj Europ mus for one year; one-man show sponsored by Fr Embassy, Amsterdam, 73. Awards: Carnegie Int. Media: Oil, Glass. Mailing Add: 2100 Linwood Ave Ft Lee NJ 07024

GROTENRATH, RUTH
PAINTER
b Milwaukee, Wis, Mar 17, 12. Study: State Teachers Col, Milwaukee, BA. Work: Philadelphia Mus Art; IBM Collection; Madison Union; Milwaukee Art Inst; Gimbel Collection. Comn: Murals, Post Off, Hart, Mich, Wayzata, Minn & Hudson, Wis & Timmerman Field Bldg. Exhib: One-man shows, Wis State Col, Stevens Point, 64, Chapman Gallery, Milwaukee, 65 & Bradley Gallery, 66, 69, 72, 74 & 77; Milwaukee Art Ctr, 62; Madison Salon, 67 & 68; Washington, Conn, 75; Univ Wis, Whitewater, 77; plus others. Teaching: Instr design, Univ Wis-Milwaukee, 61. Awards: William & Bertha Clusman Award, 63; Grand Rapids Art Gallery Award; Dayton Co Award, Minneapolis; plus others. Dealer: Bradley Galleries 2565 N Downer Ave Milwaukee WI 53211. Mailing Add: 2626A N Maryland Ave Milwaukee WI 53211

GROTH, BRUNO
SCULPTOR
b Stolp, Ger, Dec 14, 05; US citizen. Study: Otis Art Inst, Los Angeles. Work: Palm Springs Mus, Calif; Joseph H Hirshhorn Collection, New York. Comn: Bronze fountain pieces, Cities of Fresno & Crescent City, Calif; wood sculpture, Humboldt State Col. Exhib: One-man show, De Young Mus, San Francisco, 59; Brussels World's Fair; Santa Barbara Mus Art; Portland Art Mus; Mus Contemp Crafts, New York. Media: Welded Steel, Bronze, Wood. Dealer: Ankrum Gallery 657 N La Cienega Blvd Los Angeles CA 90069. Mailing Add: PO Box 3 Trinidad CA 95570

GROTH, JOHN AUGUST
ILLUSTRATOR, PAINTER
b Chicago, Ill, Feb 2, 08. Study: Art Inst Chicago; Art Students League; hon DA, Eastern Mich Univ, 76. Work: Mus Mod Art, Whitney Mus Am Art & Metrop Mus Art, New York; Brooklyn Mus, NY; Art Inst Chicago; Libr of Cong & Smithsonian Inst, Washington, DC; Mus of Mod Art, Moscow. Teaching: Instr compos, Art Students League, 46-; artist in residence, Univ Tex, 70. Pos: Art dir, Esquire Mag, 33-36; art dir, Parade Mag. Mem: Nat Acad Design; Soc Illusr; Am Watercolor Soc. Style & Technique: Impressionist; dramatic events, sport, war, etc. Media: Watercolor, Ink. Publ: Illusr, Men Without Women, 46; illusr, Grapes of Wrath, 47; illusr, War & Peace, 60; illusr, Exodus, 62; illusr, Black Beauty, 62; illusr, Short Stories of O'Henry, 65; Gone with the Wind, 68; illusr, All Quiet on the Western Front, 71; illusr, Pudden' Head Wilson, 75, The Promise Kept, 75 & Biography of the American Reindeer, 76; plus numerous others. Mailing Add: 61 E 57th St New York NY 10022

GROTZ, DOROTHY ROGERS
PAINTER
b Philadelphia, Pa. Study: Univ Berlin, 29; Columbia Univ, MS, 45; Art Students League, 47. Work: Rochester Univ Mus Art; Santa Barbara Mus Fine Arts; Norfolk Mus Arts & Sci; Evansville Mus Arts & Sci. Exhib: Avery Libr, Columbia Univ, 50, Van Diemen Lilienfeld Gallery, 62-67 & Bodley Gallery, New York, 72; Univ Wis, 67; Columbus Gallery Fine Arts, Ohio, 72. Bibliog: Archives of Am Art, Smithsonian Inst, Washington, DC. Media: Oil. Publ: Auth rev in Archit Forum, 69 & Leonardo, 72. Dealer: Bodley Gallery 787 Madison Ave New York NY 10021. Mailing Add: 7 St Lukes Pl New York NY 10014

GROVE, EDWARD RYNEAL
MEDALIST/SCULPTOR, PAINTER
b Martinsburg, WVa, Aug 14, 12. Study: Nat Sch Art, Washington, DC, 33; Corcoran Sch Art, Washington, DC, with Schuler & Weisz, 34-40; also with Robert Brackman, Noank, Conn, 46. Work: Univ Pa Grad Sch Med, Philadelphia; Mil Mus, The Citadel, Charleston, SC; Metrop Mus Art; Carnegie Inst; Imperial Palace, Tokyo, Japan. Comn: Communion of Saints (mural with Jean Donner Grove), Church of the Holy Comforter, Drexel Hill, Pa, 52-58; World War II Medal Series 30 (with Rolf Beck), Pres Art Medals, Inc, Vandalia, Ohio; Alphabet Medal, Soc Medalists, 73; portrait plaque, Rehabilitation Inst Chicago, 74; An American Eagle (bronze Bicentennial monument), Palm Beach, Fla, 76. Exhib: Watercolor Ann, Pa Acad Fine Arts, Philadelphia, 54; 14th Am Drawing Ann, Norfolk Mus Arts, Va, 58; 2nd Philadelphia Arts Festival, Philadelphia Mus Arts, 62; Nat Sculpture Soc, Lever House, New York, 67, 69 & 71; Florida Creates, Traveling Exhib, 73-74; 16th Congress FIDEM, Krakow, Poland, 75. Pos: Secy, treas & pres, Steel & Copper Engravers League, Philadelphia, 50-62; sculptor-engraver, US Mint, Philadelphia, 62-65; official sculptor-engraver, Order St John of Jerusalem, Knights of Malta Hq, Shickshinny, Pa, 67- Awards: Lindsey Morris Mem Prize, Nat Sculpture Soc, 67 & Louis Bennett Mem Prize, 71; Sculptor of Yr Gold Medal, Am Numismatic Asn, 69. Bibliog: E Williams (auth), The mural, Today Mag, Philadelphia Inquirer, 11/58; T W Becker (auth), Edward R Grove/commitment to America, Franklin Mint Almanac, 11/69; V Culver (auth), The four best, Coins Mag, 6/70. Mem: Artists Equity Asn (nat first vpres, 65-67); fel Nat Sculpture Soc; Asn Nat Acad Design; Philadelphia Sketch Club; Art Mus of Palm Beaches. Style & Technique: Medallic sculpture and bas-relief; creative work in portraiture, historical themes, etc is based on patient research and exacting craftsmanship. Media: Clay, Bronze & Silver; Oil, Watercolor. Publ: Contribr, Design Handbook, Nat Philatelic Mus, 54; co-auth & illusr, The Communion of Saints (brochure), Church of the Holy Comforter, 58; illusr, Our Christian Heritage, Morehouse-Gorham, 59; auth & illusr, Assignment: Malta, Coin World, 65; auth & illusr, The making of a medal, Am Artist Mag, 1/72. Mailing Add: Sea-Lake Studio 3215 S Flagler Dr West Palm Beach FL 33405

GROVE, JEAN DONNER
SCULPTOR
b Washington, DC, May 15, 12. Study: Hill Sch Sculpture; Corcoran Sch Art; Cath Univ Am; Wilson Teachers Col, BS, 39; Cornell Univ; Philadelphia Mus Art; travel study in Europe; also with Clara Hill, Hans Schuler, Heinz Warneke & Fritz Janschka. Work: Rosenwald Collection, Philadelphia, Pa; Fine Arts Comn, City Hall, Philadelphia. Comn: Many portrait comn, 40-; The Communion of Saints (mural with E R Grove), Church of the Holy Comforter, Drexel Hill, 52-58; garden figures, fountains & other works in pvt collections, Washington, DC, Philadelphia, Pa, NJ & NC. Exhib: Corcoran Gallery of Art, Washington, DC, 43-47; Pa Acad Fine Arts Ann, Philadelphia, 47, 48 & 51, Regional, 53; Allied Artists Am, Nat Acad Design, New York, 49; Philadelphia Mus Art Regional Art Festivals, 55, 59 & 62; Philadelphia Art Alliance, 57, 59-60 & 66; Art USA: 58, Madison Sq Garden, New York, 58; Nat Sculpture Soc Ann, New York, 57, 74, 75 & 76 & Topeka, Kans, 57; Cayuga Mus Hist & Art, Auburn, NY, 64; Civic Ctr Mus, Philadelphia, 68; Norton Gallery of Art, West Palm Beach, Fla, 74; plus others. Awards: Morris Goodman Prize, John Herron Art Mus, Indianapolis, Ind, 57; Competition Prize for Design of Artists Equity Asn Philadelphia Award, 60; Tallix Foundry Award, Nat Sculpture Soc Bicentennial Exhib, New York, 76; plus others. Bibliog: R Hagerty (auth), A Sigma Phi in the chips, Sigma Phi Gamma Int Sorority, 10/51; E Williams (auth), The mural, Today Mag, 11/58. Mem: Soc Washington Artists; Artists Equity Asn (dir, Philadelphia Chap, 64-66); Philadelphia Art Alliance; Soc Four Arts, Palm Beach, Fla. Style & Technique: Fusion of personal interpretation and traditional

techniques; realization of the personality and mood in portraiture, in addition to achieving a valid likeness. Mailing Add: Sea Lake Studio 3215 S Flagler Dr West Palm Beach FL 33405

GROVE, RICHARD
MUSEUM DIRECTOR, WRITER
b Lakewood, NJ, Feb 7, 21. Study: Mexico City Col, BA, 48; Escuela Universitaria Bellas Artes, San Miguel de Allende, Mex, with David Alfaro Siqueiros; Mexico City Col, MA, 50, with Justino Fernandez. Teaching: Lectr art hist, Wichita State Univ, 59-61; lectr museology, Sch of Art, Univ Wash, 75- Pos: Assoc cur, Taylor Mus, Colorado Springs Fine Arts Ctr, Colo, 53-58; dir, Wichita Art Mus, Kans, 58-64; mus educ specialist, Arts & Humanities Prog, US Off Educ, Washington, DC, 64-68; assoc dir, Arts Educ Prog, JDR 3rd Fund, New York, 68-70; dep asst secy for hist & art, Smithsonian Inst, Washington, DC, 70-74; dir, Henry Art Gallery, Univ Wash, Seattle, 75- Mem: Am Asn Mus (accreditation comt, 68-70); Int Coun Mus; Nat Art Educ Asn. Publ: Auth, Mexican popular arts today, 54; auth, articles in Am Educ, Mus News & Art Educ, 67-78; auth, Museums and media: a status report, 70; auth, The Arts and the Gifted, 75. Mailing Add: 5034 18th Ave NE Seattle WA 98105

GROVES, NAOMI JACKSON
WRITER, PAINTER
b Montreal, PQ. Study: Rannows Art Sch, Copenhagen; Sir George Williams Col, McGill Univ, BA & MA; Heidelberg Univ; Univ Berlin; Univ Munich; Radcliffe Col, AM & PhD; McMaster Univ, DLitt, 72. Exhib: One-man shows, Radcliffe Col, Wheaton Col, McMaster Univ & Montreal Mus Fine Arts. Teaching: Lect, Ernst Barlach as Sculptor, as Dramatist & Barlach in America, 64; lect, The Group of Seven, Another Look, Nat Gallery Can, 69; lect, McGill Univ, Wheaton Col, Carleton Col; assoc prof in charge fine arts, McMaster Univ. Pos: Vis comt fine arts, Harvard Univ; bd mem, Ernst Barlach Gesellschaft; asst to dir, Nat Gallery Can, 42-43, consult, 63-64. Awards: Gov Gen Gold Medal, McGill Univ, 33; Can Fedn Univ Women Traveling Fel, 36-37. Style & Technique: Traditional landscape. Media: Oil on Wood Panel. Publ: Auth, The Transformations of God, Hamburg, 62; auth, A Y's Canada, Toronto, 68 & 69; auth, Ernst Barlach-Leben im Werk, 72. Mailing Add: 2896 Highfield Crescent Ottawa ON K2B 6G5 Can

GRUBAR, FRANCIS STANLEY
ART HISTORIAN, LECTURER
b New Britain, Conn, June 8, 24. Study: Univ Md, BA, 48, MA(educ), 49; Johns Hopkins Univ, MA, 52, PhD(art hist), 66. Collections Arranged: Consult, William Ranney Exhib, 60-61 & Richard Caton Woodville Exhib (auth, catalogue), 67-68, Corcoran Gallery Art, Washington, DC. Teaching: Asst prof art hist, Univ Md, 48-66; assoc prof Am art, George Washington Univ, 66-73, prof Am art, 73- Pos: Chmn art dept, George Washington Univ, 72-73. Mem: Col Art Asn; Columbia Hist Soc; Conn Hist Soc; Corcoran Gallery Art; Am Studies Asn. Res: History of painting and sculpture in America during the 19th century. Publ: Auth, William Ranney, Painter of the Early West, Potter, 62; contribr, Leila Mechlin, In: Notable American Women 1607-1950, Vol 2, Harvard Univ Press, 71; contribr, Minerva Chapman, Retrospective Exhib catalogue, Adams-Davidson, 71; contribr, A J Dozar, auth, R Tait McKenzie, Sculptor of Atheletes, Univ Tenn Press, 75. Mailing Add: Dept of Art George Washington Univ Washington DC 20052

GRUBER, AARONEL DE ROY
SCULPTOR, KINETIC ARTIST
b Pittsburgh, Pa. Study: Carnegie-Mellon Univ, BS; painting & design with Samuel Rosenberg & Robert Lepper. Work: Smithsonian Inst, Washington, DC; Rose Art Mus, Brandeis Univ; Butler Inst of Am Art; DeCordova Mus, Lincoln, Mass; Norfolk Mus of Arts & Sci, Va; Palm Springs Desert Mus, Calif; Chase Manhattan Bank Am, New York; Kawamura Mem Mus Mod Art, Sukura, Japan; Grand Rapids Art Mus, Mich. Comn: Steelcityscope (16 1/2 ft steel sculpture), Loggia, City Co Bldg, Pittsburgh, Pa, 77; kinetic metal & plexiglas sculpture, Allegheny Ludlum Industs Inc, Pittsburgh; 32 ft cor-ten sculpture, Gen Mills Corp, Minneapolis, 71; geometric painting, Pittsburgh Nat Bank, 71; kinetic sculpture, Hillman Libr, Univ Pittsburgh, 71; 18ft naval brass sculpture, Grand Cent Mall, Parkersburg, WVa, 72. Exhib: Made of Plastic, Flint Inst Arts, 68-69; A Plastic Presence, Jewish Mus, New York, 69; New Am Sculpture, US Info Agency int tour of Far Eastern mus, 71-73 & Creative Am-45 Sculptors, tour of maj Far Eastern & Japanese mus, 73-75; Refracted Images, DeCordova Mus, Lincoln, Mass, 73; Sculpture Biennale, Mucsearnok Gallery, Budapest Mus, Hungary; Everson Mus, Syracuse, NY, 73; Basil Art Fair, 76-77; Vancouver Art Gallery, Vancouver Mus, BC, 77; and others. Awards: Ten Painting Awards, Six Sculpture Awards, Four Prizes & Assoc Artists Award of Distinction, Carnegie Mus, 61-66; Six Sculpture Awards, Western Pa Soc Sculptors, 62-77; Best of Show, John Elliott Mem Prize, Newport Ann, RI, 60; Award, Allegheny Ludlum Industs, Western Pa Soc Sculptors, 77. Bibliog: Alex Mogelon & Norman LaLiberte (auth), Art in Boxes, Van Nostrand Reinhold, 75; Dr Thelma Newman (auth), Plastics as sculpture, 74; What's beautiful & has a plug at the end of it? Hint: electric art, Impetus Mag, 3/75; Funderbunk & Davenport (authors), Art in Public Places; Funderbunk (auth), Pocket Guide to the Location of Art in the United States. Mem: Western Pa Soc Sculptors (pres, 74-78); Southern Soc of Sculptors; Assoc Artists of Pittsburgh (bd dirs, 67-69); Women in the Arts; Nat Soc Lit & Arts; Am Crafts Coun. Style & Technique: Monumental-size metal sculptures, welded and fabricated utilizing geometric forms such as rounded-cornered-squares or triangular forms; vacuum-formed, laminated, transparent plexiglas and lucite sculptures in combination with various metals creating kinetic or stable sculpture. Dealer: Galeria Bonino Ltd 48 Great Jones St New York NY 10012; Electric Gallery Toronto ON Can. Mailing Add: 2409 Marbury Rd Pittsburgh PA 15221

GRUBERT, CARL ALFRED
CARTOONIST
b Chicago, Ill, Sept 10, 11. Study: Chicago Acad Fine Arts, 29-30; Univ Wis, BS, 34. Exhib: Libr Cong, 41; Nat Cartoonists Soc Exhibs, 50 & 51; Metrop Mus Art, 51. Pos: Staff artist, Great Lakes Bull, 44-45. Awards: US Treas Award of Merit, 50; Freedom's Found Medal, 50. Publ: Auth, The Berrys (int syndicated cartoon), 42- Mailing Add: Woodlawn Ave Des Plaines IL 62216

GRUCZA, LEO (VICTOR)
PAINTER, EDUCATOR
b Erie, Pa, Jan 3, 35. Study: Cleveland Inst of Art, dipl, 57, with Louis Bosa, Joseph McCullough & William McVey; Tulane Univ, MFA, 61, with George Rickey, Pat Trivigno & John Taylor. Exhib: Corcoran Biennial Exhib, Washington, DC, 63; Six Americans, Ark Arts Ctr, Little Rock, 64; 23rd Am Drawing Biennial, Norfolk Mus of Arts & Sci, Va, 69; Exhib of Contemp Art, Soc of the Four Arts, Palm Beach, Fla, 72; two-person exhib, Mitchell Mus, Mt Vernon, Ill, 77. Teaching: Asst prof painting, Univ Ill, Champaign, 66-70, assoc prof painting, 70- Awards: First Prize/Painting, Ann Exhib, Delgado Mus, New Orleans, 61; Tiffany Found grant, New York, 61; First Prize/Acrylic, 4th Ann Sugar Creek Art Exhib, Wabash Col, Crawfordsville, Ind, 76. Style & Technique: Figure-related abstract style; expressionistic. Media: Acrylic on canvas. Mailing Add: 2204 Blackthorn Champaign IL 61820

GRUEN, JOHN
ART CRITIC
b Enghien-les-Bains, France, Sept 12, 26; US citizen. Study: City Col New York; Univ Iowa, BA & MA. Pos: Critic of music & art, New York Herald Tribune, 62-68; art critic, New York Mag, 69-73; art critic, Soho Weekly News, 74-; contribr ed, Art News, 76- Publ: Auth, The New Bohemia, Grosset & Dunlap, 68; auth, The Private World of Leonard Bernstein, 68, auth, Close-Up, 69, auth, The Party's Over Now—Reminiscences of the Fifties, 72 & auth, The Private World of Ballet, 74, Viking Press. Mailing Add: 317 W 83rd St New York NY 10024

GRUEN, SHIRLEY SCHANEN
PAINTER
b Port Washington, Wis, Dec 2, 23. Study: Univ Wis, BS, 45; Art Ctr Sch, Los Angeles, 46; Layton Art Sch, Univ Wis-Milwaukee Exten & Cardinal Stritch Col, 50-70. Work: Port Washington High Sch; Port Washington State Bank & First Nat Bank; Phoenix Union Area Voc Ctr, Ariz; Colonial State Bank, Thiensville, Wis. Exhib: Westchester Art Soc Exhib, White Plains, NY, 70; La Watercolor Int, Baton Rouge, La, 70 & 71; 13th & 14th Chautauqua Ann, NY, 70 & 71; Gtr New Orleans Exhib, La, 71 & 72; Mus Art, Springfield, Utah, 74. Teaching: Instr watercolor & portrait, Milwaukee Area Tech Col, Wis, 70- Awards: Slidell Art League Purchase Award, La, 70; Two Purchase Awards, Port Washington Art Fair, 70; Grumbacher Award for Best Watercolor, Chautauqua 14th Ann, 71. Bibliog: William F Schanen, III (auth), Shirley's Atelier, Ozaukee Press, 71; article in La Rev Mod, 9/72. Mem: La Watercolor Soc; Firehouse Fine Arts Asn; Wis Painters & Sculptors. Style & Technique: Vigorous style, bold color, impressionistic representational, play of light on landscapes, seascapes, buildings, figures reminiscent of Hopper. Media: Acrylic, Watercolor. Mailing Add: 6254 N Port Washington Rd Glendale WI 53217

GRUNDY, JOHN OWEN
PATRON, WRITER
b Jersey City, NJ, Mar 8, 11. Study: Cooper Union. Pos: Contrib ed, Jersey Rev, Jersey City, 28-34; free lance writer, 43-46 & 61-68; assoc ed & reporter, Villager, New York, 46-59; pres & ed, Greenwich Village News, 59-61; archivist, Jersey City Free Pub Libr, 68-72; city historian, Jersey City, 72-; mem gov bd, Washington Square Art Outdoor Art Exhib, New York, currently. Awards: Patron of the Arts Award, Hudson Artists, Inc. Mem: Jersey City Mus Asn (pres, currently); Munic Art Soc; Nat Trust Hist Preservation; Nat Soc Lit & Arts. Interest: Collector paintings, etchings, prints, autograph letters and pictures; lay member of committee to prevent demolition of artists studios in Greenwich Village; sponsor of paint the town art competition for Jersey City Bicentennial. Mailing Add: Free Pub Libr Jersey City 472 Jersey Ave Jersey City NJ 07302

GRUPP, CARL ALF
PAINTER, PRINTMAKER
b Moorhead, Minn, Sept 11, 39. Study: Minneapolis Col Art & Design, BFA, 64; Vrije Acad, Netherlands, 65; Ind Univ, MFA(with hons), 69; and with Rudy Pozzatti, Urban Couch, Marvin Lowe, William Bailey & James McGarrell. Work: Minneapolis Inst Art; Univ Minn Gallery, Minneapolis; Am Embassy, London; Chicago Art Inst; SDak Mem Art Ctr, Brookings. Exhib: Am Graphic Workshops, Cincinnati Art Mus, Ohio, 68; Joslyn Art Mus 12th Biennial, Omaha, Nebr, 72; Pratt Graphic Art Exhib, New York, 72-73; Am Printmakers, Ind Univ, US Info Agency Tour Eng, 73; Drawings USA, Minn Mus Art, St Paul, 75; plus many others. Teaching: Teaching asst lithography, Minneapolis Col Art & Design, 64-65; teaching asst intaglio printmaking, Ind Univ, Bloomington, 68-69; asst prof art, Augustana Col, 69- Awards: Gustave Krollman Award for Draftsmanship, Minneapolis Col Art & Design, 63; Vanderlip Scholar, 64; Purchase Awards, SDak Mem Art Ctr, 73 & Silvermine Guild, New Canaan, Conn. Bibliog: Spotted talents in America, Frasconi, Grupp, Tendensen, 11/65; Craig Volk (auth), Art of Carl Grupp (video tape), KUSD-TV, Univ SDak, 3/75. Mem: Graphics Soc. Style & Technique: Fantasy; imaginary figure & landscape; printmaking. Media: Oil, all drawing media. Dealer: Assoc American Artists 663 Fifth Ave New York NY 10022; ADI Gallery Inc 530 McAllister St San Francisco CA 94102. Mailing Add: 1614 S Phillips Ave Sioux Falls SD 57105

GRUPPE, CHARLES
PAINTER
b New York, NY, July 1, 28. Study: Yale Univ; Nat Univ Mex; Columbia Univ, BFA, 54, Brevoort fel & MFA, 55; Huntington Hartford Found, Pacific Palisades, 56; Fulbright fel, Italy, 56-57; Ital Govt Award, 57. Comn: Paintings, Am Pres Lines, Coolidge, Jackson & Wilson, 65; Yale Divinity Sch, New Haven, Conn, 65; Dolly O'Brien Estate, Palm Beach, 64; First Nat Bank, New Haven, 65; Apt Complexes, Palm Beach, 72-73. Exhib: Silvermine Guild Artists, New Canaan, Conn, 65 & 77; Provincetown Art Asn, 65 & 77 & Rockport Art Asn, Mass, 70 & 77; Butler Mus Am Art, Youngstown, Ohio, 72 & 75; Lord & Taylor, New York, 75. Style & Technique: Semi-abstract marines using a direct technique with limited palette. Media: Oil. Mailing Add: 20 Livingston St New Haven CT 06511

GRUPPE, EMILE ALBERT
PAINTER
b Rochester, NY, Nov 23, 96. Study: Nat Acad Design, 14-18; Art Students League, 25; La Grande Chaumiere, Paris; also with John F Carlson, Richard Miller, Charles Chapman, George Bridgeman & Chas Hawthorne. Work: Butler Mus, Youngstown, Ohio; Speed Mem Mus, Louisville, Ky; Benton Mus, Univ of Conn; Ft Wayne Mus, Ind; Montclair Mus, NJ; Springville Art Mus Permanent Collection, Utah. Comn: Gertrude Thebaud, painted for presentation to President Roosevelt, Master Mariners Asn, Gloucester, Mass, 33; Man at the Wheel (mural), Gloucester Nat Bank, 62; Judge J B Harrington (portrait), Salem Bar Asn, Mass, 65; three murals, Callaway Mills, La Grange, Ga, 66-67; Beverly Harbor (mural), MacDonald's, Beverly, Mass, 74. Exhib: Nat Acad Design Ann, New York, 16-38; N Shore Art Asn Ann, Gloucester, 22-; Allied Artists Am Ann, 34-; Audubon Artists Ann, 44-; Hudson Valley Art Asn 43rd Ann, White Plains, NY, 71. Awards: Richard Mitton Gold Medal, Jordan Marsh Exhib, Boston, 43; Ranger Fund Purchase Prize, Nat Acad Design, 53 & 69; Coun Am Arts Award, Allied Artists Am, 72; A McCarthy Award, Northshore Arts, 75; R Strisik Award, Rockport Art Asn, 76; First Prize, Meriden Arts, Conn, 76; President's Award, Am Artists Prof League, Mass, 77. Bibliog: Lawrence Dame (auth), Gruppe scores again, Sarasota Herald Tribune, Fla, 2/2/57; Judy de Turk (auth), interview with Emile A Gruppe, Naples Star, Fla, 2/3/66; Charles Movalli (auth), In Vermont with Emile A Gruppe, Am Artists, 10/75. Mem: Salmagundi Club; Allied Artists Am; N Shore Art Asn (pres, 51-52); Audubon Artists Am; Rockport Art Asn. Style & Technique: Impressionistic, realism. Media: Oil. Publ: Auth, Gruppe on Painting, Watson-Guptill, 76 & Brushwork, 77. Dealer: Grand Cent Art Gallery New York NY 10017; McNichols Gallery 1170 Third St S Naples FL 33940. Mailing Add: 9 Wonson St Gloucester MA 01930

GRUPPE, KARL HEINRICH
SCULPTOR
b Rochester, NY, Mar 18, 93. Study: Royal Acad, Antwerp, Belg, with Frans Joris; Art Students League New York; also with Karl Bitter. Work: US Vice President, in pvt collection of William Rufus King, Clinton, NC; Henry Hudson Monument, Riverdale, NY; La Joie (marble figure), Brookgreen Gardens, SC; Woman President, Adelphi Col, Long Island, NY; portrait figure in collection of Andrew Haskell Greene, New York. Comn: Bas-relief sculpture, Curtis Inst Music, Philadelphia; bronze bust of John Philip Sousa, New York Hall of Fame, 77. Exhib: Nat Acad Design Ann; Nat Sculpture Soc Ann; Int Bas-Relief Exhib. Pos: Chief sculpture, Monument Restoration Proj, New York City Dept Parks, 34-37; mem, Art Comn, New York, 44-47; mem bd dirs, Fine Arts Fedn, New York; mem adv bd, Nat Sculpture Rev; adv bd mem, Brookgreen Gardens, Myrtles Inlet, SC. Awards: Saltus Gold Medal, 52 & Elizabeth Watrees Gold Medal, 76, Nat Acad Design; Gold Medal, 75 & Theresa & Edwin Richard Mem Prize, 44th Ann Exhib, 77, Nat Sculpture Soc. Bibliog: Beatrice Gilman (auth), Karl H Gruppe-19th, Nat Sculpture Rev; Proske (auth), President-National Sculpture Society: 1950-51, 67-68. Mem: Nat Arts Club; fel Nat Sculpture Soc (pres, 49); academician Nat Acad Design (vpres, 57); Art Comn Assocs, New York; Century Asn. Media: Marble, Bronze. Mailing Add: Box 926 Southold Long Island NY 11971

GRUSHKIN, PHILIP
DESIGNER, INSTRUCTOR
b New York, NY, June 1, 21. Study: Cooper Union Art Sch. Exhib: Calligraphy, Grolier Club, 58; Art Dirs Club, 60; Int Calligraphy & Lettering, Brown Univ, 61; plus many others. Teaching: Instr lettering, calligraphy & illus, Cooper Union Art Sch, 46-68; dir bk workshop, Radcliffe Col Publ Procedures & Harvard Summer Sch, Cambridge, Mass, 66-; adj asst prof graphic design, NY Univ, 66- Pos: Cartographer, US Geol Survey, 42-43; Off Strategic Serv, USA, 43-45; designer, World Publ Co, 55-56; designer, Harry N Abrams, Inc, 57-59, art dir, 59-, vpres, 60-69; pres, Philip Grushkin Inc, Englewood, NJ. Awards: Cert of Excellence, Print for Com Exhib, Am Inst Graphic Arts, 50; plus others. Mem: Grolier Club, NY; Am Printing Hist Asn (vpres prog); Typophiles, NY. Publ: Publ & calligrapher, Aesop's Fables, 46; publ, Christmas Carols, 48; contribr, Bouquet for Bruce Rogers, 50; contribr, Calligraphics, 55; plus others. Mailing Add: 86 E Linden Ave Englewood NJ 07631

GRUSKIN, MARY JOSEPHINE
ART DEALER
b Trani, Italy; US citizen. Pos: Dir, Midtown Galleries. Specialty: Contemporary American artists. Mailing Add: 11 E 57th St New York NY 10022

GRYGUTIS, BARBARA
CERAMIST
b Hartford, Conn, Nov 7, 46. Study: Univ Ariz, BFA, 68, with Maurice Grossman, MFA, 71. Work: Tucson Mus Art, Ariz; Tucson Sch Dist 1. Comn: Fountain, Union Bank, Tucson, 71 & La Placita Shopping Ctr, Tucson, 74; mural (with Charles Hardy), Navajo Co Govt Complex, Holbrook, Ariz, 75-76; mural, Kino Community Hosp, Tucson, Ariz, 77; 12 place settings, Senate Wives Luncheon, The White House, Washington, DC, 77; fountain, Cochise Col, Sierra Vista, Ariz, 78. Exhib: Tucson Art Ctr, Ariz, 69; Univ Ariz Mus Art, Tucson, 71; Object Makers 71; Utah Mus Fine Arts, 71; Mainstreams 72, Grover M Herman Fine Arts Ctr, Marietta, Ohio, 72; Ninth, Tenth & Eleventh Southwestern Invitationals, Yuma Fine Arts Ctr, Ariz, 74, 75 & 76; Harlan Gallery, Tucson, 75; Craft Encore, Tucson Mus Art, 76; Am Crafts at the White House, Renwick Gallery, Smithsonian Inst, Washington, DC, 76; Mus Contemp Crafts, New York, NY, 76; Everson Mus of Art, Syracuse, NY, 76; Landscape, New Views, Herbert Johnson Mus, Cornell Univ, Ithaca, NY, 78; Women Artists: Clay, Fiber, Metal, Bronx Mus, NY, 78; plus numerous others. Pos: Artist in residence, Tucson Sch Dist 1, 73. Awards: Lancaster Award, Tucson Art Ctr, 70 & 71; Purchase Award, Tucson Mus Art, 73; Nat Endowment for the Arts grants, 73-74 & 77 & individual fel, 75; Pat Mutterer Mem Award & Group Show Award, Tucson Mus of Art, 76; Purchase Award, Eleventh Southwestern Invitational, Yuma Fine Arts Ctr, Ariz, 76; and others. Bibliog: Leon Nigrosh (auth), Clayworks, Davis Publ, 75; Adina Wingate (auth), article in Craft Horizons, 6/75 & article in Ceramics Monthly, 2/76; plus others. Style & Technique: Highly lustered and glazed functional and sculptural works in clay utilizing wheel thrown pieces, slabs and press molds. Media: Clay, Glass. Dealer: Hand & The Spirit 4200 N Marshall Way Scottsdale AZ 85251. Mailing Add: 273 N Main Tucson AZ 85705

GUADAGNOLI, NELLO T
ART DEALER
b Walsenburg, Colo, Dec 16, 29. Pos: Owner/dir, Kiva Gallery. Specialty: Paintings by Indian artists. Mailing Add: c/o Kiva Gallery 202 W Hwy 66 Gallup NM 87301

GUALTIERI, JOSEPH P
MUSEUM DIRECTOR, PAINTER
b Royalton, Ill, Dec 25, 16. Study: Norwich Art Sch, Conn, dipl; Sch Art Inst Chicago, Ill, dipl. Work: Pa Acad Fine Arts, Philadelphia; Wadsworth Atheneum, Hartford, Conn; RI Sch Design Mus Fine Arts, Providence; Lyman Allyn Mus, New London, Conn; Slater Mem Mus, Norwich, Conn. Comn: Wall mural, New London Co Mutual Ins Co, Norwich, Conn; portrait of Gov John Dempsey, State of Conn. Exhib: Chicago Art Inst, Ill, 41; Pa Acad Fine Arts, Philadelphia, 48 & 51; Whitney Mus Am Art, New York, 52; Corcoran Gallery Art, Washington, DC; Nat Acad Design, New York; Albany Inst Hist & Art, NY; Wadsworth Atheneum, Hartford, Conn; Calif Palace of the Legion of Honor, Lincoln Park, San Francisco. Collections Arranged: Seven or eight arranged annually. Teaching: Art teacher oil painting, figure & portrait, The Norwich Free Acad, Conn, 43- Pos: Dir, Slater Mem Mus, Norwich, Conn, 62- Awards: First Prize & Logan Medal, Chicago Art Inst, 41; Purchase Prize, Pa Acad of Fine Arts, 48 & 51; $1000 Award, Conn Artists Eastern States Expo, 51. Mem: Conn Acad Fine Arts Asn; Am Asn Mus; New Eng Conf, Am Asn Mus. Style & Technique: Figurative artist. Media: Oil, mixed media. Mailing Add: 60 Warren St Norwich CT 06360

GUDERNA, LADISLAV
PAINTER, ILLUSTRATOR
b Nitra, Czech, June 1, 21; Can citizen. Study: Tech Acad, Bratislava, Czech; Acad Creative Arts, Belgrade. Work: Nat Gallery, Prague; Nat Gallery, Bratislava; plus pvt collections in Czech, Holland, Venezuela, US, Ger, Can, Switz & Italy. Comn: Harlequin intarsia, New Theatre, Bratislava, 59; Icarus & Cosmonauts mosaic, Prague Castle, 64; Happy Prince (combined technique), Jablonec, Czech, 68; Spring (oil & enamel), Greenwin Co, Toronto, 72; Cemetery of Cars (combined technique), Greenwin Co, Willowdale. Exhib: XXIV Biennale, Venice, 48; IV Biennale, Sao Paulo, 57; Expo '57, Brussels, 57; one-man shows, Rome, Milano & Bologna, Italy, 59 & Estee Gallery, Toronto, 74; plus exhib in Zurich, New York, Vienna, Toronto & Ottawa, 75-77. Awards: Gold & Silver Medal for Display, Expo '57; First Prize for Best Stamp, Ministry of Telecommunications, Prague, 65; Gold Medal for Paneau, Int Stamps Exhib, Prague, 67. Bibliog: Articles in Art Mag, Toronto, 71 & 73; article in Int Art Bull, 73; doc film about work publ by Animette Can, 75. Mem: Soc Can Artists. Style & Technique: Imaginative and surrealistic. Media: Tempera, Oils. Mailing Add: Vancouver BC Can

GUENTHER, PETER W
ART HISTORIAN
b Dresden, Ger, Mar 29, 20; US citizen. Study: Univ Breslau; Acad Fine Arts, Stuttgart, Ger; Univ Tex, Austin, MA & PhD. Collections Arranged: Edvard Munch (assembled & auth, catalogue), Sarah Campbell Blaffer Gallery, Univ Houston, New Orelans, San Antonio & Dallas; German Expressionism, Toward a New Humanism (assembled & auth, catalogue), Sarah Campbell Blaffer Gallery, Univ Houston. Teaching: Prof art, Univ Houston, 62- Pos: Chmn dept art, Univ Houston, 62-72; scholar-in-residence, Robert Gore Rifkind Collection, Beverly Hills, 6-8/78. Awards: Teaching Excellence Award, Univ Houston, 70; Exceptional Scholar for German Expressionism Catalog, Art Libr NAm, 77. Mem: Col Art Asn Am; Tex Asn Sch Arts (pres, 71-73); SCent Renaissance Conf (pres, 73); SCent Mod Lang Asn; Mid-Am Art Hist Asn. Res: Renaissance; iconography; German Expressionism. Publ: Auth, Destruction of Art Works During the Reformation, Renaissance Explor, 77; Renaissance and Mannerism North of the Alps, Encycl World Art, suppl vol, 78. Mailing Add: 10013 Hazelhurst Houston TX 77080

GUERIN, JOHN WILLIAM
PAINTER, EDUCATOR
b Houghton, Mich, Aug 29, 20. Study: Am Acad Art, Chicago; Art Students League; Escuela Bellas Artes, San Miguel, Mex; Colorado Springs Fine Arts Ctr. Work: Dallas Mus Fine Arts; Chrysler Mus, Provincetown, Mass; Joslyn Art Mus, Omaha, Nebr; Colorado Springs Fine Art Ctr; Houston Mus Fine Arts; plus others. Exhib: One-man shows, Kraushaar Gallery, New York, 59, 63 & 68; Galeria Realities, Taos, NMex, 60; Corcoran Gallery Art, 61; Whitney Mus Am Art, New York; retrospective, Ft Worth Art Ctr, 64; plus others. Teaching: Instr painting, Dallas Mus Fine Arts, 50-52; prof art, Univ Tex, Austin, 53-; artist in residence, Skowhegan Sch Painting & Sculpture, 60. Awards: Ranger Purchase Award, Nat Acad Design, 58; Am Acad Arts & Lett Grant, 59; Univ Tex Res Inst Grant, 60 & 66; plus others. Mem: Tex Fine Arts Asn; life mem Art Students League; assoc Nat Acad Design. Style & Technique: Evocations of the landscape, both expressionistic and surrealistic in interpretation. Dealer: Carlin Galleries 710 Montgomery St Ft Worth TX 76107. Mailing Add: 3400 Stoneridge Rd Austin TX 78746

GUERRERO, JOSE
PAINTER
b Granada, Spain, 1914; US citizen. Study: Escuela Superior Bellas Artes San Fernando, Madrid, Spain, 40-44; Ecole Beaux-Arts, Paris, 45-46. Work: Guggenheim Mus & Whitney Mus Am Art, New York; Art Inst Chicago; Carnegie Inst, Pittsburgh; Mus Span Abstract Art, Cuenca, Spain; plus others. Exhib: Whitney Mus Am Art Ann, 58, 62 & 69; Carnegie Int, Pittsburgh, 58 & 62; Spanish Art Today, traveling exhib to Munich, Berlin, Copenhagen & Amsterdam, 68; Rosc '71, Dublin, Ireland, 71; one-man shows, Betty Parsons Gallery, New York, 54, 57, 60 & 63, Rose Fried Gallery, New York, 64, Juana Mordo Gallery, Madrid, Spain, 64, 67, 71, 75 & 76, A M Sachs Gallery, New York, 75 & Gruenebaum Gallery, New York, 78. Teaching: Instr painting, New Sch Social Res, 62-65. Awards: Chevalier, Order of Arts & Lett, Fr Govt, 59; Graham Found Advan Studies in Fine Arts Grant, 59; Official Cross of Isabel La Catolica, Spain, 78. Bibliog: Alberto Portera (producer), Jose Guerrero Painter (film), Madrid, 70; Paintings & sculpture, Crucible Mag, 70; monogr, Jose Guerrero, Juana Mordo Gallery, 76. Media: Oil. Dealer: Gruenebaum Gallery 25 E 77th St New York NY 10021; Juana Mordo Gallery Costello 7 Madrid Spain. Mailing Add: 406 W 20th St New York NY 10011

GUERRIERO, HENRY EDWARD
SCULPTOR
b Monroe, La, Mar 6, 29. Study: Royal Acad, London, 51-53; with Witol Klimowicz, Paris, 52; Inst Allende, Mexico, 55-56; Univ of the Americas, Mex, 56-59. Work: Univ Southern Calif; Masur Mus Art, Monroe; Santa Barbara Mus Art, Calif; La Arts & Sci Ctr, Baton Rouge; Phoenix Art Mus, Ariz; plus others. Comn: Steel & bronze sculptures, Elia Kazan Pvt Collections, 68; opera sets for Amerika, Western Opera Co, 72; bronze sculpture, Paul Heller, 74. Exhib: One-man shows, Santa Barbara Mus, Calif, 69, John Whibley Gallery, Ltd, London, 69, Phoenix Art Mus, 71 & Loyola Marymount Univ, 74; one-man retrospective, Univ Southern Calif, 70-71; plus others. Awards: Award for Institutionalization, Calif Inst Arts, 67. Bibliog: L Botto (auth), Henry Guerriero, Look Mag, 71; Henry Guerriero (art documentary film), KNOE-TV, 71-72; M Leopold (auth), Henry Guerriero, Art Int, 73-74; plus others. Style & Technique: Miriad fantasy worlds; conscious sensuous, eclectic forms; polyester cast 3 dimensional x-ray sculptures. Media: Polyester Resin, Bronze. Publ: Auth, X-Art Manifesto, 68; auth, Age of Confrontation, 71; auth, Avant-gardism & Universitarianism, 71; auth, Polarity, 75; auth, Concept, Discovery of Man Series, 75; plus others. Dealer: Ericson Gallery 963 Madison Ave New York NY 10021; Silvan Simone Gallery 11579 W Olympic Blvd Los Angeles CA 90064. Mailing Add: 3036 Veteran Ave Los Angeles CA 90034

GUGGENHEIM, PEGGY
COLLECTOR, PATRON
b New York, NY, Aug 26, 98. Pos: Dir (& financed), Gallery Guggenheim Jeune, London, 38-39, Art of This Century, New York, 43-47, Mus Palazzo Venier Leoni, Venice, Italy, 51- Awards: Hon Citizen, Venice, 62. Interest: Private collection exhibited through Europe, 51- Collection: Modern art. Publ: Auth, Out of This Century, 46 & 68, Una Collezionista Recorda, 56 & Confessions of an Art Addict, 60; auth articles & introductions. Mailing Add: Palazzo Venier dei Leoni 701 San Gregoria Venice Italy

GUIFFREDA, MAURO FRANCIS
PAINTER, PRINTMAKER
b Brooklyn, NY, Aug 25, 42. Study: Calif State Univ, Northridge, BFA; Pratt Inst, New York, MFA. Pos: Tech dir, Am Atelier, 74- Mailing Add: 260 DeKalb Ave Brooklyn NY 11205

GUILMAIN, JACQUES
ART HISTORIAN, EDUCATOR
b Brussels, Belg, Oct 15, 26; US citizen. Study: Queens Col, City Univ New York, BS, 48; Columbia Univ, MA, 52, univ fel, 57, PhD, 58, and with Meyer Schapiro. Teaching: Vis asst prof hist art, Stanford Univ, 58-59; vis asst prof, Univ Calif, Riverside, 59-60; instr, Queens Col, 60-63; from asst prof to prof art hist, State Univ NY Stony Brook, 63-, chmn art dept, 70-76; vis prof, Columbia Univ, 68 & 70. Awards: Am Philosophical Soc Grant, 60; State Univ NY Res Found Grant, 64-70. Mem: Col Art Asn Am; Int Ctr Medieval Art; Mediaeval Acad Am. Res: Early Medieval ornaments; Mozarabic manuscript illumination; Carolingian manuscript illumination; early Medieval metalwork. Publ: Contribr, American Watercolors,

Drawings & Prints, 1952, catalog, Met Mus Art, New York, 52; auth, Zoomorphic decoration and the problem of the sources of Mozarabic illumination, XXXV 60 & Illuminations of the Second Bible of Charles the Bald, XLI 66, Speculum; auth, Observations on some early interlace initials and frame ornaments in Mozarabic manuscripts of Leon-Castile, Scriptorium, XV, 61; auth, On the classicism of the Classic phase of Franco-Saxon manuscript illumination, Art Bull XLIX, 67; auth, Enigmatic beasts of the Lindau Gospels lower cover, Gesta, X, 71. Mailing Add: PO Box 363 Setauket NY 11733

GUION, MOLLY
PAINTER
Study: Grand Cent Art Sch, with Arthur Woelfle; Art Students League, with George Bridgman; portraiture with Dimitri Romanovsky; also with Grigory Gluckmann. Work: Brit Royal Navy, Portsmouth; Brit Consulate, New York; NY State Capitol, Albany; Nat Portrait Gallery, Washington, DC; many other pub & pvt collections. Comn: Portraits of many prominent persons, US & abroad. Exhib: One-man show, Seattle Art Mus, Wash; Vancouver Art Gallery, BC; Paris Salon, France; Royal Portrait Soc, London; pvt showing, Buckingham Palace; Grand Prix Int de Cote d'Azur, Cannes, France; many other exhibs in galleries & mus, US, Can & abroad. Awards: Ellerhusen Mem Prize, Allied Artists Am; Catharine Lorillard Wolfe Art Club; Gold Medals, Nat Art Club & Am Artists Prof League; plus many others. Mem: Allied Artists Am; Pen & Brush Club; Hudson Valley Art Asn; Lotos Club; fel Royal Soc Arts; plus others. Style & Technique: Color spotting of French Impressionists. Mailing Add: 10 Barberry Lane Rye NY 10580

GUITE, SUZANNE
PAINTER, SCULPTOR
b Gaspésie, Que, Dec 10, 27. Study: Inst Design, Chicago, with Moholy-Nagy & Archipenko, 49; with Brancusi, 50; Acad Belle Arte, Florence, Italy, 51; Mus Romanesque Art, Barcelona, Spain; Inst Polytechnico, Mex, 53. Work: Que Art Mus; Nat Art Gallery, Ottawa; Jewish Libr, Montreal; Seagram's Art Collection, Montreal; New Carlisle Ct House, Que; and others. Comn: Sandstone mural & granite lintel, Quebec Justice Dept, New Carlisle; granite monument, Can Pavilion, Expo 67, Montreal; wooden monument, Govt Can, Notre Dame Island, Montreal; wall tapestry, Douglass Col, Rutgers Univ, 77. Exhib: Expo Universelle, Montreal, 67; Toronto City Hall, Toronto, 67; Univ Waterloo, 69; Musée Sao Paolo, Brazil, 69; Musée d'Art Contemporain, Montreal, 70; Musée Rodin, Paris, France, 70; Musée du Que, 70; one-woman shows, Cercle Universitaire, Montreal, 52 & Quebec, 55, Galerie 60, Florence, Italy, 60, Princeton Univ, 67, Gina Bringham Gallery, Princeton, NJ, 68, Place des Arts, Montreal, 69, Boston Univ, Mass, 71, Centre National des Arts, Ottawa, 72 (twice), Douglass Col, Rutgers Univ, NJ, 74, Princeton Pub Libr, NJ, 75, Musée Régional de Rimouski, Que, 76, Wells Gallery, Ottawa, 76, Musée du Que, Quebec, 77 & numerous others. Pos: Dir, Ctr Art Perce, Que, 57- Bibliog: Shep Jacobsen (auth), Art from the Gaspe, Ottawa Citizen, 1/29/72; M F O'Leary (auth), Suzanne Guite, sculpteur, Reedition Quebec, 9/72; La sculpture de Suzanne Guite, Ed Aquila, Montreal, 73; Lovers in Onyx, Can Broadcasting Corp film, Ottawa, 76. Mem: Que Sculpture Soc; Royal Can Acad of Arts; Sculptor's Soc Can. Media: Bronze, Stone, Wood. Mailing Add: Perce Art Ctr Perce PQ G0C 2L0 Can

GULLY, ANTHONY LACY
ART HISTORIAN
b Orange, Calif, Feb 28, 38. Study: Univ Calif, Riverside, BA; Univ Calif, Berkeley, MA; Stanford Univ, PhD; also with Jean Boggs, Walter Horn, Lorenz Eitner & Albert Elsen. Teaching: Asst prof 17th-18th century art hist, Pomona Col, Claremont, Calif, 65-66; asst prof 19th-20th century art hist, Calif State Univ, Los Angeles, 66-68; assoc prof 19th-20th century art hist, Ariz State Univ, Tempe, 72- Awards: Nat Defence Educ Act Award, Stanford Univ, 68-70; Mabel McLeod Fel, Rowlandson Study, London, Stanford Univ, 70-71; Nat Endowment for the Humanities Award, Post Doctoral Studies, Yale Univ, US Govt, 76. Bibliog: J Hayes (auth), Rowlandson, Phaidon Art Bks, 72; R Paulsen (auth), Rowlandson: New interpretation, Yale Univ, 72; R Wark (auth), Rowlandson drawings in Huntington, Huntington Libr, 75. Mem: Col Art Asn; Mid-Am Col Art Asn; Rocky Mountain Conf on Brit Studies (pres, 78-79); Nat Conf on Brit Studies (mem nat exec comt); Pacific Conf on Brit Studies. Res: Concentration on 19th century British art, at present completing a monograph and catalogue raisonné on John Sell Cotman, 1782-1842. Publ: Auth, Book reviews on eighteenth century art and aesthetics, Mod Bibliog: 18th Century, 76; auth, Mr B and the cherubim: William Blake's descriptive catalog, Phoebus, 78. Mailing Add: 2618 S Country Club Way Tempe AZ 85282

GUMBERTS, WILLIAM A
COLLECTOR, PATRON
b Evansville, Ind, May 21, 12. Study: Harvard Univ; Ohio State Univ. Pos: Bd dirs, Evansville Pub Mus. Mem: Ind Arts Comn; charter mem Evansville Arts & Educ. Collection: Nineteenth century American oils; etchings of classical periods; moderns. Mailing Add: 22 Chandler Ave Evansville IN 47713

GUMPEL, HUGH
PAINTER
b New York, NY, Feb 3, 26. Study: Columbia Univ; Art Students League. Comn: Mural, State of NY Pub Works Admin Bldg, 63. Teaching: Instr painting, Nat Acad Sch Fine Arts, 59- Awards: Gold Medal of Honor, Am Watercolor Soc, 59. Mem: Nat Acad Design; Am Watercolor Soc. Media: Watercolor. Mailing Add: 335 Rushmore St Mamaroneck NY 10543

GUMPERT, GUNTHER
PAINTER,
b Krefeld, Ger, Apr 17, 19; US citizen. Study: Sch Fine Arts Krefeld; Sch Fine Arts, Wuppertal. Work: Metrop Mus Art, New York; Victoria & Albert Mus, London; Kaiser-Wilhelm Mus, Krefeld; Mus Nat Bellas Artes, Santiago, Chile; Art Mus, Princeton Univ. Comn: Mural, Inter-Am Develop Bank, Washington, DC, 68. Exhib: Kaiser-Wilhelm Mus, 48, 49 & 52; Salon Realites Nouvelles, Paris, 58-60 & 62; Int Exhib Abstr Art, Pistoia, 61; Int Exhib Contemp Art, London, 62; Salon Mai, Paris, 62. Bibliog: Jean Grenier (auth), Gumpert, Preuves, Paris, 60; Victor Summa (auth), Gumpert & The Evolution of His Art, Educ TV Asn, 63; Willy Huppert (auth), Gunther Gumpert, Kunst-und Kunstgewerbe Verein, Pforzheim, 64. Dealer: Franz Bader Gallery 2124 Pennsylvania Ave NW Washington DC 20037; Francine Seders Gallery 6701 Greenwood Ave N Seattle WA 98103. Mailing Add: 3752 McKinley St NW Washington DC 20015

GUNDELFINGER, JOHN ANDRE
PAINTER, INSTRUCTOR
b St Die, France, Oct 3, 37; US citizen. Study: Sch of Visual Arts, New York; NY Univ. Work: Chase Manhattan Bank, New York; Sara Roby Found; Int Bus Machines; Am Tel & Tel Co; Mus of Fine Arts, Caracas, Venezuela. Exhib: Galerie Simone Stern, New Orleans, La, 71; one-man shows, John Bernard Myers Gallery, New York, 71-74, Mus of Fine Arts, Caracas, 72, A M Sachs Gallery, New York, 76-77 & Sneed-Hillman Gallery, Rockford, Ill, 77; Am Drawing 1970-73, Yale Univ Art Gallery, 73; Galerie Stevenson et Palluel, Paris, France, 76; Weatherspoon Art Gallery, Univ NC, Greensboro, 77. Teaching: Instr painting & drawing, Sch of Visual Arts, New York, 63-, Parsons Sch of Design, New York, 71- Bibliog: John Bernard Myers (auth), The Gouaches of John Gundelfinger, Sachs Gallery Publ, 75 & Recent Paintings—John Gundelfinger, Sachs Gallery & Art Inst Mag, Fall 77. Style & Technique: Landscapes of Delaware River Valley; gouaches & oils on paper, singly and in series, and large oils (to 7 ft x 10 ft) on canvas. Media: Oil, gouache. Mailing Add: 10 White St New York NY 10013

GUNDERSHEIMER, HERMAN (SAMUEL)
ART HISTORIAN
b Würzburg, Ger, Apr 25, 03; US citizen. Study: Univ Munich; Univ Würzburg; Univ Berlin; Univ Leipzig, PhD, 26. Teaching: From asst prof to prof art hist, Temple Univ, 41-70, prof art hist & dir Temple Abroad, Tyler Sch Art, Rome, Italy, 70-73; guest prof, Univ Tel-Aviv, Israel, 73-74; prof, LaSalle Col, Philadelphia, 75- Pos: Cur, Mus Ulm/Danube, Kunstgewerbe Mus, Frankfurt, Ger, 27-33; dir, Rothschild Mus, Frankfurt, 33-39. Awards: Lindbach Award for excellent teaching. Mem: Col Art Asn Am; Am Acad Rome Art Libr; Philadelphia Mus Art; Pa Acad Fine Arts; Renaissance Soc Am. Res: Renaissance and Baroque art; Jewish ceremonial art. Collection: Contemporary graphics. Publ: Auth articles on fresco painting in the eighteenth century; contributor to journals & magazines & contributing editor to encyclopedias. Mailing Add: 1500 Locust St Apt 3305 Philadelphia PA 19102

GUNDERSON, BARRY L
SCULPTOR
b Baird, Tex, Feb 9, 45. Study: Augsburg Col, Minneapolis, BA; Univ NDak, Grand Forks; Univ Colo, Boulder, MFA. Work: Ball State Univ, Muncie, Ind; Minot State Col, NDak; Normandale Jr Col, Minneapolis; Augsburg Col, Minneapolis. Comn: Large outdoor sculpture, Kenyon Col, Gambier, Ohio, 77. Exhib: Colo Biennial, 71 & Denver Metrop, 72, Denver Art Mus; Drawings USA/1975, 75 & Drawings USA/1977, 77, Minn Mus of Art, St Paul; 28th & 29th Ceramic & Sculpture Exhibs, Butler Inst of Am Art, Youngstown, Ohio, 76 & 77; 10th Dulin Nat Print & Drawing Competition, Dulin Art Mus, Knoxville, Tenn, 76; one-man show, Ohio Wesleyan Univ, Del, 77. Teaching: Asst prof sculpture, Kenyon Col, 74- Mem: Col Art Asn. Style & Technique: Varied. Media: Sculpture, drawing. Mailing Add: Box 515 Gambier OH 43022

GUNN, PAUL JAMES
PAINTER, EDUCATOR
b Guys Mills, Pa, June 21, 22. Study: Edinboro State Teachers Col, BS, 57; Calif Col Arts & Crafts, MFA, 48; wood block printing with Hideo Hagiwara, Tokyo, Japan, 61-62. Work: Portland Art Mus; Seattle Art Mus; Am Info Serv Collection, Athens, Greece; Bibliotheque Nat, Paris, France; Victoria & Albert Mus, London, Eng. Exhib: Int Bordighera Biennial, Italy; Bay Printmakers 2nd Ann, Oakland Art Mus, Calif; Ann Northwest Artists, Seattle Art Mus; Western Artists Ann, Denver Art Mus; Ore Artists Ann, Portland Art Mus. Teaching: Prof painting & printmaking, Ore State Univ, 48-, chmn dept art, 64- Pos: Resident dir, Japan Studies Prog, Ore Study Ctr, Waseda Univ, Japan, 72-74. Style & Technique: Woodcut printmaking. Media: Oil. Dealer: Gallery West 4836 SW Scholls Ferry Rd Portland OR 97225. Mailing Add: Dept of Art Ore State Univ Corvallis OR 97331

GUNNING, ELEONORE VICTORIA
PAINTER
b El Reno, Okla, May 3, 16. Study: Univ Okla, BFA; also study with Milford Zornes, Rex Brandt, Mario Cooper, Millard Sheets & Robert E Wood. Work: Hacienda El Cobano, Colima, Mex. Exhib: Southwestern Watercolor Soc, Dallas, Tex, 72 & Oklahoma City, 73; Expos Colectiva de Pinturas, Govt Palace, Colima, Mex, 73; Okla Art Guild, Oklahoma City, 74; 14th Ann Artists Salon, Okla Mus Art, Oklahoma City, 75; 16th Ann Artists Salon, Okla Mus Art, Oklahoma City, 77. Teaching: Teacher art & art hist, Sec Schs, Norman, Okla, 66-72. Awards: 4th Prize & Award of Merit, Okla Chap, Southwestern Watercolor Soc, 73; First Prize in Watercolor, Norman Art League, 74; Honorable Mention, Artists Salon, 75 & 77, Okla Mus Art. Mem: Southwestern Watercolor Soc; Okla Watercolor Asn; Int Soc Artists; Am Watercolor Soc. Norman Art League. Style & Technique: Landscape and still life in watercolor. Mailing Add: 820 College Norman OK 73069

GUNTER, FRANK ELLIOTT
PAINTER, EDUCATOR
b Jasper, Ala, May 8, 34. Study: Univ Ala, BFA; Fla State Univ, MA. Work: Sheldon Swope Gallery, Terre Haute, Ind; Evansville Mus Arts & Sci, Ind; Ill State Mus, Springfield; Birmingham Mus Art, Ala; St Paul Art Ctr, Minn. Comn: Painting, Rochester State Bank, Ill, 74; painting of facade, Bank of Ind, Merrillville, 75. Exhib: Cult Ctr for Am Embassy, Paris, 71; Mus Art, Besancon, France, 72; Am Libr, Brussels, Belg, 73; Maison Descartes, Amsterdam, 73; Varieties of Visual Reality, Northern Ariz State Univ, 75; Am Exhib, Krannert Art Mus, Univ Ill, Urbana, 77. Teaching: Instr art, Birmingham Pub Schs, Ala, 56-58; asst prof art, Murray State Univ, 60-62; prof art, Univ Ill, Urbana-Champaign, 62- Awards: Second Award for Painting, Soc Four Arts, 73; Purchase Awards, Wabash Valley Ann, Terre Haute, 74 & Union League Club, Chicago, 74. Bibliog: Stephen Spector (auth), Super realists, Architectural Dig, 11/12/74; G A Rodetis (auth), Varieties of visual reality, Northern Ariz Univ Art Gallery 1-3/75. Style & Technique: Realistic interiors and urban landscapes. Media: Acrylic on canvas. Dealer: Joy Horwich Gallery 226 E Ontario St Chicago IL 60611. Mailing Add: 806 S Elm Blvd Champaign IL 61820

GUREWITSCH, EDNA P
ART DEALER, ART HISTORIAN
b New York, NY. Study: Pratt Inst; NY Univ, New York, BA; Columbia Univ, MAEd; Inst Fine Arts, NY Univ, grad studies with Richard Offner, Walter Friedlaender, Erwin Panofsky & Jose Lopez-Rey. Pos: Vpres, E & A Silberman Galleries, Inc, New York, 53-61; pres, E P Gurewitsch Works of Art, Inc, New York, 73- Mem: Alumni Asn, Inst Fine Arts, NY Univ. Specialty: Twentieth century European and American painting and sculpture. Interest: Formed collection for Rehabilitation Dept, Columbia Presbyterian Hosp, New York. Mailing Add: 55 E 74th St New York NY 10021

GURR, LENA
PAINTER, PRINTMAKER
b Brooklyn, NY, Oct 27, 97. Study: Educ Alliance, New York, 19; Art Students League, two scholars & study with John Sloan & Maurice Stern, 20-22; Maxwell Training Sch Teachers, 15-17, dipl. Work: Metrop Mus Art, New York; Brasenose Col, Oxford, Eng; Smithsonian Inst & Libr Cong, Washington, DC; Brooklyn Mus, NY; plus many others. Exhib: Painting in the USA, Carnegie Inst, Pittsburgh, 45 & 51; Contemporary American Sculpture, Watercolors & Drawings, Whitney Mus Am Art, New York, 53; Am Acad Arts & Lett, 58, 65, 66 & 69; 37 Contemporary Americans, chosen by Nat Coun Women, IBM Corp, 60; Art

in Embassies Prog from ACA Galleries, Athens, Greece, 66-68. Pos: Rec secy, Nat Soc Painters in Casein, 56-57, bd dirs, 58-67. Awards: Medal of Honor, Nat Asn Women Artists, 54 & 61 & Marcia Brady Tucker Prize, 61; Jersey City Mus Medal, NJ Painters & Sculptors Soc, 69; plus many others. Bibliog: Elizabeth Lips (auth), Artist Lena Gurr says studio should be neat like office, Brooklyn Eagle, 51; Frank Crotty (auth), Paints big city & Cape Cod scenes, Worcester Sun Telegram, 60. Mem: Artists Equity Asn New York (rec secy, 53, bd dirs, 63-65, vpres, 66-74); Nat Asn Women Artists; Soc Am Graphic Artists (mem coun, 67-68); Painters & Sculptors Soc NJ; Am Soc Contemp Artists; plus others. Style & Technique: Semi-abstract realism with cubist and expressionistic qualities. Media: Oil, Casein. Dealer: ACA Gallery 25 E 73rd St New York NY 10021. Mailing Add: 71 Remsen Ave Brooklyn NY 11212

GURRIA, ANGELA
SCULPTOR
b Mexico City, Mex. Study: Univ Mex, LittD; Mexico City Col; and with German Cueto. Work: Mus Mod Art, Mexico City; UN Orgn, New York. Comn: Puerta-celosia, Bank of Mex, 67; ruta de la Amistad, Olympic Comt, Mex, 68; fountain, Unidad Popular, Acapulco, 70; obra oculta, Cent Dept, Tenayuca, Mex, 75. Exhib: Escultura Mexicana Contemp, Alameda, Mex, 60; Biennial Mexicana de Escultura, Mus Mod Art, Mexico City, 64 & 67; Contoy Isla de Caribe, 74; Angela Gurria, Palacio Bellas Artes, Mexico, 70. Teaching: Instr sculpture, Ibero-american Univ, Mex, 61-62; instr sculpture, Univ of the Americas, 62-63. Awards: Hon mention, Inst Bellas Artes Biennial, 60, 62 & 63, First Prize, Escultura Integrada a la Arquitectura, 67; Women in the Arts Prize, Mex Inst Art, 64. Bibliog: Margarita Nelken (auth), Angela Gurria, Excelsior, 63; Justino Fernandez (auth), Arte Mexicano contemporaneo, Dept Esteticas Univ, 68; Juan O'Gorman (auth), Angela Gurria, Mex Acad Arts, 74. Mem: Mex Acad Arts. Style & Technique: Abstract; nautralistic. Media: Stone, Bronze. Mailing Add: Francisco Sosa 363 Mexico DF Mexico

GURSOY, AHMET
PAINTER
b Turkey, Mar 5, 29; US citizen. Study: Tech Univ Istanbul, Turkey, 47-52; Ill Inst Technol, 54-56; Art Students League, 58-63. Work: Chase Manhattan Collection; Cornell Univ Collection; St Lawrence Univ; Grey Gallery, NY Univ; Ulrich Mus, Wichita, Kans. Exhib: Riverside Mus, 67; Ann New Eng Exhib, Silvermine, Conn, 67-71; State Univ NY, Binghamton, 70; Univ Chicago, 71; Minneapolis Col Art & Design, 71; Fordham Univ, New York, 73; Bronz Mus Arts, NY, 75; Middletown Art Coun, NY, 76; Tyler Art Gallery, State Univ NY Col, Oswego, 76; Myers Arts Gallery, State Univ NY Col, Plattsburg, 76; Geneva Hist Soc, NY, 76; State Univ NY Col, Alfred, 77; Wells Col, Aurora, NY, 77; Niagara Arts Ctr, Niagara Falls, NY, 77; Mohawk Valley Community Col, Utica, NY, 77; Nassau Community Col, Garden City, NY, 77; Hyden Collection, Glen Falls, NY, 77. Awards: Painting Prize, 21st Ann New Eng Exhib, Silvermine, Conn, 70. Bibliog: Grace Glueck (auth), rev in New York Times, 68; C Giuliano (auth), rev in Arts Mag, 68 & Gordon Brown (auth), rev in Arts Mag, 70. Mem: Fedn Mod Painters & Sculptors (pres, 75-); Silvermine Guild Artists; Music for People (treas, 71-72). Media: Oil. Publ: Auth, Convergence of Engineering & Art, 70. Mailing Add: 490 Bellwood Ave North Tarrytown NY 10593

GUSELLA, ERNEST
VIDEO ARTIST
b Calgary, Alta, Can, Sept 13, 41; Can citizen. Study: Alberta Col of Art, dipl; Art Student League, with Will Barnet; San Francisco Art Inst, BFA & MFA; Workshop in Mod Music Compos, State Univ of New York, Buffalo, with John Cage. Work: Pompidou Art Ctr, Paris; Donnell Libr, New York; Synapse Tape Libr, Syracuse Univ, NY; Chautauqua-Cattaraugus Libr, Jamestown, NY. Exhib: Knokke-Heist, Belg, 75; Everson Mus, Syracuse, NY, 76; Ithaca Video Festival, NY, 76 & 77; Mus Mod Art, New York, 77; Gelbenkian Found, Lisbon, 77; one-man shows, Pompidou Art Ctr, 78, Lenbachhaus, Munich, 78 & Int Cult Ctr, Antwerp, Belg, 78. Teaching: Lectr art hist, City Univ New York, 73-75; lectr film & drawing, Rutgers Univ, Newark, NJ, 74- Awards: Can Coun Grant for Video, 72-73 & 77-78; New York State Coun Grant for Video, 74-75. Bibliog: Davidson Gigliotti (auth), Words & images, images & words, Soho News, New York, 11/76; Victor Ancona (auth), Ernest Gusella: Pleasing artist & public alike, Videography Mag, 2/78. Mem: Col Art Asn of Am. Style & Technique: Conceptual video performances with electronic manipulation of image and sound. Media: Video, Performance. Publ: Contribr, The video issue, Art-Rite Mag, 74; auth, Talking heads, After-Image, 75; contribr, Video art, Harcourt, Brace & World, 76; auth, Japanese twins & white man, Ear Wax Rec, 77. Dealer: Robert Freidus Gallery 158 Lafayette St New York NY 10013. Mailing Add: 118 Forsyth St Fourth Floor New York NY 10002

GUSSMAN, HERBERT
COLLECTOR, PATRON
b New York, NY, Aug 25, 11. Study: Cornell Univ, AB, 33. Collection: French impressionists; American paintings and sculpture; African primitive art; bronzes, Luristan, Africa. Mailing Add: 4644 S Zunis Ave Tulsa OK 74104

GUSSOW, ALAN
PAINTER, WRITER
b New York, NY, May 8, 31. Study: Middlebury Col, BA, 52; Cooper Union, 52-53; Atelier 17 Graphic Workshop, 52-53. Work: Portland Mus Fine Art, Maine; Guild Hall, Easthampton, NY; Sheldon Mem Art Gallery, Lincoln, Nebr; Corcoran Gallery Art, Washington, DC; Montgomery Mus Fine Art, Ala. Exhib: Maine—50 Artists of 20th Century, Am Fedn Arts Traveling Show, 64; The American Landscape—A Living Tradition, Peridot Gallery, circulated by Smithsonian Inst, 68-70; Viewpoints 7: Painters of the Land & Sky, Picker Art Gallery, Colgate Univ, 72; A Sense of Place, Joslyn Art Mus & Sheldon Mem Art Gallery, Nebr, 73; Paintings of the Delaware Water Gap, Corcoran Art Gallery, Washington, DC, 75. Teaching: Instr painting & drawing, Parsons Sch Design, 56-68, chmn dept, 59-68; instr painting & drawing, Sarah Lawrence Col, 58-59; vis critic & lectr, Ohio State Univ, 74, Md Inst, Philadelphia Col Art, Minneapolis Col Art, Univ Utah & Kansas City Art Inst, 75, Calif Col Arts & Crafts, 76 & Pace Univ, 77; vis artists & sr lectr, Univ Calif, Santa Cruz, 75. Pos: Consult arts, Nat Park Serv, US Dept Interior, 70-; chmn rev comt, Artists Environ Conserv, Am Beautiful Fund, 70- Awards: Prix de Rome in Painting, Am Acad Rome, Italy, 53-55; Artist in Residence, Cape Cod Nat Seashore, Nat Park Serv, 68 & Hudson River Valley, Cult Coun Found, 71; Award in Art, Am Acad & Inst Arts & Lett, 77. Bibliog: G Glueck (auth), Artist in residence for mother earth, New York Times, 3/12/72; Diane Cochrane (auth), Alan Gussow revives the Hudson River School, Am Artist, 3/73; P Mainardi (auth), Allen Gussow: a sense of place, Art News, 11/75. Style & Technique: Paintings for which nature is source. Media: Oil. Publ: Auth, A Sense of Place—the Artist and the American Land, Friends of Earth & Seabury Press, 72; auth, The Use of Artists as Artists in the Struggle for Population Control, Population, Environment & People, McGraw, 72; auth, We are What we See, In: Encycl of Ecol & Pollution, NAm Publ, 72. Dealer: Washburn Gallery 42 E 57th St New York NY 10022. Mailing Add: 121 New York Ave Congers NY 10920

GUSSOW, ROY
SCULPTOR
b Brooklyn, NY, Nov 12, 18. Study: With Archipenko, Chicago & Woodstock, NY, 46-47; Inst Design, Chicago, BS, 48, with Moholy-Nagy. Work: Whitney Mus Am Art, Mus Mod Art & Brooklyn Mus, New York; NC Mus Art, Raleigh; High Mus, Atlanta, Ga. Comn: Polished stainless steel sculptures, Phoenix Mutual Life Assurance Co, Hartford, Conn, 63, City of Tulsa, Munic Bldg, Civic Ctr, Okla, 68, Xerox Corp, Xerox Sq, Rochester, NY, 69, New York City Family Ct Bldg, Manhattan, 72 & Heublein Corp, Farmington, Conn, 75. Exhib: Sculpture 1951, Metrop Mus Art, New York, 51; Pa Acad, Philadelphia, 51-59; NC Artists, NC Mus Art, Raleigh, 52-61; Nat Gold Medal Exhib Bldg Arts, Archit League, New York, 62 & 65; Am Surv Sculpture Biennial, Whitney Mus Am Art, 56 & 62-68. Teaching: Instr design & sculpture, Bradley Univ, 48-49 & Colorado Springs Fine Arts Ctr, Colo, 49-51; prof design & sculpture, Univ NC Sch Design, 51-62; adj prof sculpture, Pratt Inst Sch Archit, 62-68. Awards: Hon Mention, Pa Acad Fine Arts, 58; Purchase Awards, Ford Found, 60 & 62; First Prize, New York Family Ct Sculpture Competition, 72. Mem: Sculptors Guild (pres, 76-78); Artists Equity Asn (bd dir, 77). Style & Technique: Pure plastic forms-non-objective multiple elements relationships; mirror finish; highly refined lyricism. Media: Stainless Steel, Bronze. Dealer: Borgenicht Gallery 1018 Madison Ave New York NY 10021. Mailing Add: 4040 24th St Long Island City NY 11101

GUSTON, PHILIP
PAINTER
b Montreal, PQ, June 27, 13; US citizen. Study: Boston Univ, hon DFA, 70. Work: Guggenheim Mus, Whitney Mus Am Art, Mus Mod Art & Metrop Mus Art, New York; Tate Gallery, London. Comn: Murals, facade of WPA Bldg, New York World's Fair, 39, US Treas Dept, Forestry Bldg, Laconia, NH, 41 & Social Security Bldg, Washington, DC, 42; illus, Art News Ann, 44. Exhib: One-man retrospective exhibs, 5th Bienal, Sao Paulo, Brazil, 59, 30th Biennale, Venice, 60 & Guggenheim Mus, Stedelijk Mus, Amsterdam, Mus Beaux Arts, Brussels, Whitechapel Gallery, London & Los Angeles Co Mus Art, 62; one-man shows, Jewish Mus, 66, Marlborough Gallery, New York, 70 & Mus Mod Art, New York, 73; Nat Gallery of Art, Washington, DC, 73; Hayden Gallery, Mass Inst Technol, 75. Teaching: Artist in residence, Wash Univ, 45-47; adj prof painting, NY Univ, 51-58; guest critic painting, Columbia Univ, 69-70 & 72-73; univ prof, Boston Univ, 73- Pos: Artist in residence, Brandeis Univ, spring 66; mem bd trustees, Am Acad Rome, 70-, artist in residence, 70-71. Awards: First Prize, Carnegie Inst, 45; Guggenheim Found fel, 47 & 68; Ford Found Grant, 59. Bibliog: Dore Ashton (auth), Philip Guston, Grove, 59; H H Arnason (auth), Philip Guston, Guggenheim Mus, 62; Philip Guston (film), Blackwood Prod, Inc, 72. Mem: Nat Inst Arts & Lett. Media: Oil. Publ: Auth, Statement, Stedelijk Mus Catalog, Amsterdam, 62; auth, Piero della Francesca, Art News, 5/65; co-auth, Dialogue with Philip Guston, Art & Literature 7, London, 65; auth, Statement, Art News Ann, 66; contribr, Recent Paintings & Drawings, Jewish Mus, 66. Mailing Add: Box 660 Woodstock NY 12498

GUTHMAN, LEO S
COLLECTOR
b Chicago, Ill. Mem: Gov life mem Art Inst Chicago; Soc Contemp Art, Chicago (dir); Art Collectors Club, New York; Art Club Chicago. Collection: Contemporary painting, especially by Americans; international sculpture. Mailing Add: 1040 N Lake Shore Dr Chicago IL 60611

GUTHRIE, DEREK
ART CRITIC, PAINTER
b Liverpool, Eng, May 4, 36. Study: West of England Col Art, dipl in arts & crafts; Univ Baroda, India, Commonwealth scholar; also with Szabo. Exhib: Group de Feu, Paris, 59; English Section, Sportone Festival, Italy, 62; Cornish Painters, Exchange Exhib, Osten, Belg, 65. Teaching: Instr painting & art hist, Chicago State Univ, 69-71; instr painting, Northwestern Univ, 69- Pos: Art critic, Chicago Tribune, 71-73; assoc ed, New Art Examr, 73- Bibliog: Michael McNay (auth), Interview with Derek Guthrie, Arts Guardian, 7/68; Alan Moore, New Voices, Artforum, 12/74; Sharon Kuzmicz (auth), The New Art Examiner, Chicago Journalism Rev, 11/74. Publ: Co-auth, Chicago Regionalism, Studio Int, 12/73. Dealer: Michael Wyman Gallery 233 E Ontario Chicago IL 60611. Mailing Add: 653 W Armitage Chicago IL 60614

GUTKIN, PETER
SCULPTOR
b Brooklyn, NY, 44. Study: Tyler Sch Art, Temple Univ, BFA, 66; San Francisco Art Inst, MFA, 68. Work: Temple Univ, Philadelphia; Oakland Mus, Calif; City & Co, San Francisco; plus others. Exhib: Contemp Am Sculpture Ann, Whitney Mus Art, New York, 68 & Contemp Am Painting & Sculpture Biennial, 73; one-man show, San Francisco Mus Art, 72; Contemporary American Painting & Sculpture, Krannert Art Mus, Champaign, Ill, 74; Menace, Mus Contemp Art, Chicago, 75; plus many other group & one-man shows. Teaching: Instr, Aspen Sch Contemp Art, Colo, 66 & Univ Calif, Berkeley, 72-74. Awards: Nat Endowment Humanities & Art Award, 66; Purchase Prize, San Francisco Art Festival, 72. Bibliog: Jerome Tarshis (auth), Peter Gutkin, Paul Harris, Tom Holland, San Francisco Museum of Art, Artforum, 6/70; Stacey Moss (auth), Peter Gutkin—sculptures about restraint & containment, Artweek, Vol 8 (Oct, 1977); Thomas Albright (auth), An artist who shows dramatic development, San Francisco Chronicle, 10/1/77 & Compressed constructions, spiderweb sculptures, Art News, 12/77. Publ: Co-auth, The Edge of Now, KQED-TV, San Francisco, 69. Mailing Add: 225 11th St San Francisco CA 94103

GUTMANN, JOHN
PAINTER, EDUCATOR
b Breslau, Ger, May 28, 05. Study: State Acad Arts & Crafts, Breslau, BA; State Acad Berlin, MA. Work: Boston Mus of Fine Arts; Calif Palace of Legion of Honor, San Francisco; Mus Mod Art, New York; San Francisco Mus of Art, Calif; New Orleans Mus Art. Exhib: San Francisco Mus Art; M H De Young Mem Mus Art; one-man shows, Light Gallery, New York, 74 & As I Saw It, San Francisco Mus of Mod Art, 76. Teaching: Prof art, Calif State Univ, San Francisco, 38- Mem: Am Asn Univ Prof; Col Art Asn Am. Awards: Guggenheim Fel, 78. Publ: Contribr, Life, Time, Asia, Sat Eve Post & other nat mag; producer & photographer of two documentary films on China, 50. Mailing Add: 1543 Cole St San Francisco CA 94117

GUY, JAMES M
PAINTER, EDUCATOR
b Middletown, Conn, Feb 11, 10. Study: Hartford Art Sch. Work: Wadsworth Atheneum, Hartford, Conn; Olsen Found, Guilford, Conn; Soc Four Arts, Palm Beach, Fla; Mattatuk Mus, Waterbury, Conn; Mass Inst Technol, Boston. Exhib: Whitney Mus Am Art, New York; Metrop Mus Art, New York; Mus Mod Art, New York; Art Inst Chicago; plus others. Teaching: Instr painting, Bennington Col, 45-47; head dept art, McMurray Col, 47-54; lectr art, Wesleyan Univ, 61-73, emer prof art, 74- Mem: Essex Art Asn, Conn. Media: Oil,

Acrylic. Dealer: Charles Egan Gallery 41 E 57th St New York NY 10022. Mailing Add: 82 Neptune Ave Moodus CT 06469

GUZEVICH, KRESZENZ (CYNTHIA)
PAINTER, INSTRUCTOR
b Munich, Ger, May 24, 23; US citizen. Study: Acad Art, Munich; also with Frank Gervasi, Paul Strisik, Louis Krupp, Helen Van Wyk, Ramon Froman & Ken Gore. Work: First Nat Bank, Las Cruces, NMex. Exhib: Overseas Press Club Am, New York; El Paso Mus Art Exhib, Tex; Grand Nat Exhib, New York; Southwest Intercult Exhib, El Paso; Artists Equity Show, Albuquerque, NMex. Teaching: Instr painting, workshops in var states & pvt studio, 65- Awards: Artist of Year & Best in Show Award, Black Range Artists, 68; Best in Show Award, NMex Art League, 69. Mem: Am Artists Prof League; El Paso Mus Art Asn; Artists Equity Asn; NMex Art League. Style & Technique: Old Master technique; realist and surrealistic styles. Media: Oil. Dealer: O'Briens Art Emporium 7122 Stetson Dr Scottsdale AZ 85251. Mailing Add: 1635 Country Club Circle Las Cruces NM 88001

GUZMAN-FORBES, ROBERT
PAINTER, ILLUSTRATOR
b New York, NY, July 11, 29. Study: Univ Va, with John Canaday, BFA; Art Instr, Inc, scholar; Sch Visual Arts, with Al Werner & Burne Hogarth, cert. Work: Univ Va Mus Fine Arts, Charlottesville; Baltimore City Court House, Md. Comn: Animal portraits, comn by Louis A Reitmeister, New York, 69; animal portrait, comn by Mrs Anthony Biddle Duke, Jr, New York, 69; portrait of Alan H Murrell, attorney, 72 & Solomon Liss, Judge, 73, Saints & Sinners of Baltimore; portrait of Harris T Whittemore II, comn by Harris T Whittemore III, Middlebury, Conn, 75. Bibliog: K Cassidy (auth), The fine art of Robert G Forbes, Twin Circle Cath Newspaper, 71; article in Christian Sci Monitor; Mary E Renn (auth), Animal art, My Weekly Reader, Xerox Educ Group, 75. Mem: Portraits, Inc. Style & Technique: People and animal portraiture in pastel chalk; pen and ink wash. Mailing Add: 211 Brittany Farms Rd New Britain CT 06053

GUZZARDI, BARONESS ELENA
See Wurdemann, Helen

GWATHMEY, ROBERT
PAINTER
b Richmond, Va, Jan 24, 03. Study: NC State Col, 24-25; Md Inst, 25-26; Pa Acad Fine Arts, 26-30. Work: Brooklyn Mus; Carnegie Inst, Pittsburgh; Los Angeles Co Mus, Calif; Pa Mus Art, Philadelphia; Whitney Mus Am Art, New York. Exhib: Whitney Mus Am Art & Carnegie Inst Ann; Metrop Mus Art; Corcoran Gallery Art & Pa Acad Fine Arts Biennials. Teaching: Instr drawing & painting, Carnegie Inst Technol, 38-42; instr drawing, Cooper Union, 42-68; vis prof painting, Boston Univ, 69-70. Awards: Prize, Carnegie Inst Ann, 43; Rosenwald Fel, 44; Prize, Corcoran Gallery Art, 57. Mem: Artists Equity Asn (bd mem); Nat Inst Arts & Lett; assoc Nat Acad Design. Style & Technique: Somewhat flat, dealing with color relations rather than light and shadow; decided use of line. Media: Oil. Dealer: Terry Dintenfass Inc 18 E 67th St New York NY 10021. Mailing Add: Box 108 Amagansett NY 11930

GYERMEK, STEPHEN A
EDUCATOR
b Budapest, Hungary, Nov 9, 30. Study: Rijks Akad voor Beeldende Kunsten, Amsterdam, Holland, with Heinrich Campendonk; Univ Okla. Comn: Murals, Convent at Madrid, Spain, 55 & US Embassy, Spain, 55; stained glass windows, St Gregory's Abbey, Shawnee, Okla. Exhib: Amsterdam, 52-53; Madrid, 54; Okla Art Ctr, 60. Collections Arranged: Archaeology, Europe, Near & Far East, Egypt; American Indians & Central & South American Ethnology; Paintings from the Italian Renaissance; 19th Century American Paintings; plus others. Teaching: Lectr painting methods & religious art; asst prof art hist & art, Univ Okla; instr art hist, San Joaquin Delta Col, 67- Pos: Dir, Gerrer Mus & Art Gallery, Shawnee, Okla, 57-62; actg dir, Stovall Mus Sci & Hist, Univ Okla, 62-65; dir, Pioneer Mus & Haggin Art Galleries, Stockton, Calif, 65-70. Awards: Prizes & Van Alabbe Award, Amsterdam, Holland, 52. Mailing Add: 1870 Douglas Rd Stockton CA 95207

GYRA, FRANCIS JOSEPH, JR
INSTRUCTOR, PAINTER
b Newport, RI, Feb 23, 14. Study: RI Sch Design, dipl; Parsons Sch Design, Paris, cert advert illus & X Ital Res Sch; Brighton Col Arts & Crafts, Sussex, Eng; Froebel Inst, Roehampton, Eng; Univ Hawaii; McNeese State Col; Keene State Col, BS. Work: Providence Art Mus, RI; Tenn Fine Arts Ctr, Nashville. Exhib: Int Watercolor Exhib, Art Inst Chicago, 38 & 40; 1st Int Ann, Marietta Col, Ohio, 69; 1st Art Ann, Northern New Eng, Canaan, NH, 69; Stratton Arts Festival, Vt, 70; 8th Exhib Vt Artists, Norwich Univ, 71. Teaching: Supvr, Woodstock Union & Dist Schs, Vt, 49-69; dir art workshops, Vt State Dept Educ, 54-70; art educator, Woodstock Sch Dist, 69- Pos: Chmn, Vt Educ Asn Prog, 52; adv art & art educ, Aquinas Jr Col, Nashville, 66- Awards: People's Prize, Art Asn Newport, RI, 38; First Prize, 3rd Ann Norwich Univ Art Exhib, 66; Eva Gebhard-Gourgand Found grants, 66-72. Mem: Vt Art Teachers Asn (secy-treas, 57-58); life fel Int Inst Arts & Lett. Publ: Co-auth, Vermont Art Guide for the Classroom Teacher K-6, 69. Mailing Add: 6 Linden Hall PO Box A Woodstock VT 05091

GYSIN, BRION
PAINTER
b Taplow, Buckinghamshire, Eng, Jan 19, 16. Study: Downside Col, Eng, 32-34; Univ Bordeaux, France, 49-52; Univ Seville's Archivos de India, Spain, 50-52. Work: Mus Mod Art, New York; Mus Art, Phoenix, Ariz; Boston Fine Arts Mus, Mass; Centre Pompidou, Paris; plus numerous pvt collections. Exhib: Salon des Realities Nouvelles, Paris, 60 & 61; L'Object, Musee des Arts Decoratifs, Paris, 62; The Mysterious Sign, Inst Contemp Arts, London, 63; Domain Poetique, 3rd Biennial, Paris, 63; Between Poetry & Painting, Inst Contemp Arts, London, 65; 4th Biennial, Paris, 65; Poesie Graphie, Poesie Action, Univ Rouen, France, 68; Lettre-Signe, Swedish Cult Ctr, Paris, 73; Sontemp Villa Borghese, Rome, 73; one-man shows, Museo de Bellas Artes, Las Palmas & Teneriffe, Canary Islands, 53, Inst Contemp Arts, London, 60, Verbal Theatre, LaBoheme, Paris, 60, Permutated Poems, Metrop, 65, Galerie Weiller, 73, Galerie Germain, 75 & Mollet-Vieville, 76, Paris. Awards: Fulbright Res Scholarship, 49-52. Bibliog: Articles in The Art Gallery, New York, 62 & Phantomas, Brussels, 63; Eduard Roditi (auth), article in Art Voices, New York, 64; Rolf-Gunter Dienst (auth), Vernissage, Das Kunstwerk, Baden-Baden, 64. Style & Technique: Paintings designed to produce the viewpoint of timeless space. Publ: Auth, Dreamachine, The Olympia Review, Paris, 62; auth, The Process, New York, London, 68; auth, Brion Gysin Let the Mice In, New York, 73; illusr, The William Burroughs Catalogue, London, 73; co-auth with William Burroughs, The Third Mind, New York, 78. Dealer: Galerie Stadler rue de Seine Paris France. Mailing Add: 135 rue St Martin Paris 4 France

H

HAACKE, HANS CHRISTOPH
SCULPTOR
b Cologne, Ger, Aug 12, 36. Study: Staat Werkakademie, Kassel, Ger, MFA; Atelier 17, Paris, with S W Hayter; Tyler Sch Art, Philadelphia. Work: Mus Mod Art, NY; Kaiser Wilhelm Mus, Krefeld, Ger; Mod Museet, Stockholm; Art Gallery Ont, Toronto; Milwaukee Art Ctr; Stedelijk vanAbbe Mus, Eindhoven. Exhib: Machine as Seen at the End of the Mechanical Age, Mus Mod Art, New York, 68; When Attitudes Become Form, Kunsthalle, Bern, Switz, 69; Tokyo Biennial, 70; Documenta 5, Kassel, 72; Contemporanea, Rome, 73; Venice Biennale, 76; Frankfurter Kunstverein, Ger, 76; Wadsworth Atheneum, Hartford, Conn, 77; one-man shows, Galerie Schmela, Düsseldorf, Ger, 65, Howard Wise Gallery, New York, 66, 68 & 69, Paul Maenz Gallery, Cologne, Ger, 71 & 74, Francoise Lambert Gallery, Milan, Italy, 72 & 76, Mus Haus Lange, Krefeld, 72, John Weber Gallery, New York, 73, 75 & 77, Lisson Gallery, London, Eng, 76, Max Protetch Gallery, Washington, DC, 76 & Durand-Dessert Gallery, Paris, France, 77 & 78. Teaching: Assoc prof sculpture, Cooper Union, 67- Awards: Deut Akad Austauschdienst, 60; Fulbright Fel, 61; Guggenheim Fel, 72. Bibliog: B Vinklers (auth), Hans Haacke, Art Int, Lugano, 9/69; Jack Burnham (auth), Hans Haacke's cancelled show at the Guggenheim, Artforum, New York, 6/71; Edward Fry (auth), Hans Haacke: Werkmonographie, DuMont Schauberg, Cologne, 72; Margaret Sheffield (auth), interview in Studio Int, London, 3-4/76; Framing and Being Framed, NS Col of Art & Design Press & NY Univ Press, 75; Hans Haacke: les adhérents, Skira Ann 77, Geneva, 77. Mailing Add: c/o John Weber Gallery 420 W Broadway New York NY 10012

HAAR, FRANCIS
PHOTOGRAPHER, FILM MAKER
b Csernatfalu, Hungary, July 19, 08; US citizen. Study: Nat Acad Decorative Arts, Budapest, Hungary, Master Photog. Work: Victoria-Albert Mus, London; Mus Mod Art, New York. Comn: The Arts of Japan (film), US Info Agency, Tokyo, Japan, 53; Ukiyoe, Japanese Print (film), Art Inst Chicago, 59; Hoolaulea (dance film), Honolulu Acad Arts, 60; Japan's Cultural History, Fuji TV Co, Tokyo, 64. Exhib: Ind Univ, Bloomington, 61; one-man shows, Honolulu Acad Arts, 70 & Contemp Arts Ctr, Honolulu, 71. Teaching: Lectr photog, summer courses, Univ Hawaii, 62- Awards: First Prize, Metrop City Improvement, Chicago, Ill, 59; Golden Eagle Award for Pineapple Country Hawaii, 63 & Hawaii's Asian Heritage, 66, Coun Int Nontheatrical Events, Washington, DC. Mem: Painters & Sculptors League; Honolulu Printmakers; Honolulu Acad Arts. Style & Technique: Experimental photography; documentary films on arts. Publ: Auth, Hungarian Picture Book, 40 & auth, Around Mount Fuji, 41, Benlido Publ Co, Kyoto, Japan; auth, The Best of Old Japan, 49, co-auth, Japanese Theatre in Highlights, 51 & Geisha of Pontocho, 53, C Tuttle Publ Co, Tokyo; co-auth, Artists of Hawaii, Vols I & II, Univ Hawaii, 74. Mailing Add: 4236 Carnation Pl Honolulu HI 96816

HAAS, HELEN (HELEN HAAS DE LANGLEY)
SCULPTOR
b New York, NY. Study: With Emile Antoine Bourdell. Work: Portrait head of Bourdell, Musee Bourdelle, Paris, France; Portrait Head Dorothy Gish, Mus City of NY; Portrait Head Duke of Windsor, Chartwell Home Sir Winston Churchill, Nowa Mus; Musee Jeu de Paume, Paris; Portrait Head Gen Theodore Roosevelt, Jr, Mus Natural Hist, Roosevelt Wing. Comn: The Duke of Windsor (portrait head), comn by The Late Duke of Kent; James Forrestal, Secy US Navy (portrait head), comn by Kenneth Rocky Forrestal Libr, Princeton, NJ; Marajah of Kapurthala, India (portrait head) & Michael Arlen. Exhib: Salon Jes Teuleries, Paris; Salon D'Antomne, Grand Palais, Paris; large figure on terr of US Bldg, Int Exhib, Paris, 38; one-man show, Charpentie Gallery, Paris, Jacques Seligman Gallery, New York & Knoedler Gallery, London & spec exhib Armed Forces, London, 42-43. Bibliog: Numerous articles in Harpers Bazaar, Life and other periodicals in France, England & US, 30-40. Mem: Fel Nat Sculpture Soc; fel Salon de Teuleries; fel Salon D'Antomne; Les Amis de Bourdel. Style & Technique: Classic, Rodinesque, Greek and Roman. Dealer: Joseph A C Moore 1065 Park Ave New York NY 10028. Mailing Add: 28 E 73rd St New York NY 10021

HAAS, LEZ
PAINTER, EDUCATOR
b Berkeley, Calif, Mar 10, 11. Study: San Francisco State Teachers Col; Univ Calif, Berkeley, AB & MA; Hans Hofmann Sch Art. Work: Cedar City, Utah; paintings in pvt collections. Exhib: Roswell Art Mus; Santa Barbara Mus Art; Calif Palace of Legion of Honor; NMex Fine Arts Mus; Univ Ariz Art Gallery; plus other group & one-man shows. Teaching: Asst prof, Col Fine Arts, Univ NMex, 46-47, actg dean, 47-48, dir, Taos Field Sch, 47-48, assoc prof & chmn dept art, 47-53, prof, 53-63, actg dean, 54-55; head art dept, Univ Ariz, 63-69, prof art, 63-77. Awards: Mus NMex Prize, 57. Mem: Am Asn Univ Prof; Soc Am Archeol; Prof Photogrs Am. Mailing Add: PO Box 726 El Rito NM 87530

HAAS, RICHARD JOHN
PRINTMAKER, PAINTER
b Spring Green, Wis, Aug 29, 36. Study: Univ Wis-Milwaukee, BS, 59; Univ Minn, MFA, 64. Work: Mus Mod Art, Metrop Mus Art & Whitney Mus Am Art, New York; Yale Univ Art Gallery, New Haven, Conn; Fogg Mus, Cambridge, Mass. Exhib: Whitney Mus Am Art, 72; Contemporary American Art, Herron Mus Art, Indianapolis, 72; Printmaking Biennial, Brooklyn Mus, 74; one-man shows, Hundred Acres Gallery, 72, 73 & 74, Brooke Alexander, 73, 74 & 77, Whitney Mus Am Art, 75 & Young Hoffman Gallery, Chicago, 78; plus others, 75- Harcus-Krakow Gallery, Boston, 75. Teaching: Instr art, Univ Minn, 63-64; asst prof art, Mich State Univ, 64-68; instr printmaking, Bennington Col, 68- Awards: Ford Found Purchase Prize, 64; First Prize, Mich Printmakers, 66; Creative Artists Pub Serv Grant, New York, 72 & 75. Media: Watercolor, Intaglio. Dealer: Brooke Alexander 24 E 78th St New York NY 10021. Mailing Add: 81 Greene St New York NY 10012

HABER, IRA JOEL
SCULPTOR, WRITER
b Brooklyn, NY, Feb 24, 47. Work: Nueu Gallerie, Ludwig Collection, Aachen, Ger. Exhib: Information, Mus Mod Art, New York, 70; Whitney Mus Ann Sculpture Exhib, New York, 70; three one-man shows, Fischbach Gallery, New York, 71-74; Whitney Mus Contemp Art Biennial, 73; Painting & Sculpture Today, Indianapolis Mus Art, 74; Retrospective, Kent State Univ Art Gallery, 77; Tableaux Constructions, Univ Calif, Santa Barbara, 77. Teaching: Instr sculpture, Fordham Univ, 71-74. Awards: Creative Artists Pub Serv Grant, 74-75; Nat Endowment Arts Fel, 74-75. Bibliog: Peter Sager (auth), New Forms of realism, Mag Kunst, 71 & 77-78; Lawrence Alloway (auth), Art, Nation, 6/19/72; Corinne Robins (auth), Ira Joel Haber, Arts Mag, 11/77. Style & Technique: Miniature landscapes, enclosed or open relating to the wall and floor encompassing abstract, realist, expressionist and minimal principles. Media: Mixed Media. Publ: Auth, Radio City Music Hall, 69; auth, Elizabeth (short story), Center Mag, 72; auth, Five stories of the Music Hall, St Marks Poetry Proj, 73; auth, Some

thoughts on camouflage by John Perreault, Serif-Lit Quart, Kent State Univ, 74; M E Thelen Gallery Piece, Tri-Quarterly, 75; auth, Some reasons why I do what I do, Appearances, Vol 1 (1977). Mailing Add: 105 W 27th St New York NY 10001

HABER, LEONARD
COLLECTOR, DESIGNER
b New York, NY, Aug 5, 20. Study: Parsons Sch Design; study in Paris & Italy; Univ Paris; Yale Univ, BFA. Teaching: Asst prof fine arts, Col William & Mary. Awards: Six Medals, Beaux Art Inst Design. Style & Technique: Architectural wood sculpture in lacquer. Collection: Contemporary drawings and paintings; Japanese lacquers. Mailing Add: 8 E 62nd St New York NY 10021

HABER, WILLIAM
ART DEALER, COLLECTOR
b New York, NY, Feb 4, 21. Pos: Owner, William Haber Art Collections, Inc. Interest: Since 1960, conducted art auctions and art shows in the US and Japan (Tokyo), and lectured and exhibited graphic art with presentation as an art form in itself. Publ: Ed, Moshe Gat (auth), Mexico Spain Portugal Israel, United Artists Israel, 68; ed, Rubin (auth), Story of King David, 71; ed, Rattner (auth), In the Beginning..., 72 & People in Israel, 75, Mourlot, Paris. Mailing Add: William Haber Art Collection 139-11 Queens Blvd Jamaica NY 11435

HABERGRITZ, GEORGE JOSEPH
PAINTER, SCULPTOR
b New York, NY, June 16, 09. Study: Nat Acad Design; Cooper Union, grad; Acad Grande Chaumiere. Work: Butler Mus, Youngstown, Ohio; Wilberforce Univ, Ohio; Purdue Univ, Ind; Safad Mus, Israel; Jewish Mus, London. Exhib: Albright Mus Painting Ann, Buffalo, NY, 38-40; Va Biennial, Richmond, 40; Am Watercolor Soc Ann, 47-49; Nat Asn Painters Casein, 47-74; Nat Acad Design Drawing & Painting Ann, 48-51; Univ Mont; Okla State Mus; Evansville Mus, Ind; Detroit Gallery of Fine Arts; Gallery Meindel & El Callejon Gallery, Bogota, Colombia, 74-77. Teaching: Lectr artist in Africa, SPac & India, 57-; instr painting, Art Students League, 60-64 & Friend Sch Art, 65-69; instr new media, Workshop Prof Artists, 67- Pos: Dir, Sch Continuing Art Educ, 68 Awards: Gold Medal for Drawing, Nat Acad Design, 38; Grumbacher Awards, Nat Soc Painters Casein, 68, 70, 72 & 74. Bibliog: G Klotz (auth), Two American artists, Galerie Klotz, Stuttgart, 67. Mem: Nat Soc Painters Casein (pres, 63-64). Style & Technique: Contemporary-new media assemblage and collage combines, including metal, wood, oil, findings and miscellaneous materials. Mailing Add: 150 Waverly Pl New York NY 10014

HACK, HOWARD EDWIN
PAINTER
b Cheyenne, Wyo, July 6, 32. Study: Calif Col Arts & Crafts; Mills Col; Univ San Francisco, BA(philos); San Francisco Art Inst; also with Martin Baer, San Francisco, 50-53. Work: Whitney Mus Am Art & Sara Roby Found, New York; Oakland Art Mus, Calif; Fogg Art Mus, Harvard Univ; Art Mus STex, Corpus Christi. Exhib: San Francisco Mus Art Drawing Nat, 70; Looking West, Joslyn Art Mus, Omaha, Nebr, 70; Santa Barbara Mus Art, Calif, 72; Mills Col, Oakland, Calif; Nat Acad Design, New York, 73. Awards: Ann Bremer Mem Award, San Francisco Mus Art, 65; Richard & Hinda Rosenthal Found Award for Painting, Nat Acad Arts & Lett, 66; Childe Hassam Found Purchase Award, Am Acad Arts & Lett, 69. Media: Oil, Tempera. Dealer: Gump's Gallery 250 Post St San Francisco CA 94108; Zara Gallery 553 Pacific St San Francisco CA 94133. Mailing Add: 54 Cook St San Francisco CA 94118

HACK, PHILLIP S & PATRICIA Y
COLLECTORS
Mr Hack, b Ill, Dec 8, 16; Mrs Hack, b Los Angeles, Calif, Dec 21, 26. Study: Univ Ariz; Stanford Univ; Oxford Univ; Ariz State Univ; Wabash Col; Purdue Univ. Collection: Contemporary paintings, sculpture, prints and drawings. Mailing Add: 2201 N Central Ave Phoenix AZ 85004

HACKENBROCH, YVONNE ALIX
CURATOR, WRITER
b Frankfurt, Ger, Apr 27, 12; US citizen. Study: Univ Frankfurt, 32-33; Univ Rome, 33-34; Univ Munich, PhD(summa cum laude), 36. Pos: Asst dept Brit & mediaeval antiq, Brit Mus, London, 36-45; cur, Lee Fareham Collection, Univ Toronto, 45-49; cur, Irwin Untermyer Collection & cur, Western European Arts, Metrop Mus Art, 49- Awards: Ford Found Grant, 63; Kress Found Grants, 64 & 65. Res: The decorative arts. Publ: Auth, seven catalogues of the Irwin Untermyer Collection; contribr, Connoisseur & other mag. Mailing Add: 7 E 85th St New York NY 10028

HACKLIN, ALLAN DAVE
PAINTER
b New York, NY, Feb 11, 43. Study: Pratt Inst. Work: Whitney Mus Am Art, New York; Dallas Mus Fine Arts; Allen Mus, Oberlin, Ohio. Teaching: Instr painting, Pratt Inst, 69-70; instr painting, Calif Inst Arts, 70-77; vis prof, Cooper Union, 77- Dealer: Truman Gallery 38 E 57th St New York NY 10019. Mailing Add: Jefferson NY 12093

HADEN, EUNICE (BARNARD)
PAINTER, ILLUSTRATOR
b Washington, DC, Oct 21, 01. Study: Oberlin Col, BA; Abbott Sch Art, with Hugo Inden; also with Eliot O'Hara. Work: In pvt collections only. Exhib: Miniature Painters, Sculptors & Gravers Soc, 46-; St Augustine Art Asn, 52 & 60; Nat Collection Fine Arts, 53-56; Burr Gallery, New York, 59 & 60; one-man show, Payne Gallery, Washington, DC, 64; Gallery on the Landing, Ft Wayne, Ind, 77; plus others. Awards: Art Club Washington, 56, 59, 64 & 66. Mem: Miniature Painters, Sculptors & Gravers Soc (treas, 54-59 & 77, pres, 60-64, corresp secy, 64-66); St Augustine Art Asn; Art Club Washington (exhib comt chmn, 56-57, vchmn, 57-58, vchmn prog comt, 56-59, chmn, 61-62, corresp secy, 64-68, bd gov, 64-68); Nat Registrar (interim), 77-78; Nat League Am Pen Women. Style & Technique: Impressionistic realism in painting; traditional technique in pen and ink, or sketchy style similar to Joseph Pennell. Media: Watercolor, pen and ink. Publ: Auth & ed, DAR Patriot Index, first ed, 67, suppl, 69; auth & ed, Am Clan Gregor Soc Yearbks, 68- Mailing Add: 5112 Connecticut Ave NW Washington DC 20008

HADLER, WARREN ARNOLD
ART DEALER
b Port Washington, Wis, Oct 3, 48. Pos: Owner, Hadler Gallery, New York. Specialty: Art textile, ancient and contemporary. Mailing Add: 35-37 E 20th St New York NY 10003

HADLEY, ROLLIN VAN NOSTRAND
MUSEUM DIRECTOR
b Westboro, Mass, Dec 13, 27. Study: Harvard Univ, AB, 49, 63-65. Teaching: Mem fac Eng lit, Universita Bocconi, Milan, Italy, 60-62; vis scholar, Harvard Ctr for Italian Renaissance Studies, Florence, Italy, 72. Pos: Trustee, Corning Mus of Glass, NY, 58-60; adminr, Isabella Stewart Gardner Mus, 63-70, dir, 70- Mem: Save Venice, Inc (chmn, Boston Chap, 71-74, pres, 74-); Am Asn Art Mus Dirs; Boston Fulbright Comt (mem bd dirs, 74-). Publ: Auth, Drawings/Isabella Stewart Gardner Museum, 68 & auth, sect on Renaissance & Modern, Sculpture/Isabella Stewart Gardner Museum, 77, Trustees/Isabella Stewart Gardner Mus. Mailing Add: 2 Palace Rd Boston MA 02115

HADLOCK, WENDELL STANWOOD
MUSEUM DIRECTOR
b Cranberry Isles, Maine, May 11, 11. Study: Univ Maine, AB(hist & res); Univ Pa, MA(anthrop). Pos: Admin asst, Peabody Mus, Salem, Mass, 49-50; dir, William A Farnsworth Libr & Art Mus, 51-76. Mailing Add: RFD 1 Box 645 Rockland ME 04841

HADZI, DIMITRI
SCULPTOR, PRINTMAKER
b New York, NY, Mar 21, 21. Study: Cooper Union, cert, 50; Brooklyn Mus Art Sch, 48-50; Polytechnion, Athens, Greece, 50-51. Work: Mus Mod Art, Guggenheim Mus & Whitney Mus Am Art, New York; Fogg Art Mus, Harvard Univ, Cambridge, Mass; Hirshhorn Mus, Washington, DC. Comn: K-458 (bronze with Max Abramovitz & David Rockefeller), Philharmonic Hall, Lincoln Ctr, New York, 62-66; Thermopylae (bronze with Walter Gropius & Samuel Glaser for US Govt), John F Kennedy Fed Bldg, Boston, 66-68; Arcturus (bronze with Gunnar Birkerts), Fed Reserve Bank Bldg, Minneapolis, 71-72; ecumenical doors (bronze), St Paul's Episcopal Church, Rome, 64-76; Fed Off Bldg, Portland, Ore, 76 & Alph Gallery, Boston, Mass, 77. Exhib: Recent Sculpture USA, Mus Mod Art, New York, 59; Pittsburgh Int, Carnegie Inst, Pa, 61 & 64; one-man shows, Stephen Radich Gallery, New York, 61-62, Mecklar Gallery, Los Angeles, 78 & Grunebaum Gallery, New York, 78; Two Sculptors: Two Painters, Venice Biennale, Italy, 62; Joseph H Hirshhorn Collection, Guggenheim Mus, New York, 62; Middleheim Park, Antwerp, Holland, 71; Am Acad, Rome, 74. Teaching: Artist in residence, Dartmouth Col, summer 69; Int Sculpture Symposium, Univ Ore, Eugene, 74; studio prof, Dept Visual & Environment Studies, Harvard Univ. Awards: Fulbright Fel; Guggenheim Found Fel, 57; Nat Inst Arts & Lett Grant, 62. Bibliog: Dore Ashton (auth), article in Am Sculpture; Peter Hollander (auth), Dimitri Works in Black Wax (film), Kinesis Films, 52. Mem: Col Art Asn Am. Style & Technique: Cast bronze-forms are abstract based on nature; recent work in stone (basalt), suggesting groups of ceremonial objects. Media: Bronze, Stone. Publ: Illusr, Hellas, 71. Dealer: Alpha Gallery 121 Newbury St Boston MA 02116; Richard Gray Gallery 620 N Michigan Ave Chicago IL 60611. Mailing Add: Carpenter Ctr for Visual Arts Harvard Univ Cambridge MA 02138

HAENIGSEN, HARRY WILLIAM
CARTOONIST
b New York, NY, July 14, 00. Study: Art Students League, 19. Teaching: Fac, Famous Artists Sch. Pos: Illusr columns, spec sect, art dept, NY Eve World, 19-21; mag illusr, Photoplay, Motion Picture, 22; daily cartoon series, NY World, 24-31 & King Features Syndicate, 31-37; animated cartoons, 38-39; creator comic, Our Bill, NY Herald Tribune Syndicate, 39 & Penny, 43. Mem, Nat Cartoonists Soc (exec bd); Soc Illusr; Philadelphia Acad Fine Arts; Mod Mus, New York. Publ: Our Bill, His Life & Times, 47; auth, Penny, 53; Penny Party Book, 54; Penny (TV play), 54. Mailing Add: New Hope PA 18938

HAERER, CAROL
PAINTER
b Salina, Kans, Jan 23, 33. Study: Doane Col; Univ Nebr, BFA; Art Inst Chicago; Univ Calif, Berkeley, MA. Work: Whitney Mus Am Art, New York; Brooklyn Mus, NY; Univ Kans Mus Art, Lawrence; Sheldon Mem Art Galleries, Lincoln, Nebr; Kans State Univ, Manhattan. Exhib: Salon des Realities Nouvelles, Paris, 55; West Coast Artists Traveling Show, San Francisco Art Mus, 58-60; Lyrical Abstraction, Larry Aldrich Mus, Conn, 70; Whitney Mus Am Art Ann, New York, 70 & 72; Painting & Sculpture Today, Indianapolis Mus, 72; one-artist shows, Max Hutchinson Gallery, New York, 71 & 73; Women Choose Women, New York Cult Ctr, 73; New York Artists, Portland Art Mus, Ore, 74; Report from Soho Grey Art Gallery, NY Univ, 75; Critic's Choice, Syracuse Univ Mus, NY, 77 & Munson-Williams-Proctor Inst, Utica, NY, 78. Awards: Fulbright Scholar to Paris, 54-55 & Woolley Fel, 55-56; Alpha Chi Omega Founders Fel, 66. Bibliog: Larry Aldrich (auth), Young lyrical painters, Art in Am, 11/69; articles in Art Int, 1/74 & Arts Mag, 1/74. Dealer: Max Hutchinson Gallery 138 Greene St New York NY 10012. Mailing Add: Rte 2 Hoosick Falls NY 12090

HAESSLE, JEAN-MARIE GEORGES
PAINTER, PRINTMAKER
b Alsace, France, Sept 12, 39. Study: Ecole Nat des Beaux Arts, Paris; Ecole de la Grande Chaumiere, Paris. Work: Albright-Knox Art Gallery, Buffalo, NY; Bibliot Nat, Paris, France; Nat Art Mus, China; Ill Univ, Edwarville. Exhib: Salon de la Jeune Peinture, Paris, 67; Martha Jackson Gallery, New York, 71; 9th Nat Print Exhib, Silvermine Guild, Conn, 72; Westbeth Graphic Show, Palace of Fine Arts, Mexico City, 72; Selected Graphic Show, Albright-Knox Art Gallery, Buffalo, 72; one-man show, Westbroadway Gallery, New York, 73; Young Talent Festival, Pace Gallery, New York, 77. Bibliog: Laurie Anderson (auth), reviews in Art News, 72; April Kingsley (auth), New York newsletter, Art Int, 73; Vivian Raynor (auth), review in Art in Am, 74. Style & Technique: Abstract involved with line and texture. Media: Painting: acrylic on paper or wall and acrylic and oil on canvas; printmaking. Dealer: Robert Freidus Gallery 158 Lafayette St New York NY 10013. Mailing Add: 106-112 Spring St New York NY 10012

HAFIF, MARCIA
PAINTER, INSTRUCTOR
b Pomona, Calif, Aug 15, 29. Study: Pomona Col, BA(art), 50; Claremont Grad Sch; Univ Calif, Irvine, MFA, 71. Exhib: Pasadena Art Mus, Calif, 56; VI Biennale di Roma e Lazio, Rome, Italy, 68; EAT in Process, Univ Southern Calif, Los Angeles, 70; New York Cult Ctr, 73; Artist's Bks, Moore Col Art, Philadelphia, Pa, 73; Tendences Actuelles de la Nouvelle Peinture Americaine, Mus d'Art Mod de la Ville de Paris, France, 75; Marica Hafif, La Jolla Mus Contemp Art, Calif, 75; Bilder ohne Bilder, Rheinisches Landesmuseum, Bonn, WGer, 77; one-person shows, Sonnabend Gallery, New York, 74, 75, 76 & 78 & Gallena La Salita, Rome, Italy, 64 & 68. Teaching: Instr painting & color, Sch Visual Arts, New York, 74-76; artist-in-residence drawing, Wright State Univ, Dayton, Ohio, Fall 77. Bibliog: Marisa Volpi (auth), Marcia Hafif, Data, 74; Rosalind Krauss (auth), Notes on the Index: Seventies Art in America Part II, October (mag), 10/78. Style & Technique: Monochrome paintings analysing paint pigments and materials while going beyond physicality to a personal experience of paint. Media: All traditional paint media. Publ: Auth, Odilon Redon, The New

Mortality, 62; auth, Pomona Houses, Mother Lode Ed, 72; auth, A Fusion of Real and Pictorial Space, Arts Mag, 72; auth, Words, self-publ, 76; auth, Diversificazione dell'Avanguardia, d'Ars, 77. Dealer: Sonnabend Gallery 420 W Broadway New York NY 10012. Mailing Add: 112 Mercer St New York NY 10012

HAGAN, JAMES GARRISON
SCULPTOR, INSTRUCTOR
b Pittsburgh, Pa, July 11, 36. Study: Carnegie-Mellon Univ, BFA; Iowa State Univ; Univ Pittsburgh, MA. Work: Column 5, Nat Gallery Art, Washinton, DC; Column 8, Princeton Univ, NJ. Exhib: One-man show, Zabriskie Gallery, 75; Nine Sculptures, Nassau Co Mus, NY, 76; Wood Works, Wadsworth Atheneum, Hartford, Conn, 77; Wood, Nassau Co Mus, NY, 77. Teaching: Assoc prof sculpture, Univ Va, Charlottesville, 63- Media: Wood. Dealer: Zabriskie Gallery 29 West 57th New York NY 10019. Mailing Add: Rte 1 Box 277 Charlottesville VA 22901

HAGAN, (ROBERT) FREDERICK
PRINTMAKER, PAINTER
b Toronto, Ont, May 21, 18. Study: Ont Col Art; Art Students League; also with George Miller, New York. Comn: Mural, Oakville Centennial Libr. Exhib: Ont Soc Artists; Can Soc Painters Watercolour; Can Group Painters; Nat Gallery Can; Libr of Cong; plus others. Teaching: Res artist, Pickering Col, Newmarket, Ont, 42-46; instr drawing & printmaking, Ont Col Art, 46- Mem: Can Soc Graphic Art; Can Soc Painter-Etchers & Engravers; Ont Soc Artists. Mailing Add: Ont Col of Art 100 McCaul St Toronto ON Can

HAGE, RAYMOND JOSEPH
ART DEALER, COLLECTOR
b Huntington, WVa, Nov 28, 43. Study: Univ Ky; Marshall Univ, BBA, 66; Colgate Darden Grad Bus Sch, Univ Va, TEP, 71. Pos: Pres, Raymond J Hage, Inc, currently. Specialty: Original prints and American art. Collection: Original prints, American art and sculpture. Mailing Add: 2105 Wiltshire Blvd Huntington WV 25701

HAGEMAN, CHARLES LEE
EDUCATOR, DESIGNER
b Clay Center, Kans, June 22, 35. Study: Univ of Kans, BFA, 57, MFA, 67. Work: Ill State Univ, Visual Arts Ctr, Normal, Ill; Univ of Mo, Columbia. Comn: Univ Mace, Pres Chain of Office & 6 Board of Regent's Medallions, comn by Pres of Northwest Mo State Univ, Maryville, 77. Exhib: Juried Craft Exhib, Ark Arts Ctr, Little Rock, 73 & J P Speed Art Mus, Louisville, Ky, 74; Invitational Craft Exhib, Albrecht Mus, St Joseph, Mo, 75; Prof Jewelry Exhib, Univ of Mo, Columbia, 76; Mid-Am Metalcrafts, Kansas City Pub Libr, Kansas City, Mo, 77. Collections Arranged: Mo Craftsman Exhib, Olive DeLuce Gallery, Maryville, Mo, 73. Teaching: Assoc prof of jewelry & metals, Northwest Mo State Univ, Maryville, 67- & summer jewelry workshop, NMex State Univ, Las Cruces, 74- Pos: Area rep to Mo Craft Coun, 70-75; Mo State rep to Am Craft Coun, New York, 73-76. Awards: Best in Metals, Designer-Craftsman Show, Kans, 67; Metals Award, Springfield Art Mus, 69; Best in Metals, Mo Craftsman Exhib, 70. Mem: Mo Craft Coun; Am Craft Coun; Soc of NAm Goldsmiths. Style & Technique: Construction techniques which emphasize simple forms accented with surface textures. Media: Pewter & Gold. Mailing Add: 722 W 2nd St Maryville MO 64468

HAGERSTRAND, MARTIN ALLAN
MUSEUM DIRECTOR, ART ADMINSTRATOR
b Chicago, Ill, Nov 10, 11. Study: Metrop Theological Sem; Univ Richmond; Univ Va Exten; Univ Kans; US Army Command & Gen Staff Col; US Dept of Defence Armed Forces Staff Col. Collections Arranged: Sponsored & administered numerous spec exhibs, Cherokee Nat Hist Soc & Cherokee Nat Mus since 69. Pos: Cherokee Nat Hist Soc, Tahlequah, Okla, 63-; producer, Trail of Tears Drama, Theatre at TSA-LA-GI, Tahlequah, 60-; dir, Cherokee Nat Mus, Tahlequah, 75-; vchmn, Okla Art & Humanities Coun, 76-; pres, Okla Summer Arts Inst, 77- Awards: Arts & Tourism Award, Okla Arts & Humanities Coun & State Dept of Tourism & Recreation, 72. Mem: Am Asn of Mus; Mountain Plains Mus Asn; Okla Mus Asn (pres, 76 & 77); Am Asn of State & Local Hist; Nat Trust for Hist Preserv; Board of Visitors, Univ Okla. Interest: Indian art. Mailing Add: Cherokee Nat Hist Soc Box 515 Tahlequah OK 74464

HAGGLUND, IRVIN (ARVID)
CARTOONIST
b Holt, Minn, Mar 11, 15. Work: Cartoons, Syracuse Univ Permanent Collection. Exhib: Cartoon Exhib, San Mateo, Calif, 57; San Diego Co Fair, Del Mar, Calif, 64. Pos: Assoc cartoon ed, Dow Periodicals, Chicago, 41. Publ: Contribr, Best Cartoons of the Year, 55-72; contribr, Happy Holiday, Dodd, 56; contribr, Psychiatry Book, Little, 60; contribr, Best of Best Cartoons, Crown, 61; contribr, Modern Composition, Holt, Bk 2, 69. Mailing Add: 708 N Duluth Ave Thief River Falls MN 56701

HAGUE, RAOUL
SCULPTOR
b Constantinople. US citizen. Study: Iowa State Col, 21; Beaux Arts Inst Design, New York, 26-27; Art Students League, 27-28; Courtauld Inst London, 50-51. Work: Albright Art Gallery; Mus Mod Art; Whitney Mus Am Art. Exhib: Mus Mod Art, 33 & 56; Curt Valentin Gallery, 45; Whitney Mus Am Art, 45-48, 52, 57 & 58. Awards: Woodstock Found Grant, 49; Kleinert Award, 56; Ford Found Grant, 59. Mailing Add: Woodstock NY 12498

HAHN, BETTY
PHOTOGRAPHER, EDUCATOR
b Chicago, Ill, Oct 11, 40. Study: Ind Univ, BA, 63, MFA, 66 with Henry Holmes Smith. Work: Mus of Mod Art, New York; Smithsonian Inst; Nat Gallery of Can, Ottawa; Art Inst of Chicago; Pasadena Art Mus, Calif. Exhib: Photog in the 20th Century, Nat Gallery of Can, 67; Betty Hahn & Gayle Smalley, Smithsonian Inst, 69; Photog: New Acquisitions, Mus of Mod Art, New York, 70; Photo Media, Mus of Contemp Crafts, New York, 71; Photog Into Art, Camden Arts Ctr, London, Eng, 72; Betty Hahn, Witkin Gallery, New York, 73; Féstival du Photographie, Arles, France, 75; Am Family Portraits: 1730-1976, Philadelphia Mus of Art, 76; plus others. Teaching: Asst prof photog, Rochester Inst of Technol, NY, 69-76; assoc prof photog, Univ NMex, 76- Awards: Pratt Graphics Ctr Award, Int Miniature Print Competition; New York, 71; Purchase Award, Contemp Photog, Sheldon Arts Gallery, Lincoln, Nebr, 72; Creative Artists Pub Serv Grant fel, NY State, 76. Bibliog: James N Miho (auth), More Than Real, Commun Arts, 72; R Sobieszek (auth), Photographer: Betty Hahn, Czech Photo, 74 & Russian Photo Rev, 74. Mem: Soc for Photog Educ. Style & Technique: Non-silver and mixed media photography, especially revived gum bichromate process. Media: Large scale contact prints with applied color; use of found images; photo processes on fabrics. Publ: Auth, Speaking with a Genuine Voice: Henry Holmes Smith, IMAGE Eastman House, 73; contribr of chap on Gum Bichromate Printing, In: Darkroom, Lustrum Press, New York, 77. Dealer: Witkin Gallery 41 E 57th St New York NY 10022. Mailing Add: Art Dept Univ of NMex Albuquerque NM 87131

HAHN, MAURICE & ROSLYN
ART DEALERS
b US citizen. Study: Mr Hahn, Northwestern Univ, BS(bus); Mrs Hahn, Univ Pa, BA, grad studies in art hist; Temple Univ, Tyler Sch of Art. Collections Arranged: Benton Spruance, Retrospective, William Penn Mus, Harrisburg, Pa, 77; Benton Spruance (traveling exhib; co-auth, catalogue), with Dr Ricardo Viera, Lehigh Univ, 77-78; Alfred Bendiner, The Philadelphia Years, Willaim Penn Mus, Harrisburg, 78. Pos: Dir, Hahn Gallery, Philadelphia. Mem: Philadelphia Mus Art; Pa Acad Fine Arts; Philadelphia Print Club; Prints in Progress (Mrs Hahn, bd mem, 70-77). Specialty: Twentieth century art with special emphasis on American paintings and prints; Pennsylvania artists and artists' estates. Mailing Add: c/o The Hahn Gallery 8439 Germantown Ave Chestnut Hill Philadelphia PA 19118

HAHN, STEPHEN
ART DEALER
Pos: Dir, Stephen Hahn Gallery, New York. Specialty: French paintings. Mailing Add: 817 Fifth Ave New York NY 10021

HAINES, RICHARD
PAINTER
b Marion, Iowa, Dec 29, 06. Study: Minneapolis Sch Art, 32-34; Ecole des Beaux Arts, Fontainebleau, France, 34. Work: Metrop Mus Art, New York; Corcoran Mus, Washington, DC; Los Angeles Co Mus; Dallas Mus, Tex; Kansas City Mus, Mo. Comn: Painted mural, Mayo Diag Clin, Rochester, Minn, 50; mosaic mural, Schoenberg Hall, Univ Calif, Los Angeles, 54; painted mural, 3M Res Ctr, St Paul, 58; granite inlay mural, Univ Ky Med Ctr, Lexington, 62; 3 large mosaic murals, Fed Bldg, Los Angeles Civil Ctr, 65. Exhib: Corcoran Biennial, Washington, DC, 51; Univ Ill, 50, 51 & 61; Am Painting, Metrop Mus, New York, 50; Carnegie Inst Int, 54; Third Biennial, Sao Paulo, Brazil, 55. Teaching: Teacher painting, Minneapolis Sch Art, 41-42; head dept painting, Chouinard Art Inst, Los Angeles, 45-54; head dept painting, Otis Art Inst, Los Angeles, 54-74. Pos: Pres, Calif Watercolor Soc, 50. Awards: First Prize in Oils, Los Angeles Co Mus, 45; First Prize Oils Ann, Calif State Fair, 48; Third Prize Oils, Biennial Nat, Corcoran Mus, 51. Bibliog: Feature article in, Am Artist Mag, 4/63; Prize Winning Oil Paintings, Allied Publ, 64; Louis Redstone (auth), Art in Architecture, McGraw-Hill, 68. Mem: Artists for Econ Action (bd mem). Style & Technique: Figurative, with emphasis on strong design and color relationships, symbolism; built up layers of pigment to achieve color vibration. Media: Oil, Mosaic. Mailing Add: 247 Amalfi Dr Santa Monica CA 90402

HAKANSON, JOY
See Colby, Joy Hakanson

HALABY, SAMIA ASAAD
PAINTER, EDUCATOR
b Jerusalem, Palestine, Dec 12, 36; US citizen. Study: Mich State Univ, with Abraham Rattner & Borris Margo, 59-60; Ind Univ, with William Bailey & James McGarrell, MFA, 63. Work: Solomon R Guggenheim Mus, New York; Nelson Rockhill Gallery of Art, Kansas City, Mo; Indianapolis Mus of Art; Cleveland Mus of Art; Cincinnati Art Mus. Comn: Lithograph, Cleveland Mus Print Club, 74. Exhib: One-woman shows, Phyllis Kind Gallery, Chicago, 71 & Spectrum Gallery, New York, 73; Am Drawing, Yale Univ Gallery, 73; Tamarind Prints, Nat Gallery Art, Washington, DC, 75; Recent Acquisitions, Solomon R Guggenheim Mus, 75; Susan Caldwell Gallery, New York, 77. Teaching: Assoc prof painting & drawing, Ind Univ, Bloomington, 69-72 & Yale Univ, New Haven, 72- Pos: Artist in residence, Tamarind Lithography Workshop, 72. Bibliog: Brown (auth), Recent exhibitions, Arts Mag, 5-6/73. Style & Technique: Geometric abstract. Media: Oil on Canvas. Mailing Add: 180 York St New Haven CT 06520

HALBACH, DAVID ALLEN
PAINTER, INSTRUCTOR
b Santa Barbara, Calif, Jan 12, 31. Study: Chouinard Art Inst, cert grad; with Rex Brandt, Edward Reep & Robert Uecker. Work: Permanent Collection, Bank Calif, San Francisco, San Jose & Seattle, Wash; Favell Mus Western Art, Klamath Falls, Ore. Exhib: One-man shows, Marion Lawton Galleries, Amador & Monte Serreno, 70-75, Mary Livingston Gallery, Santa Ana, 73-74, Calif & Maintrail Galleries, Scottsdale, Ariz, 75; Desert & Western, Death Valley, Calif, 69-74; Muckenthaler Cult Ctr, Whittier, Calif, 71; Chapman Col, Ontario, 72; Cowboy Hall of Fame, Oklahoma City, 75. Teaching: Art teacher (adult educ), San Gabriel, Whittier & Covina High Schs, Calif, 65-73. Pos: Illusr, US Navy, 52-54; with Walt Disney Studio, Burbank, 54-55; illusr & art ed, Cannon Elec Co, Los Angeles, 55-59; art dir, Mowinckle Advert, Los Angeles, 59-63. Awards: Silver Medalist, Nat Acad-Cowboy Hall of Fame, 75. Style & Technique: People, land, street, seascape and wildlife. Media: Watercolor. Publ: Illusr, Orange County Illustrated, 75. Dealer: Maintrail Galleries 7169 Main St Scottsdale AZ 85251; Mary Livingston Gallery Two 1211 Broadway St Santa Ana CA 92701. Mailing Add: 2722 Lema Dr Mesa AZ 85205

HALBERSTADT, ERNST
PAINTER, SCULPTOR
b Budingen, Ger, Aug 26, 10; US citizen. Work: Metrop Mus Art & Mus Mod Art, New York; New Brit Mus, Conn; Fogg Mus, Harvard Univ, Cambridge; Addison Gallery Am Art, Andover, Mass. Comn: Murals, Fortress Monroe, Va, 37, Rockingham Park, Salem, NH, 60 & Irving Trust Co, New York, 65; sculpture, Irving Trust Co, New York; 67 & 72 & Southside Hosp, Bayshore, Long Island, 74; murals (42 panels), Metrop Life Insurance Co, Warwick, RI, 77. Exhib: Photog Fine Arts III & IV, 62-63; Art Across Am New Eng Regional Competition, 65; Norfolk Bi-Ann Am Drawings, 69; Painting, Marion Art Ctr, 70; one-man shows photog, Univ NH, 70, Traveling Show, DVA Assocs, Fla, 72 & NH Col, 77. Teaching: Head dept murals, Sch Mus Fine Arts, Boston, 47-51; instr photog, Penland, NC, 73; instr painting, Mass Maritime Acad, 74. Pos: Dir, New Eng Artists Equity Asn, 49-52. Awards: Purchase Awards, US Govt, 41; Pepsi Cola Corp New Eng Area Fel Painting, 46; Medals, Art Dirs Club, Boston, 56-57. Bibliog: H Devree (auth), Newcomber, New York Times, 3/46; T Lyman (auth), E H, double vision—photographer-painter, Prof Photogr, 5/50; P S Hurd (auth), E Halberstadt—expectancy, Christian Sci Monitor, 12/68. Publ: Illusr, Shore Road to Ogunquit, 69; auth, Rites of spring, Cape Cod Compass, 73. Dealer: Marlborough Gallery 40 W 57th St New York NY 10022. Mailing Add: Sunset Island Onset MA 02558

HALBROOKS, DARRYL WAYNE
PAINTER, EDUCATOR
b Evansville, Ind, May 3, 48. Study: Univ Evansville, Ind; Murray State Univ, Ky; Southern Ill Univ. Work: Brooks Mem Art Gallery, Memphis, Tenn; Huntington Gallery, WVa; Ky Arts Comn Gallery, Frankfurt; Louisville Sch of Art, Ky. Exhib: Ind Artists, Indianapolis

Mus Art, 73, 74 & 75; Artists Biennial, New Orleans Mus Art, 74; Washington & Jefferson Nat Painting Exhib, Washington, Pa, 74 & 75; Exhib of Contemp Am Paintings, Palm Beach, Fla, 74; Dixie Ann, Ala Mus Art, Montgomery, 75; Dulin Nat Print & Drawing Exhib, Dulin Gallery, Knoxville, Tenn, 76. Teaching: Asst prof painting, Eastern Ky Univ, Richmond, Ky, 72- Awards: Purchase Award, 72 Mid-S Exhib, Brooks Mem Art Gallery, Memphis, Tenn, 72; Purchase Award, Appalachian Corridors & Exhib 280 Huntington, WVa, 74 & 77, Ky Arts Comn. Bibliog: Guy Northrop (auth), More From Mid-South, Memphis Com Appeal, 12/72; Marion Garmel (auth), Works on Paper, Indianapolis News, 5/74; Darry Halbrooks, Arts Mag, 5/77. Mem: Col Art Asn. Style & Technique: Realism, acrylic, brush and spray on paper and canvas. Media: Acrylic; lithography. Dealer: Jo-Anne Dobrick Dobrick Gallery 161 E Erie St Chicago IL 60611. Mailing Add: Box 948 Eastern Ky Univ Richmond KY 40475

HALE, JEAN GRAHAM
ILLUSTRATOR, ART ADMINISTRATOR
b Brownstown, Ind. Study: Herron Art Sch; Indianapolis Acad Art; Indianapolis Art League. Pos: Art dir, Fun Publ Co, Indianapolis, 64- Mem: Indianapolis Art League. Style & Technique: Halftone acrylic. Media: Pen and Ink. Publ: Ed & illusr, When I Think, I Get Scared, 75, I Got an Idea, 75, You Know What I Think, 75 & Stories & Stuff Like That, 76, Fun Publ; illusr, Native Americans-Traditional & Changing Cultures, Children's Mus, 77, plus others. Mailing Add: 717 E 70th Pl Indianapolis IN 46220

HALE, KENNETH JOHN
LITHOGRAPHER, PAINTER
b Philadelphia, Pa, Nov 10, 48. Study: Calif State Univ, Long Beach, BA; Univ Ill, with Dan Socha, MFA. Work: Univ Colo Fine Arts Permanent Collection, Boulder; Watson Gallery, Wheaton Col; Southwest Tex State Univ; Ill insts & mus; foreign US embassies. Comn: Three ed lithographs, US Info Agency, US Embassy Collections, 73; one ed lithograph, Ill Arts Coun, 73. Exhib: Potsdam Nat Print Exhib, NY, 72; 13th Ann Calgary Graphics Exhib, Can, 73; Color Print USA, Lubbock, Tex, 73; Drawings '74, Watson Gallery, Norton, Mass; Colo 2nd Print & Drawing Competition, Boulder, 75. Teaching: Instr lithography, Univ Tex, Austin, 73- Awards: Ford Found Grant, summer 75. Media: Mixed Media. Mailing Add: 504 E 42nd St Austin TX 78751

HALE, NATHAN CABOT
SCULPTOR, WRITER
b Los Angeles, Calif, July 5, 25. Study: Chouinard Art Inst, Los Angeles; Art Students League; Empire State Col, BS; Union Grad Sch, PhD. Work: Bronze madonna, St Anthony of Padua, East Northport, NY; bronze reliefs, Rose Assoc Bldg, Bronx, NY; also in mus & pvt collections. Exhib: Many group & one-man shows since 1947. Teaching: Mem fac, Pratt Inst, Brooklyn, 63-64; instr anat & drawing, Art Students League, 66-72. Pos: Fine arts adv, Wilson & Snibbe, 69-; dir, Ages of Man Found, 68-, sculptor, Cycle of Life Chapel Sculpture Proj, 68- Mem: Art Students League. Publ: Auth, Welded Sculpture, 69, Embrace of Life—the Sculpture of Gustav Vigelund, 70 & Abstraction in Art & Nature, 72; also contribr to archit & art mags. Dealer: Midtown Galleries 11 E 57th St New York NY 10022. Mailing Add: Ages of Man Found Sheffield Rd Amenia NY 12501

HALE, ROBERT BEVERLY
ART ADMINISTRATOR, INSTRUCTOR
b Boston, Mass, Jan 29, 01. Study: Columbia Univ Sch Archit; Fontainebleau, France; Art Students League. Work: Metrop Mus Art & Whitney Mus Am Art, New York; Univ Ariz, Tucson. Collections Arranged: Many collections arranged at the Metrop Mus Art. Teaching: Lectr & instr drawing & anat, Art Students League, 43-; adj prof anat, Columbia Univ, 45-67; lectr anat, Pa Acad Fine Arts, 69-; prof art, Cooper Union, 71- Pos: Cur Am art, Metrop Mus Art, 48-66, cur emer, 66- Awards: First Mayor's Award for Art & Cult, City of New York, 77. Mem: Benjamin Franklin fel Royal Soc Arts; Tiffany Found (pres, 56-66). Publ: Auth, Drawing Lessons from the Great Masters, 64; ed & translr, Dr Paul Richer, Anatomie Artistique, 71; co-auth, with Nike Hale, Balcomb Greene, 77; co-auth, with Terry Coyle, Anatomy Lessons from the Great Masters, 77. Mailing Add: 2 W 67th St New York NY 10023

HALEY, JOHN CHARLES
PAINTER, SCULPTOR
b Minneapolis, Minn, Sept 21, 05. Study: With Cameron Booth, Minneapolis & Hans Hofmann, Munich & Capri. Work: Phillips Mem Gallery, Washington, DC; Univ Calif, Berkeley; San Francisco Mus Art; Oakland Art Mus; IBM Collection. Exhib: San Francisco Art Asn Ann, 30-60; 19th Int Watercolors Exhib, Chicago Art Inst, 40; Contemp Am Painting, Univ Ill, 48 & 51-53; Exhibs Oil Painting, 51 & Drawing, 52, Metrop Mus Art, New York; 149th Ann Painting & Sculpture, Pa Acad Fine Arts, 54; Int Biennial, Sao Paulo, Brazil, 55 & 62; Palace of Legion of Honor Winter Invitationals, 60-64; Mus Mod Art, New York, 63. Teaching: Prof art, Univ Calif, Berkeley, 30-72, emer prof art, 72- Pos: Mem bd dirs, San Francisco Art Inst, 59-62; mem, Inst Creative Arts, Univ Calif, 63-64. Awards: Six Painting & Sculpture Awards, San Francisco Art Asn, 36-56; Watercolor Award, Calif Watercolor Soc, 56; Painting Award, Richmond Art Ctr, 56 & 58. Media: All media in painting and sculpture. Mailing Add: PO Box 31 Point Station Richmond CA 94807

HALEY, PATIENCE E (PATIENCE E HALEY GHIKAS)
PAINTER, ART CONSERVATOR
b Boston, Mass. Study: Oberlin Col, AB. Work: Addison Gallery Am Art, Andover, Mass; Smith Col Mus Art, Northampton, Mass; Ctr for Arts, Wesleyan Univ, Middletown, Conn; Mus of Art of Ogunquit, Maine; Mus of Art, Lehigh Univ, Pa. Comn: History of Manchester, Conn (mural), Manchester Savings Bank. Exhib: One-woman shows, George Walter Vincent Smith Mus, Springfield, Mass, 60, DeCordova Mus, Lincoln, Mass, 57 & Radcliffe Inst, Cambridge, Mass, 71; New England Drawings, Lyman Allyn Mus, Conn, 57; Highlights of Am Hist, Addison Gallery, Andover, Mass, 58. Teaching: Art instr, George Walter Vincent Smith Mus, Springfield, Mass, instr & cur, Middlebury Col, Vt; art instr, Abbot Acad, Andover, Mass, 56-59. Pos: Asst painting conserv, Dept Painting Restoration, Boston Mus, Mass, 73- Awards: Grant in Painting, Louis Comfort Tiffany Found, 61; Scholar in Painting, Radcliffe Inst, 69-71; Three Painting Fels, Yaddo & MacDowell Colony. Bibliog: Edward Betts (auth), Master Class in Watercolor, Watson-Guptill Publ, 75. Mem: Boston Watercolor Soc; Ogunquit Art Asn, Maine; Radcliffe Inst Fels, Inc. Style & Technique: Abstract color impressions of nature. Media: Watercolor; Ink. Mailing Add: c/o Fenway Studios Rm 402 30 Ipswich St Boston MA 02215

HALFF, ROBERT H
COLLECTOR
b San Antonio, Tex, Dec 1, 08. Study: Wharton Sch, Univ Pa, grad; New Sch Social Res; NY Univ; Univ Calif, Los Angeles Exten. Pos: Chmn spec proj & mem acquisitions comt, Mod & Contemp Art Coun, Los Angeles Co Mus Art. Collection: American contemporary and European art. Mailing Add: 1659 Waynecrest Dr Beverly Hills CA 90210

HALKIN, THEODORE
SCULPTOR, PAINTER
b Chicago, Ill, Mar 2, 24. Study: Art Inst Chicago, BFA, 50; Southern Ill Univ, MS(art), 52. Work: Art Inst Chicago; Butler Inst Am Art, Ohio. Exhib: 25th Biennial Contemp Am Oil Painting, Corcoran Gallery Art, Washington, DC, 57; Am Painting & Sculpture Ann, Pa Acad Fine Arts & Detroit Inst Arts, 58; one-man shows, Allan Frumkin Galleries, New York & Chicago, 61 & Phyllis Kind Gallery, Chicago, 70; Chicago Images Show, Mus Contemp Art, Chicago, 72. Teaching: Assoc prof art, Art Inst Chicago. Awards: 21st Ann Midyear Show Purchase Prize, Butler Inst, Ohio, 56; Chicago & Vicinity Show First Prize for Sculpture, Art Inst Chicago, 65; Cass Andran Award, 72. Bibliog: Article in Art Int, 2/64; Franz Schulz (auth), Fantastic Images, Follett, 72. Mailing Add: c/o Phyllis Kind Gallery 226 E Ontario Chicago IL 60611

HALKO, JOE
SCULPTOR, PAINTER
b Great Falls, Mont, Aug 11, 40. Study: Col of Great Falls, Mont. Comn: Mural (10ft x 250ft), comn by C A Rumford, Great Falls Sporting Goods, 70. Exhib: C M Russell Mus Art Show & Auction, Great Falls, 73, 75, 77 & 78; Spokane Ann Art Exhib, Eastern Wash Hist Soc, Cheney Cowles Mem Mus, 74; Cowboy Hall of Fame, Solon Borglum Invitational, Okla, 76; Mus of Native Am Cult, Spokane, Wash, 77-78; Fred Oldfield Show, Tacoma, Wash, 77-78; Alley Gallery, Reader's Alley, Helena, Mont, 77; Soc of Animal Artists, Sportsmans Edge, New York, 78 & Owens Gallery, Okla, 78. Awards: Spec Award for Western Art, Spokane Ann Art Exhib, Wash State Hist Soc, 74. Bibliog: Verna Lund Praast (auth), Back home to wildlife, Billings Gazette, Mont, 4/73; Denise Mort (auth), Halko gives Wildlife Seminar, Great Falls Tribune, 3/78. Mem: Soc of Animal Artists; Studio Ten. Style & Technique: North American and African wildlife sculpture; wildlife, landscapes and portraits in oil and acrylic. Media: Wax; Acrylic, Oil. Publ: Illusr, A Century in the Foothills 1876 to 1976, Fairfield Times, 76. Dealer: Gallery West Ridpath Hotel Spokane WA 99210. Mailing Add: 705 Tenth Ave SW Great Falls MT 59404

HALL, CARL ALVIN
PAINTER, INSTRUCTOR
b Washington, DC, Sept 17, 21. Study: Meinzinger Art Sch, Detroit, Mich, with Carlos Lopez. Work: Whitney Mus Am Art, New York, NY; Boston Mus Art, Mass; Springfield Art Inst, Mass; Swope Art Gallery, Terre Haute, Ind. Exhib: 66th Ann Western, Denver Art Mus, 60; 18th Artists West Miss, Colorado Springs, 61; Drawings USA, St Paul Gallery, Minn & Traveling Show, 61; Century 21, Seattle, Wash, 62; The West, 80 Contemporaries, Univ Ariz, 66; Bicentennial Exhib, Ore, 76-77. Teaching: Artist in residence, Willamette Univ, 48-72, asst prof, 72-78, assoc prof, 78-; instr adult educ, YWCA, Salem. Pos: Art critic, Ore Statesman, Salem, 53-68. Awards: Nat Inst Arts & Lett Grant, 49; Newberry Prize, Detroit Inst Art, 49. Bibliog: Collection of drawings, Northwest Rev, 63; article in Alaska J, Vol 7 (1977). Mem: Portland Art Mus. Mailing Add: 4626 Pettyjohn Rd S Salem OR 97302

HALL, JOHN A
PAINTER, EDUCATOR
b Toronto, Ont, Oct 10, 14. Study: Ont Col Art. Work: Art Gallery Toronto; Nat Gallery, Ottawa. Comn: Murals in porcelain enamel on steel panels, Delhi, Port Colborne & Simcoe, Ont & Expo '67, Montreal, PQ. Exhib: Can Group Painters; Ont Soc Artists; Royal Can Acad; New York World's Fair, 39; Rio, 44 & 46; plus others. Exhib Designed: Can Nat Exhib, Can Furniture Mart & Can Pavilion, Brussels, Belg. Teaching: Instr, Art Gallery Toronto; instr painting, Ont Dept Educ, summer courses; assoc prof drawing & painting, Dept Archit, Univ Toronto. Awards: Can Arts Coun Sr Artists' Award, 63. Mem: Print & Drawing Coun of Can; Ont Soc Artists. Style & Technique: Calligraphic working from nature in drawing, oils and watercolors. Publ: Illusr, Spirit of Canadian democracy, These English, Grandmothers, Glooscap's country, Nunny-Bag 3 & Road across Can. Mailing Add: Glencroft RR 2 Newmarket ON L3Y 4V9 Can

HALL, JOHN (SCOTT)
EDUCATOR, PAINTER
b Edmonton, Alta, Jan 17, 43. Study: Alta Col of Art, Fine Arts Dipl; Inst Allende, Mex. Work: Nat Gallery of Can, Ottawa, Ont; Montreal Mus of Fine Arts, Que; Can Coun Art Bank, Ottawa; Glenbow Alta Art Gallery, Calgary, Alta; Alta Art Found, Edmonton. Exhib: Cincinnati Biennial, Cincinnati Art Mus, Ohio, 69; Can 4&3, Can Cult Centre, Paris, France, 71; Realism: Emulsion & Omission, Agnes Etherington Art Centre, Kingston, Ont, 72; Prairies, Saidye Bronfman Centre, Montreal, 74; Alta Realists, Edmonton Art Gallery, 75; Nine Out of Ten, Art Gallery of Hamilton, Ont, 75; Eight Calgary Artists, Mendel Art Gallery, Saskatoon, Sask, 76; 17 Can Artists: A Protean View, Vancouver Art Gallery, BC, 76; What's New, Edmonton Art Gallery, 76; Albertawork, Alta Col of Art Gallery, Calgary, 77; Realism in Can, Norman MacKenzie Art Gallery, Univ Regina, 78. Collections Arranged: Rose Mus, A Maj Survey of the Rose Motif in Western Cult (co-orgn with Ron Moppett; travelling exhib), 73-74. Teaching: Vis instr painting-design, Ohio Wesleyan Univ, Del, 69-70; instr painting-design, Alta Col of Art, Calgary, 70-71; asst prof painting-drawing, Univ Calgary, 71- Pos: Pres, Alta Soc Artists, 67-68. Awards: Proj grant, 73, travel grants, 75 & 77, Can Coun. Bibliog: Ron Moppett (auth, catalogue), John Hall, Dalhousie Univ Art Gallery, 76. Mem: Royal Can Acad; Can Artists Representation; Can Asn of Univ Teachers. Style & Technique: New realist still life paintings. Media: Acrylic on canvas. Mailing Add: 19 Rosetree Rd NW Calgary AB T2K 1M8 Can

HALL, JULIE ANN
ART WRITER, COLLECTOR
b Nashville, Tenn, Sept 24, 43. Study: Univ Colo, BA(art hist), 65; Univ Ky, 69-70; Bowling Green State Univ, study ceramics with Karen Karnes. Collections Arranged: Decoys (arranged), Sheldon Mus, Lincoln, Nebr, 75. Teaching: Instr ceramics, 73-75 & seminar instr folk art, 77, Cranbrook Mus, Bloomfield Hills, Mich. Pos: Co-dir, Turn, Turn, Turn (craft gallery), Cooperstown, NY, 71; consult on crafts, Mich Crafts at Detroit Inst of Arts, Mich, 75; res consult on Decoys, Mus Am Folk Art, New York, NY, 77. Mem: Nat Coun on Educ for the Ceramic Arts; Col Art Asn of Am; Am Crafts Coun. Res: Extensive research on American Folk art, American Decoys and contemporary American crafts. Collection: American Folk art and American Waterfowl decoys. Publ: Auth, The Collectible Decoy-An Endangered Species?, NAm Decoys, 76; auth, John Schweikart, NAm Decoys, 77; auth, Portraits in Wood, Calrion Mag, Mus of Folk Art, 77; auth, Through the Collectors Eye: A Changing View of Folk Sculpture, Winterthur Mus, 78; auth, Tradition and Change: The New American Craftsman, E P Dutton, 78. Mailing Add: c/o Cranbrook Acad of Art 500 Lone Pine Rd Bloomfield Hills MI 48013

HALL, LEE
ART ADMINISTRATOR, PAINTER
b Lexington, NC, Dec 15, 34. Study: Univ NC, Greensboro, BFA; NY Univ, scholar, 65, AM & PhD; Warburg Inst, Univ London. Work: Hudson River Mus; Montclair Art Mus; Drew Univ, NJ; Greenville Mus, SC. Exhib: One-woman shows, Ruth White Gallery, 68, Drew Univ, 74 & Betty Parsons Gallery, 75; Montclair Art Mus, 73; Neuberger Mus, 75. Pos: Chmn dept art, Drew Univ, Madison, NJ, 65-74; consult, Nat Endowment for Humanities, 69-75; dean visual arts, State Univ NY, Purchase, 74-75; pres, RI Sch Design, 75- Awards: Am Philos Soc Grant, 65 & 68. Mem: Col Art Asn Am. Style & Technique: Abstract landscapes. Media: Watercolor, Polymer Tempera. Res: History and theory of symbolism in 19th and 20th century art. Publ: Auth, Women artists in the academic world, Art & Sexual Polit, 73; auth, Ruth Vollmer's sculpture (catalog), Everson Mus, Syracuse, 74; auth, Art & sullen craft of portraiture, Craft Horizons, 74. Dealer: Betty Parsons Gallery 24 W 57th St New York NY 10019. Mailing Add: RI Sch of Design Providence RI 02903

HALL, LOUISE
EDUCATOR, ART HISTORIAN
b Cambridge, Mass, July 23, 05. Study: Wellesley Col, BA, 27; Mass Inst Technol, SB, 30; Univ Paris Inst Art & Archeol, 31; Harvard Univ, PhD(archit), 54. Teaching: Prof hist art & archit, Duke Univ, 31-75; retired. Mem: Life mem Soc Archit Historians (secy-treas, 49, vpres, 51); life mem Soc Archit Historians Gt Brit. Mailing Add: Box 2871 Durham NC 27705

HALL, MICHAEL DAVID
SCULPTOR, EDUCATOR
b Upland, Calif, May 20, 41. Study: Western Wash State Col, 58-60; Univ NC, BA, 62; Univ Iowa, 62; Univ Wash, MFA(sculpture), 64. Work: Princeton Univ Art Mus, NJ; Jacksonville Art Mus, Fla; Univ Iowa Art Mus, Iowa City; J B Speed Art Mus, Louisville, Ky; Wright State Univ. Exhib: Whitney Mus Am Art Ann Sculpture Exhib, New York, 68 & 73; Sculpture of the Month, New York City Dept Cult Affairs, 68; American Sculpture, Sheldon Mus, Univ Nebr, Lincoln, 70; Hammarskjold Plaza, New York, 72; Sculpture Off the Pedestal, Grand Rapids, Mich, 73; Three Installations, Detroit Inst of Arts, 77; Scale & Environment, Walker Art Ctr, Minneapolis, 77; plus numerous one-man shows. Teaching: Instr ceramics & sculpture, Univ Colo, Boulder, 65-66; assoc prof sculpture, Univ Ky, 66-70; resident sculptor, Cranbrook Acad Art, 70- Awards: Creative Res Grant, Univ Ky, 68-69; Guggenheim Found Fel, 73; Nat Endowment Art Fel, 74. Bibliog: Articles in Arts Mag, 6/75, 11/77 & 2/78 & Art in Am Mag, 1/78. Mem: Mus Am Folk Art; NY State Hist Asn; New Detroit Arts Div; Mich Coun Arts (adv). Style & Technique: Large scale works in fabricated metal for placement in landscape; concern with interaction of site and form. Media: Steel, Aluminum. Publ: Auth, American folk sculpture-the personal & the eccentric, 71; auth, articles in, Cranbrook Mag, 71-72; Icons of John Perates, Cincinnati Art Mus, 74; auth, The Artist as Collector, Brooklyn Mus, 76. Dealer: Feigenson-Rosenstein Gallery Rm 310 Fisher Bldg Detroit MI 48202. Mailing Add: 500 Lone Pine Rd Bloomfield Hills MI 48013

HALL, REX EARL
PAINTER, EDUCATOR
b Asbury, Mo, Feb 3, 24. Study: Washburn Univ, AB; Kansas City Art Inst; Univ Wichita, MFA. Work: Wichita Art Mus; Wichita State Univ. Exhib: Kans Ann, 56-63; Kans Biennial, 59-64; one-man shows, Birger Sandzen Gallery, 63, Kansas City Pub Libr, Mo, 63 & Wichita Art Mus, 64; plus others. Teaching: Prof art, Kans State Teachers Col, 60-68; prof art & chmn dept, Emporia Kans State Col, 69- Awards: Wichita Air Capital Award, 57 & 58; Living with Art, Wichita, 60; Designer-Craftsmen Show Award, Lawrence, Kans, 62. Mem: Kans Fedn Art (vpres, 62); Kans Art Educ Asn; Col Art Asn Am; Index Art Group (founder); Wichita Art Guild (vpres, 58-); plus others. Publ: Auth, A profile, Kans Art Educ Asn J, 61; auth, three booklets for Kans Art Educ Asn, 64-65; work reproduced in Collage & Assemblage, 73. Mailing Add: Dept of Art Emporia Kansas State Col Emporia KS 66801

HALL, SUSAN
PAINTER
b Point Reues Station, Calif, Mar 19, 43. Study: Calif Col of Arts & Crafts, Oakland, 62-65; Univ of Calif, Berkeley, 65-67, MA, 67. Work: Whitney Mus, New York; Cahse Manhattan Bank, New York; Security Pacific Nat Bank, Los Angeles. Exhib: San Francisco Mus of Art Ann, 66; Spirit of the Comics, Inst of Contemp Arts, Philadelphia, 69; Twenty-six Contemp Women Artists, Aldrich Mus of Contemp Art, Ridgefield, Conn, 71; Recent Acquisitions, 71 & Am Drawings: 1963-73, Whitney Mus, New York; New Am Landscape, Vassar Col, Poughkeepsie, New York, 73; Hand Colored Prints, Brooke Alexander Gallery, New York, 73; Drawing Show (traveling exhib), Nancy Hoffman Gallery, New York, 74; Womans Work: Am Art 1974, Mus of Philadelphia Civic Ctr, 74; Aspects of the Figure, Cleveland Mus of Art, Ohio, 74; Soho Artists, Baltimore Mus of Art, Md, 75; one-man shows, San Francisco Mus of Art, 67; Whitney Mus, 72 & Univ of Colo, Henderson Mus, Boulder, 73. Teaching: Instr, Univ of Calif, Berkeley, 67-70 & Sarah Lawrence Col, Bronxville, NY, 72-75. Bibliog: Alfred Frankenstein (auth), Extraordinary Realities, San Francisco Chronicle, 11/73; Henry J Seldis (auth), The Fine Art of Food: A Feast for the Eyes, Los Angeles Times, 11/74; Lucy R Lippard (auth), article in MS Mag, New York, 75. Mailing Add: 112 Water St New York NY 10005

HALLAM, BEVERLY (LINNEY)
PAINTER, LECTURER
b Lynn, Mass, Nov 22, 23. Study: Mass Col Art, BSEd, 45; Cranbrook Acad Art, 48; Syracuse Univ, MFA, 51-53. Work: Everson Mus, Syracuse, NY; Corcoran Gallery Art, Washington, DC; Colby Art Mus, Maine; Witte Mem Mus, San Antonio, Tex; Worcester Art Mus, Mass. Exhib: Shore Galleries, Boston, 59-75; View 1960, Inst Contemp Art, Boston, Mass, circulated throughout US by Smithsonian Inst, 60-61; Mus Fine Arts, Boston, 65; Art for US Embassies, Inst Contemp Art, Boston & State Dept, Washington, DC, 66; Am Watercolor Soc Traveling Exhib, 67; Watercolor USA, Springfield Art Mus, Mo, 68; Univ Maine, 69; Fairweather Hardin Gallery, Chicago, 69-78; 15 Years in Retrospect, Addison Gallery Am Art, 71; New England Women, De Cordova Mus, Lincoln, Mass, 75; 76 Maine Artists, State Mus, 76; Collector's Collect Contemp, 77 & Hallam Monotypes, 77, Inst Contemp Art, Boston; plus many other group & one-man shows. Teaching: Chmn art dept, Lasell Jr Col, 45-49; assoc prof painting & teacher educ, Mass Col Art, 49-62; lectr & demonstr, Use of Polyvinyl Acetate as Painting Medium, throughout Eastern US, 52- Awards: Pearl Safir Award for Outstanding Painting by a Woman, Silvermine Guild Artists, 55; Blanche E Colman Found Award, 60; Edwin T Webster Award, Boston Soc Watercolor Painters, 62. Bibliog: Roul Tunley (auth), Maine and her artists, Woman's Day, 8/64; Lynn Franklin (auth), Beverly finds a roller coaster, Maine Sun Telegram, 2/77. Mem: Am Fedn Arts; Ogunquit Art Asn (pres, 64); Barn Gallery Assocs (bd dir, 70-); Archives Am Art; Boston Watercolor Soc. Style & Technique: Contemporary, semi-abstract; technique with acrylics is with mica talc highly textured; technique with oils is on paper and gesso done with gelatin rollers. Publ: Illusr, Stamping/Diemaking (cover designs), Stanger Publ, 69-72; contribr, May Sarton, auth, House by the Sea, Norton, 77. Dealer: Frost Gully Gallery 92 Exchange Portland ME 04101; Hobe Sound Gallery Hobe Sound FL 33455. Hardin Gallery 101 E Ontario St Chicago IL 60614. Mailing Add: Surf Point York ME 03909

HALLEY, DONALD M, JR
MUSEUM DIRECTOR
b New Orleans, La, Dec 17, 33. Study: Cornell Univ, BA; Tulane Univ La, MFA. Collections Arranged: Numerous temporary exhibs for Norfolk Mus Arts & Sci, Va, Des Moines Art Ctr, Iowa & Hudson River Mus, Yonkers, NY. Teaching: Instr art educ, Old Dominion Col, summer 64; adj prof art res, Drew Univ, 71. Pos: From asst dir to assoc dir, Norfolk Mus Arts & Sci, 58-62; asst dir, Des Moines Art Ctr, 62-68; dir, Hudson River Mus, 68-77. Mem: Am Asn Mus; assoc mem Int Coun Mus; Northeast Mus Conf (bd gov, 71-72, vpres, 73-); NY State Asn Mus (coun, 73-75); Mus Collaborative New York (adv coun, 71-72). Publ: Auth, Norfolk Mus Bull, 59-62, auth, German Expressionism (catalog), Norfolk Mus, 60; auth, Des Moines Art Ctr Bull, 62-68, auth, Painting: Out from the Wall (catalog), Des Moines Art Ctr, 68; auth, Catalog of the American Republic Insurance Company Collection, 65. Mailing Add: 618 N Broadway Hastings-on-Hudson NY 10706

HALLMAN, GARY LEE
PHOTOGRAPHER
b St Paul, Minn, Aug 7, 40. Study: Univ Minn, Minneapolis, BA, 66, MFA, 71. Work: Mus Mod Art, New York; Int Mus Photog, Rochester; Nat Gallery Can, Toronto; Fogg Art Mus, Harvard Univ; Princeton Univ Art Mus. Comn: Photo murals, Dayton-Hudson Corp, Minneapolis, 70. Exhib: 60's Continuum, Int Mus Photog, 72; Fight of the Image, Contemporary American Drawings, Paintings & Photographs, Mus Turin, Italy, 73; one-man shows, Int Mus Photog, George Eastman House, 74 & Light Gallery, New York, 75; Fourteen American Photographers, Baltimore Mus, 75. Teaching: Vis artist, Southampton Col, summer 72 & 73; asst prof photog, Univ Minn, Minneapolis, 70-, assoc prof photog, 76; vis adj prof photog, RI Sch Design, 77. Awards: Grad Sch Univ Minn Res Grant, 73 & 76; Nat Endowment Arts Photog Fel Grant, 75; Bush Found Fel for Artists, 76. Bibliog: E W Peterson (auth), The photography of Gary Hallman, Image, 9/75. Mem: Soc Photog Educ. Dealer: Light Gallery 724 Fifth Ave New York NY 10019. Mailing Add: 25 N Fourth St Minneapolis MN 55401

HALLMAN, H THEODORE, JR
CRAFTSMAN
Study: Tyler Sch, Temple Univ, Sen scholar, BFA & BSEd; Fontainebleau Fine Arts, Pew scholar, cert, with Jacques Villon; Cranbrook Acad Art, West scholar, MFA(painting) & MFA(textile design); Bundestextilschule, Austria, cert. Univ Calif, Berkeley, PhD(educ); self-awareness study with Kenneth G Mills, Toronto. Work: Frontispiece to Textile Collection, Smithsonian Inst, Washington, DC; Mus Contemp Crafts, New York; Victoria & Albert Mus, London; Metrop Mus Art, New York; Philadelphia Mus Art, Pa. Comn: Translucent tapestry, Nieman Marcus, Dallas; room divider, Marshall Field & Co, Chicago; garden divider, Am Chem Soc, Washington, DC; altar hanging, Lutheran Church, Allentown, Pa; window hangings, Ashbourne Country Club, Philadelphia; plus others. Exhib: Int Kunsthandwerk, Stuttgart, 67; Objects USA Traveling Show, 69-72; Contemplation Environments, Mus Contemp Crafts, 70; Woven Structures, Camden Arts Ctr, London, 72; 1st Int Exhib Miniature Textiles, Brit Crafts Ctr, London, 74; one-man show, Royal Ont Mus, 78. Teaching: Instr, Haystack Sch, Maine & Penland Sch Crafts, summers 58-69; prof textiles & chmn dept, Moore Col Art, 65-70; assoc prof textile design, San Jose State Univ, 72-75; lectr & workshop leader, US, Can & Eng (incl San Antonio, Vancouver, Ottawa & Mich, 77-78); instr design, Ont Col of Art, Toronto; guest lectr, World Craft Conf, Mex, 76. Pos: Consult, ILO Textiles, Jamaica, summer 68; textile designer, var co. Awards: Tiffany Found Grant, 62; Textile Prize, Int Kunsthandwerk Expos, Stuttgart, 67. Bibliog: Neuman (auth), Plastics as an Art Form, Chilten, 68; Regensteiner (auth), Art of Weaving, 70 & Willcox (auth), Techniques of Rya Knotting, 71, Van Nostrand Reinhold; among others. Mem: Am Craftsmen Coun; Philadelphia Coun Prof Craftsmen (treas, 68-70); Ont Craft Coun (mem bd, 77-78); hon mem Int Soc Arts & Lett; Nat Soc Lit & Arts. Style & Technique: Structurist. Media: Weaving, Textile Designing. Mailing Add: Box 81 Lederach PA 19450

HALLMARK, DONALD PARKER
ART HISTORIAN, CURATOR
b McPherson, Kans, Feb 16, 45. Study: Univ Ill, BFA(art hist), 67; Univ Iowa, MA(art hist), 70; St Louis Univ, PhD cand. Collections Arranged: Richard W Bock Sculpture Collection (with catalog), Greenville Col, 75. Teaching: Assoc prof art & fine arts, Greenville Col, 70- Pos: Cur & dir, Richard W Bock Sculpture Collection, Greenville Col, 72-; pres, Bond Co Art & Cult Asn, Ill, 71-73. Awards: Kress Found Res Grant, Univ Iowa, 69; Shell Found Fac Improv Grant, 72-73; Nat Endowment Arts & Am Asn Mus Cur Seminar Scholar, 75. Bibliog: H Allen Brooks (auth), Prairie School, Univ Toronto, 72; W R Hasbrouck (auth), Editors note, Prairie Sch Rev, Vol VIII, No 1, 71. Mem: Am Asn Mus; Mid-Am Col Art Asn; Midwest Mus Conf. Res: Late 19th and early 20th century sculpture and architecture with emphasis on the Chicago School, 1880-1915. Publ: Auth, Richard W Bock, Sculptor, Prairie Sch Rev, 71. Mailing Add: Greenville Col Greenville IL 62246

HALLMARR, ANN
COLLECTOR
b Kansas City, Kans, Jan 1, 49. Study: St. Louis Univ. Collection: Contemporary prints and sculpture. Mailing Add: 2859 E Covina Mesa AZ 85203

HALPERN, LEA
CERAMIST, PAINTER
Study: Acad in Amsterdam, drawing, painting, sculpture & ceramics with Bert Nienhuis; Reiman Art Sch, Berlin, drawing, modelling & painting; Austrian Nat Art Sch, Vienna, drawing, sculpture, painting & ceramics with Prof M Powolny; Nat Res Sch for the Clay & Ceramic Indust, Gouda, Holland, dipl, study with Dr Kurt Zimmerman. Work: Baltimore Mus of Art, Md; Metrop Mus of Art, New York; Nat Collection of Fine Arts, Washington, DC; Victoria & Albert Mus, London; Tel Aviv Mus, Israel. Comn: The City of Amsterdam; Wertheim & Gomperts Bank, Amsterdam; Synagogue, The Hague; Temple Emanu El, Birmingham, Ala; New Sch Bldg, Chizuk Amuno Congregation, Baltimore. Exhib: One-woman shows, The Stedelijk Mus, Amsterdam, Ryksmuseum, Huis Lambert Van Meerten, Delft, Phillips Collection, Washington, DC, Baltimore Mus of Art, 76, Frans Hals Mus, Haarlem, Neth, plus others. Teaching: Instr ceramics, New Art Sch, Amsterdam, Univ of NH, Westchester Co Ctr, White Plains, NY & privately. Awards: French Ministry of Fine Arts Price for Holland, Int Exhib in the Jeu de Paume, Paris. Bibliog: Article in Artnews; G Forsythe (auth), 20th Century Ceramics, London; Otto Van Tussenbroek (auth), Gebruig & Moderne Schoonheid. Mem: Am Craft Coun; World Craft Coun; Md Craft Coun; Kiln Club of Washington; Artists Equity Asn. Mailing Add: 2714 Bartol Ave Baltimore MD 21209

HALPERN, NATHAN L
COLLECTOR
b Sioux City, Iowa, Oct 22, 14. Study: Otis Art Inst, Los Angeles; Univ Southern Calif, BA, 36; Harvard Univ Law Sch, LLB(cum laude), 39. Teaching: Lectr, Annenberg Sch Commun, Univ Pa, 66. Pos: Pres, TNT Commun, Inc. Collection: Predominantly French impressionist and post-impressionist art. Mailing Add: 993 Fifth Ave New York NY 10028

HALSETH, ELMER JOHANN
PATRON, COLLECTOR
b Rutland, SDak. Study: Eastern Col, BA; Wyo Univ, MA. Pos: Art sponsor, Rock Springs High Sch, Wyo, 38-63; art dir, Rock Springs Fine Arts Ctr, 63-69; mem, Wyo Coun Arts, 65-74. Awards: Halseth Gallery established in Rock Springs in honor of work in promoting arts in schools and building Rock Springs High School collection of 200 original contemporary paintings by nationally and internationally recognized artists, 75. Collection: Contemporary American, Mexican, Canadian & European paintings. Pos: Founding mem, Western Wyo Jr Col, Rock Springs, 57; chmn of Art Train visit to western Wyo. Publ: Art in Time Mag, 11/24/52 & in state art and educ jour. Mailing Add: PO Box 506 Rock Springs WY 82901

HALSEY, WILLIAM MELTON
PAINTER, EDUCATOR
b Charleston, SC, Mar 13, 15. Study: Univ SC; Sch Boston Mus Fine Arts, Paige traveling fel, 39-41, with Alexandre Iacovleff & Karl Zerbe; Univ Mex. Work: Baltimore Mus Art, Md; SC Arts Comn State Collection, Columbia; Mint Mus Art, Charlotte, NC; Gibbes Art Gallery, Charleston; Greenville Co Mus Art, SC. Comn: Three frescoes, Berkshire Mus Art, Pittsfield, Mass, 39; murals, Beth Elohim Synagogue, Charleston, 50, Baltimore Hebrew Congregation Temple, 52 & Sears Roebuck Co, Charleston, 54; also comns from Container Corp Am & Ford Motor Co. Exhib: Cent SC Exhib Tenn Art League, Parthenon, Nashville, 67; SC State Invitational, Columbia Mus Art, 69; Contemp Artists SC, Columbia Mus, Florence Mus, Greenville Mus & Gibbes Art Gallery, 70; Springs Mills Traveling Exhibs, New York, 71-72; retrospective, four SC mus, 72-73; Art in Transition, Boston Mus Fine Arts, 77. Teaching: Asst prof painting & drawing, Col Charleston, 65-75; instr painting & drawing, Newberry Col, 68-70; artist-in-residence, Col Charleston, 76- Awards: Hughes Found res grants, 50-52; Res Grant, SC State Art Comn, 74-75. Bibliog: Jack Morris (auth), Contemporary Artists of South Carolina, 70 & William M Halsey: retrospective (monogr), 72, Greenville Co Mus Art. Mem: Guild SC Artists (pres, 58). Media: Oil, Casein, Collage. Publ: Co-auth, A Travel Sketch Book, 71; auth, Maya Journal, 77. Mailing Add: 38 State St Charleston SC 29401

HALVORSEN, RUTH ELISE
PAINTER, WRITER
b Camas, Wash. Study: Portland Art Mus Sch, Ore; Pratt Inst, Brooklyn; Columbia Univ; and with Walter Beck, Charles Martin & Albert Heckman. Work: Reed Col, Portland; Georgia-Pacific, Portland; Univ Ore, Eugene; Ft Sumner Marine Hosp, NMex; Portland Art Mus. Exhib: San Francisco World's Fair, 39; Henry Gallery, Univ Wash, 43; Rockefeller Ctr, New York, 48; Fifth Army Midwestern Travel Show, 55; Portland Art Mus Show, 71. Teaching: Instr art, Portland State Col, 40-60; art supvr, Portland Pub Schs, 43-62. Awards: Pratt Inst Alumni Award for Distinguished Serv in Art Educ, 72; Distinguished Serv Award, Nat Art Educ Asn, 74. Mem: Portland Art Mus (mem bd, 47-53); Ore Contemp Crafts Asn (mem bd, 44-71); Nat Art Educ Asn (mem bd, 47-, vpres & pres, 59-63); Pac Art Asn (vpres & pres, 55-57); Contemp Crafts. Media: Watercolor, Oil. Publ: Co-auth, Painting in the classroom, 62; contribr, Art J; also numerous articles for var art mags. Mailing Add: 422 NE Going St Portland OR 97211

HAMADY, MARY LAIRD
See Laird, Mary

HAMADY, WALTER SAMUEL
GRAPHIC ARTIST, PAPERMAKER
b Flint, Mich, Sept 13, 40. Study: Wayne State Univ, BFA, 64; Cranbrook Acad Art, MFA, 66. Work: Numerous public and private collections. Exhib: Walker Art Ctr, Minneapolis, Minn, 68; Int Bk Art Fair, Leipzig, Ger, 71; Kansas City Art Inst Bk Exhib, 71; Albion Print & Drawing Show, 72; one-man show, Grolier Club, New York, 72-73. Teaching: Assoc prof drawing, typography & papermaking, Univ Wis-Madison, 66- Pos: Proprietor, The Perishable Press Limited. Awards: Wis Alumni Res Found grants, 66-78; 50 Best Books, Am Inst Graphic Art, 67, 69 & 76; Nat Endowment for the Arts grants, 76-78. Bibliog: Joseph Blumenthal (auth), The Printed Book in America, Dartmouth/Godine, 77; Book Publishing in Wisconsin, Wis Hist Soc, 77; Paul H Duensing (auth), Type for Esoteric Languages, 77. Mem: Wis Phenological Soc; Friends of Kurt Schwitters. Style & Technique: Incised drawings; collage; assemblage; papermaking by hand; printing; books; birdfeeders. Res: Typecasting; Sequoyah Syllabary. Publ: Auth, Papermaking by hand, In: Among Friends, Detroit Pub Libr, spring 66; auth, The Plumfoot Poems, 69 & auth, Since Mary, 71, New Directions; auth, These Chairs, 71, The Interminable Gabberjabbs (ser illus poems), 74-75 & Wowa's First Book, 77, Perishable Press. Mailing Add: PO Box 7 Mt Horeb WI 53572

HAMBLETT, THEORA
PAINTER, ILLUSTRATOR
b Paris, Miss, Jan 15, 95. Study: Univ Southern Miss; Univ Miss; Famous Artists Sch, Westport, Conn. Work: Mus Mod Art, New York; Brooks Mem Art Gallery, Memphis; First Nat Bank, Jackson, Miss; also in pvt collections of Vice Pres Nelson Rockefeller, New York & Alec Guinness, Eng; plus many others. Exhib: Atlanta Art Asn, Ga, 65; 50 Artists from 50 States, Am Fedn Arts Traveling Exhib, 66-67; Sixth Nat Biennial Religious Art, Cranbrook Acad Art, Mich; 17 Naive Painters, Mus Mod Art Traveling Exhib, 66-67; Symbols and Images, Am Fedn Arts, 70-72; plus many others. Teaching: Asst to beginners, O'Tuckolota Consolidated High Sch, 24-31. Bibliog: B Oesterling (auth), Paintings of Theora Hamblett (film), Univ Miss, 67; Guy Northrop (auth), Hamblett's paintings, Sun Com Appeal, Memphis, 72; Dr L Dollarhide (auth), Hamblett's work, Jackson Daily, 72. Mem: Miss Art Asn; Oxford-Lafayette Art Asn; Kate Skipwith Geneal Soc; Miss Folklore Soc. Media: Oil, Pencil Drawing. Publ: Auth, Heaven's Descent to Earth, 60; auth, Symbols of Faith, 66; co-auth, Dreams Can Work for You, 70; co-auth, I Remember, 71. Dealer: Parsons Gallery 24 W 57th St New York NY 10019. Mailing Add: 619 Van Buren Ave Oxford MS 38655

HAMEL, BERNARD FRANKLIN
PAINTER
b Holyoke, Mass, May 29, 33. Study: Art Students League, 51-52; Pratt Inst, 56-59. Exhib: 152nd Ann Nat Exhib, Nat Acad Design, NY, 2/77; 28th Nat Exhib, Acad Artists Asn, Springfield, Mass, 5/77; 67th Ann Exhib, Conn Acad Fine Arts, Wadsworth Atheneum, 5/77; 42nd Nat Art Exhib, Cooperstown Art Asn, NY, 7/77; 24th Nat Exhib, Nat Soc Painters in Casein & Acrylic, New York, 11/77. Awards: Gold Medal of Honor, Acad Artists Asn, 77; Margaret Cooper Mem Award, Conn Acad Fine Arts, 77; Traditional Painting Award, Silvermine Guild, Conn Bank & Trust Co, 77. Mem: Nat Soc Painters in Casein & Acrylic, New York; Berkshire Art Asn, Pittsfield, Mass; Acad Artists Asn, Springfield, Mass; Nat Arts Club, New York. Style & Technique: Realistic painting. Media: Acrylic; Pen & Ink. Dealer: Genesis Gallery 41 E 57th St New York NY 10022. Mailing Add: 144 High St Holyoke MA 01040

HAMER, MARILOU HEILMAN
ART DEALER, LECTURER
b Evanston, Ill, June 19, 22. Study: Acad Fine Arts, Ill; Chicago Art Inst; Northwest Univ, BA(cumlaude), 44; Montclair State Col, MA(art hist), 75. Collections Arranged: Allegheney Corp, 72; Montclair Art Mus, 75; Va Mus of Fine Art, 75; Montclair High Sch, 76; Temple Shomrei Emunah, 77; Fairlawn Pub Libr, 78; Montclair State Col, 78. Teaching: Instr art, Montclair, NJ, 74-75; instr art hist, St Pete's Col, Jersey City, NJ, 77-78. Pos: Dir, Gallery Graphics, Upper Montclair, NJ, 67-72; dir, Discovery Art Galleries, Clifton, NJ, 72-78. Mem: Arts Coun of NW NJ; Printmaking Coun of NJ; Women's Caucus for Art, NJ; Montclair Art Mus, NJ. Specialty: Contemporary American art, espically fine original prints. Collection: Contemporary American prints. Mailing Add: c/o Discovery Galleries 1191 Valley Rd Clifton NJ 07013

HAMES, CARL MARTIN
ART DEALER, COLLECTOR
b Birmingham, Ala, July 12, 38. Study: Birmingham Southern Col, BA, 58; Samford Univ, Birmingham, MA, 71, with Cornelia Rivers & Gene Smith. Collections Arranged: Burgoyne Diller Retrospective, Birmingham Southern Col, 65; Five Ala Draftsmen—Survey of Contemp Drawing in Ala, Town Hall Gallery, Birmingham, 69; Artists of Ala, Ferrum Col, Va, 70; Five Women Artists of Ala, 70, Decade of Effective Painting in Ala, Birmingham Centennial, 71, Eye Found Art—The Collection of the Eye Found Hosp (auth, catalogue), 75-77, Rx Art: The collection of the Spain Rehabilitation Ctr (auth, catalogue), 75, Honored Artists of Ala for the Greek-Am Bicentennial Festival of Arts, 76, Salon des Refuses (works recently refused in US juried exhib), 77, Mus Quality (auth, catalogue), 78 & Collection of Altamont Sch, Town Hall Gallery, Birmingham. Teaching: Teacher art/sci, Birmingham Pub Sch, 62-64; teacher art & organizer art dept, Birmingham Univ Sch, 64-75; asst headmaster, Altamont Sch, 75- Pos: Dir, Town Hall Gallery, Birmingham, 65-; vpres visual arts, Birmingham Festival of Arts, 65, 74 & 78; ed, Birmingham Art Asn Newsletter, 73-78; co-ed, Birmingham Mus of Art Bull, 73-75. Awards: Silver Bowl Award for Art, Birmingham Festival of Arts. Mem: Birmingham Arts Mus Art Educ Coun; Birmingham Art Asn; Birmingham Mus of Art; Ala Mus of Photog (mem bd). Specialty: Alabama and southeastern artists. Collection: Prints by 20th century European and American masters; sculptures, paintings and contemporary photographs. Publ: Auth (introd, catalogue), Short-Lived Moments of Elation, Ida Kohlmeyer Retrospective, Birmingham Mus of Art, 11/75; contirbr (introd), Patricia Gaines (auth), Soft, Morrow Co, 77; auth, Hill Ferguson: A Biography, Univ Ala, in press; auth (two television progs), Rosalie Pettus Price—The Implacable Abstraction of Objects, WBIQ, Birmingham & The World of Doris Wainwright Kennedy, WBIQ, Birmingham. Mailing Add: 3317D Old Montgomery Hwy Birmingham AL 35209

HAMILTON, FRANK MOSS
PAINTER, ARCHITECT
b Kansas City, Mo, June 26, 30. Study: With Eliot O'Hara; Stanford Univ, 2 years; Univ Kans, BA(archit), 54. Work: Favell Mus, Klamath Falls, Ore; Leanin' Tree Gallery, Boulder, Colo; Walter Bimson's Valley Nat Bank Collection. Exhib: Laguna Beach Festival of Arts, Calif, 49-68; Orange Co Fair, 51; Laguna Art Asn Gallery; Nat Orange Show, Pomona; Gold Medal Western Competition, Franklin Mint Yearly Western Show, 74. Teaching: Pvt art classes, 49-67. Awards: First Awards, Laguna Beach Art Festival, 63-65; First Prizes, Lake San Marcos Art Festival, 66, 68; Third Place, Franklin Mint Bicentennial Medal Design, 72. Style & Technique: Realism; opaque, dry brush watercolor. Media: Watercolor. Publ: Illusr, Orange Co Illus Mag, Calif, 66, 69 & Jerome Arizona Cookbook, 72. Mailing Add: PO Box 733 Cambria CA 93428

HAMILTON, GEORGE HEARD
MUSEUM DIRECTOR, ART HISTORIAN
b Pittsburgh, Pa, June 23, 10. Study: Yale Univ, BA, MA, PhD. Teaching: Mem dept hist art, Yale Univ, 36-66; Robert Sterling Clark vis prof art, Williams Col, 63-64, prof art, 66-75, emer prof, 75-; Slade prof fine arts, Cambridge Univ, 71-72. Pos: Curatorial staff, Yale Univ Art Gallery, 36-66; dir, Sterling & Francine Clark Art Inst, Williamstown, Mass, 66-77, emer dir, 77-; vpres & trustee, Hill-Stead Mus, Farmington, Conn; trustee, Mus Mod Art, New York; vchmn & trustee, Joseph H Hirshhorn Mus & Sculpture Garden, Washington, DC, 71-75. Mem: Col Art Asn Am (pres, 66-68). Res: 19th and 20th century European and American art. Publ: Auth, Manet & his Critics, 54; Russian Art & Architecture, 54; European Painting & Sculpture, 1880-1940, 67; co-auth, Raymond Duchamp-Villon, 67; auth, 19th & 20th Century Art—Painting, Sculpture, Architecture, 70. Mailing Add: 121 Gale Rd Williamstown MA 01267

HAMILTON, JOHN
PRINTMAKER
Study: Mus Art Sch, Portland, Ore; Ozenfant Sch of Fine Art, New York; Art Students League; Reed Col, Portland; San Francisco State Col, BA & MA. Work: Albright-Knox Art Gallery, Buffalo, NY; Addison Gallery of Am Art, Andover, Mass; Boston Mus of Fine Art; New Britain Mus of Am Art, Conn; Rochester Mem Art Gallery, NY. Exhib: Reed Col; Raymond Col, Stockton, Calif; Oakland Mus, Calif; Chabot Col, Hayward, Calif; Fitchburg Mus, Mass; New Britain Mus of Am Art, Conn; Albright-Knox Art Gallery; Stanford Mus, Palo Alto, Calif; Printmotif, Hong Kong; Wesleyan Univ, Conn. Awards: Ford Found Fel, 57-58; San Francisco Found Fel, 70-71. Mailing Add: c/o Francine Ullman Fidelity Arts 9000 Beverly Blvd Los Angeles CA 90048

HAMILTON, PATRICIA ROSE
ART DEALER, CURATOR
b Upper Darby, Pa, Oct 21, 48. Study: Temple Univ, BA, 70; Rutgers Univ, MA(art hist), 71. Collections Arranged: Ten Americans, Masters of Watercolor (with catalogue), 74, Edward Hicks, A Gentle Spirit (with catalogue), 75 & Malta: A Totemic World, 75, Andrew Crispo Gallery; Outdoor Sculpture 1974 (with catalogue), Merriewold West Gallery, Far Hills, NJ, 74. Pos: Curatorial asst, Whitney Mus Am Art, New York, 71-73; sr ed, Art in Am, New York, 73-74; cur exhibs, Andrew Crispo Gallery, New York, 74-75; assoc mem, Patricia Hamilton Traveling Exhibs, 75; dir, Hamilton Gallery Contemp Art, 77- Mem: Artist's Cert Comt. Specialty: Contemporary art. Mailing Add: 39 Fifth Ave New York NY 10003

HAMLETT, DALE EDWARD
EDUCATOR, PAINTER
b Memphis, Mo, Aug 15, 21. Study: Northeast Mo State Univ, BS(cum laude), 44; Am Acad Art, with William Mosby; Acad Appl Art, Chicago; Chicago Art Inst, with Charles Wilamoski; Univ NMex, with Ralph Douglass & Elaine de Kooning, MA(painting), 63; also with Robert Wood, Millard Sheets & George Post. Work: Univ NMex; State Fair Mus, Albuquerque; NMex Inst Mining & Technol; Eastern NMex Univ. Comn: Series of portraits, comn by Mrs William Givens, Socorro, NMex, 67; proposed redesigning of plaza, Mayor, City of Socorro, 68; drawings of 17 founders of Sigma Tau Gamma, Warrensburg, Mo, 71; painting, KOA Campgrounds, Las Vegas, NMex, 75. Exhib: Sun Carnival, El Paso Mus Art, Tex, 71; Eight State Regional Watercolor Exhibs, Fedn Rocky Mt States, Inc, 71-72; 23rd Grand Prix Int de Peinture, Deauville, France, 73; Gran Premio della Citta Eterna Palazzo delle Esposizioni, Rome, Italy, 73; 14th Ann Artists Salon, Nat Show, Okla Mus Art, Oklahoma City, 75. Teaching: Instr art, NMex Inst Mining & Technol, 65-69; assoc prof art, Eastern NMex Univ, 69- Pos: Package designer, Montgomery Ward & Co, Chicago, Ill, 47-51; commercial artist, Ward Hicks Advert Agency, Albuquerque, 51-64; artist in residence, NMex Inst Mining & Technol, 64-69. Awards: First for Watercolor, Int Exhib, Val d'Isere, France, 73, Gallery, Albuquerque, 75 & Ken Roberts Gallery, Albuquerque, NMex, 77; Second Grand Award/Watercolor, Panama City, Fla, 77. Mem: Artists Equity; NMex Watercolor Soc (eastern NMex rep, 72); Nat Arts Educ Asn; Int Soc of Artists; Clovis-Portales Arts Coun (mem bd dirs, 71, 73-74, vpres, 72 & 77-78, pres, 75); NMex Art League; Am Asn Univ Prof. Style & Technique: Realism and surrealism; play of light and shadow so as to create depth and mood; from wet into wet to dry brush, mostly landscapes including western subjects. Media: Watercolor, Acrylic. Mailing Add: 2104 S Ave H Portales NM 88130

HAMMER, ALFRED EMIL
PAINTER, ART ADMINISTRATOR
b New Haven, Conn, Jan 11, 25. Study: RI Sch Design, BFA; Yale Univ, BFA & MFA; and with John R Frazier, Josef Albers, Willem DeKooning, Stuart Davis, Abraham Rattner, Alvin Lustig & John Howard Benson. Work: Nat JC Mus, Israel; Cleveland Art Asn; RI Sch Design. Exhib: Providence Art Club Ann, RI, 53-67; Columbia Biennial, SC, 58; Newport Ann, RI, 60; Boston Art Festival, Mass, 60; Four Americans, La State Univ, 62. Teaching: Assoc prof painting, drawing, design & calligraphy, RI Sch Design, 53-69, chmn div grad studies, 63-65; vis lectr design & painting, Minneapolis Col Art, 67; dean inst, Cleveland Inst Art, 69-74; vis lectr design & painting, Case Western Reserve Univ, 70; dir sch art, Univ Man, 74- Awards: First Prize, RI Artists Ann, 53, Providence Art Club Ann, 54, 55 & 56 & Newport Ann, 60. Style & Technique: Semi-abstract. Media: Oil, Watercolor. Mailing Add: 130 King's Dr Ft Garry MB Can

HAMMER, ARMAND
COLLECTOR, ART DEALER
b New York, NY, May 21, 98. Study: Columbia Univ, New York, BS, 19, Col Physicians & Surgeons, MD, 21. Exhib: (Armand Hammer Collection) Brooks Mem Art Gallery, Memphis, Tenn, 69; Smithsonian Inst, Washington, DC, William Rockhill Nelson Gallery Art, Kansas City, Mo, Isaac Delgado Mus Art, New Orleans, La & Columbus Gallery Fine Arts, Ohio, 70; Ark Art Ctr, Little Rock, Calif Palace of the Legion of Honor, San Francisco, Okla Art Ctr, Oklahoma City & Fine Arts Gallery of San Diego, Calif, 71; Los Angeles Co Mus Art, Los Angeles, Calif, Royal Acad Art, London, Eng, Nat Gallery Ireland, Dublin & Hermitage Mus, Leningrad, USSR, 72; Pushkin Mus, Moscow, State Mus Fine Art of the Ukraine Soviet Socialist Repub, Kiev, State Fine Art Mus, Minsk, State Mus Foreign Fine Arts, Riga & Fine Arts Mus, Odessa, USSR, 73; Mus de Bellos Artes, Caracas, Venezuela, Mus de Arte Italiano, Lima, Peru, Seibu Mus Art, Tokyo, Japan & Kyoto Munic Mus, Japan, 75; Fukuoka Prefectural Cult Ctr, Fukuoka, Japan, Aichi Prefecture Mus, Magoya, Japan & Tenn Fine Arts Ctr Cheekwood, Nashville, 76; Palace of Fine Arts, Mexico City, Mex, Louvre Mus (drawings), Paris, France, Jacquemart-Andre Mus, Paris & J Paul Getty Mus, Malibu, Calif, 77; High Mus, Atlanta, Ga, 78. Collections Arranged: Impressionist and Post-Impressionist Paintings from the USSR, lent by the Hermitage Mus, Leningrad & the Pushkin Mus, Moscow, exhib at Nat Gallery Art, Washington, DC, M Knoedler & Co, Inc, New York, Los Angeles Co Mus Art, Art Inst Chicago, Kimbell Art Mus, Ft Worth, Tex & Detroit Inst Fine Arts, Mich, 73; Master Paintings from the Hermitage and the State Russian Mus, Leningrad, exhib at Nat Gallery Art, M Knoedler & Co, Inc, Detroit Inst Arts, Los Angeles Co Mus Art & Mus Fine Arts, Houston, Tex, 75-76; Paintings from the Nat Gallery Art, Los Angeles Co Mus Art, Detroit Inst Fine Arts, Mus Fine Arts, Houston & Buffalo Bill Mus, Cody, Wyo, sent to Leningrad, Moscow & Kiev, Russia & Jacquemart-Andre Mus, Paris, France, 75. Pos: Pres, Hammer Galleries, Inc, New York, 30-; chmn, M Knoedler & Co, Inc, 72- Awards: Comdr Order Crown, King Baudoin of Belg, 69; Comdr Order Andres Bellos, Armand Hammer Collection, Govt Repub Venezuela, 76; Order Aztec Eagle, Armand Hammer Collection, Govt Repub Mex, 77. Mem: Los Angeles Co Mus Art (mem bd trustees & mem acquisition comt, 68-); Munic Arts Comnrs City Los Angeles (mem bd, 69-73); Los Angeles Beautiful, Inc, Los Angeles Chamber Com (mem adv bd, 69-); Americana Comt of the Nat Archives; Royal Acad Arts, London (hon corresp mem, 75-). Collection: Paintings from Rubens and Rembrandt, to selected works by major American artists such as Gilbert Stuart, Harnett, Sargent, Prendergast, Mary Cassatt and Thomas Eakins; Impressionists and their precursors, including Van Gogh, Gauguin, Monet, Pissaro, Degas, Renoir and Cezanne; twentieth century works of Chagall, Picasso, Soutine and Mondigliani; master drawings by Durer, Raphael, Leonardo da Vinci, Michelangelo, Corregio, Fragonard and Watteau, among others. Publ: Ed mag, The Compleat Collector, Vols IV-VI, 44-46. Mailing Add: 10889 Wilshire Blvd Suite 1500 Los Angeles CA 90024

HAMMER, VICTOR J
ART DEALER
b New York, NY, Nov 1, 01. Study: Colgate Univ; Princeton Univ. Pos: Pres, Appraisers Asn Am, 64; dir, Hammer Galleries. Specialty: 19th and 20th century French art; Western American art, especially Charles M Russell and Frederic Remington; impressionist and post-impressionist paintings; elegant epoch paintings. Mailing Add: 781 Fifth Ave New York NY 10022

HAMMERSLEY, FREDERICK
PAINTER
b Salt Lake City, Utah, Jan 5, 19. Study: Univ Idaho Southern Br; Chouinard Art Sch, Los Angeles; Ecole Beaux Arts, Paris, France; Jepson Art Inst, Los Angeles. Work: Univ Art Mus, Univ Calif, Berkeley; Butler Inst Am Art, Youngstown, Ohio; Santa Barbara Mus Art, Calif; US Navy, Washington, DC; Corcoran Gallery, Washington, DC. Exhib: Abstract Classicists, San Francisco Mus Art, Los Angeles Co Mus Art & Inst Contemp Art, London, Eng, 59-60; Purist Painting, Am Fedn Arts Traveling Show, 60-61; Responsive Eye, Mus Mod Art, New York, 62; Geometric Abstraction Am, Whitney Mus Am Art, New York, 62; Art Across Am, Mead Corp & Traveling Show, 65-67; 35th Biennial, Corcoran Gallery, 77; Calif: Five Footnotes to Mod Art Hist, 77 & Private Images: Photographs by Painters, 77, Los Angeles Co Art Mus, Los Angeles. Teaching: Lectr painting, drawing & design, Pomona Col, 53-62; instr painting, drawing & design, Chouinard Art Inst, 64-68; vis assoc prof painting & drawing, Univ NMex, 68-71. Pos: Guest lectr, Tamarind Inst, Albuquerque, NMex, 73. Awards: Purchase Awards for Painting, Butler Inst Am Art, 61 & Los Angeles All City Ann, 64-66; Guggenheim Fel Painting, 73-74; Nat Endowment for the Arts for Painting, 75 & 77. Bibliog: Jules Langsner (auth), Four abstract classicists, Los Angeles Co Mus Art, 59; Lawrence Alloway (auth), West Coast hard edge, Inst Contemp Art, London, 60; Michel Seuphor(auth), Abstract Painting, Abrams, 62. Style & Technique: Flat shapes in oil paint with a palette knife on stretched linen canvas. Publ: Contribr, Classicism or hard-edge?, 60 & Los Angeles letter, 2/61, Art Int; auth, My first experience with computer drawings, 10/69 & My geometrical paintings, 4/70, Leonardo Mag. Dealer: Middendorf/Lane Gallery 2014 P St NW Washington DC 20036. Mailing Add: 608 Carlisle SE Albuquerque NM 87106

HAMMETT, POLLY HORTON
INSTRUCTOR, PAINTER
b Oklahoma City, Okla, Jan 31, 30. Study: Univ Okla, 48-50; Union for Experimental Cols, BA, 78; study with Richard V Goetz, Chen Chi, Milford Zornes & Millard Sheets. Work: Albuquerque Mus Art; Houston Neurosensory Ctr; Women's Hosp-Houston; Houston Power & Lighting. Exhib: Ninth, 10th & 11th Ann Artists Salon, Okla Mus Art,s 70, 71 & 72; 31st Artists Ann Exhib, Philbrook Art Ctr, Tulsa, 71; Watercolor USA, Springfield Mus Art, Mo, 72; Eight-State Exhib Painting & Sculpture, Okla Art Ctr, 74; Rocky Mt Watermedia Exhib, Foothills Art Ctr, Golden, Colo, 74, 75 & 76; Dimention Houston, 74 & 76; Audubon Artists Ann Exhib, Nat Acad Galleries, New York, 75; 100th Ann Am Watercolor Soc Ann, Nat Acad Galleries, 76; Watercolor, Southwest Two, Tucson Mus Art, 76; Am Watercolor Soc Traveling Exhib, 76-77; Nat Watercolor Soc 56th Ann, Laguna Beach Mus Art, Calif, 76. Teaching: Instr watercolor sem, Okla Arts Coun, 73; instr watercolor workshops, Okla & Tex, 69-77; originator workshop, The Art Experience, Tex Inst Child Psychiat, Houston, 74 & 75 & Houston Univ, Sch Continuing Educ, 76-77. Awards: Juror's Selection for Purchase, Eight-State Exhib Painting & Sculpture, Okla Art Ctr, 72; First Watercolor Award, 6th Ann Nat Small Painting Exhib, NMex, 76; Mus Purchase Award & Merit Award Watercolor, Southwest One, Albuquerque Art Mus, 76. Mem: Nat Watercolor Soc; Am Art Therapist Asn; Watercolor Art Soc-Houston (chmn prof stand comt). Style & Technique: Exploration of design and pattern with bold color in figure painting and landscape using wipe-out technique in watercolor. Media: Watercolor. Dealer: DuBose Gallery 2950 Kirby Dr Houston TX 77098. Mailing Add: 1314 W Alabama Houston TX 77006

HAMMOCK, VIRGIL GENE
EDUCATOR, PAINTER
b Long Beach, Calif, Aug 5, 38; Can citizen. Study: San Francisco Art Inst, BFA, 65, with James Weeks; Ind Univ, MFA, 67, with James McGarrell. Work: Ind Univ, Bloomington; Univ Alta, Edmonton; Art Bank Collection, Can Coun, Ottawa, Ont. Exhib: The 84th Ann, San Francisco Mus of Art, Calif, 65; Young Alta Painters, Alta Col of Art, Calgary, 68; West-71, Edmonton Art Gallery, 71; Olympic Exhib, Montreal, 75; one-man shows, Owens Art Gallery, Sackville, NB, 73 & Drawings, Dalhousie Art Gallery, Halifax, NS, 77; two-man show with Arnold Saper, Gallery 111, Univ Man, Winnipeg, 74. Teaching: Instr design & drawing, Univ Alta, Edmonton, 67-68, asst prof drawing & art hist, 68-70; assoc prof art criticism, Univ Man, Winnipeg, 70-75; prof & head, Dept Art Criticism, Mt Allison Univ, 75- Awards: Phelan Award, Young Calif Painters, Trustees of the James D Phelan Awards in Lit & Art, 65. Mem: Univs Art Asn of Can (pres, 73-); Int Asn of Art Critics, Can Sect (pres, 76-). Style & Technique: Realist. Media: Oil, pencil. Res: Contemporary Canadian painting. Publ: Auth, Lochead et le Pistolet, 72, Tony Tascona—La Succès Intérieur, 75, The Fly and the Elephant, 75, Retour à Magritte ou comment l'Ouest Canadien a éte conquis, 75 & Alex Colville—la Perfection dans le Relisme, 76, Vie des Arts. Dealer: Thomas Gallery 460 River Ave Winnipeg MB Can. Mailing Add: PO Box 1780 Sackville NB E0A 3C0 Can

HAMMOND, GALE THOMAS
PRINTMAKER, EDUCATOR
b Lumberton, NC, Sept 27, 39. Study: Chicago Acad Fine Arts, 57-59; ECarolina Univ, 62-64, BS & MA; Univ NC, Greensboro; Atelier 17, Paris, with S W Hayter, 77. Work: High Mus, Atlanta; NC Mus Art, Raleigh; Del Mar Col, Corpus Christi; Univ NC Sch Pub Health, Chapel Hill; Southern Ill Univ, Carbondale. Exhib: Colorprint USA, Lubbock, Tex, 72; Ann Exhib, Davidson Col, NC, 73; Boston Printmakers, Mass, 75; New American Graphics, Madison Art Ctr, Wis, 75; Galerie Liliane Francois & Galerie Seder, Paris. Teaching: Assoc prof drawing & printmaking, Univ Ga, Athens, 70- Awards: Etching Award, Southeastern Ctr for Contemporary Art, NC, 68; Drawing Award, Ga Arts Comn, Atlanta, 71; Etching Award, Southeastern Printmakers, Western Carolina Univ, NC, 75. Mem: Southeastern Graphics Coun (pres, 74-). Style & Technique: Etching techniques and aquatints, soft ground and line; drawing techniques of pen and ink, charcoal and pastel. Mailing Add: 257 Morton Ave Athens GA 30601

HAMMOND, HARMONY
PAINTER, SCULPTOR
b Chicago, Ill, Feb 8, 44. Study: Jr Sch Art Inst Chicago, 60-61; Milliken Univ, 61-63; Univ Minn, BFA, 67; Alliance Francaise, Paris, summers 67 & 69. Work: Mus Univ Mass; Western Mich Univ; Indianapolis Mus of Art, Ind; St Thomas More Chapel, Fordham Univ, Bronx, NY; Univ Mass Mus, Amherst; Univ Minn; Benjamin & Abbey Grey Found, St Paul. Exhib: One-woman shows, AIR Gallery, New York, 73 & Lamagna Gallery, New York, 76; Soft as Art, New York Cult Ctr, 73; Earth, Air & Water Presences, Bevier Gallery, Rochester Inst Technol, 74; A Woman's Group, Nancy Hoffman Gallery, New York, 74; Nancy Hoffman Gallery, New York, 74 & 77; Primitive Presence in the 70's, Vassar Col Art Gallery, 75; Touching on Nature, 55 Mercer St Gallery, New York, 77; Consciousness & Content, Brooklyn Mus, NY, 77; Out of the House, Downtown Whitney Mus, New York, NY, 78. Teaching: Instr & visiting artist painting, Art Inst Chicago, 73; lectr, Skidmore Col, 73, State Univ NY Col Purchase, 73 & Montclair State Col, 73-74; instr drawing, Richmond Col, 75; asst prof drawing, NY Inst Technol, Old Westbury, 77; vis artist, Univ Colo, Boulder, 77; asst prof drawing & painting & vis artist, Tyler Sch of Fine Art, Philadelphia, Pa, 77. Bibliog: Roberta Smith (auth), rev in Art Forum, 4/73; Paul Stitelman (auth), Suggesting a transference, Arts Mag, 9/73; Rosemary Mayer (auth), New trends in painting & sculpture, Info & Documents, Paris, 9/75; Carter Ratcliff (auth), On contemporary Primitivism, Art Forum, 11/75 & rev in Arts Mag, 3/76; Barbara Zucker (auth), rev in Art in Am, 5/76; Lucy Lippard, From the Center: Feminist Essays on Women's Art, Dutton, 76. Mem: Heresies. Media: Oil, Gouache; Cloth, Clay. Publ: Auth, Intro, Contemporary Graphics Published by Universal Limited Art Editions (catalog), Dayton's Gallery 12, Minneapolis, 68; auth, More on women's art: an exchange, Art in Am, 11/76; auth, Feminist abstract painting—a political viewpoint, Heresies, 12/77; plus others. Mailing Add: 129 W 22nd St New York NY 10011

HAMMOND, LESLIE KING
ART HISTORIAN, WRITER
b Bronx, NY, Aug 4, 44. Study: Queens Col, with Louis Finkelstein, Herb Aach, Paul Frazer, Marvin Belick & Harold Bruder, BA, 69; Johns Hopkins Univ, MA, 73, PhD, 75. Collections Arranged: 3400 on State, Baltimore Mus Art, 73; Baltimore Black Arts Calendar Retrospect, 1973-1978, Morris Mechanic Gallery, 78. Teaching: Lectr art hist, Md Inst Col Art, 73-76, dean grad studies, 76-; doctoral supvr, Dept African Studies & Res, Howard Univ, 77- Pos: Actg dir, Cult Arts, Youth in Action, Bedford, Stuyvesant, NY, 66; chmn art dept, Performing Art Workshops, Queens, NY, 67-69; feature columnist, Baltimore Afro-Am Newspaper; mem bd dir, Aura of the Arts Mag, Multi Ethnic Heritage Proj & Venice Beach Citizens Asn; guest cur & mem bd dir, Morris Mechanic Gallery. Awards: New York City SEEK Grant, 66-69; Horizon Fel, 69-73; Kress Found Fel, 74. Mem: Nat Conf Artist (Md state rep, 74-). Res: Nineteenth and Twentieth century Afro-American art, cartoon and comic strip art, African Art, Ancient—Renaissance/Baroque Survey. Publ: Contribr, National Landmarks Registry, Dept Interior, 75; Impact of roots on American society, African Directions, Fall 1977; African-American aesthetics, Aura of the Arts, 2/78. Mailing Add: 2021 Madison Ave Baltimore MD 21217

HAMMOND, NATALIE HAYS
PAINTER, MUSEUM DIRECTOR
b Lakewood, NJ, Jan 6, 04. Study: Study with Sergei Soudeikine. Work: The Luxembourg, Paris, France; Pittsfield Mus, Mass; also in pvt collections. Exhib: Royal Miniature Soc, Grieves Gallery, London, Eng, 27-29; one-man shows, Mem Gallery, Rochester NY, Brooklyn Mus, 27, Corcoran Gallery Art, Washington, DC, 29 & Philadelphia Art Alliance, 35; Pa Acad Fine Arts, Philadelphia, 28; plus others. Pos: Pres, Natalie Hammond Process Corp, 30-32; dir, Am Arbit Asn, 30; assoc mem, Royal Miniature Soc London, 27-39; founder & dir, Hammond Mus, North Salem, NY, 57- Mem: Mediaeval Acad Am. Media: Watercolor. Publ: Auth & illusr, Elizabeth of England, Kamin, 36; auth & illusr, Anthology of Pattern, Helburn, 49. Mailing Add: Hammond Mus Deveau Rd Rte 124 North Salem NY 10560

HAMMOND, RUTH MACKRILLE
PAINTER
b West Haven, Conn, Mar 19, 93. Study: Mt Holyoke Col, BA, 15; Yale Univ Grad Sch; and acrylics with Armen Gasparian, Laguna Beach, 72; also with Dante Ricci, Rome, Italy. Work: Farnsworth Mus, Rockland, Maine; Walker Art Bldg, Brunswick, Maine; Ford Collection, Detroit, Mich. Exhib: Allied Artists Am, New York; Pa Acad Fine Arts; Rockport Art Asn, Mass; Ogunquit Art Asn, Maine; Nat Asn Women Artists; High Mus, Altanta, Ga; exhib in Paris, France. Teaching: Pvt instr watercolors & oils. Awards: Awards for Gurnet & Low Tide & Ebb Tide (graphics), Brick Store Mus. Mem: Santa Barbara Art Asn & Mus. Media: Oil, Watercolor, Acrylic. Publ. Auth, Okefenokee swamp & Trip to Saguenay, Ford Times. Mailing Add: Apt 403 2663 Tallant Rd Santa Barbara CA 93105

HAMOUDA, AMY
SCULPTOR, VIDEO ARTIST
b Edinburg, Ind. Study: Boston Mus Sch, study under Karl Zerbe; Ohio State Univ, BFA; Inst Allende, Univ Guanajuato, study under David Alfaro Siqueiros, MFA; Ecole de la Grande Chaumiere, Paris; media study, Univ Colo, 75 & Buffalo, 77. Comn: Metal cross, First Methodist Church, Boulder, Colo, 61; with Jack Bice, Venitian glass mural & cast concrete fountainheads, Colo State Univ Student Ctr, Ft Collins, 62; nickel & silver art appointments, St Albans Episcopal Church, Worland, Wyo, 63; kinetic sound sculpture, Spaulding Fibre Co, Buffalo, NY, 66; acrylic mural, Univ Wash Residence Hall. Exhib: Albright-Knox Art Gallery, Buffalo, numerous exhibs; Experiments in Art & Technol, Brooklyn Mus, 68; Charlottenborg Women's Exhib, Copenhagen, Denmark, 75; Own Your Own Exhib, Denver Mus, several shows; Women's Exhib, Michael Rockefeller Mus, Fredonia, NY, 75; Eight Buffalo Women, Univ Mich Gallery, Ann Arbor, 76; Fiberous Art, Hansen Gallery, New York, 77; traveling exhib, Gallery Asn New York, 76-77; video performances, Univ Newcastle, Eng, 77. Teaching: Instr sculpture, Fine Arts (Siena Prog) NY State Univ Col Buffalo, 69-70; instr art & soc structures, Am Studies, NY State Univ Col Buffalo, 73-77 & instr art to non-majors, 73-77. Mem: Patteran Artists (mem bd, 76-78); Artists Comt Buffalo (mem bd, 77-78); A-C Gallery Adv Bd (mem bd, 77-78). Style & Technique: Mixed media sculpture. Media: Rope, Wood, Cast Plastic; Video. Dealer: Noho Gallery 542 LaGuardia Pl New York NY 10012. Mailing Add: 368 Voorhees Ave Buffalo NY 14216

HAMPTON, AMBROSE GONZALES, JR
COLLECTOR
b Statesburg, SC, July 24, 26. Pos: Mem, SC State Mus Comn, 73-; pres, Columbia Mus Art, 75- Collection: Chiefly contemporary oils, graphics and sculpture, with emphasis on South Carolina artists. Mailing Add: 2749 Laurel St Columbia SC 29204

HAMPTON, JOHN W
PAINTER, SCULPTOR
b New York, NY, 1918. Work: The Cow Punchers, Cowboy Hall Fame, Oklahoma City. Awards: First Prize, World Telegram Artist Contest, 35; Gold Medal/Sculpture, Cowboy Artist of Am Show, 77. Mem: Cowboy Artists Am (founder & second pres). Publ: Illusr in Ariz Hwys & Western Horseman & other mags & books. Mailing Add: PO Box 928 Scottsdale AZ 85252

HAMPTON, LUCILLE CHARLOTTE
SCULPTOR
b Brooklyn, NY, July 22, 22. Study: Columbia Bible Col, SC; Brooklyn Col, NY; NY Univ. Comn: The American Breed, 71, comn by Dr Alton Ochsner, New Orleans & The Bronc-5 Minutes to Midnight, 74; The Sidewinder, 71, comn by Donald C Cook, New York, Adam & Eve, 72-73 & The Rapture, 78; wildlife series, 77 & western series, 78, Lance Indust, Mass. Exhib: Hudson Valley Art Asn, Westchester, NY, 70 & 73; Nat Acad Design, 71-77; Catharine Lorillard Wolfe Art Club, New York, 72-78; Am Artists Prof League, Lever House, New York, 73-78; Pen Women of Am, New York, 75; Daughters of the Am Revolution, 76; Kennedy Gallery, New York; Grant Cent Art Gallery, New York; Main Trail Galleries, Scottsdale, Ariz. Awards: Anna Hyatt Huntington Award, Am Artists Prof League, 73 & 75; Brenner Gold Medal, Catharine Lorillard Wolfe, 76; Horsehead Trophy, Am Hackney Horse Soc, 77. Bibliog: Pat Boder (auth), Bronzes of the American West, 75. Mem: Catharine Lorillard Wolfe Art Club (treas, 74-76, financial adv, 77-78); Royal Soc Arts, London; fel Am Artists Prof League; Mont Hist Soc. Style & Technique: Sculpt in wax or clay utilizing foundry procedure, lost wax process; American West, wildlife and biblical types. Mailing Add: 2 Broadway Rm C 14th Floor New York NY 10004

HAMPTON, PHILLIP JEWEL
PAINTER, EDUCATOR
b Kansas City, Mo, Apr 23, 22. Study: Citrus Jr Col, Glendora, Calif; Kans State Univ; Drake Univ; Kansas City Art Inst, BFA, 51, MFA, 52; Univ Mo-Kansas City. Work: Liberty Nat Bank, Savannah, Ga; Lincoln Univ, Jefferson City, Mo; South Co Bank, Clayton, Mo; Tuskegee Inst, Ala; Ga Southern Col, Statesboro, Ga. Comn: Epitome of Home Economics, Savannah State Col, 56. Exhib: Nelson Gallery 2nd Mid-Am Ann, Kansas City, 52; 4th Coastal Empire Arts Festival, Savannah Art Asn, 64; 1st Nat Watercolor Competition, Dulin Gallery, Knoxville, Tenn, 64; Southeastern Exhib Prints & Drawings, Jacksonville, Fla, 64; Nat Print & Drawing Competition, 65, Dulin Gallery, 65. Teaching: Assoc prof art & dir, Savannah State Col, 52-69; assoc prof painting & design, Southern Ill Univ, Edwardsville, 69-, coordr ethnic & spec studies workshop, 71-72. Pos: Mem bd & chmn educ, Savannah Art Asn, 67-69. Awards: Teacher of Yr, Students Nat Educ Asn, 66; Award for Serv in Art to Community, Savannah Chap Links & Nat Conf Artists, Savannah Chap, 66. Bibliog: Alma Thomas (auth), Phillip Hampton, Savannah Morning News & Eve Press, 3/12/67. Mem: Col Art Asn Am; Am Fedn Art; Nat Conf Artists. Media: Acrylic. Res: Investigating synthetic media and their application to painting developments. Publ: Illusr, brochure, Greenbriar Children's Ctr, Savannah, 61; auth, An approach to art for preadult preadults, 63 & Modern art—the celebration of man's freedom, 66, Savannah State Col Faculty Res Bull; illusr, cover, Islander, 3/68. Mailing Add: 832 Holyoake Rd Edwardsville IL 62025

HAMPTON, ROY (GEORGE LEROY HAMPTON)
PAINTER
b Los Angeles, Calif, Dec 21, 23. Study: Walt Disney Studios for two yrs. Work: Nat Cowboy Hall of Fame, Oklahoma City, Okla; Bur of Indian Affairs, Washington, DC. Exhib: Western Heritage, Colo, 75-77; George Phippen Mem Western Art Show, Prescott, Ariz, 75-76. Awards: Gold Medal, Phippen Mem Western Art Show, 75 & 76; Silver Medal, Western Heritage Found, Colo, 77. Mem: Am Indian & Cowboy Artist Soc. Style & Technique: Realism. Media: Oil, colored pencil and watercolor; brush drawing. Mailing Add: 8367 Owensmouth Canoga Park CA 91304

HAMROL, LLOYD
SCULPTOR
b San Francisco, Calif, Sept 25, 37. Study: Univ of Calif, Los Angeles, BA, 59, MA, 63. Work: Pasadena Mus Mod Art, Calif; Los Angeles Co Mus Art, Los Angeles. Comn: Sculptures, Calif State Univ, Fullerton, 76, The New Gallery, Cleveland State Univ, Ohio, 77 & City of Seattle, Wash, 78. Exhib: Ann Sculpture & Prints, Whitney Mus Am Art, New York, 66; Am Sculpture of the Sixties, Los Angeles Co Mus Art, 67; West Coast Now, Portland Mus Art, Seattle Mus Art & San Francisco Mus Art, 68; Fifteen Los Angeles Artists, Pasadena Mus Mod Art, 72; Four Los Angeles Sculptors, Mus Contemp Art, Chicago, 73; Pub Sculpture/Urban Environment, Oakland Mus, Calif, 74; Three LA Sculptors, Los Angeles Inst of Contemp Art, 75; Los Angeles in the Seventies, Ft Worth Art Mus, Tex, 77; one-man shows, La Jolla Mus Art, Calif, 68, Pomona Col, Calif, 69 & Calif State Univ, Fullerton, 70. Teaching: Instr sculpture, Univ Calif, Los Angeles Exten Prog, 61-68; lectr art, San Diego State Col, Calif, 68; asst prof art, Calif State Col, Los Angeles, 69; fac, Calif Inst of the Arts, Valencia, 70-74; artist-in-residence, Western Wash State Col, Bellingham, 74, Univ Minn, Minneapolis, 75 & Calif State Univ, Fullerton, 76; lectr sculpture, Univ Calif, San Diego, 77-78. Awards: Los Angeles Co Mus New Talent Purchase Award, 65; Indiv Artist's Fel Grant, Nat Endowment for the Arts, 74. Bibliog: Ruth Iskin (auth), Public art as identity reinforcement: an interview with Lloyd Hamrol, Los Angeles Inst Contemp Art J, 1/76. Style & Technique: Monumental geometric, architectural construction techniques. Media: Multiple Media, including Wood and Stone. Mailing Add: c/o Zabriskie Gallery 29 W 57th St New York NY 10019

HAMWI, RICHARD ALEXANDER
PAINTER
b Brooklyn, NY, June 11, 47. Study: Queens Col, BA(cum laude); Univ NMex, MA; Univ Calif, MFA; also with William Dole, Leonard Lehrer, Harry Nadler, James Brooks, Louis Finkelstein & John Ferren. Work: Univ NMex; Pa State Univ; Queens Col. Exhib: Paul Klapper Art Ctr, Queens Col, 70; one-man shows, Esther Bear Gallery, Santa Barbara, 74, Pa State Univ, 75 & Parsons-Dreyfuss Gallery, New York, 76; Davidson Nat Print & Drawing Competition, 74; Parsons Truman Gallery, New York, 75; Drew Univ, 75; Truman Gallery, New York, 75; Penthouse Gallery of Mus of Mod Art, New York, 77. Teaching: Teaching asst, Univ NMex, 72-73; teaching asst, Univ Calif, 73-74; instr, Pa State Univ, 77- Mem: Col Art Asn Am. Style & Technique: Geometric abstract watercolor painting and collage. Media: Quill Pen & Ink, Watercolor. Dealer: Parsons-Dreyfuss Gallery 24 W 57th St New York NY 10019. Mailing Add: 579 83rd St Brooklyn NY 11209

HANAN, HARRY
CARTOONIST
b Liverpool, Eng, Dec 14, 16. Study: Liverpool Sch Art. Exhib: Metrop Mus Art & Mus Mod Art, New York; Walker Art Gallery, Liverpool, Eng. Pos: Ed cartoonist, Liverpool Eve Express, 36-40; ed cartoonist, The People, 46-48. Mem: Nat Cartoonists Soc. Publ: Auth & illusr, Louie, daily comic strip, newspapers in US & abroad, 47- Mailing Add: c/o Nat Cartoonist Soc 9 Ebony Ct Brooklyn NY 11229

HANBURY, UNA
SCULPTOR
b Eng; US citizen. Study: Polytech Sch Art; Royal Acad Sch Art, grad; Acad Grande Chaumiere & Acad Julian, Paris, France; and with Frank Calderon, March Brothers & Jacob Epstein. Work: Nat Portrait Gallery, Washington, DC; Carmichael Auditorium, Smithsonian Inst, Washington, DC; Bukovicka Banja Sculpture Park, Arandjelovac, Yugoslavia; Wheelwright Mus, Santa Fe, NMex; Nat Acad Sci. Comn: Compassion (stone monument), Arlington Co Jr CofC, Va, 68; symbolic wall relief (bronze), Med Examr Bldg, Baltimore, Md, 69; Family (10 ft cast stone group), St Marks Lutheran Church, Springfield, Va, 69; bronze paneled communion table, Wheaton Presby Church, Md, 70; Dato David Sung (bronze bust), Sung family, Kuala Lampur, Malaysia, 71. Exhib: Nat Sculpture Soc, Lever House, New York, 66 & 69-72; one-man retrospectives, Portrait Heads, 60- & Folger Shakespearean Libr, Washington, DC, 71; Mostra a'Arte Moderna, Camaiore, Italy, 70; Portraits of the American Stage, Nat Portrait Gallery, 71; St Johns Col, Santa Fe, NMex, 73. Pos: Nat vpres, Artists Equity Asn, 70; exhib chmn, Guild Relig Archit, 70; art ed, Faith & Form, 71-72. Awards: Best in Show, Relig Art Comn, 65; George L Erion Award, Washington Soc Artists, 66; Landseer Price for Sculpture in Archit Setting & Gold Medal for Portrait Bust, Royal Acad Art; among others. Bibliog: Andrea Cohen (auth), Una Hanbury, Washington, DC Gazette, 71; Patricia Broder (auth), Bronzes of the American West, 74; James M Goode (auth), Outdoor Sculpture of Washington, DC, 74; plus others. Mem: Soc Animal Artists; Common Cause. Style & Technique: Impressionistic realism. Media: Bronze, Stone. Mailing Add: 1108 Calle Catalina Santa Fe NM 87501

HANCOCK, WALKER (KIRTLAND)
SCULPTOR
b St Louis, Mo, June 28, 01. Study: St Louis Sch Fine Arts; Washington Univ, 18-20, hon DFA, 42; Univ Wis, 20; Pa Acad Fine Arts, 21-25; Am Acad Rome, fel, 28. Work: Pa Acad Fine Arts, Philadelphia; John Herron Art Inst, Indianapolis, Ind; Nat Portrait Gallery, Washington, DC; Parrish Art Mus, Southampton, NY; Nat Gallery Art, Washington, DC; plus many others. Comn: Eisenhower Inaugural Medal; Pa RR War Mem; Army & Navy Air Medal; portrait statue of Douglas MacArthur, US Mil Acad; portrait statue of John Paul Jones, Fairmount Park, Philadelphia; plus many other medals, monuments & portrait busts throughout US & abroad. Exhib: Nat & int mus & galleries. Teaching: Lectr on sculpture; head sculpture dept, Pa Acad Fine Arts, 29-68. Pos: Resident sculptor, Am Acad Rome, 56-57, 62-63; sculptor in charge, Stone Mountain Mem, Ga, 64. Awards: Adams Mem Award, 54; Proctor Prize, Nat Acad Design, 59; Medal of Achievement, Nat Sculpture Soc, 68; plus many others. Mem: Nat Acad Design; fel Nat Sculpture Soc; Nat Inst Arts & Lett; Architectural League; Franklin Fel Royal Soc of Arts; Nat Collection Fine Arts Comn; plus others. Style & Technique: Representational. Media: Bronze, Stone. Mailing Add: Lanesville Gloucester MA 01930

HAND, JOHN OLIVER
ART HISTORIAN, CURATOR
b New York, NY, Aug 17, 41. Study: Denison Univ, AB, 63; Univ Chicago, MA(art hist), 67; Princeton Univ, MFA(art hist), 71, PhD(art hist), 78; Samuel H Kress Found fel, 71-72, Belg Am Educ Found fel, 72-73. Teaching: Teacher art & art hist, Denison Univ, 63 & Princeton Univ, 71. Pos: Docent, Nat Gallery Art, 65-69, cur, Northern European Painting, 73- Res: Northern Renaissance painting; 15th and 16th century Northern Renaissance painting; Joos Van Cleve. Publ: Abstract painting and sculpture, In: American Arts Since 1960, Art Mus, Princeton Univ, 71; Joos Van Cleve and the Saint Jerome in the Norton Gallery and School of Art, Norton Gallery, 72; auth, Joos Van Cleve: The Early & Mature Paintings, Princeton Univ, 77. Mailing Add: Nat Gallery Art Washington DC 20565

HANDELL, ALBERT GEORGE
PAINTER
b Brooklyn, NY, Feb 13, 37. Study: Art Students League; Grande Chaumiere, Paris. Work: Syracuse Univ, NY; Brooklyn Mus Art, NY; Schenectady Mus Art, NY; Salt Lake City Mus Fine Arts; Art Students League. Exhib: One-man shows, Fitzgerald Gallery, New York, 61-64, Harbor Gallery, Cold Spring Harbor, NY, 65, 68 & 70, Schenectady Mus Art, NY, Albany Inst Hist & Art, NY & Berkshire Mus, Pittsfield, Mass; ACA Gallery, New York, 66 & Eileen Kuhlik Gallery, 72; group shows, Allied Artist Am, New York & Audubon Artist, New York; plus many other group & one-man shows. Awards: John F & Anna Lee Stacy Scholar Fund, 62-65; Ranger Fund Purchase Prize, Audubon Artist, 68; Elizabeth T Greenshields Mem Found, 72. Bibliog: Elinor Lathrop Sears (auth), Pastel Painting, Step by Step, Watson-Guptill, 68; Heather-Meredith-Owens (auth), The inner universe of Albert Handell, Am Artist Mag, 4/71; Joe Singer (auth), Pastel Portraits, Watson-Guptill. Mem: Allied Artist Am; Salmagundi Club; Art Students League. Media: Oil, Pastel. Dealer: Eileen Kuhlik Gallery 23 E 67th St New York NY 10021. Mailing Add: 10 Lower Byrdcliffe Rd Woodstock NY 12498

HANDLER, AUDREY
GLASS ARTIST, EDUCATOR
b Philadelphia, Pa, Dec 9, 34. Study: Tyler Sch Fine Arts, Temple Univ, Philadelphia, 52-54; Boston Univ Sch Fine & Appl Arts, BFA, 56, study with David Aronson; Art Students League, New York, summer 55; Univ Ill, Champaign, 62; sr res fel, Royal Col Art, London, Eng, 67-68; Univ Wis-Madison, MS, 67, MFA, 70, study with Harvey Littleton. Work: Greenville Co Art Mus, SC; Lannan Found, Palm Beach, Fla; Royal Col Art, London, Eng. Exhib: Am Glass Now, First Glass Nat, Toledo Mus Art, 66, 72 & 73; Am Glass Now, Carnegie Inst Mus Art, Pittsburgh, Pa, 73; Am Glass Now, Glass Invitational, Corning Mus Glass, NY, 73, 76 & 77; Int Glass Sculpture Show, Lowe Art Mus, Coral Gables, Fla, 73; Nat Collection Fine Art, Renwick Gallery, Smithsonian Inst, Washington, DC, 73; Am Glass Now, San Francisco Mus Art, Calif, 74; Collectors & Am Glass Now, Mus Contemp Crafts, New York, 74 & 76; Glass 1976, Bergstrom Mus, Neenah, Wis, 76. Teaching: Instr glass, Penland Sch Crafts, NC, 71-77 & Haystack Mountain Sch Crafts, Deer Isle, Maine, 73; instr painting, color & design & drawing, Madison Area Tech Col, Wis, 73-78. Pos: Deleg, US Glass Art, World Crafts Coun, Kyoto, Japan, 78. Awards: Juror's Awards, 46th & 59th Wis Designer Craftsmen Shows, Milwaukee, 66 & 71 & Madison Artists Exhib, Madison Art Ctr, Wis, 70; Master Craftsmen Apprenticeship Prog Grant, Nat Endowment for the Arts, 77-78. Bibliog: Paula Orth (auth), Blown Glass..., Milwaukee Sentinel, 72; Terri Gabriell (auth), Instructor Makes..., Hunterdon Co Dem, Flemington, NJ, 72; S K Oberbeck (auth), Glass Menagerie, Newsweek, 4/73. Mem: Glass Art Soc, Inc (mem bd, 76-78); Nat Coun on the Educ of Ceramic Arts; Am Crafts Coun; World Crafts Coun; Wis Designer Craftsmen Coun. Style & Technique: Single blown glass forms with inclusions of glass oxides, creating abstract land and seascapes; sculptures combine glass, rare wood and sterling silver to create table settings that describe a piece of life. Media: Blown glass; rare wood; cast and fabricated silver. Mailing Add: 105 S Rock Rd Madison WI 53705

HANDVILLE, ROBERT T
PAINTER, ILLUSTRATOR
b Paterson, NJ, Mar 23, 24. Study: Pratt Inst, cert, 48; Brooklyn Mus Art Sch; also painting with Rubentam, 60-64. Work: J F Kennedy White House Collection; UNICEF; Univ Denver; Syracuse Univ; Univ Okla; plus others. Comn: Design of Yellowstone Nat Park Commemorative US Postage Stamp, Presidential Citizens Adv Stamp Coun, 71-72. Exhib: 200 Yrs Am Watercolor Painting, Metrop Mus Art, New York, 66; Exhib Olympic Games, Mus Acuarela, Inst Arte Mex, 68; New Eng Silvermine Guild, Conn, 70; Butler Inst Am Art, Youngstown, Ohio; Smithsonian Inst, Washington, DC. Awards: Anonymous Prize, Audubon Artists; Ranger Fund Purchase Prize; 21st New Eng Exhib Award, Silvermine Guild Artists, 70, Am Can Co Award, 27th New Eng Exhib. Mem: Am Watercolor Soc (dir, 73-75); Westchester Art Soc; Katonah Gallery. Style & Technique: Abstract and semi-abstract; realistic. Media: Watercolor, Acrylic, Ink, Oil. Mailing Add: 99 Woodland Dr Pleasantville NY 10570

HANES, JAMES (ALBERT)
PAINTER
b Louisville, Ky, Feb 5, 24. Study: Philadelphia Sch Indust Art; US Army Univ, France; Pa Acad Fine Arts; Barnes Found, Pa. Work: Pa Acad Fine Arts, Philadelphia; Univ Tampa, Fla; Yale Univ, New Haven, Conn; La Salle Col, Philadelphia; Nat Acad Design, New York. Exhib: Pa Acad Fine Arts, 49-; Palazzo Venezia, Rome, Italy, 52; Palazzo Espozizione, Rome, 53; Nat Inst Arts & Lett, New York, 56; Univ Pittsburgh, 72. Teaching: Instr painting, Pa Acad Fine Arts, 55-58; asst prof painting & artist in residence, La Salle Col, 65- Pos: Art ed, Four Quarters, 70- Awards: Cresson & Lambert Awards, Pa Acad Fine Arts, 49; Tiffany First Award, Louis Comfort Tiffany Found, 50; Prix de Rome, Am Acad in Rome, 51-54. Bibliog: Valerio Mariani (auth), Un pittore Americano, Idea, 8/16/53. Mem: Am Acad in Rome; fel Pa Acad Fine Arts. Style & Technique: Creating true relationships of color and form in space. Media: Oil. Mailing Add: 415 W Stafford St Philadelphia PA 19144

HANFMANN, GEORGE M A
CURATOR, EDUCATOR
b Petersburg, Russia, Nov 20, 11; US citizen. Study: Univ Berlin, PhD, 34; Univ Jena; Munich Univ; Johns Hopkins Univ, PhD, 35; Harvard Univ, MA, 49. Teaching: From jr prize fel to asst prof, Harvard Univ, 35-43, asst prof, 45-49, assoc prof fine arts, 49-56, prof, 56-, John E Hudson prof archaeol, 71-; vis, classical dept, Mus Fine Arts, Boston; mem managing comt, Am Sch Classical Studies in Athens. Pos: Cur classical art, Fogg Art Mus, 46-74, emer cur, 74-; dir, archaeol exploration, Sardis, 58-78; mem Inst Advan Study, Princeton Univ, 71-72. Awards: Soc Antiquaries, London; Inst Studi Etruschi Florence; Ger Archaeol Inst; Aecheol Inst Am; Am Schs Oriental Res; plus others. Mem: Acad Manuscript Belles Lett France; Austrian Archaeol Inst. Publ: Auth, bks, monogr, exhib catalogs, articles & rev. Mailing Add: Fogg Art Mus Harvard Univ Cambridge MA 02138

HANKS, DAVID ALLEN
CURATOR
b St Louis, Mo, Dec 13, 40. Study: Washington Univ, St Louis, AB & MA. Exhibitions Arranged: American Art of the Colonies and Early Republic (auth, catalog), Art Inst of Chicago, 7/17-9/13/71 & The Arts and Crafts Movement in America, 1876-1916 (contribr, catalog), 2/24-4/22/73; The Decorative Designs of Frank Lloyd Wright, Renwick Gallery, Smithsonian Inst, 12/16/77-7/30/78. Pos: Asst cur, Art Inst of Chicago, 69-74; cur, The Philadelphia Mus of Art, 74-77; guest cur, Smithsonian Inst, 77- Mem: The Decorative Arts Chapter of the Soc of Archit Historians (pres, 74-77); The Philadelphia Chapter of the Victorian Soc (pres, 75-77). Res: American furniture of the 19th and 20th century. Publ: Auth, Isaac E Scott: Reform Furniture in Chicago, Chicago Sch of Archit Found, 74; co-auth, Daniel Pabst, Philadelphia Mus of Art, 77. Mailing Add: 2220 Twentieth St NW Washington DC 20009

HANKS, NANCY
ART ADMINISTRATOR
b Miami Beach, Fla, Dec 31, 27. Study: Duke Univ, AB, magna cum laude, 49; 21 hon degrees from various cols & univs in the US. Pos: Proj coordr, The Performing Arts: Problems and Prospects, Washington, DC, 56-69; pres, Assoc Coun of the Arts, 67-69; chmn, Nat Endowment fot the Arts & Nat Coun on the Arts, 69-78. Awards: Nat Citation, Arts & Bus Coop Coun New York Bd of Trade, 71; Nat Humanitarian Award, Nat Recreation & Park Asn, 75; Smithson Medal, Smithsonian Inst, 76; MacDowell Colony Award, 76. Mem: Fed Coun on the Arts & Humanities (chmn); hon mem, Am Inst Architects; hon mem, Am Soc Landscape Architects. Mailing Add: Nat Endowment for the Arts Washington DC 20506

HANLEN, JOHN (GARRETT)
PAINTER, INSTRUCTOR
b Winfield, Kans, Jan 1, 22. Study: Pa Acad Fine Arts, three traveling fels; independent study with George Harding, muralist; Barnes Found, Merion, Pa. Work: Pa Acad Fine Arts, Philadelphia; Libr of Cong, Washington, DC; War Dept Collection of Combat Paintings, Washington, DC; Woodmere Gallery Art, Chestnut Hill, Pa. Comn: Mural, egg tempera (collaborated with George Harding), comn by Montgomery Co, John James Audubon Shrine, Mill Grove, Pa, 54-56. Exhib: Pa Acad Fine Arts Ann, Philadelphia, 48-; Philadelphia Mus Art, 55; Detroit Inst Art, 59; one-man shows, Pa Acad Fine Arts, Peale House Gallery, 65 & Woodmere Gallery Art, Chestnut Hill, Pa, 73; Am Drawing 1968, Moore Col Art, 68; Pa 71, William Penn Mem Mus, Harrisburg, Pa, 71. Teaching: Instr & advan critic painting & drawing, Pa Acad of Fine Arts, Philadelphia, 53-; prof painting & drawing, Moore Col Art, Philadelphia, 54- Pos: Mem bd, fel of Pa Acad Fine Arts, 76. Awards: First, Tiffany Award for Painting, Louis Comfort Tiffany Found, 50; 1st Award, Edwin Austin Abbey fel for Mural Decoration, 51; Hon Mention, 160th Watercolor Ann, Pa Acad of Fine Arts, 65. Style & Technique: Non-objective; strong color, design, texture & reflective surfaces. Media: Roplex (acrylic) with dry color and collage; gold and silver Mylar. Mailing Add: 2218 St James St Philadelphia PA 19103

HANNA, BOYD EVERETT
PAINTER, PRINTMAKER
b Irwin, Pa, Jan 15, 07. Study: Univ Pittsburgh, 25-28; Carnegie-Mellon Univ, 28-30. Work: Metrop Mus Art, New York; New York Pub Libr; Libr Cong Pennell Collection, Washington, DC; Carnegie Inst, Pittsburgh; Boston Pub Libr; plus others. Comn: Presentation print, Hunt Inst, 72 & Print Club Albany, 75. Exhib: Seattle Art Mus, Wash, 41; Corcoran Gallery, Washington, DC, 42; Artists for Victory, Metrop Mus Art, 42; Denver Art Mus, Colo, 43; Brooklyn Mus, NY, 47; Nat Mus, Washington, DC, 47; Nat Acad Design 123rd Ann, New York, 49; Soc Am Graphic Artists Ann, New York, 48-56; Springfield Mus, Mo, 54; Hunt Inst, 73; Nat Acad, 73-74; Audubon Artists, New York, 73-74; one-man show, Print Club Albany, 75; Arena 76 Art Open, 76; plus others. Pos: Graphic designer, Pullman-Swindell Co, Pittsburgh, 50-70. Awards: Purchase Prize, Print Club Albany, 72, First Award, 74; Second Place, Washington Miniature Soc, 76. Mem: Print Club Albany. Style & Technique: Traditional. Media: Oil, Watercolor, Wood Engraving. Publ: Illusr, Longfellow's poems, Ltd Ed Club, 44; illusr, Compleat Angler, 47, Story of the Nativity, 49, Leaves of Grass, 51 & Sayings of Buddha, 57, Peter Pauper Press; plus others. Dealer: Bellevue Gallery 60 Schubert St Binghamton NY 13905. Mailing Add: 1475 S Jones G-16 Tucson AZ 85713

HANNA, KATHERINE
ART ADMINISTRATOR
b Cleveland, Ohio, Jan 25, 13. Study: Sweet Briar Col; Oberlin Col. Collections Arranged: Taft Art Collection; assembled, arranged & cataloged spec art & hist exhibs. Pos: Tech res, NBC-TV, Hollywood, Calif, 39-40; assoc to Harden deV Pratt, architect, Providence, RI & Tidewater, Va, 40-41; cur & dir, Taft Mus, Cincinnati, Ohio, 52- Mem: Asn Art Mus Dirs; Am Asn Mus; Int Coun Mus; Nat Trust Hist Preserv; Midwest Mus Conf. Res: History of art and architecture; art appreciation. Publ: Ed, Taft Mus catalog, 57; contribr, Let's go to an art museum, 60; ed, exhib catalogs & brochures; contribr, art magazines, mus bulletins, newspapers & periodicals. Mailing Add: 316 Pike St Cincinnati OH 45202

HANNA, PAUL DEAN, JR
PRINTMAKER, PAINTER
b Alice, Tex. Study: Austin Col, BA; Chouinard Art Inst; Tex Christian Univ, MFA. Work: Tex Tech Mus, Lubbock; Pace Collection, San Antonio; Bell Reproduction Collection, Ft Worth; Lubbock Art Asn, Tex; First Nat Bank, Hobbs, NMex. Comn: Six glass engraved windows (4 ft x 6 ft) & four stained glass windows, Covenant Presbyterian Church, Lubbock, Tex, 77- Exhib: Two-man show, Witte Mus, San Antonio, 68; Northwest Printmakers' Int, Seattle & Portland, 69; Southwestern Exhib Painting & Sculpture, Dallas, 71; Printmaking Now, Nat Print Exhib, 73; Longview Painting Exhib, 74; Tex Tech Univ, Lubbock, 77.

Teaching: Prof painting & drawing, Tex Tech Univ, 69- Awards: Eight State Painting & Sculpture Award, Okla Art Ctr, 66; Emma Freeman Award, Tex Watercolor Soc, 72; Longview Painting Award, 74. Mem: Tex Watercolor Soc; Tex Asn Schs Art. Style & Technique: Abstract, optical and figurative. Media: Acrylic, Oil; Glass Engraving; Woodcut, Silkscreen. Dealer: Electra Carlin Gallery 710 Montgomery Ft Worth TX 76107. Mailing Add: 2831 24th St Lubbock TX 79410

HANNAH, JOHN JUNIOR
PRINTMAKER, EDUCATOR
b Buffalo, NY, Mar 23, 23. Study: Univ Ill, with Lee Chesney, MFA, 55; Univ Buffalo, BFA; Albright Art Sch, with Letterio Calapai; Neth Royal Acad Painting & Sculpture, Fulbright grant, 60-61; Pratt Graphic Art Ctr, 67; also with Birgit Skijöld Workshop, London. Work: Northwest Printmakers, Seattle Mus Art, Wash; Okla Printmakers Collection, Oklahoma City; 3-M Collection, Tweed Gallery, Duluth, Minn; Bradley Univ Collection, Peoria, Ill; Joslyn Art Mus, Nebr, Omaha; plus many others. Comn: Tourist, Friends of Art, Kans State Univ, 67. Exhib: Philadelphia Print Club, 51, 54, 56 & 60, Libr, 54-55 & 57-58; Boston Printmakers, 51, 56, 59 & 61; Potsdam Prints, 67, 72 & 74; Colorprint USA, Art Dept, Lubbock, Tex, 71 & 74; 1st Int Print Exhib, Hilo, Hawaii, 76; Three Decades of Am Printmaking, Brooklyn Mus, NY, 77; Nat Color Blend Print Exhib, Univ Miss, 77; 44th Ann Miniature Printers Sculptors & Gravers, Washington, DC, 77; Six Printmakers, Loyola Univ, Los Angeles, 77. Teaching: Instr drawing, Ohio State Univ, Columbus, 56; assoc prof printmaking, Kans State Univ, Manhattan, 57-68; prof printmaking & drawing, Calif State Univ, Northridge, 69- Awards: Calif Art Coun Artist Grant, 78. Mem: Los Angeles Printmaking Soc (bd mem, 70-); Artists Econ Action (bd mem, 73-74). Style & Technique: Abstracted machine forms and atmospheres in complex compositions; photoimagery. Media: Etching, Serigraphy. Publ: Contribr, Etching, Van Nostrand, 73; contribr, American Printmakers, 74 & California Graphics, 74, Graphis Group Arcadia, 74. Dealer: Comsky Gallery 9489 Dayton Way Beverly Hills CA 90210. Mailing Add: 665 Haverford Pacific Palisades CA 90272

HANNIBAL, JOSEPH HARRY
EDUCATOR, PRINTMAKER
b Brooklyn, NY, May 4, 45. Study: Austin Peay State Univ, Clarksville, Tenn, BS, 68; Univ Tenn, Knoxville, MFA, 72. Work: Austin Peay State Univ. Exhib: First Light Nat Photog Exhib, Humboldt State Univ, Arcata, Calif, 76; Colorprint USA, Tex Tech Univ, Lubbock, 76; Drawing/Intent 1977, Edinboro State Col, Pa, 77; Brand 7 Nat Print Exhib, Brand Libr Galleries, Glendale, Calif, 77; Nat Print & Drawing Exhib, Ft Hays, Kans, 78. Teaching: Head, Dept Lithography & Photog Processes, Univ Wis-Stout, Menomonie, 72-; head lithography dept, Cent Col Art & Design, London, Eng, 75-76. Awards: First Place/Painting, 10th Southern Contemp Art Exhib, 67; Merit Award, Drawing/Intent 1977, Edinboro State Col, 77. Mem: Col Art Asn; Midwest Col Art Asn. Style & Technique: Photoprintmaking; recognizable imagery. Media: Printmaking, Photography, Various Media. Dealer: 118 Gallery 1007 Harmon Pl Minneapolis MN 55403. Mailing Add: 815 Seventh St E Menomonie WI 54751

HANSEN, ARNE RAE
MUSEUM DIRECTOR, ART ADMINISTRATOR
b Fergus Falls, Minn, Mar 4, 40. Study: Pvt study, Misawa, Japan, 59-60 & Hof/Saale, Ger, 62-63; Black Hawk Col, Moline, Ill, AA, 68; Univ Tex, Austin, BFA, 70; Univ Okla, Norman, MFA, 72. Work: Jones Art Ctr, Univ Okla; Goddard Art Ctr, Ardmore, Okla. Collections Arranged: The Hoover Collection of Pre-Columbia Art, 73 & African Art in the Collection of Illinois State University (auth, catalogue), Ill State Univ; African Textiles in the Girard Collection, 75, 20-20, Colorado-New Mexico Contemporary Art, 75 & 10 take 10, Ten Contemporary Southwestern Retrospectives, 77, Colorado Springs Fine Arts Ctr, Colo. Teaching: Asst prof design, Ill State Univ, 72-75. Pos: Asst to dir of mus, Ill State Univ, 72-73, dir mus, 73-75; dir, Colorado Springs Fine Arts Ctr, 75- Mem: Asn Art Mus Dir; Western Asn Art Mus (vpres, 77-); Am Asn Mus; Col Art Asn. Res: American primitive sculpture. Publ: Contribr, Hispanic Crafts, 77 & Ernest Blumenschein, A Retrospective, 78, Colorado Springs Fine Arts Ctr. Mailing Add: 41 W Cache La Poudre Colorado Springs CO 80903

HANSEN, FRANCES FRAKES
EDUCATOR, PAINTER
b Harrisburg, Mo. Study: Univ Denver, BFA; Art Inst Chicago; Univ Northern Colo, MA; Univ Southern Calif; Univ Denver; Ecoles Art Am, Fontainebleau, France. Comn: Painting, Alpha Gamma Delta Fraternity, Denver, Colo, 66. Exhib: Eleven Denver Art Mus Exhib, 45-73; Colo Women's Col Biennial Faculty Shows, 45-75; Joslyn Mus Biennial, Omaha, Nebr, 53 & 67; Gilpin Co Ann, Central City, Colo, 55-56, 66, 69 & 72; Mus NMex Ann Regional, Santa Fe, 59; William Rockhill Nelson Mus, Kansas City, Mo, 65; Denver Festival Arts, 69; Colo State Univ Centennial Exhib, 70; among others. Teaching: Prof art, Colo Women's Col, 45-73. Pos: Researcher & display designer, Am Indian, Denver Mus Natural Hist, 73-; artist-mem ed bd, Denver Botanic Gardens, 77-; lectr Am Indian art. Awards: Painting Prize for Oils, Paradise Cove, 60 & Canyon Pastoral, 65, Colo State Fair Prof Show; Colo Women's Col Faculty Res Grant, 69; Painting Prize for Acrylic, Lights, Univ Northern Colo Centennial Exhib, 70. Mem: Delta Phi Delta (Art Inst Chicago Chap); Denver Mus Natural Hist; Am Asn Univ Prof; Denver Art Mus; Nat Audubon Soc. Style & Technique: Abstract and decorative; semi-abstract and representational; hard-edge and loosely applied techniques. Media: Acrylic, Watercolor. Publ: Auth, Native arts in America, US Cult Bull, 66. Mailing Add: 700 Pontiac St Denver CO 80220

HANSEN, HAROLD JOHN
EDUCATOR, PAINTER
b Chicago, Ill, June 18, 42. Study: Univ Ill, BFA, 64; Univ Mich, MFA, 66. Work: SC State Art Collection; Columbia Mus Arts & Sci; Univ South; Univ Pac; Carroll Reese Mus, E Tenn State Univ. Exhib: Mainstreams, Marietta Col, Ohio, 70; 17th Ann Drawing & Small Sculpture Exhib, Ball State Univ, 71; La Watercolor Soc 4th Ann Int Exhib, Baton Rouge, 72; 9th Ann Piedmont Graphics Exhib, Mint Mus Art, Charlotte, NC, 73; Drawings USA, 73 & traveling show, 73-75, Minn Mus Art, St Paul; plus others. Teaching: Instr art, Kendall Sch Design, Grand Rapids, Mich, 66-69; asst prof art, Ferris State Col, Big Rapids, Mich, 69-70; assoc prof art, design & painting & chmn art studio div, Univ SC, Columbia, 70- Mem: Col Art Asn Am; Southeastern Col Art Asn; Guild SC Artists. Style & Technique: Abstract color oriented painting and drawing. Media: Encaustic painting. Res: Technical investigation of the encaustic media to improve working characteristics and hardness. Publ: Auth, A method for modern encaustic painting, Southeastern Col Art Asn Rev, spring 76; auth, The development of new vehicle recipies for encaustic paints, Leonardo, Vol 10 (1977). Mailing Add: 1314 Brentwood Dr Columbia SC 29206

HANSEN, JAMES LEE
SCULPTOR
b Tacoma, Wash, June 13, 25. Study: Portland Art Mus Sch. Work: San Francisco Art Mus; Seattle Art Mus; Portland Art Mus, Ore; Univ Ore Mus Art, Eugene. Comn: Talos, City of Fresno Civic Mall, 61; reliefs, Land Title Bldg, Vancouver, Wash, 63 & St Anns Church, Butte, Mont, 66; Shaman, Shate Wash Hwy Dept, Olympia, 71; Tholegvard, Seattle First Nat Bank, Lakewood, Wash, 75. Exhib: Whitney Mus Am Art Ann, 53; Artists Environ, Amon Carter Mus, Ft Worth, Tex, 62; Art of the Pacific Northwest, 1930 to Present, Nat Col Fine Art, Smithsonian Inst, Washington, DC, 74; one-man shows, Fountain Gallery, Portland, 69, Portland Art Mus, 71 & Friedlander Gallery, Seattle, 73. Teaching: Prof sculpture, Portland State Univ, 64- Awards: Norman Davis Award for Neo Shang, Seattle Art Mus, 58; Am Trust Co Award, 56 & Award for Ritual, 60, San Francisco Art Mus. Bibliog: William Davenport (auth), Art treasures in the West, Lane, 10/66; J A Schinneller (auth), Art/search & self discovery, Int Textbk, 12/67; Jinni (auth), Stars in art, NW Art, 6/70. Style & Technique: Abstract expression; cast bronze (lost wax method). Dealer: Fountain Gallery 115 SW Fourth St Portland OR 97204; Polly Friedlander Gallery 95 Yesler Way Pioneer Sq Seattle WA 98104. Mailing Add: 4115 Q St Vancouver WA 98663

HANSEN, ROBERT
PAINTER
b Osceola, Nebr, Jan 1, 24. Study: Univ Nebr, AB, BFA, 48; Escuela Univ Bellas Artes, San Miguel Allende, Mex, MFA, 49; also with Alfredo Zalce, Morelia, Mex, 52-53. Work: Mus Mod Art & Whitney Mus Am Art, New York; Los Angeles Co Mus Art; San Diego Gallery Fine Arts; Long Beach Mus Art. Exhib: Carnegie Int, Pittsburgh, Pa, 61 & 63; Painting USA: Figure, 62 & Tamarind: Homage to Lithography, 69; Mus Mod Art, New York; retrospectives, Long Beach Mus Art, Calif, 67 & Los Angeles Munic Gallery, 73; New Vein, organized & mounted in mus of nat capitols in Europe & SAm, Smithsonian Inst, 68-70. Teaching: Prof art, Occidental Col, 56- Awards: Guggenheim Fel, 61; Fulbright Sr Grant, 61; Tamarind Fel, 65. Media: Lacquer. Mailing Add: 1974 Addison Way Los Angeles CA 90041

HANSEN, WANDA
ART DEALER
b Fortuna, Calif, Feb 12, 35. Study: Univ Calif, Berkeley, BA(polit sci). Teaching: Elem sch instr, Oakland Unified Sch Syst, Calif. Pos: Co-dir, Hansen Fuller Gallery, San Francisco, Calif. Specialty: Contemporary art. Mailing Add: Hansen Fuller Gallery 228 Grant Ave San Francisco CA 94108

HANSON, BERNARD A
ART ADMINISTRATOR
b Williamsburg, Iowa, Oct 11, 22. Study: Univ Iowa, BA(Eng lit), 43, MA(art hist); NY Univ; Univ Pa. Teaching: Mem fac, Northwestern Univ, 44-45 & art hist, 57-58; mem fac art hist, Univ Fla, 46-56 & art hist, 57-58; mem fac gen educ, Univ Pa, 57-58 & art hist; mem fac & chmn arts & sci prog, Philadelphia Col of Art, 58-70. Pos: Dean, Hartford Art Sch, Univ Hartford, 70- Mem: Nat Asn of Sch of Art; Col Art Asn (chmn film comt; co-chmn studio sessions). Publ: Auth, D W Griffith: Some Sources, Art Bull, 73. Mailing Add: Hartford Art Sch Univ of Hartford West Hartford CT 06117

HANSON, CHRISTINA RAMBERG
See Ramberg, Christina

HANSON, DUANE
SCULPTOR, INSTRUCTOR
b Alexandria, Minn, Jan 17, 25. Study: Macalester Col, BA; Univ Minn; Cranbrook Acad Art, MFA. Work: Richmond Mus, Va; Neue Galerie, Aachen, Ger; Lehmbruck Mus, Duisburg, Ger; Milwaukee Art Mus; Nelson Gallery, Kansas City, Mo. Comn: Businessman, for Melvin Kaufman, New York, 71; Stormy Petrel, for Oglethorpe Univ, 62 & Yellow Jacket, for Howard Johnson Motel, 63, Atlanta, Ga. Exhib: Whitney Mus Am Art Sculpture Ann, 70 & 78; Documenta V, Kassel, Ger, 72; Whitney Mus Am Art Biennial, 73; Mus Contemp Art, Chicago, 74; retrospective, Stuttgart, Aachen, Berlin & Copenhagen, 74-75; one-man shows, Ulrich Mus, Wichita State Univ, Kans, 76, Sheldon Gallery, Univ Nebr, Lincoln, 76, Des Moines Art Ctr, Iowa, Berkeley Mus, Univ Calif, Berkeley, Portland Mus Art, Ore, Nelson Gallery, Kansas City, Mo, Colorado Springs Art Mus, Colo, Va Mus, Richmond & Corcoran Gallery Art, Washington, DC, 77 & Whitney Mus Am Art, New York, 78. Teaching: Asst prof art, Miami-Dade Jr Col, Miami, Fla, 65-69. Awards: Grant for work in sculpture, Ella Lyman Trust, 63; Sculpture Award, Fla State Fair Fine Arts Exhib, 68; Blair Award, Art Inst Chicago, 74. Bibliog: Kultermann (auth), The new realism, NY Graphic Soc, 72; Sam Hunter (auth), American Art Since 1960, Abrams, 72; Varnedoe (auth), Duane Hanson retrospective and recent work, Art News, 1/75. Media: Polyester Resin, Fiberglas; Oil, Mixed Media. Publ: Auth, Presenting Duane Hanson, 70. Mailing Add: 6109 SW 55 Ct Davie FL 33314

HANSON, JEAN (MRS JEAN ELPHICK)
PAINTER, DESIGNER
b Toronto, Ont, Sept 27, 34. Study: Ont Col Art. Exhib: Smithsonian Inst, 62-63; Art Gallery Hamilton, Ont, 63; Ont Soc Artists, 63-67; Hart House, Univ Toronto, 64; Can Soc Painters in Watercolour, 68; plus many other group & one-man shows. Mem: Ont Soc Artists; Can Soc Painters in Watercolour. Media: Oil, Wool. Mailing Add: 1378 2 Side Rd RR 3 Campbellville ON Can

HANSON, LAWRENCE
SCULPTOR, EDUCATOR
b Winona, Minn, July 28, 36. Study: Univ Minn, BA, 59, MFA, 62; Univ Calif, Santa Barbara, with Stan Reiffel, 69. Work: Walker Art Ctr, Minneapolis; Henry Gallery, Univ Wash; La Jolla Mus Contemp Art; Univ Mont; C M Russell Mus, Great Falls, Mont. Comn: LaMar's Tape (sound tape), Henry Gallery, Univ Wash, 73. Exhib: Recent Acquisitions, Walker Art Ctr, 62; An Event, Western Wash State Col, 67; Silverman II, Portland State Univ, 68; Light Works, Contemp Crafts Gallery, Portland, 70; Light Works II, Henry Gallery, Univ Wash, 70; Three From Washington State, La Jolla Mus Contemp Art, 70; Recent Works, Univ Mont, 74; one-man shows, Art Mus, Wash State Univ, 75, Mod Art Pavilion, Seattle Art Mus, Wash, 76, And/Or Gallery, Seattle, 76, Eastern Wash Gallery of Art, Eastern Wash Univ, 77 & Western Gallery, Western Wash State Col, 77; Together, Wash State Univ, Cheney Cowles Mem Mus, Spokane & Vancouver Sch of Art, BC, 75; The Experimental Performance Workshop, Western Wash Univ, Bellingham & And/Or Gallery, Seattle, 75. Arranged: George Segal, 67; Robert Irwin: Paintings, 67; Painting of the Sixties (with catalog), 68; Seven From Washington: Printmaking Today (with catalog), 69; Sculpture of the Sixties (with catalog), 69; Robert Morris: Earthworks & Projects, 74; Painting of the Seventies, 75. Teaching: Teaching asst & instr sculpture & ceramics, Univ Minn, 59-62; assoc prof sculpture & contemp art, Western Wash Univ, 63- Pos: Dir, Western Gallery, Western Wash State Col, 66-77; artist/consult, Pike St Ltd, Seattle. Mem: Western Asn Art Mus; Am Mus Asn; Wash Art Consortium (chmn, 75-77). Style & Technique: Environments, installations,

performance. Media: Light & Sound, Television Tapes and Performance. Mailing Add: Dept of Art Western Wash Univ Bellingham WA 98225

HANSON, PHILIP HOLTON
PAINTER
b Chicago, Ill, Jan 8, 43. Study: Univ Chicago, BA, 65; Art Inst Chicago, MFA, 69. Work: Mus des 20 Jahrhunderts, Vienna, Austria. Exhib: False Image I, 6 & False Image II, 69, Hyde Park Art Ctr, Chicago; Famous Artists, 69 & Chicago Imagist Art, 72, Mus Contemp Art, Chicago; Sao Paulo Biennale, 73; Extraordinary Realities, Whitney Mus, 73; one-man show, Phyllis Kind Gallery, Chicago, 74 & 76; SAm Traveling Exhib, Collection Fine Arts, Washington, DC, 75. Dealer: Phyllis Kind Gallery 226 E Ontario Chicago IL 60611. Mailing Add: 2527 W Ainslie Chicago IL 60625

HAOZOUS, ROBERT L
SCULPTOR
b Los Angeles, Calif, Apr 1, 43. Study: Calif Col Arts & Crafts, BFA. Work: Southwest Plains Mus, Anadarko, Okla; Heard Mus, Phoenix, Ariz. Exhib: Philbrook Mus, Tulsa, Okla, 72; Santa Fe Indian Market, NMex, 72-75; NMex Fine Arts Mus Biennial, Santa Fe, 73; Sculpture I & Sculpture II, Heard Mus, 73 & 75. Awards: Second Prize Sculpture, Philbrook Art Mus, 73; Best of Show, Santa Fe Indian Market, Southwest Asn Indian Art, 75; Grand Award Sculpture II, Heard Mus, 75. Bibliog: Guy & Doris Monthan (auth), Art & Indian Individualists, Northland, 75. Style & Technique: Personal style, traditional techniques. Media: Stone, Wood. Publ: Illusr, Pembrook Mag, 74. Dealer: Glenn Green Gallery Wall 7122 N Seventh St Phoenix AZ 85006. Mailing Add: Rte 4 Box 94D Santa Fe NM 87501

HAPKE, PAUL FREDERICK
PAINTER, EDUCATOR
b Chester, Ill Sept 19, 22. Study: Ill Col, BA; Calif Col Arts & Crafts, with Leon Goldin, MFA; Univ Am, with Cueto & Justin Fernandez, MA. Work: Minneapolis Mus Art. Comn: Abstract duco mural, Unitarian Ctr Mankato, Minn, 59. Exhib: Exhibition Momentum, Chicago, 54; Ball State Univ Drawing & Sculpture, 57; Walker Art Ctr, Minneapolis, 58-64; Piccolo Formato, Florence, Italy, 61; Minneapolis Inst Art, 65. Teaching: Prof painting, Mankato State Univ, 55- Awards: First Prize, Galeria Numero, Florence, 61; Bertah Walker Award, Walker Art Ctr, 64 & Ford Found Award, 64. Mem: Col Art Asn Am. Style & Technique: Abstract landscapes. Media: Oil, Watercolor. Mailing Add: 35 Ridgewood Mankato MN 56001

HARA, TERUO
POTTER, SCULPTOR
b Japan, May 26, 29. Study: Tokyo Univ Educ, 46-52. Work: Dusseldorf Mus, Ger; Corcoran Gallery Art, Washington, DC; Houston Mus Fine Arts, Tex. Comn: Ceramic murals, Carl M Freeman, Inc, Va, 63 & Md, 64. Exhib: One-man shows, Yoseido Gallery, Tokyo, Japan, 56, Design Technics, New York, 62, Art & Craft Ctr, Pittsburgh, Pa, 65 & Corcoran Gallery Art, 68; also shows in Rome, Italy, Sao Paulo, Brazil & Brussels, Belg. Teaching: Assoc prof ceramics, Corcoran Sch Art, 63-69; assoc prof art, Mary Washington Col, 69- Awards: Grand Prize, Brussels World's Fair, 58. Bibliog: Joanna Eagle (auth), Teruo Hara, Craft Horizons, 68; Paul Richard (auth), Pots of Hara, Potomac Post, 68; G Lindsey (auth), Three Washington Artists, NBC-TV, 71. Style & Technique: Modernistic. Media: Ceramic, Steel. Mailing Add: 222 East St Warrenton VA 22186

HARARI, HANANIAH
PAINTER
b Rochester, NY, Aug 29, 12. Study: Syracuse Univ Col Fine Arts; Fontainebleau Ecole de Fresque, France; also with Fernand Leger, Andre Lhote & Marcel Gromaire, Paris. Work: Whitney Mus; Univ Ariz Mus; Hudson River Mus, Yonkers, NY; Mus Mod Art, New York; Philadelphia Mus Art. Exhib: Whitney Mus Am Art Painting Ann, 42-47; American Realists & Magic Realists, Mus Mod Art, New York, 43; Int Exhib Watercolor, Art Inst Chicago, 43; Pa Acad Fine Arts Ann, 46 & 49; Contemp Am Art Ann, Toledo Mus Art, 50; Am Abstract Artists, Art Mus, Univ NMex, Albuquerque, 77. Teaching: Instr painting, New Sch for Social Res, 74 & Sch Visual Arts, New York, 74- Awards: First Hallgarten Prize, Nat Acad Design, 41; Emy Herzfeld Award, Audubon Artists, 45; Medal Award, Art Dir Club, Chicago, 50. Bibliog: Clement Greenberg (auth), Hananiah Harari, Nation, 1/43; Doris Brian (auth), Who's who, Art News, 1/43; Alexander Eliot (auth), Double trouble, Time, 5/50. Mem: Artists Equity Asn NY. Style & Technique: Realism; precisionism; spontaneous fantasy. Media: Oil. Dealer: Portraits Inc 41 E 57th St New York NY 10022. Mailing Add: 34 Prospect Pl Croton-on-Hudson NY 10520

HARBART, GERTRUDE FELTON
PAINTER, INSTRUCTOR
b Michigan City, Ind. Study: Univ Calif; Univ Ill; Art Inst Chicago; Art Students League, NY; and with Aaron Bohard, Charles Birchfield & Hans Hofmann. Work: Purdue Univ; Ind Univ; Ind State Univ; South Bend Art Inst; Indianapolis Mus Art; plus others. Comn: In many private collections. Exhib: Art Inst Chicago; Corcoran Biennial, Washington, DC; Butler Inst Am Art, Youngstown, Ohio; Indianapolis Mus Art; Michiana Biennial, South Bend. Teaching: Instr art, South Bend Art Ctr; instr art, Dunes Art Found; instr art, Michigan City Art League, 70-; pvt art classes. Awards: Indianapolis Mus Award, John Herron Mus, 60; Northern Ind Art Patrons Award, Hammond Art Ctr, 70; Sarasota Art Asn First Award, 74. Mem: South Bend Art Ctr; Ind Artists; Tucson Mus of Art; Southern Ariz Watercolor Guild; Am Pen Women. Media: Acrylic, Watercolor. Publ: Auth, articles in, Art News, 6/55 & Sch Arts, 60. Dealer: Neill Gallery 2402 E Grant Rd Tucson AZ; works also available at Indianapolis Mus of Art. Mailing Add: 2201 Maryben Ave Long Beach Michigan City IN 46360

HARDAWAY, PEARL (PEARL HARDAWAY REESE)
PAINTER
b Brooklyn, NY, Apr 11, 17. Study: Brooklyn Col, BA(fine arts); Art Students League, with Vaclav Vytlacil, Will Barnet; Acad Bildenden Kunst, Munich, Ger. Work: Queens Col Art Collection, Flushing, NY; First Methodist Church, White Plains, NY; Queens Col Print Collection; First Methodist Church of Jamaica, NY. Exhib: Am Exhib, Haus der Kunst, Munich, 54; one-woman shows, Queens Col, City Univ New York, 55, Arts Gallery, New York, 58 & Educ Testing Serv, Princeton, NJ, 76; Butler Inst Am Art, Youngstown, Ohio; Audubon Artists Ann, Acad Fine Arts, New York; New York Artists, Brooklyn Mus, NY. Teaching: Pvt teaching. Awards: Emily Lowe Award, Ward Eggleston, New York. Mem: Art Students League. Style & Technique: Abstract expressionist; mystic. Media: Oil, Watercolor. Mailing Add: 32 Norton Rd Monmouth Junction NJ 08852

HARDEN, MARVIN
PAINTER, EDUCATOR
b Austin, Tex. Study: Univ Calif, Los Angeles, BA(fine arts) & MA(creative painting); Los Angeles City Col. Work: Whitney Mus Am Art & Mus Mod Art, New York; Home Saving & Loan Asn, Los Angeles; Mus, Univ Calif, Berkeley; Metromedia Inc, Los Angeles; plus other pub & pvt collections. Exhib: Over 100 exhibs, incl Minneapolis Inst Art, 68; Drawings, Ft Worth Art Ctr Mus, 69; Irving Blum Gallery, Los Angeles, 72; Col of Creative Studies, Univ Calif, Santa Barbara, 76; Brooklyn Mus, 76; Calif State Col, Bakersfield, 77; James Corcoran Gallery, 78; 14 one-man exhibs, incl Rath Mus, Geneva, Switz, 71, Whitney Mus of Am Art, New York, 71 & Irvine Blum Gallery, Los Angeles, 72. Teaching: Instr drawing, Univ Calif, Los Angeles Exten, 64-68; instr drawing, Los Angeles Harbor Col, 65-68; assoc prof art, Calif State Univ, Northridge, 68- Pos: Co-founder, Los Angeles Inst Comtemp Art, 73, exhib comt mem, 73-74. Awards: Nat Endowment Arts Fel, 72. Media: Pencil, Oil. Dealer: James Corcoran Gallery 8223 Santa Monica Blvd Los Angeles CA 90046. Mailing Add: PO Box 353 Chatsworth CA 91311

HARDER, ROLF PETER
DESIGNER, PAINTER
b Hamburg, Ger, July 10, 29; Can citizen. Study: Hamburg Acad Fine Arts, 48-52. Exhib: Design Collaborative (int travelling exhib), with Ernst Roch, 70-78; 4th & 5th Biennale of Graphic Design, Brno, 70 & 74; Experimental Graphic Design, 36th Venice Biennale, 72. Awards: Symbol Competition First Prize, Can Asn Retarded Children, 64; numerous awards, Am Inst Graphic Arts, 65-; Spec Prize, 4th Biennale Graphic Design, Brno, 70. Bibliog: Theodore Hilten (auth), Rolf Harder, 9/64 & Hans Kuh (auth), Design Collaborative, 9/70, Gebrauchsgraphic, Munich; Hans Neuberg (auth), Rolf Harder, Ernst Roch, Graphics, Zurich, 69. Mem: Royal Can Acad Arts; Alliance Graphique Int; Am Inst Graphic Arts; Int Ctr Typographic Arts; Soc Graphic Designers Can. Mailing Add: Rolf Harder & Assoc 1460 Sherbrook W Montreal PQ Can

HARDIN, ADLAI S
SCULPTOR
b Minneapolis, Minn, Sept 23, 01. Study: Art Inst Chicago; Princeton Univ. Work: Pa Acad Fine Arts; New Britain Mus Am Art, Conn; Medallic Art Co Collection Bronzes; IBM Collection Sculptures of Western Hemisphere. Comn: Murals, Interchurch Ctr, New York & Seamen's Bank Savings, New York; reliefs, McMaster Univ, Hamilton, Ont, Lutheran Acad Asn, Appleton, Wis & Princeton Univ, NJ. Exhib: Nat Acad Design, New York; Pa Acad Fine Arts; Nat Sculpture Soc; Art Inst Chicago; one-man show, New Britain Mus Am Art. Awards: Henry O Avery Award, New York Archit League; Saltus Gold Medal, Nat Acad Design; Lindsey Morris Mem Prize, Nat Sculpture Soc. Bibliog: Frederick Whitaker (auth), The sculpture of Adlai S Hardin, Am Artist, 60; Walker Hancock (auth), Adlai S Hardin past president, Nat Sculpture Rev. Mem: Nat Acad Design; fel Nat Sculpture Soc (pres, 57-60); Old Lyme Art Asn. Media: Wood, Bronze. Mailing Add: Cove Rd Lyme CT 06371

HARDIN, HELEN
PAINTER
b Albuquerque, NMex, May 28, 43. Study: Univ NMex; Spec Sch for Indian Arts, Univ Ariz, Tucson. Comn: Illus for two children's bks, Clarke Indust, Albuquerque; Hist of the Am Indian (ser of coins), Franklin Mint. Exhib: Ann Am Indian Art Exhib, Wayne State Univ, Detroit, Mich; Inter-Tribal Indian Ceremonials, Gallup, NMex; Mus of NMex, Santa Fe; Scottsdale Nat Indian Art Exhib, Ariz. Teaching: Lectr, Civil Serv Comn Sem, Colo, 70. Awards: Grand Award, Best Art Work in the Painting & Sculpture Category & Best in Acrylic Div, 11th Nat Indian Arts Exhib, Scottsdale, Ariz; First & Second Awards, Santa Fe Indian Market; Patrick Swazo Hinds Award for Excellence in Painting. Bibliog: Picture of work in Am Artist, 65. Mem: Pinon Br, Nat League of Am Pen Women. Style & Technique: Contemporary painting using acrylic paint, ink, acrylic varnish and architects templets. Mailing Add: 805 Adams NE Albuquerque NM 87110

HARDIN, SHIRLEY G
ART DEALER
Pos: Co-dir, Fairweather-Hardin Gallery. Mailing Add: 101 E Ontario St Chicago IL 60611

HARDING, NOEL ROBERT
VIDEO ARTIST, ENVIRONMENTAL ARTIST
b London, Eng, Dec 21, 45. Work: Art Gallery of Ont, Toronto; Nat Gallery of Can, Ottawa, Ont; Univ Guelph, Can. Exhib: Minneapolis Col Art & Design & Walker Art Ctr, Minneapolis, Minn, 72; New York Avante-Garde Film Festival, New York, 73 & 75; Videoscape, 74, The Chairs Show, 75 & In Video, 78, Art Gallery of Ont; Everson Mus, Syracuse, NY, 75; Nat Gallery of Can, 77; Dalhousie Art Gallery, Halifax, NS, 77; Biennial, Sao Paulo, Brazil, 77; Mus Mod Art, New York, 78; one-man installations, Art Gallery of Ont, 76, Ctr for Experimental Art Commun, Toronto, 76, Artspace, Peterborough, 77, Ctr Cult Can, Paris, 77, Can House, London, 77 & Vancouver Art Gallery, BC, 78; one-man videotape, Alta Col Art & Design, Calgary, 76 & Ctr Georges Pompidou, Paris, France, 77. Teaching: Instr fine art video, Univ Guelph, 74-77; instr independent 74-77, instr independent study utilizing video, 72-76, instr sr independent study utilizing any/all of film slide & video, 76 & instr experiments in art performance, 77; instr creative film/video, Photo Electric Arts Dept, Ont Col Art, 77; instr creative film video, Univ Guelph & Ont Col Art, 77- Awards: Can Coun Arts Grant, 76 & 78-79, Travel Grant, 77 & Proj Grant, 78; Ont Arts Coun Grant, 77. Bibliog: Art Perry (auth), Noel Harding: once upon the idea of two, Vancouver in Rev, 1/78; Peggy Gale (auth), Temporal realities & Eric Cameron (auth), Video as painting, Parachute, spring 78. Style & Technique: Video as a narrative poetic logic, film as sculptured space from surface of image to lens; film utilized as environment space. Media: Videotape, Film, Live Video. Dealer: Peggy Gale c/o Art Metropole 241 Yonge St Toronto ON M5B 2H2 Can. Mailing Add: 101 Niagara St Toronto ON M5V 1C3 Can

HARDY, (CLARION) DEWITT
PAINTER, ART ADMINISTRATOR
b S Louis, Mo, June 25, 40. Study: Syracuse Univ, 58-62. Work: Bowdoin Col Mus Art, Brunswick, Maine; Kalamazoo Inst Art, Mich; St Lawrence Univ, Canton, NY; Mus Art Ogunquit, Maine; Butler Inst Am Art, Youngstown, Ohio. Exhib: Four New England Artists, Kalamazoo Inst Art, 63; New England Regional, Drawing Soc, 65; one-man shows, Frank Rehn Gallery, New York, 66-71 &Lehigh Univ, Pa, 71; Butler Inst Am Art, 69-70. Collections Arranged: Young American Draughtsmen, Mus Art Ogunquit, 69. Pos: Assoc dir, Mus Art Ogunquit, 64-77. Awards: First Prize for Drawing, Summit Art Ctr, NJ, 65; Purchase Award, Butler Inst Am Art, 69. Media: Watercolor. Dealer: Frank Rehn Gallery 655 Madison Ave New York NY 10021. Mailing Add: Oak Woods Rd North Berwick ME 03906

HARDY, DAVID WHITTAKER, III
PAINTER, INSTRUCTOR
b Dallas, Tex, Oct 5, 29. Study: Austin Col; Southern Methodist Univ; Univ Colo; Am Acad; Art Students League; Sch Visual Art; and with Ramon Froman, William Moseby, Joseph Van Der Brock, Robert Beverly Hale & Frank Mason. Work: Pvt collections in US & abroad. Exhib: One-man shows, Gallery Trohafole, Dallas, 62, Highland Park Town Hall, Dallas, 62, North Park, Dallas, 64 & Pantechnicon Gallery, San Francisco, 70; Hemisfair Art, Witte Mem Mus, San Antonio, 68; Soc Western Artists, De Young Mus, San Francisco, 70; San Francisco Ann, 71; Audubon Artists, Nat Acad, New York, 73; plus others. Teaching: Pvt art classes, 60-; instr art, Mendocino Art Ctr, Calif, 73-74. Pos: Guest, Wurlitzer Found, Taos, NMex, 65; owner, 13th Street Crafts Garden, Oakland, 73- Awards: Hon Mention, Soc Western Artists, 70; First Place for Painting, Alameda Co Fair, 73 & Valley Artists Asn, 73. Mem: Berkeley Art Festival Guild (pres, 72-); Soc Western Artists; Ctr for Visual Arts (bd trustees, 74-). Style & Technique: Contemporary subjects executed in classical style of realism with baroque painting techniques. Media: Oil, Pastel. Res: Old master painting techniques. Specialty: Portraits and figure paintings. Dealer: La Galleria 30 E Third Ave San Mateo CA 94401. Mailing Add: 326 13th St Oakland CA 94612

HARDY, ROBERT
GALLERY DIRECTOR, CERAMIST
b Millville, NJ, Aug 2, 38. Study: Calif State Univ, Long Beach, BA, MA; Univ Calif, Irvine; Scripps Grad Sch, Claremont, Calif. Comn: Numerous comns for interior designers in bas-relief ceramic sculptures. Exhib: Los Angeles Mus Sci & Indust, 62; Craftsmen USA, Lytton Gallery, Los Angeles Co Art Mus, Los Angeles, 66; Mus Contemp Crafts, New York, 66 & Ravinia Festival, Chicago, 67; Saginaw Art Mus, Mich, 68; Grand Rapids Art Mus, Mich, 68; Columbia Mus Art, SC, 68; Laguna Mus Art, Calif, 74. Collections Arranged: Religious Expressions in Art, 75, National Basketry Exhibition, 76, California Indian Basketry: An Artistic Overview (ed, catalogue), 76, June Wayne: Weaver of Tapestries, Painter & Printmaker, 77 & Year of the Horse: 4676, 78, Fine Arts Gallery, Cypress Col. Teaching: Prof ceramics, Cypress Col, 66- Pos: Designer; gallery dir, Fine Arts Gallery, Cypress Col, 66- Awards: Merit Award, Craftsmen USA, Lytton Gallery, 66. Mailing Add: 9200 Valley View Cypress CA 90630

HARDY, THOMAS (AUSTIN)
SCULPTOR
b Redmond, Ore, Nov 30, 21. Study: Ore State Univ, 38-40; Univ Ore, BA, 42, with Archipenko, summer 51, MFA, 52. Work: Whitney Mus Am Art, New York; Seattle Art Mus, Wash; Springfield Art Mus, Mo; Mus Art, Ogunquit, Maine; Portland Art Mus, Ore. Comn: Sculptures, Oregon Flora (screens), Portland State Univ, 62, Diving Birds, Fed Bldg, Juneau, Alaska, 64, Duck Fountain, Univ Ore, Eugene, 64, Flight, Dorothy Chandler Music Ctr, Los Angeles, Calif, 65 & wall sculpture, State Dept Agr, Salem, Ore, 68. Exhib: 3rd Biennial, Sao Paulo, Brazil, 55; Am Watercolors, Drawings & Prints, Metrop Mus Art, 56; Mus Mod Art Sculpture Exhib, 63; Whitney Mus Am Art Sculpture Ann, 64; Exhib Cand Grants, Am Inst Arts & Lett, 68. Teaching: Lectr, Univ Calif, Berkeley, 56-58; instr, Calif Sch Fine Arts, San Francisco, 56-58; assoc prof sculpture, Tulane Univ La, 58-59; resident artist, Reed Col, 60-61. Pos: Mem bd dirs, Contemp Crafts Gallery, Portland, 60-71. Awards: Award for Color Lithography, Soc Am Graphic Artists, 52; Seattle Art Mus Northwest Ann Sculpture Award, 55; Distinguished Serv Award, Univ Ore, 64. Bibliog: H Wurdemann (auth), Recent art of the West Coast, Art Am, 2/55; Metal sculptures by Tom Hardy, Am Artist, 4/55; L Jones (auth), Tom Hardy: sculptor-craftsman, Creative Crafts, 7/62. Mem: Portland Art Mus; Contemp Crafts Asn; Friends Mus Art, Univ Ore; Am Hist Train Asn; Maude Kerns Art Ctr. Style & Technique: Primarily arc welded forged bronze sculptures based on forms suggested by nature. Media: Welded Bronze, Brush & Ink. Dealer: Kraushaar Galleries 1055 Madison Ave New York NY 10021. Mailing Add: 1422 SW Harrison St Portland OR 97201

HARE, CHANNING
PAINTER
b New York, NY. Study: Art Students League; and with Robert Henri, George Bellows & William Zorach. Work: Boston Mus Fine Arts, Mass; Pa Acad Fine Arts, Philadelphia; Colo Springs Fine Arts Ctr, Colo; Davenport Munic Art Gallery, Iowa; Va Hist Soc; plus others. Exhib: Metrop Mus Art, New York, 52; Lowe Gallery Art, 55; Grand Cent Moderns, 56; Palm Beach Galleries, 64-66, 68-69 & 71-72; James Hunt BakBarker Gallery, 73-75. Awards: Prizes, Soc Four Arts, 42-44. Mem: Soc Four Arts (bd dirs). Mailing Add: c/o Broberg Box 966 Palm Beach FL 33480

HARE, DAVID
SCULPTOR
b New York, NY, Mar 10, 17. Study: Studied in New York, Ariz & Colo. Work: Long Beach Mus Art; Los Angeles Co Mus Art; Mus Mod Art, New York; Princeton Univ; Whitney Mus Am Art; plus others. Comn: Sculpture for New York City, States of RI, Mass & Ill. Exhib: Pittsburgh Bicentennial, Pa, 62; Seattle World's Fair, 62; Dada, Surrealism and Their Heritage, 68 & The New American Painting and Sculpture, 69, Mus Mod Art, New York; retrospective, Philadelphia Mus Art, Pa, 69; plus many other group & one-man shows. Teaching: Lectr extensively; guest critic & lectr, Md Inst Col of Art. Pos: Ed, VVV (surrealist mag), 42-44. Bibliog: Wayne Craven (auth), Sculpture in America, Thomas Y Crowell, 68; William S Rubin (auth), Dada, surrealism, and their heritage, Mus Mod Art, 68; Eduard Trier (auth), Form and Space: Sculpture in the 20th Century, Praeger, 68. Mailing Add: 34 Leroy St New York NY 10014

HARE, STEPHEN HOPKINS
PAINTER
b New York, NY, Dec 1, 21. Study: Yale Univ. Work: Boston Mus Fine Arts, Mass; Baltimore Mus Art, Md; Toledo Mus Art, Ohio; Mus Fine Arts, Houston, Tex; Norton Gallery Art, West Palm Beach, Fla; plus others. Exhib: Whitney Mus Am Art, New York; Corcoran Gallery Art, Washington, DC; Pa Acad Fine Arts, Philadelphia; Art Inst Chicago; Calif Palace of Legion of Honor, San Francisco; plus others. Mailing Add: c/o Broberg Box 966 Palm Beach FL 33480

HARI, KENNETH
PAINTER, PRINTMAKER
b Perth Amboy, NJ, Mar 31, 47. Study: Newark Sch Fine & Indust Arts, dipl, 66; Md Inst Art, BFA, 68; and with Leon Franks, John Delmonte & Donald Delue. Work: Newark Mus, NJ; Baltimore Mus, Md; Nat Portrait Galleries, London, Eng & Washington, DC; Vatican, Rome, Italy; Bulgarian Mus of Fine Arts; Grand Ole Opry, Nashville, Tenn. Comn: Portraits, W H Auden & M Moore, New York, 69, Pablo Casals, comn by Mrs Pablo Casals, Vt, 70, Princess Gloria Miglionico, New York, 71, Salvador Dali, New York, 72 & Ernest Hemingway, Hemingway House, Cuba. Exhib: Union Col, 69; Monmouth Col, 70; Newark Mus, 71; Trenton State Mus, 72; Va Polytechnic Inst, 74. Pos: Dir, NJ Art Festival, 64-69. Awards: Pulaski Award, Kusiosko Found, 63; Felice Found Award, 69; Trenton State Mus Award, 72. Bibliog: Art in the Hamptons, 69 & feature story, 73, New York Times; M Lenson (auth), Portrait of Casals, Newark News, 71; D Brown (auth), Poetess an artist, Home News, 72. Media: Oil, Graphite. Publ: Illusr, Prophet, 71, Lovers of Our Time, 71, Vermont, 72, Folk Singer, 72 & Time for Peace, 72, H S Graphics; Abraham, 74; Marcel Marceau, 75. Dealer: C C Price Gallery 15 E 48th St New York NY 10017; H S Graphics Box 243 Keasbey NJ 08832. Mailing Add: 228 Sherman St Perth Amboy NJ 08861

HARKAVY, MINNA
SCULPTOR
Study: Art Students League; with Antoine Bourdelle, Paris, France; Hunter Col, BA. Work: Whitney Mus Am Art & Mus Mod Art, New York; Mus Munic, St Denis, France; Mus Western Art, USSR; Ain Harod Mus, Tel-Aviv, Israel; also many pvt collections in US & abroad. Comn: Sculpture, Winchendon Post Off, Mass & Norfolk Mus Art & Sci, Va. Exhib: San Francisco Mus Art, Calif; Art Inst Chicago; Pa Acad Fine Arts, Philadelphia; Albright-Knox Art Gallery, Buffalo; Munson-Williams-Proctor Inst, Utica, NY; plus others. Awards: Medal of Honor, 62 & Prizes, 64 & 65, Nat Asn Women Artists; Prize, Audubon Artists, 65. Mem: Artists Equity Asn; Fedn Mod Painters & Sculptors; Sculptors Guild; assoc mem Int Inst Arts & Lett. Mailing Add: Hotel Ansonia 2109 Broadway New York NY 10023

HARLAN, ROMA CHRISTINE
PAINTER
b Warsaw, Ind. Study: Art Inst Chicago, Daughters Ind scholar; Purdue Univ, Lafayette; and with Ralph Clarkson, Chicago, Francis Chapin, Constantine Pougialis & Marie Goth. Comn: (Portraits) Gen Milton A Reckord, Sen Edward Martin & others, Nat Guard Asn US; Sen Kenneth S Wherry, US Capitol Bldg; Col Mildred I Clark, Walter Reed Army Med Ctr; John Davis, US Supreme Ct & Judge Bernita Mathews, US Dist Ct; plus many other prominent people. Exhib: One-man exhibs, George Washington Univ Gallery, Lake Shore Club, Chicago & Purdue Univ, Lafayette; Hoosier Salon Ind; All Ill Soc Fine Arts. Pos: DC state art chmn, DC Fedn Women's Clubs, 75. Bibliog: Eleanor Jewett (auth), article in, Chicago Tribune; Florence Berryman (auth), article in, Washington Eve Star, 67; plus others. Mem: Arts Club Washington; Ind Fedn Arts Clubs; Washington Forum Club; DC Fedn Women's Clubs; Zonta Club. Style & Technique: Classical. Media: Oil. Publ: Auth, Rembrandt, Cong Rec, 57. Mailing Add: 1600 S Joyce St Arlington VA 22202

HARLOW, FREDERICA TODD
ART HISTORIAN, ART DEALER
b Washington, DC, June 23, 44. Study: Hollins Col, BA(French; art); George Washington Univ, MA(art hist); Inst Fine Arts. Pos: Owner-dir, Frederica Harlow Gallery Inc, presently. Mem: Int Ctr of Medieval Art (publ comt). Res: Late Antique & Carolingian. Specialty: European graphics and illustrated books 1890-1930; vintage photography. Publ: Auth, William Morris: Reaction and Revolution, William Morris Soc, 69; co-auth, The Illustrations of George Barber, Dover, 77. Mailing Add: 1100 Madison Ave New York NY 10028

HARLOW, ROBERT E
PAINTER
b Philadelphia, Pa, Mar 20, 14. Study: Pa Acad Fine Arts, Univ Pa, BFA, 36; Columbia Univ; Yale Univ. Work: Albany Inst Art & Hist; Dunbarton Oaks, Washington, DC; Miami Mus Mod Art; Conn Pub Insts; in collection of John Davis Hatch. Exhib: Directions American Art, Carnegie Inst, 42; Artists & Engineers, Brooklyn Mus, 69; NJ State Mus Ann, Trenton, 71; IBM, Princeton, NJ, 73; one-man shows, Miami Mus Mod Art, 69 & Rutgers Univ, 71; Directions Am Art, Metrop Mus Art, New York. Teaching: Instr art, Manville Pub Schs, NJ, 57-72; supvr art, Am Sch, Madrid, Spain, 66-67. Pos: Supvr & artist, Fed Art Proj, Pa & Conn, 43-44. Awards: Hon mention, Nat Drawing Ann, Nat Acad Design, 42; cover design award, Nat Drawing Ann, Albany Mus Art & Hist, 43. Media: Oil. Res: Discovery and authentication of Thomas Eakins' painting, Pushing for Rail, Yale Univ. Mailing Add: Fernan Gonzoles 66 Madrid Spain

HARMAN, JACK KENNETH
SCULPTOR, EDUCATOR
b Vancouver, BC, July 31, 27. Study: Vancouver Sch Art, two yr dipl; Slade Sch Art, Univ Col, Univ London. Work: Sir George Williams Univ, Montreal, PQ; London Art Mus, Ont; Norman MacKenzie Gallery, Regina, Sask; Univ BC, Vancouver. Comn: Cast bronze fountain, Canadian Save the Children, Toronto, Ont, 64; Family (cast bronze), Pac Press, Vancouver, 66; Runners-Bannister & Landy (bronze), Empire Stadium, Vancouver, 67; Mother and Child (bronze), Queens Park, Parliament Bldgs, Toronto, 68; Family Group (bronze), Mus & Archives Bldgs, Victoria, 69. Exhib: 29th Ann, Vancouver Art Gallery, 60, 32nd Ann, 63; 46th Ann, Seattle Art Mus, 60; Nat Outdoor Sculpture Exhib, Quebec, PQ, 60; Montreal Mus Ann, 61; one-man shows, Vancouver Art Gallery, 62; two from Vancouver, D Cameron Gallery, Toronto, 62. Teaching: Instr sculpture, exten dept, Univ BC, 59-61; instr sculpture & metal casting, Vancouver Sch Art. Pos: Pres, NW Inst Sculpture, 59-60. Awards: O'Keefe Art Award, O'Keefe Breweries, 51; Can Coun Grants, 66 & 69. Bibliog: Articles in Arts in Can, 67 & Can Art Mag, summers, 62-64. Mem: Royal Can Acad Arts; Soc Sculptors. Media: Bronze. Mailing Add: 1190 Kilmer Rd North Vancouver BC V7K 1R1 Can

HARMAN, MARYANN WHITTEMORE
PAINTER
b Roanoke, Va, Sept 13, 35. Study: Univ Va, Mary Washington Col, BA; Va Polytech Inst & State Univ, MA. Work: Minn Mining & Mfg Corp, Minneapolis; Philip Morris Corp, Richmond, Va; Hunter Mus, Chattanooga, Tenn; Chrysler Corp, Detroit; Shawmut Bank, Boston. Exhib: Hunter Mus Art Ann, 64 & 69-74; Va Mus Fine Arts Biennial, 65 & 73; Irene Leach Mem Exhib, Chrysler Mus, Norfolk, 67-72; Butler Inst Art Nat Show, Youngstown, Ohio, 69 & 72; Galery Ariadne Group Show, New York, 74; one-person shows, Andre Emmerich Gallery, New York, 76 & Allen Rubiner Gallery, Detroit, 77; Meredith Long Gallery, New York, 77; plus others. Teaching: Assoc prof painting & drawing, Va Polytech Inst & State Univ, 64- Awards: Purchase Award, Roanoke Fine Arts, 73; Purchase Awards, Hunter Mus, 74; Cert of Distinction, Va Mus Fine Arts, 74. Bibliog: Article in Commonwealth, CofC, Richmond, 73; Barclay Sheaks (auth), Painting Natural Environment, Davis, 74 & Painting with Oils, Davis, 77. Mem: Col Art Asn Am; Southeastern Col Art Asn; Va Mus Fine Arts; Am Fedn Arts. Style & Technique: Lyrical abstraction, landscaped based; stained and textured surfaces. Media: Acrylic, Oil. Dealer: Andre Emmerich Gallery 41 E 57th St New York NY 10019. Mailing Add: 602 Landsdowne Dr Blacksburg VA 24060

HARMON, BARBARA SAYRE
PAINTER, CHILDREN'S BOOK ILLUSTRATOR
b Yerington, Nev, Aug 8, 27. Study: Bisttram Sch Fine Art, painting & drawing; etching with Lawton Parker; Black Mountain Col, bookbinding with Johanna Jalowitz. Bibliog: Mary Carrol Nelson (auth), Barbara Harmon: magic & mastery, Am Artist Mag, 5/75. Mem: Exhib Artist Taos Art Asn. Style & Technique: Original paintings and prints of the fairy world; floral

still lifes based on mythical and fantasy themes. Media: Watercolor, Lithograph; Mixed-Media, Oil. Publ: Auth & illusr, Tabbigail's Garden, 67, The Little People's Counting Book, 68 & Monday's Mouse, 70, The Children's Gallery Press; auth & illusr, This Little Pixie, 69 & The Tumpfee Wood Acorn Book, 77, The Children's Gallery Press & The Baker Co. Dealer: Baker Gallery of Fine Art Box 1920 Lubbock TX 79408; Stables Gallery Box 198 Taos NM 87571. Mailing Add: Box 202 Taos NM 87571

HARMON, CLIFF FRANKLIN
PAINTER
b Los Angeles, Calif, June 26, 23. Study: Bisttram Sch Fine Art, Los Angeles, Calif & Taos, NMex, with Emil Bisttram; Black Mountain Col, NC, with Joe Fiore; Taos Valley Art Sch, with Louis Ribak. Work: Mus NMex, Santa Fe; Okla Art Ctr, Oklahoma City. Exhib: NMex & Southwest Biennials, NMex Mus, 66, 70-72, Watercolor NMex, 74; 11th Midwest Biennial, Joslyn Art Mus, Omaha, Nebr, 70; 1st Four Corners Biennial, Phoenix Art Mus, Ariz, 71; Bertrand Russell Centenary Art Exhib, Rotundagallery, London, Eng, 72. Awards: First Premium for Abstract Painting, NMex State Fair, 68; Hon Mention, NMex Mus & Phoenix Art Mus, 71. Mem: Taos Art Asn (first vpres, 68-69, pres, 78-79). Style & Technique: Hard-edge. Media: Acrylic, Watercolor, Oil. Dealer: Stables Gallery Taos NM 87571; Total Arts Gallery Taos NM 87571. Mailing Add: Box 202 Taos NM 87571

HARMON, ELOISE (NORSTAD)
SCULPTOR
b St Paul, Minn, Aug 28, 33. Study: Hunter Col; Art Students League; Alfred Univ; also with Maija Grotell, Albert Jacobson & Norman La Liberte. Comn: Mural, Inn at the Landing, Kansas City, 68; mural, New York Apt, 70; murals, Park Sheraton Hotel, New York, 70; Fountain, El Conquistador Hotel, PR, 70; altar cross, Our Redeemer Lutheran Church, New York, 72. Exhib: Commission On, Worship & Fine Arts Show, Bridgeport, 69; Cranbrook Art Show, Detroit, 69; Int Exhib, Am Inst Decorators, 70; Relig Art Show, Episcopal Church Ctr, Chicago, 71; New Eng Exhib, New Canaan, Conn, 72; numerous shows, 72-78, incl Mainstreet Gallery, Nantucket, Mass, Kendall Gallery, Wellfleet, Mass, Handmakers Gallery, Houston, Tex, Virginia Barrett Gallery, Chappaqua, NY & Westlake Gallery, White Plains, NY. Awards: Int Award, Am Inst Decorators, 70. Bibliog: Art in good use, New York Times, 61; Moody (auth), Decorative Art in Modern Interiors, Viking, 65. Mem: Katonah Gallery Art Lending, NY; Soc Renewal Christian Art, New York. Style & Technique: Direct use of clay; building hollow with slabs and cylinders, carving; result is a high-fired one of a kind sculpture. Media: Clay. Dealer: Emily Bouchard 1060 Lexington Ave New York NY 10021. Mailing Add: 35 Bedford Rd Pleasantville NY 10570

HARMON, FOSTER
ART DEALER
b Judsonia, Ark, Nov 5, 12. Study: Ind Univ; Ohio Univ; State Univ Iowa, BA, 35, MFA, 36. Collections Arranged: Arrangement and presentation of twelve exhibitions annually. Teaching: Instr drama & dir univ theatre prod, Ind Univ, Bloomington, 36-42. Pos: Pub rels dir, Ringling Mus Art, Sarasota, Fla, 58-59; dir, Oehlschlaeger Galleries, Sarasota, 61-70; owner-dir, Harmon Gallery, Naples, Fla, 64- Awards: Award of Merit for Long Serv & Contrib to Art, Ohio Univ, 70. Mem: Am Fedn Arts; Fla League Arts; Ringling Mus Art (mem coun); Sarasota Art Asn (pres, 59-60); Fla Artists Group (mus & gallery adv). Specialty: Paintings, drawings and sculpture by major American artists of the 20th century. Collection: Private collection of American art. Mailing Add: PO Box 6187 St Armands Sta Sarasota FL 33578

HARMON, LILY
PAINTER, SCULPTOR
b New Haven, Conn, Nov 19, 12. Study: Yale Sch Art; Acad Colarossi, Paris; Art Students League. Work: Whitney Mus; Butler Art Inst, Youngstown, Ohio; Newark Art Mus, NJ; Tel Aviv Mus, Israel; Hirschhorn Mus, Washington, DC. Comn: Mural, Portchester Jewish Ctr, NY, 50. Exhib: Metrop Mus Art, New York, 43; Carnegie Inst, Pittsburgh, 44-49; Univ Ill, 49; 12 one-man shows, Int Salon, Palace Fine Arts, Mexico City, 44-73. Teaching: Teacher oil painting, Nat Acad Design, New York, 74- Awards: La Tausca Art Award, 47; Hallmark Art Award, 49; Pearl Safir Award, Silvermine Guild, 54; plus others. Bibliog: Sculpture of Lily Harmon, Commun Arts Mag, 72; A Lily for a Lily, Limited Ed Club, 75; Art in boxes, Norman Laliberte, 75. Mem: Provincetown Art Asn; Artists Equity; Nat Acad Design. Publ: Illusr, Jane Austin's Pride & Prejudice, 47; illusr, Jean Paul Sartre's Dirty Hands, 67, Kafka's Castle, 67 & Thomas Mann's Buddenbrooks, 67, Jap Publ; illusr, Edith Wharton's House of Mirth, Limited Eds, 75; illusr, Guy de Mauppasant, auth, Short Stories, Franklin Libr, 77. Mailing Add: 151 Central Park W New York NY 10023

HARMS, ELIZABETH
PAINTER
b Milwaukee, Wis, May 26, 24. Study: Art Inst Chicago, BFA & MFA. Work: Newark Mus, NJ. Exhib: Art Inst Chicago Ann, 61-64 & 66; one-man shows, Traverse Festival Gallery, Edinburgh, Scotland, 65, Hewlett Gallery, Carnegie-Mellon Univ, 67, Mus Art, Carnegie Inst, 69 & Fischbach Gallery, New York, 75; 7th Triennial, Newark Mus, NJ, 71; Contemp Images in Watercolor, Arkson Art Mus, Ohio, Indianapolis Mus Art, Ind & Univ Rochester, NY, 76. Awards: Third Prize Nat Watercolor exhib, Smithsonian Inst, 63; Armstrong Prize, Art Inst Chicago, 63; Tiffany Found Grant for Painting, 77. Bibliog: Hilton Kramer (auth), Art: More from Dubuffet feast, NY Times, 9/27/75. Style & Technique: Abstract. Media: Oil, Watercolor. Dealer: Fischbach Gallery 29 W 57th St New York NY 10019. Mailing Add: 240 Ogden Ave Jersey City NJ 07307

HARNETT, MR & MRS JOEL WILLIAM
COLLECTORS
Mr Harnett, b New York, NY, Dec 3, 25. Study: Mr Harnett, Univ Richmond, BA; New Sch Social Res. Mem: Friends of Whitney Mus Am Art. Collection: Works by Hopper, Burchfield, Marsh, Greene, Anuszkiewcz, Raphael Soyer, Rosenberg, Seley, Tooker, Jenkins, Pearlstein, Rickey, Lamis and Fletcher Benton. Mailing Add: 2 Sutton Pl S New York NY 10022

HAROOTIAN, KHOREN DER
PAINTER, SCULPTOR
b Armenia, Apr 2, 09; US citizen. Study: Worcester Art Mus, Mass. Work: Metrop Mus Art & Whitney Mus Am Art; Worcester Art Mus; Billy Rose Collection, Bezalel Mus, Israel; Armenian Nat Mus, Erevan, Soviet Armenia. Comn: Sculptures, Scientist, Fairmount Park Art Asn, 50, Christ, Armenian Cathedral Comt, New York, 58, Beaver, Baruch Col, 60 & saints, Armenian Apostolic Church, Wynnewood, Pa, 73; bronze monument, Armenian Bicentennial Comt, Fairmount Park, Philadelphia, 75. Exhib: Whitney Mus Am Art Ann, New York, 45-66; Pa Acad Fine Arts, Philadelphia, 45-66; Fairmount Park Int Exhib, Philadelphia Mus, 48; Am Pavilion, Brussels World's Fair, Belg, 58; Royal Acad Arts Summer Exhib, Piccadily, London, Eng, 64 & 65; plus others. Awards: George D Widener Medal, Pa Acad Fine Arts, 54; Am Acad Arts & Lett & Nat Inst Arts & Lett Award & Citation, 54; Silver Medal, Gruppo Donatello, Florence, Italy, 62. Bibliog: Dorothy Grafly (auth), Prophet of man in his eternal battle against evil, Am Artist Mag, 11/46; Ralph M Pearson (auth), article in Modern Renaissance Am Art, Harper & Row, 54; article in, Current Biog, 1/55. Media: Watercolor, Bronze, Marble. Mailing Add: RFD Rte 9-W Castle Rd Orangeburg NY 10962

HARPER, ELEANOR O'NEIL
PAINTER
b Newburyport, Mass, Dec 23, 19. Study: Radcliffe Col, AB(fine arts); Sch Practical Art, Boston; also with Donald Stoltenberg, Betty Lou Schlemm & Arthur Pope. Exhib: Jordan Marsh Ann Exhibs, Boston, 69-73; Copley Soc, Boston, 69-75; Catharine Lorillard Wolfe Art Club Exhib, Nat Arts Club, New York, 72-73; Rockport Art Asn, Mass, 74-75; Nat Exhib, Mus Fine Arts, Springfield, Mass, 75; Butler Mus, Ohio. Teaching: Pvt instr & painting workshops, Rockport, 74- Pos: Cpoywriter, Filene's, Boston, 42-43, dir advert, Br Shop, 43-45. Awards: Best of Show, Newburyport Art Asn, 74; Maurice E Goldberg Mem Award, Rockport Art Asn, 75. Mem: Rockport Art Asn (mem comt, 74-75, dir portrait figure group, secy & mem bd governors); Copley Soc. Style & Technique: Portrait, creative figure and landscape painting. Media: Oil. Mailing Add: Penzance Rd Rockport MA 01966

HARPER, JOHN RUSSELL
ART HISTORIAN
b Ont, Can, Apr 15, 14. Study: Victoria Univ Toronto, Ont, BA; Univ Toronto, MA; Univ Guelph, Ont, Can, hon DLitt. Teaching: Mem staff, Concordia Univ, Montreal, Que, 67-, currently prof fine art. Pos: Cur Can art, Nat Gallery Can, Ottawa, 58-62; chief cur, McCord Mus, McGill Univ, 63-66. Awards: Officer of the Order of Can. Mem: Fel Royal Soc Can. Res: Canadian painting, particularly in the 19th and early 20th centuries. Publ: Auth, Painting in Canada: A History, 66, Paul Kane's Frontier, 70 & A People's Art, 74, Univ Toronto Press; auth, William G R Hind, Nat Gallery Can, 76. Mailing Add: R R Three Alexandria ON K0C 1A0 Can

HARPER, ROBIN OKEEFFER
See Asante, Kwasi Seitu

HARPER, WILLIAM
ENAMELIST, EDUCATOR
b Bucyrus, Ohio, June 17, 44. Study: Western Reserve Univ, BS, 66, MS, 67; Cleveland Inst Art, cert, 67. Work: Cleveland Mus Art; Columbus Gallery Fine Art; Minn Mus Art; Mus of Contemp Crafts; Mint Mus, NC. Exhib: Art of Enamel, State Univ NY New Paltz, 73; Baroque '74, Mus Contemp Crafts, New York, 74; Goldsmith, Renwick Gallery, Smithsonian Inst, Washington, DC, 74 & one-man exhib, 77-78; Crafts of the Americas, Colo State Univ, 75; Int Enamel Biennale, Mus City Limoges, France, 75; Am Crafts 1976, Mus of Contemp Art, Chicago, 76; Landscape: New Views, Johnson Mus of Art, Cornell Univ, NY, 77. Teaching: Vis artist enamels, Kent State Univ, 70-73; assoc prof metals & enamels, Fla State Univ, 73- Awards: Beaux Arts Exhib Best in Show, Columbus Gallery Fine Art, 73; Award for Crafts & Horace Potter Award for Excellence in Craftsmanship, Cleveland Mus Art, 73-74; Medallion of Limoges, Int Enamel Biennalle, 75. Bibliog: Elizabeth McClelland (auth), Enameling on the upbeat, Craft Horizons, 5/73. Mem: Soc NAm Goldsmiths; Am Crafts Coun. Style & Technique: Cloisonne enamel/metal objects which are designed to involve the viewer in tactile participation. Publ: Contribr, The Art of Cloisonne, Lowe Art Mus, Coral Gables, Fla, 72; auth, Step by Step Enameling, Western, 73; auth, The magic of cloisonne: William Harper, Craft Horizons, 6/77. Mailing Add: 3516 Trillium Ct Tallahassee FL 32303

HARRILL, JAMES
PAINTER
b NC, Mar 21, 36. Study: NY Univ, 52-56; Parsons Sch Design, 52-56; Ogunquit Sch Sculpture & Painting, Maine, with John Laurent. Work: Mus NMex, Santa Fe; Colonial Williamsburg Found, Va; Statesville Fine Arts Mus, NC. Exhib: NC Mus Art Ann, Raleigh, 56-68; Southeastern Ann, Atlanta, Ga, 58-68; Zappeion Mus, Athens, Greece, 64; Southwest Biennial, Mus NMex, Santa Fe, 71 & 72; 30 NC Painters, Shaw Studios, New York. Teaching: Instr painting, Int Coun Europe, Greece, 63-64; instr painting & drawing, Proj Newgate, NMex State Penitentiary, 71- Awards: Thalhimer Found Award, 60; Purchase Award, NMex Biennial, Mus NMex, 71. Media: Acrylic. Mailing Add: c/o Janus Gallery 116 1/2 E Palace Ave Santa Fe NM 87501

HARRINGTON, LA MAR
ART ADMINISTRATOR, ART HISTORIAN
b Iowa, Nov 2, 17. Study: Iowa State Col, 35-36; Cornish Sch Fine Arts, Seattle, 45-50; Univ Wash, 60-65. Founded & Developed: Registry of NW Artists & Archives Northwest Art, Univ Wash, 69; Index Art in Pac Northwest, for Henry Art Gallery, publ by Univ Wash Press, 70. Exhibitions Arranged: Art and Machines: Light, Motion and Sound, 69; Across the Border, 69; Claes Oldenburg Icebag, 71; More Art for Public Places, 71; New Works from the Walker, 71; Kenneth Callahan: A Universal Voyage, 73; Adventures in Photography, 75. Pos: Staff mem, Henry Gallery, Univ Wash, 56-75, asst dir, 69-72, assoc dir, 72-75, cur arch & manuscripts div, Arch of Northwest Art, 75-; panel mem visual arts, Nat Endowment for the Arts, 76- Awards: Governor's Arts Award, Wash State Art Comn, 71; Friends of Crafts Award, 72; Woman of Achievement Award, Women in Commun Ann Matrix Table, 74. Mem: Western Asn Art Mus (bd trustees, vpres, 73, pres, 74 & 75); Allied Arts Seattle (bd trustees); Pac Northwest Arts Ctr (bd trustees); Pac Northwest Arts & Crafts Asn (life mem bd trustees, pres, 57 & 58); Pottery NW (bd trustees, vpres, 76 & 77). Res: Contemporary American art and handcrafts; ceramics of the West Coast. Publ: Auth, Letter from Seattle, 63-68, First Annual Western Craft Competition, 7/64 & Northwest Craftsmen's Exhibition, 5/65, Craft Horizons; contribr, 74th Western Annual (exhib catalog), 73. Mailing Add: 511 Galer Seattle WA 98109

HARRINGTON, WILLIAM CHARLES
SCULPTOR, EDUCATOR
b Chicago, Ill, June 20, 42. Study: Hartford Art Sch; Univ Ill, with Roger Majorowicz & Frank Gallo, BFA; Univ Hartford with Ted Behl & Lloyd Glasson, MFA. Comn: 15 ft concrete & steel, Cabot, Cabot & Forbes, Seattle, Wash, 75; 4 ft wood relief, Amalgamated Spirits & Provisions, Ames, Iowa, 75 & Cedar Rapids, Iowa, 76. Exhib: Evansville Mus, Ind, 72; Indianapolis Art Mus, Ind, 72; Brunnier Gallery, Ames, Iowa, 75; Dorsey Gallery, Roanoke, Va, 74; Red River Exhib, Morehead, Minn, 75, 76 & 77; Des Moines Art Ctr, 76. Teaching: Asst prof sculpture & drawing, Ind State Univ, Terre Haute, 70-72; asst prof sculpture, Iowa State Univ, 74- Pos: Workshop asst, George Rickey, East Chatham, NY, 65; mem, Combat Artists Team Vietnam, 68-69. Style & Technique: Carving, metal and assemblage. Media: Mixed Media, Wood. Mailing Add: RR 1 Box 128 A Bent Mountain VA 24059

HARRIS, ALFRED PETER
PAINTER, ART ADMINISTRATOR
b Toronto, Ont, Apr 4, 32. Study: Ont Col Art, Toronto, hon dipl. Work: Sir George Williams Univ, Montreal; Bronfman Collection, Montreal Mus Fine Art; Brascan Collection, Toronto; Can Coun Art Bank; Northern & Cent Gas Co. Exhib: Mem Gallery, Albright-Knox Gallery, Buffalo, 62; four-man exhib, London Pub Libr & Art Mus, 63-65; two-man exhibs, Dorothy Cameron Gallery, 64-65; two-man show, Roberts Gallery, Toronto, 70; Ann Exhib Contemp Can Art, Hamilton, 70-72. Collections Arranged: J W Morrice, J Chambers Retrospective & William Kurelec Retrospective, 66; Baker, Boyle & Hollenback, 67; John Newman, 68; Soul of Niagara, 69; John Boyle—Ed Fantinel, 70; Harvey Breverman & Niagara Now, 71; plus earlier exhibs. Teaching: Art instr, Ont Col Art, 59-60; instr gen art, Ridley Col, St Catharines, 63-65; spec lectr mod art, Brock Univ, 66. Pos: Dir, St Catharines & Dist Arts Coun, 59-; pres, Ont Asn Art Galleries, 70-71. Bibliog: Harry Malcomson (auth), Artist, Toronto Life, 69. Mem: Can Soc Graphic Art; Ont Soc Artists. Media: Oil. Publ: Contribr, Nude in Canadian Art, 72. Dealer: Roberts Gallery 641 Yonge St Toronto ON Can. Mailing Add: 109 St Paul Crescent St Catharines ON L2S 1M3 Can

HARRIS, ANN SUTHERLAND
ART HISTORIAN, ART ADMINISTRATOR
b Cambridge, Eng, Nov 4, 37. Study: Courtauld Inst Art, Univ London, BA(hon, first class), 61 & PhD, 65. Collections Arranged: Women Artist 1550-1950 (co-auth, catalogue), Los Angeles Co Mus Art, Los Angeles, 76-77; Univ Art Mus, Univ Tex Austin, 77; Mus Art, Carnegie Inst Int, Pittsburgh, 77; Brooklyn Mus, 77. Teaching: Asst prof art hist & archaeol, Columbia Univ, 66-71; asst prof art hist, Hunter Col, New York, 71-73; assoc prof art hist, State Univ NY, Albany, 73-77. Pos: Vis lectr, Yale Univ, New Haven, Conn, fall 72-73; vis assoc prof, Inst Fine Arts, NY Univ, 74-75; chmn acad affairs, Metrop Mus Art, New York, 77- Mem: Col Art Asn Am (mem bd dir, 75-79); Women's Caucus for Art (pres & founder mem, 71-74, mem exec adv bd, 74). Res: Italian and French, 16th & 17th century painting and drawing. Publ: Co-auth, Die Zeichnungen von Andrea Sacchi & Carlo Maratta, Kataloge des Kunstmuseums, Düsseldorf, III, Düsseldorf, 67; ed, Selected Drawings of Gian Lorenzo Bernini, Dover Publ, 77; auth, Andrea Sacchi, Complete Edition of the Paintings, Phaidon, Oxford, 77. Mailing Add: 560 Riverside Dr New York NY 10027

HARRIS, HARVEY SHERMAN
PAINTER, EDUCATOR
b Hartford, Conn, Aug 31, 15. Study: Hartford Art Sch, dipl; Kansas City Art Inst, with Thomas Hart Benton & John de Martelly; Yale Univ, with Josef Albers & Willem de Kooning, BFA & MFA. Work: Speed Mus, Louisville, Ky; Southern Ill Univ Mitchell Gallery, Carbondale; State Univ NY Oswego Libr Art; La State Univ, Baton Rouge Libr Art. Comn: Illustrations for Look Homeward, Angel, 45; sets & costumes for Double Trouble (opera), Rockefeller Fund for Louisville Symphony & Opera, 56, sets & costumes for School for Wives, 57. Exhib: Drawings, USA, Mus Mod Art, New York, 55; Pa Acad Nat Watercolor & Drawing Biennial, 58 & 59; Butler Inst Am Art Nat Mid-Yr Show, Youngstown, Ohio, 64; Norfolk Mus 21st Am Drawing Biennial & Smithsonian Inst Traveling Drawing Show, 65; Avanti Gallery, New York, 75. Teaching: Lectr basic studio graphic design, Louisville Art Ctr & Univ Louisville, 54-57; asst prof drawing & art hist, State Univ NY Oswego, 57-60; assoc prof, Southern Ill Univ, Carbondale, 60-67; prof painting & drawing, La State Univ, Baton Rouge, 67- Awards: Hon Mention, Conn Artist-Teachers, Yale Art Gallery, 49; Hon Mention, Nat Drawing Show, Ball State Col, 64; Robert B Tunstall Prize, Norfolk Mus 21st Am Drawing Biennial, 65. Style & Technique: Hieratic, iconic, decorative; optical color mixtures obtained by overall patterning of dots and circles. Media: All Media. Dealer: William Dale Gallery 828 Chartres St New Orleans LA 70116. Mailing Add: 2209 Glendale Ave Baton Rouge LA 70808

HARRIS, JOSEPHINE MARIE
EDUCATOR, ART HISTORIAN
b Webster Groves, Mo, Jan 20, 11. Study: Washington Univ, AB, 31, MA, 32 & PhD, 36; Am Sch Classical Studies, Athens, Greece, 37-39; Dumbarton Oaks, Harvard Univ, Washington, DC, 42-45. Teaching: Prof fine arts & chmn dept, Wilson Col, 46- Awards: Award for Distinguished Teaching, Christian R & Mary F Lindback Found, 64. Mem: Col Art Asn Am. Res: A study of Coptic architectural decorative sculpture, with special reference to material found at Oxyrhynohos. Publ: Contribr, rev in, Am J Archaeol, 60-72. Mailing Add: Wilson Col Chambersburg PA 17201

HARRIS, JULIAN HOKE
SCULPTOR, ARCHITECT
b Carrollton, Ga, Aug 22, 06. Study: Ga Inst Technol, BS, 28; Pa Acad Fine Arts, 29-34. Work: IBM Collection, New York; High Mus Art, Atlanta, Ga; Univ Va Mus; also in many pvt collections. Comn: 50 sculptures for pub & pvt bldgs; 50 portrait & mem comns; 14 commemorative medallions. Exhib: Painting & Sculpture From Sixteen Cities, Mus Mod Art, 33; Pa Acad Fine Arts Mus, 34; three one-man shows, High Mus, Atlanta, 35, 39 & 69; Jewish Mus, New York, 52; Nat Sculpture Soc Ann, 70-72. Teaching: Emer prof, Ga Inst Technol Sch Archit; prof sculpture, Atlanta Sch Art, 46-52. Pos: Pres, Asn Ga Artists, 39-42; charter mem, Atlanta Citizens Adv Comt Urban Renewal, 58-71; charter mem, Atlanta Civic Design Comn, 65- Awards: Edgar Tobin Award, Southern States Art League, 39; Fine Arts Gold Medal, Am Inst Architects, 54; Ivan Allen, Sr Award, North Ga Chap Am Inst Architects, 62. Bibliog: Many articles in, Nat Sculpture Rev, 53-72; Georgia Tech Alumnus, Ga Inst Technol, 53, 71 & 72; Julian Hoke Harris, Am Sculptors Ser, No 16, 54. Mem: Fel Nat Sculpture Soc; fel Am Inst Architects; Atlanta Art Asn (sch adv comt, 72). Publ: Auth, Sculpture can be functional, WVa State Mag, 54; auth, Sculpture in architecture today, J Am Inst Architects, 55; auth, Architectural sculpture, Dixie Contractor, 55; auth, Environment, Atlanta Pub Sch Syst, 60; co-auth, Improving the mess we live in, NGa Chap Am Inst Architects, 66. Mailing Add: 177 Fifth St NW Atlanta GA 30313

HARRIS, LAWREN PHILLIPS
PAINTER, EDUCATOR
b Toronto, Ont, Oct 10, 10. Study: Boston Mus Fine Arts; also with Lawren S Harris (father), Toronto. Work: War Records, Nat Gallery Can. Comn: Off war artist with Can Army, 43-46; prize, Atlantic Awards Exhib, 67. Exhib: Ont Soc Arts, 36-; Royal Can Acad Arts, 38-; Can Group Painters, 38-; New York World's Fair, 39; Can Soc Graphic Art, 39-41; plus others. Teaching: Instr, N Voc Sch, Toronto, 38-40; instr, Trinity Col Sch, Port Hope, Ont, 40-41; emer prof fine arts & head dept, Mt Allison Univ. Awards: Can Govt Overseas Fel, 57-58; Hon Fel, NS Col Art. Mem: Ont Soc Arts; Can Group Painters; Royal Can Acad Arts. Mailing Add: 29 Orichtons Ottawa ON K1M 1V5 Can

HARRIS, LEON A, JR
COLLECTOR, PATRON
b New York, NY, June 20, 26. Study: Harvard Col. Pos: Former trustee, Dallas Mus Fine Arts. Interest: Donor to museums. Collection: Paintings, drawings and prints. Publ: Auth, The great picture robbery, Young France, The fine art of political wit & Only to God: the life of Godfrey Lowell Cabot; articles in Esquire, Good Housekeeping, McCalls & Encycl Americana. Mailing Add: 4512 Fairfax Dallas TX 45205

HARRIS, MARGO LIEBES
SCULPTOR
Study: Art Students League; also in Italy. Work: Portland Mus, Maine; Roseman Collection; Lehman Collection; Zorach Collection; Frank Alt-Schul Collection; plus others. Comn: Sheraton Southland Hotel, Dallas; Show Mart, Dallas; portraits, Prince Aziz Elganian, Teheran; fountains, N P Hildum Interiors; Sheraton Hotel, Chicago; plus others. Exhib: Whitney Mus Am Art; Portland Mus Fine Arts; Detroit Art Inst; Sculpture Ctr, New York; Boston Arts Festival; plus others. Awards: Nat Acad Design First Prize, Nat Asn Women Artists; Sculpture Medal of Honor Prize, 71; Mr & Mrs Charles Murphy Prize, 72; plus others. Bibliog: Dona Z Meilach (auth), Contemporary Stone Sculpture, Crown, 70. Mem: New York Soc Women Artists (pres, 67-70, bd dirs & sculpture chmn, 72-74); Am Soc Contemp Artists (bd dirs, juror & vpres); Artists Equity Asn. Mailing Add: 300 E 74th St New York NY 10021

HARRIS, MARIAN D
PAINTER
b Philadelphia, Pa, Apr 22, 04. Study: Pa Acad Fine Arts, 22-26, Cresson traveling scholar, 25, Acad Summer Sch, Chester Springs, Pa, 21-24 & 32; Hugh Breckenridge Summer Sch Art, East Gloucester, Mass, 26; with Wayman Adams, Elizabethtown, NY, 33, 35 & 38. Work: Albright-Knox Art Gallery, Buffalo, NY; Fellowship Pa Acad Fine Arts; Philadelphia Art Alliance; Gov Bacon Hosp, Del; YWCA, Wilmington, Del; among others. Exhib: Pa Acad Fine Arts Ann, 32; Nat Acad Design Ann, New York, 32; Art Inst Chicago Int Watercolor Exhib, 35; Am Watercolor Soc Ann, New York, 52; Newark Mus Triennial, NJ, 64; Am Artists Prof League Ann, 73 & 74; Garden State Art Ctr, NJ, 74; Cape May Co Art League, NJ, 74; NJ Fed Art Asn Asn, NJ State Cult Ctr, Trenton, 76 & 77; plus many others. Teaching: Instr painting, Wilmington Acad Art, Del, 27-32, 36-37; instr art, Atlantic City Friends Sch, NJ, 56-57; lectr art appreciation, Jewish Community Ctr, Margate, NJ, 59. Awards: George A Rhodes Prize, Wilmington Soc Fine Arts, 30; Public Choise, Triennial, South Jersey, 64; Second Prize, Heritage Show, Smithville, 73; and others. Bibliog: Benizet (auth), French Dictionary of Artists & Painters; Fielding (auth), American Artists from 1860. Mem: Fellowship Pa Acad Fine Arts; Am Watercolor Soc; League South Jersey Artists (pres, 60-61); Atlantic City Art Ctr (pres, 65-66); Prof Artists South Jersey (treas). Style & Technique: Contemporary realism. Media: Oil, Watercolor. Dealer: Charles Bertolino Gallery 406 Harrison Ave West Berlin NJ 08091. Mailing Add: 22 N Cornwall Ave Ventnor NJ 08406

HARRIS, MURRAY A
COLLECTOR, COMMERCIAL ARTIST
b Boston, Mass, Feb 1, 11. Study: Mass Normal Art Sch; Boston Mus Fine Art; Harvard Univ Exten. Comn: Complete series of US vice presidents, Presidential Mus, Odessa, Tex. Exhib: One-man shows, Funnies, USA, City Hall Tower, Los Angeles & State Mutual Savings & Loan Asn; West Side Community Ctr; Lytton Savings & Loan Asn; Brand Libr, Glendale, Calif. Pos: Artist & cartoonist, Boston Globe, Mass, 41-46; artist, Rexall Drug Advert Dept, Los Angeles, 48-68; lectr hist comic strips, Univ Calif, Riverside. Awards: Mem Jury Hall of Fame, Mus of Cartoon Art. Bibliog: Thelma Winnie (auth), article in Western Collection, 7/65; Carol Flack (auth), Murray A Harris: Americana Collector, 6/14/72; Susan Graves (auth), article in Seminar, 12/74. Style & Technique: Graphic art. Media: Pen, Ink. Collection: Graphic art with special emphasis on original artwork of comic strips; editorials and illustrations, Uncle Sam. Publ: auth, Many Faces of Uncle Sam, World of Comic Art, Fall 1966; Terra Mag, Los Angeles Co Mus of Natural Hist, summer 74. Mailing Add: 2561 E Phyllis St Simi Valley CA 93065

HARRIS, PAUL
SCULPTOR
b Orlando, Fla Study: With Joy Karen Winslow, Orlando; Univ NMex; New Sch Social Res, with Johannes Molzahn; Hans Hofmann Sch. Exhib: Sculpture USA, 59 & Hans Hofmann & His Students, 64-65, Mus Mod Art, New York; People Figures, Mus Contemp Crafts, 66-67; Sculpture of the Sixties, Los Angeles Co Mus & Sao Paulo Biennial, 67; Soft Art, NJ Mus, 69; New Vein Show, Vienna, Cologne, Belgrade, Baden-Baden, Geneva, Brussels & Milan, 69-70; plus many one-man shows. Teaching: Instr art, Univ NMex, Knox Col, BWI, New Paltz State Col, Calif Art Inst & Cath Univ Chile; prof art, Calif Col Arts & Crafts, presently. Media: Bronze, Cloth. Dealer: Poindexter Gallery 24 E 84th St New York NY 10028. Mailing Add: Box 1 Grove Rd Bolinas CA 94924

HARRIS, PAUL ROGERS
MUSEUM DIRECTOR, EDUCATOR
b Dallas, Tex, Jan 2, 33. Study: NTex State Univ, BA, 54, MA, 56; NY Univ, 65-67. Exhibitions Arranged: Bags & Sacks, 74, The World of George W White, Jr, 75, At the Time of the House, 76, Clara McDonald Williamson, 77 & Roger Winter, 78, The Art Ctr, Waco, Tex. Teaching: Supvr art, Children's House, Dallas Mus Contemp Arts, Tex, 60-65; head dept art educ, Southern Methodist Univ, Dallas, Tex, 70-74. Pos: Coordr educ servs, Mus Mod Art, New York, 66-70; dir, The Art Ctr, Waco, Tex, 74-; chmn educ adv panel, Tex Comn on the Arts & Humanities, 75-78. Bibliog: Janet Kutner (auth), Texas small museums discovering each other, Art News, 2/77. Mem: Am Asn Mus; Nat Art Educ Asn; Tex Assembly Arts Coun (mem bd dir, 77-). Publ: Co-auth (with Janet Kutner), David McManaway (catalog introd), Contemp Arts Mus, Houston, 73; auth, Laurence Scholder: Prints, 74, Blake Hampton: Illustrator, 75, Gillian Bradshaw-Smith: Soft Sculptures & Drawings, 76 & Esta Nesbitt: Xerography Prints, 76, The Art Ctr, Waco, Tex. Mailing Add: Box 5396 Waco TX 76708

HARRIS, PAUL STEWART
ART HISTORIAN
b Orange, Mass, Mar 7, 06. Study: Antioch Col, BS; Harvard Col, SB(hist art); New York Univ Grad Sch Fine Arts. Collections Arranged: Assisted in installation of the Cloisters and gallery display, Metrop Mus Art; numerous exhibs, Des Moines Asn Fine Arts, Iowa & J B Speed Art Mus, Louisville, Ky, 33-62. Teaching: Lectr Am Art, Univ Minn, 46. Pos: Curatorial asst & asst cur, Metrop Mus Art, 33-38; dir & secy, Des Moines Asn Fine Arts, 38-40; sr cur, Minneapolis Inst Arts, 41-46; dir & cur, J B Speed Art Mus, 46-62; dep dir, H F du Pont Winterthur Mus, 62-67; dir collections, Henry Ford Mus & Greenfield Village, Mich, 67-71. Mem: Am Asn Mus; Col Art Asn Am; NH Hist Soc; Early Am Indust Asn & League NH Craftsmen. Res: Mediaeval European art, American art, European decorative arts and paintings and modern art. Publ: Auth, Fourteen seasons of art accessions, J B Speed Art Mus, 60; auth, 30 early American paintings, for Winterthur Mus; also var articles in mus bulletins, 34-64. Mailing Add: RFD Chesham Marlborough NH 03455

HARRIS, ROBERT GEORGE
PAINTER, ILLUSTRATOR
b Kansas City, Mo, Sept 9, 11. Study: Kansas City Art Inst, with Monte Crews; Grand Cent Sch Art, with Harvey Dunn; Art Students League, with George Bridgeman. Work: Portraits, Phoenix Jr Col, Dept of Justice, Washington, DC, Seabury Western Theol Seminary, Chicago, Ill, Wabash Col, Crawfordsville, Ind & Franciscan Renewal Ctr, Scottsdale, Ariz; also in many pvt collections in US. Exhib: Soc Illusr; Art Dirs Club, 43-46; New Rochelle Art Asn, 49; Westport Artists, 50; one-man show of portraits, Phoenix Art Mus, 62. Mem: Soc Illusr; Phoenix Fine Art Asn; Phoenix Art Mus. Style & Technique: Realism; careful modeling with generally smooth and painstaking technique, but without slavish detail. Media: Oil. Publ: Illusr, McCall's, 39-60, Sat Eve Post, 39-61, Good Housekeeping, 40-60, Ladies' Home J, 40-61 & other nat mags. Mailing Add: PO Box 1124 Carefree AZ 85331

HARRIS, DR & MRS S ELLIOTT
COLLECTORS
Pos: Dr Harris, gen practitioner; Mrs Harris, art dealer. Specialty: Contemporary prints, sculpture, oils. Collection: Sculptures by B Hepworth, Calder, Pol Bury, Lila Katzin, Dubuffet and H Moore; paintings by Hans Hofmann, Hartigan, Appel, Jenkins and Gilliam; about 200 prints, from Leger to Rucha. Mailing Add: 3521 Old Court Rd Baltimore MD 21208

HARRIS, WILLIAM WADSWORTH, II
PAINTER
b Hamden, Conn, Mar 26, 27. Study: Yale Univ, BA; Univ Mich, MA; also with Richard Wilt, Deane Keller & Jerry Farnsworth. Work: Galerie Moos, Geneva, Switz; Toledo Mus Fine Arts, Ohio; Yale Univ Collection; Mattatuck Mus Arts & City Nat Bank, Waterbury, Conn; and in pvt collections in Europe, Mid East & US. Exhib: Festival of Arts, Boston, 59; Ringling Mus Art, Sarasota, Fla, 61; Galerie Georges Moos, Geneva, Switz, 64-69; Hub Gallery, Pa State Univ, State College, 73; Conn Soc Fine Arts, Wadsworth Atheneum, Hartford, 74; Am Painters in Paris Exhib, France, 75-76; Berkshire Mus Fine Arts, Pittsfield, Mass, 77. Awards: Top Award, Conn Artists 23rd Ann, Slater Mus, Norwich, 66; Top Awards, Waterbury Arts Festival, Conn, 67 & 68; Northwest Conn Art Asn Winsted Award, 75. Bibliog: Prize Winning Art, Bk 7, Allied Publ, 67. Mem: New Haven Paint & Clay Club (bd dirs, 67-69); New Haven Festival Arts (bd dirs, 71-73). Style & Technique: Abstract and semi-abstract on archaeological and nature themes. Media: Oil on Canvas, Collage in Mixed Media. Mailing Add: Chestnut Hill Rd Killingworth CT 06417

HARRISON, CAROLE
EDUCATOR, SCULPTOR
b Chicago, Ill, Oct 30, 33. Study: Cranbrook Acad Art, Bloomfield Hills, Mich, BFA, MFA; Cent Sch Arts & Crafts, London, Eng, with Robert Adams. Work: Kalamazoo Inst Art, Mich; Am Fedn Art; Hackley Mus, Muskegon, Mich; Springfield Mus, Ill; Hope Col Art Gallery, Holland, Mich. Comn: Welded copper figurative (10ft x 14ft), Oak Park Pub Libr, Ill, 65; welded copper figure (8ft x 3ft), Holland High Sch, Mich, 65; fountain (15ft x 10ft x 12ft), Steinman Reality, Kalamazoo, 69; bronze figure (7ft x 3ft), Kalamazoo Inst Art, 70; welded brass figures (14ft x 16ft), Western Mich Univ, Kalamazoo, 72. Exhib: Exhib Momentum, Chicago, 57; 2nd Biennial Am Painting & Sculpture, Detroit Art Inst & Pa Acad Art, 59; New Horizon's in Sculpture, Chicago, 61; Am Fedn of Arts Traveling Exhib, 63; Contemp Painting & Sculpture, Springfield Mus, Mo, 66; Painting & Sculpture Today, Herron Mus Art, Indianapolis, Ind, 67; Mainstreams, Marietta Col, Ohio, 76. Teaching: Instr sculpture, Nat Music Camp, Interlochen, Mich, 57-60; assoc prof sculpture, Western Mich Univ, Kalamazoo, 60-74; assoc prof sculpture, State Univ NY Col, Fredonia, 75- Awards: Fulbright Award, Inst Int Educ, 57; Tiffany Found Award, 60; First Prize, New Horizons in Sculpture, 60. Bibliog: Marcia Wood (auth), Sculpture, Carole Harrison (film), Kalamazoo Col, Mich, 76; Cesta Pekstock (auth), Art & Architecture in Kalamazoo (film), Western Mich Univ, 76. Mem: Col Art Asn Am; Women's Caucus of Art. Style & Technique: Abstract figurative work; in the round and relief. Media: Copper, Plastic. Publ: Auth, Three figures, Western Mich Univ Mag, 73. Dealer: Mack Gilman Galleries 201 E Ohio Chicago IL 60611. Mailing Add: 824 Davis Kalamazoo MI 49008

HARRISON, HELEN MAYER
CONCEPTUAL ARTIST, PHOTOGRAPHER
b New York, NY. Study: Queens Col, BA; Cornell Univ; NY Univ, MA. Work: Powers Inst, Univ Sydney, Australia. Comn: Lagoon (with Newton Harrison), Hartley, Los Angeles, 73-74. Exhib: Vesuvio (with Newton Harrison), Galleria Il Centro, Naples, Italy, 73; In a Bottle, art gallery, Calif State Univ, Fullerton, 73; one-man show, Grandview Gallery, Los Angeles, 74; A Response to the Environment (with Newton Harrison), Rutgers Univ Art Gallery, 75. Bibliog: Jack Burnham (auth), Great Western Salt Works, Brazillier, 74; Newton Harrison (auth), Sea Grant and Related Projects, Studio Int, 74; Cindy Nemser (auth), Blowing the whistle on the art world, Feminist Art J, summer 75. Style & Technique: Growth systems, narrative, photo-murals, ecological proposals, planning structures. Media: Photography, collage, drawing, writing. Dealer: Ronald Feldman Fine Arts 33 E 74th St New York NY 10021. Mailing Add: 2940 Camino del Mar Del Mar CA 92014

HARRISON, JOSEPH ROBERT, JR
COLLECTOR, PATRON
b Chicago, Ill, June 20, 18. Study: Wabash Col, AB; Univ Chicago Law Sch. Pos: Pres bd trustees, Metrop Mus & Art Ctr, Miami, Fla, 74-77, chmn bd trustees, 76- Mem: Metrop Dade Co Coun of Arts & Sci; Am Asn Mus (trustees comt). Interest: Museum, art school and sculpture. Collection: Late Cubist watercolors and drawings; late 19th century watercolors and drawings. Mailing Add: 3471 Main Hwy Miami FL 33133

HARRISON, NEWTON A
ECOLOGICAL ARTIST, EDUCATOR
b New York, NY, Oct 20, 32. Study: Yale Univ Sch Art & Archit, BFA & MFA. Work: Los Angeles Co Mus Art; Hayward Gallery, London, Eng; Palais des Beaux Arts, Brussels, Belg; World Wildlife Fund, Washington, DC; Powers Inst, Univ Sydney, Australia. Comn: Lagoon (with Helen Harrison), Hartley, Los Angeles, 73-74. Exhib: Art & Technology, US Pavilion, Osaka World's Fair, 70 & Los Angeles Co Mus Art, 71; Earth, Air, Fire, Water: Elements of Art, Boston Mus Art, Mass, 71; Eleven Los Angeles Artists, Hayward Gallery, London, Eng, 71; Project '74, Cologne; Univ Art Gallery, Rutgers Univ, 75; Feldman Gallery, New York. Teaching: Asst prof art, Univ NMex, 65-67; assoc prof art, Univ Calif, San Diego, 67-71, prof & chmn dept, 73- Awards: Award for E A T: Projects Outside Art; Nat Endowment for Arts Grant, 75; US Dept Com Sea Grant, 74-76. Bibliog: R C Kenedy (auth), London letter, the icon: unmasked or unveiled—Paolozzi, Larry Bell & Newton Harrison, Art Int, Vol 15, No 10; Jack Burnham (auth), Great Western Salt Works, Brazillier; Jose Barrio-Garay (auth), Newton Harrison's fourth lagoon: strategy against entropy, Arts Mag, 11/74. Style & Technique: Growth systems, narrative photo murals, ecological proposals, planning structures. Publ: Auth, Three projects: Harrison, Mock, McGowan, Art in Am, 1/74; auth, Sea Grant & two precedent works, Studio Int, 5/74. Dealer: Ronald Feldman Fine Arts 33 E 74th St New York NY 10021. Mailing Add: 2940 Camino del Mar Del Mar CA 92014

HARRISON, PAT (BROEDER)
PAINTER
b Houston, Tex, May 3, 41. Study: Tex Tech Univ, BA(fine arts); also with Sam Smith & Milford Zornes. Work: NMex State Fair, Albuquerque; Earth Resources Co, Dallas, Tex; Am Bank of Com Collection, Albuquerque. Comn: Designs for posters, tickets, progs, etc, Albuquerque Symphony Asn, 71-75; prog & logo for convention ctr opening, Albuquerque City Comn, 72. Exhib: Santa Fe Biennial, Mus Santa Fe, 68; NMex Rocky Mountain Fedn 8-State Traveling Exhib, 69-71; Catharine Lorillard Wolfe Art Club 76th Ann Exhib, Nat Arts Club, New York, 72; Am Artists Prof League Grand Nat Exhib, New York, 73; George Phippen Ann Mem Exhib, Prescott, Ariz, 75. Pos: Co-owner, Galeria de Sol. Awards: Citation, Tex Fine Arts Asn, 68; Purchase Award Watercolor, NMex State Fair, 69; First Prize & Purchase Award, Nacimiento Mining Co Competition, Earth Resources Co, Dallas, Tex, 71. Bibliog: Jack Kirk (auth), Art and Artists of New Mexico, Your Host, 11/71; Lois Duncan (auth), How our land feels to us, NMex Mag, 10/73; Alan Weisman (auth), Prescott art scene, Ariz Living, 7/74. Mem: Am Artists Prof League; Artists Equity (secy-treas, 70); NMex Watercolor Soc (secy, 69). Style & Technique: Southwestern landscapes and depictions of southwestern cultural life in watercolor and egg tempera; traditional, representational style. Publ: Illusr, Menu Mates, 73. Dealer: Galeria de Sol 206 1/2 San Felipe NW Old Town Albuquerque NM 87102. Mailing Add: 11 Juniper Hill Rd NE Albuquerque NM 87122

HARRISON, TONY
PAINTER, EDUCATOR
b Gt Brit, Aug 18, 31; US citizen. Study: Northern Polytech Eng; Chelsea Sch Art, London, Eng; Cent Sch Arts & Crafts, London. Work: Aldrich Mus Contemp Art, Ridgefield, Conn; Achenbach Found at Calif Palace Legion Honor, San Francisco; Arts Coun Gt Brit, London; Royal Collection, Stockholm, Sweden; Nat Gallery S Australia; plus many others. Exhib: One-man shows, San Francisco Mus Art, 64, Bertha Shaefer Gallery, New York, 68-69, 72 & 74 & Soho Ctr for Visual Artists, New York, 77; Ohio Mus Art, Columbus, 69; 10th Anniversary Exhib, Westmoreland Co Mus Art, Greensburg, Pa, 69; 3rd Kent Exhib Contemp Art, Ohio, 69; Nat Inst Arts & Lett, New York, 73; plus many other group & one-man shows. Teaching: Instr drawing & printmaking, Columbia Univ, 71-; asst prof painting, NY Univ, 72; printmaking workshop, New York, 74-75. Awards: Purchase Awards, Calif Soc Etchers, 64 & Soc Am Graphic Artists, 65; Nat Endowment for the Arts, 75; Creative Artists Pub Serv, 76. Bibliog: Robert Erskine (producer), Artists proof (film), St Georges Gallery, 57; Collectors Choice, produced on ITV, London, 62; S W Hayter (auth), About Prints. Style & Technique: Nonobjective; geometric. Media: Acrylic, Mezzotint. Aquatint. Mailing Add: 42 W 30th St New York NY 10001

HARRITON, ABRAHAM
PAINTER
b Bucharest, Rumania, Feb 16, 93; US citizen. Study: Nat Acad Design, 08-15, with Emil Carlsen, Kenyon Cox, George DeForest Brush & Mielatz. Work: Whitney Mus Am Art, New York; Addison Gallery Am Art, Phillips Acad, Andover, Mass; Ein Harod Mus, Israel; Syracuse Univ Mus; Hirshhorn Mus, Washington, DC; plus others. Comn: Mural, Louisville Post Off & Agr Bldg, Ga, 36. Exhib: Five Whitney Mus Am Art Ann, 36-41; 15 one-man exhibs, ACA Galleries, 36-72; Mus Mod Art, 40; Carnegie Inst, 41, 43, 45 & 46; Artists for Victory, Metrop Mus Art, 42; Am Painting Collection, Montclair Art Mus, 77. Teaching: Instr painting & drawing, WPA Art Sch, New York, 32-36; instr painting & drawing, Great Neck Art Asn, NY, 45-50. Awards: Marine Painting Award, Silvermine Guild Artists, 63; Marjorie Peabody Waite Award, Nat Inst Arts & Lett, 68-; Mintz Mem Award, 35th Ann Exhib, Audubon Artists, 77. Bibliog: Harry Salpeter (auth), Ex-Picassoid, Esquire Mag, 1/46; Abraham Harriton discusses a system of glazing, Am Artist, 9/51. Mem: Audubon Artists (dir, 58); Artists Equity Asn. Style & Technique: Romantic symbolism encompassing modern technique. Media: Oil. Res: Technique of underpainting and glazing as based on Venetian masters. Dealer: ACA Galleries 25 E 73rd St New York NY 10021. Mailing Add: 66 W Ninth St New York NY 10011

HARSH, RICHARD
PAINTER, EDUCATOR
b Feb 6, 40. Study: Columbia Tech Inst, cert, 61; Univ Northern Iowa, BA, 65; Southern Ill Univ, scholar, 68-69, MFA, 69; also with Siegfried Reinhardt; Harvard Univ, summer 74; Emmanuel Seminary, summer 75. Comn: Bicentennial prints (ltd ed), Morania, Iowa. Exhib: 3rd Nat Cape Coral, Fla, 69; 3rd Nat Polymer Exhib, Eastern Mich Univ, Ypsilanti, 70; 2nd Washington & Jefferson Col Painting Exhib Fine Arts Festival, 70; Am Acad Arts & Lett, Hassam Found, 70; Gtr Fall River Art Asn, Mass, 70; 14th Ann Christian Art Show, Lansing, Mich; Flint Inst Art, Mich; one-man shows, Adrian Col, Mich, Grand Rapids Bible Col, Mich & Saginaw Valley State Col, Mich; plus other group & one-man exhibs. Teaching: Instr art, Community Unit II High Sch, Greenville, Ill, 66-68; asst to supvr dept painting, Southern Ill Univ, 68, instr art, Workshop, summer 69, grad asst, 69; instr art, Univ Northern Iowa, 70-71; asst prof art, Mackinac Col, 72; lectr var civic, relig & educ orgn; artist in residence, John Wesley Col, currently. Pos: Asst, Fed Bur Invest, Washington, DC, 58-61; illusr, McGregor-Werner Co, 61. Awards: Hon Mention, River Roads Exhib, St Louis, Mo, 68 & Mitchell Gallery Drawing Exhib, Southern Ill Univ, 69; Purchase Awards, 3rd Nat Polymer Exhib, Eastern Mich Univ, 70 & Am Acad Arts & Lett, Hassam Found, 70. Mailing Add: Dept of Art John Wesley Col Owosso MI 48867

HARSLEY, ALEX
GALLERY DIRECTOR, INSTRUCTOR
b Rockhill, SC, July 16, 38. Study: Prof trained color lab technician; pvt studies with Lloyd Varden, Sci Adv to photog indust. Exhib: Optional Art One & Optional Art Two, Mind, Matter & Art (series of travelling one-man shows), New York, 71; one-man show, Berkshire Mus, Pittsfield, Mass, 74; Symbols in the Mind—A Closer Look, 72 & Communications 73, Long Island Univ, NY; Communications 73, Union Carbide, New York, 73; Contemp Arts Gallery, NY Univ, 76. Teaching: Dir/instr photog, Minority Photogr, Inc, 71- Pos: Dir, Minority Photogr, 4th St Photo Gallery, 71- Bibliog: A D Coleman (auth), Shows We've Seen, Popular Photog, 7/71 & Latent Image, Village Voice, 7/71; P Henning (auth), SWN Discoveries, Soho News, 8/75. Style & Technique: Experimental photography. Media: Photography. Publ: Contribr, Looking Ahead, Harcourt Brace, 75; contribr, Creative Photography, Eastman Kodak, Javanovich Inc, 74; contribr, UNICEF Calendar, UNICEF, 76. Mailing Add: 155 Essex St New York NY 10002

HART, AGNES
PAINTER, INSTRUCTOR
b Conn. Study: Ringling Col & Sch Art; Iowa State Univ; and with Lucile Blanch, Josef Presser & Paul Burlin. Work: Metrop Mus Art; Norfolk Mus; Wichita State Univ. Exhib: Am

Painting Today, 50 & Watercolors, Drawings & Prints, 52, Metrop Mus Art; Art USA, 58; Brooklyn Mus; Pa Acad Fine Arts; Woodstock, NY; Coral Gables, Fla; Artists—Then & Now, New York Washington Proj for the Arts; New Deal for Art; plus solo exhibs, NY, Ga & Switz. Teaching: Instr, Birch Wathen Sch, New York; instr, Dalton Schs, New York, 61-63; instr painting, drawing & compos, Art Students League, 65- Mem: Woodstock Artists Asn (mem bd, 55-57); Am Soc Contemp Artists; Art Students League. Dealer: Rudolph Galleries Woodstock NY & Coral Gables FL. Mailing Add: 30 E 14th St New York NY 10003

HART, ALLEN M
PAINTER, EDUCATOR
b New York, NY, June 12, 25. Study: Art Students League, with Anne Goldthwaite, Frank Vincent Dumond & Jean Liberte; Brooklyn Mus Art Sch, with Vincent Candell. Work: Butler Inst Am Art, Youngstown, Ohio; Univ Mass, Amherst; Slater Mem Mus, Norwalk, Conn; Children's Aid Soc, New York; Union Am Hebrew Congregations. Exhib: One-man shows, Greer Gallery, 56, Roko Gallery, 59, Cober Gallery, 66 & 68, Visual Arts Ctr, 70, Boiborik Gallery, 76 & N Jersey Cult Arts Ctr, 78; Art USA, New York, 58; New York Pub Libr, 61; Articulate Subconscious, Am Fedn Arts Traveling Show, 67-68; Visual Arts Ctr, Children's Aid Soc, 70; Joseph & Betty Harlem Gallery, Union Am Hebrew Congregations, 75. Teaching: Instr painting, Samuel Field YMHA & YWHA, Littleneck, NY, 62-68; dir painting, Visual Arts Ctr, 68-; dean visual arts, Union Am Hebrew Congregations, 70-, resident artist, 72-; art consult, Bd Coop Educ Serv, 71- Bibliog: NY illustrated, NBC-TV, 70; Ned Harris (producer), In the beginning (film), 70 & Shabbat (film), 72; Doris Freedman (auth), Artists in the City, WNYC-FM, 10/12/72. Mem: Life mem Art Students League. Media: Oil, Mixed Media. Publ: Auth, articles in, Lower Manhattan Twp, 2/20/71 & Herald, 5/1/71. Mailing Add: 34 Jackson Rd Valley Stream NY 11581

HART, BETTY MILLER
PAINTER, GRAPHIC ARTIST
b East Orange, NJ, Apr 15, 18. Study: Van Deering Perrine; Syracuse Univ Sch Fine Arts; Newark Col Eng. Comn: Panoramic view of Mobile, Ala & oil field, comn by Everet Eaves, Shreveport, La, 65; self portrait, comn by James Elder, Washington, DC; landscape, Philip Desind Collection, Silver Spring, Md, 75. Exhib: Newark Mus NJ Artists, 68; Pa Acad Fine Arts 164th Ann, Philadelphia, 69; Philadelphia Mus Art Eastern Cent Regional Drawing Show, 70; Norfolk Mus Arts & Sci Am Drawing Biennial XIV, Va, 71; NJ State Mus Art from NJ, Trenton, 67-71 & 72; Hudson Artists 21st Ann, Jersey City Mus, NJ, 74; Thirteen Invited Artists, Hunterdon Art Ctr, Clinton, NJ, 74; one-person show, Capricorn Galleries, Bethesda, Md, 75; Am Drawings Nat, Tidewater Arts Coun & Portsmouth Arts Ctr, Portsmouth, Va, 76; 7th Ann State Show, Somerset Art Asn, NJ, 77; 36th Ann Nat Exhib of Audubon Artists, Nat Acad Design, New York, 78; plus others. Pos: Founding pres, Monmouth Med Art Auxiliary, Long Branch, NJ, 60-63; speaker, Red Bank Cath High Sch, NJ, 73 & Monmouth Regional High Sch, West Long Branch, 75. Awards: James R Marsh Mem Prize, Hunterdon Art Ctr, 73; Purchase Awards, Festival of Arts Tri-State Exhib, Monmouth Col, West Long Branch, NJ, 76 & Print Show by Friends of NJ State Mus, Henry Chauncey Conf Ctr, Princeton, 76. Bibliog: Feature, New York Sunday News, 61; Michael Lenson (auth), Realm of art, Newark Sunday News, 67; Florence Lonsford (auth), Spot light on Kappa artists, Key of Kappa Kappa Gamma, Vol 91 No 4. Mem: Guild Creative Art (pres, 70-71). Style & Technique: Realism; fantasy. Media: Oil, Pastel; Pencil, Ink. Dealer: Capricorn Galleries 8004 Norfolk Ave Bethesda MD 20014. Mailing Add: 60 Little Silver Point Rd Little Silver NJ 07739

HART, BILL
ART DEALER
b St Louis, Mo, Oct 17, 39. Study: Univ Loyola, Los Angeles, BA. Pos: Dir, Razor Gallery, New York. Specialty: Contemporary American abstract painting and sculpture; some realist work. Mailing Add: Razor Gallery 464 W Broadway New York NY 10013

HART, HAROLD RUDOLF
ART DEALER
b Washington, DC, May 6, 26. Study: Cath Univ; Univ Madrid. Pos: Vpres & dir, Martha Jackson Gallery, Inc, New York, 61- Specialty: Contemporary art. Mailing Add: 32 E 69th St New York NY 10021

HART, JOHN LEWIS
CARTOONIST
b Endicott, NY, Feb 18, 31. Pos: Comic strip BC nat syndicated, 58-, The Wizard of Id, 64- Awards: Outstanding Cartoonist of Year, 68; Yellow Kid Award, Int Cong Comics for Best Cartoonist, Lucca, Italy; France's Highest Award Best Cartoonist of Year, 71. Mem: Nat Comics Coun; Nat Cartoonists Soc. Publ: The Peasants are Revolting: Remember the Golden Rule: There's a Fly in my Swill; The Wonderous Wizard of Id; The Wizard's Back; plus others. Mailing Add: 639 Elm St Endicott NY 13760

HART, MORGAN DRAKE
PAINTER, INSTRUCTOR
b Shrub Oak, NY, Jan 8, 99. Study: Nat Acad Design, with Charles Webster Hawthorne & Francis C Jones. Work: Maine Harbor; Trenton State Mus; Somerset Hosp, NJ; Hillsborough NJ Libr. Comn: Portrait in old of Dr A D Dunbar & landscape mural of George Washington (in auditorium), Peekskill High Sch, NY; Frank Demster Sherman, Poet (portrait), Peekskill Mil Acad; William R O'Neal (portrait), Rollins Col, Winter Park, Fla. Exhib: Montclair Mus State Show, 53, 59 & 63; Grand Nat Show, Lever House, 60, 65, 71 & 72; Ft Worth Mus, Tex, 65; Am Artists Prof League traveling show, Prince Rainier's Palace, Monaco, 67; one-man show, Ferargi Gallery, New York, 28. Teaching: Instr art, Peekskill Eve Schs, 30-35; instr art, Peekskill Mil Acad, 34; instr drawing, Ducret Art Sch, 67-68; instr pvt classes. Pos: Color technician, Union Carbide Corp, Bound Brook, NJ, 48-64. Awards: Second Prize, All City Show, Somerville, NJ, 77; Best of Show, Raritan Valley Arts Asn, 77; First Prize, Sr Citizen's Exhib, Somerset Co, 77. Mem: Am Artists Prof League (secy nat bd, 60-72); hon mem Raritan Valley Arts Asn; Hunterdon Co Art Asn. Style & Technique: Direct landscapes; portraiture. Media: Oil, Acrylic. Dealer: M Knoedler & Co 21 E 70th St New York NY 10021; Swain Gallery 317 Front St Plainfield NJ 07060. Mailing Add: Hickory Dr Sunset Lake Pluckemin NJ 07978

HART, ROBERT GORDON
ART ADMINISTRATOR
b San Francisco, Calif, Dec 28, 21. Pos: Ed, Brooklyn Mus, NY, 59-61; gen mgr, Indian Arts & Crafts Bd, US Dept of Interior, 61- Mem: Am Asn of Mus; Conseil Int des Musees; NAm Crafts Adminrs Asn (chmn, 77); Am Crafts Coun; World Crafts Coun; Fed Interagency Crafts Comt (chmn, 74-). Mailing Add: 916 25th St NW Washington DC 20037

HARTELL, JOHN (ANTHONY)
PAINTER
b Brooklyn, NY, Jan 30, 02. Study: Cornell Univ, BArch; Royal Acad Fine Arts, Stockholm, Sweden. Work: Herbert F Johnson Mus Art, Cornell Univ; Ill Wesleyan Univ; Munson-Williams-Proctor Inst, Utica, NY; Univ Nebr, Lincoln; Wake Forest Univ; Altanta Univ; Northern Trust Co, Chicago. Exhib: Five exhibs, Mem Art Gallery, Rochester, NY, 43-71; Cincinnati Mus, 45; City Art Mus, St Louis, 45; Carnegie Inst, Pittsburgh, Pa, 45-47; four exhibs, Whitney Mus Am Art, 45-56; Munson-Williams-Proctor Inst, Utica, NY, 48-58; Chicago Art Inst, Ill, 51; Pa Acad Fine Arts, Philadelphia, 53; Mus of Fine Arts, Houston, 55; Mus of Fine Arts, Dallas, 57; Walker Art Ctr, Minneapolis, Minn, 58; Mus of Art, Indianapolis, 70; Lehigh Univ, 71; Butler Inst of Am Art, Youngstown, Ohio, 77. Teaching: Prof archit & art, Cornell Univ, 30-68, chmn dept art, 39-59, emer prof archit & art, 68- Bibliog: Rosamund Frost (auth), Hartell: builder in paint, Art News, 10/15/45; Hartell: visiting artist, Munson-Williams-Proctor Inst Bull, 1/52. Media: Oil. Dealer: Kraushaar Galleries 1055 Madison Ave New York NY 10028. Mailing Add: 319 The Parkway Ithaca NY 14850

HARTER, JOHN BURTON
CURATOR, PAINTER
b Jackson, Miss, Oct 7, 40. Study: Hanover Col, Univ Louisville, BA(art hist); Univ Vienna; Univ Pa; grad archaeol, Hebrew Univ, Jerusalem; La State Univ, MA(studio art); Williamsburg Seminar. Collections Arranged: La Folk & Naive Art, 75 & La Portrait Gallery, 77, La State Mus. Pos: Asst cur, La State Mus, 67-73; asst cur, Hist Orleans Collection, 73-74; assoc cur & cur paintings, La State Mus, 74- Mem: Am Asn Mus. Style & Technique: Photorealism. Media: Oil, Acrylic. Mailing Add: 5700 St Anthony Apt 210 New Orleans LA 70122

HARTFORD, HUNTINGTON
COLLECTOR, PATRON
b New York, NY, Apr 18, 11. Study: Harvard Univ, AB, 34. Pos: Patron, Lincoln Ctr for Performing Arts; founder, Huntington Hartford Found, 49; founder & bd dirs, Gallery Mod Art (now New York Cult Ctr), 64; ed-in-chief, Show Mag; mem, Nat Coun on Arts, 69; mem adv coun, dept art hist & archaeol, Columbia Univ. Awards: Art Man of Year, Nat Art Materials Trade Asn, 62; Am Artists Prof League Award, 64; Orgn Am States Award, 66. Mem: Hon fel Nat Sculpture Soc; Nat Arts Club; Salmagundi Club; Am Artists Prog League. Collection: Oriental and far Eastern Art. Publ: Auth, Art or anarchy?, 64. Mailing Add: 1 Beekman Pl New York NY 10022

HARTGEN, VINCENT ANDREW
PAINTER, EDUCATOR
b Reading, Pa, Jan 10, 14. Study: Sch Fine Arts, Univ Pa, BFA & MFA. Work: Mus Fine Arts, Boston; Wadsworth Atheneum, Hartford, Conn; Sheldon Swope Art Gallery, Terre Haute, Ind; Walker Art Ctr, Minneapolis, Minn; Wichita Art Mus, Kans. Exhib: One-man shows, Chase Gallery, 62 & 68, Kalamazoo Inst Art, Mich, Howard Univ Art Gallery, Washington, DC, Brooks Mem Art Gallery, Memphis, Tenn, Univ Idaho Art Gallery, Moscow, Everhart Mus, Scranton, Pa, Bermuda Art Asn, Hamilton, Bixler Art Gallery, Colby Col, Maine, Fla Gulf Coast Art Ctr, Clearwater & King's Col, Wilkes-Barre, Pa; Artists of Maine, Am Fedn Arts Traveling Exhib, 64-66; Embassies Art Prog, Dept State, Washington, DC, 66-70; 200 Yrs Watercolor Painting Am, Metrop Mus Art, 67; Landscape I, De Cordova Mus, Lincoln, Mass, 70. Collections Arranged: Contemp Schs, USA, Contemp Churches, USA, 56-57, Ceramics & Dinnerware, 68 & Boxes, Sacks & Bags, 71, Univ Maine Art Gallery. Teaching: Prof art & dir art gallery & collection, Univ Maine, Orono, 46-, Huddiston prof art, 62- Pos: Trustee, Haystack Sch Crafts, 50-55; comnr, Maine State Comn Arts & Humanities, 65-70. Awards: Hon mentions, 50 & 66, Creative Aquarelle Award, 65 & Silver Medal, 74, Audubon Artists. Bibliog: H J Seligmann (auth), Vincent Hartgen...artist & teacher, Downeast Mag, 60; Ralph Fabri (auth), Watercolorist for all seasons, Today's Art, 65; Norman Kent (auth), 100 Techniques of Watercolor Painting, 70. Mem: Am Asn Univ Prof; Col Art Asn Am; Audubon Artists; Am Watercolor Soc; hon mem Can Soc Painter-Etchers & Engravers. Style & Technique: Semi-abstract interpretation of forces of nature; expressionistic. Media: Watercolor. Publ: Auth, Watercolor, Pen & Brush, 54; auth, Defending the middle ground of the semi-abstract, Am Artist, 67 & Maine Alumnus, 75. Dealer: Chase Gallery 31 E 64th St New York NY 10021. Mailing Add: 109 Forest Ave Orono ME 04473

HARTIGAN, GRACE
PAINTER
b Newark, NJ, Mar 28, 22. Study: Pvt art classes with Isaac Lane Muse; Moore Col, Philadelphia & Md Inst Art, Baltimore, hon DFA. Work: Mus Mod Art, Whitney Mus Am Art & Metrop Mus Art, New York; Carnegie Inst, Pittsburgh, Pa; Walker Art Ctr, Minneapolis, Minn; Art Inst Chicago, Ill; Albright-Knox Art Gallery, Buffalo, NY; plus many others. Exhib: Carnegie Int, 61; American Vanguard, organized by Solomon R Guggenheim Mus for US Info Agency, Austria, Eng, Ger & Yugoslavia, 61-62; A Decade of New Talent, Am Fedn Arts Exhib, 64-65; one-man shows, Univ Chicago, 67 & Gertrude Kasle Gallery, Detroit, 68; plus many others. Teaching: Resident artist, Md Inst Grad Sch Painting, 65-75. Awards: Mademoiselle Mag Merit Award for Art, 57. Media: Oil on Canvas, Watercolor Collage, Mixed Media Collage. Dealer: Genesis Gallery 41 E 47th St New York NY 10022. Mailing Add: 1701 1/2 Eastern Ave Baltimore MD 21231

HARTLEY, PAUL JEROME
PAINTER, EDUCATOR
b Charlotte, NC, Dec 30, 43. Study: NTex State Univ, BA; ECarolina Univ, MFA. Work: Southeastern Ctr Contemp Art, Winston-Salem, NC; NC Nat Bank Collection, Charlotte; Rausch Indust Collection; NC Art Soc, Raleigh. Exhib: One-man shows, Vanderbilt Univ Fine Arts Gallery, Nashville, Tenn, 73, Southeastern Ctr for Contemp Art, Winston-Salem, NC, 75, NC Mus Art, Collectors Gallery, Raleigh, 76 & G Walker Gallery, Columbia, SC, 76; Mint Mus Art, 501 Gallery, Charlotte, NC, 73; Art on Paper, Weatherspoon Gallery, Greensboro, NC, 73; Washington & Jefferson Nat Painting Exhib, Washington, Pa, 74; Soar Nat Art Exhib, Shreveport, La, 74; NC Mus Art Traveling Exhib of NC Artists, 75; Am Inst Architects, Raleigh, NC, 75 & 76; Southeastern Artist Invitational, Southeastern Ctr for Contemp Art, Winston-Salem, NC, 75. Teaching: Asst prof painting & drawing, ECarolina Univ, 75- Awards: Rausch Indust Award, Piedmont Graphics Exhib, Mint Mus Art, Charlotte, NC, 73; Purchase Awards, Southeast Regional Graphics Exhib, Southeast Ctr for Contemp Art & NC Nat Bank, 74. Mem: Col Art Asn Am. Style & Technique: Manipulation of pattern between the illusion of 2-D and 3-D space with objective elements present. Media: Mixed media. Dealer: NC Mus Art Collectors Gallery Raleigh NC 27611. Mailing Add: 227 Woodstock Dr Greenville NC 27834

HARTMAN, ROBERT LEROY
PAINTER, EDUCATOR
b Sharon, Pa, Dec 17, 26. Study: Univ Ariz, BFA & MA; Colo Springs Fine Arts Ctr, with Vaclav Vytlacil & Emerson Woelffer; Brooklyn Mus Art Sch. Work: Nat Collection Fine Arts, Smithsonian Inst, Washington, DC; Colorado Springs Fine Arts Ctr; Oakland Mus Art, Calif; Achenbach Found Graphic Arts, San Francisco; Henry Gallery, Univ Wash. Exhib: Contemp Am Painting & Sculpture Biennial, Krannert Mus, Univ Ill, 65; Art Across Am, Traveling Show, 65-67; 4th Int Young Artists Exhib, Am-Japan, Tokyo, 67; Santa Barbara Mus Art, 73; Whitney Mus Biennial, New York, 73. Teaching: Instr art, Tex Technol Col, 55-58; asst prof art, Univ Nev, Reno, 58-61; from assoc prof to prof art, Univ Calif, Berkeley, 61- Pos: Mem, Univ Calif Inst Creative Arts, 67-68. Awards: Emanuel Walter Fund First Prize, 85th Ann San Francisco Art Inst, 67; hon mention, 4th Int Young Artists Exhib Am-Japan, 67. Media: Acrylic, Oil. Dealer: Hank Baum Gallery Three Embarcadero Ctr San Francisco CA 94111. Mailing Add: 1265 Mountain Blvd Oakland CA 94611

HARTT, FREDERICK
ART HISTORIAN
b Boston, Mass, May 22, 14. Study: Nat Acad Design; Columbia Col, BA, 35; Princeton Univ, 35-36; NY Univ, MA, 37, PhD, 49. Teaching: Vi lectr art, Smith Col, 46-47; lectr fine arts, NY Univ, 48-49; from asst prof to prof art hist, Wash Univ, 49-60; prof hist art, Univ Pa, 60-67, chmn dept art, 60-65; vis art historian, Harvard Renaissance Ctr, Florence, Italy, 65-66; McIntire prof hist art, Univ Va, Charlottesville, 67-, chmn art dept, 67-76. Pos: Asst, Yale Art Gallery, 41-42; actg dir art mus, Smith Col, 46-47; bd dirs, Am Comt for Restoration Ital Monuments, 46-49; mem exec comt, Comt to Resc ue Ital Art, 66-; dir, Univ Va Art Mus, currently. Awards: Guggenheim Fel, 48-49 & 54-55; Fulbright Res Grants, 54-55 & 65-66; Am Coun Learned Socs Fel, 65-66. Mem: Col Art Asn Am (dir, 59-62); Am Asn Univ Prof; Renaissance Soc Am (coun, 70); hon academician Acad Arts Design, Florence, Italy. Res: Italian Renais sance art. Publ: Auth, The Paintings of Michelangelo, Vol I, 64, History of Italian Renaissance Art, Vol II, 69 & Michelangelo's Drawings, Vol III, 71, In: Michelangelo, The Complete Sculpture, Abrams; Donatello, Prophet of Modern Vision, 73; Art, History of Painting, Sculpture & Architecture, 76; also many articles & rev in art periodicals. Mailing Add: 940 Locust Ave Charlottesville VA 22901

HARTWELL, PATRICIA LOCHRIDGE
ART ADMINISTRATOR
b Austin, Tex, Sept 22, 16. Study: Columbia Univ, MS; Wellesley Col, BA; Ariz State Univ; Univ Hawaii. Collections Arranged: Lew & Mathilde Davis, 72; Naive Art, Scottsdale & Honolulu, 72 & 73; Fibers '74, Dorothy Fratt Retrospective 74, 69-, continuing exhibs, Civic Ctr Gallery, Scottsdale, Ariz & Arts Coun Gallery, Prince Kuhio Fed Bldg, Honolulu, Hawaii. Pos: Dir, UN Children's Greeting Card Fund, 56-62; exec dir, Scottsdale Fine Arts Comn, 69-75; art critic & writer, Honolulu & Phoenix Mag; contribr, Southwest Gallery Art; exec dir, Hawaii Coun for Cult & the Arts, 76- Awards: Ford Found Study Arts Grant, 75- Res: Mainstreams in contemporary European, Middle European and American naive art. Mailing Add: 28 Palione Pl Kailua HI 96734

HARTWIG, CLEO
SCULPTOR
b Webberville, Mich, Oct 20, 11. Study: Western Mich Univ, AB, hon MA & hon DFA; Int Sch Art, Europe; Art Inst Chicago, summers; and carving with Jose de Creeft. Work: Detroit Inst Arts, Mich; Newark Mus, NJ; Pa Acad Fine Arts, Philadelphia; Montclair Art Mus, NJ; Chrysler Mus at Norfolk, Va. Comn: Family Group (aluminum), Facade of Continental Casualties Bldg, New York, 52; Wild Ducks (terra-cotta), Cabin Class Lounge, SS United States, 52; bronze Kneeling figure with dove, All Faiths Mem Tower, Paramus, NJ, 63; two sculpture awards, Columbia Univ Law Sch Alumni, New York, 71. Exhib: Artists for Victory, Metrop Mus Art, New York, 42; Am Paintings & Sculpture Ann, Art Inst Chicago, Ill, 42; Pa Acad Fine Arts Ann, 45-54, 58 & 62; Fairmount Park Int Sculpture Exhib, Philadelphia Mus Art, 49; Women Artists of America, Newark Mus, 65; one-person shows traveling Can, 49-50, US, 65-66 & Montclair Art Mus, NJ, 71; Whitney Mus Am Art, New York; Detroit Inst Arts, Mich; Denver Art Mus, Colo; Boston Mus Sci, Mass; Nat Acad Design; Nat Inst Arts & Lett; Smithsonian Inst Natural Hist; US Info Agency Traveling Show in Europe; Philadelphia Art Alliance. Awards: Audubon Artists First Prize for Sculpture, 52; Medal of Honor, Nat Asn Women Artists, 67; Silver Medal, Nat Sculpture Soc Ann, 69. Bibliog: Enid Bell (auth), Compatibles, Am Artist Mag, summer 68; Archives of American Art, Smithsonian Inst. Mem: Sculptors Guild (exec secy, 47-54, 63-65, exec dir, 74-76); fel Nat Sculpture Soc (mem coun, 67-73, exhib chmn, 69-72, ed bd, NaReview, 72-75); acad Nat Acad Design; Audubon Artists (vpres for sculpture, 70-73); Nat Asn Women Artists (mem sculpture jury, 72-74, first vpres, 74-76). Style & Technique: Direct carving, interpreting subjects in nature in very simplified forms. Media: Stone. Publ: Co-auth, Direct carving in stone, Nat Sculpture Rev, summer 65. Mailing Add: 5 W 16th St New York NY 10011

HARVEY, DERMOT
KINETIC ARTIST
b Amersham, Eng, June 26, 41. Study: Univ Dublin, Trinity Col, MA; Univ London, MPhil. Work: Okla Art Ctr. Comn: Muse Aurora (liquid projections exhib operated by viewer), Brooklyn Children's Mus, 70; portable, multi-image aurora, Okla Art Ctr, 73; liquid projection exhib, Arnot Mus, Elmira, NY, 75; portable muse aurora, Continuum Mus, Ft Lauderdale, Fla, 76. Exhib: 24 Hour Technicolor Dream, Alexandra Palace, London, 67; Alliance of Light Artists, Fillmore East, New York, 69; Liquid Projections, Montreux Television Festival, Switz, 69; Projected Environments, New York Avant Garde Festival, 72, 74 & 75; Light Works, Intermedia Found, Garnerville, NY, 75. Teaching: Instr kinetic & light art, Rockland Community Col, Suffern, NY, 75- Pos: Dir theater of light prog (prog of exhib, performances & workshop in light & kinetic art funded by the NY State Arts Coun & Nat Endowment Arts), Intermedia Found, 74- Awards: Creative Artists Pub Serv Grant, NY Cult Coun, 71. Bibliog: Martha Geacintov (auth), He practices his art in the light side, 3/5/74 & Michael Hitzig (auth), Theater of light, 5/4/75, Journal News; Carol Lawson (auth), Film night with a Gothic twist, New York Times, 6/18/76. Style & Technique: Liquid projection exhibits producing compositons in light and color, participant operated; gas discharge light sculpture. Mailing Add: 17 Church St Garnerville NY 10923

HARVEY, DONALD
PAINTER, LECTURER
b Walthamstow, Eng, June 14, 30; Can citizen. Study: West Sussex Col Art, nat dipl painting; Brighton Col Art Eng, art teachers dipl. Work: Nat Gallery Can, Ottawa; Montreal Mus Fine Arts; Charlottetown Confedn Gallery, PEI; Seattle Art Mus, Wash; Albright-Knox Mus, Buffalo, NY. Comn: Large mural, BC Provincial Govt, Nelson, BC, 75. Exhib: Commonwealth Exhib Prints & Drawings, Cardiff, Gt Brit, 65; Nat Gallery Can Biennial Painting, 65; Can Abstract Art, London & Edinburgh, Gt Brit, 67; Brit Print Biennial, Bradford, Eng, 68; Int Print Exhib, Seattle, 69. Teaching: Prof painting, Univ Victoria, 61- Pos: Exec secy, Sask Arts Bd, 58-61. Awards: Sadie & Samuel Bronfmann Purchase Prize, Montreal Mus, 63; First Prize, Vancouver Island Show, Art Gallery Gt Victoria, 64-66 & 69; First Prize, Exhib Can Art, Vancouver Art Gallery, 64. Bibliog: Tony Emery (auth), Canadian art today, Artscanada, 65. Mem: Academician Royal Can Acad Arts. Style & Technique: Abstract oil paintings; serigraph prints landscape; abstract landscape. Dealer: Doris Pascal Gallery Pascal 334 Dundas St W Toronto ON Can. Mailing Add: 1025 Joan Crescent Victoria BC Can

HARVEY, DONALD GILBERT
SCULPTOR, INSTRUCTOR
b Louisville, Ky, June 25, 47. Study: Dixie Col, 65; Utah State Univ, BFA, 69; Univ Hawaii, MFA, 71. Work: Honolulu Acad Arts, Hawaii; State Found Cult & Arts, Honolulu; Utah State Univ Permanent Collection; Honolulu Community Col; Advert Publ Permanent Collection, Hawaii. Exhib: Hawaii Craftsman, 69-70; Artist of Hawaii, 70; Pomona Fair Crafts Exhib, Calif, 70; Easter Art Festival, Honolulu, 70-71; one-man show, Contemp Art Ctr of the Pac, 72. Teaching: Lectr art, Univ Hawaii, 70-71; instr art, Kamehamea High Sch, 71- Awards: Outstanding Art Student in Ceramics Award, Dixie Col, 67; Outstanding Student in Sculpture & Ceramics, Utah State Univ, 69; Honolulu Acad Arts Purchase Award, 70. Mem: Hawaii Painters & Sculptors League; Nat Art Educ Asn. Media: Mixed Media. Mailing Add: 2227 Aulii Honolulu HI 96817

HARVEY, JACQUELINE
PAINTER
b La Madeleine, France, Feb 2, 27; US citizen. Study: High Sch Mus & Art, New York, 42-45; New Sch Social Res, 45-46; also silversmith apprentice with Paul Lobel, 45-46 & studio training with Morris Davidson, New York, 45-46, Fernand Leger & Leopold Survage, Paris, 46-47 & William Hayter, New York, 48. Work: Birla Acad Art & Cult, Calcutta, India; Eggers Partnership, New York; also in pvt collections. Exhib: One-man shows, Panoras Gallery, New York, 55 & 63 & Eola Gallery, Orlando, Fla, 57; First Ann Metrop Young Artists, Nat Arts Club, New York, 58; Art USA, Madison Sq Garden, New York, 58; Rose Fried Gallery, New York, 69-70. Style & Technique: Abstract-triptychs, columns, and others. Media: Oil, Acrylic. Mailing Add: 279 Park Ave Manhasset NY 11030

HARVEY, ROBERT MARTIN
PAINTER
b Lexington, NC, Sept 16, 24. Study: Ringling Sch Art, with Elmer Harmes & Georgia Warren; San Francisco Art Inst, with Nathan Oliveira & Sonia Gechtoff. Work: Corcoran Gallery Art & Hirshhorn Collection, Washington, DC; Wichita Art Mus, Kans; Storm King Art Ctr, Mountainville, NY; Crown-Zellerbach Found, San Francisco; plus others. Exhib: American Painting, Va Mus Fine Arts, Richmond, 66; Butler Inst Am Art, Youngstown, Ohio, 66; Univ Ill, 67 & 69; Phoenix Art Mus; Richard White Gallery, Seattle, 69; plus other group & one-man shows. Awards: Award of Merit, San Francisco Art Festival, 63; Western Wash State Col Purchase Prize, 65; Mead Painting of the Year, 67; plus others. Dealer: Oscar Krasner 1043 Madison Ave New York NY 10021; David Stuart Galleries 807 N La Cienega Blvd Los Angeles CA 90046. Mailing Add: La Huerta del Angel Macharaviaya Malaga Spain

HARVEY, (WILLIAM) ANDRÉ
SCULPTOR
b Hollywood, Fla, Oct 9, 41. Study: Univ Va, BA; additional study with Michael Anasse, Valauris, France & Charles Parks, Hockessin, Del. Work: Del Art Mus, Wilmington; City of Wilmington, Del; White House, Washington, DC. Comn: Four life-size figures, comn by Pan Am Airlines, Worldport, Kennedy Airport, completion date 78-79; Water Environment, comn by Rouse Corp, Baltimore for Cleveland site, completion date 78. Exhib: Artist & the Animal, Brandywine River Mus, Chadds Ford, Pa, 73; Nat Acad of Design, New York, 74; Amarillo Art Mus, Tex, 74; Nat Sculpture Soc, New York, 75-77; Images of Am, US Info Agency, Moscow, London, Paris, 76-77; Del Art Mus, Wilmington, 76; Hunter Mus, Chattanooga, Tenn, 77. Bibliog: Chris Perry (auth), André Harvey Sculpture, Del Today, 11/73; Adrienne Roos (auth), Sculptor in Wyeth Land, Philadelphia Sunday Bull, Discover, 5/75; John Caldwell (auth), The Sculpture of André Harvey, SW Art, 11/76. Mem: Nat Sculpture Soc. Style & Technique: Realistic sculpture of contemporary subjects. Media: Bronze. Dealer: Frank Fowler 1213 Ft Stephenson Oval Lookout Mountain TN 37350. Mailing Add: Box 8 Rockland Rd Rockland DE 19732

HARWOOD, JUNE BEATRICE
PAINTER, INSTRUCTOR
b Middletown, NY, June 16, 33. Study: Syracuse Univ, BFA; Univ Calif, Los Angeles, Art Ctr Sch; Calif State Univ, Los Angeles, MA. Work: Calif State Univ, Los Angeles; Home Savings & Loan, Los Angeles; Long Beach Mus, Calif; Univ Calif, Santa Barbara; Newport Harbor Mus of Art, Newport Beach, Calif. Exhib: One-man shows, Hollis Galleries, San Francisco, 66, Santa Barbara Mus Art, 67, Molly Barnes Gallery, Los Angeles, 68, Rex Evans Gallery, Los Angeles, 70-71 & David Stuart Galleries, Los Angeles, 75-78. Teaching: Instr art, Hollywood High Sch, Los Angeles, 58-70; instr design & painting & dir gallery, Valley Col, Van Nuys, 71- Pos: Organizer of seminars for teachers, Los Angeles Unified Sch Dist, 69; idea develop & proposal writer, Art & Technol Calif, 70-71. Style & Technique: Hard edge. Media: Acrylic. Publ: Contribr, Sourcebook Mag, 70-; auth, Carmean, 74. Mailing Add: 4223 St Clair Ave Studio City CA 91604

HASELTINE, JAMES LEWIS
ART ADMINISTRATOR, PAINTER
b Portland, Ore, Nov 7, 24. Study: Portland Mus Art Sch, Ore, 47 & 49; Art Inst Chicago, 47-48; Brooklyn Mus Sch, 50-51. Work: Portland Art Mus, Ore; Oakland Art Mus, Calif. Exhib: Libr Cong, Washington, DC, 51; Brooklyn Mus, NY, 51-52; Portland Art Mus, Ore, 51-58; Seattle Art Mus, Wash, 52, 53, 57 & 59; San Francisco Mus Art, Calif, 53-54. Teaching: Vis lectr art hist, Univ Utah, 64-65. Pos: Dir, Salt Lake Art Ctr, Utah, 61-67; exec dir, Wash State Arts Comn, Olympia, 67- Awards: Purchase Prize, Portland Art Mus, 53; best monogr, Mormon Hist Asn, 65. Mem: Western Asn Art Mus (pres, 64-66); Am Asn Mus; Assoc Coun Arts; Nat Assembly State & Prov Arts Agencies (exec comt, 68-70); Nat Endowment Arts (mus panel, 70-72 & visual arts policy panel, 77-). Media: Oil. Publ: Auth, 100 Years of Utah Painting, 65; contribr, Mus News, 65; contribr, Utah Hist Quart, Dialogue & American West, 66. Mailing Add: 3820 Sunset Beach Dr NW Olympia WA 98502

HASELTINE, MAURY (MARGARET WILSON HASELTINE)
PAINTER
b Portland, Ore, May 7, 25. Study: Reed Col; Mus Art Sch, Portland; Eastern NMex Univ. Work: Salt Lake Art Ctr, Utah; Univ Ore Mus; Bell Tel Co, Portland; First Nat Bank, Portland; Coos Art Mus, Ore. Comn: Assemblage collage mural, Donald Lloyd, Assoc Grocers Off, Salt Lake City, 65; Plexiglass collage, Columbian Optical Co, Seattle, Wash, 74. Exhib: 13 shows, Artists Ore, Portland Art Mus, 51-73; Intermountain Biennial Painting & Sculpture, Salt Lake Art Ctr, 63, 65 & 67; New Accessions USA, Colorado Springs Fine Art Ctr, 64; Selected Painters 65, Mulvane Art Ctr, Topeka, Kans, 65; Our Land, Our Sky, Our

Water, Spokane World's Fair, 74; Anacortes Art Festival, Wash, 75. Teaching: Instr oil painting, Salt Lake Art Ctr, 64-65; instr oil & acrylic painting, Creative Activities Ctr, State Capitol Mus, Olympia, Wash, 67-, coordr creative activities, 69-70. Awards: Southwest Fiesta Biennial Prize, Santa Fe, NMex, 66; 8th Utah Biennial Salt Lake Art Ctr Award, 66; 3rd Ann Painting & Sculpture Award, Tacoma Art Mus, 73. Bibliog: Charles Miller (producer), Way of art, KUTV, 65; Prize-Winning Graphics, Allied Publ, 66. Mem: Portland Art Mus; State Capitol Mus (chmn hist comt, 68-69, bd mem, 70-74); Ballet Northwest (bd mem, 70-76). Style & Technique: Semi-abstract landscape and seascape; abstract collage. Media: Oil, Acrylic. Publ: Contribr, Forms Upon the Frontier, Utah State Univ, 69. Mailing Add: 3820 Sunset Beach Dr NW Olympia WA 98502

HASEN, BURT STANLY
PAINTER
b New York, NY, Dec 19, 21. Study: Art Students League, 40, 42 & 46, with Morris Kantor; Hans Hofmann Sch Fine Arts, 47-48; Acad Grande Chaumiere, Paris, 48-50, with Ossipe Zadkine; Accad Belli Arti, Rome, 59-60. Work: Walker Art Ctr, Minneapolis; Worcester Art Mus; Hampton Inst, Va; Crestview Col, Allentown, Pa; Muhlenberg Col, Allentown. Comn: Mural, YMHA & YWHA, New York, 47. Exhib: Salon Mai, Mus Art Mod, Paris, 51; Metrop Mus Art, New York, 53; Berlin Acad, WGer, 56; Whitney Mus Am Art Ann, New York, 63; Walker Art Ctr, 66. Teaching: Instr painting & drawing, Sch Visual Arts, 53-; instr painting, Col Art & Design, Minneapolis, 66. Awards: Three Purchase Prizes, Emily Lowe Found, 54; Fulbright Grant to Italy, 59-66. Bibliog: Allen S Weller (auth), Contemporary American Painting & Sculpture, Krannert Art Mus, 61; The Whitney Annual, Time, 63; Eric Protter (auth), Artists on Art, Grosset & Dunlap, 64. Media: Oil, Acrylic. Publ: Illusr, Contes del'Inattendu, 59, De la Terre a la Lune, 61, Voltaire, 61 & Moliere, 61. Mailing Add: 7 Dutch St New York NY 10038

HASKELL, BARBARA
CURATOR
b San Diego, Calif, Nov 13, 46. Study: Univ Calif, Los Angeles, BA(philos & art hist), 69. Exhibitions Arranged: Claes Oldenburg: Object into Monuments (with catalog), 71-72; Larry Bell (with catalog), 72; John Mason (with catalog), 74; Arthur Dove (with catalog), 74-76; Jo Baer (with catalog), 75. Pos: Cur painting & sculpture, Pasadena Mus Mod Art, 72-74, dir exhib & collections, 74; cur painting & sculpture, Whitney Mus Am Art, New York, 75- Awards: Woman of the Year, Mademoiselle Award, 73; Leadership Among Professional Women, Los Angeles Soroptimist, 73. Mailing Add: 139 Spring St New York NY 10012

HASKELL, HARRY GARNER, JR
COLLECTOR
b Wilmington, Del, May 27, 21. Study: Princeton Univ, 40-42. Collection: Andrew Wyeth. Mailing Add: Hill Girt Farm Chadds Ford PA 19317

HASKIN, DONALD MARCUS
EDUCATOR, SCULPTOR
b St Paul, Minn, July 28, 20. Study: Univ Minn, BA, study with Tovish; Cranbrook Acad Art, MFA. Work: Yuma Art Asn, Ariz; Benicia Art Mus, Calif. Comn: Eight ft bronze figure, City of Tucson, 72; 15 ft diameter stainless steel fountain, City of Tucson, 72; 18 ft high stainless steel, Univ Ariz, 73. Exhib: Contemp Crafts Mus, New York, 61; San Francisco Mus Art, 62; Preview '65, Alamo Gallery, Benicia, Calif, 65; Southwestern Invitational, Yuma Art Asn, 72-75; Tucson Mus Art, 75. Teaching: Lectr sculpture, Univ Calif, Berkeley, 63-65; prof sculpture, Univ Ariz, Tucson, 65- Awards: First Prize, Minn State Fair, 58; Purchase Award, City of Benicia, 65; Purchase Prize Award, Yuma Art Asn, 72. Style & Technique: Cast bronze; fabricated stainless steel. Dealer: Steckler Haller Galleries 7077 E Main Scottsdale AZ 85251. Mailing Add: 3242 N Kelvin Tucson AZ 85716

HASKINS, JOHN FRANKLIN
ART HISTORIAN, EDUCATOR
b La Junta, Colo, Nov 16, 19. Study: Univ Colo, Boulder, BFA, 47; NY Univ, PhD, 61. Collections Arranged: Near Eastern & Far Eastern Art from the Collections of Jay C Leff, New York (travelling exhib; auth, catalogue), 65; Imperial Carpets form Peking (auth, catalogue), Univ Art Gallery, Pittsburgh & Duke Univ, Durham, NC, 73-74. Teaching: Instr art hist, Finch Col, New York, 57-58; asst prof Oriental art hist, Univ Pittsburgh, 64- Mem: Col Art Asn; Am Oriental Soc; Soc of Archit Historians; Asian Asn. Res: Art of Central Asia, the Far East and the Steppe nomads. Publ: Auth, Northern Origins of Sasanian Metalwork, Artibus Asiae, 52; auth, Er Targhyn—The Hero, Aq-Zhunus—The Beautiful & Peter's Siberian Gold, Ars Orientalis IV, 61; auth, The Mongolian Captivity of Lady Wen-Chi, and the Pazyryk Felt Screen, Bull of Mus of Far E, 63; auth, Nomads and Migrants in the Art of Early Europe, 22nd Cong of Art Hist, Budapest, 69. Mailing Add: 5613 Darlington Rd Pittsburgh PA 15217

HASLEM, JANE N
ART DEALER
b Knoxville, Tenn, Dec 26, 34. Study: DePauw Univ, BA; Ind State Univ. Teaching: Instr art, Mecklenburg Co, NC, 58-59. Pos: Dir, Jane Haslem Gallery, Chapel Hill, NC, 60-65, Madison, Wis, 65-71 & Washington, DC, 69-71; pres, Haslem Fine Arts, Inc, Jane Haslem Gallery, Washington, DC, 71- Mem: Washington Print Club. Specialty: Contemporary American paintings, prints and political cartoons; publisher of art catalogues. Mailing Add: 2121 P St NW Washington DC 20037

HA-SO-DE (NARCISCO ABEYTA)
ILLUSTRATOR CHILDREN'S BOOKS, PAINTER
b Canyoncito, NMex, Dec 18, 18. Study: Santa Fe Indian Sch, with Dorothy Dunn Kramer, 35-39; Am Indian Art Inst Am; Somerset Art Sch, Pa, 41-42; Univ NMex, with Johnson & Haas, BFA, 53. Work: Am Indian Art Dietrich Collection; Phil Brook Mus, Tulsa, Okla. Comn: Navajo Antelope Hunt (mural), Maisel Store Entrance, Albuquerque, NMex, 35. Exhib: Painting & Reproduction Exhib, Paris, France by Paul Coze, 35; Philbrook Mus, 35-53; Scottsdale Nat Indian Art Coun, 67-74; NMex Art & Crafts Fair, Albuquerque, 74; NMex State Fair, 75. Teaching: Instr silversmithing, Santa Fe Indian Sch, 47-48. Awards: Poster Antelope Hunt & Scholar, Indian Golden Gate Int Exposition Courts, San Francisco summer 39; First Prize Faun Hunt, NMex State Fair, 75. Bibliog: Hoffman Birney (auth), Ay-Chee Son of the Desert, Pa Publ Co, 36; J J Brody (auth), Indian Painters & White Patrons, Univ NMex, 75; Doris Monthan (auth), Up to date write up on Ha-So-De, Am Indian Art Mag. Mem: NMex Teacher-Counr Orgn. Style & Technique: American Indian art; no depth, length and width; two-dimensional designs; abstract line of rhythm movement of animals, antelope and horses, family life done in color; harmony casein tempera; Navajo creation myth paintings. Media: Shiva Casein, Chemical Paint Very Permanent. Res: Annual reports & Washington Reports of early explorers in Fort Wingate & Navajo reservation areas in New Mexico. Dealer: Kiva Gallery 202 W 66th Gallup NM 87301. Mailing Add: 102 Viro Circle Gallup NM 87301

HASSRICK, PETER H
MUSEUM DIRECTOR, ART HISTORIAN
b Philadelphia, Pa, Apr 27, 41. Study: Univ Colo, BA(hist & classics); Harvard Univ, classics; Univ Denver, MA(art hist). Exhibitions Arranged: Albert Bierstadt, 72, Frederic Remington (auth, catalogue), 73 & Peter Rindisbacher, 70, Amon Carter Mus, Ft Worth, Tex. Pos: Cur collections, Amon Carter Mus, Ft Worth, Tex, 69-75; dir, Buffalo Bill Hist Ctr, Cody, Wyo, 76- Mem: Wyo Coun on the Arts (vchmn, 77). Res: Nineteenth and early twentieth century artists of the American West. Publ: Auth, Frederic Remington, 73 & The Way West: Art of Frontier America, 77, Harry N Abrams, Inc. Mailing Add: Box 1020 Cody WY 82414

HASTIE, REID
EDUCATOR, WRITER
b Donora, Pa, Feb 14, 16. Study: Edinboro State Col, BS; WVa Univ, MA; Univ Pittsburgh, EdD. Work: Minneapolis Inst Arts; Minn Mus Arts. Exhib: State Fair Gallery, St Paul, Minn, 66; Northrop Gallery, Univ Minn, 67; Encounters with Artists, 70; Drawings, St Paul, 72. Teaching: Prof art & art educ, Univ Minn, 49-70; prof art & art educ, Tex Tech Univ, 70- Awards: Distinguished Art Educator, Minn Art Educ Asn, 66; Award of Merit, Nat Art Educ Asn, 69. Mem: Nat Art Educ Asn (pres, 57-59); Nat Soc Study Educ. Media: Acrylic, Watercolor. Res: Study of aesthetic theory and sensitivity; the creative process. Publ: Ed, Art Education, 65; auth, Encounter with Art, 69. Mailing Add: 2114 65th Pl Lubbock TX 79412

HASWELL, HOLLEE
ART LIBRARIAN, PAINTER
b Albany, NY, May 4, 48. Study: Russell Sage Col, Troy, NY, BA; Simmons Col, Boston, Mass, MLS. Work: Russell Sage Col. Pos: Art & music librn, Forbes Libr, Northampton, Mass, 73-78; librn, Worcester Art Mus, Mass, 78- Mem: Am Libr Asn (mem col & res librn fine arts group); Art Libr Soc NAm (mem New Eng chap by-law comt, 73-74; treas, New Eng chap, 76-77). Style & Technique: Oil painting; palette knife. Interest: Development of resource collections to serve researcher and artist alike; personalization of art—making art something special for each person. Mailing Add: The Library Worcester Art Mus Worcester MA 01608

HATCH, JOHN DAVIS
ART CONSULTANT, ART HISTORIAN
b Oakland, Calif, June 14, 07. Study: Univ Calif, 26-28; Harvard Univ, 32; Princeton Univ, 38; Yale Univ, 40. Collections Arranged: Traveling Exhibs for Carnegie Corp, 36-37; American Drawings, 42; Thomas Cole, 43; pioneer exhib, Negro Artist Comes of Age, 45; Painting in Canada, 46. Teaching: Vis prof, Univ Ore, 48-49; vis prof, Univ Calif, summer 49; coordr adv & actg chmn fine arts div, Spelman Col, 64-70; vis prof, Univ Mass, summer 71. Pos: Exec secy, Seattle Art Mus, 28-29, dir, 29-31; vpres, Western Asn Art Mus, 30-31; asst dir, Isabella Stewart Gardner Mus, 32-35; dir, US art projs, New Eng States, 33-34; ed, Parnassus, 37-39; founder, Am Art Depository, 38; founder, Am Drawing Ann, 40; dir, Albany Inst Hist & Art, 40-48; ed, Albany Co Hist Asn Rec, 41-48; ed, Early Am Indust Chronicle, 42-49; dir, Norfolk Mus Art & Sci, 50-60. Mem: Master Drawing Asn (trustee, founder, 62); Am Drawing Soc (adv bd); Berkshire Co Hist Soc (past treas, trustee); Col Art Asn Am; MacDowell Colonists. Interest: Life of John VanderLyn and a survey of American drawings and draughtsmen. Publ: Auth, Reproductions of paintings in the Isabella Stewart Gardner Museum; auth, Negro Artist Comes of Age & Historic Church Silver in the Southern Diocese of Virginia; co-compiler, Historic Survey of Painting in Canada. Mailing Add: Lenox MA 01240

HATCH, JOHN W
PAINTER, EDUCATOR
b Saugus, Mass, Nov 1, 19. Study: Mass Col Art; Sch Fine Arts, Yale Univ, BFA & MFA. Work: De Cordova & Dana Mus, Lincoln, Mass; Phillips Exeter Acad; Portland Mus Art; Addison Gallery Am Art, Andover, Mass; Pa Acad Art, Philadelphia. Comn: Murals, Army Map Serv Bldg, Washington, DC, Am Red Cross, Melbourne, Australia & Kingsbury Hall, Univ NH; mem window, Student Union, Univ NH; hist mural, Ledges, Durham, NH; plus others. Exhib: US Info Agency Exhib, Russia, 61; Centennial Exhib of Land Grant Cols, Kansas City, Mo, 62; De Cordova & Dana Mus, 62 & 64; Boston Mus Fine Arts, 67-69; Addison Gallery Am Art; plus others. Teaching: Prof art, Univ NH, currently. Awards: City of Manchester Award, NH, 64; NH Art Asn Award, 64; Portland Mus Art Festivals Award; plus others. Mem: NH Art Asn (pres, 58-60); Am Asn Univ Prof; Boston Watercolor Soc. Style & Technique: Interpretive images of New England mountains and sea, using watercolor on Oriental papers strengthened with sumi; also acrylic with collage and watercolor. Mailing Add: Paul Creative Arts Ctr Univ of NH Durham NH 03824

HATCH, W A S
PRINTMAKER, EDUCATOR
b Bridgeport, Conn, Mar 19, 48. Study: Syracuse Univ, BFA, 70; Pratt Inst, MFA, 72. Work: New York Community Col; Ill State Mus; US Info Agency Embassy Collection; Univ Leeds; San Diego Mus. Comn: Spec ed prints, Pratt Graphic Ctr, New York, 73. Exhib: 3rd Brit Int Biennale, Yorkshire, 72; Folio Seventh-Three, Int Exhib, Calif Col Arts & Crafts, 73; Brooklyn Mus 19th Nat Print Exhib, 74-75; 4th Nat Graphic Arts Exhib, Taiwan, 75; Yugoslavia 11th Int Biennial, Ljubljana, 75 & 77; Miami Int Biennial, Fla, 75 & 77; Premio Int Biella per l'incisione, Italy, 76; 5th Int Drawing Show, Mus Mod Art, Riejka, Yugoslavia, 76; World Print Competition, 77; Am Printmakers, Venice, 77; New Talent Show, Allied Artists of Am, New York, 77; Self-Portrait, Kyoto, Japan, 77. Teaching: Asst prof printmaking, Bradley Univ, 73- Awards: Purchase Award, 1st Ann NH Print Exhib, 73; Purchase Award, Los Angeles 2nd Nat Print Exhib, 74; Merit Award, Boston Printmakers 26th Ann Exhib, 74. Bibliog: The European Graphic Biennale, Print Rev, 77. Media: Intaglio, Lithography. Dealer: Assoc American Artists 663 Fifth Ave New York NY 10022. Mailing Add: 110 W Grand Ave Chicago IL 60610

HATCHETT, DUAYNE
SCULPTOR, EDUCATOR
b Shawnee, Okla, May 12, 25. Study: Univ Mo; Univ Okla, BFA & MFA. Work: Whitney Mus Am Art; Rochester Mem Mus, NY; Ft Worth Art Mus, Tex; Carnegie Inst, Pittsburgh, Pa; Albright-Knox Gallery, Buffalo, NY. Comn: First Nat Bank Tulsa, Okla; Trader's Nat Bank, Kansas City, Kans, 61; Tulsa Fire Dept Hq, Okla, 63; GSA-Fed Bldg, Rochester, NY, 75; Nat Endowment for the Arts, Flint, Mich, 78. Exhib: Whitney Mus Am Art Ann, 66-68; Am Sculpture of Sixties, Los Angeles Co Mus, 67; Pittsburgh Int, 67-71; 11th Int Biennial Sculpture, Middelheim Mus, Antwerp, Belg; one-man show, Albright-Knox Gallery, 74. Teaching: Assoc prof sculpture, Ohio State Univ, 64-68; prof art, State Univ NY Buffalo, 68- Style & Technique: Constructivist in form, using line, plane and volume to emphasize space and form. Media: Metal. Mailing Add: 347 Starin Ave Buffalo NY 14216

HATFIELD, DAVID UNDERHILL
PAINTER
b Plainfield, NJ, July 16, 40. Study: Miami Univ, BFA, 62; Sch Visual Arts, 63; Art Students League, 64. Exhib: Nat Acad Design Ann, New York, 70 & 73; Nat Arts Club Ann, New York, 69-72, 75 & 76; Am Artists Prof League Grand Nat, New York, 71-77; Allied Artists Am, New York, 71-77; one-man show, Nat Arts Club, 76. Awards: Julius Hallgarten Second Prize, Nat Acad Design, 70; Elizabeth T Greenshields Mem Found Grant, 73 & 74; John F & Anna Lee Stacey Found Grant, 75. Mem: Salmagundi Club; Allied Artists Am; Hudson Valley Art Asn; Am Artists Prof League; Knickerbocker Artists. Style & Technique: Traditional. Media: Oil. Dealer: Grand Central Art Galleries 40 Vanderbilt Ave New York NY 10017; Christopher Gallery 766 Madison Ave New York NY 10021. Mailing Add: 240 W 38th St New York NY 10018

HATFIELD, DONALD GENE
PAINTER, EDUCATOR
b Detroit, Mich, May 23, 32. Study: Northwestern Mich Col, AA; Mich State Univ, BA & MA; Univ Wis, MFA. Work: Montgomery Mus Art, Ala; Tuskegee Inst, Ala; Univ Wis-La Crosse; Milwaukee Pub Sch, Wis; Opelika Art Asn Collection, Ala. Exhib: 2nd Ann Juried Arts Nat Exhib, Jr League, Tyler, Tex, 63; 7th Ann Nat Exhib, Chautauqua Art Asn, NY, 64; 8th Ann Nat Exhib, Gtr Fall River Art Asn, Mass, 64; 26th Nat Watercolor Exhib, Miss Watercolor Soc, Jackson Munic Art Gallery, 67; 57th Nat Oil Painting Exhib, Miss Art Asn, Jackson, 67. Teaching: Elem art supvr, Auburndale Elem Sch Syst, Wis; instr jr & sr high art classes, Auburndale High Sch, 62-64; asst prof art, Auburn Univ, 64-71, assoc prof art, 71-; part time instr hist archit & art, Tuskegee Inst, 68-69. Awards: Awards: Purchase Award, 49th Ann Exhib Wis Art, Milwaukee Art Ctr, Milwaukee J, 63; Purchase Award, 11th Dixie Ann, Montgomery Mus Art, 70; Kelly Fitzpatrick Award, 42nd Ann, Montgomery Mus Art, Ala Art League, 71. Mem: Ala Art League (first vpres, 69-70, pres, 70-72); Opelika Arts Asn (bd trustees, 71-73); Ala Watercolor Soc; Birmingham Art Asn. Media: Watercolor. Mailing Add: 550 Forest Park Circle Auburn AL 36830

HATGIL, PAUL
SCULPTOR
b Manchester, NH, Feb 18, 21. Study: Mass Col Art, BFA; Columbia Univ, MFA; Harvard Univ, summer 50. Work: Fed Aviation Agency, Balboa, CZ. Comn: St Paul's Lutheran Church, Austin, Tex; Univ Tex Bus & Admin Bldg, Austin; Our Saviour's Lutheran Church, Victoria, Tex; Design Assocs Bldg, Dallas, Tex; Rio Bldg, Austin; plus others. Exhib: 4th-6th Int Invitational, Smithsonian Inst, Washington, DC; Int Invitational, Gulf-Caribbean Exhib, Houston, Tex; Philbrook Art Ctr Int, Tulsa, Okla; US World's Fair Pavilion, NY; Hemisphere 1969, Tex Pavilion, San Antonio, Tex; plus many others. Teaching: Instr, Columbia Univ; instr, San Antonio Art Inst; instr, Tex Fine Arts Asn, Austin; prof art, Univ Tex, Austin, 51- Awards: Univ Tex Res Inst Grants, 64 & 65. Mem: Am Craftsmen Coun; Col Art Asn Am. Style & Technique: Geometric. Media: Resin, Polyester. Publ: Auth, articles in, Ceramic Monthly, Sch Arts, Tex Trends Art Educ, La Rev Mod, Ceramic Age & Hellenic Chronicle. Mailing Add: 1401 Red Bud Trail Austin TX 78746

HATHAWAY, WALTER MURPHY
MUSEUM DIRECTOR
b Norfolk, Va, Feb 25, 39. Study: Richmond Prof Inst, BFA; Fla State Univ, MS. Exhib: Piedmont Graphics Ann, Mint Mus, Charlotte, NC, 71; Art on Paper, Weatherspoon Gallery, Greensboro, NC, 71. Teaching: Instr art, Lake City Jr Col, Fla, 64-67; asst prof art & art educ, Longwood Col, Farmville, Va, 67-70. Pos: Art consult, State Dept Pub Instr, NC, 70-72; dir, Roanoke Fine Arts Ctr, Va, 73-77; dir, Columbia Mus of Arts & Sci, 77- Mem: Am Asn Mus. Publ: Auth, On hair turning grey, Art Educ, 71. Mailing Add: Columbia Mus of Art & Sci Senate & Bull Columbia SC 29201

HAUG, DONALD RAYMOND
PAINTER, INSTRUCTOR
b Detroit, Mich, May 12, 25. Study: Mich State Univ, with Murry Jones & John De Martelly, 46 & 47; Albright Art Sch, with Philip Elliott & Peter Gileran, dipl, 52 & 53; State Univ NY Col, with Peter Busa, BS & MS, 52-60; Univ Chicago, John Hay Whitney Found fel, with Joshua Taylor & Harold Haydon, 62-63. Work: Butler Inst Am Art, Youngstown, Ohio; Ball State Univ Art Gallery; Mem Gallery, Albright-Knox Art Gallery, Buffalo, NY; also numerous pvt collections. Exhib: 10 shows, Butler Inst Am Art Ann Midyear Show, 56-74; Chautauqua Art Asn Nat Jury Show, NY, 59, 66 & 72-74; Cooperstown Art Asn Nat Ann, NY, 71-72; Drawing & Small Sculpture Ann, Ball State Univ, 72-75; 62nd Wadsworth Atheneum Ann, Hartford, Conn, 72; plus others. Pos: Chmn art dept, Eden Cent Schs, NY. Awards: Silver Medal & Patrons Award, Buffalo Soc Artists 70th Ann, Albright-Knox Art Gallery, 65; Purchase Awards, 35th Ann Midyear Show, Butler Inst Am Art, 70 & Drawing a Small Sculpture Ann, Ball State Univ, 73; First Prize Still Life, Cooperstown Art Asn, 71-72; plus others. Mem: Buffalo Soc Artists (pres, 69, coun mem, 70-72); Patteran Artists (pres, 74). Media: Oil. Mailing Add: 9267 W Lane Angola NY 14006

HAUPT, SHIRLEY ELIASON
See Eliason, Shirley

HAUPTMAN, SUSAN ANN
DRAFTSMAN
b Detroit, Mich, Dec 8, 47. Study: Carnegie Inst Technol, 65-66; Univ Mich, Ann Arbor, BFA, 68; Wayne State Univ, MFA, 70. Work: Minn Mus Art, St Paul; Univ Colo, Boulder; St Lawrence Univ; Univ NDak; NY State Univ Potsdam. Exhib: Drawing USA, Minn Mus Art, 71, 73 & 75; Nat Drawing Exhib, NY State Univ Potsdam, 73 & 75; 14th Ann Calgary Graphics Int, Alta Col Art, 74; Carnegie Mus Art, 74; Int Brit Drawing Biennale, Cleveland, Eng, 75; plus others. Teaching: Instr drawing & design, Univ Pittsburgh, 72-74, asst prof, 74; guest artist, Summer Lithography Workshop, St Lawrence Univ, 74; asst prof drawing & painting, Skidmore Col, 74- Awards: Nat Drawing Exhib Purchase Prize, Univ Colo, 74 & Univ NDak, 75; Univ Pittsburgh Grant, 74; Skidmore Col Grant, 75; plus others. Mem: Col Art Asn. Style & Technique: Line drawing. Media: Ink, Graphite, Charcoal. Dealer: Kingpitcher Gallery 303 S Craig St Pittsburgh PA 15213. Mailing Add: 365 Canal St New York NY 10013

HAUSER, ALONZO
PAINTER, SCULPTOR
b La Crosse, Wis, Jan 30, 09. Study: Layton Sch Art; Univ Wis; Art Students League, with William Zorach; also with Amedeo Merli. Work: State Capitol Grounds, Rice Park & St Paul Gallery Art, St Paul, Minn; Walker Art Ctr, Minneapolis; Wustum Mus, Racine, Wis. Comn: Five figures & four reliefs, Greendale Fed Govt, Wis, 37-40; Christ figure (16' limestone), St Paul's Evangel Church, St Paul, 52; fountain (bronze), Vet Serv Bldg, St Paul, 52-56; fountain (bronze), Rice Park Woman's League, St Paul, 68. Exhib: ACA Gallery, New York, 36; Milwaukee Art Inst, Wis, 40; one-man retrospective, Walker Art Ctr, Minneapolis, 46; Rochester Art Ctr, 62; Las Cruces Community Art Ctr, NMex, 75. Teaching: Chmn & founder art dept, Macalester Col, St Paul, 44-49; critic, Sch Archit, Univ Minn, Minneapolis, 57-69. Style & Technique: Figurative. Media: Stone, Bronze. Mailing Add: Box 12037 Mesilla Park NM 88047

HAUSMAN, FRED S
SCULPTOR, DESIGNER
b Bingen on Rhine, Ger, Apr 27, 21; US citizen. Study: Pratt Inst; New Sch Social Res, with Stuart Davis. Work: Emily Lowe Collection, Univ Miami; Mus Mod Art, Bogota, Colombia; Evansville Mus; Rutgers Univ; Fordham Univ. Exhib: NY Univ, 66; Contemporary Art USA, Norfolk Mus, 67; Columbia Univ, 68; Black & White Show, Smithsonian Inst, 69-70; 2nd Biennial, Medellin, Colombia, 70. Media: Acrylic. Collection: Fifteenth and twentieth century drawings. Dealer: Bodley Gallery 1063 Madison Ave New York NY 10028. Mailing Add: 100 Pembroke Dr Stamford CT 06903

HAUSMAN, JEROME JOSEPH
EDUCATOR
b New York, NY, May 4, 25. Study: Pratt Inst, 42-43; Cornell Univ, AB, 46; Columbia Univ, 47-48; Art Students League, 48; NY Univ, MA, 51, EdD, 54. Teaching: Instr art, Elizabeth Pub Schs, NJ, 49-53; assoc prof, Sch Fine & Appl Arts, Ohio State Univ, 53-68, actg dir, 58-59, dir, 59-68; vis lectr, Sch Art, Syracuse Univ, 57; vis prof art educ, Pa State Univ, 58; prof div creative arts, NY Univ, 68-75; pres & prof, Minneapolis Col Art & Design, 75- Pos: Mem arts & humanities panel, US Off Educ, 64-70; ed bd, J Aesthetic Educ, 68-; consult, John D Rockefeller III Fund, 69-75; pres, Minn Alliance for Arts in Eudc, 77- Mem: Nat Art Educ Asn (chmn res comt, adv res bd); Nat Comn Art Educ (chmn); Am Soc Aesthetics; Western Arts Asn; Inst for Study Art in Educ (pres). Publ: Ed, Research in Art Education (yearbk), Nat Art Educ Asn, 59; ed, Studies in art education, J Issues & Research; contribr, articles in prof jour. Mailing Add: 1772 DuPont Ave S Minneapolis MN 55403

HAUT, CLAIRE (JOAN)
DESIGNER, PAINTER
US citizen. Study: Augustana Col; Am Acad Art, Chicago; Sch Design, Chicago, Lazlo Moholy-Nagy scholarship; Inst Design; also with Hin Bredendieck, John Kearney & Gyorgy Kepes. Work: Libr Cong, Washington, DC. Comn: Screen, woven and printed drapes, rug and upholstery, Teachers Rm & Home Econ Rm, Saarinens Crow Island Sch, Winnetka, Ill, 40; libr traveling display throughout S & Cent Am, Am Libr Asn, 40; plus pvt comn. Exhib: State Dept sponsored traveling exhib of Works Progress Admin crafts to eight European countries; Traveling Exhib Works Progress Admin Crafts, Chicago Art Inst, Mus Mod Art, New York, Corcoran Mus, Carnegie Inst, San Francisco Mus, Mus St Louis & Toledo Mus; Southwest Biennial & Traveling Show, Mus NMex, Santa Fe, 68-69; NMex Biennial, Mus of NMex, Santa Fe, 71; Albuquerque 20, NMex Arts Comn, Santa Fe, 73; All American, The Gallery, Barnegat Light, NJ, 73; 1st Body Ornament Show, Southwest Crafts Ctr Gallery, San Antonio, Tex & BAU Hous Gallery, Houston, 73-74. Pos: Artist-designer, Experimental Design Workshop, Ill Art Project, Chicago, 39-42; art ed, Cudahy Packing Co, Chicago, 43-45; illusr, Sandia Labs, Albuquerque, 58- Awards: Pop Art Exhib First Prize, NMex Art League, 64; First Prize for Graphics, NMex State Fair Prof Artists Exhib, 67; First Purchase Prize for Crafts & Sculpture, Llano Estacado, 71; plus many others. Mem: Artists Equity (secy-treas, 73 & pres, 76, Albuquerque Chap); Albuquerque Designer Craftsmen; Nat League Am Pen Women (pres, Manzanita Br, 70-72; state chmn, Biennial Exhib, 74-76); Southwest Craft Ctr; NMex Art League. Style & Technique: Two and three dimensions. Mailing Add: 9836 McKnight NE Albuquerque NM 87112

HAVARD, JAMES PINKNEY
PAINTER
b Galveston, Tex, June 29, 37. Study: Sam Houston State Univ, BS; Pa Acad Fine Arts, Cresson scholar to Europe, 64, I J Henry Schiedt scholar, 65. Work: Philadelphia Mus Art; also in pvt collections. Exhib: Nat Drawing Exhib, Am Fedn Arts, 65; Nat Inst Arts & Lett, 65; Pa Acad Fine Arts, Philadelphia, 65; Germantown First Ann Exhib & Eastern Cent Exhib, Philadelphia Mus Art, 65; plus others. Awards: Mabel Wilson Woodrow Award, Pa Acad Fine Arts, 62; Purchase Prize, Eastern Cent Drawing Exhib, Philadelphia Mus Art, 65; Wechsler Prize, Cheltenham Art Ctr. Mem: Fel Pa Acad Fine Arts. Dealer: Atelier Chapman Kelley Galleries 2526 Fairmount Dallas TX 75201. Mailing Add: 237 Chestnut St Philadelphia PA 19106

HAVELOCK, CHRISTINE MITCHELL
ART HISTORIAN
b Cochrane, Ont, June 2, 24; US citizen. Study: Univ Toronto, AB; Radcliffe Col, AM; Harvard Univ, Charles Eliot Norton fel, 51-52, PhD. Teaching: Prof art hist, Vassar Col, 53- Pos: Cur classical collection, Vassar Col. Awards: Am Asn Univ Women Fel, 58-59. Mem: Col Art Asn Am; Archeol Inst Am. Res: Greek sculpture of Hellenistic period. Publ: Auth, Hellenistic art, New York Graphic Soc, 71. Mailing Add: Vassar Col Poughkeepsie NY 12601

HAVERSAT, LILLIAN KERR
ART DEALER
b New York, NY, Jan 12, 38. Study: Univ Vt; Danbury State Col; Famous Artist Sch, cert com art; Trinity Col, Vt, 78; also with David K Merrill & Patricia Reynolds. Pos: Art consult, Discovery Mus, Essex Junction, Vt, 74-; owner, Monk's House Art Serv & Gallery, Jericho, Vt, 74-; consult, Vt Educ Television Arts Auction, 75-78, state coordr, 75-76; consult, Lake Champlain CofC Regional Exhib, 77-78, coordr, 78. Mem: Northern Vt Artist Asn (pres, 73-78); founding mem Essex Vt Art League. Specialty: Contemporary American art; contemporary and antique prints, sculpture, pottery; New England representative for David K Merrill. Publ: Auth, Artfully Speaking, 74. Mailing Add: Box 189 Jericho VT 05465

HAVIS, C KENNETH
GALLERY DIRECTOR, DESIGNER
b Hubbard, Tex, Mar 11, 39. Study: NTex State Univ, BA & MA; study with Billie Leach & Marvin Lapofsky. Work: New Orleans Mus Art. Exhib: Ann Drawing, Photo & Crafts Exhib, Ark Art Ctr, Little Rock, 69, 70 & 74; Tarrant Co Ann, Ft Worth Art Mus, Tex, 71 & 77; Tex Ann Crafts Exhib, Dallas Mus Fine Art, 71, 74 & 77; NTex Painting & Sculpture Exhib, Dallas Mus Fine Art, 73; Levi's Denim Art, M H De Young Mus Art, San Francisco & Mus Contemp Crafts, New York, 74 & 75; 1975 Artist Biennial, New Orleans Mus Art, 75; Main Street, Houston, Tex, 76. Collections Arranged: Marcus, Murchison, Weiner, 72; Fashion & Art from the Twenties, 73; The Nasher Collection, 74. Teaching: Prof 3-D design, NTex State Univ, Denton, 69-, prof beginning ceramics, 73-74, prof practice for the studio artist, 77-78. Pos: Vpres, Tex Designer/Craftsman, 73-74; vpres, Greater Denton Arts Coun, Tex, 74-77; dir gallery, NTex State Univ, 69- Awards: Award of Excellence, Ten Ann Crafts Exhib, Dallas Mus Fine Arts, 71 & 74; 3rd Place, Levi's Denim Art, Levi Strauss, 74; one-man exhib award, 1975 Artist's Biennial, New Orleans Mus Art, 76; $250 Materials Award, Dallas

Mus Invitational, 77. Bibliog: American Denim, Harry N Abrams, Inc, 75. Mem: Tex Art Alliance. Style & Technique: Abstract and non-objective; intense interest in color and texture; found objects important. Media: Acrylic and found objects. Specialty: 2-D and 3-D art work and posters. Mailing Add: NT Box 5063 Denton TX 76203

HAWES, CHARLES
PAINTER, ILLUSTRATOR
b Huntington, WVa, Oct 7, 09. Study: Chicago Acad Fine Art. Exhib: Nat Acad Gallery, New York; Am Watercolor Soc Traveling Exhib, Lect Technique, 65; Rocky Mountain Nat, Foothills Art Ctr, Golden, Colo, 77; one-man shows, Island Ctr, St Croix, 63-78. Pos: Sketch artist, Maxon Inc, New York & Detroit, 53-57; art dir, Lennen & Newell, New York, 57-61 & Geyer, Morey & Ballard, New York, 61-65. Awards: Purchase Prize, Wichita Nat, Kans, 73. Publ: Illusr, Colliers Mag, Am Mag & Reader's Digest Mag; illusr bks, Putnam, 44-65, Reader's Digest Bks. Mailing Add: Box 962 Frederiksted St Croix VI 00840

HAWKINS, MYRTLE H
PAINTER, WRITER
b Merrit, BC. Study: Harnell Col, AA; San Jose State Univ; Univ Calif; West Valley Col; also with Marshall Merrit, Maynard Stewart & Thomas Leighton. Work: Nat Easter Seal Soc, Chicago; pvt collection of Austen Warburton, Santa Clara, Calif. Comn: Portrait of Rev John Foster, First Congregational Church, San Jose, Calif, 70; portrait of Rose Shenson, Triton Mus, Santa Clara, Calif, 71. Exhib: De Saisset Gallery, Santa Clara, 68; Am Artist Prof League Nat Exhib, Lever House, New York, 71; one-man shows, Triton Mus Art, 71 & Rosicrucian Mus Art, San Jose, 73; Hartnell Col, 69. Teaching: Teacher painting, Calif State Dept Vocational Rehab, San Jose & Palo Alto, 69-71; also pvt painting lessons. Awards: First Place, Nat Easter Seal Soc, Chicago, 65; Gold Seal Award, de Saisset Art Gallery, 66; Best of Show, St Mark's Art Ann, Santa Clara, 68. Bibliog: Article in Rosicrucian Digest, 11/73. Mem: Allied Artists Santa Clara Co (pres, 72-73); Am Artists Prof League; Soc Western Artists; Triton Mus Art. Style & Technique: Portraits of children and animals; still life and modern color studies in all media; representational. Media: Pastel, Oil. Publ: Illusr, The Adventures of Mimi, Books I & II, 66; auth, Art as Therapy, Recreation and Rehabilitation for the Handicapped, 74. Mailing Add: 646 Bucher Ave Santa Clara CA 95051

HAWKINS, THOMAS WILSON, JR
PAINTER, INSTRUCTOR
b Los Angeles, Calif, May 15, 41. Study: Calif State Univ, Long Beach, BA(design) & MA(drawing, painting); Calif State Univ, Los Angeles, art hist, design & ceramics. Work: Overholt & Overholt Law Off, Los Angeles; Dr Ambler Collection, Palos Verdes, Calif; Whittier Art Asn, Calif. Exhib: Southern Calif Expos, Del Mar, 67-77; Inland Exhibs, 68-77; Butler Inst Am Art, Youngstown, Ohio, 70; DaVinci Open Art Competition, New York, 70; Bertrand Russell Centenary Art Exhib, London & Nottingham, Eng, 73. Teaching: Instr drawing & design, Rio Hondo Col, Whittier, Calif, 67-; instr art, Long Beach City Col, 67-72; instr drawing, art hist & painting, Golden West Col, Huntington Beach, Calif, 72- Awards: Best Painting, Art in All Media, Southern Calif Expos, 67, Third Prize, 70; Second Award, Inland Exhib, San Bernardino Art Asn, 71 & 73; Purchase Award 25th All City Los Angeles Art, Barnsdall, 77. Mem: Los Angeles Art Asn; Whittier Art Asn; Orange Co Art Teachers Asn; Calif Teachers Asn. Style & Technique: Expression of the backyard landscape; colorist; oil brush painting on linen and figure drawing. Mailing Add: 414 Fairview Ave Arcadia CA 91006

HAWORTH, B COGILL (MRS PETER HAWORTH)
PAINTER
b Queenstown, SAfrica; Jan 20, 10; Can citizen. Study: ARCA; Univ London, grad. Work: Nat Gallery Can; Art Gallery Ont; Art Gallery Hamilton; Art Gallery of Windsor; Art Gallery, SAfrica. Exhib: Royal Can Acad; Ont Soc Artists; Can Soc Painter Watercolour; Can Group Painters. Awards: Best in Show, Can Soc Painters Watercolor; Best in Show for Watercolor, Jessie Dow; Monsanto Award. Mem: Royal Can Acad; Ont Soc Artists; Can Soc Painters Watercolour (pres, 3 yrs); Can Group Painters (vpres & treas). Style & Technique: Abstract hard edge in oil; abstract realism in acrylic. Publ: Illusr, Book of Remembrance, Guelph Agr Col; illusr, Illustrated Habitant Merchant; contribr, Book on the Saguanay; contribr, Four Decades; contribr, Canadian Watercolours. Dealer: 641 Yonge St Toronto ON Can. Mailing Add: 111 Cluny Dr Toronto ON M4W 2R5 Can

HAWTHORNE, JACK GARDNER
EDUCATOR, PAINTER
b Philadelphia, Pa, May 8, 21. Study: Philadelphia Col Art, BA, 43; Univ Pa, MSEd, 56, MFA, 58. Teaching: Dir art educ, Pub Schs, Pa & NJ, 43-50; instr drawing, Philadelphia Col Art, 43-53, asst dean & registr, 57-60; asst prof educ, Beaver Col, 60-63; assoc prof art, West Chester State Col, 65-, chmn art dept, 73-74 & 77- Awards: Award in Drawing, Pa Acad Fine Arts, 39. Mem: Peale Club, Pa Acad Fine Arts; Nat Trust for Hist Preserv; Philadelphia Art Alliance; life mem Nat Educ Asn; Inst Study Art Educ; Chester Co Art Asn. Media: Watercolor. Publ: Contribr, Course of study in art educ, Commonwealth Pa, 51. Mailing Add: 619 W Miner St West Chester PA 19380

HAY, DICK
SCULPTOR, EDUCATOR
b Cincinnati, Ohio, Nov 19, 42. Study: Ohio Univ, BFA; NY State Col Ceramics, Alfred Univ, MFA. Work: Speed Art Mus, Louisville, Ky; Butler Inst Am Art, Youngstown, Ohio; Evansville Mus Arts & Sci, Ind; Sea of Japan, Kanazawa-shi, Japan; Edinboro Col, Pa. Exhib: Clayworks: 20 Americans, Mus Contemp Crafts, New York, 71; Chicago Plates, Exhib A Gallery, Evanston, Ill, 72; Sensible Cup Int Exhib, Sea of Japan Expos, 73; Ceramics USA-Circa 1975, Playhouse Sq Gallery, Cleveland, Ohio, 74; Nat Funk Exhib, Habitat Gallery, Dearborn, Mich, 75; Contemp Ceramic Sculpture, Univ NC, Chapel Hill, 77; plus others. Teaching: Assoc prof ceramics, Ind State Univ, Terre Haute, 66- Pos: Guest lectr, Univ Iowa, 69, Alfred Univ, 72 & 74, Univ Del, 72, Ariz State Univ, 73, Sheridan Col Appl Arts, Toronto, Ont, 74, La State Univ, 76, Univ Miami, 76 & Col of Santa Fe, 77; plus others. Mem: Nat Coun Educ for Ceramic Arts (bd dirs, 70-, pres, 78-). Style & Technique: Object oriented clay sculpture. Dealer: Exhibit A 1708 Central Evanston IL 60201. Mailing Add: Dept of Art Ind State Univ Terre Haute IN 47809

HAY, GEORGE AUSTIN
PAINTER, FILMMAKER
b Johnstown, Pa, Dec 25, 15. Study: Pa Acad Fine Arts; Art Student League; Nat Acad; Univ Rochester; Univ Pittsburgh, BS & MLitt; Columbia Univ, MA; also with Robert Brackman & Dong Kingman. Work: New York Pub Libr; Dept Army; Libr Cong, Washington, DC; Metrop Mus Art; numerous pvt collections. Exhib: Philharmonic Hall, Lincoln Ctr, 65; Parrish Art Mus, Southampton, 69; Riverside Mus, 70; Carnegie Inst, Pittsburgh, 72; Duncan Galleries, NY, 73; Manufacturers Hanover Trust, 73; Bicentennial Exhib of Am Painters in Paris, 76. Awards: Prizes in regional exhibs. Mem: Am Artists Prof League; Fed Design Coun; Arts Club of Washington (trustee); Provincetown Art Asn; Allied Artists. Style & Technique: Along his path of varied responses to the world around us—figure and still life, torrid huts of the Pacific and misty castles of Scotland—the artist reflects a mysterious tranquility; rich images of life in our time. Media: Oil, Watercolor. Publ: Auth & illusr, Seven Hops to Australia, 45; auth & illusr, The Performing Arts Experience, 69; auth & dir, Visit to the Museum of Modern Art (film), 72; dir, Highways of History (film), 76. Dealer: Gallery Madison/90 1248 Madison Ave New York NY 10028. Mailing Add: 2022 Columbia Rd NW Washington DC 20009

HAY, IKE
SCULPTOR, EDUCATOR
b Atlanta, Ga, Apr 28, 44. Study: Univ Ga, BFA & MFA. Work: Indianapolis Mus Art; New Orleans Mus Art; Mint Mus Art, Charlotte, NC; Lancaster Co Courthouse, Pa; High Steel Corp, Lancaster. Comn: Architectural sculpture, Wheeler Basin Libr, Decatur, Ala, 75. Exhib: Experiments in Art & Technol, High Mus Art, Atlanta, Ga, 69, Invitational, 73; 69 Artists of the Southeast & Texas, New Orleans Mus Art, 69, one-man show, 70; Nat Sculpture 73 Traveling Show, 73. Teaching: Asst prof sculpture, Purdue Univ, West Lafayette, 69-74; asst prof sculpture, Millersville State Col, Pa, 75- Pos: Nat Endowment artist in residence, Decatur, 74-75. Awards: Rosenblatt Scholarship, Univ Ga, 68; Grant in Aid, Arts Festival Atlanta, 68; Fac Grant, Purdue Univ, 70. Bibliog: John Spofforth (auth), The Ike Hay workshop, Ala-Arts, Ala State Arts Coun, 74. Mem: Am Asn Univ Prof; Col Art Asn Am; Southern Asn Sculptors. Style & Technique: Non-representational constructions. Media: Steel, Brass, Plastic. Dealer: Image South Gallery Peachtree St Atlanta GA 30601. Mailing Add: 205 W Frederick St Millersville PA 17551

HAYDEN, FRANK
EDUCATOR, SCULPTOR
b Memphis, Tenn, June 10, 34. Study: Xavier Univ, BA; Notre Dame Univ, MFA, study with Ivan Mestrovic; Iowa State Univ; Munich Art Acad, Fulbright fel, study with Heinrich Kirchner; Am Scand fel to Copenhagen, Denmark, under Mogens Boggeld; Southern fel to Stockholm, Sweden under Asmund Arle. Work: Johnson Publ Bldg Collection Black Art, Chicago; Southside Community Art Ctr, Chicago; La Arts & Sci Ctr, Baton Rouge, Contemp Liturgical Arts Gallery, New York. Comn: Life size sculpture, St Joseph's Cathedral, Baton Rouge, 66; sculpture monument, Newman Ctr, Southern Univ, Baton Rouge, 70; bold relief mahogany sculpture, Am Bank Bldg, Baton Rouge, 74; bronze monument sculpture, City of New Orleans, 75; sculpture monument, City of Baton Rouge, 75. Exhib: New York World's Fair, 65; Spokane World's Fair, Wash, 74; one-man shows, La State Univ Union Gallery, Baton Rouge, 65, Southside Community Art Ctr, 70 & El Centro Col Gallery, Dallas, Tex, 70. Teaching: Prof sculpture & drawing, Southern Univ, 61- Style & Technique: Contemporary architectural sculptures using modern and traditional materials and idioms. Media: Bronze, Wood. Mailing Add: 353 Hillcrest Ave Baton Rouge LA 70807

HAYDEN, MICHAEL
SCULPTOR
b Vancouver, BC, Jan 15, 43. Work: Nat Gallery of Can, Ottawa, Ont; Art Gallery of Ont, Toronto; Winnipeg Art Gallery, Man; Nat Sci Libr, Ottawa; Everson Mus, Syracuse, NY; Slim Line-Hamilton Art Gallery. Comn: Flame fountain, Consumer Gas Co, Toronto, 67; audio hydrokinetic presentation, Nat Gallery of Can, Toronto, 67; electronic escalator mural, York Univ, Toronto, 69; irresolute icon (vibrating mirror piece), Arts Coun of Great Brit, Southbank, Eng, 72; arc en ciel (600ft long neon rainbow), Toronto Transit Comn, Yorkdale Subway Station, 77. Exhib: Vancouver Art Gallery, BC, 67; Nathan Phillips Square of Toronto City Hall, 67; Martha Jackson Gallery, New York, 67; Univ Calif, Los Angeles & Phoenix Art Mus, 69; Kinetics, Hayward Gallery, London, Eng, 70; Electronic Art, Mus d'Art Contemporare, Montreal, Que, 74; Kunst Bleibst Kunst, Projekt 74, Koln, Ger, 74; Opening Show, Art Gallery of Can, 74, Chair Show, 75 & Xerox Show, 76; one-man shows, Art Gallery of Ont, Toronto, 66-76, Gallery Moos, Toronto, 66, 68, 70 & 72, Univ Toronto, 67, Rodman Hall, St Catherines, Ont, 68, Queen's Univ, Kingston, Ont, 68, Southern Ill Univ, Carbondale, 68, Waterloo Univ, Ont, 68, Rothman's Art Gallery, Stratford, Ont, 68, Carnegie-Mellon Univ, Pittsburgh, Pa, 69, Electric Gallery, Toronto, 70-72 & 76, York Univ, Toronto, 70, Buffalo State Univ, NY, 70, Denise Rene/Hans Mayer Gallery, Dusseldorf, Ger, 71, Woodstock Pub Art Gallery, Ont, 72, Willistead Art Gallery, Windsor, Ont, 72, Kitchener/Waterloo Art Gallery, Ont, 72, Winnepeg Art Gallery, Man, 73 & Sculpture New Gallery, New York, 76. Collections Arranged: Mind Excursion, Univ Toronto, 67; Duplex, Art Gallery of Ont, Toronto, 68; Atmosphere, Galaxii at the Can Nat Exhib; Self Portrait, Hommage to Colonel Sanders (traveling exhib to Can & Europe). Teaching: Sculptor-in-residence creative electronics, Fanshaw Col, London, Ont, 71-73; instr & lectr interdisciplinary studies, New Sch of Art, Toronto & York Univ, Toronto & artistic adv, Brock Univ, St Catherines, 71-73. Pos: Partner, Intersystems, Toronto, Ont, 67-69; pres, Michael Hayden Assoc Ltd, 70-75, Hayden/Arn Productions Ltd, 75-77 & Hayden Systems, 77-; mem bd, Art Gallery of Ont, Toronto, 74-76; dir, Toronto Arts Coun, 76-77. Awards: Can Coun short-term grant, 66 & Bursary grant, 68 & 71; Can Coun Sr Arts Award, 74. Bibliog: The environment, a night at the feelies, Time Mag, 7/68; Michael Greenwood (auth), Hayden's light/sound escalator at York Univ, Arts Can, 8-9/71; Tadeyish Yaworski (auth), Michael Hayden (film), Can Broadcasting Corp, 71. Mem: Can Artists Representation; Royal Can Acad of Art; Alliance of Technol & Art (dir); Videoring; Softwarehouse. Style & Technique: Deal with systems; access to and with contemporary technology. Media: Mind and Hands. Publ: Contribr, What is technology, Video Tape, 12/71, 3/73 & 12/72; contribr (videotape), Michael Hayden—Technology and the Artist, Media Ctr, Univ Windsor, 72; contribr, Art in Canada 72—Dr Wiebka van Bonnin, WGer Television Network, 72; contribr (film/videotape), Technology of the Artist, Ont Educ & Commun Authority, 72; contribr (xerographic art), Sci Mag, 6/76. Mailing Add: 29241 Circle Dr Malibu Lake Agoura CA 91301

HAYDON, HAROLD (EMERSON)
PAINTER, EDUCATOR
b Ft William, Ont, Apr 22, 09; US citizen. Study: Univ Chicago, PhB, 30, MA, 31; Sch Art Inst Chicago, 32-33. Work: Pickering Col, Newmarket, Ont. Comn: Wool ark cover, Temple Beth Am, Chicago, Ill, 58; glass mosaic murals, St Cletus Roman Cath Church, La Grange, Ill, 63; mosaic & stained glass murals, Sonia Shankman Orthogenic Sch, Univ Chicago, 66-77, porcelain enamel on steel mural, 77; stained glass windows, Rockefeller Mem Chapel, Univ Chicago, 72-78; wool Ark curtain, Niles Township Jewish Congregation, Skokie, Ill, 76. Exhib: Seven Exhibs Artists Chicago & Vicinity, 37-67 & 58th Ann Am Painting—Abstr & Surrealist Art, 47, Art Inst Chicago; Options, Mus Contemp Art, Chicago, 68; 21 one-man shows, 76. Teaching: From instr art to asst prof, George Williams Col, 34-44; from instr art to prof, Univ Chicago, 44-75, emer prof, 75-; vis lectr murals, Sch of Art Inst of Chicago, 75-; adj prof fine arts, Ind Univ NW, 76- Pos: Pres, Renaissance Soc Univ Chicago, 56-65 & 74-75; mem cult adv comt, Mayor's Comt Econ & Cult Develop, Chicago, 63-; art critic, Chicago Sun-Times, 63-; chmn art comt, Nat Assessment Educ Progress, 65; accreditation examr, NCent Asn Schs, 66- Mem: Artists Equity Asn, Chicago Chap (pres, 50-52, 55-57); Chicago

Soc Artists (pres, 59-61); Nat Soc Mural Painters; hon life mem Artists Guild Chicago. Media: Oil, Mosaic, Porcelain Enamel, Stained Glass. Publ: Auth, Great Art Treasures in America's Small Museums, 67. Mailing Add: 5009 Greenwood Ave Chicago IL 60615

HAYES, BARTLETT HARDING, JR
ART ADMINISTRATOR, WRITER
b Andover, Mass, Aug 5, 04. Study: Phillips Acad, grad, 22; Harvard Col, AB, 26; studied art in US, 27-29; study in Europe, 27-33. Teaching: Instr art, Phillips Acad, 33-69; lectr fine arts & res assoc, Grad Sch Educ, Harvard Univ, 64-68; fac, Grad Sch Educ, Lesley Col, Cambridge, Mass, 76. Pos: Asst cur, Addison Gallery Am Art, 34-40, dir, 40-69; trustee, Am Fedn Arts, 40-70, Mus Fine Arts, Boston, 49-71, Old Sturbridge Village, 50-70, Boston Arts Festival, 52-65, St Gaudens Mem, 67-72 & 74-, Amon Carter Mus, Ft Worth, 68-76 & Inst Contemp Art, Boston, 69-70 & 74-; mem ed bd, Art in Am, 44-69; chmn comn to survey role of arts, Mass Inst Technol, 52-54 & 69-70, mem exec comt, Coun Arts, 74-; mem art comn, Smithsonian Inst, 54-; bd dirs, Print Coun Am, 57-63; bd ed, John Harvard Libr, 58-61; lectr, Salzburg Sem, Austria, 60 & 71, Asiatic Mus Training Prog, Honolulu Acad Fine Arts, 69-70, Nat Humanities Faculty, 69-70 & Lowell Lectures, Boston, 75; mem exec comt, Art in Am Embassies Prog, Dept State, 65-70; mem vis comt, Dept Educ, Metrop Mus Art, 70-71; dir, Am Acad Rome, 69-73; mem art adv comt, Internal Revenue Serv, 70-74; mem bd overseers, Strawbery Banke, Portsmouth, NH, 73-; consult, Learning Disabilities Found, Landmark Sch, Prides Crossing, Mass, 73-, Essex Inst, Salem, Mass, 74 & Custom House Maritime Mus, Newburyport, Mass, 75; mem art adv comt, Mt Holyoke Col, South Hadley, Mass, 75-; consult, Educ Inst, Lincoln Ctr Performing Arts, 75-76; consult, Farnsworth Mus & Libr, Rockland, Maine, 76; dir centennial exhib, Sch Mus Fine Arts, Boston, 77. Mem: Col Art Asn Am (secy, 59-64); fel Am Acad Arts & Sci; Colonial Soc Mass. Publ: Auth, Naked Truth & Personal Vision & American Drawings; auth, Intent of Art (TV series), NET; co-auth, Layman's Guide to Modern Art; co-ed, Artist & Advocate; plus others. Mailing Add: Phillips St Andover MA 01810

HAYES, DAVID VINCENT
SCULPTOR
b Hartford, Conn, Mar 15, 31. Study: Ogunquit Sch Painting & Sculpture, with Robert Laurent; Univ Notre Dame, AB; Ind Univ, MFA, sculpture with David Smith. Work: Mus Mod Art & Guggenheim Mus, New York; Mus Arts Decoratif, Paris; Mus Fine Arts, Houston; Baltimore Mus Art. Comn: Ceramics, walls, De Porceleyne Fles, Delft, Holland, 67, Lee Kolker, Stanfordville, NY, 70 & Elmira Col, 71, mural, Great Southwest Corp, Atlanta, Ga, 68 & relief, comn by David Anderson, Ardsley, NY, 69. Exhib: Salon Jeune Sculpture, Mus Rodin, Paris, 63; Salon Mai, Mus Art Mod, Paris, 66; Carnegie Int, Pittsburgh, 67; Smithsonian Organized Drawing Exhib, White House, Washington, DC, 68; Jewelry 71, Art Gallery Ont, 71; one-man shows, Harvard Univ, 72, Albany Inst Hist & Art, NY, 73 & Copley Sq, Boston, 74; De Cordova Mus, Lincoln, Mass, 72; Corcoran Gallery Art, Washington, DC, 73; plus others. Teaching: Vis artist, Carpenter Art Ctr, Harvard Univ, 72. Awards: Fulbright Res Grant, 61; Guggenheim Found Fel, 61; Nat Inst Arts & Lett Award, 64. Media: Metal, Ceramics. Dealer: Willard Gallery 29 E 72nd St New York NY 10021; Agra Gallery 1721 DeSalles St Washington DC 20037. Mailing Add: PO Box 109 Coventry CT 06238

HAYES, LAURA M
CURATOR, ART HISTORIAN
b Birmingham, Ala, Nov 28, 27. Study: Univ Wyo; Univ Idaho; Oberlin Col. Pos: Head photog section, Wyo State Art Gallery, 65-74, art registrar, 67-71, curator art, 71- Mem: Western Asn Art Mus; Wyo Press Women; Wyo Prof Photog (pres); Wyo Artist Asn; Nat Fedn Press Women. Style & Technique: Wyoming landscapes; historical paintings. Media: Watercolor. Mailing Add: Rte 3 Box 495 Cheyenne WY 82001

HAYES, ROBERT T
PAINTER, PRINTMAKER
b Bloomfield, Ind, Jan 18, 15. Study: Miami Univ, Ohio, BFA. Work: In pub & pvt collections. Exhib: Exhib Intercontinental Monaco, 65 & 66; plus over 100 nat exhibs & 15 major one-man shows. Awards: Watercolor USA Award; Knickerbocker Award; Am Watercolor Soc Award; plus others. Mem: Am Watercolor Soc; Knickerbocker Art Soc; Cincinnati Art Club; Washington Watercolor Club, DC; plus others. Style & Technique: Primarily a representational style, occasionally a non-objective abstract style. Media: Watercolor. Mailing Add: 2859 Gilna Ct Cincinnati OH 45211

HAYES, TUA
PAINTER
b Anniston, Ala. Study: Converse Col, BA; Columbia Univ Teacher's Col; also with Henry Lee McFee. Work: Wilmington Soc Fine Arts, Del; Univ Del; Chester Co Art Asn, Pa; Converse Col, Spartanburg, SC. Exhib: Nat Jury Show, Chatauqua, NY, 59; five shows, Univ Del Regional Exhib, 66-71; Philadelphia Pro-Show, Pa, 67; Nat Acad Design, New York, 70; Baltimore Mus Regional Show, Md. Awards: First Prize for Oil Painting, 65 & First Prize for Drawing, 67, Del Art Mus. Mem: Philadelphia Art Alliance; Studio Group, Inc (pres, 54-56); Wilmington Soc Fine Arts (bd dirs, 62-). Media: Oil, Watercolor. Mailing Add: 3 Carriage Rd Wilmington DE 19807

HAY-MESSICK, VELMA
PAINTER
b Bloomington, Ill. Study: Watercolor with Dong Kingman, 44; Chouinard Art Inst, 47, 48 & 50; Otis Art Inst, 49. Work: Seton Hall Univ, Newark, NJ; City of Hope, Duarte, Calif; Grumbacher Artists' Palettes, New York. Exhib: E B Crocker Gallery Art, Sacramento, Calif, 56 & 57; Fresno Art Ctr, Calif, 57; Seton Hall Univ, Newark, 58; Nat League Am Pen Women Southwest Regional, Albuquerque, NMex, 71; Long Beach Community Theatre Gallery, 75; Exhibs, Nat League Am Pen Women, 76 & 77; Messick-Hay Studio Gallery, Apple Valley, Calif, currently. Pos: Dir, Messick-Hay Studio Gallery, 52- Awards: Key Award, Seton Hall Univ, 58; Hon Mention for Drawing, Southwest Regional Conf, 71 & Second in Oils, Calif State Exhib, 71, Nat League Am Pen Women. Bibliog: John Oglesby (auth), Lively arts, Sacramento Bee, 57; Vera Williams (auth), Art is a way of life, Southland Mag, 66; Geraldine H Wheeler (ed), Profile, Ben Messick & Velma Hay-Messick, Athelings Mag, 75. Mem: Victor Valley Br of Nat League Am Pen Women (Calif S State co-art chmn, art chmn, Long Beach Br, 72-74). Style & Technique: Mystical; impressionistic. Media: Oil. Publ: Auth, Art spirit in XVII century America, Pen Woman, 6/73; auth, XVII century art, Guild St Margaret of Scotland Mag, 78. Dealer: Messick-Hay Studio Gallery 20930 Lone Eagle Rd Apple Valley CA 92307. Mailing Add: c/o Messick-Hay Studio Gallery 20930 Lone Eagle Rd Apple Valley CA 92307

HAYNES, DOUGLAS H
PAINTER, EDUCATOR
b Regina, Sask, Jan 1, 36. Study: Provincial Inst Technol & Art, Calgary, Alta, with R Spickett; Royal Acad Fine & Appl Arts, The Hague, Holland. Work: Edmonton Art Gallery, Alta; Confederation Art Gallery, Charlottetown, PEI; London Pub Mus & Art Gallery, Ont; Univ Calgary, Alta. Exhib: 5th Biennial Exhib Can Art, London, Eng & Ottawa, Can, 63 & 6th Biennial Exhib, Ottawa, 65; All Alberta '70, Edmonton, 70; West '71 Exhib, Edmonton, 71; Royal Can Acad Arts 91st Ann, Montreal, 71. Teaching: Assoc prof art & design, Univ Alta, 70- Pos: Art adv, Govt Alta, 67-70. Awards: Govt of Neth Scholar, 60; All Alta First Prize, Jacox Gallery, 65; Can Coun Sr Award, Can Govt, 67. Bibliog: N Yates (auth), Three from Edmonton, Arts Can, 10/69; K Wilkin (auth), Western Canada, a survey, Art in Am, 5-6/72. Mem: Assoc Royal Can Acad Arts; Univ Art Asn Can. Media: Acrylic, Mixed Media. Dealer: Terry Burrell 207-5210 122nd St Edmonton AB Can. Mailing Add: 14312 Ravine Dr Edmonton AB T5N 3M3 Can

HAYNES, GEORGE EDWARD
PAINTER, ILLUSTRATOR
b Hinton, WVa, Apr 29, 10. Study: Phoenix Art Inst, New York; Lockwood Sch Art, Kalamazoo, Mich; Art Inst Pittsburgh. Work: United Va Bank, Richmond; Country Club of Va, Richmond; plus numerous others. Comn: First Day Docking in America & First Clipper Built in United States Shipyard, Officers Mess, Norfolk Naval Shipyard, 60; mural, Merrimac Restaurant, Portsmouth, 65. Exhib: Irene Leach Mem, 64, Norfolk Mus, Tidewater Artists Ann, 65; Hunter Gallery Ann, Chattanooga, Tenn, 64; Va Mus Fine Art, 65; Watercolor USA, Springfield Art Mus, Mo, 72. Pos: Dir-owner, Portsmouth Artists Guild, Va, 38-66. Awards: Grumbacher Award, Norfolk Mus, 65; Best in Show, Portsmouth Jaycees, 66; Purchase Prizes, Petersburg Arts Festival, 72-74. Mem: Tidewater Artist Asn, Norfolk (pres, 63-64); James River Art League, Richmond (gallery dir, 68-). Style & Technique: Traditional in oil; contemporary overtones in watercolor and acrylic. Media: Oil, Watercolor. Dealer: Art Cove 5704 Patterson Ave Richmond VA 23226. Mailing Add: 1521 Avondale Ave Richmond VA 23227

HAYNIE, HUGH
CARTOONIST
b Reedville, Va, Feb 6, 27. Study: Col William & Mary, AB, 50; Univ Louisville, LHD, 68. Pos: Cartoonist, Richmond Times/Dispatch, Va, 50-53, Greensboro Daily News, NC, 53-55 & 56-58, Atlanta Jour, 55-56, with Louisville Courier J, 58-; ed cartoonist, Syndicated Los Angeles Times. Awards: Headliner Award, 66; Freedoms Found Award, 66. Mem: Soc Alumni Col William & Mary (dir). Mailing Add: Courier Journal 525 W Broadway Louisville KY 40202

HAYWARD, JANE
ART HISTORIAN, CURATOR
b Orange, Conn, Aug 13, 18. Study: Pa Acad Fine Arts, Philadelphia, 36-42; Cresson scholar, 40, 42; Sch Fine Arts, Univ Pa, BFA, 52, MA, 54; Yale Univ, fel 57-58, PhD, 58. Collections Arranged: Medieval Art from Private Collections (with catalog), 68-69; The Year 1200 (with catalog), 70; Ecclesiastical Vestments of the Middle Ages, 70; Stained Glass Windows of the Middle Ages & the Renaissance, 71-72; Cloisters Apocalypse Exhib, 73; The Secular Spirit: Life & Art at the End of the Middle Ages, 75. Teaching: Lectr art hist, Yale Univ, 61; asst prof art hist, Conn Col, New London, 64-67; adj assoc prof art hist, Columbia Univ, 71- Pos: Tech illusr, Am Viscose Corp, Philadelphia, 45-54; res asst, Art Gallery, Yale Univ, 58-61; cur, Lyman Allyn Mus, New London, 61-65; cur, The Cloisters, Metrop Mus Art, New York, 69- Awards: Cresson Scholar, Pa Acad Fine Arts, 40, 42; Am Coun Learned Socs Fel, 66-67. Mem: Col Art Asn; Int Ctr Medieval Art (bd dir); Soc Francaise d'Archeologie. Res: Medieval stained glass. Publ: Contribr, History of stained glass, Encycl Americana, 73; auth, Cistercian glazed windows, Gesta, Vol XII, 73; auth, Corpus Vitrearum Medii Aevi: Medieval Stained Glass in the United States of America, in prep. Mailing Add: The Cloisters Ft Tryon Park New York NY 10040

HAYWARD, PETER
PAINTER, SCULPTOR
b Keene, NH, Nov 8, 05. Study: Middlebury Col, 21-23. Work: USN Combat Art Collection, Washington, DC; Hawaii State Found for Cult & the Arts, State of Hawaii; also in pub collection in Rochester, Miami, Denver & Syracuse. Comn: Destroyers on Maneuvers, San Diego to Pearl Harbor, 60, Proteus, Guam, 66, Apollo 8 Splashdown & Recovery, 68 & Apollo 15 Splashdown & Recovery, Navy Art Coop & Liaison Comt, 72; menu covers, United Air Lines, 74. Exhib: Washington Sq Outdoor Art Show (formerly Hors de Concours), New York, 56-63; Salmagundi Fall Show, New York, 60-70; Four Easter Art Festivals, Honolulu, Hawaii, 63-71; Nat Acad Design Shows, New York, 66, 68 & 70; Artists of Hawaii, Honolulu Acad, 68-70. Teaching: Instr sculpture, Riverdale Country Sch for Girls, 46-56; instr oil painting, pvt studio, New York summers & Honolulu winters, 62-67. Pos: Treas, Am Artists Prof League, 57-58. Awards: Proctor Prize in Portrait Sculpture, Nat Acad Design, 48-49; Grand Prize All Media, Washington Sq Outdoor Art Show, 56-58; Foreign Travel Prize, Lufthansa Air Lines, 59. Mem: Salmagundi Club; Asn Honolulu Artists; Windward Artists Guild (pres, 69-70); Lahaina Art Asn. Style & Technique: Impressionistic. Media: Oil, Bronze, Clay. Dealer: Grand Central Galleries 40 Vanderbilt Ave New York NY 10017; Royal Hawaiian Gallery 2259 Kalakaua Ave Honolulu HI 96815. Mailing Add: 53-033 Kamehameha Hwy Hauula HI 96717

HAZARD, JIM (OVINGTON)
ART CRITIC, ART EDITOR
b Oak Ridge, Tenn, Aug 8, 46. Study: Tenn Technol Univ. Pos: Art ed & critic, Chattanooga News-Free Press, 67- Mailing Add: 400 E 11th St Chattanooga TN 37411

HAZEN, JOSEPH H
COLLECTOR
b Kingston, NY. Collection: Late nineteenth and early twentieth century paintings. Mailing Add: 1345 Ave of the Americas New York NY 10019

HAZLEHURST, FRANKLIN HAMILTON
ART HISTORIAN, EDUCATOR
b Spartanburg, SC, Nov 6, 25. Study: Princeton Univ, BA, 49, MFA, 52, PhD, 56. Teaching: Instr art hist, Princeton Univ, 54-56; lectr art hist, Frick Collection, New York, 56-57; asst assoc prof, Univ Ga, 57-63, prof art hist & chmn dept fine arts, Vanderbilt Univ, 67- Awards: Fulbright Fel, 53-54; Am Coun Learned Soc Grant in Aid, 67; Madison Sarratt Prize, Vanderbilt Univ, 70. Mem: Am Archaeol Soc; Col Art Asn Am; Southeastern Col Art Asn (pres, 73-74); French Soc Hist Art; Soc Archit Historians. Res: 17th and 18th century French art, especially landscape architecture. Publ: Auth, Origins of a Boucher theme, Gazette des Beaux Arts, 60; auth, Artistic origins of David's Oath of the Horatii, Art Bull, 60; auth, Jacques Boyceau and the French Formal Garden, 66; auth, Additional sources for the Medici

Cycle, Bull Musees Royal des Beaux Arts Belg, 67; ed, French formal garden, Third Colloquim Landscape Archit, Dumbarton Oaks, 74. Mailing Add: 4430 Shepard Pl Nashville TN 37205

HAZLITT, DON ROBERT
PAINTER
b Stockton, Calif, Jan 6, 48. Study: San Joaquin Delta Col, AA, 69; Sonoma State Col, with William Morehouse & Hubert Crehan, BA(art), 71; Calif State Univ, Sacramento, with Jim Nutt & Joseph Raffael, MA(art), 73. Work: Univ of the Pac Art Dept. Exhib: Crocker-Kingsley Art Ann, Crocker Art Mus, Sacramento, Calif, 73-74; one-person show, Artist Contemp Art Gallery, Sacramento, 74; Whitney Biennial Contemp Art, New York, 75; Contemp Reflections, Aldrich Mus Contemp Art, Ridgefield, Conn, 75; 15 Contemp New York Artists, Univ Denver, 75. Awards: Bank of Am Art Award, 67; Gold Key Award Art, Scholastic Mag, 67; August Ben-Day Award Art, Alpha Rho Tau, Delta Col, 69. Bibliog: F Ball (auth), revs in Artweek, 73 & 74; C Johnson (auth), rev in Sacramento Bee, 74. Style & Technique: Abstract. Media: Acrylic, Latex. Mailing Add: 198 Bowery New York NY 10012

HEAD, GEORGE BRUCE
PAINTER, DESIGNER
b St Boniface, Man, Feb 14, 31. Study: Univ Man, Dipl(fine art), 53. Work: Nat Gallery Can; London Pub Libr & Art Mus; Montreal Mus Art; Manitoba Govt DPW; Can Coun Art Bank. Comn: Oil on panels, Manitoba Teachers Col, 59. Exhib: Nat Gallery, Australian Art Tour, 67-68; 10th Winnipeg Art Gallery Biennial, 70; Montreal Spring Exhib; Nat Gallery Can Biennial; one-man show, Winnipeg Art Gallery, 73. Pos: Graphic designer, Can Broadcasting Corp, 56- Awards: Hon Mention & Purchase Prize, Winnipeg Show, Winnipeg Art Gallery; 20th Western Ont Exhib Purchase Award; Benson & Hedges Art Wall Design Award, 72. Bibliog: H Ochi (auth), article in, Ideas Mag; W Hertig (auth), Graphics annual, Graphic Press; article in, Art Director Ann; plus others. Mem: Royal Can Acad. Media: Acrylic. Dealer: Mixmedia 61 Gertie St Winnipeg MB Can. Mailing Add: 50 Brewster Bay Winnipeg MB R2C 2X3 Can

HEAD, ROBERT WILLIAM
PAINTER, EDUCATOR
b Springfield, Ill, Aug 6, 41. Study: MacMurray Col, BA(art educ), 63, with Sidman & Foresterling; Kent State Univ, MFA, 65, with Shock, Morrow, Petersham & Short; Colo Outward Bound Sch, 71. Work: J B Speed Art Mus, Louisville, Ky; Mint Mus, Charlotte, NC; Del Mar Col, Corpus Christi, Tex; MacMurray Col, Jacksonville, Ill; Massillon Mus, Ohio. Exhib: Ball State Univ Nat Drawing Show, Muncie, Ind; Bucknell Nat Drawing Exhib, Lewisburg, Pa; Mainstreams Int Painting Exhib, Marietta, Ohio; Brooks Mem Gallery Show, Memphis, Tenn; Weatherspoon Ann Drawing Exhib, Univ NC. Teaching: Chairperson & prof drawing, painting & design, Murray State Univ, 65-; assoc prof drawing & introd art, World Campus Afloat, Chapman Col, spring 70 & 72. Awards: Distinguished Alumni Award, MacMurray Col, 69; Merit Award for Excellence in Teaching, Murray State Univ, 70; First Purchase Award, Piedmont Graphic Exhib, Mint Mus. Mem: Col Art Asn; Mus Mod Art; Ky Art Educ Asn; Nat Audubon Soc; Ky Ornith Soc. Media: Mixed media. Mailing Add: Murray State Univ Dept Art Box 2438 Univ Sta Murray KY 42071

HEADLEY, SHERMAN KNIGHT
MUSEUM DIRECTOR, PATRON
b St Paul, Minn, Oct 10, 22. Study: Carleton Col; Univ Wis; Univ Iowa; Univ Minn, BA. Pos: Exec vpres & dir, Minn Mus Art, St Paul, 77- Mem: Am Asn Mus. Interest: Stability and growth of museums. Mailing Add: c/o Minn Mus of Art 305 St Peter St Paul MN 55102

HEALY, ANNE LAURA
SCULPTOR, EDUCATOR
b New York, NY, Oct 1, 39. Study: Queens Col, New York, BA, 62. Work: Mus Contemp Crafts, New York; New York Cult Ctr; Allen Art Mus, Oberlin, Ohio; City Univ Grad Ctr, New York. Comn: Solow Bldg Corp, New York; Dept Cult Affairs, New York; Mich State Univ, East Lansing; Wayne State Univ-Detroit Gen Hosp, Mich. Exhib: Mus Contemp Crafts, New York, 71 & 72; Proj, Philadelphia Col Art, Pa, 76; Art 7'76 (outdoor installation), Basel, Switz, 76; Outdoor Environmental Art, New Gallery, Cleveland, Ohio, 77; Contemp Women: Consciousness & Content, Brooklyn Mus, NY, 77; The Material Dominant, Pa State Univ, University Park, 77; one-person shows, City Univ Grad Ctr, New York, 74, Hammarskjold Plaza Sculpture Garden, 74, Contemp Art Ctr, Cincinnati, Ohio, 76 & Monumenta II, Newport, RI, 76; plus many others. Teaching: Instr sculpture, St Ann's Sch, Brooklyn, 73-; vis artist, Mich State Univ, East Lansing, 73 & Broward Col, Ft Lauderdale, Fla, 76; vis artist-in-residence, Univ Cincinnati, 76; adj asst prof, Baruch Col, City Univ New York, 76- Awards: Award for Sculpture, Asn Am Univ Women, 76-77. Bibliog: Sylvia Hochfield (auth), Sculptural grounds, 4/76 & Elizabeth Perlmutter (auth), Salton Sea to Muscle Beach, 4/76, Artnews; Lucy Lippard (auth), Art outdoors, Studio Int, 2/77. Style & Technique: Use of fabric to explore possibilities of light, color, space and form. Media: Sculpture. Dealer: Virginia Zabriskie c/o Zabriskie Gallery 29 W 57th St New York NY 10019. Mailing Add: 55 W 26th St New York NY 10010

HEALY, ARTHUR K D
PAINTER, LECTURER
b New York, NY, Oct 15, 02. Study: Princeton Univ, BA, 24 & MFA, 26; Ecole Beaux Arts, Fr Govt grant, 25; Princeton Univ, MFA, 26; Middlebury Col, Conn, hon DHumL, 77. Work: Harvard Univ; Addison Gallery Am Art, Andover, Mass; New Brit Mus, Conn; Carnajoharie Mus, NY; Norwich Univ, Northfield, Vt. Comn: Many painting comns in US, Mex & Europe. Exhib: Am Watercolor Soc, New York, 36-70; Philadelphia Watercolor Soc, 38-60; Audubon Artists, New York, 40-70; each Boston Art Festivals. Collections Arranged: Many exhibs for Middlebury Col, 44-69; early Am Painting by B F Mason 1804-71, Sheldon Mus, Middlebury, Vt, 71. Teaching: Emer prof hist fine arts, Middlebury Col, 44-49; lectr Am art, Univ Vt; lectr Am art, Shelburne Mus, Vt. Pos: Mem bd, Yaddo Found, 54-; pres & chmn bd, Sheldon Mus, 57 ; mem Bd Hist Sites Vt, State of Vt, 69-71. Awards: Zabriski Prize, Am Watercolor Soc, 38; Prizes for watercolors, Norwich Univ, 68-70 & Boston Festival Arts. Mem: Am Watercolor Soc; Audubon Artists; Boston Watercolor Soc; Boston Soc Independent Artists; Southern Vt Artists. Media: Watercolor. Res: Early American painting; subject matter of American historical museums. Publ: Co-auth, Two journeyman painters with Alfred Frankenstein, Art Am; illusr, State of Maine; illusr, Indian folklore; auth, many revs & criticisms, Middlebury Col Newslett, Art Am & other mags. Dealer: Deeley Gallery Manchester VT 05254; Gallery 7W Woodstock VT 05091. Mailing Add: c/o Sheldon Art Museum Archael & Hist Soc Inc 1 Park St Middlebury VT 05753

HEALY, JULIA SCHMITT
PAINTER, ART CRITIC
b Elmhurst, Ill, Mar 28, 47. Study: Univ Chicago, 66-70; Yale Univ Summer Sch, 69, with Mel Bochner, Bob Mangold & Bob Moskowitz; Art Inst of Chicago, BFA, 70, MFA, 72. Work: Can Coun Art Bank, Ottawa, Ont; NS Art Bank, Halifax; Confederation Art Gallery, Charlottetown, PEI; Mount St Vincent Univ Art Gallery, Halifax; Dept of Educ, Prov of NS, Halifax. Comn: Halifax Diary (print), Dept Pub Works, NS, 75. Exhib: Fel Finalists, Gunsalus Hall, Art Inst of Chicago, 72; one-person exhib, Dalhousie Art Gallery, Dalhousie Univ, Halifax, 76, Owens Art Gallery, Mt Allison Univ, Sackville, NB, 77; 100 Distinguished Alumni, Art Inst of Chicago, 76; Young Contemporaries (travelling exhib), London Art Gallery, Ont, 76-78; Atlantic Jour (travelling exhib), Nat Galler of Can, 76-77. Collections Arranged: Intercourse (co-cur with Ray Johnson), Wabash Transit Gallery, Chicago, 71; Grassroots-Nova Scotian Folk Art, Eye Level Gallery, Halifax, 75. Pos: Dir, Eye Level Gallery, 75-76. Awards: Purchase Award, Graphics Atlantic, Mount St Vincent Univ, 76; Can Coun Arts grant, 76-77 & 77-78. Bibliog: Ron Shuebrook (auth), The Atlantic Provinces: Letter, Artscanada, 3/75; Marilyn Smith (auth), Some Nova Scotian Women Artists, 12/75 & Ron Shuebrook (auth), Some Major Nova Scotian Painters, 10-11/76, Art Mag. Mem: Can Artists Representation; Visual Arts NS. Style & Technique: Figures in oil and acrylic; drawings in crayon; scratchboard technique. Media: Oil, acrylic; crayon; colored pencil. Publ: Ed, Recent Work: Julia Schmitt Healy, Dalhousie Art Gallery, 76. Dealer: Phyllis Kind Gallery 226 E Ontario Chicago IL 60611. Mailing Add: 219 E 5th St Apt 2 New York NY 10003

HEARN, M F (MILLARD FILLMORE HEARN, JR)
ART ADMINISTRATOR, ART HISTORIAN
b Lincoln, Ala, Aug 18, 38. Study: Auburn Univ, Ala, BA, 60; Ind Univ, MA(hist), 64, MA(art hist), 65, PhD, 69; Univ Calif, Berkeley, study with Jean Bony, 65-66; Courtauld Inst of Art, 66-67. Teaching: From instr to assoc prof medieval art & archit, Univ Pittsburgh, 67- Pos: Actg chmn fine arts dept, Univ Pittsburgh, 73-74, chmn, 74- Mem: Col Art Asn. Res: Romanesque and Gothic architecture of England and France; Romanesque sculpture of Germany, Italy, France and Spain. Publ: Auth, A Note on the Chronology of Romsey Abbey, J Brit Archaeol Asn, Vol 32 (1969); auth, The Rectangular Ambulatory in English Medieval Architecture, J Soc Archit Historians, Vol 30 (1971); auth, On the Original Nave of Ripon Cathedral, J Brit Archaeol Asn, Vol 35 (1972); auth, Romsey Abbey: A Progenitor of the English National Tradition in Medieval Architecture, GESTA, Vol 14 (1975); auth, Postscript: On the Original Nave of Ripon Cathedral, J Brit Archaeol Asn, Vol 39 (1976). Mailing Add: Univ of Pittsburgh 104 Frick Fine Arts Bldg Pittsburgh PA 15260

HEATH, DAVID C
ART DEALER
b Atlanta, Ga, June 6, 40. Study: Vanderbilt Univ; Univ Vienna; Columbia Univ. Pos: Pres, Contemp Art/SE Inc & Contemp Art/SE Mag & dir, Heath Gallery, currently. Specialty: 20th century American, particularly of the '60's and '70's. Mailing Add: 34 Lombardy Way Atlanta GA 30309

HEATH, DAVID MARTIN
EDUCATOR, PHOTOGRAPHER
b Philadelphia, Pa, June 27, 31. Study: Philadelphia Col Art, 54-55; New Sch, with W Eugene Smith, 59 & 61. Work: Nat Gallery Can, Ottawa; Nat Film Bd Can; Mus Mod Art, New York; Int Mus Photog, George Eastman House, Rochester, NY; Philadelphia Mus Art. Exhib: A Dialogue with Solitude, Eastman House, Rochester & Art Inst Chicago, 64; Photography in the 20th Century, Nat Gallery Can, 67, Le grand ALBUM ordinaire, 74; Beyond the Gates of Eden, Peale Galleries Fine Art, Philadelphia, 70; Photography in America, Whitney Mus Art, New York, 74. Teaching: Instr photog, Sch Dayton Art Inst, 65-67; asst prof photog, Moore Col Art, Philadelphia, 67-70; prof photog, Ryerson Polytech Inst, 70-; adj fac, Visual Studies Workshop, 76-77; artist-in-residence, Int Ctr Photog, New York, 78. Pos: Artist in residence, Univ Minn, Minneapolis, 65. Awards: Guggenheim Found Fels, 63 & 64. Bibliog: Charles Hagen (auth), Le grand ALBUM ordinaire, Afterimage Visual Studies Workshop, 2/74. Mem: Soc Photog Educ; Photog Hist Soc Can. Style & Technique: Photographic sequence. Media: Silver Print; Slide/Sound. Publ: Contribr, Infinity, A Dialogue with Solitude, Vol II No 4; contribr, Contemporary Photographer, Vol 5 No 1; auth, A Dialogue with Solitude, Community Press, 65; contribr, Photography in the 20th Century, 67; contribr, Photography in America, 75. Mailing Add: 318 Palmerston Blvd Toronto ON Can

HEATON, MAURICE
DESIGNER, CRAFTSMAN
b Neuchatel, Switz, Apr 2, 00; US citizen. Study: Ethical Cult Schs, 15-19; Stevens Inst Technol, 20-21. Work: Metrop Mus Art, Cooper Union Mus Art & Mus Contemp Crafts, New York; Newark Mus Art, NJ; Corning Mus Glass, NY. Comn: Glass mural, Polygraphic Co Am; glass mobile, Valley Cottage Free Libr, NY; stained glass windows, glass murals & lighting fixtures for pvt comns, 23- Exhib: One-man & group shows in over thirty mus & galleries in US & Can, plus traveling exhibs. Teaching: Lect on glass to art & craft orgns. Awards: Medal, Boston Soc Arts & Crafts, 56; First Prize for Glass, Wichita Art Asn, 60. Mem: Artist-Craftsmen New York; York State Craftsmen; Rockland Found; Am Crafts Coun; Boston Soc Arts & Crafts. Mailing Add: 347 Old Mill Rd Valley Cottage NY 10989

HEBALD, MILTON ELTING
SCULPTOR, PRINTMAKER
b New York, NY, May 24, 17. Study: Art Students League, with Ann Goldwaithe, 27-28; Nat Acad Design, with Gordon Samstag, 31-32; Master Inst United Arts, 31-34; Beaux-Arts Inst Design, 32-35. Work: Whitney Mus Am Art; Philadelphia Mus Art; Tel-Aviv Mus, Israel; Va Mus Fine Arts; Joyce Mus, Dublin, Ireland; plus many others. Comn: Bronze frieze, Pan-Am Terminal, Kennedy Airport, NY; Ackland Mem, Univ NC; James Joyce Monument, Zurich, Switz, 66; Marshall Field Mem, Sun Times Bldg, Chicago, Ill, 66; Tempest Group Bronze, Central Park, New York, 72; plus many others. Exhib: Arte Figurativo, Rome, Italy, 64 & 67; Carnegie Inst Pittsburgh, Pa, 67; Va Mus Fine Arts, 67; Norton Art Gallery, West Palm Beach, Fla, 69; one-man show, Mickelson Gallery, Wash, 72; plus many other group & one-man shows. Teaching: Instr, Brooklyn Mus Sch Art, 46-51; instr, Cooper Union, 46-53; instr, Univ Minn, 49; instr, Skowhegan Sch Painting & Sculpture, summers 50-52; instr, Long Beach State Univ, Calif, summer 68. Awards: Second Prize, Pa Acad Fine Arts, 51; First Prize New York City Dept Pub Works, for E Bronx TB Hosp, 52; Prix de Rome, 55-58; plus others. Bibliog: Martha C Cheney (auth), Modern Art in America, McGraw-Hill, 39; C Ludwig Brumme (auth), Contemporary American Sculpture, Crown, 48; Frank Getlein (auth), Milton Hebald, Viking, 71. Mem: Fel Am Acad in Rome; An Am Group. Style & Technique: Figurative. Media: Bronze, Wood, Lithography. Mailing Add: Via Santo Celso 22 Bracciano 00062 Italy

HEBERLING, GLEN AUSTIN
PAINTER, ILLUSTRATOR
b Ambridge, Pa, Nov 18, 15. Study: Ad Art Studio Sch, Pittsburgh, Pa, with Ray Simboli, 36; Art Inst Pittsburgh, with Milan Petrovitz & Vincent Nesbert, scholar, 36-38; Art Students League, with many famous Am & European artist instr, 46-51. Work: Old Economy Hist Mus, Ambridge; Ladycliff Col, Highland Falls, NY. Comn: World War II Mem (mural in oil) & portrait in oil for Highland Falls High Sch, comn by 50th Anniversary Comt, 50; three watercolor landscapes & a tempera, Marine Midland Bank, Highland Falls, 67; plus many pvt comns. Exhib: Assoc Artists Pittsburgh, Pa Ann Regional, Carnegie Mus, 10 times from 38-47; Am Watercolor Soc Nat Ann, Nat Acad Design Galleries, NY, 44-46; New Year's Show Regional Ann, Butler Inst Am Art, Youngstown, Ohio, 45; US Army Arts Contest Nat, Nat Gallery Art, Washington, DC, 45; ACA Gallery, New York, 46; Mus Fine Arts, Boston, 49; Kennedy Gallery, New York, 50; Artists of the Upper Hudson Regional Ann, Albany Inst Art & Hist, NY, 62; among others. Teaching: Instr & lectr painting I & II, Ladycliff Col, 61-71; Garrison Art Ctr, NY, 76, Mt St Mary Col, Newburgh, NY, 76 & Rec Serv, West Point, NY, 78. Pos: Illusr, US Mil Acad, West Point, NY, 58-71. Awards: Hon Mention for Watercolor, Assoc Artists Pittsburgh Ann, Carnegie Mus, 44; First Prize & Hon Mention for Watercolors, 2nd Serv Comd, Army Arts Contest, Art Students League, 45. Style & Technique: Classic realism, fantasy, surrealism, symbolism and abstractions expressed with highly refined techniques in all media. Publ: Illusr, Handbook on Physical Education, 44; illusr, En Busco de Oro Negro, 59; illusr, Assembly, Asn Grads, West Point, 66; illusr, Kepler & the Discovery of His Planetary Laws, 69; illusr, Engineering Fundamentals, 70. Mailing Add: 58 Church St Highland Falls NY 10928

HEBERT, JULIEN
SCULPTOR, DESIGNER
b Rigaud, PQ, Aug 19, 17. Study: Ecole Beaux-Arts, Montreal; Univ Montreal; also with Zadkine, Paris. Exhib: Int & Can Sect, Milan Triennale, 54; Design Exhibs, Can & abroad. Teaching: Instr hist of art, Ecole Beaux-Arts, Montreal; furniture design, Inst Appl Arts, Montreal. Awards: Design Awards, Nat Indust Design Coun & others, 53-58. Mem: Asn Can Indust Designers; Interior Decorating Soc Quebec; Sculptors Soc Can; Royal Can Acad Arts. Mailing Add: 430 rue du Bon-Secours Montreal PQ H2Y 3C4 Can

HECKSCHER, MORRISON HARRIS
CURATOR, ART HISTORIAN
b Harrisburg, Pa, Dec 12, 40. Study: Wesleyan Univ, BA; Univ Del, MA(early Am cult); 18th century English archit studied with Rudolf Wittkower, Columbia Univ. Collections Arranged: The Easy Chair in Am, 71 & An Architect & His Client: Frank Lloyd Wright & Francis W Little, 73, Metrop Mus of Art, New York. Teaching: Lectr Am archit, Columbia Univ, 74-75. Pos: Chester Dale fel, Print Dept, Metrop Mus of Art, New York, 66-68, from asst cur to cur, Am Wing, 68- Mem: Soc of Archit Historians (dir, 73-76; pres, NY chap, 73-75); Furniture Hist Soc. Res: Eighteenth century American architecture and decorative arts, especially furniture; Eighteenth century English architecture and furniture. Publ: Auth, Gideon Saint, an 18th Century Carver and His Scrapbook, Metrop Mus of Art Bull, 69; auth, Form and Frame: New Thoughts on the American Easy Chair, 71 & The New York Serpentine Card Table, 73, Antiques Mag; contribr, The Chase, The Capture: Collecting at the Metropolitan, Metrop Mus, 75; contribr, Essays on the Arts in America...in Honor of Robert C Smith, Am Life Found, in press. Mailing Add: 176 W 87th St New York NY 10024

HECKSCHER, WILLIAM SEBASTIAN
ART HISTORIAN
b Hamburg, Ger, Dec 14, 04. Study: Univ Hamburg, PhD, 35; NY Univ; Oxford Univ. Exhib: One-man show, Allied Arts Gallery, Durham, NC, 67. Teaching: Teacher, Univ Man, Sask, State Univ Iowa, 47-55; chmn & dir, Iconological Inst, Univ Utrecht, 55-66; chmn dept art, Duke Univ, 66-69, Benjamen N Duke Prof & dir Art Mus, 70- Pos: Mem, Inst Advan Study, Princeton, NJ, 36-40, 47-48, 52-53 & 60-61. Awards: Festschrift, Netherlands Yearbook Hist Art, 64. Mem: Fel Folger Shakespeare Libr; Benjamin Franklin Fel Royal Soc Arts, London; corresp mem Soc Indexers London. Mailing Add: 32 Wilton St Princeton NJ 08540

HEDBERG, GREGORY SCOTT
CURATOR, ART HISTORIAN
b Minneapolis, Minn, May 2, 46. Study: Princeton Univ, BA, 68; Inst Fine Arts, NY Univ, MA, 71. Collections Arranged: Barbizon School, Minneapolis Inst Arts, 75; Picasso, Braque, Leger (co-auth, with Samuel Sachs, catalogue), 75; Charles Biederman: A Retrospective (auth, catalogue), 76; Millet's Gleaners, 78; Victorian High Renaissance (cur-in-charge), Manchester City Art Galleries, Minneapolis Inst Arts & Brooklyn Mus, 78-79. Pos: Lectr, Frick Collection, New York, 71-74; curator paintings, Minneapolis Inst Arts, 74- Res: 15th century painting in Rome. Publ: Auth, The Farnese Courtyard Windows and the Porta Pia: Michelangelo's creative process, Marsyas, 71; auth, The Jerome Hill bequest: Delacroix's Fanatics of Tangiers and Corot's Silenus, 76 & In favor of Nicola di Maestro Antonio d'Ancona, 77, Minneapolis Inst Arts Bull. Mailing Add: 2400 Third Ave S Minneapolis MN 55404

HEDDEN-SELLMAN, ZELDA
PAINTER, INSTRUCTOR
b Farmington, Ill. Study: Bradley Univ, BS & MA; Ohio Univ; Harvard Univ; Western Reserve Univ; also with Ben Shahn, Arnold Blanch & Gladys Rockmore Davis. Work: Manias Manor, Peoria, Ill; Expos Bldg, Springfield, Ill; Spoon River Col, Canton, Ill. Exhib: Art Schools, USA Traveling Exhib, 50; Old Northwest Territory Show, Springfield, 52; Ohio Valley Watercolor Show, Athens, 53; Ill State Mus, Springfield, 59; three-man show, Kottler Gallery, New York, 72. Teaching: Instr art, Ind State Univ, Terre Haute, 53-54; insr art, Ill Cent Col, Peoria, 69-71; instr art, Spoon River Col, 66- Pos: Dir, Peoria Art Ctr Sch, 54-56. Awards: Cent Ill Artists Award. Style & Technique: Expressionist approach to subjects of social concern; work reflects Quaker testimony to contemporary problems. Media: Acrylic, Watercolor. Publ: Auth, Treasures in the Snow, 64. Dealer: Upstairs Gallery Lakeview Ctr for Arts & Sci 1125 W Lake Ave Peoria IL 61614. Mailing Add: 241 Timberland Metamora IL 61548

HEDMAN, TERI JO
PRINTMAKER, PAINTER
b St Paul, Minn, Oct 10, 44. Study: Univ Minn, BS(design); also with Paul Hapke, Toshi Yoshido, Pat Austin & Marge Horton. Exhib: All Alaska Exhib, 72, 74, 75 & 78; one-man show, Univ Minn, 67 & Artique Ltd, 73-78. Teaching: Traveling instr printmaking, Naknek, Bethel & Nome, Alaska, 73. Pos: Designer-draftsman, Minneapolis Housing Authority, 68-70; interior designer, Tiptons Interiors, Anchorage, 70-71. Mem: Alaska Artists Guild (prof chmn, 72, funding chmn, 73, vpres, 74, pres, 75, mem bd, 76); Anchorage Arts Coun (visual arts adv comt, 75). Style & Technique: Flat shapes and line patterns using intaglio & relief printing and acrylic painting. Dealer: Kaill Fine Crafts PO Box 2461 Juneau AK 99803; Artique 314 A St Anchorage AK 99501. Mailing Add: 2219 St Elias Dr Anchorage AK 99503

HEDRICK, WALLY BILL
SCULPTOR, PAINTER
b Pasadena, Calif, July 21, 28. Study: Otis Art Inst; Calif Sch Fine Arts, BFA, 55; Calif Col Arts & Crafts; San Francisco State Col. Work: Mus Mod Art, New York; Aldridge Mus Contemp Art, Ridgefield, Conn; Oakland Mus Art; Los Angeles Mus Art; San Francisco Art Comn. Exhib: 16 Americans, Mus Mod Art, New York, 59; Places, San Francisco Mus Art, 62; Balboa Pavilion Gallery, Newport, Calif, 67; one-man show, Sonoma State Col Gallery, 68; Poets of the Cities, Dallas Mus Art, 74; plus others. Teaching: Instr painting & drawing, San Francisco Art Inst, 60-70; instr painting & drawing, San Jose State Col, 72-74; instr painting & sculpture, Indian Valley Col, 75- Awards: Purchase Award, Los Angeles Co Mus, Los Angeles, 53; Purchase Award, San Francisco Art Comn, 58 & 76 & San Francisco Mus Mod Art, 76; Nat Endowment Arts Grant, 68. Bibliog: William Morehouse (auth), Funk Daddy (catalog), Sonoma State Col, 68; Wayne Andersen (auth), American Sculpture in Process: 1930/1970, NY Graphic Soc, 75; Dan Tooker (auth), interview in Art Inst, Vol 19 (Oct, 1975). Media: Welded Metal; Oil on Canvas. Mailing Add: PO Box 186 352 Meadow Way San Geronimo CA 94963

HEE, HON-CHEW
PAINTER, GALLERY DIRECTOR
b Kahului, Hawaii, Jan 24, 06. Study: Calif Sch Fine Arts, dipl, 32; Art Students League, 48-49; Andre L'hote & Fernand Leger, Paris, 49-51. Work: Honolulu Acad Arts; Tennent Art Found Art Gallery, Honolulu; Libr Hawaii, Kaneohe Libr & Kailua Libr; Contemp Art Gallery, Honolulu; Ala Moana Hotel, Honolulu. Comn: Mural (oil), Naval Supply Depot Cafeteria, Pearl Harbor, 43, Oakland Naval Supply Ctr, Calif, 54 & Maui Med Ctr, Wailuku, Maui, 61; mural (concrete), Hawaiian Holiday Bldg, Honolulu, 62; mural (redwood carved), Honolulu Community Church, 65. Exhib: One-man show, Galerie Ariel, Paris, France, 51; Taiwan Nat Hist Mus, 73; 140th Ann Exhib, Nat Acad Design, New York, 65; 11th Ann Exhib, Artist Hawaii, Honolulu, 66; Nat Ann Exhib, El Paso Mus Art, Tex, 72. Collections Arranged: One-man watercolor show, Honolulu Acad Arts, 48; int show, Solon de l'art Libre in Paris, 50. Teaching: Lectr watercolor, Univ Hawaii, Honolulu, 60-70; prof watercolor, Taiwan Normal Univ, Taipei, 71-72, prof serigraph, 72-73. Pos: Dir, Tennent Art Found Gallery, 67- Awards: Serigraphy for Text Book, Dr Sun Yet Sen Grant, Taiwan, 71; Ancient IBM Oil Painting & Koolau Sunrise, Oil Painting, Hawaii State Found Cult & Arts, 73. Bibliog: Demonstration of watercolor, Pau Hana Year, Univ TV Sta, 73; Haar & Neogy (auths), Artists of Hawaii, Univ Hawaii, 74; Shimeji Kanazawa (auth), Logo Hawaiian aging, Gordon Asn Inc, 74. Mem: Hawaii Painters & Sculptors League; Hawaii Watercolor & Serigraphy Soc (founder & pres, 61-); Taiwan Eastern Serigraph Asn (founder, 73). Style & Technique: Wet on wet. Publ: Ed, Serigraphy Text, H C Hee Studio, 71 & auth, Thirty Serigraphs, 73, H C Hee Studio. Mailing Add: 45-650 Kapunahala Rd Kaneohe HI 96744

HEFLIN, TOM PAT
PAINTER, DESIGNER
b Monticello, Ark, July 18, 34. Study: Northeast La State Col; Chicago Art Inst. Work: Marietta Col; Burpee Art Mus, First Nat Bank, & First Fed Savings, Rockford, Ill; Hill, Sherman, Meroni, Gross & Simpson Law Off, Chicago. Exhib: Chicago Art Inst, 71-73; House of Cong, Washington, DC, 72; Butler Inst Am Art, Youngstown, Ohio, 73; New Horizons in Art, Chicago, 75; Am Watercolor Soc, New York, 75. Teaching: Instr painting, Burpee Art Mus, 69-71; instr painting, Rock Valley Col, 70- Awards: First Prize Medal, Nat Soc Painters in Casein & Acrylic; First Prize, Ark Nationwide Bicentennial Medal Design, Franklin Mint; First Prize in Painting, Mainstreams 72, Ohio. Bibliog: Article in, Famous Artists Mag, 70. Mem: Nat Soc Painters in Casein & Acrylic; Rockford Art Asn; Fishy Whale Litho Workshop, Milwaukee. Style & Technique: Realism, transparent acrylic on crushed paper; abstractions, oil on canvas and wood. Publ: Auth, Quiet Places, 77. Dealer: Carlson Lowe Gallery Taos NM 87571; Troy's Cowboy Art Gallery 7106 Main St Scottsdale AZ 85251. Mailing Add: 2116 Springbrook Ave Rockford IL 61107

HEFNER, HARRY SIMON
PAINTER, EDUCATOR
b Kalamazoo, Mich, Nov 20, 11. Study: Western Mich Univ, BA, 36; Columbia Univ, MA, 39. Work: Kalamazoo Col; South Bend Art Ctr; Albion Col; Western Mich Univ. Exhib: Detroit Inst Arts, 63-64; Kalamazoo Inst Arts, 63-66; Grand Rapids Inst Arts, Mich, 64-65; South Bend Inst Arts, Ind, 64-66; Battle Creek Inst Arts, 66; plus others. Teaching: Teacher, Muskegon Pub Schs, Mich, 37-38; Cranbrook Boys Sch, summers 37-39; Skidmore Col, 39; mem fac, Western Mich Univ, 40-77, prof watercolor & design, 56-77, emer prof, 77-, head dept art, 63-66; teacher, Harvard Univ, summer 41 & Univ Vt, summers 54-56. Mem: Mich Watercolor Soc; Mich Art Educ Asn. Mailing Add: 1415 Sutherland St Kalamazoo MI 49007

HEIDEL, FREDERICK (H)
PAINTER, EDUCATOR
b Corvallis, Ore, Dec 29, 15. Study: Univ Ore, BS, with Andrew Vincent, David McCosh & Lance Hart; Art Inst Chicago, Anna Louise Raymond foreign traveling fel, BFA & MFA, with Boris Anisfeld & Francis Chapin. Work: World Bk Art Collection, Chicago; Portland Art Mus, Ore; Hazeltine Collection, Mus Art, Eugene, Ore; Eastern Ore Col, La Grande, Ore; Kaiser Found, Portland. Comn: Mural, Lane Co Comn, Lane Co Courthouse, Eugene, 58; fused glass wall, comn by Sally Stafford, Eugene, 70; fused glass panel, Brock Dixon House, Forest Grove, Ore, 70; laminated glass construction, Portland State Univ, Sci I Bldg, 71; laminated glass window, comn by Mr & Mrs Marvin Witt, Portland. Exhib: Drawing & Watercolor Exhib, Metrop Mus Art, New York, 51; Sao Paulo 3rd Biennial, Brazil, 56; 2nd Pac Coast Biennial, WCoast, 57; Vancouver, BC, 58; The West: 80 Contemporaries, 67. Teaching: Instr painting, Long Beach City Col, 46-49; instr painting, Univ Ore, 49-53; prof painting, Portland State Univ, 51-, head dept art & archit, 55- Pos: Chmn artist mem, Portland Art Mus, 52-53; mem bd, Albina Art Ctr, Portland, 64-67. Awards: Painting Award, San Francisco Mus Art, 48; Chapelbrook Found Fel, 67. Bibliog: Rachel Griffin (auth), Painting & Sculpture of the Pacific Northwest, Portland Art Mus, 59; painting reproduced in World Bk Encycl, 65-72; Nancy McCauley (auth), article in Artweek, Vol 13, No 15. Mem: Portland Art Asn (art comt, 53-55); Col Art Asn Am; Art Ore. Mailing Add: Dept of Art Portland State Univ Portland OR 97207

HEILOMS, MAY
PAINTER
US citizen. Study: Hunter Col; Art Students League. Work: Philadelphia Mus, Pa; Norfolk Mus, Va; Samuel Fleisher Art Found, Philadelphia; Bat Yam Mus, Israel; Kenny Int Art Found. Exhib: Pa Acad Fine Arts, Philadelphia; Denver Mus, Colo; Corcoran Gallery, Washington, DC; Okla Mus, Oklahoma City; Butler Inst Am Art, Youngstown, Ohio; also in Portugal, Italy, Greece, Belgium, Israel, Can, Mex & Arg. Teaching: Instr fine art, City Col New York, 60-62; instr indust & fine art, Fashion Inst Technol, 63-65. Pos: Vpres, Nat Asn Women Artists, 60. Awards: Ann Prizes for Oil, Painters & Sculptors Soc NJ, 50-75; Elizabeth Morse Genios Mem Watercolor Prize, Nat Asn Women Artists, 60; Prize for Oil, Nat Arts, 76; plus others. Bibliog: Archives Am Art, Smithsonian Inst. Mem: Painters &

Sculptors Soc NJ (hon life pres); Audubon Artists (vpres, 56-58); Nat Soc Painters Casein & Acrylic (dir, 65-); NY Soc Women Artists (dir & chmn mem comt, 72-75); Am Soc Contemp Artists (mem comt). Mailing Add: 340 W 28th St New York NY 10001

HEIN, MAX
PRINTMAKER, INSTRUCTOR
b Lincoln, Nebr, Dec 27, 43. Study: San Diego State Univ, AB, 66; Univ Calif, Los Angeles, MA, 68, MFA, 69. Work: Int Mus Photog, George Eastman House, Rochester, NY; Frederick S Wight Galleries, Univ Calif, Los Angeles; Newport Harbor Mus Art, Calif; Bradford City Art Gallery, Yorkshire, Eng; DeAnza Col Art Gallery, Calif; plus others. Exhib: Recent Acquisitions: Photog, Pasadena Mus Art, Calif, 69; Calif Photogr, Univ Calif, Davis, Oakland Mus & Pasadena Mus Art, 70; Works on Paper: US W Coast Artists, Govett-Brewster Art Gallery, New Plymouth, NZ, 71; Four Printmakers: Benson, Foote, Hein & Quandt, San Francisco Mus Art, 71; 3rd Brit Int Print Bienniale, Bradford City Art Gallery, Yorkshire, Eng, 72; Recent Photog, NS Col Art & Design, Halifax, 72; San Francisco Bay Area Printmakers, Cincinnati Art Mus, Ohio, 73; 8th Nat Print & Drawing Competition, Dulin Gallery Art, Knoxville, Tenn, 74-75, plus Smithsonian Traveling Exhib of show Nat Collection Fine Arts, Washington, DC, Univ Nebr Gallery, Omaha, Univ Colo, Boulder, Millikin Univ, Decatur, Ill, Pa State Univ, Univ Hawaii & elsewhere. Teaching: Instr silkscreen printmaking, Univ Calif, Los Angeles Exten, 68-69; instr art, Santa Rose Jr Col, Calif, 69-; vis artist silkscreen printmaking, Visual Studies Workshop, Rochester, NY, summer 75. Awards: Guest Ed Award, 6th Ann Los Angeles Printmaking Soc Exhib, 69; Purchase Award, 3rd Brit Int Print Biennale, 72 & Bay Area Print Exhib, DeAnza Col Gallery, 75. Bibliog: Alfred Frankenstein (auth), Photo Image in Printmaking, San Francisco Chronicle, 11/71; Carole Schuck (auth), Max Hein Prints, 9/72 & Gerry Payne (auth), Geometric Dynamics, 11/75, Art Week. Mem: The Graphics Soc. Style & Technique: Geometric abstractions on paper. Media: Silkscreen prints and drawing. Publ: Illusr, Half a Century, Nat Football League, 70. Dealer: Allrich Gallery The Embarcardero Ctr San Francisco CA 94111; Comsky Gallery 9100 Wilshire Blvd Beverly Hills CA 90212. Mailing Add: 2690 Bristol Rd Kenwood CA 95452

HEINECKEN, ROBERT FRIEDLI
PHOTOGRAPHER, EDUCATOR
b Denver, Colo, Oct 29, 31. Study: Univ Calif, MA, 60. Work: Mus Mod Art, New York; Int Mus Photog, Rochester, NY; Fogg Art Mus, Harvard Univ; Pasadena Art Mus; San Francisco Mus Art. Exhib: Persistence of Vision, George Eastman House, Rochester, 67; one-man shows, Robert Heinecken, Witkin Gallery, New York, 70, Light Gallery, New York, 73 & Int Mus of Photog, George Eastman House, Rochester, NY, 76; Photography into Sculpture, Mus Mod Art, New York, 70; Photography in America, Whitney Mus, New York, 74. Teaching: Prof art & photog, Univ Calif, Los Angeles, 60-; vis prof art & photog, Art Inst Chicago, 70; vis prof art & photog, Harvard Univ, 72. Awards: Guggenheim Mem Fel, 75; Nat Endowment for the Arts Grant, 77. Bibliog: Carl Belz (auth), Robert Heinecken, Camera, Bucher Ltd, Luzerne, Switz, 1/68; Fred Parker (auth), Robert Heinecken, Untitled Number 5, Friends of Photog, 73; John Upton (auth), Robert Heinecken (exhib catalog), Calif State Univ, Long Beach, 74. Mem: Soc Photog Educ (mem bd dir); Friends Photog (mem bd trustees). Style & Technique: Work includes etching, lithography and drawing, as well as photography. Publ: Contribr, Contemp Photogr, Vol 5, No 4; contribr, Untitled Number 7 & 8, Friends of Photog, 74. Dealer: Light Gallery 724 Fifth Ave New York NY 10019. Mailing Add: Univ Calif Los Angeles Dept of Art 405 Hilgard Ave Los Angeles CA 90024

HEINEMAN, BERNARD, JR
COLLECTOR
b New York, NY, Nov 29, 23. Study: Williams Col, BA. Collection: 20th century American art, including Prendergast, Demuth, Dove, Marin, Sheeler, Tam, Jacob Lawrence and Heliker and sculpture by Lachaise, Cook and Don Russell. Mailing Add: c/o Heineman & Co 151 W 40th St New York NY 10018

HEINEMANN, PETER
PAINTER, INSTRUCTOR
b Denver, Colo, Apr 22, 31. Study: Black Mountain Col, 1 yr, with Joseph Albers, 48-49. Comn: Multi-figure oil mural, New York Coun Arts, 71-72. Exhib: Nat Inst Arts & Lett, New York, 60, 61 & biennially 70, 71 & 72. Teaching: Instr painting & drawing, Sch Visual Arts, New York, 60- Awards: Creative Artists Pub Serv Grants, 71-72, 74-75 & 77-78. Media: Oil. Mailing Add: Dept Painting & Drawing Sch of Visual Arts New York NY 10010

HEINZ, MR & MRS HENRY J, II
COLLECTORS, PATRONS
Mrs Heinz, b Sewickley, Pa, July 10, 08. Study: Mr Heinz, Yale Univ, AB, 31; Trinity Col, Cambridge Univ, 31-32. Pos: Mr Heinz, trustee, Carnegie Inst; chmn gov bd, Yale Univ Art Gallery; trustee, Carnegie Inst Mus Art; trustee, Bus Comt for Arts, Inc; bd nat assocs, Smithsonisn Inst; Am Friends of Tate Gallery, Eng. Mailing Add: Goodwood Sewickley PA 15143

HEINZ, SUSAN
ART ADMINISTRATOR
b RI. Study: Brown Univ, BA(Am civilization); Harvard Univ, MA(int rels); Univ Calif, Los Angeles, MA(film hist & criticism). Pos: Educ coordr, Jr Arts Ctr, Los Angeles Munic Arts Dept, 68-73; mem, Los Angeles Munic Arts Comn, 73-; exec dir, Palos Verdes Art Ctr & Mus, Rancho Palos Verdes, 74-; mem, Mayor's Citizen's Adv Comt Arts, Los Angeles, currently; mem bd dirs, Harvard Club of Southern Calif; adv bd arts mgt, MBA Prog, Univ Calif, Los Angeles, currently. Awards: Am Film Inst Scholar, 72-73; Smithsonian Inst Grant res in India, 74. Mem: Am Asn Mus; Int Coun Mus. Mailing Add: 11444 Bolas St Los Angeles CA 90049

HEISE, MYRON ROBERT
PAINTER
b Bancroft, Nebr, June 30, 34. Study: Univ Omaha; Art Students League; Pratt Ctr Contemp Printmaking, New York; Acad Fine Arts, Florence, Italy; also with George Grosz, Arthur Lee, Robert Brackman & Louis Bouche. Work: Omaha Univ; Robert & Elizabeth Browning Soc, Florence, Italy; US Army Craft Serv, Ft Lewis, Wash. Comn: Portrait of John G Neihardt, J G Neihardt Found, Inc, Bancroft, 67. Exhib: 8th Ann Exhib, Pac Gallery Artists, Inc, Tacoma, Wash, 58; 2nd Ann Exhib Young Am Artists, Florence, Italy, 63; 145th Ann Exhib, Nat Acad Design, New York, 70; Contemp Graphic Artists 1st Ann, New York, 71; The New Humanists, Grace Gallery, Brooklyn, 73; Artist's Choice, Figurative Art in New York, 76; Am Acad of Arts & Lett, New York, 76. Teaching: Teacher painting & drawing, US Army Craft Serv, Ft Lewis, 58-59; teacher painting & drawing, New Sch Social Res, 77-Pos: Press dir, Bowery Gallery, New York, 74- Bibliog: Barry Schwartz (auth), The New Humanism, Praeger, 74; Barbralu Fried (auth), Figurative painter Heise in Boulder, Boulder Sunday Camera, 11/17/74. Mem: Figurative Artists Alliance (founding mem, 69-, chmn, 76-78). Style & Technique: Figurative, representational style depicting the modern metropolis and its inhabitants at night; attention to detail. Media: Oil on Canvas; Etching. Publ: Illusr, Dancescope, 71-72; illusr, Arts in Soc, 72-73; illusr, A Dance Student's Handbook, 78. Dealer: Bowery Gallery 135 Greene St New York NY 10012. Mailing Add: 102 Forsyth St New York NY 10002

HEISKELL, DIANA
PAINTER, DESIGNER
b Paris, France; US citizen. Work: Santa Barbara Mus Art, Calif; Slater Mus, Norwich, Conn. Exhib: Whitney Mus Am Art Ann, 2 yrs; Chicago Art Inst; Boston Arts Festival; De Cordova & Dana Mus, Lincoln, Mass; Southern Vt Art Ctr, Manchester; plus others. Awards: Hon Mention, Berkshire Art Asn; Grumbacher Prize, Southern Vt Art Ctr. Mem: Southern Vt Art Asn (trustee); Berkshire Art Asn. Mailing Add: Marlboro VT 05344

HEIT, STEVEN ROBERT
ART DEALER
b Ellenville, NY, June 30, 43. Study: Univ Buffalo, BA; Baruch Col, MBA; Fashion Inst Technol, AA(art & photog). Pos: Owner, Heit Galleries, Phoenix. Mem: Men's Art Coun. Specialty: Graphics, watercolors and photography. Mailing Add: Heit Galleries 3003 N Central Suite 115 Phoenix AZ 85012

HELANDER, BRUCE PAUL
PAINTER, ART ADMINISTRATOR
b Great Bend, Kans, Jan 27, 46. Study: RI Sch Design, Providence, BFA(illus), MFA(painting); Univ Kans, Lawrence, cert; RI Col, Providence. Work: Rochester Airport, Minn; RI Sch Design. Comn: Animated film, Perpetual Motion Pictures, New York, for Ohio Bell Systs, 71; Ann Exhib Poster, Exec Comt, RI State Coun Arts, 72. Exhib: Bi-Ann Fac Exhib, Mus Art, RI Sch Design, 70, 72 & 74; Botolph Gallery, Cambridge, Mass, 72; First Cancelled Art Exhib, 152 Prince Street Gallery, New York, 73; Loeb Art Ctr, Harvard Univ, 73; Int Corresp Exhib, Minihan Gallery, Depere, Wis, 74; Watson Gallery, Wheaton Col, Norton, Mass, 76; Tyler Sch of Art, Temple Univ, 77. Teaching: Lectr design, RI Sch Design, 71-; lectr painting, Inst Am Indian Art, Santa Fe, NMex, 75-; vis artist conceptual art, Art Park, Lewiston, NY, 75-; mem, Fine Arts Workshop, RI Sch of Design, summer 76. Pos: Asst dir admis, RI Sch Design, 70-72, dir summer sessions & exten sch, 72-; spec asst to coordr, Fed Graphics Improv Prog, Nat Endowment for Arts, Washington, DC, 73-; adv, Inst Am Indian Art, 75-; actg assoc provost, RI Sch of Design, 76 & provost & vpres acad affairs, 77. Awards: Purchase Prize, Providence Art Club, 71; Chairman's Grant, Intern Prog, Nat Endowment Arts, 73. Bibliog: Lisa Morrison (producer), The Art of Collage, Art Train, WPRI TV, 75; Ray Johnson, Much ado about nothing (interview), Sunday New York Times, 10/75; Perfect Pitchers/Fancy Frames, Provincetown, J, 77. Mem: Am Fed Arts; Soc for Preserv of Indust Archit; Am Asn Univ Admin; Col Art Asn Am; Provincetown Art Asn; Providence Atheneum. Style & Technique: Conceptual. Media: Collage. Publ: Illusr, Growing Up with Education, Educ Develop Corp, Cambridge, Mass, 73. Dealer: 152 Prince St New York NY 10010. Mailing Add: 151 Power St Providence RI 02906

HELBECK, DEWEES COCHRAN
See Cochran, Dewees

HELCK, (CLARENCE) PETER
ILLUSTRATOR, WRITER
b New York, NY, June 17, 93. Study: Art Students League, with Frank Brangwyn, Harry Wickey & Lewis Daniel. Work: Metrop Mus Art, New York; Carnegie Inst, Pittsburgh; Mus Am Art, New Britain, Conn; Sheldon Swope Galleries, Terre Haute, Ind; Montagu Mus, Beaulieu, Eng. Exhib: Royal Acad, London, 23; Pittsburgh Int, 35; Nat Acad Design Exhibs, 40-50; one-man shows, New York City, 24, 27, 30, 41, 54 & 61, Smithsonian Inst, Washington, DC, 47, Ark Art Ctr, Little Rock, 64, Sheldon Swope Galleries, Lincoln, Nebr, 66, Pittsfield, Mass, 66, Terre-Haute, Ind, 66 & Riverside, Calif, 67. Teaching: Mem fac illus, Famous Artists Sch, Westport, Conn, 48-73. Pos: Art ed, Bulb Horn, Boston, 50-; assoc ed, Antique Automobile, Hershey, Pa, 50-; artist & auth, Automobile Quart, New York, 62-70. Awards: Pennell Medal, Philadelphia Acad, 28; five Medals, New York Art Dirs, 31-51; Hall of Fame Gold Medal, Soc Illusr, 68. Bibliog: Walter Reed (auth), Illustrator in America, 66; Y Inomoto (auth), Auto art, Automobile Illus, Tokyo, 71; Ken Browing (auth), Autographics, Ont, Can, 77. Mem: Nat Acad Design; Am Watercolor Soc; Soc Illusr; Famous Artists Sch; Allied Artists Am. Media: Casein, Tempera. Publ: Illusr, Sat Eve Post, 35-55; illusr, Country Gentleman, 40-50; illusr, Esquire, 40-50; auth & illusr, The Checkered Flag, Scribner, 61; auth & illusr, Great Auto Races, Abrams, 76. Mailing Add: Boston Corners RD 2 Millerton NY 12546

HELD, AL
PAINTER
b New York, NY, Oct 12, 28. Study: Art Students League; Acad Grande Chaumiere, Paris. Work: Brandeis Univ; Geigy Chem Corp; Kunsthalle, Basel, Switz. Exhib: Systemic Painting, Guggenheim Mus, 66; Jewish Mus, 67; Documenta IV, Kassel, Ger, 68; one-man shows, San Francisco Mus Art & Corcoran Gallery Art, 68 & Andre Emmerich Gallery, New York, 75; Retrospective, Whitney Mus Am Art, New York, 74 & Emmerich Gallery, Zurich, Switz, 77; plus many other group & one-man shows. Teaching: Prof art, Yale Univ, 62- Awards: Logan Medal, Art Inst Chicago, 64; Guggenheim Found Fel, 66. Bibliog: Barbara Rose (auth), American Art Since 1900, a Critical History, Praeger, 67; Gregory Battcock (ed), Minimal Art: a Critical Anthology, Dutton, 68. Dealer: Donald Morris Gallery 20082 Livernois Detroit MI 48221. Mailing Add: 435 W Broadway New York NY 10012

HELD, ALMA M
PAINTER
b Lemars, Iowa. Study: State Univ Iowa, with Charles A Cumming, BA & MA; Nat Acad Design, with Sydney Dickinson; Cape Cod Sch Art, Provincetown, Mass, with Charles Hawthorne & Richard Miller. Work: Waterloo Munic Galleries, Iowa; portrait & landscape paintings, Ft Dodge Pub Schs, Iowa; landscape, YWCA, Waterloo; Nat Bank Bldg Waterloo; Garwin Pub Libr, Iowa. Comn: Portrait of Jack Logan, Logan Jr High Sch, Waterloo, 62; portrait, Cedar Falls Woman's Club, Iowa, 71; Flight Into Egypt (painting), First Congregational Church, Waterloo, 71, portraits of Rev J Richmond Morgan & Rev Charles F Jacobs, 74. Exhib: Kansas City Art Inst, Mo, 35; Joslyn Mus Art, Omaha, Nebr, 35 & 46; 16th Ann Iowa Artists Exhib, Des Moines Art Ctr, Iowa, 64; Ithaca Collects, Ithaca Col Mus Art, NY, 69; 8th Ann Waterloo Munic Galleries Show, 71; one-man retrospective, Waterloo Recreation & Arts Ctr, Iowa, 72. Teaching: Instr art & later assoc, State Univ Iowa, formerly. Awards: Iowa State Fair Gold Medal, Iowa Art Salon, 26; Purchase Prize, First Iowa TV Art Show, Waterloo, 68 & 76; First Prize, Competitive Art Show Nat Dairy Cattle Cong, Waterloo, 68 & 74. Mem: Cent Area Chap Artists Equity Asn; Waterloo Art Asn. Media: Oil, Watercolor. Mailing Add: 623 W Eighth St Waterloo IA 50702

HELD, JULIUS S
EDUCATOR, WRITER
b Mosbach, Ger, Apr 15, 05; US citizen. Study: Univ Heidelberg, 23; Univ Berlin, 23-24, 27-28; Univ Vienna, 25-26, 29; Univ Freiburg, PhD, 30; Williams Col, hon DHL, 72; Columbia Univ, hon DLitt, 77. Teaching: Lectr, NY Univ, 35-41; Carnegie lectr, Nat Gallery Can, 36-37; lectr art, Barnard Col, Columbia Univ, 37-44, asst prof, 44-50, assoc prof, 50-54, prof, 54-70, chmn dept art hist, 67-70, emer prof, 70-; vis lectr, Bryn Mawr Col, 43-44; vis prof, New Sch Social Res, 46-47; vis prof, Yale Univ, 54 & 58; Robert Sterling Clark prof art, Williams Col, 69 & 74; Andrew W Mellon prof, Univ Pittsburgh, 72-73. Pos: Asst, Staatliche Mus, Berlin, 31-33; mem ed bd, Art Bull, 42-; mem ed bd, Art Quart, 59-74; consult, Mus Arte Ponce, PR, 59-; mem, Inst Advan Study, Princeton Univ, 67; pres, Am Friends Mus Plantin Moretus, Antwerp, 69-73. Awards: Belg-Am Educ Found Spec Advan Fel, 47; Fulbright Fel, 52-53; Guggenheim Fels, 52-53 & 66-67. Mem: Col Art Asn Am (dir, 59-64, hon dir, 75, mem ed bd); Mediaeval Acad Am; Renaissance Soc Am; Soc Hist of Art Francaise; Deutscher Verein für Kunstwissenschaft. Res: Flemish and Dutch art. Collection: Old master paintings and drawings. Publ: Auth, Rubens, Selected Drawings, Phaidon, 59; auth, Rembrandt's Aristotle & Other Rembrandt Essays, Princeton, 69; co-auth, 17th & 18th century Art: Baroque & Rococo, 72, Abrams; auth, The Oil Sketches of Peter Paul Rubens, Princeton, 78. plus many earlier publ; contribr, articles in art periodicals. Mailing Add: 81 Monument Ave Bennington VT 05201

HELD, PHILIP
PAINTER, INSTRUCTOR
b New York, NY, June 2, 20. Study: Art Students League, 38-42 & 46, with Kuniyoshi, Fiene, Blanch, Lee & Vytlacil; Sch Art Studies, New York, with Moses Soyer, 47-48; Columbia Univ Teachers Col, serigraphy with Arthur Young, 49. Work: Berkshire Mus, Pittsfield, Mass; Univ Mass, Amherst; Philadelphia Mus Lending Collection; Art Students League Collection; Ringling Mus, Sarasota Fla. Exhib: Woodstock Artists, Riverside Mus, New York, 60; USA Paintings, Pa Acad Fine Arts Ann, 62; Mod Masters, Brown Univ, 63; Recent Accessions, Univ Mass, 66; Fla Mus Dir Asn Exhib, 73. Teaching: Instr fine arts, Scarborough Sch, NY, 47-52; instr fine arts, Fieldston Sch, Riverdale, NY, 52-62, chmn dept, 62-71; instr & coordr Fine Arts Prog, Booker-Bay Haven Sch, Sarasota, Fla, 71- Pos: Exhib juror, Manatee & Sarasota Co, 77-78. Awards: Second Prize for Printmaking, Am Vet Soc Artists, 49; Presentation Exhib Award, Woodstock Artists Asn, 64; H Kleinert Found Grant, 66; Sarasota Art Asn Figure Exhib Award, 75. Bibliog: Gordon Brown (auth), Art voices 1964-65, Art Voices, 65; V Donohue (auth), rev in, Philadelphia Sun Bull, 10/20/68; articles in Sarasota Herald Tribune, 7/1/76, 8/16/76 & 8/22/76. Mem: Life mem Art Students League; Woodstock Artists Asn; Sarasota Art Asn; Fla Artists Group. Style & Technique: Realism, painting the human figure in different environments. Media: Oil. Dealer: Fontana Gallery 307 Iona Ave Narberth Philadelphia PA 19072. Mailing Add: 3035 Wood St Sarasota FL 33577

HELFOND, RIVA
PAINTER, PRINTMAKER
b Brooklyn, NY. Study: Art Students League, with William Von Schlegell, Harry Sternberg, Yasuo Kuniyoshi, Morris Kantor & Alexander Brook; Sch Indust Arts, New York. Work: Mus Mod Art, New York; Libr Cong, Washington, DC; Los Angeles Mus; Newark Mus Fine Art; Springfield Mus Fine Art, Mass. Exhib: Carnegie Inst, Pittsburgh, 54; one-man show, Gallerie Collette Allendy, Paris, 57; Art USA, New York, 58 & 59; Corcoran Gallery Art, Washington, DC, 60; Newark Triennials, Newark Mus Fine Art, 64 & 67; plus others. Teaching: Instr graphics, NY Univ, 65-67; instr painting, Somerset Art Ctr, Bernardsville, 72- Awards: Pennell Purchase Prizes in Graphics, Libr Cong, 55-57; First Prize in Oil, Montclair Mus Art, 60-62 & 69; Prize in Oil, Monmouth Col Art Festival, 69; plus others. Mem: Audubon Artists; Soc Am Graphic Artists (mem coun bd); Assoc Artists NJ (pres, 66-70); Artists Equity Asn NY; Artists Equity Asn NJ (treas, 62-). Style & Technique: Abstract; expressionist; heavy impasto; painting knife; intaglio and embossing in graphics. Media: Oil; Etching. Dealer: Barrett Art Gallery 218 E Front St Plainfield NJ 07060. Mailing Add: 919 Knollwood Ct Plainfield NJ 07062

HELGOE, ORLIN MILTON
PAINTER, EDUCATOR
b Billings, Mont, July 12, 30. Study: Eastern Mont State Col, BSEd; Cornell Univ, MFA; study with John Hartell, Allan Atwell & Peter Kahn. Work: McCelland Libr, Pueblo, Colo; Penrose Libr, Colorado Springs, Colo; Judicial Bldg, Pueblo, Colo; First Nat Bank, Billings, Mont; Koshare Indian Kiva Mus, La Junta, Colo; Mont State Mus, Helena; Charles Russell Mus, Great Falls, Mont; Colorado Springs Fine Art Ctr, Colo; H F Johnson Mus, Ithaca, NY; Denver Art Mus, Colo; Sangre de Cristo Fine Art Ctr, Pueblo, Colo; Minn Mus of Fine Art, St Paul; Scotsdale Ctr for the Arts, Ariz; Yellowstone Fine Art Ctr, Billings, Mont; Mus of Fine Art, Sante Fe, NMex; J K Ralston Mus, Sidney, Mont. Exhib: One-man shows, Colo Springs Fine Art Ctr, Colo, 67, Mont State Mus, Helena, 63-72, Sangre de Cristo Fine Art Ctr, 75 & Charles Russell Mus, Great Falls, Mont, 68-77; Pac Northwest Regional, Spokane Art Ctr, Wash; Cent NY Regional, Munson-Williams-Proctor Inst Mus, Utica, NY; Nat Print & Drawing Show, Okla Fine Art Ctr, Oklahoma City; Mercyhurst Col Nat Print Show, Erie, Pa; 1st USAF Acad Fine Art Exhib, Colo; plus others. Teaching: Grad asst art, Cornell Univ, 60-62; assoc prof art, Southern Colo State Univ, 62- Awards: Merit Awards, Mulvane Eight State Show, Mulvane Fine Art Ctr, Topkea, Kans, 67 & Southwest Print & Drawing Show, Dallas Mus Fine Arts, Tex, 68; Purchase Prize, Drawings USA, Minn Mus Fine Art, 68. Bibliog: James A Schinneller (auth), Art/Search & Self-Discovery, Int Textbook Co, 67; Terry Melton (auth), If I Leave This Earth, Nat Endowment for the Humanities, 73; Jo Ann McPhail (auth), Southwest Art, Southwest Art Gallery Mag, 75. Style & Technique: Paintings of the Rocky Mountain region, landscape, animal and figure. Media: Oil paint and colored drawing. Publ: Illusr, cover design, Southwest Art Gallery Mag, 77. Dealer: Gallery A Kit Carson St Taos NM 87571. Mailing Add: 905 W Evans Pueblo CO 81005

HELIKER, JOHN EDWARD
PAINTER, EDUCATOR
b Yonkers, NY, 09. Study: Art Students League; Colby Col, hon DFA. Work: Metrop Mus Art, New York; Cleveland Mus Art, Ohio; Whitney Mus Am Art, New York, Hirshhorn Found; Philadelphia Mus Art. Exhib: Am Painting Today, Metrop Mus Art, 50; Nature in Abstraction, 58, Art of the United States 1670-1966, 66 & retrospective exhib, 68, Whitney Mus Am Art; Brussels World's Fair, 58. Teaching: Prof painting, Columbia Univ, 47-74; instr, Art Students League, 75- Pos: Vpres, Am Acad Arts & Lett, 72-74. Awards: First W A Clark Prize, Corcoran Gallery Art, 41; Prix de Rome, 48; Award of Merit Medal, Am Acad Arts & Lett, 67. Bibliog: J I H Baur (auth), New decade, 55 & L Goodrich (auth), John Heliker, 68, Whitney Mus Am Art; W Nordness (auth), Art USA now, Viking, 62. Mem: Nat Inst Arts & Lett. Media: Oil, Watercolor. Dealer: Kraushaar Galleries 1055 Madison Ave New York NY 10028. Mailing Add: Apt 3C 865 West End Ave New York NY 10025

HELIOFF, ANNE GRAILE (MRS BENJAMIN HIRSCHBERG)
PAINTER
b Liverpool, Eng; US citizen. Study: Art Students League, with Nicolaides, Homer Boss & Kuniyoshi; also pvt summer classes; Hans Hofmann Sch. Exhib: Paintings of the Year, all maj mus of the US; Pa Acad Fine Arts, Philadelphia; Dedication Exhibition, Nat Gallery Art, Washington, DC; Art USA, New York & all maj cities of the US; American Exhibition, Palazzo Uecchio, Florence, Italy & Mus Naples, Italy, 72; Bicentennial Expo Six Painters from New York, Annemasse & Cluses, France; plus five solo shows in New York galleries. Pos: Mem bd control, Art Students League; mem, US Deleg to 5th Cong, Int Asn Artists, Tokyo, 66; exec bd, Phoenix Gallery, New York, 70-72. Awards: Silver Medal & Hon Mention for oil and watercolor, Albany Mus Hist & Art, 60; Oil Award, Am Soc Contemp Artists, Riverside Mus, 62; Three Cert of Merit, Am Soc Contemp Artists, 70. Bibliog: Gordon Brown (auth), rev in Arts Mag, spec issue, 4/71; Dorothy Hall (auth), article in Park East, 11/76; C Offin (auth), article in Pictures on Exhib, 11/76; N Frachtman (auth), article in Arts Mag, 1/77. Mem: Nat Asn Women Artists (dir); Am Soc Contemp Artists (past dir); New York Soc Women Artists (past dir); Artists Equity Asn New York (past dir); life mem Woodstock Artists Asn (past dir). Media: Oil, Acrylic. Dealer: Phoenix Gallery 939 Madison Ave New York NY 10021. Mailing Add: 340 W 28th St New York NY 10001

HELLER, BEN
ART DEALER, COLLECTOR
b New York, NY, Oct 16, 25. Study: Bard Col, BA. Pos: Adv, Washington Gallery Mod Art; benefactor, Metrop Mus Art, New York; past trustee or bd mem, Int Coun of Mus Mod Art, Friends of Whitney Mus Am Art & Jewish Mus. Collection: Contemporary American painting and ancient, Eastern and primitive arts. Mailing Add: 121 E 73rd St New York NY 10021

HELLER, DOROTHY
PAINTER
b New York, NY. Study: With Hans Hofmann. Work: Univ Calif Art Mus, Berkeley; Allen Mem Art Mus, Oberlin, Ohio; Mus Mod Art, Haifa, Israel; Greenville Co Mus Art, SC. Exhib: One-man shows, Tibor de Nagy Gallery, New York, 53, Galerie Faccetti, Paris, France, 55, Poindexter Gallery, New York, 56-57, Betty Parsons Gallery, New York, 72, 76 & 78 & Fairlawn Libr, NJ, 75; Whitney Mus Am Art, New York, 56; Carnegie Int, Pittsburgh, Pa, 59; Mus Mod Art, New York, 63; Wadsworth Atheneum, Conn, 64. Bibliog: Article in, Arts Mag, 10/72; Archives of American Art, Smithsonian Inst, Washington, DC. Media: Acrylic. Dealer: Betty Parsons 24 W 57th St New York NY 10019. Mailing Add: 8 W 13th St New York NY 10011

HELLER, GOLDIE (MRS EDWARD W GREENBERG)
COLLECTOR
b Salem, Mass. Study: Mass Sch Art. Collection: Hans Hartung, Henry Botkin, Ralph Rosenborg, Byron Browne, Noel Rockmore, Andy Warhol, Francisco Larez, Jose de Creeft, Jean Marie Souverbie (School of Paris), John Ross, June Rogoff, Bolegard, Clare Romano and others. Mailing Add: 440 E 56th St New York NY 10022

HELLER, JULES
PRINTMAKER, WRITER
b New York, NY, Nov 16, 19. Study: Ariz State Univ, BA, 39; Columbia Univ, MA, 40; Univ Southern Calif, PhD, 48. Work: Long Beach Mus Art, Calif; Ariz State Univ; Allan R Hite Inst, Univ Louisville; Tamarind Inst, Univ NMex; Toronto Dom Centre; Can Coun Art Bank, York Univ. Exhib: Soc Am Etchers, 50; 2nd Int Biennial Color Lithography, Cincinnati Art Mus, 52; First Nat Exhib Prints, DePauw Univ, 59; Pa Acad Fine Arts Ann, 59 & 63; Canada, Gallery Pascal, 75; Martha Jackson Gallery, New York, 76. Teaching: Prof printmaking & art hist, Univ Southern Calif, 46-61; prof fine arts, York Univ, 72-76. Pos: Dir sch arts, Pa State Univ, University Park, 61-63, founding dean col arts & archit, 63-68; founding dean fac fine arts, York Univ, 68-72; dean, Col Fine Arts, Ariz State Univ, Tempe, 76- Mem: Col Art Asn Am; Int Coun of Fine Arts Deans; Int Asn Paper Historians. Media: Graphics. Publ: Illusr, Canciones de Mexico, 48; contribr, Estampas de la revolucion Mexicana, 48; contribr, Prints by California Artists, 54; contribr, Dictionary of Art, McGraw, 69; auth, Printmaking Today, rev ed, 72; auth, Papermaking, 5/78. Mailing Add: 6838 E Cheney Rd Scottsdale AZ 85253

HELLER, REINHOLD AUGUST
ART HISTORIAN
b Fulda, Ger, July 22, 40; US citizen. Study: St Joseph's Col, Philadelphia, BS, 63; Ind Univ, Bloomington, MA, 66, PhD, 68, with Albert Elsen, John Jacobus & Sven Loevgren. Teaching: Prof art hist, Univ Pittsburgh, 68- Awards: Foreign Area Fel Prog fel, 66-68; Guggenheim Found fel, 73-74; d'Harnoncourt fel, Mus of Mod Art, New York, 70. Mem: Col Art Asn; Mod Lang Asn. Res: Art criticism; symbolism; expressionism; German Romanticism; iconography of modern art. Publ: Auth, Iconography of Edvard Munh's Sphinx, Artforum, 60; auth, Art of Wilhelm Lehmbruck, Nat Gallery, Washington, DC, 72; auth, Munch: The Scream, Viking, 73; auth, Edvard Munch's Vision and the Symbolist Swan, Art Quart, 73; auth, Recent Scholarship on Vienna's Golden Age, Art Bull, 77. Mailing Add: 10843 Highpoint Dr Pittsburgh PA 15235

HELMAN, PHOEBE
SCULPTOR
b New New York, NY, Oct 29, 29. Study: Wash Univ, with Paul Burlin, BFA; Art Students League; also with Raphael Soyer. Work: Hampton Inst Mus, Va; Ciba-Geigy, Ardsley, NY; Fox, Flynn & Melamed, New York; Friedlich, Fearon & Strohmeier, New York. Comn: Steel wall piece, comn by Milan Stoeger, New York, 73; steel wall piece, comn by Muriel Mannings, New York, 73. Exhib: Two-woman show, Emily Lowe Gallery, Nofstra Col, 69; one-woman show, Max Hutchinson Gallery, 74, Bronson Gallery, Manhattanville Col, Purchase, NY, 76 & Gallery 101, Univ Wis, River Falls, 77; Sculpture Now, Inc, Gallery I, 74; plastics, State Univ NY Potsdam, 74; Drawing in New York Today, Hamilton Gallery of Contemp Art, New York, 77; Proj: New Urban Monuments (travelling exhib), 77; Small Works, Landmark Gallery, New York, 77. Teaching: Asst prof art, Pratt Inst, 72- Awards: Creative Artists Pub Serv Grant, 75-76. Bibliog: Phyllis Derfner (auth), Light, color, image, Art Inst, 4/76; Carter Ratcliff (auth), Notes on small sculpture, Art Forum, 4/76; Corinne Robins (auth), Phoebe Helman, Arts, 3/78. Style & Technique: Large free standing environmental pieces that can be walked through; wall pieces; drawings. Media: Laminite & Wood; Steel. Dealer: Sculpture Now Inc & Max Hutchinson Gallery 142 Greene St New York NY 10012. Mailing Add: 217 E 23rd St New York NY 10010

HELZER, RICHARD BRIAN
METALSMITH, EDUCATOR
b Hastings, Nebr, Aug 27, 43. Study: Kearney State Col, Nebr, BA, 65; Univ Kans, MFA, 69. Work: C M Russell Mus, Great Falls, Mont. Comn: Altar serv, St Elizabeth's Episcopal

Church, Nebr, 69 & Hope Lutheran Church, Kans, 70; altar cross, Univ Kans Chapel, Lawrence, 70. Exhib: Am Crafts, Am Crafts Coun Gallery, New York, 73; Body Adornment, Portland Art Ctr, Ore, 74; Hist of Gold & Silversmithing in Am, Lowe Art Mus, Univ Miami, Coral Gables, Fla, 75; NW Invitational Silversmiths, Seattle Art Mus, Wash, 76; US Off Info Goldsmiths Exhib, Melbourne, Australia, 76; NW Designer-Craftsman, Henry Gallery, Seattle, Wash, 77; 3rd Profile of US Jewelry, Tex Tech Univ, Lubbock, 77; Goldsmiths 77, Phoenix Art Mus, Ariz, 77. Collections Arranged: Metal Art in Am Exhib (auth, catalogue), Mont State Univ, 76. Teaching: Teaching asst, Univ Kans, Lawrence, 68-69, instr metalsmithing, 69-70; asst prof metalsmithing, Mont State Univ, Bozeman, 70-74, assoc prof metalsmithing, 75- Awards: Nat Endowment for the Arts fel, 76; Runner-up, Western State Arts Found fel, 77. Bibliog: Frank Potter (auth), article in NW Craftsman, 76. Mem: Soc NAm Goldsmiths; Am Crafts Coun; NW Designer Craftsmen. Style & Technique: Jewelry and metalsmithing. Media: Precious metals and acrylics. Dealer: Gallery 85 Emerald Dr Billings MT 59715. Mailing Add: RT 2 Box 242 Bozeman MT 59715

HEMENWAY, NANCY (MRS ROBERT D BARTON)
TAPESTRY ARTIST, DESIGNER
b Boothbay Harbor, Maine, June 19, 20. Study: Wheaton Col, 37-41; with Matheu, Europe, 54-56; Univ Madrid, 56; Art Students League, 57-61; Columbia Univ, MA, 66. Work: Net (Bayetage), Woodmere Art Gallery, Germantown, Pa; Sea Edge, Chase Manhattan Bank, New York; Sea Lace, Maine Savings Bank, Portland; plus many works in pvt collections in Europe, Latin Am & USA. Comn: Monkeys, Crab & Mask (Bayetages), Mrs Walter Ford, Detroit, Mich, 72; Tidal (two part screen in silk & velvet), Mr & Mrs Arthur Schultz, Chicago, Ill, 72; Amulet, Hon & Mrs Hugh Scott, 73; Milkweed (wool & organdy), Hon & Mrs Dewey Bartlett, 74; Serpent, Masque with Jaguars, William Clements, Jr, 75; Swing, Victor Borge, 75. Exhib: Woodmere Gallery Art, Germantown, 71; Copley Soc Boston, Mass, 72; McNay Art Inst, San Antonio, Tex, 73; Mus NMex, Santa Fe, 74; Mus Fine Arts, Montgomery, Ala, 75; Bowdoin Col Mus Art, Brunswick, Maine, 77; Va Mus, Richmond, 77; Seattle Mus Art, Wash, 78; Textile Mus, Washington, DC, 78. Pos: Founder, San Esteban Sch, Guadalajara, Mex, 70; pres, Hemenway Designs, Washington, DC; spec Bicentennial proj, City of Boston, 76; African lect tour, US State Dept, 76. Bibliog: Nancy Hemenway & Bayetage (film), produced by US Info Agency, 70. Mem: Art Students League; Maine Hist & Cult Soc; Maine Art Gallery; Maine Coast Artists; Corcoran Gallery Fine Arts. Interest: Originator of Bayetage, a new art form consisting of wall hangings in needlecraft and collage on handwoven wool or organdy. Mailing Add: Juniper Point West Boothbay Harbor ME 04575

HEMPHILL, HERBERT WAIDE
CURATOR, LECTURER
b Atlantic City, NJ, Jan 21, 29. Collections Arranged: Hunt for the Whale; Plenty of Pennsylvania; Occult; Tattoo!; Macrame: Hail to the Chief; Fabric of the State (with catalog), 73; Commerce in Wood; 20th Century American Folk Art & Artists, 74; Collector's Choice; America Expresses Herself, New Children's Mus, Indianapolis, Ind, 76; Missing Pieces—Georgia Folk Art (adv; intro to catalogue), 76; Japan Celebrates America's Bicentennial—The Hemphill Collection, Tokyo & Osaka, Japan, 76. Pos: Founding mem, Mus Am Folk Art, 58, cur, 61-72; guest cur, Brooklyn Mus, 74-76. Bibliog: Robert Bishop, Mary Black, Tom Armstrong, Louis Jones, et al (auth), The H W Hemphill Collection of 18th, 19th & 20th Century American Folk Art, Heritage Plantation Mus; Jack Bolton (auth), The Hemphill Collection of 20th Century American Folk Art, Contemp Arts Ctr, Cincinnati, 73. Interest: Gifts to various folk collections and museums; 18th, 19th & 20th century American folk art. Publ: Co-auth, Metal of the State, 74; co-auth, with Julia Weissman, 20th Century American Folk Art & Artists, 74; ed (catalogue), Folk Sculpture USA. Mailing Add: 108 E 30th St New York NY 10016

HEMPHILL, PAMELA
ART HISTORIAN
b Manchester, Eng, May 1, 27; US citizen. Study: Manchester Univ, BAdmin; Univ Pa, PhD(classical archaeol). Teaching: Prof classical, medieval & modern art, Women's Studies, West Chester State Col, 70- Awards: Ital Govt Fel, 65; Fulbright Travel Grant, 65; Am Philos Soc Study Grant, 74. Mem: Am Inst Archaeol; Inst Studi Romani; Univ Mus, Philadelphia; Philadelphia Art Mus; Inst Field Archaeol. Res: Surface survey in Italy to find new pottery types and land usage in Italy from prehistoric to medieval times. Publ: Auth, Survey of the Hill Country North of Rome, Exped Mag, 70; auth, Notes to slide sets on Roman Forum, Palatine and Herculaneum, Am Inst Archaeol, 73; auth, Cassia—Cladia Survey, Papers of Brit Sch, Rome, Vol 43 (1975): 118-172. Mailing Add: Cheyney PA 19319

HENDERSHOT, J L
PRINTMAKER, EDUCATOR
b Cleveland, Ohio, Nov 3, 41. Study: Cleveland Inst Art, with H C Cassill, Louis Bosa & Julian Stanczak; Syracuse Univ, NY, with George Vander Sluis & Donald Cortesse. Work: Philadelphia Mus Art; Rochester Mus Art, NY; Minn Mus Art, St Paul; Univ NDak; Pennell Fund, Libr Cong. Comn: Drawing, Alumni Asn, St John's Univ, Collegeville, Minn, 73; drawing for gift, Spira Dance Co, Portland, Ore, 74; print, St Cloud State Col, 75; 50th Anniversary lithographs (50 ed), Minn Mus; lithographs ed, Assoc Am Artist. Exhib: Int Philadelphia Print Exhib, 68; NJ State Mus, 69; 50th Ann Exhib, Soc Am Graphic Artist, Asn Am Artist Gallery, New York, 70; one-man show, RI Sch Design, Providence, 75, Assoc Am Artists Gallery, New York, 76, Red River Art Ctr Mus, Moorehead, Minn, 76 & Uptown Gallery, New York, 77; 7th Nat Biennial Drawing US Show, St Paul, Minn, 75. Teaching: Asst instr drawing & printmaking, Syracuse Univ, 68-70; asst prof drawing & printmaking, St John's Univ, 71- Pos: Art Gallery dir, St John's Univ, 75- Awards: Philadelphia Print Club Purchase Award, Philadelphia Mus Art, 68; Univ NDak Purchase Award, 15th Nat Print & Drawing Exhib, 72; Minn Mus Art Purchase Award, 7th Nat Biennial Drawing US Show, 75. Mem: Graphic Soc, Hollis, NH; Print Collector's Newslett, New York; Boston Printmakers; Pratt Graphics Print Club, New York. Style & Technique: Working in a realist manner with over lays of transparency and complexity in high value tone. Media: Intaglio, Lithography; Pencil Drawing. Mailing Add: St John's Univ Collegeville MN 56231

HENDERSON, JACK W
PAINTER, INSTRUCTOR
b Kenosha, Wis, Mar 12, 31. Study: Kansas City Art Inst, BFA & MFA, 47-52; Ecole des Beaux Arts, Paris, 52-53; Art Students League, 55-58; also with Edward Laning, Louis Bouche & Robert Beverly Hale. Work: Nat Acad Design, New York; Everhart Mus, Scranton, Pa; Am Acad Rome, Italy; Kansas City Art Inst. Comn: Murals in pvt collections, Rome & New York. Exhib: Pa Acad Fine Arts, 59 & 61; one-man show, Nat Acad Design, 68, Ranger Fund Exhib, 74; Am Watercolor Soc Ann, New York, 69-70; plus others. Teaching: Assoc prof painting, Moore Col Art, 67-75; instr life drawing & painting, Art Students League, 75- Awards: Pulitzer Traveling Fel, 55; Abbey Fel for Mural Painting, Am Acad Rome, 63-65; Ranger Fund Purchase Award, Nat Acad Design, 74; plus others. Mem: Nat Acad Design; Am Watercolor Soc; Nat Soc Mural Painters; Art Students League; Artists Equity. Style & Technique: Realist. Media: All media. Mailing Add: 118 Remsen St Brooklyn NY 11201

HENDERSON, LESTER KIERSTEAD
PHOTOGRAPHER, ART DEALER
b Abington, Mass, May 9, 06. Study: Northeastern Univ, 27; self study. Work: Photog Hall of Fame, Santa Barbara, Calif. Exhib: Wichita Art Mus, Kans, 75; Marion Koogler McNary Art Inst, San Antonio, Tex, 76; Okla Mus Art, Oklahoma City, 77; Leigh Yawkey Woodson Art Mus, Wausau, Wis, 77; Houston Mus Natural Hist, 78. Res: Exclusively Martha Mood stitcheries and Portuguese tapestries. Specialty: Athos Menakon bird paintings; Marilyn Bendell portraits. Publ: Auth, The Sublime Heritage of Martha Wood, Kierstead Publ, 78. Mailing Add: 712 Hawthorne St Monterey CA 93940

HENDERSON, MIKE (WILLIAM HOWARD HENDERSON)
PAINTER
b Marshall, Mo, June 15, 43. Study: San Francisco Art Inst, with Bob Nelson, Joan Brown & Dr Richard Miller, BA & MA(painting, film making); Skowhegan Sch Painting & Sculpture; also with Phillip Perlstine, Robert Mango & Jacob Lawrence. Work: Oakland Mus, Calif. Exhib: Human Concern/Personal Torment, Whitney Mus, New York, 69, Black Untitled, 70; Black Unlimited, Oakland Mus, 70; Third World Art, San Francisco Mus, 74-75; North East West South and Middle Drawing Show, Moores Col, Pa, 75. Teaching: Asst prof painting & film making, Univ Calif, Davis, 70-, grad adv mass commun, 74- Awards: Guggenheim Found Fel, 73. Style & Technique: Soft paintings, mutilated by fire and enhanced with color. Media: Acrylic. Mailing Add: 414 Francisco St San Francisco CA 94133

HENDERSON, VICTOR (LANCE)
PAINTER, PHOTOGRAPHER
b Cuyahoga Falls, Ohio, Nov 30, 39. Study: San Francisco State Col, BA, 63. Work: Newport Harbor Mus, Newport Beach, Calif; Chicago Art Inst; M H De Young Mem Mus, San Francisco. Comn: Beverly Hills Sidhartha, Michael Huit, Los Angeles, Calif, 69-70; Venice in the Snow, Jerry Rosen, Los Angeles, Calif, 70; Isle of Calif, Jordy Hormel, Los Angeles, 70-72; Hippy Knowhow, French Govt, Paris, France, 71; Ghost Town, Ed Janss, Thousand Oaks, Calif, 72-73 (all the above murals were executed under the name Los Angeles Fine Arts Squad). Exhib: Biannual de Paris, France, 71; LA 8, Los Angeles Co Mus Art, Calif, 76; one-man shows, Tortue Gallery, Santa Monica, Calif, 76, Grossmount Col Gallery, San Diego, Calif, 76 & Reptilian Uhual Performance Piece, Venice, Calif, 77; 100-plus, Los Angeles Inst Contemp Art, 77; Illusion and Reality, Australian Nat Gallery, Canbera, plus six other Australian galleries & mus, 77. Teaching: Lectr drawing, Univ Calif, Los Angeles, 75-77. Pos: Co-founder, Los Angeles Fine Art Squad, Calif, 69-73. Bibliog: T H Garver (auth, article), Artforum, Vol 9, 71; Peter Plagens (auth), Sunshine Muse, Praeger, NY, 73; Eva Cookcroft (auth), Towards a People Art, E P Dutton & Co, NY, 76. Style & Technique: Large illusionistic painted murals, drawings; large photographic murals. Media: Photographic mural and drawing. Publ: Auth, Mega Murals & Big Art, Running Press, Philadelphia, 77. Mailing Add: 52 Brooks Ave Venice CA 90291

HENDLER, RAYMOND
PAINTER, SCULPTOR
b Philadelphia, Pa, Feb 22, 23. Study: Acad Grande Chaumiere, Paris, France; Contemp Sch Art, Brooklyn, NY; Tyler Sch, Temple Univ; Pa Acad Fine Arts; Philadelphia Col Art; Graphic Sketch Club, Philadelphia. Work: NY Univ; Walker Art Ctr, Minneapolis; Birla Acad Mus, Calcutta, India; Univ Notre Dame; Geigy Chem Corp, New York; plus others. Exhib: One-man shows, Galerie Huit, Paris, 51, Rose Fried Gallery, New York, 62-, Minneapolis Inst Art, Minn, & others; exhibs at major mus, univs & galleries throughout US, Can & Europe. Teaching: Dir, Eve Art Sch Pratt Inst; dir, First Yr Prog Sch Visual Arts; head dept painting, Minneapolis Col Art; prof art, Univ Minn, Minneapolis, 68- Awards: Longview Found Purchase Award, 63. Bibliog: Orie (auth), Raymond Hendler, Quandrum XVII; Burton (auth), Hendler paintings, Art News, 5/67; Brown (auth), Hendler exhibition, Arts, 6/67. Mem: Artists Club, New York; Col Art Asn Am. Media: Acrylic, Polystyrene. Mailing Add: 2212 Seabury Ave S Minneapolis MN 55406

HENDRICKS, BARKLEY LEONNARD
PAINTER
b Philadelphia, Pa, Apr 16, 45. Study: Pa Acad Fine Arts, 63-67, William Cresson European Traveling scholar, 66; Yale Univ Sch Fine Art, 70-72. Work: Philadelphia Mus Art; Pa Acad Fine Arts, Philadelphia; Cornell Univ; Wichita State Univ, Kans; Nat Gallery, Washington, DC. Exhib: Fel Exhib, Pa Acad Fine Arts, 67-72; Nat Acad Design Ann, New York, 70-71 & 74-75; Contemp Black Artists, Whitney Mus Am Art, New York, 71; Childe Hassam Fund Exhib, Am Acad Arts & Lett, 71 & 75; Nat Inst Arts & Lett Ann, 71-72. Teaching: Instr painting & drawing, Pa Acad Fine Arts, 71-72; asst in painting, Yale Univ, 71-72; asst prof painting & drawing, Conn Col, 72- Awards: Julius Hallgarten Second Prize, Nat Acad Design, 71; Richard & Hilda Rosenthal Award, Nat Inst Arts & Lett, 72. Media: Oil, Acrylic. Dealer: ACA Galleries 25 E 73rd St New York NY 10021. Mailing Add: 58 State St New London CT 06320

HENDRICKS, DAVID CHARLES
PAINTER, VISUAL ARTIST
b Hammond, Ind, Mar 25, 48. Study: Skowhegan Summer Sch Painting & Sculpture, 69; Univ Ill, BFA, 70; Ox-Bow Summer Sch Painting, 70. Work: Hirshhorn Mus & Sculpture Garden, Washington, DC; NC Nat Bank, Davidson. Exhib: Davidson Nat Print & Drawing Show, Davidson Col, NC, 76; Childe Hassam Fund Show, Am Acad Arts & Lett, New York, 76; Monique Knowlton Gallery, New York, 76-78; Contemp Landscape: Image & Idea, Queensborough Community Col, NY, 77; Artists Salute Skowhegan, Kennedy Gallery, New York, 77; one-man show, Monique Knowlton Gallery, 77. Awards: Artist-in-residence, MacDowell Colony, Peterborough, NY, summer 71-75, Ossabaw Island Proj Found, Savannah, Ga, 5/76 & Yaddo, Saratoga Springs, NY, summer 77; Purchase Award, Davidson Nat Print & Drawing Show, NC Nat Bank, 76; Visual Arts Fel, Nat Endowment for the Arts, 77. Bibliog: John Russell (auth), Invigorating breezes of the fall season, New York Times, Arts & Leisure, 10/2/76; Lenore Malen (auth), David Henricks, Arts Mag, 2/77. Style & Technique: Large scale landscape drawings (up to 72in x 120in). Media: Pencil and Powdered Graphite on Plastic Panel; Oil on Canvas. Dealer: Monique Knowlton Gallery Inc 19 E 71st St New York NY 10021. Mailing Add: 652 Broadway New York NY 10012

HENDRICKS, DONALD TEVES
PAINTER, SCULPTOR
b Glen Cove, NY, Jan 1, 14. Study: Grand Cent Sch Art, New York, grad, 39; Hofstra Univ, 45-48. Work: Univ Pa; Guild Hall, Easthampton, NY; Mus Mod Art, Barcelona; Mus City Lugano; City Hamburg Kunsthalle, Ger; plus others. Exhib: Galleria Trini, Cuernavaca, Mex, 68; Galleria Ivan Spence, Ibiza, Spain, 71; Heckscher Mus, Huntington, NY, 70; one-man

show, UN Benefit, Williamsport, Pa, 72; Int Exhib, Mus Art, Lugano, Switz, 74; plus others. Teaching: Instr painting, Inst Belles Artes, Mex, 39-40; lectr art, Inst Allende, Guanajato, Mex, 69-70 & Queens Col, 74-75. Awards: First Prize, Long Island Painters, Heckscher Mus, 71. Mem: Huntington Twp Art League (bd dirs, 71-); Found for Community Artists, New York; Artists Equity. Style & Technique: Hard-edge; geometric, using gold and silver leaf and constructions. Media: Acrylic; Steel. Publ: Contribr, IBIZA Eng Press, 70, Art Workers News, New York, 73 & New York Times Mag, 73. Mailing Add: PO Box 10 Bayshore NY 11706

HENDRICKS, GEOFFREY
PAINTER, ENVIRONMENTAL ARTIST
b Littleton, NH, July 30, 31. Study: Amherst Col, BA, 53; Norfolk Art Sch, Yale Univ, scholar, summer 53; Cooper Union Art Sch, 53-56; Columbia Univ, MA, 62. Work: NJ State Mus, Trenton; Mus Mod Art & Metrop Mus Art, New York; Lehmbruck Mus, Duisburg, WGer. Exhib: Contemp Am Still Life, Mus Mod Art, New York, circulating exhib, 66-68; A Mus of Merchandise, Philadelphia Arts Coun, 67; Happening & Fluxus, Kunstverein, Köln & Stuttgart, Ger, 70-71; Image Bank Post Card Show, Univ Art Gallery, Vancouver, BC & touring, 71 & 77; Il Tronce (with Brian Buczak), Galleria d'Arte Moderna, Bologna, Italy, 77; Hermetic Images in Contemp Art, Inst for Art & Urban Resources/PS 1, New York, 78; Artwords & Bookworks, Los Angeles Inst of Contemp Art, Calif, 78; one-man shows, Bianchini Gallery, New York, 66, Tokyo Gallery, Japan, 68, Apple Gallery, New York, 71, Galerie Baecker, Bochum, WGer, 72 & 74 & Rene Block Gallery, New York, 76-77; plus numerous other group & one-man shows. Teaching: Assoc prof art, Douglass Col, Rutgers Univ, 56-; instr art, New York Fine Arts Winter Term Prog of Earlham Col, Richmond, Ind, 65-69. Awards: First Prize for Watercolors, Champlain Valley Exhib, Vt, 50; MacDowell Colony Fel, 55; Individual Fel, Nat Endowment for the Arts, 76-77. Bibliog: K Nobuyuki (auth), The art of trompe l'oeil: Hendricks & Gilardi, Bijutsu-Techo, 4/68; Ichiro Haryu (ed), Art as action & concept, Art Now, 72; Gerd Winkler (auth), Wolken und Gitarren, Kunstforum Int, 2/74; Geoffrey Hendricks, Flash Art, 2/76; and others. Mem: Col Art Asn Am; Am Asn Univ Prof; Fluxus. Media: Acrylic, Intermedia. Publ: Contribr, Film culture—expanded Cinema (spec issue 43), winter 66; auth, Sky Post Cards, Vols 1-6, Black Thumb Press, 67-68; contribr, Pop Architektur, Droste Verlag, Dusseldorf, 69; auth, Ring Piece, Something Else Press, 73; co-auth (with F Conz), A Sheep's Skeleton & Rocks, Unpublished Ed, New York, 77; co-auth (with Brian Buczak), Rulers, Ladders and Buckets, Money for Food Press, 77; and others. Dealer: Galerie Baecker Bergstrasse 54 D4630 Bochum West Germany. Mailing Add: 486 Greenwich St New York NY 10013

HENDRICKS, JAMES (POWELL)
PAINTER, EDUCATOR
b Little Rock, Ark, Aug 7, 38. Study: Univ Ark, Fayetteville, BA, 63; Univ Iowa, MFA, 64. Work: Finch Col Mus, New York; Smithsonian Inst, Washington, DC; Univ Mass, Amherst; Hudson River Mus, Yonkers, NY; Nat Gallery Art, Washington, DC. Comn: Apollo 14 Launch, Nat Gallery Art & NASA, 71. Exhib: One-man shows, Smithsonian Inst Nat Air & Space Mus, Washington, DC, 69, Hudson River Mus, Yonkers, NY, 70 & French & Co Gallery, New York, 72; Biennial Contemp Am Painting & Sculpture, Krannert Art Mus, Univ Ill, 69; Nat Gallery Art, 70; Abstract Painting, De Cordova Mus, Lincoln, Mass, 71; Warren Benedek Gallery, New York, 73; Sunne Savage Gallery, Boston, 74; Phillips Exeter Acad, Lamont Gallery, Exeter, NH, 76. Teaching: Grad instr drawing, State Univ Iowa, 63-64; instr art, Mt Holyoke Col, 64-65; asst prof painting & drawing, Univ Mass, Amherst, assoc prof & dir grad progs in art, 72- Awards: Top Prize for Painting, Soc Four Arts, 68; Painting Awards, Purdue Univ Art Gallery, 69 & Silvermine Guild Artists, 69. Bibliog: H Lester Cooke (auth), Eyewitness to Space, Abrams, 71; Van Deren Coke (auth), The Painter & the Photograph, Univ NMex, 72; Robert Ackermann (auth), Arts reviews, Arts Mag, 9/74. Style & Technique: Non-representational, painterly painting. Media: Acrylic, Oil. Publ: Illusr cover, Time, 71. Dealer: Genesis Gallery 41 E 57th St New York NY 10022. Mailing Add: Art Dept Univ of Mass Amherst MA 01002

HENKLE, JAMES LEE
SCULPTOR, EDUCATOR
b Cedar Rapids, Iowa, Mar 13, 27. Study: Univ Nebr, BA; Pratt Inst, cert indust design. Work: Okla Art Ctr, Oklahoma City; Univ Okla Art Mus, Norman; Springfield Art Mus, Mo; Okla State Art Collection, Okla Arts & Humanities Coun, Oklahoma City; Ark Arts Ctr, Little Rock. Comn: Sculpture & fountain, First Fed Savings & Loan Bldg, Ft Smith, Ark, 61; sculpture mural, Numerical Anal Res Ctr, Norman, 63; sculpture mural, Tulsa Pub Libr, Tulsa Hist Soc, Okla, 65; sculpture, Norman Pub Libr, 75th Anniversary Comt, 66; wall sculpture, Dale Hall, Univ Okla, Chi Omega Sorority, 69. Exhib: Nat Col Art Students Exhib, Andover, Mass, 49; Eight State Art Exhib, Oklahoma City Art Ctr, 61; one-man sculpture exhib, Univ Okla Mus Art, 68 & Philbrook Art Ctr, Tulsa, 70. Teaching: Prof art, Univ Okla, 53- Pos: Designer, Dave Chapman Design Firm, 52-53. Awards: Purchase Prize for Sculpture, Okla Art Ctr, 65; Purchase Prize for Painting, Springfield Art Mus; Purchase Award for Crafts, Eighth Ann Print, Drawing & Crafts Exhib, Ark Arts Ctr, 75. Style & Technique: Carved wooden constructions and welded metal sculpture generally abstract in form. Mailing Add: Sch of Art Univ of Okla Norman OK 73069

HENNESY, GERALD CRAFT
PAINTER
b Washington, DC, June 11, 21. Study: Corcoran Sch Art; George Washington Univ; Am Univ; Univ Md; also with C Gordon Harris. Work: Nat Hq Am Legion, Washington, DC; Md State Exec Mansion, Annapolis. Comn: Paintings, Gibson Bldg, Fairfax, Va, 74; paintings, United Va Bank, Richmond, 75. Exhib: Corcoran Gallery Art Area, Washington, DC; Am Art League, Smithsonian Inst, Washington, DC, 62 & 64; Baltimore Mus Art Regional, 63; New York World's Fair, 65; one-man show, Pla Gallery, McLean, Va, 67; Allied Artists of Am, New York, 75 & 76; plus many others. Pos: Advertising artist, Washington Times Herald, DC, 41-42. Awards: First Prize, Gilham Show, 66; Best West Virginia, Harpers Ferry Art Festival, 66; Watercolor Medal, Landscape Club, 74. Mem: Landscape Club Washington (treas, 73-77). Style & Technique: Realistic landscapes and seascapes. Media: Oil, Watercolor. Dealer: Via Gambaro Gallery 414 11th St SE Washington DC 20003. Mailing Add: 6811 White Rock Rd Clifton VA 22024

HENNING, EDWARD BURK
CURATOR, ART HISTORIAN
b Cleveland, Ohio, Oct 23, 22. Study: Cleveland Inst Art, cert painting; Western Reserve Univ, BSc, MA; Acad Julian, Paris, France. Collections Arranged: Paths of Abstract Art (with catalog), 60; Fifty Years of Modern Art: 1916-1966 (with catalog), 66; Landscapes Interior and Exterior: Avery, Rothko and Schueler (with catalog), 75; plus many other theme and one-man exhib. Teaching: Adj prof mod art, Case Western Reserve Univ, 68- Pos: Asst cur educ, Cleveland Mus Art, 55-56, assoc cur educ, 56-59, asst to dir, 59-70, cur mod art, 63- Mem: Col Art Asn; Am Asn Mus; Am Soc Aesthetics; ICOM. Res: Impressionism to present, especially Cezanne, symbolism, cubism, Dada and surrealism, abstract-impressionism, color-field painting and conceptualism. Publ: Auth, Patronage and Style in the Arts: A Suggestion Concerning their relations, 60; contribr, On Understanding Art Museums, 75. Mailing Add: 3325 Fairmount Blvd Cleveland Heights OH 44118

HENNING, PAUL HARVEY
PHOTOGRAPHER, ART DEALER
b Milwaukee, Wis, Dec 11, 49. Study: Studied mass commun, Univ Wis-Milwaukee, 68-73. Exhib: Beloit & Vicinity Show, Beloit Col, Wis, 77; Celebration of Sight, First Wis Ctr, Milwaukee, 77. Teaching: Instr basic photog, Cent YMCA, Milwaukee, Wis, 75-76 & Ozaukee Art Ctr, Cedarburg, Wis, 76. Pos: Pres/dir, Infinite Eye Studio/Gallery, Ltd, Milwaukee, Wis, 74-; photog ed, Cityside (bi-weekly news & arts paper), Milwaukee, 77- Specialty: Fine art photography; works of Barbara Morgan, Eva Rubinstein, Bill Owens, Charles Harbutt, Michael Labadie, Bil Leidersdorf and many others. Dealer: Infinite Eye Studio/Gallery Ltd 207 E Buffalo St Suite 303 Milwaukee WI 53202. Mailing Add: PO Box 162 Milwaukee WI 53201

HENRICKSON, PAUL ROBERT
PAINTER, WRITER
b Boston, Mass. Study: RI Sch Design, BFA; Boston State Col, ME; Univ Minn, PhD; Clark Univ; Statens Kunst Akademiet, Oslo; Statens Kunst Industriskole, Oslo. Work: La Jolla Art Ctr, Calif; Mus of NMex, Santa Fe; Statens Kunst Industriskole. Comn: Crash (canvas panel), in pvt collection, NDak. Teaching: Prof & head div fine arts, Univ Gaum, 64-68; prof res art, Univ Northern Iowa, 68-72. Pos: Exec dir, Insular Arts Coun, Gov Guam, 65-68; art critic, 74- Style & Technique: Light and space. Res: Psychology of art. Publ: Auth, Two Primitive Micronesian Art Forms, 68; Lying, Dogmatic and Creative Persons, 70; The Perceptive and Silenced Minorities, 72; auth, The Word for Cross is Cryptic, 77. Mailing Add: 428 Camino de las Animas Santa Fe NM 87501

HENRY, JEAN
PAINTER, INSTRUCTOR
b Oakland, Calif. Study: Art Acad, Amsterdam, Holland; Am Univ Berlin; Md Inst, Baltimore. Work: Triton Mus Art, San Jose, Calif; Chamber of Commerce, San Francisco; Schwartz Hall, Presidio, Calif. Comn: Portrait of Bernard Maybeck, Palace of Fine Arts, 69; portrait of Gen Letterman, Letterman Gen Hosp, 71, portrait of Gen Schwartz, 72; portrait of Sen Graham, Capitol Bldg, Frankfurt, Ky, 72. Exhib: Soc Western Artists, De Young Mus, 68; De Saisset Gallery, Santa Clara, Calif, 69; one-man show, Triton Mus Art, 70; Marin Art & Garden Show, 71; Rosicrucian Mus Invitational Show, 71. Teaching: Instr portrait painting, Md Inst, Johns Hopkins Univ, 58-60; instr painting, Jean Henry Sch Art, San Francisco, 69-; instr painting, Jean Henry Sch Art, Burlingame, 71- Pos: Dir, Jean Henry Arts & Crafts Ctr, Burlingame, 72- Awards: First Award, De Young Mus, 68; First Award, Antioch Outdoor Festival, 69; First Award for Portrait, De Saisset Gallery Ann, 70. Mem: Soc Western Artists (publicity dir, 71). Style & Technique: Impressionist. Media: Oil. Mailing Add: 5340 Geary Blvd San Francisco CA 94121

HENRY, JOHN RAYMOND
SCULPTOR
b Lexington, Ky, Aug 11, 43. Study: Univ Ky; Univ Wash; Art Inst Chicago, Edward L Reyerson fel, 69. Work: City of Rockford, Ill; Ill State Mus, Springfield; British Mus; Smithsonian Inst, Washington, DC; Ft Worth Art Mus, Tex. Comn: Sculpture, comn by Nat Endowment for the Arts, Works of Art in Pub Places, Govs State Univ, South Park Forest, Ill; Sun Target, Nat Endowment for the Arts, Mich Mus, Charlotte, NC, 75; Sculpture for City of Sioux City, Iowa, Nat Endowment for the Arts Matching Grant. Exhib: Structures, 68; Art Inst Chicago, 68; Eight American Sculptors, Chicago, 68; Painting & Sculpture Today, Indianapolis Mus, Ind, 70 & 72; Sculpture Off the Pedestal, Grand Rapids, Mich, 73; Sculpture in the Park, Chicago, 74; Monumental Sculpture, Houston, Tex, 75; Super Sculpture, New Orleans, La, 76; The Chicago Connection, E B Crocker Mus, Sacramento, Calif, 76; Sculpture Potsdam, 77, Potsdam State Univ, NY, 77; one-man shows, Riverside Park, New York, 75, Laguna Gloria Mus of Art, Austin, Tex, 76 & Springfield Mus of Art, Mo, 77. Teaching: Vis prof sculpture, Univ Iowa, summer 60; artist in residence, Univ Wis-Green Bay, 69-70; vis prof sculpture, Univ Chicago, summer 70. Pos: Vpres, Chicago Creative Arts Found, 69-; mem adv bd, Lawyers for the Creative Arts, Chicago. Mem: Sculptor's Group Inc, Chicago. Media: Metals. Dealer: Richard Gray Gallery 620 N Michigan Ave Chicago IL 60611; Dorsky Galleries Ltd 111 Fourth Ave New York NY 10003. Mailing Add: 2943 N Seminary Ave Chicago IL 60657

HENRY, ROBERT
PAINTER, EDUCATOR
b Brooklyn, NY, Aug 3, 33. Study: Hans Hofmann Sch Fine Art, New York & Provincetown, Mass; Brooklyn Col, BA, with Ad Reinhardt & Kurt Seligmann. Exhib: Hudson River Mus, Yonkers, NY, 71; Contemporary Figurative Painting, Suffolk Co Mus, Stony Brook, NY, 71; one-man show, Green Mountain Gallery, New York. Teaching: From asst prof to assoc prof art, Brooklyn Col, 60- Bibliog: L Campbell (auth), Stop, look & look & look, Art News, 2/72. Media: Oil. Publ: Auth, Horizontally oriented rotating kinetic painting, Leonardo, 69. Dealer: Green Mountain Gallery 148 Greene St New York NY 10012. Mailing Add: 803 Greenwich St New York NY 10014

HENRY, SARA LYNN
ART HISTORIAN, ART CRITIC
b Teaneck, NJ, Sept 24, 42. Study: Denison Univ, BFA; NY Univ, MA(art hist) with Robert Goldwater; Univ Calif, Berkeley, PhD with Peter Selz & Herschel B Chipp. Teaching: Lectr art hist, Goucher Col, Towson, Md, 70-71; vis instr art hist, Ohio State Univ, Columbus, 71-72; instr art hist, Carnegie-Mellon Univ, Pittsburgh, 73-76; asst prof art hist, Drew Univ, 76- Mem: Col Art Asn; Women's Caucus for Art. Res: Paul Klee; abstract expressionism; contemporary art. Publ: Contribr, New Catholic Encyclopedia, McGraw-Hill, 66; contribr, Selection 1968, Univ Art Mus, Univ Calif, Berkeley, 68-69; co-auth (with S A Longstaff), The Political Art of Duncan MacPherson, Can Dimension, 3-4/70; auth, Form-creating Energies: Paul Klee & Physics, Arts Mag, 9/77; auth, Klee's Kleinwelt & Creation, Print Rev, Fall 77. Mailing Add: Box R17 Drew Univ Madison NJ 07940

HENRY, STUART (COMPTON)
MUSEUM DIRECTOR, PAINTER
b Tufts College, Mass, 1906. Study: Phillips Acad; Harvard Col, BS & Harvard Grad Sch. Work: Fogg Art Mus; also in pvt collections. Exhib: One-man show, Fogg Art Mus; Pittsfield Art League; Berkshire Mus; Symphony Hall, Boston. Pos: Dir, Berkshire Mus, currently; trustee, Chesterwood Studio of Daniel Chester French, Shaker Community, Inc, Hancock, Mass & Berkshire Mus. Mem: Am Asn Mus. Publ: Auth catalogs of exhibs, collections, guides to collections & others, Berkshire Mus. Mailing Add: Berkshire Mus 39 South St Pittsfield MA 01201

HENSCHE, ADA RAYNER
See Rayner, Ada

HENSCHE, HENRY
PAINTER, INSTRUCTOR
b Chicago, Ill, Feb 20, 01. Study: Charles W Hawthorne's Cape Cod Sch Art; Art Inst Chicago; Nat Acad Design; Art Students League; Beaux Arts Inst Design New York. Work: Fort Wayne Art Inst, Ind; Chrysler Collection, Norfolk; Mint Mus, NC; Harvard Club, New York; Oklahoma City Mus. Exhib: Pittsburgh Int, Nat Acad Design, New York, Chicago Am, Philadelphia Ann & Corcoran Biennial, Washington, DC, 22-33. Teaching: Instr oils & watercolors, Cape Cod Sch Art, 28- Awards: Hallgarten Prize, Nat Acad Design, 30. Mem: Boston Guild Artist; Provincetown Art Asn. Media: Oil. Dealer: Grand Central Art Gallery 40 Vanderbilt Ave New York NY 10017. Mailing Add: Provincetown MA 02657

HENSELMANN, CASPAR
SCULPTOR
b Mannheim, Ger, Mar 13, 33; US citizen. Study: Art Inst Chicago, BFA; Univ Ill Col Med, MMed-Art; Northwestern Univ; Columbia Univ. Comn: Lobby sculpture (glass, steel, oil, air), Technicon Corp, Tarrytown, NY, 68-69; multiple turbine (aluminum & stainless), Southridge Shopping Ctr, Milwaukee, Wis, 69-71; wave piece (stainless), comn by A Clayburgh, Byram, Conn, 71; glass lobby piece (oil, air), Marshall-Ilsley Bank, Milwaukee, 71. Exhib: Pa Ann Am Art, 64; Kern Co Mus, Bakersfield, Calif, 65; Stamford Mus, Conn, 67; American Abstract Artists, Riverside Mus, New York, 69; Mus Contemp Crafts, 69. Awards: Tiffany Award; Ford Found Artist in Residence, Am Fedn Arts. Mailing Add: 21 Bond St New York NY 10012

HENSLEE, JACK
PAINTER, ILLUSTRATOR
b Ft Worth, Tex, Feb 16, 42. Study: Univ Tex, Arlington. Exhib: Two-man show, Baker Gallery Fine Art, Lubbock, Tex, 74 & Panhandle Plains Mus, Canyon, Tex, 75; Soc Animal Artists Ann Show, Grand Cent Gallery, New York, 75. Mem: Soc Animal Artists. Style & Technique: Wildlife, Indians, portraits, nudes, tight realism. Media: Watercolor, Oil, Acrylic for Illustrations. Mailing Add: 4116 Eldridge Ft Worth TX 76107

HERARD, MARVIN T
SCULPTOR, EDUCATOR
b Puyallup, Wash, July 4, 29. Study: Burnley Sch Art, Seattle; Seattle Univ; Univ Wash, BA; Cranbrook Acad Art, MFA; Acad Fine Arts, Florence, Italy; Fonderia Artistica Florentina, Italy. Comn: Sculpture, Renton Pub Libr; Lemieux Libr, Seattle Univ. Exhib: Palazzo Venezia, Rome, 62; Seattle Art Mus, 65-67; Gov Exhib, State Capitol Mus, 67-69; Henry Gallery, Univ Wash, 68; Cheney Cowles Mus, Spokane, Wash, 69; plus many others. Teaching: Instr, Seattle Pub Schs, 56-58; teaching fel sculpture, Cranbrook Acad Arts, 59-60; assoc prof art & chmn fine arts dept, Seattle Univ, 60-; instr painting, Pius XII Inst Art, Florence, Italy, 62. Awards: Am Craftsmen Award, Henry Gallery, 61 & 65; Spokane Pac Northwest Exhib, 63, 64 & 66; Seattle Art Mus, 65; plus others. Mem: Nat Art Educ Asn; Am Asn Univ Prof. Mailing Add: 1131 23rd Ave E Seattle WA 98112

HERBERT, DAVID
ART DEALER, COLLECTOR
b Lakewood, NJ, Jan 1, 25. Study: Syracuse Univ, BA; Univ Mich. Pos: With Betty Parsons Gallery, 51-53, Sidney Janis Gallery, 53-59, David Herbert Gallery, 59-62 & Feigen/Herbert Gallery, 63-64; dir, Graham Gallery, 68-74; art consult & pvt dealer, 74- Specialty: Twentieth century American art. Collection: Contemporary American and Latin American art. Mailing Add: 445 E 86th St New York NY 10028

HERBERT, JAMES ARTHUR
PAINTER, FILM MAKER
b Boston, Mass, Feb 13, 38. Study: Dartmouth Col, AB(art hist, magna cum laude); Univ Colo, MFA; also with Clyfford Still, Kenzo Okada & Stan Brakhage. Work: Whitney Mus Am Art, New York; Mus Mod Art, New York; NY Univ Art Collection; Royal Film Arch Belgium; Centre Beaubourg, Paris, France. Exhib: One-man shows, Babcock Gallery, New York, 67, Poindexter Gallery, 72-74 & 76, Walker Art Ctr, Minneapolis, 73 & High Mus of Art, Atlanta, Ga, 75; Westdeutsche Kurzfilmtage, Oberhausen, Ger, 70 & 72; Cineprobe: An Evening with James Herbert, Mus Mod Art, 70-77; Festival de Toulon, France, 74; Contemporary American Painting & Sculpture 1974, Krannert Art Mus, Univ Ill, 74; Whitney Mus of Am Art, New York, 74 & 75; Am Film Festival, New York, 74 & 76; 5th Int Exp Film Competition, Knokke-Heist, Belgium, 75. Teaching: Resident artist, Yale Summer Sch Art & Music, Norfolk, Conn, 65; prof painting, Univ Ga, 62- Awards: Am Film Inst Independent Filmmakers grant, 69; Guggenheim Mem Found Fel, 71; Nat Endowment Arts Independent Artist's Grant, 75 & 78. Bibliog: David Curtis (auth), The informal vision, In: Experimental Cinema, Dell, 71; Roger Greenspun (auth), Quick-Who are David Rimmer & James Herbert?, NY Times Sunday Edition, 10/8/72; Scott Hammen (auth), James Herbert: Visions of the nude, Afterimage, 2/74. Style & Technique: Expressionist nudes. Media: Acrylic on Canvas, Watercolor, 16mm Color Film (silent). Dealer: Poindexter Gallery 1160 Fifth Ave Newark NJ 10029. Mailing Add: 243 Dearing St Athens GA 30601

HERBERT, ROBERT L
ART HISTORIAN
b Worcester, Mass, Apr 21, 29. Study: Wesleyan Univ, BA, 51; Inst Art & Archeol & Ecole du Louvre, Paris, Fulbright scholar, 51-52; Yale Univ, MA, 54, PhD, 57; Am Coun Learned Soc grant, 60; Morse fel, London, Eng, 60-61; sr faculty fel, Paris, 68-69; Guggenheim fel, Paris & New Haven, Conn, 71-72. Collections Arranged: Barbizon Revisited, Mus Fine Arts, Boston, 62-63; Neo-Impressionists & Nabis in the collection of Arthur G Altschul, Yale Univ Art Gallery, 65; Neo-Impressionism (with catalog), Solomon R Guggenheim Mus, New York, 68; Retrospective J F Millet, Mus Nat, Paris & Arts Coun, London, 75-76. Teaching: Asst art, Wesleyan Univ, 50-51; asst instr art, Yale Univ, 54-55, actg instr art, 55-56, instr art & mem comt hist, arts & lett, 56-60, asst prof hist art, 60-63, assoc prof, 63-66, prof hist art, 66-74, Robert Lehman prof hist of art, 74-, dir undergrad studies, 62-64, interim dir grad studies, 65 & 66, actg chmn, 65-66, chmn, 66-68. Awards: Frank Jewett Mather Award for Barbizon Revisited, Col Art Asn, 63; plus others. Res: 19th and 20th century French art. Publ: Auth, Barbizon Revisited (book catalog), Clark & Way, 62; auth, Seurat's Drawings, Shorewood, 63; auth, The Art Criticism of John Ruskin, Doubleday, 64; auth, Neo-Impressionism (catalog), Van Nostrand-Reinhold, 69; auth, David, Voltaire, Brutus and the French Revolution, Penguin, London & Viking, New York, 72; plus many others. Mailing Add: Beacon Rd Bethany CT 06525

HERBLOCK (HERBERT LAWRENCE BLOCK)
CARTOONIST
b Chicago, Ill, Oct 13, 09. Study: Lake Forest Col, 27-29, hon LLD, 57; Rutgers Univ, hon LLD, 63; Art Inst Chicago. Comn: Designed US postage stamp commemorating 175th anniversary Bill of Rights, 66. Pos: Ed cartoonist, Chicago Daily News, 29-33, NEA Serv, 33-43 & Washington Post, 46- Awards: Pulitzer Prize, 42; Capitol Press Club Award, 63; Bill of Rights Award, 66. Mem: Fel Am Acad Arts & Sci. Publ: Auth, The Herblock Book, 52; Herblock Special for Today, 58; Herblock's Here & Now, 62; Straight Herblock, 64; plus others. Mailing Add: Washington Post Washington DC 20005

HERFIELD, PHYLLIS ANNE
ILLUSTRATOR, PRINTMAKER
Study: Art Students League, with Ernest Fiene, 65; Tyler Sch Art, Temple Univ, BFA, 69, Rome, Italy, 67-68. Comn: Etchings, comn by Michael Steinberg, Kornblee Gallery, New York, 76; multimedia canvas (5ft x 6ft), 112 Greene St Gallery, New York, 77; etching, Fred Dietzel, Orion Gallery, New York, 78. Exhib: Mus Mod Art, Paris, France, 75; Kathryn Markell Gallery, New York, 76; one-person shows, Ellen Sragow Ltd, 76 & Orion Gallery, New York, 77; Spectrum Gallery, New York, 77-; Inst Contemp Art, Philadelphia, 77. Pos: Illusr, New York Times, Esquire, New York Mag, New Times, Pyschology Today, 77-78. Bibliog: Rev in Soho News, 76 & Print Collector's Newsletter, 77; Jim Quinn (auth), article in Philadelphia Mag, 77. Mem: Illusr Guild. Style & Technique: Airy, figurative, fluid kind of motion; surreal sense of color; subject matter often deals with motion, sometimes mythical. Media: Watercolor, Pastel; Mixed-Media; Colored Pencil. Dealer: Fred Deitzel 1168 Lexington Ave New York NY 10021; Bill Goff 30 W 57th St New York NY 10019. Mailing Add: 160 Prince St New York NY 10012

HERFINDAHL, LLOYD MANFORD
PAINTER
b Emmons, Minn, June 15, 22. Study: Minneapolis Col Art & Design; also with Adolph Dehn, New York. Work: Montbard Mus Fine Arts, France; Holy Land Mus, Los Angeles; Bethany Col; Police Acad Mus, New York, NY; Stevens Co Hist Mus, Morris, Minn; Mid-East Mus Div, Eye-O-Graphic Ctr, Minneapolis. Comn: Portrait of Percy Grainger, Lutheran Sentinel Hq, Bethany Col, 67, portrait of Karl Rolvaag, 67 & portrait of King Olav V of Norway, 68; The City (mural), Eye-O-Graphic Ctr, 68; Law & Government (mural), City of Albert Lea, Minn, 70. Exhib: Salon des Independents, Grand Palais, Paris, France, 72; Bertrand Russell Peace Found Centenary, Rotunda Gallery, London, 72; Acad Soc Liberal Arts, Paris, 72; Salon de l'Ecole due Thouet, Thovars, France, 73; Mus Mod Art, Paris, 74. Awards: Queen Fabiola Gold Medal, Belgio-Hispanica, Helder Palace, Belg, 73, l'Order de Chevalier, 74; Silver Medal, Soc Encouragement Progress, Paris, 74; Gold Medal, Grand Prix de Humanitaire, Paris, 77. Bibliog: Michel Frantz (auth), Elle et Eux-La Femme, Christian Halls, 72; Vallobra (auth), L'Art Contemporain et l'Art Fantastique, Draps, Wemmel, Belg, 75. Mem: Minn Artists Asn (foreign corresp, 75-76); Int Arts Guild, Monte Carlo, Monaco (foreign corresp, 69-, co-pres, Int Grand Prix, comdr & int cult counr); Asn Belgo-Hispanica, Bruxelles, Belg; Int Platform Asn; fel Int Biog Asn; Acad Soc Liberal Arts; Soc Encouragement Progress. Style & Technique: Multiple image; actual fragments of artifacts embedded in pigments on canvas. Media: Oil, Watercolor, Acrylic. Mailing Add: 809 John Farry Pl Albert Lea MN 56007

HERIC, JOHN F
SCULPTOR
b Reno, Nev, Feb 28, 42. Study: Ariz State Univ, with Ben Goo, BFA; Southern Ill Univ, Carbondale, with Milt Sullivan, MFA, 65. Work: City of Scottsdale, Ariz; Grossmont Col; Ariz State Univ; Mus Northern Ariz, Flagstaff; Mesa Community Col, Ariz. Comn: Steel sculpture, Ridgewood High Sch, 64; courtyard, Sopori Sch, Sahaurita Sch Dist, Ariz, 71. Exhib: St Paul Mus Art, Minn, 65; one-man shows, Univ Wis-Milwaukee, 66, Grossmont Col, 69 & Elaine Horwitch Gallery, Scottsdale, 74; Southwestern Invitational, Yuma, Ariz, 69-74. Teaching: Instr sculpture, Wis State Univ-Platteville, 65-67; vis lectr sculpture, Ariz State Univ, 67-69; lectr sculpture, Univ Ariz, 69-; vis artist, Grossmont Col, 74-75. Awards: Best of Show, Ariz Designer Craftsmen, 68; First Award Sculpture, Ariz Ann, 68; Purchase Award, Southwestern Invitational, 71, 72 & 74. Style & Technique: Contemporary style combining and contrasting mixed media in an image based on primitive art and religion. Media: Stone, Plastics. Dealer: Elaine Horwitch Gallery 4200 N Marshall Way Scottsdale AZ 85251. Mailing Add: 3622 Camino Blanco Rte 5 Tucson AZ 85718

HERMAN, ALAN DAVID
DESIGNER, WRITER
b Kew Gardens, NY, Mar 8, 47. Study: Pratt Inst Sch Art & Design, Ida D Haskell scholarship & BFA(cum laude), 69. Comn: Tourist promotion & info guides, Southern Calif Tourist Coun, 71-75; promotional graphics prog, McCulloch Corp, Lake Havasu City, Ariz, 73; consumer advert promotion, Carrier Air Conditioning Co, Los Angeles, 73-; entire line soaps & beauty aids, Organic Aid Co, Los Angeles, 74-; med insurance commun & marketing prog, Johnson & Higgins, Los Angeles, 76- Exhib: 1972 Exhibit of Best Advertising & Editorial Art in the West, 72; Los Angeles Graphics Expo, 73; IAM Graphics Exhib, New York, 74; Indust Graphics Int, San Jose, Calif, 77. Pos: Pres & creative dir, Alan Herman & Assoc, Los Angeles, 70- Awards: Los Angeles Art Dirs Club Award, 72; Top Package of the Yr, Print Mag, 76; IGI Distinctive Merit, 77. Mem: Art Dir Club Los Angeles; Los Angeles Co Mus Art. Style & Technique: Bold visual concepts depicted through wide range of visual styles. Mailing Add: 3601 Chevy Chase Dr Glendale CA 91206

HERMAN, JOYCE ELAINE
ART DEALER, COLLECTOR
b Milwaukee, Wis, 45. Pos: Dir, Hansen Galleries, New York. Specialty: Contemporary paintings, drawings and sculpture. Collection: Contemporary work with emphasis on photorealism and surrealism. Mailing Add: c/o Hansen Galleries 70-72 Wooster St New York NY 10012

HERMAN, LLOYD ELDRED
MUSEUM DIRECTOR
b Corvallis, Ore, Mar 19, 36. Study: Ore State Univ; Univ Ore; Am Univ, BA. Collections Arranged: Eight exhibs inaugurating the Renwick Gallery, Smithsonian Inst, Washington, DC. Pos: Prog mgr, Off of Dir-Gen of Mus, Smithsonian Inst, 66-71, dir, Renwick Gallery, 71- Mem: Am Crafts Coun; hon mem Am Soc Interior Designers; Nat Trust for Hist Preserv; Soc Archit Historians; Victorian Soc Am. Interest: 20th century crafts and industrial design. Publ: Co-auth, Woodenworks (exhib catalog), 72; auth, Form and Fire: Natzler Ceramics 1939-1972, 73, auth, A Modern Consciousness: D J De Pree and Florence Knoll, 75, contribr, The Designs of Raymond Loewy, 75 & contribr, Craft Multiples, 75, Smithsonian Inst. Mailing Add: Smithsonian Inst Washington DC 20560

HERMAN, SUSAN L
PAINTER, PRINTMAKER
b Portland, Ore, Feb 22, 42. Study: Calif State Univ, Humboldt, BA & MA. Exhib: 63rd Tex Nat, Austin, 74; one-person show, Grandview Gallery, Los Angeles, Calif, 75; Tex, Dept of Art, Univ Tex, El Paso, 75; Fragmentation, Calif State Univ, Chico, 76; Marietta Nat, Grover M Herman, Ohio, 78. Teaching: Asst prof drawing, Univ Utah, 73-74; asst prof painting, drawing & printmaking, Calif State Univ, Fresno, 74- Mem: Col Art Asn; Women's Art Caucus; Northern Calif Women's Caucus. Style & Technique: Drawing in photorealism, using some collage and mixed-media. Media: Drawing in Charcoal; Acrylic. Mailing Add: Calif State Univ Cedar & Shaw Fresno CA 93740

HERMAN, VIC
PAINTER, ILLUSTRATOR—CHILDREN'S BOOKS
b Fall River, Mass. Study: Yale Puppeteers, Los Angeles, Calif, apprentice, with Harry Burnett; Art Students League, with George Bridgeman; New York Com Illus Sch, with Lu Kimmel; Columbia Univ, with Ed Johnson & Dr Samuel Penchansky; Mt Sinai Hosp, New York. Work: Vic Herman Collection, Syracuse Univ; Mex-Norteamericano Cult Inst, Guadalajara, Mex; Repub Mex Gallery, Los Angeles; Galeria Zamora, Veracruz, Mex; Galleria Vic Herman, Del Mar, Calif; plus others. Comn: Many Faces of Mexico, US Embassy, Mexico City & Govt Mex, US & Mex, 60; Lowrey Pines Bluff (painting), City of Del Mar, 72. Exhib: One-man shows, Munic Gallery, Veracruz, 67, Foreign Corresp Gallery, Mexico City, Mex, 68; Chicago Press Club Gallery, 72 & 76, US Embassy, Mexico City, 73 & Calif Mus Sci & Indust, 74; plus many others. Pos: Asst art dir, Warner Bros Studios, New York, 40-43; artist-field corresp, Army News Serv, US, 43-46; pres & prod chief, Vic Herman Prod, 50-60; art juror, Southern Calif Expos 74; freelance illusr & corresp, New York & Mex, 50- Awards: US Army Medal for Creation of Winnie the Wac, 46; Children's Book Coun Showcase Award, 76; Printing Indust of Am Grafic Art Award, 77. Bibliog: Cal Whipple (auth), Soldier artist makes a Wac his heroine, Life, 45; Sally Cass (auth), US artist portrays the Mexican feeling, Mexico City News, 68; Frederic Whitaker (auth), Vic Herman, ambassador with a brush, Am Artist Mag, 74. Mem: Chicago Press Club; Mexico City Foreign Corresp Club; Soc Illusr; La Jolla Art Asn; Soc Children's Book Writers, Calif. Style & Technique: Culture and heritage of the Mexican people through realistic multi-media. Media: Mixed Media. Publ: Auth & illusr, Winnie the Wac, McKay, 45; auth, My Days Are Made of Butterflies, Holt Rinehart & Winston, 70 & auth & illusr, Sunday in Zamora Park, 72, Holt, Rinehart & Winston; illusr, God and Mr Gomez, Readers Digest Condensed Books, 75; auth & illusr, Juanito's Railroad in the Sky, Golden Books, 76. Mailing Add: RR1 M-25 South Lane Del Mar CA 92014

HERNANDEZ, ANTHONY LOUIS
PHOTOGRAPHER
b Los Angeles, Calif, July 7, 47. Study: E Los Angeles Col, 66-70; Ctr of the Eye, Aspen, Colo, 69, with Lee Friedlander. Work: Univ Calif at Davis; Mus Mod Art, New York; Bibliot Nat, Paris, France; Int Mus Photog, George Eastman House, Rochester, NY. Comn: Photographs, Corcoran Gallery of Art, Washington, DC, 76. Exhib: Calif Photogr, Pasadena Art Mus & Oakland Mus Art, Calif, 70; The Crowded Vacancy, Pasadena Art Mus & San Francisco Mus Art, Calif, 71; The Nation's Capital in Photographs, Corcoran Gallery of Art, 76; Unposed Portrait, Whitney Mus Am Art, New York, 77; Contemp Am Photog Works, Mus Fine Arts, Houston, Tex, 77. Awards: Ferguston Grant, Friends of Photog, Carmel, Calif, 72; Nat Endowment for the Arts Photog Fel, 75 & 78. Bibliog: Douglas Davis (auth), Sweeping Up American, Newsweek, 7/12/76. Style & Technique: Black and white photographs. Mailing Add: 255 1/2 S Carondelet Los Angeles CA 90057

HERNANDEZ, MARIA LAGUNES
See Lagunes, Maria

HERNANDEZ-CRUZ, LUIS
PAINTER, EDUCATOR
b San Juan, PR. Study: Univ PR, BA; Am Univ, MA, with Ben Summerford. Work: Chase Manhattan Bank, New York; Ponce Mus Art, PR; Mus Am, Madrid, Spain; Univ PR Mus; Inst PR Cult Mus. Comn: Murals, PR Med Ctr, 64 & 65; mural, Santa Juanita Elem Sch, 68. Exhib: Arte Actual de America y Espana, Madrid, Spain, 63; Esso Salon of Young Artists, Washington, DC, 64; 1st Salon of Pan-Am Art, Cali, Colombia, 65; 2nd Biennial, Coltejer-Medellin, Colombia, 70; 1st & 2nd Biennial of Latin Am Prints, San Juan, 70 & 72. Teaching: Prof painting, Univ PR, Rio Piedras, 68, assoc dir dept fine arts, 68- Pos: Actg dir univ mus, Univ PR, Rio Piedras, 71. Awards: First Prize in Painting, Inst PR Cult, 63; First Prize, Esso Art Contest, 64; Nat Prize, 2nd Biennial Latin Am Prints, 72. Bibliog: Efrain Perez Chanis (auth), El arte abstracto de Luis Hernandez-Cruz, Revista Urbe, 7/64; Pintores Puertorriquenos Hernandez-Cruz, Ed Artisticas de PR, 67; Marta Traba (auth), El abstracto que se salva, Artes Visuales, 71; plus others. Mem: Ateneo Puertorriqueno (dir plastic arts sect, 67-71). Media: Oil, Silkscreen. Mailing Add: Dept of Art Univ of PR Rio Piedras PR 00931

HERO, PETER DECOURCY
ART ADMINISTRATOR, ART HISTORIAN
b Washington, DC, Sept 10, 42. Study: Williams Col, Williamstown, Mass, MA(art hist), 75, with George Heard Hamilton; Stanford Univ, Calif, MBA, 66. Collections Arranged: The Elegant Academics (joint exhib of 19th century Fr paintings; contribr, catalogue), Clark Art Inst, Williamstown, Mass & Wadsworth Atheneum, Hartford, Conn, 75. Pos: Exec dir, Ore Arts Comn, 75-; ed, Ore Arts Newsletter, 75- Awards: Kress Found Fel, 6/75. Mem: Univ Ore Art Mus (mem exhib comt, 75-); Western State Arts Found (bd dirs, 75-); Nat Assembly State Arts Agencies (bd dirs, 77-80); Nat Endowment for the Arts (mem theatre panel, 76-78; consult, City Spirit Prog, 76-). Res: Influence of Japanese prints upon evolution of perspective and space in Edgar Degas' work. Publ: Contribr, article in NW Arts, 76; contribr, %For Art: new legislation can integrate art and architecture, Western State Arts Found, 76. Mailing Add: 835 Summer St Salem OR 97301

HEROLD, DONALD G
MUSEUM DIRECTOR
b Brooklyn, NY, June 8, 27. Study: State Univ NY Albany, BA. Pos: Dir, Davenport Mus; dir, Polk Pub Mus, Lakeland, Fla; dir, Daytona Beach Mus Arts & Sci, Fla; dir, Charleston Mus, presently. Mem: Assoc Am Asn Mus. Mailing Add: Charleston Mus 121 Rutledge Ave Charleston SC 29401

HERPST, MARTHA JANE
PAINTER
b Titusville, Pa. Study: Pa Acad Fine Arts, 32; Grand Cent Sch Art, New York, with Wayman Adams, Edmund Greacen, Harvey Dunn & Georg Lober; also with Guy Pene Du Bois. Work: Nat Arts Club, New York; Titusville Woman's Club; Univ Pittsburgh, Titusville; Gannon Col, Erie, Pa; Titusville Masonic Lodge. Comn: Portrait of Charles T Evans, Titusville Masonic Lodge, 43; portraits of Mrs Edgar Doty & Mrs C Burgess, comn by Edgar Doty, Titusville Recreation Ctr, 54; portrait of Archbishop John Mark Gannon, comn by Rev C H Cooper for Gannon Col, 58. Exhib: Nat Arts Club, New York, 33-72; Butler Art Inst, Youngstown, Ohio, 38 & 45; Am Artists Prof League Grand Nat, New York, 46-70; Ogunquit Art Asn, Maine, 51-61; Catharine Lorillard Wolfe Art Club, New York, 54-62. Teaching: Instr art, St Joseph Acad High Sch, Titusville, 55-69; pvt instr painting, 70- Awards: Grand Cent Sch Art Medal, 33. Mem: Nat Arts Club; Am Artists Prof League. Style & Technique: Realist, impressionistic; oils both directly & in glazes. Media: Oil, Watercolor. Mailing Add: 118 W Main St Titusville PA 16354

HERR, RICHARD JOSEPH
SCULPTOR, INSTRUCTOR
b Sheboygan, Wis, Jan 17, 37. Study: Layton Sch Art, Milwaukee; Marquette Univ; Univ Wis-Milwaukee; also with Oscar Binder, Stuttgart, Ger. Work: Borg-Warner Collection, Chicago; Univ Wis-LaCrosse; MaDonna High Sch, Milwaukee; Prairie Sch, Racine, Wis. Comn: Relief sculpture, Northern Precision Casting, Lake Geneva, Wis, 73; door, Nafziger & Assocs, Lake Geneva, 75. Exhib: Hyde Park Art Ctr, Chicago, 72; Critic's Choice Show, Chicago Art Inst, 72; one-man show, Wustum Mus, Racine, 73; 1st Chicago Sculpture Invitational, Fed Bldg, 74; 3-D '75, Union League Club, Chicago, 75. Teaching: Instr art & chmn dept, Col Racine, 71-72; instr art, Prairie Sch, 71-; instr 3-D design, Univ Wis-Parkside, 73-74. Pos: Owner-dir, Art Independent Gallery, Lake Geneva, 68-; Johnson Wax Found grant sculptor in residence, Prairie Sch, 70-71. Awards: Award for Sculpture, Va Beach Invitational, 71; Chicago Tribune Duo Critic's Award, Chicago Art Inst, 72; Award for Sculpture, Old Orchard Invitational, Chicago, 73. Mem: Southern Asn Sculptors; Am Int Sculptors; Wis Art Educ Asn (bd mem). Style & Technique: Non-objective and social commentary. Media: Aluminum, Resin. Publ: Contribr, Sculpture Casting, 72, Collage and Assemblage, 73 & Soft Sculpture and Related Soft Art, 75, Crown; contribr, Playboy, 74. Dealer: Loft-On Strand 2118 1/2 Strand Galveston TX 77550. Mailing Add: c/o Art Independent Gallery 706 Main St Lake Geneva WI 53147

HERRERA, CARMEN
PAINTER
b Havana, Cuba, May 31, 15; US citizen. Study: Studio Federico Edelman, Havana; Marymount Col; Paris, France; Sch Archit, Havana; Art Students League. Work: Havana Mus; Cintas Collection. Exhib: Lyceum, Havana, 51; Art Cubain Contemporain, Mus Mod Art, Paris, 51; Geometric Classic & Romantic Painting, Jerrold Morris Gallery, Toronto, 62; Trabia Gallery, 63; Ctr Interam Rels, 68 & 75. Awards: Cintas Found Fel, 66 & 68; Creative Artists Pub Serv, 77-78. Mem: Women in Arts. Style & Technique: Hard-edge geometric painting. Mailing Add: 37 E 19th St New York NY 10003

HERRERA, RAUL OTHON
PAINTER
b Mexico City, Mex, Jan 16, 41. Study: Univ Nacional Autonoma de Mex, BA(polit sci, archit, philos); Iberoamerican Univ, Mex, with Matias Goertiz; also with Rudolfo Nieto, Mexican painter in Paris, France. Work: Mus Brussels, Belg; Mus Mod Art, Mex; Mus Nottingham, Eng; Casa de las Campanas, Cuernavaca. Exhib: Latin American Art, Mod Art Mus, Paris, 64; Biennial, Paris, 66; Mexican Art, Mus Tokyo, 67; one-man show, Palacio Nacional de Bellas Artes, Mexico City, 67 & Mus Mod Art, Mexico City, 75. Collections Arranged: Mexican Art, Montreal, Ont, 67; Latin American Art, Mus Nottingham, Eng, 67 & Mus Hemel, Hempstead, Eng, 67. Bibliog: Jorge A Manrique (auth), Raul Herrera, Revista de la Univ Nat de Mexico, 66; Luis Cardoza y Aragon (auth), Nuevos Pintores, Arte Contemp Mex, 74; Gioconda Tomassi (auth), Raul Herrera the Painter (film-documentary), Subsecretaria de Radiodifusion, Gov Mex, 75. Media: Collage, Acrylic on Canvas. Publ: Illusr, Histories of the Hermit Abdala, Comic Book, Prometeo Libre, Mex, 75 & 76. Dealer: Fabian Aldama Casa de las Campanas Cuernavaca Mexico. Mailing Add: c/o Galeria Pecanins Hamburgo 103 Mexico 6 DF Mexico

HERRING, JAN(ET MANTEL)
PAINTER, WRITER
b Havre, Mont, May 17, 23. Study: Northern State Teachers Col; also painting with Frederic Taubes. Work: Grumbacher Collection, New York; Lubbock Art Ctr, Tex; Univ Idaho, Pocatello; Roswell Mus, NMex. Exhib: One-man shows, El Paso Mus Art, Santa Fe Mus Art, Tulsa Art Ctr, Roswell Mus & Brigham Young Univ. Teaching: Pvt instr. Bibliog: F Taubes (auth), article in Am Artist Mag, 55; aritcle in La Rev Mod, 61; article in House Beautiful, 64. Publ: Auth, The Painters Composition Handbook, 71 & The Painter's Complete Portrait and Figure Handbook, 77, Poor-Henry Publ Co. Mailing Add: Box 156 Clint TX 79836

HERROLD, CLIFFORD H
EDUCATOR, CRAFTSMAN
b Luther, Okla. Study: Cent State Univ (Okla), BA; Univ Northern Colo, MA; Stanford Univ, EdD; Inst Design, Chicago; Sch Am Craftsmen, Rochester, NY. Exhib: Craftsmen USA, Milwaukee, Wis, 66; Craft Commitment, Rochester, Minn, 70; Northwestern Craftsmen Invitational, Brookings, SDak, 74 & 77; Int Crafts Exhib, Duluth, Minn, 75 & 77; Iowa Designer Craftsmen Invitational, Cedar Rapids, 75; Beaux Arts Designer Craftsmen, 77; plus others. Teaching: Prof jewelry, Univ Northern Iowa, 56- Mem: Am Crafts Coun; Iowa Designer Craftsmen. Style & Technique: Fabricated and cast jewelry using precious and semi-precious metals, stones, and other materials. Media: Metal. Mailing Add: 2810 Walnut St Cedar Falls IA 50613

HERSCHLER, DAVID
SCULPTOR
b Brooklyn, NY, Mar 1, 40. Study: Acad Belli Arte, Perugia, Italy, 60; Univ Rome, 60; Cornell Univ, BArch, 62; Claremont Grad Sch, MFA, 67. Work: Joseph H Hirshhorn Found, Washington, DC; La Jolla Mus Art, Calif; Storm King Art Ctr, Mountainville, NY; Palm Springs Mus, Calif. Comn: Sculptures, comn by Mr & Mrs N S Walbridge, La Jolla, 70, Sigmund Edelstone, Chicago, 71, Mr & Mrs J W Constance, Santa Barbara, 72, Mr & Mrs Marvin Smalley, Beverly Hills, 72 & Storm King Art Ctr, 72. Teaching: Instr art, San Jocquil Delta Col, Stockton, Calif, 67-69. Media: Stainless Steel, Gold. Dealer: Percival Gallery 210 Shops Bldg Des Moines IA 50309; Forum Gallery 1018 Madison Ave New York NY 10021. Mailing Add: c/o Ankrum Gallery 657 N La Cienega Blvd Los Angeles CA 90069

HERSHBERG, ISRAEL
PAINTER, INSTRUCTOR
b Linz, Austria, Nov 7, 48. Study: Brooklyn Mus Art Sch, 66-68; Pratt Inst, BFA, 72; State Univ NY Albany, MA, 73. Exhib: One-man shows, Prince Street Gallery, New York, 70 & 71 & Jacobs Ladder Gallery, Washington, DC, 74; A Sense of Place: The Artist and the American Land, Joslyn Art Mus, Omaha, Sheldon Mem Art Gallery, Lincoln, Nebr & Arts Alliance, 73; Current Trends in Contemporary American Art, Washington Co Mus Fine Arts, Hagerstown, Md, 74. Teaching: Instr painting & drawing, Md Inst Col Art, 73- Mem:

Alliance Figurative Artists. Style & Technique: Representational, landscape and figures. Media: Oil. Mailing Add: 103 W Monument St Baltimore MD 21201

HERSHMAN, LYNN LESTER
SCULPTOR
b June 17, 41. Study: Case Western Reserve Univ, BS, 63; Calif State Univ, San Francisco, MA, 72; Calif Col Arts & Crafts, Univ Calif, Los Angeles; Ohio Univ; Otis Art Inst; Cleveland Inst Art. Work: Nat Collection Fine Arts, Smithsonian Inst; Cleveland Inst Art; City of San Francisco Collection Art; Calif State Cols Collection Art; Richmond Art Ctr; plus other pub & pvt collections. Comn: Art poster, San Francisco Mus, 69; cover for Robopaths, Penguin Books, 72. Exhib: Butler Inst Am Art, Youngstown, Ohio; Ball State Univ Painting Exhib; Nat Sculpture Exhib, San Diego Mus Art, 72; Nat Sculpture Show, Del Mar Col, 73; Univ Art Mus, Berkeley, 74; Univ Nev, Las Vegas, 75; Bronx Mus, NY, 75; one-man shows, Stefanotty Gallery, New York, 75 & Circus Circus, Las Vegas, Nev, 75 plus many others. Teaching: Instr, Cleveland Mus Art, 62-63; vis asst prof drawing, Calif Col Arts & Crafts, 72-73, assoc prof, 74; instr, Melville Col, Scotland, 73. Pos: Corresp ed, Artweek, 71-73; coordr, Insights, San Francisco Mus Art, 72-74; gallery curator, Walnut Creek Civic Art Ctr, Calif, 74-76; assoc coordr, Christo's Running Fence Project, 74-76; invited artist, Int Inst Experimental Printmaking, Santa Cruz, Calif, 75. Awards: Bates & Springer Award, 62; Purchase Prize, San Francisco Art Festival, 69; Purchase Prize, Olive Hyde Drawing Competition, 72. Bibliog: Peter Selz (auth), 6 artists in search of a definition of San Francisco, Art News, 6/73 & Art in Am, 3/74; Jan Butterfield (auth), Pacific Sun, 4/74; Alfred Frankenstein (auth), Macabre roome of wax ladies, San Francisco Chronicle, 10/13/74; plus many others. Style & Technique: Surrealist, wax, sound and environment. Publ: Auth, Harold Paris, the Berkeley Years, Artweek, Vol 3, No 21; auth, Edinburgh as Oz, Vol 186, No 959 & Interview with Dennis Oppenheim, 11/73, Studio Int; co-auth, Toward light and space, City Mag, Vol 1, No 7; auth, Forming a Sculptured/Drama in Manhattan, Marginal Arts & Stefanotty Gallery, 75; plus others. Mailing Add: 3007 Jackson San Francisco CA 94115

HERSTAND, ARNOLD
PAINTER, ART ADMINISTRATOR
b New York, NY, Sept 10, 25. Study: Yale Univ, BFA; Columbia Univ, MA; Art Students League; Pratt Inst; also with Fernand Leger, Paris & T Munro. Work: Gen Mills Corp; Dayton-Hudson Corp; Northwestern Nat Life Ins Corp, Minneapolis. Exhib: Whitney Mus Am Art Ann, New York, 48; Everson Mus Art Ann, Syracuse, NY, 55-62; Munson-Williams-Proctor Inst Ann, Utica, NY, 55-62; Walker Art Ctr Biennial, Minneapolis, 64; Minneapolis Inst Arts Biennial, 66-68. Teaching: Lectr, City Col New York, 52-54; instr, Colgate Univ, 54-57, asst prof, 57-62, assoc prof music & visual art, 62-63; vis artist, Cornell Univ, 63. Pos: Dir, Minneapolis Col Art & Design, 63-69, pres, 69-74; pres, San Francisco Art Inst, 74-; consult, Danforth Regional Conf, Univ Wash, Art Inst Chicago Bd Trustees & State Univ NY Albany; hon trustee, Osaka Univ Arts, 74. Awards: Littauer Found Grant, 57-58; Danforth Found Grant, 60; Ford Found Fel, Harvard Univ, 58-59. Mem: Ben & Abby Grey Found, St Paul (bd dirs); Union Independent Cols Art (chmn bd, 74-75); Col Art Asn Am; assoc Am Asn Univ Prof; Nat Asn Schs Art (bd dirs, 71-72). Publ: Auth, articles in Art J, Eastern Arts Quart, Art News & J Gen Educ. Mailing Add: 800 Chestnut St San Francisco CA 94133

HERTZBERG, ROSE
PAINTER, PRINTMAKER
b Passaic, NJ, Dec 17, 12. Study: With Ben Benn; Hans Hoffman Art Sch; Art Students League, with Vaclav Vytlacil & Will Barnet; New York Graphics Workshop; Rockland Community Col; Fairleigh Dickinson Univ Art Seminars. Work: Edward Williams Col, Hackensack, NJ; Rockland Community Col, Suffern, NY; Bloomfield Col; Broadway Bank & Trust Co, Paterson, NJ; Hackensack Pub Libr & Ramsey Pub Libr, NJ; plus numerous pvt collections. Comn: Numerous pvt commissions. Exhib: Am Watercolor Soc, New York, 67, 69 & 71; Trenton State Mus, NJ, 69-71; Painters & Sculptors Soc NJ, Jersey City, 69-77; NJ Watercolor Soc, Morristown, 71; Nat Asn Women Artists, 71-77; one-woman shows, Hertzl Inst, New York, NY, Rockland Ctr for Arts, Lucinda Gallery, NJ, Bergen Community Mus, NJ, Centro des Artes, Mijas, Spain & others. Awards: Mary S Litt Award, Am Watercolor Soc, 67; Freylinghuysen Award, NJ Watercolor Soc, 70; Putnam Mem Award, Nat Asn Women Artists, 71 & 77; Awards, Painters & Sculptors Soc, 71 & 76; plus others. Mem: Life mem Art Students League; Nat Asn Women Artists; Mod Artists Guild; Painters & Sculptors Soc NJ; Artists Equity Asn NJ. Style & Technique: Employ oil and turpentine to create open layered areas which combine to make large organic forms; work is handled flat, with no easel. Media: Oil, Watercolor; Collage. Mailing Add: 27 Buckingham Dr Ramsey NJ 07446

HERTZMAN, GAY MAHAFFY
ART ADMINISTRATOR, ART HISTORIAN
b West Liberty, Iowa, Jan 22, 31. Study: Univ Iowa, Iowa City, BA, 60; Univ NC, Chapel Hill, MS(libr sci), 65, MA(art hist), 69. Pos: Registr-librn, NC Mus Art, Raleigh, 61-64; actg cur, Wm Hayes Ackland Art Ctr, Univ NC, Chapel Hill, 67-69; asst cur & cur European painting, NC Mus Art, 71-75, head collections res & publ, 75- Res: Western European art. Publ: Auth, Catalogue of the Collection: William Hayes Ackland Memorial Art Center, Chapel Hill, 71; auth, Corporate gifts, North Carolina, XXXI: 23f. Mailing Add: 1615 Ambleside Dr Raleigh NC 27605

HERZBRUN, HELENE MCKINSEY
PAINTER, INSTRUCTOR
b Chicago, Ill. Study: Univ Chicago, BA; Art Inst of Chicago; Am Univ, Washington, DC, with Jack Tworkov. Work: Nat Collection of Fine Arts, Washington, DC; Watkins Gallery, Am Univ; Phillips Gallery, Washington, DC. Comn: Tapestry (with Gloria Finn), Harcourt-Brace Publ Co, New York, 63. Exhib: Biennial Exhib, Corcoran Gallery of Art, Washington, DC, 53; 12 Washington Artists, Univ Ky Mus, 58; one-person shows, 8 exhibs, Jefferson Place Gallery, Washington, DC, 58-74, Poindexter Gallery, New York, 60 & Washington Room/Helene Herzbrun, Corcoran Gallery of Art, 76; Washington/20 Yrs, Baltimore Mus of Art, Md, 59 & 70; US Info Agency (Europ traveling show), 60-65; Ann Pa Acad of Art, Philadelphia Art in Embassies Prog (US State Dept traveling exhib), 72-; Drawing Show/Washington Proj for the Arts, DC, 75. Teaching: Prof painting, Am Univ, 59-, chmn art dept, 76- Style & Technique: Painterly abstraction. Media: Oil, acrylic. Mailing Add: 3539 Quebec St NW Washington DC 20016

HESKETH
SCULPTOR
b Maine. Study: Wellesley Col, BA; also with John Flannagan & Ahron Ben-Schmuel. Work: San Francisco Mus Art; Addison Gallery Am Art, Andover, Mass; Atlanta Mus Art, Ga. Exhib: Detroit Inst Art; Whitney Mus Am Art, New York; Art Inst Chicago; Carnegie Inst, Pittsburgh; Pa Acad Fine Arts, Philadelphia; plus others. Mem: Artists Equity Asn. Mailing Add: Bluehills Studio RD 1 Kempton PA 19529

HESS, EMIL JOHN
PAINTER, SCULPTOR
b Willock, Pa, Sept 25, 13. Study: Duquesne Univ, 38-39; Art Inst Pittsburgh, 46-49; Brooklyn Mus Art Sch, 50-51; NY Univ, 59. Work: Smithsonian Inst, Washington, DC; Pa State Mus, Harrisburg; Rockefeller Found, New York; Montclair Art Mus, NJ; Phillip Johnson Collection, NY. Exhib: Nat Acad Design, New York, 50; one-man show, Betty Parsons Gallery, 51, 52, 68 & 70; Metrop Mus Art, New York, 53; Stable Gallery, New York, 53 & 55; Mus Mod Art Traveling Exhibs, 59. Bibliog: New means for moderns, Life, 54; Emily Genauer (auth), Beatnik sculp in big museum show, New York Herald Tribune, 59; Sounds of Hess sculpture, WBAI, New York, 70. Mem: Life mem Art Students League; Am Fedn Arts; Int Platform Asn. Media: Oil, Metal. Dealer: Betty Parsons Galleries 24 W 57th St New York NY 10019. Mailing Add: 130 W Tenth St New York NY 10014

HESS, JOYCE
ART LIBRARIAN
b Shreveport, La. Study: Tex Christian Univ, Ft Worth, BA, 66; Grad Sch of Libr Sci, Univ Tex, Austin, MLS, 69. Pos: Art libr, Univ Tex, Austin, 67- Mem: Art Libr Soc NAm. Interest: Painting. Mailing Add: 908 Red Bud Trail Austin TX 78746

HESS, STANLEY WILLIAM
ART LIBRARIAN
b Bremerton, Wash, July 9, 39. Study: Olympic Community Col, 58-60; Univ Wash, BA, 64 & grad work, 67-71; Case Western Reserve Univ, MSLS, 76. Pos: Supvr, Photog & Slide Libr, Seattle Art Mus, Wash, 64-73; assoc librn photographs & slides, Cleveland Mus Art, 73- Mem: Art Libr Soc NAm; Col Art Asn Am; Am Mus Asn; Spec Libr Asn (Picture Div, pres elect & pres, 78-79). Interest: Publishing, lecturing and teaching about the visual resources in the fine arts. Publ: Auth, Annotated Bibliography of Slide Library Literature, Sch Info Studies, Syracuse Univ, 2/78; co-auth, with A Hoffberg, et al, Directory of Art Libraries, Neal/Schuman Publ, 5/78. Mailing Add: 2539 N Moreland Blvd B-11 Shaker Heights OH 44120

HESS, THOMAS B
ART CRITIC, WRITER
b Rye, NY, July 14, 20. Study: Yale Univ, BA. Retrospective Exhibitions Directed: De Kooning (with catalog), Mus Mod Art, New York, 68, Newman (with catalog), 71; Tate Gallery, London; Grand Palais, Paris; plus others. Pos: Assoc ed, Art News, 46-50, managing ed, 50-65, ed, 65-72; art critic, Le Monde, Paris, 66-72; art critic, New York Mag, 72- Res: Modern painting and sculpture. Publ: Auth, Abstract Painting Background and American Phase, 51; auth, Willem de Kooning, New York Graphic Soc, 59; auth, Barnett Newman, Walker & Co, 69 & Metrop Mus of Art, 74; auth, Reinhardt Cartoons, 72; auth, Siskind, 76. ed, Woman As Sex Object, 72. Mailing Add: 19 Beekman Pl New York NY 10022

HESSE, DON
CARTOONIST
b Belleville, Ill, Feb 20, 18. Study: St Louis Sch Fine Arts, Wash Univ, 36-37. Work: Libr of Cong, Washington, DC; also in pvt collections. Pos: Artist-photogr, Belleville Daily News-Democrat, 35-40; mem art staff, St Louis Globe-Democrat, 46-, ed cartoonist, 51-; nat syndicated cartoonist, Los Angeles Times Syndicate; operator, prof photog studio. Awards: Freedoms Found Awards, 54 & 64; Christopher Award, 55; Nat Headliners Award, 60; plus others. Mailing Add: 10 Country Hill Lane Belleville IL 62221

HESSING, VALJEAN MCCARTY
PAINTER, ILLUSTRATOR
b Tulsa, Okla, Aug 30, 34. Study: Philbrook Art Ctr, Tulsa, 45-47; Mary Hardin-Baylor Col, 52-54; Univ Tulsa, 54-55. Work: Philbrook Art Ctr; Heard Mus, Phoenix, Ariz; Anadarko Southern Plains Mus, Okla; Five Civilized Tribes Mus, Muskogee, Okla; Bur Indian Affairs, Washington, DC. Exhib: Indian Ann, Philbrook Art Ctr, 66-72; Cowboy Hall of Fame, Oklahoma City, 67; Five Civilized Tribes Mus, 67-72; Scottsdale Nat Indian Art Exhib, Ariz, 68-72; Heard Mus, 72. Awards: Spec Award for Traditional Indian Art, Scottsdale Nat Indian Art Exhib, 69 & 71; First Place for Choctaw Div, Five Civilized Tribes Mus, 70 & 71; Second Place Award for Woodland Div, Philbrook Art Ctr. Style & Technique: Representational and contemporary Indian art. Media: Watercolor. Mailing Add: 201 Delnor Ave St Charles IL 60174

HEUSSER, ELEANORE ELIZABETH
PAINTER
b North Haledon, NJ. Study: Cooper Union, dipl; Columbia Univ Sch Painting & Sculpture, fel, 45-46; Innsbruck Univ, Fulbright fel, 52-55. Work: Newark Mus; Lending Libr Mus Mod Art, New York. Exhib: Kunsthistorisches Inst, Innsbruck, Austria, 54; Konzerthaus Gallery, Vienna, Austria, 54; Fulbright Grantees Show, Duveen-Graham Gallery & mus throughout US, 57-58; Pa Acad Fine Arts Ann, Philadelphia, 59 & 65; NJ Artists 1972, NJ State Mus, Trenton, 72. Teaching: Instr fundamentals art, Columbia Univ Sch Painting & Sculpture, 46-52; instr drawing, City Col New York, 60-62; pvt instr painting, New York, 60-72; pvt instr painting, North Haledon, 72- Awards: Private Grant Study in Mex, provided by George Grebe, 43. Bibliog: M Finkelstein (auth), Artist in the Alps, Inst Int Educ News Bull, 6/55; article in Le Revue Moderne, 10/72. Style & Technique: Landscape painting in the expressionist tradition. Media: Ink, Oil. Mailing Add: 60 Roosevelt Ave North Haledon NJ 07508

HEWITT, FRANCIS RAY
PAINTER, EDUCATOR
b Rutland, Vt, May 12, 36. Study: Carnegie-Mellon Univ, with Balcomb Greene, BFA; Oberlin Col, with Wolfgang Strechow & Charles Parkhurst, MA; Case Western Reserve Univ, with Thomas Munro. Work: Cleveland Mus Art; Lodz Mus Fine Art, Poland; Caracas Mus Mod Art, Venezuela. Exhib: Movement II, Denise Rene Gallery, Paris, 64; Responsive Eye, Mus Mod Art, New York, 65; One Plus One Equals Three, Univ Tex, 65; Plus & Minus, a Review of Constructivism, Albright-Knox Mus, Buffalo, 67; The Square in Painting, Am Fedn Arts Traveling Exhib, 68. Teaching: Instr painting, Celveland Inst Art, 60-64; lectr design, Bath Acad Art, Corsham, Eng, 64-65; assoc prof drawing & design, Cooper Union, 65-70; assoc prof, Univ Vt, 70- Pos: Trustee, Vt Coun Arts, Montpelier, 70-74. Style & Technique: Constructivist, formal systems. Media: Acrylic on Canvas and Paper. Mailing Add: Flanders Brook Rd East Corinth VT 05040

HEWITT, JEAN CLIFFORD
ART DEALER, COLLECTOR
b Denver, Colo, Oct 22, 22. Study: Univ Denver, BA; theory & criticism of art with Dr L Longman, Univ Calif, Los Angeles. Pos: Owner-mgr, Hewitt Gallery, La Jolla, 73- Bibliog: Jan Jennings (auth), articles in San Diego Tribune; articles in San Diego Art Scene, Applause Mag; Richard Reilley (auth), articles in San Diego Union. Mem: Los Angeles Art Mus Asn.

Specialty: Limited to presenting one-man shows for juried artists who have not had deserved exposure. Collection: Rembrandt etchings, tracings; John Tenniel; George Cruickshank watercolors, etc. Mailing Add: 1844 Ocean Front Del Mar CA 92014

HEYMAN, MR & MRS DAVID M
COLLECTORS
Collection: Paintings. Mailing Add: 3 E 76th St New York NY 10021

HEYWOOD, J CARL
PAINTER, PRINTMAKER
b Toronto, Ont, June 6, 41. Study: Ont Col Art, assoc degree, 63; Atelier 17, with Hayter, Paris, France, 67-69. Work: Nat Gallery Can; Victoria & Albert Mus, London; Mus Mod Art, Paris; Royal Libr Belg; Brooklyn Mus. Exhib: Brit Int Print Biennale, Bradford, Eng, 68, 74 & 76; Int Print Biennale, Crakow, Poland, 70, 72, 74, 76 & 78; Biennale Graphic Art, Ljubljana, Yugoslavia, 71, 73, 75 & 77; Royal Can Acad; plus 26 one-man shows in three countries. Teaching: Prof drawing & painting, Univ Guelph, 73-74; prof printmaking & painting, Queen's Univ, 74- Awards: Northwest Printmakers Award, Seattle Art Mus, Wash, 69; Prix de la Serigraphie, Gallery du Haute Pave, Paris, 73; Graphex Award, Art Gallery of Brantford, 75 & 78. Mem: Royal Can Acad; Ont Soc Artists; Print & Drawing Coun of Can. Media: All Printmaking; Photography. Dealer: Godard Gallery 22 Hazelton Ave Toronto ON Can. Mailing Add: Dept of Art Queen's Univ Kingston ON K7L 3N6 Can

HIBBARD, HOWARD
ART HISTORIAN, WRITER
b Madison, Wis, May 23, 28. Study: Univ Wis, BA & MA; Columbia Univ; Harvard Univ, PhD. Collections Arranged: Florentine Baroque Art from American Collections, with participation of Columbia Univ (catalog with Joan Nissman), Metrop Mus Art, New York, 69. Teaching: Prof art hist, Columbia Univ, 59-; Slade prof, Univ Oxford, 76-77. Pos: Bk rev ed, Art Bull, 61-65, assoc ed, 73-74, ed in chief, 74-78. Awards: Am Acad in Rome fel, 56-58; Guggenheim Fel, 65-66 & 72-73; Mem: Col Art Asn; fel Am Acad Arts & Sci; Soc Archit Historians (dir, 63-65); Renaissance Soc Am; Am Asn Univ Prof. Res: Renaissance and Baroque art and architecture in Italy. Publ: Auth, Bernini, 65; auth, Carlo Maderno and Roman Architecture 1580-1630, 72; auth, Poussin: The Holy Family on the Steps, 74; auth, Michelangelo, 75; auth, Masterpieces of Western Sculpture from Medical to Modern, 77. Mailing Add: 176 Brewster Rd Scarsdale NY 10583

HIBEL, EDNA
PAINTER, LITHOGRAPHER
b Boston, Mass, Jan 13, 17. Study: Boston Mus Fine Arts Sch. Work: Mus Fine Arts, Boston; Detroit Art Inst; De Saisset Mus, Santa Clara, Calif; Flint Inst Art, Mich; Crocker Art Gallery, Sacramento, Calif. Exhib: Pa Acad Fine Arts, Philadelphia; Art Inst Chicago; Oehlschlaeger Gallery, Chicago; Galerie de Tours, San Francisco & Carmel, Calif; Harmon Gallery; plus others. Bibliog: Paintings of Edna Hibel, Jar, 74. Media: Oil. Dealer: Jar Publishers Box 9967 Riviera Beach FL 33404. Mailing Add: 2923 Lake Dr Riviera Beach FL 33404

HICKEN, PHILIP BURNHAM
PAINTER, INSTRUCTOR
b Lynn, Mass, June 27, 10. Study: Mass Col Art. Work: Metrop Mus Art, New York; Philadelphia Mus Fine Art; Brooklyn Mus, NY; Libr Cong, Washington, DC. Comn: Mural, Fed Art Proj, Fort Warren, Mass, 41; combat art, European Theatre, US Army, 42-45; combat art assignment, US Dept Mil Hist, 70. Exhib: Boston Arts Festival, 54; Nat Acad, Rome, Italy, 54; Brooklyn Ann, 59; Eastern States Expos, Springfield, Mass, 60; Boston Soc Watercolors, 60-72; DeCordova Mus, 71; Exhib, Am Painters in Paris, 76. Teaching: Instr painting, Harvard Univ Grad Sch Design, 50-53; instr painting, Boston Univ, 56-57; chmn dept fine arts, Art Inst Boston, 57- Awards: Brooklyn Mus Purchase Award, 58; Boston Soc Watercolor Painters Award, 60; Yankee Mag Award, Copley Galleries, 69. Bibliog: Patricia Wilson (auth), article in Christian Sci Monitor, 66. Mem: Boston Soc Watercolor Painters; Boston Printmakers; Cambridge Art Asn; fel Royal Soc Art; Nantucket Art Asn. Media: Acrylic. Mailing Add: 23 Pine St Nantucket MA 02554

HICKEN, RUSSELL BRADFORD
ART CONSULTANT, LECTURER
b Jacksonville, Fla, Dec 24, 26. Study: Fla State Univ, BS; Univ Fla. Teaching: Instr art, Duncan Fletcher High Sch, Jacksonville, 51-57. Pos: Dir, Jacksonville Art Mus, 57-63, 68-74, arts consult, 74-; dir, Tampa Art Inst, 63-66; dir, Mint Mus Art, Charlotte, NC, 66-68; dir, Art & Cult Ctr, Hollywood, Fla, 77-78. Mem: Southeastern Mus Conf (pres, 68-70); Am Asn Mus (Southeastern regional rep, 70-). Mailing Add: 2106 Funston St Hollywood FL 33020

HICKEY, ROSE VAN VRANKEN
See Van Vranken, Rose

HICKINS, WALTER H
SCULPTOR, GRAPHIC ARTIST
b Fürth, Ger, Mar 12, 36; US citizen. Study: City Col New York, BA, 59 & MA, 64; Columbia Univ Teachers Col, prof dipl, 67; NY Univ. Work: McKinsey & Co, New York; Laird, Inc; Celanese Corp; plus many other pvt collections. Exhib: Loeb Ctr, NY Univ, 71; New York Pub Libr, 75; Lever House, Burr Artists, 75; Cooperstown Ann Art Exhib, NY; Fall River Ann, Mass; Metrop Mus of Art, 77; plus others. Teaching: Ceramics & sculpture, Julia Richman High Sch, New York, 63-; adult educ teacher ceramics & sculpture, Hunter Col, 71- Pos: Designer, producer & seller of hand silk screened line of cards, New York. Awards: New York City Bd Educ Award, 68. Bibliog: Girls and puppets work hand in hand, New York World Telegram & Sun, 1/24/66; Mario Albertazzi (auth), Walter Hickins at Marcoleo, 11/30/70 & Something about the engraver Hickins, 7/21/71, Il Progresso Italo Americano; Lynn Lee (auth), Art review, preview and now, Our Town, 9/15/72. Mem: Nat Art Educ Asn; Composers, Artists & Writers of Am; Burr Artists. Style & Technique: Movement in abstract forms using sensitive rhythm and color. Media: Graphics. Collection: Kollwitz, Magritte, Richard Lindner, Moses Soyer, Rapael Soyer, Jack Levine, John Russell, Eugene Bierman, Maillol, Ben Shan posters and Jaques Callot. Publ: Auth, Puppets: our approach to community relations, Arts & Activities, 66; auth, Who Am I? Who Are You, New York City Educ, 68; auth, For meaningful clubs, High Points, 70; auth, Designing for living, 72 & Abstract painting as meaningful expression, 73, Art Teacher. Dealer: Marcoleo Ltd 1295 First Ave New York NY 10021. Mailing Add: 130 E 24th St New York NY 10010

HICKMAN, DAVID COLEMAN
PAINTER, EDUCATOR
b Richmond, Va, Dec 2, 37. Study: DePauw Univ, BA; Cleveland Inst Art; Northern Ill Univ, MA & MFA. Work: Houston Mus Fine Arts; Ill Arts Coun; Ill State Univ; Northern Ill Univ; Lakeview Ctr Arts, Peoria. Comn: Portrait, comn by Mrs Leonard Horwich, Chicago, 69; portrait, comn by Mrs Robert C Lanier, Houston, 70; painting, comn by Mrs Andrew W Rose, Pebble Beach, Calif, 71; painting, Larger Canvas, Houston Nat Bank, 71; painting, comn by Glenn Elliott, Houston, 72. Exhib: One-man shows, Gilman Galleries, Chicago, 69 & 70, Meredith Long, Houston, 72 & 73 & Ars Longa, Houston, 75; Painting & Sculpture Today, Indianapolis Mus, 70; Drawing Soc Nat Exhib, 71-72; Houston Area Exhib, 74-75. Teaching: Asst prof painting, Northern Ill Univ, 65-69; assoc prof painting, Univ Houston, 69- Pos: Asst chmn art, Univ Houston, 75- Style & Technique: Hard-edge shapes, color. Media: Acrylic. Dealer: Gilman Galleries 103 E Oak St Chicago IL 60611. Mailing Add: 2106 W Main Houston TX 77098

HICKMAN, RONALD DEAN
MUSEUM DIRECTOR
Study: Univ Kans, BFA, 57, MFA, 59. Collections Arranged: Francisco Zuniga (with catalog), 71; Pre-Hispanic Sculpture; Jules Berman Collection, 73; California Invitational Crafts, 73; Monumental Painting of the 60's, 74; Jose Luis Cuevas (with catalog), 74. Teaching: Asst prof art, Ottawa Univ, 59-62; asst prof design & metals, Kansas State Teachers Col, 62-65. Pos: Dir-cur, Wichita Art Asn, 65-67; exec cur, Fine Arts Gallery, San Diego, 67-74; dir, Phoenix Art Mus, 74- Publ: Co-auth, Graphics—Collection of Mr & Mrs Leslie Johnson, 72. Mailing Add: 1625 N Central Ave Phoenix AZ 85004

HICKS, HAROLD JON (JACK)
SCULPTOR
b Dubuque, Iowa, Nov 18, 39. Study: Univ Ariz, BFA; Univ Utah. Work: Utah Mus Fine Arts, Salt Lake City; Salt Lake City Art Ctr; Tucson Art Ctr, Ariz; Univ Utah, Salt Lake City. Exhib: Phoenix Ann, Ariz, 67; 73rd Western Ann, Denver, 71; three-man show, Salt Lake City Art Ctr, 72; 11th Biennial Utah Painting & Sculpture, Salt Lake City, 72; Mainstreams '72, Marietta, Ohio, 72. Pos: Mgr gallery, Tucson Art Ctr, 63-67; asst to dir, Utah Mus Fine Arts, 68-74, chief preparator, 75- Media: Steel, Aluminum, Wood. Mailing Add: Utah Mus Fine Arts 104AAC Univ of Utah Salt Lake City UT 84112

HICKS, LEON NATHANIEL
PRINTMAKER
b Deerfield, Fla, Dec 25, 33. Study: Kans State Univ, BS; State Univ Iowa, MA & MFA, study with Mauricio Lasansky; Stanford Univ, study with Albert Elsen; La Romita Sch Art, Italy; Atlanta Univ, Ga. Work: Charleston Art Gallery at Sunrise, WVa; Tuskegee Inst, Ala; Oakland Art Mus, Calif; Libr of Cong, Washington, DC; Albrecht Art Mus, St Joseph, Mo. Exhib: Am Graphic Workshops, Cincinnati Art Mus, Ohio, 68; Mid Am I, Nelson Gallery Art, Kansas City, Mo, 68; Black Untitled III, Oakland Mus, Calif, 72; Engraving Am (ed, catalogue), Albrecht Gallery, Mo Mus Art, St Joseph, 74; Directions in Afro-Am Art (co-auth, catalogue), Herbert F Johnson Mus Art, Cornell Univ, 74; Traveling Exhib, Tyler Mus Art, Tex, 76; Mus Mod Art, Cali, Colombia, 76; 20th Century Black Artists (co-auth, catalogue), San Jose Mus Art, 76. Collections Arranged: Ann Acad Design Exhib, New York, 68; Seventh Nat Print Exhib, Silvermine Guild Artists, Inc, New Canaan, Conn, 68; Blacks USA, New York Cult Ctr, 73; Art in the Embassies Abroad, US State Dept's Prog, 73; Embassy of US, Ankara, Turkey, 75. Teaching: Instr art, Concord Col, Athens, WVa, 65-67; asst prof art, Lincoln Univ, Jefferson City, Mo, 67; asst prof printmaking, drawing & hist, Lehigh Univ, Bethlehem, Pa, 70-74; assoc prof printmaking, drawing & hist, Webster Col, St Louis, Mo, 74- Pos: Chmn bd & exec vpres, Hicks Etchprint, Inc, Philadelphia, Pa. Awards: Fourth Prize, Des Moines, Iowa, 61; Second Prize, Atlanta Univ, 65; First Prize, Tuskegee Inst, Ninth Ann Beaux Arts Guild Exhib, 68. Mem: Assoc Brandywine Graphic Workshop, Philadelphia, Pa. Style & Technique: Engraving; multi-color intaglio etching and photo-etching; abstract and semi-abstract visual images. Media: Drawing; engraving; etching; photo-etching. Publ: Ed, The Afro-American Artist, Art Gallery Mag, 68; co-auth (with Samella Lewis & Ruth Waddy), Black Artists on Art, Contemp Crafts, 69. Dealer: Smith Mason Art Gallery 1207 Rhode Island NW Washington DC 20005. Mailing Add: Georgetown Apts A-2 844 Ravensridge Rd St Louis MO 63119

HICKS, SHEILA
TAPESTRY ARTIST
b Hastings, Nebr, July 24, 34. Study: Yale Univ, BFA, 57, MFA, 59. Work: Mus Mod Art, New York; Stedelijk Mus, Amsterdam; Kunstgewerbemuseum, Zurich; Mus des Arts Decoratifs, Nantes. Comn: Silk linen bas relief, Ford Found, New York, 67; silk bas reliefs, Air France Airlines, 69; linen mural, Rothschild Bank, Paris, 69; 7 prayer rugs, Mecca, Saudia Arabia, 71; stage curtain, Fiat Tour, Paris, 74. Exhib: One-woman shows, Art Inst Chicago, 63, Suzy Langlois Gallery, Paris, 69, 70, 72, 74 & 76, Mod Master Tapestries, New York, 74, Mus des Arts Decoratifs, Nantes, 74, Stedelijk Mus, 74; Bienalle de Tapisserie, Lausanne, Switz, 71, 73, 75 & 77; Kunsthal Lund, Sweden, 78; Grand Palais, Paris, 78. Teaching: The Hague, 78. Awards: Gold Medal for Craftsmanship, Am Inst Architects, 74; Hon fel Royal Acad Art, Hague, 75. Bibliog: Mildred Constantine & Jack L Larsen (auth), Beyond Craft: The Art Fabric, Van Nostrand Reinhold, New York, 73; Monique Levi-Strauss, Sheila Hicks, P Horay & Suzy Langlois, Paris, 73 & Studio Vista, London, 74. Style & Technique: Fiber, thread, textile, tapestry forms, volumes, bas reliefs. Dealer: Art Mural 266 Boulevard St Germain 75007 Paris France; Mod Master Tapestries Inc 11 E 57th St New York NY 10022. Mailing Add: 3 Bis Cour de Rohan 75006 Paris France

HIGA, CHARLES EISHO
PAINTER, INSTRUCTOR
b Honolulu, Hawaii, Feb 1, 33. Study: Univ Hawaii, BFA; NY Univ, MA. Work: Honolulu Acad Arts; State Capitol Bldg, State Found on Cult & Arts, Honolulu. Comn: Clay sculptures, Honolulu Int Airport & Chem Bldg, Univ Hawaii, 72. Exhib: Watercolor USA, Springfield, Mo, 63, 65 & 67; Crafts IV, Southwest Regional, Oakland, Calif, 68; The Excellence of the Object: Tour Exhib USA, Am Crafts Coun, 69; Northern Ill Crafts Exhib, Oakbrook, 70. Teaching: Instr art, Radford High Sch, Honolulu, 60-65; instr art educ, Univ Victoria, summer 65; instr art, McKinley High Sch, Honolulu, 65- Awards: Purchase Prize, Honolulu Acad Arts, 67; Purchase Prize, Hawaii State Found on Cult & Arts, 69; Teacher of Yr, State Dept Educ, Hawaii, 70. Mem: Hawaii Painters & Sculptors League (vpres, 63); Hawaii Craftsmen (vpres, 70); Am Craftsmen. Media: Watercolor, Clay. Dealer: Exhibit Ward Warehouse 1050 Ala Moana Blvd Honolulu HI 96814. Mailing Add: 3055 Pualei Circle Apt 306 Honolulu HI 96815

HIGA, (YOSHIHARU)
PAINTER, PHOTOGRAPHER
b Okinawa, Japan, Jan 15, 38. Study: Tama Art Univ, Tokyo, BFA; Art Students League; Pratt Graphic Ctr, New York. Work: Mus Mod Art, New York; Brooklyn Mus; Philadelphia Mus; Los Angeles Co Mus; also at the Am Embassy. Exhib: Contemp Japanese Art Exhib, Mus Tokyo, 64; 50th Ann Exhib, Soc Am Graphic Artists, 69; New Talent Printmaker, Assoc Am Artists, New York, 70; Int Engraving Biennial, Buenos Aires, Arg, 70; Am Graphics Artists traveling show to tour the East, US Info Agency, 70. Teaching: Instr drawing, painting & printmaking, Upsala Col; photogr, Mt St Vincent Col, 72- Awards: Best Print in Show, 50th

Ann Exhib, Soc Am Graphic Artists, 69; Mus Purchase Awards, Int Print Exhib, Seattle Art Mus, Wash, 70 & Nat Print Exhib, Boston. Bibliog: Original art, hot off the presses, Life, 6/23/70; Famous artist annual, a treasury of contemporary art, Famous Art Sch, 70. Mailing Add: 2 Bond St New York NY 10012

HIGGINS, DICK
DESIGNER, PRINTMAKER
b Cambridge, Eng, Mar 15, 38; US citizen. Study: Yale Univ, 55-57; Columbia Univ, 57-60; NY Univ, AM(Eng), 77; additional study with John Cage & Henry Cowell. Exhib: One-man shows, Galérie René Block, Berlin, WGer, 73, Centro de Arte y Communicacion, Buenos Aires, Arg, 74, Galerie Petri, Lund, Sweden, 74, Véhicule, Montreal, 74, Museu de Arte Contemporânea, Sao Paulo, Brazil, 76, Galérie Écart, Geneva, Switz, 77, La Mamelle, San Francisco, Calif, 77, Studio Morra, Naples, Italy, 77 & Galerie Inge Baecker, Bochum, WGer, 78; Judson Gallery, New York, 60; Stable Gallery, New York, 64; Tyler Sch of Art, Philadelphia, 66; Sch of Visual Arts, New York, 66; Mus Contemp Art, Chicago, 69; Copenhagen Mus Mod Art, 72; Museu de Arte Contemporânea, Sao Paulo, Brazil, 74 & Visual Poetry, 77; Visual Poetry Exhib, Lehigh Univ, Bethlehem, Pa; Fluxus & C, Cannariello Studio d'Arte, Rome, Italy, 77; Bookworks, Mus Mod Art, New York, 77; plus numerous other one-man & group shows. Teaching: Prof, Graphics Workshop, Calif Inst Arts, 70-71; instr, Univ Wis-Milwaukee & dir, Vis Artists Prog. Bibliog: Hugh Fox (auth), Dick Higgins—Neo-Dadaist, Studies in 20th Century, 70; Gilbert Chase (auth), New Contents for Old Shells, Arts in Soc, 70; Milli Graffi (auth), Diario su Quattro Colonne, Tam Tam, Milan, Italy, 74; Michael Nyman (auth), Experimental Music: Cage and Beyond, Studio Vista, London, 74; Richard Kostelanetz (auth), The End of Intelligent Writing, Sheed & Ward, New York, 75; and others. Media: Photo Silkscreen; Offset Camera. Publ: Auth, Towards the 1970's, 69; auth, Computers for the Arts, 70; co-auth, Fantastic Architecture, 71. Mailing Add: PO Box 842 Canal St Sta New York NY 10013

HIGGINS, EDWARD KOELLING
CRAFTSMAN, EDUCATOR
b Milwaukee, Wis, Apr 30, 26. Study: Univ Wis, Milwaukee, BS(art educ), MS(ceramics); Univ Wis-La Crosse; Northwestern Univ. Work: Mus of Contemp Crafts, New York; Theo Portney Gallery, New York, many pvt collections. Exhib: Milwaukee Printmakers, 51-52, Wis Designer Craftsman, 53-69 & Wis Painters & Sculptors, 55-68, Milwaukee Art Ctr; Am Jewelry Today, Everhart Mus, Scranton, Pa, 67; Mississippi River Art Festival, Jackson, Miss, 67-; Southern Tier Art & Craft Exhib, Corning Mus, NY, 69-; Crafts-1970, Inst of Contemp Art, Boston, 70; Appalachian Corridors Exhib, Charleston Art Gallery, WVa, 70-; Harrisburg Festival of the Arts, Harrisburg Art Gallery, Pa, 70; Cooperstown NY Festival of the Arts, 70. Collections Arranged: Headdress/A History of American Headgear & Crafts Invitational, Kohler Art Ctr, Sheboygan, Wis; Forms in Metal & Objects Are, Mus of Contemp Crafts, New York; Excellence of the Object, Honolulu Acad of Arts, Hawaii; Fantasy in Silver, Akron Art Inst, Ohio; Jewelers, USA, Calif State Col at Fullerton; Am Evolution in Art, Chambers Gallery, Pa State Univ; Box Exhib, Kohler Art Ctr; Celebration 20, Mus of Contemp Crafts, New York; Forms in Metal, Montgomery Mus of Fine Arts, Fine Arts Mus at Mobile, Ala, Philbrook Art Ctr, Tulsa, Okla, Va Mus of Fine Arts, Richmond & Huntsville Mus of Art, Ala; 100 Artists Celebrate 200 Yrs, Fairtree Gallery, New York; Xerox-Fun & Fantasy Exhib, Xerox Hall, Rochester, NY. Teaching: Asst prof jewelry, Mansfield State Col, Pa, 69-70; assoc prof jewelry, ceramics & photog, Mercyhurst Col, 71- Awards: Sculpture Award & Merit Award for Metal, Mississippi River Art Festival, Jackson Art Gallery; Silver Award, Appalachian Corridors Exhib, Charlestown Art Gallery. Bibliog: Donald Wilcox (auth), Body Jewelry, Regnery, 73; Dona Meilach (auth), Box Art Assemblages, Crown, 76. Mem: Soc NAm Goldsmiths. Style & Technique: Social comment via mini-sculpture in sterling. Media: Silver & clay. Publ: Contribr, Body Jewelry, Regnery, 73; contribr, Inventive Fiber Crafts, Prentice Hall, 75; contribr, Box Art Assemblages, 76, A New Look at Crochet, 76 & Career Opportunities in Crafts, 77, Crown. Dealer: Ed Levin Workshop 262 North St Bennington VT 05201. Mailing Add: 4210 Briggs Ave Erie PA 16504

HIGGINS, (GEORGE) EDWARD
SCULPTOR
b Gaffney, SC, Nov 13, 30. Study: Univ NC, BA, 54. Work: Mus Mod Art, Guggenheim Mus & Whitney Mus Am Art, New York; Albright-Knox Art Gallery, Buffalo, NY; Dallas Mus Fine Arts; plus others. Comn: Sculpture, Cameron Bldg, New York, 62 & NY State Theatre, Lincoln Ctr for Performing Arts, New York, 64. Exhib: New York World's Fair, 64-65; Contemporary American Sculpture, Selection 1, Whitney Mus Am Art, 66; Flint Inst Art, Mich, 66; Documenta IV, Kassel, Ger, 68; Duke Univ, 69. Teaching: Instr sculpture, Parsons Sch Design, 61-62; Philadelphia Mus Sch, 63. Awards: Louis C Tiffany Grant, 62; Purchase Prize, Flint Inst Art, 66. Bibliog: Harriet Janis & Rudi Blesh (auth), Collage: Personalities—Concepts—Techniques, Chilton, 62; Sam Hunter (ed), New Art Around the World: Painting & Sculpture, Abrams, 66; Eduard Trier (auth), Form & Space: Sculpture in the 20th Century, Praeger, 68. Mailing Add: Old Philadelphia Rd RFD 4 Easton PA 18042

HIGGINS, MARY LOU
CRAFTSMAN
b Milwaukee, Wis, June 27, 26. Study: Univ Wis-Milwaukee, BS(art educ), MS(weaving). Work: Slides of work in many mus such as Los Angeles Co Mus Art, Milwaukee Art Ctr, Mus Contemp Crafts, Art Now Series, Univ Galleries, New York; also in numerous pvt collections. Exhib: American Jewelry Today, Everson Mus, 68; Furs & Feathers, Mus Contemp Crafts, 70; Fun & Fantasy, Xerox Sq Galleries, Rochester & Fairtree, New York, 73; Miniature & Delicate Objects, Fairtree, New York & Galeria del Sol, Santa Barbara, 75; one-woman show of weaving, jewelry & ceramics, Tapestry, Denver, 75, Prairie House, Springfield, Ill, 75, Kroger Gallery, New York, 76, Ed Levin Workshop, Bennington, Vt, 77 & Sol Del Rio, San Antonio, Tex, 77. Teaching: Instr art educ & fiber & fabrics, Mansfield State Col, 69-71; asst prof ceramics, fiber & fabrics & art educ, Mercyhurst Col, 71-74. Awards: Wisconsin Designers & Craftsman Award, Milwaukee Art Ctr, 65; Textile Award, Cooperstown, NY, 70; Textile Award, 25th Pa Craftsman Award, 72. Mem: Am Craftsman Coun. Style & Technique: Art forms using craft medias: crochet soft sculpture figures, woven tapestries, drawings on ceramics, basket weave scrimshaw necklaces. Media: Weaving, Ceramics. Publ: Contribr, Elyse Sommer, auth, Wearable Crafts, Crown, 76, Inventive Fiber Crafts, Prentice-Hall, 77 & Career Opportunities in Crafts, Crown, 77. Dealer: Ed 78209. 1020 Townsend San Antonio TX 78209. Basketry, 74 & A New Look at Crochet, 75, Crown. Mailing Add: 4210 Briggs Erie PA 16504

HIGH, FREIDA
PRINTMAKER, EDUCATOR
b Starkville, Miss, Oct 21, 46. Study: Graceland Col, Lamoni, Iowa, AA, 66; Northern Ill Univ, De Kalb, BS, 68; Univ Wis, Madison, MA, 70, MFA, 71, with printmaker, Ray Gloeckler, & painter, Robert Grilley. Work: Grad Sch, Univ Wis, Madison; Afro-Am Arts Inst, Univ Ind, Bloomington; Du Sable Mus of African & Afro-Am Art, Chicago; S Side Community Art Ctr, Chicago; Afro-Am Ctr, Univ Wis. Comn: Mixed-media drawing, Afro-Am Arts Inst, Univ Ind, Bloomington, 76; prints & drawings, Wis Arts Bd, 78. Exhib: Mid-States Art Exhib, Evansville Mus of Arts & Sci, Ind, 70; Black Expo, San Francisco Bay Area Civic Ctr, Calif, 72; Sixth Concours Int de la Palme d'Or des Beaux Arts, Palmares, Monte Carlo, France, 74; Ann Print & Drawing Show, Art Guild Chicago Gallery, 74; Midwestern Artists Exhib, Burpee Art Mus, Rockford, Ill, 75; Prints & Drawings, MAMA Gallery, Madison, Wis, 76; BeloitVicinity Ann Exhib, Wright Art Ctr, Wis, 76; 15th Nat Print Exhib, Art Gallery, Bradley Univ, Peoria, Ill, 76; Midwestern Black Artist, Performing Arts Ctr, Milwaukee, Wis, 76. Collections Arranged: Cur & auth of catalogues for: Traditional African Art, 71, Traditional Art of Sub-Saharan Africa, 72, Prints & Paintings, 72, Mem Union Gallery, Univ Wis, Midwestern Black Artist, Performing Arts Ctr, Milwaukee, 76 & Contemp African Art, 77, Mem Union Gallery, Univ Wis, Madison. Teaching: Asst prof African/Afro-Am art, Univ Wis, Madison, 72-77, assoc prof African/Afro-Am art, 77- Pos: Artist-in-residence, Univ Wis, Madison, 71-72. Awards: Wis Arts Bd Art Grant, 77; City Arts Grant, Prints & Drawings, Off of the Mayor, Madison, 77. Bibliog: Interest in African art is on the increase in US, Capital Times, 7/75; James Auer (auth), PAC surveys midwestern Black art, Milwaukee J, 2/76; Shirley Carley (auth), Starkville native making name in field of art, Starkville Daily News 3/76. Mem: Wis Women in the Arts; Nat Conf of Artists (regional coordr, 74); Nat Coun for Black Studies. Style & Technique: Woodcuts which are bold and expressionistic; flat and decorative; generally black and white; vivid and dramatic when colored; multi-media drawings. Media: Woodcut prints; drawings. Publ: Illusr (cover), Ba Shiru, Univ Wis, 71 & 76-77; contribr, Center debut: a Black artist's view, Milwaukee J, 11/75. Dealer: Assoc Am Artist 663 Fifth Ave New York NY 10022. Mailing Add: 2726 Granada Way Apt 6 Madison WI 53713

HIGH, TIMOTHY GRIFFIN
PRINTMAKER, INSTRUCTOR
b Memphis, Tenn, Mar 10, 49. Study: Tex Tech Univ, BFA(printmaking), 73; Univ Wis-Madison, MA(printmaking), 75, MFA(printmaking), 76. Work: Chicago Art Inst; Elvehjem Art Ctr, Madison, Wis; De Cordova Mus, Lincoln, Mass; Col of Siskiyous, Weed, Calif; Fla Tech Univ, Orlando. Comn: New Am Graphics (60 imp ed of commemorative posters for Nat Print Competition), comn by Univ Wis-Madison, 75. Exhib: 4th-7th Ann Colorprint Nat Competition, Tex Tech Univ, Lubbock, 73-76, Miami Int Biennial, Metrop Mus Art Ctr, Fla, 75; one-person show (thesis exhib), Univ Wis-Madison, 75-76 & Pecan Sq Gallery, Austin, Tex, 77; 1st & 2nd Nat Exhib Works on Paper, Springfield Col, Mass, 75-76; Previews (co/featuring works by Tom Hunt), Focal Point Gallery, Madison, 75; show co/featuring works by Cynthia Spikes, Abilene Fine Arts Mus, Tex, 76; Potsdam Prints, State Univ NY Col, Potsdam, 76; Los Angeles Printmaking Soc Bicentennial Traveling Exhib, 76; SW Biennale of Mus NMex, Santa Fe, 76; Boston Printmakers 29th Nat Print Exhib, De Cordova Mus, Lincoln, Mass, 77; Ae Bienniale l'Invitation de l'Image, Epinal, France, 77; Eight for Tex, Univ Dallas, 77. Teaching: Asst drawing, Univ Wis-Madison, 75-76; vis artist & lectr, Univ Tex, Austin, 76, instr serigraphy & printmaking, 76- Pos: Staff artist, KTXS Television, Abilene, Tex, 69-70; illusr, Tex Ornithological Soc, Lubbock, 73. Awards: Marshall S Mayer Award, 1st Nat Exhib, Col of Siskiyous, Weed, Calif, 75; Jurors' Purchase Award, 5th Int Matmedia Exhib, Dickenson State Col, NDak, 75 & Boston Printmakers 29th Nat, De Cordova Mus, 77. Mem: Graphics Soc; Los Angeles Printmaking Soc; Boston Printmakers; Tex Fine Arts Asn. Media: Serigraph; Pencil/Ink Drawings. Publ: Contribr, New American Graphics—1975, Univ Wis-Madison, 75. Mailing Add: c/o Dept of Art Univ of Tex Austin TX 78712

HIGHBERG, STEPHANIE WENNER
INSTRUCTOR, PAINTER
b Kalamazoo, Mich, Dec 29, 41. Study: Univ Mich Col Archit & Design, BS(drawing & design); and with Guy Palazzola, Milton Cohen & Mildred Fairchild; Columbia Univ Teachers Col, MA(fine arts & fine arts educ). Exhib: Mystic Art Mus Regional Show, Conn, 68; Slater Mus, Norwich, Conn, 69; Gilman Gallery, Chicago, 72; Lord & Taylor Gallery, New York, 72; Flora & Fauna of Madeira, Funchal, Madeira, Portugal, 73. Teaching: Chmn dept art, Latin Sch Chicago, 70-72; instr watercolor & freehand drawing, Chamberlayne Jr Col, Boston, 75- Pos: Artistic consult, New Eng Conserv Music, Boston, 74- Awards: Am Cancer Soc Art Awards, 67 & 68; Lyme Art Asn Second Prize for Painting, 68. Bibliog: Susan Croce Kelly (auth), It's all in the family: sister artists display work here, St Louis Globe Dem, 70; On exhibit, Where Mag, 12/72. Style & Technique: Fantasized interpretation of realistic, natural subjects; imaginative approach to nature. Media: Impasto, Oil Wash. Dealer: Lord & Taylor Gallery 424 Fifth Ave New York NY 10018. Mailing Add: 50 Commonwealth Ave Boston MA 02116

HIGHTOWER, JOHN B
ART ADMINISTRATOR
b Atlanta, Ga, May 23, 33. Study: Yale Univ, BA, 55; Calif Col Arts & Crafts, hon DFA, 75. Teaching: Instr arts mgt, Wharton Sch of Bus, New Sch, 75-77. Pos: Asst to pub, Am Heritage Publ Co, 61-63; exec asst, NY State Coun on the Arts, 63-64, exec dir, 64-70, mem, 70-76; cult adv, Rockefeller Mission to Latin Am, 69; Am rep, UNESCO Conf on Performing Arts, Canberra, Australia, 69; dir, Mus Mod Art, New York, 70-72; pres, Assoc Councils of the Arts, 72-74; founder & chmn, Advocates for the Arts, 74-77; pres, S St Seaport, 77-; mem bd dirs, Urban Arts Corps; vis critic, Sch Drama, Yale Univ. Awards: NY State Award, 70. Mem: Century Asn; Buffalo Acad Fine Arts; Inst for Art & Urban Resources; Poets & Writers; Drawing Ctr. Mailing Add: 333 Central Park W New York NY 10025

HIGHWATER, JAMAKE
ART CRITIC, LECTURER
b Mont. Study: Univ Mont, AA; Univ Calif, Berkeley, BA & MA; Univ Chicago, PhD; spec study in comparative lit, music, cult anthrop & art hist. Teaching: Lectures extensively at universities for E Colston Leigh Lect Bur. Pos: Consult, NY State Coun on the Arts, 76-; mem art task panel, Pres Carter's Comn on Mental Health, 77-; pres cult coun, Am Indian Community House, New York, 77- Awards: Newbery Honor Award for Bk ANPAO, Am Libr Asn, 77. Mem: White Buffalo Coun of Am Indians; Nat Cong of Am Indians; Author's Guild; Dramatists Guild. Res: Concerned with all aspects of American Indian art, crafts and culture. Publ: Auth, Fodor's Indian America: A Cultural & Travel Guide, David McKay Co, 75; auth, Song from the Earth: American Indian Painting, NY Graphic Soc, 76; auth, Ritual of the Wind: American Indian Music, Ceremonies, Studio/Viking, 77; auth, ANPAO, 77 & Many Smokes, Many Moons: American Indian History thru Indian Art, 78, Lippincott. Mailing Add: c/o Fox Chase Agency 419 E 57th St New York NY 10022

HILDEBRAND, JUNE MARY ANN
PRINTMAKER
b Eureka, Calif, Nov 2, 30. Study: Calif Col Arts & Crafts; Art Students League, scholar; Queens Col, BFA; Hochschule Bildende Kunste Berlin; Hunter Col, MA; Pratt Graphic Ctr. Work: Philadelphia Mus Art, Pa; Univ Wis-Madison; New York Pub Libr; Everson Mus Art; Univ Minn; plus others. Exhib: Am Color Print Soc, 64-69; Pratt Int Miniature Print Exhib,

66 & 68; Oneonta State Univ, 67; Montclair State Col, 68; Gotham Bk Mart, New York, 69. Style & Technique: Work is based on subject matter, predominately nature. Media: Black & White Linoleum Cuts; Color Silk Screen Prints. Publ: Contribr graphics, Artists Proof Mag; Gourmet Mag. Mailing Add: 229 E 12th St Apt 2 New York NY 10003

HILDEBRANDT, WILLIAM ALBERT
PAINTER, ART ADMINISTRATOR
b Philadelphia, Pa, Oct 1, 17. Study: Tyler Sch Art, Temple Univ, BFA, BSEd & MFA; Philadelphia Col Art, cert advert design. Work: Glen-Croft Baptist Church, Folcroft, Pa. Exhib: One-man shows, Philadelphia Art Alliance, 62 & 73, Widener Col, 65, Springfield Libr, Pa, 69 & Women's Univ Club, Philadelphia, 61; Wallingford Art Ctr Ann, Pa, 65; Nat Drawing Soc Eastern Cent Regional Drawing Exhib, Philadelphia Mus Art, 65 & 70; Am Drawing Biennial, Norfolk Mus Arts & Sci, Va, 67; Nat Drawing Exhib, Bucknell Univ, Lewisburg, Pa, 67; Avanti Gallery, New York, 69; Pennsylvania 71, William Penn Mem Mus, Harrisburg, 71. Teaching: Supvr art educ, Philadelphia Pub Schs, 54- Awards: Francis Homer Award, Woodmere Gallery Earth-Sky-Water Exhib, 66; Best of Show Ann Award, Philadelphia Art Teachers Asn, 70; Philadelphia Sketch Club Medal, 113th Ann Exhib Oil Painting, 76. Mem: Philadelphia Art Teachers Asn (pres, 50-52); Temple Univ Gen Alumni Asn; Tyler Sch Art Alumni Asn (pres, 47-48); Woodmere Art Gallery; Philadelphia Asn Sch Adminr. Style & Technique: Realistic representation of subject matter adaptable to contemporary pop and surrealism. Media: Oil. Publ: Illusr, The Keystone State, 53; auth, Arthur Graeff, Winston; illusr, Humanities Curriculum, 68 & Echoes from Mount Olympus, 70, Instrnl Serv, Sch Dist Philadelphia. Mailing Add: 417 Turner Rd Media PA 19063

HILDRETH, JOSEPH ALAN
PRINTMAKER, PAINTER
b Bowling Green, Ky, Sept 2, 47. Study: Western Ky Univ, BFA, 69; Pratt Inst, with Walter Rogalski, MFA, 71. Work: Mint Mus, Charlotte, NC; Erie Fine Arts Ctr, Pa. Exhib: Western Ill Nat Print & Drawing Exhib, 70; St John's 1st Ann Drawing Show, 70; 6th Ann Piedmont Graphics, 70; Mercyhurst Nat Graphics Exhib, 70; 24th American Drawing Biennial, Norfolk Mus, 71; 35th Ann Artists of Cent NY, Munson-Williams-Proctor Inst, Utica, 72; Tex Fine Arts Asn Exhib, Laguna Gloria Art Mus, Austin, 74; Miniature Prints Exhib, Terrain Graphics Gallery, New York, NY, 74; Eight Upstate, Artists' Space Gallery, New York, NY, 74; Nat Print Exhib, Second St Gallery, Charlottesville, Va, 76; 16th Bradley Nat Print Exhib, Bradley Univ, Peoria, Ill, 77. Teaching: Asst prof printmaking, State Univ NY Col Potsdam, 71- Media: Intaglio, Lithography. Mailing Add: 7 Bicknell St Potsdam NY 13668

HILL, CLINTON J
PAINTER, EDUCATOR
b Payette, Idaho, Mar 8, 22. Study: Univ Ore, BS, 47; Brooklyn Mus Art Sch, 49-51; Acad Grande Chaumiere, Paris, 51; Inst Arte Statale, Florence, Italy, 51-52. Work: Mus Mod Art, New York; Philadelphia Mus Art; Phoenix Art Mus, Ariz; Hampton Inst, Va; Port Authority New York; plus others. Exhib: Drawing USA, Mus Mod Art, New York, 56; Collage in America, Am Fedn Arts Circulating Exhib, 58; Two Decades of American Prints, Brooklyn Mus, 68; one-man exhibs, Zabriskie Gallery, New York, 55-75 & Gallerie Darthea Speyer, Paris, 73-75. Teaching: Assoc prof, Queens Col (NY), 68- Awards: Fulbright Grant to India, 56; Caps Grant, 74-75; Fac Res Grant, City Univ New York, 75. Bibliog: Harriet Janis & Rudi Blesh (auth), Collage: Personalities, Concepts, Techniques, Chilton, 62; Leo Steinberg (auth), Other Criteria, Oxford Univ, 72; Jeremy Gilbert-Rolfe (auth), article in Artforum, 12/73; Gerrit Henry (auth), The permitting medium, Art Int, summer 74. Style & Technique: Abstract, subtly painted transparent and translucent color. Media: Handmade Paper, Acrylic. Dealer: Zabriskie Gallery 29 W 57th St New York NY 10019. Mailing Add: 178 Prince St New York NY 10012

HILL, DALE LOGAN
PAINTER, INSTRUCTOR
b Boise, Idaho, July 23, 09. Study: Minneapolis Inst Art, scholar; Am Acad Art, Chicago; Frederick Mizen Sch Art; also with Pruett Carter, Stanley Parkhouse, Harry Timmins, Haddon Sundlom & others. Comn: Many pvt comns. Exhib: Village Gallery, Taos, NMex; Jamison Gallery, Santa Fe, NMex; Desert Southwest Gallery, Palm Desert, Calif; Desert Art Mus, Palm Springs, Calif; Laguna Art Asn Gallery, Laguna Beach, Calif; plus others. Teaching: Instr art, Orange Co Art Inst; pvt instr art. Pos: Owner, dir & instr, South Coast Acad Art, Santa Ana & Newport Beach, Calif; former owner, D Logan Hill Fine Art Gallery, Carmel, Calif. Mem: Am Inst Fine Arts; Allied Artists Am; Los Angeles Art Dir Club. Style & Technique: Trompe l'oeil paintings of antique silver and crystal; brush and palette knife; Westerns and Indians. Media: Oil. Mailing Add: 23222 Caminito Andreta Laguna Hills CA 92653

HILL, DOROTHY KENT
MUSEUM CURATOR
b New York, NY, Feb 3, 07. Study: Vassar Col, AB; Johns Hopkins Univ, PhD. Pos: Res assoc, Walters Art Gallery, Baltimore, Md, 34-37, assoc cur ancient art, 37-40, cur ancient art, 40-69, cur Greek & Roman art, 70-77; ed, Walters Art Gallery Bull, 48-71; ed, bk rev, Old World, Am J Archaeol, 58- Mem: Archaeol Inst Am; Am Oriental Soc; corresp mem Deutsches Archäologisches Inst; Inst di Studi Etruschi ed Italici. Publ: Auth, Catalog of Classical Bronze Sculpture, Walters Art Gallery, 49; auth, articles in Am J Archaeol, Hesperia & others. Mailing Add: 249 W 31st St Baltimore MD 21211

HILL, DRAPER
EDITORIAL CARTOONIST, ART HISTORIAN
b Boston, Mass, July 1, 35. Study: Harvard Col, BA(magna cum laude), 57; Slade Sch Fine Arts, London, Eng, 60-63. Work: Wiggin Gallery, Boston Pub Libr; Univ Va; Lyndon B Johnson Libr, Austin; Nat Gallery Can, Ottawa; Worcester Art Mus, Mass. Exhib: View from Draper Hill, Casdin Gallery, Worcester, Mass, 66; Int Salon de Caricature, Montreal, PQ, 66-78; Editorial Art of Draper Hill, Brooks Mem Art Gallery, Memphis, 75; Image of America in Caricature and Cartoon, Amon Carter Mus, Ft Worth, 75; American Presidency in Political Cartoons, Univ Art Mus, Berkeley, 75-76. Collections Arranged: Cartoon and Caricature from Hogarth to Hoffnung, Arts Coun Gt Brit, 62, James Gillray 1756-1815, 67; exhib on hist caricature, Boston Pub Libr, 64, 66 & 70. Teaching: Instr life drawing, Sch Worcester Art Mus, 67-71. Pos: Ed cartoonist, Worcester Telegram, Mass, 64-71, Com Appeal, Memphis, Tenn, 71-76 & Detroit News, 76- Bibliog: Julian Grow (auth), A cartoon is born, Feature Parade, Worcester Sunday Telegram, 3/10/68; Lydel Sims (auth), Draper Hill, Cartoonist Profiles, 3/75; Guy Northrop (auth), The Editorial Art of Draper Hill, Brooks Gallery, Memphis, 75. Mem: Asn Am Ed Cartoonists (vpres & dir, 70-75, pres, 75-76). Style & Technique: Brush and pen on grafix board, with stress on caricature. Collection: Caricature and cartooning, with particular emphasis on 18th and 19th century English satire. Publ: Auth, The Crane Library, 62; auth, Fashionable Contrasts, London, 66; auth, Illingworth on Target, 70; co-illusr, The Decline and Fall of the Gibbon, 74; auth, The Satirical Etchings of James Gillray, 76. Mailing Add: Detroit News 615 W Lafayette Blvd Detroit MI 48231

HILL, ED
ART DEALER, COLLECTOR
b El Paso, Tex, June 23, 37. Study: Univ Tex, El Paso, BA(Eng lit), 62. Pos: Dir, Hill Gallery, currently. Specialty: Original prints of Fritz Scholder. Collection: One of largest collections of Fritz Scholder prints. Mailing Add: 4141 Pinnacle St El Paso TX 79962

HILL, J TWEED
PAINTER
b Boston, Mass. Study: Taubes Pierce Sch Art, Provincetown, Mass, 59-60; with Steven Trefonides, Boston, Marguerite Pearson & Wayne Morrell, Rockport, Mass & Roger Curtis, Gloucester, Mass. Exhib: North Shore Arts Asn, Gloucester, 66-77; Jordan Marsh Annual Exhibit of New England Artists, 67; Newburyport Art Asn Show, 71-77; Butler Art Inst Show, Youngstown, Ohio, 72; Grand National Show, Am Artists Prof League, New York, 75-76. Pos: Dir & owner, Pigeon Cove Gallery, Rockport, Mass, 68-71; mem & co-operator, Harbor Gallery, Rockport, 73- Awards: Third Prize for Oils, Newburyport Art Asn, 75 & First Prize, 77; Kiwanis Club Silver Bowl Award for Most Popular Painting, 76 & 77. Mem: North Shore Arts Asn (mem bd dir, 73-); Newburyport Art Asn; Salmagundi Club; Am Artists Prof League. Style & Technique: Traditional, still life and florals with brush; landscape and marine with knife. Media: Oil, Pen & Ink. Dealer: Harbor Gallery Main St Rockport MA 01966. Mailing Add: J Tweed Hill Studio Rockport MA 01966

HILL, JIM
SCULPTOR
b Albuquerque, NMex, Mar 24, 44. Study: Univ NMex, BFA & MA, with Charles Mattox. Work: Fine Arts Mus, Univ NMex, Albuquerque; Mus NMex, Santa Fe. Exhib: Tri-Culture Show, Mus NMex, 69; Light Sculpture, Esther Robles Gallery, Los Angeles, 70; Art Multiples, Univ Md Art Mus, Baltimore, 71; Scheid-Hill, Deson-Zaks Gallery, Chicago, Light Sculpture, Hill's Gallery, Santa Fe, 72. Bibliog: Jim Hill, light sculpture, Art Int, summer 70; Light sculpture (Jim Hill), Southwest Art Gallery Mag, 1/72; article in The Santa Fean Mag, 74. Mem: NMex Mus Found. Style & Technique: Mystical realism; cast bronze figures with detailed realism including glass eyes combined with unconscious symbols such as fish, snake and scarab. Media: Plexiglas, Metal. Specialty: Fine arts. Publ: Auth, My plexiglas & light sculptures, Leonardo, Vol 3. Mailing Add: Rte 2 Box 203 La Cienega Santa Fe NM 87501

HILL, JOAN (CHEA-SE-QUAH)
PAINTER, ILLUSTRATOR
b Muskogee, Okla. Study: Northeastern State Col, BAEduc, 52; Famous Artists Course, 53-; spec study Indian art, with Dick West, 58-63; pvt study with int artists, 58-72; extensive air-travel-study on T H Hewitt Painting Workshops, 65-75, with Dong Kingman, Millard Sheets, Robert E Wood, Rex Brandt & George Post. Work: Heard Mus, Phoenix; Dept Interior, Arts & Crafts Bd, Washington, DC; Mus of the Am Indian, Heye Found, New York; Fine Arts Mus NMex, Santa Fe; Philbrook Art Ctr Mus, Tulsa, Okla. Comn: Mural-type oil paintings of Cherokee Nation through Dept Interior, Tahlequah, Okla, 67; portrait (gouache) for book, Sam Houston with the Cherokees, comn by Rennard Strickland & Jack Gregory Collection, Tulsa, 67; portrait & illus for book poetry, Five Civilized Tribes Mus, Muskogee, 68; oil painting, USA Ctr Mil Hist for Bicentennial Collection, Washington, DC, 75; $5000 mural comn, Seattle Arts Comn, Wash, 77. Exhib: Five Ann Center Arts Indian America, Dept Interior, 64, 67-70; American Embassies Overseas, Dept Interior Traveling Exhib, 65-66; America Discovers Indian Art, Smithsonian Inst, Washington, DC, 67; Outstanding Indian Painters & Sculptors Hon Exhib, Princeton Univ, 70; Am for Indian Opportunity Hon Exhib, Washington Gallery of Art, 71; plus others. Teaching: Instr art, Tulsa Secondary Pub Schs, 52-56; instr art & adult art educ, Muskogee Art Guild, 59-60. Pos: Career day art consult, Am Asn Univ Women, 62-63; mem exec comt, Alliance Arts Educ, Bur Indian Affairs. Awards: First Award, Philbrook Art Ctr Mus, 66, 68, 71 & 75; Walter Bimson Grand Award, Scottsdale Nat Indian Arts Exhib, Ariz, 68; Grand Spec Award, All Am Indian Art Exhib, Sheridan, Wyo, 71; plus many others. Bibliog: Joan Bucklew Hale (auth), A critic views Indian art in general and painting in particular, New Dimensions in Indian Art, 65; Marion Gridley (auth), Indians of Today, Indian Coun Fire Publ, 71; Jamake Highwater (auth), Song From the Earth—American Indian Painting, NY Graphic Soc, 76. Mem: Nat League Am Pen Women; Int Platform Asn; Southwestern Art Asn; Muskogee Art Students Guild (art dir & publicity dir, 58-64); Intercontinental Biog Asn. Style & Technique: Subjective expressionism with emphasis on human figure; traditional techniques combined with experimental concepts. Media: Oil, Gouache; Collage, Acrylic. Publ: Illusr, Life en Espanol, Time-Life Int, Mex, 69; contribr, Look to the Mountain Top, 72; contribr & illusr, The American Way, Am Airlines, 72; illusr, The Cherokee People, Indian Tribal Series, Phoenix, 73; illusr, Fire & the Spirits, Univ Okla Press, 75. Mailing Add: Rte 3 Box 151 Harris Rd Muskogee OK 74401

HILL, JOHN ALEXANDER
COLLECTOR
b Shawnee, Okla, Feb 24, 07. Study: Univ Denver, AB, 28, LLD, 62. Pos: Trustee, Cheekwood Mus Art, 73-, chmn acquisitions comt, 75- Interest: American traditional. Collection: All media Western Americana, 1850 to present. Mailing Add: 105 Leake Ave Nashville TN 37205

HILL, JOHN CONNER
DESIGNER, PUBLISHER
b Philadelphia, Pa, Feb 17, 45. Study: Pratt Inst, BID, 68; Cosanti Found, Paradise Valley, Ariz, with Paolo Soleri, 72-76. Exhib: Ariz Photog Biennial, Phoenix Art Mus, 69; Southwest Biennial, Int Folk Art Mus, Santa Fe, NMex, 70, NMex Biennial, 71; Tucson Festival Crafts Exhib, Tucson Mus, Ariz, 77; Ariz Textile Exhib, Matthews Ctr, Ariz State Univ, Tempe, 77. Teaching: Instr art, Rough Rock Demonstration Sch, Navajo Nation, Ariz, 68-70. Pos: Bronze sculpture casting, Cosanti Found, 74-76; publ-owner, Kokopelli Press, Phoenix, 76- Awards: Third Award, Ariz Textile Exhib, Scottsdale Ctr for the Arts, 76. Style & Technique: Wall hangings and coverings, fabric assemblage applique, costume design applique and leather assemblage. Dealer: Hand & Spirit Gallery 4200 N Marshall Way Scottsdale AZ 85251. Mailing Add: Box 33666 Phoenix AZ 85013

HILL, MEGAN LLOYD
PAINTER, ART DEALER
b Chicago, Ill, Sept 22, 42. Study: Ind Univ, BA, 65; Univ Chicago, with Max Kuhn; Univ NMex, with Charles Mattox, MA, 69. Work: Univ NMex Fine Arts Mus, Albuquerque; Mus NMex, Santa Fe. Exhib: Intrinsic Art, Friends Contemp Art, 71, Denver; Fall Invitational, Roswell Mus & Art Ctr, NMex, 72; one-man show, Lerner Heller Gallery, New York, 72; Fine Arts Mus NMex, Biennial, 73; Seven Artists, Francis McCray Gallery, Western NMex

Univ; plus others. Pos: Owner, Hill's Gallery, Santa Fe. Awards: Honorable Mentions, Five-State Invitational, Port Arthur, Tex, 71; Southwest Biennial, Mus NMex, 72. Bibliog: Donna Meilack (auth), Leather Book, 71; article in Art in Am, 8/72; article in Southwest Art Gallery Mag, 12/72. Mem: Mus NMex Found. Specialty: Contemporary New Mexico fine arts and crafts. Style & Technique: Painted constructions on leather with ceramic portions attached. Publ: Auth, Aiming at the creative environment, Southwest Art Gallery Mag, 11/71 & 1/73; contribr, Craft Horizons, 12/71. Mailing Add: 110 W San Francisco Santa Fe NM 87501

HILL, PETER
PAINTER, EDUCATOR
b Detroit, Mich, Nov 29, 33. Study: Albion Col, AB, 56; Cranbrook Acad Art, Bloomfield Hills, Mich, MFA, 58. Work: Joslyn Art Mus, Omaha, Nebr; Sheldon Mem Gallery, Lincoln, Nebr; Springfield Art Mus, Mo; Sioux City Art Ctr, Iowa; Spiva Art Gallery, Joplin, Mo. Exhib: Max Nat Painting Exhib, Purdue Univ, Lafayette, 69; Springfield Art Mus Ann, Mo, 70 & 74; Northern Ill Univ Nat Drawing Exhib, 71; Midwest Biennial, Joslyn Art Mus, 72 & 74; Colo/Nebr Exchange Exhib, Denver, 73; one-man show, Sheldon Mem Art Gallery, Lincoln, Nebr, 78; plus others. Teaching: From instr to chmn dept, Univ Nebr, Omaha, 58- Awards: Ford Found Purchase Award, 12th Ann Mid-Am Exhib, 62; Ann Exhib Purchase Awards, Springfield Art Mus, 63 & 74, Purchase Award, Watercolor USA, 67. Style & Technique: Hard-edge abstraction. Media: Acrylic, Oil. Dealer: Gallery 72 37th & Leavenworth Omaha NE 68102. Mailing Add: 11734 Shirley St Omaha NE 68144

HILL, POLLY KNIPP
ETCHER, PAINTER
b Ithaca, NY, Apr 2, 00. Study: Univ Ill; Syracuse Univ, BP; Acad Colarossi, Paris; also painting with George Snow Hill, Paris. Work: Syracuse Mus Fine Arts, NY; Libr Cong, Washington, DC; Metrop Mus Art, New York; J B Speed Mem Mus, Louisville, Ky; New York Pub Libr. Comn: Gift print for Printmakers Soc Calif, 62. Exhib: Soc Am Graphic Artists; Chicago Soc Etchers; Libr Cong; one-man show, Smithsonian Inst; St Petersburg Main Pub Libr, Fla, 77; plus many other one-man shows. Awards: Nathan I Bijur Award, Brooklyn Soc Etchers, 29; Purchase Prize, Libr Cong, 41; Purchase Prize, Soc Am Etchers, 47; plus others. Bibliog: Fine Prints of the Year, 30, 32 & 33; Contemporary American Prints, 31; Albert Reese (auth), Prize Prints of the Twentieth Century, 49. Mem: Soc Am Graphic Artists; Mus Fine Arts St Petersburg; Ringling Mus Art. Style & Technique: Line etching and dry point, some with watercolor and plumbago added. Publ: Illusr, Woodpile Poems, 36; illusr, Bible Chillun, 39; illusr, Dark Windows, 42; illusr, Rainbow Through the Web, 44. Dealer: Wits End Highlands NC 28741; Little Art Gallery North Hills Shopping Ctr Mall Raleigh NC 27609. Mailing Add: 2233 Green Way S St Petersburg FL 33712

HILL, RICHARD WAYNE
PAINTER, PHOTOGRAPHER
b Buffalo, NY, Aug 7, 50. Study: Art Inst of Chicago, 68-71; State Univ NY, Buffalo, 77. Work: Native Am Ctr for the Living Arts, Niagara Falls, NY; Arts & Crafts Bd, Dept of Interior, Washington, DC; Woodland Indian Cult & Educ Ctr, Brantford, Ont; Int Ctr of Photog, New York. Comn: Watercolor series, Farmer's Mus, Cooperstown, NY, 71; photog, Everson Mus, Syracuse, 72; drawings series, Buffalo Courier Express, NY, 74; photog, Smithsonian Inst, Washington, DC, 75-76. Exhib: Iroquois Confederacy Arts & Crafts Exhib, Everson Mus, Syracuse, NY, 72; one-man show, Paintings by Richard Hill, Buffalo Mus of Sci, NY, 73; An Exhib of Iroquois Arts, Univ Mus, Univ Pa, 74; Exhib of Liturgical Arts, Philadelphia Civic Ctr, 76; Exhib of Iroquois Art, Dortmund, Ger, 76; 32nd Am Indian Artists Exhib, Philbrook Art Ctr, Tulsa, 77; Three Indian Artists, Roberson Ctr, Binghamton, NY, 77. Collections Arranged: Art of the Iroquois (auth, catalogue), Erie Co Savings Bank, Buffalo, 74; People of the Longhouse, Buffalo & Erie Co Hist Soc, 76; Indian Art from New York State, Native Am Ctr, Niagara Falls, 76; Iroquois Art, Artists Comt Gallery, Buffalo, 77. Teaching: Instr art & photog, Buffalo NAm Indian Cult Ctr, 74-76; lectr Indian art, State Univ NY, Buffalo, 75- Pos: Photogr, Woodland Indian Cult & Educ Ctr, Brantford, Ont, 72-73; res asst, Buffalo & Erie Co Hist Soc, Buffalo, 73-76; treas, Native Am Ctr for the Living Arts, Niagara Falls, 75-; mem bd, Int Native-Am Coun of Arts, 75-77; admin exec, Asn for Advan of Native NAm Arts & Crafts, Niagara Falls, 76-; mem expansion arts adv panel, Nat Endowment for the Arts, 77. Awards: Am the Beautiful Fund grant, NY, 74; Creative Artist Pub Serv grant, NY, 76; Hon Mention, 32rd Am Indian Artists Exhib, Philbrook Art Ctr, Tulsa, 77. Bibliog: Susan Greenwood (auth), Indian mind, 74, Rebecca Irving (auth), Indian art, 75, Niagara Falls Gazette; Anthony Bannon (auth), CAPS winners, Buffalo Evening News, 77. Style & Technique: Portraits in watercolor, realistic with traditional symbolism. Media: Watercolor, graphite; black & white photog. Publ: Illusr (series on local hist), Buffalo Courier Express, 74; illusr, 1975 Festival of American Folklife, Smithsonian Inst Prog, 75; auth, On returning cultural objects, Mus News, 77. Dealer: Native Am Ctr for Living Arts 466 Third St Niagara Falls NY 14301. Mailing Add: 3560 Stony Point Rd Grand Island NY 14072

HILL, WILLIAM MANSFIELD
ART HISTORIAN, MUSEUM DIRECTOR
b Middlesbrough, York, Eng, Dec 4, 25. Study: Calif State Univ, San Jose, BA, 49; Univ of Calif, Berkeley, MA & post grad study; Univ of Calif, Los Angeles, post grad study with Walter Horn & James Ackerman. Collections Arranged: Southern California Regional Print & Drawing Annuals, 73-78 & Four Santa Monica Artists: Stanton MacDonald Wright, John Altoon, Sam Francis, Richard Diebenkorn, 75, Santa Monica Col; plus others. Teaching: Lectr art hist, Otis Art Inst, Los Angeles, 58-71; chmn dept of art & assoc prof art hist, Calif State Univ, Northridge, 65-68. Pos: Sr cur, Los Angeles Co Mus of Art, Los Angeles, 64-65; assoc dir arts & humanities, Univ Exten, Univ of Calif, Los Angeles, 68-71; dir, Art Gallery, Santa Monica Col, Calif, 73- Awards: Four Creative Prog Awards, Nat Univ Exten Asn, 68-69. Bibliog: Walter W Horn (auth), Medieval origins of the bay system, Soc of Archit Hist J, 58. Mem: Western Asn of Art Mus; Col Art Asn. Res: Architecture of Constantine; Cathedral of St Pierre; Angoulême; history of 19th and 20th century art history and city planning. Publ: Contribr, Handbook, Los Angeles Co Mus of Art, 64. Mailing Add: 1900 W Pico Blvd Santa Monica CA 90405

HILLDING, JOHN EMIL
See Uthco, T R

HILLER, BETTY R
GALLERY DIRECTOR, CURATOR
b El Paso, Tex, Sept 25, 25. Study: Univ Tex, El Paso; Univ NMex; Univ Southern Calif, BFA, 45; Univ Nebr, Omaha; Creighton Univ; study of painting, Des Moines Art Ctr, with Jean Charlot, Georg Grosz, William Zorach & Jimmy Ernst. Collections Arranged: Ralston Crawford Exhib, Creighton Univ Gallery, Omaha, Nebr, 69; Julian Brody Collection of African Art, Univ Nebr, Omaha, 76. Pos: Original developer, Children's Mus, Des Moines Art Ctr, 52-58; gallery owner & dealer, Lubetkin Gallery, Des Moines, Iowa, 62-64; ed arts, Spectrum Page, Sun Newspaper, 68-69; gallery dir, Creighton Univ, Omaha, 68-70; original developer, Children's Mus of Omaha, 75, first mus pres, 77-78; gallery dir, Univ Nebr, Omaha, 76; dir & mgr gallery, Univ Nebr, Omaha, 76- Bibliog: George Shane (auth), Lubetkin Gallery, Des Moines Register, 62; Betty Hiller—Eugene Kingman Gallery Directors, 68, Elizabeth Flynn (auth), Betty Hiller, painter and gallery director, 76, Omaha World Herald. Mem: Omaha Artists Asn; Am Fedn Arts; Coun Art Advocates. Style & Technique: Acrylic in construction form. Specialty: Ethnic arts both ancient and modern, and 20th century American arts. Collection: American and European antiquities of the 20th century. Mailing Add: 10346 Fieldcrest Ct Omaha NE 68114

HILLES, SUSAN MORSE
COLLECTOR, PATRON
b Simsbury, Conn, July 4, 05. Study: Mus Fine Arts Sch, Boston, 24-25; Sacker Sch Design, Boston, 26-29; Univ Kings Col, DCL, 58; Wheaton Col, LittD, 67. Pos: Trustee, Yale Art Gallery Assocs, 57-; trustee, Mus Fine Arts Boston, 68-; trustee, Whitney Mus Am Art, 70; hon trustee, Wadsworth Atheneum, 71; trustee, Am Acad in Rome, 72; trustee, Boston Athenaeum. Collection: Contemporary sculpture and painting. Mailing Add: 19 Castle Rock Branford CT 06405

HILLIGOSS, MARTHA M
ART LIBRARIAN
b St Louis, Mo, Oct 28, 28. Study: Washington Univ, St Louis, BS; Univ Ill, Champaigne, MSLS. Pos: Chief art dept, St Louis Pub Libr, 65- Mem: Art Libr Soc NAm (Kans-Mo Chap). Publ: Auth, Steedman Architectural Library Catalogue, 73. Mailing Add: 1301 Olive St St Louis MO 63105

HILLIS, RICHARD K
DESIGNER, PAINTER
b Cincinnati, Ohio, Oct 3, 36. Study: Ohio Univ, BFA, 60, MFA, 62; Univ Ariz, 66; Carnegie Mellon Univ, NDEA fel, 72, DA, 73. Work: Ark Art Ctr, Little Rock. Exhib: Southwest Print & Drawing Exhib, Dallas, 65; Images on Paper, Jackson, Miss, 71; 17th Ann Delta Exhib, Little Rock, 74; Southwest Fine Arts Biennial, Mus NMex, Santa Fe, 74; 64th Ann Tex Fed Am Art Exhib, Austin, 75. Teaching: Asst prof art, Kent State Univ, 69-73; assoc prof 20th century art, Tex Tech Univ, 73-74. Awards: Eastern NMex Univ Res Grant Printmaking, 67. Bibliog: Western Rev, Western NMex Univ, 67. Mem: Col Art Asn Am. Style & Technique: Contemporary. Media: Oil, Etching. Publ: Auth, Courbet, Art Educ Mag, 68; auth, Visual aspects of Prana, Oriental Arts Mag, 69; auth, Television as idea, 72, Figure ground phenomenon, 74, Ubiquitious Mandala, 75 & Interface through process, 76, Design Mag. Dealer: Green Apple Gallery 900 Karen Ave B-116 Las Vegas NV 89109. Mailing Add: 4117 Brownfield Hwy Bel Air 33 Lubbock TX 79407

HILLMAN, ARTHUR STANLEY
PRINTMAKER, INSTRUCTOR
b Brooklyn, NY, Feb 21, 45. Study: Philadelphia Col Art, with Jerome Kaplan & Benton Spruance, BFA; Univ Mass, Amherst, MFA. Exhib: 21st & 22nd Nat Exhib, Libr Cong, Washington, DC, 69 & 71; Prize Winning Am Prints, Pratt Graphics Ctr, New York, 69, 4th Int Miniature Print Exhib, 71; one-man show, Philadelphia Art Alliance, 70; 16th NDak Ann Print & Drawing Exhib, Univ NDak, 73; one-man show, Williams Col Mus Art, 76; plus others. Teaching: Instr printmaking & chmn dept, Mass Col Art, Boston, 68-74; instr printmaking & photog, Simon's Rock Early Col, Mass, 74- Awards: Univ Mass Fel, 67; Pennell Fund Purchase Award, Libr Cong, 69; Northern Ill Univ Purchase Award, 70. Mem: Col Art Asn Am; Philadelphia Print Club. Style & Technique: Photo silk-screens and experimental photo process prints, synthesizing figurative and landscape images. Mailing Add: Box 106F RD 1 Housatonic MA 01236

HILLSMITH, FANNIE
PAINTER
b Boston, Mass, Mar 13, 11. Study: Boston Mus Fine Arts Sch; Art Students League, with Alexander Brook, Kuniyoshi, Zorach & Sloan; Atelier 17, with Stanley Hayter. Work: Mus Mod Art, New York; Boston Mus Fine Arts; Currier Gallery Art, Manchester, NH; Fogg Mus Art, Cambridge, Mass; Newark Mus Art, NJ; plus others. Exhib: Boston Arts Festival, 50-54 & 56-61; Cornell Univ, 64; one-man retrospective, Brockton Mus, Mass, 71 & Bristol Mus, RI, 72; Brattleboro Mus, 74; plus many others. Teaching: Vis critic, Cornell Univ, 63-64. Awards: Alumni Traveling Scholar, Boston Mus Fine Arts Sch, 58; Tour Gallery Award, 64; Berkshire Mus Award, 64; plus many others. Style & Technique: From Belgian linen, ground colors, various media, to projected patterns to establish a half-real and half-abstract world of vistas and tangible objects. Publ: Auth & illusr, The Ups and Downs of Needlepoint, Barnes, 76. Mailing Add: c/o Wedgewood Jaffrey NH 03452

HILSON, DOUGLAS
PAINTER, EDUCATOR
b Flint, Mich, Dec 7, 41. Study: Cranbrook Acad Art, Bloomfield Hills, Mich, BFA; Univ Wash, MFA. Work: Indianapolis Mus Art; Ill Art Mus, Springfield, DeWaters Art Inst, Flint, Mich; Decatur Art Mus, Ill; Western Mich Univ Art Mus, Kalamazoo. Exhib: One-man show, Marianne Deson Gallery, Chicago, 75; 76th Chicago Exhib, Chicago Art Inst, 76; Midwestern Artists, Ind Univ Art Gallery & Krannert Mus, 76; Midwestern Figurative, Madison Art Ctr, Wis, 76; Chicago Connection, Nat Traveling Exhib of Chicago Artists, 76-77; Retrospective 1973-77, Krannert Mus Art, 77; Nat Beauty of the Beast Animal Images in Contemp Am Art, Kohler Art Ctr, Wis, 77; Int Art Fair, Bologna, Italy, 78. Teaching: Prof painting & dir grad painting prog, Univ Ill, Champaign, 65- Awards: Atwater Kent Award-First Prize, Soc Four Arts, Palm Beach & Atwater Kent Corp, 67; First Prize, Nat Works Art on Paper, 76; Purchase Award, 29th Ill Invitational, Ill Art Mus Permanent Collection, 76. Style & Technique: Illusionism vis trompe l'oeil combined with actual physical cuts within rectangle. Media: Oil & Acrylic on Canvas; Graphite on Paper. Dealer: Marianne Deson Gallery 226 E Ontario Chicago IL 60611; Galerie Darthea Speyer 6 Rue Jacques Callot Paris France. Mailing Add: 713 W Green Champaign IL 61820

HILTON, ERIC G
DESIGNER, LECTURER
b Bournemouth, Brit, Feb 7, 37. Study: Edinburgh Col of Art, Scotland, dipl art, post-dipl art; Moray House Teachers Col, dipl educ. Work: Pilkington's Glass Mus, Liverpool, Eng; Corning Mus of Glass, NY; Lowe Art Mus, Univ Miami, Coral Gables, Fla; Univ Victoria, BC; Birmingham Col of Art, Eng. Comn: Photog design, Edinburgh Col of Art, Scotland, 60; glass exhib, Stourbridge Col of Art, London, 63 & T W IDG Inc, London, 65; archit mural, Token House, London, 67 & Sun Life Assurance Co, London, 67. Exhib: Greater Victoria Art Gallery, BC, 70; Corning Mus of Glass, NY, 70; Pilkington's Glass Mus, Eng, 71; Am Glass Now (traveling exhib), 73; Int Glass Sculpture, Miami, Fla, 73; Craft Biennal, Edinburgh, Scotland, 74; Am View—Art of Craft, Ill State Univ, 76; Mus of Contemp Art, Chicago, 76. Teaching: Lectr glass, Edinburgh Col of Art, Scotland, 60-62; prof 3-D design,

Univ Victoria, BC, 69-71; prof glass, State Univ NY Col, Alfred, 72-76. Pos: Chmn graphic arts, Univ Victoria, 70-71; co-organizer cold glass workshop, World Craft Coun of Japan, 78; designer, Steuben Glass, Corning, NY, 73-78. Awards: Open Glaziers Competition, Brit Glass Mfg, 68; Can Coun of Art Grant, Corning Mus of Glass, NY, 70 & Pilkington's Glass Mus, 71. Bibliog: Glass design, Scottishfield, 68; Trautmansdorf (auth), Capturing light, Times Educ Suppl, Eng, 68. Style & Technique: Cut and engraved glass; drawing; photography. Media: Glass, wood, plastic, metal & light. Publ: Auth, Frank J Malina, ed, Optical art in glass, Leonardo, 75. Mailing Add: Box 198 RD 1 Odessa NY 14869

HILTON, JOHN WILLIAM
PAINTER, ILLUSTRATOR
b Carrington, NDak, Sept 9, 04. Study: With Maynard Dixon, Clyde Forsythe & Nicolai Fechin; Int Inst Arts & Lett fel; Am Inst Fine Arts fel. Work: La Verne Col; Nat Park Visitor Ctrs; San Diego Mus Nat Hist; Palm Springs Desert Mus; plus many others. Comn: Mural, Desert Southwest Gallery, 37; mural, Saddleback Western Gallery, Santa Ana, Calif, 62; diorama, Living Desert Reserve, Palm Desert, 72; mural, Calif Acad Sci, 76. Exhib: Hundreds of group & one-man shows in US & abroad, 35-72. Bibliog: Dave Packwood (auth), An artist looks at Baja California, Westways, 3/56; Mason Sutherland (auth), Californians escape to the desert, Nat Geog, 57; Ed Ainsworth (auth), Painters of the Desert, Desert Mag, 60; plus many others. Mem: Grand Cent Art Gallery; Salmagundi Club; life mem Laguna Beach Art Asn; Lahaina Art Asn; life mem Twentynine Palms Artists Guild (pres, 52-55). Style & Technique: Poetic realism, with knife to produce texture perspective. Media: Oil, Wax. Publ: Auth & illusr, Sonora Sketchbook, Macmillan, 47; auth & illusr, This is my desert, Ariz Hwys, 64; auth & illusr, Hilton paints the desert, Desert Mag; contribr Ariz Hwys, 4/75 & 12/75; auth, Hardly Any Fences, Baja the Way it Was, Glen Dawson, 76; plus others. Dealer: Grand Central Galleries 40 Vanderbilt Ave New York NY 10017; Desert Southwest Galleries Palm Desert CA 92260. Mailing Add: PO Box 14 Twentynine Palms CA 92277

HILTS, ALVIN
SCULPTOR
b Newmarket, Ont, Apr 2, 08. Study: In Mex & Can. Work: Churches, Kirkland Lake, Welland & Newmarket; also in schs. Comn: Memorial, Newmarket, 36; Univ Guelph, 61; Univ Lennoxville, 70; also pvt comn, Vancouver, Toronto, Ottawa, Oshawa & St Louis. Exhib: Sculpture Soc, 31-72; Royal Can Acad; Ont Soc Artists. Mem: Sculpture Soc Can (pres, 57, 58 & 61). Media: Wood, Stone. Mailing Add: 605 Oshawa Blvd N Oshawa ON Can

HIMLER, RONALD NORBERT
ILLUSTRATOR, PAINTER
b Cleveland, Ohio, Oct 16, 37. Study: Cleveland Inst Art, dipl; Cranbrook Acad Art, Bloomfield Hills, Mich; New York Univ. Style & Technique: Realistic style for illustration in oil on acetate, blackwash oil on acetate, or pencil; abstract style for painting in oil on canvas or gesso panels. Publ: Co-auth & illusr, Little Owl, Keeper of the Trees, 74, auth & illusr, The Girl on the Yellow Giraffe, 76 & illusr, Windrose, 76, Harper & Row; illusr, The Blue Stone, Holiday House, 76; illusr, Tornado, Delacorte, Press, 77. Mailing Add: 680 West End Ave New York NY 10025

HIMMELFARB, JOHN DAVID
PAINTER
b Chicago, Ill, June 3, 46. Study: Harvard Univ, BA, 68, MAT, 70. Work: Art Inst Chicago; Nat Collection Fine Art, Smithsonian Inst, Washington, DC; Fogg Mus Art, Cambridge, Mass; Sheldon Mem Art Gallery, Lincoln, Nebr; Ill State Mus, Springfield. Exhib: Printmakers Mid-West Show, Walker Art Ctr, Minneapolis, 73; one-man show, Graphics I & Graphics II Gallery, Boston, 74, Art Gallery, Univ Nebr, Omaha, 76 & Dorothy Rosenthal Gallery, 76 & 78; 27th Ill Show, Ill State Mus, 74; 19th Nat Print Show, Brooklyn Mus, 74; Three Lithographers, Sheldon Mem Art Gallery, 75; Davidson Nat Print & Drawing Exhib, 76; 19th Ann, Okla Art Ctr, Oklahoma City, 77. Awards: Drawings USA Purchase Award, Minn Mus, St Paul, 71. Media: Oil, Pen & Ink. Publ: Illusr, Bridge Over Troubled Laughter, 70; illusr, The Family Dog, 73. Mailing Add: 908 W 19th St Chicago IL 60608

HINES, JOHN M
PAINTER
b Lanius, Tex. Study: Colo Univ, BA; Harvard Univ, MA; New Sch; Nat Acad Sch Fine Arts; with Philip Hicken. Exhib: One-man shows, Community Gallery, New York, 72-77, Little Gallery, Nantucket, 74 & Grist Mill Gallery, Vt, 75; Kenneth Taylor Gallery, Nantucket, 72-77; Nat Arts Club, New York, 73-77; Burr Artists, Union Carbide & Lever House, 74-75; Metrop Mus of Art, New York. Mem: Nat Arts Club; Burr Artists, Inc (treas); Am Artists Prof League (bd); Artists Asn Nantucket (exec comt); Artists Equity. Style & Technique: Landscapes and seascapes; brush and knife. Media: Acrylic. Mailing Add: 10 Park Ave New York NY 10016

HING, ALLAN MARK
EDUCATOR, INTERIOR DESIGNER
b San Francisco, Calif, Apr 3, 43. Study: San Francisco State Col, BA, 65; Pratt Inst, BFA, 68; Syracuse Univ, MA, 78. Teaching: Asst prof interior design, Syracuse Univ, 71-77. Pos: Interior designer, Space Design Group, New York, 68-69; interior designer, Skidmore, Owings and Merrill, New York, 69-71. Mem: Am Soc Interior Designers; Interior Designers Educr Coun. Publ: Auth, Educational parks sketches—The Space Design Group, Interiors Mag, 69 & Contract Mag, 69. Mailing Add: 69 Onondaga St Skaneateles NY 13152

HINKHOUSE, FOREST MELICK
ART CONSULTANT
b West Liberty, Iowa, July 7, 25. Study: Coe Col, AB; Univ Mex; Fogg Art Mus, Harvard Univ; NY Univ Inst Fine Arts, MA; Univ Madrid, PhD. Collections Arranged: Industrial Gouaches of John Hultberg, 57; Paintings & Portraits by Frank Mason, 58; Contemporary Arizona Painting, 58; Festival of Arts, 58; One Hundred Years of French Painting 1860-1960, 61; English Landscape Painting, 61. Teaching: Asst prof art, Albright Art Sch, Univ Buffalo, 56-57; lects, Spanish Painting, Mediaeval Art, Art of the Far East & Contemporary Art; guest lectr, Prudential Lines, 77. Pos: Pub relations, Int House Asn, New York; art critic, Buffalo Eve News, Ariz Repub & Phoenix Gazette; founding dir, Phoenix Art Mus & Phoenix Fine Arts Asn, 57-67; co-founder, Hinkhouse Gallery, Coe Col, 65; consult & adv, Phoenix Art Mus, 67-; consult, Calif Art Comn, 68-; co-founder, Hinkhouse Collection, Melick Libr, Eureka Col, 69; mem bd trustees, Coe Col, Cedar Rapids, Iowa. Mem: Claustro Extraordinario, Madrid; Col Art Asn Am; Am Asn Mus. Publ: Auth, Catalogue of the Collections of the Phoenix Art Museum; contribr, articles in Oregonian, 75- Mailing Add: 1815 Jones St Russian Hill San Francisco CA 94109

HINMAN, CHARLES B
PAINTER, SCULPTOR
b Syracuse, NY, Dec 29, 32. Study: Syracuse Univ, BFA, 55; Art Students League, with Morris Kantor. Work: Mus Mod Art, New York; Larry Aldrich Mus Contemp Art, Conn; Los Angeles Co Mus; Detroit Inst Art; Mus Mod Art, Nagaoka, Japan; plus many others. Exhib: Retrospective, Philharmonic Hall, Lincoln Ctr, New York, 69; Opening Exhib, Contemp Art Ctr, Cincinnati, Ohio, 70; Contemporary Painting & Sculpture from New York Galleries, Wilmington Soc Fine Arts, Del Art Ctr, 70; Selections from Chase Manhattan Bank Collection, Finch Col, 71; Sculpture & Shapes of the Last Decade, Aldrich Mus, Ridgefield, Conn; plus many others. Media: Acrylic. Mailing Add: 231 Bowery New York NY 10002

HIOS, THEO
PAINTER, GRAPHIC ARTIST
b Sparta, Greece, Feb 2, 10; US citizen. Study: Am Artists Sch; Art Students League; Pratt Inst; Nat Univ Athens. Work: Carnegie Inst, Pittsburgh; Nat Collection Fine Art, Washington, DC; Guild Hall Mus, Easthampton, NY; Parrish Art Mus, Southampton, NY; Tel Aviv Mus, Israel; plus others. Exhib: Long Island Artists, Brooklyn Mus, 58; Carnegie Inst Int, 61; one-man retrospective, Harpur Col, 61; Nat Exhib, Pa Acad Fine Arts, 62; one-man shows, Parrish Art Mus, 64 & 72, New Sch Social Res, 67 & 70 & Guild Hall Mus, 70; plus others. Teaching: Instr painting & drawing, City Col New York, 58-61; instr painting & drawing, Dalton Sch, 62-73; instr painting & drawing, New Sch Social Res, 62- Awards: First Prize, New Eng Exhib, Silvermine Guild Artists, 48; Purchase Prize, Riverside Mus, 62; One-Man Show Award, Guild Hall Mus, 69; plus others. Bibliog: Lawrence Campbell (auth), article in Art News, 11/63; Marshall Matusow (auth), article in Art Collector's Almanac, 65; article in Lithopinion, 6/71; plus others. Mem: Fedn Mod Painters & Sculptors (vpres, 57-62 & 66-75). Media: Oil, Acrylic. Mailing Add: 136 W 95th St New York NY 10025

HIRSCH, DAVID W (DAVE)
CARTOONIST
b New York, NY, Dec 26, 19. Study: Brooklyn Col; Art Students League; Grand Cent Art Sch; Cartoonist & Illusr Sch. Publ: Contribr cartoons, Sat Eve Post, Look, Christian Sci Monitor, Argosy, Am Legion Mag, US Info Agency Russian publ, America, Am Weekly, Wall St Jour, King Features Syndicate & MacNaught Syndicate; plus others. Mailing Add: 14 Stuyvesant Oval New York NY 10009

HIRSCH, GILAH YELIN
PAINTER, EDUCATOR
b Montreal, PQ, Aug 24, 44. Study: Univ Calif, Berkeley, BA; Univ Calif, Los Angeles, MFA. Exhib: One-woman shows, Lytton Gallery, Los Angeles Co Mus Art, 71, Tibor de Nagy Gallery, New York, 72, Calif State Col, Fresno, 74, Calif State Col, Dominguez Hills, 75 & Downey Mus, 75; Southern California Attitudes, Pasadena Mus, 72; New York Cultural Center Realist Revival, 72; Whitney Mus Ann, 73. Teaching: Asst prof painting & drawing, Calif State Col, Dominguez Hills, 73- Awards: Los Angeles Municipal New Talent Award, 70; Artist in Residence Fel, Tamarind Lithography Workshop, 73. Bibliog: Revs in New York Times, Los Angeles Times, Art News, Artforum, Village Voice & Art in Am. Mem: Artists Equity. Style & Technique: Paintings of food and ribbons on watery rich surfaces. Media: Oil on Canvas. Publ: Auth, Joan of art seminar, Artweek Mag, 73. Mailing Add: 2412 Oakwood Ave Venice CA 90291

HIRSCH, JOSEPH
PAINTER
b Philadelphia, Pa, Apr 25, 10. Study: Philadelphia Col Art, 27-31; also with Henry Hensche, Provincetown & George Luks, New York. Work: Whitney Mus Am Art, New York; Mus Mod Art, New York; Corcoran Gallery Art, Washington, DC; Boston Mus Fine Arts, Mass; Metrop Mus Art, New York; plus many others. Comn: Mural, Benjamin Franklin High Sch, Philadelphia; mural, Amalgamated Clothing Workers Bldg, Philadelphia; mural, Philadelphia Munic Court Bldg; documentary paintings for US Govt. Exhib: Many throughout US, 34- Teaching: Instr painting sem, Univ Utah, summer 59; instr painting, Art Students League, 59-67; vis artist, Dartmouth Col, 66; instr, Brigham Young Univ, 71; instr, Univ Utah, 75. Awards: Altman Prize, Nat Acad Design, 59 & 67; Purchase Prize, Butler Inst Am Art, 64; Carnegie Prize, 68; plus many others. Mem: Artists Equity Asn (founder); Nat Acad Design (first treas); Nat Inst Arts & Lett. Mailing Add: 90 Riverside Dr New York NY 10024

HIRSCH, RICHARD TELLER
MUSEUM DIRECTOR, CRITIC
b Denver, Colo, Sept 12, 14. Study: Ecole Louvre. Collections Arranged: Four Centuries of Still Life, 60; The World of Benjamin West, 62; James A Michener Foundation Collection, 63, 65-68 & 71; Arms & Armor, 64; 17th Century Painters of Haarlem, 65; History of Glass, 66; Albert Decaris, 67; Eugene Carriere, Seer of the Real, 68; Mediaeval Art in France, 72; NZ Artists, 73; Constable, The Natural Painter, 73; Dutch Pastoral, 74. Teaching: Lectr art hist. Pos: Publ graphics, Paris, 37-39 & 45-46; art critic, Palm Beach, 54-56; dir, Pensacola Art Ctr, 56-59; dir, Allentown Art Mus, 59-68; spec cur, The Michener Collection, Univ Tex, Austin, 68-71; dir, Auckland City Art Gallery, NZ, 72-74; dir Auckland Art Acad, 75- Awards: Samuel H Kress Found Museology Study Grant, 67. Mem: Am Asn Mus; Col Art Asn Am; Am Soc Aesthet; Int Coun Mus. Mailing Add: 10 Shortland Flats Auckland New Zealand

HIRSCH, WILLARD NEWMAN
SCULPTOR
b Charleston, SC, Nov 19, 05. Study: Nat Acad Design; Beaux Arts Inst Design. Work: Gibbes Art Gallery, Charleston; Columbia Mus Art, SC; Florence Mus Art, SC; SC State Art Collection, Columbia; Sculpture of Western Hemisphere, IBM Collection. Comn: Stainless steel works, Clemson Univ, 49-55 & Charleston Co Libr, 61; pulpit sculpture, Woodsdale Temple, Wheeling, WVa, 65; steel & brass sculpture, Porter Gaud Sch, Charleston, 66; bronze fountain figure, Home Fed Savings & Loan, Charleston, 70; aluminum sculptures, Newberry Col, 73. Exhib: Nat Acad Design, New York, 35-42; Pa Acad Fine Art, Philadelphia, 42; Syracuse Mus Art, NY, 48; Fairmont Park 3rd Int, Philadelphia, 49; Whitney Mus Am Art, New York, 50. Bibliog: Jack Morris, Jr (auth), Contemporary Artists of South Carolina, SC Tricentennial Comn, 70. Mem: Charleston Artists Guild; SC Artists Guild (past pres). Mailing Add: 2 Queen St Charleston SC 29401

HIRSCHFELD, ALBERT
GRAPHIC ARTIST
b St Louis, Mo, June 21, 03. Study: Nat Acad Design, New York; Julien's, Paris; London Co Coun; Art Students League. Work: Whitney Mus Am Art, New York; Mus Mod Art, New York; Metrop Mus Art, New York; Brooklyn Mus Art, NY; St Louis Mus Art. Comn: History of Cinema, Fifth Ave Playhouse, New York, 45; Personalities, Eden Roc Hotel, Miami, Fla, 55; American Theatre, Brussels World's Fair, 59; Opening Night, Playbill Room, Manhattan Hotel, NY, 60. Exhib: One-man shows, Staten Island Mus, NY, 61, Hammer Gallery, New

York, 67, Mus Performing Arts, Lincoln Ctr, New York, 68, Margo Feiden Gallery, New York, 72-74 & Seibu Gallery, Tokyo, Japan, 75; Gallery 18, London, Eng, 77. Pos: Theatre caricaturist, New York Times, 23- Awards: Specialist Grant, US State Dept. Media: Ink. Publ: Auth, The American Theatre, George Braziller, 61; auth, The World of Hirschfeld, Abrams, 71; auth, Rhythm, Touchstone, 70; auth, Kabuki, Goodstadt, 76; auth, The Entertainers, Elm Tree, London, 77. Mailing Add: 122 E 95th St New York NY 10028

HIRSHHORN, JOSEPH H
COLLECTOR
b Latvia, Aug 11, 99; US citizen. Pos: Trustee, George Wash Univ, Washington, DC; Friends of Whitney Mus, Arch Am Art, Palm Springs Mus, Calif & Aldrich Mus, Ridgefield, Conn. Bibliog: Jay Jacobs & Jean Lipman (auth), The Collector in America, Viking, 71. Interest: Donated Hirshhorn Museum and Sculpture Garden, Smithsonian Institution, Washington, DC. Collection: American nineteenth and twentieth century painting; European twentieth century painting; sculpture from antiquity to the present.

HITCH, JEAN LEASON
PAINTER
b Sydney, Australia, Oct 18, 18; US citizen. Study: Melbourne Tech Art Training Sch, Australia; Leason Sch Painting; Wayman Adams Sch Painting, Adirondacks, NY. Exhib: Allied Artists Am, Am Artist Prof League & Catharine Lorillard Wolfe Art Club, New York; Hudson Valley Art Asn, White Plains, NY; Audubon Artists, New York. Pos: Art cur, Staten Island Inst Arts & Sci, 45-51. Awards: Kathleen Grumbacher Award, 66; Anna Hyatt Huntington Horse-Head Award, 72; Bronze Medal, Cape Cod Art Asn, 77. Mem: Cape Cod Art Asn (1st vpres); Copley Soc of Boston; Allied Artists Am; Catharine Lorillard Wolfe Art Club (first vpres, 71-; Hudson Valley Art Asn; Am Artist Prof League. Media: Oil. Mailing Add: 51 Gordon Lane Yarmouth Port MA 02675

HITCH, ROBERT A
PAINTER
b Brooklyn, NY, May 12, 20. Study: Art Career Sch, New York; also painting with Wilford S Conrow, Percy Leason & Douglas Grant. Work: Hickory Art Mus, NC; Tamassee DAR Sch, SC. Exhib: Allied Artists Am & Am Artists Prof League, New York; Hudson Valley Art Asn, White Plains, NY; Staten Island Mus Arts & Sci, NY; Nat Arts Club, New York. Awards: Henry Ward Ranger Prize, Nat Acad Design, 54; Grand Nat Award, Am Artists Prof League, 54; Best Cape Cod Scene, Cape Cod Art Asn, 77. Mem: Allied Artists Am (pub rels, 69-); Cape Cod Art Asn; Copley Soc of Boston; Hudson Valley Art Asn; Am Artists Prof League. Media: Oil. Mailing Add: 51 Gordon Lane Yarmouth Port MA 02675

HITCHCOCK, HENRY RUSSELL
ART HISTORIAN, ART CRITIC
b Boston, Mass, June 3, 03. Study: Harvard Univ, AB, 24, MA, 27; NY Univ, hon DFA; Glasgow Univ, Scotland, hon LHD; Univ Pa, hon DHL. Teaching: Asst prof art, Vassar Col, 27-28; asst prof art, Wesleyan Univ, 29-41, assoc prof, 41-47, prof, 47-48; instr, Conn Col, 34-42; prof art, Smith Col, 48-61, Sophia Smith prof art, 61-68; prof art, Univ Mass, Amherst, 68; adj prof, Inst Fine Arts, NY Univ, 69-; lectr, Mass Inst Technol, 46-48; vis lectr, Yale Univ, 52-53, 59-60 & 69, Cambridge Univ, 62, Harvard Univ, 65 & Columbia Univ, 71. Pos: Dir, Smith Col Mus Art, 49-55. Awards: Soc Archit Historians Book Award, 55; Col Art Asn Book Award, 58; Am Coun Learned Soc Prize, 61; plus others. Mem: Franklin fel Royal Soc Arts; Soc Archit Historians (dir, pres, NY Chap, 70-); Victorian Soc Am (pres, 69-); Col Art Asn Am; Royal Inst Brit Architects. Publ: Auth, In the Nature of Materials, the Buildings of Frank Lloyd Wright, 42 & 69; auth, Architecture: 19th and 20th Century, 58, 69, 72 & 77; auth, Rococo Architecture in Southern Germany, 69; co-auth, with W Seale, Temples of Democracy, 76; plus others. Mailing Add: 152 E 62nd St New York NY 10021

HNIZDOVSKY, JACQUES
PAINTER, PRINTMAKER
b Pylypcze, Ukraine, Jan 27, 15; US citizen. Study: Acad Fine Arts, Warsaw; Acad Fine Arts, Zagreb, Yugoslavia. Work: Mus Fine Arts, Boston; Philadelphia Mus Art; Cleveland Mus; Nelson Rockefeller Collection. Exhib: Boston Printmakers Ann, Mus Fine Arts, Boston, 61-; Contemporary US Graphic Arts, USSR, 63; Triennale Int dellaxilografia Contemporanea, Carpi, Italy; Contemporary US Printmakers, Tokyo, Japan, 67; one-man shows, Lumley-Cazalet, London, Eng, 69 & 72; one-man retrospective, Ten Years of Woodcuts, Assoc Am Artists, New York, 71; Long Beach Mus Art, Calif, 77; Yale Univ, 77. Awards: First Prize for Woodcut, Mus Fine Arts, Boston, 62; MacDowell Colony Fel, 63; YADDO, 78. Bibliog: Slavko Nowytski (auth), Sheep in Wood (film), Am Film Festival, New York, 71. Mem: Soc Am Graphic Artists; Audubon Artists; Boston Printmakers. Style & Technique: Simplified realism, emblematic approach. Media: Oil; Woodcut. Publ: Illusr woodcuts, Poems of John Keats, 64 & Poems of Samuel Taylor Coleridge, 67, Crowell-Collier; illusr, Tree Tails in Central Park, 71; co-auth & illusr, Flora Exotica, D Godine, Boston, 72; contribr, Portfolio: Jacques Hnizdovsky: Twelve Birds, Assoc Am Artists. Dealer: Assoc Am Artists 663 Fifth Ave New York NY 10017. Mailing Add: 5270 Post Rd Riverdale NY 10471

HOARE, TYLER JAMES
SCULPTOR, PRINTMAKER
b Joplin, Mo, June 5, 40. Study: Univ Colo; Sculpture Ctr, New York; Univ Kans, BFA, 63; Calif Col Arts & Crafts, Oakland. Work: US Info Agency, Washington, DC; State Univ NY Albany; Oakland Mus, Calif; Calif Col Arts & Crafts; plus many pvt collections. Exhib: One-man shows, John Bolles Gallery, San Francisco, Calif, 69, 71 & 74, Camberwell Sch Art, London, Eng, 71 & Cent Sch Art & Design, London, 74; 4th Int Print Exhib, Pratt Graphics Ctr, New York, 71; 22nd Nat Print Exhib, Libr Cong, Washington, DC, 71; Calif Palace Legion Honor; Xerographic Art, Xerox Corp, New York; plus many others. Teaching: Guest lectr, San Francisco Art Inst, 72; guest lectr, San Francisco State Univ, 72-74; instr, Univ Calif, Berkeley, 73-74; guest lectr, Oakland Mus, Calif, 74; guest lectr, Calif State Univ, Hayward, 74. Awards: Merit Award, 22nd Ann San Francisco Art Festival, San Francisco Art Comn, 68; 2nd Ann Graphic Exhib, Olive Hyde Art Ctr, 72; Focuserie Award, Nat Photog Exhib, Erie, Pa, 74; plus others. Bibliog: Thomas Albright (auth), Funk refinement, San Francisco Chronicle, 3/69; New American Sculpture, US Info Agency, 71; Robert Cartmell (auth), Xerox is okay-but will it last?, Albany Times Union, 2/72. Mem: Los Angeles Printmaking Soc; Nat Soc Lit & Arts; Metal Arts Guild, San Francisco; Ctr Visual Arts, Oakland, Calif; Richmond Art Ctr, Calif. Style & Technique: Mixed media sculpture and prints from the 3M color in color and Xerox color machines. Media: Wood, Metal. Dealer: ADI Gallery 530 McAllister San Francisco CA 94102. Mailing Add: 30 Menlo Pl Berkeley CA 94707

HOBBIE, LUCILLE
PAINTER, ILLUSTRATOR
b Boonton, NJ, June 14, 15. Work: Montclair Art Mus, NJ; Newark Pub Libr, NJ; Colonial Williamsburg, Va; Seeing Eye, Morristown, NJ. Comn: Drawings of bicentennial historic sites, Jersey Cent Power & Light Co. Exhib: NJ State Ann, 50-72; NJ Watercolor Soc Ann, 50-72; Audubon Soc Ann, 53-72; Am Watercolor Soc Ann, Nat Acad Design Gallery, 56; 50 Artists, NJ State Mus, Trenton, 56. Pos: Admin asst, Newark Sch Fine & Indust Art, 63-75. Awards: First Prize Award for Lithography, NJ State Exhib, 51, Award for Watercolor, 52 & 62; Agnes Noyes Award, NJ Watercolor Soc, 56 & 63. Mem: NJ Watercolor Soc (pres, 50-52); Asn Artists NJ (bd dirs, 70-72); Nat Soc Arts & Lett; Am Watercolor Soc. Media: Watercolor. Publ: Illusr, A Calendar for Dinah, 69; illusr, Ecliptecs, 70. Dealer: Grand Central Galleries 40 Vanderbilt Ave New York NY 10017. Mailing Add: Talmadge Rd Mendham NJ 07945

HOBBS, (CARL) FREDRIC
SCULPTOR, FILM MAKER
b Philadelphia, Pa, Dec 30, 31. Study: Cornell Univ, BA; Acad San Fernando Belles Artes, Madrid, Spain. Work: Mus Mod Art, New York; Metrop Mus Art, New York; Finch Col Mus, New York; Oakland Mus Art, Calif; Spencer Mem Church, Brooklyn, NY; plus others. Comn: Big Sur Redwoods, Episcopal Church, 62-; Hall of Spirits (monumental environ sculpture for motion pictures), 72-78. Exhib: Biennial Exhib Am Art, Pa Acad Fine Arts, Philadelphia, 64; Nat Fine Arts Collection, Smithsonian Inst, Washington, DC, 64; The Highway Traveling Exhib, Inst Contemp Art, Philadelphia, 70; one-man shows, Calif Palace Legion of Hon, San Francisco & Mus Sci & Indust, Los Angeles, 76; plus others. Pos: Pres, Madison Hobbs Co, Inc, 71-; distinguished speaker, Progs Int Syst. Bibliog: John W McCoubrey (auth), Art & the road, Highway, 70; Thomas Albright (auth), Visuals, Rolling Stone Mag, 71; plus others. Style & Technique: Architonic; color imagist with strong expressionistic, figurative references. Media: Steel Supported Fiberglass, Latex Acrylic. Publ: Auth six original screenplays, 69-77; co-auth, The Richest Place on Earth, Houghton-Mifflin, 78. Dealer: Heritage Gallery 718 N La Cienega Blvd Los Angeles CA 90069. Mailing Add: PO Box 334 Los Altos CA 94022

HOBBS, JOE FERRELL
ART ADMINISTRATOR, SCULPTOR
b Deport, Tex, June 30, 34. Study: Univ Tex, BFA, 57; Univ Southern Calif, MFA, 60. Work: Mus Fine Arts, Houston, Tex; Ft Worth Art Ctr Mus, Tex; Mus Fine Arts, Dallas, Tex. Comn: With John Alberty, belt buckle, Ft Worth Art Ctr Mus, 75 & brand, Art Park, Lewiston, NY, 77. Exhib: Ft Worth Art Ctr Mus, 75; Art Park, NY, 77. Teaching: Instr sculpture, Univ Okla, Norman, 66- Pos: Dir, Sch Art, Univ Okla, Norman, 66- Bibliog: Jan Butterfield (art critic), article in Arts Mag, 75; Don Lipski (auth), article in Crisscross Art Commun, 76; article in Currant Mag, 76. Style & Technique: Environmental sculpture in mixed-media. Mailing Add: 719 Schulze Dr Norman OK 73071

HOBBS, ROBERT DEAN
ART ADMINISTRATOR, PRINTMAKER
b Merkel, Tex, Apr 21, 28. Study: WTex State Univ, Canyon, BA, with Emillio Caballero; Northern Colo State Univ, Greeley, MA, with Richard Ellinger; Pa State Univ, State Col, DEd, with Will Barnett. Work: WTex State Univ, Canyon; Colo State Col, Greeley; Viktor Lowenfiel Mem Collection, Pa State Univ, State College; Smithsonian Inst, Washington, DC. Exhib: Colo State Col, 57; Fac Show, WTex State Univ, 68 & 71, Clarion State Col, Pa, 71-78; one-man shows, WTex State Univ, 51-70, Amarillo Ctr, Tex, 53, Howard Co Jr Col, Big Spring, Tex, 59, Borger Co Libr, Tex, 62, Odessa Col, Tex, 63, Pa State Univ, University Park, 67 & 69, John Sloan Gallery, Lock Haven State Col, Pa, 78 & Nat Art Educ Bldg, Reston, Va, 78. Teaching: Art teacher in pub sch, Midland, Tex, 54-58; instr art, WTex State Univ, 58-63; grad asst, Pa State Univ, 65-67; assoc prof art, WTex State Univ, 67-71; prof art & chmn art dept, Clarion State Col, Pa, 71- Mem: Nat Art Educ Asn; Nat Endowment for the Arts; Pa Art Teacher Asn, Harrisburg. Style & Technique: Photo-silkscreen paintings; multi-image on canvas or Plexiglas. Media: Silkscreen. Dealer: Westbroadway Gallery 431 W Broadway New York NY 10012. Mailing Add: PO Box 605 Clarion PA 16214

HOBSON, KATHERINE THAYER
SCULPTOR
b Denver, Colo, Apr 11, 89. Study: Art Students League; also in Europe; sculpture with Walter Sintenis, Dresden, Ger. Comn: Statue, Bahnhofs Platz, Göttingen; busts, Univ Göttingen & Univ Koenigsberg; bust, Sch Technol, Dresden & univ libr, Göttingen; war mem, St James Episcopal Church, New York. Exhib: Nat Acad Design, Allied Artists Am, Am Artists Prof League, Hudson Valley Art Asn & Catharine Lorillard Wolfe Art Club, New York, 66-; also many earlier exhibs. Teaching: Lect, Roman, Greek, Renaissance & Gothic Sculpture. Pos: Secy, Fine Arts Fedn, New York, 52-69. Awards: Prizes, Allied Artists Am, Am Artists Prof League & Hudson Valley Art Asn, 68; plus others. Mem: Fel Nat Sculpture Soc; Hudson Valley Art Asn; Pen & Brush Club; Allied Artists Am; Am Artists Prof League; plus others. Mailing Add: 27 W 67th St New York NY 10023

HODGE, G STUART
MUSEUM DIRECTOR
b Worcester, Mass. Study: Sch Fine Arts, Yale Univ, BFA; Cranbrook Acad Arts, MFA; Univ Iowa, PhD. Pos: Dir, Flint Inst Arts, currently. Mem: Asn Art Mus Dir; Am Asn Mus; Am Fedn Arts. Mailing Add: Flint Inst Arts 1120 E Kearsley St Flint MI 48503

HODGE, ROY GAREY
PAINTER, INSTRUCTOR
b Moweaqua, Ill, July 27, 37. Study: Eastern Ill Univ, BS(educ), 61, MA(painting), 73; Harvard Univ Summer Sch, with William Georgenes. Comn: Pvt comns. Exhib: Tri-State Exhib, Evansville Mus, Ind, 59; Miss Valley Exhib, Ill State Mus, Springfield, 64; Ill Bell Tel Exhib, Chicago, 67; River Roads Exhib, St Louis, 69, 70 & 72; 5th Int Biennial Sport Fine Arts, La Pinacoteca, Barcelona, Spain, 75. Teaching: Instr painting, graphics & design, Lanphier High Sch, Springfield, 62-; artist in residence painting, Springfield Art Asn, 68-70. Pos: Vpres, Lahonton Valley Art Asn, Fallon, Nev, 61-62. Awards: Runner Up, New York World's Fair Sculpture Design, Int Fair Consults, 63; Second in Painting, Northside Art Asn, St Louis, 69; Grand Prize, US Hockey Hall of Fame, 76. Bibliog: I See Chicago, Ill Bell Tel TV Spec, 67. Mem: Ill Art Educ Asn (exec coun, 69-71); Ill State Mus Soc; Springfield Art Asn. Style & Technique: Semi-abstract; developing a work through washes; alla prima and mixed media using sports as subject matter. Media: Acrylic, Graphite, Watercolor. Publ: Contribr, La Rev Mod, 60. Mailing Add: 1133 N 14th St Springfield IL 62702

HODGE, SCOTTIE
ART DEALER, ART ADMINISTRATOR
b Darlington, SC, Oct 21, 40. Study: Winthrop Col, Rock Hill, SC, BS, 62; Furman Univ, Greenville, SC, MA, 73; Greenville Co Mus Art Sch, 74-75. Teaching: Dir painting &

drawing, Tempo Studios, 75- Pos: Founder & dir, Tempo Gallery (coop), 75-; founder & admin asst, SC Watercolor Soc, 78- Awards: Outstanding Young Women of Am, 77. Mem: Greenville Artist Guild (secy-treas, 76-77; pres-elect, 77-78; pres, 78-); Greenville Art Asn (bd mem, 78-). Specialty: Cooperative gallery of works by local, area artist in all media. Mailing Add: c/o Tempo Gallery 125 W Stone Ave Greenville SC 29609

HODGELL, ROBERT OVERMAN
PRINTMAKER, SCULPTOR
b Mankato, Kans, July 14, 22. Study: Univ Wis, BS & MA; Dartmouth Col; Univ Iowa; Univ Ill; Univ Michoacana, Mex; also with John Steuart Curry. Work: Joslyn Art Mus; Dartmouth Col; Libr Cong, Washington, DC; Ringling Mus Art, Sarasota, Fla; Metrop Mus Art; plus others. Teaching: Artist in residence & instr, Des Moines Art Ctr, 49-53; asst prof art, Eckerd Col, 61-67, artist in residence, 67-77; instr, Ringling Sch of Art, 77- Pos: Asst art dir & illus, Our Wonderful World, Champaign, Ill, 53-56; art dir, ed & commun serv, Exten Div, Univ Wis-Madison, 57-59; bk illusr for UNESCO in Pakistan, 60; co-owner, Hodgell-Hartman Gallery, 77- Mem: Nat Acad Design; Fla Craftsmen; Soc Am Graphic Artists. Style & Technique: Experimental in process; traditional in concept. Mailing Add: 4809 Featherbed Lane Sarasota FL 33581

HODGES, STEPHEN LOFTON
PAINTER
b Port Arthur, Tex, Oct 9, 40. Study: Univ Tex; Lamar Univ, BS; Univ Ark, MFA. Work: Isaac Delgado Mus, New Orleans; Atlanta Artist's Club, Ga. Exhib: Biennial Artists of Southeast & Texas, Isaac Delgado Mus, 71, one-man show, 72; one-man shows, Galerie Simonne Stern, New Orleans, 72 & Southwest Mo State Col, 73; First Street Gallery, New York, 75. Awards: Purchase Awards, Atlanta Artist's Club, 70; Purchase Award, Isaac Delgado Mus, 71. Mem: Col Art Asn. Style & Technique: Representational. Media: Acrylic. Dealer: Galerie Simonne Stern 516 Royal St New Orleans LA 70130. Mailing Add: 1901 NW 55th Terr Gainesville FL 32605

HODGKINS, ROSALIND SELMA
PAINTER
b Farmington, Maine, May 25, 42. Study: Univ SFla; Pratt Inst, BFA; Art Students League. Work: Southern Ill Univ, Carbondale; Bronx Mus Fine Arts, NY; Hewitt Sch, New York. Exhib: One-woman shows, Warren Benedek Gallery, New York 72 & 73 & James Yu Gallery, New York, 76; Univ Mo-St Louis, 73; State Univ NY Col Potsdam, 74; Kensington Arts Asn, Toronto, Ont, 75; PS 1 Pattern Painting Show, New York, 77; O1A Art in Pub Places Show, New York, 77. Style & Technique: Brush painted multiple painting style images juxtaposed in a collage structure. Media: Oil. Mailing Add: 325 W 16th St New York NY 10011

HODGSON, JAMES STANLEY
ART LIBRARIAN
b Detroit, Mich, Apr 26, 42. Study: Brown Univ, AB, 64; Simmons Col, MS, 67. Pos: Acquisitions librn, Fogg Art Mus, Harvard Univ, Cambridge, 68- Mem: Art Libr Soc NAm. Mailing Add: 23 Foster Rd Belmont MA 02178

HODGSON, TREVOR
PAINTER, PHOTOGRAPHER
b Bradford, Eng, Apr 27, 31. Study: Lancaster Col Art; Univ London. Work: Oxford Univ; Accrington City Art Gallery, Eng; Birmingham Univ, Eng; J B Speed Art Mus; Agnes Etherington Art Ctr, Can. Comn: Mural, First Nat Lincoln Bank, Louisville, Ky, 66; mural, York Univ, Eng, 69; fiber glass relief mural, Queen's Univ, Kingston, Ont, 71; Art & Environment (film), 71 & colourslide collection, 72, Ont Educ Commun Authority. Exhib: One-man shows, Artist's Int Asn Gallery, London, 61 & 68, Merida Gallery, US, 66 & Oxford Univ, 67; Six British Artists, US, 67; one-man show, York Univ, 68. Teaching: Asst prof found studies & art educ, Queen's Univ, 69. Awards: Fulbright Scholar to USA, 65; Best Work Award, State of Ky, 66; Teron Prize, Agnes Etherington Art Ctr, Can, 71. Mem: Can Artists' Rep; Can Soc Artists; Int Soc Educ through Art. Media: Mixed Media. Mailing Add: 206 Frontenac St Kingston ON K7L 3S6 Can

HOEVELER, MARY-GRIFFIN SMITH
See Smith, Griffin

HOFER, EVELYN
PHOTOGRAPHER
b Marburg, Ger; Brit citizen. Study: Switz. Work: Metrop Mus of Art, New York; Smith Col Mus of Art, Northampton, Mass; Univ of Colo Libr, Boulder. Exhib: Manhattan Now, New York Hist Soc, 74; Witkin Gallery, 77. Awards: Art Dir Club, 76. Media: Four by Five Camera. Publ: Co-auth, The Stones of Florence, 59, London Perceived, 63, The Presence of Spain, 64 & New York Proclaimed, 65, Harcourt, Brace, Jovanovich; co-auth, Dublin, A Portrait, Harper & Row, 67. Dealer: Witkin Gallery 41 E 57th St New York NY 10022. Mailing Add: 463 West St New York NY 10014

HOFER, INGRID (INGEBORG)
PAINTER, INSTRUCTOR
b New York, NY. Study: Meisterschule Fuer Mode, Hamburg, Ger, BA, 48; Univ Hamburg; Traphagen Sch Design, New York, 51; with A Odefey, Goettingen, Ger, Albert Bross, Jr, Pauline Lorentz, John R Grabach, Adolf Konrad & Nicholas Reale. Work: Fairleigh Dickinson Univ. Comn: Many pvt coms in Ger, Switz & US, 56-78. Exhib: Painters & Sculptors Soc NJ, Jersey City Mus, 70-72; Hudson Valley Art Asn, White Plains, NY, 70 & 71; Catharine Lorillard Wolfe Art Club, Nat Acad Design, New York, 70 & 71; Am Artist Prof League Grand Nat, Lever House, New York, 70-72; Am Watercolor Soc, 73; Rocky Mountain Nat Watercolor Exhib, Colo, 75; Scarab Club, Detroit, 75-78. Teaching: Sr instr mixed media, YWCA Adult Educ, Summitt, NJ, 67-73; instr mixed media, Acad Artists, Trailside Mus, Mountainside, NJ, 68-70; instr, Grosse Pointe War Mem, Mich, 74-78. Awards: Award for Lily Lever House, Am Artists Prof League, 72; Award for Iris, Catharine Lorillard Wolfe Art Club, Nat Acad Design, 71; Am Watercolor Soc Traveling Show Award, 73; plus others. Mem: Am Artists Prof League (dir, Am Art Week, NJ, 68-70, trustee, 69-71); Catharine Lorillard Wolfe Art Club; Mich Watercolor Soc; NJ Watercolor Soc; Scarab Club; Nat Soc Lit & Arts. Style & Technique: Realistic; semi-abstract. Media: Watercolor, Graphics. Dealer: Discovery Art Galleries Clifton NJ 07013; Charter Galleria Luisa E Grand Rapids MI 49506. Mailing Add: 25560 Lake Shore Dr Timberlake Barrington IL 60010

HOFF, MARGO
PAINTER, COLLAGE ARTIST
b Tulsa, Okla. Study: Tulsa Univ; Art Inst Chicago; Pratt Graphics Ctr; St Marys Col, Notre Dame, hon DFA, 69. Work: Whitney Mus Am Art, New York; Brooklyn Mus, NY; Art Inst Chicago; Krannert Mus, Univ Ill, Champaign; Rosenwald Found Collection; plus others. Comn: Wall design (75 canvases), Home Fed Bank, Chicago, 66; Mirror to Man (mural), Mayo Clinic, Rochester, Minn, 68; portrait of S Fairweather, Fairweather Hardin Gallery, Chicago, 67; stage set & costumes for Murray Louis Dance Co, 69; portrait of S Madeleva, St Marys Col, Notre Dame, 70; plus others. Exhib: One-man shows, UNESCO Palace, Beirut, Lebanon, 57, Wildenstein Gallery, Paris, 58, Banfer Gallery, New York, 64, 66 & 68, Fairweather Hardin Gallery, 64-75, Bednarz Gallery, Los Angeles, 67 & Babcock Gallery, New York, 74. Teaching: Teaching grant, Am Univ, Beirut, 56-57; artist in residence, Univ Southern Ill, 66-67; artist in residence, St Marys Col, Notre Dame, 69-70; teaching grant, Goretti Sch, Fort Portal, Uganda, E Africa, 71; Col St Maria, Sao Paulo, Brasil. Mem: Am Asn Univ Prof; Whitney Mus Am Art; Mus Mod Art, New York. Style & Technique: Canvas pieces, painted with acrylic color, laminated to other canvas. Media: Acrylic. Publ: Illusr, Christmas House, Coachhouse, 65; illusr, 4 Seasons & 5 Senses, 66 & Christmas Cupboard, 67, Funk & Wagnall. Dealer: Fairweather Hardin Gallery 101 E Ontario St Chicago IL 60610; Babcock Gallery 805 Madison Ave New York NY 10021. Mailing Add: 114 W 14th St New York NY 10011

HOFF, (SYD)
CARTOONIST, WRITER
b New York, NY, Sept 4, 12. Study: Nat Acad Design. Media: Watercolor, Crayon, Washes, Ink. Publ: Contribr, New Yorker, Esquire Mag, Playboy Mag & others; auth & illusr, children's bks. Mailing Add: PO Box 2463 Miami Beach FL 33140

HOFFBERG, JUDITH ANN
ART LIBRARIAN, ART CONSULTANT
b Hartford, Conn, May 19, 34. Study: Univ Calif, Los Angeles, BA(cum laude polit sci), MA(Ital lang & lit), MLS; Ital Govt grant, study of Leonardo da Vinci. Pos: Intern, Libr Cong, 65-66, cataloger, Prints & Photographs Div, 66-67; fine arts librn, Univ Pa, 67-69; bibliog in art, lit & lang, Univ Calif, San Diego, 69-71; librn, Brand Art Ctr Libr, Glendale, Calif, 71-73; founder, ed newslett, 1st chmn & exec secy, Art Libraries Soc NAm, 72-77; ed & dir, Umbrella Assoc, 78-; bd dir, Franklin Furnace & Assoc Art Publ. Mem: Women's Caucus for Art (adv bd, 77-); Int Fedn Libr Asn (secy, Art Libr Round Table); Col Art Asn Am (bd dirs, 75-); Soc Archit Historians; Int Coun Mus. Publ: Auth, Libraries, lasagna and leaning towers, Wilson Libr Bull, 6/66; auth, To preserve and to protect: a call to action, Picturescope, 71; auth, Ephemera in the art collection, Libr Trends, 1/75; auth, ARLIS/NA: The Art Libraries Society of North America, WAAM Newslett, fall 74 & winter 75. Mailing Add: PO Box 3692 Glendale CA 91201

HOFFELD, JEFFREY
ART HISTORIAN, GALLERY DIRECTOR
b Brooklyn, NY, Dec 3, 45. Study: Brooklyn Col, BA, 66; Columbia Univ, MA, 67, MPh, 73; also with Meyer Schapiro. Collections Arranged: The Year 1200, Masterpieces of 50 Centuries & Art of the Medieval Blacksmith, Metrop Mus Art. Teaching: Asst prof medieval & mod art, Brooklyn Col, 68-72; asst prof medieval & mod art, State Univ NY Col Purchase, 73-77. Pos: Asst cur, Metrop Mus Art; dir, Neuberger Mus, State Univ NY Col Purchase, 75-77; contrib ed, Arts Mag, New York, 75-77; dir, Pace Gallery, New York, 78- Publ: Auth, Adam's Two Wives, 68; co-auth, The Cloisters Apocalypse, 70; auth, An Image of St Louis and the Structuring of Devotion, 71; auth, Lucas Samaras Pastels, 75; ed, The Year 1200, Vol III, 75. Mailing Add: c/o The Pace Gallery 32 E 57th St New York NY 10022

HOFFMAN, EDWARD FENNO, III
SCULPTOR
b Philadelphia, Pa, Oct 20, 16. Study: Pa Acad Fine Arts. Work: Philadelphia Art Mus; Pa Acad Fine Arts; Brookgreen Gardens, SC; Huntington Galleries, WVa; Grand Cent Art Galleries, New York. Comn: Girl with Basin (bronze), Philadelphia Col of Physicians, 60; bronze figures, Weightlifters Hall of Fame, York, Pa, 60-72; portrait heads, Am Col Life Underwriters, Bryn Mawr, Pa, 65-70; Winnie the Pooh, Children's Libr, Hanover, Pa, 66; Fawn, Newlin Mill Park, Lima, Pa, 72; plus others. Exhib: Allied Artists Am Ann, New York, 71; Mainstreams 72, Marietta Col, 72; Nat Sculpture Soc Ann, New York, 72; Am Artists Prof League Ann, 72; Nat Acad Design Ann, New York, 72. Awards: Artists Prize, Nat Acad Design, 69, Watrous Gold Medal, 72 & Speyer Prize, 73; Gold Medal of Honor, Am Artists Prof League, 72; Silver Medal, Nat Sculpture Soc, 73. Bibliog: Proske (auth), Brookgreen Gardens Sculpture, Brookgreen Gardens. Mem: Assoc Nat Acad Design; Nat Sculpture Soc (1st vpres, 73-76); Am Artists Prof League; Allied Artists Am. Style & Technique: Character of subject expressed for emotional impact; sensitively modeled form, but positive. Media: Bronze. Dealer: Erkins Studio 14 E 41st St New York NY 10017; Galerie Int 1095 Madison Ave New York NY 10028. Mailing Add: 353 Oak Terr Wayne PA 19087

HOFFMAN, ELAINE JANET
PAINTER
b Oak Park, Ill. Study: Averett Col; Portland Art Mus; Northwest Watercolor Sch, with Irving Shapiro; Maryhurst Educ Ctr, 76-78; also with Charles Mulvey, Perry Acker, George Hamilton & Phil Austin. Exhib: Watercolor Soc Ore Traveling Tours, 68-77; Artists of Oregon, Portland Art Mus, 70; Am Artists Prof League, New York, 71; George Fox Col Invitational, Newberg, Ore, 72-75; Prof Ore Artists Invitational Exhib, Coos Bay Mus, Ore, 72-74. Teaching: Pvt classes in watercolor landscapes, 65-; instr, Portland Community Col, 75- Pos: Bd dirs, Lake Oswego Art Guild, Ore, 65-68. Awards: Grand Award, Soc Wash Artists, 68; Spec Merit Award, Watercolor Soc Ore, 69 & 70; Purchase Award, Coos Bay Mus, 73; plus others. Mem: Fel Am Artists Prof League; Portland Art Mus; Ore Watercolor Soc; Lake Area Artists (pres, 67-68, 71-72 & 75-76); Ore Soc Artists. Style & Technique: Impressionist; wild fowl in natural settings. Media: Watercolor. Dealer: Oceanside Gallery Lincoln City OR 97367; Lake Area Artist Gallery Second St Lake Oswego OR 97034. Mailing Add: 16695 Glenwood Ct Lake Oswego OR 97034

HOFFMAN, HELEN BACON
PAINTER
b San Antonio, Tex, July 14, 30. Study: Ogontz Col, Philadelphia; Parsons Sch Design. Work: NAm-Mex Inst Cult Relations, Mexico City, Mex; Wichita Art Asn, Kans. Exhib: One-man shows, North Star Gallery, San Antonio, Tex, 66-78, Grand Cent Art Galleries, New York, 69-78 & Veerhoff Galleries, Washington, DC, 64, 74 & 78; plus others. Awards: Philadelphia Award, Pa Acad Fine Arts, 69; First PlaAward, Catherine Lorillard Wolfe Art Club Show, 73; First Place Painting, Salmagundi Club, 74; plus others. Mem: Artists Equity Asn; Soc Wash Artists; Nat Soc Arts & Lett; Salmagundi Club; Catherine Lorillard Wolfe Art Club. Style & Technique: Realist; action of light on everyday subjects and figures. Media: Pastel, Oil. Dealer: Veerhoff Galleries 1512 Connecticut Ave Washington DC 20036; Grand Central Art Galleries Biltmore Hotel 40 Vanderbilt Ave New York NY 10017. Mailing Add: 6015 Lamont Court Springfield VA 22152

HOFFMAN, LARRY GENE
MUSEUM DIRECTOR
b Paola, Kans, Mar 12, 33. Study: Drake Univ, BFA; Des Moines Art Ctr, with Thomas S Tibbs. Collections Arranged: Arthur S Dayton Collection, 69; Henri Dourif Mem, 69; Mid-Mississippi Valley Ann, 71-75; Grand Wood, 72; Neiswanger Haitian Art, 74; Roy W Carver Collection, 75; plus others. Teaching: Mem & adminr vis guest artist prog, Des Moines Art Ctr, 52-67; instr art, Des Moines Pub Sch Syst, 55-60. Pos: Consult art, Des Moines Pub Sch Syst, 60-62; dir educ, Des Moines Art Ctr, 62-67; consult art, WVa Arts & Humanities Coun; collaborator, Walter Gropius Mus Bldg Addition, Huntington, WVa, 67-69; dir, Huntington Galleries, 67-71; dir, Davenport Munic Art Gallery, 71- Awards: Model jr mus, Saint Louis Conf, Am Asn Mus, 67. Mem: Am Asn Mus; Am Fedn Arts; Delta Phi Delta (past pres); Iowa State Art Educ Asn (past pres). Publ: Contribr, Sch Arts & Mus News; auth, exhib catalogs. Mailing Add: Davenport Munic Art Gallery 1737 W 12th St Davenport IA 52804

HOFFMAN, MARILYN FRIEDMAN
GALLERY DIRECTOR
Study: Brown Univ, Providence, RI, BA(hon; art hist), 67, MA(art hist), 70, PhD(art hist), 71. Teaching: Grad asst, Educ Dept, Metrop Mus Art, New York, 69; teaching asst, Brown Univ, 69-70; adj lectr, Dept Pub Educ, Mus Fine Arts, Boston, 70-71. Pos: Cur asst, Educ Dept, Mus Art, RI Sch Design, 67-68; gallery asst, Adelson Galleries, Inc, Boston, 68-69 & 70-71; cur, Brockton Art Ctr-Fuller Mem, Mass, 71-73, actg dir, 73-74, dir, 74- Mem: Am Asn Mus; Col Art Asn Am; Metrop Cult Alliance Mus Dirs Group. Publ: Auth, American Still Life Painting, 1860-1900 (catalogue), Adelson Galleries, Inc, 68; auth, Pssst!, Airbrush Painting (catalogue), 72, The Good Things in Life/19th Century American Still Life (catalogue), 73 & Unstretched Paintings (catalogue), 73, Brockton Art Ctr-Fuller Mem; auth, Museum Loans at Brockton, Art J, Vol 32 (1973). Mailing Add: 43 Walnut St Stoughton MA 02072

HOFFMAN, MARTIN (JOSEPH)
PAINTER, ILLUSTRATOR
b St Augustine, Fla, Nov 1, 35. Work: Miami Mus Mod Art; Va Mus Fine Arts, Richmond; Indianapolis Mus Art; J B Speed Mus, Louisville, Ky. Comn: Numerous pvt comns, Fla, 60-72; numerous paintings & illus, Playboy Mag, 66-72; cover, Art Direction Mag, 4/72; Ashleys, New York, 75. Exhib: Realism Now, New York Cult Ctr, 72; New American Landscape, Vassar Col, 73; The Jersey Meadows Series, OK Harris Gallery, New York, 73, Street People, 75; Our Land, Our Sky, Our Water, Int Expos, Spokane, Wash, 74; plus others. Teaching: Instr grad painting & drawing, Univ Miami, 69-71. Pos: Art dir, munerous Miami advert agencies, 57-70; designer-illusr, Graphic Arts, Inc, 60-70. Awards: Numerous painting awards in var regional shows, 69-70; Art Dir Awards, Miami Art Dirs Club, 69-70; Illus Awards, Chicago Advert Club, 71-72. Bibliog: Doris Reno (auth), var rev, 57-65 & article, 8/23/70, Miami Herald, Griffin Smith (auth), article in Tropic Mag, 9/71. Mem: Kooter Boogers Am (pres, 72-). Style & Technique: Realist. Publ: Illusr, Playboy, 67-78; illusr, Art Direction, 4/72; illusr, New York Time & Artforum, 74; illusr, Fortune, 74; plus others. Dealer: OK Harris Gallery 383 W Broadway New York NY 10012; Frank & Jeff Lavaty 45 E 51st St New York NY 10022. Mailing Add: 300 Mercer St New York NY 10003

HOFFMAN, NANCY
ART DEALER
b New York, NY, Feb 23, 44. Study: Wellesley Col, 62-64; Barnard Col, Columbia Univ, BA(art hist), 66. Pos: Asst registrar, Asia House Gallery, New York, 64-69; dir, Fr & Co Contemp Gallery, New York, 69-72; dir, Nancy Hoffman Gallery, New York, 72- Specialty: Contemporary art: paintings, drawings, sculpture and graphics. Mailing Add: 429 W Broadway New York NY 10012

HOFFMAN, RICHARD PETER
PAINTER
b Allentown, Pa, Jan 10, 11. Study: Mercersburg Acad, grad, 29; Parsons Sch Design, grad, 33. Work: Butler Inst Am Art, Youngstown, Ohio; Maravian Col, Bethlehem, Pa; Pa Power & Light Co, Allentown; Call-Chronicle Newspapers, Allentown; Liberty High Sch, Bethlehem, Pa. Exhib: Philadelphia Watercolor Exhibs, Pa; Am Watercolor Soc; Nat Soc Painters in Casein, New York; Audubon Artists Exhibs; Woodmere Art Gallery, Philadelphia; one-man shows, First Nat Bank, Allentown, Pa, 72-75, , Allentown Art Mus, Pa, 72-77, Kemmerer Mus, Bethlehem, Pa, 73, Meirhans Art Gallery, Quakertown, Pa, 74, Woodmere Art Gallery, Philadelphia, 74 & New Britain Mus Am Art, Conn, 75; plus others. Awards: Gertrude Rowan Capolino Prize, Woodmere Art Gallery, Philadelphia, 52; Grumbacher Prize for Casein, Knickerbocker Artists, 55; Com Mus Civic Ctr Award, Philadelphia, 65. Mem: Philadelphia Watercolor Soc; Woodmere Art Gallery; Allentown Art Mus; Lehigh Art Alliance. Style & Technique: Modern interpretation of and variations upon the traditional folk art of rural Pennsylvania. Interest: Photographer and lecturer. Publ: Auth article in Am Artist, 11/48 & La Rev Mod, 3/53. Mailing Add: 1035 N 30th St Allentown PA 18104

HOFFMANN, ARNOLD, JR
PAINTER, ART DIRECTOR
b New York, NY, Jan 16, 15. Study: Nat Acad Design; Art Students League. Work: Chrysler Mus, Provincetown; Corcoran Art Gallery, Washington, DC; 20th Century Fund; Honeywell Corp; Butler Inst Am Art, Youngstown, Ohio; plus others. Exhib: Allied Artists Am; Am Watercolor Soc; Stuttman Gallery, New York, 63; Angeleski Gallery, 65; Osgood Gallery, 68; Parish Art Mus, Southampton, NY, 77. Pos: Art dir, New York Times Mag, 43-; dir silk screen fine art workshop, East Hampton, 72- Style & Technique: Abstract, non-objective free brush work; developing advanced techniques for serigraphy. Mailing Add: 924 Fireplace Rd East Hampton NY 11937

HOFFMANN, LILLY ELISABETH
WEAVER, INSTRUCTOR
b Strassburg, Alsace, Nov 8, 98; US citizen. Study: With Florence House. Work: Mus Mod Art, New York; Currier Gallery Art, Manchester, NH. Comn: Hanging, Andover-Harvard Theol Sch, Cambridge, Mass; curtains, Temple Beth Abraham, Nashua, NH; 32 pieces, Holy Trinity Methodist Church, Danvers, Mass. Exhib: Designer Craftsmen USA, Brooklyn Mus, NY, 53; Nat Gold Medal Exhib Archit League New York; Fabrics Int, US & Can, 61-63. Teaching: Instr weaving, NH Asn for Blind, Concord; instr weaving, League NH Craftsman, Concord, 49-; lect, Exploring the Crafts: Weaving, Channel 11, 67. Awards: Grand Award, Designer Craftsmen USA, 53. Mem: League NH Craftsmen. Style & Technique: Loom weaving; plain, enjoyable color combinations. Media: Textiles. Mailing Add: Rte 2 Concord NH 03301

HOFMAN, KATE
ART DEALER, COLLECTOR
b Breda, Neth, Apr 15, 21; Can citizen. Study: Amsterdam, Paris & London. Collections Arranged: Int Art Exhib, Olympic Pavilion, Expo 67, Montreal, 67; Graphics by Int Masters, Gallery 1667, 77. Pos: Asst dir, Int Art Exhib, Olympic Pavilion, Expo 67, Montreal, 67; owner/dir, Gallery 1667, Halifax, 70- & Mahone Bay, 74-; commentator, Art To See (weekly show), CJCH-TV, Halifax, 70-75. Awards: Centennial Medal of Can, Int Art Exhib, Expo 67, Govt of Can. Specialty: International masters of the 20th century; contemporary Canadian artists. Collection: Dali, Miro, Chagall, Moti, Braque, Ernst & Calder; also contemporary Canadian artists such as Wylie, Bolt & Barry. Mailing Add: c/o Gallery 1667 Hist Properties 1869 Upper Water St Halifax NS B3J 1S9 Can

HOFSTED, JOLYON GENE
SCULPTOR, EDUCATOR
b San Antonio, Tex, Oct 21, 42. Study: Calif Col Arts & Crafts, Oakland; Brooklyn Mus Art Sch, NY; clay works with Anne Arnold, 77. Work: Mus Mod Art, Kyoto, Japan; Brooklyn Mus & Mus Contemp Crafts, New York; Newark Mus, NJ; Sea of Japan Expos Secretariat, Kanazawa-shi. Exhib: Monuments, Tombstones & Trophies, Mus Contemp Crafts, New York, 67; Attitudes, Brooklyn Mus, NY, 70; Contemp Ceramic Art Can, US, Mex & Japan, Mus Mod Art, Kyoto & Tokyo, Japan, 71-72; Sensible Cup, Sea of Japan Expos, 73; Distinguished Contemp Potters, New Haven, Conn, 75; Clay 77, Goddard-Riverside Ctr, New York, 77; Land, Kohler Arts Ctr, Sheboygan, Wis, 77. Teaching: Instr art, Brooklyn Mus Art Sch, 63-71; instr art, Queens Col, City Univ New York, 66-; instr ceramics, Haystack Mountain Sch Crafts, Maine, 66 & 68. Pos: Dir, Brooklyn Mus Art Sch, 70-73. Awards: Alfred Harvey Parker Ceramics Award, Brooklyn Mus, 64; Craftsmen Nat Award; Del Art Mus, 66. Mem: Ulster Co Coun for Arts (bd dirs). Style & Technique: Ceramic sculpture influenced by landscape. Publ: Auth, Ceramics, Western Publ Co, 67; auth, Pottery, Pan Bks, London, 74; contribr, Encyclopedia of Crafts, Avon Bks, 75; contribr, Craft Encyclopedia, Time-Life Publ, 75. Mailing Add: Box 66 Shady NY 12479

HOGBIN, STEPHEN JAMES
SCULPTOR
b Tolworth Surrey, United Kingdom. Study: Kingston Col Art, United Kingdom, NDD; Royal Col Art, United Kingdom, Des RCA. Work: Art Bank Can Coun, Ottawa, Ont; Australia Coun, Sydney; Melbourne State Col, Australia; Ont Crafts Coun, Toronto, Ont; Can Crafts Coun, Ottawa, Ont. Comn: Wood sculpture, Melbourne State Col, Australia, 75; wood wall screen, Metrop Toronto Libr Can, 77. Exhib: One-man shows, Aggregation Gallery, Toronto, Can, 74, York Univ, Toronto, 75, Australian Design Centre, Melbourne, 76 & Parnham House Gallery, Dorset, United Kingdom, 77; Wood, London Pub Gallery, Ont, Can, 74; Chairs, Art Gallery Ont, Toronto, 75; Language of Wood, State Univ NY Col, Buffalo, 75; Wood & Clay, NZ, 76. Teaching: Instr wood, Sheridan Sch Design, Port Credit, Ont, Can, 68-71; instr wood, Col Educ, Univ Toronto, 71-72. Pos: Craftsman-in-residence, Melbourne State Col, Australia Coun, 75-76. Awards. Best Contemp Design, One Nation Exhib, Jordan Wines Ltd, 73. Bibliog: D L McKinley (auth), The forms of Stephen Hogbin, Craft Horizons, 4/74; Tony Perryman (producer), Craftsman (film), pvt produced, 75; Peter Drummond (producer), Woodcraftsman Stephen Hogbin (film), Crafts Coun Australia, 76. Mem: Ont Crafts Coun (dir, 77-); Can Crafts Coun (vpres, 73-74); World Crafts Coun. Style & Technique: Wood-turning, milling and carving; functional and sculptural forms. Media: Wood. Publ: Auth, Sacred cows and puddling around, Craft Dimensions, 74; auth, Interrelationships, Can Craft Coun News, 74; auth, Crafts and industry, Design Australia, 75; auth, One year in Australia, Artisan, Can Crafts Coun, 77. Dealer: Aggregation Gallery 83 Front St Toronto ON Can. Mailing Add: RR1 Caledon East ON L0N 1E0 Can

HOGE, ROBERT WILSON
MUSEUM DIRECTOR, EDUCATOR
b Wilmington, Del, Jan 5, 47. Study: Univ Colo, BA(anthrop); post-grad study, Univ Colo & Univ Chicago. Collections Arranged: Tatangka Wotin Ni Sa: the Buffalo People (Plains Indian cultures), Spring 76, First Hundred Yrs (Am Hist—Bicentennial), Fall 76, Children of the Blizzard (Inuit culture), Spring 77, Interweave (materials, techniques & hist of textiles), Fall 77 & Surprising saurians (interpretation of the dinosaurs), Spring 78, Sanford Mus & Planetarium. Pos: Asst dir, Sanford Mus & Planetarium, Cherokee, Iowa, 76, actg dir, 76 & dir, 76-; instr anthrop (part-time), Buena Vista Col, Storm Lake, Iowa, Fall 76. Res: American archaeology, historical studies; Old World archaeology; numismatics. Publ: Ed, Northwest Chapter Newsletter, Iowa Archaeol Soc, Sanford Mus. Mailing Add: Sanford Mus 117 E Willow Cherokee IA 51012

HOGROGIAN, NONNY
ILLUSTRATOR
b New York, NY, Mar 7, 32. Study: Hunter Col, 53, BA; New Sch Social Res, 57. Awards: Caldecott Medal, 66 & 72. Publ: Illusr, About Wise Men & Simpletons, 71, One I Love, Two I Love, 72, The Hermit & Harry & Me, 72, Billy Goat and His Well Fed Friends, 72, Rooster Brother, 74 & other children's books. Mailing Add: East Chatham NY 12060

HOGUE, ALEXANDRE
PAINTER, LITHOGRAPHER
b Memphis, Mo, Feb 22, 98. Work: Mus Nat Art Mod, Paris; Nat Collection Fine Arts, Washington, DC; Dallas Mus Fine Arts, Tex; Okla Art Ctr, Oklahoma City; Univ Ariz Mus Art. Exhib: Int Exhib, Jeu de Paume, Paris, 38; Carnegie Inst Int Exhibs, 38 & 39; Tate Gallery, London, Eng, 46; Whitney Mus Am Art, New York; Wilderness, Corcoran Gallery Art, Washington, DC, 71. Teaching: Instr life drawing & painting, Tex State Col Women, summers 31-42; prof art & head dept, Univ Tulsa, 45-68, emer prof, 69- Awards: Purchase Award, 9th Southwest Prints & Drawings, Dallas Mus Fine Arts, 59; Grand Awards, Philbrook Art Ctr, Tulsa, Okla, 61 & 75; Purchase Award, Springfield Mus Art, Mo, 65. Bibliog: John Bauer (auth), Revolution & Tradition in Modern American Art, 51; Nouvelles acquisitions, La Revue Du Louvre, 61; Ralph K Andrist (ed), History of the 20's and 30's, Am Heritage, 70. Style & Technique: From abstract realism to hard edge non-objective. Media: Oil, Watercolor; Lithography. Publ: Auth, A portrait of Pancho Dobie, Southwest Rev, spring 65. Mailing Add: 4052 E 23rd St Tulsa OK 74114

HOIE, CLAUS
PAINTER, ETCHER
b Stavanger, Norway, Nov 3, 11; US citizen. Study: Pratt Inst; Art Students League; Ecole Beaux Arts, Paris. Work: Brooklyn Mus, NY; Norfolk Mus, Va; Butler Inst Am Art, Youngstown, Ohio; Okla Mus Art; Guild Hall Mus, East Hampton, NY. Exhib: Am Watercolor Soc Ann, New York, 60-75; Brooklyn Mus Watercolor Biennial, 63; Mus Watercolor Painting, Mexico City, Mex, 68; Pa Acad Fine Arts Ann, 69; Childe Hassam Award Exhib, Nat Inst Arts & Lett, 73; plus others. Awards: Am Artist Mag Medal, Am Watercolor Soc, 56, Gold Medal of Honor, 62, Prize, 75; Award for Painting, Nat Inst Arts & Lett, 75. Mem: Nat Acad Design; Am Watercolor Soc (vpres, 60-62). Style & Technique:

Blend of realism and fantasy. Media: Watercolor, Graphics. Publ: Auth, Technique of watercolor, Am Artist Mag, 57; auth, My views on watercolor painting, North Light Mag, 70. Mailing Add: 20 W 12th St New York NY 10011

HOKIN, GRACE E
ART DEALER, COLLECTOR
b Chicago, Ill. Study: Sch Design, Chicago, cert; Northwestern Univ, BFA. Specialty: Contemporary painting; sculpture; graphics; tapestries; African, Pre-Columbian and Oceanic art. Collection: 20th century painting and sculpture; African and other primitive art. Mailing Add: c/o Hokin Galleries 245 North Ave Palm Beach FL 33480

HOLBROOK, ELIZABETH BRADFORD
SCULPTOR
b Hamilton, Ont, Nov 7, 13. Study: Hamilton Tech Inst; Ont Col Art, Toronto; Royal Col Art, London; also with Emanuel Hahn & Carl Milles. Work: Nat Gallery Can, Ottawa, Ont; Parliament Bldgs Gallery, Ottawa; Art Gallery Hamilton; McMaster Univ. Comn: Girl with dove in stone, Bird Protection Soc, Royal Bot Gardens, Hamilton, 37; archit decoration Canadiana in stone (with Husband, Robertson & Wallace, Architects), Fed Bldg, Hamilton, 53; centennial fountain in stone, Dunnville, Ont, 67; bronze portrait, comn by Roy G Cole, Hamilton, 69; bronze portrait of Rabbi Bernard Baskin, Anshe Sholom Temple, Hamilton, 70; plus others. Exhib: Art Gallery Hamilton Ann, 45-; Sculptor's Soc Can Ann, 60-; Nat Sculpture Soc New York Ann, 62 & 69; Int Fedn Medallists, Cologne, Ger, 71, Helsinki, Finland, 73 & Cracow, Poland, 75; one-man retrospective, Art Gallery Hamilton, 74; plus others. Teaching: Instr sculpture, Dundas Valley Sch Art, 65-70. Awards: Lt Gov Medal, Ont Col Art-Govt Ont, 36; Gold Medal Award, Nat Sculpture Soc New York, 69. Bibliog: E Wyn Wood (auth), Canadian Sculpture, 48; Charles Comfort (auth), Observations on a decade 1938-48, Royal Archit Inst Can J; John Bryden (auth), Art, Hamilton Spectator, 70, 71 & 72. Mem: Sculptor's Soc Can; Ont Soc Artists; Royal Can Acad Art; life mem Art Gallery Hamilton (benefactor, 45-); Art Gallery Ont. Style & Technique: Traditional; realism; rough modelled surface; smooth stone surface; portraits, figure and animal subjects. Media: Stone, Bronze. Mailing Add: 1177 Mineral Springs Rd RR3 Dundas ON L9H 5E3 Can

HOLBROOK, HOLLIS HOWARD
MURALIST, PAINTER
b Natick, Mass, Feb 7, 09. Study: Mass Sch Art, dipl, 34; Yale Univ, BFA, 36; Univ Michoacan, Morelia, Mex, 50-51. Work: Norfolk Mus Arts & Sci, Va; Southern Col Fla; Sheldon Swope Art Gallery, Terre Haute, Ind; Natick Pub Libr, Mass; Univ Fla, Gainesville. Comn: John Eliot & Indians (egg tempera mural), Natick Post Off Bldg, 37; frescoes, Morelia Libr, Michoacan, Mex, 51; History of Florida (egg tempera), Univ Fla Libr, 53; Life in the World (collage panels with Harrison Covington), RI Col, 59; Ocala Industries (collage panels), US Post Off, Ocala, 61. Exhib: Contemporary Painting and Sculpture, Univ Ill Biennial, 61; Pa Acad Fine Arts Painting & Sculpture Ann, 64; 29th Biennial Contemp Am Painting, Corcoran Gallery Art, 65; 21st Am Drawing Biennial, Norfolk Mus Arts & Sci, 65; 22nd Southeastern Ann, High Mus Art, Atlanta, Ga, 67. Teaching: Prof art, Univ Fla, 38-78. Pos: Designer-illusr, Dennison Mfg Co, Framingham, Mass, 29-30; designer-illusr, Assoc Press, New York, 41; designer, Warren Telechron Co, Ashland, Mass, 42. Awards: Award & Purchase Prize for Winter, Walter Chrysler, Jr, 8th Ann Nat, Sarasota, Fla, 58; Purchase Prize for Protest (drawing), Norfolk Mus Arts & Sci, 65; Top Award for Figure with Blue Patch, 22nd Southeastern Ann, High Mus Art, 67. Bibliog: Jacqueline Barnitz (auth), Holbrook exhibit, New York City, Arts Mag, 12/65. Mem: Nat Soc Mural Painters. Media: Acrylic. Publ: Auth, Fresco painting, Design Mag, summer 51; auth, A media laboratory, Am Artist Mag, 9/60; auth, Development of the Plastic Arts of Central America, Univ Fla, 61; auth, Painting for non-majors, Art J, summer 70. Mailing Add: 1710 SW 35th Pl Gainesville FL 32601

HOLBROOK, VIVIAN NICHOLAS
PAINTER, ART ADMINISTRATOR
b Mount Vernon, NY, Mar 31, 13. Study: Yale Univ, BFA. Work: Univ Ga. Exhib: Butler Art Inst Ann, Youngstown, Ohio, 52; Patronato Belles Artes y Mus Nat, Havana, Cuba, 56; Columbia Mus Art, SC, 59; Purdue Univ Small Painting Show, Lafayette, 64; Ball State Univ Ann, 72; Ten Yr Retrospective, Fla Southern Col, Lakeland, 76; Prof Women Artists of Fla, Lowe Art Mus, Univ Miami & Women's Hemispheric Cong, 76; four-man show, Ctr of Mod Art, Micanopy, Fla, 77. Teaching: Instr painting & drawing, Colby Jr Col, New London, NH, 36-39; interim instr painting & drawing, Univ Fla, 42-44; instr painting, Ctr Mod Art, Micanopy, Fla, 69-70. Pos: Dir, Ctr Mod Art, 69-; designer exhibs, Fla State Mus, summer 70. Awards: Second Award, Harry Rich Competition, Miami, 57; Top Award, Soc Four Arts, 58, Atwater Kent Award, 66. Media: Oil, Ink. Mailing Add: 1710 SW 35th Pl Gainesville FL 32601

HOLCOMB, ADELE MANSFIELD
ART HISTORIAN
b Scranton, Pa, June 25, 30. Study: Univ Utah; Univ Calif, Los Angeles, BA, PhD. Teaching: Asst prof, Hamline Univ, St Paul, Minn, 66-68; asst prof, State Univ NY Col, Brockport, 68-71; asst & assoc vis prof, Univ Guelph, Ont, Can, 75-77; assoc prof & head dept, Bishop's Univ, Lennoxville, Que, 77- Awards: Univ Calif Los Angeles Art Coun Award, 65-66; State Univ NY Fac Res Fel, 69 & 70; Am Coun Learned Soc One-Yr Res Fel, 71-72. Mem: Women's Caucus for Art (nat bd mem, 74-77); Col Art Asn; Univ Art Asn of Can. Res: Romantic landscape painting; history of art history and criticism, including contributions of women. Publ: Auth, Turner & Scott, J of the Warburg & Courtauld Insts, 71; auth, The bridge in the middle distance, Art Quart, 74; auth, John Sell Cotman's dismasted brig & the motif of the drifting boat, Studies in Romanticism, 75; auth, A-F-Rio, Anna Jameson & the second volume of modern painters, Gazette des Beaux-Arts, 78; auth, John Sell Cotman, Brit Mus Publ, 78. Mailing Add: 1760 Prospect Ave 2 Sherbrooke PQ J1J 1K5 Can

HOLCOMB, GRANT
ART HISTORIAN, EDUCATOR
b San Bernardino, Calif, Sept 30, 42. Study: Univ Calif, Los Angeles, BA; Univ Del, MA & PhD. Teaching: Asst prof Am art & archit, Mt Holyoke Col, 72-, dir, Mus of Art, 76- Pos: Cur, John Sloan Collection, Del Art Mus, Wilmington, 70-72. Awards: John Sloan Mem Award, Del Art Mus, 69; Samuel H Kress Fel, Nat Gallery Art, Washington, DC, 70-71. Res: American painting; preparing the catalogue raisonne of the paintings of John Sloan; working on a monograph on the life and art of Jerome Myers. Publ: Auth, Jerome Myers, 1867-1940 (exhib catalog), Kraushaar Galleries, New York, 70; auth, The Calico Market by Jerome Myers, Currier Gallery Art Bull, 72; auth, Leonard DeLonga: Artist and Teacher (exhib catalog), 73 & William Dole (exhib catalog), 74, Mt Holyoke Col; auth, The forgotten legacy of Jerome Myers (1867-1940): painter of New York's lower east side, 5/77 & John Sloan in Santa Fe, 5/78, Am Art J. Mailing Add: 11 Minden Pl South Hadley MA 01075

HOLCOMBE, R GORDON, JR
COLLECTOR, PATRON
b Lake Charles, La, Oct 28, 13. Study: Vanderbilt Univ; Tulane Univ, BS, Sch Med, MD. Pos: Past pres, Art Assocs Lake Charles. Collection: Paintings, including works by Bernard, Derain, Buffet, Levier & Courbet; early 19th century American paintings. Mailing Add: 1607 Foster St Lake Charles LA 70601

HOLDEN, DONALD
ART EDITOR, ART ADMINISTRATOR
b Los Angeles, Calif, Apr 22, 31. Study: Parsons Sch Design, New York, 46-47; Art Students League, 48; Columbia Univ, BA, 51; Ohio State Univ, MA, 52. Pos: Dir pub rel, Philadelphia Col Art, 53-55; dir pub rel & personnel, Henry Dreyfuss, New York, 56-60; assoc mgr pub rel, Metrop Mus Art, New York, 60-61; art consult, Fortune Mag, 62; ed dir, Watson-Guptill Publ, 63-; ed dir, Am Artist Mag, 71-75. Mem: Am Inst Graphic Arts; Nat Art Educ Asn. Publ: Auth, Whistler Landscapes and Seascapes, 69; auth, Art Career Guide, 3rd ed, 72; plus articles in Am Artist, Am Inst Graphic Arts J & Intellectual Digest. Mailing Add: 128 Deertrack Ln Irvington NY 10533

HOLDEN, RAYMOND JAMES
PAINTER, ILLUSTRATOR
b Wrentham, Mass, May 2, 01. Study: RI Sch Design, 23. Work: Children's Mus, West Hartford, Conn; Mus Am Art, New Britain, Conn. Exhib: Jones Libr, Amherst, Mass, 69; Providence Pub Libr, RI, 70. Mem: Providence Watercolor Club. Publ: Illusr, Thoreau's Cape Cod, 69; illusr, The Fenwick Story, Conn Hist Soc, 74; illusr, Thoreau's A Week on the Concord & Merrimack Rivers, Limited Editions Club, 75. Mailing Add: RFD Box 130 Sterling CT 06377

HOLDER, KENNETH ALLEN
PAINTER, EDUCATOR
b Heald, Tex, Sept 11, 36. Study: Tex Christian Univ, BFA(com art), 59; Art Inst Chicago, MFA(painting), 65. Work: Ill State Mus, Springfield; Purdue Univ, West Lafayette; Ill State Univ, Normal; Quincy Art Asn, Ill; Western Ill Univ. Comn: Fresno City Col, Calif, 73; Va Commonwealth Univ, 73; Cent Mich Univ, 75; all in collab with Harold Gregor. Exhib: Made in Macomb, Hyde Park Art Ctr, Chicago, 69; Chicago Vicinity Show, Chicago Art Inst, 73; 118 Gallery, Minneapolis, 74; one-man show, Nancy Lurie Gallery, Chicago, 75; Drawings USA, Minn Mus St Paul, 75. Teaching: Asst prof drawing & painting, Western Ill Univ, 65-69; assoc prof drawing & painting, Ill State Univ, 69- Awards: Purchase Award, Purdue Univ, 73; Third Prize for Painting, Grand Galleria, Seattle; Purchase Award, Ill State Mus, Springfield. Bibliog: Henry Glover (auth), Artist (video), Ill State Univ, 72. Style & Technique: Varied in content, formal concerns and media. Media: Acrylic; Mixed Media. Dealer: Nancy Lurie 2293 N Lincoln Park W Chicago IL 60614. Mailing Add: 104 Kreitzer Bloomington IL 61701

HOLDER, TOM
PAINTER
b Kansas City, Mo, Jan 21, 40. Study: San Diego State Univ, BA; Univ Wash, MFA. Work: Metromedia Collection, Los Angeles; ITT, Los Angeles, Calif; San Diego Fine Arts Gallery, Calif; Valley Bank, Las Vegas & Reno, Nev; Las Vegas Art Mus, Nev. Comn: Mural (44'), Seattle-Tacoma Int Airport, 73; exterior wall mural, Seattle Steam Corp Plant, Seattle Arts Comn, 75. Teaching: Instr painting, Univ Wash, 67-69; assoc prof painting, Univ Nev, Las Vegas, 71- Dealer: Foster-White Gallery 211 1/2 Occidental S Seattle WA 98104; Ruth Schaffner Gallery 8406 Melrose Blvd Los Angeles CA 90069. Mailing Add: PO Box 19423 Las Vegas NV 89119

HOLEN, NORMAN DEAN
SCULPTOR, EDUCATOR
b Cavalier, NDak, Sept 16, 37. Study: Concordia Col, BA, 59; State Univ Iowa, MFA, 62; Univ Minn, Minneapolis, 72. Work: 3M Co, Minneapolis, Minn; Univ Lutheran Church of Hope & Victory Lutheran Church, Minneapolis; Gen Mills Co, Minneapolis; State Univ Iowa. Comn: Sheet steel bas relief, Augsburg Col Libr, 66; welded steel sculpture, Nativity Lutheran, Minneapolis, 69; welded steel figure, Trinity Evangelical Lutheran Church, Clear Lake, SDak, 67; half life size bronze figure, St Bridget's Catholic Church, Cavalier, NDak, 74; brazed steel bas relief, Luther Theological Seminary, St Paul, Minn, 77. Exhib: Drawing & Small Sculpture, Muncie, Ind, 65, 71, 74, 76 & 77; one-man show, Minneapolis Inst Art, 68; Nat Gallery, Washington, DC, 69; Mainstreams, Marietta, Ohio, 69, 71, 73, 74, 76 & 77; Dakota Nat, Rapid City, SDak, 75. Teaching: Instr art, Northwestern Col, Orange City, Iowa, 62-63 & Concordia Col, Moorhead, Minn, 63-64; assoc prof art, Augsburg Col, Minneapolis, 64- Pos: Guest lectr, Rochester Art Ctr, 69; exhib adv, Augsburg Col, 71-75; art consult, Richfield High Sch, 73; juror, Red River Ann, Moorhead, 75. Awards: Award of Excellence, Mainstreams, Marietta, 71 & Top Award for Sculpture, 73; Nat Drawing & Small Sculpture Award, Muncie, 71 & 77; First Prize, Dakota Nat, Rapid City, 75. Bibliog: Wendy Ross (auth), Welded steel animals and birds, Minn Tribune Mag, 72; Ms Hamilton (auth), Norman Holen is artist, sculptor, Richfield Sun Newspaper, 73; Diana Swanson (auth), Documentary on Minnesota sculpture, Midwest Educ TV, 74. Mem: Artists Equity Asn (vpres, Minn Chap, 73-74, chap pres & mem nat exec bd, 74-75); Nat Sculpture Soc; Minn Sculptors Soc. Style & Technique: Abstract and realistic subjects in a wide variety of media. Media: Welded Steel, Terra Cotta. Publ: Contribr, Nat Sculpture Rev, 72; contribr, National community arts program, HUD, 73; auth & illusr, Building a strong case for sculpture, Nat Sculpture Rev, 74; auth, Upper midwest art: Minnesota, North Dakota, South Dakota, Rev of the Arts, 77; auth, A pressing need for clay, Today's Art, 78. Mailing Add: 7332 12th Ave S Minneapolis MN 55423

HOLGATE, JEANNE
PAINTER, ILLUSTRATOR
b London, Eng, Mar 11, 20. Study: Self-taught. Work: Queen Elizabeth, the Queen Mother, Brit Mus & Royal Horticultural Soc, London; Hunt Inst for Botanical Documentation, Pittsburgh; Franklin Mint, Pa. Exhib: One-man shows, Tryon Gallery, London, Los Angeles Co Mus, 66, Incurable Collector, New York, 70, Hunt Inst for Botanical Documentation, 73, Gertrude Posel Gallery, 73, Schiele Mus of Natural Hist, 77 & Mus of Natural Hist, Raleigh, NC, 77. Teaching: Instr flower illus, Longwood Gardens, Kennett Square, Pa, 67-70. Awards: Royal Horticultural Soc Gold Medals, London, 63 & 64; Silver Trophy for Best Educ Exhib, 5th World Orchid Conf, Long Beach, Calif, 66; Silver Trophy, Del Orchid Soc, 69. Bibliog: John Dorsey (auth), Someone who cared fired her, Sunpapers, Baltimore, 73; Jeanne Holgate (film), Franklin Mint, 73; State Flowers, Hodge Podge Lodge, WPBS-TV, 75. Mem: Nat Arts Club, New York; Md Fedn Art; Artists Equity Asn. Style & Technique: Dry brush technique; assemblage using coral, shells, sand and glass. Media: Watercolor, Oil. Publ: Contribr, Royal Horticultural Soc Orchid J, 54-66; contribr, Proc Third World Orchid Conf, 60; illusr, Limited edition folio of orchid hybrids, 63; illusr, Flowers of America (limited ed folio), 74; illusr, Can the world feed its people?, Nat Geog Mag, 75. Dealer: Tryon Gallery London, Eng;

Bendann Art Gallery Towson MD 21204. Mailing Add: 700 Mill Dam Rd Towson MD 21204

HOLLADAY, HARLAN H
ART HISTORIAN, PAINTER
b Greenville, Mo, Dec 10, 25. Study: Southeast Mo State Col, BS(educ); Wash Univ, with Werner Drewes, Fred Carpenter & Fred Conway; State Univ Iowa, MA; Cornell Univ, PhD. Work: Munson-Williams-Proctor Inst, Utica, NY; St Lawrence Univ Collection, Canton, NY; Des Moines Art Ctr, Iowa; Sioux City Art Ctr, Iowa; Springfield Art Mus, Mo. Exhib: Corcoran Gallery Art Biennial, Washington, DC, 51; Whitney Mus Am Art, New York, 52; Pa Acad Fine Arts, Philadelphia, 52, 53 & 59; 61st Nat Watercolor Ann, Washington, DC, 58. Teaching: Art teacher, Poplar Bluff Pub Schs, Mo, 51-53 & Des Moines, Iowa, 53-55; from instr to asst prof drawing & painting, Univ Nev, Reno, 55-58; prof fine arts, St Lawrence Univ, 61-, head dept, 65-71, L M & G L Flint Prof, 67-; prof art & artist in residence, Am Col Switz, 68-69. Awards: Hon Mention, 61st Nat Watercolor Ann, Washington, DC, 58; Reynolds Awards, Cooperstown Art Asn, 67; First Prize Painting, NY State Fair, Syracuse, 74; plus others. Mem: Col Art Asn Am; Soc Archit Historians; Am Asn Univ Prof; Cooperstown Art Asn; St Lawrence Co Hist. Style & Technique: Realistic and abstract landscapes. Media: Oil, Acrylic. Res: 15th century art, especially Northern European painters and sculptors; 19th century art and architecture; American art and architecture. Publ: Auth, Art in the liberal arts curriculum, 64 & auth, The value of a teaching collection, 70, St Lawrence Bull; auth, Catalogue for the McGinnis Collection, St Lawrence Univ, 70. Mailing Add: Dept of Fine Arts St Lawrence Univ Canton NY 13617

HOLLAND, TOM
PAINTER
b Seattle, Wash, 1936. Study: Willamette Univ; Univ Calif, Santa Barbara; Univ Calif, Berkeley. Work: Stanford Univ; St Louis City Mus; San Francisco Mus Art; Mus Mod Art, New York; Art Inst Chicago; plus many others. Exhib: Kid Stuff, Albright-Knox Art Gallery, Buffalo, NY, 71; New Options in Painting, Walker Art Ctr, Minneapolis, 72; California Prints, Mus Mod Art, New York, 72; USA-West Coast, Hamburg, Hanover & Cologne, Ger, 72; Works in Progress, San Francisco Mus Art, 72; Corcoran Biennial, Washington, DC, 75; plus many other group & one-man shows. Teaching: Instr art, San Francisco Art Inst, currently. Awards: Fulbright Grant, Santiago, Chile, 59-60. Mailing Add: 28 Roble Rd Berkeley CA 94705

HOLLANDER, GINO F
PAINTER, ART DEALER
b Newark, NJ, Aug 4, 24. Work: Mus Bellas Artes, Madrid; Johnson Mus, Cornell Univ, Ithaca, NY; Greenville Mus, SC; Churchill Col, London; Olivetti Collection, Milan. Comn: Group Figures, Hotel Diplomat, Jerusalem, 73; Black & White Group, Palacio de Congressos, Torremolinos, Spain, 74; 7 Panels, Airlines Terminal Bldg, New York, 74; Family, Sloane Kettering Mem Hosp, New York, 74; Abstract with Blue, Int Airport, Malaga, Spain, 75. Pos: Artist-owner, Hollander Gallery, London, Marbella, New York, Toronto. Style & Technique: Abstract expressionism with figuration; black and white figuration. Media: Acrylic, Ink. Mailing Add: Pizarra Malaga Spain

HOLLERBACH, SERGE
PAINTER, INSTRUCTOR
b Pushkin, Russia, Nov 1, 23; US citizen. Study: Acad Fine Arts, Munich, Ger, 46-49; Art Students League, with Ernst Fiene, 50; Am Art Sch, with Gordon Samstag, 51. Work: St Paul Gallery Art, Minn; Bridgeport Mus Art, Sci & Indust, Conn; Ga Mus Art, Athens; Seton Hall Univ Art Gallery; Norfolk Mus Art & Scis, Va. Exhib: Am Watercolor Soc Ann Exhib; Nat Acad Design Ann Exhib; Drawings USA, St Paul, Minn; 200 Years of Watercolor Painting in America, Metrop Mus Art, New York; Am Acad Arts & Lett, New York. Awards: Childe Hassam Purchase Award, Am Acad Arts & Lett, 68-69; NJ Soc Painters & Sculptors Medal of Honor, 69; Adolph & Clara Obrig Prize, Nat Acad Design, 71 & 75. Mem: Am Watercolor Soc (dir, 72); Audubon Artists (vpres, 71); NJ Soc Painters & Sculptors; Nat Soc Painters in Casein & Acrylics; assoc Nat Acad Design. Style & Technique: Figurative. Media: Acrylic, Oil. Mailing Add: 304 W 75th St New York NY 10023

HOLLIDAY, BETTY
PAINTER, PHOTOGRAPHER
b New York, NY. Study: Barnard Col, with Julius Held, BA; Fogg Mus, Harvard Univ, with Jacob Rosenberg, MA; Art Students League, with Vaclav Vytlacil. Work: Art Students League; Nat Asn Mus Publ. Exhib: Recent Drawings: USA, Mus Mod Art, New York, 56; Drawings: The Currier Gallery, Manchester, NH, 69-72; Photographs & Photo-Sculptures, Post Col, 69; Unmanly Art, Suffolk Mus, Stonybrook, NY, 72; Traveling Exhib Drawings & Photographs, New Eng Cult Ctr, Durham, NH; Dartmouth Col, and others. Teaching: Vis lectr figure painting, Nassau Co Cult Develop Prog, Roslyn, NY, 73. Pos: Ed assoc, Art News Mag, 50-55; coordr fine arts, Dept Continuing Educ, Great Neck Bd Educ, 58-; mem, Art Adv Coun, Great Neck Libr, 70-; dir, Fine Arts Workshop, Williams Col, 74-75. Awards: Currier Award, Currier Gallery, Manchester, NH, 69. Bibliog: Dorothy Seckler (auth), Furor over Figure, Art in Am, 61; J P Sedgewick, Jr (auth), Discovering Modern Art, Random House, 66; George Kushar (auth), From Sands Point (film), 70. Mem: League NH Artists. Style & Technique: The human figure explored through visual and psychological nuances of line and infinite possibilities of a broad grey-scale; photography as an extension of imagery. Media: All Drawing Media; Acrylic on Canvas; Black & White Composite Photographs on Sculptural Supports. Mailing Add: 2 Pelham Ave Sands Point NY 11050

HOLLIDAY, JUDITH
ART LIBRARIAN
b Butler, Pa, Mar 16, 38. Study: Col Wooster, BA, 60; Columbia Univ, MSLS, 61. Pos: Head librn, Fine Arts Libr, Cornell Univ, 70- Mem: Art Libr Soc NAm; Soc Archit Historians. Interest: Nineteenth century American architectural periodicals. Mailing Add: Box 13 DeWitt Park Apts Ithaca NY 14850

HOLLINGER, (HELEN WETHERBEE)
PAINTER, LECTURER
b Indianapolis, Ind. Study: Herron Sch Art, dipl fine arts; also with Donald Mattison, Henrik Mayer & Emile Gruppe. Work: First Fed Savings & Loan Asn, Miami, Fla; Herron Sch Art; Hialeah, Miami Springs Realty Bd. Exhib: One-man exhib, Bacardi Gallery, Miami, 68 & Gables Art Gallery, Coral Gables, 70; Grand Nat Exhib, Am Artists Prof League, New York, 69-72; Am Artists Prof League, New York, 69-75; Nat Biennial Art Exhib, Nat League Am Pen Women, Salt Lake City, Utah, 70; Miami Shores Community Ctr, 73 & 75; Mus Sci Fine Art Show, Miami, Fla, 75 & 76. Teaching: Instr art, Miami Shores Community Ctr, Fla, 71-72 & 75. Awards: Nat League Am Pen Women First Prize for Portraiture, Fla State Art Exhib, 69; First Place Art Achievement Award, Wometco Enterprises, Miami, 71; Poinciana Art Exhib Best in Show, Burdine's, Miami, 72. Mem: Am Artists Prof League (pres, Miami Chap, 69-70, dir, 71-73); Nat League Am Pen Women (art chmn, Fla State Orgn, 66-68, nat art bd, 72-74); Blue Dome Art Fel; Miami Art League (pres, 66-67, dir 71 & 75). Style & Technique: Representational, with brush and palette knife. Media: Oil, Pastel, Acrylic. Dealer: Blunt Gallery 315 Fifth Ave S Naples FL 33940. Mailing Add: 80 NE 97th St Miami Shores FL 33138

HOLLINGSWORTH, ALVIN CARL
PAINTER, INSTRUCTOR
b New York, NY, Feb 25, 30. Study: Music & Art High Sch; City Univ New York, BA, 56, MA, 59; Art Students League, with Kunioshi, Ralph Fabri & Dr Bernard Myers, 50-52. Work: Chase Manhattan Bank, New York; Brooklyn Mus Permanent Collection, NY; IBM Collection, White Plains, NY; Williams Col Art Collection; Johnson Publ Permanent Art Collection, Chicago; plus others. Comn: Don Quixote limited ed lithographs, Orig Lithographs Inc, 67; Don Quixote murals, Don Quixote Apts, Bronx, NY, 69; mural, Rutgers Univ, New Brunswick, NJ, 70. Exhib: Art USA, Madison Square Garden, New York, 57; Emily Lowe Award Exhib, 63; Traveling Exhib Black Painters America, Univ Calif, Los Angeles, 66; 15 New Voices, Hallmark Gallery, New York & traveling, 69; Am Black Painters, Whitney Mus Am Art, New York, 71; plus The Women, Interfaith Coun of Churches, 78, Reflections of the Prophet, Pa State Univ, 78 & other one-man shows. Teaching: Instr graphics, High Sch Art & Design, 61-70; instr painting, Art Students League, 69-75; asst prof painting, Hostos Community Col, 71-77, assoc prof, 77- Pos: Consult art & art coordr, Harlem Freedom Sch, Off Econ Opportunity, 66-67; dir, Lincoln Inst Gallery, Lincoln Inst Psycho-Ther, 66-68; supvr art, Proj Turn-On, New York, 68-69. Awards: Emily Lowe Art Competition Award, 63; Whitney Found Award, 64; Award of Distinction, Smith Mason Gallery, 71. Bibliog: Cedric Dover (auth), American Negro Art, 61; Samella Lewis (auth), Black Artist on Art, privately publ, 71. Media: Acrylic, Collage. Res: Aesthetic use of fluorescent materials in the fine arts. Publ: Auth & illusr, I'd like the Goo-gen-heim, Regnery, 69; co-auth, Art of Acrylic Painting, Grumbacher, 69; illusr, The Sniper, McGraw, 69; illusr, Black Out Loud, Macmillan, 70; illusr, Journey, Scholastic, 70. Dealer: Lee Nordness Gallery 236 E 75th St New York NY 10021; Harbor Gallery 43 Main St Cold Spring Harbor NY 11724. Mailing Add: Hostos Community Col City Univ of New York New York NY 10021

HOLLINGWORTH, KEITH WILLIAM
SCULPTOR
b Providence, RI, Apr 21, 37. Study: RI Sch of Design, Providence, BFA, 59; Mills Col, Oakland, Calif, MFA, 64. Exhib: Sculpture Ann, Whitney Mus Am Art, New York, 66; Referendum 70, Paula Cooper Gallery, New York, 70; Drawings, Janie C Lee Gallery, Dallas & Paula Cooper Gallery, 70; Statements Beyond the 60s, Inst Art, Detroit, 72; 26 By 26, Vassar Col, Poughkeepsie, NY, 72; Kith & Kin, Univ Ky, Lexington, 72; Painting & Sculpture Today, Herron Art Inst, Indianapolis, Ind, 72; one-man shows, Univ Mass, Amherst, 65, performance, St Peter's Episcopal Church, New York, 68, performance, Loeb Student Ctr, New York, 69, Art Inst Chicago, 70, Paula Cooper Gallery, 71 & 72, St Cloud State Col, Minn, 72 & Westfield State Col, Mass, 75. Teaching: Ohio Univ, Athens, 64-65; instr, Univ Mass, Amherst, 65-67, Drexel Univ, Philadelphia, 69-71 & Pace Col, New York, 72-73; guest artist, Univ Mich, Kalamazoo, 73; instr, Queens Col, Flushing, NY, 73-74; guest artist, Univ Maine, Orono, 74. Bibliog: Marjorie Wellish (auth), Material extension in new sculpture, Arts Mag, summer 71; Gregory Battcock (auth), New York, Art & Artists, London, 9/71; Peter Schjeldahl (auth), Take wheels & feathers & fishing lines, New York Times, 1/10/72. Style & Technique: Constructions concerned with ornithology, ethnology, horticulture and other things of personal interest. Mailing Add: Lyman Rd Chester MA 01011

HOLLISTER, PAUL
PAINTER, WRITER
b New York, NY. Study: Harvard Col, BS. Exhib: Riverside Mus, NY; Whitney Mus Am Art, New York; New York City Ctr; New Sch Social Res, New York; Silvermine Guild Artists; plus others. Mem: Nat Early Am Glass Club (ed, Bull); Soc Preserv New Eng Antiquities; Glass Circle, London; Int Asn Hist Glass, Liège, Belg; Neenah Munic Mus Found, Wis. Publ: Auth, The Encyclopedia of Glass Paperweights, Potter, 69; contribr, The Collectors Encyclopedia of Antiques, Crown, 73; auth, Glass Paperweights of the New York Historical Society, Potter, 74; auth, London's Crystal Palace of 1851, Antiques Mag, 1/74; auth, The glazing of the Crystal Palace, Corning J Glass Studies, 74; plus others. Mailing Add: c/o Clarkson N Potter Inc One Park Ave New York NY 10016

HOLLISTER, VALERIE (DUTTON)
PAINTER
b Oakland, Calif, Dec 29, 39. Study: Stanford Univ, AB, 61 & MA, 65; San Francisco Art Inst, 63; Col Art Study Abroad, Paris, 64-65. Exhib: Corcoran Biennial Contemp Am Painting & Corcoran Gallery Area Show, Washington, DC, 67; Whitney Mus Ann Contemp Am Painting, 67-68; Inside/Outside, Women's Interart Ctr, New York, NY, 75; Painting 75-76-77, Sarah Lawrence Col, NY, Am Fedn of Arts, Miami, Fla & Contemp Arts Ctr, Cincinnati, Ohio, 77; one-woman shows, Jefferson Place Gallery, Washington, DC, 66-72, Madison Art Ctr, Wis, 68, Swarthmore Col, Pa, 72 & 77, Westbroadway Gallery, New York, NY, 73 & Selected Paintings Since 1965, Washington Proj for the Arts, Washington, DC, 78; plus other one-woman & group shows. Media: Acrylic. Mailing Add: 1 Whittier Pl Swarthmore PA 19081

HOLM, BILL
ART HISTORIAN, CURATOR
b Roundup, Mont, Mar 24, 25. Study: Univ Wash, BA, 49, MFA, 51. Collections Arranged: Arts of the Raven (with Doris Shadbolt, Bill Reid & Wilson Duff), Vancouver Art Gallery, 67; Northwest Coast Indian Life, Pac Sci Ctr, Seattle, 71-; Crooked Beak of Heaven, Henry Art Gallery, Univ Wash, Seattle. Teaching: Prof Northwest Coast Indian art, Univ Wash, Seattle, 68- Pos: Cur, Northwest Coast Indian art, Thomas Burke Mem Wash State Mus, Univ Wash, Seattle, 68- Awards: Governor's Writers Award, 66 & 77. Res: All aspects of Northwest Coast Indian art, with concentration on form and style and relation to ceremonialism. Publ: Auth, Northwest Coast Indian Art: An Analysis of Form, Univ Wash Press, 65; contribr-illusr, Boxes and Bowls, Smithsonian Press, 74; contribr-illusr, The Human Mirror: Material and Spatial Images of Man, La Univ Press, 74; co-auth (with Bill Reid), Indian Art of the Northwest Coast, Univ Wash Press, 76; auth, Crooked Beak of Heaven, Univ Wash Press, 72. Mailing Add: 1027 NW 190th St Seattle WA 98177

HOLM, MILTON W
PAINTER
b Rochester, NY. Study: With Edward S Siebert, Rochester. Work: Mem Art Gallery, Rochester; Rochester Inst Technol; Univ Rochester; Greenville Pub Libr, SC. Exhib: Mem Art Gallery, 24-76; Nat Acad Design Ann, New York, 35-70; Allied Artists Am, New York, 38-71 & 77; Currier Art Gallery, Manchester, NH, 40; Cincinnati Art Gallery, Ohio, 45. Awards: Ranger Purchase Award, Nat Acad Design, 40; James Hogarth Dennis Award, Mem

Art Gallery, 58-62, Rochester Art Club Award, 69-74. Mem: Allied Artists Am; Rochester Art Club (pres, 57-59); Genesee Group (pres); Rockport Art Asn, Mass. Media: Oil. Dealer: Wolfard Galleries 9 S Goodman St Rochester NY 14607. Mailing Add: 30 Hathaway Rd Rochester NY 14617

HOLMAN, ARTHUR (STEARNS)
PAINTER
b Bartlesville, Okla, Oct 25, 26. Study: Univ NMex, BFA, 51; Hans Hofmann Sch Art, Provincetown, Mass, 51; Calif Sch Fine Arts, San Francisco, 53. Work: San Francisco Mus Art; Oakland Mus, Calif; Stanford Univ Mus; Eureka Col. Exhib: One-man shows, Esther Robles Gallery, Los Angeles, 60, M H De Young Mem Mus, San Francisco, 63 & William Sawyer Gallery, San Francisco, 71, 73 & 74; Fifty California Artists, Whitney Mus Am Art, New York, 62; 1st Painting Invitational, Palo Alto Cult Ctr, Calif, 73; Calif Painting & Sculpture: The Mod Era, San Francisco Mus, 76; Smithsonian Inst, Washington, DC, 77. Awards: Purchase Award, Invitational Show, Stanford Univ, 62; Public Vote Prize, Bay Area Art, First Savings Bank of San Francisco, 64. Style & Technique: Impressions of California landscapes. Media: Oil. Mailing Add: Box 72 Lagunitas CA 94938

HOLMBOM, JAMES WILLIAM
PAINTER
b Monson, Maine, Mar 3, 26. Study: Portland Sch Art, with Alexander Bower; Univ Maine, BSA; Inst Allende, Mex, MFA, with James Pinto & Fred Samuelson. Work: Inst Allende; also in the corporate collections of Beverly Trust Corp, Mass, Union Mutual Life Ins Co, Casco Bank & Trust Corp & Maine Savings Bank, Portland. Exhib: Three-man show, Inst Allende, 67; Mainstreams USA, 70; UNICEF Invitational Exhib, 71; Bridgton Art Show, Maine, 71; Bertrand Russell Centenary Int Art Exhib, 72-73; plus others. Teaching: City art dir, Montpelier, Vt, 56-59; city art dir, Marblehead, Mass, 59-71; pvt classes, Essex, Mass, 56-71; instr landscape & studio painting, Inst Allende, 66-67. Awards: Purchase Prizes, Portland Art Festival, 69-71. Style & Technique: Landscape semi-abstraction in acrylics; chimeric imagery in oil. Mailing Add: Box 52 Hancock ME 04640

HOLMES, DAVID BRYAN
PAINTER
b London, Eng, Aug 8, 36; Can citizen. Study: Twickenham Tech Col, Eng; Harrow Sch Art, London; Queen's Univ (Ont); Art Students League, with Robert Beverley Hale; London Sch of Art & Design, Eng. Work: Willistead Art Gallery, Windsor, Ont. Comn: Many pvt comn in Eng & NAm. Exhib: Ann Spring Exhib, Queen's Univ (Ont), 64-71, two-man show, 67; Soc Can Artists Ann, Toronto, 68-71; Country Scenes in Quebec, City of Montreal, PQ, 69; one-man shows, Galerie Gauvreau, Montreal, 69 & 70 & Wally F Findlay Galleries, Inc, New York, 74 & 75, Chicago, 77, New York, 78 & Palm Beach, Fla, 79. Teaching: Instr art, St Lawrence Col Appl Arts & Technol, Kingston, Ont, 68-74. Awards: Ann Nat Spring Exhib, Queen's Univ (Ont), 67, 69 & 71; Award for Country Scenes in Quebec, City of Montreal, 69. Mem: Int Soc Artists; Print & Drawing Coun Can; Soc Can Artists; Art Students League. Style & Technique: Realism. Media: Silverpoint Drawing, Tempera. Dealer: Wally F Findlay Galleries Inc 17 E 57th St New York NY 10022. Mailing Add: RR 3 Odessa ON Can

HOLMES, PAUL JAMES & MARY E
COLLECTORS
Mr Holmes, b North Henderson, Ill, Jan 28,96; Mrs Holmes, b Chicago, Ill, Sept 12, 00. Study: Mr Holmes, Univ Mich, BS; Univ Toulouse; Mrs Holmes, Art Inst Chicago; also with Sadie M Hess, Gary, Ind. Collection: 18th century porcelains and figurines; miniatures; patch and snuff boxes; Russian enamels, porcelains and Faberge; Russian icons; rare items in porcelain, art glass and graphics; medieval and 18th century enamels of England and the Continent; wax portraits and groups; silhouettes; Verre de Nevers; momentos mori. Mailing Add: 836 Du Shane Ct South Bend IN 46616

HOLMES, REGINALD
PAINTER, PHOTOGRAPHER
b Calgary, Alta, Oct 4, 34. Study: Vancouver Sch Art. Work: Larry Aldrich Mus, Ridgefield, Conn; Art Gallery Ont, Toronto; Chase Manhattan Bank, New York; New York Bank Savings; Port Authority, Kennedy Airport, New York. Exhib: Vancouver Art Gallery, BC, 65; Isaacs Gallery, Toronto, 67, 69 & 71; Can Biennial, Ottawa, 69; Gallery 99, Fla, 70; Whitney Exp Sch, New York, 70. Teaching: Instr painting, Vancouver Art Sch, 59-68; instr design, NY Univ, 70. Awards: Can Coun Awards, 69, 70 & 72. Bibliog: Walter Klepac (auth), The contingencies of colour & form, Artscan, 2-3/72. Media: Acrylic. Mem: Royal Can Acad Arts. Mailing Add: 24 Ryerson Ave Toronto ON M5T 2P3 Can

HOLMES, RUTH ATKINSON
PAINTER, SCULPTOR
b Hazlehurst, Miss. Study: Miss State Col Women; Tulane Univ; Miss Col & Southwest Jr Col. Work: Univ La, Alexandria & Baton Rouge; Miss State Col Women, Columbus; Miss State Univ, Starkville. Comn: Mural (with Bess Dawson), Church of God, McComb, Miss; mural (with Bess Dawson & Halcyone Barnes), Progressive Bank, Summit, Miss; mural (with Bess Dawson & Halcyone Barnes), First Nat Bank, McComb; 14 Stations of the Cross, Church of Mediator, McComb, 72. Exhib: One-man shows, Ahda Artzt, New York, 64, Mary Chilton Gallery, Memphis, Tenn, 66, Brooks Mem Gallery & Mus, Memphis, 69, Univ La, Alexandria, 69 & Bryant Gallery, Jackson, Miss, 71. Awards: First Prize Pastel, Chautauqua Art Asn, NY, 62; First Prize, Miss Art Asn Nat Oil Show, Jackson, 66; First Prize, La Font Workshop, S Cent Bell Tel Co, Pascagoula, Miss, 68. Mem: Miss Art Asn (bd mem, 69); Miss Art Colony; LeFonte Art Colony. Publ: Co-auth, Camellia Magic, 50. Dealer: McComb Gallery McComb MS 39648. Mailing Add: PO Box 543 McComb MS 39648

HOLO, SELMA REUBEN
ART HISTORIAN, CURATOR
b Chicago, Ill, May 21, 43. Study: Univ Mich, Ann Arbor, 61-63; Northwestern Univ, BA, 65; Hunter Col, City Univ New York, MA(art hist), adv. Ann Sutherland Harris, 72; Univ Calif, Santa Barbara, PhD candidate. Collections Arranged: Italiote Vases in LA (co-auth, catalogue), 75 & Goya: Los Disparates (auth, catalogue), 76, J Paul Getty Mus. Teaching: Instr art hist, Art Ctr Col of Design, Pasadena, Calif, 73-77. Pos: Cur-in-charge of res & publ, Norton Simon Mus, Pasadena, 78- Awards: Univ Calif Patent Fund Grant, Spain, 76. Bibliog: Eric Young (auth), Los Disparate at Malibu, Burlington Mag, 2/77. Mem: Col Art Asn; Hispanic Art Hist; Southern Art Calif. Res: Goya prints, Velaquez. Mailing Add: Colorado & Orange Grove Blvd Pasadena CA 91105

HOLSCHUH, (GEORGE) FRED
SCULPTOR
b Beerfelden, Ger, Nov 19, 02; US citizen. Study: Indust art & archit dipl; Pa Acad Fine Arts; Univ Pa; also with Bauhaus founder, Walter Gropius. Work: Süddeutsches Mus, Darmstadt, Ger; Addisson Gallery, New York; Brookgreen Garden, SC. Comn: St Francis Monument, Yugoslav Order of St Francis, Washington, DC, 36; Murrell Dobbins Mem, Bd Educ, Philadelphia, 38; bronze sculptures (collab with Bass Studio, Philadelphia), Penn Mutual Life Ins Bldg, 39; copper sculpture, Irene Edmond Mem, Tallahassee, Fla, 67 & 10th anniversary figure, Garden Le Moyne Art Found, 72. Exhib: Pa Acad Fine Arts, Philadelphia, 36; Nat Acad Design, New York, 37; Int Sculpture Outdoor Show, Parkway Mus, Philadelphia, 39; Regional Sculpture Show, Smithsonian Inst, Washington, DC, 40. Teaching: Prof design & art hist & head dept art, Cedar Crest Col, Allentown, 36-38; prof humanities & sculpture, Fla State Univ, 46-72, emer prof, 72- Pos: Pres, Assoc Fla Sculptors, 56-59. Awards: Stimson Prize in Sculpture, Pa Acad Fine Arts, 35 & European Traveling Scholars, 35 & 36; Regional First Prize, Southern Sculptors Nat Show, 66. Mem: Asn Southern Sculptors (bd dirs, 63-65); Am Asn Univ Prof. Style & Technique: Wood assemblage and carving; brazing and reveting; build-up copper structural figures. Media: Wood, Copper. Dealer: Harmon Gallery 1258 Third St Naples FL 33940. Mailing Add: 2007 W Randolph Circle Tallahassee FL 32303

HOLSTE, THOMAS JAMES
PAINTER, INSTRUCTOR
b Evanston, Ill, Jan 12, 43. Study: Calif State Univ, Fullerton, BA, 67, MA, 68, study with Vic Smith; Claremont Grad Sch, MFA, 70, study with Guy Williams, Mowry Baden. Work: La Jolla Mus Contemp Art, Calif; Long Beach Mus Art, Calif. Exhib: Fifth, Sixth & Seventh Ann Southern Calif Exhib, Long Beach Mus Art, Calif, 68, 69 & 70; The Subtle Image, La Jolla Mus Contemp Art, Calif, 70; one-man shows, Pomona Col, Claremont, Calif, 70, Irving Blum Gallery, Los Angeles, 72 & Newspace Gallery, Los Angeles, 73-77; Contemp Am Art from Orange Co Collections, Newport Harbor Art Mus, Newport Beach, Calif, 71; The Market Street Prog, Los Angeles Co Mus Art, Los Angeles, 72; Ruth S Schaffner Gallery, 73; John Doyle Gallery, Chicago, Ill, 73; Cusack Gallery, Houston, Tex, 73; Aber, Buchanan, Holste, Newport Harbor Art Mus, Newport Beach, Calif, 76; Los Angeles, Mus Mod Art, Penthouse Gallery, New York, 76; plus others. Teaching: Assoc prof painting, Calif State Univ, Fullerton, 69- Awards: Patrons Purchase Grant, Sixth Ann Southern Calif Exhib, Long Beach Mus Art, Calif, Clement Greenberg, 69; Cash Award, 20th Ann All-Calif Exhib, Laguna Beach Mus Art, Calif, 74. Bibliog: Melinda Terbell (auth), A break for the artist, Artnews, 1/74; Betty Turnbull (auth), Aber, Buchanan, Holste (catalogue), Newport Harbor Art Mus, 76; Michael Auping (auth), Abstract Painting: A Selected Exhibition (catalogue), Long Beach City Col, Calif, 77. Style & Technique: Mixed media wall constructions (abstract). Dealer: Newspace Gallery 5015 Melrose Ave Los Angeles CA 90038. Mailing Add: Star Rte Box 796 Orange CA 92667

HOLT, CHARLOTTE SINCLAIR
MEDICAL ILLUSTRATOR, SCULPTOR
b Springfield, Mass, June 11, 14. Study: Mass Normal Art Sch & Boston Mus Fine Arts, 29-34; Child-Walker Sch Fine Arts & Crafts, Boston, 32-34, dipl; Boston Univ, 33-34, Col Med, 34-35; portrait painting with Bernard Keyes, Boston, 34; med photog with Laurence Toriello & Anthony Kuzma, 36-37 & 71-72; Sch Med Illus, cert, 37; Rush Med Col, med art with Willard C Shepard, 37-38; watercolor with Elliot O'Hara, Maine, 41; sculpture with Malvina Hoffman, New York, 39-66; plaster casting with John Pletinkx; plastic carving with Joseph Krstolich; Marquette Univ Med Col, PhD, 73. Work: Miracle of Growth, Mus Sci & Indust, Chicago. Exhib: Many nat & int exhib, 37-70. Pos: Chief med illusr & sculptor, Visual Educ Prog, Univ Ill Col Med in coop with Ill State Dept Health, 35-70; free lance med illusr, sculptor & graphic artist for advert agencies & pharmaceut co, 36-; instr, Sch Med Illus, 37-45; adv ed, J Am Med Illusr, 59-70, assoc ed, 70-; med artist, Am Med Asn, 61-63; dir, Med Audio/Visual Communications, Akron Gen Med Ctr, 72- Awards: First Award, Am Med Asn, Chicago, 63; Distinguished Serv Awards, Asn Med Illusr, 66 & 70, Presidential Award, 71; plus others. Mem: Asn Med Illusr (vpres, 60-61, bd gov, 61-66 & 71-76, corresp secy, 65-69, pres, 70-71 & chmn many comts); fel Med Artists Asn Gt Brit; Royal Photog Soc; assoc Inst Med & Biol Illus; Allied Artists Am; plus many others. Style & Technique: Medical and fine arts sculpture and plastic carving; stained glass designs and interior designs. Media: Watercolor; pen and ink. Publ: Co-auth & illusr, Obstetric and Gynecologic Nursing, Mosby, 37, rev ed, 41; co-auth & illusr, Atlas of Obstetric Complications, Lippincott, 62; illusr many jour & med bks. Mailing Add: 738 Keystone Ave River Forest IL 60305

HOLT, MARGARET MCCONNELL
PATRON, COLLECTOR
b Gastonia, NC, July 26, 09. Study: Univ NC-Greensboro, BS(music), 30; painting with Louis Bouche, New York, 40; Black Mountain Col, ceramics with Marguerita Wildenhain, Bernard Leach & Shoji Hamada, 53; watercolor with Eliot O'Hara, 55, 65 & 68; Queens Col, with Philip Moose, 65-66; Univ NC-Charlotte, Bach Creative Arts, 73. Interest: Proceeds from art work go towards collecting works by living American artists, providing art scholarships and sponsoring creativity in university art schools. Collection: Founder of the D E McConnell Collection of American Art which is housed at the Gaston-Lincoln Regional Library Headquarters, Gastonia, NC. Mailing Add: 115 Ingleside Dr SE Concord NC 28025

HOLT, NANCY LOUISE
SCULPTOR, FILM MAKER
b Worcester, Mass, Apr 5, 38. Study: Jackson Col; Tufts Univ, BS. Comn: Landscape sculptures, Univ Mont, 72, Univ RI, 72 & Artpark, Lewiston, NY, 74. Exhib: Interventions in the Landscapes, Mass Inst Technol, 74; Painting & Sculpture Today, Indianapolis Mus, 74; Collectors Video, Los Angeles Co Mus, 74; Response to the Environment, Rutgers Univ, 75; Video '75, Corcoran Mus, Washington, DC; New Am Filmmaker's Series, Whitney Mus Am Art, New York, 75 & 77; Art in Landscape (traveling exhib), Independent Cur, Washington, DC, 76; Whitney Biennial, 77; Probing the Earth: Contemp Land Proj, Hirshhorn Mus, Washington, DC, 77. Awards: Nat Endowment Arts Grant, 75; Creative Artists Pub Serv Grant, 75; Beard's Fund Inc, 77. Bibliog: David Antin (auth), Television: video's frightful parent, Artforum, 12/75; Rosalind Krauss (auth), Video: the aesthetics of narcissism, October, spring 76; Carrie Rickey (auth), Revolve, Arts, 11/77. Publ: Auth, Hydra's head, Arts Mag, 1/75; auth, Pine barrens, Avalanche, summer 75; auth, Some notes on video works, In: Video Art, Harcourt, Brace & Jovanovich, 76; auth, Sun Tunnels, Artforum, 4/77. Mailing Add: 799 Greenwich St New York NY 10014

HOLTON, LEONARD T
CARTOONIST
b Philadelphia, Pa, Sept 6, 06. Comn: Script writer, TV, stage & screen productions; designer & writer TV commercials for Bert Lahr, Nat Cleo Festival & New York Advert Club. Mem: Soc Illustrators; Writers Guild Am. Media: Pen and Ink, Wash. Publ: Illusr, mag & newspaper syndicates; co-auth &/or illusr, bks publ by Scribners, Simon & Schuster & others. Mailing Add: 129 E 82nd St New York NY 10028

HOLTZ, ITSHAK JACK
PAINTER, PRINTMAKER
b Skernewiz, Poland, Dec 14, 25; US citizen. Study: Bezalel Acad Art, Jerusalem; Art Students League; Nat Acad Design, New York. Exhib: Karlebach Gallery, Fair Lawn, NJ,

65-; Nat Acad Design & Audubon Artists of New York, 66; Tyringham Galleries, Mass, 66-75; Allied Artists Am, New York, 72. Bibliog: Articles in Art Rev Mag, 5/66 & La Rev Mod, 6/66. Mem: Art Students League. Style & Technique: Realism and impressionism. Media: Oil, Felt Pen & Ink; Lithography. Mailing Add: 118 E 28th St New York NY 10016

HOLVERSON, JOHN
MUSEUM DIRECTOR, CURATOR
b Marshfield, Wis, June 14, 46. Study: Univ Iowa, 65-66; MacMurray Col, Jacksonville, Ill, BA, 67; Univ Iowa, Iowa City, MA, 71. Collections Arranged: Tamarind: A Renaissance of Lithography, 73, Milton Avery: Prints, 1933-1955, 73, Jules Feiffer, 74, Edwin Douglas: Paintings, 74, Agnes Martin: One a Clear Day, 74, Winslow Homer, 74, Point of View: 19 Women Artists, 74, Sea & Sail (auth, catalogue), 75, 21 Prints by Living Am Artists, Nat Endowment for the Arts-Palmer Fund Collection, 76, 58 Maine Paintings, 1820-1920 (auth, catalogue), 76, Multiple Fields—William Manning, Artist-in-Residence, 77, Images of Woman (auth, catalogue), Photography Exhib, 77, Selections from the Permanent Collection: Contemp Prints, Paintings, Watercolors, 77 & The Revolutionary McLellans, 77, Portland Mus Art, Maine. Teaching: Asst dept of art, MacMurray Col, Jacksonville, Ill, 63-65 & 66-67. Pos: Summer intern, Art Inst Chicago, 68-69; grad asst, Mus Art, Univ Iowa, 68-69, head grad asst, 69-70; cur, Portland Mus Art, Maine, 70-73, cur collections, 73-, actg dir, 73-74 & 74-75, dir, 75-; ed monthly bull, Portland Soc Art, 70- Mem: Am Asn Mus; New Eng Conf, Am Asn Mus; Soc for the Preservation of New Eng Antiq; Nat Trust for State & Local Hist Soc; Col Art Asn. Publ: Auth, Rene Dubois and the cathedrals of the future, Greater Portland Landmarks Observer, Fall 73; auth, Fire buckets and bags in Portland, 1783, Clues & Footnotes Sect, Antiques, 3/74: 447. Mailing Add: Portland Mus Art 111 High St Portland ME 04101

HOLVEY, SAMUEL BOYER
SCULPTOR, DESIGNER
b Wilkes Barre, Pa, July 20, 35. Study: Syracuse Univ, BFA, 57; Am Univ, MA, 69. Comn: Bas-relief mural, Wyo Valley Country Club, Wilkes Barre, 62. Exhib: Corcoran Gallery Area Show, Washington, DC, 68; Greater Washington Area Show, 72; 2nd Ann Washington Area Sculpture Show, 74; The Am Genius, Corcoran Gallery, 76. Teaching: Asst prof design, Corcoran Sch Art, Washington, DC, 65-78; asst prof design, Univ Md, College Park, 67-78. Pos: Designer, William Fertig Interiors, Kingston, Pa, 57-58, 63-64; art dir, WFM-TV, Eatontown, NJ, 60-61; designer display exhibs, The Displayers Inc, New York World's Fair Pavilions, 61-63; designer, Robert Kayton Assocs, New York, 62. Style & Technique: Abstract, open, linear sculpture; abstract hard edge overlapped forms, kinetic, in lumia. Media: Metal Direct Construction, Lumia. Dealer: Franz Bader Gallery Inc 2124 Pennsylvania Ave NW Washington DC 20037. Mailing Add: 5100 Elm St Bethesda MD 20014

HOMAR, LORENZO
PRINTMAKER, PAINTER
b Puerta de Tierra, PR, Sept 10, 13. Study: Pratt Inst, 40-42; Brooklyn Mus, with Peterdi, Tamayo & Osver, 46-50; Inter-Am Univ PR, hon DFA. Work: Libr Cong, Washington, DC; Mus Mod Art, New York; Metrop Mus Art, New York; Klingspor Mus, Offenbach, WGer; Poster Mus, Warsaw, Poland. Comn: Mural of olympic swimming pool, Dept Parks, San Juan, 67-68; mural of pub sch, Dept Educ, San Juan, 71; portfolio, Blanco-Casals-Homar, Galeria Colibri, San Juan, 71. Exhib: Poster Biennale, Warsaw, 70 & 74; San Juan Biennale, 70; Havana Exhib Prints, Cuba, 72; Norwegian Int Print Biennale, 74; Ljubljana, Yugoslavia Biennale; plus others. Collections Arranged: First San Juan Print Biennale; Retrospective Exhib, Mus Int PR Cult, San Juan, 70. Teaching: Master printing silk-screen, Inter-Am Univ PR, summer 72; instr, Cali, Colombia, 72; instr, Sch Plastic Arts, Inst PR Cult, presently. Pos: Jewelry designer, Cartier Inc, New York, 38-50; dir graphic workshop, Div Community Educ, 50-56; dir graphic workshop, Inst PR Cult, 58-72. Awards: Guggenheim Fel, 57; Honorable Mention, Leipzig Bk Exhib, 65. Bibliog: Lorenzo Homar & Fritz Eichenberg (auth), Posters in Puerto Rico, Artist Proof, Vol 6, No 9-10; Jose Gomez Sicre (auth), 6 Puerto Rican Artists (film), Pan-Am Union, 68; Marta Traba (auth), Proposed Polemics on Puerto Rican Art, Libr Int Rio Piedras, PR, 71. Media: Silk-Screen, Woodcut. Publ: Auth, Los Renegados, 62; illusr children's bk, Harcourt Brace & World, 69; auth, Aqui en la Lucha, 70. Dealer: Galeria Santiago Calle Del Cristo San Juan PR 00901. Mailing Add: Calle Cuevillas 607 Miramar PR 00907

HOMER, WILLIAM INNES
ART HISTORIAN, EDUCATOR
b Merion, Pa, Nov 8, 29. Study: Princeton Univ, BA; Harvard Univ, MA & PhD. Teaching: Asst prof art & archaeol, Princeton Univ, 61-64; assoc prof hist art, Cornell Univ, 64-66; prof hist art, Univ Del, 66- Pos: Cur, Mus Art, Ogunquit, Maine, 55-58; actg asst dir, Princeton Univ Art Mus, 56-57. Awards: Coun Humanities Jr Fel, Princeton Univ, 62-63; Am Coun Learned Soc Fel, 64-65; Guggenheim Fel, 72-73. Mem: Col Art Asn; Soc Archit Historians; Royal Soc Arts; Wilmington Soc Fine Arts; Nat Arts Club. Publ: Auth, Seurat and the Science of Painting, 64; auth, Robert Henri & His Circle, 69; ed, Avant-Garde Painting and Sculpture in America, 1910-25, 75; auth, Alfred Stieglitz & the American Avant-Garde, 77. Mailing Add: Dept of Art Hist Univ of Del Newark DE 19711

HOMITZKY, PETER
PAINTER
b Berlin, Ger, Dec 7, 42; US citizen. Study: Art Students League, with F Reilly, J Leberte, J Hirsh, 59-63; San Francisco Art Inst, 65-66. Work: Wichita Mus Art, Kans; World Trade Ctr, New York; San Francisco Mus Art; Prudential Ins Co, Newark, NJ; Newark Mus, NJ; NJ State Mus, Trenton, NJ. Comn: Poster award, Jewish Ctr, Union, 74. Exhib: One-man shows, Goddard Col, Plainfield, Vt, 72, Roko Gallery, New York, 74 & State Mus, Trenton, NJ, 76; Maxwell Galleries, San Francisco, 65-68; Alonzo Galleries, New York, 76-77. Teaching: Instr painting, Queens Col Continuing Educ, Flushing, NY, 72-73, Morris Co Art Ctr, Morristown, NJ, 72-74 & Summit Art Ctr, NJ, 74- Pos: Apprenticed as restorer with Gordon Cope, Maxwell Galleries, 64-67; assoc dir, Forum Gallery, New York, 68-69; dir, Spectrum Gallery, New York, 70-72; dir creative arts prog, E Union Co YMYWHA, NJ, 72- Bibliog: Diane Cochrane (auth), Industrial American landscapes of Peter Homitzky, Am Artist, 5/74; Susan Myer (ed), 20 Landscape Painters, Watson-Guptill, 77; Hilton Kramer (auth), rev, New York Times, 12/9/77. Style & Technique: Landscapes, synthesizing the energy of man-made, or inorganic, forms with those produced by force of nature. Media: Oil, Pastel. Publ: Contribr, Arts Mag, 71; auth, exhib catalogs, Maxwell Galleries, 65-67. Dealer: Alonzo Gallery 26 E 63rd St New York NY 10021; Diamond Gallery 309 Millburn Ave Millburn NJ 07041 Mailing Add: 1437 Parkview Terr Hillside NJ 07205

HOMPSON, DAVI DET (DAVID ELBRIDGE THOMPSON)
CONCEPTUAL ARTIST
b Sharon, Pa, Aug 7, 39. Study: Anderson Col, BA; Indiana Univ, MFA. Exhib: Art by Telephone Show, Chicago Mus Contemp Art, 69; one-man shows, Alexandre Iolas Gallery, New York, 70, Apple Gallery, New York, 71-73, La Mamelle Inc, San Francisco, Calif, 77; Video Art '74, Galerie Impact, Lausanne, Switz, 74; Ideas at the Idea Warehouse, New York, 75. Teaching: Asst prof vis commun, Herron Sch Art, Ind Univ, 67-69; guest artist sculpture, Va Commonwealth Univ, 72-74; guest artist graphic design, RI Sch Design, summer 75. Bibliog: Jerry Bowles (auth), This Book is a Movie, Dell, 71; Richard Kostelanetz (auth), Breakthrough Fictioneers, Something Else Press, 73; George Cruger (auth), Arts in Virginia, Va Mus Art, 74. Style & Technique: Typographic presentations, printed, projected and performed. Publ: Auth, S553 Study Manual, 69; auth, Blue Light Containment, 69; co-auth, Fact and Fiction, 75; auth, Understand, This is Only Temporary, 76 & Hook, 77. Mailing Add: PO Box 7035 Richmond VA 23221

HONEYMAN, ROBERT B, JR
COLLECTOR
Collection: Contemporary art. Mailing Add: Rancho Los Serritos San Juan Capistrano CA 92675

HONIG, MERVIN
PAINTER, PAINTING CONSERVATOR
b New York, NY, Dec 25, 20. Study: Art with Francis Criss, 39-41, Amadee Ozenfant, 46 & Hans Hofmann, 47-50; Brooklyn Mus, conservation with Caroline & Sheldon Keck, 56-58. Work: Okla Mus Art, Oklahoma City; Colby Col Mus Art; Emily Lowe Gallery, Hofstra Univ; also in many pvt collections. Exhib: Portrait of America, Metrop Mus Art, New York, 44 & Carnegie Inst Fine Arts, 45; Whitney Mus Am Art Artists Ann, 49; Brooklyn & Long Island Artists, Brooklyn Mus, 60; Wadsworth Atheneum Artists Ann, 65; one-man shows, Nat Art Mus of Sport, Madison Square Garden, NY, 77 & The New Sch Social Res, New York, 78; plus many others. Teaching: Lectr life drawing, New York City Community Col, 68-70; lectr conservation of painting, Hofstra Univ, 72- Awards: Gold Medal for Best in Show, Am Vet Soc Artists, 66; First Prize for Oil Painting, Locust Valley Art Show, 66; Award of Excellence, Mainstreams '70, Marietta Col, 70. Bibliog: Article in Today's Art Mag, 67; Amy Pett (auth), Beneath suburban exterior are two dedicated artists (husband & wife), Port Washington News & other newspapers, 70; demonstr, Conservation of Paintings, Channel 21-TV, 77. Mem: Audubon Artists; Col Art Asn Am; assoc Int Inst Conserv Artistic & Hist Works; Am Inst Conserv Artistic & Hist Works. Style & Technique: Contemporary realism. Media: Oil on Canvas. Res: The use of polyurethane foam in the process of transfer. Dealer: Frank Rehn Gallery 655 Madison Ave New York NY 10021. Mailing Add: 64 Jane Ct Westbury NY 11590

HOOD, DOROTHY
PAINTER
b Bryan, Tex. Study: RI Sch Design, grad; Art Students League. Work: Mus Mod Art, New York; Whitney Mus Am Art, New York; Brooklyn Mus, NY; San Francisco Mus of Mod Art, Calif; Everson Mus, Syracuse, NY. Exhib: One-man shows, Retrospective, Contemp Art Mus, Houston, 70, Everson Mus Art, 72 & 75, Tibor de Nagy Gallery, New York, 74, Works in Progress, Univ Tex Mus, Austin, 75, Mus Fine Art, Houston, 75 & Retrospective, McNay Art Inst, San Antonio, 78; Int Kuntsmesse, Basel, Switz, 74; Exhib 75, Mus S Tex, Corpus Christi, 76; New Work in Clay by Painters & Sculptors, Everson Mus of Art, 76; Ahrenberg Collection, Kuntshalle, Dusseldorf, 76; plus others. Awards: Childe Hassam Purchase Award, Am Acad Arts & Lett, 74. Bibliog: Philippe de Montebello (auth), Dorothy Hood, Haiti, a surrealist abstraction, Mus Fine Arts Bull, 71; James Harithas (auth), Dorothy Hood, 72 & Dorothy Hood Drawings, 75, Everson Mus Art; plus others. Style & Technique: Space meeting space of the mind's eye. Media: Oil, Ink. Dealer: Meredith Long Houston Galleries 2323 San Felipe Houston TX 77006; Meredith Long Contemp 7 W 57th St New York NY 10019. Mailing Add: 1408 Missouri St Houston TX 77006

HOOD, ETHEL PAINTER
SCULPTOR
b Baltimore, Md, Apr 9, 08. Study: Art Students League; Acad Julian, Paris. Work: St Francis of the Curbs, Brookgreen Gardens, SC. Exhib: Baltimore Mus Art; Corcoran Gallery Art, Washington, DC; Nat Acad Design, New York; Whitney Mus Am Art, New York; Pa Acad Fine Arts, Philadelphia; also four one-man exhibs, New York. Mem: Fel Nat Sculpture Soc; Nat Asn Women Artists. Mailing Add: 15 E 61st St New York NY 10021

HOOD, GARY ALLEN
PRINTMAKER, CURATOR
b Wichita, Kans, Oct 22, 43. Study: Wichita State Univ, BAE, 67, MA, 72, MFA(printmaking), 75; Walker Art Ctr, Minneapolis, 72-73; Minneapolis Inst Arts, 72-73. Work: Philbrook Art Ctr, Tulsa, Okla; Wichita State Univ, Kans. Exhib: Eight State Exhib Painting & Sculpture, Okla Art Ctr, Oklahoma City, 71; Midwest Regional Exhib, Tulsa Publ Libr, Okla, 73; Western Ann Exhib Works on Paper, Western Ill Univ, 74; Nat Exhib Images on Paper, Springfield Art Asn, Ill, 74; Am Indian Ann Nat Exhib, Philbrook Art Ctr, 75; among others. Collections Arranged: Asst, American Indian Art: Form & Tradition, Walker Art Ctr, 72; Contemporary American Indian Art, Wichita State Indian Asn, 73, 74 & 75; consult, American Indian Art, Mobile Art Gallery of Kans Cult Arts Comn, 74-76; Ulrich Mus: Will Barnet Paintings; Charles Grafly Sculptures; Ernest Trova Graphics, Cork Marcheschi Electrics, 75. Teaching: Lectr Am Indian art, Walker Art Ctr & Minneapolis Inst Arts, 72; guest lectr, Wichita State Univ, 71-; guest lectr, Minn Asn State Cols, 72; lectr, Univ Santa Clara Sem, Wichita, 73; plus others. Pos: Asst cur, Ulrich Mus Art, Wichita State Univ, 73- Awards: Ford Found Grant, 72; Am Indian Grad Fel, Wichita State Univ, 71-73; Ford Found Grad Fel Grant, 73-74; plus others. Mem: Am Asn Mus; Mid-Am All Indian Ctr, Inc, Wichita. Style & Technique: Landscapes in parallel linear style and pictorgraphs in intaglio and mixed media, generally derived from Indian subject matter. Res: From realism to abstraction to nonobjectivism; tradition and change in American Indian art; contemporary American Indian art influences. Collection: Contemporary American Indian art; contemporary printmakers. Dealer: White Buffalo Gallery 3555 E Douglas Wichita KS 67218. Mailing Add: 5136 S Madison Wichita KS 67216

HOOD, (THOMAS) RICHARD
PRINTMAKER, DESIGNER
b Philadelphia, Pa. Study: Univ Pa Sch Fine Arts; Philadelphia Mus Sch Art, BFA, 53. Work: Philadelphia Mus Art; New York Pub Libr; Yale Univ Mus; Mus Mod Art, New York; Smithsonian Inst Nat Portrait Gallery, Washington, DC; Libr Cong, Washington, DC. Exhib: New Horizons, Mus Mod Art, New York, 36; Am Art Today, New York World's Fair, 39; Art Dirs Ann, Philadelphia, 52-72; Fabulous Decade, Smithsonian Inst, 64; Color Prints of Americas, NJ State Mus, Trenton & tour to mus in Hawaii, Alaska & nine cities in Japan, 70. Teaching: From instr to prof, Philadelphia Col Art, 51- Pos: Assoc dir advert design, Philadelphia Col Art, 57-60, dir exhibs, 67-; design consult, 67- Awards: Art Dirs Club Philadelphia Gold Medal, 66 & 69; Franklin Gold Medal, Printing Industs Philadelphia, 59 (twice), 69 & 70; Nat Graphic Arts Design Award, 68 (twice) & 70; plus 60 other awards. Bibliog: Gertrude Benson (auth), Tradition versus innovation, Pa Traveler, 5/59; Sam

Gamburg (auth), Professor Hood and award winning invitation, Centennial News, spring 71; Victoria Donohoe (auth), Dick Hood's timeless, abstract, balancing act, Philadelphia Inquirer, 2/25/72. Mem: Philadelphia Art Alliance (print comt, 60-, chmn, 77); Mus Mod Art; Print Club Philadelphia; Am Color Print Soc (pres, 56-); fel Int Inst Arts & Lett; Wisdom Hall of Fame. Style & Technique: Abstract silk-screen. Mailing Add: 1452 E Cheltenham Ave Philadelphia PA 19124

HOOD, WALTER KELLY
ART HISTORIAN, PAINTER
b Catawba Co, NC, Aug 19, 28. Study: Antioch Col, 48-49; Pa Acad Fine Arts, 49-53; Am Acad Rome, 53-55; Univ Pa, BFA, 57; Univ Hawaii, MFA, 61; Northwestern Univ, PhD(art hist), 66; mural studies with George Harding & Jean Charlot. Work: Pa Acad Fine Arts, Philadelphia; Fred T Foard Sch, Vale, NC. Comn: Six egg tempera murals, Christ's Life, Death & Resurrection, St Peter's Episcopal Church, Glenside, Pa, 57-58; mosaic for residence with nocturnal theme, comn by Nona Boren, Chevy Chase, Md, 60; three frescoes, Bd Regist for Engrs, Architects & Land Surveyors, Honolulu, 61. Exhib: III Mostra de Pittura Americana, Bordighera, Italy, 55; one-man exhib of mural designs, Archit League New York, 56; 152nd Ann Exhib, Pa Acad Fine Arts, 57; 62nd Ann Nat Exhib, Washington Watercolor Club, 59; 1974 Grand Nat Exhib, Am Artists Prof League, Lever House, New York, 74. Teaching: Instr drawing & painting, Honolulu Acad Art, summer 61; prof painting & art hist & head dept art, Catawba Col, Salisbury, NC, 71- Awards: Cresson European Traveling Award, Pa Acad Fine Arts, 52 & Schiedt Foreign Traveling Award, 53; Abbey Mural Fel, Am Acad Rome, 53-54. Bibliog: Frederick Williams (auth), To the Glory of God: Glimpse of a Man (biog film), 70. Mem: Nat Soc Mural Painters; Am Artists Prof League; fel Am Acad Rome. Style & Technique: Original representational style; broad technical experience: mosaic, fresco, encaustic, tempera, distemper, silverpoint, oil, watercolor, acrylic. Media: Fresco, Egg Tempera. Res: Definitive study of the art life of George Harding; study of the flora of Hawaii. Publ: Illusr, Arc Welding Instructions for the Beginner, 64; illusr, The Theory & Technique of Soldering & Brazing of Piping Systems, 71. Mailing Add: 2508 W Innes St Salisbury NC 28144

HOOK, FRANCES A
ILLUSTRATOR
b Amber, Pa, Dec 24, 12. Study: Pa Mus Sch Art, Philadelphia, with Thornton Oakley & Henry C Pitz. Work: Standard Publ, Cincinnati, Ohio; Child's World, Elgin, Ill; Concordia Publ, St Louis, Mo; Hallmark Cards, Kansas City, Mo; pvt collection of David C Cook, Elgin, Ill. Comn: Steinway Piano advert featuring children & Gen Electric advert, N W Ayer Advert, Philadelphia; illus, Northern Tissue com & article in Teens of our Times, Good Housekeeping Mag. Awards: Mead Paper Co Ann Award; NY Advert Ann Award. Style & Technique: Pastel-impressionistic with realism in drawing, watercolor. Media: Pastel. Publ: Illusr, Winter, Summer, Spring is Here, 75, My Quiet Book, 77 & My Wonder Book, 77, Child's World; illusr, My Book of Special Days, 77 & My Jesus Book (in four lang), 77, Standard Publ. Mailing Add: Ocean Point Rd East Boothbay ME 04544

HOOK, WALTER
PAINTER, PRINTMAKER
b Missoula, Mont, Apr 25, 19. Study: Univ Mont, BA, 42; Univ NMex, MA, 50, with Kenneth Adams & Randall Davey. Work: Cheney Cowles Mem Mus, Spokane, Wash; Butler Inst Am Art, Youngstown, Ohio; Springfield Art Mus, Mo; Richmond Art Mus, Va; Yellowstone Art Ctr, Billings, Mont. Comn: Stations of Cross (sculptures), St Anthony's Parish, Missoula, Mont, 63, mosaic, 64; mosaic, St Vincent de Paul Parish, Fed Way, Washington, DC, 65; low relief, Newman Ctr, Missoula, 65; low relief, Missoula Vo-Tech Ctr. Exhib: Butler Inst Am Art Ann, 64, 67 & 68; Pac Northwest Watercolor Soc Ann, Seattle, 68-77; Nat Watercolor Soc Ann, Los Angeles, 68-75; Pa Acad Fine Arts Ann, Philadelphia, 69; Am Watercolor Soc Ann, New York, 71-76. Teaching: Prof painting & drawing, Univ Mont, 55-77. Pos: Sci illusr, Western Elec AEC Prog, Albuquerque, NMex, 51-54; art dir, Gen Elec AEC Prog, Richland, Wash, 54-55. Awards: Watercolor USA Purchase Award, Springfield Art Mus, 71; Fred Marshall Watercolor Award, Northwest Watercolor Soc, Seattle, 71; Western States Art Found Cash Grant, 76. Mem: Ala Watercolor Soc; Nat Watercolor Soc; Philadelphia Watercolor Soc; Artists Equity Asn; Assoc Nat Acad. Style & Technique: Realism; surrealism; magic realism. Media: Watercolor, Lithography, Oil. Dealer: Pearl Fox 103 Windsor Ave Melrose Park Philadelphia PA 19126. Mailing Add: 400 Pattee Canyon Dr Missoula MT 59801

HOOKER, MRS R WOLCOTT
COLLECTOR, PATRON
b Missoula, Mont, Sept 28, 08. Study: Col William & Mary; Art Students League, drawing with Robert Beverly Hale; Albright Art Sch, Buffalo. Pos: Dir, Int Coun Mus Mod Art; trustee, Am Fedn Arts. Awards: First Prize, Painting Award, Garrett Club, Buffalo. Collection: Contemporary painting and sculpture. Mailing Add: 563 Park Ave New York NY 10021

HOOKS, CHARLES VERNON
ART DEALER, COLLECTOR
b Houston, Tex, Aug 8, 30. Pos: Pres, Hooks-Epstein Galleries, Houston. Mem: Houston Art Dealers Asn (pres, founder). Specialty: Prints, drawings and sculpture of 20th century; publisher and distributor of original graphics. Collection: Works on paper of 20th century American and European masters and sculpture from the 1950s. Mailing Add: 1200 Bissonnet Houston TX 77005

HOOKS, EARL J
EDUCATOR, SCULPTOR
b Baltimore, Md, Aug 2, 27. Study: Howard Univ, BAE; Cath Univ; Rochester Inst of Technol, NY, grad cert. Work: Howard Univ, Washington, DC; DePauw Univ, Greencastle, Ind; Harmon Found, New York; City of Gary, Ind; State of Tenn Arts Comn. Comn: Intaglio wall mural (10 ft x 25 ft), Mr & Mrs Roosevelt Allen, Gary, Ind, 63; ceramic sculpture, State Gift to Gov Ray Blanton, Tanzania, 77. Exhib: Howard Univ Invitational, 61; 21st Syracuse Biennial (traveling exhib), Smithsonian Inst, 61-62; Int Minerals & Chemicals, Skokie, Ill, 66; three-man show, Art Inst of Chicago, 67; Ball State Mus, Muncie, Ind, 69; Two Centuries of Black Am Art, Los Angeles Co Mus of Art, Los Angeles, 76; Dallas Mus of Fine Arts, Tex, High Mus, Atlanta, Ga & Brooklyn Mus, NY, 77. Collections Arranged: African Art (contribr), Fisk Univ Collection, 70; Amistad II: Afro-Am Art (traveling exhib), United Church of Homeland Ministries, 77; From These Roots, Fisk Univ & Tenn State Mus, 77. Teaching: Instr ceramics & drawing, Shaw Univ, Raleigh, NC, 53-54; instr & art consult, Gary Pub Schs, Ind, 59-68; instr ceramics & drawing, Ind Univ, Gary, 64-67; assoc prof sculpture & ceramics & chmn dept art, Fisk Univ, 68- Awards: Second Prize, Arts & Crafts, John Herron Art Sch, 59; Purchase Prize, Dedication of Art Bldg, Howard Univ, 60; Cert of Honor, Int Festival of Lagos, Nigerian Govt, 77. Bibliog: Cedric Dover (auth), American Negro Art, 60; Elton Fax (auth), Seventeen Black Artists, Dodd-Mead, 71; Bruno Bak (auth), The Rites of Color and Form, Fisk Univ, 74. Style & Technique: Ceramic sculpture (wheel-thrown & hand-built). Media: Ceramics; drawing; photography. Publ: Co-auth, Extended Services in Museum Science Training, 72 & Ben Jones (catalogue on artist's work), 77, Fisk Univ. Mailing Add: 935 18th Ave Nashville TN 37208

HOOPES, DONELSON FARQUHAR
MUSEUM CURATOR, ART HISTORIAN
b Philadelphia, Pa, Dec 3, 32. Study: Pa Acad Fine Arts, 50-53; Univ Pa, AB, 60; Univ Firenze, 58-59. Collections Arranged: The Private World of John Singer Sargent, 64; The Triumph of Realism, 67; The Beckoning Land: Nature & the American Artist, 71; The Düsseldorf School & the Americans, 72; American Narrative Painting, 74. Pos: Dir, Portland Mus Art, Maine, 60-62; cur, Corcoran Gallery Art, 62-64; cur painting & sculpture, Brooklyn Mus, 65-69; cur American art, Los Angeles Co Mus Art, 72-75; vis cur, M H de Young Mem Mus, San Francisco, 76-77. Awards: Notable Bk of 1969 (Homer Watercolors), Am Libr Asn, 69. Mem: Col Art Asn Am; Am Asn Mus. Res: Relating the cultural history of the nineteenth century America to its artists. Publ: Auth, Sargent Watercolors, 70; auth, Eakins Watercolors, 72; auth, The American Impressionists, 72; auth, American Watercolor Painting, 77. Mailing Add: 8262 W Norton Ave Los Angeles CA 90046

HOOTON, ARTHUR
PAINTER
b Bolton, Eng, July 27, 06; US citizen. Study: Mus Fine Arts, Boston, with tutor Florence L Spaulding; Swain Sch Design, New Bedford, Mass. Comn: Portrait of former mayor in City Hall, Danbury, Conn; relig painting, Chapel of St James Episcopal Church, Danbury. Exhib: Grand Nat, Am Artists Prof League, New York, 75; Kent Art Asn, Conn, 75; Conn Classic Arts, 75; Am Painters in Paris, France, 75; Am Artists Prof League, New York, 76 & 77; Danbury CofC, Conn. Awards: Bicentennial Art Award Bronze Medal, Richter Asn for the Arts, Danbury, 76; Second Best in Show, Conn Classic Arts Christmas Exhib, 77, Third Prize, spring 77. Mem: Conn Classic Arts Asn; Am Artists Prof League; Pomperaug Art League, Southbury, Conn; Kent Art Asn, Conn (vpres, 75, pres, 76 & 77). Style & Technique: Traditional representational, realistic. Media: Oil. Dealer: Cyvia Gallery 75 Whitney Ave New Haven CT 06510. Mailing Add: 48 Hayestown Rd Danbury CT 06810

HOOTON, BRUCE DUFF
ART DEALER, CRITIC
b Waukegan, Ill, Dec 11, 28. Study: Southwestern Col, 46-50; Memphis Acad Arts, 48-50; Harvard Univ, scholar, 51-52. Collections Arranged: Sculptors Guild Bryant Park Exhibition, in association with New York Cultural Affairs, 67; Niezvestny (modern Russian sculpture), Sculptors Guild, New York, 68; Drawing Society Regional Drawing Exhib (8 museums), Am Fedn Arts, 70-72; Venice Biennale, Castelli Gallery, 73; Benito Retrospective, New York Cult Ctr, 74. Pos: Ed & auth, Drawing Mag, 57-60; art critic, ed & reviewer, New York Herald Tribune, 62-65; head New York off, Archives Am Art, 65-66; ed, Art News, 68-69; exec dir, Save Venice, New York, 73-75; assoc, Lee Ault & Co, 71-; ed & publ newspaper, Art/World, New York. Mem: Drawing Soc (vpres, 75); Stravinsky Diaghilev Found (vpres, 72); Charles Burchfield Ctr (adv bd, 72); NY State Coun Arts (consult, 72); Cooper-Hewitt Mus (Friends of Prints & Drawings, 71-72). Specialty: 20th century paintings, sculpture and drawings; French and European masters; South American masters; young masters. Publ: Ed, Drawings of Edwin Dickinson, Yale Univ, 60; ed, Mother & Child in Modern Art, Duell, Sloan & Pearce, 64; ed, American Paintings in Reynolda House, Reynolda House, 70. Mailing Add: c/o Art/World 1295 Madison Ave New York NY 10028

HOOVER, F HERBERT
ART DEALER, WRITER
b Atlanta, Ga, June 16, 29. Study: Maryville Col, BA(cum laude); sculpture with Michael Von Meyer. Teaching: Instr hist art, Am Inst Banking, San Francisco, 69; instr art collecting, Univ Calif, Santa Cruz, 71-; lectr & instr, Univ Calif Exten & invited lectr, Univ Calif, 78. Pos: Dir, Pomeroy Galleries, San Francisco, 65-69; mem, Calif Arts Comn, 66-73; owner, Hoover Gallery, 69-; chancellor's assoc, Calif State Univ Syst, 77. Awards: Alumni Citation, Maryville Col, Tenn, 77. Mem: Sr mem Am Soc Appraisers. Res: Life of American sculptress Patience Lovell Wright and French painter Marie Laurencin; medieval and Renaissance sculpture. Specialty: 19th century American and European painters and contemporary American painters and sculptors. Publ: Auth, Taste in the Arts, 65; auth, Brushstrokes, 71; auth, Frederic C Torrey and the Infamous Nude, 74; auth, Hoover's Guide to Galleries: San Francisco, 74 & Hoover's Guide to - Galleries: Los Angeles, 74, Camaro. Mailing Add: Hoover Gallery 710 Sansome St San Francisco CA 94111

HOOVER, FRANCIS LOUIS
COLLECTOR, APPRAISER
b Sherman, Tex, Mar 12, 13. Study: NTex State Univ, BS, 33; Columbia Univ, MA, 35; Art Students League, 40-41; New Sch Social Res, 40-41; NY Univ, DEd, 41. Teaching: Asst prof art, NTex State Univ, 36-40; asst prof art, Eastern Ill State Univ, 41-44; prof art, Ill State Univ, 44-73, dir, Univ Mus, 72-73. Pos: Dir, LaSalle Art Gallery, 33-36; ed, Arts & Activities Mag, 52-67; dir, Fairway Gallery, 62-67. Awards: Award of Merit for Ed Excellence, Indust Mkt 6th Ann, 54. Mem: Appraisers Asn Am; Am Soc Appraisers; Int Platform Asn. Collection: Art of the Cuna Indians; pre-Columbian ceramics and jade; primitive arts of Africa and Oceania; folk arts of Middle America; works are in permanent collections of Philadelphia Museum of Art, Cleveland Museum of Art, Art Institute of Chicago, Field Museum of Natural History, Peabody Museum, Honolulu Academy of Art and others. Publ: Auth, Art Activities for the Very Young, 62; auth, Young Printmakers I, 63; auth, Young Printmakers II, 64; auth, Young Sculptors, 67; auth, African Art, 74; plus others. Mailing Add: 305 N University Ave Normal IL 61761

HOOVER, JOHN JAY
SCULPTOR, PAINTER
b Cordova, Alaska, Oct 13, 19. Study: Derbyshire Sch of Fine Arts, Seattle, Wash. Work: Bur Indian Affairs, Washington, DC; Seattle Art Mus, Wash; Gulf Paper Co; Heard Mus, Phoenix, Ariz; King Co & Seattle Art Comn. Comn: Mural, Tyonek Tribe, Anchorage, Alaska, 64; mobile, James Bialac, Ariz, 76; mural, City Light Co, Seattle, 77. Exhib: Sculpture I & Sculpture II, Heard Mus, Phoenix, Ariz, 73 & 74; one-man shows, Whatcom Co Mus, Bellingham, Wash & Mus of Plains Indians, Browning, Mont, 75; Sculpture Invitational, Heard Mus, Phoenix, Ariz, 77. Teaching: Artist-in-residence sculpture, Inst of Am Indian Art, Santa Fe, NMex, 72 & DOD Sch Syst, Japan, Taiwan & the Philippines, 74. Awards: First Prize/Sculpture, Cent Wash State Col, 73, Philbrook Art Ctr, Tulsa, Okla, 74 & Heard Mus, Phoenix, Ariz, 75. Style & Technique: Contemporary Indian renditioons on polychromed cedar of myths and legends. Dealer: Haines Gallery 8015 15th NW Seattle WA 98117. Mailing Add: Box 45 W Stadium Grapeview WA 98546

HOOVER, MARGARET POMEROY
COLLECTOR, RESEARCHER
b San Francisco, Calif, Mar 26, 43. Study: Univ Calif, Berkeley, BA, 65. Pos: Researcher, Pomeroy Galleries, San Francisco, 65-69; archivist, Hoover Gallery, San Francisco, 69- Res: Life of Marie Laurencin; 19th and 20th century American and European; provenance searches. Collection: Original Marie Laurencin illustrated books, drawings, watercolors and oils. Publ: Contribr (catalogue), Dorothy Brown & Marie Laurencin, Univ Calif, Los Angeles. Mailing Add: 710 Sansome St San Francisco CA 94111

HOOWIJ, JAN
PAINTER
b Hengelo, Holland, Sept 13, 07. Study: Acad Fine Arts, The Hague, Holland, BA; Acad Grande Chaumiere, Paris; also painting with Henk Meyer, Holland. Work: Brooklyn Mus; Joslyn Mem Mus, Omaha; Witte Mem Mus, San Antonio; Art Ctr, Tulsa, Okla; Honolulu Acad Art. Comn: Portrait of Mayor Wagner, New York, 55; portrait of Gov Allred, Fed Courthouse, Corpus Christi, Tex, 59; mosaic mural, Ardmore Develop Co, Phoenix, 61 & Hollywood, 62; portrait of Neil Jacoby, Sch Bus Admin, Univ Calif, Los Angeles, 71. Exhib: Rijksmuseum Nat Show, Amsterdam, Holland, 35; Brooklyn Mus Regional Show, 42; Int Marine Art Show, Palais Chaillot, Paris, 46; Carnegie Inst Nat Ann, Pittsburgh, 47; Los Angeles Co Art Mus Regional Ann, 56. Teaching: Instr figure, Acad Fine Arts, The Hague, 31-34; pvt instr painting, 52-57. Awards: Royal Subsidy for Artists, Holland, 31-34; Therese Van Duyl Schwartz Prize for Best Portrait in Holland, 36; Purchase Prize, Witte Mem Mus, 59. Bibliog: Janice Lovoos (auth), The paintings of Jan Hoowij, Am Artist Mag, 8/65. Style & Technique: Contemporary realism in portraits; semi-abstract figure and landscapes; emphasis on texture and design. Media: Oil, Acrylic, Tempera. Dealer: Emerson Gallery 18676 Ventura Blvd Los Angeles CA 91356; Serisawa Gallery 8320 Melrose Ave Los Angeles CA 90069. Mailing Add: 16614 Chaplin Ave Encino CA 91436

HOPKINS, BENJAMIN
ART LIBRARIAN
b MAnchester, NH, Apr 20, 36. Study: New Eng Conserv of Music; Univ NH, BA; Univ RI, MLS. Pos: Librn, Mass Col Art, Boston, 67- Mem: Art Librn Soc NAm. Res: Bibliography on Design Education in International Encyclopedia of Higher Education. Mailing Add: 694 Windwood Dr Tiverton RI 02878

HOPKINS, BUDD
PAINTER
b Wheeling, WVa, June 15, 31. Study: Oberlin Col, BA, 53; Columbia Univ, 53-54, with Meyer Schapiro. Work: Whitney Mus Am Art, New York; Guggenheim Mus Art, New York; San Francisco Mus Art; Joseph Hirshhorn Collection, Washington, DC; Williams Col Mus. Comn: Oil painting, WVa State Humanities Coun, 72. Exhib: Whitney Mus Am Art Ann, 58-72; Festival Two Worlds, Spoleto, Italy, 58; Young America, Whitney Mus Am Art, Baltimore Mus Art, City Art Mus St Louis & others, 60; Benjamin Collection, Yale Univ Art Gallery, 67; Young New England Painters, Ringling Mus Art, Portland Mus Art & Currier Gallery, 69; one-man shows, Zierler Gallery, New York, 72-, Weatherspoon Art Gallery, Univ NC, Greensboro, 74, Kresge Art Ctr, Mich State Univ, Lansing, 74 & Galerie Liatowitsch, Basel, Switz, 74; Free Form Abstraction, Whitney Mus Am Art, 72; Guggenheim Mus, New York, 73; New Sch Art Ctr, New York, 73; plus others. Teaching: Docent, Mus Mod Art, summers 55-56; docent, Whitney Mus Am Art, 57-60; instr, Pratt Inst, Provincetown, summer 75; instr, RI Sch Design, Provincetown, summer 75. Bibliog: Brian O'Doherty (auth), Budd Hopkins, master of a movement manque, Object & Idea, 67; April Kingsley (auth), Energy and order—the paintings of Budd Hopkins, Art Int, 4/73; Peter Frank (auth), Budd Hopkins: the works on paper, Kresge Art Ctr Bull, 4/74. Mem: Provincetown Art Asn (hon vpres, 68-70). Style & Technique: Abstract paintings, assembled from a group of retangular paintings into an assymetrical whole. Media: Oil, Acrylic. Publ: Auth, First person singular, Art Gallery Mag, 4/72; co-auth, Concept vs art object, Arts Mag, 4/72; auth, Budd Hopkins on Budd Hopkins, Art in Am, 7-8/73; contribr, Roundtable on painting, Artforum, 9/75; plus others. Dealer: William Zierler Gallery 956 Madison Ave New York NY 10021. Mailing Add: 246 W 16th St New York NY 10011

HOPKINS, HENRY TYLER
MUSEUM DIRECTOR, EDUCATOR
b Idaho Falls, Idaho, Aug 14, 28. Study: Art Inst Chicago, BAE & MAE; Univ Calif, Los Angeles. Exhibitions Arranged: 30 California Artists, 61; Reuben Nakian, 62; Josef Albers: White Line Squares (with catalog), 66; Robert Rauschenberg: Selections, 69; Milton Resnick: Large Paintings (with catalog), 71; Irwin-Wheeler, 72; Joe Goode: Work Until Now (with catalog), 73; Clyfford Still, 75; Painting & Sculpture in California: The Modern Era, 76. Teaching: Instr art hist & theory, Univ Calif, Los Angeles Exten, 58-68; instr art hist, Tex Christian Univ, 68-73. Pos: Head educ, Los Angeles Co Mus Art, Los Angeles, 61-65, cur exhib, 65-68; dir, Ft Worth Art Mus, Tex, 68-74; dir, San Francisco Mus Art, 74- Mem: Asn Art Mus Dirs; Col Art Asn; Am Asn Mus; Western Asn Art Mus (pres, 77-78). Res: 20th century art of California; modern art. Publ: Contribr, Art in Am, Art News & Artforum Mag, 61-75. Mailing Add: San Francisco Mus Art Van Ness Ave at McAllister St San Francisco CA 94102

HOPKINS, KENDAL COLES
PAINTER
b Haddonfield, NJ, Jan 6, 08. Study: Pa Acad Fine Arts; Acad Grande Chaumiere, Paris. Work: Woodmere Art Gallery, Philadelphia; plus many pvt collections. Comn: Many pvt portrait & landscape comns. Exhib: Pa Acad Fine Arts Ann, Philadelphia; Philadelphia Mus Art, Pa; Nat Acad Design, New York; Ivan Spence Gallery, Ibiza, Spain; one-man show, Farnsworth Mus, Rockland, Maine; plus 15 other one-man shows. Teaching: Instr painting, Bryn Mawr Col, Pa; head dept art, Baldwin Sch, Bryn Mawr, Pa; instr art, Fieldston Sch, New York. Mem: Pa Acad Fine Arts; Philadelphia Mus; Peal Club, Philadelphia. Dealer: Hahn Gallery 8439 Germantown Ave Philadelphia PA 19118. Mailing Add: Maisfield Rd Phoenixville PA 19460

HOPKINS, KENNETH R
MUSEUM DIRECTOR, ART ADMINISTRATOR
b Springfield, Mass, Aug 24, 22. Study: Pratt Inst; Univ Vt; Parsons Sch of Design; NY Univ, BS; Univ Wis, MS. Pos: Art dir, Univ Wis, Madison, 48-50; cur exhib, State Hist Soc Wis, Madison, 50-52; art dir, Old Sturbridge Village, Mass, 52-56; cur, Buffalo & Erie Co Hist Co, Buffalo, NY, 56-60; hist preservationist, Bethelehm Steel Co, Pa, 60-62; dir, Explorers Hall, Nat Geog Soc, Washington, DC, 62-65; dir, State Capitol Mus, 65- Mailing Add: 3001 Monte Vista Olympia WA 98501

HOPKINS, PETER
PAINTER, EDUCATOR
b New York, NY, Dec 18, 11. Study: Art Students League, 27 & 45-50, with George Bridgman, Reginald Marsh, Kenneth H Miller, Robert B Hale & sculpture with William Zorach. Work: Mus City of New York. Comn: Landscapes, Theatre Guild, New York, 49, portraits, 50; mural, comn by Stewart Chaney, New York, 54; mural, comn by Gino di Grandi, 55; illus, RCA Victor Corp, New York, 56. Exhib: Lyman Allyn Mus, 47; Art Students League, Nat Acad Design Galleries, 49; Am Acad Arts & Lett, 50; Artists Equity, Whitney Mus Am Art, 51, Contemp Painting, 52; St George's Galleries, London, Eng, 56; Ward Eggleston Galleries, New York, 58-65; Jr League of Buffalo, NY, 60; Women's Club of Westport, NY, 61; Am Mural Painters Asn, 76. Teaching: Instr drawing & painting, Moore Inst Art, Sci & Indust, 49-50; instr, Newark Acad Art, 50; instr, Cartoonists & Illusr Sch, New York, 51; instr art, New York-Phoenix Schs Design, 61-77, chmn dept fine art & dean of men; asst prof art hist, Pratt Inst, 75-77; lectr perspective, Art Students League, 75- Pos: Supvr libr, NY Univ, 53; asst dir, Mortimer Brandt Gallery, 53-58; art consult, Nabisco Co, 76; dir workshop & Old Master oil painting techniques, 76-78. Awards: Art Grant, Am Acad Arts & Lett, 50; Art Grant, Nat Inst Arts & Lett, 50. Bibliog: The artist & the Copa girls, See, 53; C B (auth), Art exhibition notes, New York Herald Tribune, 1/25/58. Mem: Life mem Art Students League. Media: Oil. Publ: Contribr, Town & Country Mag, 44; contribr, Family Circle Mag, 45; auth, The Essentials of Perspective, Resley, 64; illusr, The American Heritage History of the 1920's and 1930's, 70; contribr essays & poems, The Christian Sci Monitor, 73-; auth, Workshop Manual of Painting, 77; plus others. Dealer: Grand Central Art Galleries 40 Vanderbilt Ave New York NY 10017. Mailing Add: 36 Horatio St New York NY 10014

HOPKINSON, GLEN SPENCER
PAINTER, SCULPTOR
b Laramie, Wyo, Dec 31, 46. Study: With Harold I Hopkinson & Robert M Meyers; Brigham Young Univ, BFA; also with Don Putman. Work: Mont Hist Soc, Helena; Shoshone First Nat Bank, Cody, Wyo. Comn: Jesus and the Apostles, Latter-day Saint Chapel, Taegu, Korea, 68. Exhib: Rendezvous of Western Art, Mont Hist Soc, 73-74; Roundup of Western Art, Saddleback Inn, Santa Ana, Calif, 73-75; C M Russell Art Auction & Show, Great Falls, Mont, 75; Art Assocs Presents Western Art, Chicago & Minneapolis Athletic Clubs, 75; retrospective, Wyo Hist Soc & Mus, Cheyenne, 75. Teaching: Pvt art classes, 72-74. Awards: First Place in Oil, Cody Country Art League Regional Show, 73, 74 & 75, Sweepstakes Award, 73. Style & Technique: Realistic. Media: Oil, Acrylic; Clay. Dealer: Trailside II Galleries Jackson Hole WY 83001. Mailing Add: 1020 Alpine Cody WY 82414

HOPKINSON, HAROLD I
PAINTER, COLLECTOR
b Salt Lake City, Utah, Aug 8, 18. Study: Univ Wyo, BA & MA; Art Ctr Sch, Los Angeles; Brigham Young Univ; also with Paul Bransom, O Conrad Schwiering & Robert W Meyers. Work: Whitney Gallery Western Art, Cody, Wyo; USAF Acad, Colorado Springs, Colo; Springville Fine Arts Gallery, Utah; Univ Wyo Fine Arts Collection; Cult Ctr Am Embassy Prague. Comn: Mural, Col Bus Admin, Ariz State Univ, 71 & mural & four paintings, 71; portrait of Junius E Driggs, Western Savings & Loan, Tempe, 72; painting, McCleery-Cumming Co, Washington, Iowa, 75; painting, Mont Bicentennial Admin, Helena, 74. Exhib: Whitney Gallery Western Art, 72; C M Russell Gallery & Mus, Great Falls, 73-74; Rendezvous Western Art, Mont Hist Soc, 72-74; Western America in Paint & Bronze, Chicago, 75; West in Paint & Bronze, Minneapolis, 75. Teaching: Art dir, Reliance Pub Schs, Wyo, 49-52; art dir, Sch Dist One, Byron, 52-62; instr oil painting, Univ Wyo, 62-67. Pos: Pres, Cody Country Art League, 65-66, chmn bd, 66-69. Awards: Design Award, Wyo Activities Asn, State Wyo Educ Dept, 63; Purchase Award, Western Art Show, Wyo Nat Bank, Casper, 74. Bibliog: Ed Ainsworth (auth), The Cowboy in Art, World, 68; Lucille N Patrick (auth), Hopkinson, Wyoming Artist, Western Horseman, 68; Royal B Hassrick (auth), Western Painting Today, Watson-Guptill, 75. Mem: Life mem Nat Cowboy Hall of Fame & Western Heritage Ctr. Style & Technique: Broad brush technique to find rendering often accompanies with palette knife. Media: Oil. Collection: Paintings by Ken Riley, Robert Meyers, Harley Brown, Edward Grigware, James Bama, Ron Crook and others. Publ: Contribr & illusr, On the Wings of a Butterfly, 62 & National Federation of State High School Association, 63-70; contribr, Western Horseman, 68-74, Wyoming the Proud Land, 70 & Westerner, 74. Dealer: May Gallery Jackson WY; Thunderhorse Gallery Cody WY 82414. Mailing Add: Box 175 Byron WY 82412

HOPPER, FRANK J
PAINTER, ILLUSTRATOR
b Evansville, Ind, Oct 15, 24. Study: Ind Univ, BFA; Art Inst Chicago; Am Acad Art, Chicago. Work: Famous Am Series, Historic Mus, Washington, DC. Comn: 200 paintings, Archdiocese of Chicago, 67; two 4ft x 8ft acrylics, metal sculpture light & rug design, East Point Condominium, Chicago, 69; 10ft mural & eight major painting, Chateau Pyrenees, Denver; 26ft mural & 14 stations of the cross, St Mary Star of the Sea Catholic Church, Longboat Key, Fla, 78; mag covers, Yachting, plus others. Style & Technique: Realistic/representational. Media: Acrylic, Watercolor. Publ: Illusr, co-auth, ed or contribr to various publ including Chicago publs & newspapers, Western Publ Co, Chicago Tribune, Art Inst Chicago & books for Chicago Area Sch TV. Mailing Add: PO Box 1806 Sarasota FL 33578

HOPPER, MARIANNE SEWARD
PAINTER, ART DEALER
b Rochester, NY, June 10, 04. Study: Cleveland Sch Art; RI Sch Design; Montclair Art Mus, with Michael Lenson, also portraits with Douglas Prizer, acrylics with Tom Vincent, watercolors with Avery Johnson & sculpture with Ulric Ellerhausen. Work: Pvt collections in NJ, NMex, Calif, Fla, Ohio & Ill. Comn: Paintings for private individuals and businesses, 64-75. Exhib: Nat Miniature Art Exhib, Nutley, NJ, 72-75; NJ State Show, Ocean Co Col, Toms River, NJ, 73; Bergen Community Mus, State Show, Paramus, NJ, 74; Nat Miniature Art Show, Bellair, Fla, 75; Nat Am Artists Prof League Lever House Show, New York, 75. Awards: Best in Show, Garden State Plaza, Paramus, NJ, 64; Purchase Awards, McBride Agency, Franklin Lakes, NJ, 71 & 72; ITT Space Award, Int Tel & Tel Defense Space Group, Nutley, NJ, 73. Bibliog: Mary Clemens (auth), feature story in Herald News, Passaic, NJ, 65; Michael Lenson (auth), article in Newark Eve News, 68; article in NJ Music & Arts Mag, 73. Mem: Am Artists Prof League; Miniature Art Socs of NJ & Fla; Nutley Art Group, NJ. Style & Technique: Seascapes, landscapes, and florals in miniature and full size using palette knife technique. Media: Acrylic, Oil. Specialty: Painting in all medias; prints, serigraphs and wall sculptures are exhibited. Mailing Add: 45 Hopper Ave Pompton Plains NJ 07444

HOPPES, LOWELL E
CARTOONIST
b Alliance, Ohio, July 1, 13. Pos: In freelance cartooning for 46 yrs. Publ: Created over 30,000 cartoons in Colliers, Post, American, Esquire, New Yorker, Farm Jour, Parade, Family

Weekly, King Features Syndicate & others. Mailing Add: 642 Calle del Otono Sarasota FL 33561

HOPPS, WALTER
ART ADMINISTRATOR
Collections Arranged: Organizer and comnr United States contribution to Venice Biennale, sponsored by Nat Collection Fine Arts, Smithsonian Inst, 72. Pos: Former dir, Corcoran Gallery Art; vis cur contemp art, Nat Collection Fine Arts, Smithsonian Inst, cur 20th century painting & sculpture, currently. Bibliog: Grace Glueck (auth), US photos and movies for biennale, New York Times, 4/72. Interest: Current American art, especially wall-space experience. Mailing Add: Nat Collection Fine Arts Eighth & G Sts NW Washington DC 20560

HOPTNER, RICHARD
SCULPTOR
b Philadelphia, Pa, Apr 3, 21. Study: Univ Pa, 51-57; Cranbrook Acad Art, scholar, 60. Work: Philadelphia Civic Ctr Mus. Exhib: Detroit Inst Art, 60; Philadelphia Mus Art, 61; Pa Acad Fine Arts, 69; Haverford Col, 74; Gallerie Illien, Atlanta, Ga. Teaching: Instr 3-D design, Univ Pa, 68-70. Awards: Sculpture Grant, Louis Comfort Tiffany Found, 64. Bibliog: New forms-new materials (film), Pa Acad Fine Arts, 69; Sculpture at St Joseph College, WCAU TV, 69. Style & Technique: Direct carver. Media: Teakwood, Rare Woods. Publ: Auth, Anti-art/anti-life, Great Speckled Bird, Atlanta, Ga, 70. Dealer: Patricia McGrath RD 1 Lewisberry PA 17339. Mailing Add: 5109 Pulaski Ave Philadelphia PA 19144

HORIUCHI, PAUL
PAINTER
b Yamanashiken, Japan, Apr 12, 06. Study: Univ Puget Sound, Hon LHD, 68. Work: Harvard Univ; Denver Art Mus; Univ Ore, Eugene; Wadsworth Atheneum, Hartford, Conn; Santa Barbara Mus Art; plus others. Comn: Free-standing mural, Seattle World's Fair, 62. Exhib: American Painting, Va Mus Fine Arts, Richmond, 66; one-man shows, San Francisco, 66 & 68 & Tacoma, Wash, 67; retrospective, Univ Ore & Seattle Art Mus, 68. Awards: Ford Found, 60; Seattle World's Fair, 62; Burpee Mus, Rockford, Ill, 66; plus many others. Dealer: Gordon Woodside Gallery 803 E Union St Seattle WA 98122. Mailing Add: 9773 Arrowsmith Ave S Seattle WA 98118

HORN, BRUCE
PRINTMAKER, EDUCATOR
b Circleville, Ohio, June 30, 46. Study: Miami Univ, BFA; Ohio State Univ, with Sidney Chafetz, David Driesbach & Andrew Rush, MFA. Work: Kalamazoo Inst Arts, Mich; Doane Col, Nebr; Ohio State Univ; Miami Univ. Exhib: Nat Soc Arts & Lett Print Exhib, Shreveport, La, 71; Mid-Am 4, St Louis Art Mus, Mo, 72; Nat Print Exhib, Silvermine Guild, New Canaan, Conn, 74; Nat Print & Drawing Show, Univ NDak, 74; Young Contemp Art, Univ Sao Paulo, Brazil, 74; Nat Print & Drawing Competition, Minot State Col, NDak, 75; SW Print & Drawing Competition, NMex State Univ, 75; Int Small Print Exhib, Davidson Galleries, Seattle, Wash, 76; Arizona's Outlook, Tucson Mus Art, 78; Nat Print Exhib, Silvermine Guild, New Canaan, Conn, 78; Boston Printmakers, Mass, 78; plus many others. Teaching: Asst prof printmaking, Blackburn Col, Carlinville, Ill, 70-72 & Northern Ariz Univ, 72- Pos: Package designer, Diamond Nat Paper Co, Middletown, Ohio, summer 68; art dir, Eighth Ann Flagstaff Summer Festival, Ariz, 74. Awards: Purchase Awards, Phoenix Art Mus, Ariz, 73 & Doane Col, Nebr, 73; Northern Ariz Univ Res Grant, 75. Mem: Mid-Am Col Art Asn. Style & Technique: Environments. Media: Color Intaglio & Lithography. Dealer: Lakeside Studio 150 S Lakeshore Rd Lakeside MI 49116; Missal Gallery 7373 Scottsdale Mall Scottsdale AZ 85251. Mailing Add: 1625 N Sunset Dr Flagstaff AZ 86001

HORN, MILTON
SCULPTOR, WRITER
b Russia, Sept 1, 06; US citizen. Study: Beaux Arts Inst Design, New York; Olivet Col, Mich, hon DFA, 76; also with Henry H Kitson. Work: Brookgreen Gardens, SC; Nat Collection Fine Arts, Washington, DC; Olivet Col; Smithsonian Inst Div Numismatics; Bernard Horwich Ctr, Chicago. Comn: Three symbolic bronze groups on facade of hq bldg, Nat Cong Parents & Teachers, Chicago, 53-54; eight marble reliefs, WVa Univ Med Ctr, 54-59; symbolic bronze on facade & holy ark in sanctuary, B'nai Israel Temple, Charleston, WVa, 59-60; Hymn to Water (bronze), Central Water Filtration Plant, Chicago, 65; bronze, Nat Bank Commerce, Charleston, WVa, 68-69. Exhib: American Art Today, New York World's Fair, 39 & 40; 3rd Int Exhib Sculpture, Philadelphia Mus Fine Arts, 49; American Sculpture—1951, Metrop Mus, New York, 51; Chicago & Vicinity Exhib, Art Inst Chicago, 52; Nat Inst Arts & Lett, New York, 53, 55 & 77. Teaching: Artist in residence & prof art, Olivet Col, 39-49. Awards: Award for excellence in the fine arts allied with archit, Chicago Chap, Am Inst Architects, 55; Nat Citation Honor, Nat Conf, Am Inst Architects, Washington, DC, 57; Henry Hering Mem Medal, Nat Sculpture Soc, New York, 72. Bibliog: Avram Kampf (auth), Contemporary Synagogue Art, Union Am Hebrew Congregations, 61; Cecil Roth (ed), History of Jewish Art, 61 & 71 & Louis Redstone (auth), Art in Architecture, 68, McGraw-Hill. Mem: Founding mem Sculptors Guild; Nat Academician (elect); Col Art Asn Am; fel Nat Sculpture Soc. Style & Technique: Figural; modelling for cast bronze and direct carving in wood and stone. Media: Bronze, Wood, Stone. Publ: Contribr, Proceedings of Teachers Seminar, Col Schs Archit, Aspen, Colo, 57; contribr, The Christian Century, 2/59; contribr, New City-Men in Metropolis, 64; contribr, Indland Architect, 65; contribr, Nat Sculpture Rev, 72. Mailing Add: 1932 N Lincoln Ave Chicago IL 60614

HORN, STUART ALAN
GRAPHIC ARTIST, WRITER
b Union, NJ, Dec 18, 45. Study: Boston Univ; Drew Univ, BA, 67; Cornell Univ. Exhib: Corresp Art, Whitney Mus Am Art, New York, 70; Bootleg Exhib, Inst Contemp Art, Philadelphia, 72; Litter, Art Shows, Philadelphia, 73; Earth Art, Philadelphia Civic Ctr, 73; Exhib Degenerative Art, Southworks, Philadelphia, 74. Pos: Ed, Northwest Mounted Valise, 68-74; dir, Eat with Artists, Philadelphia, 73-; dir, Libr Art, Philadelphia, 74-76; assoc ed, Inside Philadelphia, 75-76. Awards: Coord Coun Lit Mag Publ Grant, 73. Bibliog: Thomas Albright (auth), Correspondence art, Rolling Stone, 4/72; David Zack (auth), Mail art, Art in Am, 1/73; Jim Quinn (auth), Making it, Philadelphia Mag, 11/74. Style & Technique: Offset printed editions of black and white verbal and visual collages; also events, exhibitions and narrative literature. Media: Paper, Found Objects. Publ: Co-auth, Gun Moll Talk, 68; auth, Modern Office Buildings, 73; auth, While Rome Burns, 74; auth, Rock, 75; auth, 197-, 76. Dealer: Marion Locks Gallery 1524 Walnut St Philadelphia PA 19102. Mailing Add: 44 E Riding Cherry Hill NJ 08003

HORNADAY, RICHARD HOYT
PAINTER, EDUCATOR
b Joplin, Mo, Aug 15, 27. Study: State Univ Iowa, BFA & MFA; Art Inst Chicago. Work: State Univ Iowa Collection, Iowa City; Calif State Univ, Chico; Shasta Col Collection, Redding, Calif. Exhib: Recent Painting, USA, The Figure, Mus Mod Art, New York, 65; Pavillion Gallery, Balboa, Calif, 65; 23rd Am Drawing Biennial, Norfolk Mus, Va, 69; Nat Small Painting Exhib, Univ of the Pac, Stockton, 70; Fifty Years of Crocker-Kingsley (retrospective), Crocker Art Gallery, Sacramento, 75; plus others. Teaching: Instr drawing-painting, Shasta Col, 56-63; grad adv, Calif State Univ, Chico, 68-72, prof, Grad Studios, 68-, chmn dept art, 72- Awards: Kingsley Exhib & Nat Coun Arts Exhib, Sacramento. Bibliog: Alfred Frankenstein (auth), Ruthermore Gallery—Richard Hornaday, San Francisco Chronicle, 62. Style & Technique: Still life in watercolor and drawing, trompe l'oeil technique. Media: Watercolor, Drawing. Mailing Add: Dept of Art Calif State Univ Chico CA 95929

HORNAK, IAN JOHN
PAINTER
b Philadelphia, Pa, Jan 9, 44. Study: Univ Mich; Wayne State Univ, BFA, MFA. Work: Corcoran Gallery Art, Washington, DC; Indianapolis Mus Art, Ind; Canton Art Inst, Ohio; Owens Corning Fiberglas Corp, Toledo, Ohio; Albrecht Art Mus, St Joseph, Mo. Exhib: The New Landscape, Moore Col Art, Philadelphia, 71; Painting & Sculpture Today, Indianapolis Mus Art, 72; The Realist Revival, Am Fedn of Arts (traveling exhib), 72-73; one-man shows, Tibor de Nagy Gallery, New York, 71-76, Fischbach Gallery, New York, 77 & Gertrude Kasie Gallery, Detroit, 74. Teaching: Instr drawing, Wayne State Univ, Detroit, Mich, 65-67 & Henry Ford Col, Dearborn, Mich, 66- Style & Technique: Large detailed romantic-realist landscapes, with surrealist overtones. Media: Acrylic. Dealer: Fischbach Gallery 29 W 57th St New York NY 10022. Mailing Add: Box 1371 East Hampton NY 11937

HORNE, (ARTHUR EDWARD) CLEEVE
PAINTER, SCULPTOR
b Jamaica, BWI, Jan 9, 12. Study: Ont Col Art, AOCA; also with D Dick, Eng & Europe. Work: Nat Gallery Can. Comn: Alexander Bell Mem, Brantford, Ont; War Mem, Law Soc Upper Can; Shakespeare Mem; Stratford, Ont; plus others. Exhib: Nat Gallery Can; Royal Can Acad Arts, 28-; Ont Soc Artists, 39; Sculptors' Soc Can, 35- Pos: Art adv, Ont Hydro-Elec Power Comn, St Lawrence Seaway Power House Proj, 57-58; art consult, Imperial Oil Bldg, Toronto; art consult, Can Imperial Bank Com, 61-63; mem art consult comt, York Univ, 63-; art consult, Queen's Park Proj, Ont Govt, 66-69. Awards: Allied Arts Medals, Royal Archit Inst Can, 63, Royal Can Acad of Arts & Silver Jubilee. Mem: Ont Soc Artists (past pres); Arts & Lett Club (pres, 55-57); Royal Can Acad Arts. Mailing Add: 181 Balmoral Ave Toronto ON M4V 1J8 Can

HORNUNG, CLARENCE PEARSON
DESIGNER, WRITER
b New York, NY, June 12, 99. Study: Cooper Union; Art Students League; City Col New York, BS, 20. Work: New York Pub Libr; Springfield Mus, Mass; Newark Pub Libr, NJ; NY State Mus, Albany; Nat Gallery Art, Washington, DC. Mem: Am Inst Graphic Artists; Typophiles. Publ: Auth, Early American Advertising Art, Dover, Vol I & II, 47; auth, Wheels Across America, Barnes, 59; auth, Gallery of the American Automobile, Collectors Prints, 65; auth, Treasury of American Design, Abrams, Vol I & II, 72; co-auth, 200 Years of American Graphic Art, George Braziller, 75; plus others. Mailing Add: 12 Glen Rd West Hempstead NY 11552

HORNUNG, GERTRUDE SEYMOUR
ART HISTORIAN, LECTURER
b Boston, Mass. Study: Wellesley Col, AB; Case Western Reserve Univ, MA & PhD(visual arts), 49. Teaching: Lectr art hist, Cleveland Mus Art, 37-45, supvr, 45-60; free lance writer & lectr, 60-; lectr, John Carroll Univ, 72-78, Dublin, Ireland, Rome, Italy, Honolulu & Tehran, Iran, 74-75. Pos: Founder & chmn, Jr Coun, Cleveland, 41-42; deleg, White House Conf Educ, Washington, DC, 55; pres, Adult Educ Coun Greater Cleveland, 56-58; founder & chmn, Greater Cleveland Educ TV Comt, 58-60; trustee, Cleveland Area Arts Coun, 75; consult to dir-gen, Mus Iran, 75; deleg, Int Coun Mus Cont, USSR, 77. Awards: Ital Ministry Foreign Affairs Res Grant, 62. Mem: Assoc Int Coun Mus; Cleveland Mus Art (mem adv coun); Mus Mod Art; Metrop Mus Art; Am Arts Coun. Res: History of Italian art; art of the South Seas, especially Polynesia & Melanesia; contemporary American art; interrelations arts of East and West; art of Ancient Iran. Collection: Contemporary Italian and American paintings. Publ: Auth & ed, Cultural Directory of Greater Cleveland, 47; contribr, articles on art hist & educ in art mus in mags & Jours, 50-78. Mailing Add: 2240 Elandon Dr Cleveland OH 44106

HOROWITZ, BENJAMIN
ART ADMINISTRATOR, ART DEALER
b New York, NY, Mar 13, 12. Study: Jamaica Teachers Col, cert; City Col New York, BA; NY Univ. Pos: Pres, Art Dealers Asn Southern Calif, 70-; dir, Heritage Gallery. Mem: Los Angeles Co Mus Print Coun; Univ Calif, Los Angeles Print Coun. Res: American art. Specialty: American artists: international prints. Publ: Images of Dignity-Drawings of Charles White, 67. Mailing Add: 718 N La Cienega Blvd Los Angeles CA 90069

HOROWITZ, NADIA
PAINTER, DESIGNER
b Warsaw, Poland; US citizen. Study: Warsaw Acad Fine Art, with Pruszkowski & Schultz; Acad Grande Chaumiere, Paris, with L Lefevre; Ecole Superieure Art Graphiques, Belg, with Paul Van Maas & Tilla Vandervelde; Rheiman Sch, Berlin, Ger; silver sculpture with Sliwniak. Comn: Painting in Colina medium, comn by Dr Harrison-Pollock for Gerard Croisset, Holand, 68; painting in Colina medium, comn by Vincent Lopez, 69; oil painting, comn by M Elkin for Tel Aviv Mus; Fly Me to the Moon (Colina painting), for Astronaut Neil Armstrong, to be donated to a mus in Ohio; plus murals in pvt houses in Fr Riviera, Israel, US & Holland. Exhib: One-man shows, New York Jewish Mus, New York Anthrop Soc Am, La Petite Galerie, Brussels, Belg, Sophie Ryback Gallery, Paris, Hilton Hotel, Cascais, Portugal, Barski Medical Ctr, New York, 78; Zurich, Switz, 73; Artists Equity Gallery, New York, 76; plus many others. Teaching: Asst instr art, Adam Rychtarski Art Sch, 37-38; instr pvt studio, 52- Pos: Asst stylist, M & Avon, 53-61; art exhib dir, Israeli 20th Anniversary Traveling Exhib, 68. Awards: First Prize for The Colours of My Homeland (oil), Polish Art Asn, 57; First Prize for The Spirit of Sedona, 72; Certificate of Merit, Int Who's Who in Art & Antiques, 76-77. Bibliog: J Lefevre (auth), article, 32 & A Werner (auth), article, 67, Grande Chaumiere; B Murphy (auth), article in E S Sentinel, Art Mag, 66. Mem: Nat Soc Lit & Arts, Washington, DC; Polish Am Artists Asn (vpres, 77); Artist Equity Asn New York; Nat Asn Women Artists; Artist 72 Group 8. Interest: Originator of Colina media. Mailing Add: Apt 6 E 205 W 89th St New York NY 10024

HOROWITZ, MR & MRS RAYMOND J
COLLECTOR
b US citizen. Study: Mr Horowitz, Columbia Univ, AB & LLB, 39; Mrs Horowitz, NY Univ, AB, 36; Columbia Univ, MA, 37. Bibliog: John K Howat & Dianne H Pilgrim (auth),

American Impressionist and Realist Paintings and Drawings from the Collection of Mr and Mrs Raymond J Horowitz, Metrop Mus Art, 4-6/73. Collection: American turn of the century Realist and Impressionist paintings, watercolors and drawings. Mailing Add: 930 Fifth Ave New York NY 10021

HOROWITZ, SAUL
COLLECTOR
b New York, NY. Collection: French Impressionists and Post Impressionists. Mailing Add: 35 E 76th St New York NY 10021

HORTON, CAROLYN
ART & BOOK CONSERVATOR
b Buffalo, NY, July 13, 09. Study: Wellesley Col, 27-29; Univ Vienna, 29-30; apprentice bookbinder with Albert Oldach, Philadelphia; bookbinding also at Wienen Frauen Akademip. Pos: Conservator, Am Philosophical Soc, 35-39; conservator, Yale Univ Libr, 39-41; free lance work for numerous collections. Mem: Fel Int Inst for Conservation; fel Am Inst for Conservation; Guild of Bookworkers. Publ: Auth, Treating water-soaked books, Int Inst for Conserv, Vol 2 (1964); contribr, Encyclopedia Am, 67; auth, Saving the libraries of Florence, Wilson Libr Bull, 6/67; auth, Cleaning and preserving books and related materials, Am Libr Asn, 69. Mailing Add: c/o Carolyn Horton & Assoc Inc 430 W 22nd St New York NY 10011

HORTON, JAN E
PAINTER, WRITER
b Tecumseh, Nebr. Study: Univ Nebr, BFA; Millsaps Col; Univ Miss. Work: Miss Art Asn; Miss Auth Educ TV Videotape Libr; Eastern Educ Network Videotape Libr; WNET Videotape Libr, NIT Videotape Libr. Exhib: Tri-State Exhib, Cheyenne, 55; Gulf Coast Arts Festival, Biloxi, 65; Frontal Images, Jackson, Miss, 65-70; Nat Watercolor Exhib, Jackson, 66 & 68; Monroe Competition, La, 69. Teaching: Instr art hist, Miss Col, 62-64 & summer 67; instr, Murrah High Sch, 66-67; instr watercolor & art, Univ Miss Exten. Pos: Writer, Miss Educ TV, 70-, TV producer art films, 71- Awards: First Award for Buffalo For Sale (watercolor), Shreveport, 69; Best in Show for Pyrocantha, Cleveland, 70; Peabody Award in Film/TV for Art for the Day, 72. Bibliog: Bettersworth (auth), Mississippi History, 68. Mem: Miss Art Asn. Style & Technique: Film as an art medium; photographic processes in printmaking. Media: Oil. Publ: Auth & ed, Art for the Day (educ TV ser). Mailing Add: 3203 Prytania St New Orleans LA 70115

HORWITT, WILL
SCULPTOR
b New York, NY, Jan 8, 34. Study: Art Inst Chicago, 52-54. Work: Boston Mus Fine Arts; Wadsworth Atheneum, Hartford, Conn; Yale Univ Art Gallery; Albright-Knox Art Gallery, Buffalo, NY; Guggenheim Mus; plus others. Exhib: One-man shows, Stephen Radich Gallery, New York, 63, 65 & 67, Lee Ault & Co, 72, 74 & 77 & Summer Home of Boston Symphony Orchestra, Tanglewood, Mass, 74; Sculpture Ann, 68 & Biennial of Contemp Am Painting & Sculpture, 73, Whitney Mus Am Art, New York; Dwelling for a Sculpture, State Univ NY Col, Purchase, 74-76; Construction is Alive, Gruenebaum Gallery, New York, 75, Thorne Mem Art Gallery, Keene State Col, NH, 75 & Neuberger Mus, State Univ NY Col, Purchase, 76; Painting & Sculpture Today, Indianapolis Mus Art, Ind, 76. Awards: Guggenheim Fel, 65; Louis Comfort Tiffany Found Purchase Grant, 68-69. Mailing Add: 60 Beach St New York NY 10013

HOSTETLER, DAVID
SCULPTOR, EDUCATOR
b Beach City, Ohio, Dec 27, 26. Study: Ind Univ, BS; Ohio Univ, MFA. Work: Speed Mus, Louisville, Ky; Butler Inst Am Art, Youngstown, Ohio; Ft Lauderdale Mus, Fla; Miami Mus Mod Art, Fla. Comn: Head of William McGuffey, Massillon Mus, Ohio, 65; bronze figure, One Erieview Plaza, Cleveland, Ohio, 68; wood carved head, Solon Pub Libr, Cleveland, 69. Exhib: Parke-Bernet Galleries, Bernard Davis Col, New York, 62; one-man shows, Sculpture Ctr Gallery, New York, 65-72, Downey Mus Art, Calif, 69 & Speed Mus, 71; Pa Acad Fine Arts, Philadelphia, 66. Teaching: Instr ceramics, Ind Univ, Bloomington, summer 48; instr sculpture, Ohio Univ, 50-; instr, San Miguel Allende, Mex, summer 58. Pos: Mem adv panel, Ohio Arts Coun, Columbus, 69-73. Awards: First Prize, Mainstreams '69, Marietta Col, 69; Purchase Prize, Butler Art Inst, 70; Ohio Arts Coun Award, 71. Bibliog: Dona Meilach (auth), Contemporary Art with Wood, Crown, 68; The craftsman in America, Nat Geographic Soc, 75; John Platt (auth), Step by Step Woodcraft, Western Publ Co, 78. Style & Technique: Simplified formal image of the female figure. Media: Wood, Bronze. Mailing Add: Box 989 Athens OH 45701

HOTVEDT, KRIS J
PRINTMAKER, INSTRUCTOR
b Wautoma, Wis, 1943. Study: Layton Sch Art, Milwaukee, Wis, 61-64; San Francisco Art Inst, BFA, 65; Inst Allende, Mex, with D Kortlang, MFA, 67. Work: Mus NMex; Univ Sonora, Mex; Huntington Art Alliance, Calif; Ariz State Univ Mem Union Collection; Atalya Sch, Santa Fe; among others. Exhib: One-woman exhibs, Univ Sonora, 72, Ariz State Univ, 72, Okla Art Ctr, Oklahoma City, 73, Ore Univ Mus, 74-76 & Discovery Gallery, Santa Fe, 75; plus others. Teaching: Instr painting & printmaking, Pembroke State Univ, 67-69; head art dept, Los Llanos, Santa Fe, 70-72; substitute art instr, Inst Am Indian Arts, Santa Fe, fall 71, St Johns Col (NMex), 70-78, Mus NMex, 72 & Santa Cruz Adult Educ, 73. Pos: Art ed, Pembroke Mag, 72- Awards: NMex Arts Comn Grant, Art in Pub Places, 77-78. Style & Technique: Figurative and garden prints, mostly black and white. Media: Woodcut. Publ: Southwest art, Puerto del Sol, 12/74. Dealer: Ledoux Gallery Taos NM 87571; Art Wagon Gallery 7156 Main St Scottsdale AZ 85251. Mailing Add: 125 Spruce St Santa Fe NM 87501

HOUGH, RICHARD
PHOTOGRAPHER, DESIGNER
b Roanoke, Va, Mar 1, 45. Study: Roanoke Col, BBA, 67; Rochester Inst Technol, summer 69; Hotchkiss Workshop, with Minor White, summer 71; Sch Design, Calif Inst Arts. Exhib: Virginia Photographers 1969 & 1971, Va Mus, Richmond, 69 & 71; 23rd Irish Int, Dublin, Ireland, 70; New Photographics, Cent Wash State Col, 71; Soc Photog Educ Exhib, Univ Ill, Chicago Circle, 71. Teaching: Asst prof photog, Va Western Community Col, Roanoke, 68-71; grad teaching asst photog, Calif Inst Arts. Mem: Soc Photog Educ. Publ: Contribr, Mill Mt Rev, 70 & Networks, 72. Mailing Add: 430 Burnside Ave S Los Angeles CA 90036

HOUGHTON, ARTHUR A, JR
ART ADMINISTRATOR
b Corning, NY, Dec 12, 06. Study: Harvard Univ, 25-29; Lehigh Univ, Hon LHD, 50, Univ Md, Hon LHD, 63; Univ Rochester, Hon LLD, 52; Alfred Univ, Hon LLD, 54; Wesleyan Univ, Hon LLD, 63; Washington Col, Hon LittD, 53; Hofstra Col, Hon LittD, 56; Trinity Col, Hon LittD, 55; St John's Univ, Hon LittD, 66; Beaver Col, Hon DLit, 57; Hobart & William Smith Col, Hon DSc, 58; Bucknell Univ, Hon DSc, 68; Washington & Jefferson Col, Hon DFA, 71; MacMurray Col, 71. Pos: Pres, Steuben Glass, 33-72, chmn, 73-; cur rare bks, Libr of Cong, 40-42 & hon consult, Eng bibliog; dir, Corning Glass Works, 30-; vpres, Corning Mus of Glass; emer trustee, Pierpont Morgan Libr; emer trustee, past chmn & past pres, Metrop Mus Art; hon trustee & past chmn, Parsons Sch Design; trustee & emer chmn, Cooper Union; hon cur, Keats Collection, Harvard Univ; hon trustee, Inst Contemp Art, Boston; bd gov, Fed Reserve Syst Adv Comt Arts; hon trustee, Baltimore Mus of Art. Awards: Comdr, l'Ordre des Arts et Lett; Michael Friedsam Medal in Indust Art; Gertrude Vanderbilt Whitney Award, Skowhegan Sch Painting & Sculpture; plus others. Mem: Fel Royal Col Art; Royal Soc Arts. Mailing Add: Wye Plantation Queenstown MD 21658

HOULIHAN, PATRICK THOMAS
MUSEUM DIRECTOR
b New Haven, Conn, June 22, 42. Study: Georgetown Univ, BS; Univ Minn, Minneapolis, MA; Univ Wis-Milwaukee, PhD. Teaching: Instr Am Indian art, Phoenix Col; instr primitive art, Ariz State Univ. Pos: Dir, Heard Mus, currently. Mailing Add: Heard Mus 22 E Monte Vista Phoenix AZ 85002

HOUSE, JAMES CHARLES, JR
SCULPTOR, EDUCATOR
b Benton Harbor, Mich, Jan 19, 02. Study: Univ Mich, 19-21, Law Sch, 21-23; Pa Acad Fine Arts, 23-27; Univ Pa, BSEd, 41, MA, 72. Work: Whitney Mus Am Art; Woodmere Art Gallery, Germantown, Pa. Comn: Mem tryptich (birch wood), Swarthmore Presby Church, Pa, 56-57; large head of John Dewey (oak), Penniman Libr, Univ Pa, 56-57; St Christopher & Jesus (oak lunette), St Clements Episcopal Church, Philadelphia, Pa, 58; med emblem, Norfolk Med Tower, Va, 60; teak wall relief, Philadelphia Br Libr, Bustleton, Pa, 65-66. Exhib: Whitney Mus Am Art Sculpture Biennials, 34 & 36; Kansas City Art Inst, 35; Int Sculpture Shows, Philadelphia Mus Art, 40 & 50; Artists for Victory, Metrop Mus Art, 42; Nineteen Cities, Mus Mod Art, New York, 47. Teaching: Assoc prof sculpture & drawing, Univ Pa Grad Sch Fine Arts, 27-72, emer assoc prof, 72-75; assoc prof, Philadelphia Mus Art Eve Class, 49-50; assoc prof, San Diego State Col, summer 56; vis sculpture critic, Univ Pa, 75-76; retired. Pos: Free lance caricaturist, New York Eve Post, Philadelphia Pub-Ledger, New Yorker & others, 25-32; caricaturist, Philadelphia Eve Bull, 47-54. Awards: John Frederick Lewis First Prize for Caricature, Pa Acad Fine Arts, 27. Bibliog: Dorothy Grafly (auth), article in, Am Artist, 55. Media: Wood. Publ: Illusr, Fifty Drawings, 30. Mailing Add: 810 Crum Creek Rd Media PA 19063

HOUSER, ALLAN C
SCULPTOR, PAINTER
b Apache, Okla, June 30, 14. Study: Chilocco Indian Sch, Okla; Santa Fe Indian Sch, NMex, spec study with Dorothy Dunn; mural techniques with Olle Nordmark, Okla; Utah State Univ, Logan; St Michael's Col, Santa Fe. Work: Heard Mus, Phoenix, Ariz; Philbrook Art Ctr, Tulsa, Okla; Mus of Northern Ariz, Flagstaff; Denver Art Mus, Colo; Univ of Okla, Oklahoma City; plus others. Comn: Murals, Dept of Interior, Washington, DC; dioramas, Southern Plains Indian Mus, Anadarko, Okla; medals, Soc of Medalists; illus for nine bks; portrait of Stewart Udall, Dept of Interior, Washington, DC. Exhib: New York World's Fair, 35; Exposition of Indian Tribal Arts (traveling), Col Art Asn, 31-33; San Francisco World's Fair, 39-40; Contemp Indian Painters, Nat Gallery of Art, Washington, DC, 53; Ann Am Indian Exposition, Chicago Indian Ctr, 53; Art Inst of Chicago, 53; Inter-Tribal Indian Ceremonials, Gallup, NMex, 53; Ann Indian Artists, Denver Art Mus, Colo; Fine Arts Mus NMex; Scottsdale Nat Indian Art Exhib, Ariz; Heard Mus, Phoenix, Ariz, 70; Southern Plains Indian Mus, 71; Philbrook Art Ctr, Tulsa, 72; Gallery Wall, Phoenix, Ariz, 75-78; Outdoor Sculpture Shows, Shidoni Foundry, Santa Fe, 76-77; Gov's Gallery, State Capital, Santa Fe, 77; Jamison Gallery, Santa Fe, 77; Sacred Circles Art Exhib, Kansas City, Mo, 77; Am Indian & Cowboy Exhib, San Dimas, Calif, 78; Wagner Gallery, Austin, Tex, 78. Teaching: Instr art, Intermountain Indian Sch, Brigham City, Utah; head, Dept of Sculpture, Inst of Am Indian Arts, Santa Fe; slide lect, Lake Forest Col, Chicago, Ill, 78; slide lect & sem, Thomas Burke Mem State Mus, Univ of Wash, Seattle, 78. Awards: Gold Medal in Bronze, Silver Medal in Stone & Silver Medal in Other Metal, Heard Mus Sculpture I Show, 73; Best of Show & First Place in Sculpture, Am Indian & Cowboy Show, San Dimas, Calif, 78. Bibliog: Television series, Am Indian Artists 1976, Allan Houser, Working Sculptor, Pub Broadcasting System, KAET Television, 76. Mailing Add: 1020 Camino Carlos Rey Santa Fe NM 87501

HOUSER, CAROLINE M
ART HISTORIAN
b Walla Walla, Wash. Study: Mills Col, BA; San Francisco Art Inst; Harvard Univ, AM, PhD; Am Sch Classical Studies, Athens, Greece. Teaching: Asst prof art hist, Univ Tex, Austin, 75-; Mellon Fel art hist, Harvard Univ, Cambridge, Mass, 78- Mem: Archaeol Inst of Am; Col Art Asn. Res: Greek sculpture, especially monumental work in bronze. Publ: Auth, Is it from the Parthenon, Am J Archaeol, 72. Mailing Add: 2610 McCollum Dr Austin TX 78703

HOUSER, JIM
PAINTER, EDUCATOR
b Dade City, Fla, Nov 12, 28. Study: Ringling Sch Art; Fla Southern Col, BS; Art Inst Chicago; Univ Fla, MFA; Johns Hopkins Univ. Work: Univ Notre Dame; Cornell Univ; NY Univ; Soc Four Arts Collection, Palm Beach, Fla; Syracuse Univ Art Collection; Dulin Gallery Art, Knoxville, Tenn. Exhib: Soc Four Arts, Palm Beach, Fla, 64-77; one-man shows, Grand Cent Mod, New York, 67 & Lehigh Univ, Bethlehem, 68; Peter Rudolph Galleries, Woodstock, NY & Coral Gables, Fla, 67-75; Mainstreams USA, Ohio, 68; David Findlay Galleries, New York, 76. Teaching: Asst prof painting, Ky Wesleyan Col, 54-60; prof painting, Palm Beach Jr Col, 60-, chmn dept, 64-70. Awards: Atwater Kent Award, Soc Four Arts, 64 & 76, Akston Award, 77. Verna Lammi Mem Award, Norton Gallery, 74; Merit Award, 16th Hortt Competition, Ft Lauderdale Mus Arts, 74; among others. Media: Acrylic. Dealer: Peter Rudolph Galleries 338 Sevilla Ave Coral Gables FL 33134; David Findlay Gallery 984 Madison Ave New York NY 10021. Mailing Add: 693 Jog Rd West Palm Beach FL 33406

HOUSKEEPER, BARBARA
SCULPTOR, PAINTER
b Ft Wayne, Ind, Aug 25, 22. Study: Knox Col, Ill; RI Sch Design; Art Inst Chicago. Work: Ill Bell & Tel, Chicago; Gould Found, Rolling Meadows, Ill; Kemper Ins Co, Long Grove; Mercury Rec, Chicago. Comn: Large sculptures, Exec Off Condecor Mfg, Mundelein, Ill, 72, Mr & Mrs William Goldstandt Collection, Glencoe, Ill, 72, Mr & Mrs Leonard Sax Collection, Northfield, Ill, 72 & Reception Hall, Kemper Ins Co Home Off, Long Grove, Ill, 74; Mem Sculpture, Am Bar Asn, Chicago, 75. Exhib: New Horizons in Art (wide regional ann), since 66; Theme Ecology Invitational, Univ Wis Gallery, Madison, 70; Springfield State Mus All Summer Show, 73; First Chicago Sculpture Invitational, Fed Bldg, Chicago, 74; Chicago Lyrical Abstraction traveling show, Springfield, Mo & elsewhere, 78; one-artist

shows, Michael Wyman Gallery, Chicago, 73 & 76, Zaks Gallery, Chicago, 78 & Artemesia Coop Gallery, Chicago, 79. Teaching: Teacher, Working in the Environ, Oxbow Summer Sch Art, Saugatuck, Mich, 72-75, dir, 73-74; teacher advan critique, North Shore Art League, Winnetka, Ill, 73- Pos: Cur, Univ Mo Gallery, 76-78. Awards: First Prize-Painting, New Horizons in Art Ann, 69 & First Prize-Painting, 70; Second Prize-Sculpture, Old Orchard Festival Ann, 73. Bibliog: Jane Allen & Derek Guthrie (auth), From Brave New World to Village Smithy, Chicago Tribune, 4/23/72; Dorothy Andries (auth), She Gives Opportunity to Others, Pioneer, 74. Mem: Arts Club of Chicago; Chicago Artists Coalition; WEB. Style & Technique: Sculpture for indoor and outdoor space with emphasis on interaction of environment, using transparent or reflective material; paintings on canvas using reflective color. Media: Acrylic Sheet, Stainless Steel. Dealer: Zaks Gallery 620 Michigan Ave Chicago IL. Mailing Add: 842 Holmes Ave Deerfield IL 60015

HOUSMAN, RUSSELL F
PAINTER, INSTRUCTOR
b Buffalo, NY, Jan 13, 28. Study: Albright Art Sch, Buffalo, dipl; State Univ NY Col Buffalo, BS; NY Univ, MA & PhD; also with Hale Woodruff & Revington Arthur. Work: Human Resources Ctr Collection; NY Univ; State Univ NY. Comn: Mural, USA, Kans Munic Auditorium, 52; painting, L Goodyear Collection, 57; Discovery Ctr, Human Resources Ctr, 72. Exhib: State Univ NY; Tri-State Exhib, Chautauqua, NY; one-man show, Silvermine Guild Art, Albany Inst Hist & Art & Wellons Gallery, New York; plus others. Collections Arranged: Arms & Armor, 60 & Civil War Centennial, 60, Decatur Art Ctr, Ill; George Crosz Retrospect, Firehouse Gallery, Garden City, NY, 64. Teaching: Prof art, Adelphi Univ, 56-59; prof art & chmn dept, Milliken Univ, 59-61; prof art, Nassau Community Col, 63-, dir, Firehouse Gallery, 63-70. Pos: Dir, Decatur City Art Ctr, 59-61; art consult, Human Resources Ctr, Albertson, NY, 61- Awards: Purchase Award, State Univ NY, 68; Prizes, Silvermine Art Guild & Chautauqua Art Ctr. Bibliog: Viscardi (auth), The School, Eriksson, 64; 21 Paint in Hyplar, Grumbacher, 68; Watson (auth), The Artist as a Cook, Country Art Gallery, 72. Mem: Am Fedn Art; Silvermine Art Guild; NY State Art Teachers (ed, 69); Long Island Art Teachers. Style & Technique: Abstract anatomical landscapes. Res: Core humanities curriculum for disabled children; artist in psychological warfare; the child as artist. Publ: Auth, Psychological Warfare Capabilities & Vulnerabilities as Found in Soviet Art, 54; The Design of an Art Room, 55; Utilization of Artist Personnel in Psychological Warfare, 63; Telephone Assisted Teaching Devices, 69; Core Humanities Curriculum for Disabled Children, 70. Mailing Add: 38 Hampshire Rd Great Neck NY 11023

HOUSSER, YVONNE MCKAGUE
PAINTER, DESIGNER
b Toronto, Ont, Aug 4, 98. Study: Ont Col Art, scholar; Acad Grande Chaumiere & Acad Ranson, 21, 22 & 24, with Prinet; Univ Vienna; also with Hans Hofmann & Emile Bistram. Work: Nat Gallery Can; Art Gallery Ont; London Art Gallery, Ont; Robert McMichael Collection Art; Univ Toronto; plus many others. Comn: Mural, The Canadian, Can Pac Rwy. Exhib: Royal Can Ann, Ont Soc Artists; Can Group of Painters, Nat Gallery Can; Contemporanea, Rio de Janeiro; Century of Can Art, Tate Gallery, London, Eng; plus many others. Teaching: Instr art, Ont Col Art, 20-41; also instr at Doon Sch Fine Art & Ryerson Inst. Awards: Can Nat Purchase Award; Baxter Award, Ont Soc Artists, 65. Media: Oil, Acrylic, Mixed Media, Collage, Watercolor. Mem: Royal Can Acad; Ont Soc Artists; Can Group of Painters; Heliconian Club. Mailing Add: Mont Soudan No 1002 700 Mount Pleasant Rd Toronto ON M4S 2N7 Can

HOVELL, JOSEPH
SCULPTOR
b Kiev, Russia. Study: Cooper Union Art Sch, with Brewster; Nat Acad Design, with Robert Aitken. Comn: Portrait busts & bas-reliefs of many prominent persons in pvt collections; plaques & busts, Carnegie Hall, New York; Nathan Sachs bronze mem plaque; mem plaque, Hebrew Union Col & Jewish Inst Relig, Cincinnati; medals, awards, terra-cottas, wood carvings, etc. Exhib: Nat Acad Design; Brooklyn Mus; Whitney Mus Am Art; Carnegie Hall Gallery; Jewish Mus, New York; plus others. Mailing Add: 130 W 57th St New York NY 10019

HOVEY, WALTER READ
ART HISTORIAN, LECTURER
b Springfield, Mass, July 21, 95. Study: Yale Univ, AB; Harvard Univ, AM; Wooster Col, hon PhD. Teaching: Head dept fine arts, Univ Pittsburgh, 36-68 (retired), lectr, currently. Pos: Dir, Henry Clay Frick Art Mus, Univ Pittsburgh, formerly; adv Oriental art, Carnegie Inst, Pittsburgh, currently. Collection: Chinese ceramics. Mailing Add: Cedar St Chatham MA 02633

HOVING, THOMAS
ART CONSULTANT
b New York, NY, Jan 15, 31. Study: Princeton Univ, BA(summa cum laude), 53, Grad Sch Art & Archaeol, Nat Coun Humanities fel, 55, study & travel in Europe, 56-57, Grad Sch Fine Arts, Kienbusch & Haring fel, 57, MFA, 58 & PhD(art hist), 59; Pratt Inst, hon LLD, 67; Hofstra Univ, hon LHD; NY Univ, hon DFA, 68; Princeton Univ, hon DH, 68; Middlebury Col, hon LittD, 68. Collections Arranged: Initiated and developed series of art exchanges between museums of France, Soviet Union and the US. Pos: Curatorial asst, Dept Medieval Art & The Cloisters, Metrop Mus Art, 59-60, asst cur, 60-63, assoc cur, 63-65, cur, 65-66, dir, 67-; admin, Recreation & Cult Affairs, New York, 66-67. Awards: Distinguished Achievement Award, Advert Club Am, 66; NY Univ Creative Leadership in Educ Award, 75; Woodrow Wilson Award, Princeton Univ, 77. Mem: Int Ctr Medieval Art (mem bd dir). Publ: Auth, Guide to the Cloisters, 62; auth, The Bury St Edmunds Cross, 64; auth, Italian Romanesque Sculpture, 65; auth, Branch out, Mus News, 68; auth, Discovery of Tutankhamun, fall 78. Mailing Add: 150 E 73rd St New York NY 10021

HOVSEPIAN, LEON
PAINTER, DESIGNER
b Bloomsburg, Pa, Nov 20, 15. Study: Worcester Art Mus Sch, cert; Yale Univ, Alice Kimball traveling fel, 41-42, BFA; Fogg Mus. Work: Worcester Art Mus, Mass; Fitchburg Art Mus, Mass; Fine Arts Collection, Washington, DC; Springfield Mus, Mass. Comn: Fresco, Immaculata Retreat House, Willimantic, Conn, 60; mosaics, Oblate Fathers Retreat House, Willimantic, 61; stained glass, Holy Cross Col, Worcester, 65; portraits, Leiceister Jr Col, Mass, 68-69; fresco mural, Church of the Annunciation, Washington, DC, 74. Exhib: Art Inst Chicago, 41; Albright Art Gallery, 46; Nat Gallery Art, 47; RI Sch Design, 48; Worcester Art Mus Am Biennial, 48; By the People For the People—New Eng, De Cordova Mus, Lincoln, Mass, 77; plus others. Teaching: Instr art, Bancroft Sch, 36-38; prof art, Woman's Col, New Haven, 38-40; instr art, Worcester Art Mus Sch, 40-, instr, Pub Educ Div, 41-56. Pos: Dir, Boylston Summer Art Sch, Mass, 41- Awards: St Wulstan Soc Art Award, 38-40; Painting Prize, Fitchburg Art Mus. Bibliog: Adlow (auth), Stuart gallery, Christian Sci Monitor, 46; Sandrof (auth), Artist in his studio, Feature Parade, 53; Browne (auth), Leon Hovsepian, Art News, 11/66. Mem: The Bohemians. Publ: Illusr, Worcester Fedral, Past—Present—Future, 52; illusr, Androck, 58. Dealer: Triart Studios 90 Pocasset Ave Worcester MA 01606. Mailing Add: 96 Squantum St Worcester MA 01606

HOWARD, CECIL RAY
PAINTER, SCULPTOR
b Wichita, Kans, Jan 25, 37. Study: Kans State Teachers Col, BS; Wichita State Univ, MFA. Work: Wichita Art Mus; Amarillo Col Gallery, Tex; Wichita State Univ; Glendale Community Col, Ariz; Emporia Kans State Col. Comn: Collage mural, Western NMex Univ, 69; tympanum ceramic sculpture, Church Good Shepherd, Silver City, 71. Exhib: One-man shows, Marion Koogler McNay Gallery, San Antonio, Tex, 60 & Wichita Art Mus, 67; Mid-America Show, Nelson Gallery, Atkins Mus, Kansas City, Mo, 62; Mainstreams '68 Int Exhib, Marietta, Ohio, 68; Int Designer-Craftsmen Exhib, El Paso Art Mus, Tex, 69; Mus NMex, Santa Fe; Santa Fe Mus Int Folk Art; Tucson Art Mus, Ariz. Teaching: Prof painting & sculpture, Western NMex Univ, 63- Pos: Dir, McCray Gallery, Western NMex Univ, 63-, actg chmn art dept, 77-; co-juried, Int Designer-Craftsman Exhib, El Paso, Tex; mem standards comt, NMex Arts & Crafts Fair, 77. Awards: Purchase Awards, Wichita Art Mus, 60 & 62; Juror's Award for Distinction, Mainstreams '68 Int Exhib, 68; First Place Award in Ceramics, El Paso Art Mus, 69. Mem: NMex Potters' Asn. Media: Collage, Assemblage, Ceramic. Publ: Illusr, Voyage to America, Univ Nebr, 67; contribr, Donna Meilach, auth, Collage on Construction, Crown. Dealer: Mariposa Gallery Old Town Albuquerque NM 87104. Mailing Add: Rte 10 Box 138 Glenwood NM 88039

HOWARD, DAN F
PAINTER, EDUCATOR
b Iowa City, Iowa, Aug 4, 31. Study: Univ Iowa, BA, 53, MFA, 58. Work: Joe & Emily Lowe Art Mus, Univ Miami, Fla; Parthenon Mus, Nashville, Tenn; Ark Arts Ctr, Little Rock; Masur Mus Art, Monroe, La; Sheldon Mem Art Gallery, Univ Nebr, Lincoln; Exhib: Nat Painting Exhib, Lowe Art Mus, 63; Contemporary Americans, Ark Arts Ctr, 67; Ark Pavilion, Hemis-Fair '68, San Antonio, Tex, 68; Contemp Am Painting Exhib, Palm Beach, Fla, 70; Regional Artists, Nelson Gallery, Kansas City, Mo, 72 & 73; Nebr Exhib, Joslyn Art Mus, Omaha, 75. Teaching: From instr to assoc prof painting & drawing, Ark State Univ, 58-71, chmn div art, 65-71; prof painting & drawing & head dept art, Kans State Univ, 71-74; prof art & chmn dept art, Univ Nebr-Lincoln, 74- Pos: Dir art gallery, Ark State Univ Fine Arts Ctr, 67-71; exec dir, Friends of Art, Kans State Univ, 71-74. Awards: First Prize, Nat Painting Exhib, Miami, 63; Top Award, Ark-La-Miss Show, Monroe, La, 65; Top Award, Cent South Exhib, Nashville, 68. Bibliog: Dan Howard, artist, Changing Middle South, 67; Weathersby (auth), Art in Arkansas, Ark State Mag, 67. Mem: Col Art Asn Am; Am Fedn Arts; Mid-Am Col Art Asn (vpres, 75, pres, 76, bd dir, 75-78); Nat Coun Art Adminr; Nebr Art Asn (bd trustees, 74-). Style & Technique: Tangible images in satiric contexts, using oil in expressive, coloristic application. Mailing Add: 3800 Stockwell Lincoln NE 68506

HOWARD, DAVID
PHOTOGRAPHER, INSTRUCTOR
b Brooklyn, NY. Study: Ohio Univ; San Francisco Art Inst, MFA; additional study with Ansel Adams, Duane Michaels & Jerry Ulesman. Work: Mus of Mod Art, New York; San Francisco Mus of Mod Art; Oakland Mus, Calif; City of San Francisco; de Saisset Art Gallery & Mus, Santa Clara, Calif. Exhib: One-man shows, San Francisco Art Inst, 73, Third Eye Gallery, New York, 76, Fourth St Gallery, New York, 76, Analyses of Realities, Madison Art Ctr, Wis, 76 & Photog Sculpture & Prints, Images Gallery, New York, 77; Capricorn Asunder, San Francisco Art Comn Gallery, 73; 10th & 13th Int Festivals of Contemp Art, Royan, France, 73 & 76; Oakland Mus, Calif, 74; 34th Int Salon of Japan, Tokyo, 74; de Young Mus, San Francisco, 75; Hansen Fuller Gallery, San Francisco, 75; Univ Calif, San Francisco Exten, 75; Nat Exhib, Ohio Silver Gallery, Los Angeles, 75. Pos: Vis artist art hist, San Francisco City Col, 73; dir photog, San Francisco Ctr of Visual Studies, 74- Awards: Purchase Award, 27th San Francisco Art Festival, City of San Francisco, 73. Bibliog: Alfred Frenkenstein (auth), Beauty & elegance, San Francisco Chronicle, 74; F McDonald (auth), Center page, Village Voice, 76; Joan Murry (auth), Realities, bk rev, Artweek, 76. Style & Technique: Non-verbal experience which integrates life experiences as religion, into art. Media: Photography, printmaking. Publ: Illusr, Artweek, 73; illusr, Wester D Kemp (auth), Photography for Visual Communicators, Prentice-Hall, 73; illusr, San Francisco Chronicle, 75; auth & illusr, Realities, 76 & Perspectives, 77, San Francisco Ctr for Visual Studies. Mailing Add: c/o San Francisco Ctr for Visual Studies 900 Alabama St San Francisco CA 94110

HOWARD, HUMBERT L
PAINTER
b Philadelphia, Pa, July 12, 15. Study: Univ Pa; Howard Univ Sch Fine Arts; Int Acad Arts & Lett, Rome, Italy, hon degree. Work: Howard Univ; Pa Acad Fine Arts, Philadelphia; Philadelphia Civic Ctr Mus; Libr Cong; Stanley Bernstein Collection & numerous other pub & pvt collections. Exhib: City Col New York, 67; Grabar Gallery, 68; Howard Univ; Int Acad Arts & Lett, 70; William Penn Mem Mus Exhib, 71 & 77; Gross McCleaf Gallery, Philadelphia, 77; plus others. Teaching: Fac mem, Allens Lane Art Ctr, Philadelphia, formerly. Pos: Am Found Negro Affairs Comn on Cult & Performing Arts. Awards: Silver Medal for Painting, Int Acad Arts & Lett, Rome, 70. Mem: Pyramid Club (former art dir); Artists Equity Asn; Peale Club; Philadelphia Art Alliance. Mailing Add: 3411 Hamilton St Philadelphia PA 19104

HOWARD, LINDA
SCULPTOR
b Evanston, Ill, Oct, 21, 34. Study: Univ Colo; Northwestern Univ; Chicago Art Inst, 53-55; Univ Denver, BA, 57; Hunter Col, New York, MA, 70. Work: Bradley Collection, Milwaukee Art Ctr, Wis; 1-80 State of Nebr, Ogallala; Colorado Springs Fine Arts Mus, Colo; Aldrich Mus Contemp Art, Ridgefield, Conn. Comn: Up/Over (aluminum sculpture, 20ft x 15ft x 10ft), State of Nebr, 76; Skywall (aluminum, 18ft x 9ft x 9ft), 76 & Round About (8ft x 8ft x 8ft), 76, Art Park, Lewiston, NY. Exhib: Focus, Women's Work, Am Art, Philadelphia Civic Ctr, 74; Park Sculpture, Hudson River Mus, Yonkers, NY, 74; Aldrich Mus Contemp Art, 75; NY Univ, 76; Colorado Springs Fine Arts Mus, 76; Am Artists, A Celebration, McNay Art Inst, New York, 76; Sculpture Potsdam 77, State Univ NY Col, Potsdam, 77; one-person show, Sculpture Now Gallery, New York, 78. Teaching: Asst prof sculpture, Hunter Col, New York, 69-72 & Lehman Col, New York, 73-76; asst prof sculpture, Hunter Col, New York, 76- Awards: Creative Artists Pub Serv Grant, NY State, 75; City Univ New York Fac Res Grant, 75. Bibliog: Doc films, Roll Over, New Roles for Women, Marion Hunter, 73, Linda Howard, Sculpture, 76, Constructions Sculpture, 76 & 500 Mile Sculpture Garden, 76, Nebr Educ Television. Style & Technique: Aluminum monumental sculpture. Dealer: Max Hutchinson c/o Sculpture Now Gallery 142 Greene St New York NY 10012. Mailing Add: 11 Worth St New York NY 10013

HOWARD, RICHARD FOSTER
ART ADMINISTRATOR
b Plainfield, NJ, July 26, 02. Study: Harvard Col, BS, 24; Harvard Univ Grad Sch, 27-29. Collections Arranged: For Tex Centennial, Dallas Mus, Des Moines Art Ctr & Birmingham Mus Art. Pos: Dir, Dallas Mus Fine Arts, 35-41; chief, Monuments, Fine Arts & Arch, Ger, 46-49; dir, Des Moines Art Ctr, 49-51; dir, Birmingham Mus Art, 51-74, emer dir, 74- Awards: Stella Solidarieta, Repub Italy; Order of White Lion, Czech. Mem: Southeastern Mus Conf (pres, 73-74); Am Asn Mus; Am Asn Mus Dirs. Mailing Add: 3920 Ninth Court S Birmingham AL 35222

HOWARD, ROBERT A
SCULPTOR, EDUCATOR
b Sapulpa, Okla, Apr 5, 22. Study: Phillips Univ; Univ Tulsa; with Ossip Zadkine, Paris, France. Work: NC Mus Art, Raleigh; Ackland Art Ctr & NC Nat Bank, Chapel Hill, NC. Comn: Monumental sculpture, Fed Bldg, Louisville, Ky, 76. Exhib: 153rd Ann Exhib, Pa Acad Fine Arts, Philadelphia, 58; Art 65—Young American Sculpture, New York World's Fair, 65; Sculpture of the Sixties, Los Angeles Co Mus, 67; Ann Contemp Sculpture, Whitney Mus Art, New York, 68; Contemp Am Painting & Sculpture, Univ Ill, 69. Teaching: Prof sculpture, Univ NC, 51-72 & 74-; prof sculpture, Univ Southern Calif, 72-73. Awards: Coop Prog in Humanities, Duke Univ, Univ NC & Ford Found, 65 & Univ NC, 71; Nat Endowment for the Arts, 72. Style & Technique: Multiple modular systems in spacial constructions. Media: Welded Steel, Fiberglas, Aluminum. Publ: Auth, Space as form, Col Art J, 51. Mailing Add: 1201 Hillview Rd Chapel Hill NC 27514

HOWARD, ROBERT BOARDMAN
SCULPTOR
b New York, NY, Sept 20, 96. Study: Calif Sch Arts, Berkeley, 15-16; Art Students League, 16-17; also in Europe, 20-22. Work: Acad Sci, San Francisco; San Francisco Mus Art; Oakland Mus Art; Univ Calif, Santa Cruz; Bank Am Head Off Bldg, San Francisco; Acad of Sci, San Francisco; San Francisco Mus of Mod Art; Oakland Mus, Calif; Crown & Kresge Cols, Univ of Calif, Santa Cruz; Bank of Am Hq, San Francisco. Comn: Sculpture murals, San Francisco Stock Exchange, 30 & Yosemite Park Co, 36; Whale fountain, City of San Francisco, Golden Gate Park, 40; two reliefs, P G & E Elec Sta, San Francisco, 48; Hydro Gyro, IBM Res Ctr, San Jose, Calif, 58. Exhib: San Francisco Art Inst Ann, 22-72; six Whitney Mus Am Art Ann, 48-55; Sao Paulo, Brazil, 51-55; Salon Mai, Paris, France, 62-64; San Francisco Art Comn, 71; Pub Sculpture/Urban Environment, Oakland Mus, Calif, 74; Painting & Sculpture in Calif: the Mod Era, San Francisco Mus of Mod Art, Calif, 76 & Nat Collection of Fine Arts, Smithsonian Inst, Washington, DC, 77; one-person shows, San Francisco Art Inst, 56 & 73, San Francisco Mus of Art, 63, Crown Col, Univ of Calif, Santa Cruz, 68 & Kresge Col, 71 & Capricorn Asunder Gallery, San Francisco Art Comn; plus others. Teaching: Instr sculpture, San Francisco Art Inst, 45-54; instr sculpture, Mills Col, Oakland, 46. Pos: Comnr, San Francisco Art Comn. Awards: Awards, for Eyrie, San Francisco Art Asn, 46, Night Watch, San Francisco Art Comn, 51 & Rocket, San Francisco Art Inst, 55. Bibliog: Alfred Frankenstein (auth), many articles in, San Francisco Chronicle, San Francisco Art Inst; San Francisco Mus Art; plus others. Mem: San Francisco Art Inst; San Francisco Mus Art; Univ Calif Art Mus, Berkeley; Mus Mod Art. Mailing Add: 521 Francisco St San Francisco CA 94133

HOWARTH, SHIRLEY REIFF
MUSEUM DIRECTOR, ART HISTORIAN
b Ft Benning, Ga, Oct 1, 44. Study: Dickinson Col, Carlisle, Pa, BA(art hist); Pa State Univ, University Park, MA(art hist). Collections Arranged: Recent Sculpture: Steven Urry, 76 & Marcel Breuer: Architect & Designer, 78, Hackley Art Mus, Muskegon, Mich. Pos: Asst cur, William Penn Mem Mus, Harrisburg, Pa, 69-74, cur prints, Pa Collection Fine Arts, 74-75; dir, Hackley Art Mus, Muskegon, Mich, 75- Mem: Mich Mus Asn (art mus rep, 77-); Mus Adv Bd, Mich Coun for the Arts; Am Asn Mus; Col Art Asn; Greater Muskegon Coun for Arts (vpres, 75-76 & 76-77). Res: Primarily in fields of Medieval and Northern Renaissance art; history of prints and photography. Publ: Auth, Care of Works of Art on Paper and Care, Display and Storage of Photographs, Pa Hist & Mus Comn, 73; auth, Marcel Breuer: Architect and Designer, Hackley Art Mus, 78. Mailing Add: Hackley Art Mus 296 W Webster Muskegon MI 49440

HOWAT, JOHN KEITH
CURATOR, ART HISTORIAN
b Denver, Colo, Apr 12, 37. Study: Harvard Univ, BA, 59, MA, 62. Collections Arranged: David Smith, Hyde Collection, 64; John F Kensett (with catalog), Am Fedn Art, 68; 19th Century America: Paintings & Sculpture (with catalog), 70, American Paintings & Sculpture, 71 & Heritage of American Art: Paintings from the Collection, 75, Metrop Mus Art. Pos: Cur, Hyde Collection, 62-64; asst cur Am painting, Metrop Mus Art, 67-68, assoc cur, 68-70, cur Am painting & sculpture, 70- Awards: Ford Found fel, 65; Chester Dale fel, Metrop Mus Art, 65-67. Mem: Am Fedn Arts; Arch Am Art (adv comt). Res: American paintings of 18th and 19th centuries, especially the Hudson River School. Publ: Auth, Hudson River & its Painters, 72. Mailing Add: Metrop Mus of Art New York NY 10028

HOWE, NELSON S
DESIGNER, ASSEMBLAGE ARTIST
b Lansing, Mich, Nov 5, 35. Study: Univ Mich, BA, 57, MA, 61. Work: New Orleans Mus Fine Arts, La; Libr Collections, Mus Mod Art, Finch Col Mus Art & Chase Manhattan Bank Collection, New York; Univ Calif, Berkeley; plus others. Comn: Wall I (fabric wall), Mr & Mrs Keith Waldrop, Providence, RI, 68; Fur Music (installation unit), Mus Contemp Crafts, New York, 71; Fur Score (fur wall), New Orleans Mus Fine Arts, 72. Exhib: One-man show, Little Gallery, Minneapolis Inst Art, Minn, 67; NJ Artists Triennial, Newark Mus, 68; 50 Best Books of the Year, Am Inst Graphic Arts, 69; Fur & Feathers Show, Mus Contemp Crafts, 71; Experimental Sound, ICES Festival, London, Eng, 72; plus others. Pos: Proc & founding artist mem, Participation Proj Found, 73- Awards: 50 Best Books of the Yr Award, Am Inst Graphic Arts, 69; Intermedia Found Grant for Lab Serv, 72. Bibliog: Rose De Neve (auth), Art - notation - art, Print Mag, Vol 25, No 1; Source: Museum of Avant Garde, No 9, 72; plus others. Style & Technique: Designing of scores and graphic notation systems to involve the public directly in art participation. Publ: Illusr, To the Sincere Reader, 68, illusr, Body Image, 70 & co-auth, Job Art, 71, Wittenborn; illusr & auth, Daily translating systems, Circle Press (London), 71; Harpers' Mag Wraparound Sect, 5/73; plus others. Mailing Add: 307 W Broadway New York NY 10013

HOWE, OSCAR
PAINTER, EDUCATOR
b Joe Creek, SDak, May 13, 15. Study: Dakota Wesleyan Univ, BA, 52; Univ Okla, MFA, 54. Work: Denver Art Mus; Joslyn Art Mus, Omaha, Nebr; Mus NMex, Santa Fe; Philbrook Art Ctr, Tulsa, Okla; Smithsonian Inst, New York Br; plus others. Comn: Murals, Mitchell Libr, SDak, 40, Nebraska City, Nebr, City of Mobridge, SDak, auditorium, 41 & high sch, Hillside, Ill, 56. Exhib: Mus Mod Art, New York, 36; Collectors Choice Exhib, Denver Art Mus, 63; one-man shows, Philbrook Art Ctr, Tulsa, 64, Joslyn Art Mus, 67 & Heard Mus, Phoenix, 71. Teaching: Artist in residence, Dak Wesleyan Univ, 48-52; prof art & artist in residence, Univ SDak, 57- Pos: Dir art, Pierre High Sch, SDak, 53-57. Awards: Dorothy Field Award, Denver Art Mus, 52; Mary Benjamin Rogers Award, Mus NMex, 58; Waite Phillips Trophy, Philbrook Art Ctr, Tulsa, 66. Bibliog: Robert Pennington (auth), Oscar Howe, artist of the Sioux, Dakota Territory Cent Co, 61; Panorama for Pakistan, US Info Serv, 71; John Milton (auth), Oscar Howe, The Story of an American Indian, Dillon, 72. Mem: Delta Phi Delta; fel Int Inst Arts & Lett. Media: Casein. Mailing Add: Dept of Art Univ of SDak Vermillion SD 57069

HOWE, THOMAS CARR
MUSEUM DIRECTOR
b Kokomo, Ind, Aug 12, 04. Study: Harvard Univ, AB(magna cum laude), 26, Sch Archit, 27-28, MFA, 29; Calif Col Arts & Crafts, Hon DFA, 69. Teaching: Tutor & instr fine arts, Harvard Univ, 27-28. Pos: Asst dir, Calif Palace of Legion of Honor, 31-39, dir, 39-68, dir emer, 68-; vchmn, Comt Pub Works of Art Proj, San Francisco, 34; dep chief monuments, Fine Arts & Archit Sect, US Forces, Ger & Austria, 45-46; spec art comnr, Golden Gate Int Expos, 58; mem, Fine Arts Comt for White House; mem, Smithsonian Art Comn; adv coun, Princeton Univ Art Mus, 69; mem, Calif Arts Coun, 69-74; chmn, Nat Collection Fine Arts, Smithsonian Inst, 70. Awards: Chevalier, Legion of Honor, Fr Govt, Officer, Order of Orange-Nassau, Dutch Govt. Mem: Asn Am Art Mus Dirs (pres, 60-61); Am Fedn Arts (trustee); Western Asn Art Mus Dirs (pres, 41-42). Publ: Auth, Salt Mines & Castles, 46. Mailing Add: 2709 Larkin St San Francisco CA 94109

HOWELL, CLAUDE FLYNN
PAINTER, EDUCATOR
b Wilmington, NC, Mar 17, 15. Study: With Charles Rosen, Woodstock, NY, Bernard Karfiol & Jon Corbino; Wake Forest Univ, DHL, 75. Work: NC Mus Art, Raleigh; Weatherspoon Gallery, Univ NC; NC Nat Bank, Charlotte; Wake Forest Univ; IBM Collection, New York; Wachovia Collection, Winston-Salem, NC. Comn: Illus, John F Blair Publ Co, Winston-Salem, 58; mosaics, NC Dept Arch & Hist, Mus Old Brunswick, 65 & State Ports Maritime Bldg, Wilmington, 66. Exhib: Am Watercolors 1952, Metrop Mus Art, New York; Fifth Ann Painting Yr, Atlanta Art Asn Galleries, Ga, 59; Piedmont Purchase Award Show, Mint Mus Art, Charlotte, 63; Art on Paper, Weatherspoon Gallery, 67; retrospective, NC Mus Art, 75. Teaching: Assoc prof painting & art hist & chmn dept art, Univ NC, Wilmington, 58- Awards: Rosenwald Found Fel, 48; Purchase Awards, NC Mus Art, 54 & NC Col Durham, 68. Bibliog: Senta Bier (auth), Notes on a North Carolina artist, Longview J, 71. Mem: NC Art Soc (adv coun, 69-). Publ: Illusr, Hatterasman, 58, Exploring the Seacoast of North Carolina, 70 & Beachcombers Handbook of Seafood Cookery, 71; auth, A Balkan Sketchbook, 77. Mailing Add: Box 214 Wilmington NC 28402

HOWELL, DOUGLASS (MORSE)
PAINTER, ART HISTORIAN
b New York, NY, Nov 30, 06. Study: Study in Europe & tutorials. Work: Handmade papers, Boston Mus Fine Art; Brooklyn Mus; handpress printing bks, New York Pub Libr; Huntington Mus, San Marino, Calif; Fogg Mus; plus other work in pub & pvt collections. Exhib: Phillips Exeter Acad; Huntington Mus, Long Island, NY; Univ Tex, Austin, 61; NY State Art Teachers Asn Conv, Corning, NY, 61; Univ Western Ont, London & Sheridan Col, Oakville, 72; plus other group & one-man shows. Collections Arranged: Recovery Studies of Two Albrecht Dürer Woodcuts. Teaching: Lectr, Off Cult Develop, Nassau Co Pub Schs, 71 & 72; resident artist, C W Post Col, Long Island Univ, 72; resident artist, Nassau Co, 73-74. Pos: Dir, Handmade Paper Workshop Fine Arts & Handpress of Douglass Howell, 46- Awards: Ford Found Fel Res Papers, 61. Bibliog: Helmut Becker (auth), Handmade papermaking for the Fine Arts, Artmag, Can, 3-4/77; John B Myers (auth), article in Arts, 5/77; The paper revolution, Am Artist, 8/77; plus many others. Mem: Int Inst Conserv Hist & Artistic Works, London. Interest: A correct metrology for research in the fine arts; aesthetics. Publ: Contribr, Fritz Eichenberg, auth, The Art of the Print, Abrams, 76; co-auth, with Calvin Thomas, article in The New Yorker, 6/76; auth, article in Craft Horizons, 10/76. Mailing Add: 625 Bayville Rd Locust Valley NY 11560

HOWELL, ELIZABETH ANN (MITCH)
PAINTER, ILLUSTRATOR
b Hartselle, Ala, Feb 27, 32. Study: Birmingham Southern Col, BA; Famous Artists Sch; watercolor & advan tech with John G Kramer. Work: Birmingham Mus Art, Ala; Montclaire Gallery, Birmingham. Comn: Illus & cover for bk of sermons, Rev Ralph K Bates, United Methodist Church, Hartselle, 67; portrait class mem, Morgan Co High Sch, Hartselle, 69; children's portraits, Mr & Mrs Thomas Caddell, Decatur, Ala, 70; children's portraits, Dr & Mrs William Sims, Decatur, 71; illus & cover for cook bk, Decatur Jr Serv League, Inc, 72. Exhib: Southeastern Art Exhib, Panama City, Fla, 68; Birmingham Art Asn Jury Show, 69; Williamsburg Art Exhib, Va, 70; Charleston Art Exhib, SC, 70; Int Platform Asn Art Exhib, Washington, DC, 71. Teaching: Pvt art classes, 63-68; head dept fine art, Morgan Co High Sch, 64-66. Pos: Dept head, Hubert Mitchell Industs, Inc, Hartselle, 49-55. Awards: Hannah Elliott Award, Lovemans of Birmingham, 69; Second Pl Award, Decatur Art Guild Jury Show, Decatur Art Guild, 69; Second Pl Award, Rickwood Park, Richter Bros, Cullman, Ala, 70. Bibliog: France-Amerique, Courrier Etats-Unis, New York, 69; Huida G Lawrence (auth), article in, Park East News, New York, 69; article in, Aufbau, New York, 69. Mem: Life mem Kappa Pi (pres, col chap, 53-54); founding mem Decatur Arts Coun (vpres & mem bd dirs); Decatur Art Guild (founder, actg pres, publ chmn & vpres, 67-); charter mem Birmingham Mus Asn; Birmingham Art Asn. Style & Technique: Realistic approach using loose washes combined with tightness of detail. Media: Watercolor, Acrylic. Publ: Illusr, Emmanuel-God With Us, 67 & Cotton Country Cooking, 72; co-auth & illusr, Paint a Prayer. Dealer: Lynn Kottler Gallery 3 E 65th St New York NY 10021 Mailing Add: PO Box 585 Hartselle AL 35640

HOWELL, FRANK
PAINTER
b Sioux City, Iowa, July 31, 37. Study: Univ Northern Iowa, BA. Comn: Two paintings, Breckenridge Co, Colo, 70; portrait, Sioux City Pub Libr; 25 Drawings & Paintings (series), Art Assocs, Inc, Denver & Ulrich Mus Art, Wichita, among others. Exhib: 17th Ann Mich Outstanding Artists Exhib, Ann Arbor, 69; 26th Ann Scarab Club Watercolor Show, Detroit, Mich, 69; Nat Traveling Exhib Drawings, appeared in ten states, 76-77; plus numerous one-man shows. Teaching: Instr art, W Del High Sch, Manchester, Iowa, 60-68; instr art, Detroit Pub Schs, 68-69. Pos: Founder, Breckenridge Galleries, Inc, Colo; partner, Carlson-Lowe Galleries, Inc, Taos, NMex. Awards: Critic's Choice, 17th Ann Outstanding Mich Artists, 69; first hon mention, 26th Ann Scarab Club Watercolor Show, 69. Style & Technique: Subtle detailed line work, humanistic in approach. Media: Oil, Acrylic, Watercolor, Pencil, Lithography. Specialty: Realism; Southwest contemporary art. Publ:

Illusr & artist, Many Winters, Doubleday, 74; auth, articles in High Country Mag, Southwest Art Mag & Artists of the Rockies Mag. Mailing Add: 37 Viking Dr Cherry Hills CO 80110

HOWELL, HANNAH JOHNSON
ART LIBRARIAN
b Oskaloosa, Iowa, June 22, 05. Study: Penn Col, Oskaloosa; Univ Chicago, PhD; Columbia Univ Sch Libr Serv, BLS. Pos: Head librn Frick Art Ref Libr, New York, 47-70, consult librn, 70- Mailing Add: 151 E 83rd St New York NY 10028

HOWELL, MARIE W
DESIGNER, INSTRUCTOR
b Milwaukee, Wis, July 30, 31. Study: Conn Col Women, 49-50; Philadelphia Mus Sch Art, 51; RI Sch Design, BFA, 54. Exhib: New Eng Craft Show; Haystack Retrospective Craft Show; Decorative Arts & Ceramic Exhib, Women's Int Expos; Contemp Am Textiles, Int Traveling Exhibs, 65-67 & Threads of History, 65-67; plus many others. Teaching: Instr, RI Sch Design, 55-61, asst prof textile design, 61-65; mem fac, Pa Guild Craftsmen, summer 58; mem fac weaving, Haystack Mountain Sch Crafts, 58-59; vis scholar, Univ Del, 60; mem fac, Parsons Sch Design, 65- Pos: Spec consult, Alliance for Progress in Colombia, SAm, 65; design assoc, Larson Design Corp, 65-68; designer, Carson, Lundin & Shaw, Architects, 68-70; designer, United Textile Corp, 70- Awards: Prize, Women's Int Expos, 59; Prize, RI Arts Festival, 60 & 61. Mem: Nat Home Fashions League. Publ: Contribr, Design (India), Upholstering, Handweaver & Craftsmen, Cross Country Craftsman, Decorative Art (Eng), Am Fabrics & Casa y Jardines (Arg). Mailing Add: 20 Universal Pl Carlstadt NJ 07072

HOWELL, RAYMOND
PAINTER, PHOTOGRAPHER
b Oakland, Calif, Sept 27, 27. Work: Oakland Art Mus; Anna Warden Br, San Francisco Pub Libr; Fine Am Art Calendar Collection; Julius Fleischmann Collection, Cincinnati, Ohio; also in pvt collection of Harold Zellerbach. Exhib: Negro in Am Art, Kaiser Ctr, Oakland; Univ NC, Chapel Hill; Mich State Univ; Black Am Artists/71, Ill Bell Tel, Chicago; Los Angeles Int Black Art Show, Oakland Art Mus. Awards: First Prize for Photograph, 68 & First Prize for Graphics, 69, City of Berkeley Art Festival; First Prize for Oil Painting, Univ Calif, Berkeley Black Art Festival, 70. Bibliog: Articles in, Black Artists on Art, Artforum & San Francisco Mag. Dealer: Gilbert Galleries 590 Sutter St San Francisco CA 94102. Mailing Add: 690 20th St San Francisco CA 94107

HOWETT, JOHN
ART HISTORIAN
b Kokomo, Ind, Aug 7, 26. Study: John Herron Inst, BFA; Univ Chicago, MA & PhD. Collections Arranged: Circa 1300: Paintings, Sculpture, Illum & Textiles, 65 & Mod Image, 72; Kress Study Collection Notre Dame (with catalog), 62; Renaissance Illuminations (with catalog), High Mus Art, Atlanta, 74. Teaching: Asst prof Renaissance & mod art, Univ Notre Dame, 61-66; assoc prof Renaissance & mod art, Emory Univ, 66-, chairperson dept hist art, 73- Res: Italian and Northern Renaissance painting and sculpture; contemporary art and culture. Publ: Co-auth, Modern Image, 72; co-auth, New Image, High Mus Art, 76; auth, Two panels by the master of the St George Codex in the Cloisters, Metrop Mus J, Vol 11 (1976): 85-102; auth, Edward Ross, High Mus Art, 77; auth, Boondocks Bohemias: a case for the regional avant-garde, Contemp Art/SE, Vol 1 (1977). Mailing Add: 325 Hertford Circle Decatur GA 30030

HOWLAND, RICHARD HUBBARD
ART HISTORIAN, WRITER
b Providence, RI, Aug 23, 10. Study: Brown Univ, AB, 31, hon DArts; Harvard Univ, AM, 33; Johns Hopkins Univ, PhD, 46. Teaching: Instr, Wellesley Col, 39-42; organizer dept hist art, Johns Hopkins Univ, 47, chmn dept, 47-56. Pos: Fel Agora Athens, Greece, 36-38; chief pictorial rec sect, OSS, 43-44; pres, Nat Trust for Hist Preserv, 56-60; chmn dept civil hist, Smithsonian Inst, 60-67, spec asst to secy, 68-; mem comt, Nat Cathedral; founding mem, Am Comt Int Comn Hist Sites & Monuments; trustee, L A W Fund, Sotterley Fund & Evergreen Found. Mem: Fel in Am Studies; Soc Archit Historians; Irish Georgian Soc (trustee); Archaeol Inst Am (trustee); Am Sch Classical Studies, Athens (trustee). Publ: Co-auth, Architecture of Baltimore, 54; auth, Greek Lamps & Their Survivals, 58 & 66. Mailing Add: Smithsonian Inst Washington DC 20560

HOWLETT, CAROLYN SVRLUGA
EDUCATOR, DESIGNER
b Berwyn, Ill, Jan 13, 14. Study: Art Inst Chicago, BAE, 37, MAE, 52; Northwestern Univ, MA, 53. Comn: Stained glass windows, State Ill Host House, Chicago World's Fair, 33. Exhib: Art Inst Chicago Ann, 45, 46, 52 & 55; Am Fedn Arts Print Show, 48; Newspaper Critics Shows, Findlay Galleries, Chicago, 49 & 50; Assoc Am Artists Galleries, Chicago, 50; two-man shows, Chicago Press Club, 66, 68 & 73. Teaching: Instr art educ, Oak Park & Libertyville Pub Schs, 34-37; instr design & crafts, Art Inst Chicago, 37-70, prof art educ, 52-70, emer prof, 70-; tech consult, Arts & Skills Prog, Am Red Cross, 42-45; lectr fine art & crafts, Univ Ill Exten, 67-73. Pos: Head dept art educ & Jr Sch, Art Inst Chicago, 43-63, assoc dean & educ consult, 63-68; dir, Gallery Studio, Coonley Estate, 70- Awards: Gov Art Award, Ill State Fair, 31; Gen Excellence Award, Art Inst Chicago, 32 & Conf Club Pres Award, 33 & 34; Outstanding Serv Award, Ill Art Educ Asn, 76. Bibliog: Louis Hoover (ed, Leaders in art education, Arts & Activities, 57; Edwin Ziegfield (auth), Research in art education, Nat Art Educ Asn Yearbk, 59. Mem: Arts Club Chicago; Nat Art Educ Asn (coun mem, 47-51, mem prof develop comt, 69-); Ill Art Educ Asn (pres, 62-63); Around Chicago Art Educ Asn (pres, 38-39). Style & Technique: Abstract. Publ: Contribr, Arts & Activities, Sch Arts, House Beautiful & Design, 42-70; auth, The need for art, Related Arts Serv Bull, 49; contribr, World Bk Encycl & Childcraft Encycl, 49-59; ed, Art Education Bibliography, Art Inst Chicago, 60; auth, Art in Craftmaking, Van Nostrand Reinhold, 74. Mailing Add: Gallery Studio 336 Coonley Rd Riverside IL 60546

HOWZE, JAMES DEAN
EDUCATOR, PAINTER
b Lubbock, Tex, Apr 8, 30. Study: Austin Col, BA; Art Ctr Col Design; Univ Mich, MS. Work: Del Mar Col, Corpus Christi; Hobbs Pub Schs, NMex; San Antonio Col. Exhib: 5th Nat Biennial Relig Art Exhib, Cranbrook Acad, Bloomfield Hills, Mich, 66; Southwest Biennial Exhib, Mus NMex, Santa Fe, 66; Pavilion Texan Cult, Hemisfair World's Fair, San Antonio, 68; Tex Fine Arts Asn Nat, Laguna Gloria Mus, Austin, 69 & 71; Four Art Ctr Soc of Alumni Int Competitions, 73-76; Colorprint USA, Tex Tech Univ, 74; one-man exhib, Del Mar Col, 76. Teaching: Assoc prof, Dept Archit & Allied Arts, Tex Tech Univ, 58-68, prof studio art, Dept Art, 68-, prof summer art workshop, Taos, NMex. Pos: Exhib juror & lectr, Tex, NMex & Okla. Awards: Cash Awards, Nat Drawing & Small Sculpture Exhib, Del Mar Col, 70 & 74; Best in exhib, Nat Mensa Mem Exhib, 71; Silver Award, Wichita Art Dir Club, 76. Mem: Hon mem Dallas-Ft Worth Soc Visual Commun; Am Asn Univ Prof; Tex Asn Col Teachers; Tex Asn Schs Art; Graphics Soc. Style & Technique: Personal imagery, sometimes with optical overtones, sometimes meticulously rendered in monochrome; illusory space or spatial ambiguities, often multiples, sometimes sculptural. Publ: Contribr, cartoons & humorous verse, Sports Car Graphic, 65-66; designer & illusr, var advert publ. Mailing Add: 2503 45th St Lubbock TX 79413

HOY, ANNE TAWES
ART HISTORIAN, ART EDITOR
b Baltimore, Md, Aug 8, 42. Study: Vassar Col, BA(hon), 63, with Linda Nochlin; Sarah Lawrence, Paris, with Leo Steinberg; Inst Fine Arts, NY Univ, MA, 67, with Robert Goldwater, William Rubin, Robert Rosenblum, Gert Schiff, PhD candidate. Teaching: Instr mod art, archit & sculpture, Hollins Col, Roanoke, Va, 66-68; instr mod art, archit & survey art hist, Manhattanville Col, 69-70, instr abstract expressionism, summer 75; instr mod art, archit & survey art hist, Queens Col, 70; lectr survey art hist, Barnard Col, 70-71. Pos: Copywriter, guest ed & asst travel ed, Mademoiselle Mag, 63-64; rev ed, Arts Mag, 65-66; contribr ed, Art Gallery, 68-69; managing ed, Art Bull, Col Art Asn, 70- Mem: Int Ctr Photog (docent, 77-). Publ: Auth, Modern Art Since 1945, Holt, Rinehart, (in press). Mailing Add: 54 Riverside Dr New York NY 10024

HOYT, DOROTHY (DOROTHY HOYT DILLINGHAM)
PAINTER
b East Orange, NJ, Aug 11, 09. Study: Cornell Univ, BS & MA; Art Students League; New Sch Social Res; Graphic Arts Workshop, Pratt Inst. Exhib: Whitney Mus Am Art, New York; Nat Asn Women Artists, Kyoto, Japan; Pa Acad Fine Arts, Philadelphia; one-man shows, Riverside Mus, New York & Manila, Philippines; Johnson Mus of Art, Cornell Univ, 76; plus many other group & one-man shows. Awards: Medal of Honor for Graphics, Nat Asn Women Artists, 58; First Prize, Cent Adirondack Art Asn, 66; Jane Peterson Award/Oils, NJ Soc Painters & Sculptors. Style & Technique: Semi-abstract expressionist landscapes. Media: Oil, Watercolor. Mailing Add: 92 Myers Rd Lansing NY 14882

HOYT, WHITNEY F
PAINTER, COLLECTOR
b Rochester, NY, July 7, 10. Study: New York Sch Fine & Appl Arts; Ecole Beaux Arts, Fontainebleau, with Camille Liausu, Paris & Fritz Trautman, Rochester. Work: Springfield Mus Fine Arts, Mass; Munson-Williams Proctor Inst, Utica, NY; Rochester Mem Art Gallery, NY. Exhib: Five From Rochester, 40 & Juror's Show, 46, Rochester Mem Art Gallery; Fifty Oncoming Americans, Inst Mod Art, Boston, 41; Railroad in Painting, Dayton Art Inst, 49; Iron Horse in Art, Ft Worth Art Ctr, 58. Awards: Rochester Finger Lakes Exhib Award, 46 & George L Herdle Mem Award, Rochester Mem Art Gallery; Allied Artists Prize, 51. Bibliog: Ernest Watson (auth), Paintings of Whitney Hoyt, Am Artist, 11/52; David P Morgan (auth), Railroad in painting, Trains, 6/61. Mem: Artists Equity Asn (dir); Century Asn; Allied Artists Am; Conn Acad Fine Arts; Artists Fel. Collection: Old master drawings of the 17th century; contemporary paintings. Mailing Add: 39 E 79th St New York NY 10021

HRDY, OLINKA
MURALIST, DESIGNER
b Prague, Okla, Aug 7, 02. Study: Univ Okla, Norman, BFA; Roerich Mus; New York Riverside Dr Dynamic Symmetry Scholar, with Howard Giles; also with Frank Lloyd Wright, Taliesen East. Comn: Harvest of Foods (32 door oil line), Univ Okla Women's Dorm, 24-28; Medieval murals, Copper Kettle, Norman, Okla, 25-29; mod music murals, Riverside Music Studio, Tulsa, Okla, 30; abstract stage curtain, City of Tulsa, 30; Deep Sea Magic, Lowell Jr High Sch, Long Beach, Calif, 38; Festival of Foods, Cent Jr High Sch, Los Angeles, 39. Exhib: One-man shows, Roerich Mus, Riverside Dr, New York, 32; Bullocks Wilshire, Los Angeles, 36, Gumps, San Francisco, 37, Standahl Art Gallery, Los Angeles, 38 & Hanson Music Shop, Beverly Hills, Calif, 41; Fed Art Exhib, Paris, France, 38. Pos: Chief designer, Sci & Indust Bldg, Expo Park, Los Angeles, 40-43; indust designer, Hycon Mfg Co & Swedlow Plastics, Los Angeles, 52-57; designer TV & movie backgrounds, Solar Hill Workshop, Woodland Hills, Calif, 60-69. Awards: Letzeiser Gold Medal, Univ Okla, 29; Hall Famous Oklahomans, Hist Soc, Chandler, Okla, 70. Publ: Illusr, By a Waterfall (1st bk with braille illusr), Okla State Libr for the Blind. Media: Oil, Watercolor; Lithograph, Stone. Publ: Children's books, games, post cards. Mailing Add: Box 134 Prague OK 74864

HSIAO, CHIN
PAINTER, SCULPTOR
b Shanghai, China, 35. Study: Taipei Normal Col, BA; with Li Chun-Sen, Taipei, Taiwan. Work: Mus Mod Art & Metrop Mus Art, New York; Nat Gallery Mod Art, Rome, Italy; Philadelphia Mus Art; Detroit Inst Art. Comn: Mural, Mr S Marchetta, Messina, Sicily, 71. Exhib: Carnegie Int, Pittsburgh, 61; Int Malerei 1960/61, W Eschenbach, 61; Art Contemporain, Grand Palais Paris, 63; 7th Biennial Sao Paulo, Brazil, 63; 4th Salon Galeries-Pilotes, Lausanne, Switz & Paris, 70. Teaching: Instr art, Southampton Col, Long Island Univ, 69; prof visual commun, Inst Europeo Design, Milan, Italy, 71-72; vis artist, La State Univ, Baton Rouge, 72- Awards: City of Capo d'Orlando, Italy Prize, 70. Bibliog: K Leonhard (auth), Hsiao Chin (portfolio of eight prints), 63 & Hsiao Chin, V Scheiwiller, 65; W Schönenberger (auth), Hsiao, Prearo, 72. Media: Metal Constructions; Acrylic. Dealer: Giorgio Marconi 15 Via Tadino Milan Italy. Mailing Add: 77 E 12th St New York NY 10003

HU, MARY LEE
METALSMITH, EDUCATOR
b Lakewood, Ohio, Apr 13, 43. Study: Miami Univ, Oxford, Ohio, 61-63; Sch for Am Craftsmen, Rochester Inst Technol, summer 63, with Hans Christensen; Cranbrook Acad Art, Bloomfield Hills, Mich, BFA, 65, with Richard Thomas; Southern Ill Univ, MFA, 67, with Brent Kington. Work: Goldsmith Hall, London, Eng; Mus Contemp Crafts, New York; Columbus Gallery Fine Arts, Ohio; Ill State Univ, Normal; Southern Ill Univ, Carbondale. Exhib: New York, Young Americans, 69, Face Coverings, 70, Goldsmith, 70, Forms in Metal, 75, Mus Contemp Crafts; Goldsmith, Renwick Gallery, Smithsonian Inst, Washington, DC, 74; World Silver Fair, Mexico City, Tasco, 74; Contemp Crafts of the Americas, Colo State Univ & Pan Am Bldg, Washington, DC, 75; Beaux Arts, 75 & two-person show, 77, Columbus Gallery Fine Arts, Ohio, 75; Am Crafts, Mus Contemp Art, Chicago, 76; Six Contemp Am Jewellers, Electrum Gallery, London, Eng, 76; Jewelers USA, Calif State Univ, Fullerton, 76; The Philadelphia Crafts Show, Philadelphia Mus Art, 77; Contemp Jewelry Exhib, Design Ctr Philippines, 77. Teaching: Vis artist metalsmithing, Univ Iowa, Iowa City, fall 75; instr metalsmithing, Kans State Univ, Manhattan, summer 76; lectr metalsmithing, Univ Wis, Madison, 76-77; asst prof metalsmithing, Mich State Univ, East Lansing, 77- Awards: Nat Endowment for the Arts Craftsmen's Fel, 76; Best in Show, Best in Metals & Outstanding Craftsman of N Cent Region; Purchase Award, Beaux Arts Designer/Crafts, N Cent Region of Am Crafts Coun, 75; Merit Award, The Metalsmith, 77. Bibliog: Elizabeth Breckenridge (auth), Mary Lee Hu: high on the wire, Craft Horizons, 4/77. Mem: Soc NAm Goldsmiths (vpres, 76-77, pres, 77); Am Crafts Coun; World Crafts Coun; Mich Silversmith Guild. Style & Technique: Wire-often using fiber techniques. Media: Silver, Gold & Coated Copper

Electrical Wires for Jewelry & Small Objects. Publ: Contribr, Body Jewelry—International Perspectives, Henry Regnery, 73; contribr, Wire Art, Crown, 75; contribr, Textile Techniques in Metal, Van Nostrand Reinhold, 75; contribr, Jewelry Techniques, Doubleday, 78. Mailing Add: Dept of Art Mich State Univ East Lansing MI 48824

HUBBARD, JOHN
PAINTER
b Ridgefield, Conn, Feb 26, 31. Study: Harvard Univ, Cambridge, Mass, AB, 53; Art Students League, New York, study with Morris Kantor, 56-58; study painting with Hans Hofmann, Provincetown, Mass. Work: Tate Gallery, London, England; Scottish Nat Gallery of Mod Art, Edinborough; Arts Coun of Great Brit, London; Arts Coun of Northern Ireland, Belfast; Dept of the Environment, London. Exhib: Ten Americans, Palazzo Venezia, Rome, 59; Festival of Two Worlds, Spoleto, Italy, 60; John Moores Exhib, Walker Art Gallery, Liverpool; Brit Painting in the 60's, Contemp Art Soc, London, 63; Art Spectrum-South, 71; Leas Gallery, Folkstone, England, 71; Int Kunstmussee, Basel, Switz, 73; Brit Painting, 74, Hayward Gallery, London, 74; From Brit 75, Taidemuseo & Alvar Aalto Mus, Helsinki, 75; Brit Colour (S Am tour), Brit Coun, 78; one-man shows, New Art Ctr, London, 61-73, Keele Univ, Stafford, England, 68, Dorset Co Mus, Dorchester, England, 72, Mappin Gallery Sheffield, England, 75, Aberdeen Art Gallery, Scotland, 75, Ikon Gallery, Birmingham, England, 75 & New Lyn Gallery, Eng, 78. Teaching: Vis painting instr, Camberwell Sch of Art, London, 63-65. Pos: Member, Coun of Mgt, SPACE/AIR, London, 71-75; collaborator, Mark Rothko Mem Portfolio, London, 73; chmn, Art Panel, Southwest Arts, Exeter, Devon, 73-75; mem, Arts Panel, Arts Coun of Great Brit, London, 73- Bibliog: Hilary Spurling (auth), Trailing Foliage, Fretted Rocks, The Times, London, 11/70; Marina Vaizey (auth), John Hubbard's Painting Financial Times, London, 3/73; John Hubbard: Paintings, an article in Gallery, Aberdeen, Scotland, 8/75. Style & Technique: Painted landscapes, built up through a succession of glaze-like layers. Dealer: New Art Ctr 41 Sloane St London SWI England. Mailing Add: Chilcombe Near Bridport Dorset England

HUBBARD, ROBERT
SCULPTOR
b New York, NY, Mar 27, 28. Study: Lafayette Col, BA; RI Sch Design, BFA. Work: Lafayette Col; Sara Roby Found. Exhib: Ravinia Festival, Chicago, 63 & 69; Whitney Mus Am Art, New York, 66 & 72; RI Art Mus, 67; Newport Art Asn, RI, 67; Providence Art Club, 69; plus others. Awards: RI Art Festival, 60; Providence Art Club, 69; Howard Fel, 69. Style & Technique: Abstract, simple, clear forms, precisely executed. Mailing Add: 3812 N Wayne Ave Chicago IL 60613

HUBBARD, ROBERT HAMILTON
ART HISTORIAN
b Hamilton, Ont Ont, June 17, 16. Study: McMaster Univ, BA; Univ Wis, MA & PhD; Univ Paris, cert. Collections Arranged: Can Painting, Tate Gallery, London, 64; 300 Yrs Can Art, 67 & Scottish Painting, 68, Nat Gallery Can; plus many others. Teaching. Lectr hist art, Univ Toronto, 45-46. Pos: Cur Can art, Nat Gallery Can, 47-54, chief cur, 54-; cult adv, Gov Gen of Can, Ottawa, 75- Mem: Fel Royal Soc Can; Officer of Order of Can; Col Art Asn Am; Can Hist Soc; Can Mus Asn; Royal Can Geog Soc. Res: History of Canadian art. Publ: Auth, National Gallery of Canada Catalog, Univ Toronto, Vols I-III, 56-60; auth, Development of Canadian Art, Queen's Printer, 63; auth, Rideau Hall, a History of Government House, 77; auth, Thomas Davies, Oberon, 72. Mailing Add: Government House Ottawa ON Can

HUBENTHAL, KARL SAMUEL
CARTOONIST
b Beemer, Nebr, May 1, 17. Study: Chouinard Art Inst, Los Angeles. Work: State Hist Soc Wis; Syracuse Univ; Truman Mem Libr; Eisenhower Mem Libr; Lyndon B Johnson Libr. Exhib: Am Ed Cartoonists Traveling Exhib, US, Mexico, Can & Eng, 62-77; Int Salon Caricature, Montreal, 65-77; Univ Minn, 68; Los Angeles Co Mus, 69 & 73; Madison Sq Garden Gallery Sport, 71; Univ Southern Calif, 75; Chaffey Col, Calif, 76; Calif State Univ, Northridge, 77. Pos: Political cartoonist, Hearst Newspapers, 55- Awards: Nat Headliners Award for Outstanding Achievement in Jour, 59; Nation's Best Ed Cartoonist, Nat Cartoonists Soc, 62, 67, 70 & 72; Helms Athletic Found Medal Contrib Sport in Art, 64. Mem: Marine Corps Newsmens Asn; Nat Cartoonists Soc (dir, 63-69); Los Angeles Soc Illusr (pres, 58-59); Asn Am Ed Cartoonists (pres, 63-64). Mailing Add: 16863 Marmaduke Pl Encino CA 91436

HUCHEL, FREDERICK M
MUSEUM DIRECTOR, CURATOR
b Brigham City, Utah, Aug 28, 47. Study: Brigham Young Univ, Provo, Utah. Work: Brigham City Mus-Gallery, Utah. Collections Arranged: Minerva Kohlhepp Teichert, Brigham City Mus-Gallery, 77. Pos: Dir, Brigham City Mus-Gallery, 77- Mem: Western Asn Art Mus; Utah Mus Asn; Utah State Hist Soc. Res: Study of Utah and Mormon art and artists. Specialty: Varied types of mostly representational art. Mailing Add: PO Box 583 Brigham City UT 84302

HUCHTHAUSEN, DAVID RICHARD
GLASS ARTIST, SCULPTOR, LECTURER
b Wisconsin Rapids, Wis. Study: Univ Wis, BS, study with Harvey K Littleton; Ill State Univ, MFA, study with Joel Philip Myers; Vienna Univ of Applied Arts (Fulbright scholar). Work: Chrysler Mus of Art, Norfolk, Va; Corning Mus of Glass, NY; Tweed Mus of Art, Duluth, Minn; Musee du Verre, Liege, Belg; Mus fur Kunsthandwerk, Frankfurt, Ger. Exhib: 7th, 8th & 10th Nat Sculpture Exhib, Delmar Col, Corpus Christi, Tex, 73-76; Lake Superior Int Crafts Exhib, Tweed Mus, Duluth, Minn, 75-77; Mod Glass of Europe, Am & Japan (tour of Ger mus), 76; New Am Glass, Huntington Mus, WVa, 76; 50 Am in Glass, Leigh Yawkey Woodson Art Mus, Wausau, Wis, 78; Mod Glass & Porcelain of Austria, Lugano Mus, Switz, 78; Contemp Art Glass Group, New York, 77, 79; one-man shows, J & L Lobmeyr, Vienna, Austria, 78 & SM Gallerie, Frankfurt, Ger, 78. Teaching: Instr glass, Ill State Univ, Normal, 76-77; lectr glass, Royal Col of Art, London, Eng, Univ of Prague Czechoslovakia and others. Pos: Consult, Leigh Yawkey Woodson Art Mus, Wausau, Wis, 76-; vis artist, J & L Lobmeyr, Vienna, 77-78; represenative, World Crafts Coun, Kyoto, Japan, 78. Awards: Newberry Award, Univ Wis, 73; Stein Fel, Ill State Univ, 76. Style & Technique: Furnace worked glass, fabricated sculpture, mixed-media constructions. Media: Glass. Mailing Add: Contemp Art Glass Group 806 Madison Ave New York NY 10021

HUDSON, JACQUELINE
PAINTER, GRAPHIC ARTIST
b Cambridge, Mass. Study: Sch Nat Acad; Art Students League, with Jean Liberte, Will Barnet & Michael Ponce de Leon; Columbia Univ. Work: Libr Cong (Pennell Purchase), Washington, DC. Exhib: Nat Acad, New York; Pa Acad Fine Arts, Philadelphia; Am Watercolor Soc, New York; Allentown Art Mus, Pa, 74; Bowdoin Col Mus Art, Brunswick, Maine, 75. Awards: Buell Mem Prize for Northern Lights (color lithograph), Nat Asn Women Artists Ann, 68 & Helen Turner Prize for Penobscot Bay (intaglio), 74. Mem: Nat Asn Women Artists; Rockport Art Asn; Maine Art Gallery, Wiscasset; Artists Equity Asn; Monhegan Assocs Inc, Maine (trustee, 60-63, chmn Monhegan mus comt, 62-65). Style & Technique: Landscapes and marines: graphics, acrylic and watercolor. Mailing Add: Monhegan Island ME 04852

HUDSON, RALPH MAGEE
ART HISTORIAN, EDUCATOR
b Fields, Ohio, Dec 18, 07. Study: Ohio State Univ, BA, BSc & MA; Univ Ala, EdD. Work: Univ Ark, Fayetteville; Mus Fine Arts, Little Rock, Ark. Exhib: Ark Watercolor Soc, 37-40; Grumbacher Aquarelle Travel Exhib, 38; one-man show, Hendrix Col, Conway, Ark, 40-41; Meridian Art Asn, Miss, 46-50; Miss State Col Women, Columbus, 46-68. Teaching: Instr art & actg head dept, Morehead State Col, 31-36; head dept art, Univ Ark, Fayetteville, 36-46; prof art & chmn dept, Miss State Col Women, 46-69; vis prof art, Blue Mountain Col, summers 58-60; vis prof art, Miss Valley State Col, fall 68; prof art & chmn dept, Univ Ala, Huntsville, 69-73; part time prof art, 73-; vis prof art hist, Inst Allende, Mex, 74. Awards: Univ Ala & Nat Endowment Humanities Res Grants Afro-Am Art; Distinguished Serv Award, Southeastern Col Art Conf, 74. Mem: Southeastern Col Art Conf (pres, 66-67, treas, 71-73); Nat Art Educ Asn (Ala chmn bldg fund, 71-73); Kappa Pi (int historian, 48-74, int first vpres, 74-); Ala Art Educ Asn. Style & Technique: Both representational and abstract. Media: Watercolor, Photography. Res: 19th century American art, architecture and furnishings; Afro-American art. Publ: Auth & illusr, Art in Arkansas, Ark Hist Quart, winter 44; ed, Ida Kohlmeyer, 68; auth, Afro-American Art: a bibliography, Nat Art Educ Asn, 70; Afro-American Art (slide sets with lecture scripts), Nat Endowment Humanities, 72-75. Mailing Add: 7102 Criner Rd SE Huntsville AL 35802

HUDSON, ROBERT H
SCULPTOR
b Salt Lake City, Utah, Sept 8, 38. Study: San Francisco Art Inst, BFA, 62, MFA, 63. Work: Los Angeles Co Mus; San Francisco Mus Art; Stedelijk Mus, Neth; Oakland Mus Art, Calif. Exhib: Five Whitney Mus Am Art Ann, New York, 64-72; Los Angeles Co Mus Art, 67; Philadelphia Mus Art, 67; Art Inst Chicago, 67; Walker Art Ctr, Minneapolis, 69; Retrospective, Moore Col of Art, 77. Teaching: Instr, San Francisco Art Inst, 61-65, chmn sculpture & ceramic dept, 65-66; asst prof art, Univ Calif, Berkeley, 66-73; asst prof art, San Francisco Art Inst, 76- Awards: Purchase Prize, San Francisco Art Festival, 61; San Jose State Col, 64; Nealie Sullivan Award, San Francisco, 65; Guggenheim Found fel, 76; plus others. Bibliog: Peter Selz (auth), Funk, Univ Calif, 67; Maurice Tuchman (auth), American Sculpture of the Sixties, Los Angeles Co Mus Art, 67. Dealer: Allan Frumkin Gallery 41 E 57th St New York NY 10022; Hansen-Fuller Gallery 228 Grant Ave San Francisco CA. Mailing Add: 392 Eucalyptus Ave Cotati CA 94928

HUDSON, WINNIFRED
PAINTER
b Sunderland, Eng, May 21, 05; US citizen. Study: Honolulu Acad Arts; Univ Hawaii; with Joseph Feher, Wilson Y Stamper, John Hultberg & Norman Ives; also with James Pinto, Mex. Work: Honolulu Acad Arts; State Found Cult & Arts; Contemp Arts Ctr; Castle & Cooke Ltd. Exhib: One-man shows, Recent Paintings, 67 & Winnifred Hudson Paintings, 72, Contemp Arts Ctr; Three Plus One, Ala Moana Art Ctr, 69; Honolulu Acad Arts Ann; Honolulu Printmakers Ann. Teaching: Pvt classes, 5 yrs. Awards: Purchase Award for Print, Watumull Found, 67; Purchase Award for Painting, Honolulu Acad of Arts, 72; First Prize for Painting, Ala Moana Festival. Bibliog: Nell Hutton (auth), Techniques of Collage, Batson/Watson-Guptill (London), 68. Mem: Hawaii Artists League; Honolulu Printmakers; 12 Women. Style & Technique: Semi-abstract landscapes. Media: Oil, Acrylic, Watercolor, Collage. Dealer: Downtown Gallery Merchant St Honolulu HI 96813. Mailing Add: 426-B Kekau St Honolulu HI 96817

HUEBLER, DOUGLAS
SCULPTOR
b Ann Arbor, Mich, 1924. Study: Univ Mich, Ann Arbor, MFA; Cleveland Sch of Art, Ohio; Acad Julian, Paris, France. Work: Los Angeles Co Mus Art, Los Angeles, Calif; Mus Mod Art, New York; Stedelijk Mus, Amsterdam, Neth. Exhib: 1st Columbia Biennial, Columbia Mus Art, SC, 57; Primary Structures, Jewish Mus, New York, 66; Six Sculptors, Pa State Univ, Abington, 67; When Attitudes Become Form, Kunsthalle Berne, Switz, 69; Prospect 69, Kunsthalle, Dusseldorf, 69; Software, Jewish Mus, New York, 70; Conceptual Art/Land Art/Arte Povera, Galleria Civica d'Arte Mod, Turin, 70; Earth Air Fire Water: Elements of Art, Mus Fine Arts, Boston, Mass, 71; Sossbeek, 71, Arnhem, 71; Randon, Kunsthistorisches Inst, Utrecht, 72; Documenta 5, Kassel, WGer, 72; Kunst als Boek, Stedelijk Mus, Amsterdam, 73; one-man shows, Addison Gallery, Andover, Mass, 70, Art & Proj, Amsterdam, 70 & 71, Calif Inst Arts, Valencia, 72, Mus Fine Arts, Boston, 72, Westfalischer Kunstverein, Munster, WGer, 72, Von der Heydt Mus, Wuppertal, WGer, 73, Stadische Kunsthalle, Kiel, WGer, 73, Mus of Mod Art, Oxford, Eng, 73, Israel Mus, Tel-Aviv, 73, Galerie Francoise, Lambert, Milan, 75 & Galeria Akumulatory II, Poznan, Poland, 76. Teaching: Instr, Harvard Univ, Cambridge, Mass. Bibliog: Lynda Morris (auth), Douglas Huebler, Studio Int, London, 2/73; I Leeber (auth), Douglas Huebler, Chroniques de l' Art Vivant, Paris, France, 4/73; J Gilbert-Rolfe (auth), article in Artforum, 2/74. Publ: Auth, Letter to the Editor, Art News, 9/66; auth, Untitled, Xerox-Book, New York, 68; auth, Durata/Duration, Turin, 70; auth, Statements plus Location Pieces 1, 2, VH 101/3, Paris, autumn 70; auth, Trois Travaux, VH 101/6, Paris, 72. Dealer: Galerie Konrad Fischer, Platanenstrasse 7 4 Dusseldorf 1 WGer. Mailing Add: c/o Calif Inst of the Arts Los Angeles CA 91355

HUEMER, CHRISTINA GERTRUDE
ART LIBRARIAN
b Orange, NJ, May 24, 47. Study: Mt Holyoke Col, BA, 69; Columbia Univ, MS, 70; Cornell Univ, MA, 75. Pos: Asst art librn, Cornell Univ, Ithaca, NY, 70-75; indexer, Art Index, H W Wilson Co, Bronx, NY, 75-76; art librn, Oberlin Col, 76- Mem: Col Art Asn; Art Libr Soc of NAm (regional rep to exec bd, 77-). Res: Piranesi's Vedute de Roma. Publ: Co-auth, Classification & the art library user, Art Libr Soc of NAm Newsletter, 76. Mailing Add: Clarence Wart Art Libr Oberlin Col Oberlin OH 44074

HUETER, JAMES WARREN
SCULPTOR, PAINTER
b San Francisco, Calif, 1925. Study: Pomona Col, BA; Claremont Grad Sch, MFA, with Henry Lee McFee, Albert Stewart & Millard Sheets. Work: Scripps Col, Claremont, Calif; Nat Orange Show, San Bernardino, Calif; Long Beach State Col. Exhib: San Gabriel Valley Artists, Pasadena Art Mus, 50-56 & 58; Artists Los Angeles & Vicinity, Los Angeles Co Mus, 52 & 54-59; Denver Mus Art Ann, 54 & 59; Butler Inst Am Art Midyear Ann, 55, 57-59 & 62; Long Beach Mus Art Drawing Exhib, 60; Southern Calif 100, Laguna Beach Mus, 77; one-man shows, Pasadena Art Mus, 55 & Mt San Antonio Col, Walnut, Calif, 77. Teaching:

Instr painting & drawing, Mt San Antonio Col Eve Div, Walnut, Calif, 51-; instr sculpture, Pomona Col, 59-60; instr drawing, Claremont Grad Sch, summer 63; lectr art, Pitzer Col, 72. Awards: First Prize & Purchase Award for Painting, Pasadena Art Mus, 52; First Prize for Sculpture, Los Angeles Co Mus, 55; First Prize for Painting, Frye Mus, Seattle, 57. Bibliog: A Segunda (auth), Reviews, Vol 1, No 8 & Delores Yonker (auth), James Hueter, Vol 2, No 2, Artforum. Style & Technique: Abstract symbolist; oil painting on solid mahogany, mahogany skin, glass and canvas; ink wash, pencils and charcoal on paper. Media: Wood, Oil. Mailing Add: 190 E Radcliffe Dr Claremont CA 91711

HUFF, HOWARD LEE
EDUCATOR, PHOTOGRAPHER
b Kansas City, Mo, July 18, 41. Study: Col Idaho, BA; Univ Idaho, MFA. Work: J R Simplot Co, Boise; Boise Cascade Co, Boise; State of Ore Permanent Collection, Salem; Boise Gallery Art. Comn: Photographs (five 16in x 20in), Boise Cascade Corp, 71; photomurals (three 6ft x 12ft), Simplot Co, 76-78. Exhib: Photomedia USA, San Diego, Calif, 71; La Grange Nat Competition III, Ga, 77; Photog 78, Colby, Kans, 78; 4th Ann Coos Bay Regional Photo Competition, Ore, 78; two-man show, Univ Mo, Columbia, 78. Teaching: Prof photog, Boise State Univ, 65- Awards: Judges Merit Award, 41st Ann Exhib for Idaho Arts, Boise Art Asn, 76; Best of Show, Image 2000, 76 & 3rd Ann Coos Bay Photo Competition, Coos Art Asn, 77. Style & Technique: Black and white and color photographs done in a traditional manner utilizing a landscape motif. Media: Photography. Mailing Add: 3319 Mountain View Boise ID 83704

HUGGINS, VICTOR, (JR)
PAINTER, EDUCATOR
b Durham, NC, July 23, 36. Study: Univ NC, Chapel Hill, AB & MA. Work: Ackland Art Ctr, Univ NC, Chapel Hill; B Carroll Reece Mus, ETenn State Univ; Brooks Mem Gallery Art, Memphis, Tenn; Vanderbilt Univ; Weatherspoon Art Gallery, Univ NC, Greensboro. Exhib: One-man shows, Bertha Schaefer Gallery, New York, 70, Jane Haslem Gallery, Washington, DC, 71, 20th Century Gallery, Williamsburg, Va, 71 & B Carroll Reece Mus, Johnson City, Tenn, 72; group show, Gallery Contemp Art, Winston-Salem, NC, 71. Teaching: Asst prof art, Vanderbilt Univ, 68-69; assoc prof painting & drawing, Va Polytech Inst & State Univ, 69- Awards: First Purchase Awards, NC Nat Bank, 67, Springs Art Contest, Springs Mills, 67 & Ann Southern Contemp Painting Exhib, 68. Style & Technique: Mountainscapes employing canvas collage for earth forms. Media: Acrylic. Dealer: Jane Haslem Gallery 2121 P St NW Washington DC 20037. Mailing Add: Dept of Art Va Polytech Inst & State Univ Blacksburg VA 24060

HUGHES, DONALD N
PRINTMAKER, DRAFTSMAN
b 1943. Study: San Diego State Col, 64-66; Calif Col Arts & Crafts, BFA(with high distinction), 69, MFA, 73. Exhib: Aspects of California Painting & Sculpture, La Jolla Mus Art, 65; one-man shows, Drawings & Prints, Univ Calif, San Diego, La Jolla, 65; Sun Sign Gallery, Colo, 68; Capper Gallery, San Francisco, 69; Southwestern College Gallery, Chula Vista, Calif, 74. Teaching: Instr painting & drawing, Calif Adult Educ, Coronado, 65-66; printmaking consult, Nat City Pub Schs, Calif, 74; instr art, Southwestern Col, Calif, 74-78. Awards: Calif Arts Coun Grant, 78. Publ: Writer, Clear Creek Mag, 72; Poems & Prints by Don Hughes, copyright 72, Berkeley, Calif; Linear Hymns, copyright 75, San Diego, Calif. Mailing Add: 3310 N Mountain View San Diego CA 92116

HUGHES, EDWARD JOHN
PAINTER
b North Vancouver, BC, Feb 17, 13. Study: Vancouver Sch Art. Work: Nat Gallery Can, Ottawa; Art Gallery Ont, Toronto; Vancouver Art Gallery; Montreal Mus Fine Art; Gtr Victoria Art Gallery. Exhib: Retrospective, Vancouver Art Gallery, 67. Pos: War artist, Can Army, 40-42, off war artist, 42-46. Awards: Emily Carr Scholar, Lawren Harris, 47; Can Coun Fels & Awards, 58, 63 & 67, Short Term Grant, 70. Bibliog: Doris Shadbolt (auth), E J Hughes, Can Art Mag, spring 53. Mem: Royal Can Acad Art. Style & Technique: Realistic. Media: Oil. Dealer: Dr Max Stern 1438 Sherbrooke St W Montreal PQ Can. Mailing Add: 2449 Heather St Duncan BC V9L 2Z6 Can

HUGHES, ROBERT S F
ART CRITIC, LECTURER
b Sydney, Australia, July 28, 38. Study: Sydney Univ, four yrs. Pos: Art critic & sr writer, Time Mag, 70- Publ: Auth, The Art of Australia, Penquin, 66; auth, Heaven & Hell in Western Art, Weidenfeld & Nicholson, 68; auth, The Future That Was (9-part TV series on 20th century art), Brit Broadcasting Corp & Pub Broadcasting Corp, (in prep). Mailing Add: c/o Time Mag Time-Life Bldg Rockefeller Ctr New York NY 10020

HUGO, JOAN (DOWEY)
ART LIBRARIAN, ART WRITER
b Weehawken, NJ, Jan 12, 30. Comn: Simmons Col, Boston, Mass, BLS. Collections Arranged: Artwords & Bookworks (traveling exhib; co-cur with Judith Hoffberg), Los Angeles Inst of Contemp Arts, Calif, 78. Exhib: Instr artist & the bk, Otis Art Inst, fall 77. Pos: Cataloguer, Brooklyn Mus Libr, 52-53; librn, Am Libr in Paris, Left Bank Br, 53-54; art librn, Otis Art Inst of Los Angeles Co, 57- Mem: Col Art Asn; Art Libr Soc of NAm (panelist; chap chmn, 75-76; local chmn ann conf, 77). Res: History of artists' books; history of visual communications. Interest: Contemporary art, especially the relationships between the arts and social history; also, the concept of the future and the arts. Publ: Contribr, Art & Cinema, Visual Resources, 73-; contribr, spec issue on artists' bks, Dumb Ox, 77; ed, A Guide to Art Resources in Los Angeles, Art Libr Soc NAm, 77; ed, Artwords & Bookworks: A Set of Artists' Postcards, 77; contribr, Gutenberg in the gallery: a review of artists' books & bk objects at University of California, San Diego, Artweek. Mailing Add: 2401 Wilshire Blvd Los Angeles CA 90057

HUI, HELENE
PAINTER, FILM MAKER
b New York, NY, June 24, 35. Study: Brooklyn Mus Art Sch, 57-60. Work: Hampton Col Mus, WVa. Exhib: 13 Women Artists, New York, 72; NY Women Artists, State Univ NY Albany, 72; Bard Col, Annandale on Hudson, NY, 73; 3rd Ann Contemp Reflections 1973-74, Aldrich Mus Contemp Art, Ridgefield, Conn, 74. Style & Technique: Abstract paintings using acrylic on canvas. Media: Painting; Film. Mailing Add: 136 E 26th St New York NY 10010

HUI, KA-KWONG
CRAFTSMAN, EDUCATOR
b Hong Kong, Aug 16, 22. Study: Shanghai Sch Fine Arts; New York State Col Ceramics, MFA. Work: Cooper Union Mus & Mus Contemp Crafts, New York; Everson Mus, Syracuse, NY; Johnson Wax Collection; Univ Mich Art Mus, Ann Arbor. Exhib: Everson Mus Art, 70; Nat Mus Mod Art, Tokyo, 70; Objects USA, 76; one-man show, Mus Contemp Crafts, 67. Teaching: Instr, Rutgers Univ, 57- Mem: Am Craftsman's Coun; World Crafts Coun. Mailing Add: RD 1 Deans Rhode Hall Jamesburg NJ 08831

HULDAH (HULDAH CHERRY JEFFE)
PAINTER
b Dallas, Tex. Study: Grand Cent Sch Art; Art Students League; also with Robert Brackman, New York. Work: Ga Mus Fine Arts; Columbia Mus Art; Norfolk Mus Art; Sheldon Swope Mus Art; Cornell Univ Med Club. Exhib: Salon des Artistes Francaise; Wally Findlay Galleries, New York, Chicago, Beverly Hills & Palm Beach. Pos: Artist, Hallmark Cards, ten yrs; ceramist, W Goechet & Co, Bavaria, Ger, ten yrs. Awards: Honorable Mentions, Salon des Artistes Francais, Paris, 48 & 67; Hallmark Hall of Fame Artists. Style & Technique: French impressionist; figures and still life; brush mostly; palette knife sometimes. Mailing Add: 680 S Country Rd Palm Beach FL 33480

HULDERMANN, PAUL F
ART DEALER, LECTURER
b Hamburg, WGer, June 29, 02; US citizen. Pos: Founder & pres, Scottsdale Nat Indian Art Coun, 62-72; founding mem & first chmn, Scottsdale Fine Arts Comn, 68-76; bd mem, Scottsdale Ctr for the Arts Asn. Mem: Assoc Coun Arts. Specialty: Indian art, including historic, prehistoric and contemporary. Mailing Add: 7051 Fifth Ave Scottsdale AZ 85251

HULL, MARIE (ATKINSON)
PAINTER
b Summit, Miss. Study: Pa Acad Fine Arts; Art Students League; also with John F Carlson, Robert Reid, Robert Vonnoh & George Elmer Browne; France; Spain; Morocco. Work: Witte Mus, San Antonio, Tex; Birmingham Mus, Ala; Miss Art Asn Permanent Collection; Univ Miss; plus others. Comn: Portraits, Univ Miss, Oxford, Tulane Univ La, New Orleans, Miss State Univ, Starkville, Miss Col, Clinton; plus others. Exhib: Salon Paris, 31; Art Inst Chicago Am Ann; Butler Art Inst Ann, Youngstown, Ohio; New York World's Fair, 39; Golden Gate Expos, 39; Atlanta Southeastern Ann, Ga; plus many others. Pos: Pres, Miss Art Asn. Awards: First Award, Montgomery Mus Ann, 60; First Award, Birmingham Mus Ann, 63; First Award, Ala Watercolor Soc Nat, 65. Mem: Am Watercolor Soc; Miss Art Asn; Ala Art League. Media: Oil, Watercolor, Acrylic, Casein. Mailing Add: 825 Belhaven St Jackson MS 39202

HULL, WILLIAM FLOYD
MUSEUM DIRECTOR
b Pomeroy, Wash, June 27, 20. Collections Arranged: The Art of the Manchos, 59; XXI Ceramic National, 60; The World of Hobson Pittman, 72; Manayunk and Other Places: Paintings and Drawings by Francis Speight, 74; Twenty-four British Potters, 76. Pos: Managing dir, G R Crocker & Co, Syracuse, NY, 48-57; dir, Everson Mus Art, Syracuse, 57-61; assoc dir, NY State Coun Arts, 61-66; exec dir, Ken Arts Comn, 66-71; dir, Mus Art, Pa State Univ, University Park, currently. Mem: Am Ceramic Circle. Mailing Add: Mus of Art Pa State Univ University Park PA 16802

HULMER, ERIC CLAUS
CURATOR-CONSERVATOR
b Heidelberg, Ger, Aug 4, 15. Study: Yale Univ, BA, 38; Univ Pittsburgh, PhD, 55; research: Harvard Univ; Kunst Acad, Oslo, Norway. Pos: Curator-conservator, George R Hann Collection, Sewickley Heights, Pa, currently, Westmoreland Co Mus Art, Greensburg, Pa, currently, Butler Inst Am Art, Youngstown, Ohio, currently & Pa State Univ Mus Art, currently. Mem: Fel Am Conserv Orgn. Res: Preservation materials and methods. Mailing Add: RD 1 Harmony PA 16037

HULSEY, WILLIAM HANSELL
COLLECTOR
b Carbon Hill, Ala, May 2, 01. Pos: Mem bd dirs, Birmingham Mus Art. Collection: Paintings including works by Laurencin, Modigliani, Rouault, Degas, Vlaminck, Buffet, Bezombes and Corbellini. Mailing Add: 2980 Cherokee Rd Birmingham AL 35223

HULTBERG, JOHN PHILLIP
PAINTER
b Berkeley, Calif, Feb 8, 22. Study: Fresno State Col, BA, 43; Calif Sch Fine Arts, 47-49; Art Students League, 49-51. Work: Metrop Mus Art, Mus Mod Art & Guggenheim Mus Art, New York; Albright-Knox Mus, Buffalo, NY; Stedlijk Mus, Eindhoven. Comn: Paintings of Newport News Shipyard, Fortune Mag, 57. Exhib: One-man shows, Martha Jackson Gallery, New York, 55-72, Corcoran Gallery Art, Washington, DC, 56, ICA Gallery, London, 56, Galerie Dragon, Paris, 56-71 & Oakland Mus, Calif, 60. Teaching: Instr painting, Art Students League, summer 60; instr painting, San Francisco Art Inst, 63-64; artist in residence, Honolulu Art Acad, 66-67. Awards: First Prize, Corcoran Biennial, Washington, DC, 55; Am Fedn Arts-Ford Found Grant, 64; Benjamin Altman Prize for Landscape, Nat Acad Design, 72. Bibliog: Emily Genauer (auth), article in New York Herald Tribune Mag, 55; article in Int Studio, London, 66. Media: Oil. Mailing Add: c/o Martha Jackson Gallery 521 W 57th St New York NY 10021

HUMBLE, DOUGLAS
GALLERY DIRECTOR, SCULPTOR
Study: Claremont Grad Sch, MFA. Pos: Galleries Mgr, Claremont Col, 72- Mem: Los Angeles Inst Contemp Art. Style & Technique: Working with social-political ideas, getting the physical part of ideas to wider, non-art audience; sculpture with assemblage emphasis. Mailing Add: Montgomery Art Ctr Claremont Col Claremont CA 91711

HUMES, RALPH H
SCULPTOR
b Philadelphia, Pa, Dec 25, 02. Study: Md Inst Art, with Rhinhart; Pa Acad Fine Arts. Work: Brookgreen Gardens, SC; Children's Zoo, Lincoln, Nebr; Pa Acad Fine Art, Philadelphia; plus others. Comn: Mahogany Comanche figurehead, J Price Yacht, Miami, Fla; Fountain of the Sea, Coral Gables Libr, Fla; Tony Janus Mem, St Petersburg, Fla; Padre Kino Statue, Nogales, Ariz; bird panet fountain, Fairchild Tropical Garden, Miami. Exhib: Nat Acad Design, New York; Nat Sculpture Soc Shows; Art Inst Chicago, Ill; Rosequist Galleries, Tucson, Ariz; Conn Acad Fine Arts. Awards: Speyer Mem Prize, Nat Acad Design, twice; Soc Wash Artists Gold Medal; Lindsey Morris Sterling Prize; plus others. Bibliog: Article in, Brookgreen Gardens Publ Sculptors. Mem: Assoc nat academician, Nat Acad Design; fel Nat Sculpture Soc; Soc Medalists; fel Pa Acad Fine Arts; Soc Washington Artists; plus others. Media: Bronze. Mailing Add: 2616 Azalea Pl Coachwood Colony Leesburg FL 32748

HUMLEKER, RUTH S
ART ADMINISTRATOR
b Chicago, Ill, Aug 18, 22. Study: Lawrence Col, BA. Pos: Publicity dir, Minneapolis Inst Arts, 61-69, asst dir, 75-77, assoc dir & chmn commun div, 77-; asst dir, Minn State Arts Coun, 69-74. Mailing Add: 2400 Third Ave Minneapolis MN 55404

HUMMEL, CHARLES FREDERICK
CURATOR
b Brooklyn, NY, Sept 16, 32. Study: City Col New York, BA(magna cum laude), 53; Univ Del, MA, 55. Teaching: Adj assoc prof art hist, Univ Del, 64- Pos: Curatorial asst, H F du Pont Winterthur Mus, Del, 55-58, asst cur, 58-60, assoc cur, 60-67, cur, 67- Mem: Nat Conserv Adv Coun; Early Am Indust Asn (dir, 64-); Int Rug Soc (dir, 71); Hajji Baba Soc, New York; Am Inst Conserv Hist & Artistic Objects. Publ: Auth, With Hammer in Hand, Univ Va Press, 68, 73 & 77; contribr, Furniture to 1790, Britannica Encycl of Am Art, Encycl Brit Inc, 73; auth, A Winterthur Guide to American Chippendale Furniture: Middle Atlantic & Southern Colonies, Crown/Rutledge, 76; auth, Floor coverings in 18th century America, Irene Emery Textile Roundtable, 1975, Textile Mus, 77. Mailing Add: c/o H F du Pont Winterthur Mus Winterthur DE 19735

HUMPHREY, DONALD GRAY
GALLERY DIRECTOR, LECTURER
b Hutchinson, Kans, May 3, 20. Study: Univ Kans, BFA; State Univ Iowa, MFA & PhD. Exhibs Arranged: French & American Impressionism, 67; American Sense of Reality, Contemporary Latin American Painting, 69; Texas Collects 20th Century American Art, 71; American Folk Art from the Ozarks to the Rockies, 75. Teaching: Instr art hist, State Univ Iowa, 50-51; asst prof art hist, Okla Univ, 51-57; instr art hist, State Univ Iowa, 57-58; adj prof art hist, Tulsa Univ, 67-72. Pos: Dir, Philbrook Art Ctr, 59-75, Stark Mus Art, 76-77 & Pinon Gallery, 78- Mem: Southwestern Art Asn (pres, 72-74); Am Asn Mus; Am Fedn Arts; Okla Mus Asn; Asn Art Mus Dirs. Publ: Contribr, Mus News. Mailing Add: 2405 Avenida de las Campanas Santa Fe NM 87501

HUMPHREY, RALPH
PAINTER
b Youngstown, Ohio, 1932. Study: Youngstown Univ, 51-52 & 54-56. Work: Bennington Col; Rose Art Mus, Brandeis Univ; Wadsworth Atheneum, Hartford, Conn; Mus of Mod Art, New York; Univ NC. Exhib: Abstract Expressionists and Imagists, 61 & Systemic Painting, 66, Solomon R Guggenheim Mus, New York; Ithaca Col, 67; Focus on Light, NJ State Mus, Trenton, 67; Romantic Minimalism, Univ Pa, 67; The Art of the Real, Mus of Mod Art, 68; Whitney Mus of Am Art, 69 & The Structure of Color, 71; Color and Field: 1890-1970, Albright-Knox Art Gallery, Buffalo, NY, 70; one-man shows, Tibor de Nagy Gallery, 59 & 60; Emmericah Gallery, New York, 71 & Tex Gallery, 73. Teaching: Instr, Art Students League, New York; Harley House, New York, 59-60; Bennington Col, 61-63; New Sch for Social Res & Hunter Col, New York. Mailing Add: c/o Bykert Gallery 24 E 81St New York NY 10028

HUMPHREY, S L
PAINTER, ILLUSTRATOR
b Silver City, NMex, Nov 18, 41. Study: Western NMex Univ, BA. Work: Glendon E Johnson, Am Nat Ins Co, Galveston, Tex; Gerald I Freeman, MD (corp collection), San Jose, Calif; Sen Benny Altamirano, Silver City, NMex; in pvt collection of Dennis Weaver, Calif. Comn: Cover for Frontier Days Publ, 73-75; paintings of Rio Grande Valley & settlement of Santa Fe between 1890 & 1900, comn by Clive Edgar, Colo, 75; First Place Award for the World's Champion Barrel Racer, Okla, 75; background painting depicting uses of tools & Western paraphernalia, C O Crum Tool Mus, Henderson, Nev, 75; painting of hist stage line in Southwest Ariz, comn by Juel L Bell, San Diego, Calif, 75. Exhib: Women Artists Am West, Saddleback Western Gallery, Santa Ana, Calif, 74-75; George Phippen Mem Show, Prescott, Ariz, 75; Death Valley Exhib, Furnace Creek, Calif, 75; Nat Small Paintings Show, Albuquerque, NMex, 75; NMex State Fair, Albuquerque, 75; plus numerous one-woman shows. Teaching: Instr painting, Lordsburg Pub Schs, NMex, 63-66. Awards: First & Second Place Best Show, South Western NMex State Fair, 74; First & Second Place, Women Artists Am Western Art Show, 74 & Second Place, 75. Bibliog: Mares, mules & mountain bells, Western Horseman Mag, 73; The 32nd El Paso Art Show, Sundial Sect, El Paso Times, 74; Regina Cooks (auth), article in Southwest Art Mag, 74. Mem: NMex Art League; Women Artists Am West; Grant Co Art Guild; Nat League Am Pen Women. Style & Technique: Depiction of historical Southwestern places, people, events, particularly the cowboy between 1850-1919. Media: Oil, Watercolor. Publ: Illusr, Western Horseman Mag, 73 & Appaloosa Mag, 74; paintings also reproduced on cards & stationery by Saga Publ Co, 74- Mailing Add: 815 B St Silver City NM 80061

HUNDLEY, DAVID HOLLADAY
ART DEALER, EDUCATOR
b Phoenix, Ariz, Dec 25, 46. Study: Manchester Col Art & Design, Eng, dipl art & design, 69, with Keith Murgatroyd; Allgemeine Gewerbeschule, Basel, Switz, 70, with Armin Hofmann; Brigham Young Univ, Provo, Utah, BFA, 71, MA, 72. Comn: Graphic design for UN Declaration of Human Rights Plaque, Manchester City Hall, Eng, 70. Teaching: Instr drawing & design, Brigham Young Univ, 72-73; guest lectr Bauhaus design, Chicago Educ Insts, Ill, 74-76; instr graphic design, Art Ctr Col Design, Pasadena, 77- Pos: Art critic, Ariz Daily Star, Tucson, 73-74; design consult, Ariz Inn, Tucson, 73-74; art dir graphics, Tuesday Publ, Chicago, 74-75; graphic designer, Health & Hospital Gov Comn Cook Co, Chicago, 75-76; art dealer, Andreé Stassart Assoc, 77- Mem: Arts Club of Chicago. Specialty: Twentieth century European masterpainters. Collection: Twentieth century prints and drawings. Publ: Auth, The Influence of the Bauhaus on Contemporary Swiss Graphic Design, Brigham Young Univ Press, 72. Mailing Add: 339 W California Blvd Pasadena CA 91105

HUNGERFORD, CYRUS COTTON
CARTOONIST
b Manilla, Ind. Study: Washington & Jefferson Col, Dr Arts, 45. Pos: Newspaper cartoonist, Pittsburgh Sun, 12-27, Pittsburgh Post-Gazette, 27-; European cartoon news assignments, 23, 37, 47 & 53. Awards: Nat Headliners Award, 47; Freedoms Found Award, 53; Lincoln Nat Life Found Award, 57. Mailing Add: Bigelow Apts Bigelow Sq Pittsburgh PA 15219

HUNISAK, JOHN MICHAEL
ART HISTORIAN, EDUCATOR
b Troy, NY, June 28, 44. Study: Williams Col, BA; NY Univ, MA, PhD. Teaching: Instr art hist, Middlebury Col, 70-75, asst prof Baroque & Mod art, 75- Pos: Reader, Advan Placement Exams in Art Hist, Educ Testing Serv, 76, 77 & 78. Mem: Col Art Asn. Res: Later 19th century French sculpture. Publ: Auth, The Sculptor Jules Dalou: Studies in His Style & Imagery, Garland, 77; auth, Jules Dalou: The Private Side, Detroit Art Inst Bull, Fall-Winter 77; auth, Transformations in the Figurative Tradition in Modern Sculpture, Honolulu Acad of Arts J, III, 78; auth, Rodin, Dalou, and the Monument to Labor (Festschrift for H W Janson), Abrams, 78. Mailing Add: 3 Storrs Ave Middlebury VT 05753

HUNKLER, DENNIS FRANCIS
PAINTER, PRINTMAKER
b Oakland, Calif, Mar 3, 43. Study: New Sch Art, Toronto, 65-70; with Jack Bush, 69-70; San Francisco Art Inst, BFA, 72. Work: Oakland Mus, Calif. Comn: Walks US of A (set design), Lesser Oakland Dance Theatre, 74. Exhib: One-man show, Gordon Hill Agency, Toronto, Ont, 70, Valley Art Gallery, Walnut Creek, Calif, 73 & Humboldt Galleries, San Francisco, 75; Polly Friedlander Gallery, Seattle, Wash, 74; California Printmakers, Printmakers Coun Gt Brit, London, 75; 2nd Int Text-Sound-Image Festival, Antwerp, Belg, 78. Pos: Asst dir, Artists Resource Ctr, Oakland, 73. Bibliog: Alexander Fried (auth), The fantasy of three artists, San Francisco Examr, 12/6/74; Thomas Albright (auth), Unique visions of nature, San Francisco Chronicle, 12/11/74; R F Stepan (auth), Dennis Hunkler's private world, Artweek, Vol 6 No 26. Style & Technique: Poetic fantasy. Media: Acrylic on Canvas; Felt-pen on Paper. Dealer: Humboldt Galleries 94 Fulton St New York NY 10038. Mailing Add: 3875 Castro Valley Blvd Castro Valley CA 94546

HUNT, COURTENAY
PAINTER, INSTRUCTOR
b Jacksonville, Fla, Sept 17, 17. Study: Ringling Sch Art; Farnsworth Sch Painting. Comn: Portraits, Univ Fla; Jacksonville Univ; Jacksonville City Hall; Duval Co Ct House, Jacksonville; Shrine Mem, Washington, DC. Exhib: Allied Artists Am; Sarasota Art Asn, Fla; Audubon Artists Am; Soc of the Four Arts, Palm Beach, Fla; Fla Artist Group Inc, Norton Gallery, Palm Beach. Mem: St Augustine Art Asn. Style & Technique: Contemporary academic. Media: Oil, Pastel. Mailing Add: PO Box 247 Orange Park FL 32073

HUNT, DAVID CURTIS
MUSEUM DIRECTOR, WRITER
b Oswego, Kans. Dec 7, 35. Study: Univ Tulsa, BA(com design), 58, with Alexandre Hogue, MA(art hist), 68. Exhib: Okla Artists Ann, Philbrook Art Ctr, Tulsa, 62-65. Teaching: Instr mus practices, Univ Tulsa, 70-72. Pos: Ed, Am Scene Quart, Gilcrease Mus, 65-72, cur art, Gilcrease Inst, 67-72; mem, Tulsa Artists League, 68-72; cur collections, Stark Mus, Orange, Tex, 72-76; dir, Missoula Mus of the Arts, Mont, 77- Mem: Am Asn Mus. Res: American art, with emphasis on 19th and 20th century Western regional artists and works. Publ: Co-auth, The Art of the Old West, Knopf, 71; contribr, Encyclopedia of the American West, Crowell, 76. Mailing Add: 127 Saranac Missoula MT 59801

HUNT, KARI
SCULPTOR, WRITER
b Orange, NJ, Jan 29, 20. Study: Mt Holyoke Col, 37-39; Univ Buffalo, summer 38; Cornell Univ, summer 39; maskmaking with Doane Powell, New York, 50-51. Comn: Maskmaker for TV Masquerade Party prog, 51-60. Exhib: New York Pub Libr; Morris Mus; Hunterdon Co Libr, NJ. Teaching: Lect & demonstrations, art of mask making, clubs, orgn, libr & on TV. Collection: The late Doane Powell collection of portrait masks, books, masks of Java, Bali, Tibet, Siam, Japan & others; collection is widely exhibited. Publ: Co-auth, Masks & Mask Makers, Abingdon, 61; co-auth, Pantomime—the Silent Theater, 65 & co-auth, Art of Magic, 67, Atheneum. Mailing Add: RD 1 Box 358 Glen Gardner NJ 08826

HUNT, RICHARD HOWARD
SCULPTOR
b Chicago, Ill, Sept 12, 35. Study: Art Inst Chicago, BAE. Work: Mus Mod Art, New York; Cleveland Mus Art, Ohio; Art Inst Chicago; Nat Mus Israel, Jerusalem; Mus 20th Century, Vienna, Austria. Exhib: Whitney Mus Am Art Ann, New York, 70; American Sculpture, Univ Nebr Art Gallery, Lincoln, 70; Large Scale Sculptures, Ravinia Park, Highland Park, Ill, 71; The Sculpture of Richard Hunt, Mus Mod Art, New York & Art Inst Chicago, 71; one-man shows, Southern Ill Univ, 70, Mus Mod Art, New York, 71 & Dorsky Gallery, New York, 71; 20th Nat Print Exhib, Brooklyn Mus, NY, 77. Bibliog: Lieberman (auth), The Sculpture of Richard Hunt, Mus Mod Art, New York, 71. Mem: Nat Coun Arts; Ill Arts Coun; Col Art Asn Am (bd dirs, 70-). Media: Metal. Dealer: Dorsky Gallery 111 Fourth Ave New York NY 10003. Mailing Add: 1503 N Cleveland Ave Chicago IL 60610

HUNT, ROBERT JAMES
ART ADMINISTRATOR, EDUCATOR
b Fargo, NDak, Apr 5, 21. Study: Univ Iowa, BA, 47, MFA, 50. Work: Univ Iowa; Mulvane Art Mus; Des Moines Art Ctr; Kans State Teachers Col; Wichita Art Mus. Exhib: Wichita Art Mus; Mid-America Artists; Kansas Free Fair; Am Fedn Arts; Colorado Springs Fine Arts Ctr; plus others. Teaching: Prof art & chmn dept, Washburn Univ, 50- Pos: Dir, Mulvane Art Ctr, Washburn Univ, 50- Awards: Purchase Prizes, Wichita Art Mus & Kans State Univ. Mem: Mid-West Col Art Asn; Col Art Asn Am. Mailing Add: Dept Art Washburn Univ Topeka KS 66621

HUNTER, DEBORA
PHOTOGRAPHER, EDUCATOR
b Chicago, Ill, June 16, 50. Study: Northwestern Univ, BA(Eng lit), 72; RI Sch Design, MFA(photog), 76. Work: Dallas Mus Fine Arts, Tex; Mus Art, RI Sch Design, Providence. Exhib: Women Look at Women (traveling exhib), Lyman Allyn Mus, New London, Conn, 75; Northeastern Regional Photog Exhib, Mt Holyoke Art Mus, Mass, 75; Photovision 75, Boston Ctr for the Arts, 75; one-person shows, Pa State Univ, University Park, 76, D-W Coop Gallery, Dallas, 77 & Sarah Reyonds Gallery, Univ NMex, Albuquerque, 77; Fac Show, Pollock Gallery, Southern Methodist Univ, Dallas, 76 & 77; Tarrant Co Ann, Ft Worth Art Mus, 77; Recent Photog Acquisitions, Dallas Mus Fine Art, 77; 1977 Artists Biennial, New Orleans Mus Art, La, 77. Teaching: Instr, Swain Sch Design, New Bedford, Mass, 75-76; instr photog, Southern Methodist Univ, Dallas, 76- Awards: Hon Mention, Ann Exhib, Art Asn Newport, RI, 75; Boston Ctr for the Arts Award, Photovisions, 75; First Prize in Photog, Tarrant Co Ann, Ft Worth Art Mus, 76. Bibliog: Lucy Lippard (auth), From the Center: Feminist Essays on Women's Art, Dutton, 76; Janet Kutner (auth), article in Dallas Morning News, 2/77; David Dillon (auth), From the lighthouse, D Mag, Dallas, 78. Style & Technique: Black and white, 4in x 5in, often infrared film and color in 120mm. Media: Photography. Publ: Contribr, Camera, Bucher, 8-9/75; contribr, article in Anyart J, RI, 10/75; ed, Ishmael, Brown, RI Sch Design Lit Arts Mag, 76; contribr, Women See Women, Crowell, 76; contribr, Channel 13-KERA Art Calander for 1978, KERA Television, Dallas, 78. Dealer: Witkin Gallery 41 E 57th St New York NY 10022. Mailing Add: Dept of Art Southern Methodist Univ Dallas TX 75275

HUNTER, GRAHAM
CARTOONIST
b La Grange, Ill. Study: Landon Sch Cartooning, Cleveland, Ohio; Art Inst Chicago; Art Instr, Inc, Minneapolis, Minn. Work: Ed cartoons in permanent J Edgar Hoover FBI

Collection; Peter Mayo Editorial Cartoon Collection, State Hist Soc, Columbia, Mo. Exhib: Editorial Cartoon Exhib, Wayne State Univ, Detroit, 64. Pos: Cartoonist, Nat Asn Mfrs, 49-, Indust Press Syndicated Features, 54-, Farmer-Stockman, 64-, Milk, Inc, 71- & var newspaper syndicates; free lance. Awards: Distinguished Serv Citation, US Treas, 43; George Washington Honor Medal, Freedoms Found, 59 & 62; Hon Cert Award for Cartoon, Freedoms Found, 60 & 61. Style & Technique: Humorous line drawings full of action. Publ: Auth, Creating the Busy Scene Cartoon (cartoon course lesson), Art Instr, Inc. Mailing Add: Lindenshade 42 Clonavor Rd West Orange NJ 07052

HUNTER, JOHN H
PAINTER, EDUCATOR
b Pa, Sept 26, 34. Study: Pomona Col, BA, 56; Claremont Grad Sch, MFA, 58. Work: Mus Mod Art, New York; Los Angeles Co Mus; Pasadena Art Mus, Calif; Amon-Carter Mus, Ft Worth, Tex; Scripps Col, Claremont, Calif. Comn: Poster for Tamarind Exhib, Mus Mod Art, Tamarind Lithography Workshop, Los Angeles, 69. Exhib: Western Painters Under 35, Univ Calif, Los Angeles, 58; Fulbright Artists Show, US Info Serv, Florence, Italy, 65; Painters Behind Painters, Calif Palace of Legion of Honor, San Francisco, 67; Drawings, Ft Worth Art Ctr Mus, 69; Decade of Accomplishment, Ill Bell Tel Co, Chicago, 70. Teaching: Instr fine art, Ohio State Univ, 60-63; guest artist, Ind Univ, Bloomington, summer 63; assoc prof art, Calif State Univ, San Jose, 65-; guest artist, Tamarind Lithography Workshop, 69. Awards: Fulbright Fel Painting, Florence, 63-64, Renewal Grantee, 64-65. Bibliog: Peter Plagens (auth), Possibilities of drawing, Artforum, 10/69; also rev in, New York Times, Los Angeles Times, Rome Daily Am, Art News & others. Style & Technique: Figurative. Media: Collage, Mixed Media. Mailing Add: Dept of Art Calif State Univ San Jose CA 95114

HUNTER, LEONARD LEGRANDE, III
SCULPTOR, EDUCATOR
b Washington, DC, July 3, 40. Study: Univ Miami, BA; Grad Sch Archit, Univ Pa; Univ Calif, Berkeley, MFA & study with James Melchert. Work: Hopkins Ctr, Dartmouth Col. Comn: Large outdoor hydraulic/kinetic sculpture, Crossroads Plaza, Lexington, Ky, 74. Exhib: San Francisco Art Inst Centennial, H M De Young Mem Mus, 71; Metal Experience, Oakland Mus, Calif, 71; one-man show, Univ Art Mus, Berkeley, 72; Biennial, New Orleans Mus Art, 73; Annual, Whitney Mus Am Art, 75. Teaching: Assoc prof art, Univ Ky, 72- Pos: Archit design consult, HCD Collab, San Francisco, 66-67. Awards: Chancellor's Award, Univ Calif, Berkeley, 69; Mary & Jacob Kemler Seitz Scholar, Univ Calif, 69-70; teaching fels, Univ Ky, 73-74; Golden Venus Medallion, Film Festival of the Americas, 77. Bibliog: Stanley Majka (auth), Build an Outdoor Sculpture (film), KET-TV, Lexington, Ky, 74. Mem: Col Art Asn; Southern Asn Sculptors. Style & Technique: A metaphysical style of sculpture executed in a highly precise fabrication and joining method. Dealer: Maureen E Wise 2807 Piedmont Ave Berkeley CA 94705. Mailing Add: 2105 Cactus Ct Walnut Creek CA 94595

HUNTER, MEL
PAINTER, PRINTMAKER
b Oak Park, Ill, July 27, 27. Study: Northwestern Univ. Work: Japan Trade Bank; Am Heart Asn; Gen Re-Ins Corp; plus others. Comn: Several thousand illus comn by publ such as, Life, Colliers, Nat Geog, Newsweek & Time-Life Bks, 53-68; 6 major murals, Transp Bldg, New York World's Fair, 64; 12 paintings of ecol areas, Gen Motors Corp, Detroit, 74. Pos: Dir, Gallery North Star, Atelier N Star & Mel Hunter Graphics, Grafton, Vt, 75- Bibliog: Susan Ellis (auth), Drawing color separations on surfaced Mylar, Tamarind Tech Papers, 3/74. Mem: Drawing Soc; Nat Arts Club; Salmagundi Club; Southern Vt Artists Asn. Style & Technique: Oil, gouache, and watercolor—thin washes and glazes built up to final tones, smooth surface, work lights to darks; all prints, drawing and added color. Media: Watercolor, Oil; Stone Lithographs. Specialty: Contemporary realism. Publ: Auth, Making pre-separation effective, Bk Production Indust Mag, 72; auth, Revolution in hand drawn lithography, Am Artist, 10/77. Dealer: Brentano's 586 Fifth Ave New York NY 10020. Mailing Add: Gallery North Star Box 2 Grafton VT 05146

HUNTER, MIRIAM EILEEN
EDUCATOR, ART ADMINISTRATOR
b Cincinnati, Ohio, June 6, 29. Study: Ball State Univ, BS(art), 50, MA(art educ), 56, and spec study with I Rice Perera & Margules; Wheaton Col, MA(Christian educ), 57; Sch of Art Inst Chicago, 60; Nova Univ, EdD candidate. Work: Burris Lab Sch, Ball State Univ, Muncie, Ind. Comn: Catalogue cover design, Wheaton Col, 59-, centennial mural, 60; design consult, Glen Ellyn Baptist Church, Chicago, 61. Exhib: Prize-winning Entries, Carnegie Inst Int, 46-47; Fac Fine Arts Gallery, Art Inst Chicago, 60-; Ball State Univ Alumni Show, 63. Teaching: Instr art & Eng, Hoagland Consolidated Sch, 51-52; fel instr art, Wheaton Col, 52-56, assoc prof art, 56-; guest instr art & art educ, Teacher Training Cols, Kenya, Africa, summer 63. Pos: Free lance design consult, Chicago, 52-72; chmn art dept, Wheaton Col, 69 & 75- Awards: First Place State of Ind, Nat Scholastic Art Exhib, Carnegie Inst Int, 47; Bronze Medal Award, DuPage Sesqui Centennial Design, Mayor's Off, Wheaton, 69; Outstanding Alumnus Award for Excellence in Educ, Ball State Univ, 75. Mem: Int Soc Lit & the Arts; Nat Asn Advan Christian Scholar; Nat Art Educ Asn; Am Asn Univ Prof. Style & Technique: Semi-abstract, highly textured commentary painting. Media: Oil combined with Textural Material; Clay for Stoneware. Res: Curriculum, education, policies, college governance, learning theory (Gestalt psychology and art). Publ: Auth, Color in the library, Christian Librn, Minneapolis, 59; illusr, Kenneth Taylor, auth, African Inland Mission, 63; illusr (booklet), Ensign for This Hour, Peru, Ind, 64. Mailing Add: 530 Aurora Way Wheaton IL 60187

HUNTER, ROBERT DOUGLAS
PAINTER, INSTRUCTOR
b Boston, Mass, Mar 17, 28. Study: Cape Sch Art, Provincetown, Mass, with Henry Hensche; Vesper George Sch Art, Boston; also with R H Ives Gammell, Boston. Work: Northeastern Univ, Boston; Tufts Univ; Boston Univ Med Ctr; Mass Inst Technol; Wheaton Col. Comn: Epiphany mural, Church St Mary of the Harbor, Provincetown, 56; altar frontal, Emmanuel Church, West Roxbury, Mass, 62. Exhib: Acad Artists Show, Springfield, Mass, 61; Am Artist Prof League Show, New York, 66, 67 & 70; New Eng Artists Exhib, Boston, 70 & 74. Teaching: Instr fine arts, Vesper George Sch Art, 55-; instr fine arts, Worchester Art Mus, 70- & Mt Ida Jr Col, Newton, 78- Pos: Mem adv comt, Art Ctr, Ogunquit, Maine, 65-75. Awards: 15 Richard Milton Gold Medals, New Eng Artists Exhib, 54-70; Gold Medal, 62 & Newington Prize, 66 & 67, Am Artists Prof League; Frederick Thompson Found Award, 76. Bibliog: Richard Goets (auth), Sight sized method, Am Artist, 70. Mem: Guild Boston Artists (vpres, 68-73, pres, 73-); Am Artists Prof League (dir, 60-70); Acad Artists Asn; Copley Soc Boston; Grand Cent Art Gallery. Style & Technique: Representational, impressionist landscape, still life and portraiture. Media: Oil. Dealer: Grand Central Art Gallery 40 Vanderbilt Ave New York NY 10017; Blair Gallery Santa Fe NM 87501. Mailing Add: 250 Beacon St Boston MA 02116

HUNTER, ROBERT HOWARD
PAINTER, PRINTMAKER
b Auburn, Wash, May 17, 29. Study: Ore State Univ, 47-49; Univ Ore, BS & MFA, 49-53; Univ SC, 55-56. Work: Ackland Art Ctr, Univ NC, Chapel Hill; Duke Univ, Durham, NC; Greenville Co Mus Art, SC; Beaufort Art Mus, SC; Lee Gallery, Clemson Univ, SC. Exhib: 159th Ann Painters & Sculptors, Philadelphia, 64; 7th Nat Show Art, Brockton, Mass, 64; Art on Paper, Weatherspoon Art Gallery, NC, 65; 16th Ann Drawing & Small Sculpture Show, Ball State Univ, 70; one-man show, Ackland Art Ctr, Univ NC, Chapel Hill, 68. Teaching: Instr figure drawing, Univ Ore, 52-53; prof printmaking, painting & basic design, Clemson Univ, 56-, head dept visual studies, 67-71. Pos: Gallery dir, Rudolph Lee Gallery, Clemson Univ, 58-68; Ford Found fel, Univ NC, Chapel Hill, 66-67. Awards: Guild of SC Artists Awards, 56-63; Springs Art Contest, SC, 61 & 77; 8th Ann Painting of Yr, Atlanta Art Asn, 62. Mem: Col Art Asn Am; SC Arts Comn (subcomt state art collection, 69-71, subcomt environ art, 71-73). Style & Technique: Hard edge; shape and illusion of form. Media: Mixed Media. Publ: Auth, Twenty Lithographs by Robert Hunter, 61; auth, The Shape of R Hunter, 66; illusr, The Binnacle, R Peterson, 67; contribr, Contemporary Artists of South Carolina, 70. Dealer: Hampton Gallery Wade Hampton Blvd Taylors SC 29687. Mailing Add: 21 Wilton St Greenville SC 29601

HUNTER, SAM
ART HISTORIAN
b Springfield, Mass, Jan 5, 23. Study: Williams Col, AB; Univ Florence, cert. Collections Arranged: Many exhibs at Mus Mod Art, New York, Minneapolis Inst Arts, Rose Art Mus, Jewish Mus, New York & Princeton Art Mus. Teaching: Former instr, Harvard Univ, Univ Calif, Los Angeles, Barnard Col, Columbia Univ, Cornell Univ & Brandeis Univ; prof art hist, Princeton Univ, 69- Pos: Art critic, New York Times, 47-49; cur, Mus Mod Art, 56-58; dir, Minneapolis Inst Arts, 58-60; dir, Rose Art Mus, Brandeis Univ, 60-65; dir, Jewish Mus, 65-68; consult ed, Harry N Abrams, Inc, 68-; fac cur mod art, Princeton Art Mus, 69- Awards: Guggenheim Fel, 71-72. Mem: Col Art Asn Am. Publ: Auth, Hans Hofmann, 63; auth, New Art Around the World, 66; auth, Larry Rivers, 69; auth, Avant-garde Painting in America, 70; auth, Josef Albers, 71; plus many others. Mailing Add: 451 West End Ave New York NY 10024

HUNTER-STIEBEL, PENELOPE (PENELOPE HUNTER STIEBEL)
CURATOR
b Washington, DC. Study: Barnard Col, BA; Inst Fine Art, NY Univ, MA. Collections Arranged: Twentieth Century Decorative Arts Gallery, 71-74, The Grand Gallery (int exhib; ed, catalogue), 74, Reinstallation of the Twentieth Century Decorative Arts Gallery, 78, Metrop Mus Art, New York. Pos: Asst cur, Metrop Mus Art, 75- Res: Twentieth century decorative arts; eighteenth century French furniture; European ceramics, sixteenth through eighteenth century. Publ: Auth, Art Deco and the Metropolitan Museum of Art, The Connoisseur, 4/72; auth, Art deco: the last hurrah, Bull of Metrop Mus Art, 6/72; auth, A royal taste: Louis XV-1738, J Metrop Mus Art, 73; auth, Faience prelude to porcelain, Apollo, 11/77. Mailing Add: Metrop Mus of Art Fifth Ave & 82nd St New York NY 10028

HUNTINGTON, DAPHNE
PAINTER, MURALIST
b Ketchikan, Alaska. Study: Ecole de Louvre, Paris; London Sch Arts & Crafts; Slades, London. Comn: Wave Poetry (seascape), Mary Pickford Collection, Pickfair, Beverly Hills, 64; Christ of World Peace, with Sister Venetia Epler, St Francis Chapel, Episcopal Church, Glendale, 71; 11 stained glass windows, Church of Relig Sci, Beverly Hills, Calif, 74; Life of Christ Mural, with Sister Venetia Epler, facade of Christian Heritage Mausoleum, Forest Lawn Mem Park, West Covina, Calif, 75. Exhib: Calif State Fair, Sacramento, 59; Am Inst Fine Arts Competition, Los Angeles, 69; Grand Nat Competition, Am Artists Prof League, 71; Invitational Show, Los Angeles Co Mus, 72; San Bernardino Co Mus, Redlands, Calif, 76. Pos: Art judge, San Bernardino Co Fairs, Victorville, 71-75; art judge, Norwalk & Anaheim Art Festivals, 73 & 74; art judge, Date Festival Art Show, Indio, 76. Awards: Best of Show, Calif State Fair, Sacramento, 59; Fels, Am Inst Fine Arts, 65 & Am Artists Prof League, 71. Bibliog: Walter A Bailey (auth), Epler & Huntington duo sisters, artists supreme, South Pasadena Rev, 8/74; Jackie Dashiel (auth), Artist of the Forest Lawn mosaic, Los Angeles Herald Examr, 10/74; Al Bine (auth), The Birth, Life, and Works of Jesus Christ, Calif Living, 3/75. Mem: Am Inst Fine Arts (pres, 69); Coun Traditional Artists Socs (first vpres, 69-75); Nat League Am Pen Women (Calif state art chmn, 62-64); Nat Soc Arts & Lett (pres, Los Angeles Chap, 59); Am Artists Prof League. Style & Technique: Traditional. Media: Oil, Watercolor. Res: Biblical costumes, types, architecture and history; Leonardo da Vinci; Christian art. Publ: Co-auth (with Sister Venetia Epler), Creation of the World's Largest Religious Mosaic, and the Story of Christ in Art (doc slide film), 76. Mailing Add: 1835 Outpost Dr Hollywood CA 90068

HUNTINGTON, JIM
SCULPTOR
b Elkhart, Ind, Jan 13, 41. Study: Ind Univ, Bloomington, 58-59; El Camino Col, 59-60. Work: Addison Gallery Am Art, Andover, Mass; Rose Art Mus, Brandeis Univ; Smith Col Mus, Holyoke, Mass; Whitney Mus Am Art, New York; Power Inst, Univ Sidney, Australia; plus many others. Exhib: Corcoran Gallery Art Biennial, Washington, DC & Traveling Exhib, 65 & 67; Whitney Mus Am Art Painting Ann, 68 & Sculpture Ann, 69; one-man shows, Hayden Gallery, Mass Inst Technol, 68, Max Hutchinson Gallery, New York, 71 & Parker St 470, 72; David McKee Gallery, New York, 76; Seven Sculptors, Laguna Gloria Mus, Austin, Tex, 77-78; plus many others. Awards: Grand Prize Award, Sheraton-Boston Competition & Blanche Colman Award, Boston, 65. Media: Stone, Metal, Wood. Dealer: David McKee Gallery 140 E 63rd St New York NY 10012. Mailing Add: 36 Walker St New York NY 10013

HUNTINGTON, JOHN W
COLLECTOR, PATRON
b Hartford, Conn, Oct 19, 10. Study: Yale Col, BA, 32; Sch Archit, Columbia Univ, BArch, 36. Pos: Trustee & vpres, Wadsworth Atheneum, Hartford; bd trustees, Children's Mus, Hartford. Collection: Contemporary paintings, drawings and graphic arts. Mailing Add: 159 Bloomfield Ave Hartford CT 06105

HUNTLEY, DAVID C
PAINTER, EDUCATOR
b Lenoir, NC, Oct 17, 30. Study: Univ NC, AB & MA. Exhib: City Art Mus St Louis, Mo, 66; Raymond Ducan Gallery, Paris, 66; Ligoa Duncan Gallery, New York, 67; Peoria Art Ctr, 68; Wesleyan Col, Macon, Ga, 69; plus many other group & one-man shows. Teaching: Linstr children's art, Univ NC; instr hist art, design & art, Limestone Col; prof art, Ala Col, Montevallo; prof & chmn art & design dept, Southern Ill Univ, Edwardsville, currently. Awards: Johnson Award, Birmingham Mus Art, 58; NC Mus Award, Raleigh, 60; Soc Independent Artists St Louis, 66; plus others. Mem: Col Art Asn Am; Ill Art Asn; Ala

Watercolor Soc; Nat Conf Art Admin (bd dir); Am Asn Univ Prof; plus others. Mailing Add: Sch Fine Arts Southern Ill Univ Edwardsville IL 62025

HUOT, ROBERT
PAINTER, FILMMAKER
b Staten Island, NY, Sept 16, 35. Study: Wagner Col, Staten Island, 53-57, BSc, 57; Hunter Col, grad art, New York, 61-62. Work: Torrington Manufacturing Co, Conn; Wasserman Develop Corp, New York; William Rubin Collection, New York; Doberman Collection, Munster, Ger; Mus of Mod Art, New York, NY. Exhib: Eight Young Artists, Hudson River Mus, New York; Systematic Painting, Guggenheim Mus, New York, 66; Int Young Artist Exhib, Tokyo, 67; Whitney Painting Ann, Whitney Mus, New York, 67 & 69; New Art USA, Mod Mus of Art, Minchem, WGer, 68; 557087, Seattle Art Mus, Wash, 69; Festival of Independent Avant-Garde Film, London, 73; Sense of Scale, Lowe Gallery, Syracuse, NY, 74; Autobiographical Art, Colgate Univ, Hamilton, NY, 75; one-man shows, Paula Cooper Gallery, New York, 69-73 & 74, Galerie Renee Ziegler, Zurich, Switz, 70, Millennium, New York, 75 & State Univ of NY, Albany. Teaching: Instr art, Hunter Col, New York, 63-71; asst prof painting, drawing & filmmaking, 71- Pos: Pigment chemist, Sun Chemical Co, Staten Island, 57-58 & 60-62; plant mgr, Neti Art Color, New York, 62-63. Awards: Nat Coun on the Arts Grant, New York, 66. Bibliog: Gregory Battcock (ed), Minimal Art: a critical anthology, New York, 68; Eugene C Goossen (auth), The Art of the Real: USA 1948-1968, New York, 68; Robert M Murdock (auth), Modular Painting (catalog), Buffalo, NY, 70. Style & Technique: Many films and paintings recording a personal log of events. Media: Unstretched Canvas for Painting; Film. Dealer: Filmmakers Coop 175 Lexington Ave New York NY 10016. Mailing Add: RD 1 New Berlin NY 13411

HUPP, FREDERICK DUIS
PAINTER, EDUCATOR
b Streator, Ill, Dec 21, 38. Study: Univ Ariz, BFA, 62, MFA, 66. Work: Tucson Mus Art, Ariz. Exhib: Am Fedn Arts Painting Exhib, 70-72; Western Ann, Denver, 72; Nat Small Painting Exhib, Albuquerque, NMex, 72; Arizona's Outlook, Tucson Mus Art, 74 & 76; Univ Ariz, 74; All Media Art Competition, Houston, Tex, 76; Univ Man, Winnipeg, 76; SW Biennial, Mus NMex, Santa Fe, 76; Eight State West Biennial, Grand Junction, Colo, 76; Four Corners Biennial, Phoenix, Ariz, 77. Teaching: Instr design, Univ Ariz, 68-; asst prof drawing & painting, Tucson Mus Sch, 68-, dir educ, 68-70; instr design, Pima Col, Tucson, 77- Pos: Cur, Univ Ariz Art Mus, 60-61; instr, Fenster Ranch Sch, Tucson, 64-65. Eight West State Biennial Cash Award, Grand Junction, Colo, 74; Four Corners Biennial Cash Award, Phoenix, Ariz, 75; Cash Award, Cedar City Nat, Utah, 76. Style & Technique: Nonobjective, hard-edged circular bands of color around various areas within square formats. Media: Acrylic. Mailing Add: 1023 N Perry Tucson AZ 87505

HURD, JUSTIN G (JUD)
CARTOONIST
b Cleveland, Ohio, Nov 12, 12. Study: Cleveland Inst Art; Case Western Reserve Univ, AB, 34; Chicago Acad Fine Arts, 35-36; Spencerian Bus Col, Cleveland, 40-42. Pos: Cartoonist, Charles Mintz Animated Cartoon Studio, 36-37; cartoonist, Comic Bk Cartoons, Dell Publ & others, 40-42; US Army Weekly Cartoon Bull, 42-46; dir, Jud Hurd Cartoon Studio, 46-58; founder & owner, Ticker Toons Syndicate, 59-; ed, The Cartoonist, Nat Cartoonists Soc Mag, 65-69; publ, Cartoonist Profiles, 59- Mem: Nat Cartoonists Soc (Ohio regional chmn, 57-64, regional coordr, 65, ed newslett, 65-66); Newspaper Comics Coun; Advert Club New York. Publ: Health Capsules (daily cartoon), Syndicated by United Features Syndicate, in US newspapers & in Turkey, E Pakistan, Arg, The Philippines, Chile, Brazil & other countries, 61- Mailing Add: 281 Bayberry Lane Westport CT 06880

HURD, PETER
PAINTER, WRITER
b Roswell, NMex, Feb 22, 04. Study: US Mil Acad, 21-23; Haverford Col, 23-24; Pa Acad Fine Arts, 24-26, with N C Wyeth; Tex Tech Univ, DFA; NMex State Univ, LLD, 68. Work: Metrop Mus Art, New York; Nat Gallery, Edinburgh, Scotland; Delaware Art Mus, Wilmington; Dallas Art Mus, Tex; Roswell Mus, NMex; plus many others. Comn: 16 fresco panels, Tex Tech Univ Mus; fresco murals, Big Spring Post Off Bldg, Tex; mural panel, Prudential Ins Co Bldg, Houston, Tex; portrait of President Johnson for White House Hist Asn (now in Nat Portrait Gallery); murals, Alamogordo Post Off Bldg, NMex; plus others. Exhib: Retrospectives, Amon Carter Mus Art, Ft Worth, Tex, 64 & Calif Palace of Legion of Honor, 65. Pos: War corresp, Life Mag & USAAF, 42-45, artist, Life Mag, 46-; mem, Nat Fine Arts Comn, 58-63. Awards: Wilmington Soc Fine Arts, 41 & 45; Pa Acad Fine Arts Medal, 45; Isaac Maynard Prize, Nat Acad Design, 54. Mem: Academician Nat Acad Design; Wilmington Soc Fine Arts; Am Watercolor Soc; Century Asn. Publ: Illusr, Last of the Mohicans, 26, Great Stories of the Sea & Ships, 33 & Habit of Empire, 38, plus others; auth, Count-down at Canaveral, Art in Am, 63; auth, Peter Hurd-The Lithographs, Baker Gallery, 69 & Sketch Book, Swallow, 71. Mailing Add: Sentinel Ranch San Patricio NM 88348

HURD, ZORAH
ILLUSTRATOR, PAINTER
b White Plains, NY, Jan 25, 40. Study: Parson's Sch Design, cert. Comn: Unique & limited ed engraving designs, Steuben Glass, New York, 69-75. Exhib: Silvermine Guild Artists, Conn, 69 & 70. Pos: Illusr, Am Merchandizing Corp, New York, 60-62; freelance illusr, 62- Style & Technique: Hard edge pencil and watercolor, hard edge acrylic. Media: Acrylic on Canvas. Mailing Add: Lindley Rd Rte 2 Corning NY 14830

HURLEY, WILSON
PAINTER
b Tulsa, Okla, Apr 11, 24. Study: US Mil Acad, BS, 45; George Washington Univ Law Sch, JD, 51. Work: Fairchild Hall, US Air Force Acad. Exhib: Nat Acad Western Art, Oklahoma City, 73-75. Awards: Silver Medal, Nat Acad Western Art, 73, Gold Medal, 77. Bibliog: Mary C Nelson (auth), Wilson Hurley, Landscapist, In: American Artist, Watson-Guptill, 73 & Wilson Hurley, Lowell Press, 77. Mem: Nat Acad Western Art (exec comt, 75-78). Style & Technique: Oil, usually large canvas, representational style, often from imaginary rather than actual locale-landscape. Media: Oil on Canvas. Publ: Illusr, Without Noise of Arms, Briggs, Northland, 75. Dealer: Owens Gallery Santa Fe Plaza Oklahoma City OK 73102; Baker Gallery Lubbock TX 79408. Mailing Add: 7516 Vista del Arroyo NE Albuquerque NM 87109

HURST, RALPH N
SCULPTOR, EDUCATOR
b Decatur, Ind, Sept 4, 18. Study: Ind Univ, Bloomington, BS & MFA; Ogunquit Sch Painting & Sculpture, Maine, with Robert Laurent; Fla State Univ, fac res grant, summer 61; instructional grant, summer 67; fac develop grant in Italy, 71. Work: Evansville Mus Arts & Sci, Ind; Columbus Mus Arts & Crafts, Ga; Mobile Art Asn Gallery, Ala; Gulf Life Ins Co, Jacksonville, Fla; LeMoyne Art Found Gallery, Tallahassee, Fla. Comn: Relief sculpture, Fla State Univ Col Educ, 57; wall relief sculptures (with Leon Mead), Fla State Univ Union Bldg, Tallahassee, 63; sculpture-Madonna, St Thomas More Cath Church, Tallahassee, 71. Exhib: American Sculpture 1951, Metrop Mus, New York, 51; Contemporary Sculptors Drawings, Ohio State Univ, 54; Art USA, Madison Sq Garden, New York, 58; Nat Liturgical Art Exhib, San Francisco, 60; Southeastern Art Exhib, High Mus, Atlanta, Ga, 67. Teaching: Prof art educ & constructive design, Fla State Univ, 53- Pos: Cur, Mus Art of Ogunquit, summer 53. Awards: Purchase Award, Assoc Fla Architects Art Exhib, Jacksonville, Fla, 59; Ball Gallery Award, Nat Small Sculpture Exhib, Ball State Univ, Muncie, Ind, 60; Community Purchase Award, Mobile Art Gallery, Ala, 71. Mem: Nat Art Educ Asn; Southeastern Sculptors Asn. Media: Alabaster, Wood. Dealer: Harmon Gallery 1258 Third St S Naples FL 33940; Le Moyne Art Found 125 N Gadsden Tallahassee FL 32301. Mailing Add: 1801 Skyland Dr Tallahassee FL 32303

HURT, SUSANNE M
PAINTER
b New York, NY. Study: Duke Univ; Art Students League, with Frank V Dumond & Kenneth Hayes Miller; Corcoran Sch Art; also with Wayman Adams & A Ginsburg. Work: In pvt collections. Exhib: One-man shows, Cayuga Mus Hist & Art, Auburn, NY, 71 & Grist Mill Gallery, Chester, Vt, 76; Catharine Lorillard Wolfe Art Club, Nat Acad Design, New York, 71; Hudson Valley Art Asn, Westchester Co Ctr, White Plains, NY, 72; Am Artists Prof League, Lever House, New York, 72-75; Nat Art League, Long Island, NY, 72; Mus Fine Arts, Springfield, Mass; Hammond Mus, North Salem, NY; Nat Arts Club, New York; Nat Acad Design; Grand Cent Galleries, New York; plus others. Teaching: Pvt classes & demonstrations. Awards: Spec Award for Oil, Art League Long Island, 68; Anna Hyatt Huntington First Prize for Painting, Catharine Lorillard Wolfe Art Club, 70; First Prize for Oil, Composers, Authors & Artists Am, 72; First Prize, Nat Biennial, 73. Mem: Catharine Lorillard Wolfe Art Club (corresp secy, 71-74); Am Artists Prof League; Hudson Valley Art Asn; Composers, Authors & Artists Am (nat rec secy, 71-71-75); Royal Soc Arts. Style & Technique: Realistic, traditional. Media: Oil. Mailing Add: 299 Riverside Dr New York NY 10025

HURTIG, MARTIN RUSSELL
PAINTER, SCULPTOR
b Chicago, Ill, Aug 11, 29. Study: Inst Design Chicago, BS, 52, & MS, 57; Atelier 17, Paris, 55. Work: Bibliot Nat, Paris; Philadelphia Free Libr; Carroll Reese Mus, Johnson City, Tenn; Honolulu Acad Art. Comn: Stained glass windows & mural wall, Union Church, Lake Bluff, Ill, 63; outdoor court sculpture, Waukegan Pub Libr, Ill, 64; lobby relief sculpture, Midwest Iron Works, Chicago, 67. Exhib: 11th & 16th Nat Print Exhib, Brooklyn Mus, 58 & 68; one-man shows, Flint Inst Arts, 61 & 68, Alonzo Gallery, 66 & 67 & Ecole Spec Archit, Paris, 69; 6th Am Artists Traveling Show, Paris & 12 French cities, 69-70. Teaching: Asst prof drawing & design, Mich State Univ, 57-62; prof painting & printmaking, Univ Ill, Chicago Circle, 62- Awards: Purchase Awards, Carroll Reese Mus, 67 & Honolulu Acad Arts, 71. Bibliog: F Schulze (auth), Art news in Chicago, Art News, 11/71; A Goldin (auth), Vitality vs greasy kids stuff, Art Gallery Mag, 4/72; D Guthrie & J Allen (auth), Waging polemical warfare, Chicago Tribune, 4/30/72. Dealer: Alonzo Gallery 26 E 63rd St New York NY 10021. Mailing Add: 1727 Wesley St Evanston IL 60201

HURTUBISE, JACQUES
PAINTER
b Montreal, PQ, Feb 28, 39. Study: Beaux Art Sch, Montreal. Work: Mass Inst Technol; Peter Stuyvesant Art Found, Amsterdam; Galerie Nat Can, Ont; Art Gallery Ont, Toronto; Vancouver Art Gallery; among others. Comn: Murals, Ottawa Univ, 69, Place Radio Can, Montreal, 72 & Ministry of Defense, Ottawa, 72. Exhib: 9th Int Biennial, Sao Paulo, Brazil, 67; 300 Ans d'Art Canadien, Galerie Nat Can, Ottawa, 67; Canada Art d'Aujourd'hui, Paris, France, Rome, Italy & Lausanne, Switz, 68; 7 Canadians, Mass Inst Technol & Gallery Mod Art, Washington, DC, 68; Edinburgh Festival, Scotland, 68; plus many one-man & group exhibs. Pos: Resident artist, Dartmouth Col, 67. Awards: First Prize, Concours Artistique Quebec, PQ Govt, 65; Prize, Expos Hadassah, 68; Can Coun Arts Grant, 70; among others. Bibliog: Laurent Lamy (auth), Hurtubise, Lidec, 71. Mem: Royal Can Acad Art. Dealer: Galerie Joliett 29 Place Royale Quebec PQ G1K 4G2 Can. Mailing Add: 1226 Rue St Louis Terrebonne PQ J6W 1K4 Can

HURWITZ, SIDNEY J
PAINTER, PRINTMAKER
b Worcester, Mass, Aug 22, 32. Study: Sch Worcester Art Mus; Brandeis Univ, BA; Boston Univ, MFA. Work: Libr Cong; Mus Mod Art, New York; DeCordova Mus, Lincoln, Mass; Minneapolis Mus; Fed Reserve Bank, Boston; Univ Mass, Amherst. Comn: Mosaic mural, Skowhegan Sch Art, Maine, 64; ed of woodcuts, Wellesley Col, Mass, 67; six paintings of London, Japan Int Bank, London, 73. Exhib: Am Drawing, Mus Mod Art, New York, 56; Print Biennial, Libr Cong, 62; Pa Acad, Philadelphia, 64; New Eng Artists, Boston, 71. Teaching: Prof art, Boston Univ, 62- Awards: Fulbright Fel, 59; Louis Comfort Tiffany Award, 66; Artist Award, Am Inst Arts & Lett, 69; Mass Found for the Arts Fel, 76. Mem: Col Art Asn Am. Publ: Etchings of Sigmund Abeles, 66 & auth, My woodcut technique, 67, Am Artist. Mailing Add: 202 Homer St Newton MA 02159 Boston MA 202 Homer St Newton MA 02159

HUSHLAK, GERALD MARSHALL
PAINTER
b Edmonton, Alta, Feb 15, 44. Study: Univ Alta; Univ Calgary, Alta; Univ Calif; Royal Col of Art, London, Eng, BEd, BFA & MFA. Work: Can Coun Art Bank, Ottawa, Ont; San Francisco Mus of Mod Art, Calif; Vancouver Art Gallery, BC; Norman McKenzie Art Gallery, Regina, Sask; Alta Art Found. Exhib: Western Can Art, Edmonton Art Gallery, Alta, Spectrum, Royal Acad Exhib for 1976 Olympics, Montreal, Forum, Montreal Mus of Fine Art, Que, Univ Art Gallery, Calgary, Alta & Thomas Art Gallery, Winnipeg, Man, 76; Smithsonian Traveling Exhib, 77; World Print Competition, San Francisco Mus of Mod Art, 50 Can Drawings (traveling exhib, rep Western Can), Making Marks, Norman McKenzie Art Gallery, Regina, Sask, What's New, Edmonton Art Gallery, Alta & From Computer Art to Generative Art, Int Centre, Toronto, 77. Teaching: Instr painting, Univ Calgary, Alta, 75- Awards: Purchase Award, World Print Competition, San Francisco Mus of Mod Art, 77. Bibliog: Articles in Arts Rev, 74, Art Weekly, 76, Calgary Herald, 76 & Vancouver Sun, 76. Mem: Col Art Asn; Can Artists Representation. Style & Technique: Computer generated drawings and paintings. Media: PDP-11 and plotter; acrylic. Dealer: Galerie Royale 1509 W 7th Ave Vancouver BC Can. Mailing Add: 202 11th Ave Calgary AB T2M 0B8 Can

HUTCHINS, MAUDE PHELPS MCVEIGH
SCULPTOR
b New York, NY. Study: Yale Univ, BFA, 26. Work: Libr Cong. Exhib: One-man show, Roullier Art Galleries, Chicago, 42-48; New Haven Paint & Clay Club, Brooklyn Mus. Nat Asn Women Painters & Sculptors, Chicago; World's Fair Show Mod Art; plus others. Mem:

Prof life mem Grand Cent Art Galleries. Publ: Co-auth, Diagramatics, 32; plus others. Mailing Add: 1046 Pequot Rd Southport CT 06490

HUTCHINSON, JANET L
MUSEUM DIRECTOR, COLLECTOR
b Washington, DC, May 2, 17. Exhibs Arranged: William Grant Sherry; Gene Klebe; Carmen Z Simpkins; Kan Man Shu (Diana Kan); Richard Tucker; Harry Stump, sculptor; George Curtis, sculptor; Alfred van Loen, sculptor; Scott Croft; Bruce Elliott Roberts; Harriet Arnold, photographer; Vincent Hartgen; Eda Kassel, sculptor; African sculpture on loan from Carlebach Gallery, New York. Pos: Owner-dir, Broadlawn Gallery, Camden, Maine, 57-64; cur, Old Merchants House, New York, 61-62; dir, Martin Co Hist Soc; Elliott Mus & House of Refuge, 65- Mailing Add: Elliott Mus 825 NE Ocean Blvd Stuart FL 33494

HUTCHINSON, MAX
ART DEALER
b Melbourne, Australia, Aug 25, 25. Study: Royal Melbourne Inst Technol. Pos: Dir, Max Hutchinson Gallery, New York; pres, Sculpture Now Inc. Specialty: Contemporary painting and sculpture. Mailing Add: 142 Greene St New York NY 10012

HUTCHINSON, PETER ARTHUR
CONCEPTUAL ARTIST
b London, Eng, Mar 4, 30. Study: Univ Ill, BFA, 60. Work: Mus Mod Art, New York; Mönchengladbach Mus, WGer; Krefeld Mus, WGer; Rose Mus, Boston, Mass; Chrysler Mus, Norfolk, Va. Exhib: Landscapes & Paricutin Project, John Gibson Gallery, 69-70; Images: 2 Ocean Projects, 69 & Information, 70, Mus Mod Art; Nature & Art, Krefeld Mus, Haus Lange, WGer, 72; Stedelijk Mus, Amsterdam, 74. Awards: Outstanding Grad Painter, Univ Ill, 60. Bibliog: Scheldahl (auth), Breadworks as earth works, NY Times, 69; Back to nature, Time, 6/70; James Collins (auth), Story art, New York Mag, 10/74. Media: Mixed Media, Film. Publ: Auth, Fictionalization of the past & Earth in upheaval, 68, Arts Arts Mag, 68; auth, Science fiction: an aesthetic for science, Art Int, 68; auth, Is there life on earth, 68 & Foraging: being an account of a hike through the snow-mass wilderness as a work of art, 72, Art in Am. Mailing Add: 759 Sixth Ave New York NY 10010

HUTCHISON, ELIZABETH S
PAINTER
Study: Otis Art Inst; and with Joseph Mugnaini & Aimee Bourdieu. Work: Rice Univ Permanent Collection; Utah State Univ Permanent Collection; Riverside Art Mus Collection, Calif; Am Fedn Social Settlements Permanent Collection, New York; plus many others in pvt collections. Exhib: Nat Watercolor Soc Ann, 66-75; Watercolor USA, Springfield, Mo, 69, 70 & 72-73; Southern Calif Expo, Del Mar, 69-75; Old Bergen Art Guild, 70-75; Nat Acad Design, New York, 70-72; plus many other group & one-man shows. Awards: Purchase Award, Watercolor USA, 69, 73 & 74; First Prize in Acrylic, Southern Calif Art for 75, Del Mar; Purchase Prize, Fifth Ann St Raymond's Art Show, Thousand Oaks, Calif, 71; plus many others. Mem: Nat Watercolor Soc (bd mem, 4 yrs, pres, 71-72, juror, 72-73); Women Painters West (juror, 69-72, bd mem, 8 yrs, pres, 73-75); Riverside Art Mus Asn; Los Angeles Art Asn; Pasadena Art Asn. Media: Oil, Watercolor. Dealer: Albert J Kramer Gallery 3459 Meier St Los Angeles CA 90066. Mailing Add: 26320 Rim Rd Hemet CA 92343

HUTH, HANS
ART HISTORIAN
b Halle, Ger, Nov 11, 92; US citizen. Study: Univ Vienna; Univ Berlin, PhD, 22. Collections Arranged: Relig Show, Art Inst Chicago, 54. Teaching: Lectr mus training, NY Univ, 38-39; lectr mus training, Univ Calif, Los Angeles, 68-69. Pos: Asst cur, State Mus, Munich & Berlin, 24-26; cur admin, Royal Palaces, Prussia, 27-36; consult, Nat Park Serv Br Hist, 39-50; cur, Art Inst Chicago, 44-63; consult & ed, Encycl Britannica, 54- Mem: Charter mem Nat Trust Hist Preserv; Int Coun Mus. Res: Decorative arts; preservation; conservation. Publ: Auth, Künstler und Werkstatt der Spätgotik, 23 & rev ed, 67, auth, Abraham und David Roentgen, 28 & rev ed, 74; auth, Der Park von Sanssouci, 22 & rev ed, 29; auth, Nature & the American, 59 & 72; auth, Lacquer of the West, 71; plus others. Mailing Add: PO Box 4414 Carmel CA 93921

HUTH, MARTA
PAINTER, PHOTOGRAPHER
b Munich, Ger, Dec 25, 98; US citizen. Study: State Sch Photog, Munich, Master; Acad Munich. Work: Städtisches Mus, Munich; Monterey Peninsula Mus Art. Exhib: Art Inst Chicago Regionals, 48-60; one-man shows, Calif Palace Legion of Honor & Chicago Pub Libr, 54; Naval Postgrad Sch Relig Ann, Monterey, 64-72; Interiors of Berlin (photos), Berlin Mus, 70; Ft Ord, 74. Bibliog: Painting on glass, Craft Horizons, 2/54; Gisland Ritz (auth), Hinterglas malerei, München, 72. Style & Technique: Imaginative painting in reverse on glass. Publ: Co-auth, Baroness von Riedesel & the American Revolution, Journal, 65. Mailing Add: PO Box 4414 Carmel CA 93921

HUTSALIUK, LUBO
PAINTER
b Lvov, Ukraine, Apr 2, 23; US citizen. Study: Cooper Union Art Sch, 54. Work: Palm Springs Desert Mus, Calif; Vt Art Ctr, Manchester; Bibliotheque Nat, Paris, France. Exhib: One-man shows, Galerie Norval, Paris, France, 59, Juster Gallery, New York, 50, Angle du Faubourg, Paris, 63 & Hilde Gerst Gallery, New York, 66; Galerie Royale, Paris, 76. Bibliog: P Imbourg (auth), Art d'Hutsaliuk, J Amateur Art, 64; J Hess Michel (auth), Vibrant paintings of Hutsaliuk, Am Artist, 69. Mem: Audubon Artists. Style & Technique: Semi-abstract, palette knife technique. Media: Oil; Lithograph. Dealer: Rolly-Michaux Gallery 943 Madison Ave New York NY 10021. Mailing Add: 260 Riverside Dr New York NY 10025

HUTTON, DOROTHY WACKERMAN
DESIGNER, PRINTMAKER
b Cleveland, Ohio, Feb 9, 99. Study: Minneapolis Sch Art, cert; Univ Minn, with Vytlacil, Earl Horter & Hobson Pittman; Acad Andre L'Hote, Paris. Work: Smithsonian Inst, Washington, DC; Harvard Univ; plus others. Exhib: Five Pennell Exhibs, Libr Cong, Washington, DC; Corcoran Gallery Art, Washington, DC; Philadelphia Print Club, Pa; Carnegie Exhib, Pittsburgh; Grand Cent Art Gallery, New York. Mem: Philadelphia Art Alliance (print comt, 50-); Am Colorprint Soc (corresp secy, 65-); Philadelphia Watercolor Club (dir, 65 & 68); Plastic Art Club Women. Mailing Add: 42 Rosedale Rd Philadelphia PA 19151

HUTTON, LEONARD
ART DEALER
Pos: Owner & dir, Leonard Hutton Galleries. Specialty: German Expressionism and Russian Avant-Garde art. Mailing Add: 33 E 74th St New York NY 10021

HUTTON, WILLIAM
MUSEUM CURATOR
b New York, NY, Oct 2, 26. Study: Williams Col, BA, 50; Harvard Univ, MA, 52. Pos: Asst cur, Toledo Mus Art, 52-65, chief cur, 71-; dir, Currier Gallery Art, 65-68; res staff, Victoria & Albert Mus, London, Eng, 68-71. Res: 18th century Meissen porcelain. Mailing Add: Toledo Mus of Art Box 1013 Toledo OH 43697

HUXTABLE, ADA LOUISE
CRITIC
b New York, NY. Study: Hunter Col, AB(magna cum laude); NY Univ; Fulbright fel for advan study in archit & design, Italy, 50 & 52; Guggenheim fel for studies in Am archit, 58; hon degrees, Yale Univ, Oberlin Col, Smith Col, Skidmore Col, Mt Holyoke Col, Trinity Col, Pratt Inst, Pace Col, La Salle Col & others. Pos: Asst cur archit & design, Mus Mod Art, New York, 46-50; contrib ed, Progressive Archit Art in Am, 50-63; archit critic, New York Times, 63-, mem ed bd, 73-; bd dirs, Munic Art Soc New York & Soc Archit Historians. Awards: Elsie de Wolfe Award, Am Inst Interior Designers, 69; Pulitzer Prize for Distinguished Criticism, 70; Nat Arts Club Lit Award, 71; plus others. Mem: Am Soc Archit Historians; Nat Trust Hist Preserv; Victorian Soc Am. Publ: Auth, Pier Luigi Nervi, Braziller, 60; auth, Four Walking Tours of Modern Architecture in New York City, Mus Mod Art, 61; auth, Classic New York, 64; auth, Will They Ever Finish Bruckner Boulevard?, Macmillan, 70; auth, Kicked A Building Lately?, 76. Mailing Add: New York Times 229 W 43rd St New York NY 10036

HYDE, ANDREW CORNWALL
ART ADMINISTRATOR, ART CONSULTANT
b Detroit, Mich, Apr 25, 41. Collections Arranged: Many exhibs, 69-72. Pos: Dir, Inst Contemp Art, Boston, 68-71; spec adv visual arts, Mass Bay Transit Auth, 70-; dir vis ctr, Children's Mus, Boston, 71-72; assoc publ, Boston Rev Arts, 72- Mem: Metrop Cult Alliance (exec comt, 70-); Inst Contemp Art (trustee, 71-); Boston Film Ctr (trustee, 69-); Music & Art Develop (trustee, 70-); Gov Task Force Arts Educ. Res: Art for public places; community involvement in the arts; government's role in the arts. Mailing Add: 955 Boylston Boston MA 02138

HYDE, LAURENCE
PAINTER, DESIGNER
b London, Eng, June 6, 14. Study: Cent Tech Sch, Toronto. Work: Nat Gallery Can; Art Gallery Vancouver, BC; Art Gallery Toronto; Libr Cong, Washington, DC. Comn: Design of seven stamps for Can Postal Dept. Exhib: Ont Soc Artists; Can Soc Painter-Etchers & Engravers; Can Soc Graphic Art; New York World's Fair, 39; Rio, 46. Pos: Producer & dir, Nat Film Bd Can. Mem: Can Soc Graphic Art. Style & Technique: Modern realist, incorporating lettering and signs; social comment, humor, city life; overtones of magic realism. Publ: Auth, Southern Cross, 52; illusr, Ottawa, 61; auth, Under the Pirate Flag, Houghton Mifflin, 65; illusr, History of the Bank of Montreal, 2 vols, 67; auth, Captain Deadlock, Houghton, 68; contribr to Can Arts & Can Geog Mag. Mailing Add: 15 Crichton St Ottawa ON K1M 2E3 Can

HYSLOP, FRANCIS EDWIN
ART HISTORIAN
b Philadelphia, Pa, Jan 7, 09. Study: Princeton Univ, BA, 31, MA, 33, MFA, 34. Teaching: Prof art hist, Pa State Univ, 34-74, emer prof, 75- Mem: Col Art Asn Am. Res: Nineteenth century French art and literature. Publ: Translr, Le Corbusier, When the Cathedrals were White, Reynal & Hitchcock, 47; co-auth, Baudelaire as a Critic, 64; auth, Henri Evenepoel a Paris, 72; auth, Henri Evenepoel, Pa State Press, 75. Mailing Add: Dept of Art Hist Pa State Univ University Park PA 16802

HYSON, JEAN
PAINTER
b Alvarado, Tex, Mar 4, 33. Study: NY Univ with William Baziotes, 52; Art Students League with Yasuo Kuniyoshi, George Grosz & Harry Sternberg, 52-56. Work: Walter Barrise Collection, New York; Oakland Art Mus, Calif; Int Banking Ctr, San Francisco, Calif; City of San Francisco; Levi-Strauss, San Francisco. Exhib: One-person shows, San Francisco Mus Art, 67, Calif Palace of the Legion of Honor, 69, William Sawyer Gallery, San Francisco, 72 & Richmond Art Mus, Calif, 77; Fine Arts Contemp Exhib, Northern Ill Univ, 69; Mus Mod Art Rental & Sales Gallery, New York, 71; California Artists, Western Art Mus Asn, 70. Media: Acrylic. Mailing Add: 1815 Greenwich San Francisco CA 94123

I

IACURTO, FRANCESCO
PAINTER, INSTRUCTOR
b Montreal, PQ, Sept 1, 08. Study: Fine Arts Sch Montreal; Grande Chaumiere Colarossi, Paris, France, govt scholar; and with Charles Maillard, Ed Dyonnet, John Y Johnstone & others. Work: Prov Mus Que; Can House, London, Eng; House of Senate, Ottawa; Rideau Hall, Gov Gen Can; Klincoff Gallery, Montreal. Comn: Portraits, Lord Rothermere & Lord Cromer, Eng, 53; portraits, Price Bros & Anglo Paper Que, 63; fall landscapes, Bank Montreal, London, 71; painting, Janin Construction, PQ, 71; pastel, Can Govt, Ottawa, 71. Exhib: Royal Can Acad, Toronto, Ont, 48 & 51 & Montreal, 60; Spring Exhib, Montreal Mus Art, 52 & 53. Teaching: Instr drawing, Cath Sch Comn, 29-33; instr drawing, Art & Trades Montreal, 29-38; instr painting, Libr Ste Foy, PQ, 66- Awards: First Medal for Art, 28 & Scholar to Europe, 29, Govt PQ; Silver Medal, Ministry Exterior, France, 29. Mem: Royal Can Acad Arts; Soc Artists Prof Que; Independent Art Asn. Style & Technique: Figurative portraits and landscapes. Dealer: Klincoff Sherbrooke St W Montreal PQ Can; Arts & Styles 896 Sherbrooke St W Montreal PQ Can. Mailing Add: 1232 La Vigerie Quebec PQ G1W 3W7 Can

IANNETTI, PASQUALE FRANCESCO PAOLO
ART DEALER, COLLECTOR
b Florence, Italy, Apr 10, 40; US citizen. Study: Univ Florence; Acad di Belle Arti, Florence; Univ Minn, Minneapolis. Pos: Pres, Pasquale Iannetti Inc Galleries, San Francisco & Los Angeles, Calif. Mem: Am Soc of Appraisers; Graphic Art Coun, Los Angeles Co Mus & Achenbach Found, San Francisco. Specialty: Fine original prints and works on paper from the 16th century through the 20th century. Collection: Contemporary prints and drawings, Pre-Columbian and African art. Mailing Add: 575 Sutter St San Francisco CA 94102

IANNONE, DOROTHY
PAINTER
b Boston, Mass, Aug 9, 33. Study: Boston Univ, 53-57, BA(Phi Beta Kappa), 57; Brandeis Univ, Waltham, Mass, grad studies in Eng, 58. Exhib: La Cedille qui sourit, Villefranche-sur Mer, France, 66; Dieter Roth/Dorothy Iannone, Zwirner Galerie, Cologne, 67; Erotic Art Show: Collection of Drs Phyllis and Eberhard Kronhausen (traveling), Kunsthalle, Stockholm, 69; Freunde Ausstellung, Kunsthalle, Berne & Kunsthalle, Dusseldorf, 69; Edinburgh Festival of Arts, Edinburgh, Scotland, 70; Biennale, Venice, 75; Daily Bull Exposition (traveling), Fondation Maeght, St Paul-de-Vence, France, 76; Boites (traveling), Mus of Mod Art, Paris, 76; one-man shows, Stryke Gallery, New York, 66, Galerie Wahlandt, Schwabisch-Gmund, WGer, 73, Galerie 38, Copenhagen, 75, Galerie Bama, Paris, 76, Studio Galerie, Berlin, 77, Wiener & Würthle Galerie, Berlin, 77 & Haus am Lützowplatz, Berlin, 77. Teaching: Instr open workshop, Hochschule Der Künste, Berlin, summer 77. Awards: Deutscher Akademischer Austauschdienst Grant, Berlin, 76. Bibliog: Ed Sommer (auth), article in Kunstforum Int, Mainz, spring 73; Francois Pluchart (auth), article in Artitudes, St Jeannet, France, 1/76. Style & Technique: Linear, decorative and brightly colored paintings heightened with words. Media: Gouache on Cardboard and Wood. Dealer: Herve Wurz Arrocaria Editions 34 Blvd Wilson 06600 Antibes France. Mailing Add: Käuzchensteig 10 1 Berlin 33 Germany

ICAZA (FRANCISCO DE ICAZA)
PAINTER, SCULPTOR
b Mexico, Oct 5, 30. Study: Univ Madrid, BA, BC. Work: Mus Mod Art, Mex; La Jolla Mus Art, Calif; Mus Art, San Diego, Calif; Phoenix Art Mus, Ariz; Biblioteca Luis Angel Arango, Bogota, Colombia. Comn: In Mex Pavilion, Expo '67 Can; in Mex Pavilion, Hemisphere US & Osaka, Japan, 70; mural for Hotel Casino de la Selva, Cuernavaca, Mex; sculpture in bronze, Unidad Clemente Orozco, Guadalajara, Mex. Exhib: 4th Int Exhib, Guggenheim Mus, New York, 64; Phoenix Art Mus, Ariz, 67; Long Beach Mus Art, Calif, 68; Ariz State Mus, 68; 2nd Exhib Salon Independiente, Nat Univ Mex, 69. Awards: First Prize for Nuevos Valores, 57, Second Prize for National Landscape, 60 & First Prize for Salon de la Plastica Mex, 62, Mus Mod Art, Mex. Bibliog: Margarita Nelken (auth), El expresionismo en Mexico, Bellas Artes; Luis C y Aragon (auth), Mexico pintura de hoy, Fondo Cult Econ; Raquel Tibol (auth), Historia de la pintura moderna Mexicana. Mem: Frente Nac Artes Plasticas (treas, 56); Nueva Presencia (founder, 63); Salon Independiente (founder, 68). Publ: La Fiera Malvada (ltd ed 25 bks), Barcelona, 71. Mailing Add: Adolfo Prieto 601 Col de Valle Mexico DF Mexico

IDA, SHOICHI
PRINTMAKER, SCULPTOR
b Kyoto, Japan, Sept 13, 41. Study: Kyoto Munic Univ of Art, Japan, post-grad study, 65; Govt of France scholar, study in Paris, 68. Work: Mus of Mod Art, New York; Mus of Mod Art, Paris; Victoria & Albert Mus, London, Eng; Stedelijk Mus, Amsterdam, Holland; Nat Mus of Mod Art, Kyoto, Japan. Exhib: First Int Biennial Exhib of Prints, Florence, Italy, 69; Third Salon Int de Galeries Pilotes, Mus Cantonal des Beaux Arts, Lausanne, Switz, 70; Second Int Exhib of Graphics, Frechen, Ger, 72; Third Paris Int Biennial Exhib of Prints, Mus of Mod Art, Paris, 72; one-man shows, Nat Mus of Mod Art, Tokyo & Kyoto, Japan, 76; Japan Art Festival, Nat Mus of Mod Art, Tokyo, Mod Art Pavilion, Seattle Art Mus, Wash & Los Angeles Co Mus of Art, Los Angeles, 76; 12th Int Print Biennial Exhib, Nat Mus, Ljubljana, Yugoslavia, 77; 13th Contemp Art Exhib of Japan, Tokyo City Mus & Kyoto Munic Mus, Japan, 77. Awards: Museum Prize, Norway Int Biennial of Prints, Mus of Mod Art, Friedrikstad, Norway, 74; Museum Prize, 11th Int Biennial, Ljubljana, Mus of Mod Art, Rijeka, Yugoslavia, 75; Museum Prize, Tenth Int Biennial at Tokyo, Mus of Mod Art, Tokyo, 76. Bibliog: Rand Castile (auth), Shoichi Ida, Japan House Gallery, New York, 74; Yoshiaki Inui (auth), Shoichi Ida, Bijutsu Tech Art Mag, 12/76; Thomas Albright (auth), Shoichi Ida, San Francisco Chronicle, 12/76. Style & Technique: Stone lithography with strong conceptual statement usually in muted pastel tones, especially in pink and grey. Media: Stone lithography; stone sculpture. Mailing Add: c/o Soker-Kaseman Gallery 1457 Grant Ave San Francisco CA 94133

IDEN, SHELDON
PAINTER, EDUCATOR
b Detroit, Mich, Sept 29, 33. Study: Art Inst Chicago; Wayne State Univ, BFA; Cranbrook Acad Art, with Zoltan Sepeshy, MFA. Work: Detroit Inst Arts; Cranbrook Acad Art, Bloomfield Hills, Mich; Ball State Univ, Muncie, Ind; Wayne State Unv, Detroit; Macomb Community Col, Warren, Mich. Exhib: 2nd Biennial, Pa Acad Fine Arts & Detroit Mus Art, 60; Mich Artists Ann, 60-70 & 72 & Other Ideas, 69, Detroit Inst Arts; Drawing & Sculpture Ann, Ball State Univ, 62; All Mich Show, Flint Mus Art, 72. Teaching: Instr drawing & painting, Wayne State Univ, 63-68; asst prof drawing & painting, Eastern Mich Univ, 68- Pos: Artist in residence, Mich Coun Arts, 69. Awards: Fulbright Fel to India, 62; Mus Purchase Award, 70 & Gertrude Kasle Award for Painting, 71, Detroit Inst Arts. Bibliog: Hakanson (auth), Made in Detroit, Art Scene, 67 & critical rev in Detroit News, 71; Tall (auth), critical rev in Detroit Free Press, 71. Media: Oil, Graphics, Charcoal. Mailing Add: Dept of Art Eastern Mich Univ Ypsilanti MI 48197

IERVOLINO, JOSEPH ANTHONY
ART DEALER, COLLECTOR
b Brooklyn, NY, Aug 4, 20. Study: City Col New York; Univ Miami Law Sch, LLB; Americana Art Ctr. Pos: Owner & pres, Americana Galleries, 61- Mem: Assoc Int Inst Conserv of Hist & Artistic Works; Am Soc Appraisers. Specialty: American contemporary painting, sculpture and prints. Collection: Contemporary paintings of North and South America and Europe; nineteenth century American and European. Mailing Add: Americana Galleries Inc 271 Waukegan Rd Northfield IL 60093

IERVOLINO, PAULA
ART DEALER, COLLECTOR
b NDak. Study: Art Inst Chicago; Northwestern Univ. Pos: Com artist, Advertisers Art Serv, Chicago, 39-40; com artist (catalog), Furniture Mfg, Chicago, 41-61; gallery dir, Americana Galleries, 61- Mem: Art Inst Chicago Alumni Asn; Munic Art League Chicago; Am Fedn Arts; Am Soc Appraisers. Specialty: Contemporary American artists. Collection: Contemporary artists of America; paintings, sculpture and graphics. Mailing Add: 271 Waukegan Rd Northfield IL 60093

IGLEHART, ROBERT L
EDUCATOR
b Baltimore, Md, Feb 2, 12. Study: Md Inst Art, scholar for European study; Johns Hopkins Univ; Columbia Univ, BS Educ; New Sch Social Res. Teaching: Instr sch art, Univ Wash, 38-41; chmn dept art educ, NY Univ, 46-55; prof art, Univ Mich, 55-, chmn dept, 55-71. Awards: Nat Gallery Art Medal for Distinguished Serv to Art Educ, 66. Mem: Fel Royal Soc Arts; Mus Mod Art, New York; John Dewey Soc; Col Art Asn Am; Nat Art Educ Asn. Publ: Auth, numerous articles for prof mag. Mailing Add: 117 Dixboro Rd Ann Arbor MI 48105

IHARA, MICHIO
SCULPTOR
b Paris, France, Nov 17, 28; Japanese citizen. Study: Tokyo Univ Fine Arts, BFA, 53; Mass Inst Technol, Fulbright fel, also with Gyorgy Kepes, 61. Work: Wind, Wind, Wind, Kanagawa Mus Mod Art, Kamakura, Japan. Comn: Queens sq plaza, Auckland, NZ, 77; sculpture, New Castle, Australia, 77; wind sculpture, Springfield, Mass, 77; plaza sculpture, Inner Harbor, Baltimore, Md, 78; metal screen, Rockefeller Ctr, New York, 78. Exhib: Selection 64, Inst Contemp Art, Boston, 64 & Boston Celebrations, 75; Trends Contemporary Art, Kyoto Mus Mod Art, 68; Ann Exhib, Nat Inst Arts & Lett & Am Acad Arts & Lett, 73; Japanese Artists in Americas, Tokyo Mus Mod Art & Kyoto Mus Mod Art, 73-74; one-man show, Staempfli Gallery, New York, 77. Teaching: Instr basic design, Musashino Fine Arts Univ, Tokyo, 66-68. Pos: Fel Ctr Advan Visual Studies, Mass Inst Technol, 70-75. Awards: Graham Found Fel, 64; Ann Award, Am Acad Arts & Lett & Nat Inst Arts & Lett, 73; First Prize, Fitchburg Libr Art Competition, Mass Coun Arts & Humanities, 74. Mem: Japanese Artists Asn. Style & Technique: Metals, often stainless steel welded sculptures of great detail; abstract; use of light and shadow or wind movement as element in work. Media: Stainless Steel, Brass. Dealer: Staempfli Gallery 47 E 77th St New York NY 10021. Mailing Add: 35 Buena Vista Park Cambridge MA 02140

IHLE, JOHN LIVINGSTON
PRINTMAKER, EDUCATOR
b Chicago, Ill, Feb 1, 25. Study: Univ Iowa, 49, with Maurice Lasansky; Ill Wesleyan Univ, Bloomington, BFA, 50; Bradley Univ, Peoria, Ill, MA, 51, with Ernest Freed; San Francisco State Univ, 54. Work: Libr of Cong, Washington, DC; Chicago Art Inst; New York Pub Libr; Achenbach Found for Graphic Arts, Calif Palace of Legion of Honor, San Francisco; Nat Gallery of Art, Washington, DC. Comn: Prints (210 each ed), Int Graphic Art Soc, New York, 57, 60 & 61; print, Roten Galleries, Baltimore, Md, 67; print, San Francisco Hosp Comn, San Francisco Art Comn, 73. Exhib: One-man shows, San Francisco Mus Art, 60, 66 & 77, Achenbach Found for Graphic Art, 62, Hansen Gallery, San Francisco, 64 & 68; Nat Print Exhib, Libr of Cong, Soc Am Graphic Artist, New York & Brooklyn Mus, NY; Nat Print Invitationals, Univ Ky, 61, State Univ NY, Albany, 68, Univ Ill, 70 & Cincinnati Art Mus, Ohio, 73. Collections Arranged: Prints of John Ihle (auth, catalogue), Achenbach Found of Graphic Art, 49-62; Ihle: Survey of Work, Univ NDak Art Galleries, 57-76; Traveling Exhibits, Univ NDak, Minot State Col, NDak, Univ Mont, Univ Alta, Calgary & San Francisco Mus Art, 76-77; plus others. Teaching: Prof art & printmaking, San Francisco State Univ, 55-; vis prof printmaking, Univ Alta, Edmonton, 68-69. Pos: Chmn bd, San Francisco Tapestry Workshop, 78- Mem: Calif Soc Printmakers (former pres); Color Print Soc. Style & Technique: Deep etch intaglio, color a la poupee, photointaglio. Dealer: Fountain Gallery of Art 117 NW 21st Ave Portland OR 97965. Mailing Add: Indust Ctr Bldg Sausalito CA 94965

IIMURA, TAKA
FILMMAKER, VIDEO ARTIST
b Tokyo,, Japan, Feb 20, 37. Study: Keio Univ, Tokyo, BA(political sci), 59. Work: Anthology Film Arch, New York; Centre Beaubourg des Art Plastiques, Paris; Everson Mus, Syracuse, NY; Royal Film Arch, Brussels, Belg; Neuer Berliner Kunstverein, Berlin. Exhib: Int Experimental Film Festival, Knokke, Belg, 63 & 74; First Japan Film Independent Exhib, Tokyo, 64; Japanese Experimental Films, Mus of Mod Art, New York, 66; Wandering Concert, Goethe Inst, Tokyo, 70; Tokyo Biennial, Metrop Mus, 71; First Video Festival, Kitchen, New York, 72; Open Circuit (traveling), Everson Mus, Syracuse, NY, 72; Neue Medien-Neue Methoden, Palais Thurn und Taxis, Bregenz, Austria, 73; Aktionen der Avangarde, Akademie der Kunste, Berlin, 73; Projekt 74, Kunsthalle, Cologne, 74; Video/Art, ARC 2, Musee d' Art Moderne, Paris, 74; Video Shows, Inst of Contemp Art, Philadelphia, Pa, 75; one-man shows (films with performance), Filmmakers Cinematheque, New York, 66, Inst of Contemp Arts, London, 69, Royal Film Arch, Brussels, 69, Nederlands Filmmuseum, Amsterdam, 69, Swedish Film Inst, Stockholm, 69, Finnish Film Arch, Helsinki, 69, Pacific Film Arch, San Francisco, 71, Apple, New York, 72, Kitchen, New York, 72, Mus of Mod Art, New York, 75, Centre Beaubourg des Art Plastique, Paris, 77, Anthology Film Arch, New York, 77 & Int Cult Ctr, Antwerp, Belg, 77. Teaching: Vis tutor film, Schiller Col, Berlin, 73, Univ NMex, 75-76; vis asst prof film, Kent State Univ, 76. Awards: Spec Prize (for film Onan), 3rd Int Experimental Film Festival, Knokke, Belg, 63; Artist-in-residence Grant, Deutscher Akademischer Austamschdienst, Berlin, 73-74; Creative Artist Pub Serv Grant in Film, 75-76. Mailing Add: PO Box 431 Cooper Sta New York NY 10012

IKEDA, MASUO
PRINTMAKER
b 1934. Exhib: One-man show, Mus Mod Art, New York, 65; traveling show of prints in US, 67. Awards: Grand Prize Graphics, Venice Biennale, 66. Mailing Add: PO Box 1194 East Hampton NY 11937

IMANA, JORGE GARRON
PAINTER
b Sucre, Bolivia, Sept 20, 30; US citizen. Study: Univ San Francisco Xavier, Sucre, MA. Work: Nat Mus, La Paz, Bolivia; Univ San Francisco Xavier Mus, Sucre; Nat Mus, Bogota, Colombia; Casa de la Cult, Quito, Ecuador; Bolivian Embassy, Moscow. Comn: Hist mural (9 ft x 12 ft), comn by Bolivian Govt, Junin Col, Sucre, 58; Hist of Educ in Bolivia (mural), comn by Bolivian Govt, Padilla Col, Sucre, 59; Social Hist in Peru (13 ft x 50 ft mural), Constructors Union, Lima, Peru, 61; Ciudad de Dios Sch (mural), comn by students' parents, Lima, 62; 200 Yrs in San Diego's Life (7 ft x 73 ft outdoor mural), David G Fleet, San Diego, Calif, 68. Exhib: Nat Mus, Bogota, 58-63; Nat Salon of Watercolor, Lima, 62; Nat Salon, La Paz, 62; Latin Am Show, Fine Arts Gallery, San Diego, 64; Bolivian Paintings, Mus of Mod Art, Paris, France, 73 & Nat Gallery, Warsaw, Poland, 75; House of Friendship of the Peoples, Moscow, 75; Gallery IDB, Washington, DC, 76; plus 70 one-man shows. Teaching: Prof drawing, Univ San Francisco Xavier, Sucre, 54-60; prof drawing & watercolor, Nat Acad, La Paz, 60-62; dir art dept, Inst Normal Superior, La Paz, 60-62. Pos: Owner, The Artist's Showroom, San Diego. Awards: Nat Award, Nat Show, La Paz, Bolivian Govt, 62; Watercolor Award, Nat Watercolor Show, Lima, Peru, Watercolor Soc, 62; Purchase Awards Oil & Watercolor, Ann Show, San Diego Art Inst, 64. Style & Technique: Realist, all media, main interest mural painting. Mailing Add: 3645 Argonne St San Diego CA 92117

IMMERWAHR, SARA ANDERSON
ART HISTORIAN, WRITER
b Royersford, Pa, Aug 28, 14. Study: Mt Holyoke Col, BA, 35; Bryn Mawr Col, MA, 37 & PhD, 43. Teaching: Instr hist art, Wellesley Col, 42-46; lectr archaeol, Bryn Mawr Col, 46-47; from assoc prof to prof hist art, Univ NC, Chapel Hill, 67- Mem: Archaeol Inst Am (mem

exec comt, 69-72). Res: Minoan and Mycenaean art, particularly fresco and vase painting; classical Greek sculpture. Publ: Auth, Athenian Agora, Vol XIII, Neolithic and Bronze Ages, 72; auth, Early burials from the Agora Cemeteries, Agora Picture Bk 13, 73; auth, articles and bk revs in Am J Archaeol, Archaeol & Hesperia, 45- Mailing Add: Ackland Art Center Chapel Hill NC 27514

INDECK, KAREN JOY
ART DEALER, COLLECTOR
b Chicago, Ill, May 8, 51. Study: Venice Island of Studies, Venice, Italy, spec study with Prof Pignati; Drake Univ, Des Moines, Iowa; Univ Ill, Chicago, BFA, spec studies in art hist. Collections Arranged: Mesopotamian Exhibition (assisted & assembled permanent installation), Oriental Inst Chicago, 77; Aubusson Tapestry Exhibition (arranged & assembled), 78; Paper Sculpture by William Haendel (arranged & assembled), 78. Pos: Art consult & corp cur, Collector's Showroom, Chicago, 75- Mem: Mus Contemp Art (Northside Affil; bd mem); N Shore Art League. Res: Special studies on the transitions of specific artist from non-objective to abstract expressionist, 1910-1949. Specialty: Assembling and curating corporate collections, specialty in 20th century contemporary. Collection: Emphis on Rembrandt etchings and 20th century abstract expressionist graphics. Mailing Add: 3200 N Lake Shore Dr Chicago IL 60657

INDIANA, ROBERT
PAINTER, SCULPTOR
b New Castle, Ind, Sept 13, 28. Study: John Herron Sch Art; Munson-Williams-Proctor Inst; Art Inst Chicago, BFA; Skowhegan Sch Painting & Sculpture; Univ Edinburgh & Edinburgh Col Art, Scotland. Work: Mus Mod Art & Whitney Mus Am Art, New York; Carnegie Inst Arts, Pittsburgh; Stedelijk Mus, Amsterdam, Neth; Detroit Inst Arts, Mich. Comn: Electric mural, New York World's Fair, 64-65. Exhib: Mus Mod Art, New York, 61, 63-64; Americans 1963, Mus Mod Art, New York, 63; Dunn Int, Tate Gallery, London, 63; Whitney Mus Am Art, New York, 63-67, 69 & 74; New Realism, Gemeentemuseum, The Hague, Neth, 64; White House Festival of Arts, Washington, DC, 65; 9th Sao Paulo Bienal, Brazil, 67; Documenta, Kassel, WGer, 68; Fine Arts Acad, Helsinki, 69; Jewish Mus, New York, 69; Mus de Tertulia, Cali, Colombia, 70; High Mus Art, Atlanta, Ga, 72; Va Mus Fine Arts, Richmond, 74; Hirshhorn Mus, Washington, DC, 74; Corcoran Gallery Art, Washington, DC, 75; 20th Nat Print Exhib, Brooklyn Mus, NY, 77; plus others. Bibliog: Brattinga (auth), Robert Indiana, Gebrauchsgraphik, 64; Swenson (auth), Horizons of Robert Indiana, Art News, 66; McCoubrey (auth), Robert Indiana, Univ Pa, 68. Mem: Royal Soc Arts. Media: Oil, Steel. Publ: Illusr, Numbers, 68. Dealer: Galerie Denise Rene 6 W 57th St New York NY 10019. Mailing Add: 2 Spring St New York NY 10012

INDIVIGLIA, SALVATORE JOSEPH
PAINTER, INSTRUCTOR
b New York, NY, Nov 16, 19. Study: Leonardo da Vinci Art Sch; Sch Indust Arts; Pratt Inst, BA; fresco & mural painting with Alfred D Crimi; also with Buck Ulrick, Nicholas Volpe, Earl Winslow & George Harrington, Jr. Work: USN Combat Art Collection, Washington, DC; Grumbacher & Sons Collection, New York; Mutual Benefit Life Ins Co, NJ; Annin Flag Co & Morris Davis Collection, Emily Lowe Found, New York. Comn: Assisted Alfred D Crimi with hist mural for Northampton, Mass, 40, Gen Anthony Wayne Mural for Wayne, Pa, 41 & Bowery Mission Mural for Bowery Mission, New York, 42. Exhib: Am Watercolor Soc Ann, New York, 53-72; Audubon Artists Ann, New York, 53-72; Joe & Emily Lowe Found Show, 55 & 60; Operations Palette, USN Combat Art, Smithsonian Inst, Washington, DC, 65; Nat Acad Design, New York, 65-75. Teaching: Asst & instr, City Col New York & pvt classes, 46-69; instr watercolor, East Williston Libr, New York & pvt classes, 60-72; instr fine & appl arts, Mechanics Inst, New York, 62-66. Pos: Off USN combat artist, 61-; art dir, acct exec & vpres, Vogue Wright Studios, 64-; dir art, Electrographic Corp, 69-71. Awards: Pauline Law Award in Oil, Knickerbocker Artists, 74; Honorable Mention in Watercolor, 75 & Jane Peterson Award in Oil, 76, Allied Artists of Am. Mem: Artists Fellowship (pres, 60-63); Am Watercolor Soc (dir, chmn, 53-72); Allied Artists Am (secy, 59-62); Knickerbocker Artists (vpres, 57-59); Audubon Artists (jury watercolor awards, 71). Style & Technique: Traditional to interpretive. Media: Watercolor, Oil. Publ: Contribr, Direction, Int Rels Div, Off Info, 66; contribr, Watch, USNR, 67; contribr, Naval Aviation News, 68; contribr, All Hands, Bur Naval Personnel, 69; auth, Watercolor page, Am Artist Mag, 71. Mailing Add: 974 Lorraine Dr Franklin Square NY 11010

INGALLS, EVE
PAINTER, INSTRUCTOR
b Cleveland, Ohio, Sept 29, 36. Study: Smith Col, BA; Yale Sch Art, BFA, 60, MFA, 62, with Joseph Albers; Skowhegan Sch Art; Cleveland Inst Art. Exhib: Butler Inst Am Art, Youngstown, Ohio, 66; Vassar Col Art Gallery, 70; Yale-Norfolk Exhib, 72; Trumbull Art Series, Yale Univ, 74; Contemp Reflections, Aldrich Mus Contemp Art, Ridgefield, Conn, 77; Cleveland Mus Art, 77; Yale Sch Art Gallery, 77; Conn Women Artists, Carlson Gallery, Univ Bridgeport, 77; Conn Painting Drawing & Sculpture (traveling exhib), 78. Teaching: Instr painting & drawing, Silvermine Guild Sch Art, New Canaan, 72-; instr drawing, Housatonic Community Col, Bridgeport, Conn, 74-75. Style & Technique: Large drawings (maplike) in ink and graphite on raw stretched canvas. Mailing Add: 131 Arsonia Rd Woodbridge CT 06525

INGBER, BARBARA
ART DEALER, COLLECTOR
b New York, NY, Apr 18, 32. Study: NY Univ; Feigan Dramatic Sch. Mem: Mus Mod Art; Whitney Mus Am Art; Guggenheim Mus; Metrop Mus. Specialty: A great variety of styles of painting and sculpture that has in common only that it is of very high quality. Collection: Paintings, drawings, sculpture and photographs by contemporary American artists. Mailing Add: Ingber Gallery 3 E 78th St New York NY 10021

INGRAHAM, ESTHER PRICE
PAINTER
b Needham, Mass. Study: Mt Holyoke Col, BA; Cleveland Sch Art; Montana State Univ; Famous Artists Sch, Westport, Conn, cert; also with Taubes, Earl Cordrey, John Pike, Jade Fon & Tadeshi Sato. Exhib: Maui Art Shows, Hawaii, 64-68; Easter Art Festival, Honolulu & Windward Artists Shows, Hawaii, 68-74. Teaching: Instr painting, Seabury Hall, Makawao, Maui, 64-65; pvt classes on Maui & Oahu, 65-74 & La Jolla, Calif, 75- Awards: Watercolor Prize, Maui Art Soc, 66. Mem: Windward Artists Guild (bd dirs, 68-73); Artists of Hawaii. Collection: Hawaiian landscapes and portraits; Canadian Rockies; Alaska. Mailing Add: Casa de Manãna 849 Coast Blvd La Jolla CA 92037

INGRAM, JERRY CLEMAN
PAINTER, DESIGNER
b Battiest, Okla, Dec 13, 41. Study: Inst Am Indian Arts; Okla State Univ Sch Tech Training, BA, 66. Work: Nat Gallery Art, Washington, DC; Heard Mus, Phoenix, Ariz; R C Gorman Navajo Gallery, Taos, NMex; also in collections of Jerry Bregman, New York & Dr Byron Butler, Phoenix. Comn: Mural of dancers, Okla State Univ Sch Tech Training, Okmulgee, 65. Exhib: Philbrook Art Ctr Indian Art Ann, Tulsa, Okla, 66 & 77; two-man show, 70, Indian Art Ann, 71 & one-man show, 72, Heard Mus, Phoenix, Ariz; Scottsdale Indian Art Ann, Ariz, 71 & 72; Charles W Bowers Mem Mus, Santa Ana, Calif, 72; Gallup Ceremonial & NMex State Fair, 72. Awards: Hon Mention for Vision, Heard Mus, 71; Spec Award for Buffalo Dancer, Scottsdale Indian Art Ann, 72; First Prize for Buffalo Woman Dancing, Gallup Ceremonial, 72; Wolf Robe Hunt Award, 33rd Ann Am Indian Artists Exhib, Philbrook Art Ctr, Tulsa, Okla, 77. Bibliog: Tom Bahti (auth), Southwest Indian ceremonials, K C Publ, 70; Doris Monthan (auth), Indian Individualists, Northland. Media: Watercolor, Acrylic. Mailing Add: PO Box 428 Corrales NM 87048

INGRAM, JUDITH
PRINTMAKER, COLLAGE ARTIST
b Philadelphia, Pa, Oct 12, 26. Study: Philadelphia Col Art; printmaking with Carol Summers. Work: Del Mus Art, Wilmington; Univ Pa Law Sch, Philadelphia; Philadelphia Mus Art; RCA Corp, Eastern US & PR. Exhib: Philadelphia Print Club Exhib; Boston Printmakers Ann, 70; Hooks-Epstein Gallery, Houston, Tex; Philadelphia Art Alliance; NJ State Mus, Trenton; solo exhibs, Gallery 252, Philadelphia, 67, 69, 71, 73 & 75, Community Arts Ctr, Wallingford, Pa, 76 & Guenther Gallery, Wallingford, 77. Teaching: Resident artist, Pa Title III Prog, Springfield Sch Dist, Pa, 68-69. Mem: Am Color Print Soc; Artists Equity Asn. Style & Technique: Embossed collage prints, mostly white on white, using torn paper, feathers and other found objects. Mailing Add: 5 Kenny Circle Broomall PA 19008

INGRAM, VERONICA MARIE
See Orr, Veronica Marie

INMAN, PAULINE WINCHESTER
PRINTMAKER, ILLUSTRATOR
b Chicago, Ill, Mar 3, 04. Study: Smith Col, AB; and with Allen Lewis. Work: Carnegie Inst, Pittsburgh, Pa; Libr Cong, Washington, DC; Metrop Mus Art, New York; Montclair Art Mus, NJ; Boston Pub Libr, Mass. Exhib: Nat & int exhibs incl Exchange Ital Exhib, Contemp Print Exhib, Tokyo, Japan & London, Eng. Mem: Boston Printmakers; Soc Am Graphic Artists (coun, 54-56, corresp secy, 59-61, 65-66); Conn Acad Fine Arts; Acad Artists Asn. Media: Woodcut. Publ: Illusr, How to Know American Antiques, 51, New World Writing Number 2, 52 & Down East Reader, 62, Lippincott; contribr, articles in, Antiques, 60, 69 & Artists Proof, 64; illusr, Antiques Guide to Decorative Arts in America, Dutton, 72. Mailing Add: 4 Currituck Rd Newtown CT 06470

INOKUMA, GUENICHIRO
PAINTER
b Takamatsu, Japan, Dec 14, 21. Study: Tokyo Acad Fine Arts, Ueno; also with Prof Takeji Fujushima, Japan & Matisse, France. Work: Nat Mus, Tokyo; Baltimore Mus Art; Inst Contemp Art, Boston; Bridgestone Mus, Tokyo; San Francisco Mus Art; plus one other. Comn: Murals, Keio Univ, 47, Maruei Hotel, Nagoya, 52, Tokyo Cent Sta, 53; Takashimaya Dept Store, 58 & ceramic mural, Munic Bldg, Kagawa Prefecture, 59. Exhib: Imperial Art Exhib, 27-30; Tokyo Munic Art Mus, 37; Sao Paulo Biennale, 54 & 59; Mus Mod Art, Tokyo, 64; Int Art Festival, St Louis, Mo & Maline City, Ill, 67; plus one other. Teaching: Prof oil painting, Japanese Acad Fine Arts, 37-40; established art sch in Japan, 45; lect mod art to Crown Prince before world tour, 53. Awards: Mainichi Cult & Artistic Prize for Murals, 52; First Prize, Japanese Contemp Artists Exhib, 64; First Prize, Japanese Govt, Tokyo Biennale, 69. Mem: Dainibuki. Media: Oil, Acrylic. Mailing Add: c/o Willard Gallery 29 E 72nd St New York NY 10021

INOUE, KAZUKO
PAINTER, LECTURER
b Fukuoka City, Japan, Jan 14, 39; US citizen. Study: Mich State Univ, BFA & MFA. Work: Wichita State Univ Mus Fine Arts, Kans; Mich State Univ. Exhib: Toledo Mus Art, Ohio, 69; Chautauqua Exhib Am Art, NY, 70; Detroit Inst Arts, 72; Flint Inst Art, Mich, 73; one-woman show, Razor Gallery, New York, 74. Teaching: Vis artist painting & drawing, Mich State Univ, 73; lectr drawing, Eastern Mich Univ, fall 74. Awards: Awards, Chautauqua Art Ctr, 70 & Detroit Inst Arts, 72. Bibliog: David Shirley (auth), rev in New York Times, 69; rev in Art News, 72; Joseph Dreiss (auth), rev in Arts Mag, 74. Mem: Col Art Asn Am. Style & Technique: Geometric abstraction. Media: Acrylic, Mixed Media. Dealer: Bill Hart c/o Razor Gallery 464 W Broadway New York NY 10013. Mailing Add: 543 Broadway New York NY 10012 Ann Arbor MI 543 Broadway New York NY 10012

INSEL, PAULA
ART DEALER, ART ADMINISTRATOR
b Paris, France, Jan 13, 03; US citizen. Study: City Col New York, cert, 54; NY Univ, cert, 55; New York Sch Interior Design, cert, 57. Pos: Dir, Artravelrama, NY State 20 Shows in Tex, 58; dir, Stuyvesant Outdoor Art Festival, Union Square Savings Bank, New York, 59; dir, Galerie Paula Insel, New York, 60-; dir, Coney Island Art Show, CofC, Brooklyn, NY, 70. Awards: Grumbacher Art Co Award of Merit for Var Nat Exhibs, 57; Citation for Original Art Exhibs, Murray Hills, New York, 57; Citation, State Mus City of New York by Police Athletic League Comnr, 59. Mem: Am Fedn Art; Mod Mus Art. Specialty: Mostly contemporary. Publ: Auth column in Art World, 54-55; auth, New York galleries, Arts Mag, 4/71; plus others. Mailing Add: Galerie Paula Insel 987 Third Ave New York NY 10022

INSLEE, MARGUERITE T
PAINTER, COLLECTOR
b Grand Rapids, Mich, June 17, 91. Study: Univ Mich Exten, Grand Rapids Art Mus; Colorado Springs Fine Arts Ctr, with Emerson Woelfer; Inst Allende, San Miguel de Allende, Mex, Western Mich Show grant, 59; Escuela Bellas Artes, Taxco, Mex; Int Summer Acad Fine Arts. Salzburg, Austria. with Oscar Kokashka. Exhib: Grand Rapids Art Mus, 59; Sch Fine Arts, Taxco, Mex; one-woman shows, Steel Case, Inc, Women's Club & Fountain Street Church, Grand Rapids. Awards: Prize for Oil, Grand Rapids Art Mus, 59. Mem: Grand Rapids Art Mus; Mus Mod Art, New York; Smith Col Mus Art; Grand Rapids Print Club. Media: Oil. Collection: Les Yeux Clos, Redon; Peasant Girl with Kerchief, Picasso; Vienna, Oskar Kokaschka; Young Bather Standing (bronze), Maillol. Mailing Add: 909 Floral Dr SE Grand Rapids MI 49506

INSLEY, WILL
PAINTER
b Indianapolis, Ind, Oct 15, 29. Study: Amherst Col, BA; Harvard Univ Grad Sch Design, MArch. Comn: Great Southwest Indust Park, Atlanta, Ga, 68. Exhib: One-man shows, Stable Gallery, 65, Weatherspoon Art Gallery, Univ NC, Greensboro, 67, Allen Mem Art Mus, Oberlin, Ohio, 67, Walker Art Ctr, Minneapolis, 68, Albright-Knox Art Gallery, Buffalo, NY, 68, John Gibson Gallery, 69, New York, Will Insley: Space Diagrams, Inst Contemp Art,

Univ Pa, Philadelphia, 69, Will Insley: Ceremonial Space, Mus Mod Art, New York, 71, Documenta 5, Kassel, WGer, 72, Hause Lange Mus, Krefeld, WGer, 73, Fischbach Gallery, New York, 73, Württembergischer Kunstverein, Stuttgart, WGer, 74, Mus Contemp Art, Chicago, 76 & Max Protech Gallery, New York, 77. Teaching: Artist in residence, Oberlin Col, 66; art critic, Univ NC, 67-68; art critic, Cornell Univ, 69; instr art, Sch Visual Art, 69-78. Awards: Nat Found Arts & Humanities Award, 66; Guggenheim Fel, 69. Bibliog: The greater context, Tracks, Vol 1 (Nov, 1974); Alison Sky & Michelle Stone (auth), Unbilt America, McGraw-Hill, 76; Abstract Space—The architectural space—the empty building, Tracks, Vol 3 (spring 77). Dealer: Max Protech 21 W 58th St New York NY 10019; Paul Maenz Lindenstrasse 23 5 Köln 1 West Germany. Mailing Add: 231 Bowery New York NY 10002

INUKAI, KYOHEI
PAINTER, SCULPTOR
b Chicago, Ill, July 13, 13. Study: Art Inst Chicago; Nat Acad Design; Art Students League. Work: Brandeis Univ Mus Fine Art, New York; Portland Mus, Maine; Wichita Univ Mus Art, Kans; Atlantic Richfield Collection, New York; Chase Manhattan Bank Collection, New York; plus many others. Comn: Sculptures for shopping malls, Knoxville, Tenn, Monmouth, NJ & North Riverside, Ill. Exhib: US Info Agency Print Exhib, Osaka World's Fair, 70; White House Rotating Exhib; Screenprints 1970, Int Silk Screen Asn, 70; Dixon White Art Ctr, Cornell Univ, 70; ann print exhib, Brooklyn Mus, NY, 71; Am Fedn Arts Traveling Print Show. Style & Technique: Primarily geometric; some figurative. Media: Oil, Acrylic; Steel, Aluminum. Mailing Add: 884 West End Ave New York NY 10025

INVERARITY, ROBERT BRUCE
DESIGNER, MUSEUM DIRECTOR
b Seattle, Wash, July 5, 09. Study: Univ Wash, BA, 46; Fremont Univ, MFA, 47, PhD, 48; and with Kazue Yamagishi, Blanding Sloan & Mark Tobey. Work: Univ Wash; US Naval Collection, Washington, DC; also in pvt collections. Comn: Two mosaics, Univ Wash, 40; cut aluminum decorations, US Naval Airstation, Seattle, 40; six panels, Wash State Mus. Exhib: One-man shows & numerous group exhibs, US & Can, 29-39. Teaching: Dir sch creative art, Vancouver, Can, 31-33; instr, Univ Wash, 33-37; asst dir, Fred Archer Sch Photography, 47-49; assoc, Sch Am Res, 49-54; res asst, Yale Univ, 51-53. Pos: State dir, Works Progress Admin Art Proj, Seattle, 37-41; off war artist, USN, 43-45; art dir, Boeing Aircraft Co, Seattle, 46-47; dir, Mus Int Folk Art, 49-54; dir, Adirondack Mus, 54-65; dir, Philadelphia Maritime Mus, 69-76. Awards: Meritorious Civilian Serv Award, USN, 45; Wenner-Gren Found Grant for Anthrop Res, 51. Publ: Auth & illusr, Art of the Northwest Coast Indians, 50; ed, Winslow Homer in the Adirondacks, 59; auth & illusr, Visual Files Coding Index, 60; auth, Accessioning & Cataloguing, 65; co-auth, Early Chinese Art & Its Possible Influence in the Pacific Basin, 72. Mailing Add: 2610 Torrey Pines Rd C22 La Jolla CA 92037

INZERILLO, GIAN DEL VALENTINO
ART DEALER, COLLECTOR
b Milan, Italy, Jan 1, 29. Study: Univ of Rome, MA. Pos: Owner, Gian Del Valentino Galleries, Geneva, Los Angeles, Milan, Montecarlo, New York & Rome. Specialty: Original oil painting, sculptor, lithography of European and Israeli masters of contemporary art. Collection: Sironi, Picasso, Dali, Calder, Lafer, DeChirico, Sciltian, Annigoni, Guttuso, Marini, Manzo, Mago, Ferrelli, Elron and Gilboa. Mailing Add: c/o Gian Del Valentino Galleries Inc 235 Fifth Ave New York NY 10016

IOLAS, ALEXANDER
ART DEALER
Pos: Owner & dir, Alexander Iolas Gallery. Mailing Add: 52 E 57th St New York NY 10022

IPCAR, DAHLOV
ILLUSTRATOR, PAINTER
b Windsor, Vt, Nov 12, 17. Work: Metrop Mus Art, New York; Whitney Mus Am Art, New York; Newark Mus, NJ; Brooklyn Mus, NY; Univ Maine, Orono & Portland-Gorham. Comn: US Post Off Murals, LaFollette, Tenn, 37 & Yukon, Okla, 39, comn by Sect Fine Arts, US Treas Dept, Washington, DC. Exhib: Corcoran Biennial, 37; one-woman shows, Young People's Gallery, Mus Mod Art, 39 & Dalzell-Hatfield Galleries, Los Angeles, 70, Portland Mus of Art, Maine, 59, 63 & 70, Univ Maine, 65, Del Art Mus Libr, 76 & Frost Gully Gallery, Portland, Maine, 77; 14 Outstanding Women Artists, Detroit Inst, 43; two-man show, Colby Col, 74; Maine Artists, Maine State Mus, 76; plus others. Awards: Clara A Haas Award, Silvermine Guild, Conn, 57; Maine State Award, Maine Comn Arts & Humanities, 72; Juror Merit Award, Bridgton Ann, Maine, 73. Bibliog: Margaret Hammel (auth), Dahlov Ipcar's Peaceable Kingdom, Down East Mag, Camden, Maine, 4/74; John Clayton (producer), Vision Series Number 47, (doc film), US Info Agency, 75. Style & Technique: Decorative realism; recent work includes many intricately patterned jungles, animal subjects, stylized, sharp. Media: Oil, Tempera, Watercolor; Cloth. Publ: Auth & illusr, Brown Cow Farm, 59 & The Song of the Day Birds and the Night Birds, 67, Doubleday; auth & illusr, Calico Jungle, 65 & Bright Barnyard, 66, Knopf; auth & illusr, The Land of Flowers, Viking, 74. Mailing Add: Star Rte 2 Bath ME 04530

IPPOLITO, ANGELO
PAINTER, EDUCATOR
b S Arsenio, Italy, Nov 9, 22; US citizen. Study: Ozenfant Sch Fine Arts, New York; Brooklyn Mus Art Sch, with Ferren; Meschini Inst, Rome, Italy; also with Afro, Rome. Work: Whitney Mus Am Art, New York; Munson-Williams-Proctor Inst, Utica, NY; Phillips Gallery, Washington, DC; Norfolk Mus Arts & Sci, Va; Milwaukee Mus, Wis. Comn: Mural (oil painting), comn by Singer & Sons, now in collection of Montreal Trust Co, PQ, 67. Exhib: Carnegie Inst Int, Pittsburgh, 56-59; Young America, Whitney Mus Am Art, 57; Abstract Impressionism, Arts Coun, London, 58; Sao Paulo Bienal, Brazil, 61; American Collages, Mus Mod Art, New York & Beuningen Mus, Rotterdam, 66; Retrospective, State Univ NY Col, Binghamton, 75; plus others. Teaching: Instr painting, Cooper Union, 56-66; artist in residence, Mich State Univ, 66-71; assoc prof painting, State Univ NY Binghamton, 71- Awards: Fulbright Fel to Florence, Italy, 58; Ford Found Artist in Residence to Arnot Gallery, 65. Bibliog: Dore Ashton (auth), Arte Americana contemporanea, Commentari, Lionello Venturi Rome, 55; Irving Sandler (auth), Angelo Ippolito Landscapes, Provincetown Advocate, 7/4/57; Alfred Frankenstein (auth), Professors tell a story at Bolles, San Francisco Chronicle, 10/1/61. Media: Oil. Publ: Contribr, Italy Rediscovered (catalog), Munson-Williams-Proctor Inst, 55; contribr, It Is, spring 58; contribr, Nature in Abstraction, Whitney Mus. Dealer: Grace Borgenicht Gallery 1018 Madison Ave New York NY 10021. Mailing Add: Friendsville Stage Binghamton NY 13903

IPSEN, KENT FORREST
GLASSWORKER, EDUCATOR
b Milwaukee, Wis, Jan 4, 33. Study: Univ Wis-Milwaukee, BS; Univ Wis-Madison, MS & MFA; also with Harvey K Littleton. Work: Milwaukee Art Ctr, Wis; Toledo Mus Art, Ohio; Corning Glass Mus, NY; Chrysler Mus, Norfolk, Va; Objects USA, Chicago Art Inst. Exhib: Toledo Art Glass Nat, 66, 68, 70 & 72; Vidrios, Estudio Actual, Caracas, Venezuela, 74; Wis Directions, Milwaukee Art Ctr, 75; Looking Forward, Fairtree Gallery, New York, 75. Teaching: Asst prof glassworking, Mankato State Col, Minn, 65-68; assoc prof glassworking, Chicago Art Inst, 68-72; assoc prof glassworking & chmn dept crafts, Va Commonwealth Univ, 72- Awards: Nat Endowment Arts, US Govt, 72 & 75. Bibliog: Lee Nordness (auth), Objects USA, Viking, 71; Ray Grover (auth), Contemporary Art Glass, Crown, 75. Mem: Am Craft Coun (Ill State rep, 71-72); Ill Craft Coun (pres, 70-72); Nat Coun Educ in Ceramic Arts; Nat Coun Art Adminr. Style & Technique: Offhand methods of blowing, casting molten glass. Media: Glass. Dealer: Exhibit A Gallery 1708 Central St Evanston IL 60002. Mailing Add: 11761 Bollingbrook Dr Richmond VA 23235

IRELAND, PATRICK (BRIAN O'DOHERTY)
ARTIST
b Ballaghaderrin, Ireland, 34. Exhib: One-man shows, Betty Parsons Gallery, Los Angeles Co Mus of Art, Corcoran Gallery of Art, La Jolla Mus of Contemp Art & Seattle Art Mus; The Golden Door: Artist-Immigrants of Am 1876-1976, Hirshhorn Mus, Washington, DC, 76; PS 1, New York, NY, 76; Rosc, Dublin, Ireland, 77; Documenta, Kassel, WGer, 77. Pos: Dir, Visual Arts Progs, Nat Endowment Arts, 69-; ed, Art in Am, 71- Mailing Add: 15 W 67th St New York NY 10023

IRELAND, RICHARD WILSON (DICK)
PAINTER, INSTRUCTOR
b Marion, Ind, Mar 31, 25. Study: Ind Univ, BA & MA; Art Students League. Work: Mus Mod Art, New York. Exhib: John Herron Art Inst, 48, 51 & 53; Ind Printmakers, 52; one-man show, Ind Univ, 52; Mus Mod Art, New York, 56; Baltimore Mus Art; plus others. Teaching: Instr fine arts, Md Inst Art, currently. Mailing Add: Md Inst Col Art 1300 Mt Royal Ave Baltimore MD 21217

IRIZARRY, CARLOS
PAINTER, PRINTMAKER
b Santa Isabel, PR, Aug 26, 38. Study: Sch Art & Design, New York. Work: Mus Mod Art, New York; Ponce Mus, PR; Inst PR Cult, San Juan, PR; Assoc Am Artists, New York; also in collection of Harry N Abrams, New York. Exhib: Artists as Adversary, Mus Mod Art, New York, 71; Int Exhib Prints, Tokyo, Japan & Yugoslavia, 70, Cracow, Poland & Norway, 72; Drawings, Int Riejka, Yugoslavia, 72. Awards: Hon Mention, Primera Bienal de Grabado Latino Americano, San Juan, 70; Prize, Print Biennale, Vienna, Austria. Media: Mixed Media. Dealer: Harry N Abrams Ed 110 E 59th St New York NY 10022. Mailing Add: c/o Galeria Colibri 156 Cristo San Juan PR 00901

IRVIN, FRED MADDOX
ILLUSTRATOR, PAINTER
b Chillicothe, Mo, Nov 19, 14. Study: Kansas City Art Inst; Chicago Acad Fine Arts; Art Students League, New York. Teaching: Artist-in-residence, Fine Arts Fair, Chillicothe Fine Arts Coun, Mo State Coun on the Arts & Nat Endowment for the Arts, 75. Pos: Treas, Santa Barbara Art Asn, 74-75. Mem: Soc Illusr, Los Angeles. Style & Technique: Representational line and wash. Media: Pencil with Watercolor; Acrylic with Brush & Palette Knife. Publ: Illusr, Sea Lion Island, Creative Educ Soc, 72; illusr, Hit the Bike Trail, Albert Whitman Co, 74; illusr, Dictionary for Children, Macmillan, 75; illusr, Hurry Up Christmas, Garrard, 76; illusr, Hurry Home, Addison-Wesley, 76. Dealer: Kirchoff/Wohlberg Inc 433 E 51st St New York NY 10022. Mailing Add: 1702 Hillcrest Rd Santa Barbara CA 93103

IRVINE, BETTY JO
ART LIBRARIAN, INSTRUCTOR
b Indianapolis, Ind, July 13, 43. Study: Ind Univ, AB, 66, MLS, 69, ABD, 75. Teaching: Instr art bibliog, Dept of Fine Arts, Ind Univ, Bloomington, 69- Pos: Fine arts slide librn, Dept of Fine Arts, Ind Univ, Bloomington, 66-68, asst fine arts librn, 68-69, fine arts librn, 69- Awards: Officer's Grant, Coun of Libr Resources, Washington, DC, 71. Mem: Art Libr Soc NAm (mem standards comt, 75-76; co-founder, Ill-Ind Chap, 74); Col Art Asn (mem steering comt, 71-73); Am Libr Asn (vchmn/chmn-elect art sect, 78-79); Midwest Art Hist Soc (session chmn, 76). Res: Organization and management of slide libraries, art library planning and design. Interest: Library management, slide and photograph preservation. Publ: Auth, Slide classification, Col & Res Libr, Vol 32 (1/71); auth, Slide Libraries, Colo Libr Unltd, 74; auth, Organization and management of art slide collections, Libr Trends, 1/75; co-auth (with W Freitag), Slides, In: Non-print Media in Academic Libraries, Am Libr Asn, 75. Mailing Add: RR 2 Box 206 Burma Rd Gosport IN 47433

IRVING, DONALD J
ART ADMINISTRATOR, WRITER
b Arlington, Mass, May 3, 33. Study: Mass Col Art, BA, 55; Columbia Univ Teachers Col, MFA, 56, EdD, 63. Teaching: Teacher art, White Plains High Sch, NY, 58-60; instr art, State Univ NY Col Oneonta, 58-60; prof art & dean, Moore Col Art, Philadelphia, 63-67. Pos: Chmn dept art & dir, Peabody Mus Art, George Peabody Col Teachers, Nashville, Tenn, 67-69; dir sch, Sch of the Art Inst Chicago, 69- Mem: Nat Asn Schs Art (treas & mem bd dirs, 72-75); Union Independent Cols Art (bd dirs, 72-); Nat Coun Art Adminr (bd dirs, 73-); Fedn Independent Ill Cols & Univs (bd dirs, 74-); Res: Application of industrial materials and techniques to contemporary sculpture. Publ: Auth Sculpture: Material and Process, Van Nostrand Reinhold, 70. Mailing Add: Sch of the Art Inst Chicago Michigan Ave at Adams St Chicago IL 60603

IRWIN, ARTHUR
See Riley, Art

IRWIN, GEORGE M
PATRON, COLLECTOR
b Quincy, Ill, May 2, 21. Study: Univ Mich, BA, 43. Pos: Chmn bd, Assoc Coun Arts, 62-72; chmn bd, 63-71 & mem, Ill Arts Coun; former mem bd, Ill State Mus & Mus Contemp Art, Chicago; pres, Quincy Soc Fine Arts. Mem: Am Craftsmen Coun; Am Fedn Arts; Am Symphony Orchestra League; Nat Trust Hist Preserv; plus others. Collection: 20th century American artists. Mailing Add: 428 Maine St Quincy IL 62301

IRWIN, ROBERT
PAINTER
b Long Beach, Calif, 1928. Study: Otis Art Inst, 48-50; Jepson Art Inst, Los Angeles, 51; Chouinard's Art Inst, Los Angeles, 51-53. Work: Art Inst Chicago; Cleveland Mus; San Francisco Mus; Vancouver Art Mus; Mus of Mod Art, New York; Whitney Mus, New York; Walter Art Ctr, Minneapolis; Des Moines Art Ctr, Iowa; plus others. Comn: 37 sight line works, executed in Calif, Ariz, Utah & NMex. Exhib: Los Angeles Co Mus Art, 67; Vancouver Art Ctr, BC, 68; Stedelijk Mus, Amsterdam, Holland, 70; Fogg Mus, Harvard Univ, Cambridge, Mass, 72; one-man shows, Jewish Mus, New York, 68, Mus of Mod Art,

New York, 70, Chicago Mus of Contemp Art, 76, Walker Art Ctr, Minneapolis, 76 & Retrospective, Whitney Mus of Am Art, New York, 77. Teaching: Instr, Chouinard Art Inst, 57-58; instr, Univ Calif, Los Angeles, 62; instr, Univ Calif, Irvine, 68-69. Bibliog: Jan Butterfield (auth), articles in Arts Mag. Style & Technique: Working with intervals and space. Mailing Add: 10966 Strathmore Dr Los Angeles CA 90024

ISAACS, AVROM
ART DEALER
b Winnipeg, Can, 26. Study: Univ Toronto, BA (polit sci & econ). Pos: Dir & owner, Isaacs Gallery, 56-; owner, Innuit Gallery, 70-; assoc fel, Calumet Col, York Univ, 70- Specialty: (Isaacs Gallery), Contemporary Canadian art; (Innuit Gallery) art of the Eskimo. Mailing Add: 832 Yonge St Toronto ON Can

ISAACS, CAROLE SCHAFFER
COLLECTOR, PATRON
b New York, NY, May 10, 31. Collection: Bruce Backman Turner, Tom Nicholas, Emile Gruppé, Henry Gasser, Stow Wengenroth, Michael Stoffa & Aldro Hibbard. Mailing Add: 41 E Sherman Ave Colonia NJ 07067

ISAACS, CLAIRE NAOMI
GALLERY DIRECTOR
b San Francisco, Calif, Feb 12, 33. Study: Pomona Col, BA, 54; Ohio State Univ, 54-55; Univ Calif, Berkeley, 62-64; Claremont Grad Sch, MA(20th century art hist), 69; Univ Southern Calif, 71; Harvard Univ, cert in art mgt, 77. Collections Arranged: Children's Book Illustrators (artmobile exhib), 67; Art of the African (traveling exhib), 69; Children's Art From Three Countries: Japan, Iran, USSR, 76. Teaching: Lectr art for deaf, Univ Calif Exten, Los Angeles, 72. Pos: Asst, Art Gallery, Univ Calif, Berkeley, 61-63; educ supvr, San Francisco Mus Mod Art, 63-66; asst dir & coordr, Visual Art Proj, PACE (Proj to Advance Creativity in Educ), San Bernardion, Inyo & Mono Co Sch, 66-69; dir, Jr Arts Ctr, Munic Arts Dept, Los Angeles, 70- Mem: Am Asn Mus; Am Asn Youth Mus; Nat Art Educ Asn. Res: The Tribulations of St Anthony by James Ensor in the Museum of Modern Art. Collection: Contemporary art of the Los Angeles & Bay Area. Publ: Auth, Paul Klee and Galke Scheyer, Artforum, 62; auth, The Art of Borrowing and Distributing Art for the Small Community, Visual Arts Proj, 70; ed, Proceedings of the Conference on Art for the Deaf, Jr League of Los Angeles, 75; contribr, The Museum and the Visitor Experience, Western Regional Conf Am Asn Mus, 77. Mailing Add: 6704 Hillpark Dr No 403 Los Angeles CA 90068

ISAACS, RON
PAINTER, INSTRUCTOR
b Cincinnati, Ohio, Oct 14, 41. Study: Art Acad Cincinnati, summer 62; Berea Col, BA, 63; Ind Univ, MFA, 65, with James McGarrell, Robert Barnes, William Bailey, Leland Bell & Rudy Pozzatti. Work: Berea Col, Ky; Col of Mount St Joseph, Cincinnati, Ohio; AT&T Collection, New York; Chase Manhattan Bank Collection, New York; Kemper Ins Co Collection, Chicago, Ill. Exhib: Mid-States Ann Exhib, Evansville Mus Arts & Sci, Ind, 68, 69, 70, 71, 73 & 75; Second Cincinnati Biennial, Cincinnati Art Mus, Ohio, 69; Regional Fine Arts Biennial, J B Speed Art Mus, Louisville, Ky, 71; one-man shows, Deson-Zaks Gallery, Chicago, Ill, 74 & Monique Knowlton Gallery, New York, 77; Selections from the Weller Collection, Krannert Art Mus, Univ Ill, Urbana-Champaign, 75; Painting and Sculpture Today, Indianapolis Mus Art, Ind, 76; Boston Permanent Collections, Boston Inst Contemp Art, Mass, 77. Teaching: Instr fine arts, Sue Bennett Col, London, Ky, 65-69; assoc prof painting & drawing, Eastern Ky Univ, Richmond, 69- Awards: John Y Brown Award, Regional Fine Arts Biennial, J B Speed Art Mus, 71; First Purchase Awards, Preview 73, Col of Mount St Joseph, Cincinnati, Ohio, 72 & Fifth Berea Drawing Biennial, Berea Col, Ky, 73. Bibliog: W T Williams (auth), Ron Isaacs: in admiration of individualism, Ky Artists & Craftsmen Mag, 4-5/77. Mem: Ky Guild Artists & Craftsmen; Nat Art Educ Asn. Style & Technique: Realistic; recent work has taken the form of 3-D painted relief constructions of birch plywood, primarily trompe l'oeil articles of clothing; earlier work usually dealt with figures and multiple imagry. Media: Acrylic painting on jigsawed constructions of birch plywood. Dealer: Monique Knowlton Gallery 19 E 71st St New York NY 10021; Marianne Deson Gallery 226 E Ontario Chicago IL 60611. Mailing Add: Rte 10 Stateland Richmond KY 40475

ISAACSON, MARCIA JEAN
DRAFTSMAN, EDUCATOR
b Atlanta, Ga, Sept 25, 45. Study: Univ Ga, Athens, BFA & MFA. Work: Minn Mus Art, St Paul; High Mus Art, Atlanta, Ga; Southeastern Ctr Contemp Art, Winston-Salem, NC; Potsdam Col Collection, State Univ NY Col Potsdam; Greenville Co Mus Art, Greenville, SC. Exhib: Drawings USA, Minn Mus Art, St Paul, 71 & 73; Davidson Nat Print & Drawing Show, Davidson Col, NC, 73-75; 2nd NH Int Graphics Ann, Nashua, 74; Invitational Group Exhib, Jacksonville Art Mus, Fla, 74; Potsdam Drawing Exhib, NY, 74 & 75; 35 Artists in the SE (traveling exhib), High Mus Art, Atlanta, Ga; Prof Women Artists Fla, Lowe Art Mus, Univ Miami, Coral Gables, Fla, 76; Southeast 7, Nat Endowment for the Arts & Southeastern Ctr Contemp Art Fel Recipients, Winston-Salem, NC, 76. Teaching: Instr printmaking & drawing, Wesleyan Col, Macon, Ga, 70-73; asst prof drawing, Univ Fla, Gainesville, 73- Awards: Purchase Awards, Minn Mus Art, 73, Davidson Col, 73; Mem: Southeastern Graphics Coun. Style & Technique: Drawings and prints on paper, combining realism with fantasy. Media: Pencil/Chalk & Etchings on Paper. Mailing Add: Dept of Art Univ of Fla Gainesville FL 32611

ISAACSON, PHILIP MARSHAL
ART CRITIC, WRITER
b Lewiston, Maine, June 16, 24. Study: Bates Col, BA, 47; Harvard Law Sch, LLB, 50. Pos: Art critic, Maine Sunday Telegram, Portland, 68; mem fed-state adv panel, Nat Endowment for the Arts, 77-; second vpres & mem bd dir, Nat Assembly of State Arts Agencies, 77- Mem: Maine State Comn Arts & Humanities (chmn, 75-). Res: The American eagle as a decorative device; architecture of Maine since 1920. Publ: Auth, The American Eagle, NY Graphic Soc, 75. Mailing Add: 2 Benson St Lewiston ME 04240

ISAAK, NICHOLAS, JR
PAINTER, PRINTMAKER
b Manchester, NH, July 5, 44. Study: Boston Univ, BFA, 67, MFA, 69; spec study with Walter Murch, Robert Gwathmey & Karl Fortress. Work: Va Mus Fine Arts, Richmond; Western Ill Univ, Macomb; Fitchburg Mus Art, Mass; Northern Ill Univ, DeKalb; Bradley Univ, Peoria, Ill; plus others. Exhib: Pa Acad Fine Arts 164th Ann, 69; three-man show, Exeter Acad, NH, 71; one-man show, Va Mus Fine Arts, Robinson Gallery, 71; Chrysler Mus Art, Norfolk, Va, 72; Print Invitational, Pratt Grahics Ctr, New York, 73; Berkshire Mus, Pittsfield, Mass, 73; 19th-22nd Ann, Ball State Univ, Muncie, Ind, 73-76; Mod Printmakers, Rochester Inst Technol, NY, 74; 2nd Graphics Biennial, Metrop Mus, Miami, Fla, 75; Fitchburg Mus Art, Mass, 76. Teaching: Instr printmaking, Norfolk State Col, Va, 69-72; asst prof painting, Boston Univ, Mass, 72-77; assoc prof printmaking & chmn dept, Keene State Col, NH, 77- Awards: Nat Teaching fel, Dept Health, Educ & Welfare, 69; Cert of Distinction, Va Artists Biennial, Va Mus Art, 71. Mem: Col Art Asn Am. Style & Technique: Representational, landscape, still life and figure. Media: Oil on canvas; drawing; etching. Dealer: Assoc Am Artists 663 Fifth Ave New York NY 10022. Mailing Add: Rte 63 Westmoreland NH 03467

ISELIN, LEWIS
SCULPTOR
b New Rochelle, NY, June 22, 13. Study: Art Students League, 34-38, with Mahonri Young, John Stuart, Curry, George Bridgman & Gleb Derujunshy. Work: Columbus Gallery Fine Arts, Ohio; Fogg Art Mus, Cambridge, Mass; Colby Col Mus, Waterville, Maine; Yale Univ. Comn: Sculpture, US Mil Cemetery, Suresnes, France, 50; portraits of John Wanamaker & Marshall Field, Merchandise Mart, 54; figure of Gen Nathaniel Greene, City of Philadelphia, 60; figure of St Vincent de Paul, Vincent Astor Found, 65; sculpture mural, Midland Mutual Life Ins, 71. Exhib: Metrop Mus Art, 45; Pa Acad Fine Arts, 40-60; Whitney Mus Am Art, 40-60. Awards: Helen Foster Badnet Prize, Nat Acad Design, 38; Guggenheim Fel, 52. Media: Bronze. Mailing Add: Belfast Rd Camden ME 04843

ISENBURGER, ERIC
PAINTER
b Frankfurt am Main, Ger, May 17, 02; US citizen. Study: Frankfurt Art Sch. Work: Mus Mod Art, New York; Corcoran Gallery Art, Washington, DC; Pa Acad Fine Arts, Philadelphia, Pa; M H De Young Mem Mus, San Francisco, Calif; John Herron Art Inst, Indianapolis, Ind. Exhib: Art of Today, 1951, Metrop Mus Art, New York; Pa Acad Fine Arts, Philadelphia; Art Inst Chicago, Ill; Carnegie Inst, Pittsburgh, Pa; eight one-man shows, Knoedler's, New York. Teaching: Instr painting, Nat Acad Sch Fine Arts, 59- Awards: Third Prize, Carnegie Inst, 47; First Prize & Gold Medal, Corcoran Gallery Art, 49; Edwin Palmer Mem Prize, Nat Acad Design, 57 & 70. Mem: Academician Nat Acad Design; Audubon Artists. Style & Technique: Neo-impressionistic. Media: Oil. Publ: Auth, article in, Am Artist, 48. Mailing Add: 140 E 56th St New York NY 10022

ISHAM, SHEILA EATON
PAINTER
b New York, NY, Dec 19, 27. Study: Bryn Mawr Col, BA(cum laude), 50; Hochschule Fiü Bildende Künste, Berlin, Ger, 50-54. Work: Mus Mod Art, New York; Nat Collection Fine Arts, Washington, DC; Philadelphia Mus Art, Pa; Corcoran Gallery Art, Washington, DC; San Francisco Mus Art. Exhib: One-man shows, Jefferson Place Gallery, 68-70, French & Co Gallery, New York, 70 & Brockton Art Ctr, Mass, 72; Am Cult Ctr, Paris, 73; Corcoran Gallery, Washington, DC, 74; Albright-Knox Gallery, NY, 74. Teaching: Instr art hist & graphics, Chinese Univ, Hong Kong, 63-65. Awards: Print Award, Corcoran Gallery Art, 58; Print Award, Libr Cong, Pennell Comt, Wash Soc Printmakers, 60 & 61. Bibliog: New images, Art Mag, summer 70; Sidra Stich (auth), Five new Washington artists, Art Int, 12/71; Edward Fry (auth), article in Arts Int, 76. Publ: Co-auth, I Ching (portfolio of eight lithographs with poems); Marakech (portfolio of four lithographs). Dealer: Pyramid Gallery 2121 P St NW Washington DC 20037; Fendrick Gallery 3059 M St NW Washington DC 20007. Mailing Add: 1601 19th St NW Washington DC 20009

ISHIKAWA, JOSEPH
MUSEUM DIRECTOR, LECTURER
b Los Angeles, Calif, July 29, 19. Study: Univ Calif, Los Angeles, AB, 42; Univ Nebr. Collections Arranged: Beloit & Vicinity Exhib, ann, 62-74, Nathan Cummings Collection Ancient Peruvian Ceramics, 63; Figure in the 60's, 69; Art Beyond, 69; Black Experience, 70; Harvey Littleton: Glass, 71; Chicago Five, 71. Pos: From asst cur to cur, Univ Nebr Art Galleries, 43-51; chief cur to asst dir, Des Moines Art Ctr, 51-58; dir, Sioux City Art Ctr, 58-61; dir, Wright Art Ctr, Beloit Col, 61-74; dir, Kresge Art Gallery, Mich State Univ, 74- Awards: Scandinavian Sem, Am Asn Mus & Fulbright Fels, 65; Beloit Col & Ford Found Humanities Grant, 69. Mem: Int Coun Mus; Am Asn Mus; Midwest Mus Conf (vpres, 70, pres, 73-74); Wis Fedn Mus (chmn, 70-). Res: Influence of Puvis de Chavannes on 20th century painting. Publ: Auth, University as tastemaker, Palette, 58; auth, Puvis de Chavannes: Moderne Malgre Lui, Art J, 68. Mailing Add: Kresge Art Gallery Mich State Univ East Lansing MI 48824

ISKIN, RUTH EVELYN
ART HISTORIAN, EDUCATOR
b Jerusalem, Israel, Sept 15, 45. Study: Hebrew Univ, Jerusalem, BA(art hist); Johns Hopkins Univ, MA(art hist). Teaching: Lectr women's art, Univ Calif, Los Angeles, 73-74; lectr mod art & women's art, Otis Art Inst, Los Angeles, 73-75; fac mem feminist art hist, Feminist Studio Workshop, Woman's Bldg, Los Angeles, 74- Pos: Ed, Womanspace J, 73; co-dir, Womanspace, Los Angeles, 73-74; dir, Woman's Bldg Galleries, 76-78; ed, Chrysalis Mag, 77- Mem: Los Angeles Inst Contemp Art; Women's Caucus for the Arts (adv bd, 73-77); Woman's Bldg (bd dir, 73-). Res: Monographic study of art of Mary Cassatt; research and curator of documentary exhibition of Woman's Building, Chicago World's Fair 1893; research and curator of exhibitions of contemporary women's art and feminist art. Publ: Auth, Sexual—and self—imagery in art, male & female, Womanspace J, 73; auth, Public art as identity reinforcement: an interview with Lloyd Hamrol, Los Angeles Inst Contemp Art J, 76; auth, Female experience in art: the impact of women's art in a work environment, Heresies, 77; auth, Joan Snyder: toward a feminist imperative, 77 & Anita Steckel's feminist fantasy: the making of a new ideology, 77, Chrysalis. Mailing Add: c/o Chrysalis 1727 N Spring St Los Angeles CA 90012

ISKOWITZ, GERSHON
PAINTER
b Kelce, Poland, Nov, 1921; Can citizen. Study: Munich Acad Fine Arts; also with Oscar Kokschka. Work: Art Gallery Ont, Toronto; Nat Gallery Can, Ottawa; Ft Lauderdale Art Mus; Simon Fraser Univ; also in pvt collection of Joseph H Hirshhorn, Greenwich, Conn. Exhib: 6th Can Biennial, Nat Gallery Can, 65; Tel Aviv Mus, Israel, 70; Man and His World, Montreal, 71; 36th Venice Biennale, Italy, 72; one-man retrospective, Glenbow-Alberta Art Inst, Calgary, 75; Nat Gallery Can, Ottawa, 73; Mus d'Arte Contemporain, Montreal, 74. Awards: Senior Arts Grant, Can Coun, Ottawa, 74. Bibliog: Peter Mellen (auth), Gershon Iskowitz, Arts Can, 71 & Standing Apart (film from 36th Venice Biennale), 72; Gershon Iskowitz (film), Can TV. Mem: Royal Soc Can Artists. Style & Technique: Abstracted landscapes. Media: Oil, Watercolor. Mailing Add: c/o Gallery Moos 138 Yorkville Ave Toronto ON M5R 1C2 Can

ISPANKY, LASZLO
SCULPTOR, DESIGNER
b Budapest, Hungary, Nov 3, 19. Study: Budapest Fine Arts Acad; Cranbrook Acad of Art, Bloomfield, Mich. Work: Vatican Mus, Rome, Italy; Peking Mus, China; Buckingham Palace, London, Eng; Shrevesport Mus, La; NJ State Mus, Trenton. Comn: Dance & music mural (60 ft x 20 ft), Grinnell Music Store, Birmingham, Mich, 58; bust of Eugene Ormandy, comn by Eugene Ormandy, Philadelphia Philharmonic, 59; Basketball players (sculpture), Basketball Hall of Fame, Springfield, Mass, 74; George Washington at Prayer (sculpture), Freedom Found, Valley Forge, Pa, 76; Spring Wind—Autumn Wind, Soc of Medalists, New York. Exhib: Religious Sculpting, Catholic Diocese, Detroit, Mich, 58; 29th Ann Exhib, 62 & 32nd Ann Exhib, 65, Nat Sculpture Soc, New York; Porcelain in Retrospect, NJ State Mus, Trenton, 73; one-man show, Squibb Int Hdq, Princeton, NJ, 74; Reality Reflected, Nat Sculpture Soc, New York, 77. Collections Arranged: Little Gallery, Birmingham, Mich, 58; Lynn Kottler Galleries, New York, 63; Delancy Gallery, Philadelphia, 64-; Norton Gallery of Fine Art, West Palm Beach, Fla, 74-; Hungarian Festival, Garden State Arts Ctr, Holmdel, NJ, 74. Teaching: Instr sculpting, Int Inst, Detroit, 57-58. Pos: Chief sculptor, Cybis Porcelain Studio, Trenton, NJ, 61-66; pres, Ispanky Porcelains Ltd, Pennington, NJ, 66-76; sculptor, adv & consult, Goebel Art (GmbH), Rodental, WGer, 66- Awards: Grand Cross of Malta, Contrib to Art & Cult, Knights of Malta, 77. Bibliog: J Wendell Sether (auth), For your information, Newsweek Mag, 9/57; Annette Barshay (auth), Porcelain approach to US history, Trenton Evening Times, 8/68; Miriam Leinwoll (auth), '56 Refugee now master of sculpture in porcelain, New York Times, 2/73. Style & Technique: Realistic, classical modern. Media: Bronze and porcelain. Mailing Add: Van Dyke Rd Hopewell NJ 08525

ISRAEL, MARVIN
DESIGNER, PAINTER
b Syracuse, NY, July 3, 24. Study: Syracuse Univ, BFA, 50; Yale Univ, MFA(graphic design), 55. Work: Whitney Mus Art & Mus Mod Art, New York; Art Inst Chicago; Galerie Ostergren, Sweden; J L Hudson, Detroit. Exhib: One-man shows, Cordier & Ekstrom, New York, 66, 69, 71 & 74, Staatliche Kunsthalle, Baden-Baden, Ger, 67, Brusberg Gallery, Hanover, Ger, 71 & Richard Feigen, Chicago, 72; Baltimore Mus Art, 68; Whitney Mus Art, 69; Pasadena Mus Art, Calif, 69; Indianapolis Mus Art, Ind, 70 & 72. Teaching: Instr design & painting, Parsons Sch Design, 59-64, Sch Visual Arts, 65-67 & Cooper Union, 68-69. Pos: Art dir, Seventeen Mag, 57-59 & Harper's Bazaar, 60-62. Style & Technique: Realist. Media: Acrylic, Pastel, Charcoal, Paint. Dealer: Cordier & Ekstrom Gallery 980 Madison Ave New York NY 10021. Mailing Add: 273 W 14th St New York NY 10011

ISSERSTEDT, DOROTHEA CARUS
ART DEALER, ART HISTORIAN
Study: Univ Munich; Univ Freiburg, PhD(art hist); Wheaton Col. Pos: Dir, Carus Gallery. Mem: Art Dealers Asn Am. Res: Medieval art, mainly 12th and 13th century sculpture. Specialty: Art of the German Expressionists and art of the twenties. Mailing Add: 1044 Madison Ave New York NY 10021

ITALIANO, JOAN NYLEN
SCULPTOR, EDUCATOR
b Worcester, Mass. Study: Siena Heights Col, PhB, Studio Angelico, MFA; Barry Col, Fla; Nino Caruso, Rome, Italy. Work: Little Gallery, Siena Heights Col, Adrian, Mich; Botolph Gallery, Boston; Anna Maria Col, Paxton, Mass; Int Ctr for Ceramics, Rome, Italy; plus pvt collections in US & Can. Comn: Stations of the Cross, Navy Base, Chapel, Key West, Fla, 57; Our Mother of Joy Fountain, comn by John Cardinal Wright, St Vincent Hosp, Worcester, Mass, 59; Stations of the Cross, comn by architect, Our Lady of Lourdes Church, Milbury, Mass, 62; Last Supper Mural, Passionist Monastery, Shrewsbury, Mass, 64; Tree of Life Fountain, Mary Manning Walsh Home, New York, 71. Exhib: Detroit Inst Art, 50 & 56; Toledo Mus, Ohio, 50, 52 & 57; Norton Gallery, Palm Beach, Fla, 54-57, one-man show, 56; Sarasota Nat, Fla, 56 & 57; Worcester Art Mus, 62 & 72); Eastern States Ann, Springfield, Mass, 62; Rochester Relig Arts Festival Nat, NY, 71; WEB at the PRU, Prudential Ctr, Boston, 74; Fitchburg Art Mus, Mass, 75 & 77; Attleboro Mus, Mass, 76; plus many others. Teaching: Instr sculpture, Barry Col, Miami, Fla, 56-58; assoc prof sculpture, Col of the Holy Cross, 69, chmn fine arts dept, 77- Pos: Dir, Art Gallery, Barry Col, 56-58; consult liturgical art, Dick Bros Archit Interiors, 62-72. Awards: First Prize in Sculpture, Fla Craftsmen Ann, 55 & Palm Beach Art League Ann, 55 & 56; Best of Show, Artist's Guild Show, Palm Beach, 55; plus others. Mem: New Eng Sculptors Asn; Mass Asn Craftsmen; WEB; Southern Asn Sculptors. Style & Technique: Architectural sculpture and liturgical art. Media: Clay, Metal; Enamel, Wood. Mailing Add: Dept of Fine Arts Col of the Holy Cross Worcester MA 01610

ITCHKAWICH, DAVID MICHAEL
PRINTMAKER
b Westerly, RI, Aug 18, 37. Study: RI Sch Design, BFA. Work: John Sloane Study Collection, Univ Del; Charles Dana Mus, Colgate Univ; New York Pub Libr; Munson-Williams-Proctor Inst, Utica, NY. Exhib: Nat Print Exhib, Brooklyn Mus, NY, 70 & 72; one-man show, Horizon Gallery, New York, 71; two-man show, Michael Wyman Gallery, Chicago, 72; Davidson Nat Print Show, Davidson Univ, 73-75; Martin Sumers Graphics, 76. Teaching: Artist lecturer in residence, Appalachian State Univ. Bibliog: The visions of David Itchkawich, Intellectual Digest, 2/72. Style & Technique: Ersatz reportage in representational basic line etching. Dealer: Horizon Gallery 45 Christopher St New York NY 10014. Mailing Add: 1428 Lexington Ave New York NY 10021

IVES, ELAINE CAROLINE
PAINTER
b New York, NY, Oct 20, 22. Study: Jacksonville Art Sch, with Paul Toleffson & William Pachner; Inst de Allende, with Jim Pinto. Exhib: Soc Four Arts, Palm Beach, 66-68 & 76; Sarasota Art Asn, 67-71; Butler Inst Am Art, Youngstown, Ohio, 69; Fla Artist Group, 72-74 & 76; Loch Haven Art Ctr, Orlando, 74 & 77; Tampa Bay Art Ctr, Fla, 75-77; Retrospective, Winter Haven Cult Art Ctr, Fla, 76. Awards: Best in Show for Causway Gale, Fla Fedn Art, 64; Second Prize for Wipe Out, Sarasota Art Asn, 70; Best in Show for Transition, Latin Quarter Gallery, 74. Bibliog: Currios and Ives, then & now, Nationwide Ins Mag, 65; plus others. Mem: Fla Artist Group; Loch Haven Art Ctr; Latin Quarter Gallery (pres, 75-76); Ridge Art Asn (pres). Style & Technique: Abstract image; hard edge; emphasis on design and color; brush. Media: Oil, Acrylic, Ink. Dealer: Ringling Art Rental & Sales Gallery PO Box 1838 Sarasota FL 33578. Mailing Add: 2115 18th St NW Winterhaven FL 33880

IVEY, JAMES BURNETT
CARTOONIST, COLLECTOR
b Chattanooga, Tenn, Apr 19, 25. Study: Univ Louisville; George Washington Univ; Nat Art Sch. Work: Libr Cong, Washington, DC; Syracuse Univ, NY; Albert T Reid Collection, Univ Kans; Mo State Hist Soc; State Hist Soc Wis, Madison. Collections Arranged: Cartoons from Gillray to Goldberg, San Francisco Mus Art, 62; Cartoon Museum, Madeira Beach, Fla, 67-68; Cartoon from Hogarth to Herblock, Lock Haven Art Ctr, Orlando, Fla, 71. Pos: Political cartoonist, Washington Star, DC, 50-53, St Petersburg Times, 53-59, San Francisco Examr, 59-66, Rothco Syndicate, 63- & Orlando Sentinel, 67-77; cur & dir, Cartoon Mus, Madeira Beach, Fla, 67-68 & Orlando, Fla, 75-; ed & publ, Cartoon, 71- Awards: Reid Found Fel, 59. Bibliog: John Chase (auth), Today's Cartoon, Haiser Press, 63; Dorothy MacGreal (auth), World of Comic Art, 66. Mem: Nat Cartoonist Soc (chmn Fla chap, 72-); Am Asn Ed Cartoonists. Style & Technique: Black and white with color overlays. Media: Ink. Collection: Original cartoon art, approximately 2000 cartoons representing entire history of the art in twenty countries. Publ: Contribr, Freedom & Union: European Cartoonists, 61; contribr, Freedom & Union: US & European Cartoon Compared, 62; contribr, Cartoonist Profiles, 70; contribr, Cartoon: Pen Mightier than Suit, 71. Mailing Add: 561 Obispo Ave Orlando FL 32807

IVY, GREGORY DOWLER
PAINTER
b Clarksburg, Mo, May 7, 04. Study: Cent Mo State Col, BS; St Louis Sch Fine Arts, Wash Univ; Columbia Univ, MA; NY Univ. Exhib: Art Inst Chicago; Brooklyn Mus; Metrop Mus Art, New York; High Mus Art, Atlanta; Mint Mus Art, Charlotte, NC; plus others. Teaching: Instr art, State Teachers Col, Indiana, Pa, 32-35; prof art & head dept, Woman's Col, Univ NC, Greensboro, 35-61, dir, Burnsville Sch Fine Arts, 52-53; dir summer session fine arts, Beaufort, NC, 54; chmn dept art, Calif State Univ, Fullerton, 65-67, prof 65-74. Pos: Bd dirs & exec comt, NC Mus Art, 56-58; mem policy comt, Col Art Asn Am, 56-58; vpres, Southeastern Col Artists Conf, 57-58; mem policy comt, Nat Art Educ Asn, 57-59; mem exec comt, Assoc Artists NC, 59-60; bd mem, NC State Artists Soc, 60-62. Publ: Auth & illusr, An Approach to Design (monogr). Mailing Add: 2522 Brentwood Ave Springfield MO 65804

IWAMASA, KEN
EDUCATOR, ARTIST
b Manzanar, Calif, Apr 28, 43. Study: Calif State Univ, Long Beach, BA(drawing & painting), 66 & MA(printmaking), 72. Work: El Camino Col; City of Los Angeles; J S Scott Found; Rio Hondo Col. Exhib: Young Am Printmakers (Europ traveling exhib), 73; Prints of the 70s, Calif State Univ, Sacramento, 74; Spree 76, Denver Mus Natural Hist, Colo, 76; World Print Competition, San Francisco Mus Mod Art, Calif, 77; Haward Exhib, Boulder Fine Arts Ctr & Impressions, Colo, 77; 10th Ann Graphics Int, New York, 77; Fantasies, Colo Women's Col, Denver, 78; one-man shows, Univ Colo, Boulder, 75, Wash State Univ, Pullman, 76, Rio Hondo Col, Whittier, Calif, 76 & Old Dominion Univ, Norfolk, Va, 77. Teaching: Asst prof drawing & printmaking, Univ Colo, Boulder, 72- Awards: Grants & Purchase Awards from Scott Found, Japan Found, Univ Colo, Canon City & City of Los Angeles. Style & Technique: Basically prints, screen, lithography, photography, drawing & mixed-media. Dealer: Martha Jackson Gallery 521 W 57th St New York NY 10022. Mailing Add: Dept of Fine Arts Univ Colo Boulder CO 80309

IWAMOTO, RALPH SHIGETO
PAINTER
b Honolulu, Hawaii, Sept 13, 27. Study: Community Col, New York, 49-51; Art Students League, 48-49 & 51-53. Work: Butler Inst Am Art, Youngstown, Ohio; Sheldon Swope Art Gallery, Terre Haute, Ind; Herbert F Johnson Art Mus, Cornell Univ; State Found on Cult & Arts, Honolulu; Honolulu Advertiser Collection. Exhib: Pa Acad, Philadelphia, 58; Whitney Mus Ann, New York, 58; one-man shows, Columbia Mus Art, SC, 59, Watson Art Gallery, Elmira Col, NY, 68 & Westbeth Gallery, New York, 73 & 74; Am Abstract Artists, New York, 76; Paterson Col, NJ, 77; plus many others. Awards: Purchase Prize, Butler Inst Am Art, 57; Fel, John Hay Whitney Found, 58. Bibliog: James Mellow (auth), Art rev, New York Times, 2/17/73. Mem: Am Abstract Artists. Style & Technique: Abstract geometric octagon concept. Media: Pencil/Ink, Acrylic. Mailing Add: 463 West St A-1110 New York NY 10014

IZACYRO (ISAAC JIRO MATSUOKA)
PAINTER
b Honolulu, Hawaii, Mar 17, 30. Study: Baker Univ; Univ Hawaii, BFA; Art Students League New York; St Olav's, Malmo, Sweden, hon DFA, 69. Work: St Paul Art Ctr Mus, Minn. Exhib: Drawings USA, St Paul, 63; Galerie Int, New York, 64-69; Am Artists, Salon de Prix Paris, 71; two-man show, East-West Art Cult Ctr, 68; Dyptch, Honolulu Acad Arts Ann, 75. Awards: Ink Painting Award, Artists of Hawaii, 60. Style & Technique: Modern abstract. Mailing Add: c/o Galerie Int 1095 Madison Ave New York NY 10028

IZUKA, KUNIO
SCULPTOR
b Tokyo, Japan, Mar 2, 39. Study: Otis Art Inst of Los Angeles Co; Art Students League. Work: Otis Art Inst of Los Angeles Co; Mus Mod Art of Tokyo, Japan; Mus Mod Art of Kyoto, Japan. Comn: Monumental sculpture, Warner Commun, Los Angeles, 72. Exhib: 1st Int Exhib Mod Sculpture, Hakone Open-Air Mus, Japan, 69; Exhib Contemp Japanese Art, Mus Mod Art of Rio de Janeiro, 71 & Milan, Italy, 72. Teaching: Asst instr sculpture, Art Students League, 68-69. Awards: Purchase Prize, 50th Anniversary Show of Otis Art Inst of Los Angeles Co, 68; Second Prize, Exhib Contemp Japanese Art, New York, 72. Mem: Sculptors Guild; Japanese Artist Asn New York. Style & Technique: Metal sculpture, motion and sound. Mailing Add: 80 Amsterdam Ave 4-B New York NY 10023

IZUMI, KIYOSHI
ARCHITECT, EDUCATOR
b Vancouver, BC, Mar 24, 21. Study: Univ Man, BArch; Mass Inst Technol, MCP. Teaching: Mem fac environ studies, Univ Waterloo, currently. Pos: Mem, Sask Arts Bd, 60; mem bd trustees, Nat Mus Can, Govt Can, 68-74; chmn vis comt, Nat Art Gallery Can, Ottawa, 70-74. Mem: Academician Royal Can Acad Arts. Publ: Auth, Some considerations on the art of architecture and art in architecture, Structurist, Univ Sask, Modern Press, No 2, 61-62. Mailing Add: Sch Urban & Regional Plan Univ of Waterloo Waterloo ON Can

J

JACHMANN, KURT M
COLLECTOR
Collection: African, Pre-Columbian and Oceanic art; French abstract-expressionist; calligraphic paintings; German expressionists. Mailing Add: 215 E 68th St New York NY 10021

JACHNA, JOSEPH DAVID
PHOTOGRAPHER, EDUCATOR
b Chicago, Ill, Sept 12, 35. Study: Univ Mo Photo-Jour Workshop, 57; Ill Inst Technol Inst Design, BS(art educ), 58, MS(photog), 61, with Aaron Siskind, Harry Callahan & Frederick Sommer. Work: George Eastman House, Int Mus Photog, Rochester, NY; Art Inst Chicago; Photog Collection, Exchange Nat Bank of Chicago; Mass Inst Technol Permanent Collection; Univ Kans Art Mus, Lawrence. Exhib: One-man shows, Art Inst Chicago, 61 & Nikon Salon (two galleries), Tokyo, Japan, 74; Photog in the 20th Century, Nat Gallery Can, 67; Photog: Midwest Invitational, Walker Art Ctr, Minneapolis, 73; Univ Notre Dame Art Galleries, Ind, 75; plus 22 one-man shows & 50 group shows. Teaching: From instr to asst prof photog, Inst Design, Ill Inst Technol, 61-69; from asst prof to assoc prof photog, Univ Ill, Chicago Circle Campus, 69-; workshops, Peninsula Sch Art, Door Co, Wis, summers 69-71. Awards: Fac Res Grant, Ill Inst Technol, 69; Fac Grant Color Photog, Univ Ill, Chicago Circle Campus, 72; Ferguson Grant, Friends of Photog, Carmel, Calif, 73. Bibliog: Fred R Parker (auth), Joseph Jachna, Untitled No 4, Friends of Photog, 73; Landscape illusions, In: Photography Year 1974, Time/Life Bks, 74; John B Turner (auth), Joseph D Jachna, Photo-Forum, Auckland, NZ, 75. Mem: Soc Photog Educ; assoc George Eastman House-Int Mus Photog. Style & Technique: Photography, mostly black and white. Publ: Contribr, Aperture, 61; contribr, Art in America, New Talent Issue, 62; contribr, Photography in the 20th Century (catalog), Eastman House, 67; contribr, Exposure, 73; contribr, Camera Mainichi '74-9, 74. Dealer: Visual Studies Workshop Gallery 4 Elton St Rochester NY 14607. Mailing Add: 5707 W 89th Pl Oak Lawn IL 60453

JACKARD, JERALD WAYNE
See Jacquard

JACKSON, A B
EDUCATOR, PAINTER
b New Haven, Conn, Apr 18, 25. Study: Yale Norfolk summer fel, 52, with Josef Albers, Nicholas Marsicano & Gabor Peterdi; Yale Univ Sch Art & Archit, BFA, 53, MFA, 55. Work: Yale Univ, New Haven, Conn; Dartmouth Col, Hanover, NH; Univ Mass. Amherst; Mint Mus, Charlotte, NC; Chrysler Mus, Norfolk, Va. Exhib: Int Figure Painting Traveling Show, 69-70; Smithsonian American Drawing Traveling Show, 69-72; Black Artists in Review, Cleveland State Univ, 72; Va Mus Traveling Exhibs. Teaching: Instr art, Southern Univ, 55-56; asst prof art, Norfolk State Col, 56-67; prof art, Old Dom Univ, 67- Pos: Artist in residence, Living Arts Ctr, Dayton, Ohio, summer 69; artist in residence, Dartmouth Col, Spring 71; vis artist, Humanities Ctr, Richmond, Va, 71; vis artist, Roanoke Fine Arts Ctr, Va, spring 72. Awards: Purchase Award, Va Biennial, Va Mus Fine Arts, 64; Purchase Award, Graphics Ann, Mint Mus, Charlotte, 67; Purchase Award, Am Drawing Exhib, Chrysler Mus, Norfolk, 71. Bibliog: Sidney Hurwitz (auth), A B Jackson: his porch people, Am Artist, 2/68. Publ: Illusr several issues of Red Clay Reader, 65-70; illusr, Randolph Bourne, Legend & Reality, 66. Dealer: Eric Schindler Gallery Broad St Richmond VA 23233. Mailing Add: Dept of Art Old Dom Univ Norfolk VA 23508

JACKSON, BILLY MORROW
PAINTER
b Kansas City, Mo, Feb 23, 26. Study: Washington Univ, BFA; Univ Ill, Urbana, MFA. Work: Metrop Mus Art, New York; Calif Palace Legion of Honor, San Francisco, Calif; Butler Inst Am Art, Youngstown, Ohio; Nat Collection, Smithsonian Inst & Nat Gallery Art, Washington, DC; plus many others. Exhib: McClung Mus, Univ Tenn, 65 & 66, two-man show, 67; Fine Arts Gallery San Diego, Calif, 66; Lehigh Univ, Bethlehem, Pa, 66; Decatur Art Ctr, Ill, 66; 4 Arts Gallery Evanston, Ill, 67; plus many other group & one-man shows. Teaching: Prof art, Univ Ill, Urbana, currently. Awards: Purchase Prize, Evansville Mus Arts & Sci, 66; Butler Inst Am Art, 66; Union League Club, Chicago, 67; plus many others. Style & Technique: Representational. Media: Oil, Watercolor. Dealer: Jane Haslem Gallery 2121 P St NW Washington DC 20037. Mailing Add: Dept of Art Univ of Ill Urbana IL 61801

JACKSON, EVERETT GEE
PAINTER, ILLUSTRATOR
b Mexia, Tex, Oct 8, 00. Study: Tex A&M Univ; Art Inst Chicago; San Diego State Col, BA; Univ Southern Calif, MA; also study in Mex. Work: Houston Mus Art, Tex; Fine Arts Gallery, San Diego, Calif; Los Angeles Co Mus Art; Pa Acad Fine Arts, Philadelphia. Exhib: Am Painting Exhib, Art Inst Chicago, Ill, 27; Whitney Mus Am Art, New York; Pa Acad Fine Arts, Philadelphia; Los Angeles Co Mus Art; San Francisco Mus Art; plus others. Teaching: Prof art, Calif State Univ, San Diego, 30-63; prof art, Univ Costa Rica, 62. Pos: Bd trustees, Fine Arts Soc, San Diego, 35-, chmn Latin-Am arts comt, 65-70, acquisitions comt; mem adv bd, Calif State Univ, San Diego, 63-70. Awards: First Anne Bremer Prize, San Francisco Art Asn, 29; First Prize, 30 & Leisser Farnham Prize, 30, Fine Arts Gallery, San Diego; Los Angeles Co Mus Art Award, 34. Mem: San Diego Art Guild; Am Asn Univ Prof. Media: Oil. Res: Maya sculpture. Publ: Illusr, Wonderful adventure of Paul Bunyon, Ugly Duckling, Popol Vuh, Ramona & American Indian legends, Limited Ed Club & Heritage. Mailing Add: 1234 Franciscan Way San Diego CA 92116

JACKSON, HARRY ANDREW
PAINTER, SCULPTOR
b Chicago, Ill, Apr 18, 24. Study: Art Inst Chicago, 31-38; with Ed Grigware, Cody, Wyo, 38-42; Brooklyn Mus Art Sch, with Hans Hofmann, 46-48; Fulbright & Ital Govt grants, 57. Work: Whitney Gallery Western Art. Cody; Amon Carter Mus, Ft Worth, Tex; Ft Pitt Mus, Pittsburgh; Woolarac Mus, Bartlesville, Okla; Am Mus Gt Brit, Bath, Eng. Comn: Stampede, 60 & Range Burial, 66 (oil murals), Whitney Gallery Western Art; Sor Capanna (monument), Piazza dei Mercanti, Rome, 62; painted sculpture of John Wayne (for cover), Time Mag, 8/8/69; Mem Bronze of Adm Lord Cochrane, comn by Douglas Cochrane, Plaza Cochrane, Valdivia, Chile, 70; River, Road & Point (mosaics, bronzes & mural), Ft Pitt Mus, Pittsburgh. Exhib: Tate Gallery, London, 45; Nat Collection Fine Arts, Washington, DC, 64; Nat Acad Design, New York, 64, 65, 67, 68 & 70; XVII Nostra Int Arte, Premio Fiorino, Florence, Italy, 66; Nat Cowboy Hall of Fame, Oklahoma City, 66 & 70-72. Pos: Off combat artist, USMC, 44-45. Awards: Interstate Gold Medal, Pennational Artists Ann, 67; Samuel Finley Breese Morse Gold Medal, Nat Acad Design, 68; Silver Medal, Nat Cowboy Hall of Fame, 71. Bibliog: D Seiberling (auth), Painter striving to find himself, Life Mag, 56; D G Lowe (auth), Death on the range, Am Heritage, 67; J McGuire (auth), Harry Jackson a man & his art, Barbre Prod, 72. Mem: USMC Combat Corresp Asn; Nat Sculpture Soc; Bohemian Club; fel Am Artists Prof League. Media: Oil; Bronze. Publ: Contribr monograph catalog, Kennedy Galleries, 69; auth, Lost Wax Bronze Casting, Northland Press, 72. Dealer: Kennedy Mailing Add: 801 Sheridan Ave Cody WY 82414

JACKSON, HAZEL BRILL
SCULPTOR
b Philadelphia, Pa. Study: Boston Mus Fine Arts; Scuola Rosatti, Florence, Italy; also with Angelo Zanelli, Rome & with Bela Pratt & Charles Grafly. Work: Concord Art Mus; Wellesley Col; Vassar Col; Dartmouth Col; Calgary Mus, Can. Exhib: Nat Acad Design; Nat Acad Rome; Nat Acad, Firenze, Italy; one-man shows, Boston Guild Artists & Corcoran Gallery Art, Washington, DC. Mem: Fel Nat Sculpture Soc. Style & Technique: Animal sculpture, especially horses and dogs. Mailing Add: Twin Oaks 83 Balmville Rd MO 25 Newburgh NY 12550

JACKSON, HERB
PAINTER, EDUCATOR
b Raleigh, NC, Aug 16, 45. Study: Davidson Col, BA; Phillips Univ, Marburg, WGer; Univ NC, MFA. Work: Calif Palace of Legion of Honor, San Francisco, Calif; Libr Cong, Washington, DC; Philadelphia Mus Art, Pa; Smithsonian Inst, Washington, DC; Whitney Mus Am Art, New York. Exhib: NC Artists Exhib, NC Mus Art, Raleigh, 62 & 69-71; Piedmont Graphics Exhib, Mint Mus, Charlotte, NC, 68 & 70-71; Artists of the Southeast & Tex, Isaac Delgado Mus, New Orleans, La, 71; Western Ill Univ Drawing & Print Show, 72; Drawings USA, Minn Mus Art; 200 Yrs of Art in NC, NC State Art Mus, 76; 35 Artists of the Southeast, High Mus, Atlanta, Ga, 76; 30 Yrs of Am Printmaking, Brooklyn Mus, NY, 77. Teaching: Asst prof studio art, Davidson Col, 69- Mem: Col Art Asn Am; Southeastern Col Art Conf. Style & Technique: Heavy-textured color fields. Media: Acrylic, Graphics. Dealer: Nielsen Gallery 179 Newbury St Boston MA 02116. Mailing Add: Box 2495 Davidson NC 28036

JACKSON, LEE
PAINTER
b New York, NY, Feb 2, 09. Study: NY Univ, 1 yr; Art Students League; also with John Sloan & George Luks. Work: Metrop Mus Art, New York; Corcoran Gallery Art Art, Washington, DC; Walker Art Ctr, Minneapolis, Minn; Nebr Art Asn, Lincoln; Los Angeles Co Mus Art, Calif. Exhib: 56th Ann Paintings, Art Inst Chicago, 46; Whitney Mus Am Art, New York, 49-50; Am Painting Today 1950, Metrop Mus Am, 50; 23rd Biennial, Corcoran Gallery Art, 53; 140th Ann, Nat Acad Design, New York, 65. Teaching: Instr painting & drawing, Sch Art Studies, 47-48; instr painting & drawing, City Col New York, 48-54. Awards: Guggenheim Fel, 41; Univ Nebr Art Gallery Purchase Prize, 43; Thomas B Clarke Prize, Nat Acad Design, 51. Mem: Art Students League; Audubon Artists Am (dir & chmn ways & means); Am Watercolor Soc; Artists Equity Asn; Nat Soc Painters in Casein. Style & Technique: Under painting and over glazes. Media: Oil. Publ: Contribr, Drawings by American Artists, 47; contribr, Am Artist Mag, 9/53. Mailing Add: Strong's Lane Water Mill NY 11976

JACKSON, RICHARD NORRIS
PAINTER
b Sacramento, Calif, Aug 6, 39. Study: Sacramento City Col, Calif, 58-59; Sacramento State Univ, 60-61. Work: Corcoran Gallery Art, Washington, DC; Los Angeles Co Mus Art, Los Angeles, Calif. Exhib: Crocker Art Gallery, Sacramento, Calif, 61; 32nd Biennial, Corcoran Gallery Art, Washington, DC, 71; Los Angeles Co Mus Art, Los Angeles, Calif, 71; Houston Mus Mod Art, Tex, 73; Stedlijk Mus, Amsterdam, 74; Los Angeles Inst Contemp Art, Calif, 75; Brown Univ, Providence, RI, 77; PSI, New York, 77. Style & Technique: Acrylic on canvas. Mailing Add: 167 N Orange Grove Pasadena CA 91103

JACKSON, RUTH AMELIA
CURATOR
b Paterson, NJ; Can citizen. Study: Parsons Sch, Ridgewood, NJ; Holton Arms, Washington, DC; Maret French Sch, Washington, DC; Miss Spauldings, Queensgate, London, Eng. Collections Arranged: Auguste Rodin, 63, Mains et Merveilles, 72, Gold for the Gods, 77, The Decorative Scene—Montreal 1860-1914, 77, Treasures of London, 77 & Spider Woman and the Navajo, 78, Montreal Mus Fine Arts. Pos: Dir, Can Guild of Crafts, 72-; registrar & cur dec arts, Montreal Mus Fine Arts, 72- Publ: Auth, Galerie Hosmer-Pillow-Vaughan, 69 & Clutch of Curiosities, 70, Can Collector; auth, Mobel, Silber und Keramik aus Quebec, Weltkunst, 74; auth, Canada's Heritage of Silver, Antique Monthly, 76; auth, Traditional Furniture from the Province of Quebec, Apollo, 76. Mailing Add: 3500 Mountain St Apt 27 Montreal PQ H3G 2A6 Can

JACKSON, SARAH
SCULPTOR, GRAPHIC ARTIST
b Detroit, Mich, Nov 13, 24. Study: Wayne State Univ, BA, 46, MA, 48. Work: Joseph H Hirshhorn Collection, Washington, DC; Nat Gallery Can, Ottawa; Montreal Mus Fine Arts; Montreal Mus Contemp Arts; Art Gallery Ontario, Toronto. Comn: Dancer (bronze), Cloverdale Shopping Ctr, Toronto, 66; Metamorphosis (bronzes) & Mindscape (bronze hanging), Student Union Bldg, Dalhousie Univ; plastic & bronze sculpture, Mt Sinai Hosp, Toronto. Exhib: Montreal Mus Fine Arts; Ontario Graphic Artists; Gadatsy Gallery, Toronto; Mt St Vincent Univ; one-man show, St Mary's Univ; plus many others. Teaching: Lectr, Mexico City Col, 48, London Univ, 54-55, Tate Gallery, London, 54-55, Thomas More Inst, 56, Nat Gallery, Ottawa, 57, Toronto Univ, 60-61, YMCA Adult Educ, Toronto, 62, St Mary's Univ, 63, Nova Scotia Col Art, 70 & Dartmouth Adult Educ Div, 72-73. Pos: Artist-in-residence, NS Tech Col. Awards: Sculpture Award, Winnipeg Art Gallery; Ontario Arts Coun Grant, 74. Bibliog: Sarah Jackson/sculpture, xerography & drawing, Moving Out, Vol 4, No 1; Brian Charent (auth), An interview with Sarah Jackson, Art Mag, winter 74; Guy Robert (auth), Eros et humour chez Sarah Jackson, Vie Des Arts, spring 75. Mem: Can Artists Rep. Media: Bronze, Plastic; Drawings. Dealer: Gadatsy Gallery 112 Yorkville Toronto ON Can; Gallery Danielli 336 Dundas St W Toronto ON Can. Mailing Add: 1411 Edward St Halifax NS Can

JACKSON, SUZANNE FITZALLEN
PAINTER, WRITER
b St Louis, Mo, Jan 30, 44. Study: San Francisco State Col, BA; Otis Art Inst, Los Angeles, with Charles White. Work: Joseph Hirshhorn Mus Mod Art, Smithsonian Inst, Washington, DC; Palm Springs Desert Mus, Calif; Mafundi Inst, Watts, Calif; Daniel, Mann, Johnson & Mendenhall, Co, Los Angeles. Comn: Peace Bird, Secy State Edmund G Brown, Jr, Sacramento, 72; Stephen Chase, Arthur Elrod & Assoc, Palm Springs, 74; Sonny Bono, Bel Air, 75; Artful Living, William Chidester Co, Pac Design Ctr, Los Angeles, 75. Exhib: Joseph Hirshhorn Collection, Palm Springs Desert Mus, 70; Black Untitled II/Dimensions of the Figure, Oakland Mus, 71; Blacks: USA: Now, New York Cult Ctr, 73; Directions in Afro-American Art, Herbert F Johnson Mus Art, Cornell Univ, 74; Pioneer Mus, Haggin Art Galleries, Stockton, Calif, 75; plus others. Collections Arranged: Coordr art exhibs & ed catalog for San Francisco Bay Area Black Expo, 72. Teaching: Art instr, St Stephens Sch, San Francisco, 65-66; guest educ aide, Black Arts Coun Exhib, Los Angeles Pub Schs, 69-70; instr dance & crafts, Watts Towers Art Ctr, 70; lectr art, Stanford Univ, summer 72; lectr, Univ of the Pac, 72, 73 & 75; lectr, Scripps Col, 74; lectr, Calif Inst Women, 74; lectr, San Diego Fine Arts Soc, 75. Pos: Owner-dir, Gallery 32, Los Angeles, 68-70; bd dirs, Los Angeles Black Arts Coun, 69-70; mem, Mayor Alioto's Screening Comt for St Artists, San Francisco Art Comt, 72-74; mem, Calif Arts Comn, 75-78; artist/coordr, CETA Prof Artists

Pub Art Prog, Brockman Gallery Productions, 77-78. Awards: Int Latham Found Humane Kindness & World Peace Scholar, 61; Univ of the Pac & Pioneer Mus Artists Merit Award, 75. Bibliog: Alfred Frankenstein (auth), Ironic contrasts in Black Expo '72 Art Exhibition, San Francisco Chronicle, 9/72; Henry J Seldis (auth), Art walk, Los Angeles Times, 9/74; Gordon Hazlitt (auth), Creating her own world, Art News, 11/74; plus others. Mem: Nat Conf Artists; Advocates for Arts; Nat Soc Lit & Arts. Style & Technique: Figurative fantasy and reality, translucent and opaque acrylic washes; mixed media drawings. Media: Acrylic Wash. Publ: Contribr, Black Artists on Art, Vol 2, 71; auth & illusr, What I Love, Contemp Crafts, 72; auth & illusr, Animal, 77; contribr, Contributions of Women-Art, Dillon, 77; contribr, Samella Lewis (ed), African-American, Brace Harcourt, 77; plus others. Mailing Add: c/o Ankrum Gallery 657 N La Cienega Blvd Los Angeles CA 90069

JACKSON, VAUGHN L
PAINTER, ILLUSTRATOR
b Raymond, Ohio, Jan 7, 20. Study: Am Univ, AA, BA, 69; Corcoran Sch Art, with Richard Lahey, 47-50; Ohio State Univ, 42-43; Columbus Art Sch, 39-40; with Hans Hofmann, Provincetown, summer 55; also with Eliot O'Hara. Work: Many in pvt collections. Comn: Over 900 design & illus in advert, tech & mil publ, displays, visual presentations for art studios, advert agencies, govt & com accts. Exhib: Am Artists Prof League, 50-52 & 57; Washington Watercolor Club Ann Nat Exhibs, 54-58; Am Art League, 58; Soc Tech Writers & Publ Ann, 71; one-man show, Washington, DC, 56 & 58; plus others. Pos: Advert artist, Kal, Ehrlich & Merrick Advert Agency, 47-52; artist-illusr, Opers Res Off, Johns Hopkins Univ, 52-55, asst art dir, 55-63; publ art dir, Res Anal Corp, 63-67, visual & graphics mgr, 67-72; visual & graphics mgr, Gen Res Corp, 72, tech publ dir, 72-76; visual dir, System Planning Corp, 76- Awards: Silver Medal, Landscape Club Washington, DC, 55; Award for Outstanding Achievement in Tech Commun, Soc Tech Writers & Publs, 71. Mem: Soc Tech Commun; Am Inst Graphic Arts; Art Dirs Club Metrop Washington (charter mem, bd dirs); Washington Watercolor Asn (bd mgrs, vpres). Style & Technique: Traditional; naturalistic with abstract compositional structure; realistic; expressionistic, nonobjective; some hard-edge. Media: Watercolor, Acrylic, Ink. Publ: Work in Ed & Publ, Printers Ink, Aviation Age, Electronics Mag, Agr Chemicals, point of sale & direct mail campaigns, Washington Post, Eve Star & other newspapers. Mailing Add: Ten Penny Studio PO Box 54 Fairfax Station VA 22039

JACKSON, VIRGIL V
CARTOONIST, ILLUSTRATOR
b Peoria, Ohio, Sept 17, 09. Study: Columbus Art Sch, scholarships. Comn: Murals, US Govt, Marysville High Sch, Ohio; portrait comns in Ohio. Exhib: Columbus Art Gallery. Teaching: Instr drawing & cartooning, Columbus Art Sch. Pos: Com artist & dir, Columbus Citizen & Washington Post; vpres & treas, Com Art Studios, Inc & Graphic Craftsmen, Inc, Washington, DC. Mem: Art Dir Club, Washington, DC; Advert Club, Washington, DC. Style & Technique: Contemporary to abstract. Publ: Contribr, cartoons & illus, Columbus Dispatch, Columbus Citizen, Nat Educ Asn, Signs of the Times, Ohio State J, Washington Post & US Army, Dept Defense. Mailing Add: 611 F St NW Washington DC 20004

JACKSON, WARD
PAINTER, EDITOR
b Petersburg, Va, Sept 10, 28. Study: Richmond Prof Inst of Col William & Mary, BFA & MFA; Hans Hofmann Sch Fine Arts, scholar, 52. Work: Nat Collection Fine Arts, Smithsonian Inst, Washington, DC; Riverside Mus Collection, Rose Art Mus, Brandeis Univ; Elvehjem Art Ctr, Univ Wis-Madison; Va Mus Fine Arts, Richmond; Wilhelm Lehmbruck Mus der Stadt Duisberg, Ger. Exhib: One-man shows, Fleischman Gallery, New York, 58-60 & Stowe Galleries, Cunningham Art Ctr, Davidson Col, NC; Va Mus Fine Arts, Richmond, 71 & Graham Gallery, New York, 72; Fine Arts Ctr Gallery, Ocean Co Col, Toms River, NJ, 73; three-man exhib, Atrium Gallery, Seattle, Wash, 65. Teaching: Instr art hist, Rollins Col, Winter Park, Fla, 54-55. Pos: Co-ed, Folio, 49-51; co-ed, Art Now: New York, 69-72, adv ed, Art Now Gallery Guide, 69-; archivist & head viewing prog, Solomon R Guggenheim Mus, New York, 55- Awards: Fel, Va Mus Fine Arts, 48 & 49; First Prize for painting, New York Ctr Gallery, 56; Artists Fel, Nat Endowment for Arts, 75-76. Bibliog: George Cruger (auth), Ward Jackson, Va Mus Bull, 2/71 & 5/73; Siegfried Salzmann (auth), Ward Jackson Zeichnungen, Lehmbruch Mus, 73; Ward Jackson Watercolors, Davidson Col, 75. Mem: Am Abstract Artists; Col Art Asn Am. Publ: Auth, Art in glass (works of Art by Louis Comfort Tiffany), Rollins Col Lit Mag, 55; auth, George L K Morris: forty years of abstract art, Art J, 72. Dealer: Buecker & Harpsichords 465 Broadway New York NY 10012. Mailing Add: 32 Union Sq Rm 918 New York NY 10003

JACKSON, WILLIAM DAVIS
SCULPTOR, DESIGNER
b Philadelphia, Pa, Feb 1, 46. Study: Shop asst to J C McLauchlin, cabinetmaker, 61-63; Univ NH, BA(painting & graphic arts), 68, Gladys & Charles Edgecomb Found grant for music & art, 67; Ind Univ, MFA(sculpture), 72, sculpture fel, 70. Exhib: Sculpture at Ind Univ, Ind Univ Fine Arts Mus, Bloomington, 71; Arts: USA 2, Northern Ill Univ, DeKalb, 71; 15th Nat Exhib, Greater Fall River Art Asn, Mass, 72; Sculpture Exhib, Studio San Giuseppe, Col Mt St Joseph, Cincinnati, Ohio, 72; William Jackson/Arla Patch: Sculpture, Art Acad Cincinnati, Cincinnati Mus Art, Ohio, 74; William Jackson: Sculpture/Arthur Hillman: Prints, The Williams Col Mus Art, Williamstown, Mass, 76; Copper, Brass & Bronze, Univ Ariz Mus Art, Tucson, 77; Nat Drawing Exhib, State Univ Col, Potsdam, NY, 77. Teaching: Instr painting, drawing & graphics, The Phillips Exeter Acad, Exeter, NH, 68-70; instr sculpture, jewelry & drawing, Simon's Rock Early Col, Great Barrington, Mass, 72- Pos: Shop asst, George Rickey, East Chatham, NY, 71-72. Bibliog: David J Jacobs (auth), Confessions of a leaf-peeper, Diversion Mag, 10/76. Mem: Col Art Asn. Style & Technique: Functional aesthetic and aesthetic devices and objects using wood, air, electronics, metals. Media: Mixed media constructions. Mailing Add: 125 Main St Stephentown NY 12168

JACOB, NED
PAINTER, SCULPTOR
b Elizabethton, Tenn, Nov 15, 38. Study: Pvt studies with Robert Gilbert, Robert Lougheed & Bettina Steinke. Work: Denver Art Mus; Indianapolis Mus of Art; Whitney Gallery of Western Art, Cody, Wyo; Albrecht Art Mus, St Joseph, Mo; Pac NW Indian Ctr, Spokane, Wash. Exhib: One-man shows, Univ Sask, Saskatoon, 56, C M Russell Gallery, Helena, Mont, 56, Nat Cowboy Hall of Fame & Western Heritage Ctr, Oklahoma City, 66, Colo Coun on Arts & Humanities, Colo Gov's Mansion, Denver, 74, Boise Gallery of Art, Idaho, 75, Birger Sandzen Mem Gallery, Lindsborg, Kans, 76 & Whitney Gallery of Western Art, 76; group exhib, Kennedy Galleries, New York, 60. Awards: John F & Anna Lee Stacy Fel, 74. Bibliog: Cover story, Am Artist Mag, 8/75; Royal B Hassrick (auth), Western Painting Today, Watson-Guptill, 75; James K Howard (auth), Ten Years with the Cowboy Artists of America, Northland Press, 76. Mem: Salmagundi Club, New York. Style & Technique: Traditional realism. Mailing Add: Denver CO

JACOBS, DAVID (THEODORE)
SCULPTOR, EDUCATOR
b Niagara Falls, NY, Mar 1, 32. Study: Orange Coast Col, AA; Los Angeles State Col, AB & MA. Work: Guggenheim Mus & Assyrian Embassy, New York; Mus Art, Richmond, Va; Otterbein Col, Ohio; Valley Mall, Hagerstown, Md. Comn: Cloud Fountain (sculptured fountain), Valley Mall Assoc, Hagerstown, Md, 74; bronze relief, Paul Radin Mem, Hofstra Univ Libr, 74; Raingate (sculptured fountain), A Dworkin, Westbury, NY, 75; Ventura High, Deer Park High Sch, NY, 76; Rainframe (sculptured screen), Dawn-Joy Corp, New York, 76. Exhib: The Art of Assemblage, Mus Mod Art, New York, 61; 68th Am Exhib, Art Inst Chicago, 66; Sound, Light, Silence, Art That Performs, W R Nelson Gallery, Atkins Mus, Kansas City, 66; Inflatable Sculpture, Jewish Mus, New York, 69; Sound Sculpture, Vancouver Art Gallery, 73; plus many one-man shows, 61-71. Teaching: Assoc prof sculpture, Hofstra Univ, 62-; vis critic sculpture, Cornell Univ, New York Prog, 69 & 70. Awards: Res grant, Hofstra Univ, 68; Creative Artists Pub Serv grant, 73 & 76. Bibliog: D J Irving (auth), Sculpture: Materials & Processes, Van Nostrand Reinhold, 68; Wayne Craven (auth), Sculpture in America, Crowell, 68; Chichura & Stevens (auths), Super Sculpture: Using Science, Technology and Natural Phenomena in Sculpture, Van Nostrand Reinhold, 74. Media: Aluminum, Rubber, Sound. Mailing Add: Div of Humanities & Fine Arts Hofstra Univ Hempstead NY 11550

JACOBS, HAROLD
PAINTER, SCULPTOR
b New York, NY, Oct 29, 32. Study: Cooper Union, 53; NY Univ; New Sch Social Res; Sorbonne, Fulbright scholar, 61. Work: Whitney Mus Am Art, New York; Portland Art Mus, Ore; Kalamazoo Art Ctr; McCory Corp. Teaching: Prof painting, Moore Col Art, 66- Awards: Nat Endowment Arts Collaboration Grant Visual & Performing Arts, 75. Style & Technique: Timed inflated sculpture in performance exhibition. Media: Mixed Media; Inflatable Structures. Mailing Add: 632 South St Philadelphia PA 19147

JACOBS, HELEN NICHOLS
PAINTER
b Kent, Conn, Feb 16, 24. Study: With Spencer B Nichols & Arthur Maynard. Exhib: Catharine Lorillard Wolfe Arts Club, Nat Arts Club, 74-75; Am Artists Prof League, New York & NJ, 75; Audubon Artists, 75 & 77; Kent Art Asn, Conn, 75 & 77. Teaching: Instr oil painting, Ridgewood Adult Sch, NJ, 68-72 & Ridgewood Art Asn, 71- Awards: Tercentenary Award, Closter, NJ, 70; First Prize in Oils, NJ Am Artists Prof League, 73 & Kent Art Asn, Conn, 75. Mem: Ridgewood Art Asn; Am Artists Prof League; Bergen Co Artists Guild; Kent Art Asn. Style & Technique: Traditional oil painting. Media: Oil. Mailing Add: 684 Terrace Dr Paramus NJ 07652

JACOBS, JAY
ART WRITER, CRITIC
b New York, NY, Apr 19, 23. Study: Art Students League, 45-46. Pos: Sr ed, Portfolio, Artnews, Inc, New York, 62-63, managing ed, Artnews Ann, 63; exec ed, Arts Mag, 65-66; ed, The Art Gallery Mag, Hollycroft Press, Ivoryton, Conn, 71-75. Res: Interviews with contemporary artists. Publ: Ed, Horizon Book of Great Cathedrals, Am Heritage Publ, 68; contribr, Art in Am, 64-73 & Art Gallery, 66-; auth, Color Encyclopedia of World Art, Crown, 75. Mailing Add: 32 Oakview Hwy East Hampton NY 11937

JACOBS, JIM
PAINTER
b New York, NY, May 26, 45. Study: Boston Univ, BA; Bryn Mawr Col, study with Richmond Lattimore; Harvard Univ; Boston Mus of Fine Arts. Work: Rose Art Mus, Brandeis Univ, Waltham, Mass; Fogg Art Mus, Harvard Univ, Cambridge, Mass; City of New York; Nat Gallery of Art, Washington, DC. Comn: Large wall piece, comn by Arman, Paris, 77; wall piece, comn by Yves Fernandez, New York, 77; wall piece comn by Jean Martin, New York, 78. Exhib: O K Harris Works of Art, 76 & 77; Salon des Jeunes et des Grands, Paris, 77; Lillian Vinci Gallery, Paris, 78; Expressions of the Seventies, New York, 78; Sam & Esther Minsiloff Cult Art Ctr, New York, 78; Lowen Adler Gallery, Stockholm, Sweden, 78. Teaching: Instr vase painting, Boston Univ, 65; instr painting techniques, Harvard Univ, 66; instr vase painting, Bryn Mawr Col, 67. Pos: Archivist, Leo Castelli Gallery, 67. Style & Technique: Color field painting. Media: Lacquered on Board. Dealer: Ivan Karp 383 W Broadway New York NY 10013. Mailing Add: 112 W 13th At New York NY 10011

JACOBS, PETER ALAN
ART ADMINISTRATOR, PRINTMAKER
b New York, NY, Jan 31, 39. Study: State Univ NY Col New Paltz, with Ilya Bolotowsky, BS(art educ), 60, MA(art), 62; George Peabody Col, EdD(fine arts), 65. Work: Bloomsburg State Col, Pa; Col of the Mainland, Texas City, Tex; Muskingum Col, New Concord, Ohio; George Peabody Mus, Nashville, Tenn. Exhib: New Directions in Art, Beloit Mus, Wis; Wis Designer-Craftsman, Milwaukee Art Ctr & Wis Painters & Sculptors, 68 & 69; Southwest Invitational, Yuma, Ariz, 73 & 74; one-man shows, Work on Tour by Ariz Arts & Humanities Comn, Ariz, Tex, Ohio & Wis, 74-75 & Univ Ohio, Univ Colo, Grand Canyon Art Ctr & Univ Wyo Art Mus. Collections Arranged: Ilya Bolotowsky Retrospective, Crossman Gallery, Univ Wis-Whitewater, 68 & Northern Ariz Univ Mus, 73. Teaching: Chmn dept art, Univ Wis-Whitewater, 65-70; chmn dept art, Northern Ariz Univ, 70-74; chmn dept art, Cent Mich Univ, 74-76; chmn art dept, Colo State Univ, 76- Mem: Nat Coun Art Adminr (founder & chmn bd dirs, 72-77); Col Art Asn Am; Mich Soc Arts, Lett & Sci (chmn fine arts div, 75); Nat Art Educ Asn; Coun Art Dept Chmn State Wis (pres, 65-70). Style & Technique: Use of photo-offset technique on aluminum; sculpture using leather and other natural materials. Mailing Add: 2643 Silver Creek Dr Ft Collins CO 80521

JACOBS, RALPH, JR
PAINTER
b El Centro, Calif, May 22, 40. Study: With Evelyn Nadeau, Frederic Taubes & Abel G Warshawsky. Work: Beirut Art Mus, Lebanon. Comn: Many pvt collections. Exhib: Coun Am Artists Soc Nat Exhib, New York, 64; Nat Exhib, SpringVille Mus Art, Utah, 65; Soc Western Artists Ann Exhibs, de Young Mus, San Francisco, 65 & 69; Armenian Allied Arts Ann, Los Angeles, 66. Awards: State Ann Exhib First Awards, Art League Galleries, Santa Cruz, 63 & 64; Soc Western Artists Ann Second Award for Silhouette in Morning Light, 64; Klumpkey Mem Award for Classic Nude, 65. Mem: Soc Western Artists. Style & Technique: Realism and impressionism; brush and palette knife techniques. Media: Oil. Mailing Add: PO Box 5906 Carmel CA 93921

JACOBS, TED SETH
PAINTER
b Newark, NJ, June 11, 27. Study: Art Students League, 43-47. Work: Mus Mod Art & Finch Col Mus, New York. Comn: Portraits in oil, Dr Theodor Reik, 62, Jane Fonda, 64 & Mrs Mary Ellen Fahs, 71; portrait drawing, Thomas Hoving, 66; murals, St Regis-Sheraton Roof,

New York, 74 & Venetian Room, Copley Plaza, Boston, 75; plus over 200 portrait comns & many murals. Exhib: One-man shows, St Vincents Col, Latrobe, Pa, 65, Drawing Exhib, Drawing Shop, New York, 65 & 66, paintings, Noah Goldowsky Galleries, New York, 66, Drawing & Painting Exhib, Adelson Galleries, Boston, 67 & 68, Coe Kerr Gallery, New York, 77 & Galerie Mouffe, Paris, France, 77; Reyn Galleries, New York, 72. Awards: Bridgeman Prize, Art Students League New York, 44; First Prize, John F & Anna Lee Stacey Award, 52. Style & Technique: Contemporary realism based on a philosophy of perception. Media: Oil. Dealer: Coe Kerr Gallery 49 E 82nd St New York NY 10021; Reyn Gallery 680 Madison Ave New York NY 12208. Mailing Add: 523 E 83rd St New York NY 10028

JACOBS, WILLIAM KETCHUM, JR
COLLECTOR
b Brooklyn, NY, Mar 17, 08. Collection: Late 19th and 20th century sculptures and paintings. Mailing Add: 895 Park Ave New York NY 10021

JACOBSEN, MICHAEL A
ART HISTORIAN
b Pasadena, Calif, June 4, 42. Study: Univ Calif, Santa Barbara, BA, 65, MA, 70; Columbia Univ, PhD, 76. Teaching: Asst prof Renaissance art, Cleveland State Univ, Ohio, 73-77; asst prof Renaissance art, Univ Ore, 77- Mem: Col Art Asn; Mid-West Art Hist Asn; New Orgn for the Visual Arts. Res: Renaissance art history; 15th century in Italy. Publ: Auth, Vulcan forging Cupid's wing, Art Bull, 72; auth, A Sforza miniature, Burlington Mag, 74; auth, Savoldo & northern art, Art Bull, 74. Mailing Add: Dept of Art Hist Univ of Ore Eugene OR 97403

JACOBSHAGEN, N KEITH, II
PAINTER, PHOTOGRAPHER
b Wichita, Kans, Sept 8, 41. Study: Kansas City Art Inst, Mo, BFA; Art Ctr Col Design, Los Angeles; Univ Kans, MFA. Work: Sheldon Mem Gallery, Lincoln, Nebr; Univ Kans Mus Art, Lawrence; Mus Art Okla Univ; Oakland Mus, Calif; Pasadena Art Mus, Calif. Exhib: 34th Ann Contemp Am Painting, Palm Beach, Fla, 72; Festival of the Image, Am Ctr Paris, France, 72; Selections from the Collection, Pasadena Art Mus, Calif, 72; Seven by Seven, Univ Kans Mus Art, 73; A Sense of Place: the Artist and the American Land, Sheldon Mem Gallery, 74; Charles Campbell Gallery, San Francisco, Calif, 76; Am Painterly Realism, Univ Mo Art Gallery, Kansas City, 76; Eye of the West, Hayden Gallery, Mass Inst Technol, Cambridge, 77; Alexander Calder Mem & Hassam Fund Purchase Exhib, Am Acad & Inst of Arts & Lett, New York, 77; Instant Image, Camerawork Gallery, San Francisco, 77. Teaching: Assoc prof art, Univ Nebr-Lincoln, 68- Awards: Owen H Kenan Award, 34th Ann Contemp Am Painting, 72; Frank Woods Fel, Univ Nebr, 75. Bibliog: Alan Gussow (auth), A Sense of Place: the Artist and the American Land (film), Nebr Educ TV, 74. Style & Technique: Landscape. Media: Oil. Publ: Contribr, Creative Camera, 71; contribr, 35mm Photography, 71; contribr, Camera, 71; contribr, A Sense of Place: the Artist and the American Land, Vol II, 74; contribr, Young American Photography, Vol I, 74. Dealer: Dory Gates PO Box 7264 Kansas City MO 64113; Charles Campbell Gallery 647 Chestnut St San Francisco CA 94133. Mailing Add: 1945 E St Lincoln NE 68510

JACOBSON, ARTHUR ROBERT
PAINTER, PRINTMAKER
b Chicago, Ill, Jan 10, 24. Study: Univ Wis, BS, MS(art); Madrid Print Workshop, Spain; London, Eng, 72. Work: Dallas Mus Art, Tex; Pa Acad Fine Arts, Philadelphia; Mus NMex, Santa Fe; Ariz State Univ, Tempe; Hastings Col, Nebr. Comn: Exterior mural in marblecrete, Phoenix Jewish Community Ctr, Ariz, 62. Exhib: Corcoran Biennial of Painting, Corcoran Gallery Art, Washington, DC, 57; Libr Cong Print Exhib, Washington, DC, 65; Minn Mus Art Exhib Drawings, St Paul, 71; Graphics USA, Clarke Col, Iowa, 71; Drawings USA, Minn Mus Art, 75. Teaching: Prof painting & printmaking, Ariz State Univ, 56-; guest prof painting, Univ Wis, 67-68. Awards: Purchase awards, Pa Acad Fine Arts & Dallas Mus Art, 65; First Prize for painting, Phoenix Art Mus, 71. Mem: Phoenix Art Mus. Style & Technique: Caligraphic expressionist. Media: Oil. Mailing Add: 5618 E Montecito Phoenix AZ 85018

JACOBSON, URSULA MERCEDES
PAINTER, SCULPTOR
b Milwaukee, Wis, Mar 26, 27. Study: Univ Wis-Milwaukee, BS, 48; Univ Wis-Madison, MS, 50, grad study, 50-51. Exhib: Int Biennial Contemp Color Lithography, Cincinnati, 54; 7th & 10th Southwest Prints & Drawings, Dallas Mus, 57 & 59; 64th Ann, Denver Mus, Colo, 58; 154th Ann, Pa Acad, 59; Four Corners Biennial, Phoenix Art Mus, 73 & 75; plus many others. Awards: State of Ariz Awards, Ariz State Fair, var times, 56-70; Purchase Award, Art on Paper, Weatherspoon Ann, NC, 67; Prints & Drawings Award, Phoenix Art Mus, 74. Style & Technique: Hard edge expressionist; acrylic; sheet steel and bronze sculpture. Media: Ink Drawing, Sheet Metal, Bronze. Publ: Contribr, Collins, auth, Women Artists in America II, Univ Tenn, 75. Mailing Add: 5618 E Montecito Phoenix AZ 85018

JACOBSON, YOLANDE (MRS J CRAIG SHEPPARD)
SCULPTOR
b Norman, Okla, May 28, 21. Study: Univ Okla, BFA; also study in Norway, France & Mex. Work: Gilcrease Mus Art, Tulsa, Okla; Jacobsen Mus Art, Norman; State Hist Soc, Reno, Nev; Hist Mus, Carson City, Nev. Comn: Sen Patrick McCarran (bronze statue), Statuary Hall, Washington, DC, 61; president's portrait bust, Univ Nev, Reno, 62; bronze sculpture, Gov Mansion, Carson City, 65. Exhib: Denver Mus Art, 41; Okla Ann, Tulsa, 42-45; Mid-West Ann, Kansas City, 51; Oakland Mus Art, 56; Silver Centennial, Virginia City, Nev, 61. Pos: Asst ed & bk designer, Univ Nev Press, 63-66. Awards: Mid-West Ann, Kansas City, 41; Denver Mus Art, 41; Silver Centennial, Virginia City, 61. Style & Technique: Representational portraiture; figurative; semi-abstract. Media: Bronze, Wood. Mailing Add: 1000 Primrose St Reno NV 89502

JACOBSSON, STEN WILHELM JOHN
DESIGNER, SCULPTOR
b Mar 28, 99. US citizen. Study: Sweden, Ger, France, US. Work: Swedish Art Exhib, Metrop Mus Art & Detroit Inst Art. Teaching: Instr sculpture, painting & design & examnr MA degree prog, Wayne State Univ; instr, Detroit Country Day Sch; head dept art, Artisan Guild, Henry Ford Art Sch; asst to Prof Carl Milles, Cranbrook Acad Arts. Pos: Archit examr & construction analyst, Fed Housing Admin; founder & pres, Contemp Backgrounds, Inc. Awards: First Prize in Sculpture & First Prize in Medalist Competition, US Govt; Honorable Mention, US War Dept Bd & Fed Bldg World's Fair. Bibliog: Articles in Archit Forum, 8/73 & Pittsburgh Glass Co Publ, New York Times; Free Press & Detroit News. Mem: Soc Medalists. Style & Technique: Contemporary. Mailing Add: 7666 Chatham St Detroit MI 48239

JACQUARD (JERALD WAYNE JACKARD)
SCULPTOR, EDUCATOR
b Lansing, Mich, Feb 1, 37. Study: Mich State Univ, BA & MA. Work: Mus Am Art, Andover, Mass; Detroit Inst Arts, Mich; Kresge Mus, Mich State Univ, East Lansing; Kalamazoo Inst Art, Mich. Comn: Sculpture, Chicago Transit Authority, 74. Exhib: One-man shows, Detroit Inst Art, 65, Ill Inst Technol, 69, Univ Chicago, 70 & Indianapolis Mus, 75; Bicentennial Sculpture for a New Era, Chicago, 75. Teaching: Assoc prof sculpture, Univ Ill, Chicago Circle Campus, 66-75; prof sculpture, Ind Univ, Bloomington, 75- Awards: Fulbright Scholar, 63; Founders Award, Detroit Inst Art, 64; Guggenheim Fel, 73. Style & Technique: Large architectural sculpture fabricated with steel. Media: Fabrication, Casting. Mailing Add: 132 Lexington Rd Bloomington IN 47401

JACQUEMON, PIERRE
PAINTER
b Lyon, France, Aug 6, 35; US citizen. Study: Self-taught. Work: Gotesborg Mus, Sweden; Magdalene Col, Cambridge, Eng; Mus d'Art Mod, Paris, France; St Paul Sch, NH; Ika-Shika Nat Univ, Tokyo, Japan. Exhib: Autagouismes, Palais du Louvre, Paris, 60; Ft Worth Art Ctr, Tex, 63; Charleroy Mus, Belg, 65; Inst Contemp Art, Boston, 70; one-man shows, Temple Gallery, London, 62, Bianchini Gallery, New York, 63, Weeden Gallery, Boston, 68, Berkshire Mus, Mass, 69 & Atrium Gallery, Geneva, Switz, 74. Style & Technique: Abstract image with emphasis on texture. Media: Oil. Dealer: Phoenix Gallery 31 W 57th St New York NY 10019. Mailing Add: 62 E Seventh St New York NY 10003

JACQUES, MICHAEL LOUIS
PRINTMAKER, EDUCATOR
b Barre, Vt, Apr 12, 45. Study: Boston Univ, BFA, 67; Univ Hartford Art Sch, MFA, 71; and with David Aronson, Walter Murch & Paul Zimmerman. Work: Nat Collection Fine Arts, Smithsonian Mus, Washington, DC; Springfield Mus, Mass; Philadelphia Mus Art; William Rockhill Nelson Mus, Mo; Worcester Art Mus, Mass. Comn: Painting of Georgetown waterfront, Kiplinger Letters, Washington, DC, 70. Exhib: Davidson Nat Print & Drawing Competition, NC, 72 & 74; Boston Printmakers Exhib, Mass, 72, 74 & 75; Audubon Artists Exhib, New York, 72, 74 & 75; Nat Acad Design, New York, 74; Living American Artists & The Figure, Mus Art, Pa State Univ, 75. Teaching: Instr art, Emmanuel Col, Boston, 71-73, assoc prof art, 73-, chmn dept, 75-77. Awards: Bronze Medal of Honor for Graphics, Arts Atlantic, Gloucester, Mass, 72; First Prize Graphics, 72nd Virginia Beach Outdoor Exhib, Va, 73; First Prize Graphics, John Taylor Arms Award, Audubon Artists Nat Exhib, 75. Mem: Acad Artists Asn, Springfield Mus (coun mem, 73-); Coopertown Art Asn, NY; Conn Acad Fine Arts; Boston Printmakers; Hudson Valley Art Asn. Style & Technique: Realistic figurative line etchings with aquatint. Dealer: Pucker Safrai Gallery 171 Newbury St Boston MA 02116. Mailing Add: 13 Wethersfield St Rowley MA 01969

JACQUETTE, YVONNE HELENE (YVONNE HELEN BURCKHARDT)
PAINTER, EDUCATOR
b Pittsburgh, Pa, Dec 15, 34. Study: RI Sch Design, 52-56, with John Frazier & Robert Hamilton; also with Herman Cherry & Robert Roche. Work: Weatherspoon Gallery, NC; Whitney Mus Am Art, New York; Metrop Mus Art, New York; Colby Col Mus, Waterville, Maine. Comn: Five panel painting in oil, NCent Bronx Hosp, NY, 73; five color lithograph, Horace Mann Sch, Riverdale, NY, 74. Exhib: Skying, Rutgers Univ Art Gallery, 72; Whitney Painting Ann, Whitney Mus Am Art, 72; Women Choose Women, New York Cult Ctr & US Traveling Show, 72-73; New Image in Painting, Int Biennial, Tokyo, Japan, 74; Small Scale in Contemporary Art, Art Inst Chicago, 75. Teaching: Vis artist painting, Moore Col Art, 72; vis artist & instr painting, Univ Pa, 72-76; vis artist, Nova Scotia Col Art, 74; instr, Parsons Sch of Design, 76- Bibliog: Hilton Kramer (auth), Extreme cross purposes, New York Times, 12/10/72; Linda Nochlin (auth), Some women realists, Arts Mag, 2/74; Greg Battcock (auth), Super Realism, Dutton, 75. Mem: Artists Equity. Style & Technique: Realist, urban and aerial landscape; originally smooth flat style, presently in short stroke technique. Media: Oil, Watercolor. Publ: Illusr, Country Rush, Adventures in Poetry, 72. Dealer: Brooke Alexander Gallery 20 W 57th St New York NY 10019. Mailing Add: 50 W 29th St New York NY 10001

JAFFE, IRA SHELDON
EDUCATOR, ART ADMINISTRATOR
b New York, NY, Aug 19, 43. Study: Columbia Univ, AB, 64, MFA(film, radio & television), 67, with Erik Barnouw; Univ Southern Calif, PhD(cinema), 75, with Arthur Knight. Exhib of Films: The Producer, SW Theatre Conf, Univ NMex, 74; Interference, The Best of Canyon Cinema Nat Film Festival, San Francisco Art Inst, 77. Teaching: Lectr cinema, Univ Southern Calif, Los Angeles, 70-72; lectr cinema, Univ NMex, Albuquerque, 72-75, asst prof cinema, 75- Mem: Univ Film Asn. Style & Technique: Non-narrative but representational. Res: Analysis of spatial organization or spatial plot in narrative and non-narrative films. Publ: Auth, Masculine—Feminine: Film, Fun & Games, Columbia Daily Spectator, 66; auth, The clowns, Film Quart, 71; auth, Film as the Narration of Space: Citizen Kane, Col Art Asn, 77; auth, Patterns of Reflexivity in the Documentary Film, Univ Film Asn, 77; auth, Films: little boy, ARTSPACE, 78. Mailing Add: Dept of Theatre Arts Univ NMex Albuquerque NM 87131

JAFFE, IRMA B
ART HISTORIAN
b New Orleans, La. Study: Columbia Univ, BS, MA, PhD. Teaching: Prof art hist, Fordham Univ, 66- Pos: Res cur, Whitney Mus Am Art, New York, 64-65. Mem: Col Art Asn Am; Am Studies Asn. Res: American art. Publ: Auth, Cubist elements in the painting of Marsden Hartley: a phenomenological view, Art Int, 70; ed, Baroque art: the Jesuit Contribution, Fordham Univ, 72; auth, John Trumbull: Patriot-Artist of the American Revolution, NY Graphic Soc, 75; auth, Trumbull: The Declaration of Independence, Viking-Penguin, 76; auth, Copley's Watson and the Shark, Am Art J, spring 77; plus others. Mailing Add: Dept of Fine Arts Fordham Univ Bronx NY 10458

JAFFE, NORA
SCULPTOR, PAINTER
b Urbana, Ohio, Feb 25, 28. Study: Dayton Art Inst, Ohio; also with Samuel Adler & David Hare, New York. Work: Brooklyn Mus, NY; Pa Acad Fine Arts, Philadelphia; Univ Art Mus, Berkeley, Calif; MacDowell Colony, Peterborough, NH. Exhib: Mus Mod Art, New York, 61; Village Art Ctr, New York, 62; Baltimore Mus Art, Md, 63; Pa Acad Fine Arts, 63-67; A M Sachs Gallery, New York, 65; Univ Art Mus, Univ Calif, Berkeley, 67; Finch Col Mus, New York, 67-71; Brooklyn Mus Art, 68; New Sch Art Ctr, New York, 69-73; Va Mus Fine Arts, Richmond, 70; Gallery Lasson, London, Eng, 70; ArnolFini Art Ctr, Rhinebeck, NY, 78. Awards: Second Prize, Gymnasium Show I, New York, 64; MacDowell Colony Residency, 69-70. Style & Technique: Plaster & wood reliefs, oil on canvas. Publ: Illusr, Snapshots of a Daughter-in-Law—Adrianne Rich, Norton, 67; illusr, Caterpillar 2, 68 &

Caterpillar 13, 70, Caterpillar; illusr, Realignment, 74 & The Name Encanyoned River, 78, Treacle Press. Mailing Add: 285 Central Park W New York NY 10024

JAFFE, MRS WILLIAM B
COLLECTOR
Collection: Paintings, contemporary art. Mailing Add: 640 Park Ave New York NY 10021

JAGGER, GILLIAN
PAINTER, SCULPTOR
b London, Eng, Oct 27, 30. Study: Carnegie Inst Technol, BFA; Colorado Springs Fine Arts Ctr, scholar, 52, with Vytlacil; Univ Buffalo; Columbia Univ; NY Univ, MA. Work: Finch Col Mus, New York; Brompton's, Montreal, Que; Carnegie Inst, Pittsburgh. Comn: Portrait comns, 47-51. Exhib: Two-man & group shows, Loft Gallery, 55-57; one-man shows, Ruth White Gallery, New York, 61, 63 & 64; Finch Col Mus, 64; Lerner-Heller Gallery, 71, 73, 75 & 77; The Horse: Light & Motion, Lerner-Heller Gallery, New York, 75. Teaching: Lectr art, Radio Free Europe, cols & prof art schs; instr painting, NY Univ, Post Col & New Rochelle Acad; formerly asst prof hist & philos art, Post Col. Pos: Display artist, 53-55; textile designer, Wamsutta Mills, Fruit of the Loom, 55-57. Mailing Add: 418 Central Park W New York NY 10025

JAGMAN, ED
PAINTER
b Chicago, Ill, Nov 29, 36. Study: Am Acad Art, Chicago; Community Col, Denver, Colo. Work: Park Forest Pub Libr, Ill: Cent Bank Denver; Johns-Manville Corp, Colo; United Bank Denver; Nat City Bank Denver; Pub Serv & Mt Bell of Colo. Exhib: One-man show, Chicago Pub Libr, 66; Nat Watercolor Exhib, Erie, Pa, 69; Painters & Sculptors NJ 28th Ann, 69; Am Watercolor Soc 102nd Ann, 69; Mainstreams 74, 75 & 76, Marietta, Ohio. Awards: Purchase Award, Park Forest Libr, 63-64; hon mention, Ill Festival Arts, 64; Spec Purchase Award, Colo Coun Arts & Humanities, 73. Style & Technique: Both wet into wet and dry brush techniques; realism; impressionistic. Media: Watercolor. Publ: Cover, Compact Mag, 4/69; cover & article, Up Date Mag, 10/71; auth, Watercolor page, Am Artist Mag, 12/75. Dealer: DeColores Gallery 2817 E Third Ave Denver CO 80206; Blair Galleries Ltd PO Box 2342 Santa Fe NM 87501. Mailing Add: 3991 E Orchard Rd Littleton CO 80121

JAGOW, ELLEN T
PAINTER
b Wisconsin Rapids, Wis, Sept 21, 20. Study: Concordia Teachers Col, BS; Art Inst Chicago. Work: Butler Inst Am Art, Youngstown, Ohio; Riverview Sch, Milwaukee, Wis; Fox-Richmond Gallery, Keuka Park, NY; Lincoln Col, Ill; Galesburg Civic Art Ctr, Ill. Exhib: Cent Ill Exhib, Peoria, 65; Miss Valley Artists, Ill State Mus, Springfield, 66; Butler Inst Am Art, Youngstown, 69; Massillon Mus Show, Ohio, 69; Allied Artists Am, 74. Awards: Purchase Award, Midyear Show, Butler Inst Am Art, 69. Mem: Am Fedn Art; hon life mem Galesburg Civic Art Ctr (pres, 64); Cleveland Mus Art; Butler Inst Am Art; Artists Equity Asn. Style & Technique: Structural basis for the development of subject matter, especially abstract values and simplicity of color. Media: Acrylic. Dealer: Bonfoey Gallery 1710 Euclid Ave Cleveland OH 44115. Mailing Add: Box 7 Garfield Rd Hiram OH 44234

JAIDINGER, JUDITH C (JUDITH CLARANN SZESKO)
PRINTMAKER, PAINTER
b Chicago, Ill, Apr 10, 41. Study: Art Inst Chicago, BFA. Work: Minot State Col, NDak; Washington & Jefferson Col, Washington, Pa; Ill State Mus, Springfield; Brand Libr, Glendale, Calif; Hunterdon Co Art Clinton, NJ. Exhib: Nat Acad Design Ann, New York, 67, 68, 70, 73-75 & 77; 39th Int, Northwest Printmakers, Seattle, 68; 51st Print Exhib, Soc Am Graphic Artists, New York, 71; Graphics '71, Western NMex Univ, Silver City, 71; 12th Midwest Biennial Exhib, Joslyn Art Mus, Omaha, 72; 29th Exhib, Ill State Mus, 76; A Selectio Recent Am Prints, State Univ Col, Oneonta, NY, 76; 66th Exhib Tex Fine Arts Asn, Laguna Gloria Art Mus, Austin, 77. Awards: Graphics Award, Mercyhurst Col, Erie, Pa, 70; Smithsonian Traveling Exhib Award, Contemp Am Drawings V, Norfolk Mus Arts & Sci, 71-74; Graphics Award, Okla Mus Art, 75. Mem: Painters & Sculptors Soc NJ, Inc; Miniature Art Soc NJ. Style & Technique: Surrealism. Media: Wood Engraving; Opaque Watercolor, Mixed Media. Mailing Add: 6248 N Bell Chicago IL 60659

JAKSTAS, ALFRED JOHN
MUSEUM CONSERVATOR
b Boston, Mass, Oct 30, 16. Study: Harvard Col, AB, 38; Fogg Mus Dept Conservation, with George Stout, Murray Pease & Richard Buck. Pos: Conservator, Isabella Stewart Gardner Mus, Boston, Mass, 41-61; conservator, Art Inst Chicago, 61-; consult in conservation, numerous collections. Mem: Int & Am Insts Conserv Artistic Objects. Res: Study of materials and techniques of painting of various periods. Publ: Auth, Problems of Museum Conservation, 63. Mailing Add: 125 E Monroe St Chicago IL 60603

JAMEIKIS, BRONE ALEKSANDRA
DESIGNER, INSTRUCTOR
b Vilnius, Lithuania; US citizen. Study: Univ Vilnius, dipl; Ecole Arts et Metiers, Freiburg, Ger, dipl; Art Inst Chicago, BFA & MFA; Univ Hawaii, MA. Comn: Mosaic, Holy Cross Church, Chicago, Ill, 52; leaded stained glass, St Philomena Church, Chicago, 60; mosaic & faceted slab glass, Holy Cross Church, Dayton, Ohio, 64; faceted slab glass windows, Springdale Mausoleum, Peoria, Ill, 66; leaded & faceted slab glass, O'Hare Int Airport, Chicago, 68. Exhib: Artists of Lithuania, Windsor Mus, Can, 57; Artists of United States, Denver Mus Art, 57; Nat Biennial Relig Art Exhib, Cranbrook Acad, Detroit, Mich, 60-69; Artists of Hawaii, Honolulu Acad Arts, 61 & 72; Ecumenical Art Show, St Benet Gallery, Chicago, 65. Teaching: Instr art, Univ Hawaii, 58-61. Pos: Art dir, Valeska Art Studios, Chicago, 51-58 & 62-71; keeper, AV educ, Honolulu Acad Arts, 71- Awards: Award for Leaded Stained Glass, Relig Art Exhib, Chicago, 56; Award for Stained & Slab Glass, Am Inst Designers, 60; Award for Faceted Slab Glass, Madonna Theme in Art Exhib, Honolulu, 61. Bibliog: David Asherman (auth), Rare gift from Europe to Hawaiian art, Honolulu Advertiser, 60; J Dainauskas (auth), Brone Jameikis-stained glass artist, Aidai-Echoes, Brooklyn, NY, 69; D J Anderson (auth), An artist brings light to dark corners, Vol 9, No 4, Chicago. Mem: Inst Lithuanian Artists. Style & Technique: Amalgamation of semi-abstract tendencies and folkloristic expressions; slab glass used in faceted manner, producing a full scale of lighting effects and color values. Mailing Add: PO Box 4212 Honolulu HI 96813

JAMES, CATHERINE
See Catti

JAMES, CHRISTOPHER P
PHOTOGRAPHER
b Boston, Mass, May 8, 47. Study: Cummington Community for the Arts, 68; Mass Col Art, BFA, 69; RI Sch of Design, MAT, 71. Work: Mus Mod Art, New York; Int Mus Photog, George Eastman House, Rochester, NY; Bibliot Nat, Paris; Boston Mus Fine Arts, Mass; Minneapolis Inst Arts Mus. Exhib: One-man shows, Eastman Kodak, Rochester, NY, 73, Archetype Gallery, New Haven, Conn, 74-77, Carl Siembab Gallery, Boston, 75, 76 & 78, Minneapolis Inst Arts Mus, 77, Rosa Esman Gallery, New York, 77-78 & Int Mus Photog, George Eastman House, 77; USA/USSR, Mus Francais de la Photographie, 76; Mass Inst Technol, Cambridge, 78. Teaching: Asst prof photog & design, Greenfield Community Col, 71; Nat Endowment for the Arts artist-in-residence, Keene State Col, 77- Awards: Daguerre, Niepce Medal, Phot-Univers USA/USSR, Minister of Foreign Affairs, Paris, 76. Bibliog: Peggy Sealfon (auth), The strip, 35mm Summer Ed, 77; Hilton Kramer (auth), New York Review, Esman, New York Times, 9/23/77; David Bourdon (auth), New York Review, Esman, Village Voice, 10/10/77. Mem: Soc Photog Educ; Friends of Photog. Style & Technique: Hand-dyed and enameled photographs. Media: Photography. Publ: Contribr, Camera 35, 73 & Photog Ann, Ziff-Davis, 75 & 77; auth, Meniscus, Addison House, 78; contribr, Alternative Photographic Process, Morgan & Morgan, 78. Mailing Add: c/o Rosa Esman Gallery 29 W 57th St New York NY 10019

JAMES, FREDERIC
PAINTER
b Kansas City, Mo, Sept 28, 15. Study: Col Archit, Univ Mich, BDes; Cranbrook Acad Art. Work: Nelson Gallery Art, Kansas City, Mo; Denver Art Mus; Univ Mo, Columbia; Cranbrook Acad Art, Bloomfield Hills, Mich. Comn: Murals, Trinity Lutheran Church, Mission, Kans, Overland Park State Bank, Kans & Consumer's Coop Asn, Kansas City; Wildflowers in America (print series), New York Botanical Garden. Exhib: Milch Gallery, New York; Nelson Gallery Art; Mid-Am Ann; Springfield Mus Art, Mass; Maynard Walker Gallery, New York; plus others. Awards: Prizes, Denver Art Mus & Nelson Gallery Art. Mem: Am Watercolor Soc. Dealer: Graham Gallery 1014 Madison Ave New York NY 10021; Kachina Gallery 112 Shelby St Santa Fe NM 87501. Mailing Add: 850 W 52nd St Kansas City MO 64112

JAMES, GEOFFREY
ART ADMINISTRATOR
b St Asaph, Wales, Jan 9, 42; Can citizen. Study: Wadham Col, Oxford, Eng, BA & MA(mod hist). Pos: Dir visual arts, Film & Video Sect, Can Coun, 75- Mailing Add: 255 Albert St Ottawa ON K1P 5V8 Can

JAMESON, DEMETRIOS GEORGE
PAINTER, PRINTMAKER
b St Louis, Mo, Nov 22, 19. Study: Corcoran Sch Art, Washington, DC, 46; Washington Univ Sch Fine Arts, BFA, 49; Univ Ill Sch Fine & Appl Arts, Urbana, MFA, 50. Work: Portland Art Mus, Ore; Seattle Art Mus, Wash; Denver Art Mus, Colo; Victoria & Albert Mus, London, Eng; Am Embassy, Athens, Greece; plus others in pub & pvt collections. Exhib: Younger Am Painters, Guggenheim Mus, New York, 54; 4th Int Print Show, Bordighera, Italy, 58; Northwestern Art Today, Seattle World's Fair, Wash, 62; Corcoran Mus, Washington, DC; San Francisco Mus Oakland Art Mus, Calif; Tacoma Art Mus, Wash; Butler In Am Art, Youngstown, Ohio; Seattle Art Mus; Portland Art Denver Art Mus; Kraushaar Gallery, New York; New Forms Gallery, Athens, Greece; one-man show, Portland Art Mus, 52 & 60; plus many others. Teaching: Prof art, Ore State Univ, 50- Awards: J T Millican foreign Travel Award, Washington Univ, 50; Awards, Coos Art Mus, Ore & City Art Mus, St Louis, Mo; plus many others. Mem: Portland Art Asn (pres, 57-58); Corvallis Art Ctr; Salem Art Asn. Style & Technique: Contemporary figure-landscape. Media: Oil. Mailing Add: 725 NW 28th St Corvallis OR 97330

JAMIESON, MITCHELL
PAINTER
b Kensington, Md, Oct 27, 15. Study: Washington, DC & Mexico City, Mex. Work: White House, Washington, DC; Whitney Mus Am Art & Metrop Mus Art, New York; Brooklyn Mus; Seattle Art Mus; Ft Worth Art Ctr, Tex; plus others. Comn: Murals, Interior Bldg, Washington, DC, Comptroller Gen Suite, Washington, DC, Post Off Bldgs, Upper Marlboro, Laurel, Md & Willard, Ohio; paintings for Life Mag, 57. Exhib: One-man shows, Santa Barbara Mus Art, Calif, Des Moines Art Ctr, Iowa, Calif Palace of Legion of Honor, San Francisco, Norton Gallery Art, Washington, DC; plus many other nat exhibs. Teaching: Head painting dept, Cornish Sch, Seattle, 49-51; instr painting, Madeira, Sch, Greenway, Va, 52-55; vis instr, Norton Gallery & Art Sch, 52-53 & 56-57. Awards: Bronze Star for Work as Navy Combat Artist, 46; Guggenheim Fel, 46; Am Acad Arts & Lett Grant, 47. Mailing Add: 1108 Prince St Alexandria VA 22314

JAMISON, MARGARET CONRY
ART DEALER
b Winfield, Kans, July 3, 17. Pos: Founder & former owner, Jamison Galleries. Specialty: Western and Southwestern art. Mailing Add: Jamison Galleries 111 E San Francisco Santa Fe NM 87501

JAMISON, PHILIP (DUANE, JR)
PAINTER
b Philadelphia, Pa, July 3, 25. Study: Philadelphia Mus Sch Art, grad. Work: Pa Acad Fine Arts, Philadelphia; Wilmington Soc Fine Arts, Del; Nat Acad Design, New York; Flint Inst Art, Mich; Frye Art Mus, Seattle, Wash. Exhib: Pa Acad Fine Arts, 49-69; Nat Acad Design, 56-77; Am Watercolor Soc, New York, 56-77; 200 Yrs of Watercolor Painting in Am, Metrop Mus Art, New York, 67; one-man shows, Hirschl & Adler Galleries, New York, 59-77, Sessler Gallery, Philadelphia, 63 & 72, Duke Univ, 69, Del Art Mus, Wilmington, 73, Janet Fleisher Gallery, Philadelphia, 77 & Grand Gallery, Wilmington, 77. Teaching: Instr watercolor, Philadelphia Col Art, 61-63. Pos: Artist, Apollo Soyuz Space Launch, Kennedy Space Ctr, Fla, Nat Aeronautics & Space Admin, 75. Awards: Dana Medal, Pa Acad Fine Arts, 61; Gold Medal of Honor, Allied Artists Am, 64; Nat Acad Design Prize, 67. Mem: Nat Acad Design; Am Watercolor Soc; Philadelphia Watercolor Club; Wilmington Soc Fine Arts. Media: Watercolor. Publ: Contribr, Am Artist Mag, 62. Dealer: Hirschl & Adler Galleries Inc 21 E 67th St New York NY 10021. Mailing Add: 104 Price St West Chester PA 19380

JANELSINS, VERONICA
ILLUSTRATOR, PAINTER
b Riga, Latvia, May 20, 10; US citizen. Study: State Acad Fine Arts, Riga, grad, 40. Work: State Hist Mus Riga; State Art Mus Riga; Baumgarten-Schuler Collection, Stuttgart, WGer; Vitols Collection, Venezuela, Caracas. Exhib: Latvian State Art Mus, 40; Expos des Artistes en Exile, Paris, 49; Madonna Festival, Los Angeles, Calif, 55; Los Angeles Co Mus, 56; one-man show, Stockholm, 70; plus many others. Awards: Madonna Festival Awards, 53 & 55. Style & Technique: Contemporary and semi-abstract oil painting. Publ: Many book covers and illus for Gramatu Draugs, Brooklyn. Mailing Add: 1298 Monument St Pacific Palisades CA 90272

JANIS, CONRAD
ART DEALER, COLLECTOR
b New York, NY, Feb 11, 28. Collections Arranged: Participated in arranging all exhibitions at Sidney Janis Gallery from New Realism, 62 through Sharp Focus Realism, 72. Pos: Co-dir, Sidney Janis Gallery. Specialty: All historic movements in 20th century art to the present. Collection: Contemporary American art. Mailing Add: Sidney Janis Gallery 6 W 57th St New York NY 10019

JANIS, SIDNEY
ART DEALER, WRITER
b Buffalo, NY, July 8, 96. Exhibs Arranged: Les Fauves, 50; Futurism, 54; Analytical Cubism, 56; New Realists (Pop Art), 62; Sharp Focus Realism, 72; plus many one-man shows, including Henri Rousseau, Dada, Delaunay, Kandinsky, Mondrian, deKooning, Pollock, Rothko & Kline; plus many others. Pos: Owner, Sidney Janis Gallery. Mem: Art Dealers Asn Am (bd dir, 69-71). Specialty: Presentation of work by three generations in 20th century art from cubism to pop art and sharp focus realism. Collection: Sidney and Harriet Janis Collection of 20th century art given to Museum of Modern Art, New York. PLAuth, School of Paris comes to US, Decision, 11-12/41; auth, They Taught Themselves, XXth Century American Primitive Painting, Dial Press, 42; auth, Abstract & Surrealist Art in America, Reynal Hitchcock, 44; co-auth, Picasso: the War Years 1939-46, Doubleday, 46; auth, Aims of the Janis Gallery, Arts Mag, 4/71; plus others, 40-75. Mailing Add: 6 W 57th St New York NY 10019

JANKOWSKI, JOSEPH P
PAINTER, EDUCATOR
b Cleveland, Ohio, Jan 12, 16. Study: St Mary's Col, Mich; John Huntington Polytech Inst; Art Students League; Cleveland Inst Art, BFA. Work: Akron Art Inst, Ohio; Univ Ala; Cleveland Print Club; USAF Collection; Cleveland Mus Art; plus others. Comn: Stations of the Cross, St Mary's Church, McKeesport, Pa; mural, Jewish Community Ctr, Cleveland; St Mary's Col, Orchard Lake, Mich. Exhib: Art Inst Chicago; Albright-Knox Art Gallery, Buffalo, NY; Audubon Artists, New York; Isaac Delgado Mus Art, New Orleans; High Mus Art, Atlanta; plus others. Teaching: Assoc prof art, Univ Ala, 49-53; instr art, Notre Dame Col, Ohio, 54; instr painting, Cleveland Inst Art, 53-, dir eve sch, 55- Awards: Prizes, Albright-Knox Art Gallery, Akron Art Inst, Butler Inst Am Art & Cleveland Mus Art; plus many others. Mem: Col Art Asn Am; Mid-Am Col Art Asn; Art Students League. Mailing Add: Cleveland Inst Art 11141 East Blvd Cleveland OH 44106

JANOWSKY, BELA
SCULPTOR, INSTRUCTOR
b Budapest, Hungary, 1900. Study: Ont Col Art; Pa Acad Fine Arts; Cleveland Sch Art; Beaux-Arts Inst Design. Comn: Bust, Queens Univ, Kingston, Ont; Gold Medal, Royal Soc Can; bronze reliefs, US Dept Com Bldg, Washington, DC; bronze mem, Post Off, Cooperstown, NY; bronze 150th anniversary plaque, Naval Shipyard, Brooklyn, NY. Exhib: Allied Artists Am Ann, 39-; Am Artists Prof League; Nat Acad Design; Nat Sculpture Soc; Pa Acad Fine Arts, Philadelphia; plus others. Pos: Instr sculpture, Craft Students League, YWCA, New York, 52- Awards: Lindsey Morris Mem Prize, Allied Artists Am, 51 & 64. Mem: Allied Artists Am; Nat Sculpture Soc. Mailing Add: 52 W 57th St New York NY 10019

JANSCHKA, FRITZ
PAINTER, GRAPHIC ARTIST
b Vienna, Austria, Apr 21, 19. Study: Acad Fine Arts, Vienna, with A Paris Guetersloh. Work: Albertina, Vienna; Mus XXth Century, Vienna; Philadelphia Mus Art, Pa; Grafische Sammlung, Zurich, Switz; James Joyce Ctr, London. Exhib: Art Club Exhib, Vienna, Turin, Rome, 47-51; Acad Fine Arts, Philadelphia, 51-54; Print Club, Philadelphia, 56; Graphische Sammlungen, Zurich, 72; Fantastic Realists, Wiener Schule, Near East & Far East countries, 72-74; Finnegan's Wake, Univ Tulsa, Okla, 77. Teaching: Artist in residence in graphics & painting, Bryn Mawr Col, Pa. Pos: Bd mem, Int Art Club, Vienna, 46-51. Bibliog: Gerhard Meyer (auth), Fritz Janschka, Pheitner-Lichtenfels, Vienna, 69; J Norton-Smith (auth), A Tribute to James Joyce's Ulysses, Reading Univ, Eng, 73; Johan Muschik (auth), Janschka Monograph & Vienna school of fantastic realism, Jugend & Volk, Vienna/Munich, 74. Style & Technique: Fantastic realism, mixed media, welded sculpture, graphics, etching. Media: Oil, Watercolor. Publ: Auth, 26 etchings to James Joyce's Ulysses, Rizet, 72; ed, 6 poems & 6 drawings, 72; contribr, After Surrealism, 72, auth, Ulysses Alphabet, 73 & contribr, After Clacicism, 73, Propylaen. Mailing Add: Bryn Mawr Col Bryn Mawr PA 19010

JANSEN, ANGELA BING
PRINTMAKER, PHOTOGRAPHER
b New York, NY, Aug 17, 29. Study: Brooklyn Col, BA; NY Univ, MA; Atelier 17, New York with S W Hayter; Brooklyn Mus Art Sch. Work: Mus of Mod Art, New York; Philadelphia Mus of Art; Art Inst of Chicago; Victoria & Albert Mus, London, Eng; Worcester Mus, Mass. Exhib: Brooklyn Mus Nat Print Exhib, 50, 70 & 76; Nat Exhib of Prints, Libr of Cong, Washington, DC, 69 & 71; Ljubljana Int Print Biennale, Yugoslavia, 71-77; Venice Biennale, Italy, 72; Biennale of Graphic Art, Vienna, 72 & 77; Lang of Print, Pratt Ctr, New York, 73; Individual Exhib, Gimpel & Weitzenhoffer, New York, 74; Five Printmakers, Martha Jackson Gallery, New York, 75. Teaching: Teacher, New York high schs, 55- Awards: Assoc Am Artists Gallery Award, Int Miniature Print Exhib, 71; George Roth Prize, Philadelphia Print Club, 71 & 74; Grant for Printmaking, Nat Endowment for the Arts, 74-75. Style & Technique: Photoetching, photography and painting. Media: Etching. Dealer: Gimpel & Weitzenhoffer 1040 Madison Ave New York NY 10021. Mailing Add: 1646 First Ave New York NY 10028

JANSEN, CATHERINE SANDRA
PHOTOGRAPHER, INSTRUCTOR
b New York, NY, Dec 14, 45. Study: Cranbrook Acad of Art, Bloomfield Hills, Mich, BFA, 68; Acad di Belle Arti, cert, 69; Temple Univ, MFA, 73. Work: Philadelphia Mus of Art. Exhib: Unique Photographs: Multiple Sculpture, Mus of Mod Art, New York, 73; Stuffed, Stitched & Sewn, Mus of Contemp Crafts, New York, 73; Light & Lens, Hudson River Mus, Yonkers, NY, 73; Photo Transfer, Akron Art Inst, Ohio, 73; Three Centuries of Am Art, Philadelphia Mus of Art, Pa, 76; Soft Sculpture, Living Arts Ctr, Dayton, Ohio, 76; Am Family Portraits, Philadelphia Mus of Art, 76; Breath of Vision, Smithsonian Inst Traveling Exhib, 76-77. Teaching: Instr photog, Bucks Co Community Col, Newtown, Pa, 73- Style & Technique: Photographic images on cloth, stuffed, stitched, embroidered; often 3-D or environmental. Publ: Illusr, Frontiers in Photography, Time Life, 73; illusr, Photography, Upton & Upton, 76; illusr, Three Centuries of American Art, Philadelphia Mus of Art, 76; illusr, Design Through Discovery, Holt Rinehart & Winston, 77; illusr, Photography Catalogue, Harper & Row, 77. Mailing Add: 152 Heacock Lane Wyncote PA 19095

JANSON, ANTHONY FREDRICK
ART HISTORIAN
b St Louis, Mo, Mar 30, 43. Study: Columbia Univ, BA; Inst Fine Arts, NY Univ, MA; Fogg Mus, Harvard Univ, PhD. Teaching: Asst prof, State Univ NY, Buffalo, 73-75; asst prof, Col Charleston, SC, 75- Res: Dutch 17th century and American 19th century painting, including Washington Allston. Publ: Auth, The western landscapes of Worthington Whittredge, Am Art Rev, 76; auth, Worthington Whittredge: two early landscapes, Detroit Inst Arts Bull, 77; auth, Review of Peter Bermingham, American art in the Barbizon mood, Col Art J, 77; co-auth, The Story of Painting From Cave Painting to Modern Times, Harry N Abrams, 77; auth, Instructor's Manual to H W Janson's History of Art, Prentice-Hall, 78. Mailing Add: 25 Gadsen St Charleston SC 29401

JANSON, HORST WOLDEMAR
ART HISTORIAN
b Leningrad, USSR, Oct 4, 13; US citizen. Study: Univ Hamburg, 32-33; Univ Munich, 33-34; Univ Hamburg, 34-35; Harvard Univ, MA, 38, PhD, 42. Teaching: Asst fine arts, Harvard Univ, 36-38; docent & lectr fine arts, Worcester Art Mus, 36-38; instr fine arts, State Univ Iowa, 38-41; asst prof fine arts, Washington Univ, 41-48; prof fine arts, NY Univ, 49-, chmn dept, 49-75. Awards: Guggenheim Fel, 48-49 & 55-56; Charles Rufus Morey Award, Col Art Asn Am, 52 & 57. Mem: Col Art Asn Am (pres, 70-72). Res: Italian renaissance sculpture; iconography; 19th and 20th century art. Publ: Auth, Apes & Ape Lore in the Middle Ages & the Renaissance, 52; co-auth, Story of Painting for Young People, 52; auth, Sculpture of Donatello, 57; auth, Key Monuments of the History of Art, 59; auth, History of Art, 62. Mailing Add: 29 Washington Sq W New York NY 10011

JANSS, EDWIN, JR
COLLECTOR
Collection: Painting, contemporary art. Mailing Add: 100 E Thousand Oaks Blvd Thousand Oaks CA 91360

JANZEN, LOREN GENE
PRINTMAKER, EDUCATOR
b Wichita, Kans, July 20, 38. Study: Wichita State Univ, BFA & MFA; Kansas City Art Inst. Work: Bibliot del Ist Tecnol Regional, Juarez, Mex; Philbrook Art Ctr, Tulsa, Okla; Ark Arts Ctr, Little Rock. Exhib: 4th Ann Prints, Drawings & Crafts Exhib, Ark Arts Ctr, 70; 3rd Biennial Nat Exhib Prints & Drawings, Dickinson State Col, NDak, 72; Southwest Graphics Invitational, San Antonio, Tex, 72; IV Int Painting Competition, Italia 2000, Via L Giodano, Naples, 74; Int Painting Competition, Galleria Schettini, Naples, 74. Teaching: Asst prof printmaking, Univ Tex, El Paso, 67- Awards: Purchase Award, 4th Ann Prints, Drawings & Crafts Exhib, Ark Arts Ctr, 70; Purchase Award, IV Int Painting Competition, Italia 2000, Associazone Artists e Professionist Vanvitelli, 74; Premio Marc' Aurelio, Club Marc' Aurelio, Rome, 75. Bibliog: Salvatore Bartolomeo (auth), Loren Janzen e il recupero del reale, Le Arti, Milan, Italy, 75. Mem: Tex Printmakers Soc; Western Asn Art Schs & Mus; Western Asn Art Mus; Southwest Col Art Conf; Col Art Asn. Media: Lithography, Intaglio. Mailing Add: c/o Art Dimensions 808 Montana El Paso TX 79902

JAQUE, LOUIS
PAINTER
b Montreal, PQ, May 1, 19. Study: Inst Appl Arts, Montreal. Work: Nat Gallery Can, Ottawa; Montreal Mus Fine Arts; Mus Quebec; Mus d'Art Contemporain, Montreal; Societe Publicite Editoriale Collection, Milan, Italy. Comn: Mural, Quebec Pavilion, Expo 70, Osaka, Japan, 70; mural, Maison de Radio-Canada, Montreal, 72; mural, Place de la Bourse, Montreal, 74. Exhib: 6th Biennial Exhib Can Painting, Nat Gallery Can, 65; Hemisfair Can Pavilion, San Antonio, Tex, 68; one-man shows, New York, 69 & 70, Milan, 70 & 73, Paris, 71, 73 & 75 & Rome, 73; Europa 72, 3rd Int Exhib Painting, Milan, 72; Salon Int d'Art Contemp, Paris, 74 & 75. Awards: Jessie Dow Award, Montreal Mus Fine Arts, 60; Can Art Coun Grant to Artist, 64 & 72; Europa 72 Bronze Medal, City of Milan, 72. Mem: Soc Prof Artists of Quebec (founder, pres, 64-65). Style & Technique: Abstract of cosmic dimension with major aim at dimensional light and spirituality. Media: Oil on Canvas, Drawings, Tempera. Dealer: Galerie Bernard Desroches 1194 Sherbrooke St W Montreal PQ Can. Mailing Add: 1760 Ducharme Ave Outremont PQ H2V 1H3 Can

JARAMILLO, VIRGINIA
PAINTER
b El Paso, Tex, Mar 21, 39. Study: Otis Art Inst, 58-61. Work: Long Beach Mus Art, Calif; Pasadena Art Mus, Calif; Aldrich Mus Contemp Art, Ridgefield, Conn; Schenectady Mus, NY. Exhib: Whitney Mus Am Art Ann, New York, 72; Contemporary Reflections 1971-72, Aldrich Mus Contemp Art, Ridgefield, 72; group exhib, Douglas Drake Gallery, Kansas City, Kans, 75 & one-man show, 76; traveling exhib contemp art throughout Eastern Europe, 76; plus others. Pos: Assoc dir & aesthet adv, Hybrid Inc, 72-74. Awards: Ford Found Grant, 62; Nat Endowment Arts, 72-73; Creative Artists Pub Serv Prog Grant, 75. Mem: Nat Soc Lit & Arts. Bibliog: F Bowling (auth), Outside the galleries: four artists, Arts Mag, 11/70; Deluxe show, Houston Chronicle, 8/71; C Ratcliff (auth), The Whitney Annual, Part I, Artforum, 4/72. Media: Acrylic, Oil. Res: Religious architecture throughout Europe. Publ: Post-minimal artists, Arts Mag, 9/75. Mailing Add: 109 Spring New York NY 10012

JARDINE, DONALD LEROY
ART EDITOR, EDUCATOR
b Idaho Falls, Idaho, July 7, 26. Study: Weber Col, Ogden, Utah, CA, 48, Assoc Sci, 49; Univ Utah, BS, 50 & MS, 62; Univ Minn, Minneapolis, PhD, 75; studied with Farrell R Collett, Alvin Gittens, Arnold Friberg, Walter Wilwerding, Peter Busa & Reid Hastie. Work: Salt Lake Art Barn; Univ Utah; Weber State Col; Univ Minn. Exhib: Utah Artists' Invitational, Ogden, 54-58 & 61; Instructor's Exhib, Salt Lake Art Ctr, 57-60; Asn Prof Artists Ann, Minneapolis, 64-66; People-to-people Exhib, Santiago, Chile, 66; Studio Arts Fac Show, Univ Minn, 68 & 70. Teaching: Art teacher, Bountiful Sr High Sch, Utah, 51-62; assoc dir art educ, Westminster Col, Salt Lake City, 58-60; assoc educ dir art, Art Instr Sch, Minneapolis, 62-; asst prof career art, Univ Minn, 68- Pos: Pres, Utah Art Educ Asn, 58-60; ed, The Illustrator, 65- Awards: Distinguished Art Award, Weber State Col. Mem: Asn Prof Artists (dir, 65-67); Art Instr Schs (vpres, 77); Art Dir Club; Nat Art Educ Asn (lectr, 74-75). Publ: Illusr, The children's friend, 55-62; illusr, Tell Me a Story, 60; contribr, Art Instruction School's Textbooks, 62-75; auth, How to Sell Your Artwork, 63. Dealer: Treehouse Art Gallery Farmington UT 84025. Mailing Add: 2390 Wisconsin Ave N Golden Valley MN 55427

JARKOWSKI, STEFANIA AGNES
PAINTER, EDUCATOR
b Gdansk, Poland, US citizen. Study: Liberal Col, Torun, Poland, dipl; Acad Fine Arts, Warsaw, Poland; art study in Paris, France; Nat Mus Poland, restoration study with Dr J Burshe. Work: George Washington Carver Mus, Tuskegee, Ala; Bochnia Mus, Poland; Argonne Nat Lab, Chicago; Milenium Art Gallery, Warsaw. Comn: (Restoration of works)

Yucca Gloriosa, 66 & Still Life, 67 (oils by George Washington Carver), Tuskegee Inst; Nobleman (14th century oil), Nat Mus, Warsaw, 67; oil by Roederstein, Alice Pike Barney Collection, Smithsonian Inst/Tuskegee Inst, 69; oil portrait by Shieffelin, Tuskegee Inst, 71. Exhib: One-man shows, George Washington Carver Mus, 63, Polish Artists Asn Zacheta, Warsaw, 65 & Polish Ctr, Hamilton, Can, 67; Burr Artists Group Show, New York; Ala Watercolor Soc Traveling Exhib. Teaching: Lectr & instr art, Tuskegee Inst, 62- Pos: Dir art gallery, George Washington Carver Mus, Tuskegee Inst, 62- Awards: Hon Mention, Kalamazoo Art Festival, 61 & Milenium Art Show, Warsaw, 65; Nat Art Festival Award, Beaux Arts Guild, 64. Mem: Am Asn Univ Prof; Art Educ Asn; Ala Watercolor Burr Artists; Polish Artists Asn. Media: Oil, Watercolor. Mailing Add: 410 Parker Ave Tuskegee Institute AL 36088

JARMAN, WALTON MAXEY
COLLECTOR
b Nashville, Tenn, May 10, 04. Study: With Philip Perkins & Gus Baker. Collection: Abstracts in oils, acrylics and collages. Mailing Add: Box 941 Nashville TN 37202

JARVAISE, JAMES J
PAINTER
b Indianapolis, Ind, Feb 16, 31. Study: Carnegie Inst Technol; Ecolue Art, Biarritz, France, with Leger; Univ Southern Calif, BFA, 53, MFA, 55. Work: Larry Aldrich Mus, Ridgefield, Conn; Mus Mod Art, New York; Albright-Knox Art Gallery, Buffalo, NY; Los Angeles Mus Art; Butler Inst Am Art, Youngstown, Ohio; plus others. Exhib: Carnegie Int, Pittsburgh, 59 & 65; Va Mus Fine Arts, Richmond, 61 & 67; Director's Choice, New York World's Fair, 64; Calif Inst of the Arts, Los Angeles, 66 & 67; plus many other group & one-man shows. Teaching: Instr, Univ Southern Calif, 55-62; instr, Pa State Univ, summer 63; instr, Univ Madrid Int Art Expos, 63; instr, Occidental Col, 65, 66 & 67; instr, Calif Inst of the Arts, 65-68; instr, Univ Southern Calif, summers 66 & 67. Mailing Add: 233 E Islay Santa Barbara CA 93101

JARVIS, DONALD
PAINTER, INSTRUCTOR
b Vancouver, BC, 23. Study: Vancouver Sch Art, with hon, 48; also with Hans Hofmann, New York, 48 & 49. Work: Nat Gallery of Can, Ottawa, Ont; Art Gallery of Greater Victoria, BC; Vancouver Art Gallery; London Pub Libr & Art Mus; Can Coun Art Bank, Ottawa. Exhib: Biennial, Nat Gallery of Can, 55-65 & 69; Nat Gallery Traveling Exhib, Australia, 57; Int Exhib of Painting & Graphic Art, Mexico City, 58; One Hundred Yrs of BC Art, 58, Images for a Can Heritage, 66 & Twenty-Nine Yr Retrospective, 77, Vancouver Art Gallery; Six Ways with Figure Painting, London Art Gallery, Ont, 63; Nat Gallery Can Artist Series VI, Ottawa, 64; Some Painters of the BC Mainland, Art Gallery of Greater Victoria, 65; Int Exhib of Drawings & Prints, Lugano, Switz, 66; one-man show, Vancouver Art Gallery, 49 & 55. Teaching: Instr painting & drawing, Vancouver Sch of Art, 58- Awards: Emily Carr Scholar, Vancouver Sch Art, 49; Sr Arts Fel, Can Coun, 61. Mem: Royal Can Acad Arts. Style & Technique: Abstraction from nature; finding metaphors for the landscape. Media: Acrylic; Graphite; Ink; Watercolor. Mailing Add: c/o Bau-Xi Gallery 1876 W First Ave Vancouver BC V6G 1G5 Can

JARVIS, JOHN BRENT
PAINTER
b American Fork, Utah, Nov 28, 46. Study: Snow Col, AS, 65; Utah State Univ, BS(biology), 71; Brigham Young Univ. Work: Brigham City Mus, Utah. Exhib: Mormon Art Show, Brigham Young Univ, Provo, 73-77; Utah Painting Show, Utah Mus Fine Arts, Salt Lake City, 74-76; Am Watercolor Soc (traveling nat), 76; Salt Lake Art Ctr Regional Show, 76; Am Watercolor Soc, New York, 76; one-man shows, Brigham Young Univ, Provo, Brigham City Mus, Bertha Eacles Gallery, Ogden, Utah & Trivoli Gallery, Salt Lake City. Awards: Merit Award, Utah Painting & Sculpture, Utah Inst Fine Arts, 74; Ann Noye Watercolor, Salt Lake Art Ctr Intermountain, 76; Merit Award, Mormon Art Show, Brigham Young Univ, 77. Style & Technique: Western landscape, figures, watercolor, gouache and oil. Mailing Add: 1150 N 200 W No 22 Lehi UT 84043

JARVIS, LUCY
COLLECTOR, FILMMAKER
b New York, NY, June 23, 27. Study: Cornell Univ; Columbia Univ; New Sch for Social Res, New York. Pos: Exec producer, Nat Broadcasting Corp, New York, 60-76; pres, Creative Proj Inc, 76- Awards: Emmys for The Kremlin & The Louvre (films), Nat Asn Television Arts & Sci, 63; Golden Mike Award for Kremlin Film, Am Women in Radio & TV, 64; Chevalier de l'Ordre des Arts et des Lettres for Museum Without Walls, Louvre & Picasso (films), Fr Govt, 69. Interest: Promotion of painting and sculpture and all other related art forms through the use of film. Collection: Contemporary, universal in origin; emphasis on surrealism. Mailing Add: c/o Creative Proj Inc 45 Rockefeller Pl New York NY 10020

JAUDON, VALERIE
PAINTER
b Greenville, Miss, Aug 6, 45. Study: Miss State Col Women, Columbus; Univ Am, Mexico City; St Martin's Sch Art, London, Eng; Memphis Acad Art, Tenn. Work: Hirshhorn Mus, Washington, DC; Aldrich Mus Contemp Art, Ridgefield, Conn. Comn: Tile work (with Romaldo Giurgola, architect), State Off Complex, Harrisburg, Pa, 76; entrance courtyard (with Giurgola), Salk Inst, La Jolla, Calif, 76; courtyards & fountains (with Giurgola), Wainwright Bldg, St Louis, Mo, 76; ceiling mural (90ft x 22ft; with Giurgola), Insurance Co NAm, Philadelphia, Pa, 77. Exhib: Aldrich Mus Contemp Art, Ridgefield, 75; Mus Mod Art, New York, 75; Albright-Knox Art Gallery, Buffalo, NY, 76; Selections 1977, Aldrich Mus Contemp Art, 77; Recent Acquisitions, Hirshhorn Mus & Sculpture Garden, 77; Basel Art Fair, Switz, 77; Pattern Painting, PS 1, Queens, NY, 77; Painting, Contemp Arts Ctr, Cincinnati, Ohio, 75-77; Critics Choice-Contemp Paintings, New York Gallery Season 1976-1977, 77; Lowe Art Gallery, Syracuse, NY, 77. Bibliog: Jeff Perrone (auth), Approaching the decorative, Artforum, 12/76; John Perreault (auth), More patterns, Soho News, 5/77 & Pattern Painting, Artforum, 77; Sally Webster (auth), Spacial geometry, Arts Exchange, 77. Style & Technique: Oil painting. Dealer: Holly Solomon Gallery 392 W Broadway New York NY 10012. Mailing Add: 139 Bowery New York NY 10002

JAUSS, ANNE MARIE
PAINTER, ILLUSTRATOR
b Munich, Ger, Feb 3, 07; US citizen. Study: Art Sch State Munich. Work: New York Pub Libr Print Rm, NY. Exhib: Group shows, Ger, before 32; one-man shows, Portraits of Pets, Portraits Inc, New York, 47, Old Custom House, Philadelphia, Pa, 51, graphics, Netherwood Arts, Hyde Park, NY, 71 & watercolors, Larcada Gallery, New York, 74. Awards: Author's Award for Pasture, NJ Asn Teachers Eng, 68. Bibliog: R C (auth), Anne Marie Jauss, Panorama, 42; Eugen Guerster (auth), Anne Marie Jauss, Am-Ger Rev, 6/51; Bruno Werner (auth), Anne Marie Jauss, Die Kunst, 1/52. Style & Technique: Romantic realism. Media: Oil, Watercolor, Linoleum, Dry Point. Publ: Auth, Legends of Saints & Beasts, 54, Discovering Nature the Year Round, 55, River's Journey, 57, Under a Green Roof, 60 & Pasture, 68; co-auth, Little Horse of Seven Colors & other Portuguese folk tales, 70; illusr of over 60 bks, mostly for children. Dealer: Larcada Gallery 23 E 67th St New York NY 10021; Portraits Inc 41 E 57th St New York NY 10019. Mailing Add: RD 1 Box 82H Stockholm NJ 07460

JAVACHEFF
See Christo

JAWORSKA, TAMARA
PAINTER, DESIGNER
b Archangelsk, Russia; Can citizen. Study: State Acad Fine Arts, Poland, BFA, Fac Art Weaving, MFA; Royal Can Acad Arts, fel academician. Work: Nat Mus, Warsaw, Poland; Nat Mus Hist Weaving, Lodz, Poland; Pushkin Gallery Europ Art, Moscow, USSR; Art Gallery Col Arts, Gallashields, Scotland; pvt collections. Comn: Tapestries-Gobelin, Olympia & York Co, Place Bell Can, Ottawa, 71 & Bank Montreal, Toronto, 75, Metrop Life Ins Co, Ottawa, 77, JDS Finch 1000, Toronto, 76 & var pvt collections in US, Can, Switz, Eng & Sweden. Exhib: Ther Hermitage, Leningrad; one-man shows, Warsaw Art Gallery, 65, Lodz Art Gallery, Poland, 65, Pushkin Mus Europ Art, Moscow, 66, Richard Demarco Art Gallery, Edinburgh, Scotland, 68, Scottish Woolen Art Gallery, Galashields, 68, Fine Art Mus, Plymuth, Eng, 68, Merton Gallery, Toronto, Ont, 71; Rothman's Art Gallery of Stratford, Can, 71, plus others in Poland, Italy, Switz, WGer, Holland, Mex, Can & Iran. Teaching: Lectr design for gobelins & textiles, State Acad Fine Arts, Lodz, Poland, 52-58. Pos: Artistic dir, Artist Guild Lad, Warsaw, 54-59; artistic dir, Lab for Design of Linen Indust, Poland, 59-63; artistic dir, Polish Guild Arts & Crafts, Warsaw, 63-68; dir pvt design-weaving art studio, Toronto. Awards: Gold Medal, Trienale de Milano, Italy, Int Exhib Interior Design & Archit, 57; Award for Excellence, Wool Gathering, Can Guild Crafts, Montreal, 73. Bibliog: Tad Jaworski (auth; films), Textures, Film Indust, Poland, Czech & Ger, 67, Tapestries by Tamara Jaworska, CBS Toronto, 70 & Tamara's Tapestry World, CBS Arts & Sci Prog in Film, Toronto, 75. Mem: Royal Can Acad Arts. Style & Technique: Abstract-realistic; gobelin technique. Media: Acrylic, Oil, Watercolor; Handspun Wool & Artificial Materials. Mailing Add: 49 Don River Blvd Willowdale ON M2N 2M8 Can

JAY, BILL
PHOTOGRAPHIC HISTORIAN, ART CRITIC
b Maidenhead, Berkshire, Eng, Aug 12, 40. Study: Berkshire Col Art, dipl; Univ NMex, MA & MFA; spec study with prof Van Deren Coke & prof Beaumont Newhall. Work: Int Mus Photog, Rochester, NY; Bibliotheque Nat, Paris, France; Art Mus, Univ NMex, Albuquerque; plus many pvt collections. Exhib: Mod Art, var locations in Brit & Europe, 67; Art Mus, Univ NMex, 76; one-man shows, Micro-Gallery, Phoenix, Ariz & Northlight Gallery, Tempe, Ariz, 77. Collections Arranged: Brit Documentary Photog 1850-1970, Brit Coun, 71; The English Scene, Tony Ray-Jones & Sir Benjamin Stone 1864-1914, 71, The Inst for Contemp Arts, London; plus others. Teaching: Asst prof art hist, 19th century & 20th century photog, Ariz State Univ, Tempe, Ariz, 74- Pos: Ed/dir, Album Mag, London, Eng, 69-71; dir photog, Inst Contemp Arts, London, Eng, 69-71. Mem: Soc for Photog Educ (mem bd dir, 71-); Royal Photog Soc Gt Brit (mem Royal comn, 72). Style & Technique: Photographic journalism. Res: Photography of the 19th and 20th centuries, especially British topographical work of the wet-plate era. Publ: Auth, Views on Nudes, Focal Press, 71; auth, Customs and Faces: Sir Benjamin Stone, 72 & Robert Demachy: Photographs and Essays, 74, Acad Ed; auth, Victorian Cameraman: Francis Frith 1822-1898, 73 & Victorian Candid Camera: Paul Martin 1864-1944, 73, David & Charles. Mailing Add: Dept of Art Ariz State Univ Tempe AZ 85281

JECT-KEY, ELSIE
PAINTER
b Koege, Denmark; US citizen. Study: Art Students League, with Bridgman; Nat Acad Art Sch, with Olinsky; Beaux Arts Inst. Work: Butler Inst Am Art, Youngstown, Ohio; Norfolk Mus, Va. Exhib: Butler Inst Am Art, 71; Nat Acad Design Ann, 71; Am Watercolor Soc Ann, 72; Charles & Emma Frye Mus, Seattle, Wash, 73; Panhandle Plains Mus, Canyon, Tex, 74; among others. Awards: William Church Osborne Mem Award, Am Watercolor Soc, 72; Frank Monaghan Mem Award, Nat Soc Painters in Casein & Acrylic, 73; Knickerbocker Artists Bicentennial Medal, 75. Mem: Nat Asn Women Artists (first vpres, 67-69, finance chmn); Allied Artists Am (corresp secy, 61-64, treas, 67-68); Knickerbocker Artists (corresp secy, dir, 70, rec secy, 74-); Am Watercolor Soc (treas, 70); Nat Soc Painters in Casein & Acrylic (treas, 74-76, dir, 76-78). Media: Oil, Watercolor. Mailing Add: 333 E 41st St New York NY 10017

JEFFE, HULDAH CHERRY
See Huldah

JEFFERS, WENDY JANE
PAINTER, CURATOR
b Providence, RI, Sept 5, 48. Study: Univ Mass, BFA, 71; Pratt Inst, MFA(painting), 74. Work: Port Authority of NY & NJ; Chase Manhattan Bank, New York; Shah of Iran, Gift of Nelson Rockefeller. Exhib: Westfield State Ann Art Exhib, Mass, 71; Nat Soc of Acrylic & Casein Painters, New York, 72; Easthampton Mus Guild Hall Show, NY, 72; Western Carolina Exhib, NC, 76. Collections Arranged: Cataloguer of First Nat City Bank Art Collection, New York, 73-74; registr, Seven Decades at the Colony (auth, catalogue), New York, 76. Pos: Art cur, Citibank, New York, 73-74. Awards: Max Beckman fel, Brooklyn Mus, 72; MacDowell fel, 77. Style & Technique: Abstract linear imagery, investigating the relationship of scale to color and light; poured paint on horizontal surface, drying into a 3-D skein. Media: Acrylic paint, agglutinated rag paper. Dealer: Kathryn Markel Gallery 50 W 57th St New York NY. Mailing Add: PO Box 419 Canal St Sta New York NY 10013

JELINEK, HANS
GRAPHIC ARTIST, EDUCATOR
b Vienna, Austria, US citizen. Study: Acad Appl Arts, Vienna; Univ Vienna. Work: Metrop Mus Art, New York; Victoria & Albert Mus, London, Eng; Libr Cong, Washington, DC; Philadelphia Mus Art, Pa; Boston Mus Fine Arts, Mass. Comn: Prints in color, Int Graphic Art Soc, 53 & 61 & Soc Am Graphic Artists, 56. Exhib: Am Watercolors, Drawings & Prints, Metrop Mus Art, New York, 52; First Int Exhib Woodcuts Xylon, Kunsthaus Zurich, Switz, 53; First Expos Int Gravure, Gallery Mod Art, Ljubljana, Yugoslavia, 55; Art from the US, De Beyerd Cult Ctr, Breda, Holland, 57; Contemp Am Prints, Tokyo, Japan, 67. Teaching: Prof graphic art, City Col New York, 48-; instr graphic art, New Sch Social Res, 45-50; instr graphic art, Nat Acad Sch Fine Arts, 73- Awards: First Prize for Woodcut, Artists for Victory, Nat Graphic Art Exhib, 43; Pennell Prize, Third Nat Exhib Current Am Prints, Libr Cong, 45; Paul J Sachs Prize, 15th Ann Exhib, Boston Printmakers, 62. Bibliog: A Reese (auth), American prize prints of the 20th century, Assoc Am Artists; H C Pitz (auth), A Treasury

of American Book Illustration; Lynd Ward (auth), Hans Jelinek, Soc Am Graphic Artists, 56. Mem: Academician Nat Acad Design (mem coun); Royal Soc Arts, London (Benjamin Franklin fel); Soc Am Graphic Artists (mem coun, treas); Audubon Artists (dir, vpres). Style & Technique: Mostly black line woodcuts executed with knife only. Mailing Add: Dept of Art Eisner Hall City Col of New York New York NY 10031

JELLICO, JOHN ANTHONY
ART DIRECTOR, PAINTER
b Koehler, NMex, June 26, 14. Study: Art Inst Pittsburgh, dipl; Univ Pittsburgh, teaching cert; Phoenix Sch Design; Grand Cent Sch Art, New York. Comn: Seven relig murals, St Patricks Cath Church, Raton, NMex, 37; 62 chapel murals, Third Air Force, Tampa, Fla, 43-45. Exhib: Raton Ann Art Show, NMex, 37; Phoenix Art Inst Ann, New York, 38; Art Inst Pittsburgh Exhib, Pa, 40; Taos Art Colony Ann Show, NMex, 41; Gallery Santa Fe, NMex. Teaching: Head illus, Art Inst Pittsburgh, 46-56; dir drawing, Colo Inst Art, 56- Pos: Asst dir, Art Inst Pittsburgh, 50-56; dir, Colo Inst Art, 56-62, pres, 62-72. Mem: Hon mem Eugene Fields Soc; Mark Twain Soc. Publ: How to Draw Horses for Commercial Art, 46; co-auth, Land of the Southwest, Naylor, 50; auth, textbks, Int Correspondence Schs, 59-60; auth, articles, 59-68, contribr ed, 68-, Am Artist Mag; auth, articles in, Westerner Mag, 72; assoc ed, Southwestern Art Mag, 74- Mailing Add: 1 Martin Lane Englewood CO 80110

JENCKS, PENELOPE
INSTRUCTOR, SCULPTOR
b Baltimore, Md. Study: With Hans Hoffman; Skowhegan Sch Painting & Sculpture; Boston Univ, BFA. Work: MacDowell Colony Collection. Exhib: Nat Inst Arts & Lett, New York, 66; Young Talent, Mass Coun Arts & Humanities, Boston, 68; 21 Alumni, Boston Univ, 69; 14 Aspects of Realism, Boston Visual Artist Union, 74; Living Am Artists & the Figure, Mus Art, Pa State Univ, 74. Teaching: Instr sculpture, Art Inst Boston, 75. Awards: Colonist, MacDowell Colony, 75. Bibliog: Profile in Boston Globe, 9/14/71; Marian Parry (auth), Interview with P Jencks, Am Artist Mag, 8/73. Style & Technique: Figures, portraits and self portraits built hollow and fired, lifesize. Media: Terra-Cotta. Dealer: FAR Gallery 746 Madison Ave New York NY 11221. Mailing Add: 202 Homer St Newton MA 02159

JENKINS, DONALD JOHN
MUSEUM DIRECTOR, ART HISTORIAN
b Longview, Wash, May 3, 31. Study: Univ Chicago, BA & MA. Collection: The Woodcut in Japan, 1700-1969, Portland Art Mus, Ore, 69; Ukiyo-e Prints & Paintings, The Primitive Period, 1680-1745 (auth, catalogue), Art Inst of Chicago, 71; Louis V Ledoux, Collecting of Ukiyo-e Master Prints (auth, catalogue), Japan House Gallery, New York, 73; Masterworks in Wood: China and Japan (auth, catalogue), Portland Art Mus & Asia House Gallery, New York, 76. Teaching: Instr art hist, Mus Art Sch, Portland, Ore, 63-65; lectr hist art, Univ Mich, Ann Arbor, 74; vis instr, Dept of Art, Univ Chicago, 74. Pos: Asst cur, Portland Art Mus, 66-68; assoc cur Oriental art, Art Inst of Chicago, 69-74; cur, Portland Art Mus, 74-75, dir, Portland Art Asn, 75- Mem: Arts Club of Chicago; Int Hajji Baba Soc; Asia House Gallery Adv Comt; Soc Japanese Arts & Crafts. Res: Japanese prints and paintings of the Ukiyo-e School. Publ: Co-auth, Near Eastern Art in Chicago Collections (catalogue), Art Inst of Chicago, 74. Mailing Add: Portland Art Mus 1219 SW Park Portland OR 97205

JENKINS, MARY ANNE K
PAINTER, INSTRUCTOR
b Pitt Co, NC, Nov 20, 29. Study: Ferree Sch Art, Raleigh, dipl fine arts, with Donald Nolan; NC State Univ Sch Design, with Joseph H Cox; San Carlos Art Sch, Mexico City. Work: NC Mus Art, Raleigh; Minn Mus Art, St Paul; NC A&T State Univ; NC State Fair Collection, Raleigh; WITN TV Collection of Eastern NC Artists; plus others. Comn: Interior mural, Radio Station WPTF, Raleigh, 71. Exhib: Southeastern Ctr for Contemp Art, Winston-Salem, NC, 64-69 & 74; Exhib Contemp Art, Soc Four Arts, Palm Beach, 69; 5th Dulin Nat Print & Drawing, Dulin Gallery Art, Knoxville, Tenn, 69; Frontal Images 70 & Traveling Show, 60th Nat Competitive Exhib Am Art, Jackson, Miss, 70; 7th Ann Small Sculpture & Drawing Show, Western Wash State Col, 70; Nat Painting Show, Washington & Jefferson Col, Washington, Pa, 71; 9th Ann Drawing & Small Sculpture Show, Delmar Col, Corpus Christi, Tex, 75; 24th Nat Acad Galleries Ann, New York, 77; plus others. Teaching: Instr painting, Continuing Educ, Sch Design, NC State Univ, 75- Awards: Third James River Art Exhib First Patron Award, Mariners Mus, Newport News, Va, 69; Drawings USA Purchase Award, Minn Mus Art, St Paul, 71; Purchase Award & Hon Mention, Piedmont Exhib, Mint Mus, Charlotte, NC, 77. Mem: Assoc Artists NC; Artists Equity. Style & Technique: Non-objective; realism. Media: Oil, Watercolor, Acrylic. Dealer: Collector's Gallery 107 E Morgan St Raleigh NC 27611. Mailing Add: 2600 Oxford Rd Raleigh NC 27608

JENKINS, PAUL
PAINTER
b Kansas City, Mo, July 12, 23. Study: Kansas City Art Inst & Sch Design, 38-41; Art Students League, 48-51; DH, 73. Work: Mus Mod Art, Whitney Mus Am Art & Solomon R Guggenheim Mus, New York; Tate Gallery, London, Eng; Mus Art Mod, Paris; Stedelijk Mus, Amsterdam, Holland; Mus Western Art, Tokyo, Japan; plus many others. Exhib: Art Inst Chicago; Carnegie Inst, Pittsburgh; Corcoran Gallery Art, Washington, DC & watercolor traveling show; Arthur Tooth Gallery, London; Tokyo Gallery; Tate Gallery, London, Eng; Smithsonian Inst, Washington, DC; Inst Contemp Art, Boston; Whitney Mus Am Art, New York; Retrospective, San Francisco Mus Art, Calif, 72; plus many other group & one-man shows. Awards: Silver Medal, Corcoran Biennial, 67; Golden Eagle Award for Ivory Knife (film), 67. Bibliog: Jean Cassou (auth), Paul Jenkins, Abrams Inc, Thames & Hudson, 63; Gerald Nordland (auth), Paul Jenkins, Universe Bks, 71; Albery Elsen (auth), Paul Jenkins, Abrams, New York, 73. Publ: Co-ed, Observations of Michael Tapie, Wittenborn, 56. Dealer: Gimpel-Weitzenhoffer Gallery 1040 Madison Ave New York NY 10021; Karl Flinker Gallery 25 rue de Tournon Paris France. Mailing Add: 31 E 72nd St New York NY 10021

JENKINSON, GEOFFREY
PAINTER
b Leeds, Eng, Aug 31, 25; US citizen. Study: Yorkshire Art Class, Eng, 41-48. Work: Leeds City Art Gallery; also pvt collections. Exhib: Bradford City Art Gallery, Eng, 41; Royal Cambrian Acad, 45; Royal Acad, London, 47-49 & 55; Mission Gallery, Taos, NMex, 68-; Hutchinson's Headrow Gallery, Leeds, 71-; Knox Campbell Gallery, Tucson, Ariz, 71- Mem: Royal Cambrian Acad Art. Awards: Saxton Barton Prize, Royal Cambrian Acad Art, 47. Media: Oil, Watercolor, Pencil. Publ: Contribr oil painting reproduction, Western Painting Today; contribr watercolor reproduction, Royal Acad Illus, 49. Mailing Add: Gen Delivery Tubac AZ 85640

JENNERJAHN, W P
EDUCATOR, PAINTER
b Milwaukee, Wis, June 15, 22. Study: Univ Wis-Milwaukee, BS, 46; Univ Wis-Madison, MS, 47; Black Mountain Col, 48-50, with Josef Albers, 48 & 49; Acad de la Grande Chaumiere, Paris, 50; Acad Julian, Paris, 50-51. Work: NY Univ; Dulin Gallery Art, Tenn; Univ Mass, Amherst; Adelphi Univ. Comn: Stained glass panel, Long Island Jewish Hosp, NY; stained glass mural, comn by Dr Fredrick Lane, Great Neck, NY; stained glass mural, with John Urbain, JFK Airport Int Hotel; murals for eight ships, with Elizabeth Jennerjahn for Mil Sea Transport Serv; painting, Avis World Hq, Garden City, NY. Exhib: Exhib Momentum, Chicago; Milwaukee Ann, Univ Wis-Milwaukee; Birmingham Ann, Ala; Dulin Ann, Tenn; Black Mountain Col Invitational, Johnson City, Tenn. Teaching: Art teacher, Black Mountain Col, NC, 49-50, Cooper Union, 52-54 & Hunter Col, 53; prof art, Adelphi Univ, 54- Awards: Tiffany Found Grant, 52; Adelphi Univ Humanities Grants, 62 & 68. Style & Technique: Painting in all major media; drawings in reed and graphite on gesso; landscapes; heads. Media: Oil, Watercolor. Publ: Illusr, Respect for Life, Morey & Gilliam, eds, 74. Mailing Add: 120 Brixton Rd Garden City NY 11530

JENNINGS, FRANCIS
SCULPTOR, PAINTER
b Wilmington, Del, Feb 27, 10. Study: Wilmington Acad Art; Fleischer Mem Sch Art. Work: Mural, Del Indust Sch Boys. Exhib: One-man show, Phoenix Gallery, New York, 62; Brandt Gallery, New York, 62; Whitney Mus Am Art, New York, 62; Baltimore Mus Art, Md, 63; four shows, Makler Gallery, Philadelphia & Rose Fried Gallery, New York, 60-66; Tenth St Anniversary, Ward Nasse Gallery, New York, 77; Landmark Gallery, New York, 77; plus others. Teaching: Lectr, Nat Art Teachers Asn Conv, 4/69. Publ: Contribr, The Artist in New York (radio series), 67; contribr, You and the Artist (TV series), 69. Mailing Add: 55 Greene St New York NY 10013

JENNINGS, FRANK HARDING
LECTURER, PAINTER
b Can; US citizen. Study: Phoenix Art Inst, New York, grad; Meyer-Both Col Art, Chicago, grad; with Norman Rockwell, 8 months; also with Robert E Wood, Jr, Calif, Mario Cooper, New York, Marc Moon, Ohio & George Post, Calif. Work: Many pvt collections. Comn: Oil landscapes, comn by McOsker of Miami Herald, 67; watercolor landscapes, pvt comns, 74 & 75; watercolor landscapes, Flagler Fed Savings & Loan, 75. Exhib: One-man show, Bacardi Gallery, Miami, 69, group show, 75; Am Artists Prof League, New York, 71-72 & 74-75; Am Watercolor Soc, New York, 74; Miami Watercolor Soc, 74 & 75. Teaching: Instr fine art, Miami-Dade Community Col, 64-67 & 72-; instr fine art, Merrick Demonstration Sch, Miami, 68-; instr fine art, Ponce Jr High Sch, Miami, 73-; instr fine art, Grove House, Coconut Grove, Fla, 75-; instr fine art, Metrop Mus of Art, Miami, Fla, 77; instr, demonstrations & workshops, Opportunity House, Hendersonville, NC, 77. Pos: Art dir, Platt-Forbes, Inc, New York & Hartford, 42-45; commercial artist & agency dir, New York & Miami, 45-60; art dir, Miami Herald, 60- Awards: First Prize for Violets in Snow, Blue Dome Art Fel, 72; Best in Show for Iris, Coral Gables Art Club, 73; First Prize for Seagrapes, Miami Watercolor Soc, 75; Spec Award of Distinction, Fla Watercolor Soc, 77; Spec Award, Int Soc of Artists, 77. Bibliog: Sorlot (auth), Aux Etats-Unis, La Rev Mod, 3/75. Mem: Miami Watercolor Soc (pres, 76-77); Prof Artists Guild; Int Soc of Artists; Am Artists Prof League (pres, Miami, 72); Coral Gables Art Club (dir, 71-73); Blue Dome Art Fel (treas, 71); assoc Am Watercolor Soc. Style & Technique: Imaginative realism; strong technique mixed with softness; wet in wet and dry brush. Media: Watercolor; Aquarelle. Dealer: Miller & King Gallery Commodore Plaza Coconut Grove FL 33133; Schoolhouse Gallery Sanibel Island FL 33957. Mailing Add: 12710 SW 17th Terr Miami FL 33175

JENNINGS, JAN
ART CRITIC, WRITER
b Chicago, Ill, Apr 4, 43. Study: Northwestern Univ, Evanston, BSJ; Univ Mo-Columbia, grad studies jour & art. Pos: Art ed, Eve Tribune, San Diego, Calif, 71- Mem: Fine Arts Soc of San Diego. Publ: Free-lance writer with contributing features to Southwest Art Mag & Am Artist, including articles (on Frederic Whitaker, Eileen Monaghan Whitaker, Mary Lehman, Paul Detlefson, Robert Watson, Ken Eberts, Charles Kinghan, Francis Woodahl, Robert E Wood & John Marsh) & feature interview articles (on Olaf Wieghorst, Francisco Zuniga, Leroy Nieman, June Wayne, Francoise Gilot, Ted DeGrazia, Jose Luis Cuevas, Paul Jenkins, Malcolm Alexander, Christo, John McLaughlin, Newton Harrison, Guy Dill, Donald Roller Wilson, Corita Kent, Maus Palmer, Norman Rockwell, Martha Alf, Robert Miles Parker, Lawrence Brullo, Kwan June, Beverly Pepper, Zultan Szabo & others). Mailing Add: 350 Camino de la Reina PO Box 191 San Diego CA 92112

JENNINGS, THOMAS
PAINTER, PRINTMAKER
b Superior, Wis, Feb 7, 14. Study: Los Angeles City Col, AA; Chouinard Art Inst; Univ Calif, Los Angeles, EdB; Univ Calif, Berkeley, MA. Work: Cult Arts Found, Honolulu, Hawaii. Exhib: Sixth Nat Print & Drawing Competition, Dulin Gallery, Knoxville, Tenn, 70; 55th Nat Orange Show, San Bernardino, Calif, 70; one-man shows, Santa Monica Libr Gallery, Calif, 70 & 74, Roberts Gallery, Santa Monica, Calif, 71, Sunset Recreation Ctr, 72 & Wetzler Weiss Gallery, Encino, Calif, 77; The Foundry Gallery, Honolulu, Hawaii, 71 & 72. Teaching: Instr art, Kann Inst Art, Beverly Hills, Calif, 46-53 & Chouinard Art Inst, 53; prof graphic design, Univ Calif, Los Angeles, 53- Pos: Tech illusr, NAm Aviation, 42-43; visual aids specialist, Lockheed Aircraft, 43-44; animation designer, United Productions Am, 44-46. Awards: Creative Arts Inst Appointment, 72 & Regents Fac fel creative arts, 77, Univ Calif. Bibliog: C W Anderson (auth), Art Critic, Honolulu Advertiser, 8/71 & 9/72; Judy Owyang (auth), Art Critic, Santa Monica Outlook, 1/71. Mem: Art Dir Club Los Angeles (secy, 63). Style & Technique: Application of technological possibilities to creative expression with the human figure in painting and printmaking. Media: Offset lithography on metal and plastic; oil painting; manipulative photography. Publ: Auth, The Female Figure in Movement, Watson-Guptill, 71. Mailing Add: 21267 Entrada Rd Topanga CA 90290

JENRETTE, PAMELA ANNE
PAINTER, COSTUME DESIGNER
b Ft Bragg, NC, Aug 24, 47. Study: Univ Tex, BFA, 69. Exhib: Clean, Well-lighted Place (two-artist show), Austin, Tex, 71; Whitney Biennial, New York, 75; Cologne Art Festival, Ger, 75; one-artist show, Artists Space, New York, NY, 75. Pos: Studio asst, Lawrence Poons, New York, 71-75. Awards: Competition Award, Conde Nast, 69. Bibliog: Martha Utterback (auth), Texas, Artforum, 1/71. Style & Technique: Abstract, painterly. Media: Acrylic, Watercolor. Mailing Add: 30 Bond St New York NY 10003

JENSEN, ALFRED
PAINTER
b Guatemala City, Guatemala, Dec 11, 03. Study: San Diego Fine Arts Sch, 25; Hofmann Sch, Munich, Ger, 27-28; Ecole Scandinave, Paris, 29-34; also with Charles Despiau, Charles Dufresne, Othon Firesz, Marcel Gromaire & Andre Masson. Work: Guggenheim Mus & Mus Mod Art, New York; Dayton Art Inst, Ohio; Rose Art Mus, Brandeis Univ; Galerie Beyeler, Basel, Switz; plus others. Comn: Mural, Time, Inc. Exhib: Post Painterly Abstraction, Los Angeles Co Mus Art, 64; Int Biennial Exhib Paintings, Tokyo; Plus by Minus, Albright-Knox

Art Gallery, Buffalo, NY, 68; Documenta IV & V, Kassel, Ger, 68 & 72; Whitney Biennial, 73; plus many other group & one-man shows. Teaching: Md Inst, 58. Awards: Tamarind Fel, 65. Mailing Add: 152 Hawthorne Ave Glen Ridge NJ 07028

JENSEN, CECIL LEON
CARTOONIST
b Ogden, Utah, Jan 17, 02. Study: Chicago Acad Fine Arts. Work: Syracuse Univ; Univ Mo. Pos: Editorial cartoonist, Daily News, Los Angeles, 24-28 & Daily News, Chicago, 28- Awards: Christmas Safety Cartoon Award, Nat Safety Coun, 51; Ed Cartooning Award, Sigma Delta Chi, 53. Media: Brush, Ink. Mailing Add: Hwy 265 S Fayetteville AR 72701

JENSEN, CLAUD
CRAFTSMAN
b Sprague, Wash. Study: Wash State Univ, BS; Carnegie Inst Technol, jewelry & metalsmithing; Willimantic State Col, Enameling on metal. Work: Permanent collections, Ind State Teachers Col, Pa; stained glass windows, Church of St Mary of the Harbor, Provincetown, Mass; silver sacristan's cross & brass flower urns, Calvary Episcopal Church, Pittsburgh; enameled copper plaques, Provincetown Hist Asn; oval brass flower bowls, Church of the Ascension, Pittsburgh. Exhib: WVa Univ, Morgantown, 54; Stamford Mus, Conn, 66; Things, Regional Craft Show, Brockton Mus, Mass, 72; Peary-MacMillan Arctic Mus, Bowdoin Col, Brunswick, Maine, 73; one-man show, Attleboro Mus, Mass, 74. Pos: Pres, Assoc Artist of Pittsburgh, 47-49; bd dirs, Soc Conn Craftsmen, 67; chmn govt comt, Fine Arts Work Ctr, Provincetown, Mass, 68-70. Awards: Assoc Artists of Pittsburgh Craft Award, Mrs Roy Arthur Hunt, 44 & 60; Craftsmen's Guild of Pittsburgh Enamel Award, Thomas C Thompson Co, 60; Jewelry Award, Soc Conn Craftsmen, 66. Bibliog: Roger Hawthorne (auth), Cape craftsman now in stained glass & ceramics, Cape Cod Standard Times, 63. Mem: Provincetown Art Asn (treas, 69-70). Media: Jewelry & Enamels. Publ: Auth, Art, artists & the Thirty-Eighth Annual Exhibition, 48 & auth, Our local artists, this year, 49, Carnegie Mag. Mailing Add: 7 Anthony St Provincetown MA 02657

JENSEN, DEAN N
ART WRITER, ART CRITIC
b Milwaukee, Wis, Oct 9, 38. Study: Univ Wis, BA, Roosevelt Univ, Chicago; Univ Chicago. Pos: Art ed & critic, The Milwaukee Sentinel, Wis, 67- Res: Ashcan School; Circus as a theme in art. Publ: Auth, The Biggest, The Smallest, The Longest, The Shortest, Wis House, 75; contribr to numerous publ incl New York Times, Art News & Midwest Art. Mailing Add: 5484 Monches Rd Colgate WI 53217

JENSEN, GARY
PAINTER, FILM MAKER
b Great Falls, Mont, Mar 27, 47. Study: Mont State Univ; Col of Great Falls, Mont; Calif Col of Arts & Crafts, BFA & MFA. Work: Mont State Univ; San Jose Mus of Art. Exhib: Calif Col of Arts & Crafts Grads: Past & Present, Kaiser Ctr, Oakland, 72; Water Works, Berkeley Art Ctr, Calif, 75; Realism in Painting & Ceramics, De Anza Col, Calif, 75; Oakland Mus Collectors Gallery Invitational, Calif, 77; Bay Area Artists Exhib/Sale, Oakland Mus, 77; one-man shows, Zoomfauk Gallery, San Francisco, 71, William Sawyer Gallery, San Francisco, 75, San Jose Mus of Art, Calif, 77, Redding Mus & Art Ctr, Calif, 77, Mont Hist Soc Mus, 77 & C M Russell Mus, Great Falls, Mont, 78, plus others. Bibliog: Judith Dunham (auth), Water Works, Artweek, 75; Charles Shere (auth), Artists tap water in Berkeley Show, Oakland Tribune, 75; Norma Ashby (auth), Interview with Gary Jensen, Today in Mont (television show), 78; Martha Catlin (auth), Gary Jensen, Art W, 78. Style & Technique: Paintings utilizing water in various manifestations as the imagery which acts as doorway to allow viewer to enter into painting, with his/her imagination and experience composition, colors and spatial illusions. Dealer: William Sawyer Gallery 3045 Clay St San Francisco CA 94115. Mailing Add: 37 Yosemite Ave Oakland CA 94611

JENSEN, HANK
SCULPTOR
b Pittsburgh, Pa, Apr 29, 30. Study: Carnegie Mellon Univ; Pratt Inst, BID; additional study with Hans Hofmann. Work: Hirshhorn Mus, Washington, DC; Provincetown Mus of Art, Mass; Roswell Mus & Art Ctr, NMex. Comn: Stage construct for dance theater piece Sanctum, Nikolais Dance Co, Henry St Playhouse, New York, 64; Cor Ten steel sculpture, Lyndon State Col, Lyndonville, Vt, 69; two fiberglassed plywood sculptures, Roswell Mus, 72; pressure-treated wood sculpture, Goddard Col, Plainfield, Vt, 76. Exhib: One-person shows, Lyndon State Col, 69 & Roswell Mus, 72. Teaching: Goddard Exp Prog in Further Educ, Goddard Col, 69-71 & 73, vis artist, 74. Pos: Artist in residence, Roswell Mus & Art Ctr, 72-73 & Goddard Col, 76. Awards: Fulbright Grant to Florence, 64-65; two Grants in Aid to Ind Artists, Vt Arts Coun, 74-76; CETA Grant, Goddard Col, 76; and others. Style & Technique: Large, outdoor, permanent or expendable constructions. Media: Cor Ten Steel, Pressure Treated Wood. Mailing Add: RFD Box 31F Worcester VT 05682

JENSEN, JOHN EDWARD
PAINTER, DESIGNER
b New London, Conn, June 12, 21. Study: McLane Art Inst, New York, scholar, 40-42; Art Students League, 45-47. Work: Bergen Mall, Bergen Co Mus; Passaic Co Courthouse; Riveredge Boro Hall; Broadway Bank, Paterson, NJ. Exhib: Nat Arts Club, 72; Allied Arts Am, 73; Am Artists Prof League, Lever House, 74; Chaffee Art Ctr, Vt, 75; Norwich Univ, Vt, 76 & 77; Am Watercolor Soc, 77. Awards: Oehler Award, Am Watercolor Soc, 74; Gold Medal for Graphics, Hudson Valley Art Asn, 74; Council Award for Watercolor, Am Artists Prof League, 74. Mem: Am Watercolor Soc; Allied Artists Am; Am Artists Prof League; Hudson Valley Art Asn. Style & Technique: Dry brush technique on very high finish illustration board. Media: Watercolor. Mailing Add: Rte 1 Box 108 Orwell VT 05760

JENSEN, LEO (VERNON)
SCULPTOR, PAINTER
b Montevideo, Minn, July 10, 26. Study: Walker Art Ctr, scholar, 46-48. Work: Rose Art Mus, Brandeis Univ; New Britain Mus Am Art, Conn; Phillip Morris Traveling Collection; US Info Agency, Washington, DC; Brown Univ. Comn: Mural, Sheraton Hotels, Minneapolis, 63; bronze musicians, United Artists Corp, New York, 67; construction, Macmillan Publ Co, New York, 68; polychrome relief, Gulf & Western Corp, New York, 69; polychrome relief, Med World News, New York, 70. Exhib: One-man shows, Creative Gallery, New York, 53, Amel Gallery, New York, 64 & 65 (twice), Young & Rubicorn, New York, 66, Sculpture of Leo Jensen, New Britain Mus, 67 & Far Gallery, New York, 73; Butler Inst Am Art, Ohio, 53; Mus Mod Art Lending Collection, New York, 64-65; Pop Art & American Tradition, Milwaukee Art Ctr, 65; Contemporary Art USA, Norfolk Mus, Va, 66; Phillip Morris Int, Am Fedn Arts, 66-67; Yale Univ Art Gallery, 67; Artist & the Athlete, Nat Art Mus Sport, New York, 68; Fourth Int Exhib Sport in Art, Madrid, 73. Awards: First Prize for Wood Carving, Silvermine Guild Artists Ann, 58; First Prize for Sculpture, John Slade Ely House Invitational, 63. Bibliog: L Lippard (auth), Pop Art, Praeger, 66; M B Scott (auth), The Art & the Sportsman, Renaissance, 68; D Z Meiloch (auth), Contemporary Art With Wood, Crown, 68. Style & Technique: Hand wrought bronze figures by welding and grinding; polychrome wood construction of imaginative nature. Media: Bronze, Wood. Mailing Add: PO Box 264 Ivoryton CT 06442

JENSEN, MARIT
PAINTER, SERIGRAPHER
b Buffalo, NY. Study: Carnegie Inst Technol Sch Painting; Hans Hofmann Sch Fine Art, Provincetown. Work: Va Mus Fine Arts, Richmond; Pittsburgh Bd Pub Educ; Univ of the South; Cult Div, US Info Agency; Provincetown Heritage Mus. Exhib: Cincinnati Art Mus, 37 & 45; Carnegie Inst, 40-46; Butler Art Int, Youngstown, Ohio, 43-46 & 59; DeYoung Mus, San Francisco, 45; Houston Mus, Tex, 45; Corcoran Gallery Art, Washington, DC, 47; Pa Acad of Fine Arts, 52; Brooklyn Mus, 54; Serigraph Int, Riverside Mus, 59; Int Cult Ctr, New Delhi, 67; Nat Print & Drawing Exhib, Provincetown Art Asn & Mus, 75, 76 & 77; Gallerie Dubini, Locarno, Switz, 74; plus others. Pos: Dir bd, Assoc Artists Pittsburgh, 45-47; trustee bd, Nat Serigraph Soc, 51-59; dir bd, Arts & Crafts Ctr, Pittsburgh, 60-61. Awards: Carnegie Inst Prize, 45; Purchase Prize, Va Mus Fine Arts, 47; Grumbacher Prize, Nat Asn Women Artists, 60. Bibliog: Frances Walker (auth), Artist paints space about us, 5/7/56 & Jeannette Jena (auth), Marit Jensen's recent work, 5/9/56, Pittsburgh Post Gazette; Eleanor Meldahl (auth), One man show opens in Provincetown, Cape Cod Standard Times, 6/28/69. Mem: Provincetown Art Asn (trustee, 75-77 & hon vpres, 71-74); Provincetown Group Inc (bd dir, 74-77). Style & Technique: Abstract and semi-abstract; loose and flowing. Media: Oil. Dealer: Provincetown Group Gallery Provincetown MA 02657. Mailing Add: 7 Anthony St Provincetown MA 02657

JENSEN, PAT
PAINTER
b Montevideo, Minn, Mar 17, 28. Study: Pasadena City Col, 49-50; with Leo Jensen, 54-57; Univ Ga & Aberham Baldwin Col, 57-59. Work: Gertrude Herbert Inst Art, Ga; plus many others in pvt collections. Comn: Tennis, comn by Stan Smith; Hockey, comn by Rod Gilbert. Exhib: Nelson Atkins Mus, Kansas City, 63; Albright-Knox Gallery, Buffalo, 63; O K Harris Gallery, New York, 71; Beth El Temple, Hartford, Conn, 72; Far Gallery, New York, 72; plus many others. Awards: First Prize for Oil & Watercolor & Second Prize for Watercolor, 5th Ann Mystic Outdoor Art Festival, 62; First Prize for Oil Painting, Mitchel Pappas Mem Award, Beth El Temple, 72. Bibliog: Ralo T Coe (auth), Popular art, Nelson Gallery 4/63; B Brooks (auth), article in Saybrook Pictorial, 3/72. Style & Technique: Realistic; smooth surface style. Mailing Add: PO Box 162 Deep River CT 06417

JERGENS, ROBERT JOSEPH
PAINTER, EDUCATOR
b Cleveland, Ohio, Mar 18, 38. Study: Cleveland Inst Art; Skowhegan Sch Painting & Sculpture; Yale Univ, BFA & MFA; Am Acad in Rome. Work: Cleveland Mus Art; NAm Col, Rome, Italy; Newman Relig Art Gallery; Skowhegan Sch Painting & Sculpture; Sem Archivescovile, Bari, Italy. Exhib: Cleveland Mus Art, 57-64; Exhibs by Cleveland Mus & US Info Agency; Mus Mod Art, New York; Corcoran Gallery Art, Washington, DC; Mostra Univ, Rome; plus others. Teaching: Instr design, Cooper Union; instr drawing, Sch Art & Archit, Yale Univ; instr design, Cleveland Inst Art, currently. Awards: Mary C Page Grant, 61; Johnson Award for Printmaking, 61; Prize, Cleveland Mus Art, 61; plus others. Mailing Add: 2324 Brookdale Ave Parma OH 44134

JERRY, MICHAEL JOHN
EDUCATOR, CRAFTSMAN
b Grand Rapids, Mich, Aug 18, 37. Study: Sch for Am Craftsman, Rochester Inst Technol, AAS, BFA & MFA, 58-60 & 62-63; Cranbrook Acad Art, 60-62. Work: Wustum Mus Fine Art, Racine, Wis. Exhib: Objects USA, Smithsonian Nat Collection Fine Arts, Washington, DC, 69; Int Trade Fair Jewelry Exhib, Munich, Ger, 71; The 6th Goldsmiths Expos, Kersnikova, Yugoslavia, 72; Goldsmiths, Renwick Gallery, Washington, DC, 74; Contemporary Crafts of the Americas, Colo State Univ, 75. Teaching: Assoc prof metalsmithing, Wis State Univ, Menomonie, 63-70; assoc prof metalsmithing, Syracuse Univ, 70- Mem: Am Crafts Coun; Soc NAm Goldsmiths. Media: Metal. Publ: Contribr, American jewelry, Design Quart, 59; contribr, Philip Morton, Contemporary Jewelry, Holt, 69; contribr, Objects: USA, Viking, 70; contribr, Contemporary Crafts of the Americas: 1975; contribr, The Craftsman in America, Nat Geog Soc, 75. Mailing Add: 208 Dewitt Rd Syracuse NY 13214

JERVISS, JOY
PRINTMAKER
b Palmerton, Pa, Feb 14, 41. Study: C W Post Col, also with Ruth Leaf. Work: Colgate Univ Libr, Hamilton, NY; Bibliot Nat, Paris; Syracuse Univ Art Collection, NY; Ariz State Univ, Tempe; Princeton Univ Art Mus, NJ. Exhib: Okla Printmakers Nat Travel Exhib, 65; Port Washington Pub Libr Group, 65; Huntington Twp Art League, 72. Teaching: Asst instr printmaking, NShore Community Arts Ctr, Great Neck, NY, 66-68; instr printmaking, Union Free Sch Dist 4, Northport, NY, 70-72. Pos: Art exhib dir, Winston Must Corp, New York, 66-73; pres, Joy J Indust Graphic Supplies, Northport, 68-; sponsor, Washington Square Outdoor Art Exhib, NY, 70-72; founder & dir, Northport Art League, 71- Awards: Hon Mention, Mineola Mem Libr, 65; Purchase Award, Talens & Son Corp, 66; First Prize Award, NY Bank for Savings, 67. Mem: NShore Community Arts Ctr; Silvermine Guild Artists; Huntington Twp Art League. Media: Etching. Mailing Add: c/o Bermond Art Ltd 3000 Marcus Ave Lake Success NY 11040

JESS (JESS COLLINS)
PAINTER, COLLAGE ARTIST
b Long Beach, Calif, Aug 6, 23. Study: Calif Sch Fine Arts, with Clyfford Still, Edward Corbett, David Park, Elmer Bischoff & Hassel Smith. Work: Mus Mod Art, New York; Art Inst Chicago; Dallas Mus Fine Arts; Wadsworth Atheneum, Hartford, Conn; San Francisco Mus Mod Art. Exhib: Assemblage, Mus Mod Art, New York, 61; Pop Art USA, Oakland Art Mus, 63; The Spirit of the Comics, Inst Contemp Art, Univ Pa, Philadelphia, 69; 70th Am & 71st Am, Art Inst Chicago, 72 & 74; Extraordinary Realities, Whitney Mus Am Art, New York, 73; Poets of the Cities, Dallas Mus Fine Arts, 74; Matrix Two, Wadsworth Atheneum, 75; Calif Painting & Sculpture, Mus Mod Art, San Francisco, 76; Perceptions of the Spirit, Ind Mus Art, 77; one-man shows, Mus Mod Art, San Francisco, 68, Mus Contemp Arts, Chicago, 72, Mus Mod Art, New York, 74 & Dallas Mus Fine Arts, 77. Awards: Individual Artist Fed Grant, Nat Endowment for the Arts, 73. Style & Technique: Paste-ups and paintings romantically conceived; juxtaposes meticulous line with expressionist texture and composition; arrangement by spiritual chance. Publ: Illusr, Caesar's Gate, Divers Press, Mallorca, 55; illusr, Ballads, Acadia Press, New York, 64; illusr, A Book of Resemblances, Henry Wenning, Hartford, 66; illusr, The Cat and the Blackbird, White Rabbit Press, San Francisco, 67; illusr & translr, Gallowsongs, auth, Christian Morgenstern, Black Sparrow

Press, Los Angeles, 70. Dealer: Federico Quadrani c/o Odyssia Gallery New York NY. Mailing Add: San Francisco CA

JESWALD, JOSEPH
PAINTER
b Leetonia, Ohio, May 17, 27. Study: Acad Julian, Paris; with Fernand Leger, Paris; Columbia Univ. Work: Hirshhorn Collection; Addison Gallery Am Art; Colby Col; Simmons Col; Rockefeller Univ. Exhib: Anna Herb Mus, Augusta, Ga, 54; Grippi Gallery, New York, 59 & 60; Cober Gallery, New York, 63; Art Galleries, Ltd, Washington, DC, 63; Gallery 7, Boston, 64-65; plus many other group & one-man shows. Pos: Bd dirs, Land's End Cult Ctr, Rockport, Mass; chmn dept fine arts, New Eng Sch Art, Boston; dir, Montserrat Sch Visual Art, Beverly, Mass, 70- Awards: Prize, Beverly Farms Regional, 61. Mem: Rockport Art Asn. Mailing Add: Revere St Gloucester MA 01930

JETER, RANDY JOE
DRAWER, EDUCATOR
b Longview, Tex, Dec 25, 37. Study: Univ Tex, Austin; Stephen F Austin Univ, BA & MA; spec study with Robert J Martin. Work: Ark Art Ctr, Little Rock; Bank of Austin, Tex; Fellowship Church, Baton Rouge, La; Hudson Printing Co, Longview, Tex. Exhib: Marymount Col Nat Christmas Exhib, Union Carbide Bldg, New York, 67; 12th Nat Exhib Prints & Drawings, Okla Art Ctr, Oklahoma City, 69; 15th Mid-South Exhib, Brooks Mem Art Gallery, Memphis, Tenn, 70; one artist exhibs, Southwestern Univ, Georgetown, Tex, 73, Univ Tex Med Sch, San Antonio, 73, Ouachita Univ, Arkadelphia, Ark, 76, Longview Mus & Arts Ctr, Longview, Tex, 76 & Univ Cent Ark, Conway, 77. Teaching: Instr art, Gladewater, Tex Pub Schs, 65-72; instr drawing, Longview Mus & Arts Ctr, Tex, 73-75; instr art, Univ Cent Ark, Conway, 75-77; instr art, Coleman Pub Schs, Tex, 77- Awards: Mus Dirs Award, Beaumont Art Mus, Tex, 69; Award, 4th Nat Drawing & Small Sculpture Show, Del Mar Col, Corpus Christi, 69; Juror's Choice, Tex Fine Arts Asn Ann Fall Invitationals, 69 & 71. Mem: Longview Mus & Fine Arts Ctr; Tex Fine Arts Asn (mem bd dirs, Region 8, 70-72); Nat Asn Educators in Art. Style & Technique: Drawing, magic realism. Media: Pen & Ink, Silverpoint. Dealer: L&L Gallery 1107 N Fourth Longview TX 75601. Mailing Add: 2517 Tryon Rd Longview TX 75601

JEWELL, KESTER DONALD
CURATOR
b Terre Haute, Ind, Sept 1, 09. Study: John Herron Art Inst; Nat Acad Design, with Arthur Covey; Art Students League, with Dumond & Bridgman; Newark Mus Assocs, mus training. Collections Arranged: Ancient Treasures of Peru (with catalog, 60; cataloged Worcester Art Mus Collection. Teaching: Head adult art workshop, Newark Mus Art, Sci & Indust, 35-38. Pos: Dir, Fitchburg Art Mus, 38-41; adminr, Worcester Art Mus, 41-71, cur pre-Columbian art, 71-76. Awards: Carnegie Found Grant for Europ Studies, 38. Mem: Am Asn Mus; Nat Soc Arts & Lett. Mailing Add: 606 Hibiscus Dr Hallandale FL 33009

JEWELL, WILLIAM M
EDUCATOR, PAINTER
b Lawrence, Mass, Dec 9, 04. Study: Harvard Col, AB, 27, Archit Sch, 27-29. Work: Fogg Mus, Cambridge, Mass; Farnsworth Mus, Rockland, Maine; De Cordova Mus, Lincoln, Mass. Comn: Ralph Taylor, dean (portrait), Dean's Off, Boston Univ, 55; Col Israel Putnam (portrait), Putnam Mason Lodge, Conn, 58; Gov Milliken (portrait), State of Maine, Augusta, 62. Exhib: One-man shows, Doll & Richards, Boston, 53-59, Guild of Boston Artists, 42-73 & Currier Gallery Art, Manchester, 42; Boston Watercolor Soc, 36-; Am Watercolor Soc, 40- Teaching: Prof, col lib arts, Boston Univ, 34-72, chmn fine arts dept, 55-68, prof emer fine arts, 72-; instr, Harvard Univ Exten, 58-75. Pos: Archit designer, ETP Graham, Boston, 29-31; trustee, Boston Arts Festival, 55-62; asst ed, Speculum, 56-62. Awards: Mitton Gold Medal & Cash Award, North East Artists, 41, 46, 47 & 62; Am Coun Learned Socs grant-in-aid, 60; Hon Phi Beta Kappa, 65. Mem: Am Asn Univ Profs; fel Am Acad Arts & Sci; Am Watercolor Soc; Boston Watercolor Soc (auditor, 40-70); Guild of Boston Artists (treas, 50-57). Style & Technique: Landscapes. Media: Watercolor, Oil. Res: History of American landscape; all aspects of American art. Publ: Auth, Modern Architecture, Frontier Press, 60; auth, Lucia Fairchild Fuller, In: Biog of Notable Am Women, 1607-1950, 67; auth, A Note on artistic interdependence, In: Festschrift in Honor of Samuel Montefiore Waxman, 65, Radcliffe Col, Boston Univ Press, 68; auth, George DeForest Brush, 70 & auth, Helen Gardner, Art Historian, 73, Dict Am Biog. Dealer: Guild of Boston Artists 162 Newbury St Boston MA 02116. Mailing Add: 37 Dana St Cambridge MA 02138

JEWESSON, KENNETH R
ART ADMINISTRATOR
b Nov 23, 39; US citizen. Study: San Fernando Valley State Col, BA, 61; Fashion Inst Technol, 62; Chouinard Art Inst, 62-64; Univ Calif, Santa Barbara, MFA, 69. Exhib: San Francisco Mus Art, 73; New Talent, Martha Jackson Gallery, New York, 73; one-man show, Tom Brotolazzo Gallery, Santa Barbara, 73; Santa Barbara Mus Art, 74; Fountain Gallery, 74. Teaching: Lectr, Santa Barbara Mus Art, 74. Pos: Liaison off, Western Asn Schs & Cols, Santa Barbara Art Inst, 72-75; dir, Santa Barbara Inst Art, 74-75; dir, Sch Art, Mus Fine Arts Houston, 75- Mem: Nat Coun Art Admin. Mailing Add: 3720 Albans Houston TX 77005

JIMENEZ, LUIS ALFONSO, JR
SCULPTOR
b El Paso, Tex, July 30, 40. Study: Univ Mexico City, BS(art), 64; asst to Semore Liptin, 66. Work: Long Beach Mus, Calif; New Orleans Mus, La; Roswell Mus & Art Ctr, NMex; Univ NMex Art Mus, Albuquerque; Alfonso Ossorio Collection, The Creeks, Easthampton, NMex. Comn: Southwest Monument, comn by D Anderson & Roswell Mus, 71-75; glass goggles, Sea-Girl, Steuben, New York, 71; City of Houston, Tex & Nat Endowment Arts, 77; City of Fargo, NDak & Nat Endowment Arts, 77. Exhib: Human Concern Personal Torment, Whitney Mus, New York, 69; Recent Figure Sculpture, Fogg Art Mus, 71; Whitney Mus Biennial, New York, 71; Richard Brown Baker Collects, Yale Univ Art Mus, Hartford, Conn, 75; Jimenez Retrospective, Contemp Arts Mus, Houston, Tex, 75; Amon Carter Mus of Western Art, Ft Worth, Tex, 77; Nat Collection, Washington, DC, 77; Centre Culturale Americaine, Paris, France, 77; Palacio de Bellas Artes, Mexico City, Mex, 78. Awards: Personal grant fel, Nat Endowment Arts, 77. Bibliog: Hilton Kramer (auth), Sculpture Emphasising Poetry, New York Times, 5/2/70; Quirarte (auth), Mexican American Artists in the US, Univ Tex, 73; Hunter-Jacobus (auth), American Art of 20th Century, Abrams, Abrams, 73. Style & Technique: Life size and overlifesize contemporary Icons, with a monumental impact; drawings. Media: Fiberglass Sculpture With a Jazzy Metal-Flake Epoxy Finish & Neon & Lights; Colored Pencil Drawings; Lithographs. Dealer: Ad Jimenez PO Box 3458 Sta A El Paso TX. Mailing Add: 1511 W Mescalero Rd Roswell NM 88201

JOACHIM, HAROLD
MUSEUM CURATOR
Pos: Cur prints & drawings, Art Inst Chicago. Mailing Add: Art Inst of Chicago Michigan Ave at Adams St Chicago IL 60603

JOCDA (JOSEPH CHARLES DAILEY)
PAINTER
b Reynoldsville, Pa, Mar 4, 26. Study: Youngstown Univ, AB, with Margaret Evans, David P Skeggs, John Naberezny & Robert Elwell. Work: Youngstown Col; Westmar Col; Sioux City Art Ctr; Mo Synod; Des Moines Art Ctr; plus others. Exhib: Butler Inst Am Art, 52 & 53; Siouxland Watercolor Exhib, 55-57; Six State Exhib, 55-58; Life of Christ Show, Iowa, 57 & 58; Laas-George Gallery, San Francisco, 61; plus others. Pos: Designer, Crest Johnson Studios, Youngstown, Ohio, 53; staff artist, Warren, Ohio, 54; asst dir, Sioux City Art Ctr, 55-61, instr & actg dir, 57-59; arts & crafts coordr, Cent Community Ctr, Columbus, 64-68; free lance artist, 69- Awards: Awards, Trumble Co, 50 & Mahoning Co, 51; Youngstown Col Purchase Award, 52; 11th Iowa Artist Ann Purchase Award, 59. Mem: Midwest Mus Conf; fel Inst Arts & Let; Nat Soc Lit & Arts. Style & Technique: Experimentalist. Media: Oil, Watercolor, Acrylic. Mailing Add: 4164 Commander Lane Columbus OH 43224

JOFFE, BERTHA
DESIGNER
b Leningrad, Russia; US citizen. Study: New York-Phoenix Sch Design; City Col New York, BS(educ); Teachers Col, Columbia Univ, MA; NY Univ Inst Fine Arts; Art Students League, with William Zorach, Winold Reiss & Oronzo Malderelli. Work: Drapery designs in leading hotels; design on drapery fabric, UN Staff Dining Rm. Exhib: Provincetown Art Asn, Mass, 40; Artists for Victory, Metrop Mus Art, New York, 42; Art in Business Exhib, New York, 42; Int Textile Exhib, Weatherspoon Art Gallery, Univ NC, 44. Teaching: Instr textile & costume design, City Col New York, 40-43; docent art hist, Metrop Mus Art, 41. Pos: Free lance textile designer, 42- Style & Technique: Drapery, home furnishings and other fabric designs, primarily modern floral, geometric and abstract. Mailing Add: 77 Parker Ave Maplewood NJ 07040

JOHANSEN, ANDERS DANIEL
PAINTER
b Denmark; nat US. Study: Pratt Inst, 22; also with Charles Hawthorne & Daniel Garber. Work: Yale Univ; J H Vanderpoel Mus Collection, Chicago; Reading Pub Mus, Pa; Tiffany Found, Long Island; plus many pvt collections. Exhib: Pittsfield Mus; Nat Acad Design; Allied Artists Am; Nat Arts Club. Awards: Pratt Alumnae Award. Mem: Berkshire Artists Asn; Allied Artists Am; Nat Arts Club; Columbia Co Arts & Crafts. Media: Oil, Watercolor. Mailing Add: 50 Hudson Ave Chatham NY 12037

JOHANSEN, ROBERT
PAINTER
b Kenosha, Wis, Mar 30, 23. Study: Layton Sch Art, Milwaukee, Wis. Work: Wustum Mus & Johnson's Wax Art Collection, Racine, Wis; Univ Wis Collection, LaCrosse, Wis; Continental Bank of Chicago; NY CTA Chem Collection, Brooklyn. Exhib: Watercolor Wisconsin, Racine, 72; Am Watercolor Soc Show & Traveling Exhib, New York, 72; Mainstreams '74, Marietta, Ohio; Watercolor USA, Springfield, Mo, 75; Nat Acad Design 150th Ann Exhib, New York, 75; plus several one-man shows. Teaching: Instr painting, Wustum Mus Fine Arts, 70-73. Pos: Aquarellist & advert artist, Eisenberg Studios, Milwaukee, Wis, 53- Awards: Top Award, Watercolor Wisconsin, 72; Watercolor Award, Wis Painters & Sculptors; Best of Show, Springfield, Ill Exhib, 74. Bibliog: Stephan Bellgraph, Watercolor Wisconsin (film), George Richards, 73. Mem: Wis Watercolor Soc (treas, 70-75). Style & Technique: Pure, transparent watercolor landscapes. Publ: Contribr, Watercolor Page, Am Artist, 3/75. Mailing Add: 3017 Taylor Ave Racine WI 53405

JOHANSON, GEORGE E
PAINTER, PRINTMAKER
b Seattle, Wash, Nov 1, 28. Study: Portland Mus Sch, Ore; Atelier 17, New York. Work: Nat Collection, Washington, DC; Chicago Art Inst; New York Pub Libr; Victoria & Albert Mus, London, Eng; Oldham Co Coun, Eng; Seattle Art Mus, Wash; Portland Art Mus, Ore; Civic Auditorium, Portland, Ore; State of Ore Collection, Salem; Henry Gallery, Univ of Wash, Seattle. Exhib: Northwest Printmakers; Henry Gallery, Seattle; Int Printmakers Exhib; Smithsonian Inst, Washington, DC; Denver Art Mus; Calif Palace of the Legion of Hon, San Francisco; Am Embassy, London, Eng; Seattle Art Mus; Portland Art Mus, Ore; Univ of Ariz, Tucson; Univ of Ill; Western NMex Univ. Teaching: Instr painting & printmaking, Portland Mus Art Sch, 55- Awards: Purchase Prizes, Northwest Printmakers, 55 & 63; Award, Seattle Art Mus, 63; Awards, Portland Art Mus, 67 & 72; Artists of Ore Award, Corvallis Art Ctr, Ore, 75; First Ed Award, Ore Arts Comn, 76; Award, Ore State Fair, Salem, 77. Publ: Creator, Etching and Color Intaglio, 73 & Printmaker, 76, films. Mailing Add: 2237 SW Market St Portland OR 97201

JOHANSON, PATRICIA (MAUREEN)
SCULPTOR, ARCHITECT
b New York, NY, Sept 8, 40. Study: Art Students League; Bennington Col, with Paul Feeley, Tony Smith & E C Goossen, BA; Hunter Col, MA; City Col Sch Archit, BS & BArch. Work: Detroit Inst Arts; Storm King Art Ctr, Mountainville, NY; NY State Coun on Arts Film Collection, Syracuse, NY; Crawford & Chester St Park, Cleveland, Ohio. Comn: Stephen Long (sculpture), Buskirk, NY, 68; Ixion's Wheel, State Univ NY Albany, 69; gardens, House & Garden Mag, 69; Cyrus Field (landscape sculpture park), Buskirk, 70-75; Mitchell/Giurgola Assoc Architects, 72-75. Exhib: One-man shows, Tibor de Nagy Gallery, New York, 66-68; Art of the Real, Mus Mod Art, New York, Grand Palais, Paris, Kunsthaus, Zurich & Tate Gallery, London, 68-69; Concept, Vassar Col, 69; Projected Art: Artists at Work, Finch Col Mus, 71; Art in Space, Detroit Inst Arts, 73; Interventions in Landscapes, Mass Inst Technol, 74; Work of Venturi & Rauch & Mitchell/Giurgola Assocs, Pa Acad Fine Arts, 75; City Proj: Outdoor Environ Art, New Gallery Contemp Art & Cleveland State Univ, 77; Women in Am Archit, Brooklyn Mus, NY, 77. plus others. Teaching: Vis prof art, State Univ NY Albany, 69; vis artist, Mass Inst Technol, 74; vis artist, Oberlin Col, 74; vis artist, Alfred Univ, 74. Pos: Design consult, Consolidated Edison Corp, NY, 72; design consult, Yale Univ, 72; design consult, Bartholomew Consolidated Sch Corp, Columbus, Ind, 73; plus others. Awards: Guggenheim Fel, 70-71; First Prize, Environ Design Competition, Montclair State Col, 74; Artist's Fel, Nat Endowment Arts, 75; plus others. Bibliog: Stephen Long (film), Mus at Large, NY, CBS-TV, 68; E C Goossen (auth), The art of the young, Vogue, 8/1/68; Colin Naylor (ed), Contemporary Artists, St Martin's Press, NY, 77. Mem: Women's Caucus for Art; Soc Archit Historians. Publ: Auth, Patricia Johanson, A Selected Retrospective: 1959-1973 (catalog), Bennington Col, 73; auth, Patricia Johanson: Some Approaches to Landscape, Architecture, and the City (catalog), Montclair State Col, 74; co-auth (with Peter Blake), Patricia Johanson: Plant Drawings for Projects (catalog), Rosa Esman Gallery, 78.

Dealer: Rosa Esman Gallery 29 W 57th St New York NY 10019. Mailing Add: RFD 1 Buskirk NY 12028

JOHN, NANCY REGINA
ART LIBRARIAN
b Brooklyn, NY, Feb 1, 48. Study: Stanford Univ, AB(psychol), 69, study of art hist, 70-71; Univ Calif, Los Angeles, MLS with specialization in art librarianship. Pos: Libr asst, Catalog Dept & Art Libr, Stanford Univ, Calif, 69-72; libr asst, Elmer Belt Libr of Vinciana, Univ Calif, Los Angeles, 72-73; cataloger, Nat Gallery Art Libr, Washington, DC, 74-77. Mem: Art Libr Soc NAm (co-chmn cataloging & indexing spec interest group, 74-75; chmn comt on cataloging, 75, vchmn, 76, chmn, 77 & past chmn, 78); Col Art Asn; Am Libr Asn. Res: Leonardo da Vinci bibliography; entry of artist monographs; entry of exhibition catalogs. Interest: Italian Renaissance, chiefly Leonardo da Vinci. Publ: Auth, ARLIS/NA CISSIG Clearinghouse, 74-75, ARLIS/NA Conference Hotline, 76 & From the Chair, 77, Art Libr Soc NAm Newsletter; auth, ALA Yearbook—Art Libraries (in press). Mailing Add: 1222 E 52nd St Chicago IL 60615

JOHNS, JASPER
PAINTER
b Augusta, Ga, 1930. Study: Univ SC. Work: Tate Gallery Art, London; Mus Mod Art & Whitney Mus Am Art, New York; Albright-Knox Art Gallery, Buffalo, NY; Wadsworth Atheneum, Hartford, Conn; Mod Mus, Stockholm, Sweden. Exhib: Jewish Mus, New York, 57, 63 & 66; Mus Mod Art, New York, 59, 61-62, 66 & 68; Whitney Mus Am Art Ann, 60-65, Biennial, 73 & Am Pop Art, 74; Documenta Kassel, WGer, 64 & 68; Retrospective, Jewish Mus, New York, 64, Whitechapel Art Gallery, London, Eng, 64 & Pasadena Art Mus, Calif, 65; 7th Int Print Exhib, Gallery Mod Art, Ljubljana, Yugoslavia, 67; one-man shows, Mus Mod Art, New York, 68, 70 & 72, Fendrick Gallery, Washington, DC, 72, Mus Fine Arts, Houston, 72, Hofstra Univ, 72, Mod Art Agency, Naples, Italy, 74 & Mus Mod Art, Oxford, Eng, 74; New York 13, Vancouver Art Gallery, BC, 69; The Development of Modernist Painting: Jackson Pollock to the Present, Washington Univ, St Louis, 69; Rose Art Museum Collection, Scudder Gallery, Univ NH, Durham, 69; New York: The Second Breakthrough, 1959-1964, Univ Calif, Irvine, 69; Robert Hull Fleming Mus, Univ Vt, Burlington, 69; Mus Contemp Art, Chicago, 71-72; Inst Contemp Art, Univ Pa, 72; Seattle Art Mus, Wash, 73; Art Mus STex, Corpus Christi, 74; Art Inst Chicago, 74; Walker Art Ctr, Minneapolis, 74; plus many other group & one-man shows. Bibliog: C Kelder (auth), Prints: Jasper Johns at Hofstra, Art in Am, 3/73; D Ward (auth), Jasper Johns drawings, Arts Rev, 9/74; J Reichardt (auth), The rendering is the content, Archit Design, 12/74. Mailing Add: 225 E Houston St New York NY 10002

JOHNSEN, MAY ANNE
PAINTER, ETCHER
b Port Chester, NY. Study: With John Carroll. Work: St Mary's Church, Hudson, NY; also in pvt collection of Philip Schyler, Albany, NY. Comn: Fire Equipment 1890's (painting), Tsaawassa Fire Dept, Brainard, NY, 53. Exhib: Nat Art Exhib, Oqunquit, Maine, 59; Drawing Int, Barcelona, Spain, 60; Knickerbocker Artists Nat, New York, 61; Miniature Painters, Sculptors & Gravers Soc of Washington Nat, 62-72; Catharine Lorillard Wolfe Nat Art Show, New York, 64; Miniature Art Soc of Fla Exhib; Bertrand Russel Int Peace Found Exhib, Nottingham, Eng; Women Artists in Am from 18th Century to Present. Awards: Silvermine Guild Marine Award, 59; First Prize, Columbia Co Fair, 59; Ohio Marine Award, Ohio Miniature Soc, 69. Bibliog: Article in La Rev Mod, 68. Mem: Assoc mem Miniature Painters, Sculptors & Gravers Soc of Washington, DC; Miniature Art Soc NJ. Style & Technique: Color impressionist. Media: Silver Point, Oil. Dealer: Squillaci Gallery 524 Summit Ave Schenectady NY 12307. Mailing Add: Box 5 Brainard NY 12024

JOHNSON, ARTHUR HAROLD
CURATOR
b Pine Bluff, Wyo, Dec 2, 98. Study: Univ Ore, BA. Pos: Cur, Jonson Gallery, Univ NMex, 65- Mailing Add: Jonson Gallery Univ of NMex 1909 Las Lomas Rd NE Albuquerque NM 87106

JOHNSON, AVERY FISCHER
PAINTER, INSTRUCTOR
b Wheaton, Ill, Apr 3, 06. Study: Wheaton Col, BA, 28; Art Inst Chicago, grad. 33. Work: Newark Mus, NJ; Montclair Art Mus, NJ; Philbrook Mus, Tulsa, Okla; Holyoke Mus, Mass; Libr of Cong, Washington, DC. Comn: Post Off murals, North Bergen, NJ, Bordentown, NJ, Catonsville, Md, Lake Village, Ark & Liberty, Ind. Exhib: 200 Years of Watercolor Painting in America, Metrop Mus Art, New York, 67; Mus Aquarelle, Mexico City, 68; also numerous ann exhibs, Am Watercolor Soc, New York, Montclair Art Mus, NJ & NJ Watercolor Soc. Teaching: Instr painting, Montclair Art Mus, 40-70; instr painting, Newark Sch Fine & Indust Arts, 47-60. Awards: First Watercolor Award, Montclair Art Mus, 60; Sen George Hammond Watercolor Award, Mus Fine Arts, Springfield, Mass, 64; Winsor-Newton Award, Am Watercolor Soc, 65. Mem: Assoc Nat Acad Design; Am Watercolor Soc; Audubon Artists; NJ Watercolor Soc. Style & Technique: Romantic realist; transparent watercolor. Media: Watercolor, Miscellaneous Media. Publ: Auth, Suburban life (art column), NJ, 66-68; auth, Watercolor page, Am Artist, 10/67; illusr, Factory & Mod Mfg, 67-71. Dealer: Grand Cent Art Galleries 40 Vanderbilt Ave New York NY 10017. Mailing Add: 38 Cooper Rd RFD Denville NJ 07834

JOHNSON, BUFFIE
PAINTER, LECTURER
b New York, NY, Feb 20, 12. Study: Art Students League; Acad Julien, Paris; S W Hayter Atelier, with Francis Picabia; Univ Calif, Los Angeles, MA. Work: Boston Mus Fine Arts; Yale Univ Art Gallery; Nat Collection Fine Arts, Washington, DC; Whitney Mus Am Art, New York; Walker Art Ctr, Minneapolis; plus many others. Comn: Murals, Astor Theatre, New York, 59. Exhib: 31 Int Women Painters, Peggy Guggenheim's Art of This Century, Wakefield Gallery; Contemp Am Art Biennial Exhib, Whitney Mus Am Art, 73; one-woman shows, Howard Putzel's 67 Gallery, New Sch Social Res, Betty Parsons Gallery, Max Hutchinson Gallery, New York, 73 & Stamford Mus, Conn, 77; plus others. Teaching: US Dept State lectr, Greece, Yugoslavia, Ger & Italy; instr, Univ Calif, Los Angeles; instr Parsons Sch Design, 46-50. Awards: Yaddo Fel; Bollingen Found Award; Edward Albee Found Fel; plus others. Bibliog: Parker Tyler (auth), On Buffie Johnson: the city as cosmic mural, 10/60 & Horace Gregory (auth), The transcendentalism of Buffie Johnson, 11/65, Art Int; Ellen Lubell (auth), Arts reviews: Buffie Johnson at Palm Beach, 5/75; plus others. Mem: Group Espace, Paris; Women in the Arts, New York. Style & Technique: Single image frontal plant forms, sacred in origin, in a realistic style with evidences of brushwork, greatly enlarging each against a single color ground. Media: Oil on Canvas. Dealer: Max Hutchinson Gallery 127 Greene St New York NY 10012. Mailing Add: 102 Greene St New York NY 10012

JOHNSON, CECILE RYDEN
PAINTER, PUBLISHER
b Jamestown, NY. Study: Augustana Col, AB; Pa Acad Fine Arts; Art Inst Chicago; Am Acad Fine Arts; Univs Colo & Wis. Work: Chicago Mus Sci & Indust; Davenport Munic Mus; Augustana Col; US State Dept; USN; Wagner Col. Comn: Ford Motor Co; Trans World Airlines; Rockefeller Resorts; Jamaican Govt; Bank of Bermuda; Memorable Mountain (six yr series watercolors), Skiing Mag; Broadmoor Hotel; Princess Hotels; Napa Valley vintners; US Am Hockey Asn. Exhib: Am Watercolor Soc; Washington Watercolor Soc; Art Dirs Ann, Chicago; US Info Agency & State Dept Traveling Exhib to Europe, Asia, Africa & SAm; one-man shows, Davenport Munic Mus & Hudson River Mus; plus many others. Awards: Catharine Lorillard Wolfe Art Club Gold Medal; Prizes, Am Watercolor Soc, Knickerbocker Artists & others. Bibliog: Featured on ABC Wide World Sports painting World's Figure Skating Championship, 77; also featured on Eurovision & BBC. Mem: Am Watercolor Soc; Nat Arts Club. Style & Technique: Production and publication of folios of own work. Media: Watercolor. Publ: Auth, Creating in Watercolor (1 film & 4 filmstrips), Crystal Productions, Aspen, Colo. Dealer: Grand Cent Galleries Biltmore Hotel New York NY 10017; Newman Gallery 1625 Walnut St Philadelphia PA 19103. Mailing Add: Des Artistes One W 67th St New York NY 10023

JOHNSON, CHARLES W, JR
ART HISTORIAN, EDUCATOR
b New York, NY, Apr 7, 38. Study: Westminster Col, BMEd; Union Theol Seminary, MSM; Ohio Univ, PhD, 70. Teaching: Asst prof, State Univ NY Col New Paltz, summer 66; asst prof art hist, Univ Richmond, 67-70, assoc prof art hist, 70-, chmn dept fine arts, 67- Mem: Col Art Asn Am; Col Art Adminr Am; Vi Mus Fine Arts; Smithsonian Inst; Soc Arts & Lett. Res: Comparative studies between art and music; contemporary music and art. Mailing Add: Modlin Fine Arts Ctr Univ of Richmond Richmond VA 23173

JOHNSON, CHARLOTTE BUEL
ART HISTORIAN, EDUCATOR
b Syracuse, NY, July 21, 18. Study: Barnard Col, BA, 41; Inst Fine Arts, NY Univ, MA, 51. Teaching: Instr art hist, Hollins Col, 47-48; asst prof art & art hist, Maryville Col, 48-52; mus instr, Worcester Art Mus, 52-57; lectr & res asst, Albright Knox Art Gallery, 57 58, cur educ, 58- Pos: Contrib ed, Sch Arts Mag, 63-70. Mem: Am Asn Mus. Res: 19th century American art; contemporary European and American art. Publ: Auth, Alvan Fisher and the European tradition, Art in Am, Vol 41, No 2; auth, Man from Eden by Walt Kuhn & Two contemporary French abstractionists, Vol 21, No 2 & auth, Optical illusion & Antonio Tapies, Vol 27, No 2, Gallery Notes; auth, New art, Instr, 9-10/69; auth, articles for prof journals, 53- Mailing Add: 1985 Delware Ave Buffalo NY 14216

JOHNSON, CLETUS MERLIN
SCULPTOR, PAINTER
b Elizabeth, NJ, Nov 19, 41. Study: Bard Col; Parsons Sch Design; Sch Visual Arts. Exhib: Small Scale in Contemp Art, Art Inst Chicago, 75; Spring Ann, Weatherspoon Gallery, Univ NC, Greensboro, 75; Collector's Choice XV, Philbrook Art Ctr, Tulsa, Okla, 75; one-man shows, Neuberger Mus, Purchase, NY, 75 & Arts Club of Chicago, 76. Bibliog: Richard Martin (auth), Cletus Johnson, Arts Mag, 9/74; Barbara Thomsen (auth), Cletus Johnson, Art in Am, 12/74. Style & Technique: Painted and electrified shadowbox constructions of imaginary facades. Dealer: A M Sachs Gallery 29 W 57th St New York NY 10019. Mailing Add: Stony Point NY 10980

JOHNSON, DANA DOANE
EDUCATOR, PAINTER
b Beverly, Mass, Apr 22, 14. Study: Dartmouth Col, AB; Boston Univ, MEd & EdD. Work: State of Tenn Art Collection, Nashville. Exhib: Vt Artists Exhib, Burlington, 49; Painting of the Year, Atlanta, 58; Delta Art Exhib, Little Rock, Ark, 58; Hunter Gallery, Chattanooga, Tenn, 60; Mid South Art Exhib, Memphis, Tenn, 62. Teaching: Prof art educ & chmn dept art, Johnson Teacher's Col, Vt, 45-54; prof art hist & chmn dept, Memphis State Univ, 54- Awards: Honorable Mention, Atlanta, Ga, 58. Style & Technique: Mixed media, expressionistic. Media: Drawing. Res: Prehistoric and primitive. Mailing Add: 3522 Midland Ave Memphis TN 38111

JOHNSON, DANIEL LARUE
SCULPTOR, PAINTER
b Los Angeles, Calif, Feb 18, 38. Study: Chouinard Art Inst, BFA. Work: Mus Mod Art & Bathome Tower, New York; Martin Luther King Park; Robert Hastings, Detroit; Smith Haven Mall. Comn: Some Am Hist, De Menil Found, 70; Peace Form One Monument, UN for Ralph Bunche, 72. Exhib: Paintings in Homage to Dr Ralph Bunche, Noah Goldowsky, New York, 75. Awards: Statan Art Fel, 60; John Hay Whitney Fel, 63; Guggenheim Found Fel, 65. Bibliog: Article in Look Mag, 1/7/69; articles in Time Mag, 4/6/70 & 4/12/71. Mailing Add: PO Box 101 Prince St Sta New York NY 10012

JOHNSON, DIANE CHALMERS
ART HISTORIAN
b Dubuque, Iowa, Jan 3, 43. Study: Harvard Univ, Radcliffe Col, BA(fine arts), 65; Univ Kans, MA(art hist), 67, PhD(art hist), 70. Teaching: Asst prof art, Col of Charleston, 70-75, assoc prof art & chmn dept, 75- Mem: Col Art Asn Am; SC Artists Guild (pres, 75). Res: European and American art transformations 1850-1920, especially Art Nouveau. Publ: Co-auth, Art as confrontation: the Black man in the art of Gericault, Mass Rev, 69; auth, The studio: a contribution to the nineties, Apollo Mag, 70; auth, Art Nouveau in America: three posters by Will H Bradley, Register Mus Art, Univ Kans, 71; auth, Odilon Redon's apocalypse de Saint-Jean, Arts Va, 72. Mailing Add: 59 Smith St Charleston SC 29401

JOHNSON, DONALD MARVIN
METALSMITH
b Billings, Mont, Jan 24, 47. Study: SDak State Univ, Brookings, BS(fine arts); Mont State Univ, Bozeman, MAA(jewelry & metalsmithing). Work: C M Russell Gallery, Great Falls, Mont; Renwick Gallery, Smithsonian Inst, Washington, DC. Exhib: Craft Multipules, 75 & The Object as Poet, 76, Renwick Gallery, Smithsonian Inst, Washington, DC; Contemp Crafts Exhib 1976, Del Art Mus, Wilmington, 76; Goldsmith 77, Phoenix Art Mus, Ariz, 77; Lake Superior 77, Tweed Mus Art, Duluth, Minn, 77; Third Profile of US Jewelry 1977, Art Mus, Tex Tech Univ, 77; Copper, Brass, Bronze Competition, Univ Ariz, 77. Teaching: Instr film, SPICE Prog fed grant, SDak State Univ, 69-70; instr metalsmithing, Dept of Art, State Univ Col Oneonta, NY, 73- Awards: Purchase Awards, Crafts & Craftsmen, C M Russell Gallery, 73 & Craft Multipules, Lloyd E Herman, 75; Juror's Award, Craft Forms, Brockton Art Ctr, 76. Mem: Soc NAm Goldsmiths; NY State Craftsman; Am Crafts Coun; Col Art Asn Am. Style & Technique: Mixed material metalsmithing fabrication with precious and semi-precious metals, plastics, woods, silicone, nylon and others. Publ: Auth, Stretched texture, 70 & Canteen forms adapted from stones, 71, Ceramics Monthly; auth,

Non-soldering techniques for the metalsmithing craftsman, Casting & Jewelry Craft, 76. Mailing Add: RD Box 388 Oneonta NY 13820

JOHNSON, DONALD RAY
ART HISTORIAN, PRINTMAKER
b Poteau, Okla, Jan 14, 42. Study: Northeast Okla State Col, BA, 63; Univ Okla, MFA, 70 & MA, 71. Comn: Lithograph, Kans Cult Arts, 73. Exhib: 10th Eight State Exhib Painting & Sculpture, Oklahoma City, 68; 2nd Nat Exhib Prints & Drawings, Dickinson State Col, 69; Lithography 1969, Fla State Univ, 69; Images on Paper, Jackson, Miss, 71; Graphics 71, Western NMex Univ, 71. Teaching: Asst prof art hist, Emporia Kans State Univ, 70- Awards: Emporia Kans State Univ Grants, 73, 75 & 76. Mem: Col Art Asn. Res: American West during the 19th century. Mailing Add: 1009 Rural Emporia KS 66801

JOHNSON, DORIS MILLER (MRS GARDINER JOHNSON)
PAINTER
b Oakland, Calif, Dec 8, 09. Study: Calif Col Arts & Crafts, 32-33; Univ Calif, Berkeley, BA, 34, grad study, 34-36. Work: Piedmont High Sch Art Gallery & Collection, Calif. Exhib: Golden Gate Int Expos, Fine Arts Bldg, Calif, 39-40; Portland Art Mus Invitational, Ore, 40; Carnegie Traveling Show from San Francisco Mus Art, 40-41; Nat Drawing Exhib, San Francisco Mus Art, 70; one-man show, Lucien Labaudt Art Gallery, San Francisco, 73; plus others. Teaching: Instr art, Oakland Art Mus, 39-52. Pos: Founder children's art classes, Art League East Bay, 39; dir, Oakland Art Mus, 39-52, chmn art rental gallery, 56-59; chmn acquisitions comt of activities bd, San Francisco Mus Art, 57-64; mem bd trustees, Calif Col Arts & Crafts, 70-; juried San Francisco Women Artists Painting Show, Zellerback Gallery, San Francisco & Print, Drawing, Sculpture, Photog Show, Col of Marin Art Gallery, Kentfield, Calif, 77. Awards: 13th Ann San Francisco Women Artists Pres Purchase Prize, San Francisco Mus Art, 38, San Francisco Art Asn Ann Artists Fund Prize, 40; San Francisco Women Artists Ann Painting & Sculpture Show Honorable Mention in Painting, Kaiser Ctr Gallery, Oakland, 74; plus others. Mem: San Francisco Women Artists (pres, 46-48, mem artists coun, 70-); hon life mem Art League East Bay. Style & Technique: Line drawing. Media: Oil, Ink, Pencil. Mailing Add: 329 Hampton Rd Piedmont CA 94611

JOHNSON, DOUGLAS WALTER
PAINTER
b Portland, Ore, July 8, 46. Study: Self-taught. Work: Permanent Collection, Mus NMex, Santa Fe; Am Nat Collection, Am Nat Ins Co, Galveston, Tex. Exhib: The Cassidy Collection, 70, Eight From Santa Fe, 71 & NMex Biennial, 71 & 73, Mus NMex, Santa Fe; one-man show, Retrospective from 1969-1975, Jamison Gallery, 75. Awards: Jurors Award, NMex Biennial, Mus NMex, 73; Second Prize Award, Watercolor NMex, NMex Watercolor Soc, 74. Bibliog: Douglas Johnson, painter, Santa Fean Mag, 2/74; Robert Ewing (auth), The eye dazzlers of Douglas Johnson, Southwest Art Mag, 3/74. Style & Technique: Mystical realist or surrealist dealing with Southwestern landscape and Indian scenes. Media: Casein on Paper. Dealer: Jamison Gallery 111 E San Francisco St Santa Fe NM 87501. Mailing Add: PO Box 111 Abiquiu NM 87510

JOHNSON, EDVARD ARTHUR
PAINTER, EDUCATOR
b Chicago, Ill, Dec 18, 11. Study: Chicago Acad Fine Arts; Art Inst Chicago; Univ Ga, BFA; Inst Design, Ill Inst Technol, with L Moholy-Nagy & Alexander Archipenko, also MS. Work: Nat Mus, Vaxiö, Sweden; Ga Mus Art, Univ Ga, Athens; Univ Rochester Mem Art Mus, NY. Exhib: Eastern States Ann, Springfield, Mass, 59; New Eng Exhib, New Canaan, Conn, 61; Watercolor USA, Springfield, Mo, 66; Nat Acad Design, New York, 70; Southbury Libr Gallery, Conn, 77; one-man show, Silvermine Gallery, New Canaan, Conn, 73. Teaching: Asst prof advan design, illus & drawing, Univ Ga, 47-51; instr visual fundamentals, Inst Design, Ill Inst Technol, 52; instr painting & drawing, Famous Artists Schs, 60-73 & Heritage Village, Southbury, Conn, 73-78. Pos: Art dir for mags, Holt, Rinehart & Winston, New York, 53-58. Awards: Nat Swed-Am Art Asn Purchase Award, 41; Miss Art Asn Watercolor Prize, 50; Rockefeller Fel, 51-52. Mem: Conn Watercolor Soc; Silvermine Guild Artists; Col Art Asn Am. Style & Technique: Abstract. Publ: Designer, American sculptor series, Univ Ga Press, 49; designer, Israel re-visited, Ralph McGill, 50. Mailing Add: 755A Heritage Village Southbury CT 06488

JOHNSON, ELLEN HULDA
ART HISTORIAN, ART CRITIC
b Warren, Pa, Nov 25, 10. Study: Oberlin Col, BA & MA; post-grad studies at Harvard Univ, Sorbonne, Uppsala & Stockholm Univs. Collections Arranged: Three Young Americans, Allen Art Mus, Oberlin Col, 63, 65 & 68; India Triennale of Contemporary World Art, American Collection, New Delhi, 68; Expression in Fiber: The Art of Eleanor Merrill, Allen Art Mus, 75. Teaching: From instr to prof modern & contemp art & Scandinavian art, Oberlin Col, 45-77; vis prof, Univ Wis-Madison, 49-50; vis prof, Uppsala Univ, 60. Pos: Mus staff mem, Toledo Mus Art, Ohio, 36-39; art librn, Oberlin Col, 39-45; hon cur modern art, Allen Art Mus, 73- Awards: Sr Fel, Nat Endowment Humanities, 73; Guggenheim Fel, 75; Distinguished Teacher of Art Hist, Col Art Asn of Am, 78. Bibliog: Linda Nochlin (auth), Ellen Johnson of Oberlin: Mainstream in Middle America, Art in Am, 3-4/75; Lawrence Alloway (auth), Art, The Nation, 3/29/75; Jay Gorney (auth), Oberlin's Tribute to Ellen Johnson, Art News, 4/75; Richard Morphet (auth), rev of Modern Art and the Object, Studio Int, 3-4/77. Mem: Col Art Asn Am (mus ed, Col Art J, 58-60 & mem bd dirs, 77-); Am Scandinavian Found. Res: Art since World War II. Publ: Auth, Cezanne, The Masters Series, London, 67; auth, Claes Oldenburg, Penguin Bks, Ltd, London, 71; auth, Modern Art and the Object, Thames & Hudson, Ltd, London, Harper & Row, Inc, New York, 76. auth numerous articles in Artforum, Art News, Art Int, Arts Mag, Studio Int, Art & Artists, etc. Mailing Add: Dept of Art Oberlin Col Oberlin OH 44074

JOHNSON, EUGENE JOSEPH
ART HISTORIAN
b Memphis, Tenn, May 22, 37. Study: Williams Col, BA, 59; NY Univ, MA, 63, PhD, 70. Teaching: Assoc prof art, Williams Col, Williamstown, Mass, 65-, chmn art dept, 78- Publ: Auth, S Andrea in Mantua, the Building History, 75. Mailing Add: Dept of Art Williams Col Williamstown MA 01267

JOHNSON, EVERT ALFRED
ART ADMINISTRATOR, PAINTER
b Sioux City, Iowa, Mar 2, 29. Study: Morningside Col, BA, 53; Univ Iowa, MA, 54. Collections Arranged: National Drawing Invitational, Southern Ill Univ, Carbondale, 71, WPA Revisited, 72; Iron, Solid Wrought/USA 1776-1976 (with catalogue), 76. Teaching: Asst prof art & head dept, Westmar Col, 56-61; instr painting, Hampton Inst, 65-66; lectr art hist & mus technol, Southern Ill Univ, Carbondale, 66- Pos: Dir, Sioux City Art Ctr, 61-65; dir, Col Mus, Hampton Inst, 65-66; cur, Univ Galleries, Southern Ill Univ, Carbondale, 66-, cur art & exhib, Univ Mus & Art Galleries, 75- Publ: Auth, Animal sculpture, Sch Arts Mag, 59; auth, Unfired clay, Craft Horizons Mag, 70. Mailing Add: Univ Mus & Art Galleries Southern Ill Univ Carbondale IL 62901

JOHNSON, FRIDOLF LESTER
DESIGNER, WRITER
b Chicago, Ill, Feb 24, 05. Study: Art Inst Chicago, 23-25. Work: Calligraphy, Victoria & Albert Mus, London; specimens of printing in New York Pub Libr, Newark Pub Libr, NJ & Fine Arts Gallery, San Diego, Calif; plus others. Exhib: Pvt Press Shows, Int Inst Graphic Arts, 59 & 62; Pvt Press Printing: a Fine Art, Fine Arts Gallery, San Diego, 60; Printers at Play, Newark Pub Libr, 60; Two Thousand Years of Calligraphy, Peabody Libr, Baltimore, Md, 62. Teaching: Lectr, New York, Boston, Pittsburgh & Baltimore. Pos: Art dir, Frankel-Rose Co, Chicago, 25-34; owner, Contempo Art Serv, Hollywood, Calif, 48-50 & Mermaid Press, 58-; exec ed, Am Artist Mag, New York, 62-70. Bibliog: John Ryder (auth), Miniature Folio of Private Presses, Ryder, London, 60; Roderick Cave (auth), The Private Press, Faber & Faber/Watson-Guptill, 71. Mem: The Typophiles, New York (vpres, 71-72); Woodstock Art Asn, NY. Res: Graphic arts; calligraphy; printing. Publ: Auth, Ornamentation & Illustrations for the Kelmscott Chaucer, 73 & auth, Illustrations of Rockwell Kent, 76, Dover; co-auth, 200 Years of American Graphic Art, Braziller, 75; illusr, Mythical Beasts Coloring Book, Dover, 76; auth, A Treasury of Bookplates from the Renaissance to the Present, Dover, 77. also graphic arts bk rev for Am Artist Mag, currently. Mailing Add: 34 Whitney Dr Woodstock NY 12498

JOHNSON, HARVEY WILLIAM
PAINTER
b New York, NY, Apr 9, 21. Study: Art Students League, 46-49; with Howard Trafton & Robert Johnson; also with Annetta St Gaudens, Cornish, NH. Work: Favell Mus, Klamath, Ore; Zool Bldg, Oklahoma City; Ariz Bank, Tucson; Pac Northwest Indian Ctr, Spokane, Wash; Boatmen's Nat Bank, St Louis. Exhib: Cowboy Artists of America, Oklahoma City, 66-72, Phoenix, Ariz, 73-78; Shriver Gallery Ann Exhib, Taos, NMex, 72-78; two-man show, Troy's Cowboy Art Gallery, Scottsdale, Ariz, 74. Teaching: Instr com art, Famous Artists Sch, Inc, 53-72. Bibliog: Ed Ainsworth (auth), The Cowboy in Art, Bonanza Bks, 68; Don Hedgpeth (auth), Harvey Johnson: historian with a paint brush, Southwest Art Mag, 3/74; Royal B Hassrick (auth), Western Painting Today, Watson-Guptill, 75. Mem: Cowboy Artists of Am (vpres, 75-76 & pres, 76-77). Style & Technique: Realistic, story-telling. Media: Oil. Dealer: Shriver Gallery Taos NM 87571; Troy's Cowboy Art Gallery 7106 Main St Scottsdale AZ 85251. Mailing Add: PO Box 5733 Santa Fe NM 87502

JOHNSON, HOMER
PAINTER
b Buffalo, NY, Dec 24, 25. Study: Pa Acad Fine Arts with Julius Bloch & Hobson Pittman, 46-52. Work: Butler Inst Am Art, Youngstown, Ohio; Smith, Kline & French Labs, Philadelphia; Pa Acad Fine Arts. Exhib: Pa Acad Fine Arts Regional, 64; Mus Fine Arts, Springfield, Mass; Pa 71, Harrisburg, 71; one-man show, Philadelphia Art Alliance, 71; Philadelphia Earth Show, Philadelphia Civic Ctr, 73. Teaching: Teacher, Pa Acad Fine Arts, Fleisher Art Mem & Allens Lane Art Ctr. Awards: Tiffany Grant, 59; Cresson Europ Scholar, Pa Acad Fine Arts, 61; Purchase Prize, Am Watercolor Soc, 72. Mem: Am Watercolor Soc; Artists Equity. Media: Watercolor, Acrylic, Pen and Ink. Dealer: Pearl Fox Gallery 103 Windsor Ave Melrose Park PA 19126. Mailing Add: 2120 Spring St Philadelphia PA 19103

JOHNSON, IVAN EARL
EDUCATOR, DESIGNER
b Denton, Tex, Sept 23, 11. Study: NTex State Univ, BA; Columbia Univ, MA; NY Univ, PhD. Teaching: Dir art, Ind Sch Dist, Dallas, Tex, 46-52; prof art educ, Fla State Univ, 52- Pos: Secy-treas, Nat Seminar Res in Art Educ, 75-77. Awards: Founders Day Award, NY Univ, 60; Fla State Univ Grant for Study in Denmark, 71. Awards: Distinguished Serv Award, Nat Art Educ Asn, Philadelphia, 77. Mem: Nat Art Educ Asn (Western regional vpres & pres, 48-52, nat pres, 55-57, southeast regional chmn higher educ, 75-77); Fla Art Educ Asn (mem bd, 60-61); Fla Coun Arts (mem bd, 65-66); Am Inst Designers. Media: Fabrics, Wood. Res: Investigation of evaluation instruments on basic color knowledge. Publ: Co-auth, Design for Living, Laidlow, 52; auth, Preparation of Art Teachers, Report of Commission on Art in Education, Nat Art Educ Asn, 69; auth, Relevance in art education, J Art Educ, 71. Mailing Add: Arts Educ Dept Fla State Univ Tallahassee FL 32304

JOHNSON, J STEWART
CURATOR
b Baltimore, Md, Aug 31, 25. Study: Swarthmore Col, BA; Univ Del, MA, Winterthur Prog in Early Am Cult. Pos: Cur decorative arts, Newark Mus, 64-68; cur decorative arts, Brooklyn Mus, 68-73, vdir for collections, 70-72; consult contemp glass, Corning Mus Glass, 73-74; cur decorative arts, Cooper-Hewitt Mus Design, 75-76; cur design, Mus of Mod Art, 76- Mem: Victorian Soc Am (pres, 66-69); Am Friends of Attingham Park (dir); Lockwood-Mathews Mansion, Norwalk, Conn (adv). Mailing Add: Mus of Mod Art 11 W 53rd St New York NY 10019

JOHNSON, JAMES ALAN
PAINTER, EDUCATOR
b Malden, Mass, Apr 2, 45. Study: Mass Col Art, Boston, BFA, 67; Wash State Univ, Pullman, MFA, 70. Work: Wash State Univ; Nebr Wesleyan Univ, Lincoln; Otis Art Inst Arch, Calif; Franklin Furnace Arch, New York. Exhib: Spokane Ann, Cheney Cowles Mus, Wash, 68 & 69; Ball State 16th Ann Drawing, Ball State Univ, Muncie, Ind, 70; Denver Metrop Exhib, Denver Art Mus, Colo, 72; Exchange Exhib, Joslyn Art Mus, Omaha, Nebr, 73; Exchange Exhib, Friends of Contemp Art, Denver, 73; one-man show, Nebr Wesleyan Univ, 75; Artwords & Bookworks, Los Angeles Inst Contemp Art, Calif, 78; 5th Colo Ann, Denver Art Mus, 78. Teaching: Asst prof painting & drawing, Univ Colo, Boulder, 70-; instr graphics, Dept of Archit, Wash State Univ, Pullman, 70. Style & Technique: Abstract oil paintings; acrylic objects; concrete poetry books and drawings. Media: Oil; Pencil; Ink; Drawings; Acrylic Objects. Publ: Auth, Squares root two rectangles—matinal muses, Criss-Cross Art Column, Vol 1 (1976). Mailing Add: 2344 Mapleton Ave Boulder CO 80302

JOHNSON, JAMES EDWIN & SANDRA KAY
GRAPHIC DESIGNERS
b Minneapolis, Minn, James E, Feb 18, 42, Sandra K, Mar 3, 44. Study: James E, Col of St Thomas, Minneapolis, Minn Col Art & Design, BFA, with Robroy Kelly & Joe Luca; Sandra K, Minneapolis Col Art & Design & Fed Regional Design Assembly Western States, Denver. Work: Minneapolis Col Art & Design; James E, Nat Gallery of Fine Arts, Washington, DC. Comn: Bicentennial pinwheel (outdoor graphic wind piece), Ft Worth Art Mus, Tex, 76. Exhib: James E, Exhib of Graphics, Minneapolis Col Art & Design, 66; Exhib of Int Bus Machines Graphics, Rochester, Minn, 71; Making the City Observable, Int Design Conf, Aspen, Colo, 72; World Crafts Coun, Oaxtepec, Mex, 76; Images of an Era: The Am Poster 1945-1975, Int Traveling Exhib, 76; Exhib of Design Process, Clara M Eagle Gallery, Murray

State Univ, 77; Sandra K, Alumni Exhib, Minneapolis Col Art & Design, 74. Teaching: James E, instr graphic design, Minneapolis Col Art & Design, 71-75, instr first yr graphic prog, 74; instr interdisciplinary pilot prog, Hamlin Univ & five-col consortium, 74; Sandra K, asst to chmn graphic design, Minneapolis Col Art & Design, 76- Pos: James E, graphic designer, Gen Mills, Sacred Design & Int Bus Machines Corp, 66-70; head graphic design dept, Walker Art Ctr, Minneapolis, 70-; partners, James E & Sandra K Johnson, Graphic Designers, 70- Awards: James E, Awards of Excellence, Int Typographic Competition, 75 & Fed Design Coun, 76; Award of Merit (with Sandra K), Soc Publ Designers, 77. Bibliog: James E, Graphics for exhibit, nine artists/nine spaces, Landscape Archit, 71; Design Quart, 94/95, Graphics USA, 75; The Show awards exhib, Format Mag, 76; Sandra K, Publication design awards 1977, Soc Publ Designers, 77. Mem: Minn Graphic Designers Asn (James E, mem coun, 77); Am Inst Graphic Arts; James E, Soc Publ Designers; Fed Design Registry. Publ: James E (designer), American Indian art: form and tradition, Walker Art Ctr, 72; co-designer with Sandra K, The great American rodeo, Ft Worth Art Mus, 75; designer format & masthead, Architecture Minnesota, Minn Soc, Am Inst Architects, 75-77; co-designer with Sandra K, Dan Flavin/drawings, diagrams, prints 1972-1975, Ft Worth Art Mus, 77; Sandra K, designer, The rivals of D W Griffith, Walker Art Ctr, 76; designer, Art train (account of Nat Endowment for Arts-funded travels through rural areas of the upper Midwest), Affil State Arts Agencies of Upper Midwest, 76. Mailing Add: 1800 Emerson Ave S Minneapolis MN 55403

JOHNSON, JAMES RALPH
PAINTER, WRITER
b Ft Payne, Ala, May 20, 22. Study: Howard Col, BS. Exhib: Death Valley Invitational, Calif, 73-77; one-man shows, NMex State Fair Fine Arts Gallery, Albuquerque, 73, 74 & 75; Art Barn Gallery, Ft Worth, Tex, 74; Saddleback Ann Roundup of Cowboy Art, Santa Ana, Calif, 74-78. Awards: Award of Merit, Prof Div, NMex State Fair, 73; Gov Purchase Prize, 75 & 77 Bibliog: Marian Love (auth), James Ralph Johnson, artist & author, Santa Fean Mag, 4-5/75; Royal Hassrick (auth), Western Painting Today, Watson-Guptill, 75. Mem: Artists Equity Asn (vpres, Santa Fe, 73); Am Indian & Cowboy Artists Soc; Grand Cent Art Galleries. Style & Technique: Realistic landscapes, historical westerns. Media: Acrylic, Oil. Publ: Auth & illusr, The Last Passenger, Macmillan, 56; auth & illusr, Utah Lion, Follett, 62; auth & illusr, Camels West, McKay, 64; auth & illusr, Animal Paradise, 69; auth & illusr, The Southern Swamps, 70; plus many others. Mailing Add: Box 5295 Santa Fe NM 87501

JOHNSON, JOYCE
INSTRUCTOR, SCULPTOR
b Newton, Mass, July 12, 29. Study: Escuela de Artes Oficios y Tecnicos, Madrid, Spain, cert, study with Don Ramon Mateu; Sch of Mus Fine Arts, Boston, cert, study with Harold Tovish & Oscar Jespers. Work: Cushing Acad, Ashburnham, Mass; Cape Cod Conserv, Barnstable, Mass. Exhib: One-woman exhib, Annhurst Col, South Woodstock, Conn, 74; Retrospective (20 yr), Wellfleet Art Gallery, Mass, 77; Art in Transition—A Century of the Mus Sch, Mus of Fine Arts, Boston, Mass, 77. Teaching: Instr sculpture from life, Cape Cod Conserv, Barnstable, Mass, 73- & Truro Ctr for the Arts, Truro, Mass, 74- Pos: Asst dir, Beaupre Arts Ctr, Stockbridge, Mass, 59-62; dir/founder, Nauset Sch Sculpture, North Eastham, Mass, 68-71; dir/co-founder, Truro Ctr for the Arts, Mass, 72-; mem steering comt, City Spirit, Lower Cape Nat Endowment for the Arts Proj, Mass, 75-76. Mem: Provincetown Art Asn (trustee, 76-78); Lower Cape Arts Coalition (mem steering comt, 77-). Media: Wood carving; modeling in clay for bronzing. Mailing Add: Box 756 Truro MA 02666

JOHNSON, KATHERINE KING
ART ADMINISTRATOR, PAINTER
b Lincoln, Nebr. Study: Univ Nebr Col Fine Arts, with Dwight Kirsh, Francis Colburn, Darwin Dunkin & Marshel Merritt. Work: Lyndon B Johnson Mem Libr, Austin, Tex; Bennington Mus Art & Hist, Vt; Fleming Mus, Burlington, Vt; Southern Vt Art Ctr, Manchester; Rutland Hosp Mem Collection, Vt. Exhib: Southern Vt Artists Nat Traveling Show, 56; Nat League Am Pen Women Regional, 65-71; Indio Date Festival, Calif, 68; Hale Galleries Exhib, Palm Springs, Calif, 70; Stratton Art Festival, Vt, 70; Nat Biennial Art Exhib, Nat League Am Pen Women, Miami Beach, Fla, 74. Collections Arranged: Loan exhib of Currier & Ives Prints; Humor in Art, commemorating 75th yr of the comicstrip & Honduras Art Loan Exhibit, 71; Gottlob Briem Mem Exhib, 72; Indian Art from Coast to Coast, 73; Living Arts from Africa, 74; Frederick Chaffee Mem Stamp Collection, 74. Pos: Founder, Rutland Area Art Asn Inc, 61, pres & exec dir, 61-74, chmn bd, 77; exec dir, Chaffee Art Ctr, Rutland, 61-; parliamentarian, Shadow Mountain Palette Club, Palm Desert, Calif, 71; Vt state pres, Nat League Am Pen Women. Awards: President's Citation for Quality of Serv Rendered, Nat League Am Pen Women, 74; Recognition Award/Art & Bus, Am Asn Univ Women, 77; Award of Merit, Vt Coun on Arts, 77. Bibliog: M Farnsworth (auth), articles, 62 & Doris Goodhue (auth), article, 68, Pen Women; article in Restorer, 71. Mem: Nat League Am Pen Women (br pres & state art chmn, 65, state pres, 73-74); Rutland Area Art Asn Inc, Vt; Southern Vt Artists Asn Inc; Shadow Mountain Palette Club. Media: Oil. Mailing Add: 40 Piedmont Pkwy Rutland VT 05701

JOHNSON, KENN ELMER
PAINTER, CURATOR
b Seattle, Wash, Nov 13, 14. Study: Pac Lutheran Col; Art Inst of Chicago; study of oils with F Mason Holmes & Abel G Warshawsky & watercolor with Elliott O'Hara & Rex Brandt. Work: Tacoma Pub Libr, Wash; Mt Tacoma High Sch, Wash; Pierce Co Law Libr, Wash; Wash State Hist Soc Mus, Tacoma; State Capitol Mus, Olympia, Wash. Comn: Voyage of Discovery (mural), comn by S A Perkins, Wash State Hist Soc Mus, Tacoma, 56; Indians of Columbia Basin (diorama), comn by L M McDonald, Wilson Carey Mus, Cashmere, Wash, 60; Tumwater 1858 (mural), comn by I Burford, State Capitol Mus, Olympia, Wash, 60. Teaching: Instr oils & watercolors, pvt classes in Olympia, Tacoma, Burien, Port Orchard, Chehalis & Auburn, Wash, 45-; instr watercolors, Tacoma Community Col, 68. Pos: Cur of art & exhib, Wash State Hist Soc Mus, Tacoma, 49- Mem: Life mem Puget Sound Group Northwest Painters Inc; Northwest Watercolor Soc; life mem Pac Gallery Artists, Inc (past pres). Style & Technique: Landscape and still life watercolors; palette knife and brush in oils; landscape, portrait and still life. Media: Oil, Watercolor. Mailing Add: 3079 Horsehead Bay Dr NW Gig Harbor WA 98335

JOHNSON, LEE
PAINTER, EDUCATOR
b Albion, Nebr, Nov 9, 35. Study: Minneapolis Col Art & Design, BFA; Skowhegan Sch Painting & Sculpture, with Alex Katz; Univ NMex, MA. Work: Denver Art Mus, Colo; Roswell Mus & Art Ctr, Roswell, NMex; Mus of NMex, Fine Arts, Santa Fe; Jonson Gallery, Univ NMex, Albuquerque, NMex. Exhib: Watercolor USA, Springfield, Mo, 64; 1st Ann Painting Invitational, Mus of NMex, 68; Masterpieces from the Mus of NMex, McNay Art Inst, San Antonio, Tex, 70; Rocky Mountain Coun on Arts Traveling Exhib, Eight Western States, 72; 8 West Biennial, Grand Junction, Colo, 72-74. Teaching: Instr drawing & painting, Eastern NMex Univ, Roswell, 62-67; asst prof drawing & painting, Western State Col, Gunnison, Colo, 68- Pos: Asst dir-cur, Roswell Mus & Art Ctr, NMex, 62-68; dir, Gunnison Coun on Arts & Humanities, Colo, 73-75. Awards: Five Artists from Colo Traveling Exhib, Rocky Mountain Coun on Arts, 71-72; First Prize Painting, 8 West Biennial, W Co Art Ctr, 74; Artist in Residence Grant, Roswell Mus & Art Ctr, 75. Style & Technique: Abstraction of land and animal forms; watercolor with taping. Media: Acrylic. Dealer: Motif Gallery 300 Fillmore Denver CO 80206. Mailing Add: 310 S Wisconsin Gunnison CO 81230

JOHNSON, (LEONARD) LUCAS
PAINTER, ILLUSTRATOR
b Hartford, Conn, Oct 24, 40. Work: Mus Mod Art, New York; Mus Art San Francisco; Mus Mod Art, Tel-Aviv, Israel; Nat Mus, Warsaw, Poland; Ponce Mus, PR. Comn: Four color lithographs, Masonite Co, Fibracel SA, Mexico City, Mex, 72. Exhib: Salon Independiente, Mexico City, 68 & 70; Galeria Arte Misrachi, Mexico City, 70 & 72; Gotham Gallery, New York, 71; Image of Mexico Traveling Exhib, Gen Motors Permanent Collection; Pratt Inst Lithography Collection, traveling. Bibliog: Tom Cranfield (auth), article in Tex Quart, 70; Ann Holmes (auth), Fantastic artists, Southwest Arts Mag, 72. Media: Oil. Publ: Illusr, Loss of Rivers, Azazel, 67; illusr, Moonshots, 67 & Pablo Neruda-early poems, 69, New Rivers; illusr, Master of Knives, Harmon, 70; illusr var works, Antaeus. Dealer: Galeria de Arte Misrachi Genova 20 Mexico DF Mexico. Mailing Add: c/o Janus Gallery 116 1/2 E Palace Ave Santa Fe NM 87501

JOHNSON, LESTER F
PAINTER, EDUCATOR
b Minneapolis, Minn, Jan 27, 19. Exhib: Carnegie Int, Pittsburgh, 64, 68 & 72; Rosc '67, Dublin, Ireland; L'Art Vivant aux Etats-Unis Fondation, Maeght, France, 71; 10 Independents, Guggenheim Mus, New York, 72; Chicago Biennial, 72; 70th Am Exhib, Art Inst Chicago, 72; Minn Mus Art, 73; Whitney Mus Am Art, 73; Nat Acad Design, 74. Teaching: Prof painting & dir grad painting, Yale Univ, 65- Awards: Guggenheim Fel, 72. Mailing Add: Sch of Art Yale Univ New Haven CT 06520

JOHNSON, LESTER L
PAINTER, INSTRUCTOR
b Detroit, Mich, Sept 28, 37. Study: Wayne State Univ. Work: Detroit Inst Arts; Nat Bank Detroit; Johnson Publ Co, Chicago; Sonnenblick-Goldman Corp, New York; City of Hope Med Ctr, Los Angeles; plus one other. Comn: Urban Wall Mural, New Detroit, Living With Art Comt, 73. Exhib: One-man exhib, Gallery 7 Detroit, 70 & Detroit Artists Mkt, 72; Contemporary Black Artists in America, 71, Contempor ary American Painting, 72 & Whitney Biennial, 73, Whitney Mus Am Art; Nat Afro-Am Exhib, Carnegie Inst, Pittsburgh, Pa, 71-72. Teaching: Instr drawing & painting, Summer Workshop, Neighborhood Youth Corps, Detroit, 66; instr drawing, Genesee Community Col, Flint, Mich, 71- Awards: John S Newberry Purchase Prize, 54th Exhib Mich Artists, Detroit Inst Arts, 64; First Prize Painting, Mich State Fair Art Exhib, 69; Gallery Purchase Award, Harlem Gallery Sq, 72. Mem: Nat Watercolor Soc; Mich Watercolor Soc; Founders Soc, Detroit Inst Arts; Arts Extended Gallery; hon mem Laguna Beach Art Asn. Media: Acrylic. Publ: Contribr, Seven Black artists, 69 & Misalliance, 69, Detroit Artists Mkt; contribr, Black reflections, Flint Community Schs, 69-70. Mailing Add: 8350 E Morrow Circle Detroit MI 48204

JOHNSON, LINCOLN FERNANDO
EDUCATOR, ART WRITER
b Lynn, Mass, May 21, 20. Study: Bowdoin Col, AB, 42; Harvard Univ, MA, 47, PhD, 56. Teaching: Vis prof art hist, Wellesley Col, 49-50; prof art hist, Goucher Col, 50-, chmn fine arts dept, 60-71. Pos: Mem bd trustees, Md Inst Col of Art, Baltimore, 56-; mem, Munic Arts Comn, Baltimore, 60-61 & 77-; mem visual arts panel, Md Arts Coun, Baltimore, 69-; surveyor art in fed bldgs, US Gen Serv Admin, 72. Awards: Bacon fel, Harvard Univ, 48-49; Fulbright scholar, 62; Award of Merit, Artists Equity Asn, 76. Mem: Col Art Asn of Am; Artists Equity; Univ Film Asn; Film Studies Asn; Baltimore Film Forum (chmn prog comt, 76-77). Res: International art, 1885-1910, history of film and 20th century art. Publ: Auth (catalogues), Four Paris Painters, 62 & Art in 1914, 64, Baltimore Mus; auth, Amelie Rothschild Drawings, Goucher Col, 68; auth of weekly art column, Baltimore Sun, 71-; auth, Film: Space, Time, Light, Sound, Holt, Rinehart & Winston, 74. Mailing Add: 759 Bridgeman Terr Towson MD 21204

JOHNSON, LOIS MARLENE
PRINTMAKER, EDUCATOR
b Grand Forks, NDak, Nov 17, 42. Study: Univ NDak, BS, 64; Univ Wis-Madison, MFA, 66. Work: Philadelphia Mus Art; Elvehjem Art Ctr, Madison; McCray Gallery, Univ NMex, Albuquerque; Univ NDak, Grand Forks; Adolph Behn Mem Collection, New York. Comn: Poster, Philadelphia Mus Art, 72. Exhib: Soc Am Graphic Artists, New York, 65-67, 70 & 71; Northwest Printmakers Int, Seattle, 68; Am Color Print Soc, 68-72; Silk Screen, Philadelphia Mus Art, 72; 18th Biennial Exhib, Brooklyn Mus, NY, 72; plus many others. Teaching: Asst prof printmaking & chmn dept, Philadelphia Col Art, 67- Awards: Abraham Hankins Award, Am Color Print Soc, 68; Award, Prints in Pa, 69; Eyre Medal, Philadelphia Watercolor Club, 71. Mem: The Print Club (prints in progress, 67-72); Am Color Print Soc (coun, 68-72); Philadelphia Watercolor Club (bd dirs, 72); Soc Am Graphic Artists; Philadelphia Art Alliance (print comt), 72. Media: Intaglio, Silkscreen. Publ: Contribr, Artist proof, Pratt Graphic Ctr, 67. Dealer: The Print Club 1614 Latimer St Philadelphia PA 19102. Mailing Add: 5800 Race Philadelphia PA 19139

JOHNSON, MARIAN WILLARD
ART DEALER
b New York, NY, Apr 20, 04. Pos: Founder, East River Gallery, 36-38; assoc, Neumann-Willard Gallery, 38-40; owner & dir, Willard Gallery, 40-; chmn ad comt, Mus Mod Art, New York, 44-46, bd trustees & acquisitions comt, 44-46; chmn, Asia House Gallery, 59-, trustee, 61-, exec comt, 63-67; vpres, Mus Am Folk Art, 62-69, trustee, 62- & hon trustee, 74, secy, 71-73; bd overseers, Rose Art Gallery, Brandeis Univ, 65-69. Specialty: Contemporary American art. Mailing Add: Willard Gallery 29 E 72nd St New York NY 10021

JOHNSON, MIANI GUTHRIE
ART DEALER
b New York, NY, July 14, 48. Study: Barnard Col. Pos: Dir, Willard Gallery, currently Specialty: Contemporary painting and sculpture. Mailing Add: 31 E 72nd St New York NY 10021

JOHNSON, PAULINE B
EDUCATOR, WRITER
b Everett, Wash. Study: Columbia Univ, MA; Moore Col, Hon DFA. Exhib: Calif Palace of Legion of Honor, 33; Oakland Art Gallery; Ann Watercolor, Seattle Art Mus, 37; Henry Art Gallery, 66; Art Louie Gallery, 72. Teaching: Prof art, Univ Wash, 41-77, emer prof, 77- Pos:

Mem ed bd, Art Educ J, 62-73; mem ed bd, Sch Arts Mag, 63-67. Awards: First Prize for Watercolor Painting, Seattle Art Mus, 37. Bibliog: Reproduction of ink painting, Argus, 6/66. Mem: Nat Art Educ Asn (mem coun, 56-60); Pac Arts Asn (vpres, 58-60); Wash Art Asn (pres, 54-55). Media: Watercolor. Publ: Auth, Creating with Paper, 58; co-auth, Crafts Design, 62; auth, Creative Bookbinding, 63; contribr, 64th Yearbook NSSE, Nat Soc Study Educ, 65; contribr, Christ & the Modern Mind, 72. Mailing Add: 527 Eastlake Ave E Seattle WA 98109

JOHNSON, PHILIP CORTELYOU
COLLECTOR, ARCHITECT
b Cleveland, Ohio, July 8, 06. Study: Harvard Univ, AB, Grad Sch Design, BArch. Comn: Design of Mus Mod Art Annex & Sculpture Ct, NY State Theatre, Lincoln Ctr, New York, Glass House, New Canaan, Conn & Plaza of Seagram Bldg; plus many others. Teaching: Design critic, Cornell Univ & Yale Univ; instr, Pratt Inst; vis comt, Sch Design, Harvard Univ, 50-51; coun comt, Sch Art & Archit, Yale Univ, 59- Pos: Dir dept archit & design, Mus Mod Art, 30-36 & 46-54, trustee, 58-73; architect, Neuberger Mus. Awards: First Prize, Sao Paulo Bienal, 54; Progressive Archit Design Award, 64; Elsie DeWolfe Award, NY Chap, Am Inst Interior Designers, 65; plus many others. Mem: Nat Inst Arts & Lett (coun). Collection: Young Americans. Publ: Auth, Machine Art, 34; auth, Mies Van Der Rohe, rev ed, 53; auth, Architecture, Nineteen Forty-Nine to Nineteen Sixty-Five, 66; co-auth, The International Style, rev ed, 66. Mailing Add: 375 Park Ave New York NY 10022

JOHNSON, RAY
PAINTER
b Detroit, Mich, Oct 16, 27. Study: Art Students League; Black Mountain Col, 45-48, with Josef Albers, Robert Motherwell, Mary Callery & Ossip Zadkine. Work: Art Inst Chicago; Dulin Gallery; Houston Mus Fine Arts; De Cordova Mus, Lincoln, Mass; Mus Mod Art, New York. Exhib: Chicago Mus Contemp Art, 67; Finch Col, 67; Am Fedn Arts Circulating Exhib, 67; Hayward Gallery, London, 69; two-man show, Univ BC, 69; Univ BC, 69; Ft Worth Art Mus, Tex, 69; one-man shows, Whitney Mus Am Art, New York, 70, Art Inst Chicago, 72 & NC Mus Art, Raleigh, 76; Mus Fine Arts, Dallas, 74; plus other group & one-man shows. Pos: Founder, New York Corresp Sch Art, 62- Awards: Nat Inst Arts & Lett Award, 66. Bibliog: Becker et al (auth), Happenings, fluxus, pop, nouveau realism, Rowohlt Verlag GMBH, 65; Al Hansen (auth), A primer of happenings and time/space art, Something Else Press, 65; John Russell & Suzi Gablik (auths), Pop Art Redefined, Praeger, 69; plus others. Publ: Auth, The paper snake, 65. Mailing Add: 44 W Seventh St Locust Valley NY 11560

JOHNSON, ROBERT FLYNN
CURATOR, ART HISTORIAN
b Jersey City, NJ, Mar 20, 48. Study: McGill Univ, Montreal, Que, grad art hist cum laude, 72; Inst Fine Arts, New York, grad work in Northern Renaissance art with Colin Eisler & mod art with Robert Goldwater, 72-73. Exhibitions Arranged: Whistler & His Circle, Worcester Art Mus, 72; The Antique as Inspiration, 73, Am Prints 1870-1950 (catalogue), Toulouse-Lautrec Posters, Animals: Real & Imagined, 20th Century Prints & Drawings & Max Klinger: Selections from His Graphic Work, 74, The Inspired Copy: Artists Look at Art (catalogue), 20th Century Am Drawings from the Mus Collection, 74 & Matt Phillips: Monotypes, 76, Baltimore Mus Art; Jennifer Gibbar: Drawings, Univ Md, Baltimore Campus, 75; Artists' Portraits & Self Portraits, 75, Edgar Chahine: Selections from His Graphic Work, Turn of the Century Am Posters: The Arthur W Barney Collection, James Torlakson: Prints, Am Observed: Etchings by Edward Hopper, Photographs by Walker Evans (catalogue), David Lance Goines Posters: 1968-1976, The Frank M Carlson Mem Collection, Artists' Portraits and Self Portraits: Part II, 76 & William Nicholson: Selections from His Graphic Works, 77, Fine Arts Mus San Francisco. Pos: Cur asst, Worcester Art Mus, Mass, summer 72; asst cur prints & drawings, Baltimore Mus Art, 73-75; cur in chg, Achenbach Found Graphic Arts, Fine Arts Mus San Francisco, 75- Awards: Mus prof fel, Nat Endowment Arts, 75. Mem: Print Coun Am (trustee mem); Print & Drawing Soc of Baltimore Mus Art (vpres, 74-75); Bay Area Graphic Arts Coun (adv). Res: American prints of the 19th and 20th century; 19th century French drawings. Publ: Auth, American Prints, 1870-1950, Univ Chicago Press, 76. Mailing Add: Achenbach Found Graphic Arts Fine Arts Mus San Francisco Lincoln Park San Francisco CA 94121

JOHNSON, RUTH CARTER
COLLECTOR, PATRON
b Ft Worth, Tex, Oct 19, 23. Study: Sarah Lawrence Col, BA, 45. Pos: Chmn bd, Amon Carter Mus Western Art; emer trustee, Ft Worth Art Mus; founder, Ft Worth Art Coun; vpres, Int Coun Mus Mod Art, 67-72; trustee, Nat Trust Hist Preservation, 68-74; nat chmn collector's comt, Nat Gallery of Art, 74-78; mem vis comt, Fogg Mus, Cambridge, Mass, 77- Mem: Nat Endowment of the Arts; Ft Worth City Art Comn (chmn, George Rickey Sculpture Comt, 74-75). Interest: Trinity River beautification program with Lawrence Halprin and Robert Zion, Ft Worth; commissioned Philip Johnson for Ft Worth Water Gardens. Collection: French 19th century; European and American sculpture and graphics. Mailing Add: 1200 Broad Ave Ft Worth TX 76107

JOHNSON, SELINA (TETZLAFF)
MUSEOLOGIST, MUSEUM HISTORIAN
b New York, NY. Study: Hunter Col, AB(cum laude); City Col New York, MS(educ); Ctr Human Relations Studies, NY Univ, PhD(museology); Work: Bergen Community Mus Art & Sci, Paramus, NJ; Mus Natural Sci, Nantucket Island, Mass. Comn: Mem plaque for Hans Christian Andersen Madison, Bergen Mall, 59; Report on Mus Needs & Resources, Bd Chosen Freeholders, Bergen Co, NJ, 68. Exhib: Nat Tour Nature Photog, Photog Soc Am, 52; Fine Arts in Com Art, 3rd Ann Exhib, Freedom House, New York, 59; Painting & Sculpture Ann, Bergen Co Artist's Guild, 60; Photographic Art of Selina Johnson & Louis Davidson, Art Asn, Nantucket Island, Mass, 61; Books Illustrated by NJ Artists, Johnson Libr, Hackensack, NJ, 69. Collections Arranged: Driftwood Designs, Flower Paintings & Fresh Arrangements, 60; The Fine Art of Color Photography, 61; Excavating Our Hackensack Mastodon, 62-64; 1st NJ Junior Historians' Fair, 64-69; New Arts in Old County Home: Bergen Community Museum Opens B Spencer Newman Gallery, 70; plus others. Teaching: Instr kinesiology & phys educ, Hunter Col; instr comp anat & biol, NY Univ & City Col New York; guest lectr landscape archit, Columbia Univ. Pos: Biol staff artist, City Col New York; founder, dir & trustee, Youth Mus, Leonia, NJ, 50-56; founder, dir & first pres, Bergen Community Mus, 56-70, trustee, 70-; dir, Mus Natural Sci, Nantucket Island, Mass, 59-65; archit consult hist hall, Bd Freeholders, 68-69; Bergen Co (NJ) Cult & Heritage Comnr & historian, 72-; curator, Greater Light, Nantucket Island, 75-; biol & med illusr, City Col New York & Harvard Univ. Awards: First Prize in Art (Silver Orchid), NJ State Fedn Women's Clubs, 51, First Prize for Photog, 65, 67 & 69. Bibliog: Editorials & articles in New York Times, Bergen Bull, Record & Press-J, 50-77 & Bergen News, 76-; Clifford Misché (auth), Museum in Overpeck Park, Bergen Co Park Comn, 56; Georgianne Ensign (auth), The Hunt for the Mastodon, Watts, 71. Mem: Nat Trust Hist Preservation; Mus Coun NJ; North Jersey Opera Theatre (founding trustee & pres, 69-); life mem Nantucket Hist Asn (field archaeologist, 73-); Caduceus Soc; hon life mem Maria Mitchell Asn; Phi Beta Kappa. Res: Museology as practiced in developing museums, including study of their origins, relationships and cultural effects. Publ: Illusr, Adventures With Living Things, Heath, 38; auth, Creating a Community Museum, 54; auth & illusr, Museums for Youth in the United States, Univ Microfilms, 62; ed, Greater Light on Nantucket, Hill House, 73. Mailing Add: 24 Hawthorne Terr Leonia NJ 07605

JOHNSON, UNA E
CURATOR, WRITER
b Dayton, Iowa. Study: Univ Chicago, PhD, 28; Western Reserve Univ, MA, 37. Collections Arranged: All exhibs of prints & drawings, Brooklyn Mus, 41-68. Pos: Cur prints & drawings, Brooklyn Mus, 41-68. Awards: Rockefeller Found Award, 52. Publ: Auth, Ambroise Vollard, 44 & rev ed, 77; auth, American Prints, 1660, 50; auth, What is a Modern Print, 56; auth, Twentieth Century Drawings, 1900-, 2 Vols, 64; plus numerous monogr on mod artists including Bonnard, Rouault, Louise Nevelson & others, 46-74. Mailing Add: 341 W 24th St New York NY 10011

JOHNSTON, HELEN HEAD
ART DEALER
b Atlanta, Ga. Study: Univ Ga, AB(jour). Pos: Dir publicity, M H DeYoung Mem Mus, Golden Gate Park, San Francisco, 53-65; dir, Focus Gallery, 66- Awards: Award for outstanding contribution to photography in Calif, Prof Photogr Northern Calif, 68; Second Ann Dorothea Lange Award, Oakland Mus, 72. Mem: Western Asn Art Mus; San Francisco Art Dealers Asn. Specialty: Photographs. Mailing Add: Focus Gallery 2146 Union St San Francisco CA 94123

JOHNSTON, RICHARD M
SCULPTOR, EDUCATOR
b Kankakee, Ill, Sept 22, 42. Study: El Camino Jr Col; Calif State Col, Long Beach, BA; Cranbrook Acad Art, MFA. Work: Utah Mus Fine Art; Cranbrook Acad of Art; Salt Lake Art Ctr. Comn: Steel wall sculpture, Western Airlincs, Los Angeles, 69; bronze wall sculpture, Telemation Inc, Salt Lake City, Utah, 71; gold leaf/steel sculpture, Sun Valley Ski Corp, Idaho, 71; Temple Kol Ami, Salt Lake Int Ctr. Exhib: Craftsman USA, Los Angeles Co Mus Art, 66; Nat Crafts Exhib, Univ NMex, 68; Inter-Mountain Biennial, Salt Lake Art Ctr, 70; 73rd Western Ann, Denver Art Mus, 71; Nat Small Sculpture & Drawing Show, San Diego State Col, 72. Teaching: Assoc prof metal & basic design & sculpture, Univ Utah, 68- Awards: First Prize, Sterling Silversmiths, 68; Purchase Award, Utah Mus Fine Art, 69; Purchase Award, Salt Lake Art Ctr, 70. Mem: Col Art Asn Am; Am Crafts Coun. Media: Metal. Mailing Add: Dept of Art Univ of Utah Col Fine Arts Salt Lake City UT 84112

JOHNSTON, ROBERT HAROLD
ART ADMINISTRATION, ART HISTORIAN
b Reading, Pa, July 1, 28. Study: Kutztown State Col, BS(art educ), 51; Columbia Univ, MA(fine arts & fine arts educ), 54; Pa State Univ, PhD(ceramic archaeol), 70. Teaching: Vis lectr art, Grad Sch, Rutgers Univ, 54-58; asst prof art, Lock Haven State Col, Pa, 58-65, chmn & head dept, 58-70, assoc prof, 64-; prof ceramics, Sch for Am Craftsmen, Rochester Inst Technol, 70. Pos: Dean, Col Fine & Appl Arts & dir, Sch for Am Craftsmen, Rochester Inst Technol, 70; art ed, Biblical Archaeologist, 72- Awards: Grant-in-aid res, Am Schs Oriental Res, 73; affil Fulbright scholar, Afghanistan, 73-74; John D Rockefeller Third Found Ceramic & Glass res grant, Afghanistan, 74. Mem: World Crafts Coun (mem mkt comt); Am Crafts Coun; Nat Asn Schs Art; fel Am Anthrop Asn; Am Asn Univ Profs. Res: Ceramic archaeology; glass and clay technology. Publ: Auth, The aborigines of Cawichnowane, Lock Haven Bull, Ser 1(2); auth, The aboriginies of Cawichnowane II, Pa Archaeologist, 12/61; auth, A statistical approach to archaeology, New World Antiquity, Vol 11(11-12), Markham House Press Ltd, London, Eng; auth, A statistical analysis of 1113 weapon points from the area related to Cawichnowane, Lock Haven Bull, Ser 1(4); auth, The School for American Craftsmen, Handweaver & Craftsman, 3-4/72. Mailing Add: 80 Washington Rd Pittsford NY 14534

JOHNSTON, ROBERT PORTER
SCULPTOR, ART HISTORIAN
b Philadelphia, Pa, Oct 25, 24. Study: Pa State Univ, BA & MA; Pa Acad Fine Arts; Philadelphia Print Club Workshop; Graphic Sketch Club, Philadelphia; Univ Wyo, MA; Univ Pa; Mich State Univ; also with Francis Speight, Walker Hancock, Harold Dickson, Francis Hyslop & Robert Russin. Work: Numerous private collections. Comn: Christ the King (bronze), Martin Luther Chapel, East Lansing, Mich, 64; Dr Dwight Rich (two bronzes), Lansing Community Col & D Rich Jr High Sch, Mich, 66; Drs Dunbar, Friedmann & Knauss, Western Mich Univ, Kalamazoo, 72 & Dr James W Miller, 74; Wacky Olson (bronze), Olson Hockey Arena, Marquette, Mich, 75. Exhib: Denver Ann, Denver Art Mus, 58; one-man shows, Beardsley Art Gallery, Omaha, Nebr, 60 & King Gallery, Kalamazoo, in coop with Western Mich Univ, 75; Small Sculpture & Drawing Ann, Ball State Univ, Ind, 63; 5th Minn Artists' Biennial, Minneapolis Inst Arts, 67; Kalamazoo Art Ctr, 75 & 78. Teaching: Instr art, Northwood Sch, Lake Placid, NY, 48-49; asst prof, Hastings Col, Nebr, 58-63; instr, Lansing Community Col, Mich, 64-66; asst prof, Mankato State Col, Minn, 66-67; assoc prof, Western Mich Univ, 67-; vis prof, Kalamazoo Col, 71 & St Mary's Col, Notre Dame, Ind, 74-75. Awards: Hon Mention, All-Nebr Exhib, Univ Nebr, 59; Recommended for Purchase, Springfield Art Mus, Mo, 62. Mem: Col Art Asn Am; Artists Equity Asn, Chicago Chap; Nat Asn Schs Art (rep accrediting comn, 72-75); fel Pa Acad Fine Arts; Mich Acad Sci, Arts & Lett (treas fine arts sect, 70-74). Style & Technique: Bronze reliefs; scratchboard technique for drawings. Media: Sculptor, Printmaker. Res: American and Afro-American art. Publ: Auth, Six major figures in Afro-American art, 71 & rev, The buildings of Detroit by W Hawkins Ferry, 71, Mich Academician; Quotations from student examination papers, 71 & co-auth, The teaching of art history in Michigan's two-year colleges, 73, Art J; auth, William Ellisworth Artis, Afro-American sculptor, ceramist & teacher, Minority Voices, 6/77. Dealer: Michigan Multiples Richland MI 49083. Mailing Add: Dept of Art Western Mich Univ Kalamazoo MI 49001

JOHNSTON, THOMAS ALIX
PRINTMAKER, PAINTER
b Oklahoma City, Okla, June 4, 41. Study: San Diego State Col, BA, 65, with Robert Baxter; Univ Calif, Santa Barbara, MFA, 67, with Kurt Kranz. Work: Henry Art Gallery, Univ Wash, Seattle; Univ NDak, Grand Forks; Seattle Art Mus, Wash; Mod Art Mus, Kobe, Japan; Cheney Cowles Mus, Spokane, Wash. Exhib: Seven from Washington, Printmaking Today (traveling exhib to Japan), 70; one-man show, Whatcom Mus, Bellingham, Wash, 71; 52nd Biennial, Libr Cong, Washington, DC; NW Ann, Seattle Art Mus, Wash, 72; W Coast Prints, Univ Calgary, Alta, 75. Collections Arranged: Evergreen Col Print Collection, Olympia, Wash; Western NMex Univ Print Collection; Whatcom Co Libr, Bellingham, Wash. Teaching: Assoc prof printmaking, Western Wash Univ, 67- Pos: Vis artist, Univ Lethbridge, Can, 70 & Univ Calgary, Alta, 75; vis prof, Intercambio Cult, Guadalajara, Mex, spring 76.

Awards: Purchase Award, 18th NW Printmakers Ann, Henry Gallery, Univ Wash, 67; First Place/Graphics, 14th Northern Calif Ann, Calif State Univ, Chico, 70; Purchase Award, 57th NW Ann, Seattle Art Mus, Wash, 72. Bibliog: William Ritchie (video interview), Thomas Johnston, Univ Wash, 70; L Hanson (auth), Seven from Washington, Wash State Arts Comn, 71; M Randlett (auth), Living Artists of the NW, Univ Wash Press, in press. Style & Technique: Organic geometry. Media: Intaglio, drawing. Publ: Illusr, Concerning Poetry, Western Wash Univ, 73 & 76; illusr, The Ventriloquist. R Huff, Univ Press Va, 77. Mailing Add: PO Box 2398 Bellingham WA 98225

JOHNSTON, WILLIAM EDWARD
PAINTER, EDUCATOR
b Salem, Ohio, June 12, 17. Study: Ala State Univ, BS, 63; John Herron Art Inst, dipl, 64; Auburn Univ, with Dr J D Kiser; Rochester Inst Technol, MFA, 70. Work: Ark Arts Ctr Gallery, McArthur Park, Little Rock. Comn: The Resurrection, Wesley Chapel Methodist Church, Greenwood, Miss, 65. Exhib: Frontal Images, Munic Gallery, Jackson, Miss, 69; 6th Ann Art Exhib, Masur Mus, Monroe, La, 69; Discovery 70, Ams Gallery, Univ Cincinnati, 70; USA 1971-72, Carnegie Inst, 71; 15th Ann Delta Art Exhib, 72. Teaching: Chmn dept printmaking, Miss Valley State Univ, 63- Awards: Hon Mention & Purchase Award, Beaux-Art Guild, Tuskegee Inst, Ala, 60; Hon Mention, USA 1971-72, Carnegie Inst, 71. Bibliog: Dr Lee Cannon (auth), Todays Home, ETV, Auburn Univ, 5/31/73. Mem: Nat Asn Schs Art; Miss Art Asn; Southeastern Art Conf. Style & Technique: Style related to an order of values, close to the esthetic of form in space. Media: Plexiglas. Publ: Auth, Black Rebuttal, Hampton Assocs, 75. Mailing Add: Art Dept Miss Valley State Univ Box 121 Itta Bena MS 38941

JOHNSTON, WILLIAM MEDFORD
PAINTER, EDUCATOR
b Atlanta, Ga, Mar 2, 41. Study: Ga State Univ, BA, 65; Fla State Univ, MFA, 67. Work: High Mus Art, Atlanta, Ga; Chase Manhattan Bank, New York; Ft Worth Nat Bank, Tex; Hunter Gallery Art, Chattanooga, Tenn; Omni Int Hotel, Atlanta, Ga & Miami, Fla. Comn: Paintings, Barton & Ludwig, Atlanta, 71-75; three panel paintings (4ft x 8ft each), 77 & 350 graphics, 77, Omni Int Hotel, Miami, Fla; six panel paintings (3ft x 6ft each), Int City Corp, Norfolk, Va, 77. Exhib: 23rd Southeastern Exhib, 68 & Selected Southeastern Artist From the Permanent Collection, 75, High Mus Art; 10th Hunter Ann, Hunter Gallery Art, Chattanooga, 69; Soc of Four Arts Ann Exhib of Contemp Am Art, Palm Beach, Fla, 70 & 71; 8th Ann Graphics Exhib, 71, 12th Ann Painting & Sculpture, 72 & 1975 Biennial Piedmont Painting & Sculpture, Mint Mus, Charlotte, NC; 18th Ann Drawing & Small Sculpture Show, Ball State Univ, Muncie, Ind, 72; Tex Fine Arts Asn 61st Ann, Laguna Gloria Art Mus, Austin, 75; LaGrange Nat Competition, LaGrange Col, Ga, 74, 75 & 77; three-man show, Ga State Univ, Atlanta, 76. Teaching: Assoc prof painting, Ga State Univ, 67- Awards: Purchase Award, 10th Hunter Ann, Chattanooga Art Asn, 69; Soc of Four Arts Award, 32nd Ann Exhib of Contemp Am Painting, 70. Bibliog: Clyde Burnett (auth), var rev in The Atlanta J, 72-78; John Howett (auth), Medford Johnston, Art Voices S, 1/78. Style & Technique: Modernist abstraction, paint. Media: Acrylic.

JOHNSTON, WILLIAM RALPH
ART HISTORIAN, ART ADMINISTRATOR
b Toronto, Ont, Feb 15, 36. Study: Univ Toronto Trinity Col, Hon BA, 59; NY Univ Inst Fine Arts, MA, 66. Collections Arranged: Anatomy of a Chair: Regional Variations in 18th Century Furniture Styles, Metrop Mus, New York, 62; J W Morrice (with catalog), Montreal Mus Fine Arts, Nat Gallery Can, 68; William & Henry Walters, Collectors & Patrons, Walters Art Gallery, 74-75. Pos: Cur, Robert Lehman Collection, New York, 64-66; gen cur, Montreal Mus Fine Arts, 66-68; asst dir, Walters Art Gallery, 68- Awards: Fel, Am Wing, Metrop Mus Art, 63-64. Mem: Am Ceramic Circle; Victorian Soc Am (pres, Baltimore Chap, 71-72); Am Fedn Arts. Res: 18th and 19th century painting and decorative arts. Publ: Auth, W H Stewart, the American patron of Mariano Fortuny, Gazette des Beaux-Arts, 71; auth, American paintings in the Walters Art Gallery, Antiques, 75; co-auth, Japonisme, Cleveland Mus. Mailing Add: Walters Art Gallery 600 N Charles St Baltimore MD 21201

JOHNSTON, YNEZ
PAINTER, PRINTMAKER
b Berkeley, Calif, May 12, 20. Study: Univ Calif, Berkeley, MFA, 46. Work: Mus Mod Art, New York; Whitney Mus Am Art, New York; Metrop Mus Art, New York; San Francisco Mus Art; Los Angeles County Mus Art; plus others. Comn: Etchings, Int Graphic Arts Soc, New York; etchings, Roten Galleries, Baltimore, Md, 66-67; drawings, Washington Gallery Mod Art, DC, 65. Exhib: One-man retrospective, San Francisco Mus Art, 67; Mostra Int della Grafica, Unione Fiorentina, Florence, Italy, 68-69; Four Printmakers, Calif Inst Technol, 69; Wiener Gallery, New York, 77; Mitsukoshi Galleries, Tokyo, Japan, 77; plus others. Teaching: Instr etching, Colorado Springs Fine Arts Ctr, 54-56; instr etching, Univ Judaism, 67; instr painting, Calif State Univ, Los Angeles, 66-67, 69 & 72-73. Awards: Guggenheim Grant, 52; Tiffany Award in Painting & Graphics, 55 & 56; Tamarind Wookshop Grant, Ford Found. Bibliog: Jules Langsner (auth), Ynez Johnston, Arts & Archit, 51; Gerald Nordland (auth), West Coast in review, Arts Mag, 61; John Berry (auth), View from the wind palace, Mankind Mag, 75. Media: Oil, Watercolor; Etching. Dealer: Mekler Gallery 651 N La Cienega Los Angeles CA 90069; Ericson Gallery 963 Madison Ave New York NY 10021. Mailing Add: 579 Crane Blvd Los Angeles CA 90065

JOLLES, ARNOLD H
ART ADMINISTRATOR, CONSERVATOR
b US, Jan 9, 40. Study: Univ Chicago, BA(hist of art); Art Inst Chicago, 6 yr apprenticeship in conservation of paintings with Alfred Jakstas. Pos: Asst conservator, Art Inst Chicago, 67-68; conservator, Minneapolis Inst of Arts, 68-74; asst dir for art, Philadelphia Mus Art, 74-77, actg dir, 77- Mailing Add: Philadelphia Mus Art 26th & Pkwy Philadelphia PA 19101

JOLLEY, GEORGE B
SCULPTOR, DESIGNER
b Washington, NC, Aug 18, 28. Study: E Carolina Univ, BFA; Inst Allende, MFA. Work: Hirshhorn Mus, Washington, DC; Mod Mus, Banjaluka, Yugoslavia. Comn: Abstract, Salem Steel Co, Winston-Salem, NC, 66; abstract, Appalachian State Univ, Boone, NC, 66; abstract, Duke Univ, Durham, NC, 69; recirculating fountain, Nat Acad Sci, Washington, DC, 69 & fountain, 75. Exhib: NC Artist Ann, Raleigh, 68; 9th Rio Grande Art Fiesta, Laredo, Tex, 70; Celebration of the Artist, Washington, DC, 75; one-man shows, Garden Gallery, Raleigh, 70 & Galeria, San Miguel de Allende, Gto, Mex, 71-75. Teaching: Instr sculpture, Inst Allende, San Miguel de Allende, 70-77; instr sculpture & painting, Western Carolina Univ, Cullowhee, 77-78. Awards: Award, High Mus Art, Atlanta, Ga, 66; First Award Sculpture, Rio Grande Art Fiesta, 70. Style & Technique: Free-form abstract metal sculpture, often including water as part of design. Mailing Add: c/o PO Box 158 Babylon NY 11702

JOLLEY, GERALDINE H (JERRY)
PAINTER, SCULPTOR
b Rochester, NY, June 14, 11. Study: Rochester Inst Technol, with Margaret Weston & Ehrich; Rochester Mem Art Mus, with Francis Denny; Univ Wash; also with Cora Scofield Johnson, New York, Richard Yip & Eliot O'Hara. Work: Rochester Inst Technol. Exhib: Rochester Mem Mus NY State Sculpture Exhib, 39; Western Painters Show, Oakland Art Mus, 54, Alameda Art Asn 11th Ann, 55; Henry Gallery, Univ Wash, 55; New York Int Art Exhib, 70. Awards: Award for Tribulation (sculpture), Rochester Mem Art Mus, 33; Alameda Art Asn 11th Ann Award, Oakland Art Mus, 54, Award for Carriage Ride in Central Park (painting), 55. Bibliog: A J Bloomfield (auth), Art previews in San Francisco, News-Call Bull, 60; Felice T Ross (auth), Gallery previews in New York, Pictures Exhib, 67; Interesting Personalities, WROC-TV, Rochester, 6/67. Mem: Artists Equity Asn (mem bd Northern Chap, 70); Marin Soc Artists Ross Calif; Soc Western Artists; Eight Women Watercolorists of West (pres, 53-57). Style & Technique: Impressionism which evokes sensitivity to life; heavily textured; palette knife. Media: Oil. Publ: Auth, Palette Knife Painting Instruction (rec), 68. Mailing Add: 1009 Ripple Ave Pacific Grove CA 93950

JONAS, JOAN
VIDEO ARTIST, CONCEPTUAL ARTIST
b New York, NY, July 13, 36. Study: Mount Holyoke Col, Mass; Boston Mus Sch, Mass; Columbia Univ, New York, MFA. Work: Mus of Mod Art, New York. Exhib: Documenta V, Kassel, WGer, 72; Festival d'Automne, Paris, 73; Some Recent Am Art, Australia (toured), 73; Xerox Corp Show, Rochester, NY, 74; Bienniale de Sao Paulo, Brazil, 74; Art Now 74, Washington, 74; Project 74, Cologne, WGer, 74; The Video Show, Serpentine Gallery, London, 75; Van Abbe Mus, Eindhoven, 75; Mus of Mod Art, New York, 75; Assoc Students, Univ Calif, Los Angeles, 75; one-woman shows, Univ Calif, San Diego, 70, Leob Student Ctr, New York, 71, The Kitchen, New York, 74, Walker Art Ctr, Minneapolis, Minn, 74, Anthology Film Archives, New York, 75, San Diego State Univ, Calif, 75, Inst of Contemp Arts, Los Angeles, 75, Womanspace, Los Angeles, 75 & And/Or Gallery, Seattle, Wash, 75. Awards: Creative Artists Pub Serv Prog, 72, 73 & 75; Nat Endowment for the Arts Grant, 73 & 75. Bibliog: Laurie Anderson (auth), Joan Jonas, Art Press, Paris, 11-12/73; Wulf Herzgenrath (auth), Video Ein Neue Medium in der Bildenden Kunst, Mag Kunst, Mainz, 7/74; Marcus Guterich (auth), Art Presented According to the Evolution Principle, Kunst Kunst Kunst, Cologne, WGer, 74. Style & Technique: Performance and video art; conceptual. Media: Mirrors; Videotape. Publ: Auth, Organic Honey's Visual Telepathy, Drama Rev, New York, 72; co-auth with Simone Forti, Show Me Your Dance, Art & Artists, London, 10/73. Dealer: Leo Castelli Gallery 420 W Broadway New York NY 10013. Mailing Add: 112 Mercer St New York NY 10012

JONES, ALLAN DUDLEY
PAINTER, EDUCATOR
b Hampton, Va, Feb 25, 15. Study: Pa Acad Fine Arts, Univ Pa, BFA; Barnes Found, with Arthur B Carles, Daniel Garber & George Harding. Work: Chrysler Mus, Norfolk, Va; Philadelphia Mus Art; Va Mus Fine Arts, Richmond; High Mus, Atlanta, Ga; Ford Found. Comn: 27 ft dining room mural, US Presidents Line, SS Pres Monroe, 39; historical, Athens, Pa Post Off, US Govt Competition, 41; 30 ft mural-historical, Newport News Pub Libr, Va, 56; Merrimac-Monitor Diorama, Mariner's Mus, Newport News, 64; St Stephen Sculpture, St Stephen's Church, Newport News, 70; relief sculpture, Newport News City Hall, 75; St Francis mural, Presbyterian Church, Newport News, Va, 77. Exhib: Philadelphia Watercolor Club; Drawing USA, Chrysler Mus, 71; Mainstreams, 71; Pa Acad Fine Arts; Va Mus. Teaching: Vis artist painting, Univ Va, 59-60; instr mural design, Pa Acad Fine Arts; vis artist drawing, Va Wesleyan Col, 71. Awards: Philadelphia Watercolor Club Prize; Leache Mem Top Ten Award, Chrysler Mus, 68; Purchase Prize, Drawing USA, 71. Mem: Va Mus Fine Arts; Peninsula Arts Asn; Philadelphia Watercolor Club; fel Pa Acad Fine Arts. Style & Technique: Acrylic, realism and dry-brush ink drawings. Publ: Illusr, Introduction to Parasitology, 72. Mailing Add: 44 Claremont Ave Hampton VA 23661

JONES, AMY (AMY JONES FRISBIE)
SCULPTOR, PRINTMAKER
b Buffalo, NY, Apr 4, 99. Study: Pratt Inst, scholar; also with Peppino Mangrarite, Xavier Gonzales, Ippolito, Carlus Dyer & Roger Prince. Work: New Britain Mus Am Art, Conn; Chrysler Mus, Norfolk, Va; Wharton Sch Finance, Univ Pa; Standard Oil Co NJ presented to State of Md; New York Hosp; Hudson River Mus. Comn: Mural (oil on canvas), Winsted, Conn, 39, mural (underpainted & glazed), Painted Post, NY, 40 & mural (egg tempera on canvas), Scotia, NY, 41, Fine Arts Sect, US Treas Dept. Exhib: Galleria S Stefano, Venice, 58, 72 & 74; one-man shows, Philadelphia Art Alliance, 62, New Britain Mus Am Art, Conn, 63, Norfolk Mus Arts & Sci, Va, 67, Briarcliff Col, 76 & Wave Hill, Riverdale, NY, 77. Padova, Galleria Il Sigillo, 74; Gallery of Glory Be, Jamaica, 75; plus others. Teaching: Instr art, Bedford Art Ctr, 62-; instr printmaking, Col New Rochelle, summer 72; pvt studio, Mt Kisco, NY & Venice, Italy. Awards: Purchase Award, Wash Co Mus, Hagerstown, Md, 58; First Prize for Graphics, Northern Westchester Artists, 61; Baltimore Watercolor Club Purchase Prize. Bibliog: Norman Kent (auth), Amy Jones, Am Artist Mag, 54 & Amy Jones, Watson-Guptill, 56. Mem: Silvermine Guild Artists; Katonah Gallery; Philadelphia Watercolor Club; The Print Club, Philadelphia; Audubon Artists; Am Watercolor Soc. Media: Oil, Watercolor. Mailing Add: Byram Lake Rd Mt Kisco NY 10519

JONES, ANTHONY
EDUCATOR, PAINTER/SCULPTOR
b Mountain Ash, Wales, Gt Brit, Aug 3, 44. Study: Newport Col Art, Gt Brit, dipl art, 66; Tulane Univ, New Orleans, MFA, 68. Work: Arts Coun Gt Brit: Contemp Arts Soc Gt Brit; Univ Ark Collection: Ft Worth First Bank Collection. Comn: Interior design (three floors of new restaurant), comn by John Kraska, Edmund Smith & K C Grierson, Langs, Glasgow, Scotland, 70-72; large fiberglass structure, Livingston New Town, Scotland, 71. Exhib: Art in Wales Today, Nat Mus, Cardiff, Wales, 71; New Art in Scotland, Touring Exhib, Scotland, 72-73; Tex Fine Arts, Laguna Gloria Mus, Austin, Tex, 73 & 74; one-man show new works painting & sculpture, Tex Christian Univ, 74 & Welsh Chapel Archit, Touring Exhib, Gt Brit, 76-77; Southwest Ann, Ft Worth Art Ctr, 75; Ark Invitational, Little Rock Art Ctr, 75; Change & Decay, Victoria & Albert Mus, London, Eng, 77. Collections Arranged: Welsh Chapel Archit, 150 color & black & white photographs designed, mounted & written descriptions, introd, etc, toured six locations in Gt Brit, 76-77. Teaching: Lectr sculpture, Glasgow Sch Art, Scotland, 69-72; chmn dept art, Tex Christian Univ, Ft Worth, Tex, 72-; vis prof, Univ Wales, 78. Pos: Artist-in-residence, Loyola Univ, New Orleans, 67-68; fel, Gloucestershire Sch Art, Wheltenham, Eng, 68-69. Awards: Fulbright scholar, US, US Govt, 66-68; Major Sculpture Bursary, Scottish Arts Coun, 71; Tex Fine Arts Asn Prize, 75. Mem: Nat Coun Art Adminrs; Col Art Asn; Tex Asn Schs Art. Style & Technique: Large-scale fiberglass sculpture for exterior location; paintings in gouache-tempera. Media: Fiberglass; gouache-tempera collage. Res: Architecture of nonconformist religions in Britain and Wales from the late 1600's to the early 20th century. Publ: Auth, Chapel Architecture, Merthyr Libr, 63; auth, Interview with Robert Gordy, Bumpy Days, 74; auth, Chapels: The Forgotten

Heritage, Ninnau, 77. Dealer: Carlin Gallery 710 Montgomery Ft Worth TX 76107. Mailing Add: 4024 Clarke Ave Ft Worth TX 76107

JONES, BARBARA NESTER
PAINTER
b Oklahoma City, Okla, Feb 14, 23. Study: Phillips Univ, BFA; Univ Calif, Fullerton, MA; Okla Univ, postgrad; also with Ken Tyler, Gemini GEL, Los Angeles. Work: Laguna Beach Mus Art, Calif; Riverside Art Ctr & Mus, Calif. Comn: Mural, Community Bank of Enid, Okla, 66. Exhib: 26th Ann Exhib, Philbrook Art Ctr, Tulsa, Okla, 66; Art in Politics, Lytton Ctr of Visual Arts, Los Angeles, 68; 11th Art Unlimited, Downey Mus Art, Calif, 68; 13th Ann Purchase Prize Competition, Riverside Art Ctr & Mus, 74; 21st All Calif Show, Laguna Beach, 75; one-person shows, Riverside Mus Art, Calif, 76 & Arnold Gallery, Newport Beach, Calif, 77. Teaching: Lectr, var mus & art alliances, Calif. Awards: Painting Award, Downey Art Mus, 68; Painting Award, Laguna Beach Mus Art, 73; Painting Award, Harry Hopkins, San Francisco Mus Art, 75. Mem: Artists for Econ Action; Laguna Beach Art Gallery (exhib comt, 71-74). Style & Technique: Non-representational abstract paintings related to large color-field work. Media: Acrylic on Canvas. Mailing Add: 3080 Nestall Rd Laguna Beach CA 92651

JONES, BEN
PAINTER, SCULPTOR
b Paterson, NJ, May 26, 42. Study: Sch Visual Arts; NY Univ, MA; Pratt Inst; Univ Sci & Technok, Kumasi, Ghana. Work: Newark Mus, NJ; Howard Univ; Studio Mus, New York, NY; Johnson Publ, Chicago. Exhib: Mus Mod Art; Studio Mus in Harlem; Princeton Mus; New York Cult Ctr; Black World Arts Festival, Lagos, Nigeria; Newark Mus, 77; Fisk Univ, 77; Ala A&M Univ, 78; Bishop Col, Dallas, Tex, 78; plus others. Teaching: Prof fine arts, Jersey City State Col, 68- Pos: Art dir, Urban League Essex Co Exhib, 72. Awards: Nat Endowment Arts Grant, 74-75; NJ Arts Coun Grant, 77-78. Bibliog: Articles in Art in Am, 71; articles in New York Times, 72; included in Black Perspectives & Black Contemporary Artists. Res: African art and culture in WAfrica and Paris, France. Mailing Add: 15 Goldsmith Ave Newark NJ 07112

JONES, BILL
PAINTER, ASSEMBLAGE ARTIST
b Antioch, Calif, Aug 15, 46. Study: Univ Ore, BA, 68. Work: Vancouver Art Gallery, BC; Art Gallery Ont, Toronto; Burnaby Arts Coun, BC; Henri Gallery, Washington, DC; Can Broadcasting Corp, Vancouver. Exhib: A Plastic Presence, Jewish Mus, New York & San Francisco Mus Art, 69-70; one-man show, Vancouver Art Gallery, 72; Canada Trajectoires 73, Mus Art Mod de la Ville de Paris, 73; Pacific Vibrations, Vancouver Art Gallery, 73; The Canadian Canvas, Traveling Exhib, 75-76. Awards: Can Coun Arts Grants, 73-75. Bibliog: Geoffrey James (auth), The Canadian Canvas: a broad sweep, Time Mag (Can), 1/27/75; Charles Shere (auth), Four days in Vancouver & Victoria, Artscanada, 3/75; Judy Heviz (auth), The Canadian Canvas, Art Mag, spring 75. Style & Technique: Photographic assemblages combining color and black and white mural photographs in special mounting technique. Dealer: A Space 85 St Nicholas St Toronto ON Can. Mailing Add: 2340 Haywood Ave West Vancouver BC V7V 1X7 Can

JONES, (CHARLES) DEXTER (WEATHERBEE), III
SCULPTOR
b Ardmore, Pa, Dec 17, 26. Study: Pa Acad Fine Arts & Chester Springs Art Sch, with Charles Rudy & Walker Hancock; Accad Belli Arti, Florence, Italy. Work: Pa Acad Fine Arts, Philadelphia; Woodmere Art Gallery. Comn: Clinical Meeting Gold Medal, Am Med Asn, 60; A C Storz Tribute Tablet, Omaha Airport, 61; two hist relief panels, New Bradford Nat Bank Bldg, 61; Newcomb Cleveland Medal, Am Asn Advan Sci, 64; Great Seal of Philadelphia, Munic Serv Bldg, Philadelphia, 65; plus many other portraits, plaques & medals. Exhib: Pa Acad Fine Arts, Nat Acad Design, Nat Sculpture Soc, Allied Artists Am & Nat Art Club, many exhib, 49-65. Awards: Silver Medal, DaVinci Alliance, 60; Gregory Award, 61; Art Dir Club Philadelphia Award, 66; plus many others. Mem: Fel Nat Sculpture Soc; Allied Artists Am; Nat Art Club; Academician Nat Acad Design; fel Pa Acad Fine Arts; plus others. Mailing Add: 2124 Lombard Philadelphia PA 19146

JONES, CLAIRE (DEANN BURTCHAELL)
PAINTER, INSTRUCTOR
b Oakland, Calif. Study: Stanford Univ, AB; Otis Art Inst; Univ Calif, Irvine; Laguna Beach Sch Art; San Diego Acad Fine Arts, Calif; also with Dong Kingman, Mario Cooper, Rex Brandt. Work: Hunt Wesson, Fullerton, Calif; Copley Found, San Diego; HEAR Found, Pasadena, Calif. Comn: Many pvt comns. Exhib: Southern Calif Expos, Del Mar, 69-72; Death Valley Invitational, Furnace Creek, Calif, 71-77; Watercolor West, Riverside, Calif, 72-75; Cedar City Invitational, Utah, 74; West Coast Americana Realists, Fullerton. Teaching: Teacher dry brush watercolor, Jade Fon Watercolor Workshop, 7/75; teacher dry brush watercolor, Merced Col Watercolor Workshop, 8/75. Awards: First Award Watercolor, Southern Calif Expos, 69; Hon Mention, Watercolor West, 72 & 75; Best of Show, Hillcrest Invitational, 74. Bibliog: Arte unica, Life en Espanol, 11/3/69; R P Spencer (auth), Dramatis Personnae, Aesthetic Enterprises, 11/72; Fielding Greaves (auth), Nostalgia and old country houses, Southwest Art, 6/75. Mem: Watercolor West (scholar comt, bd mem, ed, 71-); Asn Western Artists; San Diego Art Inst (secy); San Diego Watercolor Soc. Style & Technique: Combining negative areas of paper with images produced by both wet and dry brush methods of watercolor. Publ: Illusr, Leanin' Tree, 72 & 76; illusr, Pictorial Publ; illusr (cover), SW Art, 9/76. Mailing Add: c/o Art Ctr of Rancho Santa Fe PO Box 80 Rancho Santa Fe CA 92067

JONES, DAN BURNE
ART HISTORIAN, PAINTER
b Dalzell, Ill, Aug 16, 08. Study: Art Inst of Chicago; Univ Chicago; Univ Ill; Northern Ill Univ. Comn: Mural, Top Hat Club (with M Waskowsky & William Seymour), Chicago, 39, W Side Tavern Club (with M Waskowsky & Rudolph Pen), Chicago, 39. Exhib: Art Inst of Chicago, 28; one-man show, Northern Ill Univ, 30; Brooks Mem Art Gallery, Memphis, Tenn, 37-38; United Am Artists, Chicago, 39; Print Club Philadelphia, 39; New York World's Fair, 39; Nat Artists Cong, Rockefeller Plaza, New York, 39; Peninsula Art Asn, Ephraim, Wis, 40; Nat Art Week, Chicago, 40; State Teachers Cols, Millersville, Pa & Kirksville, Mo, 39-40; USAF Exhib, l'Hotel de Ville, Casablanca, French Morocco; MAFD-ATC Insignia Exhib, Casablanca, French Morocco, 44-45; Thomas Wolfe Exhib, Acorn Bookshop & Gallery, Oak Park, Ill, 46; Village Art Fair, Oak Park, Ill, 47; 1973 World's Ex Libris Exhib, Copenhagen, Denmark, 73; Int Ex Libris Exhib, Lugano, Switz, 78. Teaching: Staurday Sch, Art Inst Chicago, 28-30 & 40-41; asst principal, Jr High Sch, Ladd, Ill, 32-36; instr design & drawing, State Teachers Col, Kirksville, Mo, 32-36; head dept of design, Lee Art Acad, Memphis, Tenn, 36-39; asst etching, lithography & anatomy, Art Inst of Chicago, 40-42; lithographic draftsman, US Coast & Geodetic Survey, Washington, DC, 43-44. Pos: Free-lance fine & com artist, Midwest, 25-78. Awards: Blow Scholar, LaSalle, Ill, 27; Ricketts Scholar, Art Inst Chicago, 28-30; Supervisory Cert, Art Inst of Chicago, 31; Ill State Supervisory Cert, 33; First Prize, Art Students League, Art Inst of Chicago, 28; First Prize, Peninsula Art Asn, Ephraim, Wis, 40-41; Second Prize North African Theatre Oper, Casablanca, French Morocco, 45; travel grant, Smithsonian Inst, Washington, DC, 71. Bibliog: D Hight & J Baima (co-auths), Bookplates of Dan Burne Jones, Am Bookplate Soc, Washington, DC, 36; Rockwell Kent (auth), It's Me O Lord, Dodd, Mead, New York, 55; Audrey S Arellanes (auth) Bookplates, A Selected Annotated Bibliog, Gale Res, Detroit, 71; Fridolf Johnson (auth), Prints of Rockwell Kent, Publ Weekly 7/75; Chandler P Granniss (auth), Prints of Rockwell Kent, Publ Weekly, 7/75. Mem: Delta Phi Delta (nat hon art fraternity); Am Bookplate Soc for Collectors & Designers; Fedn Ill Archaeol; Ill State Archaeol Soc; Smithsonian Assocs; Emergency Civil Liberties Comt. Media: Oil, watercolor, wood engraving, lithography, pen-ink-brush. Publ: Auth, Who's Who: Indian Relics Number 3 (bibliog), Parks & Thompson, St Louis, Mo, 72; auth, The Prints of Rockwell Kent, Univ of Chicago Press, 75; auth, Prehistoric Indians and their artifacts, chap in: Lar Hothem (auth), The Indian Artifact Collector, Columbus, Ohio, 78; auth, Lynd Ward: A Descriptive Bibliography, in progress. Mailing Add: 816 North Blvd Oak Park IL 60301

JONES, DAVID LEE
PAINTER, SCULPTOR
b Columbus, Ohio, Feb 26, 48. Study: Kansas City Art Inst, BFA, 70; Univ Calif, Berkeley, Marion Davies Fel, 72, MFA, 73; studio asst to Peter Voulkos, 70-72. Work: San Francisco Mus Art; Univ Art Mus, Berkeley; DeSaisset Mus & Art Gallery, Univ Santa Clara, Calif. Exhib: Recent Acquisitions, Univ Mus, Berkeley, 73; Market St Prog, Pasadena Mus Mod Art, Calif, 73; Whitney Biennial Am Painting & Sculpture, Whitney Mus Art, New York, 75; Calif Painting & Sculpture—the Mod Era, San Francisco Mus of Art & Nat Collection of Fine Arts, Washington, DC, 76-77; one-man shows, Soc Encouragement Contemp Art, San Francisco Mus Art, 74 & Michael Walls Gallery, New York, 75. Awards: Soc Encouragement Contemp Art Grant, 74; Individual Artists Grant, Nat Endowment Arts, 74. Bibliog: Ellen Lubell (auth), David Jones, Art Mag, 6/74; Al Frankenstein (auth), numerous reviews in San Francisco Chronicle & Examr. Media: 20th Century Media. Mailing Add: 746 Arguello San Francisco CA 94118

JONES, DOUGLAS MCKEE (DOUG)
PAINTER, ART DEALER
b Sewell, Chile, Oct 16, 29; US citizen. Study: San Diego Fine Arts & Crafts; San Diego State Col; Los Angeles Art Ctr Col Design, grad; also with Lorser Feitelson, Audubon Tyler, Leon Franks & Sergei Bongart. Comn: Portraits of Mayor Charles Dail, San Diego & Mayor Kiyoshi Nakarai, Yokohama, comn by San Diego Chap, Am Inst Architects, 63; 43 portraits, Int Aerospace Hall of Fame, San Diego, 64-72; portrait of Gen Claire Chenault, Flying Tigers Asn, 71; portrait of Marie Winzer, Scripps Hosp; also many portraits of prominent people and children. Pos: Owner & dir, The Jones Gallery, 64- Media: Oil, Pastel. Specialty: Paintings, sculpture and ceramics by distinguished 19th and 20th century American artists. Mailing Add: The Jones Gallery 1264 Prospect St La Jolla CA 92037

JONES, EDWARD POWIS
PAINTER, SCULPTOR
b New York, NY NY, Jan 8, 19. Study: Harvard Univ; Art Students League; Acad Ranson, Paris. Work: Mus Mod Art, New York; Libr Cong, Washington, DC; Riverside Mus, New York; Philadelphia Mus Art; Brooklyn Mus; plus others. Exhib: Libr Cong; Modern Religious Prints, Mus Mod Art Circulating Exhib, 63; Tokyo Print Bienale, Japan, 68; New York World Trade Ctr, 75; plus others. Teaching: Lectr, The Modern Illustrated Book; instr art, Loyola Sch, New York, 70-72. Mem: Philadelphia Print Club; Century Asn; Munic Art Soc; Artists Equity Asn; Fels Pierpont Morgan Libr (chmn coun, 72). Style & Technique: Representational expressionist. Media: Oil, Watercolor; Bronze. Publ: Contribr, Art in Am; illusr, Liturgical Arts. Mailing Add: 925 Park Ave New York NY 10028

JONES, ELIZABETH
SCULPTOR, MEDALIST
b Montclair, NJ, May 31, 35. Study: Vassar Col, BA, 57; Art Students League, 58-60; Scuola Arte Medaglia, The Mint, Rome, Italy, 62-64; Acad Brasileira Belas Artes, Rio de Janeiro, hon dipl, 67. Work: Creighton Univ. Comn: Portrait of Albert Schweitzer, Franklin Mint, Pa, 66; gold sculptures with precious stone, Govt Italy, 68; portrait of Picasso, comn by Stefano Johnson, Milan, Italy, 72; Gold Medal Award for Archeol, Univ Mus, Univ Pa, 72; Holy Year Jubilaeum; plus many others. Exhib: Tiffany & Co, New York, Houston, Los Angeles, Chicago & San Francisco, 66-68; Montclair Art Mus, NJ, 67; many int medallic art shows, Rome, Madrid, Paris, Athens, Prague & Cologne; Smithsonian Inst & Nat Sculpture Soc, New York, 72; USIS Consulate, Rome, Italy, 73. Awards: Outstanding Sculptor of the Year, Am Numismatic Asn, Colorado Springs, Colo, 72. Bibliog: Mario Valeriana (auth), Medalists in Italy, Editalia, Rome, 72; plus articles in Women's Wear Daily, Coin World & other mags & newspapers in the US & Italy. Mem: Nat Sculpture Soc; Am Numismatic Asn; Fedn Int Medaille; Ital Soc Medalists. Style & Technique: Non-figurative silver sculptures evolve from organic forms; medals in high relief. Media: Wax, Plaster; Silver, Gold. Mailing Add: Via Giuseppe Ceracchi 29 Rome Italy

JONES, ELIZABETH ORTON
ILLUSTRATOR, WRITER
b Highland Park, Ill, June 25, 10. Study: Univ Chicago, PhB, 32; Ecole Beaux Arts, Paris, dipl, 32; Art Inst Chicago, 32; Wheaton Col, Hon MA, 55. Comn: Murals, Crotched Mountain Ctr, Greenfield, NH; panel, Univ NH Libr. Exhib: O'Brien Galleries, Chicago; Smithsonian Inst; plus others. Awards: Charles Muller Prize, Chicago Soc Etchers, 39; Caldecott Medal for Illus, 44; Lewis Carroll Shelf Award, Univ Wis, 58. Publ: Auth & illusr, Maminka's Children, Twig, Big Susan & How Far Is It to Bethlehem?; illusr, The Peddler's Clock, Small Rain, Prayer for Little Things & others. Mailing Add: Mason NH 03244

JONES, FRANCES FOLLIN
CURATOR
b New York, NY, Sept 8, 13. Study: Bryn Mawr Col, AB, 34, MA, 36, PhD, 52; Am Sch Class Studies at Athens, 37-38. Pos: Secy & asst cur class art, Art Mus, Princeton Univ, 43-46, asst to dir & cur class art, 46-60, chief cur & cur class art, 60-71, cur collections & cur class art, 71- Publ: Contribr to prof journals & publ. Mailing Add: Art Mus Princeton Univ Princeton NJ 08540

JONES, FRANKLIN REED
PAINTER, ART WRITER
b Needham, Mass, May 18, 21. Work: Mus of Art, Sci & Indust, Bridgeport, Conn; Conn Audubon Soc, Fairfield. Exhib: Nat Acad of Design, New York, 74; Conn Watercolor Soc, New Britain, 74; Univ of Utah Invitational Exhib, 76; Am Watercolor Soc, New York, 77; De Cordova Mus, Lincoln, Mass, 77; Berkshire Mus, Pittsfield, Mass, 77; Ellsworth Nat Exhib, Simsbury, Conn, 77. Teaching: Instr painting, Famous Artists Sch, Westport, Conn,

53-58. Pos: Asst to dir, Famous Artists Sch, 58-74. Awards: Purchase Award, Mus Art, Sci & Indust, Famous Artists Schs, 64; Gold Medal of Hon, Am Watercolor Soc, 75; Award of Excellence, Ellsworth Gallery, Simsbury Cult Comt, 77. Bibliog: Fred Whitaker (auth), The Paintings of Franklin Jones, Am Artist Mag, 66. Mem: Am Watercolor Soc. Style & Technique: New Eng landscapes in realistic style; fluid washes with watercolor; acrylic used in the manner of egg tempera. Media: Acrylic, watercolor. Publ: Contribr, Acrylic Watercolor Painting, 70 & Complete Guide to Acrylic Painting, 71, Watson-Guptill; auth, The Pleasure of Painting, North Light, 75; illusr, Gray's Sporting J, 77; auth, Painting nature: solving landscape problems, North Light, 78. Mailing Add: RFD 1 West Stockbridge MA 01266

JONES, FREDERICK GEORGE
PRINTMAKER, EDUCATOR
b Llanymymech, Wales, Mar 6, 40. Study: Cardiff Col Art, Wales; Univ Pittsburgh; Univ Wis-Madison. Work: Ill State Mus; Lakeview Ctr for Arts, Peoria, Ill; Laura Musser Mus, Muscatine, Iowa; Westmoreland Co Mus, Greensburgh, Pa; Western Ill Univ Permanent Collection, Macomb. Exhib: Int Print Biennale, Seoul, Korea, 71; Mid-Am Exhib, Montreal, Can, 71; Nat Image on Paper Show, Springfield, Ill, 72; Nat Print & Drawing Show, Macomb, 75; Gov Invitational, Gov Mansion, Springfield, 75. Teaching: Lectr design drawing, Chester Col Art, Eng, 66-68; assoc prof printmaking, Western Ill Univ, 68-, gallery dir, 69-71. Awards: Painting Award, Container Corp Am, 70; Best of Show, Tri-State Exhib, Muscatine, Iowa, 73; Purchase Award, Ill State Mus, 74. Mem: Royal Cambrian Acad, Wales; Col Art Asn Am; NH Print Soc. Style & Technique: Landscape, prints, drawings and watercolors describing environmental violence. Media: Serigraphy, Drawing. Dealer: Van Stratten 646 N Michigan Ave Chicago IL 60611; Prairie Gallery Springfield IL. Mailing Add: RR 4 Macomb IL 61455

JONES, GEORGE BOBBY
PAINTER, SYNAESTHETIC ARTIST
b Louisville, Ky, Oct 30, 43. Study: Syracuse Univ, with Larry Bakke & Jim Ridlon, BFA, 72, MFA, 73. Work: Finch Mus Art, New York; Herbert F Johnson Mus Art, Ithaca, NY; Roberson Art Mus & State Univ NY, Binghamton; Noyles Art Gallery, Antioch Col, Yellow Springs, Ohio. Exhib: Everson Art Mus 15th & 21st Regional Art Exhibs, Syracuse, NY, 67 & 74; J B Speed Mus Biennial Exhib Nat, Louisville, Ky, 69 & 71; Mem Art Gallery Regional Art Exhib, Rochester, NY, 73; GVW Smith Art Mus 55th Nat Exhib, Springfield, Mass, 74; Washington & Jefferson 10th Nat Paint Exhib, Washington, Pa, 74; plus many one-man & group shows. Teaching: Vis artist, Northern Ky Voc Tech High Sch, Covington, 68-69; instr fine & commercial arts, Ahrens High Sch, Louisville, Ky, 69-71; vis artist, Syracuse Univ Summer Exchange Prog, 73; vis artist, Pelham Sch Dist, NY, spring 74; art supvr, West Chester, Pa, fall 74; prof, Studio, Concord Col, Athens, WVa, 74-75; prof art, Marshall Univ, Huntington, WVa, 75. Awards: Spec Art Grants, Syracuse Univ, 71-72 & Art Assistantships & Scholars, 72-73. Mem: Col Art Asn Am; Nat Art Educ Asn; Am Asn Univ Prof. Style & Technique: A manifestation of synaesthetic art process through multi-sensory approaches using interactions of the environment as the media. Publ: Auth, Synaesthetic process thru film, Cent New Yorker, Inc, spring 73. Dealer: Alan Brown c/o Alan Brown Gallery Hartsdale Ave Hartsdale NY 10530. Mailing Add: 401 Elliott St Syracuse NY 13204

JONES, HAROLD HENRY
ART ADMINISTRATOR, PHOTOGRAPHER
b Morristown, NJ, Sept 29, 40. Study: Newark Sch Fine & Indust Arts, dipl, 63; Md Inst Art, BFA, 65; Univ NMex, MFA, 72. Work: George Eastman House, Rochester, NY; Univ Art Mus, Univ NMex. Exhib: Mus Mod Art, New York, 70; Photog Invitational 71, Ark Art Ctr, Little Rock, 71; Continuum, George Eastman House, 72; New Images 1839-1973, Smithsonian Inst, 73; one-man show, Soho Photo Gallery, New York, 74, Spectrum Gallery, Tucson, Ariz, 76, Light Gallery, New York, 76, Kresge Art Ctr, Mich State Univ, East Lansing, 77 & Hang-Up Gallery, Tucson, 77. Exhibitions Arranged, George Eastman House; Light Gallery, New York. Teaching: Assoc prof art hist, Queens Col, 74-75. Pos: Assoc cur, George Eastman House, 70-71; founding dir, Light Gallery, 71-75; founding dir, Ctr Creative Photog, Univ Ariz, 75-77; coordr photog prog, Univ Ariz, Tucson, 77. Awards: Nat Endowment for the Arts Photogr Fel, 77. Mem: Soc Photog Educ (bd mem, 71-75). Res: Aspects of the history of photography. Collection: Contemporary photography and related material. Mailing Add: Ctr for Creative Photog Univ of Ariz Tucson AZ 85721

JONES, HERB (LEON HERBERT JONES, JR)
PAINTER, PRINTMAKER
b Norfolk, Va, Mar 25, 23. Study: William & Mary Col. Work: Univ Va, Charlottesville; NC Nat Bank, Raleigh; Cong Off of William G Whitehurst, Washington, DC; Chrysler Mus at Norfolk; State Univ NY, Buffalo. Comn: Paintings, Comdr Deveraux, Atomic Submarine USS Skipjack, 69, comn by Va Nat Bank for State Secy Fed Repub of Ger, 70, O M Stevenson Bonds Div, US Treasury Dept, Richmond, Va, 70, Conn Mutual Life Ins Co, 70 & VAdm W P Arentzen, Surgeon Gen of the Navy, Washington, DC, 74. Exhib: Seventh Ann Exhib of Realistic Art, Mus of Fine Art, Springfield, Mass, 66; First-Seventh Ann James River Art Exhibs, Mariners Mus, Newport News, Va, 67-73; one-man shows, Recent Work by Herb Jones, Norfolk Mus of Arts & Sci, 68 & Portsmouth Naval Hosp for returning prisoners of Vietnam War, sponsored by Surgeon Gen of the Navy Arentzen, 72; Va Biennial, Va Mus, Richmond, 69 & 71; Realists, Gallery of Contemp Art, Winston-Salem, NC, 70 & 72; Tidewater 12, Columbia Mus of Art, SC, 72; two-man exhib, Tidewater Arts Festival, Chrysler Mus at Norfolk, 74. Awards: Citation of Excellence, 22nd Tidewater Artists Exhib, Chrysler Mus at Norfolk, 73; Best-in-Show (representational), Va Beach Boardwalk Show, 73; Cert of Award, Graphic Arts Award Competition, Printing Indust of Am, 75 & 76. Bibliog: Tony Burden (auth), Christmas with Herb Jones, WVEC-TV film, 70-74; Barclay Sheaks (auth), Drawing & Painting the Natural Environment, Davis Publ, 74; Mary Timmins (auth), Portrait of the artist—conversation with Herb Jones, Metro Mag, 10/76. Mem: Tidewater Artist Asn; Nat Soc of Arts & Lit. Style & Technique: Moody realism. Media: Egg tempera and watercolor. Publ: Illusr (covers), Va Wildlife Mag, 64-68; illusr, Outdoor scenes from original by Herb Jones, Va Wildlife Mag, 11/64; illusr (covers), Virginia Beach Art Center Calendar, 66, Peninsula Symphony Orchestra Prog, 67 & Fifteenth Dimension, Tidewater Pub Television Mag, 11/71. Mailing Add: 238 Beck St Norfolk VA 23503

JONES, HOWARD WILLIAM
PAINTER, SCULPTOR
b Ilion, NY, June 20, 22. Study: Toledo Univ; Columbia Univ; Syracuse Univ, BFA; Cranbrook Acad Art. Work: Jewish Mus, New York; Walker Art Ctr, Minneapolis; Knox-Albright Mus, Buffalo, NY; Milwaukee Art Inst, Wis; St Louis Art Mus. Comn: Time Columns: The Sound of Light (wall of light & sound), Whitney Mus Am Art, New York, 68; Retinal Bypass I (sound environment), NJ State Mus, Trenton, 75; Retinal Bypass II (sound environment), Brooks Mem Art Gallery, Memphis, Tenn, 77. Exhib: Light, Motion, Space, Walker Art Ctr, Minneapolis, 67 & Mus Contemp Art, Chicago, 68; Magic Theater, Nelson-Atkins Mus, Kansas City, Automation House, New York, Montreal & others, 68-70; Moon Show, Mass Inst Technol, Boston & Newark Mus Fine Arts, NJ, 69 & 70; Art of the 60's, Princeton Univ, NJ, 70; Kinetic Art, Rockefeller Univ, New York, Arts Coun Gt Brit & Hayward Gallery, London, 70; one-man shows, Electric Gallery, Toronto, Ont, 71, St Louis Art Mus, Mo, 73, Nelson-Atkins Mus, Kansas City, Mo, 73, Wadsworth Atheneum, Hartford, Conn, 74 & Forbes Found Mus, NJ, 76; Multiples, Philadelphia Mus of Art, 71; Responsive Environment, NJ State Mus, Trenton, 72; Recent Media—Ten Yrs, Brooks Mem Art Gallery, Memphis, 77; Art of the Space Era, Huntsville Mus of Art, Von Braun Civic Ctr, Ala, 78. Teaching: Instr painting & design, Tulane Univ La, 51-54; asst prof painting & design, Fla State Univ, 54-57; prof multi-media, Wash Univ, 57- Awards: Graham Found Fel & Grant, 66-67; New Talent: USA, Art in Am Mag, 66-67; Nat Endowment for the Arts fel & grant, 77. Bibliog: Ralph Coe (auth), Post pop possibilities: Howard Jones, Art Int, 1/66 & Breaking the sound barrier, Art News Mag, summer 71; Nat Endowment Arts (producer), Artist in America: Howard Jones (film), KETC-TV, 71. Media: Sound & Light. Mailing Add: 12 N Newstead St St Louis MO 63108

JONES, JACOBINE
SCULPTOR
b London, Eng. Study: Regent St Polytech; also with H Brownsword, London & in Denmark. Work: Kelvin Mus, Glasgow, Scotland; Confederation Life Bldg, Toronto, Ont; Nat Gallery Can; Hamilton Art Gallery, Ont; plus many others. Comn: Seven figures in bronze, Facade of Bank of Can, Ottawa, Ont; four figures in stone, Facade of Sigmund Samuel Mus, Toronto; mural in stone, Confederation Life Bldg, Toronto; Facade of Gen Hosp, Toronto; mural in marble, N Wall of Main Banking Rm, Bank of NS, Toronto. Exhib: Paris Salon, 32; Royal Can Acad Arts, 32-; Tate Gallery, London, Eng, 38; Hamilton, Ont, 66-69; one-man show, Rodman Hall Art Ctr, St Catharine's, 69; plus many others. Teaching: Lect on sculpture; dir sculpture & ceramics, Ont Col Art, 51-58. Awards: Gold Medal, Regent St Polytech, London. Mem: Royal Can Acad Art; Sculptors' Soc Can; Am Soc Animal Artists. Media: Stone, Bronze. Dealer: Laing Galleries 194 Bloor W Toronto ON Can. Mailing Add: 209 Davey St Niagara-on-the-Lake ON L0S 1J0 Can

JONES, JAMES EDWARD
PRINTMAKER, PAINTER
b Paducah, Ky, Jan 27, 37. Study: Philadelphia Col Art, with Henry Pitz & Benton Spruance, dipl, 60, fel, 56-61, BFA, 61; Univ Pa, with Barnett Newman, Angelo Seveili, David Smith, Richard Stankiewicz & Adja Yunkers, MFA, 62. Work: Morgan State Univ; McDonosh Sch, Md; Dennison Univ; Univ S Ala. Exhib: 16th & 18th Area Exhib, Baltimore Mus Art, 63-64; Wilmington Soc Fine Arts, Del, 64; Corcoran Mus Art, Washington, DC, 64; Printmakers Exhib, Spelman Col, Paine Col, LeMoyne Col & Ga Southern Col, 69. Teaching: Assoc prof art educ, painting & printmaking, Morgan State Univ, 62- Awards: Stewart Art Award, NJ State, 56; Univ Pa Fel & Thorton Oakley Creative Achievement Award, 62. Mem: Artists Equity Asn. Style & Technique: Mixed media; abstractionist. Media: Assemblage, Oil, Etching, Engraving, Aquatints, Mezzotints. Mailing Add: 2930 Silver Hill Ave Baltimore MD 21207

JONES, JERRY
SCULPTOR, PAINTER
b Pineville, Ky, Apr 9, 47. Study: Cooper Sch Art, cert fine art; Cleveland Inst Art, BFA. Work: El Paso Mus Art, Tex; Allen Mem Mus Art, Oberlin, Ohio; Mus Contemp Art, Sao Paulo, Brazil. Exhib: Prospective 74, Mus Contemp Art, Sao Paulo, 74; Biennial Contemp Am Art, Whitney Mus Art, New York, 75; Open to New Ideas, Ga Mus of Art, Athens, 77; Painting 75, 76 & 77, Sarah Lawrence Col, NY, 77; Franklin Furnace, New York, NY, 77; Queensboro Col, Queens, NY, 78; one-man shows, Cult Ctr, Washington, DC, 75-76 & Holly Solomon Gallery, 76 & 78. Awards: Painting grant, Creative Artists Pub Serv (CAPS), 78. Bibliog: R Welchans (auth), Biotic Series, John Carroll Univ, 69; Museums, New Yorker, 2/17/75. Style & Technique: Works and writings for special installations. Media: Mixed. Dealer: Holly Solomon Gallery 392 W Broadway New York NY 10012. Mailing Add: 140 Grand St New York NY 10013

JONES, JOHN PAUL
PAINTER, PRINTMAKER
b Indianola, Iowa, Nov 18, 24. Study: State Univ Iowa, BFA, 49, MFA, 51, with Mauricio Lasansky. Work: Mus Mod Art, New York; Brooklyn Mus; Libr Cong, Washington, DC; Los Angeles Co Mus Art; Nat Gallery Art, Washington, DC. Exhib: Art of America in Spain, Madrid, 63; Pittsburgh Int, Carnegie Inst, 64-67; American Painting, Va Mus Arts & Sci, Richmond, 66-70; Tamarind: Homage to Lithography, Mus Mod Art, New York, 69; The New Vein—Europe, toured in Europe by Smithsonian Inst, 69-70. Teaching: Asst prof prints, Univ Calif, Los Angeles, 53-63; prof prints & drawings, Univ Calif, Irvine, 70- Awards: Graphics Award, Tiffany Found, 51; Creative Printmaking Award, Guggenheim Found, 60. Bibliog: Una Johnson (auth), John Paul Jones, Prints & Drawings 1948-1963 (monogr), Brooklyn Mus, 63; Henry Hopkins (auth), John Paul Jones, Painting & Sculpture 1955-1965 (monogr), Los Angeles Co Mus Art, 65; Eugene Anderson (auth), John Paul Jones (monogr), Felix Landau Gallery, Los Angeles, 67. Dealer: Mekler Gallery 651 N La Cienega Blvd Los Angeles 90069. Mailing Add: 22370 Third Ave South Laguna CA 92677

JONES, LOIS MAILOU (MRS V PIERRE-NOEL)
PAINTER, DESIGNER
b Boston, Mass, 1905. Study: Boston Mus Sch Fine Arts, scholar, 4 yrs; Boston Normal Art Sch; Designers Art Sch; Harvard Univ; Columbia Univ; Howard Univ, AB; Acad Julien, Paris, with Berges, Montezin, Maury & Adler; Acad Grand Chaumiere, Paris; Colo State Christian Col, PhD(hon), 73. Work: Brooklyn Mus; Phillips Collection, Washington, DC; Palais Nat, Haiti; Corcoran Gallery Art, Washington, DC; Mus Fine Arts, Boston; Hirshhorn Mus; plus others. Comn: Designed AKA Commemorative Stained Glass Window, Andrew Rankin Chapel, Howard Univ, 78. Exhib: Nat Acad Design, New York; Rhodes Nat Gallery, SRhodesia; Trenton Mus, NJ; San Francisco Mus Art; Salon Artistes Francais, Grand Palais Champs-Elysees, Paris; plus 40 one-man shows & numerous other group shows. Teaching: Emer prof design & watercolor painting, Howard Univ, 30- Awards: Gen Educ Bd Foreign Fel for Study in France & Italy, 37-38; 8th Ann Area Exhib Oil Painting Award, Corcoran Gallery Art, 53; Chevalier, Nat Order Merit of Honor, Govt Haiti for Achievement in Art; Alumni Award, Howard Univ, 78; plus others. Bibliog: Cedric Dover (auth), American Negro art, NY Graphic Soc, 60; Dr Samella S Lewis & Ruth G Waddy (auth), Black artists on art, Contemp Crafts Publ, Vol 1, 69; Elsa H Fine (auth), The Afro-American artist: a search for identity, Holt, Rinehart & Winston, 72; Karen Peterson & J J Wilson (auths), Women Artists, Harper & Row, 76. Mem: Fel Royal Soc Arts; Artists Equity Asn; Soc Washington Artists; Art Dirs Club Metrop Washington; Nat Conf Artists. Style & Technique: Haitian and African themes, with decorative trend in a highly keyed palette; from realism to abstract. Media: Oil, Acrylic. Publ: Auth, Lois Mailou Jones penitures—1937-1951, Georges Frere, Tourcoing, France, 52. Mailing Add: 4706 17th St NW Washington DC 20011

JONES, LOIS SWAN
ART HISTORIAN, LECTURER
b Dallas, Tex, July 3, 27. Study: Univ Chicago, PhB, 47, BS, 48, MS, 54; NTex State Univ, PhD, 72; Ctr Univ d'Ete des Pyrenees, Univ Toulouse, summer 75. Teaching: Lectr art hist, Univ Tex, Arlington, 69-70; from asst prof to assoc prof art hist, NTex State Univ, Denton, 72- Pos: Conductor, Le Petite Cercle d'Art, Dallas, 60-; auth, narrator & photogr, Five Nights in Europe, Dallas Country Club, 63-75. Mem: Art Libr Soc NAm (mem standards comt); Col Art Asn; Am Asn Mus. Res: Art museum educational programs; art library research; medieval art. Publ: Auth, Let Your Fingers Do the Walking, 5/74 & Where to Publish? Where to Index?, 1 & 2/75, Mus News; auth, Volunteer-Guides & Classroom Teachers in School-Visitation Programs in European and North American Art Museums, Studies in Art Educ, 77; auth, Art Research Methods and Resources, Kendall/Hunt, 78. Mailing Add: 3801 Normandy Dallas TX 75205

JONES, LOUIS C
MUSEUM DIRECTOR
b Albany, NY, June 28, 08. Study: Hamilton Col, AB, 30, hon LHD, 62; Columbia Univ, AM, 31, PhD, 41. Teaching: Instr, State Univ NY Albany, 34-36; instr, Cooperstown Grad Prog, State Univ NY, 73- Pos: Exec dir, NY State Hist Asn & Farmers Mus, 46-72, emer dir, 72-; chmn, NY State Hist Trust, 66-72; mem NY State Coun on Arts, 60-72; state liaison off, Nat Regist Hist Places; mem ed bd, Am Heritage; ed, NY Hist, 47-52. Awards: Guggenheim Fel, 46; Award of Distinction, Am Asn State & Local Hist, 69; Rochester Mus Fel; plus others. Mem: Fel Am Folklore Soc; Am Asn Mus (coun, 52-70); Am Asn State & Local Hist (exec coun, 50-58); NY State Hist Asn (trustee, exec dir); Folklore Soc (co-founder, ed quart, 45-50); plus others. Interest: American folk art. Publ: Co-auth, American Folk Art, 52; auth, Things That Go Bump in the Night, 59; co-auth, New Found Folk Art of the Young Republic, 60; auth, Growing Up in the Cooper Country, 65; co-auth, Queena Stovall, Artist of the Blue Ridge Piedmont, 75; plus others. Mailing Add: 11 Main St Box 351 Cooperstown NY 13326

JONES, MARVIN HAROLD
PRINTMAKER, PAINTER
b Flora, Ill. Study: Univ Ill, Urbana; Roosevelt Univ, Chicago; Anderson Col, Ind, BA; Univ Calif, Davis, MA, with Roy DeForest, William Wiley & Peter Saul. Work: Libr of Cong, Washington, DC; Confederation Art Gallery, Charlottetown, PEI, Can; Osaka Univ of Arts, Japan; Edmonton Art Gallery, Alta; Univ Dallas, Irving, Tex. Exhib: Royal Can Acad of Art Ann Exhib, Montreal Mus of Fine Arts, 71; Brit Int Print Biennale, Bradford City Art Gallery, 72 & 76; Drawings/USA, Minn Mus of Art, St Paul, 73, 75 & 77; Nat Print Invitational, Brooklyn Mus, NY, 74; Perth Int Drawing Exhib, Western Australian Art Gallery, 75; Miami Int Print Biennial, Miami Art Ctr, Fla, 75; Biennial Int Print Exhib, Print Club of Philadelphia, 77; plus numerous others both international and domestic. Teaching: Asst prof printmaking, Univ Alta, Edmonton, 70-72; assoc prof printmaking, Cleveland State Univ, 76- Awards: Purchase Award, Miami Int Print Biennial, 75; Coun Award, Am Color Print Soc, 76; Purchase Award, Miami Univ Nat Print & Drawing Exhib, 77. Bibliog: C S McConnell (auth), Marvin Jones, Middle American, Artscanada, 4/71; Derek M Besant (auth), Satirical graphics by Marvin Jones & John Will, Art Mag, 10/75. Mem: Am Color Print Soc, Style & Technique: Traditional and photographic intaglio and relief techniques and color Xeroxing. Media: Print (intaglio and relief); acrylic. Dealer: Graphics Gallery 3 Embarcadero Ctr San Francisco CA 94111. Mailing Add: 2924 E Overlook Rd Cleveland Heights OH 44118

JONES, REITA
PAINTER
b Lawton, Okla. Study: Univ Okla, BA(Phi Beta Kappa), 66; Art Inst San Miguel de Allende, Mex; study with Millard Sheets, Rex Brandt, Ed Whitney, Robert E Wood & Charles Reid. Exhib: 8th Ann Artists Salon, Mus Art, Oklahoma City, 69; Philbrook Art Ctr, Tulsa, Okla, 70; Southwestern Watercolor Soc Ann, Dallas, Tex, 71; Ann Eight-State Exhib, Okla Art Ctr, Oklahoma City, 72; 11th Ann Benedictine Art Awards, New York, 73. Pos: Pres, Oklahoma City Chap, Southwestern Watercolor Soc, 71-72. Awards: Honorable Mention, Benedictine Art Awards, 73. Mem: Okla Watercolor Asn (pres, 72-74). Style & Technique: Portraits, figures, still life and landscapes in transparent watercolor, wet-in-wet, dry brush; non-objective in hard edge. Dealer: Legend's 1313 Lindsay St Norman OK 73069. Mailing Add: 136 W Silver Meadow Dr Midwest City OK 73110

JONES, ROBERT CUSHMAN
PAINTER
b West Hartford, Conn, Oct 15, 30. Study: RI Sch Design, BFA, 53, MS, 59. Exhib: Drawings USA, St Paul Mus, 61-71; 17th Ann Exhib Am Painting & Sculpture, Pa Acad Fine Arts, 62; 82nd Ann Exhib, 63 & Far West Regional Exhib of Art Across Am, 65, San Francisco Mus Art; The West—80 Contemporaries, Univ Ariz, 67. Teaching: Instr drawing & painting, RI Sch Design, 56-60; assoc prof drawing & painting, Univ Wash, 60-; instr drawing & painting, Univ BC, summers 66 & 71. Media: Oil. Dealer: Francine Seders Gallery 6701 Greenwood Ave N Seattle WA 98103. Mailing Add: 5412 21st St NE Seattle WA 98105

JONES, RUTHE BLALOCK
PAINTER
b Claremore, Okla, June 8, 39. Study: Bacone Col, with Dick West, AA; Univ Tulsa, with Carl Coker, BFA, grad study. Work: Mus Am Indian, Heye Found, New York; Indian Arts & Crafts Bd, US Dept Interior, Washington, DC; Heard Mus, Phoenix; Philbrook Art Ctr, Tulsa; Five Civilized Tribes Mus, Muskogee, Okla. Exhib: US Dept Interior Invitational Indian Exhib, Washington, DC, 65; Indian Ann, Philbrook Mus, Tulsa, 68 & 72, Okla Ann, 72; Indian Ann, Five Civilized Tribes Mus, Muskogee, 69 & 70; Scottsdale Indian Nat Art Exhib, Ariz, 72. Awards: First for Traditional Indian Painting, Philbrook Mus, 68; Spec Award, US Dept Interior, Okla State Soc; Second for Watercolor Painting, Scottsdale Nat Indian Art Exhib, 72. Bibliog: J Snodgrass (auth), Handbook American Indian Artists, Mus Am Indian, 67; Forum, Christian Sci Monitor, 6/67; Ruth B Jones—something a bit different, Ariz Repub, 7/67. Style & Technique: American Indian; impressionistic; non-objective; fantasy. Media: Watercolor, Acrylic, Graphics. Publ: Illusr, Nimrod (Am Indian issue), Univ Tulsa J, spring 72. Mailing Add: 517 S Woodlawn St Okmulgee OK 74447

JONES, THEODORE JOSEPH
SCULPTOR, PRINTMAKER
b New Orleans, La, Sept 14, 38. Study: Xavier Univ, BA; Mich State Univ, MA; Univ Mont, MFA; Fla A&M Univ, cert; Fisk Univ, cert. Work: Johnson Publ Co, Chicago; Mus African Art, Washington, DC; Fisk Univ, Afro-Am Slide Depository, Univ South Ala; First Am Nat Bank, Nashville; slide collections of Cleveland State Univ, Upper Iowa Col, Ky State Univ, Ft Steilacoom Community Col, New York Pub Libr, Agua Frin Union High Sch, Mass Col of Art, Manchester Col, Jacqueline McRoth Collection & Univ of Mass at Amherst. Exhib: 7/2 Exhib, Zerbe, Gunn, Hurst, Jones, White, Milton, Tallahassee, Fla, 68; 9th Ann Dixie Exhib, Montgomery, Ala, 68; 11 Black Printmakers, Spelman Col, 70; Cent South Exhib, Parthenon Gallery, Nashville, 75; Amistad II: Afro-American Art Traveling Exhib, Fisk Univ, 75; Tenn Bicentennial Invitational Art Exhib, War Mem Plaza, Nashville, 76; 17th Tenn All-State Artists Exhib, Centennial Park Galleries, Nashville, 77; From These Roots Exhib, Tenn State Mus, Nashville, 77; Smith-Mason Galleries, Washington, DC, 77; one-man exhibs, Ala A&M Univ, Normal, 75, Tenn State Mus, Nashville, 75 & Creatadrama Art Gallery, Bloomington, Ind, 75. Teaching: Instr art, Fla A&M Univ, 65-68; assoc prof art, Tenn State Univ, 68-, actg chmn, Dept of Art, 78. Pos: Touring artist, Tenn Arts Comn, 70-; lyceum comt mem, Tenn State Univ, 74-; bd mem, Tenn Art League, 74-; art consult, Claiborne Ave Design Team Symp, New Orleans, La, 74-; mem, Alex Haley Day in Tenn Comt, Nashville, 77; mem & chmn, Art & Lecture Series Comt, Tenn State Univ, 78. Awards: Tenn State Univ Grant, 70; Third Place Sculpture, Tenn Art League, 74; Lyzon Galleries Award Graphics, Cent South Exhib, 75; Hon Mention, 17th Tenn All-State Artists Exhib, Centennial Park Galleries, Nashville, 77. Bibliog: Clara Hieronymus (auth), Ted Jones Exhibition, Tennessean Newspaper, 75; Kenneth Weedman (auth), article in Sculpture Quarterly, 75. Mem: Tenn Lit Arts Asn; Southern Independent Artists Asn; Southern Asn Sculptors; Southeastern Graphics Coun; Tennessee Art League. Style & Technique: Sculpture woodcarving and casting, the human figure is used as a point of departure. printmaking, Masonite cuts, expressionistic human forms are utilized as visual imagery. Publ: Contribr, Galaxy III Communication Arts Seminar Basic Holography, 74; ed, Faculty exhibition catalogs & brochures, Tenn State Univ, 74-75; auth, Thoughts and Verses (poetry and prints), 75 & Masonite-Printing: A New Approach in Relief Printing, 77, New Dimension Studio, Nashville. Mailing Add: 3872 Augusta Dr Nashville TN 37207

JONES, TOM DOUGLAS
KINETIC ARTIST, LECTURER
b Kansas City, Mo. Study: Kansas City Art Inst; Teachers Col, Columbia Univ; NY Univ; Ecole Beaux-Arts, Fontainebleau, France, dipl, 35; Univ Kans, BFA, 36; Univ Iowa, MA, 43; Bethany Col, hon DFA, 60. Teaching: Asst prof design, Univ Kans, 36-44; res prof, Long Island Univ, 64-71. Pos: Artist & designer, Kansas City Star, Brooklyn Eagle & New York World, 26-34; dir, IBM Gallery Arts & Scis, 52-62. Awards: Nat Acad Sci Grant, 43. Res: Color and light; inventor of Chromaton (color organ) and other devices. Publ: Auth, The Art of Light and Color, Van Nostrand Reinhold, 72. Mailing Add: 411 Lakewood Circle Colorado Springs CO 80910

JONES, W LOUIS
PAINTER, SCULPTOR
b Durham, NC, Feb 22, 43. Study: Pa Acad Fine Art; E Carolina Univ, BS; Cranbrook Acad Art, MFA. Work: Butler Inst Am Art, Youngstown, Ohio; Kalamazoo Inst Art, Mich; NC Mus Art, Raleigh; Mint Mus Art, Charlotte, NC; Flint Inst Art, Mich. Exhib: US Art in Embassies, 67; Butler Inst Am Art, 67; Nat Soc Painters in Casein, Washington, DC, 68; Northwest Artists Ann, Seattle, 68; Nat Realists Exhib, Gallery Contemp Art, Winston-Salem, NC, 71; New Realism, Jacksonville Art Mus, Fla; Photo Realist Painters, traveling show to three states. Teaching: Instr painting, Atlanta Sch Art, Ga, summer 65; instr painting, Univ Idaho, 67-69; asst prof drawing & painting, Skidmore Col, 69-74; asst prof grad painting, Russell Sage Col, Troy, NY, 75-77. Awards: Purchase Awards, NC Mus Art, 63, Butler Inst Am Art, 67 & Mint Mus Art. Mem: Nat Soc Painters in Casein; Am Asn Univ Prof. Style & Technique: Close focus acrylic realism. Media: Acrylic; Wood. Dealer: Arwin Galleries 222 Grand River W Detroit MI 48226; Kornblee Gallery 20 W 57th St New York NY. Mailing Add: 19 Elsmere Ave Delmar NY 12054

JONES, WILLIAM EZELLE
CURATOR, LECTURER
b Los Angeles, Calif, Aug 6, 36. Study: Univ Calif, Berkeley, archit; Univ Calif, Los Angeles, BA(art) & MFA; Univ Bristol, Eng, grad cert. Collections Arranged: Gilbert Collections: Monumental Silver (auth, catalogue) & The Art of Mosaics. Teaching: Lectr decorative arts & archit, Newport Beach Art Mus, Calif, 71-74 & Long Beach Art Mus, Calif, 75. Pos: Cur decorative arts, Los Angeles Co Mus Art, 68-; actg dir, Skirball Mus, Hebrew Union Col, Los Angeles, 71-72. Awards: Fulbright Scholar, 62-63; Nat Endowment Arts Visiting Specialist, 72; Kress Found, 72. Mem: Am Asn Mus; Soc Archit Hist. Mailing Add: Los Angeles Co Mus Art 5905 Wilshire Blvd Los Angeles CA 90036

JONSON, RAYMOND
PAINTER, GALLERY DIRECTOR
b Chariton, Iowa, July 18, 91. Study: Portland Mus Art Sch; Chicago Acad Fine Arts; Chicago Art Inst; Univ NMex, hon LHD, 71. Work: Rose Art Mus, Brandeis Univ; William Rockhill Nelson Gallery Art, Kansas City; Dallas Mus Fine Arts; Cincinnati Art Mus; Jonson Retrospective Collection of 704 Works, Univ NMex. Comn: Mural panels, A Cycle of Science, Univ NMex, 34; murals, Art & Science, East NMex Univ, 36. Exhib: Art Inst Chicago; Minneapolis Inst of Art; Milwaukee Art Ctr; Kansas City Art Inst, Mo; Albright-Knox Art Gallery, Buffalo, NY; Houston Mus Fine Arts; Denver Art Mus; Guggenheim Mus, New York; Los Angeles Co Mus of Art, Los Angeles; Dallas Mus of Fine Arts; Cincinnati Art Mus; Brooklyn Mus, NY; San Francisco Mus of Art; Philadelphia Mus of Art; Teaching: Prof painting, Univ NMex, 34-54. Pos: Dir, Jonson Gallery, Univ NMex, 50- Awards: Laureate, Delta Phi Delta, 46; Hon Fel Sch Am Res, 56. Bibliog: Ben Wolf (auth), Raymond Jonson, New Mex Artists, 52; Ed Garman (auth), The Art of Raymond Jonson, Painter, 76; Nicholai Cikovsky, Jr (auth), The art of Raymond Jonson, Am Art Rev, 76. Style & Technique: Representational moving into abstraction; non-objective. Media: All Media. Mailing Add: 1909 Las Lomas Rd NE Albuquerque NM 87106

JONYNAS, VYTAUTAS K
SCULPTOR, PAINTER
b Alytus, Lithuania, Mar 16, 07. Study: Nat Art Col, Kaunas, Lithuania; Conservatoire Nat Arts et Metiers & Ecole Boulle, Paris. Work: Nat Mus in Lithuania, Latvia, Estonia, Weimar & Hamburg, Ger, Antwerp, Belg; Amsterdam City Mus; Metrop Mus Art, New York; Libr Cong, Washington, DC; Brooklyn Mus Art; and others. Comn: Mosaics in Chapel, Nat Shrine of the Immaculate Conception, Washington, DC; decorator bas-relief sculptures, Chapel of Our Lady of Vilnius, St Peter's Basilica, Rome; sculpture, Brooklyn Col, 72; monument, Sidney, Australia, 73; mosaic murals, City of New York, 74-75; plus others. Exhib: One-man shows, Gallery Zack, Paris, 35, Gallery Ariel, Paris, 49, Weyhe Gallery, New York, 54 & Augustiner Mus, Freiburg, Ger; Am Watercolor Soc Traveling Exhib, 56-58; Am Fedn Arts Traveling Exhib, 58-60; Int Art Gallery, Cleveland, 64; USA Traveling Exhib, SAm; USA Int Traveling Exhib by Xylon, Europe; Kunst Geboide, Mus Tubingen, Ger; plus others. Teaching: Instr drawing, painting & graphic arts, cols & insts in Europe, 35-51; instr, Catan-Rose Inst Fine Arts, 52-57; asst prof, Fordham Univ, 56-73. Awards: Gold Medal, Paris World's Fair, 37; Medal Honor & Purchase Prize, Audubon Artists, 57 & 58; Prize, Print Club of Philadelphia, 58; Best Print of Drawing Award, Springfield Art League, 59; Print & Drawing Prize, Conn Acad Fine Arts, 59; Purchase Prize, Calif Soc Etchers, 61; Winner, Int Stained Glass Window Competition, Wilton, Conn; plus many others. Style & Technique:

Contemporary. Publ: Contribr, illus in Das Kunstwerk, 47, 50 & 57 & Am Artist Mag, 52. Mailing Add: 218-45 Sawyer Ave Queens Village NY 11429

JOOST-GAUGIER, CHRISTIANE L
ART ADMINISTRATOR, ART HISTORIAN
b Ste Maxime, France; US citizen. Study: Radcliffe Col, BA(hon) & MA; Harvard Univ, PhD. Teaching: Asst prof Renaissance art, Tufts Univ, 69-75; prof Renaissance art & head art dept, NMex State Univ, 75- Awards: Fulbright fel, Univ Munich; res grants, NMex State Univ. Res: Venetian drawings; Quattrocento art in Florence and Venice. Publ: Auth of var articles in Gazette des Beaux Arts, Art Bull, Zeitschrift für Kunstgeschichte, Commentari, Antichita Viva & Acta Historiae Artium. Mailing Add: Dept of Art NMex State Univ Las Cruces NM 88003

JORDAN, BARBARA SCHWINN
PAINTER, ILLUSTRATOR
b Glen Ridge, NJ. Study: Parsons Sch Design; Grand Cent Art Sch; Art Students League, with Frank DuMond, Luigi Lucioni & others; Grande Chaumiere & Acad Julian, Paris, France. Work: Holbrook Collection & numerous pvt collections. Exhib: One-man exhibs, Soc Illustrators, Barry Stephens Gallery, Bodley Gallery, New York, 71, CC of AC, 73, & Duquesne Univ, Pa, 73; Ga Mus of Art, Univ of Ga; Nat Acad Design, 55; Royal Acad, London, Eng, 56; Guild Hall, 69. Teaching: Lectr illus & portrait painting, instr illus, Parsons Sch Design, 52-54; adv coun, Art Instr Schs, 56-70. Pos: Founder & chmn art comt, UNICEF, 50-61. Awards: Prizes, Guild Hall & Art Dirs Club. Mem: Cosmopolitan Club, New York; Soc Illustrators. Publ: Auth, The technique of Barbara Schwinn & World of fashion art, Art Instr Schs, 68; contribr, Ladies Home J, Good Housekeeping, Colliers, Cosmopolitan, McCalls, Saturday Eve Post & French, Brit, Belg, Danish & Swed mag & other publ, 40-60. Mailing Add: RFD 550 Mecox Rd Watermill NY 11976

JORDAN, CHRISTINE
PAINTER
b Washington, DC, Dec 10, 40. Study: Art Students League, with Will Barnet & Peter Golfinopoulos. Exhib: Contemporary Reflections, Aldrich Mus, Ridgefield, Conn, 74; New Talent Festival, Gimpel & Weitzenhoffer Gallery, New York, 74; 19 Creative Women, Portland Mus, Maine, 74; two-person show, NJ State Mus, Trenton, 76-77; Old Bergen Art Guild Traveling Exhib, 76-77; two-person show, Soho Ctr for Visual Arts, New York, NY, 77; group show, 74 & one-woman show, 75, Aames Gallery, New York. Awards: Ford Found Scholar. Mem: Art Students League. Style & Technique: Abstractions. Media: Acrylic & Pastel on Canvas. Mailing Add: 489 Broome St New York NY 10013

JORDAN, GEORGE EDWIN
ART CRITIC, ART HISTORIAN
b Ky, Oct 29, 40. Study: Univ Ky; Ringling Sch Art, Sarasota, Fla, BFA; E Tenn State Univ, grad study in painting & art hist. Teaching: Guest instr hist contemp painting, Adult Educ, Tulane Univ, 76- Pos: Cur, Reece Mus, Johnson City, Tenn, 66-69; cur Am art & registrar, New Orleans Mus Art, La, 69-72; art critic, New Orleans Times-Picayune, La, 74-77, ed world of art column, 77- Bibliog: Justine McCarthy (auth), Louisiana Artist 19th Century, WYES-Educ Television, New Orleans, 72-73. Res: Specialist on artists who worked in New Orleans and the southeast, from Europe and American, late 18th, 19th and early 20th century. Publ: Contribr, Kenneth Lindsay, auth, Works of John Vanderlyn, Univ Art Gallery, Binghamton, NY, 70; contribr, Louisiana Paintings 19th Century, The William Groves Collection, Groves Press, 71; contribr, Two Centuries of Black American Art, Los Angeles Co Mus Art & Alfred A Knopf, 76; contribr & co-auth, Louisiana portraits, Colonial Dames of Am in La, 76. Mailing Add: 519 St Ann New Orleans LA 70116

JORDAN, JACK
ART ADMINISTRATOR, SCULPTOR
b July 29, 27; US citizen. Study: Langston Univ, BA; Univ Iowa, MA; Ind Univ, MS; State Univ Iowa, MFA; Okla Univ; Ind Univ, DEd. Work: Ind Univ Mus, Bloomington; State Univ Iowa Mus, Iowa City; Atlanta Univ Art Mus, Ga; Okla Art Ctr, Oklahoma City; Golden State Ins Co, Calif. Comn: Christ (ornamental sculpture), Lutheran Church, New Orleans, 70; Come Ye Children (sculpture), Bethany United Methodist Church, New Orleans, 71; Contrib of Black to La Hist (25 ft mural), Southern Univ New Orleans, comn by State of La, 75; bust of A P Tureau (sculpture), Local Nat Asn Advan Colored People, New Orleans, 77. Exhib: New York Archit League & Nat Sculpture Soc; Joslyn Art Mus, Omaha, Nebr; Nat Competitive Art Show, Walker Art Ctr, Minneapolis, Waterloo Art Gallery, Iowa & El Mira Art Gallery, Pismo Beach, Calif; Nat Art Show, Carnegie Inst Int, Pittsburgh, Pa; one-man shows, Philbrook Art Mus, Tulsa, Okla & Matrix Art Gallery, Bloomington, Ind. Collections Arranged: Emmanicpation Centennial Nat Art Exhib (exec chmn), 63; New Orleans Bicentennial Art Exhib (exec chmn), Bicentennial Comn of New Orleans, 74; Black Family Bicentennial Art Show, 75. Teaching: Head art dept, Claflin Univ, Orangeburg, SC, 49-50, Allen Univ, Columbia, SC, 52-55 & Langston Univ, Okla, 57-61; prof & head art dept, Southern Univ New Orleans, 61- Bibliog: Cedric Dover (auth), American Negro Art, New York Graphic Soc, 60; Kaye Teall (auth), Black History of Oklahoma, Okla Pub Sch Title III, Elem & Sec Educ Act, 71; Judith W Chase (auth), Afro-American Arts & Crafts, Van Nostrand Reinhold, 71. Mem: Okla Art Asn (historian, 59-61); Nat Conf Artists (vpres, 65, pres, 66-67, mem bd dirs); Creatadrama Soc (mem bd dirs). Mailing Add: Southern Univ New Orleans Dept of Art 6400 Press Dr New Orleans LA 70126

JORDAN, JAMES WILLIAM
ART HISTORIAN, PAINTER
b Memphis, Tenn, Nov 27, 40. Study: Univ Tex, BFA(summa cum laude), 63, with George Bogart & C Forsyth; Univ Ill, MFA, 65, MA(art hist), 65, with Peter Bodnar, Lee Chesney & M Franciscono; Harvard Univ, fel, 65-66, with F Deknatel, Michael Fried & James Ackerman. Work: Univ Tex, Austin; Univ Tex, Arlington; Ft Worth Mus Fine Arts; Univ Ill; Dayton Art Inst, Ohio. Exhib: All-Ohio Painting & Graphics, Dayton Art Inst, 67, 70 & 74; Ohio Drawings, Columbus Gallery of Fine Arts, 70, Antioch Arts, Contemp Art Ctr, Cincinnati, Ohio, 72; plus others. Collections Arranged: Robert Whitmore, American Impressionist Retrospective (auth, catalogue), 74 & Sid Chafetz, Thirty Years in Ohio Retrospective 1948-1978 (auth, catalogue), 78, Noyes Gallery Art, Antioch Col, Yellow Springs, Ohio; plus others. Teaching: Assoc prof art hist, painting & drawing, Antioch Col, 66- Pos: Chmn art dept, Antioch Col, 66-; dir, Noyes Gallery Art, 73; vis artist, Univ Southern Calif, Los Angeles, 75; bk rev ed, Antioch Rev, Antioch Col, 78. Mem: Col Art Asn Am; Midwestern Col Art Asn Am; Nat Coun Art Adminr; Am Fedn Arts; Soc Archit Historians. Style & Technique: Expressionist, figurative and non-objective. Media: Oil; Charcoal, Pastel. Res: Nineteenth century French painting and contemporary American art. Publ: Ed, Bibliography of Victoriana, 65 & auth, Edouard Manet's Paintings Prior to 1870, Univ Ill, 68. Mailing Add: Dept of Art Antioch Col Yellow Springs OH 45387

JORDAN, ROBERT
PAINTER, EDUCATOR
b Floral Park, NY, Sept 22, 25. Study: Dartmouth Col, BA; Columbia Univ, MA. Work: Addison Gallery of Am Art, Andover, Mass; Nat Air & Space Mus, Washington, DC; St Louis Art Mus; Boston Pub Libr; Washington Univ Art Gallery, St Louis, Mo. Exhib: Seven Decades, Addison Gallery, 69; The New Landscape, Moore Col Art, Philadelphia, 73; A Sense of Place, Joslyn Mus, Omaha, Nebr, 74; one-man shows, Far Gallery, New York, 74, 76 & 77, Hopper House, Nyack, NY, 77; Am 1976 (traveling exhib), US Dept Interior Bicentennial, 76; Butler Inst Am Art Ann, Youngstown, Ohio, 77. Teaching: Prof painting & Am art hist, Washington Univ, 56- Style & Technique: Landscapes in oil and pastels. Dealer: Far Gallery 746 Madison Ave New York NY 10021. Mailing Add: General Delivery Center Conway NH 03813

JORDAN, WILLIAM B
MUSEUM DIRECTOR, ART HISTORIAN
b Nashville, Tenn, May 8, 40. Study: Washington & Lee Univ, BA, 62; NY Univ, MA, 64, PhD, 67. Teaching: Assoc prof Span art hist, Southern Methodist Univ, 68-75, prof Span art hist, 75- Pos: Chmn div fine arts, Meadows Sch of the Arts, Southern Methodist Univ, 67-73, dir, Meadows Mus, 67- Mem: Asn of Art Mus Dirs; Am Soc of Hispanic Art Hist Studies (pres, 76-78); Hispanic Soc of Am. Publ: Auth, Juan van der Hamen y Leon: a Madrilenian still life painter, Marsyas, 65; auth, Murillo's Jacob laying the peeled rods before the flocks of Laban, Art News, 68; auth, A museum of Spanish painting in Texas, 68 & The Meadows School of the Arts at Southern Methodist University: Progress..., 70, Art J; auth, The Meadows Museum: A Visitor's Guide to the Collection, Meadows Mus, 74; auth, Dallas Collects: Impressionist and Early Modern Masters, Dallas Mus of Fine Arts, 78. Mailing Add: Meadows Mus Southern Methodist Univ Dallas TX 75275

JORGENSEN, FLEMMING
PAINTER
b Aalborg, Denmark, May 29, 34; Can citizen. Study: Art Sch Denmark. Work: Nat Gallery Can, Ottawa, Ont; Can Coun, Ottawa; McGill Univ; Univ Victoria; Winnipeg Art Gallery, Man. Exhib: 2nd Biennial Int Prints, Paris, France, 70; one-man shows, Marlborough-Godard, Montreal, Que, 72, Gallery Allen, Vancouver, 74, Bau-Xi Gallery, Victoria, 75 & Gallery Mira Godard, Toronto, 76; Young Artists 1973, New York, 73. Awards: Can Coun Arts Bursary, 69 & 71. Mem: Royal Can Acad Arts. Dealer: Gallery Mira Godard 22 Hazelton Ave Toronto ON Can. Mailing Add: 1180 Clovelly Terr Victoria BC Can

JORGENSEN, SANDRA
PAINTER, EDUCATOR
b Evanston, Ill, Apr 21, 34. Study: Lake Forest Col, with Franz Schulze, BA, 57; Akademie der Bildenden Kunste, Vienna; Art Inst Chicago, with Paul Wiegardt & Whitney Halstead, MFA, 64. Exhib: Chicago Print Show, Allan Frumkin Gallery, Chicago, 69; Black & White Show, Kovler Gallery, Chicago, 69; New Talent '74, Richard Gray Gallery, Chicago, 74 & Three Painters, 77; Contemp Still Life, Renaissance Soc, Univ Chicago, 74. Teaching: Assoc prof art & art hist, Elmhurst Col, 66-; vis lectr drawing, Art Inst Chicago, 66 & 73, Lake Forest Col, Ill, 73-74 & Univ Ill, Chicago Circle, 73-74. Bibliog: Franz Schulze, Alan Artner & Harold Haydon (auths), articles in Chicago Daily News, 6/69, Chicago Sun Times, 6/69 & Chicago Tribune, 6/74. Style & Technique: Landscape realist, surrealist. Media: Oils on Canvas. Mailing Add: 245 Elm Park Elmhurst IL 60126

JORGENSON, DALE ALFRED
ART ADMINISTRATOR, AESTHETICIAN
b Litchfield, Nebr, Mar 20, 26. Study: Harding Col, Ark, philos with J D Bales, BMus, 48; George Peabody Col, Tenn, MA, 50; Ind Univ, aesthetics with John Mueller, PhD, 57; Harvard Univ, cert arts admin, 72. Teaching: Prof aesthetics, Bethany Col WVa, 59-62; dir fine arts, Milligan Col, Tenn, 62-63; head fine arts div & teacher aesthetics, Northeastern Mo State Univ, 63- Mem: Am Soc Aesthetics; Midwest Col Art Asn. Res: Aesthetics and elementary aesthetics for contemporary students. Publ: Auth, Toward a biblical aesthetic, Christianity Today, 60; auth, The campus and the arts, Proceedings of the Nat Asn Sch Music, 70; auth, Preparing the educator for related arts, Music Educr J, 5/70; auth, The French lieutenant's woman, or to forego manipulation, Christianity Today, 5/11/73. Mailing Add: 1512 S Cottage Grove Kirksville MO 63501

JOSEPH, CLIFF (CLIFFORD RICARDO)
PAINTER, ART THERAPIST
b Panama, CZ, June 23, 22. Study: Pratt Inst, BFA. Exhib: San Francisco Mus Art, 69; Afro-American Artists 1869-1969, Mus Fine Arts, Boston, 70; Blacks, USA, New York Cult Ctr, 73; FESTAC, 2nd World Black & African Festival of Arts & Cult, Lagos, Nigeria, 75; Mus Mod Art, Paris, France, 75. Teaching: Instr psychol of art, 69-70, asst prof group art ther, Pratt Inst, 70- Bibliog: Elsa Honig Fine (auth), The Afro-American Artist, Holt, Rinehart, Winston, 73; Barry Schwartz (auth), The New Humanism: Art in a Time of Change, Praeger, 74; Samella Lewis (auth), Art: African American, Harcourt Brace, 75. Mem: Black Emergency Cult Coalition (co-chmn, 69-); New York Art Ther Asn (mem exec coun, 72-); Comt for the Third World Am Revolution in Art Inc (chmn, 74-); Am Art Ther Asn (ATR, 74-). Style & Technique: Social realist, figurative and semi-abstract brush and knife paintings and pen and ink drawings. Media: Oil. Publ: Contribr, The Urban Reader, Cahill & Cooper, Prentice Hall, 71; contribr, Arts in Society, summer 73 & fall 73; contribr, Freedomways Mag, 73; co-auth, Murals of the Mind, Int Univ Press, New York, 74; contribr, The Attica Book, Artists & Writers in Protest & Black Emergency Cult Coalition, 74. Mailing Add: 463 West St New York NY 10014

JOSIMOVICH, GEORGE
PAINTER, DESIGNER
b Mitrovica, Yugosalvia, May 2, 94; US citizen. Study: Art Inst Chicago, 14-19; also with George Bellows, Randall Davey & Herman Sachs, 19-20. Work: Joslyn Art Mus, Omaha, Nebr. Exhib: One-man show, Galerie d'Art Contemporain, Paris, 27; 28th Int Exhib, Carnegie Inst, Pittsburgh, 29; Selected Paintings by Contemp Am Artists, Toledo Mus Art, 30; nine ann exhibs, Artists of Chicago & Vicinty, Art Inst Chicago, 33-49; Three Rivers Art Festival, Pittsburgh, 68 & 70. Teaching: Supvr craft shop, Dayton Mus Art, 21; instr parents' ceramic class, Pine Grove Pre-Sch, Chicago, 53-55. Pos: Vpres, Chicago Soc Artists, 42-43, pres, 43-44; worked in Paris, 26-27. Awards: Silver Medal, Chicago Soc Artists, 29. Bibliog: J Z Jacobson (auth), The Chicago independent, The Arts, 6/31 & Art of Today, L M Stein, 33; C J Bulliet (auth), Six Chicagoans, Art Digest, 5/50. Media: Oil, Acrylic, Watercolor. Mailing Add: 1800 Walker Ave Union NJ 07083

JOSKOWICZ, ALFREDO
FILM MAKER, ART CRITIC
b Mexico City, Mex, Aug 16, 37. Study: Politech Inst, 55-58; Univ Mex, 66-70; INSAS, Belg, 71-72. Work: Univ Mex. Comn: Crates, El Cambio & Meridiano 100 (35mm color feature films), UNAM, 71-74; doc films (16mm color), Ministry Educ, Govt Mex, 75-76. Exhib: Quinzaine des Realizateurs, Cannes, France, 73; Cinematheque Royal de Belgique, Belg, 73; Mus Mod Art, New York, 74; Venice Film Festival, Italy, 74. Teaching: Acad chief, Univ Ctr Cinematic Studies, Univ Mex, 70-, film makers workshop staff, 72- Pos: Art critic, El Heraldo J, Mexico City, 66-70; dir cinematographics areas, Centro de Capacitación Cinematogràfica, Banco Nac Cinematogràfico & Res, Univ Mex, 77- Awards: First Prize Gold Sea-Horse, Int Cinematic Festival of the Sea, 73. Bibliog: Jorge Ayala Blanco (auth), La busqueda del cine Mexicano, Univ Mex, 74; Louis Marcorelles (auth), Le renouveau Mexicain, Rev Cinema, 11/74. Mem: Int Asn Art Critics. Publ: Ed, Artes Visuales, Mus Mod Art, Mexico City, 75; co-auth, Antonio Pelaez, Pintor, Secy Educ Publ, Mex, 75. Mailing Add: Fuente de Jupiter 48 Mexico 10 DF Mexico

JOSTEN, MRS WERNER E
COLLECTOR
Collection: Contemporary paintings. Mailing Add: 944 Fifth Ave New York NY 10021

JOUKHADAR, MOUMTAZ A N
ART DEALER, PAINTER
b Damas, Syria, Apr 29, 40; US citizen. Study: Accademia di Belle Arti, Rome, Italy, MS, with Mario Mafai & Prof Gottuso; Art Students League, 69-72. Work: Damascus Mus. Exhib: Group Exhib for Foreign Artists, Rome, Italy, 68; Joukhadar Gallery, New York; one-man shows, Nat Mus Damascus, Syria, 64, Nader Art Gallery, New York, 74 & Joukhadar Gallery, 76. Teaching: Prof fine art, Pub Sch Syst, Homs, Syria, 60-62. Pos: Art dir, Adalia Anstalt, Rome, Italy, 64-68, Medical Tribune, New York, 70-73, Media Properties, New York, 73-75 & Physics Today, New York, 75-; owner, Joukhadar Gallery, New York. Awards: Biennial Venezia, Int Exhib, 66; Medal of the City of Rome, Group Exhib for Foreign Artists, Italy, 68. Media: Oil. Res: History of the Islamic architecture in Spain and the Alhambra of Granada. Specialty: Modern and naive art. Mailing Add: c/o Joukhadar Gallery 440 E 85th St New York NY 10028

JOY, NANCY GRAHAME
ILLUSTRATOR, EDUCATOR
b Toronto, Ont, Jan 15, 20. Study: Ont Dept Educ, sr matriculant, 38; Ont Col Art, assoc, dipl & hon grad, 42; Univ Toronto Fac Med, spec study with Dr J C B Grant & Dr William Boyd, 42-44; Univ Ill, spec study med illus & asst to Prof Tom Jones. Exhib: Contrib to permanent exhib human growth & develop, Mus Sci & Indust, 45-48. Teaching: Asst prof, Dept Surgery, Univ Man, 56-62; prof & chmn art appl to med, 62- & dir BSc Art Appl to Med, Univ Toronto, 68- Awards: Hughes Owens Grad Prize, 42; Biocommun '70 Med Educ Film Award & Asn Med TV Broadcasters Second Film Award, 70. Mem: Asn Med Illusr (bd gov, 56-61); Can Asn Med Illusr (bd gov, 71); Acad Med, Toronto. Media: Ink; Watercolor. Publ: Auth, Pictured fact & fancy in current medical literature, Ann of Surg, Vol 156, No 3; auth, Dean's reports, BSc Art Appl to Med, 68-; auth, Medical illustrations & copyright, Med & Biol Illus, 4/64; ed, Medical illustration (cumulative bibliog), Asn Med Illusr, 67; co-auth (with R H Thorlakson & T K Thorlakson), Synchronous abdomino-perineal excision for carcinoma of the rectum, Surgical Techniques Illus, Vol 2, No 1, winter 77. Mailing Add: Dept of Art as Appl to Med Univ of Toronto Toronto ON Can

JOYCE, MARSHALL WOODSIDE
PAINTER, INSTRUCTOR
b Medford, Mass, Mar 12, 12. Study: Sch Practical Art, Boston. Work: Paintings, Plymouth Five Cents Bank, Mass; painting of Mayflower, Plymouth Plantation, Mass. Comn: Painting & carving, Plymouth Home Nat Bank, 65; painting, Plymouth Pub Libr, 67. Exhib: Marine Painting Nat Competition, Franklin Mint, Philadelphia, 74; Rockport Art Asn, Mass, 74; NShore Art Asn, Gloucester; Cape Cod Art Asn. Teaching: Instr design illus, Butera Sch Art, Boston, 61-70; pvt art classes, 70- Pos: Free lance artist & illusr, Boston, 36-60; art dir, Gunnar Myrbeck, Quincy, Mass, 61-64. Awards: Marine Painting Prize, Franklin Mint, 74; Gold Medal of Honor, Rockport Art Asn, 74; Waters of the World Award, NShore Art Asn; Watercolor Awards, Cape Cod Art Asn. Mem: Rockport, NShore, Braintree, Cape Cod & Brockton Art Asns. Style & Technique: Marine, seascapes, ships. Media: Oil, Watercolor. Publ: Illusr, Skipper Mag, 67; illusr calendars, Davis-Standard Co, Pawcatuck, Conn, 56-57. Dealer: Orleans Art Gallery Orleans MA 02653. Mailing Add: 5 River St Kingston MA 02360

JU, I-HSIUNG
PAINTER, EDUCATOR
b Kiangyin, China, Sept 15, 23. Study: Nat Univ Amoy, China, AB(Chinese art), 47; Univ Santo Tomas, Manila, BFA, 55, MA(hist), 68. Work: Philippine Cult Ctr, Manila; Nat Mus Hist, Taipei, Taiwan; Int Ctr, Univ Conn; DuPont Art Gallery, Washington & Lee Univ; F&M Ctr, Richmond, Va; plus others. Comn: 14 paintings, Gulf States Paper Corp Nat Hq, Tuscaloosa, Ala, 70-71; plus many others. Exhib: South-East Asian Art Contest, Manila, 57; Asian Arts Festival, Univ Philippines, Manila, 65; Philippine & Japan Joint Art Exhib, Nat Mus Hist, Taipei, 66; 10th Japan Nan-ga-in Exhib, Tokyo, Kyoto & Osaka Mus, 70; Nat Painting & Calligraph Exhib, Nat Gallery, Taipei, 70 & 74. Teaching: Lectr Chinese arts, Univ Maine, Univ NH, Univ Vt & Univ Conn, 68-69; lectr Chinese arts, Va Mus Fine Arts, Richmond, 69-71; prof art, Univ Va & Washington & Lee Univ, 69- Awards: Nan-ga-in Awards, Japan Nan-so-ga Soc, 66-67; Ring-Tum-Phi Award, Washington & Lee Univ, 71; Art Educator of the Year, Taiwan, 74. Mem: Va Mus Fine Arts; Col Art Asn Am; Nat Mus Philippines (hon curator, 64-). Style & Technique: Chinese brush and tradition Oriental technique. Media: Ink, Acrylic, Watercolor. Publ: Illusr, The Children of Light, 56; auth, About Art, 59; Book of Bamboo, second ed, Book of Orchids & A Collection of Recent Landscape Paintings by Ju, Nat Mus of Hist, Taipei, 76 Mailing Add: Dept of Fine Arts Washington & Lee Univ Lexington VA 24450

JUDD, DE FORREST HALE
PAINTER, EDUCATOR
b Hartsgrove, Ohio, Apr 4, 16. Study: Cleveland Inst Art, grad, 38, post grad scholar, 39; Colorado Springs Fine Arts Ctr, scholar, also with Boardman Robinson, 39-42. Work: Cleveland Mus Art, Ohio; Dallas Mus Fine Arts, Tex; Beaumont Mus Art, Tex; Univ Tex, Austin; Southern Methodist Univ. Exhib: American Painting Today, Metrop Mus Art, 50; Texas Contemporary Artists, Knoedler Gallery, New York, 52; New Accessions, USA, Colorado Springs Fine Arts Ctr, 52; Ten Texas Painters, Frank Perls Gollery, Beverly Hills, Calif, 53; Texas Painting & Sculpture, 20th Century, Southern Methodist Univ, 71. Teaching: Prof painting, Southern Methodist Univ, 46- Awards: First Prize, Cleveland Mus Art, 41; E M Dealey Purchase Award, Tex Painters & Sculptors Exhib, 50; First Prize, 2nd Ann Exhib, Beaumont Mus Art, 53. Style & Technique: Semi abstraction emphasizing color and organization. Media: Oil, Acrylic. Mailing Add: 11039 Tibbs St Dallas TX 75230

JUDD, DONALD CLARENCE
SCULPTOR
b Excelsior Springs, Mo, June 3, 28. Study: Art Students League, 47-53; Columbia Univ, BS(philos), 53, grad study, 58-61. Work: Mus Mod Art, New York; Whitney Mus Art, New York; Walker Art Ctr, Minneapolis, Minn; Los Angeles Co Mus; Albright-Knox Art Gallery, Buffalo. Comn: Art Gallery of SAustralia, 74, Northern Ky Univ, 77, Linz, Austria, 77 & Muenster, WGer, 77. Exhib: One-man shows, Whitney Mus Am Art, 68, Stedelijk Van Abbemuseum, Eindhoven, Holland, 70, Pasadena Art Mus, Calif, 70, one-man retrospective, Nat Gallery Can, Ottawa, 75, Kunst Halle, Bern, 76, Heiner Friedrich Galleries, New York, NY & Cologne, WGer, 77, Mus of STex, Corpus Christi, 77 & Watari Gallery, Tokyo, Japan, 78; New York Painting & Sculpture: 1940-1970, Metrop Mus Art, New York, 69-70. Pos: Contrib ed, Arts Mag, 59-65. Awards: US Govt grants, 67 & 76; Guggenheim grant, 68. Bibliog: William Agee (auth), Don Judd, Whitney Mus Am Art, 68; John Coplans (auth), Don Judd, Pasadena Art Mus, 71. Media: Metal, Wood, Plexiglas. Mailing Add: c/o Leo Castelli Gallery 420 W Broadway New York NY 10013

JUDKINS, SYLVIA
PAINTER
b New York, NY. Study: Pratt Inst; Sch Visual Arts, New York; China Inst, New York; also painting tours with Edgar Whitney & Barse Miller; Nat Acad Fine Arts, scholar, 68-70. Exhib: Am Artists Prof League Grand Nat Exhib, Lever House, New York, 67 & 70; Parrish Mus Ann Exhib, Southampton, NY, 70; Nat Art League Spring Exhib, Adelphi Univ, 71 & 77; Am Watercolor Soc Ann, Nat Acad Design, New York, 73-75; Painters & Sculptors Soc NJ, Nat Arts Club, 75; plus others. Pos: Display artist, 50-60; tech illusr, 60-65. Awards: High Winds Medal, Am Watercolor Soc, 75; Medal of Honor, Painters & Sculptors Soc NJ, 75; First Prize for Watercolor, Manhasset Art Asn, State Univ NY Col, Westbury, 77; plus others. Mem: Am Artists Prof League; Island Art Guild (vpres, prog chmn, 74-75); Jackson Heights Art Club (exhib chmn, 69, publicity chmn, 70 & ed, newsletter, 71-); Am Watercolor Soc; Manhasset Art Asn. Style & Technique: Mysterious overlays of color. Media: Watercolor, Acrylic. Mailing Add: 35-36 76th St Jackson Heights NY 11372

JUDSON, JEANNETTE ALEXANDER
PAINTER
b New York, NY, Feb 23, 12. Study: Nat Acad Design, with Robert Phillip & Leon Kroll; Art Students League, with Vaclav Vytlacil, Charles Alston, Carl Holty & Sidney Gross. Work: Joseph H Hirshhorn Collection; NY Univ Collection; Brandeis Univ; Brooklyn Mus; Columbia Univ, New York, NY; US Embassy, Stockholm, Sweden; Fordham Univ; plus many other pub & pvt collections. Exhib: One-man shows, Bodley Gallery, New York, 67-73, Laura Musser Mus Art, Muscatine, Iowa, 69, Pa State Univ, 69, NY Univ, 69 & Syrasuce Univ House, New York, 75. Awards: Grumbacher Award, Nat Asn Women Artists, 67; D Feigen Mem Award, Am Soc Contemp Artists, 77. Mem: Nat Asn Women Artists (exten comt, 69 & oil jury, 78-79); Am Soc Contemp Artists; NY Soc Women Artists; Artists Equity New York. Style & Technique: Abstract; hard edge geometric; transparent overlaps of color. Media: Oil, Acrylic. Dealer: Bodley Gallery 787 Madison Ave New York NY 10021. Mailing Add: 1130 Park Ave New York NY 10028

JUDSON, SYLVIA SHAW
SCULPTOR
b Chicago, Ill, June 30, 97. Study: Art Inst Chicago, with Albin Polasek; Acad Grande Chaumiere, Paris, with Antoine Bourdelle. Work: Art Inst Chicago; Nat Acad Design, New York; First Lady's Garden, White House, Washington, DC; Brookgreen Gardens, Ga; Kosciaseo Park, Milwaukee. Comn: Mem fountain to Theodore Roosevelt, Brookfield Zoo, 54; Violinist, Norman Ross Mem, Ravinia Park, Chicago, 55; monument to Mary Dyer, State House, Boston, Mass Art Comn, 59; group of granite animals, Fairmount Park Asn, Philadelphia, 65; gate posts & drinking fountain, Morton Arboretum, Lisle, Ill, 70. Exhib: One-man shows, Art Inst Chicago, 38, Arden Gallery, New York, 40 & Sculpture Ctr, New York, 57; Int Sculpture Exhib, Philadelphia Mus; American Shows, Art Inst Chicago, Mus Mod Art, New York & Whitney Mus Am Art, New York. Teaching: Instr sculpture, Am Univ, Cairo, 63. Pos: Pres, Chicago Pub Sch Art Soc, 48-50; vpres women's bd, Art Inst Chicago, 53-54; mem humanities vis comt, Univ Chicago, 62- Awards: Logan Prize, Art Inst Chicago, 29; Purchase Prize, Int Sculpture Show, Philadelphia Mus, 49; Millbrook Garden Club Medal, 57. Bibliog: What is good sculpture, House Beautiful, 57. Mem: Nat Acad Design; fel Nat Sculpture Soc; hon mem Nat Acad Interior Decorators; Art Club Chicago; Cosmopolitan Club, New York. Media: Bronze, Stone. Publ: Auth, The Quiet Eye, 54 & For Gardens & Other Places, 68, Regnery. Mailing Add: 1230 N Green Bay Rd Lake Forest IL 60045

JULES, MERVIN
PAINTER, EDUCATOR
b Baltimore, Md, Mar 21, 12. Study: Baltimore City Col; Md Inst Fine & Appl Arts; Art Students League. Work: Metrop Mus Art, New York; Art Inst Chicago; Mus Fine Arts, Boston; Portland Art Mus; Libr Cong, Washington, DC; plus many other pub & pvt collections. Exhib: Carnegie Inst Int, Pittsburgh; San Francisco World's Fair; Artists for Victory, sent to Eng; Corcoran Gallery Art, Washington, DC; Whitney Mus Am Art; plus many others. Teaching: Fieldston Sch, Mus Mod Art, War Vet Art Ctr & Peoples Art Ctr, New York; Highfield Art Workshop, Falmouth, Mass, summer 50; Univ Wis, 51; George Walter Vincent Smith Art Mus, 53; Univ Mass; Univ Mich, summer 62; vis artist, Smith Col, 45-46, assoc prof, 46-63, prof, 64-69; prof art & chmn dept, City Col New York, 69- Pos: Adv ed, Sch Arts Mag; trustee, Cummington Sch Music & Art & Provincetown Art Asn; gov bd, Inst for Study of Art in Educ. Awards: Asian-African Study Prog Grant to Japan, 67; Alfred Vance Churchill Found Grant, 67; City Col New York Medal, 73; plus others. Publ: Auth, many articles in nat art publ. Mailing Add: Dept of Art City Col of New York New York NY 10031

JULIAN, LAZARO
PAINTER, DESIGNER
b Guadalajara, Mex, Mar 12, 45. Work: Mus del Estado de Jalisco. Exhib: One-man show, Relieve Mecanico, Galeria de Arte Munic, Guadalajara, 71, Constructions, Rhoda Sande Gallery, New York, 76 & 77; Iman New York, Mod Art Mus, Ponce de Leon, PR, 76 & Ctr Inter-Am Relations, New York, 76; Primera Muestra de la Plastica Jalisciense, Guadalajara, 77; Artists 77 Int Exhib, Union Carbide Bldg, New York, 77. Pos: Dir graphic design dept, Departamento de Bellas Artes del Gobierno del Estado de Jalisco, Mex, 72-73. Bibliog: Diana Loercher (auth), Art posing a riddle, Christian Sci Monitor, 3/8/76; Abraham Kein (auth), Conceptual constructions, The Eastsider, New York, 5/26/77; Howard Katzander (auth), Mexican art, Archit Digest, 1/78. Style & Technique: Surrealistic, three-dimensional work,

lights. Media: Acrylic, Cardboard. Mailing Add: c/o Rhoda Sande Gallery 61 E 57th St New York NY 10022

JULIO, PAT T
EDUCATOR, CRAFTSMAN
b Youngstown, Ohio, Mar 1, 23. Study: Wittenberg Col, BFA, with Ralston Thompson; Univ NMex, MA, with Raymond Jonson & Lex Haas; Univ Colo, with Robert Lister; Ohio State Univ, with Edgar Littlefield; Tex Western Col, with Wiltz Harrison. Work: Pvt collections only. Comn: Stained glass windows, Episcopal Good Samaritan Church, Community Church & pvt collections. Exhib: Denver Art Mus, 50 & 63; Pueblo Art Mus, 60; Pueblo Col, 60 & 69; one-man shows, Pueblo Art Mus, 64 & Western State Art Gallery, 69. Teaching: Lectr Indian art, American art and the Kachina Doll; assoc prof art, Western State Col, 56-71, prof, 71- Pos: Ed, Colo Art Educ Asn Bull. Mem: Col Art Asn Am; Western Art Asn; Am Ceramic Soc; Am Crafts Coun; Inst Indian Studies; plus others. Mailing Add: Dept of Art Western State Col Gunnison CO 81230

JUNG, KWAN YEE
PAINTER
b Toysun, China, Nov 25, 32; US citizen. Study: Chinese Univ Hong Kong New Asia Col, BA(painting), 61; San Diego State Univ, postgrad studies, 68. Work: Springville Mus Art, Utah; Utah State Univ Galleries, Logan; IBM Corp, Austin, Tex; Southern Utah State Col, Cedar. Exhib: Calif Nat Watercolor Soc Ann, 72-74; Watercolor USA, 72 & 75; Am Watercolor Soc Ann Exhib, 73-75; Nat Acad Design Ann, 74; one-man show, Univ Hong Kong, 75. Awards: Clare Stout Award, Am Watercolor Soc, 73; First Award, San Diego Watercolor Soc, 73; Nat Watercolor Soc Award, Watercolor West Soc, 75. Mem: Nat Watercolor Soc; Am Watercolor Soc; Watercolor West Transparent Soc; San Diego Watercolor Soc (dir, 70-71). Style & Technique: True escape scene for landscape paintings; bold and wet style for flower and bird paintings. Media: Watercolor. Dealer: Jung's Gallery 1006 Torrey Pines Rd La Jolla CA 92037. Mailing Add: 5468 Bloch St San Diego CA 92122

JUNG, YEE WAH
PAINTER
b Canton, China, Sept 4, 36; US citizen. Study: Chung Man Art Sch, WuHun, China, 56-57; Chinese Univ Hong Kong New Asia Col, 59-62. Comn: The Tours of Confucius (mosaic painting), Facade of Ambassador Hotel, 59 & The Sacred Text (mosaic painting), Facade of Tai Sing Mid Sch, Kowloon, Hong Kong, 65, both with Chiu Fung Poon. Exhib: Calif Nat Watercolor Soc, 73-74; Watercolor USA, 73-75; Nat Acad Design, 74; Butler Inst Am Art, 74; Am Watercolor Soc, 74-75. Awards: First Place, Southern Calif Expo Art, Del Mar, 71; Calif Nat Watercolor Soc Award, Watercolor USA, 73; Watercolor USA Award, Calif Nat Watercolor Soc, 74. Mem: Nat Watercolor Soc; Watercolor West Soc; San Diego Watercolor Soc. Style & Technique: Modern linear abstract painting and decorative figure mural. Media: Oil, Watercolor. Dealer: Jung's Gallery 1006 Torrey Pines Rd La Jolla CA 92037. Mailing Add: 5468 Bloch St San Diego CA 92122

JUNGWIRTH, IRENE GAYAS (I GAYAS JUNGWIRTH)
PAINTER, STAINED GLASS ARTIST
b McKees Rocks, Pa. Study: Cass Tech, Detroit; Marygrove Col, BFA; Wayne State Univ; Mich State Univ; also study abroad. Work: Detroit Inst Arts; Marquette Univ Art Collection; Marygrove Col Art Collection; CSSP Seminary Collection, Ann Arbor. Comn: Station of Cross (with Leonard D Jungwirth), Churches, Detroit, 55-62; crown in gold, topaz & diamonds, St Mary's Church, Detroit, 57-58; crucifixion (with Leonard D Jungwirth), St John's Church, East Lansing, 60; stained glass windows, YMCA-Children's Chapel, Methodist Church, 60-63; mural painting, Dept Hort, Mich State Univ, 67. Exhib: Michigan Artists, Detroit Art Inst, 43-63; Flint Art Inst, 51; Int Ecclesiastical Show, 55-62; Va Biennial; Butler Inst Am Art, Youngstown, Ohio; plus exhibs in Md. Awards: Painting of Child, Detroit Inst Arts, 43, Nocturne with Figure & Peacocks, 57; Whitcomb Prize, Spring Nocturne, Butler Art Inst, 52. Style & Technique: Like Flemish or early Italian figures; handground; glazes; religious; metaphysical; surrealist. Media: Egg Tempera & Oil. Mailing Add: Westwinds Studio 2022 Byrnes Rd Lansing MI 48906

JUSTUS, ROY BRAXTON
CARTOONIST
b Avon, SDak, May 16, 01. Study: Morningside Col, 20-23, hon LLD, 56. Work: Syracuse Univ, NY. Pos: Political cartoonist, Sioux City Tribune, 24-41; ed cartoonist, Sioux City Jour, 41-44; ed cartoonist, Minneapolis Star & Tribune, 44- Awards: Nat Headliner's Club Award, 44; Freedoms Found Awards, 49-56; Christopher Award, 55; plus others. Mem: Asn Am Ed Cartoonists (pres, 58-59). Mailing Add: 17 S First St Minneapolis MN 55401

JUSZCZYK, JAMES JOSEPH
PAINTER
b Chicago, Ill, Jan 30, 43. Study: Univ Ill, 60-62; Cleveland Inst Art, Ford Found grant & BFA, 66; Univ Pa, univ fel, 68, MFA, 69. Work: Chase Manhattan Bank, New York; Art Co Int SA, Geneva, Switz; Harry Abrams Inc, New York; Swiss Bank Corp, New York; Citicorp, New York. Exhib: Theodor Ahrenberg Collection, Kunsthalle, Düsseldorf, 77; Some Attitudes About Painting in the Seventies, Inst of Contemp Art, Univ Pa, Philadelphia, 78; The Geometry of Color, Andre Zarre Gallery, New York, 78; one-man shows, Galleriaforma, Genova, Italy, 74, Rosa Esman Gallery, New York, 74, 75, 77 & 78 & Gimpel & Hanover Galerie, Zurich, Switz, 75-77. Teaching: Instr drawing, Case Western Reserve Univ, 66-67. Pos: Printer's asst, Studio Angelo Savelli, Springtown, Pa, 70-71; preparator, Inst Contemp Art, Univ Pa, 70- Style & Technique: Geometric color abstraction using extensive glazing technique for fine, hand brushed surface, plus various paper techniques. Media: Acrylic on Canvas. Dealer: Rosa Esman Gallery 29 W 57th St New York NY 10019. Mailing Add: 367 Greenwich St New York NY 10013

K

KADAK, ROBERT
PAINTER, EDUCATOR
b New York, NY, Feb 15, 30. Study: Brooklyn Col, BA(cum laude), 52; Yale Univ, MFA(painting), 54. Work: Mus of Mod Art, New York; John D Rockefeller III Collection, New York; John Rewald Collection, New York; Helene Wurlitzer Found, Taos, NMex. Exhib: New Talent, 56 & Recent Acquisitions, 57, Mus of Mod Art, New York; Painting Ann, Whitney Mus of Am Art, New York, 56 & 58; Carnegie Int, Carnegie Mus of Art, Pittsburgh, 67; A New Look at an Ancient Land, NMex Mus of Fine Arts, Santa Fe, 77; plus over 30 one-man shows. Teaching: Instr art, Brooklyn Col, 60-62; asst prof design, Univ Calif, Berkeley, 62-67; assoc prof painting & design, Northern Ill Univ, 68-74; prof design, Univ Mo, Columbia, 74- Awards: Painting grants, MacDowell Colony, 56-68, Inst for Creative Arts, Univ Calif, 65-66 & Wurlitzer Found, Taos, NMex, 69-72 & 76. Bibliog: James Smith Pierce (auth), Robert Kabak's big landscapes, Art Int, 69. Style & Technique: Abstract; landscape motifs; 10 ft x 6 ft is typical size of paintings. Media: Oil on canvas. Mailing Add: 142C Stanley Hall Univ of Mo Columbia MO 65201

KABOTIE, FRED
PAINTER, DESIGNER
b Shongopavy Village, Second Mesa, Ariz, Feb 20, 1900. Study: Alfred Univ, New York. Comn: Hopi Indian legendary designs, Fred Harvey Co, Watch Tower, Grand Canyon, Ariz, 34; Hopi Social Dances, Fred Harvey Co, Painted Desert Inn, Ariz, 39; Reproduction of Pre-Columbian Kiva Murals, Indian Arts & Crafts Bd, Washington, DC, 40; Indian & Tourists, Fred Harvey Co, Bright Lodge, Grand Canyon, 56. Exhib: San Francisco World's Fair, 39; Mus Mod Art, New York, 40; Ariz State Fair in Fine Art, Phoenix, 49; Chicago Art Inst, 49; Inter-Tribal Indian Ceremonial, Gallup, NMex. 50. Teaching: Teacher fine art, graphic art, silversmithing, High Sch, Oraibi, Ariz, 37-59; teacher silversmithing & art, Univ Southern Calif, 75. Pos: Mgr, Hopi Arts & Crafts, Silver Coop Guild, Second Mesa, 37-59; arts & crafts specialist, Under Indian Arts & Crafts Bd, Washington, DC, 60-71; pres, Hopi Cult Ctr, Second Mesa, 71- Awards: Medallion Achievement Award, Indian Coun Fire, Chicago, 49; Medallion & Cert Republique Francaise, Ministere de l'Educ Nat, 59; Medallion & Cert, Univ Ariz, 61; Cert Appreciation, Univ Southern Calif, 76. Mem: Assoc of Sci & Art Asn, Mus Northern Ariz; Assoc Inter-Tribal Indian Ceremonial; Louis Comfort Tiffany Found (trustee); Indian Arts & Crafts Asn (bd dir). Style & Technique: True life style and abstract; self expression, painting from nature; reviving of old pre-historic designs and murals paintings; using old designs on Hopi jewelry. Media: Earth Color & Oil; Acrylic. Publ: Auth, Designs with my Interpretations from Mimbrennos; illusr, many books of the Southwest Indians. Mailing Add: PO Box 37 Second Mesa AZ 86043

KACERE, JOHN C
PAINTER
b Walker, Iowa, June 23, 20. Study: Mizen Acad of Art, Chicago, Ill, 38-42; State Univ of Iowa, Ames, 46-51, BFA, 49 & MFA, 51. Work: Stedelijk Mus, Amsterdam; Wadsworth Atheneum, Hartford, Conn; Mt Holyoke Col, Mass; Yale Univ, New Haven, Conn; Brandeis Univ, Waltham, Mass. Exhib: Walker Art Ctr (traveling), Minneapolis, Minn, 49; Corcoran Gallery, Washington, DC, 63; Radical Realism, Mus of Contemp Art, Chicago, 71; The Realist Revival, Mus of Mod Art, New York, 72; Relativierend Realismus, Stedelijk van Abbemuseum, Eindhoven, Holland, 72; Amerikanisher Fotorealismus, Kunstverein, Wurttemberg, Ger, Frankfurt & Wuppertal, 72; Super-realist Vision, DeCordova Mus, Lincoln, Mass, 73; Hyperrealistes Americaans Fotorealisme, Grafick, Hendendaagse Kunst, Utrecht & Palais van Schone Kunst, Brussels, Belg. Art Inst of Chicago; one-man shows, Univ of Fla, Gainesville, 53 & 57, La State Univ, Baton Rouge, 57, Allan Stone Gallery, New York, 63 & Harris Gallery, New York, 73. Teaching: Grad asst instr, State Univ of Iowa, 49-50; instr, Univ Manitoba, 50-53 & Univ Fla, Gainesville, 53- Bibliog: I Narp (auth), Rent is the only Reality or the Hotel instead of the Hymn, Arts, New York, 12/71; P Sager (auth), Relativierend Realismus, Kunstwerk (Baden-Baden), 3/72; Linda Chase (auth), Les Hyperralistes Americanins (catalogue), Paris, 73. Style & Technique: Photorealist painter. Publ: Auth, The End is Art, Oui, Paris, 5/74. . Mailing Add: c/o Allan Stone Gallery 48 E 86 St New York NY 10028

KACHADOORIAN, ZUBEL
PAINTER, EDUCATOR
b Detroit, Mich, Feb 7, 24. Study: Meinzinger Art Sch Detroit, 43-44; Saugatuck Summer Art Sch, Mich, 44-45; Skowhegan Sch Painting & Sculpture, Maine, 46; Colorado Springs Fine Arts Ctr, summer 47. Work: Detroit Inst Art; Art Inst Chicago; Worcester Mus, Mass; Smithsonian Inst, Washington, DC; William Rockhill Nelson Gallery, Kansas City. Comn: Gold leaf & oil altar painting, St John's Amenian Church Greater Detroit, 67. Exhib: Univ Ill, Urbana, 61; Am Ann, Art Inst Chicago, 61; Art USA Now, Johnson Wax Collection, 62; Butler Inst Am Art Ann, Youngstown, Ohio, 64; Ball State Univ, 73 & 74. Teaching: Artist in residence, Sch Art Inst Chicago, 60-61; instr painting & drawing, Skowhegan Sch Painting & Sculpture, summer 64; prof drawing, Wayne State Univ, 67-73. Pos: Adv, Common Grounds Detroit, 65-66; art dir, Detroit Repertory Theatre, 70-76. Awards: Pepsi-Cola Midwest Fel, 46; Prix-de-Rome, Am Acad Rome, 56-59; Richard & Hinda Rosenthal Award, Nat Inst Arts & Lett, 61. Bibliog: A S Weller (auth), Art USA Now, C J Bucher, 62. Mem: Fel Am Acad Rome. Style & Technique: Under and over painting; high keyed palette. Media: Oil, Charcoal. Mailing Add: 1214 Beaubien Detroit MI 48226 Detroit MI 48226

KACHEL, HAROLD STANLEY
MUSEUM DIRECTOR, EDUCATOR
b Elmwood, Okla, Jan 25, 28. Study: Panhandle State Univ, Goodwell, Okla, BS; Okla State Univ, Stillwater, MS; Univ Northern Colo, EdD. Collections Arranged: Arrangement & cataloging of a minimum of nine exhibs annually. Teaching: Instr crafts, Yarbrough Sch, Eva, Okla, 52-57; prof copper tooling & head, Indust Arts Dept, Panhandle State Univ, Goodwell, Okla, 57- Pos: Asst cur, No Man's Land Hist Mus, Goodwell, Okla, 66-68, cur & mus dir, 68- Awards: Distinguished Serv Award, Area Artists Studio, Amarillo, Tex, 76; Teacher of Yr at Panhandle State Univ, Okla Educ Asn, 76. Bibliog: Lee Tucker (auth), A Salute to No Man's Land Hist Mus, Old Timer's News, Keyes, Okla, 6/76. Mailing Add: PO Box 307 Goodwell OK 73939

KAEP, LOUIS JOSEPH
PAINTER
b Dubuque, Iowa, Mar 19, 03. Study: Loras Col; Art Inst Chicago; Julian Acad, Paris. Work: Loras Col; City of Chicago; Kalamazoo Inst Arts; Soc New York Hosps; Am Acad Arts & Lett, New York. Exhib: Royal Watercolor Soc, London, 62; 200 Years of Watercolor Painting in America, Metrop Mus, New York, 66; Am Watercolor Soc 100th Ann, New York, 67; 50 Am Watercolor Soc Watercolors, Mus Aquarelle, Mexico City, Mex, 68; Nat Acad Design 147th Ann, New York, 72. Teaching: Instr painting, Art Inst Chicago, 24-26; instr watercolors, Chicago Acad Fine Arts, 36-42. Pos: Vpres, Vogue Wright Studios, New York, 52-56, pres, 56-65; pres, Electrographic Corp, New York, 65-71, vchmn, 71- Awards: Olsen Award for Sampans & Junks, Hong Kong, Am Watercolor Soc 95th Ann, 62; Assoc Mem Award for the Old Quarry, Allied Artists Am, 69; Gold Medal for Fiesta, Toledo, Spain, Hudson Valley Art Asn, 70. Bibliog: Developing Paintings From Sketches (film), 71. Mem: Am Watercolor Soc (first vpres, 62); Salmagundi Club (bd dirs, 65); Artists & Writers Asn; Nat Acad Design; Allied Artists Am. Media: Watercolor. Publ: Contribr, Fairfield watercolor group, Am Artists Mag, 7/72. Mailing Add: 14 Anderson Rd Greenwich CT 06803

KAERICHER, JOHN CONRAD
PRINTMAKER, EDUCATOR
b Springfield, Ill, June 6, 36. Study: Millikin Univ with David Driesbach, BFA, 59; Univ Iowa, with Mauricio Lasansky, Stuart Edie, James Lechay & Robert Knipschild, MFA, 63. Work: Univ Iowa; Millikin Univ; Dordt Col; Northwestern Col Iowa; Bethesda Midwest Clin, Orange City, Iowa; plus pvt collections. Comn: Medal, Northwestern Col, 66. Exhib: Cent Ill Ann, Decatur Art Ctr, 61-; Gov Off, State Capitol, Des Moines, Iowa, 71; Paper Works, 9th Ann, Waterloo Munic Gallery, 73; Kottler Galleries, New York, 73; Va Polytech Inst Ann, 74; Benjamin Galleries, Chicago, 76. Teaching: Assoc prof printmaking & drawing & chmn art dept, Northwestern Col Iowa, 63- Pos: Gallery dir, Northwestern Col, 63-, chmn fine arts coun, 68- Awards: Creative Prod Grants, Northwestern Col Iowa, 66, 68, 75 & 77. Bibliog: Rev of NY exhib in Park East Periodical, 10/25/73. Mem: Mid-Am Col Art Asn; Cols Mid-Am Art Fac Group; Iowa Print Group. Style & Technique: Personal fantasy, figurative. Media: Intaglio Prints; Drawing. Mailing Add: 615 Arizona SW Orange City IA 51041

KAGY, SHEFFIELD HAROLD
PAINTER, SCULPTOR
b Cleveland, Ohio, Oct 22, 07. Study: Cleveland Sch Art; John Huntington Sch Art; Corcoran Sch Art; also with Oley Nordmark, Robert Laurant & Ernest Fiene. Work: Cleveland Mus Art. Comn: Agriculture & Industry, Walterboro Post Off, SC, Sect Fine Arts, Treas Dept & Luray 1840, Luray, Va Post Off, 40. Exhib: Int Watercolor Exhib, Art Inst Chicago, 34; Int Painting Competition, Greenbriar Hotel, WVa, 36; Libr of Cong Pennell Show, 43; Venice Bicentennial, 44; US State Dept, 66. Teaching: Prof fine arts & printmaking, Abbott Art Sch, 36-37; head art dept, Chevy Chase Jr Col, 40-43; prof fine arts, Nat Art Sch, 46-56. Pos: Exhib officer & designer, Agency Int Develop, US State Dept, 59-73. Mem: Artists Guild Washington (vpres, 44); Soc Washington Artists (pres, 49-51); Landscape Club Washington (pres, 52-54); Washington Watercolor Asn; Arts Club Washington (exhibs chmn, 74-75, mem admis comt, 75-). Style & Technique: Realistic with abstract undertones. Media: Oil, Watercolor; Metal, Wood, Lithostone. Mailing Add: 5515 Carolina Pl NW Washington DC 20016

KAHAN, ALEXANDER
ART DEALER
Study: State Univ NY. Pos: Owner, Alexander Kahan Fine Arts Ltd, New York. Mem: Appraisers Asn Am. Specialty: Paintings and graphics of 19th and 20th century. Collection: Appel, Matta, Dubuffet, De Chirico, Riopelle Bombois, Calder, Dufy, Arp, Francis, Chagall and Picasso. Mailing Add: 25 E 73rd St New York NY 10021

KAHANE, ANNE
SCULPTOR
b Vienna, Austria, Mar 1, 24; Can citizen. Study: Cooper Union Art Sch, 45-47. Work: Nat Gallery Can, Ottawa; Montreal Mus Fine Arts, PQ; Winnipeg Art Gallery, Man; Art Gallery Hamilton, Ont; Vancouver Art Gallery, BC. Comn: Interior sculpture (mahogany), Winnipeg Int Airport, Man, 63; interior sculpture (mahogany), Place de Arts, Montreal, 65; exterior sculpture (mahogany), Expo 67, Montreal, 67; interior mural (pine), Can Chancery, Islamabad, Pakistan, 72; interior sculpture (pine), Great Lakes Forest Res Ctr, Sault Ste Marie, Ont, 75; plus others. Exhib: Can Pavilion, Brussels Worlds Fair & Venice Biennial, Italy, 58; Pittsburgh Int, Carnegie Inst, 59; 30 Years of Canadian Art, Nat Gallery Can, 67; Sculpture 67, Toronto, 67. Awards: Award for Unknown Political Prisoner, Eng, 53; Grand Prix for Sculpture, Concours, Que, 56; Can Coun sr arts grant, 77. Bibliog: Charles Spencer (auth), Anne Kahane, The Studio, Vol 160, No 807; Dorothy Cameron (auth), People in the park, Art & Artists, Vol 4, No 8; Alma de Chantal (auth), Anne Kahane: marees de pin, Vie des Arts 69, winter 72-73; plus others. Style & Technique: Lamination and carving. Media: Wood and Metal. Dealer: Merton Gallery 68 Merton St Toronto ON Can. Mailing Add: 3794 Hampton Ave Montreal PQ H4A 2K8 Can

KAHANE, MELANIE (MELANIE KAHANE GRAUER)
DESIGNER
b New York, NY, Nov 26, 10. Study: Parsons Sch Design, grad, 31; Paris, 32. Comn: Designer, Reid Hall, Paris, 48, Children's Mus, Ft Worth, Tex, 55, Gov Shriver's Mansion, Austin, Tex, 57, Playbill Restaurant, New York, 58 & Ziegfield Theatre, New York, 63; plus others. Teaching: Lectr, Parsons Sch Design, 50- Pos: Illusr, Tobias Green Advert Co, 31-32; designer, Lord & Taylor, 33-34; founder & pres, Melanie Kahane, Inc, 35-52; founder & pres, Melanie Kahane Assocs, Interior & Indust Design, 52-; designer, Charles of Ritz Beauty Salons throughout US, 57-; dir styling & design, Sprague & Carleton Furniture Co, 62- Awards: Decorator of the Year Award, 53; Career Key Award, Girls' Clubs Am, 61; one of 100 Am Women of Accomplishment, Harper's Bazaar, 67; plus others. Mem: Fel Am Inst Interior Designers (past nat secy, bd dirs, past pres, NY Chap, nat treas, 71-75); Munic Art Soc; Decorator's Club New York; Inter-Soc Color Coun; Inst Practising Designers, Eng; plus others. Publ: Producer, Decorating, a Way of Life (doc film), 49; auth, There's a Decorator in Your Doll House, 68; also contribr to bks & encycl. Mailing Add: 29 E 63rd St New York NY 10022

KAHLENBERG, MARY HUNT
ART HISTORIAN, CURATOR
b Wallingford, Conn, Oct 19, 40. Study: Simmons Col, Boston, 58-60; Scand Sem, 60-61; Boston Univ, 61-62, BA(art hist), 62; Austrian Acad Applied Arts, 62-63; Berlin Acad Fine Arts, Ger, 63-64; Master Sch & Craft, Berlin, 64-65; Art Inst Chicago, scholar, 65-66. Collections Arranged: The Smart Set (with catalog), 69, Huene and the Fashionable Image, 70, Patterns in Fashion (with catalog), 70, Japanese Textiles of the Edo Period (with catalog), 70, From the Bosporus to Samarkand, 70, Ornamental Costumes from the John Wise Collection of Peruvian Textiles (with catalog), 71, Tapestry, Tradition and Technique (with catalog), 71, Body Shells and Shadows (with catalog), 72, Abstract Design in American Quilts, 72, If the Crinoline Comes Back (with catalog), 73, Anatomy in Fabric (with catalog), 73, Fabric and Fashion (with catalog), 74, The Tapestries of Helena Hernmarck (with catalog), 74 & The Grand Tour, 75, Textile & Costume Galleries, Los Angeles Co Mus Art; Eighteenth Century English and French Costumes, Huntington Galleries, Pasadena, Calif, 71; The Navajo Blanket (with catalog), Los Angeles Co Mus Art circulating exhib, 72-76; L A Flash, Mus Contemp Crafts, New York, Philadelphia Mus Art, Univ Kans Mus Art & Fashion Group, Chicago, 73. Pos: Instr textile design, Univ Tenn, 65; conservationist, Karen Finch Lab, London, 66-67; asst cur, Textile Mus, Washington, DC, 67-68; vis prof hist textiles, Univ Calif, Los Angeles, 75; cur, Los Angeles Co Mus Art, 68- Awards: Prof Travel Grant & Grant for Mus Storage Facil, Nat Endowment for the Arts, 74. Mem: Costume Soc Am (bd); Pacific 21 Coun (bd); World Folk Art Mus & Slide Collection (bd); Am Mus Asn (bd & Western Regional rep); Southern Calif Int Folk Art Mus (bd & consult). Res: Islamic textiles; fabrics from West Malaysia & Indonesia; folk textiles on the Island of Kushya, Japan; European textiles. Publ: Auth, A 17th century Indian figurative velvet, Burlington Mag, 12/73; auth, An Indian floral velvet, Los Angeles Co Mus Art Bull, 73; auth, Islamic textiles, Apollo Mag, 8/75; auth, Navajo Blanket, New York Graphic Soc; plus others. Mailing Add: Los Angeles Co Mus Art 5905 Wilshire Blvd Los Angeles CA 90036

KAHN, A MICHAEL
PAINTER, DESIGNER
b Russia, July 4, 17; US citizen. Study: Pratt Inst, Brooklyn, MFA; Art Students League, cert; Univ Mex, dipl; Univ Lima Bellas Artes, dipl; also with Robert Brackman, Ogden Pleisner, Chaves Morado; fresco with Mexico's foremost painters. Work: Judah L Magnes Mus, Berkeley, Calif; Los Angeles Mus; Matson Navig Co Collection, San Francisco; Peruvian Cult Ctr, Lima; Pomeroy Collection; also in pvt collections around the world. Comn: Graphics for Europe & Far East, Off of Surgeon Gen, USA, Pentagon, Washington, DC. Exhib: One-man shows, US Info Serv Cult Ctr, sponsored by US Info Serv, Lima, Peru, 51 & On Israel, Pomeroy Gallery, San Francisco, 68; Exhib, Judah L Magnes Mus, Berkeley, 57 & Art of Israel, 70; US Info Serv Hellenic Am Exhib, Athens, Greece. Bibliog: E M Polley (auth), Sacred Cows, Art & Artist Mag, San Francisco, 69; Alexander Fried (auth), A Michael Kahn, Lively Arts-San Francisco Examr, 70; Allen Gadol (auth), A Michael Kahn, Directions in Art, Miami, 72. Mem: Am Artists Group, New York; Artists Club of San Francisco; Art Dirs Club of San Francisco. Style & Technique: Allegorical, Surrealistic, easel painting; also murals. Media: Oil, Acrylic & Tempera. Mailing Add: 1030 Venetian Way Miami FL 33139

KAHN, ANNELIES RUTH
CERAMIST, INSTRUCTOR
b Dresden, Ger, Aug 17, 27; US citizen. Study: RI Sch Design, BFA; Tex Woman's Univ, MA. Exhib: 7th Int Exhib Ceramic Art, Smithsonian Inst, Washington, DC, 58; Ann Area Competition, Corcoran Gallery, Washington, DC, 59; 22nd Ceramic Nat Traveling Show, Everson Mus, Syracuse, 62 & 68; Am Craftsmen's Coun Exhib, Oakland, Calif, 63; Form and Quality, Int Exhib, Munich, Ger, 64-69. Teaching: Instr ceramics, Md Art Inst, Baltimore, 57-59; instr ceramics, Southern Methodist Univ, 64-69; instr ceramics & sculpture, Mountain View Col, Tex, 70-74. Pos: Designer & glaze analyst, Calif Art Tile Co, Richmond, 51-52; asst to dir, Gump's Gallery, San Francisco, 52-53; asst to dir, Fine Art Gallery, Dallas, 64-66. Awards: Craft Horizons Award, Smithsonian Inst, 58; First Prize, Corcoran Gallery, 59; 16th Tex Crafts Exhib Top Award, Dallas Mus Fine Arts, 74; plus others. Bibliog: Creation in Clay, KERA TV, 68. Mem: Tex Designer Craftsmen (secy, 71, vpres, 74-75); Dallas Craft Guild; World Crafts Coun; Am Craftsmen Coun. Style & Technique: Large slab built sculptural ceramic pieces, welded metal sculpture, cast bronzes and cast polyester resin works; abstract. Dealer: Contemporary Gallery 2800 Routh St Dallas TX 75201. Mailing Add: 10808 Snow White Dr Dallas TX 75229

KAHN, PETER
PAINTER, DESIGNER
b Leipzig, Ger, July 5, 21; US citizen. Study: With Hans Hofmann, 47-49; NY Univ, BS & MA. Work: Utica Mus; Va Mus; White Mus; Cornell Univ; Univ Notre Dame Gallery. Exhib: Art USA 1954, Va Mus, 54; Artists of Central New York, Utica, 59-61; New Graphic Art Traveling Show, Holland, 65; Natural Vision, Columbia Univ, 68; Retrospective, Hobart Col. Teaching: Asst prof graphic design, La State Univ, Baton Rouge, 51-53; assoc prof graphic design & chmn dept, Hampton Inst, Va, 53-57; prof graphics & paintings, Cornell Univ, 57-68, lectr art hist, 69-72, prof art hist, 72- Awards: Gov Award, Va Mus, 56; First Prize for Graphics, Binghamton Mus, 58; First Prize, Utica Mus, 59 & 60. Media: Graphics. Mailing Add: Dept of Art Hist Cornell Univ Ithaca NY 14853

KAHN, RALPH H
ART DEALER, LECTURER
b Trier, Ger, Aug 17, 20; US citizen. Study: Spec study with W Baumeister. Collections Arranged: Ten exhibs annually, Contemp Gallery, 65- Teaching: Guest lectr 20th century art, art collecting & art processes, for mus, cols & pvt art groups. Pos: Dir, Contemp Gallery, Dallas, 65- Bibliog: American Printmaking in the '70's, Oklahoma City TV. Mem: Terra Linda Art Asn (asst dir, 63); Tex Fine Arts Asn (pres, 72 & 75); Am Soc Appraisers; Assoc Art Gallery Dir, Dallas. Res: W Baumeister and other 20th century contemporary artists. Specialty: Twentieth century contemporary paintings, prints and sculpture. Collection: Baumeister, Braque, Chagall, Klee, Miro & Picasso. Mailing Add: Contemporary Gallery 2425 Cedar Springs Dallas TX 75201

KAHN, SUSAN B
PAINTER
b New York, NY, Aug 26, 24. Study: Parsons Sch Design; also with Moses Soyer. Work: New York Cult Ctr; Montclair Mus, NJ; Butler Inst Am Art, Youngstown, Ohio; Reading Mus, Pa; Joslyn Art Mus, Omaha. Exhib: Audubon Artists, New York, 69; one-person shows, Sagittarius Gallery, New York, 60, ACA Galleries, New York, 64, 68, 71 & 76, Charles B Goddard Art Ctr, Ardmore, Okla, 73, Albrecht Art Mus, St Joseph, Mo, 74 & New York Cult Ctr, 74; Nat Acad Design, 70; Butler Inst Am Art, 73; Albrecht Gallery Mus, St Joseph Mo, 74; New York Cult Ctr, 74; plus others. Awards: Knickerbocker Artists Medal of Honor, 64; Nat Arts Club Award, 67; Famous Artists Sch Award, Nat Asn Women Artists, 67. Bibliog: Marshall Matusow (auth), Art Collectors Almanac, Jerome E Treisman, 65. Mem: Artists Equity Asn; Nat Asn Women Artists; Knickerbocker Artists. Style & Technique: Humanist. Media: Oil. Publ: Contribr, How to Paint a Prize Winner, 65. Dealer: ACA Gallery 25 E 73rd St New York NY 10021. Mailing Add: 870 United Nations Plaza New York NY 10017

KAHN, WOLF
PAINTER
b Stuttgart, Ger, Oct 4, 27. Study: New Sch Social Res, with Stuart Davis; Hans Hofmann Sch; Univ Chicago, BA. Work: Whitney Mus Am Art, New York; Mus Mod Art, New York; Brooklyn Mus; Houston Mus Fine Arts; City Art Mus, St Louis, Mo. Exhib: Ann, Whitney Mus Am Art, 58 & 59, Young America, 61; Univ Ill Biennial, 58-60; Americans in Europe 11E, circulated by Am Fedn Arts, 71-72; New England Art, Inst Contemp Art, Boston, 72; Bloedel Bequest, Whitney Mus Am Art, 77. Teaching: Vis assoc prof painting, Univ Calif, Berkeley, 60-61; adj assoc prof painting, Cooper Union Art Sch, 60-77. Awards: Purchase Award, Ford Found, 63; Fulbright Scholar to Italy, 63-65; Guggenheim Fel, 66. Bibliog: L Campbell (auth), In the mist of life, Art News, 2/69; Gussow (auth), Sense of place, Friends of the Earth, 72; D Cochrane (auth), Updating landscape painting, Am Artist, 11/74; M Sawin (auth), W Kahn's Landscape Paintings, Arts Mag, 4/77. Style & Technique: Impressionist; landscapist. Media: Oil, Pastel. Publ: Auth, Uses of painting today, Daedalus Mag, 69. Dealer: Grace Borgenicht 1018 Madison Ave New York NY 10021; Harkus Krakow Gallery 7 Newbury Boston MA 02116. Mailing Add: 813 Broadway New York NY 10003

KAINEN, JACOB
PAINTER, PRINTMAKER
b Waterbury, Conn, Dec 7, 09. Study: Art Students League, with Nicolaides; NY Univ Eve Sch Archit; Pratt Inst, grad. Work: Mus Mod Art, New York; Art Inst Chicago; Phillips Collection, Washington, DC; Corcoran Gallery Art, Washington, DC; Carnegie Inst, Pittsburgh; Hirshhorn Mus & Sculpture Garden, Washington, DC; Nat Collection of Fine Arts, Washington, DC; Whitney Mus of Am Art; Brooklyn Mus of Art; Metrop Mus of Art; Yale Univ Mus of Art; Nat Gallery of Art; Kunsthalle, Hamburg, WGer; plus numerous others. Exhib: Painting Retrospective, Cath Univ Am, 52; Corcoran Gallery Art Painting Biennial, 57; Phillips Collection, Washington, DC, 73; Three Contemp Printmakers, Nat Collection of Fine Arts, 73; Prints, a Retrospective, Nat Collection of Fine Arts, Baltimore Mus of Art, Univ of Pittsburgh & Univ of Ore, 76-78; one-man shows, Roko Gallery, New York, 64-66, Pratt Manhattan Ctr, New York, 72, Lunn Gallery, Washington, DC, 76-78 & Print Retrospective 1938-1978, Assoc Am Artists, New York, NY, 78. Media: Oil. Mailing Add: 27 W Irving St Chevy Chase MD 20015

KAISER, CHARLES JAMES
PAINTER
b Milwaukee, Wis, Mar 10, 39. Study: Layton Sch Art, Milwaukee; Univ Wis-Milwaukee, BFA, MS & MFA, painting with John Colt & Robert Burkert. Work: Wustum Mus, Racine, Wis; Union Art Gallery, Univ Wis-Milwaukee; Civic Art Collection, Munic Bldg, Springfield, Ill; Marquette Univ, Milwaukee. Exhib: Five shows, Watercolor USA, Springfield, Mo, 62-72; Northwest Miss Valley Artists Invitational, Ill State Mus, Springfield, 66; Calif Nat Watercolor Soc, Laguna Beach, 70 & 72-73; Exhib Contemp Am Painting, Palm Beach, Fla, 70; Chicago & Vicinity, Chicago Art Inst, 71; Wis Directions, Milwaukee Art Ctr, 75. Awards: Calif Nat Watercolor Soc Purchase Award, Butrijamp Found, 70; Madison Salon Graphic Art Drawings & Prints Award, Wis State J & others, 70; Wis Watercolor Soc Award for Excellence, 71. Mem: Calif Nat Watercolor Soc (Wis hon rep, 70-); Wis Watercolor Soc. Style & Technique: Watercolors, surreal juxtapositions of images in high key pencil renderings and subtly tinted washes; Oils: surreal images subdued by soft blends of color on highly refined surfaces. Media: Oil, Watercolor. Dealer: Bradley Galleries 2565 N Downer Ave Milwaukee WI 53211. Mailing Add: 5028 N Diversey Blvd Milwaukee WI 53217

KAISER, DIANE
SCULPTOR, EDUCATOR
b Brooklyn, NY, May 27, 46. Study: Brandeis Univ, BA; Columbia Univ, MFA; additional study with Peter Grippe & Sahl Swarz. Exhib: Rose Art Mus, Waltham, Mass, 74; Contemp Reflections, Aldrich Mus of Contemp Art, Ridgefield, Conn, 75; Meadow Brook Art Gallery, Rochester, Mich, 75; one-person shows, Women Artists Series: Yr 5, Douglass Col, New Brunswick, NJ, 75, Soho 20 Gallery, New York, 77 & 78; Artists Space, New York, 75; Flint Inst of Art, Mich, 76; This Doesn't Look Like a Work of Art, Parsons-Truman Gallery, New York, 76; New Talent, Parsons-Dreyfuss Gallery, New York, 77. Collections Arranged: Drawings & Prints, Independent Exhib Prog, Comt for the Visual Arts, Inc, New York, 77. Teaching: Chmn & instr art dept, Chapin Sch, New York, 70-; vis artist, Dwight-Englewood Sch, NJ, 76. Awards: MacDowell Colony Fel, 73. Mem: Found for the Community of Artists. Style & Technique: Abstract sculpture and drawing. Media: Ceramic sculpture, ink wash drawing. Dealer: Soho 20 Gallery 99 Spring St New York NY 10012. Mailing Add: 225 W 106th St New York NY 10025

KAISER, VITUS J
PAINTER
b Erie, Pa, May 3, 29. Study: NC State Col; Veterans Sch, Erie, with Joseph Plavcan; Univ Pittsburgh. Work: Erie Pub Libr. Exhib: Nat Watercolor Competition, Galerie 8, Erie, 69; Chautauqua Nat Juried Show, NY, 69; Am Drawing Biennial, Norfolk Mus, Va, 71; Albright-Knox Art Gallery, Mem Gallery, Buffalo, 72; Butler Inst Am Art, 73. Teaching: Instr art, Tech Mem High Sch, 70- Mem: Erie Art Ctr (adv bd, 70); Chautauqua Art Asn. Style & Technique: Realism. Media: Acrylic, Oil, Watercolor. Mailing Add: 551 W 26th St Erie PA 16508

KAISH, LUISE
SCULPTOR
b Atlanta, Ga. Study: Syracuse Univ, with Ivan Mestrovic, BFA & MFA; Escuela Pinture y Escultura, Mexico City, Mex, with Taller Grafico. Work: Whitney Mus Am Art, New York; Jewish Mus, New York; Rochester Mem Art Gallery, NY; Continental Grain Co, NY; UAHC, Jerusalem, Israel. Comn: Ark of Revelations (bronze), Temple B'rith Kodesh, Rochester; Great Ideas of Western Man & Walter Paepke Award Sculpture, Container Corp Am; Christ in Glory (bronze), Holy Trinity Mission Sem, Silver Spring, Md; ark doors, menorahs, eternal light (bronze), Temple Beth Shalom, Wilmington, Del; Wall of Martyrs (bronze), Beth El Synagogue Ctr, New Rochelle, NY. Exhib: Sculpture USA, Metrop Mus Art, New York; Recent Sculpture USA, Mus Mod Art, New York; Albright-Knox Mus, Buffalo; K x 2, US Info Serv, Rome, Italy; Hopkins Ctr, Dartmouth, NH; Whitney Biennials, Whitney Mus Am Art, New York; one-man shows, Minneapolis Mus Art, Staempfli Gallery, New York, Rochester Mem Art Gallery & Jewish Mus, New York; plus others. Pos: Artist in residence, Hopkins Ctr, Dartmouth Col; lectr sculpture, Columbia Univ, New York. Awards: Guggenheim Fel Creative Sculpture; Louis Comfort Tiffany Grant Creative Sculpture; Rome Prize Fel in Sculpture. Mem: Sculptors Guild. Dealer: Staempfli Gallery 47 E 77th St New York NY 10021. Mailing Add: 610 West End Ave New York NY 10024

KAISH, MORTON
PAINTER, EDUCATOR
b Newark, NJ, Jan 8, 27. Study: Syracuse Univ, BFA; Acad de la Grande Chaumiere, Paris; Ist d'Arte, Florence; Accad delle Belle Arti, Rome. Work: Brooklyn Mus, NY; Syracuse Univ; Philadelphia Print Club; Atlantic Richfield Corp, New York; J C Penney Co, New York. Comn: Poster, Dartmouth Col, 74. Exhib: Young American Printmakers, Mus Mod Art, New York, 53; one-man shows, Staempfli Gallery, New York, 64, 67, 71, 73 & New Sch Social Res, 74; Biennial of American Painting, Krannert Art Mus, Univ Ill, 65 & 67; Whitney Mus Ann of Am Painting, 66; Am Inst Arts & Lett, 66, 73 & 74. Teaching: Instr painting & drawing, Fashion Inst Technol, State Univ NY, 73-, New Sch Social Res, 74-77 & Art Students League, 74- Awards: H H Sullivan Award, Everson Mus Art, Syracuse, NY, 50; Jurors Show Award, Rochester Mem Art Gallery, 52; artist in residence, Dartmouth Col, 74. Bibliog: Guitierrez & Roukes (co-auths), Painting with Acrylics, Watson-Guptill, 65; Wendon Blake (auth), Complete Guide to Acrylic Painting, Watson-Guptill, 71; Z M Pike (auth), Roman light, Roman ladies, Art Int, 4/73; M L Kelly (auth), Kaishes find Dartmouth fruitful, Christian Sci Monitor, 8/23/74. Style & Technique: Figures, landscapes, interiors. Media: Oil, Acrylic. Dealer: Staempfli Gallery 47 E 77th St New York NY 10021. Mailing Add: 610 West End Ave New York NY 10024

KAKAS, CHRISTOPHER
PRINTMAKER, PAINTER
b Dayton, Ohio, Dec 11, 41. Study: Miami Univ, Ohio, with Robert Wolfe, Jr, BFA, 66; Univ Iowa, with Maurico Lasansky, MA, 68, MFA, 69. Work: Cleveland Mus Art, Ohio; Cincinnati Mus Art, Ohio; Herbert F Johnson Mus Art, Cornell Univ; Kans State Univ Mus Art; Ga Comn Arts, Atlanta. Comn: Group of five prints, Lakeside Studios, Mich, 75. Exhib: 9th Nat Print Exhib, Silvermine Guild Artists, New Canaan, Conn, 72; Midwest Graphics, Univ Wis-Oshkosh, 73; Five Printmakers, Grinnell Col, 74; All Ohio Painting & Sculpture, Dayton Art Inst, 74; US Info Serv Ctrs, Istanbul, Ankara & Izmir, Turkey, 75. Teaching: Asst prof drawing, George Mason Col, Fairfax, Va, 69-70; asst prof printmaking & painting, Dayton Art Inst, 70-75; asst prof printmaking, Syracuse Univ, 75-76; prof art, Western Ky Univ, 76- Pos: Resident artist, Living Arts Ctr, Dayton, Ohio, 70. Awards: Print Purchase Awards, San Diego State Col, 68, Ga Comn Arts, 71 & Kans State Univ, 72. Mem: Col Art Asn Am; Mid-Am Art Asn. Style & Technique: Figurative prints, using color, done in intaglio and lithograph methods; paintings are abstract, color field. Media: Intaglio. Mailing Add: 604 E Main St Bowling Green KY 42101

KALAVREZOU-MAXEINER, IOLI
ART HISTORIAN
b Athens, Greece, Dec 15, 45. Study: Univ Calif, Berkeley, PhD. Teaching: Asst prof late Roman & Byzantine art, Univ Calif, Los Angeles, 76- Mailing Add: Dept of Art Univ Calif 405 Hilgard Ave Los Angeles CA 90024

KALB, MARTY JOEL
PAINTER
b Brooklyn, NY, Apr 13, 41. Study: Mich State Univ, BA, 63; Yale Univ, BFA, 64; Univ Calif, Berkeley, MA, 66. Work: J B Speed Mus, Louisville, Ky; Univ Mass; Ohio Wesleyan Univ. Exhib: Art Ctr Ann, J B Speed Mus, 67 & Fine Arts Biennial, 69; Cincinnati Biennial, Cincinnati Mus of Art, 68; 23rd Am Drawing Biennial, Norfolk Mus of Arts & Sci, 69; All-Ohio Artists, Dayton Art Inst, 70 & 76; Small Paintings, Purdue Univ, 70; Ohio Artists, Canton Art Inst, 72; Centenary Exhib for B Russell, London, Eng, 73; Ann Columbus Gallery of Fine Art, 74 & 75; Nat Drawing Invitational, Univ Southern Ill, 75; Forms of Color, Akron Art Inst, 75; Ten From the File, Columbus Gallery of Fine Art Invitational, 77; Nat Drawing 77, Rutgers Univ, NJ, 77; one-man show, Akron Art Inst, 75; plus others. Teaching: Instr, Univ Ky, 66-67; assoc prof painting, Ohio Wesleyan Univ, 67- Mem: Col Art Asn Am. Style & Technique: Geometric/organic abstraction. Media: Acrylic on Canvas. Dealer: Allan Stone Gallery 48 E 86th St New York NY 10028. Mailing Add: 165 Griswold St Delaware OH 43015

KALINA, RICHARD SETH
PAINTER
b New York, NY, May 21, 46. Study: Univ Pa, BA, 66. Exhib: Inst Contemp Art, Boston, 70, Albright-Knox Gallery, Buffalo, 70; Aldrich Mus, Ridgefield, Conn, 70; Brazilian-Am Cult Inst, Brazil, 75; Mus Mod Art, New York, 75; PS 1, New York, NY, 77; Mus of the Am Found for the Arts, Miami, Fla, 77. Style & Technique: Pattern/decorative painting. Media: Oil on Canvas. Mailing Add: 139 Bowery New York NY 10002

KALINOWSKI, EUGENE M
PAINTER, SCULPTOR
b Pittsburgh, Pa, Jan 19, 29. Study: Carnegie-Mellon Univ, BFA, 52, MFA, 65. Work: In pvt collections only. Exhib: Inst Contemp Art, Boston, 62; Albright-Knox Art Gallery, Buffalo, 62; Butler Inst Am Art, Youngstown, Ohio; Carnegie Inst, Pittsburgh; one-man show, Slippery Rock State Col, Pa, 66. Teaching: Instr painting & drawing, Pittsburgh Pub Sch Syst; instr, Arts & Crafts Ctr, Pittsburgh, 68. Awards: Second Prize for Sculpture, Assoc Artists Pittsburgh, 58, Jury Award for Distinguished Painting, 60 & Award for Distinguished Work in Watercolor, 61; First Prize, Pittsburgh Playhouse Show, 60. Mem: Assoc Artists Pittsburgh (bd dirs, 62-64); Pittsburgh Watercolor Soc; Soc Sculptors. Mailing Add: RD 1 Box 268 Apollo PA 15613

KALISCHER, CLEMENS
PHOTOGRAPHER, GALLERY DIRECTOR
b Hoyren, Bavaria, Mar 30, 21; US citizen. Study: Cooper Union, New York; New Sch for Social Res, New York, with Bernice Abbott. Work: Libr of Cong, Washington, DC; Metrop Mus Art, New York; Williams Col, Lawrence Art Mus; Brooklyn Mus. Exhib: In and Out of Focus & Family of Man, Mus Mod Art, New York; Camera as a Witness, Expo 67, Montreal, Que, 67; Photog in the Arts, Metrop Mus Art, New York; Beacon Hill, Boston 200, 76; Portrait of Am Traveling Show, Smithsonian Inst, Washington, DC, 76-79; NE Photovision, Cycloram, Boston, 75; Photo-League Traveling Exhib, 78-79. Teaching: Vis lectr art photog, Williams Col, Williamstown, Mass, 74-77; instr photog, Berkshire Community Col, Pittsfield, Mass, 73-; vis instr print collecting, Simon's Rock Col, Great Barrington, Mass, 78. Pos: Pres, Millay Art Colony, Austerlitz, NY, 76-; mem, Govt Task Force on the Arts, Mass; mem visual arts adv, Mass Coun for the Arts; dir, Image Gallery, Stockbridge, Mass. Style & Technique: Straight photography. Specialty: Contemporary art, not limited to specific style, only critieria is quality; Mazur, Alice Neel, Mary Miss, Benigna Chilla, Julian Casado, Philip Grausman, Alex Markhoff, V Longo & Julio Granda. Mailing Add: Main St Stockbridge MA 01262

KALLEM, HENRY
PAINTER
b Philadelphia, Pa, May 2, 12. Study: Graphic Sketch Club, Philadelphia, Pa; Nat Acad of Art, New York; Hans Hoffmann Sch. Work: Corcoran Gallery of Art, Washington, DC; Newark Mus, NJ; Chrysler Mus of Norfolk, Va; Colby Col Mus; Matatuck Mus of Art, Waterbury, Conn. Exhib: Carnegie Inst Int, Pittsburgh, Pa, 51; Pa Acad of Design, Philadelphia, 51 & 57; Nat Acad of Design, New York, 56; Audubon Artists, New York, 74; Int Watercolor Soc, Brooklyn Mus, NY, 60; New York World's Fair, 65; Corcoran Biennial, Washington, DC, 65; Affect/Effect Exhib, La Jolla Mus of Art, Calif, 70; New York Work Progress Admin Artists, Then & Now, Parsons Sch of Design, New York, 77. Teaching: Instr painting, Craft Students League, YWCA, New York & Springfield Art Mus, Mo. Awards: First Prize, Pepsi Cola Paintings of the Yr, 47; Third Prize, Hallmark Exhib, 54 & 56; Hon Mention, Casein Soc Ann, 59. Mem: Audubon Soc. Style & Technique: Semi-abstract. Media: Oil painting. Mailing Add: 250 Mt Hope Pl Bronx NY 10457

KALLEM, HERBERT
SCULPTOR
b Philadelphia, Pa, Nov 14, 09. Study: Nat Acad Design; Pratt Inst; Hans Hofmann Sch Fine Arts. Work: Whitney Mus Am Art, New York; Wadsworth Atheneum, Hartford, Conn; NY Univ Loeb Collection; Newark Mus Art, NJ; Chrysler Mus, Provincetown, Mass; also in pvt collections. Exhib: Whitney Mus Am Art, New York; Carnegie Inst, Pittsburgh; Univ Ill, Urbana; plus others. Teaching: Instr sculpture, Sch Visual Arts & NY Univ, formerly. Mem:

Sculptors Guild; Am Abstract Artists. Dealer: Roko Gallery 90 E Tenth St New York NY 10003. Mailing Add: 45 W 28th St New York NY 10001

KALLER, ROBERT JAMESON
ART DEALER
Study: Columbia Univ; Harvard Univ; NY Univ. Pos: Owner, Galerie de Tours, San Francisco, Carmel & Beverly Hills, Calif, 60-; art critic; art consult to mus & corps; cert appraiser; pres, Arts & Humanities Coun, Monterey, Calif, 63-64. Specialty: 19th and 20th century American art; German expressionists; French impressionists; 17th century Dutch. Mailing Add: PO Box 413 Pebble Beach CA 93953

KALLIR, OTTO
ART DEALER, ART HISTORIAN
b Vienna, Austria, Apr 1, 94; US citizen. Study: Univ Vienna, PhD, 31. Pos: Dir art dept, Rikola Verlag, Vienna, 20-22; founder-owner, Neue Galerie, Vienna, 23-72; founder-owner, Johannes Press, Vienna & New York, 23-; founder-owner, Galeries St Etienne, Paris, 38-39, New York, 39-; pres, Grandma Moses Properties, Inc, New York, 50- Awards: Grosses Ehrenzeichen (Grand Medal of Honor for Merit in the Field of Art), Repub of Austria, 60; Silbernes Ehrenzeichen (Silver Medal of Honor for Fostering Relations in Art Between Austria and the US), City of Vienna, 68. Mem: Art Dealers Asn Am. Res: Austrian expressionist art, especially Egon Schiele; Kaethe Kollwitz; American primitive art, especially Grandma Moses; history of aeronautics. Specialty: Austrian & German expressionists; American primitive art. Collection: Austrian 19th & 20th century art; American primitive art; history of aeronautics. Publ: Auth, Egon Schiele (catalogue raisonne of the paintings), 30, rev & enlarged ed, 66; auth, Grandma Moses: American Primitive, 46 & 47; ed, My Life's History by Grandma Moses, 52; auth, Egon Schiele (catalogue raisonne of the graphic work), 70; auth, Grandma Moses (catalogue raisonne), 73; plus others. Mailing Add: 24 W 57th St New York NY 10019

KALTENBACH, STEPHEN JAMES
PAINTER, SCULPTOR
b Battlecreek, Mich, May 5, 40. Study: Univ Calif, Davis, BA & MA. Work: Allen Art Mus, Oberlin Col, Ohio. Exhib: One-man shows, San Francisco Mus Art, 67, Whitney Mus Am Art, New York, 69 & Reese Palley Gallery, San Francisco, 70 & 72; When Attitudes Become Form, Kuntshalle, Berne, Switz, 69; Information, Mus Mod Art, New York, 70; Conceptual Art, Conceptual Aspects, New York Cult Ctr, 70; Tokyo Bienale, Japan, 70; Sacramento Sampler, E B Crocker Art Gallery, Calif, 72; Seattle Art Mus; plus many others. Teaching: Assoc prof, Calif State Univ, Sacramento, 77- Bibliog: Germano Celant (auth), Art povera, 70; Cindy Nemser (auth), An interview with Stephen Kaltenbach, Artforum, 11/70; article in Art Now, 3/72. Mailing Add: 2131 51st St Sacramento CA 95817

KAMEN, GLORIA
ILLUSTRATOR, PAINTER
b New York, NY, Apr 9, 23. Study: Pratt Inst, New York; Art Students League, with Robert Brackman, Will Barnett & Kuniyoshi. Work: Kerlan Collection, Univ Minn; de Grummond Collection, Univ Southern Miss. Awards: Ed Press Award for Publ Art, Outstanding Covers, Syracuse Univ, NY, 69 & 74; Ohio State Award, Best Educ Television for Children, 75-77. Mem: Children's Bk Guild of Washington, DC (pres, 75-76); Artist Equity Asn; Washington Watercolor Soc. Style & Technique: Modern representational, watercolor, line and wash; figure studies. Publ: Illusr, Betty Crocker Cookbook for Boys & Girls, Golden Press, 60; illusr, When Shoes Eat Socks, 71 & Hawkins, 77, Abingdon Press; illusr, Lisa & Her Soundless World, Human Sci Press, 74. Mailing Add: 8912 Seneca Lane Bethesda MD 20034

KAMIHIRA, BEN
PAINTER
b Yakima, Wash, Mar 16, 25. Study: Art Inst Pittsburgh; Pa Acad Fine Arts, 48-52, J Henry Schiedt traveling scholar, 52. Work: Whitney Mus Am Art, New York; Pa Acad Fine Arts, Philadelphia; Ringling Mus, Sarasota, Fla; Colorado Springs Fine Arts Ctr, Colo; Dallas Mus Fine Arts; plus others. Exhib: One-man exhib, Galleria La Medusa, Rome, Italy & throughout Italy (tour), 78; Nat Acad Design; Pa Acad Fine Arts; Corcoran Gallery Art, Washington, DC; Butler Inst Am Art, Youngstown, Ohio; Mus Mod Art, New York; plus many others. Teaching: Instr drawing & painting, Pa Acad Fine Arts & Pa State Univ. Awards: Johnson Prize, New Eng Ann, 61; First Altman Prize, Nat Acad Design, 62; First Prize, Chatauqua Nat Exhib, 62; plus many others. Mem: Fel Pa Acad Fine Arts; academician Nat Acad Design. Style & Technique: Oil on Canvas. Mailing Add: c/o Forum Gallery 1018 Madison Ave New York NY 10021

KAMINISKY, JACK ALLAN
EDUCATOR, PHOTOGRAPHER
b New Brunswick, NJ, Sept 8, 49. Study: Brooklyn Mus Art Sch, 71; Brooklyn Col, BS, 72, MFA, 75, with Walter Rosenblum; Pratt Inst, 73, with Marvin Hoshino. Work: LaGrange Col, Ga. Comn: Graphic designs, Off of Neighborhood Govt & New York Mass Transit Authority for Eastern Pkway Subway Sta, 74; artist-in-residence, Am the Beautiful Fund, Palisades Interstate Park, 77. Exhib: New York Eyes, Third Eye Photog Gallery, 76; The First Picture Show, Greenwich House, New York, 77; Works on Paper, Katonah Gallery, NY, 77; 23rd Ann Long Island Art Exhib, Heckscher Mus, Huntington, NY, 78; one-man shows, Jamaica Bay Wildlife Refuge, Gateway Nat Park, New York, 74 & Aunt Len's Doll & Toy Mus, New York, 75. Teaching: Instr photog, Midwood Adolescent Proj, Brooklyn, NY, 73-76; head graphics dept, Brooklyn Mus Art Sch, 73- Pos: Photogr, Aunt Len's Doll & Toy Mus, 74- & Mus Archaeol, Staten Island, NY, 76. Awards: Teaching Fel, Brooklyn Col, 74. Mem: New York Photog Forum; Soc Photog Educ. Style & Technique: Photography—360 degree panoramas as well as straight forward traditional images; graphics—etchings and screen prints based on photographic images. Media: Photography. Mailing Add: 855 E 19th St Brooklyn NY 11230

KAMMERER, HERBERT LEWIS
SCULPTOR
b New York, NY, July 11, 15. Study: Apprentice to Charles Keck & C Paul Jennewein; asst to Paul Manship; Nat Acad Design; Art Students League; New Yale Univ, BFA, 41; Am Acad Rome, 49-52. Work: Va Mil Inst; Eisenhower Collection; pvt collection of Queen Elizabeth, Eng. Comn: Many medals, portraits & archit sculpture. Exhib: Pa Acad Design Ann, 41, 48 & 52-; Fairmont Int Show, 49; Nat Acad Design, 49, 51 & 52; Palazzo Venezia Int, 50 & 51; plus many others. Teaching: Prof sculpture, State Univ NY Col New Paltz, 62- Awards: George D Widener Gold Medal, Pa Acad Design Ann, 48; Prix d'Rome, Am Acad Rome, 49; Grant in Sculpture, Nat Inst Arts & Lett, 52. Mem: Fel Nat Sculpture Soc (pres, 63-65); Century Asn. Media: Bronze, Stone, Terra-Cotta. Mailing Add: RFD 1 Box 582 Plains Rd New Paltz NY 12651

KAMPEN, MICHAEL EDWIN
ART HISTORIAN, ILLUSTRATOR
b Webster, SDak, July 12, 39. Study: Univ Minn, BA, 61; Tulane Univ, MA, 64; Univ Pa, PhD, 69. Work: Latin Am Studies Collection, Univ Fla, Gainesville. Exhib: El Tajin, Drawings & Phorographs, Univ Gallery, Univ Fla, 76; Photography in Anthropology, Heard Mus, Phoenix, Ariz, 77. Teaching: Vis prof hist of art, Philadelphia Col of Art, 65-67 & 74-75; vis prof hist of art, Univ Fla, 69-70; vis lectr, Yale Univ, New Haven, Conn, 70-71; asst prof hist of art, Salem Col, Winston-Salem, 72-74; assoc prof hist of Art, Ariz State Univ, Tempe, 76- Style & Technique: Pen & ink drawing and lithographic reconstructions of ancient Mesoamerican monuments. Res: History of art and architecture in Veracruz, Mexico, the Maya Guatemala, Honduras and the Yucatan; hist of North America. Specialty: Indian Art. Publ: Auth, The Sculptures of El Tajin, Veracruz, Mexico, Univ Fla, 72; co-auth, Maya Cities of the Gods, Univ Fla, 74; auth, The Graffiti of Tikal, Guatemala, Inst Nat Mex, 78; auth, The Grotesque Gods of El Tajin, Man, 78; auth, Iconography of Maya Religion, Vols I & II, E J Brill, 78. Mailing Add: 2045 E Broadway Tempe AZ 85281

KAMROWSKI, GEROME
PAINTER, EDUCATOR
b Warren, Minn, Jan 29, 14. Study: St Paul Sch Art; Art Students League; New Bauhaus; Hans Hofmann Sch, New York. Work: Flint Inst Arts, Mich; Detroit Inst Art; Guggenheim Mus, New York; Phillips Mem Gallery; Albion Col; plus others. Exhib: Blood Flames, Hugo Gallery, New York, 45; Int Expos Surrealism, Gallerie Maegt, Paris, 46; Surrealism & Abstract Art, Sydney Janis Gallery; one-man shows, Betty Parsons, New York, 42, Galerie Creuze, Paris, 51 & Monique Knowlton Gallery, New York, 78; Dada & Surrealism Reviewed, Hayward Gallery, London; Surrealism, Rutgers Univ Mus of Art, 77; Am Abstract Artists, Univ NMex Mus of Art, 77; plus many others. Teaching: Prof art, Sch Art, Univ Mich, Ann Arbor, 46- Awards: Founders Prize, Detroit Inst Art; Guggenheim Fel, 37; Racknam Fel, 72. Bibliog: Andre Breton (auth), Surrealisme et la peinturu, Brentano's. Manupilii (auth), Celestial Rythms (film). Mailing Add: 1501 Beechwood Dr Ann Arbor MI 48103

KAMYS, WALTER
PAINTER, EDUCATOR
b Chicago, Ill, June 8, 17. Study: Art Inst Chicago, 43, with Hubert Ropp & Brois Anisfeld; also with Gordon Onslow-Ford, Mex, 44. Work: Yale Univ; Mt Holyoke Col; Smith Col; Fogg Art Mus; Regional Contemp Art Collection, Fargo, ND; plus others. Exhib: One-man shows, Bertha Schaefer Gallery, New York, 55, 57 & 60, New Vision Centre Gallery, London, Eng, 60 & East Hampton Gallery, NY, 70; Recent Drawings, USA, Mus Mod Art, 56; 22nd Int Watercolor Biennial, Brooklyn Mus, 63; Inst Contemp Art, Boston, 66; Smithsonian Inst, 68; plus others. Teaching: Instr art, Putney Sch, Vt, 45; instr art, G W V Smith Art Mus, Springfield, Mass, 47-60; prof painting & drawing, Univ Mass, 60-, dir, Art Acquisition Prog, 62- Awards: Boston Art Festival Award, 55; Award, Amherst, Mass, 57 & 58; Westfield State Col Purchase Prize, 68; plus others. Bibliog: Harriet Janis & Rudi Blesh (auth), Collage: Personalities, Concepts, Techniques, Chilton, 62. Style & Technique: Organic, poetic aspects of nature; swift linear strokes that energize the surface so that the total effect is one of contained action. Mailing Add: N Main St Sunderland MA 01375

KAN, DIANA
PAINTER, LECTURER
b Hong Kong, Mar 3, 26; US citizen. Study: With Chang Dai Chien, China, 46; Art Students League, 49-51, with Robert Johnson & Robert B Hale; Ecole Beaux Arts, Paris, 52-54, with Paul Lavelle. Work: Metrop Mus Art, New York; Philadelphia Mus Art; Nelson Gallery, Atkins Mus, Kansas City, Mo; Nat Hist Mus, Taiwan; Elliott Mus, Stuart, Fla. Comn: Lotus painting, Nat Hist Mus, Taiwan, 71. Exhib: Royal Acad Arts, London, Eng, 64; Royal Soc Painters, London, 64; Nat Acad of Design, New York, 67-77; one-man shows, Elliott Mus, 67 & 74, Nat Hist Mus, Taiwan, 71 & New York Cult Ctr, 72; Hobe Sound Galleries, Fla, 76; Nat Arts Club, 78; plus others. Awards: Am Watercolor Soc Traveling Award, 68, 73 & 75; Barbara Vassillieff Mem Award, Allied Artists Am, 69; Anna Hyatt Huntington Bronze Medal, Catharine Lorillard Wolfe Art Club, 70 & 74. Bibliog: Robert Harris (auth), Pictures by a Chinese artist, London Times, 64; Barbara Wright (auth), Diana Kan, Arts Rev, London, 64; Daniel Su (auth), Chinese Paintings, Cosmorama Pictorial, 72. Mem: Am Watercolor Soc (dir, 75-77); Allied Artists Am (corresp secy, 75-78); Pen & Brush Club (dir, 68-70, 72-77); Salmagundi Club; Catharine Lorillard Wolfe Art Club. Style & Technique: Combination of Chinese traditional impressionist and abstract modern using vibrant mineral colors based on a writing brush stroke technique. Media: Watercolor. Publ: Auth, White Cloud; auth, How and Why of Chinese Painting, 74; auth, article in Am Artists Mag, 74. Dealer: Grand Central Art Galleries 40 Vanderbilt Ave New York NY 10017; Hobe Sound Galleries 739 Bridge Rd Hobe Sound FL 33455. Mailing Add: 26 W Ninth St New York NY 10011

KAN, MICHAEL
ART HISTORIAN, ART ADMINISTRATOR
b Shanghai, China, July 17, 33; US citizen. Study: Columbia Col, BA(art hist & archeol), 53; State Univ NY Agr & Tech Col Alfred, MFA(ceramics & sculpture), 57; Columbia Univ, MA(art hist), 69, MPhil, 74. Collections Arranged: African Art & Simpson Collection, Brooklyn Mus, 70; guest cur, Ancient Art of West Mexico, Los Angeles Co Mus Art, 70; curatorial consult, African Art Tribal Art from West Africa, Portland Mus, 71; curatorial consult, Pre-Columbian Art in the Collection of Jay C Leff, Allentown Mus, 72. Teaching: Lectr art hist, Univ Calif, Berkeley, 64-66; lectr art Eastern Asia, Finch Col, 66-67; lectr African art, NY Univ, 70- Pos: Assoc cur primitive art, Brooklyn Mus, 68-70, cur, 70-73, chief cur, 73-76; cur African, Oceanic & New World cult, Detroit Inst of the Arts, 77- Mem: Mus Collaborative Inc (trustee, 75); Am Asn Mus. Res: The art of early cultures of pre-Columbian Peru and pre-Columbian Mexico; African art education. Publ: Contribr, Early Chinese Art and the Pacific Basin, 68; auth, African Sculpture, 70; co-auth, Ancient Art of West Mexico, 70. Mailing Add: Detroit Inst of the Arts 5200 Woodward Ave Detroit MI 48202

KANE, BOB PAUL
PAINTER
b Cleveland, Ohio, July 11, 37. Study: Cornell Univ; Art Students League, with Will Barnet; Pratt Inst. Work: Cincinnati Art Mus; Mus Munic St Paul de Vence, France; Joseph H Hirshhorn Collection; Palm Springs Desert Mus. Exhib: Lytton Mus, Los Angeles, 67; Joslyn Art Mus, Nebr, 68; Collector's Choice, Okla Art Ctr, 68; American Painting on the Market Today, Cincinnati Art Mus, 68; 20 Painters of Southern California, Palm Springs Desert Mus, 70; Mus Munic St Paul de Vence, 72 & 76; Palais de la Mediterranee, France, 73; Ft Wayne Art Mus, 68; Biennial of the Painters of the Mediterranean, Nice, France, 73; Biennial of Mention, France, 73; Bertha Schaefer Gallery, New York, 68, 70, 72 & 74; Galerie Marcel Bernheim, Paris, 70, Albright-Knox Mus, 73; Ankrum Gallery, Los Angeles, 69 & 74; plus many other group & one-man shows. Teaching: Instr painting & art hist, Mt Clair Col, 69-70; instr painting & art hist, NY Univ, 69-70. Bibliog: Richard Boyle (auth), Bob Kane, Mus Munic St Paul de Vence, 72. Media: Oil. Dealer: Bertha Schaefer Gallery 41 E 57th St New

York NY 10022; Ankrum Gallery 657 N La Cienega Blvd Los Angeles CA 90069. Mailing Add: 125 Riverside Dr New York NY 10024

KANE, MARGARET BRASSLER
SCULPTOR
b East Orange, NJ, May 25, 09. Study: Syracuse Univ; Art Students League; Colo State Christian Col, hon PhD, 73; also with John Hovannes. Work: US Maritime Comn; Limited Ed Lamp Co. Comn: Plague for Burro Monument, Fairplay, Colo. Exhib: Lever House, New York, 59-77; Chicago Art Inst; New York Metrop Mus; Whitney Mus Am Art, New York; Philadelphia Mus Int Sculpture Exhibs; Pa Acad Fine Arts; plus others. Teaching: Lectr, Creative Approach to Sculpture. Pos: Juror, Am Mach & Foundry Co, 57. Awards: First Anna Hyatt Huntington Prize, 42 & Medal of Hon for Sculpture, 51, Nat Asn Women Artists; Henry O Avery Prize, NY Archit League, 44; plus others. Mem: Charter mem Sculptors Guild (past pres); Nat Asn Women Artists; Pen & Brush Club; Greenwich Art Soc; Silvermine Guild Artists; fel Int Inst Arts & Lett. Style & Technique: Representational; bronze castings. Media: Wood, Marble. Publ: Contribr ann reproductions, Greenwich Time Publ, 50-77; auth, article in Am Artists, 1/70; reproductions, In: Contemporary Stone Sculpture, Crown, 71; reproductions of wood carvings used by McGraw-Hill, 73. Mailing Add: 30 Strickland Rd Cos Cob CT 06807

KANEE, BEN
COLLECTOR
b Melville, Sask, Oct 12, 11. Pos: Former chmn permanent collection comt & former vpres, Vancouver Art Gallery. Mem: Hon life mem Vancouver Art Gallery. Collection: Contemporary West Coast artists; British works including drawing by Augustus John; sculpture by Rodin, Valentine and Maillol; Canadian art including works by Turner, Cox and Osterle; graphics including works by Picasso, Chagall, Miro, Renoir, Bonnard, Vlaminck, Villon, Moore, Dali, Uchima, Braque and Albers; Canadian Eskimo carvings and prints, Haida Indian carvings including a totem pole by Bill Reid; Etruscan antiquities, Luristan bronze, early Hebrew art, pre-Columbian and early Peruvian art. Mailing Add: Apt 103-5455 Vancouver BC V6M 4B3 Can

KANEGIS, SIDNEY S
ART DEALER
b Winthrop, Mass, Sept 6, 22. Study: Boston Mus Fine Art Sch. Pos: Owner & dir, Kanegis Gallery, Boston, 50- Specialty: Contemporary art; modern master graphics. Mailing Add: 244 Newbury St Boston MA 02116

KANEMITSU, MATSUMI
PAINTER, LECTURER
b Ogden, Utah, May 28, 22. Study: Painting with Fernand Leger, Paris, France; Art Students League, with Kuniyoshi, Sternberg, Auston & Browne; also sculpture with Karl Metzler, Baltimore. Work: Galleria Civica Arte Mod, Turin, Italy; Honolulu Acad Arts, Hawaii; Mus Mod Art, New York; San Francisco Mus Art; Corcoran Gallery Art, Washington, DC. Comn: Watercolor, Shinwa Bowl, Kawasaki City, Japan, 72. Exhib: In Memory of My Feelings, Mus Mod Art, New York, 67, Tamarind: An Homage to Lithography, 69; Trends in 20th Century Art, Univ Calif, Santa Barbara, 70; Black & White Drawings & Watercolors, San Francisco Mus Art, 71; one-man show, Michael Smith Gallery, Los An art, Chouinard Art Sch, 65-72; artist in residence, Univ Calif, Berkeley, 66; artist in residence, Honolulu Acad Arts, 67-68; instr, Calif State Col, Los Angeles, 69; Art Ctr Col Design, Los Angeles, 70; Univ Calif, Berkeley, 70-71; Otis Art Inst, 71; Calif Inst Arts, Valencia, 71-72. Awards: Ford Found Awards, 61 & 64; Longview Found Award, 62; Japan Cult Forum Award, 4th Int Young Artists Exhib, 67. Media: Oil, Duco, Watercolor. Dealer: Janus Gallery 21 Market St Venice CA 90291. Mailing Add: 854 S Berendo St Los Angeles CA 90005

KANGAS, GENE
SCULPTOR, COLLECTOR
b Painesville, Ohio, May 22, 44. Study: Miami Univ, BFA; Bowling Green Univ, MFA; Univ Ky, sculpture sem. Hall. Work: Butler Inst Am Art, Ohio; Univ NC, Chapel Hill; Bowling Green Univ; Ackland Art Ctr, Chapel Hill. Comn: Sculpture, Cuyahoga Co Justice Ctr, Cleveland, Ohio, 77. Exhib: Toledo Glass Nat II, Ohio, 68; NC Sculpture Invitational, 69; Young Americans 1969, Am Crafts Coun, New York, 69-71; one-man show, Royal Marks Gallery, New York, 70; Ohio Sculpture Invitational, Dayton, 74. Teaching: Instr sculpture, Univ NC, 68-71; asst prof sculpture, Cleveland State Univ, 71-75, assoc prof, 75- Awards: Fulbright-Hays Scholar, 68; Univ Res Grant, Univ NC, 68-70, Smith Fund Grant, 70; First Prize in Sculpture, Cleveland Mus Art, 75. Bibliog: Hargrove (auth, film), The History of Public Sculpture in Cleveland & Public Art at the Justice Center, 78; Hollander (auth), Plastics for Artists and Craftsmen. Style & Technique: Hybrid mixture of geometric and organic life forms made from large pieces of structural metals. Collection: American folk art. Mailing Add: 6852 Painesville-Ravenna Rd Painesville OH 44077

KANIDINC, SALAHATTIN
DESIGNER, CALLIGRAPHER
b Istanbul, Turkey, Aug 12, 27. Study: Defenbaugh Sch Lettering, under Roger I Defenbaugh; Zanerian Col Penmanship, text lettering under John P Turner; State Univ Iowa, cert lettering, under Prof Meyer; Univ Minn, cert lettering; Univ Calif, cert advert. Work: The White House, Washington, DC; Independence Hall, Philadelphia; Franklin Mint Mus Medallic Art, Franklin Center, Pa; Peabody Inst Libr, Baltimore, Md. Comn: Monogram design for King of Morocco, Tiffany & Co, New York, 70; 60 calligraphs for Genius of Michelangelo Medals, Franklin Mint, 71, 37 calligraphic lettering for White House Hist Asn Presidential Plates, 72, 4 calligraphic designs for Official Bicentennial Commemorative Plates, 73 & 24 calligraphic lettering for The Old Testament by Monti Medals, 73; commemorative medal design for 50th Anniversary of the Turkish Repub, Fedn Turkish-Am Socs, New York, 73; Christmas Card Design, UNICEF, New York, 73; postage stamp design (one cent definitive), UN, 78. Exhib: 1000 Yrs of Calligraphy & Illumination, Baltimore, 59; Bertrand Russell Centenary Int Art Exhib, London, 72-73. Pos: Chief calligrapher, Deniz Basimevi MD, Istanbul, Turkey, 50-61; lettering artist, Buzza-Cardozo, Anaheim, Calif, 62-64; asst art dir, Rust Craft Publ, Dedham, Mass, 64; lettering specialist-designer, Tiffany & Co, New York, 64-72; owner-creative dir, Kanidinc Int, New York, 72- Awards: Distinguished Serv to Art of Calligraphy Cert of Merit, 69; Distinguished Achievement Dipl, 71; Summo Cum Honore, Honors Regist, 71; First Prize, Ann McKay Christmas Card Contest, 74. Mem: Int Asn Master Penmen & Teachers of Handwriting; Int Ctr for Typographic Arts; Queens Coun on Arts; Soc Scribes & Illuminators; Nat Soc Lit & Arts. Media: Ink, Gouache. Res: Historical development of letter forms. Publ: Contribr, Alphabet Thesaurus, Vol II, III, 65-71; contribr, Turkish-Am Encycl Dig. Mailing Add: 62-34 99th St Rego Park NY 11374

KANNEGIETER, KATSKO SUZUKI
See Suzuki, Katsko

KANOVITZ, HOWARD
PAINTER
b Fall River, Mass, Feb 9, 29. Study: Providence Col, BS, 49; RI Sch Design, 49-51; also with Franz Kline, 51-52. Work: Whitney Mus Am Art, New York; Wallraf-Richartz Mus, Cologne, Ger; Neue Galerie Stadt Aachen, Ger; Mus Contemp Art, Utrecht, Holland; Göteborgs Konstmuseum, Göteborg, Sweden. Comn: The Opening, 180 Beacon Corp, Boston, 67; A Death in Treme, Florists Transworld Delivery Collection, Detroit, 71; Collector's Wall, F K Johnssen, Essen, Ger, 71. Exhib: Mus Contemp Art, Chicago, 71; Hayward Gallery, London, Eng, 71; Am Inst Arts & Lett, 72; Whitney Mus Am Art Ann, New York, 72; Dokumenta 5, Kassel, Ger, 72. Teaching: Instr painting & design, Brooklyn Col, 61-64; instr 2-D design, Pratt Inst, 64-66. Bibliog: B H Friedman (auth), Focus on physical reality, Art News, 10/66; Rosalind Constable (auth), Style of the year: the inhumanists, New Yorker Mag, 12/16/68; Peter Sager (auth), Neve Formen des Realismus, Mag Kunst, 71. Media: Acrylic. Mailing Add: c/o Galerie M E Thelen Lindenstrasse 20 Cologne West Germany

KAO, RUTH (YU-HSIN) LEE
FIBER ARTIST, EDUCATOR
b Peking, Repub of China; US citizen. Study: Univ N Iowa, Cedar Falls, BA & MA; Univ Kans, Lawrence; Haystack Mountain Sch of Crafts; also with Philip Evergood & Chunghi Choo. Comn: Weaving, Univ N Iowa Libr, Cedar Falls, 77. Exhib: Marietta Col Crafts Nat, Ohio, 75; InnerSpace, Mano Galleries, Chicago, 77; Ruth Kao Weavings & Paintings, Bradley Galleries, Milwaukee, 77; Focus on Crafts, Univ Minn, St Paul, 77; Lake Superior 77, Tweed Mus Art, Duluth, 77; Fibers, Hadler Galleries, New York, 77; Currents 77, Mid Tenn State Univ, Murfreesboro, 77; Fiber Arts, Paul Waggoner Gallery, Chicago, 77. Teaching: Instr fibers, Univ N Iowa, 70-74; asst prof fibers, Univ Wis, Milwaukee, 74- Pos: Juror, 4th Biennial Int Crafts Exhib, Tweed Mus Art, 77 & 5th Wis Union Crafts, Univ Wis, 77. Awards: Craftsmen's Fel, Nat Endowment for the Arts, 74; res grant, Grad Sch, Univ Wis, Milwaukee, 75. Bibliog: James Auer (auth), Her artistry looms large, Milwaukee J, 3/13/77; Joan Zyda (auth), A show of Ravioli, Chicago-Tribune, 12/18/77; Sonia Katz (auth), Eighteen fiber artists, New Art Examr, Chicago, 1/78. Mem: Am Crafts Coun; Surface Design Asn. Style & Technique: Geometric brocade loom weaving, with color emphasis; organic metaphors in watercolor. Media: Weaving, Fiber Contruction; Watercolor. Dealer: Hadler Galleries 35-37 E 20th St New York NY 10003. Mailing Add: 2906 N Downer Ave Milwaukee WI 53211

KAPLAN, ALICE MANHEIM
PATRON, COLLECTOR
b Budapest, Hungary, Nov 27, 03; US citizen. Study: Teachers Col, Columbia Univ, BS, 24, MA(art hist), 66; Cedar Crest Col, hon DFA, 68. Pos: Trustee, J M Kaplan Fund, 44-, vpres, 58-; trustee, Am Fedn Arts, 58-, pres, 67-77; co-chmn, 50th Anniversary Exhib, Armory Show, 63; mem adv bd, Mus Am Folk Art, 63 & trustee, 77; mem adv coun, Dept Art & Archaeol, Columbia Univ, 65-, chmn, 72-; mem adv coun, Inst Fine Arts, NY Univ, 65-; mem, Fine Arts Comn, New York, 69-; co-chmn. Comt to Save Cooper-Hewitt Mus, 65; coun fels, Morgan Libr. Awards: Ford Found Grant, 66. Mem: Munic Arts Soc. Collection: Diversified with emphasis on drawings; 19th and 20th century American paintings and sculpture; Oriental, pre-Columbian and African. Mailing Add: 760 Park Ave New York NY 10021

KAPLAN, JACQUES
COLLECTOR
b Paris, France, Oct 22, 22. Collection: Contemporary American art, 19th century European art and the Old Masters. Mailing Add: 4 E 70th St New York NY 10021

KAPLAN, JEROME EUGENE
PRINTMAKER
b Philadelphia, Pa, July 0. Study: Philadelphia Col Art, dipl; also with Paul Froelich & Benton Spruance. Work: Libr Cong, Washington, DC; Philadelphia Mus Art; Nat Gallery Art, Washington, DC; New York Pub Libr; Rosenwald Collection. Exhib: 4th Int Prints, Ljubjana, Yugoslavia, 61; Am Prints Today, Print Coun Am, 62; First Biennial Int l'Estampe, Epinal, France, 71; 25th Nat Exhib, Washington, DC, 77; 55th Nat, Soc Am Graphic Artists, New York, 77. Teaching: Prof printmaking, Philadelphia Col Art, 48-, chmn dept, 64-72. Awards: Guggenheim Fel, 61; Fel, Tamarind Lithography Workshop, 62. Mem: Print Club Philadelphia; Artists Equity Asn; Soc Am Graphic Artists. Media: Intaglio, Lithography. Publ: Illusr, The Ballad of the Spanish Civil Guard, 64 & 75; illusr, The Bucket Rider, 72. Dealer: The Print Club 1614 Latimer St Philadelphia PA 19103. Mailing Add: 7029 Clearview St Philadelphia PA 19119

KAPLAN, JOSEPH
PAINTER
b Minsk, Russia, Oct 3, 00; US citizen. Study: Educ Alliance, New York; Nat Acad Design, New York. Work: Butler Inst Am Art, Youngstown, Ohio; Decatur Art Ctr; Newark Mus; Univ Ky; Tel Aviv Mus; Mus of Western Art, Moscow, USSR; and others. Exhib: Nat Acad of Design, 46-49; Pa Acad, 46-49, 52, 55 & 56; Carnegie Inst, 48; Audubon Artists, 48-59; Univ Ill, Urbana, 48-53; Am Watercolor Soc, 49-50; Corcoran Gallery, Washington, DC, 49, 53 & 55; Boston Arts Festival, 54-57; Nat Soc Casein Painters, 55-59; one-man shows, Salpeter Gallery, New York, NY, 47-52, 55, 56 & 57, Massilon Mus, Ohio, 51, Butler Art Inst, Youngstown, Ohio, 51, Dayton Art Inst, Ohio, 52, Univ Miss, 52, East End Gallery, Provincetown, Mass, 60 & 61, Summit Gallery, New York, NY, 77, Tirca Karlis Gallery, Provincetown, Mass, 77 & others. Collections Arranged: Traveling Show, five Midwest mus; also exhibs for Art Alliance, Philadelphia & Cape Cod Art Asn, Hyannis, Mass. Awards: Awards, incl Gold Medal for Oil & two Medals of Hon, Audubon Artists, 55, 59, 60, 67 & 70; Prizes, Nat Soc Casein Painters, 60 & 65; Award for Oil, Cape Cod Art Asn, 62, plus other awards; Prizes, incl Purchase Prize for Oil & Award for Self Portrait, Nat Acad Design, 67, 69 & 70; Chapelbrook Found grant, 69; plus others. Bibliog: Carl Fortes (interviewer), tape interview, Mus Arch, 68. Mem: Provincetown Art Asn (hon vpres & trustee, 55-); Audubon Artists (trustee & vpres); Artists Equity, New York. Media: Oil, Gouache. Mailing Add: 638 Commercial St Provincetown MA 02657

KAPLAN, JULIUS DAVID
ART HISTORIAN
b Nashville, Tenn, July 22, 41. Study: Wesleyan Univ, Middletown, Conn, BA; Columbia Univ, MA & PhD. Teaching: Lectr, Colby Col, Waterville, Maine, 66; asst prof, Univ Calif, Los Angeles, 69-77; assoc prof art hist, Calif State Col, San Bernardino, 77- Awards: Fulbright fel, Paris, 67 & 68; Regents' Fac Fel in Humanities, Univ Calif, Los Angeles, 76-77; grant-in-aid, Am Coun of Learned Socs, 77. Mem: Col Art Asn; Art Historians of Southern Calif. Res: Academic and official art in France, 1850-1900. Publ: Auth, The religious subjects

of James Ensor 1877-1900, Revue Belge d'Archaeol et d'Histoire de l'Art, 66; auth, Gustave Moreau, Los Angeles Co Mus of Art, 74. Mailing Add: 3414 Troy Dr Los Angeles CA 90068

KAPLAN, LEONARD
ART DEALER, PAINTER
b New York, NY, Jan 15, 22. Study: Art Students League. Work: Los Angeles Co Mus Art, Los Angeles; Laguna Beach Mus Art, Calif; James S Copley Libr, La Jolla, Calif. Comn: Mural, Goldwater's, Scottsdale, Ariz; mural, Stix-Baer-Fuller, St Louis; sculpture, Beverly Hilton, Beverly Hills. Exhib: Retrospectives, Univ Ariz Art Gallery, Tucson, 67; Edward Dean Mus, Cherry Valley, Calif, 72; Laguna Beach Mus Art, 74. Teaching: Lectr life drawing, Laguna Beach Sch Art, 74-; lectr life drawing, Univ Calif, Irvine, 75; vis artist-in-residence, Calif State Univ, Fullerton, 76-77. Awards: Los Angeles Co Purchase Award, 56. Style & Technique: Drawings, figures. Media: Conte, charcoal. Specialty: Oriental and pre-Columbian. Mailing Add: 860 Glenneyre Laguna Beach CA 92651

KAPLAN, MARILYN
PAINTER
b Brooklyn, NY. Study: Syracuse Univ, BFA; Columbia Univ Teachers Col, MA(art educ); Art Students League, with Harry Sternberg. Work: New York Port Authority; Publ Clearing House, Port Washington, NY; Nat Collection of Fine Arts, Smithsonian Inst, Washington, DC; Lanvin-Charles of the Ritz Collection, New York; United Mutual Savings Bank, Great Neck. Comn: Poster, No More War by Personality Posters, New York for Nat Peace Movement, 69. Exhib: Audubon Artists, New York, 66, 70 & 71; Allied Artists of Am, New York, 69; Hecksher Mus Ann Competition, Huntington, 69-72 & 75; Nat Acad Design, New York, 70, 72 & 75; New Eng Ann Exhib, Silvermine, Conn, 72-73; Images of an Era: The Am Poster 1945-1975, Smithsonian Inst Bicentennial Art Exhib, traveling to Corcoran Gallery of Art, Washington, DC, Contemp Arts Mus, Houston, Tex, Mus of Sci & Indust, Chicago, Ill, Inst of Contemp Art, London, Eng, Henie-Onstad Mus, Oslo, Norway, Stedelijk Mus, Amsterdam, Neth, Hamburg Mus für Kunst und Gewerbe, Hamburg, WGer & Musee des Arts Decoratifs, Paris, France, 76-78. Teaching: Art coordr elem & jr high sch art, Croton-Harmon Schs, NY, 54-56; instr painting, Mid Island Art League, Hicksville, 59-63; instr painting, Jericho Adult Educ, 63-69. Pos: Vpres, Mid Island Art League, Nassau Co, NY, 62-65. Awards: Award, Invitational Show, Hofstra Univ, 66; Second Prize Oils, Hecksher Mus, 72; Benjamin Altman Landscape Prize for Painting, Nat Acad Design, 75. Bibliog: Gary Yanker (auth), Prop Art; Images of an Era: The American Poster 1945-1975 (catalogue), Nat Collection of Fine Arts, Smithsonian Inst; Robert Carlsen (auth), Encounters: Themes in Literature, McGraw-Hill. Mem: Artists Equity Asn; Prof Artists Guild (treas, 73-76). Style & Technique: Abstract and semi-abstract landscapes; collages of paint and newsprint on canvas depicting city life. Media: Oil & Acrylic on Canvas. Mailing Add: 26 Birchwood Park Dr Jericho NY 11753

KAPLAN, MURIEL SHEERR
SCULPTOR, DESIGNER
b Philadelphia, Pa, Aug 15, 24. Study: Cornell Univ, BA, 46; Norton Art Sch, Fla, study of stone carving with Jose de Creeft, 51; grad work in welding, Sarah Lawrence Col, 60; study of medieval art & archit, Oxford Univ, Eng, 71; study of Renaissance art, Univ Florence, Italy, 73. Work: Law Libr Collection, Columbia Univ, New York; John F Kennedy Sch Collection, Jerusalem, Israel; Univ Tex Collection, Austin; Brandeis Univ Collection, Waltham, Mass. Comn: Nine ft stainless steel rotating sculpture, Trans-Lux Corp, Harrisburg, Pa, 66; two & one-half ton, 17 ft Corten steel sculptures, Empire State Co, Tarrytown, NY, 72. Exhib: Sculptor's Guild, New York, 61; Engineers & Artists in Technol, Brooklyn Mus, NY, 68; Allied Artists of Am, 69, 70, 74 & 75; Nat Asn of Women Artists, 69-75. Teaching: Instr sculpture portrait, pvt students, New York, 66-70. Pos: Pvt dealer, New York, 77-; consult for contemp art collectors, 77- Awards: Sculpture Prize, Nat Asn Women Artists, 66 & Allied Artists of Am, 69. Mem: Affil Am Fedn of the Arts; Nat Asn Women Artists; Am Crafts Coun. Style & Technique: Large, minimal, architectural steel sculptures and portrait busts. Media: Corten or stainless steel for architectural sculptures; bronze or polyester resin for portraits. Specialty: Contemporary art. Collection: Trova, Gallo, Mallory, Theibaud, Milne, Epstein, Robus & other contemp Americans. Dealer: Portraits Inc 47 E 57th St New York NY 10022; C C Price Portraits 15 E 48th St New York NY 10017. Mailing Add: 150 E 69th New York NY 10021

KAPLAN, STANLEY
PRINTMAKER, EDUCATOR
b Brooklyn, NY, Sept 4, 25. Study: Cooper Union Sch of Art, cert fine arts, 49; NY Univ, BS, 52; Pratt Inst, New York, MS, 68. Work: Metrop Mus of Art, New York; Br-oklyn Mus, New York Pub Libr; Columbia Univ; Philadelphia Mus Art. Comn: Murals, Int Tel & Tel Community Develop Corp, New York & Fla, 73 & 74; mural, Manuche's Restaurant, New York, 62. Exhib: Libr of Cong, Washington, DC, 51; one-man shows, ACA Galleries, New York, 55, Hofstra Univ, 57, Port Washington Libr, 67 & Nassau Community Col, Garden City, NY, 71; Audubon Artists, 66, Nat Acad of Design, New York, 71, Kennedy Gallery, 71 & Assoc Am Artists Gallery, 72. Teaching: Art teacher, Levittown Pub Schs, NY, 54-59; prof art, Nassau Community Col, Garden City, 66- Awards: Award, Sixth Ann Competition, Port Washington Pub Libr, 71; Purchase Award, Soc Am Graphic Artists 55th Nat Print Exhib, 77. Mem: Soc Am Graphic Artists (vpres, 72-74, pres, 76-). Mailing Add: 47 Trapper Lane Levittown NY 11756

KAPLINSKI, BUFFALO
PAINTER
b Chicago, Ill, May 25, 43. Study: Art Inst Chicago; Am Acad Art. Exhib: 140th Ann, Nat Acad Design, New York; 98th Ann, Am Watercolor Soc, New York; 162nd Ann, Pa Acad Fine Arts, Philadelphia; 27th Exhib, Audubon Artists, New York; 15th-18th Ann, Nat Soc Painters in Casein; plus many others. Awards: 15th Ann Exhib Hon Mention, Nat Soc Painters in Casein; Southwestern Watercolor Soc Purchase Award, Southern Methodist Univ Fine Arts Ctr; Southwestern Biennial Hon Mention, NMex Arts Mus, Santa Fe. Bibliog: Article in Am Artist Mag, 8/72. Mailing Add: PO Box 44 Elizabeth CO 80107

KAPPEL, PHILIP
WRITER, ETCHER
b Hartford, Conn, Feb 10, 01. Study: Pratt Inst, 24; Trinity Col, Conn, Hon DFA, 66. Work: Metrop Mus Art, New York; Boston Pub Libr, Mass; Corcoran Gallery, Washington, DC; Univ Col West Indies, Jamaica; Wadsworth Atheneum, Hartford, Conn. Exhib: Retrospective exhib, Corcoran Gallery, Washington, DC, 31, Montclair Art Mus, 48, New Britain Mus Am Art, Conn, 56; Austin Art Ctr, Trinity Col, 66 & Washington Art Asn, Conn, 69. Awards: Wunderlich Award, Soc Am Etchers, 52; Numerous Jury Awards, Salmagundi Club; Awards, Hudson Valley Art Asn. Bibliog: Eugene Ettenberg (auth), article in Am Artist Mag, 65; Elton Hall (auth), article in Am Art Rev, 75; Archives Am Art, Smithsonian Inst, Washington, DC. Mem: Wash Art Asn (pres, 55-70); Salmagundi Club; Conn State Comn Arts (comnr, 66-); Hudson Valley Art Asn; Soc Am Etchers. Style & Technique: Realistic, specializing in etching. Media: Drypoint, Aquatint. Publ: Auth & illusr, Boothbay Harbor, privately publ, 24; illusr, Louisiana Gallery, Putnam, 50; illusr, Jamaica Gallery, 60 & New England Gallery, 66, Little-Brown. Mailing Add: Church St Roxbury CT 06783

KAPPEL, R ROSE (MRS IRVING GOULD)
PRINTMAKER
b Hartford, Conn, Sept 23, 10. Study: Pratt Inst, New York, 30; NY Univ, BS, 47, MA, 50, EdD, 54; Wash Univ; Univ Wis; Yale Univ. Work: Metrop Mus Art, New York; Cleveland Mus Art, Ohio; New Britain Mus Fine Arts, Conn; Mt Holyoke Mus, Mass; Fogg Mus, Cambridge. Comn: Murals on educ, Cult & Health Sch, Brooklyn, 50. Exhib: Nat Acad of Art, 60-67; Washington Art Asn. Teaching: Art specialist, Bur for Educ of Phys Handicapped Children, New York, 31-75. Pos: Art dir, Great Detective Mag, 35-40. Awards: Beth Creedy Hamm Prize/Watercolor, Nat Acad, 69; Watercolor Award, Nat Asn Women Artists, 62 & Nat Acad, 61. Mem: Am Asn Univ Women; Queens Pres Coun (gen vpres, 68-). Style & Technique: Semi-traditional, creative. Publ: Illusr, Ships & Sails, 47. Mailing Add: 35-36 76th St Jackson Heights NY 11372

KAPROW, ALLAN
PAINTER, EDUCATOR
b Atlantic City, NJ, Aug 23, 27. Study: Hans Hofmann Sch Fine Arts, 47-48; NY Univ, BA, 49, postgrad study, 49-50; Columbia Univ, MA, 52; also with John Cage, New York, 56-58. Exhib: Inst Contemp Arts, Boston, 66; Central Park, New York, 66; Westchester Art Soc, White Plains, NY, 66; State Univ NY Stony Brook, 67; retrospective, Pasadena Art Mus, Calif, 67; one-man show, John Gibson Gallery, 69; Jewish Mus, New York, 69 & 70; Calif Inst Arts, Valencia, 70-73; Mus Fine Arts, Dallas, Tex, 74; plus many others. Teaching: Instr fine arts, Rutgers Univ, 53-56, asst prof, 56-61; lectr aesthetics, Dept Fine Arts, Pratt Inst, 60-61; assoc prof fine arts, State Univ NY Stony Brook, 61-66, prof, 66; assoc dean sch art, Calif Inst Arts; prof art, Univ Calif, San Diego, 76- Pos: Co-founder, Hansa Gallery, New York, 52, Reuben Gallery, New York, 59; dir, Judson Gallery, New York, 60, co-dir, 61; dir criticism & exp res, Inst Contemp Arts, Boston, 65-66. Awards: Copley Found Award, 62; Off Foreign Area Studies, State Univ NY, 65; Guggenheim Found Fel, 67; plus many others. Bibliog: Mirella Bandini (auth), article in Data, Milan, Italy, 6-8/75; Jonathan Gray (auth), article in Arts Mag, 9/76. Publ: Auth, Assemblage, Environments and Happenings, Abrams, 65; auth, var bks & articles. Mailing Add: c/o John Gibson Gallery 392 W Broadway New York NY 10028

KAPSALIS, THOMAS HARRY
PAINTER, SCULPTOR
b Chicago, Ill, May 31, 25. Study: Sch Art Inst Chicago, BAE, 49, MAE, 57; Fulbright grant, Ger, 53-54. Exhib: Pa Acad Fine Arts Ann Watercolor & Print Exhib, Philadelphia, 46; Contemp Drawings From 12 Countries, Art Inst Chicago, 52; Barone Gallery Group Show, New York, 56; 27th Biennial Exhib Contemp Painting, Corcoran Gallery Art, Washington, DC, 61; Ill Arts Coun Traveling Exhib, 71; Visions/Painting & Sculpture: Distinguished Alumni 1945 to Present, Art Inst of Chicago, 76; one-man exhib, One Ill Ctr, Chicago, 77. Teaching: Assoc prof drawing & painting, Sch Art Inst Chicago. 54-; lectr painting, Northwestern Univ, Chicago & Evanston, 58-71. Awards: Huntington Hartford Found Grant, 56 & 59; Pauline Palmer Prize, Art Inst Chicago, 60, Jule F Brower Prize, 69. Bibliog: Meilach & Seiden (auth), Direct Metal Sculpture, Crown, 66; Meilach & Hinz (auth), How to Create Your Own Designs, Doubleday, 75. Style & Technique: 20th century style. Media: Oil; Brazed & Welded Metals. Mailing Add: 5204 N Virginia Ave Chicago IL 60625

KARAWINA, ERICA (MRS SIDENY C HSIAO)
PAINTER, STAINED GLASS ARTIST
b Ger; US citizen. Study: Study in Europe; also with Frederick W Allen & Charles J Connick, Boston. Work: Metrop Mus Art, New York; Mus Mod Art, New York; Boston Mus Fine Arts; Libr Cong, Washington, DC; Honolulu Acad Arts. Comn: 20 lancents of faceted glass in concrete, Robert Shipman Thurston, Jr Mem Chapel, Punahou Sch, Honolulu, 67; Crux Gemmata (glass in concrete), Manoa Valley Church, Honolulu, 67; six windows of sculptured glass, St Anthony's Church, Kailua, Oahu, Hawaii, 68; This Earth is Ours (sculptured glass), News Bldg Foyer, Honolulu Advertiser, 72; translucent glass moasic murals, Hawaii State Off Bldg, Honolulu, 75; plus others. Exhib: Dance Int, Rockefeller Ctr, New York, 37; Competition of State of Mass, New York's Fair, 39; Protestant Orthodox Ctr, New York World's Fair, 64; one-man shows, China Inst Int, Taipei, Taiwan, 56 & Contemp Arts Ctr, Honolulu, 77; plus others. Pos: Draftsman stained glass, Co Studios, Boston, 30-33; designer stained glass, Burnham Studios, Boston, 35-38. Awards: John Poole Mem Prize, Honolulu Acad Arts, 52; James C Castle Award, Narcissus Art Festival, Honolulu, 61. Bibliog: Jean Charlot (auth), Exhibition of stained glass, 5/53; Joanne Shaw (auth), Echoes of universality, Vol 72, No 9, Paradise of Pac; Francis Haar & Murray Turnbull (ed), Artists of Hawaii, Vol II, 77. Mem: Honolulu Print Makers; Honolulu Acad of Arts; Hawaii Artists League. fel Int Inst Arts; Nat League Am Pen Women. Style & Technique: Contemporary; leaded and faceted sculptured glass. Media: Stained Glass. Publ: Contribr, From Maui to Mainz, 56-57 & From Hawaii to Holland, 63, Stained Glass. Mailing Add: 3529 Akaka Pl Honolulu HI 96822

KARDON, JANET
CURATOR, ART HISTORIAN
b Philadelphia, Pa. Study: Temple Univ, BS(educ); Univ Pa, MA(art hist). Collections Arranged: Line, Sch of Visual Arts, New York; cur & catalogue auth, Artists Maps, 76, Time, 77, Artists Sets & Costumes, 77 & Duane Michaels, 77, Philadelphia Col of Art. Teaching: Lectr Am art & 20th century art, Philadelphia Col of Art, 68- Pos: Mem 20th century comt, Philadelphia Mus of Art, 74-; dir exhib, Philadelphia Col of Art, 76-; consult panelist, Visual Arts Prog, Nat Endowment for the Arts, 76- Mem: Col Art Asn; Am Asn of Mus. Res: Twentieth century; post-World War II; earthworks performance sculpture. Publ: Auth, Janet Kardon interviews some modern maze makers, Arts Int, 76. Mailing Add: 118 E 60th St New York NY 19021

KARESH, ANN BAMBERGER
PAINTER, SCULPTOR
b Bamberg, Ger; US citizen. Study: Willesden Tech Col, London, Eng; Hornsey Col Art, London. Work: Gibbes Art Gallery, Charleston, SC; Home Fed Savings & Loan Asn Collection, SC; Jewish Community Ctr Collection, Charleston; Columbia Mus Art, SC. Exhib: Watercolor USA, Nat Watercolor Exhib, 62; 23rd Ann Contemp Am Painting, Palm Beach, Fla, 62; Directors Choice, 10 SC Artists Traveling Exhib, 65; Contemp Artists, SC Invitational, 70-71; one-man show, Columbia Mus Art, 72 & B'nai B'rith Mus, Washington, DC, 75; plus others. Awards: First Prize in Painting, SC Artists Ann, 63; Best in Enamel, SC Craftsmen, 68, Best in Metal, 70. Bibliog: Jack A Morris, Jr (auth), Contemporary artists of South Carolina, SC Tricentennial Comn, 70. Mem: Guild of SC Artists (vpres, 65-66, pres, 66-67); SC Craftsmen; Carolina Art Asn (exhib comt, 55-59). Style & Technique:

Representational. Media: Acrylic; Metal, Wood. Mailing Add: 1 Chalmers St Charleston SC 29401

KARLSTROM, PAUL JOHNSON
ART HISTORIAN, ART ADMINISTRATOR
b Seattle, Wash, Jan 22, 41. Study: Stanford Univ, BA(Eng lit), 64; Univ Calif, Los Angeles, MA(art), PhD, 73. Collections Arranged: Venice Panorama (auth, catalogue), Grunwald Ctr for Graphic Arts, Univ Calif, Los Angeles, 69; Archives of American Art, California Collecting, (auth, catalogue), Oakland Mus, Calif, 77; Louis M Eilshemius in the Hirshhorn Museum (traveling exhib; auth, catalogue), Hirshhorn Mus & Sculpture Garden, Smithsonian Inst, Washington, DC, 78. Teaching: Instr Renaissance to mod art, Calif State Univ, Northridge, 72-73; vis instr mus practices, Calif Col Arts & Crafts, Oakland, 76. Pos: Asst cur, Grunwald Ctr for the Graphic Arts, Univ Calif, Los Angeles, 67-70; guest cur, Smithsonian Inst Traveling Exhib Serv, Washington, DC, 77; dir, West Coast Area Ctr, Arch Am Art, Smithsonian Inst, San Francisco, 73- Res: American art history, late 19th to early 20th century: Americans abroad; Victorian painters; Louis M Eilshemius. Publ: Auth, Americans Abroad: Painters of the Victorian Era, San Jose Mus Art, Calif, 75; Louis Michel Eilshemius, Harry N Abrams, 78. Mailing Add: c/o de Young Mus Arch of Am Art Golden Gate Park San Francisco CA 94118

KARN, GLORIA STOLL
PAINTER, INSTRUCTOR
b New York, NY, Nov 13, 23. Study: Art Students League; also with Eliot O'Hara & Samuel Rosenberg. Work: Yale Univ; Carnegie Inst Mus, Pittsburgh; Brooklyn Mus; Pittsburgh Pub Schs. Exhib: Assoc Artists Pittsburgh Ann, 49-; Butler Inst Am Art Ann, 61; one-man shows, Pittsburgh Plan for Art, 65, Carnegie Inst Mus, 66 & North Hills Art Ctr, 78; Sacred Arts Show, St Stephens, Pittsburgh, 66. Teaching: Instr painting & collage, North Hills Artists' & Craftsmen's Guild, 65-; instr, Community College of Allegheny Co, 73- Awards: Purchase Prize, Brooklyn Mus Nat Print Ann, 49; Carnegie Inst Purchase Prize, 60; Westinghouse Purchase Prize, 66. Mem: Assoc Artists of Pittsburgh; Group A, Pittsburgh (pres, 66-70); Arts & Crafts Ctr, Pittsburgh (bd mem, 69-72); North Hills Artists's & Craftsmen's Guild (bd mem, 70-72). Style & Technique: Impasto painting combined with many layers of glaze; reflects spiritual and psychological dimensions of life. Media: Oil. Mailing Add: 151 Louise Rd Pittsburgh PA 15237

KARNIOL, HILDA
PAINTER, INSTRUCTOR
b Vienna, Austria, Apr 28, 10; US citizen. Study: With Olga Konetzny-Maly & A F Seligman, Vienna, 25-28; Acad for Women, 26-30. Work: St Vincent Abbey, Latrobe, Pa; Del Art Ctr, Wilmington; Lycoming Col; Lincoln Sch, Honesdale, Pa; US Dept Health, Educ & Welfare; Pa State Col, Bloomsburg. Comn: Portrait of Dr Gustave Weber, Pres of Susquehanna Univ, 68; and of Mrs Gustave Weber, 77; plus many other pvt portraits. Exhib: Pa State Mus, Harrisburg, 54; Adha Artzt Gallery, New York, 60; Drexel Inst Technol, 60; La Salle Col, 64; La State Univ, New Orleans, 71; plus many others. Teaching: Instr painting, Susquehanna Univ, 58-75. Pos: Artist in residence, Fed Govt Cult Enrichment Prog for Clearfield, Clinton, Centre & Lycoming Cos, 67; art adv, Bicentennial Comn, Sunbury, Pa, 73. Awards: First Prize in Portraiture, Berwick Art Ctr, Pa, 65; First Merit & Purchase Prize, Lewisburg Art Asn, 75. Bibliog: L E L (auth), Art & artists, gallery guide, New York-J Am, 11/60; Sigmund Stoler (auth), Upstate artist's 14th show, Harrisburg Patriot, 67; Michael Lenson (auth), The realm of art, culture mirror, Newark Sun News, 11 /67. Mem: Midstate Artists; Nat Forum Prof Artists; Art Alliance Cent Pa; Soroptimist, Sunbury, Pa. Style & Technique: Neo-realism; abstract-expressionism. Media: Oil. Publ: Illusr, Melusine & illusr, The Nose, 29, Adolf Synek; auth, From the Sketchbook of Hilda Karniol, Standard, 70. Dealer: Rembrandt Art Gallery Inc 1051 Madison Ave New York NY 10028; Millbrook Art Gallery Mill Hall PA 17751. Mailing Add: 960 Race St Sunbury PA 17801

KARP, IVAN C
ART DEALER, LECTURER
b June 4, 26; US citizen. Teaching: Instr art hist, Finch Col, 66-67; instr art hist, Sch Visual Arts, 70-71; lectr. Pos: Pres, Anonymous Arts Recovery Soc, 60-; dir, OK Harris Gallery. Mem: Nat Trust Hist Preservations; Soc Indust Archeol. Specialty: Contemporary painting and sculpture. Publ: Contribr, Artforum & Arts Mag. Mailing Add: 383 W Broadway New York NY 10012

KARP, RICHARD GORDON
PAINTER
b Brooklyn, NY, May 17, 33. Study: City Col New York, BBA(advert) & MA(fine art); Brooklyn Mus Art Sch, with John Bageris. Work: Aankoop Gemete, Stedlijk Mus, Amsterdam, Neth; Northern Ill Univ, DeKalb. Exhib: Ten American Artists Living in the Netherlands, Amsterdam, 68; Traveling Exhib, Benelux Countries, 69; Stedlijk Mus, Amsterdam, 70; RAI Exhib, Amsterdam, 70; Heckscher Mus, Huntington, NY, 74; Viridian Gallery, New York, 77. Bibliog: Julie Attkiss (auth), Karp, riding his intuition, Holland Herald, 3/69. Mem: Asn Artist Run Galleries (exec comt, 75). Style & Technique: Abstract expressionistic paintings utilizing mathematical symbols and quasi grid; chalk, ink and pencil. Media: Oil & Mixed Media. Dealer: Viridian Gallery 24 W 57th St New York NY 10019; Kunsthandel K 276 Keizersgracht 276 Amsterdam Netherlands. Mailing Add: 8 E 12th St New York NY 10003

KARPEL, BERNARD
ART LIBRARIAN, ART EDITOR
b Brooklyn, NY, Feb 10, 11. Study: City Col New York, with Prof George W Eggers, BA, 32; Pratt Inst, BLS, 37; Columbia Univ, Carnegie Corp grant, 41. Teaching: Instr art librarianship, Grad Libr Sch, Columbia Univ, 67-69; lectr art librarianship, Sch Libr Sci, Pratt Inst, 69; assoc prof art librarianship, Sch Libr Sci, Queens Col, 70. Pos: Reader in art, Dept Art, City Col New York, 34-36; art librn, 58th St Br, New York Pub Libr, 37-41; chief librn, Mus Mod Art, New York, 42-73; ed, Bicentennial Bibliog Am Art, Smithsonian Inst, 73-76; consult, Soho Ctr Visual Artists, New York, 74-77; consult, Chadwyck-Healey Microfiche, London, 75-; consult, Art Assocs, Poughkeepsie, NY, 78- Awards: John D Rockefeller III Fund Grant, 66-67; Thomas Jefferson High Sch Alumni Achievement, 70; Award of Merit, Philadelphia Col Art, 69. Mem: Archons Colophon; Art Ref Librn NAm; Col Art Asn Am; Int Coun Mus Mod Art (exec dir, Libr Overseas Prog, 67-75). Res: Bibliography of art in the 20th century, both European and American, visual and verbal as expressed in teaching, publication and international dissemination. Publ: Contribr, Bibliog, Mus Mod Art Publ, 42-73; contribr, Documents of Modern Art, Wittenborn, series 48-72; ed, Contemporary Art, Arno, series 68-72; assoc ed, Documents of Twentieth Century Art, Viking, series 71-78; ed, The Arts in America: An Anthology of Bibliographies, Smithsonian Inst, 78. Mailing Add: 12-16 160th St Beechhurst NY 11357

KARPEL, ELI
SCULPTOR, INSTRUCTOR
b New York, NY, Oct 25, 16. Study: City Col New York, BA; Univ Calif, Los Angeles, MA; Univ Southern Calif; Ohio State Univ; with Chaim Gross. Work: Palm Springs Desert Mus; Hirshhorn Mus, Washington, DC; Storm King Mountain Mus, Mountainville, NY. Exhib: Newport Harbor 19th Ann Art Exhib, 64; 50th Nat Orange Show, San Bernardino, Calif, 65; 4th Ann Southern Calif Exhib, Long Beach Mus Art, 66. Teaching: Lectr art, Univ Calif, Los Angeles, 50-53; prof art, Los Angeles Pierce Col, 58- Style & Technique: Abstractions in polished bronze; occasional realistic human figurative patinated bronze. Media: Bronze & other materials. Dealer: Ankrum Gallery 657 N La Cienega Los Angeles CA 90069. Mailing Add: 689 Brooktree Santa Monica CA 90402

KARSH, YOUSUF
PHOTOGRAPHER
b Armenia, Dec 23, 08; Can citizen. Study: With John H Garo, Boston; hon degrees from nine univs. Work: Metrop Mus Art, New York; Mus Mod Art, New York; Nat Portrait Gallery, London, Eng; St Louis Art Mus, Mo; Nat Gallery Can, Ottawa, Ont. Exhib: One-man shows, Men Who Make Our World, Expo 67, Montreal, PQ, 67, Boston Mus Fine Arts, Mass, 68, Corcoran Gallery Art, Washington, DC, 69, Seattle Art Mus, 70, Mus Mod Art, Tokyo, 71, 72, 73, 74, 75 & 76 & all over Europe, Wichita State Mus, Ulrich Art Gallery, Kenosha Pub Mus, Wis & Mus Sci & Indust, Chicago, 77-78; plus many others, including Nat Gallery of Australia & Prov Alta, Can. Teaching: Vis prof photog & fine arts, Ohio Univ, 68-70; vis prof photog & fine arts, Emerson Col, 72-73. Pos: Photog adv, Expo 70, Osaka, Japan, 69-70; trustee, Photog Arts & Sci Found, 65-72. Awards: Can Coun Medal, 65; Order of Can, Can Govt, 68; Rochester Sci Mus Fel, 72. Bibliog: Faces of Our Time, Telescope Diary of a Portraitist, Can Broadcasting Co, 68; Liptak (auth), Interview with Karsh, Honolulu Mag, 70; Forsee (auth), Yousuf Karsh, In: Five Famous Photographers, 70; featured article, Reader's Digest, 2/77; featured on Sixty Minutes, Columbia Broadcasting Syst, 5/77. Mem: Hon fel Royal Photog Soc; Dutch Treat Club, New York; Rideau Club, Ottawa; Royal Can Acad Arts; Prof Photog Asn Can; Century Club; hon fel Prof Photog Am. Publ: Auth, Faces of Destiny, 46; auth, Portraits of Greatness, 59; auth, In Search of Greatness, 62; auth, Karsh Portfolio, 67; auth, Faces of Our Time, 71; auth, Karsh Portraits, 76. Mailing Add: Karsh Photog Studio 6th Floor Chateau Laurier Ottawa ON Can

KARWELIS, DONALD CHARLES
PAINTER, LECTURER
b Rockford, Ill, Sept 19, 34. Study: Univ Calif, Irvine, with Robert Irwin, BA, 69, with Robert Morris, MFA, 71. Work: Long Beach Mus Art, Calif; Orange Coast Col, Costa Mesa, Calif; Atlantic Richfield Corp; Brand Art Ctr, Glendale, Calif; Riverside City Col, Calif. Exhib: Los Angeles 72, Sidney Janis Gallery, New York; Brand Art Ctr, 72; Collage & Assemblage, Los Angeles Inst Contemp Art, 75; Southland Video Anthology, Long Beach Mus Art, 75; The Irvine Milieu, La Jolla Mus Contemp Art, Calif, 75. Teaching: Lectr sculpture, Univ Calif, Irvine, 69-71; lectr drawing & painting, Riverside City Col, 71-72. Awards: Nat Defense Educ Act Res Grant, US Govt, 70; Nat Endowment for the Arts grant, 76. Bibliog: Barbara Rose (auth), California here it comes, New York Mag, 6/5/72; Peter Plagens (auth), article in Artforum, 11/72; Lynn Gamwell (auth), article in Artweek, 1/78. Mem: Los Angeles Inst Contemp Art. Style & Technique: Acrylic painter; video; film; performance (multi-media). Publ: Contribr, 3/70, 70; contribr, Los Angeles Artists' Publ, 73; auth, Color, 75. Dealer: Ruth S Schaffner 8406 Melrose Ave Los Angeles CA 90069. Mailing Add: 202-K E Stevens Santa Ana CA 92707

KASAK, NIKOLAI (KAZAK)
SCULPTOR-PAINTER, THEORETICIAN
b Lushtcha, Russia, Sept 24, 17; US citizen. Study: City Col Arts, Warsaw, BFA; Acad Fine Art, Vienna, MFA; Acad Fine Art Sch Advan Study, Rome, dipl. Work: Mus Fine Art, Minsk; Mus Fine Art, Baranowicze; Arte Madi Collection, Buenos Aires, Arg. Comn: Sgraffito, City Hall Warsaw; mural, City Hall Baranowicze. Exhib: Palazzo Venezia, Rome, 47; Neue Galerie, Vienna, 48; Quadrienale Arte Rome Rassegna Naz, Galleria Naz Arte Moderna, Rome, 48-49; Palazzo Carignano, Torino, 49; Mus Mod Art, Dallas, Houston & San Antonio, 51; Guggenhiem Mus, New York; Bonino Gallery, Buenos Aires, Arg, 56; Riverside Mus, NY, 58-68; Betty Parsons Gallery, New York, 59-74; Arte Madi Int, Mus Mod Art, Buenos Aires & Denis Rene Gallery, Paris, 61; IBM Gallery, New York, 62; NC Mus of Art, Raleigh, 69; Int Housing & Urban Develop (HUD) Competition Exhib, Washington, DC, 72; plus others. Awards: First Prize for Warsaw Emblem, City Hall Warsaw; First Prize for Mural, City Hall Baranowicze; Prize for Painting-Construct, Art Club Rome. Bibliog: The World of Abstract Art, Wittenborn, 57; The Art of Kasak (monogr), October House, New York, 68; Robert Kramer (auth), Nikolas Kasak, Int Regist of Profiles, Cambridge, 78; plus others. Mem: Am Abstr Artists; Smithsonian Inst. Style & Technique: Essential geometrical constructions of positive and negative space. Res: Originator of Physical Art, a concept of art based on action between (opposing but complementary) material and anti-material reality. Publ: Auth, Physical art—action of positive & negative elements, Manifesto, 46-47; contribr, Storia de Pitture Contemporanee, Domani, Rome, 48; auth, Negative and positive physical space, 51 & auth, Arte fisico-constructivo, 52, Arte Madi, Buenos Aires; auth, Three Decades of Physical Art, New York, 78. Mailing Add: 5648 Delafield Ave Riverdale NY 10471

KASHDIN, GLADYS S
PAINTER, EDUCATOR
b Pittsburgh, Pa, Dec 15, 21. Study: Art Students League, with Stefan Hirsch; Univ Miami, BA(magna cum laude), 60; Fla State Univ, with Karl Zerbe, MA, 62, PhD(humanities), 65. Work: Otterbein Col, Ohio; Hillsborough Aviation Authority, Tampa, Fla; Columbus Mus Arts & Crafts, Ga; Pensacola Art Ctr, Fla; Futan Univ, Shanghai, China. Comn: Silkscreen eds, LeMoyne Art Found, Tallahassee, Fla, 70, 71 & 73. Exhib: 28th Ann Brooklyn Mus, 44; 2nd & 3rd Southeastern Ann, High Mus, Atlanta, 47, one-woman show, 48; Palm Beach Art League, Norton Gallery, West Palm Beach, 48-63, one-woman show, 62; LeMoyne Art Found, Tallahassee, 66-74, one-woman shows, 69 & 74, one-woman show, Columbus Mus Arts & Crafts, Ga, 73. Teaching: Instr & dir oil painting, Adult Educ, Palm Beach Co, Fla, 56-60; instr watercolor, Thomasville Art Guild, Ga, 61-62; prof humanities, Univ S Fla, Tampa, 65-, Humanities Visual Arts Workshops, 66-71. Pos: Photogr, Shafran Co, NY & Fla, 38-60. Awards: Awards of Merit, Palm Beach Art League, 58, 60 & 63, Gold Medals, Univ Miami, 60; One-Person Exhib, Bank of Clearwater, Fla, 66. Bibliog: Charles Benbow (auth), Creators, St Petersburg Times, Fla, 70; Dr Hans Juergensen (auth), Kashdin's Everglades series, 73 & Herb Allen (auth), Local rivers series theme, 75, Tampa Tribune. Mem: LeMoyne Art Found. Style & Technique: Nature subjects; ink drawings, paper and cloth collages, acrylics, serigraphs. Media: Ink, Acrylic. Publ: Auth, A new approach to a humanities-visual arts workshop, Humanities J, fall 70; auth, Life long education for women—general & liberal studies...from their point of view, Perspectives, winter 74. Dealer: LeMoyne Art Found 125 N Gadsen Tallahassee FL 32301. Mailing Add: 441 Biltmore Ave Temple Terrace FL 33617

KASLE, GERTRUDE
ART CONSULTANT, COLLECTOR
b New York, NY, Dec 2, 17. Study: Art STudents League, with John Barber; NY Univ; Univ Mich; Soc Arts & Crafts, Detroit; Wayne State Univ, BS(art educ). Pos: Assoc dir & partner, Franklin Siden Gallery, 64-65; pres, Gertrude Kasle Gallery, 65-; mem comt visual arts & mus, Mich Coun Arts, 71. Awards: Distinguished Alumni Award, Wayne State Univ, 68; President's Cabinet Award, Univ Detroit, 77. Mem: Art Dealers Asn Am; Detroit Art Dealers Asn (vpres, 71-72, pres, 73-75); patron Detroit Inst Arts (Founders' Soc); Nat Soc Lit & Arts; Artists Equity Asn; plus others. Specialty: Contemporary paintings, sculpture and graphics with emphasis on living American artists. Mailing Add: Gertrude Kasle/Colby Art Consults 251 Merrill Birmingham MI 48011

KASPE, VLADIMIR
ARCHITECT, EDUCATOR
b Harbin, China, May 3, 10; Mex citizen. Study: Sch Fine Arts, Paris, dipl, study with Georges Gromort; Nat Univ Mex, dipl. Comn: French Lyceum in Mexico City, French Govt & Colony of Mexico, 50; Monument in Camerone, 65; Jewish Sport Club in Mexico City, 50-73; Grupo Roussel, Pharmacal Lab, Mexico City, Grupo Roussel, SA, 61 & Sumesa, Cent Off, Mex, Super Mercados SA, 61. Exhib: Several exhibs of Mex mod archit in Mex and different countries of Am and Europe. Teaching: Prof archit & adv, Nat Univ Mex, 43-73; prof archit & adv, Univ La Salle, 72-; adv, Univ Autonoma Metropolitana, 75. Awards: Grand Medal, Soc Archit Diplomes par le Gouvernement, French Govt, 39; First Prize, Competition for Temple in Torreon, Mex Asn, 45; Ordre des Palmes Acad, French Govt, 57. Bibliog: I E Myers (auth), Mexico's Modern Architecture, Arch Bk Publ, 52; Alberto Sartoris (ed), Encyclopedia de l'architecture nouvelle, ordre et climat Americains, U Hoepli Editeur, Milan, 54. Mem: Int Soc Critics Art; Soc Archit Diplomes par le Gouvernement; Soc Mex Archit; Cercle Etudes Architecturales, Paris. Res: Theory of architecture. Publ: Numerous articles and constructions in Mexican, American, European and Asian Mag, 45-; contribr, Living Architecture, In: Ancient Mexican, 67. Mailing Add: Ave Ruben Dario 17 Mexico DF Mexico

KASS, RAY
PAINTER
b Rockville Centre, NY, Jan 25, 44. Study: Univ NC, BA(philos), 67, MFA(painting), 69; also painting with Keith Crown. Work: Addison Gallery Am Art, Andover, Mass; Smith Col Mus, Northampton; Boston Pub Libr; Griffith Art Ctr, St Lawrence Univ, Canton, NY; Tufts Univ Med Ctr, Boston. Exhib: One-man shows, Calif State Univ, Humboldt, 70, Allan Stone Gallery, New York, 72, 75 & 77 & Addison Gallery Am Art, 74; 4 Artists Sponsored by Inst Contemp Art, Boston City Hall, 72; Contemp Landscape, Brockton Art Ctr, Fuller Mem, 74. Teaching: Asst prof painting, Calif State Univ, Humboldt, 69-71; guest lectr, Landscape Workshop, Univ NH, Durham, summer 73; asst prof painting, Va Polytechnic Inst, Blacksburg, Va, 76- Awards: Sch Pub Health Purchase Award, Univ NC, 68; Norfolk Biennial Painting Prize, Norfolk Mus, Va, 68; Blanche E Colman Found Award, 73-74. Bibliog: John Canaday (auth), Ray Kass at Allan Stone Gallery, New York Times, 6/3/72. Mem: Boston Visual Artists Union; Col Art Asn Am. Style & Technique: Landscape and environmental abstraction, much of work done in nature. Media: Watercolor, Encaustic. Dealer: Allan Stone Gallery 48 E 86th St New York NY 10028. Mailing Add: Rte 2 Yellow Sulphur Springs Christiansburg VA 24073

KASSOY, BERNARD
PAINTER, PRINTMAKER
b New York, NY, Oct 23, 14. Study: City Col New York, BSS(cum laude), MSE(fine arts); Cooper Union Art Sch, grad, 37; also with John Ferren, Isaac Soyer & Arthur Osver. Work: Workmans Circle Community House, Bronx, NY; pvt collections, Ceylon, England, Italy & US. Comn: Birdiness (film photog & editing), Bd Educ, High Sch Music & Art, New York, 57. Exhib: Art USA 1958, New York, 58; Nat Acad Design, New York, 68 & 75; Showcase, Bronx Coun Arts, New York, 68 & 69; 28 Contemporaries, Bronx Mus Arts, New York, 71; Int Sculpture Exhib, Pietrasanta, Italy, 76 & Forte dei Marmi, Italy, 76; one-man shows, United Fedn Teachers Gallery Invitational, 65, Caravan House Gallery, 75 & Steindler Gallery, 62- (eleven shows to 75); plus others. Teaching: Instr fine arts, High Sch Music & Art, 39-72; instr lithography, City Col New York, 66-67; instr lithography, Nat Acad Design, 68; instr painting & mem fac, Harriet FeBland Advan Painters Workshop, New Rochelle, NY, 74- Pos: Deleg to US comt, Int Asn Artists, UNESCO. Mem: Artists Equity Asn New York (bd dirs, ed, Newsletter, 62-, secy, 75-78); League Present Day Artists (bd dirs, 70-); Contemp Artists Guild. Style & Technique: Figurative. Media: Oil, Watercolor; Woodcut; Lithography, Etching. Publ: Illusr, ed drawings, NY Teacher News, 50-60. Mailing Add: 130 Gale Pl Bronx NY 10463

KASSOY, HORTENSE
SCULPTOR, PAINTER
b Brooklyn, NY, Feb 14, 17. Study: Pratt Inst, grad; Columbia Univ Teachers Col, with Oronzo Maldarelli, BS & MA; Am Artists Sch, with Chaim Gross. Comn: Maternal Force (marble sculpture), Amalgamated Housing Coop Towers, Bronx, NY, 71. Exhib: Nat Acad Design, New York, 71; 28 Contemporaries, Bronx Mus Art, 71, Ann, 72, Year of the Woman, 75; Sculpture Today, Toledo Mus & Toronto Mus, 74; Brooklyn Mus, Contemp Artists Guild, 74; 150th Ann, Nat Acad Design, 75; Int Sculpture Exhib, Forte dei Marmi, Italy, 76 & Pietrasanta, Italy, 76; one-man show, Caravan House Gallery, New York, 75; plus others. Teaching: Instr sculpture, painting & 3D design, Evander Childs High Sch, Bronx, 61-72; instr sculpture, Harriet FeBland Advan Workshop, 75- Pos: Chmn visual arts, Bronx Coun Arts, 73-76. Awards: Grumbacher First Prize in Watercolor, Painters Day at World's Fair, 40. Mem: Artists Equity Asn New York (vpres, 75-77); League Present Day Artists; Contemp Artists Guild; Am Soc Contemp Artists. Style & Technique: Figurative, with elements of abstraction. Media: Wood, Marble; Watercolor, Batik. Mailing Add: 130 Gale Pl Bronx NY 10463

KASTEN, KARL ALBERT
PAINTER, PRINTMAKER
b San Francisco, Calif, Mar 5, 16. Study: Marin Col; Univ Calif, AB & MA; Univ Iowa, with Lasansky; Hans Hofmann Sch Art. Work: Victoria & Albert Mus, London, Eng; Mus MRd Art, New York; Auckland City Mus, New Zealand; Mus Beaux-Arts, Rennes, France; Los Angeles Co Art Mus. Exhib: Int Biennial, Sao Paulo, Brazil, 55; 5th Contemporary Printmakers, Univ Ill, Champaign, 56; Art Inst Chicago Am Painting Ann, 60; Contemporary American Painting & Sculpture, Univ Ill, 69; Achenbach Found Graphic Arts, San Francisco, 75; plus others. Teaching: Instr painting & drawing, Univ Mich, 46-47; asst prof painting & drawing, San Francisco State Col, 47-50; prof painting & graphics, Univ Calif, Berkeley, 50- Awards: Oakland Art Mus Women's Bd Purchase Prize, Western Painters Exhib, 54; Creative Arts Inst Fel, 64 & 71; Tamarind Lithography Fel, 68; plus others. Bibliog: S Minamora (auth), On Collography, Educ Films, 69; L Edmondson (auth), Etching, Van Nostrand Reinhold, 73; Meilach & Ten Hoor (auth), Assemblage & Collage, Crown, 73; A Kurasaki (auth), Modern Woodcut Techniques, Kyoto, Japan, 78; plus others. Mem: Calif Soc Printmakers (coun mem, 72-76). Style & Technique: Abstract, emphasis on color and textural qualities. Dealer: Arlene Lind Gallery 435 Jackson St San Francisco CA 94111; Van Straaten Gallery 646 N Michigan Ave Chicago IL 60611. Mailing Add: 1884 San Lorenzo Ave Berkeley CA 94707

KASUBA, ALEKSANDRA
ENVIRONMENTAL ARTIST
b Lithuania, Jan 10, 23; US citizen. Study: Art Inst Kaunas, Lithuania, 41-42; Acad Fine Rrts, Vilnius, Lithuania, 42. Work: Atlanta Univ Collection; Delgado Mus Art, New Orleans; Mus Contemp Crafts, New York; Johnson's Wax Collection. Comn: Mural (cement), New York Hilton Hotel, 63; four brick walls, Rochester Inst Technol, NY, 67-69; marble wall, Bank of Calif, Portland, Ore, 69; white marble wall, Container Corp Am, Chicago, 69; 20th Century Environment, Carborundum Mus Ceramics, Niagara Falls, 73; plus others. Exhib: One-man show, Waddell Gallery, New York, 66; Experiments in Art & Technology, Brooklyn Mus Art, 68; Contemplative Environments, Mus Contemp Crafts, New York, 70; Space Shelters for Senses, New York, 71-72; Spectral Passage, DeYoung Mem Mus, San Francisco, 75; Cranbrook Acad of Art Mus, 76; Women in Am Archit, Brooklyn Mus, 77; plus others. Teaching: Instr creative processes & elements art in archit scale, Sch Visual Arts, 71-72; instr stretched fiber structures, Cranbrook Acad of Art, 76. Awards: Am Inst Archit Citation, Artist-Archit Collab, 71; Citation for Innovative Space Treatment, Women's Archit Auxiliary & New York Chap Am Inst Archit, 72. Bibliog: Rita Reif (auth), article in New York Times, 5/11/71; James D Morgan (auth), article in Archit Rec, 8/71; Ronald Najman (auth), Saturday Revue, 8/12/72; plus many others. Style & Technique: Space definitions. Publ: Contribr, Report on Art & Technology Program of the Los Angeles County Museum of Art, 71; contribr, Underground Interiors, Quadrangle, 72; contribr, Women in American Architecture & Design, Whitney Pub, 77. Mailing Add: 43 W 90th St New York NY 10024

KATAOKA, MITS
DESIGNER, VIDEO ARTIST
b Los Angeles, Calif, Mar 12, 34. Study: Univ Calif, Los Angeles, BA, 57, MA, 59. Work: Design of City of Irvine 2-way interactive cable TV as a mosaic, decentralized, creative, aural-visual access system. Exhib: Tokyo 2nd Ann Video Exhib, 72; Am Ctr Exhib, Brussels, 75; Exhib, Aarhus, Denmark, 76. Teaching: Assoc prof design & video, Univ Calif, Los Angeles, 68-, vchmn dept art & head design, 75- Pos: Dir, Univ Calif, Los Angeles Dickson Video Lab, 70-75; dir & designer, Irvine City-Wide Sch & Community Cable Syst, 74- Awards: Concord Res Grant, 70; Univ Calif Art Coun Grant, Los Angeles, 71; Sr Fulbright Res Fel, 72. Mem: Col Art Asn Am. Style & Technique: Videotape real time aural-visual imagery. Media: Video, Offset, Silkscreen. Mailing Add: 1747 Kelton Ave Los Angeles CA 90024

KATAYAMA, TOSHIHIRO
DESIGNER, EDUCATOR
b Osaka, Japan, July 17, 28. Study: Self-taught. Work: Mus Mod Art, New York; Seibu Mus Art, Tokyo, Japan; Mus Mod Art, Olta, Japan; Rose Art Mus, Brandeis Univ, Waltham, Mass. Comn: Banners (6ft x 18ft), Grad Sch Design, Harvard Univ, 73; two murals (8ft x 8ft), BP, Alaska Bldg, 74; mural (12ft x 40ft), Metrop Boston Transit Authority, State St Sta, 76; Super Graphic Mural, Goshen Col, Ind, 76. Exhib: Graphic Image, Cent Mus Mod Art, Tokyo & Kyoto Nat Mus, Japan, 73 & 74; Identity, Seibu Mus Art, Tokyo, 76; one-man shows, Visual Construction Series, Herman Miller, Basel & Zurich, Switz, 65, Am Inst Graphic Art Gallery, New York, 68, Plaza Dick Gallery, Tokyo, 71, Sq & Movement Series, Rose Art Mus, Brandeis Univ, 71, Gallery Art Asia, Cambridge, Mass, 76, Kunstler Haus, Wine, Austria, 77 & Nantenshi Gallery, Tokyo, 78. Teaching: Sr lectr graphic design, Carpenter Ctr for Visual Arts, Harvard Univ, Cambridge, 66- Pos: Art dir, Nippon Design Ctr, Tokyo, 60-63; grpahic designer, Geigy, Basel, Switz, 63-66. Bibliog: Max Huber, Eugen Gomringer (auth), Toshi Katayama & his colored constellations, Graphis, 64 & 66; George Kepes & Ivan Number 114, 64 & Number 124, 66; George Kepes & Ivan Chermaeff (auth), Graphic work by Toshi, Graphic Design, Number 50, 73; Shutaro Mukai, Susumu Shingu, Koji Taki & Tsunehisa Kimura (auth), World of Toshi Katayama, Design, Number 7, 74. Mem: Alliance Graphique Int (head official, Zurich, 75); Am Inst Graphic Art, New York. Style & Technique: Concrete art, topological expression. Media: Collage; Silkscreen Print; Acrylic on Canvas; Metal with Magnet. Publ: Co-auth, Twelve Persons in Graphic Design Today, Bijutsu Shuppan-Sha, 69; co-auth, Three Notations, Rotations with Mr Octavio Paz, Harvard Univ, 74. Dealer: Nantenshi Gallery 3-7-13 Kyobashi Chuo-Ku Tokyo Japan. Mailing Add: 16 Mystic Bank Arlington MA 02174

KATO, KAY
CARTOONIST, ILLUSTRATOR
b Budapest, Hungary. Study: Art Acad, Budapest; Pa Acad Fine Arts; also with Janos Vaszary. Comn: Cover, Am Tel & Tel Mag, 54; book jacket for The Television-Radio Audience and Religion, 55; cover, Today's Living, New York Herald-Tribune, 57; also covers for Christian Sci Monitor, Sat Eve Post & others. Exhib: White Mountains Art Festival, 63; one-man shows at Pa Acad Fine Arts, Montclair Art Mus, Boston Pub Libr & Newark Pub Libr; At Man and His World, Int Salon of Cartoons, Montreal, Que, 75, 76, 77 & 78; plus others. Teaching: Lect on art of cartooning & other subjects, women's clubs, prof groups, cruises & others; instr, Cambridge Cte Adult Educ, Mass, 44-47; instr, South Orange & Maplewood Adult Sch, 63. Pos: Cartoonist, Am Cyanamid Co; cartoonist, Nat Asn Home Economists Convention, 63; spec featured appearance, New York World's Fair, 64. Awards: Best Cartoons of the Year, 43; Foremost Woman in Commun, 70; Heart Asn Award for Cartoon Column, 75; First Prize Award for Cartoons, NJ State Fedn Women's Clubs, 77 & 78; plus others. Mem: Essex Watercolor Club; Overseas Press Club Am (chmn graphic arts comt, mem bull comt). Style & Technique: Brush and ink and halftone for magazine covers in color; pen and ink. Publ: Contribr, This Week, Nation's Bus, New York Times Mag, Am Weekly & others; contribr, Bicentennial July 4th souvenir ed, Philadelphia Bull, 76; contribr, Staten Island Advance, 77; auth, weekly cartoon column, Star Ledger, Newark. Mailing Add: 60 Chapman Pl Glen Ridge NJ 07028

KATSIFF, BRUCE
PHOTOGRAPHER, EDUCATOR
b Philadelphia, Pa, Dec 10, 45. Study: Philadelphia Col of Art, 64-65; Rochester Inst of Technol, BFA, 68; Pratt Inst, MFA, 73. Work: George Eastman House, Rochester, NY; Am Arts Doc Ctr, Exeter, Eng. Exhib: Photog as Printmaking, Mus of Mod Art, New York, 68; 164th Ann Printmaking & Drawing, Pa Acad of Fine Arts, 69; Vision & Expressionism, George Eastman House, 69; Philadelphia Mus of Art, 70; Christmas Invitational, Philadelphia Art Alliance, 71; Lumberville, Peale House Gallery, Pa Acad of Fine Arts, 73. Collections Arranged: Underground Gallery, New York; Riverside Gallery, Rochester, NY. Teaching: Assoc prof photog, Bucks Co Community Col, 69- & Thomas Edison Col, 76- Pos: Asst producer, Darcey Assoc, 67-69; chmn fine arts, Bucks Co Community Col, 73- Bibliog: Gene Thorton (auth), Photography Review, Village Voice, 70. Mem: Col Art Asn; Arts

Alliance of Bucks Co (mem bd). Style & Technique: Worked as both a straight and crooked photographer. Mailing Add: River Rd Lumberville PA 18933

KATZ, ALEX
PAINTER
b New York, NY, July 24, 27. Study: Cooper Union; Skowhegan Sch, Maine. Work: Mus Mod Art, New York; Art Inst Chicago; Whitney Mus Am Art, New York; Detroit Inst Arts; Wadsworth Atheneum, Hartford, Conn; Metrop Mus, New York. Exhib: Twenty Years of American Painting, Mus Mod Art, New York, 66; Figures and Environments, Walker Art Ctr, Minneapolis, 70; Retrospective Exhib, Wadsworth Atheneum, 71, Whitney Mus & Va Mus, 74-75; 32nd Biennial Exhib Contemp Am Painting, Corcoran Gallery Art, Washington, DC, 71; American Collage, Mus Mod Art, New York. Awards: Guggenheim Fel, 72. Bibliog: Nicol Calas (auth), Art in the Age of Risk, 68 & Nicol & Elena Calas (auth), Icons and Images of the Sixties, 71, Dutton; Sam Hunter (auth), American Art Since 1945, Abrams, 69; Irving Sandler & William Berkson (ed), Alex Katz,Praeger, 71. Style & Technique: Representational; modern imagery. Media: Oil. Mailing Add: 435 W Broadway New York NY 10012

KATZ, EUNICE
PAINTER, SCULPTOR
b Denver, Colo, Jan 29, 14. Study: Art Student League, with Harry Sternberg; Sculpture Ctr, with Dorothea Denslow; also with Angelo di Benedetto, Frederick Taubes, Donald Pierce & Edgar Britton. Work: US State Dept Art for Embassies Prog, Washington, DC; Temple Emanuel Collection, Denver, Colo; Denver US Nat Bank; Hillel House, Boulder; Children's Hosp, Pittsburgh, Pa. Comn: Stained glass window, BMH Congregation, Denver, 67 & 13' walnut & bronze tablet, 75; stained glass window, East Denver Orthodox Congregation, 68; four figure sculpture (bronze), Beth Israel Hosp, 70; two stained glass windows, Hebrew Congregation, Wichita, Kans, 72. Exhib: Allied Artists Am, Nat Acad, 49-66; Nat Soc Painters & Sculptors, NJ, 64; one-man shows, Pietrantonio Gallery, New York, 65 & La Salle Univ, Philadelphia, 65; Int Soc Designers & Craftsmen, El Paso, Tex, 72. Teaching: Instr drawing & painting, Studio Classes, 57-65. Pos: Adv, KRMA Channel 6 Educ TV Ann Art Auction, Denver, 70-74. Awards: Award of Merit, Rocky Mountain Liturgical Arts, 58; Patron's Award, Art Mus NMex Biennial, 66; First Place Award, Am Asn Univ Women, 66. Bibliog: KRMA TV Fine Artist Series, Educ TV, 66; Woman artists of the Southwest, Artist Mag, 73. Mem: Allied Sculptors Colo; Artists Equity (secy, Denver Chap, 63-64); Rocky Mountain Liturgical Arts; Greater Denver Coun Arts & Humanities; Am Fedn Arts. Style & Technique: Expressionistic painter, figurative; figurative sculptures in clay and wax for lost wax casting. Media: Oil; Bronze. Dealer: Saks Galleries 3019 E Second Ave Denver CO 80206. Mailing Add: 3131 E Alameda Ave Denver CO 80209

KATZ, HILDA (HILDA WEBER)
PAINTER, PRINTMAKER
b June 2, 09; US citizen. Study: Nat Acad Design; New Sch Social Res, scholar, 40 & 41. Work: In spec collections of Nat Gallery Art, Washington, DC, Metrop Mus Art, New York, Libr Cong, Washington, DC, Nat Collection Fine Arts, Washington, DC & Nat Air & Space Mus, Washington, DC. Exhib: Venice Biennial, US Pavilion, Italy, 40; Corcoran Gallery Art Biennial, Washington, DC; Boston Pub Libr Invitations to Turin, Venice, Florence & Naples, Italy & France & Israel; US Info Agency Exhib to Europe, Asia, MidE & Africa; Soc Am Graphic Artists-Japan Invitational Exchange; plus others. Teaching: Lectr demonstrations in painting & graphics for art asns, until 51. Awards: Six Purchase Awards, Libr Cong; Prize; Soc Am Graphic Artists; Honor Award Plaque, Exec & Prof Hall of Fame, 66; plus others. Bibliog: Article in Metrop Mus Art Bull, 66; Report & studies in history of art, Nat Gallery Art, 67-69; article in Nat Air & Space Catalog, 71. Mem: Soc Am Graphic Artists (jury-award selection bd); Nat Asn Women Artists (jury-award selection bd); Int Platform Asn; fel Metrop Mus Art; hon mem Acad Sci, Lett & Arts, Milano, Italy; plus others. Mailing Add: 915 West End Ave Apt 5D New York NY 10025

KATZ, JOSEPH M
COLLECTOR, PATRON
b July 7, 13. Study: Univ Pittsburgh, 31-34. Collection: 19th and 20th century paintings and sculpture; gold and enamel snuff boxes of 17th, 18th and 19th centuries; Chinese snuff bottles; antiquities; ancient glass of the Roman era; French and English porcelain; 18th century French furniture. Mailing Add: Gateway Towers Pittsburgh PA 15222

KATZ, LEO
PAINTER, WRITER
b Roznau, Austria, Dec 30, 87; US citizen. Study: Acad Fine Arts, Vienna, grad, 08; Acad Fine Arts, Munich, 09. Work: Whitney Mus Am Art; Print Dept, Metrop Mus Art & Print Dept, Mus Mod Art, New York; Print Dept, Lessing Rosenwald Collection, Nat Gallery, Washington, DC; Bibliot Nat, Paris; plus others. Comn: Murals, comn by Baron W Von Gutmann, Tobitschau Castle, Czech, 13-15, Give Us This Day Our Daily Light, Century Prog Expos, Johns-Manville Bldg, Chicago, 33-34, Crossroads, Works Prog Admin, Frank Wiggins Trade Sch, Los Angeles, 35-36 & Metamorphosis 1942, comn by Dr & Mrs Bela Schick, Garrison, NY; sect of Orozco frescoes, Dartmouth Col, NH, 32. Exhib: One-man shows, Old Nat Gallery, Smithsonian Inst, Washington, DC, 24 & Fine Arts Mus, San Diego, Calif, 27; Nat Print Shows, Long Beach, Calif, 38 & Libr of Cong, Washington, DC, 46; US Embassy-Cult Attache Exhib, Paris, 51 & Traveling Exhib New York, France, Italy, Egypt, India, Pakistan & others, 51-52. Teaching: NY Univ lectr, Metrop Mus Art, 27-33; vis lectr, New Sch Social Res & Univ Calif, Los Angeles, 29-33; lectr, Cooper Union Art Sch, 36-46; assoc prof hist art, painting, photog, graphics & design, Brooklyn Col, 42-45. Pos: Chmn dept art, Hampton Inst, 46-53; dir, Atelier 17, New York, 46 & 50-55; pres & trustee, Va Art Alliance, Richmond, 51-52; Whitney prof artist in residence, Spelman Col, 55-57. Awards: First Prize for Lithography, Nat Print Soc, Long Beach, 38; Pennell Purchase Prize for Engraving & Etching, Libr of Cong Print Dept, 46; MacDowell Fel, 60-62. Bibliog: F E Washburn Freund (auth), Leo Katz: Freud of the easel, Int Studio, 4/23; Meyer Levin (auth), Myth & cosmos & Adolph Rosenberg (auth), Leo Katz, 11/27/59, Southern Israelite; Stanley & Lelie Krippner (auth), Dreams, creativity & prophetic art, Psychic, 7/72; plus one other. Mem: Soc Am Graphic Artists; Found Mind Res (adv bd); Am Soc Psychical Res; plus others. Media: Watercolor, Tempera, Fresco. Res: Pre-Columbian art and mythology; comparative religions, parapsychology; astro-mythological psychology; competitive and creative thinking; dimensional dynamics. Publ: Contribr chap in Encycl Social Sci, Columbia Univ, 30; auth, Understanding Modern Art, Vols I-III, 36-40; contribr, Miniature Camera Work, Morgan & Lester, 38; contribr four chaps in Encycl Photog, 42-72; contribr, Art & archeology in the Aztec figure of Coatlicue, Mag Art, 4/45. Dealer: Allan Stone Gallery 48 E 86th St New York NY 10028; Lotte Jacobi Studio of Art & Photog Hillsboro NH 03244. Mailing Add: 1125 Grand Concourse Bronx NY 10452

KATZ, MORRIS
PAINTER
Study: Ulm, WGer & Gunsburg; with Hans Facler; Art Students League. Work: Evansville Mus Arts & Sci, Ind; Jr Col Albany, NY; Butler Inst Am Art, Youngstown, Ohio; St Lawrence Univ Gifffiths Art Ctr, Canton, NY; Univ Art Gallery, State Univ NY Binghamton. Exhib: Instant Art Shows, more than 3500 throughout the world. Mem: Am Guild of Variety Artists; Int Platform Asn; Artists Equity Asn; Int Arts Guild Monaco. Style & Technique: Instant art-combined use of palette knife, tissue paper and liberally applied amounts of paint. Media: Oil, Pencil. Mailing Add: 406 Sixth Ave New York NY 10011

KATZ, THEODORE (HARRY)
EDUCATOR, PAINTER
b Philadelphia, Pa, July 29, 37. Study: Franklin & Marshall Col, AB, 59; Philadelphia Col Art, 59-60; Art Students League, 61-65; Acad Grande Chaumiere, Paris, 64-65; Boston Mus Sch Arts, 68-71; Carpenter Ctr, Harvard Univ, 69, Grad Sch Educ, 68-70, EdM, 69, EdD, 72. Exhib: Salem Col, Winston-Salem, NC, 67; Harvard Univ, Cambridge, Mass, 70; Inst Am Indian Arts, Santa Fe, NMex, 72; John F Kennedy Ctr for Performing Arts, Washington, DC, 73; Moore Col of Art, Philadelphia, Pa, 77. Teaching: Master instr & curric developer, NC Advan Sch, Winston-Salem, 65-67 & Skidmore Col, 67; dir commun prog, Pa Advan Sch, Philadelphia, 67-68; lectr & consult classroom Renaissance arts, Humanities Leadership Inst, State of NJ, 68-70. Pos: Field reader, Off Educ, Arts & Humanities, Dept Health, Educ & Welfare, 67-71; res asst proj, Grad Sch Educ, Harvard Univ, 69-71; consult, Northwest Regional Educ Lab, Portland, Ore, 71-74; dir, Ford Found Proj, Inst Am Indian Arts, Santa Fe, NMex, 72-74; dir, Outreach Prog, Appalachian Regional Libr, North Wilkesboro, NC, 76; mem exec bd, Nat Exhib of Art by the Blind, Philadelphia, Pa, 77-78; chief, Div Educ, Philadelphia Mus of Art, Pa, 77- Bibliog: The Advancement School for boys who could do better, Carnegie Quart, Vol 14, No 3; Howard Taubman (auth), Awakening the defeated, New York Times, 11/12/66; Henry S Resnik (auth), Turning on the System: War in the Philadelphia Public Schools, Pantheon, 70. Mem: Phi Delta Kappa; Nat Art Educ Asn; Am Asn of Mus; Archives of Am Art; Asn for Supv & Curric Develop. Media: Oil, Watercolor; Pen and Ink. Mailing Add: 411 E Rydal Apts Jenkintown PA 19046

KATZEN, HAL ZACHERY
ART DEALER
b Baltimore, Md, July 16, 54. Study: San Francisco Col Art; Johns Hopkins Univ; Md Inst Col Art, BFA. Pos: Asst dir, B R Kornblatt Gallery, Baltimore, Md, 76- Specialty: Contemporary art, American painting and sculpture. Mailing Add: 3410 Vargas Cir Baltimore MD 21207

KATZEN, LILA (PELL)
SCULPTOR, EDUCATOR
b New York, NY. Study: Art Students League; Cooper Union; also with Hans Hofmann, New York & Provincetown, Mass. Work: Nat Collection Fine Arts, Smithsonian Inst, Washington, DC; Everson Mus of Art, Syracuse, NY; Milwaukee Art Ctr, Wis; Nat Gallery of Art, Washington, DC; Mus of Art, Univ Iowa, Iowa City; plus others. Comn: Light-floors, Archit League New York, 68; Universe as Environment, State Univ NY Stony Brook, 69; Laterna Magika, Czech Theatre Facade, Expo '70, Eurofilm Ltd, 70; media-wall (with James R Edmunds, III, Architect), Chesapeake & Potomac Tel Co, Baltimore, MD, 72; and others. Exhib: Ga Mus of Art, Athens, 68 & 69; Nat Collection of Fine Arts, Smithsonian Inst, Washington, DC, 68; Explorations 70, Sao Paulo Biennale, Smithsonian Inst, 70; Gedok, Kunsthaus, Hamburg, Ger, 72; Biennial of Contemporary Painting and Sculpture, Whitney Mus Am Art, New York, 73; Newport Monumenta '74; Sculpture and Site '75, Everson Mus, Syracuse, NY & Baltimore Mus, 75; plus others. Teaching: Instr 2-D design-media, sculpture, art & perception, Md Inst Col Art, 62- Awards: Nat Endowment Grant, 73; Goodyear Fel, 74; Creative Arts Award, Am Asn Univ Women, 74; plus others. Bibliog: Lawrence Alloway (auth), Directions I: Options (catalog), Milwaukee Art Ctr, 68-; Cindy Nemser (auth), Lila Katzen: A human approach to public sculpture, Arts Mag, 75 & Art Talk, 75; Alessandra Comini (auth), Aspects: Lila Katzen (catalogue), Mus of Art, Univ Iowa, Iowa City, 77. Mem: Archit League, New York; College Art Asn; Municipal Art Soc, New York. Style & Technique: Environmental, broad open gestures of curved steel, in weathered metal combinations. Media: Steel, Plastics and Various Metals. Dealer: Gloria Cortella Gallery 41 E 57th St New York NY 10022; Barbara Kornblatt Gallery, 326 N Charles St Baltimore MD 21201. Mailing Add: 345 W Broadway New York NY 10013

KATZEN, PHILIP
ART DEALER, CURATOR
b Baltimore, Md, Apr 24, 22. Study: St Louis Univ, Mo, BS. Collections Arranged: Bobst Library Art Collection, NY Univ. Pos: Cur, Martha Jackson Gallery, New York. Specialty: Contemporary American and European painting, sculpture and graphics. Mailing Add: c/o Martha Jackson Gallery 521 W 57th St New York NY 10019

KATZENBERG, DENA S
CURATOR
b Baltimore, Md. Study: Johns Hopkins Univ; New York Sch of Interior Design. Collections Arranged: Great Am Cover-Up: Counterpanes of the 18th & 19th Century (auth, catalogue), 71, Contemp Egyptian Folk Tapestries, 73, Blue Traditions: Indigo Dyed Textiles & Related Cobalt Glazed Ceramics from the 17th Century through the 19th Century (auth, catalogue), 73-74 & And Eagles Sweep Across the Sky: Indian Textiles of the NAm W (auth, catalogue), 77, Baltimore Mus of Art. Pos: Cur, Baltimore Mus of Art. Mem: Centre Int d'Etude des Textiles Anciens, Lyon, France; Needle & Bobbin Club, New York. Res: History of Indigo dye, Irish textile printing and manufacturing; North American Indian weaving; American quilting. Collection: Textiles. Publ: Auth, Copper plate-printed Irish textile, Antiques, 4/77. Mailing Add: Baltimore Mus of Art Art Mus Dr Baltimore MD 21218

KATZIVE, DAVID H
ART ADMINISTRATOR
b San Francisco, Calif, Mar 23, 42. Study: Brown Univ, BA; Univ Chicago, MA. Teaching: Instr art hist, Univ Chicago Exten, 66-68; instr art hist, Ill Inst of Technol, Chicago, 68-70. Pos: Chief educ div, Philadelphia Mus of Art, 70-76; consult, Art Park, Lewiston, NY, 74-; asst dir, Brooklyn Mus, 76- Mem: Am Asn of Mus (mem coun, 77-80); Col Art Asn. Mailing Add: c/o Brooklyn Mus Eastern Pkwy & Washington Ave Brooklyn NY 11238

KATZMAN, HERBERT
PAINTER, INSTRUCTOR
b Chicago, Ill, Jan 8, 23. Study: Art Inst Chicago, cert. Work: Mus Mod Art & Whitney Mus Am Art, New York; Art Inst Chicago; Hirschorn Mus, Washington, DC; Crocker Art Ctr, Sacramento, Calif. Exhib: Fifteen Americans, Mus Mod Art, New York, 52; New Decade, Whitney Mus, 54; Venice Biennial, Italy, 57; Carnegie Biennial, Pa Acad Fine Arts. Teaching: Instr painting & drawing, Sch Visual Arts, New York, 69- Awards: Grants, Nat Acad Arts

& Lett, 58, Nat Coun Arts & Humanities, 66, Guggenheim, 68 & New York Coun Arts, 76. Bibliog: Art USA, Viking, 63; Eric Protter (auth), Painters on Painting, Dunlap, 63. Style & Technique: Landscape and figures. Media: Oil. Dealer: Dintenfass Gallery 50 W 57th St New York NY 10021. Mailing Add: 463 West St Apt 919C New York NY 10014

KATZMAN, LAWRENCE
See Kaz

KAUFFMAN, (CAMILLE) ANDRENE
PAINTER, MURALIST
b Chicago, Ill, Apr 19, 05. Study: Art Inst Chicago, BFA; Univ Chicago, MFA; Ill Inst Technol; Univ Ill, Chicago; also with Andre Lhote, Paris. Work: Art Inst Chicago; Vanderpoel Gallery, Beverly Art Ctr, Chicago; Rockford Col; Mt Mary Col (Wis); also many easel paintings in schs throughout Midwest. Comn: Murals (oil on canvas), Works Progress Admin & US Treas Dept, Burbank & Hirsch High Sch, Cook Co Hosp, Ida Grove & Iowa Post Off Bldgs, 34-42; bas reliefs (wood or stone), Works Progress Admin, schs & field houses, Oak Park & Evanston, Ill, 34-42; murals (ceramic tile), Sci Bldg, Rockford Col, 51-52; murals (ceramic) & stained glass window, Third Unitarian Church Chicago, 55-69; mural (acrylic), Forest Park Pub Libr, Ill, 72. Exhib: One-woman shows, San Diego Mus, 50, La Jolla Fine Arts Gallery, Calif, 50, Bernard Gallery, Chicago, early 60's, Vanderpoel Gallery, 70 & Univ Club Chicago, 74; one-woman retrospective, Third Unitarian Church Chicago, 67. Teaching: Prof, Art Inst Chicago, 27-67, emer prof, 67- Awards: John Quincy Adams Fel to Europe, Art Inst Chicago, 27, Chicago & Vicintiy Exhib Honorable Mention for Drawing, 46; Second Prize for Block Print Calendar, 73, Chicago Soc Artists, 72. Bibliog: Robert B Johnson (auth), Sermon results in murals, Unitarian Register, 1/59; Prof John Hayward (narrator), Third Church Trilogy (TV prog), Channel 11, Chicago, 8/59; Donald Key (auth), Kauffmann show rich in color, Milwaukee J, 9/17/61. Mem: Arts Club Chicago; Nat Soc Mural Painters; Chicago Soc Artists. Media: Acrylics, Ceramic Glaze; Oil, Watercolor. Dealer: Art Rental & Sales Gallery The Art Institute of Chicago Michigan Blvd at Adams St Chicago IL 60603. Mailing Add: 411 N West Ave Elmhurst IL 60126

KAUFFMAN, ROBERT CRAIG
PAINTER, SCULPTOR
b Los Angeles, Calif, Mar 31, 32. Study: Univ Southern Calif Sch Archit, 50-52; Univ Calif, Los Angeles, MA, 56. Work: Whitney Mus Am Art, New York; Tate Gallery Art, London, Eng; Art Inst Chicago; Los Angeles Co Mus Art; Pasadena Art Mus, Calif; plus others. Exhib: The New Aesthetic, Washington Gallery Mod Art, 67; 5th Paris Biennale, Paris & Pasadena, 67; The 1960's, Mus Mod Art, New York, 67; Kompas IV, Holland, Ger & Switz, 69; one-man show, Pasadena Mus, Calif, 70; California Prints, Mus Mod Art, New York, 72; Corcoran Biennial, 73; 71st Am Exhib, Art Inst Chicago, 74; Whitney Downtown, 74; Univ Ill, 74; Inst Contemp Arts, Los Angeles, Calif, 75; plus others. Teaching: Assoc prof painting & sculpture, Univ Calif, Irvine, 67-72; instr painting & sculpture, Univ Calif, Berkeley, 69; instr painting & sculpture, Sch Visual Arts, New York, 70-71. Awards: US Govt Fel for the Arts, 67; 69th Am Exhib First Prize, Art Inst Chicago, 70. Bibliog: Barbara Rose (auth), Craig Kauffman (catalog for New Aesthetic), 67; Jane Livingston (auth), Recent works by Craig Kauffman, 69 & Review of Kauffman show, 70, Artforum. Style & Technique: Literal structural; semi-expressionist. Media: Acrylic, Plastic. Publ: Co-auth, Transparency, Reflection, Light, Space, 71. Dealer: Pace Gallery 32 E 57th St New York NY 10022. Mailing Add: 160 La Brea Laguna Beach CA 92651

KAUFMAN, EDGAR, JR
DESIGNER, WRITER
b Pittsburgh, Pa, Apr 9, 10. Study: Painting in New York, Vienna, Florence & London; apprentice with Frank Lloyd Wright. Collections Arranged: Dir, Good Design, thrice-yearly exhibs sponsored by Merchandise Mart, Chicago & Mus Mod Art, New York; dir two exhibs, US Consumer Wares, circulated by US Govt in Europe, 50-55; dir, Int Competition for Low-Cost Furniture Design, 54-55; dir exhib, Textiles & Jewelry from India, 54-55; US Coordr, The Arts of Denmark Exhib, Metrop Mus Art, 60; traveling exhibs organized for Smithsonian Inst on work of Fulbright designers & for US Info Agency on Am designers. Teaching: Bemis lectr, Mass Inst Technol, 56; lectr, NY Univ Inst Fine Arts, 61; lectr, Mus Mod Art; plus others. Pos: Dir dept indust design, Mus Mod Art, 46-50; adv dept design in indust, Parson's Sch Design, 55-61; mem comt on 20th century painting & sculpture, Art Inst Chicago; dept ed applied arts, Encycl Britannica, 58-; chmn design comt & adminr Kaufman Int Design Award, 59- Mem: Fel Royal Soc Arts; Int Design Inst; Am Inst Interior Designers; Chicago Art Club. Publ: Auth, Prize Designs for Modern Furniture, What is Modern Design?, What is Modern Interior Design & Taliesin Drawings, Mus Mod Art; auth, Frank Lloyd Wright, Writings and Buildings, 60; plus others. Mailing Add: 278 First Ave New York NY 10009

KAUFMAN, IRVING
PAINTER, EDUCATOR
b New York, NY, Oct 4, 20. Study: Art Students League; NY Univ, BA & MA. Work: Univ Mich Mus Art; Saginaw Mus Art; Ohio State Univ; Parke-Davis Co; Columbia Univ Law Libr. Exhib: Various group shows and one-man exhibs. Teaching: Assoc prof art, Univ Mich, Ann Arbor, 56-64; prof art, City Col New York, 64- Mem: Inst Study Art in Educ (pres, 72); Col Art Asn Am; Univ Coun Art Educ. Style & Technique: Colorfield abstraction; landscape impressionist. Media: Oil. Publ: Auth, Art & Education in Contemporary Culture, 66; contribr, Concepts in Art Education, 70; contribr, New Ideas in Art Education, 72; ed, Arts Issue, Curriculum Theory, Network, 74; contribr, Arts in Society, 75; plus others. Dealer: Rehn Gallery 655 Madison Ave New York NY 10021. Mailing Add: 34 Corell Rd Scarsdale NY 10583

KAUFMAN, JANE A
PAINTER, INSTRUCTOR
b New York, NY, May 26, 38. Study: Cornell Univ; NY Univ, BA; Hunter Col, MA. Work: Whitney Mus Am Art, New York; Aldrich Mus, Ridgefield, Conn; Corcoran Gallery, Washington, DC. Exhib: One-man shows, A M Sachs Gallery, New York, 58 & 70, Whitney Mus Am Art, 71, Henri Gallery, Washington, DC, 73 & Alessandra Gallery, New York, 76; The Structure of Color, Whitney Mus Am Art, 71; Paley & Lowe Gallery, New York, 72. Teaching: Instr art, Lehman Col, 69-70; instr art, Bard Col, 71-; instr, Queens Col, 73-74. Awards: Guggenheim Fel, 74. Style & Technique: Sprayed metal flake on canvas. Media: Acrylic. Dealer: Alessandra Gallery 489 Broome St New York NY 10013. Mailing Add: 262 Bowery St New York NY 10013

KAUFMAN, JOE
ILLUSTRATOR
b Bridgeport, Conn, May 21, 11. Study: Lab Sch Indust Design; also with Herbert Bayer. Exhib: Art Dirs Club, 43-60; Soc Illustrators, 45; one-man show, Fleisher Art Mem, Philadelphia, 50. Mem: Soc Illustrators. Publ: Auth & illusr, Christmas Tree Book, 68, Words; auth & illusr, What Makes It Go, Work, Fly, Float?, 71 & illusr, Eddie's Moving Day, 69, Western Publ; illusr, I Spy With My Little Eye, McGraw, 70; auth & illusr, Busy People, 73; auth & illusr, How We Born, How We Grow, Work, Learn, 75; auth & illusr, About the Big Sky, High Hills, Rich Earth, Deep Sea, 78; plus others. Mailing Add: 18 W 70th St New York NY 10023

KAUFMAN, MICO
SCULPTOR
b Romania, Jan 3, 24; US citizen. Study: Acad Fine Arts, Rome & Florence, Italy, 47-51. Work: Bas relief, Rivier Col, Nashua, NH; Andover Gallery Fine Arts, Mass; Kiski Acad, Saltburg, Pa; Weltman, Weltman Conserv Music, Malden, Mass. Comn: Official Ford VPres Commemorative Medal; Official Ford Pres Commemorative Medal Obverse; 200 Bicentennial Medals, Danbury Mint; Official NC Bicentennial Medal; 12 Legendary Americans, Am Sculpture Soc; plus many others. Exhib: Rockport Artits Asn, 67; Prudential Art Festival, New Eng Sculpture Soc, 69; Nat Sculpture Soc, New York, 70-71; Audubon Artists, 71; Allied Artists Am, 71. Teaching: Instr sculpture, Boston Ctr Adult Educ, 59-62; instr sculpture, New Eng Sch Art, Boston, 69-70; instr sculpture, Nashua Arts & Sci, 70-71. Awards: Alma & Ulysses Ricci Award for Best Conservative Sculpture or Painting, Rockport Artists Asn, 67, R V T Steeves Award for Most Outstanding Work in Sculpture, 69 & 72; Bronze Medal of Honor, Concord Art Asn, 69; First Prize, NShore Art Asn, Gloucester. Bibliog: Ann Schecter (auth), Vivid sculptural works, 11/19/67 & Perlinax (auth), Maggie Walker Medal, 11/11/71, Lowell Sun, Mass; Brenda Badolato (auth), The sculpture of Mico Kaufman, Lawrence Eagle Tribune, Mass, 6/18/68. Mem: Nat Sculpture Soc; New Eng Sculpture Asn; Cambridge Art Asn; Rockport Artists Asn. Style & Technique: Representational and semi-abstract. Media: Bronze, Stainless Steel. Publ: Auth, The Making of Mold Block and Case, 60; auth, Your most penetrating portrait ever, Nat Sculpture Rev, 72. Mailing Add: 23 Marion Dr North Tewksbury MA 01876

KAUFMAN, NANCY
ART ADMINISTRATOR
b Woonsocket, RI. Study: Boston Univ, AB(art hist), 60; Univ Calif, Berkeley, art & archit hist. Exhibitions Arranged: Halahmy & Howard, Manhattan, summer 75; West Side Sculpture Show, 76; Coop City Sculpture Show, summer 77. Pos: Dir visual arts referral serv, Creative Artists Pub Serv prog, 74-; bd dir, Ctr for Arts Info, 78. Mailing Add: 305 W 86th St New York NY 10024

KAUFMANN, ROBERT CARL
ART LIBRARIAN
b Birmingham, Ala, Apr 27, 37. Study: Birmingham Southern Col, Ala, BS(Fr & hist), 61; Sch Libr Serv, Columbia Univ, New York, MSLS, 65, MA candidate in art hist, 65-69. Pos: Asst librn, Fine Arts Libr, Columbia Univ, New York, 64-68, fine arts librn, 68-69; librn, Cooper-Hewitt Mus, Smithsonian Inst, New York, 65-; art libr, Div Art, Donnell Br, New York Pub Libr, 69; art & archit librn, Yale Univ, New Haven, Conn, 71-74. Awards: Joe Delmore Langston Award, Ala Libr Asn, 63; Comt to Rescue Italian Art Res Fel, Bibliot Naz Centrale, Florence, Italy, 69-71. Mem: Victorian Soc Am; Art Libr Soc NAm. Res: Nineteenth century furniture and decorative arts; subject headings for twentieth century decorative arts. Mailing Add: 220 W 93rd St Apt 11-A New York NY 10025

KAULITZ, GARRY CHARLES
PAINTER, PRINTMAKER
b Rapid City, SDak, Oct 6, 42. Study: Rochester Inst Technol, BFA & MFA. Work: Brockport State Col; Gallery Today Collection, Indianapolis, Ind; State of Ky; City of Louisville, Ky. Exhib: Images on Paper, Int Print Show, SC, 69; one-man shows, J B Speed Art Mus, Louisville, 71 & Gallery Today, 71; Corp Collections, Citizens Fidelity Bank, Louisville, 72; Univ SDak, 74; Univ Ind, 74; World Print Competition, San Francisco, 77; plus others. Teaching: Assoc prof printmaking, Louisville Sch Art, 68- Awards: Brockport State Col Purchase Award, 67; Evansville Mus Ann Exhib Award, 68; Arthur D Allen Mem Award, Regional Fine Arts Biennial, 71. Bibliog: New printmaker, 68, Sarah Lansdell (auth), Review of work, 2/71 & Linda Bousch (auth), A printmakers excursion into fact & fantasy, 2/75, Courier-J & Times. Publ: Auth, A Portfolio of Prints & Poems, pvt publ, 73. Style & Technique: Figurative; philosophic; designed environment; image maker; fantasy. Media: Acrylic, Serigraphy. Mailing Add: PO Box 3 Sulphur KY 40070

KAUPELIS, ROBERT JOHN
PAINTER, WRITER
b Amsterdam, NY, Feb 23, 28. Study: State Univ NY Col Buffalo, BS; Albright Art Sch, cert; Teachers Col, Columbia Univ, MA & DEd. Work: Univ Mass, Amherst; Mich State Univ; State Univ NY Col Potsdam; NY Univ Art Collection; Montclair State Col. Exhib: New Eng Ann, Silvermine Guild, Conn, 68, 70 & 71; Crosscurrents USA, Detroit Inst Art, 69-70; one-man shows, Bertha Schaefer Gallery, New York, 69, 70, 72 & 74, Katonah Gallery, NY, 70, 75 & 78, State Univ NY Col Oneonta, 71, Galeria Arvil, Mexico City, Mex, 71, Circle Gallery, New Orleans, La, 72, Elwood Mus, Amsterdam, NY, 72, Springfield Col, 74, Col of St Rose, Albany, NY, 76 & Andre Zarre Gallery, New York, 77; plus others, including Image South Gallery, Atlanta, Ga. Teaching: Prof art, NY Univ, 56- Awards: Prize, Int Drawing Competition, 60; Artists of Northern Westchester First Prize, Pace Col, 68; Prize for Sculpture, New Eng Ann, 69; Painting Prize, Silvermine New Eng Ann, 73; plus others. Bibliog: Ellen Zeifer (auth), Robert Kaupelis teaches a personal approach to drawing, Am Artists, 3/72; Herbert Livesey (auth), The Professors, Charterhouse, 75. Mem: Nat Art Educ Asn; NY State Art Teachers Asn; Silvermine Guild Artists; Univ Coun on the Arts; Inst Study Art & Educ. Media: Acrylic, Oil. Publ: Auth, Learning to Draw, Watson-Guptill, 66. Dealer: Andre Zarre Gallery 41 E 57th St New York NY 10022. Mailing Add: 988 Barberry Rd Yorktown Heights NY 10598

KAWA, FLORENCE KATHRYN
PAINTER
b Weyerhauser, Wis, Feb 24, 12. Study: Minneapolis Sch Art, 30-34; Univ Wis-Milwaukee, BS, 40; La State Univ, Baton Rouge, MA, 44; summers, Black Mountain Col, 44, Columbia Univ, 46-48, Cranbrook Acad Art, 51, Mass Inst Technol, 56 & Leeds Col Art, Eng, 70. Work: Univ Wis-Madison; La Art Comn, Baton Rouge; US Info Agency for Am Embassies; Pub Bldgs Admin for Marine Hosps. Exhib: Int Watercolor Biennial, Brooklyn Mus, 51, 55, 57, 59 & 61; Ann Exhib Contemp Am Sculpture, Watercolor & Drawings, Whitney Mus Art, New York, 53; Nat Competition Watercolors, Drawings & Prints, Metrop Mus Art, New York, 53; Contemp Watercolor in the US, sponsored by US Embassy Cult Div, France, 53; 20th Century American Graphic Arts, US Info Agency Touring Foreign Mus, 56-57. Teaching: Asst prof painting & design, Fla State Univ, 46-62; prof painting & design, Drake Univ, 64- Awards: Edith & Esther Younker Prize for Creative Painting, Des Moines Art Ctr, 69, Edmundson Award for Best Work in Any Medium, 70; 13th Midwest Biennial Purchase Award & Best in Show, Joslyn Mus, Omaha, 74; plus others. Media: Oil, Watercolor. Mailing Add: 1545 29th St Des Moines IA 50311

KAWABATA, MINORU
PAINTER, INSTRUCTOR
b Tokyo, Japan, May 22, 11. Study: Tokyo Acad Fine Art, grad, 34; also study in Paris & Italy, 37-39. Work: Albright-Knox Art Gallery, Buffalo, NY; Everson Mus Art, Syracuse, NY; Elder Art Gallery, Nebr Wesleyan Univ; Mus Mod Art, Sao Paulo, Brazil; Mus Mod Art, Tokyo. Exhib: Guggenheim Int, New York, 59 & 64; Betty Parsons Gallery, NY, 60-; Venice Biennial, 62; Everson Mus Art, 74; Mus Mod Art, Kamakura, Kamakurashi, Japan, 75. Teaching: Prof painting, Tama Univ Art, Japan, 50-58; prof painting, drawing & compos, New Sch Social Res, 60- Awards: Rhythm of Brown, Guggenheim Mus, 59; Work, Mus Mod Art, Sao Paulo, 60; Work B, Mus Mod Art, Kamakura, 61. Style & Technique: Abstract. Dealer: Betty Parsons Gallery 24 W 57th St New York NY 10019. Mailing Add: 463 West St New York NY 10014

KAWARA, ON
CONCEPTUAL ARTIST
b Aichi Prefecture, Japan, Jan 2, 33. Study: Self-taught in art. Work: Kaiser Wilhelm Mus, Krefeld, Ger. Exhib: 557087, Seattle Art Mus, Wash, 69; Konception, Staditisches Mus, Leverkusen, Ger, 69; Conceptual art & Conceptual Aspects, New York Cult Ctr, 70; Information, Mus of Mod Art, New York, 70; Andre: Broodthaers: Buren: Burgin: Gilbert & George: Kawara: Long: Richter, Palais des Beaux-Arts, Brussels, Belg, 74; one-man show, Kunsthalle, Berne. Bibliog: Lucy R Lippard (auth), Six Years: The Dematerialization of the Art Object, New York, 73; J Bodolai (auth), Borderlines in Art & Experience, Artscanada, Toronto, spring 74; B M Reise (auth), Carl Andre, Marcel Broodthaers, Diel Buren, Victor Burgin, Gilbert and George, On Kawara, Richard Long, Gerhard Richter, Art in Am, New York, 1/75. Mailing Add: Sperone-Westwater-Fischer 142 Greene St New York NY 10012

KAWECKI, JEAN MARY
SCULPTOR, GALLERY DIRECTOR
b Liverpool, Eng, June 24, 26; US citizen. Study: Liverpool Col Art, Eng; Art Career Sch, New York; also with Douglas Prizer. Exhib: Art Ctr NJ Regional, 74; Nat Miniature Soc, Nutley, NJ, 75; Hudson Artists Ann, Bergen Mus, NJ, 76; Nat Coun Jewish Women, West Orange, NJ, 77; Audubon Artists, Nat Acad Design, New York, 78. Pos: Free lance illusr mag, London, Eng, 46-51, Sol Vogel & Am-Mitchell Publ, New York, 51-53, Tobias Meyer & Nebenzahl, New York, 58-66; co-founder & dir, Doubletree Coop Art Gallery, Upper Montclair, 74- Awards: Patrons Award, Regional Show, Ringwood Asn Arts, 71; Art Ctr Combined Award, Tri-State Ann, Art Ctr NJ, 74; Patrons Award, Hudson Artists at the Bergen Mus, 76. Bibliog: Anne Betty Weinshenker (auth), M & A on Art, NJ Music & Arts, 12/76. Mem: Artists Equity Asn NJ; Doubletree Coop Gallery (dir & chmn hanging comt & spec shows, 74-). Style & Technique: Bonding of metal to stone; foundstone and copper; concerned with universal themes, man's relation to animals, and dance. Media: Natural Found Wood & Bones combined with Plaster & Cellulose Fiber. Dealer: Doubletree Art Gallery 5 Alvin Pl Upper Montclair NJ 07043. Mailing Add: 28 Mountainside Park Terr Upper Montclair NJ 07043

KAY, REED
EDUCATOR, PAINTER
b Boston, Mass, Mar 29, 25. Study: Sch Mus Fine Arts, Boston, dipl, 49, with Karl Zerbe; also with Oskar Kokoschka. Exhib: New Eng Regional Drawing, Smith Col Mus Art, 65; Am Fedn Arts Nat Exhib, 66; Urban Aesthetics, Queens Mus, New York, 76; A Selection of Am Art, Inst Contemp Art, Boston, 76; Art in Transition, Mus Fine Arts, Boston, 77. Teaching: Instr painting, Sch of Mus Fine Arts, Boston, 51-56; instr painting techniques, Skowhegan Sch Painting, Maine, 52-60; prof painting, Boston Univ, 56- Awards: Painting Prize, Silvermine Guild, New Canaan, Conn, 55. Style & Technique: Landscapes of city. Media: Oil, Gouache. Res: Effects of painter's materials and media on aesthetic qualities of pictures and on way they change with age. Publ: Auth, The Painter's Companion, Webb Bks, 61; auth, The Painter's Guide to Studio Methods & Materials, Doubleday, 72; contribr, World Bk Encycl, 71-77. Dealer: Alpha Gallery 121 Newbury St Boston MA 02116. Mailing Add: 109 Rawson Rd Brookline MA 02146

KAYE, DAVID HAIGH
TEXTILE ARTIST, DESIGNER
b Kingston, Ont, 1947. Study: Ont Col Art, Toronto, AOCA; Univ Guelph, BA. Work: Jean A Chalmers Collection of Contemp Can Crafts, Ont Crafts Coun, Toronto; Permanent Collection of Dept of External Affairs, Ottawa; Nat Mus Mod Art, Kyoto, Japan. Comn: Linen & Jute (tapestry), comn by P Farlinger, Glouchester Mews, Toronto, 74. Exhib: Contemp Crafts of the Americas: 1975, Colo State Univ, Ft Collins, 75; one-man shows, Merton Gallery, Toronto, 75 & 78; Spectrum Can, Royal Can Acad Arts, Montreal, Que, 76; 100 Yrs: Evolution of Ont Col of Art, Art Gallery of Ont, Toronto, 76; Fiberworks, Cleveland Mus Art, Ohio, 77; Fiberworks: Americas & Japan, Nat Mus Mod Art, Kyoto & Tokyo, Japan, 77 & 78. Awards: Lt-Gov's Medal, Grad Medal, Ont Col of Art, 72; Can Coun Short-Term Grant, Ottawa, 75 & 78. Bibliog: S Himel & E Lambert (auth), Handmade in Ontario, Van Nostrand Reinhold Ltd, Toronto, 76; M E Bevlin (auth), Design Through Discovery, Holt, Rinehart & Winston, 77. Style & Technique: Textiles in woven and non-woven techniques, work is subtle, textural in both flat and relief. Media: Natural fibers. Dealer: Merton Gallery 68 Merton St Toronto ON M4S 1A1 Can. Mailing Add: 4 Follis Ave Toronto ON M6G 1S3 Can

KAYE, GEORGE
PAINTER
b Malden, Mass, Nov 21, 11. Study: Swain Sch Design; Brooklyn Mus Art Sch; Brooklyn Col, BA; City Col New York Grad Sch; NY Univ, MA. Work: Philathea Col Mus, London, Ont; Dept Educ Film Libr, Mus Mod Art, New York. Exhib: One-man shows, Artzt Gallery, New York, 66, Bronx Community Col, NY, 67-69, Community Ctr, Newark, Del, 71, Univ Del, Newark, 71, Philadelphia Art Alliance, 72, Friday Gallery, 75 & Gallery CSA, 75-76. Teaching: Instr art, New York City Pub Schs, 34-53; chmn dept art, High Sch Music & Art, New York, 53-59; lectr art educ, NY Univ, 60-62; lectr hist art, Pratt Inst, 65-66; lectr hist art, Bronx Community Col, 67-68. Pos: Asst dir art, Bd Educ, New York, 59-68, mem coun dirs, 60-73, dir art, 68-73; consult art, Mayor's Off, New York, 65-66; consult art, Dept Pub Events, New York, 66-73; cult dir, Coun Supt & Adminr, 75- Awards: Cert Commendation, Park Asn New York, 66; Cert Appreciation, New York City Soc Osteopathic Physicians & Surgeons, 70; Citation, NY State Educ Dept, 72. Bibliog: J M McCormick (auth), Gallery reviews in New York, Pictures on Exhib, 3/66; J Gollin (auth), Reviews & previews, Art News, 3/66. Mem: Nat Art Educ Asn (local chmn, 72); NY State Art Teachers Asn (New York City liaison, 59-72); NY State Coun Adminr Art Educ (vpres, 63-72); New York Sch Art League, NY (trustee, 60-); NY Soc Exp Study Educ (chmn art sect, 63-72). Style & Technique: Expressionist. Media: Watercolor, Pastel, Mixed Media. Publ: Contribr, Color in education, Color Eng, 64; ed, Art & the Young Child, 68; ed, Creative Crafts for Today, 70; co-auth, A Child's Story of Vincent Van Gogh, 70; Pastels, 74. Mailing Add: 3333-F Henry Hudson Pkwy Bronx NY 10463

KAYSER, STEPHEN S
EDUCATOR, WRITER
b Karlsruhe, Ger, Dec 23, 00. Study: Class State Sch, Karlsruhe; Univ Heidelberg, PhD. Teaching: Lectr, Univ Calif, Berkeley, 41-44; prof hist art, San Jose State Col, 45-62; prof art, Univ Judaism, Los Angeles; vis prof art, Univ Calif, Los Angeles, 66-70, lectr art & integrated arts, 66-76; lectr, Univ Calif Los Angeles Exten, 76-; lectr hist of painting & synagogue art & architecture. Pos: Former cur & dir exhibs, Jewish Mus, New York. Publ: Auth, Jewish Ceremonial Art, 55; auth, The Book of Books in Art, 56; contribr, Parnassus, Rev of Relig, Pacific Art Rev, Art Quart & Art News. Mailing Add: 220 San Vicente Blvd Santa Monica CA 90402

KAZ (LAWRENCE KATZMAN)
DESIGNER, CARTOONIST
b Ogdensburg, NY, June 14, 22. Study: Univ Pa, BS; Art Students League, with Reginald Marsh. Pos: Pres & chmn bd, Kaz Mfg Co, 47-; bus mgr, Cartoonist; chmn, Int Cong Comics. Awards: Silver Cup of City of Bordighera, Italy, 59; Palma d'Oro, 66; Silver T-Square, Nat Cartoonists Soc. Mem: Art Students League; Nat Cartoonists Soc (spec proj chmn & mem comt, Overseas Tours); Cartoonists Guild (mem exec bd). Style & Technique: Single panel gag cartoons; pen and ink plus shading pencils, smudge. Publ: Auth & illusr, Nellie the Nurse, 58, Calling Nurse Nellie, 61 & Nellie's Laff-In, 68; auth & illusr, For Doctors Only, Eng, 60; auth & illusr, Prima y Dopo i Pasti, Italy, 60; plus other bks & cartoons in mags & newspapers throughout the world; illusr, greeting cards & bks, Gibson-Buzza. Mailing Add: 101 Central Park W New York NY 10023

KAZ, NATHANIEL
SCULPTOR, INSTRUCTOR
b New York, NY, Mar 9, 17. Study: Art Students League, with George Bridgman. Work: Brooklyn Mus; Whitney Mus Am Art & Metrop Mus Art, New York; also in pvt collections. Comn: Limestone carving, Fine St Temple, Nashville, Tenn; bronze sculpture, Pub Sch 59, Brooklyn; two colored aluminum reliefs to Thespians Tragedy & Comedy, Jr High Sch 164, Queens; sculpture, Temple Beth Emeth, Albany, NY, 65; plus others. Exhib: Whitney Mus Am Art, New York; Metrop Mus Art, New York; Mus Mod Art, New York; Art Inst Chicago; Philadelphia Mus Fine Arts; plus others. Teaching: Instr sculpture, Art Ctr of Northern NJ & Art Students League. Awards: Prize, Audubon Artists, 47, Medal of Honor, 60; Brooklyn Soc Artists Award, 48 & 52; Nat Inst Arts & Lett Grant, 57. Mem: Sculptors Guild. Mailing Add: 160 W 73rd St New York NY 10023

KAZOR, VIRGINIA ERNST
CURATOR
b Detroit, Mich, Sept 28, 40. Study: Univ Southern Calif, BA, MA. Collections Arranged: Separate Realities (catalog), 73; 24 From Los Angeles (with catalog), 74; Peter Krasnow (with catalog), 75; Ron Davis/Tom Holland: Works from the Collection of Mr & Mrs Robert Rowan (with catalog), 75. Pos: Curatorial asst mod art, Los Angeles Co Mus Art, 65-68; cur, Los Angeles Munic Art Gallery, 70- Mem: Los Angeles Bicentennial Orgn (chmn mus comt, 74-). Mailing Add: Los Angeles Munic Art Gallery 4804 Hollywood Blvd Los Angeles CA 90027

KEANE, BIL
CARTOONIST
b Philadelphia, Pa, Oct 5, 22. Work: Bil Keane Original Cartoon Collection, Syracuse Univ; Mus Cartoon Art, Greenwich, Conn. Pos: Staff artist, Philadelphia Eve Bull, 45-59; creator & nat syndicated cartoonist, The Family Circus & Channel Chuckles. Awards: Best Syndicated Panel Cartoonist, Nat Cartoonists Soc, 69, 71 & 74. Mem: Nat Cartoonists Soc; Newspaper Comics Coun; Cartoonists Guild. Media: Pen and Ink. Publ: Co-auth, Just Wait Till You Have Children of Your Own, Doubleday, 71; auth, When's Later, Daddy?, 74; auth, I Can't Untie My Shoes, Fawcett, 75; auth, Deuce and Don'ts of Tennis, O'Sullivan Woodside, 75. Mailing Add: 5815 E Joshua Tree Lane Paradise Valley AZ 85253

KEANE, LUCINA MABEL
PAINTER, PRINTMAKER
b Gros, Nebr, 04. Study: Ashland Col; Ohio State Univ, BS(educ); Teachers Col, Columbia Univ, MA; Pa State Univ; Temple Univ; NY Univ. Exhib: Allied Artists WVa; Clarksburg Art Ctr, WVa; Centennial Exhib, Huntington Art Gallery, WVa. Teaching: Lect, Sculpture & Art Appreciation; instr art, Univ NDak, 26-29; instr art, Ill State Normal Univ, 30-31; assoc prof art & head dept, Morris Harvey Col, 36-72. Pos: Pres bd & mem steering comt, Charleston Art Gallery, 63-66; mem, Centennial Art Comt WVa, 63; mem, Kanawha Valley Bicentennial Comn, 76. Awards: Five Prizes, Allied Artists WVa, 36-59. Mem: Col Art Asn Am; Tri-State Art Asn; Allied Artists WVa; plus others. Collection: Print collector, Europe, SAm & Japan. Mailing Add: 2908 Noyes Ave Charleston WV 25304

KEARL, STANLEY BRANDON
SCULPTOR
b Waterbury, Conn, Dec 23, 13. Study: Yale Univ, BFA, 41, MFA, 42; Univ Iowa, PhD, 48; study in Rome, Italy, 9 yrs. Work: Iowa State Univ; Univ Minn, Duluth; Naz Galeria, Rome, Italy; Nat Mus, Stockholm, Sweden; Mus Goteborgs, Sweden; plus others. Exhib: Penthouse Exhib, 60 & Art Lending Libr Exhib, 65, Mus Mod Art, New York; Whitney Mus Am Art Ann, New York, 62; Hudson River Mus, Yonkers, 63; Grand Cent Mod, New York, 65 & 68; Art in Am Embassies Abroad, selected by Mus Mod Art, New York, 68; Inst Int Educ, Graham Gallery, New York, 69; Selected Artists Show, Ingber Gallery, New York, 74; one-man shows, Gallery of Mod Art, Basel, Switz, 51, Hudson River Mus, Yonkers, 64 & Benson Gallery, Bridgehampton, NY, 76; plus others. Teaching: Lectr, Univ Minn, Duluth, 47-48; lectr, Pratt Inst, 67. Pos: Fulbright exchange prof to Univ Rome, Italy, 49-50. Awards: Sculpture Award, Painters & Sculptors Soc of NJ, 59; Hudson River Mus Sculpture Award, 63; Silvermine Guild Asn Ann Award, 67; plus others. Bibliog: Torsten Bergmark (auth), Palettes, Swed Art J, 52; Michel Seuphor (auth), The Sculpture of This Century, Dictionary of Modern Sculpture, A Swemmer, Ltd, London, 59. Mem: Col Art Asn Am. Media: Cast Bronze. Dealer: Ingber Gallery 3 E 78th St New York NY 10021. Mailing Add: 344 Sprain Rd Scarsdale NY 10583

KEARNEY, JOHN (W)
SCULPTOR, ART ADMINISTRATOR
b Omaha, Nebr, Aug 31, 24. Study: Cranbrook Acad Art, Bloomfield Hills, Mich, 45-48; Univ Stranieri, Perugia, Fulbright grant Itlay & Ital Govt grant sculpture, 63-64. Work: Norfolk Art Mus, Va; Detroit Children's Mus; Minn Mus, St Paul; Edwin A Ulrich Mus of Art, Wichita, Kans; Canton Art Inst, Ohio; plus others. Comn: Wichita State Univ; City of Chicago, Chicago Park District; Wichita Coliseum; Springfield Art Asn, Ill. Exhib: Corcoran Biennial, Washington, DC, 55; Am Fulbright Artists, Palazzo Venezia, Rome, 64; Painting & Sculpture Today, John Herron Mus, Indianapolis, 65; Soc Contemp Am Art Exhib, Art Inst Chicago, 66; one-man shows, Ill Inst of Technol, 76 & Ulrich Mus of Art, Wichita, 76;

two-man show, Art Inst of Chicago, 77. Teaching: Instr sculpture, Mundelein Col, 70-71. Pos: Dir, Contemp Art Workshop, Chicago, 51- Awards: S J Wallace Truman Prize, Nat Acad Design, 53; Ringling Mus Award, 60; Man of Year, Adult Educ Coun Chicago, 62. Mem: Provincetown Art Asn (vpres, 62-70); Fine Arts Work Ctr, Provincetown (adv bd); Arts Club Chicago. Style & Technique: Involved with figure or figurative ideas, often animals; most quite large; usually comments on the times. Media: Bronze, Steel. Dealer: ACA Gallery 25 E 73rd St New York NY 10021; Galleria Schneider Rampa Mignanelli Rome Italy. Mailing Add: 830 Castlewood Terr Chicago IL 60640

KEARNS, JAMES JOSEPH
SCULPTOR, PAINTER
b Scranton, Pa, Aug 7, 24. Study: Art Inst Chicago, BFA, 51. Work: Mus Mod Art & Whitney Mus Am Art, New York; Newark Mus Art; NJ State Mus, Trenton; Nat Collection Fine Arts, Smithsonian Inst, Washington, DC. Exhib: Nat Inst Arts & Lett, 59; Whitney Mus Am Art Ann, 59-61; Johnson Wax Collection, World Tour, 62-67; Pa Acad Fine Arts, Philadelphia, 64-65; San Diego Nat Print Show, Calif, 64, 66 & 69. Teaching: Instr drawing, painting & sculpture, Sch Visual Arts, 60-; instr sculpture, Fairleigh-Dickinson Univ, 62-63; instr painting & sculpture, Skowhegan Sch Painting & Sculpture, summers 62-65. Pos: Mem bd gov, Skowhegan Sch Painting & Sculpture, 64-70. Awards: Nat Inst Arts & Lett Grant, 59. Bibliog: Selden Rodman (auth), Conversations with artists, Devin Adair, 57 & The Insiders, La State Univ, 60; Lee Nordness (auth), Art USA Now, Viking, 63. Media: Bronze, Fiberglas. Publ: Illusr, Can these bones live, New Directions, 60; illusr, The Heart of Beethoven, Shorewood Press, 62. Dealer: Sculpture Ctr 167 E 69th St New York NY 10021. Mailing Add: 452 Rockaway Rd Dover NJ 07801

KEATS, EZRA JACK
ILLUSTRATOR, WRITER
b Brooklyn, NY, Mar 11, 16. Exhib: Assoc Am Artists Gallery, New York, 50-54. Teaching: Teacher, Sch Visual Arts, 47-48 & Workshop Sch, New York, 55-57. Pos: Mag advert illusr, 47- Awards: Newberry-Caldecott Medal, 63; Boston Globe-Horn Book Award, 70. Mem: PEN; Authors Guild; Soc Illusr. Publ: Auth & illusr, The Snowy Day, 62, Hi, Cat, 70, Pet Show, 72 & Skates, 73; ed & illusr, God is in the Mountain; plus others. Mailing Add: 444 E 82nd St New York NY 10028

KECK, SHELDON WAUGH
EDUCATOR, ART CONSERVATOR
b Utica, NY, May 30, 10. Study: Harvard Univ, BA, 32; Fogg Art Mus, apprentice in restoration, 32-33. Teaching: Dir art conserv, NY Univ Conserv Ctr, 61-65, prof fine arts, 64-66; prof art conserv, Cooperstown Grad Progs, State Univ NY Col Oneonta, 69- Pos: Conservator, Brooklyn Mus, 34-61. Awards: Fulbright Fel, 59; Guggenheim Fel, 59-60. Mem: Brooklyn Mus (gov comt); Cooperstown Art Asn (bd dirs); Int Inst Conserv Hist & Artistic Works (mem coun, pres, 74-); Int Coun Mus (conserv comt); Am Inst Conserv Hist & Artistic Works (pres, 72-74). Publ: Auth, numerous articles in prof jour & art periodicals on exam & conserv of paintings. Mailing Add: River St Cooperstown NY 13326

KEEFE, KATHARINE LEE
CURATOR
b Detroit, Mich, Dec 12, 41. Study: Vassar Col, BA(art hist, magna cum laude), 63; Harvard Univ, MA, 66. Collections Arranged: Prairie School Furniture: Wright, Elmslie, Maher, 72, Art Deco: Trends in Design, 73, Islamic Prayer Rugs, 73, Photographs by Aaron Siskind in Homage to Franz Kline, 75, Contemporary Art from the Robert B Mayer Collection, 76, from Artists View the Law of the 20th Century (auth, catalogue), 77, Collection of Contemporary Art of Mid-America Club, Chicago, 76-78, Renaissance Soc & Smart Gallery, Univ Chicago. Teaching: Mus course in hist mus & collection inst, Univ Chicago, 78. Pos: Asst cur, Toledo Mus Art, Ohio, 68-70; dir exhib, Renaissance Soc, Univ Chicago, 71-73, cur collections, Smart Gallery, 73-; bd mem, Friends Vassar Col, 74- Awards: Fulbright Scholar, 63-64; Ford Found Grant in Mus Curatorial Training Internship, 66-68. Publ: Ed, The Documentary Photograph as a Work of Art: Photographs of the American Civil War and the Exploration of the Western Frontier 1876-1880, 77 & Hsieh Shih-ch'en: A Ming Dynasty Painter Reinterprets the Past, 78 & auth, Meaning in Dutch 17th Century Flower Pieces, 78, Univ Chicago Libr Soc. Mailing Add: 1765 E 55th St Chicago IL 60615

KEELER, DAVID BOUGHTON
ART ADMINISTRATOR, PAINTER
b Cleveland, Ohio, Feb 11, 31. Study: Cleveland Inst Art, dipl; Case Western Reserve Univ, Cleveland. Work: Cleveland Inst Art, Ohio; Cleveland Art Asn; Nat Collection of Fine Arts, Washington, DC. Exhib: Cleveland Mus Art Regional, 60-63, 65, 67, 74 & 76; Butler Inst Am Art Nat, Youngstown, Ohio, 60 & 62; Corcoran Gallery of Art, Washington, DC, 65 & 69; one-man shows, 323 Gallery, Alexandria, Va, 65; Studio Gallery, Alexandria, 66; Barbara Fielder Gallery, Washington, DC, 76 & Wolfe St Gallery, Alexandria, 77. Pos: Prepator & exhib designer, Cleveland Mus Art, 61-64; tech asst to cur, Nat Collection Fine Arts, Washington, DC, 66-71 & chief exhib & design, 72- Bibliog: Newspaper critiques, Andrew Hudson (auth), Washington Post, 10/65 & 10/66 & Ben Forgey (auth), Washington Evening Star, 4/76. Mem: Col Art Asn; Am Mus Asn. Style & Technique: Abstract and figure compositions, oils and mixed-media collage. Dealer: Barbara Fiedler Gallery 1621 21st St NW Wasington DC 20009. Mailing Add: 1308 Namassip Rd Alexandria VA 22308

KEELING, HENRY CORNELIOUS
PAINTER, EDUCATOR
b St Albans, WVa, Sept 4, 23. Study: Pratt Inst, BFA(interior design); NY Univ; Hans Hofmann Sch Fine Art, New York; Art Students League; Marshall Univ, MA(fine art); also with Bernard Klonis, Reuben Tam, Leo Manso & Victor Kandell. Work: Parkersburg Art Ctr, Parkersburg, WVa; Charleston Art Gallery of Sunrise, WVa; WVa Arts & Humanities Coun, Charleston; Herbert M Rothchild Collection, New York; WVa State Col. Comn: Three paintings & mural, Consolidated Gas Corp, Clarksburg, WVa, 67; two paintings, Roanoke Indust Savings & Loan Corp, Va, 68. Exhib: Brooklyn Mus Art Sch Ann, 54 & 55; New York City Ctr Gallery Monthly Shows, 55-57; Exhibs 180, 65-68 & Exhibs 280, 75-77, Huntington Galleries; Three West Virginia Artists, Charleston Art Gallery, 68; Invitational, Parkersburg Art Ctr, 76-77; Invitational Relig Show, WVa State Col, 77; one-man shows, Huntington Galleries, 72, Gallery 4, Charleston, WVa, 78 & Morris Harvey Col, 78. Teaching: Head dept, Morris Harvey Col, 73- Awards: First Prize, WVa Allied Artist Ann, 70; Purchase Awards for Graphics, Charleston Art Gallery, 71 & WVa Arts & Humanities, 71; Merit Award, Parkersburg Art Ctr, 77. Mem: Provincetown Art Asn; WVa Allied Artists. Style & Technique: Abstract; paper and cardboard collages; wet in wet watercolors. Media: Watercolor, Collage. Mailing Add: 406 Park St St Albans WV 25177

KEEN, HELEN BOYD
PAINTER, COLLECTOR
b Tacoma, Wash. Study: Calif Sch Fine Arts; with Mark Tobey, 8 yrs; Art Students League, with Cobino, Hale & Vytlacil, 4 yrs. Work: Seattle Art Mus; Addison Gallery Am Art, Andover, Mass; Art Gallery Greater Victoria, BC; Tacoma Art Mus; Archives Am Art, Smithsonian Inst. Exhib: US State Dept Show (selected by Mus Mod Art), France, 56-57; Pa Acad Fine Arts, 57; Brooklyn Mus, 57; Norfolk Mus Arts & Sci, 63; Avanti Gallery, New York, 72; Nat Arts Club Graphics Show, Gramercy Park, NY, 76; plus others. Awards: First Award, Tacoma Art Mus, 45. Mem: Art Students League; Art Gallery Greater Victoria; Tacoma Art Mus. Media: Oil on Japanese Paper and Canvas. Collection: Mark Tobey, Pehr, Vytlacil, John Ford, Mario Bambagini, Judith Rothschild, Toko Shinoda & Ethel Schwabacher. Dealer: Avanti Galleries 145 E 72nd St New York NY 10021. Mailing Add: 201 E 79th St New York NY 10021

KEENA, JANET LAYBOURN
PAINTER
b St Joseph, Mo, Sept 11, 28. Study: William Woods Col; Univ Kans; Univ Calif, Los Angeles; also with Sergei Bongart. Work: Albrecht Mus, St Joseph, Mo; Park Col, Parkville, Mo; Dart Drug Hq, Los Angeles; Regional Comnr, Gen Serv Admin, Washington, DC. Comn: Painting, Phoenix Art Mus, Ariz; painting, Weight Watchers Hq, Kansas City, Mo, 74; Designs for Miniature Gallery, Hallmark Cards, Kansas City, 74. Exhib: 13th Ann Delta Art Exhib, Little Rock, Ark, 70; Nelson Art Gallery, Kansas City, 70; Albrecht Art Mus, 72; Ft Smith Art Ctr, Ark, 72; Int Traveling Show Americana, Am Art by Mid-West Artists, 72. Teaching: Teacher, Kansas City Art Guild & Studio Delaware, Mo, 70-74; artist in residence, William Jewell Col, 73. Pos: Free-lance artist, Hallmark Cards, Kansas City, 74. Awards: First Prize & Best in Show, Parkville Festival of Arts, 70; First Publ Award, Fine Arts Discovery Mag, 70; First Prize, Kans State Fair, 54 & Mo State Fair, 71 & 72. Bibliog: Donald Hoffmann (auth), Art in Mid-America, Kansas City Star, 5/69 & 5/74; Jean Trusty (auth), Art, Kansas City Squire Mag, 4/71; R C Seine (ed), Contemporary American Artists, La Rev Mod, Paris, 11/71. Mem: Md Fedn Art. Style & Technique: Emphasis on lighting and color; landscapes, figure, and abstracts in oil. Media: Oil. Dealer: Washington Gallery of Art 1531 33rd St NW Washington DC 20007; Gallery One 7307 Arlington Blvd Falls Church VA 22042. Mailing Add: 7501 Range Rd Alexandria VA 22306

KEENE, PAUL
PAINTER
b Philadelphia, Pa, Aug 24, 20. Study: Philadelphia Mus Sch & Univ Pa, 39-41; Tyler Sch Art, Temple Univ, 45-48; Acad Julien, Paris, 49-51; Whitney fel, 52-54. Work: Pa Acad Fine Arts, Philadelphia; Philadelphia Mus; Howard Univ; Morgan State Col; Bowdoin Col. Comn: History of University (mural), Johnson C Smith Univ; medal for Am Negro Commemorative Soc, Philadelphia; Exhib: Salon de Jeunes Pientres, Paris, 51; Pa Acad Fine Arts, 52-53 & 68-69: Lagos Mus, Nigeria, 61; San Jose State Col, 69; Master Series, Carnegie Libr, Pittsburgh, 70. Teaching: Prof painting & dir course, Centre D'Art, Port-au-Prince, Haiti, 52-53; assoc prof drawing & painting, Philadelphia Col Art, 54-68, chmn basic art prog, 63-66; prof drawing & design, Bucks Co Community Col, Newton, 68-, chmn dept art, 70- Awards: Alumni Award in Art, Temple Univ. Bibliog: Briskin (auth), New talent art in America, Art in Am, 54; Lewis/Waddy (auth), Black artists on art, Contemp Crafts, 71. Style & Technique: Abstract colorist. Media: Mixed Media. Mailing Add: 2843 Bristol Rd Warrington PA 18976

KEENER, ANNA ELIZABETH
PAINTER, PRINTMAKER
b Flagler, Colo, Oct 16, 95. Study: Bethany Col (Kans), BFA & BA; Art Inst Chicago; Kansas City Art Inst; Univ NMex, MA; also graphics with George Miyasake & mural painting with James Pinto. Work: Rare Bk Sect, NMex State Libr; Mus NMex Fine Arts; Birger Sandzen Mem Gallery, Lindsborg, Kans; US Nat Monument, Los Alamos, NMex; current seal for Sul Ross State Univ, Alpine, Tex. Comn: Zuni Pottery Making (mural), McKinley Co Courthouse, Gallup, NMex; Baptistry, Bd Dirs, Baptist Church, Portales. Exhib: Mus NMex Biennial, Santa Fe, 68; Rocky Mountain States Print Collection, 69; Southwestern Art Festival, Tucson, Ariz, 70; 47th Ann, Springville, Utah, 71; 5 State Exhib, Port Arthur, Tex, 71; Tex Fine Arts Ann, 72; Ex Patriots Exhib, Kansas City Art Inst, 73. Teaching: Supvr art, Ariz Pub Schs, Globe; instr art, Kansas City High Sch; head dept art, Eastern NMex Univ. Pos: Bd dirs, NMex Art Educators Asn; juror, Mus NMex Art Exhibs; juror, NMex Pub Schs Exhibs, State Fair; Fine Arts Prog, Am Asn Univ Women; State Chmn Fine Arts, NMex Fed Women's Clubs. Awards: Bronze Medal for Barn on the Hill, Kansas City Art Inst; Poorbough Press Award for Giraffes, 56; award for collagraph, Mus NMex Fine Art, 62. Mem: Artists Equity Asn. Style & Technique: A creative approach to the environment in which I life; an interest in numerous media. Media: Acrylic. Mailing Add: 312 Cadiz Rd Santa Fe NM 87501

KEHDE, MARTHA ELIZABETH
ART LIBRARIAN
b Topeka, Kans, Apr 2, 42. Study: Univ Mo, BA, 68, MALS, 69. Teaching: Instr art hist bibliography, Univ Kans, Lawrence, 74- Pos: Art Librn, Univ Kans, 70- Mem: Art Libr Soc NAm(regional chairperson, 76-77). Res: Art serials; art museums. Publ: Contribr, Magazines for Libraries, Bowker, New York, 78. Mailing Add: c/o Art Library Univ Kans Lawrence KS 66045

KEITH, EROS
ILLUSTRATOR, PAINTER
b Fulton, Mo, June 24, 42. Study: Art Inst Chicago; Denver Univ; Univ Chicago, BA & BFA. Exhib: Shepard Gallery, New York, 69. Style & Technique: Varied, watercolor, black & white gouaches, predugreirs scratch board and oil. Publ: Auth & illusr, A Small Lit, 68, auth, The King's Falcon, 69 & auth & illusr, Rrra-ah, 69, Bradbury; auth & illusr, Nancy's Backyard, Harper & Row, 73; auth & illusr, The Biggest Noise, Doubleday, 78. Mailing Add: 105 W 73rd St New York NY 10023

KELDER, DIANE M
ART HISTORIAN, ART CRITIC
b New York, NY, May 23, 34. Study: Queens Col, AB, 55; Univ Chicago, MA, 57; Bryn Mawr Col, PhD, 66. Collections Arranged: Drawings by the Bibiena Family, Philadelphia Mus Art, 68 & Finch Col Mus, 68; Five Centuries of Stage Design, Finch Col Mus, 71. Teaching: Instr art hist, Queens Col, 60-; instr art hist, Finch Col, 67-71; prof art hist, Richmond Col, 71- Pos: Asst cur prints & drawings, Philadelphia Mus Art, 66-67; ed, Art J, currently. Awards: Fanny Workman Fel, Am Asn Univ Women, 62-63; Jr Humanist Fel, Nat Endowment Humanities, 71; Ingram Merrill Found Award, 72. Mem: Int Art Critics Asn; Col Art Asn. Interest: Baroque stage design; late 18th century painting; graphic art from the 16th through the 20th centuries. Publ: Auth, Rembrandt, McGraw-Hill, 70; auth, The French Impressionists and Their Century, 70 & ed, Stuart Davis, 71, Praeger; contribr, Ferdinando Galli Bibiena's Architettura Civile, Blom, 71; plus others. Mailing Add: 178 E 95th St New York NY 10028

KELEMEN, PAL
ART HISTORIAN
b Budapest, Hungary, Apr 24, 94; US citizen. Study: Univ Ariz, DHL; Univ Budapest; Univ Munich; Univ Paris; mus res in Budapest, Vienna, Florence, London, Madrid & Seville. Teaching: Lectr, Nat Gallery Art, Metrop Mus Art & other mus & univs; spec lect tour, US Dept State, Europe & the Near East. Pos: Survey trips, US Dept State, Mex, Cent Am & Europe, 33-; mem comn for protection & salvage of artistic & hist monuments in war areas, World War II. Awards: Comdr, Order of Merit, Ecuador. Mem: Fel Royal Anthrop Inst; mem var sci socs in US, Latin Am & Europe. Res: Early Christian art; pre-Columbian and colonial art in Latin America. Publ: Auth, Ancient, Colonial Art of the Americas, Dutch, 62, Ger, 64, Fr, 65, Span, 67, Port, 69; auth, Art of the Americas, 69 & 70; auth, Peruvian Colonial Painting, 71; contribr, Folk Baroque in Mexico, 74, Vanishing Art of the Americas, 77, Encycl Britannica, Stauffacher's World Art History & others. Mailing Add: Box 447 Norfolk CT 06058

KELLEHER, DANIEL JOSEPH
PAINTER, INSTRUCTOR
b Erie, Pa, Nov 15, 30. Study: Edinboro State Col, BS, 53; Syracuse Univ. Work: Washington & Jefferson Col, Washington, Pa; Hemingway Collection, New York; First Nat Bank, Erie; Erie Pub Libr. Exhib: Nat Soc Painters in Casein, New York, 67; Butler Inst Am Art, Youngstown, Ohio, 67 & 68; Audubon Artists 26th Ann, New York, 68; Mainstream 69, Marietta Col, Ohio, 69; Watercolor USA, Springfield, Mo, 71. Teaching: Art educator, Erie Sch Dist, 61- Awards: Hon mention, Four Art Soc, Palm Beach, Fla, 67; Purchase Award, Washington & Jefferson Col, 68; Award of Excellence, Mainstream 69, 69. Bibliog: Clyde Singer (auth), Butler midyear show, 67; Connie Kienzle (auth), Washington & Jefferson Show, Pittsburgh Press, 68; Group show Erie artist, Cleveland Plain Dealer, 69. Mem: Erie Art Ctr (mem bd dirs, 68-72); Chautauqua Inst Art, NY; Pa Art Educ Asn. Style & Technique: Concerned in giving meaning to objects through texture and color; style and technique is collage assemblage. Media: Acrylic, Collage. Publ: Contribr, articles in, Sch Arts Mag, 68 & 72; auth, Art From Found Objects, Davis Publ, 74. Dealer: Galerie 8 1100 State Erie PA 16501. Mailing Add: 427 E Eighth St Erie PA 16502

KELLEHER, PATRICK JOSEPH
ART HISTORIAN, ART CONSULTANT
b Colorado Springs, Colo, July 26, 17. Study: Colo Col, AB, 39; Princeton Univ, MFA, 42 & PhD, 47; Am Acad Rome, fel, 47-49; fine arts specialist off, Ger, 45-46. Collections Arranged: Art Mus, Princeton (new bldg), 66 & numerous spec exhibs, incl European & American Painting & Sculpture in Princeton Alumni Collections, 72. Teaching: Lectr art hist, Univ Buffalo, 50-51; res prof art hist, Univ Mo, 56-59; prof art hist, Princeton Univ, 60-73. Pos: Chief cur art, Los Angeles Co Mus, 49; cur collections, Albright-Knox Art Gallery, 50-54; cur European art, Nelson Gallery-Atkins Mus, 54-59; dir, Art Mus, Princeton Univ, 60-73; juror, regional exhibs. Publ: Auth, The holy crown of Hungary, Am Acad Rome, 50; auth, Expressionism in American art, Albright-Knox Art Gallery, 53; co-auth, The century of Mozart, Nelson Gallery, 56; auth, Living Modern Sculpture, Princeton Univ Press, 78; auth, The Holy Crown & The Royal Insignia of Hungary, (in prep). Insignia of Hungary, in prep. Mailing Add: 176 Parkside Dr Princeton NJ 08540

KELLER, ANDREA MILLER
CURATOR
b Los Angeles, Calif, Mar 19, 42. Study: Radcliffe Col, BA, 63; Columbia Univ, 66-67. Pos: Yale Univ-Atheneum catalogue coordr, Wadsworth Atheneum, Hartford, 69-75, auth & cur MATRIX, Changing Exhib of Contemp Art, 74- Mem: Am Asn Mus; Col Art Asn. Res: Contemporary art. Mailing Add: Wadsworth Atheneum Hartford CT 06103

KELLER, DEANE
EDUCATOR, PAINTER
b New Haven, Conn, Dec 14, 01. Study: Art Students League, with George Bridgman; Yale Univ Sch Fine Arts; with Eugene F Savage & E C Taylor; Am Acad Rome, 26. Work: Hq, US Post Off, Washington, DC; Portrait of Sen Robert Taft, Senate Reception Chamber, Capitol Bldg, Washington, DC; Conn Ct Errors, Hartford; Yale Univ, New Haven; New York Hosp, Cornell Univ. Comn: Two murals, Shriver Hall, Johns Hopkins Univ, Baltimore, Md, 57; mural (with Bauncel La Farge), Pub Libr, New Haven. Exhib: Portraits, Inc, New York, 60's; Yale Univ; Hartford, Conn; Harrisburg, Pa; plus others. Teaching: Prof art, Yale Univ Sch Art & Archit, 30-70; prof art, Paier Sch Art. Pos: Chief fine arts sect, Fifth Army, Italy, 43-46. Mem: New Haven Paint & Clay Club (pres, 36-39). Media: Oil. Dealer: Portraits Inc 41 E 57th St New York NY 10022. Mailing Add: 18 Brookhaven Rd Hamden CT 06517

KELLEY, CHAPMAN
PAINTER, ART DEALER
b San Antonio, Tex, Aug 26, 32. Study: Hugo D Pohl Art Sch, San Antonio; Trinity Univ; Pa Acad Fine Arts, with Franklin Watkins, Hobson Pittman, Walter Steumpfig, Abraham Rattner, Morris Blackburn, Julius Bloch, Harry Rosin, Francis Speight & Roswell Weidner. Work: Mulvane Art Ctr, Topeka, Kans; Okla Art Ctr, Oklahoma City; Witte Mem Mus, San Antonio; Dallas Mus Fine Arts; Tex Instruments, Inc, Dallas; Colorado Springs Fine Arts Ctr. Exhib: Southwestern Art Exhib, Dallas Mus Fine Arts, circulated nationally by Am Fedn Art, 57; 157th Ann Am Painting & Sculpture, Pa Acad Fine Arts, Philadelphia, 62; Childe Hassam Fund Exhib, Am Acad Arts & Lett, New York, 63; Butler Inst Am Art Midyear Shows, 64 & 66-67; 11th Midwest Biennial, Joslyn Mus, Omaha, Nebr, 70; Artists Southeast & Tex Biennial, Delgado Mus, New Orleans, 71; plus many other group & one-man shows. Teaching: Pvt instr, Dallas, 57-68; instr painting & drawing, Dallas Mus Fine Arts, 59-67; sem instr, Northern Ill Univ, 71. Pos: Partic Matrix for Arts Symp, Ctr Advan Studies, Urbana, Ill, 67; panelist, Nat Sculpture Conf, Univ Kans, 70; dir, Atelier Chapman Kelley. Awards: Top Purchase Award, Okla Art Ctr, 65; El Paso Mus Art Purchase Prize, Sun Carnival Nat, 69. Bibliog: Sold out art, Life Mag, 9/20/63; article in Burlington Mag, 64. Media: Oil, Pastel. Specialty: Contemporary, major twentieth century and impressionist works. Collection: Twentieth century and contemporary works. Mailing Add: 2526 Fairmount St Dallas TX 75201

KELLEY, DONALD CASTELL
GALLERY DIRECTOR, ART LIBRARIAN
b Boston, Mass. Study: Sch of Mus Fine Arts, Boston, dipl; Yale Univ, BFA & MFA. Pos: Asst art librn, Boston Atheneum, 68-, gallery dir, 74- Interest: Work of contemporary artists, photographers and craftsmen. Mailing Add: Boston Atheneum 10 1/2 Beacon St Boston MA 02108

KELLEY, DONALD WILLIAM
PRINTMAKER, SCULPTOR
b Tulsa, Okla, July 20, 39. Study: Univ Tulsa, with Alexandre Hogue & Duayne Hatchett, BA, 62; Claremont Grad Sch, MFA, 66; Univ NMex with Garo Antreasian, 66; Tamarind Lithography Workshop, Los Angeles, 66-69. Work: Art Inst Chicago; Cincinnati Art Mus; Los Angeles Co Mus Art, Los Angeles; Mus Mod Art, New York; Pasadena Art Mus. Exhib: One-man show, Univ Tulsa, 72, Not in New York Gallery, Cincinnati, 75, Antioch Col, 75 & Cincinnati Invitational Awards Exhib, Cincinnati Art Mus, 75; Alternative Landscape, Contemp Art Ctr, Cincinnati, 72; Environ Sculpture—Proposals for Sawyer Point Park, Contemp Arts Ctr, Cincinnati, Ohio, 77. Teaching: Asst prof printmaking, Univ Cincinnati, 69-75; vis artist lithography, Antioch Col, 75. Bibliog: Jules Engel & Ivan Dryer (auth), Look of a lithographer (film), Tamarind Lithography Workshop, 69; Kristin L Spangenberg (auth), Cincinnati Invitational Awards Exhibition: Drawings and Prints, Midwest Art, 3/75. Style & Technique: Landscape related imagery. Media: Lithography and Blueprint Processes, Three Dimensional Mixed Media. Mailing Add: 801 Pond Run Rd New Richmond OH 45157

KELLEY, RAMON
PAINTER
b Cheyenne, Wyo, Feb 12, 39. Study: Colo Inst Art. Work: Santa Fe Art Mus, NMex; Mus of Native Am Cult, Spokane, Wash; George Amos Mem Libr, Gillette, Wyo; Charles & Emma Frye Mus Fine Art. Exhib: One-man show, Charles & Emma Frye Mus Fine Art, Seattle; Ann Exhib, Am Watercolor Soc, 71-76; Mainstreams, Marietta, Ohio, 72, 75 & 76; Allied Artists Am, 72, 73 & 74; Nat Arts Club Pastel Exhib, 74; Pastel Soc Am, 75-77; plus others. Awards: Betty & Leon Peters Award, Nat Arts Club, 74; Award of Distinction, Mainstream, 75 & 76, Cook Mem Award & Purchase Award, 76; Pope Found Award, 75, Pastel Soc Am, Trump Award for Exceptional Merit, 76 & Columbus Citizen Found Award for Best Portrait, 77. Mem: Nat Arts Club; Am Watercolor Soc (nat juror); Allied Artists Am; Pastel Soc Am. Style & Technique: Impressionist, in all medias. Media: Oil, Watercolor, Pastel. Publ: Contribr, Am Artist Mag, 3/69 & 12/72 & Southwest Art Mag, 11/73; contribr, Joe Singer, auth, How to Paint Figures in Pastel, Watson-Guptill, 76; co-auth (with Mary C Nelson), Ramon Kelley Paints Portraits & Figures, Watson-Guptill, 77. Dealer: Canyon Rd Art Gallery 710 Canyon Rd Santa Fe NM 87501. Mailing Add: 180 Franklin St Denver CO 80218

KELLOGG, MAURICE DALE
PAINTER, LECTURER
b Wellington, Kans, Dec 15, 19. Study: Univ Kans, AB; Harvard Univ, MA. Work: W H Over Dakota Mus, Vermilion, SDak; Southeast Arts & Sci Ctr, Pine Bluff, Ark; SArk Arts Mus, El Dorado; Secy of State, State Capitol, Little Rock; Dept Parks & Tourism, State Capitol, Little Rock. Comn: Paintings, comn by Mrs Jeanette Rockefeller, Petit Jean, Ark, 69, First Nat Bank, Little Rock, 71, Mickey Rooney, Ft Lauderdale, Fla, 73, Winthrop Paul Rockefeller, Petit Jean, Ark, 74, Johnny Cash, 77 & Gregory Peck, 77; mural comn by Maumelle Community Ctr, Little Rock, Ark, 77. Exhib: Mid-South Exhib, Memphis, 72; Shreveport Nat, La, 73; Delta Exhib, Little Rock, 74; one-man show, Univ Tenn, Memphis, 74; Univ Ark Purchase Invitational, Little Rock, 74. Teaching: Lectr painting, Univ Ark, Little Rock, 74-; instr painting, Southeast Ark Arts & Sci Ctr, 74- Pos: Assoc dir, Graphics & Design Div, Ginn & Co, Boston, 49-67. Awards: Award of Merit Contemporary Painting, Shreveport Nat, 73; Distinguished Ark Artist, Montessori Soc, Little Rock, 75; Best of Show Contemporary Painting, Ark Festival Arts, Ark Arts Ctr, Little Rock, 75; Senate Resolution of Commendation, 77. Style & Technique: Contemporary painting and realistic historical subjects. Media: Acrylic. Dealer: Konrad Toch Corp 1734 W Shady Grove Irving TX 75060. Mailing Add: 5804 Scenic Dr Little Rock AR 72207

KELLY, ARLEEN P
See Schloss, Arleen P

KELLY, ELLSWORTH
PAINTER, SCULPTOR
b Newburgh, NY, May 31, 23. Study: Boston Mus Sch, 46-48. Work: Metrop Mus Art; Mus Mod Art; Guggenheim Mus; Whitney Mus Am Art, New York; Tate Gallery, London. Comn: Sculpture, Penn Ctr Transp Bldg Lobby, Philadelphia, 56; wall sculpture, comn by Philip Johnson, New York World's Fair, New York Pavilion, 64; mural, UNESCO, Paris, 69. Exhib: 16 Americans, 59 & Art of the Real, 68, Mus Mod Art, New York; Paintings, Sculpture & Drawings by Ellsworth Kelly, Washington Gallery Mod Art, 63; Documenta III, IV & VI, Kassel, Ger, 64, 68 & 77; Venice Biennale Int Art, 66; New York Painting & Sculpture, 1940-1970, Metrop Mus Art, 69; retrospective, Mus Mod Art, New York, 73. Awards: Carnegie Int Prizes, 62 & 64; Brandeis Creative Arts Award, 63; Tokyo Int Educ Ministry Award, 63. Bibliog: Eugene Goossen (auth), Derriere le miroir, Paris, Maeght Ed, 58 & (auth), Ellsworth Kelly, Mus of Mod Art, New York, 73; Diane Waldman (auth), Ellsworth Kelly drawings, collages, prints, New York Graphic Soc, 71; John Coplans (auth), Ellsworth Kelly, Abrams, 72. Mailing Add: c/o Leo Castelli Gallery 4 E 77th St New York NY 10021

KELLY, ISAAC PERRY
CRAFTSMAN, EDUCATOR
b Orlando, Fla, June 2, 25. Study: Univ Hawaii; Univ Fla, BD, 53, MEd, 55; Peabody Col, EdD, 65. Comn: Tapestry (woven), comn by Mrs Ed Buerk, Delray Beach, Fla, 75; tapestry (woven), comn by Dr William Chovan, Cullowhee, NC, 75. Teaching: Assoc prof art educ & weaving & dir exhib, Western Carolina Univ, 68- Pos: State supvr art, Dept Pub Instr, Raleigh, NC, 63-68. Mem: Assoc Artists NC (pres, 73-75); NC Art Educ Asn (pres, 77-); Southeast Col Art Conf; Handweavers Guild of Am; Int Soc for Educ in the Arts; NC Crafts Asn; Nat Art Educ Asn; Col Art Asn Am. Media: Weaving, Pottery. Publ: Auth, Art Education in North Carolina, 65. Mailing Add: Box 755 Cullowhee NC 28723

KELLY, JAMES
PAINTER
b Philadelphia, Pa, Dec 19, 13. Study: Pa Acad Fine Arts, Philadelphia; Barnes Found, Merion, Pa; Calif Sch Fine Arts, San Francisco. Work: San Francisco Mus Art; Mus Mod Art, New York; Los Angeles Mus Art; Univ Mass, Boston; Westinghouse Corp, Salem, NC & Pittsburgh, Pa. Exhib: San Francisco Mus Art Painting Ann, 55-58; Minneapolis Inst Art, Minn, 57; Am Fedn Arts Traveling Exhib, 58-59; Los Angeles Co Mus Art, 68; Smithsonian Inst, Washington, DC, 77; Huntsville Mus of Art, Ala, 77; one-man shows, Albright Col, Reading, Pa, 66, Long Island Univ, Brooklyn, NY, 68, East Hampton Gallery, New York, NY, 69 & Westbeth Galleries, New York, 71-72. Teaching: Lectr painting, Univ Calif, Berkeley, summer 56. Awards: Ford Found grant lithography, 63; Nat Endowment Arts grant painting, 77-78. Mailing Add: 463 West St New York NY 10014

KELLY, LEE
SCULPTOR
b McCall, Idaho, May 24, 32. Study: Mus Art Sch, Portland, Ore. Work: Univ Houston; Portland Art Mus; Seattle Art Mus; Univ Ore Mus, Eugene. Comn: Welded steel play piece, Unthanr Park, Portland, 68; welded steel fountain, Milwaukee Ore Libr, 69; welded stainless

steel wall piece, Pac Northwest Bell, Portland, 71; welded stainless steel water piece, Univ Houston, 72; welded steel gateway, Candlestick Park, San Francisco, 72. Exhib: Ore Centennial Invitational, 60; Denver Mus Ann Invitational, 61 & 71; Pacific Profile, Pasadena Mus, Calif, 62; West Coast Now, Portland Art Mus, 68. Teaching: Instr art, Mt Angel Col, 68-71; prof art, Reed Col, 76- Awards: Seattle Art Mus Purchase Award, 60-61; Ford Found Purchase Award, 63; Art Advocates Proj Award, 70. Media: Metal. Dealer: Foster/White Gallery Seattle WA. Mailing Add: 13099 S Warnock Rd Oregon City OR 97045

KELLY, LEON
PAINTER
b Perpignan, France, Oct 21, 01; US citizen. Study: Pa Acad Fine Arts, traveling scholar, 24; Acad Grande Chaumiere, Paris; also with Jean Auguste Adolphe, Alexandre Portinoff, Arthur Carles & Earl Horter. Work: Mus Mod Art, Whitney Mus Am Art & Metrop Mus Art, New York; Wadsworth Atheneum, Conn; Tel Aviv Mus, Israel; plus many others. Exhib: Retrospective 1920-65, Int Gallery, Baltimore, Md, 65, Pa Acad Fine Arts, 57; Long Beach Found, NJ, 68; Exhibs, Richard Feigen Gallery, Chicago, 68 & 70; Newark Mus, NJ, 69; plus many other one-man & group shows. Teaching: Instr, Pa Acad Fine Arts. Awards: William & Nora Copley Award, 58. Media: Oil. Mailing Add: 268 Pompano Dr Loveladies NJ 08008

KELLY, WALTER W
ART DEALER
b Chicago, Ill, Jan 14, 41. Study: Roosevelt Univ, BA, 63. Pos: Dir, Walter Kelly Gallery. Specialty: Contemporary American large-scale sculpture. Mailing Add: 620 N Michigan Ave Chicago IL 60611

KELLY, WILLIAM JOSEPH
EDUCATOR, PAINTER
b Buffalo, NY, May 4, 43. Study: Philadelphia Col Art, BFA; Prahran Col Adv Educ; Nat Gallery Sch, Australia, MA. Work: Lehigh Univ, Pa; Accad di Belle Arti, Perugia, Italy; Melbourne Univ, Australia; Westminster Col, Pa; Victorian Arts Ctr: Performing Arts Collection, Melbourne, Australia. Exhib: Ann Exhib, Albright-Knox Art Gallery, Buffalo, 63; Benalla Mus Art, Australia, 70; Seven Young Artists, Del Mus Art, Wilmington, 72; Watergate, Odense Mus, Denmark, 74; Kelly: Drawings, Accad di Belle Arti, Perugia, 75; The Figure in Recent Am Painting (traveling exhib), 75; Corio Invitational, Gaelong Gallery of Art, Australia, 77; Am Figure Drawing, Lehigh Univ, 76. Teaching: Instr painting & perceptual psychology, Victorian Col of Arts, Melbourne, 75- Pos: Dean sch art, Victorian Col of Arts, Melbourne, 75- Awards: S M Egnal Painting Award, Grad Exhib, Philadelphia Col of Art, 68; Fulbright Fel, Inst for Int Studies, 69. Bibliog: Elwyn Lynn (auth), Proving that realism is alive and well in the American scene, The Bull, Sydney, 6/69. Style & Technique: Figurative painter, work primarily with overhead views of figures and objects against a floor plane; work employs forshortening but avoids use of perspective. Media: Acrylic on Canvas; Charcoal on Paper. Publ: Auth, The Melbourne Balthus: a footnote, Art & Australia, 6/69; auth, Two Who Responded, Art & Artists, London, 4/76. Mailing Add: c/o Victorian Col of Arts 234 St Kilda Rd Melbourne 3004 Australia

KELPE, PAUL
PAINTER
b Minden, Ger, 1902; US citizen. Study: Art Sch, Hanover, Ger; Univ Chicago, MA & PhD. Work: Detroit Inst Arts, Mich; Mus of Mod Art, New York; Towson State Col, Md; Univ NMex Art Mus, Albuquerque; Kresge Art Ctr, Mich State Univ, East Lansing. Exhib: Geometric Abstraction of 1930s, Zabriskie Gallery, New York, 72; Constructivists of the 20's & 30's, Carus Gallery, New York, 75; The Emergence of Modernism in Illinois 1914-1940, Ill State Mus, Springfield, 76; Am Abstract Artists, Univ NMex Art Mus, Albuquerque, 77; plus many others. Bibliog: Jacobson (auth), Art of Today, Stein Publ, 33; M Candler Cheney (auth), Modern Art in America, McGraw, 39; The World of Abstract Art, Wittenborn, 57. Mem: Am Abstr Artists. Media: Oil, Watercolor. Mailing Add: 705 Texas Ave Austin TX 78705

KELSEY, MURIEL CHAMBERLIN
SCULPTOR
b Milford, NH. Study: Univ NH, BS, 19; Univ Vt, 21; Teachers Col, Columbia Univ, 33; New Sch Social Res, 34; Sculpture Ctr New York, with Dorothea Denslow. Comn: Dancing Pickaninny (bronze statuette), Brookgreen Gardens Mus, SC, 37; plus many others in pvt comns. Exhib: Sculpture Ctr New York, 34-; Audubon Artists, New York, 58-62; Nat Acad Design, New York, 59-62; Harmon Gallery, Naples, Fla, 64-; 3rd Sculpture Int, Fairmount Park Art Asn, Philadelphia. Teaching: Asst zool lab, Univ NH, 20; asst zool lab, Univ Vt, 21. Awards: Sarasota Festival Arts, 53; Art League Manatee Co, 59; First Prize, Longboat Key Art Ctr, 65. Mem: Sculpture Ctr New York. Media: Stone. Dealer: Oehlschlaeger Galleries 107 E Oak St Chicago IL 60611. Mailing Add: c/o Harmon Gallery 1258 Third St S Naples FL 33940

KEMBLE, RICHARD
PRINTMAKER, SCULPTOR
b Erie, Pa, Nov 7, 32. Study: Trenton State Col, NJ, BA; Pratt Graphics Art Ctr, study with Carol Summers, Clare Romano & Al Blaustein. Work: NJ State Mus, Trenton; Mus Mod Art, Sao Paulo, Brazil; Allentown Art Mus, Pa; Newark Pub Libr, NJ; Trenton State Col, NJ. Comn: Sculpture, Mercer Hosp, Trenton, NJ; altarpiece & vestments, St Andrews Church, Yardley, Pa, 72; cake, Mus Contemp Crafts, New York, 73; ed of prints for publicity, Circle F Indust, Trenton, 73; sculpture, Gloucester Co Col, 75. Exhib: The Bakers Art, Mus Contemp Crafts, New York, 67; Art from New Jersey, NJ State Mus, 68-73; Albright-Knox Art Gallery, Buffalo, NY; Pratt Graphics Ctr, New York; Allentown Art Mus, Pa; Art in Embassies, 71-; Exposicao de Cinco Gravados Contempores Americanos, Brazil, 73; Pratt on Paper, Phoenix Gallery, New York, 75; Suzuki Gallery, New York, 77-78. Teaching: Instr printmaking, Long Beach Island Found Arts & Sci, Loveladies, NJ, 73; artist in residence, North Country Sch, 73 & NJ State Coun Arts, 74-75. Awards: Purchase Award, NJ State Mus, 70; Printmaker's Fel, Nat Endowment Arts, 74-75. Bibliog: Peggy Lewis (auth), If he knows you're coming, he'll bake cake, Trenton Times, 5/68; Mary Midura (auth), Renaissance man leads the good life, Trentonian, 12/71; Burton Wasserman (auth), Kemble's woodcuts, Camden Courier Post, 10/73. Mem: Pratt Graphic Arts Ctr; Artists Equity; Soc Am Graphic Artists; Am Color Print Soc. Style & Technique: Woodcuts in usual manner, then paper is sprayed with solvent causing ink to permeate the paper and reflect print from both sides of the paper; bold abstract shapes sometimes reflecting landscapes and Mayan motifs as found in ruins; welded steel sculpture in abstract forms, some painted, others left to rust. Dealer: Fendrick Gallery 3059 M St NW Washington DC 20007; Int Print Soc New Hope PA 18938. Mailing Add: c/o Forager House Studio Box 82 Washington Crossing PA 18977

KEMENYFFY, STEVEN
CERAMIST, EDUCATOR
b Budapest, Hungary, Aug 8, 43; US citizen. Study: Augustana Col, Rock Island, Ill, BA, 65; Univ of Iowa, Iowa City, MA, 66 & MFA, 67. Work: Mus of Contemp Crafts, New York; State Univ of NY, Geneseo; Butler Inst of Am Art, Youngstown, Ohio; Univ of NDak Grand Forks. Comn: Ceramic wall murals with Susan Kemenyffy, 8 (3ft x 4ft), 41st Int Eucharistic Congress Exhib of Liturgical Arts, Philadelphia, Pa, 76, (4ft x 6ft), Fairtree Gallery, 76 & (4ft x 8ft), comn by Dr David Doupe, Erie, Pa, 77. Exhib: Wis Designer Craftsman, Milwaukee Art Ctr, 67-71; Objects USA, Smithsonian Inst, Washington, DC, 69; Ceramics 70 plus Woven Forms, Everson Mus of Art, Syracuse, NY, 70; Scripps Col Invitational, Claremont, Calif, 71, 77; Cleveland May Show, Cleveland Mus Art, 71-72; Salt Glaze Ceramics, Mus of contemp Crafts, New York, 72; Ceramic Art of the World, Calgary, Alta, Can, 73; Int Pottery Competition, Nagoya, Japan, 73; This Plastic Earth, John Michael Kohler Art Ctr, Sheboygan, Wis, 73; Baroque 74, Mus of Contemp Crafts, 74; Ceramic Invitational, Philadelphia Mus of Art, 77 & Pratt Sch of Art, 77; Drinking Companions, John Michael Kohler Art Ctr, 78. Teaching: Prof ceramics, Edinboro State Col, Pa, 69-; lectr, Univ Chicago, Ill, 75, Temple Univ, Tyler Sch of Art, Pa, 76, Univ of Manitoba, Winnipeg, Can, 77, Rochester Inst of Tech, New York, 78 & Vancouver Sch of Art, BC, Can, 78. Awards: Cash Ceramic Award, Cleveland May Show, Cleveland Mus of Art, Ohio, 72; Hon mention, Ceramic Art of the World, Calgary, Alta, Can, 73; Fel Grant, Nat Endowment for the Arts, 77. Mem: Nat Coun on Educ for Ceramic Arts; Pittsburgh Craftsman Guild; Pa Guild of Craftsmen; Am Crafts Coun; Minn Crafts Coun. Style & Technique: Work in collaboration with wife Susan on Raku process. Media: Clay. Dealer: The Elements 766 Madison Ave New York NY 10021; Sylvia Ullman American Crafts 13110 Woodland Cleveland Heights OH 44120. Mailing Add: 4570 Old State Rd McKean PA 16426

KEMENYFFY, SUSAN B HALE
CERAMIST, PRINTMAKER
b Springfield, Mass, Oct 4, 41. Study: Syracuse Univ, New York, BFA, 63, study with Robert Marks; Univ of Iowa, Iowa City, MA, 66, study with Mauricio Lasansky, MFA(with hons), 67. Work: Butler Inst of Am Art, Youngstown, Ohio; Chrysler Mus, Province Town, Mass; Cleveland State Univ, Ohio; Marietta Col, Ohio; Hope Col, Holland, Mich. Comn: Ceramic wall murals with Steven Kemenyffy, 8 (3ft x 4ft), 41st Int Eucharist Congress Exhib of Liturgical Arts, Philadelphia, 76; (4ft x 6ft), Fairtree Gallery, New York, 76; (4ft x 8ft), comn by Dr David Doude, Erie, Pa, 77. Exhib: This Plastic Earth, John Michael Kohler Art Ctr, 73; Int Pottery Competition, Nagoya, Japan, 73; Ceramic Art of the World, Calgary, Alta, Can, 73; Baroque 74, Mus of Contemp Crafts, New York, 74; Crafts Invitational, Skidmore Col, Saratoga Springs, NY, 76; East Coast Ceramics, Philadelphia Col of Art, 75; The Box Show, 76 & Drinking Companions, 77, John Michael Kohler Art Ctr, Sheboygan, Wis; Scripps Col Ceramic Invitational, Claremont, Calif, 77; Pratt Sch of Art, Brooklyn, NY, 77; The Am Hand, Raku Exhib-1978, Washington, DC, 78. Teaching: Asst prof art, Mercyhurst Col, Erie, Pa, 74-; lectr, Temple Univ, Tyler Sch of Art, Philadelphia, 76, Univ of Manitoba, Winnipeg, Can, 77, Rochester Inst of Tech, New York, 78, Vancouver Sch of Art, BC, Can, 78 & Univ of NMex, Silver City, 78. Awards: 2nd Prize, cash, Ceramic Art of the World, Calgary, Alta, Can, 73; Fel Grant, Nat Endowment for the Arts, 73. Style & Technique: Work in collaboration with husband Steven on Raku process. Dealer: The Elements 766 Madison Ave New York NY 10021; Sylvia Ullman 13010 Woodland Cleveland Heights OH 44120. Mailing Add: 4570 Old State Rd McKean PA 16426

KEMOHA (GEORGE W PATRICK PATTERSON)
PAINTER, ART HISTORIAN
b Centralia, Ill, Dec 29, 14. Study: Univ Okla. Comn: Murals, Our Lady of Guadalupe, Dewey, Okla, 50; murals, St John's Cath Church, Bartlesville, Okla, 60; murals, St Charles Borromeo, Oklahoma City, 70; plus hundreds of pvt portrait commissions. Pos: Dir, Woolaroc Mus, 38-70. Media: Oil. Mailing Add: 418 Texas Ave Woodward OK 73801

KEMP, PAUL ZANE
PRINTMAKER
b Apache Creek, NMex, Nov 6, 28. Study: NMex Highlands Univ, BA, 50, MA, 54; Cranbrook Acad Art, MFA, 60. Exhib: 3rd Ann Prints, Drawings & Crafts, Ark Arts Ctr, Little Rock, 69; Am Graphics 69, Col of the Pac, 69; Nat Graphic Arts & Drawing Show, Wichita Art Asn, Kans, 69; Northwest Printmaker's Int, Seattle, 69; Tex Fine Arts Asn Ann Citation Show, Austin, 69 & 70. Teaching: Asst prof art, Baylor Univ, 61-64, assoc prof, 64-69, prof, 69- Awards: Jurors Choice, Tex Fine Arts Asn Citation Show, 69 & 70; Purchase Entry, Ark Art Ctr, 69. Mem: Tex Designer-Craftsmen; Print Coun Am; Tex Fine Arts Asn; Am Crafts Coun; Col Art Asn Am. Media: Intaglio, Metal. Publ: Contribr & illusr, Tex Trends Art Educ, spring 69. Dealer: Ed Hill 5736 Trobridge Dr El Paso TX 79925. Mailing Add: Dept of Art Baylor Univ Waco TX 76706

KEMPER, JOHN GARNER
PAINTER, DESIGNER
b Muncie, Ind, June 3, 09. Study: Ohio State Univ, BFA; Columbia Univ, MA; Chicago Acad Fine Arts. Exhib: Ann Exhibs Mich Artists, 44 & 46 & Relig Christmas Card Competition, 55, Detroit Inst Arts; 11th Ann New Yr Show, Butler Inst Am Art, Youngstown, Ohio, 46; Ogunquit Art Ctr, Maine, 58-62. Teaching: Prof art, Western Mich Univ, 42-70, prof emer, 70- Pos: Designer, Ohio Wax Paper Co, 34-36; designer, Dell Publ Co, 36-41; graphic designer, Western Mich Univ, 70-77. Awards: Awards, for Three Houses (serigraph), Friends Am Art, Grand Rapids, 46 & The Experiment Station (oil), Ohio Valley Oil & Water Show, 54; Report of Pres, Am Col Pub Rel Asn, 69. Style & Technique: Abstract, usually landscape motifs. Media: Oil, Graphic Design. Publ: Illusr, var articles and covers, Design Mag, 31-33; auth & illusr, A portable marionette stage, Indust Arts & Voc Educ Mag, 43; auth & illusr, Marionettes, Sch Arts Mag, 46; co-auth, Art consciousness comes to Kalamazoo, Design Mag, 47. Mailing Add: 605 W Lovell St Kalamazoo MI 49007

KEMPTON, GRETA
PAINTER
b Vienna, Austria, Mar 22, 03. Study: Nat Acad Design; Art Students League. Work: The White House, The Pentagon, US Treas Dept, US Supreme Court, Nat Portrait Gallery, Apostolic Delegation & Georgetown Univ, Washington, DC; plus many other mus & pvt collections in US & abroad. Exhib: One-woman shows, Corcoran Gallery Art, Washington, DC, Canton Art Inst, Ohio, Col Wooster, Ohio, Art Asn Harrisburg, Pa, Akron Art League, Ohio & Circle Gallery, Cleveland, Ohio; plus many others. Mem: Fel Royal Soc Arts; Burr Artists. Mailing Add: 14 E 75th St New York NY 10021

KENDA, JUANITA ECHEVERRIA
PAINTER, WRITER
b Tarentum, Pa, Nov 12, 23. Study: Stephens Col; Art Students League; Temple Univ, BFA; Univ Hawaii; also with Jon Corbino, Sam Hershey, Boris Blai, Raphael Sabatini, Jean Charlot, George Bridgman & others. Comn: Murals, Straub Clinic & Children's Hosp, Honolulu.

Exhib: The Gallery, Honolulu, 60; Honolulu Painters & Sculptors, 60 & 61; Moorestown Friends Sch, 61; Univ Hawaii, 65; Galeria Santiago, San Juan, PR, 67; plus many others. Collections Arranged: Organized Exhib, Art of Hawaii Children, circulated by Smithsonian Inst, 60-64. Teaching: Lectr, art educ; instr workshop, Hawaii Summer Sch, 51; chmn art teaching conf, 51-52, 53, 55, 56 & 58; instr, Univ Hawaii Sch Educ, 65-66. Pos: Adv, Art Teachers Asn, 50-; chmn sch art exhib, Honolulu Acad Arts, 50-, head creative art sect, 49-63; state prog spec, State Dept Educ, Honolulu, 63-64; community relations officer, East-West Ctr, 68-70; pres, Downtown Gallery Ltd, 69-; Hon Consul of Mex in Hawaii. Mem: Honolulu Printmakers; Hawaii Painters & Sculptors League; Asn Art Mus; Pac Art Asn; Nat Art Educ Asn; plus others. Publ: Auth & illusr, Art education in Hawaii, Hawaii's children exhibit their art, Art and art education in Hawaii & Art guide for Hawaii, Sch Arts Mag; auth & illusr, Curriculum outline—elementary art and curriculum outline—secondary art, Dept Educ, State of Hawaii; contribr to Paradise of the Pacific; auth, Art guide for pre-school and kindergarten, San Diego Schs, Calif, 71. Mailing Add: 125 Merchant St Honolulu HI 96813

KENNEDY, J WILLIAM
PAINTER
b Cincinnati, Ohio, Aug 17, 03. Study: Art Acad Cincinnati; Carnegie Inst Technol, AB; Univ Ill, MFA. Work: Portraits, Ind Univ, Bloomington & Univ Ill, Champaign; A E Staley Co, Decatur, Ill; Withrow High Sch, Cincinnati. Comn: Portraits: Pres Herman B Wells, 62, VPres Joseph Franklin, 63 & Dean Edmundson, 64, Ind Univ, Bloomington & Dean Carl Brandley, 67 & Col Leslie A Bryan, 69, Univ Ill, Champaign. Exhib: 1st, 2nd & 3rd Nat Exhibs, Rockefeller Ctr, New York; San Francisco World's Fair; Corcoran Biennial; two Pa Acad Fine Arts Ann; Richmond Biennial, Va. Teaching: Prof art, Univ Ill, Champaign, 26-70. Awards: Award of Merit, Fla Gulf Coast Art Ctr, 72; hon mention, Milwaukee Art Gallery; First Prize in painting, Decatur Art Ctr. Mem: Provincetown Art Asn; Fla Gulf Coast Art Ctr; Midwest Col Art Conf. Media: Vinyl. Dealer: Secrest Gallery Wellfleet MA 02667. Mailing Add: 1414 Monte Carlo Dr Clearwater FL 33516

KENNEDY, JAMES EDWARD
PAINTER, SCULPTOR
b Jackson, Miss, Sept 30, 33. Study: Ala State Univ, BS; Ind Univ, MAT(painting); Spring Hill Col. Work: Johnson Publ Co Collection, Chicago. Exhib: Atlanta Univ Nat Exhib, 60-64; Eastern Shore Art Gallery, 67; Birmingham, Ala Festival Arts Centennial Exhib, 72; Ala State Univ, 72; Univ WFla, 73. Teaching: Asst prof art hist & painting, Univ S Ala, Mobile, 68-; guest instr Afro-Am art, Morehead State Univ, Minn, summer 72. Awards: Afro-Am Art Slide Grant, 69 & Ethnic-Am Minority Art Slide Libr Grant, 71, Samuel H Kress Found. Bibliog: Afro-American Artists, publ by Boston Pub Libr, 73. Mem: Nat Conf Artists (regional mem chmn); Col Art Asn Am. Style & Technique: Expressionism, sometimes abstract, sometimes fragmented realism. Publ: Co-auth, An Afro-American Slide Project, Art J, 70-71 & An Afro-American Art and Artist's Finders Index, Am Revolution Bicentennial Comn, Washington, DC, 73. Mailing Add: 2073 Tucker St Mobile AL 36617

KENNEDY, LETA MARIETTA
CRAFTSMAN
b Pendleton, Ore, July 4, 95. Study: Mus Art Sch, Portland, Ore; Columbia Univ Teachers Col, BS; Colorado Springs Art Ctr; also with Arthur Wesley Dow, Herman Rosse, Hans Hofmann, Maholy-Nagy, Arthur Baggs, Dorothy Wright Liebes, Frances Senska, Marian Hartwell & Minor White. Work: Portland Art Mus; Seattle Art Mus. Exhib: Northwest Printmakers, Seattle Art Mus, 38; Philadelphia Art Alliance, Pa, 39; Contemp Crafts Asn, Portland, 62; 10 Artists Ore, Portland Art Mus, 67; Univ Ore, Eugene. Teaching: Head dept, Mus Art Sch, Portland, 22-71; retired. Mem: Portland Art Asn; Contemp Crafts Asn. Mailing Add: 2545 SW Terwilliger Portland OR 97201

KENNEY, ALLEN LLOYD
EDUCATOR, MUSEUM DIRECTOR
b Salt Lake City, Utah, July 19, 33. Study: Colo Inst Art; Univ Wyo, BA; studied design with Robert Russin. Comn: Three hist landscapes, Sweetwater Co Mus, Green River, Wyo, 70; Western design, Antler Hotel, Newcastle, Wyo, 60. Exhib: One-man shows, Wyo Artists's Asn, 60 & Community Fine Arts Ctr, 67. Collections Arranged: 256 original art works owned by Sch Dist Number One, Sweetwater Co, Wyo. Teaching: Instr art, Weston Co Pub Schs, 57-60; chmn dept art, Sch Dist Number One, Sweetwater Co, Wyo, 60- Pos: Asst dir, Community Fine Arts Ctr, 66-69, dir, 70- Mem: Wyo Art Educ Asn (vpres, 68-69, pres, 69-70); Nat Art Educ Asn; Colo & Wyo Mus Asn; Wyo Artist's Asn. Style & Technique: Expressionist. Media: Oil; sculpture. Collection: Early 20th century, 1900-1950, North American art. Mailing Add: 400 C St Rock Springs WY 82901

KENNEY, ESTELLE KOVAL
ART THERAPIST, PAINTER
b Chicago, Ill, Feb 15, 28. Study: Sch Art Inst Chicago, BFA, 76, MFA, 78, with Joshua Kind; registred art therapist, ATR. Work: Ill State Mus, Springfield; Union League Club Chicago. Exhib: Ill State Mus, Springfield, 75; Naive Painting in Ill 1830-1976, Ill State Mus & Ukranian Inst Mod Art, Chicago, 76-77; The Chicago Connection, E B Crocker Art Gallery, Sacramento, Calif, Newport Harbor Art Mus, Newport Beach, Calif, Phoenix Art Mus, Ariz & elsewhere, 76-77; Contemp Issues—Works on Paper by Women, Woman's Bldg, Los Angeles, plus others, 77-78. Teaching: Art therapist, Grove Sch Handicapped, Lake Forest, Ill, 72-77; art therapist, N Shore Inst Therapy Through Arts, Winnetka, Ill, 77- Pos: Art therapist lectr, Univ Ill Circle Campus, Chicago, 77 & Nat Col Educ, Evanston, Ill, 77; art therapist, New Triar E & C, Spec Educ, Winnetka, 77- Awards: First Purchase Prize, Union League Club of Chicago, 74 & Ill State Mus, Springfield, 75. Bibliog: Marla Paul (auth), Kenney gives retarded a start through art, Lener Newspapers, Chicago, 76. Mem: Am Col Art Asn; Ill Art Educ Asn; Nat Art Educ Asn; Am Art Therapy Asn; Ill Art Therapy Asn (mem chmn). Style & Technique: Use of rich colors and black outlines; expressionistic images of a personal world. Media: Enamel Paint on Aluminum Sheets; Watercolor on Heavy Paper. Dealer: Sonia Zaks Gallery 620 N Michigan Ave Chicago IL 60611. Mailing Add: 1344 W Greenleaf Ave Chicago IL 60626

KENNY, BETTIE ILENE CRUTS (BIK)
PAINTER, WRITER
b Longmont, Colo, June 5, 31. Study: Pac Lutheran Univ, with George Roskos; design with James Marta; Univ Wash, BA(Eng, with hons); with Norman Lundin, Everett Du Pen, Edward L Praczukowski & George Tsutakawa; also with Florence Gould, Jack Cady, E H Smith, Prof Yaggy & Prof Hudson. Work: Commemorative portrait of President J F Kennedy on glass, Smithsonian Inst; drawing into crystal & slides of diamond-point work, Corning Mus Glass, NY & Smiling Abraham Lincoln (portrait); Gov Evans (portrait), Gov Mansion, Olympia; Henry Art Gallery Arch of Artists, Seattle, Wash; plus numerous other pvt & pub collections. Comn: Joan French (oil portrait), Gilbert & Sullivan Operetta Co, Seattle, 58; Anniversary Commemorative (drawing in diamond-point), Church of God, 71; diamond-point drawing (32 percent glass lead), Baptist Church, Seattle, 72; Ski Scene (drawing in diamond-point), State of Wash to be presented at Heavenly Valley Ski Races, 72. Exhib: 10th Ann Puget Sound Area Exhib, Charles & Emma Frye Art Mus, Seattle, 68; Lambda Rho Art for Collectors' Sale, 71 & Women in Art, 72, Henry Art Gallery, Seattle; Mus Hist & Indust, Seattle; State Capitol Mus, Olympia, Wash, 73 & 74; DBA/SEAFAIR Exhib, Seattle; Pac Gallery Artists of Tacoma, 74; Fidelity Mutual Savings & Loan, 74; and numerous others. Awards: Creative thinking merit awards, Boeing Co, Seattle, 58-59; letter of commendation from Gov Daniel J Evans, State of Wash, 72; commendation for portrait on glass, Lawrence Welk, 72. Bibliog: Guest artist demonstration of diamond-point engraving on full percent lead glass, Channel 5, King TV Telescope Prog, 5/31/72. Style & Technique: Eclectic; drawing procedure in which lead crystal is my canvas or paper. Media: Oil on Linen Canvas, Lead Glass. Mailing Add: PO Box 30049 Seattle WA 98103

KENNY, LISA A
PAINTER, SCULPTOR
b Mineola, NY. Study: Studied with Thomas Henry Kenny. Work: Mus Mod Art, Miami, Fla; Madison Art Ctr, Wis; Print Collection, Philadelphia Pub Libr; Univ Mo Mus of Art, Columbia; Nassau Community Col Firehouse Gallery, Garden City, NY. Exhib: Graphics 1971, Miami Mus Mod Art. Style & Technique: Modern geometrics in lithography and hard line geometrics painted in acrylics. Media: Lithography, Sculpturing. Mailing Add: Oak Ridge Lane North Hills Roslyn NY 11576

KENNY, PATRICK GERALD
PAINTER, ILLUSTRATOR
b Waterford, PEI, May 18, 12. Study: NAm Sch Art, Toronto; Ottawa Tech, with Henri Masson & E H Cabeldu; also with Roger Curtis, Gloucester, Mass. Work: Elliott Mus Gallery, Stuart, Fla; Univ PEI; Confederation Gallery, Charlottetown; City Hall, Summerside; House of Refuge, Martin Co, Fla. Comn: Seascape (oil), Heritage Found, PEI, 71; Marine (oil), comn by Dr R S Grober, Ft Pierce, Fla, 72; Seascape (oil), Dr John B Sullivan, Vero Beach, Fla, 73; House of Refuge Portrait (oil), Martin Co Hist Soc, Stuart, Fla, 74; Illustrations (marine), Eastern Graphic Mag, 74. Exhib: St Lucie Hilton, Port St Lucie, Fla, 69; New Eng Art Festival, Westerly, RI, 71; Confederation Gallery, Charlottetown, 73; Elliot Mus Gallery, 75. Style & Technique: Seascapes and marine with brush. Media: Oil on Convas; Pencil & Felt Tips. Mailing Add: 2302 Sunrise Blvd Apt 1-208 Ft Pierce FL 33450

KENNY, THOMAS HENRY
PAINTER
b Bridgeport, Conn, Jan 12, 18. Study: Knox Col; Ohio Christian Univ, MA. Work: Metrop Mus Art, New York; Philadelphia Mus Art; Stedelijk Mus, Amsterdam, Neth; Mus Mod Art, Mexico City; plus 367 mus collections in 27 countries. Exhib: Kenny-Retrospect, Mus Mod Art, Miami, Fla, 70; 246 Years of Am Art, New Brit Mus, 70; Int Graphics, Neue Galerie der Stadt Linz, Austria, 70; New Acquisitions, Mus Arte Moderna, Rio de Janeiro, Brazil, 71; Mod Art Mus Eilat Israel; Nat Inst Fine Arts, Mexico City; Nat Mus of Wales; plus others. Mem: Life fel Royal Soc Arts, London; Col Art Asn Am; Am Fedn Arts; Inst Contemp Arts, London. Interest: Lithography. Mailing Add: Oak Ridge Lane North Hills Roslyn NY 11576

KENOJUAK (KENOJUAK ASHEVAK)
PRINTMAKER, SCULPTOR
b S Ikerasak Baffin Island, NT, Can, Dec 25, 33. Work: Nat Gallery of Ottawa, Ont; Mus of Man, Ottawa; Toronto Dominion Bank Collection, Ont. Comn: Metal plaque, Alcan Can, 64; mural, Expo 67, 67, Expo 70, Osaka, 70, Japan. Exhib: Cape Dorset Collection Ann. Awards: Order of Can, Govt Can. Mem: Royal Can Acad of Arts. Media: Drawing; Stone Sculpture. Publ: Auth, Kenojuak, Nat Film Bd, 61. Mailing Add: Cape Dorset NT X0A 0C0 Can

KENT, H LATHAM
GALLERY DIRECTOR, PAINTER
b Mass, June 20, 30. Study: Vesper George Sch Art, Boston, Mass; study with Artie McKenzie, Fla. Exhib: Am Artists Prof League, New York; The Copley Soc, Boston, Mass; The Bicardi Gallery, Miami, Fla; The Grove Group Gallery, Coconut Grove, Fla; Beaux Arts, Lowe Art Gallery, Miami, Fla; Artists Unlimited Gallery, Key West, Fla; Coral Gables Art Gallery, Coral Gables, Fla; Int Boat Show Art Exhibs, Miami Beach, Fla; Gingerbread Sq Garden, Key West, Fla. Pos: Artist, Steve Hannagan, New York 51-54 & Bronzini of New York, 54-57; owner, Dodge House Art Gallery, Chatham, Mass, 60- Mem: Copley Soc, Boston, Mass; Soc Marine Painters, Fla; Am Artists Prof League, SFla (vpres, 77, pres, 78). Style & Technique: Landscape and seascape paintings; representational realist in oils. Media: Oil. Mailing Add: 5800 SW 51st St Miami FL 33155

KENT, JACK
ILLUSTRATOR
b Burlington, Iowa, Mar 10, 20. Work: Kerlan Collection, Univ of Minn. Exhib: Children's Book Art, Contemp Arts Mus, Houston, Tex, 75. Pos: Free-lance cartoonist for various mag, 34-50; Comic Strip artist for King Aroo, 50-65. Awards: Top Honor Book, 22nd Ann Exhib, Chicago Book Clinic, 71; one of the New York Times Outstanding Picture Bks of the Yr, 76. Mem: Nat Cartoonist Soc; Am Inst of Graphic Arts. Style & Technique: Pen and ink with watercolor, tempera or acrylic. Media: Pen and Ink, Watercolor. Publ: Auth, The Fat Cat, Parent's Mag Press, 71; auth, illusr, Dooly and the Snortsnoot, Putnam, 72; auth, illusr, There's No Such Thing As A Dragon, Golden Press, 75; auth, illusr, The Egg Book, MacMillian, 75; auth, illusr, Jack Kent's Happy-Ever-After Book, Random House, 76. Mailing Add: 103 W Johnson St San Antonio TX 78204

KEPALAITE, ELENA
See Kepalas

KEPALAS (ELENA KEPALAITE)
SCULPTOR, PAINTER
b Vilnius, Lithuania; US citizen. Study: Ont Col Art, Toronto; Brooklyn Mus Sch Art. Work: Pa Acad Fine Arts, Philadelphia; Univ Mass Art Gallery, Amherst; Libr & Mus of Performing Arts, Lincoln Ctr, NY; Lithuanian Mus, Adelaide, Australia; Mus Mod Art Lending Serv, New York. Comn: Bronze bust, Mr Louis Horst, New York, 62; bronze bust, Mrs Gunilla Kessler, New York, 71. Exhib: Pa Acad Fine Arts, Philadelphia, 68; Silvermine Guild Artists Ann, New Canaan, Conn, 69; Jersey City Mus, NJ, 69-71; Phoenix Gallery, New York, 70, 72, 74, 76 & 78; one-man show, Brooklyn Mus, NY, 64. Awards: 1970 Sculpture House Award, Jersey City Mus, 70; Am Soc Contemp Artists First Prize Award, Union Carbide, New York, 74. Mem: Am Soc Contemp Artists. Style & Technique: 1961-1970: Symbolic sculptures (lost wax process for bronze casting); 1971-1978: Architectural structures (metal welded). Mailing Add: c/o Phoenix Gallery 30 W 57th St New York NY 10019

KEPES, GYORGY
PAINTER, EDUCATOR
b Selyp, Hungary, Oct 4, 06. Study: Royal Acad Fine Arts, Budapest, MFA, 28. Work: Univ Ill; Dallas Mus Fine Arts; Albright-Knox Art Gallery, Buffalo, NY; Mus Mod Art & Whitney Mus Am Art, New York; plus many others. Comn: Murals, Grad Ctr, Harvard Univ, Travelers Ins Co, Los Angeles, Sheraton Hotel, Dallas & Chicago, Children's Libr, Fitchburg, Mass & Church of Redeemer, Baltimore; plus many others. Exhib: Art Inst Chicago; San Francisco Mus Art; Mus Fine Arts, Houston; Nat Collection Fine Arts, Washington, Whitney Mus Am Art, New York; Carnegie Inst, Pittsburgh; plus others in mus in the US & Rome, London, Copenhagen, Amsterdam & other cities. Collections Arranged: Designed exhib, Arts of the United Nations, Art Inst Chicago, 64; designer sect of Triennale de Milano, 68. Teaching: Head light & color dept, New Bauhaus, 37-38; Inst Design, 38-43; prof visual design, Mass Inst Technol, 46-, dir, Ctr Advan Visual Studies, 67-, Inst prof, 70. Awards: Guggenheim Fel, 60-61; Medaglia d'Oro, Convengo Int Artisti Critici e Studiosi d'Arte, 66; Fine Arts Award, Am Inst Architects, 68. Mem: Nat Inst Arts & Lett; fel Am Acad Arts & Sci. Publ: Auth, Language of Vision, 44 & The New Landscape, 56; ed, Visual Arts Today, 60; ed, Vols I-VII, In: Vision & Value Series, Braziller. Mailing Add: 90 Larchwood Dr Cambridge MA 02138

KEPETS, HUGH MICHAEL
PAINTER
b Cleveland, Ohio, Feb 6, 46. Study: Carnegie-Mellon Univ, BFA; Ohio Univ, MFA. Work: Metrop Mus Art, New York; Philadelphia Mus Fine Arts; Cleveland Mus Art; Libr of Cong, Washington, DC; Yale Univ Art Gallery. Exhib: One-man shows, Fishbach Gallery, New York, 74 & 75, Vick Gallery, Philadelphia, 74 & Michael Berger Gallery, Pittsburgh, 75; Davidson Nat Print & Drawing Competition, 75; Biennial Int Open Competition, 75; Philadelphia Print Club; May Show, Cleveland Mus Art, six times, 68-75; 20th Nat Print Exhib, Brooklyn Mus, NY, 77. Awards: Award for Graphics, 55th May Show, Cleveland Mus Art, 74; Bertha von Moschzisker Prize, 1975 Biennial Int Open Competition, Philadelphia Print Club. Style & Technique: Representational. Mailing Add: c/o Fischbach Gallery 29 W 57th St New York NY 10019

KERKOVIUS, RUTH
PAINTER
b Berlin, Ger, June 9, 21; US citizen. Study: Munich, Ger, 46-49; New Sch Social Res; Art Students League; Pratt Graphic Art Ctr, scholar; Sch Visual Arts. Work: New York Pub Libr; Mus Fine Arts, Boston; Mus Western Art, Ft Worth, Tex; White House; Ford Found; plus others. Exhib: Print Club, Philadelphia, 67; Asheville Art Mus, NC, 68; Assoc Am Artists, New York, 69; Tenn Fine Arts Ctr, Nashville, 68; C Troup Gallery, Dallas, 70; plus others. Awards: Second Prize for intaglios, Jersey City Mus, 62 & Wesleyan Univ, 67; Soc Am Graphic Artists Prizes, 63, 67 & 73. Mem: Print Club Philadelphia; Soc Am Graphic Artists (past coun mem). Mailing Add: Mas Le Paladium Rte de Raphele 13200 Arles France

KERMES, CONSTANTINE JOHN
PAINTER, PRINTMAKER
b Pittsburgh, Pa, Dec 6, 23. Study: Carnegie-Mellon Univ, BFA; also with Victor Candell, Leo Manso & Frank Lloyd Wright. Work: Storm King Art Ctr, Mountainville, NY; Notre Dame Art Mus, South Bend, Ind; Indiana Univ Pa; Pa State Univ, University Park; Hershey Med Ctr, Pa. Comn: Icon paintings, Holy Cross Greek Orthodox Church, Pittsburgh, 55; two murals, Pa Hist & Mus Comn, Cornwall Mus, 68; assemblage panels, Hain Wolf Assocs, Harrisburg, Pa, 70; assemblage murals, Sperry Rand Corp, Pa. Exhib: Ten one-man exhibs, Jacques Seligmann Gallery, 50-73, Des Moines Art Ctr, Iowa, 53; Pa State Univ, University Park, 71-72; Butler Inst Am Art Ann, Youngstown, Ohio, 64; Design Rev, Smithsonian Inst, Washington, DC, 69. Teaching: Instr printmaking, Millersville State Col, summer 69; prof art adv, Lancaster Co Tech Schs, 70-72. Awards: Ann Design Rev Awards, Indust Design Mag, 62, 64, 68 & 72; Design Awards, Am Iron & Steel Inst, 65, 69, 73 & 75; Traveling Exhib Painting Prize, Petrol Industs, 71. Bibliog: Emily Genauer (auth), Icons of American saints, This Wk, 5/17/53; D Yoder (auth), Painter of the Amish, Pa Folklife, summer 66; George Swetnam (auth), Search for simplicity, Pittsburgh Press, 9/6/70. Style & Technique: Simplified pattern and color, echoing forms of American folk art and Byzantine iconography. Media: Oil, Acrylic; Woodcut, Lithography. Publ: Auth & illusr, There is a season, 69; Shaker Architecture, 70; painting reproduced in 1972 UNICEF Art Calendar; American Icons, 75; Folk images of rural Pennsylvania, Pa Folklife, 6/75. Dealer: Jacques Seligmann Gallery 5 E 57th St New York NY 10022. Mailing Add: 981 Landis Valley Rd Lancaster PA 17601

KERN, ARTHUR (EDWARD)
EDUCATOR, SCULPTOR
b New Orleans, La, Oct 27, 31. Study: Tulane Univ La, BA, 53 & MFA, 55. Exhib: One-man shows, Ariz State Univ, 74 & Int Sculpture Conf, Tulane Univ, 76; South Houston Gallery, New York, 75. Teaching: Asst prof drawing, Univ Southwestern La, 67-69; assoc prof painting & sculpture, Tulane Univ La, 69-, assoc chmn dept art, 72- Style & Technique: Figurative expressionism; lost wax molding of polyester resin. Mailing Add: 1730 Pine St New Orleans LA 70118

KERNS, ED (JOHNSON, JR)
PAINTER
b Richmond, Va, Feb 22, 45. Study: Va Commonwealth Univ, BFA; with Grace Hartigan, Md Inst Col Art, Baltimore, MFA. Work: Aldrich Mus Art, Ridgefield, Conn; Chase Manhattan Bank Collection, New York; Edward Albee Found Collection, New York; Citicorp Collection, New York; Corcoran Collection, Washington, DC; Univ Mass Art Collection, Amherst; Dallas Mus Collection, Tex. Exhib: One-man shows, A M Sachs Gallery, 72 & 74, Rosa Esman Gallery, 75, 76, 77 & 78 & Suzette Schochet Gallery, 77; Contemporary Reflections, Alrich Mus Art, 72; Art Acquisitions, Univ Mass, 72; Image of Movement, Stamford Mus, Conn, 73. Awards: Artist of the Year, Larry Aldrich Assoc, New York, 71; Art Achievement Key, Va Commonwealth Univ, 67. Bibliog: Rev of 72 show at A M Sachs Gallery, A Mikotajuk in Arts Mag, 4/72, B Schwartz in Arts News Mag, 4/72 & H Gerard, Art Int Mag, 5/72; reviews in Arts Mag, 12/77 & Artforum, 1/78. Style & Technique: Painted collage (abstract). Media: Acrylic Polymer and Collage Materials. Dealer: Rosa Esman Gallery 29 W 57th St New York NY 10019. Mailing Add: 343 E 18th St New York NY 10003

KERR, BERTA BORGENICHT
ART DEALER, COLLECTOR
b New York, NY, Nov 27, 43. Study: Boston Univ, BA. Pos: Asst dir, Grace Borgenicht Gallery, New York, 65- Specialty: Contemporary American painting and sculpture. Collection: Picasso, Klee, Seurat, Avery, Marsden Hartley, José de Rivera, Valladon, Bolotowsky, Vasarely, Matisse, Gris & Kupka. Mailing Add: c/o Borgenicht Gallery 1018 Madison Ave New York NY 10021

KERR, JAMES WILFRID
PAINTER, LECTURER
b New York, NY, Aug 7, 97. Study: Poppenhusen Inst, College Point, NY, 14; New York Sch Fine & Appl Art, 20-2 Social Res, 33-34; study with Howard Giles & Camilio Egas, Ecuador, Jacques Maroger, Louvre, Paris. Work: Mus City New York; Joslyn Art Mus, Omaha; Newark Mus, NJ; NMex State Fair Permanent Art Collection, Albuquerque; Fla Southern Col Fine Art Collection, Lakeland. Exhib: Painting in the United States, Carnegie Inst, Pittsburgh, 49; Art USA, Madison Sq Garden, New York, 58; Allied Artists Am Ann, New York, 61, 62 & 63; Albuquerque Exhib, Mus NMex, Santa Fe, 61; 47th Ann Nat Art Exhib, Mus Art, Springville, Utah, 71. Teaching: Asst instr art, NY Sch Fine & Appl Art, summer 21; dir art educ, Kerr Summer Sch Art, Detroit, summers 23-24; spec lectr art educ, Syracuse Univ, summer 32. Pos: Founder & owner, Fairbairn Publ, New York, 25-40; art dir, Harry Doehla Co, Fitchburg, Mass, 45-50. Awards: First Altman Prize, Nat Acad Design, New York, 45; Purchase Prize, NMex State Fair, Albuquerque, 63; Silver Medal, Am Vet Soc Artists, New York, 63. Mem: Salmagundi Club; Allied Artists Am; Am Vet Soc Artists; Artists Equity Asn; Mus Albuquerque Asn. Style & Technique: Modern and traditional style of painting with a meticulous technique. Media: Oil. Publ: Contribr, Art recovery, Sch Arts Mag, 33; co-auth, Historic design for modern use, 38; auth, Modern lettering, 39. Dealer: Grand Central Galleries 40 Vanderbilt Ave New York NY 10017. Mailing Add: 7017 Bellrose Ave NE Albuquerque NM 87110

KERR, JOHN HOARE
ART ADMINISTRATOR, ART HISTORIAN
b Newport, RI, Apr 19, 31. Study: Art Students League; Yale Univ & Sch Fine Arts; Boston Mus Sch Fine Arts. Collections Arranged: Planned exhibs on American Art Collection for Nat Collection Fine Arts; planned extensive exhibs on American & Europ Art at Huntington Galleries. Pos: Dir interpretation, Sleepy Hollow Restorations, 61-63; spec consult Am art & mus collection planning, Nat Collection Fine Arts, 63-64; dir, Huntington Galleries, 64-67; cult consul, US Consulate Gen, Madras, India, 67-69; dir educ, Nat Endowment Arts. Mem: Am Asn Mus; Nat Trust for Hist Preserv; Soc Archit Historians; Am Foreign Serv Asn. Res: American art from earliest days through 1540's; South Indian bronzes (India). Collection: Small personal specimen collection of European, American and Asian (Indian) paintings, sculpture, prints and decorative arts with emphasis on the 19th and 20th centuries. Publ: Auth, Museum Collections of the Trirandrum Museum, Kerala, South India, 68; auth, South Indian Bronzes in the Madras Government Museum, Tamilnadu, 70. Mailing Add: 2804 P St Washington DC 20007

KERR, KENNETH A
PAINTER, DESIGNER
b Pittsburgh, Pa, Feb 10, 43. Study: San Diego City Col, AA; Art Ctr Col, BA; also with Robert E Wood, Lorser Feitelson & Harry Carmean. Comn: Paintings, US Financial Corp, San Diego, 72; US Air Force Collection/Smithsonian Inst, Washington, DC. Exhib: Calif 200th, 70; Calif-Hawaii Regional, 71; Del Mar Fair, 71 & 74; Watercolor West, 71, 74, 75, 76 & 77; Art Inst 14th Ann, 73; Nat Watercolor Soc, 73, 74, 75 & 76. Teaching: Instr life drawing & watercolor, San Diego Community Cols, 70- Pos: Illusr, Gen Dynamics, San Diego, 61-64; designer, Collage Studios, Los Angeles, 66-68; art dir, Art Assocs, San Diego, 68-69; art dir & owner, Daisy Studio, San Diego, 69-75; vpres, Group West Inc, 75-; proj dir/graphics, W E D Div, Walt Disney Productions (in chg all graphic design for Disneyland & all Disney projs). Awards: First for Watercolors, San Diego Art Inst Ann, 71 & Southern Calif Expo, 71; Distinctive Merit, Soc Communicating Arts, 73; Soc Illusr, 74, 75, 76 & 77 & Zellerbach Award, 77. Mem: San Diego Watercolor Soc (vpres, 70, pres, 71); San Diego Art Inst (pres, 70-71); Nat Watercolor Soc; Soc Illusr (bd mem, 75); Los Angeles Art Asn (bd mem). Dealer: Fireside Gallery Carmel CA 93921; The Art Connection 8407 Melrose Pl Los Angeles CA 90069. Mailing Add: 7201 Floramorgan Trail Tujunga CA 91042

KERSLAKE, KENNETH ALVIN
PRINTMAKER, EDUCATOR
b Mt Vernon, NY, Mar 8, 30. Study: Pratt Inst, 50-53, with Calvin Alberts & Philip Guston; Univ Ill, Urbana, with Lee Chesney, BFA, 55 & MFA, 57. Work: Libr Cong, Washington, DC; Boston Mus Fine Arts, Mass; De Cordova Mus, Lincoln, Mass; Seattle Art Mus, Wash; Univ Nebr, Lincoln; plus others. Exhib: 2nd & 3rd Brit Int Print Biennial, Bradford, Eng, 70; Four Printmakers, Sheldon Mem Gallery, Univ Nebr, Lincoln, 70; Photo/graphics, George Eastman House, Rochester, NY, 71; one-man traveling exhib, Ringling Mus, Sarasota, Fla, 74-75; New American Graphics, Univ Wis & Madison Art Ctr, 75. Teaching: Prof printmaking, Univ Fla, 58- Awards: Award, Fla Mus Dirs & Fla Gas Co, 71; Intag One Best of Show, San Fernando Valley State Col, 71. Bibliog: H Williams (auth), Notes for a Young Painter, Prentice-Hall, 63. Mem: Southeastern Graphic Coun; Boston Printmakers; Nat Soc Lit & Arts. Style & Technique: Extensive exploration of halftone and photo-intaglio techniques combined with traditional intaglio methods, generally conceived from personal photographs, collage and drawing. Media: Intaglio and Photo Intaglio. Dealer: Drexler Gallery 1062 Madison Ave New York NY 10028; ADI Gallery 538 McAllister St San Francisco CA 94102. Mailing Add: 1114 NW 36th Dr Gainesville FL 32601

KERSTETTER, BARBARA ANN
PAINTER, INSTRUCTOR
b Kokomo, Ind, Mar 20, 28. Study: Art Inst Pittsburgh; Univ Hawaii; Univ Pittsburgh, BA(cum laude); Seton Hill Col, with Frank Webb. Work: Air Force Mus Art Collection, Dayton, Ohio. Exhib: Three Rivers Art Festival, 72 & 75; Hoosier Salon Indianapolis, 72; Am Artists Prof League Exhib, New York, 74 & 75; Washington & Jefferson Nat Painting Exhib, Washington, Pa, 75; one-man show, Clarion State Col, Pa, 75. Teaching: Instr oil painting, Boyce Community Col, Riverview High Sch Campus, 69- Awards: Gold Medallion Award, Twin Towers Art Exhib, Ingomar, Pa, 72; Best of Show Award, Indiana Co Fair Art Exhib, Pa, 73; Mus Award, Greensburg Art Asn, Pa, 73. Mem: Am Artists Prof League; Indiana Art Asn, Pa; Holiday Park Artists League, Pittsburgh (pres, 74-75). Style & Technique: Landscapes, particularly city scapes with emphasis on brickwork and lights and shadows, very realistic; rural landscapes more vignette; prints, black and white preferred working in linocut and etching. Media: Oil, Watercolor. Publ: Auth, Painting on black velvet, Today's Art, 7/66. Mailing Add: Box 251 RD 1 Apollo PA 15613

KERSWILL, J W ROY
PAINTER
b Bigbury, Eng, Jan 17, 25; US citizen. Study: Plymouth Col Art, Eng; Bristol Col Art, scholar. Work: Wyo State Art Gallery; Mus Mountain Man; Grand Teton Natural Hist Asn Nat Park, Wyo; Jefferson Nat Expansion Mem, St Louis, Mo; Dept Interior Nat Collection, Washington, DC. Comn: Hist murals, Alpenhof Teton Village, Wyo, First Nat Bank, Englewood, Colo & Cheyenne Nat Bank, Wyo. Exhib: Am Artists Prof League Ann, New York, 50- Mem: Am Artists Prof League; Artist Equity Asn. Style & Technique: Traditional. Media: Watercolor, Oil. Dealer: May Gallery PO Box 1972 Jackson WY 83001. Mailing Add: Teton Village Jackson Hole WY 83025

KERTESS, KLAUS D
ART DEALER, ART HISTORIAN
b New York, NY, July 16, 40. Study: Yale Univ, BA(art hist, magna cum laude), 62, MA(art hist), 64; Univ Bonn & Univ Cologne, 62-63. Pos: Dir, Bykert Gallery, New York. Mailing Add: Leonard B Stern & Co 274 Madison Ave New York NY 10016

KESSLER, ALAN
PAINTER, SCULPTOR
b Philadelphia, Pa, Oct 15, 45. Study: Philadelphia Col Art, BFA; Yale Univ Summer Sch, Norfolk, Conn, Yale fel, 66; Md Inst Col Art, Baltimore, Hoffberger fel painting, 68-69, MFA. Work: Am Fedn Arts, New York; NY Univ Collection; Brockton Art Mus, Mass; Rose Art Mus, Brandeis Univ; State Univ NY Col Cortland. Exhib: One-man shows, Bernard Danenberg Galleries, New York, 73, A B Closson Co, Cincinnati, 73, James Yu Gallery, New York, 75 & 76, Brown Univ, 77, O K Harris Gallery, New York, 77, Everson Mus of Arts, Syracuse, NY, 78 & Morgan Gallery, Kansas City, Mo, 78; Still Life Today, Am Fedn Arts Traveling Exhib, 72; New Realism, Revisited, State Univ NY Col Potsdam, 74. Teaching: Instr painting & drawing, Md Inst Col Art, 68-69; instr, Hudson River Mus, 74; asst prof art, Brown Univ, 77- Awards: First Prize in Painting, Acad Arts, Easton, Md, 68; Elizabeth T Greenshields Mem Found Grant in Painting, Montreal, 74; Artist in Residence Grant, Nat Endowment Arts, Del State Arts Coun, 75-76. Bibliog: Gregory Battcock (auth), Super Realism a Critical Anthology, Dutton, 75; Vivian Radnor (auth), Art: while waiting for tomorrow, New York Times, 10/23/77; Kim Levin (auth), Preview exhibition wood sculpture, O K Harris Gallery, Arts Mag, 10/77. Style & Technique: Realistic sculpture; polychrome wood sculpture laminated, shaved, pegged and assembled in crates; illusionistic painting to look like real thing. Dealer: O K Harris Gallery 383 W Broadway New York NY 10021. Mailing Add: 45 Bond St New York NY 10012

KESSLER, EDNA LEVENTHAL
PAINTER, PRINTMAKER
b Kingston, NY. Study: Parsons Sch Design, teaching cert; NY Univ; Columbia Univ; Queens Col, Inst San Miguel, Mex, also with Joseph Margulies, Paul Puzinas, Edgar A Whitney, Charles Kinghan, Dong Kingman, Victor D'Amico & George Post. Work: In pvt collections in Eng, Can & throughout US. Exhib: Dallas Mus of Fine Arts, 62; Witte Mus, San Antonio, Tex, 62; Smithsonian Inst, Washington, DC, 63; Hudson Valley Art Asn, White Plains, NY, 64-69; Travel Show, USA, Am Watercolor Soc-Nat Acad Design, New York, 65; Am Artists Prof League Grand Nat, New York & Dallas, 62-69; Fine Arts Festival, Parrish Mus, Southampton, NY, 65-69; La Biennale Int, Vichy & Clermont-Ferrand, France, 66-68; Metrop Mus & Art Ctr, Miami, Fla, 75, 76 & 77; plus 16 one-artist shows. Teaching: Instr costume design & illus, Parsons Sch Design, 29-31; instr oils & watercolors, Temple Sholom, Glen Oaks, NY, 60-69; instr pvt classes, Hallandale & Hollywood, Fla, 69- Pos: Pres, Edna L Kessler-Interior Designs, NY, 46-69, Fla, 69-78; free lance artist, New York & Miami Beach, Fla, 58-78. Awards: More than 125 awards, incl Gold Medal, Nat Art League, 61; Arbogast Mem Award, Fine Arts Festival, Parrish Mus, 65; Grand Prix d'Aquerelle, La Biennale Int, 66. Mem: Nat Art League (dir, 58-69); Am Artist Prof League; Women's Caucus for Art; Artists Equity Asn; Allied Arts North Miami (dir, 71-78). Media: Oil, Watercolor, Graphic. Publ: Contribr, La Rev Mod, 65-67 & Rev des Beaux Arts, 70; auth, Prize Winning Art, 65, 66 & 67; contribr, Enciclopedia Internazionale Degli Artisti, 70-71; contribr, Artists USA, 72-73. Dealer: Deligny Art Galleries 709 E Las Olas Blvd Ft Lauderdale FL 33301. Mailing Add: 1050 93rd St Bay Harbor Islands FL 33154

KESSLER, LEONARD H
ILLUSTRATOR
b Akron, Ohio, Oct 23, 21. Study: Carnegie Inst of Tech, BFA(painting & design), 49. Awards: New York Times 10 Best Illus Children's Books, 54, 55 & 57. Mem: Soc of Illusr; Graphic Artists Guild; Author's League; Authors Guild. Style & Technique: Strong line, humerous, direct. Media: Pen and Ink, Watercolor, Gouache. Publ: Auth-illusr, What's in a Line? Willam R Scott, 51; auth-illusr, Art is Everywhere, Dodd/Mead, 58; auth-illusr, Here Comes the Stike-out, Harper & Row, 65; auth-illusr, Ghosts and Crows and Things with O's, Scholastic Books, 76; co-auth-illusr, What do You Play on a Summer Day? Parent's Press, 77. Mailing Add: 6 Stoneham Ln New City NY 10956

KESSLER, SHIRLEY
PAINTER, INSTRUCTOR
b New York, NY. Study: Art Students League. Work: Iowa State Mus, Iowa City; Nashville Mus Art, Tenn; Asheville Mus Art, NC; Norfolk Mus Art, Va. Exhib: Museo Nacional Bellas Artes, Buenos Aires, 63; Am Watercolor Soc Ann, 64 & Audubon Artists, 65, Nat Acad Design, New York; 1st Int Exhib Women Painters, Cult Ctr, Cannes, France, 66; Int Peinture de Saint Germaine-des-Pres, Paris, 70. Teaching: Instr painting, adult div, Bd Educ, New York, 48- Awards: Art Laureate, Dipl & Rosette, Medal of Honor, Soc D'Encouragement au Progress, Paris, 70; Palmes d'Or Promotion Queen Fabiola, Belg, 75; Grand Prix Humanitaire de France & Medaille d'Argent with Laureate Dipl, Int Arts Festival, De Saint Germain-des-Pres, France, 75. Bibliog: Vallobra (auth), Man and the arts, Paul Verlaine Ed, 69 & article in Apollo Defenseur des Arts, 69-70; Archives of American art, Smithsonian Inst, 70. Mem: Nat Asn Women Artists (pres, 67-70, permanent adv bd, 71-); Nat Soc Painters Casein & Polymer (bd dirs, 70-); Soc D'Encouragement au Progress (USA permanent officer, 70-); NJ Painters & Sculptors Soc; Audubon Artists. Style & Technique: Impressionistic; expressionism in varied applications of brush, palette knife and spray. Media: Oil, Watercolor, Acrylic Polymer. Mailing Add: 185 E 85th St New York NY 10028

KESTENBAUM, LOTHAR J
SCULPTOR, EDUCATOR
b Berlin, Ger, July 3, 26. Work: Mutual Trust & Savings Asn, Los Angeles; Senate of Berlin, Ger; Mus Fine Arts, Hagerstown, Md; Public Park, Mexico City; Altos Hornos de Mex, Monclova, Mex. Exhib: One-man shows, Galeria Antonio Souza, Mexico City, 58, Mus Santa Barbara, Calif, 58, Gallery Silvan Simone, Los Angeles, 58, 60 & 61, Milwaukee Jewish Ctr, Wis, 67, Palacio Bellas Artes, Mexico City, 67; Galeria Pecanins, Mexico City, 70, Phoenix Gallery, Baltimore, 70, Thompson Gallery, Phoenix, Ariz, 73 & many others. Teaching: Instr sculpture, Inst Allende, San Miguel de Allende, Mex, 57-62; guest prof sculpture, Univ Calif, Santa Barbara, 64; asst prof sculpture, drawing & metal casting, Univ Wis-Milwaukee, 64-71; prof sculpture, Ctr Cult San Miguel de Allende, Inst Nac Bellas Artes, 71- Awards: Huntington-Hartford Found Fel Grant, 55; Rome Prize, Ger Acad, Villa Massino, Ger Govt, 62-63; Travel Grant, Ger Acad Exchange Serv, Ger Govt, 74. Bibliog: Margarita Nelken (auth), Esculturas de Lothar Kestenbaum, Excelsior, 8/13/67; Henry J Seldis (auth), Sculptor emerges as powerful imagist, 10/13/61; Thomas Goldwaite (auth), Sculptor in Phoenix debut, Ariz Repub, 11/22/71. Mailing Add: Calle Quebrada 113 Guanajuato San Miguel de Allende Mexico

KESTER, LENARD
PAINTER
b New York, NY, May 10, 17. Work: Brooklyn Mus, NY; Toledo Mus, Ohio; Denver Mus, Colo; Boston Mus Fine Arts, Mass; Everson Mus Art, Syracuse, NY. Comn: First Nowell (painting), Life, 47; Pictorial Record of Pacific Northwest, Louis Comfort Tiffany Found, 49; Man's Musical Heritage (mural), Mayo Clin, Rochester, Minn, 53; stained glass windows, Billy Rose Mausoleum, NY, 67. Exhib: Five exhibs, Los Angeles Mus, 43-55; Art Inst Chicago, 47; Carnegie Inst, Pittsburgh, 47-49; six exhibs, Nat Acad Design, New York, 51-66; Corcoran Gallery Art, Washington, DC, 57. Teaching: Pvt instr & pub lect. Awards: First Prize, Storm in the Canyon, Los Angeles Mus, 43; Saltus Gold Medal for Merit, November 7th, Nat Acad Design, 58; First Prize, Venice Reflections, Calif State Expos, 71; plus many others. Bibliog: Janice Lovoos (auth), The art of Lenard Kester, Am Artist, 2/59. Mem: Assoc Nat Acad Design; Am Watercolor Soc; Soc Western Artists. Style & Technique: Representational realism. Media: Oil, Watercolor, Gouache. Mailing Add: 1117 N Genesee Ave Los Angeles CA 90046

KESTNBAUM, GERTRUDE DANA
COLLECTOR
b Boston, Mass. Study: Wellesley Col, BA, 16; Simmons Col, BS, 19. Collection: Contemporary painting and sculpture; antique silver, porcelain and furniture; Chinese and Japanese porcelain, jade. Mailing Add: 209 E Lake Shore Dr Chicago IL 60611

KETCHAM, HENRY KING (HANK)
CARTOONIST
b Seattle, Wash, Mar 14, 20. Study: Univ Wash, 38. Work: Albert T Reid Collection; William Allen White Found, Univ Kans; Achenbach Found for Graphic Arts, Calif Palace of Legion of Honor; Boston Univ Libr. Pos: Animator, Walter Lantz Prod, 38-39, Walt Disney Prod, 39-42; co-designer, Dennis the Menace Playground, Monterey, Calif, founder, Playart Found, 69. Awards: Billy De Beck Award as outstanding cartoonist, 52; Cert for Best Comic Mag, Boys' Club Am, 56. Mem: Nat Cartoonists' Soc. Interest: Donor, Hank Ketcham Collection to Boston University Libraries. Publ: Auth & illusr, Dennis the Menace ann bk collection, 51-; auth & illusr, daily syndicated cartoon, Dennis the Menace, US & foreign newspapers, 51-; contribr, cartoons to nat newspapers; auth, I Wanna Go Home, McGraw-Hill, 65. Mailing Add: PO Drawer BB Carmel Valley CA 93924

KETTNER, DAVID ALLEN
ARTIST, EDUCATOR
b Sunman, Ind, Oct 19, 43. Study: Skowhegan Sch of Painting and Sculpture, 64; Cleveland Inst of Art, BFA, 66; Ind Univ, MFA, 68. Work: Philadelphia Mus of Art, Pa; Rutgers Univ, Col of Arts & Sci, Camden, NJ. Exhib: North, South, East, West & Middle, nat traveling show, 75; Six Self-Portraits 1975 Series, Whitney Mus of Am Art, New York, 76; 41st Int Eucharistic Congress, Liturgical Arts Exhib, Civic Ctr, Philadelphia, 76; Philadelphia Houston Exchange, Inst of Contemp Art, Philadelphia, 76; Recent Acquisitions, Philadelphia Mus of Art, 77; Am Drawing Show, Fine Arts Gallery, San Diego, Calif, 77. Teaching: Assoc prof painting & drawing, Philadelphia Col of Art, 68- Style & Technique: Radical Realism, various micro-focal, particle-binding methods. Media: Variety of Wet and Dry. Mailing Add: 7430 Ardleigh St Philadelphia PA 19119

KEVORKIAN, RICHARD
PAINTER
b Dearborn, Mich, Aug 24, 37. Study: Pa Acad of Fine Arts, Philadelphia, 58; Richmond Prof Inst, BFA(painting), 61; Calif Col of Arts & Crafts, Oakland, MFA(painting), 62. Work: Philip Morris, USA, Richmond, Va; Walter Rawls Mus, Courtland, Va; Southeastern Ctr for Contemp Art, winston-Salem, NC; First & Merchants Nat Bank, Richmond; Bank & Trust of Wachovia, NC. Exhib: The 15th Irene Leach Mem Exhib, Chrysler Mus at Norfolk, Va, 70; Drawing Exhib, Mint Mus of Art, Charlotte, NC, 70; Va Biennial, Va Mus of Fine Arts, Richmond, 73; 35 Southeastern Artists, High Mus, Atlanta, Ga, 76; Southeast 7, Southeastern Ctr for Contemp Art, Winston-Salem, 77. Teaching: Instr painting, Richard Bland Col, Petersburg, Va, 61-64; prof & chmn dept of painting & printmaking, Va Commonwealth Univ, Richmond, 64- Awards: Va Mus of Fine Arts traveling fel, 60; Nat Endowment for the Arts, Individual Sr Artists Grant/Painting, 72 & Southeastern Ctr for Contemp Arts Grant/Painting, 76. Bibliog: Articles in Artforum, summer 76 & Art in Am, summer 76. Mem: Nat Coun of Art Adminr; Col Art Asn. Style & Technique: Large formalist paintings, expansive field of color working with edge considerations. Media: Oil, acrylic. Mailing Add: 325 N Harrison St Richmond VA 23220

KEY, DONALD D
ART CRITIC, WRITER
b Iowa City, Iowa, Jan 30, 23. Study: Univ Iowa. Pos: Ed asst, Daily Iowan, Iowa City, 48-50; asst to ed, Cedar Rapids Gazette, 50-59; art ed, Milwaukee J, 59-72. Awards: Cert of Merit for bk on multiple sclerosis, Multiple Sclerosis Soc, 72. Mem: Cedar Rapids Jaycees; Milwaukee Press Club. Publ: Auth, Future unknown, Views & Rev; auth, Printmaking impressions (booklet). Mailing Add: 7519 N Crossway Rd Milwaukee WI 53217

KEY, TED
CARTOONIST
b Fresno, Calif. Study: Univ Calif, Berkeley. Pos: Creator, Hazel, daily panel syndicated by King Features; auth, Gus, Walt Disney Prod; auth, So'M I. Publ: Auth & illusr, 18 Hazel bks, The Biggest Dog in the World, Phyllis, Many Happy Returns & Squirrels in the Feeding Station; auth, Cat From Outer Space; auth, Million Dollar Duck, Walt Disney Prod. Mailing Add: 1694 Glenhardie Rd Wayne PA 19087

KEY-OBERG, ELLEN BURKE
SCULPTOR
b Marion, Ala, Apr 11, 05. Study: Cooper Union, grad. Work: Norfolk Mus, Va; Univ Wis. Exhib: Nat Acad Design, New York, 43; Nat Ceramic Ann, Syracuse Mus & Traveling Shows, 43-54; Pa Acad Fine Arts Ann, Philadelphia, 53; Whitney Mus Am Art Ann, 53. Teaching: Instr painting & sculpture, Chapin Sch, 37-70, head dept art, 65-70; instr sculpture, Arts Workshop, Newark Mus, NJ, 55-65. Awards: First Prize & hon mentions, Audubon Artists, 44; Pauline Law Prize, Nat Asn Women Artists, 59. Bibliog: Jacques Schnier (auth), Sculpture in Modern America, Univ Calif Press, 48; John B Kenny (auth), Ceramic Sculpture, Greenberg, 53 & Ceramic Design, Chilton, 63. Mem: Sculptors Guild; Audubon Artists; Nat Asn Women Artists. Style & Technique: Direct carving in wood and stone; exploration in form and space. Mailing Add: Chateau Girard 935 Genter St La Jolla CA 92037

KEYSER, ROBERT GIFFORD
PAINTER, EDUCATOR
b Philadelphia, Pa, July 27, 24. Study: Univ Pa, 42-47; Atelier Fernand Leger, 49-51, cert. Work: Munson-Williams-Proctor Inst, Utica, NY; Lyman Allyn Mus, New London, Conn;

Phillips Gallery, Washington, DC; Vassar Col Art Gallery, NY; Philadelphia Mus. Exhib: Salon Mai, 50; Salon Autome, 50; Salon Realities Nouvelles, 51; Pa Acad Fine Arts Ann, 51-70; Collage Am, 58-60, Am Fedn Arts Traveling Show; Corcoran Gallery Art, Washington, DC, 75. Teaching: Assoc prof painting & drawing & chmn, Philadelphia Col Art, 63-75; Temple Abroad, Rome, 75- Style & Technique: Abstract/surrealist. Media: Oil, Watercolor. Dealer: Marian Locks Gallery 1524 Walnut Philadelphia PA 19102. Mailing Add: 2103 Locust St Philadelphia PA 19103

KEYSER, WILLIAM ALPHONSE, JR
CRAFTSMAN, EDUCATOR
b Pittsburgh, Pa, July 30, 36. Study: Carnegie-Mellon Univ, Pittsburgh, BS, 58; Sch for Am Craftsman, Rochester Inst of Tech, MFA(furniture design), 61. Work: Univ Collection, Univ of Nebr, Lincoln; Am Crafts Coun, New York; Interfaith Chapel, Univ of Rochester; State Univ of NY, Brockport; Sybron-Ritter Corp, Rochester, NY. Comn: Window Screen sculpture (20ft x 14ft), 68 & sculpture wall shelf, 78, Rochester Inst of Tech; complete office comn by Mr J Kevin Mahoney, 75, altar, lecturn, chair & cross, St John Evangalist, 77; altar, lecturn & cross, Risen Christ Lutheran, 77, Rochester. Exhib: Objects USA, Mus of Contemp Crafts, New York, 69; Nat Crafts Invitational, Wis State Univ, Oshkosh, 73; A Comment on Contemp Crafts, Univ Wis, Milwaukee, 73; Radila 80, Xerox Square Exhib Ctr, Rochester, 74; Contemp Crafts of the Americas, Colo State Univ, Fort Collins, 75; Rochester Finger Lakes Exhib, Mem Art Gallery, 75; Bed & Board, DeCordova Mus, Lincoln, Mass, 75; Contemp Works by Master Craftsman, Mus of Fine Arts, Boston, 78. Teaching: Instr, industrial design, Ohio Univ, Athens, 61-62; prof furniture design, Sch for Am craftsman, Rochester Inst of Tech, 62- Awards: Young Americans Award, Am Crafts Coun, 62; Gertrude H Moore, Rochester Finger Lakes, 72; Craftsmen's Fel, Nat Endowment for the Arts, 75. Bibliog: Donald J Wilcox (auth), Wood Design, Watson-Guptill Publ, 68; Lee Nordness (auth), Objects USA, Viking Press, 70; Dona Z Meilach (auth), Creating Mod Furniture: Trends, Techniques, Application, Crown Publ, 75. Mem: Am Crafts Coun; NY State Craftsmen. Style & Technique: Individually expressive functional pieces and sculpture using traditional woodworking techniques, as well as vacuum forming, steam bending, ship bldg techniques. Publ: Auth, Steam Bending—Heat and Moisture Plasticize Wood, Fine Woodworking Taunton Press, 77. Mailing Add: 6543 Rush-Lima Rd Rush NY 14543

KHENDRY, JANAK KUMAR
ART ADMINISTRATOR, SCULPTOR
b Amritsar, India, Sept 26, 35. Study: Col Fine Arts, Hyderabad, India, dipl, 61; Ohio State Univ, MA(sculpture), 63. Exhib: One-man show, Ohio State Univ, 63; Va Mus, 67; Philbrook Art Ctr, Tulsa, Okla, 75. Pos: Dir, The Sculpture Ctr, 65- Style & Technique: Figurative. Media: Wax for Bronze Casting. Res: Indian art. Dealer: The Sculpture Ctr 167 E 69th St New York NY 10021. Mailing Add: 208 E 70th St New York NY 10021

KIAH, VIRGINIA JACKSON
PAINTER, MUSEUM DIRECTOR
b East St Louis, Ill, June 3, 11. Study: Philadelphia Mus & Sch Art, 27-31, dipl; Art Students League, 29-32, study with Louis Bouche, Robert Brackman & Vincent Damonde; Columbia Univ, AB, 49 & MA, 50. Comn: Portrait of Congressman Adam Powell, Community Ctr, Abbysinia Baptist Church, New York, 37; portrait of Finley Wilson, Elks, Washington, DC, 40; portrait of Judge Thomas L Griffith, comn by self, Los Angeles, Calif, 41; two portraits of Mrs Thomas Dyett, comn by Thomas Dyett, New York, 52; portrait of Rev Harry Hoosier, Washington Delaware Conf, Methodist Church, Gulfside, Miss, 54. Exhib: Philadelphia Mus & Sch Art Ann Exhib, 30; Baltimore Mus Art Ann Md Artists Show, 35; Nat Columbia Motion Pictures Portrait Painting Contest Prizewinners Exhib, Eggleston Galleries, New York, 37; Art Students League Ann Show, 37; Southern Regional Art Show, Williamsburg, Va, 69. Collections Arranged: Marie Dressler Exhib, Kiah Mus, Savannah, Ga; African Art & William H Johnson Pastel & Print Collection, Found, New York. Teaching: Instr art & chmn dept, Cuyler, Beach & Scott Jr High Schs, 51-62. Pos: Founder & dir, Kiah Mus, 59-; chmn, Comt for the Ga United Nations Arts, 74-75; founder & dir, Lillie Carroll Jackson Mus, Baltimore, Md, 74- Awards: First Prize Life Drawing, 30 & Second Prize, 31, Philadelphia Mus & Sch Art; Honorable Mention Anna Lucasta Portrait Painting, Columbia Motion Pictures, 37; Nat Conf of Artists Distinctive Merit, 60-62, 68 & 70-72. Bibliog: Dr K B Raut (auth), Mrs Virginia Kiah—artist, Kiah Mus, Savannah Mag, Joseph Chauhan Publ, 1/71; Burchart, Denilov, Naeve & Taylor (auths), Treasures of America, Reader's Digest Asn, 74; Helen C Smith (auth), She couldn't go to museums so she started one, Atlanta Constitution Newspaper, 11/9/74. Mem: Nat Conf Artists (dir student div, 59-69); Du Sable Mus (mem bd); Savannah Ga 36th St Improv Asn (past pres, 64-71); Mus Asn Savannah. Style & Technique: Portraits with palette knife or brush. Media: Oil. Publ: Auth, Gone fishing, Afro-Am Newspaper Mag, 55; auth, Black artists, Savannah Mag, 72. Mailing Add: 2010 Highview Rd SW Atlanta GA 30311

KIDD, STEVEN R
ILLUSTRATOR, INSTRUCTOR
b Chicago, Ill, June 27, 11. Study: George Bridgman Scholar, Art Students League; Art Inst of Chicago with Henry Varnum Poor; Grand Cent Sch of Art, New York, with Harvey Dunn; additional study with Dean Cornwell; graphics at Pratt Inst. Work: Casey at the Bat, Baseball Hall of Fame, Cooperstown, NY; 37 paintings & drawings as US Combat Artist, US Army Hist Sect, Pentagon Bldg, US Army Art Mus & USAF Mus, Washington, DC. Exhib: US Army Hist War Art White House Exhib, 45; US Army Hist War Art (traveling exhib), 46-; USAF Hist War Art, USAF Mus & Smithsonian Inst, Washington, DC; Art Students League Yearly Prof Exhib, 62-; Retrospective Show, Soc of Illusrs, New York, 63; 200 Yrs of Am Illus Bicentennial Show, New York His Mus, 76. Teaching: Instr illus, Art Students League, 62- Pos: Illusr, New York Sunday News-Chicago Tribune Syndicate, 31-69; court reporting artist, Famous Hines Trial, New York Daily News, 38 & Watergate Verdict for Assoc Press, 76. Awards: Gold Medal of Honor, Hudson Valley Art Asn, 60; Second Prize, New York Sports Show, Abercrombie & Fitch, New York, 66; Theodore Croslin Award, Warwick Murals, 68. Bibliog: Articles in Life Mag, 51 & Am Artist, summer 67; Henry Pitz (auth), The Brandywine Tradition. Publ: Contribr, Bob Crozier (ed), Two Hundred Years of American Illustrations, Random, 77; contribr (auth, Walter Reed), The Illustrator in America, 73. Mailing Add: c/o Art Students League 215 W 57th St New York NY 10019

KIEFERNDORF, FREDERICK GEORGE
PAINTER, EDUCATOR
b Milwaukee, Wis, May 12, 21. Study: Univ Wis, BA & MS. Work: Springfield Art Mus, Mo; Mo State Hist Soc Permanent Collection (painting requested 75); Wis Salon Art, Madison; Sch Ozarks, Point Lookout, Mo; Pittsburgh State Col, Kans. Exhib: Five Painters of the Ozarks, Traveling Exhib, 53; Watercolor USA, Springfield, Mo, 67, 68 & 71; Ann Delta Show, Little Rock, 67 & 74; Ten Painters of Missouri, Traveling Exhib, Mo State Coun Arts, 68; Springfield Art Mus Midwest Exhib, 72. Teaching: Prof art, Southwest Mo State Univ, 53- Awards: Purchase Award, Springfield Art Mus, 56 & 65 & Award of Merit, 67; Purchase Award, Sch Ozarks, 70. Media: Polymer, Vinyl Cement. Mailing Add: 1748 Madaline Springfield MO 65804

KIELKOPF, JAMES ROBERT
PAINTER
b St Paul, Minn, July 13, 39. Study: Minneapolis Sch Art, 61-65, BFA; Grand Marias Art Colony, summer 63; Skowhegan Sch Painting, summer 64. Work: Walker Art Ctr, Minneapolis. Exhib: Walker Art Ctr Biennial, 64 & 66; Minneapolis Inst Art Biennial, 67; Interchange, Dallas Mus Fine Arts, Tex, 72. Style & Technique: Tonal paintings on canvas and wood. Media: Oil, Graphite. Dealer: Eye Corp 214 S Clinton St Chicago IL 60606; Friends Gallery Minneapolis Inst of Arts 2400 Third Ave S Minneapolis MN 55404. Mailing Add: 1963 Ashland St Paul MN 55104

KIENBUSCH, WILLIAM AUSTIN
PAINTER
b New York, NY, Apr 13, 14. Study: Princeton Univ, BA(magna cum laude), with Henry Varnum Poor, Abe Rattner, Anton Refregier & Stuart Davis. Work: Metrop Mus Art, Mus Mod Art & Whitney Mus Am Art, New York; Philadelphia Mus, Pa; Boston Mus Fine Arts, Mass. Exhib: New Decade, Whitney Mus Am Art, 55; Brussels World's Fair, 58; Masters Am Watercolors, 60-62, Six Int Tokyo, 62-63 & Maine Artists, 64-66, Am Fedn Arts. Teaching: Instr art, Brooklyn Mus Art Sch, 48-69. Awards: Metrop Mus Art Prize for Drawing, 52; Guggenheim Found Fel, 58; Ford Found Purchase Award, 61; Cash Award, Nat Inst Arts & Lett, 76. Bibliog: E Eliot (auth), 300 years of American painting, New York Times, 57; Maine and its Role in American Art 1740-1963, Viking Press, 63; Alan Gussow (auth), A Sense of Place—the Artist and the American Land, Sat Rev Press, 72. Media: Casein, Oil. Dealer: Kraushaar Galleries 1055 Madison Ave New York NY 10028. Mailing Add: 120 E 80th St New York NY 10021

KIENFIELD, NITA
ARTIST
b Phoenix, Ariz, Sept 28, 49. Study: Ariz State Univ, BA; Univ of Ariz, Tucson, MFA; Art Students League. Work: Ariz State Univ, Tempe; Univ of Ariz, Tucson; Phoenix Art Mus, Ariz; City of Scottsdale Collection, Ariz. Exhib: Ft Worth Contemp Art Mus, Tex; Southern Ill Univ Drawing Show, Carbondale; Matthews Ctr, Univ of Ariz; Phoenix Art Mus. Mailing Add: 12812 N 68th St Scottsdale AZ 85254

KIJANKA, STANLEY JOSEPH
PAINTER
b Ansonia, Conn, Oct 17, 37. Study: Hartford Art Sch; Univ Hartford, Conn. Exhib: Audubon Artists, New York, 74; Allied Artists, New York, 74; Knickerbocker Artists, New York, 74; Hudson Valley Art Asn Ann, White Plains, NY, 74, 75 & 76; Am Watercolor Soc, New York, 74, 75 & 76. Awards: Best in Show, New Haven Paint & Clay Club, 74; Arthur T Hill Award, Salmagundi Oil Exhib, 76; Best in Show, NW Conn Ann Exhib, Soc of Creative Arts of Newtown, 77. Mem: Salmagundi Club; Mamaroneck Artists Guild; Am Watercolor Asn; New Haven Paint & Clay Club; Soc of Creative Arts of Newtown. Style & Technique: Representational landscape and wildlife. Media: Oil, watercolor. Dealer: Douglas Gallery 1117 High Ridge Rd Stamford CT 06905. Mailing Add: RD 2 Brushy Hill Rd Newtown CT 06470

KILGORE, AL
CARTOONIST
b Newark, NJ, Dec 19, 27. Study: Art Career Sch, New York, grad, 51. Pos: Illusr children's books, Pageant Press, 52-55; gag cartoons for weekly trade paper, 52-62; auth & illusr, Bullwinkle comic strip, Bell McClure Syndicate, 62-65; advert comics, Quaker Oats Co, 65; Storyboards for Underdog, TV show, 66-67; weekly caricature puzzle feature, TV Star-Screen, 69-; co-producer, dir, auth & lyrics, animated cartoon, World of Hans Christian Andersen, 70-71. Mem: Nat Cartoonists Soc. Publ: Auth, Bullwinkle Comic Books, Western Publ Co, 60-62; illusr, Pink Panther Books, Lion Press, 68. Mailing Add: 216-55 113th Dr Queens Village NY 11429

KILIAN, AUSTIN FARLAND
PAINTER, EDUCATOR
b Lyons, SDak, Sept 19, 20. Study: Augustana Col (SDak), BA, 42; Univ Iowa, MFA, 49; Acad Montmartre, Paris, 51, with Fernand Leger; Mexico City Col, 52; Ohio State Univ, 55; Univ Calif, Los Angeles, 66. Work: D D Feldman Collection, Dallas; Univ Iowa Galleries, Iowa City. Exhib: Terry Nat Art Exhib, Miami, 52; Laguna Gloria Mus Citation Regional, Austin, Tex, 58; Art Asn New Orleans, Delgado Mus, 59; Made in Tex by Texans, Dallas Mus Contemp Arts, 59; San Diego Art Instr Show, Art Ctr La Jolla, Calif, 61. Collections Arranged: Waco Art Forum Mus Regional Shows, 59; San Diego Art Guild Shows, Fine Arts Gallery, 61; Art In All Media, Southern Calif Expos, Del Mar, 63-70; Col of the Desert Shows, 70- Teaching: Instr photog, Univ Idaho, 49-50; head dept art, Dillard Univ, 50-53; asst prof, Baylor Univ, 53-59; chmn dept art, Calif Western Univ, 59-64; assoc prof, Col of the Desert, 70- Awards: Art Asn New Orleans Third Award, Delgado Mus, 52; Sons of Herman Award, San Antonio, Tex, 55; Purchase Award, D D Feldman Exhib, 68. Mem: San Diego Art Guild; Palm Springs Desert Mus; Fine Arts Soc San Diego; Col Art Asn Am; Am Fedn of Arts. Style & Technique: Structured form, modified contemporary total visual effect, fantasy, social commentary, psychological color. Media: Collage, Oil. Publ: Auth, Catalog loan exhibition of notable works from the Metropolitan, 52, Culture makes a face, KABC-TV, Hollywood, 62, The two Californias (catalog), 63, Southern California exposition, art in all media (catalogs), 63-70 & article in San Diego Eve Tribune, 6/14/64. Mailing Add: 3720 Wawona Dr San Diego CA 92107

KILIATT, JUNE LEE
COLLECTOR, PAINTER
b Columbus, Ohio, July 4, 45. Study: Univ Kans, Lawrence, BFA, 69; Art Student League. Work: Nelson-Atkins Gallery of Art, Kansas City, Mo; Dallas Mus of Fine Arts, Tex. Exhib: Art Students League; Univ Kans, Lawrence; William Rockhill Nelson Gallery of Art, Kansas City, Mo. Collection: Contemporary American painting. Mailing Add: 323 E Dunbar Dr 33 Tempe AZ 85282

KILLAM, WALT
PAINTER, ART DEALER
b Providence, RI, June 18, 07. Study: RI Sch Design. Work: Millbrook Sch, NY; Lyman-Allen Mus, New London, Conn; South Co Art Asn; plus many in pvt collections. Comn: Many pvt commissions. Exhib: US, Mex, Hawaii & Can, 32-70. Teaching: Instr art, Millbrook Sch; guest instr advan drawing & painting, Minneapolis Sch Fine Art. Pos: Head

supvr projs, Works Proj Admin, New York, owner, Fine Oriental Arts, Chester, Conn, 65- & Golden Hotei Bonsai Gardens. Awards: First Prize, First H two O Exhib, Hartford Art Asn, Conn, 34; Silvermine Guild Artists Award, 54; Essex Art Asn Award, 56. Mem: Hon mem South Co Art Asn; hon mem Essex Art Asn (past pres); hon mem Mystic Art Asn (past pres). Style & Technique: Works varying from early surrealism (c 1930) to works abstracted from natural sources. Media: Oil, Gouaches. Specialty: Oriental porcelains and allied arts. Collection: Small art objects of world-wide arts. Mailing Add: 122 Middlesex Pike Chester CT 06412

KILLMASTER, JOHN H
PAINTER, MURALIST
b Allegan, Mich, Dec 2, 34. Study: Soc Arts & Crafts, Detroit, Mich; Hope Col, BA; Univ Guanajuato, Mex, Cranbrook Acad Art, MFA. Work: Braithwaite Gallery, Southern Utah State, Cedar City; Boise Gallery of Art Collection; Boise Cascade World Hq Collection Fine Art, Idaho; Northwestern Col, Orange City, Iowa; FMC Corp, Chicago World Hq Collection. Comn: Enameled sculpture, Portland Ore Arts Comn, 76. Exhib: First Nat Acrylic Show, Eastern Mich Univ, 67; Mainstreams, 68 & 76 & Int Art Exhib, 68 & 70, Marietta, Ohio; Juried Arts Nat Exhib, Tyler, Tex, 68; one-man show, Hackley Art Mus, Muskegon, Mich, 70; 31st Ann Northwest Watercolor Exhibs, Seattle Art Mus, 71; 36th Ann Spokane Art Exhib, Cheney Cowles Mus, Wash, 74; Am Watercolor Soc Exhib, New York, 75; Ten State Bicentennial Art Exhib, C M Russell Mus, Great Falls, Mont, 76. Teaching: Asst prof painting, Ferris State Col, 69-70; assoc prof art, Boise State Col, 70- Pos: Illusr & designer, Ladriere Art Studio, Detroit, 58-61. Awards: Purchase Awards, Idaho Artists Ann, Boise Art Mus, 70, 74, 76 & 77; Idaho Arts & Humanities Grant, 74; Western States Art Found fel & grant, 74. Bibliog: Idaho landscape painter (film), Idaho Arts Comn, 72. Mem: NW Designer Craftsman Asn; Col Art Asn Am; Idaho Art Asn. Style & Technique: Abstractionist and realist in oil and acrylic; large acrylic abstractions; large outdoor steel assemblage murals in porcelain and exterior enameled sculpture. Publ: Illusr, Gen Motors Stockholders Publ, 59 & Ford Times Mag, 78. Dealer: Gallery Madison 90 1248 Madison Ave New York NY 10028. Mailing Add: 2723 N 36th St Boise ID 83703

KIM, BONGTAE
PAINTER, PRINTMAKER
b Pusan, Korea, July 23, 37; US citizen. Study: Col of Fine Arts; Seoul Nat Univ, BFA; Otis Art Inst, Los Angeles, BFA & MFA. Work: French Govt; Univ of Southern Calif; Chase Manhattan Bank; Contemp Mus of Art, Seoul, Korea; Seoul Nat Univ Gallery. Comn: Geometric image murals, Lathem & Watkins, 70, Paul Hastings, Janofsky & Walker, 71, Allison Co, 72, Baker, Ancel & Redmond, 72 & K T Color Lab, 77, Los Angeles. Exhib: 3rd Exhib of Biennial de Paris, 63; The Graphics Gallery Exhib, Kaiser Ctr, Oakland Mus, 69; Exhib of Graphics, San Jose Mus of Art, 74; 2nd British Int Print Biennial, Bradford City Art Mus, 70; Nat Mus of Korea Invitational Exhib of Five Graphic Artists, 63; one-man shows, Graphics Gallery, San Francisco, 70, Pacific Culture Asia Mus, Pasadena, 73 & Jean's Art Gallery, Seoul, 77. Teaching: Senior lectr printmaking, Univ Southern Calif, 71-; instr, drawing, West Los Angeles Col, 70- Pos: Co-dir & co-founder, Triad Graphic Workshop, 67- Awards: Purchase awards, 4th & 5th Ann Print Show, San Diego State Col, 71, 72 & Ink & Clay Show, Calif State Politech Univ, 75; cash award, 3rd Nat Print Show, Univ of Southern Calif, 75. Bibliog: Innovative Printmakers (article) Southwest Art Mag, 72; Leonard Edmondson (auth), Etching, Van Nostrand Reinholt Co, 73; Thelma R Newman (auth), Innovative Printmaking, Crown Publ, 77. Mem: Los Angeles Printmaking Soc (pres, 72); Los Angeles Inst of Contemp Art. Style & Technique: Post op. Media: Painting, Printmaking. Mailing Add: 11162 McCormick St North Hollywood CA 91601

KIM, ERNIE
CERAMIST, ART ADMINISTRATOR
b Manteca, Calif, Sept 2, 18. Study: Los Angeles City Col, 40-42; also design with Marian Hartwell, 50-53. Work: Smithsonian Inst, Washington, DC; Everson Mus Art, Syracuse; St Paul Art Ctr, Minn; Utah State Univ; San Francisco Arts Comn. Exhib: Cannes Festival, France, 55; Fiber Clay & Metal Nat, St Paul, 57 & 58; Wichita Ceramic Nat, 59 & 62; Buenos Aires Invitational, Arg, 62; Syracuse Ceramic Nat, 62, 64 & 66. Collections Arranged: Multi-Media Exhibition: Featuring Black Artists and Craftsmen, Richmond Art Ctr. Teaching: Ceramic instr, Palo Alto Adult Educ, Calif, 52-56; instr ceramics & head dept, San Francisco Art Inst, 57-62; ceramics instr & supv art instr, Richmond Art Ctr, 62-70. Pos: Dir, Richmond Art Ctr, 70- Awards: First Award, 6th Int Exhib Ceramic Art, Washington Kiln Club, 57; Purchase Awards, Wichita Nat Ceramic Exhib, 59 & 62; Helen S Everson Mem Award, Syracuse Nat Ceramic Exhib, 66. Mem: Asn San Francisco Potters; Am Crafts Coun. Media: Stoneware. Mailing Add: 5920 McBryde Ave Richmond CA 94805

KIMBALL, WILFORD WAYNE, JR
DRAFTSMAN, LITHOGRAPHER
b Salt Lake City, Utah, July 15, 43. Study: Southern Utah State Col, BA, 68; Univ Ariz, MFA, 70; Tamarind Inst, Albuquerque, NMex, fel printing, 70-71, Master Printer, 71. Work: Tamarind Collection, Albuquerque, NMex; NY Univ; Libr Cong, Washington, DC; Lessing J Rosenwald Collection, Alverthorpe Gallery, Jenkintown, Pa; The Philadelphia Mus of Art, Pa. Comn: Madison Print Club, Wis, 76. Exhib: One-man shows, Tyler Mus Art, Tex, 77 & Univ Dallas, Irving, Tex, 78; 25th Nat Exhib Prints, Libr of Cong, 77; Biennial Int Open Competition, The Print Club, Philadelphia, Pa, 77; Nat Print Invitational, Univ SDak, Vermillion, 78; Nat Print Invitational, Albion Col, Mich, 78. Teaching: Lectr lithography, Univ NMex, fall 71; vis lectr lithography & drawing, Univ Wis, Madison, 72-73 & summers 73 & 74; asst prof lithography & drawing, San Diego State Univ, 73-74; asst prof lithography, Calif State Univ, Long Beach, 74-75; asst prof lithography & drawing, Univ Tex San Antonio, 75-77; lectr lithography & serigraphy, San Diego State Univ, 77-78. Pos: Artist in residence, Roswell Mus & Art Ctr, NMex, 72. Awards: Louis Comfort Tiffany Found Grant, 74; Purchase Awards, 1st Nat Print & Drawing Show, Univ Colo, Boulder, 74 & Invitational Print Show, Univ Dallas, Tex, 74. Mailing Add: 7681 Loma Vista Dr La Mesa CA 92041

KIMBALL, YEFFE
PAINTER
b Mountain Park, Okla, 1914. Study: Art Students League, 35-39; study & work in France & Italy, 36-39; also with Leger in Paris & New York. Work: Nat Gallery Art, Washington, DC; Boston Mus Fine Arts; Dayton Art Inst, Ohio; Portland Art Mus, Ore; Norfolk Mus Arts & Sci, Va; plus many others in pub & pvt collections. Exhib: Nat Gallery Art, 70; Smithsonian Inst, Washington, DC, 70; Princeton Univ, NJ, 70; Northern Va Fine Arts, Alexandria, 71; Trinity Col, Hartford, Conn, 71; plus many other group & one-man shows. Collections Arranged: Expertised & catalogued 6000 art objects of Pacific Northwest Coast Indians, Portland Art Mus, 49; American Indian Exhibition, Mattuck Mus, Waterbury, Conn, 50; asst, Northwest Indian Art Exhibit, Brooklyn Mus, NY, 51; selected American Indian art objects for US Dept of State Exhib Tour abroad, 53; exhib asst, American Indian Exhibit, Isaac Delgado Mus, New Orleans, 64; plus others. Teaching: Am Forum Int Study, Spec Am Indian Prog, Inst Am Indian Arts, Santa Fe, 70; panel mem, Convocation Am Indian Scholars, Princeton Univ, 70. Pos: Tech adv, Americana Found, New York, 51-56; Juror, Nat Am Indian Exhib, Scottsdale, Ariz, 70; consult & adv to mus, publ & US govt on Indian hist & art. Awards: First Hon Mention, Nat Exhib Am Indian Painting, Philbrook Art Ctr, 47 & 51; First Prize, Nat Indian Exhib, Philbrook Art Ctr, 59. Mem: Nat Conf Am Indian; Artists Equity Asn; Nat Acad Design; Audubon Artists; Native NAm Artists. Publ: Illusr, Story of the Totem Pole, 51, Some People are Indians & The world of Manaboze, 65, Vanguard Press; illusr, The Story of the Pueblo Indians, Caedmon Records, 55; co-auth & illusr, The Art of American Indian Cooking, Doubleday, 65 & Avon Press, 70. Dealer: Frank Rehn Gallery 655 Madison Ave New York NY 10021. Mailing Add: 11 Bank St New York NY 10014

KIMBROUGH, (SARA) DODGE
PAINTER
b New York, NY. Study: Cooper Union; Grand Cent Art Sch, scholar; also with William DeLeftwich Dodge, Henry Lee McFee, Jerry Farnsworth & Frederick MacMonnies. Work: Phoenix Pub Libr, Ariz; Leflore Co Courthouse, Greenwood, Miss; US Sen Pat Harrison Libr, Univ Miss; Mem Rm, Davison Speech Sch, Atlanta, Ga; Beauvoir, Jefferson Davis Shrine, Biloxi, Miss. Comn: Many portrait commissions of prominent persons, 30-72. Exhib: Mellon Gallery, Washington, DC; Ariz State Fair, Phoenix, 51-57; Nat Asn Women Painters & Sculptors; Am Artists Prof League; one-man shows, Phoenix Art Ctr, Meridian Mus Art, Miss, Harrison Co Pub Libr, Gulfport, Miss & Wright Art Gallery, Cleveland, Miss; plus many others. Awards: League Am Pen Women, 36; Grand Nat Finalist, Am Artists Prof League, 53; Award, Ill Valley Art Exhib, 60. Mem: Miss Art Asn; Gulf Coast Art Asn; regional mem Portraits, Inc; Nat Soc Lit & Arts. Style & Technique: Portraits in oils, pastels, watercolors and conté crayon; still lifes and landscapes. Publ: Auth, Drawn From Life, Univ Miss, Jackson, 76. Dealer: Vztop Gallery E Zaragossa Pensacola FL 32503. Mailing Add: 806 North Beach Bay St Louis MS 39520

KIMMEL-COHN, ROBERTA
ART DEALER, DESIGNER
b Milwaukee, Wis, Feb 1, 37. Study: Sophie Newcomb Col, with George Rickey; Univ Wis; Boston Univ Sch Fine & Appl Arts, BFA. Pos: Art dir, McGraw-Hill Publ Co, New York, 61-62, Macmillan & Co, 64-65 & Walker & Co, 65-67; pres, Roberta Kimmel Advert, New York, 67-; partner, Kimmel/Cohn Photog Arts, New York, 74- Bibliog: Surrealism in advertising, Art Dir Mag, 70; article in Art Dir Ann, 72; People in the news, New York Times, 74. Specialty: Photography; Man Ray; 19th and 20th century. Mailing Add: 41 Central Park W New York NY 10023

KIMMELMAN, HAROLD
SCULPTOR
b Philadelphia, Pa, Feb 20, 23. Study: Cape Sch Art, Provincetown, Mass; Pa Acad Fine Art, Philadelphia. Comn: Giraffe, Philadelphia Dept Recreation, 68; Decline & Rise, Westmill Creek Greenway, Philadelphia, 69; Wind Chime, Crawford Mem Park, Norristown, Pa, 70; Butterfly, Penn Tower Corp, 71; Parabolic Fountain, Granite Run Mall, Media, Pa, 75; Helios Flame, Sun Oil Corp Hq, Radnor, Pa, 76; Burst of Joy, The Gallery, Philadelphia, 77; Marino Monument, Casa Enrico Fermi Corp, Philadelphia, Pa, 77. Exhib: Pa Acad Fine Arts, 68; Philadelphia Civic Ctr Show, 71. Awards: Braverman Karp Prize for sculpting, 68; May Audubon Prize for sculpting, 69. Mem: Artists Equity Asn (pres, Philadelphia Chap, 72); fel Pa Acad Fine Arts. Style & Technique: Forged, welded and polished metal abstract shapes derived from natural forms. Media: Stainless Steel, Bronze. Publ: Auth, Sculpture of a City, Walker Publ Co, 74. Mailing Add: 538 W Carpenter Lane Philadelphia PA 19119

KIMURA, RIISABURO
PAINTER, PRINTMAKER
b Yokosuka, Japan, Oct 13, 24. Study: Yokohama Univ, 47; Hosei Univ, Tokyo, 54. Work: Mus Mod Art, New York; Nat Mus Mod Art, Kyoto, Japan; US Info Agency; City of Hamburg, WGer. Comn: Print ed, Brooklyn Mus, 75. Exhib: One-man shows, Long Island Univ, NY, 69, Downtown Gallery, Honolulu, 72, Fuma Gallery, Tokyo, 74, Michido Gallery, Tokyo, Osaka & Nagoya, 74 & Gallery of Mod Art, Munchen, WGer, 77; USA Pavillion Expo 70, Osaka, Japan; two-man show, Gimpel Gallery, New York, 71; Japanese Artists in the Americas, Nat Mus Mod Art, Kyoto, 74; Wiener Gallery, New York. Awards: Int Biennal of Print, Tokyo, 70. Mailing Add: c/o Dorothy Nakamura 207 E 85th St New York NY 10028

KIMURA, SUEKO M
PAINTER, EDUCATOR
b Hawaii. Study: Univ Hawaii, BA & MFA; Chouinard Art Inst; Columbia Univ; Brooklyn Mus Sch Art; Art Students League. Work: State Found Cult & Arts; Contemp Arts Ctr; State Dept Educ Artmobile; Int Savings & Loan; Kaiser Hawaii-Kai Develop Co; Bilger Hall, Univ Hawaii; Honolulu Acad Art. Exhib: One-man shows: George Hall Gallery, Gimas Gallery, Contemp Arts Ctr & Crossroads Gallery; group exhibs: Brooklyn Mus, Long Island Art Gallery, San Diego Art Mus, Biblioteca Americana, Bucharest, Kyoto Mus Mod Art & Honolulu Printmakers Easter Art Show. Teaching: Emer prof art, Univ Hawaii, 52- Awards: Honolulu Printmakers, 62; Easter Art Show, 62, 65 & 68; Purchase Prizes, State Found Cult & Arts, 68, 69 & 72; plus others. Mem: Hawaii Painters & Sculptors League; Honolulu Printmakers. Style & Technique: Hard edge, currently (with overtones of expressionists idioms at times). Publ: Illusr, cover design & drawings, Philosophy and Culture, East & West, 62. Mailing Add: 2567B Henry St Honolulu HI 96817

KIMURA, WILLIAM YUSABURO
PAINTER
b Seattle, Wash, June 28, 20. Study: Hollywood Art Ctr, 39; Cornish Sch Art, Seattle, 40; also with Adolph Kronengold, Danny Pierce, Junichiro Sekino, Bill Richie & Evan Phoutrides. Work: Anchorage Fine Art Mus, Alaska; Alaska Methodist Univ, Anchorage; Color Ctr Gallery, Anchorage. Exhib: Ann Exhib Northwest Artists, Seattle, 53, 58 62 & 63; Smithsonian Traveling Exhib, USA & Europe, Washington, DC, 62; one-man shows, Alaska Methodist Univ, 63, Mel Kohler Gallery, 64, Anchorage Fine Art Mus, 71, prints, The Gallery, Anchorage, 77 & Painting & Prints, Anchorage Fine Arts Mus, 78; Ann All Alaska Exhib Artists & Craftsmen, 65-72; Wenatchee Apple Blossom Festival, Wash, 71. Teaching: Instr painting, Anchorage Community Ctr, 59-60; instr painting, Anchorage Community Col, 61-63; artist in residence, Alaska Methodist Univ, 66 & assoc prof art, 73, artist in residence, Visual Arts Ctr of Alaska, 77. Pos: Mem coun, Alaska Coun Arts, 64-68; chmn exhibs, Ann All Alaska Art Exhib, 65- Awards: First Award in Painting, Fur Rendezvous Exhib, 60; Best of Show, SCent Alaska Exhib, 62; Mel Kohler Award in Painting, Ann All Alaska Exhib, 66; Prints Alaska Award, Alaska Coun Arts, 76; First Award in Prints, All-Alaska Juried Art Exhib, 76 & 77. Bibliog: Paintings & Prints, Alaska Methodist Univ, 63; Woodcuts & Prints, Mel Kohler Gallery, 64; Paintings & Prints, Anchorage Fine Art Mus, 71. Mem: Life mem Alaska Artist Guild (pres, 63-65). Dealer: Color Ctr Gallery 111 Fireweed Lane Anchorage AK 99503. Mailing Add: 1025 W 11th Ave Anchorage AK 99501

KINCADE, ARTHUR WARREN
COLLECTOR, PATRON
b Chillicothe, Mo, Aug 14, 96. Collection: About 100 paintings from 16th century Italian Baroque to artists of the southwest; Henri, etc. Mailing Add: 255 N Roosevelt Wichita KS 67208

KIND, JOSHUA B
EDUCATOR, ART CRITIC
b Philadelphia, Pa, Nov 5, 33. Study: Univ Pa, Philadelphia, BA, 55; Columbia Univ, PhD, 67. Teaching: Instr art hist, Northwestern Univ, Evanston, Ill, 59-62; instr humanities, Univ Chicago, 62-65; vis prof art hist, Sch of Art Inst Chicago, 64-76; asst prof art hist & humanities, Ill Inst Technol, Chicago, 65-69; assoc prof art hist, Northern Ill Univ, DeKalb, 69- Pos: Chicago ed, Art News, New York, 64-70; dir, Oxbow Summer Sch Art, Saugatuck, Mich, 67-68; contrib ed, New Art Examr, Chicago, 75-; contribr, World Bk Year Book, 70-78. Awards: Nat Endowment for the Arts Critics Fel, 77. Mem: Col Art Asn; Soc Architectural Historians. Res: Modernism; creativity and the avant-garde; Renaissance inconography; modern architecture. Publ: Auth, Humanist of decay: Ivan Albright, Art News, 11/64; auth, Rouault, Tudor, 69; auth (catalogue), Naive Painting in Illinois, Ill Arts Coun, 76; auth, Art and the Corps of Women, New Art Examr, 3/78. Mailing Add: 3828 N Keduale Ave Chicago IL 60641

KIND, PHYLLIS
ART DEALER
b New York NY. Study: Univ Pa, AB; Univ Chicago, MA. Pos: Dir, Phyllis Kind Gallery. Specialty: Representing major Chicago artists; acquiring prints and drawings by modern and old masters; introducing exhibitions and selected works by other major contemporary American artists. Mailing Add: 226 E Ontario Chicago IL 60611

KINDERMANN, HELMMO
PHOTOGRAPHER, EDUCATOR
b Lancaster, Pa, Oct 11, 47. Study: Tyler Sch Fine Art, Temple Univ, BFA, 69; study of photog with Nathan Lyons, Visual Studies Workshop, Rochester, NY, 71-73; State Univ NY Buffalo, MFA, 73. Work: Miss Art Asn, Jackson; Visual Studies Workshop, Rochester, NY. Exhib: Color Print USA, Tex Tech Univ, Lubbock, 70; Images on Paper, Miss Art Asn, Jackson, 71; Light and Lens-Methods of Photog, Hudson River Mus, New York, 73; Images, Dimensional, Movable, Transferable, Akron Art Inst, Ohio, 73; New Approaches, Ctr for Exploratory and Perceptual Arts, Buffalo, NY, 75; New Photographics/76, Cent Wash State Col, Ellensburgh, 76; Photo/Synthesis, Herbert F Johnson Mus of Art, Ithaca, NY, 76. Teaching: Asst prof photog, Lake Placid Sch Art, Ctr for Music, Drama & Art, NY, 73- Pos: Co-dir & instr, W Alton Jones Cell Sci Ctr, Lake Placid, NY, 76-; mem adv bd, Soc Adirondack Photogr, Lake Placid, NY, 77- Awards: Purchase Prize, Images on Paper, Miss Art Asn, 71. Mem: Soc for Photog Educ; Col Art Asn Am; Photog Instr Asn; Friends of Photog. Style & Technique: Transformation of found photographic images into humorous satire using collage, photography and painting. Media: Photography; painting. Publ: Contribr, Frontiers of Photography, Time-Life Bks, 72; contribr, Light and Lens—Methods of Photography, Hudson River Mus, 73; New Photographics/76, Cent Wash Col, 76; contribr, Works and Process, CMDA Publ Co, 76; contribr, Photo/Synthesis, Herbert F Johnson Mus Art, 76. Mailing Add: 32 Park Ave Saranac Lake NY 12983

KING, CLINTON BLAIR
PAINTER, PRINTMAKER
b Ft Worth, Tex, Oct 3, 01. Study: Broadmoor Art Acad, Colorado Springs; with Randall Davey, Santa Fe, NMex; with Hayter, Paris, France. Work: Bibliot Nat, Paris, France; City of Paris; Nat Collection Fine Arts, Smithsonian Inst, Washington, DC; Victoria & Albert Mus, London, Eng; Kalamazoo Inst Art, Mich; plus many others. Exhib: Contemp Painting from France, Johannesburg, SAfrica, 64; one-man show, Lakeview Ctr Arts & Sci, Peoria, Ill, 66; Salon d'Automne, Paris, 67; plus many others. Awards: Clyde F Carr Landscape Prize, Chicago Art Inst, 44. Mem: Arts Club of Chicago. Style & Technique: All subjects; intaglio etching, all colors on one plate, viscosity method. Media: Oil, Gouache. Dealer: Jean Seth's Canyon Road Gallery 710 Canyon Rd Santa Fe NM 87501. Mailing Add: Main St Lakeside MI 49116

KING, EDWARD S
ART HISTORIAN
b Baltimore, Md, Jan 27, 00. Study: Johns Hopkins Univ; Princeton Univ, AB & MFA; Harvard Univ. Teaching: Lect art hist; instr, Bryn Mawr Col, Pa, 24 & Princeton Univ, 28; mem fac, Md Inst & Johns Hopkins Univ, Baltimore. Pos: Assoc cur paintings & Far Eastern art, Walters Art Gallery, 34-41, cur, 41-51, actg adminr, 45-46, adminr, 46-51, dir, 51-66, res assoc, 66-78. Publ: Contribr, Apollo, Art Bull & Walters Art Gallery J. Mailing Add: 4520 N Charles St Baltimore MD 21210

KING, ELAINE A
CURATOR, PHOTOGRAPHY CRITIC
b Oak Park, Ill, Apr 12, 47. Study: Northern Ill Univ, BA(20th century art hist), MA with Robert Bonnhuetter, Jan Swenson & Joshua Kind; Columbia Col, Chicago, photog hist with Arthur Siegel. Collections Arranged: Womens' Photog Invitational Exhib, 10/75, Retrospective on David Driesbach's Prints, 3/76, J D Sloan & David Avison, 6/76, Perspective on Quilts, 1/77, Photographs 1963-1977 James Newberry, 6/77, Contemp Color Photog, 7/77 & Art Fac Show, Dittmar Mem Gallery, Northwestern Univ; A Number of Instructions on How to Make Certain Drawings by Irene Siegel, 4/77; Eve Sonneman Photographs, 3/77 & Work by Naomi Savage, 5/77, Artemisia Gallery; Focus on Chicago, 11/77 & David Avison & Annie Noggle—Photographs, 3/78, Wesleyan Univ. Teaching: Asst prof photog, Northwestern Univ, 75- Pos: Craft studio supvr, Northwestern Univ, 74-75; dir, Artemisia Photo Gallery, Artemisia Gallery/Fund, Chicago, 76-77; cur, Dittmar Mem Gallery, Northwestern Univ, 77- & guest cur & consult, Ill Wesleyan Univ, Bloomington, 77- Awards: Chicago Art Award, Best Interview of Yr, Richard Hunt Art Award, 5/77. Mem: Soc for Photog Educ; Col Art Asn; Chicago Artists Coalition. Publ: Auth, Bernice Abbott, Midwest Art, 10/76; auth, Elaine A King Talks with Alice Adam at the Frumkin Gallery, winter 76, City Families—Chicago & London, 3/77, ...a kind of life Conversations in the combat zone, summer 77 & Garry Winogrand—Public Relations, spring 78, Exposure; auth, Five Chicago Photojournalists, Afterimage, 6/77. Mailing Add: 1522 Davis St Evanston IL 60201

KING, ETHEL MAY
COLLECTOR, PATRON
b New York, NY. Study: Columbia Univ. Mem: Mus Primitive Art; life fel Metrop Mus Art. Collection: Religious art and Americana. Publ: Auth, Darley, the most popular illustrator of his time. Mailing Add: 720 Lenox Ave New York NY 10039

KING, HAYWARD ELLIS
GALLERY DIRECTOR
b Little Rock, Ark, Mar 28, 28. Study: San Francisco Art Inst, BFA, 55; Sorbonne, 55-57, Fulbright scholar, 55; also lithography with Gaston Dorfinant, Paris, 55-57. Exhib: Many ann, San Francisco Art Asn & San Francisco Mus Art; two Winter Invitationals, Calif Palace Legion of Honor; Fulbright Painters Traveling Show; Rolling Renaissance; Underground Arts of San Francisco, 1945-68. Collections Arranged: Richmond Art Ctr solo & group exhibs, including drawings of Richard Diebenkorn & Elmer Bischoff, paintings of Richard Fiscus, John Kalamaras, Fred Martin & Theodore Polos, ceramics of Howard Whalen & others; John Bolles Gallery exhibs, Karl Kasten, Peter Shoemaker, John Battenberg, Lee Kelly, Gurdon Woods & others. Teaching: Lectr gallery design & mus training, Calif State Univ, San Francisco, 71- Pos: Grad eve sch registr, San Francisco Art Inst, 58-62; registr, San Francisco Mus Art, 63-66; cur dir, Richmond Art Ctr, Calif, 66-70; cur, John Bolles Gallery, San Francisco, 70-74; gallery dir, Calif State Univ, San Francisco, 74- Mem: Int Child Art Ctr (mem adv bd, 68-69); Univ Art Mus Coun, Berkeley (mem bd dirs, 69-70); Western Asn Art Mus (second vpres, 68-70). Mailing Add: Calif State Univ Gallery 19th & Hollaway San Francisco CA 94132

KING, HENRI UMBAJI
PAINTER, ILLUSTRATOR
b Detroit, Mich, Sept 9, 23. Study: Detroit Inst Arts; Soc Arts & Crafts Sch; Art Res West Africa. Work: Cent Mich Univ; Lewis Artists Supply Gallery, Detroit; Univ S Ala Slide Collection; Alma Lewis Sch Fine Art Slide Collection, Boston; Johnson Publ Bldg Collection, Chicago. Comn: Oil paintings, Plymouth Congregational Church, Detroit, 51-53, Charade Supper Club, Detroit, 65 & Patmon, Young & Kirk Corp, Detroit, 69. Exhib: Michigan Artists Ann, Detroit Inst Arts, 58-69; Atlanta Univ Ann, 67-68; Midwest Black Artists, Ind State Univ, Evansville, 74; one-man shows, Black Reflections, Cent Mich Univ, 75 & Recent Work, Henri Umbaji King, Kent State Univ, 75. Teaching: Instr painting & drawing, Downtown YMCA Adult Educ, Detroit, 61-68. Pos: Pres & gallery dir, Contemp Studio Inc, 58-65; vpres & gallery dir, Kumasi Mart-Art Gallery, Inc, 68-70; chmn & convenor, Mich Festival Comt, NAm Zone Festac, Nigeria, 74- Awards: First Painting Award, Russell Woods Ann, Detroit, 67; Gold Medal Painting, Fremont Mich Ann, 70; First Painting Award, Ind State Univ, Evansville, 74. Bibliog: Hoyt Fuller (auth), Nigerian Art Festival, Black World Mag, 72; Dean Cusino (auth), Reflections, Cent Mich Line, 75; Wendell Harrison (auth), Henri Umbaji King, Tribe Mag, 75. Mem: African Gallery Comt Detroit Inst Arts (bd dirs); NAm Zone Comt Festac Nigeria (bd dirs). Style & Technique: Figures, landscapes, semi-abstract, brush, knife. Media: Oil, Pastel-Charcoal, Ink. Publ: Illusr & contribr, A quest for ancestral land, 67 & contribr, How to appreciate African art, 67, Detroit Free Press; illusr, Perennial Paraders, Fairfield Butler, Jr, 67; contribr, About becoming an artist, Mich Chronicle, 70; illusr, Black American echoes of the past, Eckrich Meat Co, 70. Dealer: Arts Extended Gallery 1549 Broadway Detroit MI 48226. Mailing Add: 2223 Virginia Park Detroit MI 48206

KING, JOSEPH WALLACE (VINCIATA)
PAINTER
b Spencer, Va, May 11, 12. Study: Corcoran Sch Art; also in Italy & France. Work: Wake Forest Col; NC Mus Art, Raleigh; Va Mil Inst; Gov Mansion, Raleigh, NC; Lotos Club, New York; also in pvt collections. Comn: Mural, Community Ctr Bldg, Winston-Salem, NC; portrait of Pres Nixon, Duke Univ; portrait of Queen Elizabeth, London, 71. Exhib: Corcoran Gallery Art, Washington, DC; Fra Angelico Salon, Rome, Italy; Royal Soc Brit Art Exhib, London; one-man show, Bernheim-Jeune, Dauberville, Paris, France; five shows, Hammer Galleries, New York, 60-68; plus others. Mem: Am Int Acad New York; Int Fine Arts Coun, Paris; Lotos Club, New York. Publ: Contribr, Newsweek, 2/72, Time & Tide Mag, 3/72, Town & Country, 10/72, The Connoisseur, London, 10/72 & Visitors East, NY, 11/72. Mailing Add: 1201 Arbor Rd Winston-Salem NC 27104

KING, MYRON LYZON
ART DEALER
b Hampton Bays, NY, Oct 22, 21. Study: David Lipscomb Col, Peabody Col, BA. Pos: Lyzon Pictures & Frames, Inc, Nashville. Specialty: Contemporary American art; Sterling Strauser. Mailing Add: 411 Thompson Lane Nashville TN 37211

KING, WARREN THOMAS
CARTOONIST
b New York, NY, Jan 3, 16. Study: Fordham Univ, BS, 38; Grand Cent Sch Fine Arts, 38, with Ivan Olinsky, Grelian, Maura & Biggs; Phoenix Art Inst, 38-41, with Franklin Booth & others. Work: The Pentagon, Washington, DC; Air Force Acad, Colorado Springs, Colo; Metrop Mus Art, New York. Exhib: Collection of ed cartoons toured in nat mus; int exhibs. Teaching: Lectr fundamentals of art & editorial cartooning, in schs, art orgn & clubs. Pos: Ed cartoonist, Nat Asn Mfrs, New York, 51-; ed cartoonist, Daily News, New York, 55- Awards: Nat Headliners Club Award, 68; Nat Art Dirs Club Award, 68; Overseas Press Club Citation, 68; plus others. Mem: Soc Illustrators; Nat Cartoonist Soc; Soc Silurians; Am Asn Ed Cartoonists. Publ: Contribr, Chicago Tribune News Syndicate & nat newspapers & mag. Mailing Add: Captain's Lane Wilton CT 06897

KING, WILLIAM ALFRED
EDUCATOR, PAINTER
b Tulsa, Okla, Nov 11, 25. Study: Univ Tulsa, BA & MA; Okla State Univ; Inst Statale d'Arte, Florence, Italy; Int Univ Art, Florence. Work: Vrije Acad, Amsterdam, Holland; US Consulate, Stuttgart, Ger; Volkshochschule, Erlangen, Ger; Univ Wis-Green Bay; Univ Tulsa. Exhib: One-man shows, Galerie am Dom, Frankfurt am Main, Ger, 57, Galerie Vigna Nuova, Florence, Italy, 64 & Univ Wis-Madison, 65; Nat Print & Drawing Exhib, Galerias Biosca, Madrid, Spain, 57; Inst Auslandsbiezhungen, Stuttgart, Ger, 61. Teaching: Asst prof painting, Nebr State Col, 53-56; prof art & chmn fac art, Univ Tex, Permian Basin, 73-76. Pos: Dir arts & crafts, Spec Serv Div, US Dept Army, Ger & Italy, 56-64; pres, West Tex Chap, Artists Equity Asn, 75. Awards: One of Ten Outstanding Artists in Wis, Marquette Univ, 67. Mem: Col Art Asn Am; Nat Coun Art Adminr; Tex Asn Schs Art; Am Fedn Arts. Media: Etching; Oil. Publ: Toward Design in the Vernacular; The Museum as Anti-environment. Mailing Add: c/o Blair Print Collectors Gallery 225 E DeVargas Santa Fe NM 87501

KING, WILLIAM DICKEY
SCULPTOR
b Jacksonville, Fla, Feb 25, 25. Study: Univ Fla, 42-44; Cooper Union Art Sch, 45-48; Brooklyn Mus Art Sch, 49; Skowhegan Sch Painting & Sculpture, 48; also in Rome. Work: Univ Calif; Cornell Univ, Ithaca, NY; Univ NC; Syracuse Univ, NY; Addison Gallery Am Art, Andover, Mass. Comn: SS United States; Bankers Trust Co, New York. Exhib: Whitney Mus Am Art, Mus Mod Art & Guggenheim Mus, New York; Philadelphia Mus Art; Los Angeles Co Mus Art; Mus Contemp Crafts, New York; Retrospective, San Francisco Mus Art, Calif, 70 & 74; Am Acad Arts & Lett, 70 & 74; New Sch Social Res, New York, 72;

Harvard Univ, 72; 2nd Int Biennial Small Sculptures Exhib, Art Gallery of Budapest, Hungary, 73; Cranbrook Acad Art, Bloomfield Hills, Mich, 74; plus other group & one-man shows. Teaching: Instr sculpture, Brooklyn Mus Sch Art, 53-59; lectr sculpture, Univ Calif, Berkeley, 65-66; instr sculpture, Art Students League, 68-69. Awards: Fulbright Fel, 49; Brooklyn Mus, 49; St Gaudens Medal, Cooper Union, 64; plus others. Bibliog: S Schwartz (auth), New York letter: William King, Art Int, 11/72; John Sanders (auth), Photography Year Book 1973, London, 72; Hilton Kramer (auth), The Age of the Avant-Garde, London, 74. Dealer: Terry Dintenfass Inc 18 E 67th St New York NY 10021. Mailing Add: 17 E 96th St New York NY 10028

KINGHAN, CHARLES ROSS
PAINTER
b Anthony, Kans, Jan 18, 95. Study: Am Acad Art; Art Inst Chicago. Work: Philadelphia Mus Art, Pa; Nat Acad Design, New York; Smithsonian Inst, Washington, DC. Exhib: Wichita Art Asn, Kans, 56; Allied Artists Am, New York, 57-; Am Watercolor Soc, 57-; Nat Acad Design, New York, 57- Teaching: Instr art, Am Acad Art; instr watercolor, pvt classes, 37-; instr oil & watercolor, Huguenot Sch Art, 45-51. Pos: Sketch man, Maxon Advert Agency, New York, 51-53; sketch man, Batton Barton Durstin Advert Co, New York, 53-62. Awards: Gold Medal, 56 & Gold Medal for portrait, 64, Allied Artists Am; Gold Medal, Hudson Valley Art Asn, 60. Bibliog: Rendering techniques, 58 & Ted Kautzky, Master of Pencil and Watercolor, 59, Reinhold. Mem: Nat Acad Design (academician); Am Watercolor Soc; Hudson Valley Art Asn; Allied Artists Am; Acad Artists Asn; plus one other. Style & Technique: Realistic. Media: Acrylic, Oil, Watercolor. Interest: Portraits. Dealer: Blair Gallery Ltd Santa Fe NM 87501; Grand Central Galleries 40 Vanderbilt Ave New York NY 10017. Mailing Add: 775 D Laguna Canyon Rd Laguna Beach CA 96251

KINGMAN, DONG M
PAINTER, ILLUSTRATOR
b Oakland, Calif, Mar 31, 11. Study: Lingnan Sch, Hong Kong, with Sze-To-Wai, 26; Fox & Morgan Art Sch, Oakland. Work: Metrop Mus Art, Mus Mod Art & Whitney Mus Am Art, New York; Boston Mus Fine Arts, Mass; M H De Young Mus, San Francisco. Comn: Murals for Works Progress Admin Proj, San Francisco, 42, Hilton Hotel, New York, 63, mosaic, Pres Hotel, Hong Kong, 64, Bank Calif, San Francisco, 68 & Boca Raton Hotel, Fla, 70; tapestry designed for Ambassador Hotel, Hongkong, 74. Exhib: Am Watercolor Soc; San Francisco Art Asn; Metrop Mus Art Watercolor Exhib; Whitney Mus Am Art Ann; Columbus Mus Arts & Crafts, Ga. Teaching: Instr art, Columbia Univ, 46-54; instr watercolor & hist Chinese art, Hunter Col, 48-53; fac mem, Famous Artists Sch, Westport, Conn, 54- Pos: Art dir, Greatest Amusements Mag, currently. Awards: Prizes at San Francisco Art Asn Ann Exhib, 36, Metrop Mus Art Watercolor Exhib & Am Watercolor Soc Ann. Bibliog: Dong Kingman (film), directed by James Wong Howe, 54; Alan D Gruskin (auth), The Watercolors of Dong Kingman, Crowell Co, 58; Hongkong Dong (film), directed by Dong Kingman, 75. Mem: Am Watercolor Soc; West Coast Watercolor Soc; Dutch Treat Club. Media: Watercolor, Lacquer. Publ: Illusr, The bamboo gate, 46; illusr, China's Story, 46; illusr, Johnny Hong in Chinatown, 52; illusr, City on the golden hill, 67; illusr, The effect of gamma rays on man-in-the-moon marigolds, 71. Dealer: Hammer Gallery 51 E 57th St New York NY 10022. Mailing Add: 21 W 58th St New York NY 10019

KINGREY, KENNETH
DESIGNER, EDUCATOR
b Santa Ana, Calif, Dec 23, 13. Study: Univ Calif, Los Angeles, BE & MA. Exhib: 50 Best Books, Am Inst Graphic Arts, 58; Traveling Exhib, US, Europe, Cent Am & Russia; Univ Hawaii, ann; Ann State Fair; plus others. Teaching: Prof advert art, Univ Calif, Los Angeles, 40-53; prof art, Univ Hawaii, 50-51 & 53- Awards: 50 Best Bks Award, Am Inst Graphic Arts, 58 & 61; Western Bks Awards, 58-63. Mem: Los Angeles Art Dirs Club; Hawaii Painters & Sculptors League; Nat Art Dirs Club; Nat Art Educ Asn. Publ: Ed, Design Quart, Walker Art Ctr, 60; contribr, Idea, 61; contribr, Graphic design, Eur-Asian Graphics. Mailing Add: 5959 Kalanianaole Hwy Honolulu HI 96816

KINGSLEY, APRIL
ART CRITIC, LECTURER
b New York, NY, Feb 16, 41. Study: NY Univ, BA(art hist) & MA. Collections Arranged: Rafael Ferrer Exhibition (with catalog), Pasadena Art Mus; Chronology for Frank Stella (with catalog), Mus Mod Art. Teaching: Instr ideas in art, Sch Visual Arts, 73-; instr mod art, Castle Hill Ctr Arts, Truro, Mass, summer 75. Pos: Asst cur, Mus Mod Art, New York, 70-71; assoc cur, Pasadena Art Mus, Calif, 71-72; regular critic, Soho Weekly News, NY, 75-77 & Village Voice, 77- Mem: Int Art Critics Asn. Res: Conceptual art. Publ: Auth, Douglas Huebler, Artforum, 72; auth, Budd Hopkins: energy & order, 72, Jack Tworkov, 74 & Ronald Bladen, 74, Art Int; auth, James Brooks dialogue & critique, Arts Mag, 75. Mailing Add: 246 W 16th St New York NY 10011

KINGSTON, EMILY FULLER
See Fuller, Emily

KINGTON, LOUIS BRENT
SCULPTOR, EDUCATOR
b Topeka, Kans, July 26, 34. Study: Univ Kans, BFA, 57; Cranbrook Acad Art, MFA, 61. Work: Mus Contemp Crafts, New York; Johnson Collection, Racine, Wis; St Paul Art Ctr, Minn; Krannert Art Mus, Univ Ill, Urbana; Univ Wis-Milwaukee. Exhib: Objects USA, Racine, 69; Goldsmith 70, St Paul, 70; Wichita Nat, Kans, 70; Design in Steel, New York, 71; Acquisitions, New York. Teaching: Prof metal smithing, Southern Ill Univ, Carbondale, 61- Awards: Spec recognition, St Paul Art Ctr, 65; Nat Merit Award, Am Craftsmen Coun, 65, Design in Steel Award for Excellence, Am Iron & Steel Inst, 71. Mem: Soc NAm Goldsmiths (pres, 70-); Am Craftsmen Coun. Style & Technique: Blacksmithing forging jewelry as large scale work. Media: Iron, Steel, Silver, Gold. Dealer: Gilman Galleries 103 E Oak Chicago IL 60611. Mailing Add: Sch of Art Southern Ill Univ Carbondale IL 62901

KINIGSTEIN, JONAH
PAINTER, DESIGNER
b New York, NY, June 26, 23. Study: Cooper Union Art Sch, 41-43; Grande Chaumiere, Paris, 47-51; Belle Arte, Rome, 53-54. Work: Mus Mod Art, New York; Albright-Knox Art Gallery, Buffalo, NY; Nelson Gallery Art; Washington Mus; Ain Herod Mus, Tel-Aviv, Israel; also in pvt collections. Exhib: Butler Inst Am Art, Youngstown, Ohio, 56; Young Americans, Whitney Mus Am Art, New York, 57; Nat Acad Arts & Lett, 68; one-man shows, Grippi Gallery, New York, 61, Kinematic Art, Nordness Gallery, 64, ACA Gallery 68 & Rittenhouse Gallery, Philadelphia, 75; plus others. Teaching: Brooklyn Mus Art Sch, 70. Awards: First Prize, Silvermine Guild, 59; Louis Comfort Tiffany Found Award, 62; Perkins-Elmer Prize, 62; plus others. Mailing Add: 105 E Ninth St New York NY 10003

KINNAIRD, RICHARD WILLIAM
PAINTER, EDUCATOR
b Buenos Aires, Arg, Nov 19, 31; US citizen. Study: Univ Mich, Ann Arbor, 49-51; Carleton Col, Northfield, Minn, BA, 53; Art Inst of Chicago, 52; Univ Ill, MFA, with Lee Chesney, 58. Work: Seattle Mus of Art; NC Mus of Art, Raleigh; Aldrich Mus of Contemp Art, Ridgefield, Conn; Hanes Knitting Corp & R J Reynolds Corp, Winston-Salem, NC. Comn: Thomas Wolfe Mem Sculpture, class gift to Univ NC-Chapel Hill, 66; pediment sculpture, Mint Mus of Art, Charlotte, NC, 72. Exhib: Award Winners Exhib of Chicago No-Jury Show, Art Inst of Chicago, 57; Dirs Choice, Birmingham, Ala, 61; Southeastern Ann Painting & Sculpture, High Mus, Atlanta, Ga, 66; Ann NC Artists, NC Mus of Fine Art, Raleigh, 68, 74 & 76; Experimental Media, Corcoran Gallery of Contemp Art, Washington, DC, 70; Painting & Sculpture Exhib, Mint Mus of Art, 71; Modern Maxis II, New Britain Mus of Am Art, Conn, 73; Third Ann Contemp Reflections, Aldrich Mus of Contemp Art, 73; Southeastern Ctr for Contemp Art, Winston-Salem, 77. Collections Arranged: Recent Abstract Paintings, Pratt Inst Gallery, 74; Univ Evansville Fine Arts Exhib, Ind, 73; Exhib of Candidates for Am Acad of Arts & Lett, New York, 74; Invitational Group Exhib, Carleton Col, 69; NC Sculpture Invitational Exhib, Duke Univ; Chicago Award Winners tours France for US Info Agency, 57; Libr of Cong Print Exhib sent to Munich, Ger, 57. Teaching: Instr printmaking & etching, Auburn Univ, Ala, 60-64; from instr to assoc prof painting, Univ NC, 64-76, prof painting, 76- Awards: Purchase Award, Dillard Collection Art on Paper, Dillard Found, 72; Purchase Award, Third Ann Contemp Reflections, Aldrich Mus of Contemp Art, 74; First Painting Award, Spring Mill Ann Art Exhib, Spring Mills Corp, Lancaster, SC, 76; First Award, 40th Ann NC Artists, NC Mus of Fine Art, Raleigh, 77. Style & Technique: Abstract painting analogue to structural color. Media: Acrylic and oil. Mailing Add: 402 Hillsborough St Chapel Hill NC 27514

KINNEY, GILBERT HART
COLLECTOR, ART ADMINISTRATOR
b New York, NY, May 11, 31. Study: Yale Univ, BA, 53 & MA, 54; John F Kennedy Sch, MPA, 73. Pos: Trustee, 74-77 & chief exec officer, 77-, Corcoran Gallery of Art, Washington, DC; trustee & vpres, Archives of Am Art, 74; trustee, Am Federation of the Arts, 78. Collection: Major emphasis post-war American painting and sculpture, also European 20th century painting and sculpture and Far Eastern ceramics and sculpture. Mailing Add: 1231 31st St NW Washington DC 20007

KINOSHITA, GENE
ARCHITECT
b Vancouver, BC, Jan 18, 35. Study: Univ BC, BArch (honors), 59; Yale Univ, MArch, 62. Comn: Res Ctr, Fed Govt, 71; Bldg Expansion, Royal Ont Mus, Toronto, 74; Detention Ctr, Ont Govt, 74; Humber Col Master Planning, 75; Ont Col of Art expansion & renovations, 77-; High Park Libr, Toronto, 77. Archit Exhib: Travelling Exhib Can Art Mus, Royal Can Acad Arts, 67; Can Unit Masonry Awards Prog Travelling Exhib Can, 72; Ont Masons Rels Coun, Travelling Prov Exhib, 73. Pos: Partner design, Moffat, Moffat & Kinoshita, Architects, 65- Awards: Residence in Toronto Award Excellence, Can Housing Design Coun, 71; Manta Sound Co Award Excellence & Crystaplex Plastics Award Merit, Nat Design Coun, 72; Leather Medals Award for Great W Beef Co Restaurant & Lounge, Waterloo, Ont, 76; Metrop Toronto Regional Detention Centre, Award of Excellence from Ont Asn of Architects Design Awards, 77 & Award of Excellence from Ont Masons' Rels Coun, 77. Mem: Can Conf Arts; life mem Royal Ont Mus; Royal Archit Inst Can; Ont Asn Archit. Mailing Add: 278 Sheldrake Blvd Toronto ON Can

KINSTLER, EVERETT RAYMOND
PAINTER, INSTRUCTOR
b New York, NY, Aug 5, 26. Study: Nat Acad Design, New York; Art Students League, with DuMond; also with Wayman Adams & John Johansen. Work: Metrop Mus Art, New York; Carnegie Inst, Pittsburgh; Brooklyn Mus; Smithsonian Inst, Washington, DC; Mus City New York. Comn: Portraits of Astronaut Scott Carpenter, 63 & Astronaut Alan Shepard, 65, USN Combat Art, Washington, DC; Gov John Connolly, 75; portraits of John Wayne, Roy Rogers & Dale Evans; official White House Portrait of Pres Gerald R Ford. Exhib: One-man shows, Grand Cent Art Galleries, New York, 58, Columbia Mus Art, SC, 70 & Lotos Club, New York, 72. Teaching: Instr painting & drawing, Art Students League, 70-75. Awards: Gold Medal for painting, Nat Arts Club, New York, 64; Purchase Prize, Ranger Fund, Nat Acad Design, 71; Gold Medal, Lotos Club, New York, 72. Bibliog: H Rogoff (auth), The pro's nest, Palette Talk, M Grumbacher Inc, 70; Norman Kent (auth), The artists studio, Am Artist Mag, 1/70; Wendon Blake (auth), Acrylics, Am Artist Mag, 1/72. Mem: Nat Acad Design; Am Watercolor Soc; Century Club; Nat Arts Club (vpres); life mem Lotos Club; Players' Club (art chmn); Pastel Soc Am; Allied Artists; Audubon Artists; plus others. Publ: Illusr, Opera Companion, Dodd, 61 & Verdi, 63; auth, Painting Portraits, Watson-Guptill, 71; auth, Painting Men's Portraits, Singer-Watson-Guptill, 77. Mailing Add: 15 Gramercy Park New York NY 10003

KIPNISS, ROBERT
PAINTER, LITHOGRAPHER
b New York, NY, Feb 1, 31. Study: Art Students League; Wittenberg Col; Univ Iowa, BA & MFA. Work: Whitney Mus Am Art, New York; Chicago Art Inst; Yale Univ Art Gallery; Libr Cong, Washington, DC; Albright-Knox Mus, Buffalo, NY; Nat Collection of Fine Arts, Smithsonian Inst, Washington, DC; Cleveland Mus Ohio. Exhib: One-man shows, Allen R Hite Inst, Univ Louisville, 65, Museo de Arte Moderno La Tertulia, Colombia, 75 & Hirschl & Adler Galleries, New York, NY, 77; Recent Acquisitions, Whitney Mus Am Art, 72 & New York Pub Libr; Am Acad Design, New York; Int Exhib of Original Drawings, Mus of Mod Art, Rijeka-Dolac, Yugoslavia, 76; III Bienal Americana de Artes Graficas, Museo La Tertulia, Cali, Colombia, 76; Retrospective, Assoc Am Artists, New York, NY, 77. Awards: Purchase Prize, Ohio Univ, 65; Audubon Artists Hon Mention, 74; Prize, Nat Acad of Design. Mem: Audubon Artists (dir graphics). Media: Oil. Publ: Illusr, Poems of Emily Dickinson, Thomas Y Crowell, 64; illusr, Collected Poems of Robert Graves, Anchor Doubleday, 66. Dealer: Merrill Chase Galleries 620 N Michigan Ave Chicago IL 60611; Hirschl & Adler Galleries 21 E 70th St New York NY. Mailing Add: 5 Hillside Pl Tarrytown NY 10591

KIPP, LYMAN
SCULPTOR
b Dobbs Ferry, NY, Dec 24, 29. Study: Pratt Inst, 50-52; Cranbrook Acad Art, 52-54. Work: Whitney Mus Am Art, New York; Albright-Knox Art Gallery, Buffalo; High Mus of Art, Atlanta, Ga; Univ Ala, Huntsville; State NY Albany Mall. Comn: Sculpture for Post Off & Fed Off Bldg, Van Nuys, Calif. Exhib: Four Whitney Mus Am Art Sculpture Ann, 64-70; Primary Structures, Jewish Mus, New York, 66; Sculpture in Environment, New York, 67; Art of the Real, Mus Mod Art, New York, 68; Cool Art, Larry Aldrich Mus, Conn, 68, Highlights of the Season, 68 & Change of View, 75; Art of the Real, Mus Mod Art, New York & London, 68, Paris & Berlin, 69; Sculpture in the Constructivist Tradition, Hamilton

Gallery, NY, 77; Urban Structures/Monumental Sculpture, Nat Endowment for the Arts Traveling Exhib originated in Akron, Ohio, 77; plus many others. Teaching: Instr sculpture, Bennington Col, 60-63; asst prof sculpture, Hunter Col, 63-66, prof & chmn dept, 75-; prof sculpture & chmn dept, Lehman Col, 66-75. Awards: Guggenheim Fel, 66; Fulbright Grant, 66. Mailing Add: 11 Worth St New York NY 10013

KIPP, ORVAL
PAINTER, EDUCATOR
b Hyndman, Pa, May 21, 04. Study: Stetson Univ; Carnegie Inst, AB(with hon); Teachers Col, Columbia Univ, AM; Univ Pittsburgh, PhD. Work: Latrobe High Sch, Aspinwall High Sch, Greensburg Pub Schs, Indiana Pub Schs & Uniontown High Sch, Pa. Exhib: Provincetown Art Asn; Assoc Artists Pittsburgh; Am Fedn Arts Traveling Exhib; Am Artists Prof League Grand Nat, 72; Three Rivers Arts Festival, Pittsburgh; plus others. Teaching: Instr art, Indiana Univ Pa, 36-41, dir art dept, 41-60, chmn, 60-64, prof, 60-69, prof emer, 69-; artist-in-residence, Kiski Sch, 64-69; instr, Ivy Sch of Prof Art, 64-69; lectr, Trick or Treat in Art Education, Ind State Art Teachers, Indianapolis; lectr & demonstrations, The Mystery of The Masters. Awards: Prizes, Indiana Art Asn, 47-57; Spec Jury Award, Pittsburgh Soc Art, 68. Mem: Eastern Art Asn; Assoc Artists Pittsburgh (vpres & pres); Indiana Art Asn (pres); Pa Art Educ Asn (coun); Pittsburgh Watercolor Soc (vpres & pres). Style & Technique: Abstract & realistic. Media: Watercolor, Oil. Mailing Add: 635 Church St Indiana PA 15701

KIRBY, KENT BRUCE
PRINTMAKER, PHOTOGRAPHER
b Fargo, NDak, Dec 31, 34. Study: Carleton Col, with Albert Elsen, BA, 56; Univ NDak, with Robert Nelson, MA, 59; Univ Mich, MFA, 70. Work: Art Inst Chicago; Guggenheim Mus, New York; Philadelphia Mus Art. Comn: Prints, comn by Joseph Kinnebrew. Exhib: Oklahoma City Art Ctr Nat Watercolor Exhib, 60; Soc of Four Arts Nat Exhib, 62; Eastern Mich Univ, Nat Polymer Show, 67; Mich Arts Biennial, Detroit Art Inst, 69; Hunterdon Nat Print Exhib, Clinton, NJ, 75. Teaching: Instr drawing & painting, Muskingum Col, 59-61; instr, Wilkes Col, 61-62; prof printmaking & photog & chmn dept art, Alma Col, 62-, chmn fine arts div, 73- Pos: Organizer & first dir, Alma Arts & Crafts Coun, 64; chmn mus comt, Mich Coun Arts, 66-67; printing consult, Hersig-Sommerville, Ltd, Toronto, Ont, 78. Awards: Newberry Libr Res Fel, 74; Mich Coun Arts Grant, 75; Nat Endowment Arts grant, 76. Bibliog: Richard Lyons (auth), Kent Kirby, Minn Rev, 60. Mem: Nat Coun Art Adminr; Col Art Asn Am. Style & Technique: Interest in relationship between art and technology, exploring various qualities of supposed reality. Res: Light print press to revive collotype technique, publishing works by American artists. Publ: Auth, Art, technology & the liberal arts college, Art J, spring 70. Dealer: Lantern Gallery Ann Arbor MI 48104. Mailing Add: 4100 Riverview Alma MI 48801

KIRK, JEROME
SCULPTOR
b Detroit, Mich, Apr 3, 23. Study: Mass Inst Technol, BS. Work: Phoenix Art Mus, Ariz; Storm King Art Ctr, Mountainville, NY; plus others. Comn: Outdoor mobile sculptures, Quest, TRW Inc, Redondo Beach, Calif, 68; 69; Phoenix Bird Ascending & Tiered Orbits, Civic Plaza, Phoenix, 71; Silver Orbit, Storm King Art Ctr, 73; Waves, Monterey Conf Ctr, Calif, 77. Exhib: De Young Mus Collectors Show, 65; Contemporary American Painting & Sculpture, Krannert Art Mus, Champaign, Ill, 67; Or 67; Santa Barbara Mus, 69; Storm King Art Ctr, 73; Painting & Sculpture Today, Indianapolis Mus of Art, 76; plus many others. Bibliog: Mary Lou Loper (auth), article in Los Angeles Times, 3/17/71; Michael Leopold (auth), rev in Art Int, 1/74. Style & Technique: Constructivist school; kinetic sculptures; wind driven and/or achieve infinitely random patterns via pendular motions. Media: Stainless Steel, Aluminum, Brass. Mailing Add: 874 41st St Oakland CA 94608

KIRK, MICHAEL
PRINTMAKER
b New York, NY, Oct 31, 47. Study: Rutgers Univ, NJ, BA(art hist), 69; Pratt Inst, MFA(printmaking), 73. Work: Philadelphia Mus of Art; Boston Mus of Fine Arts; Nat Collection of Fine Arts, Washington, DC; Brooklyn Mus; Libr of Cong, Washington, DC. Exhib: The 18th & 19th Nat Print Exhib, Brooklyn Mus, 72 & 73; Drawings, Marion Koogler Mus, San Antonio, Tex, 74; First Bienale of Graphika of Finland, 75; Color Print USA, Tex Tech Univ, Lubbock, 75; one-man shows, Gimpel-Weitzenhoffer, New York, 75 & 77, Colgate Univ, 75, Philadelphia Print Club, 75 & Marilyn Meyers, Washington, DC, 78; III Bienal Am de Artes Graphicas, Cali, Colombia, 76; Bienale Int de la Gravure, Krakow, Poland, 76; Prints in Sequence, State Mus of NJ, Trenton, 77; Manscape, Okla Arts Ctr, Oklahoma City, 77; Primera Bienal del Grabado de America, Maracaibo, Venezuela, 78. Teaching: Instr printmaking, Parsons Sch of Design, Manhattan, 73- Style & Technique: Figurative etchings and drawings. Dealer: Gimpel & Weitzenhoffer Gallery 1040 Madison Ave New York NY 10021. Mailing Add: 307 Canal St New York NY 10013

KIRKLAND, VANCE HALL
PAINTER, COLLECTOR
b Convoy, Ohio, Nov 3, 04. Study: Cleveland Sch Art, BEA; Cleveland Col Educ, Western Reserve Univ, with Henry Keller, Frank Wilcox, William Joseph Eastman & Albert Olson; also study in Europe, Africa & Asia. Work: Denver Art Mus; Art Inst Chicago; Nelson Gallery Art, Kansas City, Mo; Columbus Gallery Fine Arts, Ohio; Norton Gallery Fine Arts, West Palm Beach, Fla. Comn: Ceiling in Drawing Room, comn by Mrs Gerald Hughes, Denver, 36; Hist of Costume (five murals), Neusteter's, Denver, 37; mural room & ranch bar, Albany Hotel, Denver, 37; Cattle Round-Up, US Treas Dept, Eureka, Kans, 38 & Land Rush, US Treas Dept, Sayre, Okla, 40. Exhib: International Watercolors, Art Inst Chicag, 30-46; Contemporary American Painting, Univ Ill, 52; Artists West of Mississippi, Colorado Springs Fine Arts Ctr, 65; 73rd Western Ann, Denver Art Mus, 71; Color Exp Space Retrospective, Denver Art Mus, 72. Teaching: Prof art & dir sch art, Univ Denver, 29-32 & 46-69; instr art & dir, Kirkland Sch Art, Denver, 32-45. Awards: Awards for Watercolors, Mountain Climbers, Friends Art, Nelson Gallery 41 & Gwydenmanders, Denver Art Mus, 45. Media: Oil, Watercolor. Collection: Contemporary art; Oriental art. Mailing Add: 1311 Pearl St Denver CO 80203

KIRKWOOD, LARRY THOMAS
DESIGNER, PRINTMAKER
b Knoxville, Iowa, Oct 4, 43. Study: Univ Iowa; Univ Mo, BA; Univ Kans. Work: City Hall, Kansas City, Kans; Simpson Col, Indianola, Iowa. Comn: Patrons print, Jewish Community Ctr, Kansas City, Mo, 73; 1000 prints for Ocho Rios Jamaica Hotel, Playboy Enterprises, Jacklyn Interiors, Miami, Fla, 74. Exhib: Am Contemp Arts & Crafts Slide Libr, Palm Beach, Fla, 75; 2nd Ann Nat Exhib, Ga Tech Univ, 75; 17th Ann Nat Print & Drawing Exhib, Oklahoma City Art Ctr, 75; 6th Greater New Orleans Int Exhib, 76; 20th Nat Print Exhib, Hunterdon Art Ctr, Clinton, NJ, 76; 3rd Ann Nat Exhib, Ga Tech Univ, 76; 19th Ann Nat Print & Drawing Exhib, Oklahoma City Art Ctr, Okla, 77; Arena 77 4th Ann Art Open, Binghamton, NY, 77. Teaching: Norton Mus of Art, 78- Awards: First Place, Winter Arts Exhib, 74; Third Place, Rock Springs Art Ctr, 77; Third Place, 9th Ann La Junta Art Exhib, 77. Mem: Am Graphics Soc. Style & Technique: Realistic and semiabstract subject matter; hand prepared stencils; exploring textures. Media: Hand prepared Serigraph; Brushed Acrylic. Mailing Add: 1850 Seventh Ave N Lake Worth FL 33460

KIRKWOOD, MARY BURNETTE
PAINTER
b Hillsboro, Ore, Dec 21, 04. Study: Univ Mont, BA; Univ Ore, MFA; Harvard Univ Sch Fine Arts, art hist with Prof Paul J Sachs; Royal Art Sch, Stockholm, Sweden, with Prof Otte Sköld; Art Students League, with Reginald Marsh; also with Joseph Stefanelli & Robert Goldwater, Paris. Work: Cheney Cowles Mus, Spokane, Wash; Boise Art Gallery, Idaho; IBM Corp; Bank of Idaho; Boise Cascade Corp. Comn: Murals for agr sci bldg, 48 & libr, 52, Univ Idaho. Exhib: West Coast Juried, Seattle Art Mus, 62; West of the Mississippi Exhib, Colorado Springs, 63; Intermountain Exhib, Salt Lake City Art Ctr, 63 & 65; Fifty States Exhib, Burpee Art Mus, Rockford, Ill, 66; Western States Exhib, Denver Art Mus, 71; plus others. Teaching: Prof art, Univ Idaho, 30-70. Awards: Third Prize for Miercoles Santo, Pac Coast Ann, Wenatchee, Wash, 63; Best of Show for El Cristo de la Columna, 63 & Second Prize for Trampoline, 66, Cheney Cowles Mus, Spokane, Wash. Mem: Portland Art Asn; Idaho Art Asn; Boise Art Asn. Style & Technique: Primarily a figure painter; truth of character sought through color shapes seen as form, structure and abstraction all in one, in free brush, direct painting. Media: Oil. Mailing Add: 812 Apple Lane Moscow ID 83843

KIRSCHENBAUM, BERNARD EDWIN
SCULPTOR
b New York, NY, Sept 3, 24. Study: Cornell Univ; Inst Design, Chicago, BA. Work: Storm King Art Ctr, Mountainville, NY. Comn: Sculptures, Spectrum II, Mass Inst Technol, Cambridge, 68 & Walkthrough, J Patrick Lannan Found, Palm Beach, Fla, 69. Exhib: Sculpture in Environment, Cent Park, New York, 67; Cool Art: Abstraction Today, Newark Mus, NJ, 68; Painting & Sculpture Today, Indianapolis Mus Art, 70; Three New York Artists, Corcoran Gallery Art, Washington, DC, 73; Sculpture in the Fields, Storm King Art Ctr, 74. Awards: Guggenheim Fel Sculpture, 72. Style & Technique: Constructed forms, large scale. Dealer: Sculpture Now Inc Max Hutchinson 142 Greene St New York NY 10012. Mailing Add: 180 Park Row New York NY 10038

KIRSCHENBAUM, JULES
PAINTER, EDUCATOR
b New York, NY, Mar 25, 30. Study: Brooklyn Mus Art Sch. Work: Butler Inst Am Art, Youngstown, Ohio; Whitney Mus Am Art, New York; Weatherspoon Art Gallery; Univ NC; Des Moines Art Ctr, Iowa; Everhardt Mus, Scranton, Pa. Comn: Hist of Iowa, Cent Nat Bank, Des Moines, 64. Exhib: Drawings USA, Mus Mod Art, New York, 34, Painting USA The Figure, 63; Whitney Mus Am Art Ann, 55; Artists Abroad, Paintings from Whitney Collection, 69; Gov Exhib Nine Iowa Artists, 71. Teaching: Artist in residence, Des Moines Art Ctr, 63-67; prof painting, Drake Univ, 67-; vis prof art, Temple Univ, 72-73. Awards: Fulbright Fel, 56; First Prize for Figure Painting, Nat Acad Design, 57; First Prize for Oils, Butler Inst Am Art, 60. Bibliog: The figure, Time, 62. Media: Acrylic. Dealer: Forum Gallery 1018 Madison Ave New York NY 10021. Mailing Add: 2829 Forest Dr Des Moines IA 50312

KIRSTEIN, MR & MRS LINCOLN
COLLECTORS
Mr Kirstein, b Rochester, NY, May 4, 07. Study: Mr Kirstein, Harvard Univ, BS, 30. Publ: Auth, Pavel Tchelitchew Drawings, 47; auth, Elle Nadelman Drawings, 49; auth, Elie Nadelman, Eakins Press, 73. Mailing Add: 128 E 19th St New York NY 10003

KIRSTEN-DAIENSAI, RICHARD CHARLES
PAINTER, PRINTMAKER
b Chicago, Ill, Apr 16, 20. Study: Art Inst Chicago; Univ Wash; also study in Japan, 58-69. Work: Seattle Art Mus; Bell Tel Co; Libr of Cong, Washington, DC; Metrop Mus Art, New York; Tokyo Mus Mod Art, Japan; also in pvt collections. Exhib: Seattle Art Mus, numerous shows, 45-69; Frye Mus, Seattle, 60-65 & 69; Gov Invitational, 67; Collector's Gallery, Bellevue, Wash, 67; Richard White Gallery, Seattle, 68; plus many others. Pos: Art ed, Seattle Post-Intelligencer, 48- Awards: Ordination as Zen Buddhist priest (with Zen name Daiensai), Zuisenji Temple, Kamakura, Japan, 67; Purchase Prize, Univ Ore, 68; Purchase Prize, Seattle First Nat Bank, 69; plus others. Mem: Am Fedn Arts; Northwest Watercolor Soc (pres, 68 & 69); Artists Equity (pres, Seattle Chap, 52-56); Northwest Printmakers. Media: Watercolor. Dealer: Kirsten Gallery WA. Mailing Add: 900 N 102nd St Seattle WA 98133

KISCH, GLORIA
SCULPTOR
b New York, NY, Nov 14, 41. Study: Sarah Lawrence Col, BA, 63; Boston Mus Sch, 64-65; Otis Art Inst, Los Angeles, BFA & MFA, 69. Work: Mildura Art, Victoria, Australia; Palm Springs Desert Mus, Calif; Downey Mus Art, Calif; Otis Art Inst, Los Angeles. Exhib: One-woman shows, Suzanne Saxe Gallery, San Francisco, 73, Newport Harbor Art Mus, Newport Beach, Calif, 74, Calif State Univ, Los Angeles, 77 & Los Angeles Inst of Contemp Art, 78; Cirrus Gallery, Los Angeles, 74, 75 & 77; Wade Stevenson Gallery, Paris, 75; Recent Int Forms in Art, Biennale of Sydney Art Gallery, Australia. Teaching: Instr drawing & design, Southwestern Col, 70; Santa Monica Col, 72-75. Dealer: Cirrus Gallery 708 N Manhattan Pl Los Angeles CA 90038. Mailing Add: 117 Brooks Ave Venice CA 90291

KISELEWSKI, JOSEPH
SCULPTOR
b Browerville, Minn, Feb 16, 01. Study: Minneapolis Sch Art, 18-21; Nat Acad Design, 21-23; Beaux-Arts Inst Design, 23-25; Am Acad in Rome; Acad Julian, Paris, France. Comn: Harold Vanderbilt (statue), Nashville, Tenn, 65; Moses (statue), Law Col, Syracuse Univ, 66; Sylvanus Thayer bronze bust for Hall of Fame for Great Americans, NY Univ, 66; groups, Bronx Co Ct House, NY; fountain, Huntington Mus, SC; plus others. Awards: Beaux Arts Paris Prize, 25-26; Prix de Rome, 26-29; Elizabeth N Watrous Gold Medal, 37; plus others. Mem: Nat Acad Design; assoc fel Am Acad Rome; fel Nat Sculpture Soc; Archit League New York. Mailing Add: 246 W 80th St New York NY 10024

KISH, MAURICE
PAINTER
b Russia; US citizen. Work: Hermitage Mus, Leningrad, Russia; Brooklyn Mus, NY; Maurice Kish Mus, Ohalo, Israel; Ein Horod Mus, Israel; Mus City of New York; Smithsonian Inst, Washington, DC; Springville Mus, Utah; plus twelve other mus. Exhib: Nat Acad Design, since 32; Corcoran Gallery Art, 37; Pa Acad Fine Arts, 38; Carnegie Inst Fine Arts, 41; Detroit Inst Fine Arts, 59. Awards: Prize for outstanding painting, Coal Towers, 45; Gold Medal for Hills of Sorrow, Am Vet Soc Artists, 63; Minnie R Stern Medal for Street of Forgotten Men, Audubon Artists, 64; Emily Lowe Cash Award for Painting (The Great

Eclipse), 75; Cash Prize, Painters & Sculptors Soc, 76; plus many others. Mem: Allied Artists Am; Audubon Artists; Painters & Sculptors Soc NJ; Conn Acad Fine Arts; Am Vet Soc Artists. Media: Oil. Publ: Auth, The World is My Song, Ykuf, 68. Mailing Add: 417 Brightwater Ct Brooklyn NY 11235

KISKADDEN, ROBERT MORGAN
PAINTER, EDUCATOR
b Tulsa, Okla, Dec 6, 18. Study: Univ Kans, BFA; Ohio Wesleyan Univ, MA. Work: Wichita Art Mus, Kans; Birger Sandzen Mem Gallery, Lindsborg, Kans; Bloomfield Collection, Wichita State Univ; Univ Tex, El Paso Gallery; Kans State Univ Gallery, Manhattan; also in other pub & pvt collections. Exhib: Many local, regional and nat exhibs. Teaching: Prof art, Wichita State Univ, 49-, asst dean, Col Fine Arts, 71- Style & Technique: Paintings of the west. Media: Oil, Watercolor. Mailing Add: 301 N Old Manor Rd Wichita KS 67208

KISNER, BERNARD
COLLECTOR
b Winnipeg, Man, Sept 9, 09; US citizen. Study: Univ Calif, Los Angeles, BA. Pos: Pres, Dice Inc, Decorative Displays, Los Angeles, 56- Collection: Quartzite plates to 36 inches square dated over one billion years, rare find of most colorful patterns yet seen in nature. Publ: Contribr, Terra Calendar, Los Angeles Co Mus Natural Hist, 75. Mailing Add: 1201 S Ogden Dr Los Angeles CA 90019

KISSEL, WILLIAM THORN, JR
SCULPTOR
b New York, NY, Feb 6, 20. Study: Harvard Univ, BA, 44; Pa Acad Fine Arts, 51-53; Barnes Found, Menon, Pa, grad, 53; Rinehart Grad Sch Sculpture, grad, 58, with Sidney Waugh, Cecil Howard & Bruce Moore. Comn: Granite Mem, Montclair, NJ, 56; many bronze animal sculptures, Eastern US, 65-70. Exhib: Mass Sculptor's Exhib, Beverly, Mass, 58; Am Artists Prof League Grand Nat, Lever House, New York, 64 & 66; Nat Acad Design Exhibs, New York, 65-68 & 71; Nat Sculpture Soc Exhibs, Lever House, 67 & 70; Md Arts Coun Exhib & State Tour, 71 & 72. Awards: Speyer Awards, Nat Acad Design, 66 & 68; Am Artists Prof League Award, 66. Bibliog: Article in Am Art Stone, 59; article in La Rev Mod, Paris, 66. Mem: Nat Sculpture Soc; fel Am Artists Prof League; fel Pa Acad Fine Arts; Munic Art Soc New York. Style & Technique: Interpretation of nature and of its forms which I try to arrange onto a harmonious and aesthetic composition. Media: Bronze, Marble. Mailing Add: Owings Mills MD 21117

KITAJ, R B
PAINTER, PRINTMAKER
b Chagrin Falls, Ohio, 32. Study: Ruskin Sch, Univ Oxford, dipl, 60; Royal Col Art, grad, 62. Work: Mus in the US & Europe. Exhib: One-man shows, Los Angeles Co Mus Art, 65, Stedelijk Mus, Amsterdam, 67, Cleveland Mus, 67, Gemeente Mus, Hague, 68, Univ Calif, Berkeley, 68; plus others. Teaching: Vis lectr, Slade Sch, Univ London; vis prof, Univ Calif, Berkeley & Univ Calif, Los Angeles. Mailing Add: c/o Marlborough Gallery 40 W 57th St New York NY 10019

KITNER, HAROLD
EDUCATOR
b May 18, 21; US citizen. Teaching: Prof painting & drawing, Kent State Univ, 47-, chmn painting & sculpture dept, 50-67, chmn sch art, 64-65. Pos: Art critic, Akron Beacon Jour, 48-61; dir, Blossom-Kent Art Prog, 67- Mailing Add: Sch Art Div Painting & Sculpture Kent State Univ Kent OH 44242

KITTA, GEORGE EDWARD
PRINTMAKER, GRAPHIC ARTIST
b Omaha, Nebr, Jan 1, 53. Study: Kansas City Art Inst, BFA. Work: Nelson/Atkins Mus, Kansas City, Mo; Springfield Art Asn, Ill; Stowe Gallery, Davidson Col, NC; Univ NDak, Grand Forks. Exhib: 1st Ann Nat Print Exhib, Municipal Art Gallery, Los Angeles, Calif, 73; 23rd & 24th Nat Exhib of Prints, Smithsonian Inst, Washington, DC, 73 & 75; MidAmerica Five, Nelson/Atkins & St Louis Mus, Mo, 74; Summer Invitational, 74 & 75 & 30 Miles of Art, 75 & 76, Nelson/Atkins Mus, Mo; Strange Sensibilities, Stowe Gallery, Davidson, NC, 75; Spokane Nat Drawing Competition, Chaney Cowles Mus, Wash, 76; Drawing Missouri, Albrecht & Springfield Art Mus, Mo, 76. Awards: Purchase Prize, Mid-America Five, Nelson/Atkins Mus, 74; Jurors Purchase Awards, Davidson Nat, Davidson Col, 74 & 17th NDak Ann, Univ NDak, 74. Bibliog: Benjamin Forgey (auth), A Printmakers Print Show, Art News, 9/76. Style & Technique: Lithographs and recently drawings on paper emphasizing the subtalties of color values through black and white. Media: Pencil and Conte on Paper; Stone Litography. Dealer: Dorry Gates 5321 Belleview Kansas City Mo 64110. Mailing Add: 105 E 41st St Apt 2W Kansas City MO 64111

KITTELSON, JOHN HENRY
PAINTER, SCULPTOR
b Arlington, SDak, July 5, 30. Work: Riversedge Found, Calgary, Alta; Favell Mus, Klamath Falls, Ore. Exhib: Cowboy Artists Am, 66-73; Death Valley Ann Western Art Show, 72-74; Post Tex Ann Western Art Show, 72-74; Nebr Land Days Western Art Show, 72-75; Kansas City Soc Western Art, 74; O S Ranch Art Exhib, 77. Bibliog: Ed Ainsworth (auth), Cowboys in Art, World, 68; John Matthews (auth), How to Become One, Hawthornes of Nottingham, Eng, 73; Patricia Broder (auth), Bronzes of the American West, Abrams, 74. Style & Technique: Western and wildlife sculpture in bronze and wood. Dealer: Husbergs Fine Art Gallery PO Box 966 Sedona AZ 86336. Mailing Add: 3708 Ideal Dr Ft Collins CO 80521

KITZINGER, ERNST
ART HISTORIAN
b Munich, Ger, Dec 27, 12; US citizen. Study: Univ Rome, 31-32; Univ Munich, PhD, 34. Teaching: A Kingsley Porter univ prof, Harvard Univ. Pos: Asst, Brit Mus, London, Eng, 35-40; with Dumbarton Oaks Ctr for Byzantine Studies, Washington, DC, 41-67; mem, Inst Advan Study, Princeton Univ, 66-67. Mem: Medieval Acad Am; Col Art Asn Am; Archeol Inst Am; Ger Archaeol Inst; Am Philos Soc; plus others. Res: Early Christian, Byzantine and medieval art. Publ: Auth, Early Medieval Art in the British Museum, 40; auth, The Mosaics of Monreale, 60; auth, The Art of Byzantium and the Medieval West, Selected Studies, 76; auth, Byzantine Art in the Making, 77. Mailing Add: 7 Waterhouse St Cambridge MA 02138

KIVA, LLOYD
See New, Lloyd H

KJARGAARD, JOHN INGVARD
PAINTER, PRINTMAKER
b Denmark, Sept 13, 02; US citizen. Study: Cooper Union; Calif Sch Fine Arts, San Francisco; Univ Calif, Berkeley; Univ Hawaii, with Joseph Albers. Work: Mint Mus Art, Charlotte, NC; Honolulu Acad Arts, Hawaii; Libr of Cong, Washington, DC; Hawaii State Found Cult & Arts. Comn: Glass mosaic mural, Honolulu Int Airport, Hawaii State Dept Transportation, 72. Exhib: One-man shows, 58, 69 & 74 & First Hawaii Nat Print Exhib, 71, Honolulu Acad Arts, Hawaii; print exhib, Rochester, NY, 62; Mex-Hawaii Exchange Exhib, 68; Pac Cities Loan Exhib, Auckland City Art Gallery, NZ, 71; Contemp Art of Hawaii, Bucharest, Romania, 77. Awards: Watumull Found Purchase Award, 58; Elsie Das Mem Award, 63; Honolulu Printmakers, 66. Mem: Hawaii Painters & Sculptors League; Honolulu Printmakers; Honolulu Acad Arts. Style & Technique: Abstract. Media: Acrylic. Publ: Contribr, mag sect, Los Angeles Times, 54 & 56; contribr, Paradise of the Pacific, 12/58 & 59; contribr, Design Quarterly, 60; contribr, The Hawaii Book, Ferguson, 61; contribr, The technique of collage, 68. Dealer: Downtown Gallery 125 Merchant St Honolulu HI 96813. Mailing Add: 2080 Mauna Pl Honolulu HI 96822

KLABUNDE, CHARLES SPENCER
PRINTMAKER, PAINTER
b Omaha, Nebr, Oct 1, 35. Study: Univ of Nebr at Omaha, BFA, 58; Univ of Iowa, Iowa City, MFA, 62, also studied with Mauricio Lasansky. Work: Mus of Mod Art, New York; Metrop Mus of Art, New York; Whitney Mus of Am Art, New York; Art Inst of Chicago; Philadelphia Mus of Art. Comn: Ed of Prints, Assocs Am Artist, New York, 71, 72 & 74. Exhib: Five Printmakers, Whitney Mus, 70; The Boston Printmakers Exhib, 73-75; Int Compositional Print Exhib, The Print Club, Philadelphia, 75; Vatican Exhib of Am Graphic Artist, Borgia Palace, 76; Int Biennial Exhib of Prints, Tokyo, 76; one-man shows, Sheldon Mem Art Gallery, Nebr, 72, Philadelphia Art Alliance, 73, St Mary's Col of Maryland, 75, Univ of Main at Orono, 75, Assoc Am Artists, New York, 75, Van Straaten Gallery, Chicago, 76 & Franz Badger Gallery, Washington, DC, 76. Teaching: Asst prof printmaking, The Cooper Union, New York, 68-75. Awards: John Simon Guggenheim Fel, 71-72; Purchase Award, Davidson Nat Print and Drawing Competition, 73 & The Print Club, Philadelphia, 75. Style & Technique: Intaglio four color print technique and oil glaze painting technique in surealistic fantasy. Media: Copper Etching and Engraving; Oil on Canvas. Dealer: Assoc American Artists 663 Fifth Ave New York NY 10022. Mailing Add: 68 W Third St New York NY 10012

KLARIN, WINIFRED ERLICK
PAINTER
b Portland, Maine, Dec 8, 12. Study: Portland Mus Fine Art, Hayloft scholar, 30; Vesper George Sch Art, grad, 33; Soc Arts & Crafts, Detroit, 58-60; Wayne State Univ, 58-62; Cranbrook Grad Sch Art, 63. Work: US Libr, State Dept, Washington, DC; Owens-Corning Fiberglass Corp, Toledo, Ohio; Steel Case Corp, Grand Rapids, Mich; First Fed Savings & Loan, Detroit; Masco Corp, Ypsilanti, Mich. Exhib: One-woman shows, Pace Gallery, 66, J B Speed Art Mus, Louisville, Ky, 69, Forsythe Gallery, Ann Arbor, Mich, 67, 69 & 71, Clossons Gallery, Cincinnati, Ohio, 69-71, Main Libr, St Petersburg, 75 & Long Boat Key Art Ctr, Fla, 78; Henry Ford Col, 66; Rackham Gallery & Univ Mich, Ann Arbor, 66-67; Showcase Gallery, Southfield, Mich; Weir Gallery of Fine Arts, Vero Beach, Fla; plus others. Pos: Vis artist, Eckerd Col, St Petersburg, 74-75. Awards: Outstanding Mich Artist, Nat Bank Detroit, 65; two Top Awards—Best in Show, Scarab Club & Palette & Brush, 67. Bibliog: Jean Paul Susser (auth), Art in review, Ann Arbor News, 4/7/67; Jeanette Crane (auth), St Petersburg Independent, 4/10/75; Darcy Arpke (auth), The Islander, Long Boat Key, 1/5/78. Media: Acrylic. Mailing Add: 3947 35th Way 130 St Petersburg FL 33711

KLAVANS, MINNIE
PAINTER, SCULPTOR
b Garrett Park, Md, May 10, 15. Study: Wilson Teachers Col, BSEd, 35; pvt instr in silversmithing, 51-55; painting with Laura Douglas, 58-60; Am Univ, 60-64; with Luciano Penay, 65-70; Corcoran Gallery Art, plastics with Ed McGowin, 70-71. Work: Nat Collection Fine Arts, Smithsonian Inst, White House, Corcoran Gallery Art & Nat Endowment Arts, Washington, DC; Mus Contemp Art, Madrid, Spain; Baltimore Mus Art, Md. Exhib: Corcoran Gallery Art, 65 & 67; Baltimore Mus Art, Md, 67 & 72; Cisneros Gallery, New York, 67; Mus Mod Art, Bilbao, Spain, 69; Chrysler Mus Art, Norfolk, Va, 72. Awards: First Prize for silversmithing, Smithsonian Inst, 53 & 55; Spec Award, Baltimore Mus Art, 67. Mem: Artists Equity Asn. Dealer: Mickelson Gallery 707 G St NW Washington DC 20001. Mailing Add: 2135 Bancroft Pl NW Washington DC 20008

KLAVEN, MARVIN L
PAINTER, EDUCATOR
b Alton, Ill, Apr 8, 31. Study: State Univ Iowa, BA & MFA. Work: Univ Iowa; Millikin Univ; Mayer Collection, Gilman Collection & Ill Bell, Chicago. Exhib: 24 Illinois Artists, 67; Chicago Sun Times Exhib, 68; 21st NMiss Valley Art Exhib, 68; Artists Who Teach, 69; Contemp Am Painting & Sculpture, 69. Teaching: Asst prof drawing, Northern Ill Univ, 59-61; chmn art dept, Millikin Univ, 61- Pos: Dir, Decatur Art Ctr, Ill, 61-69; dir, Kirkland Art Gallery, 69- Awards: Tiffany Found Grant, 64. Media: Acrylic, Silk Screen. Dealer: Gilman Gallery 201 E Ohio St Chicago IL 60611. Mailing Add: Art Dept Millikin Univ Decatur IL 62522

KLEBE, GENE (CHARLES EUGENE)
PAINTER, WRITER
b Philadelphia, Pa, Sept 18, 07. Study: Philadelphia Col Art; Univ Pa. Work: US Navy & Marine Art Gallery, Washington, DC; Farnsworth Mus, Rockland, Maine; Nat Acad Design, New York; Univ Maine, Orono; Maine Nat Bank, Portland. Comn: Combat art, US Navy, 59-77; Maine State series, Maine Nat Bank, Portland, 60-72; Expo '67 mural, State of Maine, 67; sesquicentennial seal, Maine Sesquicentennial Comn, 70. Exhib: Salmagundi Club, 45-77; Am Watercolor Soc, 50-76; Allied Artists Am, 50-74; Acad Artists Asn, 64-76; Nat Acad Design, 69-76. Pos: Pres, Pemaquid Group Artists, 55-; mem, Gov Coun Art & Cult, 65-69; chmn, Maine State Art Comn, 66-71. Awards: Wu-Ject-Key Award, Am Watercolor Soc, 69; Salmagundi Club Award, 71; Franklin Mint Gold Medal, 74. Bibliog: Lew Deitz (auth), Gene Klebe—Maine artist, Down East Mag, 69. Mem: Acad Artists Asn; Am Watercolor Soc; Allied Artists Am; Salmagundi Club; Nat Acad Design. Media: Watercolor. Publ: Co-auth, Penguin family, 64; contribr, Maine through the eyes of her artists, 65; contribr, US Navy combat art, 63-77; auth, Gene Klebe watercolor page, Am Artists Mag, 3/72. Mailing Add: Pemaquid Rd Bristol ME 04539

KLEEMANN, RON
PAINTER
b Bay City, Mich, July 37. Study: Univ Mich, BS(design), 61. Work: Mus of Mod Art, New York; Solomon R Guggenheim Mus, New York; Hirschhorn Mus, Washington, DC; Indianapolis Mus of Art; Univ Va Art Mus. Exhib: Ann Sculpture & Painting Show, San Francisco Mus of Art, 61; Mus of Contemp Art, Chicago, 71; Aldrich Mus of Contemp Art, Ridgefield, Conn, 72; Addison Gallery of Am Art, Andover, Mass, 74; Butler Inst of Am Art, Youngstown, Ohio, 74; Wadsworth Atheneum, Hartford, Conn, 74; Brooks Mem Art Gallery, Memphis, Tenn, 74; Wichita Mus, Wichita State Univ, Kans, 75; New Acquisitions,

Mus of Mod Art, New York, 77; Flint Inst of Fine Arts, 78. Pos: Official Artist, Indianapolis 500, 77- Bibliog: Judy Beardsall (auth), Stuart M Speiser Photorealist Collection, Art Gallery Mag, 10/73; Martin Ries (auth), Ron Kleemann, Arts Mag, 6/74; Andrea Mikotajok (auth), American Realists at Louis K Meisel, Arts Mag, 1/75; Indianapolis News, 4/77; Chicago Tribune, 10/77. Style & Technique: Photo-realist painting. Mailing Add: c/o Louis K Meisel Gallery 141 Prince St New York NY 10012

KLEIDON, DENNIS ARTHUR
EDUCATOR, DESIGNER
b Chicago, Ill, Sept 20, 42. Study: Bradley Univ, Peoria, Ill, 60-61; Univ Ill, Champaign, 61-64; Ill Wesleyan Univ, Bloomington, BFA(com art), 66; Ill State Univ, Normal, MS(sculpture), 67. Work: Massillon Mus, Ohio; Northern Ill Univ, DeKalb; Ill State Univ; Numa Ltd, Akron. Comn: 25 ft commemorative sculpture wall piece (wood, assemblage), Akron Nat Bank & Trust, Tuchman, Canute, Ryan & Wyatt, Architects, Rolling Acres Shopping Ctr, 76; promotional design, Scheeser & Buckley, Inc, Akron, 76; illustration, Hesselbart & Mitten Advert, Akron, 75 & Alsides, Inc, Akron, 75. Exhib: Third Ann Nat Print & Drawing Competition, Northern Ill Univ, 70; Color Print USA, Tex Tech Univ, Lubbock, 71; All-Ohio Exhib, Canton Art Inst, 71 & 72; Images, Nat Drawing Competition, Baldwin Wallace Col, Berea, Ohio, 72; Cleveland Invitational Exhib, Cooper Sch of Art, 72 & Lake Erie Col, 73; one-man shows, Gallery 200, Columbus, Ohio, 75, Massillon Mus, 75 & Akron Art Inst, 76. Teaching: Instr drawing, Univ Ill, Champaign, 67-69; asst prof graphic design, Univ Akron, 69- Pos: Designer/deliniator, Wight & Assoc, Downers Grove, Ill, 65-66 & Richard R Cramer, Architects, Hinsdale, Ill, 67; dir, Kleidon & Assoc, 75- Awards: Res grants, Univ Akron, 70 & 77; First Place/Painting, All-Ohio Exhib, Canton Art Inst, 71; Merit Award/Design, Nat Univ & Col Designers Asn Design Competition, 75. Bibliog: Tex Tech Univ, Color Print USA (filmstrip), 71. Style & Technique: Flat patterned graphic paintings incorporating both figurative and modular geometric subjects. Media: Polymer acrylic and vinyl polymer acrylic on film and board. Dealer: Gallery 200 200 W Mound Columbus OH 43223. Mailing Add: 26 Waterside Dr Medina OH 44256

KLEIMAN, ALAN
PAINTER, SCULPTOR
b Brooklyn, NY, Feb 20, 38. Study: Richmond Prof Inst, BFA; Cranbrook Acad Art, MFA; study with Oscar Kokoschka, Salzburg, Austria. Work: Mus Mod Art, Whitney Mus Am Art & Metrop Mus Art, New York; Carnegie Mus, Pittsburgh, Pa; Boston Mus Fine Art, Mass. Comn: Abstract fresco, Richmond City Fathers, Va, 57; rubber paint pool mural, comn by Mr & Mrs Pechenik, York, Pa, 60; abstract painted wall, Detroit Archit League, Mich, 65; abstract painted wall, City Walls, New York, 72. Exhib: Momentum, Chicago, 56-60; Boston Arts Festival, 59; Biennale, Sao Paulo, Brazil, 68; Silvermine, Conn, 70; Carnegie Inst Int, Pittsburgh, 71. Pos: Asst publicity dir, Artist Tenents Asn, 60-67; vpres, Grand St Artist Group, 70-75; chmn, Soho Artifacts, 71-75. Awards: First Prize for Print, Boston Arts Festival, 59; Creative Artists Pub Serv fel & CETA grant, 78. Bibliog: Hans Van Deljen (auth), Alan Kleiman paints Europe, Frie Folkes, Amsterdam, 56. Style & Technique: All over limitless surface, color involved; sculpture made of oil paint. Media: Watercolor, Oil. Publ: Auth, Painting Provincetown Water, The Beacon, 61; auth, Investigations into the Light of Red Color, Arts, 76; auth, Light Dazzle and Glow, The Soho Artist. Dealer: Area Code Gallery 31 Wooster St New York NY 10013. Mailing Add: 70 Grand St New York NY 10013

KLEIN, BEATRICE T
PAINTER, PRINTMAKER
b Lynchburg, Va, Feb 7, 20. Study: Md Inst Art, cert fine arts; Art Students League, with Yasuo Kuniyoshi; Va Commonwealth Univ; also with Hans Hofmann, Provincetown. Work: Va Mus Fine Arts; Rocky Mount Art Ctr, NC; Philip Morris Co; First & Merchants Nat Bank, Richmond. Comn: Portrait of prof med, Med Col Va, 70; portrait of pres of Va Commonwealth Univ, 75. Exhib: One-man show, Va Mus, 57, Va Printmakers, 75; Anderson Gallery, Va Commonwealth Univ, 73; one-man show of prints, Fells Point Gallery, Baltimore, 75; Va Artist Biennials. Awards: Cert of Distinction, Va Mus Fine Arts, 55 & 57; Third Prize, Anderson Gallery, Va Commonwealth Univ, 73. Mem: Richmond Artists Asn (pres, 65-66). Style & Technique: Poetic realism & semi-abstract realism. Media: Oil, Watercolor; Silk Screen. Dealer: Scott-McKennis Fine Arts 3465 W Cary St Richmo nd VA 23221. Mailing Add: 6401 Three Chopt Rd Richmond VA 23226

KLEIN, CECELIA F
ART HISTORIAN, EDUCATOR
b Pittsburgh, Pa, June 5, 38. Study: Oberlin Col, BA, 60, MA, 67; Columbia Univ, PhD with Douglas Fraser, 72. Collections Arranged: Art of Pre-Columbian Am, Meadow Brook Art Gallery, Oakland Univ, Rochester, Mich, 76. Teaching: Asst prof art hist, Oakland Univ, Rochester, 72-76; asst prof art hist, Univ Calif, Los Angeles, 76- Mem: Col Art Asn. Res: Pre-Columbian art history, with empahsis on Aztec art/iconography. Publ: Contribr, Death and the Afterlife in Pre-Columbian America, Dumbarton Oaks, 75; auth, The Face of the Earth: Frontality in Two-Dimensional Mesoamerican Art, Garland, 76; contribr, The Identity of the central deity on the Aztec calendar, Art Bull, 76. Mailing Add: 4237 Sunnyslope Ave Sherman Oaks CA 91423

KLEIN, DORIS
PAINTER
b New York, NY, Nov 10, 18. Study: Art Students League, with Sidney Gross; Works Progress Admin Sch, with James Leschay & Anton Refregier; also sculpture with Maurice Glickman. Work: Univ Maine Permanent Collection; New Sch Permanent Collection, New York, NY. Exhib: Mus Belles Artes, Arg, 63; Alley Gallery, Houston, Tex, 66; Maxwell Gallery, San Francisco, 67; Audubon Artists, 68; Roko Gallery, New York, 68-72. Awards: Best of Show, Jersey City Mus, 63-66; Marion K Haldenstein Mem Prize, Nat Asn Women Artists, 68; Grumbacher Award, Mamaroneck Artists Guild, 69. Bibliog: Hilton Kramer (auth), Rev of Roko show, New York Times, 68; Betty Chamberlain (auth), Philharmonic Hall program, 72. Mem: Nat Asn Women Artists. Media: Oil. Dealer: Phoenix Gallery 939 Madison Ave New York NY 10021. Mailing Add: 235 W 76th St New York NY 10023

KLEIN, ESTHER M
PATRON, COLLECTOR
b Philadelphia, Pa, Nov 3, 07. Study: Temple Univ, BS; Univ London. Pos; Ed, Philadelphia Art Alliance Bull; art critic, WPEN daily radio prog; founding dir, Long Beach Island Found Arts & Sci, NJ. Awards: Award for art talks on radio, Artists Equity Philadelphia; Gimbel Award, 75; Art Alliance Award of Merit, given jointly to Esther & Philip Klein, 75. Mem: Life mem Pa Acad Fine Arts; life mem Philadelphia Print Club; Philadelphia Art Alliance (comt mem); Color Print Soc (vpres); contrib mem Art Inst Chicago; plus others. Interest: Donor of annual prizes to Print Club and Clothesline Exhibit to encourage young Philadelphia artists. Collection: Philadelphia artists. Publ: Auth, Fairmount Park, History & Guidebook; chap in American Art History Intertwines Park. Mailing Add: 1520 Spruce St Philadelphia PA 19102

KLEIN, MEDARD
PAINTER
b Appleton, Wis, Jan 6, 05. Study: Var art schs, Chicago. Work: Pvt collections in Chicago, New York, Boston, Detroit, Mexico City & others. Exhib: Int Watercolor Show, Art Inst Chicago; Salon Realities Nouvelles; Joslyn Mem Mus, Omaha, Nebr; San Francisco Mus Art; Ill State Mus, Springfield; plus many other group & one-man shows. Media: Oil, Watercolor. Mailing Add: 807 N Wabash 14 Chicago IL 60611

KLEIN, PATRICIA WINDROW
See Windrow, Patricia

KLEIN, SANDOR C
PAINTER, SCULPTOR
b New York, NY, Oct 27, 12. Study: Nat Acad Design; Acad Julien, Paris; Beaux-Arts, Paris; Acad Fine Arts, Vienna; Royal Acad Art, Budapest; Am Acad Rome, fel, 31. Work: Nat Gallery Art, Washington, DC; Albany State Mus, NY; Luxembourg Mus; Coast Guard Acad, New London, Conn; Pentagon, Washington, DC. Comn: Portraits of Hon Schuyler Otis Bland, Chmn Maritime & Fisheries Comn, 46, Gen Nathan F Twining, Chmn Joint Chiefs of Staff, 61 & Gen Curtis E LeMay, USAF Chief of Staff, 62, comn by US Govt; portrait of Eleanor Roosevelt, comn by Am Cancer Soc, 63; portrait of Pres Armand Hammer, Occidental Petrol Co, 67. Exhib: Paris Salon; Carnegie Inst Int; plus others in the US & abroad. Teaching: Instr painting, Nat Acad, New York, Beaux Arts & Acad Julien, Paris. Awards: Pulitzer Prize for Painting, 31; Silver Medal, Paris Salon; medal, Int Biennale, Venice, 32. Style & Technique: Impressionistic, realism. Media: Oil. Mailing Add: 33 W 67th St New York NY 10023

KLEINBAUER, W EUGENE
ART HISTORIAN
b Los Angeles, Calif, June 15, 37. Study: Univ Calif, Berkeley, with Walter Horn, BA & MA, 59; Princeton Univ, with Richard Krautheimer & Kurt Weitzmann, PhD, 67. Teaching: Asst prof hist of art, Univ Calif, Los Angeles, 65-72; prof hist of art, Ind Univ, 77-; Sam & Ayala Zacks vis prof hist of art, Hebrew Univ, Jerusalem, 78. Pos: Chmn dept fine arts, Ind Univ, 73-76, chmn arts admin prog, fall 78; chmn visual arts adv panel, Ind State Art Comn, 75-76. Awards: Nat Endowment for the Humanities Fel for Independent Study & Res, 76-77. Mem: Col Art Asn of Am (mem nominating comt, 75); Int Ctr of Medieval Art (mem bd dir, 70-73 & 74-77); Medieval Acad of Am; US Nat Comt for Byzantine Studies; Soc for Armenian Studies; Archeol Inst of Am, Cent Ind Soc (pres, 77-78). Res: Specialist in late antique and Byzantine art and architecture; historiography of Western art. Publ: Ed, Modern Perspectives in Western Art History, Holt Rinehart, 71; ed, E Kitzinger, Art of Byzantium & Medieval West, Ind Univ, 76. Mailing Add: 2002 Greenbriar Lane Bloomington IN 47401

KLEINHOLZ, FRANK
PAINTER, WRITER
b Brooklyn, NY, Feb 17, 01. Study: Fordham Univ, LLB, 23; Colby Col, Hon DFA; also with Alexander Dobkin, Yasuo Kuniyoshi & Sol Wilson. Work: Metrop Mus Art, New York; Brooklyn Mus, NY; Marquette Univ, Milwaukee, Wis; Mus Mod Art, Tel-Aviv, Israel; Fine Arts Mus, Moscow. Comn: Outdoor mural, Blankman Found, Sands Point, NY, 58. Exhib: Directions in American Painting, Carnegie Inst, Pittsburgh, 41; Artists for Victory, Metrop Mus Art, 42; one-man shows, Assoc Am Artists, New York, 42 & ACA Gallery, Rome, Italy, 65; American Painting Today, Metrop Mus Art, 50. Awards: Sixth Purchase Prize for Back Street, Hearn Fund, Metrop Mus Art, 42; First Prize for Bright Lights, Manhasset Art Asn, 53; First Prize for Prints for Sunflower, YMHA, Miami, 72. Bibliog: Edwin Alden Jewell (auth), Frank Kleinholz holds art show, New York Times, 42; Donald Bear (auth), Contemporary American painting, In: Encycl Britannica, 46; August L Freundlich (auth), Frank Kleinholz, the Outsider, Univ Miami, 69. Style & Technique: Social comment-expressionist. Media: Oil. Publ: Auth, Frank Kleinholz, a Self Portrait, Shorewood Press, 64; auth, Abstract art is dead, Am Dialog, 7/64; auth & illusr, Ile de Brehat—the Flowering Rock, Univ Miami, 71. Dealer: ACA Galleries 25 E 73rd St New York NY 10021. Mailing Add: 21 Second Ave Port Washington NY 11050

KLEINSMITH, BRUCE JOHN
See Nutzle, Futzie

KLEMENT, VERA
PAINTER, EDUCATOR
b Danzig, Poland, Dec 14, 29; US citizen. Study: Cooper Union Sch Art & Archit, grad, 50. Work: Mus Mod Art, New York; Philadelphia Mus Art; Ill State Mus, Springfield; Univ Tex. Comn: Ed of etchings, NY Hilton/Rockefeller Ctr, 61; 27 & 1/2 ft painting, Kemper Ins Co, Long Grove, Ill, 75. Exhib: Modern Art in US, Mus Mod Art Traveling Exhib, New York, 56; NC Mus Art, Raleigh, 60; Print Club, Philadelphia, 62; Art Inst Chicago, 67; Ill State Mus, 74; Walker Art Ctr Invitational, Minneapolis, Minn, 76. Teaching: Instr painting, Univ Ill, 68-69; asst prof art, Univ Chicago, 69- Awards: Emily Lowe Award, NY, 50; Louis Comfort Tiffany Found Award, 54; Longview Found Purchase Award, 61. Bibliog: William S Lieberman (auth), Printmaking & the American woodcut today, Perspectives USA, 53; Museum of Modern Art Calendar, 62; Amy Goldin (auth), Vitality vs greasy kid stuff, Art Gallery Mag 4/72; article in Artists' Writings, publ by NAME, 77. Mem: Participating Artists of Chicago (treas, 66-70); Chicago Artists Coalition; Renaissance Soc (exec bd mem, 75-); Adv Arts Coun, Ill Ctr; The Five. Style & Technique: Abstract, lyrical. Media: Oil on Canvas. Dealer: Marianne Deson Gallery 226 E Ontario Chicago IL 60611. Mailing Add: 5542 S Blackstone Chicago IL 60637

KLEP, ROLF
MUSEUM DIRECTOR, ILLUSTRATOR
b Portland, Ore, Feb 6, 04. Study: Univ Ore, BA; Art Inst Chicago; Grand Cent Sch Art. Work: Baseball Hall of Fame; Univ Ore Mus Art; Haseltine Collection of Northwest Art; Mariner's Mus, Newport; Maritime Mus, City Hall & Pub Libr, Astoria, Ore; plus others. Teaching: Lectr with slide illus throughout Ore, incl Univ Ore Mus Art, 60. Pos: Bd dirs, Friends of the Mus, Univ Ore; bd dirs, Univ Ore Develop Fund, 59-65; founder, pres & dir, Columbia River Maritime Mus, Astoria, Ore, 62- Awards: Watzek Award; Outstanding Citizen Award, Lewis & Clark Col, 77. Style & Technique: Watercolor (with india ink and airbrush for effects in technical illustrations). Publ: Auth & illusr, Album of the great, 37 & The children's Shakespeare, 38; illusr, Beowulf, 41; contribr & illusr, Across the space frontier, 52 & Conquest of the moon, 53; also illusr for nat mag & advert agencies. Mailing Add: Columbia River Maritime Mus Astoria OR 97103

KLINDT, STEVEN
ART ADMINISTRATOR, PHOTOGRAPHER
b Davenport, Iowa, Dec 18, 47. Study: Sch of Art, Univ Iowa, BA(studio art), 70, MA(photog), 74. Work: Art Inst Chicago; Ill State Mus, Springfield; Knox Col, Galesburg,

Ill; Monmouth Col, Ill. Exhib: One-man shows, Davenport Munic Art Gallery, Iowa, 69, Mus Art, Univ Iowa, Iowa City, 74 & Knox Col Gallery, 76; City of Man, Univ Chicago, 70; Contemp Photog, Sheldon Art Gallery, Univ Nebr, Lincoln, 72; Third Ann Photog, Kansas City Art Inst, 73; Ill Photogr 75, Ill State Mus, 75; Photographs by Steven Klindt & Gretchen Garner, St Xavier Col Gallery, Chicago, 76. Collections Arranged: Photograph Invitational, Galesburg Civic Art Ctr, Ill, 76; Proposals for Lake Sculpture, Evanston Art Ctr, Ill, 77. Pos: Dir, Galesburg Civic Art Ctr, 74-76; dir, Evanston Art Ctr, 76- Style & Technique: Sequential and multiple black and white photographs. Media: Photography. Mailing Add: 1028 Wesley Evanston IL 60202

KLINE, ALMA
SCULPTOR
b Nyack, NY. Study: Radcliffe Col, AB; also sculpture with Jose De Creeft. Work: Cronkhite Grad Ctr, Cambridge, Mass; Norfolk Mus Arts & Sci, Va; St Lawrence Univ, NY. Exhib: Women's Int Art Club, London, 55; Nat Asn Women Artists, Mus Bellas Artes, Buenos Aires, 63; one-man shows, Travel Art Guild, 64 (ten shows), Thomson Gallery, New York, 69 & Caravan House Gallery, New York, 76; Soc Animal Artists, Natural Hist Mus, Smithsonian Inst, 71. Awards: Grumbacher Purchase Award, Audubon Artists, 60; Medal of Honor, Knickerbocker Artists, 64; Patrons of Art Award, Painters & Sculptors Soc NJ, 69. Bibliog: Nat Wildlife, 67; Nat Sculpture Rev, 69; The Arthur & Elizabeth Schlesinger Library on the History of Women in America, Cambridge, 74. Mem: Audubon Artists (chmn ways & means, 73); Nat Asn Women Artists (adv, 74); Soc Animal Artists (treas, 73); Knickerbocker Artists; Silvermine Guild Artists. Style & Technique: Simplified realism achieved by carving directly into the stone or wood. Mailing Add: 225 E 74th St New York NY 10021

KLINE, HARRIET
PAINTER, PRINTMAKER
b New York, NY, Sept 25, 16. Study: Hunter Col, BA; also with Isaac Soyer, 45-59; Art Students League, with Robert Philipp & Morris Kantor; China Inst, NY, with Prof Y C Wang. Work: Art Collection, NY Univ; State Univ NY Col Oswego; Western New Eng Col. Exhib: Art USA, 58; Silvermine Nat Exhib, Silvermine Guild, New Canaan, Conn, 59; Nat Asn Women Artists, Nat Acad, New York, 59 ; 38th Ann, Butler Inst Am Art, 74; var one man shows, 60- Awards: Gene Alden Walker Prize Watercolor, Ann Nat Asn Women Artists, 70; Alice Standish Buell Prize Graphics, Ann Nat Asn Women Artists, 72 & Aileen O Webb Prize Watercolor, 75; Laura M Gross Prize Watercolor, 24th Ann Silvermine Exhib, New Eng, 73. Mem: Nat Asn Women Artists (mem graphics jury, 75-76, chmn mem juries, 76-); Silvermine Guild Artists; Artists Equity Asn; Greenwich Art Soc; Am Soc Contemp Artists; Hudson River Contemp Artists; life mem Art Students League; Mamaroneck Artists Guild. Style & Technique: Landscapes in watercolors with geometric forms, on canvas with Plexiglas and in etching. Media: Oil, Watercolor, Etching. Dealer: Contemp Masters Galleries 655 Madison Ave New York NY 10021. Mailing Add: 390 Heathcote Rd Scarsdale NY 10583

KLITGAARD, GEORGINA
PAINTER, MURALIST
b New York, NY, July 3, 93. Study: Barnard Col, Columbia Univ; Nat Acad Design; Art Students League. Work: Metrop Mus Art & Whitney Mus Am Art, New York; Newark Mus, NJ; New Brit Mus Art, Conn; Dayton Art Mus, Ohio. Comn: Old Poughkeepsie, Poughkeepsie Post Off, NY; painting, Goshen Post Off, NY; landscape, Pelham Post Off, Ga; two landscapes, Chesapeake & Ohio RR. Exhib: Six one-man shows, Rehn Galleries, New York, 29-61, Woodstock, NY, 56-60 & one-man traveling show, Col Art Asn Am, 45; Pan-Am Exhib, San Francisco, 33; Pa Acad Fine Arts, 33-45. Teaching: Instr painting, Durham Sch Painting, 45-46. Awards: Guggenheim Fel, 35; Huntington Fel, 65-66; Wirlitzer Found Award, 68-70; plus others. Bibliog: J P Slusser (auth, G K, 38; Ray Bethers (auth), How Paintings Happen, Norton, 51; Kay Klitgaard (auth), Through the American Landscape, Univ NC Press. Mem: Audubon Artists; Woodstock Artists Asn; MacDowell Colony. Media: Oil, Watercolor. Publ: Contribr, Meet the artist & The art of the artist. Dealer: Rehn Galleries 655 Madison Ave New York NY 10021. Mailing Add: Bearsville NY 12409

KLITZKE, THEODORE ELMER
ART HISTORIAN
b Chicago, Ill, Nov 4, 15. Study: Art Inst Chicago, BFA, 40; Univ Chicago, BA, 41, PhD, 53. Teaching: Instr art hist, Univ Chicago, 46-47; asst prof art hist, State Univ NY Col Ceramics, Alfred Univ, 53-59; prof art hist & chmn dept art, Univ Ala, Tuscaloosa, 59-68. Pos: Vpres acad affairs & dean, Md Inst Col Art, 68-77, actg pres, 77- bd dirs, Nat Asn Schs Art, 71-74; chmn planning comt, Union of Independent Col of Art, 77- Mem: Am Studies Asn; Col Art Asn Am; Soc Archit Historians; Southeastern Col Art Conf. Res: Social history of American art; 19th century French art; history of prints and drawings. Publ: Contribr, reviews in Col Art J & Art Bull, 59-; contribr, Alexis de Tocqueville and the arts in America, Festschrift Ulrich Middeldorf, 68; auth, Melville Price retrospective: 1920-1970, Frame House Gallery, 70; contribr, Hermann Wilhelm (catalog), 72. Mailing Add: 1300 Mt Royal Ave Baltimore MD 21217

KLONER, JAY MARTIN
ART HISTORIAN, ART ADMINISTRATOR
b New York, NY, Sept 14, 38. Study: Yeshiva Univ, BA & BHL; Columbia Univ, MA & PhD. Teaching: Assoc prof art hist & humanities, Col Arts & Sci, Univ Louisville, Ky, 64-, actg dir, Allen R Hite Art Inst, 72-73 & dir, 73-77. Res: The influence of Japanese prints on modern art; history of photography. Mailing Add: Allen R Hite Art Inst Univ Louisville Louisville KY 40208

KLONIS, STEWART
PAINTER, ART DIRECTOR
b Naugatuck, Conn, Dec 24, 01. Study: Art Students League. Work: IBM Collection & many pub & pvt collections. Exhib: Am Watercolor Soc; Century Asn. Teaching: Instr, Queens Col, 40-45; exec dir, Art Students League, 46- Awards: Gari Melchers Award, Artists Fellowships Inc, 75. Mem: Munic Art Soc; Nat Arts Mus Sports (trustee, 63-); Benjamin Franklin fel Royal Soc Arts (hon corresp secy of State NY, 75); MacDowell Colony (bd dirs); Inst Int Educ (adv comt for arts, 61-). Media: Watercolor. Mailing Add: 215 W 57th St New York NY 10019

KLOPFENSTEIN, PHILIP ARTHUR
PAINTER, ART ADMINISTRATOR
b Lake Odessa, Mich, Apr 28, 37. Study: Mich State Univ, with Abraham Ratner & Linsey Decker, BFA; Western Mich Univ, with Harry Hefner, MFA; Harvard Univ, Arts Admin Cert. Work: Russellville Pub Schs, Ark. Exhib: State Ark Educ Dept Traveling Exhib, 76-; Mid Southern Watercolor Soc Ann. Collections Arranged: John Henry Byrd (1840-1880), Southeast Ark Arts & Sci Ctr, Pine Bluff, 70; Ernest Trova One-Man Exhib, 71. Teaching: Instr, Paw Paw Pub Sch, Mich, 63-65; instr painting, watercolor & art educ, Little Rock Univ, 65-68. Pos: TV writer & teacher, Ark Educ TV, Conway, 68-69; dir, Southeast Ark Arts & Sci Ctr, 70-; exec dir, Augusta Richmond Co Mus, Ga, currently. Mem: Am Asn Mus; Southeastern Mus Conf (regional rep, 74-75); Mid Southern Watercolor Soc (exhib chmn, 73); Jefferson Co Hist Comn (trustee, 73-76). Style & Technique: Landscape painter after the style of John Marin. Media: Watercolor. Res: John Henry Byrd. Publ: Auth, John Henry Byrd (1840-1880), 71; auth, Childrens Gallery Education: A Report, 75. Mailing Add: 405 Brookside Rd Augusta GA 30904

KLOSS, GENE (ALICE GENEVA GLASIER)
ETCHER, PAINTER
b Oakland, Calif, July 27, 03. Study: Univ Calif, Berkeley, AB(hon in art), 24; Calif Sch Fine Arts, 24-25; Calif Sch Arts & Crafts. Work: Libr of Cong, Washington, DC; Metrop Mus Art, New York; Carnegie Inst, Pittsburgh; Pa Acad Fine Arts, Philadelphia; Nat Gallery, Washington, DC; Smithsonian Inst, Washington, DC; NY Pub Libr; Honolulu Mus Fine Arts; WTex Mus; Mus NMex; San Francisco Art Mus; San Diego Mus Fine Arts; Mus Tokyo, Japan. Comn: Prints, Soc Print Connoisseurs, New York, 49; prints, Print Club Albany, NY, 52; prints, Soc Am Graphic Artists, New York, 53; prints, Print Makers Calif, Los Angeles, 56. Exhib: Three Centuries of Art in United States (in collab with Mus Mod Art, New York), Paris, 38; Nat Acad Design Ann, New York, 50-; Embassy Bldg, New Delhi, India, 61; Soc Am Graphic Artists, yearly; The West by Members of the National Academy of Design, Phoenix Art Mus, Ariz, 72; Three Am Regionalist Printmakers, Pratt Graphic Ctr, NY, 76; plus one-man shows. Awards: Eyre Gold Medal, Pa Acad Fine Arts, 36; Henry B Shope Prize, Soc Am Graphic Artists, 51; First Prize, Chicago Soc Etchers, 52; Purchase Award, Libr of Cong, 53; Fower Prize, Print Club of Albany, 60 & Purchase Prize, 61; anonymous prize, Nat Acad Design, 61. Bibliog: Mary Carrol Nelson (auth), Intaglios by Gene Kloss, Am Artist, 2/78. Mem: Nat Acad Design (academician); Soc Am Graphic Artists; Philadelphia Watercolor Club; Albany Print Club. Media: Oil, Watercolor, Etchings. Mailing Add: Box 33 Taos NM 87571

KLOSTY, JAMES MICHAEL
PHOTOGRAPHER, WRITER
b New York, NY, Feb 9, 43. Study: Brandeis Univ, BA; Sch Arts, NY Univ, MFA. Exhib: Photographs 1968-1972, Leo Castelli Gallery, 75; MC equals E squared, Traveling Photo Exhib, Independent Curators Inc, 75; one-man exhibs, Int Ctr Photog, New York, 76, Art Gallery Ont, Toronto, 77, Am Cult Ctr, Paris, France, 77 & Harcus Krakow Gallery, Boston, Mass, 78. Pos: Cinematographer, House Party, 74 & Dune Dance, 75. Style & Technique: Straightforward photography. Publ: Auth, Cunningham & the critics, Ballet Rev, 71; photogr-ed, Merce Cunningham, Sat Rev Press/Dutton, 75; plus photog in var publ including New York Times, America & numerous bks; auth, Venice Waltzes (film), 78. Mailing Add: Mountain House Springhill Farm Millbrook NY 12545

KLOTZ-REILLY, SUZANNE RUTH
PAINTER, SCULPTOR
b Shawno, Wis, Oct 15, 44. Study: Washington Univ, St Louis, 62-64; Kansas City Art Inst, 64-66, BFA, 66; Univ Mo, Kansas City, 66-67; Tex Tech Univ, 70-72, MFA, 72. Work: Minn Mus Art, St Paul; Minneapolis Mus Art, Minn; Mus of Art, La Grange, Ga; Lannan Found, Palm Beach, Fla; Okla Art Ctr, Oklahoma City; Tulsa City Co Libr; Abilene Fine Arts Mus, Tex; Fred & Mary Marer Collection of Contemp Ceramics, Los Angeles, Calif. Exhib: Scripps Col, Claremont, Calif, 72; Artists Biennial, New Orleans Mus Art, City Park, New Orleans, 73; Drawings USA, Minn Mus Art, St Paul, 73; Drawings, Dallas Mus of Fine Arts, Tex, 73; Group Exhib, Fairtree Contemp Crafts, New York, NY, 74 & Folk Roots in Contemp Art, Fairtree Gallery, New York, 75; NY State Craftsman, Inc, I Miller Co, New York, 75; Boxes, John Michael Kohler Art Ctr, Sheboygan, Wis, 77; Magical Mystery Tour, Barnsdale Munic Art Gallery, Calif, 77; Women Painters, Loyola Mus of Art, Ariz & Calif, 78; one-woman show, Scottsdale Ctr for the Arts, Ariz, 78. Teaching: Instr painting, drawing & design, Angelo State Univ, San Angelo, Tex, 72-75; asst prof drawing & design, Scripps Col, Claremont, Calif, 76-78. Awards: Circuit, Zeul, Dallas Mus Fine Arts, 72; Purchase Award, At Leisure, Ga Asn Advan Art, 73; Purchase Award, The Pet Shop, La Grange, Ga Nat Sculpture Competition, 75; Craftsman Fel, Nat Endowment Arts, 76; Award, Nat Crafts Exhib, Scottsdale Ctr for the Arts, Ariz, 77. Bibliog: Hubert Crehan (auth), Dream houses & fanciful creatures of Suzanne Klotz, St Louis Post Dispatch, Mo, 74; Berman & Pinto (auths), Creative Exploration Series, Merrick, 75. Style & Technique: Painting and patches of stitchery; sculptures consist of clay, wood, cloth, acrylic, bird wings, animal legs and teeth. Media: Acrylic, Mixed Painting Media; Clay, Wood in Sculpture. Publ: Co-auth (with Jeffrey Powers), Everything's the Same, Country Western Press, 77. Mailing Add: Art Off Scripps Col Claremont CA 91711

KLUVER, BILLY (JOHAN WILHEM KLUVER)
ART ADMINISTRATOR, TECHNICAL CONSULTANT
b Monaco, Nov 13, 27; Swedish citizen. Study: Royal Inst Technol, Stockholm, EE; Univ Calif, Berkeley, PhD(elec eng). Collaborative Work: Mus Mod Art, New York; Kunsthaus, Zurich, Switz; Centre George Pompidou, Paris, France; Mus Ludwig, Cologne, WGer. Collections Arranged: Four Americans, Mod Museet, Stockholm, 62; Art 1963—A New Vocabulary (cur), Arts Coun YMHA, Philadelphia, 62; American Pop-Art, Mod Museet, Stockholm, 64; Some More Beginnings (cur), Brooklyn Mus, NY, 68; The New York Collection for Stockholm, Mod Museet Stockholm, 73. Pos: Mem tech staff, Bell Tel Lab, Murray Hill, NJ, 58-68; co-founder & pres, Experiments in Art and Technol, 66- Awards: Royal Order of Vasa, New York Collection for Stockholm, Govt Sweden, 74. Bibliog: Jill Johnston (auth), Marmelade Me, E P Dutton, 71; Douglas Davis (auth), Art and The Future, Praeger, 73; Calvin Tomkins (auth), The Scene, Viking Press, 76. Activities: Ongoing technical consultation and collaborations with painters, sculptors, dancers, musicians and theater performers. Publ: Ed, International Anthology of Contemporary Engraving, Galleria Schwarz, Vol 5 (1964); contribr, The Machine, Mus Mod Art, New York, 68; contrib, Scienza Tecnica 71, In: Enciclopedia Della Scienze E Della Tecnica, 72; contribr & ed, Pavilion, Dutton, 72; ed, Experiments in Art and Technology Bibliog 1966-1977, 78. Mailing Add: 49 E 68th St New York NY 10021

KNAPP, SADIE MAGNET
PAINTER, SCULPTOR
b New York, NY, July 18, 09. Study: NY Training Sch Teachers, lic; City Col New York; Brooklyn Mus Art Sch; Atelier 17; Sculpture Ctr. Work: Ga Mus Art, Athens; Norfolk Mus Art, Va; Riverside Mus, New York. Exhib: Corcoran Gallery Art, Washington, DC; Baltimore Mus; Pa Acad Fine Arts, Philadelphia; Butler Inst Art, Youngstown, Ohio; plus others in Can, Eng, France, Switz, Arg, Mex, Japan, India, Scotland & Italy. Collections Arranged: Exchange exhibs arranged for women artists of Japan, 60 & artists of Argentina, 65 & Nat Asn Women Artists—both exhibs shown in var foreign & domestic mus. Teaching: Instr enamels, Worcester Crafts Ctr, 63. Awards: Awards for Paintings, Baltimore Mus, 56, 58 & 61; Award for Painting, Silvermine Guild Artists, 65; Grumbacher Award for Painting,

Nat Acad Design, 68; Awards (two), Am Heritage Art Exhib, 77. Mem: Nat Asn Women Artists (vpres, 61-65, pres, 65-67); Nat Soc Painters in Casein & Acrylics (treas); Am Soc Contemp Artists; Artists Craftsmen New York; Artists Equity Asn. Mailing Add: 162 Somerset H West Palm Beach FL 33409

KNAPP, TOM
SCULPTOR, PAINTER
b Gillette, Wyo, Sept 28, 25. Study: Santa Rosa Jr Col, Calif; Calif Col Arts & Crafts, Oakland; Art Ctr Sch, Los Angeles. Work: Whitney Gallery Western Art, Cody, Wyo; Indianapolis Mus Art; Heritage Libr, Bank of Alaska, Anchorage; Mescelero Tribe, Mescalero Indian Reservation, NMex; Midland Nat Bank Collection, Tex. Comn: Paul Stock Mem, Stock Found, Cody, Wyo, 72; Bronze Plaque of Sen Quinn, Quinn Mem Auditorium, Mass, 73; Larry Mahan, Oil City Brass Works, Beaumont, Tex, 74. Exhib: Davidson Col Nat Print & Drawing Competition, Davidson Col, 73; Jinx Gallery, El Paso, Tex, 74; Maxwell Gallery, San Francisco, 74; Wichita Art Asn, Kans, 75; Kermizaar Prof Invitational, El Paso, 75. Teaching: Instr painting, Carrizo Lodge Workshop, Ruidoso, NMex, 72-74, instr sculpture, 73-75; instr, Las Cruces Art Asn Sculpture Workshop, NMex, 73. Pos: Owner, Buckhorn Bronze Foundry, Ruidoso Downs, NMex, 71- Awards: Best of Show Bronze, Sacramento Indian Art Show, 74; First Place Indian Art, Great Western Exhib Ctr, Los Angeles, 74; First Place Bronze, San Diego Indian Art Show, 74. Bibliog: Ellen Wetzal (auth), Sculptor at Work, TV Doc, NMex State Univ, 73; Barbara Funkhouser (auth), A sculptor casts his bronzes, El Paso Sun Dial Mag, 74; Marilyn Watson (auth), Pouring in the Hondo Valley, NMex Mag, 2/78. Style & Technique: Recording the modern Western, Indian and Alaska scene searching for new approaches to old problems, both in sculpture and painting. Media: Bronze; Drawing. Dealer: Maxwell Gallery 551 Sutter St San Francisco CA 94102; Peterson Gallery 9433 Wilshire Blvd Beverly Hills CA 90212. Mailing Add: Box 510 Ruidoso Downs NM 88346

KNAUB, RAYMOND L
PAINTER, INSTRUCTOR
b Gering, Nebr, July 6, 40. Study: Baylor Univ, 58-60; Univ Nebr, Lincoln, BFA, 63; Univ Colo, Boulder; also with Frederick Mizen, David Seyler & Frank Sampson. Comn: United Bank of Colo; Dixon Paper Co; Empire Savings & Loan, Denver, Colo; WTex Mus Asn Collection. Exhib: Denver Art Mus, 72 & 73; 20th Nat Soc Painters Acrylic & Casein, New York, 73; 61st Allied Artists Am, New York, 74; Rocky Mountain Nat Watermedia Exhib, Golden, Colo, 75; Colo Exhib, Aruada Cult Ctr, Colo, 77. Teaching: Instr art, Jefferson Co Schs, Lakewood, Colo, 68-; instr art, Community Col Denver, 71-73. Style & Technique: Landscapes, figures and animals. Media: Watercolor; Acrylic. Mailing Add: 859 S Miller Ct Lakewood CO 80226

KNEE, GINA (MRS ALEXANDER BROOK)
PAINTER, ETCHER
b Marietta, Ohio, Oct 31, 98. Work: Guild Hall, East Hampton, NY; Johnson Collection, Univ NMex, Albuquerque; Denver Art Mus, Colo; Phillips Art Gallery, Washington, DC; Buffalo Fine Arts Acad, NY. Exhib: Guild Hall Ann, 50-71; Willard Gallery, New York & Pyramid Gallery, Washington, DC, 55; Metrop Mus Art, New York, 59; Newark Mus, NJ, 65; Larcada Gallery, New York, 73; Skidmore Col, Saratoga Springs, NY, 73. Awards: First Prize, Calif Watercolor Soc, 38; First Prize, Nat Oil Exhib, New Orleans, La, 47; First Prize, Guild Hall Exhib, 63. Bibliog: Sidney Janis (auth), Abstract and Surrealist Art in America, Reynal & Hitchcock, 44; Van Deren Coke (auth), Taos and Santa Fe, 1882-1942, Amon Carter Mus, 63. Mem: Artists Equity Asn; Guild Hall. Media: Watercolor, Oil, Etchings. Dealer: Rehn Gallery 655 Madison Ave New York NY 10021. Mailing Add: Box 1092 Sag Harbor NY 11963

KNERR, SALLIE FROST
PAINTER, PRINTMAKER
b Plattsburg, Mo, Apr 7, 14. Study: Univ Mo; Cincinnati Acad Com Art; Corcoran Sch Art; Canal Zone Jr Col; Nat Acad Design; Am Univ; George Washington Univ, BA, 64; Univ Ga, scholarship for travel-study in Mex & Guatamala, 67, MFA, 68. Work: Biblioteca Nac, Panama; Greenville News Piedmont, SC. Exhib: Contemporary Artists of South Carolina, Greenville Co Mus Art & Gibbes Gallery Art, Charleston, SC, 70; La Watercolor Soc 3rd Int Show, 71; 13th Dixie Ann Montgomery Mus Fine Arts, Ala, 72; Prints from the Persian Suite (travelling exhib, including Iran), Iran-Am Soc, 77; Old Masters & Contemp Printmakers, Huntsville Mus of Art, Ala, 77. Teaching: Asst prof art, Baptist Col Charleston, 68-70; instr, Gibbes Gallery Sch. Awards: First in watercolor, Marshall Award Show, Art League Northern Va, 62; hon mention for woodcut, SC Guild Artists Show, Greenville, 65; Award of Merit, Coastal Carolina Fair, 70. Bibliog: Jack Morris & Robert Smeltzer (auths), Contemporary artists of South Carolina, Greenville Co Mus Art, 70; Louise & Paul Trescott (auths), Sallie Frost Knerr, printmaker, Sandlapper Mag, 2/70; John D Morse (auth), Prints of America, Winterthur Mus, 70. Mem: Carolina Art Asn; Charleston Artists Guild; Southeastern Graphics Coun. Style & Technique: Simplicity, clarity, simplest means for technique. Media: Watercolor, Serigraph. Publ: Illusr, The student pilot's training primer, Knerr, 41. Mailing Add: c/o Knerr Corp Box 335 Isle of Palms SC 29451

KNIEF, JANET (HELEN JEANETTE)
PAINTER
b Brooklyn, NY, July 16, 09. Study: Art Students League, with Bridgeman, l'Olinsky & S Dickinson; Brooklyn Mus Art Sch, with Victor Candell, David Stone Martin; Nat Acad Sch, with Robert Phillip; Phoenix Sch Design; Pratt Inst. Work: Work in over 200 private collections. Comn: Portraits, pres of Flushing Savings Bank, NY, 54, police comnr, Nassau Co Police Dept, 55, seven grandchildren, comn by Mrs John Ryan, Baldwin, NY, 64-74, Phillip Chasin, shown in his honor at Waldorf Astoria Dinner, 74 & Mr B C Cobb, comn by Mrs Carl Miller, New York, 74. Exhib: Brooklyn Mus, NY, 57; Long Beach Arts Asn, NY, 69-70; Nat Acad Gallery, New York, 70-71; Lever House, Union Carbide, NY, 71-72; Garden City Galleries, Kans, 75; plus several one-man shows. Teaching: Pvt adult classes, 68-72. Awards: Numerous, including First Prize, Kathy, Malverne Artists Long Island, 68; First Prize, Walled Garden & Second Prize, The Garden, Long Beach Art Asn, 70. Bibliog: Catharine L Wolfe (auth), Jeanne Paris, Long Island Press, 71. Mem: Catharine Lorillard Wolfe Art Club; Malverne Artist Long Island; Art League Nassau Co; Long Beach Art Asn (bd dirs). Style & Technique: Landscapes in oils; palette knife and brush portraits in pastels and oils; graphics touch of impressionism with realism and abstract combined. Media: Oil, Pastel. Publ: Articles in Long Island Press, 58, Long Island New Owl, 58-75, Malverne Herald, 68, Long Island Entertainer & Nassau Star & Independent, 71. Dealer: Mrs Harry Glosner 345 E 81st St New York NY 10028. Mailing Add: 154 Fonda Rd Rockville Centre NY 11570

KNIFFIN, RALPH GUS
PEN AND INK ARTIST
b San Carlos Reservation, Ariz, Nov 21, 46. Study: Inst Am Indian Art, Santa Fe, NMex, degree of completion; study with Allan Houser, Charles Loloma, Otellie Loloma & Fritz Scholder. Work: Gila Co Court House, Globe, Ariz; Sentry Ctr, Scottsdale, Ariz; San Carlos Indian Hosp, Ariz; Universal Homes, Phoenix, Ariz; United Bank, Tempe & Phoenix, Ariz. Exhib: All Indian Art Show, Gallery La Luz, Alamagordo, NMex, 74; Scottsdale Nat Indian Art Exhib, Scottsdale, Ariz, 75 & 76; Nat Indian Art Show, Heard Mus, Phoenix, Ariz, 76; Invitational in Drawing, Heard Mus, Phoenix, Ariz, 77. Awards: Best of Show, Gallery La Luz, Alamagordo, NMex, 74; First Place, Scottsdale Nat Art Exhib, Ariz, 76; First Place Spec in Graphics, Heard Mus, Phoenix, Ariz, 76. Bibliog: Articles in Carefree Enterprise, 74 & Phoenix Cent News, 75; Maggie Wilson (auth), New Artist Stunned by Limelight Status, Ariz Repub, 76. Style & Technique: Figurative spirit faces and animals in sensitive lines with dramatic design. Media: Pen and ink drawings with prisma color highlights on 100% rag board. Mailing Add: c/o Gallery 3 3819 N Third St Phoenix AZ 85012

KNIGHT, FREDERIC CHARLES
PAINTER
b Philadelphia, Pa, Oct 29, 98. Study: Pa Mus Sch Indust Art, cert; State of Pa scholar, 16, cert grad, 20; also in France & Italy, 26. Work: Rockefeller Collection, Dartmouth Col, NH; Everhart Mus, Scranton, Pa; Univ Ariz Mus, Tucson; Berkshire Mus, Pittsfield, Mass; Schenectady Mus, NY. Comn: Murals in lobby of post off, Johnson City, NY, Treas Art Proj, Washington, DC, 38. Exhib: Contemp Am Art, Whitney Mus Am Art, New York, 33-48; Biennial Exhib Contemp Am Oil Paintings, Corcoran Gallery Art, Washington, DC, 35-51; Pa Acad Fine Arts Ann, 38-62; Painting in the US, Carnegie Inst Int, Pittsburgh, Pa, 41-45; one-man shows, Berkshire Mus, Pittsfield, Mass, 67, 72 & 78, Albany Inst Hist & Art, NY, 68, Boyer Col, Tucson, Ariz, 70, Simon's Rock Col, Barrington, Mass, 74 & Caravan House Galleries, New York, 77. Schenectady Mus, 75. Teaching: Asst prof drawing & painting, Newcomb Sch Art, Tulane Univ La, 43-46; from lectr to asst prof drawing & painting, Columbia Univ, 46-64. Pos: Pres, An Am Group, Inc, New York, 33-40; chmn, Artists Coord Comt, New York, 37-40; chmn exhib comt, Columbia Univ, 54-64, dept rep painting & sculpture, 60- Awards: First Prize for drawing & spec award for gen excellence, Pa Mus Sch Indust Art, 20; First Prize for painting, Woodstock Artists Asn, 33. Bibliog: Edward Bruce & Forbes Watson (auths), Art in federal buildings, Vol I, Art Fed Bldgs, 36. Mem: Am Asn Univ Prof. Style & Technique: Figurative, landscape and still life, also drawings of the nude. Media: Oil. Publ: Contribr, The Art of the Artist, Crown, 51. Mailing Add: RD Box 124B Canaan NY 12029

KNIGHT, HILARY
ILLUSTRATOR, DESIGNER
Study: Art Students League. Publ: Illusr, Sunday Morning, 68, auth & illusr, Sylvia the Sloth, 69 & illusr, Angie, 71, Harper & Row; illusr, Child's Book of Natural History, Platt, 69; auth, Mother Goose, Western, 73; plus others. Mailing Add: 300 E 51st St New York NY 10022

KNIGHT, JACOB JASKOVIAK
PAINTER, ILLUSTRATOR
b Worcester, Mass, Feb 26, 38. Study: Self-taught. Work: West Point Pepperell, New York; General Electric Co; Rockefeller Collection, New York; Hugh Heffner Collection; Exxon, New York. Exhib: One-man shows, Peterson Gallery, Nantucket, Mass, 69, Green Mountain, Green St, New York, 70, Irvin Brenner, New York, 71, Fairfield Univ, Conn, 72, Maison Bernard Gallery, Caracas, Venezuela, 73, Soc of Illusr, New York, 73, Worcester Art Mus, 74, Art Dir Club, New York, 74, Main St Gallery, Nantucket, Mass, 75 & Hubris Gallery, New York, 78. Bibliog: Fred Karden (auth), The Artist as His Own Man, Worcester Telegram & Gazette, Mass, 69; Leslie Powell (auth), Art: Primative, The Villager, Greenwich Village, 70; Valerie Brooks (auth), Love & Magic: The Naive Style in Illus, Print Mag, Washington, DC, 74. Style & Technique: Primative, surreal, dream fantasies; oil and acrylic on canvas and wood. Media: Oil and Acrylic. Publ: Illusr, What's gone right with the United Nations, Vista, UN Mag, 73; illusr, All things bright and beautiful, McCalls, 74; illusr, We must decide which species will go on forever, Smithsonian, 76; illusr, A very quiet horror, Playboy, 77. Mailing Add: Wigwam Hill West Brookfield MA 01585

KNIGHT, THOMAS LINCOLN, JR
EDUCATOR, PHOTOGRAPHER
b Oakland, Calif, June 17, 25. Study: Humboldt State Col, with Reese Bullen & Melvin Schuler, BA, 50, MA, 56; Calif Col Arts & Crafts, with Louis Miljarak; Mexico City Col, with Madame C Cueto. Work: Humboldt State Univ. Exhib: Focus Gallery, San Francisco, 66, 67 & 73; US Arts Comn Photog Exhib, Smithsonian Inst, Washington, DC, 68; one-man show, Photography Europe, Univ Nev, Reno, 70 & Ameka Gallery, Arcata, Calif, 77; US Arts Comn Int Traveling Exhib, 70; The Variety Show, Western Asn Art Mus Traveling Exhib, 73-74. Teaching: Prof photog & art, Humboldt State Univ, 56-; vis prof photog, Univ Nev, Reno, summers 68 & 69; vis prof photog, Grand Valley State Col, summer 71. Awards: Earthquake Feature Photog, Assoc Press, West Coast, 56; Smiling Man Photograph, Mex Govt, 74; Mexico Photog, Redwood Arts Asn, Eureka, Calif, 75. Bibliog: Judy Vaughn (auth), Get a girl-teach a class, Bonanza Mag, San Francisco Chronicle, 2/2/64; Margery Mann (auth), Process or pure trends in photography, Popular Photog, 6/74. Mem: Soc Photog Educ; Humboldt Arts Coun. Style & Technique: Straight and process photography. Publ: Photog Prize winning homes by Wm Van Fleet, AIA, Archit Rec, 11/64; photog, Anza's bones in Arizona, J of the West, Vol VII, No 3; photog (back cover), Imogene Cunningham & Margery Mann's Imogene Cunningham-Photographs, Univ Wash, 70; photog, Travel Guide to Mexico, Sunset Bks, 74; contribr (cover & portfolio), Brit J Photog, 3/77; plus others. Dealer: Focus Gallery 2146 Union St San Francisco CA 94123. Mailing Add: 76 California St Arcata CA 95521

KNIGIN, MICHAEL JAY
PAINTER, PRINTMAKER
b Brooklyn, NY, Dec 9, 42. Study: Tyler Sch Art, BFA. Work: Whitney Mus Art, New York; Nat Collection Fine Arts, Washington, DC; NY Univ; Albright-Knox Art Gallery, Buffalo; Mus Graphic Arts, New York. Exhib: Smithsonian Inst, Washington, DC, 69; Osaka World's Fair, Japan, 70; Albright-Knox Art Gallery, 70; Mus Mod Art Lending Serv, New York, 71; Recent Acquisitions, Whitney Mus Am Art, New York, 71. Teaching: Asst prof graphics, Pratt Inst. Awards: Ford Found Grant, Tamarind Lithography Workshop, 64; MLA-ALA Lithographic Tech Inst Award, 69. Bibliog: A note on the frontispiece, Artists Proof, 71. Publ: Co-auth, The Technique of Fine Art Lithography, 70; auth, Local Choice, Pratt Graphics Ctr, 72; auth, Lithographics Workshops Around the World. Mailing Add: 832 Broadway New York NY 10003

KNIPSCHER, GERARD ALLEN
PAINTER
b New York, NY, July 9, 35. Study: Calif Col Arts & Crafts, BFA (with honors); Acad Art, San Francisco; Sch Fine Art, San Francisco; Sch Visual Arts; also with Richard Diebenkorn, David Leffel. Work: Calif Col Arts & Crafts, Oakland, Calif; NACAL Operation Palette, US Navy Combat Art Collection. Comn: Launch US second moon shot, Apollo XII, US Navy Combat Art, Washington, DC, 69; Navy Amphibious Exercise Operation Exotic Dancer,

Onslow Beach, NC, 74; portrait & drawings of Lt Al Cisnernos, first pilot of Mex-Am heritage to fly with US Navy Blue Angels flight demonstration team, 75; portraits Mario, Gala & Ronnie Broeders, comn by Mr Mario Broeders, Buenos Aires, Arg, 75; portrait Laura Buddington, comn by Mrs Madeleine Buddington, Ft Lauderdale, Fla & Berwick, NS, 74. Exhib: Nat Acad Design Ann Exhib, New York, 67 & 71; 60th Ann Exhib Allied Artists Am, Inc, New York, 73; Nat Arts Club Open Oil Exhib, New York, 75; Am Artists Prof League, Lever House, NY, 75; Am Fortnight Exhib, Hong Kong, 75. Teaching: Instr figure painting, Salmagundi Club, currently. Awards: Allied Artists Am Award, 73; Macown Tuttle Mem Prize, Salmagundi Club, 74; Grand Street Boys Asn First Prize, 74. Mem: Salmagundi Club (co-chmn scholarship comt, 72-, vchmn art comt, currently, co-chmn spec exhib comt, 74-75); Artists Fellowship (vpres, 73-); Hudson Valley Art Asn; Am Artists Prof League. Style & Technique: Realistic portraits and figure situations with strong composition in light; brushes on canvas. Media: Oil on Specially Self Prepared Canvas; Graphite Pencil on Fabriano Paper. Dealer: North Light Studio PO Box 454 Berwick NS Can. Mailing Add: PO Box 45 Glen Cove NY 11377

KNIPSCHILD, ROBERT
PAINTER, EDUCATOR
b Freeport, Ill, Aug 17, 27. Study: Univ Wis, BA, 49; Cranbrook Acad Art, MFA, 51. Work: Pa Acad Fine Arts, Philadelphia; Baltimore Mus Art, Md; Phillips Gallery & Libr Cong, Washington, DC; Cranbrook Mus, Bloomfield Hills, Mich. Exhib: American Painting Today, Metrop Mus Art, New York, 51; Pa Acad Fine Arts Ann, 51; Carnegie Inst Int, Pittsburgh, 52; Container Corp Am, 63; 50 Artists from 50 States, Am Fedn Arts, 65. Teaching: Vis artist, Am Univ, 52; instr painting, Univ Conn, 54-56; asst prof, Univ Wis-Madison, 56-60; assoc prof, Univ Iowa, 60-66; prof painting, Univ Cincinnati, 66- Awards: Purchase Awards, Libr Cong, 51, Pa Acad Fine Arts, 51 & Am Fedn Arts, 63. Bibliog: Patricia Boyd (auth), Exhibition of Robert Knipschild, Christian Sci Monitor, 11/3/69. Mem: Mid Am Col Art Asn; Nat Asn Schs Art. Media: Oil. Dealer: Yares Gallery 3625 Bishop Lane Scottsdale AZ 85252. Mailing Add: Dept of Art Univ Cincinnati Cincinnati OH 45221

KNOBLER, LOIS JEAN
PAINTER
b New York, NY, Feb 2, 29. Study: Syracuse Univ Col Fine Arts, BFA; Fla State Univ, MA. Exhib: Art for US Embassies, Inst Contemp Art, Boston, 66; Contemp Women Artists, Skidmore Col, Saratoga Springs, NY, 70; one-man show, Jorgensen Gallery, Univ Conn, Storrs, 70; St Lawrence Univ Acquisition Exhib, NY, 74; William Benton Mus, Univ Conn, Storrs, 75; two-person show, Hillyer Gallery, Smith Col, Northamton, Mass, 76. Awards: Greater Hartford Civic Arts Festival Award, 72. Style & Technique: Non-representational. Mailing Add: 2041 Wallace St Philadelphia PA 19130

KNOBLER, NATHAN
SCULPTOR, EDUCATOR
b Brooklyn, NY, Mar 13, 26. Study: Newark Sch Fine & Indust Art; Ohio State Univ; Syracuse Univ, BFA, 50; Fla State Univ, MA, 51. Work: US Info Agency; Smith Col Mus, Northampton, Mass; Munson-Williams-Proctor Mus, Utica, NY; Fla State Univ. Slater Mus, Norwich, Conn. Comn: Silver Award Sculpture, Int Silver Co, Meriden, Conn; Bronze Award Sculpture, G Fox & Co, Hartford, Conn. Exhib: Pa Acad Fine Arts Nat Print Show, Philadelphia; Brooklyn Mus Nat Print Show, NY; Drawing Soc Traveling Nat; Selection 1964, Inst Contemp Art, Boston; Surreal Images, De Cordova Mus, Lincoln, Mass & Smith Col. Teaching: Dean fac & prof art, Philadelphia Col Art. Mem: Col Art Asn Am. Media: Stone, Wood, Bronze. Res: Art appreciation; drawing. Publ: Auth, The Visual Dialogue, rev ed, 70; auth, El Dialogo Visual, 70. Mailing Add: Philadelphia Col of Art Broad & Spruce Sts Philadelphia PA 19102

KNORR, JEANNE BOARDMAN
CRAFTSMAN, EDUCATOR
b Chambersburg, Pa. Study: Indiana Univ Pa, BS; Columbia Univ Teachers Col, MA; Art Students League, scholar; Ohio State Univ, PhD(painting). Work: Dallas Theol Sem, Tex; Lakeview Ctr Arts, Peoria, Ill; Ohio State Univ Mus Collections, Columbus; First & Merchants Bank Collection, Richmond, Va. Comn: Fabric wall hanging, St Paul's Episcopal Cathedral, Peoria, 69; fabric wall, Computer Ctr, Norfolk & Western Railroad, Roanoke, Va, 78; plus many fabric wall hangings in pvt collections in Ill, NY & Va. Exhib: Madison Art Asn Regional Crafts Exhib, 68; Indiana Univ Nat Craft Exhib, 69; Nat Drawing Biennial, Chrysler Mus, Norfolk, Va, 70; one-man exhib, Robinson House, Va Mus, Richmond, 72; Peninsula Art Asn, Va Mus Exhib, 75; Crafts Invitational, Bank of Va, Norfolk, 77; Artists Invitational, Hermitage Found, Norfolk, Va, 77. Teaching: Assoc prof art, Norfolk State Col, 69- Awards: Artist of Distinction in crafts, 70 & in sculpture, 71, Va Mus; 3rd & 4th Ann Crafts Fabric Award, Norfolk, Va, 73 & 74. Bibliog: Dona Meilach (auth), Creative stitchery, 8/71, Craft Horizon Mag & Soft sculpture, 74; Cornelia Justice (auth), rev of exhibs at Studio Gallery, 4/66; Elyse & Mike Sommer (auth), A new look at crochet, 75. Mem: Am Craftsmen Coun; Tidewater Artists Asn. Publ: Contribr, Directions, Ill Art Educ Asn, 70. Mailing Add: 730 Maury Ave Norfolk VA 23517

KNOWLES, ALISON
PERFORMANCE ARTIST, PRINTMAKER
b New York, NY, Apr 29, 33. Study: Middlebury Col, Vt, 52-54; Pratt Inst, 54-57, BFA(hon); Manhattan Sch of Printing, 62. Work: Mus of Mod Art Bk Collection, New York; Oakland Mus, Calif; Jean Brown Archives, Tyringham, Mass. Comn: The Identical Lunch (two self-portraits), comn by Alberto Zopellari, 77; Leone D'oro (silkscreen edition), comn by Francesco Conz, 78. Exhib: Solo exhib silkscreen paintings, Judson Gallery, 62; Fluxus Performances, London, Wiesbaden, Copenhagen, Paris & New York, 62; Artypo Exhib, Stedelijk Mus, 67; The Big Book, Mus of Contemp Art, Chicago, 67; Happening & Fluxus Exhib, Kunstverein, Cologne, 70; The Identical Lunch solo exhib, Galerie Inge Baecker, Bochum, Ger, 73; Collections from the Full Moon, Galerie Rene Block, Berlin, De Appel, Amsterdam, 74; SumTime, Everson Mus, Syracuse, NY, 74; Objects in Hand, De Appel, Amsterdam, 76; The Bean Garden, New Sch, New York, 76; 03 23 03, Mus of Fine Art, Montreal, Can, 77. Collections Arranged: The Big Book, Something Else Gallery, New York, Phase Two Gallery, Toronto & Mus of Contemp Art, Chicago, 67, Frankfurt Buchmesse, Ger, Kunsthalle Exhib, Cologne & Nikolaj Kirche, Copenhagen, 68, Univ of San Diego, Calif & Jewish Mus, New York, 69; The House of Dust (outdoor installation), The Garment Workers Coop Apts, New York, 69, Calif Inst of the Arts, Burbank & Valencia, 70. Teaching: Dir graphics lab, Calif Inst of the Arts, Valencia, 70-72. Awards: Guggenheim Fel, 68. Bibliog: William Wilson (auth), The Big Book, Art in Am, 7-8/68; Women in Communications, The Big Book, 68; Tom Johnson (auth), Shoes, Shoestrings & Gertrude Stein, Village Voice, 78. Mem: Fluxus; Sounds Out of Silent Spaces; Printed Ed; The Performance Workshop. Style & Technique: Portable environments which include performances alone or in collaboration with others. Media: Graphics and Silkscreen Prints Based of Found Objects and Aspects of Performances. Publ: Auth, The Canned Bean Rolls, Fluxus, 63; auth, By Alison Knowles, Something Else Press, 65; co-auth (with James Tenney), The House of Dust, Gerb Konig Verlag, 69; auth, More By Alison Knowles, Unpublished Ed, 76; auth, Gem Duck, Pari & Dispari, 78. Dealer: Wies Smals of De Appel Brouwersgracht 196 Amsterdam Holland. Mailing Add: 122 Spring St New York NY 10012

KNOWLES, DOROTHY ELSIE (DOROTHY ELSIE PEREHUDOFF)
PAINTER
b Unity, Sask, Apr 7, 27. Study: Univ Sask, BA, with Eli Bornstein & Reta Cowley; workshops, Emma Lake, with Will Barnet, Clement Greenberg, Ken Noland, Jules Olitski, Lawrence Alloway & Michael Steiner. Work: Edmonton Art Gallery; Kitchener-Waterloo Art Gallery; Winnipeg Art Gallery; Willisted Art Gallery at Windsor, Ont; Norman MacKenzie Art Gallery, Regina, Sask. Exhib: Nat Gallery Biennial, 68; Sask Art & Artists, Norman MacKenzie Art Gallery, 71; 22nd Ann Exhib Paintings, Hamilton, Ont, 71; West 71, Edmonton, Alta, 71; Watercolour Painters from Saskatchewan, Nat Gallery Traveling Show, 71-72. Bibliog: Karen Wilkin (auth), Canada—a report from the West, Art in Am, 6/72; Terrence Heath (auth), Dorothy Knowles, Arts Can, autumn 72. Media: Oil, Acrylic, Watercolor. Dealer: Waddington Galleries 1456 O Sherbrooke W Montreal PQ Can. Mailing Add: 1131 Second St E Saskatoon SK S7H 1R4 Can

KNOWLES, RICHARD H
PAINTER, WRITER
b Evanston, Ill, June 29, 34. Study: Grinnell Col; Northwestern Univ, Evanston, BA, 56; Ind Univ, MA, 61. Work: Ind Univ, Bloomington; Ark State Univ; State of Tenn Collection, Reece Mus, Nashville; Brooks Mem Art Gallery, Memphis, Tenn. Exhib: 22nd Artists West Miss Ann, Colorado Springs, 63; Six Americans, Ark Art Ctr, Little Rock, 64; 50 States Exhib & Tour, Rockford Art Asn & Am Fedn Arts, 65-67; 40 Tenn Artists Exhib & Tour, 68-69; Am Painters & Sculptors, Colgate Univ, 75; plus other group & one-man shows. Teaching: Asst prof art, Univ Ark, 61-65; prof art, Memphis State Univ, 66- Pos: Ed, Untitled (an art jour). Awards: Best Entry for Ark Artist, Delta Ann, 61 & 62; painting prize, Mid-South Exhib, 72. Style & Technique: Abstract organic forms in acrylic on canvas. Mailing Add: 386 Elwood Lane Memphis TN 38117

KNOWLTON, DANIEL GIBSON
BOOKBINDER
b Washington, DC, Nov 14, 22. Study: With Marian U M Lane, Washington, DC; Boston Arts & Crafts, grad. Work: Univ Chicago Libr; Brown Univ Libr, Providence, RI; Dumbarton Oaks Libr, Washington, DC; Harvard Univ Libr; Cornell Univ Libr. Comn: Epistle (gold & leather binding), Grace Church, Providence, 56; The Anguish of the Jews (gold & leather binding), comn by Ciro Scotti, Vatican Libr, 68. Exhib: Hand bookbinding exhibs, Corcoran Gallery Art, 58; one-man shows, Ann-Mary Brown Mem Libr, Providence, 67, Handicrafts Club, Providence, 68, Bristol Hist Soc RI, 69, RI Sch of Design, 71 & 75 & Ctr for Bk Arts, New York, 75. Teaching: Instr bookbinding, Brown Univ Exten Div, 58-73. Pos: Owner & bookbinder, Longfield Studio, 47- & Markey & Asplund Inc, Providence, 74; bookbinder, Brown Univ, 56- Bibliog: Yankee Damon (auth), article in Yankee Mag, 62; Ann Banks (auth), article in Brown Alumni Monthly, 71; WSBE-TV Showcase, Bookbinding. Mem: Miniature Painters, Sculptors & Gravers Soc Washington, DC. Style & Technique: Hand bookbinding in leather and gold tooling, period binding and decitification. Mailing Add: 1202 Hope St Bristol RI 02809

KNOWLTON, GRACE FARRAR
SCULPTOR
b Buffalo, NY, Mar 15, 32. Study: Smith Col, BA; Corcoran Sch Art; Am Univ; painting with Kenneth Noland & Vatclav Vitlacil; drawing & sculpture with Lothar Brabanski, welding steel with Martin Chirino. Work: J Patrick Lannan Mus, Palm Beach, Fla; Lloyds of London, Washington, DC; Newark Mus, NJ; Storm King Art Ctr, NY. Comn: Pottery prototypes for Appalachian Workshops, Am Fedn Arts, New York, 71. Exhib: One-man shows, Hinckley & Brohel Gallery, Washington, DC, 69, Spectrum Gallery, New York, 71, Henri Gallery, Washington, DC, 73, Razor Gallery, New York, 74. Teaching: Instr art, Arlington Co Pub Schs, 57-60. Pos: Asst to cur graphic arts dept, Nat Gallery Art, Washington, DC, 54-57. Bibliog: E Brohel (auth), Midnight Raku (film), Hinckley & Brohel Gallery, 69. Mem: Am Fedn Art (trustee, 72). Style & Technique: Groups of spherical objects up to eight ft diameter, built with clay, concrete, steel and polyester resin. Dealer: Bonino Gallery 48 Great Jones St New York NY 10012; Henri Gallery 1500 21st St NW Washington DC 20036. Mailing Add: Sneden's Landing Palisades NY 10964

KNOWLTON, JONATHAN
PAINTER
b New York, NY, Feb 22, 37. Study: Yale Univ, BA; Univ Calif, Berkeley, MA. Work: Mus Mod Art, New York; Los Angeles Co Mus Art; Victoria & Albert Mus, London; Univ Calif Art Mus, Berkeley; La Jolla Mus Fine Art, Calif. Exhib: Survey '68, Montreal Mus Fine Arts, 68; 17th Nat Print Exhib, Brooklyn Mus, 70; Edmonton Art Gallery, 72; John Bolles Gallery, San Francisco, 73; Latitude 53, Edmonton, 75. Teaching: Asst prof fundamentals design & painting, Univ Alta, 66- Awards: Purchase Award, Los Angeles Co Mus Art, 61; Fulbright Grant, 64-65; Can Coun Grant, 68-69. Style & Technique: Hard-edged synthesis of organic and geometric forms. Media: Acrylic. Dealer: Latitude 53 Edmonton AB Can. Mailing Add: c/o Dept Art & Design Univ Alta Edmonton AB T6G 2M7 Can

KNOWLTON, MONIQUE
ART DEALER, COLLECTOR
b Karlsruhe, Ger, May 24, 37; French citizen. Study: Ecole Polyglotte, Montreaux, Switz, interpreter's dipl, Eng, French & Ger; NY Univ, cert(decorative arts), 65-69. Pos: Dir & pres, Monique Knowlton Gallery, New York, 75- Specialty: Twentieth century and contemporary American painting and sculpture. Collection: Willem de Kooning, Robert Beauchamp, Balthus, Oscar Bluemner, Alexandra Exter, Tom Wesselmann, Gerome Kamrowski, Frank Faulkner, Carol Anthony, Betye Saar, Bert Stern, Saul Steinberg, Robert Smithson. Mailing Add: c/o Monique Knowlton Gallery 19 E 71st St New York NY 10021

KNOX, ELIZABETH ANN
PAINTER
b Miami, Fla, June 13, 44. Study: Parsons Sch Design, cert (honors); New Sch Social Res; Art Students League, with Robert Beverly Hale. Comn: Symposium Erotic Art, Univ Notre Dame, 69; Whitney Biennial, Whitney Mus, 75; Davidson Nat Print & Drawing Competition, Davidson, NC, 76; The Figure in Drawing Now, Bennington, Vt, 77. Mem: Art Students League; Salmagundi Club. Style & Technique: Representative symbolism oil paint. Media: Oil; Conte Lead on Paper. Mailing Add: RFD 2 Box 81A Richmond ME 04357

KNOX, GEORGE
ART HISTORIAN
b London, Eng, Jan 1, 22. Study: Courtauld Inst Art, Univ London, BA, MA & PhD. Collections Arranged: Tiepolo Bicentenary Exhib, Fogg Art Mus, Cambridge, Mass, 70;

Tiepolo Drawings, Staatsgalerie, Stuttgart, 70. Teaching: Instr, Slade Sch Art, Univ London, 50-52; instr, King's Col, Newcastle, Univ Durham, 52-58; instr, Queen's Univ (Ont), 69-70; prof fine arts & head dept, Univ BC, 70- Interest: Venetian 18th century art, particularly the drawings of the Tiepolo family. Publ: Auth, Catalogue of the Tiepolo drawings in the Victoria & Albert Museum, 60; auth, Domenico Tiepolo: raccolta di teste, Udine, 70. Mailing Add: Dept Fine Arts Univ Brit Columbia Vancouver BC Can

KNOX, KATHARINE MCCOOK
ART HISTORIAN, COLLECTOR
b Washington, DC. Collections Arranged: (Voluntary Services) Chmn, Washington Loan Exhibition of Early American Paintings, Miniatures & Silver, Nat Mus, 25; chmn portrait comt, Robert E Lee Memorial Foundation Loan Exhibition, 31 & Primarily American Exhibitions, 59, Textile Mus; chmn portrait comt, The George Washington Bicentennial Commission Exhibition of Portraits, 32 & The George Washington Sesquicentennial Commission Exhibition of Portraits, 39, Corcoran Gallery Art; co-chmn, Privately Owned Exhibition, Corcoran Gallery Art, 52; chmn, Mus Mod Art Loan Exhibition, Washington, DC, 38; spec consult, American Processional, 50 & Our Town, 56, Alexandria, Va; spec consult, Profiles of the Time of James Monroe, Smithsonian Inst, 58; plus many others. Pos: (Voluntary Services) Hon mem, Lincoln Sesquicentennial Comn; adv coun, Civil War Centennial Comn; mem, President's Adv Comt on Arts, John F Kennedy Ctr for Performing Arts; DC comt, R E Lee Mem Found; trustee, Frick Art Ref Libr, New York. Awards: Bronze Medallion, Lincoln Sesquicentennial Comn, 60; Bronze Medal of Merit, Corcoran Gallery Art, 66. Bibliog: Helen Cooke & Evelyn Dent Boyer (auth), Distinguished Women of Washington, 64; plus many acknowledgments & comments in other publ. Interest: During the Hoover Administration, the director of the Frick Art Reference Library, New York, suggested that Mrs Knox list and describe the paintings then in the White House. This was accomplished without remuneration and with the cordial cooperation of Mrs Hoover. Collection: Extensive collection of Washingtoniana and Lincolniana, as well as modern paintings and sculpture. Publ: Auth, The Sharples: Their Portraits of George Washington & His Contemporaries, Yale Univ, 30 & Da Capo Press, 72; auth, Portraits of Adams-Clement Collection & Their Painters, Smithsonian Inst, 51; auth, Healy's Lincoln No 1, 56, rev ed, 59 & Surprise Personalities in Georgetown, DC, 58 & 59, privately publ; contribr, 1861-1865, Vol III, In: Lincoln Day by Day: A Chronology 1809-1865, Lincoln Sesquicentennial Comn, 60; plus others. Mailing Add: 3259 N St NW Washington DC 20007

KNOX, SEYMOUR H
PATRON
b Buffalo, NY, Sept 1, 98. Study: Yale Univ, BA, 20; Univ Buffalo, hon DFA, 62; Syracuse Univ, hon LHD, 66; St Lawrence Univ, hon DFA, 67. Pos: Chmn, NY State Coun on the Arts; pres bd dir, Buffalo Fine Arts Acad; fel Rochester Mus & Sci Ctr. Awards: Buffalo & Erie Co Hist Soc Red Jacket Medal, 62; Buffalo Club Medal, 62; Michael Friedsam Archit Award, 66; Yale Medal. Mailing Add: 57 Oakland Pl Buffalo NY 14222

KNUDSON, ROBERT LEROY
PAINTER
b Wadena, Minn, Nov 16, 29. Study: Minneapolis Art Inst Sch of Art, 50. Work: William Penn Mem Mus, Harrisburg, Pa; Tex Tech Univ, Lubbock; Mus Northern Ariz, Flagstaff; Orme Ranch Sch, Mayer, Ariz. Exhib: 7th Ariz Ann, Yuma, 65; Southwestern, Yuma, 67, 68 & 71; Panhandle Plains Mus-WTex State Univ, Canyon, 68; William Penn Mem Mus, 69; Northern Ariz Univ, Flagstaff, 69 & 70; The West—Artists & Illusrs, Tucson Art Ctr, 71; 3rd Ann Phippen Mem, Prescott, Ariz, 77. Teaching: Instr oil painting, Kachina Sch Art, Phoenix, 63-65; instr oil & acrylic painting, Sedona Arts Ctr, Ariz, 67-68. Awards: Purchase Award, 3rd Southwestern, Valley Nat Bank, 68; Purchase Award, 6th Southwestern, Ariz Pub Serv, 71. Bibliog: Jean Micuda (auth), Knudson, Ariz Living, Vol 3 (1972) & Magnetic—Rishell & Knudson at Troy's, Vol 4 (1973). Style & Technique: Representational, landscape; primarily Southwest, emphasizing light and mood of land and sky. Media: Oil, Watercolor. Publ: Contribr, They Came to Jerome, Jerome Hist Soc, 72; contribr, Ariz Hwy Mag, 7/72, 9/73 & 6/75; contribr (cover painting), SW Art Mag, 10/74. Dealer: Baker Gallery of Fine Art 13th & Ave L Lubbock TX 79408. Mailing Add: 929 W Myrtle No 2 Phoenix AZ 85021

KO, ANTHONY
PRINTMAKER, EDUCATOR
b Hong Kong, Dec 8, 34; US citizen. Study: Nat Taiwan Univ, BA; Univ Nev, with James McCormick, Charles Ross & Craig Sheppard; Univ Calif, Davis, MA, with Ralph Johnson, Roland Petersen & William Wiley; Univ NMex & Tamarind Lithography Workshop, with Garo Antreasian. Work: Mus Mod Art, New York; Art Inst Chicago; Los Angeles Co Mus Art; Achenbach Found for Graphic Arts, San Francisco; Hong Kong City Mus Art Gallery. Comn: 6 Impressions (suite of six lithographs), Univ Nev, Reno, 68; Return to Harmony (edition of 50 multicolor lithographs), Erie Art Ctr, 69. Exhib: Nat Lithography Exhib, Fla State Univ, Tallahassee, 69; Brooklyn Mus 17th Ann Print Exhib, New York, 70; Color Print USA, Tex Tech Univ, Lubbock, 70 & 71; Soc Am Graphic Artists, Kennedy Gallery, New York, 71; 20 American Printmakers, State Univ NY Col Oneonta, 72. Teaching: Asst prof printmaking, Edinboro State Col, 68- Awards: Ford Found Fel, Tamarind Lithography Workshop, 66. Bibliog: Six Impressions, Univ Nev Press, 68; Color Print USA (film slides), Art Libr, Tex Tech Univ, 72. Mem: Col Art Asn Am; Pittsburgh Print Group (co-chmn adv & res comt, 72). Media: Lithography. Mailing Add: RD 2 Box 620 Edinboro PA 16412

KOBAYASHI, KATSUMI PETER
PAINTER, LECTURER
b Hiroshima, Japan, Feb 5, 35. Study: Univ Hawaii, BFA, 64, MFA, 66. Comn: Oil paintings, Cent Pac Bank, Honolulu, 71 & Manoa, C S Wo & Sons, Honolulu, 71. Exhib: Two-man show, Libr Hawaii, 65; Artist Hawaii Exhib Acad Arts, Honolulu, 65, 66, 69 & 71; one-man shows, Gateway House, Honolulu, 66 & Advertiser Contemp Arts Ctr, Hawaii, 72; Hawaii Painters & Sculptors Exhib, 69-72. Teaching: Instr oil painting, Adult Educ, Farrington High Sch, Honolulu, 64-71; instr oil painting, Unitarian Church, Honolulu, 66. Pos: Visual Aid Media Specialist, Univ Hawaii, 66- Awards: Found Cult & Arts Purchase Award, State of Hawaii, 70-72, Dept Educ Award, 71-72; Purchase Award, Honolulu Advertiser, 72. Mem: Hawaii Painters & Sculptors League (vpres, 70-72, pres, 73-74); Hawaii Art Educ Asn. Media: Oil, Watercolor, Pastel. Dealer: Downtown Gallery 125 Merchant St Honolulu HI 96813. Mailing Add: 5304 Malu Pl Honolulu HI 96816

KOBER, ALFRED JOHN
EDUCATOR, SCULPTOR
b Great Bend, Kans, June 3, 37. Study: Dodge City Col, AA, 58; Ft Hays State Col, BS(art), 60 & MS(art), 66. Work: Boise Gallery Art, Idaho; Ft Hays State Col; Grover M Hermann Fine Arts Ctr, Marietta, Ohio. Comn: Two outdoor sculptures, Boise State Univ, 71 & 72; complete altar & accessories (cast bronze), St Michaels Cathedral, Boise, 72; sculptured steel & stained glass lamps, Congregational Church, McCall, Idaho, 73; sculpture (cast bronze), Continental Life & Accident Co, Boise, 73; welded steel sculpture, Boise Cascade World Hqs, Boise, 74; sculpture for Veterans Park, Boise, comn by Idaho Veterans, 76. Exhib: Ann Exhib Northwest Artists, Seattle, Wash, 69-74; Mainstreams, 72 & 77; LaGrange Nat Competition II, Ga, 75; 21st Ann Drawing & Small Sculpture Show, Ball State Univ, 75. Teaching: Instr art, Hutchinson Community Jr Col, Kans, 66-68; assoc prof sculpture, Boise State Univ, 68- Awards: Purchase Award, Grover M Hermann Fine Arts Ctr, Marietta, 72; Award of Excellence, Marietta Col, 72; Award, Ball State Univ, 75. Mem: Boise Art Asn. Style & Technique: Subjective abstraction. Media: Cast Bronze; Polyester Resin. Mailing Add: 2024 Crystal Way Boise ID 83706

KOBLICK, FREDA
SCULPTOR
b San Francisco, Calif. Study: San Francisco City Col; San Francisco State Col; Plastic Indust Tech Inst, plastics engr, 43. Comn: Prismatic construct of acrylic, comn by Anshen & Allen, Int Bldg, San Francisco, 63; cast acrylic relief, Rohm & Haas Co, Independence Hall, Philadelphia, 64; cast acrylic fountain, comn by Robert Royston, City of Vallejo, Calif, 66; stage set, Pa Ballet, 78; sculpture, San Francisco Int Airport, 78. Exhib: One-woman shows, Mus Contemp Crafts, New York, 68, Ariz State Univ, Tempe, 70 & Fountain Art Gallery, Portland, 71; Pierres de Fantasie, Oakland Mus, Calif, 70 & Object USA Int Tour. Teaching: Sr res fel, Royal Col Art, London, 65-67; lectr sculpture, Calif State Univ, Hayward; also int lect & workshops. Awards: Louis Comfort Tiffany Found Grant in Aid, 69; Guggenheim Found Fel, 70-71. Bibliog: Chamberlain (auth), An interview with Freda Koblich, Craft Horizons, 3/63; article in Western Plastics, 12/64; Charles Spencer (auth), article in Art & Artists Eng, 10/67. Mem: Artists Equity Asn; Plastics Inst Gt Brit. Media: Plastic. Publ: Auth, The plastics age, Vogue, Eng, 66. Mailing Add: 401 Francisco St San Francisco CA 94133

KOCH, ARTHUR ROBERT
PAINTER, EDUCATOR
b Meriden, Conn, Feb 26, 34. Study: Wesleyan Univ; RI Sch Design, BFA, 57, with John Frazier; Univ Wash, MFA, 61. Exhib: Art: USA: 59, New York, 59; US Info Agency Painting Show, Europe, 62-66; Tex Painting & Sculpture of the 20th Century, 70-71. Teaching: Instr studio, Univ NH, 57-59; instr studio, El Centro Col, Dallas, 66-70; head dept studio art, Meadows Sch Arts, Southern Methodist Univ, 70- Pos: Chmn Acad Standards Comt, Tex Asn Schs Art, 70-71. Awards: Ft Worth Art Ctr Award, 70. Mem: Dallas Area Artists Equity Asn (pres, 70-71); Artists Equity Asn (vpres, 71); Blue Bonnets Anonymous (chmn, 71-72). Dealer: Contemp Fine Arts Gallery 2425 Cedar Springs Dallas TX 75201. Mailing Add: 11149 Lanewood Circle Dallas TX 75218

KOCH, EDWIN E
SCULPTOR, PAINTER
b New York, NY, Feb 21, 15. Study: Mus Mod Art Sch; also with E Kramer. Work: Butler Inst of Am Art, Youngstown, Ohio. Exhib: Am Watercolors, Drawings & Prints, Metrop Mus Art, 52; Int Exhib Watercolors, Prints, Drawing, Pa Acad Design, 52; Int Watercolor Exhib, Brooklyn Mus, 53; Nat Acad Design, 58-75; var one-man shows. Awards: Award, Emily Lowe Competition, 62; Framemakers Award, Silvermine Guild Artists, 62; Medals of Honor for Watercolor, 70 & Oils, 72, Painters & Sculpture Soc NJ. Bibliog: Brian O'Doherty (auth), One-man show, 62 & John Canady (auth), One-man show, 66, New York Times. Mem: Audubon Artists; Nat Soc Painters in Casein & Acrylic (bd dirs, 75-); Knickerbocker Artists (vpres, 77-78); Painters & Sculptors Soc NJ (vpres, 74-); Am Vet Soc Artists (treas, 70-75). Media: Oil, Casein. Mailing Add: 386 E 161st St New York NY 10451

KOCH, GERD (HERMAN)
PAINTER, EDUCATOR
b Detroit, Mich, Jan 30, 29. Study: Wayne State Univ, BFA; Univ Calif, Los Angeles; Univ Calif, Santa Barbara, MFA. Work: Los Angeles Co Mus Art; La Jolla Art Mus; Pasadena Art Mus; Univ NC; Santa Barbara Art Mus. Comn: Design of Ash Grove (folk music cabaret), 58. Exhib: Los Angeles Co Mus Art Ann, 59; La Jolla Art Mus Ann, 60-62; three man traveling show, Western Asn Mus, 62-65; Calif State Fair, 63; Art or Anti Art, Occidental Col, 65; Univ NC, 66; Butler Inst Am Art, Youngstown, Ohio, 66; Calif Palace of Legion of Honor, San Francisco, 67; Calif Arts Festival, 68. Teaching: Prof painting & drawing, Ventura Col, 60-61 & 67-; instr painting & drawing, Univ Calif Exten. Awards: Purchase & First Award, Los Angeles Co Mus Art, 59; Calif State Fair First Award, 63; Calif Nat Watercolor Soc Purchase Award, 67. Mem: Calif Nat Watercolor Soc (juror, 67 & 71); Ventura Art Asn. Media: Oil, Acrylic. Mailing Add: 444 Aliso Ventura CA 93001

KOCH, JOHN
PAINTER, COLLECTOR
b Toledo, Ohio, Aug 18, 09. Work: Metrop Mus Art, New York; Brooklyn Mus, NY; Boston Mus Fine Arts, Mass; Nelson Gallery Art, Kansas City, Mo; Detroit Inst Fine Arts, Mich. Exhib: One-man shows, New York Kraushaar Galleries, 39-, Va Mus Arts & Sci, Richmond, John Koch in New York, Mus of City of New York, 63, Akron Art Inst, Ohio, 71, Speed Mus, Louisville, Ky, 71 & John Koch, Models & Moments, Colgate Univ & Pa State Univ, 77; retrospective, New York Cult Ctr, 73; Contemp Am Painting, Krannert Art Mus, Univ Ill, 69 & 74; Three Centuries of the Am Nude, Minneapolis Inst & Univ of Houston Fine Arts Ctr, 75; The Chosen Object, Joslyn Art Mus, Omaha, Nebr, 77. Teaching: Instr painting, Art Students League, 44-45. Awards: Benjamin Altman Prize, 59 & 64, Saltus Gold Medal, 62, Nat Acad Design. Bibliog: Douglas Davis (auth), Art doesn't have to be new, Nat Observer, 4/22/48; Dorothy Parker (auth), John Koch and his glorious people, Esquire, 11/19/64; Emily Genauer (auth), Miracles without trickery, New York Post, 3/11/72. Mem: Nat Inst Arts & Lett; Nat Acad Design (academician); Benjamin Franklin fel Royal Soc Arts. Style & Technique: Realist. Media: Oil. Collection: Works by Tintoretto, Rubens, El Greco, Ingres, Gainsborough, Guardi, Steen, Magnasco, Solimena, Vuillard, Marsh & Burchfield. Dealer: Kraushaar Gallery 1055 Madison Ave New York NY 10028. Mailing Add: 300 Central Park W New York NY 10024

KOCH, ROBERT
ART HISTORIAN, WRITER
b New York, NY, Apr 7, 18. Study: Harvard Univ, AB, 39; NY Univ, MA, 53; Yale Univ, PhD, 57. Teaching: Prof art hist, Southern Conn State Col, 56- Awards: Fac Scholar Award, Southern Conn State Col, 74. Res: Art nouveau in France, Spain, Latin America and the US. Publ: Auth, articles in Art in Am, 62, 64 & 65 & Antiques, 74; auth, Louis C Tiffany, rebel in glass, 64; contribr, Artistic America, Tiffany glass and art nouveau, 70; auth, Louis C Tiffany's glass-bronzes-lamps, 71. Mailing Add: Dept of Art Southern Conn State Col New Haven CT 06515

KOCH, VIRGINIA GREENLEAF
PAINTER
b Chicago, Ill. Study: Yale Univ Sch Fine Arts; Am Univ; also with Ivan Olinsky, Robert Brackman & Gene Davis. Exhib: Mariners Mus, Newport News, Va, 70 & 71; Phillips Collection, Washington, DC, 71; one-man shows, Studio Gallery, Washington, DC, 71 & Main St Gallery, Nantucket. Mem: Artists Equity Asn. Style & Technique: Lyric abstractionist; staining and glazing technique. Media: Acrylic. Dealer: Haller Gallery New York NY; Main St Gallery Nantucket MA 02554. Mailing Add: 26 Pleasant St Nantucket MA 02554

KOCH, WILLIAM EMERY
ART DEALER, COLLECTOR
b Brooklyn, NY, Jan 7, 22. Pos: Owner-dir, Koch Galleries. Specialty: Graphics, all periods; paintings, including American, early and 20th century, also continental; minor impressionist. Collection: American impressionist; School of Paris and some Barbizon artists; 20th century French and English. Mailing Add: Koch Galleries 162 S Lawrence St Mobile AL 36602

KOCHER, ROBERT LEE
PAINTER, EDUCATOR
b Jefferson City, Mo, Dec 19, 29. Study: Univ Mo-Columbia, AB & MA, also with Fred Shane & Paul Brach. Comn: Religious Feasts, Culver-Stockton Col Dining Hall, 57; outdoor sculpture, Duane Arnold Residence, Cedar Rapids, Iowa. Exhib: Mid-Am Ann, Kansas City, Mo, 60; All Iowa Artists, Des Moines Art Ctr Ann, 63-75. Teaching: Prof art, Coe Col, 59- Pos: Bd dirs, Cedar Rapids Art Ctr, 61-; Cedar Rapids, Marion Coun Arts, 71-74; exhib judge, Iowa, Mo & Ill. Awards: First Prize for painting, All Iowa Artists, Des Moines Art Ctr, 69; Yonkers Award. Media: Dye. Mailing Add: 1955 Park Ave SE Cedar Rapids IA 52403

KOCHERTHALER, MINA
PAINTER
b Munich, Ger; US citizen. Study: Columbia Univ; Art Students League, with Mario Cooper; Nat Acad Design Sch Fine Art, with Ralph Fabri. Work: Norfolk Mus Arts & Sci; also in many pvt collections. Exhib: Royal Soc Painters Watercolours, London, 62; 200 Yrs Watercolor Painting Am, Metrop Mus Art, New York, 66-67; Mus Acuarela, Mexico City, 68; Butler Inst Am Art, 70; Can Soc Painters Watercolour, 71-72. Pos: Deleg, US Comt Int Asn Arts, New York, 60-62. Awards: John J Karpick Mem Medal, Audubon Artists, 62; Prizes, Nat Soc Painters Casein & Acrylic, 58, 63, 64, 68, 71, 76 & 77; Grumbacher Polymer Award, Catharine Lorillard Wolfe Art Club, 71. Mem: Am Watercolor Soc (rec secy & coordr chmn, 62-); Audubon Artists; Nat Soc Painters Casein & Acrylic (vpres, 62-); Allied Artists Am (rec secy, 74-); Catharine Lorillard Wolfe Art Club. Media: Acrylic. Mailing Add: 124 W 79th St New York NY 10024

KOCHTA, RUTH (MARTHA)
PAINTER
b Ridgewood, NY. Study: Art Students League, with Rudolf Baranik & Julian Levi; also with E B Whitaker & Leo Manso. Work: Philathea Col Mus, Ont; First & Merchants Bank, Richmond, Va; Fairleigh Dickenson Univ, Teaneck, NJ; Nat Bank NAm, New York. Exhib: Nat Acad Design Ann, New York, 68; Heckscher Mus, Huntington, NY, 69 & 71; Wadsworth Atheneum, Hartford, Conn, 71; Elizabeth Ney Mus, Austin, Tex, 71; New Brit Mus, Conn, 72. Awards: Best in Show, Manhasset Art Festival, 70; First in oils, Bedford Art Show, 71; First in oils, Gracie Sq Art Show, 74. Mem: Conn Acad Fine Arts; Queens Coun Arts. Style & Technique: Large textural lyrical abstractions. Media: Oil. Dealer: Guild Gallery Ltd 1145 Madison Ave New York NY; Robley Gallery Roslyn Long Island NY. Mailing Add: 156-09 45th Ave Flushing NY 11355

KOCSIS, ANN
PAINTER
b New York, NY. Study: Nat Acad Design, New York. Work: Fla Southern Col; Seton Hall Univ; Am Hungarian Inst; Sq & Compass Crippled Children's Clin; Sonora Desert Mus, Ariz. Exhib: Allied Artists Am, Audubon Artists & Am Artists Prof League Grand Nat, New York; Fairleigh Dickinson Univ Exhib, NJ; Europ Tour & Japan Exchange Exhib. Awards: Hon Mention & Merit Citation, Fla Int Art Exhib, Fla Southern Col, 52; Gold Key & Grambacher Award, Seton Hall Univ, 58; Hon Mention, Am Artists Prof League, 62. Mem: Life mem Nat Arts Club (chmn arts comt); Nat Asn Women Artists (nominating comt); Knickerbocker Artists (corresp secy & 2nd vpres, 66); life fel Royal Soc Arts, London; life fel Int Inst Arts & Lett, Switz. Mailing Add: 327 W 76th St New York NY 10023

KOEBBEMAN, SKIP
EDUCATOR, SCULPTOR
b Cleveland, Ohio, Nov 11, 43. Study: Northern Ill Univ, 61-64; Univ Ill, Champaign, BFA(indust design), 67, with Frank Gallo, MFA(sculpture), 71. Exhib: J B Speed Art Mus, Louisville, Ky, 72; one-man shows, Krannert Art Mus, Champaign, 73 & Billy Son Gallery, Iowa City, 74, Dead Dog Prod 1st & 2nd Ann Corresp Art Show, Louisville Sch Art Gallery, 73 & 74; Mid-States Exhib, Evansville Mus Art, Ind, 74 & 75; 22nd Ann Drawing & Small Sculpture Show, Ball State Univ, Muncie, Ind, 76; Dayton Collection 77, Ohio. Teaching: Asst prof art & chmn dept sculpture, Louisville Sch Art, 71- Style & Technique: Polyester resin cast into blow formings; figurative bronzes. Dealer: Gilman Galleries 103 E Oak St Chicago IL 60611. Mailing Add: 1405 Elm Rd Anchorage KY 40223

KOEHLER, HENRY
PAINTER
b Louisville, Ky, Feb 2, 27. Study: Yale Univ, BA, 50. Work: Calif Palace of Legion of Honor, San Francisco; Speed Mus Art, Louisville, Ky; Parrish Art Mus, Southampton, NY. Comn: Baseball murals, NY Mets, Shea Stadium, 64. Exhib: One-man shows, Calif Palace of Legion of Honor, 66, Speed Art Mus, 67, Parish Art Mus, 70, Betty Parsons Gallery, 72 & Lad Lane Gallery, Dublin, Ireland, 77; Wildenstein & Co Ltd, London, 71, 73 & 76; The Horse in Art, Santa Barbara Mus Art, Calif, 74. Pos: Trustee, Parrish Mus of Art, Southampton, NY. Style & Technique: Sporting paintings; series of giant artichokes; portraits. Media: Oil on Canvas, Oil on Paper, Drawings. Dealer: Betty Parsons Gallery 24 W 57th St New York NY 10019; Wildenstein & Co Ltd 147 New Bond St London WI Eng. Mailing Add: 38 E 73rd St New York NY 10021

KOENIG, JOHN FRANKLIN
PAINTER
b Seattle, Wash, Oct 24, 24. Study: US Army Univ, France, 45; Univ Wash, grad, 48. Work: Mus Art Mod, Paris, France; Ctr Nat Art Contemp, Paris; Mus Western Art, Tokyo; Seattle Art Mus; Mus Art Contemp, Montreal. Comn: Mural & glass windows (with Wogenscky), CHU Hosp, St Antoine, Paris, 65. Exhib: Ecole Paris, Tate Gallery, London, 62; Carnegie Inst Int, Pittsburgh, 64; Aventure Art Abstrait, var French mus, 67-69; Retrospective, Seattle Art Mus, Wash, 70; Salon des Realities Nouvelles, Fr, 73; Galerie Arnaud, 74; Recent Paintings, Foster/White Gallery, Seattle; Menton Biennale de Tapisseries, 75; plus others. Pos: Ballet critic, Cimaise, Paris, 68-; ballet critic, Art Vivant, Paris, 70-71. Awards: Student Show Prize, Univ Wash, 48; Third Prix Artistes Etrangers, Mus Art Mod, Paris, 59; Prix Critiques Art de Presse Parisienne, 1st Biennale Paris, 59. Bibliog: Pierre Restany (auth), John Franklin Koenig, Galerie Arnaud, Paris, 60; Rene Deroudille (auth), John Franklin Koenig, Tete d'Or, Lyon, 61; Sylvie Nikitine (auth), Le regard du peintre, TV Scolaire, Paris, 68. Media: Oil, Acrylic. Publ: Co-auth, John Franklin Koenig, 65 & 70. Mailing Add: 10 rue Richer Paris France

KOEPNICK, ROBERT CHARLES
SCULPTOR, EDUCATOR
b Dayton, Ohio, July 8, 07. Study: Dayton Art Inst, dipl; Cranbrook Acad Art; also with Carl Milles. Comn: Facade sculpture, St Michael Church, Houston; portrait of Max Rudolf (bronze sculpture) plus screen, St John's Chapel, Dayton, 67; sculpture, St James of the Valley Church, Wyoming, Ohio, 67; aluminum panel, Valentine Match Plate Co, Dayton, 68; Johnny Appleseed Mem, Springgrove Cemetery, Cincinnati, Ohio, 68; plus many others. Exhib: Pa Acad Fine Arts, Philadelphia; Art Inst Chicago; Metrop Mus Art, New York; Nat Acad Design, New York; Syracuse Mus Fine Arts, NY; plus others. Teaching: Instr sculpture, Dayton Art Inst, 36-41 & 46-; vis sculptor, Mt St Joseph Col, 51-55; vis sculptor, Antioch Col, 53-54. Pos: Tech adv, Ohio Art Coun, 68- Mem: Dayton Soc Painters & Sculptors; Cincinnati Liturgical Art Group. Mailing Add: Dayton Art Inst Forest & Riverview Ave Dayton OH 45401

KOERNER, DANIEL
PAINTER, CARTOONIST
b New York, NY, Nov 16, 09. Study: Art Students League; Educ Alliance Art Sch. Work: Metrop Mus Art, New York; Queens Col, New York; City Art Mus St Louis, Mo. Comn: Textbook illus; illus for var co & Encycl Am. Teaching: Pvt instr, 38-41; cartoon instr, Cartoonist & Illustrators Sch, 48-52. Publ: Contribr cartoons, Colliers, New York Times, Sat Rev, Nation's Bus; King Features, This Week & other nat mag. Mailing Add: 422 E Tenth St New York NY 10009

KOERNER, HENRY
PAINTER, DESIGNER
b Vienna, Austria, Aug 28, 15; US citizen. Study: Acad Appl Art, Vienna; also with Victor Theodore Slama, Vienna. Work: Whitney Mus Am Art; Mus Mod Art; Art Inst Chicago; Munson-Williams-Proctor Inst, Utica, NY. Comn: 65 Time Mag cover portraits. Exhib: Nat Cancer Poster Competition, 39; Nat War Poster Competition, Mus Mod Art, 42; Philadelphia Mus Art, 50; Artist of Yr, Pittsburgh, 63; Westmoreland Co Mus Art, Greensburg, Pa. Teaching: Instr art, Munson-Williams-Proctor Inst, 47-48; artist in residence, Chatham Col, 52-53; instr art & head dept, Washington Univ, 56. Pos: Head graphic div, Off Mil Govt, Berlin, Ger, 45-47. Awards: First Prize, Nat Cancer Asn, 39 & First & Second Prize, Nat War Poster Competition, 42, Mus Mod Art; Temple Award, Art Inst Philadelphia, 50. Bibliog: His own tragedy spurs artist to paint moving post war paintings, Life, 48; Alexander Eliot (auth), Story teller, 3/27/50 & 300 years of American painting, 59, Time. Mem: Nat Acad Design; Assoc Artists Pittsburgh; Pittsburgh Watercolor Soc. Style & Technique: Peter Brueghel contents with after Cézanne appearance. Media: Ink, Watercolor, Oil. Publ: Illusr, Tracy's tiger, 49, A sense of purpose, Col Art J, 51; The Living God, Jewish Commentary, 59 & CBS Yearbook, 59; auth & illusr, University of Pittsburgh in Drawings, 65; plus others. Mailing Add: 1055 S Negley Ave Pittsburgh PA 15217

KOERNER, JOHN MICHAEL ANTHONY
See Korner, John

KOESTNER, DON
PAINTER
b St Paul, Minn, Nov 28, 23. Study: Minneapolis Sch Art, four yrs. Comn: Mural, St Olaf's Church, Minneapolis, 50; diorama-mural, Goodhue Co Hist Soc, Red Wing, Minn, 69. Exhib: Twin Cities Show, Minneapolis Inst Art, 48-56; Red River Regional Show, Minn, 60; Ogunquit Art Ctr Nat Art Exhib, 64; Minn State Fair Fine Arts Ann, 66; Am Artists Prof League, 68. Teaching: Instr painting, art instr schs, Minneapolis, 60-69; instr oil painting & drawing, Minn Mus Art Sch, 70-75 & Atelier Lack, Minneapolis, 75- Awards: Grumbacher Award, Ogunquit Art Ctr Nat Exhib, 64; First Prize for oil painting, Minn State Fair, 66; Award, Am Artists Prof League, 68. Style & Technique: Representational painting in the impressionist mode. Media: Oil. Mailing Add: 9501 123rd St E Rte 2 Hastings MN 55033

KOGA, DEAN
ART LIBRARIAN, CRAFTSMAN
b Ogden, Utah, Jan 24, 51. Study: Weber State Col, BS(art), 73; Boise State Col, ceramics workshop with Toshiko Takaezu, 72. Exhib: Fourth Ann Printmaking W, Utah State Univ, Logan, 73; Buddhist Churches of Am 75th Anniversary, Bank of Tokyo, San Francisco, Calif, 74; one-man show, Atrium Gallery, Salt Lake City Pub Libr, 75; Utah Painting & Sculpture, Utah Mus of Fine Arts, Salt Lake City, 75 & 76; Young Artists, Bertha Eccles Community Art Ctr, Ogden, Utah, 75; Utah Designer/Craftsman, Harris Art Ctr, Birgham Young Univ, Provo, 77; Interiors, Mus of Natural Hist, Salt Lake City, 77. Pos: Artists in the Sch Prog, Logan & Ogden Sch Dists, 74; fine arts librn II, Salt Lake City Pub Libr, 74- Awards: First Place, Arts Festival, Salt Lake City Pub Libr, 73. Mem: Am Crafts Coun; Utah Designer/Craftsman; Mary M Atwater's Weavers Guild. Style & Technique: Abstract hard-edge painting; hand-weaving of textiles; mixed media tapestry. Media: Painting, textile. Interest: Atrium Gallery at the library, contemporary art in craft media. Dealer: Salt Lake Art Ctr 54 Finch Lane Salt Lake City UT 84102. Mailing Add: 413 Herbert Ave Apt 4 Salt Lake City UT 84111

KOGA, MARY
PHOTOGRAPHER
b Sacramento, Calif, Aug 10, 20. Study: Art Inst Chicago, MFA; Univ Chicago, MA; Univ Calif, Berkeley, BA; also with Ken Josephson, Art Sinsabaugh, Aaron Siskind & Harry Callahan. Work: Ill Art Coun, Chicago; San Francisco Mus of Mod Art; Exchange Nat Bank, Chicago; J P Seagram Collection, New York. Exhib: One-man shows, Art Inst Chicago, 71, Evanston Art Ctr, 72 & Shado Gallery, Ore, 77; Friends of Photography, Carmel, Calif, 71, 73, 75 & 76; Art Inst Chicago, 73; Smithsonian Traveling Exhib, 75; Silver Image, Wash, 77; SW Ctr of Photog Travelling Exhib, Austin, Tex, 77, Women of Photography, San Francisco Mus Art, San Diego Mus Art, Sidney Janis Gallery, Mus NMex, Wellesley Col Mus & Univ Wis, 75. Teaching: Asst prof, Univ Chicago, 59-69; mem fac, Columbia Col, 73. Awards: Nine Women Photogrs, Ill Art Coun, 75; Festival of the Arts, Univ Chicago, 70. Bibliog: Women of Photography, An Historical Survey, San Francisco Mus Art, 75; Margery Mann (auth), Women of Photography, Camera 35, 75. Mem: Soc Photog Educ; Friends Photog; Int Ctr Photog; George Eastman House; Artists League of the Midwest. Style & Technique: Abstractions from nature; people in their own environment. Media: Black and White and

Color Photography. Dealer: Douglas Kenyon Gallery 154 E Erie St Chicago IL 60611; Second St Gallery Charlottesville Va. Mailing Add: 1254 Elmdale Ave Chicago IL 60660

KOHL, BARBARA
COLLECTOR, PAINTER
b Milwaukee, Wis, Feb 10, 40. Study: Univ Wis Madison, BS(art hist); Univ Wis Milwaukee. Work: Milwaukee Art Ctr. Comn: Painting, comn by Golda Mier, 77. Exhib: Wis Painters & Sculptors, Milwaukee Art Ctr, 65; Washington Art, Washington Armory, DC, 77 & 78; New York Show, Allen Park Gallery, 77; Janus Gallery, Washington, DC, 78. Teaching: Asst trainer of docents in art hist, Milwaukee Art Ctr, 78- Awards: Pub Television Auction Award for Best in Show, 77. Style & Technique: Naive ink paintings and collages, homemade paper, direct human approach. Media: Color and Fabric on Paper. Collection: Milton Avery oils, Morris Lewis, Dubuffet, Hockney, Ralph Fasanella, Wayne Thiebold, Hepworth, Suttman, Saul Steinberg. Dealer: Judith L Posner & Assoc Inc 7945 N Fairchild Rd Milwaukee WI 43217. Mailing Add: 1440 W Dean Rd Milwaukee WI 53217

KOHLER, MEL (OTTO)
ART DEALER
b Wilcox, Sask, Dec 7, 11; US citizen. Study: Univ Wash, BA, 35; Calif Sch Fine Arts, 36, with Maurice Sterne; Columbia Univ Teachers Col, MA, 42. Collections Arranged: Western Wash Fair, Puyallup, 40, 46 & 51; Fur Rondezvous Exhibs, Anchorage, Alaska, 58-66; Alaska Music Festival, Anchorage, 65-66. Teaching: Instr & asst prof art & head dept & galleries, Univ Puget Sound, 34-37; assoc prof art & head dept art & galleries, Alaska Methodist Univ, 58-66. Pos: Founder & dir, Tacoma Art Asn, 34-37; cur & dir, Henry Gallery, Univ Wash, 48-52; cur, Eastern Wash State Hist Soc, 67-69; cur, Wichita Art Mus, 69-70; dir, Mel Kohler Gallery & Design Studio, Seattle, 71-74, semi-retired. Mem: Capitol Hill Community Arts Coun (bd mem). Specialty: Contemporary artists, especially local artists. Mailing Add: 400 Melrose Ave E Seattle WA 98102

KOHLER, RUTH DEYOUNG
MUSEUM DIRECTOR, CURATOR
b Chicago, Ill, 41. Study: Smith Col, Northhampton, Mass, BA; Univ Hamburg, Ger; Kunsthochschule, Hamburg, Ger; Banff Sch of Fine Arts; Univ Wis, Madison. Collections Arranged: Curated & designed, The Plastic Earth/a nat ceramics invitational, Civilizations/an exhib of the work of 6 Am sculptors dealing with the concept of civilizations (Robert Arneson, David Gilhooly, Doug Baldwin, Richard Lang, Art Morrison & Clayton Bailey), Headdress/A History of American Headgear, Skin/A Survey of Man's Use of Leather & Rawhide, 1370-1970, The Human Image in the 70's, 8 Artists in Industry, ceramic sculpture produced in an extended residency program, Box/containers made in NAm, 17th century to present, John Michael Kahler Arts Ctr, Sheboygan, Wis. Teaching: Instr printmaking, Univ Alta, Calgary, Can, 64-66. Pos: Dir & mem, Kohler Found, Inc, Wis, 60-; asst dir, John Michael Kohler Arts Ctr, Sheboygan, Wis, 68-76 & dir, 72-; mem, Wis Arts Bd, Madison, 74-77 & chmn, 73-; mem, Wis Am Revolution Bicentennial Commission, Madison, 74-77; mem crafts panel, Nat Endowment for the Arts, Washington, DC, 75- & mem mus panel, 76- Mailing Add: 608 New York Ave Sheboygan WI 53081

KOHLHEPP, NORMAN
PAINTER, PRINTMAKER
b Louisville, Ky. Study: Univ Cincinnati; Grande Chaumiere, Paris; Acad Colorossi; Andre L'Hote Acad, Paris. Work: J B Speed Art Mus; Univ Louisville; Seagram Collection; Devoe & Raynolds Collection; Howard Steamboat Mus. Exhib: Mid-States Exhib, 65-67; Cincinnati Mus, Ohio, 67; J B Speed Art Mus, 68; Pa Acad Fine Arts, 66; Latin-Am Festival, 69; Liberty Bank Gallery, 76; Jr League of Louisville, 78; plus others. Pos: Treas, Louisville Art Ctr Asn, 58-59, secy, 60-61, bd mem, 62-72, hon bd mem, 72-; co-chmn, Downtown Salutes the Arts, Louisville, 64 & 65; bd mem, Jr Art Gallery, 71-72. Awards: Va-Intermont Exhib, 58; First Prize, Ky State Fair, 67 & 68; Corporate Purchase, Eight State Ann, 77; plus others. Dealer: J B Speed Art Mus 2035 S Third Louisville KY 40208. Mailing Add: 2116 Lauderdale Rd Louisville KY 40205

KOHLMEYER, IDA (R)
PAINTER
b New Orleans, La, Nov 3, 12. Study: Newcomb Col, BA, 33, MFA, 56; also with Hans Hofmann, 56. Work: Mus Fine Arts, Houston, Tex; High Mus Art, Atlanta, Ga; Corcoran Gallery Art & Nat Collection, Smithsonian Inst, Washington, DC; plus many others. Exhib: Biennial Contemp Am Painting, Corcoran Gallery Art, Washington, DC, 63 & 67; An Anthology of Modern American Painting, from collections of High Mus, Atlanta & Whitney Mus Am Art, New York, 66; 3rd Bienal de Arte Coltejer, Medellin, Colombia, 72; American Women: 20th Century, Lakeview Ctr Arts & Sci, Peoria, Ill, 72; North, East, West, South & Middle, Moore Col Art, Philadelphia, 75; plus many other group & one-man shows. Teaching: Instr drawing & painting, Newcomb Col, 56-64; assoc prof painting, Univ New Orleans, 73- Awards: Ford Found Purchase Award, 28th Corcoran Biennial Am Art, 63; Mus Purchase Award, High Mus, Atlanta, 63 & 66; Artists of SE & Tex Biennial Award, New Orleans Mus Art, 75; plus many others. Media: Oil. Dealer: Galerie Simonne Stern 516 Royal St New Orleans LA 70130; David Findlay Galleries 984 Madison Ave New York NY 10021. Mailing Add: 11 Pelham Ave Metairie LA 70005

KOHN, MISCH
PAINTER, PRINTMAKER
b Kokomo, Ind, Mar 26, 16. Study: John Herron Art Inst, BFA, 39; also with Jose Clemente Oroszco & Leopoldo Mendez, Mexico City, 43. Work: Bezalel Nat Mus, Jerusalem; Bibliot Nat, Paris; Victoria Mus, Melbourne, Australia; Mus Mod Art & Metrop Mus Art, New York; Nat Gallery Art, Libr Cong & Smithsonian Inst, Washington, DC; plus many others. Exhib: Art Inst Chicago, 51 & 60; Los Angeles Co Mus Art, 58-60; Mus Nat Art Mod & Bibliot Nat, Paris, 59; retrospective, Ford Found & Am Fedn Arts, 61; plus many others. Teaching: Assoc prof art, Ill Inst Technol, 53-65, prof art, 65-70. Awards: Tamarind Fel, 61; prizes, Brooklyn Mus, 68; prize, Philadelphia Print Club, 69; plus many others. Bibliog: Gabor Peterdi (auth), Printmaking: Methods Old and New, Macmillan, 59; S W Hayter (auth), About Prints, Oxford Univ Press, 62. Mem: Soc Am Graphic Arts; Acad Florence; Print Coun Am; Philadelphia Print Club. Mailing Add: 1860 Grove Way Castro Valley CA 94546

KOHN, WILLIAM ROTH
PAINTER, EDUCATOR
b St Louis, Mo, Aug 23, 31. Study: Wash Univ, John T Milliken traveling grant, 53, BFA; Atelier 17, Paris, with S W Hayter; Mills Col. Work: Springfield Art Mus, Mo. Exhib: 79th & 81st Ann Painting & Sculpture Show, San Francisco Mus, 60 & 62; Print & drawing Show, Los Angeles Mus, 61; Mid Am Show, Nelson Gallery, Kansas City & St Louis Art Mus, 65-67; one-man shows, Loretto Hilton Gallery, Webster Col, 70 & Terry Moore Gallery, St Louis, 76; Int Exhib Graphic Art, Mus Art, Ljubljana, Yugoslavia, 71; Midwest Invitational, Kranert Mus, Univ Ill, 76. Teaching: Assoc prof painting-design, Wash Univ, 63- Awards: Fulbright Hays Grant Painting in India, 65; grant for individual artist, Mo State Coun Arts, 77. Mem: Art Coord Coun (co-chmn, St Louis Area, 75). Style & Technique: Realistic paintings of small solid objects in strong light and shadow, usually seen from above, high chroma. Media: Acrylic on Canvas, Silkscreen Prints. Mailing Add: c/o The Graphics Gallery Three Embarcadero Ctr San Francisco CA 94111

KOHUT, LORENE
PAINTER
b La Port, Tex, Nov 16, 29. Study: With Coulton Waugh & John Gould. Work: Court Gen Sessions, Washington, DC; Pa State Univ; Fred Clark Mus, Carversville, Pa; Del State Col; Wesley Col. Exhib: 72nd Catharine Lorillard Wolfe Nat, New York, 69; Ogunquit Arts Ctr 49th Nat, Maine, 69; Nat Arts Club, NY, 69; Hudson Valley Art Asn, 42nd & 43rd Nat, White Plains, NY, 69-70; Nat Acad Design, NY, 70. Awards: Gold Medal Oils, Catharine Lorillard Wolfe Nat, 69; Gold Medal Oils, Hudson Valley Art Asn, 69; Ralph Metzer Award, Ogunquit Art Ctr, 69. Mem: Artists Equity Asn; Philadelphia Art Alliance. Style & Technique: Landscapes; seascapes; realistic manner. Media: Mixed Media, Acrylic, Pastel. Dealer: Chadds Ford Art Gallery Chadds Ford PA. Mailing Add: Rte 3 Andrews Lake Felton DE 19943

KOLAWOLE, LAWRENCE COMPTON
PAINTER, SCULPTOR
b Beaumont, Tex, Aug 20, 31. Study: Calif Art Inst, with Hassell Smith, Elmer Bischoff, Ernest Mundt, Clyfford Still, David Park, Richard Diebenkorn & Ed Corbett. Work: Leinbach Mus-Gallery, Munich, Ger; Stadt Witten Mus, Witten, Ger; Insel Film GmbH, Munich, Ger; Muiska Mus, Munchen, WGer; Nigerian Art Asn, Lagos, Nigeria. Exhib: USA Nat Shows, San Francisco Mus, 53; Herbstsalon Haus der Kunst, Munchen, 66; one-man show, Mark Mus Der Stadt Witten, 71; Salon Int Art Actuel, Brussels, 74; Int Art Market-Paint Show, Dusseldorf, 74. Style & Technique: Motion art. Media: Prints & Oil, Graphics. Mailing Add: 357 Scott Apt B San Francisco CA 94117

KOLBA, TAMARA
See St Tamara

KOLBERT, FRANK L
ART DEALER
b Detroit, Mich, Oct 17, 48. Study: Yale Univ, BA, 70. Pos: Cur asst, Detroit Inst Arts, 70-72; assoc dir, Inst Art & Urban Resources, 73-74; dir, Bykert Gallery, 74-76; dir, Droll/Kolbert Gallery Inc, New York, 76- Specialty: Twentieth century painting and sculpture, especially of living Americans. Mailing Add: 724 Fifth Ave New York NY 10003

KOLIN, SACHA
SCULPTOR, PAINTER
b Paris, France, May 9, 11; US citizen. Study: Wiener Kunstgewerbe Schule, Acad of Fine Arts, Vienna; Studio Naoum Aronson, Paris; Soc de la Soc Nat des Beaux Arts, Paris, 33 & 34. Work: Nat Galleries, Smithsonian Inst, Washington, DC; Southampton Col of Long Island Univ, NY; Neuberger Mus, State Univ NY Col, Purchase. Comn: Monumental sculpture (25ft diameter; with Donald Lippencott), comn by David Kluger, New York, Everson Mus, Syracuse, 73; two monumental sculptures (9ft 3in; with Bob Schacht), comn by Andre Boesch, New Fairfield, Conn, Johnson Mus, Cornell Univ, Ithaca, NY, 77; two monumental sculptures (12ft high; with Joe Navedo), comn by Joseph Szoecs, New York, Colgate Univ, Hamilton, NY, 77. Exhib: One-man shows, Univ Ctr of Long Island Univ, Brookville, NY, 69, Southampton Col of Long Island Univ, 72, Everson Mus, Syracuse, 73, Johnson Mus, Cornell Univ, 75, Colgate Univ, Hamilton, NY, 76; Whitney Mus of Am Art, New York; Brooklyn Mus; Salon des Realites Nouvelles, Paris; Kuenstlerhaus, Vienna. Awards: Soc de la Soc Nat des Beaux Arts, Paris, 33 & 34. Bibliog: Mariette Pathy Allen (auth, videotape), Sacha Kolin, An Artist, 75; Richard Cuomo (auth, film), Sculpture, Sacha Kolin, 77 & An Artist and A Nude, 77. Style & Technique: Hardline action painting; minimal optical illusion sculpture. Media: Oil, Watercolor; Mixed Media Drawing; Metal, Wood & Formica. Dealer: Davlyn Gallery 975 Madison Ave New York NY 10021. Mailing Add: c/o Chet Stoner 751 St Marks Ave Brooklyn NY 11216

KOLLIKER, WILLIAM AUGUSTIN
PAINTER, GRAPHIC ARTIST
b Bern, Switz, Oct 12, 05; US citizen. Study: Berner Secundar Schule, Bern; Nat Acad Design, Md Inst; Boston Sch Art, Grand Cent Art Sch; Art Students League; Univ Tex, El Paso. Work: El Paso Mus Art, Tex; Univ Tex, El Paso; Grumbacher Col, New York; El Paso Nat Bank; El Paso Fed Savings & Loan; El Paso Chamber of Com; Kemp Ford, El Paso, Tex; Johnson Libr, Austin. Comn: Mosaic mural, El Fed Savings & Loan, El Paso, 64; design of bronze eagles, Amistad Dam, Del Rio, Tex, 68; gold medal, 69 & bronze plaques, 70, Chamisal Settlement. Exhib: El Paso Mus Art, 64 & 74; Univ Tex, Austin, 64 & 65; Abilene Mus Fine Arts, 74; Juarez Mexico Museo de Artes, 75; Dept Interior, Washington, DC, 75; one-man shows, Santa Fe Mus of Art, Midland Pub Libr, Int Trade Fair at El Paso, James Bute Gallery, Houston, El Paso Nat Bank, Alamogordo Pub Libr, NMex, NMex State Univ, Olivetti Bldg, El Paso, Las Cruces Art Ctr & El Paso Mus of Art. Teaching: Instr com art, Univ Tex, El Paso, 60-63; mem fac staff, El Paso Mus Art, 73-75. Pos: Dir art, Cunningham & Walsh Advert Agency, New York, 52-54; dir art, White & Shuford, El Paso, 54-65; pres, Watercolor Soc (Rio Bravo Watercolorist), El Paso, 74- Style & Technique: Impressionist. Media: Watercolor. Collection: Pre-Columbia artifacts and graphic collection. Publ: Illusr, Street & Smith Publs, 40-45; illusr, Aesop's Fables, 40; illusr, Adventures in puddle muddle, 41; illusr, Coronet, 42; illusr, 34-44; art dir & art ed, 44-52, Am Weekly. Dealer: Jinx Galleries 6513 N Mesa El Paso TX 79912. Mailing Add: 3812 Hillcrest Dr El Paso TX 79902

KOLODNER, NATHAN K
ART DEALER
b Baltimore, Md, Sept 10, 50. Study: Brandeis Univ, BA; NY Univ, MA(sociol); Inst Fine Arts, NY Univ. Specialty: Modern and contemporary painting and sculpture. Mailing Add: Andre Emmerich Gallery 41 E 57th St New York NY 10022

KOLTUN, FRANCES LANG
COLLECTOR, LECTURER
b New York, NY. Study: Brooklyn Col, BA; Columbia Univ, MA. Pos: Writer & broadcaster, NBC Syndicated Radio on Collecting, 70-; lectr on collecting. Mem: Drawing Soc. Collection: 19th and 20th century drawings. Publ: Numerous articles on art. Mailing Add: 45 E 66th St New York NY 10021

KOMODORE, BILL
PAINTER, SCULPTOR
b Athens, Greece, Oct 23, 32; US citizen. Study: Tulane Univ La, BA, 55 & MFA, 57; Hans Hofmann Sch, Provincetown; also with George Rickey, Mark Rothko & David Smith. Work:

Whitney Mus Am Art, New York; Des Moines Art Ctr, Iowa; Nat Gallery Art, Washington, DC; Walker Art Ctr, Minneapolis. Exhib: The Responsive Eye, Mus Mod Art, New York, 64 & Traveling Show, 66; Contemp Am Painting & Sculpture, Krannert Art Mus, Univ Ill, Champaign, 65; Art in Motion, Cincinnati Art Mus, 65; Optical & Kinetic Show, 65, Plus by Minus, 68 & Today's Half Century, 68, Albright-Knox Art Gallery, Buffalo, NY; Young Am, 65, Artists for CORE, SEDF, 66, 67 & 68 & Artists Under Forty, 68, Whitney Mus Am Art, New York; Op Art & Its Antecedents, Am Fedn of Arts Traveling Show, 66-67 & The Square in Painting, Am Fedn of Arts Exhib assembled by Richard Anuszkiewics, 68-69; Marcia Tucker's The Art of the Invisible, Visual Arts Gallery, New York, 70; one-man shows, Haydon Calhoun Gallery, Dallas, 61 & Automation House, New York, 73; retrospective show, Mary Washington Col, 75. Teaching: Vis artist, Northwood Inst, Cedar Hill, Tex, spring 69; vis artist, Mary Washington Col, Fredericksburg, Va, 73-76 & Richland Col, Arts Magnet High, Dallas, 77-78. Awards: Bausch & Lomb Sci Award, 50; Houston Mus Award, Dallas Mus of Fine Arts, 60. Bibliog: Robert Trout (interviewer), Op art, CBS News with Walter Cronkite, 64; Cyril Barrett (auth), An introduction to optical art, Studio Vista, 71. Style & Technique: Complex compositions combining past and present, classical and romantic, intricate and powerful, figure and landscape, real and unreal. Media: Acrylic, Watercolor, Ink, Pencil. Publ: Illusr, Fishes of Lake Pontchartrain, Tulane Univ Press, 54; contribr, Contemporary American Painting and Sculpture, Univ Ill Press, 65; contribr, Young America, 1965, Whitney Mus Am Art, 65; Bill Komodore Retrospective, Mary Washington Col, 75. Mailing Add: 6024 Lewis St Dallas TX 75206

KOMOR, MATHIAS
ART DEALER
b Jan 24, 09; US citizen. Study: Univ Grenoble, Dr Univ, 29. Specialty: Antiquities, Greek, Egyptian, Far East and others. Mailing Add: 19 E 71st St New York NY 10021

KONI, NICOLAUS
SCULPTOR, LECTURER
b Hungary, May 6, 11; US citizen. Study: Acad Fine Art, Vienna, Austria, dipl anat fine art; Masters Sch, Paris; Masters Sch, Florence, Italy. Work: Bronze sculptures, Fountain of the Night, Okla Art Ctr, Oklahoma City, bust of F V Forrestal, Forrestal Bldg & bust of Marian Anderson, Kennedy Ctr Performing Art, Washington, DC; Seminole Club, Palm Beach, Fla & Nat Mus Jerusalem, Israel. Comn: Bronze sculpture of C Walter Nichols, NY Univ Bus Admin Sch. Exhib: Whitney Mus Am Art, New York; Birmingham Mus Fine Art, Ala; Parrish Art Mus, South Hampton, NY; Milch Galleries, New York. Teaching: Instr sculpture, Graham-Eckes Sch, Palm Beach; lectr, Univ Bridgeport; instr fine art, Univ Mo-Columbia. Awards: First Prize in art, 8th Ann Art Festival, Parrish Art Mus. Bibliog: Nicolaus Koni; a sculptor bringing out the spirit asleep in matter (film), NY Fine Arts Coun; Classical influence and values in modern art (slide prog). Mem: Nat Sculpture Soc; Quilleis Art Soc (past chmn). Style & Technique: Modern classic; Konilite process of etched and carved multi-dimensional forms which reflect light. Media: Wood, Marble, Bronze, Jade, Gold. Dealer: Milch Art Gallery 1014 Madison Ave New York NY 10021; Palm Beach Gallery 336 Worth Ave Palm Beach FL 33480. Mailing Add: 146 Australian Ave Palm Beach FL 33480

KONIGSBERG, HARVEY
PAINTER
b New York, NY, Sept 23, 40. Study: Univ Miami, 60-64; NY Univ. Work: Nat Art Mus of Sport, Madison Square Garden, New York; Joe & Emily Lowe Art Mus, Coral Gables, Fla; Sperry Rand Corp, Midland, Tex; Midland Oil Corp, Tex; Mitsukoshi Permanent Collection, Tokyo, Japan. Bibliog: Jared Finesmith (auth), The artist at home-work, Nat Film Bd Can, 68. Style & Technique: Figurative; impressionistic; action. Media: Oil, Acrylic. Dealer: M Elson Gallery 463 W Broadway New York NY. Mailing Add: 26 W 20th St New York NY 10011

KONOPKA, JOSEPH
PAINTER
b Philadelphia, Pa, Oct 6, 32. Study: Cooper Union, grad, 54; Columbia Univ, 55. Work: NJ State Mus, Trenton; Newark Mus, NJ; Ct Gen Sessions Art Trust, Washington, DC; Morris Mus of Arts & Sci, Morristown, NJ; Cooper Hewitt Mus, Nat Mus of Design, Smithsonian Inst, New York. Exhib: Am Fedn Art Traveling Exhib, 67-69; Newark Mus, 68-76; NJ State Mus, 68, 70, 71 & 76; Butler Inst Am Art, 74 & 76; Silvermine Guild Conn, 67-69 & 74; Montclair Art Mus, NJ, 72; Morris Mus of Arts & Sci, Morristown, 73, 76-77; Rutgers Univ, Camden, NJ, 75; RI Col, Providence, 76; Brooklyn Mus, NY, 76 & 78; Kosciuszko Found, New York, 76; Summit Art Ctr, NJ, 77. Awards: Purchase Awards, Newark Mus, 68 & NJ State Mus, 70; Medal of Honor, NJ Painters & Sculptors Soc, 71. Bibliog: Articles in Soho News, 75, Sunday New York Times, 76 & Viva Mag, 4/77. Mem: Assoc Artists NJ (vpres); NJ Painters & Sculptors Soc; United Scenic Artists, NY. Style & Technique: Realist paintings (subject matter, figure in the urban landscape). Dealer: Capricorn Gallery 8004 Norfolk Ave Bethesda MD 20014; Razor Gallery 464 W Broadway New York NY 10012. Mailing Add: 26 Snowden Pl Glen Ridge NJ 07028

KONRAD, ADOLF FERDINAND
PAINTER
b Bremen, Ger; US citizen. Study: Newark Sch Fine & Indust Art, NJ; Cummington Sch, Mass; Newark State Col, hon DFA. Work: Newark Mus; Springfield Mus Fine Art, Mass; Montclair Art Mus, NJ; Nat Acad Design, New York; NJ State Mus, Trenton. Exhib: Am Painting Today, Metrop Mus Art, 50 & Whitney Mus Am Art Ann, 52, New York; Butler Inst Am Art, Youngstown, Ohio, 56; Pa Acad Fine Arts Painting Exhib, 64; Mainstream 70, Marietta Col, Ohio, 70. Teaching: Adj instr painting, Newark State Col, 72. Awards: Louis Comfort Tiffany Found Fel creative painting, 61; Andrew Carnegie Prize, Nat Acad Design, 67; NJ Symphony Ann Arts Award, 69. Bibliog: An artist looks at Newark, Newark Mus, 66; Henry Gasser (auth), Adolf Konrad, painter of the American scene, Am Artist, 11/68. Mem: Nat Acad Design; Audubon Artists; Artists Equity Asn; Assoc Artists NJ. Style & Technique: Realist over a strong abstract structure. Media: Oil. Mailing Add: Asbury NJ 08802

KONZAL, JOSEPH
SCULPTOR
b Milwaukee, Wis, Nov 5, 05. Study: Beaux-Arts Inst Design, New York; Art Students League, with Max Weber & Robert Laurent, 26-31. Work: Tate Gallery Art, London; Whitney Mus Am Art & New Sch Social Res, New York; Canton Art Inst, Ohio; NJ State Mus, Trenton. Comn: Sculpture, comn by Blossom-Kent Univ Comt, Blossom Music Ctr, Cuyahoga Falls, Ohio, 72; Outdoor Sculpture, Gen Servs Admin, Art & Archit Prog, Fed Off Bldg, Dayton, Ohio, 77. Exhib: Six Ann Shows, Whitney Mus Am Art, 48-68 & Geometric Abstraction in America, 62; Recent Sculpture, Mus of Mod Art, New York, 58; five one-man shows, Bertha Schaefer Gallery, 60-71; NJ State Mus Ann, 65-71; May Show for Ohio Artists, Cleveland Mus Art, 72 & 75; Canton Art Inst, Ohio, 74; Boston Mus; NJ State Mus; Larry Aldrich Mus, Conn; one-man show, Andre Zarre Gallery, New York, 78. Teaching: Newark Sch for Fine & Indust Arts; Queens Col, New York; Adelphi Univ; Malloy Col; Brooklyn Mus Art Sch; Kent State Univ. Awards: Guggenheim Fel for Creative Work in Sculpture, 65-66; Sculpture Competition Prize for Nassau Co Ct House, John F Kennedy Mem Cult Ctr, 68. Mem: Life mem Art Students League. Arts. Media: Metals, Wood, Constructions. Publ: Auth, Who are the tastemakers, spring 69 & auth, Art, technology and liberal art colleges; a reply, winter 70-71, Art J. Dealer: Andre Zarre Gallery 41 E 57th St New York NY 10022. Mailing Add: 360 W 21st St New York NY 10011

KOOCHIN, WILLIAM
SCULPTOR, INSTRUCTOR
b Brilliant, BC, Dec 15, 27. Study: Vancouver Sch Art; Sevres Ceramics, Paris. Work: Vancouver Art Gallery; Univ Ore Mus; High Park, Toronto, Ont. Comn: Welded steel mural and free standing pieces, Can Govt, Brussels World's Fair, 57; wood carving wall hanging & crucifix, Redemptorist Col, 59; wood carved mace, Vancouver Int Arts Festival, 61; cast bronze trophy, Vancouver Maritime Festival, 62; carved granite fountain, Pacific Press Bldg, 66. Exhib: One-man shows, Agnes Lefort Gallery, Montreal, 57; Gallery Contemp Art, Toronto, 58, Vancouver Art Gallery, 59 & Victoria Art Gallery, 61; BC Sculptors, Mido Gallery, Vancouver, 75. Teaching: Instr sculpture, Vancouver Sch Art, 64- Bibliog: Arla Sarre (auth), Sculpture Koochin (film), Can Broadcasting Corp, 64. Mem: BC Sculpture Soc; Royal Can Acad Arts. Style & Technique: Figurative. Media: Carved Stone & Wood, Cast Bronze. Mailing Add: 3400 Moyne Dr West Vancouver BC Can

KOONS, DARELL J
PAINTER, INSTRUCTOR
b Albion, Mich, Dec 18, 24. Study: Bob Jones Univ, BS, 51; Western Mich Univ, MA, 55; Eastern Mich Univ. Work: Butler Inst Am Art, Youngstown, Ohio; Mint Mus Art, Charlotte, Gibbes Gallery, Charleston, Greenville Co Mus Art & Florence Mus Art, SC. Comn: Hist mural of Homer, Mich, for Homer Community Schs, 55. Exhib: Southeastern Exhibs, Atlanta, Ga, 63-65; Acquavella Galleries, New York, 64 & 66; Springfield Mus Art Nat, Mass, 65; Soc Four Arts Nat, Palm Beach, Fla, 67; Chico State Col Invitational, Calif, 72. Teaching: Instr art, Homer Community Schs, 52-54; instr art, Bob Jones Univ, 55- Awards: Purchase Awards, Guild SC Artists, 63, Davis Assocs, Chattanooga, Tenn, 65 & Wake Forest Univ Gallery Contemp Art, 65. Bibliog: Steve Yates (auth), Greenville's noted barn painter, Sandlapper, 3/68. Mem: Greenville Art Asn & Guild; Guild SC Artists. (mem bd); Int Platform Asn. Media: Watercolor, Printmaking, Polymer. Mailing Add: 6 Yancy Dr Greenville SC 29615

KOPMANIS, AUGUSTS A
SCULPTOR
b Riga, Latvia, Mar 17, 10. Study: Acad Fine Arts, Riga. Exhib: Colour & Form Soc, 53-64; Nat Gallery Can, 63; Confedn Art Gallery & Mus, Charlottetown, PEI, 64; Hamilton, Ont, 64 & 65; Albert White Gallery, Toronto, 65; plus others. Mem: Sculptors Soc Can; Ont Soc Arts; fel Int Inst Arts & Lett; Royal Can Acad Arts. Publ: Illusr, Season in Latvian Folk Songs, 56. Mailing Add: 19 Millbrook Crescent Toronto ON M4K 1H2 Can

KOPPELMAN, CHAIM
PRINTMAKER, EDUCATOR
b New York, NY, Nov 17, 20. Study: Am Artists Sch; Art Col Western Eng, Bristol; Ozenfant Sch Fine Arts; also with Eli Siegel. Work: Victoria & Albert Mus, London; Mus Fine Arts, Caracas, Venezuela; Mus Mod Art, Metrop Mus Art & Whitney Mus Am Art, New York; Libr Cong, Washington, DC; Los Angeles Co Mus, Calif; plus others. Exhib: 2nd Nat Print Invitational, Purdue Univ, 72; 2nd Ann Print Int, Utah State Univ, 72; one-man shows, Assoc Am Artists Gallery, 73 & Terrain Gallery, 74, New York; Warwick Gallery, Eng, 75; plus many others. Teaching: NY Univ, 47-55; Brooklyn Col, 50-60; State Univ NY Col New Paltz, 52-58; Sch Visual Arts, 59- Pos: Consult, Aesthet Realism Consultations, 71- Awards: Tiffany Found Grant, 56 & 59; Soc Am Graphic Artists Prize, 66; 3rd Int Miniature Print Exhib Prize, 68; plus others. Bibliog: Ralph Shikes (auth), The Indignant Eye, Beacon Press, 69; Barry Schwartz (auth), The New Humanism, Praeger, 74. Mem: Soc Aesthet Realism; Soc Am Graphic Artists (former pres). Style & Technique: People as a drama of opposites, visual and ethical at once. Publ: Contribr, Liberation Mag, 69; co-auth, Aesthetic Realism: We Have Been There, 69; auth, This Is the Way I See Aesthetic Realism, 69; illusr, Damned Welcome, Definition, 72. Mailing Add: 498 Broome St New York NY 10012

KOPPELMAN, DOROTHY
PAINTER, GALLERY DIRECTOR
b New York, NY, June 13, 20. Study: Brooklyn Col; Am Artists Sch; Art Students League; also with Eli Siegel. Work: Yale Univ, New Haven, Conn; Hampton Inst, Va. Exhib: Mus Mod Art, New York, 62; San Francisco Mus Art, Calif; Pratt Graphics Traveling Exhib, 62-63; two-man show, Terrain Gallery, 69 & three-man exhib, The Kindest Art, 70; plus many others. Teaching: Instr art, Adult Educ, Brooklyn Col, 52; consult, Aesthet Realism, 71- Pos: Dir, Terrain Gallery, 55- & Visual Arts Gallery, 63-64; pres, Aesthetic Realism Found, Inc, 73- Awards: First Prize for Painting, City Ctr Gallery, 57; Prize for Painting, Brooklyn Soc Artists, 60; Tiffany Found Grant, 65-66. Mem: Soc Aesthet Realism. Style & Technique: I consider relation an object; also, in keeping with aesthetic realism, I see feelings as objects. Media: Oil. Publ: Co-auth, Aesthetic Realism: We Have Been There, 69; illusr, Children's Guide to Parents & Other Matters, 71. Mailing Add: 498 Broome St New York NY 10012

KORAS, GEORGE
SCULPTOR
b Florina, Greece, Apr 1, 25; US citizen. Study: Sch Fine Arts, Athens, Greece, dipl, 55; study in Paris & Rome, 55; Art Students League, 57; with Jacques Lipchitz, 55-59. Work: W P Chrysler Collection; Provincetown Mus, Mass; Norfolk Mus, Va; Pnevmatikon Centron Florinis, Greece. Comn: Cast bronze sculptures, G Moffett, Edgartown, Mass, 69-70, Bd Educ, Queens, NY, 71, Bd Educ, Bronx, 72 & 74 & Marcus Asn, Hauppauge, NY, 72. Exhib: Panhellenios Zapeion, Athens, Greece, 49; Brooklyn Mus, NY, 60; Pa Acad Fine Arts, Philadelphia, 64; Silvermine Guild Artists, New Canaan, Conn, 67; Art Inst, New York, 68. Teaching: Prof art, State Univ NY Stony Brook, 66- Awards: Brooklyn Mus, 60, Pa Acad Fine Arts, 64 & Hofstra Univ, 65. Bibliog: Radio interview, produced on Voice of Am, New York, 72; G Koras Sculptor (TV film), produced by NY State Coun Arts, 72. Mem: Audubon Artists (dir sculpture, 63-66 & 68-71). Style & Technique: Mostly non-objective expressionism of abstract feelings of the subconscious, done in the lost wax process. Media: Bronze. Mailing Add: 43-44 149th St Flushing NY 11355

KOREN, EDWARD B
CARTOONIST, ILLUSTRATOR
b New York, NY, Dec 13, 35. Study: Columbia Univ, BA, 57; Atelier 17, Paris, with S W Hayter; Pratt Inst, MFA, 64. Work: Fogg Mus, Cambridge, Mass; Princeton Univ Mus; RI Sch Design Mus; US Info Agency; Swann Collection Cartoon & Caricatures. Exhib:

Exposition Dessins d'Humeur, Soc Protectrice d'Humeur, Avignon, France, 73; Biennale Illusr, Bratislav, Czech, 73; Art from the New York Times, Soc Illusr, New York, 73; Art from the New Yorker, Grolier Club, 75; Terry Dintinfass Gallery, New York, 75-77. Teaching: Adj prof art, Brown Univ, 64- Awards: Third Prize, Biennale Illusr, Bratislava, Czech, 73; Ten Best Childrens Books of the Year, New York Times, 73; Prix d'Humour, Soc Protectrice d'Humour, Avignon, France, 76. Mem: Authors Guild; Soc Am Graphic Artists; Cartoonists Guild. Style & Technique: Cartoons and illustrations; etching, wooden sculpture. Media: Pen & Ink. Publ: Illusr, The People Maybe, Duxbury, 74; illusr, Cooking for Crowds, Basic Bks, 75; auth, Do You Want to Talk About It?, Pantheon, 77; illusr, Noodles Galore, Basic Bks, 77 & Dragons Hate to Be Discrete, Knopf, 78. Mailing Add: c/o The New Yorker 25 W 43rd St New York NY 10036

KORJUS, VERONICA MARIA ELISABETH
PAINTER, LECTURER
b Tallinn, Estonia; US citizen. Study: Prof Women's Col, Higher State Acad Art, Estonia, dipl, 42; Univ Stockholm, 43-45; Columbia Univ, MA, 52; Phoenix Sch Art, 53-56; Nat Acad Design, New York, 60-61; La Grande Chaumiere, Paris, 61 & 69-70; also pvt studies in Mus Louvre, Mus Jeu Paume & others. Work: Yasuda Art Collection. Comn: Portraits, UN Ambassador Dr Jan Papanek, Scarsdale, NY, 63; Dr Richard Fafara, 69, Susan Bell, 70, Countess Maria Therese Perez de Cavanillas, 70 & Ingrid Bergman, 72; three comn portraits, World Coun Churches. Exhib: Ctr Art Gallery, New York, 64; Int Art Gallery, Toronto, 64-66; one-man shows, IBM Country Club, Poughkeepsie, NY, 64 & 69 & Las Mimosas, Tangier, Morocco, 66; Barnard Col Art Asn, New York, 69. Teaching: Lectr & demonstr portraits, IBM Country Club, 64, Riverside Arts, New York, 65-67, Mus Louvre & Mus Jeu Paume, 70 & Cape Coral Art League, Fla, 72. Mem: Am Artists Prof League; Fraternitas Artis; Int Platform Asn. Style & Technique: Abstract art in impressionistic realist tradition; from strong construction building up towards dimension with actual color in oil without diluting agents. Media: Oil, Pastel. Mailing Add: 5350 Del Monte Ct Cape Coral FL 33904

KORMAN, BARBARA
SCULPTOR, INSTRUCTOR
b New York, NY, Apr 8, 38. Study: Art Students League; NY State Col Ceramics, Alfred Univ, BFA, cum laude, 59, grad fel, 59-60, MFA. Work: In many pvt collections throughout the world. Exhib: Rochester Mem Art Gallery, NY, 59; Albright-Knox Art Gallery, Buffalo, NY, 60; Hartford Mus Gallery Shop, Conn, 61; Hudson River Mus, Yonkers, NY, 73, 74 & 76; Nat Acad Design, New York, 73-77; Metrop Mus of Art, New York, 76; Bronx Mus, NY, 77. Teaching: Teaching fel painting & basic 2-D design, NY State Col Ceramics, 59-60; teacher & dir ceramics, Ceramic Workshop, Berkshires, summer 59; teacher sculpture, New York Bd Educ, 61- Awards: Int Women's Yr Award, 75-76; House of Heydenryk Prize for Sculpture, 74. Mem: Nat Asn Women Artists; Bronx Coun Arts; Yonkers Art Asn; Int soc of Artists. Style & Technique: Mixed media two- & three-dimensional constructions. Dealer: Mari Galleries Ltd Mamaroneck NY 10543. Mailing Add: 357 E 201st St New York NY 10458

KORMAN, HARRIET R
PAINTER
b Bridgeport, Conn, Dec 10, 47. Study: Skowhegan Sch Painting & Sculpture, summer 68; Queens Col (NY), BA, 69. Work: Weatherspoon Art Gallery, Univ NC, Greensboro; Solomon R Guggenheim Mus, New York. Exhib: Solomon R Guggenheim Mus, 71; Whitney Ann Exhib Painting, Whitney Mus Am Art, New York, 72; one-person shows, Copley Gallery, Los Angeles, 74, 112 Greene St Gallery, New York, 75 & Daniel Weinberg Gallery, San Francisco, 76; Willard Gallery, New York, 75 & 76. Awards: Theodoron Found Award, 71; Nat Endowment for the Arts Fel Grant, 74. Bibliog: Robert Pincus Whitten (auth), article in Artforum, 71; Jeanne Siegel (auth), article in Art News, 72; Roberta Smith (auth), article in Artforum, 75. Dealer: Willard Gallery 29 E 72nd St New York NY 10021. Mailing Add: 72 Franklin New York NY 10013

KORN, ELIZABETH P
PAINTER, ILLUSTRATOR
US citizen. Study: Inst Fine & Appl Arts, Univ Breslau, Berlin; Mus Fine & Appl Arts, Masterclass, Berlin; study in Rome & Madrid; Columbia Univ; New Sch Social Res; NY Univ Inst Fine Arts; Art Students League, with Morris Kantor. Work: Newark Mus, NJ; Drew Univ, Madison, NJ; Prudential Ins Co Am, Newark; Stevens Inst Technol, Hoboken, NJ; Arch Am Art, Smithsonian Inst, Washington, DC; plus others. Exhib: Galleria Bragaglia, Rome, 65; Theol Sem, Drew Univ, 69; Cols & Univs Traveling Exhib, Emory & Henry Col, Va & King Col, Bristol, Tenn, 69; one-man shows, Roko Gallery, New York, 69-71; Genesee Community Col, Batavia & Cornell Univ, Ithaca, NY, 70; plus many group & one-man shows. Collections Arranged: Drew Univ Exhibits. Teaching: Fla Presby Col, St Petersburg; artist in residence & vis scholar, Emory & Henry Col & King Col, Tenn; prof art & chmn dept, Drew Univ, 58-65, artist in residence, 66; vis prof art, Newark Col Eng; studio fac, Stevens Inst Technol; vis prof, Sacred Heart Acad; Summit Art Ctr, NJ; also lectr art in cols, univs, clubs & groups in Eastern & Southern US. Awards: Grumbacher Award; Prize for Oil, Six-State Eastern Col Exhib; Windsor & Newton Award; plus others. Mem: Col Art Asn Am; Nat Asn Women Artists; Am Asn Univ Prof; life mem Art Students League; plus others. Media: Mixed Media, Assemblage. Publ: Co-auth & illusr, At Home with Children, Holt; co-auth & illusr, Trailblazer to Television, Scribner; co-auth & illusr, Apple Pie for Lewis, Aladin Bks; co-auth & illusr, Nando of the Beach, Bruce Publ; also reports, rev & articles in var publ, US & abroad. Dealer: Roko Gallery 90 E Tenth St New York NY 10003. Mailing Add: 1500 Manhattan Ave Union City NJ 07087

KORNBLATT, BARBARA RODBELL
ART DEALER
b Baltimore, Md, Jan 25, 31. Study: Goucher Col, with Hilton Brown, BA; Community Col of Baltimore, AA. Pos: Dir, B R Kornblatt Gallery, Baltimore, Md, 75- Specialty: Contemporary American sculpture, prints and painting. Mailing Add: 326 N Charles St Baltimore MD 21201

KORNER, JOHN (JOHN MICHAEL ANTHONY KOERNER)
PAINTER
b Novy Jicin, Czech, Sept 29, 13; Can citizen. Study: With F Kausek, Prague & Othon Friesz, Paul Colin & Victor Tischler, Paris. Work: Nat Gallery Can, Ottawa; Montreal Mus Fine Arts; Vancouver Art Gallery; Seattle Art Mus; Toronto Art Gallery; plus others. Comn: Murals, comn by D J Simpson, Vancouver, 66, King's Daughters Hosp, Duncan, BC, 67, A B Cliff, Palm Springs, Calif, 68, CHQM Radio Sta, Vancouver, 69 & H B McDonald, Vancouver, 70; plus others. Exhib: Nat Gallery Can Biennials, 54-64; World's Fair, Seattle, 62; Art Inst, Minneapolis, 63; San Francisco Mus Art, 65; Commonwealth Inst, London, 68; plus others. Teaching: Instr painting, Vancouver Sch Art, 53-58 & Univ BC, 58-62. Awards: Winnipeg Show Award, 55, 57 & 61; Vancouver Art Gallery Centennial Award, 59; Govt Can Centennial Medal, 67. Dealer: Bau-Xi Gallery 3003 Granville St Vancouver BC Can. Mailing Add: 5816 Kingston Rd Vancouver BC V6T 1J3 Can

KORNMAYER, J GARY (JOHN)
PAINTER, PHOTOGRAPHER
b Omaha, Nebr, July 10, 34. Study: San Diego State Univ, 59-61; Nat Univ, San Diego, BA, 70, MA(audio-visual commun), 74. Work: Riverside Art Mus, Calif. Comn: Tex Hist, Nat Univ, San Diego, 73 & Am Hist of Slavery, 74. Exhib: Joslyn Art Mus, Omaha, Nebr, 53; La Jolla Mus Contemp Art, Calif, 64; The Brooks Found, Santa Barbara, Calif, 64; Fine Arts Gallery, San Diego, Balboa Park, 67; Painting of Yr, Jewish Community Ctr, 67, 68, 72 & 78; Fine Arts Gallery San Diego, 68, 69 & 71; Ann Art Show, Riverside Art Mus, 69 & 70; Univ San Diego, 71; Eastern Mennonite Col, Harrisonburg, Va, 71; Americana Show, Pace Bicentennial, Pace Univ, New York, 75; Noho Gallery, New York, 75-78; Calif-Hawaii Biennial, Fine Arts Gallery San Diego, 76; Ann Small Image Art Show, Span Village Art Ctr, San Diego, 76-78. Pos: Photogr, Gen Dynamics Corp, San Diego, 58-60, sr audio-visual commun, 60-69. Awards: Distinctive Merit, San Diego Art Director's Soc, 65; Second Place, Fine Arts Gallery San Diego, 68; First Place Purchase Award, Riverside Art Mus, 70. Bibliog: Hedy O'Beil (auth), J Gary Kornmayer, artist, Arts Mag, 10/77; Hal Gray (auth), Horizons, Channel 39, 12/77; In the Public Interest, City of San Diego, Channel 2, 1/78. Mem: San Diego Fine Arts Soc-Art Guild (mem bd dirs, 68-70); Span Village Art Asn (mem bd dir, 72-74, pres, 74-78). Style & Technique: Surreal; unique media incorporating paint, art collage and photographic montage. Dealer: Studio 38 Span Village Art Ctr Balboa Park San Diego CA 92101. Mailing Add: 3436 Park W Lane San Diego CA 92117

KOROT, BERYL
VIDEO ARTIST
b New York, NY, Sept 17, 45. Study: Univ Wis, 63-65; Queens Col, BA, 67. Exhib: Art Now, Kennedy Ctr, Washington, DC, 74; Video Art, Inst Contemp Arts, Philadelphia, 75; Sao Paulo Biennial, Brazil, 75; Dachau 1974, Documenta VI, Kassel, Ger, 77; one-man shows, Dachau, 74, The Kitchen, New York, Everson Mus, Syracuse, NY, 75 & Text & Commentary, Leo Castelli Gallery, New York, 77. Awards: NYSCA Grant for Radical Software, 72-75; Creative Artists Pub Serv Grant, 72 & 75; Nat Endowment for the Arts Grant, 75 & 77. Bibliog: Jeff Parrone (auth), Text and Commentary (rev), Art Forum, 5/77; Grace Glueck (auth), New York Times, 3/18/77. 6/75. Mem: The Raindance Found (secy-treas, 73-). Style & Technique: Multi-channel video work; exploring relationship between ancient technology of loom and modern technology of video. Media: Videotape, Weaving. Publ: Ed, Radical software, Vol I & Vol II, Gordon & Breach Sci Publ, 72-74; ed, Video Art, Harcourt, Brace, Jovanovich (in press). Dealer: Castelli/Sonnabend Film/Video Distribution Inc 420 W Broadway New York NY 10012. Mailing Add: 16 Warren St New York NY 10007

KOROW, ELINORE MARIA
PAINTER
b Akron, Ohio, July 31, 34. Study: Cleveland Inst Art, with Rolf Stoll, Paul Riba & John Teyral; Sienna Heights Womens Col. Comn: Portraits of Richard Oberlin, Dir, Play House Gallery Collection, Cleveland, Louis Triscaro, Pres of Teamsters Local 436, George Hilden, Pres of Osco Drugs, Chicago, Jerome Weinberger, Pres Gray Drugs, Charles Walgreen, Pres Walgreen Drugs, Sarah & Peggy Gries of Shaker Heights, and others. Exhib: Butler Inst Am Art, Youngstown, Ohio, 68-70; Massillon Mus Juried Regional Exhib, 69; Pan Am Galleries, New York, NY, 71; Canton Art Inst All Ohio Show, 71; Mt Sinai Int Exhib, 72; Ohio State Fair Fine Arts Exhib, 72; Virginia Beach Nat Art Show, Va, 73; Am Watercolor Soc, New York, 73; Rocky Mountain Nat Watermedia Exhib, Golden, Colo, 74; Lynn Kottler Galleries, New York, 74; Octogon Galleries-Patterson Libr, Westfield, NY, 74; Nat Small Painting Exhib, Hadley & Philadelphia, Pa, 74; Washington & Jefferson Col Nat Painting Show, 75; Kennedy Ctr Art Gallery, Hiram Col, Hiram, Ohio, 76. Pos: Staff artist & designer, Am Greetings Corp, Cleveland, 71-73. Awards: Best in Oils, Cleveland Press Club, 66; Award of Excellence, Jewish Community Ctr, 72. Style & Technique: Portraits and figures in oil, acrylic and pastel; technique is relatively loose and contemporary. Dealer: Strongs Gallery 33 Public Square Blvd Cleveland OH 44113. Mailing Add: 3441 Lee Rd Suite 206 Shaker Heights OH 44120

KORTHEUER, DAYRELL
PAINTER, CONSERVATOR
b New York, NY, July 25, 06. Study: Art Students League, with Frank DuMond, George Bridgman & John Carroll; Nat Acad Design, with Charles Hawthorne. Work: Portraits, Merchant's Asn, New York; Mint Mus Art; Emory Univ; Univ NC; Davidson Col; plus others. Exhib: Blowing Rock Art Asn, 55; Statesville, NC, 57 & 64; Hickory, NC, 58; Carson-McKenna Gallery, Charlotte, NC, 69; Mint Mus Art, 74. Awards: Nat Arts Club Prizes, 28; Mint Mus Art Awards, 41 & 42; Gold Medal, Blowing Rock Art Asn, 54 & Award, 55. Mem: Portraits, Inc; Am Inst Conserv Hist & Artistic Works; NC State Art Soc; Mint Mus Art. Mailing Add: 1924 Sharon Lane Charlotte NC 28211

KORTLANDER, WILLIAM (CLARK)
PAINTER
b Grand Rapids, Mich, Feb 9, 25. Study: Mich State Univ, BA; Univ Iowa, MA & PhD. Work: Columbus Gallery Fine Arts, Ohio; Chubu Inst, Nagoya, Japan; Zanesville Art Inst, Ohio; Huntington Galleries, WVa; WVa State Col. Exhib: Des Moines Art Ctr, Iowa, 52 & 54; Dallas Mus of Fine Arts, Tex, 58, 59 & 61; Dallas Mus of Contemp Art, Tex, 59; Witte Mus, San Antonio, Tex, 61; Huntington Galleries, WVa, 62-66; Columbus Gallery of Fine Arts, Ohio, 62-66; Dayton Art Inst, Ohio, 63-65 & 74; Pa Acad of Fine Arts, Philadelphia, 65; Knoedler Gallery, New York, NY, 65; Toledo Mus of Art, Ohio, 65; Cleveland Art Inst, Ohio, 65; Wadsworth Atheneum, Hartford, Conn, 65; Isaac Delyado Mus, New Orleans, La, 65; Brooks Mem Art Gallery, Memphis, Tenn, 65; J B Speed Art Mus, Louisville, Ky, 65; Corcoran Gallery, Washington, DC, 68; Baltimore Mus, Md, 68; Drawings of the Sixties, New Sch Art Ctr, New York, NY, 69; Am Embassies, Bogota, Colombia & Cotonon, Dahomey, 70; Philbrook Art Ctr, Tulsa, Okla, 72, 73 & 75; Govett Brewster Art Gallery, New Plymouth, NZ, 72; Far Gallery, New York, 77; one-man shows, Denison Univ, Granville, Ohio, 65, Battelle Mem Inst, Columbus, Ohio, 66, WVa State Col, Institute, 66, A M Sachs Gallery, New York, NY, 67 & 68, Mont State Univ, Bozeman, 69, Springfield Art Ctr, Ohio, 74, Gallery 200, Columbus, Ohio, 74 & Ohio Univ, Zanesville, 76. Teaching: Instr art hist, Lawrence Univ, 54-56; asst prof art hist, Univ Tex, Austin, 56-61; vis asst prof art hist, Mich State Univ, summer 61; prof painting, Ohio Univ, 61- Awards: Painting of Year, Mead Corp, 65; Baker Award, Ohio Univ, 67. Style & Technique: Essentially figurative and landscape paintings; drawings and paintings range, however, from representational to non-objective. Media: Acryic, Oil, Watercolor. Publ: Auth, Painting with Acrylics, Van Nostrand Reinhold, 73. Dealer: Far Gallery 22 E 80th St New York NY 10021. Mailing Add: Angel Ridge Rte 4 Athens OH 45701

KOS, PAUL JOSEPH
SCULPTOR, EDUCATOR
b Rock Springs, Wyo, Dec 23, 42. Study: San Francisco Art Inst, BFA, 65, MFA, 67. Work: Ft Worth Art Mus, Tex; San Francisco Mus Mod Art; Mus Conceptual Art, San Francisco; Inst Contemp Art, Univ Pa; Austrian Govt, Ganz, Austria; de Saisset Art Gallery, Univ Santa Clara, Calif. Comn: Floating (sculpture), Winery Lake, Napa, Calif, 68, Wind (sculpture), 69 & Performance (sculpture), 70. Exhib: One-man show, M H De Young Mem Mus, San Francisco; Bienal Sao Paulo, Brazil, 73 & 75; Trigon 74, Neue Galerie am Landesmuseum Joanneum, Ganz, Austria, 74; Art Now '74, John F Kennedy Ctr for Performing Arts, Washington, DC, 74; Whitney Biennial, Whitney Mus Am Art, New York, 75; Paris Biennial, 77. Teaching: Asst prof, Univ Santa Clara, 69-77. Pos: Artist mem bd trustees, San Francisco Art Inst, 73-76. Awards: Nat Endowment Fel, 74. Style & Technique: Video art and sculpture. Mailing Add: 1215 Waller St San Francisco CA 94117

KOSCIELNY, MARGARET
SCULPTOR, PAINTER
b Tallahassee, Fla, Aug 13, 40. Study: Tex Woman's Univ, with Toni Lasalle; Univ Ga, BA(art hist) & MFA, with Irving Marantz & Charles Morgan. Comn: Plexiglas sculpture, John Portman, Atlanta, Ga, 69 & 70; Plexiglas sculpture, Maurice D Alpert, Int City Corp, Atlanta, 72 & 75; Omni, Norfolk, Va, 75. Exhib: Fla State Fair, Tampa, 65; American Drawing 1968, Philadelphia, 68; Drawing USA, St Paul, Minn, 69; Cummer Gallery, Jacksonville, 72; Art Celebration, Jacksonville, 73, 74 & 76; two-man exhib, Contemp Gallery, St Petersburg, 75; Four Jacksonville Artists, Cummer Gallery, Fla, 76; one-person show, Vanderbilt Univ, Nashville, Tenn, 77. Teaching: Instr printmaking, Jacksonville Art Mus, 68; Jacksonville Univ, 67. Awards: Fine Arts Coun of Fla grant, US State Dept of Cult Affairs & Nat Endowment for the Arts, 76. Style & Technique: Engraved and lighted Plexiglas structures utilizing drawing, reflection, floating forms. Media: Plexiglas. Mailing Add: 4207 Confederate Point Rd No 87 Jacksonville FL 32210

KOSHALEK, RICHARD
MUSEUM DIRECTOR
b Wausau, Wis, Sept 20, 41. Study: Univ Wis, Madison; Univ Minn, Minneapolis, BA(archit), MA(art hist). Exhibitions Arranged: 9 Artists/9Spaces (auth, catalogue), 9/1-10/15/70; Stephen Antonakos: Outdoor Neons, 11/10-1/5/75; Dan Flavin: Drawings, Diagrams & Spaces, 12/6-1/11/75; Larry Bell: The Iceberg & Its Shadow, 10/20-12/1/75; Robert Irwin: Continuing Responses, 7/13/75-7/23/76; The Great American Rodeo (auth, catalogue), 1/25-4/76 & 77; Ronald Bladen: Outdoor Sculpture Proposals, 11/20-1/8/78; Warburton Ave: The Architecture of a Neighborhood, 1/22-3/19/78; John Mason: Installations From the Hudson River Series, 5/14-7/9/78. Pos: Cur, Walker Art Ctr, Minneapolis, 67-72; asst dir, Nat Endowment for the Arts, 72-73; dir, The Ft Worth Art Mus, 74-76; dir, The Hudson River Mus, 76- Mem: Am Asn Mus Dir. Publ: Auth, Midwest Photographers, Walker Art Ctr, 72. Mailing Add: 2727 Palisades Ave New York NY 10463

KOSS, GENE H
SCULPTOR, EDUCATOR
b La Crosse, Wis, Nov 17, 47. Study: Univ Wis, River Falls, BS; Tyler Sch of Art, Temple Univ, Philadelphia, MFA. Work: The Lannan Found, Palm Beach, Fla; Univ Wis, La Crosse; Tyler Sch of Art, Temple Univ, Philadelphia. Comn: Ceramic sculpture, Schie Eye Inst, Philadelphia, 76. Exhib: 3rd Biennial Lake Superior Int Craft Exhibit, Tweed Mus of Art, Wis, 75-77; Glass Arts Soc Conf, Corning Glass Mus, NY, 76; Nat Glass Exhib, New American Glass, Focus: West Virginia, Huntington, 76; Marietta Col Crafts Nat, Ohio, 76; 55th Ann Exhibit, The Meadows Mus of Art, Shreveport, La, 77; one-man shows, Univ Southwestern La, Lafayette, 76 & Newcomb Art Sch, Tulane Univ, New Orleans, La, 77; two-man show, Glass & Ceramic Sculpture, Circle Gallery, New Orleans, La, 78. Collections Arranged: Louisiana Craftsmen Show, 77-78 & Glass & Ceramics Student Show, 77-78, Newcomb Art Sch, Tulane Univ, New Orleans. Teaching: Instr glass, Tyler Sch of Art, Temple Univ, Philadelphia, summer 76; asst prof ceramics & glass, Newcomb Art Sch, Tulane Univ, New Orleans, 76- Awards: Best of Show, Five State Ceramic Exhib, Minn Clay Co, 74; Sculpture Award, Marietta Col Crafts Nat, 77; Award of Excellence, La Craftsmen Show, La Craft Coun, 77. Bibliog: Joel Myers (auth), New American glass, Craft Horizons, 8/76; Fred Adams (auth), Glass, Glass Mag, 6/77; Michael Flaherty (auth), Ceramic activities, Ceramics Mo, 9/77. Mem: Glass Art Soc; Am Crafts Coun; Nat Coun on Educ in Ceramic Arts; Contemp Art Ctr; La Crafts Coun (mem standards comt bd, 77-78). Style & Technique: Glass, sculptural, blown and cast hotglass; clay, sculptural, thrown and handbuilt. Media: Glass, Ceramics. Publ: Auth, The techniques of manufacture, In: Vasilike Ware: An Early Bronze Age Pottery Style in Crete, Paul Aströms Förlag, Sweden, 77. Dealer: Circle Gallery 1072 St Charles Ave New Orleans LA 70130. Mailing Add: 1939 S Carrollton Ave Apt B New Orleans LA 70118

KOSTER, MARJORY JEAN
PRINTMAKER
b Grand Rapids, Mich, Feb 9, 26. Study: Univ Mich Exten Night Sch, 47-64; Pratt Graphic Workshop, New York, summer 64. Work: Metrop Mus Art, New York; Brooklyn Mus Art, NY; Art Inst Chicago; Detroit Art Inst, Mich; Grand Rapids Art Mus & Kalamazoo Inst Art, Mich. Exhib: 9th Ann Exhib Prints & Drawings, Oklahoma City Art Ctr, 67; 7th Ann Mercyhurst Col Nat Graphics Exhib, Erie, Pa, 67; 3rd Nat Print & Drawing Exhib, Western Mich Univ, Kalamazoo, 68; 16th Nat Print Exhib, Brooklyn Mus, 68; 1st Nat Print Exhib, Honolulu, 71. Mem: Nat Inst Arts & Lett. Style & Technique: Relief printing by hand, using plastic, metal and cardboard found-objects from our society which are embedded in a matrix of cut wood. Media: Woodcut. Mailing Add: 940 Maynard NW Grand Rapids MI 49504

KOSTYNIUK, RONALD P
SCULPTOR, EDUCATOR
b Sask, Can, July 8, 41. Study: Univ Sask, BSc & BEd; Univ Alta, BFA; Univ Wis, MS & MFA. Work: Edmonton Art Gallery, Alta; Saskatoon Art Gallery, Sask; Kresge Art Found, Detroit, Mich; Can Coun Art Bank, Ottawa, Ont; Dalhousie Univ, Halifax, NS. Exhib: One-man shows, Edmonton Art Gallery, 69, Mendel Art Gallery, Saskatoon, 71, Glenbow Art Gallery, Calgary, Alta, 72, York Univ, Toronto, Ont, 73, Beaverbrook Art Gallery, Fredericton, NB, 73, Dalhousie Univ, Halifax, NS, 73, Mem Univ, St John's Nfld, 73, Sarnia Art Gallery, Ont, 74, Univ Moncton, NB, 74, Mt St Vincent Univ, Halifax, NS, 75 & Univ Calgary, Alta, 78. Teaching: Prof design & sculpture, Univ Calgary, Alta, 71- Bibliog: Jan Van der Marck (auth), Relief sculpture, 69; John Stocking (auth), Relief sculptures, Arts Mag, 75; John Graham (auth), Kostyniuks reliefs, Vie des Arts, 75. Mem: Royal Can Acad Art; Univ Art Asn; Can Conf of the Arts; Alta Soc of Artists. Style & Technique: Relief structure (construction). Mailing Add: 4907 Viceroy Dr Calgary AB T3A 0V2 Can

KOSUTH, JOSEPH
CONCEPTUAL ARTIST
b Toledo, Ohio, Jan 31, 45. Study: Toledo Mus Sch of Design, 55-62; Cleveland Art Inst, 63-64; Sch of Visual Arts, New York, 65-67. Work: Mus of Mod Art, New York; Nat Gallery of Can, Ottawa, Ont; Tate Gallery, London, Eng; Solomon Guggenheim Mus, New York; Whitney Mus of Am Art, New York. Exhib: Art by Telephone, Mus of Contemp Art, Chicago, 69; one-man shows, Pasadena Art Mus, Calif, 70, Aarhus Kunstmuseum, Denmark, 70, Kunstmuseum Luzer, Ger, 73 & Mus van Hedendaagse Kunst, Gent, Belg, 77; Practice Praktijk Pratique, Int Cult Ctr, Antwerp, Belg, 75; Art Now, John F Kennedy Ctr for Performing Arts, Washington, DC, 74; New York/Downtown: Soho, Louisiana Mus, Humlebak, Denmark, 76. Teaching: Fac mem, Sch of Visual Arts, New York, 68; lectr, Univ Chile, Santiago, 71. Pos: Rev critic, Arts Mag, New York, 67; Am ed, Art-Lang J, New York, 69. Bibliog: Catherine Millet (auth), Joseph Kosuth, Flash Art, 2-3/71; Elizabeth Baker (auth), JK: Information Please, Art News, 2/73; Bruce Boice (auth), Kosuth: two shows, Artforum, Vol 11 (1973). Publ: Co-auth, Germano Celant, ed, Function, Ed Sperone, 70; auth, Art after philosophy, Art Press, 72; co-auth, Art & Language, DuMont Int, 72; auth, Dopo la filosofia l'arte, Data, 72; auth, Un Texte de Joseph Kosuth, Art Press, 74. Dealer: Leo Castelli Gallery 420 West Broadway New York NY 10012. Mailing Add: 591 Broadway New York NY 10012

KOTALA, STANISLAW WACLAW
PAINTER, ART LIBRARIAN
b Boleslawiec, Poland, Sept 27, 09; US citizen. Study: Inst Design, Poland, dipl, 37; Acad Fine Arts, Cracow, Poland, with K Sichulski & P Dadlez, 38-39; Acad Fine Arts, Dusseldorf, Ger, with T Champion & W Heuser, BA, 49; Rutgers Univ, New Brunswick, MLS, 65. Work: Dom Wojska Polskiego, Warszawa, Poland; Mus Slaskie, Katowice, Poland. Exhib: Int Festival, Polish Arts Exhib, Edinburgh, Gt Brit, 47; Polish-Am Artist Exib, Kosciuszko Found, New York, 50; Nat Exhib Paintings by Am Artists of Polish Descent, Alliance Col, Cambridge Springs, Pa, 51; Plastyka za Drutami, Warszawa, 63; one-man show, Samuel Fleisher Art Mem, Philadelphia, 60. Teaching: Dir art hist, Inst Art Teachers, Dossel, Ger, 43-44; inst com art, Com High Sch, Lippstadt, Ger, 46-47. Pos: Artist-painter, Cordey China Art Studio, Philadelphia, 52-59; art ref librn, Free Libr Philadelphia, 59- Awards: First Award, Off Club, 45; First Prize, Acad Fine Arts, Dusseldorf, 48. Bibliog: W Borzecki (auth), W zwierciadle sztuki, Nowy Swiat, 10/15/50; W Denkowski (auth), S W Kotala lecture, Gwiazda, 2/6/69. Mem: Am Libr Asn. Style & Technique: Impressionism. Media: Watercolor, Oil. Publ: Illusr, Nasz Plomyczek, 46; illusr, Wiadomosci, 46. Mailing Add: 8147 Revere St Philadelphia PA 19152

KOTIN, ALBERT
PAINTER, EDUCATOR
b Russia, Aug 7, 07; US citizen. Study: Art Students League; Nat Acad Design; with Charles Hawthorne, Provincetown, Mass, 24-29; Acad Julian & Acad Grande Chaumiere, Paris, 29-32; Atelier de Fresque, with Paul Baudouin; also with Hans Hofmann, New York & Provincetown, 46-50. Work: Syracuse Mus Fine Art, NY; Kalamazoo Inst Art, Mich; Brooklyn Pub Libr; Newark Bd Educ, NJ; Long Island Univ. Comn: Mural, Sociol Dept, NY Univ, 34; two murals, US Treas Dept, Arlington, NJ, 37; mural, Ada Post Off, Ohio, 38. Exhib: One-man show, Grand Cent Mod, NY, 58; Tanager Gallery, NY, 59; Galerie Iris Clert, Paris, 60; Byron Gallery, 61; Mus Univ, Mex, 74-75; plus many group & one-man shows. Teaching: Distinguished vis artist, Southern Ill Univ, Carbondale, 61; artist in residence, Stout State Univ, 64-66; assoc prof art, Long Island Univ, 66-75. Pos: Juror of murals, New York Art Exhib, 38; color consult, Cult Comn Mex Olympic Orgn, 68. Awards: First Prize, NJ Post Off Competition, US Treas Dept, 37; Purchase Award, Longview Fund, 62. Bibliog: Friedeberg (auth), Kotin, Archit Mag Art Suppl, 62; Prampolini (auth), El Arte Contemporaneo Editorial Pormaca, Macmillan, 64; Rodriguez (auth), Que ha pasado con la pintura?, Inst Investigaciones Esteticas, 68. Style & Technique: Expressionist; also work in diptychs and polyptychs. Media: Oil, Acrylic. Publ: Contribr, It Is, 60. Mailing Add: 42 E 12th St New York NY 10003

KOTTEMANN, GEORGE & NORMA
COLLECTORS
Dr Kottemann, b St Louis, Mo, Aug 17, 31; Mrs Kottemann, b Springfield, Ill, Jan 1, 32. Collection: Contemporary paintings, prints and sculpture. Mailing Add: 3300 N Bigelow Peoria IL 61604

KOTTLER, HOWARD WILLIAM
SCULPTOR, EDUCATOR
b Cleveland, Ohio, Mar 5, 30. Study: Ohio State Univ, BA, 52, MA, 56, PhD, 64; Cranbrook Acad of Art, Bloomfield Hills, Mich, MFA, 57. Work: Victoria & Albert Mus, London, Eng; Nat Mus of Mod Art, Kyoto, Japan; Cleveland Mus of Art; Mus of Contemp Crafts, New York; Detroit Inst of Art, Mich. Exhib: Int Exhib of Contemp Ceramic Art, Tokyo, Japan, 64; Am Studio Pottery, Victoria & Albert Mus, London, Eng, 66; Objects USA: Johnson Collection of Contemp Crafts, Smithsonian Inst, Washington, DC, 69; Contemp Ceramic Art, Nat Mus of Mod Art, Kyoto, Japan, 71; A Decade of Ceramic Art, 1962-72, San Francisco Mus of Art, 72; Int Ceramic Exhib, Calgary, Alta, Can, 73; Sensible Cup Int Exhib, Kanazawa-shi, Japan, 73; Illustionistic-Realism Defined in Contemp Ceramic Sculpture, Long Beach Mus, Calif, 77. Teaching: Instr art hist, Ohio State Univ, 61-64; prof ceramics, Univ of Wash, 64- Awards: Horace E Potter Award, Cleveland May Show, Cleveland Mus of Art, 64; William Ruben Award, Miami Nat Ceramic Exhib, Coral Gables Mus, Fla, 65; Purchase Award, Ceramic Conjunction, Brand Libr, Glendale, Calif, 74. Bibliog: Nancy McCauley (auth), Artist explores six concepts, Sunday Oregonian, 67; Sally Hayman (auth), Crafts enter 20th century, Seattle Post-Intelligencer, 68; C E Licka (auth), A prima facie clay sampler, Current Mag, 75. Mem: Am Craftsman's Coun. Style & Technique: Ceramic sculpture. Media: Clay. Mailing Add: Sch of Art Univ of Wash Seattle WA 98195

KOTTLER, LYNN
ART DEALER
b New York, NY. Study: Columbia Univ; NY Univ; City Col New York; New Sch Social Res. Pos: Founder, Acad Galleries, 40-44; founder, Portrait Painters Guild, 45-48; dir, Lynn Kottler Galleries, 49- Specialty: Paintings, sculpture and all media by leading contemporary artists, both American and foreign. Mailing Add: 3 E 65th St New York NY 10021

KOTUN, HENRY PAUL
MUSEUM DIRECTOR
b Uniontown, Pa, July 31, 31. Study: Mus Art Sch, Hagerstown; Syracuse Univ; Corcoran Sch Art, Washington, DC, with Teruo Hara-Potter; George Washington Univ, MA, 66. Comn: Stage sets for hist pageant, Rogers Co, Ohio, 62-63. Exhib: Cumberland Valley Exhib, Co Mus, Hagerstown, Md, 56-68; Md Craft Coun Traveling Exhib, 65; Land of Pleasant Living, WCBM Gallery, Baltimore, Md, 69; Easton Acad Fine Arts, Md, 69. Collections Arranged: An American Heritage-Silhouettes, 73; John Wellington, C&O Canal Painter, 73;

Henry L Hillyer, 1840-1886; John Chumley, Rural Americana, 73; Regional American Quilts, 74; American Pressed Glass, 74; plus others. Teaching: Art instr, Washington Co Bd Educ, Md, 55-70; instr ceramics & sculpture, Mus Art Sch, Hagerstown, 66-68; instr art appreciation, ceramics & sculpture, Hagerstown Jr Col, 66-69; instr crafts, Shepherd Col, 67-68. Pos: Color designer & consult, Jurica Bros Biol & Zool Charts, Chicago, 50-52; coun mem, Md Art Asn, 58-72; dir, The Gallery, Hagerstown, 66-70; dir, Washington Co Mus, 70- Awards: Mus Award Sculpture, Washington Co Mus, 68. Mem: Am Asn Mus; Nat Art Educ Asn (regional deleg, 64-68); Washington Co Arts Coun (pres, 67-70). Mailing Add: 428 N Potomac Hagerstown MD 21740

KOTZKY, ALEX SYLVESTER
CARTOONIST
b New York, NY, Sept 11, 23. Study: Art Students League, 41. Pos: Free-lance commercial artist, 46-57; cartoonist syndicate strip Duke Hand, 58-59, syndicate strip Apt 3-G, Field Enterprises, 61- Mem: Nat Cartoonists Soc. Mailing Add: 203-17 56th Ave Bayside NY 11364

KOUBA, LESLIE CARL
ART DEALER, PAINTER
b Hutchinson, Minn, Feb 3, 17. Study: Art Instruction Inc. Pos: Dir, Am Wildlife Art Galleries, Minneapolis. Style & Technique: Wildlife. Media: Oil and Watercolor. Specialty: American wildlife artists. Mailing Add: Am Wildlife Art Galleries 926 Plymouth Bldg Minneapolis MN 55402

KOUWENHOVEN, JOHN A
WRITER, EDUCATOR
b Yonkers, NY, Dec 13, 09. Study: Wesleyan Univ, AB; Columbia Univ, AM & PhD. Collections Arranged: Backgrounds of Modern Design, for Modern Living Exhib, Detroit Inst Arts, 49; Art Out of the Attic Exhib, Vt Coun Arts, Johnson Art Ctr, Middlebury, Vt, 70. Teaching: Prof vernacular in Am arts of design, Barnard Col, Columbia Univ, 46-75, emer prof, 75- Pos: Trustee, Vt Coun Arts, Montpelier; mem adv bd, Arch Am Art, Smithsonian Inst; trustee, Park-McCullough House Assocs. Publ: Auth, Made in America: the Arts in Modern Civilization, 48; auth, The Columbia Historical Portrait of New York, 53; auth, The Beer Can by the Highway: Essays on What's American about America, 61; auth, Design & Chaos, Shaping of Art & Architecture in Nineteenth Century America, Metrop Mus, 72. Mailing Add: Dorset VT 05251

KOVACHEVICH, THOMAS
PAINTER
b Detroit, Mich, 42. Study: Mich State Univ, BA, 60-64. Exhib: Penthouse Gallery, Mus of Mod Art, New York, 71; Detroit Inst of Art, Mich, 71; White on White, 71, Rooms and Shadows, 73, Chicago Abstract Art, 76 & Performance Week-Paper Comes Alive, 77, Mus of Contemp Art, Chicago, Ill; Documenta V, Kassel, WGer, 73; Mus of Painting & Sculpture, Grenoble, France, 73; 8th Bienniale de Paris, 73; Small Scale in Contemp Art, Art Inst of Chicago, 75; Paper Comes Alive at the Drawing Ctr, New York, 77; Paper Comes Alive, Midway Studio, Univ Chicago, 77. Mailing Add: c/o Droll/Kolbert Gallery Inc 724 N 5th Ave New York NY 10019

KOVATCH, JAK GENE
PRINTMAKER, EDUCATOR
b Los Angeles, Calif, Jan 17, 29. Study: Univ Calif, Los Angeles, 46; Chouinard Art Inst, Los Angeles, 47-49; Calif Sch of Art, Los Angeles, 49-50; Univ Southern Calif, Los Angeles, 51; Los Angeles City Col, 55-56; Art Students League, spec study with Michael Ponce de Leon, 72 & 75. Work: Fogg Mus of Art, Harvard Univ, Cambridge, Mass; Libr of Congress, Washington, DC; Joseph Hirshhorn Collection, Greenwich, Conn; Fairfield Art Collection, Town Hall, Conn; The John Slade Ely House Collection, New Haven, Conn. Exhib: Los Angeles Co Mus of Art, Los Angeles, 49, 54 & 55; Boston Mus of Fine Arts, 54; Libr of Congress, Washington, DC, 54; Smithsonian Inst, Washington, DC, 54; Butler Inst of Am Art, Youngstown, Ohio, 54; M H de Young Mem Mus, San Francisco, Calif, 54; Mus of Mod Art, New York, 56; Wadsworth Antheneum, Hartford, Conn, 58 & 72-76; Audubon Aritsts Inc, Nat Acad Galleries, New York, 73-78; Nat Acad of Design Exhib, 77; Boston Ctr for the Arts, 76; Honolulu Acad of Arts, Hawaii, 77; The Print Club, Philadelphia, Pa, 78; plus others. Teaching: Instr drawing & anatomy, Famous Artists Schs Inc, Westport, Conn, 57-59; instr art, New York City Col Exten Div, 59-60; accoc prof two-dimensional visualization, Univ Bridgeport, Conn, 62- Pos: Student asst, Lynton Kistler Lithography Studio, Los Angeles, 52-53; animation dept, Walt Disney Prod Inc, Burbank, Calif, 53-54. Awards: Purchase Prize, Gift to Fogg Mus of Art, Boston Mus of Fine Arts, 54; Purchase Prize for Collection of John Slade Ely House, 76th Ann Exhib, New Haven Paint & Clay Club, 76; Purchase Prize for Permanent Collection at Town Hall, Gen Electric Co, Fairfield, Conn, 77. Mem: Audubon Artists Inc, New York (exhib mem); Artists Equity Asn of New York; Conn Acad of Fine Arts, Hartford (exhib mem); Westport-Weston Arts Coun, Conn (exhib mem); Los Angeles Printmaking Soc (exhib mem). Style & Technique: Semi-realism, occasionally approaching abstract expressionism; printmaking, painting, sculpture. Media: Lithography, Etching; Mixed-Media & Gouache Painting. Dealer: Silvermine Guild of Artists Inc 1037 Silvermine Rd New Canaan CT 06880. Mailing Add: 34 Sasco Creek Rd Westport CT 06880

KOVINICK, PHILIP PETER
RESEARCHER, WRITER
b Detroit, Mich, July 4, 24. Study: Calif State Univ, Chico, BA & MA. Mem: Collegium Western Art. Res: Art and artists of the American West, 1819 to present. Publ: Auth, South Dakota's other Borglum, SDak Hist, 71; auth (catalog), The Woman Artist in the American West, 1860-1970, 76; co-auth, Women artists: the American frontier, Art News, 12/76. Mailing Add: 4735 Don Ricardo Dr Los Angeles CA 90008

KOVNER, SAUL
PAINTER
b Russia, Jan 13, 04; US citizen. Study: Nat Acad Design, with Ivan Olinski, Charles W Hawthorne & William Auerbach-Levy, 20-28. Work: Libr of Cong, Washington, DC; Metrop Mus Art, New York; Montpelier Mus Art, Vt; Tel-Aviv Mus Art, Israel; State Teachers Col, Indiana, Pa. Comn: Mural, Evavder High Sch, Bronx, NY, 38. Exhib: Pa Acad Fine Arts, Philadelphia, 32; Art Inst Chicago, 38; Whitney Mus Art, New York, 38; Corcoran Gallery, Washington, DC, 41; Am Printmakers, Downtown Gallery, New York; plus many others. Awards: Pa Acad Fine Arts Award for Child With Instrument, 32; Soc Am Etchers Award for Picnic; Art Inst Chicago Award for Day of Rest, 39. Bibliog: Walter Gutman (auth), Saul Kovner, Art in Am & Elsewhere, 31; Janice Lovoos (auth), Art of Saul Kovner, Am Artist, 68. Mem: Am Watercolorists (first pres, 38); Soc Am Etchers & Lithographers. Media: Oil, Watercolor; Lithograph. Mailing Add: 11733 La Maida St North Hollywood CA 91607

KOWAL, DENNIS J
SCULPTOR, WRITER
b Chicago, Ill, Sept 9, 37. Study: Art Inst Chicago; Univ Ill, Chicago Circle; Southern Ill Univ, BA, 61, MFA, 62. Work: A Robbins Off, Chicago; N Dehann Archit Off, Chicago; Gillett Corp, Boston; AAA Plastics, Boston; also in many pvt collections. Comn: Monuments, comn by Dr N Giarretta, Md, 69, Sacred Heart Hosp, Md, 70, Allegheny Col, Md, 71, Krannert Performing Arts Ctr, Univ Ill, 71 & Mass Bay Transportation Authority, Boston. Exhib: 66th Artists Chicago Ann, Art Inst Chicago, 63 & Soc Contemp Am Art, 64; Ill Sculptors, Smithsonian Traveling Exhib, Washington, DC, 69-70; Plastics in Sculpture, Boston Univ Galleries, 72; Dorsky Gallery, NY, 74; Harkos-Krakow Gallery, Boston, 75; one-man shows, Portland Sch of Art, Maine, 74, Mead Art Mus, Amherst Col, Mass, 78 & NC Mus of Art, Raleigh, 78; plus many other group & one-man shows. Teaching: Asst prof sculpture, Columbus Col Art, Ohio, 63-64, Univ Ill, Champaign, 66-70 & Mass Col Art, Boston, 71-72; vis lectr, Univ Ga, 73. Awards: Artist in Residence Fel, MacDowell Colony, NH, 65 & 72, Yaddo, NY, 70 & Dartmouth Col, NH, 71; Mat Res Award, Dow Chemical Co, 69; plus numerous others. Bibliog: Eva Jacob (auth), Portrait of the artist as a young hustler—the Boston Art Market & sculptor Dennis Kowal, The Real Paper, Boston, 3/5/77; S Olsen (auth), Dennis Kowal, Midwest Art/spring 77; John Forwalter (auth), Dennis Kowal, The New Art Examiner, 2/77; and numerous others. Mem: Art Inst Chicago; Boston Visual Artists Union; New Eng Sculptors Asn, Boston; Mus Mod Art, New York; Inst Contemp Art, Boston. Style & Technique: Classical; sensual; human scale; symbolic; intuitive; archetypical. Media: Stone, Wood, Metal. Publ: Contribr, Contemporary Wood Sculpture, 68, contribr, Contemporary Stone Sculpture, 69 & auth, Casting Sculpture, 72, Crown; auth, Artists speak, NY Graphic Soc, 76. Mailing Add: 602 Jerusalem Rd Cohasset MA 02025

KOWALEK, JON W
MUSEUM DIRECTOR, LECTURER
b Swarthmore, Pa, Dec 11, 34. Study: Kutztown State Col, BS; Pa State Univ, MArtEd; Cranbrook Acad Art, MFA; Kunstgewerbe Mus, Zurich, Switz; also studies in Eng, France & Italy. Collections Arranged: Major exhibs of Phillip Pearlstein, 68, Mark Tobey, 71, Video Tape as Fine Art, 71, Morris Graves, 72; Wood Sculpture of the Northwest, 73 & Japanese Imari, 74. Pos: Asst dir, Flint Inst Arts, Mich, 63-65; dir, Ft Lauderdale Mus Art, Fla, 66-67; dir, Art Galleries, Univ South Fla, 68-69; dir, Tacoma Art Mus, Wash, 69-; mem, Gov Adv Comn on the Arts, 78- Awards: 1974 Award Excellence in the Arts, City of Tacoma Arts Comn, 74. Mem: Int Comn Mus; Am Asn Mus; Asn Art Mus Dirs; Western Asn Art Mus (vpres, 70). Publ: Auth, Hand Blown Glass/USA, 71; auth, Morris Graves, 71; auth, Carl Lander, Lunar Landings, 72; auth, Mark Tobey, 72; auth, Video Tape as Fine Art, 73. Mailing Add: 818 N Tenth Tacoma WA 98403

KOWALKE, RONALD LEROY
PAINTER, PRINTMAKER
b Chicago, Ill, Nov 8, 36. Study: Univ Chicago, 54-56; Art Inst Chicago, 54-56; Rockford Col, BA, 59; Cranbrook Acad Art, MFA, 60. Work: Mus Mod Art, New York; Metrop Mus Art, New York; Libr Cong, Washington, DC; Nat Gallery, Washington, DC; Rockford Col, Ill. Exhib: Seven American Printmakers, Amsterdam, Holland, 67. Teaching: Instr design, Northern Ill Univ, 60-61; instr drawing, design & printmaking, Swain Sch Design, New Bedford, Mass, 61-64; prof drawing & printmaking, Univ Hawaii, 69- Awards: Faculty Res Grant, Univ Hawaii, 70 & 71. Bibliog: Sidney Horowitz (auth), White ground etchings of Ron Kowalke, Am Artist Mag, 1/66. Mem: Honolulu Printmakers (mem bd adv, 70-). Dealer: Associated American Artists Inc 663 Fifth Ave New York NY 10022; Ferdinand Roten Inc 123 W Mulberry Baltimore MD 21201. Mailing Add: Univ of Hawaii 1801 University Ave Honolulu HI 96844

KOWALSKI, DENNIS ALLEN
ARTIST
b Chicago, Ill, May 14, 38. Study: Univ of Ill, Chicago (archit), 55-57; Ill Inst of Tech, Chicago, 56; Sch of the Art Inst of Chicago, BFA(sculpture), 62; Corcoran Sch of Art, Washington, DC, 64; Sch of the Art Inst of Chicago, MFA(sculpture), 66. Work: Gov State Univ; Ill State Univ. Comn: Outdoor sculpture, Univ of Chicago, 75 & Village of Deerfield, Ill, 78. Exhib: The Art Inst of Chicago, 65-66, 75; Ill State Mus, Springfiled, 74; Mus of Contemp Art, Chicago, 76; Kalamazoo Art Inst, Mich, 77; Delahunty Gallery, Dallas, Tex, 78; Chicago Art Since 1945, Univ of Mich, Ann Arbor, 78; Artpark, Lewiston, NY, 78; Indianapolis Mus of Art, 78; one-man shows, N A M E Gallery, 76 & Marianne Deson Gallery, 78, Chicago. Teaching: Assoc prof sculpture, Univ of Ill, Chicago, 70- Awards: Fel (traveling), Sch of the Art Inst of Chicago, 66; Fel-Grant, Nat Endowment for the Arts, 75. Bibliog: Peter Schjeldahl (auth), Chicago Letter, Art in Am, summer 76; Kay Larson (auth), Rooms with a Point of View, Art News, 10/77; C L Morrison (auth), Chicago Dialect, Art Forum, 2/78. Style & Technique: Use of a variety of materials mostly wood, concrete and metal with spatial and architectural concerns. Dealer: Marianne Deson Gallery 226 E Ontario Chicago IL 60611. Mailing Add: 4134 N Damen Ave Chicago IL 60618

KOWALSKI, RAYMOND ALOIS
PAINTER
b Erie, Pa, June 21, 33. Study: Pa State Teachers Col, Edinboro; Cleveland Inst Art, BFA, 77. Work: State of Pa Educ Syst. Exhib: Watercolor USA, 68; May Show, Cleveland Mus Art, 69-71; one-man show, Bluffton Col, Ohio, 70; Preview 71, Mt St Joseph's Col, Cincinnati, 71; Butler Mus Show, Youngstown, Ohio; plus many other group & one-man shows. Teaching: Instr design, Cooper Sch Art, Cleveland, 69-70; instr painting for local art groups, 70- Pos: Designer, Am Greetings Corp, Cleveland, 59-65, art dir, 65-, managing art dir, 73- Awards: Cleveland Inst Art Students Show Award, Am Greetings Corp; Excellence in Painting, Chagrin Valley Art Asn, 70; Cert of Merit for Art Direction, Soc Illusr, 75 & 76. Bibliog: Helen Borsick (auth), article in Cleveland Plain Dealer Suppl, 68; Ray Kowalski—painter of houses, Wonderful World Ohio, 10/69; Ray Kowalski-House Painter, WKYC-TV, Cleveland. Style & Technique: Flat, decorative color over dimensional collage; strong primitive American influence; unique, descriptive titles. Media: Acrylic, Collage. Mailing Add: 2780 Berkshire Rd Cleveland Heights OH 44106

KOWING, FRANK EUGENE
PAINTER
b McMinnville, Ore, Apr 1, 44. Study: Pa State Univ, BFA, 73; Rietveld Art Acad, Amsterdam; also with M Vanderspoel. Work: Gallerie De Drie Haringen, Enkhuizen, Neth; Mus Fodor, Amsterdam. Comn: Mural, City of Enkhuizen, Neth, 69; illum manuscript, comn by M Oosterhus, Amsterdam, 69. Exhib: Mus Fodor, Amsterdam, 69; Gallerie De Drie Haringen, Enkhuizen, 69; William Penn Mus, Harrisburg, Pa, 72. Teaching: Instr drawing & painting, Pa State Univ, University Park, 72-73. Bibliog: Charles Gibbons (auth), Conversations, Pa State Univ, 73. Mem: Second Story Gallery, SoHo (dir, 73-74, secy, 74-); Asn Artist Run Galleries. Style & Technique: Lyrical abstraction; assemblage using encaustic technique. Publ: Auth, An ideological conflict, L'Albero Solitario, Arte E Politica USA, 73.

Dealer: John Remsen 167 Spring St New York NY 10012. Mailing Add: 31 Greene St New York NY 10013

KOZLOFF, JOYCE
PAINTER
b Somerville, NJ, Dec 14, 42. Study: Carnegie Inst Technol, BFA, 64; Columbia Univ, MFA, 67. Exhib: One-woman exhibs, Tibor de Nagy Gallery, New York, 70-77, Douglass Col Libr, 73, Univ RI, Kingston, 74, Kingpitcher Gallery, Pittsburgh, 75, Queens Col Libr, 76, Watson/de Nagy Gallery Houston, 77, Jasper Gallery, Denver, 77, Swarthmore Col, 77, Univ NMex, 78 & Kathryn Markel Gallery, New York, 78; Women Choose Women, New York Cult Ctr, 73; New Acquisitions, Mus Mod Art, 73; Woman's Work: American Art 1974, Mus of Philadelphia Civic Ctr; Ten Approaches to the Decorative, Alessandra Gallery, New York, 76; Pattern Painting, PS 1, 77; Contemp Women: Consciousness & Content, Brooklyn Mus, 77; plus other group & one-man shows. Teaching: Instr ACE prog, Queens Col, Flushing, NY, 72-; instr, Sch Visual Arts, 73-74, Art Inst Chicago, 75, Syracuse Univ, 77 & Univ NMex, 78. Awards: Creative Artists Pub Serv Grant, NY State Coun Arts, 73 & 75; Am Asn Univ Women Grant, 75; Nat Endowment for the Arts Grant, 77. Mem: Heresies Collective. Media: Acrylic. Dealer: Tibor de Nagy Gallery 29 W 57th St New York NY 10019. Mailing Add: 152 Wooster St New York NY 10012

KOZLOFF, MAX
ART CRITIC
b Chicago, Ill, June 21, 33. Study: Univ Chicago, BA, 53, MA, 58; Inst Fine Arts, NY Univ; Fulbright scholar, France, 62-63. Teaching: Cooper Union, 60-61; Wash Sq Col, NY Univ, 61-62; Calif Inst Arts, 70-71; Yale Univ, 74. Pos: Art critic, The Nation, 61-69; NY corresp, Art Int, 62-64; contrib ed, Artforum, 63-74, exec ed, 75- Awards: Pulitzer Fel in Critical Writing, 62-63; Frank Jewett Mather Award in Art Criticism, 66; Guggenheim Fel, 68-69. Publ: Auth, Renderings: Essays on a Century of Modern Art, 68; auth, Jasper Johns, 69 & new text, 72; auth, Cubism/Futurism, 74; contribr art & photography criticism to major journals. Mailing Add: 152 Wooster St New York NY 10012

KOZLOW, RICHARD
PAINTER, LECTURER
b Detroit, Mich, May 5, 26. Study: Soc Arts & Crafts, Detroit. Work: Detroit Inst Arts; Butler Art Inst, Youngstown, Ohio; Int Nickel Corp, New York; Miami Herald, Fla; Art Gallery Windsor, Ont. Comn: Mural, Am Savings & Loan. Exhib: Contemporary Art USA, Los Angeles, 56; Group Teix, Palma de Mallorca, Spain, 62; Transatlantics, US Embassy, London, Eng, 66; 20th Century Am Art Invitational, San Diego, 68; Hudson River Mus Exhib Lithographs from Mourlot Graphics, New York 70; plus one-man exhibs in New York, Los Angeles, Detroit, Palm Beach & Mex. Teaching: Instr design, Soc Arts & Crafts, Detroit, 50-60; instr painting, Inst Allende, San Miguel de Allende, Mex, 61; instr advan acrylic painting, Bloomfield Art Asn, Mich, 66-71. Awards: Purchase Award, Butler Art Inst, 50; Founders Award, Detroit Inst Arts, 63. Bibliog: Louise Brunner (auth), The landscape painting of Richard Kozlow, Am Artist Mag, 5/56; Jose Gutierrez & Nicholas Roukes (auth), Painting with Acrylics, 65 & Wendon Black (auth), Complete Guide to Acrylic Painting, 71, Watson-Guptill. Media: Acrylic. Publ: Auth & illusr, Of Man's Inhumanity to Man, Lark Publ, 65. Mailing Add: c/o Arwin Gallery 222 W Grand River Detroit MI 48226

KOZLOW, SIGMUND
PAINTER, INSTRUCTOR
b New York, NY, Dec 7, 13. Study: Nat Acad Design; Fontainbleau Sch Fine Arts, France. Work: Indiana Univ Pa; Munson-Williams-Proctor Inst, Utica, NY; Univ Ga; Mus Fine Arts, Springfield, Mass. Exhib: Everhart Mus, Scranton, Pa, 68 & 70; Nat Acad Design 146th Ann, New York, 71; Audubon Artists Ann, New York; Allied Artists Am Ann, New York; Rockport 70, 74 & 78; Ann, Mass, 72-78; Springfield Mus Nat Ann, Mass; Hunterdon Art Ctr, Clinton, NJ, 77; Phillips Mill Ann, New Hope, Pa; one-man show, Rockport Art Asn, Mass, 72 & 77. Teaching: Instr painting, Summit Art Ctr, Pos: Pres, Delaware Valley Artists Asn, 52-60; trustee, Hunterdon Art Ctr, Clinton, NJ, 71. Awards: Pulitzer Prize, Nat Acad Design, 36-37; S J Wallace Truman Award, 45; Marine Award, Silvermine Guild Artists, 60. Mem: Audubon Artists; Allied Artists Am; Rockport Art 75-77); Acad Artists Asn; Allied Artists NJ. Media: Oil, Pastel. Dealer: Grand Central Art Galleries 40 Vanderbilt Ave New York NY 10017. Mailing Add: Mountain Rd Finesville NJ 08865

KRAKEL, DEAN
MUSEUM ADMINISTRATOR, ART HISTORIAN
b Ault, Colo, July 3, 23. Study: Colo State Col of Educ, 46-50, BA(hist); Univ Denver, 50-51, MA; Univ Colo, advan study design, 53-54. Teaching: Asst prof archives res methods, Univ Wyo, Laramie, 52-56. Pos: Cataloger of collections, Colo Hist Soc, Denver, 51-52; dept dir, Fine Arts Div, USAF Acad, Colo, 56-61; dir, Thomas Gilcrease Inst, Tulsa, Okla, 61-64; ed, Am Scene Mag, 61-64; managing dir, Nat Cowboy Hall of Fame, Oklahoma City, 64-, ed, Persimmon Hill Mag, 72-75. Awards: Outstanding Literary Contrib, Mountain Plains Libr Asn, 55; Outstanding Non-Fiction Bk Award, Southwest Libr Asn, El Paso, 73; Trustees' Gold Medal for Contrib to Art, Nat Cowboy Hall of Fame, 75. Bibliog: Francine & Cleve Gray (auths), Thomas Gilcrease and Tulsa, Art in Am, 64; Boom in American Art, article in US News & World Report, 4/67; John Alexander (auth), Old West in Art, Saturday Eve Post, 10/75. Mem: Asn Sports Halls of Fame & Mus (vpres, 74-75); Nat Acad Western Art (trustee, 71-); Soc Western Art Appraisers (dir, 74-75); Royal Western Watercolor Competition, Nat Cowboy Hall of Fame (dir, 73-). Res: Select core of artists', living and deceased, contribution to the west. Publ: Auth, James Boren—A Study in Discipline, 69, Tom Ryan—Painter of Four Sixes, 72 & End of the Trail—James Earle Fraser Sculptor, 74. Mailing Add: Bar-O Ranch Rte 1 Box 160J Oklahoma City OK 73111

KRAKOW, BARBARA L
ART DEALER
b Boston, Mass, June 9, 36. Study: Boston Univ, BA, 58. Pos: Owner & dir, Harcus Krakow Gallery, Boston; bd mem, Brookline Arts Group, 74-77; bd of visitors, Boston Univ Art Hist Dept, 77- Specialty: American art 1945 to present, paintings, sculpture, drawings and prints. Mailing Add: c/o Harcus Krakow Gallery 7 Newbury St Boston MA 02116

KRAMARSKY, MRS SIEGRIED
COLLECTOR
Collection: Paintings. Mailing Add: 101 Central Park W New York NY 10023

KRAMER, BURTON
DESIGNER
b New York, NY, June 25, 32. Study: Inst Design, Ill Inst Technol, BSc(visual design), 54; Yale Univ Sch Fine Arts, BFA(design), 57; also with Josef Albers & Paul Rand. Exhib: Best Can Book Design, Ottawa, 71, Toronto, 73 & Montreal, 75; Aiga Communications Graphics, New York, 71 & 72; Art Dir Club, Toronto, 73; Biennial Graphic Design, Brno, Czech, 70, 74 & 78; Can Graphic Design, Tokyo, Japan, 75; Spectrum Can, Montreal, 76; VI Poster Biennale, Warsaw, Poland, 76; RCA Designers 78, Toronto, 78. Teaching: Mem design fac, Ont Col Art, 77- Pos: Chief designer, Halpern Advert, Zurich, Switz, 62-65; dir corp graphics, Clairtone Sound Corp, 66-67; pres, Burton Kramer Assocs, Ltd, Graphic Design Consult. Awards: Gold Medal Award, Int Typographic Composition Asn, 71; Gold Medal Award, Art Dir Club, 73. Mem: Royal Can Acad Art; Graphic Designers Can (pres, 75-77); Alliance Graphique Int; Am Inst Graphic Arts; Allgemein Schweizer Grafiker. Publ: Auth, Typographic eye, New York, 74; auth & contribr, Top trademarks and symbols of the world, Milan, 74; auth & ed, Idea Mag, Tokyo, 75; auth, Canadian Interiors, Toronto, 75. Mailing Add: Burton Kramer Assocs Ltd 20 Prince Arthur Ave Suite 1E Toronto ON M5R 1B1 Can

KRAMER, HILTON
ART CRITIC
b Gloucester, Mass, Mar 25, 28. Study: Syracuse Univ, BA; Columbia Univ; New Sch Social Res; Harvard Univ; Ind Univ. Teaching: Lectr art today. Pos: Assoc ed & feature ed, Arts Digest, 54-55; managing ed, Arts Mag, 55-64; chief art critic & art news ed, New York Times, currently. Publ: Auth, The Age of the Avant-Garde, Farrar, Straus & Giroux, 74; contribr, Arts Mag, Partisan Rev, Commentary, New Repub, The Progressive, Western Rev, Indust Design & others. Mailing Add: New York Times 229 W 43rd St New York NY 10036

KRAMER, JACK N
PAINTER, EDUCATOR
b Lynn, Mass, Feb 24, 23. Study: Sch Mus Fine Arts, Boston, dipl, 49, with Karl Zerbe, Albert H Whittin Traveling fel; Univ Reading, 50, with J Anthony Betts; with Oskar Kokoschka, London, 50; RI Sch Design, BFA, 54. Work: Addison Gallery Am Art; Phillips Acad, Andover, Mass; William Gurlitt Mus, Linz, Austria. Exhib: Boston City Hall, 71; Contemp Artists Gallery, Brookline, Mass, 73-75; Arts & Sci Ctr, Nashua, NH, 74; Shore Gallery, Boston, 75-76; Boston Psychoanalytic Soc & Inst, Mass, 77; Cambridge Art Asn, Mass, 78. Teaching: Prof art, Boston Univ, 57-; Sch Vision, Salzburg, Austria, 55-58. Bibliog: Portfolio of drawings, Audience Mag, 61; Portfolio of drawings, Liberal Context, 65. Style & Technique: Expressive realist; figures, interiors, landscapes. Media: Oil. Publ: Auth, Human Anatomy & Figure Drawing, 72. Mailing Add: Fenway Studios 30 Ipswich St Boston MA 02215

KRAMER, JAMES
PAINTER
b Columbus, Ohio, Oct 24, 27. Study: Cleveland Sch Art; Western Reserve Univ; Ohio State Univ; studied painting with Carl Gaertner & Frank Wilcox. Work: Monterey Peninsula Mus Art, Calif; Georgetown Hist Soc, Colo; Oklahoma City CofC, Okla. Exhib: Am Watercolor Soc, New York, 70; Calif Art Club, Los Angeles, 73; Mainstreams 74, Marietta Col, Ohio, 74; Royal Western Watercolor & Drawing Competition, Nat Cowboy Hall of Fame, Oklahoma City, 76 & Nat Acad of Western Art, 77. Teaching: Watercolor workshop, Mont Art Educ Asn, Great Falls, 74; watercolor workshop, Soc Western Artists, Fresno, Calif, 75. Awards: Robert Wolfe Mem Prize, Columbus Gallery Fine Art, 49; Best of Show, Mother Lode Art Asn, 72; Gold Medal, Calif Art Club, 73. Style & Technique: Traditional watercolor. Publ: Contribr, The Watercolor Page, Am Artist Mag, 73; contribr, 40 Watercolorists & How They Work, 76 & Executive Diary, 76, Watson-Guptill. Dealer: Shriver Gallery Taos NM; Settlers W Galleries Tucson AZ. Mailing Add: 631 Calle de Valdes Santa Fe NM 87501

KRAMER, MARJORIE ANNE
PAINTER
b Engelwood, NJ, Apr 21, 43. Study: Cooper Union, BFA, 66; New York Studio Sch, with M Matter & C Cajori. Exhib: Green Mountain Gallery, New York, 69-77; New Eng Landscapes, Fleming Mus, Burlington, Vt, 71; New Images in American Figurative Painting, Queens Mus, NY, 74-75; Portraits 1970-75, Frumkin Gallery, 75; Ten Realists, Hera Women's Gallery, RI, 75; Vt Landscape Images—A Bicentennial Event, Southern Vt Art Ctr (concurrently in five Vt mus), 76; Report from Soho, Univ Grey Art Gallery, New York, 76; Acquisition Show, Randolph-Macon Women's Col, 76; In Praise of Space—Am Landscape Painting, Parsons Sch Design, 76; Artists Choice—Figurative Art in NY, concurrently in five Soho galleries, 77. Pos: Ed, Women & Art Quart, New York, 71-72. Mem: Alliance Figurative Artists (mem steering comt). Style & Technique: Realism; landscapes and people. Media: Oil, Watercolor. Mailing Add: RFD Lowell VT 05847

KRAMER, PAUL
DESIGNER
b Düsseldorf, WGer, Sept 9, 30. Study: Prof Photog Sch, Düsseldorf, 47-50; Acad Motion & Sound, Bikla, Düsseldorf, 51-52; Werkkunstschule-Krefeld, WGer, 57-60. Comn: Contemp furniture, Cramer Indust, Kansas City, 68; contemp furniture, Drexel, NC, 70; interior, comn by H Uffner, New York, 74; showroom, Fla Condominium Info Ctr, New York, 75. Exhib: Graphics & Exhib, Cramer Indust, 69. Pos: Assoc, Knoll Planning Unit, New York, 63-65; partner, Kramer & Scott, New York, 65-70; owner, P K Design Consult, New York, 70- Awards: Nat Off Prod Asn Exhib, Chicago, Cramer Indust, Kansas City, 69. Mailing Add: 178 Atlantic Ave Brooklyn NY 11201

KRAMER, REUBEN
SCULPTOR
b Baltimore, Md, Oct 9, 09. Study: Rinehart Sch Sculpture, Europ traveling scholar, 31 & 33; Am Acad Rome; Acad Grand Chaumiere. Work: Baltimore Mus Art, Md; Corcoran Gallery Art, Washington, DC; Walters Art Gallery, Baltimore; Portland Art Mus, Ore; Western Md Col, Westminster. Exhib: Prix Rome Exhib, 36; Nat Art Week, IBM Corp, Md, 41; Int Sculpture Show, Philadelphia, 49; Nat Inst Arts & Lett, 64; 35 Years of Sculpture & Drawings, Retrospective Exhib, Jewish Community Ctr, Baltimore, Md, 74; 50-Yr Retrospective of Reuben Kramer's Art, Baltimore Mus Art, 78. Teaching: Pvt instr sculpture, 39-; instr sculpture, Adult Educ, Baltimore City Col & Polytech Inst; head dept sculpture, Am Univ. Awards: Prix de Rome, Am Acad Rome, 34; Nat Inst Arts & Lett Grant, 64. Bibliog: Alton Balder (auth), Six Maryland Artists, Balboa Publ, 55; Man the Maker, WMAR-TV, Baltimore, 61; Theodore L Low (auth), The Art of Reuben Kramer, Walters Art Gallery, 63. Mem: Artists Equity Asn (vpres, 68). Style & Technique: Expressionist-a loose handling of the medium; mainly concerned with the human figure in the art of small bronze; also line drawings in ink with same character as the bronzes. Media: Bronze. Mailing Add: 121 Mosher St Baltimore MD 21217

KRAMOLC, THEODORE MARIA
PAINTER, DESIGNER
b Ljubljana, Yugoslavia, Mar 27, 22; Can citizen. Study: Univ Ljubljana, with Prof J Plecnik; Ont Col Art, dipl, 51; graphic art with N Hornyansky & painting with Jock McDonald. Work: Nat Gallery Can, Ottawa; Art Gallery Ont, Toronto; Art Gallery Hamilton, Ont; Art Gallery Windsor, Ont; Nat Assembly Slovenia, Ljubljana. Exhib: Nat Exhib Prints, Libr of Cong,

Washington, DC, 55; Biennial, Minneapolis, Minn, 58; Can Graphic Art Biennial, Nat Gallery Can, 62; Gallery Ingenu, Toronto Hart House, Univ Toronto, 75 & 77. Bibliog: M Marolt (auth), Slovenian painters in exile, SKA, Buenos Aires, 59; Robert Fulford (auth), articles in Toronto Daily Star, 61 & 62; Giles E Gobetz, Anthology of Slovenian-American Literature, 77. Mem: Can Soc Graphic Art; Soc Can Painters, Etchers & Engravers. Media: Oil, Pastel. Mailing Add: 40 Bucksburn Rd Rexdale ON Can

KRAMRISCH, STELLA
CURATOR, EDUCATOR
b Vienna, Austria; US citizen. Study: Univ Vienna, PhD. Collections Arranged: Art of Nepal, Asia House, New York; Unknown India: Tribal & Ritual Art, Philadelphia Mus Art. Teaching: Prof Indian art, Univ Calcutta, 23-50; lectr Indian art, Courtauld Inst, Univ London, 37-40; prof SAsian art, Univ Pa, 50-69; prof Indian art, Inst Fine Arts, NY Univ, 64- Pos: Ed, J Indian Soc Oriental Art, 32-50; cur Indian & Himalayan art, Philadelphia Mus Art, 54-; ed, Artibus Asiae, 60- Awards: Bollingen Found Fel; Am Philos Soc Fel; Rockefeller Fund Grant. Publ: Auth, Indian Sculpture, 32; auth, The Hindu Temple, 46 & 76; auth, Dravida & Kerala, 46; auth, The Art of Nepal, 64; auth, Unknown India: Ritual Art in Tribe & Village, 68. Mailing Add: Philadelphia Mus of Art PO Box 7646 Philadelphia PA 19101

KRANER, FLORIAN G
PAINTER, EDUCATOR
b Vienna, Austria, June 7, 08; US citizen. Study: Kunstgewerbeschule Oesterreichischen Mus Kunst & Indust, Vienna, cert, 34. Work: Watercolor painting, Norfolk Mus Permanent Collection; illus works, Libr, Univ Minn. Comn: Pictorial murals & maps (with Richard Erdoes), Jamestown Festival, Richmond Mus Fine Arts, 57. Exhib: Audubon Soc Ann, Nat Acad Design Gallery, 52, 56 & 65, Am Watercolor Soc Ann, 67 & 68 & Allied Artists Nat, 68-71; UN Travel Show, 61-62; W W Gallery, Ringwood Manor Mus, 75; plus others. Teaching: Assoc prof art, City Col New York, 52- Pos: Art dir, Erle Racy Advert Agency, Dallas, Tex, 35-36; art dir, Baron Colliers Street & Rwy Advert Agency, 36-37. Awards: J J Newman Medal & First Award, 12th Ann Nat Soc Painters Casein, 66; First Award for Watercolor, Ringwood Manor Art Asn State Ann, 67; Digby Award for Watercolor, Nat Soc Painters & Sculptors Ann, 67. Bibliog: Article in Am Graphics Artist, 52. Mem: Nat Soc Painters Casein & Acrylic (pres, 64 & 65); Am Watercolor Soc; Nat Soc Painters & Sculptors; Allied Artists Am; Ringwood Manor Art Asn (pres, 66-70, dir, 70-). Style & Technique: Lyrical realism. Media: Watercolor, Acrylic, Oil. Publ: Illusr, covers, Time, 42 & 43; illusr, Wonder Tales of Giants & Dwarfs, 47 & Famous Myths of the Golden Age, 49, Random; illusr, King Arthur & His Knight of the Round Table, Dunlap & Grosset, 50. Mailing Add: Dept of Art City Col New York 133rd & Convent Ave New York NY 10031

KRANKING, MARGARET GRAHAM
PAINTER, INSTRUCTOR
b Florence, SC, Dec 21, 30. Study: The Nat Art Sch, Washington, DC; The Am Univ, Washington, DC, BA(summa cum laude, clendenin fellow in art hist), 52; pvt study with Edith McCartney, Sister Irenita Ecklin & Ralph Smith. Work: Fed Nat Mortgage Asn, United Nuclear Corp & Wall St J, Washington, DC; Martin Marietta Corp, Bethesda, Md; First Fed Savings, Admin Hq, Fairfax, Va; Richmond Co, Va. Comn: Portrait, Rear Admiral Harold C Train & Vice Admiral Harry D Train II, comn by Mrs Harold C Train, Washington, DC, 71. Exhib: 7th Ann Area Show, Corcoran Gallery of Art, Washinton, DC, 52; Southeastern Mus Tour of Washington Artists Equity, 72-73; Maryland Biennial, Baltimore Mus of Art, 74 & 76; 108th Am Watercolor Soc Exhib, Nat Acad Galleries, New York, 75; 1st Ann Exhib, Southern Watercolor Soc, Tenn Fine Arts Ctr, Nashville, 77, 2nd Ann, Columbus Mus of Arts & Sci, Ga, 78; 37th Ann Exhib, Watersolor Soc of Ala, Birmingham Mus of Art, 77; 54th Ann Nat April Exhib, Springville Mus of Art, Utah, 78; one-man shows, Dunbarton Col Art Gallery, Washington, DC, 72 & Spectrum Gallery Inc, 74, 76 & 78. Pos: Asst to head of publications, The Nat Gallery of Art, 52-53. Awards: Best in Show, Montgomery Co Art Asn, Mem Show, 72; Award of Excellence, Marshall Awards Show Art League, Alexandria, Va, 72; Cash award, Ann Spring Mem Show, Watercolor Soc of Ala, 78. Mem: Artists Equity; Potomac Valley Watercolorists (vpres, 77-79); Washington Watercolor Asn; Southern Watercolor Soc; Watercolor Soc of Ala. Style & Technique: Transparent watercolor; direct method on location to capture essence of a close-up or vista of nature. Media: Watercolor & Pastel. Publ: Illusr, Realtor Mag (article), Bd of Realtors, Metrop, Washington, DC, 70 & 71. Dealer: Spectrum Gallery Inc 3033 M St Washington DC 20007; Island Art Gallery, Manteo, NC, 27954. Mailing Add: 3504 Taylor St Chevy Chase MD 20015

KRASHES, BARBARA
PAINTER, INSTRUCTOR
b New York, NY. Study: Art Students League, with Reginald Marsh, Julian Levi & Vaclav Vytlacil; NY Univ, BS; Hunter Col, NY; Educ Alliance, with Chaim Gross; New Sch Social Res, New York. Work: Ulrich Mus Art, Wichita State Univ, Kans; St Lawrence Univ Mus, Canton, NY; Am Can Co, New York; Kidde Constructors, Inc, New York; Valley Bank, Springfield, Mass. Exhib: Art: 1965, Am Express Pavilion, New York World's Fair; Am Abstract Artists 32nd Anniversary Exhib, Riverside Mus, NY, 68; Fordham Univ at Lincoln Ctr, New York, 74; Bronx Mus of Arts, New York, 76; Geneva Hist Soc, NY, 77. Pos: Arts dir, Adult Educ Ctr, New York. Awards: George B Bridgman Mem Scholar, Art Students League. Bibliog: Art World Problems (tape), Today's World, Fordham Univ, 73. Mem: Int Asn Art, US Comt; Fedn Mod Painters & Sculptors, Inc (pres, 70-74); Art Students League; Artists Equity Asn. Style & Technique: Color paintings. Media: Acrylic Polymer Emulsion. Publ: Contribr, Art '65 Lesser Known & Unknown Painters, Young Am Sculpture-East to West, 65; contribr, The New York Arts Calendar (spec issue) for New York World's Fair Am Express Show, 65; contribr, The Art Gallery, 66; contribr, Feigin Memorial Collection (catalog), St Lawrence Univ, 71. Mailing Add: 77 West 85th St New York NY 10024

KRASNER, LEE
PAINTER
b Brooklyn, NY. Study: Woman's Art Sch, Cooper Union, 26-29; Nat Acad Design, 29-32; City Col New York, 33; also with Hans Hofmann, 38-40. Work: Philadelphia Mus Art; Whitney Mus Am Art, New York; also in pvt collections. Exhib: White House Traveling Exhib, organized by Smithsonian Inst, 67; Mus Mod Art, New York, 69; Marlborough Galleria Art, Rome, 72; one-man shows, Marlborough Gallery, New York, 68, 69 & 73, Retrospective Traveling Exhib, circulated by Brit Arts Coun, 65, Gallery Reese Palley, San Francisco, 69, Whitney Mus, New York, 73-74, Traveling Exhib at Miami-Dade Community Col, Miami, 74, Beaver Col, Glenside, Pa & Gibbes Art Gallery, NC, 74, Traveling Exhib at Corcoran Gallery, Washington, DC, 74, Brandeis Univ & Pa State Univ, 75, Pace Gallery, New York, 77 & Susanne Hilberry Gallery, Mich, 77. Mailing Add: The Springs East Hampton NY 11937

KRASNER, OSCAR
ART DEALER
Pos: Dir, Krasner Gallery, 54- Specialty: Contemporary American painting and sculpture. Mailing Add: 1043 Madison Ave New York NY 10021

KRATINA, K GEORGE
SCULPTOR
b New York, NY, Feb 12, 10. Study: Syracuse Univ, BS & MS; Yale Univ, BFA. Comn: Heroic pioneer monument, Chattanooga, Tenn; relief, St Bonaventure Univ, NY; statues, St Paul Cathedral, Los Angeles; sanctuary sculptures, Fac Chapel, Fr Judge Sem, Va; steel sculpture, Adath Israel Temple, Merion, Pa; plus many others, 39- Teaching: Prof design, Sch Archit, Rensselaer Polytech Inst, 63-64; former prof, Div Art & Archit, Cooper Union; lectr art and archit, collabr arts & new horizons for sculpture. Awards: Prix de Rome, 38; Nat Prize for Sculpture Competition for Cath Welfare Bldg, Washington, DC, 40; Awards for Collaboration Excellence, Am Inst Architects, 41, 58 & 60. Mem: Fel Nat Sculpture Soc. Mailing Add: RD 1 Box 76 Old Chatham NY 12136

KRATZ, MILDRED SANDS
PAINTER
b Pottstown, Pa. Study: With Edgar Whitney & Paul C Burns, Portugal. Work: Am Fine Arts Collection, Cleveland; First Federal, Pottstown, Pa; Motorola, Chicago; Del Trust Co, Wilmington; Fitchburg Mus, Mass; Mutual Ins, Philadelphia; Keystone Collection, York, Pa. Exhib: Am Watercolor Soc, New York, 66-78; one-man shows, Reading Mus Fine Art, Pa, 71, William Penn Mem Mus, Harrisburg, Pa, 74 & Fitchburg Art Mus, Mass, 75; Nat Acad Design, New York, 73-78; Saco Mus, Maine, 78; plus 32 one-woman shows. Teaching: Artist-instr, Queen Elizabeth II, New York to Eng, 75; demonstr, Am Watercolor Soc, 75; juror, Am Artists League, 76 & Am Watercolor Soc, 77. Awards: Gold Medal, Catharine Lorillard Wolfe Art Club, 69, 72 & 74 & Am Artists Prof League, New York, 73 & 76; Best of Show-Nat Winner, Nat League Am Pen Women, 74; Pa Senatorial Citation, 77. Bibliog: Jane Skinner (auth), Country life-watercolor, Palm Beach Life Mag, 73; Contemporary Artist, Univ NH, 74-; George Michael (auth), Mildred Sands Kratz, Antique Gazette & Nat Antiques Mag, 75; mentioned in: 40 Watercolorists and How They Work, Watson-Guptill. Mem: Am Watercolor Soc; Allied Artists Am; Philadelphia Art Alliance; Nat Arts Club; Pottstown Area Artists Guild (co-founder & pres, 66); Philadelphia Water Color Club. Style & Technique: Landscapes, ruralscapes in realistic style. Media: Watercolor. Publ: Illusr, Nat Antiques Rev, 71; illusr, Stories of French Creek, 73; auth, Watercolor page, Am Artist Mag, 73; auth & illusr, Dutch Porch, 72, St Peters, Pa, 73 & Hopewell, 74, Am Fine Art Collectors; plus others. Dealer: Gallery II Exton PA 19341; Piccolo Mondo Worth Ave Palm Beach FL 33480. Mailing Add: Spring Dell Studio Maple Gardens Pottstown PA 19464

KRAUSE, LAVERNE ERICKSON
PAINTER, PRINTMAKER
b Portland, Ore, July 21, 24. Study: Univ Ore, BS, 46; Mus Art Sch, Portland, 52-58; Pratt Graphic Ctr, New York, summer 66. Work: Seattle Art Mus; Portland Art Mus; Salt Lake Art Ctr, Utah; La State Univ Union, Baton Rouge; Deichmanske Bibliot, Oslo, Norway; plus others. Exhib: One-person shows, Portland Art Mus, 52, 58 & 73, Gordon Woodside Gallery, Seattle, 65, Salt Lake Art Ctr, 66, Fountain Gallery, Portland, 67, 69, 71, 74 & 78, Univ Ore, 68, La State Univ, Baton Rouge, 70, Deichmanske Bibliot, Oslo, 74, Rockford Col, Ill, 74 & Delta State Univ, 78; Artists of Oregon, Portland Art Mus Ann, 49-; six shows, Int Printmakers, Seattle Art Mus, 60-71; Northwest Art Today, Seattle World's Fair, 62; West Coast Graphics, Univ Ky, circulated by Smithsonian Inst, 71-72; Atelier Nord Exhib, Oslo, 75. Teaching: Vis artist, Mt Angel Col, Ore, summer 65; from asst prof to assoc prof painting & printmaking, Univ Ore, 66-73, prof painting & printmaking, 73-; fac res award, 70-71, summer 71, 72-73 & 77-78; vis assoc prof, La State Univ, Baton Rouge, summer 70. Pos: Juror, Int Printmakers, Seattle Art Mus, 62; mem gov, Planning Coun Arts, 65-67; juror, Redwood Art Asn 9th Ann, 67 & Artists of Oregon, 75. Awards: Seattle Art Mus Award, 60; Ford Found Purchase Prize for Painting, 64; Painting Artists Ore Award, Portland Art Mus, 69. Mem: Artists Equity Asn (pres, Ore Chap, 54-55 & 67-68, nat pres, 69-70); Col Art Asn Am; The Print Club, Philadelphia; Malaspina Printmakers, Vancouver, BC; Portland Art Asn (secy, 52, chmn exhibs, 54 & 61). Style & Technique: Poetic landscape romantic expressionist. Media: Acrylic, Etching, Oil & Woodcut. Publ: Illusr, Clouded Sea (etchings), 71 & Deady & Villard (etchings), 74, Press 22. Dealer: Fountain Gallery Art 117 NW 21st Ave Portland OR 97210. Mailing Add: 3295 W 16th Ave Eugene OR 97402

KRAUSER, JOEL
INSTRUCTOR, PRINTMAKER
b Bronx, NY, June 17, 36. Study: Harvard Col, BA, 57; Cooper Union Art Sch, 60-62; NY Univ, MA, 65; Art Students League, with Frank Reilly & Lennart Anderson; Pratt Graphics Ctr, 71-72. Work: Washington & Jefferson Col, Washington, Pa. Comn: Spirit of WEVD (oil), WEVD Radio Sta, New York, 71; intaglio ed for Artists Proof Mag, Pratt Graphics Ctr, New York, 72. Exhib: Artists Pratt Graphic Ctr, 72; Washington & Jefferson Nat Painting Exhib, 72; Nat Print Show, Hunterdon Co Art Ctr, 74; Davidson Col Nat Print Show, 74; Int Miniature Print Show, 75; plus others. Collections Arranged: Washington & Jefferson Col Permanent Collection; one-man show for Bergen Community Mus, 72. Teaching: Chmn dept art, Northern Valley Regional High Sch, Demarest, NJ, 64-; instr etching, Art Ctr Northern NJ. Awards: Nat Arts Club Award, 72; Bienfang Paper Co Award for Graphics, 72; Bradlow Prize for Graphics, Pratt Graphics Ctr, 72. Mem: Italic Soc; Painters & Sculptors Soc NJ. Style & Technique: Realistic forms; color and drawing are expressionistic. Media: Intaglio, Oil. Publ: Auth, Learning to see through drawing, Sch Arts, 68; auth, Focusing on the group in art education, Design Mag, 70. Mailing Add: 139 Jefferson Ave Tenafly NJ 07670

KRAUSHAAR, ANTOINETTE M
ART DEALER
b New York, NY. Pos: Dir, Kraushaar Galleries. Specialty: Twentieth century American art. Mailing Add: 1055 Madison Ave New York NY 10028

KRAUSZ, LASZLO
PAINTER
b Pecs, Hungary, Apr 4, 03; US citizen. Study: Univ Basel; Cooper Sch Art, Cleveland; Inst Art, Cleveland; Skowhegan Sch Painting; Pratt Inst; Western Reserve Univ, MA. Work: Mus Art, Safed, Israel; Jewish Community Ctr, Cleveland. Comn: Portraits of mem Cleveland Orch, US Info Agency Cult Exchange Prog, 64-65. Exhib: One-man shows, US Embassy, London, Case Inst & Cooper Sch Art; Butler Inst Am Art & Ashtabula Fine Arts Ctr, Ohio. Teaching: Instr, Cooper Sch Art; spec lectr & head, Exp Art Studio, Case Inst Technol. Pos: Owner-dir, Laszlo Krausz Fine Arts Gallery, currently. Awards: Award, Cleveland Chap Mil Order of World War I & II, 54. Bibliog: Amerika, US Info Agency, 66; R Breuer (auth), biog in Delphian Quart, 67; Edith Carter (auth), Drawings for sterio, Am Artists, 60 & 69; program consisting of his drawings & paintings, Pub Broadcasting Serv, 1/78. Media: Ink, Oil. Publ:

Contribr, numerous articles in art mags. Mailing Add: 3429 Blanche Ave Cleveland Heights OH 44118

KRAVIS, JANIS
DESIGNER, ARCHITECT
b Riga Latvia, Oct 20, 35; Can citizen. Study: Sch of Archit, Univ of Toronto. Exhib: Royal Can Acad of Arts, Nat Gallery of Can, Ottawa, 70. Awards: Ont Tourist Accomodation Award, 67; Ont Eedee Design Award, 67. Mem: Ont Asn of Architects; Asn of Can Indust Designers; Royal Can Acad of Art; Royal Archit Inst of Can. Mailing Add: 67 Front St Toronto ON M5E 1B5 Can

KREBS, PATRICIA (PATRICIA KREBS BARKER)
ART CRITIC
b St Louis, Mo, June 13, 33. Study: Univ Wis; Wash Univ, AB; English Lang Inst, Rome, under Lionello Venturi, 55. Pos: Art writer, St Louis Post-Dispatch, 59-63; art critic, Winston-Salem J, 71-73; art critic, Charlotte Observer, Greensboro Daily News, NC, 73-; corresp, Art News, Craft Horizons, Art Voices South & Contemp Art/Southeast; partic, Sem for Critics of the Arts, Nat Endowment for Humanities, 77- Interest: Contemporary art; regional art. Mailing Add: Greensboro Daily News Greensboro NC 27420

KREBS, ROCKNE
SCULPTOR
b Kansas City, Mo, Dec 24, 38. Study: Univ Kans, BFA. Work: Corcoran Gallery Art & Nat Collection Fine Art, Washington, DC; New Orleans Mus Fine Art, La; Larry Aldrich Mus, Ridgefield, Conn; Philadelphia Mus Art. Comn: Hemisfair '68 (transparent plastic sculpture), comn by Gilbert Denman, San Antonio, 68; laser beams, Stern Line, comn by Philip Stern, Washington, DC, 70, Day Passage, Night Passage, Albright-Knox Art Gallery, Buffalo, NY, 71, Rite de Passage, comn by Mrs Edgar B Stern, New Orleans, 71 & Light is the City at Night, comn by Shepard Latter, New Orleans, 72. Exhib: Ann Exhib Contemp Sculpture, Whitney Mus Am Art, New York, 66 & 68; 69th Am Exhib, Art Inst Chicago, 70; New Arts, US Pavilion, Expo 70, Osaka, Japan, 70; Art & Technology, Los Angeles Co Mus Art, Calif, 71; Art Now '74, Kennedy Ctr, Washington, DC & Projected Images, Walker Art Ctr, Minneapolis, 74. Awards: Artist Fel, Washington Gallery Mod Art Workshop, 68; Nat Endowment Arts Fel, 70; Guggenheim Found Fel, 72. Bibliog: Walter Hopps & Nina Felshin (auth), Three Washington artists, Art Int, 5/70; James N Wood (auth), Rockne Krebs, Albright-Knox Art Gallery, 71; Jane Livingston (auth), Art & technology, Los Angeles Co Mus Art, 71. Publ: Auth, Artists on their art, Art Int, 4/68. Mailing Add: 1737 Johnson Ave NW Washington DC 20009

KREEGER, DAVID LLOYD
PATRON, COLLECTOR
b New York, NY, Jan 4, 09. Study: Rutgers Univ, AB; Harvard Law Sch, LLB. Mem: Corcoran Gallery Art (pres bd trustees); mem, US Comn UNESCO. Interest: Donor of Kreeger Annual Purchase Awards at Corcoran Gallery Biennial and area shows, Kreeger Annual Art Prize at American University and prizes in painting, sculpture and art history at George Washington University. Collection: Painting and sculptures, especially from mid-nineteenth century to the contemporary period. Mailing Add: 2401 Foxhall Rd NW Washington DC 20007

KREILICK, MARJORIE E
MOSAIC ARTIST, EDUCATOR
b Oak Harbor, Ohio, Nov 8, 25. Study: Ohio State Univ, BA, 46, MA, 47; Cranbrook Acad Art, MFA, 52; apprentice to Gulio Giovanette, Rome, 56; Am Acad in Rome, FAAR, 63. Work: Joslyn Mus, Omaha, Nebr. Comn: Marble pebble mural, comn by Louis Redstone, Wonderland Shopping Ctr, Livonia, Mich, 59; ten marble murals, comn by Karel Yasko, State Off Bldg, Milwaukee, Wis, 63; mosaic foucault pendulum, comn by Harold Spitznagel, Augustana Univ, Sioux Falls, SDak, 67; marble mosaic mural, comn by Ellerbe, Mayo Clin, Rochester, Minn, 69; marble mosaic pool, Telfair Acad Arts & Sci, Savannah, Ga, 73. Exhib: Palace of Expos, Rome; Minn Mus Art, St Paul; solo show, Archit League, New York; Fairweather Hardin Gallery, Chicago; Toledo Mus Art, Ohio. Teaching: Instr-docent design, Toledo Mus Art, 48-51; from instr to prof design-sculpture, Univ Wis-Madison, 53- Awards: Univ Wis Grant, 60; Prix de Rome, Am Acad in Rome, 61. Mem: Nat Soc Mural Painters; Arts Club, Chicago. Media: Marble Mosaic, Watercolor. Publ: Contribr, Art in Architecture, 69; illusr, Friends around the Corner (third grade reader), Lyons, Carnahan, Chicago; illusr, Inquiring about Communities, Holt Databank Syst, 72. Dealer: Fairweather Hardin E Ontario St Chicago IL 60611. Mailing Add: 2713 Chamberlain Ave Madison WI 53705

KREITZER, DAVID MARTIN
PAINTER
b Ord, Nebr, Oct 23, 42. Study: Concordia Teachers Col, BS, 65; San Jose State Col, MA, 67. Work: Santa Barbara Mus, Calif; San Diego Mus, Calif; Joseph Hirshhorn Found, Washington, DC; Sheldon Gallery, Univ Nebr. Comn: Woman's Place & US Army Corps of Engrs, covers for Atlantic Mag, 70; California & the War, cover for Motorland Mag, 70. Exhib: One-man show & American Art Since 1850, 68, Maxwell Gallery, San Francisco; Benedictine Art Awards, New York, 69; 6th Mobile Ann, Ala, 71; one-man show, Ankrum Gallery, Los Angeles, 71 & 75. Teaching: Instr painting, San Jose State Col, 68. Awards: Ciba-Geigy Award, 71. Style & Technique: Realism. Media: Oil. Dealer: Ankrum Gallery 657 N La Cienega Blvd Los Angeles CA 90069. Mailing Add: c/o Ankrum Gallery 657 N La Cienega Los Angeles CA 90069

KRENECK, LYNWOOD
PRINTMAKER
b Kenedy, Tex, June 11, 36. Study: Univ Tex, BFA, 58, MFA, 65. Work: Fine Arts Gallery San Diego, Calif; Wichita Art Asn Galleries, Kans; Northern Ill Univ, De Kalb; Springfield Art Mus, Mo; Art in Embassies Prog, US State Dept. Exhib: 20 American Printmakers, Oneonta, NY, 72; 16th Ann Exhib Prints & Drawings, Okla Art Ctr, Oklahoma City, 74; Nat Print & Drawing Exhib, Second St Gallery, Charlottesville, Va, 75; Libr of Cong Nat Print Show, 75; Miami Int Print Show, 75; New American Graphics, Madison, Wis, 75; Boston Printmakers Nat Print Exhib, 75; Printmakers & Their Students Nat Exhib, Southern Conn Col, New Haven, 76; 11 in 77 Nat Print Show, Northern Ill Univ, DeKalb, 77; 20th NDak Ann Nat Print Exhib, Grand Forks, 77; Group Graphics Exhib, Birmingham Mus, Ala, 78; plus others. Teaching: Prof printmaking, Tex Tech Univ, 65- Awards: Purchase Awards, Fine Arts Gallery, San Diego, 71, NH Graphics Int, 73 & 10th Silvermine Guild Nat Print Show, 74. Mem: Tex Watercolor Soc (dir-at-lg, 72-73); Boston Printmakers; Graphics Soc, NH. Style & Technique: Serigraphy dealing with personal imagery. Mailing Add: 5224 14th St Lubbock TX 79416

KRENTZIN, EARL
SCULPTOR, SILVERSMITH
b Detroit, Mich, Dec 28, 29. Study: Wayne State Univ, BFA, 52; Cranbrook Acad Art, MFA, 54; Royal Col Art, London, 57-58. Work: Detroit Inst Art, Mich; Cranbrook Galleries, Bloomfield Hills, Mich; St Paul Art Ctr, Minn; Jewish Mus, New York; Sumner Found, NJ. Comn: Enamel plaque, Gloria Dei Lutheran Church, Detroit, 54; Menorah, Temple Israel, Detroit, 63; metal sculpture, Westland Shopping Ctr, Detroit, 65; plus many pvt comn of silver sculptures, 54- Exhib: Mich Artists & Artists-Craftsmen's Exhib, Detroit Inst Art, 52-68; Fibre-Clay-Metal, St Paul Art Ctr, 57, 62 & 64; Mus Contemp Crafts, New York, 63 & 65; NJ State Mus, Trenton, 70; one-man shows, Kennedy Galleries, New York, 68-75. Teaching: Instr art, Univ Wis-Madison, 56-60; vis prof silversmithing, Univ Kans, 65-66; vis prof metalwork, Fla State Univ, 69. Awards: Fulbright Fel, 57-58; Tiffany Grant, 66; Nat Decorative Arts Exhib, Wichita Art Ctr, Kans, 66. Media: Silver. Publ: Auth, Centrifugal casting, Craft Horizons Mag, 11/54. Dealer: Kennedy Galleries 20 E 56th St New York NY 10022. Mailing Add: 412 Hillcrest Grosse Pointe Farms MI 48236

KRESSLEY, MARGARET HYATT
PAINTER, PRINTMAKER
b Washington, DC, Apr 14, 28. Study: Abbott Art Sch; Watercolor Sch; O'Hara Moore Col Art; Univ Munich; also with Hans Dumler, Peter Zeiler & Oskar Kocoscha, Salzburg. Work: Art in Embassies Prog; also represented in many pub & pvt collections. Exhib: One-man shows, Munich, Ger, Jefferson Place Gallery & Gallery Ten, Washington, DC; Biennale, Anderson Gallery, Richmond, Va; graphic & watercolor shows across the country. Teaching: Pvt art classes. Mem: Artists Equity Asn; Women's Art Ctr, Washington, DC; Washington Watercolor Club. Media: Acrylic, Colored Pencils. Mailing Add: 5090 Ten Oaks Rd Clarksville MD 21029

KREVOLIN, LEWIS
DESIGNER, CRAFTSMAN
b New Haven, Conn, June 21, 33. Study: Alfred Univ, BFA; also with Kja Franck, Finland. Comn: Bethlehem Steel Corp, Travelers Ins Co & pvt clients; terra cotta mural for Bethesda-Bradley Bldg, Md, 64. Exhib: Young America Exhibit, 58 & 62; Cooper Union, 61; Silvermine Guild, 63; Craftsmen of the Northeast, 63 & The Craftsmen Designs, 64, circulated by Am Fedn Arts & Smithsonian Inst. Teaching: Instr ceramics, Brooklyn Mus Sch Art & Dutchess Community Col. Pos: Design consult numerous mfrs, 55-; chief designer, Russell Wright Assocs, 59-61; owner, Earth Work Studio & Craft/Gallery. Awards: Fulbright Grant in Glass & Ceramics to Finland, 61. Mem: Am Crafts Coun; York State Craftsmen; Mus Am Indian (res assoc). Style & Technique: Unglazed terra cotta; architectural and functional wares. Res: Reconstruction of pre contact pottery technology. Publ: Auth & illusr, Poland Craft Horizons, 10/62; co-auth & illusr, Ceramics, 65; Naked Clay 4000 American Indian Pottery, 71. Mailing Add: Earth Works Old Albany Post Rd Rhinebeck NY 12572

KREZNAR, RICHARD J
SCULPTOR, PAINTER
b Milwaukee, Wis, May 1, 40. Study: Univ Wis, BFA; Brooklyn Col, MFA; Inst Allende, Mex. Work: Walker Art Ctr, Minneapolis; Milwaukee Art Ctr, Wis; Univ Wis-Madison; Colgate Univ, Hamilton, NY; First Wis Nat Bank, Milwaukee. Exhib: Pa Acad Fine Arts, 63; Butler Inst Am Art, Youngstown, Ohio, 65; Milwaukee Art Ctr, 66; Southampton Col, New York, 65-66; Wis Directions, Milwaukee Art Ctr, 75; Univ Wis-Milwaukee, 77; Brooklyn Col Art Dept Past & Present, Robert Schoelkopf Gallery, New York, 77; The Mat Dominant—Some Current Artists & Their Media, Pa State Univ, University Park, 77; one-man shows, Paley & Lowe Inc, New York, 72 & O K Harris Gallery, New York, 74 & 76. Teaching: Instr studio art courses, Brooklyn Col, 64-73, asst prof, 74-; instr, Parsons Sch of Design, 78- Awards: Ford Found Purchase Award, 62 & 64; Prizes, Milwaukee Art Ctr, 62, Wis Salon of Art, 63 & Walker Art Ctr, 64. Dealer: O K Harris Gallery 383 West Broadway New York NY 10012. Mailing Add: 104 Franklin St New York NY 10013

KRIENSKY, (MORRIS E)
PAINTER, SCULPTOR
b Glasgow, Scotland, July 27, 17; US citizen. Study: Boston Mus Fine Arts, 36-40, with Alma O LeBrecht; Art Students League, 48-49; Escuela Tech Mex, 50-51. Work: Pushkin Mus, Moscow; Alfred Khouri Mem Collection, Norfolk Mus, Va; Lincoln Ellsworth Collection; also in many pvt collections, US, China, USSR & Mex. Exhib: Am Watercolor Soc; Nat Acad Design; Inst Mex-Norte Am Relac Cult; one-man shows, Knoedler Gallery, White House, Art Inst Chicago, Frick Art Libr, Univ Conn (15 year retrospective) & many others. Awards: First Prize, Inst Mex-Norte Am Relac Cult, 50. Style & Technique: Paintings are a complete harmony of the Oriental and Western ways of painting. Media: Oil. Publ: Auth, The Way is Peace, The Road is Love (drawings, paintings & poems), Gibson, 73; auth, The art of Art (paintings & prose—formerly titled Visions of Hope & Faith), 76. Mailing Add: 463 West St New York NY 10014

KRIGSTEIN, BERNARD
PAINTER, ILLUSTRATOR
b New York, NY, Mar 22, 19. Exhib: Am Watercolor Soc Annuals; Soc Illusr Annuals; Frye Mus, Seattle; Nat Acad Design; Pastel Soc Am Annual; Painters & Sculptors Soc, NJ; Anchorage Mus, Alaska; Knickerbocker Artists Annuals; Audubon Artists Annuals; WPA Art: Then & Now, New York, 77; plus many other group & one-man shows. Teaching: Instr painting & drawing, High Sch Art & Design, New York, 62-70; asst prof fine art, painting & drawing, Fashion Inst Technol, State Univ NY, 70-71; instr painting & drawing, High Sch Art & Design, 71- Awards: First Prize for Graphic Arts, Brooklyn Soc Artists 33rd Ann; Jersey City Mus Award for Oil Painting, Painters & Sculptors Soc NJ 31st Ann; Hon Mention for Watercolor, Audubon Artists 33rd Ann. Bibliog: Jerry West, publ & John Benson, ed, Squa Tront 6, Special Issue: Bernard Krigstein, Cambridge, Mass, 75. Mem: Painters & Sculptors Soc NJ; Pastel Soc Am; WPA Artists; Artists Equity Asn of NY (mem bd dirs, 77 & 78); Audubon Artists. Media: Oil, Watercolor, Pastel. Publ: Illusr, Manchurian Candidate, McGraw; illusr, Various Fables from Various Places, Capricorn-Putnam; illusr, Buccaneers & Pirates of Our Coasts, Random; illusr, Boy's Life Mag, Harpers Mag, Saturday Evening Post & many others. Dealer: Alexander Gallery 117 E 39th St New York NY 10016. Mailing Add: 140-21 Burden Crescent Jamaica NY 11435

KRIMS, LESLIE ROBERT
CONCEPTUAL ARTIST, PHOTOGRAPHER
b New York, NY, Aug 16, 42. Study: Cooper Union, New York, BFA; Pratt Inst, Brooklyn, MFA. Work: Mus Mod Art, New York; Nat Gallery Can, Ottawa; Musee National d'Art Moderne, Centre Georges Pompidou, Paris; George Eastman House, Rochester, NY; Minneapolis Inst Art. Exhib: One-man shows, George Eastman House, 69 & 71, Galerie Delpire, Paris, 74 & Fictcryptokrimsographs, Light Gallery, New York, 75; two-man show, Witkin Gallery, New York, 69 & 72; Photographs of Women, Mus Mod Art, 71; plus others. Teaching: Assoc prof art, State Univ NY Col Buffalo, 69- Awards: State Univ NY Res Found

Grant & Grant-in-Aid, 70 & 71, Nat Endowment for the Arts Fels, 71, 72 & 76 & NY State Coun Arts Grants, 71, 73 & 75. Bibliog: Leslie Krims, Photo Image, Japan, 70; Leslie Krims, Camera, Switz, 71. Mem: Soc Photog Educ. Publ: Auth & illusr, Eight Photographs: Leslie Krims, Doubleday, 70; auth & illusr, The Incredible Case of the Stack of Wheat Murders, 72; auth & illusr, The Little People of America 1971, 72; auth & illusr, The Deerslayers, 72; auth & illusr, Making Chicken Soup, 72. Dealer: Witkin Gallery 243 E 60th St New York NY 10022; Light Gallery 1018 Madison Ave New York NY 10012. Mailing Add: 187 Linwood Ave Buffalo NY 14213

KRODY, BARRON J
DESIGNER, INSTRUCTOR
b Cincinnati, Ohio, Feb 7, 36. Study: Art Acad Cincinnati, cert; also design with Noel Martin. Work: Cincinnati Art Mus; Mus Mod Art, New York. Comn: Urban Walls: Cincinnati & Fed Reserve Bank, Carl Solway Gallery; Model Cities, Bd Educ & Model Cities Prog, Cincinnati; State Off Tower, State of Ohio. Exhib: Art Dirs Club Ann Exhib, Cincinnati, 62-71; Communication Through Typography, Harvard Univ, 64; Laser Art Exhib, Cincinnati Art Mus, 69; Urban Walls: Cincinnati Traveling Exhib Silk Screen Prints, 71-72; Communication Graphics 1971/72, Am Inst Graphic Arts, 72. Teaching: Instr graphic design, Mt St Joseph Col, Cincinnati, 64-65; instr graphic design, Art Acad Cincinnati, 66-, actg dean, 72. Awards: Cert Excellence, Art Dirs Club, Cincinnati, 67 & Am Inst Graphic Design, 71-72. Mem: Contemp Arts Ctr. Mailing Add: 2306 Park Ave Cincinnati OH 45206

KRONSNOBLE, JEFFREY MICHAEL
PAINTER, EDUCATOR
b Milwaukee, Wis, Feb 9, 39. Study: Univ Wis-Milwaukee, BS, 61; Univ Mich, Ann Arbor, MFA, 63. Work: New Orleans Mus Art; Addison Gallery Am Art, Andover, Mass; Daytona Beach Mus Art; Auburn Univ; La State Univ, Baton Rouge. Exhib: Chicago & Vicinity Exhib, Art Inst Chicago, 61-63; one-man shows, New Orleans Mus Art, 67 & Univ Fla, Gainesville, 75; Drawing Invitational, Southeastern Ctr Contemp Art, Winston-Salem, NC, 75; 1975 Artist's Biennial, New Orleans Mus Art, 75. Teaching: Prof art, Univ SFla, 63- Awards: First Prize, Eastern US Drawing Competition, Cummer Art Mus, Jacksonville, 70; Award Merit, Fla Creates, Fla Mus Dirs, 71; First Prize, Open Painting Competition, Southeast Bank, Miami, Fla, 73. Bibliog: Charles Benbow (auth), The artist is translator-poet, St Petersburg Times, 69. Style & Technique: Painting and drawing-painting on mounted paper; usually in photorealist style. Media: Drybrush Oil, Charcoal. Dealer: ACA Galleries 25 E 73rd St New York NY 10021. Mailing Add: 908 S Dakota Ave Tampa FL 33606

KROPF, JOAN R
MUSEUM DIRECTOR
b Cleveland, Ohio, Aug 4, 49. Study: Cleveland Art Inst; Cooper Sch Art; Cuyahoga Community Col, photography with Abe Frajndlich. Collections Arranged: Worked with others to assemble and arrange, Homage to Albrecht Durer, 72, Aliyah and Song of Songs, 73, Important Writings of Dali, 74, Dali's Horses, 74, Cancelled Graphic Plates, 75, Hiram College Graphics Show, 76, Dali and Classical Mythology, 76, Erotic Art by Dali, 76, Dali's Anamorphoses, 77, Dali's Surrealist Fruits and Flowers, 77, Les Diners De Gali, 78, Salvador Dali Mus. Pos: Asst dir, Salvador Dali Mus, Cleveland, 71-76, dir, 76- Mailing Add: c/o Salvador Dali Mus 24050 Commerce Park Rd Cleveland OH 44122

KRUEGER, DONALD W
PAINTER, EDUCATOR
b Tulsa, Okla, Nov 14, 28. Study: Kansas City Art Inst, BFA & MFA; RI Sch Design, MSc. Work: Pvt collections. Exhib: Great Designs in Jewelry, New York, 67-69; Providence Art Club, Graphics, 69 & Drawing, 74; Dibellardo Gallery, New York, 69 & 70; Hess Gallery, Brookline, Mass, 70 & 71; Worcester Art Mus, Mass, 72-74; plus others. Teaching: Asst prof drawing & design, RI Sch Design, 58-64, Univ Ga, 64-65 & Wash Univ Sch Fine Arts, 65-67; chmn visual & performing arts dept, Clark Univ, 72- Pos: Art dir, Southeastern Advert Agency, New Bedford, Mass, 69-72. Mem: Col Art Asn. Style & Technique: Humanistic; expressionistic. Media: Painting & Drawing. Mailing Add: Clark Univ Worcester MA 01610

KRUG, HARRY ELNO
PRINTMAKER, EDUCATOR
b Oshkosh, Wis, Aug 20, 30. Study: Univ Wis-Milwaukee, BFA; Univ Wis-Madison, MS; Nat Art Acad, Stuttgart, Ger, with Erich Monch. Work: Libr of Cong, Washington, DC; Nelson-Atkins Art Gallery, Kansas City, Mo; US Info Agency; Springfield Art Mus, Mo; Ohio Univ Galleries. Exhib: 22nd Am Color Print Exhib, Am Color Print Soc, 63; 6th Nat Print Exhib, Silvermine Guild Artists, New Canaan, Conn, 67; 19th Ann Exhib, Boston Mus Fine Arts, Mass, 68; Teacher-Artist Today, State Univ NY Col Oswego, 69; Hopman, Krug, Ecker, Galerie Feursee, Stuttgart, 70. Teaching: Assoc prof printmaking, Kans State Col, 58- Pos: Crafts dir, Spec Serv, Baumholder, Ger, 62-64; crafts dir, Spec Serv, Stuttgart, 68-71. Awards: Mid-Am Ann Purchase Award, Nelson-Atkins Art Mus, Kansas City, 60; Sonia Watter Award, Am Color Print Soc, Pa, 62; Prize for Graphics, Jersey City Mus, NJ, 68. Mem: Boston Printmakers; Philadelphia Print Club. Mailing Add: Rte 3 Box 182 Pittsburg KS 66762

KRUGER, BARBARA
CONCEPTUAL ARTIST
b Newark, NJ, Jan 26, 45. Study: Syracuse Univ; Parsons Sch Design; Sch Visual Arts. Exhib: Whitney Biennial of Contemp Am Art, 73; Audio Narratives, Los Angeles Inst of Contemp Art, 77; two-person show, Ohio State Univ, 77; Calif Ann, San Francisco Art Inst, 77; Readings, Franklin Furnace, New York, Downtown Whitney Mus, New York & 80 Langton St Gallery, San Francisco, 77-78; one-woman shows, Artist's Space, 74 & Fischbach Gallery, 75. Teaching: Vis artist, Art Inst Chicago & Univ Calif, Berkeley. Style & Technique: Narratives (written), photographs, paintings and drawings. Media: Mixed. Mailing Add: 55 Leonard St New York NY 10013

KRUGER, LOUISE
SCULPTOR
b Los Angeles, Calif. Study: Scripps Col, Calif; Art Students League; Opoku Dwumfuor, Kumasi, Ghana. Work: Mus Mod Art & New York Libr Print Collection; Mod Mus, Sao Paulo; Brooklyn Mus, NY. Exhib: Metrop Mus, Whitney Mus Am Art & Mus Mod Art, New York; Art Inst Chicago; Kunsthaus, Zurich. Style & Technique: Figurative, varied media and techniques. Media: Wood, Bronze. Dealer: Robert Schoelkopf Gallery 825 Madison Ave New York NY 10021. Mailing Add: 30 E Second St New York NY 10003

KRUGMAN, IRENE
SCULPTOR
b New York, NY. Study: Kans City Art Inst; New York Univ; New Sch for Social Res, with Yasuo Kuniyoshi. Work: Joan & Lester Avnet Collection, Great Neck, NY; Riverside Mus Collection, Brandeis Univ, Waltham, Mass; Univ Notre Dame, Ind; Kresge Art Ctr, Mich State Univ, E Lansing; NJ State Mus, Trenton. Comn: Sculptural installation, City Univ of New York, 77 & site sculpture, Queensboro Community Col, Bayside, 78, Nat Endowment for the Arts & New York Coun on the Arts. Exhib: Some More Beginnings, 68 & Works on Paper Women Artists, 75-76, Brooklyn Mus, NY; Contemporary Americans, Riverside Mus, New York, 70; O K Harris Gallery, New York, 70, 76 & 78; Contemporary Issues, Works on Paper, Woman's Bldg, Los Angeles, Univ Utah & Univ Houston, Tex, 77; one-woman shows, Warren Benedek Gallery, New York, 73, Summit Art Ctr, NJ, 74, NJ State Mus, Trenton, 75-76 & Herter Gallery, Univ Mass, Amherst, 77. Bibliog: David Shirey (auth), Irene Krugman presents 2nd sculpture exhibition, 2/71, Piri Halasz (auth), A gestural artist exhibits in Summit, 74 & Grace Glueck (auth), Review, 2/4/77, New York Times; Lenore Malen (auth), Irene Krugman, Arts Mag, 4/78. Style & Technique: Sculpture using wood, mirrors and blackboard, incorporating relief in three dimensional sculpture. Media: Wood, Blackboard, Mirrors. Dealer: Ivan Karp c/o O K Harris Gallery 383 W Broadway New York NY 10012. Mailing Add: 22 Washington Ave Morristown NJ 07960

KRUKOWSKI, LUCIAN
PAINTER, EDUCATOR
b Brooklyn, NY, Nov 22, 29. Study: Brooklyn Col, BA, 52; Yale Univ, BFA, 55; Pratt Inst, MS, 58, PhD, 77. Work: St Louis Art Mus, Mo. Comn: Outdoor wall painting, Nat Endowment Arts, St Louis, 72. Exhib: Staempfli Gallery, 58 & 62 & Cee-je Gallery, New York, 67; Loretto Hilton Gallery, 70 & Moore Gallery, St Louis, 75 & 78. Teaching: Prof art, Pratt Inst, 55-69, chmn dept fine arts, 67-69; prof art & dean, Sch Fine Arts, Wash Univ, 69- Mem: Am Soc Aesthetics; Col Art Asn. Mailing Add: 24 Washington Terr St Louis MO 63112

KRUSHENICK, JOHN
PAINTER, EDUCATOR
b New York, NY, Mar 18, 27. Study: City Col New York; Art Students League, with Johnson, Hale, Browne & Vytlacil; Hans Hofmann Sch Fine Arts, New York; Univ Wis, BFA. Work: Mus Mod Art & Bank St Col Educ, New York; Weatherspoon Gallery, NC. Exhib: Mus Mod Art, Tokyo, Hiroshima & Kyoto, 59; Homage to Camus, Esther Stuttman, 60; Martha Jackson Gallery; Green Camp, Cooper Union, 71; New York Civil Liberties Show, Leo Castelli-Downtown, 72. Teaching: Adj instr studio crafts & procedures, Cooper Union, 68-69; assoc prof mus & gallery procedures & dir, Fine Arts Gallery, Univ Wis-Milwaukee, 72- Pos: Owner-dir, House of Brata Frames & Brata Gallery Coop, 57-64; framing consult, Dain/Schiff, 65-67; dir-cur, Dorsky Gallery, 70-71; mem mus adv panel, Ind Arts Comn, 75-76; dir, Mus Art, Fort Wayne, Ind, 75- Bibliog: Fred McDarrah (auth), Artists World; John Canady (auth), Embattled Critic. Style & Technique: Contemporary personal figurative. Media: Oil. Publ: Contribr, Voice of America, 59; co-auth, Dorsky Gallery statement, Arts, 4/71; contribr, Mus News, 6/73; contribr, Mid-West Art, 12/74; contribr catalogue, First International Mail Exhibition, Bway Galleries, Milwaukee, Wis, 3/77; auth transcript lecture, Collections Users View, Asn Ind Mus, 9/77. Mailing Add: Fort Wayne Mus of Art 1202 W Wayne St Fort Wayne IN 46804

KRUSHENICK, NICHOLAS
PAINTER
b New York, NY, May 31, 29. Study: Art Students League, 48-50; Hans Hofmann Sch, New York, 50-51. Work: Metrop Mus Art, New York; Mus Mod Art, New York; Los Angeles Co Mus Art; Folkwang Mus, Essen, WGer; Stedelijk Mus, Amsterdam, Holland. Comn: Large painting, State Univ NY Albany, 69. Exhib: Whitney Mus Am Art Ann, 63, 65 & 67, Biennial, 73; Post Painterly Abstraction, Los Angeles, Toronto & Minn, 64; Systemic Painting, Guggenheim Mus, New York, 66; New Forms & Shapes of Color, Amsterdam & Basel, 66; 1960 Mus Mod Art, 66; Documenta IV, Kassel, WGer, 68; Retrospective, Walker Art Ctr, Minneapolis, 68; Princeton Univ Art Mus, 70; Aldrich Mus Contemp Art, Ridgefield, Conn, 71 & 75; one-man shows, Univ Ala, Birmingham, 73, Calif State Col, Long Beach, 73, Portland Ctr for Visual Arts, Ore, 74, Henry Gallery, Univ Wash, Seattle, 74, Calif State Univ, San Bernardino, 75, Alfred Univ, New York, 76 & Univ Ky, Lexington, 76; plus others. Teaching: Vis artist, Univ Wis, 69; art critic, Yale Univ, 69-70; artist, Cornell Univ, 70. Awards: Tamarind Lithography Award, 65; Guggenheim Found Fel, 67. Dealer: Pace Gallery 32 E 57th St New York NY 10022. Mailing Add: 168 Mercer St New York NY 10012

KRUSKAMP, JANET
PAINTER, INSTRUCTOR
b Grants Pass, Ore, Dec 10, 34. Study: Chouinard Art Inst, Los Angeles, scholars. Work: Rosicrucian Egyptian Mus, San Jose & Triton Mus Art, Santa Clara, Calif; La Grange Col, Ga. Exhib: Soc Western Artists Ann, M H De Young Mus, San Francisco, 71; Artistes USA, Salon Prix Paris, 71; Frye Mus Art, Seattle, 71; Am Artists Prof League Grand Nat, 72; Soc Western Artists, Rosicrucian Egyptian Mus, 72; Mainstreams, Marietta Col, Ohio, 75; many solo shows nationallly. Teaching: Pvt art classes, 66- Awards: Best of Show, Santa Clara Co Hist Landmarks Exhib, 69; Soc Western Artists Ann First Place Oils, 70; Trustees' Award & Andy Trophy, Grand Galleria Art Competition, Seattle, 72 & First Grand Prize, 73; plus others. Bibliog: Janice Lovoos (auth), Janet Kruskamp's America, Southwest Art, 6/75; Reva Remy (auth), Le Solon Annuel National D'Art, La Rev Mod; Ted Bredt (auth), A romantic display, Calif Today, 76; plus others. Mem: Fel Am Artists Prof League; Soc Western Artists; Los Gatos Art Asn (pres, 69). Style & Technique: Romantic realism. Media: Oil, Egg Tempera; Printmaking. Dealer: Walton-Gilbert San Francisco CA; Rubicon Gallery Los Altos CA. Mailing Add: 1627 Hyde Dr Los Gatos CA 95030

KRUST, WALTER
PAINTER, SCULPTOR
b Pforzheim, Ger, Oct 19, 20; US citizen. Study: Pa Acad Fine Arts, BFA; Art Students League; and with Paul Klee, Europe & Hans Hofmann, New York. Work: Mus Mod Art & Whitney Mus Am Art, New York. Exhib: Venice Biennale, Italy, 54; one-man shows, Milch Galleries, New York, 55 & Wellons Gallery, New York, 56; Sao Paulo Bienal, Brazil, 59; Int Exhib Contemp Art, London, 71. Awards: Second Prize, Sao Paulo Bienal, Brazil, 59. Mem: Nat Acad Design. Style & Technique: Abstract; abstract expressionism. Mailing Add: Stillwater Hills Ossining NY 10562

KUBLER, GEORGE ALEXANDER
ART HISTORIAN, WRITER
b Los Angeles, Calif, July 26, 12. Study: Yale Univ, BA, 34, MA, 36, PhD, 40. Teaching: Prof hist art, Yale Univ, 38- Res: Pre-Columbian and colonial Latin American art; art of Spain and Portugal. Publ: Auth, Religious Architecture of New Mexico, 40; auth, Mexican Architecture of the Sixteenth Century, 48; co-auth, Art & Architecture of Spain & Portugal, 59; auth, Art & Architecture of Ancient America, 62; auth, The Shape of Time, 62. Mailing Add: 56 High St New Haven CT 06520

KUBLY, DONALD R
DESIGNER, ART ADMINISTRATOR
b Los Angeles, Calif, Nov 14, 17. Study: Pasadena Jr Col, AA; Art Ctr Col Design, BPA. Exhib: NY Art Dirs Ann Exhib, 56 & 71. Pos: Sr art dir, N W Ayer & Son, Advert, 49-63; dir, Art Ctr Col Design, Los Angeles, 63-, pres, 65- Awards: Gold Medal, NY Art Dirs Ann Exhib, 56 & 71. Mem: Am Inst Graphic Arts (dir, 72); Los Angeles Art Asn; Soc Typograph Arts. Publ: Contribr, Graphics & Creative Arts, 56-71. Mailing Add: Art Ctr Col Design 1700 Lida St Pasadena CA 91103

KUBOTA, SHIGEKO
VIDEO CURATOR, VIDEO ARTIST
b Niigata, Japan, Aug 2, 37. Study: Univ Tokyo, BA(sculpture). Exhib: Video Sculpture: Duchamp's Grave, The Kitchen, New York, 75, Seattle, Wash, 75, Everson Mus, Syracuse, NY, 76 & Acad Kunste, Berlin, WGer, 76; Nude Descending a Staircase, Seattle, 76 & Dokumenta 6, Kassel, Ger, 77; Video Sculptures, Rene Block Gallery, New York, 77. Teaching: Mem video art fac, Sch of Visual Arts, New York, 78- Pos: Video cur, Anthology Film Archives, 74- Awards: Documentary video grant, Nat Endowment for the Arts, 76; grant, 3 video sculptures, Creative Artist Pub Serv, 76. Bibliog: Jonathan Price (auth), Video Visions: A Medium Discovers Itself, New Am Libr, 77; David Bourdon (auth), A Critics diary, The New York Art Yr, 7-8/77 & The young generation: a cross section, 9-10/77, Art in Am. Style & Technique: Video sculpture; moving image with video and film and object, environment. Media: Video sculpture. Publ: Auth, Marcel Duchamp & John Cage, Takeyoshi Miyazawa, 70. Dealer: Rene Block Gallery 1000 Berlin 5 Schaperstrabe 11 Berlin WGer. Mailing Add: PO Box 846 Canal St Sta New York NY 10012

KUCHAR, KATHLEEN ANN
PAINTER, INSTRUCTOR
b Meadow Grove, Nebr, Feb 4, 42. Study: Kearney State Col, BA(educ), 63; Ft Hays Kans State Col, MS, 66; Brooklyn Mus Art Sch, Max Beckmann Mem scholar, 66-67, with Reuben Tam, 67; Wichita State Univ, MFA, 74. Work: Wichita State Univ Art Gallery; Ft Hays Kans State Col Art Gallery. Exhib: 9th Midwest Biennial, Joslyn Art Mus, Omaha, Nebr, 66; Watercolor USA, Springfield Art Mus, Mo, 68; one-person show, Nat Design Ctr, New York, 68; 3rd Nat Polymer Exhib, Eastern Mich Univ, 69; Drawing & Small Sculpture Exhib, Ball State Univ, 72. Teaching: Instr art, Minden Pub Schs, Nebr, 63-65; assoc prof painting-design, Ft Hays Kans State Col, 67- Awards: Purchase Award, Kans Bank, 74. Bibliog: Rev in Art News, 68 & Art Rev, 69; Female Artists, Past & Present, Women's Hist Res Ctr, Inc, 74. Mem: Col Art Asn Am; Kans Watercolor Soc. Style & Technique: Abstractions. Media: Acrylic; Felt Markers. Mailing Add: 2202 Fort St Hays KS 67601

KUCHEL, KONRAD
ART ADMINISTRATOR
b Salem, Mass, Aug 25, 37. Study: Bowdoin Col, AB, 60; Inst of Fine Arts, New York Univ, MA, 63. Pos: Asst to dir & ed, Mus Bull, Mus of Art, RI Sch of Design, 63-64; coordr of loans, Exhib Dept, Am Fedn of Arts, 65-69 & 76-, dir of exhibs, 69-75. Mailing Add: c/o Am Fedn of Arts 41 E 65th St New York NY 10021

KUCHTA, RONALD A
MUSEUM DIRECTOR, LECTURER
b Lackawanna, NY, June 23, 35. Study: Cape Cod Sch Art, Provincetown, Mass, 53-57; Kenyon Col, Gambier, Ohio, 53-57, BA, 57; Western Reserve Univ, Cleveland, Ohio, 61-62, MA(art hist), 62. Collections Arranged: Modern Mexican Painting, 70; Tantra (with catalog), 70; Interior Vision, European Abstract Expressionism, 1945-1960 (with catalog), 70; Animals in African Art (with catalog), 73; 15 Abstract Artists—Los Angeles, 73; New Works in Clay, 76; Provincetown Painters, 77; Francisco Zuñiga, 77. Teaching: Adj prof museol, Syracuse Univ, 74- Pos: Cur, Chrysler Art Mus, 61-68; cur, Santa Barbara Mus Art, 68-74; dir, Everson Mus Art, 74- Mem: Am Asn Mus; Am Asn Mus Dir; Int Coun Mus. Mailing Add: Everson Mus Art Syracuse NY 13202

KUCZUN, ANN-MARIE
PAINTER
b Springfield, Mass. Study: Bay Path Jr Col, AS; also with William Urton. Exhib: Denver Art Mus, 76; Sangre De Christo Cultural Ctr, 77; Boulder Art Ctr, 76 & 77; Rocky Mt Nat, 76; one-person show, Foothills Art Ctr, 77. Pos: Bd dirs, publicity chmn & exhib chmn, Boulder Fine Arts Ctr, 72-73; publicity, vpres, Grant Liaison, Boulder Art Asn, 77. Bibliog: Illus feature in Colorado Mag, 9-10/77; feature with color photos in Boulder Daily Camera, 9/16/77. Style & Technique: Contemporary environmental portraits in watercolor; abstract essences of nature in watermedia; identity series in combined drawing/collage on paper. Media: Watermedia; Drawing/Collage on Paper. Publ: Contribr, Collaging with Paper, 78. Mailing Add: 930 Miami Way Boulder CO 80303

KUEBLER, GEORGE F
ART ADMINISTRATOR, EDUCATOR
b Rochester, Ind, Dec 1, 28. Study: Manchester Col, BS(art educ), Ind Univ, MAT(fine arts); also with Max Weber & Jack Tworkov. Collections Arranged: Drawings by Arshile Gorky, 73; Art from Africa, 74; Contemporary Landscape Painting, 75. Teaching: Art instr, Ind Pub Schs, 50-58; asst prof art, Purdue Univ, 58-65; assoc prof art hist, Oklahoma City Univ, 74-77. Pos: Cur exten serv, Nat Gallery Art, Washington, DC, 65-70; dir, Hathorn Gallery, Skidmore Col, 70-72; dir, Okla Art Ctr, 72- Mem: Am Asn Mus; Western Asn Art Mus; Okla Mus Asn. Mailing Add: Oklahoma Art Ctr 3113 Pershing Blvd Oklahoma City OK 73107

KUEHN, EDMUND KARL
PAINTER, LECTURER
b Columbus, Ohio, Aug 18, 16. Study: Columbus Art Sch, cert, 38; Art Students League, cert, 39. Work: Columbus Gallery Fine Arts. Collections Arranged: Paintings from Columbus Homes, 63; Jean Crotti in Retrospect, 65; The Gordian Knot, 67; Works by David Blythe, 68. Teaching: Asst prof drawing & painting, Ohio State Univ, 46-47; assoc prof drawing & painting, Columbus Col Art & Design, 52-62. Pos: Cur, Columbus Gallery Fine Arts, 39-43, asst dir, 62-67, cur collections, 67-76. Mem: Columbus Art League; Am Asn Mus. Mailing Add: 828 City Park Ave Columbus OH 43206

KUEHN, FRANCES
PAINTER
b New York, NY, Feb 16, 43. Study: Douglass Col, Rutgers Univ, BA, Rutgers Univ, New Brunswick, MFA. Work: J B Speed Art Mus, Louisville, Ky; Weatherspoon Art Gallery, Univ NC; Power Inst, Univ Sydney, Australia; Allen Mem Art Mus, Oberlin, Ohio. Comn: Portrait for private collection, 72. Exhib: Whitney Mus Ann, 72 & Biennial, 73; one-woman shows, Douglass Col Libr, 73, Max Hutchinson Gallery, 73 & 74 & Am Sachs, New York, 78; Contemporary Portraits by Well-Known American Artists, Lowe Art Mus, Coral Gables, Fla, 74; Selections in Contemporary Realism, Akron Art Inst, Ohio, 74. Bibliog: Phyllis Derfner (auth), Frances Kuehn, Art Spectrum, 2/75. Style & Technique: Figurative. Media: Acrylic. Dealer: Max Hutchinson Gallery 127 Greene St New York NY 10012. Mailing Add: RD 4 Box 550 Princeton NJ 08540

KUEHN, GARY
SCULPTOR, GRAPHIC ARTIST
b Plainfield, NJ, 1939. Study: Drew Univ, NJ, BA(art hist), 62; Rutgers Univ, NJ, MFA, 64. Work: NJ State Mus, Trenton; also in pvt collections of Richard P Kaplan, New York, Roy Lichtenstein, New York & Robert Scull, New York. Exhib: Eccentric Abstraction, Fischbach Gallery, New York, 66; Painting & Sculpture Today, Herron Mus, Indianapolis, Ind, 67; Cool Art Today, Larry Aldrich Mus Ridgefield, Conn, 68; Whitney Ann, New York, 68; Program I, 69, Program II, 70; Program III, 71, & New Graphics, 72, Galerie Ricke, Cologne, WGer; When Attitudes Become Form (toured Krefeld, London), Kunsthalle Berne, Switz, 69; New Materials, Procedures in Sculpture, Austin Arts Ctr, Tex, 70; Sculptor's Drawings, Margo Leavin Gallery, Los Angeles, Calif, 73; one-man shows, Douglass Col, NJ, 66, Kunstverein, Cologne, 67, Milwaukee Art Ctr, Wis, 68, Fischbach Gallery, New York, 69 & 74, Paley and Lowe Gallery, New York, 72 & Stefanotty Gallery, New York, 74. Teaching: Instr, Fairleigh Dickinson Univ, NJ, 65, Drew Univ, NJ, 65-68, Sch of Visual Arts, New York, 68, Hochshule fur Bildende Kunst, Braunschweig, Ger, 70, Douglass Col & Rutgers Univ, 73. Awards: Nat Coun on the Arts Grant, Washington, DC, 67; Governor's Purchase Award, NJ State Mus, Trenton, 72. Bibliog: Robert Pincus (auth), New York: Gary Kuehn, Fischbach Gallery, 1/70, K Linville (auth), Gary Kuehn, Fischbach Gallery, 5/71 & J Gilbert-Rolfe (auth), Reviews: Gary Kuehn, Stefanotty Gallery, 5/74, Artforum, New York. Dealer: Galerie Ricke Lindenstrasse 22 Cologne Germany. Mailing Add: Buffalo Hollow Rd Glen Gardner NJ 08821

KUEHNL, CLAUDIA ANN
JEWELER, EDUCATOR
b Kenosha, Wis, Aug 11, 48. Study: Philadelphia Col of Art, Pa, BFA, 70; State Univ NY Col, New Paltz, MFA, 74. Exhib: Contemp Am Gold-Silversmiths, Corcoran Gallery of Art, Washington, DC, 72; Pulsations, Loch Haven Art Ctr, Winter Park, Fla, 73; A La Baroque Exhib, Mus of Contemp Crafts, New York, 74; Southern Tier Arts & Crafts Exhib, Corning Mus, NY, 74; Contemp Crafts of the Americas Int Exhib, Ft Collins, Colo, 75; Mex Exhib, Univ Mex, Mexico City, 75; Silver & Goldsmithing in Am Exhib, Lowe Art Mus, Univ Miami, Coral Gables, Fla, 76; Contemp Crafts Exhib, Del Art Mus, Wilmington, 76; NAm Goldsmiths Exhib, Phoenix Art Mus, Ariz, 77. Teaching: Instr art appreciation, Suffolk Co Community Col, Selden, NY, 75-; asst prof jewelry, Southampton Col, NY, 76- Awards: Nat Endowment for the Arts fel/Crafts, 75-76. Mem: Soc NAm Goldsmiths; Am Crafts Coun; NY State Craftsmen Inc. Style & Technique: Cast, engraved and architectural references. Media: 18K gold, precious stone, semi-precious stone, silver. Dealer: Rosenfeld Gallery 113 Arch St Philadelphia PA 19106. Mailing Add: Quogue St Box 622 Quogue NY 11959

KUEKES, EDWARD D
CARTOONIST
b Pittsburgh, Pa, Feb 2, 01. Study: Baldwin-Wallace Col, Hon LHD, 57; Cleveland Inst Art; Chicago Acad Fine Arts. Work: Cartoon collection at Western Reserve Hist Soc, Cleveland, Ohio & Baldwin-Wallace Col, Berea, Ohio; five thousand original cartoons in collection at Syracuse Univ. Teaching: Lect, So you can't draw a straight line, either, art groups nationally. Pos: Cartoonist, Cleveland Plain Dealer, 22-49; chief ed cartoonist, 49-66, cartoonist emer, 66-; cartoonist, Metro Newspapers, Inc, Cleveland, 68- Awards: Pulitzer Prize, Cartoon Div, 53; three First Prize Awards, Freedom Found; plus many others. Mem: Asn Am Ed Cartoonists; Nat Cartoonist Soc. Publ: Auth, Funny Fables, 38; co-auth, Alice in Wonderland & Knurl the Gnome (cartoon features), United Features Syndicate; creator, All in the Week, Along the Road, Cartoonists Looks at the News & other featured cartoons. Mailing Add: 1280 Medfield Dr Rocky River OH 44116

KUH, HOWARD
PAINTER
b New York, NY, 1899. Study: Art Students League; Marine painting with Jay Conaway, Maine; painting with S M Alder, New York. Work: Procter & Gamble; Conover Nast Publ; Summit Hotel. Exhib: Audubon Artists, Nat Acad of Design, New York; Am Soc of Contemp Artists, Rvierside Mus, Lever House, Union Carbide, Nat Acad of Design, Nat Arts Club & Nat Sports Mus; New Eng Ann, Silver Mine, Conn; Avery Mem Mus, Hartford, Conn; New Sch, New York; Loeb Ctr, New York Univ; Norfolk Mus of Fine Arts; Evansville Mus of Arts & Sci; Minneapolis Mus, Duluth; Sheldon Swope Gallery, Terra Haute; Univ of Purdue; Butler Inst of Am Art, Youngstown, Ohio; Lyman Allyn Mus, New London; one-man shows, Roko Gallery & bodley Gallery. Mem: Am Soc of Contemp Artists (vpres-dir); League of Present Day Artists (dir); Artists Equity Asn of New York (vpres-dir). Style & Technique: Abstract painter. Mailing Add: 45 Christopher St New York NY 10014

KUH, KATHARINE
ART CRITIC, ART CONSULTANT
b St Louis, Mo, July 15, 04. Study: Vassar Col, BA; Univ Chicago, MA(art hist); NY Univ. Pos: Owner & dir, Katharine Kuh Gallery, Chicago, 36-42; cur mod art, Art Inst Chicago, 42-59; art ed, Sat Rev, 59-77; art consult, First Nat Bank Chicago, 68- Publ: Auth, Art Has Many Faces, 51, auth, The Artist's Voice, 61 & auth, The Open Eye, 70, Harper & Row; auth, Leger, Univ Ill, 58; auth, Break-Up: The Core of Modern Art, NY Graphic, 65. Mailing Add: 140 E 83rd St New York NY 10028

KUHLMAN, WALTER EGEL
PAINTER, EDUCATOR
b St Paul, Minn, Nov 16, 18. Study: St Paul Sch Art, with Cameron Booth; Univ Minn, BA; Calif Sch Fine Arts; Acad Grande Chaumiere. Work: Phillips Mem Gallery, Washington, DC; San Francisco Mus Art; Mus Mod Art, Sao Paulo, Brazil; Oakland Mus, Calif; Roswell Mus, NMex. Exhib: New York World's Fair, 40; Realities Nouvelles, Paris, 51; Art in 20th Century, San Francisco Mus Art, 55; Painters Behind Painters, Calif Palace of Legion of Honor, San Francisco, 67; Midyear Show 35, Butler Inst Am Art, 70. Teaching: Asst prof painting, Univ NMex, 60-65 & Univ Santa Clara, Calif, 66-69; prof painting, Sonoma State Col, Calif, 69- Awards: Tiffany Fel, 41; Cummington Found Fel, 42; Graham Found Fel, 57. Style & Technique: Land and seascape, and figurative. Media: Oil. Mailing Add: 27 Glen Ct Sausalito CA 94965

KUHN, BOB
ILLUSTRATOR, PAINTER
b Buffalo, NY, Jan 28, 20. Study: Pratt Inst, 3 yrs; Art Students League. Work: Nat Cowboy Hall Fame, Oklahoma City. Exhib: One-man show, Abercrombie & Fitch, New York, 65 & two-man show, 67; one-man show, Tyron Gallery, Nairobi, Kenya, 73; Animals in Art, Royal Ont Mus, Toronto, 75. Mem: Soc Animal Artists. Style & Technique: Realist-impressionist. Media: Acrylic on Masonite. Publ: Auth, Animal Art of Bob Kuhn, Watson-Guptill, 73;

contribr, Classic African Animals, Winchester, 73. Dealer: Sportsman's Edge New York NY. Mailing Add: Goodhill Rd Roxbury CT 06783

KUHN, BRENDA
ART HISTORIAN
b New York, NY, June 13, 11. Study: Friends Sem, New York; also art estate mgt with Walt & Vera Kuhn. Pos: Co-mgr, Kuhn Estate, 49-56, mgr, 56-66; mgr, Collection of Brenda Kuhn, 66-75; pres, Kuhn Mem Corp, 68-75, third vpres, currently; historian, Kuhnhouse. Mem: Arch Am Art; assoc Copley Soc Boston; Am Asn Mus; Am Fedn Arts; York Art Asn. Mailing Add: Kuhnhouse Cape Neddick Park Cape Neddick ME 03902

KUHN, MARYLOU
EDUCATOR, PAINTER
b South Bend, Ind, Oct 18, 23. Study: Layton Sch Art; Univ Wis; Art Inst Chicago; Ohio State Univ, univ fel, 53, BSc & PhD; Teachers Col, Columbia Univ, MA. Exhib: LeMoyne Art Found, 65-; Ind Univ, 74; Gulf Coast Jr Col, 75. Teaching: Prof art educ, Fla State Univ, 51-; guest lectr art educ, Inst Educ, Univ London, 66-67. Pos: Ed, Fla Art News, 60-62; ed, Southeastern Arts Bull, 62-64; mem ed bd, Studies in Art Educ, Nat Art Educ Asn, 62-66, regional ed, Art Educ J, 64-66, co-ed, Studies in Art Educ, 70-73, sr ed, Studies, 73-75; treas, Sem Res in Art Educ, 76-78. Mem: Int Soc Educ Through Art (deleg, 57, 63, 66 & 70); Nat Art Educ Asn (nat comts, 60-; pres-elect, Women's Caucus, 76-78 & pres, 78-79); Adult Educ Asn USA; Am Coun Arts; Am Fedn Arts. Style & Technique: Encaustic over watercolor and/or foil ground; exaggerated realism and non-objective style. Media: Encaustic, Watercolor. Res: Community and adult art education, curriculum and teacher education in art, philosophy and theory. Publ: Auth, Art education in a world context, Southeastern Arts Bull, 63; ed & auth, Continuing art education for adults, 12/65, auth, Means & meaning in art education, 3/65, auth, The relevance of art education to the future, 6/67 & INSEA XVIII, Prague, Czechoslovakia, 68, Art Educ; auth, Standards & criteria, Adult & Exten Art Educ, 66; auth chap in: Behavioral emphasis in art education, 75; auth, Priorities for arts in everyday living and education, Registry Vol 16, Studies, 76, 3/78. Dealer: LeMoyne Art Found 125 N Gadsden St Tallahassee FL 32303. Mailing Add: 1403 Betton Rd Tallahassee FL 32303

KUJUNDZIC, ZELJKO D
CERAMIST, SCULPTOR
b Subotica, Yugoslavia, Oct 23, 20; Can citizen. Study: Royal Col of Art, Budapest, Hungary, BA, 44; Inst of Fine Arts, Budapest, MFA, 46, with Jeno Barchai. Work: Nat Mus of Art, Subotica; Edinburgh Univ Col, Scotland; Pa State Univ, University Park & Fayette Campus; Univ BC, Vancouver. Comn: Thunderbirds (sculpture), Univ BC, Vancouver, 67; Reverence (mural), Prov Hosp BC, Nelson, 68; Ceramic mural, First Fed Bank, Pittsburgh, Pa, 73; libr mural, Pa State Univ, Uniontown, 74; Ancestor (sculptor), Credit Union, Vernon, BC, 75. Exhib: One-man shows, Dorothy van Arsdale Assoc Touring Exhib Serv, two yrs & US Govt Info Serv, Peru, 71; Interartex Can, SAm Touring Exhib, 71-72; W Moreland Co Mus Ann, Greensburg, Pa, 71-77; Int Ceramics Exhib, Nat Mus of Art, Poland, 73; Nat Sculpture Exhib, 7E.7 Gallery, Lawrence, Kans, 74; Int Medalist Exhib, Nat Gallery of Art, Poland, 76; Can Nat Ceramic Exhib, Glenbow Inst, Calgary, Alta, 76. Collections Arranged: Pre-Columbian Meso-American Ceramics (cur), Pa State Univ, Fayette Campus, 75-76; Sculptors Soc of Can (US touring exhib), 72. Teaching: Dir painting, Kootenay Sch of Art, Nelson, BC, 59-64; dir mural, Art Ctr, Kelowna, BC, 64-68; assoc prof ceramics, sculpture & 3-D design, Pa State Univ, Uniontown, 68- Pos: Pres, Okanagan Contemp Artists, 66-68; exec dir, Pioneer Crafts Coun, Mill Run, Pa, 70-71. Awards: Merit Awards, Expo 67 Can, Nat Crafts Coun of Can, 67 & Int Ceramics, Nat Mus of Art, Poland, 73; Purchase Award, Int Medalist Exhib, Nat Gallery of Art, Poland, 76. Bibliog: Anne Payne (auth), Kujundzic, Arts West, 66; Ray Turner (auth), Art with Zeljko, CHBC-TV, 67-68; Philip R Shepherd (auth, feature), Z Kujundzic, Onion, Toronto, 77. Mem: Int Acad of Ceramics, Switz; Sculptors Soc of Can; Sculptors Soc of BC (regional rep). Style & Technique: Expressionist, figurative, using universal symbolism; architectural art and sculpture. Publ: Auth (autobiog), Torn Canvas, Richard Patterson, 57, paperback ed, 64; auth, Paolo Soleri, Art & You, 73; auth, Experimental solar kilns, Ceramic Mo, 75; auth, Cuire au soleil, l'Atelier des Metiers d'Art, Paris, 76. Mailing Add: RD 2 RT 40 Box 533 Farmington PA 15437

KULICKE, ROBERT M
PAINTER, CRAFTSMAN
b Philadelphia, Pa, Mar 9, 24. Study: Philadelphia Mus Sch Art; Tyler Sch Fine Arts, Temple Univ; Atelier Fernand Leger, 46-50. Work: Philadelphia Mus Art. Exhib: Silvermine Guild, 64; Art Inst Chicago; Dayton Art Inst, Ohio; 100 Years of American Realism, Am Fedn Arts, 65; Whitney Mus Am Art, New York, 69; plus others. Teaching: Instr, Univ Calif, 64 & 70; Kulicke Cloisoone Workshop, New York, 64- Awards: Int Design Award, Am Inst Interior Designers, 68. Mailing Add: Kulicke-Stark Acad Jewelry Art 2231 Broadway New York NY 10024

KULTERMANN, UDO
ART HISTORIAN, EDUCATOR
b Stettin, Ger, Oct 14, 27. Study: Univ Greifswald, Ger, 47-50; Univ Munster, 50-53. Exhibitions Arranged: Monochrome Painting, Mus Leverkusen, 60, Ad Reinhardt-Lo Savio-Jef Verheyen, 61, Glass Chain, 62. Teaching: Prof hist & theory archit, Wash Univ, 67- Pos: Dir, City Art Mus, Leverkusen, Ger, 59-64. Res: Flemish-German Baroque sculpture; 19th and 20th century art and architecture; history of art history; African culture. Publ: Auth, Art Events & Happenings, Matthew, Miller & Dunbar, London, 71; New Realism, NY Graphic Soc, 72; New Architecture in the World, 2nd ed, 75 & The New Painting, 2nd ed, 77, Westview; auth, Ernest Trova, New York, 78. plus many others. Mailing Add: Wash Univ St Louis MO 63130

KUMLER, KIPTON (CORNELIUS)
PHOTOGRAPHER, LECTURER
b Cleveland, Ohio, June 20, 40. Study: Cornell Univ, BEE, 63, MEE, 67; spec study with Minor White at Mass Inst of Technol, 68-69; Harvard Univ, MBA, 69; spec study with Paul Caponigro, 70. Work: Metrop Mus Art, New York; Mus Fine Arts, Boston; Bibliot Nat, Paris; Int Mus Photog, George Eastman House, Rochester, NY; Worcester Art Mus, Mass. Comn: Essay on Danish Archit in Frederikster, St Croix, Landmark Soc, 75-76; Photog Surv, Del Water Gap, Nat Endowment Arts, 76-77. Exhib: Recent Acquisitions, Boston Mus Fine Arts, 74; Addison Gallery Am Art, 74; Carl Siembab Gallery, Boston, Mass, 74; Mass Inst Technol, Cambridge, 74; Galeria da Emenda, Lisbon, 75; Robert Schoelkopf Gallery, New York, 75; New Acquisitions, Worcester Art Mus, Mass, 76; Douglas Kenyon Inc, Chicago, Ill, 76; G Ray Hawkins Gallery, Los Angeles, 77; Cronin Gallery, Houston, Tex, 77; Jewett Arts Ctr, Wellesley Col, 77; Univ NH, Durham, 77. Collections Arranged: Traveling Exhib, Nat Endowment Arts Survey Work, NJ, 77-78. Teaching: Instr photog, Project, Inc, Cambridge, Mass, 69-72; field fac adv photog, Goddard Col, Plainfield, Vt, 76-77; instr advan photog, Maine Photog Workshops, Rockport, Maine, 77, 78. Awards: Nat Endowment for the Arts, Photog Survey grant, Peters Valley, NJ, 76-77; photog fel, Mass Coun Arts, 77. Style & Technique: Large format photography: nature, architecture and natural symbolism. Publ: Contribr, Camera, Lausanne, Switz, C Bucher, 70; contribr, Fox, Needham, Mass, Otaguro, 72; contribr, Popular Photography, Ziff Davis, 75; auth, Kipton Kumler: Photographs, David Godine, Boston, Mass, 75; contribr, Print Letter, Zurich, Misani, 77. Dealer: Robert Schoelkopf Gallery 825 Madison Ave New York NY 10016; Grapestake Gallery California St San Francisco CA. Mailing Add: 34 Grant St Lexington MA 02173

KUMM, MARGUERITE ELIZABETH
PAINTER, PRINTMAKER
b Redwood Falls, Minn. Study: Minneapolis Col Art & Design, cert design & painting, with Cameron Booth; Corcoran Sch Art, Washington, DC, painting & composition with Eugene Weisz & Richard Lahey. Work: Boston Mus Fine Arts; Calif State Libr, Sacramento; Libr Cong, Washington, DC; Metrop Mus Art, New York; Smithsonian Inst, Div Graphic Arts, Washington, DC. Exhib: Soc Am Etchers Ann, NY, 38-53; New York World's Fair, 39 & 40; Venice Biennial Am Pavilion, Italy, 40; Artists for Victory, Metrop Mus Art, New York, 42; Nat Acad Design, New York, 42-44 & 49; three-person show, Three Va Artists, Va Mus Fine Arts, Richmond, 45; one-person shows, Smithsonian Inst, 50, Mint Mus, Charlotte, NC, 51, Isaac Delgado Mus, New Orleans, 52, Butler Art Inst, Youngstown, Ohio, 52, Calif State Libr, 53 & Witte Mem Mus, San Antonio, Tex, 53. Awards: 100 Selected Prints Award, Soc Am Etchers, 38, 40, 44 & 51, 25 Selected Miniature Prints Award, 40 & 45 & Henry B Shope Prize, 43. Bibliog: Albert Reese (auth), American Prize Prints of the 20th Century, Am Artists Group, New York, 49. Style & Technique: Realistic; people at work or play. Media: Oil, Acrylic; Aquatint, Etching. Dealer: Betty Minor Duffy Bethesda Art Gallery 7950 Norfolk Ave Bethesda MD 20014. Mailing Add: 212 Noland St Falls Church VA 22046

KUP, KARL
ART HISTORIAN
b Haarlem, Holland, May 7, 03. Study: Univ Munich, with Wolfflin; Univ Berlin, with Goldschmidt; also with Diehl, Paris; Lakeside Press Sch Printing, Chicago. Teaching: Lect, Book ration, Illuminated Manuscripts & Books of the Orient; instr graphic arts, Princeton Univ Libr, 69- Pos: Contribr ed, Juvenile Dept, Oxford Univ Press, 28-34; cur, Spencer Collection, New York Pub Libr, 34-68, cur prints, 41-68, dir exhibs, 47-55, chief art & archit div, 56-65; trustee, Corning Mus Glass, Print Coun Am, Pratt Inst Print Ctr; fel, Pierpont Morgan Libr; contrib ed, Publ Weekly, 41-52 & Am Artist, 41-49. Mem: Bibliog Soc Am; Grolier Club; China Inst; Asia Soc. Publ: Auth, The Council of Constance, 1414-1418; auth, The Girdle Book; co-auth, Books & Printing; auth, The Christmas Story in Medieval Manuscripts; contribr, New York Pub Libr Bull, Am Artist, Artist's Proof, Libr J, Publ Weekly & other publ. Mailing Add: 136 E 36th St New York NY 10016

KUPFERMAN, LAWRENCE
PAINTER
b Boston, Mass, Mar 25, 09. Study: Sch Mus Fine Arts, Boston, 29-31; Mass Col Art, Boston, BScEd, 35. Work: Boston Mus Fine Arts; Mus Mod Art & Whitney Mus Am Art, New York; Wadsworth Atheneum, Hartford, Conn. Comn: Murals, Am Export Lines, SS Constitution, 48 & SS Independence, 48. Exhib: 62nd Ann, Art Inst Chicago, 57; Contemporary American Painting & Sculpture Biennial, Univ Ill, 61; 22nd Int Watercolor Biennial, Brooklyn Mus, 63; 160th Watercolors Ann, Pa Acad Fine Arts, Philadelphia, 65; retrospective, Brockton Art Ctr, 74. Teaching: Prof painting, Mass Col Art, 41-68. Awards: Saratoga Springs Victorian Purchase Prize, Assoc Am Artists, 47; Purchase Prize for Tempest, Krannert Art Mus Biennial, 53; First Prize for Painting, Odysseus, RI Arts Festival, Providence, 61. Bibliog: John I H Baur (auth), Revolution & Tradition in American Art, Harvard Univ, 51; Bartlett H Hayes (auth), The Naked Truth & Personal Vision, Addison Gallery Am Art, 55; Nathaniel Pousette-Dart (auth), American Painting Today, Hastings House, 56. Style & Technique: Abstract expressionist-abstract impressionist with poetic objectives affirming belief in life. Media: Acrylic, Tempera. Dealer: Contemp Art Consultants 200 Boylston St Chestnut Hill MA 02167. Mailing Add: 38 Devon Rd Newton Centre MA 02159

KUPFERMAN, MURRAY
PAINTER, SCULPTOR
b Brooklyn, NY. Work: St Vincent Col, Latrobe, Pa; Brooklyn Mus; New Rochelle Col, NY; Smithsonian Inst, Washington, DC; La Monte Dougherty Geol Observ. Comn: Underseas murals, Caravelle Hotel, St Croix, VI & Hotel Bonaire, Dutch W Indies. Exhib: NY Acad Sci; Seaport Mus; Seamans Church Inst; The White House, Washington, DC; Washington Co Mus Fine Arts; Children's Mus, Brooklyn, NY; Hagerstown Mus of Fine Arts; Yonkers Mus, NY; NY State Maritime Col, Ft Schuyler; US Govt Merchant Marine Acad; Conn Univ; New York City Hall of Sci; New Rochelle Col, NY; New York Col Optometry; plus others. Teaching: Instr art appreciation & painting, Brooklyn Tech, 27-65; instr painting, Educ Alliance, 65-70. Mem: Am Watercolor Soc; Allied Artists Am; League of Present Day Artists; Audubon Artists; Nat Soc Painters in Casein; plus others. Media: Casein, Acrylic. Dealer: Ctr Art Gallery 49 W 57th St New York NY 10036. Mailing Add: 1270 E 19th St Brooklyn NY 11230

KURAHARA, TED
PAINTER, EDUCATOR
b Seattle, Wash, July 16, 25. Study: St Louis Sch of Fine Arts, Washington Univ, BFA, 51, with Paul Burlin; Bradley Univ, Peoria, Ill, MA, 52, with Leon Engers. Work: NY Univ Collection, New York; Des Moines Art Ctr, Iowa; Hofstra Univ, Hempstead, NY; Springfield Art Ctr, Ill. Exhib: Artist W of the Mississippi, Colo Springs Art Ctr, Colo, 59; Midwest Painters, Grand Rapids Art Ctr, Mich, 60; one-man shows, Des Moines Art Ctr, Iowa, 60, Huntington Gallery, WVa, 61 & Mi Chou Gallery, New York, 65; E Meets W Traveling Exhib, 64-66 & Instant Creations Traveling Exhib, 65, Am Fedn of Arts; Jung Inst Benefit Show, New York, 76; Drawing Show, M/L Gallery, New York, 77; Amaganset Drawings, Pratt Inst, Brooklyn, NY, 77; Walter St Gallery, New York, 77. Teaching: Asst prof, Hofstra Univ, 67-70; assoc prof drawing, Pratt Inst, Brooklyn, 70- Pos: Dir, Emily Lowe Gallery, Hofstra Univ, 67-70. Awards: First Prize/Painting, Des Moines Ann, 58 & Purchase Prize, 59. Bibliog: John Watts (auth), Kurahara Exhibition, Manhattan E, 65; Wallace Barker (auth), Second Kurahara show, St Louis Post-Dispatch, 65. Style & Technique: Abstract, open, meditative and structural field. Media: Acrylic; watercolor and mixed media drawing. Gallery Affiliation: 9 E 19th St Gallery New York NY 10021. Mailing Add: 78 Greene St New York NY 10012

KURDIAN, HAROUTIUN HARRY
WRITER, COLLECTOR
b Aug 9, 02; US citizen. Collection: Armenian manuscripts; Irish silver; pre-Columbian art. Publ: Auth, Armenian Keutahia Pottery, 43; auth, History of Rug Weaving in Armenia, 47; auth, Armenian Silver Smithing, 49; auth, Armenian Wood Carving IX-XIV Centuries, 66; auth, Armenian Brocades Until XVII Century, 68. Mailing Add: 2924 E Douglas Wichita KS 67214

KURELEK, WILLIAM
PAINTER
b Alta, 1927. Study: Univ Man, BA, 49; Inst Allende, San Miguel, Mex. Work: Mus Mod Art, New York; Montreal Mus Fine Arts; Philadelphia Mus Art; Nat Gallery Can, Ottawa; Art Gallery Ont, Toronto; plus other pub & pvt collections. Exhib: Canadian Art, J B Speed Art Mus, Louisville, Ky, 62; Religious Art, Regis Col, 62 & 66; Invitation Show, Rochester Mem Art Gallery, New York, 63; Biennial Can Painting, Nat Gallery Can, 63, 65 & 68; Images of the Saints, Montreal Mus Fine Arts, 65; one-man shows, Art Gallery Ont Traveling Exhib, 70, Cornell Univ, Ithaca, NY, 71, Burnaby Art Gallery, BC, 73 & Isaacs Gallery, Toronto, 74; plus many other group & one-man shows. Awards: Sr Can Coun Fel, 69; New York Times Award for A Prairie Boy's Winter, 73 & Lumberjack, 74, Best Illus Children's Bk. Bibliog: Kurelek, Nat Film Bd, 67; Robert Young, David Gruben & Dr J Maas (auth), The Maze (psychol film study), Cornell Univ, 71. Mem: Royal Can Acad Arts. Publ: Auth & illusr, A Prairie Boy's Winter, 73 & illusr, Lumberjack, 74, Turndra Bks, Montreal; illusr, O Toronto, New Press, Toronto; illusr, Someone With Me, Cornell Univ, 73; illusr, The Passion of Christ, Niagara Falls Art Gallery & Mus, 74. Mailing Add: 175 Balsam Ave Toronto ON M4E 3C2 Can

KURHAJEC, JOSEPH A
SCULPTOR
b Racine, Wis, Oct 13, 38. Study: Univ Wis, BS, 60, MFA, 62. Work: New Sch Social Res, New York; Espanol Mus Contemp Art, Madrid, Spain; Mus Mod Art, New York; Chicago Art Inst; Walker Art Ctr, Minneapolis, Minn. Comn: Bronze cone, comn by Allan Stone, Purchase, NY, 71; bronze sculpture, comn by Norman Shaifer, Brooklyn Heights, NY, 71. Exhib: Am Fedn Art Traveling Exhib, 64; Sculpture Ann, Whitney Mus Am Art, New York, 64, Young America, 65; Espanol Mus Contemp Art, 69; Ten Independents, Guggenheim Mus, New York, 72. Teaching: Asst prof, Cornell Univ, 65-66; asst prof, Newark Sch Indust & Fine Art, 67-69; asst prof, Univ Wis-Stout, 71-73. Mailing Add: c/o Allan Stone Gallery 48 E 86th St New York NY 10028

KURZ, DIANA
PAINTER, EDUCATOR
b Vienna, Austria; US citizen. Study: Brandeis Univ, BA(fine arts cum laude); Columbia Univ, MFA(painting). Exhib: Rose Art Mus, Brandeis Univ, 74; Sons & Others—Women Artists See Men, Queens Mus, NY, 75; Sister Chapel, PS Inst for Art & Urban Resources, Long Island Col, NY, 78; one-artist shows, Green Mountain Gallery, New York, 72, 74 & 77, Col of Staten Island, NY, 77 & Queens Col, NY, 77. one-artist show, Green Mountain Gallery, New York, 72 & 74; Rose Art Mus, Brandeis Univ, 74; Sons & Others-Women Artists See Men, Queens Mus, NY, 75. Teaching: Lectr drawing, Philadelphia Col Art, 68-72; adj lectr art, Queens Col, NY, 71-76; vis prof art, Pratt Inst, 73; lectr art, Inst Int Educ, 76. Awards: CAPS grant, NY State Coun on Arts, 77; MacDowell fel, 77; Fulbright Grant in Painting, France, 65-66; Yaddo Fel, 68 & 69. Style & Technique: Large scale figures, nude and clothed; landscapes; expressionist use of color. Media: Oil, Watercolor. Dealer: Green Mountain Gallery 135 Greene St New York NY 10012. Mailing Add: 152 Wooster St New York NY 10012

KUSAMA, TETSUO
FIBER ARTIST
b Tokyo, Japan, Jan 7, 46. Study: Musashino Art Univ, Japan, BFA, 69; Cranbrook Acad of Art, Bloomfield Hills, Mich, MFA, 73. Work: Salt Lake Art Ctr, Utah; Weber State Col, Ogden, Utah. Comn: Fiber wall pieces (12 ft x 10 ft), Congregation Kol Ami, Salt Lake City, Utah, 76, (13 ft x 4 ft), Pac Design Ctr, Los Angeles, Calif, 77 & (13 ft x 6 ft), with Louise Allrich, Allrich Gallery, SSI Container Corp, San Francisco, 77. Exhib: Fiber structures, Mus of Art, Carnegie Inst Int, Pittsburgh, 76; Frontiers in Contemp Am Weaving, Lowe Art Mus, Univ Miami, Coral Gables, Fla, 76; Fiberworks—The Americas & Japan, Nat Mus of Mod Art, Japan, 77; Protofiber, Lowe Art Mus, New York, 77; Fiberworks, 77, Cleveland Mus of Art, Ohio, 77; 8th Int Biennial of Tapestry, Mus Cantonal des Beaux Art Switz, 77; Focus on Crafts, Univ Minn, 77; Contemp Japanese Tapestry, Allrich Gallery, San Francisco, 77. Teaching: Instr textile printing, Northern Ill Univ, DeKalb, 73-75; asst prof textiles, Utah State Univ, Logan, 75- Awards: Judge's Award, Marietta Crafts Nat, 75; Best in Show, Utah Designer/Craftsman, 76; Cash Award, Cotton Comes Home, 76. Bibliog: Michiaki Kawakita (auth), Konnichi no Zokei, Nat Mus of Mod Art, Kyoto, Japan, 77. Mem: Am Crafts Coun; Handweavers Guild of Am; Utah Designer Craftsman. Style & Technique: Abstract in fiber construction. Dealer: Allrich Gallery Two Embarcadero Ctr San Francisco CA 94111. Mailing Add: 600 W Haven Dr Logan UT 84321

KUSAMA, YAYOI
SCULPTOR, PAINTER
b Tokyo, Japan, Mar 22, 41; US citizen. Study: Kyoto Arts & Crafts Sch, Japan, 59. Work: Chrysler Mus, Provincetown, Mass, Stedelijk Mus, Amsterdam. Exhib: De Cordova Mus, Boston, 60; Stadt Mus, Schloss Morsbroish Leverkusen, Ger, 61; Whitney Mus, 62; Inst Contemp Art, 64; Chrysler Mus, 65; one-man shows, Ginza, Tokyo, 75 & 76; plus numerous other group and one-man shows. Mailing Add: 1008 Ushigome Heim 30-2 Chome Haramachi Shinjuku-Ku Tokyo Japan

KUSHNER, DOROTHY BROWDY
PAINTER, INSTRUCTOR
b Kansas City, Mo. Study: Kansas City Teachers Col, BS, 37; Columbia Univ, MA, 38; Art Students League; Art Inst Chicago; Kansas City Art Inst. Work: Pasadena Art Mus; Univ Ill; Va Mus Fine Arts; Camino Grove Sch, Arcadia. Exhib: Libr of Cong, 60; Boston Mus Fine Arts, 65; Calif State Fair, 69; Nat Acad Design, 71; Nat Watercolor Soc, 72-77. Teaching: Instr art, Kansas City Pub Schs; instr art, Grover Cleveland High Sch, New York, 40-46; instr art, Pasadena City Col, 69- Awards: Laguna Beach Art Asn, 69, Nat Watercolor Soc, 70 & Pasadena Soc Artists Awards, 70. Mem: Am Color Print Soc; Nat Watercolor Soc; Los Angeles Art Asn; Laguna Beach Art Asn; Pasadena Soc Artists. Style & Technique: Semi-abstract with emphasis on color. Media: Acrylic, Watercolor. Mailing Add: 3121 Monroe Way Costa Mesa CA 92626

KUSHNER, ROBERT ELLIS
PAINTER, DESIGNER
b Pasadena, Calif, Aug 19, 49. Study: Univ Calif, San Diego, BA. Exhib: All Calif Exhib, Laguna Beach Art Asn, 69; Artists Make Toys, The Clocktower, New York, 75; Biennial, Whitney Mus, New York, 75. Bibliog: Vicky Alliata (auth), Da New York la moda erotica e assurda di Bob Kushner, Luomo, 4/74; Amy Goldin (auth), The new Whitney Biennial: pattern emerging?, Art in Am, 5/75. Style & Technique: Object trouve costumes, decorations and wall hangings in a decorative manner. Media: Acrylic on Cotton, Found Materials. Publ: Co-auth, Conceptual art as opera, Art News, 70; contribr, Dimensions of Black, 70; contribr, Unnatural Acts 5, Unnatural Acts Press, 74. Dealer: Holly Solomon Gallery 392 W Broadway New York NY 10012. Mailing Add: 87-89 Leonard St New York NY 10013

KUSHNER-WEINER, ANITA MAY
PAINTER
b Philadelphia, Pa, Nov 30, 35. Study: Univ Pa, BA; Temple Univ, MA; New Sch Social Res, with Egas & Poussette d'Arte; Pa Acad Fine Arts. Work: Mus Mod Art, Haifa, Israel; B'nai B'rith Mus, Washington, DC; Univ Amsterdam, Holland; Picadilly Galleries, London, Eng; Grabar Galleries, Philadelphia. Exhib: Pa Acad Fine Arts Biannual Drawing & Watercolor, 67; New Talents, Whitney Mus Am Art, New York, 68; Okla Mus Traveling Art Show, 68; one-man show, B'nai B'rith Int Mus, 71; two-man show, Philadelphia Art Alliance, 71. Teaching: Art supvr elem educ, Pennsauken Bd Educ, NJ, 63-65; instr drawing, T-Square Atelier Architects, 63-68; instr voc art, Philadelphia Bd Educ, 65-71; instr studio art & art hist, Oakton Community Col. Pos: Demonstr, Print Club Philadelphia, 66-68; art dir, Jewish Community Ctr, Skokie, Ill, 71-72. Awards: First Prize Graphics, Philadelphia Civic Mus, 68, First Print Painting, 69; Critics Choice List, New York Times, 67. Bibliog: Contemporary art in America, La Rev Mod, 67; Sara Wilkinson (auth), An artist in a Tel-Aviv Show, Jerusalem Post Mag, Israel, 69. Mem: Artists Equity Asn; Ill Comt Arts; organizing mem Artists Mkt Chicago; Drawing Soc New York; Print Club Philadelphia. -Media: Watercolor. Dealer: Piccadilly Gallery 16A Cork St London England; Wanamakers Artists Gallery 137 Chestnut Philadelphia PA 19106. Mailing Add: c/o Maass 320 E Gowan St Philadelphia PA 19119

KUSPIT, DONALD BURTON
ART HISTORIAN, ART CRITIC
b New York, NY, Mar 26, 35. Study: Columbia Univ, BA; Yale Univ, MA(philos); Univ Frankfurt, PhD; Pa State Univ, MA(art); Univ Mich, PhD(art hist). Teaching: Prof, Univ NC, Chapel Hill, 70- Pos: Bk ed, Art J; contrib ed, Art in Am, Art Voices/SW & Contemp Art/SE. Awards: Can Coun Leave Fel, 68-69; Nat Endowment for Humanities Younger Humanist Fel, 73-74; Guggenheim Mem fel, 77-78. Mem: Col Art Asn Am; Am Soc Aesthet. Res: Northern Renaissance art, Dürer in particular; modern art and contemporary criticism. Publ: Auth, Melanchthon & Dürer: the search for the simple style, J Medieval & Renaissance Studies, 73; auth, The dialectic of taste, J Brit Soc Phenomenology, 73; auth, A phenomenological approach to artistic intention, 1/74; auth, Malevich's quest for unconditioned creativity, 6/74 & auth, Francis Bacon: the authority of flesh, summer 75, Artforum. Mailing Add: Art Dept Ackland Mem Ctr Univ NC Chapel Hill NC 27514

KUSSOY, BERNICE (HELEN)
SCULPTOR
b Brooklyn, NY, 1934. Study: Art Students League; Cooper Union; Western Reserve Univ, BS; Cleveland Inst Art, MFA. Work: Butler Inst Am Art, Youngstown, Ohio; Kalamazoo Art Inst, Mich; Univ Calif, Santa Barbara; Mex-Am Inst Cult Rels, Mexico City; Bundy Art Gallery, Waitsfield, Vt; plus other pub & pvt collections. Comn: Brancusi Marble Co, Los Angeles, United Res Serv, Burlingame & Temple Beth Israel, Pomona, Calif. Exhib: Laguna Beach Art Asn, 64; Otis Art Inst, Los Angeles, 64; Pioneer Mus & Haggin Galleries, Stockton, Calif, 64; Mexico City, 65; Judah L Magnes Jewish Mus of the West, Berkeley, Calif, 68; plus others. Awards: Butler Inst Am Art, 58 & Cincinnati Mus Asn Prizes, 58. Style & Technique: Figurative constructed of bronzed or welded metals, including found objects. Mailing Add: 3169 Washington St San Francisco CA 94115

KUTKA, ANNE (MRS DAVID MCCOSH)
PAINTER
b Danbury, Conn. Study: Art Students League, with Kenneth Hays Miller, Kimon Nicolaides & Eugene Fitsch. Work: Portland Art Mus, Ore; Am Red Cross, Washington, DC. Exhib: New York World's Fair, 39; Seattle Art Mus, 45; Exhib of Watercolors, Drawings & Prints, Metrop Mus Art, New York, 52; Portland Art Mus, 70, 72 & 73; Pac Northwest Art Ann, Eugene, Ore, 72; Earthworks-Artworks, Kerns Art Ctr, Eugene, 77; Mus of Art, Univ Ore, 77. Teaching: Instr painting & drawing, M I Kerns Art Ctr, Eugene, 60- Awards: Tiffany Fel, 30; G R D Traveling Scholar, 34. Mem: Art Students League; Portland Art Mus; Mus Art, Eugene. Media: Oil. Mailing Add: 1870 Fairmount Blvd Eugene OR 97403

KUTNER, JANET
ART CRITIC, LECTURER
b Dallas, Tex, Sept 20, 37. Study: Stanford Univ, 55-57; Southern Methodist Univ, BA, 59. Teaching: Lectr, Col & Univ Art Depts & regional study clubs, 73- Pos: Pub info & res dir, Dallas Mus Contemp Arts, 59-61; art critic & bk reviewer, Dallas Morning News, 70-; juror, Trinity River Festival Art Selection Comt, 74, Tex Col Art Show 1, Mountain View Col, 74 & Tex Designer/Craftsmen Exhib, NTex State Univ, 74; Dallas corresp, Art News Mag, 75. Mem: Am Asn Mus. Publ: Auth, The Houston-Dallas axis, Art in Am, 9-10/72; auth, Aesthetic povery, D the Mag of Dallas, 12/74; auth, Marden, Novros, Rothko: the urge to communicate through non-imagistic painting, Arts, 9/75; also auth of articles in Art News, Art Gallery Mag, Southwest Art Gallery & Now Mag. Mailing Add: Dallas Morning News Young & Houston St Dallas TX 75222

KUVSHINOFF, BERTHA HORNE
PAINTER
b Washington. Work: Seattle Art Mus, Wash; Phoenix Art Mus, Ariz; Evansville Art Mus, Ind; Eureka Col Mus, Ill; Miami Art Mus, Fla. Exhib: Inaugural Art Exhib, Washington State Capitol Mus, Olympia, 65; Seattle Russian Ctr, 66; Cath Ctr Gallery, Baltimore, Md, 67; Edmonds Art Gallery, Wash, 70; Eureka Col Gallery, Ill, 71. Awards: Silver Medal, 70 & Gold Medal, 71, Acad Int Tommasso Companelia, Rome, Italy. Bibliog: Visual Arts, Seattle Times, 7/30/70; article in Roanoke Rev, 9/23/71; Hartland of Nebraska Living, Grand Island Independent, 4/1/72; plus others. Style & Technique: Phantasism. Media: Oils on Canvas. Publ: Auth, Art Book & Drawings, publ in Seattle, Wash. Mailing Add: 121 1/2 Yale Ave N Seattle WA 98109

KUVSHINOFF, NICOLAI
PAINTER, SCULPTOR
b Siberia. Work: Seattle Art Mus, Wash; Phoenix Art Mus, Ariz; Evansville Art Mus, Ind; Santa Fe Art Mus, NMex; Tacoma Art Mus, Wash. Exhib: Novikoff Found Fine Arts, Seattle, 61-72; Hutzler's Westview Exhib Hall, Baltimore, Md, 65 & 67; Tacoma Allied Arts, Wash, 66; Seattle Russian Ctr, 66; Stuhr Mus, Grand Island, Nebr, 72. Awards: Silver Medal, 70 & Gold Medal, 72, Acad Int Tommasso Campanella, Rome, Italy. Bibliog: Articles in New York Herald Tribune, Paris, France, 57; articles in Monde, Paris, 57; article in Art News, New York, 60; plus others. Style & Technique: Neo-cubist. Media: Oil on Canvas. Publ: Auth, Art Book, Libr Cong, Washington, DC, 59; auth, Drawings, 66. Mailing Add: 121 1/2 Yale Ave N Seattle WA 98109

KUWAYAMA, GEORGE
CURATOR, ART HISTORIAN
b New York, NY, Feb 25, 25. Study: Williams Col, BA; Inst Fine Arts, NY Univ; Univ Mich, MA. Collections Arranged: Arts Treasures from Japan (with catalog), 65; Contemporary

Japanese Prints (with catalog), 72; Ceramics of Southeast Asia, 72. Teaching: Instr Chinese painting, Univ Calif, Los Angeles, 62; instr Far Eastern painting, Univ Southern Calif, 63. Pos: Cur Oriental art, Los Angeles Co Mus Art, 59-63, sr cur Far Eastern art, 63- Awards: Freer Fel, Univ Mich, 55; Hackney Fel, Am Oriental Soc, 56; Inter-Univ Fel, Ford Found, 57. Mem: Asn Asian Studies; Chinese Art Soc; Japan Soc; Int House Japan; Far Eastern Art Coun, Los Angeles Co Mus Art. Res: Far Eastern art and archaeology. Publ: Auth, Two Screens by Maruyama Okyo, 64; auth, Chinese Ceramics: The Heeramaneck Collection, 73; auth, Ceramics of Thailand, 73. Mailing Add: 1417 Comstock Los Angeles CA 90024

KUWAYAMA, TADAAKI
PAINTER
b Nagoya, Japan, Mar 4, 32. Study: Tokyo Univ Art, BFA, 56. Work: Albright-Knox Art Gallery, Buffalo, NY; Worcester Art Mus, Mass; Wadsworth Atheneum, Hartford, Conn; Larry Aldrich Mus, Ridgefield, Conn; Herron Art Mus, Indianapolis. Exhib: Carnegie Int, Pittsburgh, 61-67; Formalist Show, Washington Gallery Mod Art, Washington, DC, 63; Systemic Show, Guggenheim Mus, New York,66; New Forms & Shapes of Color, Stedelijk Mus, Amsterdam, 67; Plus by Minus, Today's Half-Century, Albright-Knox Art Gallery, 68. Awards: Nat Coun Arts Grant, 69. Media: Acrylic. Dealer: Galerie Denise Rene 6 W 57th St New York NY 10019. Mailing Add: 136 W 24th St New York NY 10011

KWARTLER, ALEXANDER
PAINTER, SCULPTOR
Study: Acad Beaux Arts, Paris, France. Work: Mus Contemp Art; McCord Mus, Montreal; pvt collections. Exhib: One-man shows, Art Gen Gallery, 66, Port Royal Gallery, 67 & Hart Gallery, 68, Montreal; Bognar Gallery, Los Angeles & Katz Gallery, Israel, 71; plus others. Mem: Montreal Mus Fine Arts; Que Asn Prof Artists. Mailing Add: PO Box 548 Snowdon Montreal PQ H3X 3T7 Can

KWIECINSKI, CHESTER MARTIN
MUSEUM DIRECTOR, PAINTER
b Youngstown, Ohio, July 7, 24. Study: Kansas City Art Inst, BFA & MFA; Kansas City Univ; Youngstown Univ. Work: Butler Inst of Am Art, Youngstown, Ohio; El Paso Mus of Art, Tex. Comn: Historical Murals, McSorley Colonial, Ptiisburgh, Pa, 54; murals (with Bill Rakocy), Colonial House and Congo Rm, Youngstown, Ohio, 60 & Alberini Restaurant, Niles, Ohio, 65. Exhib: Mo State Fair, 49 & 50; Albright-Knox Gallery of Art, Buffalo, NY, 52; El Paso Regional show, 76; one-man show, Butler Inst of Art, Youngstown Ohio, 62. Teaching: Instr, Warren City Schs, Ohio, 54-66; assoc prof painting, Col of Artesia, NMex, 67-71. Pos: Mus dir, Abilene Fine Arts Mus, Tex, 73- Awards: Best Local Art, New Year Show, Butler Inst of Am Art, 42; Purchase Award, Carlsbad Art Asn, NMex, 68; Purchase Award, Hobbs-LLano Estacado, Hobbs Art Asn, NMex, 69. Mem: Am Asn of Mus; Tex Asn of Mus; Permian Basin Mus Asn, 78. Style & Technique: Objective expressionist. Media: Watercolor and Oil. Publ: Guest art ed, Abilene Reporter News, 74; auth, articles in Pigment & Form, 64. Mailing Add: 4010 Potomac Abilene TX 79605

KYRIAKOS, ALEKO
SCULPTOR
b Berlin, Ger, Dec 9, 22; US citizen. Study: Sch Fine Arts, Polytechnium, Athens, Greece. Work: Philadelphia Mus Art; Allentown Art Mus, Pa; Wellesley Col, Mass. Comn: Evangelist (plastic relief), Albright Col, Reading, Pa, 63; Phylax (bronze figure), 66 & bronze double relief, 69, Franklin & Marshall Col, Lancaster, Pa; St John (bronze figure), St John Lutheran Church, Allentown, 66; Sappho (bronze figure), Swarthmore Col, Pa, 67 & Auckland City Art Gallery, NZ, 74; Nittany Lion, Pa State Univ, Reading Campus, 75. Exhib: One-man shows, Allentown Art Mus, 63 & 70; Pa Acad Fine Arts, 66. Media: Bronze. Mailing Add: RD 1 Alburtis PA 18011

L

LABICHE, WALTER ANTHONY
ART ADMINISTRATOR, INSTRUCTOR
b New Orleans, La, July 15, 24. Study: Denver Art Inst, 48. Teaching: Instr commercial, technical & fine art & dir, New Orleans Art Inst, 70- Media: Mixed Media. Mailing Add: 2926 Canal St New Orleans LA 70119

LABINO, DOMINICK
GLASS BLOWER, SCULPTOR
b Fairmount City, Pa, Dec 4, 10. Study: Carnegie Inst Technol, 29-32; Toledo Mus Art Sch Design, 47-49; Bowling Green State Univ, hon DFA, 70. Work: Toledo Mus Art, Ohio; Corning Mus Glass, NY; Smithsonian Inst, Washington, DC; Pilkington Mus Glass, St Helens, Eng; Victoria & Albert Mus, London. Comn: Hot-cast panels, Vitrana, entrance to Glass Gallery, Toledo Mus Art, 69, Columbus Gallery Fine Arts, 71 & Riverside Hosp, Toledo, 72; Long Chain Molecules, Johns-Manville Corp, Denver; Pyradon, State Off Tower, Columbus, Ohio. Exhib: Toledo Glass Nat & Traveling Exhib, 66, 68 & 70; 20th-24th Ceramic & Sculpture Show, Butler Inst Am Art, Youngstown, Ohio, 68-72; Dominick Labino—A Retrospective Exhib, Corning Mus Glass, 69; one-man exhib, Columbus Gallery Fine Arts, Ohio, 70 & 71; Dominick Labino—A Decade of Glass Craftsmanship, 1964-74, Pilkington Mus Glass, Victoria & Albert Mus & Toledo Mus Art, 74-75. Teaching: Instr hot glass, Toledo Mus Art, 66 & 67; vis prof hot glass, Bowling Green State Univ, 72-73. Pos: Hon cur glass, Toledo Mus Art, 68-; retired vpres, Johns-Manville Corp, res consult glass fibers, 74-75. Awards: First Award for Glass, Toledo Mus Art, 66, 68 & 70; Ohio Arts Coun Award for Glass, 71; Toledo Glass & Ceramic Award, Am Ceramic Soc, 72. Mem: Fel Am Ceramic Soc; World Crafts Coun; Toledo Fedn Art Socs (vpres, 51 & 52, pres, 53 & 54); Craft Club Toledo (pres, 52 & 53); Int Inst Arts & Lett. Style & Technique: Free-hand blowing; hot-glass sculpture; development of colors and color effects. Media: Molten glass. Res: Technical and creative aspects of glass-making in earliest times; technique of Eighteenth Dynasty Egyptian hollow glass vessels; glass fibers. Publ: Auth, The Egyptian sand-core vessels, Corning J Glass Studies, 66; auth, Visual Art in Glass, W C Brown, 68. Mailing Add: 23271 Kellogg Rd Grand Rapids OH 43522

LABRIE, ROSE
PAINTER, WRITER
b Boston, Mass, Aug 31, 16. Study: Univ NH, 44-45; with Robert Grant & Carroll Towle, 54-56; Univ Wis, 58-59. Work: Strawbery Banke Colonial Preserv Mus, Portsmouth, NH; Richard Morton Collection, Portsmouth; Univ NH Colonial Heritage Film Ser, Durham; John F Barker Collection, Cambridge, Eng. Comn: Mural, USS Thresher, comn by George Bergeron, New Market, NH. Exhib: Copley Soc, Boston; Crest Gallery; one-man shows, Shapely Towne House Gallery, Portsmouth, Ann, John Sedgley Homestead, York, Maine & James Hunt/Barker Galleries, Palm Beach, Fla, 77; Shayne Gallery, Montreal, Can, 76; Palm Beach Galleries, Fla, 76. Awards: First Prize for Mem Painting of USS Thresher; Works Being Reproduced for Needlepoint Kits, Early Am Soc. Bibliog: Articles in Nat Antiques Rev, 7/72 & NH Echoes, 11-12/74. Mem: Copley Soc; York Art Asn; S Street Seaport Mus; Armed Forces Writers League; Piscataqua Pens. Style & Technique: Self-taught primitive artist, frequently referred to as the Young Grandma Moses. Media: Oil. Publ: Illusr, Story of Pemaguid Light; illusr, History of Cape Neddick Light Station; contribr, Yankee, NH Profiles, 58-68 & Nat Antiques Rev, 71; contrib cover artist, Early Am Life, 73; auth & illusr, King the Leprechaun Pony, 78; plus many other articles & illus. Dealer: America's Folk Heritage Gallery 37 W 20th St New York NY 10011. Mailing Add: 127 Middle Rd Portsmouth NH 03801

LACK, RICHARD FREDERICK
PAINTER, INSTRUCTOR
b Minneapolis, Minn, Mar 26, 28. Study: Minneapolis Sch Art; R H Ives Gammell Studios, Boston. Work: Maryhill Mus Fine Arts, Washington; Elizabeth T Greenshields Mem Found Collection, Montreal, PQ; Springville Mus Art, Utah. Comn: Six portraits of Joseph P Kennedy, Jr, comn by Ambassador Kennedy & Kennedy Found, New York. Exhib: Allied Artists Am, 53; Boston Arts Festival, 53 & 54; Nat Acad Design Ann, 55; Twin City Biennial, Minneapolis Inst Arts, 62; Am Artists Prof League Nat, 67-73. Teaching: Dir & instr painting & drawing, Atelier Lack, Minneapolis, 69- Awards: Popular Prize, Ogunquit Art Ctr, Maine, 58 & 64; First Prize, Copley Soc, Boston, 62; Gold Medal, Am Artists Prof League, 67 & 73 & Margaret Fernald Dole Prize for Best Portrait, 72. Bibliog: D Jardine (auth), Richard Lack's atelier system of training painters, Am Artist Mag, 6/71. Mem: Am Artists Prof League. Style & Technique: Portrait, figure and landscape painter working in the tradition of classical-realism. Media: Oil. Mailing Add: 5827 Louis Ave Minnetonka MN 55343

LACKTMAN, MICHAEL
EDUCATOR, DESIGNER
b Philadelphia, Pa, Mar 1, 38. Study: Pa State Col, 57-61; Cranbrook Acad of Art, Bloomfield Hills, Mich, 61-63; Kunsthaandverskolen, Copenhagen, Denmark, 65-66. Work: Pa State Col, Millersville, Pa; Cranbrook Acad of Art, Bloomfield Hills, Mich. Comn: Liturgical metalry, Redeemer Lutheran Church, Livermore, Calif, 71; Kiddusch cup, Brandeis Univ, Waltham, Mass, 63. Exhib: New Tablesilver New Jewelry, Guidsmedefagets Faellesrad, Copenhagen, Denmark, 66; Europ Jewelry, Das Deutsch Goldschmied Haus, Hanau, Ger, 66; Am Jewelry Today, Everston Mus of Art, Scranton, Pa, 67; Calif Design VI, Crocker Art Mus, Sacramento, Calif, 69; Calif Design XI, Pasadena Art Mus, Calif, 71; Metal Experience, Oakland Art Mus, Calif, 71; Fourth Int Jewelry Exhib, Schmuckmuseum, Pzorheim, Ger, 72; Diamond Today: Int Jewelry Exhib, New York, 75. Collections Arranged: Nat Mus of Art, Santiago, Chile, 72 & Univ Chile, Santiago, 72. Teaching: Asst prof design, Univ Calif, Berkeley, 66-73 & Univ Chile, Santiago, 72-73; prof jewelry & metalsmithing, Univ Wis, Milwaukee, 73- Awards: Louis Comfort Tiffany Found grant metalsmithing, 63; Ford Found res grant, 72-73; Nat Endowment for the Humanities res grant, 75. Bibliog: Articles & photographs of work, Art & Archit, 71 & Playboy Mag, 75. Mem: Am Craftsman Coun; San Francisco Bay Asn; Sterling - Silversmiths Guild of Am; Scand-Am Found; Col Art Asn. Media: Jewelry and metalsmithing. Mailing Add: Dept of Art Univ of Wis Milwaukee WI 53201

LACROIX, RICHARD
PAINTER, PRINTMAKER
b Montreal, PQ, July 14, 39. Study: Montreal Inst Graphic Arts, dipl; Atelier 17, Paris; Montreal Sch Fine Art, cert pedagog. Work: Montreal Mus Fine Arts; Nat Gallery Can; Cabinet Estampes, Paris; Mus Mod Art, New York; Victoria & Albert Mus, London. Comn: Several print albums, Montreal Graphic Guild, 66-72; kinetic sculptures, Can Pavilion & Youth Pavilion, Expo 67 & Montreal Int Airport, 68; murals, Montreal Sch Bd, 71. Exhib: Color Prints Am, 70; 2nd Int Bienal Engraving, Paris, 70; Quebec Pavilion, Osaka, Japan, 70; 4th Am Bienal Engraving, Chile, 70; 2nd Brit Int Print Bienal, 70. Teaching: Instr etching, Montreal Sch Fine Art, 60-61; vis instr art hist, Univ Quebec, 69-70. Pos: Co-founder, Fusion Arts. Awards: Can Graphic Asn Prize, 64; Prize, Int Biennal, Lugano, Switz, 64; Prize for Painting, Montreal Hadassah, 65. Bibliog: Lacroix, 65 & S Raphael (auth), Richard Lacroix, 71, Vie Arts; Deroussan (auth), Richard Lacroix, Lidec, 66. Mem: Soc Prof Artists Quebec; Graphic Guild (pres, 66-75); Atelier Libre Recherches Graphiques (dir, 64-75). Media: Acrylic. Mailing Add: 4677 Rue St Denis Montreal PQ Can

LACY, BETTIE
MUSEUM DIRECTOR
b Richmond, Va, Nov 12, 24. Study: Fine arts major, Richmond Prof Inst. Pos: Dir, The Athenaeum, Northern Va Fine Arts Asn, Alexandria, Va. Mailing Add: The Athenaeum 201 Prince St Alexandria VA 22314

LACY, ROBERT EUGENE
PAINTER
b St James, Mo, Aug 29, 43. Study: Pvt study (5 years) with Earl Strebeck. Work: Works in many collections, both private and institutional. Exhib: 35th & 38th Ann Exhib, Springfield Mus of Art, Mo, 65 & 69; 61st Ann Exhib, Birmingham Art Mus, Ala, 68; Mid-America I, Nelson-Atkins Art Mus, Kansas City & City Art Mus of St Louis, 68; Tulsa Regional Art Exhib, Arts Coun of Tulsa, 68; Okla Touring Exhib, Arts Coun of Tulsa, 69; March Ann Exhib, William A Fransworth Art Mus, Rockland, Maine, 69; 34th Ann Midyear Show, Butler Inst Am Art, Youngstown, Ohio, 69; 60th Anniversary Exhib, Wadsworth Atheneum, Hartford, Conn, 70. Awards: 2nd Ann Tulsa Award for Painting, Tulsa Arts Coun, Inc, 68. Style & Technique: Subjective realist; haunting paintings of sharp-focus realism portraying the drama & mystery of life. Media: Oil, Pencil. Dealer: Nelson Sales Gallery 4525 Oak St Kansas City MO 64111. Mailing Add: 517 N Charles Ave St James MO 65559

LACY, SUZANNE
PERFORMANCE ARTIST, EDUCATOR
b Wasco, Calif, Oct 21, 45. Study: Univ Calif, Santa Barbara, BA(zool); grad study psychol, Fresno State Col; Calif Inst Arts, MFA; study with Judy Chicago, Sheila de Bretteville & Allan Kaprow. Comn: Prostitution Notes, 75 & Three Weeks in May (sociological performance structure), 77, Los Angeles Studio Watts Workshop, Calif, 77; Elderly People Proj (sociological performance structure), Comprehensive Employment & Training Act grant, 78. Exhib: Video Exhib, Long Beach Mus Art, Calif, 76; Arte Fiera, Bologna, Italy, 77; performances, Mus Contemp Art, Bologna, Italy, 77, Chicago Inst Contemp Art, 77, Col Art Asn Conf, Los Angeles Hilton, Calif, 77, De Young Downtown Ctr, San Francisco, 77 & Floating Mus, San Francisco, 77. Teaching: Mem fac performance & feminist educ, Feminist Studio Workshop, Los Angeles, 74-77; mem fac women's studies, San Francisco Art Inst, Calif, 75-77; lectr performance, Univ Calif, San Diego, La Jolla, Calif, 76-77. Pos: Mem

bd, The Woman's Bldg, Los Angeles, Calif, 74-77. Bibliog: Faith Wilding (auth), By Our Own Hands, Double X, 76; Linda Rosengarten, On the subject of rape, Los Angeles Inst Contemp Art J, 8/77; Martha Rosler, The private & the public, Art Forum, 9/77. Mem: Los Angeles Inst Contemp Art; The Woman's Bldg. Style & Technique: Personal autobiographical and sociologically oriented commentary on women's experience. Media: Work in theatrical and non-theatrical performance; conceptual photography, books and video Publ: Auth, Rape Is, 76 & Falling Apart, 76, Suzanne Lacy. Mailing Add: 28 Ave 27 Venice CA 90291

LADEN, FRIEDA SAVITZ
See Savitz, Frieda

LADERMAN, GABRIEL
PAINTER, EDUCATOR
b Brooklyn, NY, Dec 26, 29. Study: Brooklyn Mus Sch; Brooklyn Col, BA; Hans Hofmann Sch Fine Arts; Cornell Univ, MFA; Atelier 17, fel, 52. Exhib: Vassar Col, 68; Milwaukee Art Ctr, 69; State Univ NY New Paltz & traveling, 69; Ind Univ, 69; Corcoran Gallery of Art, 69; Philbrook Art Ctr, Tulsa, Okla, 69; Milwaukee Art Ctr, Wis, 69; Ind Univ Art Mus, Bloomington, 69; one-man shows, Univ RI, 70, Tyler Sch Art, Philadelphia, 71 & Harwood Gallery, Springfield, Mo, 72; Whitney Mus Am Art, New York, 70; NJ State Mus, Trenton, 70; De Cordova Mus, Lincoln, Mass, 71; Am Acad Arts & Lett, 72; Joslyn Mus Art, Omaha, Nebr, 73; Arts Club of Chicago, 73; Mus Fine Arts, Boston, 74; plus others. Teaching: Grad lectr, Yale Univ; lectr univs, art schs, cols in NY, Mass, Iowa, Ind, Ohio & other states; asst, Cornell Univ, 55-57; asst prof, State Univ NY New Paltz, 57-59; asst prof, Pratt Inst, 59-69; asst prof art, Queens Col, 69-75. Awards: Tiffany Found Award, 59; Fulbright Fel to Italy, 62-63; Yaddo Fels, 60, 61 & 65. Bibliog: L Campbell (auth), Gabriel Laderman: a world inside itself, Art News, 10/72. Dealer: Schoelkopf Gallery 825 Madison Ave New York NY 10021. Mailing Add: 760 West End Ave New York NY 10025

LADOW, JESSE
COLLECTOR, PATRON
b Fredonia, Kans, Aug 24, 18. Interest: Nineteenth century American art; Western American art; American Indian art and artifacts. Collection: Western American art, including C M Russell, J H Sharp, F T Johnson, Carl Rungius; American Indian art. Mailing Add: 1403 Monroe PO Box 192 Fredonia KS 66736

LAESSIG, ROBERT
PAINTER, ILLUSTRATOR
b NJ, 20. Study: Art Students League; also study in Ger. Work: Cleveland Mus Fine Arts, Ohio; Butler Inst Am Art, Ohio; Norfolk Mus, Va; Springfield Inst Fine Arts, Ohio; Akron Art Inst, Ohio. Comn: Official White House Christmas card, comn by President & Mrs Johnson, 64-68. Exhib: Am Watercolor Soc Exhibs, 60-72, Audubon Artists, 60-72, Nat Acad Design, 60-72 & Allied Artists, 70-72, New York; Philadelphia Watercolor Soc, 64-70. Pos: Pres, Robert Laessig Fine Arts Co, West Richfield, Ohio, 69- Awards: Nat Acad Design Prize, 68; Prizes, Am Watercolor Soc, 70 & 71 & Wichita Centennial, 70. Mem: Nat Acad Design; Am Watercolor Soc; Nat Painters in Casein; Allied Artists Am. Publ: Illusr, From Fiji to the Philippines. Mailing Add: 5026 Hawkins Rd West Richfield OH 44286

LAFAYE, NELL MURRAY
PAINTER, EDUCATOR
b Columbia, SC, Nov 9, 37. Study: Sullins Col, with Alvin Sella; Cranbrook Acad Art, BFA, 58, with Fred Mitchell, MFA, 59, with Zolton Sepeshy & Marianne Strengall. Work: SC State Art Collection; Univ SC. Exhib: Spring Mills Traveling Art Show, Lancaster, SC, 61-69; Mint Mus Crafts Exhib, Charlotte, NC, 65 & Painting Exhib, 66 & 67; Mainstreams Int, Marietta, Ohio, 68 & 69; Gardens Art Festival, Pine Mountain, Ga, 72. Teaching: Asst prof art, Univ SC, 68-75, assoc prof art, 75- Awards: First Prize, Spring Mills, 68. Bibliog: Jack Morris (auth), Contemporary South Carolina artists, SC Tricentennial Comn, 70. Mem: SC Art Educ Asn (pres, 67-69); Nat Art Educ Asn (rep to nat assembly, 67-70); Am Craftsmen Coun; SC Artist Guild. Style & Technique: Impressionistic with great influence coming from nature. Media: Oil. Mailing Add: 2630 Stratford Rd Columbia SC 29204

LAFON, DEE J
PAINTER, SCULPTOR
b Ogden, Utah, Apr 23, 29. Study: Weber State Col; Univ Utah, BFA, 60, MFA, 62; also with Francis de Erdley, Phil Paradise & Marquerite Wildenhain. Work: Utah State Fine Art Collection, Salt Lake City; Okla Art Ctr, Oklahoma City; Philbrook Art Mus, Tulsa, Okla; Univ Okla, Norman; Dillard Collection, Univ NC, Greensboro. Comn: Wood sculpture, Univ Okla, 72; copper fountain, ECent State Col, 72. Exhib: Watercolor USA, Springfield, Mo, 68; Nat Oil Painting Exhib, Jackson, Miss, 68; Am Drawing Bienniale, Norfolk, Va, 69; Int Miniature Prints Show, Pratt Graphic Ctr, New York, 70; Midwest Bienniale, Omaha, Nebr, 72; one-man shows, Springfield Art Mus, Mo, 78 & Goddard Art Ctr, Ardmore, Ore, 78. Teaching: Instr ceramics & drawing, Weber State Col, 62-64; prof painting & drawing, ECent State Col, 64- Pos: Dir, Contemp Art Found, Okla, 68-; consult, Okla Art Ctr, 70-71. Awards: Eight State Exhib Purchase Award, 70; Hon Mention, Midwest Bienniale, 72; Tulsa Regional Painting & Drawing Award, 72. Mem: Okla Designer Craftsman. Style & Technique: Social satire/realism in imagery. Media: Paintings usually in oil; sculpture in multi-media. Dealer: Oklahoma Art Ctr 3113 General Pershing Blvd Oklahoma City OK 73118; Ben Ackard Gallery 541 NW 39th St Oklahoma City OK 73118. Mailing Add: 2127 Woodland Dr Ada OK 74820

LA FON, JULIA ANNA
PAINTER, CRAFTSMAN
b New Salem, Pa, Nov 24, 19. Study: George Washington Univ; Univ NMex. Work: Santa Fe Fine Arts Mus, NMex; NMex Bank, Hobbs; Albuquerque Nat Bank, NMex; Jonson Gallery, Univ NMex; Mus Albuquerque, NMex. Exhib: Nat Sun Carnival, Mus El Paso, Tex, 70 & 72; one-man shows, Jonson Gallery, Univ NMex, 71, 73 & 75, Dord-Fritz Gallery, Amarillo, Tex, 73, Thompson Gallery, Phoenix, 74, Hoshour Gallery, Albuquerque, 78 & Mus of Albuquerque, 78; Southwest Fine Arts Biennial, Mus NMex, 71-76; ASA Gallery, Univ NMex, 72; Regional Amarillo Art Competition, Amarillo Art Ctr, 75 & 77; Colorado Springs Fine Art Ctr, 75; Four Corners Biennial, Phoenix Art Mus, Ariz, 77; Recent Acquisitions, 77 & In the Pub Interest, 78, Santa Fe Fine Arts Mus. Awards: Best of Show & Purchase Award, NMex Jr Col, Hobbs, 69; First & Second Prizes, Contemp Crafts Exhib, Albuquerque, 71; First Prize, Carlsbad Regional Art Exhib, NMex, 73. Bibliog: Article in La Rev Mod, Paris, 72; Steve Edwards (auth), The Art of Working with Leather, Chilton, 75. Style & Technique: Innovative texture/line paintings, nonobjective; suede leather constructions. Dealer: Thompson Gallery 2020 N Central Phoenix AZ 85004; A Place on Earth Vail CO 81657. Mailing Add: 803 Martingale SE Albuquerque NM 87123

LAFORTUNE, FRANCOIS
See Crouton, Francois

LAFRENIERE, ISABEL MARCOTTE
PAINTER
b Providence, RI. Study: RI Sch Design, grad; RI Univ; pvt study in Paris. Exhib: Paris, New York, Boston, Hartford, Conn, Washington, DC, Ogunquit, Maine & others. Teaching: Pvt art classes; lectr hist of art; art demonstr. Awards: Figure Award, Rockport Art Asn, Mass, 70; Grumbacher Award, Nat Art League, 70; Best in Show, Medford, Mass, 70. Mem: Nat Art League; Springfield Acad Artists; Rockport Art Asn (bd gov); NShore Art Asn. Style & Technique: Incorporate abstract theory of Hans Hofmann and bring to a more realistic conclusion using brush or painting knife. Mailing Add: 25 South St Rockport MA 01966

LAGORIO, IRENE R
PAINTER, PRINTMAKER
b Oakland, Calif, May 2, 21. Study: Calif Col Arts & Crafts, Oakland, 38-39; Univ Calif, Berkeley, AB & MA, 42; Columbia Univ, 45. Work: Monterey Art Comn Conf Ctr Collection, Calif; Monterey Peninsula Mus of Art Collection; Northern Calif Savings & Loan Collection; Germanischen Mus & Libr Collection, Nuremberg, Ger; Sunset Cult Ctr Collection, Carmel, Calif. Comn: Mosaic murals, SS President Roosevelt, Am Pres Lines, 61 & Soc Nat Bank, Cleveland, Ohio, 69; jewel painted mural, Lloyd Ctr, Portland, Ore, 60 & metal sculpture mural, Seaside, Ore, US Bancarp, 64; mosaic mural design, Episcopal Condominium, Los Gatos, Calif, 70. Exhib: 3rd Int Biennial, Sao Paulo, Brazil; Metrop Mus Art Watercolor Exhib, 53; 7th Monterey Peninsula Competitive, Monterey Mus Art, Calif, 70; Am Color Print Soc Ann, Philadelphia, 72; US Info Serv Traveling Color Print Exhib, throughout Europe, 72. Teaching: Spec lectr, Univ Calif Exten Courses, 60- Pos: Cur educ dept, Calif Palace of Legion of Honor, 50, dir, Achenbach Found Graphic Arts, 51-55; art critic, Monterey Peninsula Herald, currently. Awards: Chapelbrook Found Grand for Graphic Proj, Boston, 69; Best in Show, Monterey Peninsula Mus Art 7th Competitive, 71. Bibliog: E Loran (auth), The San Francisco scene, Art News, 53; G Dorfles (auth), Modern painters in USA, Domus Mag, 54; Exposition de San Francisco, La Rev Mod, 60. Mem: Am Color Print Soc; Carmel Art Asn (pres, 72-); Ars Assoc Found (dir, 61-). Style & Technique: Contemporary serigraph technique in printmaking and assemblage and collage technique in painting. Publ: Illusr, This Open Zoo-A Bestiary, Salamander, 71. Mailing Add: First & Mission Sts Box 153 Carmel CA 93921

LAGUNA, MURIEL
PAINTER
b New York, NY. Study: NY Univ (archit); New Sch; Brooklyn Mus Art Sch, with Reuben Tam & Manfred Scwartz; Adelphi Univ; Pratt Graphic Ctr. Work: Rockefeller Family; Brooklyn Col; also in many pvt & indust collections. Exhib: Pa Acad Fine Arts, Philadelphia, 64; Allied Artists Am Ann, 64; Nat Acad Design Ann, 64; Salvatora Rosa, Naples, Italy, 72; Pallazzo Vechio, Florence, Italy, 72; plus others. Teaching: Instr art, Baldwin, Oceanside, Rockville Centre Pub Schs continuing educ workshops, 57- Pos: Colorist, Lawrence Laguna Architect, 60-; interior designer (free lance). Awards: Gold Medal (First Prize), Hofstra Univ, 61; seven Resident Fels including The Edward MacDowell Colony, 65, 69, 73 & 75; Medal of Honor, Nat Asn Women Artists, 67. Bibliog: Numerous newspaper interviews, Taos, Long Island Press, News Day, plus others. Mem: Artist Equity of New York, Inc; Nat Asn Women Artists, Inc; New York Soc Women Artists; Contemp Artists; Metrop Artists. Style & Technique: Contemporary landscapes. Media: Oil, Acrylic. Mailing Add: 324 Christopher St Oceanside NY 11572

LAGUNES, MARIA (MARIA LAGUNES HERNANDEZ)
SCULPTOR, PAINTER
b Veracruz, Mex. Study: Univ Femenina, Veracruz, 51-53; sculpture with Francisco Zuniga & Tomas Chavez Morado; wood and linoleum engraving with Arturo Garcia Bustos, 58-61; metal engraving with Guillermo Silva Santamaria, 60-63; with Yukio Fukasawa & Isamu Ishikawa, 63; painting & drawing with Antonio Rodriguez Luna, 61-65; Fr scholar to study sculpture, archit & urban integration with Andre Bloc, Paris, 66. Work: Gen Motors Mex Collection; Lauren Rogers Libr & Mus Art, Laurel, Miss. Comn: Monument to writer Rosario Castellanos, Pub Park, Mexico City. Exhib: Mexico City, 61, Buenos Aires, 63 & Conception Univ Chile, 64; III & IV Biennial, Mod Art Mus, Mexico City, 67-69 & Selection of 13 Artists, Women's Int Year, 75; Solar, Fine Arts Palace, Mex, 68; one-woman shows, Misrachi Art Gallery, Mexico City, 69 & 72; Salon de Mai, Mod Art Nat Mus, Paris, 73-75; Grand Prix de Lyon Int Contemp Art, 75; plus many other group & one-woman shows. Teaching: Instr sculpture, Univ State Mex, 69- Awards: Second Prize of the Press for Ciudad No 6; Third Prize, Salon Pintores Veracruz. Bibliog: Article in Tex Quart & Image of Mex II. Mem: Salon Plastica Mex; Inst Nac Bellas Artes. Dealer: Galeria de Arte Misrachi Genova No 20 Mexico DF Mexico. Mailing Add: Apt Postal 44-074 Mexico DF Mexico

LAHEY, RICHARD (FRANCIS)
PAINTER, LECTURER
b Jersey City, NJ, June 23, 93. Study: Art Students League, with Robert Henri, Max Weber & John Sloan, 13-17; also traveled and studied abroad, summers 20-27. Work: Carlotta also watercolors & etchings, Corcoran Gallery Art, Washington, DC; Head of Joan, Compote with Fruit & Main Inlet, Whitney Mus Am Art, New York; Pop Hart, Mus Mod Art, New York; Fourteenth of July, Detroit Inst Art, Mich; Pont Neuf, Brooklyn Mus Art, NY; plus many other mus. Comn: Over the Alleghenies to the West (mural), Brownsville Post Off, Pa; mural (with Carlotta Gonzales), Am Battle Monuments Comn, Honolulu; portraits for US Treas Dept, US Supreme Ct & Elks Club, Washington, DC; drawing for Alexander Woollcott, New York Times, 25; Seeing NY (drawing with verse by John Farrar), Sun Mag New York World. Exhib: Metrop Mus Art, New York; Art Inst Chicago; Carnegie Inst Int, Pittsburgh; one-man shows, Corcoran Gallery Art, Washington, DC; Richmond Mus Art, Va; plus many other group & one-man shows. Teaching: Instr painting & drawing, Art Students League, 22-34; prof fine arts, Goucher Col, 35-60; from prin to emer painting & drawing, Corcoran Sch Art, 35-64; prof painting & drawing, Ga Univ, 68. Pos: Artist, camouflage corps, US Navy, Washington, DC & overseas, 18 mos; lectr art subjects, Lee Keedick Bur, 32-72. Awards: William H Tuthill Prize, Art Inst Chicago, 25; Beck Gold Medal for portraiture, Pa Acad Fine Arts, 29. Bibliog: Richard Lahey, portrait instructor, Art Students League, 33. Mem: Hon mem Art Students League; Century Asn; Am Soc Painters, Sculptors & Gravers; Am Fine Arts Soc. Media: Oil, Watercolor. Dealer: Franz Bader Inc 2124 Pennsylvania Ave NW Washington DC 20037. Mailing Add: 9530 Clark Cross Rd Vienna VA 22180

LA HOTAN, ROBERT L
PAINTER
b Cleveland, Ohio, 1927. Study: Columbia Univ, Brevoort-Eickmeyer fel, 50-53. Work: Lehigh Univ, Bethlehem, Pa; Northern Trust Co, Kansas City, Mo; Univ NC; Hirschhorn Collection. Exhib: Corcoran Biennial, 56; Dallas Mus Contemp Art, 58; Rochester Mem Art Gallery, 66; one-man show, Lehigh Univ, 69; Kraushaar Galleries, 72 & 75. Awards:

Fulbright Fel to Ger, 53-55. Media: Oil, Watercolor. Dealer: Kraushaar Galleries 1055 Madison Ave New York NY 10028. Mailing Add: 865 West End Ave New York NY 10025

LAI, WAIHANG
PAINTER, INSTRUCTOR
b Hong Kong, Jan 7, 39; US citizen. Study: Chinese Univ Hong Kong, BA, 64; Claremont Grad Sch & Univ Ctr, MA, 67. Comn: Painting of McBryde Mill, A&B, Inc, 75 & 77. Exhib: Watercolor USA, Springfield Art Mus, Mo, 69; The Best in the West, Edward-Dean Mus, Calif, 70; Philadelphia Watercolor Club Exhib, Philadelphia Civic Ctr Mus, 72; one-man shows, Phoenix Art Mus, Ariz, 67 & Kauai Mus, Hawaii, 71 & 72. Teaching: Vis prof art, Ariz State Univ, Tempe, summer 67; asst prof art, Maunaolu Col, Maui, Hawaii, 68-70; instr art, Kauai Community Col, 70- Awards: Hon Mention, Hong Kong Art Exhib, Univ Hong Kong, 59-61; First Award for Watercolor, 1st Ann Spring Festival Fine Arts, Rowland Heights, Calif, 68; First Place for Watercolor, Maui Co Creative Arts Exhib, Hawaii, 68. Mem: Am Watercolor Soc; Philadelphia Watercolor Club; Kauai Watercolor Soc (pres). Media: Watercolor, Acrylic. Publ: Auth, The Chinese Landscape paintings of Waihang Lai, 66; auth, The Watercolors of Waihang Lai, 67 & Waihang Lai, Watercolor Calendar, 78, Am Watercolor Soc. Dealer: Aho Art Gallery Kapaa HI 96766. Mailing Add: PO Box 363 Lihue HI 96766

LAINE, LENORE
PAINTER
b Philadelphia, Pa. Study: Philadelphia Col Art. Work: Nat Mus Mod Art, Tokyo; Miami Mus Mod Art, Fla; Finch Col, New York; Ohio State Univ; Phoenix Art Mus, Ariz; plus others. Exhib: Eight Americans in Paris, Am Libr, Paris; Americans in France, Mus Lyons, St Etienne; Optical Art, Am Fedn Art Traveling Show. Media: Acrylic, Oil, Watercolor. Dealer: East Hampton Gallery 305 W 28th St 13G New York NY 10001. Mailing Add: 116 Central Park S New York NY 10019

LAING, RICHARD HARLOW
ART ADMINISTRATOR, DESIGNER
b Ypsilanti, Mich, Apr 19, 32. Study: Eastern Mich Univ, BS(art); Wayne State Univ, MA(printmaking, sculpture); Pa State Univ, DEd(art educ). Comn: Fountain (8ft bronze & stainless), Paul Vortman, Denton, Tex, 62; 40ft wall sculpture, comn by Blazier Comn for Civic Ctr, Denton, Tex, 66; three stainless steel sculptures, Pa State Univ, University Park, 67-68; 8ft bronze sculpture fountain, Ewing-Miller Assoc, Terre Haute, Ind, 68; 10 piece stained glass design & construction, Elizabeth's Restaurant, Meadville, Pa, 77. Exhib: Northwestern Pa Artists Ann, Detroit Mus of Art, 60; one-man shows, Dryer Gallery, Houston, Tex, 63 & Ball State Univ, Muncie, Ind, 69; Ultimate Concerns Nat Drawing Exhib, Athens, Ohio, 65; Am Inst of Architects Exhib, Rice Univ, Houston, 67; 16th Ann Nat Drawing & Small Sculpture, Muncie, Ind, 70; Wabash Valley Regional Exhib, Terre Haute, Ind, 71. Teaching: Design shop, Col of Art & Design, Univ of Mich, 54-55; studio art & humanities, Edsel Ford High Sch, 55-60; asst prof studio art & art educ, NTex State Univ, 60-68. Pos: Head art dept, Ball State Univ Muncie, Ind, 68-71 & Edinboro State Col, 71- Awards: First Cash Prize/Painting, Eastern Ind Artist Exhib, Muncie Art Asn, 69 & 71. Mem: Col Art Asn. Style & Technique: Welded bronze and stainless steel; acrylic painting. Mailing Add: RR 1 Edinboro PA 16412

LAIRD, E RUTH
SCULPTOR
b Houston, Tex, Mar 21, 21. Study: Cranbrook Acad Art, Bloomfield Hills, Mich, with Maija Grotell, summer 51 & 53-55. Work: Mus Contemp Crafts, New York; Everson Mus & Iroquois China Collection, Syracuse, NY; Children's Mus, Detroit; Cranbrook Mus, Mich. Comn: Altar Sculpture, Meditation Chapel, Rice Univ, Houston, 63 & Mem Sculpture, 75; Fountain, New Harmony, Ind, 65; Baptismal Fountain, St Basil Church, Angelton , Tex, 65. Exhib: One-woman shows, Univ Houston, 57, NMex Highlands Univ, 59, Laguna Gloria Mus, Austin, Tex, 65 & Mus Fine Arts, Houston, 67; Syracuse Int Traveling Exhib, New York, 57. Teaching: Instr ceramic sculpture, St Thomas, Houston, 55-57 & Univ Houston, 55-58; asst dean & instr ceramic sculpture, Mus Fine Arts Sch, Houston, 58-68. Awards: Tex Swed Cult Found summer study-travel grant, Int Designers' Conf, 55; Iroquois China Award, Int Exhib, Everson Mus, 57; Woman of the Year Outstanding Contrib to Fine Arts, Theta Sigma Phi, Houston, 68. Bibliog: Dr William Pryor, The Arts in Houston (TV show), 60; Campbell Geeslin (auth), Emerging reputations, Am Artist, 62; The American ceramist, Craft Horizon (spec issue), Am Crafts Coun, 62. Style & Technique: Nature forms, essence of growing, flowing forms in nature, spiritual (religious) experiences. Media: Clay, Stone. Dealer: Handmakers The Galleria 5015 Westheimer Rd Houston TX 77027. Mailing Add: 1618 Cherryhurst Houston TX 77006

LAIRD, MARY (MARY LAIRD HAMADY)
GRAPHIC ARTIST, ILLUSTRATOR
b Milwaukee, Wis, Jan 19, 48. Study: Univ Wis, BA. Work: New York Pub Libr; Univ Calif, Berkeley & Santa Cruz; Cranbrook Acad Art Libr; State Univ NY Buffalo & Stony Brook; Bridwell Libr, Southern Methodist Univ. Exhib: Grolier Club, 72-73; Philadelphia Col Art, 72; Pvt Press in the Midwest, Northern Ill Univ, 73. Pos: Partner, Perishable Press Ltd, 69- Bibliog: J Gordon Burke (auth), The enduring Perishable Press, Am Libr, 73. Style & Technique: Detailed small scale fine line drawings of images derived from poetry and/or prose. Media: Fine Line Pen & Ink Drawing; Wood Engraving. Publ: Auth & illusr, This Gentle Strength, 69; auth, An Everyday Celebration, 71; auth & illusr, Eggplant Skin Plants, 73. Mailing Add: PO Box 7 Mt Horeb WI 53572

LALIBERTE, NORMAN
PAINTER
b Worcester, Mass, Nov 24, 25. Study: Mus Fine Arts, Montreal; Ill Inst Technol, BS, 51 & MS, 54; Cranbrook Acad Arts, 52. Work: In numerous pvt collections. Exhib: Tucson Art Ctr, Ariz, 67; Int Festival Arts, New York, 67; LaMonte Gallery, Tampa, Fla, 67; Mint Mus Art, Charlotte, NC, 67; Newton Col, 67; plus many others. Teaching: Instr, Kansas City Art Inst, 60-61; artist in residence, St Marys Col, Notre Dame, 60-62; lectr, Webster Col, 64; assoc prof, RI Sch Design, 65; artist in residence, Newton Col, 67-74. Pos: Design consult, Vatican Pavilion, New York World's Fair, 63; design consult, Sol Productions, 63 & 66. Publ: Auth, The history of the cross, 60, Banners and hangings, 66, Wooden images, 66, Painting with crayon, 67 & Silhouettes, 67; plus articles. Mailing Add: c/o Arras Gallery 29 W 57th St New York NY 10019

LAM, JENNETT (BRINSMADE)
PAINTER, EDUCATOR
b Ansonia, Conn, May 2, 11. Study: Yale Univ, BFA & MFA, with Josef Albers. Work: Mus Mod Art & Whitney Mus Am Art, New York; Brooklyn Mus, NY; Philadelphia Mus Fine Arts, Pa; Yale Art Gallery. Exhib: Carnegie Inst Int, 64; Painting Ann, 65 & Women in Permanent Collection, 71, Whitney Mus Am Art; USA Group 67, US Embassy, Paris & Mus France, 67; Selections from Chase Manhattan Collection, Finch Col Mus, 71. Teaching: Emer prof art, Univ Bridgeport, 72- Awards: MacDowell Colony Fel, 60 & 61. Bibliog: Hubert Damisch (auth), Les chaises de Jennett Lam aux couleurs de l'absence, Cahiers Art Ann XXe siecle, 6/65; Patrick Waldberg (auth), Jennett Lam, Quadrum XIX, 65. Media: Oil. Dealer: Harmon Gallery 1258 Third St S Naples Fla 33940; Le Point Cardinal 3 Rue Jacob Paris 6 France. Mailing Add: Elwood Dr Bonita Springs FL 33923

LA MALFA, JAMES THOMAS
SCULPTOR, EDUCATOR
b Milwaukee, Wis, Nov 30, 37. Study: Univ Wis-Madison, BS, 60, MS, 61 & MFA, 62; sculpture with Leo Steppat; printmaking with Alfred Sessler. Work: Memphis Acad Art; Univ Wis-La Crosse; Neville Art Mus, Green Bay, Wis. Comn: Large relief sculpture, Phillips Hall, Univ Wis-Eau Claire, 66; sacred sculpture, Wittenberg Univ, Springfield, Ohio, 68. Exhib: The States 1st Ann, Neville Pub Mus, Green Bay, Wis, 65; Springfield Art Ctr, Ohio, 67; Print & Drawing Nat, Minot State Teachers Col, NDak, 70; 29th Northeastern Wis Art Ann, Green Bay, 70; 23rd Ohio Ceramic & Sculpture Ann, Butler Inst Art, Youngstown, Ohio, 71. Teaching: Instr visual arts, Univ Wis-Eau Claire, 63-66; instr visual arts, Wittenberg Univ, 66-69; asst prof visual arts, Univ Wis-Green Bay, 69-72; assoc prof visual arts, Univ Wis Ctr-Marinette, 72- Bibliog: J J (auth), rev in Art News, 4/64; Pierre Mornand (auth), Expositions diverses review, La Rev Mod, 11/71. Mem: Wis Acad Sci, Arts & Lett. Style & Technique: Abstract but non-objective; use of all metal welded, cast, forged and riveted. Media: Iron. Mailing Add: Univ Wis Ctr-Marinette Bay Shore Rd Marinette WI 54143

LAMANNA, CARMEN
ART DEALER, ART RESTORER
b Monteleone, Avelline, Italy, May 19, 27. Collections Arranged: Carmen Lamanna Gallery at Third Int Pioneer Galleries Exhib, Musee Cantonal, Lausanne, Switzerland & Musee des Beaux Arts, Paris, 70; Carmen Lamanna at Owens Art Gallery (auth, catalog), Mt Allison Univ, Sackville, NB, Can, 75; Water on Paper, Ron Martin solo exhib, Southern Alta Art Gallery, Lethbridge, Can, 76; Carmen Lamanna Gallery at Sculpture Vancouver Art Gallery, BC, Can, 76; Carmen Lamanna Gallery at Kuntshalle, Basel, Switzerland, 78. Pos: Dir, Carmen Lamanna Gallery, 66- Awards: Queen's Silver Jubilee Medal, awards for service in the arts, 77. Bibliog: Gail Dexter (auth), Man from Montelone, Toronto Star, 9/28/68; Time ed staff, The arts: in search of innovation, Time mag, 12/7/70; Adele Freedman (auth), Art: Guarding the case for the avante-garde: the case for Carmen Lamanna, Toronto Life, 12/77. Mem: Professional Art Dealers Asn, Toronto, Ont, Can. Specialty: Experimental art including minimalist sculpture, painting, conceptual art, earthworks, environmental art (nature systems), inventions, art-language, video, films, sound, body art, poetry, performances. Interest: Art restoration. Collection: Experimental art, mainly Canadian artists. Publ: Contribr, Le 3e Salon International de Galleries-Pilotes, Musee Cantonal des Beaux Arts, Lusanna, Switzerland, 70; auth, Carmen Lamanna Gallery 1974, Queen St mag, spring/winter 76-77. Mailing Add: 840 Yonge St Toronto ON M4W 2H1 Can

LAMANTIA, JAMES
PAINTER, COLLECTOR
b New Orleans, La, Sept 22, 23. Study: Tulane Univ La, BSArch, 43; Harvard Univ Grad Sch Design, BArch, 47; Skowhegan Sch, 47. Work: New Orleans Mus Fine Art. Pos: Prof archit, Tulane Univ, currently. Awards: Prix de Rome, 48-49; Fulbright Fel, 49-50. Bibliog: Equal arts of James Lamantia, Archit Forum, 52. Media: Oil. Collection: English drawings and paintings of the second half of the 19th century. Mailing Add: 539 Bienville St New Orleans LA 70130

LAMARCA, HOWARD J
DESIGNER, EDUCATOR
b Teaneck, NJ, July 11, 34. Study: Cooper Union Art Sch, scholar, 52-56, cert graphic arts, 56; Columbia Univ, BFA, 60; Syracuse Univ, grad asst, 60-62, MFA, 62. Collections Arranged: James Gordon Irving-Painter, 71; Grant Reynard-Painter, 71; Charles Shedden, Sculptor-Ralph Didriksen, Painter, 71; Anita Friend, Paintings-Rush Cowell, Gravestone Rubbings, 71; New Jersey Designer-Craftsmen, 71; George Fish, Painting-Shirley Yudkin, Paintings, 72; Marion Lane, Painting Retrospective, 72; Arts in Parts, 72; Paul Burns, Painting Retrospective, 72; Arnoldo Miccoli-Painter, 73; Solomon Rothman-Sculptor, 73; Mod Artists Guild, 73; Lillian Marzell-Painter, 73; Paul Sisko-Sculptor, 73; Nat Asn Women Artists, 74; Sam Weinik-Painter, 74; Erna Weill-Sculptor, 74; Eleanor Smoler-Painter, 74; Elaine Hyman-Sculptor, 74; Esther Rosen-Painter, 74; Batiks—Giovanna Bellia La Marca, Co Col Morris, 76; Best of the World, 76; Art Director's Club of New Jersey, 78. Teaching: Asst prof art, Trenton State Col, 74-; assoc prof art, Co Col of Morris, 74- Pos: Advert art dir, Givandan Advert, New York, 57-; dir, Bergen Community Mus, 71-74; sem dir Europ advert, Paris, France, Dusseldorf & Frankfurt, WGer, Zurich, Switz & Milan, Italy, 78. Mem: Soc Scribes; Art Dir Club NY & NJ; Asn Am. Style & Technique: Various materials; pure, simple, hard edge style. Media: Graphics, Calligraphy. Publ: Auth, An analysis of Gauguin's-What are We? Where Do We Come From? Where Are We Going?, Artist Mag, London, 3/62; auth, An analysis of the facade of San Marco, Eleven Mag, spring 72; auth, Some Thoughts on Design, City Univ-New York, 74; auth, Ethics & aesthetics, Focus, 76. Mailing Add: 3 Crescent Ave Cliffside Park NJ 07010

LAMB, ADRIAN
PAINTER
b New York, NY. Mar 22, 01. Study: Art Students League; Julian Sch, Paris. Work: Nat Portrait Gallery & Capitol Bldg, Washington, DC; Harvard Law Sch; Supreme Court, Tallahassee, Fla; Rockefeller Found, New York. Comn: Portraits of Stillmans, Chauncey Stillman, Stillman Mem, Brownsville, Tex, 58; portrait of Charles Merrill, Merrill Lynch, Fenner & Smith, Wall St, New York, 60; founder of Buford Col, Carnation Co, Buford, SC, 65; portrait of Mr Duke, Duke Endowment, New York, 68; portrait of Gheen, father & son, Mrs Richard Hill, Baptist Sem, Louisville, Ky, 72. Exhib: Westchester, White Plains, NY; Salmagundi Club, New York; Sculpin Gallery, Edgartown, Mass; New Canaan Libr, Conn. Mem: Salgamundi Club (vpres); Nat Arts Club; Art Students League. Media: Oil. Dealer: Portraits Inc 41 E 57th St New York NY 10022; M Knoedler & Co 21 E 70th St New York NY 10021. Mailing Add: Des Artists Hotel 1 W 67th St New York NY 10023

LAMBERT, EDDIE
PRINTMAKER, PAINTER
b Atlanta, Tex, Jan 27, 49. Study: Tex Tech Univ, BFA & MFA. Exhib: 6th and 7th Ann Nat Drawing & Small Sculpture Show, Del Mar Col, 72 & 73; Pratt Graphic Ctr Int Miniture Print Exhib, 75; Mach I Int Print Exhib, Metrop Mus of Art, Miami, Fla, 75; 19th Ann Nat Print & Drawing Exhib, Oklahoma Art Ctr, 77; one-man show, Eastern NMex Univ, Corpus Christi Mus. Teaching: Asst prof printmaking, Del Mar Col, Corpus Christi, Tex, 74- Bibliog: Joseph A Cain (auth), Art News & Reviews, Corpus Christi Caller Times, 74. Style & Technique: Personal imagery, etching & serigraph. Media: Etching & Serigraph. Mailing Add: 607 Del Mar Corpus Christi TX 78404

LAMBERT, NANCY S
ART LIBRARIAN
b Southbend, Ind, June 29, 32. Study: Univ of Mich, MALS, 69, MA(art hist), 71. Pos: Art Librn, Univ of Rochester, NY, 71-73 & State Univ NY, Binghampton, 73-75; librn, Art & Archit Libr, Yale Univ, New Haven, Conn, 75- Mem: Col Art Asn; Art Libr Soc NAm. Interest: Bibliography and graphic arts. Mailing Add: 1206 Forest Rd New Haven CT 06515

LAMBERT, PHYLLIS
ARCHITECT, COLLECTOR
b Montreal, Que, Jan 24, 27. Study: Vassar Col, BA, 48; Ill Inst of Archit, MS(archit), 63, with Myron Goldsmith & Fazlur Khan. Comn: Saidye Bronfman Ctr, with Webb, Zerafa & Menkes, YWHA, Montreal, 63-68; Jane Tate House Renovation, with Arcop Assoc, Phyllis Lambert off & residence, Montreal, 74-76; Small Cinema, with Arcop Assoc, pvt house, Montreal, 75-76; Biltmore Hotel Renovation, with Gene Summers, Los Angeles, Calif, 76-77. Exhib: Sculpture, Royal Can Acad of Arts, Toronto & Montreal, 40-44; two-person show, Perspectives: Archit Heritage of Montreal, Paintings & Photographs, McCord Mus Exhib, 75. Collections Arranged: Joseph E Seagram & Sons, Inc Collection, 54-; Can Indian Exhib, 69 & Aaron Siskind Exhib, 70, Saidye Bronfman Centre, Montreal; Seagram Plaza: Its Design & Use, Seagram Bldg, New York, 77. Pos: Dir planning, Seagram Bldg, New York, 54-58; dir, Seagram Bicentennial Proj, Co Courthouse in the US, 74- Awards: Massey Medal/Archit, Saidye Bronfman Centre, Royal Archit Inst of Can, 70; Robinson's Design Award, Renovation of Biltmore Hotel, Los Angeles, 77. Bibliog: Peter Blake (auth), Neat showcase for the arts, Archit Forum, 5/69; D Gérin-Lajoie (auth), Attention! ne détruisez pas notre entité, Archit Concept, 11-12/74; Claude R Lussier (auth), L'apport des femmes à l'architecture et au design, Décormag, 1/77. Mem: Royal Can Acad of Arts; Nat Gallery of Can (vis comt, 77-); Heritage Can (gov, 76-); Mies van der Rohe Archive adv bd, Mus of Mod Art, New York (chmn, 70-). Collection: Architectural drawings from the 16th century to the 20th century; photographs of the 19th and 20th century; manuscripts and books on architecture. Publ: Contribr, Exploring Montreal, Montreal Soc of Architects, 74; co-auth, Dossier 25—Inventaire des bâtiments du Vieux Montréal, Ministry of Cult Affairs, Que, 77; contribr, Mount Royal Montreal, McCord Mus, 77; contribr, Court House, Horizon Press, spring 78. Mailing Add: 418 Bonsecours St Montreal PQ H2Y 3C4 Can

LAMIS, LEROY
SCULPTOR, EDUCATOR
b Eddyville, Iowa, Sept 27, 25. Study: NMex Highlands Univ, BA, 53; Columbia Univ Teachers Col, MA, 56. Work: Albright-Knox Mus; Des Moines Art Ctr; Whitney Mus Am Art; Joseph H Hirshhorn Collection, Washington, DC; Larry Aldrich Mus. Exhib: Whitney Mus Am Art Sculpture Ann, New York, 64, 66 & 68; Responsive Eye, Mus Mod Art, New York, 65; Art Today, Albright-Knox Art Gallery, Buffalo, 65; Artists for CORE, 65-66; Abstract Am Artists, Riverside Mus, NY, 65-67; Contemp Am Painting & Sculpture, Univ Ill, 65-69; Flint Invitational, Mich, 66-68; one-man shows, Staempfli Gallery, New York, 66, 69 & 73 & Traveling Show, 69, J B Speed Mus, Louisville, John Herron Mus, Indianapolis, Des Moines Art Ctr, La Jolla Mus Art, Calif & Tacoma Mus, Wash; Neuberger Collection, Smithsonian Inst & RI Sch of Design, 68; Plastic as Plastic, Mus Contemp Crafts, New York, 68; Milwaukee Art Ctr, Wis, 68; Am Sculpture, Univ Nebr, Lincoln, 70; Plastic Presence, Jewish Mus, New York, 70; Constructivists Tendencies, US, 70-72; Artists at Dartmouth, New City Hall, Boston, Mass, 71. Teaching: Asst prof, Cornell Col, 56-60; prof sculpture, Ind State Univ, Terre Haute, 61- Awards: Artist in Residence, Dartmouth Col, 70; NY State Coun Arts Award, 70. Media: Plastics. Mailing Add: 3101 Oak Terre Haute IN 47803

LA MORE, CHET HARMON
PAINTER, SCULPTOR
b Dane Co, Wis, July 30, 08. Study: Colt Sch Art, 26-28; Univ Wis, BA, 31, MA, 32. Work: Libr of Cong, Washington, DC; Nat Collection, Smithsonian Inst, Washington, DC; Syracuse Mus, NY; Olsen Found, Conn; Colorado Springs Mus, Colo. Comn: History of Sports (mural), comn by US Treas Dept, Polytech Inst, Baltimore, Md, 33-34. Exhib: Chicago Print Int, Ill, 37; one-man shows, Albright-Knox Art Gallery, Buffalo, NY, 43 & Rackham Galleries, Univ Mich, Ann Arbor, 75; Whitney Mus Am Art Ann, 43-48 & 50; Calif Palace of Legion of Honor, San Francisco, 45; Int Arte Mod, UNESCO & US State Dept, Paris, 47; Carnegie Inst Ann, Pittsburgh, 49. Teaching: Prof art, Univ Mich, 47-74, emer prof art, 74- Awards: Fine Prints of the Year Award, Int Selection, 38; Purchase Prize (serigraph), Mus Mod Art, 41; Rackham Creative Res Grants, 56, 60 & 68. Style & Technique: Direct method based on the particular character of the materials. Media: Acrylic, Watercolor; Steel, Bronze. Mailing Add: 503 S First St Ann Arbor MI 48103

LAMPERT, DORRIE
PAINTER, DESIGNER
b Hartford, Conn. Study: Hartford Art Sch; Yale Art Sch; Art Students League; Nat Acad Art, New York; with Jacques Maroga, 52 & Countess Zichy & Zita Davisson. Comn: 32 paintings, comn by Nathan Cummings, New York. Exhib: Burr Artists, Union Carbide, New York; Nat Arts Club; Mod Art Mus, Paris; Caravan House, New York; Goldsboro Mus, NC; Metrop Mus Art, New York; Grist Mill Gallery, Chester, Vt. Mem: Burr Artist; Nat Arts Club. Style & Technique: Impressionist. Media: Oil, Crayon, Pencil. Mailing Add: 2 Beekman Pl New York NY 10022

LANCASTER, MARK
PAINTER
b Yorkshire, Eng, May 14, 38. Study: Dept of Fine Art, Newcastle Univ, Eng, 61-65. Work: Victoria & Albert Mus & Tate Gallery, London; Arts Coun of Northern Ireland, Belfast; Allen Art Mus, Oberlin, Ohio; Art Gallery of S Australia, Adelaide; Mus of Mod Art, New York. Exhib: The New Generation, Whitechapel Art Gallery, London, 66; British Drawings: The New Generation, Mus of Mod Art, New York, 67; Six Artists (toured Britain), Victoria & Albert Mus, London, 67; John Moores Exhib, Walker Art Gallery, London, 67; Young British Artist (traveling), Mus of Mod Art, New York, 68; Marks on a canvas, Mus am Ostwall, Dortmund, W Ger, 69; Int Exhib of Graphic Art, Ljubljana, Yugoslavia, 69; British Painting and Sculpture 1945-1970, Nat Gallery, Washington, DC, 70; Contemp British Art, Nat Mus of Mod Art, Tokyo, 70; From Britain 75, Taidehalli, Helsinki; British Painting, Hayward Gallery, London, 75; one-man shows, Rowan Gallery, London, 65-75; Arts Coun Gallery, Cambridge, Eng, 69, Sch of Design, Harvard Univ, Cambridge, Mass, 70, Betty Parsons Gallery, New York, 72 & 74, Walker Art Gallery, Liverpool, Eng, 73 & Multiples, New York, 75. Teaching: Instr, Dept of Fine Art, Newcastle Univ, Eng, 65-66; Bath Acad of Art, Corsham, Wiltshire, Eng, 66. Pos: Artist-in-Residence, King's Col, Cambridge, Eng, 68-70; designer, Merce Cunningham Dance Co, New York, 74-76. Awards: Purchase Prize, British Int Print Biennale, Bradford, 70. Bibliog: Marina Vaizey (auth), Mark Lancaster, Financial Times, London, 3/73; David Shapiro (auth), Divided Spaces, Art and Artists, London, 6/73; Mark Lancaster, Betty Parsons Gallery, article in New York Times, 10/74. Dealer: Rowan Gallery 31 A Bruton Pl London WIX 7AB England; Betty Parsons Gallery 24 W 57 St New York NY. Mailing Add: 225 E Houston St New York NY 10002

LAND, ERNEST ALBERT
PAINTER
b Hamilton, Ont, Sept 21, 18; US citizen. Work: NASA Space Mus, Washington, DC: Grumbacher Collection Fine Art; IBM Collection Fine Art, New York; Marietta Col, Ohio; Butler Inst Am Art, Youngstown, Ohio. Comn: Mural, USA Corps Engrs, Seattle World's Fair, 60; nine murals on hist solid propellants, USN Mus, Indian Head, Md, 62-63; exhib, Work of Dr Leakey, Olduvai Gorge, Africa (with Robert Widder & Ken Hopkins), Nat Geog Explorers Hall, 63-64. Exhib: Butler Inst Am Art Ann, Youngstown, Ohio, 70; Mainstreams Int, Marietta Col, Ohio, 70 & 72; Allied Artists Am 58th Ann, Nat Acad Design Galleries, 71; Am Artists Prof League Grand Nat, 71. Teaching: Lectr, Chase Manhattan Bank, New York, 54-55; lectr, Am Tel & Tel, New York, 55-62. Awards: John J McDonough Award, Butler Inst Am Art, 72; Best in Show & First Prize, Mainstreams, Marietta Col, 77; Lester Cook Mem Prize, 77. Bibliog: Joseph Grumbacher (auth), Twenty-one paint in polymer, M Grumbacher, 65; Gutierrez & Roukes (auth), Painting with Acrylics, Watson-Guptill, 65; Joseph Giacalone (auth), Leonardo would have us use polymer, Syndicate Mag, 66. Mem: Life fel, Royal Soc Art, London; fel Am Artists Prof League; Art League Northern Va. Media: Oil. Publ: Illusr, US Senate Comt Aeronaut & Space Sci, US Govt Printing Off, 63. Dealer: Capricorn Galleries 8004 Norfolk Ave Bethesda MD 20014; Grand Central Art Galleries 40 Vanderbilt Ave New York NY 10017. Mailing Add: 100 N Washington St Falls Church VA 22046

LANDAU, FELIX
ART DEALER
b Vienna, Austria, Oct 24, 24. Mem: Art Dealers Asn Am. Specialty: 20th century American and European art. Mailing Add: 760 N La Cienega Blvd Los Angeles CA 90069

LANDAU, JACOB
PAINTER, PRINTMAKER
b Philadelphia, Pa, Dec 17, 17. Study: Philadelphia Col Art, cert, 38, with Earl Horter & Franklin Watkins; New Sch Social Res, 48-49 & 52-53, with Erich Fromm, Rudolf Arnheim & Eugene O'Neill, Jr. Work: Mus Mod Art, New York; Whitney Mus Am Art; Metrop Mus Art; Libr of Cong; Philadelphia Mus Art. Comn: Print for Peace, Smithsonian Inst, 67; I, John Brown (woodcut poster), Nat Park Serv, US Dept Interior, 68; suite lithographs illus work of E T A Hoffmann, Univ Chicago Press, 69; ten stained glass windows, Keneseth Israel Synagogue, Philadelphia, 71; Meditation on Love & Death (lithograph), NJ State Arts Coun, 75. Exhib: The Figure, Recent Paintings USA, 62 & Tamarind—Homage to Lithography, 69, Mus Mod Art; Smithsonian Print Show, The White House, Washington, DC, 66; Three Artists View the Human Condition, NJ State Mus, Trenton, 68; Human Concern/Personal Torment, Whitney Mus Am Art, 69; one-man shows, Jorgenson Auditorium, Univ Conn, 71, Hopkins Hall, Ohio State Univ, 73, ACA Gallery, New York, 76; Am Acad of Arts & Lett, 73; 25th Nat Exhib Prints, Nat Collection of Fine Arts, Washington, DC, 77. Teaching: From instr to assoc prof, Pratt Inst, 57-68, prof graphic art, 68-, learning coordr, Univ-Without-Walls Proj. Awards: Nat Arts Endowment Sabbatical Grant, 66; Guggenheim Found Fel, 68; Ford Found Travel-Study Grant, 75. Bibliog: H C Pitz (auth),Jacob Landau, Am Artist, 10/56; Jacob Landau, Current Biog, 12/64; Barry Schwartz (auth), Tiger of wrath—Jacob Landau, Arts Soc, spring-summer 71. Mem: Soc Am Graphic Artists; Visual Artists & Galleries Asn; Nat Acad Design. Style & Technique: Humanist expressionism. Media: Watercolor; Woodcut, Lithography. Publ: Contribr, Charades, Tamarind Lithography Workshop, 65; auth, Yes-no, art-technology, Wilson Libr Bull, 9/66; auth, Holocaust, Assoc Am Artists, 68; illusr, Out of the whirlwind, Union Am Hebrew Congregations, 68 & Selected Writings of Hoffmann, Univ Chicago, 69; plus others. Dealer: Assoc Am Artists 663 Fifth Ave New York NY 10022; ACA Galleries 25 E 73rd St New York NY 10021. Mailing Add: 2 Pine Dr Roosevelt NJ 08555

LANDAU, MITZI
ART DEALER, CURATOR
b New York, NY, Sept 18, 25. Study: NY Univ, BA, 45. Exhibitions Arranged: Organization and circulation of exhibitions of Gaston Lachaise's sculptures and drawings throughout the United States and Canada, and of photographs and prints for Edward Muybridge, Picasso Vollard Suite, Margaret Bourke-White and Joseph Albers. Pos: Cur, Gaston Lachaise Found, 67-; founder, Circulating Exhib Serv; lectr Gaston Lachaise & mod sculpture, var mus, pub groups & docents. Mem: Col Art Asn; Western Asn of Am Mus. Specialty: Art of the 20th century, both European and American (paintings and especially sculpture). Mailing Add: 1625 Thayer Ave Los Angeles CA 90024

LANDAU, SAMUEL DAVID
See Lev-Landau

LANDECK, ARMIN
PAINTER, ENGRAVER
b Crandon, Wis, June 4, 05. Study: Columbia Univ, BArch, 27. Work: Mus Mod Art, Metrop Mus Art & New York Pub Libr, New York; Toledo Mus Art, Ohio; Libr Cong, Washington, DC; Swedish Nat Mus, Stockholm; Kaiser Friedrich Mus, Berlin, Ger; plus others. Exhib: Libr Cong; Soc Am Graphic Arts; Nat Acad Design; Pa Acad Fine Arts; Int Graphic Exhib, Yugoslavia. Awards: S F B Morse Gold Medal, Nat Acad Design, 62; Wiggin Award, Boston Printmakers, 69; Purchase Prize, Soc Am Graphic Arts, 69. Mem: Soc Am Graphic Arts; Am Inst Arts & Lett; Nat Acad Design; fel Int Inst Arts & Lett. Mailing Add: RD 1 Litchfield CT 06759

LANDERS, BERTHA
PAINTER, PRINTMAKER
b Winnsboro, Tex. Study: Sul Ross Col, BSArt; Colorado Springs Fine Arts Ctr, Colo, grad study with Arnold Blanch, Adolf Dehn, Boardman Robinson & Henry Varnum Poor; Art Students League, grad study with Reginal Marsh. Work: Dallas Mus Art; Denver Mus Art; Libr Cong, Washington, DC; Witte Mem Mus, San Antonio, Tex; Ft Worth Art Ctr, Tex. Exhib: Tex Gen Exhib, 36-45; Dallas Allied Arts Show Ann, 36-45; Libr Cong Print Show, 41-45; Nat Print Ann, New York, 42-57; Nat Acad Design, New York, 43-44; Corpus Christi Nat Exhib, Tex, 45; Nat Gallery, Washington, DC, 46; Mid-Am Artists Asn Exhib, Kansas City, Mo, 53; Kansas City Univ, Mo, 53; Kansas City Art Inst, 53; Brooklyn Art Mus Exhib, 53, Laguna Beach Exhib, Calif, 55, Oakland Art Gallery, Calif, 55, Okla Art Mus, Oklahoma City, 57. Pos: Cur & cataloguer, Mrs A A Zonnie Print Collection, 42-49; pres, Tex Women Printmakers, 44-46; art librn, Dallas Pub Libr, 46-49; pres, Dallas Print Soc, 47-48; art librn, Kansas City Pub Libr, Mo, 50-58. Awards: Painting Purchase, Corpus Christi Nat Exhib, 45; Print Purchase, Libr Cong, 45; Painting Purchase, Denver Art Mus, 47. Bibliog: Albert Reese (auth), American Prize Winning Prints of the 20th Century, 49. Mem: Dallas Mus Fine Arts (mem bd dir, 42-49); Graphic Arts Coun, Los Angeles Co Mus Art; Grunwald Graphic Arts Found, Univ Calif, Los Angeles. Style & Technique: Impressionistic, with emphasis on color and drawing. Media: Printing, Etching, Aquatinting & Lithography; Oil, Watercolor. Dealer:

S/R Gallery 337 S Robertson Blvd Beverly Hills CA 90211; Kennedy Galleries 20 E 56th St New York NY 10022. Mailing Add: 7665 Woodrow Wilson Dr Los Angeles CA 90046

LANDFIELD, RONNIE (RONALD T)
PAINTER, INSTRUCTOR
b Bronx, NY, Jan 9, 47. Study: Art Students League, 62-63, with Arnold Blanche & Stephen Greene; Kansas City Art Inst, Mo, 63, with Robert Barnes & Ross Coates; San Francisco Art Inst, Calif, 64-65, with Julius Hatofsky. Work: Mus of Mod Art, New York; Whitney Mus of Am Art, New York; Hirshhorn Mus of Art, Washington, DC; RI Sch of Design Mus, Providence; Walker Art Ctr, Minneapolis, Minn. Comn: Mural (painting 11 ft x 20 ft), Westinghouse Corp & I Chermayoff, Pittsburgh, Pa, 70. Exhib: Whitney Ann & Biennial Exhib of Am Painting, New York, 67, 69 & 73; one-man shows, David Whitney Gallery, New York, 69 & 71, Corcoran & Corcoran Gallery, Miami, Fla, 73 & 76 & Andre Emmerich Gallery, New York, 73-75; Two generations of Color Painting, Inst for Contemp Art, Univ Pa, 70; Color & Field, Mus of Fine Arts, Houston, Tex, 71; Lyrical Abstraction, Whitney Mus of Am Art, 71 & Aldrich Mus of Contemp Art, Ridgefield, Conn, 71; Art for Your Collection, RI Sch of Design, Providence, 71; Recent Acquisitions, Mus of Mod Art, New York, 72. Teaching: Instr fine arts, Sch of Visual Arts, New York, 75- Awards: Gold Medal, San Francisco Art Inst, Calif, 65; Cassandra Found grant for painting, 68. Bibliog: Carter Radcliff (auth), Painterly vs painted: painterly painting, Art News Ann, 71; Willis Domingo (auth), Neo-Tachisme Americain, l'Art Vivant, 5/74; Whee Kim (auth), A personal definition of pictorial space, Arts Mag, 11/74. Style & Technique: Work on unprimed canvas on floor and continue working on paintings after being stretched. Media: Acrylic paint on canvas; watercolor and paper. Dealer: Sarah Y Rentschler 450 W 24th St New York NY 10011. Mailing Add: 31 Desbrosses St New York NY 10013

LANDIS, ELLEN JAMIE
CURATOR, ART HISTORIAN
b Chicago, Ill, May 6, 41. Study: Univ Calif, Berkeley, BA; Univ Vienna, 60-61; NY Univ, Inst Fine Arts, MA. Collections Arranged: Homage to Rodin (co-auth, catalogue), Los Angeles Co Mus Art, Los Angeles, 67; Rodin Bronzes from the Collection of B Gerald Cantor (auth, catalogue), Am Fedn Art, 70; Vincent Van Gogh, Baltimore Mus Art, 70; Four Americans in Paris: The Collections of Gertrude Stein and Her Family, Baltimore Mus Art, 71; Early 20th Century European Masterpainters (co-auth, catalogue), 77, Indian Art Today (auth, catalogue), 77, Metro Youth Art (auth, catalogue), 77 & Albuquerque Artists I (auth, catalogue), 77, Mus of Albuquerque. Teaching: Lectr introd to art, Yuba Col, Marysville, Calif, 76-77. Pos: Cur, B Gerald Cantor Art Found, Beverly Hills, Calif, 68-70; actg cur, Robert Gore Rifkind Collection, Beverly Hills, Calif, 70 & 71-72; cur art, Mus Albuquerque, NMex, 77- Awards: The Chris Award, Homage to Rodin, Film Coun Greater Columbus, 69. Mem: Col Art Asn; Am Asn Mus (mem cur comt). Res: Centralized research in areas of 19th century and 20th century art. Publ: Co-auth, The David E Bright Collection, Los Angeles Co Mus Art, Los Angeles, 67; co-auth, Matisse in Baltimore, Television Spec, 71. Mailing Add: 4401 Montgomery Blvd NE Albuquerque NM 87109

LANDIS, LILY
SCULPTOR
b New York, NY. Study: Sorbonne, France; sculpture with De Creeft; Art Students League. Work: Lobby, Merck, Sharpe & Dohme Bldg, New York. Exhib: Art Inst Chicago; Mus Mod Art, New York; Pa Acad Fine Arts; Whitney Mus Am Art; Corcoran Gallery Art. Awards: Peabody Award, 68; Tiffany Grant. Media: Bronze, Stone, Epoxy. Dealer: Miriam Redein 343 E 30th St New York NY 10016. Mailing Add: 400 E 57th St New York NY 10022

LANDON, EDWARD AUGUST
PRINTMAKER, PAINTER
b Hartford, Conn, Mar 13, 11. Study: Hartford Art Sch; Art Students League; also with Carlos Merida, Mex. Work: Bibliot Nat, Paris; Mus Mod Art & Metrop Mus Art, New York; San Francisco Mus; Nat Mus, Stockholm. Exhib: Nat Serigraph Soc, 40-60; Am Color Print Soc Ann, 45-65; Northwest Printmakers Ann, 50-60; US Info Agency Int Circulating Exhib, 52; Boston Printmakers Ann, 55-70; Univ Maine, Orono, 70. Pos: Pres, Artists Union Western Mass, 34-38; pres, Nat Serigraph Soc, 52-53. Awards: First Prize for Prints, Springfield Art League, 45; Purchase Prize, Boston Printmakers, 54; First Prize, Nat Serigraph Soc, 59; plus others. Bibliog: Making a Serigraph (film), Harmon Found, 47. Mem: Am Color Print Soc; Southern Vt Artists; Boston Printmakers; Print Coun Am; Philadelphia Print Club. Style & Technique: Work within the arrived disciplines of each medium. Dealer: Gallery 2 Woodstock VT 05091. Mailing Add: Lawrence Hill Rd Weston VT 05161

LANDREAU, ANTHONY NORMAN
ART ADMINISTRATOR, WEAVER
b Washington, DC, Apr 2, 30. Study: Cath Univ Am, with Kenneth Noland; Black Mountain Col, NC, with Kline, Fiore, Rice, BA, 54. Collections Arranged: From the Bosporus to Samarkand, Flat-woven Rugs, (with catalog), Smithsonian Traveling Exhib Serv, 69-71 & America Underfoot, (with catalog), 75-78. Teaching: Instr weaving-design, Black Mountain Col, 54-56; lectr hist of textiles, Univ Md, 75. Pos: Exec dir, Textile Mus, Washington, DC, 67-75; cur educ, Carnegie Inst Mus Art, Pittsburgh, 75- Awards: Near E Res Ctr Grant, rug studies in Turkey, 73; Nat Endowment Arts prof fels, study in Turkey, 73 & study in USSR, 75. Mem: Am Asn Mus; Archaeol Inst Am; Col Art Asn; Am-Turkish Asn (bd mem, 74-); Iran-Am Soc (bd mem, 74-). Style & Technique: Weaving; painting. Media: Photography, Textiles, Oil. Res: Folk weaving, particularly in the Middle East. Publ: Auth, From Mexico to Rumania to Sweden, 69 & auth, Kurdish Kilim weaving in the Van Hakkari region of Turkey, 73, Textile Mus J; co-auth, Flat-woven rugs of the Middle East, Antiques, 69; co-auth, Rugs Around the World, Helvetica Press, 75; auth, Yörük, The Nomadic Weaving Tradition in the Middle East, Carnegie Inst, 78. Mailing Add: Carnegie Inst Mus Art 4400 Forbes Ave Pittsburgh PA 15213

LANDRY, ALBERT
ART DEALER
b New York, NY, Oct 9, 19. Study: Columbia Univ, MA(art hist); Nat Acad Design; Atelier Leger, Paris, France. Pos: Dir, Galerie Villand-Galanis, Paris, 50-54; dir, Assoc Am Artists, 54-58; dir, Albert Landry Galleries, New York, 58-64; dir, J L Hudson Co Art Gallery, Detroit, 64; vpres, Marlborough-Gerson Gallery, 69; former dir, Landry-Bonino Gallery; dir, New York Art '73; pvt dealer & consult for corp art collections, presently. Specialty: Contemporary American and European art. Mailing Add: 22 E 36th St New York NY 10016

LANDRY, RICHARD MILES
PHOTOGRAPHER, VIDEO ARTIST
b Cecilia, La, Nov 16, 38. Study: Univ Southwestern La, with Calvin Harlan, BME. Exhib: Whitney Mus Biennial, 72; Brazil Biennial, 73; Xerox Art in Evolution, 73; Los Angeles Co Mus, 74; ICA Gallery, Philadelphia, 75. Awards: Creative Artists Award, 74; Creative Artists Pub Serv for Mixed Media, 74; Nat Endowment for the Arts for Video, 75. Style & Technique: Video art; photographs from said tapes. Media: Drawings, Photographs, Video Tapes. Dealer: Leo Castelli Gallery 420 W Broadway New York NY 10021. Mailing Add: PO Box 64 Cecilia LA 70521

LANDSMAN, STANLEY
SCULPTOR
b New York, NY, Jan 23, 30. Study: Univ NMex, 47-50, 54-55, BFA, 55, with Randall Davey, Adja Yunkers & Agnes Martin. Work: Mus Mod Art & Whitney Mus Am Art, New York; Larry Aldrich Mus, Ridgefield, Conn; Mus Mod Arte, Paris, France; Walker Art Ctr, Minneapolis, Minn; Milwaukee Art Mus, Wis; plus others. Exhib: 1st World Triennial, New Delhi, India, 68; Cleveland Mus Art, Ohio, 68; Whitney Mus Am Art Sculpture Ann & Light, Object and Image, 68; one-man shows, Inst Humanistic Studies, Aspen, Colo, 68, Univ Wis, Madison, 69 & Contemp Art Mus, Houston, 70; Electric Art, Univ Calif, Los Angeles, 69; Univ Ill, Urbana, 69; Automation House, New York, 70; plus other group & one-man shows. Teaching: Instr sculpture, Adelphi Col, Sch Visual Arts & Pratt Inst; artist in residence, Aspen Inst & Univ Wis. Dealer: Leo Castelli Gallery 4 E 77th St New York NY 10021. Mailing Add: 45 Downing St New York NY 10014

LAND-WEBER, ELLEN E
PHOTOGRAPHER, EDUCATOR
b Rochester, NY, Mar 16, 43. Study: Univ Iowa, Iowa City, BA(art hist), MA & MFA(creative photog). Work: Int Mus of Photog, George Eastman House, Rochester, NY; San Francisco Mus of Mod Art, Calif, Pasadena Art Mus, Calif; Nat Gallery of Can; Art Inst of Chicago. Comn: Bicentennial Doc Proj on Archit of Courthouses in US (in collab with 23 other photogrs with assigned geog areas), Seagrams's Inc, New York, 75-76. Exhib: Ellen & Victor Land-Weber, Int Mus of Photog, George Eastman House, Rochester, NY, 73; 3M Color-in-Color, Pasadena Art Mus, Calif, 73; Photg Unltd, Fogg Art Mus, Cambridge, Mass, 74; one-person shows, Focus Gallery, San Francisco, 74, Sheldon Mem Art Gallery, Lincoln, Nebr, 75, Susan Spiritus Gallery, Newport Beach, Calif, 77 & San Francisco Mus of Mod Art, 78; Women of Photog, San Francisco Mus of Mod Art, 75-76; Photo Synthesis Nat, Herbert Johnson Mus, Cornell Univ, Ithaca, NY, 76; Hist of Photog, Gray Hawkins Gallery, Los Angeles, 76- Teaching: Instr photog, Univ Calif, Los Angeles, 70-74; asst prof photog, Humboldt State Univ, Arcata, Calif, 74- Awards: Nat Endowment for the Arts grant to individual photogr, 75. Mem: Soc for Photog Educ. Style & Technique: Explorations of personal imagery as enhanced by visual possibilities of copy machine technologies, color and black and white. Publ: Illusr, Vision & Expression, Horizon Press, 69; illusr, California Photographers, Univ Calif, Davis Press, 70; illusr, Camera, Bucher, Lucerne, Switz, 74; illusr, Women of photography: an historical survey, San Francisco Mus of Mod Art, 75; illusr, Courthouse—Temple of democracy, Am Heritage Mag, 77. Dealer: Susan Spiritus Gallery 3336 Via Lido Newport Beach CA 92663. Mailing Add: 790 Park Pl Arcata CA 95521

LANDWEHR, WILLIAM CHARLES
MUSEUM DIRECTOR
b Milwaukee, Wis, Sept 19, 41. Study: Univ Wis-Stevens Point, BS, 63; Univ NDak, MA, 68. Collections Arranged: Barry Le Va: Six Blown Lines (Accumulation Drift), Art Ctr Gallery, Univ Wis-Menomonie, 69; Richard Hunt: Small Sculpture/Drawings/Lithographs, Quincy Art Ctr, Ill, 72 & The Art of the Early 1920's, 72; Realism in North Carolina, Mint Mus Art, Charlotte, NC, 74 & Reflections: The Sixties and Seventies, 75. Teaching: Instr art, SDak State Univ, 69-71; lectr art, Western Ill Univ, 72-73; instr art, Cent Piedmont Community Col, Charlotte, 73-75. Pos: Cur, Art Ctr Gallery, Univ Wis-Menomonie, 68-69; dir, SDak Mem Art Ctr, 69-71; artist & dir, Quincy Art Ctr, 71-73; cur exhib, Mint Mus Art, Charlotte, 73-76; dir, Springfield Art Mus, 76- Mem: Am Asn Mus; Midwest Mus Conf; Mo Mus Assoc; Western Asn Art Mus. Publ: Auth, Melvin F Spinar: figure & fantasy, SDak Mem Art Ctr, 71; auth, Richard Hunt: small sculpture/drawings/lithographs, 72 & auth, The art of the early 1920's, 72, Quincy Art Ctr; auth, Tom Mason: sculpture/ceramics 1965-1974, Mint Mus Art, 74; auth, The villain as hero, Southwest Art, 6/75. Mailing Add: c/o Springfield Art Mus 1111 E Brookside Dr Springfield MO 65807

LANDY, JACOB
ART HISTORIAN
b New York, NY, Apr 18, 17. Study: City Col New York, BSS & MSEd; NY Univ, MA & PhD. Teaching: Prof art hist, City Col New York, 45- Mem: Col Art Asn Am; Soc Archit Historians; Victorian Soc Am; Nat Trust Hist Preserv; Arch Am Art. Res: American architecture in the nineteenth century. Publ: Auth, History of Art, 65; auth introduction, The Modern Builder's Guide, 69; auth, The Architecture of Minard Lafever, 70; auth articles in Archeol, Enciclopedia Spettacolo & J Soc Archit Historians. Mailing Add: 11 Gardenia Lane Hicksville NY 11801

LANE, ALVIN SEYMOUR
COLLECTOR
b Englewood, NJ, June 17, 18. Study: Univ Wis, PhB; Harvard Univ Law Sch, LLB; New Sch Social Res, with Seymour Lipton. Pos: Chmn comt on art, New York Bar Asn, 63-65; mem bd overseers fine arts, Brandeis Univ, 66-70; mem adv bd to NY Atty Gen on Art Legis, 66-71; secy, Aldrich Mus Contemp Art, 68-76, trustee, 69-76; trustee, Soho Ctr for Contemp Artists Inc, 76. Res: Problems on authentication of sculpture and the documentation regarding authenticity. Collection: Contemporary sculpture and sculptors' drawings. Publ: Auth, How the bar can assist the art community, New York Bar Asn, 65; auth, The case of the careless collector, Art in Am, 65; Disclosure on disclosure, Print Collector Newslett, 74. Mailing Add: 60 E 42nd St New York NY 10017

LANE, H PALMER
ART DEALER
b Jacksonville, Fla, Oct 11, 51. Study: Sweet Briar Col, BA, 73; Tulane Univ, MA, 75. Pos: Co-owner, Middendorf/Lane, Washington, DC. Specialty: Twentieth century American prints and paintings. Mailing Add: c/o Middendorf/Lane 2014 P St NW Washington DC 20036

LANE, MARION JEAN ARRONS
PAINTER, INSTRUCTOR
b Brooklyn, NY. Study: Brooklyn Mus Art Sch, with Manifred Schwartz & Reuben Tam; Pratt Inst, NY; Art Students League, with Morris Kantor; William Paterson Col, NJ, BA; Rutgers Univ, MFA. Work: Bloomfield Col, NJ. Exhib: Brooklyn Mus Alumni Exhib, 58; Work by New Jersey Artists, Newark Mus Triennial, 61; Art from New Jersey, NJ State Mus, Trenton, 68; Lincoln Ctr, Philharmonic Hall, New York, 68; New Talent, Kraushaar Gallery, New York, 75; Pleiades Gallery, New York, 76 & 77. Teaching: Instr drawing & painting, Riverdell Adult Sch, Oradell, NJ, 61-71, Edward Williams Col, 72 & Ramapo Col, 78. Awards: Grumbacher Award, Brooklyn Mus Alumni Ann, 58; Hon Mention, Montclair Mus, NJ State Exhib, 60; Essex Award, Painters & Sculptors Soc, Jersey City Mus, 65. Mem: Silvermine Guild Artists, Conn; Nat Asn Women Artists; Women in the Arts; Mod Artists

Guild (pres, 70); life mem Art Students League. Style & Technique: Intimate, minimal, abstraction. Media: Acrylics, Sheetmetal. Mailing Add: 441 Hawthorne Pl Ridgewood NJ 07450

LANG, DANIEL S
PAINTER
b Tulsa, Okla, Mar 17, 35. Study: Northwestern Univ, Evanston; Univ Tulsa, BFA, with Alexander Hogue; Univ Iowa, MFA, 59, with Mauricio Lasansky. Work: Mus Mod Art, New York; Art Inst Chicago; Libr Cong, Washington, DC; Nelson-Atkins Mus Fine Art, Kansas City; Boston Pub Libr. Exhib: Boston Mus Fine Arts, 61; Art Inst Chicago, 64 & 67; Arthur Tooth & Sons Gallery, London, Eng, 70 & 74; Fairweather Hardin Gallery, 71 & 77; French & Co, New York, 72 & 73; Gallery Alexandra Monet, Brussels, Belg, 73 & 78; Il Gabiano, Rome, 75; Gimpel & Weitzenhoffer, New York, 75; Fischbach Gallery, New York, 77. Teaching: Asst prof painting, Art Inst Chicago, 62-64; asst prof painting, Washington Univ, 64-65; vis artists, Ohio State Univ, 68-69; vis artist, Univ SFla, fall 72. Media: Etching, Lithography, Oil. Mailing Add: c/o Fischbach Gallery 29 W 57th St New York NY 10019

LANG, J T
PRINTMAKER, LECTURER
b Maple Shade, NJ, Dec 24, 31. Study: Philadelphia Col Art, Cert; Tyler Sch Art, BFA, BS(educ) & MFA; Barnes Found, with Violette De Mazia; also with Toshi Yoshida, Hirooyuki Tajima & Yuji Abe, Tokyo. Work: Philadelphia Mus Art; Cincinnati Mus Art; Birmingham Mus Art; State Dept, Washington, DC; Philadelphia Libr Collection. Comn: Large ed/woodcut, Print Club Philadelphia, 65; Exodus (litho ser), Pearl Fox Gallery of Elkins Park, 71; color litho ed, La Salle Col, Philadelphia, 74. Exhib: Japan Print Soc Ann, Tokyo, 62, 63, 65 & 66; one-man print shows, Yoseido Gallery, Tokyo, 65 & Birmingham Mus, Ala, 74; USA Print Workshop Exhib, Cincinnati, 67; Am Color Print Soc Ann, Philadelphia, 68-75. Teaching: Asst prof Western cult, Aoyama G Univ, Tokyo, 63-67; vis lectr printmaking, Tyler Sch Art, Philadelphia, 68-70; lectr printmaking, La Salle Col, Philadelphia. Awards: Print Purchase Award, Cincinnati Mus Art, 67; Art/Purchase Award, Pa Acad Fine Arts, 69; Outstanding Printmaker Award, Philadelphia Bd Educ, 73. Bibliog: Dorothy Grafly (auth), Summer print show, Sun Bull, Philadelphia, 7/30/67; Richard L Bell (auth), Prints of J T Lang (video tape), Springfield High Sch, 4/71; Sally Ann Harper (auth), Lang/printmakers, La Salle Collegian, 3/27/73. Mem: Am Color Print Soc (coun mem, 72-); Philadelphia Print Club (studio demonstr, 69-72); Col Art Teacher's Asn. Style & Technique: Large black calligraphic shapes in lithos; embossed areas with rainbow rolling on collographs. Dealer: Pearl Fox Gallery 104 Windsor Ave Melrose Park Philadelphia PA 19126. Mailing Add: 251 W Somerville Ave Philadelphia PA 19120

LANG, MARGO TERZIAN
PAINTER
b Fresno, Calif. Study: Stanford Univ; Fresno State Univ; Ariz State Univ; Prado Mus, Madrid, Spain; also spec study with Edgar Whitney, Dong Kingman, Rex Brandt, George Post and others. Work: Over 50 paintings in US Embassies in Egypt, Brussels, Belg, Arg, Italy, Bulgaria, Iceland, Laos, Colombia, Guatemala, Australia, Iran, Tripoli, Malagasy, Dahomey and others; seven paintings in Nat Collection Fine Art, Smithsonian Inst, Washington, DC, Pepsi Cola Co, Dean Witter & Co & Am Collection Fine Art; New York Life Ins Co Fine Art Calendars. Comn: Sunrise Tomorrow (cross superimposed on desert sunrise) comn by J Parker Nicholson, Glass & Garden Church, Scottsdale, Ariz, 71; Arizona Scenes, Pepsi Cola Bldg. Exhib: One-person shows, Inst Cult, Guadalajara, Mex, 68, New York City, 69, Corcoran Mus, Washington, DC, 74, Brussels, Belg, 74 & Hammer Galleries, New York, 77. Grand Cent Galleries, New York, 68 & 69; Int Platform Asn, Washington, DC, 70-75 & Phoenix Art Mus, 70 & 71; plus others. Awards: Ann Competition Award, Grand Cent Galleries, 68 & 69; Best of Show Award, 70 & Silver Medal of Excellence, 71, Int Platform Asn. Mem: Nat Soc Arts & Lett (nat bd mem & nat art chmn); Int Platform Asn; Nat Soc Lit & Arts; Am Artists Prof League; Ariz Watercolor Asn. Style & Technique: Determined by the impression of mood, color and atmosphere. Media: Oil, Watercolor. Publ: Voice of Am & Radio Liberty broadcasts worldwide, 69, 74 & 75. Dealer: Hammer Galleries 51 E 57th St New York NY 10022. Mailing Add: 6127 Calle del Paisano Scottsdale AZ 85251

LANG, RODGER ALAN
CERAMIST, EDUCATOR
b Chicago, Ill, Feb 9, 42. Study: Cornell Col, BA(art); Univ Wis-Madison, with Don Reitz & Harvey Littleton, MA(art) & MFA. Work: Brooks Mem Art Gallery, Memphis, Tenn. Exhib: Young Americans: 1969, Traveling Exhib, Albuquerque, NMex & New York, 69; Objects: USA The Johnson Collection of Contemporary Crafts, Traveling Exhib, 69; Clayworks: 20 Americans, Mus Contemp Crafts, New York, 71; Phases of New Realism, Lowe Art Gallery, Coral Gables, Fla, 72; Contemporary Crafts of the Americas, Colo State Univ & Orgn Am States, 75; Civilizations, Kohler Arts Ctr, Sheboygan, Wis, 77; 20 Colo Artists, Denver Art Mus, 77. Teaching: Instr, Cleveland Inst Art, 66-70; assoc prof, Metrop State Col, 70-77, prof, 77- Bibliog: Rose Slivka (auth), Laugh-in in clay, Craft Horizons, 10/71. Mem: Am Crafts Coun. Style & Technique: Ceramic sculpture; thrown, assembled parts and mixed media assemblage. Media: Ceramics, Wood. Mailing Add: 1655 Hoyt St Lakewood CO 80215

LANGHAUSER, DAISY BLACK
See Daisy

LANGLAND, HAROLD REED
SCULPTOR, EDUCATOR
b Minneapolis, Minn, Oct 6, 39. Study: Univ Minn, BA(art), 61, MFA(sculpture), 64. Work: Univ Minn Gallery, Minneapolis; Ind Univ, South Bend. Comn: Bronze & oak relief comn by Charles Edwards, Bletchely, Eng, 67; Standing Christ (bronze), House of Hope Presby Church, St Paul, Minn, 69; 16' steel & aluminum sculpture, Bremen Metal Co, South Bend, 72; wood & steel relief, St Paul Acad, Minn, 72; 11' steel sculpture, Ind Univ, 74. Exhib: One-man shows, People & Other Objects, Art Ctr, South Bend, 72 & New Nudes, St Mary's Col, Ind, 74; 118th Exhib, New Eng Art Club, London, 65; Mid States Exhib, Evansville, Ind, 67-69; 8 Artists Under 32, Louisville Art Ctr, Ky, 68; St Catherines Col, St Paul, Minn, 77; plus others in US & Eng. Teaching: Asst lectr sculpture, Carlisle & Sheffield Cols of Art, Eng, 64-67; asst prof sculpture, Murray State Univ, 67-71; assoc prof & chmn dept fine arts, Ind Univ, South Bend, 71-; vis lectr, Stoke-on-Trent, Eng, 77-78. Style & Technique: Figurative sculpture. Media: Bronze. Mailing Add: 12632 Anderson Rd Granger IN 46530

LANGMAN, RICHARD THEODORE
ART DEALER
b Philadelphia, Pa, June 9, 37. Study: Cornell Univ, 54-55; Univ Calif, Berkeley, BA(urban design), 60. Collections Arranged: Richard Anuszkiewicz, Paintings & Prints, 73, Alice Neel, Paintings, 74, Clayton Pond, Paintings & Graphics, 74, Graphics of the 70's (Int Graphics Show), 75 & Craft Art (Nat), 77, Langman Gallery. Pos: Dir, Langman Gallery, Jenkintown, Pa. Specialty: Contemporary painting, sculpture and craft art. Mailing Add: 218 Old York Rd Jenkintown PA 19046

LANGNER, NOLA
ILLUSTRATOR CHILDREN'S BOOKS
b New York, NY, Sept 24, 30. Study: Bennington Col, graphics with Daniel Shapiro & painting with Paul Feeley; Summer Art Sch (scholar), graphics with Gobor Peterdi. Pos: Illusr & retoucher, Videocrafts Television Art Studio, New York, 54-55. Awards: Outstanding Book Award, New York Times Juvenile Bk Sect, 69; Boston Globe, Horn Book Award, 75. Mem: Author's Guild; PEN Club. Style & Technique: Pencil drawings with watercolor, acrylic, collage and even ink blots; did Rafiki using batik technique on paper. Media: Pencil, Watercolor. Publ: Auth & illusr, Miss Lucy, Macmillan & Co, 69; illusr, Scram, Kid, 74 & auth & illusr, Rafiki, 77, Viking Press; auth & illusr, Dusty, Coward, McCann & Geoghegan, 76; illusr, Half a Kingdom, Warne & Co, 77 & Ms Mag, anniversary ed, 77. Dealer: Marilyn Marlow c/o Curtis Brown Ltd 575 Madison Ave New York, NY 10012. Mailing Add: 271 Cent Park W New York NY 10024

LANGSDORF, MARTYL SCHWEIG
See Martyl

LANGSTON, LOYD H
ART DEALER, COLLECTOR
Mr Langston, b Bowers Mill, Mo, Jan 28, 91; Mrs Langston, b Passaic, NJ, Mar 3, 02. Study: Mr Langston, Maryville Col, AB, DHL, Columbia Univ, PhD; Mrs Langston, Simmons Col, AB, Columbia Univ, MA. Teaching: Mrs Langston, Instr bus, Simmons Col, 25-27, prof bus, Long Island Univ, 29-36, acad dean, Katherine Gibbs Sch, 37-67. Mem: Mr Langston, Monmouth Mus (trustee, 65-); NJ State Mus Asn for Arts (trustee, 65-); fel Frick Collection. Mrs Langston, charter mem Monmouth Mus; Chinese Snuff Bottle Asn; Maryville Col (bd mem, 60-); fel Frick Collection. Specialty: French paintings; art of the Orient; Chinese handstones and porcelains. Mailing Add: Morningside Maryville Col Maryville TN 37801

LANIER, RUTH ASAWA
See Asawa, Ruth

LANING, EDWARD
PAINTER
b Petersburg, Ill, Apr 26, 06. Study: Univ Chicago; Art Inst Chicago; Art Students League, with Max Weber, John Sloan, Thomas Hart Benton & Kenneth Hayes Miller. Work: Metrop Mus Art & Whitney Mus Am Art, New York; William Rockhill Nelson Gallery, Kansas City, Mo; Pentagon Gallery, Dept Defense, Washington, DC. Comn: Ellis Island, NY, 37; Rockingham Post Off, NC, 37; Bowling Green Post Off, Ky, 41; New York Pub Libr, 42; Sheraton-Dallas Hotel, Tex, 60. Exhib: Many Whitney Mus Ann; Corcoran Gallery Art, Washington, DC, 38; Art Inst Chicago, 40; American Drawings, Metrop Mus Art, 52; Nat Acad Design, New York, 73. Teaching: Instr painting & drawing, Cooper Union, 40-43; head dept painting & drawing, Kansas City Art Inst, 45-50; instr painting & drawing, Art Students League, 52-75. Pos: Dir, Beaux Arts Inst Design, 40-42. Awards: Kohnstamm Prize, Art Inst Chicago, 40; Guggenheim Fel, 45; Fulbright Fel, 50-52. Mem: Nat Soc Mural Painters (pres, 68-73); Nat Acad Design (rec secy, 68-75); life mem Art Students League. Publ: Auth, Perspective for Artists, 69; auth, Memoirs of a WPA artist, 10/70 & auth, Spoon River revisited, 6/71, Am Heritage; auth, The Act of Drawing, 72; auth, The Sketchbooks of Reginald Marsh, 74. Mailing Add: 30 E 14th St New York NY 10003

LANOU, TOBIE E
ART CRITIC, ART ADMINISTRATOR
b Burlington, Vt, Mar 1, 36. Study: Harvard Col, AB, 58; Univ NC, MCP, 67. Collections Arranged: Herman Maril, Paintings 1960-74 & Fourth Ann Atheneum Show, Atheneum, Alexandria, Va, spring 74. Pos: Ed & publr, What's UP IN ART, The Washington Art Marketletter, 77- Bibliog: Jo Ann Lewis (auth), Art market comes of age, Washington Post, 5/77; Tina Felluss (auth), article in Galleries Mag, 5/77; Daniel Millsaps (auth), article in Washington Int Arts Letter, 11/77. Mem: Northern Va Fine Arts Asn (pres, 73-74, vpres, 72-73). Res: Survey research on the dynamics of the Washington art market, 76-77. Mailing Add: 6122 Woodmont Rd Alexandria VA 22307

LA NOUE, TERENCE DAVID
PAINTER, SCULPTOR
b Hammond, Ind, Dec 4, 41. Study: Ohio Wesleyan Univ, BFA; Hochschule für Bildende Künste, WBerlin; Cornell Univ, MFA. Work: Roy Neuberger Mus, Purchase, NY; Corcoran Gallery Art, Washington, DC; Univ Hartford; Wadsworth Atheneum; Whitney Mus Am Art. Exhib: Art Inst Chicago; Dayton Art Inst; Albright-Knox Gallery, 71; Indianapolis Mus Art, 72; Newark Mus Art, 72; one-man shows, Nancy Hoffman Gallery, 74 & 76-78 & Galerie Farideh Cadot, Paris, 77 & 78; 9th Paris Biennial Am Art, 75; Philadelphia Mus Art, 77; 34th Corcoran Biennial of Am Painting; Kansas City Art Inst, 77; Iran-Am Soc, 78. Teaching: Asst prof art, Trinity Col, 67-72; assoc prof art & head dept, La Guardia Col, 72- Awards: Fulbright Scholar, 64-65; Nat Endowment for Arts, 72-73. Bibliog: Robert Pincus-Witten (auth), New York, 71 & 72, Artforum; Miana (auth), article in Paris Art Int, 75; articles in New York Art News, 76 & 77. Media: Rhoplex, Acrylic, Latex, Wood, Tobacco Cloth. Mailing Add: 29A S Portland Ave Brooklyn NY 11217

LANSDON, GAY BRANDT
INSTRUCTOR, PRINTMAKER
b San Antonio, Tex, Dec 6, 31. Study: Univ Houston, Tex, BFA, 65; Mus of Fine Arts Sch, Houston, 66-68, with Stella Sullivan & Pat Colville; Sam Houston State Univ, MFA, 75. Work: Univ Houston, Univ Ctr; Sam Houston State Univ; Med & Surgical Group, Baytown, Tex; Houston Post Newspaper. Comn: 16 paintings, comn by Dr Robert Stewart, Houston, 67; serigraph, comn by Jean Geeslin, Huntsville, Tex, 69; three printed fiber panels (4 ft x 9 ft), Bellville State Bank, Tex, 72. Exhib: SW Crafts Biennial, Mus of Santa Fe, NMex, 71; 15th Ann Tex Craftsman, Dallas Mus of Fine Arts, 71; Colorprint USA, Lubbock, Tex, 75; Third Nat Print Exhib, Univ Southern Calif, Los Angeles, 75; 14th Midwest Biennial, Joslyn Art Mus, Omaha, Nebr, 75; Purdue Univ Small Print Exhib, 76; plus others. Teaching: Instr art, Mus of Fine Arts, Houston, Tex, 69-71; instr printmaking, Univ Houston, 71-76, asst prof, 76- Awards: First Prize, Photog Award Exhib, Jewish Community Ctr, 70; Jurors' Merit Awards, SW Graphics Invitational, 72 & Dimension X, 76, Houston Art League. Bibliog: Kit Van Cleave (auth), Gay Lansdon: Mixed-media printmaking, Today's Art, 2/77. Mem: Artist's Equity. Style & Technique: Abstract, hard-edge, flat areas of silkscreened color combined with free-form, fantasy organic drawings on shaped etching plates. Media: Intaglio and silkscreen. Dealer: Dubose Gallery 2950 Kirby Houston TX 77098. Mailing Add: 10418 Chambers Houston TX 77034

LANSDOWNE, JAMES FENWICK
PAINTER
b Hong Kong, Aug 8, 37. Work: Ulster Mus, Belfast; Montreal Mus Fine Arts; Art Gallery of Greater Victoria; Beaverbrook Found; Audubon House, New York. Exhib: Kennedy Galleries, New York, 62; Bird Artists of the World Exhib, Tryon Galleries, London, Eng, 64; Lab Ornithol, Cornell Univ, 68; Nat Mus Natural Hist, Smithsonian Inst, Washington, DC, 69; Animals in Art, Royal Ont Mus, Toronto, 75. Mem: Can Acad Arts. Style & Technique: Gouache on watercolor paper or canvas; detailed studies of birds. Media: Gouache. Publ: Co-auth, Birds of Northern Forest, 66; co-auth, Birds of Eastern Forest, Part I, 68 & Part II, 70; auth, Birds of the West Coast, Part I, 76; illusr, Rails of the World, 76. Dealer: M F Feheley Arts Co 5 Drumsnab Rd Toronto ON Can. Mailing Add: 941 Victoria Ave Victoria BC Can

LANSNER, FAY
PAINTER
b Philadelphia, Pa. Study: Tyler Sch Fine Art, 45-47; Art Students League, 47-48; Hans Hofmann Sch, 48-50; also with Leger & Lhote, Paris, 50-51. Work: Weatherspoon Art Mus, Greensboro, NC; NY Univ Art Collection; Corcoran Gallery Art, Washington, DC; Newsweek, Washington Post Co, New York; Neuberger Mus, State Univ NY Col, Purchase; plus others. Exhib: Corcoran Gallery, Washington, DC, 67; Albright-Knox Art Gallery, Buffalo, NY, 67; Mus Mod Art, New York, 68, 69 & 71; 17th Brooklyn Mus Print Ann, NY, 70; Women in the Arts, Stamford Mus, Conn, 72. Bibliog: Harold Rosenberg (auth), Hofmann students, Art News Ann, 63; Doris Reno (auth), Lansner paintings show, Times Herald Post, 66; I H Sandler (auth), Fay Lansner, AVA Bks, 77. Mem: Women in the Arts. Publ: Auth, Barbara Riboud, Craft Horizons Mag, 4/72. Dealer: Marlborough Graphics 41 E 57th St New York NY 10022; La Demeure 6 Place St Sulpice Paris France. Mailing Add: 317 W 80th St New York NY 10024

LANTZ, MICHAEL F
SCULPTOR
b New Rochelle, NY, Apr 6, 08. Study: Nat Acad Design, 24-26; also with Lee Lawrie, 26-35; Beaux Arts Inst Design, 28-31. Work: Pan Am World Health Ctr; Architects Bldg, Albany, NY; Lynchburg Courthouse, Va; Nat Guard Mem Bldg, Washington, DC. Comn: Spring Hill Ave Synagogue, Mobile, Ala, 56; Battle Monument, St Avold, France, 59; Nat Guard Mem Bldg, Washington, DC, 59; Sculptural Outlines, Architect's Bldg, Albany, NY, 68; Thomas Jefferson Bicentennial Medal, US Mint, 76. Exhib: Philadelphia Mus Art, Pa, 40 & 48; Silver Medal Int Exhib, Madrid, Spain, 59; many exhibs, Nat Sculpture Soc, Nat Acad Design & Lever House, New York. Teaching: Prof sculpture adult educ, New Rochelle, 36-38; instr, Nat Acad Design, 65- & Old Lyme Acad Fine Arts, 77- Pos: Ed, Nat Sculpture Rev, 50-55, ed adv, 69- Awards: Medal of the City of New York, 48; J Sanford Saltus Medal, 69; Elizabeth Watrous Gold Medal, Nat Acad Design, 70 & 75. Bibliog: Sculpture by Michael Lantz, Am Artist Mag, 57 & Nat Sculpture Rev, 72. Mem: Nat Sculpture Soc (pres, 70-73, chmn honors & awards comt); Nat Acad Design (coun mem, 70-, 1st vpres, 75-); Am Acad Achievement (bd gov); Fine Arts Fedn New York (vpres, 70). Style & Technique: Contemporary and realistic. Media: Bronze; Limestone, Marble. Publ: Auth, articles in Nat Sculpture Rev. Mailing Add: 979 Webster Ave New Rochelle NY 10804

LANYON, ELLEN
PAINTER, PRINTMAKER
b Chicago, Ill, Dec 21, 26. Study: Art Inst Chicago, BFA, 48, with Joseph Hirsch; State Univ Iowa, MFA, 50, with M Lasansky; Courtauld Inst, Univ London, with Helmut Reuhman. Work: Univ Mass; Brooklyn Mus, NY; NJ State Mus, Trenton; Metrop Mus Art, New York; McNay Art Inst, San Antonio, Tex. Comn: Lithograph, Ravinnia Asn, 68; painting, Florists' Tel Delivery Asn Traveling Exhib, 70; paintings, Ill Bell for Directory Cover, 71; Container Corp Am: Great Ideas, US Dept Interior Bicentennial Exhib. Exhib: Art Inst Chicago Am Biennials, 46-61 & Vicinity Ann, 46-71; Young Printmakers, Metrop Mus Art, 53; Recent Painting USA: The Figure, Mus Mod Art, New York, 62; The Painter & The Photograph, Am Fedn Arts Traveling Exhib, 65-66; The Chicago School, Imagist Art, Mus Contemp Art, Chicago & NY Cult Ctr, 72; 36 one-woman shows. Teaching: Instr painting & dir, Ox Bow Summer Sch of Painting, Saugatuck, Mich, 60-; vis instr drawing, Art Inst Chicago, 64-65 & 73; lectr drawing, Univ Ill, Chicago Circle, 66, artist in residence, 71; vis artist-lectr, Stanford Univ, 73 & Univ Calif, Davis, 73; vis artist & fel, Inst Arts & Humanistic Studies, Pa State Univ, 74; vis artist, State Univ Iowa; vis artist-lectr, 75-; painting, State Univ NY Col, Purchase, 78- Pos: Adv, Adult Educ Coun, Chicago, 69-72; adv visual arts, Ill Art Coun, 69-; mem bd dirs, Oxbow Summer Sch Painting. Awards: Cassandra Found Award, 71; Nat Endowment Arts Award, 74; Yaddo Fel, 74-75 & 76. Bibliog: Franz Schulze (auth), Ellen Lanyon, Follett, 5/72; Ruth Iskin (auth), interview in Visual Dialog, spring 77; Joanna Fruett (auth), article in Feminist Art J, spring 77. Mem: Col Art Asn (bd dir, 77-); Art Inst Chicago Alumni Asn. Style & Technique: Realistically rendered juxtapositions of animate and inanimates in acrylic on stretched linen. Media: Acrylic, Lithography. Publ: Contribr, Art Scene, 9/68; auth & illusr, Wonder Production, Vol I, 71; Wandering Tattler, Perishable Press, 75; illusr, Jataka Tales, Houghton Mifflin, 75; auth, Transformations, Printed Matter, 77. Dealer: Richard Gray 620 N Michigan Ave Chicago IL 60611; Odyssia Gallery 775 Park Ave New York NY 14607. Mailing Add: 412 N Clark St Chicago IL 60610

LAPENA, FRANK RAYMOND
PAINTER, ART HISTORIAN
b San Francisco, Calif, Oct 5, 37. Study: Chico State Univ, AB(art); San Francisco State Univ, life credential educ(art); also with tribal elders and medicine men/traditionalists. Work: Indian Arts & Crafts Bd, Washington, DC; Southern Plains Indian Mus, Anadarko, Okla. Comn: There is Remembering (chap heading-painting, In: The Human Condition), Scott, Foresman & Co, 73. Exhib: Phelan Awards First Photog Exhib, Oakland Mus, Calif, 71; Indian Art Show, Am Arts Gallery, New York, 72; Am Indian Art Show, Linden Mus, Stuttgart, Ger, 73; one-man shows, Paintings & Photographs, Southern Plains Indian Mus, 75 & Calif Indian Days, Calif Expo, Sacramento, 77; Fetishes, San Francisco Mus Art, 75; Am Indian Art Heritage, Art Inst of Chicago, 77; Indian Images (travelling exhib), Univ NDak, Grand Forks, 77. Teaching: Instr art & photog, Shasta Community Col, Redding, Calif, 69-71; asst prof art hist, Calif State Univ, Sacramento, 71-; vis prof Indian Art hist, Lethbridge Univ, Alta, Can, summer 74. Pos: Alt mem art, Calif Comn Teacher Preparation & Licensing, State Calif, 72; bd mem, Ctr Arts of Indian Am, Washington, DC, 74- Awards: First & Purchase Graphics, 4th Am Indian Arts & Crafts Bd, 68; one oil and three sculptures, 4th Ann N Valley Show, Redding, 69 & winner in 5th & 6th Ann; Jury Mention, New Mexico 11 State Small Painting Show, Albuquerque, 70. Bibliog: Lloyd Kiva New (auth), The crafts of the Indian, House Beautiful, 6/71; Lloyd E Oxendine (auth), 25 contemporary Indian artists, Art in Am, 7-8/72; First American (contemp Indian artists), Nat & KPIX-TV, San Francisco, 73. Mem: Native Am Indian Artists; Native NAm Indian Artists; Int Soc Preserv Black & White Photog. Style & Technique: Traditions and culture of sacred circle /tribal; abstract and semi-realistic. Media: Mixed Media, Oil. Res: Culture and arts of the traditional and evolving arts and crafts of California tribal people. Publ: Contribr, Wintu Indian, In: Handbook of North American Indian, 20 vols, Smithsonian, 76. Mailing Add: 5859 Woodleigh Dr Carmichael CA 95608

LA PIERRE, THOMAS
PAINTER, PRINTMAKER
b Toronto, Ont, Dec 28, 30. Study: Ont Col Art, AA; Ecole Beaux Arts; Atelier 17. Work: Montreal Mus Fine Art, PQ; Sir George Williams Univ; Art Gallery, Hamilton, Ont. Exhib: Sao Paulo Biennial, 63; Focus on Drawing, Art Gallery Ont, 65; Price Fine Art Awards Exhib, 70; Atlantic Provinces, 74. Teaching: Instr drawing & painting, Ont Col Art, 58- Awards: Ont Soc Artists Award, 68; Price Fine Art Award, 70; Can Soc Painters in Watercolour Honour Award, 65 & 72. Bibliog: William McElcheran (auth), Dialogue with demons, Arts Can, 70; Robert Percival (auth), 20th Century mystic, Art Mag, 75. Mem: Can Soc Graphic Art; Ont Soc Artists; Can Soc Painters in Watercolour; Royal Can Acad Arts. Style & Technique: Sustained figurative works making use of symbolism. Media: Oil, Watercolor. Mailing Add: 2067 Proverbs Dr Mississauga ON L4X 1G3 Can

LAPINER, ALAN C
ART DEALER
b Palma de Mallorca, Spain, Aug 30, 33; US citizen. Study: Antioch Col, BA. Pos: Owner-dir, Arts of the Four Quarters, Ltd, New York. Specialty: Pre-Colombian art, specializing in art of ancient Peru and ancient textiles. Mailing Add: Arts of Four Quarters Ltd 111 W 13th St New York NY 10011

LAPINSKI, TADEUSZ (A)
PRINTMAKER, EDUCATOR
b Rawa Mazowiecka, Poland, June 20, 28; US citizen. Study: Acad Fine Arts, Warsaw, Poland, MFA, 55. Work: Mus Mod Art, New York; Nat Collection Fine Arts & Nat Gallery, Washington, DC; Mus Mod Art, Tokyo; Albertina Mus, Vienna; plus others. Comn: Washington Portfolio, Washington, DC Print Club & Soc of Graphic Arts, 74. Exhib: Int Prints Exhib Biennial of Venice, 73; Biennial of Prints, Ljubliana; Three Printmakers—Jacob Kainen, Albert Christ Janer & Tadeusz Lapinski, Nat Collection Fine Arts; Biennial of Prints, Fridrikstad, Norway, 73; Biennial of Prints, Cracow; Am Print in Venice, 77. Teaching: Assoc prof lithography, Univ Md, 72- Awards: Mus Art Porto Ale gre Prize, State Rio Grande du Sol, Brazil, 67; Medal of Honor, Audubon Art Soc, New York, 72, Silver Medal, 73; Medal of Honor, Printers & Sculptors Soc NJ, 73-75. Bibliog: H Cliffe (auth), Lithography, Watson-Guptill, 65; Hans Platte (auth), Color Prints International, Universe, 69; Fritz Eichenberg (auth), The Art of the Prints, Abrams, 77. Mem: Painters Sculptors Soc of NJ (vpres, 72-76); Washington Printmakers Soc. Style & Technique: Individu al lithography (auto lithography), plate multicolor lithography. Dealer: F Bader Gallery 2124 Pennsylvania Ave NW Washington DC 20037. Mailing Add: 10413 Eastwood Ave Silver Spring MD 20901

LAPLANTZ, DAVID
CRAFTSMAN, EDUCATOR
b Toledo, Ohio, June 12, 44. Study: Bowling Green State Univ, with Hal Hasselschwert, 62-66, BS(art); Cranbrook Acad Art, with Richard Thomas, 66-69, MFA; Southern Ill Univ, with Alex Bealer, 70. Work: St Paul Art Ctr, Minn; Colo State Univ. Comn: Commemorative (scale model of house), Civil Rights Group, Detroit, 67; Farewell Commemorative (scale model of bldg), Cranbrook Sci Inst, Bloomfield Hills, Mich, 67; Farewell Commemorative (pin), Fac Wives, Humboldt State Univ, 73; liturgical symbol, Women's Soc, Mad River Community Hosp Chapel, Arcata, Calif, 74. Exhib: Young Americans 1969, Mus Contemp Crafts, New York, traveling 69-71; Goldsmith '70, St Paul Art Ctr, Minn & Mus Contemp Crafts, 70-71; Exhib of Eight American Metalsmiths & Jewelers, Sheffield Polytech Sch Art & Design, Sheffield, Eng & Richard Demarco Gallery, Edinburgh, Scotland, 74; The Goldsmith, Renwick Gallery, Smithsonian Inst, Washington, DC, 74; Contemporary Crafts of the Americas, Colo State Univ, 75; Forms in Metal, Am Craftsman's Coun, Mus Contemp Crafts, New York, 75; Six Am Metalsmiths, Am Libr, Bucharest, Romania, 76; Blacksmith as Artist & Craftsman 1776-1976, Mus Contemp Crafts, New York & Renwick Gallery, Smithsonian Inst, Washington, DC, 76-77; NAm Goldsmith Biennial Exhib, Phoenix Art Mus, Ariz, 77; Copper, Bronze & Brass Competition, Univ Ariz Mus Art, Tucson, 77; 3rd Profile of US Jewelry, Tex Tech Univ, Lubbock, 77. Teaching: Instr jewelry-metalsmithing, Inst Am Indian Arts, Santa Fe, NMex, 67-68, Colo State Univ, 69-70, San Diego State Col, 70-71 & Humboldt State Univ, 71- Pos: Pres, Delta Phi Delta, Bowling Green State Univ, 65-66; vis craftsman, Hinckley Sch Crafts, Maine, summers 72 & 73 & NH League Craftsmen, Lebanon, 75. Awards: Second Place, Nat Sterling Silver Design Competition, Sterling Silversmiths Guild Am, 69; St Paul Art Ctr Purchase Award, 70; Merit Award, NAm Goldsmith Biennial Exhib, Phoenix Art Mus, 77. Bibliog: Articles in Crafts Horizons, 69-70 & 75. Mem: Am Craftsman's Coun; Friends of Calif Design. Style & Technique: Contemporary, humorous, mini-functional; smithing and fabricated methods; engraving and filing embellishments. Media: Brass, Copper & Silver. Collection: Numerous items of contemporary craft work; prints and paintings following an experimental direction. Publ: Contrib, California Design XI (catalog), Pasadena Art Mus, 71; contrib, Body Jewelry-International Perspective, 73; contrib, Contemporary Crafts of the Americas (catalog), 75; contrib, Contemporary Jewelry, rev ed, 76. Mailing Add: 899 Bayside Cutoff Bayside CA 95524

LAPOINTE, FRANK
PAINTER, PRINTMAKER
b Port Rexton, Nfld, May 11, 42. Study: Ont Col of Art, AOCA, 66. Work: Fed Dept of Pub Works, Ottawa, Ont; Can Coun Art Bank, Ottawa; Univ Ore, Corvallis; Simon Fraser Univ, Burnaby, BC; Confederation Centre for the Arts, Charlottetown, PEI. Comn: Nfld postcard ser: What do you think of Jack?, Mem Univ Art Gallery Jubilee Portfolio, St John's, Nfld, 75. Exhib: Island Imagery, Nfld, NS & PEI, 75-76; Imprint 76, Saidye Bronfman Centre, Montreal & Ont Art Gallery, Toronto, 76; Ice Report, Mt St Vincent Art Gallery, Halifax, NS, 76; Atlantic Coast, Nat Gallery Touring Show, Can & Paris, France, 76-77; Ninth Burnaby Biennial, Burnaby Art Gallery, BC, 77; Graphex 5, Art Gallery of Brant, Ont, 77; Transparent Things, Vancouver Art Gallery, BC, 77; Nfld Postcard Series, Western Can Circuit, 77. Teaching: Instr painting & printmaking, Dundas Valley Sch of Art, Dundas, Ont, 69-70. Pos: Asst cur & art specialist, Art Gallery, Mem Univ, St John's, Nfld, 70-72, cur, 72-73. Awards: Silver Medal, 67 & Bronze Medal, 68, Nfld Arts & Lett, Govt of Nfld; Purchase Award, Graphics Atlantic, Mt St Vincent Art Gallery, 76. Bibliog: Joe Bodolai (auth), Visit to Newfoundland, 75-76 & Peter Bell (auth), Frank Lapointe/Gerald Squires, 76-77, Artscanada, Toronto; Peter Bell (auth), Oberheide, Wright, Lapointe, Vie des Arts, Montreal, winter 76. Mem: Can Soc of Painters in Watercolor. Media: Watercolor & acrylic; lithography & etching. Dealer: Mira Godard Gallery 22 Hazelton Ave Toronto ON Can. Mailing Add: Tors Cove Southern Shore NF A0A 4A0 Can

LAPOSKY, BEN FRANCIS
DESIGNER, PHOTOGRAPHER
b Cherokee, Iowa, Sept 30, 14. Work: Sanford Mus, Cherokee; Univ Okla, Norman; Mus Sci & Technol, Tel Aviv, Israel. Exhib: Photog Soc Am, Chicago, 55; Art in Science, Albany Inst Hist & Art, NY, 66; Light as a Creative Medium, Carpenter Ctr, Harvard Univ, 66; Cybernetic Serendipity, Inst Contemp Art, London, 68; On the Eve of Tomorrow, Computer Art, Hannover, Ger, 69; Computer Graphics Art Exhib, Rhinelander Gallery, New York, 76; Computer Art Exhib, Univ Waterloo Galleries, Can, 77; Art for the Space Era, Huntsville Mus of Art, Ala, 78; plus others. Awards: Art Dirs Club Medal, New York, 57. Bibliog: Design by Electrons, Design, 5/53; Electronic Gayety, Fortune Mag, 12/56; H Franke (auth), Computer Graphics-Computer Art, Phaidon, London, 71. Style & Technique: Oscillons are electronic oscillograms composed for art or design, presented as photographic exhibitions or publications. Media: Kinetic Light Assemblages, Photography. Publ: Auth, Electronic abstractions, Graphis Mag, Zurich, 54; auth, Electronic abstracts: art for space age, Proc Iowa Acad Sci, 58; auth, Oscillographic design, Perspective Mag, London, 60; auth, Oscillons: electronic abstractions, Leonardo Mag, Oxford, 69 & Kinetic Art, 74; contribr, Ruth Leavitt, ed, Electronic Abstractions in Artist & Computer, Harmony Bks, 76. Mailing Add: 301 S Sixth St Cherokee IA 51012

LARCADA, RICHARD KENNETH
ART DEALER
b Brooklyn, NY, Sept 11, 35. Study: NY Univ, BA, 56. Pos: Assoc dir, Maynard Walker Gallery, New York, 61-65; dir, Larcada Gallery, New York, 65-77; dir, One Art Serv, New York, 77- Specialty: Neo-Romantics; artists of the twenties and thirties. Mailing Add: 790 Madison Ave New York NY 10021

LARIAR, LAWRENCE
CARTOONIST, WRITER
b Brooklyn, NY, Dec 25, 08. Study: New York Sch Fine & Appl Arts, 26-29; Acad Julien, Paris; Art Students League. Teaching: Dir, Prof Sch Cartooning. Pos: Com advert artist, 30-33; illusr & polit cartoonist, 33-; cartoon ed, Liberty Mag, 41-48; ed, Best Cartoons of Year, 42-; cartoon ed, Parade Mag, 57- Mem: Am Soc Mag Cartoonist (past pres, mem war comt); Author's League Am. Publ: Auth, You've Got Me From 9 to 5; auth, You've Got Me on the Rocks, 56; auth, The Real Lowdown, 56; auth, Girl Running, 56; auth, Boat & Be Damned, 57; contribr cartoons in leading nat mags & New York daily newspapers; also auth & ed many other bks. Mailing Add: 399 F Heritage Village Southbury CT 06488

LARK, RAYMOND
PAINTER, DRAFTSMAN
b Philadelphia, Pa, June 16, 39. Study: Philadelphia Mus Sch Art; Dobbins Voc, Philadelphia; Temple Univ, BS; Los Angeles Tech Col. Work: Libr of Cong, Washington, DC; Los Angeles Co Mus, Calif; Ont Col Art, Toronto. Comn: Universal City Studios, Calif, 66; Movie Land Wax Mus & Palace of Living Arts, Buena Park, Calif, 66; Blue Cross Ins Co, 67 & CBS-TV Studios, Los Angeles, 73. Exhib: Dalzell Hatfield Galleries, Los Angeles, 68-; Charles W Bowers Mem Mus, Santa Ana, Calif, 68; Cape Cod Art Asn Gallery, Hyannis, Mass, 69; Phillip E Freed Gallery Fine Art, Chicago, 70; Smithsonian Inst, Washington, DC, 71; NJ State Mus, Trenton, 72; Honolulu Acad Arts, Hawaii, 75; Guggenheim Mus, New York, 75; plus over 60 other exhibs. Collections Arranged: Black Sculpturing Exhibition, Charles W Bowers Mem Mus, Santa Ana, Calif, 69; Five Black Artists Exhibit, Florenz's Art Gallery, Hollywood, 69; Nine American Artists Exhibit, Emerald Gallery, Hollywood Beach, Fla, 70. Teaching: Lectr art, Nat Secy Asn, Hollywood, Calif, 70, EYOA Ctr Los Angeles, 71, Compton Col, Calif, 72, Los Angeles Trade Tech Col, 73, Cent City Community Ment Health Ctr, Los Angeles, 74 & others. Pos: Pres, Art West Assoc, Inc, Calif, 68-70; ed dir, Victor Bus Schs, Los Angeles, 71; plus others. Awards: Best in Show, Immanuel's Art Exhib, Calif, 67 & 68 & two additional prizes, 68; Best in Show, Florenz's Art Exhib, Calif, 69; Spec Award, San Bernardino Art Asn, Calif, 74; plus others. Bibliog: Joyce Collins (auth), Raymond Lark finds business sense makes a successful artist, NOW Mag, 3/76; Nieda Springer (auth), The only Black artist to exhib with American Bicentennial masters, Sun Reporter, San Francisco, 7/3/76; Richard Reilly (auth), Black artist Raymond Lark had pride, talent & goals, San Diego Union Newspaper, 9/26/76. Mem: Artists Equity Asn; Int Platform Asn; plus others. Style & Technique: Realism-transfer emotion and positions in life to paper and canvas with use of expressive line and light and shadow, sometimes modelled in both the details of the figure and the background. Media: Oil, Pencil. Res: History of Afro-American art; graphic art masters. Publ: Auth, A Portfolio of 6 Prints by Raymond Lark, 72; auth, Art West, 72; auth, A Monograph, Raymond Lark, 75; auth, One Hundred & One, 75-76; plus others. Mailing Add: PO Box 8990 Los Angeles CA 90008

LARKIN, EUGENE
DESIGNER, EDUCATOR
b Minneapolis, Minn, June 27, 21. Study: Univ Minn, BA & MA. Work: Mus Mod Art, New York; Nat Gallery Art & Libr Cong, Washington, DC; Art Inst Chicago; Addison Gallery Am Art, Andover, Mass; Nat Collection of Fine Arts, Smithsonian Inst, Washington, DC; plus others. Comn: Int Graphic Arts Soc; Gen Mills Corp; Bus Wk; Minneapolis Soc Fine Arts; US Info Agency. Exhib: US Info Agency Traveling Exhib to Iran, Italy, France, Spain & Ger; one-man shows, Minneapolis Inst Art, 68 & Hamline Univ, 68; State Univ NY Albany, 69; Univ Calif, Long Beach, 69; Univ Minn, 74 & 78; plus others. Teaching: Instr, Kans State Col, Pittsburg, 48-54; head printmaking dept & chmn fine arts div, Minneapolis Sch Art, 54-69; prof, Design Dept, Univ Minn, Minneapolis, 69- Awards: Walker Art Ctr, 60 & Washington Watercolor & Print Exhib, 63; plus many others. Mem: Am Asn Univ Prof; Col Art Asn Am. Style & Technique: Contemporary, powerful, classical forms, many based on plant forms. Media: Woodcuts, Lithographs, Oil. Mailing Add: 64 Groveland Terr Minneapolis MN 55403

LARKIN, JOHN E, JR
COLLECTOR, PATRON
b St Paul, Minn. Study: Univ Minn, BS & MD; Harvard Univ. Collection: American art, works by W Homer, A Wyeth, Benton, Cameron Booth, Wanda Gag, Adolf Dehn, E Lawson, Homer Martin, George Catlin, Seth Eastman, Hans Hoffman and many others. Mailing Add: 7 Yellow Birch Rd Dellwood White Bear Lake MN 55110

LARMER, OSCAR VANCE
PAINTER, EDUCATOR
b Wichita, Kans, July 11, 24. Study: Minneapolis Sch of Fine Arts, cert painting; Univ Kans, BFA; Wichita State Univ, MFA. Work: Nelson Gallery of Art, Kansas City, Mo; Kans State Univ, Manhattan; Wichita State Univ, Kans; Wichita Art Asn Gallery; Kans Univ, Lawrence. Comn: Medallion, Kans State Col Centennial, Manhattan, 61; President's Medallion, Kans State Univ, 74; painting, Kans 4-H Found, Kans State Univ, 77. Exhib: Mid-Am Exhib, Nelson Gallery of Art, Kansas City, Mo, 52-70; Watercolor USA, Springfield Art Mus, Mo, 57 & 68; New Talent, Madison Gallery, New York, 63; Rocky Mountain Exhib, Denver Art Mus, Colo, 65; 45th Ann 17-State Exhib, Springfield, Mo, 75; Nat Watercolor Exhib, La Watercolor Soc, 76; Works of Art on Paper, Nat-Western Ann, Western Ill Univ, Galesburg, 76; Summer Invitational, Nelson Gallery of Art, Kansas City, Mo, 77. Teaching: Prof drawing & painting, Kans State Univ, Manhattan, 56- Pos: Asst dir, Wichita Art Mus, Kans, 53-55; head art dept, Kans State Univ, Manhattan, 67-71. Awards: Purchase Awards, Biennial Exhib, Kans State Univ, 60, Smoky Hills Art, Hadley Med Ctr, 77 & Kans Watercolor Soc, United Bank & Trust, 77. Bibliog: V W Bell (auth), The Kansas Art Reader, Univ Kans Press, 76. Mem: Nat Col Art Asn; Mid-Am Col Art Asn; Kans Watercolor Soc; Kans Fedn of Art. Style & Technique: Landscapes in watercolor and oil; simplification of nature. Media: Watercolor, oil. Mailing Add: 2441 Hobbs Dr Manhattan KS 66502

LARRAZ, JULIO FERNANDEZ
PAINTER
b La Habana, Cuba, Mar 12, 44. Study: Drawing and painting with Burton Silverman. Work: Westmoreland Co Mus Art, Greensburg, Pa. Exhib: Artists & Space, Nat Gallery, Washington, DC, 70; one-man show of drawings, New Sch Social Res, New York, 72; Childe Hassam Fund Purchase, Am Acad Arts & Lett, New York, 74; 39th Ann Midyear Show, Butler Inst Am Art, Youngstown, Ohio, 75; Art in the Kitchen, Westmoreland Co Mus Art, 75. Awards: Cintas Found Fel, Inst Int Educ, 75; Am Acad Arts & Lett Award, 76. Bibliog: David L Shirey (auth), Julio Fernandez, New York Times, 72; Doreen Mangan (auth), Julio Fernandez and his rogues gallery, Am Artist, 74. Style & Technique: Still life, landscapes and figures; dramatic handling of light with metaphorical intent. Media: Oil, Pastel, Charcoal, Watercolor. Publ: Contrib, The Eye Witness to Space, Abrams, 70; illusr, The Perfect Wagnerite, Time-Life Bks, 72; illusr, The Whitehouse Enemies, New Am Libr, 73; contribr, Still the flypaper of politics, New York Times Mag, 74; contribr, New York Mag. Dealer: Hall Gallery 4719 Camp Bowie Blvd Ft Worth TX 76107; FAR Gallery 22 E 80th St New York NY 10021. Mailing Add: 6 Van Houten St Upper Nyack NY 10960

LARSEN, D DANE
CERAMIST, SCULPTOR
b Oct 21, 50. Study: Harvard Univ, BA, study with William Reimann, Rudolf Arnheim & Buckminster Fuller; Univ Calif, Study with Ron Nagle; San Francisco State Univ, MA, study with Charles McKee, Hayward King, Dale Roush, Daniel Rhodes & Paul Soldner. Work: San Francisco State Univ Ceramics Collection; Carpenter Ctr for the Visual Arts, Harvard Univ, Cambridge, Mass; Oakland Mus, Calif; Prieto Gallery, Mills Col, Oakland. Exhib: Calif Ceramics & Glass, Oakland Mus, 74; Third Ann Ceramics & Glass Exhib, San Jose Mus of Art, Calif, 76; The Calif Craftsman, Monterey Peninsula Mus of Art, Monterey, Calif, 76; Marietta Col Crafts Nat, Grover M Hermann Fine Arts Ctr, Mairetta, Ohio, 76; Designer-Craftsman Nat, Richmond Art Ctr, Calif, 76 & 77; Calif Crafts X, E B Crocker Gallery & Mus, Sacramento, 77; Nat Cone Box Show, Kans Univ Union Gallery, Lawrence, 77. Collections Arranged: Introductions 76, Studio Seven Gallery; Light in Black, The Forum Gallery, 12/76; Three in Clay, The Art Resource Ctr, 2-4/77; Seeking the Inside, Meyer, Breier, Weiss Gallery, 10-12/77. Teaching: Instr ceramics, Col of Marin, Kentfield, Calif, 76- & Columbia Jr Col, Calif, summer 77. Pos: Consult & dir of ceramics prog, San Rafael City Recreation Dept, 77- Awards: Cash Award, The Calif Craftsman, Monterey Peninsula Mus, 76, Third & Fourth Ann Ceramics & Glass, San Jose Mus of Art, 76 & 77 & Calif Crafts Media, Civic Arts Gallery, 77. Mem: San Francisco Potters Asn; Am Crafts Coun; Col Art Asn. Style & Technique: High-fired ceramics, specializing in raku firing and low-fire, lusters, burnishing, underglaze and decals. Media: Clay and Wood. Dealer: Meyer, Breir & Weiss 3044 Fillmore St San Francisco CA 94123. Mailing Add: PO Box 973 San Rafael CA 94901

LARSEN, ERIK
ART HISTORIAN, EDUCATOR
b Vienna, Austria, Oct 10, 11; US citizen. Study: Inst Superieur Hist Art & Archeol, Brussels, Belg, BA; Cath Univ Louvain, MA & PhD; restoration with Jef Lammens, Ghent & Jules Defort, Brussels. Teaching: Lectr, Belg; res prof art, Manhattanville Col Sacred Heart, 47-55; instr, Sch Gen Studies Exten Div, City Col New York, 48-55; from lectr to vis prof, Georgetown Univ, 55-58, assoc prof fine arts, 58-63, prof fine arts, 63-67, head dept fine arts, 60-67; prof hist art, Univ Kans, 67-, dir, Ctr Flemish Art & Cult, 70- Pos: Dir & ed-in-chief, Pictura; Belg Govt Cult Mission in Brazil, 46-47; Am ed, Artis. Awards: Knight's Cross, Order of Leopold & Order of the Crown, Belg; Laureate, Inst France, Prix Thorlet, 62; mem, Jury Taras Shevshenko Mem, Washington, DC. Mem: Appraisers Asn Am; Am Asn Univ Prof; Asn Dipl Hist Art & Archeol, Cath Univ Louvain; plus others. Res: History of Northern Baroque and Northern Renaissance art. Publ: Auth, P P Rubens, with a Complete Catalogue of His Works in America, 52; auth, Les Primitifs Flamands au Musee Metropolitain de New York, 60; auth, Frans Post, Interprete du Bresil, 62; auth, Rembrandt & the Dutch School, Tudor, 67; ed, La vie, les ouvrages et les élèves de Van Dyck Manuscrit inédit des Archives du Louvre, Par un auteur anonyme, Acad Royale de Belg, 75; plus others. Mailing Add: 3103 Trail Rd Lawrence KS 66044

LARSEN, JACK LENOR
DESIGNER, WEAVER
b Seattle, Wash, Aug 5, 27. Study: Univ Wash, BFA, 50; Cranbrook Acad Art, MFA, 51. Work: Mus Mod Art, New York, NY; Victoria & Albert Mus, London, Eng; Stedelijk Mus, Amsterdam, Holland; The Am Archive, Detroit, Mich; Cooper-Hewitt Mus Decorative Arts & Design, New York. Comn: Wall Panels, comn by Louis Khan for Unitarian Church, Rochester, NY, 66; act curtain for Filene Ctr, comn by Mrs Jouett Shouse for Wolf Trap Farm Found, 71; theatre curtain, comn by Charles Luchman Assocs for Phoenix Civic Plaza, Concert Hall, Ariz, 72; silk banners, comn by Skidmore, Owings & Merrill for Sears Bank & Trust Co, Chicago. Exhib: One-man shows, Cranbrook Acad Art, Bloomfield Hills, Mich, 63 & Mus Decorative Art, Copenhagen, Denmark, 75; retrospectives, Stedelijk Mus, Amsterdam, 68, Mus Fine Arts, Boston, Mass, 71 & Renwick Gallery, Washington, DC, 72. Collections Arranged: Co-dir, Wall Hangings, Mus Mod Art, New York, 70. Teaching: Dir fabric design dept, Philadelphia Col Art, 61-63; artist in residence, Royal Col Art, London, 75. Pos: Chmn, US Sect, World Crafts Coun, 70-71, chief US del Gen Assembly, 73-; pres, World Crafts Coun, USA, Inc. 73- Awards: Gold Medal for design dir US Pavilion, Triennale, Milan, Italy, 57; Elsie DeWolfe Award, Am Inst Interior Designers, 71; Gold Medal, Int Furnishings Show, Monza, Italy, 73. Bibliog: Mildred Constantine (auth), Biography, 76. Mem: Haystack Mountain Sch (bd trustees, 54-, vpres, 70, chmn bd, 75-); Am Crafts Coun (bd trustees, 54-); Archit League NY (vpres, 65-66); Royal Soc Art, London. Publ: Co-auth, Elements of Weaving, Doubleday, 67; co-auth, Beyond Craft: the Art Fabric, Van Nostrand; co-auth, Fabrics for Interiors, 75; auth, The Dyer's Art, 76. Mailing Add: 41 E 11th St New York NY 10012

LARSEN, OLE
PAINTER, ILLUSTRATOR
b Mainistee, Mich. Study: Chicago Acad Fine Arts; Art Inst Chicago; Am Acad Art; also landscapes with Edward Timmons. Work: Michigan City Pub Libr, Ind; Riveredge Found, Calgary, Alta; Am Saddle Horse Mus, Lexington, Ky. Exhib: West Suburban Artists Guild,

Hillside, 72, Naperville Woman's Club Art Fair, 72 & 74, Hinsdale Fine Arts Festival, 74, Lyon's Club Ann Horse Show & Art Exhib, Oak Brook, 74 & DuPage Hosp Auxillary Ann Art & Crafts Fair, Glen Ellyn, Ill, 75; plus others. Awards: For Sir Dudly, Ky State Fair Animal Artists Exhib, 37 & Early Days of a Thoroughbred, Ill State Fair, 56. Bibliog: Articles in Globe Dem Tempo Mag, 51, Chicago Tribune, 51 & 52 & State J Regist, 67. Mem: Soc Animal Artists; Hinsdale Community Artists. Style & Technique: Realistic; honest portrayal of animal life; purity of form and color. Media: Oil, Pastel. Dealer: Findlay Galleries 814 N Michigan Ave Chicago IL 60611. Mailing Add: 441 S Adams Hinsdale IL 60521

LARSEN, PATRICK HEFFNER
PAINTER, SCULPTOR
b Port Arthur, Tex, July 11, 45. Study: Lamar Univ, BBA, 68; Sam Houston State Univ, teacher cert, 69; Stephen F Austin State Univ, MA, 70 & MFA, 73. Work: Southeastern Ark Art Ctr, Pine Bluff; Stephen F Austin State Univ, Nacogdoches, Tex; First Nat Bank of Ark, Little Rock; Univ Cent Ark, Conway. Exhib: 12th & 14th Eight-State Exhib, Okla Art Ctr, Oklahoma City, 70 & 72; 11th & 12th Midwest Biennial, Joslyn Art Mus, Omaha, Nebr, 70 & 72; First Contemp Int, John Morehead Gallery, Chico, Calif, 71; 16th & 17th Ann Delta Exhib, Ark Art Ctr, Little Rock, 73 & 74; 43rd & 45th Ann Exhib, Springfield Art Mus, Mo, 73 & 75; one-man shows, Ft Smith Art Ctr, Ark, 75 & SArk Art Ctr, El Dorado, 76; 54th Ann Exhib, Meadows Mus of Art, Shreveport, La, 76; Rocky Mountain Ann Watercolor Exhib, Foothills Art Ctr, Golden, Colo, 77; Ariz Nat Painting Exhib, Scottsdale Art Ctr, Ariz, 77. Teaching: Asst prof painting, drawing, sculpture, watercolor & design, Univ Cent Ark, Conway, 70- Pos: Chmn art dept, Univ Cent Ark, 71-72. Awards: First Place & Purchase Award, Fifth Ann Ark Artist Exhib, SE Ark Art Ctr, 72; First Place in 19th Invitational Exhib of Ann Ark State Festival, 76; Top Award, 18th Ann Ark Oil Painting Exhib, 77. Mem: Nat Art Educ Asn; Ark Art Educ Asn. Style & Technique: Hard-edged within an objective style of interpretation. Media: Acrylic and watercolor for painting; wood for sculpture. Mailing Add: Univ Cent Ark Box U1724 Conway AR 72032

LARSEN, SUSAN C
ART HISTORIAN, ART CRITIC
b Chicago, Ill, Oct 3, 46. Study: Knox Col, Galesburg, Ill, 64-66; Northwestern Univ, BA, 68, MA, 72, PhD, 75. Collections Arranged: The Montages of Charles Shaw, Washburn Gallery, New York, 77; The Gallery of Art Revisited (a re-creation of Albert E Gallatin's Gallery of Living Art at New York Univ, 1927-43; auth, catalogue), Grey Gallery & Study Ctr, NY Univ, 11/78. Teaching: Asst prof hist of art, Carleton Col, Northfield, Minn, 74-75; asst prof hist of art, Univ Southern Calif, Los Angeles, 75- Pos: Regular contribr, Art News Mag, New York, 60- & Artweek (W Coast art weekly), Oakland, Calif, 76-; reviewer, Choice, 75-; guest lectr, series of lectures on Richard Diebenkorn, Los Angeles Co Mus Art, Los Angeles, 77. Mem: Col Art Asn Am; Am Studies Asn; Southern Calif Art Historians Asn. Res: Abstract art of the 1930's; WPA in New York City; contemporary art in California. Publ: Auth, The American Abstract Artists: A Documentary History, 1936-41, Arch Am Art J, winter 74-75; co-auth, Going Abstract in the Thirties: An Interview with Ila Bolotowsky, Art in Am, 9-10/76; auth, Two Centuries of Black American Art, MS Mag, 1/77; co-auth, A Conversation with Richard Diebenkorn, J Los Angeles Inst Contemp Art, summer 77. Mailing Add: Dept of Fine Arts Watt Hall Univ of Southern Calif Los Angeles CA 90007

LARSON, BLAINE (GLEDHILL)
PAINTER, INSTRUCTOR
b Salt Lake City, Utah, July 13, 37. Work: Corcoran Gallery Art, Washington, DC; Rochester Art Mus, NY; Corcoran Gallery, Washington, DC. Exhib: Seven one-man shows, Jefferson Place Gallery, Washington, DC & Diane Brown Gallery, 77 & 78; Ten Washington Artists, Edmonton Art Mus, 70; Int Art Wash Exhib, 77. Teaching: Chmn painting, Corcoran Sch Art, 70-75. Pos: Co-chmn, Dupont Ctr for Advan Study, Corcoran Sch Art, 75- Bibliog: Andrew Hudson (auth), critiques in Washington Post, Art Int & Art Forum. Style & Technique: Calligraphic painting. Media: Acrylic on Paper. Mailing Add: Box 54 Point of Rocks MD 21777

LARSON, JANE (WARREN)
CERAMIST, ART WRITER
b San Francisco, Calif, June 2, 22. Study: Mem Art Gallery, Rochester Inst of Technol, NY; Swarthmore Col; Univ Rochester, BA(Eng, cum laude); Univ Calif, Los Angeles, sculpture with Anna Mahler. Work: Wash Co Mus of Art, Hagerstown, Md; Oak Ridge Community Art Ctr, Tenn. Comn: Outdoor mural (clay tile, 11 ft x 4 ft), Oak Ridge Community Art Ctr, Tenn, 65; fireplace hearth, home of owner of Appalachiana, Inc, Bethesda, Md, 73; fireplace hearth, comn by Mr & Mrs Grant Heilman, Buena Vista, Colo, 77. Exhib: Mississippi River Craft Show, Brooks Mem Art Gallery, Memphis, Tenn, 69; 1971 Exhib of Ceramics, George Washington Univ Dimock Gallery, Washington, DC, 71; 10th Biennial Exhib, Creative Crafts Coun, Washington, DC, 72; Technol & the Artist-Craftsman, Nat Show, Octagon Art Ctr, Ames, Iowa, 73; Now It's Clay, Northern Va Fine Arts Asn, 74 & The Kiln Club Fall Invitational, 74; Stoneware—New Forms & Ancient Glazes, Wash Co Mus of Art, Hagerstown, Md, 77. Collections Arranged: A New Look in Stoneware, The Artists Mart, Georgetown, Washington, DC, 72 & Ridgeway Gallery, Oak Ridge, Tenn, 77; Natural Themes & Ancient Glazes, McLean Gallery, Va, 74; Natural Themes & Glazes II, The Am Spirit Gallery, The Watergate, Les Champs, Washington, DC, 76. Teaching: Instr ceramics, Oak Ridge Community Art Ctr, Tenn, 63-66. Pos: Pres & mem bd, Oak Ridge Community Art Ctr, Tenn, 62-69. Awards: Hon Mention, Tenth Biennial Creative Crafts Coun of Md, 72; Purchase Award, Objects 73, Western Colo Ctr for the Arts, 73; Jurors' Mention for Excellence, New It's Clay, Kiln Club of Washington, DC, 74. Bibliog: Kathie M Smith (auth), Art pace changes, Oak Ridger, Tenn, 7/67; Gretchen Larson & Joyce Inderbitzin (auths), Ceramics at the torpedo factory, Ceramics Mo, 9/76; Libbie Powell (auth), Crafts reach fine arts realm as shown at museum this month, Daily Mail, Hagerstown, Md, 10/77. Mem: Artists Equity; Kiln Club of Washington, DC; Va Art League. Style & Technique: Work in reduction-fired, high-fire clays, chiefly on a flat board using plant materials; bottles are put together and glazed with an ancient Chinese glaze palette. Media: Stoneware. Res: Collection of ceramics; ceramics of Japan and the roots of modern ceramics, particularly American. Publ: Auth, A Tennessee mural, 6/68, Ceramics at Expo 70, 6/70, Hamada legacy, 10/70 & Collecting ceramics, 5/72, Ceramics Mo; auth, Can we consider beauty?, Crafts Horizons, 6/73. Dealer: Am Spirit Gallery The Watergate Washington DC; c/o Dir Paul Kotun Washington Co Mus of Art City Park Hagerstown MD 21740. Mailing Add: 6514 Bradley Blvd Bethesda MD 20034

LARSON, ORLAND
GOLDSMITH, DESIGNER
b Shaunavon, Saskatchewan, Can, Mar 6, 31. Study: Univ Saskatchewan, 50-51; Univ Wis, BSc, 59 & MFA, 60; Columbia Univ, 63-64; Sch for Am Craftsmen, 65; apprenticed in London, England with Michael Murray, 74. Work: NS Art Bank, Halifax, 77; NS Designer Craftsmen, Halifax; Ont Craft Coun, Toronto; Govt of Can Craft Collection, Ottawa; Univ of Wis, Madison. Comn: Presentation Ladle in Silver, Dalhousie Art Gallery, Halifax, NS, 74; Eastern Provincial Airways, Halifax Placque for Swissair, Eastern Provincial Airways, Halifax, 75; Int Fencing Awards with Herbert Hatt, NS Fencing Asn, Halifax, 75; Presentation Medal, Sch of Bus Adminis, Dalhousie Univ, 76; Anniversary ring, comn by Stephen Peterson, Armdale, NS, 77. Exhib: Can Govt Traveling Exhib, 65-66; Craft Dimensions, Ont Sci Ctr, Toronto, 69; Designer Craftsmen, Art Gallery of NS, Halifax, 73-76; Metal Four, Ont Craft Coun Craft Gallery, Toronto, 74; Soc of NAm Goldsmiths, Humber Col, Toronto, 74; Crafts of the Americas, Univ of Colo, 75; Crafts at the Olympics, Montreal, Que, 76. Collections Arranged: NS Designer Craftsmen 74, Mount Saint Vincent Univ, 74; Crafts Seventy-Eight, 78; Artisian 78, traveling, 78. Teaching: Assoc prof jewelry, NS Col of Art & Design, Halifax, 68-77; lectr art educ, Ottawa Teachers Col, summers 62-64. Pos: Art supervisor, Govt of the Southwest Territories, N Can, 61-63; vis instr, Saskatchewan Arts Bd, Fort Qu'Appelle, Saskatchewan, summer, 71; ed, NS Designer Craftsman Newletter, Halifax, 74-76; juror, Can Nat exhib, 72-77. Awards: Senior Award, Outstanding Work, Can Coun, Ottawa, Ont, 74; Production Award, Designer Craftsman, 76, NS Designer Craftsmen, Halfax, 76; Jubilee Medal, Contribution to Crafts, Queen Elizabeth II, 77. Bibliog: Shelia Stevens (auth), Focus on Orland Larson, Craftsman/L'Artisian, 70; Marilyn MacDonald, (auth), Take Thirty: NS Goldsmith, CBC Documentary (film), 74; Charles Atkinson (auth), Craft as Work, CBC (film series), 75. Mem: Can Crafts Coun (provincial dir, 74-76 & pres, 76-78); NS Designer Craftsmen (pres, 74-76); Can Conf of the Arts (dir, 75-77); Soc of NAm craftsmen (vpres, 71-73). Style & Technique: Metal & stones, mostly jewelry. Publ: Auth, Five Eskimo Readers, Queen's Printer, 60-66; auth, Craftsmen and the Government of Nova Scotia, 76, auth, Report from the President, 77 & auth, The Massey's Collect, 78, Artisian. Mailing Add: Box 316 Mahone Bay NS B0J 2E0 Can

LARSON, PHILIP SEELY
ARTIST, ART HISTORIAN
b Ventura, Calif, July 21, 44. Study: Univ Minn, Minneapolis, BA, 66; Columbia Univ, PhD, 71. Exhib: Bethel Col, St Paul, 76; Hanson-Cowles Gallery, Minneapolis, 77; one-man show, Madison Art Ctr, Wis, 75. Exhibitions Arranged: Burgoyne Diller, 71; DeKooning: Drawings & Sculptures (with catalog), 74; Naives/Visionaries (with catalog), 74. Pos: Cur, Walker Art Ctr, Minneapolis, 70-75; assoc prof, Minneapolis Col of Art & Design, 75-; contributing ed, Arts Mag, 75-; frequent contribr, Print Collector's Newsletter. Media: Cast Iron, Forged Steel, Metal Compound & Metal Fabric on Paper. Mailing Add: Minneapolis Col Art & Design 133 E 25th St Minneapolis MN 55404

LARSON, SIDNEY
PAINTER, CONSERVATOR
b Sterling, Colo, June 16, 23. Study: Univ Mo, AB & MA; Univ Okla; also with Thomas Hart Benton & Fred Shane. Work: State Hist Soc, Mo. Comn: Life Along the Missouri River, Mo State Training Sch Boys, Boonville, 50; Social History of Phelps Co, Rolla Daily News, Mo, 52; Social History of Insurance, MFA Ins Co, Columbia, Mo, 59; Social History of Ceramics & Metal, Riback Industs, Columbia, 67; Historical Architecture, First Bank Com, Columbia, 71. Exhib: St Louis People's Art Ctr, 64; Mo Pavilion, New York World's Fair, 65; one-man & group shows, Oklahoma City, Univ Mo, Columbia Col, Spiva Art Ctr & others. Collections Arranged: Missouri Masters, Mo Pavilion, New York World's Fair, 64-65; George Caleb Bingham Exhibs, 65; Thomas Hart Benton Drawings & Lithographs, 69; Benton Retrospective, Spiva Art Ctr, Joplin, Mo, 72. Teaching: Instr, Oklahoma City Univ, 50-51; instr, Univ Mo-Columbia, summers; dir art, Columbia Col, 51- Pos: Mus cur, State Hist Soc, Mo, 61-; dir cult exhib, New York World's Fair, 64 & 65. Awards: Ittner Fine Arts Prize, Univ Mo, 50; Okla Ann Award, Philbrook Art Mus, 51; Huntington Hartford Found, 62. Mem: Nat Soc Mural Painters; Mo Mus Assocs. Style & Technique: Realistic and abstract. Res: Private, federal, state and municipal restorations; conservation of art, especially of the Nineteenth and Twentieth Centuries. Publ: Auth, Introduction to Fred Shane Drawings, 64; auth articles on Thomas Hart Benton, 69, 74 & 75 & auth, Conservation of a Bingham, 72, Mo Hist Rev. Mailing Add: 2025 Crestridge Dr Columbia MO 65201

LARSON, WILLIAM G
PHOTOGRAPHER
b North Tonawanda, NY, Oct 14, 12. Study: State Univ NY, Buffalo, BS(art), 64; Inst of Design of Ill Inst of Technol, Chicago, MS(photog), with Aaron Siskind & Wynn Bullock, 67. Work: Mus of Mod Art, New York; Philadelphia Mus of Art; New Orleans Mus of Art, Am Arts Doc Ctr, Univ Exeter, Eng, Photog Archives, Univ Louisville, Ky. Exhib: Vision & Expression, Int Mus of Photog, Rochester, NY, 68; Portraits in Photog, Mus of Mod Art, New York, 69; The Expanded Photograph, Philadelphia Mus of Art, 72; Photo/Media, 72 & Sewn, Stitched & Stuffed, 73, Mus of Contemp Crafts, New York; Unique Photographs, Sculpture Multiples, Mus of Mod Art, New York, 73; Light & Lens, Hudson River Mus, Yonkers, NY, 73; Three Centuries of Am Art, Philadelphia Mus of Art, 76; Locations in Time, Int Mus of Photog, Rochester, 77. Collections Arranged: Moholy-Nagy Photographs (75 photographs with monogr; picture ed), Claremont Col, 75. Teaching: Assoc prof & dept chmn photog, Tyler Sch of Art, Temple Univ, Philadelphia, 67- Awards: Nat Endowment for the Arts, 71. Bibliog: Rourke & Davis (auths), New Frontiers in Color, Newsweek, 4/76; Skip Atwater (auth), William Larson—Time & Structure, Afterimage, Rochester, 12/76; David Featherstone (auth), Tension through color, Artweek, San Francisco. Style & Technique: Black and white, color photography and generative systems employed to synthesize images. Publ: Contribr, Great themes & art of photog, Time-Life Libr of Photog, 70-72; contribr, Three Centuries of American Art, Philadelphia Mus of Art, 76; auth, Fire Flies, Gravity Press, 76; ed, Quiver, Temple Univ, 77. Dealer: Light Gallery 724 Fifth Ave New York NY 10019. Mailing Add: 152 Heacock Lane Wyncote PA 19095

LASANSKY, LEONARDO DA IOWA
EDUCATOR, PRINTMAKER
b Iowa City, Iowa, Mar 29, 46. Study: Univ Iowa, BGS, 71, MA, 72 & MFA, 72; also with Byron Burford & 15 Stuart Edie. Work: Minn Mus Art, St Paul; Albrecht Art Mus, St Joseph, Mo; Laguna Gloria Mus Art, Austin, Tex; Norfolk Mus Art, Va; Davenport Munic Mus Art, Iowa. Exhib: Smithsonian Traveling Exhib Am Drawing Biennial, 69-72; Doane Col Nat Exhib, Crete, Nebr, 73; Young Am Graphic Arts, Bayreuth, Ger, 73-74; Contemp Am Engravers, Albrecht Art Mus, 74; Nat Print Exhib, Cent Wash State Col, 75; Smithsonian Traveling Exhib, 76-78; Mod Galerija, Ljubljana, Yugoslavia, 77; 500 Yrs of Printmaking, Metrop Mus Art, Manila, Philippines, 77; De Cordova Mus Art, Boston, Mass, 77; Minneapolis Inst Art, Minn, 77; Am Drawing 1927-1977 (travels one yr under US Info Agency), Minn Mus Art, St Paul, 77; Miami Graphics Biennial, Metrop Mus, Fla, 77; Santa Barbara Mus Art, Calif, 78; Norwegian Print Biennale, Fredrikstad Art Soc, Norway, 78. Teaching: Asst prof printmaking, Hamline Univ, 72- Pos: Nat Sci Found grant as field artist & ethnographer, under Dr Thomas Charlton, Teotihuacan Valley, Mex, 69-70. Awards: First Prize, Tex Fine Art Asn, 74; Purchase Awards, Midwestern Printmaker's Ann, Tulsa, Okla, 75, Boston Printmaker's, De Cordova Mus, 77 & Bradley Univ Mus, Peoria, Ill, 77; Print Award, Colorprint USA, Lubbock, Tex, 76. Media: Intaglio. Mailing Add: 1536 Hewitt Hamline Univ Print Dept St Paul MN 55104

LASANSKY, MAURICIO L
PRINTMAKER
b Buenos Aires, Arg, 1914; US citizen. Study: Superior Sch Fine Arts, Arg; Iowa Wesleyan Col, Hon DA, 59; Pac Lutheran Univ, Hon DFA, 69. Work: Art Inst Chicago; Seattle Mus, Wash; Libr of Cong, Washington, DC; Uffizi Gallery, Florence, Italy; Mus Arte Contemp, Madrid, Spain; plus over 100 univs & galleries, US & abroad. Exhib: One-man shows, Mauricio Lasansky: Selections from 30 Years of Printmaking, Iowa State Univ, Ames, 67, The Nazi Drawings, Palace Fine Arts, Mexico City, 69, Mus Art, Univ Iowa, 70, Dickinson Col, Carlisle, Pa, 72 & 74, Athens, Ga, 73 & Blanden Art Gallery, Ft Dodge, Iowa; Whitney Mus Am Art, New York, 71; 2nd & 3rd Int Biennial Exhib, San Juan, PR, 72 & 74; Int Print Biennale, Fredrikstad, Norway; American Prints 1973, Ames, Iowa; 2nd Am Biennial Graphic Arts, Cali, Columbia, 73; plus many others. Teaching: Dir, Free Fine Arts Sch, Villa Maria Cordoba, Arg, 36; dir, Taller Manualidades, Cordoba, 39; vis lectr, Univ Iowa, 45, asst prof art, 46, assoc prof art, 47, prof art, 48-, res prof, 65-67, Virgil M Hancher Distinguished Prof art, 67-71, res prof art, 71-72; Lucas lectr, Carleton Col, 65. Pos: Mem fine arts jury, Guggenheim Mem Found, 65. Awards: Guggenheim fels, 43-44, to Spain & France, 53 & 54, to Spain & Latin Am, 65; Bertha von Moschzisker Prize, Philadelphia Print Club Ann, 71; Dickinson Col Arts Award, 74-75; plus many others. Bibliog: L Edmondson (auth), Etching, Van Nostrand Reinhold, 72; Barry Schwartz (auth), Humanism in 20th Century Art, Praeger, 72; Jules Heller (auth), Printmaking Today, Holt, 72; plus many others. Mem: Col Art Asn Am (bd dirs, 70-). Mailing Add: Print Dept Univ Iowa Sch Art & Art Hist Iowa City IA 52242

LASCH, PAT
PAINTER
b New York, NY, Nov 20, 44. Study: Queens Col, City Univ of New York, BA. Work: Queens Col of City Univ of New York. Exhib: One-person exhib, AIR Gallery, New York, 73 & 77 & Zabriskie Gallery, New York, 75; Grids, Inst of Contemp Art, Philadelphia, 72; Options 73, Contemp Art Ctr, Cincinnati, Ohio; traveling exhibs, Walker Art Ctr, Minneapolis, 73, Inst of Contemp Art, Boston, 73, Wadsworth Atheneum, Hartford, Conn, 73 & Calif Inst of Arts, Valencia, 73; Clocktower Gallery, New York, 75; Private Notations: Artist's Sketchbook II, Philadelphia Col of Art, 76; Collection of M Britton & H Hedrick, Moore Col of Art, Philadelphia, 77. Pos: Guest panelist, Soho Ctr for Visual Arts, New York, 77. Bibliog: Corinne Robins (auth), articles in Art in Am, 3-4/74 & Arts Mag, 6/77; Jeff Perrone (auth), article in Artforum, summer 77. Style & Technique: Thread on muslin, impasto oil paint and photos on muslin related to genealogy. Media: Paint, thread. Dealer: AIR Gallery 97 Wooster St New York NY 10013. Mailing Add: 463 West St 228G New York NY 10014

LASH, KENNETH
EDUCATOR, WRITER
b New Britain, Conn, July 27, 18. Study: Yale Univ, BA, 39; Univ NMex, MA, 48; Univ Lille, 51. Teaching: Lectr art hist, San Francisco Art Inst, 59-64, chmn dept humanities, 64-70; head art dept, Univ Northern Iowa, 70-76, dir humanities prog, 76- Pos: Consult art & humanities progs; lectr changing concepts of cult, Conf on the Arts & Human Needs, Univ Wis-Madison, 75; mem, Role of the Arts Task Force, President's Comn on Mental Health, 77-78. Awards: Fulbright scholar, France, 50-51; Rockefeller Found travel grant in arts, Latin Am, 54-55; chief planner & adminr, Carnegie Corp grant for teaching the humanities in art sch, 64-67. Mem: Nat Coun Art Adminr; Nat Art Educ Asn. Res: Researching, planning, consulting and working on art programs based on changing concepts in culture. Publ: Ed & co-auth, Report on a Three-Year Experiment in the Teaching of Humanities, 68; auth, Children of turmoil, Change, 71 & In: TLE Six, Holt, 72; auth, Notes toward a new curriculum in art, NY State Coun on the Arts, 71; auth, The Elitist, the Populist and Mr Phillips, Leonardo, 73; auth, Art: saved by the infantry?, Arts in Soc, 75. Mailing Add: 2725 Rainbow Dr Cedar Falls IA 50613

LASKER, MRS ALBERT D
COLLECTOR
b Watertown, Wis. Study: Radcliffe Col, AB(cum laude); Oxford Univ; Univ Wis, hon LLD; Univ Southern Calif, hon LHD; Bard Col; Womens Med Col; NY Univ; New York Med Col; Jefferson Med Col. Pos: Former art dealer, Reinhardt Galleries. Awards: Chevalier, Legion of Honor, Fr Govt; Presidential Medal Freedom, 69. Collection: Paintings. Mailing Add: 870 United Nations Plaza 24E New York NY 10017

LASKER, JOSEPH (L)
PAINTER, ILLUSTRATOR
b Brooklyn, NY, June 26, 18. Study: Cooper Union Art Sch, cert, 39. Work: Whitney Mus Am Art, New York; Philadelphia Mus Art; Springfield Mus, Mass; Joseph H Hirshhorn Collection, Washington, DC; Calif Palace of Legion of Honor, San Francisco. Comn: Murals, US Pub Works Admin, Post Off, Calumet, Mich, 41, Milbury, Mass, 42 & Henry St Settlement Playhouse, New York, 48. Exhib: Pa Acad Fine Arts Ann, 47-53; Whitney Mus Am Art Ann, 47-58; Nat Acad Design Ann, New York, 47-72; plus many others. Teaching: Assoc prof painting, Univ Ill, 52-53. Awards: Prix de Rome Fel, Am Acad Rome, 50 & 51; Nat Inst Arts & Lett Grant, 68; Cert of Excellence for Merry Ever After, New York Times Best Illus Children's Bk Awards, 77. Bibliog: 19 Young Americans, Life, 3/20/50; An American painter looks at art boom, Parade, 9/1/63. Mem: Nat Acad Design. Style & Technique: Realist. Media: Oil. Dealer: Kraushaar Galleries 1055 Madison Ave New York NY 10028. Mailing Add: 20 Dock Rd Norwalk CT 06854

LASKEY, DR & MRS NORMAN F
COLLECTORS
Collection: Twentieth century primitives, fauve-non objective, op; American primitive sculpture. Mailing Add: Croton Lake Rd Mt Kisco NY 10549

LASKIN, MYRON, JR
CURATOR, ART HISTORIAN
b Milwaukee, Wis, Apr 7, 30. Study: Harvard Univ, AB, 52, AM, 54; Inst Fine Arts, NY Univ, PhD, 64. Collections Arranged: Fountainebleau, Nat Gallery Can, 73. Teaching: Asst prof art hist, Washington Univ, 61-66. Pos: Res cur Europ art, Nat Gallery Can, 68. Awards: Italian Govt Grant, NY Univ, 59-60; Villa Itatti Fel, Harvard Univ, 65-67, Kress Fel, 66-67. Res: Italian 16th and 17th century painting. Publ: Contribr, Burlington Mag, Art Bull, Arte Illustrata & others. Mailing Add: Nat Gallery Can Ottawa ON Can

LASLO, PATRICIA LOUISE
SCULPTOR, INSTRUCTOR
b Park Ridge, Ill, Feb 22, 30. Study: De Paul Univ; Univ Ill; Univ Wis; Northern Ill Univ, MA. Comn: Sculpture, Landsmiths, Co, 72. Exhib: One-man shows, Janus Gallery, New York & Benjamin Gallery, 70, 73-75 & 78, New Horizons in Art, Chicago, 67, 68, 70 & 71; 51st Ann Show Wis Artists, Milwaukee Art Ctr, 68; Woman's Art Show, Kohler Art Ctr, Wis, 71; 51st Ann Rockford & Vicinity, 75 & Lakehurst Union League, Chicago, two-person show, Kingscott Gallery, 78. Teaching: Instr sculpture & painting, Countryside Art Ctr, 66-70, gallery dir, 67-68; instr life drawing & 3D design, Chicago Acad Fine Art, 68-70; instr art, Maine N High Sch, 70-75. Awards: Countryside Art Ctr, 68; Award for War God, Milwaukee Art Ctr, 68 & for Cyrano, Evanston Art Ctr, 69. Bibliog: H Haydon (auth), Review of show, Chicago Sun Times, 70-72; D Anderson (auth), Review of show, Chicago Today, 72; F Schultz (auth), Review of show, Chicago Daily News, 72; article in New Art Examr, 75. Mem: Art Inst Chicago; Mus Contemp Art; Kalamazoo Art League. Style & Technique: Highly polished non-objective forms concerned with spatial relationships and precarious balance. Media: Bronze, Aluminum. Dealer: Habatat Gallery 1820 N Telegraph Dearborn MI 48128; Benjamin Gallery 900 N Michigan Ave Chicago IL 60611. Mailing Add: Rt 2 Box 152D Lawton MI 49665

LASSAW, IBRAM
SCULPTOR
b Alexandria, Egypt, May 4, 13; US citizen. Study: Sculpture Ctr, 26-30; Beaux Arts Inst Design, 30-31; City Col New York. Work: Albright-Knox Art Gallery, Buffalo; Baltimore Mus Art; Whitney Mus Am Art & Mus Mod Art, New York; Mus Mod Art, Rio de Janeiro, Brazil; plus many others. Comn: Sculpture, comn by Percival Goodman for Beth El Temple, Springfield, Mass; Baldachin & altar screen, House of Theology of Franciscan Fathers, Centerville, Ohio; hanging sculpture for lobby, Hilton Hotel, New York; sculpture for Beth El Temple, Providence, RI, Temple of Aaron, St Paul, Minn & Temple Anshe Chesed, Cleveland, Ohio, plus others. Exhib: One-man shows, Drawings, Vanderbilt Univ, Nashville, Tenn, 70 & Zabriskie Gallery, New York, 77; Modern Sculpture, Sheldon Mem Art Gallery, Univ Nebr, Lincoln; Parrish Art Mus, Southampton, NY; Recent Acquisitions, Whitney Mus Am Art, New York; Artists of Suffolk County, The Abstract Tradition, Hecksher Mus, Huntington, NY, Retrospective, 73; Twenty-one Artists Over Sixty, Guild Hall, East Hampton, NY, 73; Contemp Am Sculpture, Soc of the Four Arts, Palm Beach, Fla, 74; Work of Candidates for Art Awards, Acad Art Gallery, Nat Inst Arts & Lett, New York, 74; Sculpture—Am Directions 1945-75, Nat Collection Fine Arts, Smithsonian Inst, Washington, DC, 75; Sculptors of the 1950s, Art Gallery, Univ Calif, Santa Barbara, 76; The Golden Door: Artist-Immigrants 1876-1976, Hirshhorn Mus, Washington, DC, 76; Two Hundred Yrs of Am Sculpture, Whitney Mus Am Art, New York, 76; plus many others. Teaching: Instr sculpture, YMHA, 92nd St, New York, 35 36; instr sculpture, Am Univ, 50; artist in residence, Duke Univ, 62-63; vis artist, Univ Calif, Berkeley, 65-66; adj fac, Southampton Col, 66-; vis prof, Brandeis Univ, Waltham, NY, 72; also pvt classes in studio. Pos: Fed Arts Proj, Pub Works Admin, 33-42. Bibliog: Dore Ashton (auth), Modern American Sculpture, Abrams, 70; George M Cohen (auth), A History of American Art, Laurel-Dell, 71; Bazin (auth), A history of world sculpture, Graphic Arts Soc; plus many others. Mem: Am Abstract Artists (founder, pres, 46-49); Artists Club. Dealer: Kennedy Galleries 20 E 56th St New York NY 10022. Mailing Add: PO Box 487 East Hampton NY 11937

LASSITER, VERNICE (VERNICE LASSITER BROWN)
PAINTER
b Millry, Ala, Nov 6, 27. Study: Univ Ala, with August Trovoahe; Famous Artist Sch; Art Students League; also with Joseph Hirsch, Robert Brackman & Valdi Maris. Comn: Portraits of each Jr Miss, comn by United Air Lines, 70; mural, Sci Med Bldg, Univ S Ala, 74. Exhib: Southeastern Ann Exhib, Atlanta, Ga, 57; 26th & 27th Miniature Painters, Sculptors & Gravers Soc, Washington, DC, 59 & 60; Mobile's Cult Exchange Prog, Malagna, Spain, 65; Sears Vincent Price Traveling Show, 70; plus many other one-man & group shows. Teaching: Pvt classes, lect & demonstrations in painting. Awards: First & Best of Show & Gold Cup, Mobile Art Asn Azales Trail Exhib, 61; First & Best of Show & Gold Cup, Mobile Art Asn Outdoor Art Exhib; First Watercolor Gold Plaque, Ala State Fair, 65. Bibliog: Donald A Burrows (auth), rev in Ft Worth Art Mus Catalog; Sterling McIlhany (auth), article in Am Artist. Mem: Mobile Art Asn; Birmingham Art Asn; Eastern Shore Art Asn. Media: Mixed Media. Mailing Add: 4951 Winslow Dr Mobile AL 36608

LASTRA, LUIS
ART DEALER
b Cuba, May 5, 30. Study: Univ Havana. Pos: Art ed, Visual Arts Bull, Orgn Am States, 63-69; art dealer, Pyramid Galleries, Washington, DC, 69- Specialty: Contemporary art; Latin American art. Mailing Add: 2121 P St NW Washington DC 20037

LASUCHIN, MICHAEL
PRINTMAKER, PAINTER
b Kramatorsk, Russia, July 24, 23; US citizen. Study: Rostow Col Art, Russia, 40-41; Philadelphia Col Art, BFA; Tyler Sch Art, Temple Univ, MFA. Work: Libr Cong, Washington, DC; Philadelphia Mus Art; William Penn Mem Mus, Harrisburg, Pa; Springfield Art Mus, Mo; Allentown Art Mus, Pa. Comn: Print, Print Club Philadelphia, 74. Exhib: Nat Exhib Prints, Libr Cong, 73 & 75; Biennial Open Competition, Print Club Philadelphia, 73, 75 & 76; 1st Int Biennial Exhib Graphic Art, Segovia, Spain, 74; New American Graphics, Univ Wis-Madison, 75; 11th Int Exhib Graphic Arts, Mus Mod Art, Ljubljana, Yugoslavia, 75; 3rd Int Drawing Biennale, Cleveland, Eng, 77; 4th Hawaii Nat Print Exhib, Honolulu Acad of Art, 77; Watercolor USA, Springfield Art Mus, Mo, 77. Teaching: Asst prof printmaking, Philadelphia Col Art, 72- Awards: Medal of Honor, Painters & Sculptors Soc NJ, 73; Stella Drabkin Mem Prize & Mem Award Medallion, Am Color Print Soc, 74; Gallery de Silva Award, Nat Watercolor Soc, 77. Bibliog: Cynthia B Frost (auth), Paintings suggest..., Daily Pennsylvanian, 11/20/74; Bill Southwell (auth), Exhibiting new talent, Drummer, 4/22/75; Dorothy Grafly (auth), Art contrasts, Art in Focus, 4/75. Mem: Boston Printmakers; Audubon Artists; Nat Watercolor Soc; Artists Equity Asn; Am Color Print Soc. Style & Technique: Abstract geometrics; all printmaking media and airbrush. Media: Printmaking, Watercolor. Publ: Contribr, Folio '76. Dealer: Venable-Neslage Gallery 1742 Connecticut Ave NW Washington DC 20009; McCleaf Gallery 1713 Walnut St Philadelphia PA 19103. Mailing Add: 120 E Cliveden St Philadelphia PA 19119

LATHAM, BARBARA
PAINTER, ILLUSTRATOR
b Walpole, Mass, June 6, 96. Study: Norwich Art Sch, Conn; Pratt Inst; Art Students League; also with Andrew Dasburg. Work: Metrop Mus Art Print Collection; Libr of Cong, Washington, DC; Santa Fe Mus; Philadelphia Mus; var Tex mus. Exhib: Three Whitney Mus Am Art Ann; Brooklyn Mus Watercolor Int, 40; Prints, Carnegie Inst, 44; Prints, Nat Acad Design, 46, 48 & 49; Chicago Mus Watercolor Int; Gov's Gallery, Capitol Bldg, Santa Fe, NMex, 77; plus others. Awards: Several Purchase Prizes. Media: Oil. Publ: Illusr, Pedro, Nina & Perrito, Harper & Row, 39; illusr, Calling South America, Ginn, 45; illusr, Perrito's Pup, Knopf, 46; illusr, Tales of Old Time Texas, Little, 55; illusr, Flying Horseshoe Ranch, Viking Press, 55. Dealer: Allied Artists Gallery A Taos NM 87571. Mailing Add: 250 E Alameda Apt 137 Santa Fe NM 87501

LATHAM, CATHERINE DORIS
GALLERY DIRECTOR, PAINTER
b Willow Springs, Mo, Apr 5, 20. Study: Springfield Art Mus Sch Art, 69-72, with Robert Johnson, Bill Armstrong & Seigfried Rhinehardt; Spiva Art Ctr, Joplin, Mo, 71, with Edgar A Whitney. Exhib: Watercolor USA, Springfield Art Mus, Mo, 70-72 & 74, exhib, 71; Little Rock Fine Arts Ctr, Ark, 71-74; 6th Greater New Orleans Int, La, 76; Shreveport Parks and Recreation Nat, Barnwell Art Ctr, La, 76; one-man show, Seven E Seventh Gallery, Lawrence, Kans, 76; Southern Watercolor Soc Ann, Memphis, Tenn, 77; Laguna Gloria Art Mus, Austin, Tex, 78; Columbus Mus of Arts and Sci, Ga, 78. Pos: Founding mem, part-owner, art coordr & dir installations, Park Cent Gallery, Springfield, 72-; owner, Latham's Far-Out Gallery, Strafford, 72- Awards: First Place Cash Award, Prof & Fac, State Mo, 70 & 71, Outstanding Work, 77. Bibliog: Edgar A Albin (auth), The Arts, article in Springfield News & Leader, 5/76; Mary Petersen (auth), Different strokes, Lawrence J World, Kans, 7/2/77; Edgar A Albin (auth), cover of The View, Springfield, 3/11/78. Mem: Kans City Artists Coalition, Mo; Southern Watercolor Soc. Style & Technique: Lyrical abstraction; abstract expressionism; color field and some realism. Media: Acrylic, Charcoal. Mailing Add: RR 3 Box 161 Strafford MO 65757

LATHROP, CHURCHILL PIERCE
ART HISTORIAN
b New York, NY, Aug 26, 00. Study: Rutgers Univ, LittB, with John C Van Dyck; Princeton Univ, AM, with Rufus Morey; Dartmouth Col, Hon AM, 37. Teaching: Prof Medieval, Renaissance & Mod Art, Dartmouth Col, 28-70, chmn dept art, 37-47 & 64-68. Pos: Dir art galleries, Dartmouth Col, 40-66, dir emer, 66-, actg dir, 73-74; art consult, Dartmouth Col, 68. Mem: Am Asn Mus; Col Art Asn Am; Mus Mod Art, New York; Soc Archit Historians; Am Asn Univ Prof. Publ: Co-auth, The Individual & the World, 42; auth, Paul Sample, 48; auth, The Story of Art at Dartmouth, 51. Mailing Add: 7 Sargent St Hanover NH 03755

LATHROP, DOROTHY P
ILLUSTRATOR, WRITER
b Albany, NY, Apr 16, 91. Study: Teachers Col, Columbia Univ; Pa Acad Fine Arts; Art Students League; also with Henry McCarter & F Luis Mora. Work: Libr Cong, Washington, DC; Albany Inst Hist & Art; Woodmere Art Gallery, Philadelphia; Holyoke Mus, Mass. Exhib: Nat Acad Design & Soc Am Graphic Artists, New York; Pa Acad Fine Arts, Philadelphia; Libr Cong, Washington, DC; Woodmere Art Gallery. Awards: Caldecott Medal for Animals of the Bible, 38; Eyre Medal, Philadelphia Watercolor Exhib, 39; Pennell Purchase Prize, Libr Cong, 46; plus others. Mem: Assoc Nat Acad Design; Soc Am Graphic Artists; Albany Print Club; Philadelphia Watercolor Club; Kent Art Asn; plus others. Publ: Illusr, Puppies for Keeps, 43; auth & illusr, Who Goes There, 63 & Let Them Live, 66, Macmillan; illusr, Bells and Grass, Viking Press, 64 & Animals of the Bible, Lippincott, 69; plus many others. Mailing Add: Undermountain Rd Falls Village CT 06031

LATHROP, GERTRUDE K
SCULPTOR
b Albany, NY, Dec 24, 96. Study: Art Students League; Sch Am Sculpture; also with Solon Borglum & Charles Grafly. Work: Houston Pub Libr, Tex; Albany Pub Libr, NY; NY State Teachers Col; Smithsonian Inst, Washington, DC; Brookgreen Gardens, SC. Comn: War Mem, Mem Grove, Albany, NY; commemorative half-dollar, Albany & New Rochelle, NY; medals, Garden Club Am, 42 & 50, Hispanic Soc Am, 50, Mariners' Mus, 54, NY State Univ Hall of Fame, 62 & 66 & Nat Steeplechase & Hunt Asn, 64; plus others. Exhib: One-man shows, Albany Inst Hist & Art, 57 & 66 & Woodmere Art Gallery, Philadelphia, 63. Awards: Medal of Honor, Allied Artists Am, 64; Silver Medal, Pen & Brush Club, 67; Saltus Gold Medal for merit, Nat Acad Design, 70; plus others. Mem: Nat Acad Design; Nat Inst Arts & Lett; Nat Sculpture Soc; Soc Medalists; Am Numis Soc; plus others. Mailing Add: Under Mountain Rd Falls Village CT 06031

LAUB-NOVAK, KAREN
PAINTER, PRINTMAKER
b Minneapolis, Minn, Aug 25, 37. Study: Carleton Col, Northfield, Minn, BA; State Univ Iowa, with Mauricio Lasansky, MFA; Sch Vision. Salzburg, Austria, with Oskar Kokoschka. Work: Carleton Col; Yale Univ; St Vincent's Archabbey; Union Theol Sem. New York; Pac Sch Relig. Comn: 12-ft bronze tribute to Norman Borlaug, 1971 Nobel Peace Prize Winner, Cresco, Iowa. Exhib: One-woman shows. Des Moines Art Mus, 66, Union Court Gallery, San Francisco, 66-68, Los Robles Gallery, 68, Rochester Art Ctr, Minn, 70, Rockefeller Found, 74, Univ Tenn, 74, Pac Sch Relig, 74 & Yale Univ, 75; plus others. Teaching: Instr drawing, Carleton Col, 61-62; lectr at various cols & univs throughout the country, 68- Bibliog: L P Ruotolo (auth), A new apocalypse, Motive Mag, 66. Style & Technique: Abstract combined with detailed figures showing muscle structure; intense color. Publ: Auth, Religious & Artistic Imagination, 71; illusr, Skunk Named Zorrie (children's bk), 72; auth, Art & Mysticism are a Journey, 73; auth & illusr, article, Anima Mag, Spring 1976; contribr, Momentum Mag, 75, Lexington Theological Quart, 77, Creative Living, 77, The New Rev of Bks, 77 & Parabola Mag, 78. Mailing Add: c/o AEI 1150 17th St NW Washington DC 20036

LAUCK, ANTHONY JOSEPH
SCULPTOR, EDUCATOR
b Indianapolis, Ind, Dec 30, 08. Study: John Herron Art Sch, Indianapolis, dipl prof grade in sculpture; Corcoran Sch Art, Washington, DC, cert advan study in sculpture & painting; also with Oronzio Maldarelli, Ivan Mestrovic, Carl Milles, Hugo Robus & Heinz Warneke. Work: Pa Acad Fine Arts, Philadelphia; Corcoran Gallery Art, Washington, DC; Butler Inst Fine Arts, Youngstown, Ohio; Indianapolis Mus Art; Gary Art Ctr, Ind. Comn: Set of facet windows, Congregation of Holy Cross, Ind Prov, Moreau Sem Chapel, Univ Notre Dame, 53; limestone image of Our Lady of the Univ, Univ Notre Dame, 63; 12 stained glass windows, Ursuline Motherhouse, Chatham, Ont, Can, 64. Exhib: Fairmount Park Art Asn Int Exhib, Philadelphia, 48; Nat Exhib Art, Pa Acad Fine Arts, 49 & 53; Ind Artists' Exhib, Indianapolis Mus Art, 50, 51, 54 & 56; Audubon Artists', Nat Acad Arts, NY, 52-75. Collections Arranged: The Work of John B Flannagan, Art Gallery, Univ Notre Dame, 61, The German Impressionists, 70 & The Graphic Work of Georges Rouault (with introd), 72. Teaching: Prof drawing & sculpture in var media, Univ Notre Dame, 50-73. Pos: Conf planning comt, Mid-Am Col Art Asn, 67-72. Awards: For St John Beside the Cross in carved walnut, Fairmount Park Art Asn, 48; Monk at Prayer in limestone, Pa Acad Art, 53; The Wife of Lot in terra cotta, Indianapolis Mus Art, 54. Bibliog: Dean A Porter (auth), Anthony Lauck: sculptor, 70 & Edward Fischer (auth), The many facets of Anthony Lauck, 73, Univ Notre Dame Art Gallery Publ. Style & Technique: Variance between impressionistic form and abstract expressionism. Media: Wood, Stone. Dealer: Jacques Seligman & Co Inc 5 E 57th St New York NY 10022. Mailing Add: Moreau Sem Notre Dame IN 46556

LAUFFER, ALICE A
PAINTER, PRINTMAKER
b Mokena, Ill, Oct 25, 19. Study: Chicago Acad Fine Art, cert; Art Inst Chicago; also with Paul Weighardt. Work: Art Inst Chicago; Minn Mus Art, St Paul. Exhib: Drawings USA, Minn Art Mus, St Paul, 68, Traveling Exhib, 73-75; Nat Print & Drawing Competition, Dulin Gallery, Knoxville, 70 & 73; Contemporary American Drawings V, Smithsonian Traveling Exhib, 72-74; Nat Collection Fine Arts, Washington, DC & Smithsonian Traveling Exhib, 73-75; Nat Print & Drawing Show, Second St Gallery, Va, 75; one-person shows, Ill Arts Coun, Chicago, 75 & Artemisia S Gallery, Chicago, 77; Critics Choice, 1134 Gallery, Chicago, 76; Hyde Park Art Ctr, Chicago, 78; plus others. Awards: James Broadus Clarke Award, Art Inst Chicago, 69; Drawings USA Purchase Award, Minn Mus Art, 73. Mem: Arts Club Chicago. Style & Technique: Abstract paintings and drawings in a spray technique. Media: Acrylic, Watercolor, Lithography. Mailing Add: 4 E Ohio St Studio 36 Chicago IL 60611

LAUFMAN, SIDNEY
PAINTER
b Cleveland, Ohio, Oct 29, 91. Study: Cleveland Sch Art; Art Inst Chicago; Art Students League. Work: Metrop Mus Art, Mus Mod Art & Whitney Mus Am Art, New York; Art Inst Chicago; Corcoran Gallery Art, Washington, DC; plus others. Exhib: One-man shows, Galerie Devambez, Paris, 22, Marie Sterner Gallery, New York, 22, Arts Club Chicago, 27, Galerie Katia Grahoff, Paris, 29 & De Haucke Gallery, New York, 31; Retrospective, Forum Gallery, New York, 62, George Peabody Col, Nashville, Tenn, 63, Lowe Gallery, Univ Miami, Fla, 64 & Ft Lauderdale Mus, Fla, 64; plus many others. Teaching: Instr painting, Art Students League, 38-50; vis lectr painting, Brandeis Univ, 59-60. Awards: Mr & Mrs Frank G Logan Prize, Art Inst Chicago, 32; Third Prize, Carnegie Int, 34; First Altman Prize, Nat Acad Design, 37; plus others. Mem: Nat Acad Design; Woodstock Artists Asn. Media: Oil. Dealer: Forum Gallery 1018 Madison Ave New York NY 10021. Mailing Add: 1038 S Osprey Ave Sarasota FL 33577

LAUGESEN, MADELYN A
ART DEALER, PATRON
b Duluth, Minn, Oct 10, 18. Study: Univ of Rochester, NY, BM, Univ of Louisville, Ky, MM. Pos: Dir, Young Artists Promotions, Inc, Louisville, 59-64; owner-dir, Thor Gallery, Louisville, 64- Specialty: Contemporary American and European artists. Interest: African sculpture; contemporary works by serious young artists from universities and art schools; prints by established world artists. Mailing Add: 734-736 S First Louisville KY 40202

LAURENT, JOHN LOUIS
PAINTER, EDUCATOR
b Brooklyn, NY, Nov 27, 21. Study: With Walt Kuhn, 46-48; Syracuse Univ, BFA, 48; Acad Grande Chaumiere, Paris, 48-49; Ind Univ, MAT, 54. Work: Univ Nebr; Univ Ill; First Nat Bank, Boston; De Cordova & Dana Mus, Lincoln, Mass; Addison Gallery Am Art, Andover, Mass. Comn: Great Bay Area Mural, Univ NH; Dove & Fish (two panels), St George's Church, York, Maine, 68. Exhib: One-man shows, Kraushaar Galleries, New York, 57-69, Mus Art, Ogunquit, Maine, 68 & Addison Gallery Am Art, Andover, Mass, 72; Father & Son, Sweat Mus, Portland, Maine, 69; American Paintings & Sculpture, Univ Ill, Champaign, 71; Frost Gully Gallery, Portland, Maine, 77; St Paul's Sch, Concord, NH, 78. Teaching: Asst dir drawing & painting, Ogunquit Sch Painting & Sculpture, summers 46-60; asst prof drawing & painting, Va Polytech Inst, 50-53; prof drawing & painting, Univ NH, 54- Awards: Louis Comfort Tiffany Found Grant, 62; Nat Coun Arts Award, 66-67; City of Manchester Prize, Currier Gallery, NH, 70. Bibliog: Rev in Time, 67; Peter Cox (auth), A talk with John Laurent, 69 & The best of Maine at Frost Gallery, 69, Maine Times. Mem: Barn Gallery (bd dirs, 68-71); York & NH Art Asns. Media: Acrylic, Oil. Dealer: Hobe Sound Galleries 739 Bridge Rd Hobe Sound FL 33455; Shore Gallery 8 Newbury St Boston MA 02171. Mailing Add: Mill Lane Rd York ME 03909

LAURER, ROBERT A
EDUCATOR
b Rochester, NY, Mar 10, 21. Study: Univ Rochester, BA; Harvard Univ, MA. Teaching: Asst prof art, Univ Colo, 49-53, Univ Ark, 54-55 & Skidmore Col, 55-56; asst prof & actg chmn dept art, Fairleigh Dickinson Univ, 62-68, dep chmn dept art, 72-, assoc prof art, 68-75, prof, 75- Pos: Asst dir, Mus Contemp Crafts, 56-60, assoc dir, 60-62. Mailing Add: Fine Arts Dept Fairleigh Dickinson Univ Rutherford NJ 07070

LAURY, JEAN RAY (JEAN RAY BITTERS)
DESIGNER, WRITER
b Doon, Iowa, Mar 22, 28. Study: Northern Iowa Univ, BA; Stanford Univ, MA. Work: Crocker Gallery, Sacramento; Fresno Arts Ctr, Calif. Comn: Wood panel, Fresno Redevelop Agency, 70; mural, stitchery & wood panels, Fresno State Univ Student Union, 70; mural, stitchery, United Calif Bank, Fresno, 70 & 72. Exhib: Five Craftswomen, Fresno State Univ, 71; Quilts & Dolls, Egg & Eye Gallery, Los Angeles, 71; Mus Contemp Crafts, New York; de Young Mus, San Francisco; Fresno Arts Ctr, Calif; also numerous one-woman & group shows. Teaching: Instr art, Fresno State Univ; instr art, Univ Calif, Davis; lectr & workshops throughout the country. Media: Fabric. Publ: Auth, Applique Stitchery, 68, Quilts and Coverlets, 70, Dollmaking: a Creative Approach, 70 & Cut and Painted Wood, 72, Van Nostrand-Reinhold; co-auth, Handmade Rugs, Doubleday, 71; auth, The Creative Woman's Getting-It-All-Together Handbook, Van Nostrand, 77. Mailing Add: 25090 Auberry Rd Clovis CA 93612

LAVATELLI, CARLA
SCULPTOR, WEAVER
b Rome, Italy, Aug 21, 29; US citizen. Study: Nat Gallery, Rome, Italy; Phillips Collection, Washington, DC; Stanford Univ New Law Bldg; H E Leone, Pres Repub Italy; Freidburgh Univ, Ger. Comn: Lobby Spingold Theater, Brandeis Univ, 69; New Bldg Upjohn Pharmaceuticals, Kalamazoo, Mich, 70; portrait group of S A S Ranier, III Prince of Monaco & his family, 71; Imperial Majesties Shah & Shahbanou Iran, 74; Kasser Found, NJ, comn by Mr & Mrs A Kasser & Mr & Mrs S Mouchary, 74-75. Exhib: Spoleto, Palazzo Collicola, Italy, 66; Palazzo della Quadriennale, 67; one-man shows, Hakone Mus, Japan, 72-73 & Phillips Collection, Washington, DC, 74; San Francisco Mus Art, 75-76. Bibliog: Lorenza Trucchi (auth), Lavatelli at Carpine, Momento Sera, 65; Ruggero Orlando (auth), Contemporary Art From NY (film), Rai Italian TV, 70; Gene Baro (auth), Carla Lavatelli Ritmi Spaziali, Washington Post, 74. Style & Technique: Simple organic forms and polished surfaces. Media: Stone, Bronze, Stainless Steel, White & Black Yarns. Dealer: Iolas 15 E 55th St New York NY 10022. Mailing Add: Vado Di Camaiore Lucca Italy New York NY Vado di Camaore Lucca Italy

LAVENTHOL, HANK
PAINTER, PRINTMAKER
b Philadelphia, Pa, Dec 22, 27. Study: Yale Univ, with Robert Georges Eberhard, BA(sculpture); Acad Belli Arti, Florence, Italy. Work: Yale Univ Art Mus, New Haven, Conn; Rosenwald Collection, Nat Gallery Fine Arts, Washington, DC; Print Collection, New York Pub Libr; Lowe Mus Art, Univ Miami, Coral Gables, Fla; Bibliot Nat, Paris, France; plus others. Comn: Island Mists (five-color lithograph), 69 & Image du Rose (etching), 72, Assoc Am Artists, New York; Ruth (four-color etching), Commentary Bk Soc, New York, 71; seven color etchings, George Visat, Paris, 72; 9 ed (color etching), New York Graphic Soc, Greenwich, Conn, 72-78; 12 ed (color etching), Original Print Collection Group, New York, 75-78. Exhib: Salon de Otono, Palma de Mallorca, 63-65; Festival Cult, Pollensa, Mallorca, 64; Philadelphia Mus Art, 68; Bodley Gallery, New York, 68, 69 & 71; Print Club Philadelphia, 69-74; Westchester Art Soc, 72; Atheneum of Philadelphia, 73; Mickelson Gallery, Washington, DC, 73; Nat Arts Club, New York, 75; plus many other group & one-man shows in US & Europe. Mem: Artists Equity Asn New York; Circulo Bellas Artes, Palma de Mallorca. Publ: Le Miroir aux alouettes', Ed Georges Visat, Paris, 72. Dealer: Bodley Gallery 1063 Madison Ave New York NY 10028. Mailing Add: RFD 1 Hanover St Yorktown Heights NY 10598

LA VIGNE, ROBERT CLAIR
PAINTER, DESIGNER
b St Maries, Idaho, July 15, 28. Work: Joseph Hirshhorn Collection, Smithsonian Inst. Exhib: One-man shows, Paula Cooper, New York, 64, Gotham Book Mart Gallery, New York, 69, Star-Turtle, New York, 72, Calif Inst of Arts, Los Angeles, 74; Art as a Muscular Principal, Amherst Col, 75. Pos: Resident designer, San Francisco Actor's Workshop, 58-63; art dir, Auerhahn Press, San Francisco, 59-64; assoc producer, Baby Blue Marine, Columbia Pictures, Los Angeles, 75. Awards: Obie for best design, New York, 67-68. Bibliog: Allen Ginsberg (auth), Preface to Lion Gallery exhib, San Francisco, 58; Herbert Blau (auth), The Black Art of Robert La Vigne, 61. Mem: Artist's Equity. Style & Technique: Mutable discussions of style and self; drawings by the surrealist method in all techniques; paintings in oil applied with soft brush. Media: Oil; Graphics, Stage & Screen. Publ: Illusr, Philip Whalen's Memoirs of an Interglacial Age, 60; illusr, Allen Ginsberg's Kral Majales, 65; illusr, Charles Olsen's Human Universe, 66; illusr, Allen Ginsberg's The Moments Return, 68; illusr, Allen Ginsberg's Howl, 71. Dealer: Andreas Brown 41 W 47th St New York NY 10036. Mailing Add: 11107 Aqua Vista North Hollywood CA 91602

LAVIN, IRVING
ART HISTORIAN
b St Louis, Mo, Dec 14, 27. Study: Cambridge Univ, Eng, 48-49; Washington Univ, BA, 49; New York Univ, MA, 52; Harvard Univ, MA, 52, Sheldon Fel, 53-54 & PhD, 55; Matthews Lectr, Columbia Univ, 57; Dumbarton Oaks, 57-59; Franklin Jasper Walls Lectr, Pierpont Morgan Libr, New York, 75. Teaching: Lectr hist art, Vassar Col, 59-62; assoc prof to prof, New York Univ, 63-73; prof, Sch Hist Studies, Inst for Adv Study, 73- Pos: Mem vis comt, Dept Art & Archaeol, Princeton Univ, 73-; mem vis comt, Dept Fine Arts, Harvard Univ, 77- Awards: Fulbright Fel, 61-63; Am Coun Learned Soc Fel, 65-66; Guggenheim Found Grant, 68-69. Mem: Corpus Ancient Mosaics Tunisia (mem steering comt, 69-); Nat Comt for the Hist of Art; Comite int d'histoire de l'art. Res: Art of late antiquity; Renaissance and Baroque sculpture. Publ: Auth, The hunting Mosaics of Antioch and their sources. A study of compositional principles in the development of Early Mediaeval style, Dumbarton Oaks Papers, 63; auth, Bernini and the crossing of Saint Peter's, Archaeol Inst of Am & Col Art Asn of Am, New York, 68; auth, Five new youthful sculptures by Gianlorenzo Bernini and a revised chronology of his early works, 68, Bernini's death, 72 & Divine inspiration in Caravaggio's two St Matthews, 74, Art Bull. Mailing Add: Sch Hist Studies Inst for Adv Study Princeton NJ 08540

LAVOY, WALTER JOSEPH
JEWELER, EDUCATOR
b Glens Falls, NY. Study: State Univ NY Buffalo, BA(art educ); Albright Art Sch, cert; Columbia Univ, MFA; Pa State Univ, DEd. Comn: 18K gold & diamond engagement ring, comn by Bruce Edgerton, Plainville, Conn, 73; 14K gold & diamond engagement ring, comn by Joseph Roberts, New Britain, Conn, 74; sterling silver & filled gold constructed necklace with pirite nuggets, comn by Mr Bertram N Carvalho, Jr, Ft Lauderdale, Fla, 74; sterling silver forged & fused pendant, comn by Mrs Reba M Hille, Ft Lauderdale, 75; sculptured sterling silver dinner ring (with large fragment of rare Tiffany glass), Mrs Celeste LeWitt, West Hartford, Conn, 77. Exhib: Conn Watercolor Asn 36th & 37th Ann Show, Wadsworth Atheneum, Hartford, 74 & 75. Teaching: Instr, State Univ NY Plattsburg, 52-54; instr home arts, Pa State Univ, 56-57; prof jewelry, Cent Conn State Col, 57-, chmn dept art, 67- Pos: Supvr art, K-12 Chappaqua Pub Sch Syst, NY, 48-52 & Clarkstown Pub Sch Syst, NY, 54-56. Mem: Am Crafts Coun; Conn Watercolor Soc (bd mem, treas, currently); Nat Art Educ Asn; Conn Art Educ Asn (pres-elect). Style & Technique: Elegant structured contemporary, usually involving forging and fusing; watercolor resist technique on board or fabric. Media: Sterling Silver and Gold with Rough Crystals. Mailing Add: Fairview Dr Farmington CT 06032

LAW, C ANTHONY
PAINTER
b London, Eng, Oct 15, 16; Can citizen. Study: With Franklin Brownell, RCA, OSA, Ottawa, Ont, Frederick Varley, RCA, OSA, Percyval Tudor-Hart, Quebec & expeditions with Frank Hennessey, RCA, OSA, Ottawa. Work: Nat War Mus, Ottawa; Que Mus; Dalhousie Univ Art Gallery, Halifax, NS; Univ of NB Art Gallery, Fredricton; Heritage Mus, Dartmouth, NS. Comn: Two paintings (40in x 68in), New Court House, NS, 75. Exhib: Royal Can Acad, 39-71; Nat Art Gallery, London, Eng, 44; Nat Gallery of Can, 46; NS Soc of Artist, 51-71; Biennal 1970, Atlantic Provinces Art Circuit; Can Soc of Watercolour; Retrospective, Centennial Art Gallery, NS Mus of Fine Art, 68. Pos: Artist-in-residence, St Marys Univ, Halifax, NS, 68-; vchmn bd of dir, Art Gallery, NS, 75-78, chmn bd of dir, 78-; dir to bd, Talent Trust of NS, 75- Awards: Jessier Dow Award, Montreal Mus of Fine Arts, 39-50. Mem: NS Soc of Artists, 52. Style & Technique: Landscape and seascape, expressionist and colourist. Media: Oil and occasionally Watercolor. Dealer: Zwicker's Gallery 5415 Doyl St Halifax NS B3J 1H9 Can; Kastel Gallery 1366 Greene Montreal PQ H3Z 2B1 Can. Mailing Add: 8 Halls Rd Boulderwood Halifax NS B3P 1P3 Can

LAW, CAROL L
PRINTMAKER, PERFORMANCE ARTIST
b Temple, Tex, July 21, 43. Study: Univ of Tex, Austin, BFA, 65; San Francisco State Univ, Calif, MA, 70. Work: Kansas City Art Inst Collection; Contemp Arts Ctr, NY Univ; Joslyn Art Mus, Omaha, Nebr; Grafisch Atelier Collection, Amsterdam, Holland. Comn: Mugicians Union Performance (with Betsy Davids, Jim Petrillo & Charles Amirkhanian), The Kitchen, New York, sponsored in part by NY Coun for the Arts, 75, San Francisco Mus of Art, 75 & Walker Art Ctr, Minneapolis, Minn, 77; Performance (with composer Charles Amirkhanian), Gallery Ghislain, Mollet-Vieville, Paris, France, 76 & Santa Barbara Mus of Art, Calif, 77. Exhib: Women USA, Laguna Beach Art Mus, Calif, 73; Works of Art on Paper, San Francisco Art Inst Gallery, 74; Interstices, San Jose Mus of Art, Calif, 75; three person show, San Francisco Sampler, Women's Inter-Art Ctr, NY, 76; Americana, San Francisco Mus of Mod Art, 76; Contemp Issues: Works on Paper by Women, Women's Building, Los Angeles, traveling, 77; one-person shows, Mills Col Art Gallery, Oakland, Calif, 76, four shows, Univ of NDak Art Gallery, Grand Forks, 76 & Don't Rock the Boat & Other Scenic Trips, Univ of Calif Art Mus, Santa Barbara, 77. Collections Arranged: California Society of Printmakers, Nat traveling exhib, 74-76; Art and Marginal Communication (with catalogue), Paris, France, exhibited at Galerie Herve Alexandre, Brussels, Belgium, Galery Ecart, Geneva, Switz, Galerie Bertesca, Geneva, Italy & Inst de l'Environ, Paris, France, 74; Bay Area Regional Graphics Competition, Helen Euphrat Gallery, de Anza Col, Curpertino, Calif, 78. Teaching: Lectr printmaking, San Francisco State Univ, Calif, 75; lectr printmaking, Univ of Calif, Santa Barbara, 76-77. Pos: Coun mem, Calif Soc of Printmakers, 71-75; co-founder & mgr, Brooklyn Brewery Printmaking Studio, Oakland, Calif, 74-75. Bibliog: Judith McWillie (auth), Exploring Electrostatic Print Media, Print Rev, Pratt Graphics Ctr, New York, Vol 7 (1977); Tom Cervenak (auth), Bay Area Printmakers, Visual Dialogue, Vol 3 No 3 (1978). Mem: Col Art Asn; Calif Soc of Printmakers; Women's Caucus for Art. Style & Technique: Recognizable imagery with a combined conceptual and surrealistic approach, altered photo source material, works with photo-printmaking and new media such as color Xerox, color 3M and blueprint as well as doing slide art performance works, and mixed media. Media: Performance; Print, Mixed Media. Publ: Auth, The artist, society & electronic imaging: a personal note, All Xerox (catalogue), The Arts Ctr, San Francisco, 76; auth, The Liberation of the Rubber Stamp (spec catalogue ed), Front, Vol 1 No IV, la Mamelle, Inc, San Francisco, 76. Mailing Add: 7722 Lynn Ave El Cerrito CA 94530

LAW, PAULINE ELIZABETH
PAINTER
b Wilmington, Del, Feb 22, 03. Study: Art Students League; Grand Cent Art Sch; with John F Carlson, Henry Snell, Margery Ryerson, Aldro Hibbard, John Pike, Wayman Adams, John Conaway & George Bridgman. Work: Norfolk Mus Arts & Sci, Va; Mus Athens, Greece; Ringwood Mus, NJ; Lyndon B Johnson Collection, Tex. Comn: Amon Carter Peak, Big Bend Nat Park, Tex, 61. Exhib: Allied Artists Am, 72; Nat Asn Women Artists, 72; Nat Arts Club, 72; Am Artists Prof League, 72; Knickerbocker Artists, 72. Awards: Allied Artists Am Prize, 60; Southern Vt Art Asn Prize, 62; First Prize, Catharine Lorillard Wolfe Art Club, 75. Mem: Pen & Brush Club (2nd vpres); Nat Asn Women Artists (first vpres, 55-57); Nat Arts Club; Catharine Lorillard Wolfe Art Club (chmn finance comt); Salmagundi Club. Style & Technique: Traditional landscapes. Media: Oil, Watercolor. Mailing Add: 15 Gramercy Park New York NY 10003

LAWRENCE, HOWARD RAY
DESIGNER, EDUCATOR
b San Francisco, Calif, Mar 21, 36. Study: Univ Calif, Berkeley, BArchit, 62, MA(sculpture), 64. Exhib: Light, Pa State Univ, 74, Space, 74, Systems, 75, Movement, 75 & Structure, 75. Teaching: Asst prof archit, San Francisco City Col, 69-70, Hampton Inst, Va, 70-71, Univ Kans, 71-72 & Pa State Univ, 72- Pos: Archit apprenticeship to var architects, Calif, 65-69. Awards: Harry Lord Ford Sculpture Prize, Univ Calif, 64. Style & Technique: Constructivist sculpture. Media: Wood, Metal. Res: Basic design process and visual communication products; color theory. Publ: Auth, Basic Design Process & Visual Communication Products, 74; auth, Visual Communication Products: Black, Gray & White Drawing Media, 75; auth, Visual Communication Products: Structure, 75; auth, Visual Communication Products: Movement, 75; auth, Visual Communication Products: Systems, 75. Mailing Add: Dept of Archit Pa State Univ University Park PA 16802

LAWRENCE, JACOB
PAINTER, EDUCATOR
b Atlantic City, NJ, Sept 7, 17. Study: Harlem Art Workshop, 34-39; Am Artists Sch, 38; Denison Univ, hon DFA, 70; Pratt Inst, hon DFA, 72. Work: Metrop Mus Art, New York; Mus Mod Art, New York; Phillips Mem Gallery, Washington, DC; Am Acad Arts & Lett, New York; Whitney Mus Am Art, New York. Comn: Three paintings, Fortune Mag, 8/48; painting, Container Corp Am, 53; lithograph, Benrus Watch Co, 67; portrait of Jesse Jackson for cover, Time Mag, 4/70; Olympic poster, Ed Olympia 1972, Munich, Ger, 72; plus others. Exhib: Migration Series (sixty paintings), Mus Mod Art, New York, 44 & M'Bari Artists & Writers Club, Lagos, Nigeria, 62; John Brown Series, Am Fedn Art Traveling Exhib, 47; retrospective, Brooklyn Mus, 61; Toussaint L'Overture Series, Fisk Univ, 68; Retrospective (travelling exhib), Whitney Mus Am Art, New York, 74; one-man shows, Brandeis Univ, Waltham, Mass, 65, Seattle Art Mus, Wash, 74, Birmingham Mus of Art, Ala, 74, St Louis Art Mus, Mo, 74 & New Orleans Mus of Art, La, 75. Teaching: Instr painting, Black Mountain Col, summer 47; instr painting, Pratt Inst, 56-71; prof painting, Univ Wash, 71- Pos: Mem, Wash State Arts Comn, 74 & 77; mem app by pres, Nat Endowment for the Arts Coun, 77- Awards: Guggenheim Fel, 46; Nat Inst Arts & Lett Grant, 53; Brooklyn Art Bks Children Citation for Harriet and the Promised Land, 73. Bibliog: Alain Locke (auth), And the migrants kept coming, Fortune Mag, 41; Aline B Saarinen (auth), Jacob Lawrence, Am Fedn Arts, 60; Bearden & Henderson (auth), 6 Black Masters of American Art, Zenith, 72. Mem: Artists Equity Asn New York (past pres); Nat Inst Arts & Lett; Black Acad Arts & Lett. Style & Technique: Figurative abstract painter. Media: Gouache, Casein, Tempera. Publ: Illusr, One Way Ticket, 49; illusr, Harriet and the Promised Land, 68; illusr, Aesops Fables, 70. Dealer: Terry Dintenfass Gallery 18 E 67th St New York NY 10021. Mailing Add: 4316 37th Ave NE Seattle WA 98105

LAWRENCE, JAMES A
PAINTER, PHOTOGRAPHER
b San Mateo, Calif, May 23, 10. Study: Univ Calif, Davis, grad, 33; Art Ctr, Los Angeles, art & photog, with Barse Miller, Will Connell & Charles Kerlee, 35-37; Chouinard Art Inst, Los Angeles, with Phil Paradise & Ricco Lebrun, 38; Art Students League, 40; New York Sch Mod Photog; also with illusr Louis J Rogers, San Francisco, 34. Work: Ford Collection, Dearborn, Mich. Exhib: One-man shows, Reed Galleries, New York, 41, Gump Galleries, San Francisco, 43 & Univ Nev, 53; Golden Gate Int Exhib, San Francisco; Art Inst Chicago; Metrop Mus Art, New York; Los Angeles Co Mus Art. Teaching: Guest instr watercolor, Stanford Univ, spring 48; also pvt students in watercolor at var periods. Pos: Tech photogr, Pagano Inc, New York, 40-41; mem, Nev State Coun Arts, 67-71. Awards: Cert Merit and Gold and Silver Medals, Golden Gate Int Exhib, 40-41; Am Artists Prof League, 42; Terry Art Inst Award; plus others. Mem: Nat Watercolor Soc. Style & Technique: Landscape and wildlife. Media: Watercolor. Publ: Contribr, Ford Times, Sunset Mag, US Camera & Carson Valley-Historical Sketches. Mailing Add: Rock Creek Ranch Gardnerville NV 89410

LAWRENCE, JAYE A
SCULPTOR
b Chicago, Ill, Jan 8, 39. Study: Univ Ariz, BFA, 60; Ariz State Univ, MFA, 75. Work: Ariz State Univ Collection, Tempe; Pac Lutheran Univ Collection, Tacoma, Wash; Yuma Fine Arts Asn Collection, Ariz. Exhib: Jaye Lawrence, Pac Lutheran Univ, 70 & 73 & Mercer Univ, Macon, Ga, 74; Fiber Art, Fairtree Gallery, New York, 72 & Laguna Beach Mus Art, Calif, 74; Objects '75 Designer Craftsman Show, Western Colo Ctr Arts, Grand Junction, 75; Americana, 76 & Gifts That Artists Give, 76, Mus Mod Art, San Francisco, Calif; 29th Allied Craftsmen Exhib, Fine Arts Gallery, San Diego, Calif, 77. Awards: Best of Show, 3rd Ann Phoenix Jewish Community Ctr Show, 69; Purchase Award, 4th Ann SWestern, 69; 12th Ariz Ann Award, 69. Bibliog: Marilyn Hagberg (auth), Jaye & Les Lawrence, 10/73 & Erik Gronborg (auth), Jaye Lawrence, 8/74, Craft Horizons; Kathlyn Russell (auth), Rope forms sculpture, Daily Times Advocate, 4/28/74. Mem: Am Crafts Coun; Allied Craftsmen San Diego (corresp secy, 74); Creative Weavers San Diego. Style & Technique: Organic sculptures constructed with wet formed rawhide, various weaving, non-weaving and basketry techniques; form and surface decoration, utilizing a variety of organic materials. Media: Manilla Rope & Jute, Dog Hair. Dealer: Spectrum Gallery 4011 Goldfinch San Diego CA 92103. Mailing Add: 2097 Valley View Blvd El Cajon CA 92021

LAWRENCE, LES
CERAMIST, SCULPTOR
b Corpus Christi, Tex, Dec 17, 40. Study: Southwestern State Col, Okla, BA, 62; Tex Tech Univ; Ariz State Univ, MFA(ceramics), 70. Work: Whitty Mus, San Antonio; Phoenix Art Mus, Ariz; E B Crocker Art Gallery, Sacramento, Calif; Pac Lutheran Univ, Tacoma, Wash; Ariz State Univ Collection, Tempe; among others. Exhib: Southern Sculpture 67, Pembroke, NC, 67 & Smithsonian Traveling Exhib, 68-70; Les Lawrence-Angels & Indians, Ariz State Univ Art Collections, 73; Les Lawrence, Elaine Horwitch Gallery, Scottsdale, Ariz, 74; California Ceramics & Glass, Oakland Mus, Calif, 74; Baroque 74, Mus Contemp Crafts, New York, 74; 28th Allied Craftsman Exhib, Fine Arts Gallery, San Diego, Calif, 76; Photo/Synthesis, Johnson Mus, Cornell Univ, Ithaca, NY, 76; Americana, San Francisco Mus Mod Art, Calif, 76; New Photographics/76, Cent Wash State Col, Ellensburg, 76; 100 Artist Commemorate 200 Yrs, Xerox Corp Exhib Ctr, New York, 76; Les Lawrence, Contemp Crafts Asn, Portland, Ore, 77; Ceramic Conjunction, Long Beach Mus Art, Calif, 77; Great Am Foot, Mus Contemp Crafts, New York, 78. plus others. Teaching: Instr ceramics-sculpture, Hardin-Simmons Univ, Abilene, Tex, 66-68; instr ceramics, Grossmont Col, El Cajon, Calif, 70- Awards: Tex Watercolor Soc 16th Ann First Purchase Award, San Antonio Art League, 67; First Purchase Award, Region 20 Tex Fine Arts Asn, 68; Calif Crafts IX Purchase for E B Crocker Art Gallery, 75. Bibliog: Marilyn Hagberg (auth), Jaye & Les Lawrence, 10/73 & Erik Gronborg (auth), Les Lawrence, 6/75, Craft Horizons; Les Lawrence, Ceramics Monthly, 4/74. Mem: Am Crafts Coun; Allied Craftsmen San Diego (secy, 74). Style & Technique: Organic clay handling with emphasis on surface decoration combining drawn and photographic images. Media: Clay, Cast Metal. Dealer: Elaine Horwitch Gallery 4200 N Marshall Way Scottsdale AZ 85251. Mailing Add: 2097 Valley View Blvd El Cajon CA 92021

LAWRENCE, MARION
ART HISTORIAN
b Longport, NJ, Aug 25, 01. Study: Bryn Mawr Col, AB, 23; Radcliffe Col, AM, 24 & PhD, 32. Teaching: Asst art, Wellesley Col, 24-25; instr art hist, Bryn Mawr Col, 27-28; from instr to prof art hist, Barnard Col, Columbia Univ, 29-67, prof emer, 67- Awards: Radcliffe, Carnegie Corp, Fulbright & Inst Advan Study Fels, 25-50. Mem: Col Art Asn Am; Archaeol Inst Am; Mediaeval Acad Am. Res: Late antique and early Christian art. Publ: Auth, The sarcophagi of Ravenna, Col Art Asn, 45, republ, Brettschneider, Rome, 70; also numerous articles in jours, 28- Mailing Add: 88 Morningside Dr New York NY 10027

LAWSON, EDWARD PITT
ART ADMINISTRATOR
b Newton, Mass, Sept 12, 27. Study: Bowdoin Col, BA; Inst Fine Arts, NY Univ, AM. Teaching: Instr, Toledo Mus Art Sch of Design, 54-56; vis lectr, Sir George Williams Univ, 63-67; lectr, Univ Ariz, 68-69; lectr, Northern Va Community Col, 73 & Smithsonian Assocs, 74-; spec vis lectr, George Washington Univ, 74- Pos: Curatorial asst, Toledo Mus Art, 56-57, supvr art educ, 57-59; asst cur, The Cloisters, 59-62; asst dir, Montreal Mus Fine Arts, 62-67; dir, Tucson Art Ctr, 67-69; admin asst, Int Exhibs Found, 69-70; asst dir, Am Asn Mus, 70-72; chief, dept educ, Hirshhorn Mus & Sculpture Garden, 73- Awards: Belg-Am Summer Fel, 56; Metrop Mus Art Travel Grant, 61; Montreal Mus Travel Grant, 65. Mem: West Mus League (vpres, 68-69); Am Asn Mus; Can Mus Asn (coun mem, 63-67); PQ Mus Asn (vpres, 63-65, pres, 65-67). Mailing Add: 1216 Raymond Ave McLean VA 22101

LAWTON, JAMES L
SCULPTOR, EDUCATOR
b Louisville, Ky, July 28, 44. Study: Louisville Sch of Art, Ky; Murray State Univ, Ky, BSc; Kent State Univ, Ohio, MFA. Work: Western Mich Univ, Kalamazoo; City of Detroit, Mich. Comn: Three Trusses Plus (painted steel sculpture), Cass Park, comn by City of Detroit, 77-78. Exhib: Louisville Art Ctr Ann, J B Speed Mus, Ky, 67; Mich Art Exhib, Detroit Art Inst, 70; 35th Ann Cedar City Nat, Braithwaite Gallery, Utah, 76; All Mich Bicentennial, East Lansing, Mich, 76; Seven for 76, Seven State Exhib, Eastern Ill Univ, Charleston, 76; Nat Sculpture 76 (travelling exhib), Univ Ga, 76-77. Teaching: Assoc prof sculpture, metal casting & ceramics, Kresge Art Ctr, East Lansing, 68- Awards: Third Place, Nat Metal Sculpture, Wis State Univ, 67; Hon Mention, Nat Small Sculpture, Ball State Univ, Muncie, 68; First Place, Mich State Fair, 74. Mem: Nat Asn Southern Sculptors. Style & Technique: Self-cast bronze, aluminum and iron; welding in brass, steel and aluminum. Media: Casting and welding from wax and stock material. Mailing Add: 3485 Zimmer Rd Williamston MI 48895

LAX, DAVID
PAINTER
b Peekskill, NY, May 16, 10. Study: Ethical Cult Sch, scholar, 24-28, with H R Kniffen, Victor D'Amico & Victor Frisch, CFA; Archipenko Art Sch, with Alexander Archipenko. Work: Gallery Mod Art, New York; Clearwater Mus, Fla; Laguna Gloria Mus, Austin; Pentagon War Art Collection; State Univ NY Collection; plus others. Comn: Several hundred genre paintings, Irving Mills Collection, 32-42; combat paintings, USA, Pentagon, 42-45; Denunciation (paintings), Grossman Mem, NY, 45-50; murals, Vet Admin Regional Off Bldg, New York, 50-52; paintings of New York in the 50's, comn by group of New Yorkers, Dutchess Community Col, 52-57. Exhib: Grand Cent Founders Show, New York, 39-46; Corcoran Gallery 18th Biennial, 43; Painting in the US, Carnegie Inst, Pittsburgh, 46; Nat Arts Club 20th Ann, New York, 70; 60th Anniversary Exhib, Tex Fine Arts Asn, 71, one-man tour, 74-75. Teaching: Chmn dept art, Dutchess Community Col, 58-73, prof, 73-77; emer prof, State Univ NY, 77- Awards: Mills Artists Fel, 32-42; Silver Medal for Painting, Int Inst Arts & Lett, 60. Bibliog: Swerdlow (auth), Denunciation Series, Laurel Press, 49; Valente (auth), 60 Paintings Since Denunciation, Hamilton Reproductions, 70; Brass (auth), Raunchy dogs of defeat, J Am Med Asn, 72. Mem: Grand Cent Art Galleries; Assoc Am Artists; Dutchess Co Art Asn; Int Inst Arts & Lett. Style & Technique: Social symbolism. Media: Oil, Polymer. Publ: Co-auth, Lax Paintings, TC in the Battle of Europe, 45, Denunciation, Paintings Concerning Man's Fate, 49, David Lax, Portraits, 51, David Lax, Paintings of New York in the Fifties, 72 & One Man Show, 75; plus others. Dealer: Washington Irving Gallery 126 E 16th St New York NY 10003. Mailing Add: Box 94 Red Hook NY 12571

LAY, PATRICIA ANNE
SCULPTOR
b New Haven, Conn, Aug 14, 41. Study: Rochester Inst Technol, MFA; Pratt Inst, BS. Work: NJ State Mus, Trenton. Exhib: 25th Ceramic Nat, Everson Mus Art, Syracuse, NY, 68-69; Warren Benedek Gallery, New York, 73; one-person show, NJ State Mus, 74; Contemporary Reflections, Aldrich Mus, Ridgefield, Conn, 75; Whitney Mus Am Art Biennial, 75. Teaching: Asst prof sculpture, State Univ NY Buffalo, 68-69; instr ceramics, Wagner Col, 69-71; lectr ceramics, Hunter Col, 71-72; asst prof ceramics, Montclair State Col, 72- Bibliog: Leon Nigrosh (auth), Claywork, Davis Publ, 75. Style & Technique: Topographical abstract landscapes. Media: Fired Clay, Metal, Wood. Mailing Add: 423 Broome St New York NY 10013

LAYCOX, (WILLIAM) JACK
PAINTER, DESIGNER
b Auburn, Calif, Mar 11, 21. Study: Univ Calif, Berkeley; San Francisco State Univ, BA, 48. Work: Holy Names Col Gallery, Calif; Gen Tire Int Collection, Akron, Ohio; Naval Hosp Collection, Oakland; Latter Day Saints Collection, Salt Lake City; Rosicrucian Egyptian Art Mus, San Jose, Calif; plus others. Comn: Paintings for calendars, Zellerbach Paper Co, San Francisco, 63 & Gen Tire Int Corp, 71, 72 & 75; paintings, Thompson Aircraft Corp, San Francisco, 65 & 66; Watercolor Series, Williamhouse-Regency, Van Nuys, Calif, 69-75; oil paintings, Delta Air Lines, Atlanta, Ga, 75-76; DeAnza Bicentennial (theme painting), City of Monterey, Calif, 76. Exhib: Gallery Americana, Carmel, Calif, 73-75; Crocker Art Mus, Sacramento, 74; Fresno Art Ctr, 75; West Coast Watercolor Soc Ann, San Francisco, 75; Royal Watercolor Soc-West Coast Watercolor Soc Joint Exhib, London, Eng, 75; one-man shows, Gallery Americana, Carmel, Calif, 76 & 77; Wortsman-Stewart Galleries, San Francisco, 77; Marjorie Evans Mem Gallery, Carmel, 77; Fresno Art Ctr, Calif, 77; Briand Galleries, Glendale, Calif, 77; plus others. Teaching: Instr watercolor, Jade Fon Watercolor Workshop, Asilomar, Calif, summers 71-73. Pos: Tech illusr, AEC, Oak Ridge, Tenn, 43-46; art dir, Bacon Am Corp, Muncie, Ind, 49-56; designer, Mission-Regency Cards, Van Nuys, 66- Awards: Best of Show, Diabolo Pageant Arts, 61; Second Award for Watercolor, Soc Western Artists, 63; Second Award for Oils, Calif State Fair, 65. Bibliog: Robert Miskimon (auth), From engineer to artist, Carmel Pine Cone, 73; Bold themes of American artists, Eastern Daily Press, Holt, Eng, 10/17/75; Eugenia West (auth), The fine art of travel posters, Sky Mag, 6/76; plus others. Mem: Soc Western Artists; West Coast Watercolor Soc. Style & Technique: Impressionistic; conveys strong color interpretation and maximum emotional content to the subject. Media: Oil, Watercolor. Publ: Auth, Dramatic Paintings From Familiar Scenes, Walter Foster Bks, 72. Mailing Add: PO Box 5054 Carmel CA 93921

LAYTON, RICHARD
PAINTER
b Wilmington, Del, Apr 15, 29. Study: With Frank E Schoonover & Carolyn Wyeth; Philadelphia Mus Col Art. Work: In many bus and pvt collections in US and abroad. Comn: Ten murals, incl Univ Del & E I du Pont de Nemours & Co; designer of 1973 Am Revolution Bicentennial Comn Medal. Exhib: Corcoran Gallery Art, Washington, DC; Am Watercolor Soc; Audubon Artists; Pa Acad Fine Arts, Philadelphia; Del Art Mus; plus many others. Collections Arranged: Sixteen regional & nat exhibs incl N C Wyeth Exhib, Pa State Mus, Harrisburg, 65, Brandywine Heritage, 71 & N C Wyeth Exhib, 72, Brandywine River Mus. Pos: Former cur, Brandywine River Mus, Chadds Ford, Pa; pres, Del Arts Soc, currently; pres, Brandywine Editions, Ltd. Bibliog: Del Today Mag, 5/71. Mem: Wilmington Soc Fine Arts; Nat Soc Mural Painters; Int Platform Asn. Publ: Auth, introd to N C Wyeth, Crown, 72. Mailing Add: 2600 W 19th St Wilmington DE 19806

LAZARUS, MARVIN P
PHOTOGRAPHER
b Albany, NY, June 1, 18. Study: Union Col, BA; Harvard Univ, LLB. Work: Mus of Mod Art, New York; Chrysler Mus at Norfolk, Va; Mabel Brady Garvan Gallery, Yale Univ, New Haven, Conn. Exhib: One-man shows, Portraits of Marcel Duchamp, East Hampton Gallery, New York, 63, Am Artists, New York State Coun on Arts, 64 & Faces, Marilyn Pearl Gallery, New York, 77; Artists, UNESCO, Paris, 65; Portrait in Photog, Fogg Art Mus, Cambridge, Mass, 67; Marcel Duchamp, Mus of Mod Art, New York, 74; Galerie Zabriskie, Paris, 77. Bibliog: N French-Frazier (auth), Artists and other famous people, Art News, 2/77; R Tessier (auth), Marvin Lazarus, Arts, 12/77. Style & Technique: Interpretive portraits of artists and sculptors in studio atmosphere. Publ: Illusr, The World of Marcel Duchamp, Time-Life; illusr, Documents of 20th Century Art, Dialogues with Marcel Duchamp, Viking. Dealer: Marilyn Pearl Gallery 29 W 57th St New York NY 10019. Mailing Add: 16 Sherman Ave White Plains NY 10605

LAZZARI, PIETRO
SCULPTOR, PAINTER
b Rome, Italy, May 15, 98; US citizen. Study: Ornamental Sch Rome, Master Artist, 22. Work: Art Inst Chicago; Miami Mus Mod Art; Nat Collection Fine Arts, Washington, DC; San Francisco Mus Art; Whitney Mus Am Art, New York. Comn: Bronze bust of Eleanor Roosevelt, pvt comn & in collection of FDR Libr, Hyde Park, NY, 65; frieze in high relief, Watergate West, Washington, DC, 69; bronze monument to Ed M Gallaudet, Gallaudet Col Alumni, Washington, DC, 69; bronze monument to Walter Reuther, United Auto Workers, Family Educ Ctr, Black Lake, Mich, 70; polychrome concrete murals & bronze fountain, Embassy Row Hotel, Washington, DC, 71. Exhib: Venetian Biennial, Italy, 47; Baltimore Mus, 52; Art Inst of Chicago, 52; Corcoran Gallery Art, Washington, DC, 59; Whitney Mus Am Art, New York, 65; Galerie Schindler, Berne, Switz, 67; Nat Collection Fine Arts, 70. Teaching: Instr sculpture & drawing, Am Univ, 48-50; head dept art, Col Holy Cross, 48-50; instr sculpture, Corcoran Sch Art, 65-69. Awards: Baltimore Mus Lord Prize in Sculpture, 52; First Prize for Sumi Drawing, Washington Watercolor Asn, 64; Soc Washington Printmakers Prize, 72. Bibliog: Seuphor (auth), A Dictionary of Abstract Painting, Paris Bk Ctr, 58; Washington Artists Today, Acropolis, 67; The outdoor sculpture of Washington, DC, Smithsonian Inst Press, 74. Mem: Washington Watercolor Soc; Soc Washington Printmakers. Media: Concrete, Bronze; Oil, Sumi Drawing. Publ: Auth & illusr, I Carbonizzati (series of 42 plates), 67; auth & illusr, Adam & Eve (series of 12 plates), 70. Dealer: Franz Bader 2124 Pennsylvania Ave NW Washington DC 20037. Mailing Add: 3609 Albemarle St NW Washington DC 20008

LEA, STANLEY E
PRINTMAKER, PAINTER
b Joplin, Mo, Apr 5, 30. Study: Kans State Col, BFA; Univ Ark, MFA. Work: Smithsonian Inst & Libr Cong, Washington, DC; Brit Mus, London; Inst Mex Norteamericano, Mexico City; Mus Fine Arts, Houston. Comn: Collagraphs, Hyatt Regency Hotel, Houston, 72; paintings, Ft Worth Nat Bank, 73, Citizens Bank, Richards, Tex, 74, Am Nat Bank, Austin, 74 & USAA Bldg, San Antonio, 74. Exhib: 48th Ann Soc Am Graphic Artists, New York, 67; Mainstreams Int, Marietta, Ohio, 68; Watercolor USA, Springfield, Mo, 69; 148th Ann Nat Acad Design, New York, 73; Nat Color Print USA, Lubbock, Tex, 74. Teaching: Prof printmaking, Sam Houston State Univ, Huntsville, Tex, 61-; vis prof, Mus Fine Arts, Houston, 68-71. Awards: Arts Nat, Tyler, Tex, 62; 20th Ann Tex Watercolor, Witte Mus, 69; 4th Ann Print & Drawing, Ark Art Ctr, 70. Style & Technique: Collage and ink viscosity in printmaking and painting; abstractions. Media: Collagraphs, Mixed Media Collage. Dealer: Moody Gallery 2015-J W Gray Houston TX 77019; Valley House Gallery 6616 Spring Valley Rd Dallas TX 75240. Mailing Add: 2118 Pleasant Huntsville TX 77340

LEA, TOM
PAINTER, ILLUSTRATOR
b El Paso, Tex, July 11, 07. Study: Art Inst Chicago, 24-26; study in Italy, 30 & NMex, 33-35; Baylor Univ hon LittD, 67; Southern Methodist Univ, hon LHD, 70. Work: Dallas Mus Fine Art, Tex; El Paso Mus Art, Tex; State Capitol, Austin, Tex; Pentagon War Art Collection; Humanities Res Ctr, Univ Tex, Austin; also in pvt collections. Comn: Murals, Court House & Pub Libr, El Paso, US Post Off Bldg, Pleasant Hill, Mo, Odessa, Tex & Washington, DC. Exhib: One-man shows, Ft Worth Art Ctr, Tex, 61 & El Paso Mus Art, 63 & 71; Inst Texan Cult, San Antonio, 69. Pos: Artist & war corresp, Life Mag, 41-46. Publ: Auth & illusr, The Wonderful Country, 52, The King Ranch, Vols I & II, 57, The Primal Yoke, 60, The Hands of Cantu, 64 & A Picture Gallery, 68, Little; plus others. Mailing Add: 2401 Savannah St El Paso TX 79930

LEACH, FREDERICK DARWIN
PAINTER, ART HISTORIAN
b Arkansas City, Kans, Sept 19, 24. Study: James Millikin Univ, BA; Univ Wis, with Carlos Lopez; State Univ Iowa, MA, MFA & PhD. Work: State Univ Iowa; Ball State Univ; Minn Mus Art. Exhib: Old Northwest Territory, Springfield, Ill, 46-57; Ohio State Fair, Columbus, 56 & 57; Ball State Univ Drawing & Small Sculpture; Exhibition 180, Huntington, WVa, 56-62; Encounter, Minn Mus Art, St Paul. Collections Arranged: National Print & Drawing Exhibition: Ultimate Concerns, Ohio Univ, 60. Teaching: From instr to asst prof art hist, State Univ Iowa, 48-56, actg head dept, 55; prof art hist & drawing & dir, Sch Art, Ohio Univ, 56-68; prof art hist & drawing, Hamline Univ, 68-, actg head dept art, 71-72, chmn fine arts div, 72-73, chmn art dept, 75- Awards: Juror's Exhib Award, Huntington, WVa, 57; Drawing Prize, Ball State Univ, 63. Mem: Col Art Asn Am; Midwest Col Art Asn; Minn Art Historians. Style & Technique: Representational; expressionist. Media: Oil, Arcylic; Bronze, Steel. Publ: Auth, Speculation on an artistic common denominator, Topic: 5, 63; auth, The Found Object, State Univ NY Col Buffalo, 65; auth, Review of Nathan Lyons', Photographers on Photography, Aperture, 67; auth, Paul Manship: An Intimate View (monogr), Minn Mus, 72; auth, The Ketuba: variations within a consistent Jewish imagery, In: The Ketuba, Hamline Univ Press, 75. Mailing Add: Dept of Art Hamline Univ St Paul MN 55104

LEADER, GARNET ROSAMONDE
ART ADMINISTRATOR
b Bessemer, Ala. Study: Maryville Col, Tenn, cert fine arts; Columbia Univ, MA(fine arts); Peabody Col, Tenn; Univ Tenn; Univ Ala; Art Students League, New York. Exhib: Birmingham Asn Art, Ala; Ala State Fair Art Exhib, Birmingham; Miss Univ for Women, Columbus. Teaching: Instr arts & crafts, Birmingham Pub Schs, 28-71. Pos: Pres, Bessemer Art Club; vpres, Kappa Pi Int Hon, 38-68, pres, 69- Mem: Birmingham Art Club (past pres & treas); Watercolor Soc Ala (past treas); Nat Art Educ Asn; Birmingham Art Asn; Southeastern Art Asn. Dealer: Lassetter & Co Birmingham AL 35203. Mailing Add: 5117 Main St Bessemer AL 35020

LEAF, JUNE
PAINTER, SCULPTOR
b Chicago, Ill, Aug 4, 29. Work: Art Inst Chicago; Mus Mod Art, New York; Carbondale Mus, Ill. Exhib: Contemp Am Artists, Chicago Art Inst, 69. Teaching: Instr visual fundamentals, Art Inst Chicago, 52-58, instr painting & drawing, 54-58; instr drawing, Parsons Sch Design, New York, 67-69. Awards: Fulbright Scholar, 59. Bibliog: Franz Schulze (auth), Fantastic Art, Follett, 72. Mailing Add: Box 18 Mabou NS B3J 1T5 Can

LEAF, RUTH
PRINTMAKER, INSTRUCTOR
b New York, NY. Work: Libr Cong; NY Univ; US Info Agency; Bowdoin Col Mus Art; Colgate Univ. Exhib: Sala Exposiciones, Escuela Nac Artes Plasticas, 67; Boston Mus, 70; De Cordova Mus, Mass, 71; Soc Am Graphic Artists, New York, 71; Galerie Art & Gravure, Paris, 72. Teaching: Dir pvt studio, 63-; instr intaglio, NShore Community Art Ctr, 69- Awards: Purchase Awards, Libr Cong, 46, Hofstra Univ, 63 & Olivet Col, 67. Bibliog: Ron Perkins (auth), Artists at Work—Filmstrip 4, Jam Handy Sch Serv, 70. Mem: Soc Am Graphic Artists; Boston Printmakers; Silvermine Artists Guild; Print Club, Philadelphia; Am Color Print Soc. Style & Technique: Contemporary. Media: Graphics. Mailing Add: c/o Bermond Art Ltd 3000 Marcus Ave Lake Success NY 11040

LEAKE, EUGENE W
PAINTER
b Jersey City, NJ, Aug 31, 11. Study: Yale Univ Sch Art & Archit; Art Students League. Work: Baltimore Mus Art; J B Speed Art Mus, Louisville, Ky. Pos: Trustee, Guggenheim Mus, New York & New York Studio Sch Drawing, Painting & Sculpture. Dealer: Green Mountain Gallery 135 Greene New York NY 10012. Mailing Add: Monkton MD 21111

LEATHERS, WINSTON LYLE
PAINTER, PRINTMAKER
b Miami, Man, Can, Dec 29, 32. Study: Univ of Man, BFA, 56, studied art educ, 59; Univ of Mex, 57-58; Man Teachers Col, 60; Univ of BC, 61. Work: Can Coun Collection; Winnipeg Art Gallery; Univ of Fife, Scotland; Edmonton Art Gallery. Comn: Environmental wall mural, Roghmans Ltd, Winnipeg, 73; low relief concrete wall mural, Porv of Man, Portage La Prarie, 77; mural, IKOY Archit Partnership, Winnipeg, Man, 77; low relief wall mural, BACM Co Ltd, Winnipeg, 78. Exhib: 38th Northwest Printmakers Int, Seattle, Wash, 70; 69th Int, Washington, DC, 71; Paris Int Print Exhib, France, 72; Monaco Biennial, 72; Bermuda Biennial, 72; Brit Fedn Int, 73; Int Print Exhib, Zurich, Switz, 74; Manisphere Int, Moorehead, Minn, 75. Collections Arranged: Univ of Mex, Contemp Gallery of Art, Mexico City, 57; University of BC, 61; Western Canadian Art Circuit (traveling), Winnipeg Art Gallery, 66-67; British Fedn of Artist Gallery, London, Eng, 68; Winnipeg Art Gallery, 74. Teaching: Assoc prof design & drawing, Univ of Man, 69- Pos: Man art curric revision comt, Prov of Man, 61-66; art adv, Manitoba Asn of Art Ed, 67-68; prog chmn, Manitoba Asn of Art Ed, Winnipeg, 70-72; art adv, Libr Comn, City of Winnipeg, 76- Awards: Sr Can Coun Grant for Printmaking, 67-68 & Proj Grant for Printmaking, 73, Can Coun; Purchase Award, Man Soc Artists, Winnipeg, 76. Bibliog: Prof Vann (auth), Perspective-Winston Leathers, Univ of Man, 69; Philip Fry (auth), Manitoba Artists, Winnipeg Art Gallery, 72; Ann Davis (auth), Cosmic Variations-Winston Leathers, Winnipeg Art Gallery, Bulletin Mag, 6/75. Mem: Can Artists Representation (pres, 72); Royal Can Acad of the Arts; Brit Fedn of Artists, Eng; Can Soc of Printmakers; Can Soc of Graphic Artists. Style & Technique: Deals with light and space; low relief and impasto. Media: Painting and Printmaking, with Emphasis on Drawing. Dealer: Thomas Gallery Osborne St Winnipeg MB Can. Mailing Add: 1215-2080 Pembina Hwy Winnipeg MB R3T 2G9 Can

LEAVITT, THOMAS WHITTLESEY
MUSEUM DIRECTOR, ART HISTORIAN
b Boston, Mass, Jan 8, 30. Study: Middlebury Col, AB, 51; Boston Univ, MA, 52; Harvard Univ, PhD, 58. Collections Arranged: New Renaissance in Italy (with catalog), Pasadena, Calif, 58; Piet Mondrian (with catalog), Santa Barbara, Calif, 65; American Portraits in California Collections (with catalog), Santa Barbara, 66; Brücke (with catalog), Cornell Univ, 70, George Kolbe, 72; Seymour Lipton, 73; Directions in Afro-American Art, 74. Teaching: Lectr Am art, Univ Calif, Santa Barbara, 64-65; prof hist art, Cornell Univ, 68- Pos: Asst to dir, Fogg Art Mus, 54-56; exec dir, Fine Arts Comn, People to People Prog, 57; dir, Pasadena Art Mus, 57-63; dir, Santa Barbara Mus Art, 63-68; dir, Andrew Dickson White Mus Art, Cornell Univ, 68-72, dir mus prog, Nat Endowment for Arts, 71-72, mem mus adv panel, 72-75; trustee, Am Fedn Arts, 72-; dir, Herbert F Johnson Mus Art, Cornell Univ, 73-; mem mus panel, NY State Coun Arts, 75- Mem: Col Art Asn Am; Am Asn Mus (coun mem, 76-); Asn Art Mus Dirs (mem int exhib comt, 77-; pres, 77-78). Res: American 19th century painting. Publ: Auth, The Crisis in Museums, 71; auth, George Loring Brown (catalog), 73; auth, Let the dogs bark, George Loring Brown and the critics, Am Art Rev, 1-2/74; plus others. Mailing Add: H F Johnson Mus of Art Cornell Univ Ithaca NY 14853

LEAX, RONALD ALLEN
SCULPTOR
b Pittsburgh, Pa, June 5, 47. Study: RI Sch Design; Brown Univ, BA(art), 69; printmaking with Walter Feldman. Exhib: New England New Talent, De Cordova Mus, Lincoln, Mass, 73; 61st Ann Am Art Exhib, Art Asn Newport, RI, 73; Nashua Arts & Sci Ctr Inaugural Exhib, NH, 74; Am Images, Goethe Inst, Boston, 74; one-man show, Smith Art Mus, Springfield, Mass, 75. Awards: Gilbert Stuart Art Award, Brown Univ, 69; Small Sculpture Award, Providence Art Club, 72; Blanch E Colman Found Award, 74. Mem: Am Int Sculptors Symp. Style & Technique: Construction with wood, found and bought objects. Mailing Add: 9 Forest Ave Natick MA 01760

LEBECK, CAROL E
CERAMIST
b Spokane, Wash, Sept 8, 31. Study: Univ Calif, Los Angeles, MA(ceramics); Swed State Sch of Design, Stockholm, Sweden, HKS(ceramics). Work: Los Angeles Co Cult Art Asn, Brand Libr, Los Angeles; Marietta Col, Ohio. Exhib: Young Americans, 58 & The Great American Foot Exhibit, 78, Mus of Contemp Crafts, New York; Contemporary Crafts of the Americas, Fort Collins, Colo, 75; Objects 75 & 77, Western Colo Ctr for the Arts, Grand Junction, 75 & 77; California Design 76, Pacific Design Ctr, Los Angeles, 76; 34th Concorso Int della Ceramica d Arte Contemporanea, Faenza, Italy, 76; California Women in Crafts, Craft & Folk Art Mus, Los Angeles, 77; California Crafts X, Crocker Art Gallery, Sacremento, 77. Teaching: Instr ceramics, Grossmont Col, El Cajon, Calif, 62- Awards: Fel, Swed Am Found Grant, 58; Purchase Award, Marietta Crafts Nat, 75; Award of Merit, California Crafts X, 77. Bibliog: H Storr-Britz (auth), Ornaments & Surfaces on Ceramics, 77 & Concepts of Contemporary Ceramics, 78, An Kunst & Handwerk. Mem: Am Crafts Coun; Allied Craftsmen of San Diego (corresp secy, 75). Style & Technique: Realism and illusionism on two dimensional wall pieces using casts of papers, etc; surface developed with photo silkscreen, airbrush and underglaze. Media: Clay, Underglaze Color; Mixed Media. Mailing Add: 7108 Stanford Ave LaMesa CA 92041

LEBEDEV, VLADIMIR
PAINTER
b Moscow, Russia, June 17, 10; US citizen. Study: Tech Indust Art, grad; Acad Arts, Leningrad, with Bernstein & Filanov, grad; also with V Favorski & El Lisitski, Moscow. Work: Acad Arts, Leningrad; Kunstkabinett Keterer, Stuttgart, Ger; Berry Hill Gallery, New York; Far Gallery, New York; also mus in Moscow & Khazan, Russia. Comn: Interior decoration, USSR Bldg, New York World's Fair, 39. Exhib: Expos Artistes Exile, Paris, 48; Expos Stedelijk Mus, Amsterdam, 49; Expos Artistes, Mus Nat Belg, 49; one-man show, Charles Barzansky Gallery, New York, 57; Nat Acad Design, New York, 65-66. Awards: Honorable Mention, New York World's Fair, 39; First Prize, Art Exhib, Block Island, RI, 61. Mem: Artists Equity Asn; Am Fedn Arts; Int Inst Conserv. Media: Oil. Dealer: Far Gallery 746 Madison Ave New York NY 10021. Mailing Add: 144 E 36th St New York NY 10016

LEBER, ROBERTA (ROBERTA LEBER MCVEIGH)
CERAMIST, INSTRUCTOR
b Hoboken, NJ. Study: NY State Col Ceramics, Alfred Univ, BS; Columbia Univ. Exhib: Five Nat Ceramic Shows, Everson Mus, Syracuse, NY; Vision, George Jensen New York, 60; Environ Gallery, New York; Contemp Crafts, Worcester Mus, Mass; Rockland Ctr Arts-Craft Award Show, 72. Teaching: Instr ceramics, NY Art Workshop, New York, 34-47; head dept ceramics, Craft Students League, 35-; instr ceramics, Rockland Ctr Arts, West Nyack, NY, 57-; instr continuing educ, Rockland Community Col, 75- Pos: Art coordr, Community Resources Pool South Orangetown Cent Sch, 62 & 63. Awards: Ceramic Stoneware Vase Award of Merit, Rockland Ctr Arts, 72. Mem: Artist Craftsmen NY (bd dirs, 68-70, 72, 75-76 & 78, first vpres, 75-76); Rockland Ctr Arts (bd dirs, 68-69 & 71-74, chmn bd, 71 & 72, emer bd mem); Worlds Craft Coun; Mus Am Folk Art. Mailing Add: 117 Leber Rd Blauvelt NY 10913

LEBISH, HARRIET SHILLER
ART DEALER
b Kew Gardens, NY, Feb 8, 39. Study: Univ of Wis, George Washington Univ; Univ of Bridgeport, BS(art, cumme laude); Silvermine Col of Art, study with Carlus Dyer. Pos: Owner, dir & instr, Bauhaus II Art Gallery, Green Farms, Conn, 72-76; owner-dir, Genesis Galleries Ltd, New York, 76- Bibliog: Mary des Champs (auth), 8 Blind Children Take Tour of Sculpture, New York Times, 3/78; Sally G Devaney (auth), That the Blind May See, Art Gallery Mag, 2-3/77; Gloria Cole (auth), The Bauhaus that Harriet Built, Fairpress Newspaper, 75. Specialty: Contemporary painting and sculpture, strong inclination to realism. Mailing Add: 1 Sea Spray Rd Westport CT 06880

LEBKICHER, ANNE ROSS
PAINTER, ART ADMINISTRATOR
b New York, NY. Study: Univ Wash; Univ Mont; Columbia Univ; Chouinard Art Sch; Univ Wis; Univ Southern Calif; Otis Art Inst; Marymount Col; Palos Verdes Peninsula, Calif; also with Ejnar Hansen & Robert Frame, Pasadena, Joseph Mugnaini & Kero Antoyan, Los Angeles, Leonard Edmundson, Claremont & Francis De Erdley. Exhib: Los Angeles Regional, 60-66; Mont Inst Arts at Kalispell, 69; Flathead Co Art Asn Int Art Festival, 70; Great Falls Juried Show, Charles Russell Gallery, 73; Missoula Festival of the Arts Show, 75; plus others. Collections Arranged: Several hundred exhibs, including G Roualt, Francis De Erdley, Paul Darrow, Douglas Parshal, Edgar Ewing, Amen, Connor Evarts, Keith Crown, Ted Gilien & Frederic Taubes. Awards: Second Award in Oils, Great Falls Juried Show, 73. Bibliog: June Lee Roddan (auth), Silhouette, Palos Verdes Soc Rev, 6/66; Alan Garrett (auth), Meet our artists, Gallery Manual, 70; Neva D Baker (auth), Art in action, Golden Days Reporter, 8/71. Mem: Flathead Co Art Asn (exhib chmn, 69-72, bd dirs, 70-, vpres, 73-75); Nat League Am Pen Women; Mont League Prof Women Artists; Palos Verdes Community Arts Asn (exhib chmn, 45-65, pres, 55-56); Mont Inst Arts. Style & Technique: Direct painting with palette knife; collage; modern representational. Media: Oil, Gouache, Conte. Dealer: Hockaday Art Gallery Second Ave at Third St Kalispell MT 59901; Northwest Artists Gallery 7 First Ave E Kalispell MT 59901. Mailing Add: Flathead Lake Rollins MT 59931

LECHAY, JAMES
PAINTER
b New York, NY, July 5, 07. Work: Art Inst Chicago; Brooklyn Mus; Des Moines Art Ctr; Pa Acad Fine Arts, Philadelphia; Mus Art, Univ Iowa; plus others. Exhib: Metrop Mus Art, New York; Art Inst Chicago; Pa Acad Fine Arts; Carnegie Inst, Pittsburgh; Toledo Mus Art; plus others. Teaching: Instr art, Stanford Univ, summer 51; instr art, Skowhegan Sch Painting & Sculpture, summer 63; prof art, Univ Iowa, 45-75; vis prof, Chinese Univ of Hong Kong, 76. Awards: Norman Wait Harris Medal, Art Inst Chicago, 42; Purchase Award, Pa Acad Fine Arts; Childe Hassam Fund Purchase Award, Am Acad Arts & Lett, 74; Benjamin Altman Landscape Prize, Nat Acad Design, 77; plus others. Dealer: Kraushaar Galleries 1055 Madison Ave New York NY 10028. Mailing Add: Box 195 Wellfleet MA 02667

LECHTZIN, STANLEY
CRAFTSMAN, EDUCATOR
b Detroit, Mich, June 9, 36. Study: Wayne State Univ, BFA; Cranbrook Acad Art, Bloomfield Hills, Mich, MFA. Work: Mus Contemp Crafts, New York; Detroit Inst Arts; Schmuckmuseum Pforzheim, Ger; Philadelphia Mus Art; Goldsmiths Hall, London. Comn: Silver mace, Temple Univ, 66; Longwood Col, 74; paten, 41st Int Eucharistic Cong, Philadelphia, 76. Exhib: Contemp Jewish Ceremonial Art, Jewish Mus, New York, 61; Jewelry 71, Art Gallery of Ont, Toronto; one-man shows, Mus Contemp Crafts, New York, 65, Lee Nordness Galleries, NY, 69, Int Jewelry Exhib, Tokyo, Japan, 73, Rand Show, Johannesburg, SAfrica, 75 & Goldsmiths Hall, London, 75; Philadelphia: Three Centuries of Am Art, Philadelphia Mus Art, Pa, 76; plus others. Teaching: Prof metalsmithing, Tyler Sch Art, Temple Univ, 62-, chmn dept crafts, 65- Awards: Founders Soc Prize, Detroit Mus Art, 66; Louis Comfort Tiffany Found Award in Crafts, 67; Nat Endowment for Arts Craftsmen's Grant, 73. Bibliog: Lee Nordness (auth), Objects USA, 70 & Graham Hughes (auth), The Art of Jewelry, 72, Viking; Karl Schollmayer (auth), Neuer Schmuck, Ernst Wasmuth-Verlag, Ger, 74. Mem: Soc Nam Goldsmiths (mem bd dirs, 70-); Am Crafts Coun. Style & Technique: Organic forms used in creating jewelry employing contemporary technology and materials such as acrylic casting, electroforming and photo fabrication. Media: Metal, Plastic. Publ: Auth, Electrofabrication of metal, Craft Horizons, 64; contribr, Metal Techniques for Craftsmen, 68; auth, Museum of Contemporary Crafts (brochure), 69; contribr, Contemporary Jewelry, 70; auth, rev of occupational brief, Chronicle Guid Publ, 72. Dealer: Helen Drutt Gallery 1625 Spruce Philadelphia PA 19103. Mailing Add: Temple Univ Tyler Sch Art Beech & Penrose Ave Elkins Park PA 19126

LECKY, SUSAN
PAINTER
b Los Angeles, Calif, July 19, 40. Study: Univ Southern Calif, BFA; also European travel. Work: Los Angeles Co Mus. Exhib: Los Angeles Vicinity, 61 & 62; Midwest Ann, Decatur, Ill, 68 & 69; Univ Southern Calif, 70; Joslyn Mus, Omaha, 72; one-man shows, Urbana, Ill, 66 & Univ Ill, 77. Pos: Art critic, New Art Examr, 76- Mem: WEB-Women's Art Registry. Media: Acrylic, Watercolor. Mailing Add: 306 S Orchard St Urbana IL 61801

LE CLAIR, CHARLES
PAINTER, EDUCATOR
b Columbia, Mo, May 23, 14. Study: Univ Wis, BS & MS, 35; Acad Ranson, Paris, 36; Columbia Univ, 40-41. Work: Beaver Col; Temple Univ; Chatham Col; Albright-Knox Art Gallery; Pittsburgh Hundred Friends of Art. Exhib: Butler Inst Am Art, Youngstown, Ohio, 51, 56 & 71; Whitney Mus Am Art, New York, 51-56; Int Watercolor Exhib, Brooklyn Mus, 59; Nat Acad Design Ann, 60; Pa Acad Fine Arts, Philadelphia, 63 & 65. Teaching: Assoc prof painting, Chatham Col, 46-52, chmn dept art, 46-60, prof painting, 52-60; dean, Tyler Sch Art, Temple Univ, 60-74, prof painting, 60- Awards: Ten Awards, Assoc Artists Pittsburgh, 46-; Ford Found Fel Advan Educ, 52-53; Pennell Mem Award, Pa Acad Fine Arts, 65. Media: Oil, Acrylic, Watercolor. Publ: Co-auth, Integration of the Arts, Harper, 54; co-auth, Meeting student needs through the humanities, In: Current Issues in Higher Educ, Asn Higher Educ, Washington, DC, 55; auth, A Salute to William Pitt (catalog), Chatham Col, 58; auth, Humanities, In: Principles of Eval & Measurement for Higher Educ, Rochester Inst Technol, 61; auth, Education of the artist, Alumni Rev, Temple Univ, 1/62. Mailing Add: 7614 Lafayette Ave Philadelphia PA 19126

LECOQUE
PAINTER, WRITER
b Prague, Czech, Mar 21, 91; US citizen. Study: Acad Beaux Arts, Zagreb, with Crnic; Acad Julian, Paris, with Baschett & Emile Bernard; also with Auguste Renoir. Work: Mus Old Montmartre, Paris; Collection Beaux-Arts Ville Paris; Mus Prague; Mus Davenport, Iowa; Mus Mod Art, Haifa, Israel; plus pvt collection of US Presidents Eisenhower, Kennedy, Nixon & Ford. Comn: Rooftops of Prague, comn by Pres Jan Masaryk for Pres Eisenhower, 45; portrait of Adlai Stevenson, Chicago, 52. Exhib: Gallery Charpentier, Paris, 12; Anglo-Ger Exhib, Crystal Palace, London, Eng, 13; Int Sect, Biennale Venice, 26 & 28; Galleries Bergen, Oslo, 35; Munic Tower Gallery, Los Angeles, 58; plus many other one-man shows, 60-75. Pos: Sculptor, studios of Rodin & Bourdelle, Paris. Awards: First Prize of Archit Architect Turek, Prague, 14; Soc Arts, Sci, Lett, Paris Gold Medal, 66. Bibliog: H Adam (auth), article in Lett Françaises, 61; Maximillien Gauthier (auth), Paris, 61; Pierre Cailler (auth), Documents, Cahiers Art, 66; plus others. Mem: Soc Arts, Sci, Lett, Paris; Club Culturel Français, Los Angeles. Style & Technique: French impressionist. Media: Oil, Tempera. Publ: Auth, La Ragazza Dalla Gamba di Legno, 51; auth, Tragic Weekend, 65; auth, Renoir My Friend—Renoir Mon Ami, 68; auth, Capri Unfinished Portrait, 68; auth, Monography, 72. Dealer: Alred Loeb 11 Rue Chauchat Paris France. Mailing Add: 8079 Selma Ave Los Angeles CA 90046

LEDERER, KURT
COLLECTOR
b Vienna, Austria, Feb 10, 97; US citizen. Collection: Modern prints. Mailing Add: Hillsboro MD 21641

LEDERER, WOLFGANG
DESIGNER, EDUCATOR
b Mannheim, Ger, Jan 16, 12. Study: Akad Graphische Kuenste und Buchgewerbe, Leipzig, Ger; Acad Scandinave, Paris, France, with Othon Friesz; Officina Pragensis, Prague, Czech, with H Steiner-Prag. Work: San Francisco Mus Art, Calif; Klingspor Mus, Ger. Comn: Bk design, Univ Calif Press; and others. Exhib: One-man show, Vienna, Austria, 37; Elder Gallery, San Francisco, 41; San Francisco Mus Art, 42; San Francisco Art Asn, 43. Teaching: Lect, Design, Illus & the Work of H Steiner-Prag, to art Socs; prof graphic design & illus & chmn dept design, Calif Col Arts & Crafts, 45-, dir, div design, 70. Style & Technique: Book design; pen & ink illustrations. Mailing Add: Div of Design Calif Col of Arts & Crafts Oakland CA 94618

LEDYARD, WALTER WILLIAM
SCULPTOR
b Rockford, Ill, Mar 6, 15. Study: Rockford Col, with Marquis Reitzel; Univ Ill, AB, Col Med, MD; Univ SC; also with Gil Petroff. Work: SC State Art Collection; Columbia Mus Art, SC. Exhib: SC Artists Guild Ann, 62-71; SC Invitational, 69; one-man shows, Columbia Mus Art, SC, 65 & 73, Newberry Col, SC, 76 & Sumter Mus Art, SC, 77; plus others. Pos: Mem bd trustees, Columbia Mus Art, 63-66, vpres, 66-68, pres, 68-70, mem comn, 76- Awards: SC State Art Comn Purchase Prize, 69. Mem: SC Artists Guild (exec bd). Style & Technique: Representational; abstract. Media: Marble, Alabaster, Wood. Collection: Etchings and lithographs from 17th century to contemporary and contemporary sculpture. Mailing Add: 3900 MacGregor Dr Columbia SC 29206

LEE, AMY FREEMAN
PAINTER, LECTURER
b San Antonio, Tex, Oct 3, 14. Study: St Mary's Hall, San Antonio, grad, 31; Univ Tex, Austin, 31-34; Incarnate Word Col, 34-42, hon LittD, 65; critiques from Charles Rosen, Ralph Pearson & Edward John Stevens. Work: D D Feldman Collection, Univ Tex Mus, Austin; Smith Col Mus Fine Arts, Mass; Ft Worth Art Ctr, Tex; Norfolk Mus Arts & Sci, Va; Nat Saltonstall Collection, Boston; plus others. Comn: Camellia Award Painting, Joskes of Texas, San Antonio, 71. Exhib: Tex Watercolor Soc Exhib, McNay Art Inst, San Antonio, 50-62, 64-69, 73-74, 76 & 77; Am Watercolor Soc, Nat Acad, New York, 59, 65, 69 & 74-75; Nat Soc Painters in Casein, Nat Arts Club & Nat Acad, New York, 64-77; Nat Watercolor Soc, Los Angeles, 67-75; 20th Century, Tex Painters & Sculptors Traveling Exhib, 71-72; Calif Nat Watercolor Soc, Los Angeles, 67-77; Tex Fine Arts Asn Ann Nat, Austin, 75. Teaching: Lectr comp cult, Trinity Univ, 54-57; lectr contemp art, San Antonio Art Inst, 55-57; lectr expansion of perception, Our Lady of the Lake Col, 69- Pos: Art critic, San Antonio Express, 39-42; art critic, KONO Radio Sta, San Antonio, 47-52; mem adv coun, Col Fine Arts, Univ Tex, Austin. Awards: Tex Watercolor Soc Trevira Purchase Prize, McNay Art Inst, 74, Ann Local Artists Exhib Frost Purchase Prize, 75, Drought Award, 77; two Merit Awards, San Antonio Watercolor Soc Ann, Univ Tex Health Sci Ctr, 76. Bibliog: Reverence for Life (exhib catalog), Univ Tex Art Mus, 73; She's no queen of the May, San Antonio Mag, 74; Reality is becoming, Today's Art, 1/75. Mem: Tex Watercolor Soc (founder-pres); Nat Watercolor Soc; Nat Soc Painters in Casein; SW Watercolor Soc. Style & Technique: Experimental; multi-dimensional, kinetic; Oriental; abstract; non-objective. Media: Watercolor. Publ: Auth, The Desert is Blooming, Tex Philosophical Soc Proceedings, 75; auth, Mary Smith, Tom Brown & Dow Jones, Incarnate Word Col, San Antonio, 76; auth, The taste of art is bittersweet, San Antonio Mag, 77. Dealer: L & L Gallery 1107 N Fourth St Longview TX 75601; Sol Del Rio Art Gallery 1020 Townsend Ave San Antonio TX 78209. Mailing Add: 127 Canterbury Hill San Antonio TX 78209

LEE, BRIANT HAMOR
SCENOGRAPHER, ART HISTORIAN
b New Haven, Conn, May 6, 38. Study: Carnegie-Mellon Univ; Adelphi Univ, BA; Acad de Belle Arti, Rome, Cert de Frequenza; Univ Italiana per Stranieri-Perugia; Ind Univ, MA; NY Univ; Mich State Univ, PhD. Comn: Two theatrical productions (in collaboration with staging dir), Mich State Univ, East Lansing, 64-67; Eight theatrical productions (in collaboration with staging dir), Enchanted Hills Playhouse, Wawasee, Ind, 65. Teaching: Instr scenography, Am Int Univ, San Diego, Calif, 62-63; asst prof scenography, Bradley Univ, Peoria, Ill, 67-68; assoc prof scenography, Bowling Green State Univ, Ohio, 68- Pos: Designer/scenographer, Am Int Univ, San Diego, Calif, 62-63; design engineer, Kliegl Lighting, New York, 63-64; designer/scenographer, Univ Theatre, Bradley Univ, Peoria, Ill, 67-68 & Univ Theatre, Bowling Green State Univ, Ohio, 68- Mem: Am Theatre Asn; Speech Commun Asn; Am Soc for Theatre Res; Ohio Theatre Alliance; Ohio Community Theatre Asn (vpres-tres, 76-). Style & Technique: Scenography renderings in watercolor and pen and ink; scenery realized in wood, canvas and distemper painting technique. Res: Late 18th century European theatre architecture and scenography. Publ: Auth, Anything can be made out of corrugated, Theatre Design & Technol, 73; auth, Theatrical Visual Arts Ephemora, In: Performing Arts Resources, 75; auth, Pierre Patte, Late 18th century lighting innovator, Theatre Survey, 75-76; auth, To the Novice Scenographer, In: The OCTA Manual, ACT, Inc, 76; auth, The origins of the box set in the late 18th century, Theatre Survey, 77-78. Mailing Add: 336 S Church St Bowling Green OH 43402

LEE, DORA FUGH
PAINTER, SCULPTOR
b Peking, China, Aug 16, 30; US citizen. Study: With Prince Pu Ju, Chao Meng-chu & Yen Shao-Hsiang, Peking, China; additional study with sculptor, Pietro Lazzari, Washington, DC. Work: China Inst, New York; Pearl Buck Found, Philadelphia, Pa; Smithsonian Inst, Washington, DC. Exhib: Watercolor USA, Springfield, Mo, 75; one-woman show, Franz Bader Gallery, Washington, DC, 76; Mainstreams, Marietta Col, Ohio, 76; Md Acad of Arts, Easton, 77; Northern Va Fine Arts Asn (traveling exhib), Washington, DC, Va, Md & WVa, 77. Teaching: Pvt lessons in Chinese traditional painting & calligraphy, Bethesda, Md, 70- Awards: Best of Show, 68, First Prize/Watercolor, 71 & 72, Montgomery Co Art Asn. Mem: Washington Watercolor Asn; Potomac Valley Watercolorists; Montgomery Co Art Asn; Northern Va Fine Arts Asn. Style & Technique: Portraiture sculpture only; traditional Chinese literati style, using all Chinese traditional material depicting cityscapes in a contemporary way. Media: Chinese Watercolor; Clay, Plaster and Bronze. Dealer: Franz Bader Gallery 2124 Pennsylvania Ave NW Washington DC 20037. Mailing Add: 6305 Orchid Dr Bethesda MD 20034

LEE, DORIS
PAINTER, ILLUSTRATOR
b Aledo, Ill, Feb 1, 05. Study: Rockford Col, AB, 27; Kansas City Art Inst, 28-29; study in Europe, 31; Calif Sch Fine Arts, San Francisco, 31, with Arnold Blanch; also with Andre Lhote, Paris; Rockford Col, LLD, 48, Russell Sage Col, 54. Work: Art Inst Chicago, Metrop Mus Art, New York; Libr Cong, Washington, DC; Albright-Knox Art Gallery, Buffalo; Cranbrook Mus, Bloomfield Hills, Mich; plus others. Comn: Mural, US Post Off Bldg, Washington, DC; designed curtain for Oklahoma (play); design & illus for Rodgers & Hart Songbook, Tough Blue & Gone is my Goose; paintings for Life Mag. Exhib: Carnegie Mus, Pittsburgh; Whitney Mus Am Art, New York; New York & San Francisco World's Fairs; Asn Am Artists; World House, New York; plus others. Teaching: Guest artist, Univ Hawaii, 57. Pos: Mem fine arts adv bd, Famous Artists Schs. Awards: Gold Medal, Art Dirs Club New York, 57; Berkshire Painting Prize, New Eng Show, 64; First Prize, Art & Sci Exhib, 66; plus others. Bibliog: Paintings presented in Metro-Goldwyn-Mayer picture, The Pirate; monogr of paintings, Am Artists Group, 46. Mem: An Am Group; Woodstock Art Asn; Am Soc Painters, Sculptors & Gravers; Am Artists Cong. Publ: Illusr, The great Quillon, Hired man's elephant, St John's River & Mr Benedict's lion; co-auth, Painting for enjoyment. Mailing Add: Rte 212 Woodstock NY 12498

LEE, ELEANOR GAY
PAINTER
b Atlanta, Ga. Study: Nat Acad Design Sch Fine Art. Work: Mus City of New York; Mus Fine Art, Hickory, NC; Mus Fine Art, Greenville, SC; River Edge Mus, Can; Nat Daughters Am Revolution Hq. Exhib: Parrish Mus, Southampton, NY, 60; Guild Hall, East Hampton, NY, 63; Burr Galleries, New York, 71; Nat Biennial Composers, Authors & Artists Am, 71; Catharine Lorillard Wolfe Art Club Open, 71. Pos: Dir one-man shows, Burr Galleries, 57-64; attendant, Thompson Gallery, New York, 66-69. Awards: First Prize for oils, NY Co Fair, 55 & Composers, Authors & Artists, 71. Mem: Burr Artists (founding pres, 71); Catharine Lorillard Wolfe Art Club; Composers, Authors & Artists Am (vpres, 71); Nat League Am Pen Women, New York Br; Gotham Painters. Media: Oil, Pastel. Mailing Add: Nat Arts Club 15 Gramercy Park S New York NY 10003

LEE, MANNING DE VILLENEUVE
ILLUSTRATOR, PAINTER
b Summerville, SC, Mar 15, 94. Study: Pa Acad Fine Arts, Europ traveling scholar, 21. Work: Six Marine Paintings, US Naval Acad, Annapolis; William S Hart Co Mus, Los Angeles, Calif; Cranbrook Acad, Birmingham, Mich; Presidential Palace, Monrovia, Liberia; also in pvt collections. Comn: Portraits, of Jacob H Lowrey, 22, F Styers, Supt US Mint, Philadelphia, 22 & Lawrence Lafore, 23; Sea Plane PN9, Adm Rodgers, 23; five paintings, Philadelphia Wk Engraving Co, US Naval Acad Yearbk, 25; plus others. Exhib: Gibbs Art Gallery, Charleston, SC, 20; Pa Acad Fine Arts Watercolor Show, 31; N W Ayer & Co, Philadelphia, 45. Teaching: Instr illus, Pa Acad Fine Arts Summer Sch, 47. Awards: Gold Medal, Charleston Expos, 07; second Toppan Prize, Pa Acad Fine Arts, 21. Mem: Fel Royal Soc Arts, London; Philadelphia Art Alliance. Media: Oil, Watercolor, Ink. Publ: Illusr, From Star to Star, 44, Cadmus Henry, 49, Colt of Destiny, 50, Night Watch, 52 & Buffalo Trace, 55; plus 195 others. Mailing Add: The Kenilworth Alden Park Manor Philadelphia PA 19144

LEE, MARGARET F
PAINTER
b South St Paul, Minn, May 19, 22. Study: Rochester Art Ctr, with Adolph Dehn, Arnold Blanch & Robert Birmelin, 60-74; John Pike Watercolor Sch, Woodstock, NY, 72; watercolor with Zoltan Szabo, 74; Japanese woodblock with Toshi Yoshida, 74; Univ Minn, BA(art), 75. Work: YMCA-YWCA Permanent Collection, Rochester, Minn. Exhib: Minn State Fair Exhibs, St Paul, 71-73; one-man show, Augsburg Col, Minneapolis, 73; 17th & 18th Int, Galerie Int, New York, 73-74; Mainstreams USA, Marietta Col, Ohio, 74; American Painters in Paris, French Ministry & Paris City Coun, 75; Arts of Asia Gallery, Rochester, Minn, 75-77. Teaching: Lectr Japanese Sumi-e, Winona Art Ctr, Minn, 74; instr Japanese painting, Rochester Art Ctr, 74. Awards: First Place, Northern Lights 75, St Paul, 75; Award of Excellence, Arts Omnibus, 76, St Paul; Award, Midwest Watercolor Soc Exhib, Minn Mus of Art, St Paul, 77. Mem: Minn Artists Asn; Minn Artists Gallery; Sky Gallery, St Paul; Sumi-e Soc Am, New York; Fine Arts Soc Dakota Co, St Paul. Style & Technique: Acrylic on nylon over sculptured polystyrene and Japanese brush painting with sumi ink. Dealer: Sky Gallery 950 S Robert St Paul MN 55118. Mailing Add: 145 E Eighth St Zumbrota MN 55992

LEE, RAYMOND MAN
DESIGNER, LECTURER
b Canton, China, Aug 12, 35; Can citizen. Study: Hong Kong Sch of Fine Art; Nat Art Sch, Sydney, Australia. Work: The Nat Collection of Currency Mus, Bank of Can; Mus of the Mint, Spain; Mus of the Mint, Portugal; Smithsonian Inst, Washington, Dc. Comn: One Hundred Dollar Jubilee Gold coin, Royal Can Mint of Can, 77. Exhib: Int Typographical Compos Asn, 70 & 73-76; Am Inst of Graphic Arts, 72, 74 & 75; Toronto Art Dirs Club, 72-77; Bienale Int Exhib, Brno, Czech, 74, 76 & 78. Collections Arranged: Mod Publicity Eng (contribr, catalog), 70, 72 & 75-77; Creativity, New York, 72, 74-76; New York Type Dirs Club, 72, 74 & 75; Graphics Switzerland (contribr, catalog), 73, 75 & 76; Top Trade Marks of the World, Italy 74. Teaching: Instr commun design & concept, Ont Col of Art, Toronto, Can, 75- Pos: Sr art dir, George Patterson Pty Ltd, Sydney, Australia, 62-64 & McKim Advert Co Ltd, Toronto, Ont, 66-68; pres & creative dir, Raymond Lee & Assocs Ltd, 68-; vpres, Art Dirs Club of Toronto, 72-73. Awards: Am Inst of Graphic Arts, 72, 74 & 75; Andy Award, New York, 72, 74 & 76; Marketing Award, Can, 74-76. Mem: Am Inst of Graphic Arts; Inst of Can Advert. Publ: Contribr, New York Art Dirs Club Ann, 72, 74 & 75; contribr, Am Inst of Graphic Arts, 72, 74 & 75; Commun Arts, 72, 73, 76 & 77. Mailing Add: 170 Lytton Blvd Toronto ON M4R 1L6 Can

LEE, RENSSELAER WRIGHT
ART HISTORIAN
b Philadelphia, Pa, June 15, 98. Study: Princeton Univ, AB, 20, PhD, 26. Pos: Prof hist art, Northwestern Univ, Evanston, 31-40; prof hist art, Smith Col, 41-48; prof hist art, Columbia Univ, 48-54; prof, Inst Fine Arts, NY Univ, 54-55, mem adv comt; prof hist art, Princeton Univ, 55-66; chmn adv comt, Yale Ctr Brit Art. Mem: Renaissance Soc Am (pres, 77-78); Col Art Asn Am (pres, 44-46); Am Acad Rome (pres, 70-72). Res: Theory of art, especially in its relation to literature; influence of Italian Renaissance literature on painting. Publ: Auth, An English Gothic Embroidery in the Vatican, 30; auth, Ut Pictura Poesis: the Humanistic Theory of Painting, 40 & 67, Ital trans, 74; auth, Poetry into Painting: Tasso and Art, 70; auth, Names on Trees: Ariosto Into Art, Princeton Univ Press, 76. Mailing Add: 120 Mercer St Princeton NJ 08540

LEE, RICHARD ALLEN
PAINTER, COLLECTOR
b Warren, Pa, June 22, 49. Study: Pa Acad Fine Arts, cert, Cresson traveling scholar, 71; Philadelphia Col Art, BFA. Work: In pvt collections in Pa, Ohio, NY, NJ, Calif, Tenn & London, Eng. Exhib: Cresson Exhib, 71; Fel Pa Acad Fine Arts, 71 & 72; Woodmere Gallery, Philadelphia, 72. Awards: Hallmark Prize, 69; First Prize, Fel Pa Acad Fine Arts, 71. Mem: Fel Pa Acad Fine Arts. Media: Acrylic. Collection: American and European sculpture and porcelain antiques; American and European 20th century painting. Mailing Add: c/o Pa Acad Fine Arts Broad & Cherry Sts Philadelphia PA 19103

LEE, ROBERT J
PAINTER, EDUCATOR
b Oakland, Calif, Dec 26, 21. Study: Acad Art, San Francisco, with Richard Stephens, Hamilton Wolf & Richard Guy Walton. Work: US Air Force Hist Soc; Mt Holyoke Mus, Mass; Springfield Mus Fine Arts, Mass; Evanston Mus, Ill; Columbia Mus Art, SC. Exhib: Palace Legion of Honor, San Francisco, 46; Art Inst Chicago, 47-49; Butler Inst Am Arts, Youngstown, Ohio; Conn Acad Fine Arts, Hartford; Smithsonian Inst, Washington, DC, 71; 200 Yrs Am Illus, New York Hist Soc, 77; one-man show, Bristol Mus Fine Arts, RI, 76. Teaching: Instr illus, Pratt Inst, 55-57; assoc prof painting & design, Marymount Col (NY), 62- Awards: Purchase Award, Springfield Mus Fine Art, 55; First Prize Gold Medal of Honor, Allied Artists, 60; Award of Excellence, Soc Illusr, 67. Style & Technique: Soft feathery; use of imagery, myths, legends. Publ: Illusr, Men and Women, the Poetry of Love, Am Heritage, 70; Old Devil Wind, 70 & Exploring Music, 71, Holt Rinehart & Winston; illusr ltd ed, Our Town, 76; illusr, A Fable, Franklin Press, 76. Dealer: Christopher Gallery 766 Madison Ave New York NY 10021. Mailing Add: Seminary Hill Carmel NY 10512

LEE, ROGER
EDUCATOR, CURATOR
b Vancouver, BC, Dec 1, 42. Study: Inst Allende, San Miguel Allende, Mex, 63; Univ BC, BA, 64, fel, 65, MA, 66; Alliance Francaise, 74; also with George Riviere, Paris, 73-74. Collections Arranged: Line in Chinese and Japanese Art, Norman Mackenzie Art Gallery, Univ Regina, Sculpture in Movement, Evelyn Roth; plus others. Teaching: Asst prof art hist, Univ Regina, 66- Pos: Former cur, Norman Mackenzie Art Gallery. Awards: Grant for Exhib, Sask Arts Bd, 71. Mem: Univ Art Asn Can. Res: Contemporary international art trends; conceptual art. Publ: Auth, Jack Sures: organic pottery, Arts Can, 68; auth, Hans Hofmann acquisition, 69 & China and Japan: a comparison, 70, Norman Mackenzie Art Gallery News Lett. Mailing Add: Dept Visual Arts Univ Regina Regina SK Can

LEE, RUSSELL
PHOTOGRAPHER, EDUCATOR
b Ottawa, Ill, July 21, 03. Study: Lehigh Univ, ChE, 25; Calif Sch Fine Arts; Art Students League; study with John Sloan. Work: Farm Security Admin Collection, Libr of Cong, Washington, DC; Med Survey Solid Fuels Admin Collection & Air Transport Command Army Air Forces Collection, Nat Archives, Washington, DC; Univ Louisville Photo Archives, Ky; Mus Mod Art, New York. Exhib: First Inst Photog Exhib, Grand Cent Palace, New York, 38; Family of Man, 55, The Bitter Years, 62, Mus Mod Art, New York; Russell Lee Retrospective, Univ Tex, Austin, 65, Witte Mem Mus, San Antonio, 65 & Smithsonian Inst, 66; Just Before the War, Newport Harbor Art Mus, Newport Beach, Calif & Libr of Cong, Washington, DC, 68. Teaching: Dir & mem staff photog, Univ Mo Photog Workshop, 49-76; lectr photog, Univ Tex, Austin, 65-73. Bibliog: F Jack Hurley (auth), Russell Lee, Image, Int Mus Photog, 73; Roy Stryker & Nancy Wood (co-auths), In This Proud Land, New York Graphic Soc, 73; Hank O'Neal (auth), A Vision Shared, St Press, 76. Style & Technique: Documentary photographs. Media: Black and white silver prints. Publ: Illusr, Image of Italy, Tex Quart, Univ Tex, 61. Dealer: Witkin Gallery 41 E 57th St New York NY 10022. Mailing Add: 3110 West Ave Austin TX 78705

LEE, SHERMAN EMERY
MUSEUM DIRECTOR
b Seattle, Wash, Apr 19, 18. Study: Am Univ, BA & MA; Case Western Reserve Univ, PhD. Teaching: Lectr art hist, Univ Wash, 48-52; lectr art hist, Case Western Reserve Univ, 58, prof art, 62- Pos: Cur Far Eastern art, Detroit Inst Art, 41-46; with dept arts & monuments div, Civil Info & Educ Sect, Gen Hq, Supreme Comdr, Allied Powers, Tokyo, 46-68; asst dir to assoc dir, Seattle Mus Art, 48-52; cur Oriental art, Cleveland Mus Art, 52-, asst dir, 57, assoc dir, 58, dir, 58-; consult comt, Artibus Asiae. Awards: Legion of Honor; Order of the North Star. Mem: Am Asn Mus; Asn Art Mus Dirs (past pres); Am Acad Arts & Sci. Publ: Auth, Chinese Landscape Painting, 54, rev ed, 62; co-auth, Streams and Mountains Without End, 55; auth, Japanese Decorative Style, 61; auth, History of Far Eastern Art, 64; co-auth, Chinese Art Under the Mongols, 68. Mailing Add: 2536 Norfolk Rd Cleveland OH 44106

LEEBER, SHARON CORGAN
SCULPTOR
b St Johns, Mich, Oct 1, 40. Study: Univ Wyo; Cent Mich Univ; Nat Open Univ, Washington, DC; Trinity Univ. Work: Shreveport Mus, La; Dallas Mus Fine Arts; Las Cumbres, Acapulco, Mex; Univ Tex, Dallas, Tex. Comn: Univ Tex, Arlington, 76; Arlington City Hall, Tex, 76; large welded male, Incarnate Word Col, San Antonio, Tex, 77. Exhib: Tex Fine Arts Nat, Austin, 69; one-man retrospective show, Elizabet Ney Mus, Austin, 71; Tex Sculpture & Painting, Dallas, 71; Okla Painting & Sculpture, Oklahoma City, 71; Tex Ann Erotic Show, San Antonio, 71 & 72. Teaching: Instr sculpture, El Centro Col, Tex, 72- Awards: Purchase Award, Shreveport Mus, 69; Purchase Award, Del Mar Col. Bibliog: L Haacke (auth), Bumpers form Leeber sculpture, Dallas Times Herald, 5/2/71; J Kutner (auth), article in Art News, 4/77; Thelma Neuman (auth), The Mirror Book, 78. Mem: Nat Sculptor's Asn; Artists Equity Asn (secy, Dallas Chap, 71-72); Engrs, Artists & Technologists; Tex Fine Arts Asn; Tex Soc Sculptors (bd dir). Style & Technique: Abstracting the human figure to express inner form. Media: Steel, Aluminum, Marble. Dealer: Contemporary Gallery 2800 Routh St The Quadrangle Dallas TX 75201. Mailing Add: 6410 Dykes Way Dallas TX 75230

LEECH, MERLE EUGENE
SCULPTOR, PRINTMAKER
Study: Kans State Col, BFA & MA; NY Univ; Pratt Inst. Work: Smithsonian Inst; Cooper Hewitt Mus, New York; New York Pub Libr Collection. Exhib: 12th Ann Nat Exhib Prints & Drawings, Oklahoma City, 70; 30 Yrs of Am Printmaking, Brooklyn Mus, NY; World Print Competition, San Francisco Mus Art, Calif; Soc Am Graphic Artist Traveling Exhib; NDak Nat Print & Drawing Exhib. Teaching: Prof printing, Sch Visual Arts, 70- Awards: Outstanding Printing Award, Metrop Printing Indust, New York, 74; Purchase Award, Soc Am Graphic Artist. Style & Technique: Solid planes of color, which are juxtaposed to each other. Dealer: Peter Rose Gallery 200 E 58th St New York NY 10022. Mailing Add: 27 Greene St New York NY 10013

LEEDS, ANNETTE
PAINTER
b Boston, Mass, May 2, 20. Study: Mass Col Art, grad; Art Students League; Brooklyn Mus, with Moses Soyer; also with Paul Puzinas & Howard Boesendahl. Exhib: Catharine Lorillard Wolfe, Nat Acad Design-Nat Arts Club, 73, 74 & 77; Burr Artists, Lever House, 73 & 77; Caravan House Gallery, 74 & 77; Garden City Gallery, 75; Metrop Mus of Art, New York, 77; Goldsboro Art Ctr, 77; Union Carbide, 77; Cork & Arsenal Galleries, 78; plus others. Teaching: Pvt instr, 68- Awards: First Prize & Gold Medal, Art League Long Island, 63, Spec Award, 64; Third Prize, Art League Nassau Co, 65; First Prizes, Nat League Am Pen Women, 76 & Assoc Artists, 77. Mem: Catharine Lorillard Wolfe Art Club (chmn publicity, 69-, exhib chmn, 72); Burr Artists (chmn publicity, 69-); Pen & Brush. Style & Technique: Traditional; free use of lots of color. Media: Oil. Mailing Add: 116-17 Union Turnpike Forest Hills NY 11375

LEEPA, ALLEN
PAINTER, EDUCATOR
b New York, NY, Jan 9, 19. Study: Am Art Sch New York, scholar; Art Students League; New Bauhaus, Chicago, scholar; Columbia Univ, scholar, dean's fel, 47, BS, MA & EdD; Sorbonne & Grande Chaumiere, Paris; Fulbright Award to France, 50-51; Ford Found grant, Brazil, 70. Work: South Bend Mus Art, Ind; Royal Acad, Scotland; Grand Rapids Mus, Mich. Exhib: Mus Mod Art, New York, 53; Sao Paulo Biennale, Brazil, 63; one-man show, Galerie La Cour d'Ingres, Paris, 63; Mus Art Mod, Paris, 64 & 65; Retrospective, Hofstra Univ, 65; plus many others. Teaching: Instr art, Hull Sch, Chicago, 37-38; instr art, Brooklyn Art Ctr, 39-41; instr art, Brooklyn Mus & Metrop Mus Art, 40-41; instr art, Mus Mod Art, New York, 40-41; prof art, Mich State Univ, 45-; artist-in-residence, Ferris State Col, Big Rapids, Mich, 77- Awards: First Prizes in Painting, Grand Rapids Mus, 58 & 65; Am Fedn Arts Printmakers Award, 67; Childe Hassam Painting Award, Am Acad Arts & Lett, 69; plus others. Bibliog: Michael Seuphor (auth), Abstract Painting, 62 & Dictionary of Abstract Art, 63, Abrams. Mem: Am Asn Univ Prof; Mich Acad Arts, Sci & Lett. Style & Technique: Abstract; correlation of expressional idea and existential forming processes. Media: Acrylic on Canvas. Publ: Auth, The Challenge of Modern Art, 49 & 61; contribr, articles in Humanities in Contemp Life, 60, New Art, 66, Minimal Art, 68 & New Ideas in Art Educ, 73; auth, Abraham Rattner, 74; plus others. Dealer: Forsythe Galleries 201 Nickels Ann Arbor MI 48108. Mailing Add: 540 E South St Mason MI 48854

LEEPER, DORIS MARIE
PAINTER, SCULPTOR
b Charlotte, NC, Apr 4, 29. Study: Duke Univ, BA, 51. Work: Nat Collection Fine Arts, Washington, DC; Mint Mus Art, Charlotte; Loch Haven Art Ctr, Orlando, Fla; 180 Beacon Collection, Boston, Mass; Wadsworth Atheneum, Hartford, Conn. Comn: Fiberglass sculpture, comn by patron for Jacksonville Art Mus, 70; fiberglass sculpture, Alpert Investment for Forum 303, Arlington, Tex, 71; fiberglass sculpture, First Nat Bank, Tampa, Fla, 72-73; 160 modular unit wall sculpture, Hunter Mus Art, Chattanooga, Tenn, 73-75; enamel painting, Int Bus Machines, Atlanta, Ga, 76. Exhib: Painting: Out from the Wall, Des Moines Art Ctr, Iowa, 68; Recent Trends in American Art, Westmoreland Co Mus Art, Greensburg, Pa, 69; Contemporary Women Artists, Nat Arts Club, New York, 70; Artrain, Southeastern Tour, 74; one-person shows, High Mus Art, Atlanta, 75, Hunter Mus Art, Chattanooga, 75, Jacksonville Art Mus, Fla, 76, Greenville Co Mus Art, Greenville, SC, 76, Columbia Mus Art, SC, 76, Ringling Mus Art, Sarasota, Fla, 76 & SE Ctr for Contemp Art, Winston-Salem, NC, 77. Awards: Nat Endowment for Arts Grant, 72; Artist-in-Residence Fel, Rockefeller Found, 77; Fine Arts Coun of Fla Grant, 77. Bibliog: Edith Neely (auth), The world of Doris Leeper, Jacksonville Fine Arts Illus, 69; An interview with Doris Leeper, Enjoy, 73; The Floridian, St Petersburg Times, 76. Style & Technique: Non-objective, geometric works that derive primarily from a concern with color and space relationships. Media: Enamel; Fiberglass, Metal, Concrete. Dealer: Art Sources Inc 2101 Gulf Life Tower Jacksonville FL 32207. Mailing Add: PO Box 2093 New Smyrna Beach FL 32069

LEEPER, JOHN P
PAINTER
b Dandridge, Tenn, Apr 23, 09. Study: Los Angeles Co Art Inst. Work: IBM Collection; Long Beach Mus; Calif State Fair Colection; Ahmanson Collection. Comn: Mural, Ariz State Univ. Exhib: Calif Watercolor Soc; Los Angeles Mus Art; Calif & Can Traveling Exhib; Santa Barbara Mus Art; Long Beach Mus Art; Southern Calif 100, Laguna Beach Mus of Art, 77; one-man shows, Adele Bednarz Galleries, 66, 69, 71, 73 & 75 & Challis Galleries, 78; plus others. Awards: Calif State Fair Purchase Prize, 64; Los Angeles Festival Arts Purchase Prize, 64; Nat Orange Show, San Bernardino, 64. Media: Acrylic. Dealer: Challis Galleries 1390 S Coast Hwy Laguna Beach CA 92652. Mailing Add: 624 W 46th Ave Los Angeles CA 90065

LEEPER, JOHN PALMER
MUSEUM DIRECTOR
b Denison, Tex, Feb 4, 21. Study: Southern Methodist Univ, BS, 42; Harvard Univ, MA. Teaching: Instr art hist, Dexter Sch, Boston, 46; instr art hist, Univ Southern Calif, 51; instr art hist, Pasadena Sch Fine Arts, 52; instr art hist, Trinity Univ, 56-57. Pos: Keeper W A Clark Collection, Corcoran Gallery Art, 48-49, asst dir, 49-50; dir, Pasadena Art Mus, 50-53; dir, McNay Art Inst, 54- Mem: Am Asn Mus; Asn Art Mus Dirs. Publ: Auth, Everett Spruce, 59; auth, Otis Dozier, 60; ed, The autobiography of Jose Clemente Orozco, 62; auth, A Caribbean sketchbook by Jules Pascin, 64. Mailing Add: 6000 N New Braunfels San Antonio TX 78209

LEE-SMITH, HUGHIE
PAINTER, LECTURER
b Eustis, Fla, Sept 20, 15. Study: Art Sch Detroit Soc Arts & Crafts, Scholastic Mag scholar; Cleveland Inst Art, cert, 38; Wayne State Univ, BS(art educ), 53. Work: Detroit Inst Arts, Mich; Parrish Mus, Southampton, NY; Lagos Mus, Nigeria; USN Art Ctr, Washington, DC; Univ Mich, Ann Arbor. Exhib: Cleveland Mus Art Regional, 35-40; Detroit Inst Arts Regional, 48-57; Nat Acad Design Nat, New York, 57-72; Boston Mus Nat, 70; Whitney Mus Am Art Nat, New York, 71 & 75. Teaching: Instr painting, Grosse Pointe War Mem, Mich, 56-66; instr drawing & painting, Princeton Country Day Sch, NJ, 63-65; instr painting, Vt Acad, summer 68; artist in residence, Howard Univ, 69-71; instr, Art Students League, currently. Awards: Emily Lowe Award, 57; Allied Artists Am Prize, 58; Clarke Prize, Nat Acad Design, 58. Mem: Nat Acad Design; Artists Equity Asn; The Players, New York. Media: Oil, Watercolor, Pencil. Dealer: Grand Cent Art Galleries 40 Vanderbilt Ave New York NY 10017. Mailing Add: H6 Avon Dr East Windsor NJ 08520

LEET, RICHARD EUGENE
MUSEUM DIRECTOR, PAINTER
b Waterloo, Iowa, Sept 11, 36. Study: Univ Northern Iowa, BA, 58, MA, 65, with Ansei, Uchima, Ted Egri, Paul R Smith & John Page; Univ Iowa, 61-64, with Stuart Edie & Robert Knipschild. Work: Mus Art, El Paso; Charles H MacNider Mus, Mason City, Iowa; Iowa State Fair Asn Ann Purchase Award Collection, Des Moines; Iowa Artist Collection, Salisbury Labs, Charles City; Des Moines Art Ctr. Exhib: Ann Iowa Artists Echib, Des Moines Art Ctr, 58-72; Ann Nat Watercolor Exhib, Miss Art Ctr, Jackson, 67 & 68; Ann Midyear Show, Butler Inst Am Art, Youngstown, Ohio, 69, 75 & 77; Ann Sun Carnival Exhib, Mus Art, El Paso, 71; Midwest Biennial, Joslyn Art Mus, Omaha, 72, 74 & 76; Percival Galleries, Des Moines, 74, 76 & 78; Spiva Art Ctr, Joplin, Mo, 77. Teaching: Instr art, Oelwein Community Schs, Iowa, 58-65; instr painting & drawing, C H MacNider Mus, Mason City, Iowa, 65- Pos: Mus dir & founding dir, C H MacNider Mus, 65- Awards: Purchase Award for Watercolor & First Award in Graphics, Iowa State Fair Art Salon, 70; Purchase Award, Mus Art, El Paso, 71; Wallace Agr Bldg Purchase Award, State Iowa, 77. Bibliog: Nick Baldwin (auth), Visual arts, Des Moines Register, 8/24/69, 2/17/74 & 3/28/76; article in Iowan Mag, summer 74; plus others. Mem: Am Asn Mus; Midwest Mus Conf (vpres from Iowa, 69-71, exec vpres & prog coord, 71-72, pres, 72-73); Iowa Arts Coun (mem coun, 70-76). Style & Technique: Subjective, primarily landscape; abstract qualities; transparencies; glazes. Media: Watercolor, Oil. Publ: Auth, Monthly column in Mason City Globe Gazette, 68- Mailing Add: 1149 Manor Dr Mason City IA 50401

LEETE, WILLIAM WHITE
PAINTER
b Portsmouth, Ohio, June 12, 29. Study: Yale Univ, BA, 51, BFA, 55 & MFA, 57. Work: De Cordova Mus, Lincoln, Mass; Cleveland Mus, Ohio; Worcester Mus, Mass; Univ Mass. Exhib: New Eng Contemp Artists, Boston, 63 & 65; Silvermine Guild, Conn, 66; Art in Embassies, Inst Contemp Arts, Boston, 66; Structured Art, De Cordova Mus, 69; Young New England Painters, John & Mabel Ringling North Mus, Fla; Portland Mus & Currier Gallery, Manchester, 69. Teaching: Assoc prof art, Univ RI, 57-74, prof, 74- actg chmn art dept, spring 68 & 69-70. Pos: Comt mem, RI Arts Festival, 61-68; bd trustees, RI Gov Sch, 69- Media: Acrylic. Dealer: Lenore Grey 15 Meeting St Providence RI 02903; Ward-Nasse Gallery 178 Prince St New York NY 10013. Mailing Add: Univ RI Dept Art Kingston RI 02881

LEFCOURT, IRWIN
ART DEALER
b New York, NY, Jan 15, 10. Study: Nat Acad of Design, New York; Art Students League. Pos: Asst cur graphic art div, Smithsonian Inst, Washington, DC, 39-41; owner & dir, Art Fair Gallery, Larchmont, 57- Mem: Appraisers Asn of Am. Specialty: Modern and old master graphics; Japanese prints; Fin de Siecle posters. Mailing Add: 3 Washington Sq Larchmont NY 10538

LEFEBRE, JOHN
ART DEALER
b Berlin, Ger; US citizen. Study: Univ Berlin, with Deri. Pos: Dir, Lefebre Gallery. Specialty: Contemporary European artists. Mailing Add: 47 E 77th St New York NY 10021

LEFEBVRE D'ARGENCÉ, RENÉ-YVON
MUSEUM DIRECTOR
b Plouescat, France, Aug 21, 28. Study: Col St Aspais, Fontainebleau; Lycée Albert Sarraut, Hanoi; Ecole Libre des Sci Polit, Sorbonne; Pembroke Col; Brêveté de Ecol Nat Langues Orientales Vivantes, Licencie et Lettres. Collections Arranged: Avery Brundage Collection, 63-; Chang Dai-Chien (with catalog), 72; Hans Popper Collection (with catalog), 73; Exhib Archaeol Finds People's Repub China, 75. Teaching: Prof art hist, Univ Calif, Berkeley, 62-65. Pos: Cur, Musee Cernuschi, Paris, 53; mem, Ecole Francaise d'Extreme-Orient, 54; cur, Blanchard de la Brosse Mus, Saigon & Louis Finot Mus, Hanoi, 54-58; Quai d'Orsay grant, Taiwan, 59; cur, Asiatic Collections, M H De Young Mem Mus, San Francisco, 64; dir, Avery Brundage Collection, 65-68; dir & chief cur, Asian Art Mus San Francisco, 69- Awards: Médaille de la Reconnaissance Francaise, 57; Chevalier de l'Etoile du Nord, Sweden, 68; Order of Merit, Avery Brundage Found, 68. Mem: Ecole Francaise San Francisco (founder & bd mem); Asiatic Soc Arg; Asn Art Mus Dirs; Soc Asian Art (adv comt); French-Am Bilingual Sch (pres). Publ: Auth, Avery Brundage Collection, Chinese, Korean & Japanese Sculpture, 74; auth, Bronze Vessels of Ancient China in the Avery Brundage Collection, 77; ed & co-auth, Museum & University Collections of Asian Art in the San Francisco Bay Area, 77; auth, A Decade of Collecting. Mailing Add: Asian Art Mus San Francisco Golden Gate Park San Francisco CA 94118

LE FEVRE, RICHARD JOHN
PAINTER, DESIGNER
b Rochester, NY, Feb 11, 31. Study: Rochester Inst Technol, BS, 55, MFA, 67. Work: State of Tenn, Nashville; Fall Creek Falls State Park, Tenn; E Tenn State Univ; Univ Tenn, Knoxville; Nat Bank NC, Charlotte. Comn: Oil, St Stephen's Church, Rochester, 60; acrylic on Plexiglas, Church of Epiphany, Rochester, 65; polymer, Marine Midland Bank, Rochester, 65; acrylic on Plexiglas, Capital Cadillac Corp, Atlanta, Ga, 70; acrylic on Plexiglas altarpiece, Tyson Episcopal Ctr, Knoxville, Tenn, 71. Exhib: Appalachian Corridors Exhib 1, Va, 68; Experiments in Art and Technology, High Mus, Atlanta, 69; Midsouth Competition, Parthenon Mus, Nashville, 70; Art USA 2, Univ Northern Ill, 71; Tenn Arts Comn, Dulin Gallery, Knoxville, 72. Teaching: Dir arts & graphic arts, Rochester Inst Technol, 65-67; asst prof design, Univ Tenn, Knoxville, 67- Pos: Designer, Todd Co, Rochester, 54-55; designer, S M Crossett, Rochester, 55-58; pres, Le Fevre Studios, Rochester, 58-65. Awards: First Place for Mixed Media, Huntsville Art League & Mus Asn, Ala, 68; Purchase Award, Carroll Reece Mus, 71; Purchase Award, Mint Mus, 71. Style & Technique: Abstract. Media: Acrylic, Watercolor. Dealer: Gallerie Illien 123 14th St Atlanta GA 30309. Mailing Add: Rte 20 Lancelot Dr Knoxville TN 32921

LEFF, JAY C
COLLECTOR
b Brownsville, Pa, Jan 7, 25. Collections Arranged: Exotic Art from Ancient and Primitive Civilizations, Carnegie Inst Int, Pittsburgh, 59-60; African Sculpture from the Collection of Jay C Leff, Mus Primitive Art, New York, 64-65; Faces and Figures: Pacific Island Art, Am Mus Natural Hist, New York, 65; Ancient Art of Latin America from the Collection of Jay C Leff, Brooklyn Mus, NY, 66-67; The Art of Black Africa: Collection of Jay C Leff, Carnegie Inst Int, 69-70. Mem: Pa Coun on the Arts (chmn, 71-); Carnegie Inst Art Comt. Collection: Art from ancient Latin America, sculpture from Africa and Oceania and objects from the Far and Near East. Publ: Auth, The Art of Black Africa, Carnegie Inst Int, 69. Mailing Add: c/o Pa Council Arts 2001 N Front St Harrisburg PA 17102

LEFF, JULIETTE
PAINTER, EDUCATOR
b New York, NY, Mar 20, 39. Study: City Col of New York, BA(art, honors), 62; Hunter Col, MA, 76, with Rothko, Tony Smith & Eugene Goossen; Max Beckmann Painting Fel, Brooklyn Mus, NY; Lowengrund Scholar, Pratt Graphic Ctr, Work: Chase Manhattan Bank Collection, New York; US Info Agency Print Collection; Aubrey Cartwright Gallery, Cathedral Mus of Religious Art. Exhib: Max-24-64, Purdue Univ, 64; Occlectix, Columbia

Univ, 69; Butler Inst of Am Art, Youngstown, Ohio, 70; two-person show, NY Univ, 71; Year of the Woman: Reprise, Bronx Mus of the Arts, NY, 76; What is Feminist Art? Writings of 200 Women Artists, Women's Bldg, Los Angeles, Calif, 77. Teaching: Artist-in-Residence Teaching Grant, Nat Endowment for the Arts, Bronx Mus, 76-77; Studio-in-the-Sch Teaching Grant, NY Found for the Arts, 77-78. Pos: Art educ coordr, Bronx Mus of the Arts, 76-77. Awards: Nat Grant in Painting, Louis Comfort Tiffany Found, 66-67. Mem: Col Art Asn; Women's Caucus. Style & Technique: Figurative, expressionistic; concerned with psychological aspects of personality. Media: Pastel, Conte crayon, acrylic paintings. Mailing Add: 98 Riverside Dr New York NY 10024

LEFF, RITA
PRINTMAKER, PAINTER
b New York, NY. Study: Art Students League; Brooklyn Mus; Parsons Sch Design; also with Abraham Rattner, Louis Shanker, Adja Yunkers, Worden Day & Louis Calapai. Work: Metrop Mus Art, New York; Libr Cong, Washington, DC; Brooklyn Mus; Pa Acad, Philadelphia; Dallas Mus. Exhib: Libr Cong Print Ann; Pa Acad Design Print & Watercolor Ann; one-man shows, Esterhazy Gallery, Palm Beach, 71, Gallery Cassell, Palm Beach, 73 & Lighthouse Gallery, Tequesta, Fla, 75; plus others. Awards: Medals of Honor, Nat Asn Women Artists, 64, 66, 68 & 69; Grand Prix, Salon Int De Femme, Cannes, France, 69; First Prize Norton Gallery, Palm Beach, 71 & 72. Mem: Soc Am Graphic Artists (coun mem); Audubon Artists (juror); Nat Asn Women Artists (chmn prints); Boston Printmakers. Style & Technique: Contemporary. Media: Oil, Collage, Watercolor. Mailing Add: 1707 Consulate Pl West Palm Beach FL 33409

LEFRANC, MARGARET (MARGARET LEFRANC SCHOONOVER)
PAINTER, ILLUSTRATOR
b New York, NY. Study: Art Students League, NY; Kunstschule des Westerns, Berlin, Ger; Acad Grande Chaumiere, Paris, France; Acad Russe Paris; study with Andre l'Hote, Charles Bissiere, Antoine Bourdelle & Richard Merrick. Work: Hall of Fame, Oklahoma City; Univ Okla Press, Norman; Lowe Gallery, Univ Miami, Fla. Exhib: Solo shows, Mus NMex, Santa Fe, 48, 51 & 53, Okla Art Ctr, 50 & Philbrook Art Ctr, Tulsa, 52; Pa Acad Fine Arts, Philadelphia, 36; New York World's Fair Fine Arts Exhib, 39; Southwestern Ann, Tulsa, 52; Ann Exhib NMex Artists, Mus NMex, 56; Lowe Gallery Ann, Univ Miami, Fla, 62. Pos: Founder/dir, Guild Art Gallery, New York, 35-37; designer, colorist & stylist, Gilman Fabrics, Inc, New York, 38-42; liaison secy to cur, Cooper Union Mus, New York, 43-45. Awards: Illustration Award, 50 Best Bks of Yr, Libr of Cong, Washington, DC, 48; Hon Mention, Rodeo of Santa Fe, Mus NMex, 55; Hon Mention, Invitational Exhib, Temple Beth Am, Miami, 72. Mem: Artists Equity Asn (mem bd dirs, 60-76, pres, 61-63 & 65-67); Fla Artists Group. Style & Technique: Color expressionist with classical training. Media: Oil, Watercolor; Black & White Line Drawings & Wash Drawings. Res: Pueblo pottery design for synoptic series of San Ildefonso pottery. Publ: Illusr, Maria, the Potter of San Ildefonso, Univ Okla Press, 48; illusr, Indians on Horseback, T Y Crowell, 48; illusr, Indians of the Four Corners, T Y Crowell, 52; ed, Songs of the Tewa, Sunstone Press, 76; illusr, Dance Around the Sun, T Y Crowell, 77. Winter: 3734 Matheson Ave Miami FL 33133. Mailing Add: 627 Camino de la Luz Santa Fe NM 87501

LEHMAN, ARNOLD L
MUSEUM DIRECTOR, ART HISTORIAN
b New York, NY, July 18, 44. Study: Johns Hopkins Univ, BA, 65, MA, 66; Yale Univ, MA, 68, PhD, 73. Collections Arranged: Archit of World Fairs (auth, catalog), Dallas Mus Fine Arts, Tex, 72; Boom or Bust, Am Painting from World War I through 1939, 74, Judaica from Am Collections, 75; Am Magic Realists, 76 & World of Haitian Printing, (auth catalog), 77, Metrop Mus Art Ctr, Miami, Fla. Teaching: Lectr art hist, Cooper Union Sch Art & Archit, New York, 69-71; lectr art hist, Hunter Col, City Univ New York, 71-72. Pos: Chester Dale fel, Metrop Mus Art, New York, 69-70; dir, Urban Improvements Prog, New York, 70-72; dir, Metrop Mus & Art Ctr, Miami, Fla, 74- Mem: Soc Archit Historians; Col Art Asn; Fla Art Mus Dirs Asn; Cult Execs Coun. Res: American architecture and urban planning; American painting, 20th century; late 19th century French painting. Publ: Auth, Jazz Modern, Neo-American, Beautilitarian Style, Metrop Mus Bull, 70. Mailing Add: Metrop Mus & Art Ctr 1212 Anastasia Coral Gables FL 33146

LEHMAN, IRVING
PAINTER, SCULPTOR
Study: Cooper Union, 20-24; Nat Acad, 25-30. Work: St Edmund's Hall, Oxford Univ; Ein Harod, Israel; Nat Mus Bezalel, Israel; John H Vanderpoel Mem Collection, Chicago; Mus Art Populaire Juif, Paris; plus others. Exhib: Albany Inst Hist & Art; Ala Watercolor Soc; Brooklyn Mus; Charleston Art Gallery; Art Inst Chicago; Cordy Gallery, New York, 77; plus others. Teaching: Instr, Brooklyn Col Adult Educ; instr, New York Bd Educ; pvt instr. Awards: Kellner Award, Brooklyn Soc Artists 42nd Ann, 59; Am Soc Contemp Artists 44th Ann Distinctive Merit Award, 61; Lafayette Nat Bank Award, Am Soc Contemp Artists 47th Ann, 64; plus others. Bibliog: Articles in Am Abstr Art, 36-66; articles in Univ Syracuse Libr Mss; articles in House & Garden Decorating Guide, fall-winter, 68-69; plus others. Mem: Am Abstr Artists; Am Soc Contemp Artists. Mailing Add: RD Box 122 East Chatham NY 12060

LEHMAN, LOUISE BRASELL
PAINTER
b Orwood, Miss, Oct 15, 97. Study: Miss State Col Women; George Washington Univ; Corcoran Sch Art; Teachers Col, Columbia Univ, BS. Work: Nat Bank of Com; Montgomery Mus Fine Arts; Miss State Col Women; Brooks Mem Art Gallery. Exhib: Southern Art Festival, 67; Brooks Mem Art Gallery, 68, one-person show, 70; Miss Art Asn, 68; Tenn Art Comn Traveling Exhib, 68; Smithsonian Inst Traveling Exhib to Europe, 68; plus others. Awards: Prizes, Brooks Mem Art Gallery, 68; Tenn All-State Art Exhib, Nashville, 68; Tenn Art Comn Purchase Prize, 68; plus Asn; others. Mailing Add: 476 N Willett St Memphis TN 38112

LEHMAN, MARK AMMON
EDUCATOR, SCULPTOR
b Philadelphia, Pa, Apr 12, 30. Study: Philadelphia Col Art, BFA, 60; Tyler Sch Art, MFA, 62; Columbia Univ, Doctoral Work, 64- Comn: Head of J F Kennedy, Students of Trenton State Col, 65. Exhib: NJ Tercentenary Exhib, 63; New York World's Fair, 65; NJ State Mus Ann, 66 & 67; Columbia Univ, 66 & 77; Pa Guild Craftsmen Traveling Exhib, 67; NJ Designer Craftsmen, NJ State Mus, 68; Centenary Col, 76. Teaching: Asst prof art hist, ceramics & sculpture, Trenton State Col, 63- Awards: NJ Tercentenary Exhib Award, 64. Mem: NJ Designer Craftsmen. Style & Technique: Ceramic sculpture; forms are abstract, utilizing simple ceramic shapes, attached, then beaten or changed throughout; sizes range from 12 inches high to about four feet high. Media: Clay. Publ: Auth, Article pertaining to ceramic kiln burners, Studio Potter, 75. Mailing Add: Trenton State Col Pennington Rd Trenton NJ 08625

LEHR, JANET
ART DEALER
b New York, NY, June 7, 37. Study: Brooklyn Law Sch, Doctorate of Law, 58. Res: Photographically illustrated books of the 19th century. Specialty: The role of the photomechanical reproduction processes as used in book illustration; Fine vintage photographs of both the 19th and 20th century. Publ: Auth, Talbot's Role in the History of Photography, Antiquarian Bookman, J Chernofsky, 78. Mailing Add: PO Box 617 Gracie Sta New York NY 10028

LEHRER, LEONARD
PAINTER, EDUCATOR
b Philadelphia, Pa, Mar 23, 35. Study: Philadelphia Col Art, BFA, 56; Univ Pa, MFA, 60. Work: Mus Mod Art, New York; Nat Gallery of Art, Washington, DC; Libr Cong, Washington, DC; Yale Univ Art Gallery, New Haven, Conn; Sprengel Mus Mod Art, WGer. Exhib: One-man shows, Brooklyn Mus Print Show, 72; 1st Biennial of Graphics & Multiples, Segovia, Spain, 74; Marian Locks Gallery, Philadelphia, 74 & 77; Marion Koogler McNay Art Inst, San Antonio, Tex, 75; Tibor De Nagy, Houston, 75; Galerie Kühl, Hannover, Ger, 77; Art Fair, Cologne, Ger, 77 & Basel, Switz, 77. Teaching: Assoc prof, Philadelphia Col Art, 56-70; prof art & chmn dept, Univ NMex, 70-74; prof art, Univ Tex, San Antonio, 74-77; prof art & chmn art dept, Ariz State Univ, Tempe, 77- Pos: Pres Philadelphia Chap, Artists Equity Asn, 60-62. Awards: George Roth Prize, Philadelphia Print Club, 66; Print Award, Cheltenham Art Ctr Exhib, 67; fac summer grant, Union Independent Cols Art, 69; fac res grant, Univ NMex, 73. Bibliog: V D Coke (auth), The Painter and the Photograph, Univ NMex Press, 72; Fritz Eichenberg (auth), The Art of the Print, Abrams, 76. Mem: Col Art Asn Am. Media: Lithography, Watercolor, Oil. Dealer: Marian Locks Gallery 1524 Walnut St Philadelphia PA 19102; Galerie Kühl 3 Kaiser Wilhelm Strasse Hannover WGer. Mailing Add: 12221 N 70th St Scottsdale AZ 85254

LEIBER, GERSON AUGUST
PRINTMAKER, PAINTER
b Brooklyn, NY, Nov 12, 21. Study: Art Students League; Brooklyn Mus Art Sch. Work: Metrop Mus Art, New York; Whitney Mus Am Art, New York; Nat Gallery Art, Washington, DC; Libr Cong, Washington, DC; Boston Mus Fine Arts. Comn: Print eds, Assoc Am Artists & Int Graphic Arts Soc. Exhib: Am Prints Today, USA, New York, 59; Cincinnati Int Biennial, 60; American Prints, in Russia, Rome, Italy, Mexico City, Mex & Salzburg, Ger; Libr Cong Exhibs; plus many others. Teaching: Instr graphics & illus, Newark Sch Fine & Indust Art, 61-68. Awards: Tiffany Fels, 57 & 60; Audubon Medals of Honor for Graphics, 63-65; Am Nat Print Exhib Prize, Assoc Am Artists Gallery. Bibliog: Frank Getlein (auth), Bite of the Print, Potter, 63; Hooten & Kaiden (auth), Mother and Child in Modern Art, Meredith Corp. Mem: Soc Am Graphic Artists (treas, 69-72, coun mem); Audubon Artists; Boston Printmakers. Style & Technique: Semi-abstract. Media: Intaglio. Publ: Illusr, Crisis (poem), Oxhead Press, 69. Mailing Add: 20 E 32nd St New York NY 10016

LEIGHTON, CLARE
ENGRAVER, WRITER
b London, Eng, Apr 12, 01. Study: Slade Sch, Univ London, 21-23; Colby Col, hon DFA, 40. Work: British Mus, London; Victoria & Albert Mus, London; Nat Gallery Stockholm; Nat Gallery Can; Metrop Mus, New York; plus others. Comn: Designed 33 stained glass windows, St Paul's Cathedral, Worcester, Mass; mosaic, Convent Holy Family of Nazareth, Monroe, Conn; windows, Lutheran Church, Waterbury, Conn; windows, Methodist Church, Wellfleet, Mass. Exhib: Represented Gt Brit in Venice Biennale. Mem: Royal Soc Painters, Etchers & Engravers, London; Nat Acad Design; Soc Am Graphic Artists; Soc Wood Engravers, London; Nat Inst Arts & Lett. Publ: Auth & illusr, The Farmer's Year, Four Hedges, Country Matters, Southern Harvest & Where Land Meets Sea; plus others. Mailing Add: Woodbury CT 06798

LEIGHTON, DAVID S R
ART ADMINISTRATOR
b Regina, Sask, Feb 20, 28. Pos: Dir, Sch Fine Arts, Banff Ctr, 70- Mailing Add: Box 1020 Banff AB Can

LEIGHTON, THOMAS CHARLES
PAINTER, INSTRUCTOR
b Toronto, Ont, Sept 3, 13; US citizen. Study: London, New York & Chicago; with John Russell, Toronto; also gallery study in Paris, Rome, Madrid, Athens, Amsterdam, Vienna, Florence & Venice. Work: Portraits, still-life & flowers represented in pub & pvt collections in Can, Eng, US & Denmark. Exhib: Royal Can Acad Arts; Nat Gallery Art, Ottawa, Ont; Nat Acad Design, New York; Am Watercolor Soc, New York; Smithsonian Inst, Washington, DC; plus many others. Teaching: Asst, Russell Acad, Toronto, 33-35; dir fine arts, Ridley Col (Ont), 36-42; dir voc art, Niagara Falls Inst, 38-42; dir fine arts, Arts & Lett Club Toronto, 48; instr drawing & painting & lectr anat & art hist, Art League Calif, San Francisco, 48-55; dir, Leighton Studio, San Francisco, 55-; lectr art & art hist, TV, Radio & forums; also guide lectr on tours of Europe. Pos: Pres, Niagara Art Asn, 36-42. Awards: Klumke Award, De Young Mus, San Francisco, 64; First Award, Coun Am Artist Socs Ann, New York, 64; Newington Award, Am Artists Prof League Grand National, New York, 73, Gold Medal, 74; plus others. Bibliog: Articles in La Rev Mod, Paris & Les Images, Cairo, 66; plus others. Mem: Soc Western Artists (dir & bd trustees, 51-, pres, 52-); Bohemian Club San Francisco; Am Artists Prof League (nat bd dirs, 57-); fel Int Inst Arts & Lett. Style & Technique: Representational; broken color in full values. Media: Pastel. Mailing Add: 471 Buena Vista Ave E San Francisco CA 94117

LEIN, MALCOLM EMIL
ART ADMINISTRATOR, DESIGNER
b Havre, Mont, July 19, 13. Study: Univ Minn, BArch. Collections Arranged: Fiber, Clay and Metal Biennial, 52-; Drawings USA, Biennial, 61-; Goldsmith, 70; The Introspective Italian, 71. Pos: Pres, Minn Mus Art, 73- Mem: Am Asn Mus. Mailing Add: 361 Summit Ave St Paul MN 55102

LEISHER, WILLIAM RODGER
CONSERVATOR
b Alden, Mich, Feb 9, 41. Study: Mich State Univ, BA(Eng lit), 67, MA(medieval Eng lit), 67 & BFA(painting, printmaking & art hist), 72; Intermuseum Conserv Lab, Oberlin, Ohio, with Richard Buck, 72-74. Pos: Conserv of Paintings, Nat Gallery of Art, Washington, DC, 74- Mem: Am Inst for Conserv of Hist & Artistic Works; Int Inst for Conserv of Hist & Artistic Works; Am Asn of Mus Energy Comt; Nat Conserv Adv Coun, Energy Comt. Publ: Contribr, Protection of cultural properties during energy emergencies, Energy Info Clearing House, Am Asn of Mus, 78. Mailing Add: Nat Gallery of Art Constitution Ave at 6th St Washington DC 20565

LEITMAN, NORMAN
ART DEALER
b New York, NY, June 24, 33. Study: H S Mus & Art; Cornell Univ, BA; NY Univ Inst Fine Arts, 54-57. Collections Arranged: Old Master Drawings, 60 Anonymous Drawings, The Neglected 19th Century & 17th Century Dutch Paintings, H Shickman Gallery. Pos: Dir, H Shickman Gallery, New York. Mem: Art Dealers Asn; Col Art Asn. Specialty: Old master paintings and drawings. Mailing Add: 240 E 79th St New York NY 10021

LEITMAN, SAMUEL
PAINTER
b New York, NY, Feb 12, 08. Study: Art Students League, with Anne Goldthwaite & Bernard Klonis; Nat Acad Design, with John Pellew; also with Edgar Whitney. Work: West Point Mus; Norfolk Mus, Va; Charles & Emma Frye Mus, Seattle. Exhib: Am Watercolor Soc Ann, 60-; Salmagundi Club Ann, 61-; Am Artists Prof League, 65-; Allied Artists Ann, 67-; Knickerbocker Artists, 71-72. Teaching: Instr watercolor, Salmagundi Club. Awards: Gold Medal of Honor, Am Artists Prof League, 67; John Young Hunter Mem Award, Am Watercolor Soc, 72, Washington Sch Art Award, 75 & D'Arches Papers Award, 76. Mem: Am Watercolor Soc (vpres, 73, 1st vpres, 76); Salmagundi Club (chmn art comt, 72); Knickerbocker Artists (dir, 70-). Style & Technique: Wet in wet. Media: Watercolor. Mailing Add: 31-22 56th St Woodside NY 11377

LEJA, MICHAEL JOSEPH
CURATOR, ART CRITIC
b Woonsocket, RI, Dec 2, 51. Study: Swarthmore Col, BA (hist art); independent study prog, Whitney Mus Am Art; Helena Rubenstein fel art hist & mus studies. Collections Arranged: Gaslight Phenomena Kinetic Light Works by Alejandro Sina, 77, New Boston Filmmakers, 77, Fred Wiseman Retrospective, 77 & Wit & Wisdom: Works by Baldessari, Hudson, Levine, Oppenheim, 78 & Narrative Art, 78, Inst Contemp Art, Boston. Pos: Cur & film programmer, Inst Contemp Art, Boston, Mass, 76- Mailing Add: 62 Dartmouth St Somerville MA 02145

LEKAKIS, MICHAEL NICHOLAS
SCULPTOR
b New York, NY, 1907. Work: Mus Mod Art, Whitney Mus Am Art & Guggenheim Mus, New York; Dayton Art Mus, Ohio; Portland Art Mus, Ore; plus many others. Exhib: One-man show, Whitney Mus Am Art, New York, 53-54; Seven Sculptors, Guggenheim Mus, 58; Mus Mod Art, New York; Dayton Art Mus, Ohio; Sculpture Acquisition, Philadelphia Mus Art, 77; Drawing Collection Acquisition, Univ Lexington Mus, Ky; Weatherspoon Gallery, Univ NC Mus, Greensboro; Univ Nebr Mus, Lincoln; plus others. Awards: Ford Found Sculpture Purchase Grant for Mus Mod Art, New York. Mailing Add: 57 W 28th St New York NY 10001

LEKBERG, BARBARA HULT
SCULPTOR
b Portland, Ore, Mar 19, 25. Study: Univ Iowa, BFA & MA, with Humbert Albrizio; Simpson Col, hon DFA, 64. Work: Montclair Mus Art, NJ; Des Moines Art Ctr, Iowa; Knoxville Art Ctr, Tenn; Simpson Col, Indianola, Iowa. Comn: Three interior sculptures, Beldon-Stratford Hotel, Chicago, 53; three interior sculptures, Socony-Mobil Co, New York, 55; lobby relief, Riedl & Freede Advert, Clifton, NJ, 64; life-size figure, Bayfield Clark, Bermuda, 71. Exhib: Five Pa Acad Fine Arts Ann, Philadelphia, 50-62; New Talent, Am Fedn Arts Traveling Show, 59-60; Recent Sculpture USA, Mus Mod Art, New York, 59; one-man shows, Sculpture Ctr, New York, 59, 65 & 71; traveling one-man show, Birmingham Mus Art, Ala & Columbia Mus Art, SC, 73. Awards: Am Inst Arts & Lett Grant, 56; Guggenheim Found Fels, 57 & 59. Mem: Sculptors Guild. Media: Bronze, Steel. Dealer: Sculpture Ctr 167 E 69th St New York NY 10021. Mailing Add: 911 Stuart Ave Mamaroneck NY 10543

LELAND, WHITNEY EDWARD
PAINTER, EDUCATOR
b Washington, DC, Apr 12, 45. Study: Memphis Acad Arts, BFA; Univ Tenn, Knoxville, MFA. Work: Montgomery Mus Arts, Ala; Dulin Gallery Art, Knoxville, Tenn; Memphis Acad Art, Tenn. Exhib: 25th Ann Nat Watercolor Exhib, Jackson, Miss, 69; Box Top Art, Univ Ill, 71; Dixie Ann, Montgomery, 71; Tenn Printmakers, Knoxville, 72. Teaching: Asst prof painting, Univ Tenn, Knoxville, 70- Awards: Purchase Prize, Montgomery Mus Arts, 71; Purchase Award, Dulin Gallery Art, 72; Hon Mention, Montgomery Mus Arts, 72. Media: Acrylic, Watercolor. Dealer: Gilman Galleries 103 Oak St Chicago IL 60611. Mailing Add: Dept Art Univ Tenn 1505 W Cumberland Ave Knoxville TN 37916

LEM, RICHARD DOUGLAS
PAINTER
b Los Angeles, Calif, Nov 24, 33. Study: Univ Calif, Los Angeles, BA; Calif State Univ, Los Angeles, MA; Otis Art Inst; Calif Inst Arts; also with Rico LeBrun & Herbert Jepson. Work: San Diego Fine Arts Gallery. Exhib: 3rd Ariz Ann, Phoenix Art Mus, 61; Calif State Univ, Los Angeles, 65; California: South, San Diego Fine Arts Gallery, 65; two-man show, Palos Verdes Art Gallery, 68; Lynn Kottler Galleries, New York, 73; Galerie Mouffe, Paris, France, 76; plus others. Awards: Los Angeles Fine Arts Soc & Art Guild Award for Painting, 65. Style & Technique: Impressionism. Media: Oil, Watercolor. Mailing Add: 1861 Webster Ave Los Angeles CA 90026

LEMBECK, JOHN EDGAR
PAINTER
b St Louis, Mo, Dec 25, 42. Study: Univ Kans, BFA, 66; Yale Univ, univ scholar, 68 & 69, State Conn scholar, 69, MFA, 70. Exhib: United Gallery, New Haven, 69; Joseloff Gallery, Univ Hartford, 72; one-man shows, Spectrum Gallery, New York, 72 & Louis K Meisel Gallery, New York, 75; Butler Inst Am Art, Youngstown, Ohio, 75; Taft Mus, Cincinnati, Ohio, 76; Indianapolis Mus Art, Ind, 76; Sewall Gallery, Rice Univ, Houston, Tex, 77; State Univ NY Col, Potsdam, 77; Union Col, NJ, 77; Louis K Meisel Gallery, New York, 78; plus others. Teaching: Asst lectr art, St Louis Art Mus, 69, lectr art, 70; instr design & drawing, Yale Univ Sch Art & Archit, 70-, instr drawing, Yale Summer Sch Music & Art, 71 & 72, dir, Gallery, 71. Bibliog: Allen Ellenzweig (auth), Jack Lembeck, Arts Mag, 3/75; James Mills (auth), Metroline 75 a look at New York artists' work, Denver Post, 3/21/75; var articles in Village Voice, 76, Houston Chronicle, 9/77, Die Zeit, Ger, 12/77 & Art News, 1/77. Mailing Add: c/o L K Meisel Gallery 141 Prince St New York NY 10012

LEMIEUX, IRENEE
PAINTER
b Quebec, Can, Aug 3, 31. Study: Laval Univ; Conserv de Musique de Quebec, Montreal; Fontainebleau, France. Work: La Minerve, Quebec. Exhib: 3rd Salon Int de la Riviera, Grasse, France; 3rd Salon Int de la Cote d'Azur, Chateau des Requiers; 2nd Salon Int du Carnaval de Nice; 2nd Salon Int de Baden-Baden, Allemagne, 73; 7th Grand Prix Int Painting & Sculpture, Antibes, 74; among others. Awards: First Prize with Gold Medal, 3rd Salon Int de la Cote d'Azur, 73; Spec First Prize with Gold Medal, Acad de Lutece, Paris, 73; Second Prize with Silver Medal, 7th Grand Prix Int Painting & Sculpture, 74; plus others. Bibliog: Irenee Lemieux (autobiog), Ed Garneau, Quebec, 70; Roland Laznikas (auth), 3/73 & Raymond Clermont (auth), 6/74, rev in La Rev Mod, Paris; among others. Mem: Asn Beaux-Arts Cannes. Style & Technique: Poetic realism. Media: Acrylic with Airbrush. Compos: Musical works include six symphonies, seven cantatas & three ballets based on Huron Folklore. Mailing Add: 5 Ave du Pont Scott Quebec PQ Can

LEMIEUX, JEAN PAUL
PAINTER
b Quebec, PQ, Nov 18, 04. Study: Beaux-Arts, Montreal; Acad Colarossi, Paris; Laval Univ, Quebec, hon Dr, 69. Work: Collection of Queen Elizabeth; Art Gallery Toronto, Ont; Mus Prov Quebec. Exhib: Warsaw, 62; Tate Gallery, London, Eng, 63; Mus Mod Art Traveling Exhib through Can, 63; Mus Galliera, Paris, 63; retrospective, Montreal & Ottawa, 67; plus others. Teaching: Instr, Beaux-Arts Montreal, 33-34 & Ecole du Meuble, Montreal, 35-36; instr, Beaux-Arts, Quebec. Awards: Prize, Quebec Prov Painting; Govt Overseas Award, 54-55; Companion, Order of Can, 68; plus others. Mem: Royal Can Acad Arts. Mailing Add: 2008 Dickson Sillery PQ G1T 1C5 Can

LENNEY, ANNIE
PAINTER
b Potsdam, NY. Study: Art Students League; Grand Cent Art Sch, New York; NY Univ; Fordham Univ; Syracuse Univ; St Lawrence Univ; Col St Elizabeth, BA; also with John Grabach & Haley Lever. Work: Butler Inst Am Art, Youngstown, Ohio; Munson-Williams-Proctor Inst, Utica, NY; Newark Mus, NJ; Oklahoma City Art Ctr; Brook Mem Art Gallery, Memphis; plus many others. Exhib: Audubon Artists, Allied Artists & Nat Asn Women Artists, Nat Acad Design, New York; Assoc Artist Exhibs & Mus Ann, Montclair Mus, NJ; one-person shows, Robbins Art Gallery, South Orange, NJ, 75, Caldwell Col, NJ, 76, Mt Aloysius Col, Cresson, Pa, 77, Bluffton Col, Ohio, 77, Martin Arts Comn, Tenn, 77, Purdue Univ, West Lafayette, Ind, 78 & Centenary Col, Hackettstown, NJ, 78. Teaching: Instr art, Sch Fine & Indust Arts, Newark, 46-63; supvr, Sat Jr Art Sch, Newark, 53-55; instr art, Newton Pub Sch Syst, NJ, 63-71. Awards: Elizabethan Award for Distinguished Achievements in the Arts, Col of St Elizabeth, NJ, 74; Gene Alden Walker Prize for Oil, Pen & Brush Club, New York, 75; Ray A Jones Award, Hudson Artists NJ, 76; plus others. Bibliog: Gerry Turner (auth), The magic of a home town, Design Mag, 1-2/60; M J R Arthur (auth), Blairstown's Annie Lenney is renowned artist, Family Forum, 3/30/71. Mem: Audubon Artists (dir oils, 71, rec secy, 72-73); Allied Artists Am; Nat Asn Women Artists; Salmagundi Club; Painters & Sculptors Soc NJ. Style & Technique: Romantic realism. Media: Oil, Watercolor. Publ: Auth, American watercolor, Am Artist, 2/51. Mailing Add: Gaisler Rd Blairstown NJ 07825

LENNIE, BEATRICE E C
SCULPTOR, DESIGNER
b BC. Study: Vancouver Sch Art; Calif Sch Fine Art; pvt study in Rome & Florence; also with Frederick H Varley, J W G Macdonald, Ralph Stackpole, Carlo Marega & Harry Taüber, Vienna. Work: Winnipeg Art Gallery; pvt collections, Can & USA. Comn: Vancouver Labor Temple, Dom Construct Stone; Shaughnessy Mil Hosp, Fed Govt, Mercer & Mercer; Ryerson Mem Ctr United Church Can, P Underwood; Acad Med Libr, BC Med Soc; St John's Mem Church, C Thornton Sharp; plus others. Exhib: Many shows, Royal Can Acad, Toronto, Ont & Montreal, Que, Can Nat Exhib, Sculptor's Soc Can & Seattle Art Mus, Wash; one-man show, Toronto Picture Loan, Queen's Univ; plus others. Teaching: Head dept sculpture, BC Col Art, Vancouver; instr sculpture & theatre arts & creative puppetry, Univ BC; spec art lectr, Crofton House Sch, Vancouver. Pos: Dir, Child Art Ctr, Vancouver Art Gallery; broadcaster art subj, Can Broadcasting Corp Trans Can. Awards: Award, Sculptor's Soc Can. Bibliog: Archit rev in Can Rev Mus & Art, Vancouver Prov, Toronto Sat Night & others. Mem: Life mem BC Soc Art; Sculptor's Soc Can; Vancouver Art Gallery. Mailing Add: 4011 Rose Crescent West Vancouver BC Can

LENNON, TIMOTHY
PAINTING CONSERVATOR
b Chicago, Ill, Sept 18, 38. Study: Loras Col, BA; Univ of Notre Dame, MA. Pos: Assoc conserv, The Art Inst of Chicago, 76- Mem: Am Inst for Conserv of Artistic & Hist Works; Int Inst for Conserv of Artistic & Hist Works. Mailing Add: 835 Forest Oak Park IL 60302

LENSSEN, HEIDI (MRS FRIDOLF JOHNSON)
PAINTER, LECTURER
b Frankfurt, Ger; US citizen. Study: Uffizi, Florence, Italy, copy degree, 25; Berlin State Acad Fine Arts, cert, 29; pvt study in Paris, France; also with Count Merveldt, Rome, 32-33; Acad Rossi, Florence; Ecole Arts et Metiers, Paris. Work: Berlin Mus; Kunsthalle, Mannheim. Comn: More than 100 comns, US & Europe. Exhib: Kunsthalle, Mannheim, 31; Pavilion of Today, New York World's Fair, 39; Schoneman Gallery, 40; Audubon Artists, 44 & 45; one-man show, Lynn Kottler Gallery, 54 & 70; plus others. Teaching: Instr art & co-dir, Am Sch Design, New York, 37-42; lectr art, City Col New York Adult Educ, 45-58; instr art & lectr, Hunter Col, 49-51; lectr art, Franklin Sch Prof Arts, 52-57. Bibliog: Marthe Davidson (auth), article in Art News, 37; Emily Genauer (auth), article in World Telegram New York, 40. Mem: Woodstock Artists Asn. Style & Technique: Representational. Media: Oil, Pastel, Tempera. Publ: Auth & illusr, Art and Anatomy, J J Augustin, Inc & Barnes & Noble, 44; auth, Hands in Nature and Art, Studio Publ. Mailing Add: 34 Whitney Dr Woodstock NY 12498

LENT, BLAIR
ILLUSTRATOR, WRITER
b Boston, Mass, Jan 22, 30. Study: Boston Mus Sch, Cummings Mem travel fel to Switz & Italy, 1 yr, Bartlett travel fel to USSR, grad(hons). Work: Boston Pub Libr. Comn: Why the Sun and the Moon Live in the Sky (animated film), ACI Films, New York, 71; Christmas card design, UNICEF. Exhib: Children's Books, Am Inst Graphic Arts, New York, 68; The Work of Blair Lent 1965-1970, Wiggin Gallery, Boston, 70; Work by Five Major American Illustrators, Univ Art Gallery, Albany, NY, 72; Contemp Am Illusr Children's Bks, Rutgers Univ, 74-75. Awards: Silver Medal, Bienal Int Arte Grafice, Sao Paulo, Brazil, 65; Bronze Medal, Bienale Illustrators, Bratislava, Czech, 69; Caldecott Medal, Am Libr Asn, 73. Bibliog: Lee Hopkins (auth), Books Are By People, Citation, 69; Selma Lanes (auth), Down the Rabbit Hole, Atheneum, 71; Anne Commire (auth), Something About the Author, Gale, 72; plus others. Style & Technique: Drawing with brush and ink with acrylic wash. Publ: Auth & illusr, Pistachio, 63, John Tabor's Ride, 66 & From King Boggen's Hall to Nothing-at-all, 67, Little; auth (pseud Ernest Small) & illusr, Baba Yaga, Houghton Mifflin, 66; illusr, The Funny Little Woman, Dutton, 72. Mailing Add: Box 122 East Killingly CT 06243

LEON, DENNIS
SCULPTOR
b London, Eng, July 27, 33; US citizen. Study: Temple Univ, BSc(educ), 56; Tyler Sch Art, MFA, 57. Exhib: Pa Acad Fine Arts, 56, 64 & 68; Kraushaar Galleries, New York, 66, 68 & 70; Curator's Choice, 72 & Bicentennial Exhib, 76; Philadelphia Mus Art; James Willis Gallery, 73; Univ Calif, Davis, 74; JPL Fine Arts, London, Eng, 75; Am 76, San Francisco Mus Mod Art, 77; Hanson-Fuller Gallery, San Francisco, 77. Teaching: Prof sculpture, Philadelphia Col Art, 60-72; prof sculpture, Calif Col Arts & Crafts, 72-; vis artist, Sheffield Polytech, Eng, 75 & 76. Awards: Guggenheim Fel, 67; Nat Inst Arts & Lett Award, 67. Media: Mixed Media. Publ: Auth, Paul Harris, 73. Dealer: Hanson-Fuller Gallery 228 Grant Ave San Francisco CA 94108. Mailing Add: 3143 Eton Ave Berkeley CA 94705

LEON, RALPH BERNARD
PAINTER, ILLUSTRATOR
b Atlantic City, NJ, Mar 10, 32. Study: Pratt Inst, BFA, 57; Ecole de Musique et Beaux Arts de Fontainebleau, Walter Damrosch Scholar, 58; La Grande Chaumiere, Paris, France, with Henri Goetz. Work: Found, State Univ NY Binghamton; Pentagon Art Collection, Washington, DC. Exhib: Montclair Art Mus Ann, NJ, 56 & 58; Butler Inst Am Art Ann, Youngstown, Ohio, 56, 73 & 74; Nat Acad Design Ann, New York, 56, 74 & 76; Newark Today in Painting & NJ Artists, Newark Mus, 57 & 58; one-man shows, Atelier Christa Moering, Wiesbaden, Ger, 61 & 64, Engel Gallery, Jerusalem, Israel, 71 & Somerset Art Asn, Bernardsville, NJ, 76; three-man show, Monmouth Park System, Lincroft, NJ, 75; Santa Fe Six, Fenn Gallery, NMex, 77; Armory Show, Santa Fe, 77. Pos: Illusr & art dir, Airscoop (flight safety mag), USAFE, Wiesbaden, 59-69. Awards: Benjamin Altman Prize & Ranger Fund Purchase Prize, Nat Acad, New York, 74; Leon Lehrer Mem Award, Allied Artists Am Ann Exhib, New York, 75. Bibliog: Ana Schwarz (auth), Introd, Catalogue for Atelier Ana, Munich, 69; Review in Maiariv, Tel Aviv Daily, 71; Adolf Konrad (auth), Introd, Catalogue for one-man show, Gallery 9, 74. Style & Technique: Landscape and people in textured palette knife technique. Media: Oil. Dealer: Avantaos Gallery South Plaza PO Box 2886 Taos NM 87571. Mailing Add: 333 Otero St Santa Fe NM 87501

LEONARD, LEON LANK, SR
PAINTER, SCULPTOR
b Waco, Tex, June 18, 22. Study: Univ Denver, BFA; with Vonce Kirkland, Marion Buchan & John Billmeyer; Tex Col, with Forney Mumford, BA. Work: Prairie View A&M Col, Tex; Southside Community Ctr, Chicago; Atlanta Univ Mus, Ga; Coun House of Jewish Women, Los Angeles. Comn: Doris Miller (painting), YMCA, Waco, Tex, 58; Rev Harold Perry (drawing), comn by Mr E P Ford, New Orleans, 65; Pride of Eight (painting), Johnson Publ Co, Chicago, 71; Black History (mural), Thomas Edison Jr High Sch, Los Angeles, 71; Bishop John Adams (painting), Waco, Tex, 75. Exhib: Nat Negro Artists, Atlanta Univ, 60 & 66; Tex Watercolor Soc Ann, San Antonio, 66; USSA & Prague, Czech Circuit Exhib, 66; Watercolor USA, Springfield, Mo, 73 & 77; Nat Watercolor Soc Ann, Mt San Jacinto Col, San Jacinto, Calif, 77; Munic All-City Show, 77. Collections Arranged: A Great Evening of African-American History with Music, Songs, Drama, Art Exhibit, and Slides (with William E Smith). Teaching: Art teacher, Booker T Washington High Sch, Wichita Falls, Tex, 48-54; instr art educ, Prairie View A&M Col, 55-56; A J Moore High Sch, Waco, 56-67; art instr, Studio Gallery, Waco, summer 65; art teacher, Aububon Jr High Sch, Los Angeles, 67- Pos: Art dept chmn, Edison Jr High Sch, Log Angeles, 67-73; art dir, Art Workshop-Watercolors & Cramics, summer 75. Awards: John Hope Prizes, Atlanta Univ, 60-66; Bronze Medal, Los Angeles Home Saving Asn, 69; Winslow Homer Mem Award, Springfield Art Mus, 73. Bibliog: John H Johnson (auth), Leading young artists, Ebony Mag, 58-73; Cederic Dover (auth), American Negro art, New York Graphic Soc, 60. Mem: Tex & Nat Watercolor Soc; Nat Conf Artists (regional dir, 61); Art West Assoc Inc (secy, 74); Black Arts Coun. Style & Technique: Pointillism, resists, divisionism are definite disciplines expressed in paintings. Media: Clay; Watercolor. Res: An investigation into African art: Ashanti Coffle, rendered, triptych. Dealer: Heritage Gallery 718 N La Ciénega Blvd Los Angeles CA 90069. Mailing Add: 4043 Buckingham Rd Los Angeles CA 90008

LEONARDI, HECTOR
PAINTER, INSTRUCTOR
b Waterbury, Conn, Jan 18, 30. Study: RI Sch Design, BFA; Yale Univ, MFA. Work: Univ Notre Dame; Univ Bridgeport. Exhib: New York World's Fair, 64; Albright-Knox Art Gallery, Buffalo, 66; The Contemporaries, New York, 66 & 67; Critics Choice Exhib, Tokyo, 67; Obelisk Gallery, Boston, 68 & 69; plus others. Teaching: Instr color, design, drawing & painting, Univ Bridgeport; instr color, Parsons Sch Design, presently. Mailing Add: 334 W 20th St New York NY 10003

LEONG, JAMES CHAN
PAINTER
b San Francisco, Calif, Nov 27, 29. Study: Calif Col Arts & Crafts, BFA & MFA; San Francisco State Col, MA; Univ Oslo. Work: Mus Mod Art, New York; Whitney Mus Am Art, New York; Tate Gallery, London, Eng; Nat Inst Arts & Lett, New York; Mus Naz, Rome, Italy. Comn: Mural, Chung Mei Home for Boys, El Cerrito, Calif, 51; mural, Ping Yuen Housing Proj, San Francisco, 52; mural, San Francisco State Col, 54; prologue sequence, John Huston's Movie Freud, 62. Exhib: Inverse Illusionism, Am Fedn Arts Traveling Exhib, 71-72; Pa State Univ, 71; Istanbul, Izmir, Ankara, Turkey, 74; Larcada Gallery, New York, 75; plus others. Teaching: Vis prof painting, Univ Ga, 71. Bibliog: Robert Craft & Igor Strawinsky (auth), Themes and Episodes, Doubleday. Style & Technique: Lyric-romantic abstract; cosmic landscapes. Media: Mixed Media. Mailing Add: Piazza del Biscione 95 Rome Italy

LEOPOLD, BARRY FRANCIS
See Barry, Frank

LEOPOLD, MICHAEL CHRISTOPHER
ART CRITIC
b Wichita Falls, Tex, July 22, 29. Study: Univ Ariz. Pos: Dir pagina ingles, El Gran Mundo, Mex, 59-60; Los Angeles ed, Artnews, 71 & Artgallery Mag, 72-73, New York; Los Angeles contribr, Art Int, Lugano, Switz, 73- Awards: Fel, Huntington Hartford Found, 50. Res: 20th century sculpture; Guerriero—his conscious, subconscious and unconscious, six-volume fiction work of psychological development of artist. Publ: Auth, Artists of Mexico, El Gran Mundo, Mex, 59; auth, Guerriero, Santa Barbara Mus Art, Calif, 69; auth, The Art of Henry Guerriero, Univ Southern Calif, 70. Mailing Add: 3036 Veteran Ave Los Angeles CA 90034

LE PELLEY, GUERNSEY
CARTOONIST
b Chicago, Ill, May 14, 10. Study: Principia Col, 28-29; Art Inst Chicago; Acad Fine Art, Northwestern Univ; Northeastern Univ; Harvard Univ, BA. Pos: Free lance writer & artist, 32-; auth, daily comic strip Tubby, Christian Sci Monitor, 35-, ed cartoonist, 61- Mem: Asn Am Ed Cartoonists (past adv bd); Nat Cartoonists Soc. Mailing Add: 1 Norway St Boston MA 02115

LEPPER, ROBERT LEWIS
EDUCATOR, SCULPTOR
b Aspinwall, Pa, Sept 10, 06. Study: Carnegie Inst Technol, BA; Harvard Univ Grad Sch Bus Admin, cert. Work: Butler Mus Am Art, Youngstown, Ohio; Carnegie Mus Art, Pittsburgh, Pa; Ind Univ, Bloomington; Mus Mod Art, New York, NY; Stedelijk Mus, Amsterdam, Holland. Comn: Mural, WVa Univ, Morgantown, 40 & Airport, Charlestown, WVa, 50; sculpture, Pittsburgh Hilton Hotel, Pa, 59; windows, Convent Immaculate Conception, Washington, Pa, 61; sculpture, New York World's Fair, 64. Exhib: Pittsburgh Int, 61; Artist-Teacher Today-USA, State Univ NY Col Oswego, 69; Blossom, Kent Third Invitational, 70. Teaching: Prof design, Carnegie-Mellon Univ, 30-75. Awards: Medal, Pa Soc Architects, 61; Purchase Award, Carnegie Mus Art, 63; Honored Artist, Assoc Artists Pittsburgh, 70. Bibliog: Student projects, Indust Design, 2/57; T R Newman (auth), Plastics as an Art Form, Chilton, 64; N Roukes (auth), Sculpture in Plastics, Reinhold, 69. Mem: Assoc Artists Pittsburgh (mem bd, 64). Media: Mixed Media. Publ: Auth, The problem of the creative artist in America today, Col Art J, 54; auth, Signs & symbols, Archit Record, 56; co-auth, Transit vehicle design & rider satisfaction, Urban & Social Change Rev, 70; co-auth, Ride on, Indust Design, 71. Mailing Add: 5732 Kentucky Ave Pittsburgh PA 15232

LERMAN, DORIS (HARRIET)
PAINTER, SCULPTOR
b Newark, NJ. Study: Peoples Art Ctr, Inst Mod Art; Napeague Inst Art; also with Victor D'Amico & William Baziotes. Comn: Poster, Guild Hall, Exhib, Mus Mod Art, 55; one-man shows, Gallery 84, New York, 71, 73 & 75 & Georgetown Graphics Art Gallery, Washington, DC, 74; Artists of Springs, East Hampton, 73-77; Circulating Exhib, Suffolk Co Schs, 75; Recycled Art, Guild Hall, East Hampton, 77; Greenwich Art Barn, Conn, 77. Awards: Hon Mention, Guild Hall, 65 & 74. Mem: Napeague Inst Art (mem bd dirs & treas, 73-); Asn Artist Run Galleries (bd mem, 74-75); Metrop Painters & Sculptors; Guild Hall; Parrish Mus, Southampton, NY. Style & Technique: Mixed media, particularly transformation of various materials into an aesthetic expression concentrating on surface and form. Media: Found materials. Dealer: Gallery 84 1046 Madison Ave New York NY 10021. Mailing Add: 200 E 16th St New York NY 10003

LERMAN, LEO
WRITER, ART HISTORIAN
b New York, NY, May 23, 14. Teaching: Lectr, TV & radio; lectr art of biog & writing of children's bks, NY Univ. Awards: Lotus Club Award for the Museum—100 Years of the Metropolitan Museum of Art, 69. Res: Italian Renaissance; international 19th century art especially 1830-1914; art of the 1920's. Publ: Auth, Leonardo da Vinci: Artist & Scientist, Bobbs-Merrill, 40; auth, Michelangelo: A Renaissance Profile, Knoff, 41; auth, The Museum—100 Years of the Metropolitan Museum of Art, Viking, 69; contribr, Vogue, New York Times, Atlantic Monthly, Sat Rev & others; feature consult, Vogue. Mailing Add: 205 W 57th St New York NY 10019

LERMAN, ORA
PAINTER, SCULPTOR
b Campbellsville, Ky, Mar 14, 38. Study: Antioch Col, BA; Pratt Inst, with Calvin Albert, MFA; Art Students League, with Theodoros Stamos; Brooklyn Mus, with Reuben Tam. Work: Nat Collection Fine Arts, Smithsonian Inst, Washington, DC. Exhib: One-woman shows, Prince St Gallery, 71, 72, 74 & 76; Contemporary Sculpture, Suffolk Mus, Stony Brook, NY, 74; 20 Fulbright Artists, Inst Int Educ, NY, 75; Works on Paper, Brooklyn Mus, 75; Sons & Others, Women See Men, Queens Mus, 75. Teaching: Mem fac sculpture, New Sch Social Res, 67-69; assoc prof sculpture & painting, Suffolk Co Community Col, 71- Awards: Fulbright Fel to Japan, 63-65; Mae Pomerantz Award, Brooklyn Mus, 75-76; MacDowell Colony Fel. Bibliog: Lawrence Campbell (auth), articles in Art News, 4/71 & 10/73; John Gruen (auth), article in Soho Weekly News, 10/75. Mem: Col Art Asn Am; Women in the Arts. Style & Technique: Figurative painting. Media: Oil, Watercolor; Wax, Clay. Dealer: Prince St Gallery 106 Prince St New York NY 10012. Mailing Add: 463 West St New York NY 10014

LERNER, ABE
BOOK DESIGNER, PHOTOGRAPHER
b New York, NY, Sept 14, 08. Exhib: Cooper Union (bk designs), 48; YMCA (photographs), Newburyport, Mass, 74-75; New York Community Col, 75. Collections Arranged: Exhib of art bks, Every Home a Museum, Assoc Am Art Gallery, Am Inst Graphic Arts, 51. Teaching: Lect series on design problems and their solution for young bk designers, Am Inst Graphic Arts; instr bk design & prod, Am Inst Graphic Arts, 41-42; instr bk design & prod, Columbia Univ, 53-54. Pos: Asst prod mgr, Viking Press, 37-42; art dir & prod mgr, World Publ Co, Cleveland & New York, 42-50 & 54-64; chmn, Trade Bk Clin, Am Inst Graphic Arts, 53-54; chmn, 50 Bks of Yr Comt, 55; dir design & prod, The Macmillan Co, 64-71, ed art bks, 71-74; free lancing currently.Awards: Bks included in Fifty Books of the Year, eight yrs, 38-54; Trade Bk Clin monthly selections, 38- Mem: The Grolier Club; The Typophiles (vpres); Am Printing Hist Asn (bd trustees). Publ: Contribr, articles on typography & bk prod to Fine Print, Publisher's Weekly & Bk Prod; also articles in The Writer. Mailing Add: 101 W 12th St New York NY 10011

LERNER, ABRAM
MUSEUM DIRECTOR
b New York, NY, Apr 11, 13. Study: NY Univ, BA; also var art schs, New York & Florence. Exhib: One-man exhib, Davis Gallery, New York; Brooklyn Mus; Pa Acad Fine Arts; ACA Gallery, New York; Peridot Gallery, New York. Pos: Asst dir, ACA Gallery, 45-55; asst dir, Artists Gallery, 55-56; cur, Hirshhorn Collection, 56-67, dir, Hirshhorn Mus & Sculpture Garden, Smithsonian Inst, 67- Mem: Arch Am Art (adv bd). Mailing Add: 135 E 65th St New York NY 10021

LERNER, ALEXANDER
COLLECTOR
Collection: Impressionist thru hard edge avant garde art. Mailing Add: 785 Fifth Ave New York NY 10022

LERNER, MARILYN ANN
PAINTER
b Milwaukee, Wis, Sept 19, 42. Study: Univ Wis, BS, 64; Pratt Inst, 66. Exhib: Two-man show, Kasle Gallery, Detroit, 70, Gallery Selections, 72; Whitney Mus Am Art Ann, New York, 71; Am Women Artists, Gedok, Ger, 71; Drawings, Corcoran Mus, Washington, DC, 73; Max Hutchinson Gallery, New York, 73; plus others. Teaching: Instr printmaking, Brooklyn Mus, summer 69; instr environ sculpture, Newark Sch Fine & Indust Arts, 69-71; adj lectr

art, Hunter Col, 71-72; adj lectr art, La Guardia Community Col, 73-75; vis artist, Fla Int Univ. Mailing Add: 262 Bowery New York NY 10012

LERNER, NATHAN BERNARD
PHOTOGRAPHER, PAINTER
b Chicago, Ill, Mar 30, 13. Study: Nat Acad of Art, Chicago; Art Inst of Chicago; New Bauhaus, Chicago; Sch of Design in Chicago, BA; also with Archipenko, Moholy-Nagy and G Kepes. KMus Nat Mod Art, George Pompidou Centre, Paris, France; Mus of Mod Art, New York; Bauhaus-Archiv, Berlin, Ger; Nihon Univ, Tokyo, Japan; Art Inst of Chicago. Exhib: Bauhaus, Weimar 1919-25, Dessau 1925-28, Mus of Mod Art, New York, 38; Bauhaus, Int Traveling Exhib, 68; one-man shows, Mus of Sci & Indust, Chicago, 73, Bauhaus-Archiv, Berlin, Ger, 74; Pentax Gallery, Tokyo, Japan, 75; Emergence of Modernism in Ill, 1914-1940, Ill State Mus, Springfield, 75; Photogr & the City, Mus of Contemp Art, Chicago, 76; Lazlo Moholy-Nagy Exhib, Georges Pompidou Centre, Paris, 77; Recent Acquisitions, Int Mus of Photog, George Eastman House, Rochester, NY, 77. Teaching: Instr photogr, Sch of Design in Chicago, 39-43; instr product design, Inst of Design, Chicago, 45-49. Pos: Head photog dept, Sch of Design in Chicago, 41-43; head of product design, Inst of Design in Chicago, 45-49, dean fac & students, 45-49, actg educ dir, 46-47. Bibliog: Gerald Fromberg (auth), Nathan Lerner - The Bauhaus Years (film), Bradley Univ, Peoria, Ill, 74; Elaine A King (auth), Nathan Lerner - photographer, Midwest Art, 76. Mem: Artists Guild of Chicago. Publ: Auth, Space in Your Pictures, Minican Photog, 42; co-auth with Gyorgy Kepes, Light as a medium of expression, Encyclopedia of Arts, 45. Dealer: Allen Frumkin Gallery 520 N Michigan Ave Chicago IL 60611. Mailing Add: 849 W Webster Chicago IL 60614

LERNER, RICHARD J
ART DEALER
b New York, NY, Feb 23, 29. Study: Univ Denver, BA. Pos: Dir, Lerner-Heller Gallery. Specialty: Twentieth century art. Mailing Add: 956 Madison Ave New York NY 10021

LERNER, SANDY R
PAINTER, LITHOGRAPHER
b Pa, May 13, 18. Study: Pratt Inst; Art Stud League; Nat Univ Mex; Wahington Univ; also with Diego Rivera, Orozco, Fred Conway, Frank Reilly, Hans Hofmann & Zorach. Work: Smithsonian Inst & Navy Mus, Washington, DC; Brooklyn Navy Yard, NY; Tel Aviv Mus, Israel; Pratt Inst, Brooklyn; plus others. Exhib: Nat Arts Club; Burr Artists; Audubon Artists; Salmagundi Artists; NJ Prof Artists; plus others. Pos: Exec dir, Art Restoration Tech Inst. Mem: Salmagundi Club (vchmn, 70-); Burr Artists (house comt co-chmn, 71-); Col Art Asn Am (vpres, 69-70); Am Inst Art & Conserv; Int Inst Conserv Hist Works & Fine Arts; plus others. Style & Technique: Western and abstract painting. Media: Oil, Mixed Media. Mailing Add: Art Restoration Tech Inst 13 W 36th St New York NY 10018

LERNER LEVINE, MARION
PAINTER, INSTRUCTOR
b London, Eng, Oct 31, 31; US citizen. Study: Univ Chicago, 47-50; Art Inst of Chicago, BFA, 54, study with Paul Wieghardt, Max Kahn, Vera Berdich; Calif State Col, Los Angeles, 67. Exhib: Chicago Graphic Workshop, Chicago Art Inst, 54; Downey Mus, Calif, 65; Oils & Watercolors, Prince St Gallery, New York, 71, 73, 75 & 77; Women Choose Women, New York Cult Ctr, 73; Report from Soho, Grey Gallery, NY Univ, 75; Contemp Reflections, Aldrich Mus, Ridgefield, Conn, 76; Close to Home, Genesis Galleries, New York, 76; Fugurative Art in New York, Soho Ctr for Visual Arts, 77; Whitney Counterweight, Rabinowitch & Guerra Gallery, 77; Marion Lerner Levine Oil Paintings 1972-78, Contemp Arts Gallery, NY Univ, 78. Teaching: Lectr watercolor, Sch Gen Studies, Brooklyn Col, 76-78; instr drawing, Univ Calif, Los Angeles, 77. Pos: Chmn, Exhib Momentum, Chicago, 52-53. Awards: First Prize, Champaign County Art Fair, 59; Hon Mention, Downey Mus Juried Exhib, 65. Bibliog: K D Schnapper (auth), Marion Lerner Levine, Feminist Art J, 77; Lawrence Alloway (auth), Art, The Nation, 77; Barbara Cavalieri (auth), Marion Lerner Levine, WomanArt, 77. Mem: Col Art Asn; Womens Caucus on Art; Women in Arts. Style & Technique: Still life paintings, painted thinly with luminous tones, in which juxtapositions of scale and images hint at symbolic meanings. Media: Oil; Watercolor. Publ: Contribr, How real is realist painting?, Women Artists Newsletter, 76; co-contribr, Artists do it themselves at Prince Street Gallery, Women Artists Newsletter, 77. Dealer: Prince Street Gallery 106 Prince St New York NY 10012; Gilbert Einstein Assocs 243 E 82nd St New York NY 10028. Mailing Add: 140 Park Pl Brooklyn NY 11217

LE ROY, HAROLD M
PAINTER, LECTURER
b New York, NY, Dec 12, 05. Study: Columbia Univ, BA; Brooklyn Mus Art Sch; Art Students League; Hans Hofmann Art Sch. Work: Butler Inst Am Art, Youngstown, Ohio; Chrysler Mus at Norfolk, Va; Slater Mem Mus, Norwich, Conn; Smithsonian Inst, Washington, DC; Skirball Mus Art, Los Angeles, Calif. Exhib: Societe de L'Ecole Francaise, Mus Artes Mod, Paris, France, 69 & 70; Audubon Artists Ann Exhibs, Nat Acad Galleries, New York, 70-72; Spring Arts Festival, Elec Indust Ctr, Flushing, NY, 72; Am Soc Contemp Artists 57th Ann, Lever House, 75; Artists Equity Exhib, Union Carbide Gallery, 75. Awards: Thomas Jefferson Silver Medal, Thomas Jefferson High Sch, 24; Heydenryk Award for Graphic Art, 77. Bibliog: Eleanor Marko (auth), The palette of Le Roy, Daily Register NJ, 66; Barbara Consolas (auth), Harold M Le Roy, artist, 66 & Le Roy & the World of Art, 72, Plotinus Press; Robert S Orlove (auth), The Mind of Le Roy, W T M Publ, 73. Mem: Artists Equity Asn New York (bd dir, 67-); Metrop Painters & Sculptors; Am Vet Soc Artists; Am Soc Contemp Artists (1st vpres, 75); Contemp Circle (vpres, 75). Style & Technique: Abstract surrealism usually in brilliant colors. Media: Oil, Serigraph. Dealer: Lexington Art Gallery 968 Lexington Ave New York NY 10021. Mailing Add: 1916 Ave K Brooklyn NY 11230

LESCH, ALMA WALLACE
TEXTILE CRAFTSMAN, EDUCATOR
b 1917, McCracken Co, Ky. Study: Murray State Univ, BS, 41; Louisville Sch Art, 59-61; Univ Louisville, MEd, 62. Work: Objects: USA, Johnson Collection; J B Speed Art Mus, Louisville, Ky; Evansville Mus of Art, Ind; Mint Mus, Charlotte, NC; Flint Inst Art, Mich; Macauley Theater, Louisville. Comn: Draperies, Bernheim Forest Nature Mus, Clermont, Ky, 62; wall hangings, First Nat Bank, Louisville, 67, First Presby Church, Columbus, Ind, 70, Educ Bldg, Okla Christian Col, 71 & Citizens Fidelity Bank, Louisville, 72. Exhib: Nat Decorative Arts Wichita, Kans, 62, 66 & 70; Fabric Collage, Mus Contemp Crafts, New York, 65; Fine Art of Collage, Kunstegewerbemus, Zurich, Switz, 68; Objects: USA, Smithsonian Inst, 70; 1st World Crafts Exhib, Toronto, Ont, 74; plus others. Teaching: Assoc prof textiles, Louisville Sch Art, 61-; instr vegetable dyeing, Haystack Mountain Sch Crafts, Deer Isle, Maine, summers 66 & 70; instr vegetable dyeing, Philadelphia Col Textiles; instr vegetable dyeing, Memphis Acad Art, summer 67; instr vegetable dyeing, Indian Sch, Santa Fe, 72; instr Arrowmont Sch Crafts, Gatlinburg, Tenn, 70-77; adj prof, Univ Louisville, 75- Awards: Merit & Craft Awards, J B Speed Art Mus, 68, 70 & 72; Nat Competition Award, Wichita, Kans, 72; Best of Show, Evansville Mus of Art, 78. Bibliog: Rose Slivka (auth), Craftsmen of the Modern World, Horizon, 68; Lee Nordness (auth), Objects: USA, Viking, 70; Portraits without Faces, Ky Arts Comn film, 77-78. Mem: World Crafts Coun; Am Crafts Coun (Ky State Rep, 64-69); Ky Guild Artists & Craftsmen; Louisville Craftsmen Guild. Style & Technique: Needlework; fabric collage portraits are made from clothing; other types of abstract needlework wall hangings. Media: Textiles. Publ: Auth, Vegetable Dyeing, Watson-Guptill, 70. Mailing Add: PO Box 67 Shepherdsville KY 40165

LESH, RICHARD D
PAINTER, INSTRUCTOR
b Grand Island, Nebr, May 3, 27. Study: Univ Nebr; Univ Denver, BA & MA; Mexico City Col. Exhib: Midwest Biennial, 58; Nebraska Centennial, Joslyn Mus, Omaha, 67 & Sheldon Gallery, Lincoln, 68; Nebr Wesleyan Univ Painting Ann, Lincoln, 78. Teaching: Instr painting & head dept art, Wayne State Col, 51- Pos: Pres, Nebr Art Coun, 68-69. Awards: Second Prize for Painting, Midwest Biennial, Joslyn Mus, 55; First Prize for Painting, May Show, Sioux City Art Mus, 58. Mem: Col Art Asn Am; Nebr Art Teachers Asn (vpres, 56-58); Kappa Pi (sponsor, 51-). Mailing Add: 505 E Tenth St Wayne NE 68787

LESHER, MARIE PALMISANO
SCULPTOR
b Reading, Pa, Sept 20, 19. Study: Art Students League; Berte Fashion Studio, Philadelphia, Pa; Mus of Fine Arts Sch & Univ, Houston, Tex. Work: Beaumont Art Mus, Tex; Laguna Gloria Art Mus, Austin, Tex; Carver Mus, Tuskegee, Ala; Reading Pub Mus, Pa. Exhib: One-person shows, Houston Libr, Tex, 67 & 71, Joske's Gallery, Houston, 71, Beaumont Art Mus, Tex, 73, Longview Mus of Arts, Tex, 73, Hooks-Epstein Galleries, Houston, 73 & 76, Houston Baptist Univ, 74 & McAllen Int Mus, Tex, 76; Seventh Ann Eight State Exhib, Okla Art Ctr, Oklahoma City, 65; 12th Ann Exhib, Denver Art Mus, Colo, 68; Knickerbocker Artists 19th Ann, New York, 68; Audubon Artists 27th Ann, New York, 68; US State Dept Art in Embassies, 68-78; 28th Ann Nat Exhib, Jersey City Mus, NJ, 69; 22nd Ann, Butler Inst of Am Art, Youngstown, Ohio, 70; Catherine Lorillard Wolfe Art Club 77th Ann, New York, 73; Nat Sculpture Soc 40th & 41st Ann, New York, 73 & 74; Int Women's Arts Festival, New York, 76; 14th Biennial, Joslyn Mus of Art, Omaha, Nebr, 76. Teaching: Instr sculpture, Sculptors Workshop, Houston, 72-73. Pos: Advert mgr & art dir, Lowensteins, Memphis, Tenn, 45-46, Levy's, Houston, Tex, 46-50, Sakowitz, Houston, 50-52, Battelstein's, 59-60. Awards: Purchase Award, Ninth Ann Tuskegee Inst, Carver Mus, 68; First Award, Tex Fine Arts Asn, 73; First Purchase Award, Tri-State Exhib, Beaumont, Tex, Mobile Found, 75. Bibliog: Reva Remy (auth), L'Art a l'estranger, La Revue Mod, Paris, 6/68; Helen Anderson (auth), The sculptress, Houston Post, 3/68; Marie David (auth), Please do touch!, Houston Chronicle, 6/69. Mem: Artists Equity of New York; Tex Soc of Sculptors Int (dir, 73-); Artists Equity of Philadelphia; Fashion Group (secy-treas, 47-48); Watercolor Art Soc, Houston. Style & Technique: Realistic to abstracted; spontaneity and control best preserved by working directly in wax for bronze casting. Media: Bronze, wood and clay. Dealer: Hooks-Epstein Galleries 1200 Bissonnet Houston TX 77005. Mailing Add: 10130 Shady River Rd Houston TX 77042

LESLEY, PARKER
ART HISTORIAN, MUSEUM CURATOR
b Baltimore, Md, Aug 31, 13. Study: Stanford Univ, AB, 34; Univ Paris, cert, 35; Princeton Univ, MFA, 37; Univ Brussels, cert, 37; NY Univ, 47-48; with C R Morey, Erwin Panofsky & Marcel Aubert. Collections Arranged: Assembled, catalogued & arranged numerous exhibs, Cooper Union Mus Arts of Decoration, 50-54. Teaching: Asst prof art & archit, Univ Minn, 39-42; from asst prof to prof art, Old Dom Univ, 59- Pos: Cur Europ art, Detroit Inst Arts, 38-39; keeper, Dept Exhibs, Cooper Union Mus Arts of Decoration, 50-54; cur decorative arts, Nat Gallery Art, 74- Awards: Chevalier, Order Polonia Restituta, Poland, 46; Hon Medal Art & Sci of House-Order of Orange-Nassau, Neth, 47. Mem: Col Art Asn Am. Publ: Auth, Early Christian, Byzantine & Romanesque Art, Detroit Inst Arts, 39; auth, Handbook & Catalogue of the Lillian Thomas Pratt Collection of Russian Imperial Jewels, Va Mus Fine Arts, 60; auth, Renaissance Jewels & Jeweled Objects, Baltimore Mus Art, 68. Mailing Add: Old Dominion Univ Norfolk VA 23508

LESLIE, ALFRED
PAINTER
b New York, NY, Oct 29, 27. Study: Study with Tony Smith, William Baziotes, Hale Woodruff & John McPherson; NY Univ, 56-57. Work: Mus Mod Art & Whitney Mus Am Art, New York; Mus Mod Art, Sao Paulo, Brazil; Nat Mus, Stockholm, Sweden; Kunsthalle, Basel, Switz; Walker Art Ctr, Minneapolis; plus others. Exhib: White Mus, Cornell Univ; Am Fedn Arts Traveling Exhib; Univ Nebr; Jewish Mus; Carnegie Int, Pittsburgh; plus others. Teaching: Great Neck Adult Educ Prog, New York, 56-57; San Francisco Art Inst, summer 64. Awards: Guggenheim Fel, 69. Publ: Ed, The Hasty Papers, 60; co-dir, co-producer, ed & publ, Pull My Daisy (film). Mailing Add: c/o Martha Jackson Gallery 521 W 57th St New York NY 10019

LESNICK, STEPHEN WILLIAM
PAINTER, INSTRUCTOR
b Bridgeport, Conn, Mar 22, 31. Study: Silvermine Col Art; Art Career Sch; also with Revington Arthur, Jon McCleand, Jack Wheat & Gail Symon. Work: Boulder City Hosp Art Collection, Nev. Comn: Indust paintings, Burndy Libr Art & Sci, 59; portrait of Gov mansion, comn by Gov Paul Laxalt, Carson City, 68; commemorative coin for Boulder Dam, Elks Lodge, Las Vegas, 71-78; medallion series, Nev State Mus, 77- Exhib: All New Eng Art Exhib, Conn, 55; Layout & Design Int Art Competition, Japan, 63; Ann Conn Relig Art Exhib, 63 & 64; Ann Am Watercolor Soc Show, 68; Helldorado Western Art Exhib, Nev, 68. Teaching: Instr art, Desert Art League, Boulder City, 65-66; instr art, Las Vegas Art League & Artists & Craftsmans Guild, Nev, 65-68 & Clark Co Community Col; owner & instr, Lesnick Art Studio, Las Vegas, 65- Pos: Layout designer, Vacart Art Studio, Stamford, Conn, 60-65; art dir, Kelley & Reber Advert, Las Vegas, 65-66; illusr, E G & G, Inc, Las Vegas, 66-73; art ed, Las Vegas Sun, 70-; syndicated newspaper columnist, Art for Everyone. Awards: Int Design Show, Japan, 63; Conn Relig Show, Hallmark Greeting Cards, 63 & 64; First Prize, Nev Bicentennial Commemorative Medallion, Franklin Mint, 72. Bibliog: Articles in Desert Scope, 69-71. Mem: Nev State Watercolor Soc (chmn bd). Media: All Media. Interest: Inventor and manufacturer of The Funny Brush. Mailing Add: 1127 Westminster Ave Las Vegas NV 89119

LETENDRE, RITA
PAINTER
b Drummondville, Que, Nov 1, 28. Study: Ecole Beaux Arts, Montreal; P E Borduas, Montreal. Work: Mus Art Contemporain, Montreal; Mus Beaux-Arts, Montreal; Long Beach Mus Fine Arts, Calif; Rose Art Mus, Brandeis Univ, Waltham, Mass; Mus Que. Comn: Wall painting, Calif State Col, Long Beach, 65; mural, Greenwin of Toronto, 71; wall painting, Benson & Hedges, Neil-Wyick Col, Toronto, 71; mural, J D S Investment, Sheridan Mall,

Pickering, Ont, 72. Exhib: Internationalism des Arts, Mus Beaux-Arts, 60; 5 Festival di due Mondi, Spoleto, Italy, 62; IV Biennale Can Painting, Tate Gallery, London, Eng, 63; Can Pavilion Expo 67, Montreal, 67; Que Pavilion, World's Fair, Osaka, Japan, 70; plus others. Awards: Le Prix de Peinture, Concours Artistique Que, 61; Que Bourse de Recherche, 67; Can Arts Coun Sr Grant Award, 71. Bibliog: C Delloye (auth), Rita Letendre, Art Aujourdhui, 62; D Travers (auth), Rita Letendre wall painting, Arts & Archit, 66; Jules Heller (auth), Printmaking Today, Holt, Rinehart & Winston, 71. Mem: Royal Can Acad Art. Media: Acrylic. Mailing Add: 288 Sherbourne St Toronto ON M5A 2S1 Can

LEVEE, JOHN H
PAINTER, SCULPTOR
b Los Angeles, Calif, Apr 10, 24. Study: Art Ctr Sch & Chenard Sch, Los Angeles; Univ Calif, Los Angeles, BA, 48; New Sch Social Res, with Stuart Davis, Abe Rattner & Kunyoshi, 48-49; Acad Julian, Paris, 49-51; Grand Prix, 51. Work: Mus Mod Art, New York; Whitney Mus Am Art, New York; Guggenheim Mus, New York; Corcoran Gallery Art, Washington, DC; Mus Mod Art, Paris; plus many others in pub & pvt collections. Comn: Wall, Architects, Chateau Vaudreuil, Paris, 71-72; walls, Bank Credit Com, Paris, 72-73; inside-outside floor design (3600 sq ft), Sch in Marne-le-Vallée, Paris, 75; 24 walls & 15 banners, Prudential Life Insurance Co, Los Angeles, Calif, 77. Exhib: Salon Realities, Paris, 54-; Carnegie Inst Int, 55-58; Corcoran Gallery Art, 56-58; New Acquisitions, Mus Mod Art, New York, 57, Young Am Painters, 57-58; Whitney Mus Am Art, 57, 58 & 66; Haifa Mus Art, Israel, 63; Phoenix Art Mus, Ariz, 64; Krannert Art Mus, Univ Ill, 65; Walker Art Ctr, Minneapolis, 65; Tel Aviv Mus, Israel, 69; Palm Springs Mus, Calif, 77; plus many others. Teaching: Vis prof art, Univ Ill, 64-65; vis prof art, Wash Univ, 67; vis prof art, NY Univ, 67-68; vis prof art, Univ Southern Calif, 70. Awards: Grand Prix, 1st Biennial Paris, 59 & Int Woll Found, 75; Ford Fel, Tamarind Workshop, 69; Woolmark Found Prix, 74; plus others. Bibliog: Seuphor (auth), Dictionary of Abstract Art, 57; Reed (auth), A Concise History of Modern Art, 60; Ragon & Seuphor (auth), History of Modern Painting, 69. Style & Technique: Soft edged color geometry based on the containment and opposition of forms and colors. Media: Acrylic on Canvas or Cardboard, Plexiglas. Collection: African, pre-Columbian and contemporary painting and sculpture. Dealer: Andre Emmerich Gallery 41 E 57th St New York NY 10022; Leavin Margo Gallery 812 N Robertson Blvd Los Angeles CA 90035. Mailing Add: 119 rue Notre Dame des Champs Paris France

LEVEN, ARLINE CLAIRE
MUSEUM CURATOR
b St Louis, Mo, May 2, 36. Study: Univ Mich, BA(Eng lit); Washington Univ, St Louis, MA (art hist); Summer Inst, Boston Univ; Attingham Summer Sch, London. Collections Arranged: Rape of the Sabine Women, 71 & Hugh Ferris Drawings: An Architect's Vision, 76, Washington Univ Gallery of Art. Pos: Cur, Washington Univ Gallery of Art. Mailing Add: Washington Univ Gallery of Art St Louis MO 63130

LEVEN, RUTH ANN
ART ADMINISTRATOR
b Canton, Ohio, Nov 1, 40. Study: Brown Univ, AB, 62; studio work at RI Sch of Design; Harvard Bus Sch, MBA, 64. Pos: Asst treas, 70-72 & treas, 72-, The Metrop Mus of Art, New York; Mus Aid Panel (mem), New York State Coun on the Arts, 77. Mem: Am Asn of Mus. Mailing Add: c/o The Metrop Mus of Art Fifth Ave at 82nd St New York NY 10028

LEVENTHAL, RUTH LEE
PAINTER, SCULPTOR
b New York, NY, Oct 5, 23. Study: Art Students League; Nat Acad Design; also with John Terken, Robert Tompkins, Maxim Bugaster & Frank Eliscu. Work: Fedn Jewish Philanthropies, New York; Mus Mod Art, Israel; Tel Aviv Univ, Israel; Goldsmith's Hall, London, Eng; Riverside Mem Chapel, New York. Comn: Three paintings, New York World's Fair, 64-65; sculpture, Riverside Mem Chapel, 70, six sculptures, 72; portrait of Golda Meir, pvt comn, 72. Exhib: Nat Acad Design, New York; New York World's Fair, 64-65; Parke Bernet Galleries; Nat Arts Club, New York; one-man shows, Kottler Galleries, New York, 70, Temple Sinai, Roslyn, Long Island, 71 & Chapman Sculpture Gallery. Sculptured Gold Jewelry, Bergdorf-Goodman, New York, 72. Awards: Salmagundi Award, 75 & 76; Allied Artists Am Award, 75; Award for Portraiture Sculpture, Nat Acad Design, 78. Mem: Fel Royal Soc Arts; Nat Soc Arts & Lett (co-chmn lit, 72, bd dir, 74-77); Catharine Lorillard Wolfe Art Club (bd dir, 74-77); Allied Artists Am; Salmagundi Club; plus others. Style & Technique: Carve in slate. Media: All Media. Publ: Co-auth, Take One of My Pills, 65 & Our Romance is Over, 66, New Recording; illusr, cover, NATA Quart, fall-winter 70. Mailing Add: 425 E 58th St New York NY 10022

LEVERING, ROBERT K
PAINTER, ILLUSTRATOR
b Ypsilanti, Mich, May 22, 19. Study: Univ Ariz, AB; Art Inst Chicago; Brooklyn Mus Sch Art; Art Students League. Work: USAF Collection, Washington, DC; UN We Believe Collection; also in pvt collections. Comn: Portraits of Kennedy, Eisenhower, U Thant, Martin Luther King & Dag Hamerskjold; plus pvt comns. Exhib: Seven exhibs, New York City Ctr Gallery; Soc Illustrators Gallery, New York; Mikelson Gallery, Washington, DC, 68; Art Dirs Exhib, 69. Teaching: Guest lectr & critic, Parsons Sch Design, 65- Awards: Citations, Soc Illustrators, 62-64, Gold Medal, 69; Citation, NJ Art Dirs Club, 69; Soc Publ Designers Award, 69. Mem: Graphic Artists Guild. Style & Technique: Representational; abstract and biomorphic fantasy. Publ: Illusr, leading nat mag, bks & Newspapers. Mailing Add: 330 E 79th St New York NY 10021

LEVI, JOSEF
PAINTER
b New York, NY, Feb 17, 38. Study: Univ Conn, BA, 59; Columbia Univ, 60. Work: Mus Mod Art, New York; Albright-Knox Gallery, Buffalo; Aldrich Mus Contemp Art, Ridgefield, Conn; Krannert Art Mus, Univ Ill, Urbana; Des Moines Art Ctr. Exhib: Highlights of the 65-66 Art Season, Aldrich Mus Contemp Art, 66; Sound, Light, Silence, Art that Performs, Nelson Atkins Gallery, Kansas City, 67; Light, Motion, Space, Walker Art Ctr, Minneapolis, 67; Whitney Mus Am Art Ann, New York, 68; Smithsonian Inst Near East & SAsia Traveling Exhib, 71. Awards: Purchase Award, Univ Ill, Urbana, 66; Selected for New Talent USA, Art in Am, 66. Bibliog: William Wilson (auth), In the eye of the beholder, Art News, 2/70; J Patrice Marandel (auth), Preface for Silkscreen Portfolio, Domberger, 71; Allen Ellenzweig (auth), Still life with art history: the collage paintings of Josef Levi, Arts Mag, 12/76. Mailing Add: 171 W 71st St New York NY 10023

LEVI, JULIAN (E)
PAINTER, EDUCATOR
b New York, NY, June 20, 00. Study: Pa Acad Fine Arts. Work: Metrop Mus Art, Mus Mod Art & Whitney Mus Am Art, New York; Nat Collection Fine Arts, Washington, DC; Pa Acad Fine Arts, Philadelphia; plus many others. Exhib: Nat Acad Design; Pa Acad Fine Arts; Detroit Inst of Art; Butler Inst Am Art, Youngstown, Ohio; Venice Biennial; Pittsburgh Int; Krannert Art Mus, Univ Ill, 61; Art: USA, Smithsonian Inst, 61; Retrospective, Boston Univ, 62, New Britain Mus Am Art, Conn & Rehn Galleries, New York, 74; Whitney Mus Am Art Ann, 64. Teaching: Instr painting, New Sch Social Res, 45-66, dir art workshop; instr painting, Art Students League, 46-; instr painting, Pa Acad Fine Arts, 64-77. Pos: Dir art workshops dept, New Sch Social Res, 60- Awards: Hon Mention, Carnegie Inst, 45; Grant in Art, Nat Inst Arts & Lett, 55; Temple Gold Medal, Pa Acad Fine Arts, 62. Mem: Nat Inst Arts & Lett (mem coun, 68-71). Media: Oil. Interest: Color lithography. Publ: Auth, Modern Art: an Introduction, Pitman, 61. Dealer: Frank Rehn Gallery 655 Madison Ave New York NY 10021. Mailing Add: 79 W 12th St New York NY 10011

LEVICK, MR & MRS IRVING
COLLECTORS
Collection: Contemporary American and European artists, including Gatch, Weber, Dove, Hartley, Rivers, Levine, Marin, Weinberg, King, Knaths, Shahn, Roth, Tam, Greene, Guerero, Avery, Dubuffet, Levee, Nikos, Nicolson, Sutherland, Marini, Fraser, Francis, Wiley, Buggiani, Kinley, Lawrence, Appel, Corneille, Severini, Kinigstein, Katzman, Rouault, Graves, Brice, Heerup, Wols, Bauermeister, Jimmy Ernst, James Wines, Lynn Chadwick, Saul Steinberg, Davies, Seymour Drumlevitch, Harriet Grief and others. Mailing Add: 227 Nottingham Terr Buffalo NY 14216

LEVIN, GAIL
CURATOR, ART HISTORIAN
b Atlanta, Ga, Feb 10, 48. Study: Simmons Col, BA, 69; Sorbonne, Paris, 68; Tufts Univ, MA, 70; Rutgers Univ, PhD(art hist), 76. Exhib Arranged: Morgan Russell: Synchromist Studies, 1910-1922, Mus Mod Art, New York, 76; Synchromism and Am Color Abstraction, 1910-1925, 78. Teaching: Instr art hist, Conn Col, New London, 75-76. Pos: Assoc cur, Edward Hopper Collection, Whitney Mus Am Art, 76- Mem: Am Asn Mus; Women's Caucus for Art; Col Art Asn Am. Publ: Auth, Morgan Russell's Notebooks: an American Avant-Garde Painter in Paris, RACAR (Can Art Rev), 76; auth, Morgan Russell: The Avant-Garde Dilemma, In: California: Five Footnotes to Modern Art Hist, Los Angeles Co Mus, Los Angeles, 77: auth, Introduction & Edward Hopper: Chronology, In: Edward Hopper at Kennedy Galleries, Kennedy Galleries, New York, 77; auth, The Tradition of the Heroic Figure in Synchromist Abstractions, Arts Mag, 77; auth, Synchromism and American Color Abstraction, 1910-1925, George Braziller, 78. Mailing Add: Whitney Mus Am Art 945 Madison Ave New York NY 10021

LEVIN, JEANNE
PAINTER, COLLECTOR
b Cleveland, Ohio, Dec 13, 01. Study: Cleveland Sch Art; Wells Col, BA; Cranbrook Acad Art; Soc Arts & Crafts, Detroit; Norton Gallery & Sch Art; pvt study with Gerald Brockhurst, Ernest Fiene, Bruce Mitchell & Zubel Katchadoorian. Work: Hirshhorn Mus & Sculpture Garden, Washington, DC; Norton Gallery, West Palm Beach; plus others. Exhib: One-man shows, Contemp Gallery, Palm Beach, Fla, 60, 63, 65 & 68, Norton Gallery, West Palm Beach, 67, Hokin Gallery, Palm Beach, 73, Palm Beach Jr Col, Lake Worth, Fla, 76, Flagler Art Ctr, West Palm Beach, 76, Fla Artists Group featured artist, Lighthouse Gallery, Tequestra, Fla, 78 & Wells Col, Aurora, NY, 78; Contemp Am Painting, Soc Four Arts, Palm Beach, 64-69 & 71; Benson Gallery, Bridgehampton, NY, 67; Compass Gallery, Nantucket, Mass, 67; Artists of the Hamptons, Guild Hall, East Hampton, NY, 75; Artists of the Region, Ashwaugh Hall, East Hampton, 75-77; Fla Artists Group, Norton Gallery, 75; Lighthouse Gallery, 77. Pos: Chmn Friends of Modern Art, 58-63; assoc trustee, Detroit Inst Arts, 58-63, chmn, Futurists Exhib, 61 & chmn, Acquisition Comt Mod Art; founding mem, Gallery Contemp Art, Palm Beach, 63; trustee, New York Studio Sch, 65-69. Awards: Hon Mention, Soc Four Arts, Palm Beach, 66, Four Arts Award, 67; First Prize, Lighthouse Gallery, 77. Mem: Artists Equity; Nat Soc Arts & Lett; Fla Artists Group Inc. Collection: Post-impressionists paintings and sculpture; contemporary paintings and sculpture; primitive sculpture, Greek, African and pre-Columbian; the complete collection was exhibited at Cranbrook Academy of Art, Detroit Institute of Arts and Norton Gallery of Art. Mailing Add: 316 Garden Rd Palm Beach FL 33480

LEVIN, KIM (KIM PATEMAN)
ART CRITIC, PAINTER
US citizen. Study: Vassar Col, AB; Yale-Norfolk Summer Sch Art; Columbia Univ, MA. Exhib: One-man shows, Suffolk Mus, Stony Brook, Long Island, 63, Poindexter Gallery, NY, 64 & 67 & Vassar Col Art Gallery, 65. Teaching: Lectr drawing, Philadelphia Col Art, 67-70; lectr drawing & painting, Parsons Sch Design, New York, 69-72. Pos: Ed assoc, Art News, New York, 64-73; contrib ed, Arts Mag, 73-; NY corresp, Opus Int, 73-; contribr, Los Angeles Inst Contemp Art J, 76- Bibliog: Jane Holtz Kay (auth), For art's sake, Mademoiselle, 68. Publ: Contribr, Am J Archaeol, 64; contribr, Art News, 64-73; contribr, Light in Art, Collier, 69; contribr, Super Realism, Dutton, 75; auth, Lucas Samaras, Abrams, 75. Mailing Add: 52 W 71st St New York NY 10023

LEVIN, MORTON D
PRINTMAKER, PAINTER
b New York, NY, Oct 7, 23. Study: City Univ New York, BS(art educ); studies in Paris, France; painting with Andre Lhote, sculpture with Ossip Zadkine, etching & engraving with Stanley W Hayter & etching with Federico Castellon; studied lithography, Pratt Graphic Arts Ctr, New York. Work: New York Pub Libr; Libr of Cong, Washington, DC; Hist of Med Div, Nat Libr Med, Md. Exhib: Northwest Printmakers 18th & 21st Ann, Seattle Art Mus, 46-49; 4th-7th Ann Nat Exhib of Prints, Libr of Cong, 46-49; Nat Acad Design & Soc Am Etchers, Gravers, Lithographers and Woodcutters, Inc, 46-48; 46th Ann Watercolor & Print Exhib, Pa Acad Fine Arts, 48; Salon de Mai, Musee D'Art Mod, Paris, France, 51; Biennale Int d'Arte Marinara, Pallazzo del Academia, Genoa, Italy, 51; one-man shows, Galerie Breteau, Paris, France, 52 & Winston Gallery, San Francisco, 77; plus others. Teaching: Founder, dir & instr printmaking & painting, Morton Levin Graphics Workshop, San Francisco, Calif, 72- Awards: Hon Mention, 21st Ann Northwest Printmakers, Seattle Art Mus, 49; Bryan Mem Prize, The Villager Travel Exhib, New York, 64; Third Prize, Washington Sq Art Exhib, Inc, 64. Style & Technique: Expressionism and fantasy in treating the figure; all intaglio techniques; etching, aquatint, engraving and others. Media: Etching; engraving; oil; watercolor. Dealer: Winston Gallery 681 Sutter St San Francisco CA 94102. Mailing Add: 683 Sutter St San Francisco CA 94102

LEVINE, DAVID
ILLUSTRATOR, PAINTER
b Brooklyn, NY, Dec 1926. Study: Tyler Sch Fine Arts; Hans Hoffman Sch. Work: Hirshhorn Mus & Sculpture Garden, Washington, DC; Cleveland Mus, Ohio; Brooklyn Mus, NY; Fogg Art Mus, Cambridge, Mass; Nat Portrait Gallery, Washington, DC. Exhib: Whitney Mus Am Art Sculpture & Drawing Ann, 60 & 63; David Levine & Aaron Shikler, Brooklyn Mus, 71; Butler Inst Am Art, 58, 60, 72; Satirical Drawings, Hirshhorn Mus, spring 76. Awards: Tiffany

Found Award, Julius Hallgarten Prize, 60; Thomas B Clarke Prize, Nat Acad Design, 62. Bibliog: P A Dreyfus (auth), The double image of David Levine, Am Artist, 71. Style & Technique: Satirical of political, literary and art figures. Media: Ink Drawings, Watercolor. Publ: Illusr, The Man from MALICE, 66; illusr, Pins and Needles, 69; illusr, No Known Survivors, David Levine's Political Plank, 70; illusr, New York Rev Books; illusr, NY Mag. Mailing Add: c/o Forum Gallery 1018 Madison Ave New York NY 10021

LEVINE, JACK
PAINTER
b Boston, Mass, Jan, 3, 15. Study: Study with Dr Denman W Ross, 29-31; also with Harold Zimmerman; Colby Col, hon DFA, 46. Work: Metrop Mus Art, New York; Mus Mod Art, New York; Walker Art Ctr, Minneapolis; Art Inst Chicago; Whitney Mus Am Art, New York; plus others. Exhib: Retrospectives, Inst Contemp Art, Boston, 53, Whitney Mus Am Art, New York, 55 & Palacio Bellas Artes, Mexico City, Mex, 60; annually, Carnegie Inst, Pittsburgh & Art Inst Chicago; Corcoran Gallery Art, Washington, DC; Mus Mod Art, New York; Mus Fine Arts, Boston; Pa Acad Fine Arts; one-man show, De Cordova Mus, Lincoln, Mass, 68; plus many others. Teaching: Lectr, Art Inst Chicago, Skowhegan Sch Painting & Sculpture, Univ Ill, Pa Acad Fine Arts, Am Art Sch, New York & Cleveland Mus Art Sch. Awards: Guggenheim Fel, 45 & 46; Corcoran Gallery Art Award, 59; Altman Prize, Nat Acad Design, 75; plus others. Mem: Nat Inst Arts & Lett; Artists Equity Asn; Am Acad Arts & Sci; Nat Acad Arts & Lett. Dealer: Kennedy Galleries 20 E 56th St New York NY 10022. Mailing Add: 68 Morton St New York NY 10014

LEVINE, LES
SCULPTOR, CURATOR
b Dublin, Ireland, Oct 6, 35; Can citizen. Study: Cent Sch Arts & Crafts, London, Eng. Work: Nat Gallery Can, Ottawa, Ont; Metrop Mus Art, New York; Whitney Mus Am Art, New York; Mus Mod Art, New York; Philadelphia Mus Art. Comn: Iris (sculpture), comn by Mr & Mrs Robert Kardon, 67; Contact (sculpture), Gulf & Western Indust, 69. Exhib: Sao Paolo Biennale, Brazil, 68; Biennale Paris, France, 69; Sydney Biennale, Australia, 76; Documenta, Kassel, WGer, 77. Collections Arranged: Open To New Ideas (organizer), Jimmy Carter Collection, Ga Mus Art, Athens, 77. Teaching: Artist in residence, Aspen Inst, Colo, 67 & 69; assoc prof commun, NY Univ, 72; assoc prof video art, William Paterson Col, 74-75. Pos: Pres, Mus Mott Art, Inc, 71- Awards: Can Coun Arts Fel, 65 & 66; First Prize for The Star Machine, Sculpture Biennale, Art Gallery Ont, 68; Nat Endowment Arts Fel, 74. Bibliog: John Perreault (auth), Plastic man strikes, Art News, 3/68; David Bourdon (auth), Plastic art's biggest bubble, Life Mag, 8/69; Van Schley (producer), Les Levine Movie, 69. Mem: Archit League New York (vpres, 68-70, exec comt, presently). Style & Technique: Media sculpture; use mass media and information processing devices to create conceptual works. Media: Gold. Publ: Ed, Culture Hero, 70; contribr, Collected Essays, Dutton, 72; contribr, Newsday, Village Voice & Studio Int. Mailing Add: 20 E 20th St New York NY 10003

LEVINE, MARILYN ANNE
SCULPTOR, EDUCATOR
b Medicine Hat, Alta, Dec 22, 35. Study: Univ Calif, Berkeley, MA, 70, MFA, 71. Work: Montreal Mus Fine Arts; Nat Mus Mod Art, Kyoto & Tokyo; Australian Nat Gallery, Canberra; William Rockhill Nelson Gallery Art, Kansas City; Univ Art Mus, Berkeley. Exhib: One-man shows, Hansen-Fuller Gallery, San Francisco, 71 & 75 & O K Harris Gallery, New York, 74 & 76; Sharp Focus Realism, Sidney Janis Gallery, New York, 72; Canada Trajectories, Mus Art Mod, Paris, 73; Retrospective, Norman McKenzie Art Gallery, Regina, 74. Teaching: Asst prof sculpture & ceramics, Univ Utah, 73-76; vis lectr, Univ Calif, Berkeley, 75- Awards: Gold Medal, XXVII Concorso Int della Ceramica Arte, 69; Ceramics Int Medal, 73; Nat Endowment for the Arts Fel, 76. Bibliog: Nancy Foote (auth), The photo realists—12 interviews, Art in Am, 11-12/72; Susan Peterson (auth), The ceramics of Marilyn Levine, Crafts Horizons, Vol 37 (Feb 1977). Mem: Col Art Asn Am; Can Guild Potters (western vpres, 67-69); Can Artists Representation; Am Crafts Coun; Can Craftsmen's Asn (dir, 71-73). Media: Clay. Dealer: O K Harris Gallery 383 W Broadway New York NY 10012; Hansen Fuller Gallery 228 Grant Ave San Francisco CA 94108. Mailing Add: 951 62nd St Oakland CA 94608

LEVINE, MARTIN
PRINTMAKER
b New York, NY, May 14, 45. Study: Calif Col of Arts & Crafts, MFA(printmaking); State Univ New York, Col at Buffalo, BS(art educ). Work: Libr of Cong, Smithsonian Inst, Washington, DC; Brooklyn Mus; Mus of Fine Arts, Boston; Achenbach Found, Calif Palace of the Legion of Honor, San Francisco; New York Pub Libr, plus others. Comn: Two etchings of hist landmark (with ADI Gallery, San Francisco, Calif), The Clorox Co, Oakland, Calif, 76. Exhib: Boston Printmakers 27th Ann, Mus of Fine Arts, Mass, 75; 24th Nat Exhib of Prints, Libr of Cong, Nat Collection of Fine Arts, 75; 5th Brit Int Print Biennale, Bradford Art Galleries, Eng, 76; 111th Bienal Americana de Artes Graphicas, Mus La Tertulia, Cali, Colombia, 76; 30 Years of American Printmaking, Brooklyn Mus, NY, 76; Recent Acquisitions, Achenbach Found for Graphic Arts, 77; Primera Bienal del Grabado de America, Mus Municipal, Maracaibo, Venezuela, 77; 7th Int Print Biennale, Cracow, Poland, 78; plus many others. Collections Arranged: Calif Printmakers Invitational, Philadelphia Print Club, 73; Calif Printmakers Exhib, Brit Printmakers Coun, Ely House, London, 75; Los Angeles Printmaking Socs 75 Foreign Exchange Exhib, Seoul, Korea, 75; 7th & 8th Printmaking West Invitational, Utah State Univ, 75 & 76; Nat Invitational Drawing Exhib, Emporia State Univ, 77 & 78. Awards: Spec Purchase Award, Davidson Nat Print & Drawing Competition, 73; Purchase Award, 24th Nat Exhib of Prints, Libr of Cong, 75; Nat Endowment for the Arts Printmaking Fel Grant, 77, plus others. Bibliog: Reviews in Graphics Mag, 75 & Art Week, 76. Mem: Boston Printmakers; Calif Soc of Printmakers. Style & Technique: Realistic intaglio (combination of etching, aquatint, engraving and soft-grounds); lithography; drawing. Media: Intaglio; lithography. Dealer: ADI Gallery 530 McAllister San Francisco CA 94102. Mailing Add: 484 36th St Oakland CA 94609

LEVINE, REEVA (ANNA) MILLER
PAINTER, INSTRUCTOR
b Los Angeles, Calif, Nov 23, 12. Study: With Emil Bistrom & Alexander Rosenfeld. Work: Temple Israel, Long Beach; E Madison YMCA, Seattle; Mt Zion Baptist Church, Seattle; Temple De Hirsch Sinai, Seattle; Beth Sholom Temple, Richland, Wash, 74. Comn: Stained glass windows, Temple Beth Sholom, Santa Monica, 44; stained glass windows, Temple Sinai Wedding Chapel, Oakland, 48; ceiling of dome, Al Jolson Mem, Los Angeles, 51; mosaic, Temple Beth Sholom, Anchorage, 66; relig arks, Temple Beth Israel, Aberdeen, Wash, 66; plus numerous portraits. Exhib: One-man shows, Santa Monica Art Asn, 48, Olympia Art League, 70 & Unity Church Tacoma, 75; Seattle World's Fair Liturgical Conf, 62; Seattle Art Mus, 67. Pos: Art dir, Camp Ben Swig, Saratoga, Calif, 52-58. Awards: First in Drawing, Santa Monica Art Asn, 45, Second in Watercolor, 48; Artist of Year, Music & Art Found, Seattle, 70. Mem: Artists Equity Asn. Media: Oil, Acrylic, Watercolor. Publ: Illusr, Holy Mountain, 53; illusr, Wild Branch on the Olive Tree, 75. Mailing Add: 16 Skagit Key Bellevue WA 98006

LEVINE, RUTH GIKOW
See Gikow, Ruth

LEVINE, SEYMOUR R
COLLECTOR
b Russia, May 28, 06. Study: Sch Law, Wash Square Col, NY Univ, JD. Collection: Includes works by de Creeft, Elkan, Rubin, Blum, Neujean and others. Mailing Add: Carhart Ave Peekskill NY 10566

LEVINE, SHEPARD
PAINTER, EDUCATOR
b New York, NY, June 21, 22. Study: Univ NMex, BA & MA; Univ Toulouse, France. Work: Prints in Parnassus Hall, Athens, Greece, sponsored by US Info Serv Collection of US Embassy in 1960; Univ Ore; Ore State Univ; Arkia Airlines, Israel. Exhib: Am Graphic Arts Asn; Brooklyn Mus; Henry Gallery, Univ Wash; San Francisco Mus Art; Portland Art Mus, Ore; Spokane Art Mus; plus others. Teaching: Lect, Roots of Contemporary Expression, The Artists Vision, Motif in the Work of Three American Jewish Artists, Icons of Jewish Art, The Mind Symbol & Reflections in the Presence of Medusa; to mus & pvt groups; sem, movement & style in art & mus; prof art, Ore State Univ, currently. Awards: Purchase Award, Univ Ore. Mem: Am Asn Univ Prof. Mailing Add: Dept of Art Ore State Univ Corvallis OR 97331

LEVINSON, FRED (FLOYD)
DESIGNER, CARTOONIST
b New York, NY, May 23, 28. Study: Syracuse Univ, BFA. Exhib: Cartoon Exhib, Eng, 53, Italy, 54 & France, 54; all NY state exhibs; Cannes Film Festival, 60; New York Film Festival; Edinburgh Film Festival, 60. Pos: Pres, Wylde Productions. Awards: Hollywood Film Festival, 60; Edinburgh Film Festival, 60; New York Film Festival, 61. Interest: Industrial films, live and animated TV commercials. Publ: Contribr cartoons, Best Cartoons from True, Cartoon Cavalcade & Best Cartoons of the Year, 54; contribr cartoons in Sat Eve Post, Colliers, Look, True, This Week & many others. Mailing Add: 157 E 63rd St New York NY 10021

LEVINSON, MON
SCULPTOR
b New York, NY, Jan 6, 26. Work: Whitney Mus Am Art, New York; Joseph H Hirshhorn Collection, Washington, DC; NY Univ Art Collection; Rose Art Gallery, Brandeis Univ; Columbia Broadcasting Syst, New York. Comn: Objects, Mus Mod Art, New York, 64, 66 & 69; sculpture, Pub Sch 166, New York, 67; mural-sculpture, Great Southwest Atlanta Corp, Ga, 68; mural-sculpture, Housing & Redevelop Bd, Demountable Vest Pocket Parks, New York, 69. Exhib: Kornblee Gallery, New York, 61-72; Plus by Minus, Albright-Knox Gallery, Buffalo, 68; A Plastic Presence, Milwaukee Art Ctr, Wis, New York & San Francisco, 69-70; Whitney Mus Am Art Sculpture Ann, 70 & 73; Maeght Found, Art Vivant aux Etats Unis, France, 70; Storm King Arts Ctr, Mountainville, NY, 72 & 75; John Weber Gallery, New York, 73; Hirshhorn Collection, 74; Renwick Gallery, 76 & Nat Collection, 77, Smithsonian Inst, Washington, DC; Rosa Esman Gallery, New York, 76 & 77; plus others. Teaching: Vis artist, C W Post Col, 70-72 & 76-77. Awards: Cassandra Found Award, 72; CAPS Award, NY State Coun Arts, 74; Nat Endowment for the Arts fel, 76. Mailing Add: 309 W Broadway New York NY 10013

LEVIT, HERSCHEL
PAINTER, ILLUSTRATOR
b Shenandoah, Pa, May 29, 12. Study: Pa Acad Fine Arts, Cresson traveling scholar, 33; Barnes Found. Comn: Mural, Recorder of Deeds Bldg, Washington, DC; 33 portrait drawings of Red Seal Artists, RCA Victor, 58; photographs for Mus Mod Art. Exhib: Pa Acad Fine Arts, 66-69; Art Inst Chicago; Springfield Art Mus, Ill; Brooklyn Mus, NY; Metrop Mus Art & Whitney Mus Am Art, New York; Boston Mus Fine Arts; Columbia Univ, 78; plus others. Teaching: Prof art & advan design, Pratt Inst, currently. Publ: Illusr, Horizon Book of Great Cathedrals, 68 & Master Builders of the Middle Ages, 69; auth & illusr, Just Point, 72; contribr (photographs), Great Historic Places of Europe, Horizon, 74; auth & photogr, Views of Rome—Then & Now, 76; plus others. Mailing Add: 220 W 93rd St New York NY 10025

LEVITAN, ISRAEL (JACK)
SCULPTOR, LECTURER
b Lawrence, Mass, June 13, 12. Study: Arts & Crafts, Detroit; Chicago Art Inst; also with Amedee Ozenfant & Hans Hofmann, New York, Ossip Zadkine, Paris, France, Ramamurti S Mishra, San Francisco, Monroe, NY & Ashrams. Mus, East Hampton, Long Island; Temple Beth El, Great Neck, Long Island. Comn: Merle Armitage sculpture, Yucca Valley, Calif, 59; dancing figures, Forest Hills Apt Lobby, New York, 60; abstr ceiling narthex of chapel, Interchurch Ctr, New York, 62; head of Ben Gurion, comn by Maurice Dershowitz, 64; bronze of Moses' hands, comn by Murray Reiter, 65. Exhib: Realites Nouvelle, Mus Art Mod, Paris; Am Abstr Artists, Mus Mod Art, Tokyo, Japan; retrospective, Barone Gallery, 60 & Univ Calif, Berkeley, 62; Am Sculptors; Galerie Claude Bernard, Paris, 62; Elliot Gallery, Eckerd Col, St Petersburg, Fla, 78. Teaching: Lectr sculpture, Brooklyn Mus, 55-59; lectr sculpture, Greenwich House, New York, 58; lectr sculpture, Cooper Union, 59; instr sculpture, Univ Calif, Berkeley, 62; instr sculpture, Philadelphia Mus Col Art, 67-68; instr sculpture, NY Univ, 68; lectr sculpture, Guild Hall Mus, 71; instr sculpture, Fla Humanistics Inst, Largo, 75-, Temple of Living God, St Petersburg & Yoga Soc Fla, Redington Beach; pvt instr. Awards: First Prize, Guild Hall Mus, 58. Bibliog: A Baker's Dozen in Sculpture, CBS Camera Three, 62; Fred McDarrah (auth), chap, In: Artists' World, 64; Michel Seuphor (auth), chap, In: Sculpture of the 20th Century, 66. Publ: Contribr, Life Mag, 58; contribr, portfolio, Art News Ann, 64; contribr, Evergreen Rev, 65; contribr, Das Kunst, 66; contribr, Look Mag, 67. Mailing Add: 1348 High Bluff Dr Largo FL 33540

LEVITINE, GEORGE
ART HISTORIAN
b Kharkoff, Russia, Mar 17, 16; US citizen. Study: Univ Paris, PCB, 38; Boston Univ, MA, 46; Harvard Univ, Edward R Bacon scholar & PhD, 52. Teaching: From instr to prof hist art, Boston Univ, 49-64; prof hist art, Harvard Univ Exten, 59-64; prof & head dept art, Univ Md, College Park, 64- Pos: Mem, Inst for Advanced Study, Princeton, NY, 77-78. Awards: Am Coun Learned Socs grant, 61; Am Philosophical Soc Grant, 74; Nat Endowment for the Arts, 77-78. Mem: Col Art Asn Am (chmn Porter Prize comt, bk rev ed, Col Art J); Am Soc Aesthet. Res: European art of the eighteenth and nineteenth century, particularly romanticism. Publ: Auth, The influence of Lavater & Girodet's Expression des sentiments de l'ame, 54 & auth, Vernet tied to a mast in a storm: the evolution of an episode of art historical romantic folklore, 67, Art Bull; auth, Some emblematic sources of Goya, J of Wartburg & Courtauld Inst, 59; auth, The 18th century rediscovery of Alexis Grimou and the emergence

of the Proto-Bohemian Image of the French artist, Eighteenth Century Studies, Vol 21, No 1; auth, The sculpture of Falconet, New York Graphic Ltd, 72. Mailing Add: Dept of Art Univ of Md College Park MD 20742

LEVITT, ALFRED
PAINTER, PREHISTORIAN
b New York, NY, Aug 15, 94. Study: Columbia Univ; Art Students League; Acad Grand Chaumiere, France; also with Hans Hofmann, New York. Work: Neveh-Sha'anan Mus, Haifa, Israel; plus many other pvt collections in Europe & US. Exhib: Butler Inst Am Art, Youngstown, Ohio, 46; Pa Acad Fine Arts, Philadelphia, 48; Brooklyn Mus Exhibs, 47-59; Whitney Mus Am Art, New York, 49, 53 & 55; one-man shows, Babcock Galleries, New York, 45 & 46 & Art Alliance Philadelphia, 47; plus many others. Teaching: Lectr cave art, NY Univ, Cooper Union, Archaeol Inst Am at Wagner Col, North Shore Soc Archaeol Inst Am, New York Pub Libr, Philadelphia Art Alliance & also in France; lectr mod art. Pos: Coord chmn, Mod Artists Cape Ann, Mass, 47; founder, dir & instr, Ecole Mod de Provence, St Remy de Provence, France, 49-50 & 59-62. Awards: Chevalier de L'Order des Arts et Lettres for Outstanding Studies of Stone Age Cave Art, Fr Govt, 75. Bibliog: Artist returns from fifth trip to prehistoric caves, Villager, 11/5/70. Mem: Fel MacDowell Colony; Archaeol Inst Am; Soc Prehistorique L'Ariege; Soc Amis Mus Chateau St Germain-en Laye; Soc Prehistorique L'Ardeche; life mem Archaeol Soc Staten Island. Res: Various researches of cave art and prehistory; extended visits and studies of the drawing, engraving, painting and sculpture of Stone Age artists in France, Spain and Italy. Mailing Add: 505 W Broadway New York NY 10012

LEV-LANDAU (SAMUEL DAVID LANDAU)
PAINTER
b Warsaw, Poland, Apr 17, 95; US citizen. Study: Graphic Sketch Club, Philadelphia; also with Sol Wilson & Phil Reisman. Work: Butler Inst Am Art, Youngstown, Ohio; Norfolk Mus Arts & Sci, Va; Adelphi Univ, Garden City, NY; Menninger Mus, Topeka, Kans; Mus Tel Aviv, Israel; plus others including pvt collections. Exhib: Carnegie Inst, Pittsburgh; Pa Acad Fine Arts, Philadelphia; Corcoran Gallery Art, Washington, DC; Nat Acad Design, New York; Dayton Art Inst, Ohio; plus many other group & one-man shows. Awards: First Prize for Oil, Brooklyn Soc Artists Ann, 54; Second Purchase Prize, Abraham Lincoln High Sch, 64; Albert Dorn Prize, Audubon Artists, 65. Mem: Artists Equity Asn (mem bd, 71-72); Am Soc Contemp Art. Media: Oil, Casein. Mailing Add: Hotel Chelsea 222 W 23rd St New York NY 10011

LEVY, DAVID CORCOS
PHOTOGRAPHER, EDUCATOR
b New York, NY, Apr 10, 38. Study: Columbia Col, BA, 60; NY Univ, MA, 67. Work: Guggenheim Mus, New York. Teaching: Dean, Parsons Sch Design, New York, 70- Res: Photographic essays in Gothic Architecture. Mailing Add: Parsons Sch of Design 66 Fifth Ave New York NY 10011

LEVY, HILDA
PAINTER
b Pinsk, Russia. Study: Univ Calif, Berkeley, AB; Pasadena City Col; Jepson Art Inst; Univ Calif, Los Angeles; also with Adolph Gottlieb. Exhib: Nat Gallery Can, Ottawa, Ont; Libr of Cong, Washington, DC; Butler Inst Am Art, Youngstown, Ohio; San Francisco Mus Art & M H de Young Mem Mus, San Francisco; also exhib in Ger, Sweden, Japan, plus many others. Awards: 40 local & nat awards. Mem: Nat Watercolor Soc; Bay Printmakers; San Francisco Art Inst. Mailing Add: 2411 Brigden Rd Pasadena CA 91104

LEVY, JULIEN
EDUCATOR, WRITER
b New York, NY, Jan 22, 06. Study: Harvard Univ, 27. Teaching: Instr art hist, Sarah Lawrence Col, Lacoste, France, 75- & State Univ NY Col, Purchase, 76- Pos: Owner, Julien Levy Gallery, New York, 31-48. Publ: Auth (film), Max Ernst, 30; auth, Surrealism, Black Sun Press, 36 & World Wide & Arno, 74; auth, Eugene Berman, Viking 47 & Arno, 69; auth, Arshile Gorky, Abrams, 62; auth, Memoir of an Art Gallery, Putnam, 77; auth (film), Surrealism Is..., 72. Mailing Add: Hemlock Ridge Farm Bridgewater CT 06752

LEVY, MAYRA PHYLLIS
ART ADMINISTRATOR
b Perth Amboy, NJ, Apr 5, 55. Study: Goddard Col grad. Collections Arranged: Working Notebooks, Franklin Furnace, New York & Ont Col of Art, Toronto, Can. Pos: Cur & adv, Heiner Friedrich Inc & DIA Art Found, New York; proj dir, 112 Workshop Inc, New York. Bibliog: Barry Gadensohn (auth), Bread and Puppet, Iowa Rev; Soho, Galleries, article in The Los Angeles Times; Annette Kuhn (auth), article in Village Voice. Mem: Col Art Asn. Mailing Add: 140 A W Houston St New York NY 10012

LEVY, STUART D
GALLERY DIRECTOR, ART DEALER
b Brooklyn, NY, Feb 24, 50. Study: Brooklyn Col, BA. Pos: Gallery Director, Images...A Gallery of Photographic Art, New York. Specialty: Contemporary color photography. Mailing Add: 11 E 57 St New York NY 10022

LEVY, TIBBIE
PAINTER
b New York, NY, Oct 29, 08. Study: Cornell Univ, with Arshile Gorky, AB; Art Students League; Acad Grand Chaumiere & Acad Andre Lhote, Paris, France; NY Univ, JD. Work: Contemp Art Soc Gt Brit; Mus Mod Art, Madrid, Barcelona & Bilbao, Spain; Princeton Univ Mus; Cornell Univ Mus; Brandeis Univ; plus many others. Exhib: Bodley Gallery, New York, 60-70; Galerie Ror Volmar, Paris, 61; Sala Nebli, Madrid, 62; Galeria Forum, Madrid, 63; Portal Gallery, London, Eng, 63 & 65; plus others. Teaching: Lectr art. Media: Oil. Dealer: Bodley Gallery 787 Madison Ave New York NY 10021. Mailing Add: 2 Sutton Pl S New York NY 10022

LEW, WEYMAN MICHAEL
PAINTER, PRINTMAKER
b San Francisco, Calif, Feb 17, 35. Study: Univ Calif, Berkeley, BS, 57; San Francisco Art Inst, with Jay deFeo, 65-66. Work: M H de Young Mem Mus, San Francisco; Univ Calif Mus, Berkeley; Inst Arte Contemporaneo, Lima, Peru; Santa Barbara Mus Art, Calif; Oakland Art Mus, Calif. Exhib: One-man shows, M H de Young Mem Mus, 70, Inst Arte Contemporaneo, 70, Western Asn Art Mus Circulating Exhib, 70-71, Santa Barbara Mus Art, 71, Bonython Art Gallery, Sydney, Australia, 72-75, Wallnuts Gallery, Philadelphia, 76 & ADI Gallery, San Francisco, 76. Teaching: Guest instr painting, drawing & serigraphy, M H de Young Mem Mus Art Sch, 70-71; guest lectr. Pos: Dir, Kelley Galleries, San Francisco, 68. Style & Technique: Figurative line drawings, nudes. Media: Ink, Watercolor, Acrylic. Mailing Add: San Francisco CA

LEWANDOWSKI, EDMUND D
PAINTER, ART ADMINISTRATOR
b Milwaukee, Wis, July 3, 14. Study: Layton Sch Art, 32-35. Work: Addison Gallery Am Art, Andover, Mass; Brooklyn Mus, NY; Boston Mus Fine Arts; Mus Mod Art, New York; Mus Fine Arts, Krakow, Poland; plus many others. Exhib: Art Inst Chicago; Carnegie Inst, Pittsburgh; Corcoran Gallery Art, Washington, DC; Pa Acad Fine Arts, Philadelphia; Phillips Collection, Washington, DC; plus others. Teaching: Prof, Layton Sch Art, 45-49; prof painting, Fla State Univ, 49-54, head dept, 52-54; dir, Layton Sch Art. Awards: Award, Gimbel Centennial; Award, Hallmark Int Competition; Award, Milwaukee Art Inst; plus many others. Bibliog: Andrew C Ritchie (auth), Abstract painting and sculpture in America, Mus Mod Art, 51; Nathaniel Pousette-Dart (ed), American Painting Today, Hastings House, 56; John I Baur (auth), Revolution and Tradition in Modern American Art, Harvard Univ, 59. Mem: Wis Painters & Sculptors; Polish-Am Artists; Chicago Fine Arts Club. Publ: Contribr, covers & reproductions, Fortune Mag. Mailing Add: 537 Meadowbrook Ln Rockhill SC 29730

LEWEN, SI
PAINTER
b Lublin, Poland, Nov 8, 18; US citizen. Study: With Adron, 28 & Klaus Richter, Berlin, 30; Ecole Vaucanson, Grenoble, France, 34-36; Nat Acad Art & Design, New York, 36-38; Art Stud League, 46-50. Work: Columbia Mus Fine Arts, SC; Peabody Col, Tenn; Univ Miami, Coral Gables, Fla; Hudson River Mus, Yonkers, NY; Syracuse Univ, NY. Exhib: New York World's Fair, 40; Pa Acad Fine Arts, Philadelphia, 48; Butler Inst Am Art, Youngstown, Ohio, 54; Libr Cong, Washington, DC, 56; Whitney Mus Am Art, New York, 57 & 59. Style & Technique: Serial progression. Media: Collage, Painting. Publ: Auth, The Parade, Bittner, 57; illusr, Poems of the Ghetto, Twayne, 69. Mailing Add: 9 Pine Crest Rd New Paltz NY 12561

LEWICKI, JAMES
ILLUSTRATOR, EDUCATOR
b Buffalo, NY, Dec 13, 17. Study: Albright Art Sch; Art Sch Detroit Soc Arts & Crafts, scholar; Pratt Inst, cert. Exhib: Audubon Artists Ann; Am Watercolor Soc Ann; Pop Prints, Adelphi Univ, 64; Christmas Paintings, Dartmouth Col, 64; one-man show, Golden Bough Paintings, C W Post Col, Long Island Univ, 70; 200 Yrs of Am Illus, 77. Teaching: Instr art, Pratt Inst, 46-52; chmn dept art, C W Post Col, Long Island Univ, 63-69, prof art, 63-, chmn grad prog art, 69- Awards: Christmas Card Competition Second Prize, Am Artists, 43; New Masters Award for Sunflowers (painting), Audubon Artists 25th Anniversary Exhib, 67. Bibliog: Articles in Am Artist Mag, 62; articles in North Light Mag, 71; 200 Years of American Illustration, 77. Mem: Am Watercolor Soc; Audubon Artists. Style & Technique: Historical and nature subjects. Publ: Ed & illusr, Christmas Tales, Golden, 56; ed & illusr, Life Treasury of American Folklore, 61; illusr, Tales of Old Russia, Garrard, 64; illusr, Little Christmas, Houghton Mifflin, 64; illusr, The Golden Bough, Vols I & II, 68 & 69; illusr, nat mags, 39- Mailing Add: 5 Hawthorne Ct Centerport NY 11721

LEWIN, BERNARD
ART DEALER, COLLECTOR
b Ger; US citizen. Study: With Kurt Wagner, Berlin. Pos: Art dir, B Lewin Galleries, Beverly Hills, 60- Mem: Art Dealers Asn. Specialty: Mexican masters, Tamayo, Siqueiros, Merida, R Martinez, R Coronel and others. Collection: Mexican masters, American and European. Mailing Add: B Lewin Galleries 266 N Beverly Dr Beverly Hills CA 90210

LEWIN, KEITH KERTON
PAINTER, INSTRUCTOR
b Jamaica, West Indies; Apr 19, 31; US citizen. Study: Jamaica Sch Arts & Crafts, dipl; Brooklyn Mus Art Sch, New York, cert; London Art Col, dipl; Art Students League, Univ West Indies fel; Hunter Col (NY), cert med art; Univ West Indies. Work: Nat Fine Art Collection of Jamaican Artists, Inst Jamaica; Univ West Indies Fine Art Collection; Hector Wynter Fine Art Collections; William L Lassiter Collection. Comn: Hope Gardens, A O Scott, Univ West Indies; Hospital Waiting Room, comn by Sir Horald & Lady Allen, Minister Finance, Jamaican Govt. Exhib: Bertrand Russell Centenary Int Art Exhib, London; one-man shows, Findley Students Ctr, City Col New York, 62 & Hospitality Comt of Wives of UN Diplomats, UN Church Ctr, 63; Int Friends Art Guild Int Art Exhib; Nat Print & Drawing Exhib, Brooklyn Mus. Teaching: Art teacher, Waltann Sch Creative Arts, 66-67; art teacher, Dept Extra-Mural Studies, Univ West Indies; art dir, Jamaica Arts Club, West Indies; art teacher, tutorial col preparing students for gen cert educ, London Univ Overseas Exam. Pos: Pres, Int Friend Art Guild, 62-64. Awards: Cert of Honor, Int Art Competition, Govt PR & Art News, USA, 52. Bibliog: Charles Wagner & Francesca Byrnes (auth), rev in World of Art; Brian O'Doherty (auth), rev in New York Times, 62. Mem: Int Soc Educ through Art; fel Royal Soc Arts; Jamaica Arts Club (dir fine arts). Style & Technique: Landscape, portrait and figures. Media: Watercolor, Oil, Ink & Graphic Art. Mailing Add: 1865 52nd St Brooklyn NY 11204

LEWIN, MR & MRS ROBERT L
ART PUBLISHERS
Pos: Owners, Mill Pond Press Inc, Venice, Fla. Specialty: Wildlife, western, marine and floral art prints by nineteen prominent artists. Mailing Add: c/o Mill Pond Press Inc 204 S Nassau St Venice FL 33595

LEWIS, DON
POTTER, SCULPTOR
b Greenville, SC, July 26, 35. Study: Charles Counts Workshop, 60; Furman Univ, BA, 61; Pond Farm Workshop, with Marguerite Wildenhain, summer 61. Work: Ceramics Monthly Collection, Columbus, Ohio; Guignard Collection, Columbia, SC; Asheville Art Mus, NC; Appalachian State Univ, Boone, NC; Southern Highlands Handcraft Guild, Ashville, NC. Comn: Stoneware baptismal font, Chas Sappenfield, Architect, Burnsville Church, NC, 67; ceramic/cast stone font, Weigman/Hall, Architects, St Eugene's Church, Asheville, NC, 69. Exhib: Young Americans, Mus Contemp Crafts, New York, 62; Craftsmen of the Eastern States, Smithsonian Traveling Exhib, 64; 12-Designer Craftsmen, Baltimore Mus, Md, 67; Don Lewis, American Craftsman, Int Textile Expos, Greenville, SC, 73; Craftsman Exhib, SE Ctr Contemp Art, Winston-Salem, NC, 74; 34th Concorso Int Della Ceramica d'Arte Contemporanea, Faenza, Italy, 76. Teaching: Vis Scholar, Voorhees Col, Denmark, SC, 68; instr ceramics, Univ SC, Spartanburg, 73. Awards: First in Ceramics & Purchase Awards, SC Craftsmen, 67; Distinguished Alumni Award, Furman Univ, 70. Bibliog: Declan Haun (auth), A Potter (photo essay), Int Harvester World, 64; Chas Arisman (auth), Don Lewis Pottery (film), Voorhees Col, 67; Don Brimberry (auth), Don Lewis: Professional Potter, Harding Col, Searcy, Ark, 73. Mem: 12 Designer-Craftsmen (pres, 70, 73 & 74); Southern Highland

Handcraft Guild; Piedmont Craftsmen. Style & Technique: Figurative and abstract stoneware panels and pottery decoration, primarily in salt-glazed earth colors; sculpture in clay and clay combined with other materials. Media: Pottery, Wheel-thrown and hand-built stoneware; Sculpture, Clay; Stoneware wall panels, Salt-glazing. Publ: Auth, Graveyard pots, 67, Measuring techniques for wheel work, 68 & Architectural commissions for craftsmen, 75, Ceramics Monthly. Mailing Add: PO Box 345 Cleveland SC 29635

LEWIS, DON S, SR
ART DEALER, PAINTER
b July 21, 19; US citizen. Study: Carnegie Mus, Pittsburgh; painting with Virginia Cuthbert. Exhib: One-man show, Gallerie Int, New York, 67. Pos: Pres, dir & lectr on investment art & conserv, Aushew Gallery, Norfolk, Va, 54- Mem: Nat Soc Lit & Arts; Am Asn Mus; Am Fedn Arts; Int Inst Conserv Hist & Artistic Works. Style & Technique: Metals and plastics nailed to boards. Media: Metal, Acrylic. Specialty: Nineteenth and Twentieth Century American paintings. Mailing Add: 1419 Runnymede Rd Norfolk VA 23505

LEWIS, DONALD SYKES, JR
ART HISTORIAN, ART DEALER
b Norfolk, Va, Dec 13, 47. Study: Randolph-Macon Col, Ashland, Va, BA(fine arts); Univ Va, MA(hist of art). Teaching: Instr Am art, Hermitage Mus, Norfolk, 75 & Old Dom Univ, 75-76. Pos: Vpres, Auslew Gallery, Inc, Norfolk, 73-76, dir, 76- Mem: Archives of Am Art; Assoc Int Inst Conserv Hist & Artistic Works. Res: Cataloging works of Herman Ottomar Herzog and his son, Lewis E Herzog. Specialty: 19th & 20th century American art. Publ: Contribr, Herman Herzog (catalog), Chapellier Galleries, New York, 73; auth, Emily Nichols Hatch (catalog), 74 & auth foreword, In: Carolyn Wyeth (catalog), 12/74, Auslew Gallery, Inc; auth, Herman Herzog, Southwest Art Rev, 75; contribr, Carolyn Wyeth Exhibition Catalogue, R W Norton Art Gallery, Shreveport, La, 1/76; auth, Herman Herzog (1831-1932), German landscapist in America, Am Art Rev, 7-8/76. Mailing Add: 5951 Glenhaven Crescent Norfolk VA 23510

LEWIS, DOUGLAS
ART HISTORIAN, ART CURATOR
b Centreville, Miss, Apr 30, 38. Study: Lawrenceville Sch, NJ, dipl, 56; Yale Col, BA, 59 & 60; Clare Col, Cambridge Univ, BA, 62, MA, 66; Yale Univ, MA, 63, PhD, 67; Am Acad Rome, Chester Dale fel, 64, dipl, 66. Collections Arranged: African Sculpture, 70 & The Far North (American Eskimo and Indian Art), 73, Nat Gallery Art. Teaching: Asst prof baroque & romantic art, Bryn Mawr Col, 67-68; asst prof renaissance & baroque art, Univ Calif, Berkeley, spring 70; sem leader renaissance archit, Folger Inst, Renaissance Sem, Washington, DC, spring 72; adj prof, Renaissance & baroque art, Johns Hopkins Univ, 73-77. Pos: David E Finley fel Venetian art, Nat Gallery Art, Washington, DC, 65-68; cur sculpture, Nat Gallery Art, 68- Mem: Fel Am Acad in Rome; Soc Archit Historians; Col Art Asn Am; Belg-Am Educ Found (Am fel comt, 72-); Consiglio Sci, Centro Palladiano, Vicenza. Res: Art and architecture and their patronage in Renaissance Venice; monographic studies on Michele Sanmicheli, Andrea Palladio, Baldassare Longhena & Francisco Muttoni. Publ: Auth, The Late Baroque Churches of Venice, 67; auth, The Villa Cornaro at Piombino, Corpus Palladianum, 76. Mailing Add: Nat Gallery of Art Washington DC 20565

LEWIS, ELIZABETH MATTHEW
ART LIBRARIAN, PAINTER
b Charleston, SC. Study: Richmond Prof Inst, Va; Purdue Univ, Lafayette, Ind, BA; sculpture course at Barry I, Wales, Glamorgan Educational Comt; Univ London; Pratt Inst, MLS; Teachers Col, Columbia Univ, EdD; Inst Arts Admin, Harvard Univ, Cert. Work: Ball State Univ Art Gallery, Muncie, Ind; Miami Mus Mod Art. Comn: Fourteen four ft sq bronze reliefs, George's Restaurant, Indianapolis, Ind, 51; Five Panoramic Scenes (largest black light mural), Riverside Amusement Park, Ind, 52; History of the Theater (50 ft painted mural), Loeb Playhouse, Mem Union, Purdue Univ, 52; Community Life (47 ft ceramic bas relief mural), First Fed Savings & Loan, Lafayette, Ind, 58; 5 ft x 14 ft ceramic relief with cathedral glass, Evangelical United Brethren Church, Lafayette, Ind, 61. Exhib: Ind Ann, John Herron Art Mus, Indianapolis, 50; Audubon Artists Ann, Indianapolis, Ind, 51; Mich Ann, Detroit Art Inst, 52; Ohio Valley Oil & Watercolor Show, three states, 54; Pa Ann, Univ Pa, Indiana, 55; Drawing & Print Show, Ball State Univ Art Gallery, Muncie, Ind, 55; one-man shows, Lafayette Art Ctr, Ind, Ft Wayne Union Bank, Ind, Miami Mus Mod Art, Fla & Ft Lauderdale Art Ctr, Fla, 64. Collections Arranged: Four Generations of Waughs: An American Family of Artists 1827-1970, 70, Illustrators of the American West, loan from the collection of George Goodstadt, 75, Drawings by Al Hirschfeld, 76 & Military Medicine and the Wound Man (with Gordon E Mestler), 76, US Military Acad. Teaching: Instr painting, Ind Univ Extension, Kokomo, 50-52. Pos: Co-partner, Lewis Workshop Studios, Kokomo, W Lafayette, Ind, 50-62; sr lectr & fine arts librn, US Military Acad, West Point, NY, 67-; cur slides, Dept Art, City Col New York, 71. Mem: Art Librn Soc NAm (visual resources moderator); Spec Libr Asn (mem bd dir, Picture Div; chmn, 74-75); Col Art Asn Am; Victorian Soc Am; Asn Educ Commun & Technol. Res: Continuing investigations in retrieval of graphics, classification of slides and transparencies and computer automated indexes. Interest: Research in medieval architecture and experimental models of contemporary cathedral glass set in aluminum. Publ: Auth, Four how-to articles, Ceramics Mo, 53-54; auth, A Summer School in Wales, Art Educ, 66; auth, A Cost Study of Library Color in Microimage Storage and Retrieval, DC Col, 74; ed, Military Medicine and the Wound Man: A Graphic Display of the Wound Man Through History, US Military Acad, 76; auth, Rev: a collection in the making (Phillips collection on microfiche) May & Art Exhibition Catalogs on Microfiche, Sept, Microform Rev, 77. Mailing Add: 43 W 54th St Apt 5A New York NY 10019

LEWIS, ELMA INA
ART ADMINISTRATOR
b Boston, Mass, Sept 16, 21. Study: Emerson Col, BLI, 43; Boston Univ, MEd, 44; Emerson Col, Hon LHD, 68; Anna Maria Col, Hon LHD, 71; Boston Col, Hon LHD, 71; Colby Col, Hon DFA, 72; Harvard Univ, Hon ArtD, 72. Teaching: Founder & dir, Elma Lewis Sch Fine Arts, Boston, 50- Pos: Founder & dir, Nat Ctr Afro-Am Artists, Boston, 68- Awards: Outstanding Woman's Award, Campfire Girls Am, 70; Mayor's Citation, City of Boston, 70; Henry O Tanner Award, Black Arts Coun Calif, 71; plus others. Bibliog: Margo Miller (auth), Black Boston's Miss Lewis: art czarina with a needle, Boston Globe, 4/18/68; Caryl Rivers (auth), Black America's Barnum, Hurok & Guthrie, New York Times, 11/17/68; editorial in Vogue, 5/69. Mem: Fel Black Acad Arts & Lett; Gov Task Force on Arts & Humanities; Boston Int Platform Artists; Metrop Cult Alliance, Boston; Mass State Dept Educ Adv Bd. Publ: Contribr, Who Took the Weight, Little, 72; auth, At the crossroads: doom or bloom, Forum Mag, 72; auth, Celebrating us little people, Boston Rev of Arts, 9/72. Mailing Add: Nat Ctr of Afro-Am Artists 122 Elm Hill Ave Dorchester MA 02121

LEWIS, GLENN ALUN
See Flakey Rose Hip

LEWIS, GOLDA
ASSEMBLAGE ARTIST, PAPERMAKER
b New York, NY. Study: With Vaclav Vytacil, Hans Hofmann & Jack Tworkov; Papermaking with Douglass Howell. Work: Ciba-Geigy Chem Co, Ardsley, NY; Madden Corp, New York; Hercules Powder Co, Wilmington, Del; Foundations of Paper Hist, Haarlem, Holland; Cheney Pulp & Paper Co, Franklin, Ohio; plus other pub & pvt collections. Exhib: Landmark Gallery, New York, 73; Women Choose Women, New York Cult Ctr Mus, 73; Weatherspoon Art Gallery, Univ NC, Greensboro, 74; Kresge Art Ctr Gallery, Mich State Univ, 74; one-woman shows, Court Gallery, Copenhagen, Denmark, 70, Alonzo Gallery, New York, 74, Peter M David Gallery, Minneapolis, 74 & Benedicta Arts Ctr Gallery, Col St Benedict (Minn), 74; Handmade Paper, Prints & Unique Works, Mud Mod Art, New York, 76; New Ways with Paper, Nat Collection Fine Arts, Smithsonian Inst, Washington, DC, 77-78; Women's Caucus for the Arts, Grad Ctr, City of New York, 78; plus many others. Teaching: Instr, Ballard Sch, New York, 61-71; lectr, Marymount Manhattan Col, 71; Am Fedn Arts rent an artist workshop on paper and artists working in paper, 74. Awards: NY State Coun Arts Grant, 71. Bibliog: Rosalind Browne (auth), article in Art News, 71; Meilich & Ten Hoor (auth), Contemporary Collage and Construction, 73; Innovative Printmaking, Crown, 78; plus others. Mem: Women in the Arts. Style & Technique: Painting and reliefs in handmade paper called assemblage/time; bringing together of the old consciousness of time with the individual and the new consciousness of time with the universal. Media: Paper Made on Paper Moulds and Papes Used as Paint on Canvas. Publ: Auth, 77 Hand Papermaker's Conf, Women Artists Newsletter, 1/78. Dealer: Alonzo Gallery 30 W 57th St New York NY 10019. Mailing Add: 31 Union Sq W New York NY 10003

LEWIS, JACKSON PITTMAN
SCULPTOR
b Wilmington, NC, Dec 27, 45. Study: E Carolina Univ, BFA; Univ Ga, MFA; also studied bronze casting, Rome, Italy. Work: E Carolina Univ Permanent Collection; NC State Univ; Ky Arts Comn Collection. Comn: Wood wall relief, E Carolina Univ Student Govt, 68; garden sculpture in stone, Athens Regional Libr, Ga, 71; bronze baptismal font, St Joseph's Church, Athens, 71; sculptural screen, comn by Dutch Miller, Huntington, WVa, 73; sculpture fountain, Morehead State Univ, 74. Exhib: NC State Mus Exhib, 68 & 70; Mint Mus Show, Charlotte, NC, 70; Huntington Art Mus, WVa, 73; one-man show, Swearingen/Byck Gallery, Louisville, Ky, 74; Univ Ga Exhib, Cortona, Italy. Teaching: Instr sculpture, Morehead State Univ, 72-74; artist-lectr, Western Carolina Univ, 74-75. Awards: Best in Show, NC State Univ, 68; First Sculpture Award, Univ Ga, 71; Purchase Award, Ky Arts Comn, 73. Style & Technique: Stone construction applied with different removal technique. Media: Stone, Bronze. Mailing Add: PO Box 1381 Cullowhee NC 28723

LEWIS, JOHN CONARD
SCULPTOR, GLASSBLOWER
b Berkeley, Calif, Mar 13, 42. Study: Univ Calif, Berkeley, BA, 68, MA, 72, studied with Peter Voulkos, Marvin Lipofsky & Ron Nagle. Work: Corning Mus Glass, New York; Ariz State Univ Art Mus, Tempe; Tacoma Art Mus, Wash; Univ Wis-Madison Mus Art. Exhib: First Invitational Glass Exhib, Tacoma Art Mus, Wash, 71; Design XI, Pasadena Art Mus, Calif, 71; Reflections in Glass, Long Beach Mus Art, Calif, 72; Am Glass Now, Toledo Mus Art, Ohio, 73; Statements, Oakland Mus Art, Calif, 73; Collectors Exhib, Mus Contemp Crafts, New York, 74; Contemp Crafts of the Americas, Colo State Univ, Boulder, 76; Nat Glass Invitational III, Univ Wis-Madison, 76. Collections Arranged: New American Glass Focus WVa, Huntington Art Gallery, WVa, 76. Awards: Purchase Awards, Corning Mus Glass, NY, 70, Designer-Craftsman Ann, Richmond Art Ctr, 70 & Blown Glass Invitational, Tacoma Art Mus, Wash, 71. Mem: Am Crafts Coun; Glass Art Soc. Style & Technique: Hand blown glass. Media: Blown glass, cast glass. Mailing Add: 1677 Eighth St Oakland CA 94607

LEWIS, MARCIA
JEWELER-METALSMITH, INSTRUCTOR
b Washington, DC. Study: Corcoran Sch, Washington, DC; San Diego Univ, Calif; Calif State Univ, Long Beach. Work: Mus of Contemp Crafts, New York. Exhib: Int Handwerks Messe, Munich, Ger 71; Am Metalsmiths, DeCordova Mus, Lincoln, Mass, 73; Kunstindustri Mus, Copenhagen, Denmark, 73; Goldsmiths 74, Smithsonian Inst, Washington, DC 74; Crafts of the NAmericas, Colo State Univ & Smithsonian Inst, 75; Wis Directions, Wis Art Mus, Milwaukee, 75; Calif Design 12, Los Angeles, 76. Teaching: Instr metalsmithing & gen crafts, Univ Wis, Whitewater, 73-75 & San Jose State Univ, Calif, 75-76. Pos: Apprentice goldsmith, Ingrid Hansen, Zurich, Switz, 71-72; asst silversmith, Tony Laws Studio Ltd, Londin, Eng, 72-73. Awards: Sterling Silversmiths Award, Design Competition, Silversmiths Guild, 69; George C Marshall Mem Fel, Denmark-Amerika Fondet, 72; Nat Endowment for the Arts Award, Washington, DC, 76. Bibliog: Beverly Edna Johnson (auth), Biographical, Los Angeles Times Home Mag, 72; Thelma Newman (auth), Containers, Crown Publ, 77; Oppi Untracht (auth), Jewelry Techniques for Craftsmen, Doubleday, New York, 78. Mem: Pro-mem, Soc of NAm Goldsmiths. Style & Technique: Wearable metal ornaments designed to conform to and inhance the body of the wearer. Media: Metal. Publ: Auth, Wearable aluminum ornaments, Calif State Univ, Long Beach, 77. Mailing Add: 745 Myra Ave Chula Vista CA 92010

LEWIS, MARY
SCULPTOR, ILLUSTRATOR
b Portland, Ore, June 18, 26. Study: Univ Ore, 45-50, BS(sculpture), 49; Ore Div Am Asn Univ Women Mabel Merwin fel, 50, Syracuse Univ, with Ivan Mestrovic, tech asst to Mestrovic, 51, MFA, 52. Work: In pvt collections. Comn: Four-ft mahogany & hammered copper bird & 28 inch Carrara marble skunk cabbage, comn by Joseph Stein & Waterbury Club, Conn, 64; small stone carving, Prouty Garden, Children's Hosp Med Ctr, Boston, 65; Madonna and Child (walnut relief; 10 by 20 by 30 inches), St Louis de Montfort Sem Chapel, Litchfield, Conn, 66; Madonna & Child (maple relief; 4ft diameter x 5 inches deep), St Joseph's Church Chapel, Roseburg, Ore, 77. Exhib: Artists of Ore, Portland Mus Art, 51 & 69; 12th & 14th Ann New Eng Exhibs, Silvermine Guild Artists, New Canaan, Conn, 61 & 63; 62nd & 63rd Ann Exhib, New Haven Paint & Clay Club, John Slade Ely Ctr, New Haven, 63 & 64; Plaza Seven 3rd Ann Arts Festival Regional Exhib, Hartford Nat Bank & Trust Towers, 67. Teaching: Grad asst elem sculpture, Univ Ore, 49-50; asst prof sculpture, Nat Col Arts, Pakistan, 58-60; pvt classes, 61-67. Pos: Oceanog Mus, Ore State univ, summer 65; staff artist, GAF Corp Photo Div, Portland, Ore, 70-75. Awards: Tiffany Traveling Scholar, 53; Fulbright Lectr, 58-59; Assoc, Nat Col Arts, Pakistan, 59. Style & Technique: Simplified, interpretive objective forms, large and small; traditional and experimental techniques; direct carving. Media: Most sculptural media; Ink, Watercolor. Publ: Co-auth & illusr, The Little Yellow Dinosaur (21 stereo pictures), 71, illusr, In the Beginning—The Bible Story of Creation, Adam & Eve, Cain & Abel (21 stereo pictures), 72 & illusr, Jesus Christ, His Youth,

Disciples, Miracles (21 stereo pictures), 75, GAF View-Master. Mailing Add: Rte 3 Box 1097 Rainier OR 97048

LEWIS, MICHAEL H
PAINTER, EDUCATOR
b Brooklyn, NY, Aug 10, 41. Study: State Univ NY Col New Paltz, painting with Ben Bishop, George Wexler & Henry Raleigh, BS, 63, MFA, 75; Mich State Univ, printmaking with John DeMartelly, MA, 64. Work: Mich State Univ Art Dept Collection. Exhib: Artists of Upper Hudson, Albany Inst Hist & Art Ann, 66; New York Int Art Competition, 70; one-man show of paintings & drawings, Gallery I, Univ Maine, Orono, 72 & 75; Thin Webs (film), 13th Ann Ann Arbor Film Festival, 75; Nat Drawing Exhib, Univ Galleries, Southern Ill Univ, Carbondale, 75; Appalachian Nat Drawing Competition, Appalachian State Univ, Boone, NC, 76; Ann Graphics Competition, Provincetown Art Asn, Mass, 76; Ann Nat Painting Competition, Washington & Jefferson Col, Washington, Pa, 77; Nat Drawing Competition, Edinboro State Col, Pa, 77; Ann NDak Nat Print & Drawing Competition, Univ NDak, Grand Forks, 77; plus others. Teaching: Instr art, Kingston City Pub Schs, NY, 64-66; assoc prof painting, drawing & filmmaking, Univ Maine, Orono, 66-77, prof, 77- chmn dept art, 75- Pos: Mem, Maine Comn Arts & Humanities, 72- Awards: Coughtry Prize for Representational Painting, Albany Inst Hist & Art, 66; Silver Medal, New York Int Art Show, 70; Purchase Prize, Appalachian Nat Drawing Competition, 76. for TV, Univ Maine, Orono, summer 71. Bibliog: Rob Ellowitch (auth), Films: Michael Lewis, Maine's leader, Maine Times, 9/26/69; Toby Mussman (auth), The artist as filmmaker, 9/28/69 & Lynn Franklin (auth), Life at 30 is a painting, 6/18/72, Maine Sun Telegram. Style & Technique: Representational; based on personal myths and dreams and popular mythology; films are experimental and allegorical. Media: Oil, Film. Mailing Add: 104 Bennoch Rd Orono ME 04473

LEWIS, NAT BRUSH
PAINTER, INSTRUCTOR
b Boston, Mass, Dec 17, 25. Study: Pembroke Col, Brown Univ & RI Sch Design, AB; Art Students League; watercolor with Mario Cooper; also with Henry Gasser & Ray Ellis. Work: Am Asn Univ Women, Somerset Hills, NJ; Bloomfield Art League, NJ. Exhib: NJ Watercolor Soc, Morris Mus, Morristown, NJ, 67-74; Am Watercolor Soc, Nat Acad Design Galleries, 68 & 72 & Traveling Exhib, 72; Monmouth Mus; Am Artists Prof League Grand Nat, Lever House, 75 & 76 & Grand Cent Galleries, 77; Salmagundi Club Exhib, 75; plus others. Teaching: Instr watercolor, The Artery, Caldwell, NJ. Awards: Art Ctr Oranges Mem Award, 74; Winsor & Newton Award, Am Artists Prof League Grand Nat, 75; Salmagundi Club Award, Auction Exhib, 75; plus others. Mem: NJ Watercolor Soc (corresp secy, 69-71, vpres, 71-73, pres, 73-75); Am Artists Prof League, (third vpres, NJ Chap, 71-); Port Clyde Arts & Crafts Soc; Salmagundi Club. Media: Oil, Egg Tempera, Watercolor. Mailing Add: 51 Overlook Rd Caldwell NJ 07006

LEWIS, NORMAN WILFRED
PAINTER, INSTRUCTOR
b New York, NY. Study: Columbia Univ. Work: Art Inst Chicago; Munson-Williams-Proctor Inst, Utica, NY; Mus Mod Art, New York; IBM Collection; John D Rockefeller Collection; plus others. Comn: Mural, New Boys High Sch, Brooklyn, 75; painting, New Lincoln Hosp, NY, 75. Exhib: Venice Biennale, Italy; Sao Paulo, Brazil; Pa Acad Fine Arts, Philadelphia; Grenoble, France; Libr Cong, Washington, DC; Retrospective, City Univ Grad Ctr, New York, 76; plus many others. Teaching: Instr art, Jr High Sch 139, New York; instr art, Fed Art Proj, New York; supvr art ctr, A & T Col & Bennett Col, NC; instr art, Harlem Art Ctr & Thomas Jefferson Sch, New York; instr art, Indian Hill Music Sch, Stockbridge, Mass; supvr, Haryou-Act, Inc; instr art, Art Students League, 71- Pos: Bd dirs, Cinque Gallery, New York. Awards: Am Acad Arts & Lett Award, 70; Nat Inst Arts & Lett Award, 71; Guggenheim Fel, 75; plus others. Style & Technique: Abstract expressionist. Media: Oil. Mailing Add: 64 Grand St New York NY 10013

LEWIS, PHILLIP HAROLD
CURATOR
b Chicago, Ill, July 31, 22. Study: Art Inst Chicago, BFA, 47; Univ Chicago, MA, 53; Fulbright grant, Australian Nat Univ, 53-54; Univ Chicago, PhD, 66. Collections Arranged: Anthrop, geol & hist exhibs, Grout Hist Mus, Waterloo, Iowa, 55; What is Primitive Art, Field Mus Natural Hist, 58, estab Hall of Primitive Art, 61, with exhibs Primitive Artists Look at Civilization, The Human Image in Primitive Art & Australian Aboriginal Art: Arnhem Land, from collection of Louis A Allen, Palo Alto, Calif. Teaching: Lectr anthrop, Univ Chicago, 67-71; lectr, Eve Div, Northwestern Univ, Chicago, 73. Pos: Fied res proj primitive art, New Ireland, 53-54 & 70; asst cur primitive art, Field Mus Natural Hist, 57-59, assoc cur, 60, cur, 61-67, cur primitive art & Melanesian ethnol, 68- Awards: Chicago Natural Hist Mus Fel, 50-51, 54-55; Wenner-Gren Mus Res Fel, 68; Nat Sci Found Res Grant, 69-71. Mem: Am Anthrop Asn; fel Royal Anthrop Inst Gt Brit & Ireland; fel Am Authors Asn. Publ: Auth, A Definition of Primitive Art, Vol 36, 61 & The Social Context of Art in Northern New Ireland, Vol 58, 69, In: Fieldiana, Field Mus Nat Hist; auth, Changing memorial ceremonial in Northern New Ireland, J Polynesian Soc, Vol 182, No 2. Mailing Add: Field Mus Natural Hist Roosevelt Rd & Lake Shore Dr Chicago IL 60605

LEWIS, RONALD WALTER
PAINTER, INSTRUCTOR
b Atlanta, Ga, Jan 27, 45. Study: Ala Col, BS(art & bus), 67. Work: Birmingham Mus of Art, Ala; Fayette Art Mus, Ala; Jefferson State Col, Birmingham; Sylacauga Civic Ctr, Ala. Exhib: Ala Watercolor Soc, Birmingham Mus of Art, 71-77; Am Watercolor Soc, New York, 73; La Watercolor Soc, Old State Capitol, Baton Rouge, 73; Dixieland Watercolor & Drawing Show, Montgomery Mus of Art, Ala, 73; Watercolor USA, Springfield Art Mus, Mo, 73-74; Rocky Mountain Nat Watercolor, Golden, Colo, 76; Mainstreams, Marietta Col, Ohio, 76-77; Southern Watercolor Soc, Nashville, Tenn, 77. Teaching: Instr drawing, Birmingham Mus of Art, 73-; instr watercolor & oil, Mountain Brook Community Sch, Ala, 76- Awards: Twenty-nine awards including Ala Watercolor Soc. Bibliog: Stevens (auth), Ronald Lewis Paintings, La Revue Mod, Paris, 9/73. Mem: Ala Watercolor Soc (vpres, 73-74); Birmingham Art Asn (mem bd, 76-); Southern Watercolor Soc; Am Watercolor Soc. Style & Technique: Realism; landscape with a strong abstract pattern. Media: Drybrush watercolor, oil and tempera. Dealer: Ringland Galleries 2709 Cahaba Rd Birmingham AL 35223; Sloan-McKinney Galleries 5926 S Lewis London S Tulsa OK 74105. Mailing Add: 3228 Ridgely Ct Birmingham AL 35243

LEWIS, SAMELLA SANDERS
PAINTER, ART HISTORIAN
b New Orleans, La, Feb 27, 24. Study: Hampton Inst, BS; Ohio State Univ, MA & PhD; Tunghai Univ, Taiwan; Fulbright fel, 62; Univ Southern Calif, NDEA grant, 64-66; NY Univ Inst Fine Arts, 65. Work: Oakland Mus, Calif; Baltimore Mus Fine Arts; Va Mus Fine Arts, Richmond; High Mus, Atlanta, Ga; Atlanta Univ Mus Contemp Art. Comn: Mural Fla hist, comn by pres, Fla A&M Univ, 55; paintings, comn by dean, Hampton Inst, 67. Exhib: Joseph Hirshhorn Collection, Palm Springs Mus, 69; Dimensions of Black, La Jolla Mus Art, 70; Two Generations of Black Artists, Calif State Univ, Los Angeles, 70. Collections Arranged: Five Black Artists, 70 & The Renaissance in Harlem, 71, Lang Art Gallery, Scripps Col; The Art of African Peoples, Ankrum Gallery, 73. Teaching: Prof fine arts & head dept, Fla A&M Univ, 53-58; prof humanities & art hist, State Univ NY, 58-68; prof art hist, Scripps Col, 69. Pos: Coordr educ, Los Angeles Co Mus Art, 69-70; pres, Contemp Crafts Publ, 69; owner, Multi-Cul Gallery, 71; art ed, Black Art Mag, 78. Awards: NY State-Ford Found grant, 65. Bibliog: The Black Artists (film), Afrographics, 68; Focus, KNBC-TV, 68; article, In: Los Angeles Times, 70. Mem: Col Art Asn Am; Nat Conf Artists (co-chairperson, 70-73); Am Soc Aesthetics. Res: African, Asian and Afro-American art. Collection: Rare African works, including Bakuba in the 1890's; sand paintings of the American Indian; contemporary Asian and African-American works. Publ: Co-ed, Black Artists on Art, Vols I & II, 69 & 71; auth, Art: African American (textbk), Harcourt, 76. Dealer: Ankrum Gallery 657 N La Cienega Blvd Los Angeles CA 90069. Mailing Add: 1237 Masselin Ave Los Angeles CA 90019

LEWIS, STANLEY
SCULPTOR, PRINTMAKER
b Montreal, Que, Mar 28, 30. Study: Montreal Mus Fine Arts, 48-51; Inst Allende, San Miguel, Mex, scholars, 52-55; Elizabeth T Greenshields Mem Found grant, Florence, Italy, 56-59. Work: Que Prov Mus; Nat Gallery Can, Ottawa; Montreal Mus Fine Arts; Jerusalem Mus, Israel; Samuel Zacks Collection. Comn: Sleeping Spirit (lava boulder), Inst Allende, 53, standing nude (white marble), 53 & The Corngrinder (gray marble), 54; late Samuel Bronfman, Can Jewish Cong, 66. Exhib: One-man shows, Montreal Mus Fine Arts, 52 & 59, Israel Art Auction Gallery, Tel Aviv, 65 & Nat Gallery Can, 71; Celestial Lights Exhib, Man & His World, Montreal, Atelier J Lukacs, Montreal, 75 & 76. Teaching: Instr modeling, McGill Univ Sch Archit, 52; instr sculpture, Montreal Mus Fine Arts, 61-63; instr sculpture, Saidye Bronfman Art Ctr, Montreal, 68-; lect, The Eskimo Artist, Nat Film Bd, Montreal, 75. Awards: Prize, Concours Artistiques, Que, 59; Prize for Sculpture, Nat Art & Photog Exhib, PQ, 60, Prize for Stone-Cut Prints, 62. Bibliog: Peter Olwyer (auth), article in Can Art, fall 55; Earle Birney (auth), article in Sat Night, 55; Folch (auth), article in Vie Arts, summer 59. Mem: Founding mem Que Sculptors' Asn; hon rep Int Acad Leonardo da Vinci. Style & Technique: Unique technique in multi-colored stone cut printing. Res: Contributed original research on Michelangelo's childhood and marble carving techniques to writing of Irving Stone's The Agony and the Ecstasy. Publ: Auth, The Stone Speaks, 53; auth, Hands to Create Wonders, 61; auth, Space, Man and Stone, 69. Mailing Add: Apt 4 4131 Cote des Neiges Rd Montreal PQ Can

LEWIS, VIRGINIA ELNORA
MUSEUM DIRECTOR, ART HISTORIAN
b Sault Ste Marie, Ont, Apr 7, 07; US citizen. Study: Wellesley Col, 26-28; Univ Pittsburgh, AB, 31, with Walter Read Hovey, AM, 35; Carnegie Inst Technol, cert, 33; Harvard Univ, with Jacob Rosenberg, summer 37, with Kenneth Conant, summer 40; Brit Mus Dept Prints, with Arthur M Hind, summer 38. Collections Arranged: Exhibitions organized, arranged & catalogued independently & in collaboration with Dr Walter Read Hovey, Henry Clay Frick Fine Arts Gallery & other mus & galleries, 37-67. Teaching: Lectr & instr fine arts, Univ Pittsburgh, 34-50, instr eng compos & civil air regulations, ASTP Prog, 42-43, instr eng, 44-46, asst prof fine arts, 50-54, assoc prof fine arts, 54-57, prof fine arts, 57-67, emer prof, 67- Pos: Proofreader, Carnegie Inst Press, 31-33; cur slides & photographs, Univ Pittsburgh, 34-43, cur exhibs, 46-47, actg head, Frick Fine Arts Dept, 40-63, head librarian, Frick Fine Arts Libr, 63-65, asst dir, Frick Fine Arts Bldg, 65-67, res, Frick Found, 68-69; dir, Frick Art Mus, 70-; dir, Dennis Art Gallery, Raymond Moore Found, Mass, summer 53; consult dir, Westmoreland Co Mus Art, Woods Marchand Found, Greensburg, Pa, 54-56. Mem: Am Asn Mus (Pittsburgh comt, 59); Int Coun Mus; Col Art Asn Am; Soc Archit Hist (bd dirs, nat secy, chmn Pittsburgh Chap, 56, chmn session, Washington, DC, 58); Nat Trust Hist Preservation (chmn 14th ann session, 60). Res: Antoine Houdon, French 18th century sculptor. Publ: Auth, Andrey Avinoff: The Man, Carnegie Inst Press, 53; auth, Russell Smith: Romantic Realist, Univ Pittsburgh Press, 57; ed, Walter Read Hovey, auth, The Arts in Changing Societies: Reflections Inspired by Works of Art in the Frick Art Museum, 72 & Treasures of the Frick Art Museum, 75, Frick Art Mus, Pittsburgh. Mailing Add: Frick Art Mus 7227 Reynolds St Pittsburgh PA 15208

LEWIS, WILLIAM ARTHUR
PAINTER, ART ADMINISTRATOR
b Detroit, Mich, Mar 20, 18. Study: Col Archit & Design, Univ Mich, BDesign, 48. Work: Butler Inst Am Art, Youngstown; St Paul Art Ctr; Grand Rapids Mus Art; Univ Mich Grad Sch; Grinnell Col. Comn: Two groups of watercolors, Detroit Bank & Trust Co, Detroit & London, 63 & 69; watercolor series, Bohn Aluminum Co, Detroit, 70; oil painting, Grand Rapids City Hall, 71; acrylic painting, Soc Mfg Engrs, Dearborn, Mich, 71. Exhib: Five ann, Butler Inst Am Art, 54-65; Drawing USA, Mus Mod Art, 56; Corcoran Gallery Biennial, Washington, DC & Am Fedn Art Tour, 57; one-man show, The Last Year of the Civil War, Univ Mich, Detroit Hist Soc, Mint Mus, Madison Col (Va), Eastern Mich Univ, Dearborn Hist Mus & others, 62-65; Drawing USA, St Paul Art Ctr, 63 & 66. Teaching: Prof art, Sch Art, Univ Mich, Ann Arbor, 64-, Rackham Sch Grad Studies fac res grants, Last Year of the Civil War, 60-62 & J M W Turner, 64. Pos: Assoc dean, Sch Art, Univ Mich, Ann Arbor, 66-75; dir, Comn Accreditation, Nat Asn Schs Art, 72-75. Awards: St Paul Art Ctr Purchase Award, Drawing USA, 63. Bibliog: Hazen Schumacher (auth), The Painting Professor, Univ Mich TV Studios, 62; Louise Bruner (auth), Feelings of an artist, Toledo Blade, 64. Mem: Col Art Asn Am; Mich Watercolor Soc. Media: Watercolor. Publ: Auth & illusr, The Civil War-a contemporary approach, Dimension, spring 62; illusr, cover & article, Limnos, summer 69. Dealer: Arwin Galleries 222 Grand River Detroit MI 48226; Forsythe Gallery 201 Nickels Arcade Ann Arbor MI 48104. Mailing Add: 1106 S Forest Ave Ann Arbor MI 48104

LEWIS, WILLIAM R
INSTRUCTOR, PAINTER
b Osceola, Iowa, Sept 23, 20. Study: Drake Univ, BFA, 49; Univ Wash; Ariz State Univ, MA, 52. Work: Ariz Western Col, Yuma; Glendale Community Col, Ariz; Scottsdale Civic Ctr, Ariz. Exhib: Ariz Ann, Phoenix Art Mus, 61-68; Butler Art Mus Ann Midyear Show, 62; Am Watercolor Soc Ann, 63-65; Southwestern Invitational, Yuma, 67-72; Watercolor USA Traveling Show, 68. Teaching: Chmn dept art, S Mountain High Sch, Phoenix, 64- Awards: Ariz Ann First in Watercolor, Phoenix Art Mus, 62. Mem: Ariz Watercolor Asn (pres, 63-64). Style & Technique: From cubistic pattern to large soft edge washes. Media: Watercolor. Mailing Add: 313 E 15th St Tempe AZ 85281

LEWISON, FLORENCE (MRS MAURICE GLICKMAN)
WRITER, ART DEALER
b Jersey City, NJ. Study: Sch Art Studies, 45-49, art hist & criticism with Maurice Glickman; also study in Eng, France & Italy, 56 & 61. Pos: Art critic, feature writer & art news ed, Design Mag, 49-51; founder & dir, Florence Lewison Gallery, 61- Res: Revival and reevaluation of

19th and early 20th century American artists. Specialty: A program of exhibitions devoted solely to the reintroduction and reevaluation of 19th and early 20th century American artists. Publ: Auth, Theodore Robinson: America's first impressionist, 2/63, The uniqueness of Albert Bierstadt, 9/64, John Frederick Kensett: a tribute to man and artists, 10/66 & G P A Healy: a success at home and abroad, 12/68, Am Artist Mag; auth, Theodore Robinson and Claude Monet, Apollo Mag, London, Eng, 9/63. Mailing Add: 30 E 60th St New York NY 10022

LE WITT, SOL
SCULPTOR
b Hartford, Conn, 1928. Study: Syracuse Univ, BFA, 49. Work: Stedelijk Mus, Amsterdam, Holland; Albright-Knox Art Gallery, Buffalo, NY; Art Gallery Ont, Toronto; Los Angeles Co Mus Art, Los Angeles, Calif; Mus Mod Art, New York; work also in Ger mus. Exhib: Sculpture Ann, Whitney Mus Am Art, New York, 67; Minimal Art, The Hague, 68; Documenta, Kassel, WGer, 68 & 72; Prospect '68, Dusseldorf, 68; Stadtische Kunsthalle, Dusseldorf, 69; Univ BC, 69; La Jolla Mus, Calif, 70; Tokyo Biennale, 70; Guggenheim Int, New York, 71; one-man shows, Guggenheim Mus, 71, Mus Mod Art, New York, 71, Walker Art Ctr, Minneapolis, 72, Mus Mod Art, Oxford, Eng, 73, Stedelijk Mus, 74 & Visual Arts Mus, New York, 76; San Francisco Mus Art, 75; plus many others. Teaching: Instr, Mus Mod Art Sch, 64-67; instr, Cooper Union, 67. Bibliog: Gregory Battcock (ed), Minimal Art: a Critical Anthology, Dutton, 68; E C Goosen (auth), The Art of the Real USA 1948-1968, Mus Mod Art, 68; Lucy R Lippard (auth), Minimal Art, Haags Gemeentemuseum, 68; plus others. Publ: Auth, American sculpture, Artforum Spec Issue, summer 67; auth, Lines and combinations of lines, 69, Drawings Series 1968 (Fours), 4/69 & I am still alive: on Kawara, 7-8/70, Studio Int; auth, Sentences on conceptual art, 7/71 & Sol Le Witt, 6/73, Flash Art, Milan; auth, All wall drawings, Arts Mag, 2/72; auth, Sentences on conceptual art, Uber Kunst, Cologne, WGer, 74. Dealer: John Weber Gallery 420 W Broadway New York NY 10012. Mailing Add: 117 Hester St New York NY 10022

LEWTON, JEAN LOUISE
ART EDITOR, ART ADMINISTRATOR
b Michigan City, Ind, Sept 7, 39. Study: Pomona Col, BA(with honors), 61; Claremont Univ Col, 62; Catholic Univ, 64-67. Collections Arranged: Alice Pike Barney & Her Friends & Alice Pike Barney, 78, Nat Collection of Fine Arts, Smithsonian Inst. Pos: Cur & registr, Alice Pike Barney Collection, Washington, DC, 64-; auth, articles in DC Gazette, 70-75; producer & moderator, Washington Review of the Arts on the Air, 75-; managing ed & auth articles, Washington Review of the Arts, 75-; admin dir, Capitol Hill Arts Workshop, 71- Res: Art's politics and taxes; research Alice Pike. Mailing Add: 404 10th St SE Washington DC 20003

LEWTON, VAL EDWIN
DESIGNER, PAINTER
b Santa Monica, Calif, May 23, 37. Study: Claremont Univ Col, Calif, MFA, 62; also with Dr David W Scott. Work: Towson State Col, Md. Exhib: Ann Southern Calif Drawing Competition, Long Beach State Col, Calif, 61; Eastern Regional Exhib, Nat Drawing Soc, Philadelphia, 65; Corcoran Area & Vicinity Exhib, Washington, DC, 66-68; one-man shows, Dimmok Gallery, Georgetown Univ, 70 & Studio Gallery, 75-77; Cross Roads of America, Am Seating Co, NEOCON, Chicago, 75. Collections Arranged: Exhib designer for Nat Collection Fine Arts-Smithsonian Inst, Washington, DC, Man Made Mobile, 74-75, Made in Chicago, 74, Mark Toby, 74 & Academy, 75; also Art-Now '74 & Art Now Cartoons '75, Kennedy Ctr; Robert Rauschenburg Retrospective, Nat Collection Fine Arts, 76 & Decorative Designs of Frank Lloyd Wright, 77, Renwick Gallery, 77, Smithsonian Inst, Washington, DC; among others. Teaching: Lectr art, Univ Calif, Riverside, 62-63. Pos: Asst chief for exhibs design, Nat Collection Fine Arts-Smithsonian Inst, 63- Bibliog: Ben Forgey (auth), Visions of suburbia from Val Lewton, Washington Star Calendar Sun Suppl, 75. Style & Technique: Representational painting, suburbscapes. Media: Acrylic on Canvas. Publ: Auth, Washington review of the arts (column), 73-75 & 78. Dealer: Studio Gallery 802 F St NW Washington DC 20004. Mailing Add: 404 Tenth St SE Washington DC 20003

LI, CHU-TSING
ART ADMINISTRATOR, ART HISTORIAN
b Canton, China, May 26, 20; US citizen. Study: Univ Nanking, China, BA (Eng lit), 43; Univ Iowa, MA(Eng), 49, PhD(art hist), 55; post-doctoral res, Harvard Univ, 59 & Princeton Univ, 60. Teaching: From instr to prof art hist, Univ Iowa, Iowa City, 54-66; prof Oriental art, Univ Kans, Lawrence, 66-, chmn dept hist art, 72- Mem: Col Art Asn; Midwest Art Hist Soc. Res: Painting of the Yuan Dynasty in China (13th to 14th century) and of the modern period. Publ: Auth, The Autumn Colors on the Ch'iao and Hua Mountains, 65 & A Thousand Peaks and Myriad Ravines: Drenwatz Collection, 74, Artibus Asiae; auth, Liu Kuo-sung, Development of a Modern Chinese Artist, 69 & contribr, Five Chinese Painters: Fifth Moon Exhibition, 70, Nat Gallery Art, Taipei, Taiwan. Mailing Add: Dept of Art Hist Univ of Kans Lawrence KS 66045

LIBBY, GARY RUSSELL
MUSEUM DIRECTOR, ART HISTORIAN
b Boston, Mass, June 7, 44. Study: Univ Fla, AA, BA, studied with Jerry Uelsmann, MA, studied with Philip Hultman; Tulane Univ, MA, studied with Leo Steinberg, PhD, 78. Collections Arranged: Masterpieces of Middle Am Art (auth catalog), Inst of Middle Am Studies, New Orleans Mus Art, 69; Audubon: Birds and Animals, 75, The Third Empire Porcelains and Silver, (auth catalog), 77 & Artistic Taste in Pre-Castro Cuba, (auth catalog), 77, Mus Arts & Sci, Daytona Beach, Fla; 400 Years of Prints, Eight Cuban Masters, Sampson Hall Gallery, Stetson Univ, Deland, Fla, 77. Teaching: Instr, Tulane Univ, New Orleans, La, 68-71; vis prof, Univ Mexico, Merida, Yucatan, 71-72; asst prof humanities-art hist, Stetson Univ, 72-73, asst prof art hist surv, 72-77. Pos: Dir, Mus Arts & Sci, Daytona Beach, Fla, 77- Mem: Southeast Col Art Conf; Col Art Conf; Col Art Asn. Res: Latin American: Cuban and Caribbean, 19th century English and American painting; Pre-Columbian ceramics. Collection: Pre-Columbian, etchings, engravings, 19th century painting. Publ: Auth, 19th Century Romanticism, 68, The 18th Century, 68 & Victorian Novel, 69, Univ Fla Press. Mailing Add: 221 W Michigan Ave Deland FL 32720

LIBBY, WILLIAM C
PAINTER, WRITER
b Pittsburgh, Pa. Study: Univ Pittsburgh; Carnegie-Mellon Univ, BA; Univ Tex; Colorado Springs Fine Arts Ctr; Acad Grande Chaumiere; Atelier 17, with Stanley W Hayter. Work: Pennell Collection, Libr of Cong, Washington, DC; Brooklyn Mus, NY; Carnegie Mus Art, Pittsburgh; Butler Inst Am Art, Youngstown, Ohio; Metrop Mus Art, New York. Comn: Presentation print, Print Club, Rochester, NY, 56; bicentennial dir cover, Bell Tel Co Pa, Pittsburgh, 57; commemorative hist painting, Pa RR, Pittsburgh, 58; History of Pittsburgh (hist illus), 60; altar piece, Carnegie-Mellon Chapel, Pittsburgh, 63. Exhib: Painting in the US, Carnegie Mus Art, 48; Nat Acad Design, New York, 51; US Info Agency Overseas Exhib Am Graphic Art, 61; 6th Int Graphics Exhib, Ljubljana, Yugoslavia, 65; 1st Biennial Graphic Art, Krakow, Poland, 68. Teaching: Prof drawing & painting, Carnegie-Mellon Univ, 45- Awards: Purchase Award, Nat Print Exhib, Brooklyn Mus, 52; Jury Award of Distinction, Assoc Artists Pittsburgh, 66; Purchase Award, Nat Print Exhib, Kutztown, Pa, 66. Bibliog: Norman Kent (auth), William Libby, Am Artist Mag, 59. Mem: Soc Am Graphic Artists; Assoc Artists Pittsburgh (pres, 55-57); Nat Acad Design. Media: Oil. Publ: Illusr, The Story of an American City, Doubleday, 59; auth, They know what they like, Eastern Arts Asn Bull, 59; auth, A look at printmaking, Carnegie Mag, 60; auth, Offset lithography as a fine art, 67 & auth, Marco de Marco, 70, Am Artist Mag. Mailing Add: Box 135 Carnegie-Mellon Univ Pittsburgh PA 15213

LIBERI, DANTE
PAINTER, SCULPTOR
b New York, NY, Oct 15, 19. Study: Acad Fine Arts, Montecatini, Italy. Exhib: Group shows, Knickerbocker Artist, New York, 52 & Premio Nazionale di Pittura, Quarrata, Tuscany, Italy; one-man shows, Galleria Vannucci, Pistoia, Italy, 70, Galleria Ghelfi, Montecatini, Italy, 72 & Bottega D'Arte, Quarrata; plus others. Awards: First Prize for Sculpture, Oper Democracy. Media: Oil. Publ: Illusr, New Yorker Mag, 43. Dealer: Country Art Gallery The Plaza Locust Valley NY 11560. Mailing Add: 15 Ardis Lane Plainview NY 11803

LIBERMAN, ALEXANDER
PHOTOGRAPHER, WRITER
b Kiev, Russia, 1912; US citizen. Study: Painting with Andre Lhote, Paris, France, 29-31; archit with August Perret & at Ecole Beaux-Arts, Paris, 30-32. Work: Addison Gallery Am Art, Andover, Mass; Albright-Knox Art Gallery, Buffalo; Art Inst Chicago; Tate Gallery, London, Eng; Nat Collection Fine Arts, Washington, DC; plus many others. Exhib: One-man shows, Mus Mod Art, New York, 66, Jewish Mus, New York, 66, Emmerich Gallery, New York, 67-69 & 73 & Honolulu Acad Arts, 72; Mus Mod Art, New York, 62, 64, 65, 68 & 69; Contemp Am Sculpture Ann, Whitney Mus Am Art, 69; Pure and Clear, Philadelphia Mus Art, 69; Retrospectives: Painting and Sculpture, Corcoran Gallery Art, Washington, DC & Mus Fine Arts, Houston, 70; plus others. Pos: Ed dir, Conde Nast Publ, 62- Publ: Auth, The Artist in His Studio, 60 & Greece, Gods and Art, 68, Viking. Dealer: Andre Emmerich Gallery 41 E 57th St New York NY 10028. Mailing Add: 173 E 70th St New York NY 10021

LIBHART, MYLES LAROY
ART ADMINISTRATOR, ART WRITER
b Marietta, Pa, Mar 8, 31. Study: Brooklyn Mus Art Sch; pvt instr with Nicholas Marsicano. Work: Newark Mus, NJ. Comn: Painted enamel murals, Grace Shipping Lines, New York, 61. Exhib: Arts & Crafts Regional, Newark Mus, NJ, 59; Enamels, Mus of Contemp Crafts, New York, 60. Collections Arranged: International Watercolor Biennial, 61 & Fine Printmaking, 62, Brooklyn Mus, NY; Contemporary Sioux Painting, (auth, catalog) & Photographs and Poems by Sioux Children, Sioux Indian Mus, Rapid City, SDak, 71; Contemporary Indian Artists, Montana, Wyoming, Idaho, Mus of the Plains Indian, Browning, Mont, 72; Contemporary Southern Plains Indian Painting (ed, catalog), 72 & Painted Tipis by Contemporary Plains Indian Artists (co-auth, catalog), 73, Southern Plains Indian Mus, Anadarko, Okla. Teaching: Instr painted enamels, Brooklyn Mus Art Sch, NY, 61-63. Pos: Dir of exhibs & publ, Brooklyn Mus, NY, 60-63; dir of mus, exhibs & publ, Indian Arts & Crafts Bd, US Dept of the Interior, Washington, DC, 63- Bibliog: David Cambell (auth), New Talent, USA, Art in Am, Vol 1, No 1, 60. Mem: Am Asn of Mus; Am Craftsman's Coun. Style & Technique: Abstract works in oil and vitreous enamels. Media: Oil. Res: Development of contemporary Native American arts of the United States. Mailing Add: Indian Arts & Crafts Bd Rm 4004 US Dept of the Interior Washington DC 20240

LICHTENBERG, MANES
PAINTER
b New York, NY. Study: Art Students League; with Fernand Leger, Paris; Acad Grande Chaumiere, Paris. Exhib: Philadelphia Acad Fine Arts; Nat Acad Design, New York; Mus Mod Art, Paris; Allied Artists Am, New York; Mus l'Ile de France, Paris. Awards: Prix Othon Friesz, Paris, 61; Gold Medal of Honor, Allied Artists Am, 64; Prix Maurice Utrillo, Utrillo Found Int, Paris, 64. Mem: Allied Artists Am; Am Watercolor Soc. Media: Watercolor, Oil and Pastel. Mailing Add: 835 Mix Ave Hamden CT 06514

LICHTENSTEIN, ROY
PAINTER, SCULPTOR
b New York, NY, Oct 27, 23. Study: Ohio State Univ, BFA, 46, MFA, 49. Work: Solomon R Guggenheim Mus, New York; Whitney Mus Am Art, New York; Tate Gallery, London, Eng; Stedelijk Mus, Amsterdam, Holland; Pasadena Mus Art, Calif; plus others. Comn: Outside wall for Circarama, NY State Pavilion, New York World's Fair, 63; billboard for Expo '67, Montreal. Exhib: Retrospective, Pasadena Art Mus, 67 & Tate Gallery, 68; Documenta IV, Kassel, Ger, 68; Print Biennial, Brooklyn Mus, 68; Solomon R Guggenheim Mus, 69; one-man shows, Nelson-Atkins Art Gallery, Kansas City, Kans, 70, Mus Contemp Art, Chicago, 70, Seattle Art Mus, Wash, 70, Univ Calif, Irvine, 70, Contemp Arts Mus, Houston, 72 & Centre Nat d'Art Contemporain, Paris, 75; Whitney Mus Am Art Ann, 70, 72 & 73, Am Pop Art, 74; Mus Fine Arts, Osaka, Japan, 70; Va Mus Art, Richmond, 70; Contemp Arts Ctr, Cincinnati, 70 & 74; Corcoran Biennial, Washington, DC, 71; Albright-Knox Art Gallery, Buffalo, NY, 71; Art Inst Chicago, 72 & 74; Detroit Inst of Arts, 73; Art Mus STex, Corpus Christi, 74; Mus Mod Art, New York, 74; plus many others. Teaching: Instr, Ohio State Univ, 46-51; instr, State Univ NY Col Oswego, 57-60; instr, Douglass Col, Rutgers Univ, 60-63. Bibliog: Nicolas Calas (auth), Roy Lichtenstein: insight through irony, Arts Mag, 9-10/69; Michael Compton (auth), Pop Art, Feltham, Middlesex, 70; Diane Waldman (auth), Roy Lichtenstein, London, 71; plus many others. Dealer: Leo Castelli Gallery 4 E 77th St New York NY 10021. Mailing Add: PO Box 1369 Southampton NY 11968

LICHTY, GEORGE M
CARTOONIST
b Chicago, Ill, May 16, 05. Study: Art Inst Chicago; Univ Mich, BA. Work: Truman Libr, Independence, Mo; Presidential Mus, Austin, Tex; Mus Cartoon Art, Greenwich, Conn; Tate Gallery, London, Eng. Pos: Syndicate cartoonist, United Features Syndicate, 34-40 & Field Newspaper Syndicate, 40-74. Awards: Best Syndicate Panel Award, Nat Cartoonists Soc, 59, 63, 65 & 73. Bibliog: Greer William (auth), Does Lichty hate people, Saturday Eve Post, 52; news article in Time Mag, 56. Mem: Nat Cartoonists Soc. Style & Technique: Loose. Media: Brush & Ink, Oil. Mailing Add: 5440 Thomas Rd Sebastopol CA 95472

LIDDLE, NANCY HYATT
ART ADMINISTRATOR, GALLERY DIRECTOR
b Martinsville, Ind, Aug 27, 31. Study: Ind Univ, AB. Pos: Vpres, 327 Gallery, Albany, NY, 59-63; art critic, Knickerbocker News, Albany, NY, 64-65; asst dir, Univ Art Gallery, State

Univ NY, Albany, 66-67; dir univ art gallery, State Univ NY, Albany, 77- Mem: Albany Inst Hist & Art; Hist Albany Found. Mailing Add: 34 Willett St Albany NY 12210

LIDOV, ARTHUR HERSCHEL
PAINTER, SCULPTOR
b Chicago, Ill, June 24, 17. Study: Univ Chicago, BA, 36, study art hist, 38-39. Comn: Mural, Post Off, Chillicothe, Ill, 39 & J W Thompson, New York, 64; series of Bible paintings, Christian Art Tours, Huntsville, Ala, 77. Exhib: One-man shows, Art Inst Chicago, 41, Pineapple Gallery, Brooklyn, 43 & J Walter Thompson Gallery, 64; Art Inst Chicago, 33 & 34; Nat Acad Art, 58; Mus Mod Art, 62; plus others. Pos: Creative consult & mem exec comt, Sudler & Hennessey Advert Agency, New York, 50-52; gen partner & prin exec officer, SWP3, New York, 72-75. Awards: Art Dirs Club Awards, 52, 53 & 59; Illusr Club New York Award, 63, 73 & 74; Am Inst Graphic Arts Award, 63. Style & Technique: Developed new bas-relief technique; developed and extended Namias methods of photo-sculpture. Mailing Add: Pleasant Ridge Rd Poughquag NY 12570

LIEB, VERED (VERED SHAPIRO-LIEB)
ART WRITER, PAINTER
b Haifa, Israel, Apr 2, 47; US citizen. Study: Queens Col, City Univ, NY, BA(philos); Westminister Col, Oxford Eng(archaeol); Arts Students League (painting), study with Macabee Greenfield. Exhib: Nat Woman's Art Exhib, SOHO 20 Gallery, New York, 76; First Ann New York Salon Show, Echo Gallery, 76; Group Installation, Cayman Gallery, New York, 77; Art in Pub Spaces, Fed Hall, Nat Mem, New York, 77. Collections Arranged: The Thomas Chapis Collection (consult cur), New York, 75-76; Personal Visions: Place-Spaces (consult cur; ed, catalog), Bronx Mus of the Arts, 2/78-4/78. Pos: Art ed, Appearances Mag, New York, 76-77; ed & publ, Re-View: artists on art Mag, New York, 77-; consult cur, Bronx Mus of the Arts, New York, 78- Mem: Orgn of Independent Artists, New York. Style & Technique: Abstract expressionism (third generation), acrylic paint on canvas, primary interest in color relationships and surface texture. Interest: The roots of American painting in particular abstract expressionism and its ramifications for painting today. Publ: Contribr, Essay on art, Unmuzzled Ox, Michael André, 78. Mailing Add: 85 Mercer St New York NY 10012

LIEBER, FRANCE
PRINTMAKER, PAINTER
b Newark, NJ. Study: Art Students League; Pratt Graphic Ctr, New York; Kean Col, NJ. Exhib: 16th Nat Print Exhib, Montclair Art Mus, Bergen Mus & Hunterdon Art Ctr, 72; Airlift 549, Women's Interart Ctr, NY, 73; Women Printmakers, Philadelphia Focuses on Women in the Visual Arts, Del Art Mus, Wilmington & Print Club, Philadelphia, 74; Nat Asn Women Artists 86th Ann Exhib-Int Women's Year, Nat Acad Design, 75; Nat Asn Women Artists Traveling Graphic Exhib, USA, 75-76; Ward-Nasse Gallery, New York, 75-; Cayuga Mus, Auburn, NY, 76; Cent Wyo Mus Art, Casper, 76; Old Bridge Art Guild Traveling Exhib, 77-78; 1st Biennial NJ Artists, Newark Mus & NJ State Mus, 77; two-person show, Cornell Club of New York, 77; Women Artists 78, Grad Ctr, City Univ New York; among others. Teaching: Instr painting, Kenilworth Recreation Ctr, NJ, 70-73; instr painting & printmaking, Cranford Community Ctr, NJ, 72-74; instr printing & printmaking, ArtMakers Art Sch, 73-; lect demonstr in graphics for art asns, prof groups, women's clubs & Cranford, NJ schs. Pos: Owner-photogr, France Lieber Portrait Studio of Photog, Newark, 50-65; staff photogr, YMHA-YWHA, Essex Co, Newark, 70-71; artist in residence, State Mus Cult Ctr, Trenton, 73-74; co-owner & dir, ArtMakers Gallery & Art Sch, Garwood, 73- Awards: First Prize (oils & graphics), Cranford Art Asn, 65, 70 & 73; First Prize (graphics), Somerville Art Asn, 73; Nat Asn Women Artists Medal of Honor for Graphics, Nat Acad Gallery, NY, 75; plus many others. Bibliog: S Weinstock (auth), Diverse interest make her swing, Newark Star Ledger, NJ, 69; R A Williams (ed), Plumbing the depths of art, NJ Music & Arts Mag, 73; Artmakers of Garwood, New York Sunday Times, 76; plus over 100 others. Mem: Nat Asn Women Artists, Inc; Nat Painters & Sculptors Soc; Philadelphia Print Club; Women's Caucus for Art; Cranford Art Asn (pres, hon pres & trustee, 60-74). Style & Technique: Inventive forms fused with minimal reality; impressionistic abstracts; magic realism. Media: Silkscreen, Intaglio; Oils, Pen & Ink. Mailing Add: 56 Nomahegan Ct Cranford NJ 07016

LIEBERMAN, HARRY
PAINTER
b Gnieveshev, Poland, Nov 15, 76; US citizen. Work: Joseph H Hirshhorn Collection, Washington, DC; Mus Boymans-Van Beuningen, Rotterdam, Holland; Seattle Mus Art; Palm Springs Desert Mus, Calif; Judah Magnes Mem Jewish Mus, Berkeley. Exhib: Of Time and the Image, Phoenix Art Mus, 66; one-man shows, Judah Magnes Mem Mus, 69, St Andrew's Priory, Valyermo, Calif, 71, Morris Gallery, New York, 73 & Great Neck Pub Libr, 75; plus others. Bibliog: William Mordecai Kramer (auth), Harry Lieberman, KCOP-TV; The holidays (greeting card), Jewish Bk Club Commentary Mag; Herbert W Hemphill, Jr & Julia Weissman (auth), 20th Century American Folk Art and Artists, Dutton, 74. Media: Oil. Publ: Illusr, cover design, Moise, Mont-Blanc, Geneva, Switz; illusr, Great Ideas Western Man Series, Container Corp Am, 65; The Holidays (full color lithograph), Commentary Libr/Jewish Bk Club Ltd Ed, 72. Dealer: Ankrum Gallery 657 La Cienega Blvd Los Angeles CA 90069. Mailing Add: 9 Birch St Great Neck NY 11023

LIEBERMAN, MEYER FRANK
PAINTER, PRINTMAKER
b New York, NY, Aug 28, 23. Study: Art Students League, with Reginald Marsh; Pratt Graphics Ctr, with Andrew Stasik. Work: Jewish Mus, New York; Flatbush Jewish Ctr, Brooklyn. Exhib: Coney Island, Mus City New York, 55; Drawing USA, Mus Mod Art, New York, 56; one-man shows, Jewish Mus, New York, 55, Herzl Inst, New York, 69 & La Salle Col, 70. Teaching: Instr drawing, painting & composition, Art Life Craft Studios, New York, 64-68; instr drawing, collage painting & composition, Temple Emanu-El, Yonkers, NY, 66-; instr drawing, painting & composition, Flatbush Jewish Ctr, Brooklyn, 67- Mem: Artists Equity Asn (dir, 68-71). Style & Technique: Neo-impressionist. Media: Pastel, Oil, Watercolor. Mailing Add: RFD 421 Zena Rd Woodstock NY 12498

LIEBERMAN, WILLIAM S
ART ADMINISTRATOR
b Paris, France, Feb 14, 24. Study: Swarthmore Col, BA(hons), 43; Harvard Univ, with Paul J Sachs, 44-45. Collections Arranged: Amedeo Modigliani, 51; Picasso: 75th Anniversary Exhibition, 57; German Art of the 20th Century, 58; Joan Miro, 59; Max Ernst, 61; The New Japanese Painting & Sculpture, 66; Jackson Pollock, 67; Jean Dubuffet, 68; Julio Gonzalez, Kandinsky Watercolors, Tamarind: Homage to Lithography, George Grosz: Drawings & Watercolors, Archipenko: The Parisian Years & The Sculpture of Richard Hunt, 69-71; plus many other exhibitions & permanent collections at the Mus Mod Art. Pos: Mem staff, Dept Exhibs & Publ, Mus Mod Art, New York, 43, asst to dir mus collections, 45-49, assoc cur prints & illus bks, 49-53, cur prints, 53-66, dir drawings & prints, 66-, cur painting & sculpture, 67-71; staff adv, Jr Coun, 54-64. Awards: Chevalier de l'Ordre des Arts et des Lett, Repub France. Mem: Grolier Club; Am Fedn Arts (trustee); Cassandra Found (trustee); Drawing Soc (trustee); Int Graphic Arts Soc (trustee); plus others. Collection: Eighteenth century silver boxes, Japanese prints of the Meiji ear and first ed tions of one British and two American authors. Publ: Auth, Picasso: Blue & Rose Periods, Abrams, 54; auth, Matisse: 50 Years of His Graphic Art, Braziller, 56; auth, Edvard Munch, Los Angeles Co Mus Art, 69; Redon: Prints & Drawings & Jacques Villon, Mus Mod Art; plus many other bks & catalogues, bulletins & articles in the US & abroad. Mailing Add: Mus of Mod Art 11 W 53rd St New York NY 10019

LIENAU, DANIEL CLIFFORD
ART DEALER, COLLECTOR
b Sturgeon Bay, Wis, May 30, 43. Study: Univ Wis-Madison, studied sculpture for four yrs; studied with Leo Steppat & David Smith. Collections Arranged: Daisy Chan photographs, Diana Rainbo sculpture, Cristine Dimaggio drawings, Milo Needles recent works on paper, Gustave Baumann gouaches and woodcuts, Raymond Barnhart drawings and collage, Robert K Gronendyke nostalgia revisited & Elizabeth Quandt homage to boudin, Annex Gallery, 77, plus many others from 72- Teaching: Instr conserv framing, Riley St Annex, Santa Rosa, Calif, 77- Pos: Owner-dir, Annex Galleries, Santa Rosa, Calif, 70-; gallery dir, Santa Rosa Jr Col Gallery, Calif, 74-75, wholesale rep, The Roten Collection, Brentano. Awards: Santa Rosa Civic Art Award, City of Santa Rosa, Calif, 74. Mem: Santa Rosa Arts Coun (vpres, 73); Collectors, Artists & Dealers for Responsible Equity. Specialty: Prints, traditional through experimental, photography and selected painting and sculpture. Collection: Oils, Paul Beattie, Jim Rosen; prints, Goya, Lautrec, Baumann, Quandt, Tooker; drawings, Rosen, Marquet, minor masters; sculpture, Ewing, Baumann. Mailing Add: 604 College Ave Santa Rosa CA 95404

LIGARE, DAVID H
PAINTER
b Oak Park, Ill, 1945. Study: Art Ctr Col Design. Work: Mus Mod Art, New York; Univ Kans Mus Art, Lawrence; Sara Roby Found Collection; Atlantic-Richfield Corp; Weatherspoon Art Gallery, Greensboro, NC. Exhib: Am Watercolor Soc Ann, 67-72; ACA Galleries, New York, 69-73, Calif Portraits, Civic Art Ctr, Walnut Creek, 71, Drawings USA & Traveling Exhib, Minn Mus Art, St Paul, 71-73; Realism, Cleveland Inst Art, Ohio, 72; Andrew Crispo Gallery, New York, 73-78; Krannert Art Mus, Univ Ill, 74; Santa Barbara Mus Art, Calif, 74 & 77; William Benton Mus Art, Univ Conn, 76; Mus Mod Art, New York, 77; Phoenix Art Mus, Ariz, 77; Mus Contemp Art, Chicago, 78. Teaching: Hartnell Col, Salinas, Calif. Pos: Critic (David Rush), Artweek. Awards: Mary S Litt Award, Am Watercolor Soc, 69; Monterey Peninsula Mus Art Award, 70. Bibliog: Article in Artforum, 4/77. Mem: Am Watercolor Soc. Mailing Add: c/o Andrew Crispo Gallery 41 E 57th St New York NY 10022

LIJN, LILIANE
SCULPTOR, ART WRITER
b New York, NY, Dec 22, 39. Study: Ecole de Louvre, Paris, Sorbonne, Paris. Work: Tate Gallery, London, Eng; Mus de la Ville de Paris, France; Centre Nat d'Art Contemporain, Paris; Arts Coun Great Brit, London; Victoria & Albert Mus, London. Comn: Liquid Reflections (4ft kinetic sculpture), Curtis & Davis Architects, New Orleans, La, 69; Spiral Spectrum Foundatain (50ft diameter), Bebington Civic Ctr, Liverpool, Eng, 71; 20ft Kinetic sculpture, Peter Stuyvescent Corp & Arts Coun Great Brit, Warwick Univ, Coventry Eng, 72; etchings, Alecto Print Comn Award, Bradford Print Biennale, 76. Exhib: Kunsthalle, Bern, Switz, 66; Mus d'Art Mod, Paris, 67; Sci Fiction, Kunsthalle, Bern, Switz & Mus d'Art Decoratif, Paris, 67; 5th Biennale de Paris, 67; Prospect 68, Dusseldorf Mus, WGer, 68; Art Vivant Found Maeght, St Paul de Vence, France, 68-70; Kinetic Art, Hayward Gallery, London, 70; Serpentine Gallery, London, 75 & 76; Hayward Ann, Hayward Gallery, 78. Bibliog: Cyril Barrett (auth), Art as research: the experiments of L Lijn, Studio Int, Vol 173 (June, 1967); Vera Lindsay (auth), Liliane Lijn in discussion with Vera Lindsay, Studio Int, Vol 177 (May, 1969); Alastair Mackintosh (auth), Functionalism of art, Art & Artists, Vol 7 (Mar, 1973). Style & Technique: Formal work with light and motion in numerous materials and in collaboration with technological processes used in industry. Media: Kinetic Sculpture; Etching; Metal, Glass. Publ: Auth, The inside of a work is to find out, Art & Artists, 1/71; auth, Inside & out; notes on anti-gravity koans, Flash Art, Milan, Italy, 2/71; auth, All people are artists, Ink, London, 9/71; auth, Reflections; Three Poems; Time Zone, Grosseteste Rev, 71; auth, What is art?, Ostrich No 9, Northumberland, 9/73. Mailing Add: 28 Camden Sq London NW1 9XA England

LIKAN, GUSTAV
PAINTER, INSTRUCTOR
b Srb, Yugoslavia, May 1, 12; US citizen. Study: Akad der Bildenden Kunste, Munich, Ger; Franz Hals Mus, Haarlem; Louvre, Paris. Work: Moderna Galerija & Strossmayer Mus, Zagreb, Yugoslavia; Mestrovic Mus, Split, Yugoslavia; Kunstlerhaus Mus, Salzburg, Austria; Kunstmuseet, Copenhagen, Denmark. Comn: Murals of schs, comn by Eva Peron, Buenos Aires, 50, Cordoba, 51 & Mendoza, Arg, 51, mural of a hosp, comn by Eva Peron, 50 & mural of a church, Buenos Aires, 51. Exhib: Georges Petit Gallery, Paris, 32; Kunstmuseet, Copenhagen, 38; Kron Prinz Palais, Berlin, 41; Nat Mus Vienna, 41; one-man shows, Merrill Chase Galleries, Chicago, 64, Laguna Gloria Art Mus, Austin, Tex, 76 & Abilene Fine Arts Mus, Tex, 76. Teaching: Prof fine art, Chicago Acad Fine Art, 60-67 & Laguna Gloria Mus Fine Art, Austin, Tex, 69- Style & Technique: Glazing process. Media: Graphic & Acrylic Painting. Publ: Auth, Art Classes 2,5: Meaning, Method & Media, 72; auth, Likan Drawings, 73; also auth articles in bks & newspapers in Austria & Yugoslavia. Dealer: Merrill Chase Galleries Ltd 620 N Michigan Ave Chicago IL 60611. Mailing Add: 1407 Ridgecrest Dr Austin TX 78746

LILES, RAEFORD BAILEY
PAINTER, SCULPTOR
b Birmingham, Ala, July 20, 23. Study: Birmingham-Southern Col; Auburn Univ, BSEE, 49; Atelier Fernand Leger, Paris, France, 49-51. Work: Musee d'Art Mod, Eliat, Israel; Andrew Dickson White Mus Art, Cornell Univ; Corcoran Gallery Art, Washington, DC; Amos Andersons Konstmuseum, Helsingfors, Finland; Alfred Khouri Collection, Norfolk Mus, Va; plus others. Comn: Silk screen series, East Hampton Gallery, NY, 67; fomaca sculpture series, comn by Silvia Pizitz, New York, 70; collage series, comn by Mrs D O'Kennedy, Long Island, 71; painted plastic series, comn by Dr Bill Lipscomb, Boston, 72. Exhib: Salon d'Art Independent & Art Libre, Paris, 51; Salon Nouvelle Reality, Moma, Paris, 55; Mirco Salon d'Avril, Iris Clert, Paris, 56; Carroll Reece Mus 11 Ann Purchase Exhib, Johnson City, Tenn, 68; Art for Peace, New York, 70; plus others. Awards: Prize, Students of Leger, 51; First Prize, Alpine Gallery, 58. Bibliog: Turpin (auth), L'Orleanais Dans Les Art, 52; Orinese (auth), Tour D'Expositions Combat, 55; Brown (auth), Review of expositions, Art Mag, 68. Mem: Birmingham Art Asn; Ala Watercolor Soc. Mailing Add: 446 W 38th St New York NY 10018

LILIENTHAL, MR & MRS PHILIP N, JR
COLLECTORS
Collection: Paintings and contemporary art. Mailing Add: 2275 Summit Dr Burlingame CA 94010

LILJEGREN, FRANK
PAINTER, INSTRUCTOR
b New York, NY, Feb 23, 30. Study: Art Students League, with John Groth, Dean Cornwell & Frank J Reilly. Work: Manhattan Savings Bank, New York; Am Educ Publ Inst, New York; New Britain Mus Am Art, Conn. Exhib: Hudson Valley Art Asn, White Plains, NY, 62-68; Allied Artists Am, Nat Acad Design, New York, 62-75; Coun Am Artists Soc, Lever House, New York, 64 & 67; Salmagundi Club, New York, 64-68; Acad Artists Asn, Springfield Fine Arts Mus, Mass, 66-70; O S Ranch Exhib, Tex, 77. Teaching: Instr painting, Westchester Co Art Workshop, White Plains, 66-; instr, Art Students League, 73- Awards: Allied Artists Am Awards; Frank V Dumond Award, Salmagundi Club, 65 & 67; Medal of Merit for Oil Painting, Today's Art Mag, 71. Bibliog: Jo Mary McCormick-De Guyton (auth), Frank Liljegren and his old friends, Am Artist Mag, 2/72; Ralph Fabri (auth), Medal of merit winner in 58th A A A annual, Today's Art Mag, 3/72. Mem: Allied Artists Am (corresp secy, 67, exhib chmn, 68-76, pres, 70-72, dir, 72-76); Artists Fellowship; Salmagundi Club; life mem Art Students League. Style & Technique: Realism in the traditional manner. Media: Oil. Mailing Add: 64 Lispenard Ave New Rochelle NY 10801

LI MARZI, JOSEPH
PAINTER, INSTRUCTOR
b Chicago, Ill. Study: Art Inst Chicago. Comn: Historical, Fed Govt, Fed Bldg, Wapokeneta, Ohio, 37; mil hist of army co, Fed Govt, Staten Island, NY, 42; story of food, Royal Scarlet Foods, New York, 51; indust uses of Gen Cables, Inc, New York, 52. Exhib: Art Inst Chicago Nat; Brooklyn Mus Nat; Pa Acad Fine Arts Nat; one-man shows, Contemporary Arts, New York, Simon's Rock, Mass & Lehman Gallery, Red Rock, NY, 75. Teaching: Instr painting, High Sch Art & Design, New York, 52-73. Awards: Hon Award, Mural Competition, Fed Govt, 37. Mem: Painters & Sculptors Soc NJ; Audubon Artists New York. Style & Technique: Figurative-romantic non realistic; combining direct application of paint, glaze and scumble. Media: Oil, Graphics. Dealer: Ella Lerner Gallery 17 Franklin St Lenox MA 02140. Mailing Add: Box 144 East Chatham NY 12060

LIMBER, TRUDY C
ART DEALER
b Detroit, Mich. Pos: Dir, Limber Galleries, 68- Specialty: Originals multiplex single; all media; international and time scope. Mailing Add: 648 Cannery Row Monterey CA 93940

LIMONT, NAOMI CHARLES
PRINTMAKER, INSTRUCTOR
b Pottstown, Pa. Study: Pa Acad Fine Arts, BFA; Pratt Graphic Ctr, with Michael Ponce de Leon; Barnes Found; Univ Pa, BFA; Tyler Sch Art, with Romas Viesulas, MFA; also with Jerome Kaplan. Work: Philadelphia Mus Art & Pa Acad Fine Arts; Yale Univ; Harvard Univ; Goshen Col, Ind. Comn: Mural, St Christopher's Children's Hosp, Philadelphia, 65; Creation (folio of prints), Philadelphia Print Club, 67; Folio '76 (bicentennial folio), Graphics Guild, Cheltenham, Pa, 75. Exhib: Int Miniature Print Show, New York, 73; Nat Acad Design, 73; Am Color Print Soc Ann, 74; Graphics of the Seventies, Langman Gallery, 74; The Earth Art Show, Philadelphia, 75. Teaching: Instr graphics, Cheltenham Art Ctr, 65- Awards: Cresson Foreign Traveling Scholar, Pa Acad, 48; Phillip Klein Award, Am Color Print Soc, 72; Sun Oil Award, Earth Art Exhib, 75. Bibliog: Bagnell & Sosin (coordrs), The Tyler Show Working Women Artists from Tyler School of Art, Samuel Paley Libr, Temple Univ, 73. Mem: Philadelphia Print Club; Philadelphia Art Alliance (gallery comt, 75-); Artists Equity Asn (rec secy, 68-69); Am Color Print Soc (on coun as rec secy, 67-); Philadelphia Watercolor Club. Style & Technique: Deeply etched, embossed prints; collagraph in color with nature images. Dealer: Richard Langman Gallery Jenkintown PA 19046. Mailing Add: 137 Harvey St Philadelphia PA 19144

LINCOLN, FRED CLINTON
DESIGNER, CERAMIST
b Cape Girardeau, Mo, July 9, 43. Study: Southeast Mo State Univ; Memphis Acad Arts, BFA. Work: Tenn Crafts Collection, Carroll Reece Mus. Exhib: Miss Valley Crafts Exhib, Brooks Mem Art Gallery, Memphis, 70, 73 & 77; Memphis Acad Arts, 70 & 76; one-man show, Southeast Mo State Univ, 70 & Paducah Art Guild, Ky, 70; Mixed Media Gallery, Memphis, 74. Teaching: Instr pottery, Memphis Acad Arts, 73- Pos: Sign designer, Memphis, 73- Style & Technique: Stoneware utilitarian; drafting and watercolor illustrations. Mailing Add: 4985 Ruthie Cove Memphis TN 38127

LINCOLN, RICHARD MATHER
CERAMIST, EDUCATOR
b Ann Arbor, Mich, Mar 1, 29. Study: Potters Guild, Ann Arbor, with Rhoda Le Blanc Lopez & J T Abernathy. Work: Dallas Mus Fine Arts; Witte Mus, San Antonio, Tex; Univ Mich Mus, Ann Arbor; Detroit Inst Arts; Davenport Art Ctr, Iowa. Comn: Mural, Apparel Mart, Dallas; mural, Ft Worth Children's Hosp, Tex; light fixtures, The Quadrangle, Dallas. Exhib: Eight Ceramic Nat & Int Exhibs, Everson Mus, Syracuse, NY, 54-68; Young Americans, New York, 56; Fiber, Clay & Metall, St Paul, Minn, 60; Miami Ceramic Nat, 60; five SCent Regional Exhibs, Santa Fe, NMex, 62-71. Teaching: Assoc prof ceramics, Tex Christian Univ, 63- Awards: Third Pottery Prize, Young Americans, 56; Purchase Award, Univ Mich Mus, 56; First Pottery Award, SCent Regional Exhib, 62. Bibliog: Texas potter—Richard Lincoln, Designers W, 11/70. Mem: Am Craftsmen Coun. Mailing Add: 4759 Westcreek Ft Worth TX 76133

LINDEMANN, EDNA M
MUSEUM DIRECTOR, EDUCATOR
b Buffalo, NY. Study: Univ Buffalo, BS(art); Albright Art Sch; Northwestern Univ, MA(magna cum laude), 40; Cranbrook Acad Art; Columbia Univ, Augusta Larned fel, 41, EdD. Collections Arranged: Wallpapers, Charles E Burchfield Ctr, 73, George William Eggers Arch, 74 & Facets of the Artist's Expression, 74. Teaching: Instr art educ, NY Univ, 49-56; prof design, State Univ NY Col Buffalo, 56- Pos: Dir cult affairs, State Univ NY Col Buffalo, 65-68; dir, Charles Burchfield Ctr, 68-; chmn, Gallery, Asn NY State, 70-72, mem bd dirs, 72-77. Awards: Honorary, Creative Leadership Coun, Creative Educ Asn, 69. Mem: Hon mem Patteran Artists; hon mem Buffalo Soc Artists; hon mem Assoc Artists; hon mem Creative Educ Asn; Buffalo State Col Alumni Found. Res: Charles Burchfield, particularly his Buffalo years, 1921-1968. Publ: Auth, Our Legacy of Art in Western New York, 72; ed, Martha Visser't Hooft, 73; ed, Six Corporate Collectors, 75; ed, Edwin Dickinson, 77; ed, Roycroft: Spirit for Today, 77. Mailing Add: 52 Behm Rd West Falls NY 14170

LINDER, STASIA
PAINTER, EDUCATOR
b New York, NY, Apr 2, 22. Study: Adelphi Univ; Hofstra Univ; also with Hsiung-Ju, Bing-Sun Chen, Tseng Hou-Hsih & Ryukyo Saito. Work: Nat Libr, Manila, Philippines; Mus Fine Arts, Taipei; Am Embassy, Baghdad, Iraq. Exhib: Nat Mus Art Taipei, Repub China, 63; one-man shows, Hong Kong City Hall, 64 & Nat Libr Philippines, 64; Am Embassy, Baghdad, Iraq, Beirut, Lebanon & Warsaw, Poland, 65-70; Planting Fields, Locust Valley, NY, 75. Teaching: Instr painting Oriental brush, Adelphi Univ, 75- Mem: Sumi-e Soc Am; Nat Arts Club; Nat Art League. Style & Technique: Chinese classical Oriental brush; palette knife. Media: Watercolor, Oil. Collection: Mesopotamian pottery on loan to Metropolitan Museum of Art; African masks IBO of Nigeria; Budha sculptures from Far East. Mailing Add: c/o Studio One 99 Seventh St Garden City NY 11530

LINDGREN, CHARLOTTE
WEAVER
b Toronto, Ont, Feb 1, 31. Study: Univ Mich, BS; with Jack Lenor Larsen; Can Coun studies in Finland, Sweden & Eng. Work: Can Coun Art Bank; Can Dept External Affairs, Ottawa; York Univ; Winnipeg Art Gallery; Confederation Ctr Art Gallery, Charlottetown, PEI; Can Dept External Affairs, Ottawa. Comn: Ten woven cylinders, Queen's Col, Nfld, 68; tabernacle veil, St Michael's Church, Spryfield, NS, 68; woven sculpture, Expo '70, Can Dept External Affairs, Osaka, Japan, 69; cylinder, CBC Bldg, Montreal, 74; wall sculpture, Fed Fisheries Bldg, 77. Exhib: Mus Fine Arts, Montreal, 66; Nat Gallery, Ottawa, 66; Am Fedn Arts Threads of History Traveling Show, 66-69; NB Mus, 67; Confedn Gallery, PEI, 67; Competition Perspective 67, Art Gallery Ont, Toronto, 67; Expo '67, Can Art Gallery Pavilion, Montreal, 67; Int Biennial Tapestry, Lausanne, Switz, 67 & 69; Vancouver Art Gallery, BC, 68; Art Gallery of Ont, 74; Olympia Art Centre, Jamaica, 75; Can House, London, 76; Can Cult Centre, Paris, France, 76; NS Fine Art Gallery, 77. Pos: Juror arts bursaries, Can Coun, 70, consult art panel, 71-72; mem adv panel, Can Coun Arts. Awards: Haystack Sch Scholar Award, 64; Can Coun Arts Award, 65; First Prize Award, Perspective Competition Centennial Comn, Govt Can, 67. Bibliog: C Fraser (auth), article, 6/66 & J Graham (auth), article, 7/71, Arts Can; L Rombout (auth), article in Vie Art, winter 67. Mem: Royal Can Acad Artists; Can Artists' Representation (NS rep). Media: Fibers. Mailing Add: 1557 Vernon St Halifax NS B3H 3M8 Can

LINDLOF, EDWARD AXEL, JR
ILLUSTRATOR, LECTURER
b Long Beach, Calif, Nov 6, 43. Study: Southern Methodist Univ, 62-63; Univ Tex, Austin, BFA(studio art), 66; Art Ctr Col Design, with Lorser Feitelson, 66-67. Exhib: NY Soc Illusr Ann, 73-74 & 76-78. Teaching: Lectr illus, Univ Tex, Austin, 74- Awards: Gold & Two Silver Medals, New Orleans Art Dirs Club, 71; Two Silver Medals, Houston Art Dirs Club, 73; Cert of Merit, New York Soc Illusr, 73 & 74. Style & Technique: Illustrations in various styles and techniques, appropriate to the problem. Media: Pencil & Ink. Publ: Illusr, John Dewey, The Early Works, Univ Southern Ill, Vols 1-5, 74; illusr, Dramatists in Revolt, The New Latin American Theater, 75, Jorge Luis Borges, Other Inquisitions 1937-1952, 75, The Comic Spirit of Federico Gardia Lorca, 75 & The Great Frontier, 75, Univ Tex. Mailing Add: 603 Carolyn Ave Austin TX 78705

LINDMARK, ARNE
PAINTER, LECTURER
b Poughkeepsie, NY, Oct 26, 29. Study: Pratt Inst; also watercolor with Edgar Whitney. Work: Huntington Gallery, WVa. Exhib: Am Watercolor Soc Traveling Exhibs, 66-75; Nat Arts Club Ann, 69-71; 50 American Watercolorists, Mexico City Olympics, 70; Allied Artists Am, 71-72; Mainstreams 72, Marietta, Ohio, 72. Teaching: Instr painting & watercolor, Huntington Gallery, summer 71; instr painting & watercolor, Beckley Art Group, WVa, summer 72. Awards: Herb Olsen Award, Am Watercolor Soc, 68, William Church Osborne Award, 70, Samuel J Bloomingdale Mem Award, 73 & Edgar A Whitney Award, 74; Silver Medal of Horor, Nat Arts Club, 71. Bibliog: Wendon Blake (auth), Acrylic Watercolor Painting, Watson-Guptill, 70; Margit Malstrom (auth), Arne Lindmark, master of the watercolor scene, Am Artist Mag, 1/71. Mem: Am Watercolor Soc; Allied Artists Am (jurist, 72); Hudson River Art Asn; Duchess Co Art Asn. Style & Technique: Realism, distorted and abstracabstracted; heavy on composition. Media: Watercolor. Mailing Add: 101 Forbus St Poughkeepsie NY 12603

LINDNER, ERNEST
PAINTER
b Vienna, Austria, May 1, 97; Can citizen. Study: Univ Sask, hon LLD, 72. Work: Nat Gallery Can, Ottawa; Art Gallery Ont, Toronto; Winnipeg Art Gallery, Man; Mendel Art Gallery, Saskatoon; Beaver Brook Art Gallery, Fredericton, NB; plus others. Exhib: One-man show, Banfer Gallery, New York, 64; 7th Biennial of Can Painting, Nat Gallery, Ottawa, 68. Pos: Dir dept art, Saskatoon Tech Inst, 31-62; free lance artist, 62- Bibliog: Article in Time Mag, 7/19/68; Paul Duval (auth), High Realism in Canada, Clarke & Cougar Ltd, 74. Mem: Can Artists Representation. Mailing Add: 414 Ninth St E Saskatoon SK S7N 0A8 Can

LINDNER, RICHARD
PAINTER
b Hamburg, Ger, Nov 11, 01; US citizen. Study: Acad Munich. Work: Mus Mod Art & Whitney Mus Am Art, New York; Mus Nat Arte Mod, Paris; Tate Gallery Art, London; Art Inst Chicago. Exhib: Walker Art Ctr, Minneapolis; Brooklyn Mus, New York; Art Inst Chicago; Whitney Mus Am Art, New York; Mus Mod Art, New York; Corcoran Gallery Art, Washington, DC; Ringling Mus, Sarasota, Fla; Retrospective, Mus Nat d'Arte Mod, Paris, 74. Teaching: Prof painting, Pratt Inst, 52-64; vis artist, Yale Univ, 62-63. Awards: Lichtwerk Award, Hamburg, 70. Bibliog: Dore Ashton (auth), R Lindner, Abrams, 70; R G Dienst (auth), R Lindner, Thames & Hudson, London, 70; S Tillim (auth), R Lindner, William & Noma Copley Found, Chicago. Mem: Nat Inst Arts & Lett. Media: Oil, Watercolor. Mailing Add: 3 E 71st St New York NY 10021

LINDQUIST, EVAN
PRINTMAKER, EDUCATOR
b Salina, Kans, May 23, 36. Study: Emporia Kans State Univ, BSE; Univ Iowa, MFA. Work: Whitney Mus Am Art, New York; Uffizzi, Florence, Italy; Albertina Mus, Vienna, Austria; Nelson-Atkins Art Mus, Kansas City; Art Inst Chicago. Exhib: Prints by Seven, Whitney Mus Am Art, New York, 71; Boston Printmakers Ann Exhib, 71-75; one-man circulating exhib, Mo Coun Arts, 73-75. Teaching: Distinguished assoc prof art, Ark State Univ, Jonesboro, 63- Awards: More than 60 awards including Boston Printmakers, 71-74 & Potsdam Prints, NY State Univ Potsdam, 72. Mailing Add: Box 846 State University AR 72467

LINDSAY, KENNETH C
ART HISTORIAN, WRITER
b Milwaukee, Wis, Dec 23, 19. Study: Univ Wis, PhB, 41, scholar, 47, MA, 48, PhD, 51; Ecole du Louvre, Fulbright fel, 49. Collections Arranged: Marshall Glasier, An Exhibition of Paintings & Drawings, 59; Jean Lappien, Paintings, Watercolors, Graphic Works, 64; Architectural Process, Works of James Mowry, 67; The Works of John Vandelyn, 70; Angello Ippolito, Retrospective, 75. Teaching: Asst surv, Univ Wis, 47-49; instr, Williams Col, 50-51; prof, State Univ NY Binghamton, 51- Pos: Mem, NY State Comn Arts, 66-67; coun archit & urban design, Binghamton, 67-68. Awards: NY State Res Found Grants, 67, 69 & 72. Res: Modern American painting. Publ: Co-auth, Method in Breughel's paintings, J Aesthet & Art Criticism, 15: 376-386; auth, Kandinsky in 1914 New York, Art News, 55: 32-33; auth, Kandinsky in Russia (catalog), Guggenheim Mus, 63; auth, Les themes de l'inconscient, XXe Siecle, 27: 46-52; auth, Millet's Winnower rediscovered, Burlington Mag, 74; plus others. Mailing Add: Dept of Art State Univ of NY Binghamton NY 13901

LINDSTROM, GAELL
PAINTER, EDUCATOR
b Salt Lake City, Utah, July 4, 19. Study: Univ Utah, BS; Calif Col Arts & Crafts, MFA; also with Roy Wilhelm, Gloucester, Mass. Work: Utah State Univ; Southern Utah State Col. Comn: Murals, Southern Utah State Col & Cedar City Pub Libr; mosaic mural, Utah State Univ Forestry Bldg, 61. Exhib: Am Watercolor Soc, 53 & 57; Calif Watercolor Soc, 57. Collections Arranged: Maynard Dixon Exhibition, Southern Utah State Col, 55; Nat Ceramic Exhibition, 57 & 58 & Nat Painting Exhibition, 58, Utah State Univ. Teaching: Prof art, Southern Utah State Col, 53-56; prof art, Utah State Inst Fine Arts, 57-61; prof art, Utah State Univ, 57- Awards: Prizes & Purchase Awards, Utah State Fair, 52-54; Utah State Art Inst, 54; Am Watercolor Soc, 57. Mem: Am & Nat Watercolor Socs. Mailing Add: Dept of Art Utah State Univ Logan UT 84322

LINHARES, PHILIP E
PAINTER, CURATOR
b Visalia, Calif, Aug 8, 39. Study: Calif Col of Arts & Crafts, BFA, MFA, 66; post-grad study in Florence, Italy, 72. Exhib: San Francisco Mus of Art, Calif, 65; San Jose Mus of Art, Calif, 77; Nev Art Gallery, Reno, 77; La Mus, Copenhagen, Denmark, 77; one-man shows, Berkeley Gallery, San Francisco, 70 & Lone Mountain Col, San Francisco, 77. Pos: Curatorial asst, Oakland Mus of Art, Calif, 67; dir exhib, San Francisco Art Inst, Calif, 67-77; artist-in-residence, South of Market Cult Ctr, San Francisco, 77-; assoc ed, Visual Dialog Mag, 77- Style & Technique: Abstract, symbolist painter. Media: Enamel on canvas/cardboard. Publ: Auth, articles in Currant Mag, 75-76; auth, California Communication, Sydney Biennale Exhib catalogue, Australia, 76. Mailing Add: 1218 Folsom St San Francisco CA 94103

LINK, HOWARD ANTHONY
CURATOR
b Rochester, NY, Dec 18, 34. Study: Pa State Univ, BAppArts, MA(art hist); Univ Pittsburgh, PhD(art hist). Collections Arranged: Utamaro & Hiroshige (int travelling exhib), 76-77 & The Theatrical Prints of the Torii Masters, Japan, 77, Honolulu Acad of Arts. Teaching: Instr art hist, Sophia Univ, Tokyo, Japan, 66-67, asst prof art hist, 67-70; assoc prof art hist, Univ Hawaii, Hilo, 70-71. Pos: Assoc cur of Oriental art, Honolulu Acad of Arts, 71-74, keeper of Ukiyo-e Print Ctr, 71-, cur Asian art, 74- Awards: Nat Best Lect Series Award, Cherry Blossom Festival, Univ Hawaii, 71. Mem: Oriental Art Soc of Hawaii. Res: Torii Sch of Ukiyo-e, Rimpa paintings and Nikuhitsu. Publ: Co-auth, Torii Kiyonaga in the Honolulu Acad of Arts, Zaigai Hiho, 72; auth, Utamaro & Hiroshige, Otsuka Kogeisha, 76; auth, Theatrical Prints of the Torii Masters, Dobi Insatsu, 77; co-auth, Japanese Prints in the Honolulu Academy of Arts—The Primitives, Univ Hawaii Press, 78; contribr, Dictionary of Ukiyo-e Prints and Paintings, Japan Ukiyo-e Soc, (in press). Mailing Add: Honolulu Acad Arts 900 S Beretania Honolulu HI 96814

LINK, VAL JAMES
JEWELER, EDUCATOR
b Shreveport, La, Apr 28, 40. Study: Cranbrook Acad Art, Bloomfield Hills, Mich, MFA; Univ Tex, Austin, BFA; Del Mar Jr Col, Corpus Christi, Tex, AA. Work: Ark Art Ctr Mus, Little Rock; Sarah Campbell Blaffer Gallery, Univ Houston; Mus Contemp Crafts Touring Exhib, NY; Denver Art Mus & Am Crafts Coun Touring Exhib. Comn: Sic Holloware & jewelry works, comn by Mr C A Harlan, Birmingham, Mich, 67-68; commemorative cup, comn by Univ Houston for Mrs Sarah Blaffer, 73; sculptural awards, Am Petrol Inst, Washington, DC, 73 & 74; seven major jewelry pieces, comn by Kenneth Helfand, Mill Run, Pa, 74-75; plus many others. Exhib: The Goldsmith 70 Exhibition, Minn Mus Art, St Paul; Profiles in Jewelry, Tex Tech Univ, 73; International Design in Opal, McNeish Gallery, Pittsburgh, 73-74; Inter-D III, Crafts 74 Int, McAllen Int Mus, Tex, 74; Reprise, Int Exhib Metalsmithing Work, Cranbrook Acad Art, 75; Contemp Metalcrafts, Clifford Gallery, Pittsburgh Arts & Crafts Ctr, Pa, 77; Soc NAm Goldsmiths Nat Metalsmith 77, Phoenix Art Mus, Ariz & Henry Gallery Fine Arts, Wash Univ, Seattle, 77; among many others. Teaching: Instr jewelry & metal, Interlochen Arts Acad, Mich, 67-70; assoc prof & head jewelry & metal area, Univ Houston, 70- Awards: First & Second Place Hon Mention, Sterling Silversmiths Guild Am Exhib, New York, 67; First Place, 15th Tex Crafts Exhib, Dallas Mus Fine Arts, 71; Ark Art Ctr Mus Purchase Award, 71-72. Bibliog: Lisa Hammel (auth), Thank technology, New York Times, 6/20/70; Murray Bovin (auth), Photographic representation of work, In: Silversmithing, Bovin Publ, 4th ed, 73. Mem: Soc NAm Goldsmiths; Sterling Silversmiths Guild Am; Am Contemp Arts & Crafts Slide Libr; Am Crafts Coun; Tex & Houston Designer Craftsmen. Style & Technique: Simplicity of both form and surface treatment; all metal techniques primarily construction, forging and other hand wrought techniques. Media: All Metal Media, primarily Gold & Silver. Dealer: Robinson Gallery of Art 1100 Bissonnet Houston TX 77005. Mailing Add: 5531 Darnell Houston TX 77035

LINN, JOHN WILLIAM
ART ADMINISTRATOR, ART WRITER
b Shanghai, China, May 25, 36; US citizen. Study: Art Inst Chicago; San Diego State Univ, BA & MA; Univ Ga, PhD; worked with Edmund B Feldman and Albert Christ-Janer. Work: San Diego State Univ Gallery, Calif; Paul Sargent Gallery, Eastern Ill Univ, Charleston; First Nat Bank, Springfield, Ill. Exhib: La Jolla Mus Art, 65 & 66; San Diego Fine Arts Gallery, 66; Second Ann Nat Contemp Arts & Crafts Exhib, Fla, 75; Wabash Valley Exhib, 77; Ill State Fair Exhib, Springfield, 77; Provincetown Nat Print & Drawing Exhib, Mass, 77; plus others. Collections Arranged: Seven State Bicentennial Exhibition, Paul Sargent Gallery, Eastern Ill Univ, 9/77. Teaching: Assoc prof art hist, Eastern Ill Univ, 67-77; prof art hist, Henderson State Univ, 77- Pos: Dir & owner, Art Cellar Gallery, San Diego, Calif, 65-67; chmn dept art, Eastern Ill Univ, 75-77; dean fine arts, Henderson State Univ, 77- Awards: Best in Show, All San Diego Co Collegiate Exhib, San Diego State Univ, 63 & Del Mar Southern Calif Exhib, Del Mar Co Fair, 67; First Place, San Diego Co Exhib, San Diego Art Guild, John Paul Jones, 66. Bibliog: Naomi Baker (auth), John Linn, San Diego Union, 64; Charlotte Steen (auth), Art Review, Art Forum, 65; Donovan Mailey (auth), Art Cellar Gallery, San Diego Mag, 65. Mem: Nat Coun Art Adminrs; Am Coun For Arts. Style & Technique: Painting and drawing highly textured surfaces, e. g. creases and wrinkles of paper. Media: Mixed media for painting; pencil for drawing. Res: Using the phenomenological method of art criticism in the analysis of art, particularly Chinese landscape painting. Publ: Auth, The Old Realism, 74, Painting The Timeless, 75, The Smiling Face of the Universe, 76 & Marriage of Arnolfini by Jan Van Eyck, 77, Christian Sci Monitor; auth, Wu Tao-Tzu: The Man of T'Ang, Arts of Asia, 75. Mailing Add: PO Box H2260 Arkadelphia AR 71923

LINN, STEVEN ALLEN
SCULPTOR
b Chicago, Ill, May 3, 43. Study: Univ Ill, BS(floricult & ornamental hort). Exhib: Painting & Sculpture Ann, Berkshire Mus, Pittsfield, Mass, 67-68; Sculpture, Contemp Arts Found, Oklahoma City, 71; one-man shows, Univ Calif, Santa Cruz, 72 & Louis K Meisel Gallery, New York, 74 & 76; Experimental Prints, Santa Barbara Mus, Calif, 74; Rothman's Int Traveling Exhib, Can, 76-78; Flint Inst Fine Arts, Mich, 78. Teaching: Lectr theatre design, Smith Col, Northampton, Mass, 68-69; tech instr sculpture, Univ Calif, Santa Cruz, 71-74. Awards: Design Fel, Ford Found-Arena Stage, 65; Ward Sculpture Prize, Berkshire Mus, 68; Rome Prize, Am Acad in Rome, 75. Bibliog: Exhib rev in Arts Mag, 75 & 77. Style & Technique: Large figure vignettes and landscapes; historical fragments. Media: Bronze & Wood Combined. Publ: Graphics designer, Courselector Mag, 75. Mailing Add: 101 Crosby St New York NY 10012

LINSKY, MR & MRS JACK
COLLECTORS
Mr Linsky, b Russia, Jan 1, 97; US citizen. Collection: Ancient art and paintings. Mailing Add: 927 Fifth Ave New York NY 10028

LINTAULT, ROGER PAUL
EDUCATOR, SCULPTOR
b New York, NY, June 13, 38. Study: State Univ NY New Paltz, BS(art) with distinction, 60; Southern Ill Univ, MFA(sculpture & ceramics), 62. Work: Honolulu Acad Arts, Hawaii; Mus Contemp Crafts, New York; Warner Brothers Records, Los Angeles, Calif. Exhib: Artists of Hawaii, Honolulu Acad Arts, 66 & 67; Craftsmen USA 66, Los Angeles Co Mus Art, Los Angeles, Calif, 66; Mus Contemp Crafts, New York, 69; Looking West 1970, Joslyn Art Mus, Omaha, Nebr, 70; All Calif Art Exhib, Nat Orange Show, San Bernardino, 74, 75 & 77; one man show, Esther-Robles Gallery, Los Angeles, 75. Teaching: Asst prof art, Univ Hawaii, Honolulu, 65-68; lectr art, Calif State Univ, Long Beach, 68-69; prof & chmn dept art, Calif State Col, San Bernardino, 69- Awards: First & Purchase Prizes, All Calif Art Exhib, Nat Orange Show, 74. Bibliog: Don Woodford (auth), Truth, Illusion and Roger Lintault, 4/26/75 & Jim Rosen (auth), Exhibition Review, 10/5/74, Artweek. Mem: Col Art Asn. Style & Technique: Ambiguity and illusion; wall constructions of sheet acrylic plastic, floor based works and small architecturally oriented miniature-scale constructions. Media: Acrylic plastic and various other media suitable for three-dimensional constructions. Dealer: Lonny Gans 9353 W Third St Los Angeles CA 90210. Mailing Add: 1434 Parkside Dr San Bernadino CA 92404

LIONNI, LEO
SCULPTOR, PAINTER
b Amsterdam, Holland, May 5, 10; US citizen. Study: Univ Genoa, Italy, PhD(econ). Work: Philadelphia Mus Art; Mus Mod Art & Metrop Mus Art, New York. Exhib: Four American Graphic Artists, Mus Mod Art, New York, 53; one-man shows, Worcester Mus, Mass, 58 & Portland Mus, 59; Galleria Del Milione, 72; Venice Biennale, 72; Klingspor Mus, Ger, 73; Baukunst Gallery, Cologne, Ger, 74; Staempfli Gallery, New York, 77. Pos: Art dir, NW Ayer & Son, Philadelphia, 39-48; art dir, Fortune, 48-60. Awards: Art Dir of the Year, Nat Soc Art Dirs, 55. Media: Bronze; Oil. Publ: Auth & illusr, Little Blue & Little Yellow, 59, Swimmy, 63, Frederick, 66, Alexander & with Wind-Up Mouse, 69, Taccuino di Lionni, 72 & Parallel Botany, 77. Dealer: Staempfli Gallery 47 E 77th St New York NY 10021. Mailing Add: Via San Bernardo Lavagna Italy

LIPINSKY DE ORLOV, LINO S
PAINTER, ILLUSTRATOR
b Rome, Italy, Jan 14, 08; US citizen. Study: Brit Acad Arts, Rome; Lipinsky Art Acad, Rome; Accad Belle Arti, Rome. Work: Metrop Mus Art, New York; New York Pub Libr; Detroit Inst Art; Galleria Naz Arte Mod, Rome; Mus Revoltella, Trieste, Italy. Comn: Mosaic, The Grenadier, Hq Second Regiment, Rome, 37; Christ the King, Christ the King Church, St Louis, Mo, 41; etchings, Libr of Cong, Washington, DC; diorama, Verrazzano's Landing in New York Bay in 1524, 57 & mural, New Amsterdam, 1660, 66, Mus City New York. Exhib: Int Biennale, Venice, Italy, 34-36; Libr of Cong, Washington, DC, 42-54; Cleveland Art Mus, 43; Nat Acad Design, New York, 43-49; Am Watercolors, Drawings & Prints, Metrop Mus Art, 52. Teaching: Prof graphic arts, Lipinsky Art Acad, 25-39. Pos: Founder & dir, Garibaldi & Meucci Mem Mus, Staten Island, NY, 56; exhibs dir, Mus City New York, 59-67; admis comt, Huntington Hartford Found, 62-65; cur hist, John Jay Homestead, Katonah, NY, 67- Awards: Order of Merit, Italy, 58; Gold Medal & Cert of Merit, Order Sons of Italy Am, 61; L L Huttleston Staff Award, State Coun Parks & Recreation, 74. Bibliog: Elena Canino (auth), Clotilde tra due guerre, Longanesi & Co, Milan, Italy, 57; Rita Reif (auth), To the state, it's a historic trust; to two young boys, it's home, New York Times, 9/22/70; Nancy Rubin (auth), Jay Homestead: a curator's dream, New York Times, 9/18/77. Mem: Audubon Artists (chmn exhib, 52); Soc Am Graphic Artists; NY State Asn Mus; Bedford Hist Soc (bd dirs, 68-); Coun Arts Westchester; plus others. Media: Etching, Oil. Publ: Auth, Pocket Anatomy in Color for Artists, Int House Publ, 47; auth, Giovanni da Verrazzano, the Discoverer of New York Bay, 1524, 58; illusr, Roman People, Houghton Mifflin Co, 59; illusr, The Ghost of Peg-leg Peter, Vanguard, 65; contribr, Giovanni da Verrazzano, Yale Univ, 70. Dealer: James St L O'Toole 667 Madison Ave New York NY 10021. Mailing Add: Jay St John Jay Homestead PO Box AH Katonah NY 10536

LIPMAN, HOWARD W
COLLECTOR
b Albany, NY, July 11, 05. Pos: Trustee, Whitney Mus Am Art, 67-, pres, 74-77, chmn bd, 77- trustee, Arch Am Art, 56-, pres, 72-74; trustee, Phoenix Art Mus, 71- Mem: Smithsonian Inst; Guggenheim Found; Mus Mod Art, New York; Whitney Mus Am Art; Metrop Mus Art. Collection: Sculpture through the Howard and Jean Lipman Foundation for the Whitney Museum of American Art; sculpture of the 1960's with special accent on Alexander Calder and Louise Nevelson. Mailing Add: 120 Broadway New York NY 10005

LIPMAN, JEAN
ART EDITOR, WRITER
b New York, NY, Aug 31, 09. Study: Wellesley Col, BA; NY Univ, MA. Pos: Ed-in-chief, Art in Am, 41-71; ed publ, Whitney Mus Am Art, 71-74. Collection: American folk art and

contemporary American sculpture. Publ: Co-auth, The Flowering of American Folk Art, Viking, 74; auth, Provocative Parallels, Dutton, 75; auth, Bright Stars, Dutton, 76, Calder's Universe, Viking, 76 & Art About Art, 78. Mailing Add: 226 Cannon Rd Wilton CT 06897

LIPMAN, STAN
SCULPTOR, INSTRUCTOR
b Lancaster, Pa, Mar 18, 31. Study: Temple Univ, Millersville State Col, BS(educ); Univ Southern Calif. Work: Nat B'nai B'rith Traveling Show & Smithsonian Fine Arts Gallery, Washington, DC; Los Angeles Co Art Mus; Sperry Rand Collection, Cincinnati, Ohio & Lancaster, Pa. Comn: Phoenix (large copper fountain sculpture), Park City Asn, Lancaster, 71; Abstract (aluminum pouring, mural), comn by Dr Kahn, Clinic, Cincinnati, 73; The Wall (steel blocks arranged to form wailing wall), Jewish Community Ctr, Lancaster, 74; Millstones (mural, steel), Millersville State Col, 74; Film (steel mural), Cinema Dept, Univ Southern Calif, 75. Exhib: Two-man show, Nat B'nai B'rith Gallery, Washington, DC, 69; Sculptured Small Table, New York Sch Design, 71 & 73; Los Angeles Co Art Mus Nat Exhib, 72; Philadelphia Mus Art Contemp Art Show, 73; Lancaster Open Nat, 74. Teaching: Instr spec educ, Manheim Twp High Sch, Lancaster, 62-75. Awards: Small Table Sculpture Award, New York Sch Design, 71 & 73; Los Angeles Co Art Mus Award, 72; Best over All, Lancaster C of C, Lancaster Open Nat, 74. Bibliog: Articles in Life Mag, 61, The Millstone, 74 & Nikon World, 75. Style & Technique: Contemporary, impressionistic; making use of casting, welding and brazing. Media: Steel, Bronze. Mailing Add: 2407 Helena Rd Lancaster PA 17603

LIPMAN-WULF, PETER
SCULPTOR, PRINTMAKER
b Berlin, Ger, Apr 27, 05; US citizen. Study: State Acad Fine Arts, Berlin, with Ludwig Gies. Work: Metrop Mus Art & Whitney Mus Am Art, New York; Nat Gallery Art, Washington, DC; Brit Mus, London; Nat Mus, Berlin. Comn: Stone fountains, Berlin, 32; bronze busts of Bruno Walter & Karl Böhm, Metrop Opera, New York, 58 & 72; St Andrew (ceramic), St Andrew Lutheran Church, Chicago, 67; Joy of Life (ceramic relief), Mill Lane High Sch, Farmingdale, Conn, 68; bronze bust of Pablo Casals, Corcoran Gallery Art, Washington, DC, 74. Exhib: Pa Acad Fine Arts Ann, 50-64; Whitney Mus Am Art Ann, 50-68; Int Sculpture Exhib, Philadelphia, 52; Ceramics Int, Syracuse Mus, NY, 59; Jewish Mus, NY, 60; Goethe House, New York, 69 & 74; Guild Hall, East Hampton, NY, 74. Teaching: Prof sculpture, Adelphi Univ, 61-77, emer prof, 77- Awards: Gold Medal, World Exhib, Paris, 37; Guggenheim Fel, 49-50; Olivetti Award, Silvermine Guild Artists, 62. Mem: Artists Equity Asn; Am Soc Contemp Artists; Silvermine Guild Artists. Style & Technique: Semi-abstract sculpture in multimediae; semi-abstract illustrations in graphics; classical and mythological themes. Publ: Auth, Wall and space, 71, Artist as teacher in America, 72, On teaching a fundamental course of sculpture, 73, On my illustrations of Goethe's Faust, 75 & Artist-in-residence in a Secondary Sch, 77, Leonardo Mag. Dealer: Harbor Gallery Cold Springs Harbor Long Island NY 11724; Rizzoli Int Galleries 712 Fifth Ave New York NY 10019. Mailing Add: Whitney Rd Sag Harbor NY 11963

LIPOFSKY, MARVIN B
SCULPTOR, GLASS BLOWER
b Barrington, Ill, Sept 1, 38. Study: Univ Ill, Urbana, BFA; Univ Wis-Madison, MS & MFA. Work: Mus Art Contemp, Skopje, Yugoslavia; Mus Contemp Crafts, New York; Mus Boymans-Van Beuningen, Rotterdam; Stedelijke Mus, Amsterdam, Holland; Oakland Art Mus, Calif; Corning Mus Glass, NY. Comn: Glass, plastic, metal twin panels, Metro Media Bldg, Los Angeles, 69; Frank Lloyd Wright, Calif Col Arts & Crafts Founders Award, 72. Exhib: One-man shows, San Francisco Mus Art, 67, Hansen Gallery, San Francisco, 68, Mus Contemp Crafts, New York, 69, Stedelijke Mus, Amsterdam, Holland, 70 & AO Gallery, Tokyo, Japan; Glass Today, Mus Bellervie, Zurich, Switz. Teaching: Asst prof design, Univ Calif, Berkeley, 64-72; prof glass dept, Calif Col Arts & Crafts, Oakland, 67-; vis prof Bazalel Acad Art, Jerusalem, Israel, 71. Awards: Purchase Awards, Toledo Mus Art, 68 & Northern Ill Univ, 69; Nat Endowment Arts Fel, 74; plus others. Bibliog: John Coney (producer), Marvin Lipofsky Blows Glass (film), KQED, San Francisco, 68; E Marc Treib (auth), Marvin Lipofsky—just doing his thing, Craft Horizon Mag, 69. Mem: Int Comt Artists in Glass; Glass Art Soc. Media: Glass. Mailing Add: 1012 Pardee Berkeley CA 94710

LIPPARD, LUCY ROWLAND
WRITER
b New York, NY, Apr 14, 37. Study: Smith Col, BA, 58; NY Univ Inst Fine Arts, MA, 62; Moore Col Art, hon DFA, 72. Awards: Guggenheim Fel, 68; Nat Endowment Grant, 72-73 & 76-77. Mem: Ad Hoc Women Artists Comt; West-East Bag; Heresies Publ Collective; Printed Matter Inc. Publ: Auth, Pop Art, 66, The Graphic Work of Philip Evergood, 66, Changing: essays in art criticism, 70, Tony Smith, 70; ed, Dadas on art, 71 & Surrealists on art, 71; auth, Six years: the dematerialization of the art object, 73, Eva Hesse, 76, From the Center, 76; plus others. Mailing Add: 138 Prince St New York NY 10012

LIPPINCOTT, JANET
PAINTER
b New York, NY, May 16, 18. Study: Colorado Springs Fine Art Ctr; Art Students League; San Francisco Art Inst; also with Emil Bisttram, Taos, NMex. Work: Utah Fine Arts Mus, Salt Lake City; NMex Fine Arts Mus, Santa Fe; Columbia Fine Arts Mus, SC; Denver Art Mus, Colo; Roswell Mus & Art Ctr, NMex. Exhib: Denver US Nat Ctr, Colo, 63; Colo State Col, Greeley, 61; St John's Col, Santa Fe, 68; Columbia Fine Arts Mus, SC, 72; Arts & Crafts Mus, Columbus, Ga, 72; plus many others. Awards: Atwater Kent Award, Palm Beach, Fla, 63; Southwestern Biennial Award, Santa Fe, 66; Arts in Residence, Durango, Colo, 68. Bibliog: Artist of the month, Southwest Art Gallery Mag, 5/72. Mem: Friends of Art, Albuquerque, NMex (mem bd). Dealer: Hoshour Gallery 471 Second St SW Albuquerque NM 87102; Gallery of Contemp Art Taos NM 87571. Mailing Add: 1270 Canyon Rd Santa Fe NM 87501

LIPPOLD, RICHARD
SCULPTOR
b Milwaukee, Wis, May 3, 15. Study: Art Inst Chicago, BFA, 37; Univ Chicago; Univ Mich. Work: Metrop Mus Art & Mus Mod Art, New York; Va Mus Fine Arts, Richmond; Des Moines Mus Fine Arts, Iowa; Mus Vin, Cauillac, Gironde, France. Comn: Outdoor sculpture, Hyatt Regency Hotel, Atlanta, Ga; Baldacchino, Cathedral of St Mary, San Francisco, 70; retiring room, King of Saudi Arabia, Riyadh, 76; Ad Astra (115ft high), Nat Air & Space Mus, Washington, DC, 76; seven sculptures, Shah of Iran, 77-78. Exhib: Origins of Modern Sculpture, St Louis Mus, Mo & Detroit Art Inst, Mich, 45; Unknown Political Prisoner (competition finalists), Tate Gallery Art, London, 52; Fifteen Americans, Mus Mod Art, New York, 52; Salute to France, Mus Arte Mod, Paris, 55; The New Decade, Whitney Mus Am Art, New York, 55; Portraits of Speakers, Arts Club Chicago, 75; Post-War Am Sculptors, Nat Collection Fine Arts, Washington, DC, 75; Am Directions, Smithsonian Inst, Washington, DC, 75; 200 Yrs Am Sculpture, Whitney Mus Am Art, New York, 76; Art in Archit, Meadow Brook Art Gallery, Rochester, Mich, 77; Pvt Images: Photographs by Sculptors, Los Angeles Co Mus Art, Los Angeles, Calif, 78. Teaching: Head art dept, Trenton Jr Col, 47-52; prof art, Hunter Col, 52-65. Pos: Vpres, Nat Inst Arts & Lett, 63. Awards: Creative Arts Award, Brandeis Univ, 58; Silver Medal, Architects League New York, 60; Fine Arts Medal, Am Inst Architects, 70. Bibliog: Brian O'Dougherty (producer), Richard Lippold (TV film), Boston Educ TV, 60; The sun and Richard Lippold (TV film), New York TV, 69. Media: Wire, Metals. Mailing Add: c/o Willard Gallery 29 E 72nd St New York NY 10021

LIPSCHULTZ, MAURICE A
COLLECTOR
b Chicago, Ill, Aug 5, 12. Pos: Mem bd gov, Mus of Contemp Art, Chicago; mem art vis comt, Smart Gallery, Univ Chicago; mem art adv comt, Spertus Mus & D'Arcy Gallery, Loyola Univ. Collection: Primarily contemporary; specializing in structurist art and large scale sculpture. Mailing Add: 214 S Clinton St Chicago IL 60606

LIPSKY, PAT
PAINTER
b New York, NY, Sept 21, 41. Study: Brooklyn Mus Art Sch, summers 60 & 61; Cornell Univ, BFA, 63; Art Students League, 64; Hunter Col, MA, 68, with Tony Smith. Work: Whitney Mus Am Art; Fogg Mus; Walker Art Ctr; Ft Worth Mus; San Francisco Mus Art. Exhib: Lyrical Abstraction, 69, Highlights 1969-70 & exhibs, 72, Aldrich Mus; Pat Lipsky Recent Paintings, Everson Mus, 70; Lyrical Abstraction, Whitney Mus Am Art, 71. Bibliog: Kramer Hilton (auth), Art: 2 interesting talents make debut, New York Times, 6/13/70; Hodgson Moira (auth), A question of survival, Soho Weekly News, 7/10/75. Media: Acrylic, Oil. Mailing Add: 42 Wooster St New York NY 10013

LIPTON, BARBARA B
ART WRITER, CURATOR
b Newark, NJ. Study: Univ Iowa, Iowa City, BA(art hist, Eng lit); Univ Mich, Ann Arbor, MA(Eng & Am lit) & studies in Oriental art with Prof James Plummer; Rutgers Univ, New Brunswick, NJ, MLS. Collections Arranged: Newark Long Ago (auth, catalog), 74 & Whaling Days in New Jersey (auth, catalog), 75, The Newark Mus, NJ; Photographs of Eskimo Whaling, The Bryggens Mus, Bergen, Norway, 76; Survival: Life and Art of the Alaskan Eskimo (auth, catalog), The Newark Mus, NJ, The Bowers Mus, Calif, The Heard Mus, Ariz, The Ill State Mus, Huntington Art Gallery, WVa, Anchorage Hist & Fine Arts Mus, Alaska & Witte Mem Art Mus, San Antonio, Tex, 77-78. Pos: Art libr dir, Newark Mus, NJ, 70-75, guest cur, 76-77, spec proj consult 77- Mem: Am Asn Mus; Art Librn Soc NAm (treas, NJ Chap, 75); Arctic Inst NAm. Res: Whaling history; life and art of the Alaskan Eskimo; New Jersey history and photography; Tibet. Collection: Eskimo art and artifacts. Publ: Co-auth, Westerners in Tibet, 73 & Bibliography of Mayan Architecture, 74, The Newark Mus. Mailing Add: 282 Scotland Rd South Orange NJ 07079

LIPTON, SEYMOUR
SCULPTOR
b New York, NY, Nov 6, 03. Study: City Col New York, 21-22; Columbia Univ, 23-27. Work: Mus Mod Art & Metrop Mus Art, New York; Brooklyn Mus, NY; Hirshhorn Mus, Washington, DC; Whitney Mus Am Art, New York; Nat Collection Fine Arts; plus many others. Comn: Lincoln Ctr for the Performing Arts, New York; Dulles Int Airport, Washington, DC; Milwaukee Ctr for Performing Arts, Wis, 69; City of Philadelphia, Pa; plus others. Exhib: Whitney Mus Am Art Ann, Art Inst Chicago, 66; Mus Mod Art, New York, 68 & 69; Smithsonian Inst, Washington, DC, 68; one-man shows, Milwaukee Art Ctr, Wis, 70, Mass Inst Technol, 71, Va Mus Fine Arts, 72, Cornell Univ, 73 & Everson Mus, Syracuse, NY, 73; plus many others. Teaching: Instr sculpture, Cooper Union, 42-44; instr sculpture, New Sch Social Res, 40-64. Pos: Vis art critic, Yale Univ, 56; mem art curriculum adv bd, NY Univ; sculptor chmn, Art Comn New York City, 67. Awards: Ford Found Grant, 62; Archit League Award, 63; Widener Gold Medal, Pa Acad Fine Arts, 68; plus many others. Bibliog: Barbara Rose (auth), American Art Since 1900, a Critical History, Praeger, 67; Allen S Weller (auth), The Joys & Sorrows of Recent American Art, Univ Ill, 68; Albert E Elsen (auth), Seymour Lipton, Abrams, 69; plus many others. Dealer: Marlborough Gallery 41 E 57th St New York NY 10022. Mailing Add: 302 W 98th St New York NY 10025

LIPTON, SONDRA (SAHLMAN)
PAINTER, SCULPTOR
b New York, NY. Study: NY Univ, sculpture with Vincent Glinsky. Work: Pres Lyndon B Johnson Libr & in private collections of Mrs Pierre du Pont II, Paul Mellon, Mrs. Seward Mellon, Jacqueline Kennedy Onassis, Gov Winthrop Rockefeller; Mrs Vincent Astor, Lord & Lady Dunsany, H E Ambassador & Mme Guy de Keller, Gerald Van der Kemp, Richard Rodgers & Adele Astaire Douglass. Style & Technique: Flemish still-life. Media: Oil on wood. Mailing Add: 501 E 87th St New York NY 10028

LIPZIN, JANIS CRYSTAL
FILM MAKER
b Colorado Springs, Colo, Nov 19, 45. Study: Ohio Univ, with Clarence H White, Jr, BFA; NY Univ, with Irving Sandler, Robert Kaupelis & Howard Conant; Univ Pittsburgh, MLS; San Francisco Art Inst with James Broughton, Gunvor Nelson, Larry Jordon & Don Lloyd, MFA; Pittsburgh Filmmakers Workshop, with Bruce Baillie. Comn: Doc film (with Stephanie Beroes), People's Oakland, Model Cities of Pittsburgh, 74. Exhib: One-woman show, Slippery Rock Col, 72; Assoc Artists Pittsburgh Ann, Carnegie Mus, 72-74; two-woman show, Photo-Imagery, Sewickley Acad, Pa, 73; Pa Women Artists, Pittsburgh, 74; Seven by Four, Canyon Cineatheque, San Francisco, 75. Collections Arranged: Coordr, film-video prog, Pa Women Artists, 6/74. Teaching: Lectr, Contemp Women Artists, Carlow Col, 73; student-teacher filmmaking, San Francisco Art Inst, 75- Pos: Fine arts librn, Henry Clay Frick Arts Libr, Pittsburgh, 71-74; co-juror, Lewisburg Arts Festival, Bucknell Univ, 73; slide-curator, Anne Bremer Mem Libr, San Francisco Art Inst, 74-; mem, Women's Res & Bibliog Comt, Womens Studies Prog, Univ Pittsburgh, 74. Awards: Festival Photography Award, Three Rivers Art Festival, Pittsburgh, 74. Bibliog: Donald Miller (auth), rev, 74 & Margie Carlin (auth), Era of computer art joins city's cultural circle, 74, Pittsburgh Post-Gazette; Michael Reynolds (auth), Seven visions by four, Berkeley Barb, 75. Mem: Canyon Cinema Coop; Pittsburgh Filmmakers Asn; Assoc Artists Pittsburgh; NOW Task Force Women in Arts; Women's Caucus of Col Art Asn. Media: Mixed; Film. Dealer: Canyon Film Coop Rm 220 Indust Ctr Bldg Sausalito CA 94965. Mailing Add: San Francisco Art Inst 800 Chestnut St San Francisco CA 94133

LIS, JANET CHAPMAN
PAINTER
b Cleveland, Ohio, Jan 9, 43. Study: Cleveland Inst Art, scholar, 57-61; Ohio Univ Sch Fine Arts, BFA, 61-65; Western Reserve Univ, 66; also with David Driesbach, Gary Pettigrew & Dave Hostetler. Work: Hollywood Mus Art, Fla; Int Inst Human Rights, Strasbourg, France; Nat Red Cross, Cleveland; Ft Lauderdale Symphony Orch, Fla; Holy Cross Hosp, Ft

Lauderdale. Comn: Poster, Cleveland Inst Art, 61; painting of New River Hist Soc Ft Lauderdale, 74; portrait of Charles Bachman, Football Hall of Fame, comn by Charles Bachman, Jr, Pompano Beach, Fla, 74; Hist Silver Thatch Bldg (charcoal drawing), Gen Builders Corp, Pompano Beach, 75; mural, First United Methodist Church, Pompano Beach, Fla, 76. Exhib: Ann Nat Art Exhib, Springville Mus Art, Utah, 75 & 76; Ann Nat Exhib Paintings, Ogunquit Art Ctr, Maine, 75; NMex Int Art Show, Univ NMex, Portales, 75; Women Artists, Metrop Mus Dade Co, Miami, 75; Univ New Orleans, La, 75-77; Perspectives Two, Womanart Gallery, New York, 76; Artists in Quotations, Lincoln Ctr, New York, 76; Artists Equity Exhib, Hollywood Mus Art, Fla, 76; Ann Painting & Sculpture, Mus Great Plains, Lawton, Okla, 76; Ponce Mus Art, PR, 77; Southeastern Painting & Sculpture Competition, Arts Assembly of Jacksonville, Fla, 77; Festival of Women in the Arts, Coun Arts & Sci, Orlando, Fla, 77; Fla Artists Exhib, Daytona Mus Arts & Sci, Fla, 78. Awards: C Duaine Dillin Award, 11th Ann Southeastern Art Exhib, 75; Hon Mention, NMex Int Show, Univ Eastern NMex, Portales, 75; Int Women's Yr Award, Int Women's Arts Festival, Ford Found, New York, 75-76. Bibliog: Shubert Jonas (auth), Color in Janet Lis' paintings impressive with boldness, Ft Lauderdale News, 9/28/75; Lorraine Huber (auth), The colorful world of Janet Lis, Fiesta Mag, 9/75; Pamela Peters (auth), Meet artist Janet Lis—Outstanding Woman in Contemp Art, The Herald, 10/20/77. Mem: Artists Equity Asn; Broward Arts Coun (visual arts task force); Fla Artists Group; Women's Caucus for the Arts; Women in the Arts Found. Style & Technique: Semi-realistic; a colorist, strong use of light and shadow, limited pallet, paint wet into wet-rapidly-giving painting spontaneous feeling. Media: Acrylic on Canvas, Charcoal. Publ: Contribr, Sunshine Artists USA, 10/72, Miami Herald, 3/1/74, Tribune Publ, 10/14/76 & Ft Lauderdale News, 3/20/77; illusr cover, Hi-Riser, 1/30/75. Mailing Add: 12 Sunset Lane Pompano Beach FL 33062

LISSIM, SIMON
PAINTER, DESIGNER
b Kiev, Russia, Oct 24, 00; US citizen. Study: In Russia & Paris, France. Work: Mus Nat du Jeu de Paume, Paris; Metrop Mus Art, New York; Nat Collection Fine Arts, Washington, DC; Victoria & Albert Mus, London; Albertina Mus, Vienna, Austria; plus 63 other mus in US, Can & Europe. Exhib: Int Exhibs, Paris, 25 & 37; Int Exhib, Barcelona, Spain, 28; Theatre Exhib, Vienna, 33 & Mus Gallera, Paris, 33; plus over 60 group & one-man shows. Teaching: From asst prof to prof painting & design, City Col New York, 44-71, emer prof, 71- Pos: Chmn, Nat Selecting Comt Fulbright Awards in Painting, Sculpture & Graphic Arts, 56. Awards: Silver Medal, 25 & two Diplomes d'Honneur, 37, Int Exhib, Paris; Gold Medal, Int Exhib, Barcelona, 28. Mem: Societe de Salon d'Autonme, Paris; Societe des Artistes Decorateurs Francais; Audubon Artists; Soc Miniature Painters, Eng; Royal Soc Arts Eng (hon corresp mem in US, vpres coun). Media: Gouache. Publ: Monogrs and many forewords for exhibs and articles published in Paris, Eng and US, 28-58. Mailing Add: 55 Magnolia Dr Dobbs Ferry NY 10522

LIST, VERA G
PATRON, COLLECTOR
b Boston, Mass, Jan 6, 08. Study: Simmons Col. Pos: Chmn art ctr comt & trustee, New Sch Social Res; hon chmn bd gov, Jewish Mus; dir, List Art Posters, New York. Awards: Solomon Schechter Medal, Jewish Theol Sem Am, 59; Louise Waterman Wise Award, 64; NY State Coun on Arts Award to Albert A List Found for List Art Poster Prog, 69. Interest: Financed establishment of New School Art Center, 1960, and purchase fund, 1962, for purchase of art for Lincoln Center, New York; established List Art Posters Program; many gifts of art to New York museums and others. Collection: Contemporary sculpture and painting. Mailing Add: Byram Shore Rd Byram CT 10573

LISZT, MARIA VERONICA
PAINTER, DESIGNER
b Boston, Mass. Study: Scott Carbee Sch Art, grad; Boston Mus Sch Fine Art, grad; Art Students League; landscape painting with Aldro Hibbard, Rockport, Mass, Carl Nordstrom, Ipswich, Mass, Emile Gruppe, Gloucester, Mass & Lester Stevens, Conway, Mass. Comn: Murals for hotels in Boston, NY & Fla, comn by Carl Abbott; murals comn by Carl Gundlach & Emile Coulon, Boston, for leading hotels, ballrooms, dining rooms & foyer entrances; also many portrait comns. Exhib: NShore Arts Asn Exhibs, Gloucester; Nat Asn Women Painters, Acad Design, New York; Acad Artists, Springfield, Mass; Grand Cent Art Galleries, New York; NJ Art Asn. Teaching: Instr pvt classes. Awards: Elizabeth T Greenshield's Mem Award, 61. Mem: North Shore Art Asn; Acad Artists Asn; Nat Asn Women Painters. Media: Oil. Mailing Add: c/o Grand Cent Art Galleries 40 Vanderbilt Ave New York NY 10017

LITTLE, JOHN
PAINTER, SCULPTOR
b Sanford, Ala, Mar 18, 07. Study: Buffalo Fine Arts Acad; Art Students League, with George Grosz; Hans Hofmann Sch Fine Arts, New York & Provincetown, Mass. Work: Ball State Univ; Guild Hall, East Hampton, NY; Berkeley Art Mus, Calif; Dillard Univ; Bruce Mus, Greenwich, Conn. Exhib: Major one-man shows, Calif Palace of Legion of Honor, San Francisco, 46, Betty Parsons Gallery, New York, 48, Bertha Schaefer Gallery, New York, 57 & 58, A M Sachs Gallery, New York, 71 & Tower Gallery, Southampton, NY, 77; Osaka Festival (Gutai Group), Japan, 58; G David Thompson Collection, exhibited Kunstmuseum, Duseldorf, Ger, Munic Mus, The Hague, Holland & Guggenheim Mus, New York, 59; Panorama, Gallerie Beyeler, Basle, Switz, 61. Teaching: Lectr painting, Univ Calif, Berkeley, spring 63 & Long Island Univ, summer 67. Pos: Founder & treas, Signa Gallery, East Hampton, NY, 57-61. Awards: Anne Bremer Mem Prize, San Francisco Mus Ann, 48; Purchase Prize, Longview Found, 62. Bibliog: Hans Namuth (auth), Image from the sea, Film Images, New York, 54-55. Mem: Smithsonian Inst. Style & Technique: Abstract color formalist painting. Media: Oil, Bronze. Publ: Auth, Statement of the artist, It Is, 59. Mailing Add: 367 3-Mile Harbor-Hog Creek Hwy East Hampton NY 11937

LITTLE, NINA FLETCHER
COLLECTOR, ART HISTORIAN
b Brookline, Mass, Jan 25, 03. Pos: Trustee, consult & chmn curatorial comt, Old Sturbridge Village; cataloger & res consult, Abby Aldrich Rockefeller Folk Art Collection, 54-57. Awards: Art Res Award, Hist Soc Early Am Decoration, 53; Rotary Club Brookline for distinguished pub serv, 56; Crowninshield Award, Nat Trust for Hist Preserv, 64. Res: New England painting, architecture and decorative arts. Collection: American decorative arts, especially folk paintings and furniture. Publ: Auth, American decorative wall painting, 52, Abby Aldrich Rockefeller Folk Art Collection (catalog), 57, Maine's role in American art (1700-1865 sect), 63 & 72 & Country art in New England, 65; Country arts in early American homes, 75. Mailing Add: 305 Warren St Brookline MA 02146

LITTLETON, HARVEY K
SCULPTOR, EDUCATOR
b Corning, NY, June 14, 22. Study: Univ Mich, BDesign; Brighton Sch Art, Eng; Cranbrook Acad Art, MFA. Work: Toledo Mus Art, Ohio; Victoria & Albert Mus, London; Mus Mod Art, New York; Kunstmuseum, Dusseldorf, WGer; Mus Contemp Crafts, New York. Exhib: Form & Qualitat, Handwerkskammer, Munich, WGer, 68-69; Vrij Glas, Boymans Mus, Rotterdam, Neth, 69; Objects USA, Johnson Wax Collection, 69-72; Artist Produced Glass, Bellerive Mus, Zurich, Switz, 72; 15th Triennale Exhib Archit & Decorative Art, 74; one-man show, Contemp Art Glass Gallery, New York, 76 & 77. Teaching: Instr ceramic art, Toledo Mus Art Sch Design, 49-51; prof art, Univ Wis-Madison, 51-77, emer prof, 77-, chmn dept art, 64-67 & 69-71, univ res grants, 54, 57, 62, 72 & 75. Awards: Toledo Mus Art Res Grant, 62; Louis Comfort Tiffany Found Grant, 70-71; Corning Glass Works, 74. Bibliog: Colescott (auth), Harvey Littleton, 59 & Dido Smith (auth), Off hand glassblowing, 64, Craft Horizons; Hot glass, WTMJ-TV & Milwaukee Art Ctr, 66. Mem: Fel Am Crafts Coun (trustee, 57 & 59-64); hon mem Nat Coun Educ in Ceramic Arts. Style & Technique: Minimal and abstract; work in furnace worked glass and combinations with metals; also series of color intaglio prints from glass plates. Media: Glass. Publ: Auth, Erwin Eisch, 63 & auth, Glass in the Ozarks, 73, Craft Horizons; auth, Glassblowing—a Search for Form, Van Nostrand Reinhold, 72. Dealer: Contemp Art Glass Gallery 806 Madison Ave New York NY 10021; Kunsthaus am Mus Drususgasse 1-5 Koln 1 West Germany. Mailing Add: Rte 1 Box 843 Spruce Pine NC 28777

LITTMAN, ROBERT R
ART ADMINISTRATOR, ART HISTORIAN
b New York, NY, Oct 27, 40. Study: Antioch Col, BA(hist); NY Univ Inst Fine Arts, MA(art hist). Collections Arranged: Diaghilev/Cunningham: The Arts of Dance (with catalog), 74; Wish You Were Here: The History of the Picture Postcard 74; Art Pompier: Late Nineteenth Century French Salon Painting 74; Three Unrelated Works, 75; Bradley Walker Tomlin: A Retrospective View, 75; Fashion Photography: Six Decades, 75; Peter Rabbit & Other Tales; Art from the World of Beatrix Potter; Panoramic Photography. Pos: Dir, Emily Lowe Gallery, Hofstra Univ, 69-76; consult, Asn Better New York, 70-; dir, Grey Art Gallery & Study Ctr, NY Univ, 76- Publ: Auth, Hanging & Leaning (catalog), 70; co-auth, Universal Limited Art Editions in Long Island Collections (catalog), 70. Mailing Add: 125 E 87th St New York NY 10028

LIU, HO
COLLECTOR, PAINTER
b Canton, China, Mar 20, 17; US citizen. Study: Lingnan Univ, Canton, BA; George Washington Univ, MA. Collection: Chinese calligraphy and painting. Mailing Add: 1946 Hopewood Dr Falls Church VA 22043

LIVESAY, THOMAS ANDREW
MUSEUM DIRECTOR
b San Francisco, Calif, Feb 1, 45. Study: San Francisco Art Inst, 63-65; Univ Tex, Austin, BFA, 68, MFA, 72. Collections Arranged: Five Austin Artists (with catalog), 74; The Amarillo Competition, 75 & 77; Charles Burchfield Selected Works (with catalog), 75; Henri Matisse Etchings, 75; American Masters, 75; Warren Davis Retrospective (with catalog), 75; American Images, 76, with Nat Endowment for the Humanities; Young Texas Artists Series, 76-78. Pos: Tech staff, Univ Tex Art Mus, Austin, 66-70; cur, Elisabet Ney Art Ctr, Austin, 70-73; dir, Longview Mus & Art Ctr, Tex, 73-75; cur, Amarillo Art Ctr, 75-77, dir, 77- Awards: Roy Crane Award Fine Arts, Univ Tex, Austin, 68. Mem: Am & Tex Asns Mus. Res: 20th century American art with particular emphasis on sculpture. Publ: Auth, Texture, Form & Color, 72; co-auth, Larson/Walsh/Sculpture, 74. Dealer: Harvey Bott 2118 Strand Galveston TX 77550. Mailing Add: 1013 S Bryan Amarillo TX 79102

LIVINGSTON, CHARLOTTE (MRS FRANCIS VENDEVEER KUGHLER)
PAINTER, ART ADMINISTRATOR
b New York, NY. Study: Nat Acad Design; Art Students League; Columbia Univ; Realgymnasium, Kassel, Ger. Work: Ford Mus, Dearborn, Mich; Jumel Mansion, New York; Tamassee DAR Schs, SC; Hickory Mus Art, NC; Greenville Mus, NC. Exhib: Hotel Monmouth, Spring Lake, NJ, 72, 73 & 74; Nat Arts Club, 72; Authors, Artists & Writers, Pacem in Terris, 72; Grand Cent Art Gallery, New York; Hudson River Mus, Ridgewood, NJ. Pos: Dir, Kingsbridge Hist Soc, 59-; pres, Bronx Artists Guild; pres, Gotham Painters. Awards: Mary Yates Medal, 70; Eva Rappleye Medal, 71; Anna Morse Medal, 72; plus other hon mentions. Mem: Bronx Mus; Salmagundi Club; Burr Artists; Nat Arts Club; Staten Island Inst Arts & Sci. Style & Technique: Aquarell, impressionistic. Media: Watercolor. Mailing Add: 2870 Heath Ave New York NY 10463

LIVINGSTON, JANE S
ART CRITIC, CURATOR
b Upland, Calif, Feb 12, 44. Study: Pomona Col, BA(art hist), 65; Harvard Univ, MA(fine arts), 66. Exhibitions Arranged: Bruce Nauman, 1972-73 (with catalog), Los Angeles Co Mus Art, Los Angeles; Five Washington Artists (auth, catalogue), 76; Andre/Leva/Long, 76; The Nation's Capital in Photographs, 76; Norman Bluhm, Gabriel Kohn, Howard Mehring (auth, catalogue), William Eggleston, Corcoran Biennial, 77; The Collection of Sam Wagstaff, Norman Zammitt, Manuel Alvarez Bravo (auth, catalogue), 78. Pos: Cur mod art, Los Angeles Co Mus Art, 67-75; corresp ed, Art in Am, 70-; chief cur, Corcoran Gallery Art, 75-; mem mus adv panel, Nat Endowment for the Arts, 77- Mem: Asn Am Mus; Col Art Asn (chmn studio panels, 78-); Int Coun Mus. Publ: Co-auth, Art & Technology, Viking Press & Los Angeles Co Mus Art, 70; auth, Ed McGowin's True Stories, Corcoran Gallery Art, 75. Mailing Add: Corcoran Gallery Art New York Ave & 17th St Washington DC 20006

LIVINGSTON, SIDNEE
PAINTER
b New York, NY. Study: Nat Acad Design. Work: Princeton Univ; Everhart Mus, Pa; Univ Miami, Fla; Univ Miss; Columbus Mus, Ga; plus pvt collections in Eng, France, Sweden & Italy. Exhib: Art Inst Chicago; Butler Art Inst; Philadelphia Acad Fine Arts; St Louis Mus, Mo; Libr of Cong, Washington, DC; plus solo monotype exhib, 75-78. Awards: First Prize for Watercolor, Painters & Sculptors NJ, 65; Mildred Tommy Atkins Prize, Nat Asn Women Artists, 71, Award/Oil, 77. Mem: Artists Equity Asn New York. Media: Oil, Watercolor. Mailing Add: 50 E 89th St New York NY 10028

LIVINGSTON, VIRGINIA (MRS HUDSON WARREN BUDD)
PAINTER, ILLUSTRATOR
b Baltimore, Md. Study: Md Inst Art; Cooper Union Art Sch; Art Students League; Nat Acad Design; Beaux Art Am, Fontainbleau, France; with Fernand Leger, Paris Acad, France; also with Brackman, Ryerson, Kroll, O'Hara & Phillip, New York. Work: Draped Figure, Home Fed Bank Bldg, Charleston, SC. Exhib: Salon de L'Arte Libre, Paris, 51; Miniature Painters, Sculptors & Gravers Soc, Smithsonian Inst, Washington, DC, 52; Am Watercolor Soc Ann

& Allied Artists Am Ann, Nat Acad Art, New York, 54-60; Corcoran Gallery Art, Washington, DC, 55; one-man show, Mus City New York, 60; plus many others. Awards: First Prize, Ann Studio Club, YWCA, New York, 52; Hon Mention, Smithsonian Inst, 52; Medal of Honor, Ann Artists Prof League, New York, 56; plus others. Bibliog: Article in La Rev Mod, Paris, 56. Mem: Copley Soc of Boston; Carolina Art Asn; Charleston Artists Guild (planning comt chmn, 69-). Interest: Organized new gallery, LaPetite Louve, to promote young artists. Media: Watercolor. Publ: Illusr fashions & by-line, Chicago Tribune Synd, 24-26; illusr textbks, Scribners, 24-25; co-auth & illusr ann calendar, Am Cyanamid Co, 59-60. Dealer: Blue Knight Gallery 82 Broad St Charleston SC 29401. Mailing Add: c/o Sherrill House 1359 Huntington Ave Boston MA 02130

LIVINGSTONE, BIGANESS
PAINTER, EDUCATOR
b Cambridge, Mass, May 17, 26. Study: Mass Col Art, BFA, 51; Boston Univ, drawing with Walter Murch, 66; Newton Col, MP, 72. Work: Chase Manhattan Bank Collection, New York; Cranwell Sch Comn, Lenox, Mass; Radcliffe Col, Cambridge; Sheraton Corp, Boston. Exhib: De Cordova Mus, Lincoln, Mass, 58 & 63; Mus Mod Art, New York, 62; Harvard Univ, 62; Carl Siembab Gallery, New York, 74; Fitchburg Art Mus, Mass, 76; Sunne Savage Gallery, Boston, 76; Art & Sci Ctr, NH, 77. Teaching: Asst prof art, Newton Col, 70-75, artist in residence, 72-75, lectr studio art & dir exhibs, Colby Jr Col, NH, 69-70; asst prof art, Univ Wis, Fox Valley, 76- Awards: Radcliffe Inst Fel, 63-65; First, Silvermine Guild Artists 11th; painting grant, Inst Independent Study, Radcliffe Col. Bibliog: Ted Farah (auth), Art collecting for pleasure and profit; James Collins (auth), Women Artists in America, Vol 2 (1975). Style & Technique: Front of the canvas is cut out creating a space, the space is treated as a volume. Media: Oil, Charcoal and acrylic on cut canvas. Dealer: Sunne Savage Gallery Boston MA. Mailing Add: 1500 Palisades Lane Appleton WI 54911

LLORENTE, LUIS
PAINTER, DESIGNER
b Santander, Spain; US citizen. Study: Sch Indust Arts & Sch Visual Arts, Columbia Univ; also with Anthony Thieme & Umberto Romano. Work: USN Combat Art Collection, Washington, DC; Neighborhood Med Ctr, Bronx, NY; also in many pvt collections. Comn: Bathyscaph Trieste, San Diego Naval Base, USN, 61; atomic submarine, Rota Naval Base, Spain, 64; Gemini V Recovery, Aboard USS Lake Champlain, 65; USS New Jersey, Philadelphia Navy Yard, 68; US Marines Distributing candy to children, 69. Exhib: Audubon Artists, Nat Acad Design, 60-61 & Am Watercolor Soc, eight times & six travel awards, 60-75; Mus de la Marine, Paris, 63; Smithsonian Inst & Dept of State Exhib Hall, Washington, DC, 65; museums, universities & embassies, US & abroad, 61- Pos: Free-lance commercial artist for agencies, studios & pharmaceutical cos, 63-; juror, Washington Square Outdoor Show & Art Orgns, 66- Awards: Citation from Mayor John V Linsay, New York City Pan Am Art Contest, 66; Katherine M Howe Mem, Knickerbocker Artists, New York, 73; Ford Times Award, Am Watercolor Soc, 75. Bibliog: John Smee (auth), Portrait of an artist, Chronicle, New York, 61; Mann Sierra (auth), American-Spaniard paints in Rota Naval Base, Alerta, Santander, Spain, 64; plus others. Mem: Artists Fel (chmn nominating comt & trustee, 65-); Am Watercolor Soc (asst corresp secy, 71-); Knickerbocker Artists (2nd vpres, 73-); Salmagundi Club (art & nominating comts, 64-, chmn art comt, 74-); Navy Combat Art (art comt, 63-). Style & Technique: Expressionist; glazing. Media: Watercolor, Oil. Mailing Add: 245 Fort Washington Ave New York NY 10032

LLOYD, GARY MARCHAL
SCULPTOR, EDUCATOR
b Los Angeles, Calif, Aug 27, 43. Study: Art Ctr Col Design, 63-65; Otis Art Inst Los Angeles Co, BFA & MFA, 70. Work: Los Angeles Co Mus Art, Los Angeles, Calif; Tyler Mus Art, Tex. Comn: Site work, Univ Southern Calif, 73; site work, Univ Calif, Irvine, 74; performance, Immaculate Heart Col, 74; installation with Connie Zehr, Otis Art Inst Los Angeles Co, 75. Exhib: 8th Tyler Nat, Tyler Mus Art, 72; Pasadena Mus Mod Art, 73; Installation of New Acquisitions Prints & Drawings, Los Angeles Co Mus Art, 75. Teaching: Asst prof intermedia sculpture, Otis Art Inst Los Angeles Co & Univ Calif, Los Angeles, 75- Pos: Dir, Nat Conf, Innerdependence Art & Sci, Calif State Univ, Los Angeles, 71-72; co-prin, Mellow Productions: Video & 16mm doc for the arts, 71-74; mem bd dirs, Los Angeles Inst Contemp Art, 74-75. Awards: Purchase Award, Tyler Mus Art, 72. Bibliog: Peter Plagens (auth), rev, Artforum, 11/72; Joe Young (auth), Reevaluating the tradition of the book, Art News, 3/75. Media: Mixed. Res: Objects and installation with space and light displacement. Publ: Co-auth, Bob went home, 73. Mailing Add: 3742 Jasmine Ave Apt 4 Los Angeles CA 90034

LLOYD, MRS H GATES
COLLECTOR, PATRON
b Devon, Pa, July 19, 10. Pos: Trustee, Philadelphia Mus Art, Am Fedn Arts & Washington Gallery Mod Art. Collection: Contemporary painting and sculpture. Mailing Add: Darby Rd Haverford PA 19041

LLOYD, TOM
SCULPTOR
b New York, NY, Jan 13, 29. Study: Pratt Inst, with Gottlieb, McNeil, Guston & Nakian; Brooklyn Mus scholar, 61, pvt study with Peter Agostini. Work: In pvt collections only. Exhib: Studio Mus in Harlem, 68; Dr Martin Luther King Benefit Exhib, 68; C W Post Col, Greenvale, NY, 69; Univ Calif, Los Angeles, 69; Phoenix Art Mus, Ariz, 69; plus many others. Teaching: Dir painting & sculpture, Adult Creative Arts Workshop, Dept Parks, New York, 67-70; instr light media, Sarah Lawrence Col, 69-71; instr three dimensional design, Cooper Union, 69-71. Pos: Art consult, group serv agencies & educ div, Lincoln Hosp, New York, 66. Mailing Add: 195-45 107th Ave Jamaica NY 11433

LOAR, PEGGY A
CURATOR, ARTS ADMINISTRATOR
b Cincinnati, Ohio, May 14, 48. Collections Arranged: Ind Stoneware (auth, catalogue), Indianapolis Mus Art, 72. Teaching: Lectr art hist, Indianapolis Mus Art, 71-75 & numerous mus & conf, 71- Pos: Cur educ, Indianapolis Mus Art, 72-, asst to dir, 75-; mem state supt adv comt, State Plan for the Arts in Educ, Ind, 75-; prof dir, Learning Mus, Nat Endowment for the Humanities, Washington, DC, 75-, mem nat bd consult, 77-; mem comt on ethics, Am Asn Mus, 76-; prog dir, Inst Mus Serv, Washington, DC, 77- Awards: Nat Endowment for the Arts Grants, Ind Pottery, 75 & Role of Humanities in Art Mus Educ, 76. Bibliog: Adele Silver (auth), Issues related to museum education: curators/directors and educators interface, Midwest Mus Cont, Vol 36, No 4; Priscilla Brouillette (auth), Loar adds new enthusiasm, Vision, The Ind Comt for the Humanities, 77. Mem: Ind Comt for the Humanities (mem exec comt; chmn mem subcomt, 73-; vchmn, 76); Am Asn Mus; Indianapolis Art League Found (adv bd). Res: Museum education; Indianapolis Museum of Art accessions and collections; humanities curriculum. Publ: Auth, Pre-Columbian Gold Pendant: LaVoile Jaune/Fenetre Gothique, Indianapolis Mus Art, 72; auth, Museums Are a Resource, Art Educ Asn Ind, 75; auth, Arts and the three Rs/43, Mus News, 9-10/76; auth, Issues, Midwest Mus Conf, Vol 36, No 4. Mailing Add: 4150 46th St NW Washington DC 20016

LOBDELL, FRANK
PAINTER
b Kansas City, Mo, 21. Study: St Paul Sch Fine Art, Minn; Calif Sch Fine Art; Acad Grande Chaumiere, Paris. Work: Pasadena Art Mus, Los Angeles Co Mus, Stanford Mus, San Francisco Mus Art & Oakland Mus Art, Calif. Exhib: Salon du Mai, Paris, 50; 3rd Biennial of Sao Paulo, Brazil, 55; International Art of a New Era, Osaka, Japan, 58; Kompas 4, West Coast USA, Van Abbemuseum, Eindhoven, 70; 32nd Biennial Am Painting, Corcoran Gallery Art, Washington, DC, 71. Teaching: Prof art, Stanford Univ, 66- Bibliog: Michel Tapie (auth), Frank Lobdell, David Anderson (Paris), 66; Walter Hoppe (auth), Frank Lobdell 1948-1965, Pasadena Art Mus, 66; Gerald Nordland (auth), Frank Lobdell, San Francisco Mus Art, 69. Dealer: Martha Jackson Gallery 32 E 69th St New York NY 10021. Mailing Add: 340 Palo Alto Ave Palo Alto CA 94301

LOBERG, ROBERT WARREN
PAINTER, INSTRUCTOR
b Chicago, Ill, Dec 1, 27. Study: City Col San Francisco, AA; Univ Calif, Berkeley, BA & MA; San Francisco State Univ; Hans Hofmann Sch Art, Provincetown, Mass. Work: Art Inst Chicago; San Francisco Art Comn; Portland Art Mus, Ore; Oakland Art Mus, Calif; Gallery Mod Art, Washington, DC; plus others. Exhib: Richmond Art Ctr, Oakland Art Mus & San Francisco Mus Art, ann, 55-; US Info Agency Exhib, Paris, France, 64; Ithaca Col Art Mus, NY, 68; Henry Gallery, Univ Wash, 68; Calif Col Arts & Crafts, Oakland, 69; Both-Up Gallery, Berkeley, Calif, 72-78; Berkeley Art Ctr, 77; San Jose Art Mus, Calif, 78; plus others. Teaching: Art lectr; instr painting & drawing, Calif Col Arts & Crafts, 61-63; instr art, San Francisco Art Inst, 63-66; instr art, Univ Calif, Berkeley, 65; vis fac, Dept Art, Univ Wash, 67-68. Awards: Yaddo Found Scholar, 57; MacDowell Colony Scholar, 59 & 60; La Jolla Art Mus Prize, 62; plus others. Mailing Add: 2020 Vine St Berkeley CA 94709

LOCHRIDGE, SUDIE KATHERINE
ART ADMINISTRATOR, ART HISTORIAN
b Miss, Feb 6, 46. Study: Miss State Col Women, Columbus, BFA(studio), 68; Univ NC, Chapel Hill, with Joseph Sloane, MA(art hist), 70; Univ Del, Am art hist with William I Homer. Collections Arranged: Organized exhibs & wrote catalogs for Art, Man & Mechanization, 73, Paintings, Drawings & Prints by Rockwell Kent, 74, Patriotism & Persuasion: World War I & II Posters, 74, Wm O Partridge: American Sculptor, 74 & Portraits & Painters of the Early Champlain Valley, 75. Teaching: Instr art hist, Miss State Col Women, 70-71. Pos: Cur collections, Univ Del, Newark, formerly; cur art gallery, State Univ NY Col Plattsburgh, currently. Mem: Am Asn Mus (comt on univ & col mus, 74-75); Col Art Asn Am; Coun Arts (bd mem, 73-); Gallery Asn NY State. Mailing Add: 151 S Catherine St Plattsburgh NY 12901

LOCHRIE, ELIZABETH DAVEY
PAINTER, SCULPTOR
b Deer Lodge, Mont, July 1, 90. Study: Pratt Inst, life cert, normal art, 11; study with Weinold Reiss, summers 33 & 34; secco with Dorothy Pucinneli, summer 46; fresco with Victor Arnitoff, 46. Comn: Murals, State of Mont for Galen Hosp, 24-25; murals, comn by US Treas Dept for Post Off Bldgs, Burley, Idaho, 37, St Anthony, Idaho, 38 & Dillon, Mont, 39; bronze mem portrait palen, comn by Cummerford-Walker family, Washington, DC, 48; Indian portraits, five Butte schs, Mont, 50-72; bronze bas-relief portrait, James Finlen, Fort Lauderdale, 70. Exhib: One-man shows, State Hist Gallery, Helena, Mont, 44 & 73; Arthur Newton Gallery, New York, 59, Stadtler Hotel Gallery, Los Angeles, 60 & Marquette Nat Bank Gallery, Minneapolis, 63; Whitney Mus Art, Cody, Wyo, 68; Butt Silver Bow Art Chateau, 77. Bibliog: Local watercolor scenes, IBM Ann, 44; Gamers Confectionary, Ford Motor Co Cookbook, 72; Dale Burk (auth), New Interpretations, Bk Mont Artists, 72. Mem: Life fel, Int Inst Arts & Lett; Mont Inst Arts; Mont Hist Soc; Nat Soc Lit & Arts. Style & Technique: Realistic; Western art. Collection: Indian and mining artifacts covering 150 years. Mailing Add: 4900 Telegraph Rd G94 Ventura CA 93003

LOCK, CHARLES K
ART DEALER
Pos, Dir, Lock Galleries. Mailing Add: 44 E 67th St New York NY 10021

LOCK, CHARLES L
PAINTER, ILLUSTRATOR
b Chiswick, London, Eng, June 15, 19. Study: Polytech Sch of Art, Chiswick, London, Eng; further studies with George Ayling & Kenneth Washburn. Work: Air Force Art Collection, Art & Mus Branch, Pentagon, Washington, DC; Naval Aviation Mus, Pensacola, Fla. Pos: Art dir, Aero-Marine Specialties, Washington, DC, 74-77; partner, LTD Fine Art Prints, Vienna, Va, 77- Mem: Guild of Aviation Artists; Royal Soc of Marine Artists; Am Soc of Marine Artists. Style & Technique: Aviation and marine subjects and portrait artist. Media: Water Media, Pen and Ink; Pastel Oil. Publ: Illusr, Airways to Airlines-A 50 Year History of Commercial Aviation, John Meyers, 75; illusr, Fundamentals of meteorology, United Air Lines, 76; illusr, These were the ugliest airplanes, Aircraft Owners & Pilots Asn Mag, 77; illusr, The three musketeers, Am Aviation Hist Soc, 77; illusr, Allegheny Aircraft (ltd ed prints), Moore & Moore, 78. Mailing Add: 1080 N Fairoaks 105 Sunnyvale CA 94086

LOCKE, CHARLES WHEELER
PAINTER, PRINTMAKER
b Cincinnati, Ohio, Aug 31, 99. Study: Ohio Mechanics Inst; Cincinnati Art Acad; Art Students League, with Joseph Pennell; study in Paris, 28. Work: Metrop Mus Art & Whitney Mus Am Art, New York; Nat Gallery, London, Eng; Corcoran Gallery Art & Phillips Collection, Washington, DC; plus other pub & pvt collections. Teaching: Lect on lithography; instr lithography, Art Students League, 22-37. Awards: Logan Award, 36; Am Acad Arts & Lett Grant; Ranger Fund Purchase Award, Nat Acad Design, 74; plus others. Mem: Nat Acad Design; Century Club. Publ: Illusr, Tale of a Tub, Walden; illusr, Capt Stormfield's Visit to Heaven; contribr, Freeman Mag. Mailing Add: Old Post Rd Garrison NY 10524

LOCKE, MICHELLE WILSON
CURATOR, ART HISTORIAN
b Dallas, Tex, June 10, 47. Study: Trinity Univ, San Antonio, Tex; Univ Tex, Austin, BFA. Pos: Lectr-librn, Art Mus of STex, Corpus Christi, 72-76, cur, 76- Mem: Am Asn of Mus; Col Art Asn. Res: Fifteenth Century French illuminated manuscripts. Mailing Add: PO Box 1010 Corpus Christi TX 78403

LOCKER, THOMAS
PAINTER
b New York, NY, June 26, 37. Study: Univ Chicago, with Joshuah Taylor; Am Univ. Work: John Herron, Indianapolis; Chicago Arts Coun. Exhib: Banfer, NY, 64; Gilman Galleries, Chicago, 64, 67 & 68; Rex Evans, Los Angeles, 70; Vincent Price Gallery, Chicago, 70 & 71; R S Johnson Int Gallery, Chicago, 72; Oehschlaeger Galleries, Chicago, 75. Style & Technique: Hudson River School, a updated 19th century Romanticism. Dealer: Merril Chase Galleries Water Tower Place 835 Michigan Ave Chicago IL 60611. Mailing Add: RR 1 Elizabeth IL 61028

LOCKHART, JAMES LELAND
ILLUSTRATOR, PAINTER
b Sedalia, Mo, Sept 26, 12. Study: Univ Ark; Am Acad Art; Art Inst Chicago, with Edmund Giesbert. Comn: Container Corp Am; Baseball Hall of Fame Mus, Cooperstown, NY; Ferry Hall Sch; Lincoln Rm, Gettysburg Mus, Pa; R R Donnelley Co; plus others. Exhib: One-man shows, Art Guild Chicago, 58, Ferry Hall Sch, 58, Great Lakes Naval Base, 58, Lake Forest Pub Libr, 58 & 61 & Lake Forest Acad, 68. Teaching: Lectr wild life painting & mag illus. Awards: Nat Graphic Arts Award, 68 & 70; Printing Indust Award, 70-71. Mem: Art Guild Chicago; fel Int Inst Arts & Lett; Arts Club Chicago. Publ: Portfolio of Upland Game Bird Prints, 60; Portfolio of Cats, 61; Prints of Waterfowl & Game Birds, 64; auth & illusr, Portrait of Nature, Crown, 67; illusr, Sat Eve Post, Colliers, Coronet, Sports Afield & others. Mailing Add: 980 E Walden Lane Lake Forest IL 60045

LOCKS, MARIAN
ART DEALER, COLLECTOR
b Philadelphia, Pa, June 24, 15. Pos: Dir, Marian Locks Gallery, Philadelphia. Mem: Moore Col Art, Philadelphia (bd mem, 75-); Pa Acad Fine Arts; Inst Contemp Art, Univ Pa. Specialty: Contemporary Delaware Valley Art; development of local talent. Collection: Largely Philadelphia art of the seventies; also special group of works by Beauford Delaney, an American artist now living in Paris and recently acclaimed as one of the twenty major Black artists; a few small works by European Masters. Mailing Add: 1524 Walnut St Philadelphia PA 19102

LOEB, MR & MRS JOHN L
COLLECTORS
Collection: Paintings. Mailing Add: 730 Park Ave New York NY 10021

LOEFFLER, CARL EUGENE
ART PUBLISHER, ART ADMINISTRATOR
b Cleveland, Ohio, Nov 14, 46. Exhib: Introductions, San Francisco Art Inst, 75; Art Magazines, Victoria & Albert Mus, London, 76; Recordings, Ctr for Experimental Art & Commun, Toronto, 77; Book Works, Los Angeles Inst of Contemp Art, 78. Collections Arranged: International Rubber Stamp Exhibition, 76; West Coast Conceptual Photographers, 76; Photography & Language, 76; Recorded Works, 76; Use Value of the Gallery, 77. Pos: Pres, La Mamelle Inc, San Francisco, 75- Mem: Assoc Art Publ (asst chmn, 77-); Western Asn of Art Mus. Res: Contemporary art. Mailing Add: PO Box 2123 Rincon Annex San Francisco CA 94119

LOEHR, MAX
MUSEUM CURATOR, EDUCATOR
b Chemnitz, Ger, Dec 4, 03; US citizen. Study: Univ Berlin, 33-34; Univ Munich, PhD, 36; Harvard Univ, Hon MA. Teaching: Assoc prof, Tsinghua Univ, Peking, 47-48; lectr Far Eastern art, Univ Munich, 50-51; prof Far Eastern art, Univ Mich, 51-60; Abby Aldrich Rockefeller prof Oriental art, Harvard Univ, 60- Pos: Asst cur, Mus Volkerkunde, 36-40, cur, 50-51; dir, Sino-Ger Inst, Peking, 41-45; ed, Sinologische Arbeiten, Peking, 43-45; hon res assoc, Freer Gallery Art, 52-60; Far Eastern ed, Arts Orientalis, 54-60; cur Oriental art, Fogg Art Mus, Harvard Univ, 60-74; co-ed, Harvard J Asian Studies. Awards: Guggenheim Found Grant, 57-58. Mem: Fel Am Acad Arts & Sci; Am Oriental Soc; Chinese Art Soc Am. Res: Chinese art and archaeol. Publ: Auth, Chinese Bronze Age Weapons, 56; auth, Relics of Ancient China, 65; auth, Chinese Landscape Woodcuts, 68; auth, Ritual Vessels of Bronze Age China, 68; auth, Ancient Chinese Jades, 75; also contribr to Artibus Asiae, Ars Orientalis, Oriental Art, J Asian Studies & others. Mailing Add: 14 Loring Rd Cambridge MA 02173

LOEW, MICHAEL
PAINTER
b New York, NY, May 8, 07. Study: Art Students League, 26-29, with Richard Lahey & Boardman Robinson; Acad Scandinave, Paris, France, 29, with Dufresne; Hans Hofmann Sch Fine Arts, New York, 46-49; Atelier Leger, Paris, 50. Work: Whitney Mus Am Art, New York; Philadelphia Mus Fine Arts; Sheldon Swope Mem Mus, Lincoln, Nebr; Univ Art Mus, Univ Calif, Berkeley; Joseph H Hirshhorn Mus, Washington, DC. Comn: Evolution of Textile Making (mural), Works Progress Admin, Charles E Hughes High Sch, New York, 33; mural (with Wilhelm DeKooning), Hall of Pharm, New York World's Fair, 39; murals, comn by US Treas Dept Sect Fine Arts for Post Off Bldgs, Amherst, Ohio, 41 & Belle Vernon, Pa, 42. Exhib: One-man shows, Univ Calif, Berkeley, 60 & 66, Landmark Gallery, New York, 73 & 76 & Marilyn Pearl Gallery, New York, 77; Whitney Mus of Am Art, New York, 61, 62, 75 & 77; Hans Hofmann & His Students, Mus of Mod Art Travelling Show, 63; Maine: 50 Artists of the 20th Century, Fedn of Arts Travelling Show, 65; Ciba-Geigy Collection, Hudson River Mus, NY, 71 & Univ Tex Art Mus, 73; Monhegan Artists, Allentown Mus, Pa, 74; Works on Paper, Mus Art Ctr, Wichita Falls, Tex, 76; Selections from the Permanent Collection, Hirshhorn Mus, Washington, DC, 76-77; New Deal Art, Gallery Asn of NY State Travelling Exhib, 77; Works on Paper, Neuberger Mus, NY, 77; plus many others. Teaching: Sr instr painting, Sch Visual Arts, 58-, co-chmn dept fine arts, 62-70; vis prof painting, Univ Calif, Berkeley, 60-61, vis lectr painting, 65-66. Pos: Pres & secy, Artists Union, New York, 34-35; mem, Mayor LaGuardia's Art Comt of 100, 35-36; selecting juror, Int Asn Plastic Arts European Touring Exhib, 57 & Contemp Am Painting. Awards: Sadie A May Fel, 29; Honorable Mention for Murals, Treas Dept, 41 & 42; Ford Found Purchase Award, Art Inst Chicago Exhib, 64, Nat Endowment for the Arts grant, 76-77. Bibliog: Thomas B Hess (auth), Art, New York Mag, 1/73; Hilton Kramer (critic), New York Times, 11/11/77; Deborah Rosenthal (critic), Arts Mag, 11/77; plus others. Mem: Am Abstract Artists; Fedn Mod Painters & Sculptors. Style & Technique: Color abstractionist; combines and synthesizes geometric and expressionist concepts. Media: Oil. Publ: Auth, statement in Realities Novelles, Paris, 50; auth, statement in It Is, autumn 58; contribr, Josef Albers, impersonalization in perfect form, 56 & Academy, 59, Art News; auth, Artists and critics, a letter, Arts Mag, 10/62. Mailing Add: 280 Ninth Ave New York NY 10001

LOEWER, HENRY PETER
ILLUSTRATOR, PRINTMAKER
b Buffalo, NY, Feb 13, 34. Study: Albright Art Sch, Univ Buffalo, with Lawrence Calcagno & Anne Coffin Hanson, BFA, 58. Work: Hunt Inst for Botanical Doc, Carnegie-Mellon Univ, Pittsburgh, Pa; Catskill Art Soc, Hurleyville, NY. Exhib: Int Exhib of Botanical Drawings, Hunterdon Art Ctr, Clinton, NJ, 77; 4th Int Exhib of Botanical Art, Carnegie-Mellon Univ, Pittsburgh, Pa, 77-78; one-man show, Horticultural Soc of New York, 77. Style & Technique: Realistic renderings of plant and animal life. Media: Pen & Ink, Watercolor. Publ: Auth & illusr, Bringing the Outdoors In, 74, Seeds and Cuttings, 75 & Growing and Decorating with Grasses, 77, Walker; illusr, Wildflower Perennials for Your Garden, Hawthorn, 76. Mailing Add: PO Box 43 Cochecton Center NY 12727

LOGAN, DAVID GEORGE
EDUCATOR, METALSMITH
b Milwaukee, Wis, June 14, 37. Study: Univ Wis-Madison, BS, 63, with Arthur Vierthaler, MFA, 68; Univ Ill-Urbana, with Robert von Neumann, Jr, MA, 67. Comn: Art in Worship (slide series), Am Crafts Coun. Exhib: Jewelry 64, Plattsburg, NY, 64; Icasals Nat Jewelry Competition, Lubbock, Tex, 70; Michigan Competitive, Midland, 71; Michiana Crafts Competition, Lafayette, Ind, 72; Exhib of Relig Art, Assention Lutheran, East Lansing, Mich, 73. Teaching: Art teacher, Oregon Pub Schs, Wis, 63-66; asst prof art, Mich State Univ, 68-; vis artist metalsmithing, Northern Mich Univ, summer 71 & 74. Awards: Jewelry Award, Westchester Art Soc, NY, 70; Assention Lutheran Church Award for Liturgical Jewelry, East Lansing, 73; Col Art Teacher of Year, Mich Youth Arts Festival Comt, 74. Mem: Mich Art Educ Asn (pres, 71-72, ed newslett, 73-74); Nat Art Educ Asn; Am Crafts Coun. Style & Technique: Classical, unromantic with emphasis on the austere, the mechanistic and the understated. Media: Gold, Sterling, Gem Stones. Mailing Add: 2670 Bluehaven Ct East Lansing MI 48823

LOGAN, FREDERICK MANNING
EDUCATOR, WRITER
b Racine, Wis, July 18, 09. Study: Milwaukee State Teachers Col, BE, 32; Art Inst Chicago, 33; Columbia Univ Teachers Col, MA, 39; Northern Mich Univ, hon LLD, 74. Teaching: Head div art educ, Milwaukee State Teachers Col, 43-46; prof art, Univ Wis-Madison, 46-, chmn art dept, 47-49 & 51-58; vis lectr, Sch Art Educ, Birmingham, Eng, summer 64. Pos: Pres, Wis Artists Fedn, 34-41; mem bd, Madison Art Asn, 52-67; coun mem, Comt Art Educ, Mus Mod Art, New York, 53-63; mem bd, Western Arts Asn, 54-57; mem bd, Madison Art Ctr, 74-76. Awards: Distinguished Serv Award, Nat Art Educ Asn, 75; Fine Arts Achievement Award, Miami Univ, 75; Barkan Award, Nat Art Educ Asn, 76. Mem: Inst Study Art Educ; Nat Art Educ Asn; Wis Acad Sci, Arts & Lett; Int Soc Educ Art. Res: Aesthetics of the environment; history of American art education. Publ: Auth, Growth of Art in American Schools, 55; contribr, Report of Commission on Art Education, 65; ed, A Report for Urban America, Educ Aesthetic Awareness Environ, 66; ed, Geography and psychology of urban cultural centers, Arts & Soc, 67; auth, A challenge to art education, J Nat Art Educ, 70. Mailing Add: 2913 Waunona Way Madison WI 53713

LOGAN, GENE ADAMS
SCULPTOR, PAINTER
b Kickapoo, Kans, June 14, 22. Study: Southwest Mo State Univ, BS, 49; Univ Ore, 65; Univ Kans, MFA, 67; also with Elden Tefft & Jan Zach. Work: El Camino Col Sculpture Garden, Torrance, Calif; included in over 200 pvt collections. Comn: Sculpture, Chase Nat Ins Co, Springfield, Mo, 66, Westmont Industs, Santa Fe Springs, Calif, 75 & City of La Mirada, Calif. Exhib: All-Calif Exhib, Laguna Beach, Calif, 60 & 61; Nat Acad Design 136th Ann, New York, 61; Form & Space Show, Mus Art, Laguna Beach, 62; Nat Orange Show, All-Calif Exhib, San Bernardino, 63, 72 & 73; one-man shows, Ankrum Gallery, Los Angeles, 70-72 & 75; Pioneer Mus & Haggin Galleries, Stockton, Calif, 78. Teaching: Prof art anat, Southwest Mo State Univ, Springfield, 67-69; prof life drawing, Pasadena Sch Fine Arts, Calif, 70. Awards: Hon Mention, Los Angeles Munic Art Show, 57; First Award Sculpture, All-Calif Exhib, Laguna Beach, 60 & 61; Sculpture Gold Medal Award, Calif State Fair & Expos, Sacramento, Calif, 62. Bibliog: Michael Leopold (auth), Los Angeles, Art Gallery Mag, 11/72; Irene Lagorio (auth), Art & artists, Monterey Peninsula Herald, 2/17/74; David Braff (auth), Art, Beverly Hills Courier, 2/28/75. Media: Welded Cor-Ten Steel, Bronze; Egg Tempera, Acrylic. Dealer: Ankrum Gallery 657 N La Cienega Los Angeles CA 90069; Zantman Art Galleries Sixth & Mission Carmel CA 93921. Mailing Add: 473 Guilford Ave Claremont CA 91711

LOGAN, JUAN LEON
SCULPTOR
b Nashville, Tenn, Aug 16, 46. Study: Howard Univ; Clark Col. Work: Mus African Art, Washington, DC; Davidson Col, NC; NC Nat Bank, Mint Mus Art & Johnson C Smith Univ, Charlotte. Exhib: Benny Andrews & Juan Logan, Carlow Col Pittsburgh, 71; USA...1971-1972, Carnegie Inst, Pittsburgh, 71; National Exhibition/Black Artist, NJ State Mus, Trenton, 72; Reconstruction Period, Mint Mus Art, Charlotte, 73; Directions in Afro-American Art, Herbert F Johnson Mus, Cornell Univ, 74. Awards: Romare Bearden Award for 75; Santa Fe Festival of the Arts, NMex; Faces Exhib, St John's Col, 78. of Medium, Carnegie Inst, 71; Hon Mention PICA Award, Assoc Printing Co; Nonprocess Educ Poster-Printing Indust of the Carolinas, Inc, 74. Bibliog: Henri Ghent (auth), Quo vadis Black art?, Art in Am, 11-12/74; Dr Samella Lewis (auth), Art: African American, Harcourt, 76. Mem: Southern Asn Sculptors Inc; Nat Conf Artists. Style & Technique: Nonfigurative art concerned with formal organization of plane; expression of volume in terms of modern industrial material. Media: Wood, Steel. Dealer: Contemp Crafts Gallery 5271 W Pico Blvd Los Angeles CA 90019. Mailing Add: PO Box 836 Belmont NC 28012

LOLOMA, CHARLES
JEWELER, DESIGNER
b Hotevilla, Hopi Reservation, Ariz, Jan 7, 21. Study: Sch Am Craftsmen, Alfred Univ, NY, journeyman cert; Univ Ariz, Tucson. Work: Mus Northern Ariz, Flagstaff; Heard Mus, Phoenix, Ariz; Denver Art Mus, Colo; US Dept of Interior Gallery, Washington, DC; Mus Int Folk Art, Santa Fe, NMex. Comn: Golden Gate Expos, US Dept Interior, San Francisco, 39 & Reproduction of Awatoui Murals, Mus Mod Art, New York, 40 (both under Rene D'Harnoncourt). Exhib: Nat Ceramics Show, Syracuse, NY, 48; Dept of Interior Show, Washington, DC, 65; Scottsdale Nat Indian Arts Exhib, Ariz, 65-75; Objects USA, Johnson Wax Collection Contemp Crafts Traveling Exhib, 69; Loloma, Mus Contemp Crafts, New York, 74. Teaching: Instr pottery, Ariz State Univ, summer 54-58; instr pottery & jewelry, Rockefeller Found on Indian Youth, Tucson, Ariz, 59-61; dir dept plastic arts, Inst Am Indian Arts, Santa Fe, NMex, 61-65. Awards: Whitney Found Fel, 49-51; Award, Objects USA, Johnson Wax Found, 69. Bibliog: Articles in Ariz Highways Mag, 60-; Three Indians, KAET-TV, Ariz State Univ, Tempe, 71 & nationally aired TV prog, 4/1/74; Loloma, Pub Broadcasting Syst, 73. Mem: Ariz Comn Arts & Humanities; fel Am Craftsman Coun; Ariz Designer Craftsman. Style & Technique: Contemporary, based on Hopi background;

construction, inlay and sandstone casting. Media: Gold, Silver & Precious & Semi-precious Stones. Publ: Illusr, Hopi Hoya, 39; illusr, Indians of the Southwest, 42; contribr, Objects: USA, 69; contribr, Indian Voices, 70. Mailing Add: PO Box 185 Hotevilla AZ 86030

LOMAHAFTEWA, LINDA (LINDA JOYCE SLOCK)
PAINTER, EDUCATOR
b Phoenix, Ariz, July 3, 47. Study: Inst Am Indian Arts, Santa Fe, NMex; San Francisco Art Inst, BFA & MFA. Work: Ctr Arts Indian Am, Washington, DC. Exhib: Riverside Mus, New York, 65; Mus NMex, Santa Fe, 65-66; Ctr Arts Indian Am, 67-68; San Francisco Art Inst Spring Show, 70-71; Scottsdale Nat Indian Art Exhib, Ariz, 70-71. Teaching: Asst drawing, San Francisco Art Inst, 70; painting instr, Assoc Am Indian Arts, San Francisco, summer 72; asst prof Native Am studies, Calif State Col, Sonoma, 72- Awards: Hon Mention for Oil Painting, Mus NMex, 65; First Place in Graphic Arts Purchase Award, Ctr Arts Indian Am, 67; Third Place in Drawing, Scottsdale Nat Indian Art Exhib, 70. Bibliog: Lloyd E Oxendine (auth), 23 contemporary Indian artists, Art in Am, 7-8/72. Publ: Illusr, Indian Mag, 71; illusr, Weewish Tree, Am Indian Historian Press, 71; contribr, Art in Am, 72. Mailing Add: 2082 Golden Gate Ave San Francisco CA 94115

LOMBARDO, JOSEF VINCENT
ART HISTORIAN, EDUCATOR
b New York, NY, Nov 6, 08. Study: Cooper Union, dipl; NY Univ, BA & BFA; Columbia Univ, MA & PhD; Univ Florence, LittD; Villanova Univ, LLD. Teaching: Prof fine arts, Queens Col (NY), 38-76, emer prof, 77- Awards: Columbia Univ Res Grant Spec Study of Michelangelo, 68. Mem: Renaissance Soc Am; Soc Archit Historians; Metrop Mus Art. Res: Michelangelo; the Pieta and other masterpieces; Italian culture in the 20th century. Publ: Auth, Attilio Piccirilli, Life of an American Sculptor, Pitman, 44; auth, Chaim Gross, Sculptor, Dalton House, 49; co-auth, Italian Culture in the Twentieth Century, 52; auth, Michelangelo: the Pieta and Other Masterpieces, Simon & Schuster, 65. Mailing Add: 100-11 70th Ave Forest Hills NY 11375

LO MEDICO, THOMAS GAETANO
SCULPTOR, DESIGNER
b New York, NY, July 11, 04. Study: Beaux Arts Inst Design. Work: New York Pub Schs, 60; Deerfield Acad, 61; Seal for City of Rye, NY, 64; Alice Freeman Palmer Medal for Hall of Fame, NY, 64; Jr High Sch, Staten Island, NY, 64. Comn: Family Group, Metrop Life Ins Co, New York World's Fair, 39-40. Exhib: Metrop Mus Art; Whitney Mus Am Art; Pa Acad Art; Nat Acad Design; plus many others. Teaching: Instr, Nat Acad Design Sch Fine Arts, New York. Awards: J Stanford Saltus Medal, Am Numismatic Soc, 56; Mrs Louis Bennet Prize & Lindsey Morris Mem Prize, Nat Sculpture Soc. Mem: Fel Nat Sculpture Soc (coun); fel Am Numismatic Soc; Archit League New York; Allied Artists Am. Mailing Add: 61 Main St Tappan NY 10983

LONDON, ALEXANDER
COLLECTOR, ILLUSTRATOR
b Paris, France; US citizen. Study: Lycee Mantaigne, Paris; Univ Pa, MS(chem eng); Columbia Univ. Pos: Pres, Marstin Printing Corp, 69-; publ, Electronic & Appliance Co, 70-; exec dir, Imprimerie Centrale Commerciale, Paris, 70- Awards: Seven Typographical Awards, 56-71; Award for Illus in Kelavala, 54. Mem: Sustaining mem New York Acad Sci; assoc fel Am Inst Aeronaut & Astronaut. Collection: French Impressionists; French Montparnasse; American contemporary. Publ: Illusr, Kalevala, 54; contribr & illusr var catalogs & art mag. Mailing Add: 350 Central Park W New York NY 10025

LONDON, BARBARA
CURATOR
b Glen Cove, NY, July 3, 46. Study: Hiram Col, Ohio, BA, 68; Inst of Fine Arts, New York Univ, MA, 72. Collections Arranged: Mus of Mod Art, New York, Projects: Video I-XVII, 74-78, Loren Madsen, 75, Peter Campus, 76, Nam June Paik, 77, Bookworks, 77 (Sachs Gallery), Projects: Shigeko Kubota, 78 & Video Viewpoints, 78. Pos: Asst int prog, Mus of Mod Art, New York, 71-73, curatorial asst dept of prints & illus bks, 73-77 & cur video prog, 77- Publ: Auth, Video art in USA, Video, Mus d'Art Mod, Geneva, 77; auth, Video at the Museum of Modern Art, The New Television: A Public/Private Art, Mass Inst Technol Press, 77; auth, Independent video: a report for the Rockefeller Foundation and the Museum of Modern Art, Mus of Mod Art, 78. Mailing Add: c/o Mus of Mod Art 11 W 53rd St New York NY 10019

LONDON, ELCA
ART DEALER
b St John, NB, Can, July 11, 30. Study: Dalhousie Univ, Halifax, NS, BA; McGill Univ, Montreal, Que, MS. Pos: Dir, Elca London Gallery, 61- Mem: Prof Art Dealers Asn of Can. Specialty: International and Canadian art; separate Eskimo Gallery. Mailing Add: 770 Lucerne Rd Mount Royal PQ H3R 2H6 Can

LONDON, JEFF
DESIGNER, LECTURER
b New Haven, Conn, Dec 11, 42. Study: Philadelphia Mus Col Art. Work: Off Secy State, Capitol Bldg, Hartford, Conn; Berkeley Divinity Sch, New Haven. Comn: People That Talk Too Much (centerpiece), Nat Soc Interior Designers for Home Show, Hartford, 69; New Methods (demonstration), Assoc Coun Arts Convention, St Louis, Mo, 71; A Parentally Prescribed Children's Playground (experience structure), Conn Comn Arts, Wadsworth Atheneum, Hartford, 71. Exhib: Jeff London...Caustic Merriment, John Slade Ely House, New Haven, 67; Under 35, New Brit Mus Am Art, 69; People Furniture, US Plywood Corp, New York, 71; Artists Save Face, Parish House Gallery, New Haven, 72; People Chairs...Unusual-ity, Stamford Mus; Fairtree Gallery, New York, 75. Teaching: Vis artist Caustic Merriment, Conn State Grad Schs, 69-; vis artist Caustic Merriment, Conn High Schs, 69-; resident artist Caustic Merriment, North Haven High Sch, Conn, 71; Nat Endowment Fund resident artist, Choate Sch, Wallingford, Conn, 72-73, fac resident artist, 73- Bibliog: A Parentally Prescribed Children's Playground...re Jeff London, WTIC-TV, 71; Jeff London...Caustic Merriment, Conn Pub TV, 72; Carolyn Meyer (auth), People Who Make Things, 75; plus others. Media: Mixed Media. Res: Caustic Merriment, a trademarked, kind of hard humored therapeutic form of art that lets you laugh at things you most ordinarily don't. Interest: Company designs and produces children and adult-child Peoples Furniture (trademark). Mailing Add: 180 Thimble Islands Rd Stony Creek CT 06405

LONEWOLF, JOSEPH
POTTER
b Santa Clara Pueblo, NMex, Jan 26, 32. Work: Taylor Mus, Colo Springs. Exhib: NMex State Fair, 69-73; Heard Mus Indian Arts & Crafts Exhib, Phoenix, Ariz, 70-72; Inter-Tribal Indian Ceremonials, Gallup, NMex, 70-72; Scottsdale Nat Indian Arts Exhib, Ariz, 71-72; Portland Am Indian & Western Relic Show, Ore, 73; Ann Southwestern Indian Arts Festival, 73; Bower Mus Exhib, 73; Roadrunner Trail Exhib, Maxwell Mus of Anthrop, Univ of NMex, 75. Awards: Two First Prizes & Honorable Mention, 70, First Prize, 71, Honorable Mention, 72, Heard Mus Indian Arts & Crafts Exhib; Second Prize, 71 & First Prize, 72, Scottsdale Nat Indian Arts Exhib, Ariz; First Prize, 72 & 73, Best of Show, Pottery Past 1920, 74 & Judges Award Pottery Past 1920, 74, Am Indian Arts Show, Denver, Colo. Style & Technique: Coiled clay pots with designs etched directly onto the pots; natural materials in traditional technique. Media: Clay. Mailing Add: c/o Grace Medicine Flower Box 1037 Espanola NM 87532

LONEY, DORIS HOWARD
PAINTER
b Everett, Wash, Jan 24, 02. Study: Univ Wash, BA; Art Students League, with Robert Brackman & Yasuo Kuniyoshi; Farnsworth Sch Art; Scripps Grad Art Sch, with Henry McFee & Millard Sheets; watercolor with Dong Kingman. Comn: Portraits, three pres, Univ Wis-Superior, bd dirs, First Nat Bank, Superior, pres, Univ Ariz, Dr & Mrs Richard Harvill, Columbia Univ, Dr Robert Terry; plus other outstanding persons. Exhib: One-man show, Rosequist Gallery, Tucson, 56 & 73; two-man show, Fine Arts Gallery, Univ Ariz, 60; three-man show, Tucson Art Ctr, 62; Nat League Am Pen Women Nat Biennial, 62, 64 & 70; Tucson Festival Six State Show, 62 & 70; plus seven one-man shows in US. Pos: Pres, Tucson Nat League Am Pen Women, 66-68, state art chmn, 69-71, art chmn, 74-76. Awards: First for Figure Painting, Seattle Art Mus, 50; First Prize for Papago Today (portrait), Nat Biennial, Nat League Am Pen Women, 70; Third Prize, Nat League Am Pen Women, Flagstaff, Ariz, 77. Mem: Life mem Art Students League; Nat League Am Pen Women; Tucson Palette & Brush. Dealer: Portraits Inc 41 E 57th St New York NY 10022. Mailing Add: 2727 E Elm St Tucson AZ 85716

LONG, C CHEE
SCULPTOR, PAINTER
b Smith Lake, NMex, Dec 5, 42. Study: Inst Am Indian Arts, cert; Univ Ariz, two yrs. Work: Inst Am Indian Arts Mus, Santa Fe, NMex; Indian Arts & Crafts Collection, CofC, Gallup, NMex; Navajo Tribal Mus, Window Rock, Ariz. Comn: Navajo History (mural), Ariz State Fair Comn, 65; mural of chapel altar, design, St Michael High Sch, 68. Exhib: Scottsdale Indian Art Nat, Ariz, 66 & 71; Guild Am Indian Arts & Crafts Exhib, Heard Mus, Phoenix, Ariz, 70 & 71; Arts & Crafts Exhib, Inter-Tribal Indian Ceremonial, 71 & 72. Collections Arranged: Navajo Centennial Exhib, Navajo Tribal Mus, Window Rock, 68. Pos: Asst cur, Navajo Tribal Mus, 65-68, staff artist, 68-70. Awards: Merit Award for Paintings, 70 & First, Second, Third & Merit Awards for Sculpture, 71 & 72, Inter-Tribal Indian Ceremonial Asn. Media: Wood, Casein, Oil. Collection: Indian and Western artifacts. Publ: Contribr poems & design, Four directions, Inst Am Indian Arts, 63; illusr cover & article, Long walk 1868, Window Rock, 68; contribr, Navajo Indian (poem), Univ Chicago Mag, 68; contribr ten poems, Blue Cloud Quart, 69; contribr poems, Roberts English Series, 71. Dealer: Woodards Indian Arts 224 W Coal Ave Gallup NM 87301. Mailing Add: Box 22 Continental Divide NM 87312

LONG, FRANK WEATHERS
SCULPTOR, JEWELER
b Knoxville, Tenn, May 7, 06. Study: Art Inst of Chicago, 25-27; Pa Acad of Fine Art, 27-28; Acad Julien, Paris, 28-29. Work: Nat Collection, Smithsonian Inst, Washington, DC; Int Bus Machines Corp, New York; Berea Col, Ky. Comn: Two panels, Univ Ky Libr, Lexington, 31, ten panels, Fed Bldg, Louisville, KY, 32; three panels, US Post Office, Hagerstown, Md, 34 & one panel, US Post Office, Drumright, Okla, 36, Treas Dept, Fed Govt; one panel, Davidson Col, Libr, 35. Exhib: Jewelry 1963, Everhart Mus, Scranton, Pa, 63; Three Man Crafts Invitational, Mus of Int Folk Art, Santa Fe, NMex, 63; SW Crafts Biennial, 75; 18th Nat Decorative Arts Exhib, Wichita Mus, Kans, 65; Media 1966, Walnut Creek Mus, Calif, 66; Hemisfair Preview Exhib, San Antonio, Tex, 67; Nat Crafts Exhib, Univ NMex Gallery, 68; Crafts VII Exhib, Mus of Albuquerque, 77. Pos: Dir, Alaska Off of Indian Arts & Crafts Bd, Juneau, 51-57; field rep, SW Off of Indian Arts & Crafts Bd, Gallup, NMex, 57-59, Albuquerque, 62-69. Mem: Albuquerque Chap NMex Designer-Craftsmen (pres chap, 69; pres, 67).Style & Technique: Contemporary design jewelry and sculpture. Media: Gem material and metal. Publ: Auth & illusr, Herakles, The 12 Labors, Black Archer Press, 31; auth & illusr, The Creative Lapidary, Van Nostrand Reinhold, 77. Dealer: Mariposa Gallery 113 Romero St NW Albuquerque NM 87104; Sunrise Shop La Fonda Hotel Santa Fe NM 87501. Mailing Add: 1836 Florida NE Albuquerque NM 87110

LONG, GLENN ALAN
ART HISTORIAN, WRITER
b Cleveland, Ohio, Oct 1, 39. Study: Ohio Univ, BFA(photog & studio art), MFA(painting & printmaking) & PhD(comparative arts). Work: Baltimore Mus Art. Collections Arranged: Social Rite & Personal Delight: African Art from Baltimore Collections, 75. Teaching: Instr art hist & drawing, Bethany Col, WVa, 64-67, actg chmn dept art, 66-67; instr art hist, Md Inst Col Art, 72- Pos: Cur educ, Baltimore Mus Art, 70-72, chmn div educ, 72-; prog officer, Nat Endowment for the Humanities, Washington, DC, 77-78; exec dir, Sunrise Inc, Charleston, Wva, 78- Mem: Col Art Asn Am; Am Asn Mus; Mus Educ Roundtable. Res: African, Oceanic and pre-Columbian art generally, with a concentration of ethnoconchology, particularly the Americas. Publ: Auth, Structural & Decorative Use of Shell Images on American Furniture Before 1850, 72; auth, Shell Trumpets & Concentric Circle in Pre-Columbian Tomb Offerings, 73; auth, Frog Motifs on Archaeological Mollusks from Hohokam & Mogollon Indian Cultures, 74; auth, Spondylus: the Red Shell, 75; co-auth, Social Rite & Personal Delight: African Art from Baltimore Collection, 75. Mailing Add: Baltimore Mus Art Art Museum Dr Baltimore MD 21218

LONG, HUBERT
SCULPTOR
b Sydney, Australia, Feb 2, 07; US citizen. Study: Fawcett Sch Art, Newark, NJ, 10 yrs. Work: Guild Hall Mus Collection, East Hampton, NY; Phoenix Art Mus, Ariz; also in pvt collections of Otto Spaeth Collection, Dr & Mrs Alfred Loomis, Mr & Mrs Robert Vanderbilt & others. Comn: Cyclops (six ft wood), Hugh Horner, Scottsdale, Ariz, 74. Exhib: Martha Jackson Gallery, New York, 60-61; one-man shows, Andrew Crispo Gallery, New York, 74 & 76 & Guild Hall, East Hampton, NY, 76; Painting & Sculpture Today, Indianapolis Mus & Taft Mus, Cincinnati, 74; Tower Gallery, Southampton, NY, 77; plus others. Pos: Art dir, Reynolds Corp, New York, until 39. Awards: First Prize, Membership Exhib, Guild Hall, East Hampton, 60. Bibliog: M L D'Otrnge Mastai (auth), Intellect & emotion in contemporary sculpture, Art Voices, 10/63. Mem: Guild Hall, East Hampton. Style & Technique: Constructivist, assembles found pieces of wood. Dealer: Andrew Crispo Gallery 41 E 57th St New York NY 10022. Mailing Add: Box 166 55 The Circle East Hampton NY 11937

LONG, MEREDITH J
ART DEALER
b Joplin, Mo, Sept 14, 28. Study: Univ Tex, BA, 50, Law Sch, 50-51, 53-54. Pos: Munic arts comnr, Houston; Pres, Meredith Long & Co, Houston, 57-; mem, Davis & Long, New York; mem, Watson-de Nagy & Co, Houston. Mem: JFK Ctr Performing Arts (pres' adv bd); Contemp Arts Mus, Houston (bd trustees); Mus Fine Arts, Houston (bd trustees); Alley Theatre, Houston (mem bd); Houston Ballet Found (mem bd). Specialty: 19th and 20th century American art. Publ: Ed, Americans at Home and Abroad Catalogue, 71; ed, Tradition and Innovation—American Paintings 1860-1870, 74. Mailing Add: 2323 San Felipe Houston TX 77019

LONG, SANDRA TARDO
DESIGNER, GRAPHIC ARTIST
b Hodge, La, Apr 2, 36. Study: La State Univ, with Caroline Durieux, Paul Dufour & Tom Cavanaugh, BS & MA. Work: La State Univ Libr, Baton Rouge; Jonesboro State Bank, La. Exhib: Ark Art Ctr, Little Rock, 63; Birmingham Festival Art Graphics Competition, Ala, 63; Old Testament Nat Art Competition, Inst Art, St Louis, Mo, 63; Piedmont Graphics Ann, Mint Mus, 68 & 69; Va Polytech Inst Women in Art Traveling Exhib, 75; one-person shows, Roanoke Fine Arts Ctr, Va, Silverman Art Ctr, Radford Col, Va & Suires Student Ctr, Va Polytech Inst & State Univ, 77. Teaching: Asst art, La State Univ, 61-63, dir arts & crafts, Student Union, 63-65; instr art, Va Polytech Inst & State Univ, 71-75; pvt studio instr. Pos: Cur, Va Polytech Inst & State Univ Col Archit, 68-69; designer for advert consult, Roanoke, 78- Style & Technique: Geological forms; almost photographic in detail of textures. Media: Drawing, Acrylic. Mailing Add: 606 Woodland Dr Blacksburg VA 24060

LONG, SCOTT
CARTOONIST
b Evanston, Ill, Feb 24, 17. Study: Harvard Univ, AB, 39. Pos: Reporter & cartoonist, Zanesville News, Ohio, 39; ed cartoonist, St Paul Pioneer Press, 41 & Minneapolis Tribune, 43- Awards: Freedoms Found Award, 49; Headliner Award & Christophers Award, 53; Sigma Delta Chi Award, 57. Mem: Asn Am Ed Cartoonists. Publ: Auth, Hey! Hey! LBJ! Mailing Add: 4501 Dupont Ave S Minneapolis MN 55409

LONG, WALTER KINSCELLA
MUSEUM DIRECTOR, PAINTER
b Auburn, NY, Feb 2, 04. Study: Syracuse Univ, BFA & MFA. Work: Syracuse Univ Collection Fine Arts; Univ Fla; Lansing Cent Sch; Shotwell Park, Skaneateles, NY. Comn: Church murals; portraits for pvt comns; City of Auburn Civic Award Medal; Syracuse Univ Sch Journalism. Exhib: Syracuse Mus Fine Arts; Rochester Mem Art Gallery; New York City Galleries. Collections Arranged: Homespun Art; Shoes Thru the Ages; Cayuga County Inventions; plus others. Teaching: Instr basic art & art appreciation, Auburn Community Col; lect, Art Appreciation, World Art, Hist of Art & others to civic groups, mus, schs & study groups. Pos: Ed, Archaeol Soc Cent NY Bull; Cayuga Co Historian; secy-treas, Northeast Mus Conf; dir, Finger Lakes Art Asn; dir, Instrument Res Inst; mem, Int Coun Mus, UNESCO; dir, Cayuga Mus Hist & Art, currently. Awards: Mus Asn Fel, Rochester Mus Arts & Sci; Citizen of the Year, 63; Honor Teacher of the Year, 64. Mem: Fel Royal Soc Arts; fel Int Inst Arts & Lett; Nat Acad TV Arts & Sci; Int Platform Asn. Style & Technique: Representational; realist. Mailing Add: Cayuga Mus of Hist & Art 203 Genesee St Auburn NY 13021

LONGAKER, JON DASU
EDUCATOR, WRITER
b Davos, Switz, Jan 5, 20; US citizen. Study: Univ Pa, BA(fine arts), 41; Barnes Found, Merion, Pa, 46-47; Cinquantenaire Mus, Brussels, Belg Am Educ Found, summer 51; Columbia Univ, art hist, 47-52. Teaching: Instr art appreciation, Barnes Found, Merion, Pa, 50-51; prof art hist, Randolph-Macon Col, Ashland, Va, 53-; prof art hist, Inst Am Univs, Aix-en-Provence, France, 64-65. Pos: Art critic, Richmond Times-Dispatch, Va, 56-64, drama critic, 65-; columnist on arts, Commonwealth Mag, Richmond, 67-; mem, State Art Comn, Richmond, 70-74. Publ: Auth, Painting in the South—a Double Portrait, Inst Southern Cult, Longwood Col, 61; auth, Strive and succeed, Arts in Va, 70; auth, Art, Style and History: a Selective History of Art, Scott, Foresman, 70. Mailing Add: 133 Beverly Rd Ashland VA 23005

LONGLEY, BERNIQUE
PAINTER, SCULPTOR
b Moline, Ill. Study: Art Inst Chicago, Byron Lathrop traveling fel, 45, grad; Inst de Allende, San Miguel de Allende, Mex, 71; Santa Fe Sch Arts & Crafts, 75. Work: Mus NMex, Santa Fe; Dallas Mus. Comn: Murals, comn by Alexander Girard, Santa Fe, 59; murals, La Fonda Del Sol, NY, 60. Exhib: Int Watercolor Show, Art Inst Chicago, 48; Denver Mus Art Regional Show Sculpture, 48; Mus NMex Biennial Show, 53 & 65; NMex Mus Fine Arts Invitational Show, 68; Kermezaar Festival, El Paso, Tex, 75. Awards: Honorable Mention, Art Inst Chicago, 48; Honorable Mention, Denver Mus Art Regional Show Sculpture, 48; Purchase Prize, Mus NMex, 53, Honorable Mention, 65. Mem: Alumni Asn Art Inst Chicago; Int Liaison Network Women Artists; Artists Equity Asn; Advocates for Arts. Media: Oil, Acrylic. Publ: Auth, Suite of Lithographs, Tamarind Inst, 72. Mailing Add: 427 Camino del Monte Sol Santa Fe NM 87501

LONGMAN, LESTER DUNCAN
ART HISTORIAN
b Harrison, Ohio, Aug 27, 05. Study: Oberlin Col, AB & MA; Princeton Univ, Carnegie fel, 28-30, MFA, 30, Am Coun Learned Socs fel, 30-32, PhD, 34; Iowa Wesleyan Col, hon LHD, 55; Simpson Col, hon DFA, 61. Teaching: Prof hist art, McMaster Univ, 33-36; prof art & head dept, Univ Iowa, 36-58; prof art, Univ Calif, Los Angeles, 58-, chmn dept, 58-63. Pos: Pres, Midwestern Col Art Conf, 39, 49 & 58; ed, Parnassus, 40 & 41; bd dirs, Col Art Asn Am, 40-42; pres, Am Soc Aesthetics, 53-55. Awards: Fulbright Fel, 52-53. Mailing Add: 718 Enchanted Way Pacific Palisades CA 90272

LONGO, VINCENT
PAINTER, EDUCATOR
b New York, NY, Feb 15, 23. Study: Cooper Union Art Sch, with Leo Katz, Moris Kantor, Delevante, 42-46; Brooklyn Mus Art Sch, with Max Beckman, 49-50. Work: Corcoran Gallery Art, Libr of Cong & Nat Collection Fine Arts, Washington, DC; Whitney Mus Am Art & Mus Mod Art, New York. Exhib: Two Decades of American Prints, Brooklyn Mus, 69; Print Retrospective, 1954-1970, Corcoran Gallery Art & Detroit Inst Arts, 70; Painting Ann, Whitney Mus, 71; American Drawings, Whitney Mus, 73; 20th Nat Print Exhib, Brooklyn Mus, NY, 77. Teaching: Instr printmaking, Brooklyn Mus Art Sch, 55-56; admin asst, Yale Summer Sch Art, 55-59, dir, 69-; instr printmaking, Bennington Col, Vt, 57-67; prof art, Hunter Col, City Univ New York, 67-, chmn dept, 69-70. Pos: Contrib ed, Arts Mag, 55-59. Awards: Fulbright Scholar to Italy, 51; Guggenheim Fel, 72; Nat Endowment Grant, 74. Bibliog: Hilton Kramer (auth), Woodcuts of Vincent Longo, Arts Mag, 4/59; Judith Goldman (auth), Print criteria, Art News, 1/72. Mem: Soc Am Graphic Artists. Style & Technique: Abstract systems dealing with regularity, repetition, center, lattice patterns in paintings, prints, drawings. Media: Intaglio, Relief. Publ: Auth, Picasso in New York, Europ Art This Month, 57; auth, Printmaking today, Arts Mag, 10/58 & auth, Peterdi as printmaker, 12/59, Arts Mag. Mailing Add: 50 Greene St New York NY 10013

LONGSTAFFE, JOHN RONALD
COLLECTOR
b Toronto, Ont, Apr 6, 34. Pos: Pres, Vancouver Art Gallery, 66-68; vchmn, Nat Mus Can, 68-69, dir, 75- Interest: Aid to Vancouver Art Gallery's and National Gallery of Canada's Permanent Collection. Collection: Contemporary Canadian art; contemporary international graphics. Mailing Add: 15th Floor 505 Burrard St Vancouver BC Can

LONGSTREET, STEPHEN
PAINTER, WRITER, ART HISTORIAN
b New York, NY, Apr 17, 07. Study: New York Sch Fine & Appl Art, 27; also with Matisse & Bonnard & sketching with Pascin, Grosz, Arp & Feitelson, Paris, 27-29 & 33-38. Work: San Francisco Mus; Yale Univ; Jazz Mus New Orleans; Los Angeles Art Asn; Mus Mod Art; Memphis Music Mus, Univ Wis; plus others. Exhib: Nu-World Shows, Balbac Gallery, Paris, 40-60; San Francisco Mus Show, 65; Santa Barbara Mus Show, 67; Southern Calif Ann, 70; Paideia Galleries, Los Angeles, 71; plus others. Teaching: Lectr, Los Angeles Art Asn, 50-; prof art, Viewpoints Inst, 65-; lectr mod art, Univ Calif, Los Angeles, 69; lectr, Los Angeles Co Mus; instr at large, Univ Southern Calif, 73-78. Pos: Ed-in-chief, The Great Draftsmen (30 vols), 65-75. Awards: Winader Found First Prize for Watercolor, 30; First Prize for Oils, Am Art Festival, 46; Second Prize for Drawings, Midwest Antiwar Soc, 69. Mem: Los Angeles Art Asn (pres, 72-75); Viewpoints Inst (mem bd dir); Writers Guild Film Soc; Los Angeles Co Mus Art Graphic Soc (co-founder); Paris-Am Arts. Style & Technique: Colored paper collage; pen drawings. Media: Oil, Collage. Collection: Daumier prints; Rowlandson; Goya; Japanese prints. Publ: Auth, A Treasury of the World's Great Prints, 62 & rev ed, 78; auth, Burningman (Picasso), 58; auth, Yoshiwara, 70; auth & illusr, We All Went to Paris, 72; auth, Geisha, Pocket Bks, rev ed, 77. Mailing Add: 1133 Miradero Rd Beverly Hills CA 90210

LONIDIER, FRED SPENCER
CONCEPTUAL ARTIST, PHOTOGRAPHER
b Lakeview, Ore, Feb 19, 42. Study: San Francisco State Col, BA(sociol); Univ Calif, San Diego, MFA; also with David Antin. Exhib: One-man shows, I Sent You a Rose, Ha, Ha, Oakland Mus, Calif, 73-74, Photo Text Works: Toward a New Social Realism, and/or Gallery, Seattle, 75; Photog Exhib, Orlando Gallery, Encino, Calif, 73; Directions 74, Focus Gallery, San Francisco, 74; Southland Video Anthology, Long Beach Mus Art, Calif, 75. Teaching: Lectr photog, Univ Calif, San Diego, 72-75, asst prof, 75- Awards: Regents Fel, Regents of the Univ Calif, 71-72. Bibliog: William Wilson (auth), Art walk, Los Angeles Times, 12/14/73; Thomas Albright (auth), Art photography is out, San Francisco Chronicle, 2/19/74. Mem: Los Angeles Inst Contemp Art; Col Art Asn Am. Style & Technique: Informational, appropriate to a social realist; ad hoc techniques. Media: Photo Prints, Slides & Video. Publ: Contribr, David Antin's eight artists, Studio Int, Vol 170, 70; contribr, Autobiography/history, Los Angeles Inst Contemp Art J, No 7, 75. Mailing Add: 7224 B Fay Ave La Jolla CA 92037

LOOMER, GIFFORD C
EDUCATOR, PAINTER
b Millard, Wis, Nov 29, 16. Study: Northern Iowa Univ, BA; Univ Wis-Whitewater, BEd; Columbia Univ, MA; Univ Wis-Madison, PhD. Exhib: Fifty-six one-man shows in 27 states, 63- Teaching: Instr, High Sch, Iowa, 39-41; instr art, Ball State Univ, 47-49; asst prof art, Eastern Ill Univ, 51-54; prof art, Western Ill Univ, 54-, head dept art, 58-65. Pos: Dir five foreign art tours, Mex & Europe; jurist, State Fair Prof Art Shows, 67-; scholar dir, Kappa Pi Int Hon Art Fraternity; plus jurist other midwest & regional art shows. Awards: Certificate of Merit for Disginguished Service in Studio Art, London, Eng; plus awards in painting, photography, sculpture and commercial art. Mem: Ill Art Educ Asn; Western Arts Asn; life fel Int Asn Arts & Lett. Media: Acrylic, Oil. Publ: Auth, Learning Experiences in Art, 52 & Evaluations in Drawings, 53, Univ Wis; auth, Arts & crafts of Mexico, 63 & auth & illusr, Rubens and Rembrandt in European galleries, 72, Int Sketchbook; auth, Award Winning Art, 75. Mailing Add: 227 Western Ave Macomb IL 61455

LOONEY, NORMAN
PAINTER, INSTRUCTOR
b Seattle, Wash, Oct 31, 42. Study: East Los Angeles Col, Calif, AA; Calif State Col, Long Beach, BA(art); Calif State Univ, Long Beach, MA(drawing & painting). Exhib: One-man shows, Plaza 58 Gallery, Orange, Calif, 74, Robinson Gallery, Houston, Tex, 76 & 78, Southwestern Univ, Georgetown, Tex, 77; Rio Hondo Col, Whittier, Calif, 74; Davidson Nat Print & Drawing Competition, NC, 75; State Capitol, Austin, Tex, 75; Nat Invitational Drawing Exhib, Slocumb Gallery, Tenn, 75; Hunter Mus of Art, Chattanooga, Tenn, 76; Mus of Art, Beaumont, Tex, 76; Art Ctr, San Angelo State Univ, Tex, 76; 11th Dulin Nat Print & Drawing Competition, Knoxville, Tenn, 77; 11th Ann Nat Drawing & Small Sculpture Show, Corpus Christi, Tex, 77; 19th Ann Nat Exhib of Prints & Drawings, Okla Art Ctr, Oklahoma City, 77; The Texas Thirty, Nave Mus, Victoria, Tex, 77; The Tex Arts Alliance Exhib, Univ Tex, Austin, 77; 19th Ann Longview Mus & Art Ctr, Tex, 77. Teaching: Instr painting & drawing, Citrus Col, Azusa, Calif, 74; instr painting & drawing, SW Tex State Univ, San Marcos, 74- Mem: Col Art Asn. Awards: Resident, Yaddo (Trask Found Fel), Saratoga Springs, NY, 77. Style & Technique: Photorealism; textures in large oil paintings and small graphite drawings. Dealer: Robinson Gallery 1100 Bissonnet Houston TX 77005. Mailing Add: 1400 Highland Dr San Marcos TX 78666

LOPEZ, MICHAEL JOHN
CERAMIST
b Los Angeles, Calif, Oct 19, 37. Study: Los Angeles City Col, 56-60; Calif Col Arts & Crafts, BFA & MFA, 63. Work: Oakland Mus, Calif; E B Crocker Art Gallery, Sacramento, Calif. Comn: Leslie Ceramics Supply Co, Berkeley, Calif. Exhib: 18th Nat Decorative Arts & Ceramics Exhib, Wichita Art Asn, Kans, 64; 23rd & 24th Ceramic Nat, Everson Mus Art, Syracuse, NY, 64 & 65 & traveling show, 65; Media 72, a Western State Craft Competition, Civic Arts Gallery, Walnut Creek, Calif, 72; Calif Design 76, Pac Design Ctr, Los Angeles, 76. Teaching: Instr ceramics, Calif Col Arts & Crafts, 65-70; instr ceramics, Diablo Valley Col, 70- Awards: Am Craftsmen Coun Award of Merit, 2nd Biennial Calif Craftsman Exhib, Oakland Mus, 63; First Place Ceramics, Chicago Festival Art, 63; Asn San Francisco Potters Award, 71. Bibliog: Jacinto Quirarte (auth), Mexican American Artists, Univ Tex, 73. Mem: Asn San Francisco Potters. Style & Technique: Abstract landscapes in clay, combination wheel thrown and hand building; low fire glaze with lusters. Media: Clay. Mailing Add: 1031 Walker Ave Oakland CA 94610

LOPEZ, RHODA LE BLANC
SCULPTOR, EDUCATOR
b Detroit, Mich, Mar 16, 12. Study: Detroit Art Acad, Wayne State Univ; Cranbrook Acad Art, with Maija Crotell. Work: Detroit Inst Arts; Univ Wis-Madison; Scripps Col, Claremont, Calif. Comn: Figure of Christ (incised in concrete), Claremont Lutheran Church, 67; two sculpted brick fireplaces, 69 & one high relief fireplace, 70, Sim Bruce Richards; baptismal fountain, University City Lutheran Church, 70; wall fountain, Med Ctr, Dr Larry Fine, 71; mem wall (32ft x 48ft), Unitarian Church, San Diego, 77-78. Exhib: Syracuse Nat, 49-55; Mich Craftsmen Ann, Detroit, 49-58; five shows, Scripps Invitational, 53-66; Allied Craftsmen Ann, San Diego, 60-76; Design 8-11, Pasadena, 65, 68 & 71. Teaching: Instr ceramics, Ann Arbor Potters Guild, Mich, 50-59; instr ceramics, Univ Calif Exten, San Diego, 56-; instr ceramics, La Jolla Mus Art Ctr, 60-65; lectr, Pac Arts Conf, 67; lectr series, San Diego Co Pub Schs, 72. Pos: Med artist, Univ Mich Med Sch, 53-59; founder & dir, Clay Dimensions, San Diego, 69- Bibliog: Rhoda Le Blanc Lopez, Designers West, 71; Valerie Hatch (auth), article in Art West, 71; Marie Stanton (auth), A visit into Rhoda Lopez world of clay, San Diego Union, 1/72. Mem: Allied Craftsmen (pres, 65-68); African Arts Soc (bd dir); Southern Calif Designers Craftsmen; Am Craftsmen's Coun; Calif State Crafts Coun (secy). Media: Clay. Mailing Add: 1020 Pacific Beach Dr San Diego CA 92109

LOPINA, LOUISE CAROL
ILLUSTRATOR, PAINTER
b Chicago, Ill, Nov 24, 36. Study: Chicago Art Inst; Purdue Univ, BS; study with Lawrence Harris. Exhib: Soc of Animal Artists Shows, Grand Cent Galleries Ltd, 71-77, South Vermont Arts Ctr, 73 & Columbus Gallery of Fine Arts, 76; Int Game Coin Conf, 71, 75; Colo Springs Fine Arts Ctr, 74; Major Exhib, Air Univ Libr, Maxwell AFB, Ala, 77. Teaching: Instr drawing & painting, USAF Acad-Officer's Wives Club, 72-75. Pos: Invited illusr, Dayton Chap Nat Audubon Soc, 77- Awards: Best in Show, Purdue Student, 58 & Art Exhib, 59, Purdue Univ. Bibliog: Al Rosen & Faith Every, dirs, Louise Lopinas Animal Art (feature program), television, 2/78. Mem: Soc of Animal Artists. Style & Technique: Realistic, concerned with atmosphere, mood and correct environment. Media: Oil, Line and Wash Drawing. Publ: Illustr, A Cook's Tour of the Airforce Academy Vol II, AFA Officer's Wives Club, 72; illustr, The Complete Old English Sheepdog, Howell Book House, 76; illusr, Reptiles and Amphibians of Aullwood & Wild Flowers of Aullwood, Nat Audubon, 78. Dealer: Mabel Owens Owens Gallery 4 Santa Fe Plaza Oklahoma City OK 73102. Mailing Add: 3102 Maginn Dr Xenia OH 45385

LORAN, ERLE
PAINTER, WRITER
b Minneapolis, Minn, Oct 3, 05. Study: Univ Minn, 22-23; Minneapolis Sch Art, grad, 26; Chaloner Found scholar for study in Europe, 26-30; also with Hans Hofmann, New York, 54. Work: Univ Art Mus, Univ Calif, Berkeley; Krannert Art Mus, Univ Ill, Champaign; Smithsonian Inst, Washington, DC; San Francisco Mus Art; Denver Art Mus. Exhib: Sixteen American Cities, Mus Mod Art, New York, 33; Five shows, Contemporary American Painting, Whitney Mus Am Art, New York, 37-52; American Painting & Sculpture, Art Inst Chicago, 38, Int Exhibs Watercolors, 39-46; Carnegie Inst, Pittsburgh, 41; six shows, Krannert Art Mus, Univ Ill, 49-69. Teaching: Prof art, Univ Calif, Berkeley, 36-, chmn dept art, 52-56. Awards: Bronze Medal, Pepsi-Cola Nat, New York, 48; Artists' Coun Prize, San Francisco Mus Art, 56; Purchase Prize for Imago in Reds, Krannert Art Mus, 65. Bibliog: Forbes Watson (auth), American Painting Today, Am Fedn Arts, 39; Allen S Weller (auth), Contemporary American Painting, Univ Ill, 49-69; Nathaniel Pousette-Dart (auth), American Painting Today, Hastings House, 56. Mem: Univ Calif Arts Club, Berkeley. Media: Acrylic, Oil, Gouache. Publ: Auth, Cézannes Composition, Univ Calif, 43, 70 & 77; auth, Cezanne, Les Peintres Celebres, Ed Art Lucien Mazenod, Geneva & Paris, 48; auth, Trial by juries, Art News, 12/52; auth, Cezanne in 1952, Art Inst Chicago Quart, 2/52; auth, Cezanne and Lichtenstein; problems of transformation, Artforum, 9/63. Mailing Add: 10 Kenilworth Ct Berkeley CA 94707

LORBER, RICHARD
ART WRITER, EDUCATOR
b New York, NY, Dec 9, 46. Study: Columbia Col, BA (lit & art hist), 67, with Meyer Schapiro & Lionel Trilling; Columbia Univ, MA(art hist), 70, with Meyer Schapiro & Linda Nochlin, EdD(art & art educ), 77. Teaching: Instr art hist, Parsons Sch of Design, 74-77; asst prof art & art educ, Grad Sch of Educ, NY Univ, 77- Pos: Ed, Dance Scope Mag, 74-; contribr ed, Arts Mag, 75-; community liaison, Mus of Mod Art, 76-77; critic & contribr, Artforum, 77- Mem: Arts Resources in Collab (founder/dir, 75-77); Dance Critics Asn. Publ: Co-auth, The Gap, McGraw-Hill, 68; auth, articles in Arts in Soc & Filmmakers Newsletter, 77; contribr, Video Art, Dutton, 78. Mailing Add: One Washington Sq Village New York NY 10012

LORBER, STEPHEN NEIL
PAINTER, PRINTMAKER
b New York, NY, Aug 30, 43. Study: Pratt Inst, BFA; Brooklyn Col, MFA; Yale Univ, Stoekel fel, 64. Work: Okla Art Ctr, Oklahoma City; Western NMex Univ, Silver City; Roswell Mus & Art Ctr, NMex; Am Tel & Tel Co; Chase Manhatten Bank, New York. Exhib: Albright-Knox Gallery, Buffalo, NY; Mus Fine Arts, Baltimore, 74; A M Sachs Gallery, New York, 74 & 75; Delahunty Gallery, Dallas, 75; one-man shows, Roswell Mus & Art Ctr, 74, A M Sachs Gallery, 74-77, Delahunty Gallery, Dallas, Tex, 75 & 77 & Schacht Fine Arts Ctr, Russell Sage Col, Troy, NY, 76; Am Drawings 1927-77, Minn Mus Art, St Paul; McNay Art Inst, San Antonio, Tex, 76; Weatherspoon Art Gallery, Univ NC, Greensboro. Awards: Artist in Residence Grant, Roswell Mus & Art Ctr, NMex; Yaddo Fel, 71 & 75; Nat Endowment for the Arts Fel, 76-77. Mailing Add: 87 Franklin St New York NY 10013

LORCINI, GINO
SCULPTOR
b Plymouth, Eng, July 7, 23; Can citizen. Study: Montreal Mus Sch Art. Work: Nat Gallery Can, Ottawa; Mus Art Contemporain, Montreal; Chase Manhattan Bank, New York; Aluminum Co Can, Montreal; Fleming-Hull Mus, Burlington, Vt. Comn: Mural, Nat Arts Ctr, Ottawa, 68; mural, Montreal Forum, PQ, 69; fountain sculpture, Ste Anne's Hosp, PQ, 70; sculpture, Nat Defence Bldg, Ottawa, 72; Ontario Prov Court House, London. Exhib: Op from Montreal, Fleming-Hull Mus, 66; Sculpture 67, Toronto, 67; Surv 68, Montreal, 68; one-man traveling exhib, Atlantic Provinces Mus, Can, 69; 3-D Into the 70's, Art Gallery Ont, Toronto, 70; plus others. Teaching: Asst prof painting & sculpture, McGill Univ, 60-68; resident artist, Univ Western Ont, 69-72. Awards: Jessie Dow Award, Montreal Mus Fine Arts, 65; Arts Award, Can Coun, 68. Bibliog: M Gaulin (auth), Sculptor Lorcini, Time, 68; D Sanders (auth), Gino Lorcini, Bus Quart, 71. Mem: Assoc Royal Can Acad Arts; Nat Sculpture Conf, Univ Kans (mem adv bd). Media: Aluminum, Stainless Steel. Publ: Co-auth, Creative response, McGill J Educ, 67. Mailing Add: 282 Ramsay Rd London ON Can

LORENTZ, PAULINE
PAINTER, INSTRUCTOR
b Newark, NJ. Study: Newark Sch Fine & Indust Arts, NJ, grad; Art Students League; also with John R Grabach. Exhib: Am Artists Prof League Grand Nat, New York, 65, 67-69; Expos Intercontinentale, Monaco & Dieppe, France, 67-68; 24th Am Drawing Biennial, Norfolk Mus Arts & Sci, Va, 71; Nat Exhib, Mus Fine Arts, Springfield, Mass, 71-73; Smithsonian Traveling Exhib, US, 71-73. Teaching: Instr, Summit Art Ctr, NJ, 62-; instr, Art Ctr NJ, Orange, 73- Awards: Gold Medals for Drawing, Catharine Lorillard Wolfe Art Club, 67, 69-70, 72 & 74-75; Am Artists Prof League, 67 & 70 & Arts Atlantic, Gloucester, Mass, 72; plus many others. Bibliog: Philbrook Smith (auth), article in NJ Mus & Arts Mag, 2/64; article in Palette Talk, Vol 32 (1977). Mem: Am Artists Prof League; Catharine Lorillard Wolfe Art Club; Hudson Valley Art Asn, NY; Acad Artists Asn, Mass; Rockport Art Asn, Mass. Style & Technique: Realism; broad, vigorous brush strokes, heavy paint; marine painting and boldly drawn charcoal nudes. Media: Oil, Charcoal. Dealer: Joseph Dawley Gallery 22 North Ave W Cranford NJ 07016; Rauchbach Galleries 1007 Kane Concourse Bay Harbor Island FL 31154. Mailing Add: 20 Southview Dr Berkeley Heights NJ 07922

LORENZANI, ARTHUR EMANUELE
SCULPTOR
b Carrara, Italy, Feb 12, 86; US citizen. Study: Acad Belle Arti, Carrara, grad, 04; Rome Prize & three yr pension. Work: Acad Gallery, Carrara; Golden Age, Brookgreen Gardens; Young Mather; Kinney Direct, Kansas City, Mo. Comn: John F Kennedy (bronze portrait), M Labetti Post Vet Foreign Wars, Staten Island, 64. Exhib: Nat Acad Design, New York; Pa Acad Fine Arts, Philadelphia; Albright-Knox Gallery, Buffalo; Nat Sculpture Soc, New York. Teaching: Instr sculpture, Staten Island Mus, 51-53. Awards: First Prize, City of Parma, Italy; Honorable Mention, Garden Club Am, 29; Spec Silver Medal, Nat Sculpture Soc, 68. Bibliog: B G Proske (auth), Brookgreen Gardens Sculpture. Mem: Fel Nat Sculpture Soc; Allied Artists Am. Media: Bronze, Marble. Publ: Auth & illusr, article in Nat Sculpture Rev, summer 62. Mailing Add: 273 McClean Ave Staten Island NY 10305

LORING, CLARICE
PAINTER, MURALIST
b Vancouver, BC. Study: Vancouver Art Sch, Can; Johannesburg Art Sch, SAfrica; Art Students League; Univ Calif, Santa Barbara, BA(art); Univ Calif, Berkeley, MA(art); Univ Michoacan, Morelai, with Alfredo Salze. Work: Victoria Art Gallery, Can; Ottawa Art Gallery, Can; State Hawaii. Comn: Ceramic tile & aluminum, Aloha Airlines Admin Bldg, 61; acrylic wall mural, Unity Bldg, Honolulu, Hawaii, 66; illuminated Plexiglas (3 units), Ala Moana Hotel, Honolulu, 70. Exhib: Art Festival, Honolulu, 72-74; Artists of Hawaii, Honolulu, 74; Hawaii Painters & Sculptors League, Honolulu, 75. Awards: Prize, Hawaii Watercolor Serigraphy Soc, 75. Mem: Honolulu Acad Arts; Hawaii Painters & Sculptors League (past pres, 65); Honolulu Printmakers. Mailing Add: 1867 Vancouver Dr Honolulu HI 96822

LORING, JOHN
PAINTER, PRINTMAKER
b Chicago, Ill, Nov 23, 39. Study: Yale Univ, BA, 60; Ecole des Beaux Arts, Paris, 61-64; printmaking with Johnny Friedlaender, Paris, 62-64. Work: Mus Mod Art, New York; Art Inst Chicago; Whitney Mus Am Art, New York; Boston Mus Fine Arts; Metrop Mus Art, New York. Comn: 15ft by 26ft mural, US Customs Serv, Main Hall, US Customhouse, World Trade Ctr, New York, 74; three posters, New York Cult Ctr, 74; murals (7500 sq ft), Prudential Life Insurance Co, Eastern Home Off, Woodbridge, NJ, 76; outdoor mural proj, Nat Endowment of the Arts, Scranton, Pa, 77. Exhib: Silkscreen: History of a Medium, Philadelphia Mus Art, 71; Realism Now, New York Cult Ctr, 72; one-man shows, Baltimore Mus Art, 72 & Long Beach Mus Art, Calif, 75; Biennale of Graphic Art, Ljubljana, Yugoslavia, 73 & 77; Intergrafia 74 & 76, Krakow, Poland; Painting & Sculpture Today, Indianapolis Mus Art, 74; Silkscreen Prints, Chicago Art Inst, 75. Teaching: Distinguished vis prof art, Univ Calif, Davis, 77. Pos: Art ed, Deleg World Bull, UN, 72; contribr, Print Collector's Newslett, 73-75; assoc ed & contribr, Arts Mag, 73-; contrib ed, Archit Digest, 76-; contribr, Art in Am, 77- Awards: Fourth Prize, Intergrafia 74, Krakow. Bibliog: Gregory Battcock (auth), New York, Art & Artists, 2/73; Ellen Lubell (auth), John Loring, 2/74 & Mario Amaya (auth), John Loring, 2/78, Arts Mag. Style & Technique: Realist; extensive use of photo halftone screens in both prints and paintings. Media: Oil; Photo Silkscreens. Publ: Auth, Marisol Prints (catalog), New York Cult Ctr, 73; auth, David Hockney: Drawings (catalog), Dayton's Gallery 12, 74; co-auth, Multiples, Neuen Berliner Kunstvereins, 74. Dealer: Pace Gallery 32 E 57th St New York NY 10022. Mailing Add: 143 Prince St New York NY 10012

LORO, ANTHONY PIVOTTO
ART DEALER, PAINTER
b May 6, 34. Study: Escuela Arg de Bellas Artes; Univ Buenos Aires, Arg; Escuela Nac de Ceramica de Buenos Aires, Arg. Comn: The Car (2 meters x 3 meters), Ford Motor Arg, Gral Pacheco, 66; America (4 meters x 4 meters) Com Ctr, Buenos Aires 66; Grafismos (2 meters x 6 meters), Com Ctr, Buenos Aires, 67; Cap Correa (20 ft x 10 ft), 74 & The Education (20 ft x 10 ft), 74, Univ PR. Exhib: Italica Galleries, Montevideo, Uruguay; Galeria J F Kennedy, Asoncion, Paraguay, 67; Inst Latino-Am de Relaciones Int, Asuncion, 69; Staff Art Exhib, Metrop Mus, New York, 71; Mathews Ctr, Ariz State Univ, 71; Yvapai Art Galleries, Prescott, Ariz, 71; Pima Col Galleries, Tucson, Ariz, 71; Ponce Mus of Art, PR, 72. Collections Arranged: Presencia en la Pintura Arg, Plastica Gallery, Buenos Aires, 64; Art Show, Armada Arg, Witcomb Gallery, Buenos Aires, 64; Grande Pintores Nac, 64 & Pro Paz Mundial, 64, Ateneo Popular de Cult, Buenos Aires. Teaching: Art teacher painting & engraving, Aguadilla Art Ctr & Liga de Arte, Arecibo, 76-, US Coast Guard, Base Ramey, Aguadilla, 77- Pos: Dir, Aguadilla Art Ctr, 76- Awards: First Prize & Gold Medal, 47th & 49th Nat, Buenos Aires, Arg Govt, 58 & 60; Grant Prize, Biennal Graphics of Buenos Aires, Arg Inst of Graphic Arts, 67; Caserta Award, Int Competition of Painting, Italy 70. Bibliog: Josefina Pla (auth), Antonio Loro y nuestro paisaje, Comunidad Asuncion, 67; Vicente Gesualdo (auth), Mem: Int Soc of Artists. Style & Technique: Sysbols of the symbolic American past in semi-figurative way. Media: Oil and acrylic; engraving. Publ: Auth & illusr, La Epoca y el artista, 62 & auth, Diferencia entre el arte moderno y el antiquo, 62, Arte Color (in Spanish); auth, Camille Pissarro, el padre del impresionismo, 64 & La rebeldia en el arte y la anarquia libertaria de Matisse, 64, Planteo (in Spanish); auth & ilusr, Picasso creacion y muerte, Ultima (in Spanish), 77. Dealer: Aguadilla Art Ctr Carretera Borinquen Box 3720 Aguadilla PR 00603. Mailing Add: 286 G St Urb Marbella Aguadilla PR 00603

LOTHROP, KRISTIN CURTIS
SCULPTOR
b Tucson, Ariz, Feb 8, 30. Study: Bennington Col, BA; also sculpture with George Demetrois, 4 yrs. Exhib: Nat Sculpture Soc, 67-71; Hudson Valley Art Asn, 68; Nat Acad Design, 68-71; Allied Artists Am, 69. Awards: Mrs Louis Bennett Award, Nat Sculpture Soc, 67; Thomas R Proctor Award, Nat Acad Design, 68, Daniel Chester French Award, 70. Mem: New Eng

Sculptors Asn; Nat Sculpture Soc. Style & Technique: Representative. Media: Bronze, Wood, Stone. Mailing Add: Bridge St Manchester MA 01944

LOTTERMAN, HAL
PAINTER, EDUCATOR
b Chicago, Ill, Sept 29, 20. Study: Univ Ill, BFA, 45; Univ Iowa, MFA, 46. Work: Butler Inst Am Art, Youngstown, Ohio; Akron Art Inst; Ohio Univ; Ball State Univ; Mulvane Art Ctr, Topeka, Kans. Exhib: Metrop Mus Art, New York, 50; Carnegie Inst Int, Pittsburgh, 52; Pa Acad Fine Arts Am, Philadelphia, 53; Nat Acad Design Ann, New York, 54; Art USA 58, New York, 58. Teaching: Instr art, Univ Iowa, 47-50; instr art, Toledo Mus Art, 50-56; prof art, Univ Wis-Madison, 65- Awards: Tiffany Fund Painting Scholar, 51; Univ Iowa Purchase Award, 57. Style & Technique: Photography; innovative style. Media: Oil, Video Tape. Mailing Add: 2337 Atwood Ave Madison WI 53704

LOTTES, JOHN WILLIAM
ART ADMINISTRATOR
b Minneapolis, Minn, Apr 8, 34. Study: Concordia Jr Col, St Paul, Minn, AA, 53; Minneapolis Sch Art, BFA, 60; Die Hochschule Fur Gestaltung, Ulm, Ger, 58-59; Univ Iowa, 67; Minneapolis Col Art & Design, Hon MFA, 73. Teaching: Chmn indust design, Minneapolis Sch Art, 62-63; asst prof indust design, Kansas City Art Inst, 65-66. Pos: Dean col & registr, Kansas City Art Inst, 66-68, pres, 70-; dir planning & develop, Corcoran Gallery & Sch Art, Washington, DC, 68-69; asst to pres acad affairs, Calif Col Arts & Crafts, Oakland, 69-70. Mem: Nat Asn Schs Art (bd dirs, 72-); Union Independent Cols Art (bd dirs, 70-, chmn bd, 76-). Mailing Add: 6108 Morningside Dr Kansas City MO 64113

LOUGHEED, ROBERT ELMER
ILLUSTRATOR, PAINTER
b Gray Co, Ont, May 7, 10. Study: Ont Col Art; Ecole de Beaux Arts, Montreal; also with Frank Vincent Dumond & Dean Cornwell. Comn: Flying Red Horse, Mobil Oil; comn by US Post Off to do a Buffalo stamp for their wildlife series. Exhib: One-man show, Continental Gallery, Montreal. Awards: Gold Medal for Watercolor and Gold Medal for Mixed Media at Cowboy Artists of Am Show, Phoenix, 74; Gold Medal for Watercolor, Royal Western Watercolor Show, 75; Silver Medal for Watercolor, Cowboy Artist Show, 75; plus numerous others. Publ: Covers for Reader's Digest & many other mags & calendars. Mailing Add: Rte 3 Box 126 Old Santa Fe Trail Santa Fe NM 87501

LOUGHLIN, JOHN LEO
PAINTER, LECTURER
b Worcester, Mass, Apr 11, 31. Study: Worcester Art Mus Sch; Clark Univ, AB, 57; Bridgewater State Col, EdM, 64; also with Eliot O'Hara, Edgar Whitney & Barse Miller. Work: M & M Karolik Collection, Boston Mus Fine Art; Cumberland RI Housing for Elderly; Old Colony Savings Bank, Providence, RI; US Naval War Col, Newport, RI; Gen Elec Corp, Schenectady, NY. Exhib: Boston Arts Festival, 55; Acad Artists Show, Springfield, Mass, 59; Bristol Art Mus Show, RI, 70; Am Watercolor Soc, Nat Acad Design Galleries, New York, 71; Providence Art Club Open Watercolor Show, 72. Teaching: Pvt instr, 69-; vis lectr watercolor, Providence Col, 70-72. Pos: Illusr cartogr, Nat Geog Mag, 58-59; head dept art, US Naval War Col, 61-68; art dir, WSBE-TV, Providence, 68- Awards: W Alden Brown Mem Award, Providence Watercolor Club, 69; C Gordon Harris Award, 71; F S Beveridge Mem Award, Acad Artists, 74. Bibliog: Watercolor, WSBE-TV, 69. Mem: Assoc Am Watercolor Soc; Providence Art Club; Providence Watercolor Club (vpres, 70-72, pres, 72); artist mem Rockport Art Asn. Style & Technique: Traditional, transparent watercolor. Publ: Illusr, Nat Geog Mag, 58; illusr, Mass Wildlife Mag, 59; contribr & illusr, Salt Water Sportsman Mag, 59; illusr, Naval Rev, 67; illusr, New Eng Sch Develop Coun Publ. Dealer: Limerock Studio/Gallery Lincoln RI 02865. Mailing Add: 124 Angell Rd Lincoln RI 02865

LOURIE, HERBERT S
PAINTER, EDUCATOR
b Boston, Mass, Dec 26, 23. Study: Ind Univ; Yale Univ, BFA & MFA. Work: Munson-Williams-Proctor Inst, Utica, NY. Exhib: Wadsworth Atheneum; Farnsworth Mus; Fitchburg Art Mus; Currier Gallery Art; Inst Contemp Arts, Boston; plus many others. Teaching: Asst prof art, Nasson Col, 52-55; vis lectr, Univ NH, 53-54; instr, Univ RI, 56-58; asst prof art, Elmira Col, 58-61; assoc prof art, Keene State Col, 66-74, prof, 74- Awards: Prize, Currier Gallery Art, 55; Pruchase Prize, Arnot Art Gallery, 61. Mem: Col Art Asn Am; NH Art Asn. Mailing Add: Dept of Art Keene State Col Keene NH 03431

LOVATO, CHARLES FREDRIC
PAINTER
b Santa Fe, NMex, May 23, 37. Work: Heard Mus, Phoenix; Philbrook Art Ctr, Tulsa, Okla. Exhib: Scottsdale Nat, Ariz, 68; Heard Mus, Phoenix, 69; Washington, DC Biennial, 69; Gallup Inter-Tribal Ceremonial, NMex, 72. Awards: Most Outstanding Painting, Dr Avery, Pecos, Tex, 70 & 71; Best Artist-Best Painting, Philbrook Art Ctr, 71. Media: Acrylic. Mailing Add: Sile Star Rte 72 Pena Blanca NM 87041

LOVATO, MANUELITA
INSTRUCTOR, MUSEOLOGIST
b Santo Domingo Pueblo, NMex, Sept 5, 45. Study: Inst Am Indian Arts, 64-66; Univ Colo, (mus training). Work: Inst Am Indian Arts, Santa Fe; Mus de la Cult, Mexico City. Exhib: Ceramic Sculpture, Edinburgh Festival, Scotland, 66, Berlin Festival, Horniman Mus, London, 66, Mus Bellas Artes, Buenos Aires, 68, Nac Libr, Santiago, Chile, 68 & Horniman Mus, London, Ger, 70. Collections Arranged: Travel exhib, Smithsonian Inst, installed Museo de la Cultura; Laura Gilpin's Retrospective Show, installed Inst Am Indian Arts; Eskimo and other Case Exhibits, installed St Joseph Mus, Mo. Teaching: Asst prof casting techniques, Univ Colo, 68; instr exhib arts, Inst Am Indian Arts, 70-, instr curatorial functions, 70; workshops at Antioch Col, 72, Okla Liberal Arts Col, 73 & Univ Ariz, 74. Awards: Study Fel to Mex, Orgn Am States, Washington, DC, 73. Mem: Am Asn Mus; Southwestern Anthrop Asn; Antropologia Mex Asn. Mailing Add: Inst Am Indian Arts Santa Fe NM 87501

LOVE, FRANCES TAYLOR
MUSEUM DIRECTOR, WRITER
b Salina, Kans, Apr 25, 26. Study: Univ Tex, BA(journalism & speech); studied television writing, Univ Houston; sem in Gt Brit & other Europ study, Smithsonian Inst. Collections Arranged: Steamboats Along the Louisiana Bayous (auth, catalogue), 69, 19th Century Painters in Louisiana (auth, catalogue), 72, Louisiana French Furnishings: 1750-1830 (ed, catalogue), 74, Haitian Voodoo Art (auth, catalogue), 76 & Victorian Decorative Arts in Louisiana (auth, catalogue), 77, Art Ctr for Southwestern La. Pos: Pub relations dir, Lafayette Art Asn, 60-63; dir, Art Ctr for Southwestern La, Lafayette, 65- Res: Louisiana colonial decorative arts; Texas and Louisiana decorative art and architecture; Victorian decorative art. Publ: Auth & ed, My Home is Austin, Texas, 58 & Here is South Louisiana, 65, Tribune Press. Mailing Add: PO Box 51998 Lafayette LA 70503

LOVE, IRIS CORNELIA
ART HISTORIAN
b New York, NY. Study: Smith Col, BA; Univ Firenze, Italy; Inst Fine Arts, NY Univ; Dowling Col, Hon LittD, 71. Teaching: Instr Greek & Roman art, Cooper Union, 63 & Smith Col, 64-65; asst prof art hist & archaeol, Long Island Univ, 66-67, res asst prof, 67-; instr & coordr three lect series, NY Univ Sch Continuing Studies, 68-70; instr community educ, Hofstra Univ, 69; distinguished Froman Prof, Russell Sage Col, 72; Robert Sterling Clark lectr art hist, Williams Col, 73. Pos: Staff mem, Archaeol Exped to Island of Samothrace, New York Inst Fine Arts, 55-65; collabr with Dir Brit Sch in Rome, evcavation of Quattro Fontanile, Isola Farnese, Italy, 61; dir, Archaeol Exped to Knidos, Turkey, Long Island Univ, 67- Mem: Archaeol Inst Am; Am Asn Univ Prof; Soc Women Geographers; Turkish-Am Soc. Res: Archaeology; Greek and Roman art; art history. Publ: Auth, Greece, Gods & Art, Viking Press, 68; contribr to Bollingen Series, Marsyas, Am J Archaeol, Anatolian Studies & others. Mailing Add: 113 Willow St Brooklyn Heights New York NY 11201

LOVE, JIM
SCULPTOR
b Amarillo, Tex, 1927. Exhib: Dallas Mus Contemp Art; Mus Mod Art, New York; Mus Fine Arts, Houston; Whitney Mus Am Art, New York; Contemp Arts Mus, Houston; plus others. Dealer: Janie C Lee Gallery 2304 Bissonnet Houston TX 77005. Mailing Add: 5009 Blossom Houston TX 77007

LOVE, JOSEPH
PAINTER
b Worcester, Mass, 1929. Study: Col of the Holy Cross; Boston Col, MA; Sophia Univ, Japan; Columbia Univ. Work: Metrop Mus Art, New York; Art Inst Chicago; Allentown Art Mus, Pa; New York Pub Libr; Southern Ill Univ. Exhib: One-man shows, St Louis Univ, 63 & Alonzo Gallery, 67; Japan Print Asn Ann, 63 & 64; Hijiyama Hall, Hiroshima, Japan, 65; Col of the Holy Cross, 65; Minami Gallery, Tokyo, 72. Teaching: Instr art, Sophia Univ, Japan, 56- Publ: Contribr, Artnews & Art Int. Mailing Add: c/o Alonzo Gallery 30 W 57th St New York NY 10019

LOVE, PAUL VAN DERVEER
GALLERY DIRECTOR, ART HISTORIAN
b Long Branch, NJ, Aug 1, 08. Study: Princeton Univ, BA; Univ Pa, Am Inst Architects scholar, 45; NY Univ, scholar, 48; Columbia Univ, fel, 48, PhD, 50. Exhib: Ala Watercolor Soc, 53; Kresge Art Ctr Gallery, East Lansing, Mich, 71; 15th Nat Exhib, Fall River, Mass, 72; Butler Inst Art, Youngstown, Ohio, 72; Galeria San Miguel, Mex, 74-75; plus others. Collections Arranged: The Turn of the Century; American Nineteenth Century Painting, 66; Earl Kerkam: Paintings and Drawings, 72. Teaching: Prof Am, mod & pre-Columbian art, Mich State Univ, 53-66, prof mus training, 70-74, emer prof, 74- Pos: Dir, Kresge Art Ctr Gallery, 63-74; ed, Kresge Art Ctr, Bull, 67-74. Publ: Auth, Modern Dance Terminology, 53; co-auth, An Introduction to Literature and Fine Arts, 53; auth, Patterned Brickwork in Southern New Jersey, 55. Mailing Add: 2233 N 87th Way Scottsdale AZ 85257

LOVE, RICHARD HENRY
ART DEALER, ART WRITER
b Schneider, Ind, Dec 27, 39. Study: Univ of Md, Europe; Bloom Col, Chicago Heights, Ill; Univ of Ill, Chicago; Northwestern Univ, Evanston, Ill; Villa Schifanoia, Florence, Italy; independent study in Europe. Comn: Murals, Flak Kaserne Bldg, US Army, Augsburg, Ger, 62 & Dorchester Club, Ramada Inn, Dalton, Ill, 65. Teaching: Prof art hist, Prairie State Col, Chicago Heights, Ill. Pos: Art critic, Star-Tribune Publ, Chicago Heights; art commentator, WEFM Radio & Channel 26 Television; pres & owner, R H Love Galleries, Chicago. Style & Technique: Conceptual realism. Media: Oil. Res: French impressionism and impressionist, Pierre Prins; American impressionists, Theodore Earl Butler, Louis Ritman, Walter Griffin, Harriet Randall Lumis; John Barber. Specialty: Eighteenth and nineteenth century American. Publ: Auth, John Barber, 75, The Paintings of Louis Ritman (1889-1963), 75, Theodore Earl Butler (1860-1936), 75 & Pastels by Pierre Prins, 76, Signature Galleries; auth, Dictionary of American Impressionists: 1874-1917, R H Love Galleries, 78. Mailing Add: c/o R H Love Galleries 320 S Michigan Ave Chicago IL 60604

LOVE, ROSALIE BOWEN
PAINTER, INSTRUCTOR
b Jamestown, NY. Study: Jepson Art Sch; also with Karl Seethaler, Hayward Veal, Will Foster, J Thompson Pritchard, Bennett Bradbury & Paul Puzinas. Work: De Grimm Gallery, Detroit; Chautauqua Art Inst, NY; Fri Morning Club, Severance Salon, Los Angeles. Comn: Christ Mural, Come unto Me, Christ Church, Unity, Los Angeles, 72; portrait of Dr Norman Brill, Univ Calif, Los Angeles, 78. Exhib: Nat Orange Show, San Bernardino, Calif, 67; Frye Mus, Seattle, 68, Chautauqua, NY, 68; Tucson, Ariz, 69; Wilshire Ebell, Los Angeles, 72. Teaching: Free-lance art instr portraiture, 55- Awards: First Award, Wilshire Fed Gallery, Beverly Hills, 69; Gold Medal Award, Calif Art Club, 76; Shadow Mountain Palette Club Sweepstakes Award, 78. Mem: Life mem Am Inst Fine Arts (bd dirs, 67-68); Calif Art Club; Valley Artist Guild (bd dirs, 65-67); Laguna Beach. Media: Oil. Mailing Add: 75-365 Purple Hills Rd Indian Wells CA 92260

LOVELESS, JIM
EDUCATOR, PAINTER
b Saginaw, Mich, Apr 24, 35. Study: DePauw Univ, AB, 57, with Winsey, French & Boone; Ind Univ, MFA, 60, with Leon Golub, James McGarrell & Rudy Pozzatti. Work: Munson-Williams-Proctor Inst, Utica, NY; Itaca Col Mus of Art, NY; Oneida Valley Nat Bank, Hamilton, NY; Chase Manhattan Bank, New York. Exhib: Munson-Williams-Proctor Inst Ann, Utica; Grand Rapids Mus of Art Ann, Mich, 62; Ithaca Col Mus of Art, NY, 68; one-man shows, Olivet Col, Mich & Univ Ky, Lexington, 64, Picker Gallery, Colgate Univ & Southern Conn State Col, New Haven, 69, Root Art Ctr, Clinton, NY, 72, Herbert H Lehman Col, Bronx, NY & Little Gallery, Memphis State Univ, 74, Art Inst of Pittsburgh, 76, Kalamazoo Col, Mich & Everson Mus, Syracuse, NY, 77. Teaching: Asst prof studio & art hist, Hope Col, Holland, Mich, 60-64 & Univ Ky, Lexington, 64-66; prof studio & art hist, Colgate Univ, Hamilton, 66- Awards: Heffner Award, Grand Rapids Mus of Art Ann, 62. Mem: Col Art Asn. Style & Technique: Landscapes. Media: Watercolor and acrylic; poured acrylic lacquer and enamel on masonite panels. Mailing Add: 31 Madison St Hamilton NY 13346

LOVELL, TOM
PAINTER, ILLUSTRATOR
b New York, NY, Feb 5, 09. Study: Syracuse Univ, BFA. Work: New Britain Mus, Conn; Explorers Club, New York; US Marine Corps Hq, Washington, DC; US Merchant Marine

Acad, King's Point, NY; Nat Cowboy Hall of Fame, Oklahoma City; plus others. Comn: Series of hist paintings, US Marine Corps, 45; painting of Civil War, Life Mag, 61; series of hist paintings, Nat Geog Soc, Washington, DC, 65-68; series of hist paintings, Abell-Hanger Found, 69-73. Exhib: Soc Illustrators, New York, 63; one-man show, Syracuse Univ Centennial, Lubin House, 70; Nat Cowboy Hall of Fame, 73-75. Awards: Gold Medal for Portfolio of Western Art, Franklin Mint, 74; Silver Medal, Cowboy Artists of Am, 75, Gold Medals, 76 & 77; Gold Medal, Nat Acad Western Art Show, 76; plus others. Bibliog: Norman Kent (auth), Tom Lovell & his work, Am Artists. Mem: Soc Illustrators; Cowboy Artists Am; Nat Acad Western Art. Style & Technique: Western; traditional. Media: Oil. Publ: Auth, Persimmon Hill, Nat Cowboy Hall of Fame, Oklahoma City. Mailing Add: 3 Tano Rd RR 4 Santa Fe NM 87501

LOW, JOSEPH
PAINTER, PRINTMAKER
b Coraopolis, Pa, Aug 11, 11. Study: Univ Ill, 30-32; Art Students League, 35, with George Grosz. Work: Princeton Univ; Harvard Univ; Libr Cong; Va Mus Fine Arts; San Francisco Pub Libr; plus many others. Exhib: Boston Mus Fine Arts; New York Pub Libr; Metrop Mus Art, New York; Herron Inst Art, Indianapolis; Philadelphia Mus Art; plus many others. Media: Watercolor, Graphics. Mailing Add: Cruz Bay St John VI 00830

LOWE, HARRY
ART ADMINISTRATOR, DESIGNER
b Opelika, Ala, Apr 9, 22. Study: Auburn Univ, BA, 43, MFA, 49; Cranbrook Acad Art, 51 & 53. Collections Arranged: Stuart Davis Memorial, Nat Collection Fine Arts, Washington, DC, Art Inst Chicago, Univ Calif Art Galleries, Los Angeles & Whitney Mus Am Art, New York, 65; The Charles Sheeler Exhibition, Philadelphia Mus Art & Whitney Mus Am Art, 69. Teaching: Prof art, Auburn Univ, 49-59; fac, Sem for Hist Adminrs, Williamsburg, Va, 65, 67-71. Pos: Dir, Tenn Fine Arts Ctr, Nashville, 59-64; cur, Dept Exhib & Design, Nat Collection Fine Arts, 64-72, asst dir opers, 72-74, asst dir, 74- Mem: Am Asn Mus; Nat Trust Hist Preserv; Col Art Asn Am; Skowhegan Sch Painting & Sculpture (mem adv comt). Mailing Add: Nat Collection Fine Arts Eighth & G Sts Washington DC 20560

LOWE, J MICHAEL
SCULPTOR, EDUCATOR
b Cincinnati, Ohio, Aug 18, 42. Study: Ohio Univ, BFA; Cornell Univ, MFA. Work: Butler Inst Am Art, Youngstown, Ohio; Tyler Mus Art, Tex; State Univ NY Col Potsdam; Cornell Univ; St Lawrence Univ (NY). Exhib: Butler Inst Am Art Ann, 64, 71 & 72; Artists of Central New York, Munson-Williams-Proctor Inst, Utica, NY, 65, 67-69 & 71; Tyler Mus Art, 67, 69 & 70; Ball State Univ, 67 & 72; Sculpture 75, Philadelphia, 75; Sculpture Now, Inc, New York, 78; plus others. Teaching: Instr fine arts, St Lawrence Univ, 66-67, asst prof, 67-72, chmn dept, 71-, assoc prof, 72- Awards: Inez D'Amanda Barnell Award for Sculpture, Rochester Mem Art Gallery, 66; Purchase Awards, Tyler Mus Art, 70, Butler Inst Am Art, 72 & Clinton Co Govt Bldg, 76. Mem: Col Art Asn Am. Media: Welded Metal. Mailing Add: Dept of Fine Arts St Lawrence Univ Canton NY 13617

LOWE, JOE HING
PAINTER, INSTRUCTOR
b Canton, China, Sept 15, 34; US citizen. Study: With Lajos Markos & Dan Greene. Work: USN Combat Artist Gallery, Washington, DC; USN Air Sta, Lakehurst, NJ; Switlik Parachute Co, NJ. Comn: Portraits, comn by Rep John M Murphy, 65, Adm C E Rosendahl, 67, Adm Arleigh Burke, 70 & Adm Arnold Frederic Schade, 71. Exhib: Springfield Mus, 68; Am Watercolor Soc, Nat Acad Design Galleries, 69; Hudson Valley Art Asn, 72; Am Artists Prof League, 72; Salmagundi Club, 72. Teaching: Instr, Metrop Portrait Studio, 64-; instr, Big Six Art League, 70- Awards: Dumont Mem Fund Award for Pastel Portrait, Salmagundi Club, 69; Sterling Silver Award, Nat Art Club, 69; Mary Spreadling Mem Award, 70. Bibliog: Rep John M Murphy, Journal Am, Brooklyn Sect, 5/12/65; Jack Besterman (auth), article in Big Six Chapel & Pensioners News, 2/72. Mem: Salmagundi Club; Am Artists Prof League; Hudson Valley Art Asn; Artists Fel; Knickerbocker Artists; plus one other. Media: Oil, Pastel, Watercolor, Charcoal. Publ: Contribr, How to Do Portraits in Pastel, 72; contribr, Palette Talk, 72. Dealer: C C Price Gallery 15 E 48th St New York NY 10017. Mailing Add: 147-15 84th Dr Jamaica NY 11435

LOWE, MARVIN
PRINTMAKER, PAINTER
b Brooklyn, NY, May 19, 27. Study: Juilliard Sch Mus; Brooklyn Col, BA, 54; Univ Iowa, with Mauricio Lasansky, MFA, 60. Work: Libr Cong, Washington, DC; Brooklyn Mus; New York Pub Libr; Am Embassy, London, Eng; Nat Collection Fine Arts, Smithsonian Inst. Exhib: America-Japan Contemporary Print Exhibit, Tokyo, 67; Brooklyn Mus Nat Print Exhib, 67; Graphics, 1968; Recent American Prints, Univ Ky, 68; 1st Hawaii Nat Print Exhib, Honolulu, 71; US Info Exhib, Europe, Latin Am & Orient, 74-75; plus others. Teaching: Prof printmaking, Ind Univ, Bloomington, 68- Awards: Paul J Sachs Purchase Award, Boston Printmakers, 65; Lessing J Rosenwald Purchase Prize, Philadelphia Print Club, 66; Nat Endowment Arts Grant, 74-75; plus others. Mem: Soc Am Graphic Artists; Boston Printmakers; Philadelphia Print Club; Soc Washington Printmakers. Style & Technique: Non-objective; painted reliefs. Media: Intaglio, Silk Screen. Dealer: Zriny-Hayes Gallery 2044 N Halsted Chicago IL 60614; DuBose Gallery 2950 Kirby Houston TX 77098. Mailing Add: Dept of Fine Arts Ind Univ Bloomington IN 47401

LOWINSKY, SIMON L
ART DEALER
b Black Mountain, NC, Nov 19, 45. Pos: Owner, Phoenix Gallery, San Francisco. Specialty: American and European 20th century photography, prints, paintings and sculpture. Mailing Add: c/o Simon Lowinsky Gallery 228 Grant Ave 6th Floor San Francisco CA 94108

LOWNEY, BRUCE STARK
PAINTER, PRINTMAKER
b Los Angeles, Calif, Oct 16, 37. Study: NTex State Univ, BA; San Francisco State Univ, MA; Univ NMex, asst to Garo Antreasian; Tamarind Lithography Workshop. Work: Minneapolis Inst Art; Art Inst Chicago; Art Mus Univ NMex, Albuquerque; Oklahoma City Art Ctr; Libr Cong Collection, Washington, DC; plus others. Exhib: Whitney Mus Am Art Print Exhib, New York, 70; one-man shows, Martha Jackson Gallery, New York, 71, Hills Gallery, Santa Fe, 73 & Univ NDak, Grand Forks, 74; 23rd Nat Exhib Prints, Libr Cong, 73; plus others. Awards: Louis Comfort Tiffany Found Graphics Art Award, 69; Artist in Residence Grant, Roswell Mus & Art Ctr, 70; Nat Endowment Arts Grant, 74. Style & Technique: Supra-realism. Media: Oil, Lithography. Dealer: Martha Jackson Gallery 32 E 69th St New York NY 10021. Mailing Add: PO Box 1351 Grants NM 87020

LOWRY, BATES
ART HISTORIAN, ART CRITIC
b Cincinnati, Ohio, June 21, 23. Study: Univ Chicago, PhB, 44, MA, 53, PhD, 56. Teaching: Asst prof art, Univ Calif, Riverside, , 54-57; asst prof art, Inst Fine Arts, NY Univ, 57-59; prof art & chmn dept, Pomona Col, 59-63; prof art & chmn dept, Brown Univ, 63-67; mem, Inst Advan Study, 71; prof art & chmn dept, Univ Mass, Boston, 71- Pos: Ed, Monogr Series, Col Art Asn, 59-62, 64-67; ed, Art Bull, 64-68; dir, Mus Mod Art, New York, 68-69. Awards: RI Gov's Award for Contribution to Arts, 67; Grand Off, Star of Solidarity, Italy, 68; Guggenheim Fel, 71. Mem: Soc Archit Historians (bd dirs, 60-62, 64-66); Art Historians Southern Calif (pres, 61-63); Comt to Rescue Italian Art (co-founder, chmn nat exec comt, 66-); Am Fedn Arts (trustee, 69-71); Dunlap Soc (pres, 74-). Publ: Auth, The Visual Experience, 61; auth, Renaissance Architecture, 62; auth, Architecture of Washington, DC, 77; auth, articles in Art Bull & Col Art J. Mailing Add: Essex NY 12936

LOY, JOHN SHERIDAN
PAINTER
b St Louis, Mo, Nov 4, 30. Study: Colorado Springs Fine Art Ctr, Colo; Wash Univ Sch Fine Arts, BFA, 54; Cranbrook Acad Art, Bloomfield Hills, Mich, MFA, 58. Work: Munson-Williams-Proctor Inst, Utica, NY; Utica Col, NY; Lincoln-Rochester Bank Collection, Rochester, NY; Hayes Nat Bank, Clinton, NY; Savings Bank Utica. Exhib: Mo Show, St Louis City Art Mus, 59; Artists Cent NY, Munson-Williams-Proctor Inst, 60-70; Albany Inst Hist & Art Regional, NY, 69; Everson Mus Regional, Syracuse, NY, 70; Cooperstown Art Asn Ann, NY, 71. Teaching: Instr drawing, Wash Univ, 59; instr drawing & painting, Munson-Williams-Proctor Inst, 60- Pos: Prog dir, Peoples Art Ctr, St Louis, 59. Awards: Painting Award, St Louis City Art Mus, 59; First Painting Prize, Cooperstown Art Asn, 71, 74, 76 & 77; Best in Show Award, Arena 77 Exhib, Binghamton, NY. Style & Technique: Hard-edge abstract style using flat shapes and colors. Media: Oil. Mailing Add: 602 Tracy St Utica NY 13502

LUBBERS, LELAND EUGENE
SCULPTOR, EDUCATOR
b Stoughton, Wis, June 6, 28. Study: St Louis Univ, AB, MA, PhL & STL; Univ Paris, Docteur de l'Universite de Paris; Acad Grande Chaumiere, Paris, France. Work: Duchesne Col, Omaha, Nebr; Sheldon Gallery, Univ Nebr, Lincoln; Seattle Opera Asn, Wash; Art in Embassies Prog, US State Dept; Jacksonville Art Mus, Fla. Comn: Outdoor fountain, City of Omaha, 69; sculptured constructions (with Larry Austin), for centennial exhib at Albright-Knox Art Gallery for Canisius Col, Buffalo, NY, 70; crucifix group (wrought iron), St John's Church, Omaha. Exhib: One-man shows, Automated Junk Sculpture Exhib, Sheldon Gallery, Univ Nebr, Lincoln, 65, Jacksonville Art Mus, 67 & Frye Art Mus, Seattle, 68; Ward-Nasse Gallery, New York, 74 & 77; Sheldon Gallery, Lincoln, 74-77; SW State Univ, Marshall, Minn, 77. Teaching: Instr Latin, speech & Eng, Creighton Prep Sch, Omaha, 53-56, instr French, German & art, 63-65; assoc prof fine arts, founder & head dept, Creighton Univ, 65- Pos: Dir, Nebr Arts Coun, Omaha, 66-72; pres, Omaha Civic Ballet Asn, 68-70, dir, 70-; pres, Omaha Acad Ballet Bd, 69-72. Bibliog: Robert Reilly (auth), Jesuit junkman, Critic Mag, 2-3/68; John Wain (auth), To Lee Lubbers in Omaha, In: Letters to Five Artists, Viking, 70; Larry Austin (auth), Caritas: symphony of the gigantic hammered welded aluminum imitation earth volumes, Source, 11/70. Mem: Asn Int des Docteurs (lettres) de l'Universite de Paris; Nebr Art Educ Asn; Assoc Artists Omaha. Style & Technique: Hammered iron and logs. Style & Technique: Metals. Publ: Auth, L'image publicitaire actuelle et ses origines, Univ Paris, 63. Dealer: Ward-Nasse Gallery 178 Prince St New York NY 10012. Mailing Add: Fine Arts Dept Creighton Univ 2400 California St Omaha NE 68131

LUBNER, MARTIN PAUL
PAINTER
b New York, NY, Dec 26, 29. Study: Univ Calif, Los Angeles, BA, 52, MA, 53, with Clinton Adams, Gordon Nunes & Jan Stussy. Work: Tate Gallery, London; Los Angeles Co Mus Art; Mus Mod Art, Israel; Neuberger Mus, State Univ NY Col, Purchase; Kettering Mus, Eng. Exhib: Los Angeles Co Mus Art Ann, 56, 57 & 59; Spoleto Int, Italy, 63-64. Teaching: Instr painting & drawing, Univ Calif Exten, 56-; instr painting & drawing, Univ Calif, Los Angeles, 64; instr painting & drawing, Univ Southern Calif, 68; tutor, Royal Col Art, London, 74-75; instr, Col Creative Studies, Univ Calif, Santa Barbara, 75. Dealer: Crane Kalman Gallery 178 Brompton Rd London England. Mailing Add: 916 Stonehill Lane Los Angeles CA 90049

LUCAS, CHARLES C, JR
COLLECTOR
b Charlotte, NC, Mar 4, 39. Study: Duke Univ, BA. Pos: Trustee, Mint Mus Art, Charlotte, 67-68; controller, Juilliard Sch, New York, 68- Mem: Am Asn Mus. Collection: American art—Ashcan School, abstract and realist contemporary painting and sculpture; pre-Columbian. Mailing Add: c/o Juilliard Sch Lincoln Ctr Plaza New York NY 10023

LUCCHESI, BRUNO
SCULPTOR
b Lucca, Italy, July 31, 26; US citizen. Study: Inst Arte, Lucca, MFA, 53. Work: Pa Acad Fine Arts, Philadelphia; Dallas Mus Fine Arts; Ringling Mus, Sarasota, Fla; Hirshhorn Mus, Washington, DC; Whitney Mus Am Art, New York. Comn: Sculpture for Trade Bank, New York & Willard Strait Hall, Cornell Univ. Exhib: Whitney Mus Am Art, New York; Pa Acad Fine Arts; Corcoran Gallery Art, Washington, DC; Nat Inst Arts & Lett; Brooklyn Mus, NY; plus others. Teaching: Instr, Acad Fine Arts, Univ Florence, Italy, 52-57; instr, New Sch Social Res, 62- Awards: Watrous Gold Medal, Nat Acad Design, 61; Gold Medal, Nat Arts Club, 63; S F B Morse Medal, Nat Acad Design, 65; plus others. Mem: Sculptors Guild; Artists Equity Asn; Nat Acad Design; Am Asn Univ Prof. Dealer: Forum Gallery 1018 Madison Ave New York NY 10021. Mailing Add: 14 Stuyvesant St New York NY 10003

LUCIONI, LUIGI
PAINTER, ETCHER
b Malnate, Italy, Nov 4, 00; US citizen. Study: Cooper Union Eve Sch, 16-20; Nat Acad Design, 20-25; also with William Starkwether, 18-25. Work: Pears with Pewter, Metrop Mus Art, New York; Two Willows & Jo, Whitney Mus Am Art; Rose Hobart, Pa Acad Fine Arts, Philadelphia; Vermont Pastoral, Carnegie Inst, Pittsburgh. Exhib: Carnegie Inst Int; Art Inst Chicago; Venice Biennale, Italy; Pa Acad Fine Arts; Corcoran Gallery Art Biennial, Washington, DC; 75th Anniversary Exhib of Complete Etchings, Assoc Am Artists, New York, 76. Teaching: Instr portrait painting, Art Students League, 32-33. Awards: First Popular Prize, Carnegie Inst Int, 39; First Popular Prize, Corcoran Biennial, 47-49; Purchase Prize, Nat Acad Design, 57. Bibliog: The Art of Luigi Lucioni (film), Vt Educ TV, 68. Dealer: Milch Gallery 1014 Madison Ave New York NY 10021. Mailing Add: 33 W Tenth St New York NY 10011

LUCK, ROBERT
EDUCATOR, CURATOR
b Tonawanda, NY, Oct 31, 21. Study: Univ Buffalo, BFA, 47; Harvard Univ, MA, 49; Inst Meschini, Rome, Italy, cert painting, 50. Teaching: Instr, Toledo Mus Art, 52-54; teacher art hist, Parsons Sch Design, 73- Pos: Cur, Cincinnati Art Mus, 54-55; dir, Akron Art Inst, 55-56; dir, Telfair Acad Arts & Sci, Savannah, Ga, 56-57; asst dir, Am Fedn Arts, 58-72; cur, Contemp Wing, Finch Col Mus Art, 73- Mem: Am Asn Mus; Col Art Asn Am. Mailing Add: 150 E 27th St New York NY 10016

LUCKNER, KURT T
CURATOR
b Stafford Springs, Conn, Dec 29, 45. Study: Georgetown Univ, AB(art hist); Stanford Univ, MA(art hist). Exhibitions Arranged: Silver for the Gods: 800 Years of Greek and Roman Silver (int loan exhib), Toledo Mus Art, Ohio, Nelson Gallery, Kansas City, Mo & Kimbell Mus Art, Ft Worth, Tex, 77-78. Pos: Asst cur ancient art, Stanford Univ Mus, summer 69; curatorial asst, Toledo Mus Art, Ohio, 69-70, asst cur, 70-73, cur ancient art, 73- Mem: Col Art Asn; Archaeol Inst Am (pres, Toledo Chap, 71-75). Publ: Auth, Art of Egypt-part I, Vol 14, No 1 & II, Vol 15, No 3, auth, Greek vases: shapes & uses, Vol 15, No 3, auth, African art, Vol 16, No 2 & auth, Greek gold jewlery, Vol 17, No 1, Mus News; co-auth, Corpus Vasorum Antiquorum, Toledo Mus Art, 76. Mailing Add: 3452 Kenwood Blvd Toledo OH 43606

LUDEKENS, FRED
PAINTER, ILLUSTRATOR
b Hueneme, Calif. Exhib: Contemp Am Illus, Int Gallery, New York; Palm Springs Desert Mus, Calif, 78. Teaching: Co-founder, chmn bd & mem fac, Famous Artists Schs, Westport, Conn. Mem: Soc Illustrators; Art Dir Club, New York. Publ: Illusr, Ghost Town & The Ranch Book; contribr, Sat Eve Post, This Wk & Fawcett Publ. Mailing Add: PO Box 35 Belvedere CA 94920

LUDGIN, EARLE
COLLECTOR
b Chicago, Ill, July 22, 98. Pos: Former trustee, Am Fedn Arts; former pres, Soc Contemp Art; life trustee, Art Inst Chicago; life trustee, Univ Chicago. Mem: Arts Club Chicago. Collection: Contemporary American art. Mailing Add: 1127 Sheridan Rd Hubbard Woods IL 60093

LUDINGTON, WRIGHT S
COLLECTOR, PATRON
b New York, NY, June 10, 00. Study: Yale Univ; Pa Acad Fine Arts; Art Students League. Pos: Pres, Santa Barbara Mus Art, 50-51. Collection: Paintings and sculptures, early twentieth century; classical Greek and Roman sculpture and vases; Gothic, Romanesque, Egyptian sculpture. Mailing Add: 576 Freehaven Dr Montecito CA 93108

LUDMAN, JOAN HURWITZ
ART DEALER, ART WRITER
b Brooklyn, NY, Feb 1, 32. Study: Barnard Col, BA, 53; C. W. Post Col, Long Island Univ, MA, 71. Pos: Assoc, Mason Fine Prints, Glen Head, NY, 72- Specialty: Am and Europ original prints. Publ: Co-auth, with Lauris Mason, Print Reference Sources: A Select Bibliography 18th-20th Centuries, Kraus-Thomson Orgn Ltd, 75; contribr, Cecile Shapiro, auth, Fine Prints: Collecting, Buying and Selling, Harper & Row, 76; co-auth, with Lauris Mason, The Lithographs of George Bellows: A Catalogue Raisonne, 77 & co-ed, with Lauris Mason, Print Collector's Quart: An Anthology of Essays on Eminent Printmakers of the World, 77, Kraus-Thomson Orgn Ltd. Mailing Add: 74 Hunters Lane Westbury NY 11590

LUDMER, JOYCE PELLERANO
ART LIBRARIAN, ART HISTORIAN
b New York NY. Study: Hunter Col, BA; Univ Calif, Los Angeles, MLS(libr sci) & MA(art hist), grad study with Prof Carlo Pedretti. Pos: Humanities bibliographer, Calif State Univ, Northridge, 70-72; librn, Elmer Belt Libr of Vinciana, Univ Calif, Los Angeles, 73-75; head librn, Art Libr, Univ Calif, Los Angeles, 75- Mem: Art Libr Soc of NAm (vchmn & chmn elect, 78-79); Col Art Asn, Am Libr Asn/Asn Col & Res Libr. Res: Leonardo da Vinci studies. Interest: Renaissance, classical, baroque art history; art bibliography. Mailing Add: c/o Art Libr Univ Calif 405 Hilgard Ave Los Angeles CA 90024

LUDTKE, LAWRENCE MONROE
SCULPTOR
b Houston, Tex, Oct 18, 29. Study: Univ Houston, BS; Coppini Acad Fine Art, San Antonio, with Waldine Tauch. Comn: Charging Bronze Rams, Johnson & Johnson Inc, San Angelo, Tex, 66; Dr Denton Cooley (bronze bust), St Lukes Hosp, Houston, 69; Eddie Wokecki (bronze bas relief), Rice Univ, Houston, 69; Pieta (bronze group), St Marys Sem, Houston, 74; Fiona O'Donnell (bronze bust), comn by Dr Manus O'Donnell, Houston, 74. Mem: Nat Sculpture Soc; Coppini Acad Fine Arts. Style & Technique: Classic style. Media: Bronze, Marble. Mailing Add: 10127 Whiteside Houston TX 77043

LUDWIG, EVA
SCULPTOR
b Berlin, Ger, May 25, 23; US citizen. Study: Greenwich House Pottery, 58-62, with Lu Duble; Sculptor's Workshop, 64, with Harold Castor; Craft Students League, 68, wood sculpture with Domenico Facci. Exhib: Exhib Contemp Liturgical Art, Philadelphia, 63; Own Your Own, Denver Art Mus, 68; Rochester Festival Religious Art, NY, 71; Cooperstown Art Asn Ann, NY, 71, 73 & 74; Nonmem Exhib, Nat Sculpture Soc, New York, 72. Awards: Best in Wood, Woodstock Guild Craftsmen, 69, Bert Wangler Mem Award, 72; First Prize in Sculpture, Cooperstown Art Asn, 71. Mem: Woodstock Guild Craftsmen. Style & Technique: Semi-realistic; wood sculpture. Media: Wood, Clay. Mailing Add: 57-44 164th St Flushing NY 11365

LUEDERS, JIMMY C
PAINTER, INSTRUCTOR
b Jacksonville, Fla, July 4, 27. Study: Pa Acad Fine Arts, Philadelphia, William Emlen Cresson Mem traveling scholar, 50, Henry Schiedt Mem scholar, 51. Work: Pa Acad Fine Arts; Philadelphia Mus Art; Sch Pharm & Tyler Sch Art, Temple Univ; Moore Col Art, Philadelphia. Exhib: Butler Art Inst, Youngstown, Ohio; Am Fedn Art Traveling Exhib Art Schs, 56; Metrop Young Artist Show, Nat Arts Club, New York, 60; Nat Acad Design, New York, 60; Nat Inst Arts & Lett, New York, 69. Teaching: Instr painting, Cheltenham Twp Art Ctr, 52-; instr painting, Pa Acad Fine Arts, 57-; instr painting, Philadelphia Mus Art, 67- Awards: Third Hallgarten Prize, Nat Acad Design, New York, 60. Mem: Artists Equity Asn, Philadelphia. Media: Acrylic. Dealer: Marian Locks Gallery 1524 Walnut St Philadelphia PA 19102. Mailing Add: 6819 Greene St Philadelphia PA 19119

LUISI, JERRY
SCULPTOR, INSTRUCTOR
b Minneapolis, Minn, Oct 7, 39. Study: Nat Acad Design, cert; Art Students League. Work: Greenshields Found, Montreal. Exhib: Nat Arts Club, New York; Nat Acad Design; Allied Artists Am; Nat Sculpture Soc; Acad Artists Asn. Teaching: Instr sculpture, Fine Arts Prog, Fashion Inst Technol, 72- Awards: Walter Lantz Nat Youth Award, 72; Alvah Mus Prize, Nat Sculpture Soc, 74; Figure Study Award, Acad Artists Asn. Mem: Nat Sculpture Soc; Acad Artists Asn. Style & Technique: Figurative modeling and carving. Media: Bronze. Publ: Contribr photog, In: Nat Sculpture Rev, 69, 71 & 72. Mailing Add: 37 E 28th St New York NY 10016

LUITJENS, HELEN ANITA
INSTRUCTOR, PAINTER
b Bakersfield, Calif. Study: Univ Redlands, BA; Univ Southern Calif, MA; Univ Hawaii, scholar, 63; Univ Calif, Los Angeles; Inst Art San Miguel de Allenda. Work: Munic Art Dept, Los Angeles; Inst Mex Norteamericano de Relaciones Cult, Mexico City; Anderson Konstmuseum, Helsinki, Finland; Konst Salongen Kavaletten, Uppsala, Sweden; Union Bank, Los Angeles. Exhib: Inst Mexicano Norteamericano de Relaciones Cult, 69; Konst Salongen Kavaletten, 73; Nat Watercolor Soc, Laguna Beach, Calif, 74; Pac Cult Mus Pasadena, 74; Palos Verdes Art Mus, 75. Teaching: Chmn dept art, Paul Revere Jr High, Los Angeles, 55-72; teacher pvt classes, 72-78; lectr painting & drawing, Chapman Col World Campus Afloat; lectr art hist, E Mediterr & Black Sea Cruise, 75. Pos: Demonstr watercolors to various orgns, 71-75. Awards: 30 awards in art shows in Southern California, 65-75. Mem: Nat Watercolor Soc (mem bd, corresp secy, 75); Women Painters West (jury mem); La Watercolor Soc; Los Angeles Art Asn Watercolor West. Style & Technique: Abstract; semi-abstract; impressionistic. Media: Watercolor. Publ: Contribr, Mosaics; contribr, Drawing; contribr, Elegant Era, 75; & articles in Los Angeles Times, Sch Arts Mag & Better Homes & Gardens. Dealer: Challis Gallery Laguna Beach CA. Mailing Add: 17046 107th Ave Sun City AZ 85373

LUKAS, DENNIS BRIAN
PAINTER, EDUCATOR
b Hamilton, Ont, Can, June 21, 47. Study: St Michael's Scholar Cantorum, Toronto, Dipl(ancient music); Doon Sch Fine Art, Ont, with Henri Masson, Carl Schaefer & Tony Onley; McMaster Univ, with Tony Urquhart; Montreal Mus Sch Fine Art, grad dipl, with Arthur Lismer; Atelier 17, Paris, France, with Stanley Hayter. Work: Mus d'Art Contemporain, Montreal, Que; Art Gallery Hamilton, Ont; Bibliot Nat, Paris; Montreal Mus Fine Arts; Art Gallery Greater Victoria, BC; plus many others. Exhib: Art Gallery Hamilton Ann Touring Shows, Ont, 63, 70 & 74; 12th May Salon, Mus Mod Art, Barcelona, Spain, 68; one-man shows, Stable Gallery, Montreal Mus Fine Arts, Can, 70 & Rodman Hall Art Gallery, St Catharines, Ont, 75; Retrospective Eleven Yrs, McKenzie Gallery, Trent Univ, Peterborough, Ont, 74; Peripheries, Mus d'Art Contemporain, Montreal, 74; Young Contemporaries, Art Gallery of London, Ont, 75; Forum 76, Montreal Mus Fine Arts, 76; On View Visual Arts Ont (touring 14 mus), 76-77; Root Art Centre, Hamilton Col, Clinton, NY, 77; Sch of Art, Munson-Williams-Proctor Inst, Utica, NY, 77. Teaching: Instr drawing & painting, Montreal Mus Sch, Que, 71-74; lectr drawing & painting, Univ Toronto, Ont, 75-76; vis asst prof drawing & painting, Hamilton Col, Clinton, NY, 76- Awards: First Prize, Scope Art Exhib, McGill Univ, Montreal, 66; Seventh Ann Show Award, Rodman Hall, St Catharines, Ont, 67; Prix St Paul de Vence, Grand Prix Int de la Peinture, Cote d'Azur, France, 69. Bibliog: Michael White (auth), Lukas at Sauvegarde, the Gazette, Montreal, 71; Catharine Bates (auth), Lukas, The Montreal Star, 73; Kim Todd (auth), Dennis Lukas, The Grimsby Independent, 74. Mem: Niagara Artists Co; Can Artists Representation. Style & Technique: Drawings; works impossible to photograph. Media: Self-made Acrylic and all matter including words. Dealer: Damkjar-Burton Gallery 25 Hess St S Hamilton ON Can; Bau-XI Gallery 340 Dundas W Toronto ON Can. Mailing Add: 51 Main St W Grimsby ON L3M 1R3 Can

LUKASIEWICZ, RONALD JOSEPH
PRINTMAKER, ART ADMINISTRATOR
b Pittsburgh, Pa, Apr 20, 43. Study: Carnegie-Mellon Univ, BFA; Univ Ga, MFA. Work: Pittsburgh Pub Schs, Pa; Dow Chemical Co, Midland, Mich; City of Athens, Ga; Bankers Trust Co, NC. Comn: Suite of serigraphs, 73 & bound book of serigraphs, 73, Dow Chemical Co, Midland, Mich; modular sculpture, Scorpio Rising Workshop, Farmington, Ga, 73; modular sculpture, City of Athens, Ga, 77. Exhib: Multiples, Three Rivers Arts Festival, Pittsburgh, Pa, 72; Appalachian Corridors III, Charleston, WVa, 72; 10th Ann Piedmont Graphics Exhib, Mint Mus of Art, Charlotte, NC, 73; Assoc Artists Ann Show, Carnegie Mus, Pittsburgh, Pa, 73; Medals, Banners, Ribbons, Pittsburgh Arts & Crafts Ctr, Pa, 74; Ga Nat, Lyndon House Galleries, Athens, 76. Pos: Dir cult activities, Athens, Ga, 74-76; preparator, Ga Mus of Art, Univ Ga, 76- Awards: Purchase Award, Assoc Artists of Pittsburgh, Pittsburgh Pub Schs, 72. Bibliog: D Miller (auth), Exhibit review, Pittsburgh Post Gazette, 74; J Chappell (producer), Scorpio Rising (16mm film doc), 74; Screen Printing Today, WGTV Television, 74. Mem: Col Arts Asn; Assoc Artist of Pittsburgh; Athens Art Asn. Style & Technique: All techniques of screen printing; color etching. Dealer: Frankenberg-Guthrie Gallery Station Athens GA 30601. Mailing Add: 1495 Milledge Ave Athens GA 30605

LUKIN, PHILIP
COLLECTOR
b New York, NY, June 25, 03. Study: NY Univ, 21-22; Brown Univ, PhB, 24. Mem: Four Arts, Palm Beach, Fla; Fel Metrop Mus Art. Collection: Catholic in scope and representative. Mailing Add: 328 El Vedado Palm Beach FL 33480

LUKIN, SVEN
PAINTER
b Riga, Latvia, Feb 14, 34. Study: Univ Pa. Work: Albright-Knox Art Gallery, Buffalo, NY; Los Angeles Co Mus Art; Larry Aldrich Mus, Ridgefield, Conn; Univ Tex, Austin; Whitney Mus Am Art, New York; plus others. Exhib: Univ Ill, Urbana, 65; Torcuato di Tella, Buenos Aires, Arg, 65; New shapes of Color, Stedelijk Mus, Amsterdam, Holland, 66; Univ Colo, Denver, 67; Painting: Out From the Wall, Des Moines Art Ctr, Iowa, 68; plus others. Awards: Guggenheim Fel, 66. Bibliog: Sam Hunter (ed), New Art Around the World, Abrams, 66; Allen S Weller (auth), The Joys & Sorrows of Recent American Art, Univ Ill, 68; Gregory Battcock (ed), Minimal Art: a Critical Anthology, Dutton, 68. Mailing Add: 807 Ave of the Americas New York NY 10001

LUKOSIUS, RICHARD BENEDICT
PAINTER, EDUCATOR
b Waterbury, Conn, Oct 26, 18. Study: Yale Univ, with Josef Albers, BFA & MFA. Exhib: New Eng Art Today, Northeastern Univ, 65; one-man shows, Lyman Allyn Mus, New London, Conn, 68 & Manwaring Gallery, Conn Col, 75; New Eng Artists, Slater Mus,

Norwich, Conn, 68; Contemp Drawings, Univ Conn, Storrs, 71; Frascati Gallery, Stonington, Conn, 77. Teaching: Prof painting, drawing & graphic design, Conn Col, 54- Media: Acrylic. Mailing Add: Dept of Art Conn Col New London CT 06320

LUMBERS, JAMES RICHARD
PAINTER, DESIGNER
b Toronto, Ont, Can, Oct 8, 29. Study: Ont Col of Art, AOCA, 50; study with William Maltman, Toronto. Exhib: Ont Soc of Artists, Oshawa, 71; Nature Can, Nat Mus of Can, 73, 76-78; Beckett Gallery, Hamilton, Ont, 75; Soc of Animal Artists, Sportsman's Edge Gallery, New York, 78; one-man shows, Royal Ont Mus, Toronto, Can, 69, 73; Ont Sci Ctr, Toronto, 70; Kennedy Galleries Inc, New York, 72, Toronto Dominion Ctr, 75, Wildlife Gallery, Toronto, 76; Le Moyne Art Found, Tallahassee, Fla, 78, plus many others. Pos: Graphic designer, James Lumbers Graphics Ltd, Toronto, 62-; artist-in-residence, Edward Ball Wildlife Found, Tallahassee, Fla, 78. Awards: Two Silver Medals, Packing Asn of Can, 67. Bibliog: Anker Idum (auth), James Lumbers, Artist, Nature Can, 75; Sharon Dg Marco (auth), James Lumbers, Artist, Pensacola New J, 77 & Prime Time Tu Show, WFSU, Public Broadcasting System, 78. Mem: Soc of Animal Artists, New York. Style & Technique: Wildlife, People, Landscapes, realistic style. Media: Acrylic, Tempra & Watercolor. Publ: Illusr, Encyclopedia Canadian, Grolier Soc, 58; illusr, The Firebirds, Queen's Printer, 74. Mailing Add: Pointe Au Baril ON P0G 1K0 Can

LUMSDEN, IAN GORDON
CURATOR
b Montreal, Que, June 8, 45. Study: McGill Univ, Montreal, BA, 68. Collections Arranged: The First Decade (with catalog), Confedn Ctr Art Gallery & Mus, Charlottetown, PEI, 75; Wallace S Bird Mem Collection (with catalog), Beaverbrook Art Gallery, Fredericton, NB, 75; Bloomsbury Painters & Their Circle (US & Can traveling exhib), 76-78; The Queen Comes to New Brunswick: Paintings & Drawings by Molly Lamb Bobak (Can traveling exhib), 77-78; Drawings by Jack Weldon Humphrey (Can traveling exhib), 77-79. Pos: Cur art dept, New Brunswick Mus, St John, NB, 69; cur & dir, Beaverbrook Art Gallery, 69- Mem: Can Art Mus Dirs Orgn (treas, 73-75, second vpres, 75-77, first vpres, 77-); Can Mus Asn (secy-treas, 73-75); Atlantic Prov Art Gallery Asn (chmn, 70-72); Secondary Art Sub-Comt for NB Schs; Am Asn Mus. Res: 19th & 20th century Canadian art. Publ: Auth, Warkov, No 66 & Forrestall: de l'expressionnisme a l'hyperrealisme, No 67, Vie des Arts; auth, Artist in New Brunswick: George Neilson Smith, Can Antiques Collector, 5-6/75. Mailing Add: Beaverbrook Art Gallery PO Box 605 Fredericton NB Can

LUNA (ANTONIO RODRIGUEZ LUNA)
PAINTER
b Montoro, Spain, June 22, 10; Mex citizen. Study: Sch Fine Arts, Seville, 23-27; Royal Acad San Fernando, Madrid, 27-29. Work: Nat Mus Mod Art, Madrid; Fine Arts Gallery San Diego; Nat Mus Mod Art, Mexico City. Exhib: One-man shows, Venice Biennial (representing Spain), 34, Nat Mus, Washington, DC, 41, Fine Arts Gallery San Diego, 67 & Mus Mod Art, Mex, 74; Retrospective, Nat Palace Fine Arts, Mexico DF, 59. Teaching: Prof painting, San Carlos Acad, Nat Univ Mex, 49-69. Awards: First Prize for Painting, Nat Contest Painting & Design, Barcelona, 38; Guggenheim Fel, 41-43; First Prize for Painting, Nat Inst Fine Arts Ann, Mex, 63. Bibliog: M Nelkin (auth), El expressionismo Mexicano, Inst Nac Bellas Artes, 64; Image of Mexico, Tex Quart, 69; Juan Rejano (auth), Antonio Rodriguez Luna, Nat Univ Mex, 71. Media: Oil. Mailing Add: c/o Wenger Gallery Box 312 La Jolla CA 92038

LUND, DAVID
PAINTER
b New York, NY, Oct 16, 25. Study: Queens Col (NY), BA. Work: Toronto Art Gallery; Whitney Mus Am Art; Chase Manhattan Bank, NY; Baltimore Mus, Md; Corcoran Gallery Art, Washington, DC. Exhib: Whitney Mus Am Art, New York, 58, 60-62 & 77; Art Ann, Univ Nebr, 58, 64 & 66; five one-man shows, Grace Borgenicht Gallery, NY, 60-76; Baltimore Mus, Md, 60; St Louis Art Mus, Mo, 61; Columbus Gallery Fine Arts, Ohio, 61; Mich State Univ Group & Traveling, 62; Washington Gallery Mod Art, 63; Albright-Knox Art Gallery, Buffalo, NY, 63; Everson Mus Art, Syracuse, NY, 63; Andrew Dickson White Mus, Cornell Univ, Ithaca, NY, 63; RI Sch Design, 64-65; Pa Acad Fine Arts, Philadelphia, 65, 66 & 69; Toledo Mus, Ohio, 66; Nat Collection Fine Arts, White House, 66-69; Am Acad Arts & Lett, 69-70, 76 & 77; Kent State Univ, Ohio, 69 & 71; Denver Art Mus, Colo, 70; Smithsonian Inst, Washington, DC, 70, 72 & 73. Teaching: Instr painting, Cooper Union Art Sch, 55-57, 59-74; instr painting, Haystack Sch, Deer Isle, Maine, summer 63; instr painting, Parsons Sch Design, NY, 63-69; asst prof painting, Columbia Univ, 69- Awards: Fulbright Grant to Italy, 57-59; Ford Found Purchase Prize, Whitney Mus Am Art, 61; Childe Hassam Purchase Award, Am Acad Arts & Lett, 69. Mailing Add: c/o Borgenicht Gallery Inc 1018 Madison Ave New York NY 10021

LUND, JANE
PAINTER, CERAMIST
Study: Pratt Inst, 56. Work: Nelson Gallery Found, Kansas City, Mo; de Saisset Mus, Santa Clara, Calif; De Cordova Mus, Lincoln, Mass. Exhib: 21st Exhib New Eng & NY State Artists, Berkshire Mus, 72; New Talent New England, 73 & New England Women 1975, De Cordova Mus, Mass; 55th Nat Exhib Springfield Art League, Mass, 74; Exhib of Paintings Eligible for Childe Hassam Fund Purchase, Am Acad Arts & Lett, New York, 74; Davidson Nat Print & Drawing Competition, NC; Worcester Mus, Mass; Women on Women, George W V Smith Art Mus, Springfield, Mass; one-person show, Pucker-Safrai Gallery, Boston. Teaching: Instr basic & pastel drawing, Cambridge Ctr Adult Educ, Mass, 72- Awards: Cini Found Summer Scholar, Venice, Italy, 66. Bibliog: Pastel paintings of Jane Lund, Mass Rev, spring 77. Style & Technique: Realism and surrealism. Media: Highly Finished Pastels & Lithographs; Hand Built Figure Ceramics. Dealer: Pucker-Safrai Gallery 171 Newbury St Boston MA 02116. Mailing Add: Norton Hill Rd Ashfield MA 01330

LUNDE, KARL ROY
ART HISTORIAN, WRITER
b New York, NY, Nov 1, 31. Study: Columbia Univ, BA, MA & PhD. Teaching: Instr art hist, Sch Gen Studies, Columbia Univ, 58-70; prof art hist, William Paterson Col NJ, 70- Pos: Dir, The Contemporaries, New York, 56-65. Res: Italian Renaissance bronzes; 19th century romantic art in Scandinavia; 20th century American painting. Publ: Contribr, Slavic Rev, 70-71; contribr, Art & Artists, 72; contribr, Arts Mag, 75-; auth, Isabel Bishop, 75 & auth, Richard Anuszkiewicz, 77, Abrams. Mailing Add: 440 Riverside Dr New York NY 10027

LUNDEBERG, HELEN (HELEN LUNDEBERG FEITELSON)
PAINTER
b Chicago, Ill, June 24, 08. Study: With Lorser Feitelson. Work: Los Angeles Co Mus Art, Calif; San Francisco Mus Art; Joseph H Hirshhorn Collection; La Jolla Mus Contemp Art; Nat Collection Fine Arts, Washington, DC. Exhib: Fantastic Art, Dada, Surrealism, Mus Mod Art, New York, 36-37; Sao Paulo Biennial, Brazil, 55; Whitney Mus Am Art, New York, 62, 65 & 67; Artist's Environment: W Coast, Amon Carter Mus, Ft Worth, Tex, 62-63; Calif Hardedge Painting, Newport Harbor Art Mus, Newport Beach, Calif, 64; Des Moines Art Ctr, Iowa, 67; E B Crocker Art Gallery, Sacramento, Calif, 68; Color in Control, St Petersburg Mus Fine Arts, Fla; Lundeberg Retrospective Exhib, La Jolla Mus Contemp Art, 71; Painting & Sculpture in Calif: The Mod Era, San Francisco Mus Mod Art & Nat Collection Fine Arts, Washington, DC, 76-77; Surrealism & Am Art, Rutgers Univ Art Gallery, 77. Bibliog: Joseph E Young (auth), Helen Lundeberg: an American independent, Art Int, 9/20/71. Mem: Los Angeles Art Asn. Media: Acrylic & Oil. Mailing Add: 8307 W Third St Los Angeles CA 90048

LUNGE, JEFFREY (ROY)
PAINTER
b London, Eng, July 20, 05; US citizen. Study: Art Ctr, Los Angeles; also with James Couper Wright. Work: Palm Springs Desert Mus; Mus Northern Ariz, Flagstaff; Joseph Hirshhorn Collection; Ariz Bank, Phoenix; Valley Nat Bank, Phoenix. Comn: Mural, comn by George Beadle, Calif Inst Technol Biol Bldg, Pasadena, Calif, 56. Exhib: Pasadena Soc Artists Ann, 52-65; San Gabriel Valley Artists Asn, Pasadena, 58; San Diego Bicentennial Celebration, 67-68; one-man show, Northland Press, Flagstaff, 68-70; Dealer's Choice, Northern Ariz Univ, Flagstaff, 69; Art Wagon Gallery, Scottsdale, Ariz, 69-71; Palm Springs Desert Mus, Calif, 70; 6th Southwestern Invitational, Yuma, Ariz, 71; Jamison Gallery, Santa Fe, NMex, 73; Main Trail Gallery, Scottsdale, 74-78. Mem: Phoenix Art Mus; Mus Northern Ariz. Media: Transparent Watercolor. Dealer: Main Trail Galleries 7169 Main St Scottsdale AZ 85251. Mailing Add: Box 853 Sedona AZ 86336

LUNN, HARRY, JR
ART DEALER
b Detroit, Mich, Apr 29, 33. Mem: Art Dealers Asn Am; Royal Photographic Soc, Eng. Pos: Pres, Lunn Gallery/Graphics Int Ltd, currently. Specialty: 19th and 20th century prints and drawings; rare photographs; the estates of Milton Avery and George Grosz. Publ: Auth, Milton Avery-Prints (catalog), 73. Mailing Add: 3242 P St NW Washington DC 20007

LUNSFORD, JOHN (CRAWFORD)
ART HISTORIAN, CURATOR
b Dallas, Tex, Apr 15, 33. Study: Harvard Univ, AB(Eng lit), 54; Columbia Univ, MA(pre-Columbian art hist & archaeol), 67. Collections Arranged: The Clark and Frances Stillman Collection of Congo Sculpture (with catalog), 69; Arts of Oceania (with catalog), 70; The Romantic Vision in America (with catalog), 71; African Art from Dallas Collections (with catalog), 72; The Gustave and Franyo Schindler Collection of African Sculpture (with catalog), 75. Teaching: Adj prof African, Oceanic, pre-Columbian art hist, Southern Methodist Univ, Dallas, Tex, 67- Pos: Curator, Dallas Mus Fine Arts, 68- Res: The arts of pre-Columbian Mesoamerica and West and Central Africa; pre-Columbian Central and South America, Oceania. Mailing Add: Dallas Mus Fine Arts Box 26250 Dallas TX 75226

LUNTZ, IRVING
ART DEALER
b Milwaukee, Wis, Jan 9, 29. Pos: Pres & dir, Irving Galleries, Inc, Milwaukee & Palm Beach, 59- Mem: Art Dealers Asn Am; Appraisers Asn Am. Res: 19th and 20th century American and European painting; sculpture and graphics. Mailing Add: 404 E Wisconsin Ave Milwaukee WI 53202

LUPORI, PETER JOHN
EDUCATOR, SCULPTOR
b Pittsburgh, Pa, Dec 12, 18. Study: Carnegie-Mellon Univ, BFA, 42; Univ of Minn, MS(educ), 47; studied with Joseph Bailey Ellis & John Rood. Work: The Walker Art Ctr, Minneapolis, Minn; Ball State Teachers Col Art Gallery, Muncie, Ind; North Hennepin Community Col Art Gallery, Fridley, Minn; Albert Lea Pub Libr, Minn; Minn Alumni Asn Art Gallery, IDS Ctr, Minneapolis. Comn: Crucifix & Madonna (aluminum), Stations (ceramic), Holy Childhood Church, St Paul, Minn, 56-58; Stations of the Cross (ceramic), The Col of St Benedict, St Joseph, Minn, 60; Ten Stained Glass Windows, First Methodist Church, Monmouth, Ill, 61; Medicine Int, Ceramic Bas-Relief (36ft long), Fairview-Southdale Hosp, Edina, Minn, 65-67; 24 Stained glass Windows, Minnehaha United Methodist Church, Minneapolis, Minn, 66. Exhib: Ann Assoc Artist of Pittsburgh, Carnegie Inst of Art, Pa, 40-62; Biennial Exhib of Paintings & Prints, Walker Art Ctr, Minneapolis, 47-49; 1st Biennial Exhib Prints & Drawing, Minneapolis Inst of Arts, 50, 52-54; Six-State Sculpture Exhib, Walker Art Ctr, 47, 51; Ann Local Artists Exhibs, Minneapolis Inst of Arts, 47-48, 50-52; 16th Ceramic Ann Nat Exhib, Syracuse, NY, 51; Fine Arts Exhib, Minn State Fair Art Gallery, St Paul, 46-; one-man show, St Paul Mus of Art, 52. Teaching: Instr sculpture, Univ of Minn, Minneapolis, 46-49; asst prof, sculpture, Col of St Thomas, St Paul, Minn, 49-51; prof sculpture, The Col of St Catherine, St Paul, 47- Awards: 2nd award in sculpture, Prix de Rome, NY, 41; Carnegie Inst Prize for Sculpture, Assoc Artists of Pittsburgh, 49; 2nd Prize Sculpture, Local Artists Exhib, Minneapolis Inst of Arts, 53. Mem: Artists Equity Asn (twin cities chap, vpres, 60-61); Soc of Minn Sculptors (pres, 47-49 & 53-55; vpres, 52-53 & 56-57); Minn Artists Asn. Style & Technique: Semi-abstract; works are content oriented. Media: Ceramic, Wood & Welded Metal Sculpture. Mailing Add: c/o The Col of St Catherine 2004 Randolph Ave St Paul MN 55105

LUPPER, EDWARD
PAINTER
b NJ, Jan 4, 36. Study: With Wesley Lea, Frenchtown, NJ; Trenton Jr Col; Parsons Sch Design, New York; Calif Col Arts & Crafts, Oakland; San Francisco Art Inst; San Francisco State Col; de Young Mus Sch, 78. Work: Works in pvt collections only. Exhib: Baltimore Mus Art, 55; Tucson Art Ctr, Ariz, 59; Fort Worth Art Ctr, 60; San Francisco Mus Art, 60; Am Embassy, Belg, 77-78. Awards: Huntington Hartford Found Fel, 64. Bibliog: Articles in San Francisco Chronicle, 60, San Francisco Examr, 62 & 65 & Seattle Times, 71. Style & Technique: Naive painting; very detailed, elaborate gardens, rainbow forests and arks inhabited by animals of every species; highly varnished surfaces. Media: Casein, Oil. Publ: Auth, articles in Psychic Mag, 73, Playgirl Mag, 74, Apartment Life Mag, 9/74, Popular Gardening Indoors, 77 & Eaton Paper Corp, 77 & 78. Lord & Taylor Gallery Fifth Ave New York NY 10018; Linda Farris Gallery 322 Second Ave S Seattle WA 98104. Mailing Add: 1255 Pacific San Francisco CA 94109

LURAY, J (J LURAY SCHAFFNER)
PRINTMAKER, DESIGNER
b Columbus, Ohio, Apr 14, 39. Study: Ohio State Univ; Columbus Col Art & Design, BFA(advert), 62. Work: Nat Educ Asn, Cleveland, Ohio; Prather, Seeger, Farmer & Doolittle, Washington, DC; Columbus Col Art & Design; Commun Satellite Corp, Washington, DC. Exhib: James River Contemp Art Exhib, Mariners Mus, Norfolk, Va, 72-73; Northern Va Fine Arts Asn Artists Exhib, Alexandria, 73-75 & 77; 1st Int Exhib of

Monoprints, Ogelthorpe Univ, Atlanta, Ga, 73; Ann Paper Works Show, Charlottesville, Va, 74-76; 19th Area Exhib, Corcoran Gallery Art, Washington, DC, 74. Pos: Advert designer, W P Simpson, Columbus, 60-62 & Paul L Devaney Studio, Columbus, 62-69. Awards: First Prize Graphics (monoprint), J Carter Brown, Washington, DC, 72; First in Graphics (monoprint), Sigsbe Gilham Award, Art League, 73-76; Jane Livingston Graphics Award, Northern Va Fine Arts Asn, Alexandria, 75. Bibliog: Martin Sharter (auth), Art & singular images, Atlanta Mag, 73. Mem: Columbus Art League; Columbus Gallery Fine Art; Springfield Art Guild, Va; Corcoran Gallery Art; Art League Northern Va, Alexandria (ed). Style & Technique: Images that can be worked over, around, under or into with texture, line and color. Media: Monoprints. Dealer: Foliograph Gallery Tyson's Corner Ctr McLean VA 22101. Mailing Add: Torpedo Factory 101 N Union St Alexandria VA 22314

LURIA, GLORIA
ART DEALER
b New York, NY. Study: Pratt Inst; Art Students League; Skidmore Col, BS. Pos: Owner-dir, Gloria Luria Gallery, Miami, Fla. Mem: Art Dealers Asn SFla (pres). Specialty: Contemporary paintings; sculpture; graphics; tapestries. Mailing Add: 1128 Kane Concourse Bay Harbor Island Miami Beach FL 33154

LUSKER, RON
PAINTER
b Chicago, Ill, Jan 28, 37. Study: Sch Art Inst Chicago, 54-60; Univ Ill, Chicago Circle, Ill State Gen Assembly scholar, 57-62; Univ Chicago, 62-63; Southern Ill Univ, Carbondale, BA, 65, MFA, 66. Work: Univ NC; Price Waterhouse, Chicago; Chase Manhattan; Southern Ill Univ; Aldrich Mus Contemp Art. Exhib: 14th Ann Painting & Sculpture Exhib, Peoria Art Ctr, Ill, 66; 70th Ann Midwest Painting Exhib, Art Inst Chicago, 67; Convocation Arts, Sculpture, State Univ NY Albany, 68; 4th Ann Art Exhib Sculpture, Staten Island, 69; Eastern Seaboard Regional 3rd Ann Sculpture Exhib, 70; plus others. Teaching: Instr art, Southern Ill Univ, Carbondale, 65-67; asst prof art, State Univ NY Stony Brook, 68-72; assoc prof art, Kingsborough Community Col, 72-74. Awards: Grad Sch for Sculpture Fel & Grant in Aid, State Univ NY Stony Brook, 69 & 70. Bibliog: Malcolm Preston (auth), Assemblages display intellectual fantasy, Newsday, 5/21/69; Claire White (auth), Exhibition review, Craft Horizons, 6/70; Albert Boime (auth), Cosmic artifacts: the work in lucite of Ron Lusker, Art J, winter 72. Mem: Am Craftsmen Coun; Col Art Asn Am; Ctr Study Democratic Insts; Mus Mod Art; Whitney Mus Art. Media: Acrylic. Publ: Auth, New York: the season in sculpture, 8/70, The green meadow school, 8/70, The jewelry of Marci Zelmanoff, 12/70 & Attitudes, Brooklyn Museum, 70, Craft Horizons Mag. Mailing Add: 85 Mercer St New York NY 10012

LUST, HERBERT
ART HISTORIAN, COLLECTOR
b Chicago, Ill, Oct 31, 26. Study: Univ Chicago, MA, 49; Fulbright scholar to France, 50. Pos: Bd trustees, Larry Aldrich Mus Contemp Art, Ridgefield, Conn. Res: Giacometti, surrealism; minimal art. Collection: Giacometti drawings; also Bellmer, Leaf, Baj & Calder; minimal art. Publ: Auth, The Twelve Principles of Art Investment, 69; auth, Giacometti: the complete graphics and fifteen drawings, Tudor 71; auth, Enrico Baj, Dada Impressionist with Catalogue Raisonne, 72. Mailing Add: 54 Porchuck Rd Greenwich CT 06830

LUST, VIRGINIA
ART DEALER
b Chicago, Ill, July 23, 30. Study: Art Inst Chicago, 46; Mundelein Col, grad, 52. Collections Arranged: Paintings, Drawings, Early Prints (first Am show of Hans Bellmer); The Complete Graphics (first world show of Delvaux); The History of Surrealism, Drawings & Paintings, 72. Pos: Dir, Gallery Bernard, Greenwich, 68-; sales dir, Collectors Press. Specialty: Surrealism; Giacometti, paintings and drawings. Mailing Add: 54 Porchuck Rd Greenwich CT 06830

LUTZ, CAROLYN B
See Gast, Carolyn Bartlett

LUTZ, DAN S
PAINTER
b Decatur, Ill, July 7, 06. Study: Millikin Univ; Art Inst Chicago, James Nelson Raymond Europ travel fel & dipl, 31; Univ Southern Calif, BFA, 34; also painting under Boris Anisfeld. Work: Phillips Mem Art Gallery, Washington, DC; Fine Arts Gallery, San Diego; Los Angeles Co Mus Art; Philadelphia Mus Art; Santa Barbara Mus Art; plus others. Comn: Portrait, Fac of Westhampton Col, Richmond, Va, 55. Exhib: Four Am Painting Exhibs, Art Inst Chicago, 38-46; five Biennial Exhibs, Va Mus Art, 40-48; Am Painting, Watercolor & Drawing Exhibs, Metrop Mus Art, New York, 42, 50 & 52; Painting in the United States, 43-49 & Int Painting Exhib, 50, Carnegie Inst, Pittsburgh; Contemporary American Painting, Whitney Mus Am Art, New York, 44 & 50. Teaching: Instr painting, Univ Southern Calif, 32-42; instr painting, Chouinard Art Inst, 44-52; instr painting-guest artist, Univ Ga, 55. Pos: Mem, Men of Art Guild, San Antonio, 55. Awards: Thomas B Clark Prize for Oils, Nat Acad Design, 41; Third Hon Mention for Oil, Carnegie Inst, 43; Wheelwright Prize for Watercolors, Pa Acad Fine Arts, 45. Bibliog: Donald Bear (auth), Recent picture by Dan Lutz, Mag of Art, 12/43; Arthur Millier (auth), Dan Lutz-a painting with a compelling gift for lyric expression, Am Artist, 12/51; Janice Lovoos (auth), Dan Lutz, Christian Sci Monitor, 67. Mem: Calif Nat Watercolor Soc; Am Watercolor Soc; Philadelphia Watercolor Club; Santa Barbara Art Asn; Art Inst Chicago Alumni Asn. Media: Oil, Watercolor, Acrylic. Dealer: Dalzell-Hatfield Galleries Ambassador Hotel PO Box K Los Angeles CA 90070. Mailing Add: 369 Hot Springs Rd Montecito CA 93108

LUTZE
SCULPTOR, CONSULTANT, ART DEALER
b Wuppertal, Ger, 1937. Study: Art Sch Wuppertal, studied graphics; Univ Berlin, Ger, MFA. Work: Wilhelm Lehmbruck Mus, Duisberg, Ger; Berson Collection, Karlsruhe, Ger; Gallwitz Collection, Frankfurt, Ger; Fischer Collection, Baden-Baden, Ger. Comn: Marble sculpture, City of WBerlin, 65 & hydrant monument, 66; 100 Kohl Koepfe, Kunstverein, Dusseldorf, 68; epoxy resin mural, Wuppertal, 70. Exhib: Junge Stadt Sieht Junge Kunst, Wolfsburg, Ger, 63; Junge Berliner, Kunsthalle, Basel, Switz, 66; Zapeion, Athens, Greece, 67; Kunst & Kunststoff, Mus Dortmund, & Mus Duisburg, Ger, 68; Villa Romana, Florence, Italy, 68; one-woman shows, Kunsthalle, Baden-Baden, 70, Haus am Luetzowplatz, Berlin, 70, Gallery Klang, Cologne, 70, Trinity Col, Hartford, Conn, 71; performance with Trisha Brown, 72. Teaching: Assoc prof sculpture, Trinity Col, 70-71; adv art & poetry, Tombs, Men's House of Detention, New York, 71-75. Pos: Gallery dir, Onnasch Gallery, New York, 73-74; organizer, Soho in Berlin, Berlin Festival, 75-76; organizer, Berlin Now, Senat Berlin & Goethe Haus, New York, 77. Awards: Maison de France, Paris, 64; Ford Found Traveling Grant for US & Mex, 65; Villa Romana Prize, Florence, Italy, 68. Bibliog: Udo Kultermann (auth), German Sculptress, Das Kunstwerk, 62; R G Dienst (auth), Young German Artists, Du-Mont-Aktuell, 66; J Russel (auth), Soho in Berlin, NY Times, 76. Mailing Add: 207 Second Ave New York NY 10003

LUTZE, HILDEGARDE
See Lutze

LUX, GLADYS MARIE
PAINTER
b Chapman, Nebr. Study: Kearney State Col, SS, 18; Univ Nebr, BFA, 25, AB, 33, MA, 35; Art Inst Chicago, SS, 29. Work: Peru State Col; Doane Col; Pub Schs, Kearney, Nebr; Artists Guild Collection, Lincoln, Nebr. Exhib: Regional shows, Omaha, Minneapolis, Kansas City, Wichita & Topeka, 27-67; Art Inst Chicago, 36; Rockefeller Ctr, 36-38; New York World's Fair, 39; Joseph Pennell Mem Print Exhib. Teaching: Instr art methods, Summer Schs, Univ Nebr, Lincoln, 23-25; instr art methods, Sioux City Pub High Sch, Iowa, 25-27; chmn dept art, Nebr Wesleyan Univ, 27-33 & 36-66, asst prof art, 36-66. Awards: Nebr Art Teachers Asn Serv Award, 69. Bibliog: Rev in Art Digest, 36-38; World's Fair exhibit, New Yorker, 39. Mem: Lincoln Artist Guild (past pres, secy); Nebr Art Teachers Asn (past pres, vpres). Style & Technique: Traditional; stylized; crafts are original designs, based on tradition; hooked rugs, quilts, doll costuming, wood toys, enamel on copper. Media: Watercolor, Oil. Publ: Auth, Symbols of Good Neighbors, Christ of the Andes, Candle Beam, 43; auth, European arts seen internationally, Western Arts Asn Bull, 55; auth, Students Exhibits, 59; illusr, In a Tall Land, 63; auth, The baby doll, an evolution, 72 & Our hobby with TLC, 74, In: United Federation Doll Clubs Book. Mailing Add: 5203 Garland St Lincoln NE 68504

LUX, GWEN (GWEN LUX CREIGHTON)
SCULPTOR
b Chicago, Ill. Study: Md Inst Arts; Boston Mus Fine Arts Sch; also study in Paris & with Ivan Mestrovic, Yugoslavia. Work: Detroit Mus; Hawaii State Found Cult & the Arts. Comn: Totem pole, bird pole (metal & wood), Northwood Shopping Ctr, Detroit, 52; chrome abstraction, Gen Motors Tech Ctr, Detroit, 56; stainless steel abstraction, Aviation Trades High Sch, New York, 58; bronze & concrete abstraction, KRON TV Bldg, San Francisco, 65; concrete abstraction, State Off Bldg, Kauai, Hawaii, 71. Exhib: Whitney Mus Am Art, New York, 35; Detroit Mus, 48; World House Galleries, New York, 62; Pomeroy Galleries, San Francisco, 68; Contemp Arts Ctr, Honolulu, 70; Downtown Gallery, Honolulu, 76; plus others. Teaching; Instr sculpture, Arts & Crafts Soc, Detroit, 45-48. Awards: Guggenheim Found Fel, 33; Detroit Inst Award, 45 & 46; Nat Indust Arts Coun Can Award, 65. Bibliog: C Ludwig Brumme (auth), Contemporary American Sculpture, Crown, 48. Mem: Hawaii Artists & Sculptors League. Media: Polyester Resin, Concrete, Metals. Dealer: Wailea Arts Ctr Kihei Maui HI 96753; Downtown Gallery 125 Merchant St Honolulu HI 96813. Mailing Add: 4340 Pahoa Ave Honolulu HI 96816

LUZ, VIRGINIA
PAINTER
b Toronto, Ont, Oct 15, 11. Study: Cent Tech Sch. Work: Robert McLaughlin Gallery, Oshawa, Ont; Can Dept External Affairs; Can Embassies; J S McLean Collection; London Art Mus; also in many pvt collections. Exhib: Ont Soc Artists, 45-75; Can Women Artists Show (travelling exhib to New York & Can), 47-49; Can Soc Painters in Watercolour, 47-75; Can Tours; Can Group Painters; Tribute to Ten Women, Sisler Gallery, Toronto, Ont, 75; plus others. Teaching: Instr illus, Cent Tech Sch, Toronto, 40-74, head dept art, 69-74. Mem: Ont Soc Artists; Royal Can Acad; Can Soc Painters in Watercolour. Style & Technique: Abstract based on natural forms. Mailing Add: 113 Delaware Ave Toronto ON Can

LYE, LEN
SCULPTOR, KINETIC ARTIST
b Christchurch, NZ, July 5, 01; US citizen. Study: Wellington Tech Col; Canterbury Col Fine Arts. Work: Albright-Knox Art Gallery, Buffalo, NY; Whitney Mus Mod Art; Art Inst Chicago; eight films, Libr, Mus Art, New York. Comn: New York films for Brit Govt. Exhib: One-man shows, Motion Sculpture, Mus Mod Art, New York, 61 & Albright-Knox Art Gallery, Buffalo, NY, 65; Cinema Art Ctr; Art in Motion, Stedelijk Mus, Amsterdam, Holland, 61-62; Whitney Mus Am Art Ann, 62; On the Move, Howard Wise Gallery, New York, 63. Teaching: Instr film technique, City Col New York; instr creative imagination, Sch Performing Arts, NY Univ. Awards: Int Film Festival for Colour Box, Brussels, Belg; Experimental Film Competition, World's Fair Int, Brussels, 58. Style & Technique: Direct film technique of painting or etching image on film itself, no camera used. Publ: Auth, No Trouble, Paris, 30; contribr, Life & Lett, London & Tiger's Eye, 49. Mailing Add: 801 Greenwich New York NY 10014

LYFORD, CABOT
SCULPTOR, PAINTER
b Sayre, Pa, May 22, 25. Study: Skowhegan Sch Art, summer 47; Cornell Univ, BFA, 50; Sculpture Ctr, New York, 50-51. Work: Lamont Gallery, Exeter, NH; Addison Gallery Am Art, Andover, Mass; Wichita Mus, Kans; Colby Col, Waterville, Maine; NEng Ctr Continuing Educ, Durham, NH; over 50 pvt collections. Comn: Wild Geese (cypress wood), Summit Lodge, Mt Sunapee, NH, 64; brass mobile, State NH Exhib, New York World's Fair, 65; granite Christ head, Christ Church, Exeter, 69, candelabra, 70 & black granite & brass flower holder, 71; Harbor Sculpture (black granite), Portsmouth, NH, 75. Exhib: Payson Mus, Portland, Maine; RI Festival, Providence; NH Art Asn, Manchester; Addison Gallery, Andover, Mass; Fitchburg Art Mus; plus others. Teaching: Instr sculpture, Phillips Exeter Acad, NH, 63- Awards: Prizes, City Manchester, 70 & NH Architects Asn, 71, 74-77. Style & Technique: Direct stone and wood carving. Media: Stone, Metal; Watercolor. Publ: Contribr, Contemporary Stone Sculpture, 71. Dealer: Frost Gully Gallery 92 Exchange St Portland ME 04101; Sunne Savage Gallery 105 Newbury St Boston MA 02116. Mailing Add: 9 Center St Exeter NH 03833

LYLE, CHARLES THOMAS
ART ADMINISTRATOR
b Duluth, Minn, July 16, 46. Study: Univ Minn, James Wright Hunt scholar, 67-68, BA(cum laude), 68; Univ Del, Hagley fel, 68-70, MA(Am hist), 71. Collections Arranged: New Jersey Arts & Crafts: The Colonial Expression (with catalog), 72; American Crafts: The New Jersey Contribution, 75; American Folk Art, 75. Teaching: Instr Am archit, Brookdale Community Col, fall 73; instr Am decor arts prior to 1900, Lincroft, NJ, spring 75. Pos: Field dir archaeol, Hagley Mus, Wilmington, 71; dir, Monmouth Co Hist Asn, Freehold, NJ, 71- Mem: Am Asn Mus; NE Mus Conf; Am Asn State & Local Hist (NJ state mem chmn, 73-); Nat Trust for Hist Preservation; Victorian Soc Am. Mailing Add: 70 Court St Freehold NJ 07728

LYNCH, JAMES BURR, JR
ART HISTORIAN
b Miona, Va, Aug 23, 19. Study: Harvard Univ, AB, AM & PhD. Teaching: Assoc prof art hist, Boston Univ, 55-66; prof art hist, Univ Md, College Park, 66- Mem: Col Art Asn Am.

Res: Latin American painting and architecture, especially Mexican and Cuban; Italian art of the sixteenth century. Publ: Auth, History of Raphael's small St George in the Louvre, 4/62 & G P Lomazzo's self-portrait in the Brera, 10/64, Gazette Beaux-Arts; auth, Lomazzo & the Accademia della Valle de Bregno, Art Bull, 6/66; auth, Siqueiros, Encycl World Art, Vol XIII; auth, An unsung artist of the Mexican renaissance, Americas, 6/70. Mailing Add: Dept of Art Univ of Md College Park MD 20742

LYNCH, JO (MARILYN BLANCHE)
PAINTER, ILLUSTRATOR
b Chicago, Ill, Aug 20, 28. Study: Iowa State Col; Art Inst Chicago; Burnley Commercial Art Sch, cert. Work: Nat Bank Com, Seattle; Assoc Grocers, Seattle; also in collections of Daniel Evans, Robert Hallowell & Mullavey, Hageman & Prout, Attorneys. Exhib: Northwest Watercolor Exhib, Seattle Art Mus, 71 & Cascade Gallery, Seattle, 75; Soc Western Artists Exhib, Pioneer Mus, Stockton, Calif, 73; Puget Sound Area Exhib, Frye Art Mus, 74; one-man show, Cherry & Terry, 74. Pos: Free lance designer/illusr. Bibliog: Tom Stockley (auth), Jo Lynch-she covers the waterfront, Pictorial Sect, 8/4/74 & Deloris Tarzan (auth), Frye Museum launches Lynch's world, 12/13/74, Seattle Times. Mem: Northwest Watercolor Soc; Soc Prof Graphic Artists. Style & Technique: Realistic; detail, often with much line work and white space; line used with planes of color; color often limited palette. Media: Miscellaneous Media, Black & Colored Inks, Acrylic. Mailing Add: 8031 Jones Ave NW Seattle WA 98117

LYNCH, MARY BRITTEN
PAINTER, INSTRUCTOR
b Pruden, Ky, Sept 30, 38. Study: Univ Tenn, Chattanooga, BA; Provincetown Workshop, Mass, studied with Leo Manso & Victor Candell; Hunter Mus, studied with Budd Bishop. Work: Anchorage Hist & Fine Arts Mus, Alaska; Tenn State Mus, Nashville; Little Rock Fine Arts Ctr, Arkansas; Watkins Art Inst, Nashville, Tenn; Senate Off Bldg, Washington, DC. Exhib: One-man shows, Anchorage Hist & Fine Arts Mus, Alaska, 71 & Miss Col for Women, Columbus, 72; USA Works on Paper, cols, mus & univs in US, 72-76; Nat Asn Women Artists—Nat Acad Design, New York, 73-76; Tenn Painters, Cheekwood Mus, Nashville, 74; Okla Arts Ctr, Oklahoma City, 74; USA Oil Exhib, cols, mus & univs in US, 74-76; Watercolor USA, Springfield Art Mus, Mo, 76. Teaching: Instr watercolor acrylics, Hunter Mus Art, Chattanooga, Tenn, 69-77 & Watercolor Workshop, Univ Tenn Chattanooga, 75. Pos: Founder, Lenoir City Arts Festival, Tenn, 63; mem visual arts panel, Tenn Arts Comn, Nashville, 72-76. Awards: Cash Award, Tenn Watercolor Soc, Am Nat Bank, 77; Award of Merit, Tenn Arts Comn, 77; Purchase Award, Tenn Watercolor Soc, 77. Bibliog: Jim Collins (auth), Women Artists II, Univ Press, 74; Southern Artisans (film for TV), 73; Mary B Lynch drawings, Am Artist Mag, 78. Mem: Mus Am; Nat Asn Women Artists; Tenn Watercolor Soc (founder, 69; treas, 70; vpres, 71; pres, 72-); Chattanooga Art Asn. Style & Technique: Contemporary impressionism with a variety of subjects using print-off techniques. Media: Watercolor; acrylic. Mailing Add: 1505 Woodnymph Trail Lookout Mountain TN 37350

LYNDE, STAN
CARTOONIST, PAINTER
b Billings, Mont, Sept 23, 31. Study: Univ Mont; Sch Visual Arts, New York, 56-57. Work: Mus Cartoon Art & Hall of Fame, Greenwich, Conn; plus other mus, limited primarily to cartoon art. Exhib: The Evolution of Rick O'Shay, Yellowstone Co Fine Arts Ctr, Billings, Mont, 63; The Paintings of Stan Lynde, Midland Nat Bank, Billings, 75. Pos: Creator, auth & artist comic strip, Rick O'Shay, Chicago Tribune-New York News Syndicate Inc, 58- Mem: Nat Cartoonists Soc; Newspaper Comics Coun. Style & Technique: Comic strip art; Western art, landscape and wildlife. Media: Pen & Ink, Oil Painting. Dealer: James Wempner Johnson Lane Billings MT 59101. Mailing Add: Box 296 Lakeside MT 59922

LYNDS, CLYDE WILLIAM
SCULPTOR
b Jersey City, NJ, June 22, 36. Study: Art Students League; Frank J Reilly Sch, New York. Exhib: Univ Ill Biennial, 69 & 74; Ind State Univ Centennial, 70; Contemporary American Painting and Sculpture, Del Art Ctr, Wilmington, 70; Light, Motion, Sound, Hudson River Mus, New York, 71; Corcoran Gallery Art, Washington, DC, 73; McIntosh Gallery, London, Eng, 76; Basel Art Fair, Switz, 77. Awards: First Prize, Monmouth Col (NJ), 68; First Prize, Union Col (NJ), 68; First Prize & Medal of Honor, Jersey City Mus, 68. Style & Technique: Light sculpture employing natural rhythmic movement in three dimensional space. Media: Acrylic on Canvas & Board. Dealer: Electric Gallery 24 Hazelton Ave Toronto ON Can; Babcock Gallery 805 Madison Ave New York NY 10021. Mailing Add: 237 Innes Rd Woodridge NJ 07075

LYNES, RUSSELL
WRITER, CRITIC
b Great Barrington, Mass, Dec 2, 10. Study: Yale Univ, BA; Union Col, hon DFA; Md Inst Col Art, hon LHD, 73; NAdams State Col, hon DLitt, 77. Pos: Managing ed, Harper's Mag, 47-67, contrib ed, 67-; pres, Arch Am Art, 64-71, trustee, presently; pres bd dirs, MacDowell Colony, formerly, trustee, presently; trustee, New York Hist Soc; vchmn, New York Found Arts; vis comt, Costume Inst, Metrop Mus Art, formerly, vis comt, Am Dept, presently; mem, New York City Art Comn, formerly. Publ: Auth, The Domesticated Americans, 63; auth, Confessions of a Dilettante, 66; auth, The Art-makers of 19th Century America, 70 & auth, Good Old Modern, 73, Antheneum; auth, Russell Lynes Observes Column, Archit Digest; also auth many articles for Harper's Mag, Life, Look, Yale Rev, Vogue & others, 45- Mailing Add: 427 E 84th St New York NY 10028

LYON, HAROLD LLOYD
PAINTER
b Windsor, Ont, Dec 18, 30. Study: Meinzinger Sch Art, Detroit; Ont Col Art, with George Ford & Fred Findlay. Exhib: At least seven one-man shows each year since 65 in Seattle, Wash, Scottsdale, Ariz, Winnipeg, Man, Victoria, BC, Vancouver, BC, Kelowna, BC, Edmonton, Alta & Calgary, Alta. Teaching: Teacher art, Ont TV Ser, 57- & wk CBC-TV series, Vancouver, BC. Pos: Art dir, CFCL TV Timmons, Ont, 56-57 & Hudsons Bay Co, Calgary, Alta, 58-60; founding pres, Western Artists Asn, 77. Style & Technique: Realistic abstracts, that is total abstract in theory and totally realistic in viewing; subject matter children, people, boats, landscapes, seascapes, unlimited. Media: Oil. Mailing Add: Box 142 Westbank BC Can

LYON, HAYES PAXTON
PAINTER
b Athol, Kans, Feb 10, 09. Study: Univ Colo, BA, 31; Univ Denver, BFA, 37; also with Andrew Dasburg, Jozef G Bakos & Dr Raymond Stites. Work: Denver Art Mus; US Marine Hosp, Carville, La. Comn: Original Fort Lupton, Pioneer Man & Pioneer Woman, Lupton High Sch, 40. Exhib: Am Paintings & Sculpture Ann, Art Inst Chicago, 38; 133rd Ann Exhib, Pa Acad Fine Arts, 38; Am Art Today, New York Worlds Fair, 39-40; Artists West of Miss, Colorado Springs Fine Arts Ctr, 40, 41, 46 & 48; Exhib of 200 Water Colors, Nat Gallery Art, Washington, DC, 41. Teaching: Instr drawing, design, oil painting, watercolor, Univ Tex, Austin, 46-51. Pos: Tech illusr, Lowry Tech Training Ctr, Denver, 54-73. Awards: Yetter Mem Prize, 45th Ann Show, Denver Art Mus, 39; Purchase Prize, First Nat Water Color Competition, Washington, DC, 40. Style & Technique: Representational landscape or figures. Media: Oil on Canvas, Watercolor. Mailing Add: 10105 W 78th Ave Arvada CO 80005

LYONS, IAN RAYMOND
ART ADMINISTRATOR, COLLECTOR
b Detroit, Mich, Aug 15, 48. Study: Hope Col, Holland, Mich, BA; Wayne State Univ, MA(Asian studies/humanities). Collections Arranged: The Tribal Arts from the Collection of Ian R Lyons (auth, catalog), 77 & The Arts from Jackson Prison (auth, catalog), 78, Pontiac Art Ctr. Teaching: Asst prof humanities, McComb Community Col, 75-77. Pos: Asst to dir of educ, Detroit Inst of Arts, 73-75; exec dir, Pontiac Art Ctr, 76- Mem: Am Asn of Mus; Art Ctr Asn. Res: The tribal arts of northern Thailand. Collection: Tribal costumes of the six major tribes; silk collection; Neolithic Ban Chang pottery. Publ: Auth, Tribal Arts of Northern Thailand, Needle/Bobbon Bull, Metrop Mus Bull, 77; auth, The Arts-Urgent Need of America, Ferris State Col, Sem Publ. Mailing Add: 358 W Iroquois Pontiac MI 48053

LYONS, LISA
CURATOR, ART HISTORIAN
b Minneapolis, Minn, Dec 13, 50. Study: Northwestern Univ, Evanston, Ill, BA(art hist), 72; Columbia Univ, New York, MA(art hist), 73. Collections Arranged: Scale & Environment: 10 Sculptures (contribr, catalog), 77, Richard Nonas: Sculpture & Drawings, 78 & Nicholas Africano, 78, Walker Art Ctr, Minneapolis. Pos: Fel, Toledo Mus of Art, Ohio, 73-74; Rockefeller Found Fel, Walker Art Ctr, Minneapolis, 75-77 & asst cur, 77- Publ: Auth, British painting, In: 100 masterpieces from the Metropolitan Museum of Art; auth, Henri Matisse: 1914-1917, Arts Mag, 5/75; auth, An interview with James Byrne, Studio Int, 5-6/76; contribr, The river: images of the Mississippi, Walker Art Ctr, 76. Mailing Add: c/o Walker Art Ctr Vineland Pl Minneapolis MN 55403

LYSUN, GREGORY
PAINTER, RESTORER
b Yonkers, NY, Oct 24, 24. Study: Art Students League, with Louis Bouche, Edwin Dickinson, John Groth, Robert Beverly Hale & Reginald Marsh, 47-53. Work: Art Students League; Berkshire Mus, Pittsfield, Mass; New Britain Mus Am Art, Conn; De Cordova Mus, Lincoln, Mass; Butler Inst Am Art, Youngstown, Ohio. Comn: Portrait of M D Safanie, Shearson, Hammill & Co, New York, 65; portrait of Wilmer Wright, Wright Assocs, New York, 67; restoration work of the Whistle & Simon Stevens, comn by Mrs D E Kastner, Chatham, Mass, 71; portrait of Ruth Taylor, Westchester Community Serv Coun, Inc, White Plains, NY, 75. Exhib: 22nd Ann Nat Realist Art, Acad Artists Asn, Mus Fine Arts, Springfield, Mass, 71; 35 Years in Retrospect, 1936-1970, Butler Inst Am Art Midyear Show, 71; Am Artists Prof League Grand Nat, 73; Conn Acad Fine Arts Exhib, New Brit Mus Am Art, 72; 64th Ann Allied Arts Am, 77; 67th Ann Exhib Conn Acad Fine Arts, Wadsworth Atheneum Mus, Hartford, Conn, 77; plus others. Teaching: Instr painting & drawing, Westchester Art Workshop, Co Ctr, White Plains, 69-; instr painting & drawing & chmn dept art, Fairview-Greenburgh Community Ctr, Greenburgh, NY, 72-; instr painting & drawing, Am Tel & Tel Co, 73- Awards: Purchase Prize, 31st Ann Nat, Butler Inst Am Art, 66; Coun Am Art Socs Award for Best Figurative or Traditional Painting, Miniature Painters & Sculptors Soc NJ Nat, 71; Allen H Newton Award for Best Landscape, 67th Ann Exhib Conn Acad Fine Arts, 77. Bibliog: R Stevens (auth), Gregory Lysun, La Rev Mod, 64 & 69; Winifred B Bell (auth), Paintings by Gregory Lysun, Berkshire Eagle, 71. Mem: Life mem Art Students League; Allied Artists Am; fel Am Artists Prof League; Conn Acad Fine Arts; Int Asn Art, UNESCO, Paris. Style & Technique: Traditional or realistic style, using techniques and methods of the old masters. Media: Oil. Mailing Add: 481 Winding Rd N Ardsley NY 10502

LYTLE, RICHARD
PAINTER, EDUCATOR
b Albany, NY, Feb 14, 35. Study: Cooper Union; Yale Univ, BFA & MFA; also with Josef Albers. Work: Mus Mod Art, New York; Yale Art Gallery; Nat Collection Art, Washington, DC; Columbia Univ Int House; Cincinnati Art Mus. Comn: Concrete relief mural, Fairfield Univ, 65. Exhib: 16 Americans, Mus Mod Art, New York, 59; Seattle World's Fair, 62; Whitney Mus Am Art Ann, New York, 63; Art: USA: Now, SC Johnson Collection, World Tour, 63-; one-man show, De Cordova Mus, Lincoln, Mass, 74; plus others. Teaching: Instr art, Yale Univ, 60-63; dean, Silvermine Col Art, 63-66; assoc prof art, Yale Univ, 66- Awards: Fulbright Grant to Italy, 58. Style & Technique: Conceptual landscape; imagery in color; expressionist. Media: Oil. Dealer: Marilyn Pearl Gallery 29 W 57th St New York NY 10019. Mailing Add: Sperry Rd Woodbridge CT 06525

M

MAAS, ARNOLD (MARCOLINO)
INSTRUCTOR, PAINTER
b Rotterdam, Holland, May 4, 09; US citizen. Study: Univ PR; Brooklyn Mus Art Sch, NY, with Rufino Tamayo, Camilo Egas, Joep Nicolas & Cristobal Ruiz. Work: Regional Mus of Alkmaar, Holland; Art Mus of Ponce, PR; Ateneo Puertorrigueno, San Juan. Comn: Mural (2700 sq ft), Cathedral, Otrabanda, New West Indies, 47; mosaic/stained glass, Dominican Monastery, Nymegen, Holland, 56; stained glass panels, Home of Jose Ferrer, 62; Three murals, Social Ctr, Harrisburgh, Pa, 67; stained glass wall (2800 sq ft), Benedictine fathers, Yabucoa, PR, 68. Exhib: Ateneo PR, San Juan, 42; Univ PR, Rio Piedras, 42, 63 & 67; Art Inst of Chicago, 53; Guatemala City Art Mus, Guatemala, 57; Inst of Cult, San Juan, PR, 63. Teaching: Prof stained glass, Inst of Cult, San Juan, 58-69. Bibliog: Rev, Newsweek, 53; Constatini (auth), Fede e arte, Roma. Italy, 54; Couturier, L'Art Religieux, Actualite, Paris, 54. Mem: Artists Equity Asn. Style & Technique: Stained glass. Media: Oil and acrylic; fresco, mosaic; enameling on glass. Mailing Add: 1519 Ridgewood Ave Maitland FL 32751

MAASS, RICHARD ANDREW
ART ADMINISTRATOR
b New York, NY, Apr 11, 46. Study: Univ Wis, Madison, BA(Am hist), 68; New Sch for Social Res, New York, MA(polit sci, Am govt), 72; Cooperstown Grad Prog, MA(mus admin), 73. Collections Arranged: Maynard Dixon—A Bicentennial Retrospective, 12/75; Calif-Texas Art Exchange, in prep, 3/76. Pos: Ecol supvr, Mus City New York, 70-71; asst prog dir, South St Seaport Mus, New York, 71-72; dir, Fresno Arts Ctr, 72- Awards: Fel, Sem

for Hist Adminr, Colonial Williamsburg, 71; Fel, Harvard Bus Sch Arts Admin Sem, 73. Mem: Am Asn Mus (pres-elect, Western Regional Coun, 77); Am Asn State & Local Hist; Nat Soc Arts & Lett; Manuscript Soc; Advocates for Arts. Mailing Add: 3033 E Yale Ave Fresno CA 93703

MABIE, DON EDWARD
MIXED-MEDIA ARTIST, PAINTER
b Calgary, AB, Can, Jan 9, 47. Study: Alta Col of Art, dipl(fine art painting), 69; Inst Allende, San Miguel de Allende, Mex, 70. Work: Art Gallery of Ont, Toronto; Glenbow Art Gallery, Calgary; Burnaby Art Gallery, BC; Dept of External Affairs, Ottawa, Ont; Univ Man, Winnipeg. Comn: Book plate etching, Mrs R Touche, Calgary, 69; card, (multipax Oxfam ed peace card), Oxfam of Can, Toronto, 71; 3rd Brit Print Biennale Int, Bradford, Eng, 72; poster, Inst on Can Soc, Univ Calgary, 72; mural (pen and ink), head off of Carma Developers Ltd, Calgary, 74. Exhib: 5th Burnaby Print Exhib, BC, 69; three-person exhib, Alta Col of Art Gallery, Calgary, 71; two-person exhib, Univ Art Gallery & Mus, Univ Alta, Edmonton, 74; two-person exhib, Confederation Art Gallery & Mus, Charlottetown, PE, 74; one-man show, Gallery 111, Univ Man, Winnipeg, 74; Oh Canada, London Art Gallery, Ont, 76; On Paper, Alta Col of Art Gallery, 76; Albertawork, Alta Col of Art Gallery, 77. Pos: Contribr ed, Queen St Mag, Toronto, 74-76; co-dir, Parachute Ctr for Cult Affairs, Calgary, 75-76; rep Calgary & Alta, Can Artists Representation, 75-76; ed, Images & Info, 75-; ed newsletter & mem exec comt, Print & Drawing Coun of Can, Calgary, 76- Awards: Purchase Award, 5th Burnaby Print Exhib, Burnaby Art Gallery, 69; Can Coun Arts Bursary (cash award for one yr in Toronto), 70-71; Prov Ont Coun for the Arts Grant (organizing 1st Ann Toronto Corresp & Junk Mail Art Exhib), 74. Bibliog: Robert Martin (auth), At the galleries, Toronto Globe & Mail, 8/72; Sarah Henry (auth), Yawn-more to bore from chuck stake enterprizes, Can Mag, 5/74; Brooks Joyner (auth), Don Mabie-an artistic enigma, Calgary Albertan, 10/77. Mem: Print & Drawing Coun of Can. Style & Technique: Drawing various lettering styles and overlaid with a meticulous filigre of lines; mixed-media paintings and drawings. Media: Pen and Ink; Acrylic on Paper or Card. Publ: Auth, The Rose Museum, Artscanada, 74; auth, Journey to the east, Queen St Mag, 76; auth, Miss Truly Amazing and friends, Calgary Albertan, 76. Mailing Add: 4236 Worcester Dr SW Calgary AB T3C 3L4 Can

MABRY, JANE
PAINTER, ART DEALER
Study: Univ NMex, BFA; Art Students League; Corcoran Sch Art; also with Jerry Farnsworth; Grand Cent Sch Art; Critcher Sch Art, with Catherine Critcher. Exhib: NMex State Fair, 40-73; Smithsonian Inst, Washington, DC, 45; Mus NMex Biennial, 64; All Am Indian Exhibition, Indianapolis, Ind, 74. Pos: Former staff artist, Nat Park Serv; charter mem, NMex Arts Comn, 66-74, chmn, 2 yrs; co-owner, Galeria del Sol. Awards: Numerous first place ribbons for pastels and oils. Mem: Pastel Soc Am. Style & Technique: Realistic, impressionist, landscapes and portraits; oils with brush and palette knife; pastels mostly portraits on acrylic washes, color and sepia. Media: Oils and Pastels over Acrylic; Lithographs. Specialty: Southwestern subjects, landscapes and portraits of Southwestern Indians, the New Mexico Pueblos and their people; sculptured tiles Indian designs. Mailing Add: c/o Galeria del Sol 206 1/2 San Felipe NW Albuquerque NM 87102

MACALISTER, PAUL RITTER
DESIGNER, COLLECTOR
b Camden, NJ, Oct 15, 01. Study: Pa Acad Fine Arts, Philadelphia; Sch Indust Design; Yale Univ Sch Archit; Ecole Beaux Arts, Fontainebleau, France, with Bourdelle & Carlu. Work: Astrasphere (celestial globe), Maritime Mus, Greenwich, Eng & White House Libr; Capellini Glassware, Mus Arts Decoratifs et Metiers, Paris, France. Comn: Amtico Showrooms, Am Biltrite Rubber Co, US, Can & Europe, 54-67; Decorama (slide film), Libbey-Owens-Ford Glass Co, Toledo, Ohio, 55; co-designer, Astrolabe Kit, 74, Trilogy of Time Instruments Kit, 76 & Macet Astrolabe, 77. Exhib: Miniature TV Room Settings, Art Inst Chicago, 50. Pos: Dir, Paul MacAlister, Inc, 26-42; designer & dir, Permanent Exhib Decorative Arts & Crafts, 33-40; comdr, USN Spec Devices Div & Navy Exhibs, 42-46; dir, Bureaus Indust & Interior Design, Montgomery Ward & Co, 46-48; dir & sr partner, Paul MacAlister & Assocs, Lake Bluff, Ill, 48-, dir, Americana Hayloft Mus, 50- Awards: Beaux Arts Medal, 24; Silver Medal, Indust Designers Inst, 56; Dorothy Dawes Award, Am Furniture Mart Press Ann, 55. Bibliog: Articles in House & Garden, 7/66 & Interior Design, 4/68, 10/68 & 9/72. Mem: Fel Indust Designers Soc Am (pres, 50 & 51, chmn design award prog, 50-60); fel Royal Soc Arts, London; Early Am Industs Asn; Midwest Tool Collectors Asn. Style & Technique: Model making. Collection: American eagle in art form; early hand tools; early scientific instruments; rare books on perspective, architecture and the arts; collections exhibited Chicago Pub Libr, Lake Forest Libr, Lake Forest Acad Antiques Show & Art Inst Chicago. Publ: Auth, Display for Better Business, 54; auth, articles in Lake Forest Acad Antiques Show Catalog, 69-71. Mailing Add: Box 157 Lake Bluff IL 60044

MACARAY, LAWRENCE RICHARD
PAINTER, EDUCATOR
b Elsinore, Calif, May 8, 21. Study: Whittier Col, BA, 51; Calif State Univ, Long Beach, MA, 55. Work: Bowers Mus, Santa Ana, Calif; Thompson Industs, Los Angeles, Calif; Bertrand Russell Peace Found, Nottingham, Eng; Spectrum Press, Orange, Calif; pvt collection of art critic, William Wilson, Los Angeles Times. Comn: Location oil paintings of Eng & Ireland, 75. Exhib: New Talent, New York, Los Angeles Co Mus Art, 71-72; Ann Juried Show, Palos Verdes Mus Art, Calif, 71 & 73-74; All California Art Exhibition, Nat Orange Show, San Bernardino, 72-74; Bertrand Russell Centenary Art Exhib, Nottingham, 73; Southern Calif Regional Print & Drawing Exhib, 73-74; plus others. Teaching: Prof drawing & painting, El Camino Col, 62- Pos: Art & travel ed, Torrance Press-Herald, Calif, 63-70. Awards: Prize for Art Unlimited, Downey Mus Art, Calif, 74; Southern Calif Exposition Prize, Del Mar, 74. Media: Oil. Mailing Add: 628 Buttonwood St Anaheim CA 92805

MACAUALY, DAVID ALEXANDER
DESIGNER, ILLUSTRATOR
b Burton on Trent, Eng, Dec 2, 46. Study: RI Sch of Design, BArchit. Work: Cooper Hewitt Mus, New York. Exhib: Children's Book Illus, Mus of Contemp Art, Houston, Tex, 75; Great Moments in Archit, SPACED Gallery of Archit, New York, 76 & ARCHIcenter, Chicago, 77; 10th & 11th Ann Int Exhib of Children's Book Illus, Bologna, Italy, 76 & 77; 200 Years of Am Illus, Mus of Hist Soc of New York, 77; Buildingbooks, 77 & Drawing the Line, 78, Montclair Art Mus, NJ; Children's Book Art, Monterey Penninsula Mus of Art, Calif & Triton Mus of Art, Santa Clara, Calif, 78. Teaching: Asst prof of illus, RI Sch of Design, 74. Awards: First runner-up, Caldecott Medal, Am Libr Asn, 74 & 78; Deutscher Jungenbuchpreis (Best non-fiction picture book), Ger, 75; Medal, Am Inst of Archit, 78. Bibliog: Paul Goldberger (auth), Schede/Libri, Abitare, Edtrice Segesta, Milan, 5/76 & How to Build a Castle, New York Times, 11/77; Stefan Kanfer (auth), Books, Time Mag, 11/77. Media: Pen & Ink. Publ: Auth & illusr, Cathedral, The Story of It's Construction, 73, City, A Story of Roman Planning and Construction, 74, Pyramid, 75, Underground, 76 & Castle, 77, Great Moments in Architecture, 78, Houghton/Mifflin. Mailing Add: RI Sch of Design Providence RI 02903

MACCLINTOCK, DORCAS
SCULPTOR
b New York, NY, July 16, 32. Study: Smith Col, AB; Univ Wyo, AM. Comn: White Rhinos (1/3 life size), metal cast, in prep, Peabody Mus of Nat Hist, New Haven, Conn, 78. Exhib: Soc of Animal Artists, Grand Central Galleries, New York, 72-74; Birds, Beasts & Fish, Slater Mem Mus, 73 & 77; Fur-Feathers-Flora, Foot of Main Gallery, Essex, Conn, 76; Soc of Animal Artists, Sportsman Edge Ltd, NY, 78. Mem: Soc of Animal Artists Inc (mem jury 76-). Style & Technique: Lifelike portrayals of mammals, especially hoofed and carnivores. Media: Plastilene, Clay. Publ: Auth, Squirrels of North America, Van Nostrand Reinhold, 70; auth, A Natural History of Giraffes, 73 & A Natural History of Zebras, 76, Scribners. Mailing Add: 33 Rogers Rd Hamden CT 06517

MACDONALD, COLIN SOMERLED
WRITER, PUBLISHER
b Ottawa, Ont, Mar 5, 25. Study: Self taught artist; also study with Mabel May & Carleton Col, eve, 47-49. Exhib: One-man show, Little Gallery, Photog Stores, Ottawa, Ont, 62; Ottawa Born Artists, Univ Ottawa, 67. Pos: Ed & publ, Dictionary Can Artists, 67-; pres-dir, Can Paperbacks Publ Ltd, 74- Awards: Res & Publ Award, Can Horizons Prog, Can Coun, 71 & Res Award, 75; Publ Award, Ont Arts Coun, 75. Bibliog: W Q Ketchum (auth), Faces of Ottawa, Ottawa J, 3/70. Style & Technique: Decorative realism, also impressionistic landscape and city scenes. Media: Oil. Res: Biographical information on living and dead Canadian artists with bibliography and critical comments. Publ: Auth, Dictionary of Canadian Artists, Vols I-V, 67-77. Mailing Add: 370 Queen Mary St Ottawa ON K1K 1W6 Can

MACDONALD, GAYLE COLEMAN
ART RESTORER, LECTURER
b Allentown, Pa, Mar 15, 54. Study: Lehigh Univ, Bethlehem, Pa, BA(Phi Beta Kappa); Art Restoration Tech Inst, cert & apprenticeship. Pos: Art conservator, Lehigh Univ, Bethlehem, Pa, 76-; freelance art restorer, Pa; partner, Coleman Art Gallery, Allentown, 76- Mem: Am Inst for Conserv of Hist & Artistic Work; Asn for Preservation Technol. Res: Microchemical analysis of art work. Mailing Add: 1509 Hamilton St Allentown PA 18015

MACDONALD, GRANT
PAINTER, ILLUSTRATOR
b Montreal, Que, June 27, 09. Study: Ont Col Art, Toronto; Art Students League; Heatherley's Art Sch, London; Queens Univ, Kingston, Ont, hon LLD, 74. Work: Redpath Libr, McGill Univ; Hart House, Univ Toronto; Art Gallery Toronto; Queen's Univ; Kingston Col Inst; also in galleries, schs, univs, libr & pvt collections, Can, USA & Eng. Exhib: Nine shows, Art Asn Montreal, 41-68; Art Asn Kingston, 48-55, 67 & 68; Royal Can Acad, 49, 51-55 & 67; Ont Soc Artists, 49, 51-55, 66 & 67; seven shows, Art Gallery Hamilton, 49-68; Retrospective, Agnes Etherington Art Centre, Kingston, 66; plus many others. Teaching: Instr figure drawing, Summer Sch, Queen's Univ, Kingston, 48, 52, 53, 64 & 65. Awards: Medal, Art Dirs Club, Toronto, 52; Kraft-Price Award, 65; Forster Award, Ont Soc Artists, 66. Mem: Royal Can Acad. Publ: Illusr, Shakespeare for Young Players, 42, Haida, 46, Behind the Log, 47, Sunshine Sketches of a Little Town, 48 & A Masque of Aesop, 52; plus others. Mailing Add: Tarquin 32 Lakeshore Rd Kingston ON K7M 4J6 Can

MACDONALD, KEVIN JOHN
GRAPHIC ARTIST
b Washington, DC, July 2, 46. Study: Montgomery Jr Col, Takoma Park, Md, 64-66; George Washington Univ, BFA, 69; Corcoran Sch of Art, Washington, DC, 69. Work: Metrop Mus of Art, New York; Corcoran Gallery of Art, Washington, DC; Phillips Collection, Washington, DC; Iowa Mus of Art, Iowa City. Exhib: Nineteenth Area Show, 74 & Am Drawings, 76, Corcoran Gallery of Art, Washington, DC; Fifth Davidson Nat, Davidson Col, NC, 76; Md Biennial, Baltimore Mus of Art, 76; Drawing Show, Phillips Collection, DC, 77. Awards: Purchase Award, Fifth Davidson Nat, Bank of NC, Davidson, 76; First Prize/Drawing, Montgomery Co Juried Art Show, Md, 77. Bibliog: Jo Ann Lewis (auth), rev in Washington Post, 10/77; Ben Forgey (auth), rev in Washington Star, 10/77; Tobie Lanou (auth), rev & interview in What's Up In Art, 10/77. Style & Technique: Realism; realist/surrealist scenes of ordinary places, generally without people. Media: Colored pencil and graphite, covering whole area. Dealer: Harry Lunn Graphics Int 3243 P St NW Washington DC 20007. Mailing Add: 8207 Georgia Ave 5 Silver Spring MD 20910

MACDONALD, THOMAS REID
PAINTER
b Montreal, Que, June 28, 08. Study: With Adam Sherriff Scott & Edmond Dyonnet. Work: Nat Gallery Can, Ottawa; Montreal Mus Fine Arts, Que; Art Gallery Windsor, Ont; Art Gallery Hamilton, Ont; Father's Confederation Art Gallery, Charlottetown, PEI. Exhib: New York World's Fair, 39; London World's Fair, Eng; Royal Can Acad. Teaching: Instr life drawing & painting, Art Asn Montreal. Pos: Head . dept fine arts, Mt Allison Univ, Sackville, NB, 45-46; dir, Art Gallery Hamilton, Ont. Mem: Royal Can Acad Arts. Media: Oil. Mailing Add: 175 Dufferin St Hamilton ON L8S 3N8 Can

MACDONALD, THOREAU
ILLUSTRATOR, DESIGNER
b Toronto, Ont, Apr 21, 01. Study: With J E H MacDonald. Work: Nat Gallery Can; Art Gallery Toronto. Exhib: Wembley; Paris; Coronation; Tate Gallery, London; New York World's Fair. Style & Technique: Simplicity and truth as far as possible, usually black and white. Publ: Illusr, Marie Chapdelaine, Macmillan, 21 & 38; auth, The Group of Seven, McGraw, 44; illusr, Thornhill: an Ontario Village, 64 & Old Time Thornhill, 70, FitzGerald; plus over 200 others. Mailing Add: Box 197 Thornhill ON L3T 3N3 Can

MACDONALD, WILLIAM ALLAN
ART HISTORIAN, EDUCATOR
b Lorain, Ohio, July 28, 11. Study: Oberlin Col, AB; Johns Hopkins Univ, AM & PhD. Teaching: Prof hist art, Western Md Col; prof art & archaeol, George Washington Univ, 59- Pos: Former asst dir, Baltimore Mus Art. Mem: Archaeol Inst Am; Brit Inst Archaeol, Ankara. Publ: Contribr, Hellenistic Art, New Cath Encycl; auth, Preliminary reports on excavations at Mucellena, Certino and Ancaiano, Etruscans, No 3, 74. Mailing Add: Dept of Art & Archaeol George Washington Univ Washington DC 20006

MACDONALD, WILLIAM L
ARCHITECTURAL HISTORIAN
b Putnam, Conn, July 12, 21. Study: Harvard Col, AB, Harvard Univ, AM & PhD; Am Acad Rome, fel. Teaching: Prof art & archit, Yale Univ, 55-65; prof art & archit, Smith Col,

Northampton, Mass, 65- Pos: Exec secy, Byzantine Inst, 50-54. Mem: Soc Promotion of Roman Studies, London; Soc Archit Historians (dir, 58-64); Soc Libyan Studies, London; Am Asn Archit Bibliogr; Am Inst Archaeol. Res: History of architecture; ancient, Early Christian, American. Publ: Auth, Early Christian & Byzantine Architecture, 62; auth, The Architecture of the Roman Empire, Vol 1, 65; auth, Northampton Massachusetts Architecture & Buildings, 75; auth, The Pantheon—Design, Meaning, & Progeny, 76. Mailing Add: 25 Henshaw Ave Northampton MA 01060

MACDONNELL, CAMERON
PAINTER, SCULPTOR
b Elmira, NY, May 29, 38. Study: State Univ NY Col Educ Buffalo, BS(art educ), studied with John Davidson, Mort Grossman, Larry Calcognio & Trevor Thomas; independent study, Santa Barbara, Calif. KIBM Collection, Oswego, NY & City of Santa Barbara, Calif. Comn: Backdrops for the Nutcracker Suite, Madam Helena Ballet Sch & New York Coun on the Arts, 66; Logo, Samuel L Clemens Performing Arts Ctr, Elmira, NY, 77. Exhib: Regional, Albright Knox Art Gallery, NY, 60; Encores Gallery, Buffalo, NY, 61; Regional, Everhart Mus, Scranton, Pa, 62; Mansfield Col Libr Gallery, NY, 67; Roberson Two River Gallery, Binghamton, NY, 67; Regional, Santa Barbara Mus Art, Calif; Our Town Gallery, Santa Barbara, 74; Goleta Galleria, Calif, 75; one-man show, 76, group show, 76, Arnot Art Mus, Elmira, NY, 76. Pos: Art dir marketing develop, Art Frame Publ, Santa Barbara, Calif, 70-76; mem staff, Off of Design & Develop, Asn for Retarded Children, Elmira, NY, 77- Awards: Silver Medalions, Bicentennials, City of Santa Barbara & Co of Santa Barbara. Bibliog: Trevor Thomas (auth), Views of Art, Buffalo Evening News, 60; Larry Griffis, Jr (auth), World of art, Buffalo Courier Express, 61; Lee Batten (auth), California Artists, Art Fame Publ, 75. Mem: Southern Tier Arts Asn (founder, 75); Arts in the Park, Elmira, NY (chmn). Style & Technique: Abstract interpretations of landscapes using transparent planes, painted with a glazing technique. Media: (Painting) watercolor, oil; (sculpture) cast resin. Publ: Illusr & contribr, Sethmaterial, Prentice Hall, 70; contribr, Reflections, 72 & illusr, Salvang, 75, Art Fame Publ. Dealer: Kate Zimmer Arnot Art Mus 235 Lake St Elmira NY 14901. Mailing Add: 510 Magee St Elmira NY 14901

MACGARVEY, BERNARD B
PAINTER
b San Francisco, Calif. Study: St Mary's Col, Calif, BA; NTex State Univ; Calif Arts & Crafts, Oakland. Work: Univ Calif Mus, Berkeley; Henry Gallery, Univ Wash, Seattle; Long Beach Mus, Calif; Victoria Mus, BC, Can; Dublin Mus, Ireland. Comn: Mural, Palmer Sch, Walnut Creek, Calif, 70. Exhib: One-man shows, Humboldt Galleries, San Francisco, 71, 73 & New York, 75; Univ Calif, Berkeley, 72. Bibliog: Judith Dunham (auth), Exhibit Rev, Art Week, 5/73; S Tarshiss (auth), Exhibit Rev, Art News, 6/73; Summer Gallery, Archit Dig, 6/73. Style & Technique: Mixed media abstractions on paper and canvas. Media: Tempera, Oil. Mailing Add: c/o Humboldt Galleries 1641 Third Ave 7K New York NY 10028

MACGILLIS, ROBERT DONALD
PAINTER, ILLUSTRATOR
b Bayonne, NJ, June 30, 36. Study: Mech Inst, New York; Newark Sch Fine Arts, NJ. Work: Grover M Hermann Fine Arts Ctr, Marietta Col; Bayonne Pub Libr; Caldwell Art Ctr, Caldwell Col. Exhib: Allied Artists Am, New York; Acad Artists, Springfield, Mass; Conn Watercolor Soc, Hartford; Am Artists Prof League, New York; plus others. Pos: Indust artist, Gen Dynamics Elec Boat Div, Groton, Conn, 60- Awards: Salmagundi Club Award, 72; Strathmore Award, Acad Artists, 75; Am Artists Prof League Top Cash Award for Graphic, 75; plus others. Mem: Salmagundi Club; Am Artists Prof League; Am Watercolor Soc; Acad Artists; Hudson Valley Artists. Style & Technique: Traditional watercolors in transparent approach of mostly New England landscapes and seascapes. Media: Watercolor. Mailing Add: 96 School St Groton CT 06340

MACGREGOR, JOHN BOYKO
PAINTER, ART ADMINISTRATOR
b Dorking, Eng, Jan 12, 44; Can citizen. Study: Cent Tech Sch, Toronto. Work: Nat Gallery of Can; Art Gallery of Ont; Owens Art Gallery, NB; Univ of Western Ont; Winnipeg Art Gallery. Comn: Sculpture (with Paul Wilson), Gallery One, Toronto, 76. Exhib: Ont Centennial Purchase Exhib, 67, The Collectors Chooses, 67, Can Artists, 68, 3-D into the 70's (traveling), 70, Signs & Symbols (traveling), 71, Contemp Ont Art, 74 & Chairs, 75, Art Gallery of Ontario; Kitchener-Waterloo, Art Gallery, Ont, 69 & 70; Survey 70-Realism (e)s, Art Gallery Ont, Montreal Mus of Fine Arts, 70; Isaacs Gallery at the Owens Gallery, NB, 74; Burnaby Print Biennial, BC, 75; McIntosh Gallery, Univ of Western Ont, 76; London Art Gallery, Ont, 77; Words & Images, MacKenzie Art Gallery, Trenton Univ, 76; Making Marks, Norman MacKenzie Art Gallery, Regina; Contemp Prints from Can, Ore State Univ, 76; one-man shows, Hart House, Univ of Toronto, 67, Isaacs Gallery, 68-77 & Gallery Graphics, Ottawa, 75. Teaching: Instr, Artist's Workshop, 67-77, Ont Col of Art, 70-72 & 75, York Univ, 71-73, New Sch, 72-75 & Hart House, Univ of Toronto, 76 & 77. Pos: Dir, The New Sch of Art, Toronto, 77- Awards: Can Coun Arts Bursary, 68-70 & 72; Can Coun Sr Grant, 74 & 76; Winnipeg Biennial Purchase Award, 70. Mem: Can Artist Representation. Style & Technique: Abstract expressionism based purely on reaching subconscious matter within own mind, Jungian in concept. Media: Acrylic, Watercolor, Oil, Canvas, Board and Paper. Mailing Add: c/o Isaacs Gallery 832 Yonge St Toronto ON M4W 2H1 Can

MACHETANZ, FRED
PAINTER, LITHOGRAPHER
b Kenton, Ohio, Feb 20, 08. Study: Ohio State Univ, AB, 30, MA, 35; Chicago Art Inst, 30-32; Am Acad, Chicago, 30-32; Art Students League, 45; Univ Alaska, hon DFA, 73. Work: Rasmuson Libr, Univ Alaska; Glenbow Found, Alta Mus, Calgary; Anchorage Fine Arts Mus; Northwest Indian Ctr, Gonzaga Univ; Frye Art Mus, Seattle. Comn: Arctic Explorer, Explorers Club New York, 63; Capt Cook in Arctic, Scripps Inst Res Ship, Alpha Helix, 63; Eskimo Whalers, Dept Interior, Washington, DC, 69; Dr Irving on Ice Field, Laurence Irving Bldg, Inst Arctic Biol, Univ Alaska, 71; The Tender Arctic, Frye Mus, Seattle, Wash, 73. Exhib: One-man shows, Univ Alaska, 64-72, Anchorage Fine Arts Mus, 68 & 74 & Frye Mus, 72. Pos: Distinguished assoc art, Univ Alaska, 64- Bibliog: W Jones Bibliog: Fred M—artist of Alaska, Am Artist Mag, 4/68; articles in Alaska Mag, 1/74 & Alaska J, winter 74; The Alaskan Paintings of Fred Machetanz, Peacock Press-Bantam Bks, 77; plus others. Mem: Soc Animal Artists. Style & Technique: Alaskan or arctic subject matter with one color underpainting to which glazes or layers of transparent oil color are added. Media: Lithography on Stone; Oil. Publ: Auth & illusr, Panuck, Eskimo Sled Dog, 39, auth & illusr, On Arctic Ice, 41 & illusr, A Puppy Names Gih, 57, Scribner. Mailing Add: Box S-885 Palmer AK 99645

MACIEL, MARY OLIVEIRA
ILLUSTRATOR, EDUCATOR
b New Bedford, Mass. Study: With Alva Glidden; Swain Sch Art; Vesper George Sch Art; Md Inst Art; Marjorie Martinett Sch Art; Art Students League, with George Bridgman; Johns Hopkins Univ, with Max Brödel. Comn: Illus for 14 textbks, Univ Cincinnati & Vet Admin; illus for many US & foreign sci jour. Exhib: Medical Illustration, Cincinnati, 48 & Medical Illustrator as Scientist, Columbus, 55, Ohio State Med Asn; Medical Visual Aids, Univ Helsinki, Finland, 58; Medical Illustration: a Select Career, Cincinnati Pub Libr, 62; Artist in Operating Room, Cincinnati Woman's Club, 65 & Cincinnati Pub Libr, 74. Teaching: Prof med illus & dir, Col Med, Univ Cincinnati, 47-72, emer prof med illus & free lance illusr, Med Ctr; illusr, Vet Hosp, 50-76; free lance med illusr. Awards: Six First Award for Best Sci Exhibs, Ohio State Med Asn, 48-65; Fulbright Prof, Univ Strasbourg, 56; Abbott Lab Award for Illus in SAfrica, 69. Mem: Asn Med Illusr (bd dirs, 55-59); Cincinnati Speakers Forum (bd dirs, 46-76); Delta Kappa Gamma; Proj Hope (bd dirs). Publ: Auth & illusr, Modern prostheses for human defects, Graphics, 55; auth, Rapport sur la realization d'une preparation a l'illustration medicale, Arch US Educ Comn France, 56; auth, The broad field of medical illustration, Cincinnati Post, 57; auth & illusr, Twenty points for creating good visual teaching aids, Univ Helsinki Arch, 58; auth, Importrance of adequate medical visual teaching aids, Univ Cape Town, 69. Mailing Add: 506 E Fourth St Cincinnati OH 45202

MACIVER, LOREN
PAINTER
b New York, NY, Feb 2, 09. Study: Art Students League, 19. Work: Mus Mod Art; Metrop Mus Art; Corcoran Gallery Art, Washington, DC; Addison Gallery Am Art, Andover, Mass; Whitney Mus Am Art; plus others. Exhib: Venice Biennale, 67; Tolouse Mus Fine Arts, 67; Mus Beaux Arts, Lyons, France, 68; Mus Art Mod Ville de Paris, 68; Mus Ponchettes, Nice, France, 68; Corcoran Gallery Art; Whitney Mus Am Art, New York; Mus Mod Art, New York; plus others. Awards: Ford Found Grant, 60; First Prize, Art Inst Chicago, 61; Purchase Prize, Krannert Art Mus, Univ Ill, 63; plus others. Mem: Nat Inst Arts & Lett. Dealer: Pierre Matisse Gallery 41 E 57th St New York NY 10022. Mailing Add: 61 Perry St New York NY 10014

MACK, CHARLES RANDALL
EDUCATOR, ART WRITER
b Baltimore, Md, May 23, 40. Study: Univ NC, Chapel Hill, AB(Europ hist), PhD(hist art). Collections Arranged: Classical Art from Carolina Collections (auth catalogue), Columbia Mus of Art, SC & NC Mus of Art, Raleigh, 74; H Robert Bonsack: Thirty-Eight Paintings and Drawings by the German Artist, Columbia Mus of Art, 75; Art and Artifacts from Antiquity (auth catalogue), Univ SC Mus, Columbia, 76. Teaching: Assoc prof Ancient & Renaissance art, Univ SC, Columbia, 70-; vis assoc prof Renaissance art, Univ NC, Chapel Hill summer 1977; Assoc prof ancient & Renaissance art, Univ SC, Columbia, 77- Pos: Intern asst, Supt of Galleries, Florence, Italy, 68-69. Awards: Comt to Rescue Italian Art Internship, Florence, 68-69; Kress Found Res Fel, Rome, Italy, 68-70. Mem: Col Art Asn; Soc Archit Historians; Int Survey of Jewish Monuments (founding mem); Southeastern Renaissance Conf; Southeastern Col Art Conf (pres, 75-76, co-ed, Review, 73-75). Res: Archival investigation of 15th century Italian architecture; Renaissance art; Etruscan and Roman art. Publ: Auth, The building programme of the Cloister of S Miniato, Burlington Mag, 73; auth, The Rucellai Palace: some new proposals, Art Bull, 74; auth, Michelangelo's Doni Madonna: a recapitualation, SECAC Rev, 75; Co-author, Art History for our Schools, 1976. Mailing Add: Dept of Art Univ SC Columbia SC 29208

MACK, RODGER ALLEN
SCULPTOR, EDUCATOR
b Barberton, Ohio, Nov 8, 38. Study: Cleveland Inst Art, BFA, 61; Cranbrook Acad Art, Bloomfield Hills, Mich, MFA, 63; Acad Belle Arti, Florence, Italy, Fulbright grant, 63-64. Work: Albrecht Mus Art, St Joseph, Mo; Munson-Williams-Proctor Inst, Utica, NY; St Lawrence Univ; State Univ NY Col Fredonia; Hamline Univ. Comn: Plaza sculpture, Mkt Plaza, North Little Rock, 68; Syra cast bronze, Dellplain Hall, Syracuse Univ, 69. Exhib: One-man shows, Galleria Arte, Florence, 64 & Krasner Gallery, New York, 70-78; Cross Currents in American Art, Humboldt State Col, 69; Everson Region, Everson Mus Art, Syracuse, NY, 70-71; Sculpture Invitational 75, Rochester Inst Technol, 75; plus others. Teaching: Instr sculpture, Arks Sch Art/Drama, Little Rock, 64-68; assoc prof sculpture, Syracuse Univ, 68-77, prof, 77-, head sculpture dept. Awards: A Kahn Assoc Artists Award, Detroit Inst Arts, 63; Nat Endowment Arts Award, Nat Coun Arts, Washington, DC, 67; CAST Grant, NY State Coun on the Arts, 77-78. Bibliog: John Canaday (auth), rev in New York Times, 1/70, 1/71 & 1/72. Style & Technique: Abstract, hybrid of mechanistic and biomorphic forms; cast metal in bonded sand. Media: Stone, Wood, Bronze. Dealer: Oscar Krasner Gallery 1043 Madison Ave New York NY 10021. Mailing Add: 2400 Euclid Ave Syracuse NY 13224

MACKAY, DONALD CAMERON
PAINTER, ART HISTORIAN
b Fredericton, NB, Mar 30, 06. Study: NS Col Art, assoc, 28, fel, 29, DFA, 70; Dalhousie Univ, cert fine arts; Chelsea Col Art, with P H Jowett & Graham Sutherland; Acad-Colorossi, Paris; Univ Toronto, with Arthur Lismer. Work: Nat Gallery Can, Ottawa; New York Pub Libr; Nat War Mus, Ottawa, Ont; Prov NS & Pub Arch NS; Dalhousie Univ. Comn: Three murals, Halifax Mem Libr, 51; first pres, Dalhousie Univ, Thomas MacCulloch, Dalhousie Senate, 53; Jacques Cartier at Stadacona, HM Can Ship Stadacona Wardroom, Halifax, 55. Exhib: Can Soc Graphic Arts, 30-40; Art of the Western Hemisphere, IBM, 40; First Post War Can Bienniele, 46; Can Sect New York World's Fair, Royal Can Acad. Collections Arranged: Halifax Bicentennial-200 Years of Art in Halifax, 49; Development of Canadian Art, Halifax Mem Libr, 51; A Century of Painting in Nova Scotia 1800-1900, NS Col Art, 65. Teaching: Instr graphic arts, Northern Voc Sch Toronto, Art Gallery Toronto, 31-35; instr, NS Col Art, 35-39; spec lectr art hist, Dalhousie Univ, 37-71; prof art & prin, NS Col Art, 45-71. Pos: War artist, RCN, 42-44. Awards: Bronze Medal, Art of the Western Hemisphere, IBM, 40; Silver Medal, Allied Arts, Royal Archit Inst Can, 53. Mem: Fel Royal Soc Arts; Can Soc Educ Through Art (pres, 57-58); Maritime Art Asn (pres, 51-53); Can Soc Graphic Art (vpres, 34-40); Can Arts Coun (vpres, 56-58); plus others. Style & Technique: Figurative. Media: Oil. Res: Topographical and portrait painters of the Atlantic Provinces; silver and silversmith of the Atlantic Provinces; Tsuba and sword furniture of Japan. Publ: Auth & illusr, Highlights of Nova Scotia History, 30; co-auth, Master Goldsmiths and Silversmiths of Nova Scotia, 48; auth & illusr, Silversmiths and Related Craftsmen of the Atlantic Provinces, 73; plus auth & contribr, many articles, 40-75 & illusr, many bks & periodicals on Maritime history, 47-67. Mailing Add: 5883 Inglis St Halifax NS Can

MACKAY, HUGH
ART DEALER
b New York, NY, July 4, 34. Pos: Pres, Nabis Fine Arts Inc, New York, 70-74; pres, HMK Fine Arts, Inc, 74- Mem: Am Fedn Arts; Mus Mod Art. Specialty: International publisher of graphics; art consultants to architects, design groups, corporations and galleries in all media. Mailing Add: 15 Gramercy Park S New York NY 10003

MACKENDRICK, LILIAN
PAINTER
b New York, NY. Study: Sculpture with Louis Keila, drawing & painting with Dorothy Block; Art Students League; Washington Sq Col, NY Univ, BS. Work: Metrop Mus Art, New York; Hirshhorn Collection, Washington, DC; Wadsworth Atheneum, Hartford, Conn; Walker Art Ctr, Minneapolis; Radcliffe Inst, Harvard Univ, Cambridge, Mass. Exhib: New York Dealers' Show, Witte Mus Art, San Antonio, Tex, 52; 3rd Biennial of American Painting, Bordighera, Italy, 55; Eleven Americans, touring Fr Mus, 56-57; plus many one-man shows. Awards: Honorable Mention, Brooklyn Soc Artists, 53; Gold Medal, 3rd Biennial American Painting, Bordighera, 55; Award for Public Service, Northside Ctr for Child Develop, 61. Bibliog: Allene Talmey (auth), More art than money, Vogue, 12/59; Dian Buchman (auth), Last of the great lady painters, Show, 4/70; Omar Del Carlo & R I Hall (auth), Lilian MacKendrick, Connoisseur, 5/74; plus others. Mem: Artists Equity Asn. Style & Technique: Naturalism with personal style. Media: Oil, Pastel, Watercolor. Publ: Illusr, Cat in My Mind, Putnam, Eng, 58; illusr, cover mag sect, New York Herald Tribune, 2/9/59. Dealer: Jacob Guttmann 180 E 73rd St New York NY 10022. Mailing Add: 230 Central Park S New York NY 10019

MACKENZIE, DAVID
PAINTER
b Los Angeles, Calif, Nov 8, 42. Study: Orange Coast Col, Costa Mesa, Calif, AA; San Francisco Art Inst, Calif, BFA & MFA; also with Ron Nagle & Tom Holland. Work: Oakland Mus Art, Calif. Exhib: San Francisco Art Inst Centennial, DeYoung Mus, 71; Off the Stretcher, Oakland Mus Art, Calif, 71; one-man shows, de Saisset Art Gallery & Mus, Univ Santa Clara, Calif, 73, Reed Col, Portland, Ore, 73, San Francisco Art Inst, Calif, 73 & Casat Gallery, La Jolla, Calif, 77; Whitney Biennial, Whitney Mus Am Art, New York, 75; 18 Bay Area Artists, Univ Art Mus, Univ Calif, Berkeley, 77. Pos: Guest cur, Los Angeles Inst Contemp Art, Los Angeles, 76 & San Francisco Art Inst, 78. Awards: Fel Grant to Individual, Nat Endowment for Arts, 75. Mem: San Francisco Art Inst (artist comt, artist trustee). Style & Technique: Cast Rhoplex paintings, systematic paintings with geometric configurations with the emphasis on painting as material. Dealer: Casat Gallery 5721 La Jolla Blvd La Jolla CA 92037; Grapestake Gallery 2876 California St San Francisco CA 94115. Mailing Add: 442 Shotwell St San Francisco CA 94110

MACKENZIE, HUGH SEAFORTH
PAINTER
b Toronto, Ont, June 19, 29. Study: Ont Col Art; Mt Allison Univ, BFA. Work: Montreal Mus Fine Arts, PQ; Art Gallery Ont, Toronto; Univ Waterloo; London Art Gallery, Ont; House of Commons, Ottawa. Comn: Portrait of L B Pearson, Ottawa Dept State, 68. Exhib: One-man shows, Morris Gallery, Toronto, 63-77 & Univ Waterloo, 75; Ont Soc Artists, Art Gallery of Ont, 58-59, 61 & 68; Mus Fine Arts, Montreal, 64; Realism in Canadian Art, Montreal Mus Fine Arts, PQ & Art Gallery Ont, Toronto, 70; Realism(e)s 70, Mus Fine Arts, Montreal & Art Gallery of Ont, 70; Ann Exhib Contemp Can Artists, Art Gallery of Hamilton, 70-72; Lithographs in collabr with NS Col Art, Nat Gallery Can, 71. Teaching: Instr art, Ont Col Art, 68- Awards: J W G Forster Award, Ont Soc Artists, 61; Can Coun Award, 70. Bibliog: Dauct (auth), review, Arts Can, spring 72; Hale (auth), review, Arts Mag, 2/70; Duval (auth), High Realism in Canada, Irwin Clarke & Co, Ltd, 74. Mem: Assoc Royal Can Acad. Media: Tempera, Watercolor. Mailing Add: c/o Jerrold Morris Gallery 15 Prince Arthur Ave Toronto ON Can

MACKLIN, ANDERSON D
ART ADMINISTRATOR, POTTER
b Luther, Okla, Jan 17, 33. Study: Lincoln Univ, Mo, BS, 54, studied with J D Parks; Univ of Mo, MA, 56, study with D Hanson, B Shane; Pa State Univ, PhD, 69, study with K Beittel, D Dontigney. Work: Oils, Lincoln Univ, Jefferson City, Mo, Atlanta Univ, Ga & Petersburg, Va, Exhib: Dallas Mus of Fine Arts Ann, 59; Atlanta Univ Ann, 60-70; Va Mus Biennial, 71; Lincoln Univ, Jefferson City, 73; Carriage House Gallery, Richmond, Va, 77; one-man show, Pa State Univ, pottery show, 67. Teaching: Prof of art & ceramics, Va State Col, 62- Pos: Vpres, Va Art Educ Asn, 72-74. Awards: First Place, Cole Co Ann, Mo, 58; Purchase Award, Atlanta Univ Ann, 68. Mem: Nat Conf of Artists (advisor, 65-72); Nat Art Educ Asn; Va Art Educ Asn (vpres, 72-74). Style & Technique: Pottery, combination of wheel thrown and slab forms, stoneware. Media: Pottery; Acrylic Painting. Mailing Add: 11200 Rosewood Lane Ettrick VA 23803

MACLEAN, ARTHUR
PAINTER
b New York, NY. Study: Nat Acad Design, New York; Art Students League; Grand Cent Art Sch. Exhib: Nat Acad Design, 60-70 & 75; Allied Artists Am, 60-77; Hudson Valley Art Asn, 60-77; Knickerbocker Artists, 60-72; Acad Artists, 60-68 & 75; plus others. Awards: William McKillop Prize, 74 & 77 & Helen C Nelson Award, 76, Kent Art Asn; Coun Am Artist Soc Award, Allied Artists Am, 75; Irene Rickenback Mem Award, Hudson Valley Art Asn, 77; plus others. Mem: Allied Artists; Hudson Valley Art Asn; Acad Artists. Mailing Add: 84 South Ave New Canaan CT 06840

MACLEAN-SMITH, ELIZABETH
SCULPTOR, LECTURER
b Springfield, Mass, Feb 18, 16. Study: Wellesley Col, AB; Belgian-Am Educ Found traveling fel, Belg, 37; Boston Mus Sch, with Frederick Warren Allen & Sturdivant traveling fel, Mex, 41. Work: Mus Fine Arts, Boston; Mus Fine Arts, Springfield, Mass; Williams Col, Williamstown, Mass. Comn: Polyester murals, Dini's Sea Grill, Boston, 62-70; fountain & garden sculptures & portraits in pvt collections. Exhib: New Eng Sculptor's Asn Exhibs at most New Eng mus, 48-72; seven Boston Arts Festivals, 55-65; New Eng Sculptor's Asn, Prudential Ctr, Boston, 68 & 70; one-man shows, G W V Smith Mus, Springfield, 50, Tufts Col, Medford, Mass, 52, Crane Mus, Pittsfield, Mass, 56 & McIver-Ready Gallery, Boston, 68. Teaching: Instr sculpture, Boston Mus Sch, 40-53; instr sculpture, Bradford Jr Col, 3 yrs. Mem: Fel Nat Sculpture Soc; New Eng Sculptor's Asn (five terms as pres). Media: Wood, Stone, Clay. Mailing Add: 92 Russell St Charlestown MA 02129

MACNELLY, JEFFREY KENNETH
CARTOONIST
b New York, NY, Sept 17, 47. Study: Univ NC. Pos: Mem staff, Richmond News Leader. Awards: Pulitzer Prize as Editorial Cartoonist, 72. Media: India Ink, Watercolor. Publ: Auth, MacNelly, The Pulitzer Prize Winning Cartoonist: a Specially Selected Collection, Westover, 72. Mailing Add: 407 Lakewood Dr Richmond VA 23229

MACNUTT, GLENN GORDON
PAINTER, ILLUSTRATOR
b London, Ont, Jan 21, 06; US citizen. Study: Sch Mus Fine Arts, Boston, 30-32; Mass Sch Art, Boston, 24-28. Work: Boston Mus Fine Arts; Mus Am Art, Hartford, Conn; Farnsworth Mus, Maine; Frye Mus, Seattle; Harvard Univ. Exhib: One-man shows, Guild Boston Artists, 40-41, 43 & 75, Whistler House, 42, Wellesley Col, Doll & Richards Gallery, 47; Metrop Mus, 41-42; Pa Acad Fine Arts, 42-52; Los Angeles Pub Libr, 54. Awards: Adolph & Clara Obrig Prize, Nat Acad Design, 63; Grumbacher Award, Am Watercolor Soc, 65, E Heiland Award, 71, Ford Times Award, 72 & C R Kinghan Award, 73; Frank Liljegren Award, Allied Artists Am, 72. Mem: Boston Soc Watercolor Painters (vpres, secy-treas, 45-48); Guild Boston Artists (bd mgrs); Am Watercolor Soc; Nat Acad Design; Allied Artists Am. Mailing Add: 129 Minot St Dorchester MA 02122

MACOMBER, ALLISON
PAINTER, SCULPTOR
b Taunton, Mass, July 5, 16. Study: Mass Col Art, 34-38; also with Cyrus Dallin, Raymond Porter & Sir Henry Kitson. Work: Statues, portrait busts, memorial tablets and medals in stone and bronze throughout this country and abroad including bronze door entrances to Trenton Cathedral, NJ, twelve foot statue of Christ in limestone, Church of the Holy Name, Taftsville, Conn, Shah and Queen Farah (coin) of Iran, Corp of Pub Broadcasting Emmy Award which was a portrait medal of Ralph Lowell. Comn: Garden Club Am Medal, 65; medals and bronze memorial plaques including Babe Ruth, Knute Rockne, Amos Alonzo Stagg, Cardinal Cushing, Comdr Shea of the Wasp, many bicentennial coins and many others. Exhib: Pa Acad Fine Arts Exhib, 38-; Nat Sculpture Soc Ann, 40; Smithsonian Traveling Exhib, 60-62. Teaching: Artist in residence & dir art workshops, Boston Col, 63- Pos: Assoc sculptor, Gorham Corp Foundry; comnr, Mass State Senate Art Comn, 73- Awards: Utopian Club Medal Honor Design, 60; Int Silver Competition Award, 60; plus others. Mem: Utopian Club Providence, RI (past pres); hon mem Fall River Art Club. Style & Technique: Gesamtkunstwerk. Publ: Auth, Adventures in Private Flying (film), 42; auth, The Doors of Trenton Cathedral (film), 62. Mailing Add: Mulberry Cottage Segreganset MA 02773

MADDEN, BETTY I
ART HISTORIAN, PAINTER
b Chicago, Ill, Nov 15, 15. Study: Am Acad Art, Chicago; Northwestern Univ; Univ Ill, BFA; Inst Design, Chicago; with Herb Olson, Spain & Italy; John Pellew, Ireland & Eng; Zornes, Vt. Work: Ill State Hist Libr, Springfield. Exhib: Ill State Fair Prof Artists Exhib, 57; Ill State Mus Invitational, 59. Collections Arranged: Annual Mississippi Valley Artists Exhibitions, 63-67; Arts & Crafts in Old Illinois, 65, Artists & Sculptors in Illinois: 1820-1945, 72. Pos: Com artist & illusr, Consolidated Bk Publ, Chicago, 44-46; fashion illusr, Evans, Work & Costa Advert, Springfield, Ill, 55-59; fashion illusr, S A Barker Co, Springfield, 59-61; tech asst art dept, Ill State Mus, 61-63, cur art, 63-78. Mem: Clayville Folk Arts Guild; Soc Archit Historians; Springfield Art Asn. Media: Watercolor. Res: Illinois art, architecture and crafts. Publ: Auth, Art, Crafts and Architecture in Early Illinois, Univ Ill Press, 64. Mailing Add: 1145 S First St Springfield IL 62704

MADDOX, JERALD CURTIS
CURATOR, ART HISTORIAN
b Decatur, Ind, June 9, 33. Study: Ind Univ, AB, 55 & MA, 60; Harvard Univ, 60-61. Work: Int Mus Photog, George Eastman House, Rochester, NY. Collections Arranged: American Photography: The Sixties, Univ Nebr Art Galleries, 66; Creative Photography 1869-1969, Libr Cong, Washington, DC. 70. Teaching: Instr art hist, NY State Univ Col New Paltz, 62-63. Pos: Asst to dir, Univ Nebr Art Galleries, 63-66; head curatorial section & cur photog, Prints & Photog Div, Libr Cong, 66-; consult photog, Northern Va Community Col, 77. Awards: Mus Prof Fel, Nat Endowment Arts, 74. Mem: Col Art Asn; Soc Photog Educ (treas, 68-73). Res: History and criticism of photography. Publ: Auth, Essay on a tintype, 1/69 & Creative photography, 1869-1969, 1/71, Quart J Libr Cong; auth, Photography in the first decade, Art in Am, 7-8/73; auth, How much is a photograph worth, After Image, 2/75. Mailing Add: 4514 Highland Ave Bethesda MD 20014

MADDOX, JERROLD WARREN
EDUCATOR, PAINTER
b Ft Wayne, Ind, Mar 6, 32. Study: Ind Univ, BS, 54 & MFA, 59. Exhib: Recent Painting USA: The Figure, Mus Mod Art, New York, 62-63; Moods of Light, Am Fedn Art, 63-64. Teaching: Asst prof humanities, Monteith Col, Wayne State Univ, Detroit, 60-63; lectr painting & drawing, Regional Col Art & Crafts, Hull, Eng, 64; asst prof painting & drawing, Univ Ky, Lexington, 64-66; asst prof drawing & painting, Amherst Col, Mass, 66-69; assoc prof drawing & painting, Reed Col, Portland, Ore, 69-70; assoc prof drawing & painting, Ind Univ, Bloomington, 70-74; head prof, Kans State Univ, Manhattan, 74- Mem: Col Art Asn Am; Nat Coun Art Adminr (bd dir, 78-, secy-treas, 78-). Style & Technique: Figurative. Media: Oil. Publ: Co-auth, Images and Imagination: an Introduction to Art, 65. Mailing Add: 320 N Delaware Manhattan KS 66502

MADIGAN, MARY JEAN SMITH
CURATOR, WRITER
b Nanticoke, Pa, Feb 26, 41. Study: Cornell Univ, BA, 62; Am Univ, MA, 68. Collections Arranged: Photography of Rudolf Eickemeyer (with catalog), 72; Eastlake-Influenced American Furniture (with catalog), 73; The Sculpture of Isidore Konti-1862-1938 (with catalog), 75. Teaching: Lectr Am antiques, Westchester Community Col, Valhalla, NY, 75. Pos: Cur Am decorative art & hist, Hudson River Mus, Yonkers, NY, 70-76, bd reviewer, Mus News, 75-, cur exhib & collections, 76-77, asst dir, 77-; consult, NY State Coun for the Arts, 77- & Nat Endowment for the Humanities, 77- Awards: Harry M Grier Scholar, Asn Art Mus Dir, 75. Mem: Am Asn Mus; Northeast Mus Conf. Res: 19th century American decorative art and design reform movement. Publ: Auth, The influence of Charles Locke Eastlake on American furniture manufacturers, Winterthur Portfolio, 75; auth, Eastlake in America, Connoisseur, 75. Mailing Add: 76 S Broadway 17D Hastings-on-Hudson NY 10706

MADIGAN, RICHARD ALLEN
ART ADMINISTRATOR
b Corning, NY, Oct 29, 37. Study: Drew Univ, AB, 59; Univ Del; Am Univ. Collections Arranged: Contemporary Japanese Painting, 64; Australian Painters, 65-67; Contemporary Peruvian Painting & Sculpture, 67; Imagist Realism (with catalog), 74. Teaching: Instr mus studies, George Washington Univ, 64-67; instr Am art, Foreign Serv Inst, US Dept State, 65-67; instr mus studies, Lehman Col, 67-69. Pos: Dir, White Art Mus, Cornell Univ, 60-63; asst dir, Corcoran Gallery Art, Washington, DC, 63-67; dir, Mus Resources Coun, Ft Worth, Tex, 67; dir, Brooklyn Children's Mus, 68; exec dir, Wave Hill Ctr, New York, 69-74; dir, Norton Gallery & Sch Art, West Palm Beach, 74- Awards: European Study Grant, NY State Coun Arts, 71. Mem: Am Asn Mus (chmn col & univ sect, 62-63); Fla Art Mus Dir Asn (vpres, 77-); Int Coun Mus. Publ: Contribr, Australian Painters, 71. Mailing Add: c/o Norton Gallery 1451 S Olive St West Palm Beach FL 33401

MADSEN, LOREN WAKEFIELD
SCULPTOR
b Oakland, Calif, Mar 29, 43. Study: Reed Col, Portland, Ore, 61-63; Univ Calif, Los Angeles, BA, 66, MA, 70. Work: Walker Art Ctr, Minneapolis, Minn; Mus Mod Art, New York.

Comn: Untitled Sculpture, Prudential Insurance Co, Florham Park, NJ, 75; Broken Ring, Los Angeles Co Mus Art, Los Angeles, Calif, 77; 12in x 12in Timber Piece, Cedars-Sinai Med Ctr, Los Angeles, Calif, 77. Exhib: Los Angeles 6, 74 & New Selections, 76, Los Angeles Co Mus Art, Los Angeles, Calif; The Condition of Sculpture, Hayward Gallery, London, Eng, 75; one man show, Mus Mod Art, New York, 75; Sculpture Made in Place, Walker Art Ctr, Minneapolis, Minn, 76; The Biennale of Sculpture, Sydney, Australia, 76. Awards: New Talent Award, Mod & Contemp Art Coun, Los Angeles Co Mus Art, 75; fel—grant, Nat Endowment for the Arts, 76. Style & Technique: Commonly available materials, brick, lumber, etc, put together using tension, gravity, friction, etc. Media: Brick and lumber. Mailing Add: 99 Prince St New York NY 10012

MADSEN, VIGGO HOLM
PRINTMAKER, CRAFTSMAN
b Kaas, Denmark, Apr 21, 25; US citizen. Study: Anderson Col, Syracuse Univ, BFA, 51 & MFA, 52; NY Univ; Columbia Univ Teachers Col; Adelphi Univ; Inst Allende, San Miguel, Mex; Det Danske Selskab, Denmark. Work: Philadelphia Ctr Older People, Pa; Nassau Community Col, Garden City, NY; Anderson Col, Ind; C W Post Col, Brookville, NY; N Shore Community Art Ctr, Great Neck, NY. Exhib: Triennial Exhib Graphics, Grenchen, Switz, 67; Xylon IV, Geneva, Switz, 68; US Senate Chambers, Washington, DC, 68; Heckscher Mus Fine Arts, Huntington, NY, 72; Nat Acad Design Show, New York, 75; Surface Design Conf Exhib, Towson Univ, Md, 77. Teaching: Instr art, Roslyn High Sch, NY, 60-; prof, adj staff, Nassau Community Col, 66-; instr, Crafts Workshops, Adelphi Univ, 74- Pos: Ed, Newslett, Long Island Art Teachers Asn, 62-64. Awards: Award of Excellence, Long Island Craftsmen's Guild, 66-68; Award of Excellence, Long Island Art Teachers Exhib, C W Post Col, 75 & Alumni House Gallery, Adelphi Univ, 77. Best in Show Award, Long Island Art, 75. Bibliog: Jeanne Paris (auth), rev in Long Island Press, 7/71; Malcolm Preston (auth), rev in Newsday, 2/72; Dona Z Meilach (auth), chap in Creating Art with Textiles, Reilly & Lee. Mem: Prof Artists Guild (exhib chmn, 73-75); Long Island Craftsmen's Guild; NY State Art Teachers Asn; Am Crafts Coun; Long Island Art Teachers Asn. Style & Technique: Expressionistic designs based on actual objects, boldly colored and with strong contrasts in value. Media: Woodcuts, Batik, Silkscreen & Acrylic. Publ: Contribr, Art in action, 61, J Nat Art Educ Asn, 63 & J Eastern Arts Asn, 64; auth & publ, three demonstration booklets: Batik, Silk screening & Woodcut prints, 70-72. Dealer: Grenvile Gallery 118 Christopher St New York NY 10014; Panoras Art Gallery 62 W 56th St New York NY 10019. Mailing Add: 5 Meldon Ave Albertson NY 11507

MADURA, JACK JOSEPH
PAINTER, INSTRUCTOR
b Chicago, Ill, Feb 6, 41. Study: Murray State Univ, BS(art), 64 & MA(art educ), 66; Northern Ill Univ, with Robert Kabak, MFA(painting), 70. Work: City of Springfield Munic Collection, Ill; Temple B'rith Sholom, Springfield; Lincoln Land Community Col; Northern Ill Univ, DeKalb; Sangamo Club, Springfield, Ill. Exhib: Ill State Mus 24th Show, Springfield, 71; Illinois Artists '74 Dedication Exhib, Ctr Visual Arts, Ill State Univ, 74; Chicago State Univ Flat Show, 74; Rocky Mountain Nat Water Media Exhib, Golden, Colo, 74; Watercolor USA, Springfield Art Mus, Mo, 75 & 77; Watercolorists of Ill, Charleston, 77. Teaching: Instr drawing & painting, Somerset Community Col, Ky, 66-68; instr watercolor, printmaking & drawing, Lincoln Land Community Col, 70- Awards: Strawn Gallery Bi-Annual First Place for Painting, Jacksonville, Ill, 71; Third Place for Watercolor, 74 & Second Place for Watercolor, 75 & 76, Ill State Fair Prof Show; Purchase Prize in Watercolor, 7 for 76 Seven State Regional Show, Paul Sargent Gallery, Charleston, Ill, 76. Style & Technique: Combination space and landscape abstracted. Media: Watercolor. Mailing Add: 4 Long Bay Springfield IL 62707

MAEHARA, HIROMU
PAINTER, DESIGNER
b Nawiliwili, Hawaii, Nov 1, 14. Study: NY Sch Design. Exhib: Honolulu Artists, 41-61. Teaching: Instr drawing & painting, Honolulu. Pos: Former art dir advan art. Awards: 9 Prizes, Honolulu Artists, 55-69; Prizes, 50th State Exhib, 60 & Hawaii Home Builders, 66; plus others. Mem: Asn Honolulu Artists. Mailing Add: 2885 Kalihi Valley Rd Honolulu HI 96819

MAESTRO, GIULIO MARCELLO
ILLUSTRATOR, PAINTER
b New York, NY, May 6, 42. Study: Cooper Union Art Sch, BFA; Pratt Graphics Ctr. Awards: Citation of Merit, 10th Nat Exhib, 68 & 16th Nat Exhib, 74, New York Soc of Illusr; Cert of Excellence, The Children's Book Show 1974, The Am Inst of Graphic Arts, 74; Cert of Merit, Art Dir Club, New York, 78. Mem: Am Inst of Graphic Arts. Style & Technique: Illustration, colorful and humorous picture-book style; paintings, semi-abstract landscapes expressionist and hard-edge. Media: Pencil, Pen, Dyes; Gouache, Acrylic. Publ: Auth & illusr, The Tortoise's Tug of War, 71 & The Remarkable Plant in Apartment Four, 73, Bradbury Press, Inc; illusr, Harriet goes to the Circus, 77 & Busy Day, 78 & numerous other titles, Crown Publs, Inc; auth & illusr, Leopard is Sick, Greenwillow Bks, 78. Mailing Add: 702 Summer Hill Rd Madison CT 06443

MAGAFAN, ETHEL
PAINTER
b Chicago, Ill. Study: Colorado Springs Fine Arts Ctr, with Frank Mechau, Boardman Robinson & Peppino Mangravite. Work: Metrop Mus Art, New York; Munson-Williams-Proctor Inst, Utica, NY; Butler Inst Am Art, Youngstown, Ohio; Mem Library, Univ Notre Dame, Ind; Evansville Mus, Ind. Comn: Cotton Pickers (murals), Post Off Lobby, Wynne, Ark, 39; Prairie Fire, Post Off Lobby, Madill, Okla, 40; Mountains in Snow (with Jenne Magafan), Social Security Bldg, Washington, DC, 41; Horse Corral, Post Off Lobby, S Denver Br, Colo, 42; Battle of New Orleans, Recorder of Deeds Bldg, Washington, DC, 43. Exhib: American Painting Today, Metrop Mus Art, New York, 50; Am Acad Arts & Lett, New York, 61, 64 & 69; Pa Acad Design, Philadelphia, 61, 62, 64, & 69; Butler Inst Am Art, 63-66 & 68-74; Nat Acad Design, New York, 65-75. Awards: Benjamin Altman Prize, Nat Acad Design, 56, 64 & 73; Childe Hassam Purchase Award, Am Acad Arts & Lett, 70; Andrew Carnegie Award, Nat Acad Design, 77. Bibliog: Ernest W Watson (auth), Magafan and mountains, Am Artist Mag, 12/57; Jean Lipman & Cleve Gray (auth), The amazing inventiveness of women painters, Cosmopolitan Mag, 10/61. Mem: Nat Acad Design (mem coun, 72-75, 2nd vpres); Am Watercolor Soc; Audubon Artists; Philadelphia Watercolor Club; Woodstock Artist's Asn. Media: Egg Tempera, Watercolor. Dealer: Midtown Galleries 11 E 57th St New York NY 10022. Mailing Add: RFD Box 284 Woodstock NY 12498

MAGAZZINI, GENE
PAINTER
b New York, NY, Nov 5, 14. Study: Siena, Italy, with pvt tutors; Brooklyn Col; Art Students League, with Ivan Olinsky. Work: Sloan-Kettering Inst, New York. Exhib: State Capitol, Albany, NY, 62; Allied Artists Am, Nat Acad Design, New York; Palais Congres, Expos Intercontinentale, Monaco; Nat Arts Club & Salmagundi Club, New York; Burr Artists, Metrop Mus Art, New York, 77. Awards: First Prize, Salmagundi Club, 69; Best in Show & Purchase Prize, Salmagundi Club, 70; Best in Show & Gold Medal, Nat Art League, 71. Mem: Salmagundi Club (cur, 70-72); Artists' Fel; Nat Art League; Art Students League; Am Artists Prof League. Style & Technique: Traditional oil and oil murals a secco. Dealer: LBAA Art Gallery 36 W 44th St New York NY 10036. Mailing Add: 249 Euclid Ave Brooklyn NY 11208

MAGEE, ALDERSON
GRAPHIC ARTIST, PAINTER, COLLECTOR
b Hartford, Conn, Oct 5, 29. Study: Univ Conn, BS; West Hartford Art League; also with Estelle Coniff & Walter Korder. Exhib: New Britain Mus Am Art, Conn, 73-74; Conn Acad Fine Arts, Wadsworth Atheneum, Hartford, 74; 55th Nat Exhib, Smith Mus, Springfield, Mass, 74; Easton Waterfowl Festival, Md, 74-78; Hudson Valley Art Asn Exhib, White Plains, NY, 74, 75 & 78; Salmagundi Club Ann Graphics Exhib, New York, 76-77; Federal Duck Stamp Art, Peabody Mus, Salem, Mass, 77; Soc Animal Artists Exhib, Sportsman's Edge Gallery, New York, 78, Grand Nat Exhib, Am Artists Prof League, 78. Awards: First Prize, Conn Acad Fine Arts, 74; Gold Medal, Hudson Valley Art Asn, 75 & Grand Nat Exhib, Am Artists Prof League, New York, 78. Bibliog: Russell A Fink (publ), Duck Stamp Prints, 76; Nelson Bryant (auth), Duck stamp art on sale, New York Times, 4/16/76; Stunning black & white engraving, Audubon Mag, 1/76. Mem: Salmagundi Club; Hudson Valley Art Asn; Soc Animal Artists; Am Artists Prof League. Style & Technique: Scratchboard drawings in realistic manner, specializing in wildlife. Collection: Seventeenth and nineteenth century Dutch painting. Publ: Illusr (cover), Ducks Unlimited Mag, 75 & 77; illusr, Federal Duck Stamp Design, US Govt, 76. Mailing Add: Toad Hall Sharon CT 06069

MAGLEBY, FRANCIS R (FRANK)
PAINTER, EDUCATOR
b Idaho Falls, Idaho, Mar 22, 28. Study: Brigham Young Univ, BA & MA, 52; Art Students League; Am Art Sch, New York; Columbia Univ, EdD, 67. Comn: Historical paintings for various church bldgs, Mormon Church, Salt Lake City, Utah & New York, 58-59; Heleman (mural), Brigham Young Univ, 65. Exhib: One-man shows, Southern Vt Art Ctr, 55-59 & 71, Grand Cent Art Gallery, 57 & Brigham Young Univ, Utah, 68 & 78. Teaching: Prof painting, Brigham Young Univ, 59- Pos: Dir, B F Larson Gallery, Brigham Young Univ, 62-69. Mem: Am Fedn Arts; Southern Vt Art Ctr; Grand Cent Art Gallery; Western Asn Mus; Art Students League. Style & Technique: Landscape and figure painting in realistic style; oil on gesso panels incorporating glazing and direct painting technique. Mailing Add: 464 E 2200 N Provo UT 84601

MAGNAN, OSCAR GUSTAV
PAINTER, SCULPTOR
b Cienfuegos, Cuba, Dec 16, 37. Study: San Alejandro, Habana, Cuba, MFA, with Mateo Dela Torriente; Oxford Univ, Eng, Master in aribus; Sorbonne, with Dufrenne, PhD(aesthet). Work: Trustees of Contemp Art Inst Boston; Kansas City Art Inst; Pittsburgh Collection; President Johnson's Collection; Galleria d'Arte Mod, Macerata, Italy. Comn: Three panel mural, Univ Autonoma, Dom Repub, 68; bronze statue, Haina, Dom Repub, 68. Exhib: One-man shows, Palazzo Strozzi, Florence, Italy, 66 & Galerie Motte, Paris, 70; Salzburg Int Biennial, 64; Int Fair, Basle, Switz, 72; Inter-Kunst-Infomaturien, Dusseldorf, Ger, 72. Teaching: Assoc prof aesthet/sculpture, St Peter's Col, Jersey City, NJ, 70- Pos: Mem, NJ State Coun Arts, 72-75; dir art gallery, St Peter's Col, 72-, cur mus, 73- Awards: Can Coun Fel, 64; Cintas Found Inst Int Educ Fel, 66; Guggenheim Found Fel, 68. Style & Technique: Geometric, assimetrical perspective. Media: Acrylic, Tempera; Aluminum, Bronze. Dealer: Alonzo Gallery 30 W 57th St New York NY New York NY 10019. Mailing Add: 2652 Kennedy Blvd Jersey City NJ 07306

MAGRIEL, PAUL
COLLECTOR
b Mar 12, 16. Study: Columbia Univ. Pos: Cur dance arch, Mus Mod Art, New York, 39-42. Collection: Sport in art; American still life paintings, numismatics, drawings, watercolors; Renaissance bronzes; has been exhibited in 84 American museums. Mailing Add: 85 East End Ave New York NY 10028

MAGRUDER, JEAN BOWMAN
See Bowman, Jean

MAH, PETER
PAINTER, INSTRUCTOR
b Oct 28, 46; Can citizen. Study: Ont Col Art; Tyler Sch Art; RI Sch Design. Work: Brantford Art Gallery; Kitchener-Waterloo Art Gallery; Am Cultural Info Ctr; Univ Guelph. Exhib: 2nd Am Exhib Graphics, Brantford Art Gallery, Ont, 74; Drawing Rediscovered, Saidye Bronfman Ctr, Montreal, 74; Group Around the Body, Kitchner-Waterloo Art Gallery, 75; Human Bondage, McLaughlin Art Gallery, Oshana, Ont, 76; Can Soc of Watercolor, Sarnia, Ont, 78. Teaching: Instr drawing, Ont Col of Art. Awards: Dorothy Stevens Scholarship, 69; Traveling Scholarship, Ont Col of Art, 70;.Brantford Art Gallery Purchase Award, 74. Mem: Can Soc of Painters in Watercolor. Style & Technique: Representational of male and female figurative subject matter. Media: Drawing & Watercolor. Dealer: Julia Gadatsy 115 Yorkville Toronto ON M5R 1C1 Can Mailing Add: 94 Dixon Ave Toronto ON M4L 1N8 Can

MAHAFFEY, MERRILL DEAN
PAINTER, INSTRUCTOR
b Albuquerque, NMex, Aug 12, 37. Study: Calif Col Arts & Crafts; Sacramento State Col, BA; Ariz State Univ, MFA, 67. Work: Ariz State Univ; PhoenixArt Mus; Tucson Fine Arts Ctr. Exhib: Joslyn Mus Biennial, Omaha, Nebr; 61; one-man exhibs, Ft Worth Art Ctr, Tex, 62 & Phoenix Art Mus, Ariz, 69 & 75; Mus NMex Biennial, Santa Fe, 67; Ace Space Co Notebook Number One, Victoria Sch Visual Arts, Can, 70. Teaching: Instr painting & art hist, Phoenix Col, 67-; fac art, Fat City Sch Finds Art, 72. Pos: Lectr & writer art hist Am West. Style & Technique: Abstract western landscape; specializing in spray painting techniques. Media: Acrylic. Mailing Add: Art Dept Phoenix Col 1202 W Thomas Rd Phoenix AZ 85013

MAHEY, JOHN A
GALLERY DIRECTOR
b Du Bois, Pa, Mar 30, 32. Study: Columbia Col, 50-52; Pa State Univ, BA & MA(art hist). Collections Arranged: Sarah Miriam Peale (with catalog), Peale Mus, Baltimore, Md, 68; Master Drawings from Sacramento (with catalog), E B Crocker Art Gallery, Calif, 71. Teaching: Adj prof art hist, Univ Rochester, 75- Pos: Asst dir, Peale Mus, Baltimore, 64-69; dir, E B Crocker Art Gallery, Sacramento, 69-72; dir, Cummer Gallery Art, Jacksonville, 72-75; dir, Mem Art Gallery, 75- Res: James McNeil Whistler & Rembrandt Peale. Publ: Auth, Letters of James McNeil Whistler to George Lucas, 67, The lithographs of Rembrandt

Peale, 69 & The studio of Rembrandt Peale, 69. Mailing Add: 2445 East Ave Rochester NY 14610

MAHLKE, ERNEST D
SCULPTOR, EDUCATOR
b Madison, Wis, Sept 15, 30. Study: Univ Wis, BS & MS; Inst Allende, Univ Guanajuato, Mex, MFA. Work: State Univ NY Oneonta; plus many pvt collections. Exhib: Smithsonian Inst Traveling Exhibs, 55, 57 & 58; Fiber-Clay-Metal Nat Shows & a traveling exhib arranged by the Smithsonian Inst, 55, 61 & 62; Cooperstown Art Asn Nat Ann, NY, 66-67; Artists of Cent NY Regional Ann, Munson-Williams-Proctor Inst, Utica, NY, 68-74; one-man shows, Two Rivers Gallery, Binghamton, NY, 72 & The Art Ctr, Albany, NY, 76; Drawing & Small Sculpture Show, Ball State Univ Art Gallery, 75; Sculpture 75 Nat, 75. Teaching: Assoc prof sculpture, State Univ NY Oneonta, 62- Pos: Pres, Wis Designer Craftsmen, Milwaukee, 62; mem bd, Oneonta Art Ctr, NY, 77. Awards: First Place in Sculpture, Art 77, Norwich, NY, 77. Mem: Southern Asn Sculptors; Am Craftsmen's Coun. Style & Technique: Work in wood, welded steel and cast bronze, generally incorporating large space in linear framework; much use of borrowed textures in bronze. Media: Wood and metal sculpture. Dealer: Caulfield Gallery 74 Front St Binghamton NY 13905. Mailing Add: 39 Spruce St Oneonta NY 13820

MAHLMANN, JOHN JAMES
ART ADMINISTRATOR
b Washington, DC, Jan 21, 42. Study: Boston Univ, BFA, 62, MFA, 63; Univ Notre Dame, postgrad work, summer 62; Pa State Univ, EdD, 70. Teaching: Grad asst, Boston Univ, 62-63; grad asst & res asst, Pa State Univ, 63-64, instr, 66-67, dir gallery, Art Educ Dept, 66-67; asst prof, Tex Tech Col, 67-69. Pos: Asst exec secy, Nat Art Educ Asn, Washington, DC, 69-71, exec dir, 71- Mem: Washington Soc of Asn Exec; Am Soc Asn Exec. Mailing Add: c/o Nat Art Educ Asn 1916 Association Dr Reston VA 22091

MAHMOUD, BEN
PAINTER
b Charleston, WVa, Oct 6, 35. Study: Columbus Art Sch, prof cert; Ohio Univ, BFA & MFA. Work: Ill State Mus, Springfield, Ill; Krannart Mus, Univ Ill, Urbana, Art Inst Chicago; Columbus Gallery Fine Arts, Ohio; Brooklyn Mus, New York. Comn: Bas-relief, Wurlitzer Co, 67. Exhib: 1st Flint Int Exhib, Flint Art Inst, 66; Violence Exhib, Mus Contemp Art, Chicago, 67; Contemp Art in Midwest, Notre Dame Univ, 68; Art Today, Indianapolis Mus Art, Ind, 70; New Horizons in Painting, Chicago, 72. Pos: Mem bd, Ill Arts Coun, 73-77. Awards: Purchase Award, Ball State Univ, 70; Purchase Award, Images on Paper '70, Miss, 70; Best of Show, New Horizons in Painting, Chicago, 72. Bibliog: Frans Schultze (auth), review, Chicago Daily New Panorama, 67; Joshua King (auth), review, Art News, 67; Kulterman (auth), New Painting, Praeger, 70. Style & Technique: Paintings and drawings based on photographic distortions. Media: Acrylic. Publ: Auth, article in Prize Winning Paintings, Allied Fla, 61 & 64; contribr, Chicago Omnibus, Chicago Midwest Art & Art Gallery Mag, 67; illusr, Motive Mag, 68. Dealer: Zaks Gallery 620 N Michigan Ave Chicago IL 60611. Mailing Add: Dept of Art Northern Ill Univ De Kalb IL 60115

MAHONEY, JAMES OWEN
PAINTER, EDUCATOR
b Dallas, Tex, Oct 16, 07. Study: Southern Methodist Univ, BA, 29; Yale Sch Fine Arts, BFA, 32; Prix de Rome, Am Acad in Rome, 32-35. Comn: Murals, Hall of State, Tex Centennial Expos, Dallas, 36, Hall of Judiciary, Fed Bldg & Commun Bldg, New York World's Fair, 38, pres suite, Adolphus Hotel, Dallas, 50 & Shriver Hall, Johns Hopkins Univ, 57; altar piece, All Saints Episcopal Church, Chevy Chase, Md, 58. Exhib: Pa Acad Fine Arts; Grand Cent Art Gallery; Mace Gallery, Dallas; Archit League; Fairmont Hotel, Atlanta, 74. Teaching: Prof art, Cornell Univ, 54-75, emer prof, 75-, chmn dept, 63-68. Mem: Nat Soc Mural Painters. Mailing Add: 45 Twin Glens Rd Ithaca NY 14850

MAHONEY, MICHAEL R T
ART HISTORIAN, EDUCATOR
b Worcester, Mass, Jan 24, 35. Style & Technique: Phillips Acad, 53; Yale Univ, BA, 59; Courtauld Inst, Univ London, PhD, 65. Teaching: Prof art hist, Trinity Col, Hartford, 69- Pos: Mus cur, Nat Gallery of Art, Washington, DC, 64-69, cur sculpture, 67, ed, 68-69. Res: Seventeenth Century art. Publ: Auth, Drawings of Salvator Rosa, Garland, 77. Mailing Add: Austin Arts Ctr Trinity Col Hartford CT 06106

MAILMAN, CYNTHIA
PAINTER
b Bronx, NY, Dec 31, 42. Study: Pratt Inst, BS, 64; Art Students League; Brooklyn Mus Art Sch. Work: Prudential Life Ins Co, Newark, NJ. Comn: Mural, Citywalls Pub Arts Coun, Staten Island, NY, 77. Exhib: The Eye of Woman, William Smith & Hobart Col, 74; one-person shows, Soho 20 Gallery, New York, 74 & 76, Mabel Smith Douglass Libr, NJ, 76 & Fox-Richmond Gallery, Keuka Col, NY, 77; 118, Landmark Gallery, New York, 75 & 77; Sons and Others, Queens Mus, Flushing, 75; Contemporary Reflections, Aldrich Mus, Ridgefield, Conn, 75; The Magic Circle, Bronx Mus, NY, 77. Pos: Lectr, 77- Awards: Creative Artists Pub Serv Grant in Painting, 76-77. Bibliog: John Gruen (auth), rev in Soho Weekly News, 10/31/74; Ellen Lubell (auth), rev in Arts Mag, 10/74 & 12/76; Michael Andre (auth), rev in Art News, 3/76. Mem: Woman in Arts; Soho 20 Gallery. Style & Technique: Representational forms; themes mainly landscapes and portraits painted in flat, light tonalities. Media: Acrylic on Canvas. Mailing Add: 49 Broad St Staten Island NY 10304

MAINARDI, PATRICIA M
PAINTER, WRITER
b Paterson, NJ, Nov 10, 42. Study: Vassar Col, AB, 59-63; Columbia Univ, 63-65; New York Studio Sch, 65-66; Brooklyn Col, City Univ New York, MFA, 76. Exhib: The Representational Spirit, State Univ NY Albany Gallery, 70; Painterly Realism, Am Fedn Arts, 69-71; New Images: Figuration in American Painting, Queens Mus, 74; one-artist show, Green Mountain Gallery, New York, 71 & 74 & Ingber Gallery, 75 & 78. Teaching: Vis lectr, Pratt Inst, Mass Col Art, 73 & 74, Brooklyn Col, 76-, Sch Visual Arts, 77, Goddard Col, 77-; dir, Goddard Summer Art Community. Pos: Ed, Coccatrice, 61-63; ed, Women & Art, 71-72; ed, Feminist Art J, 72-73, contrib ed, 73-74. Bibliog: Reviews in, Art News, 10/69, 11/71, 5/72, 10/74 & 1/76, Arts, 9/74 & 2/76 & Art Int, summer 74. Publ: Articles and reviews for Art News, Art in Am, Art Gallery Mag, Feminist Art J & Radical Am. Dealer: Ingber Gallery 3 E 78 St New York NY 10021. Mailing Add: Box 2 Crafts Bury VT 05826

MAIONE, ROBERT
PAINTER
b New York, NY, 1932. Study: Art Students League; also with Frank Dumond & Frank Mason. Exhib: Allied Artists Am, 65-; Nat Acad Design Ann, 65-; Audubon Artists, 65-; Continuing Tradition of Realism in American Art; The Realistic Tradition, State Univ NY, Albany, 74. Awards: Art Students League, 51-53; Arthur T Hill Mem Prize, 60; Allied Artists Am Award, 74. Mem: Allied Artists Am; Salmagundi Club. Style & Technique: Landscape; realist. Media: Oil. Mailing Add: c/o Harbor Gallery 43 Main St Cold Spring Harbor NY 11724

MAITIN, SAMUEL (CALMAN)
DESIGNER, PAINTER
b Philadelphia, Pa, Oct 26, 28. Study: Philadelphia Mus Sch Art, dipl, 49; Univ Pa, BA, 51; printmaking with Ezio Martinelli and Paul Froelich. Work: Libr Cong & Nat Gallery Art, Washington, DC; Mus Mod Art, New York; Philadelphia Mus Art, Pa; Victoria & Albert Mus, London. Comn: 47 posters, Major Poster Proj, Philadelphia YM/YWHA Arts Coun, 61-68; Standing Structures, Luther Brady, Acey Wolgin, Collectors, Philadelphia, 73; Philadelphia Mus Art, Print & Construction, 74; mural, Annenberg Sch Commun, Univ Pa, 75; mural, Children's Hosp, Philadelphia, 75. Exhib: Three Graphic Artists: Feldman, Maitin, Mavignier, Philadelphia Mus Art, 66; Yoseido Gallery, Tokyo, 67, 69 & 70; 3rd Int Graphic Biennale, Poland, 70; Samuel Fleisher Art Mem, 71; William Penn Mus, Harrisburg, Pa, 75. Teaching: Instr design, Moore Col Art, 49-51; instr printmaking & drawing, Philadelphia Col Art, 49-59; head visual graphic commun, Annenberg Sch Commun, Univ Pa, 64-70; instr drawing & printmaking, Philadelphia Mus Art, 64-69. Awards: John Simon Guggenheim Found Fel graphics, 68; 50 Best Bks of Yr, Minor White, 70; Salute to Philadelphia Super-Achievers, Juv Diabetes Found, 75. Bibliog: Willard Randall (auth), Is Philadelphia ready for Sam Maitin?, Philadelphia Inquirer, Today Mag, 11/18/73; Walter Plata (auth), Typografen unserer Zeit, Samuel Maitin, Heft. Style & Technique: Bright color, large form, celebrative; works in silkscreen; large structures in wood and metal. Media: Graphics, Acrylic. Interest: Book design, murals. Publ: The Appalachian photographs of Doris Ulmann, Aperture, 71; illusr, Turning of the Year, 70, Gentle Gentle Thursday, 71, Holt, Rinehart & Winston; Designer, Sculpture of a City: Philadelphia's Treasures in Bronze and Stone, FPAA, Walker Publ Co, 74; Designer, A Rising People, Am Philos Soc, 75-76. Mailing Add: 704 Pine St Philadelphia PA 19106

MAJDRAKOFF, IVAN
PAINTER, EDUCATOR
b New York, NY, June 19, 27. Study: Cranbrook Acad Art, with Wallace Mitchell. Work: Univ Minn Gallery; Minneapolis Inst Art. Comn: Black & white photographic collage, Bronx State Hosp, NY, 71; Masonite outdoor mural, San Francisco Art Comn. Exhib: Pa Acad Art, Philadelphia; Detroit Art Inst, Mich; Walker Art Ctr, Minneapolis; San Francisco Mus Art; Drawing Exhib, Mus Mod Art, New York. Teaching: Instr drawing & painting, San Francisco Art Inst, 57-; instr drawing, Stanford Univ, 57-58 & 68-69. Pos: Actg dir, univ art gallery, Univ Minn, 52-55; dir, Stanford Univ Gallery, 62. Bibliog: Al Wong (auth), Portrait of Ivan (film), 68. Style & Technique: Acrylic abstracted painting; fantasy ink drawing and object assemblage. Mailing Add: 70 Zoe St San Francisco CA 94107

MAJESKI, THOMAS H
PRINTMAKER, INSTRUCTOR
b Council Bluffs, Iowa, Sept 14, 33. Study: Univ Omaha, BFA, 60, MFA, 63, studied with Mauricio Lasansky. Work: Philadelphia Mus Art, Pa; Sheldon Mem Art Mus, Lincoln, Nebr; Joslyn Mus, Omaha, Nebr; Utah State Univ, Logan; Springfield Art Mus, Mo. Exhib: Nat Print Exhib, New York Univ, Potsdam, 64; Prints, Watercolors & Drawings, Pa Acad Fine Arts, Philadelphia, 65; Brooklyn Mus, New York, 66; Philadelphia Print Club, Pa, 67; Northwest Printmakers Int Print Exhib, Seattle, Wash & Portland, Ore, 67; Art On Paper, Univ NC, Greensboro, 68; 17 State Exhib, Springfield Art Mus, Mo, 74; Colorprint USA, Tex Tech Univ, Lubbock, 74. Teaching: Prof printmaking, Univ Nebr Omaha, 73- Awards: Purchase Awards, Philadelphia Print Club, Lessing J Rosenwald, 67, Nebr Centennial, State of Nebr, 67 & Springfield Art Mus, 74. Mem: Philadelphia Print Club; Col Art Asn; Mid-Am Col Art Asn. Style & Technique: Figurative Media: Intaglio; drawing. Mailing Add: 1730 N 106 St Omaha NE 68114

MAKARENKO, ZACHARY PHILIPP
PAINTER, SCULPTOR
b North Caucasus, Russia, Feb 20, 00; US citizen. Study: State Univ Acad Fine Arts, Kiev; also study in Ger & Italy. Work: Many pub & pvt collections worldwide. Exhib: Angelicum, Regional Ital IV Relig Exhib, Milan, 47; USA Relig Exhib, Burr Gallery, New York, 58; Am Artists Prof League Grand Nat, New York, 66; Painter & Sculptor Soc Exhib, Jersey City Mus, NJ, 71; Nat Acad Design Galleries, New York, 71. Teaching: Instr pvt studio, 20- Awards: Ann Hyatt Huntington Award, Am Artists Prof League, 66; Medal of Honor, Painter & Sculptor Soc Exhib, Jersey City Mus, 71; Allied Artists Am Gold Medal of Honor for sculpture, Nat Acad Design Galleries, 71. Bibliog: Son style est essentiellement classique dens son expression de la vie aux formes harmonieuses, La Rev Mod, Paris, 64; article in City East, New York, 71. Mem: Fel Am Artists Prof League. Style & Technique: Constructive expression techniques. Mailing Add: 7332 Kennedy Blvd North Bergen NJ 07047

MAKI, ROBERT RICHARD
SCULPTOR
b Walla Walla, Wash, Sept 15, 38. Study: Western Wash State Col, BA, 62; Univ Wash, MFA, 66; San Francisco Art Inst Summer Workshop, 67. Work: Henry Gallery, Univ Wash, Seattle; Washington Univ; State Hwy Admin Bldg, Olympia, Wash; Stanford Univ; Nat Collection of Fine Art, Washington, DC. Comn: Cent plaza sculpture, comn by Port of Seattle, Seattle-Tacoma Int Airport, 72 & Fed Off Bldg, Eugene, Ore, 74. Exhib: West Coast Now, Portland Art Mus, Seattle Art Mus Pavilion, De Young Mus, San Francisco & Los Angeles Munic Mus, 68; Robert Maki-Construction, 69 & Uses of Structure, 70, Michael Walls Gallery, San Francisco; one-man shows, Seattle Art Mus Pavilion, Wash, 73; Portland Ctr for Visual Arts, Ore, 74. Awards: Nat Endowment Individual Artist Award, 68; Limited Nat Sculpture Competition Award, 72; Nat Sculpture Comn Award, 74. Bibliog: Peter Selz & Tom Robbins (auth), West Coast report: the Pacific Northwest today, Art in Am, 11-12/68; Palmer D French (auth), San Francisco, Artforum, 9/69; Jan Van de Marck (auth), Robert Maki at Center for Visual Arts, Art in Am, 9-10/74. Style & Technique: Primarily large scale sculpture projects, welded steel, aluminum and concrete planar constructions involving site/perception/experience. Mailing Add: 8 W Florentia Seattle WA 98109

MAKLER, HOPE WELSH
ART DEALER
b Philadelphia, Pa, Mar 24, 24. Study: Drexel Univ, BS; Bryn Mawr Col & Univ Pa, MA; Barnes Found. Pos: Owner & dir, Makler Gallery, Philadelphia. Specialty: Twentieth century painting, sculpture and graphics; Indian and African art. Mailing Add: 1716 Locust St Philadelphia PA 19103

MALBIN, LYDIA WINSTON
COLLECTOR
Pos: Arts comnr & hon cur mod art, Detroit Inst Arts; mem int coun, Mus Mod Art, New York; mem bd, Vassar Col Gallery Art. Interest: Collection was exhibited as a whole in Detroit Institute of Arts & Solomon R Guggenheim Mus, in part in other museums in the United States and Europe. Collection: Twentieth century art—futurism, cubism, deStill, Dada, colorists, constructionists; also large collection of graphics of the twentieth century including drawings by Picasso, Gris, Leger, Boccioni, Severini, Balla and others; numerous prints. Mailing Add: 425 E 58th St New York NY 10022

MALDJIAN, VARTAVAR B
PAINTER, WEAVER
b Marash, Cilicia, July 12, 18; US citizen. Study: Maristes Brothers Col; Sch of Art, Paris, grad(fine painting). Exhib: Nat Aleppo for Carpet Picture, 50; Int Exhib, Damascus, Carpet Picture, 56; Nat Competition of Benedictine, New York, 66; Nat for Prof Artists, New York, 68; Davinci Int Open Art, New York Colisuem, 70; plus many others. Awards: Silver Medal, Gustod of Terra Sancta (carpet picture), 50; Gold Medal for Carpet Picture, Int Exhib, Damascus, 56; Award for Original Oil, Davinci Int, New York, 70. Bibliog: Rev V Hovhanessian (auth), article on carpet picture, Massis, Beirut, 49; Abdallah J Hallack (auth), Ad-Dad, Monthly Art, 52; article about Pres Kennedy's carpet picture, Newark Eve News, 11/26/63. Mem: Am Fedn Art, New York. Style & Technique: Realist, figurative, classical, original; carpet pictures. Media: Oil on Canvas; Weaving with Oriental Knots. Collection: V B Maljian Museum, original oils and carpet pictures. Publ: Auth & illusr, Carpet (technique of weaving). Mailing Add: 38 Oriental St Newark NJ 07104

MALDRE, MATI
PHOTOGRAPHER, EDUCATOR
b Geestacht, Ger, Apr 3, 47; US citizen. Study: Univ Ill, with Joseph Jachna, BA(design), 69; Inst Design, Ill Inst Technol, with Aaron Siskind, Arthur Siegel & Charles Swedlund, Encycl Britannica grant, 70-72, MS(photog), 72; also with Paul Caponagro, Jerry Uelsmann, Nathan Lyons & Les Krims. Work: Kalamazoo Art Ctr, Mich; Humbolt Arts Coun, Eureka, Calif; Pasadena Mus Art, Calif; Louisville Photo Archive, Ky; Visual Studies Workshop, Rochester, NY. Exhib: Photo Media USA, San Diego, Calif, 71; New Photographics, Ellensberg, Wash, 73; Magic Machines Traveling Show, Western Asn Art Mus, 73-75; Int Photo Show, Chicago, 74; First Light, Humbolt Arts Coun, 75; Ill Photogr 78 (traveling exhib), Ill State Mus, Springfield, 78; Survey of Ill Photog, Lakeview Mus, Peoria, 78; Archit Photographs, Park Forest Art Ctr, Ill, 78. Teaching: Asst prof photog, Chicago State Univ, 72-; instr photog, Beverly Art Ctr, Ill, 73- Pos: Photogr & lab technician, Encycl Britannica, Chicago, 70-73; consult photog & graphics, Chicago Urban Corps, 72- Awards: Purchase Award, Humbolt Arts Coun, 75; Purchase Award, Ill State Mus, 78. Bibliog: Michael E Bry (auth), Gallery snooping, Mod Photog, 4/74. Mem: Soc Photo Educ; Int Mus Photo, George Eastman House. Style & Technique: Experimental color photography; view camera architectural photography. Media: Black and White, Cibachrome. Publ: Illusr, Encycl Britannica & Britannica Bk of Yr, 70-74; illusr, Comptons Encycl & Comptons Yr Bk, 70-74; illusr, Great Ideas Today, 70-74. Mailing Add: 3036 W 114th Pl Merrionette Park IL 60655

MALICOAT, PHILIP CECIL
PAINTER
b Indianapolis, Ind, Dec 9, 08. Study: John Herron Art Inst; Cape Cod Sch; Cape Sch Art; also with Charles W Hawthorne & E W Dickinson. Work: Rochester Mus Art, NY; Chrysler Mus, Norfolk, Va; Provincetown Art Asn, Mass; Joseph H Hirshhorn Collection, Washington, DC. Exhib: Provincetown Art Asn, 32-72; Pa Acad Fine Arts, Philadelphia, 33; Corcoran Gallery Art, Washington, DC, 38; one-man shows, Jacques Seligmann Gallery, New York, 49, Cape Cod Art Asn, 52, Wellons Gallery, New York, 55, Shore Galleries, Boston, 59, Miami Univ, Oxford, Ohio, 60 & Graham Gallery, New York, 65; Nat Acad Design, 54 & Art USA, 59, New York. Awards: Prizes from Cape Cod Art Asn & Falmouth Artists Guild; Chapelbrook Grant, 68-69. Mem: Provincetown Art Asn (hon vpres, 47-72); Beachcombers (pres). Style & Technique: Representational. Media: Oil, Pencil. Mailing Add: 320 Bradford St Provincetown MA 02657

MALINA, FRANK JOSEPH
ART EDITOR, PAINTER
b Brenham, Tex, Oct 2, 12. Study: Study with H C Spencer, drawing & painting, College Station, Tex; study with Reggie Weston, painting, Paris. Work: Musee Nat d'Art Moderne, Paris; Peter Stuyvesant Art Found, Amsterdam; Hall of Aerospace Art, Smithsonian Inst, Washington, DC; UNESCO House, Paris; Tel Aviv Mus, Israel. Comn: Kinetic Mural with Nino Calos, Pergamon Press Ltd, Oxford, England. Exhib: Structures, Galerie Henri Tronche, Paris, 53; Light & Motion, Galerie Colette Allendy, Paris, 54; Realites Nouvelles, Paris, 54; Les Arts En France Et Dans La Monde, Paris, 56; Int Exhib of Art in Motion, Amsterdam, Stockholm & Copenhagen, 61; Lumidyne Kinetic Paintings, Galerie Na Karlove Namesti, Prague, 66; Lumiere Et Mouvement Exhib, Mousee d'Art Moderne De La Ville De Paris, 67; Cybernetic Serendipity Exhib, Washington, DC, 69; Miniatures 70 Int, Munich, 71; Mus of Decorative Art, Copenhagen, 71; Inst of Tex Cultures, San Antonio, 72; Electric Light Kinetic Art, Tex A&M Col Sta, 72; Lumidyne Kinetic Paintings, Int Trade Fair, Teheran, 73. Pos: Founder, ed, Leonardo Int J Contemp Visual Artist, Pergamon Press Ltd, Oxford, Eng, 68- Awards: Prix Yvonne Valensi, Salon Comparisons, Paris, Henri Valensi, 58; Prix Signatures, Exhib Signatures, Paris, Group Signature, 71. Bibliog: Reg Gadney (auth), Aspects of Kinetic Art and Motion, Kinetic Art, Motion Books, London, 66; Ministry of Educ (auth), Kinetic Painting of Frank J Malina, color film, France, 69; Roger Bordier (auth), The Itinerary of Magic, Cimaise, Paris, 9/72. Style & Technique: Figurative and non-figurative, representational and geometrical abstract styles; kinetic painting with Lumidyne, Reflectodyne and Polarodyne systems; pictorial electric light images in motion; static pictures in various paints. Publ: Auth, Essay in Data: Directions in Art, Theory, Aesthetics, Faber & Faber, London, 68; auth, Reflections of an Artist—Engineer on the Art—Science Interface, Impact, Paris, 74; ed, Kinetic Art: Theory and Practice, Dover, New York, 74; auth, Electric Light as a Medium in the Visual Fine Arts: A Memoir, J Leonardo, 75; ed, Visual Art, Mathematics and Computers, Pergamon, Oxford, 78. Mailing Add: 17 Rue Emile Dunois Boulogne Sur Seine 92100 France

MALINOWSKI, JEROME JOSEPH
SCULPTOR, DESIGNER
b Cleveland, Ohio, May 28, 39. Study: Cleveland Inst Art, dipl; Toyo Kaneshige Bizen, Japan; Syracsue Univ, MFA. Work: Munson-Williams-Proctor Inst Mus, Utica, NY; Kaneshige Collection, Okayama, Japan. Comn: Sculpture comn by Mr & Mrs McVey, Honolulu, 64; mural, Izmir Hotel, Kabul, Afghanistan, 66; sculpture comn by Clark Estate, Essex, Eng, 66; kinetic sculpture, Jr League of Rochester, 70. Exhib: Graphics exhib, Matsushita Elec Co, Osaka, Japan; kinetic exhib, Albright Knox Gallery, Buffalo, 70; Fingerlakes Exhib, Mem Art Gallery, Rochester, 73; Cleveland May Show, Ohio. 73; one-man shows, Fairmont State Col, 72-75, Emmaus Sch Syst, Pa, 77 & Western Ky Univ, 78. Teaching: Assoc prof design, Syracuse Univ, NY, 67-; vis prof design, Mont State Univ, 72; vis instr design, Westminster Col, New Wilmington, Pa, 68; chmn dept, EXS Studios. Pos: Indust automotive designer, Ford Motor Co, Dearborn, Mich, 61-64; indust designer consult, Int Indust Design, Tokyo, 64-65; designer consult, Dept Parks & Recreation, Syracuse, 68-69; designer consult, NY State Coun for Social Studies, 70-72; consult, Syracuse Develop Ctr, 78. Awards: Purchase Award (sculpture), Munson-Williams-Proctor Inst, 70; Distinguished Achievement Award (graphic design), Educ Press Asn Am, 72; Grant for Young Designers, Educ Facil Inc, Ford Found, 73-74. Style & Technique: Cast Bronze, Wood, Metals, Plastic. Publ: Auth, Experimental Furniture for Children, 75. Mailing Add: Rd1 Lord Rd Erieville NY 13061

MALLARY, ROBERT
SCULPTOR, EDUCATOR
b Toledo, Ohio, Dec 2, 17. Study: Escuela Artes Libro, Mexico City, 38-39. Work: Mus Mod Art & Whitney Mus Am Art, New York; Los Angeles Co Mus; Albright-Knox Art Gallery, Buffalo; Univ Calif, Berkeley. Comn: Glass and plastic mosaic (with Dale Owen), Beverly Hills Hotel, 54; NY State Pavilion, New York World's Fair, 64; welded steel mural, Albany Mall Proj, 67. Exhib: 16 Americans, 59 & The Art of Assemblage, 61, Mus Mod Art, New York; Carnegie Int, Pittsburgh, Pa, 62; Ten American Sculptors, 7th São Paulo Biennial, Brazil, 63; Cybernetic Serendipity, Inst Contemp Art, London, 68. Teaching: Asst prof art, Univ NMex, 55-59; adj prof art, Pratt Inst, 59-67; prof sculpture, Univ Mass, Amherst, 67- Pos: Dir, Arstecnica: Interdisciplinary Ctr for Art & Technol, Univ Mass, 72- Bibliog: Art crashes through the junk pile, Life Mag, 51: 60-64; Collage: personalities, concepts, techniques, Janis & Plesh, 62; Harris Rothenstein (auth), Ideoloque in lotus land, Art News, 10/66. Publ: Auth, Self interview, Location, spring 63; auth, The air of art is poisoned, Art News, 10/63; co-auth, Interview, Artforum, 1/64; auth, Computer sculpture: six levels of cybernetics, Artforum, 5/69. Dealer: Allan Stone Gallery 86th St at Madison New York NY 10028. Mailing Add: PO Box 48 Conway MA 01341

MALLORY, LARRY RICHARD
PAINTER, INSTRUCTOR
bPunxsutawney, Pa, June 18, 49. Study: Indiana Univ Pa, BS & MA. Exhib: Am Artists Prof League Ann, Pa Chap, Ebensburg, 71; Am Artists Prof League Grand Nat, New York, 72; one-man show, Carnegie-Mellon Univ, Pittsburgh, 72; Bicentennial Exhib, Daughters of Am Revolution, Lever House, New York. Teaching: Asst art, Indiana Univ Pa, 70-71; instr art, Moskannon Valley Sch Dist, 71- Awards: First Prize, Am Artists Prof League Fair Show, Ebensburg, 72; First Drawing Award, Indiana Art Asn, 72; Second Cash Award, Am Artists Prof League, Grand Nat, New York, 75. Mem: Am Artists Prof League; Indiana Art Asn. Media: Pencil. Mailing Add: RD 1 Glen Campbell PA 15742

MALLORY, MARGARET
COLLECTOR, PRODUCER
b Brooklyn, NY, Oct 30, 11. Pos: Pres, Falcon Films, Inc (doc art films); trustee, Santa Barbara Mus Art; trustee, Mystic Seaport, Conn; hon life dir, art affil, Univ Calif, Santa Barbara. Collection: American and European paintings, drawings, sculpture, predominantly 19th & 20th century. Mailing Add: 305 Ortega Ridge Rd Santa Barbara CA 93108

MALLORY, NINA A
EDUCATOR, ART HISTORIAN
b Madrid, Spain; US citizen. Study: Columbia Univ, BArchit, 56, MA, 63 & PhD, 65. Teaching: Instr art hist, Rutgers Univ, New Brunswick, NJ, 65-66; asst prof renaissance, The Cooper Union, New York, 66-68; assoc prof renaissance & baroque, State Univ New York, Stony Brook, 68- Awards: Fulbright Fel, US Govt, 63; Grant-in-Aid, Am Coun of Learned Socs, 67; Fac Res Fel, State Univ New York Res Found, 70, 72, 74 & 75. Mem: Col Art Asn; Am Soc for Hispanic Art Hist Studies. Res: Eighteenth-century Italian architecture and seventeenth-eighteenth century Spanish art. Publ: Auth, Narciso Tome's transparente in the Cathedral of Toledo, J Soc of Archit Hist, 70; auth, Spanish Baroque sculpture in Madrid, Art J, 70; auth, Notices on sculpture in 18th-century Rome Bollettino d'Arte, 74; auth, Roman Rococo architecture from Clement XI to Benedict XIV, 1700-1758, Garland, 77; auth, The rape of the daughters of Leucippus, a note on a Rubens source, GOYA, 78. Mailing Add: 4 Washington Sq Village New York NY 10012

MALLORY, RONALD
SCULPTOR
b Los Angeles, Calif, June 17, 35. Study: Univ Colo, BA, 51; Univ Fla, BArch, 52; Sch Fine Arts, Rio de Janeiro, with Roberto Burle Marx, 56; Acad Julian, Paris, 58. Work: Mus Mod Art; Whitney Mus Am Art; Univ Mus, Berkeley, Calif; Inst Contemp Art, Boston; Inst Contemp Art, Philadelphia; plus others. Exhib: Mus Mod Art, 66 & 68; Worcester Mus Art, Mass, 67; Univ Ill, 67 & 68; Larry Aldrich Mus, Ridgefield, Conn, 67 & 68; Torcuato di Tella, Buenos Aires, Arg, 69; Univ Calif, Los Angeles, 69; Whitney Mus Am Art; plus others. Mailing Add: c/o Gallery Bonino Ltd 98 Prince St New York NY 10012

MALONE, JAMES WILLIAM
ARTIST
b Savannah, NY, Apr 12, 43. Study: State Univ NY Col Oswego, BA. Work: Dallas Mus Fine Arts, Tex; Ft Worth Art Mus, Tex. Exhib: Proj S/SW II, Ft Worth Art Ctr Mus, Tex, 71; Whitney Mus Am Art Ann, New York, 72; 20th Ann Southwestern Prints & Drawings, Dallas Mus, 75. Pos: Registr, Ft Worth Art Ctr Mus, 70- Mailing Add: 310 1/2 Main St Ft Worth TX 76102

MALONE, LEE H B
MUSEUM DIRECTOR
b Las Cruces, NMex, 28, 13. Study: Univ Sch, Cleveland, Ohio; Yale Sch Fine Arts, BA; also study in Switz. Collections Arranged: Art in Colonial Mexico, Columbus Gallery Fine Arts, Ohio, 52; Translucent and Transparent, 71 & Flowing Form, 72, Mus Fine Arts, St Petersburg, Fla, 72. Teaching: Instr hist of art, Notre Dame Col, Staten Island, NY, 40-41; instr hist art, Mus Fine Arts, St Petersburg, Fla, 68- Pos: Dir, Columbus Gallery Fine Arts, Ohio, 45-54; dir, Mus Fine Arts, Houston, Tex, 53-59; art consult, New York, 59-67; dir, Mus Fine Arts, St Petersburg, Fla, 68- Awards: W L Ehrich Mem Prize, Yale Univ, 39; Cavalier Ordine de Merito, Italy, 74. Mem: Am Asn Mus (secy, 73-75); Fine Arts Coun Fla; Southeastern Mus Conf. Publ: Auth, Spiritual Values in Art, Abrams Press, 53. Mailing Add: Mus Fine Arts 255 Beach Dr N St Petersburg FL 33701

MALONE, ROBERT R
PAINTER, PRINTMAKER
b McColl, SC, Aug 8, 33. Study: Furman Univ; Univ NC, AB; Univ Chicago, MFA; State Univ Iowa. Work: New York Pub Libr; Calif Palace of Legion of Honor, San Francisco; Philadelphia Mus Art, Pa; Smithsonian Inst, Washington, DC; Libr of Cong, Washington, DC. Comn: Color etching, Int Graphic Arts Soc, New York, 66; several editions of intaglio & relief prints, Ferdinand Roten Galleries, Baltimore, Md, 66-69; two editions intaglio &

relief prints, De Cinque Gallery, Hollywood, Fla, 67; color etching, Ill Arts Coun, 1st Print Comn, 73. Exhib: 15th Nat Print Exhib, Brooklyn Mus Art, NY, 66; New Talent in Printmaking, AAA Gallery, New York, 68; Biennial Print Exhib, Calif State Col, Long Beach, 69; Bienniale Int L'Estampe 1970, Mus Mod Art, Paris, 70; 26th Ann Exhib Boston Printmakers, De Cordova Mus, 74. Teaching: Assoc prof painting & printmaking, Wesleyan Col, Macon, Ga, 61-68; assoc prof printmaking, WVa Univ, Morgantown, 68-70; assoc prof printmaking, Southern Ill Univ, Edwardsville, 70-75, prof, 75- Awards: Purchase Award, Colorprint USA, Tex Tech Univ, 71; Recent Am Graphics Purchase Award, Univ Wis-Madison, 75; Southern Ill Univ Sr Res Scholar Award, 75. Mem: Mid-Am Col Art Conf; Col Art Asn Am. Style & Technique: Development of abstract realism; images evoking sense of future time and place; photogravure, viscosity and vacuum-serigraph prints. Media: Oil. Dealer: Assoc Am Artists 663 Fifth Ave New York NY 10022. Mailing Add: 600 Chapman St Edwardsville IL 62025

MALSCH, ELLEN L
PAINTER, INSTRUCTOR
b Copenhagen, Denmark; US citizen. Study: Art Inst Chicago. Work: Univ Wis-Madison; Luther Col, Decorah, Iowa; Univ Wis-La Crosse; Waukesha Co Tech Inst, Pewaukee, Wis; Univ Wis, Rockcount Campus, Janesville. Exhib: Wis Painters & Sculptors Show, Milwaukee Art Ctr, 62; three-man show, Wright Art Ctr, Beloit Col, Wis, 64; Drawings USA, Nat Biennial Show, St Paul, Minn, 66; Ill State Fair Prof Show, Springfield, Ill, 69; Watercolor USA, Springfield, Mo, 71; plus others. Teaching: Pvt classes, 60-72; instr watercolor, Burpee Art Mus, Rockford, Ill, 67-70; lectr, watercolor techniques. Awards: Purchase Prize, Beloit Col Vicinity Show, 65; Purchase Prize, Univ Wis-La Crosse, 69; Best of ShowAward, Wis Festival of Arts, 75. Bibliog: Article in La Rev Mod, 67. Mem: Wis Painters & Sculptors. Style & Technique: Very free, wet, abbreviated style, impressionistic, imaginative statements on nature and man's part in it. Media: Watercolor. Dealer: Neville-Sargent Gallery 1515 Sheridan Rd Wilmet IL 60091; Art Independent Gallery Main St Lake Geneva WI 53147. Mailing Add: Walker Rd Rte 1 Box 298 Beloit WI 53511

MALTA, VINCENT
EDUCATOR, PAINTER
b Brooklyn, NY, Apr 9, 22. Study: Art Students League. Work: Univ of Minn; Philadelphia Mus; Immaculate Heart Col; Birmingham Mus of Art. Exhib: Brooklyn Mus Biennial Print Exhib, 52; Metrop Mus Nat Exhib of Watercolors, 52; Pa Acad of Fine Arts, 53; Brooklyn Mus Int Watercolor Exhib, 53; Nat Acad of Design, 53. Teaching: Instr fine arts, painting, Art Students League, 66- Awards: Emily Lowe Award, 52; Tiffany Award, Louis Comfort Tiffany Found Award, 54; Betti Salzman Award, Nat Arts Club, 77. Bibliog: Marlene Schiller (auth), Return of the Art Spirit, Am Artist Mag, 3/78. Mem: Artist Equity. Style & Technique: Semi-abstract realism, expressionist manner. Media: Oil, Mixed Media. Mailing Add: 1960 60th St Brooklyn NY 11204

MALTBY, HAZEL FARROW
WEAVER, DESIGNER
b San Francisco, Calif. Study: San Francisco State Univ; with Karen Melander, Ada Rominger & Berta Frey; Portland Sch Arts & Crafts, with Theo Moorman. Work: Triton Mus Art, San Jose, Menlo Park Civic Ctr & Metrop Furniture, Ice House, San Francisco; First Fed Savings & Loan Asn, Rugby, NDak. Comn: Theme Piece (rug hanging), Northern Calif Handweavers Conf, 71; seven large tapestries, Episcopal Church, San Carlos, Calif, 77. Exhib: Calif Expo, Sacramento, 69-70; Las Vegas Art League Nat, 71; Festival '70, Livermore Cult Art Coun, Calif; Tex Fine Arts League Nat, Austin, 74; Handweavers Guild Am Nat Conf, San Francisco, 74; Int Weaving Exhib, Kouvola, Finland, 77. Teaching: Pvt art classes, 67-; lectr weaving, Foothill Community Col, 73-74; lectr painting warps, Nat Conf Handweavers Guild Am, 74. Awards: State of Calif Expo, 71; twelve awards, First or Second Place, Palo Alto Art Club, 71-75; Las Vegas Art League Nat Roundup, 71. Mem: Palo Alto Art Club (vpres); Handweavers Guild Am; Bay Area Arts & Crafts Guild; Trampornus Weaving Guild (pres); Loom & Shuttle Weaving Guild. Publ: Auth, Painting Warps, 74. Dealer: The Gallery 1320 Broadway Burlingam CA 94010. Mailing Add: 118 Plazoleta Los Gatos CA 95030

MALTZMAN, STANLEY
PRINTMAKER, PAINTER
b New York, NY, July 4, 21. Work: Eisenhower Col, Salem, NY; Pleasantville Mid Sch, NY; Hudson River Mus, Yonkers, NY; Carnegie-Mellon Univ; Chicago Div AT&T Co. Comn: Tiffany Co, New York & Steuben Glass, Corning, NY. Exhib: Am Acad Arts & Lett, 69 & Nat Acad Design, 70 & [Int:], New York; Norfolk Mus Arts & Sci, Va, 71; Smithsonian Inst Traveling Exhib, 71-72; Acad Artists Asn, Mus Fine Arts, Springfield, Mass, 72; Albany Inst Hist & Art, NY, 77. Awards: Childe Hassam Fund Purchase Award, Am Acad Arts & Lett, 69; First Prize, Conn Acad Fine Arts, 76; Ball State Univ Award, 76. Style & Technique: Realistic style; watercolor: combine wet on wet with dry technique; lithography: work on stone rather than metal plates; etching: softgound, aquatint, dry point, etc. Media: Charcoal, Graphics. Dealer: Weyhe Gallery 794 Lexington Ave New York NY 10021; Assoc Am Artists Gallery 663 Fifth Ave New York NY 10022. Mailing Add: Rte 1 Box 158 Freehold NY 12431

MANAREY, THELMA ALBERTA
PRINTMAKER, PAINTER
b Edmonton, Alta, May 2, 13. Study: Inst Technol & Art, Calgary; Univ Alta; Univ Wash Summer Workshops; Banff Sch Fine Arts, with Charles Stegeman; Univ Calgary, with Shane Weare & Andrew Stasik; also at Emma Lake, with John Ferren & Ken Noland. Work: Alta Found; Mem Union, Univ Ore; Edmonton Art Gallery; Mem Univ Art Gallery, Nfld; Alta House Eng. Comn: Portrait of Roberta MacAdams, Women of Alta, Prov Legis, 67; Lt Gov Walsh, 73. Exhib: Can Landscape Painters, Stratford, 64; 10th Winnipeg Show, 66; Can Graphics, 70; one-person shows, Edmonton Art Gallery, Alta, 70 & 72; West '71; Printmakers Showcase West, Ottawa, 74. Awards: Centennial Visual Arts Award, 67; award, Pac Northwest Art Ann, 69; City of Edmonton Visual Arts Award, 73. Mem: Alta Soc Artists (prov vpres, 65, 67, 68 & 75); Print & Drawing Coun of Can. Media: Graphics. Dealer: Framecraft 7711 85th St Edmonton AB Can. Mailing Add: 12026 93rd St Edmonton AB T5G 1E8 Can

MANCA, ALBINO
SCULPTOR
b Tertenia, Italy, Jan 1, 98. Study: Acad Fine Arts, Rome, with Ferrari & Zanelli. Comn: Pieta Medallion in Gold, Off Medal Vatican Pavilion, New York World's Fair, 64-65; Pope Paul VI Peace Medallion in Gold, Treasury of St Peter, The Vatican, 65; The Diving Eagle, 2nd World War E Coast Mem, Battery Park, New York; The Gate of Life, entrance gate, Queens Zoo, New York, 68; Robert Moses Bronze Medallion, Fordham Univ, 70; plus others. Exhib: Many nat & int exhibs. Teaching: Former prof, Acad Fine Arts, Rome. Awards: Ellin P Speyer Prize, 64 & Mahonry Young Mem Prize, 66, Nat Acad Design; Winner Competition, Smithsonian Inst, 65; plus others. Mem: Nat Acad Design; fel Nat Sculpture Soc; Am Artists Prof League; Allied Artists Am. Mailing Add: 131 W 11th St New York NY 10011

MANCINI, JOHN
PAINTER, ILLUSTRATOR
b Comiso, Italy, Jan 9, 25; US citizen. Study: Scuola d'Arte, Comiso, Italy, dipl; Liceo & Accad di Belle Arti, Palermo, Italy, BA; Art Students League; Columbia Univ. Work: Galleria Della Accademi, Palermo, Italy; Triton Mus Art, San Jose, Calif; Galeria de Colecionistas, Mexico City. Exhib: Premio Naz di Terni, Rome, 50; Premio Naz di Suzzara, Italy, 51; 68th Western Ann Denver Mus, Colo, 62; Crocker Mus Art, Sacramento, Calif, 67; Palace of Fine Art, San Francisco, 68. Teaching: Art teacher painting, Scuola d'Arte, Comiso, Italy, 49-51. Pos: Art dir, Gridley Studio, New York, 51-58; art dir, Aerojet Gen Corp, Sacramento, Calif, 59-65; art dir, R W Graphics, Palo Alto, Calif, 66-70. Awards: Second Premio Naz, La Soffitta, 50; Purchase Award Western Image 71, Frontier Savings, 71; Gold Medal, Italian-Am Artists in USA, 77. Bibliog: Robert Brabski (auth), Italienishe Maler Und Bildhauer, William Herzog-Wien VI, 50; E M Polley (auth), John Mancini, Artforum, 65; Thomas Albright (auth), John Mancini, San Francisco Chronicle, 73. Style & Technique: Abstract-impressionist. Media: Oil. Dealer: Chase Sweetser 740 N La Cienega Los Angeles CA 90069; S Foster ADI Gallery Inc 530 McAllister St San Francisco CA 94102. Mailing Add: 604 Connie Ave San Mateo CA 94402

MANCUSI-UNGARO, CAROL CARUSO
CONSERVATOR
b Montclair, NJ, May 30, 46. Study: Conn Col Women, BA, 68; Inst Fine Arts, NY Univ, MA(hist art), 70; Yale Univ, with Andrew F Petryn, 71-74. Collections Arranged: Restored oil painting for the Edwin Austin Abbey Show, Yale Univ Art Gallery, 73-74. Teaching: Teacher prin painting conserv, Yale Univ, 76- Pos: Asst restoration, Yale Univ Art Gallery, 71-74; conservator paintings, Yale Ctr British Art & British Studies, 74- Mem: Int Inst Conserv Hist & Artistic Works. Mailing Add: 14 B Cedar Ct East Haven CT 06513

MANCUSO, LENI (LENI MANCUSO BARRETT)
PAINTER, INSTRUCTOR
b New York, NY. Study: Brooklyn Mus Art Sch, with Reuben Tam & William Kienbusch; Art Students League; Pratt Inst, NY. Work: Newberry Collection, Detroit, Mich; First Nat Bank Boston; Portland Mus Art, Maine; St Paul's Sch, Concord, NH. Exhib: Maine Art Gallery, Wiscasset, 70; New Eng Landscape Paintings, De Cordova Mus, Lincoln, Mass, 71; Lyman Allen Mus, Conn; Wadsworth Athenaeum, Hartford, Conn; one-man shows, Lamont Gallery, Exeter, NH, 73, Univ Maine, Orono, 77 & Deer Isle Artists Asn, Stonington, Maine, 77. Teaching: Instr painting & head art dept, Proctor Acad, Andover, NH, 55-60; instr painting & watercolor, Currier Gallery Art Sch, Manchester, NH, 62-70; instr painting & compos, St Paul's Sch, Concord, NH, 67- Awards: Watercolor Prize, Portland Mus Art, Maine, 61 & Currier Gallery Art, NH, 68. Mem: NH Art Asn; Boston Visual Artists Union; Col Art Asn. Style & Technique: Lyric expressionist interpretation of landscape and figure in direct painting, varying transparency with opacity in order to achieve the maximum range of form. Media: Watercolor, Casein. Dealer: Arnold Klein Gallery 4520 N Woodward Royal Oak MI 48072; Cape Split Place Addison ME 04606. Mailing Add: Eagle Island Sunset ME 04683

MANDEL, HOWARD
PAINTER, SCULPTOR
b Bayside, NY, Feb 24, 17. Study: Pratt Inst, New York; New York Sculpture Ctr; Art Students League; Atelier Fernand Léger, Paris; Atelier André L'Hôte, Paris; Ecole Beaux Arts, Sorbonne, France. Work: Whitney Mus Am Art, New York; Butler Inst Am Art, Youngstown, Ohio; Norfolk Mus Arts & Sci, Va; State Univ Teachers Col Mus, Oswego, NY; San Antonio Mus, Tex. Comn: Three-dimensional mural, Zenith Radio Corp, for Refregier Studio, Woodstock, NY, 58. Exhib: Whitney Mus Am Art Ann, 48-59; American Painting Today 1950, Metrop Mus Art, New York, 50 & Am Watercolors, Drawings & Prints, Metrop Mus Art, New York; Nat Inst Arts & Lett, Acad Art Gallery, New York, 55 & 61; Fulbright Painters, Whitney Mus Am Art & Smithsonian Inst, Washington, DC, 59. Pos: Graphic artist, film design, CBS-TV Studio One, 54-57; graphic artist, film design, NBC-TV Amahl and the Night Visitors, 55; art dir, Heath de Rochemont, D C Heath & Co, Boston, 63-68; art dir, Roemer-Young Assocs, New York, 69; art dir, Film Group, Inc, Cambridge, Mass, 71. Awards: Louis Comfort Tiffany Fel, 39 & 49; Hallmark Int Awards, 49, 52 & 55; Fulbright Scholar to Paris, 51-52. Bibliog: Herdeg & Rosner (auth), article in Graphics Ann, 55; The Art Comics & Satires of A D Reinhardt, George Wittenborn; Archives of American Art, Smithsonian Inst, Washington, DC. Mem: Am Watercolor Soc; Nat Soc Mural Painters; Nat Soc Painters in Casein & Acrylic; Audubon Artists; Allied Artists Am. Style & Technique: Personal style leaning to decorative realism. Media: Oil, Acrylic, Watercolor. Mailing Add: 285 Central Park W New York NY 10024

MANDEL, JOHN
PAINTER
b New York, NY, Dec 6, 41. Study: Pratt Inst, BFA, 64. Work: Nat Gallery Australia; Pa State Univ. Exhib: Whitney Mus Am Art Painting Ann, 69 & 72; The Contemporary Figure, A New Realism, Suffolk Mus & Carriage House at Stony Brook, NY, 71; In Sharp Focus, Sidney Janis Gallery, New York, 72; Indianapolis Mus Ann, Ind, 72; one-man shows, Max Hutchinson Gallery, New York, 71, 73 & 75. Teaching: Instr painting, grad & undergrad sch, Pratt Inst, 71-76; instr painting, Calif Inst Arts, 72- Bibliog: John Canaday (auth), Art: the figure as defined by Mandel, 11/21/71 & Art: in Mandel's Art, superb control, 4/28/73, New York Times. Mailing Add: c/o Art Sch Calif Inst of Arts Valencia CA 91355

MANDELMAN, BEATRICE M
PAINTER
b Newark, NJ, Dec 31, 12. Study: Art Students League. Work: NMex Mus Fine Arts; Metrop Mus, New York; Baltimore Mus. Exhib: One-woman show, Mus Fine Arts, Santa Fe, NMex & Stables Gallery, Taos, NMex; El Paso Mus, Tex; Denver Mus. Teaching: Teacher painting, Taos Valley Art Sch, 46-53. Awards: Oakes First Prize, Taos Art Asn Gallery, 62; Best Painting, Stables Art Gallery, 68; First Prize, Jury Show, 75. Bibliog: John Nichols (auth), article in NMex Mag, 72; Trisha Hurst (auth), article in Southwest Art, 74. Mem: Taos Art Asn. Style & Technique: Abstract painter. Media: Acrylic, Collage. Mailing Add: Box 891 Taos NM 87571

MANDLE, EARL ROGER
ART ADMINISTRATOR, ART HISTORIAN
b Hackensack, NJ, May 13, 41. Study: Williams Col, BA, 63; Art Students League; Inst Fine Arts, NY Univ, mus training cert & MA, 67; Metrop Mus Art; Victoria & Albert Mus. Collections Arranged: 30 Contemporary Black Artists, 68; Catalogue of European Paintings, Minneapolis Inst Arts, 70; Dutch Masterpieces from the 18th Century, 71-72. Teaching: Instr art, Phillips Acad, Andover, Mass, 63-64; instr art, McBurney Sch, New York, 64-65; vis

lectr, Univ Wis, 73. Pos: Cur, Inst Fine Arts Photog Arch, New York, 67; asst dir, Minneapolis Inst Arts, 67-71, assoc dir, 72-74; assoc dir, Toledo Mus Art, 74-77, dir, 77- Awards: Andover Teaching Fel, Phillips Acad, 63; Ford Found Mus Fel, 66-67; Nat Educ Asn Mus Fel, 74. Bibliog: J Woelm (auth), Dutch Masterpieces from the 18th century (film), Woelm-Polister Prod, 72; J Canaday (auth), Dutch masterpieces from the 18th century, New York Times, 72. Mem: Achtiendse Eeuw Werkgroep, Holland; Hendrik De Keyser Hist Soc, Holland; Int Coun Mus; Nat Educ Asn (panelist); Nat Endowment for Humanities (panelist). Res: Eighteenth century Dutch art and nineteenth century English art. Publ: Contribr, Peace concluded, Minneapolis Inst Arts Bull, 70; Jacob de Wit and the Amsterdam Town Hall, Apollo, 8/72; Mus orientation centers, Am Asn Mus News, 74; A ceiling design by Jacob de Wit, Toledo Mus Art News, 75; auth, Jacob de Wit's drawings of temperance, Register, Univ Kans, 2/77. Mailing Add: c/o Toledo Mus of Art Box 1013 Toledo OH 43697

MANDZIUK, MICHAEL DENNIS
PAINTER, SERIGRAPHER
b Detroit, Mich, Jan 14, 42. Work: Minn Mus Art, St Paul; Borg Warner Corp, Chicago; Kemper Ins Collection, Long Grove, Ill; Art Ctr Collection, Park Forest, Ill; Springfield City Collection, Ill. Exhib: Minn Mus Art Drawing Biennial, St Paul, 73; Butler Inst Am Art, Youngstown, Ohio, 73-74; Ukrainian Inst Mod Art, Chicago, 75; Mitchell Art Mus, Mt Vernon, Ill, 75; Battle Creek Art Ctr, Mich, 76. Pos: Artist-craftsman juror, Ann Arbor St Art Fair, 71; graphic artist & indust illusr, Ford Motor Co. Awards: Best of Show Award, Valparaiso Art Fair, Ind, 73; Old Capt Art Fair Award, Springfield, Ill, 73-74. Style & Technique: Symbolic abstraction, hard edge. Media: Acrylic. Mailing Add: 1924 Brookfield Canton MI 48188

MANETTA, EDWARD J
ART ADMINISTRATOR, PAINTER
b Export, Pa, Dec 26, 25. Study: Carnegie-Mellon Univ, BA, 53; Univ Pittsburgh; Herron Sch of Art, Ind Univ, Indianapolis, MFA, 55; NY Univ, EdD(creative arts), 65. Work: Ansty Col, Eng; Marygrove Col, Detroit; Ball State Art Mus, Muncie, Ind; South Bend Art Mus, Ind; HWA Kang Mus, Taipei, Taiwan. Comn: Paintings, Ford Motor Co, Detroit, 63; paintings, St Vincent's Priory, New York, 70; paintings, RCA Corp, New York, 70; mural, Mule Plastics Corp, Haupague, NY, 73; mural, Electrical Union Cult Ctr, New York, 75. Exhib: Wichita Art Mus, Kans, 52; Butler Art Inst, Youngstown, Ohio, 53; Pa Acad Fine Arts, Philadelphia, 53; Cincinnati Art Mus, Ohio, 55; Nat Acad Design, New York, 56; Royal Soc Galleries, Birmingham, Eng, 59; Herron Art Mus, Indianapolis, 60; Univ Detroit, 62; Int Petroleum Festival, Kansas City, 68; Nat Hist Mus, Taipei, 77; HWA Kang Mus, Taipei, 77. Teaching: Instr, Herron Sch Art, 55-61; Fulbright lectr art, Ansty Col, Sutton Coldfield, Eng, 58-59; prof, Marygrove Col, Detroit, 61-63; prof fine arts, St John's Univ, Jamaica, NY, 63-67, chmn fine arts dept, 68-, Fulbright exchange prof, Nat Taiwan Normal Univ, Taipei, spring 78. Awards: Fulbright Exchange fel, Gt Brit, 58-59; John Hay Humanities fel, Williams Col, Williamstown, Mass & Bennington Col, Vt, 61; vis artist fel, Col Chinese Cult, Taipei, 76-77. Mem: Col Art Asn; Nat Coun Art Adminrs; Am Asn Univ Prof; Nat Soc Skull & Circle; Am Acad Art & Lett. Style & Technique: Abstract expressionism. Media: Oil, Acrylic. Publ: Contribr, Evolution of the City, 74 & illusr, Education Textbook, 77, St John's Press; illusr, Administrators Guide to New Programs for Faculty Management and Evaluation, Parker Publ Co, West Nyack, NY, 77. Mailing Add: 52 Glenmere Lane Coram NY 11727

MANGEL, BENJAMIN
ART DEALER
b Philadelphia, Pa, Jan 12, 25. Pos: Owner, Benjamin Mangel Gallery, Bala Cynwyd, Pa. Specialty: Contemporary paintings and sculpture. Mailing Add: 202 Bala Ave Bala Cynwyd PA 19004

MANGIONE, PATRICIA ANTHONY
PAINTER
b Seattle, Wash. Study: Fleisher Art Mem, Philadelphia; Barnes Found, Merion, Pa. Work: Inst Contemp Art, Dallas; Fleisher Art Mem; Fidelity Bank, Philadelphia; Westchester State Mus, Pa; Rochester Mem Art Gallery, NY. Comn: Acrylic on wood mural, Continental Bank & Trust Co, Philadelphia, 69. Exhib: Five one-man shows, Frank Rehn Gallery, 60-74; one-man shows, Univ Pa, 64 & US Govt Gallery, Palermo, Italy, 65; Rosemont Col, Pa, 67 & 74; Philadelphia Art Alliance, 75. Teaching: Instr painting, Fleisher Art Mem, 48-61; instr painting, Suburban Art Ctr, Bryn Mawr, Pa, 59-61. Awards: Philadelphia Art Teachers Asn First Prize, 57 & 64; six Yaddo Resident Fels, 62-78; Saratoga Springs Oil Prize, 66. Bibliog: Burton Wasserman (auth), The Art of Patricia Mangione, Sims Press, Inc, 71 & Painter with flair, Courier-Post, Camden, 71. Mem: Artists Equity Asn; Philadelphia Art Alliance; Inst Contemp Art, Univ Pa. Style & Technique: Primarily a colorist working in the abstract; marked by a fluid interplay of tones producing an overall effect of both delicacy and strength. Media: Oil, Acrylic. Publ: Illusr, Sicilia, Ital Govt Quart, 66 & 68; auth, Some observations on the experience of painting, Parapsychol Found, Inc, 70; auth, Exercise in magic, Sunday Bulletin, Philadelphia, 71. Dealer: Frank Rehn Gallery 655 Madison Ave New York NY 10021. Mailing Add: 1901 Kennedy Blvd Philadelphia PA 19103

MANGOLD, ROBERT PETER
PAINTER
b North Tonawanda, NY, Oct 12, 37. Study: Cleveland Inst Art; Yale Univ, BFA & MFA. Work: Solomon R Guggenheim Mus, Mus Mod Art & Whitney Mus Am Art, New York; Stedelijk Mus, Amsterdam, Holland; Los Angeles Co Mus Art, Calif. Exhib: Artists Under Forty, 68 & Am Drawings: 1963-1973, 73, Whitney Mus Am Art; Albright-Knox Art Gallery, Buffalo, NY, 70; Solomon R Guggenheim Mus, 71; Documenta, Kassel, WGer, 72; La Jolla Mus Contemp Art, 74; Mus Contemp Arts, Chicago, 74; New York Cult Ctr, 74; Mus Mod Art, New York, 75; plus others. Teaching: Instr art, Sch Visual Arts, 63-, Hunter Col, 64-65, Cornell Univ, Skowhegan Summer Art Sch, 68 & Yale-Norfolk Summer Art Sch. Awards: Nat Coun on Arts Award, 66; Guggenheim Mem Grant, 69. Bibliog: Lucy R Lippard (auth), Silent art: Robert Mangold, In: Changing Essays in Art Criticism, Dutton, 71;Joseph 71; Joseph Masheck (auth), A humanist geometry, Artforum, 3/74. Dealer: John Weber Gallery 420 W Broadway New York NY 10012. Mailing Add: MD 1 Bull Rd Washingtonville NY 10992

MANGOLD, SYLVIA PLIMACK
PAINTER
b New York, NY, Sept 18, 38. Study: Cooper Union, cert, 59; Yale Univ Art Sch, BFA, 61. Exhib: Selections in Contemporary Realism, Akron Art Inst, Ohio, 74; New Images in American Painting, Queens Mus, New York, 74; The Herbert & Dorothy Vogel Collection, Inst Art & Urban Resources, New York, 75; 20th Century Drawings, Hawthorne Gallery, Skidmore Col, 75; 16 Realists, Fischbach Gallery, New York, 75. Teaching: Instr drawing, Sch Visual Arts, New York, 70, instr painting, 70-71, 74-75 & 76- Media: Acrylic. Dealer: Droll/Kolbert 724 Fifth Ave New York NY 10019. Mailing Add: MD 1 Bull Rd Washingtonville NY 10992

MANGRAVITE, PEPPINO GINO
PAINTER, LECTURER
b Lipari, Italy, June 28, 96; US citizen. Study: Scuole Techniche; Belle Arti, Italy; Cooper Union, cert, 24, citation, 56; Art Students League. Work: Metrop Mus Art & Whitney Mus Am Art, New York; Phillips Gallery Art, Washington, DC; Art Inst Chicago; Calif Palace of Legion of Honor, San Francisco. Comn: History of Transportation (two murals), comn by US Treas Dept, Hempstead Post Off, NY, 33; American at Rest and Play (two murals), comn by US Treas Dept, Atlantic City Post Off, NJ, 35. Exhib: Venice Biennale, Italy, 38; Art in Progress, Mus Mod Art, New York, 46; La Pintura Contemporanea Norteamericano (traveling exhib), Carnegie Inst Int, 48; La Pintura Contemporanea Norteamericano (traveling exhib), 61; most nat & int exhibs, 30-65; 48 one-man exhibs, New York, Washington, DC, Chicago, Colo, Calif & others. Teaching: Dir art dept, Sarah Lawrence Col, 30-35; instr drawing, Cooper Union, 37-42; prof painting, Columbia Univ, 42-64, prof emer, 64- Awards: Guggenheim Fel, 32 & 35; Purchase Prize for painting, Golden Gate Int Expos, 39; Silver Medal for mosaic design, Archit League New York, 55. Bibliog: Helen Appleton Read (auth), Peppino Mangravite, Parnassus, 34; Harry Salpeter (auth), Mangravite: music in art, Esquire, 39; Ralph M Pearson (auth), Peppino Mangravite: the Modern Renaissance in American Art, Harper & Row, 54. Mem: Century Asn. Media: Acrylic. Publ: Auth, The American painter and his environment, 35; auth, Aesthetic freedom and the Artists' Congress, 36; auth, Relation of creative design to an education in the humanities, 52; auth, The art of the war poster—an index to American taste, 57; auth, Dante through three artists' eyes, 65. Dealer: Frank Rehn Gallery 655 Madison Ave New York NY 10021. Mailing Add: Old Town Rd West Cornwall CT 06796

MANGUM, WILLIAM (GOODSON)
SCULPTOR
b Kinston, NC. Study: Corcoran Sch Art, Washington, DC; Art Students League; Univ NC, Chapel Hill, BA & MA. Work: NC Mus Art, Raleigh; Salem Col, Winston-Salem, NC; Carl Sandburg Mem Mus, Flat Rock, NC. Comn: Lamp of Learning Monument, Dunning Industs, Greensboro, NC, 67; portrait bust of Carl Sandburg, Greensboro CofC, 68. Exhib: Galerie Paula Insel Exhib & Bodley Gallery Nat, New York; Mass Mus Art, Springfield; Isaac Delgado Mus, New Orleans, La; Va Mus Fine Art Exhib. Teaching: Assoc prof art hist & sculpture, Salem Col, currently. Awards: Cert of distinction, Va Mus Fine Art; Isaac Delgado Mus Award; NC Mus Art Award. Mem: Southern Asn Sculptors. Style & Technique: Expressionist; direct carving, forms not imposed on but determined in part by shape, grain and texture of the wood. Publ: Auth, Marino Marini as portraitist, 70. Dealer: Southeastern Ctr Contemporary Art Marguerite Dr Winston-Salem NC 27108. Mailing Add: Dept of Art Salem Col Winston-Salem NC 27108

MANHART, THOMAS ARTHUR
EDUCATOR, CERAMIST
b Canon City, Colo, July 16, 37. Study: Univ Hawaii; Univ Tulsa, BA & MA. Work: Ark Arts Ctr, Little Rock; Fred Jones Mem Art Mus, Univ Okla, Norman; Philbrook Art Ctr, Tulsa; Okla State Art Collection, Okla Art Ctr, Oklahoma City. Exhib: Nat Decorative Arts Exhib, Wichita, Kans, 61, 64 & 66; Southwestern Crafts Bienniel, Santa Fe, NMex, 65, 72 & 75; Craftsmen USA, Dallas & New York, 66; Regional Prints, Drawings & Crafts Exhib, Little Rock, 67 & 75; Nat Craftsmen's Exhib, Wichita, 68, 70 & 72. Teaching: Instr ceramics, Univ Tulsa, 61-68, asst prof ceramics, 69-73, assoc prof ceramics, 74- Awards: Nat Decorative Arts Exhib Medal of Honor, Wichita Art Asn, 66; Nat Merit Award, Craftsmen USA, Am Crafts Coun, 66; Okla State Art Collection, Okla Arts & Humanities Coun, 73. Bibliog: Gar Bethel (auth), Manharts, Craft Horizons, 74; ODC Exhibition, Ceramics Monthly, 75. Mem: Am Crafts Coun (state rep, 66); Okla Designer Craftsmen; Tulsa Designer Craftsmen (pres, 68). Style & Technique: Ceramic forms, sometimes combined with fibers. Media: Clay and Fibers. Publ: Contribr, Profile, Am Crafts Coun, 60; contribr, Craft Horizons, 66, 68, 74 & 75; contribr, Cimarron Rev, 69; contribr, Tulsa Univ Alumni Mag, 69; contribr, Ceramics Monthly, 75. Mailing Add: c/o Univ Tulsa 600 S College Tulsa OK 74104

MANHOLD, JOHN HENRY
SCULPTOR
b Rochester, NY, Aug 20, 19. Study: Univ Rochester, BA; New Sch, with Chaim Gross & Manolo Pasqual; also with Ward Mount. Work: City of West Orange, NJ; Mem Sloan-Kettering Hosp, New York; Pyrofilm Corp, Whippany, NJ; A J Levera Assocs, Madison, NJ; Jacques Piccard Inst, Bern, Switz; plus others. Comn: Numerous bronze and stone figures; Fred Collins, 67-; bronze bust, Kallman Assocs, Jersey City, NJ; three bronze busts, Col Med & Dent NJ, Newark, 69 & 70; bronze figure, Bernard Koven, 71. Exhib: Allied Artists Am, 66; Audubon Artists Am, 67-69; Mainstreams '68 & '71, Grover M Hermann Fine Arts Ctr, Ohio, 68 & 71; Nat Sculpture Soc, 69; Am Artists Prof League, 70-72; plus others. Pos: Dir sculpture, Ringwood Manor Asn Arts, 68-70, 1st vpres, 70-71; vpres sculpture, Painters & Sculptors Soc NJ, 74- Awards: Medal of Honor for sculpture, State of NJ, 68; Second Prize Patrons Award, Painters & Sculptors Soc NJ, 71; John Subkis Award, Nat Arts Club, 71; plus others. Bibliog: David Leis (auth), pictures in Life Mag, 69; Pierre Morand (auth), La section Americaine de la Salon del'arte Française, La Rev Mod, 70; Ruth Ann Williams (auth), Art of the oranges, NJ Music & Art, 72. Mem: Acad Artists Asn; fel Am Artists Prof League; Painters & Sculptors Soc NJ; Nat Arts Club; Knickerbocker Artists. Media: Marble, Bronze. Mailing Add: 352 Shunpike Rd Chatham NJ 07928

MANILLA, TESS (TESS MANILLA WEINER)
PAINTER
b Poland; US citizen. Study: Educ Alliance, New York, with Abbo Ostrowsky; Brooklyn Mus Art Sch, with Reuben Tam, Victor Candell, Manfred Schwartz & Louis Finkelstein; Art Students League, with Morris Kantor, Sidney Gross & Morris Davidson; Pratt Graphics Ctr, with Walter Ragolsky; Provincetown Workshop, with Leo Manzo. Work: Long Island Univ. Exhib: One-person shows, Village Art Ctr, New York, 58, Long Island Univ, 65, Contemp Arts Gallery, New York, 66, Lincoln Savings Bank, 76 & Statesman's Club of New York, 77; Union Carbide Gallery, 73, Lever House, 74 & Aames Gallery, 75, Metrop Painters & Sculptors; one yr travelling watercolor show, Nat Asn Women Artists, Va Mus & State of Va; Nat Acad NY, 75. Teaching: Instr pvt classes, children & adults. Awards: Helen Hurzberger Scholar, Art Students League, 61; Nat Asn Women Artists Award, 72; Medal of Merit, League of Present Day Artists, 74. Mem: Nat Asn Women Artists (pub rels chmn, 73-75); Metrop Painters & Sculptors (pres, 68-75); Brooklyn Arts & Cult Asn (art chmn, 70-72); Avant VI (pres, 70-72); New York Soc Women Artists. Style & Technique: Abstract. Media: Oil, Collages. Mailing Add: 50 Lenox Rd Brooklyn NY 11226

MANKOWSKI, BRUNO
SCULPTOR
b Ger, Oct 30, 02; US citizen. Study: Munic Art Sch & State Art Sch, Berlin; Beaux Arts Inst, New York. Work: Am Numis Soc, Metrop Mus Art, Nat Acad Design & Soc Medalists, New York; Smithsonian Inst Div Numis, Washington, DC. Comn: Sculptured panel, by US Govt-Soc Fine Arts, Chesterfield, SC, 39; Mem plaque, Macombs Jr High Sch, NY, 49;

carvings, architect of capitol, Washington, DC, 50 & 60; designs for Steuben Glass, Corning, NY, 54-55; medal-Asa Gray, Hall Fame Great Am, NY Univ, 72. Exhib: Nat Acad Design Ann, 40-78; Pa Acad Fine Arts Ann, 47-54; Nat Sculpture Soc Ann, 47-78; Am Acad Arts & Lett, 49-50; Allied Artists Am Ann, 52-77. Daniel Chester French Award, Allied Artists Am, 64; Herbert Adams Mem Medal, 72 & Silver Medal, Bicentennial Exhib, 76, Nat Sculpture Soc. Bibliog: Articles in Am Artists Mag, 49-59; rev in Nat Sculpture Soc, 53-77; Works of Art in United States Capitol, US Govt Printing Off, 65. Mem: Nat Acad Design (mem comt, 71-73); fel Nat Sculpture Soc (coun mem, 53-58 & 71-78, chmn exhib comt, 56-58); life fel Am Numis Soc; Allied Artists Am; Archit League. Mailing Add: 2231 Broadway New York NY 10024

MANN, ANDY
VIDEO ARTIST
b New York, NY, June 19, 47. Study: NY Univ Sch Arts, BA, 73. Work: Everson Mus, Syracuse, NY; Ft Worth Mus Art, Tex; Long Beach Mus Art, Calif. Comn: Videotape broadcast, WGBH TV Workshop, 74; videotape, Contemp Art Mus, Houston, Tex, 75. Exhib: Videotape shows, Leo Castelli Gallery, New York, 73 & 74; Everson Mus, 73-75; one-man show, The Kitchen, New York, 74; Whitney Biennial, New York, 75 & 77; Video Art, Inst Contemp Art, Philadelphia, 75; The Great Am Rodeo, Ft Worth Art Mus, Tex, 77. Awards: Nat Endowment Arts Fel, 75. Style & Technique: Hand held video camera work. Media: Videotape. Dealer: Electronic Arts Intermix 84 Fifth Ave New York NY 10012. Mailing Add: c/o Castelli Sonnabend Tapes & Films 420 W Broadway New York NY 10012

MANN, DAVID
ART DEALER
b NJ, July 23, 18. Pos: Dir, Bodley Gallery. Mem: Art Dealers Asn Am. Specialty: Surrealist work, modern master drawings and exhibits of contemporary paintings and sculpture. Mailing Add: c/o Abbey 225 W 34th St 1611 New York NY 10001

MANN, KATINKA
PAINTER, PRINTMAKER
b New York, NY, June 28, 25. Study: Univ Hartford Art Sch; Pratt Graphic Arts, New York. Work: Nassau Community Col, Garden City, NY. Exhib: Soc Am Graphic Artists-Assoc Am Artists 50th Ann, 69; Light Happening, Suffolk Mus, Stony Brook, NY, 70; US Info Agency, Washington, DC, 71-73; Nat Asn Women's Artists Ital Exhib, Florence, Naples & Milan, 72; Int Miniature Print Exhib, Assoc Am Artists Gallery, New York, 72-73. Awards: Judith Leiber Co Purchase Award, Soc Am Graphic Artists, 69; Purchase Award, Nassau Community Col, 71. Bibliog: 50 years in American printmaking, Soc Am Graphics, 69; Artists of Suffolk County, Heckscher Mus, 7/72; Art in the World, Rinehart Press, 75. Mem: Nat Asn Women Artists; Prof Artists Guild (vpres-prog chmn, 69-71, mem jury co-chmn & bd mem, 72-73); Mus Mod Art; Artists Equity Asn. Style & Technique: Shaped canvas depicting aerial imagery; the shape is the force; the absence of brush marks and lack of process provide a pure look. Media: Polymers. Dealer: Central Hall Gallery 52 Main St Port Washington NY 11050. Mailing Add: 294 Pidgeon Hill Rd Huntington Station NY 11746

MANN, VAUGHAN (VAUGHAN GRAYSON)
PAINTER, PRINTMAKER
b Moose Jaw, Sask. Study: Columbia Univ, BS. Work: Royal Ont Mus. Exhib: Can Soc Painter-Etchers & Engravers, 54, 55 & 57; Moose Jaw, Sask, 56, 61 & 67; one-man shows, Kelowna, BC, 56 & Nelson, BC, 60; Vancouver Art Gallery; plus others. Teaching: Lectr, Exten Div, Univ BC & Univ Sask Summer Sch. Pos: Dir art, Teacher's Col, Regina & Moose Jaw, Sask; Vernon Art Soc, BC. Mem: Fine Arts Guild, Moose Jaw; Vernon Art Soc; Can Soc Painter-Etchers & Engravers; Nat Serigrapher Soc, NY. Publ: Auth, Picture Appreciation—Elementary School & Picture Appreciation—Junior High School, J M Dent & Sons, London. Mailing Add: 228 Stadacona W Moose Jaw SK S6H 1Z4 Can

MANNING, JO
PRINTMAKER
b Sydney, BC, Dec 11, 23. Study: Ont Col Art, Toronto, grad, 45, spec study printmaking, 60. Work: Nat Gallery Can, Ottawa; Montreal Mus Fine Art; London Libr & Art Mus, Ont; Willistead Gallery, Windsor; Univ Calgary, Alta. Exhib: Biennale Int Graphica, Florence, Italy, 70; 4th Am Biennale Engravings, Santiago, Chile, 70; Cracow Poland Biennale, 70 & 72; Expos Int Dessins, Rijeka, Yugoslavia, 70 & 72; Venice Biennale, 72. Teaching: Assoc master printmaking, Sheridan Col, Brampton, Ont, 71- Awards: Nicholas Hornyansky Award, Can Soc Painter-Etchers & Engravers, 70; Gold Medal, Florence, Italy, 70; Presidente Frei, 4th Am Biennale, Santiago, Chile, 70. Mem: Can Soc Graphic Arts (pres, 68-69); Can Soc Painter-Etchers & Engravers (exec, 63-65). Mailing Add: 19 Humewood Dr Toronto ON M6C 2W3 Can

MANNING, REG (WEST)
CARTOONIST, WRITER
b Kansas City, Mo, Apr 8, 05. Study: Phoenix Union High Sch Art Classes. Work: Cartoon Collection, Syracuse Univ; Lyndon Johnson Libr, Austin, Tex; Presidential Mus, Odessa, Tex; Univ Southern Miss, Hattiesburg. Exhib: One-man shows, Phoenix Art Mus, 61 & 73 & Pheonix Art Mus, 73. Pos: Ed cartoonist, Ariz Republic, 26- Awards: Pulitzer Prize, Columbia Univ, 51; Abraham Lincoln Award, Freedoms Found, 70 & 71. Bibliog: Alan D Covey (auth), Southwestern authors, Ariz Librn, fall 66. Mem: Asn Am Ed Cartoonists; Nat Cartoonists Soc; Phoenix Fine Arts Asn. Interest: Copper wheel crystal engraver and designer. Publ: Auth & illusr, What Kinda Cactus Izzat?, 41, From Tee to Cup, 54, What is Arizona Really Like?, 68 & Desert in Crystal, 73. Mailing Add: 5724 E Cambridge Scottsdale AZ 85257

MANRIQUE, JORGE ALBERTO
ART CRITIC, ART HISTORIAN
b Mexico City, Mex, July 17, 36. Study: Univ Nacional Autonoma, Mex, Grad; Univ Paris; Univ Rome. Teaching: Instr hist Mex art, Univ Veracruz, 59-62; instr sem hist art, El Colegio de Mexico, 64-68; instr Mexican colonial art, Univ Mex, 65- Pos: Dir, Fac Filosofia Letras, Univ Veracruz, 62; dir, Revista de la Univ, Mexico City, 69-72; dir, Inst Invest Esteticas, Univ Mex, 74- Mem: Acad Mex Hist; Comite Mexicano de Hist del Arte (secy, 74); hon mem Soc Mex Arquitectos Restauradores; Soc Int Hispanistas. Res: Mexican colonial art from 16th to 18th century; contemporary art. Publ: Auth, Los Dominicos y Azcapotzalco, 62; auth, El Neostilo: la Ultima Carta del Barroco Mexicano, 70; auth, El Rey ha Muerto, Viva el Rey: La Nueva Pintura Mexicana, 70; contribr, Latinoamerica en sus Artes, 74; auth, El Geometrismo Mexicano, 77. Mailing Add: Inst Invest Esteticas Ciudad Univ Torre Human Mexico DF Mexico

MANSARAM, PANCHAL
COLLAGE ARTIST, PHOTOGRAPHER
b Mount Abu, India, Mar 4, 34. Study: Sir J J Sch Art, Bombay, India, 54-59; State Acad Fine Arts, Amsterdam, fel, 63; Ryerson Polytech, Toronto, Can, cert motion picture prod, 70. Work: Gemeente Mus, The Hague; Nat Gallery Mod Art, New Delhi, India; Mem Univ Gallery, St Johns, Nfld; McIntosh Gallery, London, Ont; pvt collection of Dr Marshall McLuhan. Comn: Two ceramic murals for residence of D R Chhabra, New Delhi, 65-66. Exhib: Mixed Media Concert, Isaacs Gallery, Toronto, 67; Man and His World, Montreal, PQ, 68; Int Print Show, Vienna, Austria, 72; Int Original Drawing Show, Mus Mod Art, Rijeka, Yugoslavia, 74; Okeefe Ctr, Toronto, 75; New York Drawing Biennial, Bronx Mus Art, 76; 1st Brit Biennial Prints, Bradford, Eng, 76; Conceptual Mobile Miniature Show (with Bobby Jones, Los Angeles), Guggenheim Mus, New York, 77. Awards: First Prize, Bombay State Art Exhib, 59; Colour & Form Soc Award, Toronto, 75. Mem: Int Asn Educ Through Art; Colour & Form Soc; Print & Drawing Coun of Can; Can Artists Representation. Style & Technique: Electrostatic color transfer print, Collage, Serigraph, Painting, Blue Print. Media: Collage; Films, Video. Dealer: Canvas Gallery 21 Augusta St Hamilton ON Can; George Rackus 1998 Lakeshore Rd W Clarkson ON Can. Mailing Add: 298 Gardenview Dr Burlington ON Can

MANSHIP, JOHN PAUL
PAINTER, SCULPTOR
b New York, NY, Jan 16, 27. Study: Harvard Univ, AB, 48; with George Demetrios; Brera Acad, Milan. Work: Nat Collection Fine Arts, Washington, DC; Louisville Art Mus, Ky; Long Beach Art Mus, Calif. Comn: Baptism of Christ, Baptistry, St John Martyr, New York, 63; Pentecost (fresco), Chapel Sisters of St Joseph, Pawtucket, RI, 65; stations of cross, St Clements Church, Warwick, RI, 66; Resurrection (with Margaret Cassidy), St Anthony's Church, Springfield, Mass, 71; portrait of Judge O'Connor, Worcester Co Courthouse, 72. Teaching: Instr drawing & painting, Marymount Col, New York, 63. Awards: Childe Hassam Purchase Award, Am Acad Arts & Lett, 55; Watercolor Prize, Nat Arts Club, 62; Ranger Fund Purchase Award, Nat Acad Design, 65. Mem: Am Watercolor Soc; Nat Soc Mural Painters (secy, 72-75); Am Fine Arts Fedn; North Shore Art Asn (dir, 70-72); Burr Artists. Style & Technique: Realism in painting. Media: Oil, Gouache, Watercolor; Mosaics. Publ: Auth, Paul Claudel, Commonweal, 55; auth, Raphael, Cath Encycl Youth, 64. Dealer: Grand Central Art Galleries Madison Ave & 43rd St New York NY 10017. Mailing Add: 463 West St New York NY 10014

MANSO, LEO
PAINTER, EDUCATOR
b New York, NY, Apr 15, 14. Study: Nat Acad Design; New Sch Social Res. Work: Mus Mod Art & Whitney Mus Am Art, New York; Mus Fine Arts, Boston; Worcester Mus, Mass; Corcoran Gallery Art, Washington, DC. Comn: Mural, Lincoln Pub Libr, Nebr, 65. Exhib: Nat Inst Arts & Lett, 61 & 69; Mus Mod Art, New York, 61 & 65; Whitney Mus Am Art Ann, 47-66; Pa Acad Fine Arts, Philadelphia, 68; New Eng Arts Festival, 71. Teaching: Co-founder, Provincetown Workshop, Mass, 59-; prof painting & drawing, NY Univ, 50- Awards: Award for Aspects of the Harbor (oil), Urbana Ann, Ill, 50; Purchase Award for Seasons (oil), Ford Found, 63; Childe Hassam Purchase Award for Juggernaut (construct), Am Acad Arts & Lett, 69. Mem: Am Abstract Artists. Media: Oil, Acrylic, Collage, Assemblage. Dealer: Frank Rehn Gallery 655 Madison Ave New York NY 10021. Mailing Add: 460 Riverside Dr New York NY 10027

MANTON, JOCK (ARCHIMEDES ARISTIDES GIACOMANTONIO)
SCULPTOR, ART ADMINISTRATOR
b Jersey City, NJ, Jan 17, 06. Study: Leonardo da Vinci Art Sch, New York; Royal Acad Fine Arts, Rome, Italy; also with Onorio Ruutolo & Vincenzo Gemito. Work: Truman (sculptor), Truman Libr, Independence, Mo; Vincenzo Gemito (sculpture), Galleria di Arte Moderna, Rome, Italy; Grandma (sculpture), Royal Palace, Rome; Mediterranean Flower (sculpture), Mus Capitoleum, Rome. Comn: Spanish American War Soldier (sculpture), Union City, 42; Eisenhower (sculpture), West Point Mil Acad, NY, 45; Wounded Soldier (sculpture), Lincoln High Sch, Jersey City, 46; Christopher Columbus (sculpture), Jersey City Columbus Mall, 50; bust of Milton Cross, Metrop Opera. Exhib: Montclair Art Mus, 38; Metrop Mus Art, New York, 43; Nat Acad Design; Allied Artists Am; Nat Sculpture Soc. Pos: Trustee, Mus Jersey City, NJ, 32-48; reviewer arts, Am Broadcasting Co, 51-71; exec dir, Sussex Co Arts Coun, Inc, 71-77. Awards: Maynard Prize, Nat Acad Design; Dr Martin Luther King-Therese Richard Mem Award for Religious Sculpture, 76 & Joel Meisner & Co Award, 77, Allied Artists Am; Acad Artists Award, Springfield, Mass, 77. Bibliog: Truman Poses for Giacomantonio (film), produced on ABC TV. Mem: Nat Sculpture Soc; Lotos Club; Allied Artists Am. Media: Bronze, Marble. Mailing Add: 42 W 67th St New York NY 10023

MANUELLA, FRANK R
DESIGNER, PAINTER
b New York, NY. Study: Cooper Union Advan Sci & Art; also with Minoru Niizuma & James Rosati. Comn: Graphic design, Am Airlines, New York, 71; graphic design, Primary Indust, New York, 72; mural, Weis, Voisin & Co, Ft Lee, NJ, 73; graphic design, E C Ernst, Inc, Washington, DC, 74; graphic design, Caprice, New York, 75; plus many others. Exhib: Plastic Show, Jewish Mus, New York, 69; one-man shows, Avanti Galleries, New York, 70 & 72 & Young Collector, New York, 73; Director's Choice Show, Environment Gallery, New York, 71 & 74-75; plus many others. Teaching: Instr light & color, Pratt Inst, 75- Pos: Creative dir, L D Arstark & Co, New York, 66- Bibliog: Carompsun, New York Time Mag, 12/1/68; Karen Fisher (auth), Five careers, Cosmopolitan Mag, 3/69; Reviews & previews, Art News, 1/71; plus many others. Style & Technique: Shaped; dimensional; contemporary. Media: Acrylic, Reinforced Polyester. Dealer: Environment Gallery 205 E 60th St New York NY 10022. Mailing Add: 9104 96th St Woodhaven NY 11421

MANVILLE, ELSIE
PAINTER
b Philadelphia, Pa, May 11, 22. Study: Tyler Sch Fine Arts, Temple Univ, with Boris Blai, Franklin Watkins, Rafael Sabatini & Alexander Abels; also work with Leon Karp. Work: Temple Univ, Philadelphia. Exhib: Butler Inst Am Art, 56; Walker Art Ctr, 58; one-man exhibs, Kraushaar Galleries, 58, 66, 69 & 75; Dallas Mus, 63; Nat Acad Design Ann, 73. Awards: Carol Beck Medal for best portrait & Mary Smith Prize, Pa Acad, 53; Tyler Sch Fine Arts Award, 56. Style & Technique: Conceptual luminist. Media: Oil, Pastel. Mailing Add: c/o Kraushaar Galleries 1055 Madison Ave New York NY 10028

MANZO, ANTHONY JOSEPH
PAINTER, INSTRUCTOR
b Saddle Brook, NJ. Study: Sch Fine Art, Nat Acad Design; Phoenix Sch Design, New York; also with Salvatore Lascari. Work: Losurdo Foods Collection, Hackensack, NJ. Comn: Landscape and still life portraits, comn by Mr & Mrs Losurdo, Lodi, NJ, 68-74; still life portrait, Mr & Mrs Perlman, Elkins Park, Pa, 68 & 70; landscape portrait, Mr & Mrs J Lauren,

New York, 74-75; portrait of Former Middleweight Champion Rocky Graziano, 78; still life, Don & Dona Casey, Dallas, Tex, 78. Exhib: Allied Artists Am 61st Ann, Nat Acad Gallery, New York, 74; Am Artists Prof League Grand Nat, Lever House, New York, 74; Hudson Artists Inc 21st Ann, Jersey City Mus, 74; Salmagundi Club Summer Exhib, 75-77; Nat Miniature Art Show, 75; NJ Painter & Sculptor Soc, Nat Arts Club, 76; Hudson Valley Art Asn, 76. Teaching: Pvt art classes, 68-; demonstr & lectr painting, drawing & perspective for var metrop orgns, 70-; instr life painting & drawing & oil painting composition, Renaissance Sch Art, Saddle Brook, NJ, 73- Awards: Oil Awards, Hudson Artist Inc, 73-74 & Am Artist Prof League, 74; Ray A Jones Mem Award, NJ Painter & Sculptor Soc, 76. Salmagundi Club; Am Artists Prof League; Artist Fel. Style & Technique: Realism; technique based on craft and traditions handed down from the past. Mailing Add: c/o Collector's Gallery Fine Arts Box 2708 Taos NM 87571

MAPES, DORIS WILLIAMSON
PAINTER
b Russellville, Ark, June 25, 20. Study: Little Rock Jr Col; Hendrix Col, Ark; Ark Arts Ctr, Little Rock; Rex Brandt's Sch Painting, cert, Corona del Mar, Calif; also with George Post, Millard Sheets, John C Pellew, Louis Freund, Edgar A Whitney, Robert E Wood, John Pike & Robert Andrew Parker, 72. Work: Winthrop Rockefeller Gallery, Petit Jean, Ark; Ark Col Mus, Batesville; Am Found Life Ins Co, First Nat Bank & Ark Arts Ctr, Little Rock. Exhib: Mid-South Exhib, Brooks Mem Mus, Memphis, 68; Delta Exhib, Ark Arts Ctr, Little Rock, 69; Southwestern Watercolor Soc, Dallas, 68, 69, 71 & 73 & Albuquerque, 72; 107th Ann Am Watercolor Soc, New York, 74; Watercolor USA, Springfield, Mo, 75; Southern Watercolor Soc, Cheekwood Mus, Jackson, Miss, 77. Awards: Top of Show, Ark State Festival Arts, 68 & 75; First Award, Mid-Southern Watercolorists, 74; First Award, Southern Artists Asn, 72; plus many others. Mem: Mid-Southern Watercolorists (pres, 70-72); Southwestern Watercolor Soc; Am League Penwomen (vpres, Little Rock Br, 66-70); assoc mem Am Watercolor Soc; Southern Artists Asn. Style & Technique: Expanded range of colors in subtle transparencies to capture an impression and create an atmosphere; solid design and boldness. Media: Watercolor, Acrylic. Dealer: Sketch Box Gallery 5606 R St Little Rock AR 72207. Mailing Add: 622 N Bryan Little Rock AR 72205

MARADIAGA, RALPH
GALLERY DIRECTOR, DESIGNER
b San Francisco, Calif, Oct 27, 34. Study: City Col San Francisco, AA(design), 65; San Francisco State Univ, BA, 71 & MA(printmaking), 75; Stanford Univ, MA(doc film making), 75. Work: Mus Mod Art, New York. Comn: Logo, Tecolote (community newspaper), San Francisco, 72; posters, San Francisco State Univ, 72 & 75; coloring bk, Galeria de la Raza, 73 & calendario, 73, 74 & 75; logo, Southwest Network, Hayward, Calif, 74. Exhib: San Francisco Art Festival, 70-75; San Francisco Mus Mod Art MIX Exhib, 73; Philadelphia Print Club, 73; Posters and Society, San Francisco Mus Art, 74-75. Collections Arranged: Santos Exhib, 73-74; Colors of the Guatemalan Indians, 74; Mola Exhib from the Cuna Indians of Panama, 74-75; Huichol Yarn Paintings, Part 1, 75. Teaching: Instr printmaking, La Raza Art Workshop, San Francisco State Univ, 73-75 & Art Workshop, Jewish Community Ctr, summer 74. Pos: Dir, Galeria de la Raza, 70- Bibliog: Animation (2), San Francisco State Univ, 72; Incidente en Dowienville, 10 minute 16mm, Stanford Univ, 73 & Engineering as a Career, half-hour 16mm, MA Thesis, 75. Media: Serigraphy, Film Making. Mailing Add: 2851 24th St San Francisco CA 94110

MARAIS (MARY RACHEL BROWN)
PAINTER
b New York, NY. Work: J Aberbach Collection, Long Island, NY; Theodora Settele Collection, New York. Exhib: Galerie St Placide, Paris, 61; Panoras Gallery, New York, 71; Community Temple Gallery, Long Island, 72; Galerie Chantepierre, Aubonne, Switz, 72; Galerie Internationale, New York, 75. Mem: Nat Soc Lit & Arts. Style & Technique: Natural oil painter, style is very personal; intimate scenes of Paris capture ambiance completely; strong French impressionist influence. Mailing Add: c/o Mary Rachel Brown 33 W 67th St New York NY 10023

MARAK, LOUIS BERNARD
CERAMIC SCULPTOR, EDUCATOR
b Shawnee, Okla, Sept 9, 42. Study: Univ Ill, Champaign-Urbana, BFA, 65; Alfred Univ, MFA, 67. Work: Krannert Art Mus, Univ Ill, Urbana; Western Gallery, Western Wash State Col, Bellingham; Utah Mus Fine Arts, Univ Utah, Salt Lake City. Exhib: 25th Ceramic Nat Exhib, Everson Mus, Syracuse, NY, 68; Young Americans, Mus Contemp Crafts, New York, 69; Ceramics 70 Plus Woven Forms, Everson Mus, 70; Object Makers, Utah Mus Fine Arts, Salt Lake City, 71; San Francisco Art Inst Centennial Exhib, M H De Young Mem Mus, 71; Calif Ceramics & Glass, Great Hall, Oakland Mus, 74; Six Californians Exhib, Fairtree Gallery, New York, 74; Six from the North California Coast, Univ Wash Henry Gallery, Seattle, Crafts IX, E B Crocker Art Gallery, Sacramento, 75; Calif Design 76, Pac Design Ctr, Los Angeles, Calif, 76; Soup Tureens: 1976, Mus Contemp Crafts, New York, 76. Teaching: Instr art, Keuka Col, New York, 67-69; assoc prof art, Humboldt State Univ, Arcata, 69- Awards: Purchase Award, Utah Mus Fine Arts, 71; Award, E B Crocker Art Gallery, 75; Nat Endowment Arts Craftsmen's Fel Grant, 75. Style & Technique: Three-dimensional forms that deal with combining real and illusionary space. Media: Earthenware and Porcelain Handbuilt Forms. Mailing Add: Rte 1 Box 100 Eureka CA 95501

MARANDEL, J PATRICE
CURATOR
b Paris, France, Dec 13, 44. Study: Sorbonne Inst d'Art et d'Archeaologie, Paris, DES; Yale Univ. Exhibitions Arranged: The Pilavin Collection of XX Century American Art, 73; Gray is the Color, Rice Univ, Houston, 73; French Sketches from an English Collection, Mus Fine Arts, Houston, 73-75. Pos: Chief cur, Mus Art, RI Sch Design, Providence, 72-74; cur earlier painting, Art Inst Chicago, 74- Publ: Contribr, Arts Mag, Art Int, Arte Ilustrata & Super Realism, 70-75. Mailing Add: 910 Lake Shore Dr Chicago IL 60611

MARAZZI, WILLIAM C P
PAINTER
b France, Oct 5, 47. Study: Ecole du Louvre, Paris; Ecole du Louvre, Paris; Musee des Arts Decoratifs, Paris. Work: Palm Springs Desert Mus, Calif; Evansville Mus Arts, Ind; Huntsville Mus Art, Ala; Rutgers Univ Art Gallery; Metrop Mus Art, New York; plus others. Exhib: One-man shows, Avanti Galleries, New York, 73, Seamen's Church Inst Gallery, New York, 74, Greene Gallery, New Rochelle, 75 & 77, Harkness Found, New York, 75, Rowe House Gallery, Washington, DC, 76 & Bodley Gallery, New York, 77; Greene Gallery, 74; Evansville Mus Arts, 75. Style & Technique: Thought forms. Media: Flo-paque and Pastel on Paper or Canvas. Dealer: Lowell Cunningham c/o Clay Gallery 1162 Madison Ave New York NY 10028; David Mann c/o Bodley Gallery 1063 Madison Ave New York NY 10028. Mailing Add: 2 E 82nd St New York NY 10028

MARBERGER, A ALADAR
ART DEALER
b Philadelphia, Pa, June 15, 47. Study: Carnegie-Mellon Univ, BFA. Pos: Consult, Carnegie-Mellon Col of Fine Art, 75-77; spec asst to dean, NY Studio Sch, 69-70; dir-partner, Fischbach Gallery Inc, 70- Mem: Art Dealers Asn of Am Inc. Specialty: Contemporary art. Publ: Auth, Opinion: Corporate Collection, Carnegie-Mellon Ann, 77. Mailing Add: c/o Fischbach Gallery Inc 29 W 57th St New York NY 10019

MARCA-RELLI, CONRAD
PAINTER
b Boston, Mass, June 5, 13. Work: Mus Mod Art; Whitney Mus Am Art; Wadsworth Atheneum; Metrop Mus Art; Nat Collection Fine Arts, Washington, DC; plus many others. Exhib: Carnegie Inst; one-man retrospective, Whitney Mus Am Art, 67; Art Inst Chicago; Am Fedn Arts, 67-68; The New American Painting & Sculpture, Mus Mod Art, 69; New Sch Social Res, 69; Am Painting 1970, Va Mus Fine Arts, Richmond, 70; plus many other group & one-man shows. Teaching: Former vis critic, Yale Univ, Univ Calif, Berkeley & New Col, Sarasota, Fla. Awards: Logan Medal & Purchase Prize, Art Inst Chicago, 54, Kohnstamm Prize, 63; Ford Found Award, 59; Purchase Prize, Detroit Inst Art, 60. Bibliog: Parker Tyler (auth), Marca-Relli (monogr), 60; H Harvard Arnason (auth), Marca-Relli (monogr), Abrams, 62; Gerard Miracle & Harold Rosenberg (auth), Marca-Relli, Barcelona, Spain, 75; plus many others. Mailing Add: c/o Marlborough Gallery Inc 40 W 57th St New York NY 10019

MARCHESCHI, (LOUIS) CORK
SCULPTOR, EDUCATOR
b San Mateo, Calif, Apr 5, 45. Study: Col San Mateo, 63-66; Calif State Col, Hayward, 66-68; Calif Col Arts & Crafts, Oakland, MFA, 70; also with Mel Ramos & Paul Harris. Comn: Outdoor spark-gap, Walker Art Ctr, Minneapolis, 71 & 76; suspended neon sculpture, Can Broadcasting Co, Toronto, 74; fluorescent sculpture in barge in Lake Mich, Summerfest, Milwaukee, Wis, 75; environmental energy sculpture, Morgan Gallery, Kansas City, Kans, 75; fluorescent & spark relief, Ulrich Mus, Wichita, Kans, 75. Exhib: One-man shows, Minneapolis Inst Art, 71, Louis K Meisel Gallery, New York, 73, 75 & 77, Electric Gallery, Toronto, 74, Morgan Gallery, 75 & 78, Folkwang Mus, Essen, Ger, 75, Galerie M, Bochum, Ger, 74 & 78, Kunsthalle Dusseldoff, Ger, 76, Milwaukee Art Ctr, Wis, 76, Hanson-Cowles Gallery, Minneapolis, Minn, 77, Tubingen Mus, Ger, 78, Van Abbe Mus, Eindhoven, Holland, 78 & Nat Gallery, Berlin, Ger, 78. Teaching: Assoc prof art & intermedia, Minneapolis Col Art & Design, 70- Awards: Minn State Arts Coun Grant, 75; Bush Found Grant, 78; DAAD Berlin Artist Prog Grant, 78. Bibliog: Paul Owen (auth), Energy works (16mm film), 71; Merike Weiler (auth), Cork Marchseschi, Art Can, 73; Heiner Hepper (auth), Cork Marcheschi (film), Ger Pub Broadcasting, 75. Mem: Twin Cities Arts Alliance. Style & Technique: Sculpture based on electrical energy. Media: Electricity, Found Objects. Collection: Art deco objects and architectural period writings. Publ: Auth, Objects for producing visual phenomena with high-voltage electricity, 73; auth, Heat, light and motion, 74; auth, Neon, 75. Dealer: Louis K Meisel Gallery 141 Prince St New York NY 10012. Mailing Add: 2418 Stevens Ave S Minneapolis MN 55404

MARCHESE, LAMAR VINCENT
ART ADMINISTRATOR, PHOTOGRAPHER
b Tampa, Fla, Dec 11, 43. Study: Univ S Fla, BA, 64; Univ Fla, MA, 71. Exhib: Huntington Art Mus Photog, WVa, 71. Collections Arranged: Quilts from Eastern Kentucky, 72; Electric Skyline, 73; Warhol Reconsidered, 75. Pos, Prog coordr, Clark Co Libr Dist, Las Vegas, 72-; chmn, Nev Pub Radio Corp, 76- Awards: Second Prize & Hon Mention, Libr Pub Rels Coun, 75. Mem: Southern Nev Allied Arts Coun (exec bd, 73, vpres, 75); Nev Libr Media Coop (chmn, 74); Nev Libr Asn (publ chmn, 74); Am Libr Asn (film selection subcomt, 73); Southern Nev Community Arts Comt. Publ: Flicks Boffo at Book Factory, Kaleidoscope Rev, 75; Coming Soon, 75. Mailing Add: 2004 Poplar St Las Vegas NV 89101

MARCHESE, PATRICIA DAVIS
ART ADMINISTRATOR, PRINTMAKER
b Johnstown, Pa, July 12, 43. Study: Univ SFla, BA, 64; Fla Atlantic Univ, 67; Univ Fla, 68; Morehead State Univ, 70-71; Univ Nev, Las Vegas, 72; Inst Arts Admin, Harvard Univ, 76. Work: Western Div Univ Student Traveling Exhib. Exhib: Midwest Univ Student Drawing & Print Exhib, Ill State Univ, 70; Regional Fine Arts Biennial, J B Speed Mus, Louisville, Ky, 71; Eastern Regional Fine Arts Exhib, Morehead, Ky, 72. Pos: Instr humanities, Alachua Co Bd Educ, Gainesville, Fla, 66-69; supvr, City of Las Vegas Fine Arts Div, 73-; fine arts & humanities rep, Clark Co Sch Dist Career Educ Prog, 74-; vchmn, Nev Humanities Comt, 75- Mem: Assoc Coun Arts; Southern Nev Allied Arts Coun (exec bd, 73-); Asn Col, Univ & Community Arts Adminr. Media: Serigraphy. Publ: Co-auth, Soupcans to the Parthenon, Fla Schs, 69; co-auth, Humanities Curriculum Outline, 70; auth, A home for the arts, Emphasis, 75. Mailing Add: 2004 Poplar St Las Vegas NV 89101

MARCHISOTTO, LINDA A
ART DEALER
b New York, NY. Study: Wells Col, BA(fine arts); Trinity Col, Rome, Italy. Pos: Curatorial intern, Solomon R Guggenheim Mus, New York, 75; gallery asst, Andre Emmerich Gallery, New York, 75-76; co-dir, Monique Knowlton Gallery, New York, 76- Specialty: Contemporary art with a few specialized shows on American Surrealists. Mailing Add: c/o Monique Knowlton Gallery 19 E 71st St New York NY 10021

MARCUS, BETTY
COLLECTOR, PATRON
b New York, NY, Mar 6, 23. Study: Jr Col, art major. Pos: Vpres, Dallas Mus Contemp Arts; pres, Dallas Mus League; pres bd trustees, Dallas Mus Fine Arts; bd dirs, Assoc Coun Arts; panel mem, Am Assembly Arts; mem, Nat Comt Cult Resources; mem div arts comt, Community Develop of Dallas CofC. Collection: From Peruvian pre-Columbian pottery vessels to right this minute artists; paintings are either subdued in color or rather controlled in form; works by Mondrian, Henry Moore, Josef Albers, Herbin, Botero, Viera Da Silva, Camargo, Noguchi, Max Bill & others. Mailing Add: 4007 Stonebridge Dallas TX 75204

MARCUS, IRVING E
PAINTER, GRAPHIC ARTIST
b Minneapolis, Minn, May 17, 29. Study: Univ Minn, BA; Univ Iowa, MFA. Work: Minneapolis Inst Art; Allen Art Mus, Oberlin Col; Crocker Art Mus, Sacramento, Calif; Oakland Art Mus, Calif; State Univ Iowa; also in many pvt collections. Exhib: Luz Mus, Manila, Philippines, 64; Univ Wis, 64; one-man show, Crocker Art Mus, Sacramento, 74; Animal Imagery, Hayward State Univ, 75; Kaiser Ctr, Oakland, 75; plus many other group & one-man shows. Teaching: Instr art, Oberlin Col, 55-56; instr, Univ Hawaii, 56-57; instr, Blackburn Col, 57-59; prof painting & printmaking, Sacramento State Col, 59-, chmn dept art, 66-69. Awards: Prizes, Denver Mus Art, 52 & 58 & Crocker Art Mus, 63; plus others.

Bibliog: Thomas Albright (auth), An extraordinary artist, San Francisco Chronicle, 2/11/73; Thomas Albright (auth), Bay area.[y area mythmakers, Art Gallery Mag, 11/74. Mem: San Francisco Art Asn. Style & Technique: Social fantasy; oil on canvas. Publ: Contribr, A handbook for the development of art in small colleges, Col Art Asn. Dealer: Candy Store Gallery Folsom CA 95630; Zara Gallery 553 Pacific Ave San Francisco CA 94133. Mailing Add: 601 Shangri Lane Sacramento CA 95825

MARCUS, MARCIA
PAINTER
b New York, NY, Jan 11, 28. Study: NY Univ, BA, 47; Art Students League, 54, with Edwin Dickinson. Work: Whitney Mus Art, New York; Newark Mus, NJ; RI Sch Design, Providence; Phoenix Art Mus, Ariz; Randolph-Macon Jr Col, Lynchburg, Va. Exhib: Young Artists, Whitney Mus Art, 60; Four Women, Kansas City, 63; Carnegie Inst, Pittsburgh, 64; Woman Choose Women, New York Cult Ctr, 73; Everson Mus, Syracuse, 75. Teaching: Adj instr painting, Cooper Union Sch Art, New York, 70-71; assoc prof painting & drawing, La State Univ, Baton Rouge, spring 72; instr painting & drawing, NY Univ, summer 72; instr, Vassar Col, 73-74; instr, Cornell Univ, spring 75; vis artist, Syracuse Univ, 76, Purdue Univ, 77-78; asst prof, RI Sch Design. Awards: Fulbright Fel to France, 62-63; Ingram Merrill Award, 64 & 77; artist in residence, RI Sch Design, Ford Found, 66. Style & Technique: Figurative, classical balance of elements, generally subdued color painted thinly and directly. Media: Oil. Dealer: Terry Dintenfass Gallery 50 W 57th New York NY 10019. Mailing Add: 80 N Moore St New York NY 10013

MARCUS, STANLEY
COLLECTOR
b Dallas, Tex, Apr 20, 05. Study: Harvard Univ, BA, 25, Bus Sch, 26; Southern Methodist Univ, hon HHD, 65. Pos: Dir, Dallas Symphony Soc; adv dir, Ft Worth Art Asn; trustee, Eisenhower Exchange Fellowships; Bus Comt for the Arts; former pres, Dallas Art Asn; emer chmn, Neiman-Marcus Co; consult, Carter, Hawley Hale Stores, Inc. Collection: Paintings, contemporary art. Mailing Add: 4800 Republic Nat Bank Tower Dallas TX 75201

MARDEN, BRICE
PAINTER, EDUCATOR
b Bronxville, NY, Oct 15, 38. Study: Boston Univ, BFA, with Reed Kay, Arthur Hoener & Hugh Townley; Yale-Norfolk Summer Sch Music & Art, with Bernard Chaet & Jon Schueler; Sch Art & Archit, Yale Univ, MFA, with Esteban Vicente & Alex Katz. Work: Mus Mod Art, New York; Whitney Mus Am Art, New York; Walker Art Ctr, Minneapolis, Minn; Ft Worth Art Ctr, Tex; San Francisco Mus Mod Art. Exhib: Whitney Mus Am Art Ann, New York, 69; Modular Painting, Albright-Knox Art Gallery, Buffalo, 70; Painting—New Options, Walker Art Ctr, 72; 17th Am Exhib, Art Inst Chicago, 72; Documenta 5, Kassel, Ger, 72. Teaching: Instr painting, Sch Visual Arts, New York, 70-; instr painting, Skowhegan Sch Painting & Sculpture, summer 71-72. Pos: Bd govs, Skowhegan Sch Painting & Sculpture, 72. Bibliog: Harris Rosenstein (auth), Total & complex, 5/67 & John Ashberry (auth), Grey eminence, 3/72, Art News; Robert Pincus-Witten (auth), Manzoni, Ryman & Marden, Artforum, summer 72. Media: Oil. Dealer: Pace Gallery 32 E 57th St New York NY 10022. Mailing Add: 105 Bowery New York NY 10002

MARDER, DORIE
PAINTER, SERIGRAPHER
b Poland; US citizen. Study: Sorbonne; Art Students League; New Sch Social Res; also with Harry Shoulberg & Morris Kantor. Work: Norfolk Mus, Va; Butler Inst Am Art, Youngstown, Ohio; State Dept for Europ Embassies; Safed Mus, Israel; State Univ NY Binghamton. Exhib: Riverside Mus, 46-50; Northwest Printmakers, Seattle Art Mus, 50; Wichita Art Asn, Kans, 51; Audubon Artists, 64-70; Lehigh Univ, Pa, 71; Fordham Univ, 76; Equitable Gallery, 77; Women in Am Art, Summit Gallery, 77. Awards: Award for oil painting, Clendenen, 61; award for serigraph, Montag, 65; First Prize, Village Art Ctr. Mem: League of Present Day Artists (dir, 71-72); Nat Asn Women Artists; Artists Equity Asn New York; Nat Serigraph Soc. Style & Technique: Semi-abstract expressionism: unification through light passages allows me freedom of color and form. Mailing Add: 223 W 21st St New York NY 10011

MAREMONT, ARNOLD H
COLLECTOR
b Chicago, Ill, Aug 24, 04. Study: Univ Mich, Ann Arbor; Univ Chicago, PhB, 24, JD, 26. Pos: Trustee, Am Fedn Arts, 58-64; trustee, Lyric Opera of Chicago, 59-65; trustee, City Ctr Music & Drama, New York, 59-65. Mem: Gov life mem Art Inst Chicago. Collection: 20th century art. Mailing Add: Maremont Corp 200 E Randolph Chicago IL 60601

MARGO, BORIS
PAINTER, PRINTMAKER
b Wolotschisk, Russia, Nov 7, 02; US citizen. Study: Polytechnik Art, Odessa, USSR, cert; Futemas (workshop for art of the future), Moscow, USSR; Pavel Filonov Sch, Leningrad, USSR. Work: Metrop Mus Art & Mus Mod Art, New York; Nat Collection Fine Arts, Washington, DC; Art Inst Chicago; São Paulo Mus Art, Brazil. Exhib: Abstract and Surrealist Art in the United States, Cincinnati Art Mus, San Francisco Mus Art & others, 44; several São Paulo Bienales, 52-; Carnegie Inst Int, Pittsburgh, 52; Japan Print Asn 30th Anniversary Int, 62; Venice Biennales, 56 & 70; Honolulu Acad Art, 73; Rutgers Univ Art Gallery, 77. Teaching: Vis artist, Am Univ, 46-48; vis prof painting, Art Inst Chicago, 57-59; vis prof printmaking & drawing, Sch Art, Syracuse Univ, 66-67; artist in residence, Acad Art, Honolulu, 72. Pos: Res assoc (on the creative process), Psychiatric Inst, Univ Md, 57-58. Awards: Purchase Award for oil painting, Portland Mus Art, Maine, 60; six Purchase Awards, Brooklyn Mus Print Exhibs, 47-68; Award in printmaking, Nat Endowment Arts, 74. Bibliog: Laurence Schmeckebier (auth), Boris Margo, Graphic Work, 1932-1968, Syracuse Univ Press, 68. Mem: Provincetown Art Asn; MacDowell Colony Fels; Soc Am Graphic Artists. Style & Technique: Experimentation and simplicity. Publ: Auth, Boris Margo: my theories and techniques, Mag Art, 11/47; auth, Margo: is there an American school of art?, The Tiger's Eye, 12/47; auth, Surrealism and American Art, Jeffrey Wechsler, 77. Dealer: Monique Knowlton 19 E 71st St New York NY 10021. Mailing Add: 749 West End Ave New York NY 10025

MARGOLIES, ETHEL POLACHECK
PAINTER, ART ADMINISTRATOR
b Milwaukee, Wis, Aug 1, 07. Study: Smith Col, AB, 29; Silvermine Guild Artists; Umberto Romano Sch, East Gloucester, Mass; Univ Vt Summer Sch. Work: Burndy Libr, Norwalk, Conn; Gen Time Corp, Stamford, Conn; Springfield Mus, Mass; Int Petroleum Corp; New Haven Paint & Clay Club, Conn. Exhib: Silvermine Guild Artists, New Eng Exhib, New Canaan, Conn, 54-57, 60-68 & 74-75; Int Petroleum Art Festival, Tulsa, Okla, 66; Conn Acad Fine Arts, Hartford; Conn Watercolor Soc, Hartford; Audubon Artists, New York. Pos: Gallery dir, Larry Aldrich Mus Contemp Art, 64-66; gallery dir, Silvermine Guild Artists, 54-72. Awards: Awards for indust painting, Silvermine Guild, 54, 57, 60 & 64; Purchase Award, Springfield Mus, Mass, 57; New Haven Paint & Clay Club Award, 75. Mem: Artists Equity Asn New York; Silvermine Guild Artists (bd trustees, 54-75); Conn Acad Fine Arts; Conn Watercolor Soc; New Haven Paint & Clay Club. Media: Acrylic, Oil, Collage. Mailing Add: 103 Jelliff Mill Rd New Canaan CT 06840

MARGOLIES, JOHN
VIDEO ARTIST, PHOTOGRAPHER
b New York, NY, May 16, 40. Study: Univ Pa, AB, Annenberg Sch Commun, MA. Work: Pasadena Art Mus, Calif; Vancouver Art Gallery, BC; Baltimore Mus Art, Md; Art Galleries, Univ Calif, Santa Barbara. Exhib: Morris Lapidus: Architecture of Joy, Archit League New York, 70; The Television Environment, simultaneously in Pasadena Art Mus, Univ Calif Art Mus, Berkeley, Baltimore Mus Art, Vancouver Art Gallery & Fla State Univ Art Gallery, Tallahasse, 71; 1975 Biennial Exhib & Projected Video, Whitney Mus Am Art, NY, 75; Projects: Video V, Mus Mod Art, NY, 75. Teaching: Instr workshop commun, doc & environ, Calif Inst Arts, 71; instr 20th century archit, Univ Calif, Santa Barbara, 72; instr contemp TV, Univ Calif, Los Angeles, 73. Pos: Asst ed, Archit Record, 64-68; chmn current work, Archit League New York, 66-68; resident thinker, Am Fedn Arts, 69-70. Awards: Graham Found Archit Jour Grant, Walker Art Ctr Prog, 70; J Clawson Mills Scholar, Archit League New York, 70; Nat Endowment for Arts Photog Grant, 71, Archit Grant, 72 & 73 & Visual Arts Grant, 74. Bibliog: Ulrich Franzen (auth), The joy boy, Archit Forum, 11/70; John G Hanhardt (auth), Videology, Film Comment, 5-6/75; John J O'Connor (auth), The Whitney Shows New Projected Video, New York Times, 6/6/75. Mem: Archit League New York. Style & Technique: Black and white and color documentary video tapes and photographs. Publ: Auth, TV—the next medium, Art in Am, 9-10/69; ed, Design Quart spec issue on conceptual architecture, 11/70; auth, Now, one and for all, know why I did it: Morris Lapidus, Progressive Archit, 10/70; auth, Roadside mecca in California—the Madonna Inn, Progressive Archit, 11/73; co-auth, The television environment, Mus News, 1-2/74. Mailing Add: 222 W 72nd St 3-A New York NY 10023

MARGOULIES, BERTA (BERTA MARGOULIES O'HARE)
SCULPTOR, EDUCATOR
b Lovitz, Poland, Sept 7, 07; US citizen. Study: Hunter Col, BA(Phi Beta Kappa); Art Students League; Acad Colarossi & Acad Julien, Paris, France. Work: Whitney Mus Am Art, New York; Des Moines Art Inst, Iowa; Willamette Univ, Salem, Ore; Wyandotte Co Mus, Kans; Int Lithographers Union, New York. Comn: Colonial foot postman, comn by US Govt, Postmaster Gen Off, Washington, DC, 37; Woman & Deep, Garden Ct Fed Bldg, comn by US Govt, 39. Exhib: Whitney Mus Am Art, New York; Metrop Mus Art; New York; Pa Fine Arts Acad, Philadelphia; Chicago Art Inst; Archit League of NY; Nat Acad Design, New York; Corcoran Gallery, Washington, DC; Int Sculpture Exhib, Arts Coun Paramus, NJ, 75. Collections Arranged: Sculptors' Guild First Outdoor Exhib, New York, 19. Teaching: Instr sculpture, Finch Col, New York, 36-43, Five Mus & Art, Long Island, NY, 44-53 & Somerset Art Asn, Bernardville, NJ, 70. Pos: Exec secy, Sculptors' Guild, New York, 38-46. Awards: Avery Prize for Sculpture, Archit League of NY, 37; Accomplishment in Sculpture, Am Acad Arts & Lett, 44; Guggenheim Fel, 46. Bibliog: Women Artists of America, Newark Mus, 65. Mem: Sculptors' Guild; Artists Equity (founding mem); Assoc Artists NJ; Somerset Art Asn, NJ. Style & Technique: Uses architectural features to enhance composition; humanist-expressionist approach. Media: Wood, Stone, Bronze, Terra Cotta. Publ: Contribr, Jack C Rich, auth, Materials and Methods of Sculpture, Oxford Univ Press, 47; contribr, One Hundred American Jewish Artists, YKUF, 47; contribr, Contemporary American Sculpture, Crown, 48; contribr, Cecil Roth, auth, Jewish Art—An Illustrated History, McGraw-Hill, 61. Dealer: Benedict Gallery 254 Main St Madison NJ 07940; Roman Forum Art Gallery 396 Rte 17 Hasbrouck Heights NJ 07604. Mailing Add: Tinc Rd Flanders NJ 07836

MARGULES, GABRIELE ELLA
ILLUSTRATOR, PAINTER
b Tachau, Czech, May 30, 27; US citizen. Study: Cambridge Sch Art, Eng, nat dipl fine arts; Royal Acad Schs, London; New York, studies with Hans Hofmann, Camilo Egas & Norman Carton. Work: Kerlan Collection, Univ Minn Res Ctr for Children's Books, Minneapolis. Exhib: 100 Best Children's Books, Am Inst Graphic Arts, 68 & 70; Sumi-e Soc New York, 70-73; New York Ctr; Sale Collection, Jr Coun, Mus Mod Art. Awards: Two-Year Grad Scholar, Cambridge Co Coun, Eng, 48; Silver Medal-First Prize for Life Drawing, Royal Acad, London, 49; Myers Art Scholar, New Sch Social Res, 61. Mem: Artists Equity of New York (coun mem, 66-70); Hastings Creative Arts Coun. Style & Technique: Line drawings, animals and children, semi-abstract, sometimes impressionistic color. Media: Sumi-e Ink, Watercolor, Pastel. Publ: Illusr, Harper's Mag, 63; illusr, Out of the Ark, Atheneum, New York & Longman Young, London, 68; illusr, Bird Songs, Atheneum, 69. Mailing Add: 7 High St Cold Spring NY 10516

MARGULIES, ISIDORE
SCULPTOR
b Vienna, Austria, Apr 1, 21. Study: Cooper Union Art Sch, New York, 40-42; State Univ NY, Stony Brook, BA(liberal arts), 73; C W Post Col, MAA, 75; with Robert White, James Kleege & Alfred Van Loan. Exhib: Nat Art Mus Sport, Madison Sq Garden, New York, 72-73; one-man shows, Stony Brook Union Gallery, 73 & Suffolk Mus, Stony Brook, 74; Heckscher Mus, Huntington, Long Island, 73-75; Nat Acad Design, New York, 75; Harbor Gallery, Long Island, NY, 76. Mem: Huntington Twp Art League (chmn, 76-78). Style & Technique: Realist figurative sculpture; kinetic sculpture. Media: Bronze, Stone, Mixed Media. Mailing Add: 650 Washington Ave Plainview NY 11803

MARGULIES, JOSEPH
PAINTER, ETCHER
b Austria, July 7, 96; US citizen. Study: Cooper Union; Nat Acad Design; with Maynard; Art Students League, with Joseph Pennell; also study abroad. Work: Nat Portrait Gallery, Smithsonian Inst, Libr Cong & Judiciary, House of Representatives, Washington, DC; Metrop Mus Art, New York; Cleveland Mus Art, Ohio; New York Pub Libr. Comn: Portrait of John F Brosnan, regent & chancellor, Univ of State NY, 61; portrait of Sen Jacob K Javits, comn by Atty Gen, NY State Capitol, Albany; portrait of Congressman Emanuel Celler, comn by chmn Judiciary Staff, 63; portrait of Dr Bela Schick, Nat Portrait Gallery, 69; portrait of John Dewey, for Dewey Ctr, Carbondale, Ill. Exhib: Graphics, Univ Maine, Orono, 65; also yearly exhibs, Provincetown Art Asn, Audubon Artists, Allied Artists Am & Am Watercolor Soc. Awards: Gold Medal for Graphics, Acad Artists Asn, Springfield, Mass, 77; N Shore Art Asn Award, Gloucester, 77; Award, Hugh Botts Award & Seley Purchase Prize, Salmagundi Club. Bibliog: B F Morrow (auth), The Art of Aquatint, Putman, 35; Norman Kent (auth), 100 Watercolor Techniques, Watson-Guptill, 69. Mem: Audubon Artists (mem coun & secy); Allied Artists Am (mem jury); Salmagundi Club (mem jury); Am Watercolor Soc; Rockport Art Asn. Style & Technique: Work from life and try to interpret my emotional reactions of my subjects, regardless of media. Media: Oil, Watercolor, Graphics. Publ: Auth, Joseph Margulies paints a portrait in watercolor, Am Artist Mag, 60.

Dealer: Assoc Am Artists 663 Fifth Ave New York NY 10022. Mailing Add: 15 Grapevine Rd East Gloucester MA 01930

MARI (MARI M EAGERTON)
CRAFTSMAN, PAINTER
US citizen. Study: Atlanta Sch Art, BFA; Butler Univ; Ga State Univ; Principia Col. Work: Mus Contemp Crafts, Slide Libr, New York; Vogue Fabrics Libr, Conde Nast, New York. Comn: Batik tent ceiling, Decorator's Showhouse, 73 & Silkscreen Prints Indiana's Finest, 74, Editions Ltd Gallery; batik screen, comn by Mr & Mrs Samuel Shachet, Palm Springs, Calif, 73; batik & collage wallhanging, comn by Mr Stanley Paulson, Indianapolis, 74; batik wallhanging, Emory Univ, Atlanta, Ga; plus numerous hand painted fabrics for designers, Jerry Silverman & Don Day, New York, 73-75. Exhib: Midstates Painting Exhib, Evansville Mus Art, 72-74; Objects 73, IMA, Indianapolis, 73 & Crafts & Objects 75; American Fiber Art, Ball State Univ, 74; Fibers Invitational, Austin Peay State Univ, 74; Spoleto Festival, 77; The Dyers Art, Cincinnati, Ohio, 78. Teaching: Instr batik, silkscreen & fabric painting, Ind Univ, Indianapolis, 69-72, instr painting & drawing, 72-77; instr painting, Herron Sch Art, 72. Awards: Objects 71, Textile Award, IMA, 71; Purchase Award, Bardstown Invitational, Ky, 73; Southeastern Arts Festival Painting Award, Atlanta, Ga, 70. Bibliog: Dona Meilach (auth), Contemporary Batik & Tie Dying, Crown, 73; Joanifer Gibbs (auth), Batiks Unlimited, Watson-Guptill, 74. Mem: Surface Design Int; Am Crafts Coun. Style & Technique: Wall hangings and soft sculptural batik pieces in figurative and fantasy images. Media: Batik on Silk, Oil on Canvas. Dealer: Collector's Showroom 325 N Wells St Chicago IL 60654; Editions Ltd Gallery 919 E Westfield Blvd Indianapolis IN 46220. Mailing Add: 4004 Arthington Blvd Indianapolis IN 46226

MARIANO, KRISTINE
PAINTER
b Rochester, NY, Jan 16, 39. Study: Sch Fine Arts, Rochester Inst Technol, BFA; also at Mem Art Gallery, Univ Rochester. Work: Univ Mem Art Gallery, Univ Rochester, NY; Kidder-Peabody Corp, New York; Am Embassy Art Collection; Eastman Kodak Co; Xerox Corp. Exhib: Everson Mus Art, Syracuse, NY, 63; Provincetown Art Asn, Mass, 66-70; Chautauqua Nat Exhib Am Art, NY, 63 & 67; Albright-Knox Gallery, Buffalo, NY, 67; one-man shows, Kendall Art Gallery, Wellfleet, Mass, 67-76; Baracca Gallery, North Hatfield, Mass, 78. Awards: Painting Awards, Rochester Relig Arts Festival, 65-67; Painting Award, Am Asn Univ Women, Brockport Ann Regional, 67. Mem: Boston Visual Artists Union. Style & Technique: Semi-abstract landscapes in acrylic; acrylic collage figures. Dealer: Kendall Art Gallery Inc Box 742 E Main St Wellfleet MA 02667; Hambleton Gallery Nantucket MA. Mailing Add: 292 Winter St Weston MA 02193

MARIL, HERMAN
PAINTER
b Baltimore, Md, Oct 13, 08. Study: Md Inst Fine Arts, grad. Work: Whitney Mus Am Art & Metrop Mus Art, New York; Baltimore Mus Art; Inst & Acad Arts & Lett; Nat Collection Fine Arts, Smithsonian Inst, Washington, DC; plus others. Comn: Murals, West Scranton Post Off, Pa, 39 & Alta Vista Post Off, Va, 40, Pub Bldgs Admin, US Treas Dept. Exhib: San Francisco Golden Gate Expos, 39; Carnegie Inst Int Ann, Pittsburgh, Pa, 40-45; retrospective, Baltimore Mus Art, 67; Pa Acad Fine Arts, Philadelphia & Corcoran Gallery Art Biennials, Washington, DC, many yrs; Selected Works 1929-1977, Univ Md Art Gallery, 77; Forum Gallery, New York, 77; Provincetown, A Painter's World, Everson Mus, Syracuse, NY, 77; plus others. Teaching: Vis instr painting, Philadelphia Mus Col Art, 55-56; prof painting, Univ Md, 47-77. Awards: First Award, Silvermine Guild, 63; Univ Md Grant for creative & performing arts, 66; Stefan Hirsch Mem Award, Audubon Artists, 72. Bibliog: Eliot O'Hara (auth), Restraint (film), 61; Emery Grossman (auth), Art and tradition, Yoseloff, 67; Frank Getlein (auth), Herman Maril, Baltimore Mus Art, 67. Mem: Baltimore Mus Art (hon trustee, 72); Provincetown Art Asn; Col Art Asn Am; Artists Equity Asn. Style & Technique: Content and form being a oneness in the terms of color and space. Media: Oil, Casein, Acrylic. Dealer: Forum Gallery 1018 Madison Ave New York NY 10021. Mailing Add: 5602 Roxbury Pl Baltimore MD 21209

MARIN, AUGUSTO
PAINTER, EDUCATOR
b San Juan, PR, Nov 20, 21. Study: Art Students League, under Reginald Marsh, John Corbino, Ivan Olinsky & Harry Sternberg; Los Angeles Co Art Inst, under Jack Otterson; PR Inst Cult, stained glass under Arnold Maas. Work: Mus Mod Art, New York; Metrop Mus Art, New York; Ponce Art Mus, PR; San Juan Mus Art, PR; Mus Univ PR, Rio Piedras. Comn: Two murals, Juan R Jimenez Sch, Bayamon, 64; mural, Cruv Bldg, Rio Piedras, Govt of PR, 66; mural, Laguna Gardens Ctr, EHG Enterprises, 70, mural, Surfside Mansions, Atlantic Construct, 72 & mural, Searle Co Bldg, Caguas, 73, PR. Exhib: Primer Bienal Int Painting & Engraving, Mexico City, Mex, 58; Eleven Puerto Rican Painters, Bonn, Ger, 73; one-man shows, Ponce Art Mus, PR, 61, Inst Cult Puertorriquena, San Juan, 61, 65 & 73 & Mus Univ PR, Rio Piedras, 67. Teaching: Prof painting & composition, Sch Plastic Arts, San Juan, PR, 66-; prof drawing, Univ PR, Rio Piedras, 71- Pos: Art dir, Badillo Advert, San Juan, PR, 46-48, 58 & 59, illusr, 60-64. Awards: Second Prize, Oil Painting, Ateneo Puertorriqueno, 57 & 62, First Prize, Oil Painting, 61. Bibliog: John Gruen (auth), Latin American artist, New York Herald Tribune, 4/21/63; E Fernandez (auth), Testigo de su Tiempo, Avance Mag, PR, 5/14/73; Reinhard Fuchs (auth), Exhibition in Bonn, Gen Reporter, Ger, 12/3/75. Style & Technique: Neo-figurativism, neo-baroque. Media: Acrylic, Watercolor. Mailing Add: c/o Galeria Botello 208 Cristo St San Juan PR 00901

MARIN, KATHRYN GARRISON
PAINTER, PRINTMAKER
b Birmingham, Ala, July 14, 36. Study: Hollins Col, BA, 58; Univ Iowa, MFA, 64. Work: Ga Comn Arts, Atlanta; Ga State Univ; Mint Mus Art, Charlotte, NC; Columbia Mus Art, SC; Dreher High Sch, Columbia; Waccamaw Arts & Crafts Guild, Myrtle Beach, SC. Comn: Illustrations, This Issue Mag, Atlanta, 70-71. Exhib: 4th Dulin Nat Print & Drawing Competition, Knoxville, Tenn, 68; 23rd Am Drawing Biennial, Norfolk, Va, 69; 10th Hunter Gallery Ann, Chattanooga, Tenn, 69; 10th Ann Piedmont Painting & Small Sculpture Exhib, Charlotte, NC, 70; 3rd Nat Print Exhib, Atlanta, 72. Awards: Alice Collins Dunham Prize, 58th Conn Acad Fine Arts Exhib, 68; Three-Man Show Award, Columbia Artist Guild, 69; Purchase Award, Ga Comn Arts, 72. Media: Oil, Pencil. Mailing Add: 6122 N Trenholm Rd Columbia SC 29206

MARINO, ALBERT JOSEPH
COLLECTOR
b Pittsburgh, Pa, June 30, 99. Mem: Am Asn Mus. Collection: 275 original oil paintings and other medias, all subjects and also sculptures to be contributed to the community as a public art gallery. Mailing Add: 472 Ohio Ave Rochester PA 15074

MARINSKY, HARRY
SCULPTOR, PAINTER
b London, Eng, May 8, 09; US citizen. Study: RI Sch Design; Pratt Inst. Work: Metrop Mus Art, New York; Lincoln Ctr, Fordham Univ; Syracuse Univ Art Mus; York Univ Mus; Hunt Botanical Libr, Carnegie-Mellon Univ; plus others. Comn: Large bronze bird for scent & touch garden, Stanford Mus, Conn, 60; five bronze figures representing spirit of nationalism, Vet Mem Park, Norwalk, Conn, 66; wall sculpture representing Time, Gen Time Corp, Stamford, 67. Exhib: Mus Mod Art, New York; Art Inst Chicago, 47; All New England Art Exhibit, Silvermine Guild, New Canaan, Conn, 56-60; Riverside Mus; Florence Art Gallery, Italy; Redfern Gallery, London, Eng; Rolly-Michaux Galleries, Boston & New York; Buyways Gallery, Sarasota, Fla; plus others. Awards: Silvermine Guild Sculpture Award, 56. Mem: Artists Equity New York; Fel Int Inst Arts & Lett; Rowayton Art Ctr, Conn (dir, 69-72). Style & Technique: Abstracted sculpture representations in rhythmic line, bronze casted; landscape paintings in watercolor. Dealer: Kendall Art Gallery E Main St Wellfleet MA 02667. Mailing Add: Villa Capriglia Via Fornace 2 Capriglia 55045 Pietrasanta (Lucca) Italy

MARIONI, TOM
SCULPTOR, CURATOR
b Cincinnati, Ohio, May 21, 37. Study: Cincinnati Conserv Music, 54; Cincinnati Art Acad, 55-59. Work: Oakland Mus & Richmond Art Ctr, Calif; Student Cult Ctr, Belgrade, Yugoslavia; City of San Francisco. Comn: Free standing concrete wall (with Jacques Overhoff), Golden Gateway, San Francisco, 67; playground (with Jacques Overhoff), Fashion Island, Newport Beach, Calif, 67; Logo, Western Asn Art Mus, 69. Exhib: Sound Sculpture As, Mus Conceptual Art, 70; De Marco Gallery, Edinburgh, Scotland, 72; White Chapel, London, Eng, 72; Student Cult Ctr, Belgrade, Yugoslavia, 74; one-man show, Foksol Gallery, Warsaw, Poland, 75. Collections Arranged: All Night Sculptures, Mus Conceptual Art, 73; Actions by Sculptors for the Home Audience, KQED TV, 74; Chinese Youth Alternative, Mus Conceptual Art, 74. Pos: Cur art, Richmond Art Ctr, 68-71; dir, Mus Conceptual Art, 70-; ed, Vision, Oakland, 75- Bibliog: Cordelia Oliver (auth), Man of sound vision, Manchester Guardian, 6/5/72; P Juris (auth), The newer art, Studio Int, 6/72; Hilla Futterman (auth), Activity as sculpture, Art & Artists, 8/73. Mem: San Francisco Art Inst (bd dirs, 74-). Style & Technique: Actions using sound as a medium. Publ: Auth, Invisible Painting & Sculpture, 69; auth, The Return of Abstract Expressionism, 69; auth, The San Francisco Performance, 72; auth, Notes & Scores for Sounds, 72; auth, Vision (California), 75, Vision (Eastern Europe) & Vision (New York City). Mailing Add: 75 Third St San Francisco CA 94103

MARISOL, ESCOBAR
SCULPTOR
b Paris, France, 1930. Study: Ecole Beaux Arts, 49; Art Students League, 50; New Sch, 51-54; Hans Hofmann Sch; Moore Col Art, Philadelphia, hon Dr, 70. Work: Mus Mod Art, New York; Whitney Mus Am Art, New York; Albright-Knox Art Gallery, Buffalo; Mus Bellas Artes, Caracas, Venezuela; Nat Portrait Gallery, Washington, DC; plus others. Exhib: Painting and Sculpture of a Decade, Tate Gallery, London, 64; New Realism, Munic Mus, The Hague, 64; Whitney Sculptures & Prints Ann, Whitney Mus Am Art, 66; Soc Contemp Art 28th Ann, Art Inst Chicago, 68; Image of Man Today, Inst Contemp Arts, London, 68; one-person shows, Moore Col Art, Philadelphia, 70, Worcester Art Mus, Mass, 71, New York Cult Ctr, 73 & Ohio Univ, 74; Contemp Women Artists, Skidmore Col, 70 & State Univ NY Col, Potsdam, 72; Baltimore Mus Art, 73; plus others. Bibliog: Barbara Gold (auth), Portrait of Marisol, Interplay, 1/68; Don Cyr (auth), A conversation with Marisol, Arts & Activities, Vol 63, No 1; Lawrence Campbell (auth), Marisol, Art News, 11/67; plus others. Publ: Contribr, The Art of Assemblage, Doubleday; contribr, Pop Art, Praeger; contribr, The New American Arts, Collier, 67; contribr, In Memory of My Feelings, Crafton Graphic Co, 67; contribr, Stamps Indelibly, Multiples, Inc, 67; plus others. Mailing Add: c/o Sidney Janis Gallery 6 W 57th St New York NY 10019

MARK, BENDOR
PAINTER
b New York, NY, June 5, 12. Study: Cooper Union. Work: Denver Art Mus, Colo; Nat Collection Fine Arts, Washington, DC; Butler Inst Am Art, Youngstown, Ohio; Ga Mus Art, Athens; also in many pvt collections. Exhib: ACA Nat Competition, New York, 36; American Art Today, New York World's Fair, 39; Art Inst Chicago, 40; Am Fedn Art Traveling Show, 40-41; Pepsi Cola Nat Competition, Metrop Mus, New York, 45; Am as Art Bicentennial Exhib, Nat Collection Fine Arts, Washington, DC, 76; plus others. Awards: Second Prize, Cooper Union, 29; Second Prize, ACA Nat Competition, 36. Mailing Add: 5727 Chelsea Ave La Jolla CA 92037

MARK, ENID (EPSTEIN)
PRINTMAKER, PAINTER
b New York, NY, 32. Study: Art Students League; Smith Col, BA; Westchester State Col, with Victor Lasuchin (lithography). Work: Del Art Mus, Wilmington; Civic Ctr Mus, Philadelphia; Univ Del; Philadelphia Mus Art; First Pa Bank. Exhib: 4th Int Miniature Print Exhib, Pratt Graphics, Ctr, New York, 71; one-woman show, The Print Club, Philadelphia, 72; Philadelphia Art Alliance, 73; Nat Print Show, Soc Am Graphic Artists, 73; The Philadelphia Scene, Pa State Univ, 74; plus others. Teaching: Lectr and demonstr of var printmaking techniques in pub schs in the greater Philadelphia area. Pos: Artist in residence, Springfield Sch Dist, Pa, 68-69; chmn bicentennial publ, Folio '76, Cheltenham Graphics Guild, 74-76. Awards: Copeland Purchase Prize, Del Art Mus, 72; Earth Art Show Print Purchase Prize for Phoenix House, Jr League Philadelphia, 73; Wayne Art Ctr First Prize for Printmaking, 73. Mem: Am Color Print Soc; Cheltenham Graphics Guild, Pa; Artists Equity Asn; Print Club, Pa. Style & Technique: Non-objective imagery derived from geometric perceptions, often combined with naturalistic forms; silkscreen and lithography combined with photographic techniques. Media: Acrylic, Hard-edge; Silkscreen, Lithography. Dealer: Print Club 1613 Latimer St Philadelphia PA 19103; Benjamin Mangel Gallery Bala Ave Bala Cynwyd PA 19004. Mailing Add: 210 Sykes Lane Wallingford PA 19086

MARK, MARILYN
PAINTER
b Brooklyn, NY, Aug 7, 30. Study: Wash Sch Art, cert. Work: Nat Art Mus Sport, New York; Du Musee des Beaux Arts, Montbard, France; pvt collections of Bernard Grebanier & Schroeder, New York. Comn: Portraits of Ligoa Duncan & her dog Chi Chi, comn by Ligoa Duncan, Paris, 75. Exhib: Salons Helder Palace, Brussels, Belg, 71-73; Nat Art Mus Sport, Inc, New York, 72-73; Int Art Festival, St Germain des Pres, Paris, 74-75; Mus Mod Art, Paris, 74; City Hall, Paris, 75; Mus du Luxembourg, Paris; Poetry & Art, Nat Arts Club, Metrop Mus Art, New York, 77; Int Women's Art Festival Slide Exhib, Womenart Gallery, New York. Pos: First vpres, Artists League Brooklyn, Inc, 70, pres, 71-74; co-founder & pres, Visual Individualists United; mgr pub relations, Nat Art Mus Sport, 77. Awards: Bronze Medal & Citation, Fr Govt, 76; Silver Medal, NY State Pre-Biennial Competition, Nat

League of Am Pen Women, 77; Gold Medal & Global Award, Acad de Ciencas Humanisticas y Relaciones & Asn Belgo-Hispanica, Belg, 77. Bibliog: Vallobra (auth), articles in Apollo J, 71 & 73-74 & Le Vertige du Neant, 73. Mem: Nat League of Am Pen Women, Inc (publicity chairwoman, Nat Exec Bd, Manhattan & NY State Br, 72-74); Soc des Artistes de France; Eleanor Gay Lee Gallery Found, Inc (pub rels dir, 74-75); Artists Equity Asn New York, Inc; Asn Belgo-Hispanique. Style & Technique: Acrylics on canvas on wooden stretchers; use medium relative to oils; impasto technique built with paint only, textured; specialist in childern and sport paintings. Media: Acrylic, Pastels. Dealer: South Bay Art Gallery Ltd 35-60 73rd St Jackson Heights NY 11372; Art Sales & Rental Gallery Brooklyn Mus Eastern Pkwy Brooklyn NY 11238. Mailing Add: 2261 Ocean Ave Brooklyn NY 11229

MARK, PHYLLIS
SCULPTOR
b New York, NY. Study: Ohio State Univ; New Sch Social Res, sculpture study with Seymour Lipton. Work: Dickerson-White Mus, Cornell Univ; Syracuse Univ Permanent Collection; Lowe Art Mus, Univ Miami, Coral Gables, Fla; Corcoran Gallery Art, Washington, DC; RCA Corp Collection. Exhib: Light Sound Motion, Hudson River Mus, Yonkers, NY, 71; Critic's Choice, Sculpture Ctr, 72; one-woman shows, Ruth White Gallery, 66 & 68, Gimpel & Weitzenhoffer Gallery, 73, New York, DuBose Gallery, Tex, 74, Images Gallery, Ohio, 74, Benson Gallery, Long Island, NY, 75 & Camino Real Gallery, Boca Raton, Fla, 75; Women Choose Women, New York Cult Ctr, 73; Sculpture as Jewelry, Inst Contemp Art, Boston, 73; Brooklyn Mus, 75; Albright-Knox Art Gallery, Buffalo, NY, 73-76; Magic Circle, Bronx Mus Art, NY, 77; Refractions/Reflections, Ft Lauderdale Mus, Fla, 77; Marymount Manhattan Col, 78. Bibliog: Articles in New York Times, 2/1/73, 6/2/73, 11/1/75 & 1/24/78, Long Island Press, 6/23/74 & Feminist Art J, summer 77; plus others. Mem: NY Orgn Independent Artists; Archit League New York; Women In the Arts. Style & Technique: Working in motorized or wind moved sculpture, metal structures and Dacron sails; motion adds the element of time; factory fabrication is usual method. Interest: Kinetic sculpture; a leading exponent of large-scale multiple sculpture and editions of sculpture. Dealer: Dubose Gallery 2950 Kirby Dr Houston TX 77006. Mailing Add: 803 Greenwich St New York NY 10014

MARKEL KATHRYN E
ART DEALER
b Richmond, Va, Oct 19, 46. Pos: Dir, Kathryn Markel Fine Arts Inc, New York. Specialty: Specialty work on paper by contemporary American artists. Mailing Add: 50 W 57th St New York NY 10019

MARKELL, ISABELLA BANKS
PAINTER, GRAPHIC ARTIST
b Superior, Wis, Dec 17, 91. Study: Fountainbleau, France, 30; Md Inst, 33-34; Pa Acad Fine Arts, 35, O'Hara Sch, 38; Brackman Sch, 42, 43 & 46; also with Farnsworth. Work: New York Pub Libr; NY Hist Soc; Mus City of New York; Northwest Printmakers; Metrop Mus Art; plus many others. Exhib: Newark Mus Art; Northwest Printmakers; Metrop Mus Art; Baltimore Mus Art; Birmingham Mus Art; plus many others. Awards: Prizes, Pen & Brush Club, 53, 55 & 64; Prizes, Nat Asn Women Artists, 56, 58-60 & 64; Three Gold Medals, Am Artists Prof League, 60, Prize, 64; plus many others. Mem: Soc Am Graphic Artists; Pen & Brush Club; Philadelphia Print Club; Washington Printmakers; Miami Art Asn; plus many others. Mailing Add: 10 Gracie Sq New York NY 10028

MARKER, MARISKA PUGSLEY
PAINTER, COLLECTOR
b San Francisco, Calif. Study: With Leon Berkowitz, Robert Newmann, Hank Harmon & Dwight Roberts. Work: Prime Minister Domimic Mintoff, Malta; Nat Mus Fine Arts, Valletta, Malta. Exhib: Nat Sun Carnival Art Exhib, El Paso Mus, Tex, 70-72; 2nd Regional Ann, Northern Va Fine Arts Asn, Alexandria, Va, 71 & 75; two-person show, Nat Mus Fine Arts, Valletta, Malta, 76. Pos: Chmn, Pepco Art Gallery, Charles Co Arts Coun, La Plata, Md, 77. Awards: First Prize, Art League Northern Va, 69, Hon Mention, 70 & 72. Bibliog: E Fiorentino (auth), The Washington School at Valletta, Sunday Times of Malta, 10/24/76; The Markers at the Museum of Fine Arts, Times of Malta, 10/20/76; Peter Mayo (auth), Minimal representation, Malta News, 10/28/76; plus others. Mem: Appraisers Asn Am; Art League Alexandria, Va (bd mem, 69-70). Style & Technique: Stained canvas techniques. Media: Lucite, Acrylic, Oil, Ink. Res: Max Schallinger, a rediscovered artist. Collection: Seventeenth and Eighteenth century British, contemporary American, and contemporary American Indian. Publ: Auth, Korean arts have a great potential, Feel of Korea, Hollym Corp, 66; co-auth, Yung Lu and the Magic Pearl; plus feature articles in Kansas City Star and catalogs for Northern Va Fine Arts Asn. Dealer: Dame Francoise Tempra The Lodge 23 Kensington Park Gardens London W11 England. Mailing Add: 300 Queen St Alexandria VA 22314

MARKER, RALPH E
PAINTER, COLLECTOR
b Salamanca, NY, Dec 7, 25. Study: Pvt study with Leon Berkowitz; Art League of Northern Va, with Robert Newmann. Work: Nat Mus Fine Arts, Valletta, Malta. Exhib: Ann Regional Show, NVa Artists, NVa Fine Arts Asn, 70 & 71; 16th Nat Sun Carnival Show, El Paso Mus Art, 71; two-man show, Nat Mus Fine Arts, Valletta, Malta, 76. Awards: First Prize Watercolor, Gilham Award Show, Art League, Alexandria, Va, 69. Bibliog: The Markers at the Museum of Fine Arts, Times of Malta, 10/20/76; E Fiorentino (auth), The Washington School at Valletta, Sunday Times of Malta, 10/24/76; Peter Mayo (auth), Minimal representation, Malta News, 10/28/76; plus others. Style & Technique: Stained and washed abstract. Media: Acrylic, Oil. Collection: 17th and 18th English painting; contemporary American and contemporary American Indian paintings. Dealer: Dame Francoise Tempra The Lodge 23 Kensington Park Gardens London W11 England. Mailing Add: 300 Queen St Alexandria VA 22314

MARKLE, JACK M
ART DEALER, SCULPTOR
b Winnipeg, Man, July 9, 39. Study: With Jack Markel; Ont Col Art. Work: Art Bank, Fed Govt, Ottawa, Ont. Comn: Neon chandelier, comn by Mr & Mrs Sommerville, Toronto, Ont, 71; neon sculpture, United Trust, Toronto, 75. Exhib: Spring Joint Computer Conf, Atlantic City, NJ, 71; Basel Art Fair, Switz, 73-75; IKI Art Fair, Dusseldorf & Cologne, Ger, 73-75; Art Gallery Ont, Toronto, 74; Rotterdam Cult Ctr, Holland, 75. Pos: The Electric Gallery, Toronto, Ont. Awards: Autumn Festival of the Arts, Toronto, Kiwanis Club, 70. Mem: Prof Art Dealers Asn Can; IKI, Ger. Style & Technique: Neon sculptures; electrical and mechanical sculptures, whimsical. Specialty: Electric art. Mailing Add: c/o Electric Gallery 24 Hazelton Ave Toronto ON M5R 2E2 Can

MARKLE, SAM
ART DEALER, SCULPTOR
b Winnipeg, Man, 1933. Study: Self-taught. Work: Nat Art Bank, Ottawa. Comn: Neon installations (with Jack Markle), Alcan Aluminum, Head Off, Toronto, 70; United Trust, Head Off, Toronto, 72, Famous Players Theatre, Four Seasons Hotel, Toronto, 73, Sunoco Bldg, Toronto, 73 & Concourse & Plaza, Hudson Bay Co, 73, Toronto, 74. Exhib: One-man shows, Pop Sign Art, Gallery Pascal, Toronto, 64, Alpha 64, Four Seasons Hotel, Toronto, 64 & Flower & Garden Show, Electric Gallery, Toronto, 71; New Media, Art Gallery Ont, 71; Espace V Gallery, Montreal, 74. Pos: Dir, Electric Gallery, Toronto. Mem: Prof Art Dealers of Can (vpres, 75-78); Can Conf Arts. Style & Technique: Representational-absurd. Media: Neon tubing. Specialty: Electric art exclusively. Mailing Add: c/o Electric Gallery 24 Hazelton Ave Toronto ON M5R 2E2 Can

MARKMAN, RONALD
PAINTER
b Bronx, NY, May 29, 31. Study: Yale Univ, BFA, 57 & MFA, 59. Work: Brooklyn Mus, New York; Art Inst of Chicago, Ill; Hirshhorn Mus & Sculpture Garden, Smithsonian Inst, Washington, DC; Metrop Mus of Art, New York; Mus of Mod Art, New York. Exhib: Boston Arts Festival, 59 & 60; Recent Acquisitions Show, Mus of Mod Art, New York, 59 & 66; Young Am, Whitney Mus of Am Art, 60; Chicago Biennial Print & Drawing Show, Art Inst of Chicago, 64; Ball State Univ, Muncie, Ind, 66; Annual, Pennsylvania Acad of Fine Arts, Pa, 67; Anderson Ind Fine Arts Ctr, 67; Am Paintings, Butler Inst, Youngstown, Ohio, 67; Print Biennial, Brooklyn Mus, 68; John Herron Art Inst, Indianapolis, Ind, 68 & 69; Humor, Satire and Irony, New Sch for Social Research, 72; Indianapolis Mus of Art, 72 & 74; Work by Students of Josef Albers, Harvard Univ, 74; one-man shows, Terry Dintenfass, Inc, 65-76, Reed Col, 66, Univ of Manitoba, 72, Indianapolis Mus, 74, Herron Sch of Art, 76 & Tyler Sch of Art, Philadelphia, 76. Teaching: Instr, Univ of Fla, 59, Art Inst of Chicago, 60-64 & Indiana Univ, 64- Awards: Fulbright Fel, 62-63. Dealer: Terry Dintenfass Inc 50 W 57 St New York NY 10019. Mailing Add: 719 S Jordan Bloomington IN 47401

MARKMAN, SIDNEY DAVID
ART ADMINISTRATOR, ART HISTORIAN
b New York, NY, Oct 10, 11. Study: Union Col, Schenectady, NY AB, 34; Columbia Univ, MA, 36, PhD, 41. Teaching: Prof art hist, Univ Nac de Panama, 41-45; prof art hist, Duke Univ, 47-, actg chmn dept art, 61-62 & 75- Mem: Soc Archit Historians; Soc Am Archaeol; Latin Am Studies Asn. Res: Colonial art and architecture of Central America and Chiapas, Mexico. Publ: Auth, Horse in Greek Art, Johns Hopkins Univ Press, 43; auth, San Cristobal de las Casas, Escuela de Estudios Hispano Am, Seville, Spain, 63; auth, Colonial Architecture of Antigua Guatemala, Am Philos Soc, Philadelphia, 66; auth, Colonial Central America, A Bibliography, Ariz State Univ Press, 77. Mailing Add: Dept of Art Duke Univ Durham NC 27708

MARKOW, JACK
CARTOONIST, PAINTER
b London, Eng, Jan 23, 05; US citizen. Study: Art Students League, with Boardman Robinson, Richard Lahey & Walter Jack Duncan, 22-29. Work: Metrop Mus Art, New York; Libr Cong, Washington, DC; Brooklyn Mus, NY; Univ Ga; Hunter Col, New York. Exhib: Whitney Mus Am Art, New York, 36 & 40; one-man show drawing & lithographs, ACA Gallery, New York, 37, paintings, Hudson Guild Gallery, New York, 58; Carnegie Inst Int; Pa Acad Art, Philadelphia, 38; Corcoran Gallery, Washington, DC, 39; Whitney Mus San Francisco Mus Art, Calif; Denver Mus Art, Colo; Detroit Art Inst, Mich; Art Inst Chicago; Seligman Gallery, New York; Everhart Mus; plus others. Teaching: Instr drawing & cartooning, Sch Visual Arts, New York, 47-53. Pos: Cartoon ed, Argosy Mag, New York, 51-53. Awards: Fourth Prize, Int Salon of Cartoons, Montreal, 72. Mem: Life mem Art Students League; New York WPA Artists; Nat Cartoonists Soc; Mag Cartoonists Guild (mem exec bd, 68-72). Media: Oil. Publ: Auth & illusr, Drawing and Selling Cartoons, 55, Drawing Funny Pictures, 70 & Drawing Comic Strips, 72, Pitman; contribr, monthly column Artists and cartoonists Q's, In: Writer's Digest, 63-78; auth & illusr, Cartoonists and Gag Writers Handbook, Writer's Digest, 67; contribr, Encycl Am, 74. Mailing Add: 2428 Cedar St Manasquan NJ 08736

MARKOWSKI, EUGENE DAVID
PAINTER
b St Louis, Mo, Sept 16, 31. Study: Wash Univ Sch Fine Art, BFA, 60; Univ Pa Sch Fine Art, MFA, 61. Work: Minn Mus Art, St Paul; Lauren Rogers Mus Art, Laurel, Miss; Philip Morris Corp & First & Merchants Bank, Richmond, Va; New York Bank for Savings. Exhib: Corcoran Gallery Art Biennial, Washington, DC, 68; Northern Ill Univ Nat Drawing Competition, 71; Nat Drawing Competition, Minn Mus Art, 71; Int Print & Drawing Competition, Alta Col Art, 72; Regional Painting Competition, Montgomery Mus Fine Arts, 75. Teaching: Asst prof painting, Univ Pa, 61-68 & Montgomery Col, Rockville, Md, 68-70; assoc prof painting, Univ Va, Charlottesville, 70- Pos: Art critic, Cablevision, Charlottesville, 72- Awards: Yale-Norfolk Award in Painting, Wash Univ, 59; McKeen Award in Painting, Univ Pa, 61; Cert of Distinction, Va Mus Fine Art, 75. Mem: Col Art Asn Am. Style & Technique: Three dimensional geometrical painted constructions. Media: Plexiglas, Acrylic Paint. Dealer: Fontana Gallery 107 Iona Ave Narberth PA 19072. Mailing Add: 940 Locust Ave Charlottesville VA 22901

MARKS, MR & MRS CEDRIC H
COLLECTOR, PATRON
Interest: Donated works to various museums and colleges in the United States and Israel. Collection: Far Eastern, Near Eastern, pre-Columbia medieval and classical antiquities. Mailing Add: 880 Fifth Ave New York NY 10021

MARKS, CLAUDE
PAINTER, WRITER
b London, Eng, Nov 13, 15; US citizen. Study: Trinity Col, Cambridge Univ, MA(with honors in mod lang), 36; La Grande Chaumiere, Paris; State Univ Iowa, MFA(painting), 48; also with Yves Brayer, James Lechay & Mauricio Lasansky. Work: Brooklyn Mus Print Collection; New York Pub Libr Prints & Drawings Collection; Mus City New York Theatre Collection; Libr & Mus Performing Arts, New York; Detroit Inst Arts Theatre Collection. Exhib: One-man shows, Theatre Drawings & Pastels, Far Gallery, New York, 61 & Libr & Mus Performing Arts, 71; one-man shows, American and English Theatre, US Embassy, London, 65, Shakespeare in Central Park, Mus City New York, 66 & The Room (theatrical drawings), Greenwich, London, 70; Amsterdam Gallery, Libr & Mus of Performing Arts, Lincoln Ctr, 71; Dimitria Gallery, Princeton Univ, 73. Teaching: Asst prof art hist, State Univ Iowa, 48-50; instr art hist & appreciation, Juilliard Sch Mus, New York, 57-61; instr art hist, Parsons Sch Design, New York, 64-66. Pos: Scenic & costume designer, Pitlochry Festival, Scotland, 54, Theatre Workshop, London, 55 & New York Shakespeare Festival, 60; guest lectr art, Metrop Mus Art, New York, 59- Bibliog: Gordon Rogoff (auth), Artist's life, Theatre Arts, 11/61;

Don Dunn (auth), Artist on the aisle, Playbill, 5/72. Mem: United Scenic Artists' Union, New York; Col Art Asn. Style & Technique: Figurative, free style. Media: Oil, Pen-Brush & Ink. Res: Drawings and sketches of all periods; the Medici; art, literature of cultural background of medieval Provence. Publ: Auth, Calling on Gordon Craig, Theatre Arts, 9/57; auth, From the Sketchbooks of the Great Artists, Crowell, 72; auth, Pilgrims, Heretics and Lovers: A Medieval Journey, Macmillan, 75; auth, The Lute & The Sword, Camera 3, CBS-TV, 4-5/77. Mailing Add: 315 Central Park W New York NY 10025

MARKS, GEORGE B
PAINTER
b Conrad, Iowa, Sept 10, 23. Study: Univ Iowa, BFA, 50. Awards: Silver Medal in Drawing, Cowboy Artists Am Exhib, 73; Silver Medal in Sculpture, 77. Mem: Cowboy Artists Am. Mailing Add: 3153 Casa del Norte Ct NE Albuquerque NM 87111

MARKS, ROYAL S
ART DEALER, COLLECTOR
b Detroit, Mich, Sept 11, 29. Study: Wayne Univ. Pos: Owner & dir, Royal Marks Gallery, New York. Specialty: Works by Kupka, Tobey, Torres Garcia, Vasarely, Leger, Miro, Feininger & Picasso; also Delaunay, Robert, Villon, Jacques, Braque; contemporary sculptors, Robert Howard, Duayne Hatchett, David Weinrib & Richard Randell; contemporary painters, Fred Martin & Landes Levitin; also oceanic art and antiques; Egyptian sculpture: bronze, wood and faience, plus outstanding collection of scarobs; Calder tapestries and hammocks. Mailing Add: 29 E 64th St New York NY 10021

MARKS, STANLEY ALBERT
COLLECTOR
b Cincinnati, Ohio, May 25, 27. Study: Sorbonne, 47; Harvard Univ, AB, 49. Collection: 20 century American paintings and drawings; American Period furniture. Mailing Add: 950 Fifth Ave New York NY 10021

MARKUS, MRS HENRY A
COLLECTOR
Collection: Picasso, Henry Moore, Chagall, Giocometti, Miro & Max Ernst paintings and sculptures; Manzo sculpture, Jean Arp sculptures and Renee Magritte paintings; can be seen at Art Inst Chicago, Notre Dame Univ, Evansville Mus & Brandeis Univ. Mailing Add: 1300 Lake Shore Dr Chicago IL 60610

MARKUSEN, THOMAS ROY
DESIGNER, METALSMITH
b Chicago, Ill, Jan 1, 40. Study: Univ Wis, Madison, BS, 65, MS, 66. Work: Mus of Contemp Crafts, New York; Lannan Found Art Mus, Palm Beach, Fla; Wustum Mus of Fine Arts, Racine, Wis; Hand Workshop Gallery, Richmond, Va; New York State Craftsmen, New York. Comn: Sculpture, Va Nat Bank, Norfolk, 67; furniture, comm by Dr Simon Russi, Petersberg, Va, 68; lawn sculpture, comm by L E Frankenstein, Rochester, NY, 72; outside sculpture, comm by M M Reismen, Cazenovia, NY, 72; acting set, Newmen Oratory, Brockport, NY, 75-76. Exhib: Goldsmith 70, 74 & 77 (travelling exhib), Renwick Gallery, Smithsonian Inst, St Paul Mus, Minn, Mus of Contemp Crafts, New York, Phoenix Art Mus, Ariz & Henery Gallery, Univ Washington, Seattle; Contemp Am Silversmiths & Goldsmiths, Fairtree Gallery, New York & Corcoran Gallery, Washington, DC, 73; Smithing 73, State Univ NY Col, Brockport, 73; Metalsmithing, Lubin House, Syracuse Univ, NY, 73; Int Goldsmiths & Weavers, Albright-Knox Art Gallery, Buffalo, NY, 74; Profile 74, McGuire Gallery, Humber Col, Toronto, Ont, 74; Metalsmithing Invitational, Galeria Universitaria Aristos at the Univ Nac Autonoma de Mexico, 75; Forms in Metal; 275 Yrs of Am Metalsmithing, Finch Art Mus, New York, NY, Mus of Contemp Crafts, New York & Cranbrook Acad of Arts Mus, Bloomfield Hills, Mich, 75; Metals Invitational 1975 AD, Art Mus, Melbourne State Col, Carlton, Australia, 75; Lannan Found Objects, Lannan Art Mus, Palm Beach, Fla, 76; Fifth Marietta Col Crafts Nat, Fine Arts Ctr, Marietta Col, Ohio, 76; 41st Int Eucharistis Exhib of Liturgical Arts, Civic Ctr, Philadelphia, 76; Solid Wrought Iron, Southern Ill Univ Mus & Art Gallery, Carbondale, 76; Arts/Objects USA, Lee Nordness Gallery & Johnson Wax Found, New York, 76. Teaching: Instr crafts, Univ Wis, Madison, 65-66; asst prof metalsmithing, Radford Col, Va, 66-68; assoc prof metalsmithing, State Univ NY Col, Brockport, 68-; instr metalsmithing workshops in var mus & arts & crafts sch in, Wis, Tex, NC, NH, VA, Ohio, NY & NJ; Pos: Dir & organizer metal exhib, Fine Arts Gallery, State Univ NY Col, Brockport, 71-78; guest lectr metalsmithing, Univ Wash, Mont State Univ, Va Commonwealth Univ, Syracuse Univ, State Univ NY Col, New Paltz, US Embassy-Mexico & Seventh World Craft Conf, Mexico, 75-77. Awards: Fac Res fel, State Univ NY Res Found, 71; Craftsmen Fel, Nat Endowment for the Arts, 75; Tech Res Grant, Soc NAm Goldsmiths & Nat Endowment for the Arts, 77. Bibliog: Leon Nigrosh (auth), Forged iron today, Craft Horizons, 2/76; Jack O'Field (filmmaker), Hands: The Arts & Crafts of America, Raymond Lowry Int Productions, 76; Dona Z Meilach (auth), Decorative and Sculpture Ironwork, Crown, 77. Mem: World Crafts Coun; Am Craftsmen Coun; Artist/Blacksmiths Asn of NAm; Soc of NAm Goldsmiths (vpres & bd dir, 75-78); NY State Craftsmen (pres, vpres, bd dirs, 72-79). Style & Technique: Contemporary personal style in archtectural scale; ornamental blacksmithing and coppersmithing techniques. Media: All types of fabrication in ferrous and non-ferrous metal. Publ: Contribr, Contemporary Jewelry, Holt, Rinehart & Sinston, Second ed, 76; contribr, Autobiography, J Soc NAm Goldsmith, 76; auth, Application of hot smithing process to non-ferrous metals: copper, bronze & brass, Goldsmith J, No 16, 78. Dealer: Helen Drutt Gallery 1625 Spruce St Philadelphia PA 19103. Mailing Add: 17218 Roosevelt Hwy Kendall NY 14476

MARLOR, CLARK STRANG
ART HISTORIAN, COLLECTOR
b Camden, NJ, Nov 18, 22. Study: Carnegie-Mellon Univ, BFA, 45; Univ Mich, MA, 46; NY Univ, DEduc, 61. Collections Arranged: John Barnard Whittaker (with catalog), Adelphi Univ, 68, Eleanor C Bannister (with catalog), 71; Benjamin Eggleston, Long Island Hist Soc, 75. Teaching: Prof, Adelphi Univ, 56- Mem: Salmagundi Club (mem, Libr Comt & Bicentennial Comt), Res: 19th century American artists. Collection: American artists of the 19th and early 20th centuries. Publ: Auth, A History of the Brooklyn Art Association with an Index of Exhibitions, 70; auth, John B Whittaker, Brooklyn artist, Antiques, 11/71. Mailing Add: 293 Sterling Pl Brooklyn NY 11238

MAROZZI, ELI RAPHAEL
SCULPTOR, INSTRUCTOR
b Montegallo, Italy, Aug 13, 13; US citizen. Study: Univ Wash, BA; Univ Hawaii, MA; also with Mark Tobey. Work: St Andrew's Cathedral, Honolulu. Comn: Stone sun-dial with figure, Hanahauoli Sch, Honolulu, 53; stone bas-relief, Tennent Art Found, Honolulu, 55; stone lion, State Found Cult & Arts, Honolulu, 71; stone figure portrait, Vedanta Soc Sacramento, Carmichael, Calif, 72; Stone Madonna and Child, St Philomena Church, Honolulu, 75. Exhib: Seattle Art Mus Ann, 47 & 48; Artists of Hawaii Ann, Honolulu Acad Arts, 50-69; Assoc Artists Hawaii, Honolulu, 52-55; Hawaii Painter's & Sculptor's League, Honolulu, 55-70; two-man show, Contemp Art Ctr. Teaching: Art instr, Honolulu Acad Arts, 50-55; art instr, YWCA Adult Educ, Honolulu, 50-; art instr, Univ Hawaii Exten, Honolulu, 51-53. Awards: Hon mention for etching, Honolulu Acad Arts, 51; First Prize in sculpture, Honolulu Assoc Artists, 55. Mem: Hawaii Painters & Sculptors League; hon mem Windward Artists Guild; hon mem Honolulu Assoc Artists. Style & Technique: Semi-abstract to abstract; carving and pargeting. Media: Marble, Synthetic Stone. Publ: Auth, The influence of material and technique on sculptural form, 52; contribr, Times of India Mag, 53; contribr, Essays in philosophy, 62; contribr, Swami Vivekananda in East and West, 68; contribr, Prabuddha Bharata Mag, 69 & 73. Mailing Add: 1081 Young St Honolulu HI 96814

MARRIOTT, WILLIAM ALLEN
PAINTER, EDUCATOR
b Pontiac, Mich, July 17, 42. Study: Ctr for Creative Studies, Col of Art & Design; Wayne State Univ, BFA; Yale Univ, MFA; study with Lester Johnson, Irving Kriesberg, Nicholas Carone, Michael Goldberg, Robert Wilbert, David Mitchell, Gabor Peterdi & George Kubler. Work: Wayne State Univ, Detroit; Appalachian State Univ, Boone, NC; The New Mus, New York; Southeastern Ctr for Contemp Art, Winston-Salem, NC. Exhib: Drawings USA 1975, Minn Mus of Art, St Paul, 75; 5th Int Miniature Print Competition, Pratt Graphics Ctr, New York, 75; Nat Invitational Drawing Exhib, Southern Ill Univ, Carbondale, 75; 1977 Artists Biennial, New Orleans Mus of Art, 77; 45th Southeastern Competition for Painting and Sculpture, Southeastern Ctr Contemp Art, 75. Teaching: Assoc prof painting, drawing & printmaking, Univ of Ga, Athens, 67- Awards: Purchase Awards, Appalachian Nat Drawing Competition, Appalachian State Univ, 74 & 45th Southeastern Competition for Painting & Sculpture, Southeastern Ctr for Contemp Art, 77. Mem: Southeastern Graphics Coun. Style & Technique: Landscapes and objects, representational. Media: Oil Painting & Charcoal. Dealer: Mr Dean Gillette Image South Gallery 1931 Peachtree Rd NE Atlanta GA 30309. Mailing Add: Dept of Art Univ of Ga Athens GA 30602

MARRON, DONALD B
COLLECTOR
b Goshen, NY, July 21, 34. Pos: Trustee, Calif Inst of the Arts, Valencia, 71-, Mus of Mod Art, New York, 75- & Trust for Cult Resources of the City of New York, 76- Collection: Nineteenth and twentieth century American artists. Mailing Add: 792 Park Ave New York NY 10021

MARROZZINI, LUIGI
ART DEALER
b Rome, Italy, July 30, 33. Study: Univ Leonardo Di Vince, Rome, grad. Pos: Secy & tech adv, San Juan Bienal Latin Am Graphic Art, 70 & 72; jury mem, 3rd Int Miniature Print Show, Pratt Graphics Ctr, 68; dir, Galeria Colibri, San Juan, PR. Mem: Am Fedn Arts. Specialty: Original graphics by old and modern masters; publisher of the most outstanding Latin American artists. Publ: Auth, Catalog raisonne of the complete Orozco graphics, 69. Mailing Add: Box 1734 San Juan PR 00903

MARSH, ANNE STEELE
PAINTER, PRINTMAKER
b Nutley, NJ, Sept 7, 01. Study: Cooper Union Art Sch; plus others. Work: Brooklyn Mus; New York Pub Libr; NJ State Mus, Trenton; Metrop Mus Art; Mus Mod Art; plus others. Exhib: Metrop Mus Art; Nat Acad Design; Art Inst Chicago; Am Watercolor Soc; Soc Am Graphic Artists; plus others. Mem: New York Soc Women Artists; Nat Asn Women Artists; Boston, Albany & Washington Soc Printmakers; Soc Am Graphic Artists (past pres). Style & Technique: Stylized realism. Mailing Add: RD 1 Fiddlers Forge Pittstown NJ 08867

MARSH, DAVID FOSTER
EDUCATOR, PAINTER
b Salkum, Wash, Jan 24, 26. Study: Cent Wash Univ, BA; Univ Ore, MS. Work: Westminster Col, Fulton, Mo; Inst Mexicana-NAm, Guadalajar, Mexico. Exhib: NW Ann, 1963 & 1966; NW Watercolor Soc Exhib, 1958, 1962 & 1977. Teaching: Prof drawing & painting, Western Wash Univ, 57- Mem: Col Art Asn; Nat Art Educ Asn. Style & Technique: Watercolor landscapes. Mailing Add: Dept of Art Western Wash Univ Bellingham WA 98225

MARSH, (EDWIN) THOMAS
POTTER, EDUCATOR
b Winchester, Ky, Feb 11, 34. Study: Univ Louisville, BS(fine arts), 60; apprentice to Totaro Sakuma, Mashiko, Japan & Kei Fujiwara, Imbe, Bizen, 61-63; Ind Univ, MAT(ceramics), 70, also with Karl Martz. Work: Ashland Oil Collection, Louisville, Ky; Ind Univ, Bloomington; Smithsonian Inst; Columbus Gallery Fine Art; Brown Univ. Comn: 14 holy water fonts and other ceramic pieces (with David Day, architect), Abbey of Gethsemane, Trappist, Ky, 66; holy water font (with David Day), St Margaret of Cortona Church, Columbus, Ohio, 68; baptismal font, New Harmony, Ind, 74. Exhib: One-man exhibs, Shingei Gallery, Tokyo, 64, Togei Gallery, Japan, 64, Art Ctr, Louisville, Ky, 68 & 69 & The Gallery, Bloomington, Ind, 71 & 74; Notre Dame Univ, 76; Greenwich House Pottery, New York, 78. Teaching: Prof ceramics, Univ Louisville, 70-; vis prof ceramics, Purdue Univ, summers, 70 & 72. Awards: First Nat Bank Award & Aetna-Ashland Oil Purchase Prize, 60; Merit Award, Gen Elec Co, 72. Mem: Nat Coun Educ Ceramic Arts; Am Asn Univ Prof; Am Craftsmen's Coun. Style & Technique: Work in stoneware, raku, porcelain salt glaze container forms and sculpture. Media: Ceramics. Publ: Auth, The folk potters of Mashiko, 10/61, Marsh pottery, 3/74 & Bardstown pottery, 9/73, Ceramics Monthly. Mailing Add: c/o Marsh Pottery RR 2 Box 657 Borden IN 47106

MARSHALL, BRUCE
ILLUSTRATOR, PAINTER
b Athens, Tex, Dec 23, 29. Study: Univ Ariz, Tucson; Southern Ariz Sch of Art (full scholar). Work: First Cavalry Mus, Ft Hood, Tex; Confederate Res Ctr, Hill Jr Col, Hillsboro, Tex. Comn: Portrait of Gen Archibald Gracie, New York City Mayor's Mansion, 64 & portrait of Dick Dowling, Dowling Sch, Houston, 70, comn by Sons of Confederate Veterans; paintings, Inst of Texan Cult, Univ Tex, San Antonio, 70-75; Tex Citizen Soldier (mural), Tex Nat Guard for Nat Infantry Mus, Ft Benning, Ga, 76. Exhib: Smithsonian Inst, Washington, DC, 54; First Cavalry Mus, Ft Hood, Tex, 71; Old Overland Trail Mus, Ft Davis, Tex, 71 & 73; Univ of Ariz, Tucson, 72; Am Inst of Design & Archit, Houston, 74; Llano Estacado Mus, Midland, Tex, 75; Rotunda Exhib, Tex State Capitol, Austin, 75-76; Panhandle-Plains Mus, Canyon, Tex, 77; Chamizal Nat Mem, El Paso, Tex, 77; Mus of the Big Bend, Alpine, Tex, 77; San Jacinto Monument, Houston, Tex, 78; Star of the Repub Mus Washington State Park, Tex, 78. Pos: Auth & illusr, The Texas Star, 72-73. Awards: Knighted by King Peter II, Yugoslavia, 66; Artist of the Confederacy, United Daughters of the Confederacy, 74; Nat Artist, Confederate State of Am, Sons of Confederate Veterans, 76. Bibliog: Bill Warren (auth), 74 & Margaret Taylor Dry (auth), 75, articles in Austin Am-Statesman; Robert St Johns (auth), article in Argosy Mag, 78. Mem: Southwestern Watercolor Soc; Tex Fine Arts

Asn; Tex Watercolor Soc. Style & Technique: Watercolorist specializing in history of Texas and the Southwest. Media: Transparent watercolor. Publ: Illusr, Military History of Texas and the Southwest, Presidial Press, 71-78; illusr, Soldiers of Texas, Texian Press, 73; illusr, Sabers on the Rio Grande, Presidial Press, 75; illusr, The Texas Rangers: Their First 150 Years, Encino, 75; illusr, History of Hood's Texas Brigade, Ill Jr Col, 78. Mailing Add: PO Box 5512 Austin TX 78763

MARSHALL, JAMES DUARD
CONSERVATOR, PAINTER
b Springfield, Mo, Sept 29, 14. Study: Kansas City Art Inst, Mo, dipl painting, 40, with Thomas Hart Benton; Colo Col, BA(art), 45, with Boardman Robinson, Lawrence Barrett & Ricco Lebron; Univ Denver, MA(art), with Julio de Deigo & Ruth Reeves. Work: Libr of Cong, Washington, DC; Tex Fine Arts Asn, Austin. Comn: Murals, History of Mo (7 ft x 30 ft), comn by City of Neosho, Mo, for pub libr, 39, Children's Stories (500 ft long), Officer's Wives Nursery, Ft Worth, Tex, 52 & Beginning of a New Day (two 4 ft x 6 ft mosaics), Jones Store, Prairie Village, Kans, 62. Exhib: San Francisco Mus of Art Ann, Calif, 38; Midwestern, Kansas City, Mo, 38-41; Philadelphia Print Club Ann, Pa, 40, 45 & 52; one-man shows, Univ Ark, Fayetteville, 41, State Exhib Bldg, Shreveport, La, 42, Philbrook Mus, Tulsa, Okla, 43, Santa Fe Art Mus, NMex, 43 & Oklahoma City Art Ctr, Okla, 43; Carnegie Inst Int, Pittsburgh, 45; Denver Art Mus Ann, Colo, 45-47; Conn Acad of Design, West Hartford, 46; Nat Acad of Design, New York, 46; Artists West of the Mississippi, Colorado Springs, Colo, 47; Ann, Newport, RI, 57. Teaching: Mem, Fed Teaching Prog, Fayetteville, Ark, 33-34; teacher summer and Saturday classes, Kansas City Art Inst, 36-40; asst prof drawing & painting, Univ Denver, Colo, 46-51; instr summer art sessions, Kansas City Univ, 63. Pos: Chmn art dept, Ft Worth Children's Mus, Tex, 51-53; crafts dir, US Army, Ger, 54-60; asst to Thomas Hart Benton, Truman Libr & New York Power Authority Murals, 60. Awards: Honorable Mention, Denver Ann, Colo, 46 & Philadelphia Print Club, 46 & Benedictine Art Awards, New York, 70-74. Mem: Am Inst for Conservation; Appraisers Asn of Am. Style & Technique: From impressionism through realism to abstraction and back to representationalism. Media: Woodcut, lithography and egg tempera painting. Mailing Add: 5927 Brookside Blvd Kansas City MO 64113

MARSHALL, JOHN CARL
CRAFTSMAN
b Pittsburgh, Pa, Feb 25, 36. Study: Cleveland Inst Art, BFA; Syracuse Univ, MFA. Work: Everson Mus, Syracuse, NY; Objects USA. Comn: Cruets & lavabo bowl, Cathedral of Immaculate Conception, Syracuse, 67; chancellors bowl, Syracuse Univ, 69; gold bowl, Hendricks Chapel, Syracuse, 69; mace, State Univ NY Col Cortland, 71; cross, standing candle holders & baptismal bowl, Our Redeemers Lutheran Church, Seattle, Wash, 72. Exhib: American Metalsmiths, DeCordova Mus, Lincoln, Mass, 74; North American Goldsmiths, Renwick Gallery, Washington, DC, 74; Enamel Guild Show, Univ Md, 74; Spangle, Sheffield Polytechnic Sch Art & Design Gallery, Eng, 74; Forms in Metal, Mus Contemp Crafts, New York, 75. Teaching: Asst prof metalworking, design & enamel, Syracuse Univ, 65-70; assoc prof metalworking, Univ Wash, 70-75, prof metalworking, 75- Awards: Nat Merit Award, Am Craftsmen Coun, Craftsmen USA, 66; Thomas C Thompson Prize 45th Ceramic Nat Competition, 68; Am Metalcraft Award, Nat Enamels Exhib, 70. Mem: Northwest Designer Craftsmen; Am Craftsmen's Coun; Soc NAm Goldsmiths. Media: Gold, Silver. Mailing Add: 23312 Robinhood Dr Edmonds WA 98020

MARSHALL, KERRY
ART ADMINISTRATOR, INSTRUCTOR
b Palo Alto, Calif, Aug 11, 42. Study: San Francisco State Univ, sculpture; Volund Art Sch, Goteborg, Sweden, sculpture. Collections Arranged: California Portrait, 71; Los Tejedorcitos de San Isidro-Tapestries, 73; Keinholz-Oldenburg (with catalog), 74; Basketry (with catalog), 74; Twelve Exhibitions from the International Child Art Collection, 74-75. Teaching: Instr art, York Sch, Monterey, Calif, 67-68; instr art, Civic Art Ctr, Walnut Creek, Calif, 70-73; instr art & educ, Mus Training Prog, Oakland Mus, DeYoung Mus & Long Beach Mus, 74- Pos: Dir, Pacific Grove Art Ctr, Calif, 68-69; gallery coordr, Civic Arts Gallery, Walnut Creek, Calif, 69-73; exhib coordr, Western Asn Art Mus, Oakland, 73. Mem: Am Mus Asn; Am Crafts Coun; Western Asn Art Mus. Res: History of the American Jukebox, for exhibition. Publ: Sanity Test (for traveling exhib), 74 & A Workbook (for traveling exhib), 75, Western Am Art Mus Publ. Mailing Add: Mills Col PO Box 9989 Oakland CA 94526

MARSHALL, MARA
PAINTER
b Nice, France, July 21, 26; US citizen. Study: With Rosamond Gaydash, Washington, DC. Exhib: 25th Biennial Art Exhib, Nat League Am Pen Women, Salt Lake City, 70; one-man shows, First Fed Gallery, Chicago, 71, Nat League Am Pen Women, Washington, DC, 72 & Arts Club of Washington, 77; 41st Ann Exhib, Miniature Painters, Sculptors & Gravers Soc, Washington, DC, 74; Am Art League Exhib, Rehoboth Art League Galleries, Del, 75. Awards: State Art Exhib First Prize, Nat League Am Pen Women, 71, President's Citation, 74, DC Br Annual Award First Prize, 75. Bibliog: Article in Les Editions de la Revue Moderne, 6/73. Mem: Nat League Am Pen Women, Inc (corresp secy, 68-70, pres, 70-72, chmn hospitality, Nat Hq, 72-74, state pres, 74-76, co-chmn, Biennial Conv, 76); Am Art League; Artists Equity Asn; Nat Soc Arts & Lett; Miniature Painters, Sculpture & Gravers Soc. Style & Technique: Impressionist; brush and palette knife. Media: Oil, Acrylic. Mailing Add: 2929 Ellicott St NW Washington DC 20008

MARSHALL, RICHARD DONALD
CURATOR, ART HISTORIAN
b Los Angeles, Calif, May 5, 47. Study: Calif State Univ, Long Beach, BA, MA; Univ Calif, Irvine, grad studies. Collections Arranged: Clay (auth, catalogue), 74 & Continuing Abstraction in American Art (contribr, catalogue), 74, Whitney Mus of Am Art; 76 Jefferson Street, 75, Handmade Paper: Prints & Unique Works, 76 & New Work/Los Angeles, 76, Mus of Mod Art, New York; Calder's Universe (contribr, catalogue), 76-77, Robert Irwin (ed & contribr, catalogue), 77, Art About Art (co-auth, catalogue), 78 & New Painting (auth, catalogue), 78, Whitney Mus of Am Art. Pos: Consult, Art Adv Serv, Mus of Mod Art, New York, 74-76; exhib coordr, Whitney Mus of Am Art, New York, 74-76, asst cur exhib, 76- Mailing Add: Whitney Mus of Am Art 945 Madison Ave New York NY 10021

MARSHALL, ROBERT LEROY
EDUCATOR, PAINTER
b Mesquite, Nev, Dec 15, 44. Study: Brigham Young Univ, BA, 66, MA, 68; studies in Europe, primarily Spain, 75. Work: Mus of the Southwest, Midland, Tex; Brigham Young Univ, Provo, Utah; Webster Oil Co, Springfield, Mo; Springville Mus, Utah. Exhib: Nat Watercolor Soc, Los Angeles, Calif, 69-77; Watercolor West, Utah State Univ, Logan, 77; Watercolor USA, Springfield, Mo, 77; Utah 77, Univ Utah, Salt Lake City, 77. Teaching: Asst prof painting & drawing, Brigham Young Univ, Provo, Utah, 69-, chmn dept art & design, 76- Awards: Purchase Award, Watercolor USA, Webster Oil Co. Mem: Nat Watercolor Soc; Nat Coun Art Adminrs; Springville Mus Art (mem bd dirs, 77-). Style & Technique: Primarily watercolor, emphasizing transparent, representational imagery. Media: Transparent watercolor and acrylic or casein. Mailing Add: 35 N 1300 E Springville UT 84663

MARSICANO, NICHOLAS
PAINTER, EDUCATOR
b Shenandoah, Pa, Oct 1, 14. Study: Pa Acad Fine Arts & Barnes Found, 31-34. Work: Mus Mod Art; Art Inst Chicago; San Francisco Mus Art; Larry Aldrich Mus; Dallas Mus Fine Arts; plus many others. Exhib: Whitney Mus Am Art, 60-62; Mus Mod Art, 61 & 62; Larry Aldrich Mus, Ridgefield, Conn, 64; Univ Tex, Austin, 64, 66 & 68; The New American Painting & Sculpture, Mus Mod Art, 69; plus many others. Teaching: Assoc prof art, Cooper Union, 48-76, prof, 77- instr, Univ Mich, summer 50; instr, Yale Univ, summers 51-54; instr, Brooklyn Mus Sch, 51-58; instr, Pratt Inst, 57-60; instr, Cornell Univ, summer 59. Awards: Cresson Fel & Barnes Found Scholar to Europe, Pa Acad Fine Arts, 33-36; Second Prize, 5th Halmark Int Competition, 60; Guggenheim Award, 74. Publ: Contribr, It Is Mag; contribr, print of painting on cover, Art News, 60; contribr, color print, Man and His Image, 68. Dealer: A M Sachs Gallery 29 W 57th St New York NY 10019. Mailing Add: Cooper Union Dept Art Cooper Square New York NY 10003

MARSTELLER, WILLIAM A
COLLECTOR
b Champaign, Ill, Feb 23, 14. Pos: Trustee, Whitney Mus Am Art, New York. Collection: Modern American art. Mailing Add: 866 Third Ave New York NY 10022

MARTELL, BARBARA BENTLEY
PAINTER
b Trenton, NJ. Study: Philadelphia Col Art, Pa. Exhib: Philadelphia Sketch Club Ann, 68-; Philadelphia Plastic Club, 71-72; Long Beach Island Found Arts & Sci; plus many other local and regional shows. Awards: Hon for pastel portrait, Long Beach Island Found Arts & Sci, 69; hon for mixed media, Philadelphia Plastic Club, 72; second best show in oils, Willingboro Pa Art Alliance, 72. Style & Technique: Lyric realism; maritime landscapes and still life. Media: Oil, Acrylic, Mixed Media. Mailing Add: 333 Kentford Ave Beach Haven NJ 08008

MARTER, JOAN M
ART HISTORIAN, ART CRITIC
b Philadelphia, Pa, Aug 13, 46. Study: Temple Univ, BA; Univ Del, MA, PhD. Collections Arranged: Contemporary American Art at the Academy (guest cur), Pa Acad of the Fine Arts, Philadelphia, 76. Teaching: Asst prof art hist, Sweet Briar Col, Va, 74-77, Rutgers Univ, New Brunswick, NJ, 77- Awards: Chester Dale Fel, Nat Gallery of Art, Washington, DC, 73-74. Mem: Col Art Asn; Women's Caucus for Art; Women in the Arts Found Inc. Res: 20th Century art; Alexander Calder. Publ: Co-auth, In This Academy, Pa Acad of the Fine Arts Mus Press, 76; contribr, Alexander Calder: ambitious young sculptor of the 1930s, Arch Am Art J, 76; contribr, Arts Mag, 77- Mailing Add: 166 E 34th St 21K New York NY 10016

MARTIN, AGNES BERNICE
PAINTER
b Maklin, Sask, Can, Mar 22, 12; US citizen. Study: Columbia Univ; Univ NMex. Work: Mus Mod Art, Whitney Mus Am Art & Guggenheim Mus, New York; Tate Gallery, London, Eng; Kunstraum Munich, Ger. Exhib: Documenta 5, Ger, 72; Retrospective, Inst Contemp Art, 73; Mus Mod Art, prints, 73; Kumstraum Munich, Ger; Retrospective, Heyward Gallery, London, Eng, 77; Stedlelijk Mus, Amsterdam, Holland, 77. Style & Technique: Abstract painting. Media: Acrylic. Publ: Auth, The Perfection Underlying Life & The Untroubled Mind, 73, Univ Pa Press. Dealer: Pace Gallery 32 E 57th St New York NY 10022. Mailing Add: 9311 Fourth NW Albuquerque NM 87114

MARTIN, ALEXANDER TOEDT
EDUCATOR, PAINTER
b Kinderhook, NY, Mar 11, 31. Study: Albright Art Sch, cert, 52; Univ Buffalo, BFA, 57; Tulane Univ, MFA, 63. Work: Neuberger Mus, State Univ NY Col, Purchase; Schenectady Mus, NY; Union Carbide Corp, New York; Continental Transport Inc, White Plains, NY. Exhib: Schenectady Mus, NY, 55-59; Artist of the Upper Hudson Valley, Albany Inst of Hist & Art, NY, 55-76; Albright-Knox Art Gallery, Buffalo, 59; Ten Am Artists in Rome, Palazzo Venezia, Italy, 60; Rome-New York Art Found, Italy, 61; Southeastern Exhib, Delgado Mus, New Orleans, La, 63; Wadsworth Atheneum, Hartford Conn, 66; Convocation of Arts Exhib, State Univ NY, Albany, 69; Cooperstown Ann, NY, 75. Teaching: Prof painting & drawing, State Univ NY Col, New Paltz, 63- Awards: First Prize/Painting, Schnectady Mus, 58 & Cooperstown Ann, 75. Bibliog: Hitton Kramer (auth), article in New York Times, 9/23/73. Style & Technique: Romantic landscapes with emphasis on light and color structure. Media: Oil and watercolor. Dealer: Graham Gallery 1014 Madison Ave New York NY 10021. Mailing Add: 14 Watch Hill Rd New Paltz NY 12561

MARTIN, BERNARD MURRAY
PAINTER
b Ferrum, Va, June 21, 35. Study: Wake Forest Col, NC; Richmond Prof Inst, Va, BFA; Hunter Col, MA. Work: Va Mus Fine Arts, Richmond; Walter Rawls Mus, Courtland, Va; Wachovia Nat Bank, Winston-Salem, NC; Nat Collection, Washington, DC; First & Merchants Nat Bank, Richmond, Va. Exhib: Nostalgia and the Contemporary Artist, Am Fedn Arts Traveling Exhib, 68; American Painting 1970, Va Mus Fine Art, 70; Friends of the Corcoran, Corcoran Gallery Art, Washington, DC, 71; one-man show, Gallery Marc, Washington, DC, 71; 32nd Southeastern Exhib, Gallery Contemp Art, Winston-Salem, 72. Teaching: Assoc prof painting, Va Commonwealth Univ, 61- Awards: Cert distinction, Va Artists Exhib, Va Mus Fine Arts, 64, 66, 68 & 70; First Prize, Southeastern Exhib, Gallery Contemp Art, 70 & 71. Media: Oil. Dealer: H Marc Moyens Contemp Art Alexandria VA 22307. Mailing Add: 3329 Hanover Ave Richmond VA 23221

MARTIN, BERNICE FENWICK
PAINTER, PRINTMAKER
b Shelbourne, Ont, July 7, 12. Study: Toronto Tech Schs; Ont Col Art, Univ Toronto, with J W Beatty & Frank Carmichael; McMaster Univ; Univ Alta, with Toshi Yoshida. Work: In collections of Hon Mitchell Sharpe, Ottawa, Ont, Harold Smythe & Glen Bannerman; also pub bldgs, schs & many pvt collections, Can & int. Exhib: Soc Can Painter-Etchers & Engravers' Ann & Traveling, 54-71; Can Expo '67, Montreal, PQ, 67; Centennial Oper Ont Art '67, City Hall, Toronto, 67; one-man show & pub demonstration color block prints, Can Nat Exhib, Toronto, 68-69; exhibs across Can, art galleries, mus & pub libr, 47-71; also many one-man exhibs. Mem: Soc Can Painter-Etchers & Engravers (chmn presentation graphic arts print comn, 56-57); fel Int Inst Arts & Lett. Mailing Add: 150 Millwood Rd Toronto ON M4S 1J7 Can

MARTIN, CHARLES E
DESIGNER, PAINTER
b Chelsea, Mass, Jan 12, 10. Work: Mus City New York; Metrop Mus, NY. Exhib: One-man shows, Brooklyn Mus Art Sch, 54, Rockland Found, 56-57, Graham Gallery, 74 & Nicholls Gallery, 75; Ruth White Gallery, 60. Teaching: Instr watercolor painting, Brooklyn Mus Art Sch, 63-65. Pos: Cartoonist designer, New Yorker Mag, 35-; illusr, eve newspaper, 39-42; art dir, air drop newspapers, New York, London, Naples & Paris, 42-45. Mem: Mag Cartoonist Guild Am. Media: Watercolor, Acrylic, Oil, Ink. Publ: Contribr, New Yorker Mag, New York Times, Playboy, Sat Rev, Life & Time Mags, 35- Mailing Add: 41 Princeton Ave Princeton NJ 08540

MARTIN, DORIS-MARIE CONSTABLE
DESIGNER, SCULPTOR
b New York, NY, July 5, 41. Study: Miami-Dade Community Col, S Campus, Miami, Fla, AA, 71; Univ Miami; Univ NC, Asheville, BA, 76; Penland Sch Crafts, NC; Arrowmont Sch Crafts, Gattlingburg, Tenn; Goddard Col, Plainfield, Vt, grad work; spec study in fibers with Marilyn R Pappas, metal & fiber sculpture with William King, pottery & sculpture with William Wyman, fiber & sculpture with Else Regensteiner, fiber with Joan Michael Paque, weaving, fiber & sculpture with Walter Nottingham, printmaking with Sam Wang, printmaking & sculpture with Bob Huff. Work: Miami-Dade Community Col; Durham Art Guild, M Biddle Gallery for the Blind, NC State Mus, Raleigh; Chrysler Mus, Norfolk, Va; Miami Herald, Fla; Univ NC, Asheville. Comn: Soft sculpture, Unitarian/Universalist Church of Asheville, 78. Exhib: NC Ann, NC Mus Art, Raleigh, 72, 73 & 75; 22nd Biennel Tidewater Artists Exhib, Chrysler Mus, 73; 39th Semi-Ann Southern Painting & Sculpture Competition, Southeastern Gallery of Contemp Art & Salem Col Fine Arts, Winston-Salem, NC, 74; Int Tel & Tel Corp Int Art Exhib, Metrop Mus & Art Ctr, Miami, Fla, 74 & Craft Work 76, Am Crafts Coun Southeast Regional, 76; Marietta Col Int, Grover M Hermann Fine Arts Ctr, Ohio, 76 & 77; Springs Mills Traveling Show, Ft Mill, SC, 77 & 78; one-man shows, Chrysler Mus, 73 & Beyond Craft: Fiber/Form/Fabric, Univ NC, Asheville, 75. Teaching: Instr soft construction sculpture, Asheville Art Mus, 76-, instr beginning printmaking, 77- Pos: Founder, incorporator & first pres, Western NC Fibers/Handweavers Guild, Inc, Asheville, 75-76, 76-78. Awards: Best Sculpture, Craft Work 76, Am Crafts Coun, 76; Best Sculpture & One-Man Show, Durham Arts Guild, Inc, Allied Arts Ctr, NC, 76; Award for Sculpture, Springs Mills Traveling Show, 75 & 77. Bibliog: R Clermont (auth), Poloities & Expositions Diverses, Les Editions de la Revue Moderne Des Arts, Paris, France, 73; article in Miami Herald, 76. Mem: Am Crafts Coun; Fla Craftsmen, Miami; Western NC Fibers/Handweavers Guild (bd dirs); Handweavers Guild Am; NC Art Soc. Style & Technique: Fiber soft-sculptures in which transformation from hard to soft and change in scale are significant; historical motif. Media: (Sculpture) Fiber of Soft Construction; (Printmaking) Woodcut, Intaglio, Silkscreen on Fabric and Paper. Publ: Contribr, Shuttle, Spindle & Dyepot, Handweavers Guild Am, 76. Mailing Add: 65 Woodland Rd Asheville NC 28804

MARTIN, FLETCHER
PAINTER
b Palisade, Colo, Apr 29, 04. Work: Metrop Mus Art & Whitney Mus Am Art, New York; William Rockhill Nelson Gallery, Kansas City; Los Angeles Mus Art; Pa Acad Fine Arts, Philadelphia. Comn: Murals, Fed Bldg, San Pedro, Calif, 37, Post Off, LaMesa, Tex, 39 & Kellogg, Idaho, 40, Treas Dept. Exhib: Los Angeles Mus Ann, 35; Americans 1942, Mus Mod Art, 42 & Nat Acad Design Ann, 49, New York; Pa Acad Fine Arts, 47; retrospective, Roberson Mem Ctr, Binghamton, NY, 68; plus many other nat and regional. Teaching: Artist in residence, Univ Iowa, 40-41; head dept painting, Kansas City Art Inst, 41-43; vis artist, Univ Fla, 50-52; artist in residence, Roberson Mem Ctr, 67-68; plus many other appointments. Pos: War artist correspondent, North Africa, 43 & Normandy, 44, Life Mag. Awards: Van Rensselaer Wilbur Prize, Los Angeles Mus, 35; Lippincott Prize for figure painting, Pa Acad Fine Arts, 47; Altman Prize, Nat Acad Design, 49. Bibliog: Barbara Ebersole (auth), Fletcher Martin, Univ Fla Press, 54; H Lester Cooke (auth), Fletcher Martin, Abrams, 76. Mem: Woodstock Artists Asn; Academician, Nat Acad Design. Style & Technique: Descriptive and personal. Media: Oil, Watercolor, Print Media. Publ: Illusr, Tales of the Gold Rush, 44, Mutiny on the Bounty, 47, The Sea Wolf, 61, The Jungle, 65 & Of Mice and Men, 69, Limited Editions Club. Dealer: Loring Gallery 661 Central Ave Cedarhurst NY 11516; Rudolph Galleries Woodstock NY 12498. Mailing Add: Apartado 73 Guanajuato Mexico

MARTIN, FRED THOMAS
PAINTER
b San Francisco, Calif, June 13, 27. Study: Univ Calif, Berkeley, BA, 49 & MA, 52; San Francisco Art Inst, with David Park, Clifford Still & Mark Rothko. Work: Richmond Art Ctr, Va; Whitney Mus Am Art, New York; San Francisco Mus Art; Oakland Art Mus, Calif. Exhib: San Francisco Mus Art Ann, 50-60; Whitney Mus Am Art, 70 & 73; one-man shows, M H DeYoung Mus, San Francisco, 54, 64, San Francisco Art Inst, 72 & San Francisco Mus Art, 58 & 73; Hansen Fuller Gallery, San Francisco; plus others. Teaching: Dir col, San Francisco Art Inst, 66- Awards: Nat Found Arts Artists Grant, 70-71. Media: Watercolor, Acrylic, Pastel. Publ: Beulah Land, a Book of Etchings, Hansen Fuller & Crown Press, 74. Dealer: Hansen-Fuller Gallery 228 Grant Ave San Francisco CA 94108. Mailing Add: 232 Monte Vista Oakland CA 94611

MARTIN, G W
PAINTER, EDUCATOR
b Tacoma, Wash, Apr 19, 13. Study: Herron Art Sch, Millikan Europ travel scholar & BFA, 38; State Univ Iowa, with Philip Guston, Fletcher Martin & Emil Ganso, MFA; Boston Mus Art Sch, with Karl Zerbe. Work: Lithograph Libr Cong, Washington, DC; Watercolor Wadsworth Atheneum, Hartford, Conn; Conn Printers, Hartford. Comn: Mural, US Post Off, Danville, Ind; portrait, Chancellor Coffin, Univ Hartford; double mural comn, 75. Exhib: Mus Mod Art, New York, 42; Color Print Soc, Philadelphia, 42; Carnegie Inst Int, 42 & 43; Conn Acad Fine Arts, 47-57 & 62; Mus Am Art, New Brit, Conn, 68. Teaching: Prof art & head dept, Lindenwood Col, 41-43; assoc prof art, Hartford Art Sch, Univ Hartford, 57- Awards: New Eng Drawing Exhib Award, 58; mural competition, Gengras Campus Ctr, Univ Hartford, 68. Media: Oil. Mailing Add: 618 Willard Ave Newington CT 06111

MARTIN, KEITH
ART ADMINISTRATOR, PAINTER
b Perth Amboy, NJ, Jan 22, 10. Study: Harvard Univ, BA; also with Wayman Adams. Collections Arranged: Exhibition of Art of the Americas, Int Expos, Port-au-Prince, Haiti, 50; Models of Inventions of Leonardo da Vinci, 52. Teaching: Head dept art, Syracuse Univ, 46-48. Pos: Dir, Kans City Art Inst & Sch Design, 39-43; dir, Fine Arts Dept, IBM, 46-53; dir, Roberson Ctr Arts & Sci, Binghamton, 54- Mem: Am Asn Mus; NY State Asn Mus; Northeast Asn Mus; Assoc Couns Arts; Eastern Regional Inst Educ (trustee). Mailing Add: Roberson Ctr for Arts & Sci 30 Front St Binghamton NY 13905

MARTIN, KEITH MORROW
PAINTER
b Lincoln, Nebr, Jan 27, 11. Study: Univ Nebr; Art Inst Chicago. Work: Mus Mod Art, New York; Corcoran Gallery Art; Whitney Mus Am Art, New York; Nat Collection Fine Arts; Nat Gallery Art; plus others. Exhib: Whitney Mus Am Art, 55 & 59; Baltimore Mus Art, 53, 66 & 77; Norfolk Mus Am Drawing Ann, Va, 62; Santa Barbara Mus Art, Calif, 63; Int Gallery, Baltimore, 65; 159th Ann Am Painting & Sculpture, Pa Acad Fine Arts, 65; Ball State Ann, Muncie, Ind, 65, 67 69 & 70; Embassy Art Prog, State Dept, Washington, DC, 67 & 69; Art on Paper, Weatherspoon Ann, Greensboro, NC, 68 & 69; Springer Galerie, West Berlin, Ger, 77; plus many other group & one-man exhibs. Teaching: Instr, Baltimore Mus Art, 58-68. Awards: 2nd Md Exhib Acad Arts Award, Easton, 66; Benedictine Art Purchase Prize, 67; WCBM Area Exhib Prize, Baltimore, 69; plus others. Bibliog: A Breeskin (auth), New talent USA, Art Am, 2/55; A Balder (auth), Six Maryland Artists, Balboa Publ, 55; article in Baltimore Mus Art News, 67. Style & Technique: Lyrical abstraction with touches of surrealism. Publ: Auth, Keith Martin remembers Gertrude Stein, Baltimore Mus Art Rec, Vol 1, No 8. Mailing Add: 3208 St Paul St Baltimore MD 21218

MARTIN, KNOX
PAINTER, SCULPTOR
b Barranquilla, Colombia, Feb 12, 23; US citizen. Study: Art Students League, 4 yrs. Work: Corcoran Gallery Art, Washington, DC; Mus Mod Art, New York; Whitney Mus Am Art, New York; Mus Art, Austin, Tex; Univ Calif, Berkeley. Comn: 19 story wall painting, City Walls, Inc, West Side Hwy, New York, 71; wall painting, Mercor, Inc, Merritt Complex, Ft Lauderdale, Fla, 72. Exhib: Gallery Mod Art, Washington, DC, 63; Santa Barbara Mus Art, Calif, 64; Concrete Expressionism, Loeb Student Ctr, NY Univ, 65; Yale Univ Art Gallery, 66; Whitney Mus Am Art, 72; Brit Print Biennial, Bradford Mus, Eng, 74; Works on Paper, 1950-1975, Jankovsky Gallery, New York, 75; plus others. Teaching: Asst prof drawing & painting, Yale Univ, 65-70. Awards: Longview Fel, 56; Balloonist Award, Mat Wiedekehr, St Paul, Minn, 72; Nat Endowment Arts, 72. Bibliog: Knox Martin Super Creation (collage/film, color), Yale Univ Art Dept, 67; George Parrino (auth), Knox Martin, The Deadalian Work, 72. Dealer: Galeria Bonino 7 W 57th St New York NY 10019. Mailing Add: 128 Ft Washington Ave New York NY 10032

MARTIN, LANGTON
PAINTER, PRINTMAKER
b Toronto, Ont, May 15, 13. Study: Ont Col Art, Univ Toronto, with J W Beatty; Toronto Tech Schs; McMaster Univ. Exhib: Soc Can Painter-Etchers & Engravers; Ann & Traveling Exhibs across Can, art galleries, mus & pub libr, 54-71; Can Expo '67, Montreal, PQ, 67; Can Nat Exhib, Toronto, 68-69. Mem: Soc Can Painter-Etchers & Engravers (keeper of the prints, 56-60, historian, 61-72); Arts & Lett Club; fel Int Inst Arts & Lett. Mailing Add: 150 Millwood Rd Toronto ON M4S 1J7 Can

MARTIN, LORETTA MARSH
PAINTER, CARTOONIST
b Plymouth, Ind, Jan 22, 33. Study: Art Inst Chicago, BAE, 55; Univ Notre Dame, MA, 68; also with Jozef Wrobel & Ed Basker. Work: Many pvt collections in US & other countries. Exhib: One-woman show, First Unitarian Church, South Bend, Ind, 62; Northern Ind Artists; La Porte, Ind, Fine Arts Asn; Alumni Asn Art Inst Chicago; Hernando Co Fair, Fla; Artists 70 & 71, Citrus Co, Fla; El Paso Centennial Mus Arts & Crafts Show, 72. Pos: Asst cur, El Paso Mus Art. Mailing Add: Martin Studio 2521 Catnip El Paso TX 79925

MARTIN, LUCILLE CAIAR (MRS HAMPTON MARTIN)
PAINTER
b Carlsbad, NMex, June 7, 18. Study: With La Vora Norman; Frederic Taubes Workshops, Cloudcroft & Ruidoso; Merlin Enabnit Art Sch, Chicago, dipl. Work: Carlsbad Libr & Mus, NMex; Houston Med Ctr, Tex. Comn: Jordan River (mural), Hillcrest Baptist Church, Carlsbad, 62; Sacred River (mural), First Baptist Church, McCrory, Ark, 63; El Capitan (mural), Security Savings & Loan, Carlsbad, 64; NMex State Bird-Roadrunner, Young Democrats for Gov Off, State Capitol, Santa Fe, 64; roadrunner painting, comn by Gov Campbell for aircraft carrier Constellation, 64. Exhib: Fla Int Art Exhib, Lakeland, 52; Nat Palo Duro Art Show, WTex State Univ, Canyon, 64; Nat Sun Carnival Art Exhib, El Paso Mus Art, 64; Boulder City Art Festival, Nev, 70; one-man show, NMex State Univ, Las Cruces, 65. Awards: Grand Sweepstakes, Tri-State Art Exhib, El Paso, 57; First Place, Carlsbad Area Art Asn Exhibs, 64, 65 & 66; First Place, Nat Parks Show, 73, 75 & 76. Bibliog: Articles in NMex Newspaper & El Paso Times, 64 & 65; Elena Montes (auth), Lucille Martin's art, NMex Mag, 4/65. Mem: Charter mem Carlsbad Area Art Asn; Tucson Art Ctr. Style & Technique: Realistic style in oils, using both palette knife and brush, canvas underpainted (method of Old Masters), subjects predominantly western, ranch life, horses, desert, missions, old mines, windmills etc. Publ: Contribr, Ariz Highways Mag, 3/70 & NMex Mag, 54 & 65. Mailing Add: 5901 E Third St Tucson AZ 85711

MARTIN, MARGARET M
PAINTER, DESIGNER
b Buffalo, NY, Aug 15, 40. Study: Boston Univ, BFA; watercolor workshops with John Pike, Robert E Wood, John Pellew, Rex Brandt & Milford Zornes. Exhib: Am Watercolor Soc, 73 & Catharine Lorillard Wolfe Art, 74, Nat Acad Design Galleries, New York; one-woman show, Pen & Brush Gallery, New York, 75; Rocky Mountain Nat Watermedia, Foothills Art Ctr, Golden, Colo, 75; Far Away Places, Old Bergen Art Guild Travel Tour, 75-78; Allied Artists of Am, 76; Nat Acad Design, 76. Pos: Designer, Wagner Folding Box, Buffalo, NY, 62-64; art dir-designer, Concept Group, Inc, Buffalo, 64-77; free lance graphic designer & illusr, 77- Awards: Travel Award, Am Watercolor Soc, 70; Solo Show Award for Watercolor, The Pen & Brush, New York, 74 & 78; Addy Award, Am Advert Fedn, 74. Bibliog: R Stevens (auth), Contemporary Art in America, La Revue Modern, France, 3/71; John Hanchette (auth), The art of watercolor, Buffalo Eve News, 10/72. Mem: Am Watercolor Soc; Nat League of Am Pen Women; The Pen & Brush; Nat Arts Club; Buffalo Soc Artists. Style & Technique: Atmosphere and sparkling light recreated in fresh, vital, spontaneous transparent watercolor. Publ: Contribr, Designers Dictionary, 74; illusr, Buffalo & Erie County Arts Resource Directory, 74. Mailing Add: 78 Summer St Buffalo NY 14209

MARTIN, MARIANNE WINTER
ART HISTORIAN
b Vienna, Austria; US citizen. Study: Hunter Col, New York, BA, 45; Univ of Chicago, MA, 47; Bryn Mawr Col, MA, 53, PhD, 62; studied with Professors J C Sloane, R Bernheimer & A C Soper. Teaching: Asst prof art hist, Rutgers Univ, 63-65; assoc prof art hist, Bard Col, 65-66; assoc prof art hist, New York Univ, 66-77. Pos: Chmn & prof of Fine Arts, Boston Col, 77- Awards: Nat Endowment for the Humanities Senior Fel, 70-71; Am Coun Learned Soc Summer Grant, 63; Am Asn of Univ Women Fel, 56-57. Mem: Col Art Asn of Am; Jesuit Inst for the Art. Res: Modern Italian art. Publ: Auth, The Walter and Louise Arensberg Collection, Philadelphia Mus, 54; auth, Futurist Art and Theory, 1909-1915, Clarendon

Press, 68; auth, Torello Ancillotti, Leomonnier, 72; co-auth, A Modern Focus: Futurism, Guggenheim Mus, 73; co-auth, Great Drawings of All Times: The 20th Century, Shorewood, New York, 78. Mailing Add: Dept of Fine Arts Boston Col Newton Campus Newton MA 02159

MARTIN, MARY FINCH
ART DIRECTOR
b Glens Falls, NY, Sept 7, 16. Study: Pvt tutoring with Isabel La Freniere. Exhib: Rockport Art Asn, Mass, 71-; Hamilton-Wenham Art Show, S Hamilton, Mass, 74-76; Newbury Art Asn, Mass, 75-76; Gloucester & Cape Ann Exhib, Gloucester, Mass, 72. Pos: Art dir, Harbor Gallery, Rockport, Mass, 71- Mem: Rockport Art Asn; Newbury Port Art Asn. Media: Oil. Mailing Add: 8 Clark Ave Rockport MA 01966

MARTIN, RICHARD (HARRISON)
ART HISTORIAN, ART ADMINISTRATOR
b Bryn Mawr, Pa, Dec 4, 46. Study: Swarthmore Col, BA(art hist), 67; Columbia Univ, MA(art hist), 69 & MPhil(art hist), 71. Teaching: Instr art hist, William Paterson Col, 72-73; instr hist civilization & art, Fashion Inst Technol, State Univ NY, 73-76, asst prof, 76-; lectr art hist, Sch Visual Arts, 75-; adj asst prof, NY Univ, 77- Pos: Assoc curator art hist & archaeol, Columbia Univ, 68-70; exec ed, Arts Mag, 73-74, ed, 74- Mem: Col Art Asn Am; Am Soc Aesthetics; Soc Archit Historians; Int Ctr Medieval Art; Art Libr Soc NAm. Res: Contemporary art, art theory. Publ: Auth, articles in Arts Mag, Art & Artists, Art Educ, Cinema J & J Popular Cult. Mailing Add: 235 E 22nd St New York NY 10010

MARTIN, ROGER
PAINTER, GRAPHIC ARTIST
b Gloucester, Mass, Sept 3, 25. Study: Boston Mus Fine Arts Sch. Comn: Brochure, Cambridge Electron Accelerator, Harvard Univ & Mass Inst Technol, 64; graphic art, D C Heath & Co, Allyn & Bacon, Beacon Press, 65-68 & United Church Teaching Pictures; designed cases & executed carvings, C B Fisk Pipe Organs, Harvard Univ & Pohick Church, Lorton, Va, 65-69. Exhib: Boston Art Festival, 56 & 61; Rockport Art Asn, 57-75; De Cordova Mus, 66-67, 69, 72 & 75-78; one-man shows, Carl Siembab Gallery, Boston, 69, Southern Vt Art Asn, Manchester, 70, Marion Art Ctr, Mass, 75, Galleria Rosanna, Boston, 76 & Stagecoach House Gallery, Gloucester, Mass, 77; plus others. Teaching: Instr design & drawing & head freshman dept, New Eng Sch Art, Boston, 67-69; instr design & illus, Montserrat Sch Visual Art, Beverly, Mass, 69-78. Publ: Conbribr, illus in New Yorker Mag, Atlantic Monthly & New York Times; contribr, articles & illus in Child Life Mag & textbks. Mailing Add: 16 Mt Locust Ave Rockport MA 01966

MARTIN, RON
PAINTER
b London, Ont, 1943. Study: Beal Sec Sch, with Herb Ariss, John O'Henley & M Cryderman, 60-64. Work: London Pub Art Gallery, Ont; Can Coun Art Bank Collection, Ottawa, Ont; Nat Gallery Can, Ottawa; Art Gallery, Ont, Toronto; Gallery/Stratford, Ont. Exhib: Diversity-Canada East, Edmonton Art Gallery & Norman Mackenzie Art Gallery, Regina, 72; Boucherville, Montreal, Toronto, London 1973, Nat Gallery Can, Ottawa, Ont, 73; one-man shows, London Pub Libr & Art Mus, Ont, 74, Art Gallery of Ont, Toronto, 76, Southern Alta Art Gallery, Lethbridge, 76, Ctr for Inter-Am Relations, New York, 78, Venice Biennale, Italy, 78 & Michael Werner Gallery, Cologne, WGer, 78; Carmen Lamanna at the Owens Art Gallery, Mt Allison Univ, Sackville, NB, 75; The Canadian Canvas, Nat Touring Exhib, Time Can Ltd, 75; Carmen Lamanna at the Can Cult Ctr, Can Cult Ctr, Paris, 75; Art Bank: Int/Can Painters, Ottawa, 76. Teaching: Instr children's art, London Pub Art Gallery, Ont, 67- Awards: Centennial Purchase Award, Can Coun, 67, Arts Bursaries, 68, 70 & 71 & Sr Short-Term Grant, 72. Bibliog: Kenneth Baker (auth), Notes from an exploratory expedition, 3-4/73 & Ross Skoggard (auth), Ron Martin, 9-10/75, Art in Am; Walter Klepac (auth), rev in ArtsCanada, 12-1/77. Style & Technique: Unamable; freedom. Media: Acrylic on Canvas. Watercolor on Paper. Mailing Add: c/o Carmen Lamanna Gallery 840 Yonge St Toronto ON M4W 2H1 Can

MARTIN, ROSE BREYER
COLLECTOR
b Dunelle, NJ, Nov 3, 10. Study: Vanderbilt Univ, BA. Mem: Mus of Mod Art; Cheekwood Fine Art Ctr, Nashville. Interest: Contemporary Art. Collection: Eclectic, ranging from Picasso to John Clen Clark to Rauschenberg to Johns. Mailing Add: PO Box 12427 Nashville TN 37212

MARTIN, THOMAS
PAINTER, INSTRUCTOR
b Amsterdam, NY, Feb 24, 43. Study: State Univ NY Col Buffalo, BS(art educ); Syracuse Univ, MFA(painting). Work: State Univ NY Col Buffalo; Syracuse Univ. Exhib: One-man shows, Men & Animals, Hundred Acres Gallery, New York, 73, Drawings, 75 & Drawings & Paintings, 77 & Drawings, 77, Hanover Sq Gallery, Syracuse, NY; Allegorical Portraits, Univ Maine, Portland-Gorham, 74; Unordinary Realities, Xerox Corp, Rochester, NY, 75; Art on Paper, Weatherspoon Ann Exhib, Univ NC, Greensboro, 76. Teaching: Instr fine arts, Western Conn State Col, Danbury, 74-75 & New York Inst Technol, Old Westbury, 75- Pos: Cur exhibs, Mus of the Am Indian, New York, NY, 75- Bibliog: David Pascal (auth), Comics, An American Expressionism, Graphis, Zurich, 72; Rev of 77 New York Exhib, Arts Mag, 4/77. Style & Technique: Figurative drawings and paintings about heroic and romantic subjects. Media: Drawing and painting. Dealer: Hundred Acres Gallery 456 W Broadway New York NY 10013. Mailing Add: 237 Lafayette St New York NY 10013

MARTIN, WILLIAM BARRISS, II
SCULPTOR, DESIGNER
b Cleveland, Ohio, Oct 20, 23. Study: Case Inst Appl Sci, 41-43; Ohio State Univ, BIE; Sch Boston Mus. Comn: Hanging glass & stainless steel sculptures, Nat Art Ctr, Ottawa; hanging glass & stainless sculpture, Fair Park Mus Hall, Dallas, Tex; external light & menorah, Temple Reyim, Newton, Mass; bronze & copper cross, First Methodist Church, Saxonville, Mass; 15 bronze & glass sculptures, Cleveland Sheraton Hotel, Ohio. Exhib: Brockton Art Ctr; Boston Visual Artists Union Ann Exhib; Libr Cong; Cleveland May Show. Teaching: Instr sculpture, Sch Boston Mus, 61-65. Awards: First Award & Hon Mention Graphics, Cleveland May Show; Hon Mention Sculpture, Boston Arts Festival; Excellence for Design, Indust Design Mag Ann. Bibliog: Peter Bellamy (auth), Glass beauty, Cleveland Plain Dealer; Glass sculpture in Ottawa, Am Glass Rev; Patricia Boyd Wilson (auth), rev, Christian Sci Monitor. Mem: Boston Visual Artist Union. Style & Technique: Welded metal; stainless steel & glass organic forms in space; rhythmic movements in space; carved wood constructions. Media: Welded Steel, Welded Stainless with Glass, Wood. Mailing Add: 261 Robbins St Milton MA 02186

MARTIN, WILLIAM HENRY (BILL)
PAINTER, SCULPTOR
b South San Francisco, Calif, Jan 22, 43. Study: San Francisco Art Inst, BFA, 68 & MFA, 70; Acad Art Col, San Francisco. Exhib: Whitney Mus Am Art Painting Ann, New York, 72; Painting & Sculpture Today, Indianapolis Mus Art, 74; Biennial Am Painting & Sculpture, Art Inst Chicago, 74; Paris Bienniale, France, 75; one-man show, San Francisco Mus Art, 73. Teaching: Instr painting, Acad Art Col, San Francisco, 70-71; instr painting, Univ Calif, Berkeley, 72; instr painting, San Francisco Art Inst, 72-73, instr painting, Univ Calif, San Jose, fall 73. Awards: Tiffany Found Grant, 70. Bibliog: David Kolodney (auth), Paintings by Bill Martin, Ramparts Mag, 10/70; Tom Albright (auth), Visuals, Rolling Stone Mag, 9/2/71. Style & Technique: Enhanced reality. Media: Oil. Mailing Add: PO Box 761 Woodacre CA 94973

MARTINELLI, EZIO
SCULPTOR
b West Hoboken, NJ, Nov 27, 13. Study: Acad Fine Arts, Bologna, Italy, 31; Nat Acad Design, 32-36; Barnes Found, Merion, Pa, 40. Work: Whitney Mus Am Art & Solomon R Guggenheim Mus, New York; Newark Mus, NJ; Seattle Mus, Wash; Art Inst Chicago. Comn: Aluminum sculpture, Gen Assembly Bldg, UN, 60. Exhib: Salon for Younger Artists, Art of this Century Gallery, New York, 42; Abstract and Surrealist Art in America, Art Inst Chicago, 47; Survey of American Sculpture, Newark Mus, 62; Whitney Mus Am Art Sculpture, Drawings & Prints Ann, 66; Modern Sculptors, Their Drawings, Watercolors and Prints, Storm King Art Ctr, Mountainville, NY, 71; Atelier 17, Univ Wis, 77. Teaching: Prof sculpture, Sarah Lawrence Col, 47-75; artist in residence, Ford Found, Ringling Mus, Sarasota, Fla, 64; sculptor in residence, Am Acad Rome, 64-65; instr sculpture, Skowhegan Sch Painting & Sculpture, summer 69; semi-retired. Awards: Guggenheim Found Fel, 56-62; Tiffany Found Fel, 64; Nat Inst Arts & Lett Award, 66. Bibliog: G Carandente (auth), Dictionary of modern sculpture (Rome), 57; D Ashton (auth), Modern American sculpture. Mailing Add: 11 Jane St Saugerties NY 12477

MARTINET, MARJORIE D
PAINTER
b Baltimore, Md, Nov 3, 86. Study: Md Inst, 04; Rhinehart Sch Sculpture, 04-05; Pa Acad Fine Arts, Thouron prize & Cresson Europ scholar, 05-10; also with William M Chase & Cecelia Beaux and in Europe. Work: Asn Jewish Charities Bldg, Baltimore. Exhib: Peabody Inst; Pa Acad Fine Arts; Philadelphia Plastic Club; one-woman show, Baltimore Mus Art; Nat Asn Women Artists, 60-62; plus others. Pos: Dir, Martinet Sch Art, Baltimore, 12-69; chmn art comt, Lizette Woodworth Reese Mem Tablet for Pratt Libr, Baltimore; art consult, Oldfields Sch, Glencoe, Md, 62. Mem: Philadelphia Art Alliance; Nat Asn Women Artists; Am Fedn Arts; fel Pa Acad Fine Arts. Mailing Add: 621 Westview St Philadelphia PA 19119

MARTINEZ, ERNESTO PEDREGON
INSTRUCTOR, MURALIST
b El Paso, Tex, Feb 26, 26. Study: Self-taught. Work: New Bowie High Sch, El Paso; St Joseph Church, Houston; Mil Bldgs, Ft Bliss, Tex; also in pvt collections. Comn: Mural (28ft x 8ft), War Mem Honoring Recipient Recipients of Cong Medal of Honor, Vet Hosp, El Paso, Tex. Exhib: One-man shows, Mexico's Int Fair, 65, NMex State Univ, 74, Univ Tex, El Paso, 74, Chamizal Nat Mus, 74-75 & Officer's Clubs, White Sands Missile Proving Base, 75; Exhib for First Ladies of US & Mex, Chamizal Nat Mus, El Paso, 77; Ancient Roots/New Visions (traveling show), 78; plus others in Houston, New York & Univ Colo. Teaching: Art consult, Boy Scouts Am, 60-; prof Chicano art, El Paso Community Col, 74- Awards: Artist of the Year, Lulac Coun, 74. Media: Oil, Acrylic, Pen & Ink. Mailing Add: 4753 El Campo Dr El Paso TX 79924

MARTINEZ-MARESMA, SARA (SARA MARTINEZ)
PAINTER
b Havana, Cuba; US citizen. Study: San Alejandro Art Sch, Havana, with Leopoldo Romanach & Armando Menocal, prof drawing & painting (summa cum laude). Work: Cardinal's Arteaga (portrait), Cardinal's Palace, Havana; St Jose Pignatelli (painting), Church Sagrado Corazon, Havana; Holy Family (painting), Noviciado de St Stanislao's Col, Havana; John F Kennedy (portrait), White House, Washington, DC; Stephen P Clark (portrait), City Hall, Miami. Exhib: Havana Univ Gallery, 48; Cuban Mus, Daytona Beach, Fla, 63; Am Artists Prof League, New York, 71 & 72; one-woman shows, Bacardi Gallery, 70 & Big Five Club, Miami, 74. Teaching: Prof drawing & painting, Havana's Superior Sch, 48-59; prof drawing & painting, Apostolado Teacher's Sch, Havana, 49-59; vis prof painting, Havana Univ, 50-51. Awards: First Prize, Am Cancer Soc, 67; hon mention, Jordan Marsh, 69; Prestige Award, Am Artists Prof League, 69. Bibliog: Frank Soler (auth), Artist's output fills her home: roses favorite, Miami Herald, 69; Martha de Castro (auth), El Arte en Cuba, Ediciones Universal, 70. Mem: Am Artists Prof League; Fla Fedn Art; Miami Palette Club; Nat Soc Lit & Arts. Style & Technique: Impressionism, realistic. Media: Oil. Mailing Add: 2632 SW 30th Ct Miami FL 33133

MARTINO, ANTONIO P
PAINTER
b Philadelphia, Pa, Apr 13, 02. Study: Philadelphia Mus Col Art; La France Art Inst; also with Albert Jean Adolphe. Work: Nat Acad Design, New York; Pa Acad Fine Arts, Philadelphia; Butler Art Inst, Youngstown, Ohio; Springville Art Mus, Utah; IBM Collection. Comn: Portraits & landscapes, Jud & Mrs O'Neill, Chestnut Hill, Pa, 47, Joseph Harris, Philadelphia, 55, Mr & Mrs Alex Manos, Thousand Oaks, Calif, 60, Misericordia Hosp, 62 & Mrs & Mrs A Ricci, 65, Philadelphia. Exhib: Sesqui-Centennial, Philadelphia, 26; Nat Acad Design Ann, 26-; Golden Gate Int Expos, San Francisco, 40; Carnegie Inst Int, Pittsburgh, 40-44; Corcoran Gallery, Washington, DC, 40-47. Awards: Saltus Gold Medal Merit, Nat Acad Design, 64; Gold Medal, Calif State Expos, 73; First Award, 11th Traditional, San Bernardino Mus, Calif, 77. Bibliog: Joseph Finigan (auth), article in Am Artist Mag, 25; Henry Pitz (auth), Antonio P Martino, G Alan Chidsey, 1/53; Ernest Watson (auth), Composition, Landscape and Still Life, Watson-Guptill, 59. Mem: Nat Acad Design; life mem Nat Arts Club; Am Watercolor Soc. Style & Technique: Representational with a feel of the abstract, painted in a loose manner with simplification. Media: Oil, Watercolor. Publ: Auth, Prize winning watercolors, Allied Fla, 63. Mailing Add: 1864 Rutgers Dr Thousand Oaks CA 91360

MARTINO, EDMUND
PAINTER, DESIGNER
b Philadelphia, Pa, June 21, 15. Study: LaFrance Art Inst, Graphic Sketch Club & Poor Richard Club, Philadelphia. Work: Allentowns Art Mus, Pa. Exhib: Pa Acad Fine Arts, Philadelphia; Philadelphia Art Mus; Philadelphia Art Alliance; Corcoran Art Gallery, Washington, DC; Butler Inst Am Art, Youngstown, Ohio; Allentown Art Mus; one-man shows, Chester Co Art Ctr, W Chester, Pa, Universalist Church, Germantown, Pa & Pa Military Col, Chester. Pos: Freelance designer, Franklin Mint, Franklin Ctr, Pa. Awards: Two

Lloyd Van Scriver Prizes, Woodmere Art Gallery, 57, 59 & 60; First Prize, Wilmington Art Mus, 65; First Prize, Woodmere Art Gallery, 68. Style & Technique: Semi-abstract, pattern and design. Media: Oil. Mailing Add: 4920 W Chester Pike Newtown Square PA 19073

MARTINO, EVA E
PAINTER, SCULPTOR
b Philadelphia, Pa. Study: Gwynedd Mercy Col; Montgomery Co Community Col; also with Giovanni Martino. Exhib: Reading Mus, Pa, 62; Nat Acad Design, New York, 65; Pa Acad Fine Arts, Philadelphia, 66; Edinboro Teacher's Col, Pa, 67; Butler Inst Am Art, Youngstown, Ohio, 70; Allied Artists of Am, 77; William Penn Mem Mus, 77; Audubon Artists, 78. Awards: Third Prize, Philadelphia Sketch Club, 72; Second Prize, Perkiomenville Art League, 71; Second Prize, Greater Norristown Art League, 76. Mem: Nat Forum Prof Artists; Woodmere Art Gallery; Artists Equity Asn. Style & Technique: Representational, egg tempera under painting. Media: Oil, Wood. Mailing Add: 1435 Manor Lane Blue Bell PA 19422

MARTINO, GIOVANNI
PAINTER
b Philadelphia, Pa, May 1, 08. Study: Spring Garden Inst, Pa; La France Inst, Pa; Philadelphia Graphic Sketch Club. Work: Nat Acad Design, New York; Pa Acad Fine Arts, Philadelphia; Va Mus Fine Art; Springfield Art Mus, Mo; Butler Art Inst, Youngstown, Ohio. Exhib: Royal Acad Eng; Carnegie Inst Int, Pa; Whitney Mus Am Art, New York; San Francisco Int Expos; Nat Acad Design. Teaching: Instr painting, Lehigh Univ, 57-58. Awards: Elmer Fox Purchase Award, Springfield Art Mus, 72; Hallmark Award, 72 & Benjamin Altman Prize, 75, Nat Acad Design. Mem: Nat Acad Design; Am Watercolor Soc; Woodmere Art Gallery (exhib comt, 69-). Style & Technique: Traditional, casein underpainting. Media: Oil, Watercolor. Mailing Add: 1435 Manor Lane Blue Bell PA 19422

MARTINSEN, IVAR RICHARD
PAINTER, EDUCATOR
b Butte, Mont, Dec 9, 22. Study: Mont State Col; Univ Ore; Univ Wyo. Exhib: Wyo Artists Traveling Exhib, Sheridan & Laramie, Wyo; Scottsbluff, Nebr; Sheridan Inn Gallery, 75-76. Teaching: Prof art & chmn humanities div, Sheridan Col. Awards: Prizes, Wyo-Nebr Exhib, 58 & 59; Prize, Wyo State Fair, 60. Mem: Sheridan Artist Guild; Wyo State Art Asn. Mailing Add: Dept of Art Sheridan Col Sheridan WY 82801

MARTMER, WILLIAM P
PAINTER, PHOTOGRAPHER
b Detroit, Mich, Sept 25, 39. Study: Art Sch of Soc Arts & Crafts; Cranbrook Acad Art; Wayne State Univ. Work: Cranbrook Acad Mus; Gen Motors Corp. Exhib: Cranbrook Acad Art Gallery; Northern Ill Univ Art Dept; Brooklyn Mus Print Show; Wayne State Univ Alumni Exhib; Raven Gallery, Detroit. Teaching: Instr art, Detroit Inst Arts; instr art, Wayne State Univ. Awards: Lewis Art Prize, Huntington Woods Ann; Popular Prize, Kalamazoo Art Ctr & Scarab Club Detroit. Media: Oil. Dealer: Alan Rubiner 621 S Washington Royal Oak MI 48067. Mailing Add: Bundy Rd Rte 2 Coloma MI 49038

MARTONE, WILLIAM ROBERT
PAINTER, INSTRUCTOR
b Wilmington, Del, Nov 30, 45. Study: Pa Acad Fine Arts, 64-68, William Emlen Cresson Mem traveling scholarship, 67; Univ Pa, BFA, 69; also with Morris Blackburn, Walter Stuempfig & Franklin Watkins. Work: Pvt collection of Sen & Mrs William Roth, Jr, Wilmington, Del. Comn: Portrait of Fredrick Joseph Kinsman, Third Episcopal Bishop, comn by Mr & Mrs Charles Proctor, Warren, Ohio, 72; Resurrection, St Mark's Lutheran Church, Wilmington, 73; Sen J Caleb Boggs, comn by Sen & Mrs J Caleb Boggs, Wilmington, 73; Joe Frazier (portrait), comn by Joe Frazier, Philadelphia, 74. Exhib: 142nd & 150th Exhib, Nat Acad Design, New York, 67 & 75; one-man shows, Warehouse Gallery, Arden, Del, 69 & 73; Philadelphia Watercolor Club Ten by Ten Exhib, Philadelphia Art Alliance, 72; Works of Art on Paper, Pa Acad Fine Arts, 75; Cottage Tour, Rehoboth Art League, Del, 75. Teaching: Instr oil painting, Bancroft Studios, Schoonover Galleries, Wilmington, 68-70; instr art & chmn dept, Mt Pleasant Upper & Middle Schs, Wilmington, 69-74; instr oil & watercolor, Howard Pyle Studios-Studio One, Wilmington, 70-; instr portraiture, Pa Acad Fine Arts, 73-; instr art & chmn upper sch dept, Wilmington Friends Sch, 74- Awards: Portrait-Life Div First Prize, Ann Ocean City Exhib, NJ, 68; First Prize, Philadelphia Watercolor Club, 72. Mem: Del Archaeol Soc; Fel Pa Acad Fine Arts; Philadelphia Watercolor Club (mem bd mgr, 75-); Del Mus Art; Philadelphia Mus Art. Style & Technique: Portraits and landscapes; representational in nature; naturalist in essence. Media: Oil, Watercolor. Collection: 20th century realists and illustrators. Mailing Add: c/o Howard Pyle Studios-Studio One 1305 N Franklin St Wilmington DE 19806

MARTYL (MARTYL SCHWEIG LANGSDORF)
PAINTER
b St Louis, Mo, Mar 16, 18. Study: Washington Univ, AB; Colorado Springs Fine Arts Ctr, with Arnold Blanch & Boardman Robinson. Work: Whitney Mus Am Art, New York; Art Inst Chicago; Colorado Springs Fine Arts Ctr; Los Angeles Co Mus; St Louis Art Mus. Comn: Recorder of Deeds (mural), comn by Sect Fine Arts, Washington, DC, 43; Darkness into Light (mural), Unitarian Church, Evanston, Ill, 62; 22 projections for Pierrot Lunaire, N Shore Music Ctr, Ill, 62. Exhib: Painting in the USA, Carnegie Inst Int, Pittsburgh, 43-45; five Univ Ill Am Art Biennials, 51-61; Chicago Artists Exhib, circulated by US Info Serv to seven Fr cities, 58; New Accessions, 9th Biennial Exhib Contemp Paintings, Colorado Springs Fine Arts Ctr, 62; American Drawing Biennial XXIV, Norfolk Mus Arts, 71; one-person shows, Art Inst Chicago, 76, Fairweather-Hardin Gallery, 77 & Ill State Mus, 78. Teaching: Instr painting, Univ Chicago, 65-70; artist in residence, Tamarind Inst, Univ NMex, 74. Pos: Art ed, Atomic Sci Bulletin, 45-72; mem artists comt, Art Inst Chicago, 69; exec comt, Artists Equity Asn Chicago, 58-60. Awards: Logan Award & Medal, 50 & William Bartels Award, 57, Art Inst Chicago; Am Inst Architects Honor Award, 62. Bibliog: H W Janson (auth), Martyl, Kovler Gallery Publ, 67; George McCue (auth), Martyl, St Louis Dispatch, 69. Mem: Arts Club Chicago (bd dirs); Renaissance Soc (pres, 70-71). Style & Technique: Semi-abstract. Media: Acrylic, Ink. Publ: Contribr, Methods and techniques of gouache painting, 46; auth, Cliches, old and new, St Louis Post-Dispatch, 67; auth, Art scene—Fred Sweet, 68. Dealer: Fairweather-Hardin Gallery 101 E Ontario St Chicago IL 60610. Mailing Add: RR 1 Box 228 Meacham Rd Schaumburg IL 60172

MARTZ, KARL
CERAMIST, EDUCATOR
b Columbus, Ohio, June 24, 12. Study: Ind Univ, AB(chem), 33; Ohio State Univ, 33-34 & 39, grad study in ceramic art; sabbaticals in Japan, 62, Kyoto Univ Arts, with Kondo Yuzo, 71, Ateliers of Sakuma Totaro & Seto Hiroshi, Mashiko. Work: Nat Collection Art, Smithsonian Inst, Washington, DC; Mus Mod Art, Tokyo; Mus Contemp Crafts, New York; Mus Dec Arts, Lisbon, Portugal; Walker Art Ctr, Minneapolis. Comn: Communion vessels, First Baptist Church, Bloomington, 60. Exhib: 20th Int Ceramic Exhib, Syracuse Mus & Metrop Mus, New York, 59; Cult Exchange Exhib, Smithsonian Inst & many Europe Mus, 60; 9th Int Exhib Ceramic Art, Smithsonian Inst, Washington, DC, 63; Int Ceramic Exhib, Mus Mod Art, Tokyo, 64; Twenty Five Years of Art in Clay, USA, Scripps Col, Claremont, Calif, 69. Teaching: Instr ceramic art, Inst Design, Chicago, 44; prof ceramic art, Ind Univ, Bloomington, 45-77, emer prof, 77- Bingham prof humanities, Allen R Hite Art Inst, Univ Louisville, 75. Pos: Spec contribr, Ceramics Monthly, Columbus, Ohio, 59-; mem arts & crafts cert comt, Ind Dept Pub Instr, 61. Awards: First Prize, Ind Biennial Ceramic Exhib, Herron Mus, Indianapolis, 53, 55 & 57; Third Prize, Miami Nat Ceramic Exhib, Fla, 56; Award of Merit, Nat Fiber-Clay-Metal Exhib, St Paul Gallery Fine Arts, Minn, 57. Bibliog: Article in Encycl Britannica Yearbk, 54; Sally Gallaway (auth), Karl Martz, Ceramics Monthly, 10/68; Philip Terman (auth), Possibilities in Clay (film), Ind Univ Audio-Visual Ctr, 75. Mem: Nat Coun Educ for Ceramic Arts (pres, 65-66); World Craft Coun; Am Craft Coun (chmn, NCent Regional Assembly, 65-66); Ind Artist-Craftsmen (bd dirs, 64-66, vpres, 65-66). Style & Technique: Contemporary wheel thrown container forms, influenced by ancient Chinese, Persian, and 20th century Japanese pottery and porcelain. Media: Porcelain, Stoneware. Publ: Auth & demonstr, Craftsmanship in Clay (6 educ films), Ind Univ Audio-Visual Ctr, 47-54. Dealer: The Gallery 102 N Grant St Bloomington IN 47401. Mailing Add: 105 N Overhill Dr Bloomington IN 47401

MARX, NICKI D
ASSEMBLAGE ARTIST, SCULPTOR
b Los Angeles, Calif, Oct 3, 43. Study: Univ Calif, Riverside, philos; Univ Calif, Santa Cruz, independent study. Work: Palm Springs Desert Mus, Calif. Comn: Fairchild Sci Ctr, Stanford Univ, Calif, 77. Exhib: Calif Crafts IX, Crocker Art Gallery, Sacramento, 75; White, Hand & Spirit Gallery, Scottsdale, Ariz, 75; Plumage, Julie, New York, 75; Calif Design 12, 75 & 76; one-person shows, Phoenix Art Mus, Ariz, 76 & Palm Springs Desert Mus, Calif, 77; Ashton Gallery, Scottsdale, Ariz, 76; Sacred Heart Sch, Palo Alto, Calif, 77; Calif Women in Craft, Craft & Folk Art Mus, Los Angeles, 77; plus thirteen solo shows & work included in 28 competitions in last four yrs. Awards: Cal State Expo '74, 74; Calif Crafts IX, 75; MacDowell Colony Fel, NH, 75. Bibliog: Bea Miller (auth), Fine feathers, Los Angeles Times Home Mag, 6/14/73; M Gottschalk (auth), Fiery feathers, Calif Today, 10/74. Mem: Am Crafts Coun; Artists Equity Asn. Style & Technique: Natural forms, primarily feathers and shells, seeds and leather; wall works, sculpture, fetishes. Dealer: Smith-Andersen Gallery 200 Homer Palo Alto CA 94301. Mailing Add: 417 Cliff St Santa Cruz CA 95060

MARX, ROBERT ERNST
PAINTER, PRINTMAKER
b Northeim, Ger, 1925. Study: Univ Ill, BFA, 51, MFA, 53; study & travel in Ger, Austria, Italy, Switz & France, 1 yr. Work: Mus Mod Art, New York; Philadelphia Mus Art; Dallas Mus Art, Tex; Seattle Art Mus; Munson-Williams-Proctor Inst, Utica, NY; plus many others. Exhib: US Info Agency Graphics Traveling Exhib, USSR, 63-64, Rumania & Poland, 65, India, 65, Czech, 65, Eastern Asia, 66; one-man shows, Ohio State Univ, 68, Univ Maine, Orono, 71, Franz Bader Gallery, Washington, DC, 76-78, Hanover Sq Gallery, Syracuse, NY, 76-78 & Gallery 696, Rochester, NY, 77; 4th Int Exhib Graphic Art, Kunstverein zu Frechen, Ger, 76; Franz Bader Show, Baway Found, Vienna, Austria, 76; Art of Poetry, Nat Collection Fine Arts, Smithsonian Inst, 76; Premio Int Biella, l'Incisione, Italy, 76; plus many others. Teaching: Instr, Univ Wis, 53; chmn dept art, Flint Jr Col, 56; instr, Sch Art, Syracuse Univ, 58; assoc prof art, State Univ NY Binghamton, 66-69, prof, 69-70; assoc prof, State Univ NY Col Brockport, 70-72, prof, 72- Pos: Artist attached to exhib in Prague & Bratislava, Czech, 65; dir, Flint Inst Art, 57; dir, Impressions Workshop, Boston, 69. Media: Intaglio. Dealer: Davidson Galleries 702 First Ave Seattle WA 98104; Franz Bader GAllery 2124 Pennsylvania Ave NW Washington DC 20037. Mailing Add: Dept of Art State Univ NY Col Brockport NY 14420

MARZANO, ALBERT
PAINTER, DESIGNER
b Philadelphia, Pa, Aug 22, 19. Study: Philadelphia Graphic Sketch Club; Philadelphia Plastic Club. Comn: Mural for pub health, Dept Pub Health, Philadelphia, 67, mural with air pollution theme, 69. Exhib: Chautauqua Art Asn Ann Juried Show, NY, 59; 25th Ann Mid-Year Show, Butler Inst Am Art, Youngstown, Ohio, 60; 7th Ann Exhib, Nat Soc Painters in Casein, New York, 61; one-man shows, St Joseph's Col, Philadelphia, 70, La Salle Col, Philadelphia, 71, Philadelphia Sketch Club, 74, Waldron Acad, 75 & Episcopal Acad, 77; plus others. Teaching: Instr drawing & painting, Sons Italy in Am, Philadelphia, 65-70. Pos: Designer-consult, Philadelphia Asn Blind, 53-56; art dir-consult, J Cunningham Cox Agency, Bala-Cynwyd, Pa, 58; art consult & graphic designer, Philadelphia Pub Health Dept, 58-60; art dir-consult, Benn Assocs, Philadelphia, 60. Awards: Gold Medals, Philadelphia Art Dirs Club, 54, 55 & 56; Gold Medal, Haddonfield Art Ctr, NJ, 59; Gold Medal, Nat Soc Painters in Casein, 61. Mem: Watercolor Club Philadelphia; Philadelphia Art Alliance; Woodmere Art Gallery. Media: Acrylic, Oil, Watercolor. Mailing Add: 1809 Delancey Pl Philadelphia PA 19103

MARZOLLO, CLAUDIO
SCULPTOR
b Milan, Italy, July 13, 38; US citizen. Study: Columbia Col, BA. Work: Windsor Art Gallery, Ont; Neiman-Marcus Exec Off, Dallas, Tex. Comn: Kinetic piece, ARCO Hq, Philadelphia, 74. Exhib: Philbrook Art Ctr, Tulsa, Okla; Loan Exhib, Everson Mus, Syracuse, NY, 72; Critics' Choice, Sculpture Ctr, New York, 72; Collectors of Ohio, Toledo Mus Art, 73; Refracted Images, DeCordova Mus, Lincoln, Mass, 73; one-man shows, Tafts Mus, Cincinnati, Ohio, 74, US Info Serv, Milan, 75 & traveling exhib, Nat Acad Sci, Washington, DC, 77; Illum, Whitney Mus Am Art, New York, 74; New Acquisitions, Windsor Gallery Art, Ont, 75; Basel Art Fair, Switz, 75; The Logic & Nature of Color, Akron Art Inst, Ohio, 75; Cologne Art Fair, Ger, 75; Brilliance in Three Dimensions, Sculpture Ctr, New York, 75; Hudson River Mus, Yonkers, NY, 76. Teaching: St three-dimensional design, Sch Visual Arts, New York, 74 & Univ Bridgeport, Conn, 75-77; Mather vis scholar, Case Western Reserve Univ, Cleveland, 75; vis artist, US Mil Acad, West Point, 78- Bibliog: Joseph Horning (auth, film), Metamorphoses (20 minute, 16mm sound-color), Ohio Arts Coun, 75. Style & Technique: Kinetic light sculpture. Media: Plexiglas and Aluminum with Various Light Sources, Filters and Motors. Dealer: Gallery Nuki 800 25th St NW Washington DC 20037; Fischbach Gallery 29 W 57th St New York NY 10019. Mailing Add: Lane Gate Rd Cold Spring NY 10516

MASER, EDWARD ANDREW
ART HISTORIAN, EDUCATOR
b Detroit, Mich, Dec 23, 23. Study: Univ Mich, 41-43; Univ Chicago, MA, 49 & PhD, 58. Collections Arranged: German & Austrian 18th Century Painting, Sculpture & Graphics, 56, Benton, Curry, Woods Retrospectives, 57, 58 & 59 & The Pre-Raphaelites, 60, Univ Kans Mus Art. Teaching: Assoc prof art hist, Univ Kans, 53-61; prof art hist, Univ Chicago, 61-, chmn dept art, 61-64. Pos: Dir, David & Alfred Smart Gallery, Univ Chicago, 72-; mem int

comt, Franz Anton Maulbertsch Exhib, Vienna, 74. Awards: Fulbright Res Fel, 50-52 & Sr Res Scholar, 65-66; Guggenheim Res Fel, 69-70; Cross of Honor, Repub Austria, 74. Mem: Col Art Asn Am; Am Asn Univ Prof. Res: Italian, German and Austrian art of the 17th and 18th centuries. Publ: Co-auth, Il Museo del Opificio delle Pietre Dure, 53; auth, Giovan Domenico Ferretti, Florence, Marchi & Bertolli, 68; ed & auth, Baroque and Rococo pictorial imagery, Dover Press, 71; auth, Disegni inediti di Johann Michael Rottmayr, Monumenta Bergomensia Bergamo, 71. Mailing Add: 5318 Hyde Park Blvd Chicago IL 60615

MASHECK, JOSEPH DANIEL
EDITOR, ART HISTORIAN
b New York, NY, Jan 19, 42. Study: Columbia Univ, AB, 63, MA, 65, PhD, 75, doctoral study with Dorothea Nyberg & Rudolf Wittkower. Teaching: Lectr art hist, Maidstone Col Art, Kent, Eng, 68; preceptor art hist, Columbia Col, Columbia Univ, New York, 69-71; asst prof art hist, Barnard Col, 71- Pos: Ed, Artforum Mag, 77- Awards: Art Critics' Fel, Nat Endowment for the Arts, 72-73; Hon Fel, Soc Fel Humanities, Columbia Univ, 76-77; Guggenheim Mem Found Fel, 77. Res: Abstract painting and sculpture. Publ: Auth, The Panama Canal and some other works of work, 5/71 & Mondrran the New Yorker, 10/74, Artforum; ed, Marcel Duchamp in Perspective & essay, Chance is zee fool's name for fait, Prentice-Hall, 75; auth, The carpet paradigm—critical prolegomena to a theory of flatness, Arts Mag, 9/76; auth, Criciformality, Artforum, summer 77. Mailing Add: c/o Artforum Mag 667 Madison Ave New York NY 10027

MASON, ALDEN C
PAINTER, EDUCATOR
b Everett, Wash, July 14, 19. Study: Univ Wash, MFA. Work: Seattle Art Mus, Wash; Cent Wash State Col; Denver Art Mus. Exhib: Spirit of the Comics, Inst Contemp Art, Univ Pa, 69 & Am Fedn Arts, NY, 71-72; Drawing Soc Nat Exhib, Am Fedn Arts, 70-72; Pacific Cities Exhib, Auckland, NZ, 71; one-man shows, Portland Ctr for Visual Arts, Ore, 73, Denver Art Mus, 73 & Ruth Schaffner Gallery, Los Angeles, 75; Allan Stone Gallery, New York, 74 & 78; 14 Abstract Painters, Frederick Wight Art Galleries, Univ Calif, Los Angeles, 75; Univ Art Galleries, Univ NDak, Grand Forks, 78. Teaching: Prof art, Univ Wash, 47- Awards: Purchase Award, 44th Northwest Ann, 63 & 54th Northwest Ann, 68, Seattle Art Mus. Media. Oil, Watercolor. Dealer: Kilsu Gallery 818 E Pike St Seattle WA 98122; Alan Stone Gallery 48 E 86th St New York NY 10028. Mailing Add: 1916 NE 73rd St Seattle WA 98115

MASON, ALICE FRANCES
LITHOGRAPHER, PAINTER
b Chicago, Ill, Jan 16, 95. Study: Northwestern Univ, BS; Art Inst Chicago, BFA & MFA; Summer Sch Painting, Saugatuck, Mich, with Chapin, Kahn & others; Univ Chicago; study in Vienna; also with Maroger of the Louvre, Paris & others. Work: Metrop Mus Art, New York; Pa Acad Fine Arts, Philadelphia; Univ Chicago; Libr Cong, Washington, DC; Cincinnati Art Mus. Comn: Lithographs for print of the year, Chicago Soc Artists, 49. Exhib: Lithography Show & Vicinity Shows, Art Inst Chicago Int, 12 shows, 37-56; Metrop Mus Art, 42 & 52; Soc Am Graphic Artists, New York, 52-55 & 57; New Brit Art Mus, Conn, 52-53; one-man show, Chicago Pub Libr, 61; plus others. Teaching: Instr lithography. Awards: Hon mention, Print Club Philadelphia, 52 & Soc Am Graphic Artists, 53; First Prize, New Brit Mus, 53. Mem: Conn Acad Fine Arts; Chicago Soc Artists; Cordon Club Chicago (pres, 3 yrs); Arts Club Chicago; Ann Arbor Art Asn. Style & Technique: Lithography and oil painting relating to nature. Dealer: IFA Gallery 2623 Connecticut Ave NW Washington DC 20008. Mailing Add: 9775 W Huron River Dr Box 237 Dexter MI 48130

MASON, BETTE
PAINTER
b Tex. Study: Trinity Univ; Syracuse Univ; Stephens Col, BA; Art Students League; Mus Mgt Sem, Mus Mod Art, New York; Univ New Orleans, MFA candidate, 78. Work: Greater New Orleans Fedn of Churches. Exhib: Westchester Art Soc Juried Exhib Painting & Sculpture, Tarrytown, NY, 70-72; one-person shows, Christopher Gallery, New York, 71 & Scarsdale Gallery Contemp Art, NY, 72; Union Carbide Co Invited Artists Exhib, New York, 72; Galerie Int Exhib, New York, 72; New Orleans Art Asn Exhib, 73-77; 5th Int Exhib, New Orleans, 75; Univ New Orleans Downtown Gallery; Jefferson Parish Bicentenntial Exhib, La. Teaching: Dir art dept, Westchester Learning Ctr, Fleetwood, NY, 71-72; asst prof art, Delgado Col, New Orleans, presently. Pos: Dir, Assoc Artists Gallery, Syracuse, 66-68. Awards: First Award, Scarsdale Art Soc, 70; Beaux-Arts Award, Federated Woman's Clubs, New York, 71; Merit Award, Westchester Art Soc, 72; Mem: New Orleans Art Asn (vpres); Col Art Asn; Women in the Arts, New York; Artists Equity Asn, New York; Westchester Art Soc (former pres); plus others. Media: Acrylic, Oil. Mailing Add: 527 St Philip New Orleans LA 70116

MASON, FRANK HERBERT
PAINTER, INSTRUCTOR
b Cleveland, Ohio, Feb 21, 21. Study: Nat Acad Design, New York, with George Nelson, 37-38; Art Students League, with Frank Vincent DuMond, 37-49. Work: Eureka Col Mus, Ill; Butler Inst Am Art, Youngstown, Ohio; Am Embassy, London; Hall of Governors, State Capitol, Albany, NY; US War Dept, Washington, DC. Comn: Life of St Anthony of Padua (eight large canvases), 11th Century Church of San Giovanni di Malta, Venice, Italy, 64; Resurrection, Old St Patrick's Cathedral, New York, 72. Exhib: Assoc Artists Pittsburgh, Carnegie Inst Mus Art, 46; Nat Acad Design, New York, 63; Expos Intercontinentale, Palais des Congres, Monaco, 68; Nat Arts Club, New York, 73; Mood Gallery, Milan, Italy, 75. Teaching: Instr fine arts, Art Students League, New York, 50- Awards: Popular Prize, Assoc Artists Pittsburgh, Carnegie Inst Mus Art, 46; figure composition-St Anthony, Penn-National, Ligonier, 68; Prix d'Amerique du Nord, Expos Intercontinentale, Monaco, 68. Bibliog: Condon Riley (auth), Frank Mason, painter, Am Artist, 6/64; Alexander Eliot Frank Mason: Allegiance to the old masters, Am Artist, 12/73. Mem: Art Students League; Nat Soc Mural Painters; Int Inst Conserv of Hist & Artistic Works; Academician Nat Acad Design. Style & Technique: Realist in oils. Mailing Add: 385 Broome St New York NY 10013

MASON, HAROLD DEAN
PRINTMAKER, PAINTER
b Springfield, Mo, Feb 1, 37. Study: Fresno State Univ, Calif; Art Ctr Sch, Los Angeles, Calif, BFA. Work: Continental Ill Bank, Chicago; Nat Westminster Bank, London, Chicago Br; First Nat Bank, Phoenix, Ariz; United Bank, Phoenix; Gen Electric of Milwaukee, Wis. Comn: Regional paintings (25), Exchange Bank, Santa Rosa, Calif, 68; paintings (10), Lambdin Med Group Clin, West Covina, Calif, 70. Exhib: Gold Spike Centennial, Pac Railroad, Provost, Utah, 69; 29th Ann Soc Western Artist, de Young Mus, San Francisco, Calif, 71; Western Asn of Art Mus Traveling Exhib, 73; Watercolor Int, Dazell Hatfield Galleries, Los Angeles, 74; West Coast Watercolor Soc Exchange Exhib, Royal Watercolor Soc, London, 75. Teaching: Chmn art dept, Ursuline High Sch for Girls, Santa Rosa, Calif, 65-70; prof art, Santa Rosa Jr Col, 68-70. Awards: Madelyn Windweh Spec Award, Napa Wine & Art Festival, Calif, 69; Best of Show, 29th Ann Soc Western Art, de Young Mus, 71; Best Watercolor, Atrium 72, Santa Rosa, 72. Mem: West Coast Watercolor Soc (treas, 72-75). Style & Technique: Realist; etherial and soft; combination of English and Japanese techniques of painting. Media: Watercolor, Oil, Graphics; Black and White Prints plus Handcolored Watercolor/Etchings. Publ: Co-auth, Flight: Poems & Drawings, India House of Calif, 70; contribr, Transparent Watercolor: Ideas & Techniques, Davis Publ, 72. Dealer: Gallery Mack PO Box 3352 Bellevue WA 98009; Gallery Three 3819 Third St Phoenix AZ 85013. Mailing Add: PO Box 5504 Carmel CA 93921

MASON, JOHN
SCULPTOR
b Madrid, Nebr, Mar 30, 27. Study: Otis Art Inst, Los Angeles, 49-52; Chouinard Art Inst, Los Angeles, 53-54. Work: Art Inst Chicago; Los Angeles Co Mus Art; San Francisco Mus Art; Mus Contemp Crafts, New York; Nat Mus Mod Art, Kyoto, Japan; plus others. Comn: Ceramic relief, Palm Springs Spa, Calif, 59; ceramic relief, Tishman Bldg, Los Angeles, 61; ceramic doors, Sterling Holloway, South Laguna, Calif; plus others. Exhib: One-man shows, Pasadena Art Mus, Calif, 60 & 74; Whitney Mus Am Art, 64, 73 & 76; Retrospective, Los Angeles Co Mus Art, 66; Kompas 4, Van Addemuseum Eindhoven, Netherlands, 69; Nat Mus Mod Art, Kyoto, Japan, 71; plus others. Teaching: Assoc prof art, Univ Calif, Irvine, 67-73, prof art & chmn dept studio art, 73-74; prof art, Hunter Col, New York, 74- Awards: Ford Found Award, 67th Am Exhib, Art Inst Chicago, 64; Univ Calif Award, Creative Arts Inst, 69-70; plus others. Bibliog: John W Mills (auth), The Technique of Sculpture, Reinhold Corp, NY, 65; John Coplans (auth), John Mason—Sculpture, Los Angeles Co Mus Art, 66; Glenn C Nelson (auth), Ceramics, Holt, Rinehart & Winston, 71. Media: Ceramics. Dealer: Hansen-Fuller Gallery 228 Grant Ave San Francisco CA 94108. Mailing Add: 1521 S Central Ave Los Angeles CA 90021

MASON, LAURIS LAPIDOS
ART DEALER, WRITER
b New York, NY, Apr 21, 31. Study: Syracuse Univ, AB, 2; State Univ NY New Paltz, MS, 55. Pos: Dir, Mason Fine Prints, 72- Specialty: American and European original prints. Publ: Auth, Print Reference Sources: A Select Bibliography, 18th-20th Centuries, 75; co-auth (with Cecile Shapiro), Fine Prints: Collecting, Buying & Selling, co-ed, Joan Ludman, auth, Print Collector's Quarterly: An Anthology of Essays of Eminent Printmakers of the World & co-auth (with Joan Ludman), The Lithographs of George Bellows: A Catalogue Raisonne, KTO Press. Mailing Add: Quaker Ridge Dr Glen Head NY 11545

MASON, PHILLIP LINDSAY
PAINTER, PRINTMAKER
b St Louis, Mo, Sept 20, 39. Study: Calif Col Arts & Crafts, Oakland, Calif, BFA(painting) with high distinction, 69, MFA (painting). Work: Oakland Art Mus, Calif; Art Gallery, Howard Univ, Wash, DC; Art Gallery, Vincennes Univ, Ind; Art Gallery, Ind State Univ, Terre Haute; Canterbury Sch, Walnut Creek, Calif. Comn: Comissioned to illustrate the front & back covers of the jazz album, Those Who Chant, Blue Thumb Records, 72. Exhib: Int Art Exhib, Expos 70, Osaka, Japan, 70; Twelve Afro- Am Artists, Art Gallery, Howard Univ, Wash, DC, 70; Dimensions of Black, La Jolla Mus Art, Calif, 70; one-man Cameo Print Exhib, Wichita Art Mus, Kans, 70; Contemp Black Artists in Am, Whitney Mus Am Art, 71; A Delicate Balance of Soul, Berkeley Art Ctr Mus, Calif, 71; A Question of Surrealism?, San Francisco Mus Art, 72; Directions in Afro-Am Art, Herbert F Johnson Mus, Cornell Univ, 74. Teaching: Instr painting & drawing, Calif Col Arts & Crafts, 69-71; asst prof painting & drawing, Ind State Univ, 72-73; asso prof & chmn dept art, NC Cent Univ, 73- Awards: Oakland Mus Purchase Award, Recent Mus Acquisitions, Oakland Mus Founders Fund, 68 & Oakland Art Mus, Oakland Mus Founders Fund & Bay Area Links, 70; Tangley Oaks grad fel, Tangley Oaks Educ Ctr, 70. Bibliog: Lewis & Waddy (auth), Black Artists on Art, Vol 1, Contemp Crafts, 69; Samella Lewis (auth), Art: African-American, Harcourt, Brace, Jovanovich, 77. Style & Technique: Symbolic realist; acrylic paint with dry brush technique. Media: Acrylic and prismacolor pencil. Publ: Auth, Art and Black Consciousness, Negro Dig Mag, 69; auth, Black Art, Tangley Oaks Educ Ctr, 71. Mailing Add: 408 E 13th Ave Apt C Columbus OH 43201

MASON, WILLIAM CLIFFORD
FILM MAKER, PAINTER
b Winnipeg, Man, Apr 21, 29. Study: Univ Man Sch Art, dipl. Awards: Best Film, Soc Film & TV Awards; Three Blue Ribbons, Am Film Festival; plus numerous nat and int awards. Mem: Royal Can Acad Arts; ASIFA. Style & Technique: Impressionism. Media: Oil on Paper. Mailing Add: Meach Lake Rd Old Chelsea PQ J0X 2N0 Can

MASSARO, KAREN THUESEN
CERAMIST, SCULPTOR
b Copenhagen, Denmark, Oct 23, 44; US citizen. Study: State Univ NY, Buffalo, BSEd, 66; Univ Mass, Amherst, grad work in art, 67-68; Univ Wis, Maidson, MFA, 72, with Don Reitz. Exhib: Wis Directions, Milwaukee Art Ctr, 75; Porcelain Exhib, Kaplan-Baumann Gallery, Los Angeles, 76; 32nd Ann Ceramics Exhib, Scripps Col, Claremont, Calif, 76; Massaro & Krueger, Ohio State Univ, Columbus, 77; Eight Artists in Indust, John Michael Kohler Arts Ctr, Sheboygan, Wis, 77; Massaro, Synopsis Gallery, Winnetka, Ill, 77; Porcelain Art, Madison Art Ctr, Wis, 77; Clay, Fiber, Metal by Women, Bronx Mus, NY, 78. Teaching: Vis fac mem fine art & art hist, Beloit Col, Wis, 72-77; vis artist ceramic arts, Ohio State Univ, 77. Awards: Purchase Prize, 51st Exhib Wis Crafts, Milwaukee Art Ctr, 72; Best in Ceramics & Outstanding Wis Craftsman, Beaux-Arts Designer/Craftsman 72, Columbus Mus Fine Arts, 72; Bibliog: Ed, Beaux-Art Designer/Craftsman 72, Craft Horizons, 72; Robert Shay (auth), Karen Massaro, Craft Horizons, 12/75; ed, Karen Massaro, Ceramic Mo, 1/78. Mem: Nat Coun Educ in Ceramic Arts. Style & Technique: Ceramic Sculpture, stressing repetition of slip cast and hand built representational forms and wheel thrown porcelain pottery. Media: Porcelain Clay; Low-Fire Clay. Mailing Add: 5502 Mahocker Rd Mazomanie WI 53560

MASSEY, CHARLES WESLEY, JR
PRINTMAKER, EDUCATOR
b Lebanon, Tenn, Aug 21, 42. Study: Mid Tenn State Univ, BS, 64; Univ Ga, MFA, 72. Work: Philadelphia Mus Art; Art Inst Chicago; Pushkin Mus, Moscow, USSR; Bradford City Art Gallery, Eng; Libr of Cong, Washington, DC. Exhib: Ga Artists, High Mus Art, Atlanta, 71 & 72; Brit Int Print Biennale, Bradford City Art Mus, Eng, 72 & 74; Cult Exchange Graphic Exhib, Pushkin Mus, Moscow, 72; Drawings USA, Minn Mus Art, St Paul, 73; Nat Exhib Prints, Libr of Cong, 73 & 75; Premio Int Biella, Italy, 73 & 76; Group Russian/Am Cult Exchange Exhib, Atlanta, Ga, 73; 8th Dulin Nat Print & Drawing Competition, Smithsonian Inst Traveling Exhib, 73-74; 1st Bienal Int Deobra Grafica, Segovia, Spain, 74; one-man shows, Gallery 501, Mint Mus Art, Charlotte, NC, 75, Print Club, Philadelphia, 75 & Northwestern Mich Col, Traverse City, 78; Classical Revival, Selected Drawing Exhib, Ill Bell Tel & Tel, 75-76; 6th Int Print Biennale, Krakow, Poland, 76; Drawing as Process, Akron Art Inst, Ohio, 77; Nat Print Exhib, Albion, Mich, 78; Nat Drawing Exhib, Emporia State Univ, Kans, 78. Teaching: Instr art printmaking, Univ Ga, Athens, 72-74; asst prof

printmaking, Ohio State Univ, 74- Awards: Purchase Awards, 3rd Int Brit Print Biennale, Bradford City Art Gallery, 72 & 24th Nat Exhib Prints, Libr Cong, 75; Cash Award, 33rd Nat Drawing & Small Sculpture Exhib, Ball State Univ, Muncie, Ind, 77. Bibliog: Albert Christ-Janer (auth), Artist—Charles Massey, Jr, Printer (film), Univ Ga, 71. Mem: Philadelphia Print Club; Boston Printmakers; Conn Acad Fine Arts; Col Art Asn; Columbus Art League. Style & Technique: Detailed, subjective structures defining a personal, somewhat surrealistic statement about inanimate but articulate, symbolic systems and environment. Media: Lithography, Drawing. Publ: Illusr, The Complete Screenprint & Lithography, Macmillan & Free Press, 74. Dealer: Assoc Am Artists 663 Fifth Ave New York NY 10022; 1614 Latimer St Philadelphia PA 19103. Mailing Add: 93 E Lincoln St Columbus OH 43215

MASSEY, ROBERT JOSEPH
PAINTER, EDUCATOR
b Ft Worth, Tex, May 14, 21. Study: Okla State Univ, 39-47, BA, with Doel Reed; Univ Havana, 47-48; Univ Mich, fall 48; Syracuse Univ, MFA, 52; Univ Tex, Austin, PhD, 62. Work: Dallas Mus Fine Art; Syracuse Univ; Soc Am Graphic Artists; El Paso Mus Art; Univ NMex; plus others. Comn: Enamel mosaic, State Nat Bank El Paso; applique hanging (with Sally Bishop), Univ Tex, El Paso Union Bldg, 69 & polyester-coated polyurethane sculpture, 69. Exhib: Nat Small Painting Exhib, Univ of the Pac, Stockton, Calif, 70; 5th Ann Gulf Coast Art Exhib, Mobile, Ala, 70; 11 State Small Painting Show, Albuquerque, NMex, 70; 12th, 13th & 14th Ann Painting Exhib, Longview, Tex, 70-72; 5 State Art Exhib, Port Arthur, Tex, 71; plus many others. Teaching: Asst, Okla State Univ, 47; instr, Inst Cult Cubano-Norte-Americano, 48; teaching fel, Univ Mich, 48-49; vis prof art, Fla State Univ, 49-50; instr, Syracuse Univ, 52-53; prof art, Univ Tex, El Paso, 53- Pos: Juror, NMex State Fair Art Exhib, 58, Ariz Fine Arts Asn Exhib, State Fair, 69, El Paso Art Asn Ann, El Paso Art Mus, 69 & 9th Ann Art Exhib, Carlsbad, NMex, 72. Awards: Hon Mentions for Painting & Graphics, El Paso Artists Ann, 61; Purchase Award for Painting, 6th Nat Arts Exhib, Tyler, Tex, 69; Third Award, 11 State Small Painting Show, 70. Style & Technique: Hard-edge; glazes; luminosity. Media: Egg Tempera. Publ: Auth, Formulas for Painters, 67 & auth, Notes for American readers, In: Notes on the Technique of Painting, 69, Watson-Guptill; auth, Formulas for Artists, B T Batsford, London, 68; auth, Painting, drawing & printmaking supports, 9/70 & auth, The artist's ideal studio, 1/71, Am Artist. Dealer: Two-Twenty-Two Gallery 222 Cincinnati Ave El Paso TX 79902. Mailing Add: 708 McKelligon St El Paso TX 79902

MASSIN, EUGENE MAX
PAINTER, EDUCATOR
b Galveston, Tex, Apr 10, 20. Study: Art Inst Chicago; Univ Chicago, BFA, 48; Escuela Univ Bellas Artes, Mex, MFA, 49; first asst to David Alfara Sequeiros, Mex muralist. Work: Brandeis Univ, Boston; Lowe Mus, Univ Miami; Escuela Univ Bellas Artes, Mex; Ringling Mus, Fla; Norton Gallery, Palm Beach, Fla. Comn: Acrylic on acrylic sheet mural, Cafritz Co, Washington, DC, 65-66; acrylic/canvas mural, City Nat Bank of Miami, Fla, 66; acrylic sheet mural (with Julia Busch), City Nat Bank of Miami Beach, Fla, 72; acrylic mural, Southern Gen Builders Inc, 72; painting of Fla, World Bk Encycl, 72. Exhib: Metrop Mus Art, 53 & Whitney Ann, New York, 55; Art USA, 59; Am Fedn Art Traveling Exhib, 62; Southeastern Ann, Atlanta, Ga, 64. Teaching: Instr art, Univ Wis, 49-50 & Univ SC, 52; prof art, Univ Miami, 54- Pos: Pres, Artist Equity Asn, 55-58, founder, Fla Chap; adv, Arts Coun, 60-64; adv, Cafritz Found for Arts, Washington, DC, 66; juror, Nat Scholastic Art Awards, 71. Awards: Humanities Award, Univ Miami, 64 & 71; artist in residence, Univ WVa, 66; Res Award, Esso, 71. Bibliog: Julia Busch (auth), A painter's plastic sculpture, Art J, 70; Thelma Newman (auth), Plastics as design form, Chilton, 72; Julia Busch (auth), A Decade of Sculpture, Art Alliance Press, 74. Media: Acrylic Sheet. Publ: Contribr, Art Techniques, Reinhold, 65 & Lucite Spectrum, Du Pont Co Mag, 67-68. Mailing Add: 3891 Little Ave Coconut Grove FL 33133

MASSON, HENRI
PAINTER
b Spy, Belg, Jan 10, 07; Can citizen. Study: Ottawa Art Asn; Windsor Univ, LLD, 54. Work: Nat Gallery Can; Art Gallery Ont; Nat Gallery Caracas, Venezuela; Mus PQ; Bezalel Mus, Jerusalem. Exhib: Aspects of Contemporary Painting in Canada, Andover, Mass, 42; Rio de Janeiro, Brazil, 46; Can Painting, Washington, DC, 50; Biennale, Sao Paulo, 51; Colombon Int Exhib Mod Art, New Delhi, 53. Teaching: Instr painting, Queen's Univ, Kingston, Ont, 48-52. Bibliog: Painters of Quebec (film), Nat Film Bd, 42; M Barbeau (auth), Henri Masson, Ryerson Press, 45; Graham McInnes (auth), Canadian Art, Macmillan, 50. Mem: Can Group Painters; Can Soc Painter in Watercolor; Can Soc Graphic Arts. Media: Oil. Publ: Illusr, Quebec in revolt, Fortune Mag, 66. Dealer: Walter Klinkhoff Gallery 1200 Sherbrooke SW Montreal PQ Can. Mailing Add: 1870 Ferncroft Crescent Ottawa ON K1H 7B5 Can

MASUROVSKY, GREGORY
DRAFTSMAN, PRINTMAKER
b Bronx, NY, Nov 26, 29. Study: Art Students League, New York, study with Will Barnet; Parsons Sch of Design, New York; Black Mountain Col, NC, study with Ilya Bolotowsky. Work: Mus of Mod Art, New York; Minneapolis Inst of Art, Minn; Fogg Art Mus, Cambridge, Mass; Joseph Hirschhorn Mus & Libr of Cong, Washington, DC. Comn: Decor, Costumes & Lighting, Ballet Theatre Contemp d'Angers, France, 75. Exhib: II & III Biennale de Paris, France, 61 & 63; III Documenta, Kassel, Ger, 64; First Int Biennale of Graphic Art, Cracovie, Poland, 66; Minneapolis Inst of Arts, Minn, 67; Ars Multiplicata, Cologne, Ger, 68; Druck Graphic, 71, Nurenberg Nat Mus, Ger, 70; Estampe Contemp, Bibliotheque Nat, Paris, 73; Third Int Biennale Nat Graphique, Kunstverein, Frechen, W Ger, 74; one-man shows, Kestner-Gesellschaft, Hannover, Ger, 63; Kunsthalle, Bienne, Switz, 63 & Palais des Beaux Arts, Brussells, Belg, 64. Teaching: Vis prof drawing, Minneapolis Col of Art & Design, Minn, 66-67. Pos: Graphics monitor to Will Barnet, Art Students League, New York, 52-53. Awards: Grant, William & Noma Copley Found, 63; Int Jury Prize, Etching III Biennial de Paris, 63; Fel, Tamarind Lithography Workshop, Los Angeles, 69. Bibliog: Georges Boudaille (auth), Masurovsky, Cimaise, 5/65; Michel Conil Lacoste (auth), Masurovsky, an American in Paris, Studio Int, 3/65; Michel Buter (auth), Masurovsky, Opus Int, 71. Mem: Centre Georges Pompidou, Paris; Artists Equity Asn, New York. Style & Technique: Penny-pen-point & ink on paper (drawings); etchings and lithography (prints). Media: Pen & Ink; Etching. Publ: Illusr, Litanie D'Eau, La Hune, Paris, 64; illusr, Paysage De Repons, Catella, Switz, 68; illusr, Western Duo, Tamarind Litho, Los Angeles, 69; illusr, Seven Poems (Carl Sandburg), Asn Am Art, 70; illusr, Les Petits Miroirs, La Farandole, Paris, 72. Dealer: Ellen Myers Inc 19 E 76th St New York NY 10021. Mailing Add: 43 Rue Liancourt Paris 75014 France

MATHESON, DONALD ROY
PRINTMAKER, EDUCATOR
b Honolulu, Hawaii, Jan 30, 14. Study: US Mil Acad, West Point, BS; Univ Mich, AM; Ecole Louvre, Paris, France. Work: Detroit Inst Art; Cincinnati Mus Asn; Libr Cong; South Bend Art Ctr; Univ Okla. Exhib: Detroit Inst Art, 54, 55 & 57; Libr Cong, 55-57; Boston Printmakers, 55, 57 & 58; Cincinnati Mus Asn, 56 & 58; Am Color Print Soc, 58; plus others. Teaching: Instr art & dir mus, Univ Okla, 56-57; prof art, Univ Mass, Amherst, 58- Pos: Dir, West Point Mus, 52-53. Awards: Prize, Detroit Inst Art, 55; Scarab Club Award, 57; Yankee Mag Award, Boston Printmakers Nat Print Show, 63; plus others. Mem: Col Art Asn Am; Mich Acad Sci, Arts & Lett; Print Coun Am. Mailing Add: Dept of Art Univ of Mass Amherst MA 01002

MATHIS, EMILE HENRY, II
ART DEALER, COLLECTOR
b Superior, Wis, Feb 25, 46. Study: Dominican Col, Univ Wis, Superior, BFA, MFA Teaching: Instr art, Sheboygan Sch Syst, Wis, 68069. Pos: Asst dir, La Porte Gallery, Racine, 70-71; dir, New Gallery One, Racine, 71-72; Gallery owner, Mathis Gallery, Racine, 72- Specialty: Old and modern masters; contemporary graphics. Collection: American 19th and 20th century contemporary drawings and paintings. Mailing Add: 735 Center St Racine WI 53403

MATHIS, KENNETH LAWRENCE
ART HISTORIAN, EDUCATOR
b New York, NY. Study: Georgetown Univ, BA; Art Students League; Ecole des Beaux Arts; Univ London, MFA; Oxford Univ; Cambridge Univ, MA; Columbia Univ, PhD. Teaching: Vis prof grad studies art, Pratt Inst Art, 70-72; adj prof grad studies art, NY Univ, 74-75; vis prof philos & aesthetics, Univ Dayton, 76-; lectr & seminars in mus & univs throughout the world. Pos: Prog official, Dept Cult Affairs, Parks & Recreation New York, 65-69; asst dir & cur educ, Brooklyn Mus, 69-72; head mus progs, Nat Endowment Humanities, 72-74; dir, Grey Art Gallery & Study Ctr, NY Univ, 74-76; cur, Dayton Art Inst. Awards: Int Bd Learned Soc Scholar; Res Grant on Aesthetical Phenomonology. Mem: Col Art Asn; Brit Mus Asn; Int Coun Mus; Int Asn Educ Through Art. Res: Art history, including 20th century painting; art museum education; museology theory; contemporary art; aesthetic philosophy. Publ: Auth, Aesthetical phenomenology, Oxbridge Scholastic J, 69; co-auth, Teaching To See, Learning To Look, 72; plus others. Mailing Add: 1930 Philadelphia Dr Dayton OH 45406

MATISSE, PIERRE
ART DEALER
Pos: Owner & dir, Pierre Matisse Gallery Corp. Mailing Add: 41 E 57th St New York NY 10022

MATSON, ELINA
WEAVER
b Vaasa, Finland, Dec 12, 92; US citizen. Study: Norfolk Mus Art Sch; Penland Sch Handicrafts, NC. Work: Va Mus Fine Arts, Richmond; Norfolk Mus Fine Arts, Va. Exhib: Delgado Mus Art, New Orleans, La, 53; Chesapeake Craftsmen, Norfolk Mus Fine Arts, 54 & 56; Va Mus Fine Arts, 55, 57 & 59; Pen & Brush Club, New York, 56; Women's Int Exhib, New York, 56 & 57. Awards: Cert Distinction, Va Mus Fine Arts, 55; Purchase Prize, Norfolk Mus Fine Arts, 55; Weaving Prize, Pen & Brush Club, 56. Mem: Tidewater Weavers Guild (treas, 52-56, librn, 56-59, pres, 59-61); Tidewater Arts Coun; Pen & Brush Club. Style & Technique: Traditional style and Rya technique. Mailing Add: 8750 Old Ocean View Rd Norfolk VA 23503

MATSON, GRETA (GRETA MATSON KHOURI)
PAINTER
b Claremont, Va. Study: Grand Cent Sch Art, New York; also with Jerry Farnsworth, Cape Cod. Work: New Britain Mus Am Art, Conn; Va Mus Fine Arts, Richmond; Little Rock Mus, Ark; Tex Technol Col, Lubbock; Longwood Col, Farmville, Va. Comn: Portraits, Dean Grace Landrum, William & Mary Col, Williamsburg, Va, 46 & Mary Calcott, Calcott Sch, Norfolk, Va, 53. Exhib: Nat Drawing Ann, Albany Inst Hist & Art, NY, 40 & 45; Oil Nat, Carnegie Inst, Pittsburgh, 41, 44 & 45; Oil & Watercolor Nat, Art Inst Chicago, 42, 43 & 46; Oil Nat, Butler Art Inst, Youngstown, Ohio, 43, 45, 57 & 59; Oil Nat, Va Mus Fine Arts, Richmond, 53 & 57. Awards: Altman Figure Prize, Nat Acad Design, 45; Am Artist Mag Medal, Am Watercolor Soc, 55; Allied Artists Am Gold Medal, 62. Mem: Nat Asn Women Artists (pres, 61-65); Audubon Artists (corresp secy, 61-62); Allied Artists; Am Soc Contemp Artists (first vpres, 61); Am Watercolor Soc. Style & Technique: Traditional figure and portrait in direct painting technique; still life, flowers and landscape in wet in wet method. Media: Oil, Watercolor. Publ: Auth, Painting in watercolor at the seashore, Am Artist Mag, 56. Mailing Add: 8750 Old Ocean View Rd Norfolk VA 23503

MATSUOKO, ISAAC JIRO
See Izacyro

MATTA-CLARK, GORDON
SCULPTOR
b 1945; US citizen. Study: Cornell Univ, Ithaca, NY, 63-68, studied architecture. Exhib: Pier 18, Mus of Mod Art, New York, 71; Bienal de Sao Paulo, Brazil, 71; Photographic Portraits, Moore Col of Art, Philadelphia, 72; Documenta V, Kassel, WGer, 72; Artists' Books, Moore Col of Art, 73; New York in Chicago, Mies van der Rohe Plaza, Chicago, 73; Questions-Answers, Sarah Lawrence Col, Bronxville, NY, 74; Artists Make Toys, The Clocktower, New York; one-man shows, Museo de Bellas Artes, Santiago, Chile, 71, Mus Aachen, WGer, 74 & Musee d'Art Moderne de la Ville, Paris, France, 74; plus others. Bibliog: Robert Pincus-Witten (auth), article in Art Forum, New York, 9/70; Liza Bear (auth), Gordon Matta-Clark: Jacks, Avalanche, New York, fall 71; A Brunelle (auth), The Great Divide: Anarchitecture by Matta-Clark, Art in Am, 9-10/74. Publ: Auth, Twentieth Century New York, 72; auth, Wallspaper, New York, 72 & 73; auth, Splitting, New York, 74. Mailing Add: 20 E 20th St New York NY 10003

MATTERN, PENNY GREIG
ART LIBRARIAN
b Jersey City, NJ, Aug 24, 43. Study: Studied with Harvey Dash, NJ, 59-61 & Arthur Mazmanian, Worcester, 68; Clark Univ, AB, 65; Simmons Col, SM, 69, with Ruth Leonard. Pos: Asst librn, Worcester Art Mus, 70-72, librn, 72-77; head cataloger, Worcester Pub Libr, 77- Mem: Art Libr Soc NAm (treas, New Eng Chap, 75-76). Interest: Editorial assistance on the Index to Printmakers Oeuvre Catalogs of the Print Council of America. Mailing Add: 7 Congress St Worcester MA 01608

MATTESON, IRA
SCULPTOR, DRAFTSMAN
b Hamden, Conn, June 26, 17. Study: Art Students League, with Arthur Lee, 37-42, also with William Zorach, 46-51; Nat Acad, with John Flanagan, 46-47. Work: Akron Art Inst, Ohio; Cleveland Mus Art; Chrysler Mus, Provincetown, Mass; Norfolk Mus, Va; Col William & Mary, Georgetown, Va. Comn: Figure-Bend, Cascade Plaza, Akron, 77. Teaching: Fac, Sch

of Art, Kent State Univ, Kent, 68- Awards: Prix de Rome, Am Acad Rome, 53-55, Louis Comfort Tiffany, 56 & 60. Style & Technique: Works of sculpture in silhouette of the figure and of trees. Media: Wood, Metal. Mailing Add: 7 E Main St Hudson OH 44236

MATTHEWS, GENE
PAINTER, EDUCATOR
b Davenport, Iowa, Mar 22, 31. Study: Bradley Univ, 48-51; Univ Iowa, BFA, 53, MFA, 57. Work: Nat Collection Fine Arts, Smithsonian Inst, Washington, DC; Butler Inst Am Art, Youngstown, Ohio; Denver Art Mus, Colo; Joslyn Art Mus, Omaha, Nebr; Chrysler Mus, Norfolk, Va. Exhib: Am Watercolors, Drawings & Prints, Metrop Mus Art, New York, 52; Antagonismes, Int Painting Exhib, Louvre, Paris, 60; Art in the Embassies Prog, US State Dept, Finland, 67, Nepal, 68, Jordan, 68, Thailand, 73, Bulgaria, 74 & Africa, 77; Contemporary American Watercolors, Cleveland Art Inst, 68; Mus Fine Arts, Houston, Tex, 70; Chrysler Mus at Norfolk, Va, 71; Denver Art Mus, Colo, 71; Int Drawing Exhib, Perth, Australia, 73; one-man shows, Denver Art Mus, 72 & James Yu Gallery, New York, 73 & 77; Nat Prints & Drawing Exhib, Okla Art Ctr, Oklahoma City, 74; Watercolor USA Bicentennial Exhib, Springfield Art Mus, Mo, 76; Int Drawing Exhib, Mus Mod Art, Rijeka, Yugoslavia, 76; SW Biennial, Mus NMex, Santa Fe, 76; Int Drawing Biennale, Middlesbrough Art Gallery, Eng, 77. Teaching: Prof fine arts, Univ Colo, Boulder, 61- Awards: Prix di Rome Fel Painting, Am Acad Rome, 57-60; Univ Colo Fac Fel for Creative Res, Boulder, 66; Quartana Purchase Award, Int Watercolor Exhib, Baton Rouge, La, 73. Bibliog: Wendon Blake (auth), Acrylic Watercolor Painting, Watson-Guptill, 70. Media: Acrylic. Dealer: ADI Gallery 530 McAllister San Francisco CA 94102; Brena Gallery 313 Detroit Denver CO 80206. Mailing Add: 2865 Jay Rd Boulder CO 80301

MATTHEWS, HARRIETT
SCULPTOR
b Kansas City, Mo, June 21, 40. Study: Sullins Jr Col, Briston, Va, AFA; Univ Ga, BFA & MFA; with Leonard DeLonga. Work: Univ Ga Art Mus; Colby Col Art Mus. Comn: Designed awards for the Maine Arts & Humanities Comn, 69. Exhib: Two-person shows, Univ Okla Art Mus, 65 & Colby Col Art Mus, 67, 71, 75 & 77; one-man show, Vanderbilt Univ Mus, 74, Frost Gully Gallery, 75 & Univ Maine, Orono, 75; New England Women, DeCordova Mus, Lincoln, Mass, 75, 76 Maine Artists, Maine State Mus, 76. Teaching: Vis instr sculpture, Univ Okla, 64-65; from instr to asst prof sculpture & drawing, Colby Col, 66-75, assoc prof, 75- Media: All Media. Mailing Add: RFD 2 Clinton ME 04927

MATTHEWS, WANDA MILLER
PRINTMAKER
b Barry, Ill, Sept 15, 30. Study: Bradley Univ, Peoria, Ill, BFA, 52; Univ Iowa, Iowa City, with Mauricio Lasansky, MFA, 57. Work: Libr of Cong & Nat Collection of Fine Arts, Smithsonian Inst, Washington, DC; Philadelphia Mus of Art; Los Angeles Co Mus; Boston Pub Libr. Exhib: Two-artist exhib, US Info Serv Gallery, Naples, Italy, 60; 2nd Brit Int Print Biennial, Bradford, Eng, 70; one-woman shows, Lehigh Univ, Bethlehem, Pa, 73, Univ Colo Fine Arts Gallery, 76 & Univ NDak Art Gallery, 76; 11th Biennial of Graphic Art, Ljublijana, Yugoslavia, 75; Nat Print Show, Cent Wash Col, Ellensberg, 75; 6th Int Print Biennale, Cracow, Poland, 76; Int Grafik Biennale, Frechen, WGer, 76; Figura 2-Artists Print, Int Bk Fair, Liepzig, EGer, 77. Pos: Res assistantship printmaking, Univ Iowa, 56-57. Awards: Scholar Grant in Graphic Arts, Louis Comfort Tiffany Found, 57 & 58; Benton Spruance Prize, Print Club of Philadelphia, 71; Int Biella Prize for Prints, Biella, Italy, 76. Mem: Print Club of Philadelphia; Calif Soc of Printmakers. Media: Intaglio. Dealer: Jane Haslem Gallery 2121 P St NW Washington DC 20037; Assoc Am Artists 663 Fifth Ave New York NY 10022. Mailing Add: 2865 Jay Rd Boulder CO 80301

MATTIELLO, ROBERTO
PAINTER, SCULPTOR
b Montebelluna, Italy, Feb 13, 34. Study: Pvt study in Treviso, Italy; Inst Design, Buenos Aires, with Hector Cartier; Ikebana, Buenos Aires, with Tazko Niimura. Work: Mus Mod Art, Buenos Aires; Kliner & Bell Art Fund, Los Angeles; Am Fedn Art, New York; Galerie B Bischofberger, Zurich, Switz; Tel-Aviv Mus, Israel. Comn: Mural & interior design, Olivetti Arg, Buenos Aires, 58; Roads (mural), CIDAR-Ford, Buenos Aires, 60; Cosmic Voyage (mural), Varig Airline, Arg, 61; Ballad (mural on Fiberglas), Jack Parker Co, New York, 64; Fusion (wall sculpture), Parker 72nd St Bldg, New York, 65. Exhib: Primera Expos Int Arte Mod Buenos Aires, Mus Arte Mod, Arg, 61; Art Artists, Riverside Mus, New York, 63; one-man show, New York Hilton Hotel, 66; 1, 2, 3 Infinity, Contemp Gallery, New York, 67; Psychedelic Art, Galerie Boschofberger, Zurich & Dussendorf, 68. Awards: Hon Mention, Segunda Bienal Arg Arte Sagrado Mod, Hist Mus of the Church, Arg, 56. Bibliog: Kevin Sanders (auth), Surrealism, ABC-TV Eye-Witness News, 2/72. Media: Oil, Mixed Media. Publ: Contribr, Mandala, Shambala Publ, 7/72. Mailing Add: 243 E 31st St New York NY 10016

MATTIL, EDWARD L
EDUCATOR, WRITER
b Williamsport, Pa, Nov 25, 18. Study: Pa State Univ, BS, 40, MA, 46 & DEd, 53; also with Viktor Lowenfeld & Hobson Pittman. Teaching: From asst prof to assoc prof, Pa State Univ, 48-60, prof art educ & head dept, 60-70; prof art, NTex State Univ, 71-, chmn art dept, 71-76. Pos: Ed, Everyday Art, 57- Awards: Distinguished Serv Award, Nat Gallery Art, 65. Mem: Nat Art Educ Asn (pres, 63-65). Publ: Auth, Meaning in Crafts, Prentice-Hall, Inc, 59, 65 & 71; co-auth, Providing for individual differences in the elementary schools, 60 & The arts in higher education, 69; ed, A Seminar in art education for research and curriculum development; El valor educativo de las manualidades 73: The Cuna Mola, 74. Mailing Add: Dept Art NTex State Univ Denton TX 76203

MATTOX, CHARLES
PAINTER, EDUCATOR
b Bronson, Kans, July 21, 10. Study: McPherson Col, 28-29; Kansas City Art Inst, 30-31. Work: Los Angeles Co Mus; Victoria Mus, BC; Hirshorn Mus, Washington; Smithsonian Inst; Stedelijk Mus, Amsterdam. Exhib: One-man shows, Shelton Gallery, Univ Nebr, 68, Gallery Mod Art, Taos, NMex, 70, Hill Gallery, Santa Fe, 71; Univ Iowa Mus, 72 & Vancouver Mus, BC, 73; plus numerous others. Teaching: Instr, Kann Art Inst, Los Angeles, 48-49; instr, San Francisco Art Inst, 57-58; instr, Univ Calif, Berkeley, 58-61; prof art, Univ NMex, 65- Awards: Artists Equity Asn (pres, San Francisco, 53-55), Col Art Asn (nat bd dirs). Publ: West Coast ed, Leonado, Jr Art & Technol, 68- Mailing Add: 820 Hermosa St NE Albuquerque NM 87110

MAU, HUI-CHI
PAINTER
b Chekiang, China, Oct 1, 22; US citizen. Study: Hangchow Nat Art Acad; with Hsu Pei Hung & Chi Pai Shih. Work: San Diego Mus. Exhib: Chekiang Univ, 43; Chinese Embassy, Berlin, Ger, 48; San Diego Mus, 68; Wash Sq Art Exhib, New York, 69; Cocoanut Grove Art Exhib, Miami, Fla, 73; Elliot Mus, Stuart, Fla. Teaching: Art dir, Mil Acad China, 42-54. Awards: Monterey Art Exhib Award, Calif, 68; Wash Sq Art Exhib Award, New York, 73; Church of Ascension Award, New York, 74. Bibliog: Diana Kan (auth), The artist and his work, Villager, New York, 74; Ann D Browne (auth), Art circle, Directions Mag, 74. Mem: Suffolk Co Artist League, New York; Chinese Artists & Writers Soc, Taiwan. Style & Technique: Chinese brush painting. Media: Watercolor, Graphics. Mailing Add: 90-22 193rd St Hollis NY 11423

MAUGHELLI, MARY L
PAINTER, LITHOGRAPHER
b Glen Lyon, Pa, Nov 20, 35. Study: Univ Calif, Berkeley, BA & MA; Pratt Graphic Ctr. Exhib: Galleria Re Magi, Milan, Italy, 60; 85th Ann San Francisco Art Inst Exhib, San Francisco Mus, 66; 14th & 15th Ann Nat Exhib Prints & Drawings, Okla Art Ctr, 72 & 73; Fresno Artists Leland House, Taipei, Taiwan, 73; one-person shows, Grandview Gallery, Los Angeles, 74 & Annex Gallery, Santa Rosa, Calif, 77; Calif Soc Printmakers Traveling Exhib, 75-77; Drawing, Santa Rosa Jr Col, Calif, 76; Orlando Gallery, Los Angeles, 76 & 77; Fragmentation, Gallery 25, Chico State Univ, Calif, 77; Beyond the Garden Wall, Downey Mus Art, Calif, 77; Maggie Kress Gallery, Taos, NMex, 77; Fac Show, Calif State Univ, Fresno, 78. Teaching: Prof art, Calif State Univ, Fresno, 62-; lectr design, Univ Calif, Berkeley, summer 63. Awards: Ann Bremer Prize in Art, Univ Calif, Berkeley, 58-59; Helene Wurlitzer Found Fel, Taos, NMex, summer 76 & 77; Ossabaw Island Proj, Ga, 77. Mem: Col Art Asn; Calif Soc Printmakers; Los Angeles Inst Contemp Art; Artists Equity. Style & Technique: Figurative collage-like painting; photo techniques in lithography. Media: Acrylic; Lithography. Dealer: Fig Tree Gallery 1536 Fulton St Fresno CA 93721. Mailing Add: 1114 W Keats Ave Fresno CA 93711

MAULDIN, BILL
CARTOONIST, WRITER
b Mountain Park, NMex, Oct 29, 21. Study: Chicago Acad Fine Arts; Conn Wesleyan Univ, hon MA, 46; Albion Col, hon LittD, 70; Lincoln Col, hon LHD, 70. Pos: Cartoonist, Chicago Sun-Times, 62- Awards: Pulitzer Prize, 44 & 58; Sigma Delta Chi Award, 64. Mem: Nat Cartoonists Soc. Publ: Auth, What's Got Your Back Up, 61 & I've Decided I Want My Seat Back, 65, Harper-Row; auth, Up Front, 68 & Brass Ring, 71, Norton; auth & illusr, articles in Life, Sat Eve Post, Sports Illus, Atlantic Monthly, New Repub & many others. Mailing Add: Chicago Sun-Times 401 N Wabash Ave Chicago IL 60611

MAURER, EVAN MACLYN
ART HISTORIAN, CURATOR
b Newark, NJ, Aug 19, 44. Study: Amherst Col, BA, 66; Univ Minn, MA, 68; Univ Pa. Collections Arranged: MIA Portraits, Rochester & Red River, Minn, 71; Landscape Masterpieces, Grand Rapids, Minn, 72; The Human Image, Minneapolis Inst Arts, 72, Observations: The Female Image, 72. Teaching: Head teaching fel intro art hist, Univ Pa, 70-71. Pos: Cur & asst to dir, Minneapolis Inst Arts, 71-73; chmn, Vanderlip Award Jury, Minneapolis Col Art & Design, 72; cur primitive art, Art Inst Chicago, 73- Mem: Col Art Asn; Am Asn Mus. Res: Relationships between surrealism and primitivism. Mailing Add: Art Inst Chicago Michigan Ave & Adams St Chicago IL 60603

MAURICE, ALFRED PAUL
PRINTMAKER, EDUCATOR
b Nashua, NH, Mar 11, 21. Study: Univ NH, 40-42; Mich State Univ, BA, 47, MA, 49. Comn: Murals (with Raymond Pinet), Nat Youth Admin, Jr High Sch, Hudson, NH & Community Chest Bldg, Nashua, 39-40. Exhib: Brooklyn Mus 3rd & 5th Print Nat, 49 & 51; Philadelphia Print Club Nat, 54; 15th Audubon Artists Ann, 57; 54th Mich Artists Exhib, 64; 5th Ann Pratt Graphic Int Miniature Print Exhib, 75; one-man show, Kalamazoo Art Ctr, Mich, 76. Collections Arranged: 20th Century American Artists, 62, Four Artists in New England, 63, Three Mid-Atlantic Seaboard Artists, 63, George Rickey/Ulfert Wilke, 64, Miklos Suba, 64 & Oliver Chaffee, 64, Kalamazoo Art Ctr. Teaching: Instr printmaking, calligraphy & drawing, Macalester Col, 47-49; asst drawing, Mich State Univ, 49-50; from asst prof to assoc prof drawing, painting, printmaking & design, State Univ NY Col New Paltz, 50-57, actg chmn art dept, 55-56; exec dir, Md Inst Col Art, Baltimore, 57-59; chmn art dept, Univ Ill, Chicago Circle, 65-67, prof printmaking design & drawing, 65-, assoc dean faculties, 69-72, actg dean, Col Archit & Art, 75-77. Pos: Dir art ctr, Kalamazoo Inst Arts, Mich, 59-65. Mem: Col Art Asn Am. Style & Technique: Naturalistic to semi-abstract city scapes and landscapes and geometric, non-objective works. Collection: American prints of all periods and in all print media. Publ: Auth, Four Printmakers, 62; auth, Miklos Suba, 64; auth, Oliver Chaffee, 64. Mailing Add: 2725A S Michigan Ave Chicago IL 60616

MAVIAN, SALPI MIRIAM
PAINTER
b Mar 27, 08; US citizen. Study: Sch Practical Arts, Boston; Art Students League; also with Robert Brackman, Joseph Hirsch & Robert Philipp. Work: Three mus, Armenia, USSR. Comn: St John the Baptist & St Gregory the Illuminator, St John Church of Detroit, 68; Archbishop Garigin, Diocese of Armenian Church NAm, New York, 63; portrait of Archbishop Tiran Neesoyan; side altar paintings of St Nersess Shnorhali & St Gregory the Enlightener, Diocese of Armenian Church of Am, New York, 73. Exhib: Hudson Valley Art Asn, NY, 59; Knickerbocker Artists, 59-60 & Allied Artists Am, New York, 63; one-man show, Armenia, USSR; Artists Equity Asn, 65; one-man show, Panaras Gallery. Mem: Art Students League; Am Artists Prof League; Nat Soc Lit & Arts. Style & Technique: Portraits, traditional; flowers and landscapes, impressionistic. Media: Oil. Mailing Add: 435 E 57th St New York NY 10022

MAVROUDIS, DEMETRIOS
SCULPTOR, EDUCATOR
b Thasos, Greece, Nov 18, 37. Study: Jersey City State Col, BA; Teachers Col, Columbia Univ, MA & EdD. Comn: Bronze sculptures, Bus Comt for the Arts, Esquire, 73-76; 30ft sculpture, Lifestyles Mag, 77. Exhib: Albright-Knox Art Gallery, Buffalo, NY, 70 & 71; Young Artists from Around the World, UN, 71; Artists-in-Residence Traveling Exhib, Del Art Mus, Wilmington, 75 & 76; Sculpture in the Fields, Storm King Art Ctr, Mountainville, NY; one-man shows, Philadelphia Art Alliance, Pa, Anchorage Hist & Fine Arts Mus, Alaska & Alaska State Mus. Teaching: Asst prof sculpture, NY Univ, New York, 69-71 & Teachers Col, Columbia Univ, 67-69 & 73-74; assoc prof sculpture & artist-in-residence, Univ Richmond, Va, 74- Pos: Artist-in-residence, NJ Coun for the Arts, 71-73. Awards: Dow Purchase Award, Columbia Univ, 69. Mem: Am Foundrymen's Soc; Nat Art Educ Asn; Col Art Asn. Style & Technique: Expressionist. Media: Cast Metal, Wood. Mailing Add: 9712 Cherokee Rd Richmond VA 23173

MAWDSLEY, RICHARD W
GOLDSMITH, EDUCATOR
b Winfield, Kans, July 11, 45. Study: Kans State Teachers Col, BSE; Univ Kans, MFA. Work: Ill State Univ Art Gallery; Tex Tech Univ; Minn Mus Art, St Paul. Exhib: An Invitational Exhibition of Eight American Metalsmiths, Richard Demarco Gallery, Edinburgh, Scotland & Sheffield Polytech Sch Art, Eng, 74; Baroque '74, Mus Contemp Crafts, New York, 74; The Goldsmiths, Renwick Gallery, Washington, DC & Minn Mus Art, 74; Gold and Silver, Kodak Gallery, New York, 75; Contemporary Crafts of the Americas, Colo State Univ & Orgn Am States, Washington, DC & Two Year Traveling Exhib, Smithsonian Inst, 75. Teaching: Assoc prof, Ill State Univ, 69- Awards: Second Award, Nat Jewelry Competition, 70; Award, Profiles in Jewelry '73, 73; Best in Show, Ill Artists '74, 74. Mem: Am Crafts Coun; Soc NAm Goldsmiths. Publ: Contribr, Body Jewelry, Regnery, 73; contribr, Jewelry Techniques, Doubleday, 76. Mailing Add: 1721 Truman Dr Normal IL 61761

MAWICKE, TRAN
PAINTER, ILLUSTRATOR
b Chicago, Ill, Sept 20, 11. Study: Art Inst Chicago, with Louis Ritman; Am Acad Art, Chicago; Acad Fine Art, Chicago. Work: USAF Collection, Washington, DC; Williamsburg Corp, Va; Schenectady Mus, NY; Garrott Collection, Los Angeles. Comn: Portraits, Gen Elec Corp Knolls Lab, 48, NY Nat Guard, Schenectady, 53, Ingersoll-Rand, 75. Exhib: Am Watercolor Soc, 48 & 69-74; Audubon Artists; Soc Illusrs; Am Watercolor Traveling Exhib, 70 & 74. Bibliog: S Meyer (auth), Fairfield watercolor group, Am Artist, 7/72. Mem: Am Watercolor Soc (dir, 70 & 72); life mem Soc Illusrs (pres, 60-61); Fairfield Watercolor Group; life mem Joint Ethics Comn (chmn, 55-60); Artists Fel. Style & Technique: Loose realism. Media: Oil, Watercolor. Publ: Illusr, South America Illustrated, 60 & More Answers, 61, G & D; illusr, Little Britches, Norton, 62; illusr, Andre, Putnams, 67; illusr, Captain, Garrard, 75. Dealer: Cross Roads of Sport 11 E 47th St New York NY 10017; Exhibitors Gallery E Bay St Charleston SC 29401. Mailing Add: 452 Golf Villas Rt 1 Johns Island SC 29455

MAX, PETER
DESIGNER, ILLUSTRATOR
b Berlin, Ger, Oct 19, 37; US citizen. Study: Art Students League; Pratt Inst; Sch Visual Arts. Comn: Non-commercial art show, Metro Transit Advert Co, local buses across US, 68; zodiac poster ser, New York Daily News, Chicago Tribune, Detroit Free Press & other newspapers, 71. Exhib: Riverside Gallery, Shreveport, La; Munic Art Gallery, Los Angeles; The World of Peter Max, M H De Young Mem Mus, San Francisco & US Tour, 70; London Arts Gallery Peter Max Exhibs, 12 major world cities, 70; two Smithsonian Inst Peter Max Exhibs, US, 72-74; plus many others. Pos: Dir, Daly-Max Design Studio; designer, Gen Foods, Elgin Nat Industs, Takashimaya Ltd Japan, Van Heusen, UN & other major orgns. Awards: Award, Am Inst Graphic Arts; Award, Soc Illusr; Award, Int Poster Competition Poland; plus many others. Media: Mixed Media Publ: Auth, Peter Max Posterbook & Peter Max Superposterbook, Crown; auth, Peter Max Astrological Calendar, Grosset & Dunlap; auth, The New Age Organic Vegetarian Cookbook & Peter Max Crochet Book, Pyramid Publ; drawings & meditations syndicated in 176 papers in US & Can, two yrs; plus many others. Dealer: London Arts Gallery 321 Fisher Bldg Detroit MI 48202. Mailing Add: Peter Mex Enterprises 118 Riverside Dr New York NY 10024

MAXWELL, JOHN
PAINTER
b Rochester, NY, Nov 3, 09. Study: Rochester Inst Technol; Univ Rochester; Provincetown Workshop, with Candell & Manso; with other nationally known instrs. Work: Philadelphia Mus Art; Nat Acad Design; Butler Inst Am Art; Lehigh Univ; Wichita State Univ; many pvt collections. Exhib: Nat Acad Design; Pa Acad; Smithsonian Inst; Toledo Mus; Am Watercolor Soc; plus others. Awards: Am Watercolor Soc Medal of Honor; First Prize for Oil, Pa Statewide Exhib; Audubon Artists Medal for Creative Oil; plus many others. Bibliog: Articles in New York Times, Am Artist Mag, Art News, Philadelphia Inquirer & others; work feature in bks on painting. Mem: Nat Acad Design; Pa Acad Fine Arts; Philadelphia Mus Art; Philadelphia Art Alliance; Am Watercolor Soc. Style & Technique: Semi-abstract; specializing in mixed techniques; developer of multi-facet technique. Dealer: Piccolo Mondo 311 Worth Ave Palm Beach FL 33480; Fontana Gallery 307 Iona Ave Narberth PA 19072. Mailing Add: 415 Holly Lane Wynnewood PA 19096

MAXWELL, ROBERT EDWIN
PAINTER, GRAPHIC ARTISTS
b Mt Vernon, NY, Dec 31, 29. Study: Art Students League; Franklin Sch Art; Nat Acad Design, with Robert Philipp, Hallgarten travel scholarship, 51; Escuela de Bellas Artes with James Pinto, etching with Guilermo Silva Santamaria. Work: Galeria Moderna, Banjalvka, Yugoslavia; Inst Norteamericano de Relaciones Culturales, Mexico City; Vincent Price Col. Exhib: Am Watercolor Soc, New York, 49; 14th Am Drawing Ann, Norfolk Mus, Va, 56; Nat Acad Design, 57; Acapulco Pictorial Festival, Mex, 64; Galeria Moderna, 74. Teaching: Instr drawing & landscape, Inst Allende, Mex, 55-56. Awards: Stacey Found Scholarship, 52. Bibliog: Image of Mexico II, Univ Tex, Austin; Crespo de la Serna (auth), Exhibit Paintings, 67 & Erasto Cortez Juarez (auth), Color and drawing, 69, Novedades, Mexico City. Style & Technique: Figurative, expressionist. Media: Oil, Acrylic; Etching, Pastel. Publ: Contribr, Oil Painting-Traditional & New, 59; contribr, Painters Workshop, 69. Dealer: Galeria San Miguel C San Francisco San Miguel de Allende Guanajuato Mexico. Mailing Add: San Pedro 18 San Miguel de Allende Guanajuato Mexico

MAXWELL, WILLIAM C
PAINTER, PRINTMAKER
b Yonkers, NY, Sept 3, 41. Study: Wagner Col, Staten Island, NY, BFA, 70; Columbia Univ, New York, MA, 71, EdM, 72, EdD, 76; study with Paul Pollaro, Clare Romano & Deli Sacilotto. Work: Hudson River Mus, Yonkers, NY; Brooklyn Mus, NY; Arthur Wesley Dow Collection & Federico Castellon Mem Collection, Columbia Univ; Univ Mass, Amherst; State Dept of Educ, Trenton, NJ. Exhib: Printmakers 1973, Metrop Mus of Art, New York, 73; Contemp Am Painting, Lehigh Univ, Pa, 74; Copenhagen Invitational, Denmark, 74; 19th Nat Print Exhib (travelling show), Brooklyn Mus, 74-75; 1976 Can-Am Exchange Exhib, Signal Gallery, Montreal, Can, 76; Drawings & Prints 1977, Miami Univ, Ohio, 77; Miami Int Graphic Bienniale, Metrop Mus of Art, Miami, Fla, 77; Nat Color Blend Print Exhib (travelling exhib), Corcoran Galleries, Washington, DC, 78-80. Teaching: Vis assoc prof educ & printmaking, Teachers Col, Colunbia Univ, New York, 71-; assoc prof painting & printmaking, Col of New Rochelle, NY, 75- Pos: Pres, W Broadway Gallery Corp, New York, 72-75; cur, Federico Castellon Mem Collection, Columbia Univ, New York, 75- Awards: First Prize/Painting, Tri-State Show, Mamaronek Artist's Guild, NY, 71; President's Award, Nat Arts Club, New York, 75; Shields Award, New York, 75. Bibliog: Marion Lane (auth), review in Artist Rev Art, Vol 2 (Dec, 1976); Helen Thomas (auth), review in Arts, 2/77; Kathie Beals (auth), rev in Weekend, 4/77. Mem: Col Art Asn; Nat Art Educ Asn; West Broadway Gallery Corp (bd dirs, 72-77). Style & Technique: Non-objective grids utilizing process as motif; textural glazed paintings; transposition lithographs and multi-method intaglio prints. Media: Mixed and aqueous media. Publ: Contribr, Elizabeth Harris & Sue Vardin (auths), Urban Education, Open Univ, London, 74; auth, Printmaking: A Beginning Handbook, Prentice-Hall, 77. Dealer: Westbroadway Gallery 431 W Broadway New York NY 10012; Gimpel-Weitzenhoffer Gallery, 1040 Madison Ave New York NY 10021. Mailing Add: 106 Morningside Dr New York NY 10027

MAY, MORTON DAVID
COLLECTOR, PATRON
b St Louis, Mo, Mar 25, 14. Study: Dartmouth Col, BA, 36. Awards: Great Cross of Ger Govt for Interest in Ger Painting in US, 63. Collection: German expressionism; oceanic and pre-Columbian collections; other primitive sculpture; 20th century painting and sculpture. Mailing Add: 12 Brentmoor Park St Louis MO 63105

MAY, WILLIAM L
COLLECTOR
b La Grange, Ga, Apr 4, 13. Study: Columbia Univ, BS; Spencer Bus Col, art hist with Robert E Day. Pos: Prof photog participation, New York, 45-48; photog student art work via contract, Dept Art, Columbia Univ; bd dirs, La Interior Design Inst, 69. Awards: Int Patron Art, Boston Mus Fine Arts, 69. Collection: Graphic prints by old masters; works by contemporary artists; oils, watercolors, gouache, polymer, including works by Moore, Rockmore. Publ: Auth, A businessman looks at art, Register, 68; auth, brochures for artists & galleries, New Orleans, La, 68. Mailing Add: 5034 Whitehaven Baton Rouge LA 70808

MAYEN, PAUL
DESIGNER
b La Linea, Spain, May 31, 18. Study: Cooper Union Art Sch; Art Students League; Columbia Univ; New Sch Social Res. Work: Mus Mod Art. Exhib: Brooklyn Mus; Mus Mod Art; Nelson Gallery Art; Ann Adver Art. Teaching: Instr advert design, Cooper Union Art Sch; former instr advert design, Parsons Sch, New York. Pos: Design consult, var indust orgns; bk designer, leading publ, ads, booklets & others; art dir, Agfa, Inc, Orradio & NAm Philips Co; design coordr, Cadre Industs & Habitat, Inc; designer for exhibs, US Info Agency; staff designer, Intrex, Inc; furniture designer, Archit Suppl Inc. Awards: Art Dirs Club Award, NY. Publ: Contribr, Indust Design, Interiors, Progressive Archit, Art News Ann, Arts & Archit & others. Mailing Add: 61 Cedar Rd Cresskill NJ 07626

MAYER, BENA FRANK
PAINTER
b Norfolk, Va, May 31, 00. Study: Cooper Union; Hunter Col; Art Students League; portrait painting with Cecelia Beaux; also with George Luks & Kenneth Miller. Work: Norfolk Mus Arts & Sci, Va; Whitney Mus Am Art & Huntington Hartford Collection, New York; in collections of Mrs Charles Love, Rochester, NY & Mrs David Levy, New York; plus others. Comn: Portraits, comn by Mrs Edward Rohr, Norfolk, 24, World Med Asn, New York, 59, Dr Nachtigall, New York, 59, Dr William M Hitzig, New York, 70 & Katharine Trenchard, New York, 70; plus -thers. Exhib: Carnegie Inst Int, 40; New York Soc Women Artists Ann, 47-; Nat Asn Women Artists Ann, 50-; Am Soc Contemp Artists Ann, 50-; New York Watercolor Soc, 53; one-person show, Simon's Rock Col, Great Barrington, Mass, 73. Awards: Silver & Bronze Medals for Drawing, Cooper Union Art Sch, 20's; Marcia Brady Tucker Prize, 51 & Lena Newcastle Prize, 59, Nat Asn Women Artists. Bibliog: Helen Worden (auth), The artist in her studio, 49 & Ann Geracimos (auth), An odessey for art, 61, New York World Telegram, 61; J Harvey Rosenthal (auth), Bena Frank Mayer, Travel in Fashion, spring 59. Mem: Am Soc Contemp Artists (chmn var comts, 50-, bd gov, 65-); Nat Asn Women Artists (const comt, 69-); New York Soc Women Artists (pres, 52 & 53); Artists Equity Asn; Artists Tech Res Inst (admin asst, 59-). Style & Technique: Free vigorous expressionalism using recognizable forms. Media: Oil, Watercolor. Mailing Add: 207 W 106th St New York NY 10025

MAYER, GRACE M
CURATOR, COLLECTOR
b New York, NY. Study: Pvt schs & tutors, US & abroad. Collections Arranged: Currier & Ives & the New York Scene, 39, Philip Hone's New York, 40, New York Between Two Wars, 44, Stranger in Manhattan, 50, Charles Dana Gibson's New York, 50 & Currier & Ives Printmakers to the American People, 57-58, Mus of City of New York; 70 Photographers Look at New York (with Edward Steichen), 57-58, The Sense of Abstraction, 60, Steichen, The Photographer, 61 & others, Mus Mod Art, New York. Pos: Cur, New York Iconography, Mus of City of New York, 31-59; spec asst to dir dept photog, Mus Mod Art, New York, 59-60, assoc cur dept photog, 61-62, cur dept photog, 62-68, cur, Edward Steichen Arch, Dept of Photog, Mus Mod Art, 68-72, vol cur, 72- Awards: SHA, Am Soc Picture Prof. Mem: Print Coun Am (treas); resident mem Cosmopolitan Club New York. Res: New York subjects; history of photography. Collection: Posters and lithographs and autograph letter signed Toulouse-Lautrec; photographs, especially those of Edward Steichen; books on photography. Publ: Auth articles in Mus of City of New York Bull, Mus Mod Art Bull & var photog mags; auth, Once Upon a City, Macmillan, 58. Mailing Add: Mus Mod Art 11 W 53rd St New York NY 10019

MAYER, RALPH
PAINTER, WRITER
b New York, NY, Aug 11, 95. Study: Rensselaer Polytech Inst (chem); Art Students League, with Hayley Lever. Exhib: Ann Fac Exhibs, Columbia Univ Sch Painting & Sculpture, 44-65; Portrait of America, Metrop Mus Art & Traveling Show, 45; Am Soc Contemp Artists Ann, 50-78; Ann Fac Exhibs, New Sch Social Res, 58-65; one-man retrospectives, Firehouse Gallery, Nassau Community Col, 67 & Simon's Rock Col, 73. Teaching: Instr, Columbia Univ, 44-64, New Sch Social Res, 58-65 & Silvermine Col, Conn, 61-62; lectr, Art Students League & others art schs in East & Midwest. Pos: Tech ed, Art Digest & Arts, 50-55; dir, Artists Tech Res Inst, 52-; tech ed, Am Artist, 62- Awards: Guggenheim Found Fel, 52; Grumbacher Award, Am Soc Contemp Artists, 66, Samuel Mann Award, 74 & Spec Award of Merit, 75; Am Art Award, Man of Year in Art, Nat Art Mat Trade Asn, 69. Mem: Am Soc Contemp Artists (first vpres); fel Int Inst Conserv Hist & Artistic Works; fel Am Inst Conserv. Style & Technique: Hard edge, but intensely poetic. Media: Oil. Publ: Auth, The Artists Handbook of Materials & Techniques, 40, 57 & 70; auth, The Painter's Craft, 48, 67 & 75; auth, A Dictionary of Art Terms & Techniques, 70; auth, Ralph Mayer Answers 101 Questions Most Frequently Asked by Artists, 77. Mailing Add: 207 W 106th St New York NY 10025

MAYER, ROSEMARY
SCULPTOR
b Ridgewood, NY, Feb 27, 43. Study: State Univ Iowa, Iowa City, AB, 64; Brooklyn Mus Art Sch, 65-67; Sch of Visual Arts, New York, 67-69. Work: Herbert Johnson Mus, Cornell Univ, Ithaca, NY; Allen Mem Art Mus, Oberlin Col, Ohio; Hartwick Col Collection, Oneonta, NY. Comn: Spell (temp outdoor work with weather balloons), Queens Coun on the

Arts & Greater Jamaica Develop Coun, 77. Exhib: Soft as Art, New York Cult Ctr, Queens Cult Ctr, New York & Staten Island Inst of Arts & Sci, New York, 73; Women Choose Women, New York Cult Ctr, 73; Options 73/30, Contemp Arts Ctr, Cincinnati, Ohio, 73; Discussions: Words/Works, Clocktower, New York, 74; one-person show, Whitney Mus of Am Art Resources Ctr, New York, 75; Space/Matter 77, Womens Interart Ctr, New York, 77. Teaching: Vis artist painting, Art Inst of Chicago, 74; vis artist painting & drawing, Hartwick Col, Oneonta, 76. Pos: Art writer & reviewer, Arts Mag, 71-73 & Art in Am, 74-75. Awards: Creative Artists Pub Serv Grant, NY State Coun on the Arts, 76-77. Bibliog: Alan Sondheim (auth), Rosemary Mayer, Arts Mag, 9/75; Lawrence Alloway (auth), Rosemary Mayer, Artforum, Summer 1976; Barbara Cavaliere (auth), Rosemary Mayer, Arts Mag, 1/77. Style & Technique: Plethora. Media: Dyed, transparent fabric; painted metal screening; watercolor and/or photographs with texts. Publ: Auth, Attitudes towards materials, content and the personal, 73 & Performance and experience, 73, Arts Mag; auth, Passages, Part 1 & 2, Tracks, Vol 2 (1 & 3), 76; contribr, Individuals, Dutton, 76; auth & illusr, Surroundings, Art-Rite Publ, 77. Mailing Add: 55 Leonard St New York NY 10013

MAYER, SUSAN MARTIN
EDUCATOR, PAINTER
b Atlanta, Ga, Oct 25, 31. Study: Am Univ, with Robert Gates; Univ NC, BA(art); Univ Del; Ariz State Univ, with June McFee, MA(art educ); Atelier Grande Chaumier, Paris, with Yves Brayer; Kans State Univ. Teaching: Coordr mus educ, Univ Tex Art Mus, 69-, lectr art, Univ Tex, Austin, 71- Mem: Nat Art Educ Asn; Tex Art Educ Asn. Style & Technique: Oil media in expressionist style. Media: Oil. Publ: Auth, Museum education, Facets, 72; auth, What about museums?, Art Educ, 74; co-auth, Docent Manual, with D Franklin, Univ Tex Art Mus Publ, 74; co-auth, Sumer: the Story of 1st Civilization, Univ Tex Children's Catalog to Sumer Exhib, with Denise Schmandt-Besserat, 75; co-auth (with Becky Reese), A Woman's Place, 77. Mailing Add: 4816 Rollingwood Dr Austin TX 78746

MAYERS, JOHN J
COLLECTOR
b New York, NY, Aug 16, 06. Study: Univ Fla; Sch Dent & Oral Surg, Columbia Univ, DDS & cert proficiency orthodont. Awards: Univ Alumni Medal Conspicuous Serv, Columbia Univ, 49. Collection: Oils, watercolors, drawings and sculpture, including works by Braque, Picasso, Matisse, Chagall, Laurens, Maillol, Renoir, Utrillo, Prendergast, Marin & Kuniyoshi. Mailing Add: 565 Del Oro Dr Ojai CA 93023

MAYES, STEVEN LEE
ART ADMINISTRATOR, PRINTMAKER
b Los Angeles, Calif, Nov 7, 39. Study: Wichita State Univ, BFA & BAE, 62, MFA, 65. Work: SDak Mem Art Ctr, Brookings; Sioux City Art Ctr, Iowa; Wichita Art Mus, Kans; Tamarind Inst, Univ NMex, Albuquerque; Univ NDak, Grand Forks. Exhib: 11th Ann Mid-Am Exhib, Nelson-Atkins Art Gallery, Kansas City, Mo, 61; 10th & 11th Kans Artists Ann, Wichita Art Mus, Kans, 64 & 65; 34th Nat Graphic Arts & Drawing Exhib, Wichita Art Asn, Kans, 69; 33rd Ann Fall Show, Sioux City Art Ctr, Iowa, 71; 13th Midwest Biennial, Joslyn Mus, Omaha, Nebr, 72; Fourth Nat Print & Drawing Exhib, Minot State Col, NDak, 74; 12th Ann Paper Works, Waterloo Munic Galleries, Iowa, 76. Collections Arranged: MFA & MA Alumnae Centennial Exhib, Wichita State Univ, 70; SDak Art Fac Invitational, Brookings, 70, 72, 74 & 76; Portraits and Self-Portraits, Civic Fine Arts Ctr, Sioux Falls, SD, 74; The Artist-Teacher, Sioux City Art Ctr, Iowa, 75. Teaching: Assoc prof printmaking & drawing, SDak State Univ, Brookings, 71-77; assoc prof printmaking & design & head art dept, WTex State Univ, Canyon, 77- Awards: Purchase Awards, Fifth NDak Ann, Univ NDak, 61, 33rd & 35th Ann Fall Show, Sioux City Art Ctr, Iowa, 71 & 73. Style & Technique: Non-objective, totemic images in prints and drawings. Media: Intaglio and silkscreen for prints; mixed media for drawing. Mailing Add: 1405 Creekmere Dr Canyon TX 79015

MAYHALL, DOROTHY A
ART ADMINISTRATOR
b Portland, Ore, May 31, 25. Study: Univ Iowa, BFA & MFA; Ecole des Beaux Arts, Paris, Fulbright scholar. Collections Arranged: Highlights of the Season, Aldrich Mus, 65-71; John G Powers Collection, 66; Selections from the Collection of Susan Morse Hilles, 67; Cool Art, 67; Selections from the Collection of Hanford Yang, 68; Young Artists from the Collection of Charles Cowles, 69; Lyrical Abstraction, 70; Aldrich Fund Acquisitions for the Museum of Modern Art, 1959-1969, 71; Painting & Sculpture 1972; Outdoor Sculptors Indoors, 72; The Emerging Real, 73; Sculpture in the Fields, summers 73-75; Limited Editions: Dated, Numbered, Signed, 75. Pos: Exec secy, Jr Coun, Mus Mod Art, New York, 61-65; dir, Aldrich Mus Contemp Art, Ridgefield, Conn, 65-71; dir, Storm King Art Ctr, Mountainville, NY, 71-75. Mailing Add: 12 Marshall Dr E Newburgh NY 12550

MAYHEW, EDGAR DE NOAILLES
EDUCATOR, MUSEUM DIRECTOR
b Newark, NJ, Oct 1, 13. Study: Amherst Col, BA, 35; Yale Univ, MA, 39; Johns Hopkins Univ, Carnegie fel, 39-41, PhD, 41. Collections Arranged: Contents of Lyman Allyn Mus, check list published. Teaching: Instr art hist, Wellesley Col, Mass, 44-45; prof art hist, Conn Col, New London, 45- Pos: Dir, Lyman Allyn Mus, New London, 50- Awards: Am Philos Soc Grant for Res, 68. Mem: New London Co Hist Soc (bd mem, 60-); Conn Antiqn & Landmarks Soc (furnishings chmn, 68-); Conn Comn Arts (chmn, 71); plus many hist soc & preserv groups. Res: Documentary history of the American interior. Collection: Approximately one hundred Old Masters drawings. Publ: Co-auth, The Book of the Courtier, 58; auth, Sketches by Thornhill in the Victoria & Albert Museum, 67. Mailing Add: 613 Williams St New London CT 06320

MAYHEW, ELZA
SCULPTOR
b Victoria, BC. Study: Univ BC, Can, BA; Univ Ore, MFA; also with Jan Zach, Victoria, BC. Work: Univ Victoria; Art Gallery Gtr Victoria; Nat Gallery Can, Ottawa; Simon Fraser Univ, Vancouver; Meditation Ctr, Expo, Montreal. Comn: Bronze column, Victoria Arch & Mus, BC, 67; Coast Spirit (bronze), Univ Victoria, 67; bronze mural, Bank of Can Lobby, Vancouver, 68; Concordia (bronze column), Brock Univ, Ont, 68; Column of the Sea, Confederation Ctr, Charlottetown, PEI, 73. Exhib: Outdoor Sculpture, Quebec, 60; Contemporary Sculpture Show, Ottawa, 62; Canadian Pavilion, Venice Biennale, 64; Sculpture Today, Dorothy Cameron Gallery, Toronto, 65; Int Trade Fair, Tokyo, 65. Pos: Bd dirs, Nat Sculpture Ctr, Univ Kans, 68-; BC Govt Comt for Art, 74. Awards: Sir Otto Beit Medal, Royal Soc Brit Sculptors, 62; Purchase Award, BC Centennial Sculpture Exhib, 67. Bibliog: Tony Emery (auth), Elza Mayhew, Arts Can, Vol XX, No 4; Robin Skelton (auth), A language for humanity, 4/71 & Karl Soreitz (auth), Making of the Column of the Sea, 72, Malahat Rev, Univ Victoria Quart. Mem: Sculptors Soc Can, BC; Royal Can Acad Arts. Style & Technique: Bronze casting; architectural style with human reference, tending to classical. Mailing Add: 330 St Lawrence St Victoria BC V8Y 1Y4 Can

MAYHEW, RICHARD
PAINTER, ILLUSTRATOR
b Amityville, NY, Apr 3, 24. Study: Brooklyn Mus Art Sch, with Edwin Dickinson & Reuben Tam, 48. Collection: Whitney Mus Am Art; Olsen Found; Brooklyn Mus; Mus Mod Art; Nat Acad Design; also in pvt collections. Exhib: Butler Art Inst, Youngstown, Ohio, 61; Carnegie Inst, 61; Brooklyn Mus, 61; Whitney Mus Am Art Ann; Univ Ill, 63; Midtown Galleries, New York, 74; plus others. Teaching: Instr art, Brooklyn Mus Art Sch & Art Students League; instr, Smith Col, 69-70; instr, Hunter Col. Awards: Tiffany Found Fel, 63; Am Acad Arts & Lett Grant, 65; Benjamin Altman Award, Nat Acad Design, 70; plus others. Mem: Nat Acad Design, Macdowell Colony Asn. Dealer: Midtown Galleries 11 E 57th St New York NY 10022. Mailing Add: 541 S Mountain Rd New City NY 10956

MAYNARD, VALERIE
SCULPTOR, LECTURER
b New York, NY, Aug 22, 37. Study: Goddard Col. Work: Johnson Publ, Chicago; Riksutstallningar, Stockholm, Sweden; Arnot Mus, Elmira, NY; Nat Lawyers Guild, New York; IBM Corp, White Plains, NY. Comn: Ceramic mural (with Bennington Potters, Vt & Archit Renewal Comt Harlem, Inc, New York), comn by J P Resnick & Son, 75; monument for Harlem Park Plaza, A Phillip Randolph Park, New York, 75. Exhib: Millenium, Philadelphia Mus Art, 73; Herbert F Johnson Mus, Cornell Univ, 74; Riksutstallningar, Stockholm, 75; Sojourn Gallery 1199, New York, 75; Arnot Mus, 75. Teaching: Printmaker in residence, Studio Mus, 69-74; lectr sculpture, Howard Univ, 74-75. Awards: CAPS Grants, NY Coun Arts, 72 & 74. Bibliog: Valerie Maynard Artists, WNEW Black News, 3/73; Monica Freeman (auth), Valerie, Nafasi Film Prod, 75; Valerie Maynard Konstar in Harlem, Nat Film Co, Stockholm, 75. Mem: Nat Conf Artist. Style & Technique: Social expressionist. Media: Sculpture, Graphics. Mailing Add: 463 West St Apt A512 New York NY 10014

MAYNARD, WILLIAM
PAINTER, EDUCATOR
b Brookline, Mass, Dec 31, 21. Study: Mass Col Art; Sch Mus Fine Arts, Boston, dipl, 50. Work: Boston Mus Fine Arts; Springfield Mus Fine Arts, Mass; Fairleigh Dickinson Univ; Fitchburg Mus Fine Arts; Tufts Univ. Exhib: Shore Studio Galleries, Charles Childs Gallery & Vose Gallery, Boston; De Cordova Mus, Lincoln, Mass; Busche Reisinger Mus, Cambridge, Mass. Teaching: Instr drawing & painting, Sch Mus Fine Arts, 60-67; chmn dept fine arts, New Eng Sch Art & Design, 74- Mem: Boston Watercolor Soc; Provincetown Art Asn; Copley Soc; Brookline Soc Artists. Style & Technique: Cityscape; seascape; people in their environment. Media: Watercolor, Acrylic. Mailing Add: 223 Freeman St Brookline MA 02146

MAYOR, ALPHEUS HYATT
ART HISTORIAN, WRITER
b Gloucester, Mass, June 28, 01. Study: Princeton Univ, BA(with honors mod lang), 22; Christ Church, Oxford Univ, BLitt, Rhodes scholar, 27-28; Am Sch Classical Studies, Athens, 26-27. Collections Arranged: Print exhibs, Metrop Mus Art, 34 yrs. Teaching: Lectr, Sch Am Lab Theatre, New York, 27-31; instr art hist, Vassar Col, 22-23; adj prof mus work, NY Univ, 69- Pos: From asst to cur prints, Metrop Mus Art, 32-66, cur emer, 66- Awards: Boston Mus Award, 71. Mem: Grolier Club; Century Asn; Hispanic Soc Am (pres, 55-). Res: Prints and the graphic arts. Publ: Auth, Giovanni Battista Piranesi, 52; auth, Prints & People, 71; auth, Popular Prints of the Americas, 73; auth, Goya Drawings, 74; auth, American Art in the Century Association, 76. Mailing Add: 51 E 97th St New York NY 10029

MAYORGA, GABRIEL HUMBERTO
PAINTER, SCULPTOR
b Colombia, SAm, Mar 24, 11; US citizen. Study: Nat Acad Design, painting with Leon Kroll & Ivan Olinsky, etching with Aerobach-Levi & sculpture with Robert Aikin; Art Students League, with Brackman; Grand Cent Art Sch, New York, with Harvey Dunn. Work: Inst Ingenieros, Bogota, Colombia, 37; Art Gallery of Barbizon-Plaza, New York, 55; West Point Mus, NY. Comn: Many painting & portrait comns, 55- Exhib: Inst Ingenieros, Bogota, Colombia, 37; Art Gallery of Barbizon Plaza, New York, 55; Mayorga Art Gallery, 60; Int Expos, Paris, 62; Int Art Show, New York, 70. Teaching: Instr painting & fashion, Pan-Am Art Sch, New York, 60-72. Pos: Art dir, Revista Estrellas, Bogota, 37-38 & Mannequins by Mayorga Inc, New York, 40-65; art dir-illusr, Revista Temas, 53-54. Bibliog: Morton Cooper (auth), How to be an artist & still eat, Art & Photog, 57 & Gabriel Mayorga, New York angry artist, Figure, 60; J Rothschild (auth), Artists create with plastics, By Gum, 70. Media: Oil, Watercolor; Epoxy Plastic, Polyester Plastic. Publ: Illusr, Revista Estrellas, 37-38; illusr, Theory & Practice of Fencing, 37; illusr, Popular Publ, 38; illusr, Revista Temas, 53-54; illusr, Don Mag. Mailing Add: Mayorga Art Gallery 331 W 11th St New York NY 10014

MAYS, VICTOR
ILLUSTRATOR
b New York, NY, July 2, 27. Study: Yale Univ, BA, 49. Work: De Grummond Collection of Children's Book Illus, Univ Southern Miss; Kerlan Collection, Univ Minn. Comn: Illus for children's bks, major US publ, 55- & Reader's Digest, 55- Exhib: Nat Oceans Week Exhib, Washington, DC, 78. Mem: Am Soc Marine Artists. Style & Technique: Realistic, reportorial. Media: Watercolor, Casein (illus); Watercolor & Carved/Painted Wood Panels (paintings). Publ: Auth & illusr, Fast Iron, 53, Action Starboard, 55, Dead Reckoning, 65 & illusr, Battle of Quebec, 65, Houghton Mifflin; illusr, Red Cloud, Sioux Warrior, Garrard Publ, 75. Dealer: Foot of Main Gallery Main St Essex CT 06426; Ragged Sailor Block Island RI 02807. Mailing Add: Box 207 Clinton CT 06413

MAYTHAM, THOMAS NORTHRUP
MUSEUM DIRECTOR, LECTURER
b Buffalo, NY, July 30, 31. Study: Williams Col, BA, 54; Yale Univ, MA, 56. Exhibitions Arranged: Ernst Ludwig Kirchner Retrospective (148 works), Seattle Art Mus, Pasadena Art Mus & Boston Mus, 68-69; Great American Paintings from the Boston & Metropolitan Museum (100 paintings, with catalog), Nat Gallery Art, City Art Mus St Louis & Seattle Art Mus, 70-71; also numerous smaller exhibs, some with publ catalogs. Teaching: Lectr, mus, clubs, groups & art asns, Boston & Seattle areas. Pos: Asst, Wadsworth Atheneum, summer 55, res asst, Prof Carroll L V Meeks, Yale Univ, summer 56; asst in dept paintings, Mus Fine Arts, Boston, 56-57; head dept paintings, Boston Mus, 57-67, asst cur paintings, 67; assoc dir, Seattle Art Mus, 67-74; juror, nat & regional exhibs; mem airport art adv comt, Port of Seattle; mem agency coun, United Arts Coun; dir, Denver Art Mus, 74- Mem: Am Fedn Art (trustee), 77. Am Asn Mus; Int Coun Mus. Publ: Auth articles in Boston Mus Bull, Antiques & Can Art; ed, American Painting in the Boston Museum (catalog), Vols I & II, 68; auth, TV Prog for Nat Educ TV, produced by Boston Mus. Mailing Add: Denver Art Mus 100 W 14th Ave Pkwy Denver CO 80204

MAZUR, MICHAEL
PAINTER, EDUCATOR
b New York, NY, Nov 2, 35. Study: Amherst Col, BA, 58, with Leonard Baskin; Yale Univ Sch Art & Archit, BFA, 59 & MFA, 61, with Gabor Peterdi & Bernard Chaet. Work: Mus Mod Art, New York; Boston Mus Fine Arts; Fogg Art Mus, Harvard Univ; Art Inst Chicago; Nat Collection Fine Arts, Smithsonian Inst & Libr Cong, Washington, DC. Comn: Painting of Wassaw & Ossabaw Islands, Dept of Interior Bicentennial Exhib, 75-76. Exhib: Painters & Sculptors as Printmakers, Mus Mod Art, 64; Nine American Printmakers, US Info Serv Agency Traveling Exhib in Europe, 64; Young Americans, Whitney Mus Am Art, 65; Two Painters on Two Aspects of Illusion, Finch Col Mus, 71; American Landscape for Bicentennial, Corcoran Gallery, 76. Teaching: Instr prints & drawing, RI Sch Design, 61-64; asst prof prints & drawing, Brandeis Univ, 65-76; vis artist, Yale Sch Art & Archit, 71 & Harvard Univ, 76. Pos: Adv art, Edna St Vincent Millay Found, Austerlitz, 75-; alumni bd, Yale Sch Art & Archit, 75-; bd mem, Mass Arts & Humanities Found. Awards: Louis Comfort Tiffany Grant, 62; Nat Inst Arts & Lett Award, 64; Guggenheim Fel, 65. Bibliog: J Canaday (auth), rev in New York Times, 65, 66 & 68; C Belz (auth), Mazur at ICA, Art Forum, 9/70. Mem: Boston Visual Artists Union; Philadelphia Print Club. Style & Technique: Figurative, expressionist-realist; drawings, prints, paintings, monotypes, some sculpture. Publ: Auth, Prints by M Mazur, Artist Proof, 70. Dealer: Harcus-Krakow Gallery 7 Newbury Boston MA 02116; Robert Miller, New York. Mailing Add: 5 Walnut Ave Cambridge MA 02140

MAZZOCCA, GUS (AUGUSTUS NICHOLAS MAZZOCCA)
PRINTMAKER, EDUCATOR
b Boston, Mass, Jan 2, 40. Study: Univ Conn, BA, 64, BFA, 65; RI Sch of Design MFA, 70. Work: Mus of Mod Art, Munich; City of Hartford Fine Arts Collection. Exhib: Parish Art Mus, Southampton, NY, 67; RI Col, Providence, 69; Mus of RI Sch of Design, Providence, 70; New Talent, New Eng, De Cordova Mus, Lincoln, Mass, 72; Conn Col, New London, 74. Collections Arranged: Information, 75 & Notations, 77, Univ Conn, Storrs. Teaching: Art teacher, Riverhead Cent Sch Dist, NY, 65-68; instr, RI Sch of Design, Providence, 70; assoc prof lithography & drawing, Univ Conn, Storrs, 70- Awards: Purchase Award, Hartford Fine Art Festival, Conn, 70; Conn Artists, Slater Mus, Norwich, 73. Mem: Graphic Arts Tech Found, Pittsburgh. Style & Technique: Abstract, figurative; expressionistic tradition. Media: Lithography, charcoal and pastel. Mailing Add: 333 Prospect St Willimantic CT 06226

MAZZONE, DOMENICO
SCULPTOR, PAINTER
b Rutigliano, Italy, May 16, 27. Work: Mus Foggia, Italy; monument in Rutigliano; monument in Barletta, Italy; bronze plaque in S Fara Temple, Bari, Italy; UN Bldg, New York. Exhib: Nat Exhib Marble, Carrara, Italy, 62; Nat Exhib, San Remo, Italy, 63; Int Exhib Metal, Gubbio, Italy, 65; Exhib Tree State, Silvermine Conn, 66; Ital Club Exhib, UN Bldg, 67. Awards: Silver Medal, Carrara Exhib, 62; Gold Medal, Exhib Int Viareggio, 72; Bronze Medal of Copernicus, 72. Bibliog: M Pescara (auth), Mazzone sculptor, Mario Pescara Enterprise, New York, 69; Dino Campini (auth), Arte Italiana, Soc Ed Nuova Torino, 71; J Passantino (auth), Mazzone, Passantino Ed, New York, 71. Style & Technique: Classic, modern. Mailing Add: 44 Lembeck Ave Jersey City NJ 07305

MCADOO, DONALD ELDRIDGE
PAINTER, PRINTMAKER
b Chicago, Ill, Feb 8, 29. Study: Self-taught. Work: Va Mus Fine Arts; Columbia Mus Art, SC; Ga Mus Art; Mint Mus Art, NC; Springfield Mus Art, Mo; plus others. Exhib: A Brush with Realism, one-man touring exhib, nine major southeastern mus, 72-73; 22nd Am Drawing Biennial, Chrysler Mus, 67; Realists Invitational, Southeastern Ctr Contemp Art, NC, 69-72; Watercolor USA, Springfield Mus, 71 & 72; High Mus Art, 71. Teaching: Painting safaris & lectures to art groups. Awards: Purchase Award, 31st Nat Watercolor Exhib, Birmingham Mus, 70; Purchase Award, Nat Watercolor Exhib, La, 70; Purchase Award, Rogers Mus, Miss, 71. Bibliog: Reviews James Bowne, Leader Call, 2/17/73, Marshall L Reed, 4/11/73 & Julia Jordan, Eve Telegram, 2/3/73; plus others. Mem: Mem Guild, High Mus Art; Watercolor Soc La & Ala; Southeastern Ctr Contemp Art. Style & Technique: Ranges from impressionistic realism to Trompe l'Oeil. Media: Watercolor, Acrylic Tempera; Woodcut. Publ: Co-auth, Reflections, Island Publ House, 76. Dealer: Raymond J Hage 2105 Wiltshire Blvd Huntington WV 25701. Mailing Add: 5070 Sunset Trail Marietta GA 30067

MCALLISTER-KELLY
PAINTER
b Buenos Aires, Arg. Study: Munic Sch Art, Buenos Aires; Beaux Art Asn, Buenos Aires. Work: Fla State Supreme Court, Tallahassee; Clairol Collection, USA. Exhib: Brandeis Univ Pan Am Union for Latin Am Art & Contemp Painting, Washington, DC, 65; Hortt Mem Exhib, Mus Art, Ft Lauderdale, Fla, 65-66 & 69-71; Nat Sch Plastic Arts, Nat Comt Cult & Fine Arts, Guatemala City, Guatemala, 68; Miami Mus Mod Art, 71-73; Gloria Luria Gallery, Miami, 71. Awards: Atwater Kent Award, Soc Four Arts, Palm Beach, Fla, 69; Hon Mention, Hortt Mem Exhib, Ft Lauderdale Mus Art, 71; 1st Ann Pan Am Art Exhib, Miami, 69-70. Style & Technique: Non-objective, abstract expressionist painting, somber tone, loose design. Media: Acrylic. Mailing Add: 1912 SW 17th Ave Apt 13 Miami FL 33145

MCANINCH, BETH
PAINTER
b Corn, Okla, Nov 23, 18. Study: Southwestern State Col, grad; also with Jack Valle, Millard Sheets, Edgar Whitney, John Pike & others. Work: Okla Art Ctr, Okla Christian Col, Liberty Nat Bank & Westinghouse Corp, Oklahoma City; Okla Arts Coun. Exhib: Okla Nat Printmakers & Watercolor Show, 61; Southwestern Watercolor Soc Regional & Open, Dallas, Tex, 67, 69 & 71; 8 State Exhib Painting & Sculpture Ann, Okla Art Ctr, 71; Watercolor USA, Springfield, Mo, 72; Okla Artists Ann, Philbrook, Tulsa, Okla, 61-72. Teaching: Instr painting & drawing, pvt classes, 60-70; instr painting & drawing, Okla Sci & Art Found, 62-66. Awards: Southwestern Watercolor Soc Award, 67; First Painting Award, 7th Ann Artists Salon, Okla Mus Art, 68; First Award, 7th Ann Southwestern Watercolor Soc, 71. Bibliog: Numerous articles in newspapers. Mem: Oklahoma City Arts Coun Bd; Southwestern Watercolor Soc. Media: Watercolor, Pencil. Dealer: Norman Wilks Interiors 3839 NW 63rd St Oklahoma City OK 73116; Okla Art Ctr 3113 General Pershing Oklahoma City OK 73107. Mailing Add: 1409 Dorchester Dr Oklahoma City OK 73114

MCBRIDE, JAMES JOSEPH
PAINTER, WATERCOLORIST
b Ft Wayne, Ind, May 19, 23. Study: Ft Wayne Art Inst; Cape Cod Sch Art, Provincetown, Mass; Pa Acad Fine Art, Philadelphia; Barnes Found Mod Art, Merion, Pa. Work: Ft Wayne Art Inst; Ind Tri Kappa Collection, Nashville; Wabash Col. Comn: Murals, Key Largo Motel, Howards Gift Shop, Olympic Club & St Joseph Hosp, Ft Wayne. Exhib: Hoosier Salon, Indianapolis, Ind, 50- & one-man show, 69; Watercolor USA, Springfield, Mo, 62-72; Xmas Art Nat, Marymount Col, 67; Nat Soc Painters in Casein & Acrylic, New York, 70 & 74; Am Watercolor Soc, New York, 72 & 75; San Diego Watercolor Show, 77; Midwest Watercolor Soc Show, 77; Rocky Mt Nat Watermedia Exhib, 77; Blue Grass Exhib, Louisville, Ky, 77. Teaching: Instr watercolor, Ft Wayne Art Inst, 64-65; instr watercolor, St Francis Col (Ind), 69-70; instr creative watercolor, Ind Univ-Purdue Univ, Ft Wayne, 71- Pos: Art dir, WKVG TV, Ft Wayne, 53-59; art dir, Our Sunday Visitor, Huntington, Ind, 59-69; pres, Jim McBride Gallery, Inc, Ft Wayne, 69- Awards: Emily Francis Award, Nat Soc Painters Casein & Acrylic, New York; Ind Artists Exhib Award, 76; Best of Show, Van Wert, Ohio, 77; plus others. Mem: Hoosier Salon Asn; Ind Artists Club; Ft Wayne Artists Guild; Nat Soc Painters Casein & Acrylic. Style & Technique: Semi-abstract; wet and wet. Media: Watercolor. Publ: Illusr, Family Digest, 69; illusr, Schema XIII, 71. Mailing Add: 6220 Rolling Hills Dr Ft Wayne IN 46804

MCBRYDE, SARAH ELVA
PAINTER, PRINTMAKER
b Columbus, Ohio, July 2, 42. Study: Syracuse Univ, 60; Washington Univ, St Louis, Mo, BFA, 64, fel, spec study with Fred Becker & Arthur Osver, 63-64; Washington Univ scholar, Skowhegan Sch Painting & Sculpture, 64; Am Univ, Washington, DC, MFA, 76. Work: Many pvt collections. Comn: Mural on Hotel, San Blas Islands, Panama, Cent Am, 67; paintings, Mrs & Mrs Harry B Willis, Panama City, Cent Am, 67 & Mrs Hestlene Martin, Washington, DC, 77; plus others. Exhib: One-person shows, Panamanian-Am Inst, Panama, 67, Urdongs, Washington, DC, 71, Decatur House of the Nat Trust for Hist Preserv, Washington, DC, 72, Greater Washington Art Show, 72 & Batik Exhib, Martin Luther King Mem Libr, 77. Pos: Gallery asst, Stuttman Art Gallery, Washington, DC, 66; art libr, Martin Luther King Mem Libr, 68- Bibliog: Paul Richard, Art Review, Washington Post, 10/77. Mem: Artists Equity; Art Libr Soc NAm; Am Soc Picture Prof. Style & Technique: Acrylic paintings, sharp edge interiors and architecture with emphasis on light and shadow; pastels, printmaking; Batik; photography. Media: Egg Tempera, Acrylic, Watercolor; Woodcut, Etching. Publ: Illusr (covers), Nat Educ Asn Publ, Sci & Children's Mag, 65-66; illusr (cover), Weekender Mag, Washington Star Newspaper, 72-74. Mailing Add: 2647 41st St NW 3 Washington DC 20007

MCCABE, CYNTHIA JAFFEE
CURATOR, ART HISTORIAN
b New York, NY, Feb 8, 43. Study: Cornell Univ, BA, 63; Columbia Univ, MA, 67. Collections Arranged: Sculptors and Their Drawings: Selections from the Hirshhorn Museum Collection (with catalog), Lyndon B Johnson Libr, Austin, 74; The Golden Door: Artist-Immigrants of America, 1876-1976 (auth, catalogue), Hirshhorn Mus & Sculpture Garden, 76; Modern Sculptors & Their Drawings: Selected Works From the Hirshhorn Museum & Sculpture Garden, Greenville Mus Art & Tour, SC, 77-78. Teaching: Asst prof lectr, Am civilization & art, George Washington Univ, Washington, DC, 75-76. Pos: Art historian, Mus Mod Art, New York, Nakian Exhib, 66; art historian, Jewish Mus, New York, 66; art historian, NY State Coun Arts, 67; cur painting & sculpture, Hirshhorn Mus & Sculpture Garden, 67-76, cur exhib, 76- Mem: Am Asn Mus (cur comt; vchmn, 76-77, chmn, 77-); Col Art Asn Am; Int Coun Mus; Northeast Mus Conf (prog comt, 75-77); Women's Caucus for Art (Nat Adv Bd, 74-76). Res: 20th century American painting and sculpture; history of America's immigrant artists. Publ: Contribr, The Lower East Side: Portal to American Life (1870-1924), 66; contribr, Collection Mr & Mrs David Lloyd Kreeger, 70; contribr, The Hirshhorn Mus and Sculpture Garden, 74; auth (catalogue), Henry Moore at the Hirshhorn Museum & Sculpture Garden, 74. Mailing Add: Hirshhorn Mus & Sculpture Garden Eighth & Independence SW Washington DC 20560

MCCABE, LAWRENCE
SCULPTOR
b Jersey City, NJ, Nov 24, 24. Study: Newark Sch Fine & Indust Art, dipl sculpture, 52. Work: Hirshhorn Mus & Sculpture Garden, Smithsonian Inst; Temple Sholom, Greenwich, Conn. Exhib: Lawrence McCabe: Sculpture, Jacobs Ladder Gallery, Washington, DC, 74; 2nd & 3rd Ann Washington Area Outdoor Sculpture Exhib, Textile Mus, Washington, DC, 74 & 75; Invitational Sculpture Competition, Soc Four Arts, Palm Beach, Fla & New York Cult Ctr, 74-75. Pos: Chief asst to Reuben Nakian, 51-71. Bibliog: Paul Richard (auth), Museum Quality Show, Washington Post, 5/15/74; Ben Forgey (auth), In the galleries, Washington Eve Star-News, 5/13/74; Val Lewton (auth), Lawrence McCabe, DC Gazette, 6/74. Mem: Col Art Asn Am; Artists Equity Asn. Style & Technique: Constructivist attitude; linear involvement in drawing and sculpture. Media: Aluminum, Steel, Wood. Mailing Add: 3106 Dogwood St NW Washington DC 20015

MCCABE, MAUREEN M
COLLAGE ARTIST
Study: RI Sch Design, Providence, BFA, 69; Cranbrook Acad Art, Bloomfield Hills, Mich, MFA, 71. Work: RI Sch Design; Wadsworth Atheneum, Hartford, Conn; Kansas City Art Inst, Mo; Samuel Greenbaum & Kogod Collection, Washington, DC. Exhib: One-person shows, State Univ NY Col, Oneonta, 70, Jorgensen Gallery, Univ Conn, Storrs, 72, Arts & Crafts Ctr, Pittsburgh, Pa, 76; Selected Conn Artists, Wadsworth Atheneum, 73; Object as Poet Show, Renwick Gallery, Smithsonian Inst, Washington, DC, 77 & Mus Contemp Crafts, New York, 77; 14 Women Artists, NY Univ Visual Artists Coalition, 77. Teaching: Asst prof studio art, Conn Col, New London, 71- Awards: Yaddo, Saratoga Springs, NY, summer 75. Style & Technique: Collage with mixed-media. Dealer: Allan Stone Gallery 48 E 86th St New York NY 10028; Phyllis Kind Gallery 226 E Ontario Chicago IL 60611. Mailing Add: 50 Old Norwich Rd Quaker Hill CT 06375

MCCAFFERTY, JAY DAVID
VIDEO ARTIST
b San Pedro, Calif, Feb 21, 48. Study: Los Angeles State Col, BA; Univ Calif, Irvine, MFA. Work: Los Angeles Co Mus Art, Calif; Long Beach Mus Art. Exhib: One-man shows, Purcell Gallery, Chapman Col, 71 & Long Beach Mus Art, 74; Festival of Contemporary Arts, Allen Art Mus, Oberlin Col, 73; Southland Video Anthology Traveling Show, Long Beach Mus Art, 75. Teaching: Vis lectr art, World Campus Afloat, Chapman Col, 74. Awards: New Talent Award, Los Angeles Co Mus Art, 74; Nat Endowment for the Arts Fel, 76. Bibliog: Melinda Wortz (auth), Jay McCafferty, 4/74 & De Lap & McCafferty, 2/75, Artweek; Joseph Youth (auth), Los Angeles, Art Int, 1/75; Sandy Ballatore, Los Angeles Review, Art in Am, 3-4/76. Style & Technique: Solar burns in various materials using a magnifying glass, video tape, and photographs using 35mm camera. Dealer: Cirrus 708 N Manhattan Pl Los Angeles CA 90038; Galerie Krebs Bern Munstergasse 43 Bern Switzerland. Mailing Add: 383 W Sixth St San Pedro CA 90731

MCCALL, ANTHONY
FILM MAKER, CONCEPTUAL ARTIST
b London, Eng, Apr 14, 46. Study: Whitgift Sch, Croydon, Eng, 56-64; Ravensbourne Col of Art & Design Bromley, Kent, Eng, 64-68, BA(first class hons), 68. Work: Royal Belgium Film Arch, Brussels; Arts Coun of Gt Brit, London; Mus of Mod Art, New York. Exhib: Survey of the Avant Garde in Britain, Gallery House, London, 72; Biennale de Paris, Musee d'Art Moderne, Paris, 73 & 75, Millennium Film Workshop, New York, 74; Work: Words,

The Clocktower, New York, 74; New Media I, Konsthall, Malmo, Sweden, 75; Festival of Expanded Cinema, Inst of Contemp Arts, London, 76; Arte Inglese Oggi 1960-76, Palazzo Reale, Milan, 76; Biennale di Venezia, Italy, 76; Int Forum on Avant-Garde Film, Edinburgh, Scotland, 76; Documenta, Kassel, Ger, 77; Film as Film, 1910 to the Present, Kunstverein, Cologne, 78; one-man shows, Mus of Mod Art, Oxford, Eng, 74, Royal Col of Art Gallery, London, 74, Carnegie Inst, Pittsburgh, 75, London Filmmakers Co-operative Cinema, 75, Mus of Mod Art, New York, 76, Musee d'Art Moderne, Paris, 76, Kunstverein, Cologne, 76. Teaching: Instr, London Col of Printing, 70-71; vis lectr avant-garde film theory, New York Univ Dept of Cinema Studies, 77. Pos: Founder-mem, Int Local Group, New York, 76. Awards: Visual Art Fel, 74 & Film Award, 77, Nat Endowment for the Arts, Washington, DC, Marie-Josi Prize 5th Int Experimental Competition, Knokke, Belg, 75; Creative Artists Prog Serv Grant, New York State Coun on the Arts, 76. Bibliog: Malcolm Legrice (auth), Vision, 2/74 & Deke Dusinberre (auth), Expanding Cinema, 11/75, Studio Int, London; Annette Michelson & P Adams Sitney (auth), A on Knokke and the Independent Filmmaker, Artforum, New York, 5/75; Birgit Hein (auth), Catalog of Film as Film, 1910 to the Present, Kunstverein, Cologne, 77. Style & Technique: Contingent on problem. Media: Film; Photography; Performance. Publ: Auth, Line Describing a Cone (catalog), In: 5th Experimental Film Competition, Knokke, Belg, 74; auth, Longfilm for Ambient Light, In: Studio Int, London, 11-12/75; auth, Film as a Connective Catalyst, In: Parachute 5, Montreal, summer 76; auth, Formalist Cinema and Politics, In: Performing Arts Journal, New York, Vol 1, No 3, 77; auth, Sixteen Working Statements, In: Millennium Film Journal, Vol 1, No 2, New York, 78. Mailing Add: 11 Jay St New York NY 10013

MCCALL, ROBERT THEODORE
PAINTER, ILLUSTRATOR
b Columbus, Ohio, Dec 23, 19. Study: Scholar, Columbus Fine Art Sch, Ohio, two yrs. Work: Phoenix Art Mus, Ariz; Art Mus Univ NMex, Albuquerque; Collection of US Air Force, Washington, DC. Comn: Four Paintings for the film 2001 A Space Odyssey, MGM Film Corp, now in Nat Air & Space Mus, Washington, 68; five commemorative stamps, US Postal Serv, 72-76; The Space Mural, A Cosmic View (2100 sq ft, in the Lobby), Smithsonian Inst for the Nat Air & Space Mus, Washington, DC, 76; Three Decades of Achievement (10 ft x 20 ft mural in visitors ctr), Nat Air & Space Admin, Hugh L Dryden Flight Res Ctr, Edwards, Calif, 77. Exhib: Eyewitness to Space, Nat Gallery Art, Washington, DC, 64; Am Watercolor Soc, New York, 65; Space Art, Nat Gallery Art, Washington, DC, 70; Air & Space, Grand Cent Art Galleries, New York, 78; one-man show, Space Artist Robert McCall, Phoenix Art Mus, Ariz, 71. Bibliog: Pat Dryfus (auth), Space Artist Robert McCall, Am Artist, 70; Joe Stacy (auth), Worlds Premier Aerospace Artist, Ariz Highways Mag, 73. Mem: Soc Illusr, New York (Air Force chmn, 63-64, secy, 66). Style & Technique: Realism. Media: (Painting) Oil and acrylic; (illustration) watercolor and ink. Publ: Illusr many articles & covers for Life, Saturday Evening Post, Nat Geographic Mag, Popular Sci, Newsweek, Readers Digest, Colliers & others, 56-75; co-auth (with Isaac Asimov), Our World in Space, NY Graphic Soc, 74. Mailing Add: 4816 Moonlight Way Paradise Valley AZ 85253

MCCALLUM, CORRIE (MRS WILLIAM HALSEY)
PAINTER, PRINTMAKER
b Sumter, SC, Mar 14, 14. Study: Univ SC, cert fine arts, 36; Boston Mus Sch, with Karl Zerbe. Work: La State Univ, Baton Rouge; SC Arts Comn, State Collection; Mint Mus Art, Charlotte, NC; Columbia Mus Arts, SC; Ford Motor Co. Exhib: Dixie Ann, Montgomery Mus, Ala, 68; 1st South Carolina State Invitational, Columbia Mus Art, 69; Contemporary Artists of South Carolina, Greenvile Mus, Columbia Mus Art, Gibbes Art Gallery & Florence Mus, 70; one-man shows, Kunstsalon Wolfsberg, Zurich, Switz, 69 & Concourse Gallery, State St Bank, Boston, Mass, 71. Teaching: Pvt instr, until 60; cur art educ for Charleston Co, Gibbes Art Gallery, 60-69; instr painting & drawing, Newbery Col (SC), 69-71; instr painting, drawing & printmaking, Col Charleston, 71- Awards: Purchase Prize for Drawing, Mint Mus Graphics Ann, 64; Painting Award, Guild SC Artists Ann, 65; Scientific Educ Found Grant for Travel & Study Around the World, 68. Bibliog: J A Morris, Jr (auth), Contempoary Artists of South Carolina, Greenville Co Mus Art, 70. Mem: Guild SC Artists (pres, 61); Col Art Asn Am; Copley Soc, Boston. Style & Technique: Expressionist, more abstracted lithography; strong composition, sculptural and decorative figures and landscape. Publ: Illusr, Dutch Fork Farm Boy, & 50 Years Along the Way, 68, Univ SC; co-auth, A Travel Sketchbook, R L Byran Co, 71. Dealer: Kunstsalon Wolfsberg Bederstrasse 109 Zurich Switzerland. Mailing Add: 38 State St Charleston SC 29401

MCCANN, CECILE NELKEN
ART EDITOR, ART CRITIC
b New Orleans, La. Study: Vassar Col; Tulane Univ; San Jose State Univ, Calif, BA & MA; Univ Calif, Berkeley; also with Herbert Sanders, Robert Fritz, Shoji Hamada & Peter Voulkos. Work: City of San Francisco; San Jose City Col; San Jose State Univ; Mills Col, Oakland; State of Calif, Sacramento. Exhib: Everson Mus Art, Syracuse, 62 & 64; one-woman shows, Crocker Gallery, Sacrmento, 65 & Calif Col Arts & Crafts, Oakland, 66; Calif Design, Pasadena Mus Art, 65 & 68; Wichita Design Craftsmen, Kans, 66. Pos: Ed & publ, Artweek, Oakland, 69-; consult, Nat Endowment Arts, 74-76. Awards: Critic's Grant, Nat Endowment Arts, 75. Mem: Col Art Asn; Am Crafts Coun. Publ: Contribr, Craft Horizons, 71 & 73; contribr, William Wiley, Opus, France, 73; auth, Ken Friedman (catalog essay), Yugoslavia, 74. Mailing Add: 1305 Franklin St Oakland CA 94612

MCCANNEL, MRS MALCOLM A
COLLECTOR
b Minneapolis, Minn, Nov 20, 15. Study: Smith Col, BA; Minneapolis Sch Art. Pos: Bd mem, Walker Art Ctr, Minneapolis. Collection: Contemporary American sculpture and painting. Mailing Add: 1520 Waverly Pl Minneapolis MN 55403

MCCART, BETTY MOSES
See Moses, Betty

MCCARTHY, DENIS
PAINTER
b New York, NY, Feb 21, 35. Study: Cooper Union, 59-64; Yale Univ, BFA & MFA, 64-66. Work: Work in pvt collections only. Exhib: Group Exhib, Stable Gallery, New York, 69, one-man show, 70; Painting Ann, Whitney Mus Am Art, New York, 70, Biennial Exhib, 73; Group Exhib, O K Harris, New York, 72; Spring Exhib, Aldrich Mus, Ridgefield, Conn, 73; Group Exhib, Michael Wyman Gallery, Chicago, 74; Univ Maine, Portland, 75; Automation House, New York, 76; Hundred Acres Gallery, New York, 77; New York Acad Sci, 78. Teaching: Instr drawing, Sch Visual Arts, New York, 67-72; instr painting & printmaking, Hunter Col, 71-; instr drawing, NY Univ, 76- Mailing Add: 147 Spring St New York NY 10012

MCCARTHY, DORIS JEAN
PAINTER, INSTRUCTOR
b Calgary, Alta, July 7, 10. Study: Ont Col Art, 30; Cent Sch Arts & Crafts, London, Eng, with John Farleigh & John Skeaping. Work: Art Gallery Ont, Toronto; London Art Gallery, Ont; Imp Oil Collection; Ont Centennial Collection; Hudson Bay Oil. Comn: Mural, Toronto Pub Libr, 33; mem bk, Malvern Col, Toronto, 48; creche figures, Church of St Aldan, Toronto, 48; fabric banner Trinity, St James Cathedral, Toronto, 55. Exhib: Ont Soc Artists Ann, 33-; Royal Can Acad Ann, 34-; Can Soc Painters Watercolor, 38-; Can Nat Exhib, 48; Ont Centennial Art Exhib, 67; plus many others. Teaching: Instr drawing, painting & hist art, Central Tech Sch Toronto, 33-, asst head, 68-72. Mem: Royal Can Acad; Ont Soc Artists (pres, 65-68); Can Soc Painters in Watercolor (pres, 56-57); Fedn Can Artists (secy); Prof Artists Can (chmn, 67-69). Style & Technique: Landscapes; realism and poetic abstraction; specializing in high arctic. Media: Oil, Watercolor. Mailing Add: 1 Meadowcliff Dr Scarborough ON M1M 2X8 Can

MCCARTHY, FRANK C
PAINTER
b New York, NY, 1924. Study: Art Students League; Pratt Inst; also with George Bridgeman & Reginald Marsh. Pos: Free-lance artist working on mag illus & movie posters, 48- Style & Technique: Casein underpainting and glazing in oil on a gesso covered masonite panel. Media: Mixed Media, Oil. Publ: Illusr, Am Weekly; illusr paperback covers & mag including, Colliers, Am Mag, Cosmopolitan, Redbook, Argosy, True & Readers Digest. Mailing Add: c/o Phoenix Art Mus 1625 N Central Phoenix AZ 85004

MCCARTIN, WILLIAM FRANCIS
PAINTER
b New York, NY, Dec 9, 05. Study: Art Students League, with Richard Lahey, five yrs; New Sch Social Res, one yr. Exhib: Gallery Contemp Arts, Pittsburgh; Maine Coast Artists, Rockport, 70; 7 from Monhegan, Phillips Exeter Acad, NH, 70; Joseph De Meers Ltd, Hilton Head, SC, 71; one-man show, Beaumont Art Mus, Tex, 71; plus other group & one-man shows. Awards: Tiffany Found Grant, 25; John Newman Medal, Casein Soc, 60; Nat Endowment for the Arts Fel, 77. Media: Acrylic. Dealer: Alonzo Gallery 30 W 57th St New York NY 10021. Mailing Add: 381 Bleeker St New York NY 10014

MCCARTY, LORRAINE CHAMBERS
PAINTER, INSTRUCTOR
b Detroit, Mich, Aug 17, 20. Study: Detroit Art Acad, Wayne State Univ, with G Alden Smith; Meinzinger Art Acad; Stephens Col, with Albert Christ-Janer, also with Glen Michaels, Emil Weddidge, Clifford B West. Work: Butler Mus Am Art, Youngstown, Ohio; Northern Ill Univ De Kalb; Beech Aircraft Air Mus, Wichita, Kans; Northwood Inst, Midland, Mich; plus others. Comn: Painting, Bohn Copper & Brass, Detroit; painting, R L Polk Co Int Hq, Detroit, 73; painting, Truss Wall Int Hq, Troy, Mich, 74; mural, Jud Pilots, New York, 75; mural, Int Women's Air & Space Mus, Dayton, Ohio, 77. Exhib: Butler Mus Am Art Ann, 67 & 70-74; Detroit Inst Art Ann, 69; Women 71, De Kalb; Flint Inst Arts Ann, Mich, 74; Womanart, Saginaw Mus Arts, Mich, 74; Dayton Art Inst, Ohio, 78; Battle Creek Art Ctr, Mich, 78; Grosse Pointe Gallery, 78. Teaching: Instr painting, Flint Inst Arts, 70-75; instr, Grosse Pointe War Mem, Mich, 70-75; instr oil painting, Art Ctr, Mt Clemens, Mich, 75- Pos: Juror, art exhibs throughout Mich, 70-; slide lectr, throughout Mich, 70-; mem, Arts Cult Coun, Oakland Co, Mich, 75- Awards: Purchase Prize, Butler Mus, 67; Best Painting by a Woman, Detroit Inst Arts, 70; 16th Ann Midland Mich Grand Jury Award & Purchase Prize, Northwood Inst, 75. Bibliog: Joy Hakenson (auth), Womanart is a first, Detroit News, 74; James K Chase (auth), Art show less Midland Mich, Midland Daily News, 75; article in Womensports, 11/77. Mem: Mich Acad Arts, Sci & Lett; Mich Watercolour Soc; Detroit Soc Women Painters & Sculptors; Scarab Club, Detroit. Style & Technique: Imagery bordering on abstraction using space, aerodynamic forms; 50-100 layers of glazes. Media: Acrylic, Oil. Mailing Add: 1112 Pinehurst Royal Oak MI 48073

MCCASLIN, WALTER WRIGHT
ART CRITIC, WRITER
b June 26, 24. Study: Ohio State Univ, BA(lit & hist), 47, MA(theatre & drama lit), 49. Teaching: Instr Eng, Hampton Inst, Va, 49-50. Pos: Bk rev columnist, Dayton Daily News, Ohio, Ohio, 52-60; arts columnist, Jour Herald, Dayton, 70- Mailing Add: 222 Fairfield Pike Yellow Springs OH 45387

MCCAULEY, GARDINER RAE
EDUCATOR, PAINTER
b Oakland, Calif, Aug 8, 33. Study: Calif Col Arts & Crafts, studied with Hamilton Wolf, 48-51; Univ Calif, Berkeley, BA, 55, MA, 57, studied with Milton Resnick, David Park, Esteban Vicente, Erle Loran & Corrado Marca-Relli. Exhib: Ann Exhib of San Francisco Art Asn, San Francisco Mus Art, 55-57; Young Calif Painters, Forum Gallery, New York, 55; Ann Exhib, Oakland Art Mus, Calif, 56-57; Bay Area Invitational, Calif Palace of the Legion of Honor, San Francisco, 58 & James D Phelan Awards, 65; Everett Ellin Gallery, Los Angeles, 59; Berkeley Gallery, San Francisco, 63-72; Worth Ryder Gallery, Univ Calif, Berkeley, 63; The Berkeley Gallery Group, Mills Col Art Gallery, Oakland, Calif, 64; one-man show, Berkeley Gallery, San Francisco, 64; Artists of Ore, 67, 70, 72 & Spectrum 70, Portland Art Mus, Ore; Stephens Faculty, Merril Chase Gallery, Chicago, 74. Teaching: Lectr drawing, Univ Calif, Berkeley, 62-65; lectr art, Univ Santa Clara, Calif, 64; asst prof painting & drawing, Lewis & Clark Col, Portland, Ore, 66-72; head dept art, painting & drawing, Stephens Col, Columbia, Mo, 72- Pos: Crafts dir, US Spec Servs, France & Ger, 59-62. Awards: Anne Bremer Award Art, Univ Calif, Berkeley, 56 & 57; Juror's Prize, San Francisco Art Asn Ann, San Francisco Mus Art, 63; James D Phelan Found Award, Calif Palace of Legion of Honor, San Francisco, 65. Bibliog: Joanna Magloff (auth), From the Berkeley Gallery, 12/63, Elizabeth Polley (auth), San Francisco: Gardiner McCauley & Howard Margolis, 3/64, Artforum; Anita Ventura (auth), Pop, Photo & Paint, Arts Mag, 4/64. Mem: Nat Coun Art Adminrs; Col Art Asn Am; Mid-Am Col Art Asn; Am Asn Univ Profs. Style & Technique: Abstract. Media: Acrylic and oil. Mailing Add: Dept of Art Stephens Col Columbia MO 65201

MCCHESNEY, CLIFTON
PAINTER, EDUCATOR
b Gary, Ind, Feb 8, 29. Study: Am Acad Art, dipl; Ind Univ, with Jack Tworkow, BS; Cranbrook Acad Art, with Zolton Sepeshy, MFA. Work: Detroit Inst Art; Cranbrook Acad Art, Bloomfield Hills, Mich; Univ Ryuukus, Okinawa, Japan; Biwako Mus, Otsu, Japan; Ginza Nova Gallery, Tokyo, Japan. Exhib: Art: USA: 59, New York Coliseum, 59; 24th Ann, Soc Contemp Arts, Chicago Art Inst, 64; one-man shows, Feingarten Galleries, San Francisco & Los Angeles, 61, Benni Gallery, Kyoto, 67 & Ginza Nova Gallery Tokyo, Japan, 75. Teaching: Prof painting & drawing, Mich State Univ, East Lansing, 60- Pos: Vis artist, State Univ NY Albany, fall 65; guest artist, Kalamazoo Art Ctr, Mich, summer 64. Awards: First Merit & First Purchase Award, South Bend Art Asn, 58; Purchase Awards, Detroit Inst Arts,

61 & Purdue Univ, 70; Travel Grant to Japan, Ford Found, 74. Bibliog: Man and Humanity (film), Mich State Univ, 71; Spec American Issue, Arts Mag, Vol 39, No 7; article in, Geijutsu Seikatsu, No 4, 75. Style & Technique: Abstract polyptichs and permutable walls. Media: Oil, Acrylic, Pencil. Dealer: Birmingham Art Gallery Inc 1025 Haynes St Birmingham MI 48011. Mailing Add: Kresge Art Ctr Mich State Univ East Lansing MI 48824

MCCHESNEY, MARY FULLER
See Fuller, Mary

MCCHESNEY, ROBERT PEARSON
PAINTER
b Marshall, Mo, Jan 16, 13. Study: Wash Univ Art Sch, with Fred Conway; Otis Art Inst, Los Angeles. Work: San Francisco Art Comn; Chicago Art Inst; Whitney Mus Am Art; Oakland Art Mus; San Francisco Mus Art. Comn: Wall decoration, USS Monterey; mural, Social Serv Admin Bldg, San Francisco, Calif, 77. Exhib: Art Inst Chicago Ann, 47-61; Sao Paulo 3rd Biennial, 55; Corcoran Gallery Art, 57; Calif Palace of Legion of Honor, 62; Expo 70, Osaka, Japan, 70; Retrospective, San Francisco Art Comn Gallery, 74; 19 Yrs, Calif State Univ, Hayward, 77; plus many others. Awards: Purchase Prizes, San Francisco Art Comn, 50 & 69; Purchase Prize, Whitney Mus Am Art, 55; Prize, San Francisco Mus Art, 60. Mem: San Francisco Art Inst (bd trustees). Style & Technique: Lyrical abstractions in painting, based on response to nature; meticulous, controlled technique. Mailing Add: 2955 Mountain Rd Petaluma CA 94952

MCCHRISTY, QUENTIN L
PAINTER, DESIGNER
b Cushing, Okla, Jan 24, 21. Study: Okla State Univ, with Doel Reed, BA; Cincinnati Acad Art, with Helwhig & Crawford. Work: Philbrook Art Ctr, Tulsa, Okla; Joslyn Mus Art, Omaha, Nebr; Butler Inst Am Art, Youngstown, Ohio; Pa State Univ, State College; Dean Weller, Col Fine Arts, Univ Ill, Urbana. Comn: Murals, Ft Worth Children's Mus & Wesley Found, Methodist Church, Stillwater, Okla; designed decorations glassware, Bartlett Collins, mfrs domestic & export glassware; plus others. Exhib: 26th Biennial, Corcoran Gallery, Washington, DC, 59; Contemporary American Art, Oklahoma City, 60; All City Arts Festival, Los Angeles, Calif, 60-; Audubon Artist Nat Galleries, New York, 62; Pa Acad Fine Arts, Philadelphia, 63; plus others. Teaching: Instr drawing, Okla State Univ; instr art, Ft Worth Children's Mus. Pos: Art dir, Ft Worth Children's Mus, 50; Nat Artist Show judge, 65. Awards: Purchase Award, 47, Prize, 48 & Ruskin Award, 62, Philbrook Art Ctr; Butler Mus Art Friends of Art Award, 60; Painting Exhib Awards, Wind River Valley Nat Show, Dubois, Wyo, 61 & 65; plus others. Mem: Int Platform Asn. Style & Technique: Academic through almost unlimited experimentation. Media: Transparent Watercolor, Ink, Oil. Publ: Four pen drawings, Am Artist Mag, 6-8/64. Mailing Add: 932 1/2 NW 20th Oklahoma City OK 73106

MCCLANAHAN, JOHN DEAN
PAINTER, EDUCATOR
b Saline, Kans, May 2, 38. Study: Bethany Col, Lindsborg, Kans, BFA; Univ Iowa, Iowa City, MFA; studied with Steward Edie, James Lechay, Mauricio Lasansky & Robert Knipschild. Work: Art Mus, Univ Iowa, Iowa City; Weatherspoon Art Gallery, Univ NC, Greensboro; Mint Mus Art, Charlotte, NC; Second Street Gallery, Charlottesville, Va. Exhib: Weatherspoon Nat Painting Ann, Univ NC, Greensboro, NC, 65; Watercolor USA Painting Ann, Springfield Art Mus, Mo, 66-69 & 72-75; one-man exhibs, Queens Col Art Gallery, 66, McDonalds Art Gallery, 69, Mint Mus Art, 71 & Queens Col Fine Arts Ctr, 74, Charlotte, NC; 8th & 14th Hunter Painting Ann, Hunter Mus, Chattanooga, Tenn, 67 & 73; 13th & 14th Nat Casein Painting Exhib, New York, 67 & 68; 23rd Southeastern Painting Exhib, High Mus, Atlanta, Ga, 68; 32nd, 33rd, 34th & 35th Ann Painting Exhib, NC Mus Art, Raleigh, NC, 70-73; Second & third Nat Small Painting Exhib, Mount Clemens, Mich, 75-76; Second Nat Works on Paper, Springfield, Mass, 76; Tex Painting & Sculpture Exhib, Seguin, 77; Eighth Ann Int Watercolor Exhib, Baton Rouge, 78. Teaching: Instr painting, Stephen F Austin State Univ, Nacogdoches, Tex, 64-67; from asst prof to assoc prof painting, Queens Col, Charlotte, NC, 67-76, chmn dept art, 75-76; assoc prof painting, Baylor Univ, Waco, Tex, 76- Awards: Merit Award, Second Nat Small Painting Exhib, Gallery North, 75; Purchase Prize, Fourth Nat Print & Drawing Exhib, Second Street Gallery, 76; Purchase Prize, Tex Painting & Sculpture Exhib, 77. Bibliog: Rev, Les Editions de la Revue Moderne, Paris, France, 66, Art Rev Mag, Des Moines, Iowa, 66 & 69. Mem: Col Art Asn Am; Tex Asn Schs Art. Style & Technique: Recent explorations include use of spray enamel, casein, acrylic and combinations of mixed media including watercolor, collage and casein. Media: Various approaches with water media and collage. Mailing Add: 8288 Mosswood Dr Waco TX 76710

MCCLANAHAN, WILLIAM J
CARTOONIST
b Greenville, Tex, Dec 2, 07. Study: Southern Methodist Univ; Dallas Art Inst; Dallas Eve Sch. Work: Nat Mus Cartoon Art, Greenwich, Conn; Harry Truman Libr; L B Johnson Libr; Univ Ark Field House, Fayetteville; plus many pvt collections. Pos: Sports writer, sports cartoonist, Dallas Jour, 30-37; sports cartoonist-ed cartoonist, Dallas Morning News, 46-73. Awards: Freedom Found Valley Forge Award Cartooning; Dallas Press Club Award. Mem: Asn Am Ed Cartoonists. Publ: Texas-The Way It Used to Be; Scenery for Model Railroads; illusr numerous books on sports. Mailing Add: 6426 Glendora Ave Dallas TX 75330

MCCLELLAN, DOUGLAS EUGENE
PAINTER
b Pasadena, Calif, Oct 10, 21. Study: Art Ctr Sch, Los Angeles, Calif; Colorado Springs Fine Arts Ctr, study with Boardman Robinson & Jean Charlot; Claremont Grad Sch, MFA. Work: Los Angeles Co Mus of Art; Los Angeles Co Fair Asn; Pasadena Art Mus. Exhib: Libr of Cong, 48; San Francisco Mus of Art, Calif, 49-52; Los Angeles Co Art, 49-55; Metrop Mus of Art, New York, 50; Pennsylvania Acad of Fine Arts, Pa, 53; Corcoran Gallery of Art, Washington, DC, 53; Santa Barbara Mus of Art; Pacific Coast Biennial, 55; Carnegie Inst of Technol, Pittsburgh, Pa, 55 & 57; Whitney Mus of Am Art, New York, 57; one-man shows, Felix Landau Gallery, 53-59, Pasadena Art Mus, 54 & Univ of Calif, Riverside, 55. Teaching: Instr, Chaffey Col, 50-59, Otis Art Inst, Los Angeles, Calif, 59-61, Scripps Col & Univ of Calif, Santa Cruz. Awards: Painting Prize, Los Angeles Co Mus of Art, 50 & 53; Nat Orange Show, 54. Mailing Add: c/o Art Dept Univ of Calif Santa Cruz CA 95064

MCCLELLAND, JEANNE C
PRINTMAKER
b Edmeston, NY. Study: Albright-Knox Sch Fine Arts, Buffalo, dipl; State Univ NY Col Buffalo, BS(art educ). Work: Mus Fine Arts, Springfield, Mass; St John Fisher Col (NY); Holyoke Mus, Mass; Munson-Williams-Proctor Inst, Utica, NY. Exhib: Cooperstown Art Asn, NY, 53-74; Artists of Central New York, Munson-Williams-Proctor Inst, 64-73; Academic Artists, Springfield Art Mus, Mass, 65-75; Soc Am Graphic Artists, New York, 66; Arena 74, Binghamton, NY; one-person show, State Univ NY Col, Oneonta, 77; plus others. Mem: Munson-Williams-Proctor Inst; Acad Artists; Cooperstown Art Asn; Roberson Ctr-Arts & Sci. Style & Technique: Expressionistic, realistic; relief printing, using traditional and found materials. Mailing Add: 17 Sharon St Sidney NY 13838

MCCLENDON, MAXINE (MAXINE MCCLENDON NICHOLS)
PAINTER, CRAFTSMAN
b Leesville, La, Oct 21, 31. Study: Univ Tex, Austin; Tex Women's Univ; Pan Am Univ. Work: Mus Int Folk Art, Santa Fe, NMex; IBM Collection; Lauren Rogers Mus Art, Laurel, Miss; Ark Arts Ctr, Little Rock; McAllen Int Mus, McAllen, Tex. Comn: Panels, Childes/Dreyfus for Edward Durell Stone condominiums, West Palm Beach, 76; panels, Glenbrook Hosp, Glenview, Ill, 76; panels, Sr Citizen Ctr, Fort Wayne, Ind, 77; panels, First Nat Bank, Mt Prospect, Ill, 77; panels, Meridith Woodworth, Dallas, Tex, 77. Exhib: Art Mus STex, 71; 16th Tex Crafts Exhib, Dallas Mus Fine Arts, 74; Art Mus STex, Corpus Christi, 74; 16th Ann Eight-State Exhib Paintings & Sculpture, Oklahoma City, 74; 8th & 9th Ann Southwestern Area Exhibs, Mus of the Southwest, Midland, Tex, 74 & 75; 53rd Ann, R S Barnwell Art Ctr, Shreveport, 75; Fourth Nat Crafts Exhib, Marietta Col, 75; Invitational Biennial, Beaumont Art Mus, Tex, 76; 19th Nat, El Paso Mus Art, Tex, 76; McAllen Int Mus, 76. Pos: Cur Mex Folk Art, McAllen Int Mus, 74- Awards: Best in Exhib, 6th Ann Prints, Drawings & Crafts, Ark Art Ctr, 74; Award of Excellence, Houston Designer/Craftsman, 76; Judges Award, Fourth Marietta Nat, 75. Mem: Am Crafts Coun (state rep, 76-); Tex Designer/Craftsmen (pres, 73-74). Style & Technique: Wet on wet watercolor executed with acrylic on canvas; trapunto quilting. Dealer: Adelle M Fine Art 3317 McKinney Ave Dallas TX 75204. Mailing Add: Rt 4 Box 188 Mission TX 78572

MCCLOSKEY, EUNICE LONCOSKE
PAINTER, WRITER
b Ridgway, Pa, May 25, 04. Study: Columbia Univ. Work: Thiel Col; Pa State Univ; Ridgway Area Schs; Johnsonburg Area Schs. Exhib: Carnegie Mus, Pittsburgh, 50-70; Indiana Univ Art Gallery, Pa, 60; one-man shows, Upstairs Gallery, Pittsburgh, 62-72; Raymond Duncan Gallery, Paris, 70-72; Lynn Kottler Gallery, New York, 73; plus many others. Teaching: Lectr, Pa, NY & Ohio, 40-70; instr watercolor, YMCA Art Classes, 67-69. Pos: Judge, Nat League Am Pen Women, Philadelphia, 62; chmn, Clothesline Exhib, Elk Co & Potter Co, Pa. Awards: Assoc Artists Pittsburgh Prize, Carnegie Mus, 50, Henry Posner Award, 53; Eunice McCloskey Sketching & Painting Room, Thiel Col, 74; Eunice McCloskey Room, Ind Univ, Pa; plus others. Bibliog: Douglas Naylor (auth), Fame beats a path to her door, 56 & Connie Kienzee (auth), Poet and painter, 69, Pittsburgh Press; Betty Lawrence (auth), Woman in love with life, Lutheran Nat Mag, 59; plus others. Mem: Assoc Artists Pittsburgh (dir, 59-60); Nat League Am Pen Women; Philadelphia Art Alliance; fel Int Inst Art & Lett; Prof & Artistic Hall Fame. Media: Oil, Watercolor. Publ: Auth & illusr, 18 poetry & art bks, 38- Mailing Add: 403 Oak St Ridgway PA 15853

MCCLOSKEY, ROBERT
PAINTER, ILLUSTRATOR
b Hamilton, Ohio, Sept 15, 14. Study: Vesper George Sch Art, Boston; Nat Acad Design, New York; Miami Univ, LittD; Mt Holyoke Col, LittD. Work: May Massee Collection, William Allen White Libr, Emporia State Teachers Col, Kans. Awards: Caldecott Medal, Am Libr Asn, 42 & 58. Bibliog: Marc Simont (auth), Robert McCloskey, Inventor, Horn Bk, 58; Robert McCloskey (film), Weston Woods Studio, 65. Mem: Fel Am Acad in Rome; Author's League; PEN. Publ: Auth & illusr, Make Way for Ducklings, 41, Homer Price, 42, Blueberries for Sal, 47, Time of Wonder, 57 & Burt Dow, Deep Water Man, 63. Mailing Add: Scott Islands Harborside ME 04642

MCCLOY, WILLIAM ASHBY
PAINTER, PRINTMAKER
b Baltimore, Md, Jan 2, 13. Study: State Univ Iowa, BA, 33, MA, 36, MFA, 49 & PhD, 58. Work: Walker Art Ctr, Minneapolis; Joslyn Art Ctr, Omaha; Winnipeg Art Gallery; Libr cong, Washington, DC. Comn: Three figure group sculpture, Conn Col, 70. Teaching: Asst prof drawing & painting, Univ Wis-Madison, 39-48; prof drawing & art hist & dir, Sch Art, Univ Man, 50-54; prof studio & art hist, Conn Col, 54- Media: Collage. Mailing Add: 430 Kitemaug Rd Uncasville CT 06382

MCCLURE, CONSTANCE M
INSTRUCTOR, PAINTER
b Huntington, WVa, Feb 12, 34. Study: Ringling Sch of Art, Sarasota, Fla; Col of Mt St Joseph, BA; Univ Cincinnati, MFA. Work: Cincinnati Zoological Soc; Dubois Chemical Co, Cincinnati; Pocohontas Coal Mining Co, Cincinnati; Univ Cincinnati; Jewish Community Ctr, Cincinnati. Comn: Portrait of conductor, Cincinnati Symphony Orchestra, 70; 18 ft canvas mural, Ohio Nat Bank, Columbus, 76; portrait of pres, Mt St Joseph Col, Ohio, 77. Exhib: Two-person show, Tangeman Gallery, Univ Cincinnati, 66, 68 & 74; Juror's Show, Huntington Galleries, WVa, 67; one-person show, State House, Columbus, Ohio, 70; Drawing & Print Invitational, Cincinnati Art Mus, 74; Ohio Women Artists: Past & Present, Butler Inst of Am Art, Youngstown, Ohio, 76; 14 Cincinnati Artists, Tampa Bay Arts Ctr, Fla, Peachtree Ctr, Atlanta, Ga & Contemp Arts Ctr, Cincinnati, 76. Collections Arranged: Drawing & Print Awards Exhib, Cincinnati Art Mus, 75; Regional Proj, Contemp Arts Ctr, Cincinnati, 73. Teaching: Instr drawing, Art Acad of Cincinnati, 74-, portrait painting, 78. Awards: Best in Show, Cincinnati Zoo Arts Festival, 65-68 & 73; First Prize/Drawing, Exhib 180, Huntington Galleries, 66; Purchase Prize, Jewish Community Ctr Invitational, 68. Bibliog: Sally Webster (auth), Regional proj, Cincinnati Post, 10/73; Alan Wood (auth), Real class, Cincinnati Mag, 5/74. Style & Technique: Minimal and figurative; crosshatching on miniature to mural scale. Media: Oil with restrained color; silverpoint on coated paper and graphite on primed canvas. Mailing Add: 451 Ludlow Ave Apt 304 Cincinnati OH 45220

MCCLURE, THOMAS F
SCULPTOR, EDUCATOR
b Pawnee City, Nebr, Apr 17, 20. Study: Univ Nebr, BFA, 41; Wash State Col, 41; Cranbrook Acad Art, MFA, 47. Work: Seattle Art Mus; Syracuse Mus Fine Arts, NY; Detroit Inst Arts; Wright Mem Ctr, Beloit Col, Wis; DeWaters Art Mus, Flint, Mich. Comn: Large welded sculptural screen, comn by Skidmore Owings & Merrill, Ford Motor Co Cent Staff Off Bldg, Dearborn, Mich, 55; welded bronze relief, comn by Victor Gruen Assocs, Eastland Shopping Ctr, Detroit, 56; cast bronze relief, DeWaters Art Ctr, 58; welded bronze free standing sculpture, comn by Albert Kahn Assocs, Univ Mich Undergrad Libr, Ann Arbor, Mich, 59; ten cast bronze relief sculptures, comn by Congregation Shaarey Zedek, Detroit, 69. Exhib: Momentum Midcontinental, Chicago, 55; Pa Acad Fine Arts Ann, Philadelphia & Detroit, 58; 20th Ceramic Int, Syracuse, 58; Contemporary Sculpture 1961, Cincinnati Art Mus & John Herron Art Inst, 61; Drawings USA, St Paul, Minn, 61. Teaching: Instr design, Sch for Am Craftsmen, Alfred, NY, 47-48; asst prof drawing & design, Univ Okla, 48-49; prof sculpture, Univ Mich, 49- Awards: First Prize for Painting, Northwest Artists Ann, Seattle, 43; Prize in Sculpture, 12th Nat Ceramics Ann, Syracuse, 47; Founders Prize in Sculpture,

45th Mich Artists Ann, Detroit, 54. Media: Metal. Dealer: Gilman Galleries 103 E Oak St Chicago IL 60611. Mailing Add: 3361 N Maple Rd Ann Arbor MI 48103

MCCOLLEY, SUTHERLAND
CURATOR
b Philadelphia, Pa, Oct 17, 37. Study: Westminster Choir Col, BMus, 60 & MMus, 62; NY State Coun Arts Mus Training Prog, 70; Intermus Conserv Lab, 73; Harvard Univ Inst Arts Admin, 73; Int Mus Studies Prog, 74, Mus Exchange Prog, 76. Exhibitions Arranged: Art from Private Collections Series, 69, 71, 72 & 73; American Paintings From the Metropolitan Museum of Art, 70; Light, Sound and Motion, 70; James Renwick Brevoort, 72; Six Solos, 73; Sculpture for the Dance, 73; Hudson River Mus Invitational, 74-75. Pos: Researcher, M Knoedler & Co, 67-69; cur art, Hudson River Mus, Yonkers, NY, 69-76; dir, Gallery Nine, New York, 77- Mem: Am Asn Mus; Northeast Mus Conf; Nat Soc Lit & Arts. Publ: Auth, The Works of James Renwick Brevoort, 72. Mailing Add: 230 Riverside Dr New York NY 10025

MCCOON, BETTY JEAN
PAINTER, SCULPTOR
b Fresno, Calif. Study: With Glen Wessels, Univ Calif; with Ralph DuCasse, Mills Col; with Hans Burkhardt, Univ Calif, Los Angeles; Monterey Peninsula Col, with Alexander Nepate; Diablo Design Ctr, Danville, Calif, with Peter Bloss. Work: Fresno Arts Ctr; Calif State Univ, Fresno; also in pvt collection of Ben C Deane, Newport Beach, Calif; plus others. Comn: Space Weave (oil on canvas), Guarantee Savings & Loan Asn, 71; Metamorphic Bag (oil wash & ink drawing), First Fed Savings & Loan Asn, Calif, 71; portrait of Dr Fred Ness, Calif State Univ, Fresno, 72; Woven Landscape IV (oil on canvas), James Cy Mouradick, Chartered Life Underwriters, 75; portrait of Sister Gladys Marie, CSC (oil on canvas), St Agnes Hosp, Fresno, 76. Exhib: Calif Palace of Legion of Honor, San Francisco, 65; Watercolor USA, Springfield, Mo, 65; Austria Linz Exchange, 72; 1973 Art Exchange-Taiwan USA, 73; West Coast Watercolor Soc & Royal Watercolor Soc, London, 75-76. Teaching: Instr painting & drawing, Fresno Art Ctr, 61-66 & 75-; lectr art, Calif State Univ, Freno, 65-71. Pos: Organizer & actg chairperson, Artist Invitational, San Joaquin Valley, Calif, 66. Awards: First Prize for Oil, Soc Western Artists, San Francisco, 63; First Prize for Watercolor, Calif State Fair, Sacramento, 65; First Prize for Ink, San Joaquin Valley Ann, Fresno Arts Ctr, 70; plus others. Bibliog: Article in Calif Crossroads, 65 & La Rev Mod, 66; Kingsley Roberts, Jr (auth), Bee Jay (color film), 71; plus others. Mem: West Coast Watercolor Soc; Fresno Arts Ctr; Am Fedn Arts. Style & Technique: Spontaneous, creative draftsmanship weaving with paint and ink. Media: Oil & Watercolor, Drawing; Casting, Clay. Dealer: Van Ginkel & Moor 575 Sutter St San Francisco CA 94102. Mailing Add: 4657 N Harrison Fresno CA 93705

MCCORISON, MARCUS ALLEN
LIBRARIAN
b Lancaster, Wis, July 17, 26. Study: Ripon Col, BA(Eng), 50; Univ Vt, MA(Am hist), 51; Columbia Univ, MS(libr serv), 54. Exhibitions Arranged: A Society's Chief Joys (auth, catalog), Grolier Club, Newberry Libr, Univ Calif, Los Angeles, 68-70. Pos: Librn, Kellogg-Hubbard Libr, Montpelier, Vt, 54-55; chief rare bk, Dartmouth Col, Hanover, NH, 55-59; head spec collections, Univ Iowa, Iowa City, 55-60; librn & dir, Am Antiq Soc, Worcester, Mass, 60- Mem: Bibliographical Soc Am (first vpres, 78-); Rare Bk Sect, Asn Col & Res Libr (chmn, 65); Independent Res Libr Asn (chmn, 72-73, 78-); Grolier Club, Century Asn. Res: History of American printing, publishing, book trades, including American prints. Interest: American prints in all media prior to year 1877. Collection: American prints of the 18th and 19th century. Publ: Auth, Vermont Imprints, 1777-1820, Am Antiq Soc, 63; auth, 1764 Catalogue of the Redwood Library, Yale Univ Press, 65; ed, The history of printing in America, Imprint Soc, 70. Mailing Add: Am Antiq Soc 185 Salisbury St Worcester MA 01609

MCCORMICK, HARRY
PAINTER
b Bayonne, NJ, June 12, 42. Work: Newark Mus Art, NJ; Ark Art Ctr, Little Rock; Wichita State Univ Collection, Kans; Canton Art Inst, Ohio; Univ Wyo Mus Art, Laramie. Exhib: Meticulous Realism, Univ Md, 66-67; 20th Century Americs, ACA Galleries, New York, 70; Window & Doors, Weckscher Mus, Huntington, NY, 72; Trends in Realism, McCormich-Chase-Dobbs-Cigare-Sarsony, St Mary's Col, Md, 72; Candid Painting, De Cordova Mus, Lincoln, Mass. Style & Technique: Realistic. Media: Oil, Graphics, Watercolor. Dealer: Brewster Gallery 1018 Madison Ave New York NY 10021. Mailing Add: 69 Gansevoort St New York NY 10014

MCCORMICK, JO MARY (JO MARY MCCORMICK-SAKURAI)
PAINTER, ILLUSTRATOR
b New York, NY, Mar 6, 18. Study: Nat Acad Design, 47; Art Students League, scholar, 48; Columbia Univ, 55; Empire State Col, BS, 77. Comn: Painting, comn by Msgr Le Roy McWilliams, Highland Falls, NJ, 64; Mus Mod Art; Yale Univ; Columbia Univ. Exhib: Burr Gallery, 62; Graphics Show, Nat Arts Club, 63; Brazansky Art Gallery, 65; New York Pub Libr, 72-74. Pos: Art critic, Pictures on Exhib Mag, 59-75. Mem: Women's Press Club; life mem Art Students League; New York Color Slide Club. Style & Technique: Representational; neo-academic. Publ: Illusr, Art: USA Now, 64; auth, Wings of thought and art column, New York Column Newspaper, 71-72; contribr, Am Artist Mag, 71; auth, In the Artists' Studios. Mailing Add: 444 Second Ave New York NY 10010

MCCOSH, DAVID J
PAINTER
b Cedar Rapids, Iowa, July 11, 03. Study: Coe Col; Art Inst Chicago. Work: Coos Art Mus, Coos Bay, Ore; Portland Art Mus; Seattle Art Mus; First Nat Bank of Ore, Portland; Ore State Capitol Wings, Salem. Comn: Murals, Chicago World's Fair for Century of Progress, 33, Pub Bldgs Admins Sect Fine Arts, Washington, DC for Post Off Kelso, Wash, 36, Dept Interior Nat Parks, 40 & Beresford Post Off, SD, 42; paintings, US Nat Bank, Eugene, 60. Exhib: Golden Gate Int Expos, 39-40; New York World's Fair, 39-40; one-man shows, Seattle Art Mus, 51, Portland Art Mus, 64, Univ Ore Mus Art, 67, Gallery West, Portland, 70, Portland State Univ, 73, Satellite Mus, Univ Ore, 74, Fairbanks Gallery, Ore State Univ, Corvallis, 74, Coos Art Mus, 76 & Univ Ore Mus Art, 77; Seattle World's Fair, 62; Art of the Thirties, Henry Gallery, Seattle, Wash, 72; Paperwork, 72 & Artists of Ore, 73, Portland Art Mus; Art of the Pac NW, Smithsonian Inst, Washington, DC, 74. Teaching: Instr lithography, Art Inst Chicago, 33-34; prof art, Univ Ore, 34-70; vis prof, Art Inst Chicago, 36; vis prof, Mont State Univ, 47 & 53; vis prof, San Jose State Univ, 57. Pos: Juror, nat & regional exhibs. Awards: Seattle Art Mus Purchase Award; Portland Art Mus Watercolor Award, 70; Erb Mem Oil Painting Award, Univ Ore, 72. Bibliog: Edward B Rowan (auth), article in Am Mag Art, 11/37. Mem: Art Inst Chicago. Media: Oil. Publ: Illusr, The Rainbow Serpent, 62. Mailing Add: 1870 Fairmount Blvd Eugene OR 97403

MCCOY, ANN
PAINTER, DRAFTSMAN
b Boulder, Colo, July 8, 46. Study: Univ Colo, BFA, 69; Univ Calif, Los Angeles, MA, 72. Work: Whitney Mus Am Art, New York; Nat Gallery Australia; Dudley Peter Allen Mem Art Mus, Oberlin, Ohio; Los Angeles Co Art Mus. Comn: Mural in pencil, Harris Bank. Exhib: Choice Dealers-Dealers' Choice, New York Cult Ctr, 74; Woman's Work-American Art, Mus Philadelphia Civic Ctr, 74; Painting & Sculpture Today, Indianapolis Mus Art & Contemp Art Ctr, Cincinnati, 74; 71st Am Exhib, Art Inst Chicago, 74; Both Kinds: Contemporary Art from Los Angeles, Univ Calif Art Mus, Berkeley, 75; plus many others. Style & Technique: Pencil on paper mounted on canvas. Media: Pencil. Dealer: Brooke Alexander 20 W 57th St New York NY 10019; Margo Leavin Gallery 812 N Robertson Los Angeles CA 90069. Mailing Add: 24 W 76th St New York NY 10024

MCCOY, JASON
ART DEALER
b Middletown, Conn, Jan 26, 48. Study: Boston Univ. Pos: Mgr, Marlborough Graphics Gallery, New York, 68-69; asst dir, Reese Palley Gallery, New York, 69-70; dir, Tibor de Nagy Gallery, New York, 70-72; pvt art dealer. Specialty: Twentieth century American and European painting. Mailing Add: 1199 Park Ave New York NY 10028

MCCOY, JOHN W, (II)
PAINTER, EDUCATOR
b Pinole, Calif, May 11, 10. Study: Cornell Univ, BFA, 33; Am Sch, Fontainebleau, France, 30-32; also with N C Wyeth. Work: Pa Acad Fine Arts, Philadelphia; Farnsworth Mus, Rockland, Maine; Montclair Mus, NJ; Brandywine River Mus, Chadds Ford, Pa; Del Art Mus, Wilmington. Comn: Portrait of Gov Reed, State of Maine, State Capitol, Augusta, 70. Exhib: Pa Acad Fine Arts Ann, 40-68; Carnegie Inst Int, 50; Metrop Mus; Whitney Mus Am Art; Nat Acad Design, 72. Teaching: Instr painting, Pa Acad Fine Arts, 47-70. Awards: Whitmer Prize, Am Watercolor Soc, 55; Philadelphia Watercolor Club Award, Pa Acad Fine Arts, 55; W F B Morse Medal, Nat Acad Design, 72. Mem: Philadelphia Watercolor Club (vpres, 50-58); Nat Acad Design; Am Watercolor Soc; Audubon Artists; Wilmington Soc Fine Arts (trustee, 45-, vpres, 60-68). Media: Mixed Media. Dealer: Coe Kerr Gallery 49 E 82nd St New York NY 10028. Mailing Add: RFD 1 Chadds Ford PA 19317

MCCOY, WIRTH VAUGHAN
PAINTER, EDUCATOR
b Duluth, Minn, Dec 16, 13. Study: Univ Minn, BA, 37; Univ Iowa, MFA, 48; Acad Grande Chaumiere, cert painting & design, 51; Calif Sch Fine Art, 49; Acad Montmartre, 50; also with James Lechay, Maurice Lasansky, Mark Rothko, Yasuo Kunioshi & others. Work: Portland Art Mus; Seattle Art Mus; Mineral Industs Mus, Pa State Univ; Univ Iowa; Wash State Univ. Exhib: San Francisco Ann; Northwest Artists, Seattle; Artists Ore, Portland, 54; Centennial Exhib, Kansas City Art Inst, 62; Spokane Int Art Exhib, 64. Teaching: Asst prof painting & drawing, Ore State Univ, 48-53; prof painting & drawing, resident artist & dir, Wash State Univ Ctr, 53-64; head dept art, Pa State Univ, 64-71, prof art, 71- Mem: Am Fedn Arts; Col Art Asn Am; Peale Club Philadelphia; Pa Acad Fine Arts; Art Alliances Cent Pa. Media: Oil. Mailing Add: 932 E McCormick State College PA 16801

MCCRACKEN, HAROLD
ART ADMINISTRATOR, ART HISTORIAN
b Colorado Springs, Colo, Aug 31, 94. Study: Hope Col, hon DLit, 57; Univ Alaska, hon DLit, 66; Colo State Univ, hon LHD, 72; Univ Wyo, hon LLD. Pos: Dir, Whitney Gallery Western Art & Buffalo Bill Hist Ctr, Cody, Wyo, 59- Publ: Auth, Frederic Remington-Artist of the Old West; auth, The Frederic Remington Book; auth, The Charles M Russell Book; auth, George Catlin and the Old Frontier; auth, The Frank Tenney Johnson Book; plus others. Mailing Add: Whitney Gallery Western Art Cody WY 82414

MCCRACKEN, JOHN HARVEY
SCULPTOR, PAINTER
b Berkeley, Calif, Dec 9, 34. Study: Calif Col Arts & Crafts, BFA, 62, grad work, 62-65. Work: Mus Mod Art, Whitney Mus Am Art & Guggenheim Mus, New York; Los Angeles Co Mus; Pasadena Art Mus, Calif. Exhib: Primary Structures, Jewish Mus, New York, 66; American Sculpture of the Sixties, Los Angeles Co Mus Art, 67; 5th Guggenheim Int Exhib, Guggenheim Mus, 67; Art of the Real, Mus Mod Art, New York, 69, Ways of Looking, 71; 69th Am Exhib, Art Inst Chicago, 70; Mus Contemp Arts, Chicago, 70; Documenta, Kassel, WGer, 72; plus others. Teaching: Asst prof sculpture & painting, Univ Calif, Irvine & Los Angeles, 65-68; asst prof sculpture, Sch Visual Arts, New York, 68-69; asst prof sculpture & painting, Hunter Col, 71- Awards: Nat Endowment for the Arts Award, 68. Bibliog: Dennis Young & James Monte (auth), John McCracken: Sculpture 1965-1969, Art Gallery Ont, Toronto, 69; John McCracken, Sonnabend Gallery, Paris, 69. Media: Fiberglas, Wood. Mailing Add: c/o Nicholas Wilder Gallery 8225 1/2 Santa Monica Blvd Los Angeles CA 90046

MCCRACKEN, PATRICK ED
PAINTER, EDUCATOR
b Amarillo, Tex, Apr 6, 47. Study: Tex Tech Univ; WTex State Univ, BS(art educ). Exhib: WTex Watercolor Soc; Dos Bandeleros, Douglas, Ariz; Tex Fine Arts Asn & Circuit Show; one-man show, WTex State Univ. Teaching: Head teacher, Amarillo Art Ctr Asn, 71-72, cur educ, 74-; art teacher, Window Rock Sch, Ariz, 72-74. Awards: Jurors Choice, Tex Fine Arts Asn, 72; Second Place, Citation Show, Amarillo Fine Arts Asn, 72. Mem: Amarillo Fine Arts Asn; Tex Fine Arts Asn. Style & Technique: Contemporary composition, combining opaque and transparent acrylic techniques. Media: Acrylic. Dealer: Gallery A Kit Carson Taos NM 87571. Mailing Add: 1208 S Kentucky Amarillo TX 79102

MCCRACKEN, PHILIP
SCULPTOR
b Bellingham, Wash, Nov 14, 28. Study: Univ Wash, BA; with Henry Moore, Eng, 54. Work: Detroit Inst Art; Mus Art, Victoria, BC; UN, New York; also in pvt collections. Exhib: One-man shows, Seattle Art Mus, 61, Victoria Mus, BC, 64 & La Jolla Mus Art, Calif, 70; Corcoran Gallery Art, 66; Rutgers Univ, 68; Grand Rapids Art Mus, 69; plus many others. Awards: Norman Davis Award, 57; Artists of the Year, 64; Irene Wright Mem Award, Seattle Art Mus, 65. Dealer: Williard Gallery 29 E 72nd St New York NY 10021. Mailing Add: Guemes Island Anacortes WA 98221

MCCRAY, DOROTHY M
PRINTMAKER, EDUCATOR
b Madison, SDak, Oct 13, 15. Study: State Univ Iowa, BA, 37, MA, 39; Calif Col Arts & Crafts, MFA, 55; Tyler Sch Art, Temple Univ; Univ Florence; independent Europ study. Exhib: Chicago Int Watercolor Exhib, Art Inst Chicago, 40-41; 4th & 5th Int Exhib Color Lithography, Cincinnati Art Inst, 56-57; Northwest Printmakers Int, 57; Grenchen Print &

Drawing Triennial, Switz, 67; US Off Info Traveling Show, Europe, 71-72; plus others. Teaching: Assoc prof art, Western NMex Univ. Pos: Dir, Western NMex Univ Art Study Prog in Italy, 69. Mem: Am Color Print Soc; Print Coun Am; Col Art Asn Am; Mus NMex (artist's adv coun, 59-60); Am Fedn Arts. Media: Intaglio. Mailing Add: 802 N Cheyenne St Silver City NM 88061

MCCRAY, PORTER A
ART ADMINISTRATOR
Pos: Dir Asian cult prog, The JDR 3rd Fund. Mailing Add: 50 Rockefeller Plaza New York NY 10020

MCCREADY, ERIC SCOTT
MUSEUM DIRECTOR, ART HISTORIAN
b Vancouver, Wash, Mar 14, 41. Study: Univ Ore, BS, 63, BA, 65, MA, 68; Univ Pavia, Italy, BA, 65; Univ Del, PhD(art hist), 72; Wintherthur Summer Inst. Teaching: Asst prof art hist, Bowling Green State Univ, 72-75; Asst prof art hist, Univ Wis-Madison, 75- Mem: Am Asn Mus Dirs; Soc Archit Historians (mem decorative arts chap); Mid-West Art Hist Soc; Victorian Soc Am. Res: American 18th and 19th century architecture and the decorative arts. Publ: Auth, The Nebraska State Capitol: Its Design, Background and Influence, Nebr State Hist Soc, 74; auth, Tanner and Gilliam: two American black painters, Negro Lit Forum, 74; auth, Richard Taliaferro: 18th Century Virginia Architect, Univ Ore Press, 77; auth, Bertram Goodhue: master of many arts (rev), J Soc Archit Historians, 78. Mailing Add: 4133 Mandan Crescent Madison WI 53711

MCCULLOUGH, DAVID WILLIAM
PAINTER, SCULPTOR
b Springfield, Mass, Dec 28, 45. Study: Boston Inst of the Arts, Mass, 63-64; Aspen Sch of Contemp Art, Colo, summer 1968, with Wilbur Neiwald & Doris Cross; Kansas City Art Inst, Mo, BFA(printmaking, painting), 70; Univ Mich, 69, with printmaker, Emil Weddige; Calif Inst of the Arts, 70, with Allan Kaprow & Dick Higgins. Work: Ark Art Ctr, Little Rock; Univ Tex, Arlington; Richland Jr Col, Richardson, Tex; First Nat Bank, Houston; Kemper Insurance Co, Chicago. Comn: Sculptural fountain (35 ft x 26 ft x 2 ft, sand, steel and acrylic), Am Petrofina Oil Co, Dallas, 74; three monumental sculptures (acrylic and sand), comn by Tex Comn on the Arts & Humanities, Tyler Mus of Art, Tex, 74. Exhib: Dallas Mus of Fine Arts Bicentennial, 71; Okla Art Mus, Oklahoma City, 71; New Orleans Art Mus Biennial, 71, 73 & 77; South by SW Exhib, Ft Worth Art Mus, 72; two-man exhib, Tyler Mus of Art, 74; Beaumont Art Mus, Tex, 75; Joslyn Art Mus, Omaha, Nebr, 76; two-man exhib, Amarillo Art Ctr, 77. Teaching: Artist in residence video-audio, Western Wash State Col, Bellingham, 76; artist in residence painting & sculpture, Santa Fe Contemp Art Sch, NMex, 76. Awards: First Prize, Painting/Sculpture Biennial, Dallas Mus of Fine Arts; 71; First Prize, Univ Tex, Arlington, 76; Best of Show, Meadows Art Mus, Shreveport Art Guild, La, 77. Bibliog: Museum People, KERA-TV film, 74; Victoria Melcher (auth), David McCullough, Arts Mag, 1/76; David Dillon (auth), McCullough's whimsical monoliths, D Mag. Mem: Artists Collition of Tex. Style & Technique: Etched lyrical line, images from life abstracted and depicted in painting and sculpture. Media: Acrylic Metallic painting; sand acrylic and polystyrene acrylic sculpture and wall reliefs. Dealer: Douglas Drake Gallery 4500 State Line Kansas City KS 66103; Jan Cicero Gallery 433 N Clark Chicago, Ill 60610. Mailing Add: 839 1/2 Exposition Dallas TX 75226

MCCULLOUGH, JOSEPH
ART ADMINISTRATOR, PAINTER
b Pittsburgh, Pa, July 6, 22. Study: Cleveland Inst Art, dipl, 48; Yale Univ, with Lewis York, 49-50, BFA, 50, with Josef Albers, 50-51, MFA, 51. Work: Cleveland Mus Art; Dayton Art Inst; Ohio Univ; Syracuse Univ; Youngstown Pub Schs, Ohio. Comn: Stained glass windows, St Edmund Roman Cath Church, Warren, Mich, 69. Exhib: Corcoran Biennial Exhib, Washington, DC, 55; Audubon Artists Ann Exhib, New York, 56; Contemp Am Painting & Sculpture, Univ Ill, 57; All Ohio Painting & Sculpture Show, Dayton Art Inst, 67; Cleveland Arts Prize Exhib, 71. Pos: Pres, Cleveland Inst Art, 55-; secy, Cleveland Art Asn, 55-; pres, Nat Asn Schs Art, 62-65; chmn fine arts adv comt, Cleveland City Planning Comn, 65- Awards: Spec Award for Painting, Cleveland Mus Art, 58; Purchase Award for Painting, Dayton Art Inst, 67; Cleveland Arts Prize for Visual Arts, Women's City Club Cleveland, 71. Mem: Union of Independent Col of Art (bd dir); Artists for Environment, Del Water Gap (bd dir); Col Ceramics Adv Coun, Alfred Univ; Osaka Univ Arts, Japan (hon trustee); Col Art Asn (bd dirs, 63-68). Media: Acrylic, Watercolor. Publ: Contribr, Art in Cleveland Architecture, AIA Handhook to Cleveland Architecture, Reinhold, 58; contribr, The Enamelist, Kenneth Bates, World, 66. Mailing Add: 2637 Wellington Rd Cleveland Heights OH 44118

MCDARRAH, FRED WILLIAM
PHOTOGRAPHER, WRITER
b Brooklyn, NY, Nov 5, 26. Study: NY Univ, grad(jour), 54. Exhib: Gallery Exhib, Soho Photo, 73; Frank O'Hara Poet Among Painters, Whitney Mus, 74; Artists Comt to Save Tenth St, Brata Gallery, 74; Poets of the Cities (with catalog), Dallas Mus Fine Arts, 74, San Francisco Mus Art, 75 & Wadsworth Atheneum, 75; Volunteer Serv Photogr, Union Carbide Exhib Ctr, 75; Photogr & The Artist, Sidney Janis Gallery, 76; Basel Art Fair, Switz, 76; On the Move, Alfred Stieglitz Gallery, 76; Surfact, Edge & Color, Downtown Whitney Mus, New York, 77; NY Sch Painting & Sculpture, Empire State Mus, 78. Teaching: Guest lectr, Germain Sch Photog, summer 69, Concerned Photog, NY Univ, 72 & Soho Photo, 73. Pos: Writer, photogr, film & photog reviewer, Village Voice, 59-71, picture ed, 71- Awards: Best Spot News Photo Page One Award, NY Newspaper Guild, 71; Guggenheim Found Fel Photog, 72; Second Place News Photogs, Edward Steichen Mem Award in Newspaper Photog, 76; plus many others. Bibliog: Interview in Photog Column, Newsday, 7/27/75; article in Invitation to Photog, spring 76; interview with seven ed, 35MM Photog, winter 77. Mem: Munic Arts Soc (award comt); NY Press Club; Am Soc Picture Prof; Photog Soc Am; Author's Guild. Publ: Auth, The Artist's World in Picture, 61 & Museums in New York, 73, Dutton; ed, Photography Market Place, Bowker, 75, 2nd ed, 77; plus many art catalogues, by-line articles and picture essays. Posters Publ: Personality posters, Bob Dylan, 66, Allen Ginsberg, 66, Timothy Leary, 66, Andy Warhol, 67 & Charlotte Moorman, 68; plus many others. Mailing Add: 505 LaGuardia Pl New York NY 10012

MCDONNELL, JOSEPH ANTHONY
SCULPTOR
b Detroit, Mich, Oct 20, 36. Study: Univ Notre Dame, with Ivan Mestrovic, BFA & MFA; Acad Belli Arte, Florence, Italy. Work: Milwaukee Pub Mus. Comn: Play sculptured tumblers, Nanuet Mall, Homart Develop Co, NY, 69; fabricated sculptures, E & W Towne Malls, Madison, Wis, 70; stainless steel suspended sculpture, Lakehurst Shopping Ctr, Waukegan, Ill, 71; stainless steel fountain, Janesville Mall, Wis, 72; lunar scape sculpture, Fashion Square Mall, Saginaw, Mich, 72. Exhib: US Info Serv Am Artists in Florence, 63; Mostra Mercato Nat Arte Contemporanea, Florence, 63; one-man shows, McNay Art Inst, San Antonio, 64, Flint Art Inst, Mich, 64 & John Wanamaker Fine Arts Gallery, Philadelphia, 70. Awards: Dept of Housing & Urban Development Award, Nat Community Art Competition, 73. Bibliog: Rev in Philadelphia Inquirer, 11/1/70; Harriet Schiff (auth), article in Detroit News, 9/17/71; Louis G Redstone (auth), New Directions in Shopping Centers and Stores, McGraw-Hill, 73; plus others. Style & Technique: Usually strong, semi-geometric forms, executed in a refined manner which emphasizes the material such as mirror stainless steel or burnished brass. Media: Bronze, Steel, Marble. Mailing Add: Guard Hill Rd Bedford NY 10506

MCDONOUGH, JOHN JOSEPH
COLLECTOR, PATRON
b Carbondale, Pa. Study: St John's Col, Toledo, BS; Loyola Univ Med Sch, MD. Pos: Bd trustees, Friends Am Art, 63-66; gen chmn, Youngstown Fine Arts Festival for Proj Hope, 63-74; trustee, Butler Inst Am Art, Youngstown, Ohio, 68-71 & 73-76, bd dir, 77-; mem Wean lect prog comt, Youngstown State Univ, 77; rep of Butler Inst Am Art, Am Asn Mus Comt, Pittsburgh, Pa, 77. Mem: Art Collectors Club Am. Collection: 18th, 19th and 20th century American art; collection on tour throughout US, 75-76. Mailing Add: 1005 Belmont Ave Youngstown OH 44504

MCELCHERAN, WILLIAM HODD
DESIGNER, SCULPTOR
b Hamilton, Ont, July 9, 27. Study: Ont Col Art, Toronto. Work: Art Gallery Hamilton, Ont; Art Gallery London, Ont; York Univ; Univ Toronto Sch Archit. Comn: Archit design & sculpture, Divinity Col, McMaster Univ, 60; wood sculpture, Briar Cliff Col, 62; Stations of the Cross (mahogany), St Augustines Col, Scarboro, Ont, 66; plastic relief, Walkerton Fed Bldg, Ont, 70; sculpture, St Michael's Libr, Univ Toronto, 72. Exhib: Sculpture '67, Toronto, 67; one-man shows, Roberts Gallery, Toronto, 69 & Art Gallery Hamilton, 69; Fed Int Medaille, Cologne, Ger, 71; La Galerie de L'Esprit Montreal, 75; New Talent Exhib, Forum Gallery, New York, 75. Teaching: Instr carving, Ont Col Art, 63-66; artist in residence, Sch Archit, Univ Toronto, 71-72. Pos: Art dir & designer, Valley City Mfg Co, Dundas, 52-56; designer, Brown, Brisley & Brown, Architects, Toronto, 56-60. Awards: Medal, Lt Gov Ont, 49; Can Coun Sr Arts Award, 69; Aviva Sculpture Prize, Aviva Chap, Hadassah, 69. Bibliog: Paul Duval (auth), William McElcheran, The Hamilton Spectator, 11/69; Eric Freifeld (auth), William McElcheran, Artscan Mag, 4-5/71; Kay Kritzwizer (auth), article in Toronto Globe & Mail, 5/71. Mem: Royal Can Acad Arts; Sculptors Soc Can. Publ: Auth, The Revolution in Liturgical Art, Brief to the Bishops, Longmans Green, 65; illusr, By the Circus Sands, 67. Dealer: Roberts Gallery 641 Yonge St Toronto ON Can. Mailing Add: 191 Balsam Ave Toronto ON M4E 3G2 Can

MCELROY, JACQUELYN ANN
PRINTMAKER, EDUCATOR
b Rice Lake, Wis, June 28, 42. Study: Univ Minn; Univ Mont, BA, 65, MA, 66 & MFA, 67. Work: Graphics Group, Am Printmakers Mag; Dulin Gallery Art, Knoxville, Tenn; Winnipeg Art Gallery, Man, Can; Fed Reserve Bank, Minn; Peoria Art Guild Collection, Ill. Exhib: Midwest Biennial Exhib, Joslyn Mus, Omaha, Nebr, 74; 2nd Miami Graphics Int, Coral Gables, Fla, 75; Bradley Univ Nat Print & Drawing, Peoria, Ill, 75; Mich Artrain Upper Midwest Tour, 75; Midwestern Manisphere All Media Show, Winnipeg, 76; 16th Bradley Nat Print Show, Peoria, Ill, 77; Dulin Gallery Print & Drawing Show, Knoxville, 77. Teaching: Assoc prof art hist & printmaking, Univ NDak, Grand Forks, 68- Awards: Kempshall Mem Award, Peoria Art Guild, 74; Manisphere Purchase Award, Winnipeg Art Gallery, 76; Purchase Award, Dulin Gallery, 77. Style & Technique: Reorganized reality, landscape in photo serigraphy. Mailing Add: 917 Chestnut St Grand Forks ND 58201

MCELROY, NANCY LYNN
SCULPTOR, DESIGNER
b New London, Conn, July 23, 51. Study: Calif State Univ, San Diego; Univ Calif, Davis; with Roy DeForest. Work: Archiv Sohm, Markgroningen, Ger; Vancouver Art Gallery, BC. Comn: Soft zipper sculpture, comn by Terry Arnold, San Diego, 74; woven textile designs, Sammlung Maurer, Fluxus Arch, Budapest, Hungary, 75. Exhib: Vancouver Art Gallery, BC, 72; Oakland Mus, Calif, 72; Henry Art Gallery, Univ Wash, Seattle, 72; Joslyn Art Mus, Omaha, Nebr, 73. Mailing Add: 522 K St Apt A Davis CA 95616

MCEWEN, JEAN
PAINTER
b Montreal, Que, Dec 14, 23. Work: Mus Mod Art; Walker Art Ctr, Minneapolis; Albright-Knox Art Gallery; Ottawa Mus; Toronto Mus; plus others. Comn: Stained glass window, Sir George Williams Univ, 66; murals, Toronto Airport & Plase Arts, Montreal, 67. Exhib: One-man shows, Gallery Godart-Lefort, Montreal, four times, 62-69, Gallery, Montreal, 63, Gallery Moos, Toronto, four times, 63-69 & Mayer Gallery, Paris, 64; Dunn Int Exhib, Tate Gallery, London, 63; plus others. Awards: Quebec Art Competition, 62; Jessie Dow Award, Montreal Spring how, 64. Mem: Academician Royal Can Acad Arts. Publ: Illusr, La Pain Quotidien, 64. Dealer: Marlborough-Godard Ltd 1490 Sherbrooke St W Montreal PQ Can. Mailing Add: 3908 Parc Lafontaine Ru Montreal PQ H2L 3M6 Can

MCFADDEN, MARY
COLLECTOR, DESIGNER
b New York, NY, Oct 1, 38. Study: Columbia Univ: Traphagen Sch of Design, Work: Lannan Found, Palm Beach, Fla; Metrop Mus Art Costume Inst, New York. Collections Arranged: Biet Giorgis Teust, Lannan Found; Teaching: Instr fashion, Fashion Inst of Technol, New York, 76; instr chic, Hunter Col, 77 & instr style, Cooper-Hewitt Mus of Decorative Arts & Design, New York, 77. Pos: Ed, Vogue Mag, S Africa, 65-68, US, 71-74; contribr, Rand Daily Mail, 69-70; pres, Mary McFadden, Inc, 74-, Mary McFadden Jewels, 78-; pres & cur, Lannan Found, Palm Beach, Fla, 74- Awards: Coty Award, Audence Piquit Award, 76 & Bix Award, 77; State of Pa Gov's Award, 77; Legendary Women Award, Birmingham, Ala, 77. Style & Technique: Fabric designer. Media: Silk. Collection: Ancient artifacts from Egypt, Greece and Madagascar; primitive sculpture from Africa and New Guinea; Oriental artifacts and furniture; contemporary American art, including painting by Tom Wudl, Clyfford Still, Jane di Braghenti and Robert Mangold, sculpture by Mark di Suvero, Kenneth Shores & Isamu Noguchi. Publ: Auth, var articles on Iran, Haiti, Usbzcistan-Tashkent & Easter Island, Vogue USA, 71. Mailing Add: 264 W 35th St New York NY 10001

MCFARREN, GRACE
PAINTER
Study: Sch Design for Women; Graphic Sketch Club; Pierce Jr Col, Philadelphia; Cleveland Inst Art, study with Clayton Bachtel, Peter Dubaniewicz & Joseph McCullough; Del Art Ctr, Wilmington, with Robert McKinney, 60; study with Edgar Whitney, New York, 69; also study with Marion Bryson & Doris Peters. Work: Univ Del; Hagley Mus; DuPont de Nemours & Co; Hotel DuPont; three Wilmington Banks. Exhib: Ann May Show, Cleveland Art Mus; Dayton Art Mus Lending Libr of Paintings; Smithsonian Inst, Washington, DC;

Nelson Rockefeller Collection; Philadelphia Mus Art; Del Mus Art. Teaching: Lectr, Univ Del Days for Women Exten, four yrs. Pos: Founder, Wilmington Circulating Gallery of Paintings, dir, currently. Awards: Three Purchase Prizes, Univ Del Ann Regional Shows; First, Second & Hon Mention, Chester Co Art Asn; Best in Show, Nat League Am Pen Women Nat Show & Rehoboth Art League. Mem: Am Watercolor Soc. Style & Technique: Realism, abstract. Media: Watercolor, Acrylic, Oil. Mailing Add: 3 Winterbury Circle Wilmington DE 19808

MCFEE, JUNE KING
EDUCATOR, WRITER
b Seattle, Wash, June 3, 17. Study: Whitman Col, 35-37; Univ Wash, BA, 39; Cent Wash Col, MEd, 54; Stanford Univ, EdD, 57; Archipenko Sch Art; Cornish Sch Art; also with Amede Ozenfant. Exhib: Seattle Art Mus; Seattle Artists Summer Shows; Wash State Invitational; Stanford Art Gallery Fac Exhibs. Teaching: From instr to asst prof art educ, Stanford Univ, 55-63; vis assoc prof, Ariz State Univ, 64-65; from assoc prof to prof art educ & dir, Inst Community Studies, Univ Ore, 65-77, head art educ dept, 77- Pos: Pres, Pac Regional, Nat Art Educ Asn, 67-69; ed, Studies in Art Educ. Mem: Nat Art Educ Asn; Soc Res in Art Educ. Res: Study of the creative potential of academically superior adolescents, supported by a Ford Foundation grant to a secondary education project at Stanford University; study of the City for Children supported by the American Institute of Architects. Publ: Auth, Creative problem solving abilities in art of academically superior adolescents, Nat Art Educ, 68; auth, Visual Communication in Educational Media: Theory into Practice, 69, Preparation for Art, 70 & Art, Culture & Environment, 77, Wadsworth; auth, Art for academically talented, In: Encycl Educ, Macmillan, 72; contribr, articles in Res in Art Educ & Western Arts Bull; plus many others. Mailing Add: Inst Community Studies Univ Ore Sch Archit & Arts Eugene OR 97403

MCGARRELL, JAMES
PAINTER, EDUCATOR
b Indianapolis, Ind, Feb 22, 30. Study: Ind Univ, AB, 53; Skowhegan Sch Painting & Sculpture, 53; Univ Calif, Los Angeles, MA, 55; Stuttgard Acad Fine Arts, Ger, Fulbright fel, 56. Work: Whitney Mus Am Art, New York; Mus Mod Art, New York; Mus Mod Art, Paris; Mus Hambourg, Ger; Joseph Hirshhorn Mus, Washington, DC. Exhib: Dokumenta III, Kassel, Ger; Americans, Art Inst Chicago; Salons Galeries Pilotes, Lausanne, Switz, Venice Biennale, Italy, 68; Carnegie Inst Int, Pittsburgh. Teaching: Vis artist, Reed Col, 56-59; prof fine arts, Ind Univ, 59- Awards: Nat Inst Arts & Lett Citation & Grant, 63; Guggenheim Found Fel, 64; Nat Endowment Arts Award for Artists Who Teach, 66. Bibliog: Peter Selz (auth), New Images of Man, Mus Mod Art, New York, 59; Giovanni Testori (auth), McGarrell, Claude Bernard (Paris), 67; Norman Geske (auth), Venice 34, the Figurative Tradition in Recent American Art, Smithsonian, 68. Mem: Col Art Asn Am (bd dirs, 70-74). Style & Technique: Non-photo realism, reinvented, reconstructed and panoramic. Dealer: Allan Frumkin Galleries 41 E 57th St New York NY 10022; Galerie Claude Bernard 5 Rue des Beaux Arts Paris France. Mailing Add: Dept of Fine Arts Ind Univ Bloomington IN 47401

MCGARVEY, ELSIE SIRATZ
CURATOR, LECTURER
b Bethlehem, Pa, May 25, 12. Study: Philadelphia Col Art. Collections Arranged: Facts & Fads of Fashion—Exhibition of Period Costumes & Accessories, Beaver Col, 65; The Bride in Fashion—Three Centuries of Wedding Gowns, 66 & The Story of Samplers (display of samplers & embroideries from 1662 to the present), 71, Philadelphia Mus Art. Teaching: Instr-lectr fashion illus, Beaver Col Fine Art Dept, 39-68; instr-lectr fashion design, Philadelphia Col Art, 42-63. Pos: Artist, Vogue-Vogue Pattern Serv, Conte Nast Publ, Greenwich, Conn, 34-39; cur costume & textiles, Philadelphia Mus Art, 56- Awards: Citizen of Week, Willow Grove Guide, 65; Personality of Week, Times Chronicle, 67; Temple Univ Woman of Achievement, 70. Bibliog: Portrait of a professor, Beaver Col Alumni J, 2/66. Mem: Am Asn Univ Prof; Fashion Group Philadelphia; Philadelphia Art Alliance; Acad Fine Arts & Peale Club; Am Asn Mus. Publ: Auth, The fashion wing, Philadelphia Mus Art Bull, autumn 61. Mailing Add: Philadelphia Mus Art PO Box 7646 Philadelphia PA 19101

MCGEE, OLIVIA JACKSON
PAINTER, ILLUSTRATOR
b SC, Nov 19, 15. Study: Limestone Col, BA; Clemson Univ Sch Visual Arts; Rex Brandt's Sch Painting, Europe & Corona del Mar, Calif; Whitney Sch Watercolor, Maine; Art Students League; painting with Eliot O'Hara. Work: Chemstrand Corp, Empire State Bldg, New York; People's Nat Bank & Trust Co, Greenville, SC; Clemson Univ Alumni Ctr; Gov Mansion, Columbia, SC. Exhib: Greenville Co Mus Art, Greenville, SC, 69; Contemp SC Artists, 70; Picken's Co Artists, Rudolf E Lee Gallery, Clemson Univ, 71 & 72; Guild SC Artists, Columbia; Greenville Arts Festival; Clemson Univ Union Gallery, 77; Pickens Co Art Mus, Pickens, SC, 77; Sumter Co Art Mus, Sumter, SC, 78. Teaching: Instr watercolor, Clemson Univ Continuing Educ Ctr, 63-; instr, Tempo Art Gallery, Greenville, 77- Pos: Illusr, Clemson Univ Exten Serv, 50-56; state pres, Nat League Am Pen Women, 66-68; mem, Pickens Co Art Comn, 71-72. Awards: Best in Show Awards, Greenville Arts Festival, 68, Watson Village Arts Festival, 69 & Anderson Co Fair, 69. Bibliog: Jack Morris (auth), Contemporary Artists of South Carolina, Greenville Co Mus Art, 70; Charles M Israel (auth), Artists Olivia McGee, Sandlapper Mag, 71. Mem: Greenville Co Artists Guild; Guild SC Artists. Style & Technique: Romantic realist. Media: Watercolor. Mailing Add: 221 Riggs Dr Clemson SC 29631

MCGEE, WILLIAM DOUGLAS
PAINTER, EDUCATOR
b Syracuse, NY, May 11, 25. Study: Black Mountain Col; Univ NMex, BFA; Ind Univ, MFA; also with Franz Kline, Jack T Workov & Adja Yunkers. Work: Dallas Mus Fine Arts; Baltimore Mus Fine Art; Albright-Knox Mus, Buffalo, NY; Jonson Mus, Albuquerque, NMex; Tate Gallery, London. Exhib: American Abstract Art, Chrysler Mus, Provincetown, Mass, 59-60; Younger American Painters, Am Acad Arts & Lett, New York, 59-61; Seymour Knox Collection, Yale Univ, 61; one-man shows, Katonah Gallery, NY, 72 & Max Hutchinson Gallery, 72 & 74. Teaching: Asst prof painting, Brown Univ, 56-60; asst prof painting, Hunter Col, 62-68; asst prof painting, Lehman Col, 68- Awards: First Purchase Prize for Prints, Dallas Mus Fine Arts, 49; Res Awards, City Univ New York, 68 & 69. Style & Technique: Color field; paintings limited in color; particular concerns are surface, color feeling and scale. Media: Acrylic, Oil, Watercolor. Dealer: Max Hutchinson Gallery 127 Greene St New York NY 10012. Mailing Add: Rte 166 Purdy Station NY 10578

MCGEE, WINSTON EUGENE
PAINTER
b Salem, Ill, Sept 4, 24. Study: Univ Mo, BJ, 48 & MA, 49; Univ Wis; Ecole Superieure Beaux-Arts, 50-51; Atelier-M Jean Souverbie, French Nat Acad, 51. Work: Whitney Mus Am Art, New York; Calif Palace of Legion of Honor, San Francisco; Philadelphia Mus Art; Smithsonian Inst, Washington, DC; Indianapolis Mus Art, Ind. Comn: Relief painting, Mo State Hist Soc, Columbia; mural, Trinity Cathedral, Cleveland, Ohio; mural, David Leach estate, Madison, Ohio. Exhib: Eleven Artists in Europe, Int Cult Exhib, Paris, 58; one-man shows, Trabie Gallery, New York, 61 & Mitchell Mus, Mt Vernon, Ill, 74; 50th Yr Anniversary Traveling Show, Cleveland Mus, 68; Lincoln Fine Arts Ctr Dedication Exhib, 70. Pos: Head dept art, Lake Erie Col, 52-69; new mkt design rev bd, Lake Co, Ohio, 68-72; actg chmn art, Cleveland State Univ, 69-72, fac in painting, 72-76; prof & chmn art dept, Calif State Col, Stanislaus, 77- Awards: Fulbright Scholar to Paris, 51; Cleveland Mus May Show Jury Award, 68; Annie McEntree Norton Award Painting & Graphic, Univ Mo. Bibliog: Article in Graphic Artists, 72; article in Mo State Hist Soc Bulletin, 9/75. Mem: Cleveland Coun Arts; Cleveland Art Community; New Orgn for Visual Arts; fel Int Inst Arts & Lett (Switz). Style & Technique: Abstract space compositions with free spontaneous rhythms in primary color keys and symbolic shape constructions. Media: Oil, Acrylic. Mailing Add: 800 Monte Vista Turlock CA 95380

MCGEOCH, LILLIAN JEAN
PAINTER, SCULPTOR
b Sundridge, Ont, 1903. Study: Cent Tech Commercial Art Course; Ont Col Art; sculpture with Alfred Howell & Emmanuel Hahn; painting with William J Beatty. Work: Halifax Art Asn. Exhib: Maritime Art Asn, Halifax, NS, 65; NS Soc Artists, Halifax, 66; Douglas Art Gallery, Toronto, 66; Etobicoke Artists, Islington, 67-68; Lambton Gallery, Toronto, 70-71; one-artist show, York Fine Arts Gallery, 77. Teaching: Instr drawing & painting, Burnamthorpe Col, 52-; instr drawing & painting, Scarlett Heights Col, 60- Pos: Commercial artist, Brigden's Ltd, Toronto, 20-26; fashion designer, Photo Engravers, Toronto, 26-28. Awards: Etobicoke Art Group Award of Merit, 62 & 63. Mem: Women's Art Asn Toronto (vpres, 64-66); NS Soc Artists (vpres & secy, 61-63); Sculptors Nine Toronto; Civic Centre Art Comt; Prueter Art Selection Comt (chmn exhib, 78); Etobicoke Art Group (vpres & secy, 52-); Women's Art Asn Hamilton. Media: Oil, Bronze. Dealer: Lambton Gallery Dundas St Toronto ON Can; Fine Art Gallery Eatons Yonge St Toronto ON Can. Mailing Add: 15 King Georges Rd Toronto ON M8X 1K8 Can

MCGILL, ROBERT LEE
PAINTER, INSTRUCTOR
b Milwaukee, Wis, Oct 23, 41. Study: Univ Wis Milwaukee, BFA, 64; Pa State Univ, MFA, 66. Work: Crocker Art Mus, Sacramento, Calif; Downey Mus Art, Calif; Univ Wis-Madison; Pa State Univ. Exhib: Biannual of Painting & Sculpture, Walker Art Ctr, Minneapolis, 67; Chicago & Vicinity Show, Art Inst Chicago, 68; Northern California Artists, Crocker Art Mus, 69, Kingsley Show, 73; Downey Mus Art, 72. Teaching: Instr painting, Univ Wis-Milwaukee, 67-69; instr painting, Shasta Col, 69- Awards: Prize, Walker Art Ctr, 67; Purchase Prize, Downey Mus Art, 72; Kingsley Show, Purchase Prize, Crocker Art Mus, 73. Style & Technique: Color field; staining. Media: Acrylic. Mailing Add: c/o Baum Gallery Three Embarcadero Ctr San Francisco CA 94111

MCGILVERY, LAURENCE
ANTIQUARIAN BOOK DEALER, PUBLISHER
b Los Angeles, Calif, May 21, 32. Study: Pomona Col, BA, 54. Pos: Mem adv bd, Artbibliographs Mod, Santa Barbara, 73 & Who's Who in Am Art & Am Art Dir, 78. Mem: Art Libr Soc of NAm; Antiquarian Booksellers Asn Am. Res: Art periodical indexes and art bibliographies. Publ: Auth, Artforum, 1962-1968: A Cummulative Index to the First Six Volumes, McGilvery, 70. Mailing Add: PO Box 852 La Jolla CA 92038

MCGINNIS, CHRISTINE
PAINTER
b Philadelphia, Pa. Study: Pa Acad Fine Arts. Work: Mus Nat Sci, Philadelphia; Civic Ctr Mus, Philadelphia; Free Libr Philadelphia; Am Embassy, Dublin, Ireland; Pa Acad Fine Arts. Exhib: Pa Acad Fine Arts Nat Ann, 59; Philadelphia Art Mus Regional Exhib, 64; Brooklyn Art Mus 14th Nat Exhib, New York, 65; Am Express Pavillion, New York World's Fair, 66; Libr Cong 20th Nat, Washington, DC, 67. Awards: Thomas Eakins Prize, Pa Acad Fine Arts, 58, H S Morris Mem Drawing Prize, 61; Cresson Traveling Scholar, 60. Media: Acrylic, Graphics. Publ: Illusr, Mademoiselle Mag, 61; illusr, Chelsea Rev No 12, 62; illusr, Ctr City Mag, 63. Mailing Add: c/o Rodger La Pelle Graphics 5929 Devon Pl Philadelphia PA 19138

MCGLAUCHLIN, TOM
GLASSBLOWER, POTTER
b Beloit, Wis, Sept 14, 34. Study: Univ Wis, BS, 59, MS(art), 60; pottery with James McKinnell, Univ Iowa, 62; Oriental art hist, Univ Washington, 66-67. Work: Corning Mus of Glass, NY; Toledo Mus of Art, Ohio; Minn Art Mus, St Paul; Portland Mus of Art, Ore; Mus of Contemp Crafts, New York. Exhib: Objects USA, Johnson Wax Collection, Smithsonian Mus, Washington, DC, 69; Am Glass Now, Toledo Mus of Art, 72; Biennial Beaux Arts Designer Craftsman, Columbus Gallery, Ohio, 73; New Am Glass, Huntington Galleries, WVa, 76; Glass Art Soc Exhib, Corning Glass Mus, NY, 76; Int Paperweight exhib, Habatat Gallery, Dearborn, Mich, 77. Teaching: Prof art, Cornell Col, Mt Vernon, Iowa, 61-71; instr glass blowing, Toledo Mus of Art, 71- Pos: Chmn art dept, Cornell Col, Mt Vernon, 68-71. Awards: Award for Glass, Miami Nat, Lowe Gallery, Univ Miami, Coral Gables, Fla, 65; First Jury Award, Toledo Glass Nat II, Toledo Mus of Art, 68; First Award Glass, 7th Beaux Arts, Pittsburgh Glass Co, Pa, 75. Mem: Glass Art Soc; Am Crafts Coun; Col Art Asn. Style & Technique: Concerned with form of containers in hand blown glass. Media: Hand-blown glass, stained glass; pottery. Dealer: Habatat Gallery 1820 N Telegraph Dearborn MI 48128. Mailing Add: 2527 Cheltenham Toledo OH 43606

MCGONAGLE, WILLIAM ALBERT
ART ADMINISTRATOR
b Duluth, Minn, Dec 23, 24. Study: Univ Minn, BS(art educ & social studies), 48; Univ Mich, MFA, 51; Buffalo Mus Sci, NY, 48-49; Albright-Knox Art Gallery, Buffalo, 48-49. Collections Arranged: Mary Cassatt Among the Impressionists (with catalog), 69; The Thirties Decade: American Artists & Their European Contemporaries (with catalog), 71. Pos: Dir, Detroit Inst Arts, 51-61; cur, Honolulu Acad Arts, Hawaii, 61-65; cur, Joslyn Art Mus, Omaha, Nebr, 65-71, dir, 72-75; dir, Burpee Art Mus, Rockford Art Asn, Ill, 77- Mem: Asn Art Mus Dir; Am Asn Mus; Nebr Arts Coun (bd dirs); Hist Gen Dodge House, Council Bluffs, Iowa (trustee). Mailing Add: c/o Burpee Art Mus Rockford Art Asn 737 N Main St Rockford IL 61103

MCGOUGH, CHARLES E
PRINTMAKER, EDUCATOR
b Elmhurst, Ill, Aug 2, 27. Study: Southwestern Univ; Ray Vogue Commercial Art Sch, dipl; Univ Tulsa, BA & MA; NTex State Univ; also with Hardin Simmons. Work: Boston Mus; Philbrook Mus; Dallas Mus Fine Arts; Little Rock Mus Fine Arts; Mus Mod Art. Comn: Genre mural, Southern Hills Country Club, Tulsa, Okla, 56; mural, ETex State Univ, Commerce, 63; mural, Goodfellow AFB, San Angelo, Tex, 64; several graphic works, First Nat Bank, Dallas, Tex, 65; several graphic works, Southwestern Life Ins Co, Dallas, 67.

Exhib: Nat Serigraph Ann, Brooklyn Mus Art, Drawing USA, Walker Art Ctr, 63 & 66; Nat Print Ann, Boston Mus Fine Arts, 65 & 67; Southwest Print & Drawing Ann, Dallas Mus Fine Arts, 67, 68 & 70; Nat Print & Drawing Ann, Okla Art Ctr, 69-72. Teaching: Instr art, N R Crogier Tech High Sch, Dallas, 52-56; prof art & head art dept, ETex State Univ, 56- Pos: Owner, McGough Advert Co, 45-50; art dir, Crane Advert, Tulsa, 50-52. Awards: Graphic Purchase Award, Boston Univ Mus Show, 65; Southwest Print & Drawing Ann Award, Dallas Mus Fine Arts, 67; Graphic Purchase Award, Nat Print Ann, Okla Art Ctr, 71. Mem: Southwest Print & Drawing Soc; Tex Asn Schs Art. Style & Technique: Accent is on perfection of craft with a great concern for the beauty of line in graphics and watercolor. Media: Graphics. Publ: Auth, Print painting, Dallas Morning News, 67; auth, Serigraphy, Dallas Times Herald, 68; auth, Serigraph & the total image, Tex Trends Art Educ, 68. Dealer: Cushing Galleries 2723 Fairmount St Dallas TX 75201. Mailing Add: 1603 Walnut Commerce TX 75428

MCGOVERN, ROBERT F
PAINTER, SCULPTOR
b Philadelphia, Pa, Apr 1, 33. Study: Philadelphia Col Art, Pa, with Benton Spruance. Work: Philadelphia Mus Art; Free Libr of Philadelphia; Rare Bk Collection, Cornell Univ, Ithaca, NY. Comn: Portraits of Bishop Lorenz Grassel & Mathew Carey, Am Cath Hist Soc, Philadelphia, 76; 6ft carving of Bishop Neumann, Bishop Neumann High Sch, Philadelphia, 77; banner of St John Neumann, comn by Sister of St Francis for use at Canonization, Rome, Italy, 77; wood relief of St John Neumann for Daylesford Abbey, Paoli, Pa, 78. Exhib: Prints & Drawings, Philadelphia Art Alliance, 62; Print Club, Philadelphia, 63; Am Color Print Soc, Philadelphia, 73-77; Liturgical Arts, 41st Int Eucharistic Cong, 77. Teaching: Prof drawing design & anatomy, Philadelphia Col Art, 56- Pos: Co-chmn found prog, Philadelphia Col Art, 76- Mem: Philadelphia Print Club; Artists Equity (pres, Philadelphia Chap, 64-65); Am Color Print Soc. Style & Technique: Reflective realism. Media: Wood Carving, Woodcuts; Oil. Publ: Auth rev, Religious Art in 20th Century—An Understanding, Pax Romano, Fribourg, Switz, 65; co-auth, Saturday Waiting—60 Pen & Ink Drawings, Fortress Press, Philadelphia, 70; auth, A Re-emergence of religious art in the seventies, Dimension Mag, Philadelphia, 74; illusr, Uncommon Book of Prayer, Seabury Press, 78. Mailing Add: 120 Woodside Ave Narberth PA 19072

MCGOWIN, ED
SCULPTOR, PAINTER
b Hattiesburg, Miss, June 2, 38. Study: Miss Southern Col, BS; Univ Ala, MA. Work: Addison Mus Art, Andover, Mass; Corcoran Gallery Art, Washington, DC; Nat Collection Fine Arts, Washington, DC; New Orleans Mus Art, La; Whitney Mus Am Art, New York. Exhib: Whitney Ann Am Sculpture, 68; Gilliam Krebs McGowin, Corcoran Gallery, 69; Madison Art Ctr, Wis, 71; one-man shows, Baltimore Mus Art, 72 & Corcoran Gallery Art, Washington, DC, 75; Painting & Sculpture Today, Indianapolis Mus Art, 74; Artist Notebooks, Philadelphia Col Art, 76; 9th Int Painting Exhib, Cagnes Sur-Mer, France, 77; Narrative Art/Story Art, Contemp Mus Art, Houston, Tex, 77. Awards: Nat Endowment Arts Award, 67 & 76; Award, Am Ctr Students & Artists, Paris, 74; Oscar for Painting, 9th Int Painting Exhib, Cagnes Sur-Mer, France, 77. Bibliog: Rose (auth), Gallery without walls, Art in Am, 68; Hopps & Osnos (auth), Three Washington artists Gilliam Krebs McGowin, Art Int, 70. Style & Technique: Grandoise extravaganzas, involving auto crashes and chickens and dogs, alive and stuffed. Publ: Auth, Three Projects: Harrison, Mock, McGowin, Art in Am, 74. Mailing Add: 1884 Columbia Rd Washington DC 20009

MCGRATH, JAMES ARTHUR
ART ADMINISTRATOR, PAINTER
b Tacoma, Wash, Sept 2, 28. Study: Cent Wash State Col, 45-48; Univ Ore, BS, 50; Mont State Univ, summer 51; Univ Wash, 52; Staatliche Akad Bildenden Kunste, Karlsruhe, Ger, 58-59, with H A P Grieshaber; Univ NMex, MA, 73. Work: Mus NMex, Santa Fe; New Westinghouse Bldg, Oklahoma City; Panelette Corp, Skokie, Ill; Inst Am Indian Arts, Santa Fe. Comn: Hopi (painting), Bur Indian Affairs, Washington, DC, 70. Exhib: Seattle Art Mus, 51; Zimmer Galerie Franck, Frankfurt am Main, Ger, 56; Galerie Dorothea Loehr, Frankfurt am Main, 61; Mus NMex, 64-71; Butler Inst Am Arts, Youngstown, Ohio, 66. Collections Arranged: Am Indian exhibs & catalogs, Ctr Arts of Indian Am, Washington, DC, 63-70; Am Indian Dance Prog, The White House, 65; American Indian Arts, Riverside Mus, 65, Edinburgh Festival, 66, Berlin Festival, 66, Ankara, Turkey, 66, Alaskan Centennial, 67, Mus Bellas Artes, Buenos Aires, 67, Bibliot Nac, Santiago, Chile, 68 & Mexican Olympics, Mexico City, 68; Spec Am Indian Exhibs, US Dept State, 66-69; 50 Years with Laura Gilpin, Photographer, 69; Dance and Indian Children (with catalog) & Native American Musical Instruments (with catalog), Ctr for Arts of Indian Am, Washington, DC, 70- Teaching: Instr art, Richland Pub Schs, Wash, 52-55; instr & dir art, US Dept Defense Schs in Ger, France, Italy & Ethiopia, 55-62; instr written & visual arts, Inst Am Indian Arts, Santa Fe, 62- Pos: Exhib consult & designer, Ctr Arts of Indian Am, 63-70; Am Indian spec, exhibs & projs, US State Dept, 66-69; dir arts, US Dept Interior, Bur Indian Affairs, Inst Am Indian Arts, 64-72, dir spec projs, 72-73; dir arts, Dept Defense Schs in Japan, Korea, Taiwan & The Philippines, 73- Awards: First Prize for Spawning Salmon (stone sculpture), Bellevue Fair, Wash, 52; First Prize for Sequafnehma (painting), Mus NMex, 64, Honorable Mention for Bear Hunter (bronze sculpture), 69. Bibliog: Sally Hayman (auth), Shadow of Indian spirits by sun, lamp and fire, Seattle Post Intelligencer, 11/19/67; Narrative Poetry, American Indian Artists Series, PBS-KAET Television, Ariz, 74-77; Stones, Bones & Skin, Ritual & Shamanic Art, Ariz Hwy, 8/76 & Artscanada, 77. Mem: Int Soc Educ Through the Arts; UNESCO Conf on Creativity, Hamburg, Ger; Smithsonian Inst; plus others. Style & Technique: Japanese-Chinese calligraphy. Media: Oil, Earth Pigment, Bronze. Res: Native American cultures (Indian, Aleut, Eskimo) and their contributions to contemporary life styles. Publ: Auth, Powhoge: the Martinez Family of San Ildefonso Pueblo, 67; auth, Quilaut: the Art of Getting in Touch With the Spirits, 67; auth, Art and Indian Children, 70; plus others. Mailing Add: 5214 S Prospect St Tacoma WA 98409

MCGRATH, KYRAN MURRAY
ART ADMINISTRATOR
b Chicago, Ill, Aug 24, 34. Study: Georgetown Univ, BSS(cum laude), 56, LLB, 59. Pos: Dir, Am Asn Mus, 68-75. Mem: Am Soc Asn Exec; Am Asn State & Local Hist; Nat Trust for Hist Preserv; Int Coun Mus. Publ: Auth, articles in Mus News, Compact & Art in Am, 68-; auth, 1971 & 1973 Financial & Salary Surveys, Am Asn Mus, 71 & 73. Mailing Add: Suite 1000 1700 Pennsylvania Ave NW Washington DC 20006

MCGREGOR, JACK R
MUSEUM DIRECTOR
b Coffeyville, Kans, Mar 17, 30. Study: Univ Kans, BA(chem), 52; Brown Univ, 52-53: Univ Ital per Stranieri, Perugia, Italy, summer 56; Harvard Univ, 57-58; NY Univ, Metrop Mus Art fel, 57-58; also independent study in Europe. Collections Arranged: Assisted in formation & cataloging Wrightsman Collection, 63. Pos: Admin asst, Metrop Mus Art, 57-62; dir, M H de Young Mem Mus, 63-69; dir, San Antonio Mus Asn, 69- Awards: Order of the North Star, King of Sweden, 68. Mailing Add: 3801 Broadway San Antonio TX 78209

MCGREW, BRUCE ELWIN
PAINTER, INSTRUCTOR
b Wichita, Kans, Oct 20, 37. Study: Wichita State Univ, Kans, BFA; Univ Ariz, MFA, 64. Work: Nat Park Serv, Three Rivers, Calif & Haleakala Nat Park, Maui, Hawaii; Ft Hays Kans State Col, Hays; Univ Minn, Morris; Yuma Fine Arts Asn, Ariz. Comn: 8ft x 9ft oil landscape, Georgetown Leather, Washington, DC, 77; 24ft x 30ft watercolor, Pennie Edmonds Law Firm, New York, 77. Exhib: 73rd Western Ann, Denver Art Mus, Colo, 70; Nat Watercolor Exhib, Wichita Art Mus, Kans, 70; Braniff Int Invitational, Tucson, Ariz, 73; Triad, Wichita Art Mus, Kans, 75; Spectra 1975, Arizona's Outlook, Tucson Mus Art, Ariz, 75 & 78; Yuma Fine Arts Asn, Ariz, 75-78; Drawing Invitational, Santa Rosa Jr Col, Calif, 76; Hawaii in Watercolor, Honolulu Acad Arts, 77. Teaching: Instr painting & drawing, Univ Minn, Morris, 64-66; assoc prof painting & drawing, Univ Ariz, Tucson, 66- Pos: Artist-in-residence, Nat Park Serv, Sequoia & Kings Canyon Nat Park, Three Rivers, Calif, summer 75 & Haleakala Nat Park, Maui, Hawaii, summer 76; mem staff watercolor workshop, Summervail Art Workshop, Vail, Colo, summer 77. Awards: Fac Res Support in Humanities & Sociology, Univ Ariz, Tucson, 72-73; Purchase Awards, 13th Ann Cedar City Exhib, Utah, 74 & Ninth South Western Invitational Yuma Fine Arts Asn, Ariz, 75. Style & Technique: Landscape and figurative. Media: Watercolor and oil Publ: Contribr, Oracle: A Voluntary of Poems and Prints, Oracle Press, 74. Dealer: Marion Locks Gallery 1524 Walnut Philadelphia PA 19102. Mailing Add: Box E Oracle AZ 85623

MCGREW, RALPH BROWNELL
PAINTER
b Columbus, Ohio, Sept 6, 16. Study: Otis Art Inst, Los Angeles, with full scholar & spec fac awards, 4 yrs; also with Edouard Vysekal, Ralph Holmes & E Roscoe Shrader. Work: Cowboy Hall Fame Permanent Collection, Oklahoma City; Mus Northern Ariz Collection, Flagstaff; Diamond M Mus, Snyder, Tex; Anschutz Collection, Denver; Nat Acad Western Art; plus others. Exhib: Cowboy Artists Am, Cowboy Hall Fame; Death Valley Invitational, Calif; All-California Invitational, Laguna Beach, 59-62; Charles Russell Rendezvous Invitational, Helena, Mont, 72; Nat Acad Western Art; plus others. Teaching: Asst instr art, Otis Art Inst. Pos: Chmn, Stacey Scholar Found. Awards: First Prizes, Death Valley Invitational, 61-68; Gold Medal for Drawing & Silver Medal for Painting, Cowboy Hall Fame, 70, Gold Medal for Drawing, 72; Gold Medals, Nat Acad Western Art, 73 & 74 & Silver Medal, 75. Bibliog: Ed Ainsworth (auth), Painters of the desert, Desert Mag Press, 60 & 61; Dorothy Harmsen (auth), Harmsen's Western Americana, Northland, 71; Western Painting Today, Watson-Guptill, 75; McGrew, Lowell Press, 78. plus others. Mem: fel Am Inst Fine Arts; Nat Acad Western Art. Style & Technique: Classico-impressionist. Media: Oil, Charcoal. Publ: Auth, Artist on the Colorado, 61 & auth, Tewa-quaptewa, Hopi Chief, 61, Desert Mag; auth, Water of life for God's red children, This Day Mag, 65; auth, The art of R Brownell McGrew, Ariz Hwys, 7/69 & 10/77. Dealer: O'Brien's Art Emporium 7122 Stetson Scottsdale AZ 85251; Trailside Galleries Jackson WY. Mailing Add: PO Box 2 Quemado NM 87829

MCHUGH, ADELIZA SORENSON
ART DEALER, COLLECTOR
b St George, Utah, Apr 29, 12. Study: Spec study with Robert Arneson, Roy De Forest, David Gilhooly, Gladys Nilsson, Jim Nutt & Maija Peeples. Collections Arranged: Roy De Forest Drawings, San Francisco Mus & Whitney Mus, New York. Pos: Dir, Candy Store Gallery, Folsom, Calif, 62- Specialty: Contemporary American art. Collection: Californian ceramic sculpture, American primitive drawings of today; California paintings. Mailing Add: 605 Sutter St Folsom CA 95630

MCILHENNY, HENRY PLUMER
COLLECTOR
b Philadelphia, Pa, Oct 7, 10. Study: Harvard Univ, AB(magna cum laude), 33, grad study, 33-34. Collections Arranged: Degas; Daumier; Philadelphia Silver; Connelly and Haines; Tucker China; Shaker Furniture. Pos: Cur decorative arts, Philadelphia Mus Art, 35-64, trustee, 64-, vpres, 68-76, chmn bd dirs, 76; mem vis comt art mus, Harvard Col. Mailing Add: 1914 Rittenhouse Sq Philadelphia PA 19103

MCILROY, CAROL JEAN
PAINTER, ART DEALER
b Sandpoint, Idaho, Feb 21, 24. Study: Univ Colo, with John Pellew; Univ NMex, with Joe Morello, Arthur Sussman & Sam Smith. Work: Am Bank Com, Albuquerque NMex; NMex Jr Col. Exhib: Mainstreams, 69; Regional Art Exhib, Phoenix, 71; McAddo II Gallery, Prescott, Ariz, 73; Lubbock Tex Art Exhib, 74. Pos: Chmn standards comt, NMex Arts & Crafts Fair, 72-73; mem, Bicentennial Art Comt, 75; co-owner, Galeria del Sol. Awards: Grand Prize & Best of Show, Sky Country, Montrose Art Festival, Colo, 70; First Prize, RFD, NMex State Fair, 71; First Prize Landscape, 4th Regional Art Exhib, Phoenix, 71. Mem: Am Artists Prof League; Artists Equity (vpres, 71-72); NMex Art League. Style & Technique: Traditional. Media: Oil. Mailing Add: Galerie del Sol 206 1/2 San Felipe NW Albuquerque NM 87102

MCILVAIN, DOUGLAS LEE
INSTRUCTOR
b Mt Holly, NJ, July 26, 23. Study: Tyler Sch Fine Arts, Temple Univ, BFA & BS(educ); NY Univ, MA(art educ), Tyler Art Sch Rome; also with Raphael Sabatini & Jose De Creeft. Work: Monmouth Col; Georgian Court Col; Tyler Sch Rome. Comn: Portrait, Henry Hudson High Sch, 65; portrait, Stephenson Corp, 67; portrait, Hosp Picture Serv Co, 74. Exhib: Detroit Inst Art, 59; Pa Acad Art, 60; Jersey City Mus, 61; NJ State Mus, 67; Philadelphia Civic Ctr Mus, 72. Teaching: Assoc prof art, Georgian Court Col, 68- Awards: First Prize, Montclair Mus, 60; First Prize, Jersey City Mus, 61; First Prize, Red Bank Festival Arts, 61-62, 64-65, 67, 69-71 & 73. Mem: Southern Asn Sculptors; Guild Creative Arts. Style & Technique: Figurative work and abstract; woodcarving. Media: Bronze, Wood. Mailing Add: 40 Whitman Dr Red Bank NJ 07701

MCINERNEY, GENE JOSEPH
PAINTER
b Bangor, Pa, Jan 6, 30. Work: Miniature Art Soc of NJ, Nutley; Fred Clark Mus, Carversville, Pa; Meadowbrook Sch, Philadelphia, Pa. Comn: Bicentennial Calendar, Northampton Co, Pa, Bicentennial Comn, 75. Exhib: Miniature Art Soc, NJ, Nutley, 71-73; Painters & Sculptors Soc NJ, Jersey City Mus, 71, 72 & 74; Miniature Painters, Sculptors & Gravers Soc, Washington, DC Arts Club, 72 & 73; Nat Soc Painters in Casein & Acrylic, Nat Acad, New York, 72-75; Mainstreams Int, Marietta, Ohio, 72 & 73. Awards: First Prize, Atlantic City Nat Boardwalk Show, 70; Mainstreams Award of Excellence, Marietta Col, 72; Presidents Prize, Painters & Sculptors Soc NJ, 74. Bibliog: Art, Gene McInerney, LaRevue

Moderne, 11/72. Mem: Old Bergen Art Guild; Lehigh Art Alliance; Painters & Sculptors Soc NJ; Miniature Arts Soc NJ; Allentown Art Mus. Style & Technique: Magic realism and photorealism painting; speciality is miniature painting. Media: Acrylic, Watercolor. Dealer: Fred Clark Mus Aquetong RJ Carversville PA 18913; Bernard Picture Co New York NY. Mailing Add: Northlight Studio RD 4 Bangor PA 18013

MCINTOSH, HAROLD
PAINTER
b Galashiels, Scotland, Mar 1, 16; US citizen. Study: Winnipeg Sch Art; with L L Fitzgerald. Work: Berkshire Mus, Pittsfield, Mass; Sharon Hist Mus, Conn. Comn: Three paintings, Int Tel & Tel Grinnell, Providence, RI, 74. Exhib: Springfield Mus Fine Art, Mass, 62; one-man shows, Mus Hist & Art, Albany, NY, 64, Berkshire Mus, 68 & 74 & Butler Mus, Youngstown, Ohio, 71-73; Conn Acad Fine Arts, Wadsworth Atheneum, Hartford, 70-72. Awards: Best in Show, New Haven Festival Arts, 60, 64 & 69; Best in Show, Wash Art Asn, 74; Medal of Merit, Kent Art Asn, 74. Mem: Berkshire Art Asn; Wash Art Asn; Kent Art Asn (pres, 74-75). Style & Technique: Realism, tempera technique. Media: Acrylic, Silverpoint. Mailing Add: Cornwall Bridge Rd Sharon CT 06069

MCINTOSH, HARRISON EDWARD
CERAMIST, DESIGNER
b Vallejo, Calif, Sept 11, 14. Study: Art Ctr Sch, Los Angeles, 38; Univ Southern Calif study with Glen Lukens, 40; Claremont Grad Sch, Calif, 49-52; Mills Col with Bernard Leach, 50; also with Marguerite Wildenhain, 53. Work: Mus of Contemp Crafts, New York; Smithsonian Inst Washington, DC; Mus Nat de la Ceramique de Severes, Paris; Belg Royal Collection, Ostend, Belg; Kiushu Mus, Japan. Comn: Seven ft stoneware cross, Kingman Chapel, Claremont, Calif, 63; ceramic dinnerware design, 70-76 & glassware design, 77, Mikasa, Co, Secaucus, NJ; steel & stoneware wind chimes, Bank of Calif, Claremont, 72; sculpture series (ltd ed), Claremont Men's Col, 77. Exhib: Ceramic Nat, Everson Mus of Art, Syracuse, NY, 50-68; Calif Design, Pasadena Art Mus, Calif, 53-71; First Int Ceramic Festival, Cannes, France, 55; Craftsmanship in a Changing World, Mus of Contemp Crafts, New York, 56; Craftsmanship, Los Angeles Co Mus of Art, Los Angeles, 58; Int Ceramic Exhib, Syracuse Mus, New York, 58; Second Int Ceramic Festival, Ostend, Belg, 59; one-man shows, Long Beach Mus of Art, Calif, 59 & Wichita Art Asn Gallery, Kans, 73; Retrospective, Pasadena Art Mus, Calif, 63; Craftsmanship Defined, Philadelphia Mus Col of Art, 64; Int Exhib of Contemp Ceramic Art, Mus of Mod Art, Tokyo, Japan, 64-65; Acquisitions, Mus of Contemp Crafts, New York, 67; Objects: USA, The Johnson Collection of Contemp Crafts (int traveling exhib), Smithsonian Inst, 69-76; Media Survey 73, Fine Arts Gallery San Diego, Calif, 73; Calif Ceramics & Glass 1974, Oakland Mus, Calif, 74; Masters in Ceramic Art, Everson Mus & Alfred Univ, New York, 75; Am Crafts 1977, Philadelphia Mus of Art, 77. Teaching: Instr ceramics, Otis Art Inst, Los Angeles, 56-57, summer session, 59. Pos: Ceramic designer, Metlox Pottery Co, Los Angeles, 55-56; ceramic designer, Interpace Corp, Los Angeles, 64-66, designer ceramics & glass, Mikasa Co, Secaucus, NJ, 70-; consult-panelist, Nat Endowment for the Arts, Washington, DC, 76- Awards: Purchase Award, Second Int Ceramic Festival, Ostend, Belg, 59; Purchase Award, 21st Ceramic Nat, Everson Mus of Art, Syracuse, 60; Cash Prize, Calif Ceramics & Glass, Oakland Mus, Calif, 74. Bibliog: Janice LoVoos (auth), The Pottery of Harrison McIntosh, Am Artist Mag, 11/62; Richard Petterson (auth), Harrison McIntosh, Ceramics Monthly Mag, 6/69; Maggy Loyau (auth), Harrison McIntosh, Potier de Californie, Cahiers de la Ceramique, Paris, 74. Mem: Am Crafts Coun; World Crafts Coun; Am Ceramic Soc, Design Div. Style & Technique: Stoneware ceramic vessels; sculptures of pure simple forms combined with hardwoods or chrome. Media: Handthrown stoneware—cone five oxidation. Publ: Contrib, Treasury of Ceramic Art, Scripps Col, 55; contribr, California Design Number 8, 62, Number 9, 65, Number 10, 68 & Number 11, 71, Pasadena Mus; contribr, Marjorie Elliot Bevlin, auth, Design Through Discovery, Holt, Rinehart & Winston, 67; contribr, Lee Nordness, auth, Objects; USA, Viking Press, 70; contribr, Glenn C Nelson, auth, Ceramics: A Potter's Handbook, Three eds, Holt, Rinehart & Winston, 66, 71 & 77. Mailing Add: 4206 Via Padova Claremont CA 91711

MCIVER, JOHN KOLB
PAINTER
b Jacksonville, Fla, Oct 20, 30. Study: Trinity Col (Conn), AB, 53. Work: Okla Mus, Oklahoma City; Jacksonville Art Mus, Fla. Exhib: Am Watercolor Soc, New York, 64-68; Nat Acad Design, New York, 67; Watercolor USA, Springfield, Mo, 70; Mainstreams, Ohio, 71 & 75; Watercolor West, Utah, 75; plus others. Awards: John Marin Mem Award, Watercolor USA, 70. Mem: Am Watercolor Soc. Style & Technique: Direct spontaneous technique with realistic style for transparent watercolor and acrylic-opaque on panel and canvas; realistic and impressionistic style for acrylic-color wash on rice paper. Media: Watercolor, Acrylic. Publ: Contribr, Acrylic Watercolor Painting, Watson Guptill, 70. Mailing Add: 4280 Turtle Bend Apt 5 Grandville MI 49418

MCIVOR, JOHN WILFRED
PRINTMAKER, PAINTER
b Henderson, Ky, July 17, 31. Study: Murray State Univ, 49-50; Univ Ill, BFA(summa cum laude), 57, fel, 57-59, MFA, 59. Work: Albright-Knox Art Gallery, Buffalo, NY; Am Fedn Arts, New York; Libr of Cong, Washington, DC; State Univ NY Albany; Jacksonville Mus, Fla. Comn: Exterior (with David Hatchett), Buffalo Rehab Comn, 71. Exhib: 100th Anniversary Show of Land Grant Colleges, Kansas City Art Inst, 68; Master Drawings & Watercolors Since the 15th Century, Albright-Knox Art Gallery, 69; North of the Penn Line, traveling show to mus of Northeast, 69-71; Am Fedn Arts Traveling Exhib, 70-71; Watercolors Since 1900, Birmingham Mus Art, Ala, 72. Teaching: Asst prof art, Auburn Univ, 59-63; prof art, State Univ NY Buffalo, 63-; vis prof, Southern Ill Univ, spring 70. Pos: Founder, Team Workshop, Buffalo. Awards: Fac Fel, State Univ NY Res Found, 70 & 72. Bibliog: Edward Reep (auth), The Content of Watercolor, Reinhold, 69. Mailing Add: Dept of Art State Univ NY Buffalo NY 14214

MCKAY, ARTHUR FORTESCUE
PAINTER, EDUCATOR
b Nipawin, Sask, Sept 11, 26. Study: Alta Col Art; Acad Grande Chaumiere, Paris; Columbia Univ; Barnes Found, Pa. Work: Nat Gallery, Ottawa, Ont; Art Gallery Ont, Toronto; Montreal Mus Fine Arts, Que; Vancouver Art Gallery, BC; Norman MacKenzie Art Gallery, Regina, Sask. Exhib. Five Printers from Regina, Nat Gallery Ottawa, 61; Post Painter Abstraction, Los Angeles Co Mus, 64; Religious Art Today, Regis Col, 65; Images of a Canadian Heritage, Vancouver Art Gallery, 67; retrospective exhib, Norman MacKinzie Art Gallery, 68. Teaching: Asst prof art, Univ Regina, 51- Awards: Humanities Res Coun Grant, 57 & 58; Can Coun Sr Fel, 63. Bibliog: C Greenberg (auth), Art on the prairie, Arts Can Mag, 9/63; T Fenton (auth), Canada's Art McKay, Artforum, 12/68. Style & Technique: Poured and glazed enamels over flat scraped surfaces; large centralized images. Media: Flat undercoat enamels and flat oil borders on untempered hard board. Mailing Add: Dept Visual Art Univ of Regina Regina SK S4S 0A2 Can

MCKAY, JOHN SANGSTER
EDUCATOR, ART ADMINISTRATOR
b Farmers City, Ill, May 30, 21. Study: Univ Ill, Urbana-Champaign, BFA, 47; Inst Design, Chicago, Ill, cert, 48; Univ Buffalo, 50. Teaching: Instr design, Albright Art Sch, Buffalo, 47-54; asst dean design, Sch Fine Arts, Wash Univ, 54-68; prof visual arts, Univ Kans, 68-, assoc dean Sch Fine Arts, 68-75. Mem: Fel Nat Asn Schs Art (secy, 61-62, bd dirs, 61-75, vpres, 66-68, pres, 69-72); Am Coun Arts Educ (bd dirs, 69-72); Int Coun Fine Arts Deans; Lawrence Community Arts Coun (chmn, 73-74). Publ: Co-auth, Nat Asn Schs Art Bull, 72. Mailing Add: 742 Indiana Lawrence KS 66044

MCKEAN, HUGH FERGUSON
PAINTER, EDUCATOR
b Beaver Falls, Pa, July 28, 08. Study: Pa Acad Fine Arts; Art Students League; Ecole Beaux-Arts, Fontainebleau, France; Rollins Col, BA & DFA; Williams Col, MA; Stetson Univ, LHD; Brevard Col, DSpaceEd; Univ Tampa, LLD. Work: Toledo Mus Art; Univ Va. Exhib: Soc Four Arts, 48; Allied Artists Am, 49; Exhib, Atlanta, Ga, 49. Teaching: Prof art, Rollins Col, 52-69. Pos: Dir, Morse Gallery Art, Rollins Col & actg pres, Col, 51-52, pres, 52-69, chmn bd, 69-75; treas, Winter Park Land Co, 52-; trustee, Ringling Mus State of Fla; mem, Fla Arts Coun, 69-; trustee, Edyth Brush Charitable Found, 75-; pres, Charles Hosmer Morse Found (reorganization of the Morse Gallery of Art, removed from Rollins Col to Winter Park, Fla), 76- Awards: Prizes, Fla Fedn Art, 31 & 49; Cervantes Medal, Span Inst; Decoration of Honor, Rollins Col. Mem: Fla Fedn Art (pres, 51-52); Louis Comfort Tiffany Found (trustee); NH Art Asn; Orlando Art Asn; Am Fedn Arts; plus others. Mailing Add: 151 E Welbourne Ave Winter Park FL 32789

MCKEAN, JEANNETTE M
See Genius, Jeannette

MCKEEBY, BYRON GORDON
PRINTMAKER, EDUCATOR
b Humboldt, Iowa, Feb 27, 36. Study: Coe Col, BA, 59; Art Inst Chicago, BFA, 63; Tulane Univ, MFA, 65; Univ NMex, Tamarind Artist-Teacher fel, with Garo Antresian, summer 65. Work: Dallas Mus Fine Arts; Philadelphia Mus; Brooklyn Mus; Norfolk Mus Arts & Sci, Va; Ark Art Ctr, Little Rock. Exhib: Four exhibs, Northwest Printmakers, Seattle, 65-69; four exhibs, Okla Printmakers, Oklahoma City, 65-71; Potsdam Print Ann, State Univ NY Col Potsdam, 68 & 69; Print & Drawing Nat, Northern Ill Univ DeKalb, 68, 69 & 71; Nat Print Ann, Ga State Univ, Athens, 70 & 71. Teaching: Prof printmaking, Univ Tenn, Knoxville, 65- Bibliog: Edward Brohel (auth), New American Printmakers (TV prog), NY Educ TV, 66. Media: Lithography, Intaglio. Dealer: Assoc Am Artists Inc 663 Fifth at 52nd New York NY 10022; Vorpal Gallery 1168 Battery St San Francisco CA 94111. Mailing Add: Art Dept Univ of Tenn Knoxville TN 37916

MCKENNIS, GAIL
PRINTMAKER, PAINTER
b Wilmington, NC, May 12, 39. Study: Richmond Prof Inst, Va Commonwealth Univ, BFA & MFA; Royal Col Art; Visual Studies Workshop. Work: Victoria & Albert Mus, London; Southern Regional Arts Asn, Eng; NC Mus Art; Mint Mus Art, Charlotte, NC; Dillard Collection, Univ NC, Greensboro. Exhib: 3rd & 4th Brit Int Print Biennales, Bradford, Eng, 72 & 74; 4th Int Print Biennale, Cracow, Poland, 72; Mod Prints, Bethnal Green Mus, London; Paperworks, Washington Gallery Art, 74; one-person show, Va Mus Fine Arts, 68. Teaching: Instr painting, printmaking & drawing, Va Commonwealth Univ, 65-69; instr printmaking & drawing, Univ NC, Wilmington, 69-71; instr silkscreen, Univ Reading, Eng, 72-73; asst prof art, Roberts Wesleyan Col, Rochester, NY, 74-75. Pos: Gallery dir, Roberts Wesleyan Col, Rochester, NY, 75-78; co-dir, Richmond Printmaking Workshop, Inc, 77-78. Awards: Va Mus Fine Arts Biennial Exhib Awards, 67 & 69; Purchase Award, 3rd Brit Int Print Biennale, 72; Purchase Award, Gallery Contemp Art, Winston-Salem, 73. Style & Technique: Work based on photographic print processes, etching, silkscreen and lithography; also interested in commerical printing processes, bookmaking and portfolios, unlimited and limited editions. Media: Print. Mailing Add: 1502 Brookland Pkwy Richmond VA 23227

MCKESSON, MALCOLM FORBES
PAINTER, SCULPTOR
b Monmouth Beach, NJ, July 24, 09. Study: Harvard Col, AB(art), 33; Art Career Sch, 51-53; Art Students League, 55; NY Univ, MA(art educ), 56; NY State Teachers Col, New Paltz. Exhib: Composers, Authors & Artists Am, 59-72; Pen & Brush Club, New York, 65; Burr Artists, 66-72; Nat Arts Club, 65-69; Lynchburg Art Ctr, 69; plus others. Teaching: Instr art, New York Pub Schs, 56-60. Pos: Pres, Eleanor Gay Lee Gallery Found, New York, NY. Awards: Art Comt Award in Oil Painting, Nat Arts Club, 76. Mem: Composers, Authors & Artists Am; Burr Artists. Media: Watercolor, Oil, Ink; Wood. Interest: Architectural and landscape subjects. Mailing Add: 22 E 29th St New York NY 10016

MCKIE, TODD STODDARD
PAINTER, PRINTMAKER
b Boston, Mass, Apr 25, 44. Work: Addison Gallery of Am Art, Andover, Mass; First Nat Bank of Boston, Mass; Brockton Art Ctr, Mass; Wellington Mgt Co, Boston; Lincoln Ctr for the Performing Arts, New York. Comn: Mural (90 ft x 40 ft), City of Boston, 72. Exhib: Eat Art, Contemp Art Ctr, Cintinnati, Ohio, 72; Boston Collects Boston, Mus of Fine Arts, Boston, 73; Works on Paper, Fogg Art Mus, Harvard Univ, Cambridge, Mass, 74; Biennial Exhib, Whitney Mus of Am Art, New York, 75; Painted in Boston, Inst of Contemp Art, Boston, 75; Boston Watercolor Today, Mus of Fine Arts, Boston, 76; Collectors Collect Contemporary, Inst of Contemp Art, Boston, 77. Awards: Colman Award, Blanche E Colman Found, 72; Creative Artists Fel, Mass Arts & Humanities Found, 74. Bibliog: Carl Belz (auth), The grid and the buffet, Art in Am, 3/72; David Greenberg (auth), Big art, Running Press, Philadelphia, 77. Style & Technique: Cubist influenced; ironic and witty. Media: Oil, watercolor and silkscreen. Dealer: Acquavella Gallery 18 E 79th St New York NY 10021; Harcus-Krakow Gallery 7 Newbury St Boston MA 02116. Mailing Add: 462 Putnam Ave Cambridge MA 02139

MCKIM, WILLIAM WIND
PRINTMAKER, PAINTER
b Independence, Mo, May 13, 16. Study: Kansas City Art Inst, with Thomas Hart Benton & John S DeMartelly. Work: William Rockhill Nelson Gallery; Kansas City Art Inst. Comn: Wildlife panorama, Kansas City Mus, 62. Exhib: Mo Pavilion, New York World's Fair, 64-65; Art of Two Cities, Kansas City & Minneapolis, 66; one-man show, Kansas City Art Inst & Albrecht Gallery, St Joseph, Mo, 67-68; 10 Missouri Painters Traveling Exhib, 68-69; Mid Am Artists Exhib, St Louis & Kansas City, 68 & 70. Teaching: Instr drawing, Kansas City Art Inst, 45-48, instr lithography, 48-58, prof lithography, 58- Awards: D M Lighton Award, Midwestern Ann, Kansas City, 40; New York State Fair Award. Media: Tempera, Acrylic. Mailing Add: 8704 E 32nd St Kansas City MO 64129

MCKININ, LAWRENCE
EDUCATOR, PAINTER
b Yukon, Pa, Aug 24, 17. Study: Wayne State Univ, BS, 39; Soc Arts & Crafts, Detroit, Mich, with John Carroll, 39-40; Univ Wis, summer 41; Cranbrook Acad Art, with Zoltan Sepeshy, MFA, 48; Inst Design, Chicago, summer 49; Handy & Harman Silversmithing Workshop, Sch Am Craftsmen, Rochester, NY, summer 50. Work: Friends of Art, Nelson Gallery, Kansas City, Mo; Springfield Mus Art, Mo; Vera Mott Mem Collection, Mo Hist Soc & Columbia Art League, Columbia, Mo. Comn: Portrait of O M Stewart & H M Reese, Univ Mo Physics Dept, Columbia, 67. Exhib: Seven shows, Springfield Art Mus Ann, 50-76; Midwest Exhib, Joslyn Mus, Omaha, Nebr, 51 & 52; American Jewelry and Related Objects, circulated by Smithsonian Inst, 55-57; Ten Missouri Painters II, Mo Arts Coun Circulation Exhib, 68-69; Watercolor USA, 74. Teaching: Instr art, Univ Mo-Columbia, 48-50, asst prof art, 50-55, assoc prof art & chmn dept, 55-59, prof art, 59- Pos: Art ed, Archaeol Mag, 53-54. Awards: Purchase Prize for painting Exodus, Mid-Am Exhib, Friends of Art, Nelson Gallery, 50; Purchase Prize for painting White Lake, Springfield Art Mus, 50; Award for design of bk, Fred Shane Drawings, Chicago Bk Clin 16th Ann Exhib, 65. Mem: Mid-Am Col Art Asn. Style & Technique: Transforming the photographic image into a painterly image and depicting an atmosphere or mood through a specific quality of light and color. Media: Oil, Acrylic. Publ: Designer & art ed, Fred Shane Drawings, 65. Mailing Add: A126 Fine Arts Bldg Univ Mo-Columbia Columbia MO 65201

MCKINLEY, DONALD LLOYD
EDUCATOR, DESIGNER
b Bartlesville, Okla, Feb 14, 32; Can citizen. Study: Wichita State Univ, Kans, 50-52; NY State Col of Ceramics, Alfred Univ, NY, BFA(cum laude), 55, with Kurt Ekdahl; Fulbright Scholar (furniture & interior design), Taideteollinen Oppilaitos, Helsinki, Finland, 62-63; Syracuse Univ, NY, MID, 65, with Art Pulos in indust design. Work: Mus Contemp Crafts & Am Crafts Coun, New York; S C Johnson Collection, Objects USA; Can Govt Exhib Comn, Ottawa, Ont; Chalmer's Collection, Ont Crafts Coun, Toronto; Craft Bd of Australia Coun, Sydney, New S Wales. Comn: Interior of Factory Chapel, Gunlocke Chair Co, Wayland, NY, 61; three op-art metal sculptures, Alram Corp, Buffalo, NY, 65, 69 & 75; trophy, Rhododendron Soc, Toronto, 73; two archit screens (10ft x 20ft), Sheridan Col, Mississauga, 74; reception desk, Ont Crafts Coun, Toronto, 76. Exhib: Kans Designer-Craftsmen, Kans Univ, Lawrence, 54-74; Young Americans, 55 & 62, Craftsmanship in Wood, 60, Designer-Craftsmen USA, 60, Craftsmen of the Eastern States, 63, Craftsmen USA, 66 & Made with Paper, 67, Mus Contemp Crafts, New York; New York Crafts, Munson-Williams-Proctor Inst, Utica, NY, 61; Finger Lakes Exhib, Rochester Mem Gallery, NY, 62 & 64-66; Crafts 1967, Ball State Univ, Muncie, Ind, 67; Objects USA, Smithsonian Inst Traveling Exhib, 69; Craft Dimensions, Royal Ont Mus, Toronto, 69; Wood, London Art Gallery, Ont, 74; Chairs, Art Gallery of Ont, Toronto, 75; Crossroads, 76 & Made to Order, 77, Ont Crafts Coun Gallery; Artisan 78, Can Crafts Coun Traveling Exhib, 78-79. Teaching: Asst prof three-dimensional design, NY State Col of Ceramics, Alfred Univ, 64-67; master furniture design, Sch of Crafts & Design, Sheridan Col, Mississauga, Ont, 67- Pos: Chief staff designer, Gunlocke Chair Co, Wayland, NY, 58-62; dir, Sch Crafts & Design, Sheridan Col, 67-72; resident consult designer for Tasmania, sponsored by Craft Bd of Australia, Tasmanian Art Adv Bd & Timber Promotion Bd, 76-77. Awards: Best Wood Entry, Kans Designer-Craftsman, Kans Univ, Lawrence, 54-62 & 65, Entr'Acte: O'Keefe Ctr, Can Guild of Crafts, 73 & Can Nat Exhib, Can Guild of Crafts, 69 & 72-75. Bibliog: Nancy Gardiner (auth), The not-so-odd couple, Finger Lakes Chronicle, 6/65; Sketch Book of Kappa Pi, Nat Art Fraternity, spring 66; Harris Mitchell (auth), Tube chairs, Can Homes Mag, 5/69. Mem: Am Crafts Coun (trustee, 65-68); Can Crafts Coun (mem nat gen comt, 69-74); Ont Crafts Coun (mem adv comt, 68-71); World Crafts Coun (wood sem leader, 64, 74 & 76); Tasmanian Woodcraftsmen's Asn (mem steering & exec comt). Style & Technique: Usually modular, geometric, systematic; functional furniture and accessories. Media: Wood, Plastic. Publ: Contribr, Positions: The Role of Crafts in Education, US Health, Educ & Welfare, 66; auth, Feature review of the 24th Ceramic National, Craft Horizons, 12/66; auth (television show), Seat of the Matter, Metrop Educ Television Asn, 70; auth, Wood turned forms of Stephen Hogbin, Craft Horizons, 4/74; illusr, The mark of the fire, Studio Potter, winter 75. Mailing Add: 1460 S Sheridan Way Mississauga ON L5H 1Z7 Can

MCKINLEY, RUTH GOWDY
CERAMIST, DESIGNER
b Brooklyn, NY, June 14, 31; Can citizen. Study: NY State Col Ceramics at Alfred Univ, NY, Dept Ceramic Design, with Charles Harder, Daniel Rhodes & Marion Fosdick, BFA, 53, MFA, 55. Work: Munson-Williams-Proctor Inst, Utica, NY; St Paul Art Gallery, Minn; Royal Ont Mus, Toronto; Everson Mus, Syracuse, NY; Massey Found Collection, Can Crafts Coun, Ottawa. Comn: Thirty-one prototypes, Canadiana Pottery Ltd, Ingleside, Ont, 72; Making a Teapot (traveling educ exhib), Ont Crafts Coun, 74; hanging planter divider, Ont Crafts Coun Gallery, Toronto, 76. Exhib: 20th Ceramic Int, Everson Mus, 58; Kiln Club Ann Ceramic Exhib, Smithsonian Inst, Washington, DC, 59; Ceramics 1971, Royal Ont Mus, Toronto, 71; Can Guild Potters, Toronto, 71 & 75; Ceramics Int, Calgary, Alta, 73; In Praise of Hands, 1st World Crafts Exhib, Ont Sci Ctr, 74; Contemp Can Ceramics, Carborundum Mus, Niagara Falls, 74; Nat Ceramics Exhib, Glenbow-Alta Inst, Calgary, 76; one-person shows, Wood Fired, Visual Arts Ctr at Albion Col, Mich, 65, Crafts in the Garden, O'Keefe Ctr, Toronto, 69, Stoneware & Porcelain, Can Guild Potters, 71, Teapots & Wine Servers, Can Guild Potters, 75 & Functional Potter (traveling artists series), Ont Crafts Coun, 76-68; plus many other exhib in US, Can & Eng. Teaching: Instr ceramics, Ceramic Deisgn Dept, NY State Col Ceramics at Alfred Univ, summers 53 & 54; tutor ceramic design & wood firing, tutorials, 59- Pos: Grad asst, NY State Col Ceramics at Alfred Univ, 53-55; designer, potter & partner, Ossipee Pottery, NH, 55-57; studio potter, Stoneware & Porcelain, Wayland, NY, 58-67 & Mississauga, Ont, 68- Awards: First Award, Young Americans, Am Craftsman's Coun, 53; Juror's Award, Craft Dimensions Can, Royal Ont Mus, 69; Medal Award, Ceramics Int, Int Acad Ceramics, 73. Bibliog: Philip Salmon (auth), Exhibition—Ruth Gowdy McKinley, Tactile Page Publ, 71; Christopher Lowell (auth), The Compleat Potter, Tactile, Page Publ, 75. Mem: Royal Can Acad Arts; Ont Crafts Coun (mem portfolio selection comt, 75); Ont Potters Asn; Am Craftsman's Coun; World Crafts Coun. Style & Technique: Functional pottery with form and function made with wheel thrown, slab-built, drain cast and press-molded techniques. Media: Stoneware, Porcelain. Publ: Auth, The Mark of This Fire, Tactile, Page Publ, 75; auth, The Mark of This Fire, Studio Potter Book, Daniel Clark Found, 78. Mailing Add: 1460 S Sheridan Way Mississauga ON L5H 1Z7 Can

MCKINNEY, DONALD
ART DEALER
b New York, NY. Specialty: Nineteenth and twentieth century European and American art. Mailing Add: 930 Fifth Ave New York NY 10021

MCKNIGHT, ELINE
PRINTMAKER
b Yokohama, Japan, 1910. Study: Barnard Col & Teachers Col, Columbia Univ; Art Students League; Yale Sch Fine Arts. Work: Libr of Cong; New York Hilton Hotel, Rockefeller Ctr; Univ Tenn. Exhib: US Info Agency Traveling Exhib, Europe, 60-62; Soc Am Graphic Artists Traveling Exhib, 60-62; Brooklyn Mus, 60, 64 & 66; Am Haus, Stuttgart, 65; Corcoran Gallery Art, 67; plus many other nat & int exhibs. Pos: Conducted discussion groups on looking at mod art, Ford Fund Adult Educ; mem ed staff, New York Arts Calendar, 64; assoc ed, Collectors Almanac, 65. Awards: Purchase Prize, Prints for US Embassies Abroad, US Info Agency. Media: Graphics. Mailing Add: 100 Riverside Dr New York NY 10024

MCKNIGHT, THOMAS FREDERICK
PAINTER
b Lawrence, Kans, Jan 13, 41. Study: Wesleyan Univ, Middletown, Conn, BA(art); Columbia Univ. Work: Davison Art Ctr, Wesleyan Univ. Exhib: Three painters, Davison Art Ctr, Wesleyan Univ, 73; one-man shows, Rolly-Michaux Gallery, Boston & New York, 75, 76 & 77, Basel Art Fair, 75, 76 & 77, Tomic Galerie, Dusseldorf, Ger, 76, Hartmann Gallery, Munich, Ger, 77 & Deville Gallery, Los Angeles, Calif, 77. Style & Technique: Fantastic, visionary landscape painting. Media: Acrylic and Casein on Canvas. Dealer: Tomic Galerie 4 Benratherstrasse Dusseldorf WGer; Rolly-Michaux Gallery 943 Madison Ave New York NY 10021. Mailing Add: 301 E 47th St New York NY 10017

MCKOY, VICTOR GRAINGER
SCULPTOR
b Fayetteville, NC, Apr 21, 47. Study: Clemson Univ, BS(biology), 70, Sch of Archit, two years. Work: Birmingham Mus Art, Ala; Ward Found Mus, Salisbury State Col, Md. Exhib: Birds in the Wood, Am Mus Natural Hist, New York, 74; Animals in Art, Royal Ont Mus, Toronto, Can, 75; Expressions of Nature in Art, Greenville Mus Art, SC, 75 & Columbia Mus Art, SC, 75; Bird Sculpture Birmingham Mus Art, Ala, 76; The Artist and the Animal, High Mus Art, Atlanta, Ga, 77; Wild America, Kodak Gallery, New York, 78; one-man show, Hammer Galleries, New York, 76. Bibliog: Margaret Nichols (auth), Birds in the Wood, Field & Stream, 9/74; Gary Dicky (auth), Wood carving revolution, SC Wildlife, 11/75; Lucy Justus, The flight of wooden birds, Jour & Constitution, 1/77. Style & Technique: Realistic bird carvings. Media: Wood and oil paint. Mailing Add: Rte 1 Box 42 Wadmalaw Island SC 29487

MCLANATHAN, RICHARD B K
ART CONSULTANT, WRITER
b Methuen, Mass, Mar 12, 16. Study: Harvard Univ, AB, 38, grad sch, 41-43, Soc fels, 43-46, PhD, 51. Collections Arranged: The M & M Karolik Collection of American Paintings, 1815-1865, Mus Fine Arts, Boston, 49; Art Across America, Munson-Williams-Proctor Inst, Utica, 60. Pos: Secy mus, Mus Fine Arts, Boston, 52-56, ed publ, 52-57, cur decorative arts, 54-57; dir mus art, Munson-Williams-Proctor Inst, 57-61; cur art exhib, Am Nat Exhib, Moscow, 59; mem, NY State Coun on Arts, 60-64; mem, NY State Comnr Comt Art & Mus Resources, 60-66. Awards: Prix de Rome, Am Acad Rome, 48; Distinguished Serv Award, US Info Agency, 59; Sr Rockefeller Fel, Metrop Mus Art, 75. Mem: Am Asn Mus; Northeast Conf Am Mus Asn; NY State Mus Asn; Asn of Fels of Am Acad Rome. Res: Medieval art; renaissance art, especially Italian; American arts; modern art. Publ: Contribr, US Philanthropic Foundations, Their History, Structure, Management and Record, 67; auth, The American Tradition in the Arts, 68, col text ed, 70; A Guide to Civilisation, the Kenneth Clark Films on the Cultural Life of Western Man, 70; The Brandywine Heritage, 71; Art in America, A Brief History, 73. Mailing Add: 439 E 51st St New York NY 10022

MCLAREN, NORMAN
FILM MAKER
b Stirling, Scotland, Apr 11, 14; Can citizen. Study: Glasgow Sch Art, Scotland. Work: Nat Gallery Can, Ottawa. Pos: Film dir, Nat Film Bd Can, 41- Awards: Motion Picture Acad Oscar for Neighbors, 52; Award for Blinkity Blank, Grand Prix, Cannes, France, 55; Outstanding Achievement Award, Can Govt, 72. Bibliog: Gavin Miller (auth), The eye hears and the ear sees (film), BBC-TV, Eng; M E Cutler (auth), Unique genius of Norman McLaren, Can Art, 5 & 6/65; Laurence Elliott (auth), Norman McLaren, gentle genius of the screen, Reader's Digest, 8/71; Maynard Collins (auth), Norman McLaren, Can Film Inst, 76. Mem: Royal Can Acad Art (academician). Publ: Auth, Cameraless animation, 58; illusr, Six musical forms, Jeunesses Musicales, Montreal, 67; illusr, Interplay, Mutations Graphic Guild, Montreal, 71. Mailing Add: PO Box 730 Hudson PQ J0P 1H0 Can

MCLARTY, WILLIAM JAMES (JACK)
PAINTER, INSTRUCTOR
b Seattle, Wash, Apr 24, 19. Study: Mus Art Sch, Portland, Ore; Am Art Sch, NY; also with Anton Refregier & Joseph Solman. Comn: Murals, Collins-View Sch, Laurelhurst Sch, Riverdale Sch, Ridgewood Sch, Portland & Portland Civic Auditorium. Exhib: Recent Paintings: USA, Mus Mod Art, 62-63; 20 yr retrospective, Portland Art Mus, 63; 1st & 2nd Int Miniature Print Exhib, Pratt Graphic Art Ctr, NY, 64; Nat Drawing Soc Exhib, 70-72; Art of the Pacific Northwest, Smithsonian Inst, 74. Teaching: Instr advan woodcut & painting, drawing & compos, Portland Mus Art Sch, currently. Awards: Purchase Prize, Lewis & Clark Col Invitational, Portland, 65; Prize, Northwest Printmakers, Seattle, 66; Artists of Ore Award, 70. Publ: Auth, Seventeen love poems, Image Gallery, 67; contribr, Prize-winning graphics, 67, Northwest review, 67, Of Wind and Pines, 77, Image Gallery; & To his coy mistress, Marvell, 73. Mailing Add: 1525 NW 24th Portland OR 97210

MCLAUCHIAN, EBBA RAPP
See Rapp, Ebba

MCLAUGHLIN, JOHN D
PAINTER
b Sharon, Mass, May 21, 98. Work: Los Angeles Co Mus Art; Corcoran Gallery Art, Washington, DC; Mus Mod Art & Metrop Mus Art, New York; Nat Collection Fine Arts, Smithsonian Inst, Washington, DC; Wadsworth Atheneum, Hartford, Conn. Exhib: Painting & Sculpture Ann, 49, Contemporary Painting in the United States, 51 & Four Abstract Classicists, 59-60, Los Angeles Co Mus; Retrospective, Pasadena Art Mus, Calif, 56, 63, Corcoran Gallery Art, 68, La Jolla Mus Contemp Art, Calif, 73 & Whitney Mus Am Art, New York, 74; Sphere of Mondrian, Inst Contemp Art, Houston, 57; Purist Painting, Toured by Am Fedn Art, 60-61; San Francisco Mus Art, Calif, 62; Whitney Mus Am Art, 62; Art Inst Chicago, 64; Mus Mod Art, 65; Corcoran Gallery Art, 67; West Coast 1945-1969, Pasadena Art Mus, 69; Joslyn Mus, Omaha, Nebr, 70; Eleven Los Angeles Artists, Hayward Gallery, London, Eng, 71; one-man shows, Univ Calif, Irvine, 71, Corcoran & Corcoran, Coral Gables, Fla, 73 & Whitney Mus Am Art, 74; plus others. Art Gallery, Calif State Univ, Fullerton, 75. Awards: Bronze Medal, Corcoran Gallery, Washington, DC, 66; William A Clark Prize, 66; Nat Found Arts & Humanities Grant, 67. Bibliog: James Harithas (auth),

Color plus shape equals form: equation for a new aesthetic, Art Educ, 10/67 & A painting at degree zero, Art News, 11/68; Peter Plagens (auth), Los Angeles, Artforum, 9/70. Mem: Los Angeles Co Mus Art; Mus Mod Art, New York; life mem Laguna Beach Mus Art. Media: Oil, Acrylic. Dealer: Nicholas Wilder Los Angeles CA 90069. Mailing Add: PO Box 840 Dana Point CA 92629

MCLEAN, JAMES ALBERT
EDUCATOR, PRINTMAKER
b Gibsland, La, Nov 25, 28. Study: Southwestern La Inst, AB, 50; Southern Methodist Univ, BD, 53; Tulane Univ, MFA with J L Steg, 61. Work: Seattle Mus Art, Wash; The High Mus, Atlanta, Ga; Brooklyn Mus, NY; Olivet Col, Mich; Minot State Col, ND. Exhib: 33rd, 35th, 36th & 38th Northwest Printmakers Int, Seattle Mus, Wash, 62, 64, 65 & 67; 14th, 15th, 19th & 20th Nat Print Exhibs, Brooklyn Mus, 64, 66, 74 & 76; Nat Print & Drawing Exhibs, Minot State Col, 73-76; Colorprint, USA, Tex Tech Univ, Lubbock, 74-76. Teaching: Assoc prof gen art, LaGrange Col, Ga, 63-66; proof printmaking, Ga State Univ, Atlanta, 66- Awards: Purchase Award, Northwest Printmakers Int, 64, Western NMex Univ Nat Print Exhib, 73 & Minot State Col Nat Print & Drawing Exhib, 76. Bibliog: Illus in: Fritz Eichenberg (auth), The Art of the Print, Abrams, 76, Gene Baro (auth), 30 Years of American Printmaking, Watson-Guptill, 75. Style & Technique: Primarily involved with photoengraving, with final plates printed as relief etchings. Media: Photoengraving. Dealer: Heath Gallery 34 Lombardy Way Atlanta GA 30309. Mailing Add: 3509 Cold Spring Lane Chamblee GA 30341

MCLEAN, RICHARD THORPE
PAINTER, EDUCATOR
b Hoquiam, Wash, Apr 12, 34. Study: Calif Col Arts & Crafts, BFA, 58; Mills Col, MFA, 62. Work: Joslyn Art Mus, Omaha, Nebr; Whitney Mus Am Art, New York; Va Mus Fine Arts, Richmond; Utrecht Mus, Holland; Mus Boymans-Van Beuningen, Rotterdam. Exhib: 22 Realists, Whitney Mus Am Art, 70; Radical Realists, Mus Contemp Art, Chicago, 71; Sharp Focus Realism, Sidney Janis Gallery, New York, 72; Documenta 5, Kassel, Ger, 72; Working in Calif, Albright-Knox Art Gallery, Buffalo, NY, 72; Tokyo Biennale, 74; New/Photo Realism, Wadsworth Atheneum, Hartford, Conn, 74; Tokyo Biennale, Japan, 74; Contemp Images in Watercolor, Akron Art Inst, Ohio, 76; Painting & Sculpture in Calif: The Mod Era, San Francisco Mus Mod Art & Smithsonian Inst, 76; Thirty Yrs of Am Art, 1945-1975, Whitney Mus Am Art, New York, 77; plus many others. Teaching: Assoc prof painting & drawing, San Francisco State Univ, 63- Media: Oil. Dealer: O K Harris Works of Art 383 W Broadway New York NY 10012. Mailing Add: 6471 Oakwood Dr Oakland CA 94611

MCLEAN, RODDY (VERNEDA RODRIGUEZ)
PAINTER, INSTRUCTOR
b Chicago, Ill. Study: With Henry Wo, Lui-sang Wong, Ho-nien Au, I-hsiang Ju & Lou Stovall. Exhib: Tidewater Artists Biennial, Norfolk Mus, Va, 64; one-woman show, Art League, Northern Va, 69; Annapolis Fine Arts Found Ann, Md, 72; Abbott Gallery, 74 & 75; Sumi-e Soc Am Ann, New York, 73-75; Hang Up Gallery, Sarasota, 73, 74 & 76. Teaching: Instr Chinese brush painting, Art League Northern Va, 64-, Studio of Seven Bamboos, Torpedo Factory, Old Town, Alexandria, Va, 75- & Carleton Col, 75. Awards: Sumi-e Soc Award, 73, 75 & 77. Mem: Sumi-e Soc Am (ed, Sumi-e Notes, 75-78); Potomac Valley Watercolor Soc; Asian Benevolent Corp; Washington Womens Art Ctr; Art League. Style & Technique: Oriental brush strokes using Chinese ink and watercolor on rice paper; watercolor; silk screen. Dealer: Studio of the Seven Bamboos, Torpedo Factory King & Union St Alexandria VA 22301. Mailing Add: 4032 Oxford St Annandale VA 22003

MCMAHON, JAMES EDWARD
ART DEALER
b New York, NY, Jan 1, 37. Study: Hofstra Col, BA. Pos: Owner, Gallery Madison 90. Specialty: American art of the 19th and 20th centuries; American illustrators. Mailing Add: Gallery Madison 90 1248 Madison Ave New York NY 10028

MCMANUS, JAMES WILLIAM
SCULPTOR, INSTRUCTOR
b Glenwood Springs, Colo, Jan 1, 42. Study: Colo State Univ, BFA, 65; Univ Wash, MFA, 67. Work: Oakland Art Mus; San Diego Art Mus, Calif; Reading Art Ctr, Eng; Henry Art Mus, Univ Wash. Comn: Expo '74, Spokane, Wash; Admin Bldg, Wash State Hwy Comn, Olympia; Electro-Develop Corp, Seattle. Exhib: American Drawings, Philadelphia, 68; San Francisco Art Inst Centennial, San Francisco Art Mus, 71; six-man traveling exhib, Brit Art Coun, 73-75; one-man shows, Richmond Arts Ctr, Calif, 75 & Marquoit Gallery, San Francisco, 75; Allrich Gallery, San Francisco, 77; Selected Works 1967-1977, de Saisset Mus, Univ Santa Clara, Calif, 77; Calif State Univ, Fresno, 77. Teaching: Teaching asst, Univ Wash, 67, instr art, 67-68; assoc prof art, Calif State Univ, Chico, 68; vis prof art, High Wycombe Col Art, Eng, 71-72. Pos: Speaker, Int Sculpture Conf. Awards: Fac Res Grant, Calif State Univ, Chico, 69; Fulbright-Hays Grant, Eng, 72. Bibliog: Palmer French (auth), James W McManus, Artforum, 5/69; John Marlowe (auth), James W McManus, Current Art Mag, 6/75; James W McManus (30 min video tape), Calif State Univ, Chico, 77; plus others. Style & Technique: Linear, planear geometric abstraction. Media: Bronze, Steel, Aluminum. Dealer: Allrich Gallery Two Embarcadero Ctr San Francisco CA 94133. Mailing Add: 1734 Mangrove Chico CA 95926

MCMILLAN, CONSTANCE
PAINTER
b Millinocket, Maine, Mar 10, 24. Study: Bennington Col, painting with Karl Knaths & sculpture with Simon Moselsio, BA, 46; Colorado Springs Fine Arts Ctr, with Boardman Robinson, 46; Mills Col, fel, 53-55, art hist with Alfred Neumeyer & ceramic sculpture with Antonio Prieto, MA, 55. Exhib: One-man shows, Morris Gallery, New York, 56 & Panoras Gallery, New York, every two yrs, 59-; Guthrie Frankenberg Gallery, 74 & 75; The Gallery, West Cornwall, Conn, 75; Ames Gallery, New York, 75 & 76; plus others. Teaching: Instr painting, design & art hist, San Luis Sch, Colorado Springs, 49-51; instr painting, design & art hist, Emma Willard Sch, Troy, NY, 52-53; instr painting & design, Angel Sch, Ann Arbor, 62-63. Awards: First Prize, Morris Gallery, 56; First & Hon Mention Awards, Mich Watercolor Soc Ann, 67 & 68. Mem: Am Fedn Arts; Ann Arbor Art Asn. Style & Technique: Painterly technique; semi-abstract, depicting landscape and figure, with particular interest in ambiguity, disjuncture and gesture of form and shape. Publ: Illusr, Chikka, 62, Ponies for a King, 63, Reilly & Lee; illusr, Memory of a Large Christmas, Norton, 62. Dealer: Panoras Gallery 62 W 56th St New York NY 10019; Gallery 22 22 E Long Lake Rd Bloomfield Hills MI 48013. Mailing Add: 2760 Heather Way Ann Arbor MI 48104

MCMILLAN, JERRY EDWARD
PHOTOGRAPHER, SCULPTOR
b Oklahoma City, Okla, Dec 7, 36. Study: Oklahoma City Univ; Chouinard Art Inst, Los Angeles, Calif. Work: Norton Simon Mus, Pasadena, Calif; Des Moines Art Mus, Iowa; Ft Worth Art Mus, Tex; San Francisco Mus Art, Calif; La Jolla Mus Contemp Art, Calif. Exhib: Photog into Sculpture, Mus Mod Art, New York, 70; Calif Painting & Sculpture: The Mod Era, 76; one-man shows, Norton Simon Mus, Pasadena, Des Moines Art Ctr, Ft Worth Art Mus, San Francisco Mus Art, La Jolla Mus Contemp Art & Newport Harbor Art Mus, Calif. Teaching: Instr photog, Calif State Univ, Northridge, 70- & Univ Calif, Los Angeles Exten, 70- Style & Technique: Photosculpture and drawings. Media: Paper, Metal and Glass. Dealer: Margo Leavin Gallery 812 N Robertson Los Angeles CA 90069. Mailing Add: 1024 1/4 N Western Ave Los Angeles CA 90029

MCMILLAN, ROBERT W
PAINTER, EDUCATOR
b Belleville, Ill, Jan 22, 15. Study: Southern Ill Univ, BEd, 37; Columbia Univ, MA, 40; Washington Univ, 48; Univ Iowa, PhD, 58. Exhib: Brooklyn Mus, 40; Joslyn Mem Mus, Omaha, Nebr, 44; St Louis City Mus, 47; Cincinnati Mus, 56; Des Moines Art Ctr, 64; plus others. Teaching: Instr art, Univ Kansas City, 46-48; prof art, Southern Ill Univ, Carbondale, 50-60; prof art, Grinnell Col, 60-69, chmn dept, 61-68; prof art, Univ Ariz, 69-, head dept, 69-76. Pos: Dir, Schaeffer Gallery, Grinnell Col, 60-69. Mem: Am Asn Univ Prof; Col Art Asn Am; Midwestern Col Art Conf; Int Platform Asn. Mailing Add: Dept Art Univ of Ariz Tucson AZ 85721

MCMILLEN, MICHAEL CHALMERS
ENVIRONMENTAL ARTIST, SCULPTOR
b Los Angeles, Calif, Apr 6, 46. Study: Calif State Univ, Northridge, BA; Univ Calif, Los Angeles, MA & MFA. Exhib: Eight Artists from Los Angeles, San Francisco Art Inst, Calif, 75; Sounds: Environments by Four Artists, Newport Harbor Art Mus, Newport Beach, Calif, 75; Imagination, Los Angeles Inst Contemp Art, 76; Biennale of Sydney, Art Gallery of New S Wales, Australia, 76; Los Angeles in the 70s, Ft Worth Art Mus, Tex, 77; one-man shows, Traveling Mystery Mus, Venice, Calif, 73, Inner City, Los Angeles Co Mus, Los Angeles, 77 & Whitney Mus Am Art, New York, 78. Teaching: Lectr at var inst, 74- Awards: Sculpture Prize, Santa Monica Arts Festival, City of Santa Monica, 70; Fel, Univ Calif, Los Angeles Art Coun, 72; travel grant, Biennale of Sydney, Australia Coun, 76. Bibliog: Hal Glicksman (auth), Los Angeles in the 70s, Ft Worth Art Mus, 77; Melinda Wortz (auth), Inner City of the Mind, Art News, 2/78; Christopher Knight (auth), Some recent art and archit analogue, Los Angeles Inst Contemp Art J, 2/78. Mem: Los Angeles Inst Contemp Art. Style & Technique: Wide use of media & technology for environments and sculptures. Publ: Auth, True confessions, Los Angeles Inst Contemp Art J, 75; contribr, Choke, Choke Publ, 76; auth, Special effects breakdown, Los Angeles Inst Contemp Art J, 77. Mailing Add: 906 Princeton St Santa Monica CA 90403

MCNABB, WILLIAM ROSS
GALLERY DIRECTOR
b Knoxville, Tenn, Feb 21, 38. Study: Univ Tenn, BA; Vanderbilt Univ, MA. Collections Arranged: John Chumley Retrospective, 74; Architecture in Knoxville, Tenn, 1790-1940, 74; Ninth Dulin Nat Print & Drawing Competition, 75. Teaching: Vis lectr archit hist, Univ Tenn, Knoxville, 74-75. Pos: Former dir, Dulin Gallery of Art, Knoxville. Mem: Soc Archit Historians; Soc Archit Historians, Gt Brit. Res: American architecture; William Strickland; Tennessee architecture. Mailing Add: 3100 Kingston Pike Knoxville TN 37919

MCNALLY, SHEILA JOHN
EDUCATOR, ART HISTORIAN
b New York, NY, Dec 10, 32. Study: Vassar Col, BA; Univ London; Univ Kiel; Univ Munich; Harvard Univ, PhD, 65. Teaching: Mem fac art hist, Ohio State Univ & Mt Holyoke Col; prof art hist, Univ Minn, Minneapolis, currently. Pos: Prin investr, Excavations Diocletian's Palace, Split, Yugoslavia, 68- Awards: Fulbright Res Grants, Ger, 53-54 & Yugoslavia, 67-68. Mem: Col Art Asn (bd dirs, 75-, chmn comt status women, 75-); Midwest Art Hist Soc (mem bd dirs, 77-); Archaeol Inst Am; Libyan Soc; Women's Caucus Art. Res: Late Roman art. Mailing Add: Dept Art Hist 108 Jones Hall Univ Minn Minneapolis MN 55455

MCNAMARA, MARY JO
ART HISTORIAN, CURATOR
b Troy, NY, Jan 23, 50. Study: Vassar Col, AB, 72; Stanford Univ, MA, 75, PhD candidate. Teaching: Instr art hist, Vassar Col, Poughkeepsie, NY, 76- Pos: Cur, Vassar Col Art Gallery, 76- Awards: Cantor-Fitzgerald res grant, 75-76. Mem: Col Art Asn. Res: Modern Art. Publ: Co-auth, Rodin's Burghers of Calais, The Cantor-Fitzgerald Group, Los Angeles, 77. Mailing Add: Box 150 Vassar Col Poughkeepsie NY 12601

MCNAMARA, RAYMOND EDMUND
PRINTMAKER, PAINTER
b Chicago, Ill, Sept 25, 23. Study: Sch Art Inst Chicago, BAE; Univ Mich, MA; Wayne State Univ; also with Max Kahn, William Woodward, Peter Gilleran & Stanley Hayter; WVa Univ, MFA. Work: Charleston Art Gallery, Huntington Galleries & Concord Col, WVa; State House, Charleston; Gallery Akep, New York. Exhib: Twenty-five shows, Exhibition 180, Huntington Galleries, 64-69; Charleston Art Gallery Exhibs, 64-72; Appalachian Corridors, Charleston, 68; Ball State Univ Drawing & Small Sculpture Nat, Ind, 68; Am Drawing Biannual, Norfolk Mus Arts & Sci, Va, 69. Teaching: Assoc prof printmaking, WVa State Col, 64- Awards: First Award painting, Huntington Galleries, 66; seven Purchase Awards, WVa Arts & Humanities Coun, 66-74; Am Drawing Biannual Award, Norfolk Mus Arts & Sci, 69. Mem: Am Asn Univ Prof; Alumni Asn Art Inst Chicago. Media: Graphics. Mailing Add: 306 Ruffner Ave Charleston WV 25311

MCNARY, OSCAR L
PAINTER
b San Antonio, Tex, Mar 23, 44. Study: San Antonio Jr Col, Tex; Tex Southern Univ; Southern Methodist Univ; Warren Hunter's Sch Art. Exhib: 36th Ann Exhib, San Antonio Art League, Witte Mem Mus, 65; 65th Ann Tex Fine Arts Asn Exhib, Laguna Gloria Art Mus, Austin, 75; 109th Exhib of Am Watercolor Soc, Nat Acad of Galleries, New York, 76; Richardson Civic Art Soc's Regional Painting & Sculpture Show, 76; W Tex Ann Watercolor Exhib, Tex Tech Univ Mus, Lubbock, 77; State Fair of Tex, Dallas, 77; 4th Biennial, Five States Art Exhib, Gates Gallery, 77; Guest Artist, Harambee Living Arts Gallery, Atlanta, Ga, 77; Mus Dirs Choice Exhib, Univ Tex, Dallas, 77; Black SW Art Exhib, Mus of African-American Life & Cult, Dallas, 77 & 78; 15th Joslyn Biennial, Joslyn Art Mus, Omaha, Nebr, 78. Awards: First Place Citation Award, Tex Fine Arts Asn Region II, 75; Hon Mention, Int Art Exhib, Pilot Club of Golden Sands, 77; Purchase Award, 2nd Ann Black SW Art Exhib, SW Res Ctr & Mus, Bishop Col, 78. Mem: Assoc Am Watercolor Soc; Artists Coalition of Tex (bd dir); Dallas Mus Fine Arts; Southwestern Watercolor Soc; Tex Fine Arts Asn. Style & Technique: Contemporary multimedia using watercolor, oil, mixed-media, drawing and acrylics. Mailing Add: 1308 Timberlake Cir Richardson TX 75080

MCNEAR, EVERETT C
PAINTER, DESIGNER
b Minneapolis, Minn, Sept 30, 04. Study: Minneapolis Sch Art, with Cameron Booth; also with Edmund Kinzinger & Louis Marcoussis. Comn: Mosaic panels, Skiles Sch, Evanston, Ill, 59; mural, Perkins & Will Partnership. Exhib: Art Inst Chicago; Pa Acad Fine Arts; one-man shows, San Francisco Mus Art, 46; Walker Art Ctr, Minneapolis, 48; Gallery, Univ Notre Dame, 61 & Painter, Designer, Collector, 75; plus others. Pos: Chmn exhib comt, Arts Club Chicago, 53-; design consult, Art Inst Chicago, 58-; mem adv coun, Art Gallery, Univ Notre Dame. Awards: Medal, Art Dirs Club, Chicago, 50 & 55; Prizes, Art Guild, 51, 55, 57 & 58 & Ill State Mus, 60; plus others. Mem: Arts Club Chicago; 27 Designers. Style & Technique: Semi-abstract landscapes and figure pieces, bold color, strong spacial organization and design. Collection: Manuscripts, miniatures, primitive art, Cubist paintings and prints; Persian and Indian Miniatures, McNear Collection, a Promised Gift (exhib), 75. Publ: Illusr, Many a Green Isle, 41 & Young Eye Seeing, 56; contribr, Bull Atomic Scientists & Am Artist Mag. Mailing Add: 1448 Lake Shore Dr Chicago IL 60610

MCNEIL, GEORGE J
PAINTER, EDUCATOR
b New York, NY, Feb 22, 08. Study: Pratt Inst, Brooklyn, 27-29; Art Students League, 30-31 & 32-33; Hans Hofmann Sch Fine Art, 33-36; Teachers Col, Columbia Univ, MA, 43, EdD, 52. Work: Mus Mod Art; Nat Mus, Havana, Cuba; Newark Mus Art; Walker Art Ctr, Minneapolis; Whitney Mus Am Art; plus others. Exhib: Mus Mod Art, New York, 36, 51, 63-64 & 69; Whitney Mus Am Art Ann, 53, 57, 61 & 65, The 1930s, 68; US Info Agency Pan-Am Exhib, circulated Latin Am, 61-62; Yale Univ Art Gallery, 61-62; Pa Acad Fine Arts, 62; Wadsworth Atheneum, Hartford, Conn, 62; Art Inst Chicago, 63; plus many other group & one-man shows. Teaching: Vis emer prof art, Grad Dept Art & Design, Pratt Inst, presently; vis artist, Syracuse Univ. Awards: Ford Found Purchase Award, 63; Nat Coun Arts Award, 66; Guggenheim Fel, 69. Mailing Add: 195 Waverly Ave Brooklyn NY 11205

MCNITT, MIRIAM D
CRAFTSMAN, INSTRUCTOR
b Syracuse, Kans, Feb 13, 16. Study: Merced Col; Col Sequoias; Univ Calif Exten; stitchery with Jean Ray Laury; pottery with Richard Trojan. Work: Presidential Mus, Odessa, Tex; also many pvt collections. Comn: Many throughout US. Exhib: Needlework Show, Woodlawn Plantation, Mt Vernon, Va, 67; The Art Place, Yosemite Nat Park, 70; Stitchery Show, Sales Shop, Smithsonian Inst, Washington, DC, 70; stitchery, Ansel Adams Studio, Yosemite Nat Park, 74-75; Polit Exhib, Presidential Mus, Odessa, Tex, 75; plus others. Teaching: Instr creative stitchery, personal studio, 61-73; instr creative stitchery, Merced Col, 73-75. Pos: Columnist, WestArt, Auburn, Calif, 67-69; mgr, The Art Place, Yosemite Nat Park, 70-73. Awards: First, Calif Fedn Women's Clubs, 65; First & Purchase Awards, China Alley Art Show, Hanford, Calif, 68. Bibliog: Feature stories, Fresno Bee, 61- Mem: Am Craftman's Coun; Calif State Craft Cong; Fresno Arts Ctr. Style & Technique: Mixed media, fibers-stitchery, batik, acrylics, collages used as backgrounds incorporating the use of fibers. Publ: Contribr, Making Contemporary Rugs & Wall Hangings, Abelard, 70. Mailing Add: 746 N Wilson Fresno CA 93728

MCNULTY, KNEELAND
CURATOR
b Soochow, Ku, China, Oct 25, 21; US citizen. Study: Princeton Univ, AB, 43; Harvard Univ Grad Sch; Columbia Univ, MLS, 52. Collections Arranged: The Lithographs of Jean DuBuffet (with catalog), 64; Master E S: Five Hundreth Anniversary (with catalog), 67; Mauricio Lansansky: The Nazi Drawings (with catalog), 67. Teaching: Distinguished vis prof, Univ Tex, Austin, 78. Pos: Rare book cataloger, Houghton Libr, Harvard Univ, 46-47; apprentice in prints, Philadelphia Mus Art, 47-49; asst librarian, NY Pub Libr, 49-52; asst & assoc cur prints, Philadelphia Mus Art, 52-, cur prints, drawings & photographs, 64- Mem: Print Coun Am; Nat Comt Drawing Soc; Print Club Philadelphia; Artists Equity. Publ: Ed, The art of Philadelphia Medecine, 65; auth, Ben Shahn: Graphic Work, 67; ed, Suzuki Harunobu, 70; auth, Foreigners in Japan: Yokohama and Related Woodcuts, 72; ed, The Theatrical World of Osaka Prints, 73; auth, Peter Milton: Complete Etchings, 77. Mailing Add: 2130 Cherry St Philadelphia PA 19103

MCQUILLAN, FRANCES C
PAINTER, INSTRUCTOR
b Chicago, Ill, Dec 1, 10. Study: New York Sch Fine & Appl Art & Caldwell Col, BA; Art Students League; Fairleigh Dickinson Univ; Montclair Art Mus Adult Sch. Exhib: Conn Acad Fine Arts; Allied Artists Am; Expos Intercontinental Exhib, Dieppe, France & Monaco; Am Artists Prof League; Montclair Art Mus Exhib. Teaching: Instr drawing, watercolors, oils & acrylics, Montclair Art Mus, NJ, 50-; instr drawing, Montclair Adult Sch, 67-70; instr oil painting, Yard Sch Art, Montclair, 67-70. Pos: Illusr, Peerless Fashions, New York, 32-37. Awards: Silver Medal for oil painting, Knickerbocker Artists, 53; First Prize in watercolors, Am Artists Prof League, 70; First Prize in oils, Art Ctr of NJ, 72. Mem: NJ Watercolor Soc (secy, treas, vpres & pres); Conn Acad Fine Arts; Am Artists Prof League; Essex Watercolor Club; Art Ctr of NJ. Media: Watercolor, Oil, Acrylic; Sculpture. Mailing Add: 3 Godfrey Rd Upper Montclair NJ 07043

MCREYNOLDS, (JOE) CLIFF
PAINTER, INSTRUCTOR
b Amarillo, Tex, Jan 26, 33. Study: San Diego State Univ, BA, 59, MA, 60. Comn: Portrait of pres, Mesa Col, San Diego, Calif, 75. Exhib: One-man shows, La Jolla Mus Contemp Art, 60-67, San Diego City Col, 72 & Gallery Rebecca Cooper, Washington, DC, 76; Southwestern States Regional, Houston, 63; Calif-Hawaii Regional, San Diego, 72-74; Drawing USA, Minn Mus Art, St Paul, traveling throughout US, 75; Alternative Realities, Mus of Contemp Art, Chicago, Ill, 76; Mindscapes—5 Calif Artists, Oshkosh Mus, Wis, 76; Calif Painting & Sculpture—the Modern Era, San Francisco Mus Mod Art, 76; Juried Drawing Exhib, Chicago Art Inst, 77; Invitational Am Drawing Exhib, Fine Arts Gallery, San Diego, Calif, 77; New Delhi Triennial, New Delhi, India & travelling, 77-78. Teaching: Instr drawing, Mesa Col, San Diego, 69- Pos: Bd mem, Fine Arts Guild, San Diego, 63. Awards: Best in Show, Del Mar Exhib, 63; Best in Show, All Calif Exhib, 63 & First Prize, Calif-Hawaii Regional, 72, Fine Arts Gallery, San Diego. Bibliog: Marily Hagberg (auth), McReynolds-sharp satirist, San Diego Mag, 2/67; Jan Jennings (auth), One man show on view, San Diego Union, 12/71. Style & Technique: Revelation painting, very realistic and detailed. Media: Oil, Pencil. Publ: Illusr, Psychol Today, 70-73; illusr, Esquire Mag, 73; illusr, Abnormal Psychol, 74. Dealer: Rebecca Cooper Gallery 2130 P St Washington DC 20037. Mailing Add: 6311 Dowling Dr La Jolla CA 92037

MCREYNOLDS, KIRK SEYMOUR
See St Maur, Kirk

MCSHEEHY, CORNELIA MARIE
PRINTMAKER
b Floral Park, New York, Aug 10, 47. Study: Mass Col of Art, Boston, BFA, 69, study with David Bumbeck, Arthur Hillman, Lawrence Kupferman & John Thornton; State Univ NY, Albany, MA, 72, study with Thom O'Connor & Robert Cartmell. Work: Libr of Congress, Washington, DC; Univ NDak, Grand Forks; State Univ NY, Potsdam; Minot State Col, NDak; Tex Tech Univ, Lubbock. Exhib: Boston Printmakers, Rose Art Mus, Brandeis Univ, 72; Colorprint USA, Tex Tech Univ, 72, 75 & 76; Boston Printmakers, De Cordova Mus, Lincoln, Mass, 73; 18th Print Exhib, Brooklyn Mus, 73; Calif Palace of the Legion of Honor, San Francisco, 73; Print Exhib, Libr of Cong, 75; The Collograph, Graphics Exhib, Pratt Graphics Ctr, New York, 75-76; Int Print Exhib, Mus of Mod Art, Tokyo & Kyoto, Japan, 76-77. Teaching: Instr printmaking, Mass Col of Art, Boston, 72-75; asst prof printmaking, Brown Univ, Providence, RI, 76-77; asst prof lithography, RI Sch of Design, Providence, 77- Awards: Purchase Awards, Colorprint USA, Tex Tech Univ, 72 & 75; Nat Endowments for the Arts Grant in Printmaking, 75-76; Purchase Award, 20th NDak Ann Print Exhib, Univ NDak, 77. Bibliog: M Stephens (auth), Contemporary Art in America, La Revue Mod, Paris, 73. Mem: Boston Printmakers; Col Art Asn; Boston Visual Artists Union; Women's Caucus for Art. Style & Technique: Contemporary expressionist, satirical humorist, funky/pop mixture, colorist; prints and drawings; collograph, lithography, silkscreen, etc; all technical printmaking techniques. Media: (Prints) Collography, lithography and silkscreen; (Drawings) mixed media. Publ: Contribr, Art Now, Inc. 76- Dealer: Jo Miller The Print Cabinet Tiny House Cannon Crossing Wilton CT 06897. Mailing Add: 46 Singletary Lane Sudbury MA 01776

MCSHINE, KYNASTON LEIGH
CURATOR
b Port of Spain, Trinidad, Feb 20, 35. Study: Dartmouth Col, AB; Univ Mich; Inst Fine Arts, NY Univ. Teaching: Asst prof art hist, Hunter Col, New York, 68-69; lectr art hist, Sch Visual Arts, New York, 69-76. Pos: Cur painting & sculpture, Jewish Mus, New York, 65-68; 65-68, acting dir, 67-68; assoc cur painting & sculpture, Mus Mod Art, New York, 68-71, cur, 71- Mem: Am Fedn Arts (trustee & mem exhib comt); Int Asn Art Critics; Col Art Asn; Am Asn Mus. Publ: Auth, Josef Albers: Homage to the Square, 64 & Information, 70, ed & contribr, Marcel Duchamp, 73 & The Natural Paradise: Painting in American 1800-1950, 76, Mus Mod Art, New York; auth, Primary structures, Jewish Mus, 66. Mailing Add: c/o Mus of Mod Art 11 W 53rd St New York NY 10019

MCVEIGH, MIRIAM TEMPERANCE
PAINTER
b Wabash, Ind. Study: Calif Col Arts & Crafts, BFA; Acad Goetz, Paris; also with Elmer Tafflinger, Clifton Wheeler & Eugen Neuhaus. Work: Mus Monbart, Dijon, France; Musel des Beaux Arts de Montbard, Paris. Exhib: Am Vet Soc Artists, New York, 61; Artistes USA, Galeries Raymond Duncan, Paris, 72; Festival Int de Saint-Germain-des-pres, Paris, 73, 74 & 75; one-man shows, St Petersburg Jr Col, Fla, 61 & Galerie Internationale, New York, 74. Media: Oil, Acrylic. Dealer: Chimera 3400 Gulf Blvd St Petersburg Beach FL 33706. Mailing Add: 8200 14th St N St Petersburg FL 33702

MCVEIGH, ROBERTA LEBER
See Leber, Roberta

MCVEY, LEZA
SCULPTOR, WEAVER
b Cleveland, Ohio, May 1, 07. Study: Cleveland Sch Art, grad; Cranbrook Acad Art. Work: Craft Mus, New York; Smithsonian Inst, Washington, DC; Syracuse Mus, NY; Butler Inst Am Art, Youngstown, Ohio; Gen Motors. Comn: Ceramic mural (with William McVey), Fine Art Ctr, Flint, Mich, 61; tiles, Hicks Sch, Cleveland, 71. Exhib: Syracuse Mus & Nat Circuit, 45-69; Smithsonian Inst, 51-61; Int Cong Contemp Ceramics, Ostend, Belg, 60; one-man shows, Distinguished Alumni Ann Show, Cleveland Inst Art, 65, Albright-Knox Art Gallery, 65 & Pa Acad, Pomona, Calif. Awards: Ceramic Form 33 Award, Harshaw Chem Co, 51; spec awards & group awards, Cleveland Mus Art, 54-67; Ceramic Form 39 Award, Grand Prix des Nations, Ostend, Belg, 60. Bibliog: Louis G Farber (auth), Leza McVey profile, Ceramic Mo, 53; Meg Torbert (auth), Leza McVey, Every Day Art Quart, 53; Joe McCullough (auth), Leza McVey, Cleveland Inst Art, 65. Style & Technique: Large asymmetric, hand built receptacles. Media: Clay. Mailing Add: 18 Pepper Ridge Rd Cleveland OH 44124

MCVEY, WILLIAM M
SCULPTOR, EDUCATOR
b Boston, Mass, July 12, 05. Study: Rice Univ; Cleveland Inst Art; Acad Colarossi, Acad Grande Chaumiere & Acad Scandinave, Paris, 29-31; pupil of Despiau. Work: Heroic head of Winston Churchill, Smithsonian Inst, Washington, DC & Chartwell, Eng; Sister Ann (hollow built ceramic), Ariana Mus, Geneva, Switz; L'Ecrivain (bronze), Houston Mus, Tex; Rumination (Ga marble) & Waiting Woman, Cleveland Mus Art, Ohio; Beached Whale (cement fondu), Lincoln Ctr, Univ Ill, Urbana. Comn: Berry Monument, Hopkins Airport, Cleveland, 61; Long Road (aluminum relief), Jewish Community Ctr, 64; US Seals, Fed Bldg, Cleveland, 66; St Margaret of Scotland; Jan Hus, St Olga of Russia for Washington Cathedral; Entire Churchill Porch at Nat Cathedral; George Washington at Fed Bldg, Cleveland; J Edgar Hoover for FBI Acad, Quantico, Va; Senator Harry Flood Byrd (10ft statue), capital grounds, Richmond, Va, 77; and numerous others. Exhib: Grand Salon; Salon d'Automne; Pa Acad Fine Arts; Tex Ann; Cleveland May Shows. Teaching: Instr, Cleveland Mus, 32; instr, Houston Mus, 36-38; asst prof, Univ Tex, 39-46; instr, Ohio State Univ, summer 46; instr, Cranbrook Acad Art, 46-53; head sculpture dept, Cleveland Inst Art, 53-68; guest prof, Sch Fine Arts, Ohio State Univ, 63-64. Pos: Chmn, Nat Fulbright Screening Comt, four yrs; juror for most Midwest shows. Awards: Nat Syracuse Ceramic Show Award, 54; 11 spec awards, Cleveland May Shows; Purchase Award, Everson Mus, Syracuse, NY, 51 & 52; Purchase Award, Butler Inst Am Art, Youngstown, Ohio, 67. Bibliog: Helen Borsick (auth), Story of a statue (Winston Churchill at the British Embassy in Washington), Plain Dealer Mag, 66; Sculptor for today, Ohio Mag; Animals, animal sculpture and animal sculptors, Nat Sculpture Rev, 71. Mem: Col Art Asn Am; fel Nat Sculpture Soc; Int Platform Asn (bd gov). Style & Technique: Monumental. Media: Stone, Bronze. Mailing Add: 18 Pepper Ridge Rd Cleveland OH 44124

MCVICKER, J JAY
PAINTER, EDUCATOR
b Vici, Okla, Oct 18, 11. Study: Okla State Univ, BA & MA. Work: Libr Cong, Washington, DC; Dallas Mus Fine Arts, Tex; Joslyn Art Mus, Omaha; Okla Art Ctr; Philbrook Art Ctr, Tulsa. Exhib: Am Japan Contemp Print Exhib, Tokyo, 67; Rockhill-Nelson Gallery, Kansas City, Mo, 69; Dallas Mus Fine Arts, 69; Audubon Artists, New York, 71; one-man show, Fred Jones Mem Gallery, Norman, Okla, 71. Teaching: Mem art fac, Okla State Univ, 41-, prof printmaking, 59- Awards: Purchase Award, Okla Art Ctr, 67; Purchase Award, Dallas Mus

Fine Arts, 69; Purchase Award, Longview Jr Serv League, Tex, 71. Mem: Audubon Artists; Soc Am Graphic Artists; Philadelphia Print Club. Style & Technique: Color field painting. Media: Acrylic. Mailing Add: 4212 N Washington Stillwater OK 74074

MCWHINNIE, HAROLD JAMES
PRINTMAKER, EDUCATOR
b Chicago, Ill, July 15, 29. Study: Art Inst Chicago, BAE; Univ Chicago, MFA; Stamford Univ, EdD. Work: Los Angeles Mus Art, Calif; Pasadena Art Mus, Calif; Borg-Warner Collection, Chicago; Ohio State Univ Col Fine Arts. Exhib: Libr Cong Print Show, 55; Philadelphia Art Alliance Show, 71; Laguna Beach Art Asn Show, 71; Frostburg State Col, 71; Philadelphia Col Art, 74. Teaching: Asst prof art educ, Ohio State Univ, 65-70; assoc prof ceramics, Univ Md, College Park, 70- Awards: Fulbright Fel, 60; Ohio State Univ Fac Fel, 65; Nat Endowment for Arts, 74. Mem: Nat Art Educ Asn; Am Soc Aesthet; Brit Soc Aesthet; Am Crafts Coun. Dealer: Thought Gallery 76 East St Annapolis MD 21401. Mailing Add: 10111 Frederick Ave Kensington MD 20795

MCWHORTER, ELSIE JEAN
PAINTER, SCULPTOR
b Laurel, Miss, Apr 5, 32. Study: Univ Ga, BFA, 54 & MFA, 56, with Lamar Dodd, Howard Thomas, Abbott Patterson, Joseph Di Martini, Ulfert Wilkie & Dan Lutz; Brooklyn Mus Art Sch, Max Beckmann scholar, 56-57, with Reuben Tam & Yonia Fain. Work: Gibbes Art Gallery, Charleston, SC; Brooks Art Gallery, Memphis, Tenn; Greenville Co Mus Art, SC; Arts Comn SC, Columbia; Miss Art Asn, State Coliseum, Jackson; plus others. Comn: Seal for Sumter Co, SC, 65; welded bronze fountain, Tom Jenkins Realty Co, Columbia, 66; mural, US Post Off, Camden, SC, 67; mural, Baker Bldg, Southern Bell Tel Co, Columbia, 68; eight historic paintings, McDonald's Restaurant, Conway, SC, 76; plus others. Exhib: US Info Agency Show-Europe & Near East, 56-57; Mid-South Exhib, Memphis, Tenn, 62; Butler Inst Am Art Ann, Youngstown, Ohio, 63; Drawing USA, St Paul 2nd Biennial Competition, St Paul Art Ctr, Minn, 63; 23rd Ann Nat Watercolor Exhib, Miss Art Asn, 64; plus others. Teaching: Asst prof art, Morningside Col, 58-61; instr drawing, painting & sculpture, Richland Art Sch, Columbia Mus Art, 61-; instr sculpture & design, Univ SC, 66-67. Awards: First Prize, 5th Ann All-State Show, Knoxville, Tenn, 55; First Prize, 24th Nat Watercolor Show, State Coliseum, Jackson, Miss, 65; First Prize, Flower Festival, Greenwood, SC, 71; Fourth Place Cash Prize, Bicentennial Design Contest, Franklin Mint, Franklin Center, Pa, 72; First Prize Painting, Spartanburg Art Asn Ann, SC, 74; First Prize, Dutch Fork Art Asn Exhib, Cola, SC, 74; First Prize Sculpture, Art of the Carolinas, Spring Mills Ann, Lancaster, SC, 75; plus others. Bibliog: Prize winning sculpture, 63 & Prize winning watercolors, 65, Allied Fla; Jack Morris (auth), article in Contemp SC Artist, 70. Mem: Guild SC Artist; Artist Guild Columbia; SC Craftmen. Mailing Add: 5419 Sylvan Dr Columbia SC 29206

MEADER, JONATHAN GRANT (ASCIAN)
PRINTMAKER, PAINTER
b Aug 29, 43; US citizen. Work: Whitney Mus Am Art & Metrop Mus Art, New York; Nat Gallery, Nat Collection Fine Art & Hirshhorn Mus, Washington, DC. Comn: Serigraphs, Off Equal Employment Opportunity, 73; lithographs, Washington Printmakers' Workshop Proj, 74; serigraph, Washington Print Club, 75. Exhib: Seven Young Artists, Corcoran Gallery Art, Washington, DC, 72; Baltimore Mus Traveling Show, Md, 72; 2nd Ann Exhib of Washington Artists, Phillips Collection, Washington, DC, 72; Collectors Show, McNay Art Inst, San Antonio, 72; Pyramid Gallery, Washington, DC, 73 & 74; Washington Printmakers Proj, Phillips Collection, 74; Six Washington Artists, Iowa Univ Mus, 75; Plum Gallery, Md, 75, 76 & 78; Klein-Vogel, Mich, 76; Harlan Gallery, Tucson, Ariz, 77; Swearingen Gallery, Ky, 77. Awards: Wurlitzer Found Grant, 67; Stern Family grant, 70; Nat Endowment for the Arts Printmakers Grant, 74. Bibliog: Dreamtime, The Washingtonian, 4/75; Paul Richard (auth), Making it as an artist, The Washington Post, 10/77. Style & Technique: Fantasy; surrealism. Media: Serigraphy; Acrylic; Pencil, Pen & Ink. Collection: Fantasy and surrealism: Klinger, Milton, and others. Mailing Add: PO Box 21146 Washington DC 20009

MEADMORE, CLEMENT L
SCULPTOR
b Melbourne, Australia, Feb 9, 29. Study: Royal Melbourne Inst Technol. Work: Art Inst Chicago; Nat Gallery Australia; J B Speed Mus, Ky; Atlantic Richfield Collection; Chase Manhattan Bank Collection. Comn: Large outdoor sculptures, Australian Mutual Provident Soc, 68, Mexico City, 68, Columbia Univ, 68, NY State, Albany, 71 & Princeton Univ, 71. Exhib: Guggenheim Int, 67 & Riverside Mus, 68, New York; Aldrich Mus, Ridgefield, Conn, 68; Rockefeller Collection, Mus Mod Art, 69 & Whitney Mus Am Art Ann, 69, New York. Pos: Dir, Gallery A, Melbourne, Australia, 59-60; vpres of sculpture, Archit League New York, 70-72. Bibliog: McCaughey (auth), article in Art Int, 11/70; Hughes (auth), article in Time Mag, 4/71; Segal (auth), Clement Meadmore: circling the square, Art News, 2/72; Hugh M Davies (auth), Clement Meadmore, Arts Mag, 3/77. Media: Steel. Dealer: Hamilton Gallery of Contemp Art 20 W 57th St New York NY 10019. Mailing Add: 800 W End Ave New York NY 10025

MEADOWS, ALGUR H
PATRON
b Vidalia, Ga, Apr 24, 99. Study: Centenary Col Law Sch, grad, 26, hon LLD, 69; Southern Methodist Univ, hon DHL, 65. Mem: Dallas Art Asn. Mailing Add: 6601 Turtle Creek Blvd Dallas TX 75205

MEDEARIS, ROGER
PAINTER, LITHOGRAPHER
b Fayette, Mo, Mar 6, 20. Study: Kansas City Art Inst, with Thomas Hart Benton. Work: DC Munic Ct, Washington, DC. Exhib: American Painting Today, Metrop Mus Art, New York, 50; West Coast Exhib, Frye Art Mus, Seattle, 66; Midyear Show, 69-77 & Four American Artists, 74, Butler Inst Am Art, Youngstown, Ohio; Mainstreams Int, Grover Hermann Fine Arts Ctr, Marietta, Ohio, 70-75; Nat Acad Design 148th Ann, 73. Awards: Mihaly Munkacsy Award, Frye Art Mus, 66; First Award for Painting, 71, Grand Prize Award, 72 & Award of Distinction, 75, Mainstreams Int, Marietta, Ohio. Style & Technique: Realist. Media: Tempera, Acrylic. Dealer: Capricorn Galleries 8004 Norfolk Ave Bethesda MD 20014. Mailing Add: 2270 Melville Dr San Marino CA 91108

MEDICINE FLOWER, GRACE
POTTER
b Santa Clara Pueblo, NMex, Dec 13, 38. Exhib: NMex State Fair, 71; Inter-Tribal Indian Ceremonials, Gallup, NMex, 71 & 72; Scottsdale Nat, Ariz, 71; Am Indian Arts & Relic Show, Albuquerque, NMex, 71; Am Indian & Western Relic Show, Portland, Ore, 72; Am Indian Show, Los Angeles; Seven Families in Pueblo Pottery, Maxwell Mus of Anthrop, Univ of NMex, 74; one-person shows, Gila River Arts & Crafts Ctr, Sacaton, Ariz, 73. Awards: First Prize, Best of Show Award & Cert of Merit, Inter-Tribal Indian Ceremonials, Gallup, 71; First Prize, Scottsdale Nat Indian Arts Exhib, Ariz, 71; Honored at the White House, Washington, DC, 74. Style & Technique: Traditional Indian techniques using coils of clay and a polishing stone; forms range from tiny seed bowls to large water jars and tall, graceful bottles; designs are incised into the pot. Media: Clay. Mailing Add: Box 1037 Espanola NM 87532

MEDOFF, EVE
ARTIST, WRITER
b Philadelphia, Pa. Study: Pa Acad Fine Arts; Tyler Sch Art; Pratt Graphics Ctr. Work: Hudson River Mus, Yonkers, NY; Wagner Col for Women, Staten Island, NY; Holmes Pub Sch, Mt Vernon, NY; Gestetner Corp, Yonkers; Fellowship of Reconciliation, Nyack, NY. Exhib: ACA Gallery, New York, 62; Riverside Mus, New York, 65; Albany Inst Art & Hist, 66; Westchester Printmakers, Fordham Univ, 67; one-man show, Katonah Gallery, NY, 72. Pos: Ed arts page, Yonkers Rec, 66-70; ed artslett & interarts, Coun for Arts in Westchester, 68-69; exhib juror, Westchester & Conn, 61-71. Awards: Hudson River Mus Purchase Awards, 57 & 70; Hon Title, Mus Assoc in Art Res, Hudson River Mus, 64; Gestetner Corp Print Competition Award, 71. Style & Technique: Figurative in oils and watercolor to semi-abstract to abstract in acrylic; collage and graphics; frequent use of totemic images. Publ: Contribr, Am Artist Mag, 68-; free lance writing and editing. Mailing Add: Apt D9 7300 Cresheim Rd Philadelphia PA 19119

MEDRICH, LIBBY E
SCULPTOR
b Hartford, Conn. Study: NY Univ, 31; Vassar Col, 49 & 54; Silvermine Guild Sch, 51; Art Students League, 52-55; White Plains Co Ctr, 57 & 58; also with John Hovannes, Clara Fasano, Helen Beling, Domenico Facci, George Koras, Harold Castor, Albert Jacobson & others. Work: Univ Chicago; First Church Christ, Wethersfield, Conn; numerous pvt collections. Exhib: Over 200 group shows including Prix de Paris, Galerie Raymond Duncan, Paris, 67; New York Int Art Show, New York Coliseum, 70; Audubon Artists, Nat Acad Design, New York, 73 & 74; Am Soc Contemp Artists, Nat Art Mus of Sport, Madison Square Garden, NY, 74; League of Present Day Artists, Lincoln Ctr, Fordham Univ, NY, 75; five solo shows. Awards: Hon Mention for Sculpture, Nat Arts Club, 68 & 72; First Prize for Sculpture, Mamaroneck Woman's Club, 70 & 74; Am Soc Contemp Artists Third Prize, 74; plus 14 others. Bibliog: Mary Brett-Surman (auth), Everything is grist to sculptor's mill, 11/4/68 & Kathie Beals (auth), Women's club: show works, 5/16/75, Daily Times, Mamaroneck; Betsy Powell (auth), Art & artists, Park East News, New York, 3/16/72. Mem: Artists Equity Asn of NY; Mamaroneck Artists Guild (pres, 68-70); Metrop Painters & Sculptors; Am Soc Contemp Artists; League Present Day Artists. Style & Technique: Abstract expressionist; configurations with light-filtering extensions and with encrustations forming textural contrasts. Media: Bronze. Dealer: Ward-Nasse Gallery 178 Prince St New York NY 10003; Mag Gallery 424 Mamaroneck Ave Mamaroneck NY 10543. Mailing Add: 88 Carleon Ave Larchmont NY 10538

MEEHAN, WILLIAM DALE
PAINTER, DESIGNER
b Decatur, Ill, Oct 23, 30. Study: Art Inst Chicago, BFA; Bradley Univ, MA. Work: Ohio Univ; Bradley Univ; Evansville Mus Arts & Sci; DePauw Univ; Earlham Col. Comn: Mural design (with Richard Peeler & students), DePauw Univ Art Ctr, 72; Mem Sculpture to Chauncey Rose, Founder of Rose-Hulman Inst Technol for 100th Year of Sch, 75. Exhib: Artists Ill Exhibs, Peoria Art Ctr, 59-60; Syracuse Regional Exhibs, Everson Mus Art, NY, 61-63; Mid-States Art Exhib, Evansville Mus Arts & Sci, Ind, 64; Ind Artists Exhibs, Herron Mus, Indianapolis, 64-65 & 67-69; Works on Paper, Indianapolis Mus Art, 71. Teaching: Instr design & drawing, Syracuse Univ, 60-64; assoc prof design & painting, DePauw Univ, 64-, dir summer art tour to Europe, 68-70. Pos: Art dir, Southwestern Press, Ft Smith, Ark, 55-56; advert designer, Caterpillar Tractor Co, Peoria, 56-60; art dir, Nichols Advert, Decatur, summer 61; design consult, DePauw Univ, 64-; design consult for several industs. Awards: Purchase Award, Ohio Valley Oil & Watercolor Show, Athens, 59; First Prize, 22nd Ann Cent Ill Exhib, Decatur, 66; First Prize Watercolor, 62nd Ind Artists Exhib, Indianapolis, 67. Style & Technique: Designer of printed material; semi-abstract painter. Media: Oil, Gouache. Mailing Add: 411 E Seminary Greencastle IN 46135

MEEK, J WILLIAM, III
ART DEALER, COLLECTOR
b Aberdeen, Md, Nov 8, 50. Study: Fla Southern Col, BA, 72. Pos: Asst dir, Harmon Gallery, Naples, Fla, 72-77, dir, 78-; mem, Better Business Bur SFla (Collier Co), mem bd dirs, 77- Specialty: Paintings, drawings and sculpture by major American artists of the 20th century. Collection: Private collection of 20th century American art. Mailing Add: c/o Harmon Gallery 1258 Third St S Naples FL 33940

MEEKER, BARBARA MILLER
EDUCATOR, PAINTER
b Peru, Ind, Dec 31, 30. Study: DePauw Univ, BA; also with Robert Weaver, Jack Pellow, Ray Loos, Harriet Rex Smith & Gertrude Harbart. Work: DePauw Univ Art Ctr Print Collection, Greencastle, Ind; Purdue Univ, Calumet Campus & Hammond Pub Schs, Ind; Tri-State Col, Angola, Ind; Oak Park River Forest High Sch, Ill; Lake Co Pub Libr. Exhib: Ft Wayne Art Mus, 62, DePauw Univ Printmakers Exhib, Greencastle, 68, Ind Artists Club Ann, Indianapolis, Michiana Regional, South Bend & Hoosier Art Salon, Indianapolis, Ind. Teaching: Asst prof freehand drawing & painting, Purdue Univ, Calumet Campus, 65- Awards: Purchase & Merit Award, Ind Artists Club; Award for The Gold Pitcher (collage), Northern Ind Art Salon; Hon Mention, Outstanding Teacher Awards, Purdue Univ, Calumet Campus, 71, 75 & 76. Bibliog: Hawkins & McClarren (auth), Indiana lives, Hist Rec Asn, 67. Mem: Ind Artists Club; Gary Artists League; Hammond Art Ctr (adv); Artists Equity Asn. Style & Technique: From loose representational realism to abstracted realism. Media: Watercolor, Collage, Acrylic, Pastel. Publ: Auth, Freehand Drawing, 72 & 2nd ed, 75. Mailing Add: 8314 Greenwood Ave Munster IN 46321

MEEKER, DEAN JACKSON
PRINTMAKER, PAINTER
b Orchard, Colo, May 18, 20. Study: Art Inst Chicago, BFA & MFA; Northwestern Univ; Univ Wis. Work: Boston Mus Fine Arts; Libr Cong, Washington, DC; Mus Mod Art, New York; Dallas Mus Fine Arts; Denver Art Mus; plus others. Exhib: Seattle Art Mus, 53-55; Munic Mus, The Hague, 54; Boston Mus Fine Arts, 54-56; Mus Mod Art, New York, 55; La Gravure, 59; Los Angeles Mus Art, 59; Libr Cong; Art Inst Chicago; Metrop Mus Art, New York; plus others. Teaching: Assoc prof art educ, Univ Wis-Madison, 46-70, prof, 70- Awards: Medal of Honor, Milwaukee Art Inst, 52 & 56; Guggenheim Fel, 58. Bibliog: S W Hayter (auth), About Prints, Oxford Univ, 62. Dealer: Jane Haslem Gallery 1669 Wisconsin Ave NW Washington DC 20007. Mailing Add: Dept of Art Univ of Wis Madison WI 53706

MEGARGEE, LAWRENCE ANTHONY (LAURIE)
PAINTER, ILLUSTRATOR
b Philadelphia, Pa, July 10, 00. Study: Pa Acad Fine Arts; Nat Acad Design; Art Students League; Pratt Inst Art Sch; Cooper Union Art Sch; Grand Cent Art Sch. Work: Grand Cent Art Gallery, New York; Cross Roads of Sport, New York; Ackerman Gallery, New York; Harlow Gallery, New York. Pos: Bravo art work in 14 hosps through Am Theatre Wing, NY & NJ, 46-53. Media: Watercolor, Tempera, Pastel, Ink. Publ: Illusr, The Spur, Town & Country, Country Life & Sportsman Mag. Dealer: Sportsman's Eyrie Spread Eagle Village Wayne PA 19087. Mailing Add: 208 Bloomingdale Ave Wayne PA 19087

MEHRING, HOWARD WILLIAM
PAINTER
b Washington, DC, Feb 19, 31. Study: Wilson Teachers Col, BS(educ), 53; Cath Univ Am, Nat Inst Arts & Lett scholar, 53-55, MFA, 55; also with Kenneth Noland. Work: Solomon R Guggenheim Mus, Mus Mod Art, Whitney Mus Am Art & Chase Manhattan Bank Collection, New York; Nat Collection Fine Arts & Corcoran Gallery Art, Washington, DC. Exhib: Carnegie Inst Int, Pittsburgh, 62; Post Painterly Abstraction, Los Angeles Co Mus, 64; Systemic Painting, Solomon R Guggenheim Mus, 66; The Abrams Family Collection, Jewish Mus, New York, 66; Whitney Mus Am Art Painting Ann, 67; Ringling Art Mus, Sarasota, Fla, 69; Ten Washington Artists: 1950-1970, Edmonton Art Gallery, Alta, 70. Teaching: Instr art, George Washington High Sch, Alexandria, Va, 59; instr art, Montgomery Jr Col, 62-64. Awards: First Prize Purchase Award for Painting, Corcoran Gallery Art, 65, Artist Fel, 72. Media: Acrylic. Mailing Add: c/o Poster Pl 32 W 53rd St New York NY 10019

MEIER, RICHARD ALAN
ARCHITECT
b Newark, NJ, Oct 12, 34. Study: Cornell Univ, BArch, 57. Exhib: 15th Triennele de Milano Int Exhib Archit, Milan, Italy, 73; Low Rise High Density Housing, 73 & Archit Studies & Proj, 75, Mus Mod Art, New York; The New York Five, London Art Net, Eng, 75; Suburban Alternative, Biennale de Venezia, Venice, Italy, 76; Man Transforms, Cooper-Hewitt Mus, New York, 76; Cooper Union, New York, 76; Graham Found, Chicago, 77; 200 Yrs of Am Archit Drawing, Cooper-Hewitt Mus, 77; Archit I, Leo Castelli Gallery, New York, 77. Teaching: William Henry Bishop Vis Prof archit, Yale Univ, New Haven, Conn, 75-77; vis prof archit, Harvard Univ, Cambridge, Mass, 77. Pos: Resident architect, Am Acad in Rome, 73-74; mem, Town Planning Subcomt, Jerusalem Comt, Israel; mem adv coun, Col Art, Archit & Planning, Cornell Univ, Ithaca, NY, 71- Awards: Bartlett, First Honor & Nat Honor, Am Inst Architects, 65-77; Albert S Bard Civic Award First Honor for Excellence in Archit & Urban Design, City Club of New York, 73 & 77; R S Reynolds Mem Award, Reynolds Metals Co, Richmond, Va, 77. Bibliog: Yukio Futagawa, ed, Richard Meier: Douglas House, Michigan, Global Archit, Vol 34 (1975); Arata Isosaki, ed, Spatial Structure Richard Meier, Archit Plus Urbanism, 4/76; Suzanne Stephens (auth), Architecture Cross Examined, Progressive Archit, 7/77. Mem: Assoc Nat Acad Design; col fel, Am Inst Architects; Inst for Archit & Urban Studies (mem bd trustees, 72-); Century Club New York. Publ: Co-auth, Five Architects: Eisenman/Graves/Gwathmey/Hejduk/Meier, Wittenborn Co, 72; auth, Strategie di Progettazione—Design Strategies, Casabella, 5/74; auth, A lecture in Japan, Spazio, 12/76; auth, Richard Meier Architect, Oxford Univ Press, 76; auth, Richard Meier Drawings of Four Projects: A Post Card Book, Wittenborn, 77. Mailing Add: 136 E 57th St New York NY 10022

MEIGS, JOHN LIGGETT
PAINTER, ART HISTORIAN
b Chicago, Ill, May 10, 16. Study: Univ Redlands; Acad Grande Chaumiere, Paris. Work: Roswell Mus, NMex; Univ Tex, Austin; WTex Mus, Lubbock; Mus NMex, Santa Fe. Comn: Pioneer Frescoes (with Peter Hurd), Tex Tech Univ, Holden Hall, Lubbock, 51-54; murals, Nickson Hotel, Roswell, 51, F O Masten Farms, Tex, 60, N Jr High Sch, Abilene, Tex, 61 & Weatherford First Nat Bank, Tex, 71; hist archit restorations, Las Cruces, Lamy, Raton, Hermosa, Glencoe, Tinnie & Picacho, NMex; also Durango & Chapala, Mex. Exhib: One-man shows, Honolulu Acad Fine Arts, Calif Palace of Legion of Honor, San Francisco, Dayton Art Inst, Ohio, Mus NMex & Ball State Mus, Muncie, Ind; O S Ranch Exhib, Tex, 77. Pos: Cur, Robert O Anderson Collections: Indian, Spanish Colonial, Chinese. Awards: Tex Watercolor Soc, Mus NMex Biennial & El Paso Sun Carnival Exhib. Media: Egg Tempera, Watercolor. Res: American graphics, especially 1930-1950. Collection: American graphics and drawings; Peter Hurd; Henriette Wyeth; American Realists; American quilts, coverlets: books. Publ: Ed, Peter Hurd—the Lithographs, Baker Gallery, 70; ed, Peter Hurd—Sketchbook, 71 & ed, The Cowboy in American Prints, 72, Swallow; contribr, NMex Mag, Ford Times, Southwest Art Gallery Mag & Ariz Highways. Dealer: Baker Gallery 13th & Ave L Lubbock TX 79401. Mailing Add: San Patricio NM 88348

MEIGS, WALTER
PAINTER
b New York, NY, Sept 21, 18. Study: Syracuse Univ, BFA; Ecole Beaux-Arts, Fontainebleau, France, dipl; Univ Iowa, MFA. Work: Amherst Col, Mass; Denver Art Mus, Colo; Va Mus Fine Arts, Richmond; Smithsonian Inst, Washington, DC; Ohio Univ, Athens. Exhib: Boston Fine Arts Festival, 56; Carnegie Int, Pittsburgh, Whitney Mus Am Art Ann, New York, Univ Ill, Champaign & Univ Iowa, Iowa City, several yrs. Teaching: Asst prof art, Univ Nebr, 49-53; prof oil painting & chmn art dept, Univ Conn, 53-61. Awards: Purchase Prize, Birmingham Art Mus, 54; Best Exhib, Springfield Art Mus, Mass, 57; First Prize for Drawing, Boston Fine Arts Festival, 59. Bibliog: Lee Nordness (auth), Distinguished exhibition of American Art 7, 60; A J Weller (auth), Art: USA: Now, C J Bucher, 62. Style & Technique: Abstract landscape; selected areas of heavy impasto and collaged materials. Media: Plastic Paint. Dealer: Harmon Gallery Naples FL. Mailing Add: Candelaria Tenerife Canarias Spain

MEILACH, DONA Z
ART WRITER, PHOTOGRAPHER
b Chicago, Ill. Study: Univ Chicago, PhB, 46; Northwestern Univ Ill, MA(art hist), 69. Exhib: Mus Am Folk Art, New York; Fifty Women, San Diego Acad Fine Arts, Calif; Hammond Libr, Ind; Chicago Pub Libr. Teaching: Instr art hist & macrame, Purdue Univ, Hammond, Ind, 69-71; instr fundamentals of art, Moraine Valley Jr Col, 70-71; instr understanding art & writing for mag, Evergreen Park High Sch, Ill, 58-65. Pos: Ed, Sphere Mag, 73; ed adv & art critic, Fibernews, The Working Craftsman & Artweek; columnist, Creative Crafts, Crafts-Travel, Chicago Tribune & free lance, 73- Mem: Am Crafts Coun; Handweavers Guild of Am; Authors Guild of Am; Artists-Blacksmith Asn of NAm. Res: Through involvement for each of thirty-five art books--interviews, photography and travel. Publ: Auth, Contemporary Batik & Tie Dye, 72, Creating Small Wood Objects as Functional Sculpture, 76, Creating Modern Furniture, 76, Decorative & Sculptural Ironwork, 77 & co-auth, Exotic Needlework, 78, Crown, New York. Mailing Add: 3991 Crown Point Dr San Diego CA 92109

MEINIG, LAUREL
ART ADMINISTRATOR
b Seattle, Wash, July 13, 49. Study: Bard Col, BA, 71; Syracuse Univ, MFA, 73. Pos: Mgr, Lubin House Gallery, Syracuse Univ, 71-73; intern, Hudson River Mus, Yonkers, NY, 72; asst cur, Herbert F Johnson Mus Art, Cornell Univ, 73-75; dir, Yuma Art Ctr, 75- Mem: Am Asn Mus (regional rep, Curators Comt); Col Art Asn; Western Regional Conf; Western Asn Art Mus. Publ: Ed, Directions in Afro American Art, 74. Mailing Add: Yuma Art Ctr PO Box 1471 Yuma AZ 85364

MEISEL, LOUIS KOENIG
ART DEALER, ART HISTORIAN
b Brooklyn, NY, Sept 4, 42. Study: Tulane Univ; Columbia Univ; New Sch Social Res. Collections Arranged: Photo Realism 1973, Stuart M Speiser Collection (with catalog). Bibliog: Les Levine (auth), New dealer, Arts Mag, 1/74; Judy Beardsall (auth), Louis Meisel, Art Gallery Mag, 9/73. Res: Photo realism. Specialty: Photo realism; kinetics; abstract illusionism. Publ: Auth, Nathan Wasserberger, 67; auth, Watercolors and drawings, Am Realists, 74; auth, American photo realism in New Zealand and Australia, 75; auth, The Photo-Realists, Harry N Abrams. Mailing Add: 141 Prince St New York NY 10012

MEISELMAN, MARILYN NEWMARK
See Newmark, Marilyn

MEISTER, MAUREEN I
ART WRITER
b Spokane, Wash, Aug 25, 53. Study: Mount Holyoke Col, AB; Columbis Univ Advan Inst, Paris. Pos: Art critic, Pittsburgh Press, Pa, 77- Mailing Add: c/o Pittsburgh Press 34 Blvd of Allies Pittsburgh PA 15230

MEITZLER, (HERBERT) NEIL
PAINTER, DESIGNER
b Pueblo, Colo, Sept 14, 30. Study: With Kenneth Callahan. Work: Seattle Art Mus, Wash; Memphis Acad Art, Tenn. Exhib: Art in USA, New York, 59; one-man show, Seattle Art Mus, Wash, 59; Seattle World's Fair, Wash, 62; Pac Coast Exhib, Santa Barbara Mus Art, Calif, plus five other mus, 62-63; Artists of the Northwest, Japanese World's Fair, 71. Pos: Designer, Seattle Art Mus, 57-78. Awards: Katharine Baker Award, Seattle Art Mus, 58; Nat Coun Theatres Award, US Govt, 67. Media: Acrylic, Tempera, Watercolor. Dealer: Woodside Gallery 803 E Union Seattle WA 98102. Mailing Add: Box 163 Harrisville NH 03450

MEIXNER, MARY LOUISE
PAINTER, EDUCATOR
b Milwaukee, Wis, Dec 7, 16. Study: Milwaukee-Downer Col, BA; State Univ Iowa, MA; Art Students League, with Hale; Univ Minn & Bowling Green Univ, with Max Weber; Mills Col, with Yasuo Kuniyoshi; Am Sch, Fontainebleau, France; Carpenter Ctr Visual Arts, Harvard Univ. Work: Nat Am Home Econ Asn, Washington, DC; Des Moines Art Ctr, Iowa; Denison Arts Asn Gallery, Iowa. Exhib: Chapman Gallery, Milwaukee; Des Moines Art Ctr Ann, 54, 55 & 62; Mid Am Ann, Kansas City, Mo, 55; solo show, Nat Design Ctr, New York, 69; MacNider Mus Ann, Mason City, Iowa, 70-75; Red River Ann, Moorhead, NDak, 71. Teaching: Prof art hist, Milwaukee-Downer Col, 45-52; prof color, environ arts & painting, Iowa State Univ, Ames, 53-75, distinguished prof, 75- Awards: Regional exhib awards. Mem: Col Art Asn Am; Intersoc Color Coun; Mid Am Art Asn; Des Moines Art Ctr; Milwaukee Art Ctr. Style & Technique: Color quantities, abstract. Media: Oil, Acrylic. Res: Experiments in light and color: four films on additive color and dance, 1973-1978. Publ: Auth articles in Am Camping Mag, 53, 55 & 66, Art J, 53-71, Lyrical Iowa Poetry Mag, 62-78, Design Mag, 67 & 68 & Leonardo, 75. Mailing Add: 1007 Lincoln Way 4 Ames IA 50010

MEIZNER, PAULA
SCULPTOR
b Belchatow, Poland; US citizen. Study: Westchester Workshop, White Plains, NY. Exhib: New Eng Exhibs, New Canaan, Conn, 72; Critics Choice, Sculpture Ctr, New York, 72; Contemporary Reflections 1972-1973, Larry Aldrich Mus, Ridgefield, Conn; Modern Maxis, New Brit Mus Am Art, Conn, 74; Sculpture in the Fields, Storm King Art Ctr, Mountainville, NY, 74-75; plus others. Teaching: Pvt adult art classes. Awards: E C K Finch Award, 59 & Claudia & Maurice L Stone Mem Award, 72, New Eng Exhib, New Canaan; Charles N Whinston Mem Award, Nat Asn Women Artists, New York, 72. Bibliog: National community arts program, HUD, 74. Mem: Audubon Artists; Silvermine Guild Artists; Nat Asn Women Artists; Conn Acad. Style & Technique: Large scale sculpture for indoors and outdoors in contemporary style, partially welded, riveted, nutted aluminum. Media: Fieldstone, Aluminum. Mailing Add: 126 Seacord Rd New Rochelle NY 10804

MEJER, ROBERT LEE
PAINTER, EDUCATOR
b South Bend, Ind, Nov 8, 44. Study: South Bend Art Ctr, with Joseph Wrobel; Notre Dame Univ, with Ivan Mestrovic & Ted Golubic; Ball State Univ, BS, with John Cavanaugh & Ronald Penkoff; Miami Univ, MFA, with Robert Wolfe, Jr; Kent State Univ, with Nathan Oliveira & Milton Resnick, 73; Kalamazoo Art Inst, with Harvey Breverman, 75; Oxbow Summer Sch of Art, 76 & 77, with, Richard Haas, Winifred Lvtz, Leon Golub & Edith Altman. Work: Ball State Univ, Muncie, Ind; Quincy Art Ctr, Ill; Int Arts League of Youth, New York; Anderson Art Ctr, Ind. Comn: Archit design, Future City, Muncie Redevelop Show, Ball State Univ, 65; illus prog, Am Grand Premiere, Sch Pal (play), Quincy Col, 69; billboard, Progressive Playhouse, 71. Exhib: Dayton Art Inst Traveling Drawing Show, 67; one-man shows, St Mary's Col, Notre Dame, Ind, 64, 67 & 70 & Culver-Stockton Col, Mo, 74; Three Points of View-Bell, Bradshaw, Mejer, Ill State Mus, Springfield, 72; Limestone Col, Gaffney, SC, 72; Ill Arts Coun Gallery, Chicago, 75; New Am Monotypes, Smithsonian Inst Traveling Exhib, 77-80; Six Midwestern Painters, Springfield Art Asn, 78. Collections Arranged: Byron Burford Circus, 71, In Search of an Ideal Landscape-Syed J Iqbal Geoffrey, 71, Ben Mahmoud, 71, Don Crouch, American West Series, 73, Middlewestern Cardscape, 74 & Religious in the Arts, 77, Quincy Col; Director's Choice, Quincy Art Club, 77. Teaching: Instr painting & drawing, Pac Proj Title III, Ball State Univ, summers 66 & 67; instr drawing, Miami Univ, 66-68; assoc prof art & gallery dir, Quincy Col, 68-; instr, John Woods Community Col, Pittsfield, 75 & Quincy, 76. Pos: Vis artist, Muncie Artist Guild, spring 63; vis artist, Twin Rivers Art League, Pittsfield, Ill, fall 71; gallery asst, Ball State Art Gallery, 62-66; Quincy Art Ctr, Ill, 70-; recognition visitation team, Off Supt Pub Instr, Ill, 71-; NCent Eval Team, 75. Awards: Blossom-Kent Art Fel, 73; Outstanding Teacher Incentive Award, 74 & Fac Res Grant Prints, 75, Watercolor, 76 & Papermaking, 77, Quincy Col; Second Prize in Watercolor, 31st Ann Prof Art Show, Ill State Fair, Springfield. Bibliog: Thomas Carbol (auth), article, In: The Printmaker in Illinois, 71-72; Robert Evans (auth), The Living Museum-Three Points of View, 1/72 & 27th Illinois Invitational, 74, Ill State Mus; Terrence Riddell (auth), Bob Mejer an artist, Riverword 1, 77. Mem: Nat Art Educ Asn; Ill Art Educ

Asn (exec coun, 70-72 & 75-); Quincy Art Club (bd dir, 1st vpres, 76-); Am Fedn Arts; Nat Art Workers Asn. Publ: Auth, Quincy Happening, 68; illusr, Salt-Lick Mag, 68-71; contribr, Barnes' Works Provide Exciting Art Show, 71; contribr, Faulty Subjects, 73, Daily Specials, 74 & Joshua's Book, 75, Quincy Col Lit/Art Mag; illusr, Riverword Mag, Vols 1, 2, 3 (1977) & Riverun 1, 75. Mailing Add: Fine Arts Dept Quincy Col Quincy IL 62301

MEKLER, ADAM
ART DEALER, CURATOR
b Haifa, Israel, Feb 1, 41; US citizen. Study: Calif State Univ, Northridge, BA, MA; Univ Southern Calif. Exhibitions Arranged: Jack Zajac, Retrospective 1955-74, Fine Arts Gallery of San Diego; Jack Zajac, Retrospective 1955-77, Palm Springs Desert Mus; Jack Zajac, Retrospective 1966-74, Santa Barbara Mus of Art; William Dole, Retrospective, 1960-75, Munic Art Gallery of Los Angeles, Colo Springs Fine Arts Ctr, Fine Arts Gallery of San Diego & Santa Barbara Mus of Art. Pos: Owner-dir, Mekler Gallery. Specialty: Contemporary sculpture and paintings. Mailing Add: Mekler Gallery 651 N La Cienega Blvd Los Angeles CA 90069

MELAMED, ABRAHAM
COLLECTOR, PATRON
b Chicago, Ill, Nov 19, 14. Pos: Mem, Gov Coun Arts, Wis, 63-65; bd dirs, Wis Art Fedn & Coun, 65-71; trustee, Arch Am Art, Smithsonian Inst, 66- Bibliog: Cubist Prints in Collection of Dr and Mrs Abraham Melamed, Univ Wis, 72. Interest: Visual arts; contributor to art organizations and institutions. Collection: Contemporary and modern works-graphics, paintings, sculpture. Mailing Add: 1107 E Lilac Lane Milwaukee WI 53217

MELBERG, JERALD LEIGH
CURATOR, COLLECTOR
b Minneapolis, Minn, Aug 17, 48. Study: Pillsbury Col, Owatonna, Minn; Bob Jones Univ, Greenville, SC. Collections Arranged: 1977 Biennial Exhibition of Piedmont Painting & Sculpture (ed, catalogue), 5-6/77, 1978 Biennial Exhibition of Piedmont Crafts (ed, catalogue), 1-2/78, Beautiful Things, 9-10/78 & The Major Graphic Works of Rufino Tamayo, 11-12/78, Mint Mus Art, Charlotte, NC. Pos: Dir, Hampton III Gallery, Ltd, Greenville, SC, 73-74; exec dir, Anderson Co Arts Coun, SC, 75-76; cur exhib, Mint Mus Art, 77- Mem: Greenville Artists Guild, SC (pres, 75); Am Asn Mus; assoc Smithsonian Inst, Washington, DC. Res: Artists residing in South Carolina, Rufino Tamayo, Ramare Bearden. Collection: Paintings, sculpture, graphics and crafts by Southeastern United States artists, and graphics by nationally known American artists. Mailing Add: PO Box 6011 Charlotte NC 28207

MELCHERT, JAMES FREDERICK
SCULPTOR, EDUCATOR
b New Bremen, Ohio, Dec 2, 30. Study: Princeton Univ, AB; Univ Chicago, MFA; Univ Calif, Berkeley, MA; ceramics with Peter Voulkos. Work: San Francisco Mus Art; Mus Mod Art, Kyoto, Japan; Victoria & Albert Mus, London; Oakland Mus Art, Calif; Stedelijk Mus, Amsterdam. Exhib: Abstract Expressionist Ceramics, Univ Calif, Irvine, 66; Contemporary American Sculpture, Whitney Mus Am Art, New York, 66, 68 & 70; Documenta 5, Kassel, Ger, 72. Teaching: Chmn dept ceramics, San Francisco Art Inst, 61-64; prof sculpture, Univ Calif, Berkeley, 64-; vis sculptor, Univ Wis-Madison, spring 71. Awards: Louis Comfort Tiffany Found Grant, 63; Nealie Sullivan Award, San Francisco Art Inst, 70; Nat Found Arts Grant, 72. Media: Clay. Mailing Add: 6077 Ocean View Dr Oakland CA 94618

MELIKIAN, MARY
PAINTER
b Worcester, Mass. Study: RI Sch Design, Providence, BFA, 55; Columbia Univ Teachers Col. Work: Worcester Mus Art, Mass; Mint Mus, Charlotte, NC; Yerevan Mus, Armenia; Vassar Col Art Mus; Art for US Embassies, State Dept. Exhib: One-man shows, Stable Art Gallery, Scottsdale, Ariz, 70, Art Gallery Inn, Ft Lauderdale, Fla, 71 & Bodley Gallery, New York, 78; Nat Arts Club, New York, 69 & 70; Galerie de Tours, San Francisco & Ankrum Gallery, Los Angeles, 70, Calif; retrospective, Centenary Col, Hackettstown, NJ, 75. Teaching: Instr art, Nutley High Sch, 57-60. Pos: Asst designer, Fuller Fabrics, NY, 56; asst dir, Grand Cent Moderns, New York, 60-61; dir pub rels, Grand Cent Art Galleries, New York, 61-67. Awards: First Prize, Kit Kat Club, 61, Armenian Student Asn, 61 & 62 & Women's Nat Repub Club, 70, 72, 73 & 75. Bibliog: Stan Haste (auth), Mary Melikian, RI Sch Design Mag, 9/68; Colette Roberts (auth), rev in France-Am; N Stepanian (auth), Paintings of Mary Melikian, Voice of Am, 68. Mem: RI Sch Design (alumni bd gov, 67-70, trustee, 70-72); Am Watercolor Soc; Burr Artists. Media: Pastel, Watercolor, Oil. Publ: Auth articles in Ararat Mag. Mailing Add: 429 E 52nd St Rivercourt 27H New York NY 10022

MELLON, JAMES
PRINTMAKER, PAINTER
b New York, NY, Feb 14, 41. Study: Creative Graphic Workshop, with Chaim Koppleman, 56-59; Art Students League, 57-58. Work: Everson Mus Art, Syracuse; Pennell Collection, Libr Cong; Smithsonian Inst; Univ Pa. Exhib: Sch Visual Arts Gallery, NY, 62; Soc Am Graphic Artists Traveling Exhib, SAm, 62; Everson Mus Art, 68; Int Miniature Print Exhib, Pratt Inst, 67 & 68; Cranbrook Acad Art, Bloomfield Hills, Mich; plus others. Teaching: Instr media, Dept Adult Educ, Brooklyn Col, 64-67; instr graphics, Sch Visual Arts, 65- Awards: Pennell Purchase Prize, Libr Cong, 58 & 61; Warren Mack Mem Award, 65; Purchase Prize, Everson Mus Art. Mem: Soc Am Graphic Artists (coun mem). Mailing Add: Sch of Visual Arts 209 E 23rd St New York NY 10010

MELLON, PAUL
COLLECTOR, ART ADMINISTRATOR
b Pittsburgh, Pa, June 11, 07. Study: Choate Sch, Wallingford, Conn, 19-25; Yale Univ, BA, 29, Hon LHD, 67; Clare Col, Cambridge Univ, BA, 31, MA, 38; Oxford Univ, Hon LittD, 61; Carnegie Inst Technol, Hon LLD, 67. Pos: Trustee, Nat Gallery Art, 38-39 & 45-, pres, 38-39 & 63-; trustee, Va Mus Fine Arts, Richmond, Va, 38- Awards: Nat Inst Arts & Lett Award for Distinguished Serv to Arts, 62; Benjamin Franklin Medal, Royal Soc Arts, 65; Gertrude Vanderbilt Whitney Award, Skowhegan Sch Painting & Sculpture, 72. Interest: Major financial contributor to Yale Center and Paul Mellon Centre for Studies in British Art, London, England. Collection: (Mr & Mrs Paul Mellon) English paintings, 1700-1850; impressionist and post-impressionist paintings. Mailing Add: 1729 H St NW Washington DC 20006

MELLOR, GEORGE EDWARD
EDUCATOR, SCULPTOR
b Bronxville, NY, Sept 13, 28. Study: Oberlin Col, AB(fine arts), 54; Atelier Zadkine, 52-53; Tyler Sch Fine Arts, MFA, 65. Work: Nat Collection Fine Art, Smithsonian Inst; Danvers Security Nat Bank, Lynn, Mass; Southeastern Mass Univ. Exhib: Regional Exhib, Pa Acad Fine Arts, Philadelphia, 64; one-man shows, Lamont Gallery, Exeter, NH, 68, Tufts Univ, Medford, Mass, 69 & Kanegis Gallery, Boston, 70; RI Sch Design, 75. Teaching: Instr art, Solebury Sch, New Hope, Pa, 57-65; assoc prof sculpture & ceramics, Southeastern Mass Univ, 68- Pos: Dir art gallery, Exeter Acad, NH, 65-68. Bibliog: Fred Stein (dir), Sketches-Some American Sculpture (film), US Info Agency, 70. Style & Technique: Metal fabrication; casting. Mailing Add: R7 West Blvd Onset MA 02558

MELTZER, ANNA E
PAINTER, INSTRUCTOR
b New York, NY, Aug 6, 96. Study: Cooper Union Art Sch; Art Students League; also with Vincent Dumond & Alexander Brook. Work: Brooklyn Mus, NY; Berkshire Mus, Pittsfield, Mass; Joslyn Mem Mus, Oamah, Nebr; Calif Palace of Legion of Honor, San Francisco; Ga Mus Fine Arts, Athens. Exhib: Audubon Artists, Nat Acad, New York, 42, 44 & 45; one-man shows, Francis Taylor Gallery, Beverly Hills, 47, Marie Sterner Gallery, French & Co, New York, 48, Collector's Gallery, New York, 59 & Peter Cooper Gallery, New York, 64. Teaching: Pvt instr, 42-; instr painting & graphics, City Col New York Exten Div, 52-64. Awards: Audubon Artist's Award, 42; Citation for Contrib to Contemp Am Painting & Fine Arts Educ, Fla Southern Col, 50. Bibliog: Dorothy Grafly (auth), The art of Anna Meltzer, Design Mag, 48; Dan Daniels (auth), An Adventure in Casein Painting (film), Grumbacher, 51; Bess Barzansky (auth), 44 Colorgraphs From Realism to Prismatism, Lumas-Nakle-Art Publ, 69. Mem: Audubon Artists; Cooper Union Alumni; Artists Equity Asn; Kappa Pi; fel Royal Soc Encouragement Arts. Media: Oil, Graphic. Mailing Add: 326 Bleeker St New York NY 10014

MELTZER, ARTHUR
PAINTER
b Minneapolis, Minn, July 31, 93. Study: Minneapolis Sch Fine Art; Pa Acad Fine Arts, Cresson traveling scholar, 21, fel prize, 25. Work: Pa Acad Fine Arts, Philadelphia; Moore Inst; Woodmere Art Gallery, Columbus Gallery Fine Art; Art Alliance, Philadelphia. Comn: Budd Trains (murals) & Stephen Girard (murals), Girard Fed, Philadelphia. Exhib: Pa Acad Fine Arts; Nat Acad Design, New York; Art Inst Chicago. Teaching: Head fine arts dept, Moore Col, Philadelphia, 25-49. Awards: Gold Medal, Ligonier Art League, 61; Williamson Prize, Phillips Mill, New Hope, Pa, 63; First Prize, Jenkintown Art Festival, 73; plus others. Mem: Fel Pa Acad Fine Arts; Philadelphia Mus, Woodmere Art Gallery, Artists Equity Asn. Media: Oil. Mailing Add: 1521 Welsh Rd Huntingdon Valley PA 19006

MELTZER, DORIS
ART DEALER, PRINTMAKER
b Ulster Col, NY, Jan 1, 08. Study: NY Univ, BS(art educ), 33; Art Students League, 39. Work: Pennell Collection, Libr Cong, Washington, DC; Flower Hosp, New York; plus others. Exhib: Nat juried exhibs & traveling exhibs abroad, US Info Agency, 41-58. Pos: Easel painter, Fed Art Proj, Works Progress Admin, 36-38; dir & vpres, Nat Serigraphy Soc, 45-62; dir, Meltzer Gallery, 55-62; owner & dir, Doris Meltzer Gallery, 63-76; art consult, 76- Mem: Am Art Conserv Soc; Oriental Ceramic Soc, London; Am Fedn Arts. Specialty: Ukiyoe master prints and pottery; American, European and Oriental art; drawings and prints. Collection: Japanese pottery from the 15th to the 19th century; miscellaneous art objects of various periods and places. Mailing Add: 326 Bleeker St New York NY 10014

MELTZER, ROBERT HIRAM
INSTRUCTOR, PAINTER
b New Rochelle, NY, Oct 18, 21. Study: Jean Morgan Sch Art, 46-47; Sch Art Studies, 46-47; Art Students League, 46-47; Southern Methodist Univ, BFA, 50; Univ Hawaii, grad study, 52-56; also with Jean Charlot, Robert Beverly Hale, Ernest Fiene, Robert Benney. Work: Edward-Dean Mus, Cherry Valley, Calif; San Bernardino City Hall, Calif; US Naval Archives, Washington, DC; Armed Forces Pub Info Officers Inst, Ft Slocum, NY; Southern Methodist Univ, Dallas, Tex. Comn: Oil portrait of Admiral John Hoskins, Mil Air Transport Serv, 52; oil on masonite Hukilau scene, Hukilau Hotel, Hilo, Hawaii, 54; oil portrait of W A S Smith, Lethbridge Col, 63. Exhib: Am Watercolor Soc (traveling exhib), Scott-Fanton Mus, Danbury, Conn, 65; Edward-Dean Mus, Cherry Valley, 67-78; Charles & Emma Frye Mus, Seattle, Wash, 74; Watercolor USA, Springfield, Mo, 75; Rocky Mt Nat Watermedia Show, 76; Nat Acad Design Show, New York, 77; Am Watercolor Soc, New York, 77; Nat Exhib Tennis Art, Int Tennis Hall Fame, RI, 77. Teaching: Coordr, Crafton Hills Col Watercolor Sem, Yucaipa, Calif, 74-; artist-in-residence watercolor, Living-Learning Ctr, Univ Redlands, Calif, 75-76; lectr/demonstr watercolors, Wenatchee Valley Col, Wash, 77. Pos: Mem bd dir, Edward-Dean Mus, Cherry Valley, 72-74. Awards: First Prize, 5th Arrowhead Arts Coun, San Bernardino, 72; Juror's Award, San Bernardino Co Mus, 76; First Prize, Watercolor West, 77. Mem: Am Watercolor Soc (vpres Far West, 76-); Soc Western Artists; Am Artists Prof League; Watercolor West. Style & Technique: Transparent watercolor landscapes, seascapes, cityscapes and Western art. Media: Watercolor, Oil. Publ: Auth & illusr, Drawing for the Fun of It, newspaper series, Banning Record, 65. Dealer: Oak Glen Art Gallery 39576 Lincoln Cherry Valley CA 92223. Mailing Add: PO Box 2132 Beaumont CA 92223

MELVILLE, GREVIS WHITAKER
PAINTER, PRINTMAKER
b Damariscotta, Maine, Dec 23, 04. Study: Yale Sch Art & Archit; Art Students League; also with Will Barnet & William C Palmer. Work: William A Farnsworth Libr & Art Mus, Rockland, Maine; Pierson Col, Yale Univ, New Haven, Conn; Damariscotta Region Info Bur. Comn: Designed seal, co comnr, Lincoln Co, Maine, 75. Exhib: Pa Acad Fine Art, Philadelphia; one-man shows, Bowdoin Col Mus, Brunswick, Maine & Smith Col Mus, Northampton, Mass; Maine State Art Festival, Augusta; Maine Artists Shows, Portland Mus Art; Maine Art '75, Bowdoin Col Mus Art, 75; plus others. Teaching: Artist in residence, Hackley Sch, Tarrytown, NY, 41-42. Mem: Maine Art Gallery (bd dirs, 68-69); Pemaquid Group Artists (dir, 66-72). Style & Technique: Modified objective with abstract design. Media: Oil, Lithography. Publ: Illusr, Windswept, Macmillan, 42; illusr, Maine Memories, Greene, 68. Dealer: Jacques Seligmann Galleries 5 E 57th St New York NY 10022; Ogunquit Gallery US Rte 1 Ogunquit ME 03907. Mailing Add: 38 Main St Damariscotta ME 04543

MENABONI, ATHOS RUDOLFO
PAINTER
b Livorno, Italy, Oct 20, 95; US citizen. Study: Pvt study with marine painter, Ugo Manaresi, mural painter, Charles Doudlet & sculptor, Pietro Gori; Art Acad in Florence. Work: High Mus Art, Atlanta, Ga; Woodruff Libr, Emory Univ, Atlanta; Cerebral Palsy Sch-Clinic, Atlanta; Art Mus Livorno, Italy; Capital City Club, Atlanta. Comn: Canvas, woodpanels, egg-shell mosaic & glass mosaics for pvt individuals & banks in Atlanta & Albany, Ga; wood panels, Wesley Woods Retirement Home, Atlanta; glass mosaic mural, Commerce Club, N Atlanta. Exhib: Am Mus Nat Hist, New York; Nat Audubon Soc Traveling Show; St Louis Art Mus, Mo; High Mus Art, Atlanta; Jeykell Island Art Asn, Ga; Columbus Art Asn, Ga; Marietta Art Asn, Ga; Kennedy Gallery, New York; Vose Gallery, Boston, Mass. Pos: Art dir, Davis Island, Tampa, Fla, 24-26. Awards: Spec awards from Ga Writers Asn, Daughters

of the Am Revolution, Am Inst of Architects & Italian Cult Soc. Style & Technique: Easel oil paintings, mural paintings and mosaics, advertising art, illustrations and originals for reproduction. Media: Thin Transparent Oil Pigments on Treated Paper, Wood, Silk, Glass & Canvas. Publ: Co-auth, Menaboni's Birds, Rinehart & Co, 50; co-auth, American Camellia Catalogue, privately publ, 50. Dealer: Lester K Henderson 712 Hawthorne St Monterey CA 93940. Mailing Add: 1111 Crest Valley Dr NW Atlanta GA 30327

MENCHACA, JUAN
CURATOR, PAINTER
b Ft Worth, Tex, 1910. Study: Tex Sch Fine Arts, Ft Worth; also with Robert Grahm & portraiture with Dario Rapport. Work: In mus & pub bldgs in US. Comn: Portraits of western gov & hist people. Pos: Designed & built displays & exhib for Colo mus; supvr dioramas, Colo State Mus, Denver, 36; chief cur, Nat Cowboy Hall Fame & Western Heritage Ctr, 65- Mailing Add: c/o Anderson Antiques 5101 Classen Oklahoma City OK 73118

MENDELOWITZ, DANIEL MARCUS
PAINTER, WRITER
b Linton, NDak, Jan 28, 05. Study: Stanford Univ, BA, 26, MA, 27; Art Students League, scholar, 29. Comn: Mural, US Govt Post Off, Oxnard, Calif, 40. Exhib: Corcoran Biennial, Washington, DC; San Francisco Art Asn; Calif Palace of Legion of Honor, San Francisco; Toledo Art Mus, Ohio; Stanford & Palo Alto, Calif. Teaching: Prof art, Stanford Univ, 34-70. Pos: Secy-treas, Pac Arts Asn, 22-28. Style & Technique: Landscape, realist; wash and dry brush. Media: Watercolor. Res: Field of American art. Publ: Auth, Children are Artists, Stanford Univ, 53; auth, Drawing, 67, History of American Art, rev ed, 70 & A Guide to Drawing, 76, Holt, Rinehart & Winston, New York. Mailing Add: 800 Lathrop Dr Stanford CA 94305

MENDELSON, HAIM
PAINTER, PRINTMAKER
b Semiatich, Builsk, Poland, Oct 15, 23; US citizen. Study: Am Artists Sch, 36-40; Saul Baizerman Art Sch, 40-43; Educ Alliance Art Sch, 46; pvt study with Saul Baizerman, 43-52. Work: Contemp Drawing Collection, Minn Mus Art, St Paul; Print Collection of New York Pub Libr; Print Collection of St Vincent Col, Latrobe, Pa; Griffiths Art Ctr of St Lawrence Univ, Canton, NY; Edwin A Ulrich Mus, Wichita State Univ, Kans. Exhib: The Artist as Reporter, Mus Mod Art, New York, 40-41; Drawings USA, St Paul Art Ctr, Minn, 61 & 66; Pa Acad Fine Arts, 65; Butler Inst Am Art, Youngstown, Ohio, 65 & 67; Nat Acad of Design, New York, 65, 68, 75 & 77; 10th Nat Exhib of Prints & Drawings, Okla Art Ctr, 68; Fedn of Mod Painters & Sculptors (traveling exhib), Gallery Asn of New York, 76-78. Pos: Dir, Hudson Guild Art Gallery, New York, 71-72 & 73- Awards: First Prize, Graphics, Knickerbocker Artists Ann, New York, 64; Purchase Award, Drawings USA, St Paul Art Ctr, 66; Graphics Award, Painters & Sculptors Soc of NJ, 74. Mem: Fedn of Mod Painters & Sculptors (pres, 74-); Knickerbocker Artists; League of Present Day Artists (vpres, 63-65); Painters & Sculptors Soc of NJ. Style & Technique: Figurative and landscape painting. Media: Oil, Acrylic, Collage; Intaglio Graphics. Mailing Add: 234 W 21st St New York NY 10011

MENDENHALL, JACK
PAINTER, INSTRUCTOR
b Ventura, Calif, Apr 7, 37. Study: Calif Col Arts & Crafts, BFA, 58 & MFA(painting), 70. Work: Univ Calif Art Mus, Berkeley; San Francisco Art Comn; Gallery Ostergren, Malmo, Sweden; Univ of NMex, Albuquerque; Butler Inst of Am Art, Ohio; Va Mus of Fine Arts, Richmond; Am Tel & Tel, Chicago; plus numerous pvt collections, individual & industrial, US & Europe. Comn: Rainbows, Waldo Tunnels, Calif Div Hwy, San Francisco, 70. Exhib: Super-Realist Vision, de Cordova Mus, Lincoln, Mass, 73; Amerikanske Realister, Panders Kunstmuseum, Sweden, 73; Tokyo Biennale 74, Japan, 74; New Photo Realism, Wadsworth Atheneum, Hartford, Conn, 74; one-man show, O K Harris Gallery, New York, 74; Realist Painting in California, John Berggruen Gallery, San Francisco, 75; Watercolors & Drawings, American Realists, Meisel Gallery, New York, 75; plus others. Teaching: Assoc prof painting & drawing, Calif Col Arts & Crafts, 70- Awards: Purchase Award, San Francisco Art Comn, 70. Bibliog: William C Seitz (auth), The real and the artificial: painting of the new environment, Art in Am, 12/72; Linda Chase (auth), Les hyperrealistes Americans, Paris, Ed Filipacchi, 73; Ellen Lubell (auth), rev in Arts Mag, 2/75. Mem: Oakland Mus. Style & Technique: Photo realistic; refined brush technique. Media: Oil, Watercolor. Dealer: Ivan Karp c/o O K Harris Gallery 383 W Broadway New York NY 10012. Mailing Add: 66 Glen Ave Oakland CA 94611

MENDOZA, DAVID C
ART DEALER, ART WRITER
b Auburn, Wash, Sept 10, 44. Study: Univ Wash, Seattle, BFA(art hist); New Sch Social Res, New York. Collections Arranged: Pacific Northwest Bell Collection, Seattle, Wash, 76; 20th Century American Photography (auth, catalogue), Rainier Bank, Seattle, 77; Mark Tobey—Works From the Early 1940s, 74, Mark Tobey Memorial Exhibition, 76 & Sets and Costumes Designed for Merce Cunningham Dance Company by Rotuschenberg, Stella, Johns, Warhol, 77, Foster/White Gallery, Seattle. Pos: Dir, Richard White Gallery, Seattle, 68-72; dir, Foster/White Gallery, Seattle 73-78; owner-dir, Rain, Seattle & New York, 78- Mem: Allied Arts of Seattle (bd trustees, 77-78; bd mem, 76-). Res: Arts and design of the Pacific Northwest; 20th century American photography. Specialty: Contemporary Pacific Northwest art, paintings and sculpture; contemporary photography. Collection: Photography, to date primarily with 20th century European and American; focusing on fashion, still life, personalities and fantasy images. Publ: Auth, Pacific Northwest designer craftsmen, Craft Horizons, 69; auth, Morris Graves, Ore Rainbow, 76; auth, Zoe Dusanne—Seattle's pioneer art dealer, The Weekly-Seattle, 77. Mailing Add: 311 1/2 Occidental S Seattle WA 98104

MENEELEY, EDWARD
SCULPTOR
b Wilkes Barre, Pa, Dec 18, 27. Study: Murray Art Sch, Wilkes Barre, 52-56; Sch of Visual Arts, New York, 57-58; pvt study with Jack Tworkov, New York, 58-59. Work: Metrop Mus of Art, New York; Mus of Mod Art, New York; Whitney Mus, New York; Mus of RI, Providence; Chrysler Mus, Norfolk, Va; Victoria & Albert Mus, London, Can, Exhib: Tenth Street Group, New York, 57-60; Contemp Boxes & Wall Sculpture, Mus of Art, Providence, RI, 65; Recent Acquisitions, Whitney Mus, New York, 69; Machine Art, Mus Mod Art, New York, 70; Three Americans: Ed Meneeley, Don Judd Robert Graham, Victoria & Albert Mus, London, 71; Spring in the Air, Scottish Arts Coun Gallery, Edinborough, 72; Photography into Art, Camden Arts Ctr, London, Can, 72; Oliver Dowling Gallery, Dublin, Ireland 77; one-man shows, Inst of Contemp Arts, London, 71, Univ Col, Dublin, Ireland, 75 & Susan Caldwell Gallery, New York, 76. Teaching: Instr, Central Sch of Art, London, 68-73; instr, Winchester Sch of Art, England, 69-; instr, Art Students League, New York, 74. Awards: Nat Endowment for the Arts Grant, Washington, DC, 71; Arts Coun Grant, London, 71. Bibliog: Peter Schjeldahl (auth), Ed Meneeley, Art News, New York, Anthony Howell (auth), Ed Meneeley, Vogue, London, 8/75; Grace Glueck (auth), Instant Art, New York Times, Arts Coun Grant, London, 71. Bibliog: Peter Schjeldahl (auth), Ed Meneeley, Art News, New York, 4/66; Anthony Howell (auth), Ed Meneeley, Vogue, London, 8/75; Grace Glueck (auth), Instant Art, New York Times, 11/75. Style & Technique: Abstract. Media: Flesh. Mailing Add: 201 2nd Ave New York NY 10003

MENG, WENDY
PAINTER
b Fla, Feb 15, 44. Study: Seishen Daibako, Tokyo, 61-62; Kansas City Art Inst, BFA, 67; Md Inst Col Art, MFA(with honors), 69. Work: Chase Manhattan Bank, New York; Nat Gallery of the Smithsonian Inst, Washington, DC; Libr of Cong, Washington, DC. Comn: School of Fish (lithograph), Spec Proj Group for Bicentennial, Chicago, 75. Exhib: New Editions 74-75, New York Cult Ctr, 75; 1975 Potsdam Drawing Exhib, State Univ NY Col Potsdam, 75; New Talent, Alpha Gallery, Boston, 75; Invitational Exhib, James Yu Gallery, 75; Works on Paper, Alpha Gallery, Boston, Mass, 76 & 77; Sheldon Art Mus, Lincoln, Nebr, 76; 41st Ann Midyear Show, Butler Inst Am Art, Youngstown, Ohio, 77; Hodgell Hartman Gallery, Sarasota, Fla, 77; Works for Young Collectors, Wooster Mus, Mass, 77; Space/Color/Place, Brocton Art Mus, Mass, 77-78; one-woman shows, Gallery of July & August, Woodstock, NY, 75, James Yu Gallery, 76 & Alpha Gallery, Boston, Mass, 77. Teaching: Art instr, Berkeley Inst, Brooklyn, 71-74. Awards: Print Honorarium, Spec Proj Group, 75. Style & Technique: Realism. Media: Oil on Canvas, Watercolor. Dealer: Alpha Gallery Boston MA; Hodgell Hartman Gallery Sarasota FL. Mailing Add: 45 Bond St New York NY 10012

MENIHAN, JOHN CONWAY
PAINTER, DESIGNER
b Rochester, NY, Feb 14, 08. Study: Wharton Sch, Univ Pa, 30. Work: Libr of Cong, Washington, DC; Carnegie Inst, Pittsburgh; Mem Art Gallery, Rochester. Comn: Polyester mural, Xerox, Rochester, 60; glass mural, Nazareth Col Libr, 62; polyester murals, Security Trust, Rochester, 65, Rochester Tel Co, 67 & R T French, Rochester & Fresno, Calif, 68; designer, Chapel, Notre Dame, Elvira, NY; plus many portraits. Exhib: Finger Lakes Show, Mem Art Gallery, Rochester, 30 & 71; Art Inst Chicago, 39; World's Fair, New York, 39; Nat Acad Design, 48 & Am Watercolor Soc, 54, New York. Teaching: Asst prof drawing & painting, Univ Rochester, 46-65. Awards: Lillian Fairchild Award, Univ Rochester, 40; Marion Stratton Gould Award, Univ Rochester Mem Art Gallery, 46. Bibliog: Norman Kent (auth), John C Menihan/lithographer, Am Artist, 45. Mem: Fel Rochester Mus & Sci Ctr; Nat Acad Design; Am Watercolor Soc; Asn Am Inst Architects. Style & Technique: From realistic modern to abstract, mainly using synthetics. Publ: Illusr, How Scientists Find Out, Little, 65. Mailing Add: 208 Alpine Dr Rochester NY 14618

MENKES, SIGMUND
PAINTER
b Lwow, Poland, May 7, 96; US citizen. Study: Higher Inst Art Decorative, Lwow, 14; Acad Fine Art, Cracow, Poland, 19. Work: Metrop Mus Art & Whitney Mus Am Art, New York; Pa Acad Fine Arts, Philadelphia; Hirshhorn Mus, Washington, DC; Brooklyn Mus. Exhib: Carnegie Inst, Pittsburgh; Metrop Mus Art & Whitney Mus Am Art, New York; Corcoran Gallery Art, Washington, DC; Pa Acad Fine Arts, Philadelphia; plus many other group & one-man shows. Awards: Nat Inst Arts & Lett Award, 55; Medal of Honor, 65 & Silver Medal, 67, Audubon Artists; Polish Inst Arts & Sci Prize, 68; plus others. Bibliog: Emily Genauer (auth), Best of Art, Doubleday, 48; Arthur Zaidenberg (ed), The Art of Artists, Crown, 51; Nathaniel Pousette-Dart (ed), American Painting Today, Hastings, 56. Mem: Life fel Int Inst Arts & Lett; Fedn Mod Painters & Sculptors (pres, 42-43); assoc Nat Acad Design. Style & Technique: Figurative-semi-abstract. Media: Oil, Acrylic. Mailing Add: 5075 Fieldstone Rd Riverdale NY 10471

MENSES, JAN
PAINTER, PRINTMAKER
b Rotterdam, Netherlands, Apr 28, 33; Can citizen. Work: Mus Mod Art & Guggenheim Mus, New York; Art Inst Chicago; Brooklyn Mus; Munic Mus, Amsterdam, Holland. Exhib: Montreal Mus Fine Arts, 60, 65 & 76; 5th & 7th Biennial Can Painting, 63 & 68 & 1st & 2nd Biennial Can Watercolours, Drawings & Prints, 64 & 66, Nat Gallery Can, Ottawa; 20 New Acquisitions, Mus Mod Art, New York, 66; 9th & 11th Int Exhib Drawings & Engravings, Lugano, Switz, 66 & 72; Rotterdam Art Found, Netherlands, 74. Awards: Grand Prize Concours Artistiques Quebec, 65; Award, 9th Int Exhib Drawings & Engravings, City of Lugano, Switz, 66; Prize, Perspective 67, Prov of Ont, 67. Bibliog: The arts, Time Mag (Can ed), 7/19/68; Francois Gagnon (auth), La serie des k'lipoth de Jan Menses, Vie Arts, spring 72; Jerrold Morris (auth), The Nude in Canadian Painting, New Press, Toronto, 72. Mem: Royal Can Acad Arts; Print & Drawing Coun of Can; Soc Artistes Professionnels Quebec. Media: Tempera, Acrylic, Oil. Dealer: Mira Godard Gallery 22 Hazelton Ave Toronto ON M5R 2E2 Can; Mira Godard Gallery 1490 Sherbrooke Ouest Montreal PQ H3G 1L3 Can. Mailing Add: 5571 Woodbury Ave Montreal PQ H3T 1S6 Can

MENTHE, MELISSA
ART LIBRARIAN, PHOTOGRAPHER
b Hackensack, NJ, June 16, 48. Study: Montclair State Col, NJ, BA; Rutgers Univ, MLS. Pos: Reference librn, Art Dept, Newark Pub Libr, Newark, NJ, 71-76; reference librn, Rutgers Univ, New Brunswick, 76- Mem: Art Libr Soc of NAm; Col Art Asn; Spec Libr Asn; Indust Photographers of NJ. Res: Methodology in history of photography. Interest: History of photography, incunabula and fine printing, historic preservation. Mailing Add: 575 Easton Ave Apt 20H Somerset NJ 08873

MERCER, JOHN DOUGLAS
PHOTOGRAPHER, PUBLISHER
b Des Moines, Iowa, July 31, 45. Study: NW Mo State Col, BS(art, psych), 70; Ariz State Univ, MA(art educ), 72, MFA(photog), 73. Work: San Francisco Gen Hosp, Calif; Alcatraz Mus, Alcatraz Island, San Francisco, Calif. Exhib: Art Gallery, NW Mo State Univ, Maryville, 73; Photog Directions, Art Gallery, State Univ NY Col, New Paltz, 74; one-man shows, Lucas Gallery, San Francisco, Focus Gallery, San Francisco, 76, Alcatraz, Creative Eye Photo Gallery, Sonoma, Calif, 76 & Montalvo Ctr for the Arts, Saratoga, Calif, 77; Seven Bay Area Photographers, Capricorn Asunder Gallery, San Francisco, 76; Gallery F22, Santa Fe, NMex, 77. Collections Arranged: Christo's Running Fence, Petaluma Co Libr, Calif; Sonoma County-Sense of Place, Santa Rose Jr Col, Calif; Photographs of Sonoma County, Rohnert Park Libr & Sonoma City Libr, Calif. Teaching: Workshop toning photogs, ASUC-CAL, Univ Berkeley, Calif, 75; workshop doc photog, Modesto Jr Col, Calif, 76. Pos: Dir, Creative Eye Photo Gallery, 74-77; founder, Critical Focus Group, Sonoma, 75-77; dir, Creative Eye Press, 75- Awards: Assistance Grant, Photographs of Sonoma Co, Calif Arts Coun, 77. Bibliog: Alfred Frankenstein (auth), Credit where it's due, San Francisco Chronicle, 10/76; Joan Murray (auth), Bill Owens and John D Mercer, Artweek, 10/76; Rolf Koppell (auth), From the tightest corner, Santa Fe Reporter, 5/77. Style & Technique: Nature, man-made objects and nudes. Media: Black and white and color photography. Res: Photography as art; curriculum design for the college level. Publ: Contribr, Young American

Photography, Vol I, Lustrum, 74; contribr (images), Bombay Duck, Issues 1, 2 & 3, 74, contribr (quote), Issue 4, 76; auth, Island of the Pelicans, Creative Eye Press, 76; contribr (images), Combinations, A J of Photog, Issue 1, 77. Dealer: Creative Eye Press PO Box 620 Sonoma CA 95476. Mailing Add: 15551 Brookview Dr Sonoma CA 95476

MERCHANT, PAT (JEAN)
INSTRUCTOR, PAINTER
b Oklahoma City, Okla, Oct 8, 28. Study: Sch Fine Art, Univ Okla, Norman, BFA & MAEd. Work: Okla Art Ctr, State Fair Park, Oklahoma City; State of Okla Art Collection, Okla Art Ctr. Exhib: 31st Okla Ann Exhib, Philbrook Mus Art, Tulsa, 60, 61 & 71; Ann Eight-State Exhib Painting & Sculpture, Okla Art Ctr, 60, 67 & 68; Southwest Fine Arts Biennial, Mus NMex, Santa Fe, 70; 13th & 14th Ann Delta Exhib, Ark Art Ctr, Little Rock, 70 & 71. Teaching: Art teacher, Oklahoma City Pub Schs, 58-70, curriculum consult in art, 71-; educ dir gallery & children's prog, Okla Art Ctr, 70-71. Pos: Asst to dir, Okla Art Ctr, 70-71. Awards: Purchase Award, Ann Eight-State Exhib, Okla Art Ctr, 68; Painting Award, 31st Okla Ann Exhib, Philbrook Mus, 71; Purchase Selection, State of Okla Art Collection, Okla State Arts & Humanities, 72. Mem: Okla State Arts & Humanities (adv comt panel on grants to communities); Alliance for Arts, Adv Coun Arts Educ; Okla Art Educ Asn (adv coun to pres); Delta Kappa Gamma Soc Women Educators (chap pres); Okla Designer/Craftsman. Style & Technique: Hard edge technique, smooth flat areas of color; recent paintings are non-objective symbolic forms of shields, using shaped canvas over constructions. Media: Acrylic; Fiber. Res: Opening doors in educational programs, Indian and Mexican-American education, Black art and workshops for teachers. Publ: Auth, An art experience at Inverness-Boyd, Innovative Teaching in Okla, 72-73. Mailing Add: 2445 NW 47 Oklahoma City OK 73112

MERCIER, MONIQUE
PAINTER, TAPESTRY ARTIST
b Nicolet, Que, Can, Sept 21, 34. Study: Univ of Laval, Que, Can, Bac Es-Art; Ecole des Beaux-Arts, Que, Can, dipl. Work: Ecoles des Beaux-Arts, Que; Musee du Que; Institut des Arts au Saguenay, Que; Univ of Que, Trois-Rivieres; Ministere des Affaire, Inter-Gouvernementales, Que. Comn: Painting, Chubb & Son, Montreal, Que, 71; tapestry, Allendale Insurance Co, RI, 72; tapestry, Auberge des Gouverneurs, Que, 74. Exhib: Art Gallery of Ont, Toronto, 70; Agnes Etherington Art Ctr, Kingston, Ont, 70; Kitchner-Waterloo Art Gallery, Ont, 70 & 71; Contemp Tapestry of Can, 71 & Artfemme, 75, Mus of Contemp Art, Montreal; Mus of Sci, Los Angeles, 72-73; one-woman shows, Paintings & Tapestry, Cult Ctr of Verdun, Montreal, 70 & 72, Institut des Arts au Saguenay, Jonquiere, Que, 71, Societe Culturelle d'Amos, Que, 71, Mus of Que, 73, Drawings & Lithographs, Mus of Contemp Art, Havre, Montreal, 76; plus others. Teaching: Prof tapestry, Univ of Que, Trois-Rivieres. Pos: Dir, Module Beaux-Arts & Sect des Arts Plastique, Univ of Que, Troit-Rivieres, 69-71. Bibliog: Madeleine Jarry (auth), La tapisserie Art du xxe Siecle, 75; article in Vie des Arts, spring & summer 76. Mem: Asn of Prof of Fine Arts, Que; Asn of Prof Artists, Que; Asn of Artisans of Can. Mailing Add: 1391 rue St-Jean-Baptiste Nicolet PQ J0G 1E0 Can

MEREDITH, DOROTHY LAVERNE
WEAVER, EDUCATOR
b Milwaukee, Wis, Nov 17, 06. Study: Layton Sch Art, Milwaukee; Wis State Col, BAE; Cranbrook Acad Fine Art, Bloomfield Hills, Mich, MFA. Work: Objects USA, Johnson Found; Milwaukee Art Ctr; Cranbrook Acad Art; Fedn Handweavers Gallery, Wellington, NZ; Univ Wis-Milwaukee. Exhib: 22 Wis Designer Craftsmen, 46-72; Nippon Gendai Koghi Bijutsu Int, Japan, 67 & 68; 6 Midwest Designer Craftsmen; Am Crafts Coun Craftsmen of Midwest; Fiber Clay Metal; plus others. Teaching: Prof weaving, Univ Wis-Milwaukee, 53-75, emer prof, 75- Awards: Miss River Crafts Award, 62; Nippon Gendai Koghi Bijutsu Award, Japan, 66; 9 Wis Designer Craftsmen Award, Milwaukee Art Ctr, 71. Mem: World Crafts Coun; fel Am Crafts Coun (trustee, 58-61, state rep, 62-63); Am Crafts Coun NCent Regional; Midwest Designer Craftsmen; Wis Designer Craftsmen (secy & pres). Style & Technique: Weaving, space hangings, enclosing mirrors, plastics, and others; 3-D constructions, accent on color. Media: Fibers. Mailing Add: 2932 N 69th St Milwaukee WI 53210

MEREDITH, JOHN
PAINTER
b Fergus, Ont, 1933. Work: Art Gallery, Ont; Nat Gallery Can; Univ Waterloo, Ont; Mus Mod Art, New York; Montreal Mus Fine Arts; plus many others. Exhib: Canada 101, Edinburgh Festival, Scotland, 68; 10th Int Black & White Exhib, Lugano, Switz, 68; Winters Col, York Univ, Toronto, 69; Rothmans Art Gallery, Stratford, Ont, 70; Eight Artists From Canada, Tel Aviv Mus, Israel, 70; plus many others. Mem: Royal Can Acad Arts. Mailing Add: c/o Isaacs Gallery 832 Yonge St Toronto ON M4W 2H1 Can

MERFELD, GERALD LYDON
PAINTER
b Des Moines, Iowa, Feb 19, 36. Study: Am Acad Art, with William Mosby, 54-57. Work: Marietta Col, Ohio; McDonough Collection Am Art; US Navy Arch. Exhib: Hope Show, Butler Inst Am Art, 72, 74 & 76; Audubon Artists, New York, 73; Okla Mus Art 14th Ann Artists Salon, 75; Acad Artists Asn, Springfield Mus Fine Art, Mass, 75; Hudson Valley Art Asn 47th Ann, 75; Allied Artists Am Ann, New York, 75-77; Knickerbocker Artists, New York, 75; Civic Fine Arts Asn, Sioux Falls, SDak, 77; Vanishing Landmark Exhib, Springfield Art Mus, Mo, 77. Teaching: Pvt lessons painting, drawing & sculpture, studio. Pos: Studio asst, Dean Cornwell, New York, 57-60; combat artist, US Navy, Vietnam, 69 & Mediter, 71. Awards: Louis E Seley Gold Medal, Salmagundi Club, 71; Okla Mus Art Award, 75. Style & Technique: Objective, impressionism, chiaroscuro, impasto. Media: Oil, Pastel, Conte Crayon. Dealer: DeColores Art Gallery 2817 E Third Ave Denver CO 80206; George Shechtman 766 Madison Ave New York NY 10021. Mailing Add: 228 Oak St New Lenox IL 60451

MERIDA, CARLOS
PAINTER
b Guatemala City, Guatemala, Dec 2, 91. Work: Mus Mod Art, New York, San Francisco & Sao Paulo, Brazil; Mus Dallas, Tex; Mus Arte Mod, Caracas, Venezuela. Comn: Murals (colored concrete), Apts Juarez, Mexico City, 51; Champion Bougies (enameled tiles), Mexico City, 68 & Hemisfair, San Antonio, Tex, 68; murals (enamel on copper), Banco Guatemala, 69. Bibliog: Margarita Nelken (auth), Carlos Merida, Nat Univ Mex, 61; Monograph, Mus Mod Art, Mexico City, 70 & Galleria Collezionista, Rome, Italy, 75. Publ: Imagenes de Guatemala (10 stencils), Quatre Chemins, Paris, 28; Tres Motivos Huacograbados (portfolio), Mex, 36; Dances of Mexico (portfolio of 10 lithographs), Far Ed, New York, 37; Mexican Costumes (portfolio of 25 serigraphs), Pocahontas Press, Chicago, 41; Estampas del Popol Vuh (portfolio of lithographs), Mexico City, 43. Dealer: Galeria de Arte Mexicano Milan 18 Mexico City Mex. Mailing Add: Manuel M Ponce 138 Mexico City Mexico

MERKEL, JAYNE (SILVERSTEIN)
ART HISTORIAN, WRITER
b Cincinnati, Ohio, Sept 28, 42. Study: Simmons Col, BS(English), 64, with Wylie Sypher; Smith Col, MA(art hist), 68, with Henry-Russell Hitchcock; Univ Mich, 66-68, with Leonard K Eaton. Exhibitions Arranged: Early Works: Alexander Calder, Taft Mus, 72 (with catalog); Behind the Queen's Skirt (Cincinnati Photog), Taft Mus, 72. Teaching: Teaching asst art hist, Univ Mich, 66-68; instr art hist, part-time, Univ Cincinnati, 70-72; instr art hist, Art Acad Cincinnati, 73- Pos: Asst cur, Univ Mich Mus Art, Ann Arbor, 65-68; cur, Contemp Arts Ctr, Cincinnati, 68-69; dir educ, Taft Mus, Cincinnati, 68-74; archit critic, Cincinnati Enquirer, 77- Awards: Award for Excellence in Archit Writing, Am Inst Archit, Cincinnati, 73. Mem: Col Art Asn. Res: Contemporary and transitional modern architecture in relation to specific sociological aspects of its context. Publ: Auth & ed, The Fifth Moon Group, Contemp Chinese Painters, Taft Mus, 71; auth, Everything you need to know—But no more, Vt Road Signs, 72; auth, See the yellow brick-faced school box, Archit of Cincinnati Schs, 73; auth, Getting what we deserve, Archit Preserv in Cincinnati, 73; auth, What is a civil engineer anyway?, 74. Mailing Add: 1908 Dexter Ave Cincinnati OH 45206

MERKIN, RICHARD MARSHALL
PAINTER, PRINTMAKER
b Brooklyn, NY, Oct, 1938. Study: Syracuse Univ Sch Art, BFA; RI Sch Design, MFA. Work: Mus Art, RI Sch Design; Mus Mod Art; Finch Col, NY; Rose Art Mus, Brandeis Univ; Mass Inst Technol. Comn: Seven murals, Blackstone Park Pub Sch, Boston, Mass. Exhib: Whitney Mus Am Art, 69 & 72; Chicago Inst Contemp Art; Finch Col Mus; one-man shows, Terry Dintenfass Gallery, New York, Galleria del 'Ariete, Milan, Kingpitcher Gallery, Pittsburgh, Newport Art Asn, RI, Obelisk Gallery, Boston & Mass Inst Technol, Cambridge, Mass. Teaching: Teaching fel, RI Sch Design, asst prof painting, currently adj teacher painting. Awards: Tiffany Found Fel Painting; Rosenthal Found Award, Nat Inst Arts & Lett, 75. Dealer: Terry Dintenfass Gallery New York NY. Mailing Add: 500 West End Ave New York NY 10024

MERMIN, MILDRED (SHIRE)
PAINTER
b New York, NY. Study: Nat Acad Design; Art Students League, with Boardman Robinson & George Grosz; also with Charles W Hawthorne & Philip Evergood. Work: Israel Mus, Jerusalem; Chrysler Mus Art, Norfolk, Va; Springfield Mus Fine Arts, Mass. Exhib: Pa Acad Fine Arts, Philadelphia; Japanese-Am Exchange Exhib, Nat Mus, Tokyo, Japan, 61; Silvermine Guild Artists Nat Exhib, New Canaan, Conn, 62; Nat Acad Design, New York, 63; New Haven Festival Art, Conn, 69. Awards: Am Art Mag Award, 57 & Marian Haldenstein Award, 77, Nat Asn Women Artists; Grumbacher Award, Am Soc Contemp Artists, 68. Mem: Fel MacDowell Colony; Artists Equity Asn; Am Soc Contemp Artists; Nat Asn Women Artists; Silvermine Guild Artists. Style & Technique: Semi representational, done in a thin fluid technique with use of an independent linear design throughout. Media: Oil, Watercolor. Mailing Add: 100 Colony Rd New Haven CT 06511

MERRIAM, RUTH
CONSERVATOR, COLLECTOR
b Denver, Colo, May 15, 09. Study: Bryn Mawr Col, BA & MA. Pos: Asst cur, Class Sect, Univ Mus, 32-40; rec photog, Conserv Dept, assisting in cleaning, relining & in-painting & asst to conservator, Philadelphia Mus Art, 54- Collection: From old masters to contemporary art. Publ: Auth, History of the Deanery, Bryn Mawr Col. Mailing Add: Maybrook Wynnewood PA 19096

MERRICK, JAMES KIRK
PAINTER
b Philadelphia, Pa, Oct 8, 05. Study: Philadelphia Col Art, dipl; Cape Sch Art, Provincetown, Mass, with Henry Hensche. Work: Philadelphia Mus Art; State Mus Art, Harrisburg, Pa; State Mus NJ, Trenton; Lehigh Univ, Bethlehem, Pa; Du Pont Collection, Wilmington, Del. Comn: Murals, pvt home, Bryn Mawr, Pa, 73 & outside wall, Drake Hotel, Philadelphia, Pa, 74. Exhib: Pa Acad Fine Arts, Philadelphia, 35-; Philadelphia Mus Art, 40-; Nat Acad Design Watercolor Shows, New York, Audubon Artists, New York & Art Inst Chicago, 40-49. Teaching: From instr to prof art, Philadelphia Col Art, 29-60. Pos: Exec dir, Philadelphia Art Alliance, 60-70. Awards: Gold Medal, Philadelphia Col Art Alumni Asn, 54; Gold Medal Award of Merit, Philadelphia Watercolor Club, 55; Dawson Medal, Pa Acad Fine Arts, 64. Mem: Hon life mem Philadelphia Art Alliance (secy bd dirs); Philadelphia Watercolor Club (hon life pres, 60-); Am Nat Theater Acad (founding mem); Philadelphia Col Art Alumni Asn (pres, 48-52). Style & Technique: Abstract based on ethnic and nature forms. Media: Watercolor, Oil. Publ: Auth & illusr, Brian; illusr, Those Were Actors. Mailing Add: 341 S Hicks St Philadelphia PA 19102

MERRILL, DAVID KENNETH
PAINTER
b Bridgeport, Conn, Oct 18, 35. Comn: The Entrance, Univ Maine, Gorham, 71; Monroe Green, Town of Monroe, Conn, 72; ann report cover, William R Berkley Corp, New York, 73; IBM, Burlington, Vt, 74; 43 scenes of Southbury's past & present (8ft x 30ft mural), comn by Southbury, Conn Town Hall Bldg Comt, 78. Exhib: Kent Art Asn, Conn, 69, 73 & 74; Northern Vt Artists Asn, 71-74; Mainstreams '74, Marietta, Ohio; Conn Acad Fine Art, 74; Douglas Gallery, Stamford, Conn, 74 & 75. Teaching: Instr art, Southbury Training Sch, Conn, 63-67. Awards: Medal of Merit, Kent Art Asn, 69; First Place, Burlington Garden Show, 72; First Place, 72 & First & Second Place, 74, Northern Vt Artists Asn. Mem: Kent & Washington Art Asns; Northern Vt Art Asn; New Haven Paint & Clay Club. Style & Technique: Realistic renderings of rural New England, capturing the nostalgia of a passing era. Media: Acrylic. Publ: Auth article in This New Eng, Yankee Mag. Dealer: Douglas Gallery 1117 High Ridge Rd Stamford CT 06905; Lillian Haversat Jericho VT 05465. Mailing Add: PO Box 305 Southbury CT 06488

MERRILL, ROSS M
PAINTING CONSERVATOR, PAINTER
b Abilene, Tex, 43. Study: Pa Acad Fine Arts; Oberlin Col, Ohio, MA; Intermus Conserv Asn, conserv cert. Teaching: Lectr mus conserv for var mus & conserv orgns. Pos: Admin head of conserv dept, Cleveland Mus Art, 74- Mem: Am Inst Conserv; Int Inst Conserv; Nat Conserv Adv Coun (chmn energy comt). Style & Technique: Representational landscapes. Media: Oil, Watercolor. Res: Fifteenth century northern Euorpean painting techniques. Interest: Early European paintings. Publ: Co-auth, Honeycomb Core Construction for Supporting Panels, 72 & An Information Retrieval System for Painted Works of Art, 73, Am Inst Conserv; auth, Juan deFlandes, a technical study, Cleveland Mus Bull, 76; co-auth, A History of Painting Forgery From 1500 to Present, 78 & auth, Technical Investigation of

Cleveland Museum's Recent Forgery, St Catherine of Alexandria, 78, Am Inst Conserv. Mailing Add: 1643 Warrensville Ctr South Euclid OH 44121

MERRITT, FRANCIS SUMNER
PAINTER, DESIGNER
b Danvers, Mass, Apr 8, 13. Study: Vesper George Sch Art; San Diego Acad Fine Art; Mass Sch Art; Boston Mus Sch; Yale Univ Sch Fine Arts; Colby Col, Hon DFA, 71. Comn: Murals, Bd Educ, New London High Sch, NH, 43 & Knox Co Med Ctr, Rockland, Maine, 52. Exhib: Directions in American Art, Am Fedn Arts Traveling Unit, Carnegie Inst, 42; Int Watercolor Show, Art Inst Chicago, 42-43; Artists for Victory, Metrop Mus Art, 42; Butler Art Inst Ann, Youngstown, Ohio, 47; Greetings Exhib, Mus Mod Art, New York, 47; plus others. Teaching: Instr painting & drawing, Abbot Acad, Andover, Mass, 37-39, Colby Jr Col, New London, 40-44, Kingswood, Cranbrook, Bloomfield Hills, Mich, 46-47 & Bradford Jr Col, Mass, 53-57. Pos: Cur, John Esther Art Gallery, Andover, Mass, 37-39; dir, Flint Inst Art, Mich, 47-51; dir, Haystack Mt Sch Crafts, Deer Isle, Maine, 51-77, emer dir, 77- Awards: First Award Painting, Flint Inst Art Ann, 47. Bibliog: Haystack Mountain School of Crafts, Handweaver & Craftsman, 12/51; An unusual school, Dansk Kunst Haandvaerk, 4/60; Haystack-Hinckley, Craft Horizons, 5/70. Mem: Artists Equity (regional bd mem, 47-48); Am Crafts Coun (trustee, 56-62); State of Maine Comn Arts & Humanities (vchmn, 67-72); fel Royal Soc Arts; fel Am Crafts Coun. Mailing Add: Deer Isle ME 04627

MESAROS, RON
PHOTOGRAPHER
b Rahway, NJ, Sept 6, 42. Study: Rochester Inst Technol, BFA, 65; Ill Inst Technol, MS, 67; and with Minor White, 63 & Nathan Lyons, 64-65. Work: Int Mus Photog, George Eastman House, Rochester, NY. Exhib: The Farmer Today, Rochester Inst Technol, 65; Vision and Expression, George Eastman House, 69; North Light Gallery, Ariz State Univ, 75. Bibliog: Norman Schreiber (auth), On being a free lance, Pop Photog, 71; Markene Kruse Smith (auth), Ron Mesaros surprises, Petersen Photog, Los Angeles, 75. Style & Technique: Photographs and portraits, black and white; multiple printing. Publ: Contribr, Vision and Expression, Horizon, 69; contribr, Light and Film, 70, contribr, Art of Photography, 71 & contribr, Photographing children, 71, Time Life Bks; contribr, Contemporary Psychology/Behavior, Scott-Foresman, 73. Mailing Add: 2614 W Seventh St Los Angeles CA 90057

MESCHES, ARNOLD
PAINTER, EDUCATOR
b New York, NY, Aug 11, 23. Study: Art Ctr Sch; Chouinard's Art Inst; Jepson's Art Inst. Work: Philadelphia Mus Art; San Francisco Mus Art; Brooklyn Mus Art; Arco Collection, La; Palm Springs Mus, Calif. Comn: Murals, Hotel Newhouse, Salt Lake City, Utah, 50, Dr & Mrs August Maymudes, La, 70, Temple Isaiah, La, 73 & Bank of Am, Beverly Hills, Calif, 75. Exhib: One-person shows, Pasadena Mus Art, Calif, 53, Santa Barbara Mus Art, Calif, 66, Carroll Reece Mus Art, Johnson City, Tenn, 69, Palm Springs Mus, 72, Arco Ctr for Visual Arts, La, 76, plus Anhalt, Ankrum & James Willis Galleries in Los Angeles & San Francisco, Gallery Fendt in Amsterdam & Herbert Palmer Gallery in Beverly Hills, Calif. Teaching: Instr beginning painting & drawing, Univ Southern Calif, summer 50; instr advan painting, drawing & compos & dir, New Sch Art, Los Angeles, 54-57; instr advan drawing & compos, figure painting & drawing, Otis Art Inst, Los Angeles, 63-67 & 77-78; instr advan painting & drawing, Univ Calif Exten, Los Angeles, 72-78. Awards: Purchase Awards, Philadelphia Mus Art, 68, Home Savings & Loan, Los Angeles Munic Exhib, 69 & San Francisco Mus Art, 69. Bibliog: Arthur Secunda (auth), Mesches, McMenamin & Pederson Bros, Art Voices Mag, 65; Thomas Leavitt (auth), Preface to Arnold Mesches & his paintings, Santa Barbara Mus of Art, 66. Mem: Screen Actor's Guild; Artists Equity Asn; La Inst Contemp Art. Style & Technique: New Realism. Media: Acrylic. Publ: Illusr, Frontier Mag, 54-60; auth, Red, White & Rosie, 72; contribr, A Search for Form & A Book on Painting. Dealer: Herbert B Palmer Gallery 9570 Wilshire Blvd Beverly Hills CA 90210. Mailing Add: 2940 Main St Santa Monica CA 90405

MESEROLE, VERA STROMSTED
PAINTER, ART ADMINISTRATOR
b New York, NY, Aug 10, 27. Study: Wellesley Col, Mass, BA(hist art, painting), with A Abbot, B Swann & E Frisch & archit with J MacAndrew; Univ Vt, Burlington, adult educ with Francis Colburn; critique with Stan Marc Wright, Vt & father, Alf Stromsted, NY & NJ. Work: IBM, Montpelier, Vt. Exhib: Northern New Eng Artists, Univ Vt, Burlington, 54; New Eng Artists, New York World's Fair, 64; Nat League Am Pen Women, Tulsa, Okla, 66 & Salt Lake City, Utah, 70; Vt Pavilion, Expo, Montreal, 70. Teaching: Instr home design, Northern Vt Art Ctr, Burlington, 73- Pos: Supt art, Champlain Valley Expos, Vt, 67; juror, Cracker Barrel Exhib, Newbury, Vt, 67; chmn, Ann State, Fleming Mus, Burlington, 66-73; mgr art ctr exhib, Burlington, 72-74; auth, Newsletter Northern Vt Artists Asn, 67-73. Awards: First Prize, Champlain Valley Expos, 60; First Prize Portraits, Nat League Am Pen Women, Vt, 66 & 70. Bibliog: Stuart Perry (auth), TV interview, WCAX, Burlington, 71; article in Burlington Free Press, 67 & 72. Mem: Northern Vt Artist Asn (vpres, 65-67, pres, 67-74); Med Ctr Hosp Vt Art Comt (chmn, 60-70); Southern Vt Art Asn; Nat League Am Pen Women, Vt (pres north br, 74-75). Style & Technique: Loose, sketchy watercolor, more realistic conservative in oil. Publ: Contribr, Photo of art work, 66 & auth, essay, 70, Nat League Pen Women Mag; illusr, Handbook cover, Wellesley Col, 67. Mailing Add: c/o Mrs Milton D Block 4240 D'Youville Trace Atlanta GA 30341

MESIBOV, HUGH
PAINTER, INSTRUCTOR
b Philadelphia, Pa, Dec 29, 16. Study: Fleischer Mem Art Sch, Philadelphia, 34-35; Pa Acad Fine Arts, Philadelphia, 35-37; Albert C Barnes Found, Merion, Pa,36-40. Work: Metrop Mus Art & NY Univ Collection Contemp Am Art, New York; Philadelphia Mus Art; Pa Hist Mus; Can Soc Graphic Art; Carnegie Libr of Pittsburgh; Univ Wyo; Univ Ore Art Mus; Albert C Barnes Found; Pa Acad Fine Arts. Comn: Mural design, Benjamin Franklin High Sch, 37-40; mural, Work Progress Admin Art Proj, Bennet Hall, Univ Pa, 37-40; mural, Steel Indust, US Treas, US Post Off, Hubbard, Ohio, 41; color lithograph, New York Hilton Art Collection, 62; acrylic on canvas mural, Job, Temple Beth El, Spring Valley, NY, 72. Exhib: Pa Acad Fine Arts, 40, 58 & 67; Whitney Mus Am Art, New York, 46, 56 & 59; Hallmark Int Water Color Show, New York, 52; Corcoran Gallery Art, Washington, DC, 59; Am Acad Arts & Lett, New York,67. Teaching: Art therapist, Wiltwyck Sch Boys, NY, 57-66; assoc prof art, Rockland Community Col, Suffern, NY, 66- Awards: Hon Mentions, Philadelphia Print Club, 39, 41 & 46 & Thornton Oakley Mem Prize, 76; Hallmark Art Award, 52; Lambert Purchase Fund Award for Oil, Pa Acad Fine Arts, 52; May Audubon Post Prize for Oil, Fel of Pa Acad Fine Arts, 58; First Prize Oil Painting, Tappan Zee Bank, Rockland Found Award Show, 64. Mem: Philadelphia Water Color Club; fel Pa Acad Fine Arts. Media: Acrylic, Watercolor. Mailing Add: 377 Saddle River Rd Monsey NY 10952

MESSEGUER, VILLORO BENITO
PAINTER, SCULPTOR
b Mora de Ebro, Spain, Oct 27, 30. Study: Escuela Pintura y Escultura, Inst Nac Bellas Artes, 46-51 & 56; Escuela Estudiantes Extranjeros, Univ Mex, 56; Trinity Univ, 69-70. Work: Inst Nac Bellas Artes Mex; Mus Veersjeva, Israel; Mus Arte Mod Mex, Mexico City; Mus Chilpancingo, Guerrero, Mex. Comn: Acrilico sobre asbesto, Hotel Casino La Selva, Cuernavaca, Morelos, Mex, 61; acrilico sobre asbesto, Escuela Nac Economia, Univ Mex, 63; acrilico sobre base tipo Fresco, Inst Mex Audicion y Lenguage, Mexico City, 66; sobrerelieve de plastico, Inst Mex Protec a Infancia, Mexico City, 70; revestimiento de un muro lateral de edificio, Soldominio Conjunto Habitacional, Mexico City, 70; esculturas 1975 edificio de las osicirgas Naciones Unidas y Cepal, Mexico City; muro en la Col Popular Ermita Zaragoza, Mexico City. Exhib: 2nd Salon Nac Paisaje, Mexico City, 61; Bienal Jovenes Paris, France, 63 & 65; Bienal Tokyo, Japan, 65; Gilbert Salerie, San Francisco, 67. Teaching: Teacher escuela estudiantes extranjeros, UNAM, 56; teacher, Trinity Univ, San Antonio, Tex. Pos: Dir, Escuela de Pintura y Escultura Inst Nacional de Bellas Artes. Bibliog: Alfonso Newvillete (auth), Pintura actual de Mexico 1966, Artes Mex, 66; Antonio Rodriguez (auth), Der Mensch in Flamman, VEB Verlag der Kunst, 67; Antonio Rodriguez (auth), El Hombre en Llamas, Thomas & Hudson, 70. Mem: Salon Plastica Mex. Dealer: Merle Kupper Mooliere Mexico City Mexico; Jose Maria Tasende Costera Miguel Aleman Acapulco Mexico. Mailing Add: Privada Ortiz de Dominguez 18 Tizapan Mexico City DF Mexico

MESSER, BRENDA RUTH
SLIDE CURATOR
b Toronto, Ont, Can, June 15, 48. Study: Univ Toronto, hon BA(fine art); Univ de Dijon, Foreign Students Prog. Pos: Slide cur, Univ Western Ont, London, Can, 70- Mem: Univ Art Asn Can; Art Librn Soc NAm; Mid-Am Col Art Asn. Publ: Ed, Positive (newsletter for slide & photog cur of visual arts in Can), Univ Western Ont, 76. Mailing Add: Dept Visual Arts Rm 114 Univ Western Ont London ON N6A 5B7 Can

MESSER, THOMAS M
MUSEUM DIRECTOR, ART HISTORIAN
b Bratislava, Czech, Feb 9, 20; US citizen. Study: Thiele Col exchange student, Inst Int Educ, 39; Boston Univ, BA, 42; Sorbonne, Paris, France, 47; Harvard Univ, MA, 51; spec fel, Brussels, Belg, 53; Univ Mass, hon DFA, 62. Collections Arranged: Hirshhorn Collection, Solomon R Guggenheim Mus, 62, one-man shows, Vasily Kandinsky, 62, Edward Munch, 66 & Paul Klee (with catalog), 68, Thannhauser Collection, 65 & 72, Permanent Collection, 70; also first US mus shows, Egon Schiele & New Departures: Latin America, Inst Contemp Art. Teaching: Sr fel advan studies, Wesleyan Univ Ctr Advan Studies, 66; vis prof mod art, Barnard Col, 66 & 71. Pos: Dir, Roswell Mus, 49-52; asst dir, Am Fedn Arts, 52-53, dir exhibs & dir, 53-56; dir, Inst Contemp Arts, Boston, 57-61; dir, Solomon R Guggenheim Mus, 61-; pres, MacDowell Colony, Peterborough, NH, 77-; mem, Int Exhib Comt, Washington, DC, 76-79; mem, Port Authority, New York & NJ Comt Arts; vis comt art mus & fine arts dept, Harvard Univ. Awards: Knight First Class, Order of St Olaf, 66; Officer's Cross of Order of Merit, Fed Repub of Ger, 75. Mem: Asn Art Mus Dir (pres, 74-75, future direction comt, 77-78); Int Coun Mus; Am Arts Alliance (trustee); Czech Soc Arts & Sci (vpres); Century Asn; Studio Int Mag Adv Panel. Publ: Auth, Egon Schiele, 1890-1918: Work on Paper, Galerie St Etienne, 65; auth, Julius Bissier, 1893-1965: A Retrospective Exhibition, Guggenheim Found, 68; auth, Edward Munch, Abrams, 73. Mailing Add: Solomon R Guggenheim Mus 1071 Fifth Ave New York NY 10028

MESSERSMITH, FRED LAWRENCE
PAINTER, EDUCATOR
b Sharon, Pa, Apr 3, 24. Study: Ohio Wesleyan Univ, BFA, 48, MA, 49. Work: Addison Gallery Am Art, Andover, Mass; Cummer Gallery, Jacksonville, Fla; Butler Inst Am Art, Youngstown, Ohio; Springfield Art Mus, Mo; Huntington Galleries, WVa. Exhib: Am Watercolor Soc, 57-; Mid-Year Show, Butler Inst Am Art, 65; Ringling Mus Art, Sarasota, Fla, 67; Yale Univ, 71; one-man shows, Arno Gallery, Florence, Italy, 70 & Vaccarino Gallery, Florence, Italy, 78. Yale Univ, 71. Teaching: Chmn dept art, WVa Wesleyan Col, 49-59; chmn dept art, Stetson Univ, 59- Awards: Spec Watercolor Award, Mead Packaging, Atlanta, 60; First Award, Fla State Fair, 67 & Winter Park, 75. Bibliog: Norman Kent (auth), Fred Messersmith paints on rice paper, Am Artist Mag, 12/60. Mem: Am Watercolor Soc; Fla Artist Group (pres, 64-66); Ala Watercolor Soc. Style & Technique: Experimentalist in all watercolor media, chiefly casein on rice paper, collage, and large poured shapes. Publ: Auth, Pottery of Gene Bunker, 62 & Francis Chapin, 65, Am Artist Mag; contribr, 100 Watercolor Techniques, 68; contribr, Acrylic Watercolor Painting, 70; contribr, Eyewitness to Space, 71. Mailing Add: Dept of Art Stetson Univ Deland FL 32720

MESSICK, BEN (NEWTON)
PAINTER, INSTRUCTOR
b Strafford, Mo, Jan 9, 01. Study: Los Angeles Sch Art & Design, 23; Chouinard Art Inst, 25-32; anatomy with F Tolles Chamberlain. Work: San Francisco Mus Art; Springfield Mus Art, Mo; Los Angeles Co Mus Art; Long Beach Mus Art; Nat Mus, Washington, DC. Comn: Three murals,US Treas Dept, 35-40. Exhib: US Nat Mus, 44; Travel Exhib Midwest & Southwest Mus & Galleries, 50-51; E B Crocker Gallery, 57; Long Beach Art Mus, 57; Springfield Art Mus, 67; Pomona Valley Art Asn, Calif, 75. Teaching: Instr life drawing, Chouinard Art Inst, Los Angeles, 43-51; instr drawing & painting, San Diego Sch Arts & Crafts, La Jolla, Calif, 48-53 & Messick-Hay Studio, Long Beach & Apple Valley, 52- Pos: Sketch artist, Disney Studios, Los Angeles, 40; sketch artist, Metro-Goldwyn-Mayer, Culver City, Calif, 42. Awards: Calif Graphics Award, Fla Southern Col, 51; Seton Hall Univ Key Award, 58. Bibliog: Michael M Engel (auth), Sketching the spec, Design Mag, 56; Vera Williams (auth), Art is a way of life, Southland Mag, 66; Geraldine H Wheeler (ed), Ben Messick & Velma Hay-Messick, Athelings Mag, 75. Mem: Fel Royal Soc Arts; Int Arts Guild, Monte Carlo. Style & Technique: Humanist; impressionistic. Media: Oil. Mailing Add: 20930 Lone Eagle Rd Apple Valley CA 92307

MESSICK, DALE
CARTOONIST
b South Bend, Ind, 1906. Study: Art Inst Chicago. Pos: Designer greeting cards, Chicago; creator comic strip Brenda Starr, Reporter, Sunday papers, Chicago Tribune-NY News Syndicate, 40-, daily feature, 45- Mailing Add: 1310 Ritchie Ct Chicago IL 60610

METSON, GRAHAM
PAINTER, ART HISTORIAN
b London, Eng, June 24, 34. Study: Cainbridge Sch Art; Chelsea Col Art; Univ London. Work: Mus Contemp Art, Chicago; Manchester City Art Col; Ga Mus Art; Mus of d'Art Mod, Skopje, Yugoslavia; Can Coun Art Bank. Exhib: Blood Networks, Mus Contemp Art, Chicago, 69; Int Bood Blood Networks, Mus Contemp Art, Chicago, Calif Inst of Arts, Valencia & NS Col Art & Design, Halifax, 72; 76 Essex Festival of Conceptual Artists, Univ

Essex, United Kingdom; Morbus, Dalhousie Univ Art Gallery, 73; Videoslope, Art Gallery of Ont, 74; solo shows, Ga Mus Art, 67, Spectrum Gallery, New York, 69, Inst Contemp Art, London, 72, Anna Leonowens Gallery, NS, 74, Confedn Art Gallery, Confedn Art Ctr, 77, Nancy Poole Studio, Toronto, Ont, 77 & Eye Level Gallery, Halifax, NC, 78. Collections Arranged: Quilts, Yesterday, Today, Possibilities, Mt St Vincent Univ Art Gallery, 74; Gleams of Remoter Worlds, 18th Century Graphic Art, Dalhousie Univ Art Gallery, 76; Nova Scotia Folk Art, Art Gallery of NS, Halifax, 76; Halifax 0906 Dec 6 1917 (auth, illusr, catalogue), A Photodoc on the Halifax Explosion, West House Mus, 77. Awards: First Prize, 2nd Minn Print & Drawing Show, 69; Can Coun Grant, 74; Recreation Grant, NS Govt Dept of Recreation, 77. Bibliog: Karl MacKeeman (auth), Graham Metson, Art Mag, 76; Ron Shuebrooke (auth), article in Atlantic J, 78; Felicity Redgrave (auth), article in Artscanada, 78. Style & Technique: Paints deny the surface and disappear into a multitude of possibilities, an illusion of continental change. Media: Oil on Canvas; Watercolor. Res: Eighteenth century occult and metaphysical art. Publ: Auth, Halifax Explosion, McGraw-Hill, fall 78. Dealer: Nancy Poole Studio 16 Hazelton Ave Toronto ON M5R 2E2 Can. Mailing Add: c/o Sanford N Medford RR 2 Canning NS 1H0 Can

METYKO, MICHAEL JOSEPH
CURATOR, ARTIST
b Port Arthur, Tex, Feb 27, 45. Study: Houston Mus Fine Arts Sch; St Thomas Univ, Houston, with Dominique de Menil & Jermyne McAgy; Pratt Inst, Brooklyn; San Francisco Art Inst, MFA(printmaking). Comn: Tatto Parlor: Segment I (15 minute film) & Segment II (15 minute film; with architect, Thomas Burke), David Gallery, Houston, 70; participation/doc event piece, Main St 76, Houston CofC, 76. Exhib: Drawings from Nine States, The Drawing Soc, Houston Mus Fine Arts, 70; one-man shows, Houston Mus Fine Arts, 70 & Mus Mod Art, Houston, 77; Dallas-Ft Worth-Houston, Contemp Arts Mus, Houston (and three other Tex mus), 71; The Other Coast, Calif State Univ, Long Beach, 71; Tex Wk in San Francisco, San Francisco Art Inst, 72; Print Workshop, London, Eng, 73; Graphics from the Print Workshop, London, Boston Univ, Western Mich Univ, Univ Wis & Wooster State, 73-74; The Bosch Show, Univ St Thomas, Houston, 76; Contemp Icons, Mus Mod Art, Houston, 76. Collections Arranged: Texas Week in San Francisco, Festival & Exhib of Texas Art & The Artist's Archives, Exhib of Materials Collected by Artists, San Francisco Art Inst, 72. Pos: Asst to chmn, Dept of Art, Rice Univ, 66-67; cur, Grad Print & Photo Gallery, San Francisco Art Inst, 71-72, asst to dir/cur, S C Blaffer Gallery, Univ Houston, 73-; SCoast rep, Vision Mag, 76- Bibliog: Niomi Berman (auth), Interview & article in Southwestern Craftsman Mag, 76; Charlotte Moser (auth), Review of Houston Artists, Art News, 76. Mem: Artists Equity Asn (nat bd mem, 75-; pres chap, Houston, 75-77); Cult Arts Coun of Houston; Am Asn Mus; Western Asn Art Mus. Media: Various Media & Combinations of Media. Publ: Contribr & illusr, 9th Congress of European Exchange Students Journal, Int Cult Exchange Serv, 66; contribr & illusr, Conceptual Excerpts, Guano Mag, Univ Houston, 70; contribr & illusr exhib catalogues, S C Blaffer Gallery, 73-; contribr introd, exhib catalogue for Donald Thornton, Col of the Mainland, 76; illusr, New Cultural Decision Makers in Houston, Art News, 77. Mailing Add: 1634 Branard St Houston TX 77006

METZ, FRANK ROBERT
PAINTER, ART DIRECTOR
b Philadelphia, Pa, July 3, 25. Study: Philadelphia Mus Sch, with Ezio Martinelli; Art Students League, with Will Barnet. Work: Olsen Found, Guilford, Conn; Ball State Teachers Col, Muncie, Ind; Philadelphia Mus Art. Exhib: Drawing & Small Sculpture Ann, Ball State Teachers Col, 62-63 & 64-65; Am Acad Arts & Lett, Childe Hassam Fund, 66; The American Landscape—A Living Tradition, Peridot Gallery, New York, 68; one-man shows, Alonzo Gallery, 74 & 77; Monhegan Artists, Allentown Mus, Pa, 74. Pos: Art dir, Simon & Schuster, 50- Awards: Elisabeth Ball Purchase Award, Ball State Teachers Col, 64; Bibliog: Jules Perel (auth), Landscape drawings of Frank Metz, Am Artist, 5/62; Doreen Managan (auth), Landscape paintings of Frank Metz, Am Artists, 3/78 & Twenty Oil Painters and How They Work, Watson-Guptill, 78. Style & Technique: Abstract-impressionist paintings with low-keyed pallette, mainly of landscapes and seascapes of Maine, Scotland and Ireland. Media: Oil. Dealer: Alonzo Gallery 26 E 63rd St New York NY 10021. Mailing Add: Alonzo Gallery 30 W 57th St New York NY 10019

METZ, GERRY MICHAEL
PAINTER, INSTRUCTOR
b Chicago, Ill, July 22, 43. Study: Wright Jr Col, Chicago; Sch Prof Art, Chicago; with Joseph Abbrescia, Skokie, Ill, Frank Hamilton, Jerome, Ariz & Austin Deuel, Taos, NMex. Work: Mt Whitney Mus Western Art, Calif; Favell Mus Western Art, Klamath Falls, Ore. Exhib: Death Valley Western Art Show, Calif, 73-77; Ariz Artists State Competition, Phoenix, 74; Ariz State Fair, 74; George Phippen Mem Western Art Show, Prescott, Ariz, 75-77; Teton Co State Fair, Jackson, Wyo, 75. Teaching: Dir, Village Art Sch, Skokie, Ill, 68-72; instr oils & life drawing, Phoenix Art Mus, Ariz, 73- Awards: Gold Medal First Place Watercolor, George Phippen Mem Art Show, 75 & 76; Blue Ribbon First Place Watercolor, Teton Co Fair, Jackson, Wyo, 75. Style & Technique: Opaque Watercolor and Oils. Mailing Add: 8437 E Monterey Way Scottsdale AZ 85251

METZGER, EVELYN BORCHARD
PAINTER, SCULPTOR
b New York, NY, June 8, 11. Study: Vassar Col, AB, 32, with C K Chatterton; Art Students League, with George Bridgman & Rafael Soyer; also George Grosz, sculpture with Sally Farnham, Guzman de Rojas in Bolivia & Demetrio Urruchua in Arg. Work: Fine Arts Gallery of San Diego, Balboa Park, Calif; Ariz State Mus, Tucson; Lyman Allyn Mus, New London, Conn; Univ Mo-Columbia; Butler Inst Am Art, Youngstown, Ohio; also in over 40 mus including Art in the Embassies Prog. Exhib: One-man shows, Galeria Müller, Buenos Aires, 50, Gallerie Bellechasse, Paris, 63; Norfolk Mus Art, Va, 65; Mex-Am Cult Inst, Mexico City, 67; Van Diemen-Lilienfeld Gallery, New York, 66; Bartholet Gallery, New York, 73. Bibliog: Aymel Seghers (auth), New York news (and cover), Arts Rev, 4/63; M L D'Otrange Mastai (auth), An American flowering, 5/63 & Evelyn Metzger—recent works, 12/66, The Connoisseur. Mem: Artists Equity Asn; Am Fedn Art; Arch of Am Art; Cosmopolitan Club, New York; Mus Mod Art, New York. Style & Technique: Portraits, landscape, still life and abstracts. Media: Oil, Enamel, Acrylics & Mixed Media. Mailing Add: 815 Park Ave New York NY 10021

METZGER, ROBERT PAUL
CURATOR, EDUCATOR
b Detroit, Mich. Study: Wayne State Univ, BA, MA; Columbia Univ, with T Reff; Univ Calif, Los Angeles, PhD, with Fred Wight; Am Film Inst, with Jean Renoir. Collections Arranged: American Salon des Refuses, 76, My Country Tis of Thee, 76, Two Organic Women, 77, Reuben Nakian (auth, catalogue), 77, Aspects of Nature, 77, Lifelines—Two Generations, 78 & The Eye of the Collector, 78, Stamford Mus, Conn. Teaching: Asst prof art hist survey, Univ Detroit, Mich, 65-66; assoc prof Am art hist, Univ Bridgeport, Conn, 77- Pos: Adv Sen staff, Joint Legislature Comt on the Arts, Lansing, Mich, 73; cur, Lydia Winston Malbin Collection of Art, New York, 74-76; dir art, Stamford Mus, Conn, 76- Awards: Univ Calif Arts Coun Traveling Grant, 69; Clifton Webb Fel for Outstanding Student in the Arts, Univ Calif, Los Angeles, 72; Mich State Univ Art Hist Res Grant, 74. Mem: Col Art Asn Am. Res: Biomorphism in the 20th century, American painting and sculpture 18th through 20th century, Reuben Nakian. Publ: Ed, Directory of American Periodicals, Oxbridge Press, 76; auth, Karl Struss, American Cinematographer, 76, Nakian's Place in History, 77 & The Case for Pop Art as Neo-Dada, 78, Stamford Mus. Mailing Add: 39 Scofieldtown Rd Stamford CT 06903

METZKER, RAY K
PHOTOGRAPHER, EDUCATOR
b Milwaukee, Wis, Sept 10, 31. Study: Beloit Col, BA, 53; Ill Inst Technol, MS, 59, with Aaron Siskind & Harry Callahan. Work: Mus of Mod Art, New York; Art Inst of Chicago; Smithsonian Inst; Bibliot Nat, Paris; Philadelphia Mus of Art. Exhib: My Camera and I in the Loop, Art Inst of Chicago, 59; Persistence of Vision, Int Mus of Photog, George Eastman House, 67; one-man show, Mus of Mod Art, New York, 67; Wis Heritage, Milwaukee Art Ctr, 70; New Photog USA (int travelling exhib), Mus of Mod Art, New York, 70-72; Landscape/Cityscape, Metrop Mus of Art, New York, 73; Philadelphia: Three Centuries of Am Art, Philadelphia Mus of Art, 76; The Photographer and the City, Mus of Contemp Art, Chicago, 77. Collections Arranged: Variety Show, Western Asn of Art Mus, 71; Festival d'Art Contemporain, Paris, 73; Contemporary Photographers, William Hayes Fogg Art Mus, Cambridge, Mass, 76; Locations in Time, Int Mus of Photog, George Eastman House, Rochester, 77; Target Collection, Fine Arts Mus of Houston, 77. Teaching: Assoc prof photog, Philadelphia Col of Art, 62-; assoc prof photog, Univ NMex, 70-72; adj photog, RI Sch of Design, 77. Awards: Guggenheim Fel, 66; Nat Endowment for the Arts fel, 74. Bibliog: Nathan Lyons (auth), Persistence of Vision, Horizon, 67; John Szarkowski (auth), Looking at Photographs, Mus of Mod Art, New York, 73; Kelly Wise (auth), Photographers' Choice, Addison House, 75. Style & Technique: Black & White silver prints; straight and in combination. Publ: Illusr, Razerol, Janus, 73. Mailing Add: 733 S Sixth St Philadelphia PA 19147

MEW, TOMMY
PAINTER, EDUCATOR, CONCEPTUAL ARTIST
b Miami, Fla, Aug 15, 42. Study: Fla State Univ, MS & MA; New York Univ, PhD. Work: Am Tel & Tel, New York; Jacksonville Art Mus, Fla; Middleburg Netherlands Mus, Netherlands; Mildura Art Ctr, Australia; Meridian Mus of Art, Miss. Exhib: One-man shows, Montgomery Mus of Fine Arts, Ala, 70 & Meridian Mus of Art, Miss, 76; Diaryworks, Centro Documentazione, Parma, Italy, 70; Paintings, High Mus of Art, Atlanta, Ga, 71, 72 & 74; Paintings, Mus of Art, Macon, Ga, 72; Drawings, Kunst Informatie Centrum, Netherlands, 75; Drawings, 37th Venice Biennale, 76; Drawings, Nat Gallery of Can, Ottawa, 77. Teaching: Grad asst art, Fla State Univ, 64-65; asst prof art, Troy State Univ, Ala, 66-68 & Jacksonville Univ, Fla, 68-70; prof painting & chmn art dept, Berry Col, 70-; vis artist & lectr drawings, Nat Endowment for the Arts, 72. Awards: Cowperthwaite Corp grant, 72. Bibliog: Keith Colbourn (auth), Tommy New-Space-time artist, Atlanta Mag, 75; Annette Kuhn (auth), Scar art, Village Voice, 75; Peter Frank (auth), Auto-art-and how, Art News, 76; Alan Storey (auth), Tommy Mew, Art Voices S, 3/78. Mem: Col Art Asn; Southeastern Col Art Asn; Popular Cult Asn of the S; Nat Art Educ Asn; Am Fedn of the Arts. Style & Technique: Narrative diarywork, painting and post-conceptual work. Media: Acrylic paint; audio & video. Publ: Auth & ed, Le Voyage, Troy State Press, 68; ed & contribr, Dramatika, New York Press, 70; ed & contribr, Third Floor Love Poems, 66 & Scartissue, 66, Troy State Press; auth, Ray Johnson, Col Art Asn J, 77; contribr, Intermedia Mag, Can, 77. Dealer: Dean Gillette Image South Gallery 1931 Peachtree St NE Atlanta GA 30309. Mailing Add: Box 580-Art Mt Berry GA 30149

MEYER, MR & MRS ANDRE
COLLECTORS
Mr Meyer, b Paris, France, Sept 3, 98. Pos: Mr Meyer, trustee, Metrop Mus Art. Collection: Paintings and contemporary art. Mailing Add: 35 E 76th St New York NY 10021

MEYER, CHARLES EDWARD
ART HISTORIAN, CERAMIST
b Detroit, Mich, Sept 7, 28. Study: Wayne State Univ, BFA, 40 & Ma, 52; Free Univ, Berlin, Ger, 52-54; Univ Wurzburg, Ger, 58-59; Univ Mich, PhD, 67. Work: Mus Contemp Crafts, New York; Detroit Inst Arts; Boston Mus Fine Arts; South Bend Art Ctr, Ind; Ann Arbor Potters Guild, Mich. Exhib: Fiber, Glass, Clay & Metal Exhib, Wichita, 52; Midwest Crafts Exhib, Ceramics, South Bend, 53 & 54; Opening Exhib, Ceramics, Mus Contemp Crafts, New York, 57. Collections Arranged: Flemish Painting, Detroit Inst Arts (assembled, 58, presented, 59, with P Grigaut). Teaching: Assoc prof art hist, head dept & dir div fine arts, Mich State Univ, 59-66; chmn dept, Western Mich Univ, 66-77, prof art hist, 66- Awards: Purchase Award in Ceramics, Opening Exhib, Mus Contemp Crafts, New York, 57; Distinguished Alumni Award, Wayne State Univ, 67. Mem: Nat Asn Schs Art (certifying officer, Div II, 70-); Col Art Asn Am; Mid-Am Col Art Asn Am (vpres, 60-61, exec bd, 60-63, treas, 61-62); Ann Arbor Potters Guild (dir, 54-57); Nat Coun Art Adminr. Style & Technique: Ceramist, classical techniques in utilitarian stoneware. Media: Ceramics, Stoneware & Porcelain. Res: European baroque architecture. Publ: Auth, Sebastiano Riccio, 57, auth, A new group of ceramics, 57 & auth, A Rodin portrait, 58, Bull, Detroit Inst Arts; auth, Seymour Lipton and His Place in 20th Century Sculpture, 62. Mailing Add: 1116 Bronson Circle Kalamazoo MI 49008

MEYER, FELICIA
PAINTER
b New York, NY, May 15, 12. Study: Art Students League, with Kenneth Hayes Miller & Rimon Nicolaires. Work: Whitney Mus; Addison Gallery; New Britain Mus; Mus City New York. Exhib: Whitney Mus; Pa Acad; Nat Acad; Frank Rehn Gallery, 76. Style & Technique: Romantic realist. Dealer: John Clancy c/o Therehn Gallery 655 Madison Ave New York NY 10021. Mailing Add: 923 Fifth Ave New York NY 10021

MEYER, FRANK HILDBRIDGE
PRINTMAKER, INSTRUCTOR
b Fitchburg, Mass, Jan 21, 23. Study: Art Students League, with Wallace Morgan, Robert Brackman, Reginald Marsh, Will Barnet & George Grosz; City Univ New York, with Julius Portnoy, BA; Cent Conn State Col, MS(art). Exhib: 75th Anniversary Exhib Art Students League, Nat Acad Design, New York, 51; Bay Printmakers 1st Traveling Show, Oakland Munic Art Mus, Calif, 55; Soc Washington Printmakers 20th Exhib, Nat Gallery, Smithsonian Inst, 56; Fundacion Ynglada-Guillet Exposition de Obras, Palacio de la Virreina, Spain, 60; 25th Ann Nat Exhib Acad Artists Asn, Mus Fine Arts, Springfield, Mass, 74; plus many others in Conn area, 75-77. Teaching: Instr art, Eng & jour, Penasco Independent High Sch, NMex, 62-63; head art counr, Camp Tapawingo, Sweden, Maine, 64-68; instr art,

Windsor High Sch, Conn, 67- Pos: Artist, framer & restorer, Morristown Fine Arts Ctr, NJ, 54-56; state art consult, Ariz Dept Educ, Phoenix, 64; lectr-demonstr cellograph printmaking, Silvermine Guild of Artists Inc, 77 & New Eng Regional Art Educ Conf, 77. Awards: Best in Show, Fall Exhib, Springfield Art League, Mass, 52; Alice Collins Dunham Award, Conn Acad Fine Arts, 69, Sage Allen Award, 72. Bibliog: Ref shows, Art News, 9/54; Junior Jottings, Monday Afternoon Club Mag, 3/56; Janet Gaston (auth), Frank Hildbridge Meyer, Rev Moderne, Paris, 4/1/61. Mem: Conn Art Educ Asn (regional chmn, 74-76); Art Students League (bus mgr, League Mag, 50); Conn Acad Fine Arts; Artists Equity Asn (founder & 1st pres Conn chap, 76-); Conn Artist Asn. Style & Technique: Classical and abstract overtones. Media: Oil, Cellograph. Publ: Co-auth, League Mag, Art Students League, 50; co-auth, Comprehensive study on facilities, physical plot and philosophy of secondary and elementarv art departments, NJ Art Educ Asn, 57; co-auth, New Mexican Rev, 63; illusr, Our America, Ariz Dept Educ, 65; auth, Cellographic process of printmaking, Elihu Burritt Libr, 72. Mailing Add: 470 Wolcott Ave Windsor CT 06095

MEYER, FRED (ROBERT)
SCULPTOR, PAINTER
b Oshkosh, Wis. Study: Univ Wis; Harvard Grad Sch Bus Admin; Cranbrook Acad Art, BFA & MFA. Work: New York State Theatre, Lincoln Ctr Performing Arts; Everson Mus, Syracuse, NY; Munson, Williams, Proctor Inst, Utica, NY; Cranbrook Mus, Bloomfield Hills, Mich; Little Rock Mus Art, Ark. Comn: Murals, Schrafft's Motor Inn, Binghamton, NY, 58, Exec Motel, Buffalo, NY, 59 & Holiday Inn, Niagara Falls, NY, 60; two bronze sculptural groups, Lazarus Mall, Columbus, Ohio, 67; two murals, Sarah Coventry Int Hq, Newark, NJ, 71. Exhib: One-man shows, Midtown Galleries, New York, 47, 48, 69, 74 & 78, Philadelphia Art Alliance, 64 & Everson Mus, Syracuse, NY, 65; Scripps Col Ceramic Invitational, 66; Ann Arbor Film Festival Tour, 68. Teaching: Prof & grad rep, Acad Coun, Col Fine & Appl Arts, Rochester Inst Technol, 55- Awards: Ford Found Fel, 55; Carborundum Award, Western NY State Exhib, 64. Mem: Am Soc Interior Designers. Style & Technique: Modified realism; traditional technique. Media: Bronze, Gouache. Publ: Auth, Sculpture in Ceramic, Watson-Guptil, 71. Dealer: Midtown Galleries 11 E 57th St New York NY 10022. Mailing Add: 17 Church St Scottsville NY 14546

MEYER, SEYMOUR W
SCULPTOR
b Brooklyn, NY. Study: With Louise Nevelson. Work: C W Post Col, Long Island Univ, Brookville, NY; Arlen Industs, New York; Lester Avnet Collection, NY; Mus Mod Art, Rio de Janeiro, Brazil; Tel-Aviv Mus, Israel. Exhib: Sculpture House Gallery, NY, 66; Curator's Choice, C W Post Col, 66; Wiener Gallery, NY, 70-77; State Univ NY Col Plattsburg Ann, 71; Medich II Gallery, Fla, 74-75; Heath Gallery, 77-78. Mem: Am Fedn Arts; Mus Mod Art New York; Sculptors League of NY; Guggenheim Mus. Style & Technique: Abstract and figurative. Media: Bronze. Dealer: Randall Gallery 823 Madison Ave New York NY 10021; Heath Gallery Atlanta GA. Mailing Add: 495 E Shore Rd Great Neck NY 11024

MEYER, SUSAN E
ART EDITOR & WRITER
b New York, NY, Apr 22, 40. Study: Univ Perugia, 60; Univ Wis, BA, 62. Pos: Managing ed, Watson-Guptill Publ, New York, 63-70; ed in chief, Am Artist, New York, 71-; ed dir, Am Art & Antiques, New York, 78-; trustee, Artists' Fel, 78-79. Publ: Co-auth, Designing with Type and Painting Portraits, 71; co-auth, Watercolorists at Work, 73; auth, James Montgomery Flagg, 74; auth, Three Generations of the Wyeth Family, 75; auth, America's Great Illustrators, 78. Mailing Add: 13 W 13th St New York NY 10011

MEYER, THOMAS VINCENT
ART DEALER
b San Francisco, Calif, Dec 28, 43. Study: Inst Allende, San Miguel Allende, Mex, 61; Univ Denver, BSBA(marketing). Pos: Co-owner, Grapestake Gallery, 74-; vpres, San Francisco Art Dealers Asn, 77- Mem: Soc Encouragement Contemp Art. Specialty: Contemporary painting, sculpture and 20th century American photography. Mailing Add: c/o Grapestake Gallery 2876 California St San Francisco CA 94115

MEYER, URSULA
SCULPTOR, PHOTOGRAPHER
b Hannover, Ger. Study: New Sch Social Res, BA, 60; Columbia Univ Teachers Col, MA, 62. Work: Brooklyn Mus; Finch Col Mus; Newark Mus; Larry Aldrich Mus; Grad Ctr, City Univ New York. Exhib: One-person shows, Amel Gallery, 64 & 68, Hunter Col, 69, Lehman Col, 71 & Grad Ctr, City Univ New York, 74; Schemata 7, Finch Col Mus, 67; Listening to Pictures, Brooklyn Mus, 68; Cool Art of 1967, Larry Aldrich Mus, 68, Highlights of 1967-1968 Art Season; Cool Art, Abstractions Today, Newark Mus, 68. Teaching: Asst prof, Hunter Col, 66-68; assoc prof sculpture, Lehman Col, 68- Awards: Estelle Goodman Award for Best Sculpture, Nat Design Ctr, 66; City Univ New York Res Grant, Lehman Col, 70. Bibliog: Christopher Andreae (auth), Exhibition by Ursula Meyer at A M Sachs Gallery, Christian Sci Monitor, 2/26/68; Gregory Battcock (auth), Minimal Art, 68; Al Rogers (auth), Ursula Meyer, Alre-Films, 70. Mem: Women's Interart Ctr; Women in Arts. Media: Metal. Publ: Auth, De-objectification of the object, Arts Mag, summer 69; auth, Conceptual Art, 70 & The eruption of anti-art, In: Idea-Art, 73, Dutton; auth, How to explain pictures to a dead hare, Art News, 1/70; auth, Towards feminist art, Women & Art, summer-fall 72. Mailing Add: 260 Riverside Dr New York NY 10025

MEYEROWITZ, WILLIAM
PAINTER
b Ekaterinoslav, Ukraina, July 15, 98. Study: Nat Acad Design. Work: Metrop Mus Art, New York; Brooklyn Mus; Smithsonian Inst, Washington, DC; Duncan Phillips Mus, Washington, DC; Columbus Mus Arts & Crafts, Ga; plus others. Exhib: Carnegie Inst Int, Pittsburgh; Metrop Mus Art; Corcoran Gallery Art, Washington, DC; Pa Acad Fine Arts. Teaching: Instr painting & etching, E 105th St Settlement House, New York, 30-40; instr painting & etching, Mod Sch Self-Expression, 40-45, dir summer art course, 45-68. Pos: Mem Arts Coun, Gloucester, Mass, 67-70. Awards: Clair Layton Prize for Painting, Audubon Soc Artists, 58; Speyer Prize for Painting, Nat Acad Design, 65; Gold Medal of Honor for Painting, Rockport Art Asn, Mass, 70. Bibliog: Royal Cortissoi (auth), Contemporary American art, Am Art Dealers Asn, 31; Duncan Phillips (auth), A Collection in the Making, Phillips Publ, No 5, 36. Mem: Nat Acad Design; hon life mem North Shore Arts Asn, Gloucester (vpres, 68-69); Rockport Art Asn; Audubon Soc Artists (dir, 60-67); Allied Artists Am (dir, 73). Media: Oil. Publ: Contribr, Col Art Asn, 37; contribr, Menoran J, 44; auth, On the need of art, Menoran J, 55; contribr, Encycl Am Art, 70-71. Dealer: Summit Gallery of Art Ltd The Buckingham 101 W 57th St New York NY 10019. Mailing Add: 54 W 74th St New York NY 10023

MEYERS, DALE (MRS MARIO COOPER)
PAINTER, INSTRUCTOR
b Chicago, Ill, Jan 24, 22. Study: Corcoran Gallery Sch Art; Art Students League; watercolor with Mario Cooper; graphics with Seong Moy. Work: Nat Acad Design, New York; Portland Mus Fine Art, Maine; Frye Mus, Seattle, Wash; Nat Aeronautics & Space Mus, Washington, DC; Mus Acuarela, Mexico City; Univ Utah, Logan; Schumacher Gallery, Capital Univ, Columbus, Ohio. Comn: Apollo 11 Moon Flight (painting), 69 & Project Viking (landing on Mars), 75, for NASA, Nat Gallery Art, Washington, DC; ecol subj (paintings), Environ Protection Agency, Washington, DC, 72. Exhib: Smithsonian Inst, Washington, DC, 62-63; 200 Years of Watercolor Painting in America, Metrop Mus Art, New York, 66; Nat Acad Design, 68-78; Butler Inst Am Art, Youngstown, Ohio, 69-70; Eyewitness to Space, Nat Gallery Art, 70. Teaching: Instr watercolor, Kefauver Sch Art, Washington, DC, 61-62; asst instr watercolor, Art Students League, 65-; workshops in NMex, Calif & Maine, 70-77. Pos: Ed newslett, Am Watercolor Soc, 62-, chmn awards, 67- Awards: Bronze Medal of Honor, 68 & Paul B Remmey Award, 72, Am Watercolor Soc; Gold Medal of Honor, Nat Arts Club, 72; Samuel F B Morse Gold Medal, Nat Acad Exhibs, 73; Walter Biggs Mem Award, 151st Ann Exhib Nat Acad Design, 76. Mem: Assoc Nat Acad Design; Am Watercolor Soc (dir, 70-71); Allied Artists Am (pres, 75); fel Royal Soc Arts; Art Students League. Media: Watercolor. Publ: Auth articles in Am Artist Mag, 69 & Today's Art Mag, 70 & 74; contribr, Eyewitness to Space, Abrams, 71; contribr, Nat Sculpture Rev, 77. Mailing Add: 1 W 67th St New York NY 10023

MICALE, ALBERT
PAINTER, ILLUSTRATOR
b Punxsutawney, Pa. Study: Pratt Inst Fine & Applied Art, cert(illus). Work: Riveredge Found, Calgary; First Fed Savings & Loan Asn, Valley Nat Bank & Ariz Bank, Phoenix. Exhib: Mountain Oyster Club Western Art Show, Tucson, Ariz, 74-77; one-man show, Lincoln Thrift Asn Pres Club, Phoenix, 75; Cody Co Art League Ann Prof Show, Wyo, 75; Western States Art Show, Cody, 75; Nebraskaland Days Western & Wildlife Art, North Platte, Nebr, 75. Bibliog: Profile: Ariz horseman, 5/77. Awards: Outstanding Science Bks for Children Award, Nat Sci Teachers Asn, 76. Style & Technique: Realistic western subjects, semi-loose watercolors and oils; dry brush and wash. Publ: Illusr, Famous trails of the west, Coronet Mag, 3/61; illusr, The Sign of the Open Hand, Scribners, 62; illusr, The First Book of the Spanish American West, Franklin Watts, 63; illusr, Lets Go with Lewis and Clark, Putnam, 63; contribr, Western Horseman Mag, 72-76. Mailing Add: 7574 N Mockingbird Lane Paradise Valley AZ 85253

MICHAEL, GARY
ART WRITER, PAINTER
b Denver, Colo, Apr 17, 37. Study: Denver Univ, BA; Colo Univ, MA; Syracuse Univ, PhD, with Sydney Thomas. Work: Denver Pub Libr Permanent Collection, Colo; Denver Art Mus; Mus Natural Hist, Denver; Colorado Springs Fine Arts Ctr, Colo; Miron Collection, Poughkeepsie, NY. Comn: Mural (14ft x 20ft), Perlmack Corp, Regent Plaza, Denver, 75; bus panel design, Bill & Dorothy Harmsen Collection, Denver, 78. Exhib: Collector's Mart, 74; Gilpin Co Regional Ann Art Exhib, 74; Spree 75 Festival of the Arts, 75; one-man shows, First of Denver, Farraginous V, 76 & United Bank, Denver, 75. Teaching: Prof humanities, Metrop State Col, Denver, 70-73; instr painting, Colo Univ, Denver, 75-76. Pos: Demonstrating artist, Spree Arts Festival, 75-; lectr & demonstr, Grumbacher, New York, 77- Awards: First Place, Jewish Community Ctr Exhib, 74. Bibliog: Joan Gould (auth), Academician turned artist, SW Art, 5/75; Irene Clurman (auth), Farraginous artist, Rocky Mountain News, 11/76. Style & Technique: Traditional, representational painting of people and places in oil and pastel. Publ: Auth, Kent Ullberg: passion for nature, 76 & Roger McCoy: painter in the classic mode, 77, SW Art; auth, Nicolai Fechin in Santa Fe, 76 & The Hirshhorn Museum, 78, Rocky Mountain News. Dealer: Fred Rosenstock's 1228 E Colfax Denver CO 80206. Mailing Add: 1440 Columbine Denver CO 80206

MICHAELS, GLEN
SCULPTOR, PAINTER
b Spokane, Wash, July 21, 27. Study: Yale Sch Music, 50-52; Eastern Wash Col Educ, BA, 57; Cranbrook Acad Art, with Zoltan Sepeshy, 57-58, MFA, 58. Work: Detroit Inst Arts; Johnson's Wax Collection. Comn: Tile, wood & bronze mural, Int Monetary Fund, Vincent Kling, Washington, DC, 65; assemblage mural, Wayne State Univ Med Ctr, 73 & Wyandotte Gen Hosp, Mich, 74; tapestry, Henry Ford Mem Libr, Dearborn, Mich, 75; mural (167ft long), Renaissance Ctr, Manufacturer's Nat Bank, Detroit, 77; bronze fountain, Bicentennial Proj, Alpena, Mich, 77. Exhib: Thirteenth Trienale, Milan, Italy, 64; Archit League New York Gold Medal Exhib, 65; Plastic as Plastic, Mus Contemp Crafts, 68; Objects: USA, 69-70; Smithsonian Plastic Exhib, 69-70. Teaching: Supvr art for children, Cranbrook Acad Art, 59-65; asst prof sculpture, Wayne State Univ, 67-69; asst prof sculpture, Univ Windsor, 70-71. Awards: Stuttgart Handcraft Exhib Award, 66. Bibliog: Slivka (auth), The crafts in the modern world, Horizon, 68; Redstone (auth), Art in Architecture, McGraw, 68; Nordness (auth), Objects: USA, Viking Press, 70. Mem: Spec Comn Art in State Bldgs Mich. Mailing Add: 763 Lakeview Birmingham MI 48009

MICHALOVE, CARLA MARIA
EDUCATOR, CURATOR
b Columbus, Ga, Feb 2, 51. Study: Brandeis Univ, AB(fine arts), 72; George Washington Univ, MA(art hist & mus studies), 76. Teaching: Instr Eng & Am art hist, Continuing Educ, Univ Tenn, Chattanooga; instr mus educ, Covenant Col, Lookout Mountain, Tenn. Pos: Educ coordr, Mint Mus Art, Charlotte, NC, 75-76; cur educ, Hunter Mus Art, Chattanooga, 76- Mem: Am Asn Mus, Southeastern Mus Conf; Tenn Asn Mus; Am Asn State & Local Hist. Res: The diorama in 19th century America; a 15th century Flemish altarpiece panel in the collection of the Mint Museum of Art. Mailing Add: c/o Hunter Mus of Art Bluff View Chattanooga TN 37403

MICHALS, DUANE
PHOTOGRAPHER
b McKeesport, Pa, Feb 18, 32. Study: Univ Denver, BA. Work: Mus of Mod Art; Nat Libr, Paris; Mus Folkwang, Essen; Chicago Art Inst; George Eastman House, Rochester, NY. Exhib: Chicago Art Inst, 68; Mus of Mod Art, 70; Am Pavilion Osaka Fair, 70; Cologne Kunstverein, 73; Frankfurt Kunstverein, 74. Bibliog: Carol Stevens (auth), Series photographs, more is more, Print Mag, 10/70; Arnold Gassan (auth), A conversation with Duane Michals, Image, George Eastman House, 1/71; Carter Ratcliffe (auth), Duane Michals, Print Collector's Newslett, 9/75. Publ: Auth, Sequences, Doubleday, 70; auth, The journey of the spirit after death, Winterhouse, 71; auth, Things are queer, Wilde, Koln, 73. Dealer: Sidney Janis Gallery 6 W 57th St New York NY. Mailing Add: 109 E 19th St New York NY 10003

MICHAUX, RONALD ROBERT
ART DEALER
b Holyoke, Mass, Aug 8, 44. Pos: Dir, Rolly-Michaux Galleries, Boston & New York. Specialty: 19th & 20th century masters & contemporaries, including paintings, sculpture & graphics. Mailing Add: c/o Rolly-Michaux Galleries 943 Madison Ave New York NY 10021

MICHELI, JULIO
PAINTER, PRINTMAKER
b Ponce, PR, Aug 14, 37. Study: Univ Miami, BA, 62; Claremont Grad Sch, MFA, 65. Work: Mus Art Ponce; Ateneo Puertorriqueno, San Juan, PR; Instituto de Cultura Puertorriquena; Mus San Juan. Comn: Serigraphs (three ed), Hotel San Juan, 69 & (five ed), Hotel Caribe Hilton, San Juan, 71. Exhib: 1st Nat Painting Exhib, Joe & Emily Lowe Art Gallery, Coral Gables, Fla, 63; Expos Pan-Am Art Graficas, Cali, Colombia, 70; Primera Bienal San Juan Grabado Latin Am, San Juan, 70 & Segunda Bienal, 72; XII Sao Paulo Biennial. Teaching: Assoc prof art, Cath Univ PR, 65-, chmn dept, 71- Awards: First Prize in Painting, IBEC Corp, San Juan, 65; First Prize in Painting, Ateneo Puertorriqueno, San Juan, 66 & First Prize in Prints, 69. Bibliog: Nine Artists of Puerto Rico (film), Orgn Am States, 68; Pintores Contemporaneos Puertorriquenos. Mem: Col Art Asn Am. Style & Technique: Personal symbolic iconography, abstract, surrealist; small boxes, both wood and acrylic, containing assemblage and collage. Media: Assemblage. Publ: Contribr, How to Make Your Own Greeting Cards, 68. Mailing Add: 14 Baldorioty St Ponce PR 00731

MICHELSON-BAGLEY, HENRIETTA
SCULPTOR, PAINTER
b Kansas City, Mo. Study: Long Beach Jr Col, Calif; Univ Mex, Mexico City; Univ Mo, BA; Univ Caracas, Venezuela; also with Andre L'Hote, Paris & Edwiggi Poggi, Florence; Art Students League, with Morris Kantor, George Grosz & V Vytlicil; study of theater, dance & voice with Marshal Mason, Robert Thirkield, William Esper, Catherine Gaffigan, Mari Gorman, Joseph Chaikin, Kristin Linklater, Chuck Jones, Jack Wiener & Maria Duschenes. Comn: Set for play, Thomas Andros, Circle Repertory Theatre Co, New York, 73 & set for E E Cummings Play, Him, Circle Repertory Theatre Co, 74. Exhib: Sao Paulo Bienial, Brazil, 63; New Eng Ann, Silvermine Guild, New Canaan, Conn, 66 & 68; Drawings, Paintings & Theater Images, Artists Space, New York, 75. Teaching: In chg, workshops in color & movement, Univ Ill, Bard Col & Franconia Col; artist in residence, Univ Ill, Urbana, 74, 76 & 77. Pos: Set designer in residence, Univ Ill, Urbana, & actress, Circle Repertory Theatre Co, New York, 71-; dir six original theater-dance pieces, 75-77; founder, All Angels Theater Troupe, New York, NY, 77. Bibliog: Nancy Azara (auth), Found women-arts in their own image, MS Mag, 1/73; Howard Thompson (auth), Stage: Thomas Andros, New York Times, 6/2/73. Mem: Art Students League; Circle Repertory Theatre Co; Actors Equity Asn. Style & Technique: The human face and figure as environmental presences; large wood and canvas cutouts, painted; cut drawings as sculpture in paper. Media: Wood, Acrylic; Pastel & Crayon; Cloth. Mailing Add: 306 W 81st St New York NY 10024

MICHOD, SUSAN A
PAINTER
b Toledo, Ohio, Jan 3, 45. Study: Smith Col; Univ Mich, BS; Pratt Inst, MFA. Exhib: Artemisia Gallery, Chicago, 74-; Painting & Sculpture Today, Indianapolis Mus Art, 76; Watercolor USA, Springfield Mus, Mo, 77; Pattern Painting, PS1, Flushing, NY, 77; Jan Cicero Gallery, Chicago, 77- Teaching: Instr painting, Chicago Acad Fine Arts, 69-74. Pos: Pres, Artemisia, Inc, 74-75; dir, Artemisia Fund, 74- Awards: Purchase Prize, Ill State Mus, 74; Purchase Prize, Carleton Col Exhib, 75. Mem: Col Art Asn Am; Chicago Artists Coalition; West-East Bay-Nat Network of Women's Aid Registries. Style & Technique: Large pattern painting; brush, stamping, rolling. Media: Acrylic, Watercolor. Dealer: Jan Cicero Gallery 433 N Clark St Chicago IL 60610; Kathryn Markel 50 W 57th St New York NY 10019. Mailing Add: 2242 N Dayton St Chicago IL 60614

MIDDAUGH, ROBERT BURTON
PAINTER
b Chicago, Ill, May 12, 35. Study: Univ Ill, 54-55; Art Inst Chicago, BFA, 64. Work: Art Inst Chicago; Boston Mus Fine Art; Los Angeles Co Mus; Phoenix Art Mus; Worcester Art Mus, Mass. Comn: Prehistoric Project (permanent educ display, with Martyl Langsdorf & Prof Robert Braidwood), Oriental Inst, Univ Chicago, 68. Exhib: Chicago & Vicinity Show, Art Inst Chicago, 64, 66 & 73; Ill Biennial Exhib, Krannert Art Mus, Urbana, 65; Ill Exhib, Ill State Mus, Springfield, 66, 68, 69 & 71; Am Painting Exhib, Va Mus Fine Arts, Richmond, 66; 162nd Ann Exhib, Pa Acad Fine Arts, Philadelphia, 67; plus others. Pos: Asst cur, Art Collection First Nat Bank of Chicago, 71- Mem: Arts Club Chicago (men's comt, 73-78). Publ: Contribr, Buying Art on a Budget, Hawthorn, 68; contribr, Living World History, Scott Foresman. Dealer: Fairweather Hardin Gallery 101 Ontario Chicago IL 60657. Mailing Add: 1318 W Cornelia Chicago IL 60657

MIDDLEMAN, RAOUL F
PAINTER, INSTRUCTOR
b Baltimore, Md, Apr 3, 35. Study: Johns Hopkins Univ, BA, 55; Pa Acad Fine Arts, 59-61; Brooklyn Mus Art Sch, 61. Exhib: Human Concern/Personal Torment, Whitney Mus, 69; Painterly Painting, Am Fedn Arts, 70; Painters of Sea & Sky, Colby Col, 71; Sense of Peace, Nebr Mus, 71; Figurative Painting, Queens Col, 73. Teaching: Chmn painting dept, Md Inst Col Art, Baltimore, 61- Bibliog: Gerrit Henri (auth), rev in Art News, 72; Pat Mainardi (auth), rev in Art in Am, 7/74. Style & Technique: Figurative. Media: Oil, Watercolor. Mailing Add: c/o Allan Stone 48 E 85th St New York NY 10028

MIDENER, WALTER
SCULPTOR, INSTRUCTOR
b Ger, Oct 11, 12; US citizen. Study: Vereinigten Staats Schulen Fine & Appl Art; Berlin Acad, 32-36; Wayne State Univ, MA, 50. Work: Whitney Mus Am Art & House Living Judaism, New York; Detroit Inst Art & Flint Inst Art, Mich. Comn: Justice Butzel (portrait bust), Mich Supreme Court, 62; monument, Temple Bethel Mem Park, 62; sculpture, Bundy Corp, Detroit, 63; carved wood relief, Detroit Pub Libr, 64; hammered metal screen, Pontiac Motor Div, Gen Motors Corp, 68-69. Exhib: Mich Artists Shows, 46-61; Modellers, Carvers, Welders, Mus Mod Art, New York, 49-50; American Sculpture, Metrop Mus, New York, 51; Pa Acad, Philadelphia, 59; Friends of Whitney Collection, Whitney Mus Am Art, 64. Teaching: Instr sculpture, Henry St Settlement, 39-41; head sculpture dept, Soc Arts & Crafts Art Sch, 46-66, asst dir, 58-61, actg & assoc dir, 61-67, dean fac, 67-68, dir, Ctr Creative Studies, Col Art & Design, 68-76, pres, 76-77, pres emer & prof sculpture, 77- Awards: Mus Purchase Prize, Mich Artists Show, 50 & Founders Prize, 52, Founders Soc; Scarab Club Gold Medal, 60. Media: Metal, Wood, Clay, Bronze. Mailing Add: Ctr Creative Studies 245 E Kirby Detroit MI 48202

MIDGETTE, WILLARD FRANKLIN
PAINTER, PRINTMAKER
b Baltimore, Md, July 9, 37. Study: Skowhegan Sch Painting & Sculpture, with J Levine & Shahn, 53-56 & 59; Boston Univ Sch Fine & Appl Art, with David Aronson, 56-58; Harvard Col, AB, 58; Pratt Graphic Art Ctr, with Walter Rogalski, 59-60; Ind Univ, MFA, 62, with James McGarrell. Work: Reed Col & Mt Hood Community Col, Portland, Ore; Roswell Mus & Art Ctr, NMex. Comn: Illusionistic mural, Donald B Anderson, Roswell, 69; illusionistic hallway, J H Szold, New York, 72; illusionistic portraits, Edward Elson, Atlanta, Ga, 72 & Lewis Manilow, Chicago, 75. Exhib: One-man shows, Fountain Gallery, Portland, 70, Clean Well Lighted Place, Austin, Tex, 71, Allan Frumkin Gallery, New York, 71, 72 & 74 & Chicago, 71 & 73; Sharp Focus Realism, Sidney Janis Gallery, New York, 72; Contemporary American Painting & Sculpture, Krannert Art Mus, 74; Realismus und Realitat, Darmstadt, Ger, 75. Teaching: From artist in residence to assoc prof painting, drawing & printmaking, Reed Col, 63-70; lectr, Univ Wis & Univ Ill, Chicago Circle, 71, Moore Col Art & La State Univ, 72; Pratt Inst, 72 & 74 & Mont State Univ, 73; artist in residence & chmn dept painting, drawing & printmaking, St Ann's Episcopal Sch, Brooklyn, 72- Awards: Reed-Rockefeller Fac Grant, 69; Roswell Mus Residence Grant, 69-71. Bibliog: David Rosand (auth), Portrait of the artist as portrait of the artist, Art News, 3/71; David Hickey (auth), Review of Sidney Janis sharp focus show, Art in Am, 3-4/72; Dr Peter Sager (auth), Neue Formen des Realismus, Köln, Ger, 73. Style & Technique: Life size painted figures in spaces related illusionistically to the spectator's space. Media: Oil, Acrylic; Etching, Engraving. Publ: Auth, The naked truth, the work of Philip Pearlstein, Art News, 11/67. Dealer: Allan Frumkin Gallery 41 E 57th St New York NY 10022. Mailing Add: 124 Pierrepont St Brooklyn NY 11201

MIECZKOWSKI, EDWIN
PAINTER
b Pittsburgh, Pa, 1929. Study: Cleveland Inst Art, BFA; Carnegie Inst, MFA. Work: Cleveland Mus Art; Robert Hull Fleming Mus, Vt. Exhib: One-man shows, Robert Hull Fleming Mus, 74, New Gallery, Cleveland, 74, Tyler Sch Art, Pa, 74 & Mansfield Art Ctr, Ohio, 75; All-Ohio Show, 74; Cleveland Mus Art, 75; Park Ctr Show, Cleveland, 75. Mem: Founding mem Anonima Group; NOVA, Cleveland (trustee). Style & Technique: Acrylic on Paper and acrylic on Masonite and wood. Mailing Add: 268 Bowery New York NY 10012

MIEZAJS, DAINIS
PAINTER, INSTRUCTOR
b Latvia, Kaucminde, Mar 11, 29. Study: Ont Col of Art, 56. Work: Nat Gallery of Can, Ottawa, Ont; Art Gallery of Ont, Toronto; Mus Fine Arts, Montreal, Que; Art Gallery of Winnipeg, Man; Vancouver Art Gallery, BC. Comn: Series of 18 paintings, Trans-Can Pipeline, Toronto, Ont, 71. Exhib: Ann Can Soc of Painters in Watercolors, 61-78; Can Painters in Watercolor & Am Watercolor Soc Exchange Show, 73; Can Painters in Watercolor & Watercolor Soc of Japan, 77. Collections Arranged: Across Canada in Watercolor, Art Gallery of Ont, 69-71. Teaching: Instr drawing & painting, Ont Col of Art, Toronto, 60-; dir landscape, Madawaska Valley Sch Art, Maynooth, Ont, 65- Pos: Vpres, Latvis Soc of Artists, Toronto, 62-64; dir, Can Soc of Painters in Watercolor, 65-67. Awards: Merit Award, Can Soc of Painters in Watercolor Ann; Purchase Awards, Can Soc of Painters in WatercolorxAnnWatercolor. Bibliog: F Barwick (auth), Pictures from the Douglas Duncan Collection, Univ Toronto Press, 75. Mem: Can Painters in Watercolor; Latvis Soc Artists. Style & Technique: Contemporary realism. Media: Watercolor, Tempera. Dealer: Robert Art Gallery 641 Yonge St Toronto ON M4Y 1Z9 Can. Mailing Add: 380 Sackville St Toronto ON M4X 1S5 Can

MIGLIONICO, GLORIA
See G'Miglio

MIGNOSA, SANTO
CERAMIST, SCULPTOR
b Siracusa, Italy, Nov 14, 34; Can citizen. Study: Scuola d'Arte, Italy, Cert; Inst Statale d'Arte Firenze, Italy, Dipl: NY State Univ Alfred, MFA. Work: Univ Calgary Art Gallery, Can; Govt of Alta Art Found, Can; Govt of Tenn Ceramic Collection; Pall Mall of Can Art Collection; Art Centrum, Prague, Czech. Exhib: Int Ceramic Exhib, Ostend, Belg, 58, Prague, Czech, 61 & Gdansk, Poland, 73; Syracuse Nat, NY, 60, 62 & 66; Smithsonian Inst, Washington, DC; Faenza Int Concorso, Italy; Int Ceramic Exhib, Calgary, 73. Collections Arranged: Int Ceramic 73, Calgary, Can; Nat Ceramic 76, Calgary, Can. Teaching: Instr ceramics & sculpture, Kootenay Sch of Art, Nelson, BC, 60-68; assoc prof ceramics, Univ Calgary, Alta, Can, 69- Pos: C-chmn, Nat Ceramic Exhib, Calgary, Can, 75-76. Awards: Gold Medal, Int Ceramic Exhib, Ostend, 58, Silver Medal, Prague, 61 & Second Prize Ex-Aequo, Calgary, 73, Int Acad Ceramics. Bibliog: Al Riegger (auth), Featured Artist, Ceramic Mo, 63; article in, La Revue Mod des Arts et de la Vie, 67. Mem: Alta Potters' Asn (vpres, 70-71); Int Acad Ceramics, Geneva, Switz (coun mem). Style & Technique: Abstract. Media: Clay. Mailing Add: 5835 Bowness Rd NW Calgary AB T3B 0C5 Can

MIHICH, VASA VELIZAR
See Vasa

MIKUS, ELEANORE
PAINTER, LECTURER
b Detroit, Mich, July 25, 27. Study: Art Students League; study in Cent Europe; Univ Denver, BFA & MA. Work: Mus Mod Art & Whitney Mus Am Art, New York; Cincinnati Mus, Ohio; Los Angeles Co Mus Art; Indianapolis Mus Art, Ind. Exhib: One-woman shows, Pace Gallery, Boston, 63, Pace Gallery, New York, 64 & 65, O K Harris Gallery, New York, 70-74; Mus Mod Art, New York, 74; Richmond Mus, Va, 77; Weatherspoon Art Gallery, Greensboro, NC, 77. Teaching: Asst prof painting, monmouth Col, 66-70; vis lectr painting, Cooper Union, 70-72; lectr painting, Cent Sch of Art & Design, London, Eng, 73-77. Awards: Guggenehim Found Fel in Painting, 66-67; Ford Found Tamarind Fel in Lithography, 68; MacDowell Colony Fel, 69. Mailing Add: c/o O K Harris Gallery 383 W Broadway New York NY 10012

MILANT, JEAN ROBERT
ART DEALER
b Milwaukee, Wis, Dec 27, 43. Study: Univ Wis, Milwaukee, BA & BFA; Univ NMex, Albuquerque, MA; Tamarind Lithography Workshop, Los Angeles. Pos: Pres, dir & owner, Cirrus Ed Ltd, 69-; pres, dir & owner, Cirrus Gallery Ltd, 69-; mem bd, Los Angeles Inst Contemp Art, 75-77, vchmn, 77. Mem: Los Angeles Mus Art; Art Dealers Asn Southern Calif. Specialty: Contemporary painting, sculpture, performance, environments of Southern California artists; publisher of lithographs and screenprints of noted California artists. Mailing Add: 708 N Manhattan Pl Los Angeles CA 90038

MILCH, HAROLD CARLTON
ART DEALER
b New York, NY, Jan 2, 08. Study: City Col New York, BA; Sch Art, Columbia Univ. Pos: Pres, Milch & Vogel Art Gallery, New York, 29-34; assoc of Milch Galleries, 35-51; pres, E & A Milch, Inc (Milch Galleries), 51- Mem: Art Dealers Asn Am (pres, 68-70, bd dirs, presently); Metrop Mus Art; Am Fedn Arts; Arch Am Art. Specialty: American painting. Interest: Assisted in formulating some of the great American collections, both with museums and privately. Mailing Add: 1014 Madison Ave New York NY 10021

MILDER, JAY
PAINTER, SCULPTOR
b Omaha, Nebr, May 12, 34. Study: The Sorbonne; Ossip Zadkine; Andre L'Hote, Paris, France; Chicago Art Inst. Work: Tel Aviv Mus, Israel; Chrysler Mus, Norfolk, Va; Oakley Collection; Mass; Skidmore Col, NY. Comn: Sculpture, Sinai Temple, Los Angeles, Calif, 64; litho, Greenwich Light Opera, Conn, 70; etching, Rainbow Arts Found, NY, 77. Exhib: Mus PR; Dayton Art Inst, Ohio; Chrysler Mus, Norfolk, Va; Mint Mus Art, Charlotte, NC; Joslyn Art Mus, Omaha, Nebr; Art for the Olympics, Mus Mod Art, New York. Collections Arranged: Rhino Horn Exhib, New Sch for Social Res, New York; Oakley Collection, Skidmore Col; 50 American Contemporary Drawings, Ann Arbor Mus, Mich. Teaching: Asst prof art, City Col, New York, 77- Awards: Gutman Award, 60; First Prizes, All Ohio Artists, 64 & Am Figurative Artists, Bayonne, NJ, 77. Bibliog: Dorothy Beskind (auth), Jay Milder Paints (film), 67; Rudy Stern (auth), Paintings and Life of Jay Milder (film), 70; George Preston (auth), article in Arts Mag, 11/76. Style & Technique: Figure fantasy. Media: Oil paint. Dealer: Aaron Berman Gallery 50 W 57th St New York NY 10019. Mailing Add: 93 Greene St New York NY 10012

MILES, CYRIL
PAINTER, INSTRUCTOR
b Boston, Mass, June 13, 18. Study: Wayne State Univ, BS, 42, MA, 43. Work: IBM Bldg, Southfield, Mich; Metrop Fed Savings Bank, Detroit; Mfrs Bank, Detroit; Mich Acad Arts & Sci, Ann Arbor. Comn: Happening: Italian, Bloomfield Art Asn, Mich, 65; Happening: USA, Northamerican Mex Cult Inst, Mexico City, 67; Happening: USA, Detroit Artist Mkt, 67; Happening: USA, Downing Mus Art, Calif, 67. Exhib: Int Watercolor Exhib, Art Inst Chicago, 42; Drawing USA, St Paul, Minn, 65; one-man shows, Northamerican Mex Cult Inst, 67 & Downey Mus Art, 68; Premier Invenaire Int Poesie Elementaire, Paris, 68. Teaching: Instr painting, Detroit Inst Art, 42-67; supvr art, Highland Park Pub Schs, 50-64; instr art, Highland Park Community Col, 42-; ed, African Art Coloring Bk, 71- Awards: Mich Watercolor Soc Award; Mich Acad Art & Sci, Citation, 75; One of Ten Best Films at Rochester, NY, 67. Bibliog: Marie De Larson (auth), Cyril Miles, Manana/S A Lago Rasna 37, 7/29/67; Jean-Francois Bory (auth), Once again (poetry anthology), New Directions, 68; D Meilach (auth), Assemblage & Collage, 73 & Box Art, 75, Crowell. Mem: Mich Acad Arts & Sci; Mich Watercolor Soc (chmn, 55); Mus Mod Art; Detroit Inst of Art Founders Soc; hon mem Detroit Soc Women Painters. Media: Acrylic, Collage. Publ: Auth, Knee-Deep in Poetry, Rubiner Art Gallery, Royal Oak, Mich, 66; auth, Environment or happening thing, single issue newspaper, 67; contribr, Critical review of Moholy-Nagy, 6/71 & Book review, Hans Richter, 6/72, J Aesthet & Art Criticism. Dealer: Arts Extended Gallery Inc 1549 Broadway Detroit MI 48226. Mailing Add: 17711 Hamilton Rd Detroit MI 48203

MILES, ELLEN GROSS
ART HISTORIAN, CURATOR
b New York, NY, July 28, 41. Study: Bryn Mawr Col, BA, 64; Winterthur Summer Inst, 67; Yale Univ Grad Sch, MPhil, 70 & PhD, 76, with Jules D Prown. Pos: Pub relations asst & registr, Corcoran Gallery Art, Washington, DC, 64-66; asst to dir, Nat Portrait Gallery, Washington, DC, 72-77, assoc cur, 77- Mem: Col Art Asn; Women's Caucus for Art. Res: Eighteenth and nineteenth century British and American portrait painting and drawing. Publ: Co-auth, The Drawings of John Singer Sargent at the Corcoran Gallery of Art, Borden Publ Co, 67; ed, Portrait painting in America: the 19th century, Main St/Universe, 77. Mailing Add: c/o Nat Portrait Gallery Eighth & F Sts Washington DC 20560

MILES, JEANNE PATTERSON
PAINTER, SCULPTOR
b Baltimore, Md. Study: George Washington Univ, BFA; Grande Chaumiere, Paris; also with Marcel Gromaire, Paris. Work: Guggenheim Mus, New York; NY Univ Collection; Munson Williams Proctor Mus, Utica, NY; Andrew C White Mus, Cornell Univ; Santa Barbara Mus, Calif; Newberger Collection, Purchase, NY. Comn: Mural designs for Kentile Co, Kansas City, 60, Los Angeles, 62, Atlanta, Ga, 63; mural symbolic design, Chicago, 64 & rm divider in geometric design, NY, 65. Exhib: Ten Years at Betty Parsons Gallery, New York, 54; Mysticism in Art, Rome-New York Found, Rome, 57; Geometric Art, Whitney Mus Am Art, New York, 63; The Square in Art Traveling Show, Am Fedn Art, 68-69; retrospective, Three American Purists, Mus Fine Arts, Springfield, Mass, 75. Teaching: Docent, Mus Non Objective Art, New York, 45-50; dir art dept, Moravian Col Women, 48-51; docent, Guggenheim Mus, New York, 51-52; asst dir painting & life drawing, Oberlin Col, 52-53; instr painting, NY Inst Technol, 68-69. Awards: C C Ladd Study Scholar, 39-40; Am Inst Arts & Lett Emergency Grant, 69; Mark Rothko Found Grant, 71. Bibliog: Patricia Wilson (auth), Sculptor by Jeanne Miles, Christian Sci Monitor, 68; Collette Roberts (auth), Tape, NY Univ Arch, 68; article in Art Now, 69. Mem: Am Abstr Artists. Style & Technique: Geometric mandala art; oil in conjunction with, and over, gold and platinum leaf, in glazes. Publ: Auth, article in Arts Mag, 4/77 & illusr, cover, Art Gallery Guide. Dealer: Sid Deutch Gallery 43 E 80th St New York NY 10021. Mailing Add: 463 West St Apt A 1103 New York NY 10014

MILETTE, CLEMENCE M
PAINTER
b New York, NY. Study: Pratt Inst, cert teacher training; NY Univ, BS(educ), MS(educ); Columbia Teachers Col; Art Students League; Univ Wis; also with Dong Kingman, William Zorach & Pietro Montana. Exhib: Knickerbocker Artists, New York, 54; Mexican Paintings, Burr Gallery, 56; Grand Nat, Am Artists Prof League, Nat Arts Club, New York, 57 & Lever House, New York, 72; Art Chmns Asn Exhib, New York, 72. Teaching: Instr fine arts, Newton High Sch, New York, 36-55, chmn dept fine arts, 55-72. Mem: Am Artists Prof League; Art Chmns Asn, New York; Art Teachers Asn; Nat Art Educ Asn. Style & Technique: Watercolors, representational, in fluid, wet, transparent style; landscapes and seascapes in natural outdoor light; around the world scenes. Media: Watercolor, Oil; Wood. Publ: Auth, Museum atmosphere in school, Art Educ J, Vol 15, No 2. Mailing Add: 3743 90th St Jackson Heights New York NY 11372

MILEY, LES
CERAMIST, EDUCATOR
b Petersburg, Ind, Nov 1, 34. Study: Southern Ill Univ, with Nicholas Vergette & Brent Kington, MFA; Purdue Univ, ceramics with Bill Farrell; Ind State Univ, BA & MA. Work: Ceramics Monthly Mag Collection, Columbus, Ohio; DePauw Univ Permanent Collection, Greencastle, Ind; Evansville Mus Arts & Sci, Ind; Mitchell Gallery, Southern Ill Univ, Carbondale; Univ Ill, Champaign-Urbana. Comn: Archit ceramics, Robert L Blaffer Trust, New Harmony, Ind, 74. Exhib: 25th Ceramic Nat, Everson Mus, 69; Sheldon Swope Craft Exhib, Swope Gallery, Terre Haute, 69; Mid-South Craft Exhib, Murphreesboro, Tenn, 71; Ind Artists Objects & Crafts, Indianapolis Mus Art, 73; Functional Ceramics, Wooster Mus, Ohio, 75. Teaching: Prof art, Univ Evansville, 61-, chmn dept, 65-66 & 69- Pos: Dir visual art prog, Hist New Harmony, Ind, 75-; mem bd dirs, Evansville Mus Arts & Sci. Bibliog: Stanley Lee (auth), A sprigging variation, Ceramics Monthly Mag, 74; Thomas Schafer (auth), Pottery Decoration, Watson-Guptill, 75. Mem: Nat Coun Educ for Ceramic Arts; Nat Coun Art Adminr; Am Crafts Coun; Ind Artist-Craftsman. Style & Technique: Architectural ceramics and pottery, sculptural and wheel throwing techniques. Media: Clay, Metal. Mailing Add: 447 S St James Blvd Evansville IN 47714

MILEY, MIMI CONNEEN
EDUCATOR, CURATOR
b Bryn Mawr, Pa, Aug 17, 46. Study: Western Col, Oxford, Ohio, BA(art hist). Exhibitions Arranged: Winter Scenes by 19th Century Lithographers, 74; Pennsylvania Folk Art (with catalog), Allentown Art Mus, Pa, 74; Discover Texture, 75-77, Discover Color, 77-78 (touch participation exhibs); A Salute to Walter Emerson Baum, 76; Howard Chandler Christy: Artist/Illustrator of Style (auth, catalogue), 77. Pos: Cur educ, Allentown Art Mus, Pa, 70- Mem: Nat Arts Club; Am Asn Mus. Mailing Add: Box 117 Fifth & Court Sts Allentown PA 18105

MILHOLLAND, RICHARD ALEXANDER
PAINTER
b Paterson, NJ, Apr 30, 46. Study: Newark Sch Fine & Indust Arts, NJ, 64-68; Brooklyn Mus Art Sch, Max Beckman scholar, 68, and with Reuben Tam; Univ of the Americas, Mexico City, grad teaching fel, 69-70, BFA & MFA. Work: Honolulu Acad Arts, Hawaii; Gibbes Art Gallery, Charleston, SC; Grinnell Col; Ball State Univ Art Gallery. Exhib: Childe Hassam Fund Exhib, Am Acad Arts & Lett, New York, 72; Mem Gallery Exhib, Albright-Knox Art Gallery, Buffalo, NY, 72; one-man show, Babcock Galleries, New York, 72, 73 & 75; 21st Ann Drawings & Sculpture, Ball State Univ Art Gallery, 74. Teaching: Instr sculpture, drawing & painting, Univ of the Americas, 69-70; instr painting & drawing, Univ SFla, 72. Awards: Childe Hassam Fund Purchase Award, Am Acad Arts & Lett, 72. Style & Technique: Representational. Mailing Add: c/o Babcock Galleries 805 Madison Ave New York NY 10021

MILL, ELEANOR
ILLUSTRATOR, PAINTER
b Royal Oak, Mich, Mar 21, 27. Study: Art Students League, 45, with Robert Brackman; Corcoran Sch of Art, Washington, DC, 45-46, with Richard Lahey, Eugene Weiss & Kenneth Stubbs; spec study with Raphael Soyer & Aurelius Battaglia. Comn: Bus Christmas cards, comn by Margaret Mill Coldwell, Shearson Hayden Stone Inc, Hartford, Conn, 75-77. Exhib: Canton Artists Guild, Gallery-on-the-Green, Canton, Conn, 75. Awards: Best in Show, Juried Mem Exhib, Canton Artist Guild, Ohio, 75. Mem: Canton Artist Guild. Style & Technique: Children's books figure illustration in watercolors, pastel chalk and pen & ink, carbon pencil and acrylic. Publ: Illusr, What Mary Jo Shared, 66 & What Mary Jo Wanted, 68, Albert Whitman, Chicago; illusr, I Am Maria, Henry Regnery, 69; illusr, Mary Jo's Grandmother, Albert Whitman, Chicago, 70; illusr, The Wonderful Wizard of Oz, Golden Press & Western Publ, 77. Mailing Add: 211 Brittany Farms Rd 18-D New Britain CT 06053

MILLARD, CHARLES WARREN, III
CURATOR, WRITER
b Elizabeth, NJ, Dec 20, 32. Study: Princeton Univ, BA; Harvard Univ, MA & PhD. Pos: Dir, Washington Gallery Mod Art, 66-67; cur 19th century European art, Los Angeles Co Mus Art, 71-74; art ed, Hudson Rev, 72-; chief cur, Hirshhorn Mus & Sculpture Garden, 74- Res: 19th century French sculpture, particularly Degas and Preault, and various topics in modern painting and sculpture. Publ: Auth, Sculpture of Edgar Degas, Princeton Univ, 76; plus many other articles & rev in var art periodicals. Mailing Add: Hirshhorn Mus & Sculpture Garden Eighth St & Independence Ave SW Washington DC 20560

MILLER, BARBARA DARLENE
PAINTER, INSTRUCTOR
b Jarbidge, Nev. Study: Univ Wash, BA; Univ Hawaii, MEd; etching with Rudy Pozzatti & Gabor Peterdi; design with Clayton Rippey; painting with Tadashi Sato. Work: State Found Cult & Arts, Honolulu; Univ Hawaii Art Dept Etching Collection. Comn: Acrylic mural, KPOI Radio, Waikiki, Honolulu, 68; Christ with Thorns (acrylic painting), Church of Good Shepherd, Kahului, Maui, 70; Buddha (acrylic painting), Kahului Hongwanji Mission, Maui, 72; Mosaics (film), State Found & Maui Arts Coun, 72. Exhib: Volunteer Park Art Mus, Seattle, Wash, 49; Regional Hawaii Painting & Sculpture Exhib, Fort Ruger, Honolulu & State Tour, 62; Walker Art Ctr Nat, Minneapolis, 65; Painters of Hawaii Circulating Exhib, 69; Etchings, Hawaii State Libr, 70; Regional Ethel Baldwin Mem, Wailuku, 72; plus others. Teaching: Art instr, Hilo High Sch, 57-60; elem art specialist, Kahului Elem Sch, 64-68; art instr, Maui Community Col, 68- Pos: Artist, Logos Layouts, KPOI Radio, 65-67; art dir, KHVH Radio-TV, Honolulu, 67-68; free-lance muralist. Awards: Hawaii Artists Exhibs Awards & Prizes, 65-77; State Found Cult & Art Purchase Award, 72. Bibliog: Eileen Webster (auth), Milady of the week—Barbara Miller & Darrell Neilson (auth), Works of Mrs Miller, 68, Maui News; Tim Mitchell (auth), Art news—Barbara Miller painter, Honolulu Mag, 69. Mem: Maui Arts Coun (visual arts chmn, 68-77); Hui Noeau Art Soc (past pres, bd mem & mem bd dirs); Nat Art Educ Asn. Media: Acrylic, Intaglio. Publ: Illusr, Festival of Arts (cover design), 69; co-auth, Grass Roots, Poetry & Art (20 page bk), 70; illusr cover, Our Changing Times, Univ Hawaii Div Continuing Educ, 70. Dealer: Village Gallery-Whalers Village Kaanapali Maui HI 96753. Mailing Add: Maui Community Col 3100 Kaahumanu Ave Kahului Maui HI 96753

MILLER, DANIEL DAWSON
PAINTER, SCULPTOR
b Pittsburgh, Pa, July 7, 28. Study: Lafayette Col, BA, 51; Pa State Univ, summers with Hobson Pittman; Pa Acad Fine Arts, 55-59; Univ Pa, MFA, 58. Work: Pa Acad Fine Arts, Philadelphia; Philadelphia Mus Art; Rutgers Mus, New Brunswick, NJ; Wilmington Soc Fine Arts, Del; Dickinson Col, Carlisle, Pa. Exhib: 11 Modern American Artists, Rahr Mus, Manitowoc, Wis, 63; 158th-162nd Ann Exhib, Pa Acad Fine Arts, Philadelphia, 63-67; one-man shows, Peale House, Pa Acad Fine Arts, 67, Drexel Inst, 68, Rutgers Mus, Rutgers Univ, 70 & Univ Maine, 72. Teaching: Instr life & still life painting, Philadelphia Mus Art, 62-76; instr life painting, Pa Acad Fine Arts, 64-; instr art & head fine arts dept, Eastern Col, St Davids, Pa, 64- Pos: Mem bd, Fel of Pa Acad Fine Arts, 62- Awards: Prize for Oil, Del Ann, Del Soc Fine Arts, 60; May Audubon Post Prize, 61, Bertha M Goldberg Mem Award, 70 & 75 & Leona Karp Brauerman Prize, 76, Fel of Pa Acad Fine Arts. Mem: Philadelphia

Watercolor Club. Dealer: Gallery Doshi 1435-37 N Second St Harrisburg PA 17102. Mailing Add: Box 108 Christiana PA 17509

MILLER, DAVID STUART
ART DEALER
b Kalamazoo, Mich, Aug 8, 48. Study: Art Inst Chicago; Princeton Univ, BA(fine arts), 70; NY Univ, JD, 75. Collections Arranged: Don Berg, Paintings and Papers, 76, Lazaro Julian, Conceptual Constructions, 76 & 77, Siri Berg Paintings and Drawings, 77, Jane Schneider Sculpture, 77, Pierre Jacquenon Paintings, 77 & Art in Black and White, Mixed Media, 77. Pos: Asst cur of art collection, UNESCO, Paris, France, 74-75; pvt art dealer, New York, 76- Bibliog: Residential Interiors Mag, 9/77. Res: Constructivism and hyperrealism. Specialty: Contemporary American art. Publ: Auth, The current New York art scene, Princeton Univ Quart, 70. Mailing Add: 7 W 16th St New York NY 10011

MILLER, DOLLY (ETHEL B)
PAINTER
b Johnstown, Pa, June 14, 27. Study: Brooklyn Col, NY, BA(chemistry); NY Univ, MA(Fr lit); art hist, The Sorbonne & the Louvre, Paris, France; studied painting with Andre Lhote, Paris; Art Students League, with Julian Levi; also with Leo Manso, NY Univ. Work: Johnson & Johnson, Surgico, Inc, Piscataway, NJ; The Friends Acad, Locust Valley, NY. Exhib: NJ Regional, Jersey City Mus, 68-74; Butler Inst Am Art Ann, Youngstown, Ohio, 68 & 69; Regional, NJ State Mus, Trenton, 69; Regional, Mus Fine Arts, Springfield, Mass, 69; one-person shows, Friends Acad, Locust Valley, 70 & Art Exhib Consult, Princeton, NJ, 77; Award Winners of Fence Show, Brooklyn Mus Fine Arts, 75; Candidates for Art Award, Am Acad Nat Inst Art, New York, 76. Awards: Friedland Award, Art Centre of the Oranges, NJ, 69; Hon Mention, Garden State Art Ctr, NJ, 70; Barney Paisner Mem Award, Painters & Sculptors Soc NJ, 75. Mem: Audubon Artists, Inc; Painters & Sculptors Soc NJ. Style & Technique: Pouring and blotting oil color and brush painting; abstracts with biomorphic shapes; thinly painted figurative acrylics. Mailing Add: PO Box 82 Barton VT 05822

MILLER, DONALD
ART CRITIC, WRITER
b Pittsburgh, Pa, Dec 21, 34. Study: Univ Pittsburgh, AB, 56, MA(art hist), 75; Harvard Inst in Arts Admin, 76. Am Fedn Art Critics Workshop, with Barbara Novak, 70. Teaching: Lectr Rebels Mod Art, Community Col Allegheny Co, Pittsburgh, winter 72 & Westmoreland Co Mus Art, Greensburg, Pa, spring 72. Pos: Art critic, Pittsburgh Post-Gazette, 66- Publ: Auth, At Carnegie Institute, a happy occasion, 74, Optical parade, 75, Deborah Remington's portraits of objects in space, 75, & Alechinsky: a case of overkill?, 78, Artnews; auth, The man in the iron suit, Carnegie Mag, 77. Mailing Add: Pittsburgh Post-Gazette Pittsburgh PA 15230

MILLER, DONALD RICHARD
SCULPTOR
b Erie, Pa, June 30, 25. Study: Dayton Art Inst, 47-52; Pratt Inst, 55-57; Art Students League, 58-61; also with Ulysses A Ricci, 56-60. Work: Dayton Art Inst, Ohio; William Farnsworth Art Mus, Rockland, Maine; Medallic Art Co, New York; Div Numismatics, Smithsonian Inst. Comn: Thoreau Medal, Soc Medalists, 67; two bronze reliefs, Cincinnati Zoo; nickel-bronze relief, Philadelphia Zoo, 73; two gargoyles, Washington Cathedral, 76; six animal relief panels, Franklin Mint, 76. Exhib: Mus Fine Arts, Springfield, Mass, 63-70; Allied Artists Am, 63-; Nat Acad Design, 67-74; Nat Sculpture Soc, 67-; Soc Animal Artists, 68- Awards: Mrs Louis Bennett Prize, Nat Sculpture Soc, 68; Miriam B Beline Mem Award, Allied Artists Am, 69; Springfield Acad Artists Asn Award, 72. Mem: Fel Nat Sculpture Soc (chmn exhib comn; ed bd, Nat Sculpture Rev, 67); Soc Animal Artists (exhib comt, 67); fel Am Artists Prof League (bd dirs, 67); Allied Artists Am (comt mem, 63); Acad Artists Asn, Springfield, Mass. Style & Technique: Interpretive animal sculpture executed in all media. Mailing Add: 900 Riverside Dr New York NY 10032

MILLER, DOROTHY CANNING
ART CONSULTANT
b Hopedale, Mass. Study: Smith Col, BA & LHD, 59. Collections Arranged: Many exhibs, Mus Mod Art, 36-69. Pos: Asst to dir, Mus Mod Art, 34, assoc cur painting & sculpture, 35-43, cur painting & sculpture, 43-47, cur mus collections, 47-67, sr cur painting & sculpture, 67-69; mem art comt, Chase Manhattan Bank, 59; art adv, var collectors, cols & corp, 69-; dir, Mark Rothko Found; mem adv coun, Gottlieb Found. Publ: Ed, 12 Americans, 56; ed, The New American Painting, 58; ed, 16 Americans, 59; ed, Americans 1963; ed, 20th Century Art from the Nelson Aldrich Rockefeller Collection, 69; plus many others. Mailing Add: Mus Mod Art 11 W 53rd St New York NY 10019

MILLER, EVA-HAMLIN
PAINTER, EDUCATOR
b Brooklyn, NY. Study: Pratt Inst, BFA; Columbia Univ, MA; NY Univ, with Hale Woodruff; Art Students League, with Charles Austin; Villa Schifanoia Sch Art, Florence, Italy; Univ Ibadan, Nigeria. Work: NC Cent Univ, Durham; Am Fed Savings & Loan Bldg, Greensboro, NC; Johnson Publ Co, Chicago; NC A&T State Univ; also in many pvt collections. Comn: Stained glass window, St James Presby Church, Greensboro, 61; four stained glass windows, St Mathews Methodist Church, Greensboro, 71; stained glass window, Shilo Baptist Church, Greensboro, 72. Exhib: Gallery Contemp Art, Winston-Salem, NC, 69 & 70; Int Art Exhib, New York Coliseum, 70; 15 Afro-American Women, NC Taylor Gallery, Greensboro, 70; Eva-Hamlin Miller, Washington & Lee Univ, Lexington, Va, 71; NC Artists NC Mus Art, Raleigh; plus others. Teaching: Dir art, Tuskegee Inst, Ala, 33-36; dir art, Bennett Col, Greensboro, 37-41; supvr art, Greensboro City Schs, 42-53; chmn art dept, Winston-Salem Teachers Col, 59-63; assoc prof art, NC A&T State Univ, 63- Pos: Dir-cur, Taylor Art Gallery, 67- Awards: Southern Area Award, Links Inc, 67 & 72; Greensboro Artists League Award, 71. Bibliog: Lewis & Waddy (auth), Black artists on art, Contemp Crafts, 69; Afro-American women in art, Alpha Kappa Alpha Sorority, 69. Mem: Am Fedn Arts; Int Soc Educ through Art; NC State Art Soc; Am Asn Mus; Greensboro Artists League (bd mem, 70-72); plus others. Style & Technique: Colorist, abstract-expressionist. Media: Acrylic, Oil. Mailing Add: 1412 Benbow Rd Greensboro NC 27406

MILLER, MRS G MACCULLOCH
COLLECTOR
Collection: Contemporary art. Mailing Add: 10 Gracie Sq New York NY 10028

MILLER, GEORGE
CONCEPTUAL ARTIST, WRITER
b Wooster, Ohio, June 12, 44. Study: Ohio State Univ; Rutgers Univ, NJ; also with Allan Kaprow, Geoff Hendricks & Robert Watts. Work: Univ Redlands, Calif; Univ Iowa, Iowa City; Janus Gallery, Los Angeles, Calif; Robert Freidus Gallery, New York, NY; Permanent Collection of the Guggenheim Mus, New York, NY; Mt San Antonio Col, Walnut, Calif; Ohio State Univ, Columbus. Exhib: One-man shows, Eugenia Butler Gallery, 71 & Cirrus Gallery, Los Angeles, 72; Los Angeles Mus Art, 74; Whitney Mus Am Art Ann, New York, 75; Slocumb Gallery, Johnson City, Tenn, 75. Collections Arranged: The Last Plastic Show & Language and Luggage, Calif Inst Arts, 71. Teaching: Asst prof painting, Ore State Univ, Eugene 68-70; artist on theory, Calif Inst Arts, Los Angeles, 70-72; artist on painting, Univ Calif, Irvine, 72-74. Pos: Founder, Performance Co, Syntax/Space, Los Angeles, 71-72; ed/publ, The Portrait Rev, Los Angeles, 75- Awards: Walter-Russel Scholar, Rutgers Univ, NJ, 68; Graphics Award, Ohio State Univ, Columbus, 68; Drawing Show Award, Mt San Antonio, Walnut, Calif, 75. Bibliog: Gene Davis (auth), Gallery rev, Arts News Mag, Washington, DC, 69; William Wilson (auth), Gallery rev, Los Angeles Times, 72; Peter Plagens (auth), catalog, Univ Calif, Northridge, 74. Mem: Col Art Asn; Los Angeles Inst Contemp Art. Style & Technique: Literary format, short story against physical objects, content vs context. Media: Language; Sculpture. Publ: Auth, Radical Software, Newspaper on Video, 72; auth, California White Walls, Anthology, 74, contribr, 75; auth, Circa, 75; auth, Why language, Journal, 75. Mailing Add: Suite 14 1914 S Vermont Los Angeles CA 90007

MILLER, H MCRAE
SCULPTOR, PAINTER
b Montreal, PQ, Nov 3, 95. Study: Art Students League, with John Sloan; Beaux-Arts, Montreal, with Alfred Laliberte; also with C W Simpson & F S Coburn. Work: Nat Gallery Can. Comn: Portrait sculpture, Quc Prov Mus. Exhib: Montreal Mus Fine Arts, 27-30 & 35-45; Royal Can Acad Art, 27-59; Nat Gallery Can, 50; Royal Can Acad, Quebec & Winnipeg, 60. Pos: Pres, Sculptors' Soc Can, 55-56. Awards: Sculptors's Soc Can Award, 58; Royal Can Acad Art Award, 55. Mem: Academician Royal Can Acad Art; fel Int Inst Arts & Lett. Style & Technique: Specializing in snow paintings. Publ: Auth, bk of poetry. Mailing Add: RR 2 Range 6 St Agathe des Monts PQ J8C 2Z8 Can

MILLER, INGE MORATH
See Morath, Inge

MILLER, JAN
PAINTER, DESIGNER
US citizen. Study: Grand View Col, Des Moines, Iowa; Fenger Jr Col, Chicago; St Xavier Col, Chicago, BA. Work: Ill State Fine Arts Mus, Springfield; Mus Fine Arts, Ft Lauderdale, Fla; Springfield Civic Collections, Ill; Union League Club, Chicago; Kemper Ins Co, Long Grove, Ill. Exhib: 27th Ill State Exhib, Springfield, 74; Contemporary Still Life, Renaissance Soc, Univ Chicago, 74; Mainstreams in American Art, Marietta Col, 74; 75th Chicago & Vicinity Exhib, Art Inst Chicago, 75; New Horizons in Art, Chicago, 75. Awards: First Place for Prof Art, Ill State Fair, 73; Best of Show, Rockford & Vicinity, Ill, 75; First Place, Lakehurst Exhib, Waukegan, Ill, 75. Mem: Artists, Residents of Chicago (dir); NShore Art League. Style & Technique: Realistic, large scale still life paintings, painted directly from the subject; light and reflections. Media: Acrylic. Mailing Add: 9424 S Turner Ave Evergreen Park IL 60642

MILLER, JEAN JOHNSTON
ART LIBRARIAN, ART HISTORIAN
b New York, NY, Feb 19, 18. Study: Barnard Col, AB, 39. Pos: Art librn, Univ Hartford, West Hartford, Conn, 64- Mem: Art Libr Soc NAm. Interest: Twentieth century. Mailing Add: c/o Art Library Univ Hartford West Hartford CT 06117

MILLER, JOAN VITA
MUSEUM DIRECTOR
b New York, NY, Jan, 46. Study: Syracuse Univ, BA(art hist), MA(art hist); independent res in Italy. Collections Arranged: New York Eleven, 74; Louise Nevelson (auth, catalogue), 74; Gertrude Stein and Her Friends (auth, catalogue), 75; Wreck, 75; The Long Island Art Collector's Exhibit (auth, catalogue), 75; European Masters in Portraiture, 76; An Exploration of Photography 1839-1976 (auth, catalogue), 76; The Arts of China, 77. Teaching: Mus & gallery mgt, C W Post Col, Long Island Univ, 76- Pos: Asst dir, Michael Rockefeller Arts Ctr, State Univ NY Col, Fredonia, 71-72; dir gallery & cur permanent collection, C W Post Art Gallery, C W Post Col, 73- Mem: Am Asn Mus; Long Island Mus Asn; Gallery Asn NY State; Contemp Print Soc New York. Publ: Auth, Marsden Hartley 1877-1943, Long Island Univ Press, 77. Mailing Add: C W Post Col Art Gallery Greenvale NY 11548

MILLER, JOHN PAUL
JEWELER, INSTRUCTOR
b Huntingdon, Pa, Apr 23, 18. Study: Cleveland Inst Art, cert indust design; and with Baron Eric Fleming. Work: Cleveland Mus Art, Ohio; Mus Contemp Crafts, New York; Huntington Gallery, WVa; Minn Mus, St Paul; Johnson Wax Collection. Exhib: Int Jewelry Exhib, London, 61; Objects USA, traveling exhib, US, Europe & Japan, 69; 15 Jewelers, Schmuck-Objekte, Mus Bellevive, Zurich, 71; Metal Exhib, DeCordova Mus, Boston, 74; Goldsmiths '74, Smithsonian Inst, Washington, DC, 74; Am Craftsmen, Vatican Mus, Rome, Italy, 78. Teaching: Instr design & jewelry, Cleveland Inst Art, 40- Bibliog: Von Neumann (auth), Design and Creation of Jewelry, Chilton, 61; Graham Hughes (auth), Modern Jewelry, Crown; J Anderson Black (auth), Story of Jewelry, Morrow, 74. Mem: Am Craftsmen Coun. Style & Technique: Fabricated jewelry using techniques of fusion, granulation and enamel on gold. Mailing Add: 9333 Highland Dr Brecksville OH 44141

MILLER, LEE ANNE
PAINTER, PRINTMAKER
b Salt Lake City, Utah. Study: Utah State Univ, Logan, BS, 60; Cranbrook Acad Art, Bloomfield Hills, Mich, MFA, 61; Pratt Graphic Art Ctr, New York, 61-62; Slade Sch Art, London, Eng, Fulbright Grant painting, 62-63. Work: Ark Arts Ctr, Little Rock; Univ Mo-Kansas City; Utah State Univ. Exhib: Watercolor USA, 68-74; 17th Dixie Ann, Montgomery Mus Fine Arts, Ala, 76; 7 for 76 Bicentennial, Eastern Ill Univ, 76; Colorprint USA, 76-77; one-woman shows, Chicago, Salt Lake City, Cleveland, Ohio, Kansas City, Mo & Manhattan, Kans, 76-77; Contemp Issues: Works by Women on Paper, Los Angeles, Utah & Tex, 77-78; Contact: Women and Nature, Greenwich, Conn, 77; Nat Print Exhib, Honolulu Acad Arts, Okla Art Ctr, Oklahoma City, State Univ NY Col Potsdam, Bradley Univ, Peoria, Ill & Wichita Art Asn, Kans; Detroit Inst Fine Arts; Nelson Gallery Art, Kansas City, Mo; Witte Mem Mus, San Antonio, Tex; Springfield Art Mus, Mo; Dallas Mus Fine Arts. Collections Arranged: Women Printmakers, 76, Ellen Lanyon Retrospective, 76 & Painterly Realism Exhibition, 77, Fine Arts Gallery, Univ Mo-Kansas City. Teaching: Instr painting & drawing, Cleveland Inst Art, Ohio, 64-66; instr intaglio printmaking & painting, E Tex State Univ, Commerce, 66-68; assoc prof printmaking & painting & chairperson, Dept Art & Art Hist, Univ Mo-Kansas City, 68- Pos: Proj coodr, Women Artists, 77; mem curatorial panel, Contemp Issues: Works by Women on Paper, 77. Awards: Tamarind Inst Grant, 75; Purchase Award, 9th Ann Prints, Drawings & Crafts Exhib, Ark Arts Ctr, 76; Second Place Award, 36th Ann Cedar City Nat Exhib, Utah, 77. Bibliog: Kansas City Women Artists, Ms Mag,

(spring 78). Mem: Women's Caucus for Art (mem nat adv bd, 76-77, nat pres, 78-80]); Col Art Asn; Mid-Am Col Art Asn (conf prog coordr, 75-76, secy, 75-76). Style & Technique: Full range of watercolor techniques; organic imagery. Media: (Painting) Watercolor; (Printmaking) intaglio & lithography. Mailing Add: Dept Art & Art Hist Univ Mo-Kansas City Kansas City MO 64110

MILLER, LEON GORDON
DESIGNER, PRINTMAKER
b New York, NY, Aug 3, 17. Study: NJ State Teachers Col, BS; Art Students League: Newark Sch Fine & Indust Art, CFA; Fawcett Art Sch, with Bernar Gussow; Baldwin Wallace Col, Hon DFA, 71; Kean Col NJ, Hon DFA, 73. Work: Libr of Cong, Washington, DC; Gertrude Stein Collection, Yale Univ. Comn: Stained glass windows, ceremonial sculpture & tapestries, US relig insts; archit sculpture & graphics, US corps & govt insts. Exhib: Close Ups, Color Photog sponsored by US Embassy, 72; Nat Interfaith Conf Relig Arts Exhib, 75; 15 one-man shows of paintings, drawings, prints, photog & sculpture, since 50; plus others. Teaching: Instr indust design, Cleveland Inst Art, 47-50; guest lectr, US educ insts, Can Ministry Com, Design Ctr of Yugoslavia & others. Pos: Pres, Leon Gordon Miller & Assocs, Inc, 47-; founder, KV Design Int Ltd, 71; bd mem fine arts adv bd, Rose Art Mus, 72; US design rep, Sweden, 59, Italy, 61, Eng, 69, Mex, 72, Japan, 73 & Yugoslavia, 74. Awards: Silver Medal Award, Indust Designers Inst, 62; Outstanding Arts Alumnus Award, Kean Col NJ, 73; Sculpture Award, HUD Nat Community Art Competition, 73; plus others. Bibliog: V Ball (auth), Art of Interior Design, Macmillan, 60; Avram Kamph (auth), Contemporary synagogue art, Union Am Hebrew Congregations, 66; among others in art, design & archit periodicals. Mem: Fel Indust Designers Soc Am; Inst Bus Designers; Pierpont Morgan Libr; Guild for Relig Art & Archit (bd mem); Artists Equity Asn; plus others. Style & Technique: Multi-media artist engaged in painting, printmaking, sculpture, and stained glass, working in a contemporary style and technique. Publ: Co-auth, Lost Heritage of Alaska, World, 67; Light by Design, Gen Elec Co, 71; auth hist preface, Stained Glass Craft, Macmillan, 73. Mailing Add: 16250 Aldersyde Dr Cleveland OH 44120

MILLER, MARIANN (MARIANN HELM)
PAINTER
b Ancon, CZ, Mar 19, 32. Study: Ohio State Univ, BFA, 59; Cornell Univ, MFA, 62. Work: Robertson Mem Ctr, Binghamton, NY; Sneed Mus Art, Louisville, Ky; Ponce Mus, PR. Exhib: One-women show, Stefanotty Gallery, New York, 74; Directors Choice Exhib, New York Cult Ctr, 74; Women Artists, Philadelphia Mus, 74; Imagist Realist, Art Mus, Palm Beach, Fla, 74; Painting & Sculpture Today, Contemp Art Soc, Indianapolis Mus Art, 74. Teaching: Asst prof painting & life drawing, Cornell Univ, 63-66; vis artist grad painting, Univ Cincinnati, 75. Bibliog: Mariann Miller, Art Mag, 74; Painting & Sculpture Today, Speedway, 74; Gregory Battcock (auth), Super Realism, Dutton, 75. Style & Technique: Realist; with brush. Media: Oil. Dealer: Ramon O'Suna c/o Pyramid Gallery 2121 P St NW Washington DC 20037; Carlos Conde Galeria de las Americas Fortaleza 152 San Juan PR. Mailing Add: Kingstown Greathouse Brit Virgin Islands Tortola West Indies

MILLER, NANCY
SCULPTOR, GRAPHIC ARTIST
b Lancaster, Ohio, Mar 31, 27. Study: Bennett Col; Md Inst Col Art. Work: Small Sculpture, USA & Graphics USA, US Info Agency; Standard Oil of Chicago, Exxon Corp; Sears Bldg; Southeast Banking Corp; Crown Ctr; plus many others. Exhib: One-man shows, Environ Gallery, 70, 71, 73 & 75; Gilman Galleries, Chicago, 72; Peter M David Gallery, Minneapolis, 74, Hokin Gallery, Chicago, 74 & Palm Beach, 74, Columbus Gallery Fine Arts, 74 & Grafik Gallery, St Louis, 75. Awards: Gallery Prize, 67, Purchase Prize, Wittenberg Univ, 70 & Sculpture Award, 71, Columbus Gallery Fine Arts. Style & Technique: Layers of paper cut into geometric shapes and enclosed in Plexiglas. Dealer: Hokin Gallery 200 E Ontario St Chicago IL 60611. Mailing Add: 300 Scioto St Urbana OH 43078

MILLER, NANCY TOKAR
PAINTER, INSTRUCTOR
b Detroit, Mich, June 13, 41. Study: Chouinard Art Inst & Otis Art Inst, scholar, 56-59; Univ Calif, Los Angeles, AF, 64; Univ Ariz, MFA, 71. Work: Otis Elevator Co, Farmingdale, Conn; Western Savings & Loan Asn, Tucson, Ariz; Ariz State Univ Mem Union Collection, Tempe; Yuma Fine Arts Asn, Ariz. Comn: Poster, Ariz Civic Theater & Harlan Gallery, Tucson, 74; Maui Intercontinental Hotel, Hawaii, 75. Exhib: Southwestern Invitational, 71-78; Nat Small Sculpture & Drawing, San Diego State Col, Calif, 72; Four Corners States Biennial, Phoenix Art Mus, Ariz, 73, 75 & 77; one-woman shows, Mem Union Gallery Ariz State Univ, 73, Harlan Gallery, Tucson, 73 & 75; Yuma Fine Arts Asn (traveling exhib), Ariz Comn Arts & Humanities, 77-78 & Mathews Ctr, Ariz State Univ, 78; Univ Ariz Mus Art, Tucson, 77; two-person show, Harlan Gallery, 78. Teaching: Instr painting, drawing & design, Cambridge Ctr Adult Educ, Mass, 65-68; instr painting & design, Univ Ariz, 71-72; instr watercolor, Tucson Art Mus Sch, 72-78; vis artist, Ariz Western Col, 77. Awards: Purchase Award, Yuma Fine Arts Asn, 75; Fel, Western States Arts Found, 75-76; Juror's Cash Award, Four Corners States Biennial, Phoenix Art Mus, 77. Bibliog: Adina Wingate (auth), Nancy Tokar Miller, Art Week Mag, 2/75; Darryl Dobras (auth), Five local artists on their way to success, Desert Silhouette Mag, 10/75; Adina Wingate (auth), Arizona women artists, MS Mag, spring 78. Style & Technique: Large abstract paintings, acrylic wash on unprimed canvas; color-space foremost concerns, use of mixed media. Dealer: Comsky Gallery 9777 Wilshire Blvd Beverly Hills CA 90212; Elaine Horwitch Gallery 4200 N Marshall Way Scottsdale AZ 85251. Mailing Add: PO Box 49092 Tucson AZ 85717

MILLER, RICHARD KIDWELL
PAINTER
b Fairmont, WVa, Mar 15, 30. Study: Pa Acad Fine Arts; Am Univ, BA; Columbia Univ, MFA. Work: Phillips Collection, Washington, DC; Edward Joseph Gallagher, III Mem Collection, Univ Ariz, Tucson; Columbia Univ; Rochester Mus Art, NY; Albrecht Gallery, St Joseph, Mo. Comn: Painting, Plessey Corp, Gen Motors Bldg, New York, 71. Exhib: Pa Acad Fine Arts Ann, Philadelphia, 56-62; Salon Nat Paris, France, 58; Whitney Mus Am Art Ann, New York, 60; Carnegie Int, Pittsburgh, 62; Tokyo Int, Japan, 66; New Images, Martha Jackson Gallery, New York, NY, 74; Mainstream 74, Marietta Col, Ohio, 74; one-man shows, Baltimore Mus of Art, 52, Albrecht Gallery of Art, St Joseph, Mo, 69, Long Island Univ, 73 & numerous others. Teaching: Asst prof painting, Kansas City Art Inst, 68-69. Awards: Gertrude Vanderbilt Whitney Scholar, Nat Inst Arts & Lett, 48-56; Washington Times-Herald Scholar, 47; Fulbright Fel, 53. Style & Technique: Combine painted surface of canvas with recessed wood construction and collage. Media: Oil, Acrylic. Dealer: Peter Rose Gallery 320 W 52nd St New York NY 10019. Mailing Add: 222 W 83rd St Apt 8C New York NY 10024

MILLER, RICHARD MCDERMOTT
SCULPTOR
b New Philadelphia, Ohio, Apr 30, 22. Study: Cleveland Inst Art, 40-42, 49-51, grad, 51. Work: Sheldon Mem Art Gallery, Lincoln, Nebr; Univ Houston; Butler Inst Am Art, Youngstown, Ohio; Canton Art Inst, Ohio; Hirshhorn Mus, Washington, DC. Exhib: Four one-man shows, Peridot Gallery, New York, 64-69; one-man shows, Holland Gallery, Chicago, 65, Feingarten Gallery, Los Angeles, 66 & Alwin Gallery, London, 68; four one-man shows, Washburn Gallery, New York, 71-77. Teaching: Instr sculpture, Queens Col, 67- Awards: Page Scholar, Cleveland Inst Art, 52; Purchase Award, Butler Inst Am Art, 70; Gold Medal, Nat Acad Design, 74. Bibliog: Sidney Tillim (auth), Richard Miller, primary realist, Artforum, summer 67; Gabriel Laderman (auth), Unconventional realists, Artforum, 3/71; Grace Glueck (auth), A new realism in sculpture?, Art in Am, 12/71. Mem: Alliance of Figurative Artists; Sculptors Guild. Style & Technique: The human figure, observed from life, modeled in wax and cast in bronze. Publ: Auth, Figure Sculpture in Wax & Plaster, Watson-Guptill, 71. Dealer: Washburn Gallery 42 E 57th St New York NY 10022. Mailing Add: 53 Mercer St New York NY 10013

MILLER, ROBERT PETER
ART DEALER
b Atlantic City, NJ, Apr 17, 39. Study: Rutgers Col, BS & MFA. Pos: Exec vpres, Andre Emmerich Gallery, Inc, New York, NY, 75-77; pres, Robert Miller Gallery, Inc, New York, NY, 77- Mailing Add: Robert Miller Gallery Inc 724 Fifth Ave New York NY 10019

MILLER, MRS ROBERT WATT
PATRON
b Oakland, Calif, July 20, 98. Pos: Chmn, Van Gogh Show; chmn, Faberge Show; chmn, San Francisco Opera Guild, 50-52; chmn, Ital Festival, San Francisco, 59; chmn, De Young Mem Mus Soc, 61-63; co-chmn, Golden Anniversary, United Bay Area Crusade; mem bd trustees, United Bay Area Crusade; hon chmn, Golden Anniversary, San Francisco Opera Asn. Awards: Ital Cross Solidarity, San Francisco, 59. Interest: Presentation of shows in museums. Mailing Add: 1021 California St San Francisco CA 94108

MILLER, SAMUEL CLIFFORD
MUSEUM DIRECTOR
b Roseburg, Ore, May 6, 30. Study: Stanford Univ, BA; Inst Fine Arts, NY Univ, grad study; Seton Hall Univ, DFA(hon), 76; also in Japan, Europe & Mex. Pos: Asst to dir, Albright-Knox Art Gallery, Buffalo, NY, 64-67; asst dir, Newark Mus Asn, 67, mus dir, 68- Mem: Am Asn Mus; Northeast Mus Conf (mem bd gov); James Streed Adv Bd, Newark; Port Authority Comt on Art; Newark Preservation & Landmarks Comt; Mus Coun NJ; Am Fedn Arts; Asn Art Mus Dirs; plus others. Mailing Add: Newark Mus Asn 49 Washington St Newark NJ 07101

MILLER, VEL
PAINTER, SCULPTOR
b Nekoosa, Wis, Jan 22, 36. Study: Valley Col, Los Angeles; Art League of Los Angeles, with Hal Reed & Max Turner. Work: Glendale Col, Ariz; Home Savings & Loan Permanent Collection, Los Angeles; La Galeria, Sedona, Ariz; Barry Goldwater Collection, Scottsdale, Ariz; Lean'in Tree Mus, Boulder, Colo; plus others. Comn: Paintings & Drawings, Ira Roberts, Inc, Los Angeles, 70-75 & Lean'in Tree Publ Co, Boulder, Colo, 71-75. Exhib: Ann Cowboy Roundup, Saddleback Inn, Santa Ana, Calif, 71-75; Nebraskaland Invitational, North Platte, Nebr, 73-75; The Best of Ten Years, Home Savings & Loan All Calif Show, Long Beach, 73; one-woman show, Peterson Gallery, Beverly Hills, Calif, 74 & La Galeria, Sedona, Ariz, 74; plus others. Teaching: Instr oil painting, Grace Harvey Art Sch, Reseda, Calif, 63-71 & Art League of Los Angeles, 71-74; lectr art & selling, Long Beach State Col, 75. Pos: Demonstr, Art Clubs throughout Calif; judge, Woman's Western Artists, 75, plus many other Southern Calif shows. Awards: Best of Show (drawing), San Fernando Valley Art Club, 73; Gold Medal (sculpture), Calif Art Club, 74; Bronze Medal (watercolor), George Phippen Mem, Prescott, Ariz, 75. Mem: Calif Art Club; San Gabriel Fine Arts Asn; San Fernando Valley Art Asn. Style & Technique: Paintings, drawings, watercolors and bronze sculptures; realistic style Western in theme but through the eyes of a woman. Media: Oil, Watercolor; Bronze. Mailing Add: PO Box 1031 Paso Robles CA 93446

MILLIKEN, ALEXANDER FABBRI
ART DEALER, COLLECTOR
b Boston, Mass, Feb 14, 47. Pos: Owner, Alexander F Milliken Inc, 76- Mem: Solomon Guggenheim Mus; Mus Mod Art, New York; Metrop Mus Art, New York; Whitney Mus Am Art, New York; Skowhegan Sch Painting & Sculpture (mem jr comt). Specialty: Contemporary abstract painting & sculpture. Collection: Jackson Pollock, Alberto Giacometti, Robert Rauschenburg, Anthony Caro, Herbert Ferber, Joseph Cornell, Ed Ruscha & Morris Graves. Mailing Add: 141 Prince St New York NY 10012

MILLIKEN, GIBBS
PAINTER, EDUCATOR
b Houston, Tex, Dec 15, 35. Study: Scheiner Inst; Univ Colo; Trinity Univ, BSc; Cranbrook Acad Art, MFA. Work: Cranbrook Acad Art; Montgomery Mus Fine Arts, Ala; Serv League, Longview, Tex; Butler Inst Am Art. Exhib: Trinity Univ, 60, 61 & 68; San Antonio Artists, Witte Mus, 60-68; Tex Ann Painters & Sculptors, Witte Mus, Corpus Christi, Beaumont Mus & Dallas Mus Fine Arts, 62-66; Bucknell Univ, 67; Tex Fine Arts Comn, Hemisfair, San Antonio, 68; plus many others. Teaching: Instr painting & drawing, Cranbrook Acad Art, Bloomfield Hills, Mich, 64 & 65; instr art, Univ Tex, Austin, 65-69, asst prof, 69-73, assoc prof, 74- Pos: Asst, Univ Colo Mus; former artist, photographer, asst cur, cur & head dept exhibs, Witte Mem Mus, San Antonio. Awards: Grumbacher Award, Tex Watercolor Soc, Witte Mem Mus, 64, Naylor Award, 66 & Freeman Purchase Prize, 67; plus many others. Mem: Am Fedn Arts; Am Asn Univ Prof; Men of Art Guild; Contemp Artists Group. Mailing Add: Dept of Art Univ of Tex Austin TX 78712

MILLONZI, VICTOR
SCULPTOR
b Buffalo, NY. Study: Albright Art Sch, BA; Univ Buffalo, BA(art educ); Columbia Univ, MA. Work: Nat Collection Fine Arts, Washington, DC; Corcoran Gallery Art, Washington, DC; Albright-Knox Art Gallery, Buffalo; State Mus NJ, Trenton; Mus Mod Art, New York. Comn: Mural, Nat Broadcasting Co, Rockefeller Ctr, New York, 70. Exhib: Art in Process, Finch Col Mus, New York, 66; Stedelijk Van Abbemuseum, Eindhoven, Holland, 66; Light, Motion, Space, Walker Art Ctr, Minneapolis, 67; Sculpture: The New York Scene, Riverside Mus, New York, 68; Focus on Light, NJ State Mus, 69. Bibliog: Light art, Art in Am, 67. Media: Neon. Mailing Add: 127 W 87th St New York NY 10024

MILLS, AGNES
SCULPTOR, PRINTMAKER
b New York, NY. Study: Cooper Union Art Sch, grad; Pratt Inst, BFA; NY Univ Sch Archit; Art Students League; Design Lab; Am Artists Sch; and with Raphael Soyer, Yasua Kunyoshi & Ruth Leaf. Work: Hunterdon Co Mus, Clinton, NJ; Univ Maine, Amhurst; Washington Soc Painters, Sculptors & Printmakers; Calif Sch Arts & Crafts, Oakland; C W Post Col. Exhib: Audubon Ann, Nat Acad Design, 70 & 71; Butler Inst Am Art Ann, 71-72; Pa Acad Art Ann, 73; Okla Art Mus Ann Printmaking Exhib, 73 & 74; Seattle Art Mus Ann, 74. Teaching: Art coordr & art instr, NShore Community Art Ctr, Great Neck, NY, 57-75. Awards: First Prize in Printmaking, Washington Miniature Prints & Sculpture, 70; Purchase Prize, Hunterdon Co Art Mus, 72; Purchase Award, Nassau Community Col, 74. Mem: Print Club, Philadelphia; Nat Asn Women Artists; Artists Equity; Women in the Arts; Exp in Art & Technol. Style & Technique: Figure in motion; figure as landscape; dance; anthropomorphic form in two and three dimensions. Media: Etching in color, Colograph; Acrylics, Welded Steel. Dealer: Bermond Art Ltd 3000 Marcus Ave Lake Success NY 11021. Mailing Add: 323 Melbourne Rd Great Neck NY 11021

MILLS, FREDERICK VAN FLEET
ART ADMINISTRATOR, EDUCATOR
b Bremen Fairfield, Ohio, June 5, 25. Study: Ohio State Univ, BS, 49; Ind Univ, MS, 51, EdD, 56. Teaching: Prof art & art educ & chmn dept art educ, Ind Univ, Bloomington, 59-66; chmn dept related arts, crafts & interior design, Univ Tenn, Knoxville, 66-68; prof art & chmn dept, Ill State Univ, 68-; vis prof art, Univ Tex. Pos: Pres, Ind Art Educ Asn, 56; ed, Western Arts Bull, 58-62. Mem: Nat Art Educ Asn (bd dirs, 63-64); Col Art Asn Am; Western Arts Asn (pres, 62-64); Ill Art Educ Asn; Nat Coun Art Admin (bd dirs, 73-, ed res & info bull, 74-). Publ: Contribr, Sch Arts Mag, 59, 60, 69 & 70; contribr, Civil Defense, Off President US, 60; contribr, Arts & Activities Mag, 61, 66, 68 & 69; educ co-auth, As an Artist Sees, Ind Univ AV Ctr, 65; ed, Nat Coun Art Admin Report, 75, The Status of the Visual Arts in Higher Education, 76 & New Perspectives of Visual Arts Administration, 77, Nat Coun Art Admin. Mailing Add: Dept of Art Ill State Univ Normal-Bloomington IL 61761

MILLS, JAMES
ART CRITIC, COLLECTOR
b Chaseburg, Wis, Jan 17, 24. Study: Univ Wis, BS; Fordham Univ, MFA; Cent Sch Speech & Drama, London, Eng. Pos: Art ed, The Denver Post, Inc, 55- Mem: Greater Denver Coun Arts & Humanities (treas, 73-76); Larry Tajiri Mem Found (treas, 71-); Denver Art Mus. Collection: Twentieth century American and European paintings, sculpture and graphics; pre-Columbian ceramics; 18th-20th century Japanese prints. Mailing Add: The Denver Post Inc 650 15th St Denver CO 80202

MILLS, LEV TIMOTHY
PRINTMAKER, SCULPTOR
b Wakulla Co, Fla, Dec 11, 40. Study: Fla A&M Univ, BA(art educ); Univ Wis, Madison, MA & MFA; Slade Sch Fine Art, Univ London, Eng; Atelier 17, Paris, France, with Stanley W Hayter. Work: Victoria & Albert Mus, London; Brit Mus, London; Libr of Cong, Washington, DC; Bibliot Nat, Paris; Mus Mod Art, New York. Comn: Three glass mosaic designs, Ashby St Subway Sta, City of Atlanta, Metrop Atlanta Rapid Transit Authority, 78. Exhib: NC Nat Print Show, Ackland Mus, Chapel Hill, 70; Slade Centenary Exhib, Royal Col Art, London, Eng, 71; New Acquisitions, Victoria & Albert Mus, 72 & Bibliot Nat, Paris, 73; Artists in Ga, High Mus Art, Atlanta, Ga, 74; 20th Century Black Artist, San Jose Mus Art, Calif, 76; Retrospective, Studio Mus in Harlem, New York, 75; plus many one-man shows, 68-78. Collections Arranged: Black Artists Atlanta, 75; Contemporary Prints, Int Graphic Arts Soc Inc, 76; National Black Artists Fiber Exhib, 78. Teaching: Instr gen art, Everglades Jr High, Ft Lauderdale, Fla, 62-68; asst prof printmaking, Clark Col, Atlanta, 73- Pos: Mem bd trustees, Art Festival of Atlanta Inc, 77- Awards: Outstanding Postgrad Fel, Univ Wis, 69; Europ Study & Travel Fel, Ford Found, 70; Bronze Jubilee Award for Cult Achievement, City of Atlanta, 78. Bibliog: Pat Gilmour (auth), Lev Mills, Arts Rev, London, 72; Lewis & Waddy (auth), Black artists on art, Contemp Crafts Inc, Calif, 76; Samella Lewis (auth), Graphic Processes, Art: African American, Harcourt, Brace & Jovanovich Inc, New York, 78. Mem: Nat Col Art Asn; Black Artists Atlanta. Style & Technique: Combination of contemporary and traditional printmaking techniques coupled with a strong sense of humanism. Media: Printmaking, Sculpture. Publ: Contribr, Fla Art Mag, 68; auth, I Do, A Book of Etchings & Poems, Cut Chain Press, 71. Dealer: Assoc Am Artists 663 Fifth Ave New York NY 10022. Mailing Add: 3378 Ardley Rd SW Atlanta GA 30311

MILLS, MARGARET
ART ADMINISTRATOR
Pos: Exec dir, Am Acad & Inst of Arts & Lett, currently. Mailing Add: c/o Am Acad & Inst of Arts & Lett 633 W 155th St New York NY 10032

MILLS, PAUL CHADBOURNE
MUSEUM DIRECTOR
b Seattle, Wash, Sept 24, 24. Study: Reed Col, 45-48; Univ Wash, BA, 53; Univ Calif, Berkeley, MA, 61; Calif Col Arts & Crafts, Hon PhD, 71. Pos: Reporter, Bellevue Am, Wash, 48-51; asst cur, Henry Gallery, Univ Wash, 52-53; cur art, Oakland Mus, Calif, 53-70; vpres, Western Mus Conf, 56 & 59; dir, Santa Barbara Mus Art, 70-; dir, New Glory Bicentennial Flag Hist & Design Proj, 74-77. Awards: Ford Found Fel, 60-61. Mem: Western Asn Art Mus (vpres, 56-57, treas, 71-72); NAm Vexillological Asn; Heraldry Soc; Am Asn Mus (prog chmn); Am Asn Art Mus Dirs (trustee, 71-72, secy, 73-). Publ: Auth, Early Paintings of California, 56; auth, An Introduction to the Art of William Keith, 56; auth, Contemporary Bay Area Figurative Paintings, 58; co-auth, The California Missions of Edwin Deakin, 66; auth, Colonial and Revolutionary Era Flags. Mailing Add: 1042 Las Alturas Rd Santa Barbara CA 93103

MILLSAPS, DANIEL
See Nuki

MILONADIS, KONSTANTIN
SCULPTOR
b Ukraine, 1926; US citizen. Study: Art Inst Chicago, BAE, 57; Tulane Univ, MFA, 59. Work: Art Gallery, Ball State Univ; Grand Rapids Art Mus; Art Gallery, Western Ill Univ; Art Gallery, Univ Notre Dame; Swope Art Gallery. Exhib: Six shows, Chicago & Vicinity & three shows, Soc Contemp Am Art, Art Inst Chicago, 58-73; New Horizons Sculpture, Chicago, seven shows, 61-72; Nat Drawing & Sculpture, Ball State Univ, seven shows, 63-72; Indianapolis Art Mus Biennial, six shows, 63-74; Detroit Art Inst, 71. Teaching: Distinguished prof & artist in residence, Univ Notre Dame, 61-74, Valparaiso Univ, 72 & South Bend Art Ctr, 74- Awards: Palmer Award, Art Inst Chicago, 63 & Linde Award, 64; Mus Alliance Award, Indianapolis Art Mus, 63 & Goodman Award, 64; Magnavox Award, 69, Art League Award, 69 & Cash Award, 73, Ft Wayne Art Mus. Bibliog: Meilach & Seiden (co-auth), Direct Metal Sculpture, Crown, 66; article in Art J, 63 & 68; E B Feldman (auth), Varieties of Visual Experience, Abrams. Style & Technique: Kinetic sculpture; conceptual. Media: Metal. Mailing Add: 3390 Chicago Rd Niles MI 49120

MILRAD, AARON M
COLLECTOR, ART LAWYER
b Toronto, Ont, Can, May 17, 35. Study: Univ Toronto, BA & LLB; Law Soc Upper Can, grad lawyer. Teaching: Vis prof art & the law, York Univ, Toronto, Ont, 72-; instr art & the law, Banff Centre Sch Fine Arts, Alta, Can, 73-75; vis prof art & the law, Concordia Univ, Montreal, 76. Pos: Admin vpres, Prof Art Dealers Can, 72-; alternate trustee, Art Gallery Ont, 76- Awards: Can Coun Grant, Exploration Prog for bk on Can Art Law. Collection: Modern American and Canadian, 1945 to the present, primarily in the color field area, Noland, Olitski, Motherwell and others. Publ: Auth, The New Cultural Property Export and Import Act of Canada, 75 & Gifts to Museums, 75, Gazette. Mailing Add: 65 Queen St West Suite 1800 Toronto ON M5H 2M5 Can

MILTON, PETER WINSLOW
PRINTMAKER
b Lower Merion, Pa, Apr 2, 30. Study: Yale Univ, BFA, 54, MFA, 62, with Josef Albers. Work: Mus Mod Art & Metrop Mus, New York; Philadelphia Mus Art; Libr of Cong, Washington, DC; Bibliot Nat, Paris. Exhib: Primera Bienal Americana de Artes Graficas, 71 & one-man show, 72, Mus La Tertulia, Cali, Colombia; one-man show, Corcoran Gallery Art, Washington, DC, 72; Extraordinary Realities, Whitney Mus Am Art, 73; Norsk Internasjonal Grafikk Biennale, Gamlegyen, Norway, 74; 4th Int Exhib Original Drawings, Mus Mod Art, Rijeka, Yugoslavia, 74; plus many other one-man shows. Teaching: Instr drawing & basic design, Md Inst Col Art, Baltimore, 61-68; instr printmaking, Yale Univ Summer Sch Music & Art, 70. Awards: Louis Comfort Tiffany Found Grant in Graphics, 64; First Prize in Graphics, 9th Columbian Festival de Arte, Mus La Tertula, 69; Grand Prize, Int Biennial Exhib Prints, Seoul, Korea, 72. Bibliog: Irving Finkelstein (auth), Julia passing: the world of Peter Milton, Artist's Proof, 72; Harriet Shapiro (auth), All realism is visionary: a reach into the ambiguous realm of Peter Milton, Intellectual Digest, 11/72; Piri Halasz (auth), The metaphysical games of Peter Milton, Art News, 12/74. Style & Technique: Tend towards narrative fantasy. Media: Etching, Photo-Etching & Engraving. Dealer: Franz Bader Gallery 2124 Pennsylvania Ave NW Washington DC 20037; Impressions Workshop 27 Stanhope St Boston MA 02116. Mailing Add: PO Box 137 Francestown NH 03043

MINA-MORA, DORISE OLSON
PAINTER
b New York, NY, June 8, 32. Study: Art Students League, with Hale & Louis Bosa; Salmagundi Club scholar & study with Daniel Greene. Work: Southampton High Sch; William Cook Shipping Co & R Chapdelaine & Co, New York. Exhib: Brooklyn Mus Community Galleries, 68-71; Nat Arts Club Watercolor Ann; Catharine Lorillard Wolfe Art Club Exhib & Allied Artists Am, Nat Acad Design; Parrish Art Mus Spring Watercolor Show, 72; Winners Circle, Brooklyn Mus, 75; Metrop Mus Art (with Burr Artists), 77; Goldsboro Art Mus, NC, 77; one-woman & joint shows with husband, Caravan House Gallery, New York, Different Drummer Gallery, Conn, Wickford Art Gallery, RI & Stony Brook Univ; plus others. Awards: Gold Medal of Honor, Knickerbocker Artists, 68 & Nat Art League, 70; Grumbacher Award for Watercolor, Nat Arts Club, 70; Windsor & Newton Watercolor Award, Catharine Lorillard Wolfe Art Club, 72. Mem: Nat Soc Painters Casein & Acrylic; Allied Artists Am; Catharine Lorillard Wolfe Art Club; Nat Arts Club; Soc Women Artists; Am Artists Prof League; Audubon Artists. Style & Technique: Realistic but impressionistic with nature as a theme. Media: Watercolor, Acrylic. Mailing Add: 87 Central Blvd Oakdale Long Island NY 11769

MINA-MORA, RAUL JOSE
PAINTER, ILLUSTRATOR
b Santa Anna, El Salvador, Mar 13, 14; US citizen. Study: San Francisco Acad Advan Arts; Art Students League, with Howard Traffton; also with Daniel Gree, Harte, Austria. Work: South Hampton High Sch, NY; Freid Corp. Exhib: Nat Arts Club; Nat Soc Casein Painters; Salmagundi Club; Parrish Art Mus, NY; Nat Acad Design; Metrop Mus, New York, 77; Brooklyn Mus, NY; Goldsboro Mus, NC, 77. Teaching: Archit design & visual archit, Rudolph Shapher Sch Design; instr design, San Francisco Sch Design. Awards: Best of Show, Am Artist Prof League Grand Nat & Washington Square Art Show, 75; Silver Medal, Audubon Artist, 75. Mem: Salmagundi Art Club; Am Artist Prof League; Nat Soc Casein & Acrylic Painters; Allied Artists Am; Audubon Artists. Style & Technique: Contemporary. Media: Watercolor, Oil. Publ: Illusr, Fortune Mag, Rutledge, Macmillan, Cronwell-Colliers & Holt. Mailing Add: 87 Central Blvd Oakdale Long Island NY 11769

MINER, RALPH HAMLIN
ART DEALER, DESIGNER
b Los Angeles, Calif. Study: Univ Calif, Los Angeles. Teaching: Lectures on planning, mgt & design at state col & univ, 53- Pos: Pres & owner, Miner's Gallery Americana, Inc, 69-; owner, RHM Assoc, 65- Specialty: Contemporary art by fifty artists. Mailing Add: PO Box 6146 Carmel CA 93921

MINEWSKI, ALEX
PAINTER, EDUCATOR
b Detroit, Mich, Dec 13, 17. Study: Soc Arts & Crafts, Detroit; Art Students League, with Jean Charlot, George Grosz & Vaclav Vytlacil; Colorado Springs Acad Art, with Boardman Robinson; Acad Grande Chaumiere, Paris; also with Hans Hofmann. Exhib: Pa Acad Show; Nat Acad Show; Butler Inst Art; Artists of Monhegan, Maine; Vaclav Vytlacil & Selected Former Students Exhib, Montclair Art Mus, 75; Four-Artist Exhib, Schenectady Mus, 76; plus several one-man shows. Teaching: Prof drawing & painting, State Univ NY Col New Paltz, 66- Awards: Tiffany Fel, State Univ NY, 72 & 73. Mem: st Conserv Hist & Artistic Works. Media: Oil, Casein. Mailing Add: 15 Prospect St New Paltz NY 12561

MINISCI, BRENDA (EILEEN)
SCULPTOR, CERAMIST
b Gowanda, NY, June 15, 39. Study: RI Sch Design, Rome, Italy, 60-61, Providence, BFA, 61; Cranbrook Acad of Art, Bloomfield Hills, Mich, MFA, 64; Provincetown Fine Arts Workshop, with Harry Hollander. Work: Everson Mus, Syracuse, NY; Fitchburg Art Mus, Mass; Univ Mass, Amherst; Antonio Prieto Mem Collection, Mills Col, Oakland, Calif; N Adams State Col, Mass. Comn: Fiberglass fountain sculpture, Murray D Lincoln Campus & clear cast polyester resin sculpture (6ft, 350lb), Hampden Dining Commons, Univ Mass, Amherst; ceramic relief panels, Burnside Bldg, Worcester, Mass, 62; welded steel sculpture (6ft tall), Mercantile Trust Co, St Louis, Mo, 65-66; ceramic relief (7ft x 16ft), comn by the Smiths, Conway, Mass, (in progress). Exhib: Young Americans (traveling exhib), Mus Contemp Crafts, New York, 62 & 69; Wit & Whimsey in Am Art, Cranbrook Art Mus, Bloomfield Hills, 63; Craftsmen of the East (traveling exhib), Mus Contemp Crafts, New York

& Smithsonian Inst, Washington, DC, 64-65; Nat Ceramic Exhib, Everson Mus, Syracuse, 64 & 68; G W V Smith Mus Nat Exhib, Springfield, Mass, 70-72; Seven Sculptors, Boston City Hall Galleries, Mass, 74. Teaching: Instr ceramics, Craft Ctr, Worcester, 61-62; instr ceramics & sculpture, Univ Mass, Amherst, 67-71; instr ceramics & sculpture, Williston-Northampton Sch, Easthampton, Mass, 71-; instr ceramics & sculpture, Summer Grad Sch, Wesleyan Univ, Conn, 75. Awards: First Prize for Bronze Sculpture, 52nd Nat Exhib, G W V Smith Mus & Springfield Art League, 71; Juror's Award for Sculpture, Providence RI Art Club, 71; Purchase Prize for Sculpture, 22nd Exhib Painting & Sculpture, Berkshire Mus, N Adams Col, 73. Mem: Am Crafts Coun, NE Assembly (Mass state rep, 72-74; treas, 73-75); Mass Asn for the Crafts (mem nominating comt, 75-77). Style & Technique: Sculpture and fountain sculpture in stoneware, cast and laminated polyester resin/fiberglass and bronze. Dealer: Baracca Gallery 197 Pantry Rd North Hatfield MA 01066. Mailing Add: Box 85 North Hatfield MA 01066

MINNICK, ESTHER TRESS
PAINTER
b Chicago, Ill. Study: Art Students League; also with Edgar Whitney, Wong Suiling & Barbara Vassilioff. Work: Va State Col; Mem Hosp, New York; also in many pvt collections. Exhib: Nat Women's Republican Club, New York, 67; Nat Soc Painters Casein & Travel Exhib, New York, 68; Garden State Watercolor Soc, Princeton, NJ, 70; Princeton Art Asn, 71; two one-man exhibs, 74; plus others. Awards: First Award, Larchmont, 60; First & Third Prizes, Nat Women's Republican Club, 67; Princeton Bank Award, 70. Mem: Knickerbocker Artists; Catharine Lorillard Wolfe Art Club. Style & Technique: Wet and dry method. Media: Watercolor. Mailing Add: 95 Gloucester Way Jamesburg NJ 08831

MINO, YUKATA
ART HISTORIAN, CURATOR
b Kanagawa City, Japan, Oct 23, 41. Study: Keio Univ, Tokyo, Japan, BA(art hist), 65; Harvard Univ, PhD(art hist), 77. Pos: Cur asst, Royal Ont Mus, Toronto, Ont, 69-71; assoc cur, Montreal Mus Fine Arts, Que, 76-77; cur Oriental art dept, Indianapolis Mus Art, Ind, 77- Mem: Oriental Ceramic Soc, London & Hong Kong; SE Asian Ceramic Soc, Singapore; China House Gallery (mem art comt). Res: Development of Tz'u-chou type wares, important group of northern Chinese ceramics. Publ: Auth, Ceramics in the Liao Dynasty, China House Gallery, New York, 73; co-auth, An Index to the Chinese Ceramic Kiln Sites From the Six Dynasties to the Present, 73 & auth, Chinese Stoneware in the Royal Ontario Museum, Pre-Sung Dynasty, 74, Royal Ont Mus; auth, Kogo: Japanese Incense Boxes Rediscovered, Montreal Mus, 77. Mailing Add: 4200 N Michigan Rd Indianapolis IN 46208

MINTICH, MARY RINGELBERG
SCULPTOR, CRAFTSMAN
b Detroit, Mich. Study: Albion Col; Ind Univ, BA; Queens Col; Univ Tenn; Univ NC, Greensboro, MFA. Work: Everson Mus Art, Syracuse, NY; Mint Mus Art & NC Nat Bank, Charlotte; Raddisson Plaza, Charlotte, NC; R J Reynolds World Hq, Winston-Salem, NC; Sea Islands Develop Corp, Ga. Exhib: Piedmont Regional Painting, Sculpture & Craft Exhibs, Mint Mus Art; GCA Regional Painting & Sculpture Competition, Winston-Salem, NC, 73 & 75; Southeast Regional, Greenville Mus, SC, 74; Mint Mus Art 501 Garden Gallery, Charlotte, 75; Southeastern Ctr Contemp Art, Winston-Salem, 75, Invitational, 77 & one-artist exhib, 77; Springs Mill traveling exhib, 76; NC Artists Exhib, NC Mus of Art, 76. Teaching: Sacred Heart Col, 67-73; Penland Sch Crafts, 72; assoc prof sculpture, design & metals, Winthrop Col, 72- Awards: Purchase Awards, Ceramics Nat & 8th Regional Piedmont Crafts Exhib; Hon Mention, Springs Mill traveling exhib, 76. Mem: Piedmont Craftsmen (mem bd trustees); Am Crafts Coun; Southern Asn Sculptors; Artist's Adv Comt, Mint Mus. Style & Technique: Large scale acrylic, enameled and metal assembled sculptures, contrasting organic forms with the hard visual properties of the materials. Media: Metals, Plastics, Clay. Publ: Illusr, Red Clay Reader 6; illusr, Art Works for Urban Development, 73. Dealer: Gallery 501 501 Hempstead Pl Charlotte NC 28207. Mailing Add: PO Box 913 Belmont NC 28012

MINTZ, HARRY
PAINTER
b Sept 27, 09; US citizen. Work: Art Inst Chicago; New Evansville Mus, Ind; Whitney Mus Am Art, New York; Tel Aviv Mod Mus Art, Israel; Rio de Janeiro Mus Art, Brazil; plus others. Exhib: Art Inst Chicago, 34-63; Whitney Mus Am Art, New York; Venice Biennale, Italy; Denver Art Mus, 63; Corcoran Gallery Art, Washington, DC; plus many others. Teaching: Assoc prof, Art Inst Chicago. Awards: Hon Mentions, Art Inst Chicago, 38 & 53, Jules F Brower Prize, 52 & 54 & Silver's Prize, 62. Media: Oil. Mailing Add: 429 W Briar Pl Chicago IL 60657

MINUTILLO, RICHARD G
CURATOR, ART HISTORIAN
b Beverly, Mass. Study: Amherst Col, BA(art hist); Univ Calif Santa Barbara, MA(art hist). Collections Arranged: Artful Toil: Artistic Innovation in an Age of Enterprise, 77 & Brockton Photographed, 77 & Boston 78: invitational painting & sculpture, 78, Brockton Art Ctr, Mass. Teaching: Instr, Niagara Co Community Col, New York, 70-72; prof, The Western Col, Oxford, Ohio, 72-74. Pos: Cur, Brockton Art Ctr, Mass, 77- Mem: Col Art Asn Am; Am Asn Mus. Res: Contemporary art and the situation of the contemporary artist. Mailing Add: 159 Ames St Brockton MA 02402

MION, PIERRE RICCARDO
ILLUSTRATOR, PAINTER
b Bryn Mawr, Pa, Dec 10, 31. Study: George Washington Univ; Corcoran Gallery Sch of Art, With Elliot O'Hara; also privately with Norman Rockewell. Comn: Solar System Evolution (mural), Smithsonian Inst, Washington, DC; team portrait of Apollo astronauts, Nat Geographic Soc; paintings of space futures, Look Mag, 69; cover painting, Reader's Digest, Pleasantville, NY, 68; Bicentennial Flag, Nat Park Serv, Washington, DC, 76. Exhib: Nat Ann Watercolor Exhib, Smithsonian Inst, 51 & 63; Robots to the Moon, Hayden Planetarium, New York, 63; Artist & Space, Nat Gallery of Art, Washington, DC, 69; Space Art, Smithsonian Inst Air & Space Mus, 71 & Hudson River Mus, Yonkers, NY, 72; one-man shows, Acad of the Arts, Easton, Md, 72 & Metropolis Bldg Asn, Washington, DC, 76. Teaching: Instr illus, Marine Corps Inst, Washington, DC, 53-54. Pos: Art dir illus, Creative Arts Studio, Washington, DC, 57-60; vpres art-design, Northern Sci Indust Exhibs, 64-66. Awards: Third Prize, Outdoor Art Fair, Times Herald, 47; Second Prize/Drawing, Corcoran Art Sch, 56. Bibliog: Pierre Mion presents one-man show, Baltimore Sun, 72; Ev Gardner (auth), article in Washington Daily News, 72; Mary Runde (auth), Intensity brings detail to Mion's paintings, Star-Democrat, 72. Mem: Soc Illustr. Style & Technique: (Illustration) Space, oceanography, transportation, history & science; (Painting) realistic, landscapes. Media: Acrylic and gouache; acrylic and watercolor. Publ: Illusr, Night driving, Popular Sci, 67; illusr, The death of a president Part III, Look Mag, 67; illusr, The squalus is down, Reader's Digest, 68; illusr, All-girl team tests the habitat, 71 & First Colony in space, 76, Nat Geographic. Mailing Add: 6008 Cairn Terr Bethesda MD 20034

MIOTKE, ANNE E
PAINTER, INSTRUCTOR
b Milwaukee, Wis, Aug 31, 43. Study: Mount Mary Col, Milwaukee, with S Remy Revor, BA, 65; Univ Wis-Milwaukee, with Laurence Rathsack, MS, 70 & MFA, 73. Work: Univ Wis-Madison & Milwaukee; Cincinnati Art Mus; Wehr Corp & Joseph P Jansen Co, Milwaukee; Liberty Nat Bank, Louisville, Ky; plus others. Exhib: Wisconsin Painters & Sculptors Exhib, Milwaukee Art Ctr, 72-74; Of/On Paper, John Michael Kohler Arts Ctr, Sheboygan, Wis, 73; 10th Union League Art Biennial, Chicago, 74; 8-State Ann: Painting, J B Speed Art Mus, Louisville, 74; 31st Ann Wabash Valley Exhib, Swope Art Gallery, Terre Haute, Ind, 75; Cincinnati Invitational Exhib of Photographs & Watercolors, Cincinnati Art Mus, 77; Drawing & Prints 77, Miami Univ, Oxford, Ohio, 77; Watercolor USA, Springfield Art Mus, 77; Closson Gallery, 78; plus others. Teaching: Instr art, Mount Mary Col, Milwaukee, 70-72; Layton Sch Art & Design, Milwaukee, 73-74; Art Acad Cincinnati, 74- Pos: Bd mem, Milwaukee Area Teachers of Art, 67-70; contrib ed, Midwest Art, 75-77. Awards: Summer Fel, Grad Sch, Univ Wis-Milwaukee, 72; Nat Endowment Arts Vis Specialist Grant to Milwaukee Art Ctr, 75. Mem: Col Art Asn Am; Am Asn Univ Prof; Milwaukee Art Ctr; Cincinnati Art Mus; Wis Watercolor Soc. Style & Technique: Highly explorative work in mixed media paintings and drawings often incorporating silkscreen techniques, some including reverse painting on glass; imagery: mechanistic forms from 1969 to 1975; since 1975, watercolor and drawing, imagery nature. Res: Historic survey of reverse painting on glass. Publ: Contribr, Second Cincinnati invitational of painting and sculpture, 75, Johnnie Johnson..., 75 & Change of pace: contemporary furniture, 75, Midwest Art. Dealer: Bradley Galleries 2565 N Downer Ave Milwaukee WI 53211. Mailing Add: 5639 Macey Ave-N-C Cincinnati OH 45227

MIRABAL, MIGUEL ENRIQUE
CERAMIST, EDUCATOR
b Roy, NMex, Oct 3, 46. Study: NMex Highlands Univ, BA, 70 & MA, 71; also with Paul Volckening. Work: Folk Art Mus, Santa Fe, NMex; Univ Albuquerque. Comn: Dinner set, comn by Mr & Mrs Emilio Randall, Espanola, NMex, 71; tea set, comn by Mr Rudolfo Gallegos, Las Vegas, NMex, 72; giant chess set, comn by Mr James Mirabal, Austin, Tex, 72; garden set, comn by John Whitesides, Albuquerque, 73; altar pieces, Immaculate Conception Church, Las Vegas, 74. Exhib: 2nd Biennial Five State Art Exhib, Port Arthur, Tex, 73; Int Pottery Design Competition, Nagoya, Japan, 73-74; New Mexico 74, Univ Albuquerque, 74; Contemporary Crafts Americas-74, Colo State Univ, 74; Exposicion de Arte Chicano, NMex Univ, 74. Teaching: Instr ceramics & weaving, NMex Highlands Univ, 72- Pos: Guest artist, Montes y Valles Art Sch, 74. Awards: Purchase Award, New Mexico, 73; Honorable Mention, Japan Pottery Design Ctr, 74. Bibliog: New Mexico 74, Univ Albuquerque, 74; Douglas Grim (auth), Contemporary American Ceramics, pvt publ, 74. Mem: Nat Coun Educ Ceramic Arts; Am Crafts Coun; Potters Coop NMex; Nat Chicano Artists Asn; Nat Potters Guild. Style & Technique: Thrown and hand-built stoneware with incised decoration and slip glazes. Media: Native Clay Bodies. Publ: Contribr, Ceramic Art, 73, International Pottery Design Competition 1973, Craftsmans Gallery Mag, 73 & Ceramics Monthly, 74. Mailing Add: Rte 1 Box 1540 Las Vegas NM 87701

MIRALDA, ANTONI
SCULPTOR
b Barcelona, Spain, Oct 2, 42. Study: Sch Textile Engineers, Tarrasa, 56-61; Cours de Methode Comparee des Arts Plastiques; Ctr Int d'Etudes Pedagogiques, Sovres, France, 62-64. Work: Moderna Museet, Stockholm; Ctr Nat Art Cult, Paris; Musee Cantini, Marseilles, France; Art Gallery of New South Wales, Australia. Exhib: 4th Paris Bienniale, 65, 6th, 69; Juene Peinture, Musee d'Art Moderne, Paris, 66; Salons Grands et Juenes d'Aujourd'hui, Musee d'Art Moderne, 68; Les Assises du Siege Contemp, Musee des Arts Decoratifs, Paris, 68; Salon de Mai, Musee d'Art Moderne, 69; Contemp Art Festival, City Mus, Yokohama, 70; A Table, Mus des Arts Decoritifs, 70; Collection de Mme Boulois, Ctr Nat d'Art Contemp, Paris, 71; Prospective 74, Museau de Arte Contemp, Sao Paulo, 74; 11th New York Avante Garde Festival, Shea Stadium, New York, 74; one-man shows, Inst Contemp Arts, London, 66, Mus Contemp Crafts, New York, 71, Edible Landscape, Mus of Contemp Crafts, New York, 72, Int Design Conf, Aspen, Colo, 73, Art Gallery of New South Wales, Sydney, 73, Henry Gallery, Seattle, Wash, 73, Metrop Mus, New York, 73, Ctr Culture, Villeparsis, 75, Feast for Leda, Documenta 6, Kassel, Ger, 77 & Bread Line, Contemp Arts Mus, Houston, Tex, 77. Awards: City of Barcelona Bursary, 62-63; Laureate of 5th Bienniale de Paris, 67. Bibliog: Douglas Davis (auth), A new world of art, Newsweek, New York, 73; Bill Dyckes (auth), Contemproary Spanish art, Arts Mag, New York, 76; Pierre Restany (auth), Miralda artiste en tous genres, Artitudes Int, 77. Publ: Auth & ed, Album, pvt publ, Mallorca, Spain, 73 & Food Coloring Cards, pvt publ, Paris, 75; co-auth, Ceremonials, Galeria Vandres, Madrid & Centre Beaubourg, 75-78; auth, The Last Supper, Art Enlla, Barcelona, Spain, 76; co-auth, Situation-color, Galeria Vandres, Madrid, 77. Mailing Add: 24 Harrison St New York NY 10013

MIRANO, VIRGIL MARCUS
PHOTOGRAPHER, EDUCATOR
b Los Angeles, Calif, Jan 3, 37. Study: Calif State Univ, Fullerton, BA, 74; Univ Calif, Los Angeles, MA, 76. Work: Univ NMex Art Mus; Fla State Univ Fine Arts Gallery, Tallahassee. Comn: Edition, offset and color litho prints (with Robert Fichter), Fla State Univ, 74-75. Exhib: Light and Substance, Univ NMex Art Mus, 73; Photography Unlimited, Fogg Art Mus, Harvard Univ, 74; Colors, Fla State Univ Fine Arts Gallery, 75; New Photographics/75, Cent Wash State Col, 75; Summer Light 1975, Light Gallery, New York, 75; Emerging Artists, Fredrick S Wight Gallery, Univ Calif, Los Angeles, 76; New Blues, Mem Union Art Gallery, Univ NMex, 76; Emerging Los Angeles Photogr, Friends of Photog, Carmel, Calif, 76; (No Space), Fla State Fine Arts Gallery, 76; Fine Arts Festival, Fla State Univ Fine Arts Gallery, 77. Teaching: Teaching asst photog, Univ Calif, 74-76; asst prof art/photog, Fla State Univ, 76-77; vis artist, Art Inst Chicago, 78. Bibliog: Terry Huseby (auth), Light and Substance, Univ NMex Press, 74; Joan Murray (auth), New photographics/75, Artweek, 5/75. Mem: Soc Photographic Educ; Visual Studies Workshop; Int Mus Photog. Style & Technique: Ritual figurative pieces executed on photosensitive surfaces; large scale and non-lenticular. Mailing Add: 571 1/2 S Arizona Ave Los Angeles CA 90022

MIRKO (WOLODYMYR WALTER PYLYSHENKO)
COLLECTOR, PAINTER
b Ukraine, July 28, 34; US citizen. Study: Rochester Inst Technol, BFA, 58 & MFA, 63; NY State Univ Col Buffalo, teaching cert, 59. Exhib: Finger Lakes Regional, Rochester Mem Art Gallery, 63; Western NY Show, Albright-Knox Art Gallery, Buffalo, 63; Everson Mus, Syracuse, 63; Barnard Col, Columbia Univ, 65; Philadelphia Print Club, 65. Teaching: Assoc prof drawing & painting, NY State Univ Brockport, 63- Awards: First Prize Print Award, Rochester Mem Art Gallery, 62. Bibliog: Jean Reeves (auth), Ukrainian artist uses the myths,

Buffalo Eve News, 12/13/66; Dr D K Winebrenner (auth), Mirko show at Tomac Gallery, Buffalo Courier, 12/66. Style & Technique: Figurative, expressionistic. Media: Oil Paint, Relief Print. Collection: Collection of prints from Ukrainian Soviet Socialist Republic and 19th century Ukrainian folk costumes. Mailing Add: 1162 West Ave Brockport NY 14420

MIRVISH, DAVID
ART DEALER
b Toronto, Ont, Aug 29, 44. Pos: Dir, David Mirvish Gallery. Specialty: Twentieth century art. Mailing Add: David Mirvish Gallery 596 Markham St Toronto ON Can

MISCH, ALLENE K
COLLECTOR, PAINTER
b Utica, NY, Jan 27, 28. Study: Chicago Art Inst; Ind Univ; Purdue Univ; also with Tom Hill, Robert E Wood, John C Pellew & George Cherepov. Comn: Oil, Mem Hospital, Michigan City, Ind, 65. Exhib: Dunes Regional, Michigan City, 63-70; Michiana Regional, South Bend, Ind, 67; Las Vegas Art Mus, Nev, 72-78; State Capitol, Carson City, Nev, 76. Teaching: Instr oils & acrylics, Dunes Art Found, Michigan City, 65-70 & Las Vegas Art Mus, 71- Pos: Gallery dir, Dunes Art Found, 66-70 & Las Vegas Art Mus, 72-73; visual arts chmn, Festival: The Arts, Allied Arts Coun, Las Vegas, 77. Awards: Oils Award, Dunes Regionals, Dune Art Found, First Merchants Bank, 63, 65 & 68; Purchase Prize, Elkhart Art Festival, CofC, Ind, 65; Oil Award, Michiana Regional, South Bend Art Ctr, 67. Bibliog: Misch Exhibition, Michigan City News Dispatch, 68; Festival: The Arts, Las Vegas Sun, 77. Mem: Las Vegas Artists' Coop; Advocate for the Arts. Style & Technique: Contemporary expressionistic landscapes; Renaissance technique. Media: Acrylic, Oil. Collection: Watercolors, Indian art including Kachinas, pottery and weaving; Rex Brandt, Robert E Wood & Tom Hill. Dealer: Green Apple Gallery 4800 S Maryland Pkwy Las Vegas NV 89109. Mailing Add: 3806 Forest Crest Dr Las Vegas NV 89121

MISS, MARY
SCULPTOR
b New York, NY, May 27, 44. Study: Univ Calif, Santa Barbara, BA, 66; Rinehart Sch Sculpture, Md Art Inst, Baltimore, MFA, 68. Work: Allen Mem Art Mus, Oberlin Col, Ohio. Exhib: Whitney Mus Am Art Sculpture Ann, New York, 70; Twenty Six Contemporary Women Artists, Larry Aldrich Mus, Ridgefield, Conn, 71; Four Young Americans, Allen Mem Art Mus, Oberlin Col, Ohio, 73; Whitney Mus Painting & Sculpture Biennial, New York, 73; one-woman show, Salvatore Ala Gallery, Milan, Italy, 75. Teaching: Instr, Sch Visual Arts, New York, 72; vis artist, Pratt Inst, Brooklyn, NY, 73; instr, Hunter Col, New York, 72-75; instr, Sarah Lawrence Col, Bronxville, NY, 76- Awards: NY State Coun on Arts CAPS Grant, 73 & 76; Nat Endowment Awards, 74 & 75. Bibliog: Athena Spear, (auth), Some thoughts on contemporary art, Allen Mem Art Mus Bull, spring 73; Laurie Anderson (auth), Mary Miss, Artforum, 11/73; Lucy Lippard (auth), Mary Miss: an extremely clear situation, Art in Am, 3-4/74. Mailing Add: Box 304 Canal St Sta New York NY 10013

MITCHAM, GEORGIA WHITMAN
SCULPTOR
b Providence, RI, July 4, 10. Study: Slade Sch Art, Univ London; with Naum M Los, New York. Work: Am Mus Natural Hist, New York; Smithsonian Inst, Washington, DC; Bennington Mus, Vt; Norwich Univ, Northfield, Vt; Harvard Univ, Cambridge, Mass. Comn: Two champion Angus bulls, comn by Gifford Cochrane, North Salem, NY; bas-relief of dinosaur, Am Mus Natural Hist; plus others. Exhib: One-man shows, Studio Guild, New York, 38, Southern Vt Art Ctr, Manchester, 69 & Bennington Mus, 72 & 73; Audubon Artists, New York, 64; Child's Gallery, Boston, 64. Awards: First for Sculpture, Northern Vt Artists, 63, Saratoga Art Festival, NY, 64 & Norwich Show, Northfield, Vt, 75. Mem: Southern Vt Art Ctr; Northern Vt Artist; Nat League Am Pen Women; Rutland Vt Area Artist. Style & Technique: Animals in motion; realistic. Media: Aluminum, Lead, Iron. Mailing Add: Box 463 Middlebury VT 05753

MITCHELL, BERESFORD STRICKLAND
DESIGNER, ILLUSTRATOR
b Hamilton, Ont, Can, Jan 16, 21. Study: Ont Col of Art, AOCA. Teaching: Chmn dept of commun & design, Ont Col of Art, 69- Pos: Art dir, Hathaway Templeton, 63-66; design dir, Design Group, 66-67; creative dir, CDC Graphics, 67-68; art dir, F H Hayhurst, 68-69. Awards: Signs of the Times, Outdoor Signage, 60; Art Dirs Club, Montreal & Toronto, Salada Packaging, 65 & Southex Corp Mark, 67. Mem: Art Dir Club of Toronto. Style & Technique: Designer and illustrator of packaging, posters and advertising. Interest: Design complete advertising and packaging programs from concept through visual to finish; television print and point of purchase. Mailing Add: Box 53 Rockwood ON N0B 2K0 Can

MITCHELL, CLIFFORD
PAINTER, ARCHITECT
b Birmingham, Ala, Sept 22, 25. Study: Tuskegee Inst, BS, 49; Univ Hartford Art Sch, BFA, 58. Work: New Brit Mus Am Art, Univ Conn Sch Pharm, Storrs, Stamford Mus & Nature Ctr, Conn Gen Life Ins Co, Bloomfield & Mattatuck Mus, Waterbury, Conn; plus others. Exhib: Silvermine Guild Artists New Eng Exhib, New Canaan, Conn, 64; 12 New Eng Artists, Slater Mem Mus, Norwich, Conn, 68; Am Watercolor Soc Ann, New York, 69; Audubon Artists Ann, New York, 70; Galerie-8 Watercolor, Print & Drawing Nat, Erie, Pa, 70; Mattatuck Mus, Waterbury, Conn, 73; Am Int Col, Springfield, Mass, 74; Springfield Col, 76; Conn Pub Television, Hartford, Conn, 76; Univ Conn, Waterbury, 77; plus others. Teaching: Instr interior design, Univ Hartford Art Sch Eve Course, 68-69. Pos: Architect, Clifford Mitchell, Hartford, 75- Awards: Larry Aldrich Award, Silvermine Guild Artists, 60; Past Pres Prize, Conn Watercolor Soc, 70 & First Prize, 74; Hartford Arts Festival Purchase Award, 72; plus others. Bibliog: Janet Gaston (auth), Aux etats-unis/a New York salon audubon, La Rev Mod, 60; J V W B (auth), Works by Mitchell at local museum, New Brit Herald, 68; Jolene Goldenthal (auth), Look at art/an architect turns artist, Hartford Courant, 71. Mem: Conn Acad Fine Arts; Conn Watercolor Soc (pres, 70-72); Silvermine Guild Artists. Media: Oil, Watercolor, Graphics. Dealer: Silvermine Guild Artists Silvermine New Canaan CT 06840. Mailing Add: 105 W Euclid St Hartford CT 06112

MITCHELL, DANA COVINGTON, JR
COLLECTOR
b Bluefield, WVa, Feb 22, 18. Study: Univ WVa, BA & MD. Pos: Pres bd trustees, Columbia Mus Art, 60-61. Collection: Contemporary American art. Mailing Add: 600 Spring Lake Rd Columbia SC 29206

MITCHELL, DONALD
ART ADMINISTRATOR, ART DEALER
b Mt Vernon, NY, Mar 5, 22. Study: Wichita State Univ, art hist; Abbe Inst, painting with George DeGroat; Monterey Peninsula Col, painting with Fay Hopkins. Pos: Vpres, Universal Arts, Inc, Carmel, Calif, 60-; dir, Zantman Galleries, Ltd, Carmel, 60-; co-owner, Highlands Gallery, Carmel, 60- Specialty: Quality works, mostly representational, in all media, style and technique. Mailing Add: PO Box 3731 Carmel CA 93921

MITCHELL, DOW PENROSE
PRINTMAKER, EDUCATOR
b Winnipeg, Man, Nov 28, 15. Study: Art Inst Chicago, BFA, 49; Bradley Univ, MA, 50. Work: Libr of Cong, Washington, DC; US Info Serv Cult Div; Univ Kans Mus Art, Lawrence; Otis Art Inst, Los Angeles; State Univ NY Col Potsdam. Exhib: 50 Contemporary American Printmakers, Univ Ill, 52; 47 Midwestern Printmakers, Chicago, 56; Bay Printmakers Soc, Oakland, Calif, 57; St Louis Artists Guild, Mo, 64; Otis Art Inst, Los Angeles, 63. Teaching: Prof art, Bradley Univ, 50-, chmn sch art, 68-69. Awards: Putnam Award Excellence, Bradley Univ, 70. Style & Technique: Printmaker originated collagraph technique; collagraph and plastic intaglio prints. Media: Collagraph Prints & Drawing. Mailing Add: Box 55 Groveland IL 61535

MITCHELL, ELEANOR
FINE ARTS SPECIALIST, LIBRARIAN
b Orange, NJ, Apr 4, 07. Study: Douglass Col, New Brunswick, NJ, BA, 28, LittD, 68; Columbia Univ Sch Libr Serv, BS, 29; Inst Art & Archaeol, Univ Paris, Carnegie summer scholar, 32; Harvard Univ, 34; Smith Col, MA, 36; additional studies art, languages & music, Univ Florence, Carnegie Inst, Univ Pittsburgh & George Washington Univ. Pos: Asst cur bks & photog, Art Dept, Smith Col, 29-36; asst, Grad House, Florence, Italy, 36-37; librn, Dept Fine Arts, Univ Pittsburgh, 37-42; asst to dir, Bibliot Pub Estado Jalisco, Guadalajara, Mex, 42-43; chief art div, NY Pub Libr, 43-52; prog specialist, Cult Activities Dept, UNESCO, Paris, 48-49; dir libr serv, US Info Serv, Italy, 51-54; consult fine arts, Libr of Cong, Washington, DC, 54-55; consult, Montclair Free Pub Libr, 55; US specialist, Int Educ Exchange Serv, Bibliot Pub Dept, Cali, Colombia, 55-56; US specialist, Dept State, Univ Antioquia, Medellin, Colombia, 56-57; exec dir fine arts comt, People-to-People Prog, Corcoran Gallery, 57-61; specialist, Bks for the People Fund, Inc, Pan Am Union, Washington, DC, 61-62; bibliog asst, Rockefeller Found, Proj Int Rice Res Inst-Philippines, Washington, DC, 62-63; consult, Hisp Found, Libr of Cong, 63; libr consult, Univ Catolica, Quito, Ecuador, under St Louis Univ-Agency Int Develop Contract, 63-68; proj officer, Int Rels Off, Am Libr Asn, Washington, DC, 69-72. Mem: Am Libr Asn; Soc Women Geogr; Am Asn Mus. Publ: Contribr, Gazette Beaux-Arts, Col Res Libr, NY Pub Libr Bull, Art Educ Bull & Douglass Alumnae Bull, 37-61. Mailing Add: 730 24th St NW Washington DC 20037

MITCHELL, FRED
PAINTER
b Meridian, Miss, Nov 24, 23. Study: Carnegie Inst of Technol, scholar, 42-43; Cranbrook Acad of Art, 46-48, BFA, 48, MFA, 56; Acad of Fine Arts, Rome. Work: Columbus Gallery of Fine Arts, Ohio; Cranbrook Acad of Art, Bloomfield Hills, Mich; Munson-Williams-Proctor Mus of Art, Utica, NY. Comn: Cast concrete screen, Miss State Col for Women. Exhib: Younger Am Painters, Solomon R Guggenheim Mus, New York, 54; Dallas Mus of Fine Arts, Tex, 54; Vanguard 55, Walker Art Ctr, Minneapolis, Minn, 55; Cranbrook Acad of Art, Bloomfield Hills, Mich, 58; Carnegie Inst Int, 61; Painter, Sculptor & Printmaker, 72, Coenties Slip Exhib, 73, New York Ink Drawings, 73 & Abstract Watercolors, 1942-75, 75, Buecker and Harpsichords, New York; Painters in Watercolor, Hunterdon Art Ctr, Clinton, NJ, 75; one-man shows, Columbia Mus of Art, SC, 65, Wis State Univ, Platteville, 68, White Mus, Cornell Univ, Ithaca, NY, 69, Meridian Mus of Art, Miss, 72, Univ of Maine at Machias, 74, State Univ of New York at Binghamtom Art Gallery, 76 & Munson-Williams-Proctor Sch of Art Gallery, 77. Teaching: Prof drawing and painting, Cranbrook Acad of Art, Bloomfield Hills, Mich, 55-59; vis critic, Cornell Univ, Ithaca, 68-69; vis prof art, Ithaca Col, New York, 69-70; adj assoc prof art, New York Univ, 61-71; assoc prof art, Queens Col, New York, 73-74; vis prof art, Univ of Maine at Machias, 74; vis artist, Univ of Oregon, Eugene, 75; prof art, NYU Grad Sch in Venice, Italy, 75; vis assoc prof art and dir, Univ Art Gallery, State Univ NY, Binghamton, 76-77; vis artist, Munson-Williams-Proctor Sch of Art, Utica, NY, 77. Pos: Co-founder, Tanager Gallery, New York, 52-62; founder and artist-teacher, Downtown Art Ctr, FDR Inst, Battery Park, New York, 61 & South St Seaport Mus, New York; artist-in-residence, Columbia Mus of Art, SC, 65; artist-in-residence, Aspen Sch of Contemp Art, Colo, 65. Awards: Traveling Fel, Italy, 48-51; Ford Found Artist-in-Residence, Columbia Mus of Art. Media: Watercolor and Oil. Mailing Add: 92 Hester St New York NY 10002

MITCHELL, HENRY (WEBER)
SCULPTOR
b Canton, Ohio, Aug 27, 15. Study: Princeton Univ, AB; Tyler Sch Fine Arts, Temple Univ, MFA; Acad Brera, Milan, Italy, with Marino Marini. Work: Philadelphia Mus Art; Pa Acad Fine Arts; Wilmington Soc Fine Arts; Provident Nat Bank, Philadelphia; pvt collection of John Wanamaker, King of Prussia, Pa; plus others. Comn: Fountain, Philadelphia Mus Art; Impala fountain, Philadelphia Zoo; two sculptures, Philadelphia Free Libr; reliefs, Philadelphia Zoo & Cobbs Creek Park; Logos Mem to Adlai Stevenson, Ill State Univ, Normal; plus others. Exhib: Philadelphia Art Alliance; Philadelphia Mus Art; Munson-Williams-Proctor Inst, Utica, NY; Pa Acad Fine Arts; Wilmington Soc Fine Arts; plus many others. Awards: Fulbright Fel, 50-51; NY Show Gold Medal, Philadelphia Flower Show, 64. Mem: Artists Equity Asn; Philadelphia Art Alliance; Franklin Inn Club, Philadelphia. Mailing Add: Valley House Level & Arcola Rd Arcola PA 19420

MITCHELL, JAMES E
ILLUSTRATOR, PAINTER
b New York, NY, Jan 1, 26. Study: Pratt Inst, Brooklyn, NY, cert; Acad Grande Chaumiere, Paris. Work: US Navy Art Collection, Washington, DC; Mariners Mus, Newport News, Va; Submarine Mus, New London, Conn; US Merchant Marine Acad, Kings Point, NY. Comn: Operation Sea Orbit, Mariners Mus, Newport News, Va, 65; DASO-Cape Kennedy, USN, 69; Tall Ships (paintings), Texaco, 76. Exhib: One-man shows, Lord & Taylor Gallery, New York, 66-69; The Gallery, Essex, Conn, 73-74; South St Seaport Mus, New York, 76; Texaco Tall Ships Paintings traveling exhib to London, Madrid, Lisbon, Amsterdam, Copenhagen, Oslo, Goteborg & New York, 77. Awards: Cert of Award for Paintings for Shell Oil Co Series, Printing Industs Am, 68 & 69; Cert of Achievement for Paintings for Texaco Co Series, Printing Industs Metrop New York, 74-77. Style & Technique: Marine illustrations are in documentary realism; fine arts paintings are traditional and expressionistic. Media: Gouache, Oil. Publ: Auth & illusr, Hydrofoils: A sketchbook of the future, Motor Boating, 62; illusr, History in the making, 67- & auth & illusr, Block Island race week, 73-77, Boating Mag; illusr, Shell Oil Diary, 69-70; auth & illusr, Sketchbook: SORC '72, Rudder Mag, 72. Dealer: South St Seaport Mus Gallery 215 Water St New York NY 10016; Trend House Gallery 717 South Dakota Ave Tampa FL 33606. Mailing Add: Hill & Dale Club PO Box 236 Carmel NY 10512

MITCHELL, JEFFREY MALCOLM
MUSEUM DIRECTOR, PAINTER
b Hasbrouch Heights, NJ, Apr 5, 40. Study: Univ Ariz, BFA; Pratt Inst, MS. Work: Am Tel & Tel; El Paso Mus Art, Tex; Tucson Mus Art, Ariz; Univ Tenn Mus Art; Westinghouse Corp. Exhib: 2nd Four Corners Biennial, Phoenix Art Mus, Ariz, 73; Tucson Braniff Int, 74; 24th Ann Tucson Art Ctr, 74; 10th Southwestern Touring Exhib, 75; one-man show, Harlan Gallery, Tucson, 74. Pos: Dir, Millicent Rogers Mus, 77-; asst dir, Univ Ariz Mus Art, 73-77. Awards: Award of Excellence, Chicago Three, 70; Award of Excellence, New York Art Dir Club, 70; Purchase Award, El Paso Mus Art, 72. Mem: Am Asn Mus; Western Asn Art Mus. Style & Technique: Geometric, architectural, three-dimensional. Media: Mixed-Media. Publ: Contribr, Navajo Blankets, 74, Manguan in American, 75, Morris Broderson, 75, Isabell Bishop, 76 & First Flowers of Our Wilderness, 76, Univ Ariz. Dealer: Tally Richards Gallery of Contemp Art Ledoux St Taos NM 87571. Mailing Add: PO Box 2766 Taos NM 87571

MITCHELL, JOAN
PAINTER
b Chicago, Ill, 1926. Study: Smith Col, 42-44; Columbia Univ; Art Inst Chicago, BFA, 47; NY Univ, MFA, 50. Work: Basel Mus, Switz; Albright-Knox Art Gallery, Buffalo; Art Inst Chicago; Mus Mod Art, New York; Phillips Collection, Washington, DC; plus others. Exhib: Pa Acad Fine Arts, Philadelphia, 66; Two Decades of American Painting, Mus Mod Art, circulated in Japan, India & Australia, 67; Univ Ill, 67; Jewish Mus, 67; one-man shows, Galerie Fournier, Paris, 67 & 69, Everson Mus, Syracuse, NY, 72 & Arts Club Chicago, 74; Carnegie Inst Int, 70 & 72; Va Mus Fine Arts, Richmond, 70; Younger Abstract Artists of the Fifties, Mus of Mod Art, New York, 71; Women Choose Women, New York Cult Ctr, 73; Am Drawings, 1963-73, Whitney Mus Am Art, New York, 73, Retrospective, 74; Indianapolis Mus Art, Ind, 74; Corcoran Gallery Art, Washington, DC, 75; plus many others. Bibliog: Michel Seuphor (auth), Abstract Painting: 50 Years of Accomplishment, From Kandinsky to the Present, Dell, 64; San Hunter (ed), New Art Around the World: Painting and Sculpture, Abrams, 66; plus others. Mailing Add: Mailing Add: c/o Xavier Fourcade 35 E 75th St New York NY 10021

MITCHELL, JOAN ELIZABETH
See Robertson, Joan Elizabeth

MITCHELL, JOHN BLAIR
PAINTER, EDUCATOR
b Brooklyn, NY, Jan 30, 21. Study: Pratt Inst, cert, 39-43, Pratt Inst Sch Educ, 46-47; Columbia Univ Teachers Col, BS, 48, Univ, MA, 49; Pratt Graphic Arts Ctr, 60-61, with Edmondson, Rogalski & Ponce de Leon; NY Univ Sch Educ, PhD, 63. Work: Metrop Mus Art, New York; Libr of Cong, Washington, DC; Silvermine Guild Artists, Conn; Baltimore Mus Art; Notre Dame Col, Baltimore. Comn: Mural, Baltimore City Hosp, 72. Exhib: Six shows, Corcoran Gallery Art, Washington, DC, 54-63; Libr of Cong 19th Nat Exhib Prints, 63; Silvermine Guild Artists 5th Nat, 64; one-man show, Baltimore Mus Art, 64; Hochschild Kohn Md Artists Today Anniversary, 72; one-man show, Towson State Univ, 77. Teaching: Prof graphics drawing, painting & photog & coordr grad art prog, Columbia Univ Teachers Col, 49- instr art, summers 50, 53 & 54; chmn art dept, Towson State Col, 51-57 & 63-65; instr graphics, Baltimore Mus Art, 63-73. Pos: Bk reviewer, Art Educ, 59-60; chmn, Task Force, Nat 1 for Art Legislation, 77- Awards: Md Artists Today First Award, Hochschild Kohn Co, 72; First Award, Intercollegiate Art Exhib, Coppin State Col, 72; First Award, Easton Acad Art, 73; plus others. Bibliog: Lincoln Johnson (auth), Review of Baltimore Hebrew Cong Art One-Man Show, The Sun, Baltimore, 12/71 & Review of Towson State Univ One-Man Show, 2/24/77. Mem: Artists Equity Asn (pres, Md Chap, 65, ECoast rep to bd, 73-75, nat pres, 75-77); Baltimore Print Club (bd mem). Publ: Auth, Art Education, 52; co-auth, Art in Our Maryland Schools, State Manual, State Dept Educ, 53; auth, School Arts, 2/57; auth, Eastern Arts Quart, 1-2/63. Mailing Add: 9918 Finney Dr Baltimore MD 21234

MITCHELL, PETER TODD
PAINTER
b New York, NY, Nov 16, 29. Study: Acad Bellas Artes, Mexico City, Mex, with Lozano & Galvan; Groton; Yale Art Sch. Work: Metrop Mus Art, New York. Comn: Murals, Von Wrangell, Malaga, Spain, 55 & Thomas Murphy, St Tropez, France, 70. Exhib: Am Painters in Philadelphia Collections, 62; Smithsonian Traveling Show Graphics, 71; London Bridge Show, Guildhall-London, 72. Awards: First Tiffany Found Award for Painting, 52. Bibliog: Berg (auth), L'oeuvre de P T Mitchell, Jardin Arts, 69. Style & Technique: Romantic realist, using primarily Middle Eastern and North African subject matter. Media: Oil. Dealer: Eric Galleries 61 E 57th St New York NY 10022. Mailing Add: 116 E 57th St New York NY 10022

MITCHELL, ROBERT ELLIS
GOLDSMITH, EDUCATOR
b Decatur, Ill, Feb 5, 42. Study: Ill Wesleyan Univ, Bloomington, BFA, 64; Southern Ill Univ, Carbondale, MFA, 66; with Nicholas Vergette & Brent Kington. Work: Ark Art Ctr, Little Rock. Comn: Eternal Light, St John's Lutheran Church, Lafe, Ark, 72. Exhib: Young Americans, New York, 69; Nat Jewelry, Edinboro, Pa, 72; one-man shows, Concordia Sem, St Louis & Southwest Mo State Univ, 73-75; Goldsmiths, Smithsonian Inst, Washington, DC & travel tour, 75. Teaching: Instr jewelry & design, St Leo Col, Fla, 66-67; asst prof jewelry & silversmithing, Ark State Univ, Jonesboro, 67- Awards: Res Grants, State of Ark, 72 & 75. Mem: Soc NAm Goldsmiths; Am Crafts Coun; World Crafts Coun. Style & Technique: Jewelry and container objects. Media: Gold; Electroforming with Plastics. Publ: Auth, Metal Spinning and Castable Plastics, 72; auth, Periodic Reverse Cycles for Silver Electroforming, 75. Mailing Add: 1817 Colonial Rd Jonesboro AR 72401

MITCHELL, WALLACE (MACMAHON)
MUSEUM DIRECTOR, PAINTER
b Detroit, Mich, Oct 9, 11. Study: Hamilton Col, 30-33; Northwestern Univ, BA, 34; Cranbrook Acad Art, 35; Columbia Univ, MA, 36. Work: Cranbrook Acad Art Mus; Detroit Inst Art; Guggenheim Mus; Kalamazoo Art Ctr. Comn: Murals, Gen Motors Tech Ctr & Univ Ky Med Ctr. Exhib: Art Inst Chicago, 38-41; Detroit Inst Art Ann; Albright Art Gallery, 39; Univ Nebr; Old Northwest Territory Exhib; plus others. Teaching: Instr, Cranbrook Acad Art, 36-55. Pos: Registr, Cranbrook Acad Art, 44-64, dir galleries, 54-71, pres, 70- Mailing Add: Cranbrook Acad Art Bloomfield Hills MI 48013

MITRA, GOPAL C
PAINTER, PRINTMAKER
b Patna, Bihar, India, Nov 1, 28. Study: B N Col, Patna Univ, PHES & IA; Govt Sch of Arts & Crafts, Patna, Dipl FA; Univ Minn, MFA & PhD, also with Roy Chordhury, B B Mukherji in India & Edward Courbet, Lorenz Either, Cameron Booth & Malcolm Myers in US. Work: Youth Gallery, Bucharest, Rumania; Litchfield Art Gallery, London & Cambridge, Eng; Walker Art Ctr, Minneapolis, Minn; Minneapolis Art Inst; Univ Minn Art Gallery, Minneapolis; E B Gray Found Res Ctr, NY Univ. Comn: Life & Enlightenment of Lord Buddha (mural), Movie Theaters in India, 49-56; murals, All India Children Art Festivals, Bengal, Bihar & UP, India, 49-53; Indian Ways of Life (murals), Govt Bihar, Patna, New Delhi & Maddhya Pradesh, 53-57; murals, All India Cult Festivals, Bengal & Bihar, 54-57; Creation, Preservation & Destruction (mural), Edinboro State Col, Pa, 78. Exhib: Chemule & Jehangir Art Gallery, Bombay, India; Walker Art Ctr, Minneapolis; Minneapolis Art Inst; Okla Nat Art Exhib; Univ Minn, Minneapolis; Wis State Univ, Oshkosh & Eau Claire; All India Art Exhib, Patna, Calcutta & New Delhi; one-man shows, Gallery 8, Erie, Pa, Litchfield Gallery, London & Cambridge, Walker Art Ctr, Minneapolis Art Inst, Univ Minn, Minneapolis, Chicago State Univ, Lalit Kalo Akademy (Nat Gallery of Art), New Delhi, Acad Fine Arts, Calcutta, Hamline Univ, Wis, Wis State Univ, Oshkosh & Eau Claire; plus others. Collections Arranged: All India Art & Craft Exhib, Patna & Calcutta, 47, 48 & 53; All India Children Art Exhib, Patna, Calcutta & New Delhi, 54, 56 & 57; Indian Art & Culture Exhib, Worthington, Minn, 61; Indo-American Art & Crafts Exhib, Minneapolis, 62, 65 & 67; Himalayan Art, Edinboro State Col, 77. Teaching: Instr & teaching asst, Univ Minn, Minneapolis, 58-60 & 62-67; instr printmaking & drawing, Worthing Sch System, Minn, 60-61, instr creative arts, Art Educ Dept, 62-67; lectr & artist printmaking & painting, St Paul Art & Sci Ctr, Minn, 62-65 & 67; artist & lectr, Walker Art Ctr, Minneapolis, 64-65, instr painting, 65-66; assoc prof & lectr painting & printmaking, Chicago State Univ, 67-69; prof art, art hist of India & China, painting & drawing, Edinboro State Col, 69- Awards: First Prize Awards in Contemp Landscape Painting & Still Life, All India Art Exhib, Patna, Govt Show of Arts & Crafts, 53; plus others. Mem: Am Soc Aesthetics; Am Asn Asian Studies; Int Soc for Comparative Study of Civilizations. Style & Technique: Semi-abstraction with occasional mood variations; Indo-American (the best of both worlds). Media: Painting, Printmaking. Res: Art and culture of India and China, Himalayan art and Studies in Imperial attitudes. Dealer: Seigel Gallery Ltd 118 1/2 E Oak St Chicago IL 60611. Mailing Add: 12530 Cedar Dr Edinboro PA 16412

MITTLEMAN, ANN
PAINTER
b Jan 15, 98; US citizen. Study: NY Univ; New Sch Social Res; also with Tchac Basov, Robert Laurent & Philip Evergood. Work: Univ Minn; Jewish Mus; NY Univ Mus; Miami Mus; Birmingham Mus; plus 26 other mus. Exhib: Bodley Gallery; Wickersham Gallery, Traveling Mus Show, one-man retrospective exhib, Univ Minn. Mem: Nat Asn Women Artists; Am 63-64. fel Royal Soc Arts London; Arch Am Art. Media: Oil. Dealer: Madison Avenue Gallery 981 Madison Ave New York NY 10021. Mailing Add: 527 Madison Ave New York NY 10022

MIX, WALTER JOSEPH
PAINTER, EDUCATOR
b Chicago, Ill, Oct 14, 28. Study: Ariz State Col, Tempe, BAEd(fine arts), 53; Claremont Grad Sch, MFA, 57; studied with Phil Dike, Millard Sheets, Roger Kuntz & Jean Goodwin Ames. Work: Brigham Young Univ, Provo, Utah; Scripps Col, Claremont, Calif; Long Beach Munic Mus, Calif; Mt San Antonio Col, Walnut, Calif; Bakersfield Col, Calif. Exhib: Pa Acad Fine Arts & Detroit Inst of the Arts, 58 & 60; Denver Art Mus, Colo, 58 & 61; one-man shows, Comara Gallery, Los Angeles, 58-66, Palazzo delle Exposizione, Rome, Italy, 61 & Gallery 8, Claremont, Calif, 77; Los Angeles Co Mus, Los Angeles, Calif, 59-61; Contemp Urban Visions, New Sch for Social Res, New York, 66; Los Angeles Munic Art Gallery, 71. Teaching: Instr painting & drawing, Mt San Antonio Col, Walnut, Calif, 57- Pos: Cur, Mt San Antonio Col, Walnut, Calif, 57- Awards: Second Award, All Calif Invitational, Laguna Beach Art Gallery, 59; Purchase Awards, Religious Dimensions, Brigham Young Univ, 61 & Bakersfield Col, Calif, 62. Bibliog: Gerald Nordland (auth), One-man show rev, Arts, 62; R G Wholden (auth), rev of one-man show, Artforum, 63; Jules Langsner (auth), rev of one-man show, Art News, 67. Style & Technique: Semi-abstract views of cities; some landscapes; technique usually includes some impasto and glazing. Media: (Paintings) Oil and enamel; (Drawings) ink. Dealer: Comara Gallery 447 S La Cienega Los Angeles CA 90048; Gallery 8 301 Harvard Ave Claremont CA 91711. Mailing Add: 1903 Academy Ct Claremont CA 91711

MIYAMOTO, WAYNE AKIRA
PAINTER, PRINTMAKER
b Honolulu, Hawaii, Sept 6, 47. Study: Rennselaer Polytech Inst, 65-68; Univ Hawaii, BA & BFA, 70, MFA, 74. Work: State Found for Cult & the Arts, Honolulu; Univ Hawaii, Honolulu; Fine Arts Mus, Univ Alaska, Fairbanks; Univ Hawaii, Hilo; Leeward Community Col, Pearl City, Hawaii. Exhib: 1st Biennial Nat Print Exhib, Honolulu Acad of Arts, 71; Col of Siskiyous Nat Print Competition, Weed, Calif, 75; Bay Area Artists Exhib, Oakland Mus, Calif, 75; 2nd Ann Honolulu Printmakers Exhib, 77; Intent-Nat Drawing Exhib, Edinboro, Pa, 77; 11th Dulin Nat Print & Drawing Exhib, Knoxville, Tenn, 77; Eye of 25, Twenty-five Painters of Fla, Boca Raton Art Ctr, 78. Teaching: Vis asst prof art, Univ Hawaii, Hilo, 76; asst prof art, Fla Technol Univ, Orlando, 76- Pos: Dir, Hilo Nat Print Invitational, Hawaii, 76; humanities lectr, Nat Endowment for the Humanities, Hilo, 76; mem nat painting jury, Scholastic Art Awards, New York, 77. Awards: Nat Soc of Arts & Lett Prize, Nat Print Exhib, 71; Purchase Awards, 4th Col Regional Exhib, 74 & 47th Ann Honolulu Printmakers Exhib, 75, State Found for Cult & the Arts. Mem: Col Art Asn; Honolulu Printmakers Asn (mem bd & treas, 71-72). Style & Technique: Figurative abstraction, intaglio, woodblock, acrylic on canvas and paper and oil on canvas. Media: Intaglio, Acrylic. Publ: Auth, Unique art of Akaji, Honolulu Star Bull/Advertiser, 76. Dealer: Texann Ivy Inc 122-H N Orange Ave Orlando FL 32802. Mailing Add: Dept of Art Fla Technol Univ Orlando FL 32816

MIYASAKI, GEORGE JOJI
PRINTMAKER, PAINTER
b Kalopa, Hawaii, Mar 24, 35. Study: Calif Col Arts & Crafts, BFA & BAEd, 57 & MFA, 58. Work: San Francisco Mus Art, Calif; Brooklyn Mus Art, NY; Mus Mod Art, New York; Art Inst Chicago; Pasadena Art Mus, Calif. Teaching: Assoc prof painting & printmaking, Univ Calif, Berkeley, 64. Awards: John Simon Guggenheim Fel, 63-64. Mailing Add: c/o Assoc Am Artists 663 Fifth Ave New York NY 10022

MIYASHITA, TAD
PAINTER
b Puukolii, Hawaii, May 10, 22. Study: Corcoran Sch Art, Washington, DC; Art Students League. Work: State Found Cult & Arts, Honolulu; Honolulu Acad Arts; New York Times; Guggenheim Mus & Whitney Mus Am Art, New York. Exhib: Pa Acad Fine Arts Ann, Philadelphia, 52; Nebr Art Asn Ann, 54; One Hundred Works on Paper, Salzburg, Austria, 59; Whitney Mus Am Art Ann, 67 & 68; Collages by American Artists, Ball State Univ, Muncie, Ind, 71. Awards: MacDowell Colony Fel, 72-74 & Yaddo Fel, 73-74; Millay Colony for Arts Award, 75; Ossabaw Island Proj Award, 75. Bibliog: J Canaday (auth), article in New York Times, 66; J R Mellow (auth), article in Art Int, 68; W Anderson (auth), article in

Honolulu Star-Bull, 71. Style & Technique: Use of found and discarded materials with amalgamation of oils and collage. Mailing Add: 121 E 23rd St New York NY 10010

MOCHIZUKI, BETTY AYAKO
PAINTER
b Vancouver, BC. Study: Ont Col Art. Work: Art Gallery Ont, Toronto; Dept of External Affairs, Ottawa; Victoria Col, Univ Toronto. Exhib: One-man shows, Picture Loan Soc, Toronto, 55, 58 & 60; Victoria Col, Univ Toronto, 67; Sisler Gallery, Toronto, 76. Awards: C W Jeffery Award, 62. Mem: Can Soc Painters in Watercolour; Can Soc Graphic Art. Mailing Add: 175 Livingstone Ave Toronto ON M6E 2L9 Can

MOCK, RICHARD BASIL
PAINTER, ENVIRONMENTAL ARTIST
b Long Beach, Calif, Aug 2, 44. Study: Univ Mich, BSD, 65; NY Studio Sch; Univ Okla, MFA, 69. Work: Ft Worth Art Ctr, Tex; Roswell Art Mus, NMex. Comn: Ritual environ on Buffalo Bill's grave site, Lookout Mountain, Colo, Nat Endowment for Arts, 73. Exhib: One-man shows, Houston Contemp Arts Mus, Tex, 71 & 112 Greene St Gallery, 72-74; Contemp Art Exhib, Art Inst Chicago, 72; Whitney Biennial Contemp Am Art, New York, 73; New York Cult Ctr, 73. Awards: Painting Fel, Roswell Mus, 70; Nat Endowment Arts, 73. Style & Technique: Environments for the spiritually aware; art rituals that transform space. Publ: Auth, World piece, Art in Am, 1/73; auth, Missile silo melodrama, Arts in Ireland, 6/75. Mailing Add: 10 Bleeker St New York NY 10012

MOCKERS, MICHEL M
TRUE FRESCO PAINTER
b Nantes, Loire Atlantique, France, Dec 17, 22. Study: Rennes Univ, fine arts degree; Rouen Beaux Artes, with Leon Toublanc. Comn: Frescoes, Basilique de Nanterre & Hotel de Ville de Rouen; Church of St Thomas Acquinas, Brooklyn, NY; Church of St Frances de Chantal, Bronx, NY; Church of the Holy Family, Brooklyn, NY. Exhib: One-man shows, Munic Casino, Canne, France, 62, 64 & 65, Duncan Gallery, Paris, 66, Galerie de Lille, France, 66, TWA Show, New York, 69 & Felmington Gallery Arts, 77. Teaching: Lectr hist oil painting & lectr arts & humanities, Somerset Co Col, 77-78. Pos: Art critic, La Marseillaise newspaper, Marseille, France, 63-64; radio commentator on art, Semaine Radio Phonique, Paris, 74-76; art critic & commentator, Intermission Mag, NJ, 77- Awards: First Prize, Michael Angelo, Paris, 68. Bibliog: Marian Oswald (auth), Batir sa Vie, 45-min movie on work of Michel Mockers, Fr television, 68. Mem: Soc ARtistes Francais, Paris; Jury for Signature Prize. Style & Technique: Future-realist; oil on gessoed wood panels; portraits in bronze. Media: Oil; Bronze. Res: History of the process of oil painting. Interest: Curator of all drawings transferred for safekeeping from the Louvre to Valencay, 43-44. Publ: Auth, Maquis SS4, Paris, 47; auth, The Magnolias of the Emperor of China, Le Temoin, Paris, 75. Dealer: Flemington Gallery of the Arts 35 Mine St Flemington NJ 08822. Mailing Add: 1035 Brown Rd Bridgewater NJ 08807

MODEL, ELISABETH D
SCULPTOR
b Bayreuth, Bavaria; US citizen. Study: Ryksacademy, Amsterdam, with Prof Jurgens; also with Prof Walter Thor & Prof Cericioli, Munich & Moissi Kogan, Paris. Work: Corcoran Galleries, Washington, DC; Wadsworth Atheneum, Hartford, Conn; Jewish Mus, New York; Rose Collection, Brandeis Univ; Rykspreuteu Cabinet, Amsterdam Hall; plus others. Exhib: Mus Fine Arts, Philadelphia; Mus Fine Arts, Boston; Brooklyn Mus; Nedelph Mus, Amsterdam, Holland; Riverside Mus, New York; plus others. Teaching: Pvt lessons, Amsterdam, 30-38 & New York, 42-48. Awards: Gold Medal of Honor, Nat Asn Women Artists, 50; plus many awards & prizes. Bibliog: Meilach (auth), Contemporary Sculpture & Sculpture Casting, Crown. Mem: Fedn Mod Sculptors & Painters (corresp secy). Style & Technique: Direct carving. Media: Stone, Wood. Dealer: Bodley Gallery 1063 Madison Ave New York NY 10023. Mailing Add: 340 W 72nd St New York NY 10023

MOE, RICHARD D
ART ADMINISTRATOR
b Fargo, NDak, May 7, 28. Study: Concordia Col, Moorhead, Minn, BA, 51; Univ Colo, MEd, 53, EdD, 60. Pos: Dean Sch fine arts, Pac Lutheran Univ, Tacoma, Wash, 68- Mem: Tacoma Opera Soc (pres, 72-74); Tacoma Philharmonic (pres, 75-77); Tacoma Art Mus (pres, 77-); Pac Northwest Dance; Tacoma Allied Arts. Mailing Add: PO Box 44304 Tacoma WA 98444

MOELLER, ROBERT CHARLES, III
ART HISTORIAN, ART ADMINISTRATOR
b Providence, RI, Jan 22, 38. Study: Washington & Lee Univ, BA(hist art), 59; Harvard Univ, with John Beckwith, Dr Hanns Swarzenski, J M Delaisse & J H Plummer, MA(art hist), 63. Collections Arranged: Brummer Collection, Duke Univ Art Mus. Teaching: Teaching fel hist art, Harvard Univ, 64-65; instr art, Duke Univ, 68, asst prof art, 68-69; instr seminar medieval sculpture, Univ NC, Chapel Hill, spring 68. Pos: Res assoc dept art, Duke Univ, 67-68, dir, Duke Univ Art Mus, 68-69; asst cur dept decorative arts & sculpture, Mus Fine Arts, Boston, 70-71, cur decorative arts & sculpture, 71- Mem: Int Coun Mus; Am Asn Mus; Am Ceramic Circle; Soc Silver Collectors; Int Ctr Medieval Art (dir). Res: Study of mid-twelfth century sculpture in Burgundy concentrating on Narthex sculpture of Charlieu, seventeenth century sculpture and decorative arts. Publ: Contribr, The Brummer Collection at Duke University, Art J, 68; auth foreword, The Graphic Art of Edvard Munch, Duke Univ Art Mus Exhib, 12/69; auth, Sculpture from Brive & Sculpture from Savigny, RI Sch Design, 7/69; L'iconographie de la facade nord du narthex de Charlieu, Actes des Journees d'etudes d'histoire et d'archeologie, Charlieu, Soc Amis Arts, 73; Five Pieces of Delftware, 72 & An English Silver Tray by Jacob Bodendick, No 367, Boston Mus Bull. Mailing Add: Dept Europ Decorative Arts Mus Fine Arts Boston MA 02115

MOERSCHEL, CHIARA
PAINTER
b Trieste, Italy; US citizen. Study: Lindenwood Col, with Robert Hansen & Sandra Del Munch. Work: Mead Gallery, Amherst Col, Mass; First Northwest Bank, St Ann, Mo; St Charles Clin, Mo; Boonslick Med Ctr. Exhib: Springfield Art Mus, Mo, 68 & 70-72; Span Int Pavillion, 69; one-man shows, Springfield Col, Ill, 71, Galleria Il Velocipede, Venice, Italy, 72 & Lynn Kottler Gallerie, New York, 73; plus many others. Awards: Gustave Geotch Mem Prize, St Louis Artists Guild, 69; First Prize for Watercolor, Am Bar Asn, St Louis, 70; First Prize for Watercolor, Sesquicentennial Show, Northeast Mo State Col, 71. Mem: Acad Prof Artists (mem bd, 70-75); St Charles Artists' Guild (pres, 69-75); St Louis Artists' Guild (vchmn art sect, 70); Community Women Artists. Style & Technique: Figurative and abstract inspired by world wide travel and life events. Media: Watercolor, Oil. Mailing Add: 121 College Dr St Charles MO 63301

MOFFITT, JOHN FRANCIS
PAINTER, ART HISTORIAN
b San Francisco, Calif, Feb 25, 40. Study: Calif Col Arts & Crafts, BFA, 63; Calif State Univ, San Francisco, MA, 64; Fac Lett & Philos, Univ Madrid, PhD, 66. Exhib: 13th Ann NC Artists Exhib, NC State Mus Art, Raleigh, 68; 1st Biennial 5-State Exhib, Gates Gallery, Port Arthur, Tex, 71; 12th Midwest Biennial, Joslyn Art Mus, Omaha, Nebr, 72; 21st Ann Exhib, Beaumont Art Mus, Tex, 72; 50th Regional Exhib, R S Barnwell Art Ctr, Shreveport, La, 72; plus others. Teaching: Asst prof art, E Carolina Univ, Greenville, NC, 66-68; asst prof art, Sonoma State Col, Cotati, Calif, 68-69; vis prof landscape painting, Mendocino Art Ctr, Calif, 69; asst prof art, NMex State Univ, Las Cruces, 69-; vis assoc prof art, Fla State Univ, 78. Mem: Col Art Asn Am; Hispanic Art Hist Studies in US; Am Asn Univ Prof. Style & Technique: Ranges from Neo-Dada to Neo-Impressionist. Field of 16th and 17th century Spanish art. Publ: Auth, Whitechapel Gestalt, London Hosp Gazette, Vol LXVIII, No 4; auth, Art history as a pedagogical science: pot-shots at the old guard, Art Educ, Vol XIII, No 3; auth, Spanish Painting: a Critical Overview, Studio Vista, London, 73 & Dutton; auth, Observations on Ribera's poet, il Paragone, Florence, 78; plus numerous critical reviews in Art Quart, Art J, Burlington Mag, etc. Mailing Add: 1104 Luna St Las Cruces NM 88001

MOGENSEN, PAUL
PAINTER
b Los Angeles, Calif, Dec 3, 41. Work: Mus of Mod Art, New York; Hugh Mus of Art, Atlanta, Ga. Exhib: One-man shows, Bykert Gallery, New York, 67-69 & 75, Tex Gallery, Houston, 75, Esman Gallery, New York, 76 & 77 & Weinberg Gallery, San Francisco, 77; Minimalism, Inst Contemp Art, Philadelphia, 67; Cool Art, Aldrich Mus of Contemp Art, Ridgefield, Conn, 68; Modular Painting, Albright-Knox Art Gallery, Buffalo, NY, 70; Summer Exhib of 20th Century Art, Houston Mus of Fine Arts, 75; A View of a Decade, Mus of Contemp Art, Chicago, 77. Collections Arranged: Structural Art, Am Fedn of Art Traveling Exhib, 67. Awards: John Simon Guggenheim Mem Found Fel, 76. Bibliog: H Rosenstein (auth), Total and complex, Art News, 5/67; Janet Kutner (auth), Paul Mogensen show in Houston, Dallas Morning News, 4/75; Phyllis Derfner (auth), Paul Mogensen at Bykert, Art in Am, 7-8/75. Mailing Add: New York NY

MOGLIA, LUIGI (JOHN)
PAINTER, INSTRUCTOR
b Dover, NJ. Study: Pratt Inst, grad(interior design); Berkshire Summer Sch Art; also with Ernest Watson, Edgar Whitney, John Rogers & Rutledge Bate. Exhib: Am Watercolor Soc, Audubon Artists & Allied Artists, Nat Acad Galleries, New York; Knickerbocker Artists 3/4, Nat Arts Club, New York; Am Artists Prof League, Lever House, New York. Teaching: Instr interior design, Pratt Inst, Brooklyn, 10 yrs. Pos: Interior designer, W & J Sloane, New York; pvt practice, 26 yrs. Awards: Nat Art League; Manhasset Art Asn; Port Washington Art Coun. Mem: Audubon Artists; Knickerbocker Artists; Am Artists Prof League, Nat Art League; Manhasset Artists Asn. Mailing Add: 14 Baker Hill Rd Great Neck NY 10023

MOHN, CHERI (ANN)
PAINTER
b Akron, Ohio, Aug 12, 36. Study: Akron Art Inst, Ohio; Youngstown State Univ, BA. Work: Butler Inst Am Art, Youngstown, Ohio; Gallerie des Champignons, Youngstown; Phoenix Gallery, Philadelphia; Johnny Artcher's Ghost Town Gallery, Mogollon, NMex. Exhib: Mademoiselle Mag Contest, New York, 61; Peter Hurd Water Color Show, Artesia, NMex, 68; Butler Inst Am Art Midyear Show, Youngtowns & Guest Artist at Studio 09, Cleveland, 70; John Young Invitational, Youngstown, 72-77; one-woman show, Village Art Gallery, 76. Teaching: Dir/instr fine arts, Cheri Mohn Sch Arts, Youngstown, 63-67; instr fine arts, Cheri Mohn Studio, 68- Pos: Dir, Village Art Gallery, Village Market Place, Columbiana, Ohio, 76-77. Awards: Mademoiselle Mag Top Ten Women Artists in USA, 60; Gallerie des Champignons Purchase Award, 68; Butler Inst Am Art Purchase Prize, 70. Bibliog: Rakocy (auth), Artist of the month, Pigment & Form, 67; Feature artist, var publ. Mem: Copley Soc, Boston, Mass; Soc NAm Artists; Cleveland Mus Art; Friends of Am Art, Butler Inst Am Art. Publ: Ed, Niles Times, 58; auth & illusr, articles in Pigment & Form, 67-68; asst ed-feature writer & illusr, Paintin' Place News Inc, 72; illusr, Village Life Inc, 72. Mailing Add: 12691 South Ave North Lima OH 44452

MOHR, PAULINE CATHERINE
ART CONSERVATOR, RESTORER
b Sheboygan, Wis, May 7, 48. Study: Northwestern Univ, BA; Cooperstown Grad Prog, State Univ NY, MA(cert in art conserv), with Sheldon & Caroline Keck. Pos: Conservator, San Francisco Mus Mod Art, Calif, 76-; conservator, Western Regional Paper Conserv Lab, Calif Palace of Legion of Honor, San Francisco, 76- Mem: Int Inst Conserv Hist & Artistic Works; Am Inst Conserv Hist & Artistic Works. Mailing Add: San Francisco Mus Mod Art San Francisco CA 94102

MOIR, ALFRED
ART HISTORIAN
b Minneapolis, Minn, Apr 14, 24. Study: Harvard Univ, AB, 48, AM, 49; Univ Rome, 50-51; Harvard Univ, PhD, 53. Teaching: From instr to assoc prof hist art, Newcomb Col, Tulane Univ, 52-62; from assoc prof to prof hist art, Univ Calif, Santa Barbara, 62-, chmn dept art, 63-69. Mem: Col Art Asn Am; Soc Archit Historians; Renaissance Soc; Medieval Acad Am; Southern Calif Art Historians. Res: Italian baroque art, particularly Caravaggio and his followers; also drawings. Publ: Ed, Eighteenth Century Drawings, 55; contribr, Art in Italy 1600-1700, 65; auth, The Italian Followers of Caravaggio; ed, Drawings by 17th century Italian masters from the collection of Janos Scholz, 74; ed, European drawings in the collection of the Santa Barbara Museum of Art, 76; auth, Caravaggio and his copyists, 76; ed, Regional styles of drawing in Italy 1600-1700, 77. Mailing Add: Dept of Art Hist Univ of Calif Santa Barbara CA 93106

MOISE, WILLIAM SIDNEY
PAINTER
b Carlinville, Ill, Feb 22, 22. Study: Univ South, BA, 43; Cooper Union Art Sch, CFA, 49; Teachers Col, Columbia Univ, MA, 52. Work: US State Dept; Univ of South; Mas d'Aigrat, Les Baux de Provence, France; Mus Art, Columbia, SC; Univ Maine, Orono. Exhib: Jordan Marsh Juried Regional, Boston, Mass, 67; Kennebec Valley Art Asn, Hollowell, Maine, 74; Maine 75, Bowdoin Mus Art, Brunswick, Maine, 75. Teaching: Instr art, Downtown Community Sch, New York, 50-52; instr art, Mt Desert Pub Schs, Maine, 52-54; head dept art, Grovton High Sch, Fairfay Co, Va, 55-57; head dept art, Northern Conserv Music, Bangor, Maine, 60-69. Style & Technique: Abstract impressionism. Media: Oil. Publ: The taste of color, a touch of love, 72. Mailing Add: Hancock ME 04640

MOL, LEO
SCULPTOR
b Ukraine, Jan 15, 15; Can citizen. Study: Kunst Akad, Berlin, Ger; Acad Art, The Hague, Neth; Univ Winnipeg, Man, LLD. Work: Hamilton Art Gallery, Ont; McMichael Conserv Art, Kleinberg, Ont; Toronto Art Gallery, Ont; Winnipeg Art Gallery, Man; Vatican, Rome, Italy. Comn: Monument to a poet, T Shevchenko, Citizen's Comt, Washington, DC, 64; bust of Right Hon J G Diefenbaker, Senate, Ottawa, Can, 64; bust of Gen Dwight D Eisenhower, Gettysburg, Pa, 65; bust of Pope Paul VI, St Clements Univ, Rome, Italy, 67; monument to T Shevchenko, Citizen's Comt, Buenos Aires, Arg, 71. Exhib: Winnipeg Art Gallery, Man, 50-71; Royal Can Acad Arts, Montreal, Ottawa, Toronto & Winnipeg, 56-70; Art Gallery Hamilton, Ont, 56-71; Mus Fine Arts, Montreal, 59; Allied Artists Am, Nat Acad Galleries, New York, 63-64. Awards: Allied Artists Medal, Royal Archit Inst Can, 60; First Prize in Competition for Monument in Washington, DC, 62; Jacob C Stone Prize, Allied Artists Am, 63. Bibliog: Leo Mol, sculptor, Royal Archit Inst Can J, 60; Clement Greenburg (auth), View of art on the prairies, Can Art, 63; Anna Tillenius (auth), The lost wax casting, Winnipeg Free Press, 1/2/71. Mem: Royal Can Acad Arts. Media: Bronze. Mailing Add: 104 Claremont Ave Winnipeg MB R2H 1V9 Can

MOLDROSKI, AL R
PAINTER, EDUCATOR
b Terre Haute, Ind, Aug 27, 28. Study: Ind State Univ, BSc; Mich State Univ, MA; Southern Ill Univ, grant. Exhib: Pa Acad Fine Arts; Detroit Mus Art; City Art Mus, St Louis; De Waters Art Ctr; Boston Festival Arts; plus many others. Teaching: Lectr art, Southern Ill Univ; asst prof art, Glenville State Col; from instr to asst prof art, Eastern Ill Univ, 63-; exchange prof, Portsmouth Polytechnic Fine Arts, Portsmouth, Eng. Awards: Tiffany Found Grant; Purchase Award, Pa Acad Fine Art; Mary Richart Mem Award in Painting & Art Directors Award, Detroit Mus Art; plus many others. Mailing Add: Dept of Art Eastern Ill Univ Charleston IL 61920

MOLINA, ANTONIO J
PAINTER, ART CRITIC
b Cuba, Sept 2, 28; US citizen. Study: Univ Havana; Univ PR; Acad Eicholz, Bonn, Ger. Work: Mus Bellas Artes, Havana; Libr Cong; Mus Ponce, PR; Mus Mod Art, New York; Mus Mod Art Miami; Columbia Univ; Inter-Am Univ. Comn: Mural, Racquet Club Hotel. Exhib: Pan Am Union, Washington, DC, 64; Festival via Margutta, Rome, Italy; Galeria Aprag, New York, 66; Mus Mod Art Miami, Fla, 68; Int Exhib Drawings, Mayaguez, 68; plus many others. Teaching: Lectr, Mus Ponce, Cath Univ PR & Inter-Am Univ PR. Pos: Art critic, El Mundo, 69-; art critic, Artes Visuales, 70- Bibliog: Rosa Oliva (auth), Arte de Molina, El Mundo, Havana, 60; E Perez Chanis (auth), Pintura de Molina, Urbe, 70; Exhibition de Molina, El Imparcial, 71. Mem: Inst Internac Castillos Hist; Am Fedn Arts; Ateneo Puertorriqueno; Soc Escritores PR; Club Gente Prensa. Collection: Ex-libris and antique engravings; pre-Columbian ceramics. Publ: Auth, Pintura en Cuba, 60; auth, Mis versos son asi, Havana, 61; auth, Diccionario Biographico de Ciudad de Sancti Spiritus, Cuba, 61; auth, Criticas de arte, El Mundo, 69-72; plus others. Dealer: Gallery Santiago 207 Cristo St San Juan PR 00902. Mailing Add: PO Box 1361 San Juan PR 00902

MOLINARI, GUIDO
PAINTER, SCULPTOR
b Montreal, PQ, Oct 12, 33. Study: Ecole Beaux-Arts, Montreal; Sch Art & Design, Montreal Mus Fine Arts. Work: Kuntsmuseum, Basel, Switz; Mus Mod Art, Guggenheim Mus & Chase Manhattan Bank, New York; Nat Gallery Art, Ottawa, Ont. Comn: Murals, comn by Dept of Pub Works, Ottawa for Vancouver Int Airport, BC, 68 & Dept Nat Defence Hq Bldg, Ottawa, 72. Exhib: 4th Guggenheim Int Exhib, New York, 64; The Responsive Eye, Mus Mod Art, 65; Canada: Art Aujourdui, Rome, Paris, Lausanne, Bruxelles, 68; Venice 34th Biennial, Italy, 68; Can 101, Edinburgh, Scotland, 68; Retrospective Exhib, Nat Gallery, Ottawa, Montreal, Toronto & Vancouver, 76; 15th Anniversary Paris Biennial, Mus of Mod Art, Paris & traveling exhib to Seibu Art Mus, Tokyo, Japan, 77-78; Contemp Can Painters Exhib, Dept External Affairs World Tour, 77-78. Teaching: Head painting sect, Sir George Williams Univ, 70- Pos: Founder & pres, L'Actuelle, 55-57. Awards: Robertson Award, Montreal Mus Fine Arts, 65; Guggenheim Mem Found fel, 66; Bright Found Award Painting, 68. Bibliog: B Teyssedre (auth), Seven Montreal Painters (catalog), Mass Inst Technol, Cambridge, 67; David Silcox (auth), article for Can 101, Can Coun, Ottawa, 68; Gros Plan (film), Radio-Can, Montreal, 71; Pierre Théberge (ed), Guido Molinari, Nat Gallery, Ottawa. Mem: Academician Royal Can Acad Arts; Soc Esthetique Experimentale, Paris; Soc Color Res, Nat Coun Res (dir, 72). Publ: Auth, 19th Statement, Norman Mackenzie Art Gallery, Regina, Sask, 67; auth, Sculpture 67 Statement, Nat Gallery, Ottawa, 67; co-auth, Debats sur la Peinture Quebecoise, Univ Montreal, 71. Mailing Add: 1611 rue de la Visitation Montreal PQ H2L 3C2 Can

MOLLER, HANS
PAINTER
b Wuppertal, WGer, Mar 20, 05; US citizen. Study: Kunstgewerbeschule Wuppertal-Barmen, 19-27; Acad Fine Arts, Berlin, 27-28. Work: Mus Mod Art & Whitney Mus Am Art, New York; Detroit Inst Art, Mich; Joseph Hirshhorn Mus,Washington, DC; Allentown Art Mus; Minneapolis Mus; Norfolk Mus, Yellowstone Art Ctr, Billings, Mont; Art Mus, Princeton Univ, NJ; Sunrise Found, Charleston, WVa; Bennington Col, Vt; Spelman Col, Atlanta, Ga; NY Univ, NY; Univ Ga; Phillips Mem Gallery, Washington, DC; Walker Art Ctr, Minneapolis, Minn. Comn: Stained glass window, comn by Am Fedn Arts & stained glass indust of the US, 53; tapestry (executed in Aubusson, France), comn by Mr & Mrs Lawrence Buttenwieser, New York, 66; seven stained glass windows, comn by Mr & Mrs Neil Carothers, III, for Christ Church, Georgetown, Washington, DC, 69. Exhib: Seven Shows, Contemp Am Painting, Univ Ill, Urbana, 49-59; 3rd Art Int, Japan, 55; more than 26 one-man shows, including Allentown Art Mus, Pa & Norfolk Mus, Va, 69; Contemp Painting, Sculpture & Graphics, 69. Teaching: Instr painting, Cooper Union Sch Art, 44-56. Awards: Murray Kupferman Prize, Audubon Artists, 73; Andrew Carnegie Prize, Nat Acad New York, 74; A Hibbard Mem Award, 75; Purchase Prizes (three), Childe Hassam Fund-Acad Arts & Lett, NY. Bibliog: John I H Baur (auth), Nature in abstraction, Whitney Mus Am Art, 58; Abram Kampf (auth), Contemporary synagogue art, Union Am Hebrew Congregation, 66. Mem: Nat Acad Design. Media: Oil, Watercolor. Dealer: Midtown Galleries 11 E 57th St New York NY 10022. Mailing Add: 2207 Allen St Allentown PA 18104

MOMADAY, AL
PAINTER
b Mountain View, Okla, July 2, 13. Work: Philbrook Art Ctr, Tulsa, Okla; Dallas Fine Arts Mus, Tex; Mus of NMex, Santa Fe; Heard Mus, Phoenix, Ariz; Denver Art Mus, Colo. Comn: St Luke's Mission, 56 & Curtiss-Wright, 60, Albuquerque, NMex; Franklin Mint, Franklin Ctr, Pa, 75. Exhib: Mus of NMex, Santa Fe, 60; Philbrook Art Ctr, Tulsa, Okla, 63; Smithsonian Inst, Washington, DC, 65; one-man show, Heard Mus, Phoenix, Ariz, 73. Awards: Outstanding Indian Artist, Western NY Art Asn, 65; Grand Award, Gallup Indian Ceremonials, NMex, 67; Waite Phillips Trophy, Philbrook Art Ctr, Tulsa, 75. Bibliog: Joanne Snodgrass (auth), American Indian Painting, Heye Found, NY, 68; N Scott Momaday (auth), The Way to Rainy Mountain, Univ NMex Press, 69. Mem: Artists Equity; NMex Artists Asn. Style & Technique: Indian subjects; tradional and stylized, mostly realistic. Media: Windsor Newton Watercolor, Casein, Acrylics. Publ: Illusr, Rainbows in the Sky, Willoye & Brown, 62; illusr, The Way to Rainy Mountain, Univ NMex Press, 62. Dealer: Lorena E Ohl 22 E Monte Vista Rd Phoenix AZ 85004. Mailing Add: Box 67 Jemez Pueblo NM 87024

MOMENT, JOAN
PAINTER, EDUCATOR
b Sellersville, Pa, Aug 22, 38. Study: Univ Conn, BS, 60; Univ Colo, with William Wiley, MFA, 70. Work: E B Crocker Art Mus, Sacramento, Calif; Security Pac Nat Bank, San Ysidro, Calif & Loma Linda, Calif; Blue Cross of Southern Calif, Los Angeles; NY State Develop Corp, New York. Exhib: Calif Artists Drawing Show (traveling), San Francisco Art Inst, 70, Sacramento Valley, 72; Sacramento Sampler I (traveling), E B Crocker Art Gallery, Sacramento & Oakland Mus, 72; Contemp Am Art Biennial, Whitney Mus Am Art, New York, 73; one-person shows, Whitney Mus Am Art, 74, Wash State Univ, Pullman, 76, Univ Mont, Missoula, 77 & Crocker Art Mus, 78; Touching All Things, Walnut Creek Civic Arts Gallery, Calif, 77; NW Artists Workshop, Portland, Ore, 77; Santa Show, Crocker Art Mus, 77. Teaching: Assoc prof painting & drawing, Calif State Univ, Sacramento, 70-; guest lectr, Wash State Univ & Univ Calif, Davis, 74; vis artist, Univ Colo, Boulder, 75 & Ill State Mus, Bloomington, 77; vis lectr, Univ Mong, Missoula, 77 & Diablo Valley Col, Pleasant Hill, Calif, 78. Bibliog: Marcia Tucker, Joan Moment, Whitney Mus Am Art, 74; Phil Linhares, Interview: Joan Moment, Currant, 2-3/76; Fred Martin, San Francisco Letter, Art Int, summer 76. Style & Technique: Images composed of colored dots on a black background; primarily landscape. Media: Acrylic on Watercolor Board; Painted Objects on Canvas. Dealer: Manolides Gallery 89 Yesler Way Seattle WA 98104; Simone Stern Gallery 520 Royal St New Orleans LA 70130. Mailing Add: 1617 26th St Sacramento CA 95816

MOMIYAMA, NANAE
PAINTER, EDUCATOR
b Tokyo, Japan. Study: Gunka Gakuin Col, Tokyo; Tokyo Women's Col; Art Students League. Work: Nat Mus Mod Arts, Tokyo; Metrop Mus Arts, Tokyo; City Mus Kyoto, Japan; Munic Mus Osaka, Japan; Newberger Mus, Purchase, NY. Exhib: Mod Arts Asn Japan, 50-75; Grand Prix Humanitaire de France, 75; one-man shows, Seibu Gallery Tokyo, 74 & 77, Ligoa Duncan Gallery, New York, 75 & Galeries Raymond Duncan, Paris, 75; plus many others. Teaching: Instr painting, Westchester Art Workshop, White Plains, NY, 71-; instr painting, State Univ NY Col Purchase, 73-; lectr, Philadelphia Mus, Brooklyn Mus, Pittsfield Mus, Columbia Univ, Pratt Inst & numerous other institutions in US & Japan. Pos: Permanent juror, Nat Acad, New York, 68-77 & Salone Int di Pittura, Rome, 72. Awards: Jury Award, Grand Prix Int Peinture Deauville, 72; Madaille d'Argent, Grand Prix Humanitaire de P France, 75. Bibliog: Takachiyo Uemura (auth), Mizue, Bijitsu Shuppan-Sha, 54 & 74; Kaoru Yamaguchi (auth), Geijitsu Shincho, Shincho-Sha. Mem: Mod Arts Asn Japan (dir, NY Chap); Japanese Artists Asn of NY (pres, 78); Asn Int Artists Plastiques; Japanese Artist Asn; Nat Asn Women Artists; Old Greenwich Art Soc. Style & Technique: Abstract semi-representational. Media: Oil, Mixed Media. Publ: Auth, Sumi-e, an introduction to ink painting, 67; illusr, Makuro-no-shoslin of Se— Shonagon, 67; illusr, Rev Paris, 68; illusr, As I cross bridge of dreams, 71. Dealer: Ligua Duncan Gallery 22 E 72nd St New York NY 10021. Mailing Add: PO Box 44 Glenville Sta Greenwich CT 06830

MONAGHAN, EILEEN (MRS FREDERIC WHITAKER)
PAINTER
b Holyoke, Mass, Nov 22, 11. Study: Mass Col Art, Boston. Work: Hispanic Mus, New York; Norfolk Art Mus, Va; Springfield Mus Fine Arts, Mass; Okla Mus Art, Oklahoma City; Charles & Emma Frye Mus, Seattle. Exhib: Am Watercolor Soc Ann, New York, 49-77; Nat Acad Design Ann, New York, 57-70; Childe Hassam Show, Am Acad Arts & Lett, New York, 63; Calif Watercolor Soc, Los Angeles, 66; Watercolor USA, Springfield, Mo, 68-70. Awards: Adolph & Clara Obrig Prize for Watercolor, Nat Acad Design, 64; Silver Medal, 65 & Charles R Kinghan Award, 72, Am Watercolor Soc. Bibliog: Norman Kent (auth), 100 Watercolor Techniques, 68, Wendon Blake (auth), Acrylic Watercolor Painting, 70 & Susan Meyer (auth), 24 Watercolorists, 72, Watson-Guptill. Mem: Assoc Nat Acad Design; Am Watercolor Soc; Watercolor W. Style & Technique: Representational style in transparent watercolor, mostly figure painting. Dealer: A Huney Gallery 3746 Sixth Ave San Diego CA 92103. Mailing Add: 1579 Alta La Jolla Dr La Jolla CA 92037

MONAGHAN, KEITH
PAINTER, EDUCATOR
b San Rafael, Calif, May 15, 21. Study: Univ Calif, Berkeley, BA & MA. Work: Wash State Univ; plus many pvt collections. Exhib: San Francisco Mus, 46-48, 50 & 53; Contemporary American & Canadian Painting, Vancouver Art Gallery, BC, 58; Cheney Cowles Mus, Spokane, Wash, 60, 62-64 & 76; Western Art, Seattle World's Fair, 62; 29th Ann Butler Inst Am Art, Youngstown, Ohio, 64; one-man shows, Fountain Gallery Art, Portland, Ore, 66, Wenatchee Art Ctr, Wash, 67, Wash State Univ, 68 & Univ Idaho, 69. Teaching: Lectr art, Univ Calif, Berkeley, 46-47; prof art, Wash State Univ, 47- Awards: San Francisco Art Asn Award, 48; Seattle Art Mus Award, Northwest Watercolor Soc, 51; Frye Mus Casein Exhib Award, 56. Style & Technique: Semi-abstract, based on figure and/or landscape; abstract impressionist. Mailing Add: NE 1705 Lower Dr Pullman WA 99163

MONAGHAN, WILLIAM SCOTT
PAINTER, SCULPTOR
b Philadelphia, Pa, Nov 1, 44. Study: Yale Univ, BA; Harvard Grad Sch Design, MA. Work: Addison Gallery Am Art, Andover, Mass; Brockton Fuller Mem Art Mus, Mass; Fed Reserve Bank, Boston; Hyatt Hotel, Boston; Aldrich Mus Contemp Art, Ridgefield, Conn. Comn: Sculpture, Boston 200 Bicentennial Art Collection, 76. Exhib: Brockton Fuller Mem Mus, 73; Sculptors' Workshop Show, Addison Gallery Am Art, 74 & Berkshire Mus, Pittsfield, Mass, 75; one-man show, Inst Contemp Art, Boston, 75; Contemp Reflections, Aldrich Mus Contemp Art, 76; Davidson Art Mus, Wesleyan Univ, Conn, 77; two-man show, Soho Ctr for Visual Artists, New York, 77. Mem: Boston Visual Artists' Union. Style & Technique: Collages, assemblages and sculpture of metal, cloth and paint. Mailing Add: 165 Perry St New York NY 10014

MONDALE, JOAN ADAMS
CRAFTSPERSON
b Eugene, Ore, Aug 8, 30. Study: Macalester Col, St Paul, Minn, BA(hist), 52. Work: Boston Mus Fine Arts; Minneapolis Inst Arts; Nat Gallery Art, Washington, DC. Mem: Am Coun of the Arts (bd dir, 73-75); Inst Mus Serv (bd, 77-); Fed Coun on Arts & Humanities (hon chairperson, 78-). Interest: Ways the goverment can help the arts; use of contemporary

American art and craft items in federal buildings and offices. Publ: Auth, Politics in Art, Lerner, 72. Mailing Add: Office of the Vice President Washington DC 20501

MONGAN, AGNES
ART ADMINISTRATOR, ART HISTORIAN
b Somerville, Mass. Study: Bryn Mawr Col, AB; Smith Col, AM, Hon LHD, 41; Wheaton Col, Hon LittD, 54; Univ Mass, Hon DFA, 70. Teaching: Lectr fine arts, Harvard Univ; vis lectr fine arts, Mt Holyoke Col, 66-67; vis lectr fine arts, Oberlin Col, 67-; vis prof, Northwestern Univ, spring 76, Univ Louisville, Ky, fall 76 & Univ Tex, Austin, spring 77; Kress prof in residence, Nat Gallery Art, Washington, DC, 77-78. Pos: Res asst, Fogg Art Mus, Harvard Univ, 28-37, cur drawings, 37-, assoc dir, 64-69, dir, 69-71; vis dir, Timken Art Gallery, San Diego, Calif, 71-72; mem adv comt, I Tatti; mem, Coun of Fel of Pierpont Morgan Libr. Awards: Palms d'Acad, Fr Govt, 47; Cavaliere, Order of Merit, Repub Italy, 71. Mem: Col Art Asn Am; Asn Art Mus Dirs; hon fel Morgan Libr; Benjamin Franklin fel Royal Soc Arts. Res: Relation to drawings by the Masters, especially Tiepolo, Fragonard, Watteau, Ingres, Daumier and Degas. Publ: Co-auth, Drawings in the Fogg Museum, 41; co-auth, Ingres Drawings, 67; co-auth, Tiepolo Drawings, 70; auth articles in Burlington Mag, Art Quart, Art News, Gazette Beaux-Arts, Master Drawings & others. Mailing Add: Fogg Art Mus Harvard Univ Cambridge MA 02138

MONONGYE, PRESTON LEE
SILVERSMITH, GOLDSMITH
b Los Angeles, Calif, Sept 6, 27. Study: With Gene Pooyouma, 35-55; study with Fred Kabotie, 40-43. Work: Mus of Northern Ariz, Flagstaff; Heard Mus, Phoenix, Ariz; Smithsonian Inst, Washington, DC; Walter Bimpson Collection, Valley Nat Bank, Valley Ctr, Phoenix, Ariz; Fred Harvey Collection, Chicago. Comn: Altar set, St Luke's Hosp, Phoenix, Ariz, 72; woodcarvings (4ft x 5 1/2ft) Cottonwood Branch, Valley Nat Bank, Ariz, 74. Exhib: Inter-Tribal Ceremonials, Gallup, NMex, 50-76; Scottsdale Nat Indian Art Show, Ariz, 68-74; Tanners Invitational, Scottsdale, Ariz, 70-77; one-man show, Heard Mus, Phoenix, 74; Indian Art Show, Heard Mus, 75. Teaching: Guest artist, Calif Inst of the Arts, Valencia, 74; instr silversmithing, Phoenix Indian Ctr, Ariz, 75. Pos: Judge, Santa Fe Indian Market Show, NMex, 73 & Scottsdale Nat Indian Art Show, Ariz, 74. Awards: Best of Show, NMex State Fair, 68-71, Inter-Tribal Ceremonials, 70-72 & Scottsdale Nat, 71; Three Awards, Santa Monica Indian Ceremonials, 78. Bibliog: M Bedinger (auth), Indian Silver, Univ NMex Press, 73; Carl Rosnek & Joseph Stacy (co-auth), Skystone & Silver: The Collector's Book of Southwest Indian Jewelry, Prentice Hall, 76. Mem: Inter-Tribal Ceremonial Asn (bd mem, 68-71); Indian Artists of Am (pres, 74-). Style & Technique: Symbolic Indian design using sandcasting with inlay; silversmithing. Media: Silver, gold, acrylic, turquoise, shells, jet, coral and lapis. Publ: Auth, The new Indian art jewelry of the Southwest, 6/72 & After fifty-one miracles, 7/72, Ariz Hwys Mag; contribr, Southwest Indian Paintings: A Changing Art, Univ Ariz Press, 73; contribr, Hopi Silver, Northern Ariz Press, 74; contribr, Indian Silver—Navajo and Pueblo Jewelers, NMex Press, 74; contribr, Carl Rosnek & Joseph Stacy, co-auth, Skystone and Silver: The Collector's Book of Southwest Indian Jewelry, Prentice Hall, 76. Dealer: Christopher's Enterprises PO Box 25621 Albuquerque NM. Mailing Add: 10002 N 36th St Phoenix AZ 85028

MONROE, GERALD
PAINTER, EDUCATOR
b New York, NY, Aug 17, 26. Study: Art Students League; Cooper Union; NY Univ, EdD. Work: NY Univ Collection; Finch Col Mus Art; NJ State Mus. Exhib: Cooper Union, 67 & 69; Loeb Ctr, NY Univ, 71; William Paterson Col, 73; NJ State Mus, 75; Wagner Col, 76; Newark Mus, NJ, 78. Pos: Assoc prof art, Glassboro State Col, 68- Awards: Nat Endowment for Humanities Fel, 73-74, Grant, 75; Ossabaw Island Proj, 77; Va Ctr Creative Arts, 78. Style & Technique: Large, soft, romantic, espressionist abstractions. Res: Influence of left-wing politics on art and artists during Great Depression. Publ: Auth articles in Art J, fall 72, Arch Am Art J, Vol 13, No 3 & Vol 14, No 1, Studio Int, 9/74 & Art in Am, 9-10/75. Mailing Add: 463 West St New York NY 10014

MONROE, ROBERT
PHOTOGRAPHER
b New York, NY, Nov 20, 23. Study: Studied with Laotens. Work: Libr of Cong, Washington, DC; Ulster Co Community Col, Stone Ridge, NY; Bibliot Nat, Paris, France; Finch Mus Collection, New York. Exhib: Experimental Color Photog, Mus Mod Art, New York, 57; one-man shows, Finch Mus Art, 67, Ulster Co Community Col, 69, Neikrug Gallery, New York, 75 & Drew Univ, 76; Am Soc Mag Photogr 25 Yr Show, New York Cult Ctr, 70. Collections Arranged: Posters by Artists, Finch Mus Art, New York. Awards: First Prize, Cleo, 75; Award for Excellence, Andy, 75; Gold Medal, The One Show, 76. Bibliog: Charles Reynolds (auth), Robert Monroe, Infinity, 67; Ken Jacobs (auth), Robert Moore, Kodak Int Photog, 77. Mem: Am Soc Mag Photogr. Style & Technique: Various experimental styles. Publ: Contribr, Art Direction, 74, Photo Graphics, 75-76, Graphics, 76, Kodak Int Photog, Eastman Kodak Co, 77 & Popular Photog Ann. Dealer: Witkin Gallery 41 E 57th St New York NY 10022. Mailing Add: 255 W 90th St New York NY 10024

MONT, BETTY
ART DEALER
b Vienna, Austria; US citizen. Pos: Vpres, Frederick Mont, Inc, New York, currently. Mem: Art Dealers Asn. Specialty: Paintings by old masters. Mailing Add: Frederick Mont Inc 465 Park Ave New York NY 10022

MONT, FREDERICK
ART DEALER
Pos: Pres, Frederick Mont, Inc. Specialty: Old European masters. Mailing Add: 465 Park Ave New York NY 10022

MONTAGUE, JAMES L
PAINTER
b New Rochelle, NY, May 6, 06. Study: Dartmouth Col, AB, 28; Art Students League, with Kimon Nicolaides; also with Leger, Ozenfant & Galanis, Paris. Work: US Mil Acad; Southern Vt Artists Permanent Collection; Dartmouth Col. Comn: Private portrait commissions. Exhib: Various group shows & one-man exhibitions throughout New England states and New York. Pos: Dir, Sharon Art Ctr, NH, 61-63; dir, Southern Vt Art Ctr, 64-75. Awards: Fitchburg Mus Award, 62; Print Club Albany Award, 70; Award, Norwich Univ, 71. Mem: Art Students League; Nat Arts Club; Salmagundi Club, New York; Print Club Albany; Northern Vt Artists; Burr Artists. Media: Oil, Graphics. Mailing Add: PO Box 926 Manchester Center VT 05255

MONTAGUE, RUTH DUBARRY
See Criquette

MONTANA, PIETRO
SCULPTOR, PAINTER
b Alcamo, Italy; US citizen. Study: Cooper Union Art Sch, dipl; also with George T Brewster; Capital Univ, Ohio, DH, 77. Work: Am Numismatic Soc, New York; Art Gallery Mus, Ohio Northern Univ, Ada; Brookgreen Gardens, SC; Ga Mus Art, Athens; Hickory Mus Art, NC; Schumacher Gallery, Capital Univ, Columbus, Ohio. Comn: The Dawn of Glory (war mem), comn by people of dist, Highland Park, Brooklyn, NY, 24; Mem to Jose de Diego, gift of Oscar Bravo, Mayaguez, PR, 35; Stations of the Cross, Fordham Univ, New York, 47-52; garden sculpture in bot garden, Norrvikens Tragardar, Basted, Sweden, 54; four saints, comn by Kennedy, Walsh & Kennedy, Architects, Shrine Immaculate Conception, Washington, DC, 59; twelve medals of Vita Christi & twenty medals of the parables of Christ for Franklin Mint; sixty medals of saints for Rochester Art Mint. Exhib: Nat Acad Design Ann, New York, 21, 31 & others; Nat Sculpture Soc Ann, New York, 23-; one-man show, Rome, Italy, 30; Allied Artists Am Ann, New York, 32-; Hudson Valley Art Asn Ann, White Plains, NY, 37- Teaching: Instr sculpture, Master Inst Arts, New York, 31-34; instr painting & sculpture, Fordham Univ, 47-52. Awards: Elizabeth M Watrous Gold Medal for Sculpture, Nat Acad Design, 31; Herbert Adams Mem Medal & Citation for Serv to Society, Nat Sculpture Soc, 62; Gold Medal & Citation for Attainment in Sculpture & Painting, Hudson Valley Art Asn, 62. Bibliog: The work of Pietro Montana, Nat Sculpture Rev, summer 70. Mem: Nat Acad Design; fel Nat Sculpture Soc (mem coun); Allied Artists Am (treas, 12 yrs); Artist's Fel (treas, 4 yrs); Hudson Valley Art Asn. Style & Technique: Classic tradition. Publ: Auth, Memories (autobiography), Exposition Press, 77. Mailing Add: 7 Taylor Lane Bayville NY 11709

MONTENEGRO, ENRIQUE E
PAINTER
b Valparaiso, Chile, Dec 7, 17; US citizen. Study: Univ Fla, BFA, 44; Art Students League, out-of-town scholar, 44-45; Colorado Springs Fine Arts Ctr, summer 43; also with Morris Kantor, Kunioshi & Boardman Robinson. Work: Denver Mus Art; NC Mus Art, Raleigh; Colorado Springs Fine Arts Ctr; Issac Delgado Mus, New Orleans; Mt Holyoke Col Mus, South Hadley, Mass. Exhib: New Talent in the USA, Art in Am Mag Traveling Show, 55; one-man shows, NC Mus Art, 57 & Parma Gallery, New York, 59; Landau Gallery, Los Angeles, 60; The Painter & the Photograph, Art News Ann Traveling Show, 65. Teaching: Instr art, Univ NMex, Brown Univ, Pa State Univ, Colorado Springs Fine Arts Ctr, Mt Holyoke Col, Univ Fla, NC State Col & Towson State Col. Awards: Denver Mus Art Purchase Prize, 53; Catherwood Award Study in Europe, 56. Bibliog: Fred Bartlett (auth), New talent in the USA, Art in Am Mag, 2/55; Dorothy Seiberling (auth), New painters of the West, Life Mag, 11/4/57; Hiram Williams (auth), Notes for a Young Painter, Prentice-Hall, 63. Style & Technique: Figurative, expressionist. Media: Oil. Mailing Add: 306 Langley Ct Bel Air MD 21014

MONTEQUIN, FRANCOIS-AUGUSTE DE
ART HISTORIAN, WRITER
US citizen. Study: Univ Ital Stranieri, Perugia, Italy, cert art hist, 69; Accad di Belle Arti Pietro Vannucci, Perugia, cert painting & sculpture, 69; Univ NMex, BFA(magna cum laude), 70, PhD(art hist & criticism), 74; Univ Madrid, Spain, MA, 71; Universite de Provence, Aix-en-Provence, France, cert of Islamic Paleography, 73. Teaching: Instr hist art & archit, Univ NMex, 73-74; asst prof art, Hamline Univ, 74-; prof Hispanic Islamic art & group leader study-travels abroad, Upper Midwest Asn Intercult Educ, Macalester Col, 75; lectr docents of African Collection, Minneapolis Inst Arts, 75. Awards: Phi Kappa Phi, 70; Kress Found Res Fel, 72. Mem: Soc Archit Historians; Am Soc Hisp Art Hist Studies; Inst Int Africain; Mid East Studies Asn of NAm; Escuela de Estudios Arabes de Granada. Res: Spanish colonial art and its influences from the Islamic world; Islamic art and architecture of Spain; African sculpture and its influences from the Islamic world. Publ: Auth, A note on Jesus Guerrero Galvan's fresco, Union of the Americas, Bull, Univ NMex Art Mus, 73; auth, Campeche: evolution of a fortified colonial city, 74 & auth, Colonial settlements in Florida and Louisiana during Hispanic domination: documents in the Archivo General de Indias of Sevilla, 3/75, J Soc Archit Historians; auth, Maps and Plans of Cities and Towns in Colonial New Spain, the Floridas, and Louisiana: Selected Documents From the Archivo General de Indias of Sevilla, 2 vols, Univ Microfilms, 75; auth, Compendium of Hispano-Islamic Art and Architecture, Hamline Univ, 76. Mailing Add: Dept Art Hamline Univ St Paul MN 55104

MONTGOMERY, CLAUDE
PAINTER, ETCHER
b Portland, Maine, Jan 25, 12. Study: Portland Sch Fine Art, Maine, with Alexander Bower; Nat Acad New York, with Leon Kroll, Arthur Covey & Gifford Beal; Pratt Inst. Comn: Portraits of Sen Edmund Muskie & Gov Kenneth Curtis, State of Maine, Augusta; portrait of Maj Gen Fritz Borum, Hall of Fame, Oklahoma City; portrait of President J F Kennedy, Harvard Club, Boston; portrait of Dr Green, Jackson Res Lab, Bar Harbor, Maine, 75; portraits of Mr & Mrs J A Chapman for Children's Med Ctr & Chapman Found, Tulsa, Okla, 75; plus others. Exhib: Nat Acad, New York, 37-48; Paris Expos, France, 37; New York World's Fair, 64; Am Watercolor Soc, New York, 65-75; Mex Watercolor Soc, Mexico City, 70-74. Awards: Suydam Silver Medal, Nat Acad, 35; Silver Medal, Repub France, 37; Grand Prize, Mus Conserv Art, Oklahoma City, 64. Bibliog: Carmen Lopez (auth), Montgomery, his work in Spain, Diario Majorca, Spain, 67; Jenken Lloyd Jones (auth), People and portraits, Tulsa Tribune, Okla, 70; Isabel Currier (auth), Montgomery: His art, Down East Mag, 72. Mem: Am Watercolor Soc; Salmagundi Club; Royal Soc Art; Mex Watercolor Group; Southwestern Art Asn. Style & Technique: Conservative technique; impressionistic color. Media: Watercolor, Oil. Publ: Majorca Sketchbook, Spain, 57. Dealer: Vose Galleries of Boston 238 Newbury Boston MA 02116. Mailing Add: Box 225 Georgetown ME 04548

MONTHAN, GUY
PHOTOGRAPHER, EDUCATOR
b Tucson, Ariz, Apr 17, 25. Study: Syracuse Univ, BFA, 50; Calif State Univ, Los Angeles, MA, 67. Exhib: Los Angeles Co Mus Ann, 61; San Gabriel Valley Ann, Pasadena Art Mus, 61; Tucson Festival Art Show, 62 & 65; Southwestern Photog Exhibit, Dallas Mus Fine Arts, 73; Yuma Invitational, Ariz, 73 & 74. Teaching: Instr advert design, Northern Ariz Univ, Flagstaff, 68- Pos: Advert design, Los Angeles, 50-68. Style & Technique: Photography, landscape and multiple image. Publ: Designer-illusr, Art and Indian Individualists, 75. Mailing Add: PO Box 1698 Flagstaff AZ 86001

MONTLACK, EDITH
PAINTER
b New York, NY. Study: Metrop Mus Art Sch, scholar, with Michael Jacobs; Nat Acad Design, with Louis Bouche; Art Students League. Exhib: Parrish Mus; Riverside Mus, Hall of Art, Knickerbocker Artists & Nat Arts Club Gallery, New York; plus many others.

Awards: Emil Kohn Medal; St Gaudens Medal; First Prize for Watercolors, Nat Asn Women Art. Mem: Life fel Royal Soc Art, London; Nat Asn Women Artists. Style & Technique: Impressionist to expressionist in style. Media: Oil. Mailing Add: 90 Taymil Rd New Rochelle NY 10804

MONTOYA, GERONIMA CRUZ (PO-TSU-NU)
PAINTER, INSTRUCTOR
b San Juan Pueblo, NMex, Sept 22, 15. Study: Santa Fe Indian Sch; Claremont Col; Col St Joseph, Albuquerque, BS; also with Dorothy Dunn, Kenneth Chapman & Alfredo Martinez; Univ NMex; Col Santa Fe. Work: De Young Mus Art; Hall of Ethnol; Mus NMex; Indian Arts & Crafts Mkt, Washington, DC. Exhib: Mus NMex, Santa Fe; Indian Art Exhib, 54 & 55; Mus NMex Traveling Exhib Indian Paintings; one-man shows, Hall of Ethnol, Santa Fe, 59 & Philbrook Art Ctr, 65; plus others. Teaching: Lectr Indian design & painting; instr adult educ, San Juan Day Sch; instr NMex adult educ, eight norhtern pueblos. Awards: Spec Award Indian Art, NMex State Fair, 60; Purchase Prize, NMex Mus, 61; Ceremonial for Mod Indian Painting, Gallup, NMex, 61; plus others. Mem: NMex Educ Asn. Mailing Add: 1008 Calle de Suenos Santa Fe NM 87501

MOODY, ELIZABETH CHAMBERS
ART DEALER
b Memphis, Tenn, Nov 20, 44. Study: Univ Ky, Lexington, BFA, 66. Teaching: Instr, Mus of Fine Arts, 76- Pos: Gallery attendant, Univ Ky Art Gallery, 65-66; sales consult, DuBose Gallery, Houston, 69-72, asst mgr & vpres, 72-73; mgr & vpres, Ars Longa Gallery, Houston, 73-75; dir & owner, Moody Gallery, Houston, 75- Mem: Art Dealers Asn of Houston; Mus Fine Arts Sch Bd. Specialty: Contemporary art, paintings, prints and sculpture; Houston representative. Mailing Add: 2015-J West Gray Houston TX 77019

MOON, MARC
INSTRUCTOR, PAINTER
b Middletown, Ohio, Apr 6, 23. Study: Appl Art Acad; also with Roy Wilhelm & John Pike. Work: Canton Art Inst; Masillon Mus, Ohio; Richmond Mus, Va; Springfield Mus, Mo; Taylor Mem Libr, Cuyahoga Falls, Ohio. Comn: Mural, Canton Hall of Fame, Canton Hist Soc, Ohio, 70. Exhib: One-man show, Columbia Mus, SC, 66-68; Am Watercolor Soc, New York, 66-70; Nat Acad Design, 74; Watercolor USA, Springfield Mus, 74; Butler Art Inst, Youngstown, Ohio, 75. Teaching: Instr watercolor, Hilton Leech Art Sch, Sarasota, Fla, 68- Awards: Mario Cooper Award, Am Watercolor Soc; Best in Show, Va Beach Art Asn; Purchase Award, Watercolor USA. Bibliog: R Fabri (auth), Medal of Merit, Todays Art, 66. Mem: Am Watercolor Soc; Salmagundi Club; US Painters in Casein. Style & Technique: Landscapes and other subjects in watercolor and acrylic. Publ: Auth, Watercolor page, Am Artist Mag, 74. Mailing Add: 505 W Portage Trail Ext Cuyahoga Falls OH 44223

MOONIER, SYLIVA
ART RESTORER, PAINTER
b Philadelphia, Pa, Dec 13, 21. Study: Oklahoma City Univ, Norman; Acad Prof Art; also with Florinda Leighton. Work: Riverside Mus of Mission Inn. Comn: Mural, Wells Fargo Bank, San Diego, Calif, 70. Exhib: Am Fedn of Women, Corona, Calif, 66; Gibson Art Festival, Corona, 67. Teaching: Instr evening classes fine art, Garden Grove High Sch, 76- Pos: Pvt art conservator, Calif, 70- Awards: Torrana Art League Award, Merchants of Anaheim City, Calif, 64; Women's Fedn Award, Calif Fedn, Corona, 66; Gibson Art Festival Grand Trophy Award, Loral Radio Sta, Corona, 67. Mem: Int Inst of Conserv. Style & Technique: Expressionistic and knife. Media: Oil, Acrylic. Mailing Add: 340 N Newport Dr Newport Beach CA 92663

MOORE, BARBARA
ARCHIVIST
b New York, NY, Sept 30, 36. Study: RI Sch Design, BFA. Pos: Admin dir, The Archives of Experimental Art, New York, 62-; ed in chief, The Something Else Press, New York, 65-66; co-owner, Backworks, New York, 76- Mem: Am Soc Picture Prof (secy, 75-77); Art Libr Soc of NAm. Res: Experimental art from the early 1960's to the present, particularly performance art by artists. Mailing Add: 351 W 30th St New York NY 10001

MOORE, BEVERIDGE
PAINTER
b Richmond, Va, July 25, 15. Study: Univ Va, BA; Art Students League, with Yasuo Kuniyoshi, Morris Kantor & William Zorach. Work: Beveridge Moore Collection, Valentine Mus, Richmond, Va; Fordham Univ, New York; Rutgers Univ, New Brunswick, NJ; Evansville Mus Arts & Sci, Ind; Phoenix Art Mus, Ariz; plus many others. Exhib: Nat Acad Design, New York, 48; Va Mus Fine Arts, Richmond, 53, 55 & 57; Art Alliance, Philadelphia, Pa, 65; Butler Inst Am Art, Youngstown, Ohio, 67; Artist of the Mo Exhibs, Solebury Nat Bank, New Hope, 72, 73, 75 & 76; five one-man shows at Bodley Gallery, New York, 62-73, one at Artist of the Mo Exhib, Solebury Nat Bank, Pa, 78. Style & Technique: Expressionist, fantastical or romantic subjects in oil on canvas. Dealer: Bodley Gallery 1063 Madison Ave New York NY 10028. Mailing Add: Star Rte New Hope PA 18938

MOORE, E BRUCE
SCULPTOR
b Bern, Kans, Aug 5, 05. Study: Pa Acad Fine Arts, with Albert Laessle & Charles Grafly. Work: Whitney Mus Am Art; Wichita Art Mus; Pa Acad Fine Arts; Brookgreen Gardens, SC; Am Acad, Rome, Italy; plus others. Comn: Monumental sculpture, Nat Mem Cemetery of the Pac, Honolulu, 60-61; Osgood Hooker Doors & King Doors, Grace Cathedral, San Francisco; Walter H Beech Mem Doors, Wichita Art Asn; two bronze tigers, Princeton Univ; portraits & animal sculpture also in pvt collections. Exhib: Whitney Mus Am Art, 42; Meriden Arts & Crafts, 40 & 42; Whitney Mus Am Art, 42; Nat Inst Arts & Lett, 43; Va Mus Fine Arts, 58; Mostra Art Mod, Camaiore, Italy, 68; plus others. Awards: Nat Inst Arts & Lett Grant, 43; Am Numismatic Soc Medal, 52; Henry Hering Mem Medal, Nat Sculpture Soc, 68; plus others. Mem: Academician Nat Acad Design; Nat Inst Arts & Lett; Nat Sculpture Soc; fel Am Numismatic Soc. Mailing Add: 2912 Q St NW Washington DC 20007

MOORE, ETHEL
CURATOR, ART HISTORIAN
b Chicago, Ill. Study: Vanderbilt Univ, BA; Va Commonwealth Univ; Art Students League; State Univ Iowa, Yaddo Found fel, 63. Pos: Ed publ, Albright-Knox Art Gallery, Buffalo, NY, 64-70, ed publ & admin officer, 70-73; cur, Ga Mus Art, Univ Ga, 74- Publ: Ed, Wallpapers by Charles Burchfield, 73; ed, Clyfford Still: Thirty-three Paintings in the Albright-Knox Art Gallery, 66; ed, American Folk Art from the Shelburne Museum, 65; ed, Albert Christ-Janer, 76 & Open to New Ideas: A Collection of New Art for Jimmy Carter, 78; articles in Arts Mag, Mus News, Ga Mus Art Bull & others. Mailing Add: Ga Mus Art Univ Ga Athens GA 30602

MOORE, INA MAY
INSTRUCTOR, PAINTER
b Hayden, Ariz, Feb 20, 20. Study: Univ Ariz, BA(educ, art & music); Ariz State Univ, MA(art educ). Work: Phoenix Col, Ariz; Valley Nat Bank, Ariz; Ariz Bank, Phoenix; Western Savings & Loan Asn, Yuma, Ariz; First Fed Savings & Loan Asn, Yuma. Exhib: Phoenix Art Mus; Ariz Watercolor Asn Traveling Exhib Ann; Nat Art Exhib, Tubac, Ariz; Invitational Exhib, Univ SDak, 68; Nat League Am Pen Women, Salt Lake City, Utah, 71. Teaching: Part-time instr art, Elem Pub Schs, 40-50; pvt classes, 50-64; instr watercolor, Phoenix Art Mus, 65- Awards: Purchase Prizes, Valley Nat Bank, 66, Ariz Bank, 68 & Phoenix Col, 69; Award, Thunderbird Bank; Award, First Nat Bank. Mem: Ariz Watercolor Asn (pres, 66-68); Nat League Am Pen Women; Ariz Artist's Guild; Ariz Art Educ Asn. Style & Technique: Blend of traditional and experimental. Media: Watercolor. Mailing Add: 5718 N Tenth Ave Phoenix AZ 85013

MOORE, JOHN J
PAINTER, EDUCATOR
b St Louis, Mo, Apr 25, 41. Study: Washington Univ, Nat Found Arts & Humanities grant, BFA, 66; Yale Univ, Milliken foreign travel fel & MFA, 68. Work: Philadelphia Mus Art; Pa Acad Fine Arts, Philadelphia; Yale Univ Art Gallery, New Haven; Dartmouth Col; Ariz State Univ, Tempe. Exhib: Fischbach Gallery, New York, 69, 73, 75 & 78; New Realism, State Univ NY Potsdam, 71; Realist Revival, Am Fedn Arts Traveling Exhib, 72-73; Contemp Am Painting & Sculpture, Krannert Mus, Univ Ill, 74; Figure in Recent American Painting, Pa Coun Arts Traveling Exhib, 74-75. Teaching: Assoc prof painting & drawing, Tyler Sch Art, Temple Univ, 68-; artist in residence, Yale Summer Sch, 68 & 69; mem fac painting & drawing, Skowhegan Sch Painting & Sculpture, summer 74. Style & Technique: Representational. Media: Oil, Watercolor. Dealer: A Aladar Marburger c/o Fischbach Gallery 29 W 57th St New York NY 10021. Mailing Add: 111 Woodland Rd Wyncote PA 19095

MOORE, MICHAEL SHANNON
PAINTER
b Los Angeles, Calif, Mar 30, 42. Study: Stanford Univ, BA(art), 64; Yale Univ, 64-65; also with Diebenkorn, Boyle & Tworkov. Work: Stanford Univ Mus Art; Arco World Hq, Los Angeles, Calif. Comn: 1956 Ford School Bus, Anonymous Artists Am, 69; miscellaneous camouflaged vehicles & house mural, comn by Peter Breeze, Mill Valley, Calif, 69; garden mural, comn by Marshall Krause, Mill Valley, 70; interior mural, Foto Graphix, San Francisco, 71; panel painting, comn by David M Rumsey, San Francisco, 75. Exhib: California Landscape, Lytton Ctr, Los Angeles, 68; Krannert Biennial, Univ Ill, 69; Folio '73, Calif Col Arts & Crafts World Print Competition, San Francisco Mus Art, 73; ten-year retrospective, Stanford Univ Mus Art, 74; one-man shows, Smith Andersen Gallery, Palo Alto, 73, 74, 76 & 77 & San Francisco, 76, William Sawyer Gallery, San Francisco, 75, Linda Farris Gallery, Seattle, Wash, 75 & 76. Pos: Publisher & asst printmaker, Cactus Patch Press, 71-; environmental consult, DJD Properties, San Francisco, Calif, 75- Awards: Art Purchase Award, Stanford Univ, 63; Mem Bequest Excellence, Desert Art Colony, 65-66. Bibliog: C E Mayes (auth), Artist's sunlight exhilarating, Palo Alto Times, 3/23/74; A Frankenstein (auth), Michael Moore acrylic show, 3/30/74 & A master looks at the desert, 1/16/75, San Francisco Chronicle. Style & Technique: Thin watery washes of wide western wastes on canvas; minimal colorfield compositions; currently tending to harsher impressions drawn from photographs. Media: Ink on Paper, Watery Acrylic on Canvas. Publ: Illusr, Herbs and Things, Jeanne Rose's Herbal, Grosset & Dunlap, 72; auth & illusr, Trying talking with Art Banditz, Vol 1, No 1, Other bodies of water, Vol 2, No 1 & Five autobiographies, Vol 3, No 1, Place; plus others. Dealer: Paula Z Kirkeby c/o Smith/Andersen Gallery 200 Homer St Palo Alto CA 94305. Mailing Add: 219 Carl St San Francisco CA 94117

MOORE, PETER
PHOTOGRAPHER, ARCHIVIST
b London, Eng, Apr 28, 32; US citizen. Study: Mass Inst Technol; Haverford Col. Work: Int Mus Photog, George Eastman House, Rochester, NY; Archiv Sohm, Ger & Archive Jean Brown, Tyringham, Mass; Dance Collection, New York Pub Libr & Mus Perform Arts, NY; Mus Contemp Art, Chicago; Mus Mod Art, Paris. Exhib: Photography 63, Int Mus Photog, Rochester, NY & NY State Expos, Syracuse, 63-64; Photography 64, New York World's Fair, 64-65; Avant-Garde Dancers, NY State Coun Arts Travel Tour, 68-72; Environments/Permutations, Riverside Mus, New York, 68; Happening & Fluxus, Koelnischer Kunstverein, Cologne, Ger, 70. Teaching: Instr photog, New Sch, New York, 70-74; instr photog, pvt classes, New York, 70-74. Pos: Artistic dir, The Archives of Experimental Art, New York, 62- Awards: Cash Grant, Finch Col Mus Art, 74. Bibliog: Ronald Argelander (auth), Photo-Documentation, An Interview with Peter Moore, Drama Rev, NY Univ, Sch of Arts, 9/74. Mem: Am Soc Photog in Commun; Soho Photo Gallery & Found. Res: Experimental performance art, particularly that created by artists usually associated with the visual arts. Mailing Add: 351 W 30th St New York NY 10001

MOORE, ROBERT ERIC
PAINTER
b Manchester, NH, Oct 13, 27. Study: Univ NH; New Eng Sch Art, Boston. Work: Utah State Univ; Mus Fine Arts, Springfield, Mass; Headley Mus, Lexington, Ky; Hancock Col Art, Santa Maria, Calif; Union Bank, Houston. Exhib: Doll & Richards, Boston, 66 & 68; Hobe Sound Galleries, Fla, 72-; Philadelphia Art Alliance, 73; Centennial Art Mus, Corpus Christi, Tex; Am Watercolor Soc Ann, New York; Guild of Boston Artists, Mass, 77; New Eng in Winter Invitational, Decordova Mus, Lincoln, Mass, 77. Awards: Grumbacher Purchase Award, Am Watercolor Soc, 67; Windsor Newton Award, Painters & Sculptors Soc NJ, 67; Minor S Jameson Award, Miniature Painters, Sculptors & Gravers Soc, Washington, DC, 71; Manchester Bank Award, Currier Gallery of Art, NH, 76; Arches Paper Award, Nat Watercolor Soc, Calif, 77; Mustard Seed Award, Rocky Mountain Nat Watermedia Exhib, Golden, Colo, 77; First Place, Am Miniature Show (Nat), Laramie, Wyo, 77. Bibliog: Ralph Fabri (auth), History of American Watercolor Society the first 100 years, Am Watercolor Soc; Field Art Collection, Chicago, Ill, reproduced in World Bk Encycl, under Maine, 66. Mem: Am Watercolor Soc; Nat Watercolor Soc; Guild Boston Artists; Copley Soc; Boston Watercolor Soc. Style & Technique: Semi-realist. Media: Watercolor, Acrylic. Mailing Add: Cider Hill York ME 03909

MOORE, ROBERT JAMES
PAINTER, INSTRUCTOR
b San Jose, Calif, July 24, 22. Study: USAAF Photo Sch, Lowry Field, Colo, grad; San Jose State Col, BA; NY Inst Fine Arts, with Salmony, Schoenberger, Panofsky & Offner; Columbia Univ Teachers Col, MFA; Art Students League, with Brackman, Miller, Will Barnet & others. Exhib: Pa Acad Fine Arts, Philadelphia, 50; NW Printmakers Int, Seattle, Wash, 50; Soc Am Graphic Artists, Kennedy Galleries, 51; James D Phelan Awards Competition, San Francisco Art Mus, 51; Artists Equity Exhib, Riverside Mus, 53; 11 Yr Retrospective of Prizewinners, Village Art Ctr, Whitney Mus Am Art, New York, 54; NY City Ctr Gallery, 59; Audubon

Artists, Nat Acad Design, New York, 62; one-man shows, Ruth Sherman Galleries, New York, 64 & Adele Bednarz Galleries, Los Angeles, 65; Berkshire Mus, Pittsfield, Mass, 66; Art Students League & Ford Found Show, New York, 75. Teaching: Assoc prof art, Goddard Col, 54-57; instr art & photog, Battin High Sch, Elizabeth, NJ, 60-64; instr art, Julia Richman High Sch, New York, 64- Awards: Second Prize, Village Art Ctr 7th Ann Graphic Art Show, Village Art Ctr, New York, 52; Blue Ribbon, New Talent Show, Ruth Sherman Gallery, New York, 64; Berkshire Mus Award, 66. Mem: Artists Equity Asn; life mem Art Students League. Style & Technique: Semi-abstract to abstract, based on traditional picture structure and dynamics; currently involved with undersea themes. Media: Oil, Graphics. Publ: Auth, The Other Side of the Coin, League, spring 51. Mailing Add: 246 E 51st St New York NY 10022

MOORE, RUSSELL JAMES
MUSEUM DIRECTOR, ART ADMINISTRATOR
b Stockton, Calif, Jan 13, 47. Study: Univ Calif, Davis, BA, 69, Los Angeles, MA, 72; Harvard Univ Inst in Arts Admin, 77. Collections Arranged: Winslow Homer's Work in Black & White (ed, catalogue), 74-76, Ernest Haskell (1876-1925) A Retrospective Exhibition (auth, catalogue), 76, Nancy Hemenway: Textures of Our Earth (co-auth, catalogue), 77-78 & Calvert Coggeshall: Paintings, 77, all circulated nationwide, Bowdoin Col. Pos: Asst cur, Utah Mus Fine Arts, Salt Lake City, 72-74; acting dir, Bowdoin Col Mus Art, Brunswick, Maine, 74-78; dir, Long Beach Mus Art, Calif, 78- Mem: Am Asn Mus; Col Art Asn; Pejepscot Hist Soc. Res: American art history; early 20th century. Mailing Add: c/o Long Beach Mus of Art 2300 E Ocean Blvd Los Angeles CA 90803

MOOS, WALTER A
ART DEALER
b Karlsruhe, Ger, Sept 6, 26. Study: Ecole Superieure Com, Geneva, Switz, BA; New Sch Social Res, with Paul Zucker & Meyer Shapiro. Pos: Dir, Gallery Moos Ltd; vpres, Arts Mag, 77. Mem: Prof Art Dealers Asn Can (pres, 71-74); Can Eskimo Arts Coun. Specialty: Contemporary Canadian, European and American paintings, sculpture and graphics. Mailing Add: Gallery Moos Ltd 136 Yorkville Ave Toronto ON M5R 1C2 Can

MOOSE, PHILIP ANTHONY
PAINTER, ILLUSTRATOR
b Newton, NC, Jan 16, 21. Study: Nat Acad Design; Columbia Univ; Skowhegan Sch Painting; Taxco Sch Arts, Mex; Acad Fine Arts, Munich, Ger. Work: Atlanta Mus Art, Ga; Norfolk Mus, Va; NC State Mus Art, Raleigh; Colchester Mus, Eng; Mint Mus Art, Charlotte, NC. Comn: Mural, Montreat-Anderson Col, NC, 72. Exhib: Am Watercolors, Metrop Mus, New York; Corcoran Biennial, Washington, DC; Southeastern Ann, Atlanta, Ga; Fulbright Artists, WGer; Piedmont Ann, Charlotte. Teaching: Assoc prof art, Davidson Col, 51-53; assoc prof art, Queens Col, NC, 56-67. Awards: Pulitzer Award, 48; Tiffany Found Award, 49; Fulbright Award, 53-63. Media: Oil, Acrylic. Publ: Illusr, History of Catawba County, 52; illusr, Exploring the Mountains, 72. Mailing Add: Linville Rd Blowing Rock NC 28605

MOOSE, TALMADGE BOWERS
PAINTER, INSTRUCTOR
b Albemarle, NC, June 4, 33. Study: Va Commonwealth Univ, BFA. Work: Knight Publ Co, Charlotte, NC. Exhib: 24th Southeastern Ann Exhib, High Mus, Atlanta, 70; 34th Semi-Ann Southeastern Print & Drawing Show, 71; Ann NC Artists Exhib, 71, 73 & 74; Art on Paper 1972, Weatherspoon Gallery, Greensboro, 72; Davidson Nat Print & Drawing Competition, 73; Retrospective Exhib, Pfeiffer Col, Misenheimer, 78. Teaching: Instr drawing & painting, Stanly Tech Inst, Albemarle, 72-76. Pos: Mem bd dir, Stanly Co Arts Coun, 74-76; pres, Gallery Uwharrie Artists, Ltd, 74-76; dir, Artists/Writers Dialogue, 75. Awards: First Prize, 34th Semi-Annual Southeastern Print & Drawing Show, 71; Honorable Mention, 9th Ann Piedmont Graphics Exhib, 72; Honorable Mentions, 36th & 37th Ann NC Artists Exhib, 73-74. Bibliog: Clyde Burnett (auth), Limited art exhibit, Atlanta J & Constitution, 2/15/70; Elizabeth S Smith (auth), He never left Stanly County, State Mag, 7/73; mem of the issue, NLight Mag, 2-3/78. Mem: Watercolor Soc NC. Style & Technique: Realistic. Media: Watercolor, Carbon Pencil, Acrylics. Publ: Contribr, Charlotte Observer, 69; illusr, Home Life, 71; contribr, Uwharrie Rev, 74; illusr, The State Mag, 77; illusr, Sandlapper, 77. Mailing Add: Rte 2 Stony Mountain Albemarle NC 28001

MOOZ, R PETER
MUSEUM DIRECTOR
b New York, NY, Mar 6, 40. Study: Wesleyan Univ, BA(with distinction in art hist); Boston Univ, MA; Univ Pa, PhD. Collections Arranged: Twentieth Century American Watercolors, 73; Art of American Furniture, 74; The Winslows: Pilgrims, Patrons and Portraits, 74. Teaching: Asst prof art hist, Univ Del, 67-73; vis lectr art hist, Univ Bath, Eng, 69; vis asst prof art hist, Univ Vt, 71; sr lectr art hist, Bowdoin Col, 73- Pos: Teaching assoc, Winterthur Mus, Wilmington, Del, 67-73, mus coordr, Winterthur Prog, 71-73, dir, Winterthur Summer Inst, 72-73; dir, Am Painting Summer Inst, 73; dir, Bowdoin Col Mus Art, 73-77; dir, Va Mus Fine Arts, 77- Mem: Asn Art Mus Dir; Col Art Asn; Soc Archit Historians; Soc Preservation New Eng Antiquities (mem adv coun, 75); Nat Trust for Hist Preservation. Res: American art, especially colonial painting and American furniture; American painter Robert Feke. Publ: Auth, New clues to the art of Robert Feke, Antiques, 68; contribr, Country and Simple City Furniture, 69; auth, Smibert's Bermuda group—a re-evaluation, Art Quart, 70; contribr, American Painting to 1776: A Reappraisal, 71; co-auth, The Genius of American Painting, 73. Mailing Add: Va Mus Fine Arts Blvd & Grove Richmond VA 23221

MOQUIN, RICHARD ATTILIO
SCULPTOR, EDUCATOR
b San Francisco, Calif, July 1, 34. Study: City Col San Francisco, AA; San Francisco State Col, BA & MA, with Seymour Locks. Work: Sacramento State Col; Sacramento State Fair. Exhib: 24th Ceramic Nat, Everson Mus, Syracuse, NY, 66; 23rd Scripps Col Invitational, Claremont, Calif, 67; Col Marin Invitational, Kentfield, Calif, 69; M H De Young Mus Show, San Francisco, 70; Stanford Univ Sculpture Invitational, 71 & 72. Teaching: Instr sculpture, City Col San Francisco, 69- Pos: Vpres, Asn San Francisco Potters, 67-68. Awards: Purchase Awards, Sacramento State Fair, 68, San Francisco Art Fair, 69 & M H De Young Mus, 70. Bibliog: Albright (auth), Ceramic sculpture, San Francisco Chronicle, 68 & 70; A Meisel (auth), Ceramic sculpture, Craft Horizons, 72. Style & Technique: Contemporary. Media: Clay, Plastic, Fiberboard. Dealer: H Gardner Gallery Stinson Beach CA. Mailing Add: 3 Herbing Lane Kentfield CA 94904

MORA, FRANCISCO
PAINTER, PRINTMAKER
b Uruapan, Michoacan, Mex. Study: Univ Michoacan; with Diego Rivero. Work: Mus Mod Art, New York; Mus Mod Art, Mex; Nat Mus Prague, Czech; Nat Mus Zurich, Switz; Nat Mus, Bucharest, Rumania. Comn: Mural (exterior), Newspaper Sol De Toluca, Mex, 50; portrait of Adam Mickiewice, Polish Embassy Mex, 55; Portrait of Carranza for preconstructed schs, Secy Pub Educ, Mex, 57 & series of portraits of nat heroes, 58. Exhib: Traveling Exhib Mex Art, Tate Gallery, London; Mus Mod Art, Paris & others, 49-50; 1st Interam Biennial, Mex, 58; one-man shows, Prague, Czech, Dresden, Berlin, 73-74 & Nat Fine Arts Palace, Mex, 74. Teaching: Illusr, Mex Acad Educ, Mexico City, 57-; teacher mus cult, Mexico City, 73-74. Awards: Engraving Competition Award, Ministry Hydraulic Resources, Mex, 51; First Award Juarez Year, Nat Inst Fine Arts, Mex, 57; Honor Award, Mus Cult, Mex, 74. Bibliog: Armin Haab (auth), Mexican Graphic Art, Arthur Niggli Ltd, Switz, 57; Francisco Mora (film), Ignacio Marquez, Mex, 75. Style & Technique: Figurative abstract painting. Media: Oil, Watercolor; Linocut, Woodcut. Dealer: Salon de la Plastica Mexicana Havre 7 Mexico DF Mex. Mailing Add: Apartado Postal 694 Cuernavaca MOR Mexico

MORADO, CHAVEZ JOSE
See Chavez-Morado, Jose

MORALES, ARMANDO
PAINTER
b Granada, Nicaragua, Jan 15, 27. Study: Sch Fine Arts, Managua, Nicaragua; Pratt Graphic Art Ctr, New York. Work: Mus Mod Art & Guggenheim Mus, New York; Inst Art, Detroit; Mus Art, Philadelphia; Mus Fine Arts, Houston. Exhib: Bienal Mod Art, Sao Paulo, Brazil, 53, 55 & 59; Carnegie Int, Pittsburgh, 58, 64 & 67; Arte Am y Espana, Madrid, Barcelona, Rome & Berlin, 61; Guggenheim Int, New York, 60; The Emergent Decade, Cornell Univ & Guggenheim Mus, 66. Awards: Ernest Wolf Award, V Bienal, Sao Paulo, Brazil, 59; Award, Arte Am y Espana, Madrid, 63; J L Hudson Award, Carnegie Int, 64. Bibliog: Dore Ashton (auth), Visual pleasure from austerity, Studio Int, London, 2/65; Heinz Ohff (auth), Anleitnung zum optimismus: begegnung mit Armando Morales in Berlin, Der Taggespiegel, Berlin, 6/19/65; Esperanza Brault (auth), Armando Morales, El Sol Mex, Mexico City, 10/4/68. Dealer: Lee A Ault & Co 25 E 77th St New York NY 10021. Mailing Add: 59 Harrison St Princeton NJ 08540

MORATH, INGE (INGE MORATH MILLER)
PHOTOGRAPHER
b Graz, Austria, May 27, 24; US citizen. Study: Univ Berlin, BA; asst to Henri Cartier-Bresson. Work: Metrop Mus of Art, New York; Boston Mus of Fine Arts, Mass; Art Inst of Chicago; RI Sch of Design; Bibliot Nat, Paris, France; plus many others. Exhib: New York Overseas Press Club, 59; Chicago Art Inst, 64; Addison Gallery of Am Art, Andover, Mass, 71; Univ Miami, Coral Gables, Fla, 72; Neikrug Galleries, New York, 77; plus many group showings. Teaching: Guest instr photog & compos, Cooper Union, New York; plus others. Awards: Photog Excellence, (for Great Photographers: Inge Morath), Stuttgart Bkwks, Bucher Publ, Switz, 11/76. Bibliog: Article, Saul Steinberg & Inge Morath, Creative Camera, 2/69; Allen Porter (auth), Inge Morath, Camera Mag, 11/69; Olga Carlisle (auth), Great Photographers of Our Time—Inge Morath, Bucher, Switz, 75. Mem: Magnum Photos; Am Soc Mag Photogr. Style & Technique: Travelogues, reportage and portraits using 35mm cameras, both black and white and color. Publ: Illusr, From Persia to Iran, 61 & In Russia, 69, Viking Press; illusr, Boris Pasternak: My Sister Life, Harcourt, Brace, Jovanovich, 76; illusr, In the Country, Viking Press, 77. Dealer: Marge Neikrug 224 E 68th St New York NY 10021. Mailing Add: Tophet Rd Roxbury CT 06783

MOREHOUSE, WILLIAM PAUL
PAINTER, SCULPTOR
b San Francisco, Calif, May 27, 29. Study: Studied with Clyfford Still, 47-50; Calif Sch of Fine Art, cert, 50; San Francisco Art Inst, BFA, 54; San Francisco State Col, MA, 56. Work: Smith Col Mus of Art, Northampton, Mass; Oakland Art Mus, Calif; Univ Art Mus, Berkeley, Calif; San Francisco Art Comn Collection. Exhib: Younger Am Painters, Solomon R. Guggenheim Mus, New York, 54; Biennial, Whitney Mus of Am Art, New York, 59; San Francisco Mus of Art Ann, 55-60; Ill Biennial, Urbana & Art Inst of Chicago Ann, 61; 72nd Western Painters Ann, Denver Art Mus, 66; Funk, Univ Art Mus, Berkeley & Ctr for Contemp Art, 67; Interstices, San Jose Art Mus, Calif, 75 & 77 & Cranbrook Mus, Mich, 75. Teaching: Instr art, San Francisco Art Inst, 58-67; prof art, Sonoma State Col, 67- Pos: Chmn art dept, Sonoma State Col, 70-73. Style & Technique: Abstractionist; painter in oil and synthetic material; sculpture in fiberglass and foamed urethanes, printmaking; wall installations. Mailing Add: PO Box 210 Bodega CA 94922

MORETON, RUSSELL
PAINTER
b Feb 20, 29; US citizen. Study: Art Inst Chicago. Exhib: Ebell Salon Art, Los Angeles, 67-71; Lake San Marcos Invitational, Calif, 68-70; Showcase 21, Los Angeles, 68-72; 14th Ann Nat Art Round-up, Las Vegas, Nev, 70; Southern Calif Art Expos, Del Mar, Calif, 71; Calif Fine Arts Gallery, Laguna Beach; Kesler Art Gallery, San Diego, Calif; Dale Gardner Galerie, Rancho Santa Fe, Calif; Julie Gregory Gallery, Carmel, Calif. Awards: First Place Lake San Marcos Invitational, 68 & Second Place, Ebell of Los Angeles, 71. Style & Technique: Seascapes, with knife and brush. Media: Oil. Publ: Note paper and Christmas cards of paintings in reproduction, Western Tradition, Boulder, Colo, sixteen yrs; three seascapes, Donald Art Co, New York, 71; twenty landscapes, Bernard Picture Co, Chicago & New York; paintings in reproduction, Shedd-Brown Co, Minneapolis, Minn. Dealer: Showcase Gallery PO Box 2314 Prescott AZ 86302. Mailing Add: PO Box 2314 Prescott AZ 86302

MOREZ, MARY
PAINTER, ILLUSTRATOR
b Tuba City, Ariz. Study: Univ Ariz, Rockefeller Found scholar; Ray-Vogue Schs Com Art, Chicago; Maricopa Tech Col, Phoenix, Ariz. Exhib: 5 exhibs, Scottsdale Nat Indian Art Show, Ariz, 67-72; Nat Indian Art Shows, Sheridan, Wyo, 68-70; Heard Mus Ann Indian Arts & Crafts, 69-71; Red Cloud Indian Art Shows, Pine Ridge, SDak, 69-71; Trail of Tears, Cherokee Nat Hist Soc, 72. Pos: Vpres, Phoenix Indian Med Ctr, 70-72; res asst, Mus Navajo Ceremonial Arts, Santa Fe, NMex, 70-; mem, Phoenix Civic Plaza Indian Cult Comt, 71- Awards: Best of Show for Navajo Creation, Red Cloud Indian Art Show, 69; Award for Changing Woman & Her Weaving Loom, Nat Indian Art Show, Sheridan, 69; Award for Father Sky & Mother Earth, Heard Mus Ann Indian Arts & Crafts, 72. Res: Navajo baskets. Publ: Illusr, Death of an Elder Klallm, Baleen Press, 69; illusr, jacket covers, Canyon Rec, 69-71; illusr, NMex Rev & Legis J, Santa Fe, 70; illusr, Navajo Times, Window Rock, Ariz, 71; illusr, health care pamphlets, US Pub Health Serv, 72; plus others. Dealer: Hunter's Trading Post Town & Country Shopping Ctr 2035 E Camelback Rd Phoenix AZ 85016; Thompson Gallery 2020 N Central Phoenix AZ 85004. Mailing Add: 2535 N 28th Pl Phoenix AZ 85008

MORGAN, ARTHUR C
SCULPTOR
b Riverton Plantation, La, Aug 3, 04. Study: Beaux Arts Inst Design; also with Gutzon Borglum, Mario Korbel and others. Work: Centenary Col, Shreve Mem Libr & Civic Theater, Shreveport, La; Civic Ctr & Hist Libr, Thibodaux, La; plus numerous pvt collections. Comn: Heroic figure, Chief Justice Edward Douglass White, Edward Douglass White Mem Comn, US Capitol, Washington, DC, 55; Earl K Long Monument, State Parks & Recreation Comn, Winnfield, La, 63; Paul Geisler Mem, Comt Friends of Paul Geisler, Stadium Gounds, High Sch, Burwick, La, 65; Henry Miller Shreve Monument, City of Shreveport & Pub Subscription, River Pkwy, Shreveport, 66; A J Hodges Commemorative Bust, Trustees of Hodges Gardens, Hodges Gardens, Many, La, 72. Exhib: One-man shows, La State Univ, Baton Rouge, 27, La State Exhib Mus, Shreveport, 40 & 50; Philbrook Art Ctr, Tulsa, Okla, 52 & Centennial Mus, Corpus Christi, Tex, 57; Mem Exhib, Nat Arts Club, New York, 60- Teaching: Instr drawing, painting, sculpture & art hist & dir dept art, Centenary Col La, 28-34; dir sculpture & drawing, Southwestern Inst Arts, 34- Bibliog: Patsi Farmer (auth), Biographer in bronze, Shreveport Mag, 12/58; Mary Gray Morris Walker (auth), Portrait of an artist, NLa Hist Asn J, 7/65; Edwin Adams Davis (auth), Louisiana, the pelican state, La State Univ Press. Mem: Nat Arts Club. Style & Technique: Basically figurative and traditional. Media: Bronze, Marble. Mailing Add: 657 Jordan St Shreveport LA 71101

MORGAN, BARBARA BROOKS
PAINTER, PHOTOGRAPHER
b July 8, 00. Study: Univ Calif, Los Angeles, 19-23. Work: Mus Mod Art, New York; Int Mus Photog, Rochester, NY; Hist Photog, Smithsonian Inst, Washington, DC; Amon Carter Mus, Ft Worth, Tex. Exhib: One-woman show, Modern American Dance, Inter-Am Off, Nat Gallery Art for tour in Latin Am, Span & Portuguese versions; George Eastman House, Rochester, NY, 64; Smithsonian Inst, 70; Mus Mod Art, 72; Amon Carter Mus, 72; plus others. Teaching: Instr art, Univ Calif, Los Angeles, 25-30; Ansel Adams Photog Workshop, Yosemite, summers; also lect & sem. Publ: Auth, photographer & designer, Martha Graham: Sixteen Dances in Photographs, 41-42; auth, photographer & designer, Summer's Children: A Photographic Cycle of Life at Camp, 51; ed, photographer & designer, Barbara Morgan (monogr), 72. Mailing Add: 120 High Point Rd Scarsdale NY 10584

MORGAN, CHARLES H
WRITER
b Worcester, Mass, Sept 19, 02. Study: Harvard Univ, AB, 24, AM, 26, PhD, 28. Teaching: Instr fine arts, Harvard Univ, 24-27; lectr classical archaeol, Bryn Mawr Col, 29-30; prof fine arts, Amherst Col, 30-68, dir, Mead Art Bldg, 48-68. Pos: Dir, Am Sch Classical Studies, Athens, Greece, 35-38. Publ: Auth, Corinth XI, the Byzantine Pottery, 42; auth, The Life of Michelangelo, 60; auth, George Bellows, 65; auth, The Amherst College Art Collection, 72; auth, The Drawings of George Bellows, 73. Mailing Add: 22 Snell St Amherst MA 01002

MORGAN, DARLENE
PAINTER
b Salt Lake City, Utah, Feb 1, 43. Study: With Merle Olson. Work: Pac Northwest Indian Ctr. Exhib: Flathead Int Art Festival & Show, 71; Pac Northwest Indian Ctr Art Auction Ann, 71-; Charles Russell Exhib & Auction Ann, 72-74 & 77; Nat Parks Centennial Exhib, Glacier Park, Mont, 72. Awards: Best in Show, Pac Northwest Indian Art Auction, 72. Bibliog: Dave Crowell (auth), Montana's Own, Gateway, 70. Style & Technique: Intricate, realistic style. Media: Ink, Oil. Mailing Add: Woodsbay Bigfork MT 59911

MORGAN, FRANCES MALLORY
SCULPTOR
b Memphis, Tenn. Study: Art Students League; Nat Acad Design; Pa Acad Fine Arts; also with John Hovannes & Alexander Archipenko. Work: Brooks Mem Art Gallery, Memphis; IBM Corp. Comn: Neely Grant (bronze), Mrs Neely Grant, Memphis, 34; Sen Gilbert Hitchcock, 45 & bronze fountain, 49, Mrs Gilbert Hitchcock, Washington, DC; bronze fountain, Vance Norfleet, Memphis, 52; many portraits of children. Exhib: World's Fair, New York, 39-40; Whitney Mus Am Art, New York, 40; Artists for Victory, Metrop Mus, New York, 42; Philadelphia Art Alliance, 46; Pa Acad Fine Arts, 47. Awards: Anna Hyatt Huntington Award for Olympia, 41; Prize for Peace Again, 44, Nat Asn Women Artists; Award for Fish, Audubon Artists, 61. Mem: Nat Asn Women Artists; Sculptors Guild; Audubon Artists. Media: Clay, Stone, Wood. Mailing Add: Sunset Lane Rye NY 10580

MORGAN, FRANK JAMES
SCULPTOR
b Bowling Green, Ky, June 8, 16. Study: Coronado Sch Fine Arts, studied anatomy & figure modeling; five yrs personal instr in sculpture design with Donal Hord. Comn: Crucifix, comn by Mr Stensrud, Bisbee, Ariz, 46; Organ Loft Grills, St Francis Xavier Chapel, Chicago, 54; mausoleum doors, comn by Slater Family, Charleston, SC, 54; Ballerina (garden sculpture), comn by John Jacobs, San Diego, 75; Vicki (fountain piece), comn by Dr Lee Miller, San Diego, 77. Exhib: Los Angeles Co Fair, Los Angeles, Calif, 56; Tipton-Richards Gallery All Nude Show, 75 & 76 & Art Inst Ann, San Diego, 76; 44th & 45th Ann Nat Sculpture Soc Exhib, New York, 77 & 78. Teaching: Instr sculpture, Lake Co Art League, Ill, 54-55; instr life drawing, Orr Gallery, San Diego, 60-61; instr sculpture, Spanish Village Art Ctr, San Diego, 70-78. Pos: Vpres, Spanish Village Art Ctr, San Diego, 72-74. Awards: First in Pub Vote, Art Guild Ann, Fine Arts Soc, 48; First Purchase Award, Art Inst Ann, Mr & Mrs Shattuck, 68; Gold Medal, Nat Sculpture Soc 44th Ann, 77. Mem: Nat Sculpture Soc; Spanish Village Art Ctr. Style & Technique: Realist figurative sculpture in wood, stone, bronze and cold cast bronze. Media: Cold Cast Bronze, Wood. Mailing Add: 3115 Fourth Ave San Diego CA 92103

MORGAN, GLADYS B
PAINTER, INSTRUCTOR
b Houma, La, Mar 24, 99. Study: Randolph-Macon Women's Col, BA; Columbia Univ, grad work; spec study with Will H Stevens & Arthur C Morgan. Work: Centenary Col, Shreveport, La; La State Univ, Shreveport. Exhib: Regional Exhib Painting & Sculpture, Delgado Mus, New Orleans, 41; one-man shows, Old Capitol Mus, Baton Rouge, La, 42, Montgomery Mus Art, Ala, 46 & Centenary Col Libr Gallery, 71; Shreveport Art Club Regional, Barnwell Garden & Art Ctr, Shreveport, 70. Teaching: Instr & lectr hist art, drawing & painting, Centenary Col, 27-34; instr drawing, painting & graphics, Southwestern Inst Arts, Shreveport, 34- Awards: Blanche Bailey Wilde (auth), Gladys B Morgan: water colorist, NLa Hist Asn J, 1/66. Style & Technique: Lyrical realism. Media: Watercolor. Mailing Add: 657 Jordan St Shreveport LA 71101

MORGAN, HELEN BOSART
SCULPTOR
b Springfield, Ohio, Oct 17, 02. Study: Wittenberg Univ, AB; Dayton Art Inst; Art Inst Chicago. Work: Snyder Park, Springfield, Ohio; Springfield Art Ctr; Wittenberg Univ; Cincinnati Mus Art; Butler Inst Am Art. Exhib: Nat Acad Design; Nat Asn Women Artists; Cincinnati Mus Art; Columbus Gallery Fine Art; Butler Art Inst, Youngstown, Ohio. Awards: Least Imitative in Concept & Execution Award, Columbus Gallery, 63; Sculpture Prize, Ohio Liturgical Arts Guild, 71; First Prize-Sculpture, Springfield Art Asn, 71. Mem: Nat Asn Women Artists; Artists Equity Asn; Columbus Art League. Style & Technique: Geometric constructions in sheet bronze and stainless steel. Media: Bronze, Plastic. Dealer: Gallery 200 200 W Mound St Columbus OH 43215. Mailing Add: 845 E High St Springfield OH 45505

MORGAN, JAMES SHERROD
COLLECTOR
b Birmingham, Ala, Sept 11, 36. Study: Univ Ala, BA. Collection: Art Nouveau, Art Deco, American Indian, Mission furniture, contemporary painting, sculpture, prints, art pottery and Tiffany. Mailing Add: 5332 W 67th St Mission KS 66208

MORGAN, MARITZA LESKOVAR
PAINTER, ILLUSTRATOR
b Zagreb, Yugoslavia, Nov 20, 21; US citizen. Study: Cornell Univ, 42; Art Students League, 43. Work: Wilson Mus, Dartmouth Col, Hanover, NH; All Souls Unitarian Church, Tulsa, Okla; First Presby Church, Warren, Pa; St Luke's Chapel, Chautauqua, NY; Hurlbut Mem Church, Chautauqua. Comn: Murals, Smith-Wilkes Mem Libr, Chautauqua Inst, 70. Exhib: Nat Jury Show, Chautauqua, 66; Festival Arts Northwest Pa, 72; Gallery 100, Princeton, NJ, 75; Deson-Zaks Gallery, Chicago, 75; Lighthouse Gallery, Tequesta, Fla, 75. Teaching: Supvr art, Warren Co, Pa, 51-57; instr pvt classes, Chautauqua, NY, 66- Pos: Artist in residence, Chautauqua Inst, 66- Mem: Chautauqua Art Asn (bd mem). Mailing Add: Box 168 Chautauqua NY 14722

MORGAN, MYRA JEAN
ART DEALER
b Birmingham, Ala, Jan 26, 38. Study: Univ Ala, BA. Pos: Dir, Morgan Gallery, Shawnee Mission, Kans, 69- Specialty: Fine contemporary art including painting, sculpture, drawings and prints; major representation of established artists, primarily American. Mailing Add: c/o Morgan Gallery 5006 State Line Shawnee Mission KS 66205

MORGAN, NORMA GLORIA
PAINTER, ENGRAVER
b New Haven, Conn. Study: Art Students League, with Julian Levi; Hans Hofmann Sch Fine Art, New York; Atelier 17, New York, with Stanley W Hayter. Work: Nat Gallery Art & Pennell Collection, Libr of Cong, Washington, DC; Mus Mod Art, New York; Victoria & Albert Mus, London; Philadelphia Mus Art. Comn: Granite Tor (engraving on copper), Int Graphic Arts Soc, New York, 55; Moorland Sanctuary (oil mural), Old White Lion Inn, Haworth, Eng, 63; Carolina Paraquets (engraving on copper), 69 & Labrador Duck (engraving on copper), 75, Wildlife Int, Cincinnati; Moorland Sanctuary (engraving on copper), Assoc Am Artists, 72. Exhib: New York World's Fair, 65; Soc Am Graphic Artists, 67; Assoc Am Artists; one-man traveling show, Old Bergen Art Guild, Bayonne, NJ, 70-; plus other one-man shows throughout US, 70- & ann exhibs with Audubon Artists, New York. Awards: Gold Medal for Graphics, Am Artists Prof League, Smithsonian Inst, 63; Gold Medal for Graphics, Painters & Sculptors Soc NJ 26th Ann, 67; Blue Ribbon-First Prize for Graphics, Composers, Authors & Artists Conv, 69; Medal of Honor-Gold Medal, Audubon Artists, New York, 76. Bibliog: Janet Kalmine (auth), Above the crowd, Travel in Fashion, 58. Mem: Int Graphic Arts Soc; Print Coun Am; Soc Am Graphic Artists (coun mem, 74-75); Audubon Artists, New York; Assoc Am Artists; Knickerbocker Artists. Style & Technique: Inspired by natural forms in nature, erosion; realistic and abstract according to subject. Media: Acrylic, Oil, Watercolor; Engraving on Copper. Publ: Auth & illusr, Engraving, The Artist, 9/63 & Imaginative Painting, 3/64. Mailing Add: 239 W 63rd St New York NY 10023

MORGAN, THEODORA
ART WRITER
b Brooklyn, NY. Study: Packer Collegiate Inst, Brooklyn, NY; NY Univ, New York. Pos: Bd dir, Nat Arts Club, New York, formerly; pub relations dir, Crayon, Watercolor & Craft Inst, 57-60; managing ed, Nat Sculpture Review, 56- Mem: Nat Sculpture Soc (patron mem). Res: Representational sculpture, American and World wide. Mailing Add: c/0 Nat Sculpture Review 777 Third Ave New York NY 10017

MORGAN, WARREN DEAN
ART DEALER, DESIGNER
b Omaha, Nebr, Aug 16, 39. Study: Art Ctr, Los Angeles, Calif, Otis Art Inst; Oskar Kokoshka Sch of Vision, Salzburg, Austria. Work: Dawson Gallery, Dublin, Ireland; Galerie Schwarzer in der Dorotheegasse, Vienna, Austria; Gallerie d'Arte Ghelfi, Verona, Italy, Galerie Cardo-Matigon, Paris. Comn: Wall mural (10ft), Edward Dean Mus, 75. Exhib: Laguna Art Festival, Laguna Beach & Hillcrest Festival, Whittier, Calif, 77; one-man show, Gallery Bolotin, Laguna Beach, 76. Style & Technique: Graphics. Media: Acrylic on Canvas & Masonite. Specialty: Twentieth century contemporary graphics and impressionistic art. Mailing Add: c/o Achilles Contemp Arts 2285 Cahuilla Hills Dr Palm Springs CA 92262

MORGAN, WILLIAM
ART HISTORIAN, PRESERVATIONIST
b Princeton, NJ, June 13, 44. Study: Dartmouth Col, AB; Columbia Univ, MA & cert in restoration & preservation hist archit; Univ Del, PhD. Teaching: Lectr art & archaeol, Princeton Univ, 71-74; asst prof fine arts, Allen R Hite Art Inst, Univ Louisville, 74-77, assoc prof, 77- Pos: Chmn, Ky Hist Preservation Rev Bd, 75-; archit critic, Courier-J; bk rev ed, Landscape Archit Mag, currently. Awards: Nat Collection Fine Arts Vis Res Fel, Smithsonian Inst, 71. Mem: Soc Archit Historians; Nat Trust Hist Preservation; Soc Preservation New Eng Antiquities; Nat Trust Gt Brit & Northern Ireland; Nat Trust Scotland. Res: American art and architecture, primarily the Gothic revival; planning and preservation. Publ: Co-auth, Bucks County: photographs of early architecture, Horizon, 74; co-auth, Old Louisville: the Victorian Era, Courier-J, 75. Mailing Add: Dept of Fine Arts Univ of Louisville Louisville KY 40208

MORIN, THOMAS EDWARD
SCULPTOR, EDUCATOR
b Malone, NY; Sept 22, 34. Study: Mass Col Art, 52-56, BS(educ); Cranbrook Acad Art, MFA, 57; Brown Univ, basic metall cert, 66, plastics technol cert, 67. Work: Richmond Mus Art, Va; Brown Univ, Providence, RI; Barn Gallery Assoc, Ogunquit, Maine; NY Univ, Oneonta. Comn: Cast aluminum high relief, Brown Univ, 64; bronze sculpture & bronze screen, Am Tube, 72. Exhib: Inst Contemp Art Invitational, Boston, 60; Whitney Mus Am Art Ann, New York, 61; 11 New Eng Sculptors, Wadsworth Atheneum, Hartford, Conn, 63; Contemp Box & Wall Sculpture Invitational, RI Sch Design Mus Art, 65; Univ Conn Mus Art, Storrs, 70. Teaching: Head dept sculpture, Silvermine Guild Artists Col Art, 58-60; assoc

prof sculpture & head sculpture grad prog, RI Sch Design, 61- Awards: First Prize & Best in Show, Silvermine Guild Artists, 60; First Prize, RI Art Festival, 63; First Prize, New Haven Art Festival, 66. Mem: Union Independent Cols Art (dept head, 69); Am Foundrymens Soc. Style & Technique: Cast metal sculpture with multi-media fabrication. Mailing Add: 62 Waterman St Providence RI 02906

MORISHITA, JOYCE CHIZUKO
ART HISTORIAN, PAINTER
b Newell, Calif, Aug 22, 44. Study: Northwestern Univ, Evanston, Ill, BA(painting), 64, MA(painting), 65 & PhD candidate, 74-78. Work: Michael Reese Hosp & Med Ctr, Chicago, Ill. Comn: Oil-vaporous nudes (14ft x 5ft), Michael Reese Hosp & Med Ctr, 72. Exhib: Phalanx IV, 65 & Phalanx V, 66, Participating Artists of Chicago, Ill Inst Technol; Mideast Artists for Peace, Chicago, 67; one-person shows, Ordmeyer Gallery, Chicago, 70, Gov State Univ, Park Forest South, Ill, 75 & 78. Collections Arranged: Third World Art Exhib, Gov State Univ, 76 & 77. Teaching: Prof art, painting & art hist, Gov State Univ, Park Forest South, Ill, 73- Pos: Mem adv comt, Renovation of Chicago Pub Libr, 73. Awards: Artists & Lectrs Grant, 74 & Craftsman in Residence Grant, 75, Nat Endowment for the Arts; Acquisition Prog Grant, Ill Arts Coun, 76. Mem: Col Art Asn Am; Women's Caucus for Art. Style & Technique: Paintings primarily in oil, using Japanese and Western imagery. Media: Oil on Canvas; Graphite. Res: Study of J M W Turner at Petworth, 1802-1837. Mailing Add: 5125 S Dorchester Chicago IL 60615

MORLEY, GRACE L MCCANN
MUSEOLOGIST, WRITER
b Berkeley, Calif, Nov 3, 00. Study: Univ Calif, AB & MA; Univ Paris, Dr; Univ Grenoble, France, 24-25; Mills Col, LLD(honoris causa), 37; Smith Col, DHL, 57; Calif Col Arts & Crafts, DFA, 57; Univ Calif, Los Angeles, LLD, 58. Teaching: Lectr Latin Am & contemp art; instr Fr & art, Goucher Col, Baltimore, 27-30. Pos: Cur, Cincinnati Mus Asn, 30-33; dir, San Francisco Mus Art, 35-58; dir, Pac House, Golden Gate Expos, San Francisco, 39; consult, Art Comt, Off Inter-Am Affairs, 41-43; adv, Mus, UNESCO, 46, head mus, 47-49; mem ed bd, Mus; mem nat comt, UNESCO, 50-56; asst dir, Guggenheim Mus, New York, 59; dir, Nat Mus, New Delhi, India, 60-66; adv mus, Govt India, 66-68; head, Int Coun Mus Regional Agency in Asia, New Delhi, India, 67- Awards: Chevalier Legion of Honor, 49; Wattamul Award, 63. Mem: Am Asn Mus; Am Asn Art Mus Dirs; fel Mus Asn Gt Brit; fel Royal Soc Arts; Mus Asn India. Publ: Auth, Le Sentiment de la Nature en France dans la Premiere Moitie du 17e Siecle, Paris; auth, Carl Morris, Am Fedn Arts, 59; auth, Art in Museums, 63; auth, Museums Today, Univ Baroda, 67; auth, Pre-Columbian Art (introd to Heeramaneck Collection), Nat Mus, New Delhi, 67; contribr, prof periodicals, encycl & mus publ. Mailing Add: ICOM Regional Agency in Asia 3-4 Sapru House Annexe New Delhi India

MORLEY, MALCOM
PAINTER
b London, Eng, 1931. Study: Royal Col of Art, London, 54-57. Work: Whitney Mus, New York; Neue Galerie, Cologne, Ger; Wadsworth-Atheneum, Hartford, Conn; Mus Mod Art, New York; Musee d'Art Moderne, Paris; Victoria & Albert Mus, London. Exhib: Bienal de Sao Paulo, Brazil, 57-67; The Photographic Image, Guggenheim Mus, New York, 66; Patriotic Images in Art, Am Fedn of the Arts, New York, 68; Aspects of New Realism, Milwaukee Art Ctr, Wis, 69; 22 Realists, Whitney Mus, New York, 70; Kunst des 20 Jahrhunderts, Stadtische, Kunsthalle, Dusseldorf, 70; Contemp Am Painting, Whitney Mus, New York, 72; Documenta V, Kassel, Ger, 72; Projekt 74, Cologne, Ger, 74; one-man shows, Kornblee Gallery, New York, 64, 67 & 69. Teaching: Instr, Royal Col of Art, London, 56; instr, Ohio State Univ, Columbus, 65-66; Sch of Visual Arts, New York, 67-69 & State Univ of NY, Stony Brook, 72. Bibliog: Barry Lord (auth), The Eleven O'Clock News in Colour, Artscanada, Toronto, 6/70; Nicholas & Elena Calas (auths), Icons and Images of the Sixties, New York, 71; K Levin (auth), Malcolm Morley: Post Style Illusionism, Artsmagazine, New York, 2/73. Mailing Add: c/o Kornblee Gallery 58 E 79th St New York NY 10021

MORNINGSTERN, HARRY V
PAINTER, ILLUSTRATOR
b Newark, NJ. Study: Faucett Sch Indust Art, Newark; with Bernar Gussow. Work: City of Atlantic City, NJ; Atlantic Co Cult & Heritage Comn. Exhib: Living NJ Artists Series, Trenton State Mus, 52; New Jersey Artists, Newark Mus, 55; 32nd Ann Exhib, Woodmere Gallery, Philadelphia, 64 & 72; 29th NJ Watercolor Soc Exhib, Mus Arts & Sci, Morristown, NJ, 72; Ann Exhib Small Oil Paintings, Philadelphia Sketch Club, 75. Awards: Tercentenary Award, Rural New Jersey, State of NJ, 66; Talen's Award, The Big Trip, NJ Watercolor Soc, 69; Purchase Awards, Atlantic Co Cult & Heritage Comn, 75-77. Mem: Prof Artists of South Jersey (dir, 76-77); NJ Watercolor Soc; Philadelphia Watercolor Club; Atlantic City Art Ctr (vpres, 69-70); Fed Art Asns NJ (trustee, 75-). Style & Technique: Traditional transparent watercolor, gouache; combine transfer photos with acrylic; representational oil. Publ: Illusr, Capital News, Capital Financial Serv, 36-45; illusr, The Pilot, South Jersey Gas Co, 75. Mailing Add: 7 Lehigh Dr Somers Point NJ 08244

MOROZ, MYCHAJLO
PAINTER
b Ukraine, July 7, 04; US citizen. Study: Art Sch, Lviv, Ukraine; Conservatoire National des Arts et Metiers, Paris & Acad Julian, Paris, 28-29; additional study, var mus, Italy, 32. Work: State Mus, Lvov & Kiev, Ukraine; State Mus, Moscow; St Sergii et Vacci Mus, Rome; Ukrainian Inst Am, New York; White House, Washington, DC; plus many others. Exhib: Ukrainian Artists from all European Countries Exhib, Lviv, 34; Artists Exhib, Moscow, 40-41; Exhib, Regensburg & Munich, Ger, 47-48; Int Group Exhib, Locust Valley, NY, 58; one-man shows, Panoras Gallery, New York, 59-63. Teaching: Asst prof drawing & painting, Ukrainian Art Sch, Lviv, 30-35; also pvt lessons, Europe & US, 50- Awards: Silver Cap Second Award, Dem Club, Locust Valley, NY, 58; Prix de Paris, Galeries Raymond Duncan, 61; Most Artistic Christmas Card Prize, Onondaga Bank, Syracuse, NY, 62. Bibliog: Max M Rhoude (auth), M Moroz, Mittelbayerische Zeitung, Regensburg, Ger, 47 & 48; plus many articles in US, Ukrainian, Russian & French papers, 30- Mem: Orgn Ukrainian Artists Am. Style & Technique: Abstract expressionist. Media: Oil, Pastel. Mailing Add: 76 Coursen Pl Staten Island NY 10304

MORRELL, WAYNE (BEAM)
PAINTER
b Clementon, NJ, Dec 24, 23. Study: Philadelphia Sch Indust Art; Drexel Inst. Work: Sloan Kettering Cancer Res Ctr, New York; Clark Mus, Carversville, Pa. Exhib: Nat Acad Design, Allied Artist Am, 72 & Knickerbocker Artists, New York; Rockport Art Asn, Mass, 72; Expos Intercontinentale, Monoco, France; plus many others. Teaching: Pvt classes, 61-66. Pos: Art dir, John Oldham Studios, Conn, 55-61; designer, Paris & Brussels World's Fairs. Awards: Jane Peterson Prize, 69 & 74 & Coun Am Art Socs Award, 71, Allied Artist Am; Gold Medal, Rockport Art Asn, 70. Bibliog: R Kolby (auth), A stand for nature, Am Artist, 3/72. Mem: Allied Artist Am (jury mem, 72); Springfield Acad Artist (coun, 60-61); Salmagundi Club; Rockport Art Asn. Style & Technique: American impressionist; landscapes and marines. Media: Oil, Watercolor. Publ: Illusr, Readers Digest, 67. Dealer: Newman Galleries 1625 Walnut Philadelphia PA 19103; Grand Central Galleries 40 Vanderbilt Ave New York NY 10017. Mailing Add: 153 Main St Rockport MA 01966

MORRIN, PETER PATRICK
ART HISTORIAN, ART ADMINISTRATOR
b St Louis, Mo, Oct 31, 45. Study: Harvard Univ, AB, 68; Princeton Univ, MFA, 72. Teaching: Instr art hist, Vassar Col, 74- Pos: Dir, Vassar Col Art Gallery, 74- Awards: Nat Collection Fine Arts Res Fel, Smithsonian Inst, 73-74. Res: Modern and American art. Publ: Ed, Nineteenth and Twentieth Century French Drawings from the Art Museum, Princeton University: An Introduction, Princeton, 72. Mailing Add: Vassar Col Art Gallery Poughkeepsie NY 12601

MORRIS, CARL
PAINTER
b Calif. Study: Art Inst Chicago; Kunstgewerbeschule, Vienna; Akad Bildenden Kuenste, Vienna; Inst Int Educ fel for study in Paris. Work: Guggenheim Mus, Metrop Mus, Mus Mod Art & Whitney Mus Am Art, New York; Nat Gallery Art & Joseph Hirshhorn Collection, Washington, DC. Comn: Murals, US Treas Dept, Post Off Bldg, Eugene, Ore, 41; murals, Ore Centennial Comn, Hall of Relig Hist, 59. Exhib: Carnegie Int, Pittsburgh; Rome-New York Art Found Exhib; Pittsburgh Int; San Francisco Mus Art; Art USA Int. Awards: Ford Found Award, Retrospective Exhib, 60-62; Purchase Award, Nat Inst Arts & Lett; Purchase Award, Ford Found, 60. Bibliog: P Colt (auth), Carl Morris: a decade of painting in Portland, Portland Art Mus, 52; G L M Morley (auth), article for Ford Found, 60; David Wagoner (auth), The journey of Carl Morris, Malahat Rev, 10/74. Mem: Portland Art Asn. Media: Oil, Acrylic. Publ: Illusr covers & drawings, Poetry Northwest, summers 61 & 63; illusr cover & drawings, Five Poets of the Pacific Northwest, Univ Wash, 64; Ore Symphony poster, 76-77. Dealer: Kraushaar Galleries 1055 Madison Ave New York NY 10021; Fountain Gallery 115 SW Fourth Ave Portland OR 97204. Mailing Add: 919 NW Skyline Blvd Portland OR 97229

MORRIS, DONALD FISCHER
ART DEALER
b Detroit, Mich, Apr 12, 25. Pos: Owner & dir, Donald Morris Gallery, Inc, Birmingham, Mich. Mem: Art Dealers Asn Am; Mich Coun Arts; Detroit Art Dealers Asn (pres, 71-). Specialty: Twentieth century American and European painting and sculpture; African art. Mailing Add: Donald Morris Gallery Inc 105 Townsend Birmingham MI 48011

MORRIS, EDWARD A
PAINTER, ILLUSTRATOR
b Philadelphia, Pa, July 28, 17. Study: Philadelphia Col Art, with Henry C Pitz & W Emerton Heitland. Work: In many pvt collections. Exhib: Am Watercolor Soc Ann; also in numerous eastern galleries & mus. Awards: Fed Migratory Duck Stamp Design Award, 61-63. Mem: Asn Prof Artists; Ducks Unlimited. Publ: Contribr, Northwestern Banks Hunting Guide, 62, Gopher Historian, Naturalist, Linn's Weekly Stamp News & others. Mailing Add: 926 Plymouth Bldg Minneapolis MN 55402

MORRIS, FLORENCE MARIE
ART DEALER
b Detroit, Mich, Apr 30, 28. Study: Wayne State Univ, BS. Pos: Dir, Donald Morris Gallery, Detroit, 58- Mem: Art Dealers Asn Am; New Detroit (mem visual arts comt, 77-); Detroit Art Dealers Asn. Specialty: 20th century painting, sculpture and drawings; African sculpture. Mailing Add: 105 Townsend Birmingham MI 48011

MORRIS, GEORGE NORTH
PAINTER, WRITER
b Pittsburgh, Pa, May 13, 15. Study: Pa State Univ, 34-36; RI Sch Design, dipl painting, 40; Univ NH, pottery with Edwin & Mary Scheier, 44. Exhib: One-man shows, A M Sachs Gallery, New York, 64, Hudson River Mus, Yonkers, 66 & Shepherd Gallery, New York, 69; Mus Erotic Art, San Francisco, 73; Windham Col, 74; Albin-Zeglen Gallery, New York, 74; Noah Goldowsky Gallery, New York, 75; plus many others. Teaching: Teacher art, Workers Progress Admin Recreation Proj, New Bedford, Mass, 40-41; teacher art, Oglethorpe Univ, 41-43; teacher art, Pub Schs, Barton & Orleans, Vt, 43-45; art consult, Goddard Col, 45; teacher art, Vt Jr Col, 45-48; teacher ceramics, Barnstable High Sch, 49-52; teacher art, Cape Cod Art Asn, 53-55; supvr & coordr art instr, Pub Sch Union 24, Holden, Mass, 56-62; teacher adults, Worcester Mus Sch, 59-61; teacher art, Halsted Sch, Yonkers, NY, 62-68; teacher art, Horace Mann Sch, Bronx, 68-72. Pos: Art reviewer, Worcester Telegram, Mass, 58-62; art ed & critic, New Beacon, Provincetown, Mass, 61. Awards: Resident Fels, MacDowell Colony, Peterborough, NH, 69, 70 & 73; Third Prize, Cape Cod Art Asn; Honorable Mention, High Mus Art, Atlanta. Publ: Handbook for teaching art program, School Union 24, Holden, Mass, 57; 150th Anniversary Exhibition Catalog, Nat Acad Design, New York, 75. Mailing Add: 6053 Huxley Ave Riverdale NY 10471

MORRIS, HILDA
SCULPTOR, PAINTER
b New York, NY. Study: Art Students League; Cooper Union Sch Art & Archit. Work: Chase Manhattan Bank; Calif Palace of Legion of Honor, San Francisco; Munson-Williams-Proctor Inst Mus; Walter P Chrysler, Jr Collection, Va Mus; San Francisco Mus Art. Comn: Sculpture, Seattle Opera House, 63; bronze, Standard Plaza Bldg, Portland, 67; bronze, Pac Nat Bldg, Tacoma, Wash, 71; bronze, Mem Art Gallery, Univ Rochester, 75. Exhib: American Sculpture, Metrop Mus Art, 51; 3rd Pac Coast Biennial, Santa Barbara Mus Art, 60; Northwest Art Today, Seattle World's Fair, 62; Nat Print Show, Brooklyn Mus, 64; many exhibs, San Francisco Mus Art. Awards: Ford Found Fel, 60. Bibliog: Regional accent: Pacific Northwest, Art in Am, 65; Robin Skelton (auth), Sculpture as metaphor: five bronzes by Hilda Morris, Malahat Rev, 7/69; Carolyn Kizer (auth), Hilda Morris: Recent Bronzes, 73. Mem: Portland Art Asn; Portland Ctr Visual Arts. Publ: Illusr cover drawings, Poetry Northwest, spring & summer 68 & spring 69. Dealer: Fountain Gallery Art 115 SW Fourth Portland OR 97212; Triangle Gallery 251 Post St San Francisco CA 94108. Mailing Add: 919 NW Skyline Blvd Portland OR 97229

MORRIS, JACK AUSTIN, JR
MUSEUM DIRECTOR, WRITER
b Macon, Ga, Sept 29, 39. Study: Univ SC, AB, with Edmund Yaghjian, Augusta Wittkowski & Catherine Rembert; Univ SC; Harvard Univ Inst Arts Admin. Collections Arranged: Arnold H Maremont Collection (20th Century American & European Painting & Sculpture), 65; Ida Kohlmeyer (one-man exhib), 67; Jasper Johns Prints (with catalog), Harbor Town Mus, Hilton Head Island, SC, 71. Teaching: Lectr, Kress Collection, Columbia Mus Art, SC, 62-65; instr drawing & painting, Richland Art Sch, Columbia, 64-65. Pos: Curatorial assoc,

Columbia Mus Art, 62-63, asst to dir, 63-65; exec dir, Greenville Co Mus Art, 65-; exec dir, Greenville Co Art Asn, 75-; mem exec bd, Metrop Arts Coun, currently. Mem: Am Asn Mus; Guild SC Artists (pres, 68); SC Fedn Mus (founder, vpres, 71-72, pres, 73-74); SC Arts Comn (chmn exec comt, 72-73); SC Arts Found (pres, 75-); plus others. Res: Contemporary American art. Publ: Ed, Museum News, 64-65 & illusr, Two-Hundred Years of the Arts of France, 65, Columbia Mus Art; auth, Contemporary Artists of South Carolina (catalog), 70; auth, William M Halsey: Retrospective (catalog), 72. Mailing Add: 106 DuPont Dr Greenville SC 29607

MORRIS, KATHLEEN MOIR
PAINTER
b Montreal, PQ, Dec 2, 93. Study: Art Asn Montreal; also with Maurice Cullen. Work: Nat Gallery Can; Montreal Mus Fine Arts; Hart House, Univ Toronto; Art Gallery, Hamilton; Mackenzie King Mus; Can Legation, Paris, France; plus others. Exhib: One-man show, Montreal Mus Fine Arts, 39; New York World's Fair, 39; Can Club, NY, 50; Festival of Brit, 51; Royal Can Acad Exhib, Toronto, Ottawa & Halifax, 57; plus many others. Awards: Willingdon Art Competition, 30. Mem: Can Group Painters. Mailing Add: 79 Windsor Ave Westmount Montreal PQ Can

MORRIS, KYLE RANDOLPH
PAINTER
b Des Moines, Iowa, Jan 17, 18. Study: Art Inst Chicago, 35-40; Northwestern Univ, BA, 39, MA, 40; Cranbrook Acad Art, MFA, 47. Work: Albright-Knox Gallery, Buffalo, NY; Detroit Inst Arts, Mich; Guggenheim Mus & Whitney Mus Am Art, New York; San Francisco Mus Art; plus others. Exhib: Younger American Painters, Guggenheim Mus, 54; Nature in Abstraction, Whitney Mus Am Art, 58; American Painting, Am Pavilion, Brussels World's Fair, 58; American Painting, New York-Rome Found, Rome, 58; Pittsburgh Int Exhib, Carnegie Inst, Pa, 61; plus others. Teaching: Instr art hist & painting, Stephens Col, Columbia, Mo, 40-41; asst prof art hist & painting, Univ Tex, Austin, 45-46; assoc prof painting, Univ Minn, Minneapolis, 47-51; assoc prof painting, Univ Calif, Berkeley, 52-54; lectr art hist, Cooper Union, 58; vis critic, Yale Univ Grad Sch, 65; guest artist & critic, Carnegie Mellon Univ, 70; vis critic, Univ Iowa, 75. Awards: Purchase Award, Six States 2nd Biennial Exhib, Walker Art Ctr, Minneapolis, 49; Purchase Award, American Painting, San Francisco Mus Art, 53; Hon Mention, II Biennial, Belles Artes, Mexico City, 60; plus others. Media: Oil, Acrylic. Mailing Add: 173 Main St East Hampton NY 11937

MORRIS, MICHAEL
PAINTER
b Saltdean, Sussex, Eng, May 16, 42; Canadian citizen. Study: Victoria Univ, Toronto, 60-62; Vancouver Sch of Art, BC, 62-64; Slade Sch of Fine Art; London Univ, Eng, 64-65. Work: Nat Gallery, Ottawa; Art Gallery of Ont, Toronto; Montreal Mus of Fine Arts; Art Gallery of Greater Victoria, BC; Mus of Mod Art, New York. Exhib: Perspective 67, Art Gallery of Ont, Toronto, 67; Spring Show, Mus of Art, Montreal, 76; Int Print Exhib, Santiago, Chile, 67; The West Coast Now, Portland Art Mus, Oregon, 67; Survey 68, Art Gallery of Ont, 68; Prisma-Mirrored Light Environment, Vancouver Art Gallery, 68; New Art of Vancouver, Newport Harbor Mus, Calif, 69; Art From Across the Border, Henry Gallery, Univ Seattle, Washington, 69; Paris Bienniale, France, 69 & 71; Realism 70, Montreal Mus of Art, & Art Gallery of Ont, 70; Intermedia Show, Vancouver Art Gallery, 70; Photo Media, Mus of Contemp Crafts, New York, 71; Image Bank Post Card Show, Fine Arts Gallery, Univ BC, Vancouver, 71; ABC Artist's Proof of Alphabet Show, Burnaby Art Gallery, BC, 71; Trajectore Can, Musee d'Art Contemp, Paris, 73; Action Per Avante Garde, Berliner Kunstverein, Berlin, 73; Artists Postage Stamps, Simon Fraser Univ, Burnaby, 74; Word Works, Univ Gallery, San Jose, Calif, 74; Environmental Communications, Inst Contemp Arts London, 74; one-man show, Fine Arts Gallery, Univ BC, Vancouver, 67. Teaching: Instr & coordr of special events, Ctr for Communication & the Arts, Simon Fraser Univ, Burnaby, 67-68; guest lectr, Fine Arts Dept, Univ Victoria, 70; artist-in-residence, Univ Saskatchewan, Regina, 72; guest lectr, Univ BC, Vancouver, 73-74. Pos: Acting cur, Vancouver Art Gallery, 67; organiser, Media Workshops for the Nat Film Bd of Can, 69; founder, Image Bank Archives, 72. Publ: Auth, Alex and Roger, BC Almanac, Vancouver, 70; contribr, Concrete Poetry, Vancouver, 63, Space Atlas, Victoria, BC, 71, Art Work No Commercial Value, New York, 71, Pages Mag, London, England, 72, File Mag, Toronto, 72 & 73, Vice Mag, San Francisco, Calif, 73, Source, Music for Avante Garde, Sacramento, Calif, 74 & Strange Feces, Vancouver, 75. Dealer: Jytte Allen c/o Gallery Allen 3025 Granville St Vancouver BC V6H 3J9 Can. Mailing Add: c/o The Western Front 3030E 8th Ave Vancouver BC V5T 1S1 Can

MORRIS, ROBERT
SCULPTOR
b Kansas City, Mo, Feb 9, 31. Study: Kansas City Jr Col; Kansas City Art Inst, 48-50; Univ Kansas City; San Francisco Art Inst; Reed Col, 53-55; Hunter Col, MA, 66. Work: Nat Gallery of Victoria, Melbourne, Australia; Dallas Mus Fine Arts, Tex; Whitney Mus Am Art, New York; Tate Gallery, London, Eng; Mod Museet, Stockholm, Sweden. Comn: Earth Proj, Nat Planning Comn, Ottawa; Steam Piece, Western Wash Univ, Bellingham, 69; Grand Rapids Proj, City of Grand Rapids, Mich, 74; Observatory, Sonsbeek Unlimited, Oost-Flevoland, Holland, 77. Exhib: Guggenheim Int, Solomon R Guggenheim Mus, 67; Minimal Art, The Hague, 68; The Art of the Real, Mus Mod Art, 68; Philadelphia Mus Art, 68; one-man shows, Corcoran Gallery Art, Washington, DC, 69, Whitney Mus Am Art, New York, 70, Leo Castelli Gallery, New York, 72 & 76, Max Protetch Gallery, Washington, DC, 73 & Stedelijk Mus, Amsterdam, Holland, 77 & Florence Wilcox Art Gallery, Swarthmore Col, Pa, 78; Whitney Mus Am Art, 72, 73, 75 & 76; Ind Univ Art Mus, 72; Art in Evolution, Xerox Sq Exhib Ctr, Rochester, NY, 73; Princeton Univ Art Mus, NJ, 74; Art Inst Chicago, 74, 76 & 77; Ponderosa Collection, 74 & Proposals for Sawyer Point Park, 77, Contemp Arts Ctr, Cincinnati; Some Recent Am Art (traveling exhib, Australia & New Zealand), Mus Mod Art, New York, 74; Galerie Ricke, Cologne, Ger, 74; Beaubourg Centre Nat d'Art Contemporain, Paris, 74; Philadelphia Col Art, 75; Portland Art Mus, Ore, 75; Sculpture, Am Directions 1945-1975, Nat Collection Fine Arts, Smithsonian Inst, Washington, DC, 75; Mus Contemp Art, Chicago, 75 & 77; High Mus Art, Atlanta, Ga; NY State Mus, Albany, 77; Madison Art Ctr, Wis, 77; New Gallery Contemp Art, Cleveland, Ohio, 77; Kansas City Art Inst, Mo, 78; Mus Contemp Art, La Jolla, Calif, 78; plus many others. Awards: Prize, Guggenheim Mus, 67; Guggenheim Found Fel, 69; Sculpture Award, Soc Four Arts, 75. Bibliog: Annette Michelson (auth), Three notes on an exhibition as a work, Artforum, 6/70; Jack Burnham (auth), Robert Morris: retrospective in Detroit, Artforum, 3/70 & Voices from the gate, Arts Mag, Vol 46 (summer, 72); Jeremy Gilbert-Rolfe (auth), Robert Morris: the complication of exhaustion, Artforum, 9/74; plus others. Publ: Auth, The art of existence, 1/71, Some splashes in the ebb tide, 2/73 & Aligned with Nazca, 10/75, Artforum; auth, The present tense of space, Art in Am, 1-2/78; plus others. Mailing Add: c/o Castelli Gallery 4 E 77th St New York NY 10021

MORRIS, ROBERT CLARKE
PAINTER, EDUCATOR
b New York, Apr 2, 31. Study: Yale Univ, with Josef Albers, BFA; Univ Tex, MFA. Work: Allentown Art Mus, Pa; Okla Art Ctr, Oklahoma City; Mus Fine Arts Houston, Tex; Beaumont Art Mus, Tex. Exhib: Visionary Painters, Contemp Art Mus, Houston, 61; Connecticut Artist Educators, Widener Gallery, Trinity Col, 63; Nat Exhib Small Paintings, Purdue Univ, 64; Exhib, Alan Gallery, New York, 66 & 67; one-man shows, Carlson Gallery, Univ Bridgeport, 75, Washburn Gallery, New York, 76, Artist's Postcards-Drawing Ctr, New York, 77 & Conn Painting, Drawing & Sculpture, 78. Collections Arranged: Out of the Ordinary, Contemp Arts Mus, Houston, 58, Tenth St, 58 & Architectural Graphics, 59. Teaching: Instr painting, Univ Houston, 57-59; instr painting & drawing, Mus Sch, Mus Fine Arts Houston, 58-59; prof art, Univ Bridgeport, 61- Pos: Dir, Contemp Art Mus, Houston, 58-60; vis design cur, Univ Tex Art Mus, Austin, 68-69. Media: Oil, Acrylic. Dealer: Washburn Gallery 42 E 57th St New York NY 10022. Mailing Add: 81 Island Ave Madison CT 06443

MORRISON, ART JENS
CERAMIST, INSTRUCTOR
b Palo Alto, Calif, Apr 28, 43. Study: San Diego State Univ, AB, 70; Mills Col, MFA, with Fred Bauer, 72. Work: John Michael Kohler Art Ctr, Sheboygan, Wis; Leslie Ceramic Supply, Berkeley, Calif; Antonio Prieto Ceramic Collection, Mills Col; plus many pvt collections. Exhib: Ceramics 70, De Young Mus, San Francisco, Calif, 70; Objects 70, Corning Glass Ctr, NY, 70; Objects 71, Mus of Fine Art, Salt Lake City, Utah, 71; 43rd Ann, Springfield Mus of Art, Mo, 73; 200 Artists Commemorate 100 Yrs, Fairtree Gallery, New York, 76; Ceramic Conjunction, Long Beach Mus of Art, Calif, 77; Civilizations, John Michael Kohler Art Ctr, 77; 20th Anniversary Birthday Show, Mus Contemp Crafts, New York, 77. Teaching: Asst prof ceramic sculpture, Coe Col, Cedar Rapids, Iowa, 72-, asst prof 3-dimensional design, 78- Awards: Purchase Award, Civilizations, Kohler Co, Sheboygan, 77. Bibliog: Marilyn Hagburg (auth), Supermarket Ceramics, Artweek, 72; Dave Zack (auth), American zig-zag, Art & Artists, London, 74; Ruth Kohler (auth), Civilizations, Craft Horizons, 77. Mem: Nat Coun for Educ of Ceramic Arts; Col Art Asn; Mid-Am Col Art Asn; Am Crafts Coun; Iowa Craftsmen. Style & Technique: Low-fire whiteware used in combination with indigenous local clays, underglaze color and metallic lusters. Media: (Ceramics) low-fire earthenware; (Sculpture) ceramic, polychrome. Publ: Contribr, An Interview with the Farmisist, Craft Connections, 75; auth, Low-fire plate decoration, 75, auth, In search of farmounia, 76 & auth, Folk ceramics of Michoacan, 78, Ceramics Monthly; contribr, A History of American Studio Pottery, 78; co-auth, The Folk Ceramics of Michoacan, Mexico, Craft Horizons, (in press). Dealer: Kaplan-Bauman Gallery 8424 Melrose Pl Los Angeles CA 90069; Elizabeth Fortner Gallery 813 State St Santa Barbara CA 93101. Mailing Add: 936 Ninth St NE Marion IA 52302

MORRISON, BEE (BERENICE G)
WEAVER
b Florence, Italy, Jan 16, 08. Study: Self taught, also with Porfirio Lopez & Ted Hallman. Work: State Collection Found Cult & Arts, Honolulu, Hawaii. Exhib: Foundry Art Gallery, Honolulu, 72-74; Hawaii Arts & Crafts, Honolulu, 73; Hilo Arts & Crafts, 74; Volcano Art Ctr, Volcanoes Nat Park, 74-75; Wailoa Ctr, Hilo, 75. Mem: Hawaii Craftsmen; Honolulu Weavers Hui; Kiluea Weavers Guild (pres, 74); Handweavers Guild Am. Style & Technique: Wall hangings, rugs. Dealer: Volcano Art Ctr Volcano HI 96785. Mailing Add: Box 335 Volcano HI 96785

MORRISON, BOONE M
PHOTOGRAPHER, ART ADMINISTRATOR
b Berkeley, Calif, Jan 28, 41. Study: Stanford Univ, BA(hist), 62 & BA(commun), 63; Yosemite Photog Workshops, with Ansel Adams, 71-73. Work: Honolulu Acad Art, Hawaii; Bishop Mus, Honolulu; State of Hawaii Collection; US Nat Park Serv; Univ Hawaii Collection. Comn: Mural photographs, Kauau Mus, 71 & C Brewer & Co, 73; interior wall mural, State of Hawaii, Ka'u Hosp, 75. Exhib: Artists of Hawaii, 71-75; Mountains and the Shore, Honolulu Acad Traveling Exhib; Milolii, a most Hawaiian Place, travel exhib, 75; Time on the Land, Nat Park Serv traveling exhib, 76-77. Teaching: Instr photog, Univ Hawaii, Manoa Campus, 69-71, instr archit, 70-72; instr photog, Hawaii Photog Workshops, 71-; instr photog, State of Hawaii Artists in Schs, 74. Pos: Owner-founder, The Foundry Gallery, Honolulu, 69-71; dir, Statewide Photo Exhib, 70; dir, Hawaii Photog Workshops, 71-; bd mem, The Image Found, 73-; visual arts coordr, Artists in Schs Prog, 74; dir, The Volcano Art Ctr, Volcano, Hawaii, 74- Awards: Purchase Awards, Hawaii State Found Cult & Arts, 70-75. Bibliog: The eye of the camera (film), KHET-TV, Hawaii, 71; Tomi Kneaffler (auth), Fine arts photography in Hawaii, Honolulu Star Bull, 72; Joan Murray (auth), Photography in Hawaii, Art Week, 73. Mem: Image Continuum Group. Publ: Contribr, Beautiful Hawaii, Lane, 72; illusr, Hawaiian Legends, Bishop Mus Press, 75; illusr, Dillingham Corp Tide Calendar, 75; auth, Journal of a Pioneer Builder, Hawaii Nat Hist Asn, 77. Mailing Add: PO Box 131 Volcano HI 96785

MORRISON C L
ART WRITER, ART CRITIC
b Evanston, Ill, Jan 14, 46. Study: Roosevelt Univ, BA; Field Mus of Nat Hist. Collections Arranged: Ill Pub Sculpture, Fed Ctr Plaza, Chicago, 78-79; The Life and Work of Henry J Darger, 77; Ill Women Artists 77, Ill Arts Coun Traveling Collection, 77-78; Abstract Art in Chicago (auth, catalog), Mus of Contemp Art, Hyde Park Art Ctr, Chicago, 76. Teaching: Workshop, post-conceptual art, Mus of Contemp Art, Chicago, Ill, 76; seminar, art writing, Univ of Wis, Stevens Point, 77. Pos: Res ed, Inst for Philosophical Res, Chicago, Ill, 67-74; contrib ed, Midwest Art, Milwaukee, Wis, 74-77; Chicago correspondent, Artforum, New York, 76- Res: The New Bauhaus; design structure and social interaction: archaeological implications; contemporary trends in architecture. Publ: Ed, Webster's Guide to American History—500 Biographies, Merriam Webster, 71; auth, Realms of the Unreal, Hyde Park Art Ctr, 77; auth, Chicago Dialectic, Artforum, 78. Mailing Add: Seven Oaks 405 S 7th St St Charles IL 60174

MORRISON, DORIS
PAINTER, ART ADMINISTRATOR
b Alameda, Calif. Study: Calif Sch Fine Arts; Cleveland Inst Art, BFA, 49; Col of Marin, printmaking with a protege of S W Hayter, 61-62. Work: Col Fine Arts, Ohio Univ, Athens; Cleveland Mus Art; Womens City Club of Cleveland; Ross Valley Hosp, Calif; Oak Knoll Naval Hosp, Oakland, Calif. Exhib: Cleveland Mus Traveling & Ann Exhib; Butler Inst Am Art Annuals; San Francisco Art Inst Traveling & Ann Exhib; Am Fed Arts Traveling Exhib, Brooklyn; Ohio Watercolor Soc Traveling Exhib; Western Asn Art Mus Traveling Exhib; East Bay Artists Asn Traveling Exhib; Invitationals, Jack London Sq, Oakland, Calif & Casa Manana, Monterey. Pos: Vpres, Ohio Watercolor Soc, 50-53; vpres textile Arts, Cleveland Mus Art, 50-54; pres, Marin Soc of Artists, Ross, Calif, 65-66, critiquest chmn, 67, chmn Rental Gallery, 68 & prog chmn, 69; exhib chmn & pres, Santa Barbara Art Asn, 77-78; dir,

Contemporary Art Forum, 78- Awards: First, Second & Third Place Awards, Cleveland Mus Art Ann May Shows, 48-55; First in Watercolor, Soc Western Artists, 57; Honorable Mention in Watercolor Collage, San Francisco Women Artist, 68. Style & Technique: Abstract expressionist from mid-sixties to 1970, then geometric hard-edge, going now toward lyrical abstraction and some semi-abstraction. Media: (Painting) Acrylic, Transparent Watercolor, Oil; Collage, Printmaking. Mailing Add: 333 Old Mill Rd 204 Santa Barbara CA 93110

MORRISON, FRITZI MOHRENSTECHER
PAINTER, LECTURER
b Quincy, Ill. Study: Art Inst Chicago; Univ Chicago; also with Charles W Hawthorne, Anthony Thieme, Karl Knaths, Eliot O'Hara & John Pike. Work: St Louis Art Mus, Mo; Carpenter Gallery, Dartmouth Col, Hanover, NH; City Hall, Quincy, Mass; Elizabeth Sinnock Gallery, Quincy Art Ctr, Ill. Exhib: Am Fedn Arts sponsored Watercolor Traveling Show, 50-70; 50th Philadelphia Int Watercolor Exhib, Pa Acad Fine Arts, 52, Traveling Show, 53; A Century of St Louis Art & Artists, St Louis Art Mus, Mo, 60-70; Oklahoma City Mus Ann, Okla, 74; one-man show, Whatcom Mus Hist & Art, Bellingham, Wash, 75; plus others. Pos: Resident artist, Quincy Art Club, Ill, 38-53. Awards: Pulitzer Award Any Medium, St Louis Art Mus 11th Ann Exhib, 51; Watercolor First Award, Montgomery Co Exhib, Washington, DC, 53; McGavran Purchase Award & First in Watercolor, Quincy Art Show, 67. Mem: Am Watercolor Soc; Philadelphia Watercolor Club; Washington DC Watercolor Asn; Quincy Art Club & Artists Guild (vpres, art club). Style & Technique: Landscapes, portrait and figure compositions, accenting mood, time and feel of day, frequently from imagination or memory. Media: Transparent Watercolor. Mailing Add: 1845 Jersey St Quincy IL 62301

MORRISON, GEORGE
PAINTER
b Grand Marais, Minn, Sept 30, 19. Study: Minneapolis Sch of Art, MFA (hon), 69; Art Students League; Univ Aix-Marseille, Aix-en-Provence, France. Work: Whitney Mus of Am Art, New York; Philadelphia Mus of Art; Va Mus of Fine Arts, Richmond; Heard Mus, Phoenix, Ariz; Amon Carter Mus, Ft Worth, Tex. Comn: Cedar wood mural (18ft x 98ft), Minneapolis Regional Native Am Ctr, 75; redwood mural (8ft x 20ft), City of Seattle, Daybreak Star Art Ctr, 77; found wood collage (4ft x 10ft), Hennepin County Med Ctr, Minneapolis, 77. Exhib: Corcoran Biennial, Washington, DC, 50; Whitney Mus of Am Art Ann, New York, 52; Joslyn Art Mus, Omaha, Nebr, 55; Los Angeles Co Mus of Art, 58; Dallas Mus of Fine Arts, 58; Brooklyn Mus, 61; RI Sch of Design Mus of Art, Providence, 68; Mus of the Am Indian, New York, 71. Collections Arranged: Morrison Drawings (travelling exhib), Walker Art Ctr, Minneapolis, 73, Heard Mus, Phoenix, 73, Mus of STex, Corpus Christie, 73 & Amon Carter Mus, Ft Worth, 74. Teaching: Prof painting & drawing, Univ Minn, Minneapolis, 70-; assoc prof painting & drawing, RI Sch of Design, Providence, 63-70; vis prof, Cornell Univ, 62 & Pa State Univ, State College, 63. Bibliog: Dragos Kostich (auth), George Morrison: The Story of an American Indian, Dillon Press, 76; feature prog, Encounter with Artists: George Morrison, KTCA-TV, Minn Educ Television; 77. Mem: Audubon Artists; Fedn of Mod Painters & Sculptors; Advocates for the Arts; Native Am Coun for the Arts. Style & Technique: Expressionistic; layers of paint to gain textured surface. Media: Oil and collages of found weathered wood to gain textured appeal. Publ: Auth, George Longfish: Painter, Am Indian Art Mag, 78. Mailing Add: 2050 Stanford Ave St Paul MN 55105

MORRISON, KEITH ANTHONY
PAINTER, EDUCATOR
b Jamaica, WI, May 20, 42; US citizen. Study: Art Inst Chicago, BFA, 63, MFA, 65; Univ Ill; DePaul Univ; Loyola Univ. Work: Jamaica Inst, WI; Nat Collection Liberia, WAfrica; Fisk Univ; Art Inst Chicago. Comn: Painting for Liberian Govt, 64 & Dusable Mus Afro-Am Hist, 71; mural commissioned by Phyllis Kind Gallery for Main Bank, Chicago, 72. Exhib: Black & White, Kovler Gallery, 69; Chicago Prints, Allan Frumkin Gallery, 69; Nat Exhib Black Artists, Smith-Mason Gallery, Washington, DC, 71; Black American Artists 71, Ill Bell/Ill Arts Coun, 71; Biennial Chicago & Vicinity, Art Inst Chicago, 71; plus others. Collections Arranged: Toussaint L'ouverture (paintings of Jacob Lawrence, with catalog), organized for DePaul Univ, Chicago, 69; Black Experiences in Art (exhib of painting & sculpture, with catalog), Bergman Gallery Univ Chicago, 71. Teaching: Instr art, Hyde Park Art Ctr, Chicago, 65-67; asst prof drawing, Fisk Univ, Nashville, Tenn, 67-68; assoc prof printmaking & chmn dept, DePaul Univ, 68-71; assoc prof painting, Univ Ill, Chicago-Circle, 69- Awards: Second Prize, Jamaica Inst, 59. Bibliog: Doris Sanders (auth), Morrison's panel, Defender, 5/69; Robin Glauber (auth), Keith Morrison at Black Hawk, Skyline, 9/70; Kitty Kingston (auth), Keith Morrison, Gleaner, 2/71. Mem: Col Art Asn; Nat Conf Artists; Chicago Soc Artists. Media: Oil, Watercolor, Acrylic. Publ: Auth, The Probing Line, Fisk Univ, 68; auth, Jacob Lawrence's Toussaint L'ouverture, Art Scene, 69; auth, Meaningful concept of art in humanities, Musart, 70. Mailing Add: Dept Art & Design Univ Ill Chicago Circle Chicago IL 60680

MORRISON, ROBERT CLIFTON
PRINTMAKER, PAINTER
b Billings, Mont, Aug 13, 24. Study: Carleton Col, BA; Univ NMex, MA. Work: Harvard Univ Libr Print Collection, Cambridge, Mass; Ministry Art & Cult, Ghana; Rocky Mt Col, Billings; Int Col Copenhagen, Denmark. Comn: Mosaic murals, Mont State Unemployment Comn, Helena, 61 & Lucerne Pub Schs Wyo; mural, Lockwood Pub Schs, Billings; Bicentennial mural, Yellowstone Co Courthouse, Billings. Teaching: Dir art educ, Billings Pub Schs, 57-67; assoc prof art, Rocky Mt Col, 67- Pos: Ed, Rocky Mt Rev, 63-69; pres bd dirs, Yellowstone Art Ctr, Billings, 64-65. Awards: Mont Artist-Teacher of Yr, Am Artists Prof League, 64. Style & Technique: Strong light and dark patterns, moderate abstraction, in prints and paintings. Media: Wood; Acrylic, Oil. Publ: Translr & illusr, Maxims of LaRochefoucauld, 67. Dealer: Gallery '85 Emerald Dr Billings MT 59101. Mailing Add: 2815 Woody Dr Billings MT 59102

MORROW, ROBERT EARL
EDUCATOR, MURALIST
b Milan, Ohio, Mar 21, 17. Study: Cleveland Inst of Art, Ohio; Ohio State Univ, Columbus. Work: Cleveland Mus of Art; Butler Inst of Am Art, Youngstown, Ohio; Akron Art Inst, Ohio; Canton Art Inst, Ohio; Massillon Mus, Ohio. Comn: Hanging banners, Kent State Univ, Ohio, 62; murals (tile mosaic), Firestone High Sch, Akron, 63; murals (sgraffito), Temple Univ, Philadelphia, Pa, 66; mural (polyester resin, polydrome), Akron Pub Libr, 69; mural (portland cement sgraffito), II Cascade Plaza, William Ruhlman, 70. Exhib: Cleveland Mus of Art Ann Regional; Butler Inst of Am Art, Youngstown. Teaching: Prof drawing & painting, Kent State Univ, 46- Pos: Vis prof mural design, Tyler Sch of Art, Temple Univ, Philadelphia, 64-66. Awards: Second Award/Painting, Army Art Show, Nat Gallery, Washington, DC, 44; Purchase Awards, Cleveland Mus of Art, 64; Second Award, Butler Inst of Am Art, Youngstown, 50. Media: Drawing; Photography; Murals in Concrete; Constructions. Publ: Illusr, Orchestra Mice, Reilly & Lee, Chicago, 70. Mailing Add: 141 Crain Ave Kent OH 44240

MORROW, TERRY
DRAFTSMAN, PRINTMAKER
b Austin, Tex, Oct 1, 39. Study: Univ Tex, BFA; Univ Wis, grad study; Ind Univ, MS, study with Rudy Pozzatti. Work: Univ Tex, Austin; Tex Christian Univ, Ft Worth; Western Tex Col, Snyder; Odessa Col, Tex. Exhib: 14th Nat Print & Drawing Competition, Grand Forks, NDak, 71; 13th, 14th & 15th Ann Nat Drawing & Print Competition, Okalahoma City Art Ctr, 71-73; 4th Biennial Int Mat Media Exhib, Dickinson, NDak, 73; Nat Drawing Exhib-1975, Rutgers Univ, Camden, NJ, 75; 2nd Miami Graphics Biennial Int Competition, Fla, 75; 2nd & 3rd Nat Printmaking Invitational, Galveston Art Ctr on the Strand, 76 & 77; Appalachian Nat Drawing Competition, Boone, NC, 78; two-person exhibs, Sch Galleries, Houston Mus of Fine Arts, 71 & Art Dept Teaching Gallery, Univ of Tenn, Knoxville, 77; one-person exhib, Clara M Eagle Gallery, Price Doyle Fine Art Ctr, Murray State Univ, 73. Teaching: Instr painting & printmaking, Univ of Pa, Philadelphia, 65-66; asst prof drawing & printmaking, Univ Chattanooga, Tenn, 67-68; assoc prof drawing, printmaking, Tex Tech Univ, Lubbock, 68- Pos: Consult in litho printing, Tex Christian Univ, Ft Worth, 69, Western Tex Col, Snyder, 74 & San Angelo Col, Tex, 78. Awards: Helen Van Aken Purchase Award, 5th Ann Gulf Coast Art Exhib, 70; Cash award, 16th Ann Drawing and Small Sculpture exhib, 70; Cash award, Tri-State Art Exhib, 76; 12th Ann Del Mar Drawing & Small Sculpture, 78. Style & Technique: Personal forms from nature rendered in cross-hatch shading, pen & ink, intaglio & lithography. Media: Pen and Ink; Intaglio. Dealer: Dorothy Katz c/o Sol Del Rio Gallery 1020 Townsend San Antonio TX 78209. Mailing Add: 1004 Dover Ave Lubbock TX 79416

MORSE, A REYNOLDS
COLLECTOR
b Denver, Colo, Oct 20, 14. Study: Univ Colo, BA, 38; Harvard Bus Sch, MBA, 39. Pos: Pres, Salvador Dali Mus, Cleveland, 70; hon cur, Burr Collection, Denver Pub Libr. Collection: 93 oils, 117 drawings watercolors, over 500 prints, all by Salvador Dali; complete library on Dali. Publ: Auth, Dali, a study of his life and works, NY Graphic Soc, 58; auth, A Dali Primer, 70; auth, The Draftsmanship of Dali, 70; auth, Dali, the Masterworks, 71; auth, Dali, a Collection, 72; plus others. Mailing Add: 24050 Commerce Park Rd Cleveland OH 44122

MORSE, JOHN D
ART EDITOR
b Gifford, Ill, Sept 26, 06. Study: Univ Ill, AB & MA; Wayne Univ; NY Univ. Teaching: Lectr gen art hist & interpretation; instr, Univ Ill, 34-35; instr art hist, Kent Sch, 54-56. Pos: Mus instr, Detroit Inst Art, 35-41; managing ed, Art Quart, 38-41; assoc in radio, Metrop Mus Art, New York, 41-42; ed, Mag of Art, 42-47; dir publ, Art Students League, 48-50; assoc ed, Am Artist Mag, 51-53; conductor, Am Artist Mag Europ Tours, 50-52; exec secy, Kent Sch, 54-56; chief commun, Detroit Inst Arts, 59-62; ed publ, Henri Francis du Pont Winterthur Mus, Del, 62-70; ed, Am Art J, 72-77, consult, 77- Mem: Century Asn, NY. Publ: Auth, Old Masters in America, 55 & 79; producer, Flanders in the Fifteenth Century (film), 60, The Gardens of Winterthur (film), 64 & Winterthur in Bloom (film), 69; ed, Prints in and of America to 1850 (Winterthur conf report), Univ Press Va, 70; ed, Ben Shahn, Praeger, 72; contribr, Mag Art, Esquire, Am Artist & other mags. Mailing Add: 1871 Prospect St Sarasota FL 33579

MORSE, MITCHELL IAN
ART DEALER, RESTORER
b Brooklyn, NY, Mar 10, 26. Study: Himeji Univ, 45-46; City Col New York, BBA, 47. Pos: Pres, Art Gallery on Wheels, New York, 53-54; pres, Mitch Morse Gallery, Inc, 69-; pres, Mitch Morse Graphics, Inc, New York, 69-; pres, Graphic Source I, 71- Awards: Designer Official Seal, Village Lawrence, 67. Mem: Am Soc Interior Designers; Prof Picture Framers Asn; Calhoun's Collectors Soc, Inc Minneapolis, Minn (chmn, Artistic Evaluation Bd, 77). Specialty: Artists agents, publishers of limited edition, original graphics. Publ: Auth, Graphics as an original art form, Designer, 8/73. Mailing Add: Mitch Morse Gallery Inc 305 E 63rd St New York NY 10021

MORTENSEN, GORDON LOUIS
PRINTMAKER, PAINTER
b Arnegard, NDak, Apr 27, 38. Study: Minneapolis Col of Art & Design, BFA; Univ Minn. Work: Nat Collection Fine Arts, Washington, DC; Brooklyn Mus; Minn Mus of Art, St Paul; Philadelphia Mus of Art; De Cordova Mus, Lincoln, Mass. Exhib: The Biennial, Minneapolis Inst of Art, 63 & 67; Second Miami Graphics Biennial, Miami Art Ctr, Fla, 75; Biennial Int Open Competition, The Print Club, Philadelphia, 75 & 77; Bradley Nat Print & Drawing Exhib, Bradley Univ, Peoria, Ill, 75 & 77; Davidson Nat Print & Drawing Competition, Davidson Col, NC, 75 & 76; Brooklyn Print Show, Brooklyn Mus, 76; 14th Midwest Biennial, Joslyn Art Mus, Omaha, Nebr, 76; Plains Art Mus, Moorhead, Minn, 76; Boston Printmakers Nat Exhib, De Cordova Mus, 77; Tokyo Cent Mus Art, Japan, 78. Awards: Purchase Award, Davidson Nat Print & Drawing Competition, Davidson Col, 75 & 76; First Place Purchase, Miami Univ Print & Drawing Exhib, Oxford, Ohio, 77; George Bunker Award, Biennial Int Open Competition, The Print Club, Philadelphia Mus of Art, 77. Mem: Boston Printmakers. Style & Technique: Impressionist; reduction woodcut landscapes. Media: Oil, watercolor and woodcut. Dealer: Assoc American Artists 663 Fifth Ave New York NY 10022. Mailing Add: 4153 Crest Rd Pebble Beach CA 93953

MORTON, RICHARD H
PAINTER, ILLUSTRATOR
b Dallas, Tex, Aug 8, 21. Study: Pratt Inst, cert; Oklahoma City Univ, BA; Univ Tulsa, MA; Inst Allende, Mexico, MFA. Work: Okla Art Ctr & Am Petrol Co, Oklahoma City; Univ Tulsa, Okla; Northeast Mo State Univ, Kirksville. Exhib: Watercolor USA, Springfield Art Mus, Mo, 66, 70 & 74; Past Jurors Invitational, 69 & Eight State Exhib, 70, Okla Art Ctr; Bicentennial Jurored Art Show, Mus of the Great Plains, Lawton, Okla, 76; Okla Bicentennial Competition, State Capitol, Oklahoma City, 76; Bicentennial Competition Selections, Kennedy Ctr, Washington, DC, 76. Teaching: Instr design, Southern Ill Univ, Carbondale, 55-59; asst dean, Columbus Col Art & Design, Ohio, 59-60; asst prof design, Cent State Univ, 61-65; assoc prof painting, Northeast Mo State Univ, Kirksville, 65-72; art workshops, Southwest US, 72- Pos: Illusr, US Army, Ft Sill, Okla, 76 Awards: Purchase Award, Southwest Am Art Exhib, Okla Art Ctr, 62; WCoast Watercolor Soc Award for Transparent Watercolor, 70; John Marin Mem Award, Watercolor USA, 74; Distinguished Award, Bicentennial Jurored Art Show, Mus of the Great Plains, Lawton, Okla, 76; Award of Excellence, Okla Bicentennial Competition, State Capitol, Oklahoma City, 76. Mem: Okla Watercolor Asn. Style & Technique: Lyrical representational treatment of the Southwest landscape in the medium of transparent watercolor. Media: Watercolor. Dealer: New West Gallery 5908 Lomas NE Albuquerque NM 87110. Mailing Add: 2901 NW 34 Lawton OK 73505

MORTON, ROBERT ALAN
PUBLISHER, ART WRITER
b Jersey City, NJ, May 20, 34. Study: Dartmouth Col, BA, 55. Pos: Series ed, Time-Life Libr of Art, New York, 66-70; ed dir, New York Graphic Soc, Inc, 70-73; ed in chief, Harry N Abrams, Inc, 76- Res: American decorative arts. Publ: Auth, Southern Antiques and Folk Art, Oxmoore House, 76. Mailing Add: c/o H N Abrams 110 E 59th St New York NY 10022

MOSBY, DEWEY FRANKLIN
CURATOR, ART HISTORIAN
b San Augustine, Tex, Jan 2, 42. Study: Lamar Univ, BS, 63; Univ Calif, Los Angeles, MA, 69; Harvard Univ, PhD, 74. Collections Arranged: Degas in the Detroit Inst of Arts, Detroit Inst Arts, 74, French Painting 1774-1830: The Age of Revolution, 75 & Master Paintings from the Hermitage and the State Russian Museum Leningrad, 75; Cinco Siglos de Obras maestras de la pintura en colecciones norteamericanas cedidas en préstamo a Costa Rica, 78. Teaching: Asst prof art hist, State Univ NY Buffalo, 73-74; asst prof art hist, Harvard Univ, summer 74. Pos: Curator European art, Detroit Inst Arts, 74- Mem: Col Art Asn Am; Midwest Art Hist Soc (mem, Univ-Mus Rels Comt); Am Asn Mus. Res: 18th and 19th century art with an emphasis on Alexandre-Gabriel Decamps (1803-60). Publ: Contribr, Studies in Drawings: The Hebald Collection, Grunwald Found, 70; contribr, The Homburger Collection (catalog), Fogg Art Mus, 71; auth, Master Drawings, Vol 12, 74; auth, article in Arts Mag, 9/75. Mailing Add: 5200 Woodward Ave Detroit MI 48202

MOSCA, AUGUST
PAINTER, INSTRUCTOR
b Naples, Italy, Aug 19, 07; US citizen. Study: Yale Sch of Fine Arts; Pratt Inst; Art Students League; Grand Cent Art Sch. Work: Libr of Congress, Washington, DC; Butler Inst of Am Art, Youngstown, Ohio; Roy Neuberger Mus, New York; Parrish Mus, Southampton, NY; New York Pub Libr. Comn: Portrait of Heywood Brown, Newspaper Guild of New York, 55 & Newspaper Guild of Am, Washington, DC, 57. Exhib: Portrait of America, Metrop Mus of Art, New York, 43; Calif Palace of the Legion of Honor, 45; Brooklyn Mus Watercolor Int Ann, 59; Miss Art Asn Exhib, 59; Butler Inst of Am Art, Youngstown, Ohio, 62; New York Cult Ctr Exhib, 73; Nat Acad of Design Ann, 77; Am Inst of Arts & Letters Exhib, New York, 77; one-man shows, Harry Salpeter Gallery, New York, 57, Far Gallery, New York, 74, St Michaels Col, Winooski, Vt, 74; St Mary's Col, Md, 76. Teaching: Instr art & drawing, Pratt Inst, Brooklyn, NY, 55; instr art & painting, Tuxedo Park Sch, NY, 68-72; instr art, drawing & painting, Pvt Studio. Awards: Calif Palace of the Legion of Honor Silver Medal, 45; Audubon Artists Presidents Award, 76; Soc Am Graphic Artists Purchase Award, 77. Bibliog: George A Perret (auth), August Mosca, New York Cult Ctr, 73. Mem: Painters & Sculptors Soc of NJ (mem admissions comt, 72-75; pres, 75-77); Audubon Artists (pres graphics, 75-77). Style & Technique: Post-impressionism, cubism, futurism; Realistic with strong intimation of Fauvism and abstract; in drawing-realism and sensivity. Media: Oil on Canvas; Silverpoint Drawing, Pen and Ink; Lithography. Publ: Auth, Our artists and writers, Suffolk Times, 75; auth, Art of Post-impressism, M Grumbacher, 76; auth, Artist explains Lithography, Shelter Island Reporter, 77. Dealer: Far Gallery 22 E 80th St New York NY 10028. Mailing Add: Shelter Island NY 11964

MOSCATT, PAUL N
PAINTER, INSTRUCTOR
b Brooklyn, NY, July 9, 31. Study: Cooper Union Art Sch; Yale Univ Sch Fine Arts, BFA & MFA. Work: Univ Bridgeport, Conn; Yale Univ Art Dept; Earlham Col, Richmond, Ind; Cincinnati Art Mus; Allegheny Col, Meadville, Pa. Exhib: One-man shows, Aspects Gallery, New York, 62 & 63, Earlham Col, 65, Peter Cooper Gallery, New York, 68, Univ Md, Baltimore, 70, Towson State Col, Md, 70, Portrait Drawings of the American Indian, Md Inst Col Art, 73 & Interiors & Nudes, C Grimaldis Gallery, Baltimore, Md, 78. Teaching: Instr painting & drawing, Univ Bridgeport, 62-64; instr painting & drawing, Art Acad Cincinnati, 64-66; instr painting & drawing, Md Inst Col Art, 67- Style & Technique: Representational painting; self portraits; perceptual figuration; conceptual figuration. Media: Oil, Acrylic. Mailing Add: Md Inst Col of Art 1300 Mt Royal Ave Baltimore MD 21217

MOSELEY, RALPH SESSIONS
PAINTER
b Kingston, NY, June 5, 41. Study: Williams Col, BA; Hunter Col, MA. Work: Whitney Mus Am Art, New York; Aldrich Mus, Ridgefield, Conn. Exhib: Ann, Whitney Mus Am Art, 69, Lyrical Abstraction, 70; Aldrich Mus, 70; one-man show, A M Sachs Gallery, New York, NY, 78. Media: Acrylic. Mailing Add: 438 Broome St New York NY 10013

MOSELEY, SPENCER ALTEMONT
PAINTER, EDUCATOR
b Bellingham, Wash, July 18, 25. Study: Univ Wash, BA, 48, MFA, 51; Ecole Fernand Leger, Paris, 49. Work: Seattle Art Mus, Wash; Henry Art Gallery, Univ Wash. Exhib: Kobe Exchange Show, Japan, 65; Art Across America, San Francisco Mus Art, 65; The West—80 Contemporaries, Univ Ariz Art Gallery, Tucson, 67; 73rd Western Ann, Denver Art Mus, 71; Pac Cities Loan Exhib, Auckland Art Mus, NZ, 71; plus others. Teaching: Prof art hist & painting, Univ Wash, 49-, dir, Sch Art, 66- Awards: First Prize, Pac Northwest Arts & Crafts Fair, 65; Ford Found Purchase Award, 66; Purchase Prize, 54th Ann Northwest Painting & Sculpture, 68; plus others. Bibliog: Carraher (auth), Optical Illusions and the Visual Arts, 66 & Proctor (auth), Principles of Pattern, 69, Reinhold; Westphal (auth), Textiles (catalog), Mus Contemp Crafts, New York, 67. Media: Oil. Publ: Co-auth, Crafts Design, Wadsworth, 52; auth, History of Painting in the Western World, Frontier Press, 64. Mailing Add: Sch of Art Univ of Wash Seattle WA 98195

MOSER, BARRY
ILLUSTRATOR, PRINTMAKER
b Chattanooga, Tenn, Oct 15, 40. Study: Auburn Univ; Univ Tenn Chattanooga, with George Cress; also studied with Leonard Baskin & Jack Coughlin. Work: Brit Mus, London, Eng; Boston Athenaeum, Mass; Libr of Congress, Washington, DC; Harvard Univ, Cambridge, Mass; Cambridge Univ, Eng. Exhib: Boston Printmakers, Waltham, Mass, 72; one-man shows, Berkshire Mus, Pittsfield, Mass, 73 & Boston Athenaeum, Mass, 76; Los Angeles Nat Print Show, Calif, 74; Libr of Congress Nat Print Exhib, Washington, DC, 75-76; History of Printed Books, San Francisco Pub Libr, Calif, 76; 4th Int Exhibit of Botanical Art, Hunt Inst, Carnegie-Mellon Univ, Pittsburgh, Pa, 77-78. Collections Arranged: New York Pub Libr, New York; Swarthmore Col, Pa; Harvard Univ, Cambridge, Mass; Univ Iowa, Ames (collection of illus bks); Smith Col, 76. Teaching: Head studio art, Williston Acad Northampton Sch for Girls, Easthampton, Mass, 67- Awards: Second Prize, Cape Cod Ann, 71; Award of Merit, New Hampshire Int, 74. Mem: Am Printing Hist Asn. Style & Technique: Black and White. Media: Ink Drawing; Wood Engraving. Publ: Illusr, Rhode Island, an historical guidebook, RI Bicentennial Comn, 76; illusr, Chelmaxions, David R Godine, Boston, Mass, 77; illusr, Song of Songs, Harcourt, Brace & Jonvanovich, New York, 77; illusr, Thistles & Thorns, Abbatior Ed, Univ Nebr, 77; illusr, Moby Dick, Arion Press, San Francisco, Calif, 78. Dealer: J P Dwyer 44 Main St Northampton MA 01060. Mailing Add: 1 Railroad St Easthampton MA 11027

MOSER, CHARLOTTE
ART CRITIC
b Texarkana, Tex, June 19, 47. Study: Univ Tex Austin, MA, BA(art) & BA; Sweet Briar Col; Kans City Art Inst, Inst d'Art et Archeol, Paris. Teaching: Lectr new frontiers in southwestern art, Univ Houston, 77. Pos: Art critic, Houston Post, Tex, 73-74; art critic, Houston Chronicle, Tex, 74-; corresp, Art News, New York, 76- Awards: Nat Endowment for Arts Critic Fel, 77. Mem: Col Art Asn; Women's Caucus for Art. Res: Contemporary and historical art trends in Texas, Southwestern United States and the deep South. Publ: Auth, Deep in the art of Texas, Ms Mag, 2/77; auth, Houston's cultural leadership, 2/77 & auth, New Mexico: psychic elbow room, 12/77, ArtNews; auth, Richard Thompson (catalog essay), Tyler Mus, 3/78; auth, Women art patrons in Women in Texas, Univ Tex Press, 79. Mailing Add: c/o Houston Chronicle 801 Texas Ave Houston TX 77002

MOSER, JOANN
CURATOR, ART HISTORIAN
b Chicago, Ill. Study: Smith Col, BA(art hist), 69; Univ Wis, Madison, MA(art hist), 72, PhD(art hist), 76. Collections Arranged: Atelier 17 (50 yr retrospective travelling exhib to five mus; auth, catalogue), 77-78. Pos: Cur of collections, Univ Iowa Mus of Art, 76- Awards: Ford Fel, Dept Art Hist, Univ Wis, 71-73; Kress Fel, Nat Gallery of Art, Washington, DC, 75-76; Iowa Mus of Art, 77-78. Mem: Iowa Mus Asn (mem coun, 76-78); Col Art Asn. Res: Prints and 20th century art. Publ: Auth, Eaux-fortes Théâtrales pour Monsieur G.... by Louis Marcoussis, Elvehjem Art Ctr Bull, 74; contribr, Mauricio Lasansky and Intaglio Printmaking (catalogue), Univ Iowa Mus of Art, 76; auth, The impact of Stanley William Hayter on Post-war American art, Archives of Am Art J, Vol 18, No 1. Mailing Add: Univ Iowa Mus of Art Iowa City IA 52242

MOSER, JULON
PAINTER
b Schenectady, NY. Study: Binghamton Fine Arts, 25, with Frank Taylor Bowers; Chouinard Sch Art, 29-30, with Pattie Patterson; Univ Calif, Berkeley, 43-44, with Wessels; Scripps Col, 47, with Millard Sheets; pvt study with Nicolai Fechin. Work: Over 250 paintings in pvt collections. Exhib: Golden Gate Int, Treasure Island, San Francisco, 39; Calif Nat Watercolor Soc Current Exhib, Nat Acad Design, 72 & Ann Exhib, Laguna Beach Gallery, 72; Invitational Exhib touring Sweden, 72-73; one-woman shows, Pomoroy Galleries, 62 & Oxnard Art Gallery, 72. Awards: For Morning, Clearwater High Sch, Taos, NMex, 41; for Shades of Prometheus, Oxnard Art Gallery, 72; Purchase Award for Permanent Collection, City of Oxnard, Calif, 75; Purchase Award, City of Santa Paula, Calif, 76; Second Award, Oxnard Art Asn Exhib, 77. Mem: Calif Nat Watercolor Soc (rec recy, 72-73); Women Painters of the West (pres, 56-58, corresp secy, 72-73, mem bd, 78); Los Angeles Art Asn; Oxnard Art Asn; hon mem Ventura Art Club. Media: Watercolor. Dealer: Milk House Art Galleries Pacific Coast Hwy & Washington St Marina del Rey CA 90291. Mailing Add: 3700 Dean Dr 2806 Ventura CA 93003

MOSES, BETTY (BETTY MOSES MCCART)
PAINTER
b Eagle Bridge, NY, Feb 2, 17. Study: With Forrest K Moses (father) & Grandma Moses (grandmother). Work: Bennington Mus, Vt; Elaine Horwitch Gallery, Scottsdale, Ariz; Jones Gallery, La Jolla, Calif; Burk Gal'ry, Boulder City, Nev; The Gallery, Palm Springs, Calif. Exhib: Lord & Taylor Gallery, New York & Atlanta, 71-75; Lighthouse Gallery, Tequesta-Jupiter, Fla, 72; Art Wagon Gallery, Scottsdale, Ariz, 72; Elaine Horwitch Gallery, 73-78. Bibliog: Descendant artists of Grandma Moses (TV Prog CBS), nationally, 12/27/70. Style & Technique: Fluent style depicting Green Mountain farmlands, almost always with children at play and scenes of past Indian life in the regions of New York State and Vermont. Media: Oil. Dealer: Raymond J Poppelman No 40 3940 Algonquin Dr Las Vegas NV 89109. Mailing Add: RFD 1 Eagle Bridge NY 12057

MOSES, ED
PAINTER
b Long Beach, Calif, 1926. Study: Univ Calif, Los Angeles, MA; Tamarind Lithography grant. Work: Art Inst Chicago; Corcoran Gallery Art, Washington, DC; Pasadena Mus, Calif; Walker Art Ctr, Minneapolis, Minn; San Francisco Mus Art. Exhib: Int Graphics Exhib, Florence, Italy, 69; Tamarind Prints, Mus Mod Art, New York, 69; Corcoran Gallery Art Biennial, Washington, DC, 71; Current Am Artists, Art Inst Chicago Ann, 72, 70th Am Exhib, 73; Documenta 5, Kassel, WGer, 72; Kennedy Ctr, Washington, DC, 74; one-man shows, Emmerich Gallery, New York, 74 & 75, Univ Calif, Los Angeles, 76 & Los Angeles Co Mus Art, Los Angeles, 76; 20th Nat Print Exhib, Brooklyn Mus, NY, 77; plus others. Teaching: Instr art, Univ Calif, Irvine, 68-71. Bibliog: J Loring (auth), Print as surface, Arts Mag, 9/73; P Derfner (auth), article in Art Int, 4/74; article in Artforum, 5/74. Style & Technique: Abstract. Mailing Add: c/o Emmerich Gallery 41 E 57th St New York NY 10022

MOSES, FORREST (LEE), (JR)
PAINTER
b Danville, Va, May, 1934. Study: Washington & Lee Univ, BA, 56; Pratt Inst, 60-62; Houston Mus Sch Fine Arts, 63-64. Exhib: Wichita Falls Mus, Tex, 72; Mus of NMex Biennial, 74; Abilene Fine Arts Mus, Tex, 74; Tyler Mus, Tex, 74; Okla Art Ctr, Oklahoma City, 75. Teaching: Instr drawing, Pratt Inst, 61-62; instr drawing & watercolor, Univ Houston, 69. Awards: Selected Juror's Award & Museum Purchase, Mus NMex Biennial, 74. Media: Oil. Dealer: Hill's Gallery San Francisco St Santa Fe NM 87501; Tibor de Nagy 29 W 57th St New York NY 10019. Mailing Add: 837 El Caminito Santa Fe NM 87501

MOSKOWITZ, POBERT S
PAINTER
b New York, NY, June 20, 35. Work: Mus Mod Art & Whitney Mus Am Art, New York; Albright-Knox Art Gallery, Buffalo; Rose Art Mus, Brandeis Univ, Waltham, Mass. Exhib: Art of Assemblage, Mus Mod Art, New York, 61; Whitney Mus Am Art Ann, 69; one-man shows, Leo Castelli Gallery, New York, 62, French & Co, New York, 70, Hayden Gallery, Mass Inst Technol, Cambridge, Mass, 71 & Clocktower, Inst for Art & Urban Resources, 77. Awards: Guggenheim Fel, 67; Award, NY State Coun on the Arts, 73; Award, Nat Endowment Arts, 75. Mailing Add: 81 Leonard St New York NY 10013

MOSKOWITZ, SHIRLEY (MRS JACOB W GRUBER)
PAINTER, SCULPTOR
b Houston, Tex, Aug 4, 20. Study: Mus Sch Art, Houston; Rice Univ, BA, 41; Oberlin Col, MA, 42; also with Morris Davidson, New York. Work: Allen Mus Art, Oberlin, Ohio; Congregation Beth Yeshuren, Houston; Har Zion Temple, Philadelphia; Robert I Kahn Mus, Houston, Tex; Mus of Fine Art, Houston, Tex; Detroit Art Inst; Akron Art Inst; William Penn

Mem Mus, Harrisburg, Pa. Exhib: Ann Oil & Ann Watercolor, Pa Acad Fine Arts, Philadelphia, 53, 57 & 69; Am Watercolor Soc, Nat Acad Design, 63; one-man shows, Allen Art Mus, Oberlin, 46, Sullivan Libr, 48 & 56, Paley Libr, 70, Temple Univ, Philadelphia, 68 & Nocara, Italy, 77; US Info Serv, Rome, 73; William Penn Mem Mus, 74-75. Teaching: Instr art hist, Univ Tex, Austin, spring 43; lectr art, Houston Pub Schs, 43-46; dir art, Oberlin Pub Schs, 46-47. Pos: Art prog for grade schs, Oberlin Pub Schs, 47; pres, Norristown Art League, 65-66. Awards: Prize for Oil Painting, Houston Artists Exhib, Mus Fine Arts, Houston, 44; Second Prize for Sculpture, Regional Show, Cheltenham Art Ctr, Pa, 62; Charles Smith Sculpture Prize, Woodmere Art Gallery, 70. Mem: Pa Acad Fine Arts; Artists Equity Asn; Philadelphia Watercolor Club (secy, 68-70); Print Club. Style & Technique: Expressionistic use of paper, clippings, paint, etc to convey interpretation of subject. Color contrasts, mood and composition are important. Media: Watercolor, Acrylic Wood, Ink, Intaglio. Dealer: Rittenhouse Gallery 2042 Rittenhouse Sq Philadelphia PA 19103; Assoc Am Artists' Philadelphia Print Gallery. Mailing Add: 2211 Delancey Pl Philadelphia PA 19103

MOSLEY, ZACK T
ILLUSTRATOR, CARTOONIST
b Hickory, Okla, Dec 12, 06. Study: Chicago Acad Fine Arts, 26-27; Art Inst Chicago, 27-28. Pos: Creator syndicated comic strip, Smilin' Jack, Chicago Tribune-New York News. Mem: Nat Cartoonists Soc. Mailing Add: PO Box 375 Stuart FL 33494

MOSS, IRENE
PAINTER
b Eperjes, Czech; US citizen. Study: Brooklyn Mus Sch Art; also with Moses Soyer & Dmitri Romanofsky, New York. Work: Akron Art Inst, Ohio; Finch Col Mus, New York; Rose Art Mus, Brandeis Univ, Mass; New Brit Mus Am Art, Conn; Norfolk Mus, Va. Exhib: Ft Worth Art Ctr, Tex, 68; Rochester Mem Art Gallery, NY, 68; one-woman show, Suffolk Mus, Stony Brook, NY, 71; Stamford Mus, Conn, 72; Philadelphia Civic Ctr Mus, 74. Pos: Co-ed, Feminist Art J, 72-73. Bibliog: John Gruen (auth), Friday tour of art, World J Tribune, 66; Jacqueline Barnitz (auth), Images, 68 & Gordon Brown (auth), Irene Moss & the repetition of the natural image, 3/74, Arts Mag. Style & Technique: Multiple landscape views on a single canvas, using structural divisions. Dealer: Peter Rose Gallery 200 E 58th St New York NY 10022. Mailing Add: 271-16W Grand Cent Pkwy Floral Park NY 11005

MOSS, JOE (FRANCIS)
SCULPTOR, PAINTER
b Kincheloe, WVa, Jan 26, 33. Study: WVa Univ, AB, 51, MA, 60. Work: Bloomsburg Col, Pa; Huntington Galleries, WVa; Arts & Humanities Coun, Charleston, WVa; State Capitol, Charleston; Urban Coalition, Washington, DC. Comn: Johnson Mus, Ithaca, NY; kinetic sculpture, WVa Univ, Morgantown, 65; light sculpture, First Presby Church, Morgantown, 66; auditory environ sculpture, Robert & Mary Raley, Hockessin, Del, 74. Exhib: Members Exhib, Mus Mod Art, New York, 65; Mass Inst Technol Traveling Exhib, Multiple Interaction, Franklin Inst, Philadelphia, 73, Hall of Sci, New York, 74 & Calif Mus Sci & Indust, Los Angeles, 74; Sculpture 75, City of Philadelphia, 75; one-man shows, Sculpture Now, New York, 75, City Univ Grad Ctr, New York, 75, Washington Gallery of Modern Art, Washington, DC, 67- & J B Speed Mus, Louisville, Ky, 77. Teaching: Assoc prof art, WVa Univ, 60-70; vis prof art, Univ Md, summer 67; prof art, Univ Del, 70- Pos: Vis res fel, Ctr Advan Visual Studies, Mass Inst Technol, Cambridge, 73. Awards: Painting Award, Huntington Galleries, 63; Prize for Environ Design, Three Rivers Arts Festival, Pittsburgh, 68; Sculpture Award, Appalachian Corridors Exhib, Charleston, 70. Bibliog: Alan Gerstle (auth), Joe Moss, Arts Mag, 3/75; rev in Art Forum, 4/75; Emma Lila Fundaburk & Thomas Davenport (auth), Art in Public Places in the US, 75. Style & Technique: Environmental sculpture; shapes are designed to manipulate the environmental sounds of a space by blocking, reflecting and absorbing sounds. Media: Plastic, Metal. Dealer: Max Hutchinson c/o Sculpture Now Inc 142 Green St New York NY 10012. Mailing Add: 7 Woodsman Dr Newark DE 19711

MOSS, JOEL C
PAINTER, EDUCATOR
b US. Study: Ft Hays Kans State Col, BS, 38; George Peabody Col, MA, 42; Columbia Univ, EdD, 53. Work: Wichita Art Mus, Kans; Wichita Asn Gallery; Gallery Art, Hastings Col, Nebr; Hutchinson Art Asn, Kans; over 250 paintings in pvt collections. Exhib: Nelson Gallery Mid Am Exhib, Kansas City, Mo, 55; San Francisco Art Mus, 56; Joslyn Mus, Omaha, Nebr, 65; Watercolor USA, Springfield, Mo, 68; Wichita Art Mus Artist Ann, 70. Teaching: Instr art, Parsons Jr Col, Kans, 39-42; prof art, Ft Hays Kans State Col, 46-77, chmn dept, 50-73. Awards: First Prize Watercolor, 15 Kans Artist Ann, 67; First Purchase Prize, Wichita Art Asn Statewide Watercolor, 69 & 70; Amsden Award & Cult Arts Award, Kans Watercolor Soc, 71. Mem: Kans Watercolor Soc (bd dirs, 68-70); Kans Cult Arts (adv, 64-73). Style & Technique: Free and amorphic dealing with man and nature. Media: Watercolor. Dealer: Morton Gallery Colorado Springs CO; Geo Nix Gallery, Colorado Springs, CO. Mailing Add: 408 W Fourth Hays KS 67601

MOSS, MILTON
PAINTER
b New York, NY. Study: Cooper Union; Ecoles Beaux Arts, Paris. Work: Phoenix Mus Fine Arts, Ariz; Norfolk Mus Art & Sci, Va; Miami Mus Mod Art, Fla; Univ Maine; Houston Mus. Exhib: Butler Inst Am Art, Youngstown, Ohio, 63; one-man shows, Gallery Die Drie Hendricken, Amsterdam, Netherlands, 65, Harry Salpeter Gallery, New York, 67, Wickersham Gallery, New York, 69 & Syosset Pub Libr, New York, 71. Style & Technique: Non-objective abstractions applied with acrylics; rhythmic patterns of superimposed color fields. Dealer: Harbor Gallery 43 Main St Cold Spring Harbor NY 11724. Mailing Add: c/o Harbor Gallery 43 Main St Cold Spring Harbor NY 11724

MOSS, MORRIE ALFRED
COLLECTOR
b Chicago, Ill, June 2, 07. Collection: Paul Storr silver, over 1000 pieces; 66 old master paintings; 75 jades; 100 ivories; 16 Faberges; 48 pairs Dorothy Doughty bird models; exhibited in Brooks Mem Art Gallery, Memphis, Tenn, Indianapolis Mus Art & Dayton Art Inst. Mailing Add: 5050 Poplar Ave Memphis TN 38117

MOTHERWELL, ROBERT
PAINTER, PRINTMAKER
b Aberdeen, Wash, Jan 24, 15. Study: Stanford Univ, BA, 36; Harvard Univ Grad Sch Philos, 37; Columbia Univ, 40, with Meyer Schapiro. Work: Mus Mod Art, Metrop Mus Art & Whitney Mus Am Art, New York; San Francisco Art Mus; Tate Gallery Art, London; plus over 40 other mus. Comn: Mural, J F Kennedy Fed Bldg, Boston, 66; diptych, S Edelstone, Chicago, 71; A la Pintura (suite of aquatints), Universal Art Ed, Long Island, 72; mural, Univ Iowa Art Mus, Iowa City, 73; mural, Nat Gallery, Washington, DC. Exhib: Collage Exhib, Gallery Berggruen, Paris, 61; Retrospective, Mus Mod Art, New York & other galleries & mus, US & Europe, 65; Collage Exhib, Whitney Mus Am Art, 68; Recent Paintings, with Matisse Sculpture, Walker Art Ctr, Minneapolis, 72; Robert Motherwell's A la Pintura: The Making of a Book, Metrop Mus, New York, 72; Retrospective, Stadtische Kunsthalle, Dusseldorf, WGer, Kulturhuset, Stockholm, Sweden, Mus des 20, Jahrhunderts, Vienna, Austria, Mus d'Art de la Ville de Paris, Royal Scottish Acad, Edinburgh, Scotland & Royal Acad Arts, London; plus many others, including the Collages of Robert Motherwell. Teaching: Instr painting, Black Mountain Col, 45 & 51; prof painting, Hunter Col, 50-58, distinguished prof, 71-72. Pos: Conroy Fel, St Paul's Sch, NH, 70; educ adv, John Simon Guggenheim Found; adv ed, Am Scholar, Washington, DC, 68-; ed, Documents of 20th Century Art, 68- Awards: Am rep, Sao Paulo VI Biennale, Mus Mod Art, 61; Belgian Art Critics Prize, Brussels, 66; La Grande Medaille de Vermeil de la Villa de Paris, 77. Bibliog: Bryan Robertson & Octavio Paz (auth), Robert Motherwell paintings & collages 1967-70, Galerie I M Erker, 71; H H Arnason (auth), Robert Motherwell, Abrams, 77; E A Carmean, Jr (auth), American Art at Mid-Century, Nat Gallery of Art, 78. Mem: Smithsonian Inst (counr); Nat Collection Fine Arts (counr); John Simon Guggenheim Found (adv); fel Royal Soc Arts; fel in perpetuity Metrop Mus Art. Media: Painting, Collage, Aquatint, Lithography. Dealer: M Knoedler & Co 19 E 70th St New York NY 10021; André Emmerich Gallery 41 E 57th St New York NY 10022. Mailing Add: 909 North St Greenwich CT 06830

MOTTER, DEAN ROGER
ILLUSTRATOR, DESIGNER
b Berea, Ohio, May 14, 53. Study: Cleveland Mus of Art, Ohio; Cleveland Inst of Art, Ohio; Franshawe Col, London, Ont, Can; also with Michael Hayden, John Mills-Cockell and Richard Atkinson. Work: R Browning Gallery, Toronto, Ont. Comn: Labelle (poster), Concert Productions Int, Can, 75; poster, R Browning Gallery, Toronto, Ont, 76; Pagliaro (record sleeve), CBS Records, Can, 77; Spacecraft (record sleeve), Agency, Can, 77; sound sculpture, Sonics Gallery, Can, 74. Exhib: One-man show, Amphimores, London, Ont, Can, 74; Fantasy, R Browning Gallery, Toronto, Ont, 76. Teaching: Instr photo-elec explor, Ont Col of Art, Toronto, 75-77 & instr photo-elec interface, 76- Pos: Art dir, Stagelife Mag, Toronto, Ont, 75-; illusr & designer, Holt, Rinehart & Winston, Toronto, 76- Bibliog: Ron Kasman (auth), Dean Motter: Artist, York Univ, 76. Style & Technique: Airbrush, watercolor illustrations and electronically produced sound and music. Media: Watercolor, Gouache, Ink; Electronic Music Synthesizer. Publ: Contribr, Jeff Jones' IDYL, Blue Star, 76; auth & illusr, Star Reach Mag, Star Reach Publ, 77; illusr, Alice, Alice, Alice, wonderland in ten regions, Iconoclast Imageworks, 77; auth, ed & illusr, Andromeda Mag, Andromeda Publ, 77; illusr, Language Patterns Impressions Series, Holt, Rinehart & Winston, 77. Dealer: Iconoclast Imageworks 310 Queen St Toronto ON M5V 2A2 Can. Mailing Add: 20 Soho St Toronto ON M5V 2A2 Can

MOULD, LOLA FROWDE
PAINTER
b Sydney, NS, Dec, 1908. Study: Mt Allison Univ; Boston Sch Design; New York Sch Design. Work: Bank Montreal, Sydney Br; Miners Mus, Glace Bay, BC; also in many pvt collections, Can, USA & Europe. Exhib: Many one-man shows in Sydney, Halifax, Lord Beauebrooke, Art Gallery, Frederickton, NB, Boston & New York, Montreal & exhibited in traveling shows across Can. Teaching: Instr painting, Dept Educ & pvt classes; lectr hist art, IODE, Sydney, NS. Mem: NS Soc Artists (vpres); Maritime Asn Artists; fel Int Inst Arts & Lett, Switz. Mailing Add: 15 Amelia St Sydney NS Can

MOULTON, ROSALIND KIMBALL
PHOTOGRAPHER
b Buffalo, NY, Nov 25, 41. Study: Studied photog with Minor White, 66; Art Inst of Chicago, BFA, 71; State Univ NY, Buffalo, MFA, 76. Work: Mass Inst of Technol, Cambridge; Art Inst of Chicago; Int Mus of Photog, George Eastman House, Rochester, NY; Univ Art Mus, Univ NMex, Albuquerque; Apeiron Workshops, Millerton, NY. Exhib: The NES Group, 67 & Light 7, 68-71, Mass Inst of Technol; Contemp Photogrs, George Eastman House, 69-72; Camera Infinity Exhib, Lever House, New York; Octave of Prayer, Mass Inst of Technol, 72; Western New York Exhib, Albright-Knox Art Gallery, Buffalo, 74 & 75; 18th Dixie Ann, Montgomery Mus of Fine Arts, Ala, 77. Teaching: Vis instr photog, Purdue Univ, West Lafayette, Ind, 71; instr photog, Stephens Col, 76- Awards: Anna Louise Raymond Traveling Fel, Art Inst of Chicago, 71. Mem: Col Art Asn; Soc for Photog Educ; Int Mus of Photog, George Eastman House; Friends of Photog. Style & Technique: Silver and platinum photographic processes. Publ: Contribr, Minor White (ed), Light 7, Aperture, 68; contribr, Nathan Lyons (ed), Vision and Expression, Horizon Press, 69; contribr, Minor White (compiler), Octave of Prayer, Aperture, 72. Mailing Add: Dept of Art Stephens Col Columbia MO 65201

MOULTON, SUSAN GENE
ART ADMINISTRATOR, ART HISTORIAN
b Long Beach, Calif, June 7, 44. Study: Univ Calif, Davis, BA(art), 66, Study with Wayne Thiebaud; Univ Padua, Italy, 64-65; Accad, Venice, Italy, 64, with Prof Balest; Stanford Univ, Carnegie Found fel, 68-69, MA(art hist), 69, PHD(art hist), 77. Teaching: Assoc prof Renaissance & mod art, Calif State Col, Sonoma, 71-, from asst prof to assoc prof art, 77-, chairperson dept of art, 75- Mem: Col Art Asn; Women's Caucus for Art. Res: Sixteenth century Venetian painting, specifically Titian and the evolution of donor portraiture in Venice. Publ: Contribr, From Frontier to Fire, Univ Calif, Davis, 64; auth, Interdisciplinary Women's Studies Courses, Women's Caucus for Art, 77; auth, Titian and the Evolution of Donor Portraiture, Stanford Univ, 77. Mailing Add: 7736 Elphick Rd Sebastopol CA 95472

MOUNT, CHARLES MERRILL
PAINTER
b New York, NY, May 19, 28. Study: Columbia Univ; Univ Calif, Los Angeles; Art Students League. Exhib: Dublin, Ireland; Newman Galleries, Philadelphia; Hotel Barbizon, New York; plus others. Teaching: Guest lectr, numerous mus & univs. Awards: Guggenheim Fel, 56; Arch Am Art Grant, 62. Mem: Irish Portrait Soc (founder & first pres); Burr Artists (rec secy); Pacem in Terris Gallery, New York (mgt comt). Style & Technique: Portraits of classic representational mode distinguished by vivacity of expression and execution. Publ: Auth, John Singer Sargent, 55 & auth, Gilbert Stuart, 64, Norton; auth, John Singer Sargent, Cresset Press, London, 57; auth, Claude Monet, Simon & Schuster, 67; auth, John Singer Sargent, Kraus Reprint, 69. Dealer: Capricorn Galleries 8003 Woodmont Ave Bethesda MD 20014. Mailing Add: 135 Beach 145 St Neponsit NY 11694

MOUNT, MARSHALL WARD
ART HISTORIAN, ART ADMINISTRATOR
b Jersey City, NJ, Dec 25, 27. Study: Columbia Col, AB, 48; Columbia Univ, MA, 52, PhD, 66, with Paul S Wingert. Teaching: Prof & chmn art hist dept, Finch Col, New York, 58-75; vis prof art hist, Univ Iowa, Iowa City, summer 70 & Parsons Sch of Design, New York, 70-72; vis assoc prof art hist, Hunter Col, New York, 72-73; prof and chmn creative arts dept, Univ Benin, Benin City, Nigeria, 77- Pos: Leader art study tours to Mali, Cameroun, India,

Explorer Tours, Montreal, 69-; dir art hist prog, Finch Col, San Marino, Italy, 73-75; cataloguer, Zim Collection of African Art, Children's Mus, Brooklyn, NY, 77. Awards: Rockefeller Found Fel, 61, 62 & 68; Am Coun of Learned Soc Grant, 73; fac scholar in int studies, Columbia Univ, 66-67. Mem: Col Art Asn; Soc Archit Historians; fel African Studies Asn; African-Am Inst. Res: Traditional and contemporary art of sub-Saharan Africa. Collection: Moderate size collection (over 1,000 pieces), of traditional and contemporary African art. Publ: Auth, African Art: The Years Since 1920, Ind Univ Press, 73. Mailing Add: Dept Creative Arts Univ Benin Benin City Nigeria

MOUNT, PAULINE WARD
PAINTER, SCULPTOR
b Batavia, NY. Study: Art Students League; NY Univ; also with Albert P Lucas & Joseph P Pollia. Work: Jersey City Mus; Roosevelt Mus, Hyde Park, NY; Delgado Mus; Mus of Mod Art; Hudson River Mus; Montclair Art Mus; Trenton State Mus; Kearny Mus; Riverside Mus; Finch Col Mus; Marquis Biog Libr. Comn: Bronze medal, Painters & Sculptors Soc, Jersey City Mus; holiday card for 1971 (casein), Am Heart Asn, 71. Exhib: Audubon Artists, New York, 40-42, Nat Acad Design, 44 & Nat Sculpture Soc, 45-48; Pa Acad Fine Arts, Philadelphia, 49; Smithsonian Inst, Washington, DC, 51. Teaching: Head dept painting & casting sculpture, NJ State Teachers Col, 41-45. Pos: Former founder & head painting & sculpture, Jersey City Med Ctr, NJ; dir, Ward Mount Art Classes, Jersey City, 39- Awards: Clayton F Freeman Award for Sculpture, Montclair Art Mus, 45; First Prize for Sculpture, Kearney Mus, 47; First Prize Sculpture, Art Fair, New York, 50; Gold Medal, Jersey J Woman of Achievement, 71; Knight of Mark Twain. Bibliog: Peyton Boswell (auth), article in Arts Digest; articles in Cue Mag, Saturday Eve Post & Rev Mod Francaise. Mem: Founding mem Artists Equity Asn; Painters & Sculptors Soc NJ (founder & pres, 12 yrs, hon pres); fel Royal Soc Art; founding mem Audubon Artists. Interest: Contributor of collection of Louis C Tiffany to museums. Mailing Add: 74 Sherman Pl Jersey City NJ 07307

MOURE, NANCY DUSTIN WALL
CURATOR, WRITER
b Dayton, Ohio, Feb 26, 43. Study: San Diego State Col, BA; Univ Calif, Los Angeles, MA. Collections Arranged: Los Angeles Painters of the Nineteen Twenties (auth, catalogue), Pomona Col Art Gallery, 72; California Watercolor Society Prizewinners (auth, catalogue), 73, Western Scene (auth, catalogue), 75, Pertaining to the Sea (auth, catalogue), 76, Los Angeles Co Mus Art; William Wendt (auth, catalogue), Laguna Beach Mus of Art, 77. Pos: Curatorial aide, Los Angeles Co Mus Art, 68-72, asst cur Am art, 72- Res: American art executed before 1920 with an emphasis on pre-1930 Southern California art. Publ: Auth, California Watercolor Society, 73 & Artists Clubs and Exhibitions in Los Angeles, 74; co-auth, American Narrative Painting, Los Angeles Co Mus Art, 74; auth, Dictionary of Art and Artists in Southern California Before 1930, 75; co-auth, Index to Reproductions of American Paintings, Scarecrow Press, Inc, 77. Mailing Add: 935 W Mountain St Glendale CA 91202

MOVALLI, CHARLES JOSEPH
ART WRITER, PAINTER
b Gloucester, Mass, Aug 20, 45. Study: Clark Univ, BA; Univ Conn, MA & PhD; spec study with Emile Gruppe, Roger Curtis, Zygmund Jankowski & Betty L Schlemm. Pos: Contributing ed, Am Artist Mag, 76- Awards: Gorton Award, N Shore Arts Asn, 75; Goldberg Award, 77 & Cooley Award, 77, Rockport Art Asn. Mem: Acad Artists; Rockport Art Asn (mem bd dirs, 77-); N Shore Arts Asn (mem bd dirs, 76-); Rocky Neck Art Colony (pres, 76). Style & Technique: Outdoor, quasi-impressionistic. Media: Oil. Res: Contemporary and older painters working in plein-air tradition. Publ: Contribr, articles in Am Artist, 75-; contribr (preface), On Painting and Drawing, Dover, 76; ed & co-auth, Gruppe on Painting, 76; Brushwork, 77 & Color in Outdoor Painting, 77, Watson-Guptill. Mailing Add: 237 Western Ave Gloucester MA 01930

MOXEY, KEITH PATRICIO FLEMING
ART HISTORIAN
b Buenos Aires, Arg, Jan 4, 43; Brit/Arg citizen. Study: Univ Edinburgh, MA, 65; Univ Chicago, MA, 68, PhD, 74. Teaching: From instr to asst prof art hist, Tufts Univ, 71-74; from asst prof to assoc prof art hist, Univ Va, 74-, chmn art hist, 76- Mem: Col Art Asn. Res: Sixteenth century Netherlandish painting. Publ: Auth, Erasmus & The Iconography of Pieter Aertsen, JWCI, 71; auth, The fates & Brueghel's Triumph of Death, Oud Holland, 73; auth, The humanist market scenes of Joachim Beuckelaer, Antwerp JBH, 76; auth, Reflections on unusual subjects in work of Aertsen, Berliner JBH, 76; auth, Aertsen & Beuckelaer, Secular Painting & the Reformation, Garland, 77. Mailing Add: 1336 Hilltop Rd Charlottesville VA 22903

MOY, MAY (WONG)
PAINTER, LECTURER
b New York, NY, Dec 2, 13. Study: Parsons Sch Fine & Appl Arts, NY; Montclair Teacher's Col; Oriental Artists Sch. Exhib: Sumi-e Soc Am, 63, 64, 69, 70 & 75; Chung Cheng Gallery, St John's Univ, 76 & 77. Teaching: Lectr Oriental ink, Half Hollow Hills High Sch, Dix Hills, NY, 67-74; lectr Oriental brush painting, Huntington Hist Soc, NY, 74-; lectr Oriental brush painting, Artisan House, Northport, NY, 72-74. Pos: Lectr & demonstr Chinese brush painting, Sr Citizens Groups, Huntington Schs, 71- Awards: Zen, Sumi-e Soc Am, 63, Bamboo, 69 & Heart of Winter, 75. Bibliog: Sally Miller (auth), May W Moy exhibits Chinese painting, Half Hollow Hills Community Libr, 72; Hedda Friedman (auth), May Moy Chinese Exhibition, Long Islander Newspaper, 72; Rhoda Amon (auth), Long Island Sumi-e style, Newsday, 74. Mem: Sumi-e Soc Am, New York; Sumi-e East, Suffolk, Long Island; Huntington Hist Soc. Style & Technique: Landscapes, nature with use of bamboo brush with black ink and color diluted with water on rice paper; painting on paper and painting on silk. Mailing Add: 27 Maryland St Dix Hills NY 11746

MOY, SEONG
PAINTER, GRAPHIC ARTIST
b Canton, China, Oct 20, 21; US citizen. Study: St Paul Sch Art, with Cameron Booth, 36-40; Art Students League, with Vaclav Vytacil, 41-42; Hofmann Sch, with Hans Hofmann, 41-42; Atelier 17, New York, 48-50. Work: Mus Mod Art; Brooklyn Mus; Metrop Mus Art; Pa Acad Fine Arts; NY Pub Libr; plus others. Comn: Three ed, Int Graphic Arts Soc; New York Hilton Hotel. Exhib: Metrop Mus Art, 50; Whitney Mus Am Art, 50; Univ Ill, 51, 53 & 54; Carnegie Inst, 52 & 55; New York World's Fair, 64-65; plus many other group & one-man shows. Teaching: Instr, Univ Minn, 51; instr, Ind Univ, 52-53; instr, Smith Col, 54-55; dir, Seong Moy Sch Painting & Graphic Arts, Provincetown, Mass, summers 54-; instr, Univ Ark, 55; instr, Vassar Col, 55; instr, Cooper Union Art Sch, 57-70; instr, Columbia Univ, 59-70; instr, Art Students League, 63-; prof, City Col New York, 70- Awards: John Hay Whitney Found Grant, 50-51; Guggenheim Fel, 55-56. Mem: Art Students League; Am Fedn Arts; Artists Equity Asn; Col Art Asn Am; Fedn Mod Painters & Sculptors. Mailing Add: 100 La Salle St New York NY 10027

MOYER, ROY
PAINTER, ART ADMINISTRATOR
b Allentown, Pa, Aug 20. 21. Study: Columbia Col, BA, Columbia Univ, MA. Work: Rochester Mem Art Gallery, NY; Brandeis Univ Art Gallery, Waltham, Mass; Wichita Art Mus, Kans; Sara Roby Found, New York; Rockford Art Asn, Ill. Exhib: Audubon Artists, New York, 74; Nat Acad Design, New York, 77. Collections Arranged: Inverse Illusionism, traveling exhib; numerous others for Am Fedn Arts. Teaching: Lectr art hist, Univ Toronto, 53-55. Pos: Dir, Am Fedn Arts, 63-72; chief art & design, UNICEF, 72- Awards: First Prize for Painting, Butler Inst Am Art, 73; First Prize/Still-Life, Nat Acad Design, 77. Mem: Nat Coun Arts (exec comt, 65-72). Style & Technique: Realist, best known for horses and still-life. Media: Oil. Res: Byzantine art and architecture; sixteenth century painting and sculpture. Dealer: Rolly-Michaux Gallery 943 Madison Ave New York NY 10021 & 125 Newberry St Boston MA 02116. Mailing Add: 440 Riverside Dr New York NY 10027

MOYERS, WM
PAINTER, SCULPTOR
b Atlanta, Ga, Dec 11, 16. Study: Adams State Col, major fine arts; Otis Art Inst. Work: Gilcrease Inst, Tulsa, Okla (sculpture); Nat Cowboy Hall of Fame, Oklahoma City (paintings & sculpture); Adams State Col (painting & sculpture). Exhib: Cowboy Artist of Am Shows, Cowboy Hall of Fame & Phoenix Art Mus, since 68; one-man shows, Adams State Col, Alamosa, Colo, 71 & Nat Cowboy Hall of Fame, Oklahoma City, 73; group show, Mont Hist Soc, Helena, 72 & 73. Awards: Ltd Ed Club Illus Competition, 45; Gold Medals-Sculpture, Nat Cowboy Hall of Fame, 68 & 72; Gold Medal for Sculpture & Co-Winner Best of Show Award, Cowboy Artists Am Show, Phoenix Art Mus, 75. Bibliog: Ainsworth (auth), Cowboy in Art, World Publ, 68; Harmsen (auth), Western America, Northland, 71; Broder (auth), Bronzes of the American West, Abrams, 74. Mem: Cowboy Artists Am (vpres, 70-71, pres, 71-72). Style & Technique: Objective scenes of Western life in oil or watercolor, or bronze. Media: Oil, Watercolor; Bronze Sculpture. Publ: Illusr bks for nat publ, 45-62. Dealer: Taos Art Gallery Inc PO Box 1007 Taos NM 87571. Mailing Add: 1407 Morningside Dr NE Albuquerque NM 87110

MOYSSEN, XAVIER
ART CRITIC, ART HISTORIAN
b Morelia, Mex, July 10, 24. Study: Univ Nacional Autonoma, Mex, MFA; Inst Nacional de Antropologia e Histroia; Inst de Invest Esteticas. Teaching: Instr mod Mex art & mod & contemp art, Univ Nacional Autonoma, Mex, 58- Pos: Investr, Inst Invest Esteticas, 58- Mem: Asn Inst Critica Arte; Acad Arte. Publ: Auth, Mexico, Angustia de sus Cristos, Inst Nacional Antropologia Hist, 67; auth, Museo de Arte Moderno de Chapultepec, Artes Mex, 70; ed, Veinte Siglos de Plastica Mexicana, Vol 1, 70, Vol 2, 72 & Vol 3, 74; Pinacoteca Virreinal, 71; Arte popular mexicano, 75. Mailing Add: Inst Invest Esteticas Torre de Humanidades Mexico DF Mexico

MOZLEY, ANITA VENTURA
CURATOR, ART HISTORIAN
b Washington, DC, Aug 29, 28. Study: Northwestern Univ, Evanston, Ill, BA; Art Students League, with Morris Kantor, painter; San Francisco Art Inst, Calif, studio photog. Collections Arranged: Ansel Adams: The Portfolios, 72, Eadweard Muybridge: The Stanford Years, 1872-1882 (ed & co-auth, catalogue), 72, Mrs Cameron's Photographs from the Life (auth, catalogue), 74, Photography: Pre-history to the Present, 76 & Imogen Cunningham: A Celebration, 76, Stanford Univ Mus of Art, Calif; American Photography: Past into Present (auth, catalogue), Seattle Art Mus, Wash, 76. Pos: Reviewer, managing ed & West Coast corresp, Arts Mag, New York, 55-64; poster designer, Leo Castelli Gallery, New York, 55-62; film librn, Sextant, Inc, New York, 60-61; curatorial asst, San Francisco Maritime Mus, 62-67; ed, SEA Letter, San Francisco Maritime Mus, 64-67; cur & registr of photog, Stanford Univ Mus of Art, Calif, 70- Res: Nineteenth and twentieth century photography, particularly the works of Eadweard Muybridge, Julia Margaret Cameron, Thomas Annan and Imogen Cunningham. Publ: Auth, Thomas Annan, Photographs of the Old Closes and Streets of Glasgow, Dover Publ, 77. Mailing Add: 601 Laurel Ave Menlo Park CA 94025

MUCCIOLI, ANNA MARIA
PAINTER, SCULPTOR
b Detroit, Mich, Apr 23, 22. Study: Soc Art & Crafts; with Sarkis Sarkisian, Charles Culver & Hay Holland. Exhib: Scarab Club, 65, 70-71, 73 & 76-77; Mich State Fair Art Exhib, 68, 71, 73 & 76; Butler Inst, Youngstown, Ohio, 69; Birmingham Mus, Ala, 70; Nat Acad Galleries, New York, 71; Carrol Reece Mus, Tenn, 74; one-man show, Liggett Sch, 74; Mich Watercolor Soc, 76; Detroit Inst Arts, 76; Art Ctr Fibers Exhib, Mt Clemens, 77. Awards: Third Place, Scarab Club, 71, Hon Mention, Silver Medal Exhib, 76; Second Place, Ford Motor Co Art Exhib, 76, First Place, 77. Bibliog: Article in La Revue Mod Mag, Paris, France & Impresario Mag. Mem: Mich Watercolor Soc; Watercolor Soc Ala. Style & Technique: Watercolor & wax figure; still life; sculptures in hydra stone & clay. Mailing Add: c/o Muccioli Studio Gallery 85 Kercheval Ave Grosse Pointe Farms MI 48236

MUDGE, EDMUND WEBSTER, JR
COLLECTOR
b Pittsburgh, Pa, Nov 29, 04. Study: Harvard Univ, AB. Collection: Impressionist and post-impressionist paintings; English, French and German antique porcelain and pottery; antique Chinese snuff bottles and Chinese export porcelains; porcelain birds of Dorothy Doughty and Edward Marshall Boehm. Mailing Add: 5926 Averill Way Dallas TX 75225

MUEHSAM, GERD
ART LIBRARIAN, ART WRITER
b Berlin, Ger; US citizen. Study: Case Western Reserve Univ, BLS; Univ Vienna, Austria, PhD(musicology & art hist). Teaching: Instr adult coll educ arts sem, Queens Col, City Univ New York, 68-75. Pos: Assoc art librn, Cooper Union, New York, 50-65; supv art librn, New York Pub Libr, Donnell Libr Ctr, 65-67; art bibliographer, Queens Col, City Univ New York, 67- Mem: Col Art Asn Am; Am Soc Aesthetics; Am Libr Asn; Asn Col & Res Libr (chmn art sect, 75); Spec Libr Asn (chmn, Mus, Arts & Humanities Div, 70-71); Art Libr Soc NAm (chmn var comt). Res: Art librarianship; musical iconography. Publ: Auth, D Edzard, H Bittner & Co, 48; auth, A Designer's Library, Cooper Union Mus Chronicle, 54; ed, French Painters and Paintings from the 14th Century to Post-Impressionism, F Unger, 70; auth, Guide to Basic Information Sources in the Visual Arts, ABC-Clio Press, 78. Mailing Add: 400 E 58th St New York NY 10022

MUELLER, EARL GEORGE
ART HISTORIAN, EDUCATOR
b Harvard, Ill, Feb 12, 14. Study: Univ Rochester, BMusic; State Univ Iowa, MFA & PhD. Teaching: Chmn dept art, Duke Univ, formerly, prof art, 64- Res: Northern Renaissance art; graphics. Mailing Add: Duke Univ Dept of Art College Sta 6605 Durham NC 27701

MUELLER, HENRIETTA WATERS
PAINTER, SCULPTOR
b Pittsburgh, Pa, Apr 13, 15. Study: Art Inst Chicago, with Helen Gardner, BFA, 38; Univ Wyo, MA, 48, MEd, 60; Art Students League, with Will Barnet; Univ Colo, Boulder, with Wendell Black; also with George McNeil & Ilya Bolotowsky. Work: Joslyn Mus, Omaha, Nebr; New York Pub Libr, NY; William Rockhill Nelson Gallery, Kansas City, Mo; Mills Col Collection, New York; Univ Wash, Seattle. Comn: Stainless steel monument, Commemorative Wyo Women's Rights 1890-1970, Albany Co Courthouse, Laramie, Wyo, 72. Exhib: Six shows, Print Club Philadelphia, Philadelphia Mus, 52-61; Western Art Ann, 52-55 & Own Your Own Exhibs, 67, Denver Art Mus, 22nd Drawing & Print Ann, San Francisco Mus Art, 58; Metrop Mus, New York, 60 & 61; 11th Art Ann, Pioneer Mus, Stockton, Calif, 71. Teaching: Asst prof art & design, Univ Wyo, 50-61; asst prof art, Univ Nebr, 56-57; asst prof art, Univ Pac, 70-71. Awards: Int Textile Exhib Award, Univ NC, Greensboro, 48; Wilson Daly Prize, 50 Ind Prints, John Herron Art Inst, Indianapolis, 52; Purchase Award, Univ Wyo Art Mus for Permanent Collection, 73. Mem: Wyo Artists' Asn (conf ann lectr); Artists Equity Asn (secy-treas, Wyo Chap, 50-65); Laramie Art Guild. Style & Technique: Non-figuartive, with lyrical and calligraphic elements referent to nature. Media: Oil, Watercolor, Acrylic; Steel, Aluminum. Dealer: Overland Art Gallery Ivinson Ave Laramie WY 82070; Three Twenty Three Gallery 232 S David Casper WY 82601. Mailing Add: 1309 Steele St Laramie WY 82070

MUELLER, M GERARDINE
SCULPTOR, EDUCATOR
b Newark, NJ. Study: Caldwell Col, BA; Univ Notre Dame, MA & MFA, with A Lauck & K Milonadis; also with W Otto, Berlin; Inst Cult, Guadalajara, Mex. Comn: Wood high relief sculpture, St Dominic Acad, Jersey City, NJ, 62; illuminated ceremonial bk, Sisters of St Dominic, Caldwell, NJ, 59; windows, Sisters Chapel, Caldwell, 62; six-panel mosaic mural, Caldwell Col, NJ, 70; Sculpture & Design Chapel, All Saints Church, Jersey City, 73; windows, Puyo Cathedral, Ecuador, 77. Exhib: Nat Sculpture Soc Show, NY, 62; NJ Col Art Teachers Show, NJ State Mus, Trenton, 66; Joy in Religion, Old Bergen Art Guild Three Yr Tour, 68; NAm Calligraphers, Dallas, Tex, 74, Nat Miniature Art Soc, Fla, 75. Teaching: Lectr lettering & crafts, Fordham Univ, 61; prof & chmn art dept, Caldwell Col, 63- Pos: Pres, Cath Fine Arts Soc, 69-71; mem, Archdiocese Comn Div Worship (art & archit), 74-77. Awards: First Place Award for Lettering & Illumination, Miniature Art Soc NJ, 71. Bibliog: Williams (auth), articles in NJ Music & Arts, 6/71 & 12/77; Buckley (auth), article in Newark Advocate, 12/71; articles in Newark Eve News, 4/72, NJ Herald, 10/77 & NY Times, 11/77. Mem: Cath Fine Arts Asn; Col Art Asn Am; Nat Coun Art Adminr. Style & Technique: Semi-realism with symbolic overtones; stained glass, sculpture, mosaics, slab glass in portland cement. Publ: Auth, Yearbook production, Photolith Mag, 61; auth, Art in Latin America & Art in Indian Mission of US, Cath Youth Encycl, McGraw-Hill, 62; auth, New mosaic evolvement, Cath Fine Arts Soc, 68. Mailing Add: Caldwell Col Caldwell NJ 07006

MUELLER, TRUDE
SCULPTOR
b Bielsko, Poland, Jan 2, 13; US citizen. Study: County Art Ctr, White Plains; Greenwich House, New York; New Sch Social Res, New York; with H Beling, Lu Duble, M Pascual & P Graussman. Work: Palm Springs Desert Mus, Calif; also in pvt collections of Joseph H Hirshhorn, Conn, K Tamenaga, Tokyo, Japan, J Orrit, Geneva, Switz & M Moreau, Chantilly, France. Exhib: NY Univ, 68; Allied Artists Am, Nat Acad Gallery, New York, 68; Aritst-Craftsmen Am, Lever House, New York, 68-72 & 73; Bruce Mus, Conn, 74; Petits Formats des Maitres Contemporains, Chantilly, 75. Pos: Art therapist, Child Sch, New York, 73. Awards: Beaux Arts Award, Macy's, 64 & 65; Best Piece in Firing, Greenwich House, New York, 65; plus numerous prizes in Westchester Co, 64-74. Bibliog: Meditation, Beaux Arts, 65; R Stevens (auth), Aux Etats-Unis, La Revue Mod, Paris, 69; K Beals (auth), articles in Daily Times, Westchester, Mem: Artist-Craftsmen New York; Greenwich House Sculptors (treas, 68-69); Norton Gallery Artists Guild, West Palm Beach, Fla; Allied Artists Am; Mamaroneck Artists Guild. Style & Technique: Contemporary, emphasis on round form, semi-abstract, rough finish; casts in bronze and plastics. Media: Wood, Clay. Dealer: Hilde Gerst Gallery 681 Madison Ave New York NY 10021. Mailing Add: 1200 S Flagler Dr West Palm Beach FL 33401

MUENCH, JOHN
PAINTER, GRAPHIC ARTIST
b Medford, Mass, Oct 15, 14. Study: Art Students League; Acad Julian, Paris. Work: Metrop Mus Art, New York; Victoria & Albert Mus, London; Bibliot Nat, Paris; Nat Collection & Smithsonian Inst, Washington, DC; Nat Mus, Jerusalem; plus others. Exhib: Nine shows, Libr Cong, 45-56; Soc Am Graphic Artists, 47 & 50-52; Audubon Artists, 47, 48 & 56; Pa Acad Fine Arts, 49, 50 & 53-55; Cincinnati Mus, 54 & 56; plus many others. Teaching: Dir, Portland Sch Fine & Appl Arts, Maine, 58-65; assoc prof art, RI Sch Design, 65-77; artist-in-residence, Westbrook Col, Portland, Maine; dir, Maine Printmaking Workshop. Awards: Prizes, 56, 59 & 60 & John Taylor Arms Award & Medal, 65, Audubon Artists; Vis Fel, Tamarind Lithography Workshop, Los Angeles, 62; US Dept State Specialist Grant, 66; plus others. Mem: Philadelphia Watercolor Club; Soc Am Graphic Artists; Audubon Artists; Am Color Print Soc; Nat Acad Design. Style & Technique: Oil over acrylic with collage. Dealer: Assoc Am Artists 663 Fifth Ave New York NY 10019. Mailing Add: Westbrook Col Portland ME 04103 Design Providence RI 02903

MUENSTERBERGER, WERNER
COLLECTOR, WRITER
Pos: Cur asst, Stedeljk Mus, Amsterdam, Holland, 45-47. Awards: Guggenheim Fel, 69; Grant Found, 74-75. Mem: Fel Pierpont Morgan Libr; Fel Royal Anthrop Inst Gt Brit. Res: Primitive art of Oceania and Africa; relationship between artist, artistic themes and personality development. Collection: West African and Oceanic sculpture; Old Master drawings. Publ: Auth, Printkunst en Kultuur, 4 vols, 40-42; auth, Vincent Van Gogh: Drawings, Sketches, Watercolors, 47; auth, Some Elements of Artistic Creativity Among Primitive Peoples, 50; auth, Roots of Primitive Art, Psychoanal & Cult, 51; auth, Sculpture of Primitive Man, Thames & Hudson, London-Abrams (NY), 55; auth, The creative process..., Psychoanalytic Study Soc II, 62; auth & ed, Between Reality and Fantasy, Preliminary Notes on Collecting, New York, 78. Mailing Add: 9 Eaton Sq London England

MUHLBERGER, RICHARD CHARLES
MUSEUM DIRECTOR
b Englewood, NJ, Jan 20, 38. Study: Calif Concordia Col, AA; Wayne State Univ, BA(art hist); Johns Hopkins Univ, Baltimore, MA(art hist). Pos: Cur mus educ, Worcester Art Mus, Mass, 66-72; chmn educ, Detroit Inst Arts, 72-75; dir, Mus Fine Arts & George Walter Vincent Smith Art Mus, Springfield, Mass, 76- Awards: Phi Beta Kappa, 65; Woodrow Wilson Nat Fel, 65-67. Mem: Am Asn Mus (chmn comt educ, 74-76); Asn Art Mus Dirs. Res: Dutch 17th century bird painters. Mailing Add: c/o Mus of Fine Arts 49 Chestnut St Springfield MA 01103

MUHLERT, JAN KEENE
MUSEUM DIRECTOR
b Oak Park, Ill, Oct 4, 42. Study: Neuchatel Univ; Inst European Studies, Paris; Sorbonne, with Andre Chastel; Inst de Phonetique; Acad Grande Chaumiere. 62-63; Albion Col, BA, 64; Oberlin Col, with Ellen H Johnson & Wolfgang Stechow, MA, 67. Collections Arranged: H Lyman Sayen (with catalog), Nat Collection Fine Arts, 70, Romaine Brooks, Thief of Souls (with catalog), 71 & William H Johnson 1901-1970 (with catalog), 71. Pos: Asst cur collections, Allen Mem Art Mus, Oberlin Col, 66-68; asst cur contemp art, Nat Col Fine Arts, 68-73, assoc cur 20th century paintings & sculpture, 74-75; dir, Mus Art, Univ Iowa, 75- Mem: Asn Art Mus Dir; Am Asn Mus; Nat Endowment for the Arts (mem adv panel); Iowa Arts Coun (mem adv panel); Upper Midwest Conserv Asn (mem bd trustees); Advocates Arts. Res: Federal art projects, 1933-1943. Publ: Contribr, An Exhibition of Paintings, Bozzetti and Drawings by Baciccio (catalog), Oberlin Col, 67; co-auth, Tribute to Mark Tobey (catalog), Nat Collection Fine Arts, 74. Mailing Add: Dir Mus of Art Univ of Iowa Iowa City IA 52242

MUHLSTOCK, LOUIS
PAINTER
b Narajow, Poland, Apr 23, 04. Study: Montreal, PQ; Paris, France, with L-F Biloul. Work: Nat Gallery Can; Art Gallery Toronto; Mus Que; Art Mus, London, Ont; Montreal Mus Fine Arts; plus others. Exhib: Nat Gallery Art, Washington, DC, 50; one-man show, Montreal Mus Fine Arts, 51 & 54; Int Graphic Exhib, Lugano, 54; Nat Gallery Can, 55; Carnegie Inst, 55; plus many others. Mem: Can Soc Graphic Art; Can Group Painters; Fedn Can Artists; Contemp Arts Soc, Montreal. Mailing Add: 3555 St Famille St Montreal PQ H2X 2L2 Can

MUIR, EMILY LANSINGH
PAINTER, DESIGNER
b Chicago, Ill. Study: Art Students League, with Richard Lahey & Leo Lentelli; Univ Maine, LHD, 69. Work: Brooklyn Mus; US Govt; Univ Maine. Comn: Design of contemporary summer homes, year-round homes, mosaics & interior design, portraits and portrait busts for private owners. Exhib: Int Watercolor; US Govt; Maine Art Gallery; Univ Maine. Teaching: Lectr art, Asn Am Cols, 50-60. Pos: Mem, Comn Fine Arts, Washington, DC, 55-59; mem adv comt, Kennedy Ctr Performing Arts, Washington, DC, 69- Awards: Outstanding Achievement in Commercial Venture, Contrib to Visual Arts, Maine Comt Skowhegan Sch, 72. Bibliog: Martin Dibner (auth), People of the Maine Coast, Doubleday; William Caldwell (auth), article in Portland Press Herald; J R Wiggins (auth), article in Bangor Daily News. Style & Technique: Fitting houses to site; exposed framing; use of local specialties incorporated. Media: Oil. Publ: Auth, Small potatoes, Scribner, 40. Mailing Add: Muir Studios Stonington ME 04681

MULCAHY, FREDA
PAINTER, ART ADMINISTRATOR
b Staten Island, NY. Study: Am Art Sch; Nat Acad Design; New Sch Social Res; also with Jack Tworkov. Work: Staten Island Mus. Exhib: City Ctr Gallery, New York, 55; Art USA, 58; Corcoran Gallery, Washington, DC, 60; Washington & Regional Artists Show, Smithsonian Inst, 60. Pos: Educ cur, Staten Island Inst Arts & Sci, 64- Awards: Hon Mention, ACA Gallery Int Show, 55; Staten Island Mus Awards, 55-57; Hon Mention, City Ctr Gallery, 58 & 59. Media: Acrylic, Pastels. Mailing Add: Staten Island Inst of Arts & Sci Staten Island NY 10301

MULLEN, BUELL
PAINTER
b Chicago, Ill. Study: Tyler Sch, Chicago; Brit Acad, Rome; also with Petrucci, Rome & Cucquier, Belg. Work: Libr of Cong Hisp Rm, Washington, DC; Simon Fraser Univ; Bowling Green State Univ; Colo Woman's Col; Agronomy Bldg, Univ Ill; Lake Erie Col. Comn: Murals, Volta Redonda, Brazil, 60, Western Elec Foyer, 63, Int Nickel Corp, Exec Floor, New York Plaza, 65 & Int Minerals-Chem, Libertyville, Ill, 69; four panels, Paul Wolfe Chapel, Inter-Am Univ, PR, 70. Exhib: One-man shows, Smithsonian Inst, Washington, DC, Findlay Gallery, Chicago & Dayton Art Inst, Ohio; Salon, Paris; All-Ill Soc Arts, Chicago. Pos: Jury mem, NY Fedn Fine Arts Competition, 72. Awards: All-Ill Soc Arts Gold Medal. Mem: Archit League; Nat Soc Mural Painters (bd mem, 67- & secy, pres, currently); fel Royal Soc Arts; NY Fedn Fine Arts (bd mem, 67- & rep muralists); US Nat Comn UNESCO (rep for Int Asn Art, 67-). Media: Stainless Steel, Epoxy, Stained Glass. Publ: Co-auth article in Design Mag; auth article in Am Soc Testing & Mat Tech Publ; contribr, Zie & Er, Switz, Die Architekt, Ger & Archit Rec, US & Can. Mailing Add: 233 E 70th St New York NY 10021

MULLEN, PHILIP EDWARD
ARTIST
b Akron, Ohio, Oct 10, 42. Study: Univ Minn, BA; Univ NDak, MA, with Robert A Nelson; Ohio Univ, PhD. Exhib: Over 200, including 1975 Biennial of Contemp Am Art, Whitney Mus Am Art, New York & Smithsonian Inst Traveling Exhib. Style & Technique: Modules in acrylic and multi-color silkscreen on handmade paper. Mailing Add: 1611 Hollywood Dr Columbia SC 29205

MULLER, JEROME KENNETH
COLLECTOR, ART DEALER
b Amityville, NY, July 18, 34. Study: NY Univ; Marquette Univ, BS; Layton Sch of Art. Collections Arranged: Cartoon Show, Original Works by 100 Outstanding American Cartoonists, Laguna Beach Mus of Art, Calif, 72, Bowers Mus, Santa Ana, Calif, 76, E B Crocker Art Gallery, Sacramento, Calif, 77, Indianapolis Mus of Art, Ind, 77, Tweed Mus of Art, Duluth, Minn, 78, Everson Mus of Art, Syracuse, NY, 78 & Montgomery Mus of Fine Arts, Ala, 78; Mickey Mouse: 50 Golden Years (cur), Bowers Mus, 78. Teaching: Instr photog, Lindenhurst High Sch, NY, 53-54. Pos: Photogr, New York, 53-56; art dir, Orange Co Illustrated, 62-68, art ed, 70- Awards: Two Silver Medals, 20th Ann Exhib of Advert & Ed Art in the West, Los Angeles Art Dir Club, 64; Award of Merit, Illustration West, Los Angeles Illusr Club, 72-74. Bibliog: Steven Parker (auth), Comics are collectible, Acquire Mag, 7/77. Mem: Western Asn of Art Mus. Collection: Cartoons, comic art and original animation art, exhibited regularly in major museums throughout America. Publ: Ed, Country Beautiful, 61; auth, Rex Brandt, Unicorn Press, 72; auth, The comics: worth a second look, SW Art, 11/73; contribr, Mark Rothko, 74 & The Artist as Collector, 75, Newport Harbor Art Mus, Newport Beach, Calif; auth, Arts of Oceania, Shells of Oceania, Bowers Mus, 75. Mailing Add: Box 743 Costa Mesa CA 92627

MULLICAN, LEE
PAINTER, EDUCATOR
b Chickasha, Okla, Dec 2, 19. Study: Abilene Christian Col; Univ Okla; Kansas City Art Inst, dipl & study with Fletcher Martin; San Francisco Art Inst, study with Stanley Hayter. Work: San Francisco Mus Art; Phillips Mem Gallery, Washington, DC; Santa Fe Art Mus, NMex; Santa Barbara Mus Art, Calif; Mus Mod Art, New York; Oklahoma Art Ctr, Oklahoma City;

Univ Calif, Los Angeles. Exhib: Sao Paulo Biennial, Brazil, 49; Art Inst Chicago, 51; Carnegie Inst Int, Pittsburgh, 52, 64 & 67; Whitney Mus Am Art, 53 & Calif Artists, 62; Pa Acad Fine Arts, Philadelphia, 68; one-man shows, San Francisco Mus of Art, 49 & 65, Okla Art Ctr, Oklahoma City, 51 & 67, Museo Nacional de Bellas Artes, Santiago, Chile, 58, Santa Barbara Mus of Art, Calif, 58 & 73, Univ Calif Los Angeles Art Galleries, 59 & Pasadena Mus of Art, 61. Teaching: Prof painting & drawing, Univ Calif, Los Angeles, 62-78. Pos: Guest cur, Los Angeles Craft & Folk Art Mus, 75-78. Awards: Guggenheim Fel, 59; Award, Inst Creative Arts, Univ Calif, 63; Tamarind Fel, 64-65. Bibliog: Wolfgang Paalen & G Onslow Ford (auth), Dynaton, San Francisco Mus Art, 51; Langsner (auth), Mullican paints a picture, Art News, 52; Lee Mullican (catalog), Univ Calif, Los Angeles, 69; Gordon Onslow (co-auth), Lee Mullican, Univ Calif Los Angeles Art Galleries, 69; Fink Tuchman (auth), Three Footnotes to California Art History, Los Angeles Co Art Mus, 77. Style & Technique: Abstractions from nature; late abstract surrealism; cosmic morphology; precise knife technique. Media: Oil; Drawing. Dealer: Paule Anglim Gallery San Francisco CA. Mailing Add: 370 Mesa Rd Santa Monica CA 90402

MUNDT, ERNEST KARL
SCULPTOR, EDUCATOR
b Bleicherode, Ger, Oct 30, 05; US citizen. Study: Berlin Inst Technol, dipl archit, 30; Univ Calif, PhD, 61. Work: San Francisco Mus Art. Comn: Steel sculpture, Westmoor High Sch, Daly City, Calif. Exhib: Detroit Inst Art, 44; San Francisco Mus Art, 46; Calif Palace of Legion of Honor, 49; Metrop Mus Art, 50; Whitney Mus Am Art, 51; plus others. Teaching: Asst prof, Univ Mich, 41-44; instr, Brooklyn Col, 45-46; instr, Calif Sch Fine Art, 47-50, dir, 50-55; asst prof art, Calif State Univ, San Francisco, 55-59, chmn dept, 58-61, assoc prof, 59-64, prof, 64- Mem: Col Art Asn Am. Publ: Auth & illusr, A Primer of Visual Art, 50; auth & illusr, Art, Form, & Civilization, 52; auth & illusr, Birth of a Cook, 56; contribr, Arts & Archit, Col Art J, Art Quart & J Aesthet Mags. Mailing Add: Dept of Art Calif State Univ San Francisco CA 94132

MUNIOT, BARBARA KING
ART DEALER, COLLECTOR
b New Orleans, La. Study: Sullins Col, Bristol, Va, art degree; Newcomb Col, spec study with Prof Franklin Adams. Pos: Asst dir, Orleans Gallery, 68-70 & dir, 70-73; asst dir, Galerie Simonne Stern, 73-75 & dir, 75- Specialty: Contemporary art. Collection: Paintings, drawings, prints and photographs. Mailing Add: c/o Galerie Simonne Stern 516 Royal St New Orleans LA 70130

MUNO, RICHARD CARL
SCULPTOR, ART DIRECTOR
b Arapaho, Okla, July 2, 39. Study: Okla State Univ Sch Tech Training, cert com art. Work: Diamond M Mus, Snyder, Tex. Comn: Sculpture of Cavalry Man and Horse, Winchester Firearms, Hartford, Conn, 68; Western Heritage Awards Wrangler Trophy, Nat Cowboy Hall Fame, Oklahoma City, 68; Sculpture of a Lawman, Colt Firearms, Hartford, 73; Sculpture of Cowboy Branding Calf, Oklahoma City CofC, 75; Lifesize Sculpture of Pioneer Man, Bicentennial Comn of Clinton, Okla, 75. Exhib: Philbrook Mus Art Exhib, Tulsa, Okla, 67; Sci & Arts Found Exhib, Oklahoma City, 68; Oklahoma City Zool Exhib, 68; Okla Mus Art Five State Salon, Oklahoma City, 71-72; Solon Borglum Mem Sculpture Exhib, Nat Cowboy Hall of Fame, Oklahoma City, 75. Collection: Nat Acad Western Art Ann Exhibs, 73-75. Pos: Preparator, Gilcrease Inst Am Hist & Art, Tulsa, 60-64; cur, Nat Cowboy Hall Fame, Oklahoma City, 65-69, art dir, 70- Bibliog: Marcia Preston(auth), Orbit Mag, Okla Publ Co, 68; Dean Krakel (auth), End of the Trail, Okla Univ Press, 73. Style & Technique: Realistic western and animal sculpture. Media: Sculpture. Publ: Contribr, Persimmon Hill Mag, 72-75. Dealer: Phil Anderson 5111 Classen Blvd Oklahoma City OK 73118. Mailing Add: 6300 E Danforth Edmond OK 73034

MUNOZ, RIE (MARIE ANGELINA MUNOZ)
PAINTER, PRINTMAKER
b Los Angeles, Calif. Study: Washington & Lee Univ; Univ of Alaska; pvt lessons. Work: Alaska State Mus; Anchorage Hist & Fine Arts Mus; Gov Off, Alaska. Comn: Covers, Jr Scholastics, 67; Alaska Coun of Churches Mural, Univ of Alaska Libr, Fairbanks, 67; Reindeer Round-Up, Reindeer Serv of Bur of Indian Affairs, 67; Ethnic People of Alaska Mural, Alaska State Libr, Juneau, 69. Exhib: Anchorage Mus of Fine Arts, 71 & 78; Alaska State Mus, Juneau, 71 & 76; Ketchikan Mus, Alaska, 72; Charles & Emma Frye Mus, Seattle, Wash, 73 & 75; Contemp Art from Alaska, Smithsonian Inst, Washington, DC, 78. Pos: Political cartoonist, SE Alaska Empire, 52-67; cur of exhib, Alaska State Mus, Juneau, 68-72. Awards: Outstanding Alaska Artist, Anchorage Fine Arts Mus Asn, 77. Bibliog: Artist in Juneau captures Alaska, Alaska Log, 73; Yvonne Mozee (auth), An interview with Rie Munoz, Alaska J, 74; Rie Munoz-the artist from Juneau who gets around, Alaska Woman, 77. Style & Technique: Impressionistic, Eskimo legends and life as well as impressionistic animals and birds. Media: Water Base Colors for Painting; Silkscreen and Stone Lithography. Publ: Illusr, Juneau & its development, Alaska Develop Bd, 56; illusr, Alaska Camp Cook Book, Alaska Northwest, 62; illusr, Alaska Mag, 62-67; illusr, Nursing in Alaska 1867-1967, Alaska Nurses Asn, 67; illusr, Kahtatah, Alaska Northwest Publ, 76. Dealer: Mill Pond Press Inc 204 S Nassau St Venice FL 33595. Mailing Add: 622 4th St Juneau AK 99801

MUNSTERBERG, HUGO
ART HISTORIAN, EDUCATOR
b Berlin, Ger, Sept 13, 16; US citizen. Study: Harvard Col, AB, 38, Harvard Univ, PhD, 41. Teaching: Asst prof fine arts, Mich State Univ, 46-49, assoc prof, 49-52; prof art hist, Int Christian Univ, Tokyo, 52-56; prof, Hunter Col; prof art hist, State Univ NY Col New Paltz, 58-, chmn dept, 68-71. Pos: Art critic, Arts Mag, 57-60. Mem: Col Art Asn Am; Oriental Ceramic Soc London; Chinese Art Soc; Japan Soc. Res: Oriental art, China and Japan. Collection: Oriental art, especially ceramics. Publ: Auth, Art of the Far East, 68 & India & Southeast Asia, 70, Abrams; auth, Arts of China, Tuttle; auth, The Sculpture of the Orient, Dover, 72; auth, A History of Women Artists, 75; auth, The Modern Art of Japan, 78; plus others. Mailing Add: 48 Elting Ave New Paltz NY 12561

MUNTADAS, ANTONIO
MEDIA ARTIST
b Barcelona, Spain, Sept 21, 42. Study: Univ Barcelona, 59-62: Escuela Tecnica Superior Ingenieros Industriales, Barcelona, 63-67. Work: Everson Mus, Syracuse, New York; Museo Arte Contemporanea, Caracas, Venezuela; Archivo Storico Biennale Venezia, Italy; Museo Art Contemporanea Da USP, Sao Paulo, Brazil. Exhib: Art Video Confrontation 74, Musee d'Art Moderne, Paris; Impact Video Art, Musee des Arts Decoratifs, Lausanne, Switz, 74; Prospectiva 74, Musee de Artes Contemporanea, Sao Paulo, Brazil; Biennale, Paris, 75; Biennale De Venezia, 76; Documenta 6 Kassel, 77; one-man shows, Ateneo De Madrid, Spain, 70, Galeria Vandres, Spain, 71-74, Video Distribution, Steffanoti Gallery, New York, 75; Museode Arte Contemporanea, Caracas, 76; Int Cultureel Centrum, Anvers, Belgium, 76; Everson Mus of Art, Syracuse, NY, 77. Teaching: Res & Fel, Ctr for Advanced Visual Studies, Mass Inst of Technol, Cambridge, 77-78. Bibliog: A Bonito Oliva (atuh), Europa-America, The Different Avantgardes, Roma, 76; William Dickes (auth), Contemporary Spanish Art, New York, 75; Ira Schneider & Beril Korot (auths), Video Art, New York, 76. Style & Technique: Working with different media, communications systems in close relation with the social science. Media: Installations; Videotapes; Publications. Dealer: Fernando Vijande c/o Galeria Vandres Don Ramon De La Cruz 26 Madrid 1 Spain. Mailing Add: 24 Harrison St New York NY 10013

MUNZER, ARIBERT
PAINTER, EDUCATOR
b Mannheim, Ger, Jan 9, 30. Study: Syracuse Univ, BFA; Cranbrook Acad Art, MFA. Exhib: Nat & regional shows, 53-63. Teaching: Instr painting & design, Minneapolis Sch Art, 55-68, assoc prof painting, Div Fine Arts, 68- Mailing Add: 200 E 25th St Minneapolis MN 55404

MURATA, HIROSHI
PAINTER, PRINTMAKER
b Tokyo, Japan, Jan 18, 41. Study: RI Sch Design, BFA, 64; Yale Univ Sch Art, MFA, 66. Work: Larry Aldrich Mus Contemp Art, Ridgefield, Conn; Tokyo Univ Col Art; Nat Mus Mod Art, Kyoto; Nat Mus Mod Art, Tokyo; Kamakura Mus Mod Art, Japan. Comn: Print ed, Int Graphic Arts Soc, New York, 66; theater curtain, Aoyama Tower Bldg, Tokyo, 71-72; print ed, NY State Creative Artists Pub Serv Prog, 75. Exhib: Made with Paper Exhib, Mus Contemp Crafts, NY, 67; 17th Nat Print Exhib, Brooklyn Mus, 70; Contemporary Reflections, 71-72; Aldrich Mus, 72; Japanese Artists in the Americas, Nat Mus Mod Art, Tokyo & Kyoto, 73-74; Biennial Contemp Am Art, Whitney Mus, 75. Teaching: Asst prof art, Western Mich Univ, 66-70; asst prof art, Trenton State Col, 72- Awards: Creative Arts Artists Pub Serv Grant, NY State Coun Arts, 72-73; Nat Endowment Arts Grant, 75-76. Style & Technique: Geometric abstraction; brushed and sprayed acrylic on unprimed cotton duck. Media: Acrylic on Canvas; Silkscreen, Lithography. Publ: Illusr, Asahi J, 69 & Shincho-Sha Publ, 70. Dealer: Donna Schneier Inc E 71st St New York NY 10021. Mailing Add: 423 Broome St New York NY 10013

MURCHIE, DONALD JOHN
ART LIBRARIAN
b Plainfield, NJ, Nov 23, 43. Study: Univ Colo, BA; Dalhousie Univ, MLS. Pos: Libr dir, NS Col of Art and Design, Halifax, 72- Mem: Art Libr Soc/NAm (mem exec bd, 75-78 & chmn, 76). Res: Contemporary art, Canadian art history and Elkins Mathews. Publ: Auth, Interview with Ian Carr-Harris, Criteria, Spring 78. Mailing Add: 5163 Duke St Halifax NS B3J 3J6 Can

MURCHISON, JOHN D
COLLECTOR
b Tyler, Tex, Sept 5, 21. Study: Yale Univ. Collection: Contemporary American art. Mailing Add: 2300 First Nat Bank Bldg Dallas TX 75202

MURDOCK, ROBERT MEAD
MUSEUM CURATOR, ART HISTORIAN
b New York, NY, Dec 18, 41. Study: Trinity Col, BA, 63; Yale Univ, MA(hist art), 65. Collections Arranged: Arranged & cataloged Modular Painting, Albright-Knox Art Gallery, Buffalo, 70, Richard Tuttle, Dallas Mus Fine Arts, 71, Robert Graham, 72, Geometric Abstraction: 1926-1942, 72, Poets of the Cities: New York and San Francisco, 1950-65, 74 & Berlin/Hanover: the 1920s, 77. Pos: Ford Found Mus Curatorial Training Prog interne, Walker Art Ctr, Minneapolis, 65-67; cur, Albright-Knox Art Gallery, Buffalo, 67-70; cur contemp art, Dallas Mus Fine Arts, 70- Awards: Nat Endowment for the Arts Fels for Mus Prof, 73. Res: 20th century, especially constructivism, and recent American painting and sculpture. Publ: Auth, Today's half-century in Buffalo, Arts Mag, 3/68. Mailing Add: Dallas Mus of Fine Arts Box 26250 Dallas TX 75226

MURPHY, CATHERINE E
PAINTER
b Cambridge, Mass, Jan 22, 46. Study: Pratt Inst, BFA, 67; Skowhegan Sch Painting & Sculpture, with Elmar Bichoff, summer 66. Exhib: One-man show, First Street Gallery, New York, 70 & Fourcade Droll Gallery, New York, 75; Group Landscape Show, De Cordova & Dana Mus, Lincoln, Mass, 70; Group Figure Show, Suffolk Mus, Stony Brook, NY, 71; Whitney Mus Am Art Ann, New York, 71; Am Fedn Arts Group Traveling Landscape Show, 71-72. Awards: Purchase Award, Am Fedn Arts, 71. Media: Oil. Dealer: Xavier Fourcade 36 E 75th St New York NY 10021; First Street Gallery 118 Prince St New York NY 10012. Mailing Add: 390 Ogden Ave Jersey City NJ 07307

MURPHY, CHESTER GLENN
PAINTER
b Harper, Kans, May 28, 07. Study: With Clyde Keller, Portland, Ore. Comn: Mural, Little World's Fair, Damascus, Ore, 62; two murals, Lake Oswego Shopping Ctr, Ore, 67; Ore scene in oil, USS Sperry, 69; two Ore scenes in oil, Western Elec, Vancouver, Wash, 72; George Fox Col, Newberg, Ore, 75. Exhib: Four-man show, Maryhill Mus Fine Arts, Wash, 60; three-man show, Dedication, Anna Hyatt Huntington Statue, Lincoln City, Ore, 65; Coun Am Artist Soc, 66; Vis Exhib of Ore Art, NMex State Capitol Bldg, 69; Am Artists Prof League Grand Nat, 71-77. Teaching: Instr oil painting, Willamette View Manor, 69-78; instr oil painting, Summer Workshops, Ore; guest lectr oil painting, Ore & Wash Pub Schs. Awards: First Prize, Lake Oswego Ann Arts & Flowers Festival; First in Prof Div, All-Ore Art Show, State Fair; Best of Show, Oak Grove Ann, 75. Mem: Fel Am Artists Prof League (pres, Ore Chap, 71); Ore Soc Artists; Lake Area Artists (pres, 72); Coun Am Artist Soc. Style & Technique: Seascapes and landscapes in realistic style with emphasis on composition, color, lighting, and dramatizing elements of special interest. Media: Oil. Publ: Contribr, Art is For Everybody, 60; co-auth, An Artist Paints the Northwest, 71. Dealer: Old West Gallery 312 1/2 E Second St The Dalles OR 97058. Mailing Add: 19076 Midhill Dr West Linn OR 97068

MURPHY, GLADYS WILKINS
PAINTER, CRAFTSMAN
b Providence, RI, Apr 15, 07. Study: RI Sch Design. Exhib: Am Watercolor Soc; Nat Acad Design; Libr of Cong; Philadelphia Print Club; Philadelphia Art Alliance; plus others. Pos: Owner, Art Gallery Rockport, Mass, 46-74. Mem: Providence Watercolor Club; Rockport Art Asn. Mailing Add: 17 King St Rockport MA 01966

MURPHY, HASS
SCULPTOR, DRAFTSMAN
b Boston, Mass, Nov 1, 1950. Study: Pratt Inst. Exhib: Romantic Abstraction, Brandeis Univ, Waltham, Mass, 71; Works on Paper, Logic Transformations, Contemp Arts Gallery, New York, 74; Biennial Exhib, Whitney Mus Am Art, New York, 75; New Drawings, New York, Grapestake Gallery, San Francisco, 75; Spare, Cent Hall Gallery, New York, 75. Bibliog:

Interview, Seven Painters, Artrite, spring 75; Judy Rifka & Willy Lenski (dirs), Ten Studios (film), Basel Art Fair, 75. Style & Technique: Sculpture dealing with topological relationships in the form of metal and stone; projective geometry stating possibilities of flat tetrahedrons. Media: Steel; Limestone. Dealer: Leah Levy 140 20th Ave San Francisco CA 94121; Nancy Lurie Gallery 230 E Ohio St Chicago IL 60611. Mailing Add: 399 Washington St New York NY 10013

MURPHY, HERBERT A
ARCHITECT, PAINTER
b Fall River, Mass, June 13, 11. Study: RI Sch Design, 32. Exhib: Rockport Art Asn; NShore Art Asn; Providence Art Club; Providence Watercolor Club; RI Sch Design; plus others. Pos: Registered architect, pvt practice, 41-78; co-dir, Art Gallery Rockport, Mass, 44-; mem graphics jury, Rockport Art Asn, 61-62. Mem: Rockport Art Asn (vpres, 60-62, pres, 63-65); Providence Watercolor Club. Mailing Add: 17 King St Rockport MA 01966

MURRAY, ALBERT (KETCHAM)
PAINTER
b Emporia, Kans, Dec 29, 06. Study: Cornell Univ; Syracuse Univ, BFA(cum laude), 30; Eng & France, 31; also with Wayman Adams, NY & Mex, 34-38. Work: Nat Gallery Art, Washington, DC; US Military Acad, West Point, NY; Univ Ill; Stanford Univ; Columbia Univ; Lehigh Univ; Univ NC; Syracuse Univ; Sch Bus, Harvard Univ; Union Col; Boston Col; Departments of Defense, Com, Treasury & Attorney Gen, Washington, DC; Nat Portrait Gallery, Washington, DC; Smithsonian Inst, Nat Fine Arts Collection, Washington, DC; US Naval Acad Mus, Annapolis, Md; Combat Art Collection, Navy Dept, Washington, DC. Comn: Portrait of Alfred P Sloan, Mem Hosp, New York, 65; portrait of Rush Kress, Kress Found, New York, 54; portrait of Laurance Rockefeller, NY Zool Soc, New York, 60; portrait of Arthur Ochs Sulzberger, New York Times, 63; portrait of R K Mellon, Pittsburgh, 64. Exhib: Carnegie Inst Int, Pittsburgh, 37; Corcoran Gallery Biennial, Washington, DC, 37; Your Navy, Metrop Mus Art, 48; American War Paintings, Salon Marine, Paris, 48; Men Who Made Washington, Nat Gallery Art, 51. Media: Oil, Watercolor. Dealer: Grand Central Art Galleries Hotel Biltmore 40 Vanderbilt Ave New York NY 10017; Portraits Inc, 41 E 57th St New York NY 10022. Mailing Add: 33 W 67th St New York NY 10023

MURRAY, ELIZABETH
PAINTER
b Chicago, Ill, 1940. Study: Art Inst Chicago, BFA, 62; Mills Col, MFA, 64. Work: Detroit Inst Arts; Cent Rigging & Contracting Ltd, Montreal; McCrory Corp, New York. Exhib: Ann, Whitney Mus, New York, 72, Contemporary American Drawing, 73 & American Abstract Painting Today, 74; two-person show, Paula Cooper Gallery, 75; one-man shows, Jared Sable Gallery, Toronto, 75, Paula Cooper Gallery, New York, 75 & Ohio State Univ, Columbus, 78; Calif Inst Arts Fac Show, Paul Mellon Art Ctr, Wallongford, Conn, 75; Baltimore Mus Art, 76; Recent Abstract Painting, State Univ NY, Brockport, 76; Paula Cooper Gallery, New York, 76 & 77, Los Angeles, 76; New Work/New York, Calif State Univ, Los Angeles, 76; 1977 Biennial Exhib, Whitney Mus Am Art, New York, 77; Nine Artists: Theodoron Awards, Guggenheim Mus, New York, 77; Paintings 75-76-77 (traveling exhib, Am Found Arts, Miami & Cincinnati Contemp Arts Ctr, Cincinnati), Sarah Lawrence Col Gallery, Bronxville, NY, 77; RI Sch of Design, Providence; New York State Mus, Albany; Critic's Choice, Lowe Art Gallery, Syracuse Univ, NY & Munson-Williams-Proctor Inst, Utica, NY, 77; New Mus, New York, 77. Teaching: Instr painting, Bard Col, 73-; vis prof painting, Calif Inst Arts, Valencia, 75-76; instr, Princeton Univ, NJ, 77. Bibliog: Sandy Ballatore (auth), New work from New York, Artweek, 10/16/76; Roberta Smith (auth), rev in Art in Am, 3-4/77; John Russell (auth), The New Mus where small is beautiful, New York Times, 11/11/77. Media: Oil on Canvas. Mailing Add: c/o Paula Cooper 155 Wooster New York NY 10012

MURRAY, FLORETTA MAY
PAINTER, EDUCATOR
b Minn. Study: Winona State Univ, BEd; Univ Minn, MA & PhD; Minneapolis Col Art & Design; Univ Chicago; also in France, Belg & Italy. Work: Minn Sch Art, Univ Chicago; Benjamin & Abbey Grey Collection. Comn: History of Winona County (mural), Winona Co Hist Mus; pres medallion, Winona State Col. Exhib: One-artist show, Jewish Community Ctr, St Paul, Minn, 76; St Paul Gallery Art, 60; Northrup Gallery, Univ Minn, 62; Nat League Am Pen Women, 68; Smithsonian Inst, 69; Minn Mus Art, 71-74; plus others. Teaching: Prof art & chmn dept, Winona State Col, 38-; prof art & actg head dept, Bemidji State Col, 49-50; prof, Col St Teresa, Winona, 55-58; instr painting, Univ Minn, Minneapolis, 58; lectr, St Mary's Col (Minn), 70. Awards: Merit Award, Minn State Fair, 38 & Rochester Art Ctr; Purchase Award, 62. Mem: Am Asn Univ Prof (secy-treas, 69-71); Nat Art Educ Asn; Minn Sculpture Soc; Col Art Asn Am; Int Platform Asn; plus others. Media: Watercolor, Acrylic. Mailing Add: 65 W Lake Blvd Winona MN 55987

MURRAY, JOAN
ART CRITIC, PHOTOGRAPHER
b Annapolis, Md, Mar 6, 27. Study: Calif Col Arts & Crafts, San Francisco Art Inst; Ruth Bernard Insight Studio; Univ Calif Exten; also studied with Wynn Bullock. Work: Int Mus of Photog, Eastman House, Rochester, NY; San Francisco Mus Mod Art; Oakland Mus, Calif. Exhib: Brother and Sister, Focus Gallery, San Francisco, 69; Portraits of Calif Photogrs, Friends of Photog Gallery, Carmel, Calif, 72 & Photog/Film Ctr W, 72; Male Nudes—One Man, Mind's Eye Gallery, Vancouver, BC, 73. Teaching: Instr photog, Univ Calif Exten, 70-; instr photog, City Col San Francisco, 75- Pos: Photog ed, Artweek, 69-; W Coast critic, Popular Photog, 75-77. Awards: Nat Endowment for Arts Grant for Art Criticism, 78. Mem: Soc Photog Educ; Soc for Encouragement of Contemp Art of San Francisco Mus of Art. Mailing Add: 120 Blair Ave Piedmont CA 94611

MURRAY, JOHN MICHAEL
PAINTER
b Tampa, Fla, May 28, 31. Study: Univ Tampa, BA, 63; Ohio Univ, MFA, 65. Work: Staten Island Mus, NY; Bundy Art Mus, Watefield, Vt; NS Col Art, Halifax; NJ Mus. Exhib: The Apple Cut Five Ways, Univ Chattanooga, 72; New Prints, New York Cult Ctr, 72; James Yu Gallery, New York, 74; Int Print Exhib, Crakow, 75; Langsam Gallery, Melbourne, Australia, 75; 19 Nat Print Exhib, Brooklyn Mus, 75; one-man shows, Dorsky Gallery, New York, 72, NS Col Fine Art, Halifax, 72 & Blue Parrot, New York, 74. Teaching: Assoc prof fine arts, New York Inst Technol, 66- Awards: First Prize in Painting, Fla State Ann, 63. Mem: Am Asn Univ Prof. Style & Technique: Photo-documentation. Publ: Contribr, Art Work—No Commercial Value, Grossman, 72; Pratt Graphics Reprint, 74. Dealer: James Yu Gallery 393 W Broadway New York NY 10012. Mailing Add: 124 W Houston St New York NY 10012

MURRAY, RICHARD DEIBEL
PAINTER, SCULPTOR
b Youngstown, Ohio, Dec 25, 21. Study: Univ Notre Dame, BS, 42. Work: Am Col Surgeons, Chicago; Staatsoper, Vienna, Austria; Medart Collection, Youngstown; Archduke Otto Von Hapsburg, Starnbergsee, Ger. Comn: Four limestone sculptures on four seasons, Mill Creek Park, Youngstown, 62; four murals & three limestone sculptures, Youngstown Symphony Ctr, 69. Exhib: Several exhibs, Butler Inst Am Art, Youngstown; several exhibs, Canton Art Inst, Ohio; several exhibs, Ohio State Fair, Columbus; Int, Galerie Int, New York, 72. Media: Ink, Acrylic, Stone, Wood. Mailing Add: 2125 Glenwood Ave Youngstown OH 44511

MURRAY, ROBERT (GRAY)
SCULPTOR
b Vancouver, BC, Mar 2, 36. Study: Univ Sask Sch Art, 55-58; Mex, 59; Emma Lake Artist's Workshops. Work: Whitney Mus Am Art, New York; Metrop Mus, New York; Nat Gallery Can, Ottawa, Walker Art Ctr, Minn; Everson Mus, Syracuse; Hirshhorn Mus, Washington, DC; plus others. Comn: Sculpture, Vancouver Int Airport, 69, Dept Nat Defense, Ottawa, 72, Dept External Affairs, Ottawa, 72, Wayne State Univ, Detroit, 74 & Univ Mass, Amherst, 75. Exhib: Whitney Mus Ann Exhib Contemp Sculpture, 64, 66, 68 & 70; American Sculpture of the Sixties, Los Angeles Co Mus, 67; 14 Sculptors: The Industrial Edge, Walker Art Ctr, Minn, 69; X Sao Paulo Biennial, Brazil, 69; Condition of Sculpture, Hayward Gallery, London, 75; Sewall Gallery, Rice Univ, Houston. Teaching: Instr, Sch Visual Art; lectr, cols throughout US. Awards: Can Coun Bursary, 60 & Sr Grant, 69; Second Prize, X Sao Paulo Biennial, Brazil, 69. Bibliog: Brydon Smith (auth), Robert Murray/Canada, Queen's Printer, Ottawa, 69; D Shadbolt (auth), Ronald Bladen/Robert Murray, Art Gallery Vancouver, 70; Krainin-Sage (auth), ArtIs (film), NY State Coun Arts, 71. Style & Technique: Sculpture formed from heavy steel or aluminum plate, in industrial plants; painted a single color. Media: Steel, Aluminum. Dealer: Hamilton Gallery of Contemp Art 20 W 57th St New York NY; David Mirvish Gallery 596 Markham St Toronto ON Can. Mailing Add: First Floor 66 Grand St New York NY 10013

MURRAY, WILLIAM COLMAN
COLLECTOR, PATRON
b Dunkirk, NY, Mar 15, 99. Study: Cornell Univ, AB, 21; Hamilton Col, Hon LHD, 63. Pos: Trustee, Munson-Williams-Proctor Inst, Utica, NY, 49-, pres & secy, 55-, hon chmn bd, 77-; trustee, Am Fedn Arts, 55-63; trustee & vpres, Root Art Ctr, 59-; pres & dir, Cent NY Community Arts Coun, 67- Awards: Colgate Univ Civic Award, 53. Mem: Collectors Club; Am Fedn Arts; Mus Mod Art. Interest: Substantial donations to Munson-Williams-Proctor Institute. Collection: Primarily contemporary American; ancestral portraits and some French. Mailing Add: 1603 Sherman Dr Utica NY 13501

MURRAYGREEN, RYAN
PAINTER, PAPER ARTIST
b Toronto, Ont, Can, May 7, 47. Study: Univ BC, BA(oriental art hist); Vancouver Sch Art; Inst Allende, San Miguel de Allende, Mex. Work: Centennial Mus, Vancouver, BC; Folk Art Mus, Los Angeles; Zavala Gallery, San Miguel de Allende, Mex; San Francisco Mus Mod Art; Simon Fraser Univ Gallery, Burnaby, BC. Comn: Sculptures, Centennial Mus, Vancouver, BC, 75-77. Exhib: Centennial Mus, Vancouver, BC, 77; World Print Competition, San Francisco Mus Mod Art, 77 & 78; Paper shows, Vancouver Art Gallery & Univ BC Gallery, 78; one-man shows, Paper, Simon Fraser Univ Gallery, 78 & Gilson Gallery, Seattle, Wash, 78. Collections Arranged: Coloured Fiber in Paper as Art, Simon Fraser Univ Gallery, 78. Teaching: Instr papermaking as art, San Francisco Mus Mod Art, 77 & Univ BC, 75- Awards: Experimental Forms Award, Mrs Betsy Glummer, 76; Paper As Art, Tuft Fund, Los Angeles, 77. Bibliog: Chris Weills (auth), Goodfellow Catalogue, Berkeley Windhover Books, 77; Paul Watson (auth), Hang Onto Your Britches, Gerogia Straight newspaper, 9/77; Ann Petrie (interviewer), CBC Radio, CBC Broadcasting, 11/77. Publ: Auth, Paper Art, Univ BC Pamphlet, Univ BC, 76; illusr, Ipperwash, Can Mag, 78; illusr, The Cool Victorian, Kids Books, 77. Dealer: Iannetti Galleries 575 Sutter St San Francisco CA 94102. Mailing Add: c/o 3394 Blair Dr Hollywood CA 90068

MUSGRAVE, SHIRLEY H
EDUCATOR, PHOTOGRAPHER
b Lexington, Ky, Nov 28, 35. Study: Miss State Col Women, BFA, 57; Colorado Springs Fine Arts Ctr, summer 56; Univ Kans, scholar, 57-58, MS, 63; Univ Ark, 64-65; Univ Iowa, 66-67; Fla State Univ, fel, 67-69, PhD, 70. Exhib: 15th & 18th Ann Nat Watercolor Shows, Miss Art Asn, Jackson, 56 & 59; Kans Painters & Printmakers Show, Kans State Col, Pittsburg, 59; 28th Ann Am Graphic Arts Exhib, Wichita Art Asn, Kans, 59; one-artist photog exhib, Iowa City Civic Ctr, 65; two-artist photog show, Memphis State Univ Gallery, Tenn, 72. Teaching: Art supvr, Linwood Pub Schs, Kans, 58-60; assoc prof art educ, Memphis State Univ, 70-72; asst prof art educ, Fla Int Univ. Awards: Ark Artists Ann First Prize in Graphics, Little Rock Mus Fine Arts, 56. Mem: Nat Art Educ Asn; Southeastern Col Art Conf; Fla Art Educ Asn. Res: Reaction to pattern and content in creative photography by subjects with and without training in art; the development and testing of instructional modules for photographic art criticism. Mailing Add: 10710 SW 43rd Ln Miami FL 33165

MUSGROVE, STEPHEN WARD
ART ADMINISTRATOR, CURATOR
b Pittsfield, Mass, Mar 28, 49. Study: Lenoir-Rhyne Col, BA(hist), 73; State Univ NY, Oneonta, 73-74, Cooperstown Grad Progs, MA(mus studies). Pos: Dir, Creative Mus for Youth, Hickory, NC, 74-75; cur of collections, Mint Mus of Art, Charlotte, NC, 75- Mem: Am Asn Mus; Am Asn for State & Local Hist; Southeastern Mus Conf; NC Mus Coun. Publ: Auth & illusr, Making exhib labels: a mechanical lettering system, Hist News, 76. Mailing Add: PO Box 6011 Charlotte NC 28207

MUSICK, ARCHIE L
PAINTER, WRITER
b Kirksville, Mo, Jan 19, 02. Study: Northeast Mo State Univ, BS, 28; Broadmoor Art Acad, Colorado Springs, summers 27-28; Art Students League, 29-30; also with Randall Davey, Ernest Lawson, Thomas H Benton, Boardman Robinson & S MacDonald-Wright. Work: Civic Ctr Libr, Scottsdale, Ariz; Smithsonian Archives, Washington, DC. Comn: Hard Rock Miners in Colo, Washington, DC, 35; lounge, Fine Arts Ctr, Colorado Springs, 36; Loading Cattle in Nebr, Washington, DC, 40; Hunters, Red & White in Colorado, Washington, DC, 41. Exhib: Carnegie Inst Int, Pittsburgh, 41; Corcoran Biennial, 50; Chicago Art Inst; Whitney Mus; St Louis Ann. Teaching: Vis asst prof art, Mo Univ, 46-48; instr art, Columbia Col, 48-51; plus 26 yrs grade & high sch art teaching. Bibliog: Conversation with Archie Musick (audio-video tape), NBC Sta, Phoenix, Ariz, 75. Media: Egg Tempera on Gessoed Masonite. Publ: Auth, Transplanting of culture, Mag Art, 3/37; auth, Jigger Flies First, 57; auth, Musick Medley, 71. Mailing Add: c/o Saks Galleries 3019 E Second Ave Denver CO 80206

MUSSELMAN, DARWIN B
PAINTER, EDUCATOR
b Selma, Calif, Feb 16, 16. Study: Fresno State Col, AB, 38; Art Ctr Col Design, Los Angeles, 38-39; Calif Col Arts & Crafts, MFA, 50; Univ Calif, Berkeley, MA, 52; also with Lyonel Feininger, 37 & Yasuo Kuniyoshi, 49. Work: Oakland Art Mus, Calif; Fresno Arts Ctr, Calif; Reedley Jr Col, Calif; Vallejo Jr High Sch, Calif; Pittsburg Jr High Sch, Calif. Comn: Mural of cotton indust, Prod Cotton Oil Co, Fresno, 54. Exhib: 3rd Ann Legion of Honor Exhib, San Francisco, 48; Calif Watercolor Soc Exhib, Riverside Gallery, NY, 48; Calif Artists Exhib, Los Angeles Mus, 49; Denver Mus Ann, Colo, 54; Butler Inst Art Nat, Youngstown, Ohio, 56. Teaching: Assoc prof painting & art educ, Calif Col Arts & Crafts, 48-53; prof painting & commercial art, Fresno State Univ, 53- Pos: Artist & art dir, Thomas Advert, Fresno, 39-41 & 45-46; freelance artist, 54-63. Awards: First Prize Painting, San Joaquin Valley Art Contest, Rouze Gallery, Fresno, 47, Northern Calif Arts, Crocker Gallery, Sacramento, Calif, 56 & Ann Show, Fresno Arts Ctr, 61. Bibliog: Emil Kosa, Jr (auth), California painters, Am Artist Mag, 3/50; Barbara Cott (auth), Darwin Musselman, Fresno Arts Ctr, 62. Mem: Am Watercolor Soc; Calif Nat Watercolor Soc. Style & Technique: Non-objective to Trompe l'Oeil. Media: Oil, Egg Tempera. Publ: Illusr, Valley of the Yokuts, 40. Dealer: Gallery Americana Carmel CA. Mailing Add: 5161 N Sequoia Dr Fresno CA 93711

MYER, PETER LIVINGSTON
KINETIC ARTIST, MUSEUM DIRECTOR
b Ozone Park, NY, Sept 19, 34. Study: Brigham Young Univ, BA, 56; Univ Utah, MFA, 59; summers with Harry Sternberg & Joseph Hirsch. Work: Colorado Springs Fine Arts Ctr & Denver Art Mus, Colo; Univ Nev, Las Vegas; Phoenix Art Mus, Ariz; Salt Lake Art Ctr, Utah. Exhib: Lights in Orbit, Howard Wise Gallery, New York, 67; Light, Motion, Space, Walker Art Ctr, Minneapolis, 67; Some More Beginnings, Brooklyn Mus, 68; Art & Technology, High Mus Art, Atlanta, Ga, 69; Art of the 60's, Denver Art Mus, 70; Kinetic Light Show, Phoenix Art Mus, Ariz, 73; Billboard Art Invitational Exhib, 74; Tracy Collins Invitational Exhib, 74; Utah Valley Sculptors Invitational Exhib, Springvlle Art Mus, 77. Teaching: Assoc prof art & chmn dept, Univ Nev, Las Vegas, 62-72; prof art & art gallery dir, Brigham Young Univ, 72- Awards: Sweepstakes Award for Ranch Ride, 65, First Prize for Orb I, 66 & First Place/Sculpture, 67 & 70, Nat Art Roundup; Best in Show for Ars Moriendi, Spring Art Roundup, 65; Second Prize/Painting, Utah State Inst of Fine Arts Exhib, 74; Purchase Award, Utah Biennial/Salt Lake City Art Ctr, 75. Kranz (auth), Science and Technology and the Arts, Rheinhold, 74. Mem: Western Asn of Art Mus (regional rep, 74-); Am Asn of Art Mus; Utah Mus Asn (mem adv comt, 77). Bibliog: Art for Tomorrow (film), The 20th Century, CBS; Light is the medium, Time Mag 4/28/67. Style & Technique: Kinetic light artist; manipulates light sequences electronically. Media: Kinetic Light Art/Sculpture. Mailing Add: F-303 Harris Fine Arts Ctr Brigham Young Univ Provo UT 84602

MYERS, C STOWE
DESIGNER
b Altoona, Pa, Dec 7, 06. Study: Univ Pa, BFA; Grand Cent Sch Art, New York; Chouinard Sch Art, Los Angeles, Calif. Exhib: Int Exhib Indust Design, Mus Mod Art, Buenos Aires, Arg, 63; Int Exhib Indust Design, Salle Arts Decoratif, Louvre, Paris, 64; var design exhibs, USA & Abroad, 64- Teaching: Lectr design, Sch Design & Ill Inst Technol. Pos: Designer, Norman Bel Geddes, 33-35; partner, Walter Dorwin Teague, 35-49; assoc, Raymond Loewy, 49-53; owner, Stowe Myers Design, 54-72; Design Planning Group/Chicago, Ill, 72-74, consult, 74- Mem: Indust Designers Soc Am; Palette & Chisel Acad of Fine Art; Munic Art League of Chicago; Caxton Club; Am Watercolor Soc. Mailing Add: 535 N Michigan Ave Chicago IL 60611

MYERS, DENYS PETER
ART HISTORIAN, LECTURER
b Boston, Mass, Apr 23, 16. Study: Harvard Col, BS, 40; Columbia Univ, MA, 48; Fogg Art Mus, 49-50. Collections Arranged: Zanesville Sesquicentennial Exhib, 47; Adorations of the Magi, 48; The Grand Manner, Baroque Exhib, 49; Romanticism, Columbus Gallery Fine Arts. Teaching: Lectr medieval, baroque, romantic & contemp subjects; lectr, Johns Hopkins Univ, 60-64; lectr, Cath Univ Am, 66-67. Pos: Dir, Art Inst Zanesville, Ohio, 47-55; dir, Philbrook Art Ctr, Tulsa, Okla, 55-58; dir, Des Moines Art Ctr, Iowa, 58-59; asst dir, Baltimore Mus Art, 59-64; dir, Northern Va Fine Arts Asn, 64-66; historian, Nat Park Serv, US Dept Interior, Washington, DC, 66-68, prin archit historian, hist Am bldgs surv, 68- Mem: Col Art Asn Am; Soc Archit Historians (bd dirs, 62-65); Am Asn Mus; Steamship Hist Soc Am. Publ: Contribr, Soc Archit Historians J. Mailing Add: 201 N Columbus St Alexandria VA 22302

MYERS, FORREST WARDEN
SCULPTOR
b Long Beach, Calif, Feb 14, 41. Study: San Francisco Art Inst. Work: Mus Mod Art; Patric Lannon Mus, Palm Beach, Fla; Great SW Corp, Atlanta, Ga; Am Embassy, Mexico City, Mex. Exhib: Calif Sch Fine Arts, San Francisco, 59; Jewish Mus, 67; Philadelphia Mus Art, 68; Los Angeles Co Mus, 68; Whitney Mus Am Art, 68 & 72; Hamilton Gallery Contemp Art, New York, 77; plus others. Teaching: Instr sculpture, San Francisco Art Inst, 67; instr, Sch Visual Art, NY, 68; lectr art & indust, IBM Corp, 68. Pos: Dir art res, Art Res, Inc, 64-69; pres, Dynamite Lite Aura Co, 68-69. Awards: Am Steel Inst Award, 68; Aero Space Industs Design Award, 68. Mem: Exp in Art & Technol. Mailing Add: 238 Park Ave S New York NY 10003

MYERS, FRANCES
PRINTMAKER
b Racine, Wis, Apr 16, 36. Study: Univ Wis, MFA; San Francisco Art Inst. Work: Libr of Cong, Washington, DC; Victoria & Albert Mus, London; Metrop Mus Art, New York; Philadelphia Mus Art; Nat Collection of Fine Arts, Smithsonian Inst, Washington, DC. Comn: Limited ed print, Wis Arts Coun, 71. Exhib: Biennial of Prints, Mus d'Art Mod, Paris, 70; US Pavilion, World's Fair, Osaka, Japan, 70; 40 New American Prints, US Cult Ctrs, Tel-Aviv & Jerusalem, 73; Libr of Cong 24th Nat Exhib, 75; 20th Print Biennale, Brooklyn Mus, 76; Fifth Brit Int Print Biennale, 76; New Talent in Printmaking, AAA Gallery, New York, 77; Horwich Gallery, Chicago, 77. Teaching: Lectr printmaking, St Martin's Sch Art, London, 66-67; lectr printmaking, Col Art & Design, Birmingham, Eng, 66; vis lectr, Art Dept, Univ Wis-Madison, 75 & 76. Pos: Co-dir, Mantegna Press, Hollandale, Wis, 71- Awards: Wis Arts Coun grants, 73 & 77; Nat Endowment Arts Graphics Fel, 74-75; H Lester Cooke Found fel, 77. Mem: Madison Print Club, Wis. Style & Technique: Architectural themes of 1920's and 1930's period executed in tonal aquatints, a type of etching. Dealer: Assoc Am Artists Gallery 663 Fifth Ave New York NY 10022. Mailing Add: Hollandale WI 53544

MYERS, FRED A
MUSEUM DIRECTOR
b Lancaster, Pa, Dec 21, 37. Study: Harvard Univ, BA, 59, MA, 62. Pos: Asst to dir, Mus Art, Carnegie Inst, Pittsburgh, 62-70; dir, Grand Rapids Art Mus, Mich, 70- Mailing Add: Grand Rapids Art Mus 230 E Fulton Grand Rapids MI 49502

MYERS, JACK FREDRICK
PAINTER, INSTRUCTOR
b Lima, Ohio, Feb 17, 27. Study: Cleveland Art Inst, Ohio. Exhib: May Show, Cleveland Mus of Art, 49-54, 76 & 77; two-man show, Freedson Gallery, Lakewood, Ohio, 69; Cleveland Invitational, Smith Gallery, Painesville, Ohio, 73; Mid-Year Show, Butler Inst of Am Art, Youngstown, Ohio, 76. Teaching: Instr graphics & film, Cooper Sch of Art, Cleveland, 70- Awards: First Prize Art Category, Doc Film Competition, Bolex-Newsweek Mag, 69; First Prize (one minute animated film), ASIFA Festival, New York, 74. Style & Technique: Trompe l'oeil style still lifes, which include old photographs and contain hidden images and symbols. Media: Oil underpainting with whole egg emulsion, Serigraphy. Mailing Add: 187 Kraft St Berea OH 44017

MYERS, JOEL PHILIP
ARTIST IN GLASS, EDUCATOR
b Paterson, NJ, Jan 29, 34. Study: Parsons Sch Design, NY, grad with honors, 54; NY State Col Ceramics, Alfred Univ, BFA, 62, MFA, 67. Work: Corning Mus Glass, NY; Toledo Mus Art, Ohio; Ill State Mus, Springfield; Mus du Verre, Liege, Belg; Rosska Konstslojdmuseet, Goteborg, Sweden. Exhib: One-man shows, Mus Contemp Crafts, NY, 67, Lee Nordness Galleries, NY, 70 & George Walter Vincent Smith Art Mus, Springfield, Mass, 72; Glas Heute, Mus Bellerive, Zurich, Switz, 72; Enmansglas, Rosska Konstlojdsmuseet, Sweden, 74. Teaching: Prof art, ceramics & glass, Ill State Univ, Normal, 70- Pos: Dir design, Blenke Glass Co, Milton, WVa, 63-70. Awards: Capital Award, Louisville Art Ctr Asn, 68; Jury & Purchase Awards, Toledo Glass Nat, Toledo Mus Art, 68; Fed Glass Award, Columbus Gallery Fine Arts, 73; craftsmen's fel, Nat Endowment for the Arts, 76-77. Bibliog: Lee Nordness (auth), Objects USA, Viking, 70; Carolyn Meyer (auth), People Who Make Things, Atheneum, 75. Mem: Glass Art Soc (pres). Style & Technique: Contemporary works in glass, sculptural and utilitarian, architectural. Media: Glass. Mailing Add: RR 2 Bunn St Rd Bloomington IL 61701

MYERS, JOHN B
ART DEALER
Pos: John Bernard Myers Gallery, New York; ed & publ, Paranthese. Publ: Auth articles in Smithsonian, Craft Horizons, Art News & New York Times. Mailing Add: John Bernard Myers Gallery 59 E 73rd St New York NY 10021

MYERS, LEGH
SCULPTOR
b Ventnor, NJ, Nov 11, 16. Study: Pa State Univ, 35-36; Lehigh Univ, 36-39; also with J Wallace Kelly, 52-54. Work: In numerous pvt collections, New York, Philadelphia & throughout US. Exhib: 11 shows, Knickerbocker Artists Ann, Nat Arts Club, New York, 57-73; 13 shows, Audubon Artists Ann, Nat Acad Design, New York, 60-78 & Allied Artists Ann, 61 & 62; Ann Arts Festival, Cleveland Mus, 66; Sculptors Guild Ann Mem Show, Lever House, New York, 71-77; plus four one-man shows in New York. Awards: Audubon Artists Medal Creative Sculpture, 28th Ann Exhib, 70 & Margaret Hirsch Levine Mem Prize Sculpture, 30th Ann Audubon Artists Exhib, 72, Nat Acad Design. Bibliog: R Stevens (auth), Expositions diverses, La Rev Mod, 9/61; Ralph Fabri (auth), The 28th Audubon Annual, Todays Art, 7/70; plus others. Mem: Sculptors Guild (dir & secy, 72-); Audubon Artists; Knickerbocker Artists; Artists Equity Asn. Style & Technique: Abstract. Media: Marble. Dealer: Alonzo Gallery 30 W 57th St New York NY 10019. Mailing Add: 9 S Mansfield Ave Margate NJ 08402

MYERS, MALCOLM HAYNIE
PRINTMAKER, PAINTER
b Lucerne, Mo, June 19, 17. Study: Wichita State Univ, BFA; Univ Iowa, MA & MFA. Work: Libr of Cong, Washington, DC; St Louis Art Mus; Walker Art Ctr, Minneapolis; Seattle Art Mus; Brooklyn Art Mus; plus others. Exhib: Salon Mai, Paris, 51; Int Color Print Soc, Grenchen, Switz, 55; Ford Found Award, USA, 57; Am Prints Today, Print Coun; New York World's Fair Art Exhib; plus others. Teaching: Instr art, Univ Iowa, 45-47; prof art, Univ Minn, Minneapolis, 48-, chmn dept art, 65-70. Pos: Pres, Twin City Chap, Artists Equity Asn, 53-55; mem bd trustees, Minn Mus Art, St Paul, 72- Awards: Guggenheim Fels, 50-51 & 54-55; Ford Found Award, 57; Alumni Achievement Award, Wichita State Univ, Kans, 73. Bibliog: Article in Artists Proof, 60; Kenneth Campbell (auth), Malcolm Myers (film), Wis State Univ-Eau Claire, 69. Mailing Add: Dept of Studio Arts Univ Minn Minneapolis MN 55455

MYERS, RICHARD LEWIS
EDUCATOR, FILM MAKER
b Massillon, Ohio, Dec 1, 37. Study: Mex City Col, 57; Art Students League, New York, 57; Kent State Univ, Ohio, BFA, 59 & MA, 61. Comn: Doc film, Massillon Mus, Ohio, 75. Exhib: Detroit Art Inst, Mich; Walker Art Ctr; San Francisco Int Film Festival, Calif; Univ Calif Davis; Univ Calif Los Angeles; Designer Crafts Conf, Akron Art Inst, Ohio; Chicago Film Festival, Ill; Univ Calif Berkeley; Yale Univ, New Haven, Conn. Teaching: Prof art & cinematography, Kent State Univ, 64- Awards: Guggenheim Fel for Film-making, 69 & 71; Am Film Inst Grant, 70; Nat Endowment for the Arts Grants, 75 & 77. Bibliog: Amos Vogel (auth), Film as Subversive Art, Random, 75; Kevin Thomas (auth), Panorama of Imagination, Los Angeles Times, 10/14/75; other reviews in Hollywood Reporter, Los Angeles Free Press, Take One Mag, Film Makers Newsletter, Village Voice, Film Quart Mag & Variety. Mailing Add: Independent Films 1224 N Mantua St Kent OH 44240

MYERS, VIRGINIA ANNE
PRINTMAKER, EDUCATOR
b Greencastle, Ind, May 8, 27. Study: Corcoran Sch Art, Washington, DC, BA(drawing & painting), 49; Calif Col Arts & Crafts, MFA(painting), 51; Univ Ill, Champaign, printmaking & painting; Univ Iowa, Iowa City, printmaking with Mauricio Lasansky; Atelier 17, Paris, printmaking with Stanley William Hayter. Work: San Francisco Art Mus; Nelson-Atkins Mus, Kansas City, Kans; Toledo Mus Art, Ohio; Lehigh Univ Art Collection, Bethlehem, Pa; US State Dept. Exhib: Thirty-six one-woman shows, 53-73; Libr Cong Circulating Print, 60-63; Graphics USA, US Embassies in Europe, 65-66; Gov Exhib, 9 Iowa Artists, Des Moines & Travel Show, 71 & 72; Engravings America 1974, Albrecht Art Gallery, St Joseph, Mo, 74. Teaching: Teaching asst printmaking & crafts, Univ Ill, Champaign, 54-55; instr printmaking, Univ Iowa, Iowa City, 62-68, asst prof, 68-71, assoc prof, 71- Awards: Fulbright Grant to Paris, 61; Develop Leave Award, Univ Iowa, 73 & 78; Arts Endowment Grants, State Iowa Arts Coun & Nat Endowment for Arts, 74 & 77. Bibliog: David E Archie (auth),

I just love pigs, Iowan Mag, 10-11/60; Denis O'Brien Van (auth), Iowan seeks perfections in art, teaching, Des Moines Register, 8/29/72. Style & Technique: Drawing and various intaglio techniques including engraving, drypoint, etching, aquatint, and softground, in black and white, color and silver leaf. Media: Copper Plates; Oil on Canvas. Publ: Auth, From Tancah to Tulum with John L Stephens: Mayan Indian Ruins (three-projector slide show), 71; auth, Frederick Catherwood: Engraving & Lithographs from the Mayan Drawings, Books at Iowa, 72; auth, Giovanni Battista Piranesi and Le Antichità Romane, Univ Iowa Mus Art Bull, spring 76; creator, A Time of Malfeasance (21 engravings & drypoints), 77. Mailing Add: Tenacre Rte 3 Solon IA 52333

N

NADALINI, (LOUIS ERNEST)
PAINTER
b San Francisco, Calif, Jan 21, 27. Study: City Col San Francisco; Art Students League, with George Grosz; also with Martin Baer, San Francisco, 58-60. Work: Oakland Art Mus, Univ Calif, Berkeley, San Francisco Pub Sch & Wells Fargo Bank, San Francisco, Calif. Exhib: One-man shows, Village Art Ctr, New York, 53 & Am Student & Artist Ctr, Paris, 54; San Francisco Mus Art Painting Ann, 57-59 & 66; Calif Palace of Legion of Honor, San Francisco, 63-67; Pa Acad Fine Arts 161st Ann, 66; Oakland Art Mus Painting Ann, 66-69. Teaching: Instr art, San Francisco Pub Sch, 69-70. Awards: YMCA All City Art Exhib First Prize, San Francisco, 39; James D Phelan Award, Calif Palace of Legion of Honor, 65 & 67. Bibliog: A Fried (auth), article in San Francisco Examr, 58; A Frankenstein (auth), article in San Francisco Chronicle, 66; W Ramsey (auth), Paintings, KPIX-TV, San Francisco, 1/66. Mem: Artists Equity Asn. Media: Oil, Acrylic, Ink. Publ: Auth, Catalogue of the Art Bank, San Francisco Art Inst Sch, 59-60; auth, From the West, San Francisco Art Inst, 64; auth, articles & rev in Artforum, 3/66 & 5/71 & San Francisco Arts, 6/67. Dealer: Gordon Woodside Galleries 803 E Union St Seattle WA 98122; La Galerie Mouffe 67 Rue Mouffetard 75005 Paris France. Mailing Add: 154 Lynn St Seattle WA 98109

NADLER, HARRY
PAINTER, EDUCATOR
b Los Angeles, Calif, Feb 17, 30. Study: Univ Calif, Los Angeles, BA, 56, MA, 58. Work: Univ Mass, Amherst; Guild Hall Mus, East Hampton, NY; Okla Art Ctr, Oklahoma City; Detroit Inst Arts; Los Angeles Co Mus. Exhib: Int Exhib Young Artists, Tokyo, 67; Timeless Paintings from the USA, Gallery Paul Facchetti, Paris, 68; American Drawings of the Sixties, New York, 69-70; one-man shows, Bertha Schaefer Gallery, New York, 69, 72 & 74; Childe Hassam Purchase Show, Nat Inst Arts & Lett, 71 & 72; 15th Ann Eight State Invitational, Okla Art Ctr, 73. Teaching: Asst prof painting & drawing, Wesleyan Univ, 65-71; assoc prof painting & drawing, Univ NMex, 71- Awards: Childe Hassam Purchase Award, Nat Inst Arts & Lett, 72. Dealer: Bertha Schaefer Gallery Inc 41 E 57th St New York NY 10019. Mailing Add: 4820 Guadalupe Trail NW Albuquerque NM 87107

NAEGLE, STEPHEN HOWARD
PAINTER, SCULPTOR
b Toquerville, Utah, Oct 11, 38. Study: Utah State Univ, BFA, 68, MFA, 69; also with Joseph Hirsch & Joseph Mugnaini. Work: Wyo State Gallery, Cheyenne; Cent Wyo Mus, Casper; Utah State Univ; NMex Art League, Albuquerque; Southern Utah State Col. Exhib: Coun Am Artists Soc Exhib, New York, 64; Rocky Mountain Fedn Arts Traveling Exhib, Salt Lake City, 68; Watercolor USA, Springfield, Mo, 70; Int Miniature Print Exhib, New York, 71; Am Watercolor Soc, New York, 77. Teaching: Instr painting & drawing, Ark Tech, Russelville, 69-72; instr watercolor & sculpture, Casper Col, 73- Awards: First Place for Watercolor, NMex Art League, 64; Doris Dyche Purchase Award, Watercolor USA, 70; Best of Show, Cody Co Art League, 75. Mem: Am Crafts Coun; Int Soc Artists; Wyo Artists Asn. Style & Technique: Design, realism and abstract. Media: Watercolor, Oil; Metal, Wood. Dealer: Gallery 323 323 S David Casper WY 82601. Mailing Add: 1240 S Fenway Casper WY 82601

NAEVE, MILO M
ART ADMINISTRATOR, ART HISTORIAN
b Ness Co, Kans, Oct 9, 31. Study: Univ Colo, BFA; Univ Del, Winterthur Prog Am Studies & MA. Pos: Mem staff, Winterthur Mus, Del & Colonial Williamsburg, Va; dir, Colorado Springs Fine Arts Ctr, Colo; Art Inst Chicago. Mem: Col Art Asn Am; Brit Mus Asn; Royal Soc Arts; Am Asn Mus; Nat Trust for Hist Preservation. Res: American painting, sculpture, architecture, and decorative arts from the seventeenth to the twentieth century. Publ: Contribr, Art Quart, 59, New Eng Quart, 60 & Antiques Mag; ed, Winterthur Portfolio, Vols I, II & III, 64-66. Mailing Add: 1240 N Lake Shore Dr Chicago IL 60610

NAGANO, PAUL TATSUMI
PAINTER, DESIGNER
b Honolulu, Hawaii, May 21, 38. Study: Columbia Col, BA, 60; Pa Acad Fine Arts, Philadelphia, 63-67. Work: Hawaii State Found of Cult & the Arts, Honolulu; William Rockhill Nelson Gallery, Kansas City, Mo. Exhib: Cambridge Art Asn Group Exhib, Mass, 71 & Jurors' Exhib, 72; Pa Acad Fine Arts 75th Ann Fel Exhib, 72; Pucker/Safrai Gallery, 74, 76 & 77; Contemp Arts Ctr, Honolulu, 74. Awards: First Prize Landscape with Figures, Popular Photog, 63; Packard Prize Drawing, 64 & Lewis S Ware Traveling Scholar, 67, Pa Acad Fine Arts. Mem: Fel Pa Acad Fine Arts. Style & Technique: Oriental and impressionist. Media: Watercolor. Dealer: Pucker/Safrai Gallery 171 Newbury St Boston MA 02116. Mailing Add: 57 University Rd Brookline MA 02146

NAGANO, SHOZO
PAINTER
b Kanazawa, Japan Study: Kanazawa Fine Arts Univ, AB; Art Students League, with Julian Levi; Pratt Inst, New York. Work: Allentown Art Mus, Pa; Berkshire Mus, Pittsfield, Mass; Citicorp, New York; Hudson River Mus, Yonkers, NY; State Univ NY Albany. Comn: It is Finished (painting), comn by Richard Hirsch, cur James Michener Collection, 71. Exhib: One-man shows, Sato Gallery, Tokyo, 55-63, Berkshire Mus, 69 & 74, Alonzo Gallery, 71-72, 74 & 77 & Squibb Art Ctr, 76; Am Fedn Arts Traveling Exhib, 68 & 71; Nat Inst Arts & Lett, 72. Teaching: Instr painting, Seibu Gakuen, Tokyo, 60-65. Bibliog: Alvin Smith (auth), article in Art Int, 5/72; David Shirey (auth), articles in New York Times, 9/75 & 3/76. Mem: Japanese Artists Asn NY (pres, 75). Style & Technique: Three-dimensional shaped canvases painted with acrylic; geometric cube and crystal forms. Publ: Illusr, Kiristo-Kyo-Hoiku, 61-72; contribr, Haha no Hikari, 69-72. Dealer: Alonzo Gallery 30 W 57th St New York NY 10019. Mailing Add: 134 Hoyt St Brooklyn NY 11217

NAGLER, EDITH KROGER
PAINTER
b New York, NY. Study: Nat Acad Design, with Douglas Volk, Francis Jones & George Deforest Brush; Art Students League, with Frank Vincent DuMond, Kenneth Hayes Miller & Robert Henri. Work: Mus Fine Arts, Springfield, Mass; George Walter Vincent Smith Art Mus, Springfield; Wadsworth Atheneum, Hartford, Conn; Highland Park Mus, Dallas, Tex; Fed Ct House, Boston. Exhib: Corcoran Gallery Art, Washington, DC, 23; Nat Acad Design, New York, 28; Art Inst Chicago, 30; Philadelphia Arts Club; Pa Acad Fine Arts. Pos: Mem bd control, Art Students League. Awards: Crowninshield Prize, Stockbridge, Mass; First Watercolor Purchase Prize, Springfield. Mem: Am Watercolor Soc; Am Artists Prof League; Audubon Artists. Style & Technique: Landscapes, portraits, genre, still life. Media: Oil, Watercolor. Dealer: Cornell Galleries Springfield MA 01101; Grand Central Art Galleries 40 Vanderbilt Ave New York NY 10017. Mailing Add: 5742 Berkshire Lane Dallas TX 75209

NAGLER, FRED
PAINTER
b West Springfield, Mass. Study: Art Students League; also with Henri, Dumond & Bridgman. Work: Joslyn Art Mus, Omaha, Nebr; Michener Collection, Univ Tex, Austin; Am Acad Arts & Lett; Libr of Cong; Metrop Mus of Art, New York; also in many pvt collections. Exhib: Carnegie Inst Int, Pittsburgh; Corcoran Gallery Art, Washington, DC; Art Inst Chicago; Pa Acad Fine Arts, Philadelphia; Nat Acad Design, New York. Awards: Carnegie Award, Nat Acad of Design; LaMont Award & Fabri Award, Audubon Artists; Am Acad Arts & Lett grant; plus many others. Media: Oil. Dealer: Midtown Galleries 11 E 57th St New York NY 10022. Mailing Add: 5742 Berkshire Lane Dallas TX 75209

NAIMAN, LEE E
ART DEALER
b Baltimore, Md. Study: Goucher Col, BA; Sorbonne, Paris; Johns Hopkins Univ; NY Univ. Collections Arranged: Etchings of Gunter Grass. Pos: Owner, Naiman Fine Arts & Tapestry Assocs, 70- Specialty: Represent Gunter Grass in US; specialize in collections for art programs, corporations, private collectors; division of Tapestry Associates represents fibre and fabric artists. Mailing Add: 300 Central Park W New York NY 10024

NAKAMURA, KAZUO
PAINTER
b Vancouver, BC, Oct 13, 26. Study: Cent Tech Sch, Toronto. Work: Nat Gallery Can, Ottawa; Art Gallery Ont, Toronto; Mus Mod Art, New York; Winnipeg Art Gallery; R McLaughlin Art Gallery, Oshawa. Comn: Two sculptures, Toronto Int Airport, 63; mural panel, Queen's Park Complex, Toronto. Exhib: 20th Biennial Int Watercolor, Brooklyn Mus, 59; 5th Int Hallmark Art Award Exhib, New York, 61; 2nd Bienniale Mus Art Mod, Paris, 61; Recent Acquisitions, Mus Mod Art, New York, 63; Can Artists 68, Art Gallery Ont, Toronto, 68. Awards: Prizewinner, 4th Int Exhib Drawings & Engravings, Lugano, Switz, 56. Bibliog: Andrew Bell (auth), The art of Nakamura, Can Art, 8/59; J M Careless (ed), The Canadians, Macmillan Co, Can, 67. Media: Oil, Watercolor. Dealer: Morris Gallery 15 Prince Arthur Ave Toronto Ont Can. Mailing Add: 3 Langmuir Crescent Toronto ON Can

NAKATANI, CARLOS
PAINTER, PRINTMAKER
b Mexico, Aug 20, 34. Study: Studied in mus in New York, 56, 69 & 71, France & Italy, 65; printmaking at San Carlos Sch, Mexico, 70; Italian Govt fel, Italy, 70. Exhib: Belles Artes, Mexico, 73 & 75; Biennial of Graphic Art, Yugoslavia, 75; Int Exhib of Graphic Art, Frechen, WGer, 76; Premio Int Biella per l'Incisione, 76; Christchurch Art Festival, New Zealand, 78. Awards: Salon Plastica Mexicana, Etching, Inst Nac Bellas Artes, 73 & Painting, 75. Style & Technique: Painting, printmaking and etching. Media: Watercolor, Oil. Dealer: Estela Saphiro Hamburgo 112 Mexico DF Mexico. Mailing Add: Retorno No 2-41 Av del Taller Mexico 8 DF Mexico

NAKAZATO, HITOSHI
PAINTER, PRINTMAKER
b Tokyo, Japan, Mar 3, 36. Study: Tama Col of Art, Tokyo, BFA(painting); Univ of Wis, MS(art, printmaking); Univ Pa, MFA, painting with Piero Dorazio. Work: Mus of Mod Art, New York; Philadelphia Mus of Art; Nat Mus of Mod Art, Kyoto, Japan; Pa Acad of Fine Arts, Philadelphia; Brooklyn Mus, New York. Comn: Mural, Furukawa Pavilion, Expo 70, Osaka, Japan, 70. Exhib: Artists in Americas, Nat Mus of Mod Art, Kyoto, 74; Art of Surface: A Survey of Contemporary Japanese Art, Art Gallery of New South Wales, Sydney, 74; Three Hundred Years of American Art, Philadelphia Mus, 76; Contemporary Japanese Painting, Japan Art Festival 10th Anniversary, Tokyo, 77; Prints in Series: Idea into Image, Brooklyn Mus, New York, 77. Teaching: Asst prof painting, Tama Col of Art, Tokyo, 68-71; asst prof printmaking, Grad Sch of Fine Arts, Univ of Pa, Philadelphia, 71- Awards: John D Rockefeller 3rd Grant, 66-67; Creative Artists Public Service Grant, 74-75. Bibliog: Joseph Love (auth), Tokyo Letter, Art Int, 3-12/71; Ruth Lehrer (auth), Three Hundred Years of American Art: Philadelphia, Philadelphia Mus, 76; Teruazu Suenage (auth), Art 78, Bijutsu Techo, 1/78. Mem: Am Color Print Soc. Style & Technique: Painting, drawing and prints. Mailing Add: 10 Bleecker St New York NY 10012

NAKIAN, REUBEN
SCULPTOR
b College Point, NY, Aug 10, 97. Study: Robert Henri Sch, with Homer Boss & A S Baylinson; Art Students League, 12; also with Paul Manship & Gaston Lachaise. Work: Mus Mod Art; New Sch Art Ctr. Comn: Sculpture, NY Univ, 60. Exhib: Whitney Mus Am Art; Art Inst Chicago; Pa Acad Fine Arts; one-man retrospective, Mus Mod Art, 66, The New American Painting & Sculpture, 69; 34th Venice Biennial, 68; plus others. Awards: Guggenheim Found Fel, 30; Ford Found Grant, 59; Prize, Sao Paulo, 60. Bibliog: Sam Hunter (ed), New Art Around the World: Painting and Sculpture, Abrams, 66; Frank O'Hara (auth), Nakian (catalog), Mus Mod Art, 66; Wayne Craven (auth), Sculpture in America, Crowell, 68; plus others. Mailing Add: 810 Bedford Stamford CT 06901

NALDER, NAN
PAINTER, DESIGNER
b Spokane, Wash, Dec 9, 38. Study: Wash State Univ, BFA(Hons). Work: Haseltine Collection of Northwestern Art; Univ Ore Mus Art, Eugene; Crocker Collection, Sacramento, Calif; US Bank Collection, Portland, Ore; Bank of Calif, Sacramento. Comn: Two large paintings, US Nat Bank, Medford, Ore, 68; painting, City Hall, Medford, 70. Exhib: Northwest Ann, 67; Portland Art Mus Ann, 67-71 & 73; Frye Mus Ann, 69; Tacoma Art Mus, 70; Portland Art Mus, 72. Awards: First Place, Edmonds Art Festival, Community of Edmonds, Wash, 63; First Place, Ore Competition of Painting, Rogue Valley Art Asn, 65; Frye Mus Award, Henry Rashin, 69. Mem: Advocates for Contemp Art; Am Inst Architect; Delta Phi Delta. Style & Technique: Abstract expressionist, with emphasis on color and light.

Media: Acrylic, Mixed Media. Dealer: Stephen Goodyear c/o Discovery Gallery Gausteo St Santa Fe NM 87501. Mailing Add: PO Box 72 Santa Fe NM 87501

NAMA, GEORGE ALLEN
PRINTMAKER, PAINTER
b Pittsburgh, Pa, Feb 23, 39. Study: Carnegie Mellon Univ, BFA & MFA; Atelier 17, Paris, with Stanley William Hayter. Work: Philadelphia Mus Art; Smithsonian Inst & Libr of Cong, Washington, DC; Brooklyn Mus; Butler Inst Am Art, Youngstown, Ohio. Exhib: Original Prints, Calif Palace of Legion of Honor, San Francisco, 64; Pratt Graphic Art Ctr Serigraph Exhib, 65; Northwest Printmakers Int Exhib, 65-67; Contemp Am Prints, Gt Brit, 69-71; US Info Agency Exhibs, Japan Expo, 70. Awards: David Berger Mem Prize, Mus Fine Arts, Boston, 67; Stuart M Egnal Prize, Philadelphia Print Club, 68; Stella Drabkin Mem Award, Am Color Print Soc, 71. Bibliog: Leonard Slatkes (auth), Printmakers on exhibit, Art Scene, 68; Richard Shelton (auth), Journal of return, Kayak, 69; S Hazo (auth), Poets & prints, Artist Proof Mag, 71. Mem: Soc Am Graphic Artists. Style & Technique: Surrealist, energy theme. Media: Intaglio, Collograph, Casting. Publ: Illusr, Longjaunes his periplus, Kayak, 68; illusr, Journal of return Kayak, 69; illusr, Twelve Poems with Twelve Prints, 70; illusr, Monuments, 71; illusr, Seascript, 71. Dealer: Assoc Am Artists 663 Fifth Ave New York NY 10022. Mailing Add: 4 W 22nd St New York NY 10010

NAMINGHA, DAN
PAINTER, SCULPTOR, PRINTMAKER
b Keams Canyon, Ariz, May 1, 50. Study: Univ of Kans, Lawrence; Inst of Am Indian Arts, Santa Fe, NMex, advan painting with Otellie Loloma; Am Acad of Art, Chicago. Work: US Dept of Interior, Indian Arts & Crafts Bd Collection, Washington, DC; Mus of Northern Ariz, Flagstaff; Mus of Am Indian Arts & Cult, Chicago; City of Scottsdale Fine Arts Collection, Ariz. Comn: Two lithographs, Gallery Wall, Inc, Phoenix, Ariz, 76; seven lithographs, comn by Glenn & Sandy Green, Phoenix, Ariz, 78. Exhib: Sculpture & Drawing Exhib, Univ of Kans, 67; Philbrook Art Ctr, Tulsa, Okla, 72; Heard Mus Indian Arts & Crafts Exhib, 72, 73 & 75 & Sculpture III, 76; Muckenthaler Mus, Fullerton, Calif, 73; Scottsdale Nat Indian Arts Exhib, 73 & 75; Orange Coast Col Gallery, Costa Mesa, Calif, 77; Albuquerque Mus Invitational, NMex, 77; one-man shows, Gallery Wall, Inc, 73-78, Mus of Northern Ariz, 76 & twelve solo exhib, Albuquerque Mus. Awards: Special Award for Acrylic Painting, 72 & First & Second Awards for Paintings, 73, Heard Mus Indian Arts & Crafts Exhib; Second Place in Painting, Philbrook Art Ctr, 73. Bibliog: Dr Harry Wood (auth), Namingha becoming major painter, 3/76 & Barbara Perlman (auth), Freedom is the lifeblood of his art, 7/77, Scottsdale Daily Progress; Elliott Almond (auth), He preserves Indian culture on canvas, Los Angeles Times, 11/77. Style & Technique: Abstract expressionist. Media: Acrylic Painting; Pastel; Bronze and Stone Sculpture; Lithography. Dealer: The Gallery Wall Inc 7122 N 7th St Phoenix AZ 85020. Mailing Add: PO Box 845 San Juan NM 87566

NAMUTH, HANS
PHOTOGRAPHER, FILM MAKER
b Essen, Ger, Mar 17, 15; US citizen. Work: Mus Mod Art & Metrop Mus Art, New York; Tulane Univ, New Orleans; Cleveland Mus Art, Ohio; Va Mus Fine Arts, Richmond; plus others. Exhib: US Pavilion, Brussels, Belg, 58; Jackson Pollock, Mus Mod Art, 67; New York Cult Ctr, 70; Philadelphia Col Art, Pa, 72; one-man show, Artists: USA, US Dept State. Pos: Founder & secy, Museum-at-Large, New York, 70- Awards: Citation in Recognition of Pub Serv, US Dept State, 58; Grand Prix de Bergamo, 58. Collection: Prints, drawings and lithographs by Rauschenberg, J Johns, Albers, Robert Indiana, Lee Bontecou, George Segal, Constantine Nivola, Richard Lindner, Robert Morris, Robert Motherwell and W de Kooning; paintings by de Kooning, Jackson Pollock, Josef Albers, Joseph Cornell, Mary Bauermeister, Kenzo Okada, Ludwig Sander and others. Publ: Co-auth (films), Jackson Pollock, 51, Willem de Kooning, 58, Homage to the Square (Josef Albers), 69, Brancusi at the Guggenheim, 70, Matisse at the Grand Palais, 71 & The Architect Louis Kahn, 72; auth, Fifty Two Artists (portfolio of photog), 73, co-auth, Eight American Masters, 74, Early American Tools, 75, The Voice and the Myth by Brian O'Doherty: Photographed by Hans Namuth, Random; auth, Calder's Universe, 77; auth, Jackson Pollock: Photographs and Essays, 78. Mailing Add: 157 W 54th St New York NY 10019

NARANJO, MICHAEL ALFRED
SCULPTOR, LECTURER
b Santa Fe, NMex, Aug 28, 44. Study: Wayland Col, Plainview, Tex; Highland Univ. Work: Heard Mus, Phoenix, Ariz; Mus of the Horse, Patagonia, Ariz. Exhib: Heard Mus Guild Indian Arts & Crafts Exhib, 73 & 74; Scottsdale Nat Indian Arts Exhib, 74; NMex Fine Arts Biennial, 75; Southwest Indian Arts & Crafts Fair, 75. Pos: Bd mem, NMex Arts Comn, 71-73. Awards: P Tarmigan Sage Co Grand Award, 74; Gov Award for Excellence in Sculpture, NMex Arts Comn, 75; First in Sculpture, Southwest Indian Arts & Crafts Fair, 75; plus others. Bibliog: To Help You Understand, Vet Admin Cent Off, 73; Mary Carol Nelson (auth), Michael Naranjo, Dillon Press, 75; Guy & Doris Monthan (auth), Art & Indian Individualists, Northland Press, 75. Style & Technique: Impressionistic-representational; figures and nature forms, cast in bronze by lost wax method. Media: Bronze. Mailing Add: PO Box 747 Espanola NM 87532

NARDIN, MARIO
SCULPTOR
b Venice, Italy, Mar 17, 40. Study: Acad Belle Arti, Venice, with Guido Manarin. Work: Hudson River Mus, Yonkers, NY; Fordham Univ; also in pvt collections. Exhib: One-man shows, Hudson River Mus, 67 & 72, Atelier Gallery, New York, 68, Fordham Univ, 69, Lesnick Gallery, 70, Sindin Galleries, 77 & Village Gallery at Gallimafry, Croton-on-Hudson, NY, 78; State Univ NY Col Plattsburgh, 71. Pos: Asst to Jacques Lipchitz, 64-71; asst mgr, Avent-Shaw Art Foundry, 64- Awards: New Rochelle Art Asn A rd, 67 Award, 67; Greenburgh Arts & Cult Comt Award, 71 & 72; Mamaroneck Artist Guild Award, 73. Bibliog: Noel Frankman (auth), Nardin at the Hudson River Museum, Arts Mag, 3/72; Louisa Kreisberg (auth), Young artist brings collection to museum & Nardin: sculpture in bronze, Rockland & Westchester Newspapers, 3-4/72; Successo a Nuova York di uno scultore Veneziano, Gazzetino Venice, 72. Mem: Am Soc Contemp Artists; Sculptors League; Yonkers Art Asn; Hudson River Mus; Artists Equity Asn. Style & Technique: Delineated shapes in highly polished bronze cast in the lost wax technique. Media: Bronze. Dealer: Sindin Galleries 1035 Madison Ave New York NY 10021. Mailing Add: 184 Warburton Ave Hastings-on-Hudson NY 10706

NARDONE, VINCENT JOSEPH
PAINTER
b South Orange, NJ, Oct 19, 37. Study: Montclair State Col, NJ, BA, 61; Univ Southern Calif, Los Angeles, MFA, 66; Paris Am Acad of Fine Arts, France, 78, with Genieve Secord, Joseph Domareki, Robert Wendell, Mildred Taylor, Paul Harris & Lillian Calcia. Work: Newark Mus, NJ; Newark Pub Libr, NJ; Rome Daily Am News, Italy; Essex Co Hall of Record, NJ; Raymond Duncan Mus, Paris, France. Comn: Western pastel mural (15ft x 30ft), Bonanza Restaurant Chain, Bloomfield, NJ, 68; wall inserted stone carving, Music & Art Corp, NJ, 70; original litho mag insert, NJ Music & Arts Mag, 72; relig watercolor painting, Christ the King Parish, Ploughe, Sardenia, 72. Exhib: Scripps Col, Claremont, Calif, 70; Jersey City Mus, NJ, 70; Columbian Found, Fairleigh Dickinson Univ, NJ, 74; Am Painters in Paris, France, 75; Int Art Festival, Paris, 76 & 77; Salon les Surindependents, Paris, 76-78; Salon of the 50 States, New York & Paris, 77; Whitney Counterweight, New York, 77-78; Ligoa Duncan Gallery, New York, NY, 78. Teaching: Art specialist K-6 art educ, Tuscan Sch, South Orange/Maplewood Sch Dist, NJ, 61-; instr painting adult sch, Maplewood, NJ, 66-70; adj instr art educ, Seton Hall Univ, South Orange, NJ, 68-74. Pos: Mem bd dirs, Art Guild of South Orange & Maplewood, NJ, 61-; illusr & art consult, NJ Music & Art Mag, Chatham, NJ, 69-73; co cult heritage comnr, Essex Co Cult-Heritage Comn, NJ, 71-73; art film previewer, Film News Mag, New York, 72-; theatrical set designer, Village Players, South Orange, 72- Awards: First Place/Graphics, South Orange Outdoor State/Nat Exhib, Art Guild of South Orange/Maplewood, 70 & 74 & Atlantic City Nat Art Show, CofC, Atlantic City, NJ, 71 & 72; NJ State Arts Coun grant, 73; Raymond Duncan Medal, Prix de Paris, France, 77. Bibliog: Robert Vrinat (auth), Peintres Americans (critique), Paris, 76; Rene Carvalho (auth), critique, La Revue Moderne des Arts, Paris, 76; Elinor Walker (auth), Maplewood artist gains international recognition, News Record of Maplewood & South Orange, 77. Mem: Les Surindependants Soc, Paris; Art Educators of NJ; Irvington Art Assoc of NJ; Nat Art Educ Asn; Art Guild of South Orange/Maplewood, NJ. Style & Technique: Painting and graphics. Media: Watercolor and Acrylics; Lithography, Serigraphy and Ink. Publ: Illusr (16 issues), NJ Music & Arts Mag, 70-73; auth, Panning for federal funds, 12/71 & auth & illusr, Graven images, 4/72, NJ Music & Arts Mag; auth, Georges Rouault, Film News Mag, 72; auth & illusr, Ecological Genesis (portfolio), Rubicon Graphics, 72. Dealer: Ligoa Duncan Gallery 22 E 72nd St New York NY 10021. Mailing Add: 75 Essex Ave Maplewood NJ

NAROTZKY, NORMAN DAVID
PAINTER, PRINTMAKER
b Brooklyn, NY, Mar 14, 28. Study: Brooklyn Col, BA(cum laude), with Ad Reinhardt & Alfred Russell; Art Students League, with Robert Ward Johnson & Howard Trafton; Cooper Union, dipl, with Morris Kantor, Charles Seide & Nicholas Marsicano; Atelier 17, Paris, with S W Hayter; Kunstakademie, Munich; NY Univ Inst Fine Arts; also with Moses Soyer. Work: James A Michener Found Collection, Univ Tex Art Mus, Austin; Philadelphia Mus Art; Mus Contemp Art, Madrid, Spain; Mills Col Art Gallery, Oakland, Calif; Mus Arte Contemporaneo, Villanueva y Geltru, Spain. Comn: Mural, Banco de Guipuzcoa, San Sebastian, 63; ltd ed lithograph, Collectors Guild Ltd, 69 & Fine Arts 260, 72 & 76. Exhib: Nat Gallery, Oslo, 55; Palais de Beaux Arts, Brussels, 61; 6th Bienal Sao Paulo, Brazil, 61; Recent Painting USA: The Figure, Mus Mod Art, 62 & others; Whitney Mus Am Art Ann, New York, 62; Arte Am y Espana, Madrid, Barcelona, Naples, Rome, Berne & Berlin, 63-64; Downey Mus Art, Calif, 67; San Francisco Mus Art, 68; Grosse Kunstler Ausstellung, Haus der Kunst, Munich, 71; Atelier 17 Retrospective, Elvehiem Art Ctr, Univ Wis, 77; plus 27 one-man shows. Teaching: Pvt studio, Cadaques, Spain, 59-69, Barcelona, 76- Pos: Staff, Collector's Guild Inc, 69-71 & Fine Arts 260, 71-; dir art gallery, Cadaques, 73. Awards: Wooley Found fel, Paris, 54-55; French Govt Fel, Paris, 55-56; Fulbright Fel, Ger, 57-58. Bibliog: M Molleda (auth), Narotzky, Ateneo, Madrid, 62; Meilach & Ten Hoor (auth), Collage & Assemblage, Crown Publ, 73; Knigin & Zimiles (auth), The Contemporary Lithographic Workshop Around the World, Van Nostrand Reinhold, 74. Mem: Art Students League; Cercle Artistic de Sant Lluch, Barcelona. Style & Technique: Symbolic figuration combining and superimposing various images from reality to create a new and significant expression. Media: Collage; Acrylic, Oil; Etching, Lithography. Publ: Auth, Spain: a disenchantment with materia, 9-10/65, Conversation with Cuixart, 3/66 & The Venice Biennale: pease porridge in the pot nine days old, 9-10/66, Arts Mag; auth, Ibiza—from art refuge to art center, Art Voices, fall 65; auth, Form & communication in my art work, Leonardo Mag, 7/69. Mailing Add: Corcega 198-6 Barcelona Spain

NARUS, MARTA MARIA MARGARETA
ART DEALER
b Stockholm, Sweden, Dec 8, 37. Study: Lyceum, Stockholm. Pos: Gallery dir, Merrill Chase Galleries, Ltd, Aurora, Ill, 76- Mailing Add: c/o Merrill Chase Galleries Ltd 1516 Fox Valley Mall Aurora IL 60505

NASH, KATHERINE E
SCULPTOR, EDUCATOR
b Minneapolis, Minn. Study: Univ Minn, BS; Minneapolis Sch Art; Univ NMex, computer graphics with Richard Williams; Doane Col, Hon DFA. Work: Walker Art Ctr, Minneapolis; US Arts & Humanities Coun, Washington, DC; Joslyn Art Mus, Omaha, Nebr; Nebr Art Asn, Univ Nebr, Lincoln; Univ Minn, Minneapolis. Comn: Welded steel, Wright Co Ct House Foyer, Buffalo, Minn, 60 & Student Union, Doane Col, 64; welded cooper, steel & brass, Epworth Church, Council Bluffs, Iowa, 66; welded copper & brass, Edina Village Coun, Edina Libr, Minn, 69; welded copper, Fed Land Bank, St Paul, Minn, 70. Exhib: Walker Art Ctr, 50-72; Joslyn Art Mus, 50-65; World's Fair, Brussels, 58; US Embassy Exhibs, 66-69; Nebr Centennial, 67. Teaching: Asst prof sculpture, Univ Nebr, Lincoln, 47-53; vis assoc prof sculpture, San Jose State Col, 61-62; prof sculpture/computer graphics, Univ Minn, 64-77; univ grant, 65-71. Awards: Minn State Arts Coun Artists Award, 69-70; McMillan Award Travel Grant, 69 & 72. Bibliog: Marcel Brion (auth), Art fantastique, Albin Michel, 61; Paul Vogt (auth), Stand plastiken aus stahl, Herausgeber & Verlag, 62; Reichardt (auth), The Computer in Art, Van Nostrand Reinhold, 71. Mem: Hon mem Artists Equity Asn (regional dir exec bd, 57-61); Mid-Am Col Art Asn (secy, 67-68); Sculptors Guild; Int Computer Arts Soc; Am Asn Univ Prof. Style & Technique: Oxy-acetylene and arc welding. Media: Cast metals-bronze. Interest: Computer-generated graphics. Dealer: Seligman Galleries 5 E 57th St New York NY 10022. Mailing Add: 21450 Excelsior Blvd Excelsior MN 55331

NASH, STEVEN ALAN
ART HISTORIAN, ART ADMINISTRATOR
b Wadsworth, Ohio, Apr 8, 44. Study: Darmouth Col, BA; Stanford Univ, Phd. Study: Adj prof, State Univ NY Buffalo, 73- Pos: Res cur, Albright-Knox Art Gallery, Buffalo, 73-77, chief cur, 77- Awards: Mabel McCloud Lewis Found Fel, 71; Fr Govt Res Grant, 71. Mem: Col Art Asn Am; Am Asn Mus. Res: Jacques-Louis David; Picasso. Mailing Add: 613 Ashland Ave Buffalo NY 14222

NASH, VERONICA F
ART DEALER, COLLECTOR
b Leonardtown, Md, Jan 3, 27. Study: Four yrs study with John Chapman Lewis, Arlington, Va. Pos: Owner, Prince Royal Gallery, Inc. Specialty: Contemporary, original works of art in oil, watercolor, enamel and prints and sculpture. Collection: Oils, watercolors and etchings of nationally and internationally known artists. Mailing Add: c/o Prince Royal Gallery Inc 204 S Royal St Alexandria VA 22314

NATHAN, HELMUTH MAX
EDUCATOR, PAINTER
b Hamburg, Ger, Oct 26, 01. Study: Univ of Freiburg; Univ of Hamburg, BS & MD; study with Prof Jansen, Friedlander, Buschor Cassirer & Grosz. Work: Jewish Mus, New York; Hunter Col, New York; Columbia Univ, New York; Princeton Univ, NJ; Tel Aviv Univ, Israel. Comn: Stained glass window depicting the stages of man from birth to death, Albert Einstein Col of Med, New York. Exhib: Shalom Aleichem House, Tel Aviv, Israel, 73; Israel Mus, Hazorea, 73; Acad of Med, 75; Ann Frank House, Amsterdam; Post Col Mus, Long Island; Am Physicians Art Asn, Metrop Mus of Art, New York, 76; one-man shows, C W Post Col, Brooksville, NY, 72, Acad of Med, 73 & Hunter Col, 73. Teaching: Prof hist of art & med, Albert Einstein Col of Med, 55-, prof emer & chmn. Awards: Many First Prizes, Am Physicians Art Asn; plus others. Bibliog: Bock Tubingen (auth), Professor Helmuth Nathan on his 70th birthday, 10/26/71; Sandra Knox (auth), The Surge] on as artist, NY Times, 6/3/73; Susan B Graves (auth), The Physician Pvt Practice, 10/75. Mem: Am Physicians Art Asn (pres, 72); New York Physicians Art Asn (past pres, 66); hon mem New York Soc of Med Illus. Style & Technique: Impressionistic. Media: Graphic Sculpture. Publ: Auth, The physician in the carricature, Art & Medicine, Anatomy & Art, Death & the physician in the history of art & physiognomic studies on dying, Art & Med J for Experimental Med. Mailing Add: 327 Central Pk W New York NY 10025

NATHANS, RHODA R
PHOTOGRAPHER
b Detroit, Mich, May 29, 40. Study: Wayne State Univ, BS; NY Univ Sch Continuing Educ, photog under Dr Roman Vishniac. Exhib: One-woman exhib, in collab with Save the Children Fedn, Community Church Gallery, New York, 69; group show, Neidrug Gallery, New York UN Woman's Yr, 74; one-woman exhibs, Avanti Gallery, New York, 74 & Nikon House, Rockefeller Ctr, New York, NY, 78; group exhib, Mus of City of New York, 74. Style & Technique: Portraits to record how life can somehow mushroom from seemingly simple beginnings into the most astonishing and complex carnival of individual personality; portraits to record the faces of man and woman, young and old, without contrivance, to distill from the rivers of the mind, some of the fragments that make a person what he is. Publ: Contribr, Print Mag, 9/75; contribr, Camera 35, 12/75. Dealer: Mrs Frances Wynshaw c/o Avanti Gallery 145 E 72nd St New York NY 10022 Mailing Add: 141 E 89th St New York NY 10028

NATKIN, ROBERT
PAINTER
b Chicago, Ill, Nov 7, 30. Study: Art Inst Chicago, BA, 52. Work: Guggenheim Mus, NY; Whitney Mus Am Art; Los Angeles Mus Art; Mus Mod Art, New York; Mus Fine Art, Houston; Carnegie Inst; Hartford Atheneum; plus others. Exhib: Young America, Whitney Mus Am Art, 60, Ann, 66 & 68; Carnegie Inst, 63; Int Biennale, Japan, 63; Mus Fine Arts, Houston, 63; retrospective, San Francisco Mus Art, 69; plus many others. Teaching: Ford Found artist in residence, Kalamazoo Inst Arts, formerly. Dealer: Andre Emmerich Gallery 41 E 57th St New York NY. Mailing Add: 924 West End Ave New York NY 10025

NATZLER, OTTO
CERAMIST, SCULPTOR
b Vienna, Austria, Jan 31, 08; US citizen. Work: Mus Mod Art & Metrop Mus Art, New York; Art Inst Chicago; Kunstgewerbemuseum, Zurich, Switz; Victoria & Albert Mus, London. Exhib: One-man exhibs, Art Inst Chicago, 63 & San Francisco Mus Art, 63; retrospective exhibs, Los Angeles Co Mus Art, 66, M H De Young Mem Mus, San Francisco 71 & Renwick Gallery, Smithsonian Inst, Washington, DC, 73. Bibliog: R Henderson (auth), Natzler ceramics, The Studio, 1/57; B Johnson (auth), A civilized expression in ceramics, Los Angeles Times, 6/12/66; E Penney (auth), The ceramic art of the Natzlers, Film Assocs, Los Angeles, 67. Style & Technique: Glazed ceramics, with emphasis on reduction-fired glazes; mobiles; various media. Publ: Co-auth, Gertrud & Otto Natzler, Retrospective Exhibition (catalog), 66 & auth, Gertrud & Otto Natzler Ceramics, Sperry Collection, 68, Los Angeles Mus Art; co-auth, The Ceramic Work of Gertrud & Otto Natzler (catalog), De Young Mem Mus, 71; co-auth, Form & Fire—Natzler Ceramics 1939-1972 (catalog), Renwick Gallery, Smithsonian Inst, 73. Mailing Add: 7837 Woodrow Wilson Dr Los Angeles CA 90046

NAUMAN, BRUCE
SCULPTOR
b Ft Wayne, Ind, Dec 6, 41. Study: Univ Wis, Madison, 60-64, BS, 64, study with Italo Scanga; Univ Calif, Davis, 65-66, MFA, 66, study with William Wiley, Robert Arneson, Frank Owen & Stephen Kaltenbach. Work: Whitney Mus, New York; Wallraf-Richartz-Mus, Cologne, Ger; Kunstverein, Aachen, Ger; St Louis Mus, Mo; Los Angeles Co Mus of Art, Calif. Exhib: William Geis, Bruce Nauman, San Francisco Art Inst, Calif, 66; Am Sculpture of the sixties, Los Angeles Co Mus of Art, Calif, 67; Documenta IV, Kassel, 68; When Attitudes Become Form, Kunsthalle, Berne, Switz (toured Europe), 69; Kompass IV, Van Abbermuseum, Eindohoven, Netherlands, 69; Corcoran Gallery of Art, Washington, DC, 69; Anti-Illusion: Procedures/Materials, Whitney Mus of Art, New York, 69; Soloman R Guggenheim Mus, New York, 69; Holograms & Lasers, Mus of Contemp Art, Chicago, 70; Conceptual Art & Conceptual Aspects, New York Cultural Ctr, 70; Am Art Since 1960, Princeton Univ, New Jersey, 70; Information, Mus of Mod Art, New York, 71; Diagrams & Drawings, Rijksmuseum Kroller-Mueller, 72; USA West Coast, Kunstverein, Hamburg, Ger, 72; Documenta V, Kassel, Ger, 72; Gilder, Objedte, Filme, Konzepte, Stadische Galerie, Munich, 73; Art & Image in Recent Art, Art Inst, Chicago, 74; one-man shows, Sacramento State Col, Calif, 68; Los Angeles Co Mus of Art (retrospective, toured USA & Europe), Calif, 72 & Univ Calif, Irvine, 73, Stadtische Kunsthalle (retrospective), Dusseldorf, Ger. Teaching: Instr, San Francisco Art Inst, 66-68; instr sculpture, Univ Calif, Irvine, 70. Awards: Nat Endowment Grant, Washington, DC, 68; Aspen Inst for Humanistic Studies Grant, Colo, 70. Bibliog: Robert Pincus-Witten (auth), Bruce Nauman: Another Kind of Reasoning, Artforum, New York, 2/72; Jurgen Harten (auth), T for Technics, B for Body, Art & Artists, London, 11/73; J Minton (auth), Bruce Nauman: Gunslinger, Artweek, Oakland, Calif, 6/74. Publ: Auth, Pictures of Sculptures in a Room, Davis, Calif, 66; auth, Clear Sky, San Francisco, 68; auth, Bruning Small Fires, San Francisco, 68; auth, LA Air, Los Angeles, 70; auth, Body Works, Interfunktionen, Cologne, Ger, 9/71. Mailing Add: c/o Leo Castelli Gallery 4 E 77th St New York NY 10021

NAUMER, HELMUTH
PAINTER
b Ger, Sept 1, 07; US citizen. Study: Frank Wiggins Art Sch; Otis Art Inst, Los Angeles. Work: NMex State Art Mus; Bandelier Nat Monument; Univ Wyo; Univ NMex; Mus Sci & Hist, Ft Worth, Tex; plus many others in US & Venezuela, Guatemala, Mex, Can, Africa, Australia & Europe. Exhib: Am Asn Mus & Can Mus Asn Meeting, Toronto, 67. Bibliog: Articles in Am Ger Rev, NMex Mag & El Palacio. Style & Technique: Representational, historical, ethnic landscapes. Media: Oil, Pastel, Watercolor. Mailing Add: Rancho de San Sebastian Rte 3 Santa Fe NM 87501

NAVAS, ELIZABETH S
COLLECTOR, PATRON
b Coffeyville, Kans, June 29, 95. Study: Teachers Col, Columbia Univ; spec art study. Pos: Trustee, Louise C Murdock Estate, 15-; adminr, Roland P Murdock Collection, Wichita Art Mus, 39- Awards: Resolution of Honor & Commendation for Outstanding Cult Contrib & Serv to Wichita Art Mus & City & Citizens of Wichita in Compiling Roland P Murdock Collection at Wichita Art Mus, City of Wichita, 65. Mem: Life mem Am Fedn Arts (hon trustee & var offices); Munic Art Soc; Metrop Mus Art; Natural Hist Mus; Nat Coun Women. Publ: Auth, Louise C Murdock, In: Notable American Women 1607-1950, Harvard Univ, 71. Mailing Add: 250 E 63rd St New York NY 10021

NAVRAT, DEN (DENNIS EDWARD NAVRAT)
PRINTMAKER, EDUCATOR
b Marion, Kans, May 15, 42. Study: Kans State Univ, Manhattan, BA, 64; Wichita State Univ, Kans, MFA, 66; Univ Iowa, Iowa City, 69, with Virginia Myers; Photographer's Place, Derbyshire, Eng, 77, with Paul Hill & Ralph Gibson. Work: Mus of Fine Art, Houston, Tex; Atkinson Art Gallery, Metrop Bur of Sefton, Eng; Plains Art Mus, Moorhead, Minn; Univ Iowa Gallery, Iowa City. Comn: Sexist serigraph series, NDak Coun on the Arts & Humanities, Fargo, 74; logo & posters, NDak Comt of the Humanities & Pub Issues, Bismarck, 74-75; serigraph, Second Crossing Gallery, Valley City, NDak, 75; photoserigraph/workshop, Dept of Art, Univ NDak, Grand Forks, 76. Exhib: Sixteenth Mid-Am, Nelson Gallery & Adkins Mus, Kansas City, Mo, 66; Eight Nat Prints & Drawings, Okla Art Ctr, Oklahoma City, 66; 35th & 45th Ann Exhib, Springfield Art Mus, Mo, 66 & 75; Potsdam Prints, St Univ NY Col, Potsdam, 74; Manisphere 11th Int, Red River Art Ctr, Moorhead, Minn & Winnipeg Art Gallery, Man, Can, 74; two-person shows, Southport Arts Ctr, Eng, 77 & Lantern Gallery, Manchester, Eng, 77. Collections Arranged: Biennial National Exhibition of Prints & Drawings, 67, 69 & 71 & 4th & 5th Biennial International Matmedia Exhibition, (illusr, catalogue), 73 & 75, Dickinson St Col, NDak. Teaching: Instr enamel & metal, Inst of Logopedics, Wichita, Kans, 65-66; from instr to asst prof art, Dickinson State col, 66-71, assoc prof art & chmn art dept, 71-, Fulbright-Hays Exchange prof art, Southport Col of Art, Eng, 76-77. Awards: Purchase Award, 11th Biennial of Regional Art, Friends of Art, Kans State Univ, Manhattan, 70; Medal Award & Purchase Award, 17th Ann Exhib of Midwest Artists, Rourke Gallery, Moorhead, Minn, 76; Cash Award & Reproduction, Calendar Competition, Northwestern Bell Tel Co, Omaha, Nebr, 73. Bibliog: Article in La Revue Mod, Paris, 12/67; reproduction in NDak Horizons, Winter 1973. Mem: Mid-Am Col Art Asn; Graphic Soc; NDak Coun on the Arts & Humanities (Gov's appointee, 71-80). Style & Technique: Figurative design and landscapes in silkscreen and oil painting; photoserigraphs with split fountains; colorist. Media: Serigraphy and oil painting. Mailing Add: 258 E 12th St Dickinson ND 58601

NAVRATIL, AMY R
ART LIBRARIAN
b Mich, Sept 19, 50. Study: Wayne State Univ, 68-72, BA(art hist); Univ Mich, 72-73, AMLS, specializing in art librarianship. Pos: Librn, Norton Simon Mus, Pasadena, Calif, 74-; ed, Art Librs Soc of NAm Directory of Members, 75-77; contribr of articles in Art Libr Soc NAm Newsletter, 75-77. Mem: Art Libr Soc NAm (mem chmn, 75-77). Mailing Add: 1834 Seventh Ave Arcadia CA 91006

NAWROCKI, THOMAS DENNIS
PRINTMAKER, EDUCATOR
b Milwaukee, Wis, June 26, 42. Study: Univ Wis-Milwaukee, BFA, 64, MA, 66, MFA, 67. Work: Univ Wis-Madison; Northern Ill Univ; San Diego State Col; Philadelphia Mus Art; Miss Art Asn, Jackson. Exhib: Po tsdam Prints, State Univ NY Col Potsdam, 66-67, 69 & 74; Seattle Int Print Exhib, Seattle Art Mus, 68 & 71; Soc Am Graphic Artists, New York, 69; Colorprint USA, Tex Tech Univ, 69, 71 & 73; Hawaii Nat Print Exhib, Honolulu Acad Arts, 73; plus many others. Teaching: Instr printmaking, Southwest Tex State Univ, 67-70; asst prof printmaking, Miss Univ Women, 70- Awards: Wisconsin Designers & Craftsmen Exhibition Award, Milwaukee Art Ctr, 66-69; Nat Print Competition Award, Soc Am Graphics Artists, 69; Dixie Annual Print Competition Award, Montgomery Mus Art, 74; plus others. Bibliog: Artist's Proof-A Journal of Printmaking, Pratt Graphic Art Ctr, New York, 67. Mem: Graphics Soc, Hollis, NH. Style & Technique: Pure design compositions in a relief print color-blend technique. Media: Printmaking, Textiles. Mailing Add: 112 Shane St Columbus MS 39701

NAY, MARY SPENCER
PAINTER, EDUCATOR
b Crestwood, Ky, May 13, 13. Study: Art Ctr Asn Sch, Louisville, Ky, 34-40; Cincinnati Art Acad, 41; Univ Louisville, BA, 41; Art Students League, 42; with Boris Margo, Provincetown, Mass, 50-51; Univ Louisville, MA, 60. Work: Speed Art Mus, Louisville; Evansville Mus Arts & Sci, Ind; Ky Wesleyan Col, Owensboro; Univ Louisville; Ohio Univ, Athens. Comn: Mural for children's room, Louisville Pub Libr, Fed Art Proj, 34. Exhib: IBM Exhib, New York World's Fair, 40; Artists for Victory, Metrop Mus Art, 41; Contemp Color Lithography Int Biennials, 50, 52 & 54; 60th Ann Am Exhib, Art Inst Chicago, 51; Terry Nat Exhib, Miami, Fla, 52. Teaching: Instr painting & printmaking, Art Ctr Asn Sch, 40-59, dir, 44-49; prof art educ & painting, Univ Louisville, 59-71, distinguished prof art educ, 71-, Marcia S Hite prof painting, 75- Pos: Supvr, Puppet Proj, Nat Youth Admin, 37-39. Awards: Ashland Oil Co Purchase Awards, Art Ctr Asn Regsonal, 45, 50 & 58; Evansville Mus Purchase Awards, Tri-State Ann, 52, 56 & 58; Ky State Fair Bd Purchase Awards, 54, 56 & 58. Mem: Ky Arts & Crafts Guild (bd dirs, 67-70); Art Ctr Asn (libr & bd dirs, 71-72); J B Speed Art Mus; Provincetown Art Asn; Ky Art Educ Asn. Style & Technique: Semi-abstract expressionism with emphasis on organic structure using mixed media. Mailing Add: 207 S Galt Ave Louisville KY 40206

NAYLOR, ALICE STEPHENSON
PAINTER
b Columbus, Tex. Study: Univ NMex; San Antonio Art Inst, with Andrew Dasburg, Leonard Brooks, Charles Rosen, Xavier Gonzalez, Millard Sheets & Dong Kingman. Work: Beaumont Art Mus, Tex; San Antonio Art League Mus, Hemisfair; Columbus Art Mus. Exhib: Critics Choice, Cincinnati Art Mus; Libr Cong Print Show, 47; Tex Fine Arts Asn Exhibs, Laguna Gloria, Austin; Tex Watercolor Soc Exhibs, 50-72; Corpus Christi Art Mus, Tex. Teaching: Instr painting & lithography, San Antonio Art Inst, 42-58; head dept art, Incarnate Word Col, 58-64. Awards: Witte Mem Mus Award for Spring Motif, 50; Award, Beaumont Art Mus, 58; Tex Watercolor Soc Award for Nosegay, McNay Mus, 72. Mem: San Antonio Art League; Tex Fine Arts Asn (past vpres); Contemp Artists Group (past pres); San Antonio Craft Guild (past pres); Hill Country Arts Found (mem bd). Media: Acrylic, Watercolor. Publ: Illusr, D'Hanes, 61; illusr, San Pedro Springs Park, 67. Dealer: Shook-Carrington Gallery 6700 N New Braunfels San Antonio TX 78209. Mailing Add: 125 Magnolia Dr San Antonio TX 78712

NAYLOR, JOHN GEOFFREY
SCULPTOR, EDUCATOR
b Morecambe, Eng, Aug 28, 28; US citizen. Study: Leeds Col Art, nat dipl design; Hornsey Col Art, ATD; Univ Ill, MFA. Comn: Smithsonian Inst; Chase Manhattan Bank, New York; Gen Sci Admin Comn; water sculpture, Univ Fla, Gainesville; Pub Libr, Chattanooga, Tenn; Jacobs, Viscoesi & Jacobs, Winston-Salem, NC. Exhib: Gallery Contemp Art, Winston-Salem, NC, 74; Hirshhorn Mus, Washington, DC, 77. Teaching: Instr drawing, Fla Southern Col, 67-69; assoc prof sculpture, Univ Fla, 69- Pos: Cur, Ft Wayne Art Mus, Ind, 65-66. Awards: Fulbright Travel Grant, 54; Nat Found Arts Award, 67. Style & Technique: Fabricated sheet metal. Media: Aluminum, stainless steel. Dealer: Art Sources Lobby Universal Marion Bldg Church St Jacksonville FL 32202. Mailing Add: 104 NW Seventh St Gainesville FL 32601

NAZARENKO, BONNIE COE
PAINTER
b San Jose, Calif, Oct 26, 33. Study: San Jose State Col; Carmel Art Inst, under John Cunningham. Work: Mint Mus, Charlotte, NC. Exhib: Gallery Contemp Art, Winston-Salem, NC, 70; Am Artists Prof League, New York, 72; Soc Animal Artists, Grand Cent Art Gallery, New York, 72, 74 & 75. Awards: Beaufort Art Festival Award, SC, 66; Mint Mus Purchase Award, 68. Mem: Soc Animal Artists; Am Artists Prof League. Style & Technique: Impressionistic, recognizable subject matter. Media: Oil. Dealer: Anne Metcalf 3937 W Kennedy Blvd Tampa FL 33609. Mailing Add: 8314 Pocahontas St Tampa FL 33615

NEAL, (MINOR) AVON
WRITER, PRINTMAKER
b Indiana, July 16, 22. Study: Long Beach Col; Escuela Bellas Artes, Mex, MFA, with Siquieros. Work: Metrop Mus Art, New York; Libr of Cong & Smithsonian Inst, Washington, DC; Abby Aldrich Rockefeller Mus Am Folk Art, Williamsburg, Va; Winterthur Mus, Wilmington, Del. Comn: 500 original rubbings, 70, 250 original rubbings, 71 & ed 350 original rubbings, 74, Am Heritage; ed 100 original rubbings, 70 & ed 70 original rubbings, 74, for Arton Assocs (all with Ann Parker); ed 100 original rubbings, Mead Art Gallery, Amherst Col, 76. Exhib: One-man & two-man shows, New Eng Gravestone Rubbings, Am Embassy, London, 65, Know Ye The Hour, Hallmark Gallery, New York, 68, Amon Carter Mus, Ft Worth, Tex, 68 & 71, Ephemeral Image, Mus Am Folk Art, 70 & Mus Fine Arts, Springfield, Mass, 72; New Eng Gravestone Rubbings, Mead Art Gallery, 76; Gravestone Art, William Benton Mus Art, Univ Conn, 76; Molas, Art of the Cuna Indians, Alternative Ctr for Int Arts, New York, 76. Pos: Mem adv bd, Mus Am Folk Art, 68-71. Awards: Ford Found Grants, 62-63 & 63-64. Bibliog: M J Gladstone (auth), New art from early American sculpture, Collector's Quart Report, 63 & Pedestrian art, Art in Am, 4/64; Stephen Chodorov (auth), Know Ye the Hour, Camera Three, CBS-TV, 11/68. Style & Technique: Developing the ancient Oriental art of ink rubbing into a contemporary print technique. Interest: Stone rubbing and folk art. Publ: Auth, Itinerant Photographers of Guatemala, Smithsonian Inst, 75; contribr, Fritz Eichenberg, auth, Art of the Print, Abrams, 76; contribr, Ruth Andrews, ed, How to Know American Folk Art, Dutton, 77; co-auth, Molas, Folk Art of the Cunas Indians, Barre, 77; auth, Pigs & Eagles, Ginseng Press, ltd ed, 78. Dealer: Gallery of Graphic Arts 1603 York Ave New York NY 10028. Mailing Add: Thistle Hill North Brookfield MA 01535

NEAL, REGINALD H
PAINTER, EDUCATOR
b Leicester, Eng, May 20, 09. Study: Yale Univ, 29-30; Bradley Univ, BA, 32; State Univ Iowa, summer 36; Univ Chicago, MA, 39; Colorado Springs Fine Arts Ctr, summer 41. Work: Libr Cong; Mus Mod Art; Queen's Col, Kingston, Ont; Brigham Young Univ; Brooks Mem Gallery; plus many others. Comn: Two ed lithographs, AAA Gallery, New York. Exhib: Metrop Mus Art, 52; Cincinnati Mus Asn, 54; Mus Mod Art, 65; Des Moines Art Ctr, 66; NJ State Mus, 67; plus many other group & one-man shows. Teaching: Lectr, Asn Am Cols, 53 & 54; Univ Miss; instr, Southern Ill Univ, 58-59, 66 & 67; prof art, Douglass Col, Rutgers Univ, New Brunswick, 59-; instr, Yale Univ, 66. Awards: Golden Reel Award, Film Coun Am, 56. Bibliog: Albert Reese (auth), American prize prints of the 20th century, Am Artists Group, 49; Oto Bihalji-Merin (auth), Adventures of Modern Art, Abrams, 66. Mem: Col Art Asn Am. Dealer: A M Sachs Gallery 29 W 57th St New York NY 10019. Mailing Add: Circle Dr RD 1 Lebanon NJ 08833

NEALS, OTTO
PAINTER, SCULPTOR
b Lake City, SC, Dec 11, 30. Study: Basically self-taught, studied briefly at Brooklyn Mus Art Sch with Isaac Soyer; Printmaking Workshop, studied with Bob Blackburn, Robert DeLamonica & Krishna Reddy. Work: Ghana Nat Mus, Accra; NY State Harlem Off Bldg, New York; New York Health & Hospitals Corp; Prime Minister Forbes Burnham, Guyana Statehouse. Comn: Portrait of Eric Gairy (Prime Minister of Grenada), comn by Michael Caesar (Grenada's ambassador to the UN), 69; Portrait of Jackie Robinson, comn by Jackie Robinson Sch PTA, Brooklyn, 77. Exhib: Resurrection, Studio Mus, NY, 71; Millenium, Philadelphia Mus of Art, Pa, 73; Selections 73, 74, Brooklyn Mus, 74; Children of Africa, Am Mus of Nat Hist, New York, 74; 14 Black Artists, Pratt Inst Gallery, Brooklyn, 76; Colorprint USA, Tex Tech Univ, Lubbock, 75; Migrations, Museo De Arte Moderno, Cali, Colombia, S Am, 76 & Caraeas, Venezuela, 77. Bibliog: Peter Bailey (auth), Ten Black artists depict Christ, Ebony Mag, 4/71; Diane Weathers (auth), Black artists taking care of business, New York Times, 8/19/73; Elton Fax (auth), Black Artists of the New Generation, Dodd/Mead & Co, 77. Mem: Nat Conf of Artists; New York Arts Consortium (WEUSI Artists). Style & Technique: Basically representational painting, some stylization in printmaking and sculptured works. Media: Oil, Acrylic, Pastels; Sculpturing in Wood or Stone. Publ: Contribr, Ghala Mag, African J, 70; illusr, African Heritage Cookbook, MacMillian Publ, 71; illusr, The Adventures of Tony, David & Marc, Exposition Press, 76. Dealer: c/o Lawrence Dorsey Dorsey's Gallery 553 Rogers Ave Brooklyn NY 11225. Mailing Add: 138 Sullivan Pl Brooklyn NY 11225

NECHIS, BARBARA (FRIEDMAN)
PAINTER
b Mt Vernon, NY. Study: Univ Rochester, BA, 58; Alfred Univ, MS, 59. Work: CBS Records, Milford, Conn; Banco de Crefisul, Sao Paulo, Brazil; Citicorp, New York. Exhib: Ann Watercolor Exhib, Nat Arts Club, New York, 70-77; Am Watercolor Soc Exhib, Nat Acad Design, New York, 70, 73 & 75, 76 & 77; Hudson River Mus, 72; Audubon Artists Exhib, 75 & 77; Int Competitive Exhib Painting & Sculpture, Allied Artists, 76; Mainstreams, Marietta Col, Ohio, 77. Teaching: Artist in residence, New Rochelle Sch Syst, 74; instr watercolor, Ctr Continuing Educ, Mamaroneck, NY, 74- Pos: Juror & guest demonstr, League Am Pen Women, 72 & Nat Asn Women Artists, Nat Acad of Design, Design, 76; guest speaker, Westchester Art Forum, WVOX, WVIP Radio, 74-75; mem exec bd visual art, Coun Arts in Westchester, 75. Awards: Ann Traveling Exhib, Am Watercolor Soc, 70, 73, 75 & 76; Atkin Mem Award for Watercolor, Nat Asn Women Artists, 72 & Gene Alden Walker Prize for Painting, 75; Third Prize, Nat Arts Club Ann Watercolor Exhib, 77. Mem: Nat Asn Women Artists (mem watercolor jury, 75-77); Mamaroneck Artists Guild (pres, 72-74); Artists Equity (bd mem, 77-). Style & Technique: Subjective imagery in watercolor. Media: Watercolor. Publ: Illusr, American Artists Group Reproduction, 73. Mailing Add: 100 Kingsbury Rd New Rochelle NY 10804

NEDDEAU, DONALD FREDERICK PRICE
PAINTER, DESIGNER
b Toronto, Ont, Jan 28, 13. Study: Ont Col Art; also with J W Beatty, Franklin Carmichael & Archibald Barnes. Exhib: 11 shows, Royal Can Acad, 36-61; 20 shows, 42-65 & traveling exhibs, 44-48 & 51-65, Ont Soc Artists; group shows, 43 & 48-65 & traveling exhibs, 49-65, Can Soc Painters in Watercolor; Can Soc Painters in Water Colour & Calif Watercolor Exhib, 50-75; Can Group Painters, 55, 56, 58 & 61; plus others. Teaching: Head dept art & prin art summer sch, Cent Tech Sch, Toronto, Ont, 48- Awards: Scholar, 36 & Rous & Mann Award, 36, Ont Col Art. Mem: Ont Soc Artists; Can Soc Painters in Water Colour (past pres); Can Guild Potters; Arts & Lett Club, Toronto; Royal Can Acad of Arts; fel Int Inst Arts & Lett; plus others. Mailing Add: 21 Sherwood Ave Toronto ON M4G 2A6 Can

NEEL, ALICE
PAINTER
b Merion Square, Pa, Jan 28, 00. Study: Philadelphia Sch Design for Women, 21-25; Moore Col Art, hon Dr, 71. Work: Mus Mod Art & Whitney Mus Am Art, New York; Robert Mayer Collection, Winetka; Dillard Inst, New Orleans, La; Graham Gallery, New York. Exhib: Retrospectives, Moore Col Art, 71 & Whitney Mus Art, 74. Teaching: Lectr painting sem, Univ Pa Grad Sch, 71-72; lectr, Skowhegan Sch Painting & Sculpture, summer 72. Pos: Easel painter, Fed Works Agency, 35-42. Awards: Longview Found Award, 62; Am Acad Arts & Lett Award, 69; Benjamin Altman Figure Prize, Nat Acad Design, 71. Bibliog: H Crehan (auth), Introducing the portraits of Alice Neel, 10/62 & Ted Berrigan (auth), Double portraits, 1/66, Art News; Jack Kroll (auth), Curator of souls, Newsweek, 1/31/66. Mem: Artists Equity Asn. Media: Oil. Dealer: Graham Gallery 1014 Madison Ave New York NY 10021. Mailing Add: 300 W 107th St Apt 3A New York NY 10025

NEFF, EDITH
PAINTER, INSTRUCTOR
b Philadelphia, Pa, Aug 27, 43. Study: Philadelphia Col Art, BFA, 65. Work: Philadelphia Mus of Art; Pa Acad of Fine Arts; Minn Mus of Art, St Paul; Washington & Jefferson Col; Westminster Col, New Willmington, Pa. Comn: Lobby mural (7ft x 30ft), Univ City Sci Ctr, Philadelphia, 74. Exhib: Mid-Yr Show, Butler Inst Am Art, Youngstown, Ohio, 75; In Praise of Space, traveling exhib, Westminster Col & Parsons Sch of Design, 76; Am Figure Drawing, traveling exhib, US & Australia, 76; Am Family Portraits, Philadelphia Mus of Art, 76; Contemp Reflections, Aldrich Mus Contemp Art, Ridgefield, Conn, 76; Women's Work: Contemp Issues on Paper, traveling exhib, Los Angeles, Salt Lake City & Houston, 77; one-woman shows, Peale House Galleries, Pa Acad of Fine Arts, Philadelphia, 77 & Ariz State Univ, Tempe, 78; plus others. Teaching: Lectr painting, Philadelphia Col of Art, 71- Awards: Friends of Exhib Purchase, 73; Earth Art, Purchase Prize, Drawings USA, Minn Mus of Art, 73; Mus Purchase Prize, Cheltenham Award Show, painting donated to Philadelphia Mus of Art, 74. Bibliog: Barbara Whipple (auth), Edith Neff: Nostalgic New Realist, Am Artist, 1/74; Edith Neff, a portfolio, Painted Bride Quart, Summer 77. Style & Technique: Figurative, mainly figures in a landscape. Media: Oil, pastel. Mailing Add: 730 Kater St Philadelphia PA 10147

NEFF, JOHN A
PAINTER, DESIGNER
b Lebanon, Pa, May 5, 26. Study: Whitney Sch Art, New Haven, Conn, cert; Paier Sch Art, Hamden, Conn, with Herbert Gute. Work: New Brit Mus Am Art, Gtr Hartford Arts Coun & Mus Art, Sci & Indust, Bridgeport, Conn; Mus Fine Arts, Springfield, Mass; First Nat Bank Boston. Exhib: Landscape I, De Cordova Mus, Lincoln, Mass, 70 & New Eng in Winter, 78; Am Watercolor Soc, New York, 75; Watercolor USA, Springfield, Mo, 75; Allied Artists, New York, 77; Hudson Valley Nat Exhib, White Plains, NY, 77. Pos: Sr graphic designer, Muirson Label Co, North Haven, Conn, 50-71; owner, Crossmark Assocs, Wallingford, Conn, 72. Awards: Watercolor Award, Hudson Valley Art Asn, 66; Watercolor Award, Silvermine NE Exhib, 76; Salmagundi Club Award, New York, 77; Wm Church Osborne Award, Am Watercolor Soc, 75. Bibliog: T F Potter (auth), A proxy visit, Meriden Rec-J, Conn, 69. Mem: Am Watercolor Soc; Allied Artists Am; Salmagundi Club; Silvermine Artists Guild; Conn Watercolor Soc (bd dirs, 71-72). Style & Technique: Contemporary. Media: Transparent watercolor. Mailing Add: 17 Parkview Rd Wallingford CT 06492

NEGRI, ROCCO ANTONIO
ILLUSTRATOR, PAINTER
b Reggio Calabria, Italy, June 26, 32; US citizen. Study: Aurel Kessler Acad, Arg, BsAs; Art Students League; Sch of Visual Arts, New York; Pratt Graphic Ctr, New York. Work: Univ Minn, Minneapolis; Cedar Rapids Pub Libr, Iowa; Univ Tokyo, Japan; Fed Home Loan Bank, New York; Albert Einstein Sch, Bronx, NY. Exhib: Painter's Mill Gallery, Rochester, NY, 74; one-man shows, Ratafia Gallery, Ft Lauderdale, Fla, 75 & Mainstream Gallery, Westhampton, NY, 75; Studio Gallery, Greenport, NY, 76; Reece Galleries Inc, New York, 76. Awards: Sixth Place, WSOAE, Kiwanis Club, 72; Excellence Award, Long Beach Art Asn, NY, 74; Merit Award, Coconut Grove Merchants Asn, Miami, Fla, 76. Bibliog: A critic's choice of the year's best, New York Times, 12/70; June Dixon (auth), Fantasy of a better place, Chattanooga Times, 6/69; Picture books, Hornbook, 2/71. Style & Technique: Multicolor woodcuts, etchings, collages and pen drawings. Publ: Illusr, Journey Outside, 69 & Fee, Fi, Fo, Fum, 69, Viking; illusr, The One Bad Thing About Father, Harper & Row, 70; illusr, The Magic Pumpkin, Four Winds, 71; illusr, The Son of the Leopard, Crown, 74. Dealer: Reece Galleries Inc 39 W 32nd St New York NY 10001. Mailing Add: 1668 Norman St Ridgewood NY 11227

NEHER, FRED
CARTOONIST
b Nappanee, Ind, Sept 29, 03. Study: Chicago Acad Fine Arts. Work: Syracuse Univ; Butler Inst Am Art; Albright Col, Reading, Pa. Exhib: Humor Festival, World Cartoon Exhib, Knokke, Heist, Belg, 70 & 71. Teaching: Instr cartooning, Univ Colo, Boulder, 64- Pos: Cartoonist, Life's Like That, 34- Mem: Nat Cartoonist Soc; Soc Illusr. Publ: Auth, Will-yum, Hi-teens & Some punkins. Mailing Add: One Neher Lane Boulder CO 80302

NEIDHARDT, CARL RICHARD
ART ADMINISTRATOR, PAINTER
b Chattanooga, Tenn, May 4, 21. Study: Ga Sch of Tech, 39-41; Univ of Tenn, Chattanooge, 47-49, BA; Univ of Fla, 51-52, MFA; Rijksacademie, Amsterdam, Netherlands, 53-54; Ohio State Univ, 58-59, PhD, 61. Exhib: Ann & Biennial Exhibs, Delgado Mus, New Orleans, 57, 63, 64; 49th Ann Exhib, Columbus Gallery of Fine Arts, Ohio, 59; Fifty Florida Artists,

Ringling Mus, Sarasota, 60; Artist Teachers in Southeastern Univs, Jacksonville Mus, 60; Ark Art Ctr Mus, Little Rock, 61-63 & 69; Dallas Mus of Fine Arts, Tex, 63; Okla Art Ctr Mus, Oklahoma City, 64-69. Pos: Chmn dept of art, Hardin-Simmons Univ, Abilene, Tex, 60-65, dir dept of art, Angelo State Univ, San Angelo, Tex, 64-66; chmn dept of art, Austin Col, Sherman, Tex, 66- Awards: Fulbright Award to Netherlands, US Govt, 53-54; Danforth Grant (for research in painting), Danforth Foundation, 58-59. Mem: Col Art Assoc of Am; Tex Assoc of Schs of Art. Style & Technique: Geometric abstraction/pure color. Media: Acrylic on Canvas. Dealer: Red River & Co Sherman TX 75090. Mailing Add: 321 N Grand Ave Sherman TX 75090

NEIJNA, BARBARA
SCULPTOR
b Philadelphia, Pa, Sept 24, 37. Study: Philadelphia Mus Sch of Art; Syracuse Univ, BFA; Acad di Belli Arte di Brera, Italy; spec study with Marino Marini. Work: Lowe Art Gallery, Syracuse Univ, NY; Ft Lauderdale Mus of Art, Fla; Miami Mus of Mod Art, Fla; Freedom Fed Banks, Tampa, Fla; Omni Int, Miami, Fla. Comn: Ceramic facade (22ft x 40ft), City Hall of Hialeah, Fla, 69; Concrete Sculpture (5ft x 7ft), Ryder Complex, Miami, 72; Aluminum Environmental Sculpture (40ft x 20ft), Govt Ctr, City of Miami Beach, Fla, 76; Steel & Lacquer Sculpture (12ft), Palm Spring Recreation Ctr, Dade Co, 76; Steel & Polyurethan 26-ft Sculpture, Tampa-Hillsbarough Libr, Tampa, Fla, 77. Exhib: Miami 33, Metrop Mus & Art Ctr, Fla, 71; Bal du Mus, Ft Lauderdale Mus, 74; Pan Am Art Exhib, Consular Corps, Miami, Fla, 74; Yr of the Woman, Miami-Dade Com Col, 75; Hortt Mem Exhib, Ft Lauderdale, 76; Neal-Nevelson-Neijna Slide Exhib, Smithsonian Inst, Washington, DC, 76; 35 Artists in the SE, High Mus of Art, Atlanta, Ga, 76. Teaching: Instr sculpture, Univ Miami, Coral Gables, 63-67; instr sculpture, New Sch Fine Arts, Coral Gables, 63-74. Awards: Louis Comfort Tiffany Traveling fel, 59; Best in SE, Monumental Park Art, City of Atlanta & Nat Endowment for Arts, 76; Best of Show, Hortt Exhib, Ft Lauderdale Mus, 76. Bibliog: Emma Lila Fundaburk (auth), Art in Public Places in the US, Popular Press, 75; Marilyn Schmitt (auth), Did you see that huge..., Miami Mag, 77; Ellen Edwards (auth), Miami, Art News Mag, 77. Style & Technique: Planar, geometric progressions; conceptual, welded, polychromed steel; monumental and environmental in scale. Dealer: Betty Corcoran c/o Fleming-Fine Arts Inc PO Box 013838 Miami FL 33101. Mailing Add: 904 Anastasia Ave Coral Gables FL 33134

NEIKRUG, MARJORIE
ART DEALER
b New Rochelle, NY. Study: Sarah Lawrence Col. Teaching: Teacher, The Photographer's Eye (class), NY Univ, four yrs. Pos: Owner & dir, Neikrug Galleries, Inc. Mem: Am Soc Appraisers; Am Arbitration Soc; Am Soc Mag Photogr; Am Soc Picture Professionals. Specialty: Contemporary photography; photographica; rare books. Mailing Add: 224 E 68th St New York NY 10021

NEIMAN, LEROY
PAINTER, PRINTMAKER
b St Paul, Minn, June 8, 26. Study: Art Inst Chicago; Univ Chicago; Univ Ill. Work: Ill State Mus; Joslyn Art Mus; Wodham Col, Oxford, Eng; Mus Sport in Art, New York; Hermitage, Lenningrad, USSR; plus others. Comn: Murals, Continental Hotel, Chicago, 63; Mercantile Nat Bank, Hammond, Ind, 65; Swedish Lloyd Ship-Patricia, Stockholm, Sweden, 66; Madison Sq Garden, New York, 69. Exhib: American Exhibition of Oil Painting, Corcoran Gallery Am Art, Washington, DC, 57; Chicago American Exhibit of Painting & Sculpture, Art Inst Chicago, 60; Mus de Bellas Artes, Caracas, Venezuela, 72: Indianapolis Mus, 74; Tobu Gallery, Tokyo, 75; one-man shows, Knoedler Gallery, London, Eng, 76, Casagrafica, Helsinki, Finland, 77 & Galerie Renée-Victor, Stockholm, Sweden, 77; Hofstra Univ, 78; plus others. Teaching: Instr figure drawing, Art Inst Chicago, 50-60; instr painting, Winston-Salem Art Ctr, 64; instr painting, Atlanta Poverty Art Prog, 67-68; vis prof, Univ Ky, 77-78. Pos: Resident artist, New York Jets Prof Football Team, 68-; artist reporter, ABC-TV Wide World of Sports, 69-; official artist, Major League Baseball Promotions, 71-; ABC-TV official artist, XX Olympiad, Munich, Ger, 72. Awards: First Prize, Twin-City Exhib, Minneapolis Inst Art, 53; Munic Prize, Chicago Show, Art Inst Chicago, 58; Gold Medal, Salon d'Art Mod, Paris, 61. Media: Oil, Enamel; Serigraph, Etching. Publ: Time Mag covers, 3/1/68 & 1/17/72; Countdown to Superbowl (with Dave Anderson), Random, 69; This Great Game, Prentice-Hall, 71; Leroy Neiman Art & Life Style, Felicie Press, 74; Moby Dick (artist's ltd ed), 75. Dealer: Hammer Galleries 51 E 57th St New York NY 10022; Knoedler Graphics 21 E 70th St New York NY 10021. Mailing Add: 1 W 67th St New York NY 10023

NELSON, CAREY BOONE
SCULPTOR
b Lexington, Mo. Study: Wellesley Col, BA; Northwestern Univ; Univ Mo; Wagner Col, MSEd; Art Students League, with John Hovannes, Arturo Lorenzani & John Terken. Work: Wagner Col, Staten Island, NY; R F Shelare Libr, St Joseph Hill Acad, Staten Island; Sheldon Swope Mus, Terre Haute, Ind; Durban Art Mus, SAfrica; Victoria Libr, Melbourne, Australia. Comn: Mother Holding Child, comn by Dr Hugo Cimber, Zurich, Switz, 68; Portrait of Martin Luther, Wagner Col, 69; bronze of Hon Prof Emer Bernard Grebanier, 74; portrait of Daniel Boone in Later Years, Am Revolution Bicentennial, Mo State Capitol, 75; bronze of le Marquis de Lafayette, Am Revolution Bicentennial, Lafayette Co, Mo, 76. Exhib: Allied Artists Am, Nat Acad Design Galleries, 57-72; Int Art Exchange, Monte Carlo, Monaco, Paris & Cannes, 66-68; Hudson Valley Art Asn, Westchester Community Ctr, NY, 68-77; Am Artists Prof League Grand Nat, 68-77; Burr Artists, New York, 70-77; over 100 other group shows & eleven one-man shows, New York. Pos: Participating artist, USAF; mem, Sussex Co Art Coun, NJ; pres, Catharine Lorillard Wolfe Art Club; past bd mem trustee, Brooklyn Inst Arts & Sci. Awards: First Place for Sculpture, Composers, Authors & Artists Biennial Expos, 70 & 75; Anna Hyatt Huntington First Place for Sculpture, Catharine Lorillard Wolfe Art Club, 71; First Place Sculpture, Salmagundi Exhib, 75 & Solo Sculpture Award, 77; First Place Sculpture, Pen & Brush Exhib, 75; Wagner Col Achievement Award, 76; Kappa Kappa Gamma Award, 76. Bibliog: Articles in The Key, spring 69 & fall 71 & 74; article in Art News, 11/70; Nat Collection Fine Arts, Smithsonian Inst, Washington, DC. Mem: Catharine Lorillard Wolfe Art Club (chmn ann exhib, 69, co-chmn sculpture, 69-71, chmn sculpture, 71-75, chmn pub rels, 72, pres, 77-80); Nat League Am Pen Women (New York City art chmn, 76, 77 & 78); fel Am Artists Prof League; Composers, Authors & Artists Am (chmn sculpture shows, New York); Soc Illusr; fel Royal Soc Arts. Style & Technique: Bronze using cire perdu method; representational for portraiture. Media: Bronze, Marble. Mailing Add: 282 Douglas Rd Staten Island NY 10304

NELSON, HARRY WILLIAM
PAINTER, PRINTMAKER
b New York, NY, June 9, 08. Study: Yale Univ, BA, 33; New London Art Students League, with Harve Stein, 49-59; with Katherine Howe, 53; with Clarence Brodeur, 63-70; Lyman Allyn Mus, New London, Conn, with Beatrice Cuming, 64-67; Stonington Workshop, with Robert A Cale, 74 & 77. Work: Lyman Allyn Mus; also in many pvt collections. Exhib: Creative Gallery, New York, 52; Boston Mus of Fine Arts, 53; Sterling Libr, Yale Univ, 53; one-man show, Lyman Allyn Mus, 68; Lyme Art Asn, Old Lyme, Conn, 68-78; Essex Art Asn, Conn, 64-78; Conn Artists, Slater Mus, Norwich, 71; Invitational, Cummings Art Ctr, Conn Col, 73; one-man retrospective, Odyssey of a Poet-Painter, Karash Mem, Lawrence Mem Hosp, New London, Conn, 73; Bicentennial 1700-1950, Bicentennial Comn, Mystic Art Gallery, Conn, 76; Retrospective, Liberty Bank, Old Mystic, Conn, 77; plus others. Teaching: Spec demonstrations monotypes, Mystic Art Asn, 68 & 70. Pos: Pres, New London Art Students League, 65-68. Awards: Am Cancer Soc Show Silver Trophy, Mitchell Col, 68, Am Cancer Soc Show Spec Prize Design & Graphics, 71; First Prize Tech Excellence, Univ Conn, Avery Point, 69; Best in Show, Colchester Art Festival, Conn, 74. Bibliog: Tom Ingle (auth), One man show is delight, New London Day, 3/15/68; Leslie Pfeil (auth), Groton's award-winning multi-media man, Groton News, 7/27/71; Diane Santangelo (auth), Impressionistic artist reveals value of personal creativity, Scarlet Tanager, 4/6/72. Mem: Mystic Art Asn; Essex Art Asn; Lyman Allyn Mus; Lyme Art Asn. Style & Technique: Expressionistic and symbolistic abstraction; surrealism; expressionistic realism; lyricism; used palette knife. Media: Oil. Publ: Illusr, The Moon is Near, 44 & Blame the Skulk of Night, 74 & A Letter Among Friends, 78. Mailing Add: 213 Pleasant Valley Rd Groton CT 06340

NELSON, JACK D
SCULPTOR
b Chicago, Ill, Jan 26, 29. Study: Art Inst Chicago, dipl, 54; Goodman Theatre. Work: Mus Mod Art, Stockholm, Sweden; Everson Mus, Syracuse; also in pvt collections of Joseph H Hirshhorn, Malcolm S Forbes & Yves Tanquey, Kay Sage Estate. Comn: Sculptural wall, Philips Electronics Corp, Lidingö, Sweden, 63; kinetic clock sculpture, Halprin Assoc for City of Minneapolis, 66. Exhib: International Movement in Art Show, Stockholm, Paris & Amsterdam, 61; Nat Aspect '61 Show, Stockholm, 61; Retrospective Show, Everson Mus, 72; Circuit Existential Videotape Exhib, Cologne, Ger, Boston & Los Angeles, 74-75. Teaching: Assoc prof sculpture & film video, Col Visual & Performing Arts, Syracuse Univ, 66-78, emer prof, 78- Pos: Asst art dir, Visualscope, Inc, New York, 56-59; dir & designer children's TV show, G K Films Studio, Swedish TV-Radio, Stockholm, 60-63. Bibliog: Gunnar Berefelts (auth), Ord och bild, Särtryck, Stockholm, 62; article in Time Mag, 65; Lawrence Halprin (auth), The RSVP Cycles, Braziller, Inc, New York, 69. Style & Technique: Neo-dadaism; existential surrealism. Media: Vacuum Formed Plastic, Stretched Muslin Membrane; Videotape, Film. Dealer: Oscar Krasner c/o Krasner Gallery 1043 Madison Ave New York NY 13210. Mailing Add: 819 Comstock Ave Syracuse NY 13210

NELSON, JANE GRAY
ART LIBRARIAN
b Kankakee, Ill, Oct 10, 28. Study: Univ Calif, Berkeley, MLS, 63, MA(classical archeol), 71. Pos: Librn, Fine Arts Mus, San Francisco, 71-, asst cur in charge, Dept Ancient Art, 74-76, cur in charge, Images for Eternity: the Art of Ancient Egypt, 75. Mem: Am Inst Archaeol; Soc Promotion Hellenic Studies; Art Libr Soc NAm. Res: Gnathia ware. Publ: Contribr, Three Centuries of French Art, 73, Claude Monet, 73, Africa & Ancient Mexican Art: The Loran Collection, 74 & Walter Heil: in Memoriam, 77. Mailing Add: Fine Arts Mus San Francisco Golden Gate Park San Francisco CA 94118

NELSON, JON ALLEN
CURATOR, ART HISTORIAN
b Omaha, Nebr, July 9, 36. Study: Univ Nebr, Lincoln, BFA, 59; museology, Univ Minn. Collections Arranged: Etchings of J Alden Weir (auth, catalogue), 67 & Thomas Coleman, Printmaker (auth, catalogue), 72, Sheldon Mem Art Gallery, Univ Nebr, Lincoln. Pos: Pres, Nebr Mus Conf, 73; cur, Sheldon Mem Art Gallery, Univ Nebr, presently. Publ: Auth, Art of Printmaking, Univ Nebr, Lincoln, 66. Mailing Add: Sheldon Mem Art Gallery Univ Nebr Lincoln NE 68588

NELSON, LEONARD
PAINTER, INSTRUCTOR
b Camden, NJ, Mar 5, 12. Study: Pa Acad Fine Arts, 36-40; Barnes Found, 36-41; Philadelphia Col Art, BFA, 52. Work: Mus Mod Art; Philadelphia Mus Art; Dallas Mus Mod Art; Walker Mus Art; Portland Mus; plus many others. Exhib: One-man shows, New York & Philadelphia; many exhibs, Pa Acad Fine Art; Mus Mod Art; Art Inst Chicago; Maj Retrospective Exhib, Moore Col of Art, Philadelphia, 78. Teaching: Prof printmaking, Moore Col Art, 52-, head dept, 69- Awards: European Fel, Bd Fine Art, 39; Nat Wood Block Award, 42. Mem: Print Club (mem bd trustees, 52-57); fel Pa Acad Fine Arts; Am Fedn Teachers. Style & Technique: Contemporary; color field; heavy texture. Media: Oil, Metal. Dealer: Gross-McCleat Gallery Philadelphia PA. Mailing Add: 825 N 27th St Philadelphia PA 19130

NELSON, MARY CARROLL
ART WRITER, PAINTER
b Bryan, Tex, Apr 24, 29. Study: Barnard Col, BA(fine arts), 50, art hist with Julius Held & painting with Peppino Mangravite & Dong Kingman; Univ NMex, MA(art educ), 63, painting with Kenneth M Adams; art educ with Alexander Masley; grad studies art hist with John Tatschl, 69-70. Exhib: Nat Small Painting Exhib, 62, 70 & 73-75; Heidelberg Kunstverein, Ger, 65; NMex State Fair, 70 & 73; Nat League of Am Pen Women, 70; Southwestern Watercolor Soc, Dallas, 73. Pos: Pres, Livermore Art Asn, Calif, 63; vpres, Pinon Br, Nat League of Am Pen Women, 70-74, state secy, 72-74. Awards: Second in Acrylics, NMex State Fair Show, 70 & First in Mixed Media, 73; First in Mixed Media, Nat Small Painting Show, NMex Art League, 74. Bibliog: Charlotte Black (auth), She writes, paints & teaches children, Albuquerque Tribune, 75. Mem: Nat League of Am Pen Women; NMex Watercolor Soc (publicity chmn, 70-73); Nat Writers Club; Rio Grande Writers Asn; NMex Art League. Style & Technique: Waterbased media, semi abstract or realistic, also ink and collage, main theme is natural geologic forms, mountains and houses. Media: Watercolor, Acrylic, India Ink. Res: The Living and deceased outstanding artists of New Mexico and surrounding area, Indian biographies. Publ: Auth, Pablita Velarde/The Story of an American Indian, 71 & Michael Naranjo/The Story of an American Indian, 76, Dillon Press; co-auth (with Robert E Wood), Watercolor Workshop, 74 & co-auth (with R Kelley), Ramon Kelley Paints Portraits & Figures, 77, Watson-Guptill; co-auth, Pioneer artist of Taos, Am Artist, 78. Dealer: Mandala Art Gallery 6617 Snider Plaza Suite 204 Dallas TX 75205; Ken Roberts NMex Art League Gallery 3401 Juan Tabo Blvd NE Albuquerque NM 87111. Mailing Add: 1408 Georgia NE Albuquerque NM 87110

NELSON, ROBERT ALLEN
PRINTMAKER, PAINTER
b Milwaukee, Wis, Aug 1, 25. Study: Art Inst Chicago, BAE, 50 & MAE, 51, lithography with Max Kahn; John Herron Sch Art, Indianapolis, Ind, 64, lithography with Garo Antresian, NY Univ, EdD, 71. Work: Walker Art Inst, Minneapolis, Minn; Joslyn Mus, Omaha, Nebr; Sheldon Mus, Lincoln, Nebr; Butler Inst Am Art, Youngstown, Ohio; Mint Mus, Charlotte, NC; Springfield Mus, Mo; Addison Gallery Am Art, Phillips Acad, Andover, Mass. Comn: Murals, outdoor mosaics, Viking Sch, Grand Forks, NDak, 58 & Bridston

Savings & Loan, Grand Forks, 59, Univ NDak, Chester Fritz Libr, Grand Forks, 60 & State of NDak Hwy Dept Bldg, Bismarck, 68. Exhib: Butler Inst Ann, Youngtown, Ohio, 63-75; Boston Printmakers, Boston Mus, Mass, 65-78; New Vein, Smithsonian Inst, Washington, DC, 68; Watercolors USA, Springfield, Mo, 72-78; Cleveland Mus, 74-75. Teaching: Instr drawing, Art Inst Chicago, 52-53; asst prof lithography & painting, Univ Man Sch Art, 53-56; prof painting & drawing, Univ NDak, 56-72; prof printmaking, Cleveland State Univ, 72-75; assoc prof of art, Univ NC, Chapel Hill, 75- Awards: First Prizes for painting & R J Reynolds Purchase Prize, Secca Gallery, NC, 77; First Prize for drawing at Spring Mills, SC, 77; Fayetteville, NC Prize Prints, 75 & 77. Bibliog: Garo Antreasian & Clinton Adams (auth), The Tamarind Book of Lithography: Art and Techniques, Abrams, 72. Mem: Boston Printmakers; Soc Am Graphic Artists. Style & Technique: Realistic but surreal narrative based on pop and science fiction type imagery; stone lithography largely in black with limited color support; oil glaze approach to painting. Media: Stone; Oil. Publ: Illusr, cover, Rec, 71 & Supertooth, 72. Dealer: Mich Multiple Gallery 8713 Gull Rd Richland MI 49083; Rourke Gallery 523 S Fourth St Moorhead MN 56560. Mailing Add: 167 Lake Ellen Dr Chapel Hill NC 27514

NELSON, SIGNE (SIGNE NELSON STUART)
PAINTER
b New London, Conn, Dec 3, 37. Study: Univ Conn, BA, 59; Yale-Norfolk Summer Art Sch, 59; Univ NMex, MA, 60; Univ Ore, seminar with Ad Reinhardt, 63. Work: Tacoma Art Mus, Wash; Roswell Mus & Art Ctr, NMex; Univ NMex Art Mus; SDak Mem Art Ctr; Sheldon Mem Art Gallery, Lincoln, Nebr. Comn: Mural, Five Seasons Community Ctr, Cedar Rapids, Iowa, 77. Exhib: 50th Ann Exhib Northwest Art, Seattle Art Mus, 64; two-man exhibs, Yellowstone Art Ctr, Billings, Mont, 67, Johnson Gallery, 69 & Univ Ariz, 70; one-man shows, Sheldon Mem Art Gallery, 72, Sioux Falls Civic Fine Arts Ctr, SDak, 74, Augustana Col, SDak, 75, Warren Lee Ctr for the Fine Arts, Univ SDak, 76, Montgomery Mus Fine Arts, Ala, 77 & Sioux City Art Ctr, Iowa, 78; SDak Biennial, SDak Mem Art Ctr, 73, 75 & 77; plus others. Awards: Ford Found Purchase Award, 64; Nat Endowment for the Arts fel, 76-77; Purchase Prize, SDak Mem Art Ctr Biennial, 77. Bibliog: Jan Vander Marck (auth), The chromatic waves of Signe Nelson, ArtsCan, 71. Style & Technique: Abstract; acrylic pigment stains on sewn canvas constructions in serial form. Mailing Add: 719 Eighth St Brookings SD 57006

NEMEC, NANCY
PRINTMAKER
b Pinehurst, NC, Nov 30, 23. Study: Colby Jr Col, New London, NH; Vesper George Sch Arts, Boston, grad 44; Columbia Univ Sch Gen Studies, 48. Work: Libr Cong; New York Pub Libr; Philadelphia Free Libr; Greenville Mus, SC; Ga Mus Art; plus others. Comn: Print ed, Collectors Am Art, Silvermine Guild Artists, Hudson River Mus, Print Club Albany & New York Graphic Soc. Exhib: One-man shows, Hudson River Mus, 59, 62 & 65; Albany Inst Hist & Art, 62 & 63; Silvermine Guild Artists; Westfield Atheneum, Jasper Rand Mus & Fremont Found; plus many others. Teaching: Former instr, Westchester Art Workshop, White Plains, NY, Hudson River Mus & Manhattanville Col. Awards: Acad Artists Asn Award, 65-66, 67 & 73-76; NJ Painters & Sculptors Soc, 67 & 74; Miniature Art Soc NJ, 71 & 72; plus others. Mem: Am Color Print Soc; Silvermine Guild Artists; Nat Asn Women Artists; Miniature Painters & Gravers Soc; NH Art Asn; plus others. Style & Technique: Realistic fantasy. Mailing Add: Kearsarge Mountain Rd Warner NH 03278

NEMSER, CINDY
ART CRITIC, WRITER
b Brooklyn, NY, Mar 26, 37. Study: Brooklyn Col, BA, 58, MA(Eng lit), 64; Inst Fine Arts, NY Univ, with Walter Friedlander, Charles Sterling & Donald Posner, MA(art hist). Teaching: Guest lectr, Pratt Inst, Md Inst, RI Univ, NY Univ & others. Pos: Curatorial interne, NY State Coun on Arts, Mus Mod Art, 67; contrib ed, Arts Mag, 71-; ed, Feminist Art J, 72- Awards: Am Fedn Arts Tuition Grant, Art Critics Workshop, 68. Mem: Founding mem Women in the Arts; Col Art Asn Am (coordr three sessions on women artists, 72-73); Women's Caucus for Art (bd mem). Res: Position of women in the art world. Publ: Auth, Art criticism and perceptual research, Art J, spring 70; auth, Stereotypes and women artists, Feminist Art J, 4/72; auth, Art criticism and gender prejudice, Arts Mag, 3/72; auth, The Washington Women's Conference, Art in Am, 1/73; auth, Art Talks Conversations with 12 Women Artists, Scribner, 75; plus others. Mailing Add: Feminist Art Jour 41 Montgomery Pl Brooklyn NY 11215

NEPOTE, ALEXANDER
PAINTER, EDUCATOR
b Valley Home, Calif, Nov 6, 13. Study: Calif Col Arts & Crafts, BA, 39; Mills Col; Univ Calif, MA, 42. Work: San Francisco Mus Art; Oakland Art Mus; Metrop Mus Art; Pasadena Art Mus; Calif Palace of Legion of Honor; plus others. Exhib: Metrop Mus Art, 52; San Francisco Mus Art, 55; Art: USA, 58; Am Fedn Arts Traveling Exhib, 58-59; Americans, Va Mus Fine Arts, 62; Retrospective, Redwood City Munic Gallery, Calif, 74; Expo 70, Osaka, Japan; Auckland City Art Gallery, NZ, 71; Nat Watercolor Soc Ann, 73 & 74; plus many others. Teaching: Prof art & dean fac, Calif Col Arts & Crafts, 45-50; prof art, San Francisco State Univ, 50- Awards: Prizes, Jack London Square Exhib, 65 & Rio Hondo, Calif, 68; First Award, San Mateo Art Fiesta, 69; plus many others. Mem: Nat Watercolor Soc; Peninsula Art Asn. Mailing Add: 410 Taylor Blvd Millbrae CA 94030

NERI, MANUEL
SCULPTOR
b Sanger, Calif, Apr 12, 30. Study: Univ Calif, Berkeley, 51-52; Calif Col of Arts & Crafts, Oakland, Calif, 52-53 & 55-57; Bray Found, Helena, Mont, 53; San Francisco Art Inst, Calif, 57-59, study with Elmer Bischoff. Work: Oakland Mus, Calif; Mus of Art, San Francisco; Univ Calif Boulder; City of Napa, Calif. Exhib: Calif Sculpture To-Day, Kaiser Ctr, Oakland, Calif, 63; Funk Art, Univ of Calif Art Mus, Berkeley, 67; Sculpture Invitational, Univ Nev, Reno, 68; Sculpture Line, Oakland Mus, Calif, 71; Pub Sculpture/Urban Environment, Oakland Mus, Calif, 74; Sculptors as Draughtsmen, J P L Fine Arts, London, 75; four-man show, with Sam Francis, Fred Martin & Wally Hedrick, Mus of Art, San Francisco, 59; two-man show, with Wayne Thiebaud, Mus of Art, San Francisco, 65; one-man shows, St Mary's Col, Morago, Calif, 70, San Francisco Inst of Art, Calif, 70, Univ Nev, Reno 71x&71, Mus of Art, San Francisco, 71, Sacramento State Col, Calif, 72, Davis Art Ctr, Calif, 72 & San Jose State Univ, Calif, 74. Teaching: Instr, San Francisco Art Inst, 59-64; prof art, Univ Calif, Davis, 64- Awards: Neale Sullivan Award, San Francisco, 59; Sculpture Prize, San Francisco Art Inst 82nd Ann Exhib, 57; Nat Endowment for the Arts Grant, Washington, DC, 63; Nat Art Found Award, San Francisco, 64-65. Bibliog: Mary Fuller (auth), San Francisco Sculptors, Art in Am, New York, 6/64; Wayne Anderson (auth), Am Sculpture in Process, 1930-1970, Boston, Mass, 75; Thomas Albright (auth), Manuel Neri: A Kind of Time-Warp, Currant, San Francisco, 4-5/75. Publ: Auth, Four Drawings: Manuel Neri, Artforum, San Francisco, 4/64. Dealer: Gallery Paule Anglin 710 Montgomery St San Francisco CA 94111. Mailing Add: c/o Gallery Paule Anglin 710 Montgomery St San Francisco CA 94111

NESBITT, ALEXANDER JOHN
EDUCATOR, CALLIGRAPHER
b Paterson, NJ, Nov 14, 01. Study: Art Students League; Cooper Union; also with Harry Wickey. Work: Cooper Union Mus; Houghton Libr, Boston; Providence Pub Libr; Klingspor Mus, Offenbach am Main, Ger; Deutche Bucherei, Leipzig. Comn: Mem tablet, comn by Col Truman Smith, St John's Church, Stamford, Conn, 52; mem tablet, comn by John D Skilton, Trinity Chapel, Southport, Conn, 56; mem doc, Pilgrim John Howland Soc, presented to Lady Churchill, 66; designs for four gravestones, comn by John D Skilton, Monroeville, Ohio, 66; genealogical chart of Sherman family, comn by Mrs Gilbert H Sherman, 72. Exhib: Working Calligrapher & Lettering Artist, Brown Univ, 61; Calligraphy & Handwriting, Peabody Inst, 63, 2000 Years Calligraphy; Alexander Nesbitt—Lettering, Calligraphy, Typographic Design, Crapo Gallery, New Bedford, 66; Int Buchkunst-Ausstellung, Leipzig, 71; Work of the Third & Elm Press, Redwood Libr, Newport, RI, 77. Collections Arranged: Working Calligrapher & Lettering Artist, Brown Univ, 61. Teaching: Instr typography & lettering, Cooper Union, 50-57; assoc prof graphic design & chmn dept, RI Sch Design, 57-65; prof design, Southeastern Mass Univ, 65-74, emer prof, 74- Pos: Tech art dir, Jordanoff Aviation Co, 42-44; art dir, Technographic Publ, 44-45; owner, Third & Elm Press, 65- Awards: Travel & Study Grant, 59; Graphic Excellence Award, Fox River Paper Corp, 63; Bronze Medal, Int Buchkunst-Ausstellung, 71. Bibliog: Leo Joachim (auth), Nesbitt reviews recent European graphics safari, Printing News, 3/5/60; Leona G Rubin (auth), Nesbitt calligraphy exhbit praised, New Bedford Standard-Times, 2/20/66; Walter Plata (auth), Alexander Nesbitt, Polygraph, 72; William Flanagan (auth), The Third & Elm Press, Yankee Mag, 1/77. Mem: Providence Art Club (mem jury panels, 59); Type Dirs Club New York (mem bd gov, 55); Am Printing Hist Asn; Newport Art Asn; Goethe Soc New Eng. Style & Technique: Calligraphy, book design and documents. Publ: Auth, Lettering—the History and Technique of Lettering as Design, 50; ed, Decorative Alphabets and Initials, 59; ed, 200 Decorative Title-Pages, 64; ed, Color—Order and Harmony, 64; co-auth, Weathercocks and Weathercreatures, 70. Mailing Add: 29 Elm St Newport RI 02840

NESBITT, LOWELL (BLAIR)
PAINTER, LECTURER
b Baltimore, Md, Oct 4, 33. Study: Tyler Sch Fine Arts, Temple Univ, BFA; Royal Col Art, London, Eng. Work: Nat Collection Fine Arts, Smithsonian Inst, Washington, DC; Mus Mod Art, New York; NASA, Washington, DC; Nat Gallery Art, Washington, DC; Philadelphia Mus; plus others. Comn: Oil of Northern Trust Co, comn by Mr & Mrs Solomon Smith, Chicago, 67; poster, List Found, New York City Ctr, 68; Apollo 9 & 13 (oils), NASA, 69 & 70; poster of Renwick Mus, Smithsonian Inst, 71; Clearing Sky 72 (oil), Environ Protection Agency, Washington, DC, 72. Exhib: Tokyo Biennale, Japan, 67 & 74; Sao Paulo Biennale, Brazil, 67; Whitney Mus Am Art Ann, New York, 67; Int Art Fair, Basel, Switz, 70 & 74; one-man shows, Corcoran Gallery Art, Washington, DC, 73, Mus de Bellas Artes, San Juan, PR, 74, Univ Rochester, 75, New York Cult Ctr, 75 & Rochester Mus, NY, 75; Mus Mod Art, Paris, 74; Norton Gallery, West Palm Beach, Fla, 75; Univ Redlands, Calif, 75; Traveling Bicentennial Exhib, 76; plus many others. Teaching: Instr printmaking, Towson State Col, 66-67; instr printmaking, Baltimore Mus Art, 67-68; honorarium lectr, Univ Miami, Univ Richmond & Baltimore Mus Art, 68, 69 & 71; instr painting, Sch Visual Arts, 70-71. Pos: Asst set designer, Ogunquit Playhouse, Maine, 53 & 54; art dir TV, Walter Reed Med Ctr, 56-60. Awards: Purchase Awards for Oils & Prints, Baltimore Mus Art, 56; Award for Ben Berns Studio (oil), Nat Collection Fine Arts, 69, Baker Brush Co (drawing), 71. Bibliog: Coverage of Studio series, Time Mag, 69; reprod of Vab Bay (oil), Eyewitness to Space, NASA & Abrams, 71; The Ruins (film), John Huzar Prod, 71. Style & Technique: Combination of abstract looks at realist images and a hyperrealist scale and distortion of the image; image from photographs. Media: Oil on Canvas. Dealer: Andrew Crispo Gallery 41 E 57th St New York NY 10022. Mailing Add: 59 Wooster St New York NY 10013

NESLAGE, OLIVER JOHN, JR
ART DEALER
b Joplin, Mo, Mar 8, 25. Study: Univ Pittsburgh, AB, 50, Grad Sch, 51-52, Sch Law, 52-53; Oxford Univ, 51. Pos: Pres & managing dir, Venable Neslage Galleries, Washington, DC, 63-; pres, Neslage Assocs, Washington, DC, 68- Mem: Nat Press Club; Direct Mail Advert Asn; Am Soc Pub Rels. Specialty: Contemporary European and American artists in oil, graphics and drawings. Mailing Add: 1742 Connecticut Ave NW Washington DC 20009

NESS, (ALBERT) KENNETH
PAINTER, DESIGNER
b Saint Ignace, Mich, June 21, 03. Study: Univ Detroit, 23-24; Detroit Sch Appl Art, 24-26; Wicker Sch Fine Art, 26-28; Art Inst Chicago, with Boris Anisfeldt, dipl, 32. Work: NC State Art Mus, Raleigh; R J Reynolds Collection, Winston-Salem, NC; Ackland Art Ctr, Chapel Hill, NC; Duke Univ Mus Art. Exhib: Int Watercolor Exhibs, Art Inst Chicago, 34-39, Am Painting Ann, 35 & 37; Golden Gate Int Expos, San Francisco, 39; Am Painting Ann, Butler Inst Am Art, Youngstown, Ohio, 51; Pa Acad Fine Arts Ann, 53 & 54. Teaching: Resident artist, Univ NC, Chapel Hill, 41-73, assoc prof, 43-49, prof art, 49-73, emer prof art, 73- Pos: Dir, War Art Ctr, Univ NC, Chapel Hill, 42-44, actg head dept art & actg dir, Person Hall Art Gallery, 44, 45, 55, 57 & 58. Awards: Robert Rice Jenkins Mem Prize, Chicago Artists Ann, Art Inst Chicago, 34; Purchase Award, NC State Mus Ann, 54; NC Award, 73; Purchase Award, R J Reynolds Competition, 77. Mem: Hon assoc NC Chap Am Inst Architects; life fel Int Inst Arts & Lett. Style & Technique: Expressionist; abstract. Media: Oil, Tempera, and Other Media. Publ: Ed, Student Art at the University of North Carolina, Chapel Hill, 64; producer, Mona Lisa Rides Again (film), 69; producer, Art is Where You Mind It (film), 71-72. Mailing Add: PO Box 14 Chapel Hill NC 27514

NESS, EVALINE (MRS ARNOLD A BAYARD)
ILLUSTRATOR, WRITER
b Union City, Ohio, Apr 24, 11. Study: Muncie State Teachers Col, Ind, 31; Art Inst Chicago, 33; Corcoran Art Sch, 45; Art Students League, 47; Acad Belle Arti, Rome, Italy, 50. Teaching: Teacher children's art classes, Corcoran Sch Art, Washington, DC, 45-46; teacher art classes, Parsons Sch Design, New York, 59-60. Pos: Fashion illusr, Saks Fifth Ave, New York, 46-49; mag & adv illusr, 46-49; free lance illusr, 59- Awards: First Prize Painting, Corcoran Sch Art, 45; Caldecott Medal Children's Books, 67. Publ: Auth & illusr, A Double Discovery, 66, Sam Bangs and Moonshine, 66, The Girl and the Goatherd, 69, Do You Have the Time, Lydia, 71 & Yeck Eck, 73; plus others. Mailing Add: 350 S Ocean Blvd Palm Beach FL 33480

NESTOR, LULU B
PAINTER, ART ADMINISTRATOR
b Weirton, WVa. Study: WVa Univ, 55-56; West Liberty State Col, WVa, BAE; Eastern Mich Univ, MA(art), 73. Work: Pittsburgh Plate & Glass Co; Mt Lebonen Greek Orthadox Church,

Pittsburgh; WVa Univ; Mich Educ Asn, State Collection Art; Ins Com & Galleries, Michalsons Gallery, Washington, DC. Exhib: 4th Int Exhib, La Watercolor Soc, Baton Rouge, 72; Mich Watercolor Soc Exhib, Detroit Inst Art, 72-76; Butler Inst Art, Butler Mus, Youngstown, Ohio, 73 & 75; 17th Nat Jury Show, Chautauqua, NY, 74; Nat Soc Painter in Casien, Nat Gallery of Acad, NY, 76; Audubon Artist 35th Ann Exhib, Nat Acad Gallery, New York, 76; Nat Watercolor Soc 57th Ann, Calif State Univ, 77; one-woman exhibs, Univ Mich, 75 & Univ WVa, Morgantown, 75. Teaching: Instr, Richie Jr High Sch, Wheeling, WVa, 57-58, Elida High Sch, Elida, Ohio, 58-59 & South Lima Jr High Sch, Lima, Ohio, 60-62; art instr & dir art dept, Hartland High Sch, Mich, 68-77; instr adult educ classes, Hartland Consolidated Schs. Pos: Dir, Livingston Art Asn Exhib, First Fed Savings Bank, Howell, 72; dir, Hartland Regional Fine Arts Festival, 68-77. Awards: Honorable Mention, 6th Biennial Mich Painters Exhib, Grand Rapids Mus, 73; First Place, 72 & Honorable Mention, 76, Mich Watercolor Soc Ann, Birmingham; First Place, Nat Pittsburgh Watercolor Aqueous Open Competition, 74 & 76. Mem: Mich Watercolor Soc (mem bd); Midwest Watercolor Asn, Minn; Nat Watercolor Soc. Style & Technique: Unique and scientifically inventive watercolor technique-crystal formations in a surealistic and abstract presentational mode. Media: Watercolor; Casien. Mailing Add: 9865 Edwards Dr Brighton MI 48116

NETO, G REIS (GILDA REIS NETOPULETTI)
PAINTER
b Rio de Janeiro, Brazil. Study: Ceramic Tecnic Sch, Rio de Janeiro; Mod Art Mus, Rio de Janeiro, with Ivan Serpa; Andre Lhote, Atelier 17 & Gerard Passett, Paris; Acad de la Grande Chaumiere, Paris. Work: Cult Div of Brazilia; Pedro Ernesto Hosp, Rio de Janeiro; Embassy of Senegal; Bank of Brazil in San Francisco, Calif. Comn: Mural, Reception Salon of the Ministry of Educ & Cult, Brasilia, 60; Yacht Club (mural), with architect, Sergio Rodrigues, Yacht Club, Brasilia, 60; mural, Theatre of Parque Sch, Brasilia, 61. Exhib: One-person shows, Bahia, Brazil, 52, OCA Gallery, Rio de Janeiro, 61, Galerie Maywald, Paris, 65, Am Brazilian Cult Inst, Washington, DC, 68, L'Atelier, Paris, 70, Bechtel Int Ctr, Stanford Univ, Calif, 74 & Signo Galeria, Rio de Janeiro, 77; 7th Bienal of St Paulo, Brasil, 63; Orgn Pan Am States, Washington, DC, 65; La Fondation Royaumont, France, 69; Univ Calif, San Francisco, 71; Univ San Francisco, 73; Arline Lind Gallery, San Francisco, 72; Puletti Gallery, San Francisco, 75. Awards: Bronze Medal, Salon de SAPS, Brazilian Govt, 55 & Silver Medal, Salon Oficial de Paranà, 58. Publ: Roberto Pontual (auth), Dicionario das artes plasticas no Brasil, Civilizaçaô, 69. Mem: San Francisco Women Artists. Style & Technique: Figurative. Media: Oil and India ink. Mailing Add: 73 Santa Paula Ave San Francisco CA 94127

NEUBERGER, ROY R
COLLECTOR, PATRON
b Bridgeport, Conn, July 21, 03. Study: NY Univ; Univ Sorbonne. Teaching: Lectr art, Wadsworth Atheneum, Vassar Col, Brooklyn Mus, Detroit Inst Art, Mass Inst Technol Alumni Assocs, plus others. Pos: Bd dir, City Ctr Music & Drama, Inc, 57-74, finance chmn, 71-74, trustee, 74-; pres, Am Fedn Arts, 58-67, hon pres, 68-; mem, Friends of Whitney Mus Am Art, 60-62; chmn adv coun arts, New York City Housing Authority, 60-68; mem adv coun, Inst Fine Arts, NY Univ, 61-; trustee, Whitney Mus Am Art, 61-68, emer trustee, 69-; fine arts gifts comt, Nat Cult Ctr, 62; art ctr comt, New Sch Social Res, 62-69, 70-, trustee, 67-; adv comt art, Mt Holyoke Col, 63-; fine arts adv comt, Amherst Col, 63-70; nat adv comt, Washington Gallery Mod Art, 63-65; adv comt, Mus Am Folk Art, 65-; hon trustee, Metrop Mus Art, 68-; pres coun, Mus City New York, 71- Awards: Art in America Award, 59; NShore Community Arts Ctr Award, 61; Artists Equity Asn Award, 72. Mem: Benjamin Franklin fel, Royal Soc Arts; life fel, Nat Acad Design. Collection: Primarily American art, substantial part being given to the Roy R Neuberger Museum of the State University of New York College at Purchase; parts of private collection have been exhibited in musuems, universities and galleries in the United States and abroad. Publ: Contribr, Art in Am & var other art catalogs. Mailing Add: 522 Fifth Ave New York NY 10036

NEUBERT, GEORGE WALTER
SCULPTOR, CURATOR
b Minneapolis, Minn, Oct 24, 42. Study: Hardin-Simmons Univ, BS, 65; San Francisco Art Inst, 67; Mills Col, MFA, 69. Work: Oakland Mus, Calif; Richmond Art Ctr, Calif. Exhib: Contemporary Sculpture, San Francisco Art Inst, 67; Invisible Painting & Sculpture, Richmond Art Ctr, 69, one-man show, 70; 11 Bay Area Sculptors Under 35, Michael Walls Gallery, San Francisco, 69; Univ Calif, Davis, 73; Univ Calif, San Francisco, 74. Collections Arranged: Pierres de Fantaisie (with catalog), Oakland Mus, 70, Color and Scale (with catalog), 71, Off the Stretcher, 72, 4 Real, 72, Larry Bell, 73; Tropical, Oakland Mus & Santa Barbara Mus, 72. Pos: Cur art, Oakland Mus, 70-; mem adv bd, Archives Am Art, Smithsonian Inst, 72- Awards: Trefethen Found Fel, Mills Col, 68. Bibliog: T Albright (auth), Object and illusion, San Francisco Chronicle, 6/70; C McCann (auth), Six, six, six, 6/71 & J Dunham (auth), article, 4/73, Artweek; article in Washington Post, 3/13/75; plus others. Mem: Am Asn Mus; Western Asn Art Mus (regional rep, 72); Asn Art Mus Dir. Style & Technique: Non-objective. Publ: Ed, Tropical, 71; ed, Xavier Martinez, 74; ed, Public Sculpture/Urban Environment, 74. Mailing Add: Oakland Mus 1000 Oak St Oakland CA 94607

NEUGEBAUER, MARGOT
DESIGNER, CRAFTSMAN
b Göttingen, Ger, Nov 14, 29; US citizen. Study: RI Sch Design, BFA, 52, cert, 65; Syracuse Univ, MFA, 54; Haystack Mountain Sch Crafts, 57-70; Werkkunstschule, Ger, 71. Exhib: New England Invitational, DeCordova Mus, Lincoln, Mass, 62; Brockton & Fall River Ann, 63-67; RI Craftsmen, Providence, 65-66 & 69; Haystack Invitational, Flint, Mich, 69; Northeast Regional, ACC Gallery, New York, 72. Teaching: Art supvr, Cortland Pub Schs, 53-55; instr art, New Bedford Inst Technol, 55-58; asst prof art, Southeastern Mass Technol Inst, 58-72; asst prof art, Southeastern Mass Univ, 58-72, assoc prof, 72-77, prof, 77-, chmn dept design, 73- Mem: Am Craftsmen Coun; Boston Weavers Guild; Soc Arts & Crafts, Boston. Style & Technique: Jewelry designs in silver. Mailing Add: 133 State St New Bedford MA 02740

NEUMAN, ROBERT S
PAINTER, EDUCATOR
b Kellogg, Idaho, Sept 9, 26. Study: Calif Col Arts & Crafts; Calif Sch Fine Arts; Univ Idaho; Mills Col; also in Stuttgart, Ger. Work: San Francisco Mus Art; Boston Mus Fine Arts; Worcester Mus Art, Mass; Mus Mod Art; Addison Gallery Am Art, Andover, Mass; plus others. Exhib: De Cordova & Dana Mus, 60-65; New Eng Art Today, 63 & 65; Mus Mod Art, 64; Art Across America, Boston, 65; Allan Stone Gallery, New York; plus others. Teaching: Instr, Calif Cols Arts & Crafts, 51-53; instr, Brown Univ, 61-63; instr, Carpenter Ctr for Visual Arts, Harvard Univ, 64-65, lectr drawing on Osgood Hooker Endowment, formerly; prof art & chmn dept, Keene State Col, NH, 72-77. Awards: Fulbright Grant, 53-54; Guggenheim Fel, 56-57; Prize, San Francisco Mus Art; plus others. Style & Technique: Abstract. Mailing Add: 4 Gordon St Waltham MA 02154

NEUMANN, HANS
COLLECTOR
Collection: Modern paintings; antique sculpture and modern sculpture; antique jewelry and watches. Mailing Add: Apartado 5475 Caracas Venezuela

NEUMANN, WILLIAM A
EDUCATOR, GOLDSMITH
b Cleveland, Ohio, Oct 12, 24. Study: Cleveland Inst of Art, BFA, study with John Paul Miller; Syracuse Univ, MFA, study with John Marshall. Work: Cleveland Mus of Art; Dallas Mus of Fine Arts; Massillon Mus of Art, Ohio. Comn: Wedding bracelets (18K gold and enamel), Mr & Mrs Patrick Dougherty, Akron, Ohio, 77; diamond necklace (gold and silver enamel), Dr & Mrs Moshé Amitay, Kent, Ohio, 77. Exhib: One-man shows, Illums, Copenhagen, Denmark, 52 & Lowe Art Ctr, Syracuse Univ, 68; Goldsmith 70 Nat Exhib, St Paul, Minn, 70; Goldsmith 74 Nat Exhib, Renwick Gallery, Smithsonian Inst, Washington, DC, 74; Blossom-Kent Univ Art Exhib, Kent, Ohio, 75-77; Nat Jewelry Competition, Tex Univ, Lubbock. Collections Arranged: Collabr, Design & Aesthetics in Wood, 67 & Harry Wickey Drawing & Prints, 69, Lowe Art Ctr, Syracuse Univ. Teaching: Prof design, Syracuse Univ, 67-70; prof metalsmithing, Univ Akron, 70 Pos: Pres & design dir, Dimensional Design, Inc, Cleveland, 57-64; resident design dir, Aid to Int Develop, Bogota, Colombia, 66-67. Awards: Second Prize, All Ohio Show, Canton Art Inst, Ohio, 71; Special Award, 53rd Ann May Exhib, Cleveland Mus of Art, 72. Bibliog: Joseph Ordos (auth), Three American Goldsmiths (film), Univ Minn, 75. Mem: World Craft Coun; Am Craft Coun; Soc of NAm Goldsmiths; Nat Asn of Handcraftsmen (adv, 76-77). Style & Technique: Style basically pre-Columbian in influence and almost all pieces use enameling with granulated decoration. Media: Jewelry and metalsmithing. Mailing Add: Dept of Art Univ Akron Akron OH 44325

NEUSTADT, BARBARA (BARBARA MEYER)
PRINTMAKER, LECTURER
b Davenport, Iowa, June 21, 22. Study: Smith Col, BA; Univ Chicago; Ohio Univ Sch Fine Arts; Art Students League, scholar, 52; also with Ben Shahn & Arnold Blanch. Work: Metrop Mus Art, New York; Philadelphia Mus Art; Libr Cong, Washington, DC; Nat Gallery Art, Washington, DC; Permanent Collection Am Prints, Bonn, Ger. Comn: Ed of etchings, Collectors of Am Art, New York, 56, 58 & 61; ed of etchings, Int Graphic Arts Soc, 60; ed of etchings, New York Hilton, 61; ed of etchings, Woodstock Artists Asn, NY, 70. Exhib: Brooklyn Mus Nat Print Exhib, 54, 58 & 60; Soc Am Graphic Artists, 54-61, 73, 75 & 76; one-man shows, Ruth White Gallery, 58, Philadelphia Art Alliance, 59, Portland Mus Art, 65, Long Island Univ, Brooklyn Campus, 73 & Pace Univ, New York, 75-76; Nat Acad Design, New York, 56; US Nat Mus, 57 & 58 & Libr Cong, 57 & 61, Washington, DC; Mus Mod Art, New York, 58 & 59; Art Inst Chicago, 59; Whitney Mus Am Art, New York, 59; Nat Gallery Art, Washington, DC, 59; Int Exchange Exhib, Soc Am Graphic Artists Invitational, Europe & SAm, 60 & 61; two-person show, Smith's Col, 74; plus others. Pos: Art dir, Shepherd Cards, Inc, 56-63; acquisition comt, Portland Mus Art, Maine, 65-66; dir-instr, Studio Graphics Workshop, Woodstock, 70-; partic, Artist in Sch Prog, Dutchess Co Art Asn, 74. Awards: Lady Black Prize, Boston Printmakers, 57; Joseph Pennell Mem Medal, Philadelphia, 72; Nat Area Coun Grant, New York, 73. Bibliog: A Zaidenberg (auth), Prints & How to Make Them, Harper, 64; K Marsh (producer), Woodstock Community Video (interview & demonstration), 72. Mem: Soc Am Graphic Artists; Philadelphia Watercolor Club; Artists Equity. Style & Technique: Lyrical abstraction; semi-figurative; multi-color viscosity printing on deeply bitten zinc plates. Media: Intaglio. Publ: Illusr, The First Christmas, Crowell, 60. Mailing Add: California Quarry Rd Woodstock NY 12498

NEUSTADTER, EDWARD L
COLLECTOR, PATRON
b New York, NY, Mar 29, 28. Study: Ohio State Univ, BSc. Collection: Twentieth century American sculpture and oils; French, German and Spanish sculpture and oils. Mailing Add: Woodlands Rd Harrison NY 10528

NEUSTEIN, JOSHUA
PAINTER, ART CRITIC
b Danzig, Poland, Oct 16, 40; US citizen. Study: City Col New York, 57-61, BA, 61; Art Students League, 59-61; Pratt Inst, Brooklyn, NY, 60-63. Work: Mus of Mod Art & Whitney Mus of Am Art, New York; Jerusalem Mus of Israel; Tel Aviv Mus of Art, Israel; Louisiana Mus, Copenhagen, Denmark. Exhib: Concept & Info, Israel Mus, Jerusalem, 71; Earth Air Fire Water: Elements of Art, Mus of Fine Arts, Boston, Mass, 72; Ten Artists, Louisiana Mus, Copenhagen, Denmark; Artists Use Photographs, Arkwright Arts Centre, London, Eng; Yvon Lambert Gallery, Paris, France; Travel Art, Mus of Mod Art, Oxford, Eng, 71; Documenta V, Kassel, Ger, 72; Photog into Art, Camden Art Centre, London, 72; Photog Triennale, Israel Mus, Jerusalem, 76; one-man shows, Helena Rubenstein Pavilion, Tel Aviv, 70, Haifa Mus, Israel, 72, Boston Mus of Fine Arts, Mass, 72, Mus of Art, Worcester, Mass, 75 & Neustein-Ten Years, Tel Aviv Mus, Israel. Awards: Willem Sandberg Prize, Jerusalem, 74. Bibliog: Pincus Witten (auth), Sons of light, 9/75, Six propositions, 12/75 & Neustein papers, 10/77, Arts Mag. Style & Technique: Torn cut folded removed and replaced papers covered with acrylic paint; monumental scale. Media: Painting; Printmaking. Res: Art criticism. Dealer: Mary Boone 420 W Broadway New York NY 10012; B Urdang 23 E 74th St New York NY 10021. Mailing Add: 300 W 108th St New York NY 10025

NEVELSON, LOUISE
SCULPTOR
b Kiev, Russia, 00; US citizen. Work: Mus Mod Art & Whitney Mus Am Art, New York; Princeton Univ; Tate Gallery Art, London; Art Inst Chicago. Comn: Aluminum sculpture, South Mall Proj, Albany, NY, 68; Cor-ten steel sculptures, Binghamton, NY, 72 & Scottsdale, Ariz, 72; monumental wood sculpture, World Trade Ctr, New York, 72; Bicentennial Dawn (white painted wood), Fed Courthouse, Philadelphia, Pa; St Peter's Church, New York. Exhib: One-man & group exhibs all over the world, regularly for many years. Bibliog: Glimcher (auth), Louise Nevelson, Praeger, 72; Mackown (auth), Dawns & Dusks, Louise Nevelson, Scribner's, 76. Mem: Artists Equity Asn. Dealer: Pace Gallery 32 E 57th St New York NY 10022. Mailing Add: 29 Spring St New York NY 10012

NEVELSON, MIKE
SCULPTOR
b New York, NY, Feb 23, 22. Work: Colby Col; Wadsworth Atheneum; Whitney Mus Am Art; Strater Mus; Stratford Col. Exhib: Staempfli Gallery; Whitney Mus; Grand Cent Moderns; Amel Gallery; Expo 68, Montreal; plus others. Style & Technique: Personal with classical technique. Media: Various media. Mailing Add: 3 Milltown Rd New Fairfield CT 06810

NEVITT, RICHARD BARRINGTON
EDUCATOR, ILLUSTRATOR
b Montreal, Que, Aug, 36. Study: Ont Col of Art, AOCA, study with Eric Freifeld & John Alfsen; Univ of Toronto, studied Art as Applied to Medicine with Nancy Joy, Dr W Brown & Dr C Ower; York Univ, BA, studied with Dr R Jarrell, Dr H Leith. Work: Nat Gallery in Ottawa, Can; Ont Col of Art Gallery; Sch of Archit, Univ of Toronto. Comn: Drawings, Military, Can govt, Cyprus, 68 & Halifax, NS, 69; Scientific Illus of the Brain, Educ TV, 72. Exhib: Military Artist Prog, Nat Gallery of Can, Ottawa, 77; Art as Applied to Medicine, Anatomical Illus, 77-78. Teaching: Instr anatomy & drawing, Ont Col of Art, Toronto, 65-; prof drawing, Ministry of Educ, Toronto, 65- Pos: Hon appt, Art as Applied to Medicine dept, 76- Awards: Can Coun, Can govt, 69. Mem: Arts & Lett Club. Style & Technique: Pen and ink and pencil drawing. Mailing Add: RR 2 Alton ON L0N 1A0 Can

NEW, LLOYD H (LLOYD KIVA)
ART ADMINISTRATOR, DESIGNER
b Fairland, Okla, Feb 18, 16. Study: Okla State Univ; Univ NMex; Art Inst Chicago; Univ Chicago, BAE, 38; Harvard Univ; textile printing & dyeing with D D & Leslie Tillett. Work: Indian Arts & Crafts Bd Collection, Washington, DC. Exhib: 1st & 2nd Int Fashion Shows, Philadelphia Mus, 51 & 52; Textile Exhib, Mus Mod Art, New York; Am Craftsmen Coun Exhibs; World Crafts Coun Exhib, Peru; Int Touring Exhib, US Dept Interior; plus others. Teaching: Dir arts & instr arts & crafts, Int Am Indian Arts, Santa Fe, NMex, 62-67. Pos: Chmn, Indian Arts & Crafts Bd, US Dept Interior; owner-operator, Lloyd Kiva, Inc, Scottsdale, Ariz, 46-62; dir, Inst Am Indian Arts, 67- Awards: Cult Serv Medal, Univ Ariz, 59; Merit Award, Mus Mod Art, New York, 62. Bibliog: Articles in Sat Eve Post, Life Mag & Nat Geog. Mem: Am Coun Arts Educ (chmn intercult comt); Heard Mus, Phoenix (bd trustees); NMex Arts Comn; Am Crafts Coun; World Crafts Coun. Res: Indian arts research; history of architecture, crafts and performing arts; contemporary expression of the Indian artist. Interest: Textile design. Publ: Auth, The crafts of the Indian, House Beautiful, 6/71; auth, Performing arts and the American Indian, Am Way, 7/72; auth, Arts and minorities, Arts in Soc, 8/72. Mailing Add: Inst of Am Indian Arts Cerrillos Rd Santa Fe NM 87501

NEWBILL, AL
PAINTER
b Springfield, Mo, Jan 13, 21. Study: Society of Arts and Crafts, Detroit, study with John Caroll; Brooklyn Mus Sch, study with John Ferren; Hofmann Sch, study with Hans Hofmann. Work: Detroit Inst of Art; Univ of Kans; Mus of Mod Art, New York; Marist Col, Poughkeepsie, NY; Southern Ill Univ. Exhib: Detroit Inst of Art; Cleveland Mus of Art, Ohio; Mus of NMex Art Gallery, Santa Fe; one-man show, Univ of Kans, 68. Teaching: Instr, Queens Col, 47, Southern Ill Univ, Univ of Calif, Berkeley, Univ of Kans, 67-68, Ohio State Univ, 68 & privately. Pos: Dir, art prog, Rodman Job Corps, 66-67. Mailing Add: c/o Benson Gallery Bridgehampton NY 11932

NEWER, THESIS
PAINTER
b New York, NY. Study: Acad Delle Belle Arte, Florence, Italy, 4 yrs; Pratt Inst Interior Design, grad. Work: Pvt collections only. Exhib: Allied Artists Am; Knickerbocker Artists; Jersey City Mus; Hudson Valley Art Asn; Painters & Sculptors Soc NJ. Awards: Best in Show, Catharine Lorillard Wolfe Art Club, 68; Top Award for Polymer, Am Artists Prof League, 68; Nat Art League Gold Medal, Nat Arts Club, 69 & First Prizes, 72 & 75; plus others. Bibliog: Articles in La Rev Mod, Paris, 70-71. Mem: Am Artists Prof League; Catharine Lorillard Wolfe Art Club; Nat Art League; Painters & Sculptors Soc NJ; Allied Artists Am; plus others. Media: Oil. Dealer: Thomson Gallery 19 E 75th St New York NY 10021. Mailing Add: 876 Adams Ave Franklin Square NY 11010

NEWHALL, BEAUMONT
ART HISTORIAN, WRITER
b Lynn, Mass, June 22, 08. Study: Harvard Col, AB(cum laude fine arts), 30; Grad Sch Arts & Sci, Harvard Univ, MA, 31; Inst Art & Archeol, Univ Paris, 33; Courtauld Inst Art, Univ London, 34. Collections Arranged: Permanent collections of photog in Mus Mod Art, 37-45 & George Eastman House, 48-71; also collection of Exchange Nat Bank, Chicago (with Nancy Newhall). Teaching: Lectr, Philadelphia Mus Art, 32-33; lectr photog hist, Univ Rochester, 54-56; lectr photog hist, Rochester Inst Technol, 56-68; vis prof, State Univ NY Buffalo, 68-71; prof art, Univ NMex, 71- Pos: Asst in dept decorative arts, Metrop Mus Art, 33-34; librn, Mus Mod Art, 35-42, cur photog, 40-45; cur, Int Mus Photog, George Eastman House, 48-58, dir, 58-71. Awards: Guggenheim Mem Found Fel, 46 & 75; Kulturpreis, Deutsche Gesellschaft für Photographie, 70; Progress Medal, Royal Photog Soc, 75. Bibliog: Bibliography (of over 600 titles), Trustees of George Eastman House, 71. Mem: Hon fel Royal Photog Soc; hon master of photog, Prof Photogr Am; corresp mem Deutsche Gesellschaft für Photographie; fel Photog Soc Am; fel Am Acad Arts & Sci. Res: History of photography. Publ: Auth, Frederick H Evans, 64; auth, Latent Image, 67; auth, The Daguerreotype in America, 3rd rev ed, 76; auth, Airborne Camera, 69; auth, The History of Photography, 4th ed, rev 71; co-auth (with Diana C Edkins), William H Jackson, 74. Mailing Add: Rte 3 Box 126C Albuquerque NM 87501

NEWHOUSE, BERTRAM MAURICE
ART DEALER
b St Louis, Mo, Oct 15, 88. Study: Smith Acad, St Louis, grad, 06. Pos: Pres, Newhouse Galleries, New York, 28-; vpres, Art & Antique League Am, 33-38. Awards: Capital Order Alphonso X, Govt Spain, 64. Mem: Lotus Club New York (art comt, 70); Royal Soc Arts Great Brit. Publ: Auth, Paintings by William Merritt Chase, 27. Mailing Add: Newhouse Galleries Inc 19 E 66th St New York NY 10021

NEWHOUSE, CLYDE MORTIMER
ART DEALER, ART HISTORIAN
b St Louis, Mo, Jan 25, 20. Study: Yale Univ, BA(cum laude). Pos: Owner, Newhouse Galleries. Mem: Art Dealers Asn of Am, Inc (pres, 76); Nat Antique & Art Dealers Asn of Am, Inc (exec officer). Specialty: Old Masters from the 14th century through the 18th century; American paintings of the 18th and 19th centuries. Mailing Add: 19 E 66th St New York NY 10021

NEWMAN, ARNOLD
PHOTOGRAPHER
b New York, NY, Mar 3, 18. Study: Univ Miami. Work: Metrop Mus Art, New York; Mus Mod Art, New York; Art Inst Chicago; Philadelphia Mus Art; Smithsonian Inst, Washington, DC. Exhib: One-man shows, Artists Look Like This, Philadelphia Mus Art, 45-46, Photogr Gallery, London, Eng, 75, Ulrich Mus, Wichita State Univ, Kans, 76, Galerie Fiolet, Amsterdam, Holland, 77 & Del Art Mus, Wilmington, 77; Faces In American Art, Metrop Mus Art, 57; one-man retrospective, Art Inst Chicago, 53 & George Eastman House, Rochester, NY, 72; Arnold Newman Portraits, 4th Int Biennale Fotografia, Venice, Italy, 63; Camera & Human Facade, Smithsonian Inst, 70. Teaching: Vis prof, Cooper Union, 69- Pos: Actg cur & adv photog dept, Israel Mus, Jerusalem, 67- Awards: Newhouse Citation, Syracuse Univ, 61; Gold Medal, 4th Biennale Int Fotografia, 63; Life Achievement in Photography Award, Am Soc Mag Photogr, 75; plus others. Bibliog: H M Kinzer (auth), Arnold Newman biography, In: The Encyclopedia of Photography, Hawthorn, 64; Peter Pollack (auth), Arnold Newman, In: The Picture History of Photography, Abrams, 69; David R Godine (auth), One Mind's Eye—The Portraits and Other Photographs of Arnold Newman, 74; plus others. Mem: Am Soc Mag Photogr. Style & Technique: Carefully composed environmental and symbolic portraiture. Media: Multi-Media. Publ: Auth, Bravo Stravinsky, World, 67; auth, Faces USA, Amphoto, 78. Dealer: Light Gallery 724 Fifth Ave New York NY 10019. Mailing Add: 33 W 67th St New York NY 10023

NEWMAN, ELIAS
PAINTER, WRITER
b Stashow, Poland, Feb 12, 03; US citizen. Study: Nat Acad Design, 18-20; Educ Alliance Art Sch, 20-25; Acad Grande Chaumiere, Paris, France, 29. Work: Everson Mus Art, Syracuse, NY; Boston Mus Fine Arts; Brooklyn Mus; San Francisco Mus Art; Tel Aviv Mus, Israel. Exhib: One-man shows, Tel Aviv Mus, 34, 38, 49 & 62, Philadelphia Art Alliance, 46 & Jewish Mus, New York, 49; Art: USA, New York, 58; Am Acad Arts & Lett, New York, 59; Butler Inst Am Art, Youngstown, Ohio, 60; New Accessions USA, Colorado Springs Fine Arts Ctr, 62. Teaching: Instr painting, Educ Alliance Art Sch, 46-48; instr painting, YMHA 92nd St Art Sch, New York, 49-51; instr painting, Elias Newman Sch Art, Rockport, Mass, 51-64; exten lectr on Art of Israel. Pos: Art dir, Palestine Pavilion, New York World's Fair, 38-40; art consult, Palestine Sect, Int Expos, Cleveland, 41; ed, Improvisations, 50-52; art consult, Am Fund for Israel Inst, 54-55. Awards: Beatrice S Katz Award for Graphics, Am Soc Contemp Artists, 71; Medal of Merit, Nat Soc Painters in Casein, 71; Stanley Grumbacher Mem Medal & Prize, Audubon Artists, 77. Bibliog: Stephen S Kayser (auth), Elias Newman Exhibition, Jewish Mus, 49; Henry A La Farge (auth), Elias Newman exhibition, Art News, 2/49; Ralph Fabri (auth), Medal winner in casein annual, Today's Art, 7/71. Mem: Artists Equity Asn New York (pres, 70-75, hon pres, 75-); Conf Am Artists (chmn, 71-); Audubon Artists (dir, 71-74, treas, 77, dir, 78-); Nat Soc Painters in Casein (pres, 66-70, hon pres, 71-); Am Soc Contemp Artists (dir, 71). Style & Technique: Phenomena of nature and its ever changing moods. Media: Oil, Encaustic, Casein, Watercolor. Res: Art of Israel; economic and cultural problems of American artists. Publ: Auth, Art in Palestine, 39; ed, Improvisations, 50, 51 & 52; auth, Art in Israel, Reconstructionist Mag, 6/29/56; ed, Directory of Open Exhibitions, 57. Mailing Add: 215 Park Row New York NY 10038

NEWMAN, JOHN BEATTY
PAINTER, INSTRUCTOR
b Toronto, Ont, Apr 6, 33. Study: Ontario Col Art; Art Acad Cincinnati, scholarship. Work: Art Gallery Hamilton, Ont; Rodman Hall Art Ctr, St Catharines, Ont; Art Acad Cincinnati. Exhib: Surrealism in Canadian Painting Traveling Exhibition, London Pub Libr & Art Mus, 64; 20 Ontario Painters, Rodman Hall Art Ctr & Art Mus, 64, one-man show, 69; Art Gallery, Erindale Col, Univ Toronto, 73; Mem Univ Art Gallery, St John's, Nfld, 74. Teaching: Instr figure painting, Ont Col Art, 63- Pos: Exhib designer, Royal Ont Mus, Toronto, 58-63; mem gov coun, Ont Col Art, 73- Awards: Int Painting Competition First Prize, Can Soc Graphic Art, 56, John Alfsen Award for Drawing, 73; Honour Award, Can Soc Painters Watercolour, 74. Bibliog: Kay Kritzwiser (auth), A tender look at little girls, Globe & Mail, Toronto, 73; Peter Bell (auth), The transition to maturity, Evening Telegram, St John's, Nfld, 74; Henry Lehman (auth), To write a painting, Montreal Star, 75. Mem: Royal Can Acad; Can Soc Graphic Art (secy); Can Soc Painters Watercolour. Style & Technique: Fantasy realism, using human figure with an emphasis on drawing. Dealer: Galerie de L'Esprit 2122 Crescent St Montreal PQ Can. Mailing Add: 170 Hammersmith Ave Toronto ON M4E 2W8 Can

NEWMAN, (JOHN) CHRISTOPHER
SCULPTOR, EDUCATOR
b Boston, Mass, Jan 23, 43. Study: Harvard Col, BA(cum laude), 65; Univ Pa, BFA, 66, MFA, 68. Work: Univ Mass, Amherst; Cleveland Art Asn. Exhib: One-man shows, Ruth White Gallery, New York, 70 & Philadelphia Art Alliance, 71; Cleveland Mus Art, 74; Artists Equity, Philadelphia Civic Ctr, 74; Philadelphia Collects, Vendo Nubes, 74; Sculpture '75, Philadelphia Mus Art, 75; plus others. Teaching: Assoc prof art & sculpture, Bucks Co Community Col, 69-75. Awards: Nat Endowment Humanities Grant, Columbia Univ, 75. Style & Technique: Large scale abstract sculptures. Media: Aluminum, Steel. Mailing Add: 6803 Kingsbury Blvd St Louis MO 63130

NEWMAN, LIBBY
PAINTER, PRINTMAKER
b Rockland, Del. Study: Tyler Sch Fine Arts, Philadelphia, 54; Philadelphia Col Art, 62; also with Julius Block, Sam Feinstein & Victor Lauschin. Work: Nat Mus Belgrade, Yugoslavia; Philadelphia Mus Art; Mus Philadelphia Civic Ctr; Mus Mod Art, Buenos Aires, Argentina; Glassboro State Col. Comn: Woodcut print ed 50, Univ Pa Law Sch, 70; woodcut print ed 100, Circle Gallery, New York, Chicago & Calif, 73, woodcut print ed 50, 73 & 74. Exhib: Nat Watercolor & Drawing Exhib, Pa Acad Fine Arts, 64; Del Regional Watercolor Exhib, Del Art Mus, 64; Eastern Cent Drawing Exhib, Philadelphia Mus Art, 65; Benjamin Mangel Gallery, Bala Cynwyd, Pa, 70-75; Pa State Mus, Harrisburg, 71. Pos: Mem adv panel visual arts, Pa Coun Arts, Harrisburg, 72-; mem aesthetics comt, Mayor's Comt Sci & Technol, Philadelphia, 72-; chmn, Walnut St Theatre Fine Arts Comt, 73-75. Awards: Gold Medal Award, Da Vinci Art Alliance, Philadelphia, 64; Best Picture of Year Award, Philadelphia Art Alliance, 65; National Print Award, Cheltenham Art Ctr, Pa, 70. Bibliog: Burton Wasserman (auth), Fine print exhibition, Courier-Post, 71; Victoria Donohoe (auth), Gallery's finest hour, Philadelphia Inquirer, 72; Dorothy Grafly (auth), Impressions of Israel, Art in Focus, 72. Mem: Artists Equity Asn (pres, Philadelphia Chap, 68-70; nat vpres, 71-75); Philadelphia Art Alliance (vchmn oil painting com, 74-); Am Color Print Soc; Philadelphia Watercolor Soc; Pa Acad Fine Arts. Style & Technique: Lyrical abstraction in acrylic, woodcut, silkscreen and collage constructions; brush and palette knife technique. Media: Acrylic; Woodcut. Publ: Auth, Obtaining art grants, Artists Equity Nat Newslett, 74; auth, A City Sketched: A Guide to the Art and History of Philadelphia (bk). Dealer: Benjamin Mangel Gallery 202 Bala Ave Bala Cynwyd PA 19004. Mailing Add: 327 Meeting House Lane Merion Station PA 19066

NEWMAN, LOUIS
ART DEALER, GALLERY DIRECTOR
US citizen. Study: Ariz State Univ, BA(sociol), 70; Univ Southern Calif, Los Angeles, MA(urban & regional planning), 74. Pos: Art dealer, Los Angeles, Calif. Mem: Artist Equity; Am Crafts Coun; Southern Calif Art Dealers Asn. Specialty: Contemporary paintings, prints, drawings and sculpture. Dealer: Louis Newman Art Dealer 308 N Sycamore Los Angeles CA 90036. Mailing Add: Louis Newman Galleries Bonaventure Hotel 404 S Figueroa Los Angeles CA 90071

NEWMAN, RALPH ALBERT
CARTOONIST, WRITER
b Newberry, Mich, June 27, 14. Study: Albion Col, BA. Pos: Illusr, Old Timer (weekly cartoon panel), Indust Press Serv, 54-; comic bk writer, Harvey, 56- Media: Ink. Mailing Add: PO Box 1047 Darien CT 06820

NEWMARK, MARILYN (MARILYN NEWMARK MEISELMAN)
SCULPTOR
b New York, NY, July 20, 28. Study: Adelphi Col; Alfred Univ; also with Paul Brown, Garden City, NY. Comn: Hacking Home Trophy, Prof Horseman's Asn, 71 & The Gate Trophy, 77; Hobson Perpetual Trophy, Liberty Bell Race Track, Pa, 72; American Gold Cup Medallion Award, 72; Appaloosa Horse Club Medallion Award, 74; Triple Crown, comn by Sam Lehrman, 75; Majestic Light, comn by Ogden Phipps, 76; Man o' War, comn by Franklin Mint, 77; plus others. Exhib: Allied Artists Am, New York, 70-77; Nat Sculpture Soc, New York, 70-73 & 75-77; Nat Art Mus Sport, New York, 71; James Ford Bell Mus Natural Hist, Minneapolis, Minn, 71; Nat Acad Design, New York, 71, 72 & 74-77. Awards: Anna Hyatt Huntington Gold Medal Award, Catharine Lorillard Wolfe Art Club, 73; Am Artists Prof League Gold Medal Award, 74 & 77; Ellen P Speyer Award, Nat Acad Design, 74; Pen & Brush Gold Medal, 77; plus others. Bibliog: The bronze horses of M Newmark, Am Artist, 71; Life interest expressed in sculpture, Horsemen's Yankee Peddlar, 72; Horses in sculpture, Am Horseman, 72; The Horse in bronze, Horsemans J, 76; Horsewoman & artist extradinare, Horse of Course, 77. Mem: Fel Nat Sculpture Soc (mem coun, 73-75, rec secy, 76, secy, 77 & 78); Am Artists Prof League; Soc Animal Artists; Allied Artists Am; Pen & Brush. Style & Technique: Specialize in horses, hounds, foxes, equestrian figures of all sports, in style of 19th century animaliers. Media: Bronze. Publ: Contribr, Sculpturing horses, Morning Telegraph, 71. Dealer: Arthur Ackermann & Son Inc 50 E 57th St New York NY 10022. Mailing Add: Woodhollow Rd East Hills NY 11577

NEWPORT, ESTHER
PAINTER
b Clinton, Ind, May 17, 01. Study: Art Inst Chicago, BA; St Mary of the Woods Col, AB; Syracuse Univ, MFA; St Mary's Col (Ind), LLD, 56. Comn: Mosaic, Dan Blanc Sch, Washington, DC, 76. Exhib: Five shows, Hoosier Salon, 33-42; John Herron Art Inst, 38; Metrop Mus Art, 44; Contemp Relig Art, Tulsa, Okla, 49; Int Expos Sacred Art, Rome, Italy, 50. Collections Arranged: US Sect, Int Expos Sacred Art, Rome, 50. Pos: Founder, Cath Art Asn, 36, dir, 36-40, bd adv, 40-58; head dept art, St Mary of the Woods Col, 37-64; founder & ed, Cath Art Quart, 37-40; chmn US comn, Holy Yr Exhib, 49-51; mem staff, Cath Univ Am, 52-57, dir art workshop, 54, 58 & 59; mem collection comt, Children's Art Exhib, Vatican Pavilion, Brussels Worlds Fair, 58; dir art sect, Nat Cath Charities Jubilee Prog, 58-60; founder & gen chmn, Conf Cath Art Educ, 58-61, permanent exec secy, 60-63; art supvr, Bd Educ, 62-68; art supvr, Sisters of Providence, 62-; dir, Summer Inst Art Educ, Chicago, 65; speaker & consult elem art educ, Nat Cath Educ Asn Convention, New York, 65; now retired. Awards: Prizes, Hoosier Salon, 37, 39 & 42; First Place, Am & Int Needlepoint Exhib, Chicago, 74. Publ: Auth, National Liturgical Week, 57; ed, Catholic Art Educations, New Trends, 59; ed, Reevaluating Art in Education, 60; auth, Art Teaching Plans (3 bks), 60; auth, Art Appreciation and Creative Work, 61; plus many others. Mailing Add: Owens Hall St Mary of the Woods Col St Mary of the Woods IN 47876

NEWSOM, BARBARA YLVISAKER
WRITER
b Madison, Wis, July 14, 26. Study: Bethany Lutheran Col, Mankato, Minn, AA; Univ Minn, BA; Hunter Col, MA. Pos: Pub affairs consult to 100th Anniversary Comt, Metrop Mus Art, New York, 67-70, consult to vdir for educ, 70-71; study dir, Coun Mus Educ, 71-73; proj dir, Coun Mus & Educ in Visual Arts, New York & Cleveland, Ohio, 73-; staff assoc, Rockefeller Brothers Fund, 73- Mem: Am Asn Mus (coun mem, 75-78). Res: Art museum education; art museum and urban aesthetics. Publ: Auth, The museum as the city's aesthetic conscience, Metrop Mus Bull, 68; auth, The Metropolitan Museum as an educational institution, 70; ed, The art museum as educator, 76. Mailing Add: Rm 5450 30 Rockefeller Plaza New York NY 10020

NEWTON, DOUGLAS
ART ADMINISTRATOR, MUSEUM DIRECTOR
b Malacca, Malaysia, Sept 22, 20. Collections Arranged: Art Styles of the Papuan Gulf, (with catalog), 61; Art of the Massim Area, New Guinea, 64; Art of Africa, Oceania and the Americas, Metrop Mus Art, 69. Pos: Dir & trustee, Mus Primitive Art; chmn dept primitive art, Metrop Mus Art, New York. Res: Relationships of art and oral traditions in New Guinea. Publ: Auth, New Guinea Art in the Museum of Primitive Art, 67; auth, Crocodile and Cassowary, 72; auth, Art of the Massim Area, 72. Mailing Add: Mus Primitive Art 15 W 54th St New York NY 10019

NEWTON, EARLE WILLIAMS
ART ADMINISTRATOR, COLLECTOR
b Cortland, NY, Apr 10, 17. Collections Arranged: British Painting 17th-18th Centuries, 57, 62, 69 & 70; Jacob Eicholtz: Pennsylvania Painter, 58; Hogarth & His School, 59. Pos: Ed, Vermont Life, 46-50; ed, Am Heritage, 49-54; mem ed bd, Art in Am, 53-55; dir, Pa State Mus, 56-59; dir, Mus Art, Sci & Indust, Conn, 59-62; dir, St Augustine & Pensacola Hist Preserv Bd, 62-72; pres, Col Am, 72- Awards: Award of Merit, Am Inst Graphic Arts, 50-52; Comdr, Order of Isabel la Catholica, Spain, 65; Comdr, Order of Merit, Spain, 68. Mem: Am Asn Mus; Soc Archit Historians; Am Asn State & Local Hist (secy-treas, 47-53); Soc Am Historians (secy, 48-50); Nat Trust Hist Preserv. Res: Anglo-American art. Collection: Anglo-American art of the 17th and 18th centuries; pre-Columbian art; Latin American folk art; American maps; Americana. Publ: Auth, Before Pearl Harbor, 42; auth, The Vermont Story, 1749-1949, 49; ed, Gulf Coast Conf Proc, 70-72. Mailing Add: Rt 14 Brookfield VT 05036

NEWTON, FRANCIS JOHN
MUSEUM DIRECTOR
b Butte, Mont, Dec 27, 12. Study: Univ Idaho, BA, 36, MA, 39, hon LHD, 74; Univ Iowa, PhD, 51. Teaching: Vis prof art hist, Univ Ore, summer 59; vis prof, Portland State Col, summer 61. Pos: Cur asst, Worcester Mus Art, Mass, 51-53; cur, Portland Art Mus, 53-60, dir, 60-75; chief consult art, Portland Curric Study, 59; mem, Gov Planning Coun Arts & Humanities. Awards: Order of North Star, Sweden, 65; Distinguished Citizen Award, Univ Ore, 70; Award, Portland State Univ & City Portland, 75. Mem: Col Art Asn Am; Am Asn Mus; Western Asn Art Mus (pres, 60-61); Asn Art Mus Dirs; hon assoc mem Am Inst Architects (Ore chap). Mailing Add: 6805 SE 31st Ave Portland OR 97202

NIBLETT, GARY LAWRENCE
PAINTER
b Carlsbad, NMex, Jan 9, 43. Study: Art Instruction Inc, Minneapolis, Minn; Eastern NMex Univ, Portales; Art Ctr Col of Design, Los Angeles, Calif. Exhib: Preview, Dallas, Tex, 74-78; Cowboy Artist of Am 77 Show, Phoenix Art Mus, 77; Mungerson Gallery Invitational, Chicago, Ill, 78; The Enduring West, Mus of Albuquerque, 78; one-man show, Texas Art Gallery, Dallas, 75 & 76. Awards: Silver Medal, Cowboy Artist of Am Show, Phoenix Art Mus, 77. Bibliog: Staff writer, Gary Niblett, dedicated young western artist, Ariz Living, 74; Elizabeth Rigby (auth), Gary Niblett is rising star, The Illusr, 76; Ella Warren (auth), Gary Niblett, Artist of the Rockies and the Golden West, 78. Mem: Cowboy Artist of Am. Style & Technique: Representational style with painted technique. Media: Oil. Mailing Add: Box 142 Angel Fire NM 87718

NIBLOCK, PHILL
FILM MAKER, COMPOSER
b Anderson, Ind, Oct 2, 33. Study: Ind Univ, BA(econ). Work: Everson Mus, Syracuse; Kirkland Art Ctr, Clinton, NY; Wadsworth Atheneum, Hartford, Conn. Multimedia Performances: Hundred Mile Radius, Kirkland Art Ctr & Whitney Mus Am Art, 71; Ten Hundred Inch Radii, Everson Mus, 72; Cineprobe, films and music, Mus Mod Art, New York, 73; Sur, Wadsworth Atheneum, Hartford, Conn & The Kitchen, New York, 75; Trabajando, Herbert F Johnson Mus, Cornell Univ, 76. Teaching: Assoc prof film, Staten Island Community Col. Awards: NY State Coun Arts Grant, Kirkland Art Ctr, 70, Exp Intermedia Found, 72-74; Nat Endowment Arts Pub Media Prog, 75-76. Bibliog: Tom Johnson (auth), Music reviews, Village Voice, 72, 73 & 74; John Rockwell (auth), What's new, High Fidelity/Musical Am, 5/74; Abigail Nelson (auth), Who's Who in Film, Sight Lines, winter 74. Mem: Exp Intermedia Found. Style & Technique: Film and music museum installations. Mailing Add: 224 Centre St New York NY 10013

NICHOLAS, DONNA LEE
CERAMIST, EDUCATOR
b South Pasadena, Calif, Mar 30, 38. Study: Pomona Col, BA(cum laude), 59; apprentice with Kako Morino, Kyoto, Japan, 60-62; Claremont Grad Sch & Univ Ctr, with Paul Soldner & MFA, 66. Work: Flint Inst Arts, Mich. Exhib: One-person shows, Sherbeyn Gallery, Chicago, 70, Erie Art Ctr, 74 & Chatham Col, Pittsburgh, 76; For Men Only, Lee Nordness Gallery, New York, 71; Salt Glaze Ceramics, Mus Contemp Crafts, New York, 72; Brand V Ceramic Conjunction, Brand Art Ctr, Glendale, Calif, 75; Object as Poet, Renwick Gallery, Smithsonian Inst, Washington, DC & Mus Contemp Crafts, New York, 76; Clay, Fiber, Metal, Women Artists, Bronx Mus, NY, 78; plus others. Teaching: Instr ceramics, Genesee Community Col, Flint, 66-69; assoc prof ceramics, Edinboro State Col, 69-; vis artist/instr, Penland Sch Crafts, NC, summer 71; vis artist/instr, Scripps Col, 74; vis artist/instr, Moore Col Art, Philadelphia, 75. Mem: Am Craftsmen's Coun (Pa rep to NE Assembly, 75-); Nat Coun Educ Ceramic Arts. Style & Technique: Low fire ceramic sculpture; salt glazed porcelain. Media: Clay. Mailing Add: 501 Jefferson Edinboro PA 16412

NICHOLAS, THOMAS ANDREW
PAINTER
b Middletown, Conn, Sept 26, 34. Study: Sch Visual Arts, NY, scholar, 53-55. Work: Butler Inst Am Art, Youngstown, Ohio; Ga Mus, Athens; Farnesworth Mus, Rockland, Maine; Adelphi Univ; Greenshields Mus, Montreal; plus others. Comn: Four ten-colored lithographs, Franklin Mint, 77. Exhib: Major exhibs, New York, New Eng & Washington, DC, 59-Teaching: Instr, Famous Artists Schs, Westport, Conn, 58-61. Awards: Elizabeth T Greenshields Mem Found Grants, 61 & 62; Gold Medal Honor, Allied Artists Am, 68; Gold Medal Honor, Am Watercolor Soc; plus many others. Bibliog: Articles in Am Artist, 3/60 & 8/72; article in North Light Mag, fall 70; John L Cooley (auth), article in The Old Watercolor Soc, Eng, 71; plus others. Mem: Nat Acad Design; Am Watercolor Soc; Allied Artists Am; Salmagundi Club; Knickerbocker Artists; plus others. Style & Technique: Romantic realist. Media: Oil, Watercolor. Mailing Add: 7 Wildon Heights Rockport MA 01966

NICHOLS, ALICE W
PAINTER, EDUCATOR
b St Joseph, Mo, June 15, 06. Study: Tex Woman's Univ; Pratt Inst; Univ Tex, Austin, BA & MA; Teachers Col, Columbia Univ, EdD. Work: Ball State Univ Art Gallery; Anderson Fine Arts Found, Ind. Collections Arranged: 18 Ann Drawing & Small Sculpture Shows, 55-; Crafts 1967, Ball State Univ Art Gallery, 67, Collages by American Artists, 71. Teaching: Prof art, WTex State Teachers Col; prof art, Univ Denver; prof art, Ball State Univ, 47-72, head dept art, 47-73; retired. Pos: Dir art gallery, Ball State Univ, 67-73; pres, Nichols Assocs, Design Consults. Awards: Gibson Award Outstanding Contribution to Indiana Architecture, Ind Soc Architects, 72; Ind Arts Comn Award Outstanding Arts Leadership, 73. Mem: Am Asn Mus; Delta Phi Delta; Am Asn Univ Prof; Ind State Arts Comn. Media: Collage. Collection: European graphics including Braque, Picasso, Burri and others; also contemporary American unknowns. Publ: Auth, Art Vol, Jr Britannica; auth, articles in Palette; auth, articles in Hoosier Schoolmaster, 66, 69 & 70; auth, 7 Outside (brochure), Indianapolis Mus Art, 70; also numerous mus catalogs. Mailing Add: 402 N Calvert Muncie IN 47303

NICHOLS, DALE WILLIAM
WRITER, DESIGNER
b David City, Nebr, July 13, 04. Study: Chicago Acad Fine Arts, with Carl Werntz; Chicago Art Inst; also with Joseph Binder, Vienna. Work: Metrop Mus NY; Chicago Art Inst; Victoria & Albert Mus, London; Univ Ill; Miller & Paine Gallery, Lincoln, Nebr. Comn: Mural, Indust Mt Morris, Ill, 38; archit proj, Univ Ill, 39-40; color card, City Tucson, Ariz, 41; design & illusr book, Two Years Before the Mast, Heritage Press, 41; mural, Jean LaFitte, Holiday Inn, Longbeach, Miss, 57. Exhib: Chicago Art Inst; rep in New York, Chicago, San Francisco, San Diego & Dallas World's Fairs. Teaching: Lect var art asns, 37-; Carnegie vis prof art philos, Univ Ill, 39-40. Pos: Art ed, Encycl Britannica, 42-48; art dir, Planning Bd, City Tucson, 42-49; artist in residence, Northern Mich Col Educ, 54. Awards: Watson Blair Award, The Cold Wave & collection, End of the Hunt, Chicago Art Inst, 39. Bibliog: William A Kittredge (auth), Dale Nichols, London Studio, 38, Gebraughsgrafic Berlin, 38 & Travel Mag, 39. Mem: Am Artist Prof League; life fel Brownsville Art League; Int Platform Asn; Grand Cent Art Galleries. Style & Technique: Psychogenic uses of color, form and line of Pythagorean & Zoroastrian principles. Media: Tempera, Oil, Watercolor, Ink, Pencil. Res: Visual psychology; numerology, magic squares; heliotropic and geotropic psychic symbols. Publ: Auth, A Philosophy of Esthetics, 38; auth, The Pyramid Text of the Ancient Maya, 69, Magnificent Mystery, Tikal, 70 & The Mayan Mystery, 73 & 76. Dealer: Grand Central Art Galleries 40 Vanderbilt Ave New York NY 10017. Mailing Add: La Antigua Guatemala Central America

NICHOLS, DONALD EDWARD
DESIGNER, EDUCATOR
b Buffalo, NY, Nov 20, 22. Study: Albright Art Sch, grad graphic design, 47; Univ Buffalo, BFA, 49; Mass Inst Technol, summer design prog, 67. Comn: Graphics for ann catalog, NY State Coun on Arts, Albany, 62; cover design, J Creative Behavior, Creative Educ Found, 69; commun graphics, Am Acad Arts & Sci, Cambridge, Mass, 69; corp graphic prog, Amarillo Art Ctr Asn, Tex, 70-72. Exhib: Four Western NY Exhibs, Albright-Knox Gallery, Buffalo, 54-67, NY State Fair, 63 & 67; Convocation on the Arts, State Univ NY Albany, 69; Int IONALES Design Zentrum, Berlin, Ger, 70; Ciba-Geigy Corp Int Display, San Francisco, Calif, 77. Teaching: Instr art, Albright Art Sch, 49-54; prof art & head commun design option, State Univ NY Buffalo, 54- Awards: Western NY Exhib Lyman Prize & Kittinger Award, Albright-Knox Gallery, 54; NY State Expos Award, Art Today Exhib, Syracuse, 67; Fac Res Fels & Grants, State Univ NY Buffalo, 68, 69 & 73. Mem: Art Dir/Communicators of Buffalo; Am Asn Univ Prof. Publ: Illusr, CA J Commun Arts, 59; illusr, Sch Arts Mag, 59 & 67; illusr, J Creative Behavior, 69; illusr, Humanist Mag, 69. Mailing Add: 530 Mt Vernon Rd Buffalo NY 14226

NICHOLS, ELEANOR CARY
DESIGNER, SILVERSMITH
b Madison, Wis, Feb 27, 03. Study: Univ Wis, BS(appl art); Goldsmith Co, Stockholm, Sweden; Brookfield Craft Ctr, Conn. Work: Del Art Mus, Wilmington; Winterthur Mus, Wilmington. Comn: Twenty bronze medallions for door, St Mark's Lutheran Church, Wilmington, 54; commemorative plaque, Del Swedish Colonial Soc, 63; 30 chalices, 17 patens, 2 processional crosses & 8 torches, Lutheran Church Am, 74; ambry door plaque, St Peters Church, Smyrna, Del, 77; mem plaque, St Mark's Church, Wilmington, Del, 77. Exhib: Nat League Am Pen Women state & nat shows, 5 times, 66-74 & Cult Show in Mexico, 67; World Crafts Coun, Peru, SAm, 68. Teaching: Instr woodshop, Mt Pleasant Jr High Sch, 43-44; instr silversmithing, Del Art Mus, Wilmington, 43-; instr woodshop, Conrad Sr High Sch, 44-46. Awards: Second in Metals, Nat League Am Pen Women, 66, Second in Jewelry, 70 & First & Second in Jewelry, 70. Bibliog: Delta Zeta & her unusual talent bring beauty to her community, Delta Zeta Lamp, spring 56; Isabel Church (auth), Profile of the week, Town Talk, 9/71; Eileen Spracker (auth), Lutheran Convention gets Delaware touch, Eve J, 6/74. Mem: Am Crafts Coun; World Craft Coun; Nat League Am Pen Women (br treas, 67-72, br pres, 72-74, state pres, 74-76). Style & Technique: Traditional and contemporary gold-silversmithing. Media: Silver, Gold. Mailing Add: 1505 River Rd Bellevue Manor Wilmington DE 19809

NICHOLS, FRANCIS N, II
PRINTMAKER, EDUCATOR
Study: Wichita State Univ, MFA; also with David Bernard & Robert Kiskadden. Exhib: Okla Nat Print & Drawing Exhib, Oklahoma City, 68; Watercolor USA, Springfield, Mo, 69; Nat Print & Drawing Exhib, Gallery 8, Erie, Pa, 70; one-man shows, Limited Ed Gallery, Durham, NC, 75 & Duke Univ, 75. Teaching: Teaching fel, Wichita State Univ, 65-67; asst prof printmaking, Ft Hays State Col, 67-; teaching asst, Univ Kans, 72-73. Style & Technique: Intricate and carefully defined form; organic imagery. Media: Copper Plate Intaglio, Pen & Ink. Mailing Add: 2712 Walnut Hays KS 67601

NICHOLS, JAMES WILLIAM
PAINTER
b Pasadena, Calif, Nov 22, 28. Study: Univ Calif, Los Angeles, BA, 50; Univ Calif, Berkeley, with Worth Ryder & Estaben Vicente, MA, 54. Work: Mus Mod Art, New York; Long Beach Mus Art, Calif; Aldrich Mus Contemp Art, Ridgefield, Conn; Westmoreland Co Mus Art, Greensburg, Pa; Wichita Art Mus. Comn: Eight collage paintings, Henkel Factory, Dusseldorf, Ger, 66-67; two collage constructions, Singer Co, New York, 67; metal mural painting, Lombard Wall, New York, 71; four panel screen & new logo, Long Beach Mus Art, 73; metal mural painting, Gotham Audio, New York, 75. Exhib: Jim Nichols' Metal Collage Constructions, New York Cult Ctr, 74, Long Beach Mus Art, 75, Wichita Art Mus, 75, Scottsdale Ctr Arts & Civic Ctr Gallery, 75 & Everson Mus Art, Syracuse, NY, 75. Style & Technique: Painted and printed tin and aluminum on wood. Publ: Illusr, About the House, London, 3/65; illusr, Art & artists, London, Vol 2, No 7 & Vol 3, No 8; illusr, Works, New York, Vol 1, No 3; illusr & contribr, Mag 4, New York, 69. Mailing Add: 215 Bowery New York NY 10002

NICHOLS, JEANNETTIE DOORNHEIN
PAINTER
b Holland, Mich, July 27, 06. Study: Art Inst Chicago, BA; Ill Inst Technol; Univ Chicago; lithography with Francis Chapin; painting with Carl Hoeckner; mural painting with Peppino Mangravite. Work: Ind Univ Northwest; Washington Pub High Sch, Chicago; Prince William Co Pub Sch, Manassas, Va; Portage Pub Schs; Albrecht Art Mus, St Joseph, Mo. Exhib: Pa Acad Fine Arts, Philadelphia, 37; one-man shows, Crespi Gallery, New York, 59 & Kreig Art Gallery, Lombard, Ill, 71-73; Minneapolis Art Mus Invitational, 63; Ann Ceramic Show, South Bend, Ind, 66; Am Painters in Paris Exhib, France, 76; Artist Equity, Dallas, 77; Prof Artists of Dallas, Allen St Gallery, 77. Teaching: Art supvr, Belvedere Pub Sch Syst, Ill, 29-33; chmn art, Hyde Park High Sch, Chicago, 40-57; chmn art, Washington High Sch, Chicago, 57-72; instr art, Gary Art League, Ind & NVa Community Col, 75- Pos: Mem, Woodbridge Art Guild Workshop, 75; demonstr acrylic & mono-printmaking, Prince William Co Pub Sch & Woodbridge Art Guild, 77; mem art juries. Awards: Second Award for Macatawa Bay, Peaceful Harbor (watercolor), Southern Shores Ann, 56; First, Second & Third Purchase Awards for Three Christs (enamel on copper), South Bend Ceramic Show, 56; Award for Washington School Playground of 1959 (oil), Tri-Kappa, 67. Bibliog: Charles A Wagner (auth), World of art, New York Mirror, 9/20/59; Helen Ruth Huber (auth), Outstanding area artists, Gary Post Tribune, 61; Will & Jean Heidorn (auth), Art renaissance in progress, Potomac News, Va, 76. Mem: Assoc Artists & Craftsmen of Porter Co (former pres); Art Inst Chicago Alumni Asn; Artists Equity Asn; life fel Int Inst Arts & Lett; Woodbridge Art Guild (vpres, 75). Style & Technique: Interpretive expressionism, plus emotional symbolism using all media. Publ: Auth, Arts and activities, In: Mural Painting in High School, 56. Mailing Add: Rt 1 Buttonwood Village Waxahachie TX 75165

NICHOLS, MAXINE MCCLENDON
See McClendon, Maxine

NICHOLS, WARD H
PAINTER, PRINTMAKER
b Welch, WVa, July 5, 30. Work: NC Nat Bank Collection, Charlotte; Huntington Gallery Art, WVa; Springfield Mus Art, Mass. Exhib: Acad Artists Exhibs, Mus Fine Arts, Springfield, 66-70; Allied Artists Am, Nat Acad Design Galleries, New York, 68; Mainstreams, Fine Arts Ctr, Marietta Col, 69, 70 & 72; Frontal Images Exhib, Miss Mus Art, Jackson, 70. Teaching: Guest lectr, many cols in eastern US. Awards: Honorable Mention, Huntington Mus Art, 69; Grumbacher Award of Merit, El Paso Mus Art, 70; Jurors Merit Award, Miss Mus Art, 71. Bibliog: Of Heart and Hand (doc film), WVa Dept Com, 69; Matter of communication, Huntington Mag Sect, 69; articles in La Rev Mod, 70-72. Mem: Acad Artists Asn; Wilkes Art Guild; Northwest NC Artists; Soc NAm Artists. Style & Technique: Extreme realism, accenting textures; wet on wet technique. Media: Oil. Dealer: Northwest Gallery Hwy 115 at Armory Rd North Wilkesboro NC 28659. Mailing Add: Rte 5 Box 63 Beaumont Wilkesboro NC 28659

NICHOLSON, BEN
PAINTER
b Denham, Eng, Apr 10, 94. Work: In pub collections in Eng, US, Can, Switz, Arg, Australia, Italy, Belg, Brazil & Japan. Exhib: Kunsthalle, Berne, 61; Gimpel & Hanover Gallery, Zurich, 66; Marlborh Gallery, London, 67; Galerie Beyeler, 68; Studio Int, London, 69; plus others. Awards: US First Guggenheim Int Award, 56; First Prize for Painting, 4th Biennale, Sao Paulo, Brazil, 57; Decorated Order of Merit, Eng, 68. Bibliog: Sir John Summerson (auth), Penguin Modern Painters, 48; J P Hodin (auth), The Meaning of His Art, 57; John Russell (auth), Drawings, Paintings and Reliefs, 1911-68; plus others. Mailing Add: c/o Emmerich Gallery 41 E 57th St New York NY 10022

NICK, GEORGE
PAINTER, EDUCATOR
b Rochester, NY, Mar 28, 27. Study: Cleveland Inst Art, with Frank Wilcox; Brooklyn Mus Art Sch; Art Students League, with Edwin Dickinson; Yale Univ, BFA & MFA. Work: Rose Art Gallery, Brandeis Univ, Waltham, Mass; Galleria Sant' Onofrio, Rome, Italy. Exhib: Md Artists Ann Exhib, Baltimore, 66; Pa Artists Ann, Philadelphia Acad Fine Arts, 67. Teaching: Assoc prof drawing, Carnegie-Mellon Inst, 64-65; assoc prof painting, Univ Pa, 66-69; assoc prof painting, Mass Col Art, Boston. Awards: E Stanton Griggs Award Excellence in Drawing, Yale Univ, 63; Md Artists Ann Exhib Jury Awards, Baltimore Mus Art, 66; Mass Coun of the Arts grant, 74; Nat Endowment Arts Award, 76. Media: Oil. Dealer: Richard Gray Gallery 620 N Michigan Ave Chicago IL 60615. Mailing Add: 31 North St Georgetown MA 01833

NICKEL, JIM H
PAINTER, SCULPTOR
b Oak Park, Ill, Nov 30, 43. Study: Concordia Col, Ft Wayne, Ind, BA(philos); Concordia Seminary, St Louis, Mo; Washington Univ, St Louis, with Ernoe Koch. Work: St Louis City Art Mus, Mo. Comn: Outdoor sculptures, Alberta Slavin, 71, Dr Bernard Becker, 71 & Stanton Fisher, 71, St Louis Mo; wood sculpture, Mark Twain Bankshares, St Louis, Mo, 77. Exhib: One-man shows, Terry Moore Gallery, St Louis, 75, 76 & 77; Midwest Painters & Sculptors Show, Krannert Art Mus, Champaign, Ill, 76; Mo Photogr Show, St Louis Art Mus, 76; Washington Univ Fac Show, Steinberg Mus, St Louis, 77; Inaugural Art Exhib, St Louis Convention Ctr, 77; Delta Art Show, Ark Arts Ctr, Little Rock, 77. Teaching: Instr three-dimentional design, Washington Univ, St Louis, 77. Bibliog: Mary Hellen Spooner (auth), The artist myth, St Louis Post-Dispatch Mag, 77; Jack Peters (auth), Wood sculpture, New Art Examr, Chicago, 77; Mary King (auth), Sculpture in wood, St Louis Post-Dispatch, 77. Mem: Col Art Asn; Southern Asn Sculptors. Style & Technique: Large geometric abstractions, wood wall reliefs. Media: Sprayed acrylic on canvas and reassembled wood sculpture. Publ: Auth, Directed motion, The Triangle, Concordia Col, 65. Dealer: Terry Moore Gallery 612 N Second St St Louis MO 63102. Mailing Add: 2948 S Brentwood Rear St Louis MO 63144

NICKERSON, RUTH (RUTH NICKERSON GREACEN)
SCULPTOR
b Appleton, Wis, Nov 23, 05. Study: Simcoe Col Inst, Ont; Nat Acad Design; also with Ahron Ben-Smuel, New York. Work: Arlington Br, Brooklyn Pub Libr; Cedar Rapids Art Asn, Iowa; Montclair Art Mus, NJ; Interchurch Ctr, New York. Comn: Many portrait comns for pvt collectors, 32-; Learning (stone group), Fed Art Proj, Brooklyn, 34; Tympanum, Fed Govt, New Brunswick Post Off, NJ, 36; American Oriental Rug Weaving (ceramic mural), Fed Art Proj, Leaksville Post Off, NC; mem plaque, New Rochelle Art Comt for City Hall, 60. Exhib: Nat Acad Design Ann, New York, 32-; Whitney Mus Am Art, New York, 34; Mus Mod Art, New York, 39; Artists for Victory, Metrop Mus Art, New York, 42; Pa Acad Fine Arts, Philadelphia, 48. Teaching: Instr sculpture, Roerich Mus, New York, 34-35; instr sculpture, Westchester Art Workshop, 45-47 & 48-69. Pos: Charter mem & secy pro tem, White Plains Civic Art Comn, 48-60. Awards: Saltus Gold Medal, Nat Acad Design, 33; Montclair Mus Art Medal, 39; Guggenheim Fel, 46-47. Bibliog: Jacques Schneir (auth), Art in Modern America. Mem: Nat Sculpture Soc (mem coun, 60-63, rec secy, 62-63); Nat Acad Design; Audubon Artists (dir & bd mem, 55); Scarsdale Art Asn (treas, 43-44); Hudson Valley Art Asn. Style & Technique: Work created to embody the principles of simplicity, dignity and strength; uses contrasting surfaces of smooth and rough forms developed in the final medium by direct carving in stone. Mailing Add: 106 Woodcrest Ave White Plains NY 10604

NICKFORD, JUAN
SCULPTOR, EDUCATOR
b Havana, Cuba, Aug 8, 25; US citizen. Study: Acad Art, Havana, MFA, 46; Sch Archit, Univ Havana. Work: Smith Col Mus Art; Spaeth Found, New York; also in collections of Roy Neuberger, New York & Phil Berg, Los Angeles. Comn: Welded metal sculptures, Socony Oil Bldg, New York, 56; metal mural, Trade Show Bldg, New York, 56; free standing group, Philco Corp Trade Mart, Chicago, Ill, 57; screens, Grace Line, SS Santa Rosa, 60; outdoor sculpture, Tappan Town Soc, NY, 72. Exhib: American Sculpture, Metrop Mus Art, New York, 51; Whitney Mus Am Art Ann, 50-57; God and Man in Art, Am Fedn Arts Traveling Show, 59; Junior Council, Mus Mod Art, New York, 61; Man Came This Way, Los Angeles Co Mus Art, 71; Schenectady Mus, NY, 76; one-man exhibs, Sculpture Ctr, New York, 74, Ann Leonard Gallery, Woodstock, NY, 74, Rockland Ctr for the Arts, West Nyack, NY, 74, Manhattanville Col, Purchase, NY, 75 & Emanuel Col, Boston, Mass, 77. Teaching: Vis artist, Univ Hartford, 65-66; vis artist, Smith Col, 66-69; asst prof sculpture, City Col New York, 70-75, assoc prof art, 75- Pos: Mem exhib comt, Sculpture Ctr New York, 70-; mem exhib comt, City Col New York, 71- Awards: Honorable Mention, Pa Acad Fine Arts, 58; Bronze Medal, NY State Expos, 64; Inst Int Educ Grant for Creative Sculpture, Cintas Found, 71. Bibliog: Frank & Dorothy Getlein (auth), Christianity in Modern Art, Bruce, 61; Meilach & Seiden (auth), Direct Metal Sculpture, George Allen & Unwin, Ltd, London, 66; Nathan Cabot Hale (auth), Welded Sculpture, Watson-Guptill, 68; Wayne Andersen (auth), American Sculpture in Process: 1930/1970, NY Graphic Soc, 75. Mem: Sculptor's Guild; Rockland Found Art. Style & Technique: Fragmented figuration; hammered and welded copper elements contrasted against burnished brass reflecting surfaces. Media: Metal, Mixed Media. Publ: Contribr, New talent, Art in Am, 56. Dealer: Sculpture Center Inc 167 E 69th St New York NY 10021. Mailing Add: 161 Old Tappan Rd Tappan NY 10983

NICKLE, ROBERT W
PAINTER, EDUCATOR
b Saginaw, Mich, May 22, 19. Study: Univ Mich, BD; Inst Design, Chicago. Work: Art Inst Chicago. Exhib: Carnegie Inst Int, 59; Mus Mod Art, 61; Univ Ill, Urbana-Champaign, 69; Purdue Univ, 69; Art Inst Chicago; plus others. Teaching: Prof drawing & design, Univ Ill, Chicago Circle, 55- Awards: Purchase Prize, Art Inst Chicago. Mailing Add: Dept of Art Univ Ill at Chicago Circle Chicago IL 60680

NICODEMUS, CHESTER ROLAND
SCULPTOR, DESIGNER
b Barberton, Ohio, Aug 17, 01. Study: Cleveland Sch Art, grad, 25; Univ Dayton; Ohio State Univ. Work: Dayton Art Inst; Columbus Gallery Fine Arts, Ohio; Capital Univ. Comn: Wright Bros Tablet, Wilbur Wright High Sch, Dayton, 28; Francis C Sessions Tablet, Columbus Gallery Fine Arts, 32; Columbus Art League Medal, 47; Edward Orton Tablet, Unitarian Church, Columbus, 63; Butler Inst Am Art Medal, Youngstown, Ohio, 72. Exhib: Ceramic Nat, Syracuse, NY, 54; Ceramic Int, 58; Columbus Art League, 63; Butler Inst Am Art, 65. Teaching: Instr sculpture, Dayton Art Inst, 25-30; instr sculpture, Columbus Art Sch, 30-43, dean, 31-32. Mem: Nat Sculpture Soc; Columbus Art League (pres, 33-36). Media: Ceramics, Bronze. Mailing Add: 447 Clinton Heights Ave Columbus OH 43202

NIELSEN, STUART
PAINTER
b Evanston, Ill, Feb 16, 47. Study: Univ Minn, BFA, 69. Work: Walker Art Ctr, Minneapolis. Comn: Gilded panels, James Talcott Inc, New York, 74. Exhib: 1966 Biennial & 1974 Exhib, Walker Art Ctr, Minneapolis; Biennial, Whitney Mus Am Art, New York, 75; Univ Tex, Arlington. Awards: Fel, Minn State Arts Coun, 73. Style & Technique: Abstract, gilded. Media: Painting. Dealer: Glen Hanson Fine Arts 2440 Girard Ave S Minneapolis MN 55405. Mailing Add: 133 First Ave N Minneapolis MN 55401

NIEMANN, EDMUND E
PAINTER
b New York, NY. Study: Nat Acad Design; Art Students League. Work: Norfolk Mus Arts & Sci, Va; Springfield Art Mus, Mass; Storm King Art Mus, Mountainville, NY; Syracuse Univ Art Mus; Swarthmore Col. Exhib: Directions of American Painting, Carnegie Inst, Pa, 41; Pa Acad Fine Arts Watercolor & Drawing Ann, 64; Butler Inst Am Art Painting Nat, 68 & 74; Nat Acad Design Ann, 68; Watercolor USA, 72. Awards: Emily Lowe Found, 55; Ball State Univ Drawing Ann Purchase Award, 60; Watercolor USA Award, 74. Mem: Audubon Artists; Am Watercolor Soc; Conn Acad; Allied Artists Am; Nat Soc Painters Acrylic & Casein. Style & Technique: Transposes contemporary scene into original and imaginative metaphor, using structured abstract expressionism. Publ: Contribr, Todays Art, 7/68 & 8/73; auth, Drawing with unusual tool, Am Artists, 1/70. Mailing Add: 38-15 208th St Bayside NY 11361

NIEMEYER, ARNOLD MATTHEW
COLLECTOR, PATRON
b St Paul, Minn, Mar 7, 13. Pos: Trustee, Minn Mus Art. Collection: All media, especially fine graphics. Mailing Add: 1364 Summit Ave St Paul MN 55105

NIERMAN, LEONARDO M
PAINTER, SCULPTOR
b Mexico City, Mex, Nov 1, 32. Study: Nat Univ Mex, BA. Work: Boston Mus Fine Arts, Mass; Mus Arte Mod, Mexico City; The Wave, Detroit Inst of Arts; Bird in Flight, Acad Fine Arts, Honolulu; Genesis, Israel Mus, Jerusalem; plus others. Comn: Murals Sch Com, Univ City, Mex, 56 & Golden West Savings, San Francisco, Calif, 65; stained glass windows, two temples, Mexico City, 66-67; Cosmic Meditation (mural), Physics Bldg, Princeton Univ, NJ, 68; Eagle (bronze sculpture), Toronto, Can, 72. Exhib: Paris Biennale, Mus Mod Art, France, 61; Marlborough-Gerson Gallery, New York, 64; Pittsburgh Int, Carnegie Inst, Pa, 64 & 67; El Paso Mus Art, Tex, 64 & 71; Mus Arte Mod, 72; plus many one-man shows. Awards: First Prize, Art Inst Mex, 64; Palm D'Or Beaux Arts, Monaco, 69; Gold Medal, Tomasso Campanella Found, Italy, 72. Bibliog: Enrique Gual (auth), Leonardo Nierman, Ed Monterrey, 64; Jose Gomez Sicre (auth), Nierman, Artes Mex, 71; Julio Cortazar & Max Pol Fouchet (auth), Leonardo Nierman, A Capell & A Elmayan Ed, Paris, 75. Mem: Royal Soc Arts, London; Int Biog Asn: UK; Int Arts Guild, Monte Carlo; Salon Plastica, Mex. Media: Acrylic; Onyx, Bronze. Dealer: Wally F Findlay Galleries 17 E 57th St New York NY 10022. Mailing Add: Ave Nuevo Leon 160 Mexico City 11 Mexico

NIESE, HENRY ERNST
PAINTER, FILM MAKER
b Jersey City, NJ, Oct 11, 24. Study: Cooper Union, cert, with Robert Gwathmey & Morris Kantor; Acad Grande Chaumiere, cert, with Othon Friesz; Columbia Univ, BFA, with Leo Manso, John Heliker & Meyer Schapiro. Work: Whitney Mus Am Art, New York; Chrysler Mus, Norfolk, Va; Albright-Knox Mus; NJ State Mus, Trenton; Filmkundliches Arkiv, Cologne, WGer. Exhib: Young Am, Whitney Mus Am Art, 62 & 40 Artists Under 40, 64; 4th Int Exp Film Festival, Brussels, Belg, 67; New York Avant Garde Festivals, 69-75; Six Nations Mus, NY & Corcoran Gallery, 76. Teaching: Spec lectr grad humanities, NY Univ, 65-69; asst prof studio art, Ohio State Univ, 66-69; assoc prof studio art, Univ Md, 69- Awards: Pulitzer Found Traveling Fel, 55; Int Cinema Prize, Mus Arte Mod, Vitoria, Brasil, 69; Creative & Performing Arts Grant, Univ Md, 71 & 73. Style & Technique: Films about people; paintings of archetypal centralized symbols. Media: Acrylic, Oil. Dealer: Frank Rehn Gallery 655 Madison Ave New York NY 10019. Mailing Add: Rte 2 Box 12924 Glenelg MD 21737

NIGROSH, LEON ISAAC
DESIGNER, INSTRUCTOR
b Cambridge, Mass, Aug 7, 40. Study: Carnegie Inst Technol, 58-59; RI Sch Design, BFA, 63; Rochester Inst Technol, MFA, 65. Comn: Ceramic mural, Waltham Supermarket, Mass, 63; ceramic, metal & glass panels, comn by Mr & Mrs Benjamin Cooperstein, Belmont, Mass, 64; ceramic & acrylite sculpture, comn by Mr & Mrs George Klomberg, Long Island, NY, 70; ceramic wall panel, comn by Mr & Mrs Robert Massey, Holden, Mass, 70; five ceramic fountains, Group One Inc, New Seabury, Mass, 73. Exhib: One-man show, B'nai B'rith Bldg, Washington, DC, 69 & 78 & Soc of Arts & Crafts, Boston, 76; two-man show, The Galleries, Wellesley, Mass, 72; NC Mus of Art, Raleigh, 75. Teaching: Instr ceramics, Auburn Community Col, 64-65; instr ceramics & studio mgr, Greenwich House Pottery Sch, New York, 65-66; instr ceramics & head dept, Craft Ctr, Worcester, 67- Mem: Int Guild of Craftjournalists, Authors & Photogr; Am Crafts Coun; Mass Asn Crafts. Style & Technique: Contemporary. Media: Ceramic. Publ: Contribr, Craft Horizons, 71-; auth, Claywork, Davis, 75; auth, five articles in Sch Arts, 76-77. Mailing Add: 11 Chatanika Ave Worcester MA 01602

NIIZUMA, MINORU
SCULPTOR
b Tokyo, Japan, Sept 29, 30. Study: Tokyo Univ Arts, BFA. Work: Mus Mod Art, New York; Nat Mus Mod Art, Tokyo; Albright-Knox Gallery, Buffalo; Guggenheim Mus, New York; Hirshhorn Mus & Sculpture Garden, Washington, DC; plus others. Comn: Stone monuments, Metrop Tokyo, 56, Asia House, Tokyo, 58; Int Sculpture Symp, Vt, 68, St Margarethen, Austria, 69 & New York, 71. Exhib: Mus Mod Art, 65 & 66 & Whitney Mus Am Art Sculpture Ann, 66 & 68, New York; one-man shows, Howard Wise Gallery & Gimpel & Weitzenhoffer Gallery, New York, 66, 68 & 72-77 & Rockefeller Univ, 71; Carnegie Inst Int, 67. Teaching: Instr sculpture, Brooklyn Mus Art Sch, 64-69; lectr, Columbia Univ, 72- Awards: Mod Art Asn Award, Japan, 55 & 56. Mem: Mod Art Assoc Japan (permanent juror, 57-); Sculptors Guild. Media: Marble. Dealer: Gimpel & Weitzenhoffer Gallery 1040 Madison Ave at 79th New York NY 10021. Mailing Add: 463 West St New York NY 10014

NIND, JEAN
PAINTER, PRINTMAKER
b Miri, Sarawak, Borneo, June 17, 30; Can citizen. Study: Chelsea Art Sch, London, Eng; Univ Sask, Can, studied with Eli Bornstein & Otto Rogers. Work: Sask Power Corp, Regina; Court House, Edmonton, Alta, Can; Trent Univ, Peterborough, Ont; Volvo Corp, Halifax, NS; Sir Sandford Fleming Col, Peterborough, Ont. Comn: Symphony (oil), comn by mem bd, Saksatoon Symphony, Sask, 64; five serigraphs (for presentation to guest speakers), Trent Univ, Peterborough, Ont, 69. Exhib: Mendel Art Gallery, Saskatoon, Sask, 64-65; Ohio Invitational, Sask Arts Bd, 64; Soc Painters, Etchers & Engravers, Toronto, Ont, 65-67; McLaughlin Gallery, Oshawa, Ont, 68; Mackenzie Gallery, Trent Univ, Peterborough, Ont, 68, 73 & 77; Kingston Spring Exhib, Agnes Etherington Art Gallery, Kingston, Ont, 69; 99th & 101st Ann Exhib, Ont Soc Artists, 71-73; Art Gallery, Halifax, NS, 72. Collections Arranged: St Thomas More Art Gallery, Univ Sask, 66; Mackenzie Gallery, Trent Univ, Peterborough, Ont, 71; Sir Sandford Fleming Col Invitational, Peterborough, Ont, 75; Monument to Miniature (auth, catalogue), Art Space, Art Gallery, Ont, 75; Sisler Gallery, Toronto, Ont, 76. Teaching: Instr child art classes, Mendel Art Gallery, Saskatoon, Sask, 65-66; instr early childhood art, Sir Sandford Fleming Col, Peterborough, Ont, 69-71, instr painting, 73-77; instr painting, Trent Univ, Peterborough, Ont, 73-77. Awards: Prize Winner, Sask Exhib, Sask Arts Coun, 65; Purchase Award, Sir Sandford Fleming Col, Peterborough, Ont, 75; Merit Award, Ont Arts Coun, 75. Mem: Art Gallery Peterborough (mem bd, 72-78); Artspace, Peterborough, Ont (mem steering comt, 75); Can Artists Representation. Style & Technique: Oil on canvas, applied with brush and palet knife; non-objective color field based on landscape and mythology. Media: Oil on Canvas; Serigraphy. Publ: Contribr, Artipaction, Ont Arts Coun, 74; contribr, Parachute Mag, 74; contribr, Rags to Riches, Ont Arts Coun, 77; contribr, Art Mag, Heritage Press, 77. Dealer: Sisler Gallery 35 Baldwin St Toronto ON M5T 1L1 Can. Mailing Add: 29 Merino Rd Peterborough ON M5T 1L1 Can

NIRVANNO, COMET (VINCENT ROMANO)
PAINTER, PHOTOGRAPHER
b New York, NY, Aug 1, 40. Study: Sch Visual Arts, New York, 58-62. Work: Joslyn Art Mus, Omaha, Nebr; Oakland Mus, Calif; Nat Res Libr, Ottawa, Can; Hoo Hoo Archives, Gurdon, Ark; Art Lending Gallery, Mus Mod Art, New York. Comn: Backdrop for play, Judson Mem Church, New York, 62. Exhib: Repair Show, Berkeley Gallery, San Francisco, 69; Omaha Flow Systems, Joslyn Art Mus, 73; Doc-Pat Slide Show, Preview of First Art Book in Microfiche Form, A Space Gallery, Toronto, Can, 73; Can-Trajectories '73, Mus d'Arte Mod, Paris, France, 73; North, East, West, South & Middle Traveling Show, Moore Col Art, 75-76. Teaching: Pvt teacher painting, Venice, Calif, 65. Pos: Process cameraman, Corp Ann Reports, New York, 74-75; cameraman, Rolling Stone Mag, 77- Style & Technique: Pencil, tape recorder, camera, etc. Publ: Auth, Musee Lini, 73-75; contribr, West Coast Writing, 73; contribr, Box 749, 74; contribr, Quoz, 74; contribr, Da Vinci, 74. Mailing Add: 94 Chambers St New York NY 10007

NISS, ROBERT SHARPLES
ART CRITIC, ILLUSTRATOR
b Belfast, Maine, Mar 23, 49. Study: Colorado Col, BA, 71. Comn: Posters (with Palmer Peters), Fanny B Levy Day Sch Art Auction, 72; mag cover, Portland Lyric Theater, Maine, 75. Pos: Arts ed, critic & illusr, Portland Eve Express, 71-; arts ed, Guy Gannett Publ Co, Portland, Maine, currently. Bibliog: Donald Beal (auth), interview, Cue-Sheet, 74. Mem: Concept Ctr Visual Studies (consult, 72-3); Soc of Art, Portland, Maine. Style & Technique: Story illustrations and cartoons; dependent on story nature. Media: Pen & Ink; Pencil. Collection: Contemporary New England prints, paintings and drawings. Mailing Add: RFD 1 West Gray Rd Gray ME 04039

NITZ, THOMAS L
DESIGNER, EDUCATOR
b Elgin, Ill, Nov 11, 41. Study: Bradley Univ, BFA; Univ Ill, MFA. Work: Ball State Univ Art Gallery, Muncie, Ind; Ill State Mus, Dickson Mounds, Lewiston, Ill. Comn: Bk jacket designs, Zeno Publ, London, Eng, 73 & 75; wall graphics, Citizens State Bank, Hartford City, Ind, 74; 12 Bicentennial catalogs, Nat Endowment Arts, 75; ancient glass catalog, Ball Found, 77. Exhib: Dickson Mounds Mus, 70; solo show, Ball State Univ Art Gallery, 75 & fac show, 78. Collections Arranged: Three Graphic Designers—A Retrospective, Ball State Univ Art Gallery, 74 & A Show of Visual Commun, 78. Teaching: Assoc prof art in visual commun, Ball State Univ, 71- Pos: Pres, Design Servs, Inc, Muncie, Ind, 72- Awards: Award of Excellence, Ind Art Directors Club, 77; First Place, Ind Speech & Hearing Asn Logo Contest, 77; Res Grant Award, Ball State Univ, 77. Mem: Soc Environ Graphics Designers (founding officer, 74-); Art Directors Club of Ind. Res: Embedded figures and subliminal perception. Mailing Add: 3 Oak Rd Muncie IN 47306

NIVOLA, CONSTANTINO
SCULPTOR
b Orani, Sardinia, July 5, 11. Study: Inst Superiore Arte, Monaz, Italy, with Marino Marini & Marcello Nizzoli, 30-36, MA, 36. Work: Hirshhorn Mus, Washington, DC; Philadelphia Mus Art; Mus Mod Art; Whitney Mus Am Art. Comn: Murals, Motorola Bldg, Chicago, 60; 35 sculptures, Saarinen Dormitories, Yale Univ, 62; designed a mem plaza, Nuoro, Italy, 66; sculpture, Pub Sch 320, Brooklyn, 67; sculpture, 19th Olympiad Nac, Mexico City, Mex, 68; plus many others. Exhib: Whitney Mus Am Art, 57; Carnegie Inst, 58; Mus Contemp Crafts, 62; Nat Gold Medal Exhib Bldg Arts, New York, 62; American Drawing Traveling Exhib, Am Fedn Arts, 64; Inst Contemp Art, Boston; Mus Mod Art, New York; plus many others. Teaching: Instr, Columbia Univ, 61-63. Pos: Dir design workshop, Harvard Univ Grad Sch, 53-57. Awards: Gold Medal, Regional Exhib Figurative Art, Cagliari, Italy; Cert Commendation, Park Asn New York, 65; Fine Arts Medal, Am Inst Architects, 68; plus many others. Bibliog: Michel Seuphor (auth), The Sculpture of This Century, Dictionary of Modern Sculpture, A Zwemmer Ltd, London, 59; Fred Licht (auth), Sculpture, 19th and 20th Centuries, NY Graphic Soc, 67; Eduard Trier (auth), Form and Space: Sculpture in the 20th

Century, Praeger, 68; plus others. Mem: Nat Inst Arts & Lett; Archit League New York. Mailing Add: 410 Stone Rd Springs East Hampton NY 11937

NOBILI, LOUISE
EDUCATOR, PAINTER
b Detroit, Mich. Study: Wayne State Univ, BFA(painting), 39 & MA(painting), 41; Univ Wis, summers 39-41; Chicago Sch of Design, with Moholy Nagy, part-time 43-44; Chicago Inst of Art, part-time 43-44. Work: Detroit Inst of Art, Mich; Scott Hall, Wayne State Univ Med Bldg, Detroit, Mich; The Ford Times Collection of American Art, Dearborn, Mich; Steel Case Collection of Contemporary Art, Grand Rapids, Mich; The Butler Art Inst of Am Art, Youngstown, Ohio. Exhib: Fifty-ninth Nat Ann Am Exhib Watercolor, Chicago Art Inst, 48; Seventeenth Int Watercolor Exhib, Brooklyn Mus, NY, 53; First Columbia Painting Biennial, Columbia Mus of Art, SC, 57; The One Hundred & Fifty-third Ann Exhib of Am Painting & Sculpture, Pa Acad of Fine Art, Philadelphia, 58 & Detroit Inst of Art, Mich, 58; Okla Nat Exhib of Contemp Am Art, Okla Art Ctr, 60; Watercolor Panorama, An Int Survey of Watercolor, Flint Inst of Arts, Mich, 62; Ravinia Festival Exhib, Ravinia Gallery, Ill, 62. Teaching: Asst prof art, Northwestern Univ, Evanston, Ill, 43-44; prof painting, Wayne State Univ, Detroit, Mich, 44- Awards: John L Newberry Award, Mich Artist Ann Exhib, 45; Founders Soc Prize, Mich Artist Ann Exhib, Detroit Inst of Art, 56; Top Merit Award, Fifth Nat Exhib of Contemp Art, Okla Art Ctr, 63. Mem: Mich Watercolor Soc; Washington Watercolor Soc; Mich Acad of Sci, Arts & Letters; Grosse Pointe Art Asn; Am Asn of Univ Prof. Style & Technique: Oil, watercolor and acrylic paintings interpretive-contemporary. Media: Watercolor, Oil. Mailing Add: 17140 E Jefferson Ave Grosse Pointe MI 48230

NOBLE, JOHN A
PAINTER, LITHOGRAPHER
b Paris, France, Mar 17, 13; US citizen. Study: Nat Acad Design; also with father, John Noble. Work: Metrop Art Mus, New York; Carnegie Inst Int, Pittsburgh; Libr Cong, Washington, DC; New Britain Mus, Conn; Brooks Mem Mus, Memphis, Tenn. Comn: Lithograph commemorating Bayonne NY Centennial, 69; lithograph commemorating New York Diamond Jubilee, Staten Island CofC, 73; plus others. Exhib: Libr Cong, Nat Print Exhib; Comprehensive Exhib Oils & Print Mariner Mus, 65; Audubon Artists Ann; Am Soc Graphic Artists Ann; S St Seaport Gallery Exhib Oils & Lithographs, 75. Awards: Five Purchase Prizes, Libr Cong, 50-; Cannon Prize, Nat Acad Design, 72 & Samuel Findley Breeze Morse Medal of Honor, 75. Mem: Academician Nat Acad Design. Style & Technique: Representational industrial and marine interpreter. Mailing Add: 270 Richmond Terr Staten Island NY 10301 Bayonne NJ 270 Richmond Terr Staten Island NY 10301

NOBLE, JOSEPH VEACH
MUSEUM DIRECTOR
b Philadelphia, Pa, Apr 3, 20. Study: Univ Pa. Collections Arranged: Drug Scene, 71; Cityrama, 72. Teaching: Instr filmmaking, City Col New York, 46-49. Pos: Vdir, Metrop Mus Art, 56-70; trustee, Corning Mus Glass, 69-; dir, Mus of City of New York, 70- & Marine Mus, New York. Awards: Scientific Documentary Medal, Venice Film Festival, 48. Mem: Am Asn Mus (pres, 75-); NY State Hist Trust (chmn, 72-); NY State Asn Mus (pres, 70-72); Archaeol Inst Am (treas, 63-70); Brookgreen Gardens (vpres, 70-). Publ: Auth, The Historical Murals of Maplewood, 61; co-auth, An Inquiry into the Forgery of the Etruscan Terra-cotta Warriors, 61; auth, The Techniques of Painted Attic Pottery, 65. Mailing Add: Mus of City of New York Fifth Ave at 103rd St New York NY 10029

NOCHLIN, LINDA (LINDA POMMER)
ART HISTORIAN, EDUCATOR
b New York, NY, Jan 30, 31. Study: Vassar Col, BA; Inst Fine Arts, NY Univ, PhD. Teaching: Mary Conover Mellon prof art, Vassar Col, 63- Awards: Kingsley Porter Prize, best article in Art Bull, 67; E Harris Harbison Award gifted teaching, 72; Am Coun Learned Soc Fel, 72-73. Res: Painting and sculpture of 19th and 20th century. Publ: Auth, Mathis at Colmar, Red Dust, 63; auth, Realism and Tradition in Art, Eighteen Forty-Eight—Nineteen-Hundred, 66 & Impressionism and Post-impressionism, 1874-1904, 66, Prentice Hall; auth, Realism, Penguin, 72; auth, Gustave Courbet: A Study of Style & Society, 76; contribr, Art Bull, Art News, Art News Ann & Artforum. Mailing Add: c/o Garland Publ Co 545 Madison Ave New York NY 10022

NOE, JERRY LEE
SCULPTOR, EDUCATOR
b Harlan Co, Ky, Sept 27, 40. Study: Univ Ky, BA; Art Inst Chicago, MFA. Work: Although many museums, galleries and institutions have acted as patrons for the execution of installations, because of the nature of the work, the categories public collections and commissions are not applicable. Exhib: Sculpture 70, Art Inst Chicago, 70; Neon, Hallmark Gallery, 73; Forty Years of American Landscape, Gimpel-Wietzenhoffer Gallery, New York, 73; Nat Sculpture Traveling Exhib, 73-75; Contemporary Reflections, 1973-74, Aldrich Mus Art, Ridgefield, Conn, 74; Southeast 7, Southeastern Ctr Contemp Art, Winston-Salem, NC, 77; one-man shows, Henri Gallery, 77 & Mercer Gallery, 77. Teaching: Sculptor, Young Artists Studio, Art Inst Chicago, 69-71; vis lectr sculpture, Wis State Univ, Whitewater, 70-71; assoc prof sculpture, Univ NC, Chapel Hill, 71- Awards: Ford Found Scholar, Art Inst Chicago, 69-70; John Quincy Adams Traveling Fel, 71; Nat Sculpture 73 First Place Award, Southern Asn Sculptors, 73, Nat Sculpture 75 Third Place Award, 75; Nat Endowment for the Arts grant, 77 & Southeastern Artist Grant, 77. Bibliog: Noe & Sloan (auth), Neon-the artist (film), Res Coun, Univ NC, 75; B J Ott (auth), Artist builds bridge, Buffalo Courier Newspaper, 75; Fun & games at art park, New York Times Sunday Ed, 75; additional articles have appeared in Washington Star, Chicago Daily News & Chicago Sun Times. Mem: Southern Asn Sculptors (mem bd dirs, 74-75, conf chmn, 75, exhib chmn, 75); Col Art Asn; South Eastern Col Art Conf (co-chmn, Studio Demonstration, 75); Southeastern Ctr Contemp Art. Style & Technique: Materials and techniques of neon sign industry juxtaposed with other materials to create sculpture and environments. Media: Neon, Mixed Media. Dealer: Henri Gallery 1500 21st St NW Washington DC 20036. Mailing Add: 151 Windsor Circle Chapel Hill NC 27514

NOEL, GEORGES
PAINTER
b Beziers, France, Dec 25, 24; US citizen. Work: Albright-Knox Art Gallery, Buffalo, NY; Chase Manhattan Bank, New York; Aldrich Mus of Contemp Art, Ridgefield, Conn; Centre Nat d'Art,, Contemporain, Paris; Mus of Mod Art, New York. Comn: Wall relief, high sch, LeLuc, France, 68; mosaic mural, High Sch, Mulhouse, France, 69. Exhib: Dokumenta Six, Kassel, Ger, 64; Retrospective, Ludwigshafen Mus, 65; Sao Paulo, Bienal, 65; Montreal World's Fair, 67; Krannert Art Mus, Univ Ill, Champaign, 74. Bibliog: Barbara Rose (auth), Article in New York Mag, 3/12/73; Lugano rev, Art Int, Vol 23 (Feb, 1974); Hilton Kramer (auth), review in New York Times, 12/75. Media: Acrylics, sand, polymer and graphite. Dealer: Pace Gallery 32 E 57th St New York NY 10022. Mailing Add: 16 Greene St New York NY 10013

NOGGLE, ANNE
CURATOR, PHOTOGRAPHER
b Evanston, Ill, June 12, 22. Study: Univ NMex, BFA(art hist), MA(art), with Van Deren Coke. Work: Nat Gallery Can, Ottawa; Int Mus Photog, George Eastman House, Rochester, NY; Madison Art Ctr, Wis; Smithsonian Inst, Washington, DC; Fine Arts Mus, Santa Fe, NMex. Exhib: 60's Continuum, Int Mus Photog, Rochester, 72; one-person shows, Lightfall Gallery, Evanston Art Ctr, 73 & Silver Image Gallery, Ohio State Univ, Columbus, 74; Gallery Photog Hist, Smithsonian Inst, Washington, DC, 73; two-person show, Focus Gallery, San Francisco, 74. Collections Arranged: Laura Gilpin Retrospective (with catalog), 74; Women of Photography: A Historical Survey (catalog, with Margery Mann). Teaching: Lectr photog, Univ NMex, 70- Pos: Cur photog, Fine Arts Mus, Santa Fe, NMex, 70- Awards: Nat Endowment Art Fel Photog, 75. Bibliog: Van Deren Coke (auth), 60's Continuum, Image, 72; Joan Murray (auth), rev in Popular Photog, 3/75. Mem: Soc Photog Educ. Style & Technique: Photography. Res: Three years travel and research for Women of Photography: A Historical Survey. Publ: Auth, Prestidigitation, eyesight & hindsight, Album Mag, 70; auth, The long skinny photography of Captain Anne Noggle, Camera 35, 73. Mailing Add: 1204 Espanola NE Albuquerque NM 87110

NOGUCHI, ISAMU
SCULPTOR
b Los Angeles, Calif, Nov 17, 04. Study: With Onorio Ruotolo & Brancusi. Work: Metrop Mus Art; Mus Mod Art; Whitney Mus Am Art; Guggenheim Mus; Brooklyn Mus; plus many others. Comn: Relief sculpture A P Bldg, Rockefeller Ctr, New York, 38; fountain, Ford Expos Bldg, New York World's Fair, 39; fountain & sculpture, John Hancock Bldg, New York & Chase Manhattan Bank, New York; fountains & entrance sculpture, Mus Mod Art, Tokyo, 69; monumental outdoor sculpture, Art Inst Chicago, 77; plus many others. Exhib: Cordier & Ekstrom, NY, 63 & 68; Claude Bernard Gallery, Paris, 64; Gulbenkian Exhib, Tate Gallery, London, 64; retrospectives, Whitney Mus Am Art, 66 & 68; Los Angeles Co Mus Art, Los Angeles, 67; Whitney Mus Am Art, 70; Venice Biennial, Italy, 72; Pace Gallery, 75; plus many others. Awards: Guggenheim Fel; Bollingen Fel, 50-51; Soc Four Arts Sculpture Award, 75; plus others. Bibliog: Shuzo Takiguchi (auth), Noguchi (monogr), Bijutsu Shippan-Sha, Tokyo, 53; Eduard Trier (auth), Form and Space: Sculpture in the 20th Century, Praeger, 68; John Gordon (auth), Isamu Noguchi (catalog), Whitney Mus Am Art, 68; plus many others. Mem: Archit League; Nat Inst Arts & Lett; Nat Sculpture Soc. Publ: Auth, A Sculptor's World, Harper & Row, 68. Mailing Add: 33-38 Tenth St Long Island City NY 11106

NOLAND, KENNETH
PAINTER
b Asheville, NC, 24. Study: Black Mountain Col, 46-48; also with Ossip Zadkine, Paris, 48-49. Work: Mus Mod Art, New York; Tate Gallery Art, London; Mus Fine Arts, Boston; Art Inst Chicago; Los Angeles Co Mus Art. Exhib: Three American Painters: Noland, Olitski & Stella, Fogg Art Mus, Cambridge & Pasadena Art Mus, 65; Morris Louis, Anthony Caro & Kenneth Noland, Metrop Mus Art, New York, 68; New York Painting & Sculpture: 1940-1970, Metrop Mus Art, 70; Selections from the Guggenheim Museum Collection 1900-1970, New York, 70; retrospective, Visual Arts Gallery, New York, 75. Bibliog: Clement Greenberg (auth), Louis and Noland, Art Int, 5/60; Michael Fried (auth), Recent work by Kenneth Noland, Artforum, summer 69; Kenworth Moffett (auth), Noland vertical, Art News, 10/71. Dealer: Andre Emmerich Gallery 41 E 57th St New York NY 10022. Mailing Add: South Shaftsbury VT 05262

NONAY, PAUL
PAINTER
b Simeria, Rumania, May 1, 22; US citizen. Study: Royal Acad Fine Arts, Budapest, with Istvan Szönyi; Acad Fine Arts, Munich, with Hans Gött; Ludwig Maximilian Univ, Munich. Work: Larry Aldrich Mus, Ridgefield, Conn; Springfield Mus Fine Arts, Mass; Loeb Collection, NY Univ; Univ Bridgeport Permanent Collection; Southern New Eng Teacher's Col, New Haven, Conn. Comn: Hist mural, Hotel Utica, Utica, NY, 51; bas-reliefs, Nat Bank of Westchester, New Rochelle, NY, 69. Exhib: Art USA 1958, New York, 58; Conn Acad Fine Arts, Wadsworth Atheneum, Conn Watercolor Soc, Hartford, 58-64; New Eng Ann, Silvermine, Conn, 58-70; Nat Acad Design, Am Watercolor Soc, Audubon Artists Ann, New York, 61-66; Univ Fairfield, Univ Bridgeport & Quinnipiac Col Invitational Shows, 61-71. Teaching: Lectr art, Silvermine Guild Artists, 60-61; lectr art, Univ Bridgeport, 60-71; vis prof art, Trinity Col, 72. Awards: Conn Acad Fine Arts Prize, 62; Ford Found Purchase Prize, 65; New Haven Arts Festival Prizes, 66-68. Mem: Silvermine Guild Artists (bd mem, 64-70); Springfield Art League; Rowayton Art Ctr (co-dir, 60-68); Int Art Guild; Am Asn Univ Prof. Media: Oil, Watercolor, Collage. Publ: Illusr, cover designs for Grade Teacher, 55-56, Reporter, 55 & 60; Today's Living, 57, La Rev Mod, Paris, France, 59 & Science and Technology, 63. Mailing Add: 8 Hillside Rd S Weston CT 06883

NONG
PAINTER, SCULPTOR
b Seoul, Korea, Oct 10, 30; US citizen. Study: Self-taught (art). Work: Nat Mus of Hist, Taipei, Taiwan, The Republic of China; Musee Nat Des Beaux-Arts, Monte Carlo, Principauté De Monaco; Nat Gallery of Mod Art, New Delhi, India; M H De Young Mem Mus, San Francisco, Calif; Nat Mus of Mod Art, Seoul, Korea. Exhib: Nat Collection of Fine Arts, Smithsonian Inst, Wash, DC, 61; The Denver Art Mus, Colo, 65; Univ of Calif, Berkeley, 68; Salon D'Art Sacre, Musee D'Art Moderne, Paris, France, 69; Salon D'Automne, Grand Palais, Paris, 69-71; Grands Et Jeunes D'Aujourd'Hui, Grand Palais, Paris, 70-77; Oakland Art Mus, Calif, 71; San Francisco Mus of Art, 72; one-man shows, Ft Lauderdale Mus of the Arts, Fla, 65, Santa Barbara Mus of Art, Calif, 65, E B Crocker Art Gallery, Sacremento, Calif, 65, Ga Mus of Art, Athens, 67, Nat Mus of Hist, Taipei, Taiwan, 71 & Nat Mus of Mod Art, Seoul, Korea, 75. Awards: Lett of Appreciation for the Achievement in Art, Minister of Cult and Info, Repub of Korea, 71. Style & Technique: Painting, relief mixed media technique originated by Nong; sculpture, stone, wood, cast metals. Mailing Add: 999 Green St No 2701 San Francisco CA 94133

NOORDHOEK, HARRY CECIL
SCULPTOR, PAINTER
b Moers, Ger, Feb 10, 09; Can citizen. Study: Gemaelde Galerie, Kassel, Ger, 27-28. Work: Quebec Prov Mus, Quebec City; City of Alma, Que; Museo Giorgi, Florence, Italy; Elmwood Corp, Montreal; Mus Arte Mod, Milan, Italy; Buerdeke Galerie, Zurich, Switz; Mus Contemp Art, Montreal. Comn: Serenite Deux (sculpture), City of Alma, Que, 65; Cult Affairs Coun, Liberty Hill, Tex; Kreis Ostholstein, Eutin, WGer. Exhib: Confrontation 65, City of Montreal, PQ & Stratford, Ont, 65; one-man show, Mus Contemp Art, Montreal, 66; Penwith Soc, St Ives, Eng, 67-68; Circle Gallery, London, Eng, 68; 89th Ann, Royal Can Acad Arts, Hamilton & Edmonton, 68; 6th Int Open Air Sculpture Exhib, Milan, 70; Galerie Buerdeke, Zurich, Switz, 70; 1st Int Sculpture Show, Carrara, Italy, 72; Can Cult Centre, Paris, France, 77; Int Bildhauer Symp, Eutin, WGer, 77. Awards: Sir Otto Beit Medal for Sculpture of Spec

Merit in Brit Commonwealth, Royal Soc Brit Sculptors, 65; Acquisition Prize, Second Concours Artistiques, PQ, 66; President of Republic of Italy Gold Medal, Ital Nat Prize, 72; Renato Colombo Medal, 72. Bibliog: M Ballantyne (auth), A sculptor of cool serenity, Montreal Star, 2/27/65; T Krieber (auth), Violence at serenite s'opposent, Progres-Dimanche, Chicoutimi, PQ, 8/8/65; R Montbizon (auth), Harry C Noordhoek, sculptor, The Gazette, Montreal, 5/21/66; A zum Winkel & Harry Noordhoek (co-auths), Kunst ohne Kompromiz, Ostholsteiner Anzeiger, Eutin, WGer, 7/7/77. Mem: Royal Can Acad Arts. Style & Technique: Neo-classical abstract stone sculpture; modern and abstract landscape and portrait. Media: Stone, Oil. Publ: Ed, Enciclopedia Universale Seda Dell' Arte Moderna, Milan, 72; auth, Eine Dokumentation, Internationales Bildhauer Symposium, Eutin, WGer, 77. Mailing Add: PO Box 263 Carrara Italy

NORDHAUSEN, A HENRY
PAINTER
b Hoboken, NJ, Jan 25, 01. Study: NY Sch Fine & Appl Art; Royal Acad Fine Art, Munich, Ger; Kunst Geverve Schule, Munich; Mass Inst Technol; New Sch Social Res. Work: Cleveland Mus Fine Art; Columbus Art Mus, Ga; New Brit Mus, Conn; Syracuse Univ; Pentagon, Washington, DC; plus many others. Comn: Several portraits, Syracuse Univ, Pentagon, Royal Crown Cola Co, Columbus, Ga, Ga Inst Technol, Atlanta & Ga Power Co, plus many others. Exhib: Metrop Mus Art; Nat Acad Design, New York; Glass Palace, Munich; Art Inst Chicago; Corcoran Gallery, Washington, DC; plus many others. Teaching: Instr portraits, Roerich Mus; instr art, New York High Schs; instr art, Musemont, Columbus. Pos: Lectr, Metrop Mus Art & Brooklyn Mus Art; art demonstr, Columbus Mus Art. Awards: MacDowell Colony Fel; Trask Found Fel; Tiffany Found Fel; plus many others. Mem: Am Watercolor Soc; Salmagundi Club; Artist Fel (vpres); Dutch Treat Club; Explorers Club; plus others. Media: Oil. Dealer: Capricorn Gallery 8003 Woodmont Ave Bethesda MD 20014. Mailing Add: 1 W 67th St New York NY 10023

NORDLAND, GERALD JOHN
GALLERY DIRECTOR, ART CRITIC
b Los Angeles, Calif, July 10, 27. Study: Univ Southern Calif, AB & JD. Collections Arranged: Gaston Lachaise (with catalog), Los Angeles Co Mus Art & Whitney Mus Am Art, 63-64; Richard Diebenkorn Retrospective (with catalog), Washington Gallery Mod Art, Washington, DC, 64; Anthony Caro, Piet Mondrian, Josef Albers & The Washington Color Painters (with catalog), Washington Gallery Mod Art; John Altoon (with catalog), Julius Bissier (with Guggenheim Mus), Robert Natkin, Al Held, Fritz Glarner & others, San Francisco Mus Art. Pos: Dean, Chouinard Art Sch, Calif Inst Arts, 60-64; dir, Washington Gallery Mod Art, 64-66; dir, San Francisco Mus Art, 66-72; dir, Frederick S Wight Galleries, Univ Calif, Los Angeles, 73-78; dir, Milwaukee Art Ctr, 78- Mem: Nat Endowment Arts (mus adv panel, 70-73); Asn Art Mus Dirs. Res: More than thirty museum publications on 20th century artists and movements, emphasizing American painting, science and photography. Mailing Add: c/o Milwaukee Art Ctr 750 N Lincoln Mem Dr Milwaukee WI 53202

NORDNESS, LEE
ART DEALER
b Olympia, Wash, Dec 24, 24. Study: Univ Wash, 40-42; Stanford Univ, 43; Uppsala Univ, 47-48. Collections Arranged: Art: USA: 58, Madison Square Garden; Art: USA: 59, New York Coliseum; Art: USA, The Johnson Collection of Contemporary American Paintings; Objects: USA, The Johnson Collection of Contemporary Crafts. Pos: Dir, Lee Nordness Galleries, New York, 58- Publ: Auth, Art: USA Now, 63 & Objects: USA, 70, Viking. Mailing Add: Lee Nordness Galleries 252 W 38th St New York NY 10018

NORDSTRAND, NATHALIE JOHNSON
PAINTER
b Woburn, Mass. Study: Bradford Jr Col; Barnard Col; Columbia Univ; also with Jay Connaway, Roger Curtis, Paul Strisik & Don Stone. Work: First Nat Bank Boston; Am Mutual Ins Co, Wakefield, Mass; Am Tel & Tel Co, New York; Goodrich Tire Co, Mich; Pilot Life Ins Co, NC. Exhib: Acad Artists Am, 67-75; Am Watercolor Soc Ann, 69-77; Allied Artists Am, 69-77; Mainstreams 71, Ohio, 71; New England Art in Hong Kong, Am Chamber Com, 74 & 76; Nat Acad of Design, New York; De Cordova Mus, Lincoln, Mass; Butler Inst of Am Art, Youngstown, Ohio; Bombay Art Inst, India; Columbia Mus of Art, SC; Montgomery Mus of Fine Arts, Ala; Laguna Gloria Art Mus, Tex; Meridian Mus, Miss; plus others. Awards: Bronze Medal, Catharine Lorillard Wolfe Art Club, 70; Gold Medal, Am Artists Prof League, 71 & 75; 102nd Ann Watercolor & Sculpture Exhib Louis E Seley Prize, Salmagundi Club, New York, 74. Bibliog: Robert Kolbe (auth), Nathalie J Nordstrand poetry of the sea, Am Artist Mag, 9/72. Mem: Am Watercolor Soc; Allied Artists Am; Am Artists Prof League; Salmagundi Club; Guild Boston Artists. Style & Technique: Interprets nature in a realistic, yet impressionistic style with watercolors. Media: Watercolor, Oil. Publ: Contribr, La Rev Mod, Paris, 72; auth, The salt wind and I, Palette Talk, winter 73 & 74. Mailing Add: 384 Franklin St Reading MA 01867

NORFLEET, BARBARA PUGH
CURATOR, EDUCATOR
b Lakewood, NJ. Study: Swarthmore, BA, 47; Harvard-Radcliffe, MA, 50 & PhD, 51. Work: Mus of Mod Art, New York City; Harvard Univ, Cambridge, Mass. Exhib: Harvard Univ, 69, 73, 75 & 77; DeCordova Mus, 72; Smith Col Mus, 74; Women See Women, traveling show, 75. Collections Arranged: The Photography Archive on the photographic Social history of the US (collected, researched, organized); The Social Question: Social Reform at the turn of the Century, Harvard & Mus of Mod Art, 73; Wedding (auth, catalog), Harvard & Int Ctr of Photography, New York, 76 & 77. Teaching: Lectr photog, Harvard Univ, Cambridge, 70-78. Pos: Cur, Harvard Univ, 72-; consult on art, numerous organizations, 73-; auth, photo-essays, St Louis Post Dispatch, 73- Awards: Exhibition, The Social Question, Mass Coun on the Arts, 72; Photog Exhib Aid, Wedding, Nat Endowment for the Arts, 75; Res Grant, to set up photog archive, Nat Endowment for the Humanities, 75. Mem: Boston Visual Artists Union; Am Soc of Picture Professionals. Style & Technique: Black & white photog. Media: Photog. Res: Have compiled an archive of over 30,000 negatives and prints on the social history of the US from 1900-1970. Collection: Work from the files of professional photographers, emphasis on social behavior. Publ: Auth, Six Speak, Cambridge Civic Asn, 68; auth, The Head and the Heart, Harvard Press, 78. Dealer: Roger Kingston, The Photographic Eye 5 Boylston St Cambridge MA 02138. Mailing Add: Carpenter Ctr for the Visual Arts Harvard Univ Cambridge MA 02138

NORMAN, DOROTHY (S)
WRITER, PHOTOGRAPHER
b Philadelphia, Pa, Mar 28, 05. Study: Smith Col; Univ Pa. Work: Philadelphia Mus Art; Mus Mod Art, New York. Exhib: Captions, Family of Man, Mus Mod Art & Tour, 55 & Forms of Israel, Am Fedn Arts & Tour, 58-60; 60 Photographs & New Workers, Mus Mod Art; Selections from Dorothy Norman Collection, Philadelphia Mus Art, 68. Pos: Ed & publ, Twice a Yr, 37-48. Bibliog: William Wasserstrom (auth), Introd in Civil Liberties and the Arts, Syracuse Univ Press, 64. Collection: Contemporary and ancient symbolical art. Publ: Co-ed, America and Alfred Steiglitz, 34; ed, Selected Writings of John Marin, 49; auth, Alfred Stieglitz—introduction to an American Seer, 60; auth, The Hero: Myth/Image/Symbol, 69; auth, Alfred Stieglitz—an American Seer, winter 73. Mailing Add: 124 E 70th St New York NY 10021

NORMAN, EMILE
PAINTER, SCULPTOR
b El Monte, Calif, Apr 22, 18. Work: Oakland Mus. Comn: Mosaic window & marble relief, Calif Masonic Mem Temple, San Francisco, 56-58; Horse (wood sculpture), Crown Zellerbach Bldg, San Francisco, 59; St Francis (bronze sculpture), 67, Bank Calif Bldg, San Francisco, wood inlay mural, 68. Exhib: Archit Art Exhib, Pasadena Art Inst, 49; Relig Art Show, De Young Mus, San Francisco, 53; 20th Ann Soc Contemp Art, Art Inst Chicago, 60; Contemp Am Painting & Sculpture, Krannert Art Mus, Univ Ill, 61; Design & Esthetics in Wood, Lowe Art Ctr, Syracuse Univ, 67. Pos: Owner-dir, Emile Norman Gallery, Carmel, Calif. Bibliog: Eliz Gordon (auth), The flowering of our times, House Beautiful, 10/58; Janice Lovoos (auth), The art of Emile Norman, Am Artist Mag, 11/61. Mem: Carmel Art Asn; Nat Soc Mural Painters. Media: Oil, Acrylic; Wood, Bronze, Gold. Mailing Add: Mission & Sixth Ave Carmel CA 93921

NORQUIST, RYL
ART DEALER
b Los Angeles, Calif, Feb 25, 51. Pos: Dir, Droll/Kolbert Gallery, 77- Specialty: Contemporary American art. Mailing Add: PO Box 543 Bridgehampton NY 11932

NORRIS, ANDREA SPAULDING
ART HISTORIAN
b Madison, Wis, Apr 2, 45. Study: Wellesley Col, BA, 67; New York Univ, MA, 69, cert in mus training, 70, PhD, 77. Teaching: Lectr art hist, Queens Col of the City Univ of New York, 73-74; adj instr art hist, NY Univ, New York, 76-77. Pos: Asst to the dir, Yale Univ Art Gallery, New Haven, Conn, 77- Awards: Ford Foundation Mus Training Grant, 69-72. Mem: Col Art Asn of Am. Res: Italian Renaissance painting and sculpture; medals; Gian Cristoforo Romano; Lombard Renaissance suclpture. Publ: Co-auth, Medals and Plaquettes from the Molinari Collection at Bowdoin Col, Bowdoin Col, 76; contribr, Dizionario Biografico degli Italiani, Treccani, 77-; contribr, Bowdoin Col Mus of Art-Handbook of the Collections, Bowdoin Col, 78. Mailing Add: Yale Univ Art Gallery 2006 Yale Sta New Haven CT 06520

NORRIS, LEONARD MATHESON
CARTOONIST, ILLUSTRATOR
b London, Eng, Dec 1, 13; Can citizen. Study: Ont Col of Art. Work: Nat Libr of Canada; Univ Mo; Pavilion of Humor, Montreal, Que; Winnipeg Art Gallery, Man. Pos: Art dir, Maclean Hunter, Toronto, Ont, 45-50; ed cartoonist, Vancouver Sun, 50- Awards: Nat Newspaper Award, Can Newspapers, Toronto, 62; Hon LLD, Univ Windsor, 74. Bibliog: Nat Film Bd, The Hecklers, inclusion in Cartoon History of Can, 75; articles in various publ, Time Mag, Macleans Mag, Weekend Mag, Imperial Rev & Punch. Mem: Asn Am Ed Cartoonists; Roual Can Acad of Art. Style & Technique: Black and white line illustrations. Publ: Illusr, Johan's Gift to Christmas, Shriners, 75. Mailing Add: 4227 Almondel Pl West Vancouver BC V7V 3L8 Can

NORRIS, (ROBERT) BEN
PAINTER, EDUCATOR
b Redlands, Calif, Sept 6, 10. Study: Pomona Col; Harvard Univ; Inst Art & Archeol, Sorbonne, Paris; also with Stanton MacDonald Wright, Jean Charlot, Max Ernst & Josef Albers. Work: Honolulu Acad Arts, Hawaii; Nat Collection Fine Arts, Washington, DC; Am Fedn Arts Mus Collection; Ore State Univ Mus; Hawaii State Comn Cult & Arts. Comn: Murals, First Hawaiian Bank, Honolulu, Royal Hawaiian Hotel, Honolulu & Royal Lahaina Hotel, Maui. Exhib: Regional & local exhibs, West Coast & Hawaii, 36-; Chicago Int Watercolor Exhib, 38-42; Metrop Mus Mid-Century Exhib, 51; Whitney Mus, 61; Pacific Heritage, West Coast Mus & Berlin, Ger, 65. Teaching: From instr to prof art, Univ Hawaii, 37- Style & Technique: Painterly, with inputs from landscape, figure drawing, Asian art and abstraction. Media: Acrylic, Oil. Dealer: Saxon Gallery Pacific Trade Center Mall 170 S King St Honolulu HI 96813. Mailing Add: 2009-B Makiki St Honolulu HI 96822

NORTON, ANN
SCULPTOR
US citizen. Study: Nat Acad Design; Cooper Union Art Sch. Work: Detroit Art Inst; Art Inst Chicago; Los Angeles Co Mus Art; High Mus, Atlanta, Ga. Exhib: Mus Mod Art, 30; Schneider Gallery, Rome; Galleria XXII, Venice; one-man shows, Bodley Gallery, New York, 68 & 70. Media: Stone, Wood, Bronze. Mailing Add: 253 Barcelona Rd West Palm Beach FL 33401

NORTON, MARY JOYCE
PAINTER
b Tampa, Fla. Study: Akron Univ; Ariz State Univ; color theory with Dorothy Fratt. Work: Yuma Fine Arts Collections; First Nat Bank, Phoenix; Ariz Wholesale Corp, Phoenix. Exhib: Watercolor Biennial, Phoenix Art Mus, 70-72, Four-Corners Biennial, 71-73; 8 West Biennial, Colo Ctr Arts, 72-74; Southwestern Fine Arts Biennial, Mus NMex, 72-74; Joslyn Mus, Omaha, Nebr, 74; plus many others. Awards: Ariz Ann Painting Award, Phoenix Art Mus, 66 & 67, Watercolor Biennial Silver Mdal, 70; Southwestern Purchase Prize, Yuma Fine Arts Ctr, 67 & 73; 19th Nat Sun Carnival Exhib, El Paso Mus of Art, 77; Ariz Painting Nat Competition, 77 & others, Scottsdale Ctr for the Arts, Ariz. Bibliog: Barbara Cortright (auth), Meet the circle, Phoenix Mag, 2/75 & The look of nature, the flow of paint, Artweek, 5/75; Harry Wood (auth), Color flows in poetic paintings, Scottsdale Progress, 4/75. Style & Technique: Experimental work with color stains on raw canvas; pencil drawings; stain work on papers. Media: Acrylic, Woodcuts, Watercolor. Dealer: Gallery Rose 9025 Santa Monica Blvd Los Angeles CA 90069; Caulfield Gallery 74 Front St Binghamton NY 13905. Mailing Add: 2529 E Cheery Lynn Rd Phoenix AZ 85016

NORTON, PAUL FOOTE
ART HISTORIAN, EDUCATOR
b Newton, Mass, Jan 23, 17. Study: Oberlin Col, BA, 38; Princeton Univ, MFA, 47, PhD, 52. Teaching: From asst prof to assoc prof hist art, Pa State Univ, University Park, 47 58; from assoc prof to prof hist art, Univ Mass, Amherst, 58-, chmn dept, 58-71. Awards: Fel, Am Coun Learned Socs, 51-52; Fulbright Sr Res Fel, 53-54; Nat Endowment Humanities Sr Fel, 71-72. Mem: Soc Archit Historians (dir & ed jour, 59-64); Col Art Asn Am; Soc Française Archeol; Archeol Inst Am; fel Royal Soc Arts. Res: History of architecture; England and America in the 18th and 19th centuries. Publ: Co-auth, Arts in America: the Nineteenth Century, 69; auth, Amherst: A Guide to its Architecture, 75; auth, Latrobe, Jefferson and the National Capitol, 77; auth, articles in J Soc Archit Historians, Art Bull,

Britannica Encycl Am Art & Encycl World Biog. Mailing Add: Dept of Art Univ of Mass Amherst MA 01002

NORTON, ROB ROY, JR
PAINTER
b Louisville, Ky, Mar 26, 48. Study: Whitney Mus Independent Study Prog, 71-72; Dayton Art Inst, Ohio, BFA, 72; with David Diao & Gary Bower. Work: Va Mus Fine Arts, Richmond; Art Lending Serv, Mus Mod Art, New York. Exhib: New American Abstract Painting, Vassar Gallery, Poughkeepsie, NY, 72; one-man show, Lamagna Gallery, New York, 75; Contemporary Reflections Ann, Aldrich Mus, Ridgefield, Conn, 75; 15 New York Artists, Univ Denver, 75; Whitney Mus Biennial, New York, 75. Bibliog: Duncan Pollock (auth), 15 New York Artists, Rocky Mountain News, 4/13/75. Style & Technique: Non-objective drawing with acrylics using crude tools to draw with; concerned with two and three lines emphasizing line and space. Mailing Add: 305 Canal St New York NY 10013

NORVELL, PATSY
SCULPTOR, ENVIRONMENTAL ARTIST
b Greenville, SC, July 13, 42. Study: Bennington Col, Vt, BA; study with David Smith, Peter Voulkas; San Francisco Art Inst, post grad study; Hunter Col, MA. Exhib: New York Women Artists, Univ Art Gallery, State Univ NY, Albany; Focus on Women, Kent State Galleries, Ohio, 72; Of Paper, Newark Mus, NJ, 73; Painting & Sculpture Today, 1974, Indianapolis Mus of Art, Ind & The Taft Mus, Cincinnati, 74; Primitive Presence in the Seventies, Vassar Col, Poughkeepsie, NY, 75; Abstraction: Alive & Well, Art Gallery, State Univ Col, Potsdam, NY, 76; Rooms, PS1 Exhib, Inst for Art & Urban Resources, Queens, 76; Wood, Nassau Co Mus, Roslyn, NY, 77; one-woman show, A I R Gallery, 73, 75 & 78. Teaching: Instr sculpture & drawing, Rutgers Univ, Newark, NJ, 69-70; instr materials & printmaking, Montclair State Col, Upper Montclair, NJ, 70-74; assoc in sculpture, Columbia Univ, New York, 77. Pos: Panelist, lectr & workshops, Nassau Co Mus, Aldrich Mus, Sarah Lawrence Col, City Univ NY, Skidmore Col, Mount Holyoke & Grad Sch of Sculpture, Yale Univ, 71-78. Awards: Nat Endowment for the Arts Grant, 76-77. Bibliog: Jack Bodkin (auth), Fence Firms Installation Sculpture, Fence Indust, 77; Nancy Foote (auth), The Apotheosis of the Crummy Space, Artforum, 76; Connie Robins (auth), Patsy Norvell, Arts Mag, 76. Style & Technique: Large, abstract, outdoor sculpture. Media: Construction Material, Fencing, Branches. Publ: Contribr, Six Years....Lucy Lippart, Praeger, 69. Dealer: A I R Gallery 97 Wooster St New York NY 10012. Mailing Add: 78 Greene St New York NY 10012

NORWOOD, MALCOLM MARK
PAINTER, EDUCATOR
b Drew, Miss, Jan 21, 28. Study: Miss Col, BA & MEd; Univ Ala, MA; Univ Colo, painting with Mark Rothko. Work: Munic Art Gallery, Jackson, Miss; Miss Collection, First Nat Bank, Jackson; Miss Col; Belhaven Col; Jackson Country Club. Comn: Portrait, Southwestern Theol Sem, New Orleans, 63; landscapes & watercolors, First Nat Bank, Cleveland, Miss, 64 & 66; pottery, People's Bank, Indianapolis, Miss, 70. Exhib: SMU Invitational, Ft Worth, Tex, 62; Washington Watercolor Asn, Smithsonian Inst, 63; Contemp Southern Art Exhib, Weatherspoon Art Gallery, Univ NC, 66; Artists Registry Exhib, Brooks Art Gallery, Memphis, Tenn, 69; La State Art Comn, Baton Rouge, 69. Teaching: Head dept art, Delta State Univ, 62- Awards: First Prize, Nat Oil Exhib, Miss Power & Light Co, 63; Painting Award, Holiday Inns Am Arts Festival, 69; First Prize in Drawing, Edgewater Merchants Asn Ann, 71. Mem: Miss Art Asn (vpres, 54 & 60); Cleveland Arts Coun (projs chmn, 70-); Miss Arts Comn (educ adv bd, 71-); Greater Greenwood Arts Festival (adv bd, 71-72); Miss Art Colony (bd dirs, 63-66). Style & Technique: Watercolor landscapes that vary from representational to abstract, with a loose, wet handling of the media; figures and animals are employed in a series of clay reliefs handled in an expressive manner. Media: Watercolor. Publ: Auth, article in Jackson Daily News/Clarion Ledger, 64; illusr, 64 & cover, 68, Delta Rev; co-auth, The Art of Marie Hull, 75. Mailing Add: 600 Canal Ave Cleveland MS 38732

NOSOFF, FRANK
PAINTER
b Brooklyn, NY, Apr 10, 19. Study: Nat Acad Design, 38-40; Art Students League, 43-45; Art Career Sch, 53-56. Exhib: Painters & Sculptors Soc, NJ, Jersey City Mus, 67; Am Watercolor Soc Exhib & Traveling Show, New York, 68; L'Exposition Intercontinentale Traveling Show, 68; Nat Soc Painters Casein, New York, 71-74; Am Veterans Soc Artists, New York, 74. Awards: John J Newman Medal, Nat Soc Painters Casein, 71, Mildred & Tommy Atkin Cash Award, 72; Simmons Award, Am Vet Soc Artists, 74; Grumbacher Cash Award, 77. Style & Technique: Trompe l'oeil; dimensional abstractions. Media: Oil, Casein. Mailing Add: 50 Riverside Dr New York NY 10024

NOSSAL, AUDREY JEAN
PAINTER, WRITER
b London, Eng, Mar 12, 29. Study: With Tsai Pei Chiu, Siu Lap Sing & Tang Hung. Exhib: City Hall, Hong Kong, 70; YWCA, Hong Kong, 71; Sumie Soc, New York, 72; Abbott Gallery, Washington, 74 & 75. Teaching: Teacher Chinese painting, YWCA, Hong Kong, 68-71; teacher Chinese painting, Chevy Chase Community, Md, 71-; teacher Chinese painting, Am Arts Ctr, Bethesda, Md, 71- Style & Technique: Chinese painting; southern school; landscapes, bamboo and lotus. Media: Monochrome. Publ: Auth, Four Treasures, 71; auth, Creative Chinese painting, Landscapes, 76. Dealer: Abbott Gallery McLean Sq Mall 6624 Old Dominion Rd McLean VA 22101. Mailing Add: 10401 Riverwood Dr Potomac MD 20854

NOTARBARTOLO, ALBERT
PAINTER
b New York, NY, Jan 12, 34. Study: Nat Acad Fine Arts, scholar, 50; apprenticeship to mural painter Ignacio La Russa, 51-53. Work: Fort Bragg, NC; Aldrich Mus Contemp Art, Ridgefield, Conn; Nat Gallery Art, Washington, DC. Comn: Series of paintings, comn by Larry Aldrich, New York, 67; painting, Radio Corp Am, New York, 71; drawing, Newsweek, 72; tapestry, Aubusson, France. Exhib: Corcoran Gallery Art, Washington, DC, 68; Mus Mod Art, New York, 68-70; 21 Am Artists, Del Art Mus, 70; Aldrich Mus Contemp Art, 72; Aubusson Tapestry Exhib, Norton Gallery Mus, Fla; Nat Gallery of Art, Washington, DC, 76; plus others. Awards: First Prize, New York Intercult Soc, 53; Dept Housing & Urban Develop Nat Community Art Competition Award, Washington, DC, 73; Nat Award, New Glory Bicentennial Flag Design Competition (for flag for first lunar colony), Santa Barbara Mus of Art, 76. Mem: Nat Soc Lit & Arts. Style & Technique: Conceptual artist, innovator of orbital art; spaceworks for placement in orbit about the earth. Media: Acrylic, Mixed Media. Publ: Contribr, Art Workers News, 4/74; contribr, Leonardo Mag, spring 75; contribr, Art/World newspaper, 1-2/78. Mailing Add: 215 W 98th St New York NY 10025

NOTARO, ANTHONY
SCULPTOR
b Italy, Jan 10, 15; US citizen. Study: Rinehart Sch Sculpture, Md Inst, Baltimore, 39, with Malvina Hoffman; also with Harry Lewis Raul, Hans Schuler, Herbert Adams & William Simpson. Work: Hall of Fame for Great Americans; Seton Hall Univ Student Ctr; Nat Commemorative Soc. Comn: Sarah Josepha Hale Award Medal, 57; Anniversary Medallion, Geiger Eng & Mfg Co, 57; Hemerocallis Soc Medal, 60; NJ Tercentenary Medallion, 62; Univ Iowa Medal, 63; plus others. Exhib: Nat Acad Design; Nat Sculpture Soc; Providence Art Club; Allied Artists Am; Audubon Artists; Nat Arts Club; Archit League, New York; Am Artists Prof League; plus many others. Awards: John Spring Art Founder Award, Nat Sculpture Soc Bicentennial Exhib, 76; Gold Medal of Honor, Allied Artists Am, 77; Cert of Merit, Nat Acad Design, 78; plus others. Mem: Nat Sculpture Soc; Am Artists Prof League; Allied Artist Am. Media: Bronze, Marble, Wood. Mailing Add: 14 Brookfield Way Mendham NJ 07945

NOVAK, BARBARA (MRS BRIAN O'DOHERTY)
ART HISTORIAN, EDUCATOR
b New York, NY. Study: Barnard Col, Columbia Univ, BA; Radcliffe Col, MA & PhD. Teaching: Prof art hist & chmn dept, Barnard Col, Columbia Univ, 58- Awards: Belg-Am Educ Found Fel, 53; Fulbright Award to Belg, 53-54; Guggenheim Award, 74. Mem: Col Art Asn Am. Res: Nineteenth century American painting. Publ: Auth, American Painting of the Nineteenth Century, Praeger, 69; contribr, Metropolitan Museum Symposium on 19th Century American Art, 72; contribr to numerous art hist periodicals. Mailing Add: Dept Art Hist Barnard Col New York NY 10027

NOVINSKI, LYLE FRANK
PAINTER, EDUCATOR
b Montfort, Wis, June 23, 32. Study: Wis State Univ, BA; Univ Wis, MS & MFA; Marquette Univ. Comn: Thomas Aquinas Chapel, Univ Dallas, 69, Albert the Great Priory, 72. Exhib: Tex Gen, 64 & 72; Okla Eight State Exhib, 68; Okla Invitational, 70; Fort Worth Art Ctr, 71; Nat Interfaith Conf on Relig & Archit, 75; plus others. Teaching: Prof painting, art hist & design & chmn dept, Univ Dallas, 60- Awards: Purchase Award, Okla Eight State, 68; Top Award, Tex Gen, 72. Bibliog: Articles in Christian Arts, 68; articles in Liturgical Arts, 70; articles in Art Gallery, 71-72; plus many catalogues. Mem: Dallas Mus Fine Arts; Western Arts Asn; Col Art Asn Am; Fort Worth Art Ctr; Guild Relig Archit. Media: Leather, Acrylic. Dealer: Valley House Gallery 6616 Spring Valley Rd Dallas TX 75240. Mailing Add: 1101 Owenwood Irving TX 75061

NOVOTNY, ELMER LADISLAW
PAINTER, EDUCATOR
b Cleveland, Ohio, July 27, 09. Study: Cleveland Sch Art, dipl; Case Western Reserve Univ, BA; Kent State Univ, MA; Slade Sch, Univ London; Acad Zagreb, Yugoslavia; Yale Univ. Work: Cleveland Mus Art; Butler Inst Am Art, Youngstown, Ohio; Akron Art Inst; Canton Art Inst; Cleveland Munic Collection. Comn: Mural for game room, comn by John Sherwin, Jr, Waite Hill Village, Ohio, 37; History of Kent (mural), Portage Nat Bank, Ohio, 49; portrait of Gov Martin L Davey, comn by family, Kent, 50; portrait of Robert Carr, Oberlin Col, 70; portrait of James A Michener for Michener Collection, Kent State Univ, 71. Exhib: Cleveland Mus Ann May Show, 29-71; Butler Inst Am Art Ann Nat, 35-71; Canton Art Inst Ann Show, 37-65; Akron Art Inst Ann May Show, 37-71; Directions in American Painting, Carnegie Mus, Pittsburgh, 42. Teaching: Instr portraiture, Cleveland Inst Art, 33-43; prof painting & drawing, Kent State Univ, 36-46, dir sch art, 46-74, emer prof & emer dir, 74- Awards: First Prize for Nancy (portraiture), Cleveland Mus Art, 37; Purchase Award for Wingaersheer Beach, Butler Inst Am Art, 60; Jurors Award for Chateaux, Akron Art Inst, 69. Mem: Hon life mem Akron Soc Artists; life fel Int Inst Arts & Lett; Cleveland Soc Artists. Style & Technique: Realist working primarily in oil and polymer; wide range of subject matter including portraiture. Publ: Auth, Byways of Southern Europe, Kent State Univ, 69. Mailing Add: 7317 Westview Rd Kent OH 44240

NOVROS, DAVID
PAINTER
b Los Angeles, Calif, 41. Exhib: Systemic Painting, Solomon R Guggenheim Mus, New York, 66; Sound, Light & Silence, William Rockhill Nelson Gallery of Art, Kansas City, Mo, 66; A Romantic Minimalism, Inst of Contemp Arts, Univ Pa, 67; Rejective Art, Am Fedn of Art, 67; Whitney Mus of Am Art, 67, 69 & 73; Modular Painting, Albright-Knox Art Gallery, Buffalo, NY, 70; The Structure of Color, Whitney Mus of Am Art, 71; Corcoran Biennial, Washington, DC, 71; White on White, Mus of Contemp Art, Chicago, Ill, 71-72; Art Inst of Chicago, 72; Five Artists: A Logic of Vision, Mus of Contemp Art, 74. Mailing Add: 59 Wooster St New York NY 10012

NOWACK, WAYNE KENYON
PAINTER, ASSEMBLAGE ARTIST
b Des Moines, Iowa, May 7, 23. Study: Drake Univ, 43-45; State Univ Iowa, BA(summa cum laude), 47, MA, 48, MFA, 50. Work: Joseph H Hirshhorn Found, Greenwich, Conn; Yale Univ Art Gallery, New Haven, Conn; Des Moines Art Ctr, Iowa; Williams Col, Williamstown, Mass; Ft Worth Art Mus, Tex. Exhib: One-man shows, Des Moines Art Ctr, 50 & 57, Albany Inst Hist & Art, NY, 60 & Allan Stone Gallery, New York, 67, 70 & 74; Gallery Mod Art, Washington, DC, 63; Albright-Knox Art Gallery, Buffalo, NY, 63 & 71; Recent Am Drawings, Rose Art Mus, Brandeis Univ, 64; Human Concern, Whitney Mus Am Art, New York, 69; Unordinary Realities, Xerox Sq Exhib Ctr, Rochester, NY, 75; Am Drawings: 1927-1977, Minn Mus Art, St Paul, 77. Teaching: Assoc prof art hist & painting, Union Col, Schenectady, NY, 57-65. Awards: Danforth Found Grant, 63-64; Nat Endowment Arts Painting Grant, 73-74. Style & Technique: Work with and across many media, including oil, watercolor, ink and found objects, in collage and box constructions, sometimes combined or separately; painting in oil, watercolor, pastel and colored ink; also, assemblage-collage. Dealer: Allan Stone Gallery 48 E 86th St New York NY 10028. Mailing Add: RD 1 Spencer NY 14883

NOWYTSKI, SVIATOSLAV (SLAVKO)
FILM MAKER, PHOTOGRAPHER
b Oct 19, 35; Can citizen. Study: Pasadena Playhouse Col Theatre Arts, BA(theatre), 58; Columbia Univ, MFA(motion pictures), 64. Work: Educ Film Libr Asn, New York; Libr Cong; Dept Tourism, Recreation & Cult Affairs, Govt Man; Fedn Assoc Arts, Man; Ont Ministry Educ, Toronto. Comn: Reflections of the Past (film), Ukrainian Cult & Educ Ctr, Winnipeg, 74; Kite Magic (film), Fedn Assoc Arts Man, 74. Exhib: Sheep in Wood (film), Am Film Festival, New York, 71; Reflections of the Past (film), Can Film Awards, Niagara on the Lake, Ont, 75 & 11th Int Chicago Film Festival, Ill, 75. Pos: Ed, Ukrainian, Polish & Russian Sect, Cinema & TV Digest, 63-; pres, Filmart Prod, Minneapolis, Minn, 71- Awards: Blue Ribbon Award for Sheep in Wood, Am Film Festival, 71; Award of Merit for Reflections of the Past, 11th Int Film Festival, Chicago, 75. Mem: Minn Soc Fine Arts; Twin

Cities Metrop Arts Alliance. Res: Approach to films about artists showing artist at work, details of his techniques; voice-over his thoughts on art with or without narration. Mailing Add: 120 Demont Ave E St Paul MN 55117

NUALA (ELSA DE BRUN)
PAINTER
b Stockholm, Sweden, Oct 11, 96; US citizen. Study: Anna Sanstrom Sch, Stockholm; also with W S Hayter. Work: Stained glass window, Carnegie Hall, New York; 43 paintings to James Joyce's Finnegans Wake, Univ Tex, Austin; Carnegie Endowment Peace Bldg, New York; Benedictine Abbey, Glenstol Co, Limerick, Ireland; Mus Irish Art Hq, New York. Exhib: Whitney Mus Am Art Ann, New York, 49, 50 & 55; Int Watercolor Exhib, Brooklyn Mus, 52; Am Acad Arts & Lett, New York, 61, 63 & 65; Art of Organic Form, Smithsonian Inst, Washington, DC, 69; The Organic Vision, Hobart & William Smith Cols, 71; plus many others. Teaching: Artist in residence, Pocono Environ Educ Ctr, 74. Awards: Mark Rothko Found Grant, 73; Carlsberg Found Grant, 73; Royal Order of Vasa-First Class for Distinguished Contributions to Creative Arts, King of Sweden, 74; plus others. Bibliog: Abram Lerner (auth), Nuala (catalog), Hirshhorn Mus Dir, 71; Leif Sjoberg (auth), Art of Elsa de Brun, Am Scand Rev, 71; Kierkegaard's world wide TV spec of work with Malcolm Muggeridge from Either/Or Exhib, Mus Copenhagen, 74; plus others. Mem: James Joyce Soc. Media: Pastel. Dealer: Betty Parsons Gallery 24 W 57th St New York NY 10019. Mailing Add: 161 E 81st St New York NY 10028

NUGENT, JOHN CULLEN
SCULPTOR, EDUCATOR
b Montreal, Que, Jan 5, 21. Study: St Thomas Col, St Paul, Minn, 40-41; Cost House, Calgary, Alta, 46; St John's Univ, Collegeville, Minn, 47-48. Work: Norman McKenzie Gallery, Regina, Sask; Can Coun Art Bank, Ottawa, Ont; Univ Sask, Saskatoon. Comn: Hist site sculpture, comn by Can Govt, Ft Esperance, Rocanville, Sask, 62; relief in steel, Police Bldg, Prince Albert, Sask, 65; fountain, Mid Town Centre, Regina, 67; steel sculpture, Can Govt Dept Works, Grain Comn Bldg, Winnipeg, Man, 76. Exhib: Nat Gallery Exhib of Can, Brussels, Belg, 57; Christian Art Biennial, Salzburg, Ger, 57; Christian Art Today, Toronto, Ont, 66; Waddington Gallery, Montreal, Que, 69; Outdoor Sculpture, 72, Emma Lake Exhib, 73 & one-man show, 74, Norman McKenzie Gallery, Regina; Sculpture on the Prairies, Winnipeg Gallery, 77. Teaching: Prof sculpture, Univ Regina, Sask, 70- Awards: Sr Arts fel, Can Coun, 61. Bibliog: Troff-Swiston (film), Another Language, 73. Mem: Can Artists Rep; Royal Can Acad of Art. Style & Technique: Non-objective. Media: Welded steel. Mailing Add: Box 24 Lunsden SK Can

NUKI (DANIEL MILLSAPS)
PAINTER, WRITER
b Darlington, SC, June 30, 29. Study: Univ SC, AB; Art Students League, with Kuniyoshi, Sternberg, Martin Lewis & Nahum Tchbasov. Work: Va Mus Fine Arts, Richmond; US State Dept & Libr Cong, Washington, DC; Columbia Mus Art, SC; Berkshire Mus, Pittsfield, Mass. Exhib: Va Mus Fine Arts, 47; Delgado Mus, New Orleans, La, 48; Am Inst Graphic Arts, New York, 48; Univ Colo, Denver, 58; 10 yr retrospective, Columbia Mus Art, 66. Pos: Ed & publ, Washington Int Arts Lett, 62- Awards: Best woodcut & Va Mus Fine Arts Purchase Prize, 48; Am Inst Graphic Arts Award for 50 best, 48; Anthony Hampton Award, 50. Style & Technique: Completely non-objective, spiritual works in black and white and watercolor, all small and very large ones in acrylic. Media: Watercolor, Ink. Res: Patronage of the arts; critic of government and arts relationships. Publ: Auth, National Directory of Grants and Aid to Individuals in the Arts, 3rd ed, 77; auth, National Directory of Arts Support by Private Foundations, Vol 3, 77. Mailing Add: PO Box 9005 Washington DC 20003

NULF, FRANK ALLEN
PAINTER, EDUCATOR
b Lima, Ohio, Sept 23, 31. Study: Ariz State Univ, BS, 59; Mich State Univ, MA, 60; Fulbright grant, Madrid, Spain, 62-63; Ohio Univ, PhD, 69. Exhib: 4th Nat Exhib Contemp Am Art, Oklahoma City, 62; Soc Washington Printmakers 24th Int, 62; Boston Printmakers Ann, Boston Mus Fine Arts, 65; Int Miniature Print Exhib, Assoc Am Artists Gallery, 71; Can Printmakers Showcase, Ottawa, Ont, 72; Third Int Drawing Biennale, Cleveland, United Kingdom, 77. Teaching: Assoc prof art, State Univ NY Col Potsdam, 60-69; prof art & dean fine arts, Univ Regina, 69- Awards: Can Coun travel grant, 77. Mem: Fel Royal Soc Arts; Col Art Asn Am; Univ Art Asn Can. Style & Technique: Contemporary object oriented surreal style; pencil, graphite and watercolor drawings and glazed acrylics and oils. Res: Film history and film criticism. Publ: Auth, Report on the Bergamo film festival, Vol 5, No 3, ed, Network television and the personal documentary, Vol 6, No 1 & ed, The intensification of reality, Vol 6, No 1, Film Comment; auth, Luigi Pirandello and the cinema, Film Quart, winter 70-71. Mailing Add: Dept of Fine Arts Univ of Regina Regina SK Can

NUTZLE, FUTZIE (BRUCE JOHN KLEINSMITH)
GRAPHIC ARTIST, CARTOONIST
b Lakewood, Ohio, Feb 21, 42. Work: Mus Mod Art, New York; San Francisco Mus Art; Oakland Mus, Calif; Santa Cruz City Mus, Calif; Whitney Mus Am Art, New York. Comn: Anyone & Everyone's Theater, comn by Balloon Community, Santa Cruz, 71. Exhib: Empty Canoes, lithographs by F Nutzle, San Francisco Mus Art, 72; Paintings by Futzie Nutzle, Int Inst Exp Printmaking, Santa Cruz, 73; Opening, Santa Cruz Artists' Mus Proj, 73; Twin Rocker Paper Exhib, Indianapolis Mus Art, Ind, 75; Caffe Pergolesi, Santa Cruz, 75-76; Leica, Los Angeles, 78; Contemp Graphics Exhib, Santa Barbara, Calif, 78. Bibliog: Fragile, Handle with Care (film), 70; S Subtle & B Lee (auths), My art belongs to Dada, Esquire Mag, 8/74. Style & Technique: Drawings & paintings Futzie Nutzle style. Media: Pen and Ink, Wash on Paper; Acrylic on Canvas. Publ: Contribr, Balloon Newspaper, 68-, Oui Mag, 71, Rags Mag, 71, Rolling Stone, 75-, Wet Mag, 77- & Independent Newspaper, Santa Cruz, Calif, 77-78; illusr, P Bisconti (auth), Da Da Duck/Children's Bk & Morton Marcus (auth), The Armies Encamped in the Fields Beyond the Unfinished Avenues, 77; contribr, Quarry West, Number 8, 77. Mailing Add: PO Box 2481 Santa Cruz CA 95063

NYGREN, JOHN FERGUS
GLASSBLOWER
b Big Springs, Nebr, Oct 8, 40. Study: Univ Nebr, BFA, 65; Cranbrook Acad of Art, Bloomfield Hills, Mich, MFA(ceramics), 67; Penland Sch of Crafts, spec study in glass, 68. Work: Corning Mus of Glass, NY; Sheldon Art Gallery, Lincoln, Nebr; Chrysler Mus at Norfolk, Va; Mint Mus of Art, Charlotte, NC; Smithsonian Inst. Exhib: Toledo Glass Nat II, Toledo Mus of Art, Ohio, 68; Young Americans 69, Mus of Contemp Crafts, New York; one-man show, Sheldon Art Gallery, 71; NC Glass 76, Western Carolina Univ, Cullowhee, NC, 76; Contemp Art Glass 76, Lever House, New York, 76; New Am Glass, Focus WVa, Huntington Galleries, 76; Contemp Glass: John Nygren/Flora Mace, Chrysler Mus at Norfolk, 77. Awards: Vreeland Award, Univ Nebr, 64; Nat Merit Award, Craftsmen USA 66, Am Crafts Coun, 66; Purchase Award, NC Glass 76, NC Nat Bank, 76. Bibliog: Sidney Rosenblatt (auth), The Art Glass of Tomorrow-Today, Hobbies-Mag for Collectors, 3/75; John Mebane (auth), The Glass of John Nygren, Antiques J, 6/76. Mem: Am Crafts Coun; Glass Art Soc; Piedmont Crafts, Inc. Style & Technique: Blown glass with naturalistic pictorial motif done in a lampworking technique. Dealer: Contemp Art Glass Group 806 Madison Ave New York NY 10021. Mailing Add: The New Branch Walnut Cove NC 27052

O

OAKES, JOHN WARREN
PAINTER, ART ADMINISTRATOR
b Bowling Green, Ky, Feb 26, 41. Study: Art Instr Sch Minneapolis; Students League, Albert Dorne Scholar; Western Area Voc Sch; Western Ky Univ, AB, 64; Univ Iowa, MA, 66, MFA, 73; Harvard Univ, cert arts admin, 75. Work: Numerous works in pub & pvt collections. Exhib: Seventeen one-man shows. Teaching: Instr art, Western Ky Univ, 66-71, asst prof art, 71-76, assoc prof art, 76- Pos: Gallery dir, Ivan Wilson Ctr Fine Arts, Western Ky Univ, 66-, staff asst, off dean, Potter Col Arts & Humanities, 73-75, asst dean admin, 75- Mem: Kappa Pi; Ky Guild Artists & Craftsmen; Col Art Asn; Ky Alliance Arts Educ (bd mem & secy); Bowling Green-Warren Co Arts Comn (mem bd); Ky Art Educ Asn. Media: Acrylic, Photography. Dealer: Insel Gallery 987 Third Ave New York NY 10022. Mailing Add: c/o Ivan Wilson Ctr Fine Arts Western Ky Univ Bowling Green KY 42101

OBERHUBER, KONRAD J
ART HISTORIAN, CURATOR
b Linz, Austria, Mar 31, 35. Study: Univ Vienna, DrPhil, Dozent; Univ Cologne. Teaching: Instr art hist, Smith Col, 64-65; instr art hist, Cambridge Univ, Eng, winter 68; instr art hist, Univ Vienna, fall 70 & spring 72; prof, Fogg Art Mus, Harvard Univ, spring 74 & fall 75- Pos: Cur, Albertina, Vienna, 61-71; cur, Nat Gallery Art, Washington, DC, 71-75; cur, Fogg Art Mus, Cambridge, Mass, 75- Awards: Kress Fel, I Tatti, Florence, Italy, 65-66, fel, Inst Advanced Study, Princeton Univ, 74-75. Res: Prints, drawings and paintings of the 16th century in Italy and the Netherlands and 17th century France. Publ: Auth, Parmigianino und Sein Kreis (catalog), 63, auth, Die Kunst der Graphik III, Renaissance in Italien, 66 & auth, Die Kunst der Graphik IV, Zwischen Renaissance und Barock, 68, Albertina; co-auth, The Famous Italian Drawings of the Albertina, New York-Milan, 72; auth, Raphaels Zeichnungen, Berlin, 72; auth, Disegni di Tiziano e della sua cerchia, Venice, 76. Mailing Add: Fogg Art Mus 32 Quincy St Cambridge MA 02138

O'BRIEN, MARJORIE (MARJORIE O'BRIEN RAPAPORT)
PAINTER, PRINTMAKER
b Idaho Falls, Idaho. Study: Ripon Col, Wis; Univ of Wis, Madison; Traphagen Sch, New York; studied with Alexander Archipenko & Jean Liberte, New York; Ecole du Louvre, Academie Julian & with Andre Lhote and Conrad Kichert, Paris, France; Brooklyn Mus Sch with Kendall Shaw & Jan Hildebrandt; also studied with Herman Zaage; Univ of Calif, San Francisco with Erle Loran. Exhib: Metrop Mus of Art, New York, 75 & 77; Snug Harbor Cult Ctr, Staten Island, NY, 76; Avery Fisher Hall, Lincoln Ctr, New York, 76-77; one-man shows, Chez Fratellini, Paris, France, 50, Charles Allis Art Mus, Milwaukee, Wis, 59, Wis Ctr, Univ of Wis, Madison, 60, Music Branch, New York Pub Libr, 60, Donnell Art Ctr, New York, 64 & Hudson Park Branch, New York Pub Libr, 76. Collections Arranged: (collaborated with Dr Ionel Rapaport), Art by Mentally Retarded Patients, George Washington Univ in conjunction with President's Conference on Children & Youth, 61, plus others. Teaching: Instr painting, Univ of Wis, Madison, 58-59; instr art & psychopathology, New Sch for Soc Research, New York, 62-68. Pos: Research Asst, Staten Island Historical Soc, 77- Awards: Merite Artistique, City of Paris, 51. Bibliog: Edith Hare (auth), Paris Presse, 51 & Le Figaro, Paris, France, 52; Elaine Boies (auth), Staten Island Advance, NY, 76. Mem: Staten Island Fedn of Artists & Craftsmen; Staten Island Historical Soc; Archaeology Soc of Staten Island; Wis Acad of Sci, Arts, Letters. Style & Technique: Expressionist, with stress on composition, portraiture. Media: Oil, Watercolor; Pastel. Publ: Illusr, Carl Schurz, Patriot, 59 & A Soviet View of the American Past, 60, Wis Hist Soc. Mailing Add: 69 Sherman Ave Staten Island NY 10301

O'BRIEN, WILLIAM VINCENT
ART DEALER
b Chicago, Ill, Sept 16, 02. Pos: Pres, O'Brien's Art Emporium, 33- Specialty: Contemporary-realistic American art. Mailing Add: 7122 Stetson Dr Scottsdale AZ 85251

OCAMPO, MIGUEL
PAINTER
b Buenos Aires, Arg, Nov 29, 22. Study: Architecture. Work: Albright-Knox Collection, Buffalo; Mus Mod Art, New York; State Collection, France; Mus Fine Arts, Montevideo, Uruguay; Mus Fine Arts, Buenos Aires. Exhib: Stedelijk Mus, Amsterdam, 53; one-man shows, Mus Mod Art, Rio de Janeiro, 59, Galeria Aele, Madrid, 74 & Jacques Kaplan Gallery, NY, 75; Mus d'Art Mod, Paris, 73. Style & Technique: Abstract geometric and biomorphic forms sprayed. Media: Acrylic, Oil. Dealer: Jacques Kaplan 19 E 71st St New York NY 10021. Mailing Add: 135 Hudson St New York NY 10013

OCEJO (JOSE GARCIA)
PAINTER
b Cordoba, Mex, June 14, 28. Study: Nat Univ Mex; painting workshop with Diego Rivera, Mex; Bellas Artes, Madrid, dipl honor; Sommer Acad, Salzburg, Austria, with Oskar Kokoschka, dipl honor. Comn: Murals, Ciudad Univ, Inst Cult Hispanica, Madrid, 50, Casino Arte, Mexico City, 52, El Potrero, Ingenio El Potrero, Mexico City, 53 & Inst Madera, Direccion Gen Montes, Madrid, 58; Basilica Nazareth (mosaic), Inst Nac Bellas Artes Mex & Comt Tierra Santa Milan, 68. Exhib: Pinturas G Ocejo, Inst Nac Bellas Artes, Madrid, 61; Ocejo, Palacio Nac Bellas Artes, Mexico City, 66, Estancias Del Placer, 72; Obra De Ocejo, Kaigado Gallery, Tokyo, Japan, 66; Ocejo, Louisiana Gallery, Houston, Tex, 68; one-man shows, Nueva Galeria, Barcelona, Spain, 73 & Museo del Teatro, Barcelona, 73; plus many others. Awards: Medallas de Honor, Inst Cult Hispanica, Madrid, 50 & Sommer Acad, 64; Primer Premio Olimpiada Cult, Inst Elias Sourasky, Mex, 68. Bibliog: Alfonso Neuvillate (auth), Pintura actual, Artes Mex, 66; Ida Rodriguez (auth), Surrealismo y Arte Fantastico, 69 & Alfonso Neuvillate (auth), Jose Garcia Ocejo, 69, Nat Univ Mex; plus others. Mem: Inst Cult Hispanica, Madrid; Inst Cult Hispano, Mex; Inst Cult Mex-Norte Am, Mex; Mus Arte Mod, Mex; Inst Nac Bellas Artes, Mex. Media: Acrylic, Oil. Collection: Art nouveau; pieces from China and Thailand. Publ: Auth, Panorama art visuais, Brasil J, 65; auth, Artes visuales, Union Pan Am, Washington, 66; articles in Art in Am, 11/72. Dealer: Galeria Arvil Hamburgo 241 Mexico DF Mexico. Mailing Add: Colima 230 Mexico DF Mexico

OCHS, ROBERT DAVID
COLLECTOR, PATRON
b Bloomington, Ill, Mar 27, 15. Study: Ill Wesleyan Univ, AB, 36; Univ Ill, MA, 37 & PhD, 39. Pos: Trustee, Columbia Mus of Art, 66-69 & 74-77; chmn mus comt, Univ SC, Columbia, 74-76. Interest: Contemporary Art. Collection: Contemporary paintings, prints and sculpture, including Johns, Rauschenberg and Twombey. Publ: Co-ed, The Columbia art association 1915-1975, the Columbia museum of art 1950-1975, a history, Columbia Mus of Art, 75. Mailing Add: 15D Cornell Arms Columbia SC 29201

OCKERSE, THOMAS
DESIGNER, EDUCATOR
b Apr 12, 40; US citizen. Study: Ohio State Univ, BFA; Yale Univ, MFA; with Norman Ives, Herbert Matter, Walker Evans & Alvin Eisenman. Work: Mus Mod Art, New York; Stedelijk Mus, Amsterdam; Jean Brown Arch; Richard Demarco Gallery, Edinburg, Scotland; Indianapolis Mus Art. Exhib: Language & Structure, Kensington Arts Asn, Toronto; Int Omaha Flow Systems, Joslyn Art Mus, Omaha; Expo Int de Novisma Poesia, Inst Ditella, Buenos Aires, 69; ?Kronkrete Poezie, Stedelijk Mus, Amsterdam, 70; Edinburgh Festival, Richard Demarco Gallery, Scotland, 72, 74 & 75. Teaching: Asst prof graphic design, Ind Univ, Bloomington, 67-71; assoc prof graphic design, RI Sch Design, Providence, 71-, head graphic design dept, 73- Bibliog: J Bowles (auth), This Book is a Movie, Dell, 71; Kostelanetz (auth), Breakthrough Fictioneers, Something Else Press, 72; Camera Three (NY TV prog), 74. Style & Technique: Concrete language art, aesthetic systems dealing with the verbal/visual presence of language. Publ: The A-Z Book, 69, TOP (ed 500), 70, TV Documentracing (ed 300), 73, Time (ed 1000), 73 & 26 Poems?t1, 75, Tom Ockerse Editions; plus many others. Mailing Add: 37 Woodbury St Providence RI 02906

O'CONNELL, ANN BROWN
PAINTER, COLLECTOR
b Worcester, Mass, June 3, 31. Study: Bradford Col, AA; Boston Univ Exten; Sumi-e with Evalyn Aaron, Port Washington, NY; Chinese brush painting with Audrey Nossal, Potomac, Md; also Roddy McLean, Avondale, Va. Exhib: Sumi-e Soc Am Inc Ann Exhibs; 6th Ann Exhib, Bank of Tokyo Trust Co, New York, 69; 7th Ann Exhib, Nippon Club, New York, 70. Awards: President's Prize, Sumi-e Soc Am, Inc, 69. Mem: Sumi-e Soc Am, Inc (mem secy, 71-73, founder, Wash Chap, 72, nat vpres, 72-73, nat pres, 74-). Style & Technique: Oriental brush painting. Collection: Print collection specializing in early 20th century American printmakers; 19th and early 20th American and European paintings. Mailing Add: 1341 Woodside Dr McLean VA 22101

O'CONNELL, EDWARD E
PHOTOGRAPHER, PRINTMAKER
b New York, NY. Study: Hofstra Univ, BS; Pratt Inst, MFA. Work: Metrop Mus Art, New York; Brooklyn Mus, NY; Philadelphia Free Libr, Pa; Univ Mass, Amherst; Univ Tenn, Knoxville; plus others. Exhib: Photography into Sculpture, Mus Mod Art, New York, 70; 17th Nat Print, Brooklyn Mus, 70; US Pavilion, World's Fair, Osaka, Japan, 70; New Talent in Printmaking, Am Artists, New York, 70; Oversize Prints, Whitney Mus, New York, 71. Teaching: Asst prof photog & graphics, Montcla Sch Visual Arts, New York, 69-71; asst prof photog & printmaking, Fordham Univ, 70- Awards: Found Grant in Printmaking, Louis Comfort Tiffany Found, 66; Purchase Award, Brooklyn Mus, 70. Bibliog: James R Mellow (auth), Contemporary prints, the medium is not the message, New York Times, 6/28/70. Mem: Col Art Asn Am. Style & Technique: Exploration of photographic imagery, constructions. Media: Silkscreen; Acrylic. Publ: Auth, Artists proof, Photo-Graphics, Vol VII, 67. Dealer: Sylvan Cole c/o Assoc Am Artists Gallery 663 Fifth Ave New York NY 10022. Mailing Add: 119 Spring St New York NY 10021

O'CONNELL, GEORGE D
PRINTMAKER, EDUCATOR
b Madison, Wis, Oct 16, 26. Study: Univ Wis, BS, 50, MS, 51; Ohio State Univ; Rijksakademie Van Beeldende Kunsten, Amsterdam, Netherlands, Fulbright fel, 59-60. Work: Baltimore Mus Art; Smithsonian Inst, Washington, DC; Libr Cong, Washington, DC; Gemeentemuseum Van Schone Kunsten, The Hague, Netherlands; Brit Mus, London, Eng. Comn: Volunteer artist prog, Dept Hist of Army, 71. Exhib: Am Embassy, Dublin, Ireland; Baltimore Mus; John & Mabel Ringling Mus Art; Contemporary American Graphic Art, Corcoran Gallery Art, Washington, DC; US Info Agency Traveling Exhib Contemp Prints. Teaching: Assoc prof printmaking, Univ Md, 61-68; prof printmaking, State Univ NY Col Oswego, 69-, chmn dept art, 71- Awards: Creative Arts & Crafts Award, Univ Md, 68. Media: Drypoint, Lithography. Dealer: Franz Bader Gallery Pennsylvania Ave Washington DC 20176. Mailing Add: 39 Baylis St Oswego NY 13126

O'CONNOR, FRANCIS VALENTINE
ART HISTORIAN, LECTURER
b Brooklyn, NY, Feb 14, 37. Study: Manhattan Col, New York, BA(Eng lit), 59; Johns Hopkins Univ, MA(creative writing), 60, PhD(art hist), 65. Teaching: Jr instr Eng & art hist, Johns Hopkins Univ, Baltimore, Md, 59-62; lectr art hist, Univ Md, 64-66; instr 20th century art, Johns Hopkins Univ Evening Col, 66-67 & 70-71; asst prof art hist, Univ Md, 66-70; instr art, Am Univ, Paris, 71; instr symbolism of abstract art, Smithsonian Inst, Washington, DC, 72; adj prof, Union Grad Sch, Antioch Col, 74- Pos: Sr vis res assoc, Nat Collection of Fine Arts, Smithsonian Inst, Washington, DC, 70-72; pvt consultant, 73- Mem: Col Art Asn; Am Soc of Aesthetics; Am Studies Asn; Soc for the Arts, Relig & Contemp Cult (mem bd, 74-77); Soc Values in Higher Educ. Res: Twentieth century American art; New Deal Art Projects; abstract expressionism; projected history of American mural. Publ: Auth, Jackson Pollock, Mus of Mod Art, New York, 67; auth, Federal Support for the Visual Arts: The New Deal and Now, NY Graphic Soc, 69; ed, The New Deal Art Projects: An Anthology of Memoirs, Smithsonian Press, 72; ed, Art for the Millions, NY Graphic Soc, 73; co-auth & co-ed, with Eugene V Thaw, Jackson Pollock: A catalogue raisonné of paintings, drawings and other works, 4 vols, Yale Univ, 78. Mailing Add: 250 E 73rd St 11C New York NY 10021

O'CONNOR, HAROLD THOMAS
GOLDSMITH, INSTRUCTOR
b Utica, NY, Aug 23, 41. Study: Univ NMex, BUS; Nat Craft Sch, Copenhagen, Denmark; Nat Art Sch, Helsinki, Finland; Kunst und Werkschule, Pforzheim, Ger; Int Acad Fine Arts, Salzburg, Austria; Inst Allende, San Miguel de Allende, Mex, MFA. Work: The Goldsmiths Hall, London, Eng; Can Guild of Crafts, Toronto, Ont. Exhib: Int Jewelry Exhib, Munich, Ger, 70, 72, 74 & 77; Experimenta, Hamburg, Ger, 72 & Hannover, Ger, 73; Int Jewelry Arts, Tokyo, Japan, 73 & 76; The Goldsmiths, Renwick Gallery, Smithsonian Inst, Washington, DC, 74; Seven Golden Yrs, The Goldsmith Hall, London, 74; First World Silver Fair, Mexico City, Mex, 74; Contemp Crafts of the Americas, Colo State Univ, Ft Collins, 75; Schmuck 77 Trendenzen, Jewelry Mus, Pforzheim, Ger, 77. Teaching: Instr jewelry design, Alta Col of Art, Calgary, 71-73; dir jewelry making, Dunconor Design Workshops, Crested Butte, Colo, 75- Awards: First in Metals, Entr'acte, Toronto, Ont, O'Keefe Co, 73; Bronze Award, World Pearl Jewelry Design Competition, Tokyo, Japan, Japan Pearl Asn, 75; First & Second in Metals, Nat Crafts Competition, Guild of Am Craftsmen, 76. Bibliog: Development of Harold O'Connor, Goldschmiede Zeitung—Europ Jeweler, 7/73; Interview with Harold O'Connor, Craftsmans Gallery, Fall 74; Anatomishches von Harold O'Connor, Goldschmiede Zeitung—Europ Jeweler, 1/75. Mem: World Crafts Coun; Soc NAm Goldsmiths (corresp, 76-); Int Guild Craft Journalists, Auths & Photogrs. Style & Technique: Varied style over the years; currently exploring abstracted designs derived from discarded mining equipment from the gold and silver mines in the Rocky Mountain area. Media: Fabrication of micro-size works in combinations of gold, silver and copper. Res: Various uses for the flexible shaft machine in jewelry making. Publ: Auth, New Directions in Goldsmithing, 75, auth, Procedures and Formulas for Metal Craftsmen, 76, auth, The Jewelers Bench Reference, 77 & auth, The Flexible Shaft Handbook, 78, Dunconor Bks. Mailing Add: Box 2000 Crested Butte CO 81224

O'CONNOR, JOHN ARTHUR
PAINTER, EDUCATOR
b Twin Falls, Idaho, Jan 23, 40. Study: Univ Calif, Davis, AB(with honors) & scholarship, 61, with Wayne Thiebaud & William T Wiley, MA, 63; San Francisco Art Inst, scholarship, with James Weeks, 61. Work: Ringling Mus Art, Sarasota, Fla; State Calif Collection, Sacramento; Bates Gallery, Edinboro State Col, Pa; Archives of Calif Art, Oakland Art Mus; Kemper Gallery, Kansas City Art Inst, Mo. Comn: Carr Van Anda Award for New York Times, Ohio Univ, 68; triptych, comn by Mr & Mrs George Varian, Palo Alto, Calif, 71. Exhib: Over 13 one-man shows, including Santa Barbara Mus Art, 63, E B Crocker Art Gallery, Sacramento, 66 & Ringling Mus Art, 72; Dayton Art Inst, Ohio, 66 & 68-71; Cincinnati Biennial, Cincinnati Art Mus, Ohio, 67; 6th Ann Realist Exhib, Ctr Southeastern Art, Winston-Salem, NC, 74; A Pictorial History of the World, Kemper Gallery, Kansas City Art Inst, 75; Nat Invitational Drawing Exhib, Southern Ill Univ Galleries, Carbondale, Ill, 75; plus numerous others. Teaching: Instr painting & drawing, Univ Calif, Santa Barbara, 63-64; instr painting & drawing, Ohio Univ, 65-69; assoc prof painting & contemp art hist, Univ Fla, 69- Pos: Dir, Art Gallery, Univ Calif, Davis, 62-63; dir, Art Gallery, Ohio Univ, 67-68; sr investr, Ctr Creative & Optimal Design, Univ Fla, 72-; artist in residence, Col Creative Studies, Univ Calif, Santa Barbara, 74. Awards: Modular Systems Theory & Design Analysis Award, Air Force Off Sci Res, 74. Bibliog: Hariette von Breton (auth), O'Connor show, artforum Mag, 64. Style & Technique: Inverted trompe l'oeil combined with fragments of reality. Media: Acrylic on Board or Canvas. Res: Modular theory and systems theory in design; learning to design with other disciplines; three-dimensional design, process, product and behavior. Publ: Ed, Graphics 1968-Ultimate Concerns, 68; ed, David Hostetler, Yousuf Karsh, Dana Loomis, 68; co-auth, Unbottle Your Creative Ideas-A Cooperative Venture of Engineering and Art, 72; contribr, A Pictorial History of the World, 75. Dealer: Gallery K 2032 P St NW Washington DC 20036. Mailing Add: PO Box 12368 Gainesville FL 32604

O'CONNOR, STANLEY JAMES
ART HISTORIAN, EDUCATOR
Study: Cornell Univ, BA, 51, PhD, 64; Univ Va, MA, 54. Teaching: Prof art hist, Cornell Univ, 64- Mem: Col Art Asn; Asn Asian Studies (SE Asia Coun, 78-); Borneo Res Soc; Malaysian Br, Royal Asiatic Soc. Res: Early trade of Southeast Asia; Buddhist and Hindu art. Publ: Auth, Hindu Gods of Peninsular Siam, Artibus Asiae, 72; contribr, Buddhist Votive Tablest & Caves in Peninsular Siam, Nat Mus Bangkok, 74; contribr, Iron working as spiritual inquiry in Indonesia, Hist of Relig, 75; contribr, Tambralinga and the Khmer Empire, Siam Soc J, 75. Mailing Add: Dept of Art Cornell Univ Ithaca NY 14850

O'CONNOR, THOM
PRINTMAKER
b Detroit, Mich, June 26, 37. Study: Fla State Univ, BA; Cranbrook Acad Art, MFA. Work: Mus Mod Art, New York; Whitney Mus Am Art, New York; Brooklyn Mus; Philadelphia Mus Art. Comn: Witches of Salem (suite), State Coun Arts, NY, 72. Exhib: Brooklyn Print Ann, 68; San Diego Print Invitational, 72. Teaching: Prof lithography, State Univ NY Albany, 62-; vis artist, Williams Col, 70; vis artist, Vassar Col, 71 & 72. Awards: Tamarind Printer Fel, 64; State Univ NY Res Found Fel, 65 & 72. Dealer: Associated American Artists 663 Fifth Ave New York NY 10002. Mailing Add: Moss Rd Voorheesville NY 12186

OCVIRK, OTTO G
SCULPTOR, PRINTMAKER
b Detroit, Mich, Nov 13, 22. Study: State Univ Iowa, BFA & MFA. Work: Dayton Art Inst, Ohio; Detroit Inst Art, Mich; Dayton Co, Minneapolis, Minn. Exhib: Walker Art Ctr, Minneapolis, Minn, 47-49; Brooklyn Nat Print, NY, 49; Northwest Printmakers, Seattle, Wash, 49; San Francisco Ann Print & Drawing, Calif, 49-50; Libr Cong Nat Print Show, Washington, DC, 50. Teaching: Prof art, Bowling Green State Univ, 50- Awards: Sculpture Exhib, Walker Art Ctr, Minneapolis, Minn, 47; Mich Artist Exhib, Hal H Smith, Detroit, 50; Broadcast Media Award, WBGU-TV, 19th Ann Broadcasters, San Francisco. Mem: Col Art Asn Am; Mid America Col Art Asn; Mich Printmakers; Ohio Printmakers. Media: Stone; Intaglio. Publ: Co-auth, Art Fundamentals, Theory and Practice, Brown, 60, 68 & 75. Mailing Add: 231 Haskins St Bowling Green OH 43402

ODATE, TOSHIO
CONCEPTUAL ARTIST, INSTRUCTOR
b Tokyo, Japan, July 9, 30. Study: Art Sch, Tokyo, 50-54; Nat Chiba Univ, 57-58. Work: Rochester Mem Art Gallery, NY; Bundy Art Gallery, Waitsfield, Vt; Great Southwest Atlanta Corp, Atlanta, Ga; Brooklyn Mus, NY. Exhib: Waning Moon and Rising Sun—Japanese Artists, Houston Mus Art, Tex, 59; Joseph H Hirshhorn Collection, Solomon R Guggenheim Mus, New York, 63; The Artists Reality, New Sch Social Res, New York, 64; Whitney Mus Am Art Sculpture Ann, 65-66; Attitudes, Brooklyn Mus, 70. Teaching: Instr sculpture, Brooklyn Mus Art Sch, 61-; instr sculpture, Pratt Inst, 68-; guest lectr, Denver Mus Art, 67, Univ Wis, Wausa, 68 & Univ Ky, 69. Publ: Contribr, Modern sculpture from the Joseph H Hirshhorn Collection, 62; contribr, Modern American sculpture, 67. Mailing Add: c/o Stephen Radich Gallery 56 E 11th St New York NY 10021

O'DELL, ERIN (ANNE)
PAINTER, DESIGNER
b Phoenix, Ariz, Dec 7, 38. Study: Moore Col Art, BFA(textile design); Ariz State Univ; also with John Pike in Mexico, Jamaica, Ireland, Italy & Guatemala. Work: Ariz Bank, Phoenix; Colo Nat Bank, Colorado Springs; First Nat Bank, Mesa, Ariz; Valley Nat Bank, Scottsdale & Mesa, Ariz. Exhib: Ann Artists Salon, Oklahoma City, Okla, 73 & 74; Two Flags Festival Arts, Douglas, Ariz, 73-76; Nat Garden Valley Show, Colorado Springs, 74; Dagres Gallery Watercolor Show, Phoenix, 75; Phippen-O'Brien Gallery Watercolor Show, Scottsdale, 75. Teaching: Instr hist textiles, Moore Col Art, 63-65. Pos: Designer, Henry Cantor, Inc, Philadelphia, Pa, 61-64; free lance designer, C A Reed Co, Williamsport, Pa & Beach Prod, Kalamazoo, Mich, 64-75; artist, Modern Color Printing, Mesa, 69-74. Awards: Mesa Artist of the Year, Mesa Art League, 73; Watercolor Award, Douglas Art Asn, 73; Artist of the

Year, Ariz Saguaro Artists League, 77. Mem: Southwestern Watercolor Soc; Scottsdale Artists League; Mesa Art League (bd mem, 72-75, spec show chmn, 72-74, gen show chmn, 74-75); Ariz Saguaro Artists League; Valley Artists League. Style & Technique: Realistic landscapes, street scenes and florals. Media: Watercolor; Tempera, Gouache. Mailing Add: 938-D N Orange St Mesa AZ 85201

O'DOHERTY, BRIAN
See Ireland, Patrick

OECHSLI, KELLY
ILLUSTRATOR
b Butte, Mont, Feb 23, 18. Study: Cornish Sch of Art, Seattle, Washington, cert. Style & Technique: Pen and ink, watercolor for book reproduction. Media: Pen and Ink, Watercolor, Ink, Acrylic. Publ: Illusr, Peter Bull, Viking, 70; illusr, Germs Make Me Sick, Knopf; illusr, Walter the Wolf, 76 & Gobbledygook, Holiday House, 77. Mailing Add: 115 Sheridan Ave Hawthorne NY 10532

OEHLER, HELEN GAPEN
PAINTER, LECTURER
b Ottawa, Ill, May 30, 93. Study: Art Inst Chicago, honor grad; also with Elmer Browne, Provincetown, Mass & New York. Work: Ryerson Libr, Art Inst Chicago; Chrysler Art Mus, Provincetown. Comn: Many pvt commissions. Exhib: Salon D'Automne, Paris, 38; Nat Acad Design, New York, 39; Salon des Artistes Francais, 39; Am Fedn Arts traveling, 42; five exhibs, de Young Mus, San Francisco, 62-72; plus many other group & one-man shows. Teaching: Instr Sat juv summer normal, Art Inst Chicago, 14-15; instr art, supvr grade & high schs, Dixon, Ill, 15-18; instr ancient art hist, high sch, Evanston, Ill, 18-20. Pos: Dir, Art Coun NJ, 41-52; pres, Ridgewood Art Asn, NJ, 46-48; chmn, Artist Assoc Gallery, Mill Valley, Calif, 58-62. Awards: Award for September, Flax Mase, de Young Mus, 66; Degree of Honor, Soc Western Artists, 68; Award for Dated, Northern Calif Painting Competition, 72. Mem: Am Watercolor Soc (bd control, 44-); Am Artists Prof League; Soc Western Artists; Century Travel Club. Media: Oil, Watercolor. Publ: Art ed, Pen Women, 51. Mailing Add: Box 5397 Carmel CA 93921

OEHLSCHLAEGER, FRANK J
ART DEALER
b Paducah, Ky, Sept 8, 10. Study: Cornell Univ, grad, 33. Pos: Dir, Chicago Galleries of Assoc Am Artists, 45-47; dir, Marshall Fields & Co Art Gallery, Chicago, 47-49; dir & owner, Oehlschlaeger Gallery, Chicago, 49-, Sarasota, Fla, 62- Specialty: Contemporary American and European art. Mailing Add: PO Box 6108 Sarasota FL 33578

OENSLAGER, DONALD MITCHELL
STAGE DESIGNER
b Harrisburg, Pa, Mar 7, 02. Study: Harvard Univ, AB, 23; Sachs Fine Arts traveling fel; also with George Pierce Baker, Denman Ross & Maurice Sterne; Colo Col, hon DFA, 53. Work: Metrop Mus Art & Mus Mod Art, New York; Boston Mus Fine Arts; Detroit Inst Arts; Mus of City of New York. Comn: Designed over 250 theatrical productions in New York, 26-; consult on 15 new theatres incl Lincoln Ctr, Kennedy Ctr & Albany South Mall. Exhib: One-man exhibs, Marie Sterner Galleries, 36, Feragil Galleries, 49, Yale Gallery Fine Arts, 49, Detroit Inst Arts, 56 & Am Fedn Arts Traveling Exhib, 57. Teaching: Prof stage design, Sch Drama, Yale Univ, 25-70; lectr theatre, Salzburg Sem in Am Studies, 68 & 71; prof theatre, Grad Ctr, City Univ New York, 71-72. Pos: Trustee, Brooklyn Mus & Pratt Inst; pres, Art Comn City New York, 65-; trustee, Mus of City of New York, 64- Awards: Pa Ambassador Award, State of Pa, 50; Antonette Perry Award, Am Theatre Wing, 58-59. Mem: Am Fedn Arts (trustee, 66-); Brooklyn Inst Arts & Sci (trustee); Benjamin Franklin fel Royal Soc Arts; Int Exhibs Found (trustee, 72-). Collection: Books, drawings and manuscripts of the 16th to 20th century American theatre. Publ: Auth, Scenery, then and now, 36; ed, Notes on scene painting, 52. Mailing Add: 825 Fifth Ave New York NY 10021

OESTERLE, LEONHARD FREIDRICH
SCULPTOR, EDUCATOR
b Bietigheim, Ger, Mar 3, 15; Can citizen. Study: With Fritz Wotruba, Otto Huller, Hans Aeschbacher & Kunst Gewerbeschule, Zürich, Switz. Work: Staats Gallery, Stuttgart, Ger; Württembergischer Kunstverein, Stuttgart; Nat Gallery, Ottawa, Can; London Art Gallery, Ont; Kitchener Waterloo Art Gallery, Can. Comn: Playground sculpture, City of Berlin, 51; four figure group in bronze, Col McLaughlin Collegiate, Oshawa, 63; bronze statuary, St Augustin Chapel, Scarborough, Can, 64; wall sculpture & mural, Cent Labs, Toronto, 67; sculpture in lobby, Can Trust Bldg, London, Ont, 69. Exhib: Young Sculptor's Exhib, Helmhaus, Zürich, 49; Schwäbische Maler und Bildhauer, Zürich, 51. Teaching: Instr sculpture, Ont Col Art. Awards: Ont Soc Artists Spec Award, 68. Bibliog: John Sommer (auth), Leonhard Oesterle, Peter Shore, 11/71. Mem: Sculptor's Soc Can (vpres, 58 & 70-72); Ont Soc Artists; Royal Can Acad Arts. Media: Stone, Bronze. Dealer: Dunkelman Art Gallery 15 Bedford Rd Toronto ON Can. Mailing Add: 27 Alcina Ave Toronto ON M6G 2E7 Can

OFFIN, CHARLES Z
COLLECTOR, ART CRITIC
b New York, NY, Feb 5, 99. Study: City Col New York; Nat Acad Design; Art Students League; Ecole Beaux-Arts, Fontainebleau, France. Work: Metrop Mus Art, New York; New York Pub Libr. Exhib: One-man shows, Paris, Barcelona, Spain & New York. Teaching: Instr, City Col New York, 32-35. Pos: Art critic, Brooklyn Eagle, 33-36; ed & publ, Pictures on Exhibit, 37-; pres & treas, Charles Z Offin Art Fund. Collection: 20th century European art. Mailing Add: 30 E 60th St New York NY 10022

OFFNER, ELLIOT
SCULPTOR, PRINTMAKER
b Brooklyn, NY, July 12, 31. Study: Cooper Union; Yale Univ, BFA & MFA, study with Josef Albers & Rico Lebrun. Work: Brooklyn Mus; De Cordova Mus, Lincoln, Mass; Lowe Art Mus, Syracuse Univ; Metrop Mus Art, New York; Joseph Hirshhorn Mus. Comn: Eight hammered bronze sculpture, Kehilleth Israel, Brookline, Mass, 59 & canedlabra, Newton, Mass, 60; Ten Commandments (bronze facade sculpture), B'Nai Israel, Northampton, Mass, 63; St Francis of Assisi, St Charles Sem, Overbrook, Pa, 77. Exhib: Int Exhib of Liturgical Art at Eucharistic Cong, Pa Acad of Fine Arts, 76; Living Artists & the Figure, Pa State Univ; one-man exhibs, Forum Gallery, New York, 64, 67, 72 & 78, Berkshire Mus, Pittsfield, Mass, 65, Wells Col, 68, Int Fine Arts Galleries, Washington, DC, 68 & 73, DeCordova Mus, 74, Slater Mem Mus, Norwich, Conn, 76 & Smith Col Mus of Art, 77. Teaching: Instr art, Univ Mass, 59-60; prof art, Smith Col, 60-74, Andrew W Mellon prof humanities, 74- Pos: Dir, Rosemary Press, 67- Awards: Tiffany Found Grants, 64 & 65; Nat Coun on Arts & Humanities grant, 67; Ingram Merril Found grant, 71; plus others. Mem: Printing Hist Soc; William Morris Soc; Am Printing Hist Asn; Bibliog Soc. Style & Technique: Derived from nature and life; human form predominates. Media: Wood, Bronze; Woodcut, Calligraphy. Publ: Auth & illusr, The Granjon Arabesque, Rosemary Press, 69. Dealer: Forum Gallery 1018 Madison Ave New York NY 10021. Mailing Add: 74 Washington Ave Northampton MA 01060

OGILVIE, WILL (WILLIAM ABERNETHY)
PAINTER
b Cape Province, SAfrica, Mar 30, 01; Can citizen. Study: With Erich Mayer, Johannesburg, SAfrica; Art Students League, with Nicolaides. Work: Nat Gallery Can, Ottawa; Art Gallery, Toronto; Art Gallery, London; Art Gallery, Hamilton; Winnipeg Art Gallery. Comn: Mural, Chapel of Hart House, Univ Toronto, 36, stained glass windows in Massey Mem, 69. Exhib: Nat Gallery Can, Ottawa; Art Gallery Ont, Toronto; Tate Gallery, London, 38; War Art, Nat Gallery, London, 44; UNESCO, 46. Teaching: Dir drawing & painting, Montreal Mus Fine Arts, 37-41; instr painting & murals, Ont Col Art, Toronto, 47-55; spec lectr hist techniques painting, Univ Toronto, 59-68. Pos: Official Can war artist, 42-46. Awards: Mem Order Brit Empire; Can Coun Fel, Italy, 57-58. Mem: Assoc Royal Can Acad; Can Group Painters; Can Soc Painters in Watercolour. Mailing Add: c/o Roberts Art Gallery 641 Yonge St Toronto ON M4Y 1Z9 Can

O'GORMAN, JAMES FRANCIS
ART HISTORIAN
b St Louis, Mo, Sept 19, 33. Study: Washington Univ, Mo, BArch; Univ Ill, Urbana, MArch; Harvard Univ, PhD. Teaching: Grace Slack McNeil Prof of Am Art, Wellesley Col, 75- Mem: Soc of Archit Historians (pres, 70-72); Col Art Asn; Victorian Soc in Am. Res: American art and architecture. Publ: Auth, The Architecture of the Monastic Library in Italy, NY Univ Press, 72; co-auth, The Architecture of Frank Furness, Philadelphia Mus of Art, 73; auth, H H Richardson and His Office: Selected Drawings, Harvard Col, 74; auth, This Other Gloucester, pvt publ, 76. Mailing Add: Dept of Art Wellesley Col Wellesley MA 02181

O'GORMAN, JUAN
PAINTER, MURALIST
b Coyoacan, Mex, July 6, 05. Study: Sch Archit, Nat Univ Mex; also with Diego Rivera & Jose Clemente Orozco. Work: Mus Mod Art, New York; Mus Art Mod, Mexico City. Comn: Fresco painting, Mex Fed Govt, Libr of Patzcuaro, Michoacan, 40-41; mosaic murals, Cent Libr, Univ Mex, 50-53; three fresco paintings, Mex Fed Govt, Mus Hist, Mexico City, 60-72; acrylic painting, Mex Fed Govt, Social Security Sch, Mexico City, 64-65; fresco painting, Int Bank, Inc, Mexico City, 66. Exhib: One-man show, Palace of Fine Arts, Mexico City, 50 & Projects of Mural Paintings, 68. Teaching: Prof archit, Inst Politecnico Nac, Mexico City, 32-48. Pos: Head dept archit & construction, Secretaria Educ Publica, 32-35. Awards: Premio E Sourasky, Fondo de Fomento Educativo, 67; Premio Nac de Artes, Fed Govt Mex, 72. Mem: Soc Mex Archit; Soc Bolivariana de Arquitectos; Acad de Artes. Style & Technique: Fresco for murals; tempera for easel painting. Publ: Auth, Juan O'Gorman Autobiografia, Juicios Criticos y Documentacion de su Obra, 73. Mailing Add: Jardin 88 Mexico DF Mexico

O'HANLON, RICHARD E
SCULPTOR
b Long Beach, Calif, 1906. Study: Santa Barbara Art Sch, Calif; Calif Col Arts & Crafts; Calif Sch Fine Arts; pvt study in Europe, Near East, India, Japan & Mex. Work: Worcester Mus Art, Mass; Walker Art Ctr, Minneapolis; Smith Col Collection; Chicago Art Inst; Oakland Mus Art, Calif; plus others. Comn: Black granite sculpture, Mill Valley Pub Libr, 66; Clark Kerr Award Gold Medallion, Univ Calif, Berkeley, 67; granite sculpture, San Rafael, Calif, 73; granite sculpture, Oakland Mus Art, 74; granite sculpture, Lawrence Hall Sci, Univ Calif, Berkeley, 77; plus others. Exhib: Whitney Mus Am Art Ann, New York, 48; Critics Choice Exhib, New York, 50; San Francisco Art Asn Ann, 50-71; Sao Paulo Biennial, Brazil, 55; Retrospective, San Francisco Mus Art, 61; one-man shows, Carnegie Inst, Pittsburgh, 67 & Santa Barbara Mus Art, 69. Teaching: Prof sculpture, Univ Calif, Berkeley, 48-74, emer prof, 74- Awards: First Prize for Sculpture, San Francisco Art Asn, 58. Bibliog: A Frankenstein (auth), Sculpture of Richard O'Hanlon, Mag Art, 48. Mem: San Francisco Art Inst (bd dirs, 50-62). Style & Technique: Repousee; granite geometric forms, part rough and part polished; bronze abstract, organic forms. Media: Stone, Bronze. Dealer: Willard Gallery 29 E 72nd St New York NY 10021. Mailing Add: 616 Throckmorton Ave Mill Valley CA 94941

O'HARA, (JAMES) FREDERICK
PRINTMAKER
b Ottawa, Ont, Aug 16, 04; US citizen. Study: Mass Sch Art, dipl, 26; Sch Mus Fine Arts, Boston, 26-29; Inst Bellas Artes, Toledo, Spain, Paige traveling scholar, 29-31. Work: Lessing J Rosenwald Collection, Nat Gallery Art, Washington, DC; Metrop Mus Art, New York; Cincinnati Mus Art; Stadtmuseum, Karlsruhe, WGer; Achenbach Found Graphic Art, San Francisco. Comn: Four limited editions of prints, Int Graphic Art Soc, New York, 53-59. Exhib: Int Print Exhib Biennial, Cincinnati Mus Art, 58-62; Prints of the World, London Art Gallery, Camberwell, Eng, 62; Alliance for the Visual Arts, Utah State Univ Galleries, 72; one-man shows, Yoseido Gallery, Tokyo, Japan & Stadtmuseum, Karlsruhe, WGer, 56. Teaching: Vis prof art, Univ NMex, 48-50; vis prof art, Coronado Sch Fine Arts, 53 & 62; vis prof art, Highlands Univ, 58. Pos: Art adv comt, Sch Am Res, Santa Fe, NMex, 54-57. Awards: Fel & Print Purchase Awards, Tamarind Lithography Workshop, Los Angeles, 62. Bibliog: Lez Haas (auth), Frederick O'Hara, NMex Quart, 51; Kiyoshi Saito (auth), Frederick O'Hara, Japanese Art Mag, 56; Rolf Stubbe (auth), Graphic Arts in the Twentieth Century, 62. Style & Technique: Lyrical expressionism; technical resources of woodcut, lithography and monoprint are combined in one print; acid, grease resists, offsets and transfers are used to extend the range of imagery. Publ: Auth, Modern art today: El Palacio, Sch Am Res, 56; auth, Toward Technical Excellence in Printmaking, Artist's Proof, Pratt Graphic Art Ctr, 61. Dealer: Knowles Art Center 7420 Girard Ave La Jolla CA 92037. Mailing Add: 846 Forward St La Jolla CA 92037

O'HARE, BERTA MARGOULIES
See Margoulies, Berta

OHASHI, YUTAKA
PAINTER
b Kure City, Japan, Aug 19, 23. Study: Tokyo Acad Fine Art, Japan, BFA, 46; Sch Mus Fine Arts, Boston, 50-55. Work: Mus Fine Arts, Boston; Solomon R Guggenheim Mus, New York; Nat Mus Mod Art, Tokyo; Addison Gallery Am Art, Andover, Mass; Art Gallery, Yale Univ. Exhib: Carnegie Inst Int, Pittsburgh, 59; Summer Selection, 1962, Solomon R Guggenheim Mus, 62; Japanese Artists Abroad, Nat Mus Mod Art, Tokyo, 65; A Painter-A Potter, Montclair Art Mus, NJ, 70; Ohashis, Boston Athenaeum Gallery, 75; Art in Transition, Mus Fine Arts, Boston, 77; Half Century of Japanese Artist in New York, Azuma Gallery, 77; plus others. Teaching: Vis lectr critics, painting & design, Col Archit, Cornell Univ, 61, vis lectr, Col Human Ecol, 67 & 69. Awards: William Page Traveling Scholar, Mus Fine Arts, Boston,

56-57; Guggenheim Fel, 59-60. Style & Technique: Lyrical abstraction. Media: Collage, Acrylic on Canvas. Mailing Add: 5 Great Jones St New York NY 10012

OHE, KATIE (MINNA)
SCULPTOR, INSTRUCTOR
b Peers, Alta, Can, Feb 18, 37. Study: Alta Col Art, dipl fine arts; Montreal Sch Art & Design, with Dr Lismer; Sculpture Ctr, New York, with Assoc Dir Sahl Swarz, Dir Dorothy Denslow. Work: Can Coun Art Banks, Ottawa, Ont Alta Art Found, Edmonton; Visual Arts, Cult Activities, Edmonton; Shell Can Art Collection, Calgary; Univ Alta Art Collection. Comn: Michael the Archangel (cast stone sculpture relief), Church, Calgary, Alta, 64; cast stone sculpture fountain, City of Calgary, 66; chromed steel sculpture, Univ Calgary, 67 & 75; cast stone sculpture relief, Fed Western Regional Bldg, Calgary, 67; bronze sculpture, Sch Bd, City of Calgary, 75. Exhib: Sculpture Ctr, New York, 62-70; one-woman shows, Alta Col Art, Calgary, 64 & 76, Univ Sask, Saskatoon, 61, Univ Alta Art Gallery, Edmonton, 72 & Univ Calgary, 72; Brit Int Print Show, London, Eng, 71; Venice Biennial, Italy, 72; Alta Art Found (traveling exhib), Can House Gallery, London, Brussels, Paris & New York, 75-76; Changes: 11 Artists Working on the Prairies (traveling exhib), 75-76. Teaching: Instr sculpture, Mt Royal Col, Calgary, 70-; instr sculpture, Alta Col Art, Calgary, 70- Awards: Nat Gallery Study Grant, 58; Can Coun Grants, New York, 63, Europe, 68 & Verona, Italy, 74. Bibliog: Clement Greenburg (auth), View of art on the prairies, Can Art, 63; Anita Aarons (auth), Allied Art Catalogue, Vol 2, Arts and Architecture, Royal Archit Inst Can, 68; Barb Kwasney (auth), Canadian Golden West, Western Artist, Spring 76. Mem: Alta Soc Artists. Style & Technique: Source of material stems from the human figure and its facets; visual qualities of forms are determined by the concept; use of motion to create changing form and space relationship; use of cast forms, working directly for structural form. Media: Cast bronze and welded, chromed steel, moving parts are machined or hinged, forms are precision fitted or spacially assembled. Publ: Contribr, Archambault; Fournelle; Trudeau, Arts Can, 4/67. Mailing Add: c/o KO Arts Ltd 123 Waterloo Dr Sw Calgary AB T3C 3G4 Can

OHLSON, DOUGLAS DEAN
PAINTER
b Cherokee, Iowa, Nov 18, 36. Study: Univ Minn, BA, 61. Work: Corcoran Gallery Art, Washington, DC; Weatherspoon Gallery, Univ NC, Greensboro; Mus Purchase Fund Collection, Am Fedn Arts; Beacon Collection, Boston. Exhib: Art of the Real: USA 1948-1968, Mus Mod Art, New York, 68-69; Structure of Color, Whitney Mus Am Art, New York, 71; American Art Since 1960, Art Mus, Princeton Univ, 70; The Way of Color, 33rd Biennial Exhib, Corcoran Gallery Art, Washington, DC, 73; 14 Abstract Painters, Wight Gallery, Univ Calif, Los Angeles, 75; plus others. Teaching: Assoc prof art, Hunter Col, 64- Awards: Guggenheim Fel, 68; Nat Endowment for the Arts, 76. Bibliog: S Burton (auth), Doug Ohlson: in the wind, Art News, 5/68; G Battcock (ed), Minimal Art (critical anthology), Dutton, 68; Britannica Encyl Am Art, Simon & Schuster, 73; plus others. Media: Oil. Dealer: Susan Caldwell Gallery 383 W Broadway New York NY 10012. Mailing Add: 35 Bond St New York NY 10012

OHMAN, RICHARD MICHAEL
PAINTER, INSTRUCTOR
b Erie, Pa, May 8, 46. Study: Mercyhurst Col, Erie, BA; Ohio Univ, Athens, MFA. Work: Joseph J Akston Collection, Palm Beach, Fla; J Romano Collection, Cleveland, Ohio; First Huntington Nat Bank, WVa; numerous pvt collections. Exhib: 15th & 18th Nat Shows, Chautauqua, NY, 72 & 75; 18th Nat Sun Carnival, El Paso Mus Art, Tex, 74; 35th Ann Exhib Contemp Am Paintings, Soc Four Arts, Palm Beach, Fla, 74; 39th Midyear, Butler Inst Am Art, Youngstown, Ohio, 75; Drawings/USA, Minn Mus Art, St Paul, 75; Chautauqua Gallery of Art, NY, 76; Springfield Art Ctr, Ohio, 78; one-man exhib, Massillon Mus, Ohio, 77. Teaching: Instr painting & fundamentals of art, Ohio Univ, Chillicothe Br, 74- Style & Technique: Hard-edged fundamentalist; metaphorical narrative. Media: Acrylic; Ink & Graphite; Still Photography. Mailing Add: PO Box 1821 204 S Mulberry St Chillicothe OH 45601

OHNO, MITSUGI
GLASSBLOWER
b Tochigi, Japan, June 28, 26; US citizen. Work: Smithsonian Inst, Washington, DC; Independence Hall, White House, 72; Anderson Hall, Kans State Univ, 77; The Dwight D Eisenhower Libr. Pos: Full-time technician, Kans State Univ. Style & Technique: Scale models of glass; buildings, monuments. Mailing Add: 2808 Nevada St Manhattan KS 66502

OHRBACH, JEROME K
COLLECTOR
b New York, NY, Dec 17, 07. Study: Cornell Univ, AB, 29. Collection: Impressionist and post-impressionist art and sculpture. Mailing Add: 5 W 34th St New York NY 10001

OI, MOTOI
PAINTER, INSTRUCTOR
b Osaka, Japan, Nov 4, 10; US citizen. Study: Pac Fine Art Col, Tokyo, grad, 38. Work: Metrop Mus Art, New York; Nat Gallery Art, Washington, DC; Philadelphia Mus Art; Cincinnati Art Mus; Nagaoka Mus of Mod Art, Japan. Comn: Indust map mural, Foreign Dept of Govt, Tokyo, 50; indust map mural, Yokohama Expo, Japan, 51. Exhib: Nippon Bijutsuten, Japanese Govt, 36-38 & 50; Int Exhib, Educ Dept of Govt, Japan, 38; pres, Sumi-e Soc Am Ann Exhib, New York, 63- Teaching: Instr painting, Queens Col (NY), 60-72; instr painting, Brooklyn Inst Art & Sci, 67- Bibliog: Fusetsu Nakamura (auth), Upset hat, Educ Art, Japan, 38. Mem: Life mem Sumi-E Soc Am Inc. Style & Technique: Black ink painting on rice paper; graphic work for etching. Media: Tempera. Publ: Auth, Sumi-e Painting & Life, 58; auth, Step by Step in Sumi-e Painting (7 vols), 58-62; auth, Brush Strokes in Sumi-e Painting, 63-; auth, Work by Motoi Oi, 65; auth, Suiboku Landscape, 68. Mailing Add: 24-50 95th St East Elmhurst NY 11369

OKADA, KENZO
PAINTER
b Yokohama, Japan, Sept 28, 02; US citizen. Work: Metrop Mus Art & Mus Mod Art, New York; Art Inst Chicago; Solomon R Guggenheim Mus & Whitney Mus Am Art, New York; plus many others. Comn: Murals and paintings for Hilton Hotel, Tokyo, Japan, Dunn Int, Ford Found, UNESCO & Venice Biennial. Exhib: Sao Paulo Biennial, Brazil (representing the US), 55; Venice Biennial (representing Japan), 58; Albright-Knox Art Gallery, Buffalo, 65; Retrospective Traveling Exhib, Asahi-Shimbun Press, Tokyo, Nat Mus Mod Art, Kyoto, Honolulu Acad Arts, Hawaii, M H de Young Mem Mus, San Francisco & Univ Tex Art Mus, Austin, 66-67; one-man shows, Betty Parsons Gallery, 53-71; plus many others. Awards: First Prize, Columbia Biennial, SC, 57; Mainichi Art Award, 66; Award Poster, New York Coun of Arts, 69. Bibliog: J Canaday (auth), Okada's figurative style, New York Times, 3/15/69; Grace Clueck (auth), Early light, Art in Am, 3-4/69. Media: Oil. Mailing Add: 101 12th St New York NY 10011

OKAMURA, ARTHUR
PAINTER
b Long Beach, Calif, Feb 24, 32. Study: Art Inst Chicago, scholar, 50-54; Univ Chicago, 51 & 53; Yale Univ Summer Art Sem, 54; Edward L Ryerson for travel fel, 54; Univ Chicago, 57. Work: Corcoran Gallery Art, Washington, DC; Nat Collection Fine Arts, Smithsonian Inst; Nat Inst Arts & Lett; Hirshhorn Mus, Washington, DC; San Francisco Mus Art, Calif; plus many others. Exhib: Painters Behind Painters, Calif Palace of Legion of Honor, San Francisco, 67; Pittsburgh Int, Carnegie Inst, 67; one-man shows, San Francisco Mus Art, 68, Calif Col Arts & Crafts, 72, Southern Idaho Col, 72, Kent State Univ, Ohio, 73 & Honolulu Acad Arts, 73; Takashima 1970 Expos, Osaka, Tokyo, Japan, 70; Asian Artists, Oakland Mus, 71; plus many other group & one-man shows. Teaching: Instr, Cent YMCA Col, Chicago, 56 & 57; insr, Evanston Art Ctr, Ill, 56 & 57; instr, Art Inst Chicago, 57; instr, NShore Art League, Winnetka, Ill, 57; instr, Acad Art, San Francisco, 57; instr, Calif Sch Fine Arts, San Francisco, 58; instr, Calif Col Arts & Crafts, 58, 59 & 66-71; instr, Saugatuck Summer Art Sch, Mich, 59 & 62; guest lectr, Univ Utah, 64. Pos: Dir, San Francisco Studio Art, 58. Awards: Schwabacher-Frey Award, 79th Ann, San Francisco Mus, 60; Neysa McMein Purchase Award, Whitney Mus Am Art, 60; Purchase Award, Nat Soc Arts & Lett; plus many others. Bibliog: Lee Nordness (ed), Art: USA: Now, C J Bucher, 62. Mem: Am Fedn Arts. Dealer: Hansen Fuller Gallery 228 Grant Ave San Francisco CA 94108. Mailing Add: 155 Horseshoe Hill Rd Bolinas CA 94924

O'KEEFFE, GEORGIA
PAINTER
b Sun Prairie, Wis, Nov 15, 87. Study: Art Inst Chicago, with John Vanderpoel, 05-06; Art Students League, with William M Chase, 07-08; Univ Va, with Alon Bement, summer 12; Columbia Univ, with Arthur Dow & Alon Bement, 14-16; Mills Col, 52; Randolph-Macon Women's Col, 66; hon DFA, William & Mary Col, 38, Univ NMex, 64, Brown Univ, 71 & Minneapolis Col Art & Design, 72; hon LittD, Univ Wis, 42 & Mt Holyoke Col, 71; hon LHD, Columbia Univ, 71. Work: Metrop Mus Art; Mus Mod Art; Whitney Mus Am Art; Brooklyn Mus; Art Inst Chicago; plus others. Exhib: One-man retrospectives, Art Inst Chicago, 43, Mus Mod Art, 46, Worcester Mus Art, 60, Amon Carter Mus, Ft Worth, Tex, 66, Mus Fine Arts Houston, 66 & Whitney Mus Am Art, 70; Guggenheim Mus, New York; plus many others. Teaching: Supvr art, Amarillo Pub Schs, Tex, 13-16; instr art, Univ Va, summers 13-16; head dept art, WTex Normal Col, Canyon, 16-18. Awards: Creative Arts Award, Brandeis Univ, 63; Gold Medal for Painting, Nat Inst Arts & Lett, 70; M Carey Thomas Award, Bryn Mawr Col, 71, Edward MacDowell Medal, 72. Bibliog: Barbara Rose (auth), Georgia O'Keeffe's late paintings, Artforum, 11/70; plus many others. Mem: Nat Inst Arts & Lett; Am Acad Arts & Lett; Am Acad Arts & Sci. Publ: Auth, The Work of Georgia O'Keeffe (portfolio of 12 paintings), 37; auth, Georgia O'Keeffe Drawings (ltd ed of 10 drawing reproductions signed & numbered by artist), 68. Dealer: Doris Bry 11 E 73rd St New York NY 10021. Mailing Add: Ghost Ranch Abiquiu NM 87510

O'KELLEY, MATTIE LOU
PAINTER
b Maysville, Ga, 06. Study: Self taught. Work: Mus of Am Folk Art, New York; NY State Hist Asn, Cooperstown; High Mus of Art, Atlanta, Ga; Int Folk Art Mus, Santa Fe, NMex; Henry Ford Mus, Greenfield Village, Mich. Exhib: Hubert Hemphill Collection, Heritage Plantation of Sandwich, Mass (traveling exhib), US & Japan, 76-77; The All Am Dog, Mus of Am Folk Art, 77; Missing Pieces, Atlanta Hist Mus, Ga, 77; High Mus Art, Atlanta, Ga; Int Folk Art Mus, Santa Fe. Awards: Governor's Award for Outstanding Contribution to American Art, Gov of Ga, 76. Bibliog: Robert Bishop (auth), Women Folk Artists, Antique Monthly, 76 & The All American Dog (catalog), Mus Am Folk Art, 77. Style & Technique: Pointillism and realism. Media: Oil on canvas; watercolor. Mailing Add: c/o Jay Johnson Gallery 37 W 20th St New York NY 10011

OKOSHI, EUGENIA SUMIYE
PAINTER, PRINTMAKER
b Seattle, Wash. Study: St Margaret & Futaba Col, Tokyo; Seattle Univ, with Fay Chang & Nicholas Damascus; Henry Frye Mus Sch & New Sch Workshop. Work: Miami Mus Mod Art; Lowe Gallery, Univ Miami. Exhib: Bohman Art Gallery, Stockholm, Sweden, 68-69; Miami Mus Mod Art, 70; Mainstream 74 Int, Marietta Col, 74; Japanese Artists Abroad, Azuma Gallery, New York, 74-77; Hudson River Mus, Yonkers, NY, 77; Civic Art Mus, Goldsborough, NC, 77; Metrop Mus of Art, New York, 77. Style & Technique: Abstract; 3-D graphics, woodcut and etching. Media: Oil, Acrylic. Mailing Add: c/o Westbeth Studio G226 155 Bank St New York NY 10014

OKULICK, JOHN A
SCULPTOR
b New York, NY, Mar, 1947. Study: Univ Calif, Santa Barbara, BA; Univ Calif, Irvine, MFA. Exhib: New Am Graphic Art, Cambridge, Mass, 73; Options, 73, Cincinnati, Ohio, 73; Market St Exhib, Berkeley, Calif, 73; Nancy Hoffman Gallery, New York, 73 & 74; two-man show, John Okulick/Bradley Smith, Irvine, Calif, 74. Teaching: Instr art, Newport Mesa Sec Schs, 71-72; instr art, Univ Calif, Irvine, 73-74. Awards: Working Fel, Univ Calif, Irvine, 74. Bibliog: B Smith (auth), Illusion & substance, ArtWeek, 73; J Hyman (auth), Wall reliefs in full force, Daily Pilot, 74; J Russell (auth), John Okulick/Carlos Villa, NY Times, 75. Style & Technique: Loose & varied, structured & specific, visual mental images. Dealer: Nancy Hoffman 429 W Broadway New York NY 10012. Mailing Add: 706 Marine Santa Monica CA 90405

OLDENBURG, CLAES THURE
SCULPTOR
b Stockholm, Sweden, Jan 28, 29. Study: Yale Univ, BA, 51; Art Inst Chicago, 52-54. Work: Albright-Knox Art Gallery, Buffalo; Mus Mod Art, New York; Art Gallery Ont, Toronto; Art Inst Chicago; Whitney Mus Am Art, New York; plus many others. Comn: Sculptures, Oberlin Col, Ohio, 70, City St Louis, Mo, 71, Morse Col, Yale Univ, 74, Walker Art Ctr, Minneapolis, 74 & Hirshhorn Mus, Washington, DC, 75; plus others. Exhib: One-man shows, Mod Museet, Stockholm, Sweden, 66, Mus Contemp Arts, Chicago, 67, Art Gallery, Univ Calif, Los Angeles, 70 & Pasadena Art Mus, Calif, 71; Metrop Mus Art, New York, 69; Retrospective, Mus Mod Art, New York, 69, Pasadena Art Mus, Calif, 71, Walker Art Ctr, 75 & Kunsthalle, Tubingen, WGer, 75; Los Angeles Co Mus Art, Los Angeles, 71; Expo 70, Osaka, Japan; Documenta, Kassel, WGer, 72; Seattle Art Mus, Wash, 73; Am Pop Art, Whitney Mus Am Art, 74; Newport Art Mus, RI, 74; plus many other group & one-man shows. Bibliog: Barbara Rose (auth), Claes Oldenburg, Mus Mod Art, 70; Ellen Johnson (auth), Claes Oldenburg, Penguin, 71; articles in Art in Am, 5/74 & 9/74. Publ: Auth, Store Days, Something Else Press, 68; auth, Notes in Hand, Dutton & Petersburg, 71; auth, Object into monument, Pasadena Art Mus, 71. Mailing Add: 556 Broome St New York NY 10013

OLDENBURG, RICHARD ERIK
MUSEUM DIRECTOR
b Stockholm, Sweden, Sept 21, 33; US citizen. Study: Harvard Col, AB, 54. Pos: Dir publ, Mus Mod Art, New York, 69-72, dir mus, 72- Mailing Add: 11 W 53rd St New York NY 10019

OLDHAM, BERTON JEPSEN
PRINTMAKER, INSTRUCTOR
b Ross, Calif, Oct 23, 25. Study: San Francisco City Col, AA; Univ Calif, Berkeley, BA & MA. Comn: Hist base relief for freeway overpass, Cal-Trans, Redding, Calif, 73. Exhib: California Printmakers, Palace Legion Honor, San Francisco, 71; San Francisco Bay Area Print Exhib, Cincinnati, Ohio, 72; 5th & 6th Ann Printmaking West, Utah State Univ, 74 & 75; Graphics Gallery, San Francisco, 74. Teaching: Instr art, Shasta Col, 55- Mem: Los Angeles Printmaking Soc; Redding Mus & Art Ctr. Style & Technique: Hard edged simplified impressions of landscapes of the Western states. Media: Watercolor, Serigraphy. Mailing Add: c/o Graphics Gallery Three Embarcadero Ctr San Francisco CA 94111

OLDS, ELIZABETH
PAINTER, PRINTMAKER
b Minneapolis, Minn, Dec 10, 96. Study: Univ Minn, 2 yrs; Minneapolis Sch Art, 3 yrs; Art Students League, 2 yrs; also with George Luks, Paris, France, 1 yr. Work: Metrop Mus Art, New York; Brooklyn Mus; Baltimore Mus Art; Philadelphia Mus Art; San Francisco Mus Art; Hirshhorn Mus, Washington, DC; plus others. Comn: Drawings on World War II years & Pa Coal Country, New Repub, 40-49; war material paintings, Fortune Mag, 52-53, series of paintings on Lykes Indust, 54. Exhib: Artists for Victory, Metrop Mus Art, 42; Mus of Mod Art, 40s; Whitney Mus Am Art Watercolors & Drawings, 45-47; Prints & Books for Children, Mus Mod Art, New York; Brooklyn Mus Int Watercolor Exhibs, 49, 53 & 55; Seven Am Women: The Depression Decade, Vassar Col, 76; The Archives of Am Art, Smithsonian Inst, Washington, DC, 77; one-woman show, Staten Island Mus, 69; also many other one-woman shows, New York. Teaching: Pvt classes in silk screen printmaking. Awards: Guggenheim Fel for Painting in Europe, 26-27; First Prize for Lithograph, Philadelphia Print Club, 37 & Art Aliance, 38; Third Prize for Mexican Village (watercolor), Baltimore Mus Art, 44. Publ: Auth & illusr, The Big Fire, 45, Riding the Rails, 48, Feather Mountain, 51 & Deep Treasure, 58, Houghton Mifflin; auth & illusr, Plop Plop Ploppie, Scribner, 62. Mailing Add: 2221 Alvarado Ln Sarasota FL 33581

OLEKSIW, MICHAEL NICHOLAS, II
ART DEALER, SCULPTOR
b Evanston, Ill, June 4, 45. Study: St Lawrence Univ, Canton, NY, BA(fine arts); Univ Ariz, Tucson; Univ Del, Newark, MA(sculpture). Comn: Welded steel sculpture, Dr Stanley Holberg, Canton, NY, 68: Painting of nude, pvt collector, New York, 68 & Beverly, Mass, 69; sculptural environment (1500 sq ft) Del State Arts Coun, 71; welded steel sculpture, pvt collector, Weston, Mass, 74. Exhib: Steinman Art Festival, Canton, NY, 68; one-man show, Del Art Mus, Wilmington, 72; Artist Equity, Civic Ctr, Philadelphia, 74-75. Pos: Gallery dir, Green Apple Gallery, Beverly, Mass, 68; pres & chmn bd, JFO Ltd, Wilmington, Del, 74-; consult, Mass Arts & Humanities Found, Boston, 77- Awards: Fine Arts Award, Steinman Arts Festival, St Lawrence Univ, 68. Mem: Artists Equity Asn. Style & Technique: Welded steel, minimal works; Plexiglass environments to emphasize illusion, reflection and transparency; acrylic lacquerpainting, nudes, reflections. Res: Developing marketing techniques for the artist to increase the possibility of living via his art. Specialty: Emphasizes showing of modern art, provides art for architects, via ArtFinders. Publ: Ed, JFO Art Ltd, Newsletter, 74- Mailing Add: 110 Bridge St Manchester MA 01944

O'LENICK, DAVID CHARLES
ART ADMINISTRATOR, EDUCATOR
b Rockville Centre, NY, Apr 21, 47. Study: New York Univ; Hofstra Univ; New Sch for Social Res; State Univ NY. Pos: Co-dir, Mansight Educ, Full Circle Assocs, 68-69; owner/dir, Park Gallery, Brooklyn, 69-71; ed consult & field prog coordr, Projects Am Develop, US AID State Dept, 69-70; asst dir, Brooklyn Mus Art Sch, 74-77, admin head, 77- Mailing Add: 120 Park Pl Brooklyn NY 11217

OLIPHANT, PATRICK BRUCE
EDITORIAL CARTOONIST
b Adelaide, Australia, July 24, 35. Pos: Copyboy, press artist, Adelaide Advertiser, 53-55, ed cartoonist, 55-64; ed cartoonist, Denver Post, 64-; syndicated cartoonist, Los Angeles Times Syndicate, 65-; chmn, Int Salon Cartoons Jury. Awards: Second Place Award as Funniest Cartoonist, Int Fedn Free Journalists, London, 58; Second Place Award Int Cartoon Competition, Calif Newspapers Publs Asn, 60; Pulitzer Prize for Editorial Cartooning, 67. Publ: Auth, The Oliphant Book, 69; auth, Four More Years, 73. Mailing Add: 650 15th St Denver CO 80202

OLITSKI, JULES
PAINTER, SCULPTOR
b Snovsk, Russia, Mar 27, 22. Study: Beaux Arts Inst, New York, 40-42; Acad Grande Chaumiere, Paris, France, 49-50; Nat Acad Design, New York, 50-51; NY Univ, BS & MA. Work: Art Inst Chicago; Corcoran Gallery Art, Washington, DC; Whitney Mus Am Art, New York; Mus Mod Art, New York; Chrysler Mus at Norfolk, Va. Exhib: Whitney Mus Am Art Ann, 62, 64, 67, 69 & 72; Post Painterly Abstraction, Los Angeles Co Mus Art, Walker Art Ctr, Minneapolis & Art Gallery Toronto, Can, 64; Ólitski, Paintings 1963-67, Corcoran Gallery Art & Pasadena Mus, 67, Boston Mus of Fine Arts, 77 & Hirshhorn Mus, 77; Whitney Mus Am Art Ann, 69; Sculpture of Jules Olitski, Metrop Mus Art, New York, 69; Art Inst Chicago, 70; Inst Contemp Art, Philadelphia, 70; Albright-Knox Art Gallery, Buffalo, NY, 70; Abstract Painting in the 70's, Boston Mus Fine Arts, 72; Mus Fine Arts, Houston, 74; Indianapolis Mus Art, Ind, 74. Teaching: Assoc prof, State Univ NY Col New Paltz, 54-55; prof & chmn dept fine arts, C W Post Col, Long Island Univ, 56-63; instr art, Bennington Col, 63-67. Awards: Second Prize for Painting, Pittsburgh Int Painting & Sculpture, 61; 33rd Int Biennial Exhib Art, US Pavilion, Venice, Italy, 66; First Prize for Painting, Corcoran Gallery Art, 67. Bibliog: Gregory Batcock (auth), Minimal Art—A Critical Anthology, 68 & Henry Geldzahler (auth), New York Painting & Sculptures 1940-1970, 69, Dutton; Kenworth Moffett (auth), Jules Olitski's sculpture, Artforum, 4/69. Dealer: Knoedler Contemporary Art 19 E 70th St New York NY 10021; David Mirvish Gallery 596 Markham St Toronto ON Can. Mailing Add: RFD 1 Bear Island Lovejoy Sands Rd Meredith NH 03253

OLIVEIRA, NATHAN
PAINTER
b Oakland, Calif, Dec 19, 28. Study: Mills Col, Calif Col of Arts & Crafts, MFA, 52. Work: Hirshhorn Mus & Sculpture Garden, Smithsonian Inst, Washington, DC; Mus of Mod Art, New York; Larry Aldrich Mus of Contemp Art, Ridgefield, Conn; San Francisco Mus of Art; Solomon R Guggenheim Mus, New York. Exhib: Art Inst of Chicago, Ill; San Francisco Mus of Art; Annual, Corcoran Gallery of Art, Washington, DC; Annuals, Whitney Mus of Am Art, New York, 58-61 & 67-68; I Paris Biennial, 59; New Images of Man, 59 & Recent Painting USA: The Figure, 62-63, Mus of Mod Art; Solomon R Guggenheim Mus, 61; one-man shows, Univ of Ill, 61, Walker Art Ctr, Minneapolis, Minn, 61, Stanford Univ, 68, San Francisco Mus of Art, 69, Wis State Univ, Oshkosh, 70 & Fullerton Jr Col, 78; retrospectives: Univ Calif Los Angeles, 63 & Oakland Art Mus, 73. Teaching: Instr, San Francisco Art Inst, Calif Col of Arts & Crafts, 55-56, Univ of Ill, 61-62, Univ Calif Los Angeles, 63-64, Cornell Univ, 64, Stanford Univ, 64-, Univ of Colo, 65, Univ of Hawaii, 71, Cranbrook Acad of Art, Bloomfield Hills, Mich, 72, Baltimore Art Inst, 72, John Herron Art Inst, Indianapolis, Ind 72 & Kent State Univ, 73. Awards: Guggenheim Found Fel, 58; Norman Wait Harris Bronze Medal, Art Inst of Chicago, 60; Tamarind Fel, 64. Mailing Add: 785 Santa Marin Ave Stanford CA 94305

OLIVEIRA, V'LOU
CERAMIST, INSTRUCTOR
b Eureka, Calif, Nov 1, 51. Study: Calif State Univ, Humboldt, BA(art), 73; Univ Wash, Seattle, MFA(ceramics), 75, with Howard Kottler & Patty Warashina. Exhib: Sixtieth Ann Exhib of NW Artists, Seattle Art Mus, Wash, 74; Looking Ahead, Artists & Their Students, Fairtree Gallery, New York, 75; Bumbershoot Festival Fine Art Exhib, Seattle Art Mus, 75; 1975 NW Craft Exhib, Henry Gallery, Seattle, 75; Contemp Crafts of the Americas, SAm travelling exhib, Ft Collins, Colo, 75; Ceramic Conjunction, Long Beach Mus of Art, Calif, 77; Drinking Companions, John Michael Kohler Art Ctr, Sheboygan, Wis, 77. Collections Arranged: Contemporary Crafts: Clay and Metal, Univ Tex, Arlington, 77. Teaching: Instr ceramics, Univ Tex, Arlington, 75-77; asst prof ceramics, Univ Okla, Norman, 77- Awards: Merit Award, Okla Designer Craftsmen, 77. Mem: Okla Designer Craftsmen. Style & Technique: Ceramic sculpture. Media: Ceramic with non-fired painted surfaces. Mailing Add: 836 College Ave Norman OK 73069

OLIVER, RICHARD BRUCE
CURATOR
b San Diego, Calif, Sept 14, 42. Study: Univ Calif, Berkeley, BArch; Cambridge Univ, Eng; Univ Pa, MArch, with Louis Kahn. Exhib: Roosevelt Island Housing Competition Exhib, Archit League, New York, 75; Idea as Model, Inst for Archit & Urban Studies, New York, 76-77; Drawing Toward a More Mod Archit, Drawing Ctr, New York, 77 & Otis Art Inst, Los Angeles, 78. Teaching: Asst prof archit, Univ Tex, Austin, 67-70; lectr archit, Univ Calif, Los Angeles, 70-71, vis critic archit, 74-75. Pos: Cur contemp archit & design, Cooper-Hewitt Mus, Nat Mus of Design, Smithsonian Inst, New York, 77- Awards: Eisner Prize for Outstanding Achievement in Creative Arts, Univ Calif, Berkeley, 64; Fulbright Scholar, US Govt, 65-66; Arnold W Brunner Scholar, NY Chap, Am Inst of Architects, 77. Mem: Archit League of New York; Munic Art Soc, New York. Publ: Contribr, America Now: drawing toward a more modern architecture, Archit Design, London, 77; contribr, Magic, nostalgia & a hint of greatness in a workaday world of the building type studies, Archit Record, New York, 77. Mailing Add: 415 W 23rd St New York NY 10011

OLKINETZKY, SAM
PAINTER, MUSEUM DIRECTOR
b New York, NY, Nov 22, 19. Study: Brooklyn Col; Inst Fine Arts, NY Univ. Work: Philbrook Art Ctr, Tulsa, Okla; Okla Art Ctr, Oklahoma City; Mus Art, Univ Okla, Norman; Sch Bus, Okla State Univ, Stillwater; Lawton Munic Collection, Okla. Exhib: Philbrook Art Ctr Ann, 50-70; Int Painting & Sculpture Exhib, Mus Non-Objective Art, New York, 51-52; Recent Drawings, USA, Mus Mod Art, New York, 55; Momentum Midcontinental, Chicago Inst Design, 55; Southwestern Painting and Sculpture Ann, Okla Art Ctr, 60-70. Teaching: Asst prof art, Okla State Univ, 47-57; prof art, Univ Okla, 57-; vis prof art & humanities, Univ Ark, 62-67; lectr humanities, Langston Univ, 69-70. Pos: Art consult, Kerr-McGee Indust, 64-; dir, Mus Art, Univ Okla, 59-; art consult, Okla Art Ctr, 72- Awards: St Gaudens Medal for Draughtsmanship, City New York, 37; Purchase Award for Painting, Philbrook Art Ctr, 51; Purchase Award for Drawing, Okla Art Ctr, 65. Mem: Am Asn Mus; Okla Mus Asn; Am Asn Univ Prof. Media: Collage. Publ: Auth, Review of Oklahoma Designer Craftsmen Exhibition, Craft Horizons, 71. Mailing Add: Rte 1 Box 151 B Norman OK 73069

OLOFFSON, WERNER OLAF
PAINTER, PHOTOGRAPHER
b Port-au-Prince, Haiti, June 21, 05; US citizen. Study: NY Univ Guggenheim Sch Aeronautics, 31-33, practical aviation cert; study with H J Staude, Florence, Italy. Exhib: Hamburg, Ger, 58; Monte Carlo, 59; New York, 60, 62 & 74; Nat Acad Design; Philadelphia Acad Fine Arts; Audubon Artists Soc; Allied Artists of Am; Knickerbocker Artists Soc; Nat Arts Club. Awards: First Prize, NJ Painters & Sculptors, 52; Winsor & Newton Award, Nat Arts Club, 64; Second Prize, Am Art Prof League, 68. Mem: Am Watercolor Soc; Salmagundi Club; Am Artists Prof League; NJ Painters & Sculptors Soc; Jackson Heights Art Club. Style & Technique: Watercolor, pen & brush black & white; representational, micronature, abstract. Media: Watercolor; Black and White Pen and Brush. Mailing Add: 35-33 83rd St Jackson Heights NY 11372

OLPIN, ROBERT SPENCER
ART HISTORIAN, CURATOR
b Palo Alto, Calif, Aug 30, 40. Study: Univ Utah, with Vachtang Z Djobadze, BS, 63; Boston Univ, with William M Jewell, George Levitine, James B Lynch, Jr, Emily D T Vermeule, Cornelius C Vermeule & Samuel Y Edgerton, AM, 65, PhD, 71. Work: Utah Mus Fine Arts, Univ Utah. Collections Arranged: Alexander Helwig Wyant, 1836-1892 (with catalog), 68, Mainstreams of American Architecture-Reflections on Salt Lake City (with catalog), 73 & Am Painting Around 1850, 76; Contemporary Utah Artists Exhibition, Billboard Art, Tracy Collins Bank (with catalog), Salt Lake Art Ctr, 74 & The Art Life of Utah, 1776-1976 (Bicentennial, with catalog), 76. Teaching: Lectr art hist, Boston Univ, 65-67; from asst prof to assoc prof art hist, Univ Utah, 67-77, prof art hist, 77- chmn art hist prog, 68-, actg chmn dept art, 71-72 & 75-76, chmn art dept, 76- Pos: Consult cur Am art, Utah Mus Fine Arts, Univ Utah, 73- Awards: Univ Utah Spec Summer Grant, 72; Bicentennial Res Grants, Utah Am Revolution Bicentennial Comn & Univ Utah Bicentennial Comt, 75. Bibliog: Peter Bermingham (auth), Alexander H Wyant: some letters, Archives Am Am Art, 72 & American Art in the Barbizon Mood, Smithsonian Inst, 75; Jerry M Bloomer (auth), The Hudson River School: American Landscape Paintings, Norton, 73; plus others. Mem: Col Art Asn Am; Am Art, Smithsonian Inst; Salt Lake Art Ctr, Utah; Utah Acad Sci, Arts & Lett. Res: 19th and 20th century American art, with special emphasis on 19th century American landscape painting. Collection: 18th and 19th century European and American prints. Publ: Auth, Alexander Helwig Wyant, American Landscape Painter, Boston Univ-Univ Microfilms, 71; auth, Painting an environment, Southwest Art, 9/75. Mailing Add: Art & Archit Ctr 161 Univ of Utah Salt Lake City UT 84112

OLSEN, ERNEST MORAN
DESIGNER, PAINTER
b Pittsfield, Mass, May 5, 10. Study: Pratt Inst, pictorial illus; portraiture with Ivan Moschowitz; Boothbay Harbor summer sch of Art, landscape study with Frank Allen. Work: Berkshire Mus, Pittsfield, Mass; Fine Arts Mus, Asbury Park, NJ. Exhib: Int Print Exhib, Chicago World's Fair, 30; Pittsfield Art League, Berkshire Mus, 31-36; Stockbridge Art Exhib, Berkshire Playhouse, Mass, 35-38; Williams Col, Williamstown, Mass, 37; Yonkers Mus Exhib, NY, 55. Collections Arranged: Fine Arts Mus, Asbury Park, NJ, 77. Pos: Art dir, Sculpture Mag Nat Sculpture Review, Nat Sculpture Soc, 62-, Leica (House Organ), Pallard Corp, 45-50, Bolex (House Organ), E Leitz Corp, 50-55, Copper & Brass Res Asn, 45-65 & Maxwell House Messenger (House Organ), General Foods, 60-76; designer, Union Carbide Corp, New York, 52- Awards: Cert of Merit, Folmer Graflex Corp, 40 & Printing Indust of Metrop New York, 65-74. Mem: Art Dir Club of New York; Fel, Am Artists Prof League. Style & Technique: Oil painting; New England representational; commercial art: Layout, finished art in ink, wash or airbrush. Media: Oil, Wash. Mailing Add: 465 Westchester Ave Mt Vernon NY 10552

OLSEN, FREDERICK L
POTTER, SCULPTOR
b Seattle, Wash, Feb 25, 38. Study: Univ Redlands, BA; Univ Southern Calif, MFA; Kyoto City Col Fine Art, Japan; also apprenticeship with Tomimoto Kenkichi & Kondo Yuzo, Kyoto, 3 yrs. Work: Gallery New South Wales, Sydney, Australia; Contemp Craft Mus, Denmark; Sturt Collection, Mittigong, Australia. Exhib: Nat Shinsho-Ten, Japan, 61-63; Kyo-Ten, Kyoto Mus Mod Art, 62; Nat Asahi-Ten, Tokyo, Japan, 62; also one-man exhibs, Sydney, 63, 64 & 69, Melbourne, 63 & 69, Adelaide, 69, Copenhagen, 65, Seattle, 71 & 73, Portland, Ore, 71, Los Angeles, 71, 73 & 74 & Palm Springs Art Mus, 77. Teaching: Lectr kiln bldg, Univ Southern Calif, 66-68; asst prof kiln bldg, Univ Puget Sound, summer 71 & 73. Pos: Owner, Pinyon Crest Pottery & Olsen Kiln Co, 67- Bibliog: American Potter in Japan, Asahi TV Corp, 63. Media: Ceramics. Publ: Auth, The Kiln Book, Keramos, 72. Dealer: Serisawa Gallery 8320 Melrose Ave Los Angeles CA 90069; Northwest Craft Center-Seattle Center Seattle WA 98101. Mailing Add: Pinyon Crest Box 205 Mountain Center CA 92361

OLSON, DOUGLAS JOHN
PAINTER, EDUCATOR
b Wausau, Wis, Aug 26, 34. Study: Layton Sch Art, BFA; Univ Cincinnati, MFA. Work: Montgomery Mus of Fine Arts, Ala; Pope & Quint Corp; Gallery S; First Nat Bank of Ala. Exhib: 6th Ann Painters & Sculptors Show, Milwaukee Art Ctr, 63; 1st Cincinnati Biennial, Cincinnati Art Mus, Ohio, 67; 40th Ann Exhib, Springfield Mus Art, Mo, 70; 2nd Nat Arts & Crafts show, Jackson Mem Coliseum, Miss, 70; USA Nat Exhib, Mobile Art Ctr, Ala, 70; Centennial Painting Exhib, Birmingham Mus Art, Ala, 72; 10th Nat Art Exhib, Masur Mus Art, Monroe, La, 73; LaGrange Nat Competition III, Callaway Auditorium, Ga, 77. Teaching: Instr drawing, Univ Cincinnati, 67-68; instr painting & design, Auburn Univ, 68- Awards: Mus Purchase, 11th Dixie Ann Show, Montgomery Mus Fine Arts, 70; Best of Show, 6th Ann Show, First Nat Bank, 72; Purchase Award, 13th Ann Mus Exhib, Gallery S, 74. Mem: Montgomery Art Guild, Ala Art League. Style & Technique: Realistic and non-objective hardedge paintings; shape paintings are of enamel on Masonite or aluminum. Mailing Add: 302 E Thach Ave Auburn AL 36830

OLSON, GARY SPANGLER
SCULPTOR, INSTRUCTOR
b Chicago, Ill, Aug 29, 46. Study: Cent Col, Iowa, BA; Corcoran Gallery Art, Washington, DC; George Washington Univ, Washington, DC, MFA. Exhib: All-Army Arts & Crafts Exhib 1970 Sculpture; David Lloyd Kreeger Awards Competition, George Washington Univ, 73; Artist in the Schools Traveling Exhib, Iowa, 75. Pos: Artist in residence, Iowa Artist in the Schs Prog, Iowa Art Coun, Nat Endowment for Arts, Estherville, 73-74, Le Mars, 74-75, Mitchellville, 75-; artist in residence, Upper-Bound Prog, Univ Iowa, Iowa City, summer 74. Awards: Honorable Mention, David Lloyd Kreeger Awards Competition, George Washington Univ, 73. Style & Technique: Collage, assemblages; social statements through wood, canvas and found objects. Mailing Add: RR 1 Mitchellville IA 50169

OLSON, JOSEPH OLAF
DESIGNER, PAINTER
Study: Tadama Art Sch, Seattle, Wash; Nat Acad, New York; Art Students League. Work: Brooklyn Mus; also in pvt collections of Whitney, Pratt, Morgan, Harriman, Frick & Dupont families. Exhib: One-man shows, Corcoran Gallery, Washington, DC; Carnegie Inst, Pittsburgh; Chicago Art Inst. Pos: Stained glass designer, Rambusch Decorating Co, New York, 45-69. Awards: Isidor Prize, Salmagundi Club. Media: Oil, Watercolor. Mailing Add: RFD 1 Mystic CT 06355

OLSON, RICHARD W
EDUCATOR, PAINTER
b Rockford, Ill, Aug 14, 38. Study: Univ Wis-Madison, BS & study with R Knipschild, Leo Steppat & Italo Scanga, 60, MS(studio art/painting & graphics) & study with Warrington Colescott, 61 & MFA(studio art/painting & graphics) & study with Warrington Colescott, 62. Work: Univ Wis-Madison; Waterloo Art Ctr, Iowa; Univ NDak; Clarion Col, Pa. Exhib: 48th & 52nd Ann, Milwaukee Art Ctr, Wis, 62 & 66; Original Prints 1964, Pratt Graphic Arts Ctr, 64; Soc Etchers Ann, Calif Palace of the Legion of Honor, San Francisco, 64; 25th Print Nat, intaglio, Nat Collection Fine Arts Div, Smithsonian Inst, Washington, DC, 64; Max 24 64, Purdue Univ, 64; Original Prints, Univ Calif Davis, 65; Drawing & Small Group Sculpture Show, Ball State Univ, 69; Allan Stone Gallery, New York, NY, 68-69. Collections Arranged: Guest cur, Oriental Art from Beloit Permanent Collection, Wright Art Ctr, 73-74, Ger Expressionist Prints, 74, Recent Graduates, 75 & Bovine Beauty, 75. Teaching: From asst prof to assoc prof, Beloit Col, Wis, 63-77, prof art for drawing, design, painting & sem, 77- Pos: Chmn dept art, Milton Col, Wis, 61-62; chmn avant garde convocation, Beloit Col, 66 & chmn dept art, 69-77. Awards: Gimbels Award, Wis Painters & Sculptors, Gimbels-Milwaukee, 62; Gimbels-Schusters Award, Wis Salon Art, Gimbels-Schusters, 68; Purchase Award, Nat Juried, Waterloo Art Ctr, 65. Style & Technique: Non-representational. Media: Acrylic & Assemblage. Publ: Illusr cover, New Idea Mag, 62; illusr covers, Beloit Poetry J, 64 & 69. Mailing Add: Rte 1 Box 305 Beloit WI 53511

OLUGEBEFOLA, ADEMOLA
PAINTER, DESIGNER
b Charlotte Amalie, St Thomas, VI; US citizen. Study: Fashion Inst of Technol, New York, assoc degree, 61; Weusi Acad of Arts & Studies, New York, PhD, 69; Printmaking Workshop, New York, study with Krishna Reddy & Bob Blackburn. Work: VI Coun of the Arts, Caravelle Arcade, St Croix; Northern Ill Univ, Urbana Campus; Port Authority of NY & NJ, Twin Towers Main Off; New York, permanent collection, Harlem State Off Bldg; Mus of Guyana, state collection, S Am. Comn: Murals, New York Dept of Cultural Affairs, Marcus Garvey Cultural Ctr, 69, Teleprompter Cable TV Corp, Pub Access Ctr, 72 & New York Arts Consortium (lobby entrance), 78; Award, Int Benin Awards, Benin Enterprises Inc, 73-75. Exhib: Sun Festival, Corcoran Gallery, Washington, DC, 69; Millenium, Philadelphia Mus, Pa, 73; Black, USA Now, New York Cultural Ctr, Columbus Circle, 74; Group Exhibition, Am Mus of Natural Hist, New York, 74; 14 Artists, Pratt Inst, Main Gallery, Brooklyn, NY, 76; 1st Southwest Afro-Am Exhib, Mus of Bishop Col, Dallas, Tex, 77; one-man shows, Revelation, The Gallery, Los Angeles, Calif, 74, Beyond Orion, Gallery of Western Art, Washington, DC, 75, A Son Comes Home, Gem Gallery of Fine Arts, St Thomas, 75, One Man Exhib, Whitaker Gallery, SC State Col, 76 & Eyes on the Masses, Mus of Western Art, Washington, DC, 77; retrospectives, Graphics: 9 Yrs, Storefront Mus, Jamaica, 73 & Evolution in Color: 13 Yrs, New York State Harlem Gallery, 76. Teaching: Instr contemp black art, Wesleyan Univ, Middleton, Conn, 73-75 & printmaker, Art Carnival, Harlem, NY, 74-77. Pos: Consultant, Metrop Mus of Art, New York, 68-69; art dir, New Lafayette Publ, New York, 69-74 & Smithsonian Inst, Washington, DC, 6/76-9/76. Awards: Fredrick Douglas Award, First Ann Harlem, 20th Century Creators, 64; Lois Noel Award, New Directions, Carnegie Inst, 72; First Prize Printmaking, Lakeview Ann, Lakeview Art Society, 75. Bibliog: Barbara Rose (auth), Black Art in Am, Art in Am, 9/71; Calvin Wilson, The Art of Ademola, Impressions Mag of Arts, 6/76; Dick Young (filmmaker), Festac 77, US Info Agency, 2/78. Mem: New York Arts Consortium (bd of dirs, 78-); Nat Conference of Artists (nat vpres, 73-77), Harlem Cultural Coun (bd of dirs, 78-); Weusi Acad of Arts & Studies (co-dir, 78-); St Croix Arts Society. Style & Technique: Metaphysical & Surrealistic suggestion, subject matter using paint & collage as well as printmaking techniques. Publ: Illusr, The Art Gallery Magazine, Hollycroft Press, 70; illusr, The Duplex/A Love Fable, William Morrow, 71; illusr, The Reluctant Rapist, Harper & Row, 73; illusr, Natural History, Am Mus of Natural Hist, 2/74; illusr, Art: African American, Harcourt-Brace & Jovanovich, 78. Dealer: Tetrahedron 200 W 72nd St Suite 37 New York NY 10023. Mailing Add: 800 Riverside Dr Studio 5E East New York NY 10032

OMAR, MARGIT
PAINTER, EDUCATOR
b Berlin, Ger, May 17, 41; US citizen. Study: Art Inst of Chicago, Ill; Univ of NDak, Grand Forks, BA, 66; Univ of Colo, Boulder, MFA, 71. Work: Los Angeles Co Mus of Art, Los Angeles, Calif; Lloyds Bank of London, Los Angeles; Univ of Colo; Univ of NDak; Santa Monica Col, Calif. Exhib: Denver Art Mus, Colo, 72; Joslyn Art Mus, Omaha, Nebr, 73; All Calif Exhib, Laguna Beach Art Mus, 74; Spectrum, Los Angeles Co Mus of Art, 75; Newport Harbor Art Mus, Newport Beach, Calif, 77; four-man show, New Abstract Painting in Los Angeles, Los Angeles Co Mus of Art, 76; two-man show, Palos Verde Mus of Art, Calif, 75; one-man show, Janus Gallery, Venice, Calif, 77 & 78. Teaching: Instr painting & drawing, Univ of Colo, Boulder, 71-72; asst prof graduate studies, painting & drawing, Univ Southern Calif, Los Angeles, 73- Awards: New Talent Award, Los Angeles Co Mus of Art, Contemp Art Coun, 77. Bibliog: William Wilson (auth), Unfamiliar Assertiveness From A Second City, Los Angeles Times, 10/3/76; Susan C Larsen (auth), Margit Omar's High Desert Series, Artweek, 5/14/77; Henry J Seldis (auth), Art Walk, Los Angeles Times, 4/29/77. Mem: Los Angeles Inst of Contemp Art, Los Angeles. Style & Technique: Abstract painter. Media: Acrylic on Stretched Canvas. Mailing Add: c/o Janus Gallery 21 Market St Venice CA 90291

OMWAKE, LEON, JR
PAINTER, SCULPTOR
b New Rochelle, NY, June 14, 46. Study: Pa Acad Fine Arts, 64-68. Work: Whitney Mus Am Art, New York; Pa Acad Fine Arts, Philadelphia; Louis K Meisel Gallery, New York; Philadelphia Mus Art. Exhib: Philadelphia Mus Art, 70; Fischbach Gallery, New York, 72; Whitney Ann Am Painting, New York, 72; Cheltenham Ann Painting Exhib, 72; one-man show, Marian Locks Gallery, 72; Marcel Duchamp Retrospective, Philadelphia Mus of Art, 74; Tehran, Iran, 76; Duseldorf, Ger, 76; Austin, Tex, 77; plus others. Teaching: Instr painting, Pa Acad Fine Art; instr painting, Cheltenham Art Ctr, Pa; instr painting, Chaddsford Art Sch. Media: Mixed-media. Mailing Add: c/o Marian Locks Gallery 1524 Walnut St Philadelphia PA 19102

O'NEIL, BRUCE WILLIAM
PAINTER, INSTRUCTOR
b Winnipeg, Man, Can, July 14, 42. Study: Alta Col of Art, dipl(fine art painting), 59-64; Instituto Allende, San Miguel De Allende, Mex, 65. Work: Can Coun Art Bank, Ottawa, Ont, Can; Edmonton Art Gallery, Alta, Can; Shell Oil Resources Ltd, Calgary, Alta; Alta Culture (Alta govt); Mem Univ, St Johns Nfld. Exhib: Can Coun Art Bank, Paris, 73; Western Can Painting; Prairies, Saidye Bronfman Ctr, Montreal, 74; 9 Out of 10, A Survey of Can Art, Hamilton Art Gallery, 74; Landscape Abbreviations, Art Gallery of Greater Victoria, 74-75; The Can Canvas, traveling, 75-76; Abstraction West, Emma Lake & After, Nat Gallery of Can, 76; 14 Can, A Critics Choice: Hirschhorn Mus and Sculpture Garden, Washington, DC, 77; New Abstract Art, Edmonton Art Gallery, 77; one-man shows, Layola Col, Montreal, 68; Bruce O'Neil, 1973-76, traveling, Univ of Saskatchewan, Southern Alta Art Gallery, Lethbridgy, Edmonton Art Gallery, 75, Mira Godard Gallery, Toronto, 77, Montreal, 78 & Can Art Galleries, Calgary, 77-78. Teaching: Instr painting, Alta Col of Art, 68-; guest instr, painting, Mount Allison Univ, Sackville, New Brunswick, 76; guest instr painting, Emma Lake Artists Workshop, Emma Lake, Saskatchewan, 76. Pos: Chmn, Alberta Soc of Artists, Calgary, Alta, 72-73. Awards: Instituto Allende, Post Grad Exhib, Instituto Allende, Mex, 64; Can Coun Arts Grant, 75 & 78. Bibliog: Dale McConathy (auth), The Can Cultural Revolution, Art Can Art Mag, 75; Karen Wilkin (auth), Bruce O'Neil, Art Mag, 77; Mike Hepburn (producer), Alberta Character-Bruce O'Neil-Artist, Can Broadcasting Corp, 78. Mem: Alta Soc of Artists (Calgary chmn, 72-73); Can Artists Represenatives. Style & Technique: Color field abstractionist. Media: Acrylic on Canvas. Dealer: Mira Godard Gallery 22 Hazelton Ave Toronto ON M5R 2E2 Can. Mailing Add: 2006 30th Ave SW Calgary AB T2T 1R2 Can

O'NEIL, JOHN
PAINTER, EDUCATOR
b Kansas City, Mo, June 16, 15. Study: Univ Okla, BFA & MFA; Colorado Springs Arts Ctr, with Boardman Robinson, Paul Burlin & Henry Varnum Poor; Taos Sch Art, with Emil Bisttram; Studio Hinna, Rome, Italy. Work: Denver Art Mus; Dallas Mus Fine Arts; Libr Cong, Washington, DC; Univ Mich Mus Art, Seattle Art Mus. Exhib: Directions in American Painting, Carnegie Inst, Pittsburgh; Abstract & Surrealist Art, Art Inst Chicago; Contemporary American Painting, Univ Ill; Mid-Am Ann, Nelson-Atkins Gallery, Kansas City, Mo; Watercolor USA, Springfield Art Mus, Mo; SW Am Art, Kyoto Mus, Japan; Main St II Exhib, Contemp Arts Mus, Houston, Tex; Troisieme Salon Int des Realites Nouvelles, Paris, France; M-59 Exhib, Copenhagen, Denmark. Teaching: Prof painting, Univ Okla, 39-65; prof painting, Rice Univ, 65- Awards: 23 awards in regional & nat exhib. Mem: Col Art Asn Am. Style & Technique: Abstract paintings dependent upon close color and value relationships. Media: Acrylic, Pastel. Publ: Contribr, Oklahoma: a guide to the Sooner State, Art & Archit, 57; contribr, Thoughts on Light, Kunst, 63; contribr, On color, Cimarron Rev,

72. Dealer: Louisiana Gallery Houston TX 77013. Mailing Add: 2224 Wroxton Rd Houston TX 77005

O'NEIL, JOHN JOSEPH
ART ADMINISTRATOR, DESIGNER
b Brooklyn, NY, Apr 20, 32. Study: State Univ NY, Brooklyn, BA; State Univ NY, Buffalo, BS; Columbia Univ, MA, Prof Dipl EdD. Work: Florence Mus, SC; Furman Mus, Greenville, SC; Beaufort Mus, SC; SC Arts Comn. Exhib: Piedmont Ann Crafts, 68 & Ann Graphics Exhib, 69-71, Mint Mus of Art, Charlotte, NC; 24th Ann Southeastern Exhib, High Mus of Art, Atlanta, Ga; 37th Southeastern, Gallery of Contemp Art, 72. Teaching: Prof graphic design, Univ SC, 63- Pos: Assoc head, Dept of Art, Univ SC, 65-75, head, Dept of Art, 75-; mem by presidential appt, Panel on Fed Graphics Progs, Nat Endowment for the Arts. Mem: SC Craftsman (publicity dir, 65-67); Southeastern Art Conf; Columbia Artists Guild (vpres, 67, treas, 73-74); Guild of SC Artist; Southeastern Print Coun. Mailing Add: 4225 Sequoia Rd Columbia SC 29206

O'NEILL, JOHN PATTON
PAINTER, ILLUSTRATOR
b Houston, Tex, Apr 12, 42. Study: Univ Okla, Norman, BS; La State Univ, Baton Rouge, MS & PhD. Exhib: Denver Mus of Nat Hist; Houston Mus of Nat Sci. Teaching: Grad asst gen zoology, La State Univ, 64-73; asst prof ornithology, 78. Pos: Curatorial asst, La State Univ Mus of Zoology, Baton Rouge, 74-76, cur of higher vertabrates, 76-78 & acting dir & cur, 78- Bibliog: John O'Neills bird paintings; where art and sci meet, article in Southwest Art, 74; Jonathan Fisher (auth), , John O'Neill doesn't just paint birds, Int Wildlife, 77; Painting of John O'Neill, Cornell Lab of Ornithology, 77. Style & Technique: Realism, often with environment, natural history. Media: Watercolor, Gouache. Publ: Illusr, Distribution of the Birds of Honduras, Am Ornithologists Union, 68, Finding the Birds in Western Mexico, Univ Ariz Press, 69, Grouse and Quails of North America, Univ Nebr Press, 73; various illus for Encycl Britannica, 76; illusr, A Guide to the Birds of Trinidad and Tobago, Harrowood Bks, 77. Dealer: Mill Pond Press Inc 204 S Nassau St Venice FL 33595. Mailing Add: 1025 Aberdeen Ave Baton Rouge LA 70808

ONLEY, TONI
PAINTER
b Douglas, Isle of Man, Eng, Nov 20, 28. Study: Douglas Sch Art; Inst Allende, Mex. Work: Tate Gallery, London; Nat Gallery Can; Victoria & Albert Mus, London; Mus Mod Art, New York; Seattle Mus, Wash. Comn: Oil mural, Queen Elizabeth Playhouse, Vancouver, BC, 62. Exhib: Seattle World's Fair, 62; Contemporary Canadian Art, Nat Gallery Can & Africa, 62-63; Fifteen Canadian Artists, Mus Mod Art & USA, 63-64; Two Canadians, Commonwealth Inst, London, 64; 36 Venice Biennale, Italy, 72. Teaching: Asst prof fine arts, Univ BC, 67- Awards: Jessie Dow Award, Montreal Spring Exhib, 60; Sam & Ayala Zacks Award, 83rd Ann, Royal Can Acad, 63; Sr Can Coun Fel, 63. Mem: Royal Can Acad Arts. Dealer: Ban-Xi Gallery 3003 Granville St Vancouver BC Can. Mailing Add: 3506 W 28th Ave Vancouver BC V6S 1S2 Can

ONO, YOKO
FILMMAKER
b Tokyo, Japan, Feb 18, 33; US citizen. Study: Peers' Sch, Gakushuin Univ, Tokyo; Sarah Lawrence Col, New York; Harvard Univ, Cambridge, Mass. Exhib: Festival of Contemp Music, Montreal, 61; Destruction in Art Symposium, Inst of Contemp Arts, London, 66; Int Group Sculpture Show, Coventry, Eng, 68; Fluxfest Presentation of John & Yoko, New York, 70; Happening und Fluxus, Kunstverein, Cologne, Ger, 70; Fluxshoe, Sch of Art, Falmouth, Cornwall, Eng, 72; one-person shows, Alchemical Wedding, Albert Hall, London, 67, Evening with Yoko Ono, Birmingham 68, Event, Univ Wales, 69 & Everson Mus, Syracuse, NY, 71. Bibliog: P Devlin (auth), Yoko Ono, Vogue, New York, 12/71; Michael Benedikt (auth), Yoko Notes, Art & Artists, London, 1/72; E Wasserman (auth), This is not Here: Yoko Ono at Syracuse, Artforum, New York, 1/72. Publ: Auth, Six Film Scripts, Tokyo, 64, Thirteen Film Score Scores, London, 67, John & Yoko Calendar, New York, 70, Grapefruit, London, 70 & A Hole to See the Sky Through, New York, 71. Mailing Add: New York NY

ONSLOW FORD, GORDON M
PAINTER
b Wendover, Eng, Dec 26, 12; US citizen. Study: Fernand Leger, Paris; Surrealist Group, 38-43. Work: Tate Gallery, London; Solomon R Guggenheim Mus, New York; Whitney Mus of Am Art, New York; San Francisco Mus of Mod Art; Oakland Mus, Calif. Exhib: Karl Nierendorf Gallery, New York, 46; Retrospective, 48, Drawings and Watercolors, 64 & Large Paintings, 71, San Francisco Mus of Mod Art; Rabow Gallery, 56-73; Paintings 1950-1962, M H de Young Mem Mus, San Francisco, 62; Gallery of Art, Victoria, BC, 71; Pyramid Galleries Ltd, Washington, DC, 75; Retrospective of 100 paintings, Oakland Mus, 77. Teaching: Lectr surrealist painting, New Sch Social Res, NY, 40. Bibliog: Madeline Tourtelot (contribr), Island Time (20 minute film), Oakland Mus, 66. Style & Technique: Inner realism. Publ: Contribr, Minotaure Number 12 & 13, Skira, 39; contribr, London Gallery Bull, 40; auth, Towards a New Subject in Painting, San Francisco Mus of Art, 48; auth, Painting in the Instant, Thames & Hudson, London & Harry Abrams, New York, 64; co-auth, The Dynaton 25 Years Later (catalogue), Los Angeles Co Mus, 77. Mailing Add: Marin Co CA

OPIE, JOHN MART
PAINTER, PRINTMAKER
b Sandusky, Ohio, Dec 10, 36. Study: Kent State Univ, BFA, MA. Work: Allentown Art Mus, Pa; Akron Art Inst, Ohio; Fordham Univ, NY; New Orleans Art Mus, La; St Lawrence Univ, NY. Exhib: Pa Acad of Fine Arts, 65; Butler Mus Mid-Year Ann, 76; In Praise of Space, Westminster Col, Corcoran Gallery, 76; Artists Choice, Figurative Art in New York, The Green Mountain, Bowery, Prince Street, Soho Ctr for the Visual Arts and the First Street Gallery, 76; Personal Visions, Places, Spaces, Bronx Mus, 78; one-man shows, New Orleans Art Mus, 68, Galerie Simonne Stern, New Orleans, 69, 70, 72 & 75 & Bowery Gallery, New York, 73 & 76. Teaching: Instr painting, Pasadena City Col, Calif, 63-65; assoc prof painting, La State Univ, Baton Rouge, 65-70. Awards: Nat Endowment for the Arts Award, 67. Bibliog: Leonard Edmondson (auth), Etching, Van Nostrand Reinhold, 73. Style & Technique: Figurative paintings in acrylic. Media: Acrylic on Paper and Canvas; Etching. Dealer: Bowery Gallery 135 Greene St New York NY 10012. Mailing Add: Pleasant Valley Star Rt Quakertown PA 18951

OPPENHEIM, DENNIS A
SCULPTOR
b Mason City, Wash, Sept 6, 38. Study: Calif Col Arts & Crafts, BA; Univ Hawaii; Stanford Univ, MA. Work: Mus Mod Art, New York; Oakland Art Mus, Calif; Stedelijk Mus, Amsterdam, Holland; Ont Art Mus, Toronto; Tate Gallery, London. Comn: Ocean proj, De Menil & List Founds, Tobago, WI, 69; ground mutations, Armand & Celeste Bartos, Aspen, Colo, 70. Exhib: Earthworks, Dwan Gallery, New York, 68; When Attitude Becomes Form, Kunsthalle, Bern, Switz, 69; A Report Two Ocean Projects, Mus Mod Art, New York, 69, Information, 70; Documenta, Kassel, Ger, 72; Am Drawings 1963-73, Whitney Mus Am Art, 73; Mass Inst Technol, 74; Retrospective, Palais des Beaux-Arts, Brussels, Belg, 75 & Mus Boymans-van Beuningen, Rotterdam, Holland, 75; plus others. Teaching: Guest artist sculpture, Yale Univ, 69; guest artist, Pratt Inst Art, Brooklyn, 69; guest artist, Calif Col Arts & Crafts, 70; guest artist, RI Col Design, 70; guest artist, Univ Wis-Whitewater, 70; guest artist sculpture, Art Inst Chicago, 71-72; guest artist sculpture, NS Col Art, 71-72. Awards: Newhouse Found Grant, Stanford Univ, 65; John Simon Guggenheim Found Fel, 71-72; Nat Endowment Arts Grant for Sculpture, 74. Dealer: Galleria Alessandra Castelli Milano Italy. Mailing Add: D'Arc Gallery 15 E 57th St New York NY 10022

OPPENHEIM, SAMUEL EDMUND
PAINTER
Study: Nat Acad Design; Art Students League. Work: Chrysler Mus Art, Va; White House; West Point Mil Acad, NY; Nat Acad Design, New York; Pentagon, Washington, DC; plus many others. Exhib: Nat Acad Design; Audubon Artists; Allied Artists Am; Hudson Valley Art Asn; Grand Cent Art Galleries; plus many others. Teaching: Instr art, Art Students League, 67- Awards: Prizes, Allied Artists Am, Hudson Valley Art Asn & Am Artists Prof League. Mem: Salmagundi Club; Allied Artists Am; Grand Cent Art Gallery; Artists Fel; Hudson Valley Art Asn. Media: Oil. Mailing Add: 580 E Lake Dr Naples FL 33940

OPPENHEIMER, SELMA L
PAINTER
b Baltimore, Md, Jan 13, 98. Study: Goucher Col, AB; Md Inst Col Art. Work: Baltimore Pub Schs; Loyola Col. Exhib: Two-person show, Goucher Col, Towson, Md, 63; Nat Asn Women Artists Travelling Exhib, Scotland, Eng, France & US, 63-64; Retrospective, Jewish Community Ctr, Baltimore, Md, 67; Mus Art Ann & Invitational, 68; one-person show, Has Sinai Synagogue, 77; Corcoran Gallery Art Biennials, Washington, DC; Western Md Col; Art Inst Chicago; Va Mus Art, Richmond; Mus Mod Art, New York. Awards: Wilson Levering Smith Medals, Baltimore Mus Art, 35-38; Lillian Cotton & Susan Kahn Awards, Nat Asn Women Artists, 52, 60 & 65; Purchase Award, Loyola Col, 67. Mem: Artists Equity Asn (past pres, Baltimore Chap), Nat Asn Women Artists; Baltimore Watercolor Club; Am Fedn Art; Baltimore Mus Art (bd trustees, 61-72). Style & Technique: Semi-abstract. Media: Oil. Mailing Add: 7121 Park Heights Ave Baltimore MD 21215

OPPER, JOHN
PAINTER
b Chicago, Ill, Oct 29, 08. Study: Cleveland Sch Art; Case Western Reserve Univ, BS; Columbia Univ, MA & EdD; also with Hans Hofmann. Work: Mus Mod Art, New York; James Michener Found Mus, Austin, Tex; Milwaukee Art Ctr, Wis; NY Univ Collection; Montclair Mus Art, NJ. Exhib: Int Watercolor Exhib, Art Inst Chicago, 60; Int Watercolor Exhib, Brooklyn Mus; Int Exhib Paintings, Carnegie Inst, Pittsburgh, 61; American Drawings, Moore Inst, 68; Recent Acquisitions, Mus Mod Art, New York. Teaching: Assoc prof art, Univ NC, 52-57; prof art, NY Univ, 57-74. Awards: First Prize for Oil Painting, High Mus Art, 55; Guggenheim Fel, 69; Nat Endowment for Arts Fel in Painting, 74. Mem: Col Art Asn; Am Asn Univ Prof. Style & Technique: Abstract; juxtaposition of color and shape to its simplified element of esthetic meaning. Media: Oil, Watercolor, Acrylic. Dealer: Borgenicht Gallery 1018 Madison Ave New York NY 10021. Mailing Add: Box 347 Amagansett NY 11930

ORDER, TRUDY
PAINTER
b Munich, Ger, Nov 22, 44; US citizen. Study: Akad Malkunst, Munich; Scoula di Pictura, Ancona, Italy; Nat Acad Design, New York, with Maxwell Starr & Umberto Romano. Work: Columbia Mus Art, SC; Mt St Vincent Col; Ft Tyron Jewish Ctr, New York; Holy Rood Episcopal Church, New York. Comn: The Gift (oil), comn by Mme Trau, Antwerp, Belg, 70; Bar Mitzwa (oil), comn by Signora Cagli, Ancona, 72; Bar Mitzwa (graphic), comn by Mme Tilli le Brewster, Paris, 73; In the Park (oil), comn by Ernest Raaschou, St Thomas, VI, 73. Exhib: Audubon Artists, New York, 61; Allied Artists, New York, 62; Knickerbocker Artists, New York, 64; one-man shows, Mt St Vincent Col, 66-74 & Pietrantonio Gallery, New York, 68. Awards: First Prize for Oil, Twilight Park Artists, 63, Second Prize for Pastel, 63 & First Prize for Watercolor, 63. Bibliog: Peggy London (auth), Trudy Order, Nat Soc Arts & Lett, 64. Mem: Nat Soc Arts & Lett; Kappa Pi; fel Royal Soc Arts. Style & Technique: Figure and flower paintings; landscapes; brush and palette knife; impressionistic. Media: Oil, Watercolor. Dealer: Town Gallery 1036 Lexington Ave New York NY 10021. Mailing Add: 250 Cabrini Blvd New York NY 10033

ORDONEZ, EFREN
PAINTER, SCULPTOR
b Chihuahua, Mex, Aug 20, 27. Study: Univ Nuevo Leon. Work: Mus Mod Art, Mexico City. Comn: Cristo Rey (stained glass), 63, Maria Reina (mural), 64 & Twelve Apostles, 65, Sem Sch, Monterrey, Mex; Morelos, Govt Montemorelos, Mex, 68; Sagrado Corazon (fiber glass), Sagrado Corazon Church, Mexico City, 70. Exhib: One-man show, Dreyer Gallery, Houston, Tex, 65; Confrontacion, 66 & Solar Show, 68, Palacio Bellas Artes, Mexico City; Six Mexican Artists, Ariz State Univ, 68; 50 Ordonez Works, Govt Palace, Monterrey, 72. Teaching: Instr drawing, Univ Nuevo Leon, 53-55; instr watercolor, Monterrey Inst Technol, Mex, 55-57. Pos: Juror, Chapultepec Gallery, Inst Nat Bellas Artes, Mexico City, 67. Awards: Medal of Honor for oil painting, Mex, 59. Media: Oil, Watercolor; Concrete, Iron. Publ: Illusr, Soc Artistica Technol (covers), 57-70; illusr, Esther M Allison Poetry, 69; illusr (cover), Soc & Trabajo Soc, 70. Mailing Add: Rio Nazas 106 Col Mexico Monterrey Nuevo Leon Mexico

ORENSTEIN, GLORIA FEMAN
WRITER, ART HISTORIAN
b New York, NY, Mar 8, 38. Study: Brandeis Univ, BA(romance lang & lit), 59; Radcliffe Col, MA(Slavic lang & lit), 61; NY Univ, Danforth fel, 66-71, PhD(comp lit), 71. Teaching: Lectr women of surrealism, Cornell Univ, 73, Pa State Univ, 74, Inst 20th Century Studies, Univ Wis, 75, Sheridan Col, 75 & Artists Space, New York, 75; asst prof women in contemp arts, Douglass Col, 74-, asst prof Eng, 75-, chairperson women's studies prog. Pos: Contrib ed, Womanart & Chrysalis Mag; co-founder, The Woman's Salon. Bibliog: Article in Female Artists: Past & Present, Women's Hist Res Ctr, 74. Mem: Mod Lang Asn; Am Folklore Soc; Soc Rel Higher Educ; NEMAL; Nat Women's Studies Asn; Am Soc French Prof; Comparative Lit Am; Int Asn Study Dada & Surrealism. Res: Surrealism; women's art history; women in the arts; art and psychic phenomena. Publ: Auth, 13 Ways of looking at a portrait: Dotty Attie, Fall 1976, The Woman's Salon, Fall 1976 & The sister chapel, Winter 1977; auth, Leonora Carrington's visionary art for the new age, Chrysalis, Fall 1977; auth, Exorcism/Protest/Rebirth: modes of feminist expression in France, Womanart, Winter 77-78; plus others. Mailing Add: 711 Amsterdam Ave New York NY 10025

ORKIN, RUTH (MRS MORRIS ENGEL)
PHOTOGRAPHER, FILM MAKER
b Boston, Mass. Work: Mus Mod Art, New York; Metrop Mus Art, New York. Exhib: Little Fugitive, Edinburgh Film Festival, 54, Montevideo Film Festival, 55 & Melbourne Film Festival; Lovers & Lollipops, Venice Film Festival, 55; One-Woman Show of 175 Photos, Nikon House, NY, 74. Awards: Silver Lion of San Marco for Co-Direction of Little Fugitive, Venice Film Festival, 53; Academy Nomination for Co-Writing Little Fugitive, 53; Top Ten Women Photographers in US, Prof Photogr Am, 59. Bibliog: The incredible Ruth Orkin, Photog Workshop, winter 53; Saul Bellow (auth), Movies, Horizon Mag, 9/62; Frontier Woman, Camera 35, 5/75; plus others. Mem: Acad Motion Picture Arts & Sci; Am Soc Photogr in Commun. Style & Technique: Still photos of classical musicians, New York views, children, photo-reportage and personalities; fiction films in documentary style. Publ: Ed, Tanglewood Souvenir Guidebook, 47 & 48; contribr, Family of Man; plus many others. Mailing Add: 65 Central Park W New York NY 10023

ORLING, ANNE
ART CONSULTANT, PAINTER
b New York, NY. Study: Art Students League; Empire State Univ, Old Westbury, NY, BA(art admin). Work: UN, New York; C W Post Col. Exhib: NY World's Fair, Fine Arts Pavilion, 64; Heckscher Mus, Huntington, NY, 67; Osgood Gallery, New York, 70; Fordham Univ, Bronx, NY, 74; C W Post Art Gallery, Hillwood Commons, Greenvale, NY, 77; Silvermine Guild, New Canaan, Conn; Univ Ariz, Tucson; Baldwin Wallace Col, Berea, Ohio. Teaching: Instr art & art hist, North Shore Community Arts Ctr, Great Neck, NY, 63-69. Mem: Prof Artists Guild (vpres, 70, pres, 76-). Style & Technique: Non-objective painting; graphics with silk screen; collage. Media: Oil; Acrylics. Interest: Service as art consultant to help collectors acquire 19th and 20th century paintings, sculpture and graphics; work with museums, dealers and artists plus corporate consultations. Mailing Add: 69 Shelter Lane Roslyn Heights NY 11577

ORR, ELLIOT
PAINTER
b Flushing, New York, June 26, 04. Study: Grand Cent Art Sch, with George Luks & Charles W Hawthorne. Work: Brooklyn Mus; Whitney Mus Am Art, New York; Addison Gallery, Andover, Mass; Detroit Inst Arts; Springfield Mus, Mass; Community Fine Arts Ctr, Rock Springs, Wyo; Ill State Mus, Springfield, Ill; Chrysler Mus, Norfolk, Va. Exhib: Romantic Painting in America, Mus Mod Art, New York, 43; Painting in the United States, Carnegie Inst, Pittsburgh, 48; American Painting Today, Metrop Mus Art, New York, 50, Am Watercolors Drawings & Prints, 52; Golden Anniversary, Provincetown Art Asn, 64; By the People, For the People: New Eng, DeCordova Mus, Lincoln, Mass, 77. Awards: Joseph Lewis Weyrich Mem Prize, Baltimore Mus, 30; Crossett First Prize, Cape Cod Art Asn, 48. Bibliog: F F Sherman (auth), Notes on Elliot Orr, Art in Am, 40; Rosamund Frost (auth), Contemporary Art, Crown, 42; John I H Baur (auth), Revolution and Tradition in Modern American Art, Harvard Univ, 51. Mem: Life mem Provincetown Art Asn. Style & Technique: Traditional and figurative; uses of var methods. Media: All Media. Mailing Add: 442 Broad Ave S Naples FL 33940

ORR, VERONICA MARIE (VERONICA MARIE INGRAM)
JEWELER, COLLECTOR
b Omak, Wash, Jan 12, 45. Study: Inst Am Indian Arts, grad; painting study with Allen Houser. Work: R C Gorman Collection, Taos, NMex; C F Louato Collection, Sile, NMex; Dr Jack Adams Collection, Albuquerque, NMex; Elaine LaBoutilaire Collection, Paradise Valley, Ariz. Exhib: Gallery Wall, Phoenix, Ariz, 73; Heard Mus, Phoenix, 73-77; Navajo Gallery, Taos, NMex, 74 & solo, 76; Southwest Indian Arts & Crafts Show, Santa Fe, NMex, 74, 75 & 77; Many Horses Gallery, Marina Del Rey, Calif, 75; Thompson Gallery, Phoenix, 76; Ashton Group Show, Scottsdale, Ariz, 76; Carl Gorman Mus, Univ Calif Davis, 77; Philbrook Indian Art Exhib Mus, Tulsa, Okla, 77. Teaching: Teaching asst jewelry, Inst Am Indian Arts, Santa Fe, 62-64; art teacher, Albuquerque Indian Sch, 71-72. Awards: First, Second & Third Prizes Fabric Design, Heard Mus, Phoenix, 73 & Hon Mention Jewelry, 74; Third Place Jewelry, Southwest Indian Arts & Crafts, Santa Fe, 74 & 75. Bibliog: Carl Rosnek & Joseph Stacy (auth), Sky Stone & Silver, Prentice-Hall, 76. Style & Technique: Northwest Coast style Indian designs, stories and pictographs depicted in sandcast silver and gold with inlay. Media: Silver & Gold with Abalone, Ivory, Jade & Turquoise Inlay. Collection: Indian artist paintings; Indian pottery; North American tribes baskets. Mailing Add: PO Box 428 Corrales NM 87048

ORR-CAHALL, ANONA CHRISTINA
CURATOR, ART HISTORIAN
b June 12, 47. Study: Mt Holyoke Col, BA; Oxford Univ; Ecole du Louvre; Yale Univ, MA, MPhil, PhD cand. Exhibitions Arranged: Am Drawing 1970-1973, Yale Univ Art Gallery, 73; Addison Mizner Architect of Dreams & Realities & Contemp Views of the Am Family, Norton Gallery of Art, 77. Teaching: Head teaching asst introd hist art, Yale Univ, New Haven, Conn. Pos: Consult cur, Norton Gallery Art, West Palm Beach, Fla, 73- Mailing Add: 1064 Somera Rd Los Angeles CA 90024

ORSINI
See Anderson, Gwendolyn Orsinger

ORTIZ, RALPH
SCULPTOR
b New York, NY, Jan 30, 34. Study: Brooklyn Mus Art Sch; Art Students League; Pratt Inst, BS & MFA; Columbia Univ. Work: Mus Mod Art; Whitney Mus Am Art, New York; Finch Mus, New York; Chrysler Mus Fine Art, Provincetown, Mass; Oxford Mus Mod Art, Eng. Exhib: Traveling Assemblage Exhib, Mus Mod Art, New York, 63; Young America Exhibition, Whitney Mus Am Art, New York, 65; The Destruction in Art Symposium, London, Eng, 66; Celebration-Eros-Thanatos, Youth Pavilion, Expo '67, Montreal, Can, 67; Theater Ritual, Am Educ Theater Asn Conf, Temple Univ, Philadelphia, 70. Teaching: Instr graphic plastic forms, mixed media, intermedia, color & design, Columbia Univ Teachers Col, 67; asst prof art, Livingston Col, Rutgers Univ, 72- Pos: Dir & cur, El Museo del Barrio, New York, 69-70; comt mem, Ghetto Arts Panel, NY State Coun Arts, 70-71; vchmn, Planning Corp Arts, New York, 71- Awards: John Hay Whitney Fel Grant, 65. Bibliog: Barry Farrell (auth), The other culture, Life Mag, 2/17/67; Kurt Von Meier (auth), Violence art & the American way, Artscanada, 4/68; Charlotte Willard (auth), Violence & art, Art in Am, 1-2/69. Media: Mixed Media. Publ: Auth, Disassemblage, Art & Artists, 66; ed & auth, Ritual theatre, Aspen Mag, 69; auth, Culture and the people, Art in Am, 71. Mailing Add: 118 W 73rd St New York NY 10023

ORTIZ MACEDO, LUIS
ARCHITECT, ART HISTORIAN
b Mexico City, Mex, Apr 4, 33. Study: Escuela Nac de Arquit, Univ Nac Autonoma de Mex. Work: (Restoration works), Alcazar Bldg, Chapultepec Castle & mus in Oaxaca; compiler, Alvar & Carmen Carrillo Gil Collection for mus installation. Comn: Nat monument restorations, Mex Govt, 60-75; dir regional restoration, Govt Guanajuato State, Mex, 62-66; restoration, Nat Mus Hist, Mex Govt, 68-70. Teaching: Prof hist archit, Sch Archit, Univ NAM, Mex, 54-66 & Iberoamerican Univ, 63-74; dir, Sch Archit, Univ Guanajuato, Mex, 65-67. Pos: Dir, Restauration Inst, Govt Guanajuato State, Mex, 62-66; Mex Govt Rep, Cong Int Union Archit, 63-74; rep, Int Union Art Critics, 63-74; dir hist monuments, gen secy & gen dir, Nat Inst Anthrop & Hist, Mex, 67-71; jury, Nat Awards in Arts, Sci & Lit, 70, 72 & 73; gen dir, Nat Inst Fine Arts, Mex, 72-74. Awards: Hon Fel, Am Inst Archit, 72 & 73. Bibliog: 4,000 Years of Mexican Art, Colonial Epoch, Herrero Edit, 70. Mem: Int Comt Art & Hist (pres). Publ: Illusr, Popular Art in Guanajuato, 64; contribr, 4,000 Years of Mexican Art, Colonial Epoch, 70; auth, Art of Virreinal Mexico, 71. Mailing Add: Rio Amazonas 7 Colonia Cuauhtemoc Mexico DF Mexico

ORTLIEB, ROBERT EUGENE
SCULPTOR, GRAPHIC ARTIST
b San Diego, Calif, July 4, 25. Study: Univ Southern Calif, with Merrell Gage, Francis de Erdely & Glen Lucens, BFA & MFA; independent study, Europe, Mex & SAm; San Francisco State Col. Work: Palace of Legion of Honor Mus, San Francisco; Laguna Beach Art Mus; Riverside Art Mus. Comn: Wood Head of Christ, Congregation, First Presby Church, Culver City, Calif, 52; Monumental Head, Students, Los Angeles High Sch, 53; terra-cotta of Mother & Child, Community Church, Palos Verde of mayor, Civic Ctr, Palos Verdes, 68; bronze apothecaries, Dr MacFarlane, Univ Southern Calif, 75. Exhib: Graphic Arts, Int Graphic Exhib, Cincinnati, Ohio, 53; sculpture, Los Angeles Co Mus Calif; sculpture, Western States Exhib, Denver Art Mus, Colo; one-man shows, Ill State Mus, Springfield, 64 & Dean Mus, Cherry Valley, Calif, 75; Western States Graphic Art Exhib, Dallas Mus, Tex. Teaching: Instr sculpture, Riverside Art Ctr, Univ Calif, 62-75, Univ Southern Calif, Idyllwild, 64-75 & Inst Prof de Statoperl Industris el' Artigianto del Marmoin, Carrara, Italy, 72. Pos: Chmn art comt to estab art & exhib policy, Calif State Fair, Sacramento, 58-60. Awards: First Awards, Calif State Fair & Expos, 57, Long Beach Art Mus, 57 & 50th Nat Orange Show, San Bernardino, 65. Bibliog: Robert Ortlieb, La Rev Mod, Paris, France, 62; Janice Lovoos & Felice Paramore (co-auth), Wood carving and wood mosaic, In: Modern Mosaic Techniques, Watson-Guptill, 65; Betje Howell (auth), Twelve California artists, Am Artist, R Riedinger, 68; plus others. Mem: Hon life mem Inglewood Art Asn, Calif. Style & Technique: Expressionism, abstract, in terra-cotta, bronze and graphics; direct carving, marble, wood and plastics. Media: Stone & Wood Carving. Mailing Add: 11111 Jerry Lane Garden Grove CA 92640

ORTLIP, PAUL DANIEL
PAINTER
b Englewood, NJ, May 21, 26. Study: Houghton Acad; Art Students League; with Louis Bouche, 47, Reginald Marsh, 48, Robert Brackman & Edwin Dickinson, 49; Acad Grande Chaumiere, 50. Work: US Navy Art Collection, Pentagon, Washington, DC; Bergen Community Mus, Paramus, NJ; Air & Space Mus, Smithsonian Inst, Washington, DC; Am Col Clin Pharmacology, NY Acad of Med, New York; Fairleigh Dickinson Univ; Bergen Co Court House, Hackensack, NJ; Col Med NJ. Comn: Mem portrait of JFK, Fairleigh Dickinson Univ Libr, 64; Gemini 5 Astronauts, Off Info, USN, 65, Vietnam (painting), 67, Apollo 12 Astronauts, 69 & Apollo 17 Astronauts, 72; mural, Hist Mus, Palisades Interstate Park Comn, Ft Lee, NJ. Exhib: Salon L'Art Libre Ann, Paris, France, 50; Allied Artists Am Ann, 60-71; Collection of Fine Arts, Smithsonian Inst, Washington, DC; Galerie Vallombreuse, Biarritz, France, 74; La Galerie Mouffe, Paris, 75; plus others. Teaching: Instr painting, Montclair Acad, NJ, 57-58; artist in residence, Fairleigh Dickinson Univ, 57-67; instr painting, Montclair Mus, 58-59 & 76- Pos: Off US Navy artist, Off Info, Washington, DC, 63-; art cur, Fairleigh Dickinson Univ, 67-70. Awards: First Prize in Oils, NJ State Am Artists Prof Award, 60; Franklin Williams Award, Salmagundi Club, 67; Oil Painting Award Outstanding Achievement, US Navy, 68; Artist of the Year Award, Hudson Artists, Jersey City Mus, 70. Bibliog: Marg Dulac (auth), Odyssey of an artist, NJ Mus & Arts, 5/71; Int Naval Rev, 76. Mem: Life mem Art Students League; Allied Artists Am; Salmagundi Club; US Navy Liaison Comt (off artist); Nat Soc Mural Painters. Media: Oil, Mixed Media. Dealer: Portraits Inc 41 W 57th St New York NY 10022. Mailing Add: 95 Main St Ft Lee NJ 07024

ORTMAN, GEORGE EARL
PAINTER, SCULPTOR
b Oakland, Calif, Oct 17, 26. Study: Ariz State Univ; Calif Col Arts & Crafts; Atelier 17, New York; Acad Andre Lhote, Paris; Hans Hofmann Sch, New York. Work: Mus Mod Art & Whitney Mus Am Art, New York; Walker Art Ctr, Minneapolis, Minn; Albright-Knox Art Gallery, Buffalo; Milwaukee Art Ctr. Comn: Relig banners, Christian Theol Sem Indianapolis, Ind, 66; mural, comn by Bd Educ, PS 192, New York, 67; Reredo, Unitarian Church, Princeton, NJ, 68; banners, Ind Univ Opera House, 71; Oracle (three panels), Mfrs Hanover Trust, 71. Exhib: Carnegie Inst Int, Pittsburgh, 60, 64 & 70; Toward a New Abstraction, Jewish Mus, New York, 63; Tokyo Biennial, Japan, 64; 100 Years of Amerian Art, Whitney Mus Am Art, 64 & Two Decades of Geometric Abstraction, 65. Teaching: Sr fel painting, Princeton Univ, 66-69; head painting dept, Cranbrook Acad Art, 70- Awards: Guggenheim Fel, 65; First Prize for Religion in Art, Birmingham Mus Art, 66; First Prize, NJ State Mus Second Ann, 67. Bibliog: J Borgzingler (auth), Analytical art, Time Mag, 4/64; Martin Friedman (auth), Symbols, Art News, 10/65; J Brown (auth), Introduction for catalog to one-man show, Indianapolis Mus Art, 4/71. Media: Constructions. Dealer: Gimpel-Weitzenhoffer Galleries 1040 Madison Ave New York NY 10021. Mailing Add: Box 192 Castine ME 04421

ORTMAYER, CONSTANCE
SCULPTOR, EDUCATOR
b New York, NY, July 19, 02. Study: Royal Acad Fine Arts & Royal Acad Master Sch, Vienna, Austria, MFA. Work: Am Numismatic Soc, New York; Brookgreen Gardens, SC. Comn: Bronze group, State of SC, Brookgreen Gardens, 34; US Half Dollar, Stephen Foster Commemorative, 36; bas reliefs, US Post Off, Arcadia, Fla, 39 & Scottsboro, Ala, 41; Award Medals, Fla Acad Sci & Rollins Col, 52-62. Exhib: Vienna Secession, 32; Nat Asn Women Painters & Sculptors, New York, 35; Allied Arts, Brooklyn Mus, 36; Nat Sculpture Soc, Whitney Mus Am Art, New York, 40; Pa Acad Fine Arts, Philadelphia, 41. Teaching: Prof sculpture, Rollins Col, 37-68, head dept art, 60-68, emer prof, 68- Awards: Anna Hyatt Huntington Prize, Nat Asn Women Painters & Sculptors, 35; Henry O Avery Archit Prize, Nat Sculpture Soc, 40; Award of Metit, Fla Fedn Art, 48. Mem: Morristown Art Asn; Nat Sculpture Soc; Fla Fedn Art; hon mem Orlando Ceramic Soc. Style & Technique: Modified representational. Media: Wood, Ceramic. Mailing Add: 617 W Second N St Morristown TN 37814

ORZE, JOSEPH JOHN
ART ADMINISTRATOR, SCULPTOR
b Exeter, Pa, Dec 11, 32. Study: Syracuse Univ, BFA(magna cum laude), 55, MS, 56; George Peabody Col, EdD, 70. Work: Munson, Williams, Proctor Inst, Utica, NY; Sch Benedictine Fathers, Rome, Italy. Exhib: One-man & two-man shows, Southern Ind Studio Gallery, New Albany, 65, J B Speed Art Mus, Louisville, Ky, 65, Int Gallery, Memphis, Tenn, 66, Clark Mem Libr, Bethany, Conn, 67, Dana Arts Ctr, Colgate Univ, Hamilton, NY, 69 & Cecil Davis Clark Gallery, Marion, Mass, 71; Brooks Mem Gallery, Memphis; Hunter Gallery, Univ Chattanooga; J B Speed Art Mus; Syracuse Univ, NY; Colgate Univ; Univ Ala; Univ Ga; Conn Acad Fine Arts, Wadsworth Atheneum, Hartford; Munson-Williams-Proctor Inst, Utica, NY; Everson Mus Fine Art, Syracuse; plus others. Teaching: Instr art & educ, Syracuse Univ, 56-59; assoc prof sculpture & art educ, State Univ NY Col New Paltz, 59-61; assoc prof art & head dept, Middle Tenn State Univ, 61-66; prof art & chmn dept, Southern Conn State Col, 66-69; dean, Col Fine & Applied Arts, Southeastern Mass Univ, 69-75; pres, Worcester State Col, 75- Pos: Vpres & dir, Southern Asn Sculptors, 64-66; chmn, Conn Col Coun Arts, 67-69; vpres & dir, Marion Art Ctr, Mass, 73-75; dir & treas, Pub Art Proj, Inc, New Bedford, Mass, 74- Awards: Purchase Award for Sculpture, Munson, Williams, Proctor Inst, 58; R A Rathbone Best in Show Award, New Haven Print & Clay Club, 66; First Prize in Sculpture, New Eng Arts Festival, Waterbury, Conn, 67 & 68. Mem: Col Art Asn; Nat Art Educ Asn. Publ: Auth, Understanding children's art, Instr Mag, 5/64; auth, Engma of modern art, Peabody Reflector, 5/66; auth, Role of the Fine Arts in the University, Middle Tenn State Univ, 69; auth, Visual arts in higher education, Mass Art Educ Asn, 70; co-auth, Art From Scrap, Davis, 2nd ed, 73. Mailing Add: Worcester State Col 486 Chandler St Worcester MA 01602

OSBORN, ELODIE C (MRS ROBERT C OSBORN)
ART ADMINISTRATOR
b Brooklyn, NY, Dec 6, 11. Study: Packer Col Inst; Wellesley Col, BA; Sch Fine Arts, NY Univ; Sorbonne, cert. Collections Arranged: Many exhibs at Mus Mod Art, New York, for tour to other mus, cols & schs; Klee Memorial Exhibition, Mus Mod Art, New York, 41. Pos: Dir traveling exhibs, Mus Mod Art, New York, 33-48; dir, Salisbury Film Soc, 51- Mem: Cosmopolitan Club, New York; Am Fcdn Arts (adv comt, 41-56); Mus Mod Art; Int Film Seminars (bd trustees, 68-); MacDowell Colony (mem bd dirs, 70-, secy bd, 72-, vpres, 73-75, pres, 75-77, dir exhib: Seven Decades of MacDowell Artists, New York, 10/76); Am Fedn Film Socs (vpres, 57-58). Publ: Auth, Modern Sculpture (portfolio), 47 & auth, Texture and Pattern (portfolio), 49, Mus Mod Art; auth, Manual of Traveling Exhibitions, UNESCO, 53; contribr, Art in Am, 66; contribr, Film Quart, 68; contribr, Film Libr Quart, 72. Mailing Add: Salisbury CT 06068

OSBORN, ROBERT
ILLUSTRATOR, SATIRIC ARTIST
b Oshkosh, Wis, Oct 26, 04. Study: Yale Univ; Brit Acad, Rome; Acad Scandinav, Paris; also with Friesz, Varoquier & Despiau; Md Inst Art, hon DFA, 63. Work: Mus Mod Art, New York; Addison Gallery Art, Andover, Mass; Paine Art Mus, Oshkosh, Wis; Corcoran Gallery Art, Washington, DC; Wadsworth Atheneum, Hartford, Conn. Comn: Mural, Quinta da Bacalhoa Azeitao, Port, 38-39; mural, Am Mus Natural Hist, New York, 55; mural, comn by Stonoroff for Planning Comn Philadelphia, 56; two murals, comn by Ivan Chermayeff for Puerto Rico Planning Comn, 70; three murals, comn by Ivan Chermayeff for Smithsonian Exhib on Productivity, 72. Exhib: Wartime Posters, Art Inst Chicago, 46; Va Mus Fine Arts, Richmond, 52; Wadsworth Atheneum, 58; Whitney Mus Am Art, New York, 60; Brooklyn Mus, 61. Teaching: Founder & head dept art, Hotchkiss Sch, Lakeville, Conn, 29-35; chmn Yale Coun, Sch Art & Archit, Yale Univ, 60-65, alumni exec coun, 70- Pos: Presented first show of Edward Weston in the East, Hotchkiss Sch, 31. Awards: Gov Medal, Wis. Bibliog: Leo Lionni (auth), Osborn, Print, Vol 5; Russell Lynes (auth), Osborn's Americans, Horizon, 9/60; Fritz Eichenberg (auth), Osborn, Am Graphic Artist, 65; plus others. Mem: Elizabethan Club; Scroll & Keys; Century Asn. Style & Technique: Simple, strong, flowing line. Media: Pen, Crayon, Watercolor. Collection: Despiau, Miros, Klees, Calders, Marinni, MacIver, Hartley, Picasso, Dubuffets, Friedmans, Shahns and others. Publ: Auth & illusr, War Is No Damn Good, The Vulgarians, Low and Inside, An Osborn Festival of Phobias & Mankind May Never Make It; plus others. Dealer: Edith Halpert 57th St & Park Ave New York NY 10022. Mailing Add: Salisbury CT 06068

OSBORNE, ROBERT LEE
PAINTER, EDUCATOR
b Chandler, Ind, June 24, 28. Study: Ind Univ, with Pickens, Marx, Engel, Ballinger & Hope, MA; Univ Iowa, with Lechay, Hecksher, Longman, Ludens & Tomasini, MA. Exhib: Fla Artist Group, Norton Gallery, Palm Beach, Fla; Fac Shows, Ringling Sch Art, Sarasota, Fla; Venice Art League, Fla; one-man shows, Beaux Arts Gallery, St Petersberg, Hilton Leech Gallery, Sarasota, South Fla Col, Lakeland & Manatee Art League, Bradenton, Fla. Teaching: Lectr, Evansville Mus; asst prof art & head dept, Evansville Col; instr, Evansville Mus; instr, Ringling Sch Art, currently. Pos: Former designer, Olszewski Art Glass Co, St Louis; dir, Manatee Art League, Bradenton, 71-72; mem bd dirs, Fla Artists Group, 72-; dean fac, Ringling Sch Art, currently. Awards: Gold Key Award, Evansville, Ind, 46; Prize, Ind Univ, 52. Mem: Tri-State Art Guild (pres, 58-66). Style & Technique: Portrait and fantasy; personal expression, social satire and ecology themes. Media: Oil, Acrylic, Multi-Media. Publ: Illusr, Organization of Aquatic Clubs, 55; var illus in Image Mag. Mailing Add: Ringling Sch Art Sarasota FL 33580

OSBY, LARISSA GEISS
PAINTER
b Artemowsk, Russia, June 7, 28; US citizen. Study: Lyceum & Univ Goettingen, Ger; Univ Munich; Acad Fine Arts, Munich, Ger. Work: Carnegie Inst, Pittsburgh; Alcoa Collection; US Steel Collection; Westinghouse Elec Co Collection; plus others. Comn: Am for Democratic Action, 69; Koppers Co & First Fed Savings & Loan Asn, Pittsburgh, 72; United Steelworkers of Am, 73; Nat Steel Corp, 77. Exhib: One-man shows, Pittsburgh Plan for Art Gallery, 63, 68 & 71, Carnegie Inst Mus of Art, 72 & Pa State Unit, New Kensington, 73; Walker Art Ctr Biennial, Minneapolis, 66; Pennsylvania 71, William Penn Mem Mus, Harrisburg, 71; Herzog Anton Ulrich Mus, Braunschweig, WGer, 51; Carnegie Inst Int, 55-77, Mid-Yr Nat, Butler Inst Am Art, Youngstown, Ohio, 58 & 59, Contemp Arts Ctr, Cincinnati, 59; Guest of Hon Exhib, Birmingham Arts Festival, Mich, 61; Boston Inst Contemp Art, 61; Drawings USA, St Paul Art Ctr, Minn, 63; Chautaugua Art Ctr Ann, NY, 64; Mainstreams, Marietta Col, Ohio, 67; Am Artists in France, Palais des Congres, Paris, 75-76; plus others. Awards: Carnegie Inst Purchase Award, Assoc Artists of Pittsburgh Ann, 58; Jury Award of Distinction, Mainstreams Int, 68 & Assoc Artists Pittsburgh Ann, 69. Mem: Arts & Crafts Ctr Pittsburgh, Pittsburgh Plan for Art; Assoc Artists Pittsburgh. Style & Technique: Romantic abstract expressionist. Mailing Add: 4218 Maple Ln Allison Park PA 15101

OSCARSSON, VICTORIA CONSTANCE GUNHILD
ART DEALER, ADMINISTRATOR
b Stamford, Conn, Dec 18, 51. Study: Cours De Civilisation Francaise, the Sorbonne; Trinity Col, Hartford, Conn, BA(art hist & languages); Sotheby's Works of Art Course, London. Pos: Researcher, Guggenheim Mus, New York, summer 73; personal asst to Richard Nathanson, pvt dealer, London, 74-76; manager Noonday Graphics, London, 76-77; dir, Landmark Gallery, New York, 77. Specialty: Contemporary, all media. Mailing Add: Landmark Gallery 469 Broome St New York NY 10013

O'SHEA, TERRENCE PATRICK
PAINTER, SCULPTOR
b Los Angeles, Calif, Sept 8, 41. Study: Holy Cross Col; Boston Mus Sch; Chouinard Art Inst. Work: Los Angeles Co Mus Art; Patrick Lannan Mus, Palm Beach, Fla; Am Tel & Tel Collections, Chicago; Metromedia Collection, Los Angeles. Exhib: A Plastic Presence, Jewish Mus, New York, 69-70; Permutation, Light & Color, Mus Contemp Art, Chicago, 70; Pierres de Fantaisie, Oakland Mus, 70; Temple Street, Long Beach Mus, 71; 1st Int Biennial Small Sculpture Show, Budapest, Hungary, 71. Awards: Contemp Art Coun Purchase Award, Los Angeles Co Mus Art, 65. Bibliog: Jerry Rosen (auth), Terry O'Shea (video taped interview), 74. Style & Technique: Highly polished polyester resin sculpture utilizing many and varied inlayes. Media: Polyester Resin; Methane Base Liquid Pigment on Paper. Dealer: Cirrus Editions 708 N Manhattan Pl Los Angeles CA 90038. Mailing Add: 555 Rose Ave Venice CA 90291

O'SICKEY, JOSEPH BENJAMIN
PAINTER, EDUCATOR
b Detroit, Mich, Nov 9, 18. Study: Cleveland Sch Art, cert, with Paul Travis, Henry G Keller, Carl Gaertner, Frank N Wilcox & Hoyt L Sherman. Work: Cleveland Mus Art; Pepsi Cola Collection, New York; Cleveland Arts Asn; Mus Mod Art Poster Collection 1949-50 Exhib. Exhib: Fourteen exhibs, Cleveland Mus Art, 38-77; Pa Acad Fine Art, Philadelphia; Columbus Gallery Art Exhib; Akron Art Inst; Blossom Exhib; All-Ohio Exhibs, 74 & 77; plus other group shows & many one-man shows. Teaching: Instr art, Ohio State Univ, 46-47; instr art, Akron Art Inst, 49-52; lectr art, Case Western Reserve Univ, 56-64; prof art, Kent State Univ, 64-, coordr painting & sculpture, 68- Pos: Art dir & graphic designer, pvt co, 49-64. Awards: Spec jury mention & awards, Cleveland Mus Art, 62-67; spec jury mention, Akron Art Inst; Cleveland Arts Cash Prize for Outstanding Achievement in the Arts, 74; Medal, Cash Award & Purchase Award, Butler Inst of Am Art, Ohio, 74; First Prize Cash Wards, All-Ohio Exhibs, 74 & 77 & Best in Show Cash Prize, 74. Media: Oil. Mailing Add: Dept Art Kent State Univ Kent OH 44240

OSRIN, RAYMOND HAROLD
CARTOONIST
b Brooklyn, NY, Oct 5, 28. Study: Art Students League, 45-47. Pos: Free-lance cartoonist, comic book illusr, comic strip ghost artist & TV animator, W R Smith, Inc, Pittsburgh, 57-58; staff artist, Pittsburgh Press, 58-63; staff artist, Cleveland Plain Dealer, 63-66, polit cartoonist, 66- Awards: Freedom Award, 66 & 67; Nat Headliners Award, 70. Mem: Am Asn Ed Cartoonists. Mailing Add: 1801 Superior Ave Cleveland OH 44114

OSSORIO, ALFONSO A
PAINTER, SCULPTOR
b Manila, Philippines, Aug 2, 16; US citizen. Study: Harvard Col, AB, 38; RI Sch Design, 38-39. Work: Philadelphia Mus Art; NY Univ Art Collection; Guggenheim Mus, New York; Mus Mod Art; Whitney Mus Am Art; plus many others. Comn: Murals, Church St Joseph, Victorias, Negros, Philippines, 50-51 & Washington Square Village, New York, 54; large circular assemblage, New York Hilton Hotel, 64. Exhib: Whitney Mus Am Art Painting & Sculpture Ann, 53-; Osaka Art Festival, Japan, 58 & 60; Structure & Style, Turin, Italy & Bochum, WGer, 62; Documenta, Kassel, WGer, 64; The New American Painting & Sculpture, Mus Mod Art, 69; plus many others. Pos: Dir exhibs, Exec House, New York, 56-57; co-founder & dir, Signa Gallery, East Hampton, NY, 57-60. Bibliog: Jean Dubuffet (auth), Peintures Initiatiques d'Ossorio (monogr), La Pierre Volante, Paris, 52; Michel Tapie (auth), Ossorio (monogr), Ed Arte Fratelli Turin, 61; B H Friedman (auth), Ossorio (monogr), Abrams, 72. Collection: Contemporary painting and sculpture; art brut, primitive and Oriental. Dealer: Cordier & Ekstrom 980 Madison Ave New York NY 10021. Mailing Add: The Creeks Bridgehampton Rd East Hampton NY 11937

OSTENDORF, (ARTHUR) LLOYD, JR
PAINTER, INSTRUCTOR
b Dayton, Ohio, June 23, 21. Study: Dayton Art Inst; Lincoln Mem Univ, Lincoln Dipl Hon, 66, hon ArtD, 74; Lincoln Col (Ill), LittD, 68. Work: Gov William Lee De Ewing (oil portrait) & Speaker W Robert Blair (oil portrait), Ill State Capitol, Springfield; Msgr Harry Ansbury (oil portrait), Parish Recreation House, Corpus Christi; Msgr Joseph D McFarland (oil portrait), Holy Angels Sch, Dayton, Ohio; Dr Herbert Y Livesay (oil portrait), Lincoln Mem Univ; Gen George Rogers Clark (oil), Restored Gov Mansion, Springfield. Comn: The Jesuit Martyrs (oil), Jesuit Retreat Chapel, Milford, Ohio, 49; six religious oil paintings, Hoyne Funeral Chapel, Dayton, 55. Exhib: Dayton Art Inst, 41. Teaching: Instr com art & painting & dir, Ostendorf Art Acad, 69- Pos: Art ed, Lincoln Herald, 57- Awards: Winner in Design for Chicago Lincoln (statue), Lincoln Sq C of C, 58. Mem: Montgomery Co Hist Soc (vpres, 56); Civil War Round Table of Dayton (pres, 55-56 & 58-59). Media: Watercolor, Ink, Oil. Publ: Auth, Mr Lincoln Came to Dayton, 59; auth & illusr, A Picture Story of Abraham Lincoln, 62; co-auth, Lincoln in Photographs, An Album of Every Known Pose, 63; auth, The Photographs of Mary Todd Lincoln, 69. Mailing Add: 225 Lookout Dr Dayton OH 45419

OSTER, GERALD
PAINTER, GRAPHIC ARTIST
b Providence, RI, Mar 24, 18. Study: Brown Univ, ScB; Cornell Univ, PhD. Work: Milwaukee Art Ctr; San Francisco Mus Art; Tel Aviv Mus. Exhib: Mus Mod Art, 64; Walker Art Ctr, Minneapolis, 67; Milwaukee Art Ctr, 68; Inst Contemp Art, Chicago, 68; Tel Aviv Mus, 71; plus others. Style & Technique: Superposition of families of curves to give moire patterns; phosphorescent abstractions to depict phosphenes. Publ: Auth, The Science of Moire Patterns, 64 & 69; contribr, Art Int & Sci Am. Mailing Add: 241 W 11th St New York NY 10014

OSTIGUY, JEAN-RENE
PAINTER, CURATOR
b Marieville, PQ, Aug 14, 25. Study: Univ Montreal, BA; Ecole des Beaux-Arts, Montreal; Sch Art & Design, Montreal, dipl. Work: Carleton Univ, Ottawa; Ottawa Univ. Exhib: Montreal Spring Exhib, 51 & 52. Collections Arranged: Leon Bellefleur, 68, Adrien Hebert, 71 & Ozias Leduc, 74, Nat Gallery Can. Teaching: Prof, Ecole des Beaux-Arts, Montreal, 53-55; prof Can art, Ottawa Univ, 66-71; vis prof Can art, Laval Univ, 71-72. Pos: Cur Can art, Nat Gallery Can, 64-; adv bd, J Can Art Hist. Awards: Chriss Award, 62. Mem: Can Mus

Asn (councillor, 63-65); Int Comt Mus. Res: 19th and early 20th century Canadian art. Publ: Auth, Un Siecle de Peinture Canadienne, 71; auth, Ozias Leduc-Peinture Symboliste et Religleuse, 74; auth, Rodolphe Duguay-Quarantes Gravures, 75. Mailing Add: Nat Gallery Can Ottawa ON Can

OSTROW, STEPHEN EDWARD
ART HISTORIAN, MUSEUM DIRECTOR
b New York, NY, May 7, 32. Study: Oberlin Col, BA, 54; NY Univ Inst Fine Arts, MA, 59, PhD, 66. Collections Arranged: Baroque Painting: Italy and Her Influence (with catalog), 68; Visions and Revisions (with catalog), 68; Raid the Icebox I, with Andy Warhol, 69-70; Days Gone By, 71. Teaching: Lectr art hist, Rutgers Univ, New Brunswick, 58-62; asst prof art hist, Univ Mo-Columbia, 62-66; vis lectr art hist, Brown Univ, 70, 71, 74- Pos: Cur collections, Herron Mus Art, 66-67; chief cur, Mus Art, RI Sch Design, 67-71, dir, 71- Mem: Col Art Asn Am; Am Asn Mus; Asn Art Mus Dirs; Alliance Arts Educ, RI (exec comt, 74-); RI Hist Preserv Comn, 75. Publ: Auth, Annibale Carracci and the Jason frescoes: toward an internal chronology, Art Bull, 64; auth, Diana or Bacchus in the Palazzo Riario, Marsyas, 65; auth, A drawing by Annibale Carracci for the Jason frescoes and the S Gregorio baptism, Master Drawings, 70. Mailing Add: 224 Benefit St Providence RI 02903

OSTROWITZ, JUDITH MAURA
SCULPTOR, ART ADMINISTRATOR
b Brooklyn, NY, Feb 25, 53. Study: Sch of Visual Arts, 74, studied photog; Pratt Inst, BFA(painting & printmaking; with honors), 74, study with Joseph Stapleton, Charles Shucker & Jack Sonenberg; New Sch for Social Research, anthropology, 76- Exhib: Amos Eno Gallery, New York, 77; Gallery 91, Brooklyn, NY, 77; Galerie Signal, Montreal, Can, 77; Brooklyn 1978, Brooklyn Mus, 78; one-person show, Amos Eno Gallery, New York, 77. Teaching: Instr photog, Project Contact/Educational Alliance, 1/75-5/75. Pos: Playground asst, Arts & Crafts Mobile Unit Dept Parks, New York, 72-73; dir, Amos Eno Gallery, New York, 75- Bibliog: Eileen Blair (auth), Deja Vu at Gallery 91, The Phoenix, 1/77; John Perreault (auth), rev in Soho Weekly News, 2/77; Janice Glander-Bandyk (auth), rev in Arts mag, 5/77. Mem: Asn of Artist-Run Galleries (delegate, 75- & apprenticeship supervisor, 77). Style & Technique: Three dimensional constructions. Media: Natural Materials; Wood; Glass; Mortar; Fabric. Res: Reviews of artist's exhibitions for Artists Review Art. Specialty: Co-operative gallery, all media. Publ: Contribr, Artists Review Art, Asn of Artist Run Galleries, 76-77. Dealer: Amos Eno Gallery 101 Wooster St New York NY 10012. Mailing Add: 283 Washington Ave Brooklyn NY 11205

OSTUNI, PETER W
PAINTER
b New York, NY, Oct 9, 08. Study: Cooper Union Sch Art & Archit, cert. Comn: Vitreous enamel mural, SS United States, US Steamship Lines, 51; enamel murals, Children's Mus, Ft Worth, 52; laminated stained glass, Prudential Life Ins Main Off, Newark, NJ, 59; seven cast stone bas-reliefs, for Grace Lines SS Santa Maria, 65; six windows in laminated plastics, Phipps Plaza, Atlanta, Ga, 70. Exhib: New Work in Stained Glass, Am Fedn Arts, 53; Craftsmen USA, 63 & Enamels USA, 65, Mus Contemp Crafts, New York; New York State Artists, Munson-Williams-Proctor Inst, 70; retrospective, List Arts Ctr, Kirkland Col, 70. Teaching: Instr painting, Cooper Union Sch Art & Archit, 37-38; instr painting & sculpture, Simon's Rock Col, 66-68; prof painting & sculpture, Kirland Col, 68-73, emer prof, 73- Bibliog: Eugene Clute (auth), Murals in vitreous enamels, 12/52 & Priscilla Ginsberg (auth), Peter Ostuni, 1/61, Craft Horizons. Style & Technique: Architectural art. Media: Oil, Vitreous Enamel, Glass, Metals. Publ: Contribr, Dimensions of design, 58 & The craftsmans world, 59. Mailing Add: 40 Harrison St Apt 22K New York NY 10013

O'SULLIVAN, DANIEL JOSEPH
PAINTER
b Brooklyn, NY, Aug 18, 40. Study: Fordham Col; Brooklyn Mus Art Sch; Pratt Graphics Ctr. Work: Commerce Trust Co, Kansas City, Mo; Wichita Art Mus; Mus of Albuquerque, NMex; also in pvt collections of Hirshhorn & Neuberger. Exhib: Brooklyn Mus, 64; New Talent Exhib, Kraushaar Galleries, New York, 73; Kalamazoo Inst Art, Mich, 74; US Dept State Art in Embassies Prog, Korea, 75; Am Acad Arts & Lett, New York, 75 & 76; one-man show, Kraushaar Galleries, New York, 75. Teaching: Instr, Brooklyn Mus Art Sch, formerly; instr, New York City Cath High Schs, presently. Awards: Purchase Award, Am Acad Arts & Lett, New York, 76. Style & Technique: Realistic. Media: Oil, Acrylic. Dealer: Kraushaar Galleries 1055 Madison Ave New York NY 10028. Mailing Add: 38 Lake St Setauket NY 11733

OSVER, ARTHUR
PAINTER
b Chicago, Ill, July 26, 12. Study: Northwestern Univ, 30-31; Art Inst Chicago, with Boris Anisfeld, 31-36. Work: Mus Mod Art; Whitney Mus Am Art; Davenport Munic Art Gallery; Peabody Mus, Salem, Mass; plus many others. Comn: Cover, Fortune Mag, 60. Exhib: Whitney Mus Am Art, 44, 45 & 63; one-man shows, Univ Fla, 52; Art: USA: Now, 64-65 & Coe Col, Cedar Rapids, Iowa, 66; retrospective, Iowa State Col, Ames, 68; plus many other group & one-man shows. Teaching: Instr painting, Brooklyn Mus Art Sch, 49-51; instr, Columbia Univ, 52 & Univ Fla, 54-55; instr painting, Cooper Union Art Sch, 55 & 58; vis critic painting, Yale Univ, 56-57; painter in residence, Am Acad Rome, 57-58; instr, Washington Univ, 60- Awards: Medal, Art Dirs Club, Chicago, 61; J Henry Schiedt Mem Prize, Pa Acad Fine Arts, 66; Sabbatical Grant, Nat Endowment Arts, Washington, DC, 66; plus many others. Bibliog: Ray Bethers (auth), How Paintings Happen, Norton, 51; Lee Nordness (ed), Art: USA: Now, C J Bucher, 62. Mailing Add: 465 Foote Ave St Louis MO 63119

OSYCZKA, BOHDAN DANNY
PAINTER, ILLUSTRATOR
b Herkimer, NY. Study: Vesper George Sch Art; Col Fine Arts, Syracuse Univ, BFA; Art Students League; also with Edward Christiana & Anthony Toney. Work: Syracuse Univ, NY; Pepsico World Hq, Purchase, Purchase, NY; Hoffman-La Roche, Nutley, NJ; Am Tel & Tel Co, New York; Int Bus Machines, New York; Pitney, Hardin & Kipp, New York; Mfrs Hanover Trust Co, Rockefeller Ctr Inc, New York. Comn: Religious murals, St Peter & Paul Ukranian Orthodox Church, Utica, 48; Painting (watercolor), Pepsico World Hq, NY, 71. Exhib: One-man shows, Ward Eggleston Galleries, New York, 65, The Katonah Gallery, NY, 71 & Silvermine Guild of Artists, New Canaan, Conn, 71; Am Watercolor Soc Ann, 70; Hudson River Mus Invitational, Yonkers, NY, 74. Pos: Juror, Westchester Art Soc, Tarrytown, NY, 71; Lectr-demonstr, The Katonah Gallery, 71-74, Kirkland Col, Clinton, NY, 74 & Hudson River Mus, Yonkers, NY, 74; instr, Parsons Sch of Design, New York, 75- Awards: Agusta Hazard Fel, Syracuse Univ, NY, 43; Andrea Gail Prize of Watercolor, Am Vet Soc Artists NY, Inc, 66; Sindin Harris Gallery Award, Hudson River Mus, Yonkers, 71 & Mus Purchase Award, 76. Bibliog: Joan Hanauer (auth), Osyczka watercolors are a Maine event, NY J Am, 3/6/65; Noel Frackman (auth), Process: earthy and oozing, Patent Trader, 4/1/71; Bella O'Hara (auth), World of arts, Stamford Advocate, 9/23/71. Mem: The Katonah Gallery, Art Lending; Silvermine Guild of Artists; Artist Equity Asn, New York; Hudson River Contemp Artists; Soc of Illustr. Style & Technique: Watercolor painting non-objective, wet on wet flow application; illustration, objective, line and multi-media. Publ: Contribr, Am Artist, 9/65. Dealer: Gallery Nine 9 E 19th St New York NY 10003. Mailing Add: Summit Ave Peekskill NY 10566

OSZE, ANDREW E
SCULPTOR, PAINTER
b Nagykanizsa, Hungary, Jan 14, 09; US citizen. Study: Acad Art, Budapest; Acad D'Unpheria, Rome, fel, 47-49. Work: Denver Art Mus; Hanley Collection, Pa; Mus Budapest; and numerous others. Comn: St John of Cross, Church, Budapest, 42; Arpad Toth, comn by Nyugat, 43; Veronica (gravestone), Budapest, 43; fountain, Rome, 48; St Francis Chapel, New York, 67. Exhib: Montclair Art Mus, 61; Far Gallery, New York, 64 & 70; De Young Mus, San Francisco, 73; Denver Art Mus, 75. Teaching: Prof sculpture, Fra Angelico Art Sch, 59-60; prof sculpture & dir, Acad Mus Arte, Lima, 63-64; prof sculpture, Cath Univ, Peru, 63-64. Awards: Grant, Peru, 62-64; Grant, France & Greece, 67. Bibliog: Arthur Elek (auth), A Osze, UJSAG, 43; William Yuhasz (auth), A Osze, Hungarian Quart, 62; George Szabo (auth), A Osze, New Horizons, 70. Mem: Col Art Asn Am. Style & Technique: Neo-figurative; synthesis of the 20th century. Media: Stone, Bronze, Wood. Publ: Auth, Universal Thought and the Arts in Modern Time, Philos Question Series 10, Learned Publ, Inc, New York. Mailing Add: 652 W 163rd St Apt 37 New York NY 10032

O'TOOLE, JAMES ST LAURENCE
ART DEALER, ART HISTORIAN
b Baltimore, Md, Nov 5, 95. Study: Md Art Inst; Loyola Col, Baltimore; Trinity Col, Dublin, Ireland, Celtic archaeol. Pos: Jacques Seligmann et Fils, Paris, France, 21-25; De Hauke et Cie, New York & Paris, 25-35; co-dir, James St L O'Toole Art Gallery, New York, 35- Mem: Sr mem Am Soc Appraisers; Fel Royal Soc Antiq of Ireland, Dublin. Specialty: American, European and Asian pre-17th to 20th century paintings, prints, drawings, sculpture and photographs. Mailing Add: 667 Madison Ave New York NY 10021

OTT, JERRY DUANE
PAINTER
b Albert Lea, Minn, July 31, 47. Study: Mankato State Col, 65-70; Univ Minn, 71. Work: Walker Art Ctr, Minneapolis; Minneapolis Inst Art; Mus Contemp Art, Tokyo, Japan; Univ Kans Mus; Stuart M Speiser Traveling Collection. Exhib: Mit Kamera, Pensil, und Spritzpistol, Reckling Hausen, Ger, 73; one-man shows, Louis K Meisel Gallery, New York, 73 & 75 & Smith Fine Art Gallery, Monte Carlo, Monaco, 74; Tokyo Biennale '74, 74; Three Centuries of American Nudes, New York Cult Ctr, 75. Style & Technique: Photo-realist figure painter. Media: Airbrush, Acrylic. Dealer: Louis K Meisel Gallery 141 Prince New York NY 10012. Mailing Add: 210 County Rd B2 East St Paul MN 55117

OTT, WENDELL LORENZ
MUSEUM DIRECTOR, PAINTER
b McCloud, Calif, Sept 17, 42. Study: San Francisco Art Inst, 60-61; Trinity Univ, San Antonio, Tex, BA, 68; Univ Ariz, Tucson, MFA, 70. Work: Witte Mem Mus, San Antonio, Tex. Exhib: Tex Painting & Sculpture, Dallas Mus Fine Arts, 66; Witte Mem Mus Ann, 68; Graphics 69, Western NMex Univ, 69; 11th Ariz Ann, Phoenix Art Mus, 69; Yuma Fine Arts Asn, Ariz, 69; Juarez Mus Art, Mex, 73; one-man shows, George Walter Vincent Smith Art Mus, Springfield, Mass, 73 & Eastern NMex Univ, Portales, 74. Pos: Dir, Roswell Mus & Art Ctr, NMex, 70- Awards: Onerdonk Award, Witte Mem Mus Ann, 68; Purchase Award, 11th Ariz Ann, Phoenix Art Mus, 69; Nat Mus Act Travel Grant, 73. Mem: Am Asn Mus; NMex Asn Mus (chmn, 73-75). Media: Oil. Mailing Add: PO Box 907 Roswell NM 88201

OTTIANO, JOHN WILLIAM
EDUCATOR, SCULPTOR
b Medford, Mass, July 23, 26. Study: Mass Col Art, BS, 54; Boston Univ, MFA, 60; Pa State Univ, DEd, 63. Work: Viktor Lowenfeld Mem, Pa State Univ; Univ Western Ill; Gloucester Co Col; Glassboro State Col. Comn: Mimosa & The Age of Miracles (murals) & two other large exterior murals, Glassboro State Col, 67, sculpture, 74; Art Educator Award, Sculpture, NJ Art Educ Asn, 69. Exhib: Pa Acad Fine Arts, Philadelphia, 64; Nat Acad Galleries, New York, 65; Art From NJ, NJ State Mus, 66-70; Sculpture in the Park, Van Suan Park, Paramus, NJ, 71; Artists Equity, Philadelphia Civic Ctr, 72. Teaching: Instr three-dimensional design & jewelry, Boston Univ, 54-60; asst prof, Mass Col Art, 61-62; prof, Pa State Univ, University Park, 62-63; prof, Glassboro State Col, 63- Awards: First for Sculpture, NJ Tercenternary, 64; Award for Sculpture, Somerset Art Asn, 73. Bibliog: Artist/Educator, Sch Arts, 2/66; article in La Rev Mod, 3/1/66. Mem: Am Asn Univ Prof; NJ Art Educ Asn (pres, 70-); NJ Designer-Craftsmen Asn (Pres, 70-72, NJ state pres, 75-); Artists Equity Asn; Nat Art Educ Asn (NJ state rep, 63-). Style & Technique: Angulated and curvilinear forms, designed in a complex and yet minimal manner, reflecting a contemporary visual statement and timeless dialogue; Cire Perdue method of casting; sheet metal fabrication. Media: Bronze, Gold, Silver. Res: The relationship between surface texture preference, personality characteristics and three-dimensional art performance. Mailing Add: 1115 Glen Lake Blvd Pitman NJ 08071

OUBRE, HAYWARD LOUIS
SCULPTOR, EDUCATOR
b New Orleans, La. Study: Dillard Univ, BA; Univ Iowa, MFA; also with Hale Woodruff, Nancy E Prophet, James Lechay, Mauricio Lasansky & Humbert Albrizio. Work: Univ Iowa Gallery, Iowa City; Atlanta Univ Gallery, Ga. Comn: Ram (wire sculpture), Winston-Salem State Univ Libr, 65. Exhib: Six States Exhib, Joslyn Mem Mus, Omaha, Nebr, 47; Northwest Printmakers, Seattle Art Mus, Wash, 48; John & Mable Ringling Mus, Sarasota, Fla, 48; Ball State Ann Exhib, Muncie, Ind, 60-62; Madison Gallery Exhib, New York, 62; plus many others. Teaching: Chmn painting & sculpture, Fla A&M Univ, Tallahassee, 48-49; chmn drawing & painting, Ala State Univ, Montgomery, 49-65; chmn drawing & painting, Winston-Salem State Univ, 65- Awards: First Prize for Trailerview (oil), Iowa State Fair, 47; First Prize for Crown of Thorns (wire), Atlanta Univ, 58 & Second Prize for Equivocal Fox (painting), 68; plus many others. Bibliog: Art of wire sculpture, Design Mag, 62, 68 & 71. Mem: Southeastern Art Asn; Nat Conf Artists. Style & Technique: Wire sculpture non-welded technique. Res: Designed & copyrighted, Colorwheel with Four Intensity Bands, 62, Colorchart with Three Intensity Bands, 66; corrected color triangle devised by Johann Wolfgang Von Goethe, 76; designed Four Intensity Bank Color Wheel, 77. Publ: Auth, Directions of modern art, Art Rev Mag, 66. Mailing Add: 2422 Pickford Ct Winston-Salem NC 27101

OUTTERBRIDGE, JOHN WILFRED
ART ADMINISTRATOR, PAINTER, SCULPTOR
b Greenville, NC, Mar 12, 33. Study: Agr & Tech Univ, Greensboro, NC; Am Art Acad, Chicago, with Vernon Stakey. Work: Oakland Mus, Calif; Mills Col, Oakland; Calif State Col,

San Jose; Compton Community Col, Calif; Med Facility, Watts, Univ Southern Calif, Los Angeles. Comn: Mural collages (mixed-media), Communicative Arts Acad, Compton, 70; ceramic mural (with John Riddle, Jr), pvt physician, Compton, 70; Oh Speak, Speak (sculptural concept; photog doc destroyed by fire), Studio Watts Endowment Fund & Exxon Corp, 71; Ethnic Heritage Doll Ser (five units), Studio Watts Endowment Fund, 77. Exhib: Oakland Mus, 67; 6th & 9th Southern Calif Ann, Long Beach Mus Art, 68 & 70; Los Angeles Co Mus Art, Los Angeles, 69; Dimensions in Black Art, La Jolla Mus Contemp Art, Calif, 70; St Art by Black Am, Merabash Mus, Willingboro, NJ, 75; W Coast Artists, Studio Mus of Harlem, New York, 77. Teaching: Instr assemblage & sculpture, Pasadena Art Mus, 67-70; lectr art hist, Calif State Col, Dominguez Hills, 67-71. Pos: Painter/designer, Art Craft, Div Traid Corp, Burbank, 64-68; artistic dir, Communicative Arts Acad, Compton, 69-75, mem bd dir, presently; dir, Watts Towers Arts Ctr, Munic Arts Dept, City of Los Angeles, 75-; mem bd artists, Brockman Gallery, Productions, Inc, Los Angeles, presently; mem, Nat Conf Artists, Va Commonwealth Univ, Richmond, presently. Awards: First Place/Sculpture, Westwood Art Asn, 67; Our Auth Study Club Award, Los Angeles Area Artists, 67; Nat Conf Artists Award, 75. Bibliog: Samella Lewis (auth), John Outterbridge/Black Artist (film), Contemp Crafts Inc, 68; article in Wilson Libr Bull, 4/69; Elton C Fax (auth), Black Artists of the New Generation, Dodd, Mead & Co, 77. Mem: Calif Confedn of Arts, Los Angeles; Advocates for the Arts. Style & Technique: A great variety of materials used in a mixed-media approach, in confirmation of the belief that all things in life have value; sculptural concepts have an appeal because of the solution of technical problems. Mailing Add: PO Box 1445 South Pasadena CA 91030

OVERLAND, CARLTON EDWARD
CURATOR, ART HISTORIAN
b Stoughton, Wis, Feb 28, 42. Study: St Olaf Col, BA; Univ Wis-Madison, MA. Collections Arranged: 20th Century Graphics: The Hollaender Collection, 74. Teaching: Instr art hist, Univ Northern Iowa, Cedar Falls, 68-70. Pos: Cur prints & drawings, Elvehjem Art Ctr, Madison, Wis, 72-77, cur collections, 77- Mem: Am Asn Mus. Mailing Add: 5113 Sherwood Rd Madison WI 53711

OWEN, BILL
PAINTER, SCULPTOR
b Gila Bend, Ariz, Jan 23, 42. Work: Whitney Mus, Buffalo Bill Hist Ctr, Cody, Wyo; Phoenix Art Mus; Leanin' Tree Mus, Boulder, Colo. Exhib: Cowboy Artists Am, Phoenix, Ariz, 74-77; Tex Art Gallery, Dallas, 74 & 75; Marlboro Bicentennial Traveling Show, Louisville, Ky, 75; Whitney Mus, Buffalo Bill Hist Ctr, 75; Trailside Gallery, Scottsdale, Ariz, 75-77; Tex Art Gallery, Dallas, 76; Renaissance W Premier, Minneapolis, 77; plus others. Awards: Franklin Mint Gold Medal for Western Art, Pa, 74. Bibliog: Bill Owen, Franklin Mint, 74; Cowboy Artists of America 1974, 75-77 & Ten Years with the Cowboy Artists of America, 76, Northland Press. Awards: Cowboy Artists of Am Mem Award, 76 & Men's Arts Coun Award, 77, Cowboy Artists of Am Exhib. Mem: Cowboy Artists Am (secy-treas, 74-75, bd dir, 76-77, pres, 77-78). Style & Technique: Realistic rendition of contemporary cowboy in oil, with preliminary pencil sketching for all paintings; brush technique; finished sculpture cast in bronze. Media: Oil; Wax, Clay. Mailing Add: PO Box 95 Flagstaff AZ 86001

OWEN, FRANK (FRANKLIN CHARLES OWEN)
PAINTER
b Kalispell, Mont, May 13, 39. Study: Antioch Col; Calif State Univ Sacramento; Univ Calif, Davis, BA & MA. Work: Corcoran Gallery of Art, Washington, DC; Albright-Knox Art Gallery, Buffalo, NY; St Louis Art Mus, Mo; Des Moines Art Ctr, Iowa; Madison Art Ctr, Wis; plus others. Exhib: 32nd Corcoran Biennial, Washington, DC, 71; Madison Art Ctr Exhib, 73; Greenburg Gallery, St Louis, 73; 15th Nat Exhib of Contemp Am Painting & Sculpture, Univ Ill, 74; 71st Ann Exhib, Art Inst Chicago, 74; Soho in Berlin, Berlin Kunstmuseum, WGer, 76; one-man shows, Leo Castelli Gallery, 72, 75 & Sable-Castelli Gallery, Toronto, 77. Teaching: Instr painting, Calif State Univ, Sacramento, 67-68; instr instr fine arts, Sch Visual Arts, New York, 70- Bibliog: Peter Schedjahl (auth), Six painters of the 70s, Ackland Art Ctr, NC, 73; Douglas Davis (auth), Painter's painters, Newsweek, 5/13/74. Style & Technique: Abstract paintings. Dealer: Leo Castelli Gallery 420 W Broadway New York NY 10012. Mailing Add: 450 Broadway New York NY 10013

OWENS, AL CURTIS
PAINTER, DRAFTSMAN
b San Angelo, Tex, May 29, 33. Study: San Bernardino Valley Col; Allied Inst Japan; art instr (corresp), Minneapolis, Minn; Allied Inst Technol, Chicago. Work: Albuquerque High Sch, Albuquerque Pub Schs, NMex. Comn: Mural, African Methodist Episcopal Church, San Angelo, Tex, 51; St Mark Baptist Church, 55 & Temple Baptist Church, 63, San Bernardino, Calif. Exhib: Nat AAA Poster, 51; Mus NMex Biennial, Santa Fe, 67; Newman Ctr, Univ NMex, 67; NMex Highlands Univ, Las Vegas, NMex, 72; 23rd Grand Prix Int de Peinture de Deauville, France, 72. Awards: Nat AAA Auto Poster, 51; Liturgical Arts Festival, First Methodist Church, Redlands, Calif, 65; 23rd Grand Prix Int, Deauville, France, 72. Mem: San Bernardino Art Asn; NMex Art League; Friends of Art; Albuquerque Art Coun; NMex Arts Comn. Style & Technique: Informal, figurative & non-objective; light; work source, the Holy Bible, King James Version. Publ: Illusr, Insight Out, 65; contribr, New Mexico Mag, 1/68; contribr, Mod Rev Mag, France, 72; illusr, cover design, NMex Arts Comn Ann Report, 73. Mailing Add: 602 Broadway SE Albuquerque NM 87102

OWENS, MARY (MARY LOUIS SCHNORE)
PAINTER
b Des Moines, Iowa, Dec 4, 35. Study: State Univ NY, Buffalo, BS, 57; Albright-Knox Art Sch, with Sam Amato, Buffalo, 53-54. Work: Los Angeles Water & Power Credit Union Corp Hq, Los Angeles; Citybank Int, San Francisco; Fluor Corp Hq, Irvine, Calif; State Univ NY, Buffalo. Exhib: Watercolor Calif Ann Exhib of Artists, Los Angeles Co Mus Art, Los Angeles, 61; 56th Ann Nat April Art Exhib, Springville Mus Art, Utah, 77; Watercolor USA, Springfield Art Mus, Mo, 77; Rocky Mt Nat Watermedia Exhib, Golden, Colo, 77; 57th Ann Traveling Exhib, Nat Watercolor Soc, 77; one-person shows, Pac Basin Ser, Janus Gallery, Venice, Calif, 76 & Watercolor Exhib, Brand Libr Art Galleries, Glendale, Calif, 77. Awards: Golden CofC Award, Rocky Mt Watermedia Exhib, 77. Mem: Nat Watercolor Soc. Style & Technique: Universality in subject matter-strong feelings towards nature often bordering on the mystical. Media: Watercolor, Oil. Dealer: Janus Gallery 21 Market St Venice CA 90291. Mailing Add: 2436 Langdale Ave Los Angeles CA 90041

OWENS, TENNYS BOWERS
ART DEALER
b Washington, DC, June 25, 40. Study: St Mary's Jr Col, Raleigh, NC; Eastern Carolina Univ, Greenville, NC. Pos: Owner, Artique Ltd, 71- Specialty: General art merchandise, prints, paintings, sculpture and pottery. Mailing Add: c/o Artique Ltd 314 G St Anchorage AK 99501

OWINGS, MARGARET WENTWORTH
PAINTER, COLLAGE IN STITCHERY
b Berkeley, Calif, Apr 29, 13. Study: Mills Col, AB, 34; Radcliffe Col, 35. Exhib: One-woman shows, painting, Santa Barbara Mus Art, 40, Stanford Art Gallery, 51 & Feingarten Gallery, San Francisco, 58 & 60; stitchery, M H De Young Mus, San Francisco, 63; stitchery, Int Folk Art Mus, Santa Fe, 65. Mem: Fel Calif Acad Sci. Mailing Add: Big Sur CA 93920

OWSLEY, DAVID THOMAS
MUSEUM CURATOR
b Dallas, Tex, Aug 20, 29. Study: Harvard Col, AB, 51; Inst Fine Arts, NY Univ, MFA, 62. Collections Arranged: Decorative Arts Collection & Ailsa Mellon Bruce Collection, Carnegie Inst Mus Art. Pos: Fel, Am Wing, Metrop Mus Art; asst cur decorative arts & sculpture, Mus Fine Arts, Boston; visitor, Victoria & Albert Mus, London, Eng; cur antiquities, Oriental & decorative arts, Carnegie Inst Mus Art, presently. Mailing Add: Carnegie Inst Mus Art 4400 Forbes Ave Pittsburgh PA 15213

OWYANG, JUDITH FRANCINE
ART CRITIC
b Sacramento, Calif, Feb 9, 40. Study: Univ Southern Calif, BA, with Edward S Peck & jour with Jack C Searles. Pos: Art ed & columnist, Santa Monica Eve Outlook, 70- Mem: Kappa Pi. Mailing Add: c/o Santa Monica Evening Outlook 1540 Third St Santa Monica CA 90406

OZONOFF, IDA
PAINTER
b La Crosse, Wis, July 27, 04. Study: State Teachers Col, Milwaukee, grad, 24; Milwaukee Downer Col, 58 & 59; Univ Wis-Milwaukee, 60-64 & 69-70. Work: Print Div, Smithsonian Inst, Washington, DC; Milwaukee Pub Schs; Univ Wis, Fond du Lac Campus; Abilene Fine Arts Mus, Tex; Carleton Col, Northfield, Minn. Exhib: Walker Art Ctr Exhib, Minn, 64; Butler Inst Am Art, Ohio, 65, 67 & 68; Audubon Artists Exhib, New York, 66, 68 & 69; Nat Acad Design Exhib, New York, 68 & 69; Allied Artists Am Exhib, New York, 70; West Bend Gallery Fine Arts, Wis, 76 & 77; Univ Wis Alumni Exhib, 78. Awards: Purchase Award, Western Publ, 66; Benjamin Altman First Prize, Nat Acad Design, 68; Carleton Col Purchase Award, Charles E Merrill Trust Fund, 75. Mem: Wis Arts Coun; Collectors Gallery, Milwaukee Art Ctr. Style & Technique: Oil painting with collage on Masonite; collagraphs. Mailing Add: 500 W Bradley Rd-C217 Milwaukee WI 53217

P

PABLO (PAUL BURGESS EDWARDS)
PAINTER, EDUCATOR
b Moulton, Iowa, Feb 18, 34. Study: Iowa Wesleyan Col, with S Carl Fracassini, BA, 55; Wichita State Univ, with Robert Kiskadden, MA, 59. Work: Iowa Wesleyan Col Art Dept; Wichita State Univ Art Dept; Wichita Art Mus; Miami Beach Pub Libr; Citizens Libr, Washington, Pa. Comn: Mosaic mural, Halstead Hosp Lobby, 59. Exhib: 29th Ann Nat Graphics Art Show, Wichita Art Asn, 60 & 19th Ann Nat Decorative Arts Show, 66; Ann Juror's Award Show, Huntington Gallery, WVa, 65; Max 24, Nat Small Painting Show, Purdue Univ, 66; 2nd Nat Polymer Exhib, Eastern Mich Univ, 68. Teaching: Instr ceramics, Wichita State Univ, summer 62; asst prof sculpture & ceramics, West Liberty State Col, 63-66; chmn dept painting & drawing, Washington & Jefferson Col, 66- Pos: Co-dir, Bottega Art Gallery, Wichita, 60-62; pres, Wichita Artists Guild, 61-62; dir, Gallery 319, Wichita, 62-63. Awards: E D Caldwell Award First Prize, Bethany Col Ann, 64; First Prize, Oglebay Inst Summer Show, 64; Juror's Best of Show Award, Huntington Gallery, 65. Mem: Col Art Asn Am; Arts Coun Washington Co (pres & founding mem, 69-73); Nat Asn Arts Adminr. Style & Technique: Pop hard-edge realism. Media: Acrylic, Oil. Publ: Illusr, Nonverbal Communication, Vol 5, In: Communication Science & Technology Series, Marcel Dekker, Inc, 74. Dealer: Jean & Bob Kline c/o The Country Studio RD 1 Hadley PA 16130. Mailing Add: 268 E Wheeling Washington DC 15301

PACE, MARGARET BOSSHARDT
DESIGNER, PAINTER
b San Antonio, Tex, Dec 9, 19. Study: Newcomb Col, BFA; Trintiy Univ; Univ Tex; also with Will Stevens, Etienne Ret & Xavier Gonzalez. Work: In pvt collections. Comn: Murals, Victoria Plaza, Golden Age Ctr, 60; mosaic murals, St Lukes Episcopal Church, San Antonio, 59, Episcopal Diocesan Ctr, Diocese of WTex, 61 & Episcopal Cathedral, 65; designed & executed chalice, pattern & pix, ordination of Father Braun, Pinckneyville, Ill, 69. Exhib: Tex Ann, 58, 59 & 69; Contemp Artists Group, Mexico City Consulate, 65 & 68; Religious Art, Hemisfair, 68; Trinity Univ, San Antonio, 69; Artists Inst Tex Cult, 69; Univ Gallery, Auckland, NZ; San Antonio Artists Ann, 75-77; SW Craft Ctr, San Antonio, 75-78; Contemp Women in Tex Art Int Exhib, Laguna Gloria Mus, Austin, 76; Tex Watercolor Soc Ann, 76 & 77; Sol Del Rio Gallery, San Antonio, 77; Women Who Influenced the Art Community of San Antonio, Tex Health Sci Ctr, 77; plus many other group & one-man shows. Teaching: Instr, Incarnet Word Col, 64-65; asst prof art, San Antonio Col, 65-72; design-watercolor, Hill Country Found, 70- Pos: Bd mem & vpres, San Antonio Art Inst; bd mem, Friends of McNay Mus, San Antonio, 67-72; Southwest Craft Ctr, 69-78; nat pres alumni bd, Newcomb Col, Tulane Univ, mem pres coun, 76-78, mem alumni bd, 77-; 1st vpres design & planning, Pace-Picante Inc. Awards: Henry Steinbomer Award, Tex Watercolor Soc, 49 & 66; Grumbacher Purchase Award, 60; Richard Kleberg Purchase Award, 62; plus many others. Mem: San Antonio Art League (bd mem, 67-68); Tex Fine Arts Asn; Tex Watercolor Soc; Contemp Artists Group; San Antonio Craft Guild; plus others. Mailing Add: 208 Morningside Dr San Antonio TX 78209

PACE, STEPHEN S
PAINTER, PRINTMAKER
b Charleston, Mo, Dec 12, 18. Study: Inst Allende, San Miguel Allende, Mex; Acad Grande Chaumiere, Paris; Inst Arte Statale, Florence, Italy; Art Students League, with Cameron Booth & Morris Cantor; Hans Hofmann Sch. Work: Whitney Mus Am Art, New York; Univ Calif, Berkeley; James Michener Found, Univ Tex, Austin; Walker Art Ctr, Minneapolis; Des Moines Art Ctr. Exhib: Int Watercolor Exhib, Brooklyn Mus, 53 & 55; Whitney Ann, 53, 54, 57, 58 & 61; Carnegie Int, Pittsburgh, 55; Int Biennial, Japan, selected by Mus of Mod Art, New York, 57; Recent Am Watercolors, circulated by MOMA, France, 57 & 58; Paths of Abstract Art, Cleveland Mus, 60; Walker Art Ctr, 62; Columbus Gallery of Fine Arts, 62; Kalamazoo Art Ctr, Mich, 62; James Michener Collection, traveling exhib to Australia, 64 & to Ger & Rumania, 73; Abstract Watercolors by 14 Americans, Mus of Mod Art, tour of Europe, Asia & Australia, 64-66; 10-Yr Retrospective, Des Moines Art Ctr, 70; Univ Tex Art

Mus, 70; Recent Acquisitions, Boston Mus of Fine Arts, 77; one-man shows, Howard Wise Gallery, New York, 60, 61, 63 & 64 & A M Sachs Gallery, New York, 74, 76 & 78. Teaching: Artist in residence, Washington Univ, spring-summer 59; instr art, Pratt Inst, 61-68; instr art sem, Univ Calif, Berkeley, spring 68; prof art, Am Univ, 75- Awards: Dolia Lorian Award to promising painters, 54; Hallmark Co Purchase Award, 61. Bibliog: Hubert Crehan (auth), A change of pace, Art News, 4/64; Russell Arnold (auth), Paintings by Stephen Pace, Crucible, fall 65; Denver Lindley (auth), In a landscape (film), 69-71. Media: Oil, Watercolor, Monotype, Prints. Mailing Add: 345 W 29th St New York NY 10001

PACHECO, MARIA LUISA
PAINTER
b La Paz, Bolivia, Oct 22, 19; US citizen. Study: Acad de Bellas Artes, La Paz; Real Acad San Fernando, Madrid, Spain; also with Daniel Vazquez, Diaz, Madrid. Work: Guggenheim Mus, New York; Mass Inst Technol; Pan-Am Union, Washington, DC; Mus Mod Art, Sao Paulo & Rio de Janeiro, Brazil; Mus Art, Dallas. Comn: Triptych, Mobil Oil Labs, Princeton, NJ, 71. Exhib: 2nd, 3rd & 5th Biennial, Mus Mod Art, Sao Paulo, 51, 53 & 57; Contemporary Painting & Sculpture, Urbana, Ill, 63; Tredicesimo Premio Lissone, Italy, 63; Magnet: New York, 65; Emergent Decade, Guggenheim Mus, New York, 66. Awards: Guggenheim Fel Award, 58 & 60; Award for Painting, Biennial Sao Paulo, 59; Acquisition Prize, Pan-Am Union, 59. Bibliog: Jorge Romero Brest (auth), Art and architecture, L'art de L'Amerique Latine, Art Int, 64; Leopoldo Castedo (auth), History of Latin America, Praeger World Art Series, 69; Jackeline Bernitz (auth), Review 75, Ctr Inter-Am Rel, New York, 75. Mem: Mus Mod Art, New York. Style & Technique: Archeological and mountain shapes translated into semi-abstract shapes; techniques of collage. Media: Wood & Sand, Acrylic & Oil on Canvas. Dealer: Lee Ault & Co 25 E 77th St New York NY 10021. Mailing Add: 65-10 99th St Rego Park NY 11937

PACHNER, WILLIAM
PAINTER
b Brtnice, Czech, Apr 7, 15; US citizen. Study: Acad Arts & Crafts, Vienna, Austria. Work: Whitney Mus Am Art, New York; Butler Inst Am Art, Youngstown, Ohio; Fort Worth Art Ctr, Tex; Iowa State Teacher's Col. Exhib: Carnegie Inst Int, Pittsburgh; Whitney Mus Am Art Ann; Corcoran Gallery Art Biennial, Washington, DC; Pa Acad Fine Arts, Philadelphia; US Fine Arts Pavilion, New York World's Fair, 65. Teaching: Instr painting & drawing, Art Students League, 69-70. Awards: Am Acad Arts & Lett Award, 49; Ford Found Awards, 59-64; Guggenheim Fel, 60. Bibliog: Kenneth Donahue (auth), William Pachner, Am Fedn Arts, 59. Media: Oil, Watercolor, Ink. Mailing Add: 962 Ohayo Mountain Rd Woodstock NY 12498

PACIFIC, GERTRUDE
PAINTER, DESIGNER
b Victoria, BC, July 21, 42. Study: Univ Wash, BA(painting), 64 & MFA(painting), 65; additional study with Alden Mason. Work: Whatcom Mus of Hist & Art, Bellingham, Wash; Seattle City Light, City of Seattle, Wash; Wash State Dept of Hwys, Olympia. Exhib: Art of the Pac NW, Smithsonian Inst, Washington, DC, 74; Skagit Valley Artists, Seattle Art Mus, Wash, 74; Am Landscape, Trenton Art Mus, NJ, 76; Gertrude Pacific, Art Gallery of Greater Victoria, BC, 77. Pos: Cur design, Thomas Burke Mem, Wash State Mus, 69- Bibliog: Tom Robbins (auth), Goddess of the on-ramp, Seattle Post-Intelligencer, 73; Martha Kingsbury (auth), Art of the Pacific Northwest, Smithsonian Inst, Washington, DC, 74; Charles Cee Brown (auth), Gertrude Pacific—oyster light, Art Gallery of Greater Victoria, BC, 77. Style & Technique: Realism from multiple sources. Media: Acrylic Paint on Canvas. Dealer: Foster-White Gallery 311 1/2 Occidental S Seattle WA 98102. Mailing Add: No 41 1907 First Ave Seattle WA 98101

PACILEO, DOLORES MARGARET
ENVIRONMENTAL ARTIST, ART ADMINISTRATOR
b Queens, NY, July 2, 44. Study: Pratt Inst, BFA, 71; Art Students League, 66; Goddard Col, MA, 72; Antioch Univ, PhD(fine arts), 74, with Nancy Graves & Louise Bourgeois. Work: Neue Galerie, Aachen, Ger; Helene Wurlitzer Found, NMex; Mus am Ostwall, Dortmund, Ger. Comn: Environmental Sculpture, Maryhaven Home for Exceptional Children, NY, 74; Environment & Dance, Univ Chicago, 74; Environmental Sculptures, Lighthouse for the Blind, New York, 75 & Columbia Presby Hosp, New York, 76. Exhib: Art Today: USA, Iran-Am House, Tehran, Iran, 75; Botanische Kunst, Mus am Ostwall, Dortmund, Ger, 75; Environment 76, Denver Mus, Colo, 76; Playground on the Sea, Brooklyn Mus, NY & Boston Children's Mus, 76; Der Ball, Neue Galerie, Aachen, Ger, 77; Documenta 6, Kassel, Ger, 77. Teaching: Peer PhD comt, Union Grad Sch, Yellow Springs, Ohio, 76-77; adj prof fine arts, Southampton Col, NY, 76-77. Pos: Exec dir & founder, Children's Inst of Res & Design Inc, New York, 76- Awards: Fulbright-Hayes Res Grant, DAAD, Dusseldorf, Ger, 72-73; Three Awards for Environmental Design, Environment 76, Denver Mus, 75; Prof Res Grant in Environmental Design, Archit & Environmental Arts Div, Nat Endowment for the Arts, 76-77. Bibliog: Joseph Gatto (auth), Cities, Davis Publ, Worcester, Mass, 77. Mem: Nat Children's Island, Washington, DC (bd dir, 76-78); Children's Inst Res & Design Inc (pres bd, 77-78). Style & Technique: Multisensory participatory environmental art/design, with emphasis on the theory of loose parts through mixed-media. Media: Interplay between Soft and Hard Materials through Technological Advances. Res: Affects of environmental arts on education, therapy and play through interdisciplinary approaches of the arts, sciences and technology. Mailing Add: PO Box 432 Sound Beach NY 11789

PACKER, CLAIR LANGE
PAINTER, WRITER
b Geuda Springs, Kans, Aug 27, 01. Study: Univ NMex, Taos, with Millard Sheets & Barse Miller; also with Harry Anthony De Young, San Antonio, Tex & Paul Barr, Grand Forks, NDak. Work: Gilcrease Mus, Tulsa, Okla. Exhib: Philbrook Mus, Tulsa; Houston Mus; Gilcrease Mus, Tulsa; Elizabet Ney Mus, Austin; Dallas Mus. Teaching: Instr pvt art classes, San Antonio & Tulsa. Pos: Artist, San Antonio Express, 46-48; instr art, Littlehouse Gallery, San Antonio, 47-48; artist, Tulsa World, 48-65. Awards: Honorable Mention for Watercolor, Houston Mus; Gilcrease Mus Purchase Prize for Watercolor, Fourth Nat Bank, Tulsa. Style & Technique: Action sketches of rodeo contestants; landscapes, Indians, cowboys and marines. Media: Watercolor, Oil, Crayon. Publ: Auth & illusr, articles in Western Publ; auth & illusr, articles in Tulsa World Sunday Mag & Tulsa World Ranch & Farm World; auth, articles in Lapidary J & Gun Report Mag. Mailing Add: RR4 Box 173A Chandler OK 74834

PADOVANO, ANTHONY JOHN
SCULPTOR, LECTURER
b Brooklyn, NY, July 19, 33. Study: Carnegie Inst Technol; Pratt Inst; Columbia Univ, with Oronzio Maldarelli. Work: Whitney Mus Am Art, New York; Nat Collection Fine Arts, Washington, DC; Univ Ill; John Herron Art Inst; Storm King Art Ctr, NY. Comn: Sculpture In The Park, Parks Dept, New York, 68; design, NY State Art Awards, NY State Coun Arts, 69; sculpture, World Trade Ctr, Port Authority NY & NJ, 70; three arcs, donated by Trammel & Crow Co for City of Dallas, 72; sculpture, Nebr Bicentennial Sculpture Corp, 76. Exhib: 3rd Mostra Arte Figurative Int, Rome, Italy, 61; Young Am, Whitney Mus Am Art, 65; Am Sculpture, Mus Mod Art, 66; Am Express Pavilion, New York World's Fair, 66; Inauguration of Nat Collection Fine Arts, Washington, DC, 67. Teaching: Asst prof sculpture, Columbia Univ; asst prof sculpture, Univ Conn, 72; adj asst prof sculpture, Queens Col (NY), 72. Pos: Adv mem, NJ State Coun Arts, 65-67. Awards: Prix de Rome, Am Acad Rome, 60; Guggenheim Found Fel, 64; Ford Found Purchase Award, 66. Bibliog: Young talent, Art Am, 65; James Mellow (auth), article in New York Times Sun Rev, 4/70. Mem: Sculptors Guild (vpres, 68-69); Silvermine Guild Artists. Media: Metal, Concrete. Dealer: James Graham Gallery 1014 Madison Ave New York NY 10021. Mailing Add: RD 1 Box 219 Putnam Valley NY 10579

PADULA, FRED DAVID
FILM MAKER, PHOTOGRAPHER
b Santa Barbara, Calif, Oct 25, 37. Study: Univ Calif, Santa Barbara; Calif State Univ, San Francisco, BA(music), with Jack Welpott, Don Worth & Wynn Bullock, MA(art). Work: George Eastman House, Rochester, NY; San Francisco Mus Art; Oakland Mus Art; Kalamazoo Art Ctr, Mich; Crocker Mus Art, Sacramento, Calif. Comn: Photo murals, George Stevens, Hollywood, Calif, 64; Children's Letters to God (film), Lee Mendelson, San Francisco, 68; Navaho (film), Pub Broadcast Lab, KQED-TV, San Francisco, 68; S F Mix (film), Ford Found, 70; film, Am Film Inst. Exhib: 30 Photographers Nat Exhib, Buffalo, NY, 64; one-man shows, San Francisco Mus, 64, George Eastman House, 68 & DeYoung Mus, San Francisco, 69; Mus Mod Art, New York, 67; completion & premiere showing of El Capitan (film), San Francisco Mus of Mod Art, 78. Teaching: Lectr photo & film making, San Francisco State Univ, 63- & Univ Calif, San Francisco, 66-71; resident artist, Univ Minn, Minneapolis, 70. Pos: Judge, Int Color Slide Exhib, 67, San Francisco Int Film Festival, 68 & Foot Hill Int Independent Film Makers Festival, 68; mem selection comt, US Art in the Embassies, 68; mem bd dirs, Canyon Cinema Coop, 71- Awards: Zellerbach Award, San Francisco Int Film Festival, 65; Popoli Ethnographic Film Festival Religious Experience, 66; Am Film Inst Grant. Bibliog: Callenbach (auth), Ephesus, Film Quart, Univ Calif, winter 66-67; Winston (auth), American film maker, Melbourne Art Rev, fall 68; Hoffmann (auth), Ephesus, Weg Zum Nachbarn, Oberhausen, Ger, 68. Style & Technique: Color abstract; impressionistic. Dealer: Canyon Cinema Coop Rm 220 Indust Ctr Bldg Sausalito CA 94941. Mailing Add: 47 Shell Rd Mill Valley CA 94941

PAEFF, BASHKA (BASHKA PAEFF WAXMAN)
SCULPTOR
b Minsk, Russia, Aug 12, 93. Study: Boston Mus Sch Fine Arts, with Bela Pratt, 14; also in Paris, France. Work: Mass Inst Technol; Grad Ctr, Radcliffe Col, Cambridge; Boston Mus Fine Arts; Harvard Univ; Rockefeller Inst, NY; plus others. Comn: Life size bas-relief, Justice Oliver Wendell Holmes, Harvard Law Libr; bas-relief, Jan Addams, Addams House, Philadelphia; bronze reliefs, Dr Southard, Harvard Med Libr, Dir Augusta Bronmer, Judge Baker Found, Boston & Dr Martin Luther King, Jr, Boston Univ, 69; plus others. Exhib: One-man show, Boston Guild Artists, 59; Nat Acad Design; Nat Sculpture Soc; Johns Hopkins Art Ctr. Pos: Mem bd, Cambridge Art Asn. Awards: Medal, Tercentenary Expos, Boston, 33; Daniel Chester French Medal, Nat Acad Design, 69. Mem: Guild Boston Artists; fel Nat Sculpture Soc. Media: Bronze, Marble. Mailing Add: 21 Foster St Cambridge MA 02138

PAGE, ADDISON FRANKLIN
MUSEUM DIRECTOR
b Princeton, Ky, Oct 9, 11. Study: Wayne State Univ, BFA & MA. Collections Arranged: 19 Canadian Painters, 62; Reg Butler: A Retrospective Exhibition, 63; Treasures of Chinese Art, 65; The Figure in Sculpture 1865-1965, 65; Treasures of Persian Art, 66; Indian Buddhist Sculpture, 68; The Sirak Collection, 68; Ciechanowiecki Collection of Gilt and Gold Medals and Plaquettes, 69; 19th Century French Sculpture: Monuments for the Middle Class, 71. Teaching: Instr sculpture, Wayne State Univ, 47-55, instr hist sculpture, 55-58; instr hist mod art, Cranbrook Acad Art, 58-62. Pos: Jr cur educ, Detroit Inst Arts, 47-58, cur contemp art, 58-62; dir, J B Speed Art Mus, 62- Mem: Mich Sculpture Soc (chmn, 50); Mich Watercolor Soc (bd mem, 60); Asn Art Mus Dirs. Publ: Auth, Modern Sculpture: a Handbook, 50 & Diego Rivera's Detroit Frescoes: a Handbook, 55, Detroit Inst Arts. Mailing Add: J B Speed Art Mus 2035 S Third St Louisville KY 40208

PAGE, BILL
PAINTER, EDUCATOR
b Lumberton, NC, Sept 25, 48. Study: Pembroke State Univ, BA; Univ Ga, MFA; also with Graham Collier, Lamar Dodd, Albert Christ-Janer & James Herbert. Work: Tomme Call Mem Collection, Delmar Col; Montgomery Mus Fine Arts, Ala; Am Contemp Arts & Slide Libr, Palm Beach, Fla. Exhib: 34th Ann Exhib Contemp Am Paintings, Palm Beach, 72; 6th Washington & Jefferson Univ Nat Painting Show, 74; one-man show, Rabinovitch & Guerra Gallery, New York, 76; 67th Ann Exhib, Birmingham Mus Art, 75; 39th Ann Midyear Show, Butler Inst Art, Youngstown, Ohio, 75. Teaching: Asst prof art, Jacksonville State Univ, 72- Pos: Painting exhib juror, 6th Ann SC Festival Flowers, Greenwood, 73. Awards: Atwater Kent Award, Soc Four Arts, Palm Beach, 72; Second Award, Birmingham Art Asn, 74; Honorable Mention, Dakota Art Gallery, Rapid City, 75. Mem: Col Art Asn; Ala Watercolor Soc; Birmingham Art Asn. Style & Technique: Female figures; animals; landscape; fantasy imagery; full color palette. Media: Acrylic on Canvas; Gouche & Watercolor. Publ: Contribr, Soundings '75 (literary mag), Jacksonville State Univ, 75. Dealer: Nonson Gallery 133 Wooster St New York NY 10012; Dick Jemison Gallery 929 1/2 S 22nd St Birmingham AL 35205. Mailing Add: PO Box 758 Jacksonville AL 36265

PAGE, JOHN HENRY, JR
PRINTMAKER, PAINTER
b Ann Arbor, Mich, Jan 18, 23. Study: Minneapolis Sch Art; Art Students League; Univ Mich, BDesign; Univ Iowa, MFA. Work: Libr Cong, Washington, DC; Walker Art Ctr, Minneapolis; Des Moines Art Ctr, Iowa; Joslyn Art Mus, Omaha, Nebr; Carnegie Inst, Pittsburgh. Comn: Memberships Print, Des Moines Art Ctr, 69. Exhib: Young American Printmakers, Mus Mod Art, New York, 53; 10th Nat Print Show, Brooklyn Mus, 56; Art USA, Northern Ill Univ, 71; Nine Iowa Artists, Gov Exhib, 71-72; Midwest Printmaker Invitational, Walker Art Ctr, Minneapolis, 73; plus others. Teaching: Prof printmaking, Univ Northern Iowa, 54-; chmn dept art, Univ Omaha, 60-61. Awards: Pennell Purchase Prize, Libr Cong, 64; Younker Prize for Prints, Des Moines Art Ctr, 71; Nat Endowment Arts, Individual Artist Fel, 74; Purchase Prize & Cash Award, Fourth Ann Midwestern Printmaking & Drawing Competition, Tulsa, Okla, 77; plus others. Mem: Col Art Asn Am. Dealer: Jane Haslem Gallery 2121 P St NW Washington DC 20034; Suzanne Kohn Gallery 1690 Grand St Paul MN 55105. Mailing Add: 1615 Tremont Cedar Falls IA 50613

PAGE, ROBIN
PAINTER
b London, Eng, Nov 2, 32. Study: Vancouver Sch of Art, BC, 52-54. Work: Mus Folkwang, Essen. Exhib: Young West Coast Painters, Vancouver, 53; W Coast Hard Edge, Seattle, Wash, 54; Festival of Misfits, Gallery One, London, 62; Fluxus Festival, Nice, France, 63; Cross Section, City Mus, Leicester, 64; Form & Image, City Mus, Leeds, 66; Concert of Experimental Music, Commonwealth Inst, London, 68; Amadou in A, Antwerp, Belg, 69; Happening & Fluxus, Kunstverein, Cologne, 70; Documenta 5, Kassel, WGer, 72; 6th Int Triennial of Coloured Graphic Prints, Grenchen, Switz, 73; Holz-Kunst-Stoff, Staatliche Kunsthalle, Baden-Baden, WGer, 76; one-man shows, Kunstverein, Cologne, 73 & Salon de Mai, Paris, 70, 71 & 74. Teaching: Guest lectr, High Wycombe Col for Further Educ, Buckinghamshire, Leicester Col of Art & Coventry Col of Art, 63-65; sr lectr, Leeds Col of Art, 65-70. Bibliog: J A Thwaites (auth), Everybody invited, Art & Artists, London, 11/73; Art Perry (auth), Artist dips his brush in Canadian wry, Vancouver Prov, 11/74; Marq de Villiers (auth), I Am a unique idiot, Weekend Mag, Montreal, 2/75. Publ: Auth, Robin Page, Flash Art, Milan, 5/72. Dealer: Galerie Vallois 20 Rue St Denis Paris 75001 France. Media: Mailing Add: c/o Dan Page 1330 Hasting St Victoria BC V8Z 2W2 Can

PAHL, JAMES ROBERT, II
MUSEUM DIRECTOR
b Orange, Calif, Dec 10, 43. Study: St Mary's Col, Calif, BA; Calif State Polytech Univ, post grad work. Collections Arranged: Contemp Relig Textile Art, 74; Recordings in Clay-Tomb Sculpture of Ancient West Coast Mexico (with catalog), 74; Portrait of the Earth, Art of the Pueblo Potter (aith catalog), 75. Teaching: Teacher mus study, tour & appreciation, Chaffey Community Col, 74-75. Pos: Asst dir, Fine Arts Dept, Los Angeles Co Fair, Pomona, Calif, 70-71; dir, Griswold's Foothill Gallery, Claremont, Calif, 71-73; dir, Rex W Wignall Mus Gallery, Chaffey Col, Alta Loma, Calif, 73- Mem: Am Asn Mus; Smithsonian Assocs; Natural Hist Soc; Am Mus Natural Hist. Res: Catalogue research for Southwest pottery; religious textile arts; Lolima, Nayarit, Jalisco pre-Colombian tomb sculpture. Mailing Add: 4436 Via Padova Claremont CA 91711

PAIK, NAM JUNE
VIDEO ARTIST
b Seoul, Korea, 1932. Study: Univ Tokyo, grad, 56. Teaching: Artist-in-residence, WGBH-TV, Boston, 69 & GNET-TV, New York, 71. Exhib: Fluxus Festival, Mus Wiesbaden, WGer, 62; Cybernetic Serendipity, Inst Contemp Arts, London, Eng, 68; The Machine as Seen at the End of the Mechanical Age, Mus of Mod Art, New York, 68; Vision & Television, Rose Art Mus, Brandeis Univ, Waltham, Mass, 69; St Jude Video Int, de Saisset Art Gallery & Mus, Univ Santa Clara, Calif, 71; Circuit: a Video Invitational, Everson Mus of Art, Syracuse, NY, 73; Open Circuits: The Future of Television, Mus of Mod Art, New York, 74; one-man shows, Mus of Mod Art, New York, 72 & The Kitchen, New York, 73. Bibliog: Patricia Sloane Discusses the Work of Nam June Paik, article in Art & Artists, London, 3/72. Mailing Add: c/o Galeria Binino Ltd 48 Great Jones St New York NY 10012

PAJAUD, WILLIAM ETIENNE
PAINTER
b New Orleans, La, Aug 3, 25. Study: Xavier Univ, New Orleans, BFA; Chouinard Inst, Los Angeles, grad; also with Tyrus Wong & Charles White. Work: Norton Simon Collections, Los Angeles; Pushkin Mus, Moscow; Atlanta Univ, Ga; Westside Jewish Community Ctr, Los Angeles; Golden State Mutual Afro-Am Art Collection. Exhib: National Watercolor Soc; Watercolor USA; Carnegie Inst; Los Angeles Co Art Mus; Butler Art Inst. Awards: Westside Jewish Community Ctr; Atlanta Univ Ann; Calif Watercolor Soc. Mem: Nat Watercolor Soc (pres, 74-75), Los Angeles City Art Asn; Tutor Art, Los Angeles (pres). Style & Technique: Contemporary figurative in approach, emphasis on design; watercolors have same figure concept, wet into wet, transparent watercolors. Media: Oil. Publ: Contribr, Black American Art Encyclopedia; contribr, Black Artists on Art, vol 1; contribr, Eminent Blacks Past & Present; contribr, Black Dimensions in Contemporary American Art. Dealer: Heritage Gallery 718 La Cienega Los Angeles CA 90048. Mailing Add: 3767 Grayburn Ave Los Angeles CA 90018

PAL, PRATAPADITYA
CURATOR, ART HISTORIAN
b Sylhet, Bangladesh, Sept 1, 35. Study: Delhi Univ, BA(hons), 56; Calcutta Univ, MA, 58, DPhil, 62; Cambridge Univ, PhD, 65. Collections Arranged: Ragamala Paintings (with catalog), Mus Fine Arts, Boston, 67, Lamaist Art: The Aesthetics of Harmony (with catalog), 69; The Art of Tibet (with catalog), Asia House, New York, 69; The Art of India, Nepal & Tibet, 70; Nasli & Alice Heeramaneck Collection, Los Angeles Co Mus, 70, Islamic Art: Palevsky-Heeramaneck Collection (with catalog), 73; Sacred & Secular in Indian Art (with catalog), Univ Calif, Santa Barbara, 74; Nepal: Where the Gods are Young (with catalog), Asia Soc, New York, 75. Teaching: Lectr Indian art, Harvard Univ, 68-69; lectr Nepali art, Univ Calif, Los Angeles, 70; adj prof SE Asian art, Univ Southern Calif, 70- Pos: Sr res assoc, Am Acad Benares, 66-67; keeper of Indian collections, Mus Fine Arts, Boston, 67-69; curator Indian & Islamic art, Los Angeles Co Mus Art, 70- Mem: Asia Soc; Nat Soc Arts & Lett. Res: Arts, architecture and cultural history of India, Islamic countries, Nepal, Tibet & Southeast Asia. Publ: Auth, The Arts of Nepal, I, Sculpture, 74; auth, Bronzes of Kashmir, 75. Mailing Add: Los Angeles Co Mus Art 5905 Wilshire Blvd Los Angeles CA 90036

PALADIN, DAVID CHETHLAHE
See Chethlahe

PALAU, MARTA
TAPESTRY ARTIST, PAINTER
b Albesa, Lerida, Spain, July 17, 34. Study: La Esmeralda, Inst Nat Bellas Artes, Mex; San Diego State Col; Barcelona Escuela de Artes y Oficios. Work: Univ San Diego Med Sch; Mus Mod Art, Mexico City; Ctr Mod Art, Guadalajara, Mex; Hebrew Home, San Francisco. Comn: Mural, Ctr Mod Art, Guadalajara, 71. Exhib: Univ Tex Art Mus, 70; Bienal Cali, Colombia, 70; Bienal Santiago, Chile, 70; Bellas Artes Palace, Mex, 74; Biennale Int de la Gravure, Krakow, Poland, 74; Mod Art Mus, Tokyo & Mod Art Mus, Kyoto, Japan, 77; Eighth Biennial Int de la Tapiserie, Lausanne, Switz, 78; one-woman show, Mod Art Mus, Mexico City, Mex, 78; plus others. Awards: Exhibit Purchase Award, Inter-Am Mus Graphic Art, San Juan, PR, 73. Bibliog: Raquel Tibol (auth), Marta Palau renueva el arte del tapiz, Excelsior Sunday Mag, Mexico City, 1/74 & Los tejidos multi-multidimensionales de Marta Palau, Del Tapiz a la Excultura, Inbal, Mexico City, 74; Juan Acha (auth), El tapiz a la busqueda del espacio, Diorama de la Cultura, Mexico City, 74. Style & Technique: Weaves both on and off loom. Media: Oil, Etching. Dealer: Wenger Gallery 1730 Torrey Pines Rd La Jolla CA 92037; Galeria Pecanins Hamburgo 103 Mexico DF Mexico. Mailing Add: Hermosillo 630 Col Chapultepec Tijuana Mexico

PALAZZOLA, GUY
ART ADMINISTRATOR, EDUCATOR
b Kalamazoo, Mich, Mar 16, 19. Study: Art Sch, Soc Arts & Crafts, Detroit, cert, study with Sarkis Sarkisian & John Carroll. Work: Corcoran Gallery Art, Washington, DC; Butler Inst Am Art, Youngstown, Pa; Detroit Inst Art; Grand Rapids Art Inst. Exhib: Mich Artists Exhib, Detroit Inst Art, 38-70; Recent Mus Acquisitions Show, Chicago Art Inst, 56; other group shows in Can & SAm; one-man shows in Detroit, Chicago, Ann Arbor, 38- & Detroit Inst Arts, 61. Teaching: Prof painting & drawing, Art Sch of Soc Arts & Crafts, Detroit, 38-56; prof painting & drawing, Art Sch, Univ Mich, 56- Pos: Asst dir, Art Sch of Soc Arts & Crafts, 50-56; assoc dean, Art Sch, Univ Mich, 75- Awards: Founders Award, Mich Artists Exhib, Detroit Inst Art, 51 & 60; Purchase Award, Am Painting, Butler Inst Art, 57. Style & Technique: Geometric visual organization; acrylic spray techniques. Media: Painting, Drawing. Dealer: Detroit Artists Market Gilman Galleries Chicago IL 60611. Mailing Add: 510 Maple Ridge Ann Arbor MI 48103

PALEY, ALBERT RAYMOND
GOLDSMITH, DESIGNER
b Philadelphia, Pa, Mar 28, 44. Study: Tyler Sch Art, Temple Univ, BFA, 66, with Stanley Lechtzin, goldsmithing, MFA, 69. Work: Minn Mus Art, St Paul; Wilmington Soc Fine Arts, Del; Temple Univ; Univ Ill; Mem Art Gallery, Univ Rochester. Comn: Wrought iron portal gates, Renwick Gallery, Smithsonian Inst, Washington, DC, 74; wrought iron fence, Hunter Art Mus, Chattanooga, Tenn, 75. Exhib: Tendencies, Schmuchmuseum un Reuchlinhaus, Pforzheim, Ger, 70; Jewelry 71, Art Gallery Ont, Toronto, 71; Goldsmiths' 74, Smithsonian Inst, 74; one-man shows, Cornell Univ, 74 & Goldsmiths' Hall, London, Eng, 76. Teaching: Asst prof goldsmithing, Sch Am Craftsmen, Rochester Inst Technol, 69-72; assoc prof goldsmithing, State Univ NY Col Brockport, 72- Awards: Purchase Award, Goldsmiths' 74, Minn Mus Art, 74; Nat Endowment Arts Master Apprentice Grant, 75; Am Iron & Steel Inst Design in Steel Award, 75. Bibliog: A Peterson (auth), Metalwork of Albert Paley, Craft Horizons, 73; H Hollander (auth), Plastics for jewelry, 74; Craftsman in Am, Nat Geog Soc, 75. Mem: Soc NAm Goldsmiths; Am Crafts Coun. Media: Ferrous & Nonferrous Metals. Publ: Contribr, Goldschmiede Zeitung, 1/69 & 10/70, Body Jewelry, 73 & Jewelry Making, 75. Mailing Add: 335 Aberdeen St Rochester NY 14619

PALEY, MR & MRS WILLIAM S
COLLECTORS
Mr Paley, b Chicago, Ill, Sept 28, 01. Study: Mr Paley, Univ Chicago, 18-19; Univ Pa, BS, 22; hon LLD, Adelphi Univ, 57, Bates Col, 63, Univ Pa, 68, Columbia Univ, 75, Brown Univ, 75 & Pratt Inst, 77. Pos: Mr Paley, trustee, Mus Mod Art, New York, pres, 68-72, chmn, 72- Collection: Contemporary paintings. Mailing Add: 51 W 52nd St New York NY 10019

PALL, DR & MRS DAVID B
COLLECTORS
Dr Pall b Ft William, Ont, Apr 2, 14; US citizen. Study: Dr Pall, McGill Univ, BSc, 36; Brown Univ, 36-37; McGill Univ, PhD, 39. Collection: Contemporary art. Mailing Add: 5 Hickory Hill Roslyn Estates NY 11576

PALLEY, REESE
ART DEALER
b Atlantic City, NJ, Jan 26, 22. Study: New Sch Social Res, BA(econ), 48, postgrad studies, 48-49; postgrad studies, London Sch Econ, 49-52. Pos: Owner, Reese Palley Gallery, San Francisco, Atlantic City & Palm Beach, Fla. Specialty: Avant-garde American art plus porcelain objet d'art. Publ: Auth, The Boehm Experience, Syracuse Univ Press & Grosset & Dunlap, 72; auth, The Porcelain Art of Edward Marshall Boehm, Abrams. Mailing Add: Reese Palley Inc 1911 Boardwalk Atlantic City NJ 08401

PALMER, FRED LOREN
COLLECTOR, PATRON
b Richmond Hill, NY, Sept 12, 01. Study: Hamilton Col, AB. Pos: Trustee, Am Fedn Arts, 55-63, mem exec comn, 57-63; chmn bd adv, Edward W Root Art Ctr, Hamilton Col, 58-; mem adv coun, State Mus NJ, 60-63; trustee, Summit Art Ctr, NJ, 70-, chmn, 75- Collection: Watercolors by Robert Parker, Kingman, Fredenthal and others; drawings by Baskin, Kuniyoshi, Tam, Shahn, Hirsch, Liberman, Thomas George and others; oils by William Palmer, Rattner, Kerkam, Venard, Meigs and others; prints and etchings by Isabel Bishop, Matisse, Picasso and Beckmann; sculpture by Maldarelli and Hardy. Mailing Add: Apt 75F Troy Ct Summit NJ 07901

PALMER, LUCIE MACKAY
PAINTER, LECTURER
b St Louis, Mo, May 23, 13. Study: Boston Mus Fine Arts Sch; St Louis Sch Fine Arts, Washington Univ; Art Students League, with Rapheal Soyer, J N Newell & Robert Brackman. Exhib: One-man shows, Am Mus Natural Hist, 43 & 58-59, Nat Asn Women Artists, 44-46, Rochester Mus Arts & Sci, 59, Chicago Nat Hist Mus, 60, Calif Acad Sci, San Francisco, 61, Palomita Blanca Gallery, Cuernavaca, Morelos, Mex, 73 & Akari Gallery, Cuernavaca, 76; spec group show for Pres of Mex Portillo, Plastica de Morelos Gallery, Cuernavaca, 78; plus others. Teaching: Lectr painting above & below the sea. Awards: Prize, Nat Asn Women Artists, 44; hon mention, Art League Orange Co, 61; Governor's Award for Best Landscape, Morelos State Art Exhib, 77. Mem: Nat Asn Women Artists; St Louis Art Guild; Orlando Art Asn; Art League Orange Co. Res: Underwater painting. Mailing Add: 5399 Lindell Blvd St Louis MO 63112

PALMER, MABEL (EVELYN)
PAINTER
b Denver, Colo, Oct 19, 03. Study: With Richard Yip, Warren Brandon, Vernon Nye & Michael Green. Work: Revue Studios Hollywood; Nat Cowgirl Hall of Fame, Hereford, Tex; City Santa Rosa; Bank Am Regional Off, Santa Rosa; Security Bank Antioch, Calif; Napa Co Fair Bd, Calistoga, Calif. Comn: First Telegraph Line, Union Pac Gold Spike Centennial, Calif & Nev, 69. Exhib: M H De Young Mem Mus, San Francisco, 65-66, 68-69 & 71; Watercolor USA, Springfield, Mo, 69; 141st Ann Exhib, Nat Acad Design, New York, 66; Charles & Emma Frye Mus, 71; 105th Ann & other shows, Am Watercolor Soc, New York, 72-77; Los Angeles Mus of Sci & Indust, 76; Nat Cowgirl Hall of Fame, Tex, 77; Trails W, Calif Secy of State Off, 77; plus many others. Pos: Dir mem, Occidental Art Gallery, Calif, 68-; mem adv coun, Artists Round Table, Santa Rosa, 72-; mem art comt, Sonoma Co Fair, Santa Rosa, 75; dir & prog chmn, Santa Rosa Art Guild, 75- Awards: Villa Palette Award, De Young Mus, 66; First Award, Mother Lode Nat Art Show, 67 & 70; Best of Show & First Award, All Western Art Show, Ellensburg, Wash, 72; plus many others. Bibliog: Allen Ottley (auth), Biographical, Calif State Libr, 66; Cathy Mitchell (auth), Western Artist, Sebastopol Times, 74. Mem: Soc Western Artists; assoc Am Watercolor Soc; Women Artists Am West (historian); Marin Soc Artists, Inc; East Bay Watercolor Soc. Style & Technique: Western action scenes with animals and horse racing in impressionistic realism style. Media: Acrylic,

Transparent Watercolor. Publ: Illusr, cover of La Revue Mod, 66. Dealer: Depot Gallery Vintage 1870 PO Box 2041 Yountville CA 94599. Mailing Add: 10395 Barnett Valley Rd Sebastopol CA 95472

PALMER, WILLIAM C
PAINTER, EDUCATOR
b Des Moines, Iowa, Jan 20, 06. Study: Art Students League; Ecole Beaux-Arts, Fontainebleau, France; Hamilton Col, hon DFA, 75. Work: Whitney Mus Am Art, New York; Metrop Mus Art, New York; Des Moines Art Ctr; Munson-Williams-Proctor Inst, Utica, NY; Cranbrook Acad Art, Bloomfield Hills, Mich; plus others. Comn: Murals, Post Off Bldg, Washington, DC, First Nat City Bank New York, Queens Gen Hosp, Jamaica, NY & Homestead Savings & Loan Asn, Utica, NY. Exhib: Corcoran Gallery Art, Washington, DC; Va Mus Fine Arts, Richmond; Carnegie Inst, Pittsburgh; one-man shows, Midtown Galleries, New York, 63-69, 74 & 77, Two Decades of Painting, Munson-Williams-Proctor Inst, 71, Cummer Art Gallery, Jacksonville, Fla, 71 & Root Art Ctr, Hamilton Col, 75; plus others. Teaching: Dir, Munson-Williams-Proctor Inst Sch Art, 41-73, emer dir, 73- Awards: Prize, Nat Acad Design, 46; Medal, Audubon Artists, 47; Am Acad Arts & Lett Grant, 53; plus others. Mem: Nat Acad Design; Architects League; Audubon Artists; Nat Soc Lit & Arts. Publ: Contribr, Am Artist Mag. Mailing Add: Glen House 109 College Hill Clinton NY 13323

PALMGREN, DONALD GENE
PAINTER, PHOTOGRAPHER
b Moline, Ill, Nov 22, 38. Study: Augustana Col, BA; Lutheran Sch Theol, Chicago, MDiv; Detroit Soc Arts & Crafts; Cranbrook Acad Art, with George Ortman, MFA. Work: St John's Univ; Anoka-Ramsey Col; Gustavus Adolphus Col. Exhib: Davidson Nat Print & Drawing Competition, 72; Drawings USA, 73; Magic Silver Show, Murray State Univ, Ky, 77; Appalachian Nat Drawing Competition, Appalachian State Univ, Boone, NC, 77; one-man show, St John's Univ, 74; plus many others. Teaching: Vis asst prof drawing & design, Murray State Univ, 72; asst prof drawing & photog, Gustavus Adolphus Col, 72- Awards: Res grants, Gustavus Adolphus Col, 73, 75 & 76. Media: Charcoal, Oil; Black & White Film. Mailing Add: Dept of Art Gustavus Adolphus Col St Peter MN 56082

PANABAKER, FRANK S
PAINTER
b Hespeler, Ont. Study: Ont Col Art, Toronto; Grand Cent Sch Art; Art Students League. Work: Art Gallery Toronto; Art Gallery, Hamilton; Art Gallery, London, Ont. Exhib: Royal Can Acad; Ont Soc Artists; Can Nat Exhib, Toronto; Salmagundi Club, NY; Can Painting Exhib, London, Eng, 55; plus others. Pos: Trustee, Nat Gallery Can, 59-66. Awards: Jessie Dow Prize, Art Asn Montreal, 30. Mem: Royal Can Acad. Publ: Auth, Reflected lights, 57. Mailing Add: 375 Wilson St Ancaster ON L8L 1S8 Can

PAONE, PETER
PRINTMAKER, PAINTER
b Philadelphia, Pa, Oct 2, 36. Study: Philadelphia Col Art, BFA, 53. Work: Libr Cong; Philadelphia Mus Art; Mus Mod Art; Tamarind Inst, Albuquerque, NMex; Victoria & Albert Mus, London, Eng; plus others. Exhib: Brooklyn Mus, 62 & 64; Butler Inst Am Art, 65; Contemp Art Overseas; New York World's Fair, 65; Otis Art Inst, Los Angeles, 64 & 66; one-man shows, Contemp Art Mus, Houston, 76, Roswell Mus, NMex, 77 & Hooks-Epstein Galleries, Houston, 78; plus many others. Teaching: Instr, Philadelphia Col Art, 59; instr, Pratt Inst, 59-66; instr art hist, Positano Art Sch, Italy, 61. Awards: Tiffany Found Grant, 62 & 64; Purchase Prize, Syracuse Univ, 64; Guggenheim Fel, 65-66; plus others. Bibliog: Selden Rodman (auth), The Insiders, La State Univ, 60. Mem: Soc Am Graphic Artists. Publ: Auth & illusr, Paone's Zoo, 61; auth & illusr, Five Insane Dolls, 66; auth & illusr, My Father, 68; auth, Kachina—Paone, 76; plus others. Mailing Add: 1027 Westview St Philadelphia PA 19119

PAPAGEORGE, TOD
PHOTOGRAPHER
b Portsmouth, NH, Aug 1, 40. Study: Univ NH, BA. Work: Mus Mod Art; Art Inst of Chicago; Bibliot Nat, Paris; Boston Mus Fine Arts; Seagrams Inc, New York. Comn: The American Courthouse Bicentennial Doc, Seagrams, Inc, 75. Exhib: Recent Acquisitions, Mus of Mod Art, 71 & 73 & Pub Landscapes, 74; 14 Am Photogr, Baltimore Mus of Art, 75; Ten Am Photogr, Galene Zabriskie, Paris, France, 77; Recent Am Photog, Edinburgh Festival, Scotland, 77; one-man exhibs, Light Gallery, New York, 73, Cronin Gallery, Houston, 77 & Art Inst of Chicago, 78. Teaching: Lectr on vis studies, Harvard Univ, 75- Awards: Guggenheim Found Fel Photog, 70 & 77; Nat Endowment Arts Fel Photog, 73 & 75. Publ: Contribr, Vision & Expression, George Eastman House, 69; contribr, On Time, Mus Mod Art, 74; contribr, The snapshot & auth, On snapshots and photography, Aperture, Vol 19, No 1; contribr, 14 American Photographers, Baltimore Mus Art, 75; auth & ed, Public Relations, The Photographs of Garry Winogrand, Mus Mod Art, 77. Mailing Add: 50 White St New York NY 10013

PAPO, ISO
PAINTER
b Sarajevo, Yugoslavia, May 2, 25; US citizen. Study: Polytech Milan; Brera Acad Fine Arts, Milan, Italy, grad, 51; Boston Mus Sch; also with Carlo Carra. Comn: Paintings for films & posters, United Church of Christ, 64-65. Exhib: Inst Contemp Art, Boston, 68; Brockton Art Ctr, 70; Tanglewood, 71; one-man shows, Boston Athenaeum, 73 & Boston Psychoanal Soc & Inst, 75. Teaching: Instr art, Kirkland House & Quincy House, Harvard Univ, 64-69; vis assoc prof painting, Boston Univ, 67-75; instr painting & drawing, Pine Manor Jr Col, 68- Awards: Nat Scholastic Competition First Prize, Govt of Italy, 50. Mem: Boston Visual Artists Union. Style & Technique: Watercolor landscapes, figure painting and portraits, small pen and inks, large drawings. Media: Watercolor, Oil. Mailing Add: 212 Aspinwall Ave Brookline MA 02146

PAPPAS, GEORGE
EDUCATOR, PAINTER
b Boston, Mass, Jan 25, 29. Study: Mass Col of Art, BS, 52; Harvard Univ, MA, 53; Mass Inst of Technol, with Gyorgy Kepes, 52-53; Pa State Univ, PhEduc, 57. Work: De Cordova Mus, Lincoln, Mass; St Paul Gallery of Art, Minn; Tampa Bay Art Ctr, Fla; Pa State Univ, University Park. Exhib: Corcoran Biennial, Washington, DC; De Cordova Mus Art, Lincoln, Mass; Ringling Mus Art, Sarasota, Fla; Detroit Inst of Art, Mich; Boston Mus Fine Arts, Mass; Kanegis Gallery, Boston; Nordness Gallery, New York. Teaching: Asst prof painting & art educ, Pa State Univ, 55-56; prof painting, Univ Southern Fla, 66- Awards: Purchase Awards, Drawing USA, St Paul Gallery of Art, Chautaqua Nat, Chautaqua Art Asn & Tampa Bay Art Ctr, Fla. Mem: Col Art Asn; Nat Conf of Art Adminr; Nat Art Educ Asn. Style & Technique: Painting and abstract. Media: Oil. Publ: Co-auth, Design, It's Form and Function, Pa State Univ, 65; auth, Concepts in Art & Education, McMillian, 70. Mailing Add: Dept of Art Univ S Fla Tampa FL 33620

PAPPAS, MARILYN
COLLAGE ARTIST, EDUCATOR
b Brockton, Mass, Jan 1, 31. Study: Mass Col Art, BSEd; Pa State Univ, MEd. Work: Objects USA, Mus of Contemp Crafts, New York, NY; Viktor Lowenfeld Mem Collection, Pa State Univ; Krannert Art Mus, Univ Ill; Dayton Traveling Mus, Ohio. Comn: Wall covering, comn by Lee Nordness, New York, 67; theater curtain, Temple Israel, Miami, 68; fabric collage, Pan Am Int, 70; wall relief, Musa Isle Residence for the Elderly, Miami, Fla, 76. Exhib: Craftsmen of the Eastern States, 63, Fabric Collage, 65 & Craftsmen USA, 66, Mus Contemp Crafts; History of Collage, Kunstgewerbemus, Zurich, Switz, 68; Objects USA, Smithsonian Inst, 69. Teaching: Asst prof art educ, Pa State Univ, 59-64; assoc prof art, Miami-Dade Jr Col, 65-74; asst prof art & art educ, Mass Col Art, 74- Awards: Fla Craftsmen Ann Awards, 66, 67 & 71; Miami Art Ctr Award, 71 & 72; Nat Endowment of Arts Craftsman Grant, 73. Bibliog: Bartlett Hayes (auth), Drawings of the Masters: American Drawings, Shorewood Publ, 65; Nik Krevitsky (auth), Stitchery: art and craft, Art Horizons, 66; Lee Nordness (auth), Objects USA, Viking Press, 70. Mem: Am Crafts Coun. Media: Collage. Publ: Contribr, Sch Arts Mag, 62-67. Mailing Add: 743 Country Way North Scituate MA 02060

PARADISE, PHIL (HERSCHEL)
PAINTER, SCULPTOR
b Ontario, Ore, Aug 26, 05. Study: Chouinard Art Inst, grad; also with F Tolles Chamberlain, Rico Lebrun & Leon Kroll. Work: Libr Cong, Washington, DC; Philadelphia Watercolor Club; San Diego Fine Arts Soc. Exhib: Los Angeles Co Mus Art, 40; San Francisco Art Asn, 41; Art Inst Chicago, 43; Carnegie Inst Int, Pittsburgh, 43-44; Whitney Mus Am Art, New York, 45. Teaching: Prof painting, Chouinard Art Inst, 31-40; lectr painting & drawing, Univ Tex, El Paso, 52; lectr painting & drawing, Scripps Col, 56-57. Pos: Dir fine arts, Chouinard Art Inst, 36-40; art dir & prod designer, Sol Lesser Prod, Paramount Studios, 41-48; dir, Greystone Galleries, 62-75. Awards: Purchase Award for Goleta, Philadelphia Watercolor Club, 39, Dana Medal for Suburban Supper, 43; Purchase Award for Landscape, San Francisco Int Exhib, 41. Bibliog: Janice Lovos (auth), Guatemala journey, 50 & Phil Paradise serigraphys, 69, Am Artist Mag; Beverly Johnson (auth), Phil Paradise and his works, Los Angeles Times Home Mag, 67. Mem: Assoc Nat Acad Design. Media: Graphics. Publ: Illusr, Fortune Mag, Westways Mag, True Mag & others, 40-60. Mailing Add: 1402 Prefumo Canyon Rd San Luis Obispo CA 93401

PARDINGTON, JOYCE ELIZABETH
WEAVER, DESIGNER
b Detroit, Mich, Feb 25, 39. Study: Albion Col, BFA, 60; Fashion Inst Technol; also with Glen Kaufman, Alice Parrott & Trude Guermonprez. Work: Textile Workshops, Inc, Santa Fe, NMex; Bill Murphy, Inc, NJ. Comn: Tapestry woven quilt, comn by Fritz Scholder, Galisteo, NMex, 70-73, outdoor wall flag, 74; outdoor wall flag, Selective Eye, Santa Fe, NMex, 73-74; vegetable dyed woven quilt, comn by Mrs L Friedman, Springfield, Ill, 74; vegetable dyed wall hanging, comn by R McCormick, Santa Fe, 74. Exhib: First Northern Savings & Loan, Santa Fe, 71; Fine Art Exhib, Mus NMex, Santa Fe, 72-75, Folk Art Exhib, 73-74; Hand & Spirit Gallery, Scottsdale, Ariz, 73; Hills Gallery, Santa Fe, 74. Teaching: Instr weaving, Inst Am Indian Art, 63-65; instr pub schs & privately, 73- Mem: Am Crafts Coun; Santa Fe Weavers Guild (prog dir, 74). Style & Technique: Woven fabrics with special interest in quilts and rope off-loom weaving. Media: Sculptural Woven Forms. Mailing Add: Box 751 Hyde Park Estates Santa Fe NM 87501

PARDINGTON, RALPH ARTHUR
CERAMIST, SCULPTOR
b Highland Park, Mich, June 14, 38. Study: Albion Col, BFA, 60; Alfred Col Ceramics, summers 61 & 65; Cranbrook Acad Art, MFA, 62; with Hal Reiger & Palo Soleri, 64 & Dominic Labino, 67. Work: Inst Contemp Arts, Washington, DC; Mus Int Folk Art, Santa Fe; Mus Fine Arts, Div Mus NMex, Santa Fe; Mus Albuquerque; Mus Fine Art, Univ Okla. Comn: Bas-relief wall sculpture of patron saint, Christ Desert Monastery, Albuquerque, 69, holy water fountain, 69; sculpture, comn by Fritz Scholder, Galisteo, NMex, 70; outdoor planters, comn by A J O'Brien, Harbor Springs, Mich, 73; two large punch bowls, Int Folk Art Mus, Santa Fe, 73. Exhib: 25th Ceramic National, Syracuse, NY, 68; Object Makers, Univ Utah, 71; Inst Am Indian Arts Fac Exhib, Smithsonian Inst, Washington, DC, 73; Christmas Exhib, ACC Gallery, New York, 74; NMex Exhib, Univ Albuquerque, 74. Teaching: Chmn dept applied arts, Inst Am Indian Arts, 62-; instr ceramics, Penland Sch Crafts, summers 67 & 69. Pos: Advisor, NMex Arts Comn, 72-73. Awards: First Prize, Int Folk Art, 68; Outstanding Work Award, Mus Albuquerque, 70; Commission Prize, Mus NMex, 71. Bibliog: Article in NMex Mag, winter 71. Mem: NMex Potters Asn; Am Crafts Coun (state rep & mem regional coun, 73-); NMex Designer Craftsmen (pres, Santa Fe Chap, 64-65; state pres & vpres, 65-66). Style & Technique: Ceramic bas-relief or free standing sculpture; functional ceramics; architectural bas-relief murals. Media: Clay, Wood. Publ: Auth, 30-minute demonstration prog, KNME TV, 66. Mailing Add: PO Box 751 Hyde Park Estates Santa Fe NM 87501

PARDON, EARL B
CRAFTSMAN, EDUCATOR
b Memphis, Tenn, Sept 6, 26. Study: Memphis Acad Art, BFA; Syracuse Univ, MFA. Work: Mus Contemp Crafts; St Paul Mus & Sch Art; Lower Art Ctr, Syracuse; Memphis Acad Art; Skidmore Col. Comn: Mus Contemp Crafts & Prudential Life Ins Co, Newark, NJ. Exhib: Mus Contemp Crafts; Wichita Craft Biennial; Syracuse Ceramics Nat; Skidmore Col; Schenectady Mus Art; plus others. Teaching: Lectr painting, jewelry & design, art schs, craftsmens orgns & col alumni groups; prof art & chmn dept, Skidmore Col, currently. Mailing Add: Dept Art Skidmore Col Saratoga Springs NY 12866

PAREDES, LIMON MARIANO
ENGRAVER, PAINTER
b Veracruz, Mexico, July 26, 12. Study: Acad San Carlos, Nat Univ of Mex, Sch of Arts of the Book, SEP. Work: Nat Inst Fine Arts; Mus Mod Art; Salon Plastica Mexicana. Pos: Prof art studies, Nat Inst Fine Arts, SEP, Mexico, DF, 44-; dir, Ctr Popular Artes Plasticas, Chapultepec, Mexico, DF, 60- Mem: Soc Engravers of Mex; Ctr Mex Contemp Art; Int Asn Art Critics, Paris, France; Taller de Grafica Popular (founder). Publ: Illusr of 50 books poetry, literature, religion and textbooks. Dealer: Salon de la Plastica Mexicana Havre 7 Mexico DF Mex. Mailing Add: Playa Tambuco 81 Mexico 13 DF Mexico

PARELLA, ALBERT LUCIAN
PAINTER, DESIGNER
b Youngstown, Ohio, Mar 21, 09. Study: Cleveland Sch Art, dipl art; Am Acad, Chicago. Work: Butler Inst Am Art; Hoyt Inst; Westminster Col; Youngstown Pub Libr. Comn: Set designs, Youngstown Playhouse, 33; emblem design, Youngstown YMCA, 60; emblem

design, Youngstown Symphony Soc, 70; plague design, Choffin Voc Sch, 73; medal design, Butler Inst Am Art, 73. Exhib: Am Vet Art Soc, 74; Nat Acad, 74; Am Watercolor Soc, 74; Audubon Artists, 75; Soc Painters Casein, 75. Teaching: Teacher art, Butler Inst Am Art, 46-48; teacher art, Youngstown State Univ, 65-67. Pos: Cartoonist, Youngstown Telegram, 32-34; art dir, Wearstler Advertising, Youngstown, 34-45; advertising dir, Century Foods, Youngstown, 45-50; art dir, WKBN TV, Youngstown, 50- Awards: Gold Medal, Butler Inst Am Art, 73; Gold Medal, Am Vet Soc Artists, 73; President's Award, Audubon Artists, 74. Mem: Am Watercolor Soc; Audubon Artists; Artists in Casein & Acrylic; Knickerbocker Artists; Am Vet Soc. Style & Technique: Strong design patterns; strong color; unusual subject, loosely painted, Media: Casein, Watercolor. Publ: Auth, Art in television, Today's Art, 73. Mailing Add: 208 Evergreen Dr Poland OH 44514

PARFENOFF, MICHAEL S
EDUCATOR, PRINTMAKER
b Gary, Ind, Aug 8, 26. Study: Art Inst of Chicago, BFA, MFA, with Boris Anisfeld & Max Kahn. Exhib: Print Exhib, Libr of Cong, Washington, DC; Momentum, Art Inst Chicago; Philadelphia Print Club. Teaching: Instr lithography, Art Inst of Chicago, 58-65; prof art, Chicago City Col, 58- Pos: Dir, Blackhawk Mountain Sch of Art, 63- Mem: Am Asn Univ Prof; Ill Art Educators. Media: Printmaking, Stone Lithography. Mailing Add: 453 W Roslyn Chicago IL 60614

PARIS, HAROLD PERSICO
SCULPTOR
b Edgemire, Long Island, Aug 16, 25. Study: Akademie Bildenden Kunst, Munich, Ger; Atelier 17, New York. Work: Philadelphia Mus Art; Mus Mod Art, New York; Univ Calif Art Mus, Berkeley; Milwaukee Art Ctr; Art Inst Chicago. Comn: Fountain, Southridge, Taubman Industs, Milwaukee, 72. Exhib: American Sculpture in the Sixties, Los Angeles Co Mus Art, 67; Human Concern & Personal Torment, Whitney Mus Am Art, New York, 69; L'Art Vivant aux Etats-Unis, Fondation Maeght, St Paul, France, 70; Salon Int de Galeries-Pilotes, Lausanne, Switz, 70; The California Years, 12 yr Retrospective, Univ Calif Art Mus, Berkeley, 72. Teaching: Prof sculpture, Univ Calif, Berkeley, 60- Awards: Guggenheim Fel, 53-55; Creative Arts Inst Award, Univ Calif, Berkeley, 67; Linus Pauling Peace Prize, 70. Bibliog: Peter Selz (auth), The final negation, 3-4/69 & John Fitzgibbons (auth), Paris in Berkeley, 5-6/72, Art in Am; Robert Hughes (auth), Souls in Aspic, Time, 5/22/72. Media: Plastic, Bronze, Graphics. Dealer: Hansen-Fuller Gallery 228 Grant Ave San Francisco CA 94108. Mailing Add: 326 Athol Ave Oakland CA 94606

PARIS, JEANNE C
ART CRITIC, WRITER
b Newark, NJ. Study: Newark Sch Fine Arts; Tyler Sch Art, Temple Univ; Columbia Univ; NY Univ. Collections Arranged: Organized & directed The Artist of the Month, providing lecturers & demonstrators in all the arts for organizations & school; organized exhibs of American art for Latin America, Italy & USA. Teaching: Lectr art, univs, cols, art leagues, women's clubs, mus asns, radio & NBC-TV series, You're a Part of Art. Pos: Assoc dir, Valente Gallery, New York; art critic, Long Island Press, 63-; art critic, Newsday, 77- Mem: Overseas Press Club; Fine Arts Mus of Nassau Co (mem bd trustees); Glen Cove Pub Libr (mem bd trustees); Glen Cove Cult Asn (mem bd trustees); New York Reporters Asn; Newspaper Women's Club; Friends of Hofstra Mus (bd dirs). Collection: Twentieth century painting & sculpture. Publ: Auth articles for Weekly Newspaper Chain, Record Pilot & Newsday; auth, Art feature, in Cue Mag, 7/72. Mailing Add: 21 Whitney Circle Glen Cove NY 11548

PARIS, LUCILLE M
PAINTER
b Cleveland, Ohio, Apr 8, 28. Study: Univ Calif, Berkeley, BA, Taussig traveling fel, 50-51, McEnerney grad fel, 52 & MA; Atelier 17, Paris. Work: Butterfield Collection; NJ State Mus of Contemp Art; Newark Mus Collection of Contemp Art. Exhib: San Francisco Mus of Art, 50, 51, 53, 54, 55, 61 & 62; SFW Annuals, San Francisco, 52, 53, 56, 57 & 58; Oakland Mus of Art, Calif, 52, 53 & 54; Artist-Bay Area Graphics, 64; Univ Minn Art Gallery, 65; NJ State Mus, 68, 72 & 73; Newark Mus Triennial, 71; Yr of the Woman, Bronx Mus, 76; one-person shows, Aegis Gallery, New York, 65, NJ State Mus, Trenton, 73 & Bronx Mus of Art, New York, 76; plus others. Teaching: Prof painting & graphics, Ball State Univ, 55-57; prof art, William Paterson Col, 59- Mailing Add: Dept Art William Paterson Col Wayne NJ 07470

PARISH, BETTY WALDO
PAINTER, WRITER
b Dec 6, 10; US citizen. Study: Art Students League, with Kenneth Hays Miller & John Sloan; Acad Julian, Paris; Grand Cent Sch, New York; Chicago Acad Fine Arts. Work: Metrop Mus Art, New York; Libr of Cong, Washington, DC; Brit Mus, London; Mus d'Art, Brussels, Belg; Pa Acad Fine Arts, Philadelphia; plus others. Comn: Pvt comn, 42. Exhib: Pa Acad Fine Arts Ann, 39-41; Nat Asn Women Artists, 39-45; Libr of Cong; Nat Acad Design, New York; Nat Arts Club, 68-72; plus many others including one-man shows. Awards: Second Prize, Am Artists Prof League, 64; Nat Arts Graphic Prize, 70; David Humprys Mem Prize, Allied Artists Am, 72; plus many others. Mem: Audubon Artists (bd dirs, 60-); Allied Artists Am; Nat Asn Women Artists; Art Students League; Pen & Brush; plus many others. Publ: Auth, Rome, 58, England Again, 59 & Paris, 60. Mailing Add: 69 Fifth Ave New York NY 10003

PARISH, JEAN E
PAINTER, EDUCATOR
b Oneonta, NY. Study: Ohio State Univ, BS; Parsons Sch Design; Art Students League, with Kunyioshi, Zorach & Sidney Gross; Drake Univ, MFA; Arrowmont Sch Crafts, Univ Tenn; Mass Inst Technol, summer scholar & cert. Work: Munson-Williams-Proctor Inst, Utica; Fox Hosp, Oneonta. Comn: Paramonts & Cloths, United Methodist Church, Oneonta, 71; murals, Goldman Theater, Philadelphia & Ritz Carleton, Montreal. Exhib: Art Today, NY State Fair, 67, Graphics Nat, 69; 19th Ann New Eng Exhib, Silvermine Guild Artists, 68; Nat Exhib Contemp Am Painting, Soc Four Arts, Palm Beach, 69; Miss Nat Ann Art Asn, Jackson, 70; Invitational, Munson-Williams-Proctor Inst, 76; one-person shows, State Univ at Oneonta Gallery, 77 & State Univ at Cobleskill Gallery, 77. Teaching: Assoc prof design, color & textile design, State Univ NY Col Oneonta, 66- Pos: Designer, various interior design firms, New York, 50- Awards: Purchase Award, Munson-Williams-Proctor Inst, 67, 73 & 74; Juror's Choice Award, 33rd Regional Artists Upper Hudson, 68; First Prize Drawing, Roberson Ctr Ann, 71; First Prize Painting, Cooperstown Nat, 76; Juror's Award, Upper Catskill Coun Arts Exhib, 77; Hon Mention, Norwich Exhib, NY, 77. Mem: Oneonta Community Art Ctr (gallery chmn, 68); Upper Catskill Community Coun Arts (pres bd, 72); Col Art Asn Am; Cooperstown Art Asn; Berkshire Art Asn. Style & Technique: Colorist. Mailing Add: 71 Maple St Oneonta NY 13820

PARKE, WALTER SIMPSON
PAINTER, ILLUSTRATOR
b Little Rock, Ark, Dec 30, 09. Study: Art Inst Chicago; Am Acad Art; also with Wellington Reynolds. Work: Univ Ill Col Dentistry; Union League Civic & Arts Found; plus others in pvt collections. Exhib: Union League Club Art Show, Chicago; Allied Artists Am 52nd Ann, New York; Munic Art League, Chicago; Am Artists Prof League, New York; Denver Art Mus; plus many others. Teaching: Instr portrait painting, Palette & Chisel Acad. Awards: Five Purchase Awards, Union League Club Exhib, 55-69; Gold Medal, Chicago Asn Painters & Sculptors, 57; Gold Medal, Munic Art League, 71; Gold Medal, Diamond Medal & Silver Medal, Palette & Chisel Acad. Mem: Brown Co Art Guild; Palette & Chisel Acad; Munic Art League; Oak Park Art League. Media: Oil, Watercolor, Etching. Mailing Add: 30 W 225 Argyll Ln Naperville IL 60540

PARKER, ALFRED
ILLUSTRATOR
b Saint Louis, Mo, Oct 16, 06. Study: St Louis Sch Fine Arts, Wash Univ, 23-28. Comn: Creator mother & daughter covers, Ladies Home J, 38-51. Exhib: Exhibs in major cities of US & Can. Teaching: Lectr, major cities US & Can; mem grad fac, Illus Dept, Acad of Art Col, San Francisco, 78- Pos: Founder & mem, Famous Artists Schs, Westport, Conn, 47- Awards: Citation, Wash Univ, 53; Award of Honor, Philadelphia Art Dirs Club, 62; Named to Hall of Fame, Soc Illusr, 65; plus others. Mem: Fel Int Inst Arts & Lett; hon mem Soc Illusr; St Louis Art Dirs Club; Art Dirs & Artists Club San Francisco; Westport Artists Group (founder & past pres). Publ: Contribr, illus in Ladies Home J, Good Housekeeping, Town & Country, McCalls & Cosmopolitan; plus others. Mailing Add: 56 Rancho Rd Carmel Valley CA 93924

PARKER, ANN (ANN PARKER NEAL)
PHOTOGRAPHER, PRINTMAKER
b London, Eng, Mar 6, 34; US citizen. Study: RI Sch of Design; Yale Univ, BFA. Work: Metrop Mus Art, New York; Libr of Cong, Washington, DC; Smithsonian Inst, Washington, DC; Mus Mod Art, New York; Mus Int Folk Art, Santa Fe, NMex. Comn: (With Avon Neal) Ed of 500 original rubbings, Am Heritage, 70, ed of 250, 71 & ed of 350, 74; ed of 100 original rubbings, Arton Assoc, 70 & ed of 70, 74; ed of 100 original rubbings, Mead Art Gallery, Amherst, Mass, 76. Exhib: Rubbings of New Eng Gravestones, Am Embassy, London, 65; Fenimore House, Cooperstown, NY, 66; Know ye the Hour, Hallmark Gallery, New York, 68; Ephemeral Image, Mus Am Folk Art, New York, 70; Worlds Beyond the Echo, Friends of Photog, Carmel, Calif, 71; Portuguese Portfolios, 73 & Guatemalan Portfolio, 76, Siembab Gallery; Flowering of Am Folk Art, Whitney Mus Am Art, New York, 74; Molas, Art of the Cunas Indians, Alternative Ctr for Int Arts, New York, 76; plus many others. Awards: Fifty Best Books Award, Am Inst Graphic Artists, 57; Ford Found Grant in Arts & Humanities, 62-64; First Prize in Photog, Americana Bicentennial Photog Contest, 76 & Mass Open, 77. Bibliog: M J Gladstone (auth), New art from early American sculpture, Collector's Quart Report, 63 & Pedestrian art, Art in Am, 4/64; Stephen Chodorov (producer), Know ye the Hour, Camera Three, CBS-TV, 11/68. Mem: Friends of Photog. Style & Technique: Developing the ancient Oriental art of ink rubbing into a contemporary print technique; stone rubbing and folk art. Media: Photography. Publ: Photogr, Ephemeral Folk Figures, Potter, ltd ed, 69; photogr, Portuguese Photographs, In: Life, The Year in Pictures, 75; photogr, Itinerant Photographs of Guatemala, Smithsonian Inst, 75; co-auth & photogr, Molas, Folk Art of the Cuna Indians, Barre, 77; photogr, Los Ambulantes, Itinerant Photographers of Guatamala, Ginseng Press, ltd ed, 78; plus others. Dealer: Gallery of Graphic Arts 1603 York Ave New York NY 10028. Mailing Add: Thistle Hill North Brookfield MA 01535

PARKER, BILL
PAINTER
b Josephine, Tex, Mar 2, 24. Study: San Francisco Sch Fine Arts; Acad Grande Chaumiere, Paris, France; also with Fred Hocks, La Jolla, Calif & Hans Hoffman, New York. Work: Mus Mod Art, Paris; Stedelijk Mus, Amsterdam; Whitney Mus Am Art, New York; Moscow Mus, USSR; Eisenhower Col; NY Univ; and many others. Exhib: Five American Painters, Stedelijk Mus, Amsterdam, 55; Salon Mai, Paris, 56; Nat Exhib Contemp Am Painting & Sculpture, Univ Ill, 57; Summer Arts Festival Int Exhib, Univ Maine, 63; Chase Gallery, ten times since 62. Awards: Burhle Prize, Gallery Kaganovitch, Paris, 52. Bibliog: R Nacenta (auth), School of Paris, New York Graphic Soc, 57; L Durand (auth), article, Newsweek, 3/31/58; Y Taillandier (auth), American in Paris, Connaissance Arts, 3/58. Media: Acrylic, Oil. Dealer: Chase Gallery 31 E 64th St New York NY 10021. Mailing Add: 2 rue Gathelot Clamart France

PARKER, HARRY S, III
MUSEUM DIRECTOR
b St Petersburg, Fla, Dec 23, 39. Study: Harvard Univ, BA; Inst Fine Arts, NY Univ, MA. Teaching: Lectr mus educ. Pos: Asst to dir, Metrop Mus Art, New York, 63-67, vdir educ, 68-73; dir, Dallas Mus Fine Arts, 74- Mem: Am Asn Mus; Am Fedn Arts; Int Coun Mus. Publ: Contribr, Metrop Mus Art Bul. Mailing Add: 9612 Rockbrook Dr Dallas TX 75220

PARKER, JAMES
PAINTER
b Butte, Mont, Oct 20, 33. Study: Columbia Col, BA, 55; independent study, Spain, 60-62. Work: Whitney Mus Am Art, New York; Aldrich Mus, Ridgefield, Conn; Carnegie Inst; Chase Manhattan Bank Collection, New York; Santa Barbara Mus. Exhib: Whitney Mus Am Art; Aldrich Mus, 72 & 74; Soho Ctr Visual Artists, 74; Schaffner Gallery, 74; Univ Calif, Santa Barbara, 74; plus others. Teaching: Instr art, Metrop State Col, 65-67; instr color theory, Parsons Sch Design, New York, 74- Media: Acrylic, Pencil, Pastel. Publ: Auth, Pop's ancestors, Denver Quart, 67. Mailing Add: 547 Riverside Dr New York NY 10027

PARKER, JAMES VARNER
ART ADMINISTRATOR, DESIGNER
b Senath, Mo, June 27, 25. Study: Phoenix Community Col, AA; Ariz State Univ, BFA & MA. Work: Southeast State Teachers Col; City of Phoenix Civic Art Collection; Alhambra High Sch Art Collection, Ariz; Heard Mus, Phoenix; Scottsdale Art Collection. Comn: Carl Hayden High Sch Student Body, Phoenix, 60; Greater Ariz Savings Bank, Tucson; Heard Mus; also pvt comn by Mr & Mrs Eugene Pulliam & Dr & Mrs Dean Nichols, Phoenix. Exhib: Tucson Art Ctr, 66; Phoenix Art Mus, 66; Stanford Res Inst, Palo Alto, Calif, 66; Yuma Art Asn, Ariz, 70; Into White, Scottsdale, Ariz; plus others. Collections Arranged: African Art, Heard Mus, 6 & 9/72; Indian Art Collection, 68 & 72; Indian Art of the Americas. Teaching: Instr art, Phoenix Col, 68-70; instr art, Glendale Community Col, 71-72. Pos: Curator educ, Heard Mus, 58-68, curator art, 68-75; consult adminr, Phoenix Mus Hist, 75-77; mus dir, Southeast Mo State Univ Mus, 77- Awards: Nat Vet Award, Santa Monica Recreation Dept, 53; O'Brien Art Award, Ariz State Fair, 60; UNICEF Award, 68. Bibliog: Design/Crafts/Education (film), NAET TV, Ariz State Univ, 60. Mem: Ariz Art Asn (secy, 60); Nat Art Educ Asn; Ariz Watercolor Asn (founder & pres, 59); Ariz Art Asn (pres, 60).

Style & Technique: Collage and stitchery. Publ: Illusr, Heard Mus, 58 & 71; illusr, The Story of Navaho Weaving, 61; illusr, Pima Basketry, 65; illusr, Women in 1970, 70. Mailing Add: 445 Marie Cape Girardeau MO 63701

PARKER, JOHN WILLIAM
PAINTER, EDUCATOR
b Chicago, Ill, June 20, 22. Study: Art Inst Chicago, BA(art educ), 52, MA(art educ), 60; DePaul Univ; Univ Ill; Nat Col Educ; Univ Chicago; Northwestern Univ. Work: Textile Mus, Washington, DC; Chicago Sun Times; Lake Shore Nat Bank, Chicago; Union League Club Chicago. Comn: Youths Conversing, Sister Stanisia, SSND, Acad Our Lady, Longwood, Chicago, 55. Exhib: French Co Sculpture Exhib, New York, 53; Chicago & Vicinity Exhib, Art Inst Chicago, 54, Art Rental & Sales Gallery, 62-75; one-man shows, Univ Club Chicago, 67, 69 & 72; plus many others. Teaching: Raymond Fund asst lectr, Art Inst Chicago, 50-53; teacher high sch, Chicago, 53-56; mus educ lectr, Art Inst Chicago, 56-57, adult lectr, 57-74, asst dir adult educ, 74- Awards: Fulbright Fel, US-Fr Govt Exchange, 53-54; Purchase Prize, Sun Times & Art Inst Women's Bd, 63; Purchase Prize, Union League Club Chicago, 65. Bibliog: Articles in Daily News, 57 & Sun Times, 63. Mem: Soc Archit Historians (pres local chap, 68); Am Asn Mus; Artist Equity. Style & Technique: European architectural style; human figures; found object sculpture. Media: Oil, Watercolor, Mixed Media. Publ: Over 30 articles on collections of Art Inst Chicago, transl into Japanese, Kodansha Publ, Tokyo. Dealer: Art Rental & Sales Gallery Art Inst Chicago Mich at Adams Chicago IL 60603. Mailing Add: 116 N Ardmore Villa Park IL 60181

PARKER, NANCY WINSLOW
ILLUSTRATOR, PAINTER
b Maplewood, NJ, Oct 18, 30. Study: Mills Col, Calif, BA, 52; Art Students League & Sch Visual Arts, New York. Exhib: 3rd Ann Art Exhib, Mills Col, 69; Audubon Artists 29th Ann Exhib, New York, 71; Webb & Parsons, Bedford Village, NY, 76. Pos: Art dir, Appleton, Century, Crafts, New York, 68-70; graphic designer, Holt Rinehart & Winston, New York, 70-72. Awards: Christopher Award for Illus of Willy Bear, Soc of Christophers, 76; Am Inst Graphic Arts Best Books Award for Illus of Willy Bear, 76. Style & Technique: Houses and barns in hard-edge for oil painting; wood constructions; illustrations in India ink, watercolor. Publ: Auth & illusr, The Party at the Old Farm, Atheneum, 75; illusr, Willy Bear, Parents Mag Press, 76; auth & illusr, Love From Uncle Clyde, Dodd, Mead & Co, 78; auth & illusr, The President's Cabinet, Parents Mag Press, 78. Mailing Add: 51 E 74th St New York NY 10021

PARKER, RAYMOND
PAINTER
b Beresford, SDak, Aug 22, 22. Study: Univ Iowa, BA, 46, MFA, 48. Work: Solomon R Guggenheim Mus, Mus Mod Art, Whitney Mus Am Art, & Metrop Mus Art, New York; Tate Gallery, London, Eng. Exhib: One-man exhibs, Walker Art Ctr, Minneapolis, Minn, 50, Kootz Gallery, New York, 60-66 & Solomon R Guggenheim Mus, 61; Retrospective, Dayton Art Inst, Ohio, 65, San Francisco Mus Art, Calif, 67 & Sch Visual Arts, New York, 71; Mus Mod Art, New York, 68 & 71; Univ Tex, 72; plus others. Teaching: Prof art, Hunter Col, 55- Awards: Ford Found Purchase Award, Corcoran Biennial, 63; Nat Coun on the Arts Award, 67; Guggenheim Fel, 67. Bibliog: L Campbell (auth), Parker paints a picture, Art News, 11/62; G Nordland (auth), exhib catalog, San Francisco Mus Art, 67. Media: Oils. Publ: Contribr, Student, teacher, artist, Col Art J, 53; contribr, Direct painting, spring 58 & Intent painting, fall 58, It is. Dealer: Fischbach Gallery 29 W 57th St New York NY 10019. Mailing Add: 101 Prince St New York NY 10012

PARKER, ROBERT ANDREW
PAINTER
b Norfolk, Va, May 14, 27. Study: Art Inst Chicago, BAE, 52; Skowhegan Sch Painting & Sculpture; Atelier 17, New York, 52-53. Work: Los Angeles Co Mus; Metrop Mus Art; Morgan Libr, New York; Mus Mod Art; Whitney Mus Am Art; plus others. Comn: Designer sets, William Shuman Opera, Mus Mod Art, 61. Exhib: Brooklyn Mus, 55; Mus Mod Art, 57; Laon Mus, Aisne, France, 56; New Sch Social Res, 65; Sch Visual Arts, NY, 65; plus many others. Awards: Rosenthal Found Grant, Nat Inst Arts & Lett, 62; Tamarind Lithography Workshop Fel, 67; Guggenheim Fel, 69-70; plus others. Publ: Illusr, hand colored ltd ed poems, Mus Mod Art, 62; illusr poetry, The days of Wilfred Owen (film), 66. Dealer: Terry Dintenfass Inc 50 W 57th St New York NY 10021. Mailing Add: Parsonage Lane Washington CT 06793

PARKER, SAMUEL MURRAY
PRINTMAKER, PAINTER
b Madison, Wis, Aug 6, 36. Study: Wis State Univ, Eau Claire, BA(art), 63; Univ Wis, MS(painting & drawing, 64, MFA(painting), 65. Work: Springfield Mus; Playboy Club; Laura Musser Mus, Muscatine, Iowa; Container Corp Am. Comn: Serigraphy, Ill Print Comn, Ill Arts Coun, 73. Exhib: Univ Pac Nat Small Painting Show, 71; 3rd Nat Invitational Drawing Show, Oshkosh, Wis, 71; New Talent: Midwest USA, Gallery 1640, Montreal, PQ, 72; Dong a Ibo Korean International Invitational Print Show, Seoul, 72; Nat Print Invitational, Artists Contemp Gallery, Sacramento, Calif, 73. Teaching: Assoc prof painting & drawing, Western Ill Univ, 65- Awards: First Prize for Painting, Ill State Fair Show, 72; 25th Ill Invitational First Prize for Painting, Ill State Mus, 72; First Prize for Painting, Laura Musser Mus, 73. Style & Technique: Reverse painting. Media: Photo Serigraphy; Acrylic on Plexiglas. Mailing Add: 216 E Jefferson Macomb IL 61455

PARKHURST, CHARLES
GALLERY DIRECTOR, CURATOR
b Columbus, Ohio, Jan 23, 13. Study: Williams Col, BA, 35; Oberlin Col, MA, 38; Princeton Univ, MFA, 41. Collections & Exhibitions Arranged: Albright-Knox Art Gallery, 47; Princeton Art Mus, 48; Oberlin Col, 49-62; Baltimore Mus Art, 62-71; Nat Gallery Art, Washington, DC, 71- Teaching: Asst prof art & archaeol, Princeton Univ, 47-49; prof hist & art appreciation & head dept art, Oberlin Col, 49-62; vis lectr, Univ Minn, Univ Calif, Los Angeles & Johns Hopkins Univ. Pos: Asst to dir, Albright Art Gallery, Buffalo, 45-47; dir, Allen Mem Art Mus, Oberlin Col, 49-62; dir, Baltimore Mus Art, 62-70; asst dir & chief curator, Nat Gallery Art, 71- Awards: Chevalier, Legion of Honor, Fr Govt, 47; Ford Found Fel, 52-53; Fulbright Res Fel, Univ Utrecht, 56-57; plus others. Mem: Col Art Asn Am (past pres); Intermus Conserv Asn (co-founder & past pres); Asn Art Mus Dirs (vpres); Am Asn Mus (pres). Res: 16th and 17th century scientific color theories and their relationship to visual arts. Publ: Co-auth, French Painting from the Chester Dale Collection (catalog), Nat Gallery Art, 41; auth, Ancient and Medieval Gold, Oberlin Col, 61; auth, A color theory from Prague: Anselm de Boodt, 1609, Allen Mem Art Mus Bull, 71; auth, Red-yellow-blue/a color triad in 17th century painting, Baltimore Mus Art Ann IV, 72; plus others. Mailing Add: Nat Gallery of Art Washington DC 20565

PARKINSON, ELIZABETH BLISS
PATRON, COLLECTOR
b New York, NY, Sept 25, 07. Pos: Trustee, Mus Mod Art, New York, 39-, pres int coun, 57-65, pres mus, 65-68. Collection: Paintings and modern art. Mailing Add: 215 E 72nd St New York NY 10021

PARKS, CHARLES CROPPER
SCULPTOR
b Va, June 27, 22. Study: Pa Acad Fine Arts. Comn: Boy and dogs, H B du Pont, Wilmington, Del, 69; James F Byrnes, Byrnes Found, Columbia, SC, 70; Boy with Hawk, Brandywine River Mus, 73; Boy with Gulls, Mystic Seaport Mus, 75; Sunflowers, Equitable Bldg, New York, 76. Exhib: Nat Sculpture Soc Ann, 62-77; Nat Acad Design, 65-77; six-city tour, Equitable Life Assurance Soc, 76-77. Pos: Mem adv comt, John F Kennedy Ctr, 68- Awards: Wemys Found Travel Grant, Greece, 65; Am Artists Prof League Gold Medal, 70; Nat Sculpture Soc Gold Medal, 71. Bibliog: Nancy Mohr (auth), The Parks family, Del Today Mag, 72. Mem: Fel Nat Sculpture Soc (pres, 76-78); Allied Artists Am; Nat Acad Design; Del State Arts Coun. Publ: Contribr, Sights and sounds of Easter, TV film produced by Wilmington Coun Churches, 64. Mailing Add: RD 1 Box 214 Southwood Rd Hockessin DE 19707

PARKS, CHRISTOPHER CROPPER
SCULPTOR, PAINTER
b Wilmington, Del, July 29, 49. Study: With Charles Parks. Exhib: Nat Acad Design, New York, 68; Allied Artists Am, New York, 71; Nat Sculpture Soc, 72; plus others. Awards: Helen Foster Barnett Prize, Nat Acad Design, 68; Lindsey Morris Mem Prize, Allied Artists Am, 71; C Percival Dietsch Prize, Nat Sculpture Soc, 72. Mem: Nat Sculpture Soc; Soc Medalists. Mailing Add: RD 2 Box 144B Southwood Rd Hockessin DE 19707

PARKS, ERIC VERNON
SCULPTOR
b Wilmington, Del, Mar 8, 48. Study: Cornell Univ, BS; Pa Acad Fine Arts; also sculpture with Charles Parks. Comn: Bronze portrait, pvt comn, Wilmington, 69; bronze heron, pvt comn, Wilmington, 71; two bronze equestrians, pvt comn, Chadds Ford & Unionville, Pa, 72. Exhib: Allied Artists Ann, New York, 70 & 71; Nat Acad Design Ann, New York, 72; Nat Sculpture Soc Ann, 72; Three Sculptors of American Realism, Hewlett-Packard Instrument Div Ann, Avondale, Pa, 72. Awards: Hon Mention, Allied Artists Ann, 70; Silver Medal with Patrons Prize, Arts Atlantic Nat Exhib, Gloucester, Mass, 72. Mem: Brandywine Valley Art Asn (mem planning comt, spring 72); Nat Sculpture Soc. Media: Bronze, Steel. Mailing Add: Box 130 Green Valley Rd Unionville PA 19375

PARKS, JAMES DALLAS
ART HISTORIAN, PAINTER
b St Louis, Mo, Aug 25, 07. Study: Bradley Univ, BS; State Col Iowa, MA; Chicago Art Inst; also with Jean Charlot, Philip Guston & Thomas Hart Benton. Work: Howard Univ; Tex Southern Univ; Springfield Art Mus, Mo; Dunbar Sch, Kansas City. Comn: Early presidents mural, Lincoln Univ (Mo). Exhib: Mid-America; Atlanta Ann; Joslyn Six State Show; Ill State Fair; Mo State Fair. Teaching: Head dept art, Lincoln Univ (Mo), 27-77, emer prof, 77- Pos: Art ed, Sphinx Mag, 26-50. Awards: First Prize for Lithographs, Springfield Mus, Mo, 45; Second Prize for Oils, Mo State Fair, 45; First Prize for Watercolors, Nat Conf Artists, 63. Bibliog: Cedric Dover, American Negro art, Graphic Arts, 65; Wadder & Lewis (auth), Black Artists on Art, 70. Mem: Nat Art Educ Asn; Col Art Asn Am; Mo Col Art Asn (pres, 55-56); Nat Conf Artists (pres, 55-56); Mid-West Col Art Asn. Style & Technique: Influenced by Thomas Hart Benton in painting regional scenes in realistic style. Media: Oil, Watercolor. Publ: Co-auth, Comprehensive Examination for Undergraduate Majors in Art, Educ Testing Serv, Princeton, NJ. Mailing Add: 923 E Dunklin St Jefferson City MO 65101

PARNALL, PETER
DESIGNER, ILLUSTRATOR
b Syracuse, NY, May 23, 36. Study: Cornell Univ; Pratt Inst. Exhib: Contemp Illusr, Rutgers Mus, Newark, NJ, 75; Int Illusr Show, Bratislava, Czech, 76; Alphabets, Mus Fine Arts, Houston, Tex, 78. Teaching: Instr design, Lafayette Col, Easton, Pa, 66-76. Pos: Art dir, ed & advert consult, 58-67. Awards: Caldecott Honor Bk, Am Libr Asn, 76 & 77; Horn Bk Award, Boston Globe, 76. Style & Technique: Negative space most important element of design; contrast details with mass of space. Media: Pen & Ink; Watercolor Wash. Publ: Auth & illusr, The Mountain, 71 & The Great Fish, 73, Doubleday; illusr, The Nightwatchers, Four Winds, 71; auth & illusr, Alfalfa Hill, Doubleday, 75; auth & illusr, The Dogs Book of Birds, Scribners, 77. Dealer: Greenwich Workshop 61 Unquowa Rd Fairfield CT 06430. Mailing Add: RD 3 Waldoboro ME 04572

PARRA, THOMAS (GARCIA)
PAINTER, INSTRUCTOR
b Mexico City, Mex, Dec 29, 37. Study: Art Introd Sch, 49-51; Nat Sch Painting & Sculpture; also with Juan Soriano, Manuel Rodriguez Lozano & Rufino Tamayo. Work: Mus Mod Art, Mexico City; Mus Mod Art, Tel-Aviv; Mus Mod Art, Buenos Aires, Arg; Mus Mod Art, Bogota, Colombia; Contemp Art Mus,- Santiago, Chile. Comn: Mural, Mex Embassy, Santiago, Chile, 64; mural, Mod Art Ctr, Guadalajara, Mex, 71. Exhib: Antonio Souza Gallery Art, Mexico City, 58-62; Proteo Gallery Art, Mexico City, 62; Carmen Waugh Gallery Art, Santiago, 63-65; Pecanins Gallery Art, Mexico City, 71; Arvil Gallery Art, Mexico City, 73-75. Teaching: Instr painting, Nat Sch Painting & Sculpture, Mexico City, 73-; instr painting, Mex Autonomous Nat Univ, 74- Bibliog: Margarita Nelken (auth), Tomas Parra, Excelsior J, 60; Luis Cardoza y Aragon (auth), Mexico, Pintura de Hoy, FCE, Mex, 66 & Pintura Contempora nea de Mexico, Era, Mex, 74. Mem: Independent Group, Mex, 71. Style & Technique: Surrealist. Media: Oil, Watercolor. Res: Prehispanic cultures in Mexico and Latin America. Mailing Add: Pomona 34 Mexico 7 DF Mexico

PARRISH, DAVID BUCHANAN
PAINTER
b Birmingham, Ala, June 19, 39. Study: Univ Ala, with Melville Price & Richard Brough, BFA. Work: Brooks Mem Art Gallery, Memphis; Wadsworth Atheneum, Hartford, Conn; Partheon, Nashville; Monsanto Chem Co, Decatur, Ala. Exhib: One-man shows, French & Co, New York, 72, Galerie Francois Petit, Paris, 73 & Sidney Janis Gallery, 75; Sharp Focus Realism, Sidney Janis Gallery, New York, 72; Painting & Sculpture Today, Indianapolis Mus Art, 72; Phases of New Realism, Lowe Mus, Coral Gables, 72; Realists Revival, Am Fedn Arts Traveling Show, 72-73; New/Photo Realism, Wadsworth Atheneum, Hartford, Conn, 74; Six Americans, Sidney Janis Gallery, New York, 75; Super Realism, Baltimore Mus, 75. Awards: Award of Merit, 23rd Southeastern Ann Exhib, High Mus, Atlanta, 68; Top Award, 61st Ann Jury Exhib, Birmingham Mus Art, 69; Top Award, Mid-South Ann, Brooks Mem Art Gallery, 70. Media: Oil. Dealer: Nancy Hoffman Gallery New York NY 10012. Mailing Add: 700 Cleermont Dr Huntsville AL 35801

PARRY, ELLWOOD COMLY III
ART HISTORIAN
b Abington, Pa, Aug 9, 41. Study: Harvard Univ, AB, 64; Univ Calif, Los Angeles, MA, 66; Yale Univ, PhD, 70. Collections Arranged: American Paintings: A Gathering from Three Centuries, Hist Soc of Princeton, NJ, 75. Teaching: Asst prof, Dept Art Hist & Archaeol, Columbia Univ, 69-75; assoc prof, Sch Art & Art Hist, Univ Iowa, 76- Awards: Nat Endowment for Humanities Fel, 75-76. Mem: Col Art Asn; Mid-Am Col Art Asn; Mid-West Art Hist Soc. Res: Special interest in the iconography of American art and the interface between 19th-century painting and the popular arts, such as panoramas and photography. Publ: Auth, The Image of the Indian and the Black Man in American Art, 1590-1900, George Braziller, 74; co-auth, Reflections of 1776: The Colonies Revisited, Viking/Studio, 74; auth, Gothic elegies for an American audience: Thomas Cole's repackaging of imported ideas, Am Art J, 76; auth Thomas Eakins and the everpresence of photography, Arts Mag, 77. Mailing Add: Sch Art & Art Hist Univ Iowa Iowa City IA 52242

PARRY, MARIAN (MARIAN PARRY FELD)
ILLUSTRATOR, PRINTMAKER
b San Francisco, Calif, Jan 28, 24. Study: Univ of Calif, BA, 46; Contemporaries Gallery, etching & lithography with Michael Ponce de Leon, stone engraving with Ben Shahn. Work: Houghton Libr, Harvard Univ, Cambridge, Mass; Metrop Mus of Art Print Collection, New York; Smith Col Rare Bk Collection; Wellesley Col Rare Bk Collection; Univ of Mass Rare Bk Collection, Northampton. Exhib: Boston Visual Artists Union, 74; Cambridge Art Asn; one-man show, Smith Col Rare Bk Rm, 77; Los Angeles Inst of Contemp Art, 78. Collections Arranged: Books Collected by Hannah Duston French (with catalog), Wellesley Col Libr, 72. Teaching: Lectr illus & writing, Radcliffe Sem Prog, 74-, lectr hist of the bk, 77-; lectr writing, Emmanuel Col, 74- Awards: Scholar, Radcliffe Inst, 65-67; Best Illus Bk Award for Birds of Basel, New York Times Bk Panel, 69; One of 50 Bks of the Yr (Birds of Basel), Am Inst of Graphic Arts, 69. Mem: Soc of Children's Bk Writers; New England Authors & Illusrs of Children's Bks. Style & Technique: Pen and ink and pen and ink with watercolors. Media: Pen and Ink; Watercolor; Printmaking with Linoleum; Xerox Watercolor. Publ: Illusr, Space Child's Mother Goose, Simon & Schuster, 58; illusr, Birds of Aristophanes, Heritage Press & Limited Eds, 59; auth & illusr, Birds of Basel, Pharos Verlag, 67 & Knopf, 69; auth & illusr, Roger & the Devil, Knopf, 72; auth & illusr, King of the Fish, MacMillan, 77. Mailing Add: 60 Martin St Cambridge MA 02138

PARSHALL, DOUGLASS EWELL
PAINTER
b New York, NY, Nov 19, 99. Study: Art Students League; Santa Barbara Sch Arts. Work: De Young Mus, San Francisco; Santa Barbara Mus Art; Richmond Mus Fine Arts, Va; Springfield Art Mus, Mo; Detroit Mus; plus others. Exhib: Carnegie Inst Mus Art, Pittsburgh, 24-34; Pa Acad Fine Arts, Philadelphia, 24-41; Chicago World's Fair, 35; San Diego Expos, Calif, 35; San Francisco World's Fair, 40. Teaching: Instr portraits, Santa Barbara Art Inst, 67- Awards: Hallgarten Prize, Nat Acad Design, 24-27; Calif Watercolor Soc Purchase Awards, 62, 64 & 65; Purchase Awards, Watercolor USA, 69. Mem: Nat Acad Design; Nat Watercolor Soc; West Coast Watercolor Soc; Soc Western Artists. Style & Technique: Realist. Media: Oil, Watercolor. Publ: Contribr, Am Artist Mag. Dealer: Gallery de Silva 1470 E Valley Rd Santa Barbara CA 93108; Challis Galleries 1390 S Coast Blvd Laguna Beach, CA 92651. Mailing Add: 245 Santa Rosa Lane Santa Barbara CA 93108

PARSONS, BETTY BIERNE
PAINTER, ART DEALER
b New York, NY. Study: Study with Bourdelle, Paris; sculpture with Archipenko & Zadkine; summers in Brittany studying watercolor with Arthur Lindsey. Work: Montclair Art Mus, NJ; Nat Collection Fine Arts, Washington, DC; Whitney Mus Am Art, New York; plus many pvt collections. Exhib: Pa Acad Fine Arts Jury Meeting, 57; Nat Coun Women of the US, 59; Am Abstract Artists, 62; Soc Four Arts, 64; Artists of Suffolk County, Part II: Abstract Tradition, Heckscher Mus, 70; plus many other group & one-woman exhibs. Teaching: Creativity sem, Sarah Lawrence Col, spring 72. Pos: Owner & dir, Betty Parsons Gallery. Bibliog: Dora Z Meilach (auth), Creating Art from Anything, 68; Calvin Tomkins (auth), Profile on Betty Parsons, New Yorker, 6/9/75; Helene Aylon (auth), Interview with Betty Parsons, Womanart, 9/77. Specialty: Exclusively contemporary art. Collection: Predominantly contemporary art. Mailing Add: 24 W 57th St New York NY 10019

PARSONS, DAVID GOODE
SCULPTOR, EDUCATOR
b Gary, Ind, Mar 2, 11. Study: Chicago Art Inst, 30; Univ Wis, Experimental Col, BS, 34 & MS(art & art hist). Comn: Christus Rex (welded steel, iron, bronze, porcelain & gold), St Michael & All Angels Church, Lake Charles, La, 57-58; Birdforms (welded steel, plated & covered with gold; 28ft x 4ft x 14ft), Moody Nat Bank, Galveston, Tex, 62-63; Compassion (bas-relief & crushed quartz; 20ft x 6ft), Chapel Vet Cemetary, Houston, 64-65; Patterned Brick for Space Sci (carved wood patterns & brick), Space Sci Bldg, Rice Univ, 65-66; Large Cellist (cast in bronze), Sheppard Sch of Music, Rice Univ, 74-75. Exhib: Wis Painters & Sculptors Show, Milwaukee Art Inst, 36-42; Chicago & Vicinity Exhib, Chicago Art Inst, 37-39, 40 & 44; Am Sculpture, Carnegie Inst Int, 39; The Sculpture Int, Philadelphia Mus, 39; Am Exhib, Chicago Art Inst, 38-40; Six State Sculpture Exhib, Walker Art Ctr, Minneapolis, 45; Pa Acad Fine Arts Ann Exhib, 45; The Artist & His World, Denver Art Mus, Colo, 49; Houston Mus Fine Arts Ann, 53 & 54; Gulf Int, Mus Fine Arts, Houston, 58; 11th Ann Midwest Exhib, Joslyn Art Mus, Omaha, Nebr, 67; one-man shows, Beaumont Mus, Tex, 53-67 & Witte Mus, 56. Teaching: Dir mus sch, Denver Mus Art, Colo, 47-49; asst prof sculpture, drawing & ceramics, Bradley Univ, Peoria, Ill, 49-52; assoc prof sculpture, drawing & art educ, McNeese State Univ, Lake Charles, La, 52-53; prof sculpture & drawing, Rice Univ, Houston, 53- Pos: Sculptor, Pub Works of Art, 33-34, Fed Art Proj, Milwaukee, Wis, 38-42; sculptor & visual educ aid designer, US Army, Camp Lee, Va, 24-44; surgical artist asst in plastic surgery, Civil Serv US Army Valley Forge Gen Hospital, 44-47. Awards: First in Sculpture, Va Biennial, Va Mus Art, Richmond, 42; Sculptor Award, Houston Mus Art Ann, 54; Mus Dir Award, Beaumont Regional, Beaumont Mus Art, Tex, 70. Mem: Col Art Asn Am; Tex Soc Sculptors (pres, Gulf Coast Sect, 75-76); Artists Fedn of Wis (pres, 40-42); Houston Munic Art Comn. Style & Technique: Work in wood, stone, marble, bronze, welded steel, hammered copper, terrazo, ceramic sculpture, fiber glass, organic abstraction; most all work relates to human figures or natural forms. Media: Wood, Bronze. Mailing Add: 645 Mulberry Lane Bellaire TX 77401

PARSONS, MERRIBELL MADDUX
CURATOR, ART ADMINISTRATOR
b San Antonio, Tex. Study: Newcomb Col, BFA; Ecole du Louvre, cert; Inst Fine Arts, NY Univ, MA; Metrop Mus & Inst Fine Arts, dipl (mus training). Pos: Contribr, Minn Inst Arts Bull, 69-74; Bell Mem cur of dec arts, Minn Inst of Arts, 69-74, chief cur & cur sculpture & dec arts, 74- Awards: Longhi Fel; Ford Found Fel; Nat Endowment for the Arts Fel. Mem: Col Art Asn; Dec Arts Chap, Soc Archit Hist; Ceramic Circle; Am Asn Mus; Int Asn for the Study of Textiles. Res: European sculpture, 1600-1900. Publ: Auth, Sculpture in the David Daniels Collection, Minn Inst Arts Bull, (in prep). Mailing Add: c/o Minn Inst of Arts 2400 Third Ave S Minneapolis MN 55404

PARTCH, VIRGIL FRANKLIN, II
CARTOONIST, ILLUSTRATOR
b St Paul Island, Alaska, Oct 17, 16. Study: Chouinard Art Inst, Los Angeles. Pos: Illusr, syndicated comic strip & daily panel Big George. Awards: First Prize, Brussels Cartoon Exhib, 64. Publ: Auth, It's hot in here; auth & illusr, Hanging way over; auth & illusr, VIP tosses a party, S&S, 59; auth & illusr, New faces on the bar room floor, 61; contribr, VIP's Quips, 75; contribr, cartoons in Look & True Mags; plus others. Mailing Add: Box 725 Corona Del Mar CA 92625

PARTIN, ROBERT (E)
PAINTER, EDUCATOR
b Los Angeles, Calif, June 22, 27. Study: Univ Calif, Los Angeles, with Clinton Adams, Gordon Nunes & S Macdonald-Wright, BA, 50; Yale-Norfolk Art Sch, fel & study with Conrad Marca-Relli, 55; Columbia Univ, with Andre Racz, John Heliker, Meyer Shapiro, Paul Tillich, MFA, 56; Tamarind Lithography Workshop, Herron Art Sch, fel & study with Garo Antreasion, 63. Work: Solomon R Guggenheim Mus Art, New York; NC Mus Art, Raleigh; Picker Art Gallery, Dana Arts Ctr, Colgate Univ; Jonson Gallery, Univ NMex; Weatherspoon Art Gallery, Univ NC. Exhib: Whitney Mus Am Art Ann, New York, 63; California South Seven, Fine Arts Gallery San Diego, 69; San Francisco Art Asn Centennial Exhib, De Young Mus, 71; Viewpoints Five, Dana Arts Ctr, Colgate Univ, 71; two-man show, 58-F Plaza Gallery, Orange, Calif, 73; Union Gallery, San Jose State Univ, Calif, 76. Teaching: Assoc prof art, Univ NC, Greensboro, 57-66; vis assoc prof art, Univ NMex, 63-64; prof art, Calif State Univ, Fullerton, 66- Awards: Ford Found Purchase Prize, Whitney Mus Am Art Ann, 63; Purchase Prize, NC Mus Art Ann, 64 & 65; Purchase Award, Viewpoints Five, Colgate Univ, 71. Bibliog: Mortimer Guiney (auth), The art of Robert Partin, in Vol 1, 63, Analects, Univ NC Press; Van Deren Coke (auth), Robert Partin, The Painter and Photograph, 65. Style & Technique: Rubbed-on atmospheric fields, grids, scenes. Media: Oil, Acrylic. Dealer: Space Gallery 6015 Santa Monica Blvd Los Angeles CA. Mailing Add: Dept Art Calif State Univ 800 N State College Blvd Fullerton CA 92634

PARTON, NIKE
PAINTER, SCULPTOR
b New York, NY, June 23, 22. Study: Ringling Sch Art, fine art cert; also sculpture with Lesley Posey & painting with Jay Connaway. Work: Univ Fla; Stetson Univ. Exhib: One-man shows, Southern Vt Art Ctr, 63, Tampa Prof Artist, 68, Sarasota Art Asn, 69 & Longboat Art Ctr, 72; Art League of Manatee Co, 73. Teaching: Instr painting, Art League Manatee Co, 54-74; instr pvt studio, 63- Awards: Award for Thru the Trees (watercolor), Sarasota Art Asn, 67; award for Ducks (woodcut), 70 & First Prize for Relaxed (oil), 75, Art League Manatee Co. Mem: Fla Artist Group; Sarasota Art Asn; Art League of Manatee Co; Fla Watercolor Soc. Style & Technique: Paint on location in an emotional response to what I see and feel of natures beauty. Media: Watercolor. Dealer: Ralph Wells 1322 Fourth Ave W Bradenton FL 33505. Mailing Add: 840 Edgemere Lane Sarasota FL 33581

PARTON, RALF
SCULPTOR, INSTRUCTOR
b New York, NY, July 2, 32. Study: Albright Art Sch, Buffalo, Dipl, 53; NY Univ Col Buffalo, BS(art educ), 54; Columbia Univ, MA(art), 55. Work: Civic Ctr, Turlock, Calif; City Hall, Turlock, Calif; Northwestern Mich Col Gallery, Traverse City, Mich. Comn: Reredos bronze wall (24ft x 18ft), Our Lady of Fatima Church, Modesto, Calif, 72; sculptured fountain, comn by Dr & Mrs Lemings, Modesto, Calif, 74; wall sculpture (24ft x 6ft), comn by Dr & Mrs Tripi, Turlock, Calif, 77; cast aluminum locomotive, comn by Paul Volpp, Buena Park, Calif, 77; cast nickel-silver sculpture, comn by Frank Lockwood, San Lorenzo, Calif, 77. Exhib: 3rd Ann Ball State Small Sculpture & Drawing Show, Muncie, Ind, 57; Sisti Gallery Ann, Buffalo, NY, 57; Calif State Fair Art Exhib, Sacramento, Calif, 64; San Francisco Mus Art, San Francisco, Calif, 72; Art Fac Exhib, Calif State Col Stanislaus, Turlock, Calif, 73, A Piece (one-man show), 74 & one-man show, 75; Calif State Col Stanislaus Art Fac Exhib, Univ of the Pac, Calif, 76. Teaching: Chmn dept painting & sculpture, Northwestern Mich Col, 58-62; prof sculpture, Calif State Col, chmn dept art, 63-70, Stanislaus, 63- Awards: Horohoe Prize for originality in Sculpture, Sisti Gallery, Buffalo, NY, 57; Reynolds Prize for Sculpture, Stockton Art Show, Calif, 66. Bibliog: David Otth (auth), Monoliths to Miniatures, Toy Train Operating Soc Bull, Vol 2, Number 2, 76. Style & Technique: Techniques applicable to the solving of aesthetic concerns, technological balance, geometric-organic forms. Media: Bronze; steel, stone, wood and plastic. Mailing Add: 1900 Clemson Ct Turlock CA 95380

PARTRIDGE, DAVID GERRY
PAINTER, SCULPTOR
b Akron, Ohio, Oct 5, 19; Can citizen. Study: Univ Toronto, BA; Queen's Univ, Kingston, Ont; Art Students League; Slade Sch, London; Atelier 17, Paris, with W S Hayter. Work: Tate Gallery, London; Nat Gallery Can, Ottawa; Libr of Cong, Washington, DC; Art Gallery Ont, Toronto; Gallery NSW, Sydney, Australia. Comn: Nail mural & stone, Royal Trust Co of Can, Ottawa, 61; nail murals, Hiram Walker & Co, Windsor, Ont, 65, 67, York Univ, Toronto, 70, Westminster Cathedral, London, 71 & foyer, Toronto City Hall, 77. Exhib: Montreal Mus Spring Show, 62; Int Print Exhib, Cincinnati, 62; Art of the Americas & Spain, Madrid & Barcelona, 63; Carnegie Int, Pittsburgh, 65; Sculpture '67, Toronto. Teaching: Art master, Ridley Col, St Catharines, Ont, 46-56; instr art, Queens Univ, Ont, summers 56-60; instr art, Ont Col Art, 74-75. Awards: Brit Coun Scholar to Slade Sch, 50-51; Sculpture Prize & Purchase Award, Montreal Mus Fine Arts, 62; Hon Mention, Royal Can Acad, 64. Bibliog: Alan Jaruis (auth), Configurations, Can Art, autumn 60; Charles S Spencer (auth), David Partridge's Nail Mosaics, Studio Int, 7/65; Kenneth Coutis-Smith (auth), David Partridge, Quadrum, 65. Mem: Fel Royal Soc Arts; Royal Can Acad. Style & Technique: Relief sculpture with wood and nails; abstract; oil painting; intaglio prints. Media: Wood and Nails. Dealer: Roberts Gallery 641 Yonge St Toronto ON Can. Mailing Add: 77 Seaton St Toronto ON M5A 2T2 Can

PARTRIDGE, ROI
LANDSCAPE ETCHER
b Centralia, Territory Wash, Oct 14, 88. Study: Nat Acad Design, NY. Work: Libr Cong, Washington, DC, Smithsonian Inst, Washington, DC; Honolulu Acad of Art; Calif Legion of Honor Mus, San Francisco; Mills Col Art Gallery, Oakland, Calif. Teaching: Instr art, Mills Col, 20-23, prof art, 23-46. Awards: Los Angeles Gold Medal, Los Angeles Print Makers Soc, 28; Joseph Pennell Purchase Prize, Libr Cong, 43; Henry B Shope Prize, Soc Am Etchers, New York, 48. Bibliog: D W Prall (auth), Aesthetic Judgement, Crowell, 29; Aline Kistler (auth), Roi Partridge, Etcher, Prints, New York, 34; Frederic Whitaker (auth), The etchings of Roi Partridge, Am Artist Mag, 11/73. Mem: Nat Acad Design, New York. Style & Technique: Conservative traditional. Media: Etchings; Drawings, Pen & Ink. Publ: Contribr,

articles in Sierra Club Bull & Am Mag of Art. Mailing Add: 1601 Skycrest Dr No 2 Walnut Creek CA 94595

PASCAL, DAVID
PAINTER, CARTOONIST
b New York, NY Study: Am Artists Sch. Exhib: One-man shows, Mus Art, Sao Paulo, Brazil, Mus Mod Art, Rio de Janeiro, Brazil, Graham Gallery, New York, 73 & Man and His World, Montreal, 74. Teaching: Instr graphic journalism, Sch Visual Arts, 55-58. Pos: Int rep, Newspaper Comics Coun, New York, 69-; US rep of Phenix Mag, France, Comics, Italy & RanTanPlan, Belg, 70- Awards: Dattero D'Oro, Salone Int dell Umorismo, Italy, 63; Award for Illus Excellence, Nat Carttonists Soc, 69, Silver T-Square, 72. Bibliog: Sergio Trinchero (auth), Visit to fundland, Sgt Kirk Mag, 68; Rinaldo Traini (auth), Incontro con David Pascal (slide prog), Immagine, 3/15/69; Claude Moliterni (auth), David Pascal, Phenix Mag, 70. Mem: Nat Cartoonists Soc (foreign affairs secy, 64-); Mag Cartoonists Guild; Int Comics Orgn (USA rep, 70-). Style & Technique: Aesthetic dynamics of comics analyzed and used in painting to express serious subject content. Media: Ink, Acrylic, Oil. Publ: Illusr, Fifteen Fables of Krylov, 65; auth & illusr, The Silly Knight, 67; auth, Comics: An American Expressionism, Mus Arts, Brazil, 70; ed, Graphis Mag, 72; auth, Goofus, Paris, 75; plus others. Dealer: Graham Gallery 1014 Madison Ave New York NY 10024. Mailing Add: PO Box 31 Villate Sta New York NY 10014

PASCHKE, EDWARD F (ED)
PAINTER, ILLUSTRATOR
b Chicago, Ill, June 22, 39. Study: Art Inst Chicago, BFA, 61 & MFA, 70. Work: Art Inst Chicago; Mus des XX Jahrhundert, Vienna, Austria; Darthea Speyer Gallery, Paris, France; Mus Contemp Art, Chicago; Mus Mod Art, Vienna, Austria; Mus Boymans, Rotterdam; Musee d'Art Moderne Nationale, Paris; Baltimore Art Mus, Md; Ill Bell Tel, New York & Chicago. Exhib: Soc for Contemp Art, Art Inst Chicago, 70-72; Whitney Annuals, Whitney Mus Am Art, New York, 72-74 & Biennial Contemp Am Art, 73; XII Bienal de Sao Paulo, Sao Paulo, Brazil, 73; Made in Chicago, Mus Contemp Art, Chicago, Mexico City & Washington, DC, 74 & 75 & View of a Decade, 77; Am Show, Art Inst Chicago, 74; Ottawa Royal Mus of Art, Can, 74; Nat Collection of Fine Arts, Washington, DC, 75; Ed Paschke Retrospective, Contemp Art Ctr, Cincinnati, Ohio, 75. Teaching: Instr painting, Art Inst Chicago, 74-76; instr painting, Columbia Col, Chicago, Ill, 76-78; prof drawing, Northwestern Univ, Evanston, Ill, 77-78. Awards: Raymond Fel/Ponte del Arte Fel, Art Inst Chicago, 61 & 70; Cassandra Grant, Cassandra Found, 72; Logan Medal, Art Inst Chicago, 73. Bibliog: Barry Schwartz (auth), Humanism in 20th Century American Art, Praeger, 72; Franz Schulze (auth), Fantastic Images, Follet, 73; Sheldon Williams (auth), Made in Chicago, Art & Artists, 75; Peter Schjeldahl (auth), Letter from Chicago, Art in Am, 76. Style & Technique: Theatrical figurative paintings, excessively dramatic. Media: Oil; Pencil. Dealer: Phyllis Kind Gallery 226 E Ontario Chicago IL 60611. Mailing Add: 1927 E Estes Chicago IL 60626

PASCUAL, MANOLO
SCULPTOR, INSTRUCTOR
b Bilbao, Spain, Apr 15, 02; US citizen. Study: Acad Fine Arts, San Fernando, Madrid, Spain, MA. Work: Mus Fine Arts, Santo Domingo, Dominican Repub; Emily Lowe Gallery, Miami Univ, Coral Gables, Fla; Hofstra Univ, New York; Mus, World Univ, Tucson, Ariz; plus others. Comn: Miguel de Cervantes (sculpture), Govt of Santo Domingo, 40; Thri Relieves (sculpture), Dominican Party Bldg, 45; Trinidad Sanchez (sculpture), Santo Domingo, 46; Duarte (sculpture), Cathedral of Santo Domingo, 48; The Goddess of Pete, Harlan Collection, Mich, 58. Exhib: Int Art, Paris, 25; Royal Acad Fine Arts, Madrid, 36; Int Biennal of Venice, 37; Nat Acad Fine Arts, Santo Domingo, 44; Retrospective, 50 Years of Sculpture, Hofstra Univ, NY, 68; plus many others. Teaching: Dir & teacher sculpture, Nat Acad Fine Arts, Santo Domingo, 40-50; instr sculpture, New Sch Social Res, New York, 51- Awards: Gold Medal, Acad San Fernando, Madrid, Spain, 18; Grand Prix de Rume, Spanish Govt, 31; First Prize & Gold Medal, Biennial Santo Domingo, Dominican Repub, 45. Style & Technique: Modern, figurative and surrealist. Media: Iron, Stone. Publ: Co-auth, Album of the Victory, 45. Dealer: New Bertha Schaefer Gallery 41 E 57th St New York NY 10022. Mailing Add: 84-26 Homelawn St Jamaica NY 11432

PASSUNTINO, PETER ZACCARIA
PAINTER, SCULPTOR
b Chicago, Ill, Feb 18, 36. Study: Art Inst Chicago, scholarships, 54-58; Oxbow Sch Painting, summer 58; Inst Art Archeologie, Paris, 63; Fulbright fel, 63-64 & Guggenheim fel, 71. Work: Walter P Chrysler Mus; Hirshhorn Mus, Washington, DC; Norfolk Mus, Va. Exhib: Sherman Gallery, Chicago, 60-61; Zabriskie Gallery, New York, 62; New Sch Social Res, 70; Sonraed Gallery, New York, 71; Galerie B, Paris, 72; Corcoran Mus, Washington, DC; NJ State Mus; Knowlton Gallery, New York; Gallery K, Washington, DC; Joseph Gallery, New York; Gallery 187, Englewood, NJ. Pos: Chmn, Momentum, Chicago, 57-58. Bibliog: Articles in Art News, 1/71, Artforum, 2/71, Arts Mag, 1/72 & Humanism, 72; article in Urban Explorations 1975, Currânt, 3/76. Dealer: Gallery Marc Alexandria VA 22313; Gallery Bienville 539 Bienville New Orleans LA 70130. Mailing Add: 530 La Guardia Pl New York NY 10012

PATCH, PEGGIE (MARGARET THOMPSON WILLIAMSON)
PAINTER, ART DEALER
b St Paul, Minn. Study: Univ Minn, 36-39; Johns Hopkins Univ, Art as Applied to Med Cert; also with Paul Penczner, Marilyn Lehman, Ray Ridaback, Jason Williamson & Max Broedel. Exhib: Tenn Watercolor Soc, 71-75; 12th Tenn All State Exhib, 72. Pos: Chmn-docent, Brooks Mem Art Gallery, Memphis, Tenn, 65-66; free lance med illusr, 66-; vpres, Brooks Mem Art League, 72-73; owner-dir, Golden Fleece Art Gallery, Memphis, 72-75, Carefree, 76- Awards: First Prize in Watercolor, Tenn All State Exhib, 72; Fowler Purchase Prize, Tenn Watercolor Soc, 73. Mem: League Am Pen Women & Artists. Style & Technique: Semi-abstract; realism; impressionistic. Media: Watercolor, Oil; Pen & Ink. Specialty: Prints, watercolor, oils and acrylics. Publ: Illusr (Margaret T Guthrie, pseudonym), Memphis Med J, 67-69. Mailing Add: PO Box 1943 Cave Creek AZ 85331

PATCHETT, DANIEL CLAUDE
ART ADMINISTRATOR, PAINTER
b Easton, Md, Sept 12, 47. Study: Md Inst Col Art, Yale-Norfolk scholar, 69, MFA, 70; Univ Iowa, MA, 72; also with Salvador Scarpitta, Lila Katzen, Maricio Lasansky & Peter Milton. Exhib: Acad Arts, Easton, 65; Washington Co Mus Fine Arts, Md, 69; Myers Fine Arts Gallery, State Univ NY Col Plattsburg, 73; Washington-Jefferson Nat Painting Exhib, Washington, Pa, 76. Pos: Dir, Lake Placid Sch Art, 71-; assoc managing dir, Ctr Music, Drama & Art, 72- Style & Technique: Figurative realist; printmaker. Media: Oil. Mailing Add: 18 Academy St Saranac Lake NY 12983

PATÉ, LEE
PRINTMAKER
b Medina, Ohio, Apr 22, 52. Study: Howard Univ, Washington, DC, 71-73; Md Inst, Baltimore, 73-76; Jerome Found Grant for Bob Blackburns Printmaking Workshop, New York, 77. Exhib: Henri Gallery, Washington, DC, 72; two-person show, John O'Rourk Gallery, 77; one-person show, Howard Univ, 73, B R Kornblatt, Baltimore, 76 & Studio Mus, New York, 77- Awards: Spec Drawing Award, Howard Univ, 72. Style & Technique: Lines with flat color. Media: Etching on Metal Plates; Drawing on Lithographic Plates & Paper. Collection: Mostly drawings and small paintings on paper and prints. Mailing Add: 1360 Ocean Ave Brooklyn NY 11230

PATERNOSTO, CESAR PEDRO
PAINTER
b La Plata, Buenos Aires, Arg, Nov 29, 31. Study: Nat Univ La Plata, Sch Fine Arts, 57-59, Inst Philos, 61. Work: Mus Mod Art, New York; Nat Fine Arts Mus, Buenos Aires; Plastic Arts Mus, La Plata; Albright-Knox Gallery, Buffalo; Hirshhorn Mus, Washington, DC; plus others. Exhib: Latin American Art Since Independence, Yale Univ, Conn, 65; 3rd Biennial Am Art, Cordoba, Arg, 66; The 1960's, Mus Mod Art, New York, 67; 2nd Biennial Coltejer, Medellin, Colombia, 70; one-man shows, Dusseldorf, WGer, 72, New York, 73 & Paris, 74; plus others. Awards: First Prize, 3rd Biennial Am Art, Cordoba, 66; Acquisition Award, 15th Exhib, Mar Del Plata, Arg, 66. Bibliog: Sam Hunter (auth), The Cordoba biennial, Art Am, 4/67; J R Mellow (auth), New York letter, Art Int, 11/68; K Kline (auth), Reviews, Art News, 1/70. Style & Technique: Geometric shapes, solid colors, deployed on outer side edges of single canvases of panel groups, with fronts almost blank. Media: Acrylic on Canvas. Dealer: Galerie Denise Rene 6 W 57th St New York NY 10019 & Hans Mayer Dusseldorf West Germany. Mailing Add: 135 Hudson St New York NY 10013

PATERSON, ANTHONY R
SCULPTOR, EDUCATOR
b Albany, NY, Dec 17, 34. Study: Sch of Mus Fine Arts, Boston, dipl & grad dipl; study with Harold Tovish, Ernest Morenon, Peter Abate; La Grande Chaumier Sch Drawing, Paris; Mass Inst Technol, welding; Univ Guadalajara, Mex. Work: Sch Mus Fine Arts, Boston; Kalamazoo Inst Arts, Mich. Comn: Portrait of Phil Eliot (bronze head), comn by State Univ NY Buffalo, 75-76. Exhib: Dark Mirror, Am Fedn Arts Travel Exhib, 64; Young Talent Show, Mass Coun Arts, Boston, 67; Mainstreams, Marietta Col, Ohio, 69; Small Sculpture & Drawing, Ball State Univ, 71; Nat Drawing, Pottsdam, NY, 73. Teaching: Instr sculpture, Sch Mus Fine Arts, Boston, 62-65; instr sculpture, Mr Ida Jr Col, Newton Ctr, Mass, 64-68; asst prof sculpture, State Univ NY Buffalo, 68-71, assoc prof, 71- Awards: Alumni Travel Fel, Boston Mus Fine Arts, 69; MacDowell Colony Fel, NH, 71; Fac Res Fel, State Univ NY, 70-73. Mem: Artists Comt, Buffalo, NY (pres); Am Fedn Arts; Artists Equity; Patteran Soc, Buffalo. Style & Technique: Sculpture, deriving from figure, metal, plastic, stone and wood. Media: Bronze. Dealer: Lee Norness 236-238 E 75th St New York NY 10021. Mailing Add: 530 Norwood Ave Buffalo NY 14222

PATNODE, J SCOTT
PRINTMAKER, LECTURER
b Seattle, Wash, Oct 19, 45. Study: Gonzaga Univ, AB, 68; Pratt Inst, fel, 68, MFA, 70; also with George McNeil, Walter Rogalski & Clare Romano. Work: Cheney Cowles Mem Mus, Spokane; Honolulu Acad Art; Kalamazoo Inst Arts, Mich; Evergreen State Col, Olympia, Wash; Pac Nat Bank of Wash, Seattle. Exhib: 24th Ann Art Exhib, Spokane Art Mus, 71; Hawaii Nat Print Exhib, Honolulu Acad Art, 71 & 73; CCAC World Print Competition, San Francisco Art Mus, 73; New Generation Drawings Exhib, circulated by Western Asn Art Mus, 73-75; 59th Ann Exhib Northwest Artists, Seattle Art Mus, 74. Teaching: Assoc prof printmaking, Gonzaga Univ, 70- Pos: Dir, Ad Art Gallery, Gonzaga Univ, 71- Awards: Print Purchase Award, Honolulu Acad Art, 71; Fremont Lane South Award for Painting, Spokane Art Mus, 72. Mem: Western Asn Art Mus; Spokane Allied Arts. Style & Technique: Minimal expressionist. Media: Lithography, Serigraphy. Mailing Add: 901 E Nora Spokane WA 99207

PATRICK, ALAN K
POTTER
b Richmond, Ind, June 16, 42. Study: Ball State Univ, Muncie, Ind, BS, 64, MA, 66, with Byron Temple. Work: Ball State Univ Art Gallery; Earlham Col, Richmond, Va; Richmond Art Asn Gallery. Exhib: Mus Contemp Crafts, New York, 69; St Mary's Col, Notre Dame, Ind, 73; Ind Univ Bicentennial Craft Exhib, Bloomington, 76; Ball State Univ Art Gallery, 76; Beaux Arts Designer Craftsman Exhib, Columbus, Ohio, 75 & 77; Functional Pottery, Wooster Col, Ohio, 78. Bibliog: Ruth Chin (auth), Bethel Pike Potters, Ceramics Mo, 74. Mem: Am Crafts Coun. Style & Technique: Thrown and decorated porcelain, much brushwork and overglaze lusters. Media: Stoneware, Porcelain. Mailing Add: Rt 1 Box 80-B Albany IN 47320

PATRICK, GENIE H
PAINTER, INSTRUCTOR
b Fayetteville, Ark, Nov 25, 38. Study: Miss State Col Women, 56-58; Univ Ga, BFA; Univ Ill, Urbana-Champaign, 60-61; Univ Colo, MA, 62. Exhib: Mid-South Ann, Memphis, Tenn, 59, 60 & 64; Walker Ann, Minneapolis, 66; Iowa Artist Exhib, Des Moines Art Ctr, 66, 70 & 71; Drawing Exhib, Benedicta Arts Ctr Gallery, St Joseph, Minn, 70; two-man exhib, Drawing & Painting, Coe Col Galleries, Cedar Rapids, Iowa, 71. Teaching: Instr art, Northeast Miss Jr Col, Booneville, 62-64; instr art, Radford Col, Va, 64-65; instr children's art classes, Cedar Rapids Art Ctr, Iowa, 65-70; instr drawing & painting, Univ Iowa Exten, 74-, instr life rawing, Sch Art & Art Hist, Univ Iowa, Iowa City, 74. Pos: Fel in Residence, Huntington Hartford Found, Pacific Palisades, Calif, summer 64. Style & Technique: Realist. Media: Oil. Mailing Add: 1190 E Court St Iowa City IA 52240

PATRICK, JOSEPH ALEXANDER
PAINTER, EDUCATOR
b Chester, SC, Feb 10, 38. Study: Univ Ga, BFA, 60; Univ Colo, Boulder, MFA, 62. Work: Univ Colo, Boulder; Univ Nebr, Omaha; Davenport Munic Art Gallery & Coe Col, Cedar Rapids, Iowa; Fairfield Co Hist Soc, Winnsboro, SC; State Univ NY Col Plattsbrugh. Exhib: Midwest Biennial, Joslyn Art Mus, Omaha, 65; Nat Small Painting Show, Univ Nebr, Omaha, 66; Container Corp 6th Ann Fine Arts Exhib, Rock Island, Ill, 67; Dedication Exhib, Fine Arts Ctr, State Univ Col Plattsburgh, 70; Drawing Exhib, Benedicta Arts Ctr Gallery, St Joseph, Minn, 71. Teaching: Asst art, Univ Colo, Boulder, 60-62, instr drawing & painting, 61-62; instr drawing & painting & head dept, Northeast Miss Jr Col, Booneville, 62-64; instr drawing & painting, Radford Col, 64-65; instr drawing & painting, Univ Iowa, 65-68, asst prof drawing & painting, 68-71, assoc prof drawing, 71- Pos: Mus asst, Univ Ga Mus Art, Athens, 58-60; instr art, Davenport Art Ctr, Iowa, 68, 69 & 72; instr art, Keokuk Art Asn, Iowa, 72. Awards: Residence Fel, Huntington Hartford Found, 64; Summer Fac Fel, 69 & Fac Grant,

73, Univ Iowa Found. Mem: Mid-Am Art Asn; Col Art Asn Am. Style & Technique: Realist. Media: Oil. Mailing Add: 1190 E Court St Iowa City IA 52240

PATTEE, ROWENA
SERIGRAPHER, PAINTER
b Ft Wayne, Ind, Oct 29, 35. Study: Lewis & Clark Col; Edinburgh Col Art, Scotland; Univ Ore, BA & MFA; Univ Calif, Berkeley. Work: Nat Gallery Israel, Jerusalem. Comn: Marcus Whitman Mural, Presbyterian Church, Portland, Ore; six mosaic murals, Cave-of-Dawning, Montecito, Calif. Exhib: American Artists in Britain, New Vision Ctr Gallery, London, 58; one-woman show, Marylhurst Col, 59; two-man shows, Seligmann Gallery, Seattle, 66 & Coos Art Mus, 68; Portland & Seattle Art Mus, 67-70. Teaching: Instr vis commun, Univ Portland, 70-71; instr drawing & painting, Clackamas Community Col, 70-72; lectr myths & symbols, Univ Calif & Juno Inst, 73-74. Awards: Art Award, Lewis & Clark Col, 53-54; Art Award, Coos Art Mus, Ore, 68. Style & Technique: Symbolic work on archetypal themes, using serigraphs, woodcuts and paintings. Res: Archetypal themes in cross-cultural manner. Publ: Auth & illusr, Song to Thee: Divine Androgyne, Celestial Arts, 73; auth & illusr, Our living earth, Maitraya, Shambhalla, 74; films include Song to Thee: Divine Androgyne, Interspace & Metamorphosis I. Mailing Add: 760 Ayala Lane Montecito CA 93108

PATTEN, DAVID JOHN
EDITOR, ART LIBRARIAN
b Bancroft, Iowa, May 14, 38. Study: Univ Nebr Omaha, BFA; Univ Iowa, Iowa City, MA, study with Chu-Tsing Li; Univ Mich Ann Arbor, AMLS, study with Oleg Graber & Walter Spink. Pos: Design, art & archit librn, Univ Cincinnati, 66-68; art & archit librn, Wash Univ, St Louis, 68-70; ed, Art Index, H W Wilson Co, Bronx, NY, 70- Mem: Col Art Asn Am; Art Libr Soc NAm (secy, 73-74, chmn NY chap, 73-74). Res: Iranian architecture, art reference works, indexing in the visual arts. Interest: Islamic art; India art; Old Master prints; Japanese prints. Publ: Ed, Art Libraries Society of North America Directory of Members, 1973-74, Art Libr Soc NAm, 73-74; ed, Library Classification Systems and the Visual Arts, Art Libr Soc NAm, 76. Mailing Add: Art Index H W Wilson Co 950 University Ave Bronx NY 10452

PATTERSON, CURTIS RAY
SCULPTOR, INSTRUCTOR
b Shreveport, La, Nov 11, 44. Study: Grambling State Univ, BS, 67; Ga State Univ, MVA, 75. Comn: Coretin steel (20ft x 48ft), Bur of Cult & Int Affairs, 77; mild steel (40ft x 60ft), Atlanta Rapid Transit Authority, 78. Exhib: Thirty-five Artists in the SE (contribr, catalogue), High Mus Art, Atlanta, Ga, 76; 35 Artists in the SE (traveling show), 77-78; Festival of Arts & Cult, Lagos, Nigeria, 77; Fourteen Sculptors, High Mus of Art, Atlanta, 77. Teaching: Teacher sculpture & pottery, Therrell High Sch, Atlanta, 70-76; instr sculpture & pottery, Atlanta Col of Art, 76- Pos: Vpres, Thirteen Minus One, 76-77; mem cult events adv funding comt, Bur of Cult & Int Affairs, Atlanta, 77- Mem: Black Artist of Atlanta; Thirteen Minus One. Style & Technique: Contemporary mainstream; sculpture (foundry and fabrication), and pottery. Media: Metal, Clay. Mailing Add: 1091 Flamingo Dr SW Atlanta GA 30311

PATTERSON, GEORGE W PATRICK
See Kemoha

PATTERSON, PATRICIA
FILM CRITIC, PAINTER
b Jersey City, NJ, Mar 17, 41. Study: Parson's Sch of Design, grad cert. Exhib: Mills Col, Oakland, Calif, 77; Houston Mus Contemp Art, Tex, 77; La Jolla Mus Contemp Arts, Calif, 78; Inst for Art & Urban Resources, PS 1, New York, 78; Cleveland Mus Art, Ohio, 78; Fine Arts Gallery, Univ Calif, Irvine, 78. Teaching: Asst prof painting, drawing & art criticism, Univ Calif, San Diego, 76- Pos: Contrib writer, Film Comment Mag, New York, 75- Style & Technique: Narrative painting with casein or tempera serial panels, tableaux of free standing figures and one-of-a kind books. Media: Casein Paint or Enamel Paint on Masonite; Watercolor on Paper. Publ: (With Manny Farber) Co-auth, Werner Herzog; the cinema of Fata Morgana, 75 & The new breed of filmmakers: a multiplication of myths, 75, City Mag; auth, Fassbinder, 75 & co-auth, Gun crazy—Part II, 76 & Beyond the new wave: I (Kitchen without Kitsch), 77, Film Comment; auth, Aran kitchen, aran sweaters, Heresies, 78. Dealer: Ellie Blankfort Gallery 2341 Ronda Vista Dr Los Angeles CA 90027. Mailing Add: 1320 Ocean Ave Del Mar CA 92014

PATTERSON, WILLIAM JOSEPH
EDUCATOR, PRINTMAKER
b Albany, NY, Mar 16, 41. Study: Hartford Art Sch, BFA, 65; Am Acad Rome, Abbey Found fel, 65-67; Syracuse Univ, MFA, 69. Work: Libr of Cong; Honolulu Acad Art; New Britain Mus; State Univ NY Col Potsdam; Northern Ill Univ. Comn: Five drawings, Third Nat Bank, Springfield, 75; ed of prints, Mass Bar Asn. Exhib: One-man show, Nat Acad Design, New York, 68; New Talent in Printmaking, Assoc Am Artists, New York, 70; Artist Choice, NY State Univ & Assoc Am Artists, 72; 23rd Nat Exhib Prints, Libr of Cong & Nat Col Fine Arts, 73; Am Printmakers Bi-ann, Brooklyn Mus, 64. Teaching: Instr printmaking, Hartford Art Sch, Univ Hartford, 69-71; assoc prof printmaking & drawing, Univ Mass, Amherst, 71- Awards: Mass Coun Arts Fel, 75; Prize for Best Work of Art, Conn Acad Fine Arts Exhib. Bibliog: Florence Berlman (auth), Prints of Patterson, Hartford Courant, 7/71; Tom Hart (auth), Bank commissions painting, Springfield Daily News, 75. Mem: Boston Printmakers. Style & Technique: Figurative. Media: Intaglio. Publ: (Prints), Young Man, 71, Four Artists, 72, After Rembrandt, 73 & Daumier, 75, Assoc Am Artists; Self Portrait Near a Window, 74. Dealer: Assoc Am Artists 663 Fifth Ave New York NY 10021. Mailing Add: 24 Applewood Lane Amherst MA 01002

PATTISON, ABBOTT
SCULPTOR, PAINTER
b Chicago, Ill, May 15, 16. Study: Yale Col, BA, 37, Yale Sch Fine Arts, BFA, 39. Work: Whitney Mus Am Art; Israel State Mus, Jerusalem; San Francisco Mus; Buckingham Palace, London; Art Inst Chicago; plus others. Comn: Sculpture, Cent Nat Bank, Cleveland; Ill State Capitol, Springfield; Lincoln Libr, Springfield; Chicago State Univ; US State Dept; plus others. Exhib: Art Inst Chicago, 40-69; Metrop Mus Art, 51 & 52; four shows, Whitney Mus Am Art, 53-59; one-man shows, Holbrook Mus, Univ Ga, 54 & Sculpture Ctr, NY, 56; plus many other group & one-man shows. Teaching: Instr, Art Inst Chicago, 46-52; sculptor-in-residence, Univ Ga, 54, instr, Skowhegan Sch Art, 55-56. Awards: First Logan Prize, Art Inst Chicago, 42; Prize, Metrop Mus Art, New York, 50; Prize, Bundy Mus, Vt, 67. Mem: Chicago Art Club. Mailing Add: 334 Woodland Ave Winnetka IL 60093

PAUL, BERNARD H
CRAFTSMAN
b Baltimore, Md, Apr 22, 07. Study: Md Inst, Baltimore. Comn: Christmas shows, Colonial Williamsburg, 56-57 & 60-; marionettes for opera, Peabody Conservatory Music, 57; miniature model sets, Hutzler's Dept Store's 100th Anniversary, 58; puppets used by US Dept Health, Educ & Welfare for series of motion pictures for Social Security TV spots. Teaching: Instr puppetry, Md Inst Col Art; puppet shows, Hutzler's Br Store. Pos: Dir TV prog, Paul's Puppets, WBAL-TV, Baltimore, 48-57 & WMAR-TV, 57-58. Awards: Prizes, Md Inst, 29, 33 & 37. Mailing Add: 414 Hawthorne Rd Linthicum Heights MD 21091

PAUL, KEN (HUGH)
PRINTMAKER, PAINTER
b Ogden, Utah, Apr 24, 38. Study: Univ Utah, 58-59; Univ Wyo, BA(with honors), 61, MA, 65. Work: Art Gallery SAustralia, Adelaide; Art Gallery Tasmania, Hobart, Australia; Univ Adelaide; Univ Wyo; Coos Art Mus, Ore. Comn: Translucent painting, Adelaide Arts Festival, 67; ceiling panel restoration, Sacred Heart Chapel, Geelong, Australia. Exhib: 1st Springfield Col Nat Print Exhib, Mass, 65; Denver Art Mus Nat Show, 65; Calif Soc Printmakers Ann, Richmond, 71; Seattle Print Int, 71; Ore Artists Ann, Portland, 72-73 & 75. Teaching: Lectr art, Gordon Inst Technol, Geelong, 66-67; lectr printmaking, SAustralian Sch Art, Adelaide, 67-69; assoc prof printmaking, Univ Ore, 70-; vis instr, M I Kerns Art Ctr, Eugene, Ore, summer 71; vis instr, Pac Northwest Graphics Workshop, Cheshire, Ore, 74. Awards: Printmakers Ore Exhib First Prize, M I Kerns Art Ctr, 72; Prize for Painting, Ore Col Educ, Monmouth, 72; Graduate School Summer Res Grant, Univ Ore, 73. Mem: Contemp Art Soc SAustralia (vpres, 68-69); Maude Kerns Art Ctr (mem bd, 72-74); Portland Art Mus. Style & Technique: Synthesizing geometric structures with form fragments abstracted from nature, primarily landscape. Media: Lithography, Silkscreen; Oil, Acrylic. Dealer: Art Works Gallery Sunriver OR 97701. Mailing Add: 2585 Taylor St Eugene OR 97405

PAUL, WILLIAM D, JR
MUSEUM DIRECTOR, PAINTER
b Wadley, Ga, Sept 26, 34. Study: Atlanta Art Inst, BFA; Univ Ga, AB & MFA; Emory Univ; Ga State Col; Univ Rome, Italy. Work: General Mills, Inc, Minneapolis; Hallmark Cards, Kansas City, Mo; Little Rock Art Ctr, Ark; Ga Mus Art, Atlanta; Univ Ga, Athens; plus others. Exhib: Southeastern Ann, Atlanta; Va Intermont Col, Bristol; Birmingham Ann, Ala; Corcoran Gallery Art, Washington, DC; Art of Two Cities, Nat Traveling Exhib, Am Fedn Arts, plus many others. Collections Arranged: Sixty small original exhibs, Charlotte Crosby Kemper Gallery, Kansas City Art Inst, 61-65; Art of Two Cities, Am Fedn Arts Traveling Exhib, 65; The Visual Assault, 67, Drawings by Richard Diebenkorn, Selections: The Downtown Gallery, Drawing and Watercolors by Raphael Soyer, Recent Collages by Samuel Adler, 20th Anniversary Exhibition & Art of Ancient Peru, The Paul Clifford Collection, Ga Mus Art; American Painting: the 1940's, 68; American Painting, the 1950's, 68; American Painting: the 1960's, 69; Philip Pearlstein, Retrospective Exhibition, 70. Teaching: Instr art & art hist, Kansas City Art Inst, Park Col & Univ Ga. Pos: Dir exhibs & cur study collections, Kansas City Art Inst, 61-65; cur, Ga Mus Art, 67-69; dir, Ga Mus Art, 69- Awards: Macy's Ann, Kansas City, 59, 61, 63 & 64; Atlanta Paper Co Ann, 61; Hallmark Award, Mid-Am Ann, 62; plus others. Mem: Am Fedn Arts (trustee); Col Art Asn; Am Asn Mus. Mailing Add: Ga Mus Art Univ Ga Athens GA 30601

PAULIN, RICHARD CALKINS
MUSEUM DIRECTOR, CRAFTSMAN
b Chicago, Ill, Oct 25, 28. Study: DePauw Univ, BA; Univ Denver, MA; Inst Fine Arts, NY Univ; also in Guadalajara, Mex. Exhib: Univ Ill, 60; Rockford Art Asn, 61; Beloit Col, 61-63 & 65; two-man show, Nat Col Educ, Evanston, Ill, 64. Collections Arranged: Teachers Who Paint, 59; Chicago Painters, 60; Six Chicago Painters, 61; Picasso Preview, 62; George Rouault-His Aqua Tints and Wood Engravings, 63; Collectors Showcase, 64; 30 Contemporary Living American Painters, 64; First National Invitational Painting Exhibition: Fifty States of Art, 65; Swedish Handcraft, 61. Teaching: Instr arts & crafts, Roosevelt Jr High Sch, Rockford, Ill; former instr basic & intermediate art courses, Rockford Art Asn. Pos: Dir, Harry & Della Burpee Art Gallery, Rockford, Ill, formerly; dir mus art & asst prof art hist, Univ Ore, currently. Awards: Canfield Award, Rockford Art Asn, 61. Mem: Nat Educ Asn; Nat Coun Art Educ; Mus Dirs Asn NAm; Western Art Asn; Mid-Western Mus Dirs Asn; plus others. Mailing Add: Mus of Art Univ Ore Eugene OR 97403

PAULLEY, DAVID GORDON
PAINTER
b Midwest, Wyo, May 31, 31. Study: With Pawel Kontney, Denver. Work: Buffalo Bill Hist Ctr, Cody, Wyo; Cheyenne Nat Bank, Wyo; Wyo State Mus, Cheyenne; Nat Bank Omaha, Nebr; First State Bank, Newcastle, Wyo. Comn: Illustrated bank checks, Rocky Mountain Bank Note Co, 73 & 78; Rocky Mountain Fed Savings & Loan, Cheyenne, Wyo; Union State Bank, Upton, Wyo; First Cheyenne Bank N, Cheyenne. Exhib: Wyo State Mus, 71; 3rd & 4th Regional Competition, Cheyenne, 71 & 72; Saks Art Gallery, Denver, 71-72; Thorne Gallery, Scottsdale, Ariz, 74. Awards: 4th Regional Seven-State Competition Purchase Award, Cheyenne Nat Bank, 72. Style & Technique: Western paintings; brush and palette knife. Media: Oil, Tempra Watercolor. Mailing Add: 2862 Pine Dr Cheyenne WY 82001

PAULSEN, BRIAN OLIVER
PAINTER
b Seattle, Wash, Mar 29, 41. Study: Univ Wash, BA, 63; Wash State Univ, MFA, 66. Work: S S Kresge Inc, Detroit, Mich; Col of the Pac, Stockton, Calif; Rothmans Art Gallery, Stratford, Ont; Western Ill Univ; Pioneer Mus & Haggin Galleries, Stockton. Exhib: San Francisco Art Int Centennial Exhib, San Francisco Art Mus, 70; Extraordinary Realities, Whitney Mus Am Art, New York, 73; touring exhib, 5 Atlantic Provincial Can Mus, 74; Images on Paper, Springfield, Ill, 74; Artrain Traveling Art Exhib, Cent US, 75. Teaching: Asst prof printmaking & drawing, Calif State Univ, Chico, 66-71; asst prof painting & drawing, Univ Calgary, 71-73. Awards: Best of Show, Walnut Creek Art Asn, 69; Purchase Award, Col of the Pac, 69; Purchase Award, Western Ill Univ, 74. Style & Technique: Surrealistic fantasies with acrylic paint. Mailing Add: 320 N 16th St Grand Forks ND 58201

PAULSON, ALAN
SCULPTOR
b Philadelphia, Pa, Oct 6, 38. Study: Temple Univ, 59; Philadelphia Col Art, BFA, 63; Univ Pa, MFA, 65. Exhib: One-man shows, J B Speed Art Mus, Louisville, Ky, 68, Munson-Williams-Proctor Inst, Utica, NY, 74, West Broadway Gallery, New York, 76 & Touchstone Gallery, New York, 77; Ann Exhib, Artists of Cent NY, 73, 75 & 77; New Talent Show, Allan Stone Gallery, New York, 73; Cooperstown Art Asn Nat Ann Competition, NY, 75, 76 & 77. Teaching: Instr sculpture, Louisville Sch Art, Ky, 65-70, dir, 68-70; instr sculpture & chmn dept, Layton Sch Art, Milwaukee, 70-71; asst prof sculpture, Colgate Univ, Hamilton, NY, 71-78. Awards: Hon Mention, Competition Tour SE, Southern Asn Sculptors, 68; Second Prize, Regional Ann, Kirkland Art Ctr, Clinton, NY, 76; Selected for Sculpture Space, Utica Steam Engine & Boiler Works, Utica, NY, 77. Style & Technique: Direct carving and construction-polished. Media: Wood, Bronze. Dealer: Touchstone Gallery Inc 118 E 65th St New York NY 10021. Mailing Add: 19 University Ave Hamilton NY 13346

PAYNE, JOHN D
SCULPTOR, EDUCATOR
b Pontotoc, Miss, Sept 17, 29. Study: Beloit Col, BA, studied with Franklin Boggs, OV Shaffer & A D Popinsky; Univ Wis-Madison, MS, studied with Dean Meeker, W Colescott & A Sessler, MFA, Danforth Study Grant, studied with Ed Higgins, L E Moll & Arne Jacobson; Univ Kans, Lawrence, studied with Elden Teft. Work: Univ Wis Union Collection, Madison; Beloit State Bank, Adams Collection, Wis; Atlanta Univ, Ga; Loyola Univ, New Orleans; La State Univ, Union Collection, Baton Rouge. Comn: Steel sculpture (6ft high), Comn by John Pyros, Tarpon Springs, Fla, 67; Wood sculpture (10ft high), Baton Rouge, La, 68; The Sculptor, The Campus & The Prairie (three steel works, 10ft to 19ft), Govs State Univ, Park Forest South, Ill, 76-70. Exhib: Rock River Ann, Beloit Col, Wis, 58; Atlanta Univ Nat Ann, Ga, 58, 62, 64, 65 & 66; Wis State Fair Ann, Milwaukee, 61; Okla Ann, Okla Art Ctr, Oklahoma City, 62; Mid-America, Mulvane Mus, Topeka, Kans, 62; Oklahoma City Univ, 63; La Art Comn Ann, Old State Capital Mus, 64-66; Gulf States Ann Drawings & Prints, Delgado Mus, New Orleans, 64; Univ Kans Nat/Int Casting Conf, Lawrence, 66; one-man shows, Baton Rouge Gallery, La, 67-70, La State Univ, 68 & Beloit Col, 68; Twelve Afro-Am Artists, Univ Wis, 69; Discovery 1970, Univ Cincinnati, Ohio, 70; The Sculptor, The Campus, The Prairie, Govs State Univ, Park Forest, South, Ill, 76. Teaching: Chmn dept art, Langston Univ, Okla, 61-63; assoc prof sculpture & 3-D design, Southern Univ & La Inst Interior Design, 63-71; prof art, Southern Univ, New Orleans, La, 63-65 & Southern Univ, Baton Rouge, 66-71; sculptor in residence, chmn dept art & coordr art, music & theatre, Governors State Univ, 71- Awards: Top Award, State Fair, Milwaukee, Wis, 61 & All Wis Exhib, Class of 1930, 61; Second Award, Atlanta Univ Ann, Ga, 64, 65 & 66. Bibliog: American Printmaker, Graphic Group, Calif, 74; Afro-American Artist 1800 to Present, Boston Univ Libr, Mass, 75; Art: African American, Harcourt Brace Jovanovich, Inc, 78. Mem: Col Art Asn (mem host comt, 76); Nat Coun Art Adminr. Style & Technique: Sculpture steel; various techniques wood sculpture; welded plastics. Media: Steel and bronze; wood and plastics combined. Mailing Add: 41 S Arbor Trails Park Forest IL 60466

PAYNE, LAN
PAINTER, FILMMAKER
b South Bend, Ind, May 11, 48. Study: Webster Col; Cleveland Inst Art; San Francisco Art Inst, BFA, 72. Work: Western Asn Art Mus Circulating Exhib, Mills Col. Exhib: Civic Ctr Art Festival, San Francisco, 72; I C Nelson Gallery, Univ Calif, Davis, 74; Phoenix Gallery, San Francisco, 74; Whitney Mus Am Art Biennial, New York, 75; Information Show, San Francisco Art Inst, 75. Bibliog: Peter Plagens (auth), rev in, Artforum, 10/74; Sylvia Brown (auth), 74 Debut, City Mag, 8/7/74; A Frankenstein (auth), Art world, San Francisco Chronicle, 6/26/75. Media: Oil on Wood; Film. Mailing Add: 102 Forsyth 11 New York NY 10002

PAYOR, EUGENE
PAINTER, ILLUSTRATOR
b New York, NY, July 28, 09. Study: Univ Calif, BFA; Calif Sch Fine Arts, with Harold Von Schmidt, Judson Starr & Gertrude Partington Albright, dipl; Art Students League; also with John Stuart Curry, Jean Charlot & Raphael Soyer. Work: Birobijan Mus, USSR; B'nai B'rith Mus, Washington, DC; Gen Motors, Detroit, RCA Corp, New York; P Lorillard Co Inc, New York. Comn: Children's mural, Orphanage Hosp Nursery, San Mateo, Calif, 29; two rehab murals, Daytop Village Inc, New York, 74-75; also many poster comn by industrial corps, 50-69 & portrait comn, 60-75. Exhib: Whitney Mus Am Art, New York, 40; Univ Ga, 44; Va Mus Fine Arts, Richmond, 45; Parrish Mus, Southampton, NY, 46-75; B'nai B'rith Mus, Washington, DC, 71. Teaching: Prof art, Univ Ga, 43-45. Pos: Art dir, Einson-Freeman Corp, New York, 45-53; art dir, Consolidated Lithographing Corp, New York, 53-61; dir art, P Lorillard Co Inc, New York, 61-66. Awards: Eight First Awards & Prizes, Nat Lithographers Asn; First Award, Art Dir Club, New York, 49-50; First Prize, Guild Hall, Southampton, 53. Bibliog: Alex Kruse (auth), Murals in Georgia, Brooklyn Eagle Sun, 45; Angus Perkerson (auth), Camouflage art, Atlanta J, 45; Mary Burliuk (auth), Eugene Payor and his art, Color & Rhyme, 51. Mem: Artists Equity; Allied Artists Am. Style & Technique: Modern realist, overtones of pop and decorative; portraits, figures, flowers and still life. Media: Oil, Watercolor, Pastel. Publ: Illusr, Les Jours Heureux, Cordon, 39; illusr, Charlot Murals in Georgia, Univ Ga, 45; auth, Aerial camouflage, Atlanta J Mag Section, 45; illusr, Reunion En Mexico, Dryden. Dealer: Ella Lerner Gallery 17 Franklin St Lenox MA 02140; Capricorn Gallery 8004 Norfolk Ave Bethesda MD 20014. Mailing Add: 515 West End Ave New York NY 10024

PAYSON, MR & MRS CHARLES S
COLLECTORS
Mr Payson, b Portland, Maine, Oct 16, 98. Study: Mr Payson, Yale Univ, grad, 21; Harvard Univ, LLB, 24. Collection: 19th Century art. Mailing Add: Manhasset NY 11030

PAYSON, DALE CONSTANCE
ILLUSTRATOR, PAINTER
b White Plains, NY, June 3, 43. Study: Endicott Jr Col, Mass, grad, 63; Sch Visual Arts, New York, 64-69; also with John Gundelfinger. Style & Technique: Realist, figurative. Media: Watercolor, Pencil. Publ: Illusr, Ann Aurelia & Dorothy, Harper & Row, 68; auth, Almost Twins, 75, co-auth, Sleepy Time Treasury, 76 & illusr, My Turn Your Turn, 78, Prentice-Hall; illusr, Magic Castle Fairy Tale Book, Random House, 78. Mailing Add: 149 Franklin St New York NY 10013

PEABODY, AMELIA
SCULPTOR
b Marblehead, Mass, July 3, 90. Study: Boston Mus Fine Arts Sch, with Charles Grafly; Northeastern Univ, hon DFA. Work: End of an Era (marble), Mus Fine Arts, Boston; Boy with Cat (stone), Children's Med Ctr, Boston; plastic fox, Audubon Soc Laughing Brook Reservation. Comn: Victory Medal, Joslin Clin, Boston; baptismal font, church in Oxford, Mass; portrait plaque of Dr Hsein Wu, Harvard Med Sch, Cambridge; Woodchucks and Pheasants, cast stone for entrance gate of Groton Mem Park, Mass; granite setter in animal graveyard for Mrs Frank C Paine, Wayland, Mass. Exhib: New York World's Fair, two yrs; Whitney Mus Am Art, New York, 40; Carnegie Inst Int, 41; Nat Asn Women Artists, 53. Teaching: Chmn arts & skills, Am Red Cross, Boston. Awards: Mrs Oakleigh Thorne Medal, Garden Club Am. Mem: Guild Boston Artists; Nat Asn Women Artists; Nat Sculpture Soc; New Eng Sculptors' Asn; Copley Soc. Media: Stone, Bronze, Ceramics. Dealer: Guild Boston Artists 162 Newbury St Boston MA 02116. Mailing Add: 120 Commonwealth Ave Boston MA 02116

PEACE, BERNIE (KINZEL)
PAINTER
b Williamsburg, Ky, Oct 20, 33. Study: Berea Col, AB(art), 54; Ind Univ, MFA(painting), 57. Work: Berea Col; Ind Univ; WVa Univ; State WVa, Charleston; Washington & Jefferson Col. Comn: Painting, WVa Arts & Humanities Coun, Charleston, 72. Exhib: 11th Ann Piedmont Painting & Sculpture Exhib, Mint Mus, Charlotte, NC, 71; Max 24-72, Nat Small Painting Competition, Purdue Univ, 72; 1973 Artists Biennial, New Orleans Mus Art, 73; Washington & Jefferson National Painting Show, 74; Appalachian Corridors Biennial 4, Charleston, 75; Aqueous Open 76, Pittsburgh Watercolor Soc, Pa, 76; Ann Exhibs, Allied Artists of WVa, Charleston Art Gallery, 76 & 77 & Retrospective Exhib, 78; XII & XIII Invitational Regional Exhibs, Westmoreland Co Mus of Art, Greensburg, Pa, 76 & 77; 45th Southeastern Competition-Painting & Sculpture, Southeastern Ctr for Contemp Art, Winston-Salem, NC, 77; 77 Invitational, Parkersburg Art Ctr, WVa, 77; 54th Ann, Erie Art Ctr, Pa, 77. Teaching: Prof drawing & painting, West Liberty State Col, 60- Awards: First Prize Watercolor, Huntington Galleries, WVa, 67; Purchase Award, Washington & Jefferson Col, 71; Purchase Awards, WVa Arts & Humanities Coun, 72, 73 & 75; Judge's Choice Award, Bethany Col Fall Ann & Hon Mention, Bethany Col Bicentennial Exhib, Bethany, WVa, 76. Mem: Col Art Asn WVa; Allied Artists WVa; Nat Coun Art Adminr. Style & Technique: Hard-edge, geometric; non-objective, abstract, shaped picture planes. Media: Acrylic, Watercolor. Mailing Add: Washington Farms Wheeling WV 26003

PEAKE, CHANNING
PAINTER
b Marshall, Colo, Oct 24, 10. Study: Calif Col Arts & Crafts, 28; Santa Barbara Sch Art, 29-31; Art Students League, with Rico Lebrun, 35-36. Work: Santa Barbara Mus Art. Comn: Murals (with Louis Rubenstein), Germanic Mus, Harvard Univ, 36 (with Rico Lebrun), Pa Sta, New York, 36-38 (with Howard Warshaw), Santa Barbara Pub Libr, 58. Exhib: Pa Acad Fine Arts; Univ Ill, 53 & 55; three-man show, Santa Barbara Mus Art, 53 & 56; Colorado Springs Fine Arts Ctr; Los Angeles Co Mus Art; plus others. Pos: Founder, Santa Barbara Mus Art. Mailing Add: Box 662 Santa Ynez CA 93460

PEARL, MARILYN
ART DEALER
b Akron, Ohio. Study: Hunter Col, BA; Columbia Univ, MA. Exhibitions Arranged: Yale School of Art Faculty Drawing Show, 76 & American Geometric Abstract Painting of the 1950s, 77, Marilyn Pearl Gallery. Teaching: Asst prof hist, New York Inst of Technol, New York & Old Westbury, NY, 68-74. Pos: Dir & pres, Marilyn Pearl Gallery, 76- Specialty: Contemporary American painting, sculpture, drawing. Collection: Stephen Greene, Michael Loew, Bernard Chaet, Lawrence Fane, David Hockney, Miro, Lucas Samaras and 19th century Dutch. Mailing Add: 29 W 57th St New York NY 10019

PEARLMAN, ETTA S
PAINTER
b New York, NY, Mar 30. Study: Brooklyn Col, BA, 60; Brooklyn Mus Art Sch. Work: Power Gallery Contemp Art, Univ Sydney, Australia; Brooklyn Mus. Exhib: One-woman shows, Brooklyn Mus Little Gallery Series, painting, 73 & collages, 74 & Pleiades Gallery, 75, 76 & 78; Gallery 91, Brooklyn, 75; Brooklyn Mus Art Sales & Rental Gallery, 75. Style & Technique: Collages (words, graphite, threads, pins); large loose canvases in mixed media (denim, threads, nails, wood, words). Dealer: Pleiades Gallery 152 St New York NY 10012. Mailing Add: 2934 Clubhouse Rd Merrick NY 11566

PEARLSTEIN, PHILIP
PAINTER, EDUCATOR
b Pittsburgh, Pa, May 24, 24. Study: Carnegie Inst, with Sam Rosenberg, Robert Lepper & Balcomb Greene, BFA, 49; Inst Fine Arts, NY Univ, MA, 55. Work: Whitney Mus Am Art; Mus Mod Art, New York; Corcoran Gallery Art, Washington, DC; Hirshhorn Collection, James Michener Found; Art Inst Chicago; also in pvt collections. Exhib: Eight Ann Group Shows, Whitney Mus Am Art, 55-72 & 22 Realists, 70; Univ Ill, 65, 67 & 69; Vassar Col, 68; Smithsonian, ciruclated Latin Am, 68-70; Aspects of a New Realism, Milwaukee Art Ctr, 69; Retrospective, Univ Ga, 70; Hayden Gallery, Mass Inst Technol, 71; Philadelphia Acad Fine Arts, 71; Am Fedn Artists, 72; 25 Yrs Am Painting 1948-73, Des Moines Art Ctr, Iowa, 73; Ars 74, Helsinki Mus Art, Finland, 74; 1st Biennial Figuratuve Paintings, Tokyo, Japan, 74; Contemp Am Painting, Randolph-Macon Woman's Col, Lynchburg, Va, 75; plus many others. Teaching: Instr, Pratt Inst, 59-63; from asst prof to prof art, Brooklyn Col, 63- Awards: Fulbright Fel to Italy, 58-59; Nat Endowment Arts Grant, 69; Guggenheim Fel, 71 & 72. Bibliog: Allen S Weller (auth), The Joys and Sorrows of Recent American Art, Univ Ill, 68; Udo Kultermann (auth), The New Painting, 69 & Radical Realism, 72, Praeger; Ellen Schwartz (auth), A conversation with Philip Pearlstein, Art in Am, 9-10/71; plus others. Dealer: Allan Frumkin Gallery 41 E 57th St New York NY 10022. Mailing Add: 163 W 88th St New York NY 10024

PEARLSTEIN, SEYMOUR
PAINTER, EDUCATOR
b Brooklyn, NY, Oct 14, 23. Study: Pratt Inst; Art Students League; also pvt study with Jack Potter, New York. Work: Mus of NMex, Santa Fe; Mint Mus Art, Charlotte, NC; Nat Acad of Design, New York; Fine Arts Gallery of San Diego, Calif. Exhib: Springfield Art Mus, Mo, 72; Ball State Univ, Muncie, Ind, 75; Butler Inst Am Art, Youngstown, Ohio, 75; Art in Embassies Prog, Nicaragua, 76-78; Am Watercolor Soc, New York, 77; Nat Arts Club, Nat Acad of Design & Queens Mus, New York, 78; one-man shows, Silvermine Guild of Artists, New Canaan, Conn, 73, Far Gallery, New York, 73, 75 & 78, New York Community Col, 74 & De Mers Gallery, Hilton Head, SC, 75. Teaching: Prof art, City Univ New York & New York City Community Col, Brooklyn, 70- Awards: Childe Hassam Purchase Award, 69 & 77 & Grant, 75, Am Acad of Arts & Lett; Henry Ward Ranger Purchase Award, Nat Acad of Design, 71. Bibliog: Diane Hines (auth), Seymour Pearlstein paints the figure, Am Artist Mag, 2/71; Andrea Mikotajuk (auth), Seymour Pearlstein rev, Arts Mag, 3/73; Gordon Brown (auth), Seymour Pearlstein rev, Arts Mag, 3/75. Mem: Nat Acad of Design; Allied Artists of Am (dir, 76-78); Alliance of Figurative Artists (chmn, 76-77); Am Watercolor Soc (dir, 78). Style & Technique: Figures in interiors painted in a broad expressionistic manner, basic concerns are mood and attitude and how form is effected by light and shade and atmosphere. Media: Oil, Acrylic, Watercolor. Dealer: Far Gallery 22 E 80th St New York NY 10021. Mailing Add: 52 Dartmouth St Forest Hills NY 11375

PEARMAN, SARA JANE
ART HISTORIAN, ART LIBRARIAN
b Dallas, Tex, Sept 6, 40. Study: Univ Wichita, BAE; Univ Kans, MA(art hist); Case-Western Reserve Univ, PhD(art hist). Collections Arranged: Glass Collection of the Univ Kans (auth, catalogue). Teaching: Instr art hist, Kearney State Col, 64-66; lectr art hist, Akron State Univ, 68- & Cleveland State Univ, 77- Pos: Slide librn, Cleveland Mus of Art. Mem: Col Art Asn; Midwest Art Asn; Cleveland Medieval Soc; Arlis/NA. Res: Specialist in iconography, of all periods; art historical interest in late medieval, Northern Renaissance. Publ: Auth, Mirror of Art, Ralph, Vol 4 (1977); auth, Otto Dix, a Self Portrait, Univ Kans Exhib. Mailing Add: 4419 Sheraton Dr Parma OH 44134

PEARSON, CLIFTON
SCULPTOR, EDUCATOR
b Birmingham, Ala, June 24, 48. Study: Ala A&M Univ, BS, 70; Ill State Univ, MS, 71, EdD, 74; also with Joel Myers, Timothy Mather, Ruddy Audio, Thomas Malone, Max Rennels, M M Chambers. Work: Ill State Mus, Springfield; Peoria Art Guild, Ill. Comn: Salt glaze sculptures, comn by Dr & Mus E W Womack, Huntsville, Ala & Wayman AME Church, Bloomington, Ill; Celebrated Lady (mural), comn by Mrs Jane Rhinehart, Huntsville; Slavery Chains (ceramic bust), Ala A&M Univ, Normal. Exhib: Mid-States Crafts Exhib, Evansville Mus Arts & Sci, Ind, 71; Black Expo 71, Chicago; Afro-Am Exhib, Birmingham Mus Art, Ala, 72; Craftmen 73, Ill State Mus, Springfield, 73; Cent South Exhib, The Parthenon, Nashville, Tenn, 75. Collections Arranged: 21 exhibs, Ala A&M University Gallery of Art. Teaching: Doctorate teaching asst ceramics & art educ, Ill State Univ, 71-73; asst prof ceramics, drawing & art educ, Ala A&M Univ, 73-74, assoc prof, 74-76. Awards: Purchase Award, Ill State Mus, 73; Southern Fel Grant, 74; House of Bamboo Award in Sculpture, Tenn Art League, 75. Bibliog: C Pearson (auth), 14 programs on ceramics, Educ TV/Ala A&M Univ TV Commun, 8/75. Mem: Nat Conf Artists; Am Crafts Coun; Nat Educ Asn; Ala Craftsmen Coun (trustee, 75). Style & Technique: Free style, relates to primitive art, includes Black elements, incorporates slab and throwing ceramic techniques, functional and non-functional glass blowing, sculptural works. Media: Clay Stoneware, Salt Glaze. Mailing Add: 6315 Matic Rd Huntsville AL 35810

PEARSON, HENRY C
PAINTER
b Kinston, NC, Oct 8, 14. Study: Univ NC, BA, 35; Yale Univ, MFA, 38; Art Students League, 53-56. Work: Mus Mod Art, Metrop Mus Art & Whitney Mus Am Art, New York; Albright-Knox Art Gallery, Buffalo; NC Mus Art, Raleigh. Comn: World University Service (poster), List Art Posters, 65; 6th New York Film Festival—Lincoln Center (poster), List Art Posters, 68; Five Psalms (book), Women's Comt, Brandeis Univ, 69. Exhib: Workshop Gallery, New York, 58; Stephen Radich Gallery, New York, 60-70; The Responsive Eye, Mus Mod Art, New York, 65; 29th Biennial Exhib, Corcoran Gallery Art, Washington, DC, 65; Drawings USA, Minn Mus Art, St Paul, 71-73; Betty Parsons Gallery, New York, 71-76; Color Painting, Amherst Col, Mass, 72; Art Students League Centennial Exhib, 75; Truman Gallery, New York, 76- Teaching: Instr painting, New Sch Social Res, currently; gen critic, Pa Acad Fine Arts. Awards: Tamarind Lithography Workshop, Ford Found, 64; Kreeger Purchase Prize, Corcoran Gallery Art, 65; J Henry Scheidt Award, Pa Acad Fine Arts, 69. Bibliog: Lippard (auth), Henry Pearson, Art Inst, 65. Mem: Am Abstract Artists. Style & Technique: Single flat shape on wash ground. Media: Acrylic, Oil, Watercolor. Dealer: Truman Gallery 38 E 57th St New York NY 10022. Mailing Add: 1601 Cambridge Dr Kinston NC 28501

PEARSON, JAMES EUGENE
INSTRUCTOR, SCULPTOR
b Woodstock, Ill, Dec 12, 39. Study: Northern Ill Univ, BS(educ), 61, MS(educ), MFA, 64; Tyler Sch Art, Temple Univ; Ithaca Col. Work: Northern Ill Univ, DeKalb; Palais des Beaux Arts, Charleroi, Belg; Taft Field Campus, Northern Ill Univ, Oregon; Dixon State Sch, Ill; Sch Dist 15, McHenry, Ill. Comn: Lorado Taft (bronze relief plaque), Taft Field Campus, Northern Ill Univ, 67; Vicki Unis (oil portrait), Sarasota, Fla, 69; Mae Stinespring (oil portrait), comn by Harry Stinespring, McHenry, Ill, 69; portraits in oils of Mr & Mrs Francis Hightower, comn by Mrs Nancy Langdon, Woodstock, Ill, 71. Exhib: 21st Am Drawing Biennial, Norfolk Mus Arts & Sci, Va, 65; 54th Ann Exhib, Art Asn Newport, RI, 65; 2 eme Salon Int de Charleroi, Palais des Beaux Arts, Belg, 69; 5th Int Grand Prix Painting & Etching, Palais de la Scala, Monte Carlo, Monaco, 69; one-man show sculpture, Mitchell Art Mus, Mt Vernon, Ill, 75. Teaching: Instr art, Woodstock High Sch, Ill, 61-; instr art, McHenry Co Col, Crystal Lake, Ill, 70- Awards: Best of Show Award, William Boyd Andrews, 61; Purchase Prize, Mr & Mrs Allen Leibsohn, 63; Mary E Just Art Award, Waukegan News-Sun, 69. Bibliog: F Tramier (auth), James E Pearson, La Rev Mod, 65; Sally Wagner (auth), Volume tells McHenry history, Chicago Tribune, 69. Mem: Col Art Asn Am; Ill Art Educ Asn; Ill Craftsmen's Coun; Am Fedn Arts; Centro Studi E Scambi Internazionali, Rome. Publ: Illusr, McHenry County 1832-1968, 68; auth, A dream never realized, 69 & Eagle's nest colony, 70, Outdoor Ill; auth, Perspective: outdoor education from an artists point of view, J Outdoor Educ, 71; illusr, The rectangle, 72. Mailing Add: 5117 Barnard Mill Rd Ringwood IL 60072

PEARSON, JOHN
PAINTER, INSTRUCTOR
b Boroughbridge, Yorkshire, Eng, Jan 31, 40. Study: Harrogate Col Art, Yorkshire, nat dipl design, 60; Royal Acad Schs, London, cert, 63, with Ernst Geitlinger; Northern Ill Univ, MFA, 66. Work: Mus Mod Art, New York; Bochumer Mus, Stuttgart, WGer; Pasadena Mus Fine Art, Calif; Kleye Collection, Doertmund, WGer; Kunstverien, Hannover, WGer. Exhib: American Drawing 1963-73, Whitney Mus Am Art, New York; one-man show, Galerie Muller, Stuttgart, 64, Gray Gallery, Chicago, 67-68, Paley & Lowe Gallery, 71 & Fischbach Gallery, 74 & 76, New York. Teaching: Instr painting, Univ NMex, 66-68; assoc prof painting & head dept, NS Col Art & Design, Halifax, 68-70; int artist in residence, Cleveland Inst Art, Ohio, 70-72; assoc prof art, Oberlin Col, 72- Awards: Austin Abbey Traveling Fel, Brit Arts Coun, 63; Can Coun Grant, 70; Cleveland Arts Prize, 75. Bibliog: Jock Wittet (auth), Editorial, Studio Int, 3/68; Harry Borden (auth), John Pearson, Artforum, 2/72; James R Mellon (auth), article in New York Times, 2/3/75; Edward Henning (auth), The art of John Pearson: an analogy of works of art & general systems, Art Int, 4-5/77. Style & Technique: Reductivist, minimal, systemic, geometric abstractions utilizing mathematical systems to investigate color and structure. Publ: Contribr, Art: the measure of man, Directions 66/67, 66; contribr, article in Mus Educ J, 66. Dealer: Fischbach Gallery 29 W 57th St New York NY 10010. Mailing Add: Dept Art Oberlin Col Oberlin OH 44074

PEARSON, LOUIS O
SCULPTOR
b Wallace, Idaho, Apr 28, 25. Work: Storm King Art Ctr, Mountainville, NY; Univ NMex, Albuquerque. Exhib: Crocker Art Gallery, Sacramento, 66; Joslyn Art Mus, Omaha, 66; Northern Ariz Univ Art Gallery, 66. Media: Stainless Steel. Mailing Add: 224 12th St San Francisco CA 94103

PEARSON, MARGUERITE STUBER
PAINTER
b Philadelphia, Pa. Study: Sch Mus Fine Arts, Boston, figure painting & portraiture with William James & Frederick Bosley, landscape with Aldro T Hibbard & Harry Leith-Ross, design with Henry Hunt Clark & Howard Giles & illus with Harold N Anderson & Chase Emerson. Work: Springville Art Mus, Utah; Beach Mem Art Mus, Storrs, Conn; Case Inst Technol; Salem Ct House Portrait Collection & Somerville City Hall Portrait Collection, Mass. Exhib: Nat Acad Design, New York, 34; Corcoran Biennial Exhib, Washington, DC, 35; Pa Acad Fine Arts Ann, Philadelphia, 36; Allied Artists Am, New York, 71; Jordan Marsh Co Ann Exhib of New Eng Artists, Boston, 72. Awards: Gold Medal of Honor, Rockport Art Asn, 73; Huntington Prize, Hudson Valley Arts Asn, 73; Prize for best still life, Am Artists Prof League, 75. Mem: North Shore Arts Asn; Rockport Art Asn; Acad Artists Soc; Portraits Inc; Hudson Valley Arts Asn. Media: Oil. Mailing Add: 47 Marmion Way Rockport MA 01966

PEART, JERRY LINN
SCULPTOR
b Winslow, Ariz, Feb 26, 48. Study: Ariz State Univ, BFA(sculpture); Southern Ill Univ, Carbondale, MFA(sculpture). Work: Large-scale pub sculpture, purchased by Nat Endowment for the Arts for City of Park Forest South, Ill. Comn: Three large-scale pub sculptures, comn by Dayton Hudson Properties of Minneapolis, Minn for Novi, Mich, Grand Forks, NDak & Las Vegas, Nev. Exhib: One-man shows, Walter Kelly Gallery, Chicago, 74-76; Sculpture for a New Era, Fed Plaza, Chicago, 75; The Chicago Connection, E B Crocker Art Gallery, Sacramento, Calif, 76; The Sculptor, the Campus, and the Prairie, Governors State Univ, Park Forest South, Ill, 76; Masterpieces of Recent Chicago Art, Chicago Pub Libr Cult Ctr, 77. Awards: Jeannette Sacks Art Achievement Medal, Ariz State Univ, 70; First Chicago Art Awards for Best Body of Work Over the Yr, Chicago Art Asn, 76-77. Style & Technique: Large scale painted aluminum and steel constructions. Dealer: Walter Kelly Gallery 620 N Michigan Ave Chicago IL 60611. Mailing Add: 1544 N Sedgwick St Chicago IL 60610

PEASE, DAVID G
PAINTER, INSTRUCTOR
b Bloomington, Ill, June 2, 32. Study: Univ Wis-Madison, BS, 54, MS, 55, MFA, 58. Work: Whitney Mus Am Art, New York; Philadelphia Mus Art; Pa Acad Fine Arts, Philadelphia; Power Gallery, Univ Sydney, Australia; Des Moines Art Ctr, Iowa. Exhib: Carnegie Int Exhib Painting & Sculpture, Carnegie Inst, Pittsburgh, 61; Corcoran Biennial Painting, Corcoran Gallery Art, Washington, DC, 61 & 63; Whitney Ann Exhib Painting, Whitney Mus Am Art, New York, 63; Nat Drawing Exhib, San Francisco Mus Art, Calif, 69; Drawings USA, Minn Mus Art, St Paul, 71, 73 & 75. Teaching: Prof painting & chmn dept painting & sculpture, Tyler Sch Art, 60- Awards: William A Clark Award, Corcoran Gallery Art, 63; Guggenheim Fel, 65-66; Childe Hassam Fund Purchase Award, Am Acad Arts & Lett, 70. Mem: Col Art Asn Am; Am Asn Univ Prof. Media: Acrylic. Dealer: Terry Dintenfass Inc 18 E 67th St New York NY 10021. Mailing Add: 1497 Huntingdon Rd Abington PA 19001

PEASE, ROLAND FOLSOM, JR
ART CRITIC, COLLECTOR
b Boston, Mass, Dec 11, 21. Study: Dartmouth Col; Columbia Univ, BS. Pos: Reporter, United Press Int, 52-55; exec ed, Art Voices, 52, assoc ed, 62-63, contrib ed, 63; managing ed, Harry N Abrams, Inc, 63-64; mem, Denhard & Stewart, Inc, New York. Collection: Works by Grace Hartigan, Larry Rivers, Robert Goodnough, Fairfield Porter, Jane Wilson, Sherman Drexler, Red Grooms, Gorchov, Jane Freilicher, George L K Morris and Diego Rivera. Publ: Contribr, art criticisms in Art Int, Metro, Pictures on Exhib & Auth Guild Bulletin. Mailing Add: 11 E 71st St New York NY 10021

PECHE, DALE C
PAINTER
b Long Beach, Calif, Nov 28, 28. Study: Long Beach City Col, BPA; Art Ctr Col Design, Los Angeles; also with Reckless, Tyler, Legakes, Feitelson, Polifka, Williamaoski & Kramer. Comn: California City, 73 & Off Highway One, 75, Glendale Fed Savings & Loan Permanent Collection; Wild Blackberries & Hay Barn, McCleary-Cummings, Artists Am Collection, 74. Exhib: One-man shows, Challis Galleries, Laguna Beach, Calif, 72, 73 & 74; 149th Nat Acad Design, New York, 74; 206th & 207th Summer Exhib, Royal Acad Arts, London, 74 & 75; 61st Ann Exhib, Allied Artists Am, New York, 74. Awards: Two awards, Los Angeles Art Dirs Show, 63 & 70; Pageant of the Oaks Award, 74; Brea Art Asn Award, 75. Mem: Nat Watercolor Soc; Allied Artists Am; Royal Soc Arts. Style & Technique: Representation realism; tempera and oil on gesso panels made to my specifications. Media: Gouache. Mailing Add: c/o Challis Galleries 1390 S Coast Hwy Laguna Beach CA 92651

PECK, JAMES EDWARD
PAINTER, DESIGNER
b Pittsburgh, Pa, Nov 7, 07. Study: Cleveland Inst Art, cert. Work: Cleveland Mus Art, Ohio; US Govt, Carville, La; Dayton Art Inst, Ohio; Am Acad Arts & Lett, New York; Seattle Art Mus, Wash. Exhib: Am Watercolor Soc, New York; Seattle Art Mus Northwest Ann; Pepsi-Cola Drawing & Watercolor Exhib, Metrop Mus Art, New York; Dayton Art Inst. Teaching: Head dept art, Cornish Sch, Seattle, 47-52; instr painting & graphic design, Burnley Sch Art, Seattle, 66-76. Pos: Illusr, Fawn Art Studios, Cleveland, 36-46; art dir, Miller, McKay, Hoeck & Hartung, Seattle, 54-60; graphic designer, 60-66; graphic designer, Boeing Co, 66-70. Awards: Awards for watercolors, Dayton Art Inst, 42-45; award for painting, Guggenheim Found, 42 & 46; Seattle Art Mus Awards, var shows & yrs. Mem: Puget Sound Group Northwest Painters (past Pres). Media: Watercolor, Enamel; Wood. Publ: Illusr, Ford Times Mag. Mailing Add: 19155 130th Ave NE Bothell WA 98011

PECK, JUDITH
SCULPTOR, EDUCATOR
b New York, NY, Dec 31, 30. Study: Adelphi Col, BA; Art Students League; Sculpture Ctr, New York; Columbia Univ, MA & EdM. Work: Yale Univ; Ghetto Fighters Mus, Acco, Israel. Comn: Monuments, Temple Beth El, Spring Valley, NY, 71, James Richard Elster Mem Courtyard, Tenafly High Sch, NJ, 72 & Temple Oheb Sholom, Baltimore, Md, 75. Exhib: 23rd Ann Md Exhib, Baltimore Mus Art, 55; Art USA 58, Madison Sq Garden, 58; 2nd Biennial of Am Painting & Sculpture, Detroit Inst Arts, 60; 155th Ann Exhib Am Painting & Sculpture, Pa Acad Fine Arts, 60; NJ 33rd Ann State Exhib, Montclair Art Mus, 64; 53rd Ann Nat Exhib, Allied Artists of Am, Nat Acad Galleries, NJ, 66; Audubon Artists 21st Ann Nat Exhib, Nat Acad Galleries, New York, 66; solo sculpture shows, Barzansky Galleries, New York, 65, Unicorn Gallery, New York, 75 & 76 & NJ State Mus, Trenton, 78. Teaching: Asst prof art & art in inst, Ramapo Col NJ, Mahwah, NJ, 71- Pos: Mem archit rev bd, Mahwah, 73-; designer/dir, Art on Outside, Ramapo Col NJ, 75-78; mem bd dirs, Arts Coun Rockland, Rockland Co, NY, 76- Awards: Merit Scholar, Art Students League, New York, 53; First Prize Sculpture, 33rd Ann NJ State Exhib, 64; First Prize Sculpture, Art in the Park, Paterson, NJ, 69. Bibliog: Margaret Harold (auth), Prize Winning Sculpture, Book II, Allied Publ, 65; Jackie Kohn (auth), Sculpt-In, Arts & Activities Mag, 11/73; Mildred Jailer (auth), Ramapo Project Helps Institutionalized, New York Times, 12/75. Mem: Mod Artists Guild Inc, Bergen Community Mus, Paramus, NJ (pres, 71-73 & 76-78); Col Art Asn; Art Students League; Women's Caucus on Art. Style & Technique: Semi-abstract figures either cast in bronze via lost-wax process and in bonded bronze for large outdoor pieces, or carved in wood and stone. Media: Wax, Wood, Stone. Mailing Add: 60 Armour Rd Mahwah NJ 07430

PECK, LEE BARNES
JEWELER, EDUCATOR
b Battle Creek, Mich, Sept 21, 42. Study: Kellogg Community Col, AA, 63; Western Mich Univ, BS(art educ), 65; Univ Wis, MFA(art metal), 69. Work: Johnson Wax Collection: Objects USA; Mus of Art, Carnegie Inst, Pittsburgh; Mus of Contemp Crafts, New York; Minn Mus Art, St Paul; Detroit Inst Arts; Oak Park-River Forest Pub Sch Syst, Ill. Comn: Pvt comn, 68- Exhib: Jewelry '71, Int Exhib, Art Gallery Ontario, 71; Profile of US Jewelry, Tex Tech Univ, 73, 75 & 77; Technology and the Artists/Craftsman, Ames Soc Arts, Iowa, 73, Traveling Show, 74-75; Beaux Art Designer Craftsman, Columbus Gallery of Fine Arts, Ohio, 73, 75 & 77; The Goldsmith, Renwick Gallery, Smithsonian Inst, Washington, DC & Minn Mus Art, 74; Contemporary Crafts of the Americas, Colo State Univ, 75; Copper, Brass, Bronze Exhib, Univ of Ariz Mus of Art, Tucson, 77. Teaching: Assoc prof jewelry & metalwork, Northern Ill Univ, 70-; lectr in jewelry, Rosary Col, 72- Awards: Alton Box Co 4th Prize, Galex IX Show, Galesburg, Ill, 75; Best of Show, Art Group Kalamazoo, Mich, 75; Lakefront Festival Art Prize, Milwaukee Art Ctr, 75; The Metalsmith Award, Phoenix Art Mus, Ariz, 77; First Prize in Metal, Cooperstown Art Asn, NY, 77. Mem: Am Crafts Coun (Ill rep, 72-74); Wis Designer Craftsman; Soc NAm Goldsmiths. Style & Technique: Cast and electroformed rings, pendants, vessels and hollow ware. Media: Silver, Gold. Publ: Auth & illusr, Jewelry Making, Vol 3, In: Illustrated Libr of Arts & Crafts, 74. Mailing Add: 121 Mason Ct Sycamore IL 60178

PECK, STEPHEN ROGERS
INSTRUCTOR, PAINTER
b Cortland, NY, Dec 18, 12. Study: Syracuse Univ, BFA(painting), 34; Acad Julian, Paris, 38; also fresco painting with Unterstellar. Comn: Many portraits. Teaching: Instr drawing, Col Fine Arts, Syracuse Univ, 37-42, asst prof drawing & painting, 46-47; instr anat & life drawing, Parsons Sch Design, New York, 47-55; instr anat, Pratt Inst, 52-60; instr drawing, painting & anat, Westchester Art Workshop, White Plains, NY, 62- Mem: Artists Equity Asn. Style & Technique: Portrait painting in traditional style. Media: Oil, Pastel. Publ: Auth, Atlas of Human Anatomy for the Artist, Oxford Univ, 51. Mailing Add: 55 Sarles Lane Pleasantville NY 10570

PECK, WILLIAM HENRY
CURATOR, ART HISTORIAN
b Savannah, Ga, Oct 2, 32. Study: Ohio State Univ, 50-53; Wayne State Univ, BFA, 60, MA, 61. Collections Arranged: Mummy Portraits from Roman Egypt (with catalog), Detroit Inst Arts, 67, Detroit Collects: Antiquities, 73 & Akhenaten and Nefertiti, 73-74; plus many others. Teaching: Lectr art hist, Cranbrook Acad Art, 63-65; adj prof art hist, Wayne State Univ, 66- Pos: Jr cur educ, Detroit Inst Arts, 60-62, asst cur educ, 62-64, assoc cur, 64-68, cur ancient art, 68-; mem, Brooklyn Mus Theban Exped, 78. Awards: Travel Grant, Ford Motor Co, Eng, 62; Travel Grant, Smithsonian Inst, 75. Mem: Am Asn Mus; fel Am Res Ctr Egypt; Cranbrook Acad Art (mem bd gov, 74-); Archaeol Inst Am. Res: Ancient Near East and classical world with a particular specialty in Egypitan art. Publ: Auth, The present state of Egyptian art in Detroit, 12/70 & The arts of the Ancient Near East in Detroit, 7/73, Connoisseur; auth, A seated statue of Amun, J Egyptian Archaeol, 71; auth, The problem of restoration in teaching ancient art, Art J, summer 73; auth, Drawings From Ancient Egypt, Thames & Hudson, 78; plus others. Mailing Add: Detroit Inst of Arts 5200 Woodward Ave Detroit MI 48202

PECKHAM, NICHOLAS
ARCHITECT, DESIGNER
b Teaneck, NJ, Apr 11, 40. Study: US Merchant Marine Acad, BS, 62; Univ Calif, Berkeley, 63; Univ Pa, BArch, 67, MArch, 73, with Louis Kahn, PhD cand with R Buckminster Fuller. Teaching: Prof design, Stephens Col, Columbia, 75- Mem: Am Inst Architects. Style & Technique: Comprehensive anticipatory design science. Res: Optimization in architecture. Publ: Auth, Evolution in architecture, Pass-Age, summer 75. Mailing Add: 1500 Walnut St Columbia MO 65201

PEDERSON, MOLLY FAY
PAINTER, SCULPTOR
b Waco, Tex, Apr 26, 41. Study: Pvt study with Carl Cogar, Las Cruces, NMex, James Woodruff, Houston, Mary Berry, McKinney, Tex, Ramon Froman, Dallas, Tex, Ken Gore, Mass, Stewart Matthews, Arnold Vail & H E Fain, Dallas. Exhib: Richardson Civic Arts Soc Ann, Tex, 68-70; Artists Market, Dallas, 68-72; Bond's Alley Art & Craft Show, Hillsboro, Tex, 69-70; Tex Fine Arts Asn Exhib, Dallas, 70; Temple Emanu-El Ann Brotherhood Art Festival, Dallas, 70-72. Teaching: Instr oil painting, Richardson Recreation Ctr, 72; art instr, Air Am Sch, Udorn, Thailand, 72-73. Pos: Com artist, Goldstein-Migel Co, Waco, Tex, 58-59; layout artist, Sun Printing Co, El Paso, 60-64. Awards: Award for Manarola, Texans Asn Art Show, 68; Richardson Community Fair Award, 69; Award for Black & White Abstract, Bond's Alley Arts & Crafts Show, 70. Bibliog: Articles in Dallas Morning News, 4/5/69, Waco Citizen, 5/30/70 & Richardson Daily News, 12/3/71. Mem: Tex Fine Arts Asn; Richardson Civic Arts Soc (vpres, secy, treas, 68-70); Arlington 200 (bd mem, show chmn); Tex Starving Artists. Media: Oil, Acrylic; Brass, Copper. Mailing Add: 1228 Briarcove Richardson TX 75080

PEELER, RICHARD
POTTER, SCULPTOR
b Indianapolis, Ind, Aug 8, 26. Study: De Pauw Univ, AB, 49; Ind Univ, MA, 60. Work: Int Minerals, Skokie, Ill; Armstrong Cork Co; Ind State Univ; Taylor Univ; Ind Cent Univ; plus others. Comn: Sculpture in stone, Gobin Methodist Church, Greencastle, Ind, 63; portrait busts in stone, Pres & Mrs William Kerstetter, Greencastle, 65; sculpture in fiberglas & epoxy, First Christian Church, Greencastle, 68; portrait bust in ceramic, Harrison Johnson, Cleveland, Ohio, 71; ceramic mural, De Pauw Univ, 72. Exhib: Syracuse Nat Ceramic Show, 64; Ceramics USA 1966, Int Minerals Corp, 66; one-man shows, Ind Cent Col, Goshen Col & Univ Evansville. Teaching: Instr art, Indianapolis Pub Schs, 51-58; assoc prof art, De Pauw Univ, 58-72; vis lectr, Kyoto City Col Fine Arts, Japan, 66. Mem: Nat Coun Educ Ceramic Arts (vpres & dir, 66-70, pres, 70-71); Ind Artist Craftsmen; Ind Potters Guild (bd dir, coun fel, 73). Style & Technique: Wide range of expression; functional stoneware pottery. Publ: Auth, articles in Ceramics Monthly Mag, 62-65; eight films on ceramic art, McGraw-Hill, 66-68. Mailing Add: Rte 1 Box 320 Reelsville IN 46171

PEEPLES, MAIJA GEGERIS ZACK
See Woof, Maija

PEERS, GORDON FRANKLIN
PAINTER, EDUCATOR
b Easton, Pa, Mar 17, 09. Study: RI Sch Design, BFA, 33; Art Students League; Beaux-Arts Inst Design; also with John R Frazier. Work: RI Sch Design. Exhib: Provincetown Art Asn, 58; Dept Interior, Washington, DC; Univ Ill; Rockford Art Asn, Ill; Boston Art Festival, 58; plus many others. Teaching: Head dept painting, RI Sch Design, 34-36 & 38-69, prof painting & chmn div fine arts, 69-73, artist in residence, 74- Pos: Chief critic, RI Sch Design Europ Hons Prog, Rome, 61-62. Awards: Prizes, Boston Art Festival, 55 & Newport Art Asn, 56 & 58. Style & Technique: Drawing and oil painting, all styles, figurative presently. Mailing Add: 65 Halsey St Providence RI 02906

PEHAP, ERICH K
PAINTER, GRAPHIC ARTIST
b Viljandi, Estonia, Apr 10, 12. Study: State Sch Arts & Handicrafts, Tallinn, Estonia, 32-33; Estonia Acad Fine Arts, Tartu, grad painting, 37, grad graphic art, 39; Didactic-Methodical Teaching Col, Tartu Univ, grad, 38; Montreal Inst Mech Drafting, dipl, 52. Work: Estonian Nat Mus; Art Gallery Hamilton. Exhib: Estonian Art Exhib, Montreal, 51-55, 60, 62 & 65-71; four shows, Royal Can Acad, 54-68; Exhib Estonian Art, Cleveland, 68; Laurentian Univ Art Gallery, 68; Toronto Nat Exhib Art Gallery, 68; also exhib numerous group shows, US, Can & abroad. Awards: Estonian Govt Ministry Educ Awards, 40 & 41; Int Acad Award, Rome, 72; Estonian Cult Award, 75. Mem: Fel Int Inst Arts & Lett; Soc Estonian Artists in Toronto (pres, 61-65); Estonian Artist Soc; Can Soc Graphic Art; Graphics Soc USA. Media: All Media. Publ: Illusr, The country life (album), 43; illusr, album in New Direct Method, 61; illusr, Memories from Estonia (album), 72; illusr, Erich Pehap selected prints 1932-1972; One endless journey (portfolio), 71. Mailing Add: 14 Ozark Crescent Toronto ON Can

PEI, I M (IEOH MING PEI)
ARCHITECT
b Canton, China, Apr 26, 17. Study: Univ Pa, archit, 35; Mass Inst of Technol, Cambridge, BArch, 40; Harvard Univ, Cambridge, MArch, 46. Comn: US Nat Bank of Denver, Mile High Ctr, Colo, 52-55; Sch of Journalism, Syracuse Univ, NY, 61-64; Everson Mus of Art, Syracuse, NY, 61-68; Herbert F Johnson Mus of Art, Cornell Univ, Ithaca, NY, 68-73; East Wing, Nat Gallery of Art, Washington, DC, 68- Teaching: Instr, Harvard Grad Sch of Design, 45-48. Pos: Head Archit division, Webb & Knapp Inc, New York, 48-55; archit, New York, 55-; mem, Nat Coun on Humanities, 66-70. Mem: Nat Endowment for the Arts (Task Force on Fed Archit, 73-). Mailing Add: c/o I M Pei & Partners 600 Madison Ave New York NY 10022

PEIPERL, ADAM
KINETIC ARTIST
b Sosnowiec, Poland, June 4, 35; US citizen. Study: George Washington Univ, BS, 57; Pa State Univ, 57-59. Work: Nat Mus Hist & Technol, Nat Collection Fine Arts & John F Kennedy Ctr Performing Arts, Washington, DC; Pa Acad Fine Arts, Philadelphia; Boymans-Van Beuningen Mus, Rotterdam, Holland. Exhib: Corcoran Gallery Art, 68; one-man shows, Marlborough-Gerson Gallery, New York, 69, Baltimore Mus Art, 69, Pa Acad Fine Arts, 69 & Nat Mus Hist & Technol, 72-73; Philadelphia Art Alliance, 78. Bibliog: Frank Getlein (auth), He defied tradition and made it work, Sun Star, 7/21/68; Victoria Donohoe (auth), Something old, new show at academy, Philadelphia Inquirer, 11/23/69; Diane Chichura & Thelma Stevens (auths), Super Sculpture, Van Nostrand-Reinhold, 74. Media: Light, Water, Plastic. Mailing Add: 1135 Loxford Terr Silver Spring MD 20901

PEKAR, RONALD WALTER
PAINTER, EDUCATOR
b Cleveland, Ohio, Oct 9, 42. Study: Cleveland Inst Art; Wash Univ, BFA, fel, 66-67, MFA. Work: Ark State Univ; Miss Art Asn, Jackson; Carroll Reece Mus, ETenn State Univ; State Tenn Arts Comn Collection, Nashville; Brooks Mem Art Gallery, Memphis. Comn: Tommy stage design, Memphis State Univ, 70; illuminated painting, Gen Pub Utilities, Pa, 72; two 3-story illuminated sculptures, Lemoyne-Owen Col, 73; mural, St Jude Children's Res Hosp, 74; two urban wall graphics, CofC, Memphis, 74-75. Exhib: Young Light Artists 68, Gallery Loretto-Hilton Ctr, Webster Col, St Louis, 68; one-man shows, Miss Art Asn, 69 & Brooks Mem Art Gallery, Memphis, 73; EAT/ATL 69 & 70, Exp in Art & Technol, High Art Mus, Atlanta, Ga, 69-70; Artrain-Southeastern Tour, Nat Endowment Arts Southern Growth Policies Bd, Research Triangle Park, NC, 74; Memphis Pink Palace Mus Commemorative Painting, 77; Spirit of the River (audio/visual environment), Brooks Mem Art Gallery, 77-78. Teaching: Studio asst to Prof Arthur Osver, Wash Univ, 65-67, teaching asst, 66; dir workshop oil painting, Tenn Arts Comn, Jackson, 70, dir workshop watercolor, Arts & Crafts Guild, Helena, Ark, 74; assoc prof painting, Memphis Acad Arts, 67- Pos: Floor dir, KMOX-TV CBS, St Louis, 64-67; visual arts lectr, WKNO-TV, Memphis, 73-; mem bd dirs, Grace-St Luke's Episcopal Sch, 76-; mem bd dirs, Untitled (arts mag), 76- Style & Technique: Representational images combined with designed, symbolic passages in traditional paint applications, combined with plastic fabrications, metals, light and sound components. Media: Photography; Audio/Visual. Publ: Illusr, Air poster, Memphis Acad Arts, 69; illusr, rec label, Ardent Rec, 72; ed & illusr, Homage to the Land and Sky, 73; illusr rec label, Privilege Rec, 74; Spacemakers of Beverly Hills, Calif, 78. Mailing Add: 1500 Court Ave Memphis TN 38104

PEKARSKY, MEL (MELVIN HIRSCH)
PAINTER, EDUCATOR
b Chicago, Ill, Sept 18, 34. Study: Art Inst of Chicago; Northwestern Univ, BA, MA. Work: Cleveland Mus of Art, Ohio; Corcoran Gallery of Art, Washington, DC; Indianapolis Mus of Art; Columbus Gallery of Fine Arts, Ohio; Weatherspoon Mus, Univ NC. Comn: Exterior murals, Lafayette & Bleecker St, New York, City Walls, Inc, comn by Kaplan Fund, 70, Houston & Mulberry St, New York, City Walls, Inc, comn by Nat Endowment for the Arts, 71, Houston & Crosby St, New York, City Walls, Inc, comn by Nat Endowment for the Arts & Bernhard Found, 72, 37th & Third Ave, New York, City Walls, comn by bldg owner, 73 & Work No 5, Doyle Park, Yonkers, NY, Abel & Bainnson, Landscape Architects, comn by US Dept Housing & Urban Develop, 74. Exhib: Artists of Chicago & Vicinity, Art Inst of Chicago, 54 & 60; Butler Inst of Am Art 31st Ann, Youngstown, Ohio, 66; Oversize Prints, Whitney Mus of Am Art, New York, 71; City Walls, Lever House, New York, 72; Recent Acquisitions, Indianapolis Mus of Art, 74; Am Prints, Brooklyn Mus, NY, 74-75; Am Prints, San Diego Fine Arts Gallery, Calif, 75; New Editions 74-75, New York Cult Ctr, 75; Drawings by Seven Am Artists, Cleveland Mus, 78; one-man shows, Gimpel, Weitzenhoffer, New York, 74, Lehigh Univ, Bethlehem, Pa, 75, Mus of Ball State Univ, 75 G W Einstein, New York, 75, 77 & 78. Teaching: From asst to assoc dean art, Sch of Visual Arts, New York, 67-69; dir studio progs art, State Univ, NY, Stony Brook, 75- Pos: Founding mem & mem bd, City Walls, Inc, 69-, vpres, 70-75. Bibliog: Lawrence Alloway (auth), Art, The Nation, 9/70; Russell Connor (dir), Art in Public Places (film), Metrop Mus of Art, 74; Gilbert Bovay (dir), Filmed interview, Television Suisse de Geneve, 76. Mem: Col Art Asn. Style & Technique: Landscapes in various media. Media: Oil and mixed media drawings. Interest: Painting, public art. Publ: Illusr, The Curious Cow, 60, Little Quack, 61, The Three Goats, 63, & The Little Red Hen, 63, Follett; illusr, Handbook of Gestures, Mouton, The Hague, 72. Dealer: G W Einstein Co Inc Fine Art 243 E 82nd St New York NY 10028. Mailing Add: 48 W 22nd St New York NY 10010

PELADEAU, MARIUS BEAUDOIN
ART WRITER, MUSEUM DIRECTOR
b Boston, Mass, Jan 27, 35. Study: St Michael's Col, Winsoski Park, Vt, BA(cum laude), 56; Boston Univ, Mass, MS, 57; Georgetown Univ, Washington, DC, MA(fel recipient), 61. Pos: Dir, Maine League of Hist Soc & Mus, 72-76; dir, William A Farnsworth Libr & Art Mus, 76- Mem: Am Asn Mus; New Eng Coun of Am Asn Mus; New Eng Doc Conserv Ctr (adv coun). Res: American art and the decorative arts. Publ: Ed, The Verse of Royall Tyler, Univ Va Press, 68; ed, The Prose of Royall Tyler, Vt Hist Soc, 72; auth, Chansonetta: The Photographs of Chansonetta Stanley Emmons, 1858-1937, Morgan & Morgan, 77. Mailing Add: Box 466 Rockland ME 04841

PELHAM-KELLER, RICHARD MONROE
ART DEALER, DESIGNER
US citizen. Study: Univ Chicago; Oberlin Col; with Wolfgang Stechow; mus training with Ellen Johnson. Pos: Dir, Pelham-Von Stoffler Gallery, Houston, Tex, currently. Awards: Cert of Recognition, Mus Fine Arts, Indianapolis, 72. Specialty: American Purist painting; surrealist drawings, graphics. Interest: Established Alice Trumbull Mason Collection, Museum of Fine Arts, Springfield, Mass; donor, Museum of Fine Arts, Indianapolis, Indiana and Museum of Fine Arts, Springfield. Publ: Auth, Art of Collecting, Jr League Mag, Chicago, 67; auth, The collector speaks, Kurt Seligmann Graphic, Mus Fine Arts, Springfield, 74. Mailing Add: 2000 Peden St Houston TX 77019

PELLAN (ALFRED)
PAINTER
b Quebec City, Can, May 16, 26. Study: Ecole des Beaux Arts, Quebec City, grad, 20. Work: Mus Nat d'Art Mod, Paris; Mus Grenoble, France; Que Mus, Quebec City; Nat Gallery Can, Ottawa; Montreal Mus Fine Arts, PQ. Comn: Painting, Winnipeg Airport, Man, 63; stained glass, La Place des Arts, Montreal, 63; stained glass, Church Saint Theophile, Laval-Quest, PQ, 64; two paintings, Nat Libr & Archives, Ottawa, 67; polychromy of bldgs, Vt Constructions Inc, Laval City, 68. Exhib: Galerie Jeanne Bucher, Paris, 39; retrospectives, Mus Nat d'Art Mod, Paris, 55, Hall of Hon, Montreal, PQ, 56 & Nat Gallery Can, Art Gallery Toronto & Montreal Mus Fine Arts, 60-61; Voir Pellan, Mus d'Art Contemporain, Montreal, 69. Teaching: Instr painting, Ecole Beaux Arts, Montreal, 43-52; instr painting, Art Centre Sainte Adele, PQ, summer 57. Awards: First Prize, First Great Exhib Mural Art Paris, 35; First Prize, 65th Ann Spring Exhib, Montreal Mus Fine Arts, 48; First Prize, PQ Competition, 48. Bibliog: Donald W Buchanan (auth), Alfred Pellan, McClelland & Stewart, 62; Guy Robert (auth), Pellan, Centre Psychologie Pedagogie, Montreal, 63; Voir Pellan, Nat Film Bd Can, 69. Mem: Soc Artistes Prof Que; Royal Can Acad Arts. Media: Oil. Publ: Contribr, Les iles de la nuit, Parizeau Ed, 44; contribr, Le voyage d'Arlequin, Cahiers File Indienne, 46. Mailing Add: 649 Des Mille Iles Blvd Auteuil Laval City PQ H7S 1Z0 Can

PELLEW, JOHN CLIFFORD
PAINTER
b Heamoor, Eng, Apr 9, 03; US citizen. Study: Penzance Sch Art, Eng. Work: Metrop Mus Art, New York; Butler Inst Am Art, Youngstown, Ohio; Ga Mus Fine Arts, Athens; Adelphi Col, NY; New Brit Mus Am Art, Conn. Exhib: Nat Acad Design, New York, 48-72; Butler Inst Am Art, Youngstown, Ohio, 64; 200 Years of Watercolor Painting in America, Metrop Mus Art, New York, 67; Landscape 1, De Cordova & Dana Mus, Lincoln, Mass, 70; Am Watercolor Soc Exchange Exhib, Can, 72. Awards: Adolph & Clara Obrig Prize, Nat Acad Design, 61; First Award for watercolor, Butler Inst Am Art, 64; Silver Medal, Am Watercolor Soc, 70. Bibliog: Norman Kent (auth), Watercolor Methods, Watson-Guptill, 55; Wendon Blake (auth), Complete Guide to Acrylic Painting, Watson-Guptill, 71. Mem: Nat Acad Design; Am Watercolor Soc; Allied Artists Am; Southwestern Watercolor Soc. Style & Technique: Impressionist. Media: Watercolor, Oil. Publ: Auth, Acrylic landscape painting, 68; Painting in watercolor, 69; Oil painting outdoors, 71; Painting maritime landscapes, 73. Dealer: Grand Central Art Galleries 40 Vanderbilt Ave New York NY 10017. Mailing Add: 123 Murray St Norwalk CT 06851

PELLI, CESAR
ARCHITECT
b Tucuman, Arg, Oct 12, 26; US citizen. Study: Univ Tucuman, Dipl in Archit(cum laude), 49; Univ Ill, MS(archit). Comn: Pac Design Ctr, Los Angeles, Calif, 71; The Commons, City of Columbus, Ind, 72; Am Embassy, Tokyo, Japan, US Dept of State, 72; Mus Mod Art, New York, 78; Wintergarden, City of Niagara Falls, NY, 78. Exhib: Ten Am Architects Biennale, Venice, Italy, 76; A View of Calif Archit 1960-1976, San Francisco Mus Mod Art, 76; Los Angeles Twelve Traveling Exhib, 76. Teaching: Vis prof archit design, Sch of Archit, Yale Univ, New Haven, Conn, 72-74, dean archit sch, 77-; vis prof archit design, Univ Calif, Los Angeles, 75-76. Pos: Designer, Eero Saarinen & Assoc, 54-64; dir & vpres design, Daniel Mann, Johnson & Mendenhall, 64-68; partner in charge of design, Gruen Assoc, Los Angeles & New York, 68-77; principal, Cesar Pelli & Assoc, New Haven, 77- Awards: First Prize, Int Archit Competition, United Nations City, Repub of Austria, City of Vienna, 69; Honor Awards, San Bernardino City Hall, Calif, 75 & Pac Design Ctr, 76, Southern Calif Charter, Am Inst Archit. Bibliog: Articles in Archit & Urbanism, 3/71 & 11/76; Moholy-Nag Moholy-Nagy, Sybil (auth), Cesar Pelli: Public Architect, Spec Publ; Walter Wagner (ed), Architectural Record, US Embassy, Tokyo, 4/77. Mem: Am Inst Archit (mem urban planning & design comt, 76-). Publ: Auth, Relfective glass, Archit & Eng News, 11/69; auth, Open line city, Progressive Archit, 6/70; auth, Third generation architects, Archit & Urbanism, 3/71; auth, Design process, Kenchiku Bunku, 7/72. Mailing Add: 1056 Chapel St New Haven CT 06510

PELLICONE, MARIE
GALLERY DIRECTOR
b New York, NY. Study: Fordham Univ, BA(Eng). Pos: Dir, 47 Bond St Gallery, 76- Specialty: Paintings, sculptors, drawings and contemporary prints. Mailing Add: 47 Bond St Gallery New York NY 10012

PELLICONE, WILLIAM
PAINTER
b Philadelphia, Pa, Apr 12, 15. Study: Pa Acad Fine Arts, Philadelphia; Barnes Found, Merion, Pa. Work: Boston Mus, Mass; Smithsonian Inst, Washington, DC; Am Broadcasting Co, NY. Comn: Murals, Abraham & Strauss, Brooklyn, NY, 69 & 70. Exhib: Pa Acad Fine Arts, 39; Nat Acad Design, New York, 39; Woodmere Art Gallery & Art Alliance, Philadelphia; group show, Baltimore Mus, 71. Style & Technique: Main characteristics are the inner light that emanates; technique between a Renaissance and an impressionist. Media: Oil. Dealer: Capricorn Gallery 8003 Woodmont Ave Bethesda MD 20014; Allan Stone Gallery 48 E 86th St New York NY 10028. Mailing Add: 47 Bond St New York NY 10012

PELS, ALBERT
PAINTER, ART ADMINISTRATOR
b Cincinnati, Ohio, May 7, 10. Study: Art Acad Cincinnati; Univ Cincinnati; Beaux Arts Sch; Art Students League, six scholarships, also with Thomas Hart Benton, Kenneth Hayes Miller & Bridgeman. Work: Butler Inst Am Art. Comn: The Landing of the Swedes, Courthouse, Wilmington, Del, 42; Early History of Normal, Ill, in post off; Africa scene for ship, North African Line, 50; History of Norfolk, Va, for naval base; gen hist of Anniston, Ala area, YMCA. Exhib: Whitney Mus Am Art Ann, 40-50; Carnegie Int Exhib, 42-48; Nat Acad Design, 45-52; Butler Inst Am Art Ann, 45-55; Chicago Ann, 49; Cincinnati Mus world tour; plus many other group & one-man shows. Teaching: Instr art, Jones Mem Sch & Hessian Hills Sch; instr fine art, Albert Pels Sch Art, Inc, 46- Pos: Dir, Albert Pels Sch Art, Inc, 72-; demonstr oil painting on educ TV. Awards: First Prize for Sea Disaster, Butler Inst Am Art, 46; Schackenberg Scholar, 49. Media: Oil, Watercolor, Graphics. Publ: Contribr, Art News, 46; illusr, Easy puppets, 52 & Water pets, 56. Dealer: Gorwit Galleries Roslyn NY 11576. Mailing Add: 2109 Broadway New York NY 10023

PEN, RUDOLPH
PAINTER
b Chicago, Ill, Jan 1, 18. Study: Art Inst Chicago; BFA; also Europe, SAm, Mex & NAfrica. Work: Davenport Mus, Iowa; Libr of Cong, Washington, DC; Philadelphia Mus, Pa; Vincent Price Collection; Art Inst Chicago. Exhib: Carnegie Inst, Pittsburgh, 46; Contemp Artists Exhib, Art Inst Chicago, 61-; Watercolor Print Exhib, Pa Acad Fine Arts, Philadelphia; Am Watercolor Soc, Nat Acad Design, New York; Corcoran Gallery Art, Washington, DC. Teaching: Asst prof painting, Art Inst Chicago, 48-63; dir pvt sch, 63- Pos: Pres, Alumni Asn, Art Inst Chicago, 60-62; dir, Summer Sch Painting, 64-65. Awards: Huntington Hartford Found Grant, 58; Ryerson Traveling Fel, 63; plus many others. Bibliog: Marilyn Hoffman (auth), Art, Christian Sci Monitor, 1/3/51; Kay Loring (auth), Pen named director of art school, 7/24/64 & Edith Weigle (auth), Art critic, 11/28/65, Chicago Tribune. Mem: Am Watercolor Soc; Arts Club Chicago; hon mem Union League Civic & Arts Found; Nat Soc Lit & Arts. Style & Technique: Representational in impressionist style, often giving illusion of motion; aspect of technique is contained in use of trapezoidal frame enhancing illusion of dimension and the directing of the viewers eye. Media: Oil, Watercolor. Publ: Auth, Whipping boy or cultural spokesman, 54 & The tongue is quicker than the mind, 66, Art League; auth, Artist-teacher blasts tycoons and pretenders, Chicago Sun Times, 71. Dealer: Art Inst Sales & Rental Gallery S Michigan & E Adams Chicago IL 60603. Mailing Add: 55 W Schiller St Chicago IL 60610

PENA, AMADO MAURILIO, JR
PAINTER, ILLUSTRATOR
b Laredo, Tex, Oct 1, 43. Study: Tex A&I Univ, BA(art), 65, MA, 71. Work: Tex A&I Univ; Dept Foreign Lang, Univ Ky; Univ Tex, Austin; Juarez-Lincoln Univ, Austin; Los Pinos, Pres Palace, Mexico. Comn: Mural, Laredo Independent Sch Dist, Serv Ctr, 70; mural, City Hall, Crystal City, 72; painting, City Coun Crystal City, 72. Exhib: TFAA Citation Show, Laguna Gloria Art Mus, Austin, 68; Corpus Christi Art Found, 68; Chicago Art Exhib, Nat Lulac Conf, Washington, DC, 73 & Univ Tex Student Ctr, 74; Chicano Artists of the Southwest, Inst Mex Cult, San Antonio, 75. Teaching: Teacher art, Laredo Independent Sch Dist, 65-71, Crystal City Independent Sch Dist, 71-73 & L C Anderson High Sch, Austin, 73- Awards: Citation Award, Laguna Gloria Art Mus, 68; Corpus Christi Art Found Award, 69; Rio Grande Art Festival Award, Laredo Art Asn, 71, 72 & 74. Bibliog: Kelly Fearing (auth), Art & the Creative Teacher, Univ Tex, 69; Jacinto Quirarte (auth), The Art of Mexican Americans, The Humble Way, Exxon Oil Co, 69 & Mexican American Artists, Univ Tex, 72. Mem: Laredo Art Asn (pres, 68-69); Austin Art Teachers Asn (treas, 74-75). Style & Technique: Serigraphy; peoplescapes in watercolor; drawings. Media: Serigraphy; Watercolor. Publ: Contribr & auth, Chicano Art of the Southwest, Chicano Slide Collection, 73; contribr, Tejidos, Magazin & Calendario Chicano; illusr, Cuenots, 75. Mailing Add: 11511 Catalonia Austin TX 78759

PENCZNER, PAUL JOSEPH
PAINTER
b Hungary, Sept 17, 16; US citizen. Study: In Hungary & Austria. Work: Vatican, Rome; Capitol Bldg, Jefferson City; Univ Tenn, Memphis; Univ Mo, Cape Girardeau; Fla State Univ, Talahassee. Comn: Works comn by Mayor Walter Chandler, City of Memphis, Sen McKinney, Capitol Bldg, Jefferson City, Univ Tenn, Memphis State Univ; Gov Winfield Dunn; United Press & Scripps; Jack Howard, Howard Newspapers. Exhib: Pa Acad Fine Arts, Philadelphia; Brooks Mem Art Gallery, Memphis; Jersey City Mus; Smithsonian Inst, Washington, DC; El Delgado Mus, New Orleans. Teaching: Owner & dir, Penczner's Fine Art Sch, Memphis. Mem: Nat Soc Painters Casein; Tenn Watercolor Soc; Am Artist Prof League. Style & Technique: Originator of the oil graphic technique used in his casual and free impressionistic style. Media: Oil, Acrylic, Ink. Dealer: Round Corner Gallery 1684 Poplar Ave Memphis TN 38104; Layman's 964 June Rd Memphis TN 38117. Mailing Add: 1436 Poplar Ave Memphis TN 38104

PENDERGRAFT, NORMAN ELVEIS
MUSEUM DIRECTOR, ART HISTORIAN
b Durham, NC, Mar 4, 34. Study: Univ NC, Chapel Hill, AB & MACT; Conservatorio di Musica G Rossini, Pesaro, Italy, with Maestra Raggi-Valentini. Teaching: Asst prof art hist, NC Cent Univ, Durham, 66- Pos: Dir art mus, NC Cent Univ, Durham, 76- Mem: Am Asn Mus; Am Asn Univ Prof; Col Art Asn; NC Asn Art Galleries; NC Mus Coun. Res: Main interest in Italian Renaissance, Afro-American and American art. Publ: Auth, Durham Chautauqua: the Black man in art, Durham Co Libr, 74; auth, art rev in The Durham Sun, 75-; auth rev, Theresa D Cederholm's Afro-American artists: a bio-bibliographical dir, Art J, 2/76; auth, Heralds of Life: Artis, Bearden & Burke, NC Cent Univ Mus Art, 77; auth, Tracing the rise of Afro-American art in North Carolina, Art Voices/South, 3/78. Mailing Add: 208 Watts St Durham NC 27701

PENDLETON, MARY CAROLINE
HANDWEAVER, WRITER
b Rochester, Ind. Study: Dayton Art Inst, Ohio; Cranbrook Acad Art; also with Lili Blumenau, New York & Mary Meigs Atwater. Comn: Over the years, many pieces for pvt homes, bus & churches such as drapery fabrics, upholstery, dividers & paraments. Exhib: Int Textile Exhib, Woman Col, Univ NC, 52 & 54; Ann Women's Int Expos, New York, 59 & 60; Crafts Western US, Southern Calif Expos, Del Mar, 61; one-man show, Charles W Bowers Mem Mus, Santa Ana, 65; two-man show, Stanford Med & Res Inst, 63; Six Craftsmen Exhib, Heard Mus, Phoenix, Ariz, 63. Teaching: Teacher handweaving, Pendleton Fabric Craft Sch, 58-; weaving instr, Northern Ariz Univ, Flagstaff, 76-; teach workshops all over the country. Pos: Mem bd dirs, Handweavers Guild Am, 70; auth & ed, The Looming Arts, Nat Handweavers. Awards: Int Textile Exhib, Women's Col, Univ NC, 52; Contemporary Craftsmen Far West, Mus Contemp Crafts, 62; Ariz State Fair, 62. Bibliog: Isabel Stroud (auth), Couple finds weaving and full-time career, Christian Sci Monitor, 1/6/75. Mem: Nat

League Am Pen Women; Ariz Designer Craftsmen; Am Crafts Coun. Publ: Auth, Navajo & Hopi Weaving Techniques, Macmillan, 74; auth, Double Weave Series, 74 & Overshot Weave Series, 77. Mailing Add: PO Box 233 Sedona AZ 86336

PENKOFF, RONALD PETER
EDUCATOR, PRINTMAKER
b Toledo, Ohio, May 18, 32. Study: Bowling Green State Univ, BFA, 54; Ohio State Univ, MA, 56; Stanley William Hayter's Atelier 17, Paris, 65-66. Work: Libr of Cong, Washington, DC; Columbus Gallery Art, Ohio; Munson-Williams-Proctor Inst, Utica, NY; Montclair Mus, NJ; Ball State Art Gallery, Muncie, Ind. Exhib: Pennell Int Exhib Prints, Libr of Cong, Washington, DC, 55-57; Indiana Artists, John Herron Art Mus, Indianapolis, 60-64; Conn Acad Fine Arts Ann, Hartford, 61-62; Soc Washington Printmakers, Smithsonian Inst, Washington, DC, 62; Nouvelles Realities, Paris, 66; Skylight Gallery, 73; Madison Art Ctr, 75; Alvejihem Mus, 77. Teaching: Asst prof art, State Univ NY Col Oneonta, 56-59; asst prof art, Ball State Univ, 59-67; prof art, Univ Wis-Waukesha, 67-, chmn, Ctr Syst art dept, 70- Pos: Vis prof, Bath Acad Art, Corsham, Eng, summer 66. Awards: First Award in painting, NY State Fair, 57; Munson-Williams-Proctor Inst Award, Cent NY Artists, 58-59; First Award in painting, Eastern Ind Artists, 64. Bibliog: W Fabricki (auth), Prints and drawings of Ronald Penkoff, Quartet, 63; Donald Key (auth), Color printing is an elusive endeavor, Milwaukee J, 71. Style & Technique: Primarily based upon the argon school of visual communication. Media: Intaglio. Publ: Auth, The eye and the object, Forum, 62; auth, Roots of the Ukiyo-E, 65; auth, Sign, signal, symbol, 70. Mailing Add: 1500 University Dr Waukesha WI 53186

PENN, IRVING
PHOTOGRAPHER
b NJ, 17. Work: Mus Mod Art & Metrop Mus Art, New York; Smithsonian Inst, Washington, DC. Exhib: One-man shows, Mus Mod Art, New York, 75, Galleria Civica D'Arte Moderna, Torino, 75 & Metrop Mus of Art, New York, 77. Publ: Auth, Moments Preserved, 60; auth, Worlds in a Small Room, 74. Mailing Add· Box 934 FDR Station New York NY 10022

PENNEY, BRUCE BARTON
PAINTER
b Laconia, NH, Aug 9, 29. Study: Worcester Mus Sch; Cleveland Woodward, illusr; with Eldon Rowland, Well Fleet, Mass; New York-Phoenix Sch Design. Work: Worcester Polytech Inst, Mass; Stockholm Mus, Sweden; Dartmouth Col, Hanover, NH. Exhib: Hanover Gallery, NH; Southern Vt Art Asn, Manchester, 67; one-man shows, Wiener Gallery, New York, 68, Center St Gallery, Winter Park, Fla, 69 & Gallery 2, Woodstock, Vt, 69-71. Awards: Creative Communication's Award, Art Inst of Boston, 76. Media: Oil. Dealer: Wiener Gallery 963 Madison Ave New York NY 10021. Mailing Add: Stone Rd Kennebunkport ME 04046

PENNEY, CHARLES RAND
COLLECTOR, PATRON
b Buffalo, NY, July 26, 23. Study: Yale Univ, BA; Univ Va, LLB & JD. Collections Arranged: Prints From the Charles Rand Penney Foundation, Duns Scotus Gallery, Rosary Hill Col, Buffalo, NY, 64 & 74, Niagara Co Hist Soc, Lockport, NY, 65, Bridwell Libr, Southern Methodist Univ, Dallas, Tex, 66, Kenan Ctr, Lockport, NY, 67, 72 & 74, Patterson Libr Art Gallery, Westfield, NY, 73, Mem Art Gallery of Univ Rochester, NY, 73 & Niagara Art Ctr, Niagara Falls, NY, 74; Works of Charles Burchfield, 66 & Selected Works by Emil Ganso, 69, Kenan Ctr; Selections from the Charles R Penney Collection, Lakeview Gallery, NY, 70; Prints From the Charles Rand Penney Foundation, Niagara Co Community Col Mus, 71; Staffordshire Pottery Portrait Figures, Niagara Co Hist Soc, 72; Decade, Graphics in the Sixties, 74; NY State Photographers, 74; Victorian Staffordshire Figurines, Carborundum Mus of Ceramics, Niagara Falls, 74 & Columbus Gallery of Fine Arts, Ohio, 76; Charles Burchfield: The Charles Rand Penney Collection, Mem Art Gallery, Univ Rochester, 78. Mem: Niagara Coun of Arts; Assoc Art Orgn of Western NY; Niagara Co Antiques Club; Gallery Asn NY; Buffalo Soc Artists (trustee). Collection: International contemporary art; works of Charles E Burchfield and Emil Ganso; Western New York artists; Spanish-American Santos and Retablos; Victorian Staffordshire pottery portrait figures; American antique historic glass and textiles; American antique pressed glass; international primitive art. Mailing Add: 343 Bewley Bldg Lockport NY 14094

PENNEY, JAMES
PAINTER, EDUCATOR
b St Joseph, Mo, Sept 6, 10. Study: Univ Kans, BFA, 31, with Albert Bloch & Karl Mattern; Art Students League, 31-34, with George Grosz, Von Schlegell, John Sloan & Thomas Benton. Work: Wichita Art Mus, Kans; New Brit Mus Am Art, Conn; Des Moines Art Ctr; Hirshhorn Collection; Univ Nebr; plus others. Comn: Mural, comn by Works Progress Admin, Flushing High Sch Lobby, NY, 38; murals, Fed Art Proj, Post Off Bldgs, Union & Palmyra, Mo, 40-43; Hamilton: Four Seasons (mural), Bristol Ctr, Hamilton Col, 59; Nebraska Settlers (three murals), Main Vestibule, Nebr State Capitol, 63; Fields in Spring (painting), comn by Omaha Nat Bank for Joslyn Mus, Nebr, 66. Exhib: Artists for Victory, Metrop Mus Art, New York, 41; Pa Acad Fine Arts Ann, Philadelphia, 51-68; Am Inst Arts & Lett Ann, New York, 53, 59 & 71; Nature in Abstraction, Whitney Mus Am Art, New York, 57, 59 & 63; Nat Acad Design Ann, New York, 72-78; New Deal for Art, Carnegie Internationals Traveling Shows, originated in Pittsburgh, Pa, 75-77; Am Fedn of Art Traveling Shows to Corcoran Gallery, Washington, DC, San Francisco Mus, Los Angeles Museum, Chicago Art Inst, mus in Tokyo, Japan, and elsewhere; one-man shows, Kraushaar Galleries, New York, 50, 54, 55, 57, 61, 65, 69 & 74 & Retrospectives, Munson-Williams-Proctor Inst, Utica, NY, 55 & 77; plus others. Teaching: Instr painting, drawing & graphics, Bennington Col, 46-47; instr painting, drawing & graphics, Munson-Williams-Proctor Inst, 48-55; prof painting & drawing, Hamilton Col, 48-55 & 56-76; vis prof art, Vassar Col, 55-56; Yaddo fel, 56 & 61; vis artist, Calif Col Arts & Crafts, 60. Pos: Bd control & vpres, Art Students League, 41-46; trustee, Am Fine Arts Soc, 44-48. Awards: Midwestern Artists Ann Medal, Kansas City Art Inst, 31; medal & award, Paintings of the Year, Pepsi-Cola, 48; prize, Audubon Artists Ann, 67-78; Minnie Sterne Medal, 77; Emily Lowe Award, 78. Bibliog: James Penney paints an interior, In: Oil Painting, Watson-Guptill, 53; John I H Bauer (auth), Nature in Abstraction, Whitney Mus Am Art, 58; Nebraskaland masterpiece, Nebr Land Mag, 64; plus others. Mem: Nat Acad Design; Audubon Artists; Nat Soc Mural Painters; life mem Munson-Williams-Proctor Inst; Am Fedn Arts; Century Asn, New York, NY; plus others. Media: Oil. Publ: Auth, Cross section New York '72, Hamilton Col, 72; ed, Mural designs—James Penney, Utica Col, 72; auth, Albert Bloch, Munson-Williams-Proctor Inst, 74. Dealer: Kraushaar Galleries 1055 Madison Ave New York NY 10028. Mailing Add: 312 College Hill Rd Clinton NY 13323

PENNUTO, JAMES WILLIAM
MIXED-MEDIA ARTIST
b Joliet, Ill, June 15, 36. Study: Art Students League. Work: Oakland Mus, Calif; San Francisco Mus Mod Art. Exhib: Butler Inst Am Art, Youngstown, Ohio, 66-67; Oakland Mus, 69-70; Mus Mod Art, New York, 70; St John's Univ, New York, 70; Joslyn Art Mus, Omaha, Nebr, 70; San Francisco Mus Mod Art, 71. Bibliog: Palmer French (auth), San Francisco, Artforum, 2/70; New dimensions, Time, 4/13/70; Carter Ratcliff (auth), Report from San Francisco, Art in Am, 5-6/77. Style & Technique: From oil painting of industrial images, vacuum formed plastic and neon sculpture, abstract forms and photography, to paper constructions. Media: Film with Acoustical Sound Generations. Dealer: Simon Lowinsky Gallery 228 Grant San Francisco CA 94108. Mailing Add: 500A Cole San Francisco CA 94117

PENNY, AUBREY JOHN ROBERT
PAINTER
b London, Eng, July 30, 17; US citizen. Study: Univ Calif, Los Angeles, BA(art & art hist), 53, MA(art), 55; also with Dr Danes. Work: Contemp Art Soc, London; Edward Dean Mus, Cherry Valley, Calif. Exhib: Corcoran Gallery Art, Washington, DC, 57; Am Watercolor Soc, New York, 57-58; two-man shows, Madison Gallery, New York, 63 & Int De Deauville, France, 72; one-man show, Mt San Jacinto Col, Calif, 72. Pos: Owner, No-os Gallery, Los Angeles, 55-; mem art coun, Univ Calif, Los Angeles, 55- Awards: Prize for drawing, Emanual Sch, London, 31; award of merit, Nat Watercolor Soc, 55; hon mention, Los Angeles City Art Festival, 58. Mem: Contemp Art Soc, London; Victoria Inst, London; Am Soc Aesthetics & Art Criticism; Los Angeles Inst Contemp Art. Style & Technique: Non-objective; drawing and paint on canvas. Media: Acrylic. Publ: Auth, The Mind-Line Approach of Aubrey Penny, 76; auth, numerous series incl Amarant Series, Bootstrap Series, Ethos Series & Emancipation of Line Series. Mailing Add: c/o No-os Gallery Penny Studio 16134 Sherman Way Van Nuys CA 91406

PEPPER, BEVERLY
SCULPTOR, PAINTER
b Brooklyn, NY, Dec 20, 24. Study: Pratt Inst; Art Students League; also with Fernand Leger & Andre L'hote, Paris. Work: Albright-Knox Art Gallery, Buffalo, NY; Mass Inst Technol, Boston; Fogg Art Mus, Cambridge, Mass; Walker Art Ctr, Minneapolis; Indianapolis Mus Art, Ind; plus others. Comn: Sudden Presence (Cor-ten), City of Boston, New Chardon St, 71; Phaedrus (painted steel), Philadelphia Fed Reserve Bank, 73; Excalibur (painted steel), San Diego Fed Courthouse, Calif, 74; Amphisculpture 75 (site sculpture), Bedminster, NJ, 75; Thel (site sculpture), Dartmouth Col, 77. Exhib: Sculpture in the City, Festival dei due Mondi, Spoleto, Italy, 62; Plus by Minus, Today's Half Century, Albright-Knox Art Gallery, 68; Outdoor Sculpture, Jewish Mus, New York, 68; Sculpture, Mus Contemp Art, Chicago, 69; 23rd Biennale, Venice, Italy, 72; Hammarskjold Plaza Sculpture Garden, New York, 75; San Francisco Mus Art, Calif, 76; Documenta 6, Kassel, WGer, 77; Qadriennale Naxionale, Rome, Italy, 77; Seattle Mus Contemp Art, 77; Indianapolis Mus Art, 78. Awards: Best Art in Steel, Iron & Steel Inst, 70; Nat Endowment for the Arts Grant, 75; Gen Serv Admin Grant, 75. Bibliog: Wayne Andersen (auth), Sculpture Today, Mass Inst Technol Press, 70; Vittorio Armentano (auth), B P Making Sculpture (film), G Ungaretti, narrator, 70; Amphisculpture (film), Barbara Rose & Beverly Pepper, narrators, 77. Style & Technique: Metal, welded as well as monumental land works using the natural environments contained in metal or concrete. Media: Steel. Dealer: Andre Emmerich Gallery 41 E 57th St New York NY 10022. Mailing Add: Torre Gentile Di Todi (PG) Italy

PEREHUDOFF, WILLIAM W
PAINTER
b Saskatoon, Sask, Apr 21, 19. Study: Colorado Springs Fine Arts Ctr; Ozenfant Sch Art, New York; Univ Sask, Emma Lake, workshops with Cherry, Noland & Greenberg. Work: Norman MacKenzie Art Gallery, Regina; Mendel Art Gallery, Saskatoon; Edmonton Art Gallery; London Art Gallery, Ont; Univ Calgary, Alta. Comn: Mural, Toronto Dominion Bank, Regina, 75. Exhib: Mendel Art Gallery, 65; Edmonton Art Gallery, 72; Waddington Art Gallery, Montreal, 73; Noah Goldowsky Inc, New York, 74. Bibliog: Clement Greenberg (auth), Painting and Sculpture in Canada, Can Art, 63; Karen Wilkin (auth), W Perehudoff recent paintings, Arts Can, 72. Mem: Royal Can Acad Art. Style & Technique: Color field painting. Media: Acrylic on Canvas. Dealer: Noah Goldowsky Inc New York NY; Waddington Art Gallery Montreal Can. Mailing Add: 1131 Second St E Saskatoon SK S7A 1R4 Can

PEREZ, VINCENT
PAINTER, INSTRUCTOR
b Jersey City, NJ, July 17, 38. Study: Pratt Inst, BFA; Univ Am, Mex; Calif Col Arts & Crafts, MFA. Work: San Francisco Mus Art; Achenbach Collection, Palace Legion Honor, San Francisco; Oakland Art Mus, Calif; Playboy Enterprises, Chicago; Time, Inc, New York. Comn: Mural, Arleigh Gallery, San Francisco, 69; portrait of State Supreme Court Judge Peters, comn by Clerks of Supreme Court for Univ Calif, Berkeley Law Sch, 74; woodcuts, Civic Arts Asn, Walnut Creek, Calif, 74. Exhib: Smithsonian Nat Portrait Gallery, Washington, DC, 69; Affect Effect, La Jolla Mus Art, Calif, 69; World's Fair, Osaka, Japan, 70; Fine Artists, Otis Art Inst, Los Angeles, 71; California Printmakers, Chicago, 74. Teaching: Assoc prof drawing & printmaking & chmn dept drawing, Calif Col Arts & Crafts, 66-; instr anat, Univ Calif, Berkeley, 73- Awards: First Prize for Graphics, Northern Calif Arts, Sacramento, 66; Union Independent Col Art Res Grant, 70; Best of Show, Tech Writers Convention, Los Angeles, 72. Bibliog: Fred Martin (auth), San Francisco letter, Art Int, 66; Cecille McCann (auth), Vincent Perez, FMb Fine Arts, 69; Palmer French (auth), San Francisco artists, Artforum, 69. Mem: Oakland Art Mus; Artists Equity; Union Independent Col Art. Style & Technique: Figurative-fantasy realist. Media: Acrylic on Polyester Resin, Woodcut. Publ: Illusr, cover of Time, 69; illusr, Art & Tools, 72; illusr, Archives of Institutional Change Humanizing Technology, 73; illusr, Psychol Today, 73; illusr, Playboy, 74. Mailing Add: 1279 Weber St Alameda CA 94501

PERHAM, ROY GATES
PAINTER
b Paterson, NJ, Apr 18, 16. Study: Grand Cent Art Sch; also with Frank V Dumond & Frank J Reilly. Work: Americana Mus, Univ SC; Plimoth Plantation, Plymouth, Mass; Salisbury Pub Libr, Md; Maywood Pub Libr, NJ. Comn: Portrait of Dr O Howard, comn by friends at Diocesan Col, McGill Univ, 56; Jordan River (mural), Rutherford Baptist Church, NJ, 57; portrait of Dr Arthur Armitage, South Jersey Col, Rutgers Univ, 61; portrait of Dr Milton Hoffman, Cent Col, Iowa, 66; portrait of H Bruce Palmer, Conf Bd, New York, 71. Exhib: Allied Artists Am, New York, 66; Fairleigh Dickinson Univ, NJ, 67; Fair Lawn Art Asn, NJ, 68; Bergen Mall Exhib, Paramus, NJ, 70. Awards: Purchase Prize, Bergen Mall, 64. Mem: Hackensack Art Club; Bergen Co Artists Guild. Media: Oil. Dealer: Portraits Inc 41 E 57th St New York NY 10022. Mailing Add: 268 Raymond St Hasbrouck Heights NJ 07604

PERINE, ROBERT HEATH
PAINTER
b Los Angeles, Calif, Nov 30, 22. Study: Univ Southern Calif; Chouinard Art Inst, cert; watercolor with Rex Brandt & Phil Dike. Work: Butler Inst Am Art, Youngstown, Ohio; Univ Mass, Amherst; Brigham Young Univ; Utah State Univ; Fine Arts Gallery, San Diego. Exhib: Nat Watercolor Soc Ann, 49-53 & 71-77; San Diego Art Inst Ann, 71-; Butler Inst Ann, 72; Nat Orange Show Ann, 73-; Brand Libr Art Ctr, Glendale, Calif, 75. Awards: First Place & Purchase Award, 58th Ann Nat Orange Show, San Bernardino, 73; First Place in Watercolors & Purchase Award, 21st Ann San Diego Art Inst Show, 74; Purchase Award, 13th Ann Riverside Art Ctr Show, 75. Bibliog: Donovan Maley (auth), The delicate balance, San Diego Mag, 2/73 & A one-man renaissance for watercolor, Southwest Art Mag, summer 73; Fran Preisman (auth), Robert Perine's Geoglyphica revisited, Artweek, 4/75. Mem: Nat Watercolor Soc; Watercolor West; West Coast Watercolor Soc; San Diego Art Inst; San Diego Art Guild. Style & Technique: Large format; abstract. Media: Watercolor. Mailing Add: 628 San Dieguito Dr Encinitas CA 92024

PERKINS, A ALAN
PRINTMAKER, ENAMELIST
b Toronto, Ont, Nov 30, 15. Study: Danforth Tech Sch, Toronto, dipl; Ont Col Art, Toronto, scholar; Brookfield Craft Ctr, Conn, with Margaret Seeler & Francis Felton. Work: Ont Inst of Studies, Toronto; Ont Craft Coun Permanent Collection, Toronto, Confedn Centre Gallery & Mus, Charlottetown, PEI, Can; Jean A Chalmers Can Collection, Toronto. Comn: Mural, Cochran Murray Co, Toronto, 69; modular assemblage, Cadillac Develop Corp, Toronto, 72, Crown Life Insurance Head Off, Toronto, 73 & Inst Bicentric Psychology, Los Angeles, Calif, 73. Exhib: Expo/Can, Can Bldg, Montreal, Que, 67; Craft Dimensions Can, Royal Ont Mus, Toronto, 69; Permanent Collection, Confedn Centre Gallery, PEI, 69; MAKE, Ont Sci Centre, Toronto, 71; Jean L Chalmers Permanent Collection, Ont Craft Coun, Toronto, 74; First World Craft Exhib, Ont Sci Centre, Don Mills, 74; Design Can Award, Can Gov, Ottawa, 74; Visage du Can, Guilde Can des Metiers d'art Que, 76; Ont Craft Coun Traveling Exhib, 77-78; plus other one-man shows. Teaching: Instr enameling & jewelry arts, George Brown Col, Toronto, 68-; instr glazes on metal, Toronto Bd Educ, 68-78. Pos: Tread bd dirs, Ont Craft Found, Toronto, 68-69. Awards: Can Coun Study & Travel Grant, 68; Adelaide Merriot Award of Excellence, Can Nat Exhib, 70; Award of Excellence, MAKE Exhib, Ont Can Guild of Crafts, 71. Bibliog: Una Abrahamson (auth), Crafts Canada, The Useful Arts, Clarke Irwin & Co Ltd, Toronto, 74; David Piper (ed), Canadian Interiors, Maclean Hunter Publ, 74; J Hartley Newman (auth), Wire Art, Crown Publ, New York, 75. Mem: Soc Can Artists (chmn exhib comt, 76-77); Ont Soc Artists; Ont Crafts Coun (secy-treas bd dirs, 68-70); Can Craftsmen's Coun. Style & Technique: Vitreious enamels on metals; abstract enamel paintings; mixed-media; pen & ink drawing. Media: Enamel Painting; Printmaking. Mailing Add: 29 Glen Davis Toronto ON M4E 1X6 Can

PERKINS, ANN
ART HISTORIAN
b Chicago, Ill, Apr 18, 15. Study: Univ Chicago, AB, 35, AM, 36, PhD, 40. Teaching: Res assoc ancient art, Yale Univ, 55-65; assoc prof ancient art, Univ Ill, Urbana, 65-69, prof ancient art, 69- Awards: Guggenheim Fel, 54-55. Mem: Archaeol Inst Am; Col Art Asn Am. Res: Chiefly art of the Eastern Roman Empire. Publ: Auth, The Art of Dura-Europos, 73. Mailing Add: 1009 W Clark St Champaign IL 61820

PERKINS, CONSTANCE M
EDUCATOR, ART WRITER
b Denver, Colo, Dec 20, 13. Study: Univ Denver, BA, 35; Mills Col, MA, 37. Collections Arranged: Pacific Profile, Pasadena Art Mus, Calif & Western Asn Art Mus, 61; Jose Louis Cuevas, 64 & The Edge of Pop, 65, Western Asn Art Mus; The New Vein: The Figure 1963-1968 (traveling Latin Am), 68-70, The New Vein: The Figure 1964-1968 (traveling Europe), 69-70 & Variaciones Fotograficas, 75, Smithsonian Inst, Washington, DC. Teaching: Instr art, Univ Denver, 37-42; prof art hist, Occidental Col, Los Angeles, 47- Pos: Contribr articles in Los Angeles Times, 63-65 & Artforum 62-64; auth, Fact or fiction? the legacy of Oriental art, 65 & Los Angeles: the way you look at it, 66, Art in Am. Mailing Add: 1540 Poppy Peak Dr Pasadena CA 91105

PERKINS, G HOLMES
ARCHITECT, EDUCATOR
b Cambridge, Mass, Oct 10, 04. Study: Harvard Univ, AB, 26, MArch, 29, LLD, 72. Teaching: Chmn dept archit & dean grad sch fine arts, Univ Pa, 51-71, chmn grad prog archit & prof archit & urbanism, 71- Pos: Ed, J Am Inst Planners, 50-52; chancellor col fels, Am Inst Architects, 64-66. Mem: Fel Am Inst Architects; hon corresp mem Royal Inst Architects Can. Publ: Auth, Comparative outline of architectural history, 37; contrib, articles in prof jour. Mailing Add: Dept of Archit Univ Pa Philadelphia PA 19104

PERKINS, ROBERT EUGENE
ART ADMINISTRATOR
b Pittsfield, Mass, Oct 20, 31. Study: Sioux Falls Col, BA, 56; Columbia Univ, MA, 57; Univ SDak; Sioux Falls Col, LHD, 74. Pos: Asst prin, Canton High Sch, SDak, 59-61; dir admis, Sioux Falls Col, 61-63, dean students, 63-70; pres, Ringling Sch Art, Sarasota, Fla, 71- Publ: Co-auth, Profile of the South Dakota high school graduate of 1968, 69; auth, The Maestro, 70. Mailing Add: 3424 S Lockwood Ridge Rd Sarasota FL 33579

PERLESS, ROBERT
SCULPTOR
b New York, NY, Apr 23, 38. Study: Univ Miami, Coral Gables, Fla. Work: Whitney Mus Am Art, New York; Aldrich Mus Contemp Art, Ridgefield, Conn; Chrysler Mus at Norfolk, Va; Everson Mus, Syracuse, NY; Phoenix Art Mus, Ariz. Comn: Am Tel & Tel, Atlanta, Ga; Taupman Co, Lake Forest Shopping Mall; Guggenheim Int, New York; Avon Corp, New York; Nat Chemsearch, Irving, Tex. Exhib: Bodley Gallery, New York, 68 & 74; New Acquisitions Exhib, Whitney Mus Am Art, New York, 70; Bernard Danenberg Gallery, New York, 72; Houston Gallery, Tex, 75; Forum Gallery & Galleria Bonino, New York, 75; Aldrich Mus Contemp Art, 78. Style & Technique: Monolithic kinetic wind constructions. Media: Aluminum, Stainless Steel, Corten Steel, Bronze. Mailing Add: 43 Greenwich Ave New York NY 10014

PERLIN, BERNARD
PAINTER, ILLUSTRATOR
b Richmond, Va, Nov 21, 18. Study: Nat Acad Design, with Leon Kroll, 36-37; Art Students League, with Isabel Bishop, William Palmer & Harry Sternberg, 36-37; also in Poland. Work: Mus Mod Art; Tate Gallery, London; Nat Collection Fine Art, Smithsonian Inst, Washington, DC; Whitney Mus Am Art, New York; Va Mus Fine Arts; plus others. Comn: US Post Off Dept, 40; US Treas Dept. Comn: Cincinnati Mus Asn, 58; Brussels World's Fair, 58; Detroit Inst Art, 60; Pa Acad Fine Arts, 60; retrospective, Univ Bridgeport, 69; plus many other group & one-man shows. Teaching: Instr, Wooster Community Art Ctr, Danbury, Conn, 67-69. Awards: Fulbright Fel, 50; Guggenheim Fels, 54-55 & 59; Nat Inst Arts & Lett Award, 64; plus others. Bibliog: Lloyd Goodrich & John I H Baur (auth), American Art of Our Century, Whitney Mus Am Art, 61; Daniel M Mendelowitz (auth), A History of American Art, Holt, 61; Selden Rodman (auth), Conversations with Artists, Capricorn Press, 61; plus others. Publ: Contribr, illus, Life & Fortune Mags. Mailing Add: 56 Shadow Lake Rd Ridgefield CT 06877

PERLIN, RAE
PAINTER
b St John's, Nfld. Study: With Samuel Brecher, 41, 42 & 46 & Hans Hofmann, 47 & 48, New York; Acad Grande Chaumière, Paris; Acad Ranson, Paris. Work: Mem Univ Nfld Permanent Collection, Can. Exhib: Mem Univ Nfld Art Gallery, 71; plus others from 62-72. Pos: Art critic, St John's Daily News, 60-71; art critic, St John's Eve Telegram, 64-67. Awards: Arts & Lett, Nfld Govt, 56 & 62-67; Can Coun Grant, 70. Style & Technique: Whether drawing or painting, a feeling for form and structure; fond of all drawing media. Media: Oil, Acrylic. Collection: Contemporary works of Canadian artists; prints, drawings, constructions and paintings. Publ: Contribr, A history of art in Newfoundland, In: Book of Newfoundland, Vol 4, 67; illusr, Spindrift and morning light, 68. Mailing Add: 11A Monkstown Rd St John's NF Can

PERLMAN, JOEL LEONARD
SCULPTOR, INSTRUCTOR
b New York, NY, June 12, 43. Study: Cornell Univ, BFA, 65; Cent Sch of Art & Design, London; Univ Calif, Berkeley, MA, 68. Work: Larry Aldrich Mus of Contemp Art, Ridgefield, Conn; Storm King Art Ctr, Mountainville, NY. Comn: Large outdoor sculpture, RTKL, Inc, Baltimore, Md, 71; Night Traveler (large outdoor sculpture), Storm King Art Ctr, 77. Exhib: Axiom Gallery, London, 69; Bennington Col, Vt, 70; Whitney Mus of Am Art Biennial, New York, 73; Contemp Reflections, Aldrich Mus of Contemp Art, 73; Andre Emmerich Gallery, New York, 73, 76 & 78, Zurich, 77; Storm King Art Ctr, 74 & 75. Teaching: Instr sculpture, Sch of Visual Arts, 73-; adj prof sculpture, Lincoln Ctr Campus, Fordham Univ, 74- Awards: Guggenheim Found fel, sculpture, 74. Bibliog: Barbara Zucker (auth), Review of Exhibition, Artnews, Summer 1976. Style & Technique: Welded steel, large outdoor sculpture. Mailing Add: c/o Emmerich Gallery 41 E 57th St New York NY 10022

PERLMAN, RAYMOND
EDUCATOR, ILLUSTRATOR
b Sheboygan, Wis, May 17, 23. Study: Univ Ill, Champaign, BFA, 48 & MFA, 53; Art Ctr Col Design, Los Angeles, MPA, 52. Work: Watercolors, Univ Ill, Champaign. Exhib: Creativity on Paper, Mead Paper Co, New York, 65; Chicago 3, Ill, 70; Art Dir Club New York 49th Ann, 70; Printing Job of the Year, 3M Co, 70; TDC 17, Type Dir Club New York, 71; since 75, numerous group & one-man shows in the media of photog & printmaking. Teaching: Prof art & in charge graphic design, Univ Ill, Champaign, 49- Pos: Illusr, World Book & Childcraft, Field Enterprises, 58- Awards: UN Int Poster Competition, 49; 8th Ann Watercolor & Drawing Exhib Award, Artists Guild Chicago, 66; Center for Advan Study Fel, Univ Ill, 75. Mem: Soc Typographic Arts, Chicago. Style & Technique: Varies according to medium, from realism to abstraction; increasing experimentation with photography and printmaking techniques. Media: Watercolor, Collage, Photography. Publ: Illusr, Our Wonderful World, Grolier, 53-59; illusr, Rocks and minerals, 57, Fossils, 62, Light and Color, 71, Geology, 72 & Ecology, 73, Golden Guides. Mailing Add: RR 3 Park Hills Mahomet IL 61853

PERLMUTTER, JACK
PAINTER, PRINTMAKER
b New York, NY, Jan 20, 20. Work: Nat Gallery Art, Phillips Collection & Corcoran Gallery Art, Washington, DC; Metrop Mus Art, New York; Nat Mus Mod Art, Tokyo. Comn: First Saturn Moon Rocket Launching (painting), 67 & Saturn V, Apollo 6 (painting), 68, NASA, Kennedy Space Ctr, Fla; Woodcuts for Apollo 16, Mission Control Ctr, Houston, Tex, 72. Exhib: Four Corcoran Gallery Art Am Biennials, 49-61; American Prints Today, Print Coun Am, exhibited in ten cities, 59-60; 3rd & 4th Expos Gravure, Ljubljana, Yugoslavia, 59 & 61; 3rd Nat Exhib Printmaking, Univ Wis, 71; 2nd Nat Print Show, Fine Arts Gallery, San Diego, 71. Teaching: Chmn dept graphics, Corcoran Sch Art, 61-, prof art. Pos: Dir, Dickey Gallery Art, DC Teachers Col, 56-68; contrib ed, Art Voices/South. Awards: Fulbright Grant in art & printmaking to Tokyo, 59-60; Print Prize, 1st Int Exhib Fine Arts Saigon, 62; also numerous purchase awards. Bibliog: A Perlmutter original, Washington Star Sun Mag, 11/62; reproduction, In: Art Today, Holt, Rinehart & Winston, 4th ed; Eyewitness to Space, Abrams, 72. Mem: Soc Am Graphic Artists; Cosmos Club (art comt, 63-). Publ: Contribr, Transactions of 5th International Conference of Orientalists (Toho Gakkai), In: Japanese Prints Today, 7/60; auth, Western art influences in Japan, In: Today's Japan Orient/West, 8/60; auth, Painting in a land of transition (with reproductions), Inst Int Educ Mag, 1/61. Mailing Add: 2511 Cliffbourne Pl NW Washington DC 20009

PERLMUTTER, MERLE
PRINTMAKER, INSTRUCTOR
b London, Eng, Apr 16, 41; US citizen. Study: Art Students League, with Ethel Katz; Pratt Inst, Brooklyn, NY; Ruth Leaf Graphic Workshop, Douglaston, NY. Work: Hudson River Mus, Yonkers, NY; Dulin Galleries of Art, Knoxville, Tenn; NY State Facilities Develop Corp; Nassau Community Col, NY; Silvermine Guild of Artists, Conn. Exhib: Laguna Beach Mus, Calif, 73; Boston Printmakers Nat Competition, Mass, 74 & 76; 11th Int Biennial of Graphic Art, Mus of Mod Art, Ljubljana, Yugoslavia, 75; Pratt Int Miniature Graphics Exhib, 75 & 77; Premio Internazionale Biella Por L'Incisione, Italy, 76; Am Graphics in Venice, Opera Bevilaqua La Masa, Italy, 77; Print Club Int Biennial, Philadelphia, Pa, 77; Miami Int Biennial, Met Mus & Art Ctr, Fla, 77; 55th Soc of Am Graphic Artists Nat Print Exhib, New York, 77; Hudson River Mus, Yonkers, NY, 77; plus others. Teaching: Instr etching & printmaking, Ruth Leaf Graphic workshop, Douglaston, NY, 76-; guest printmaker prints & techniques, Grey Art Gallery & Study Ctr, NY Univ, New York, 76. Awards: Gold Medal of Honor, Audubon Artist Nat Competition, New York, 75 & 77; CAPS Fel, Creative Artist Pub Serv Prog, NY State Coun of the Arts & Nat Endowment for the Arts, 76; Purchase Award, Silvermine Guild of Artists Nat Competition, 76. Bibliog: News of the print world: people and places, Print Collectors Newsletter, 5-6/75; Robert Taylor (auth), Boston Globe, 76; Ruth Leaf (auth), Intaglio Printmaking Techniques, Watson-Guptill, 77. Mem: Boston Printmakers, Mass; The Print Club, Philadelphia, Pa; Audubon Artists, New York; Soc Am Graphic Artists, NY. Style & Technique: Multiple soft ground etching techniques; unique and mysterious vision of interior spaces. Media: Intaglio, etching. Mailing Add: 20 Cherry Ave New Rochelle NY 10801

PERLS, KLAUS G
ART DEALER
b Berlin, Ger, Jan 15, 12; US citizen. Study: Univ Basel, Switz, PhD, 33. Pos: Partner, Perls Galleries, 37- Mem: Art Dealers Asn Am. Specialty: Modern masters. Publ: Auth, Complete works of Jean Fouquet, 40; auth, Maurice de Vlaminck, 41. Mailing Add: 1016 Madison Ave New York NY 10021

PERREAULT, JOHN
ART CRITIC, MULTI-MEDIA ARTIST
b New York, NY, Aug 26, 37. Performances: (Real time performances involving artist as a presence, sculpting time and space) Wadsworth Atheneum; NY Univ; Archit League New York; Univ Iowa; Univ Mich, Ann Arbor; Critical Mass, Whitney Mus Am Art. Comn: Co-coordr & partic, Streetworks, Archit League New York, 69. Exhib: One-man show, Word Room, Gain Ground Gallery, New York, 69; Dwan Gallery, New York, 69; 957,087, Vancouver Art Gallery, Can, 69; 557,087, Seattle Art Mus, 69; Art in the Mind, Oberlin Col, 70. Exhibitions Arranged: Male Nude, Gallery Sch Visual Arts, New York; Tokyo Biennale New Figuration Art, 74; Sharp Realism: Painting from Photos, William Patterson Col Gallery, 75, Some Women Artists, 75. Teaching: Instr mod art, Grad Sch, Univ Iowa, summer 70; instr mod art, Sch Visual Arts, New York, 70-74; instr mod art, William Paterson Col, NJ, 74- Pos: Dir, Gallery, William Paterson Col NJ, 75-; art ed, Soho Weekly News, New York, 75- Awards: Nat Endowment Grant for Art Criticism, 73. Bibliog: Spec issue on John Perreault, Serif, Kent State Univ Libr Quart, fall 74. Mem: Inst Asn Art Critics. Publ: Contribr, Minimal Art, 68, Conceptual Art, 72 & Idea Art, 73, Dutton; co-ed, Anti-Object art, Tri-Quart, fall 74. Mailing Add: 105 W 27th St New York NY 10001

PERRET, GEORGE ALBERT
WRITER, LECTURER
b New York, NY. Study: Munson-Williams-Proctor Inst, Utica, NY; Utica Col, Syracuse Univ; Art Students League; Nat Acad Design Sch Art, New York. Collections Arranged: Artists of the South Fork, 65, The Wyeth Family, 66 & Mary Cassat, 67, Parrish Mus, Southampton, NY. Teaching: Instr art hist, Southampton Col, Long Island Univ, 63-68. Pos: Dir, Parrish Art Mus, 63-68; cur, Am Contemp Artists Gallery, 68-72; dir publ, Assoc Am Artists, 72-; cur, Andrew Crispo Gallery, New York & dir, Metrop Art Appraisers of Am, New York, 73- Mem: Westbeth Graphic Artists Group (prog dir). Res: American painting, 1860-1950. Publ: Contribr, Art news and reviews (weekly column), Suffolk Sun, 65-68; auth, Levon West, 66; auth, George Elmer Browne, 66; co-auth, Tully Filmus Drawings, 71; auth, Moses Soyer Drawings, 71. Mailing Add: Indian Wells Hwy Amagansett NY 11930

PERRET, NELL FOSTER
PAINTER
b Brooklyn, NY. Study: Pratt Inst; Art Students League; Design Lab. Work: Southampton Col, Long Island Univ; East Hampton Guild Hall; St Mary's Univ; Wichita State Univ. Exhib: Audubon Artists, Nat Acad Design Gallery, 71-77; Westbeth Graphics Workshop, Palacio Bellas Artes, Mex, 71-72; East Hampton Guild Hall Ann; Chung Hsing Galleries, Taiwan, 73; Assoc Am Artists, 74; Roko Gallery, New York, 76. Teaching: Instr graphics, Parrish Art Mus, Southampton, 60-68; adj prof graphics, Southampton Col, 68-70. Awards: Two awards, East Hampton Guild Hall, 61 & 62; three awards for graphics, Parrish Art Mus, 63, 64 & 67. Bibliog: Jean Paris (auth), Review of my work, Newsday, 63; Gordon Brown (auth), Review, Arts Mag, summer 71 & 76. Mem: East Hampton Guild Hall; Westbeth Graphic Artists Workshop (publ dir, 70-71); Painters & Sculptors Soc; Audubon Artists; Artists Equity Asn. Style & Technique: Painting: Under-painting, egg tempera, oil and varnish glaze; Graphics: Etching and aquatint. Dealer: Roko Gallery 90 E Tenth St New York NY 10003. Mailing Add: 463 West St 628A Westbeth New York NY 10014

PERRIN, C ROBERT
PAINTER, ILLUSTRATOR
b Medford, Mass, July 13, 15. Study: Sch Practical Art, scholar, also with John Wharf & Lester Stevens, four yrs. Work: Ford Motor Co Collection Am Watercolors; Lyman Allyn Mus, New London, Conn. Exhib: Mus Fine Arts, Boston, 52; Am Watercolor Soc, 58-; US Info Agency World Tour, 59; Boston Watercolor Soc, 60-; Nat Acad Design; Boston Arts Festival. Teaching: Artist, lectr & demonstr, Boston & Nantucket Island, Mass, 50. Pos: Freelance illusr, Boston, 39-42 & 46-68. Awards: Richard Mitton Mem Award, 32nd Ann Exhib Painting by Contemp New Eng Artists, 61; First Award, Copley Soc, 65; First Prize, Artist Asn of Nantucket, 73, 76 & 77. Bibliog: James S Geggis (auth), Art studio on wheels, United Press, 47; Patricia Boyd Wilson (auth), The home forum, Christian Sci Monitor, 66; Norman Kent (auth), 100 Watercolor Techniques, Watson-Guptill, 68. Mem: Am Watercolor Soc; Boston Watercolor Soc; Artist Asn Nantucket; Rockport Art Asn; Guild Boston Artists. Style & Technique: Watercolor in a realistic style; in some recent paintings, have introduced ghosts to some historic spots. Publ: Co-auth, Watercolor page, 59 & Making a rug mural, 66, Am Artist Mag; contribr, The folk arts and crafts of New England, 65 & Creating art from anything, 68. Mailing Add: 50 Washington St Nantucket Island MA 02554

PERROT, PAUL N
ART ADMINISTRATOR, LECTURER
b Paris, France, July 28, 26; US citizen. Study: Inst Fine Arts, NY Univ, 46-52. Collections Arranged: Three Great Centuries of Venetian Glass, 58; most exhibs shown at The Corning Mus Glass, 60-72. Teaching: Instr glass hist, Corning Community Col & Alfred Univ. Pos: Asst, The Cloisters, Metrop Mus Art, 48-52; asst to dir, Corning Mus Glass, 52-55, asst dir, 55-60, dir, 60-72; ed, J of Glass Studies, 59-72; asst secy mus progs, Smithsonian Inst, 72- Mem: Am Asn Mus (coun mem, exec comt, secy); US Int Coun Mus (past chmn); Am Archaeol Inst; Int Asn for Hist of Glass (vpres); Int Ctr for Study of Preserv & Restoration Cult Property (coun mem); Int Coun Mus (vpres). Publ: Auth, Three great centuries of Venetian glass, 58; auth, articles in Antiques, Apollo, Arts in Va, Col Art J & others. Mailing Add: Smithsonian Inst Washington DC 20560

PERRY, CHARLES O
SCULPTOR
b Helena, Mont, Oct 18, 29. Study: Yale Univ, BArch. Work: Art Inst Chicago; Oakland Mus, Calif; San Francisco Mus Art, Calif; Mus Mod Art, New York; de Young Mus, San Francisco. Comn: Univ SC, 73; Gen Elec Hq, Conn, 74; Ministry of Defense, Riyadh, Saudi Arabia, 75; Nat Air & Space Mus, Washington, DC, 76; City of Miami Beach, Fla, 78. Exhib: Hansen Gallery, 64; Milwaukee Art Ctr, Wis; Chicago Mus Contemp Art; Jewish Mus, New York; Santa Barbara Mus, Calif; Whitney Mus Am Art, New York, 64 & 66; Spoleto Art Festival, Italy, 69; Venice Bienale, 70; Quadriennale di Roma, Italy, 77; one-man shows, Axiom Gallery, London, 66, Waddell Gallery, 67 & 70, Alpha Gallery, 70, Hopkins Art Ctr, Dartmouth, 72, Arts Club of Chicago, 72. Pos: Sculptor-in-residence, Am Acad in Rome, 68 & Hopkins Art Ctr, Dartmouth, 72. Awards: Prix de Rome in Archit, 64-66; AISD, 68 & 70. Style & Technique: Mathematical, large scale, metal. Mailing Add: Shorehaven Rd Norwalk CT 06855

PERRY, EDWARD (TED) SAMUEL
ART ADMINISTRATOR
b New Orleans, La, June 4, 37. Study: Baylor Univ, BA, 61; Univ Iowa, MA, 66, PhD, 68. Teaching: Prof cinema & chmn dept, Univ Iowa, Univ Tex & NY Univ, 69-75; Luce vis prof cinema, Harvard Univ, spring 75. Pos: Dir film dept, Mus Mod Arts, New York, 75- Mem: Soc Cinema Studies; Speech Commun Asn (mem res bd, 74-). Res: Early cinema history; Italian cinema. Publ: Ed, Performing Arts Resources, 75; co-auth, New Film Index, Dutton, 75; auth, Filmguide to 8-1/2, Ind Univ, 75; auth, The passenger, Film Comment, Vol 2, No 4; auth, Formal strategies as an index to the evolution of film history, Cinema J, 75. Mailing Add: Mus Mod Art 11 W 53rd St New York NY 10019

PERRY, FRANK
SCULPTOR
b Vancouver, BC, Jan 1, 23. Study: Univ BC, BA, 56; Cent Sch Arts & Crafts, London, Eng; Regent Poly, Chelsea Sch Art, London. Work: Nat Gallery, Ottawa; Vancouver Art Gallery; Univ BC Sch Archit; Art Gallery Gtr Victoria, BC; Univ Victoria. Comn: Sculptures, granite carving, Burnaby Munic Hall, BC, 58, bronze fountain, Crescent Apts, West Vancouver, 61, cor-ten welded, Fed Govt Bldg, Victoria, 66, bronze cast, Playhouse Theatre, Vancouver, 67 & BC Govt for Prov Bldgs, 73. Exhib: Montreal Mus Fine Arts, 58; Winnipeg Show, 58; BC Centennial Outdoor Show, 58; BC Centennial Outdoor Sculpture Show, 67. Pos: Pres, Northwest Inst Sculpture, 59-60. Awards: First Prizes, Montreal Mus Fine Arts, Winnipeg Show & BC Centennial Outdoor Show, 68; Grand Prize, BC Centennial Outdoor Sculpture Show, 67; Rothman Award, 67. Mem: Sculptor's Soc Can; Sculptor's Soc BC; Royal Can Acad Art. Style & Technique: Abstract, with expressionistic qualities. Media: Bronze, Welded Steel. Dealer: Gallery Allen Granville St Vancouver BC Can. Mailing Add: 3526 Everglade Pl North Vancouver BC V7N 3T9 Can

PERRY, KATHRYN POWERS
PAINTER
b Chico, Calif, Mar 13, 48. Study: Concordia Col, seminar in Italy with Barbara Glasrud, 69, with Cy Running, BA(art, Eng), 70; Stanford Univ, 68; Art Students League, with Will Barnet, Earl Mayan, Knox Martin & Gregory d'Alessio, 71-74, Emily Ferrier-Spear scholarship, 73-74; Sch of Visual Arts, 78. Comn: Stage design for var festivals, Concordia Col, 68-69, posters & bk covers, 69-70. Exhib: Berkshire Art Asn 21st Spring Exhib, Berkshire Mus, Pittsfield, Mass, 75; Aames Gallery, New York, 76; Am Drawing Exhib, Portsmouth, Va, 77; Old Bergen Art Guild traveling exhib, NJ, 77-78; solo exhib, Berg Art Ctr, Moorhead, Minn, 77. Bibliog: Review of four Concordia College artists, Fargo Forum, 5/70; Rob Edelman (auth), Three Brooklyn artists probe their role in society, Courier-Life, 7/74. Mem: Art Students League; Women's Mus Group, New York; Berkshire Art Asn. Style & Technique: Abstract form of interior still lifes; paintings with brush. Media: Acrylic, Oil; Pen & Ink, Charcoal & Pencil. Mailing Add: 748 Carroll St Brooklyn NY 11215

PERRY, MARY-ELLEN EARL
CURATOR
b Newark, NJ, Feb 23, 32. Study: Western Md Col, BA; Cooperstown Grad Prog, State Univ NY, Oneonta, MA. Pos: Cur, Montclair Art Mus, NJ, 59-63; dir, Arnot Art Mus, Elmira, NY, 65-72; cur fine arts, M W Strong Mus, Rochester, NY, 73- Mem: Am Asn Mus; NE Mus Conf. Res: The Victorian woman in the home. Publ: Auth, William Bartlett and his imitators, Arnot Art Mus, 66; contribr, A Scene of Adornment: Decoration in the Victorian Home, M W Stront Mus, 75. Mailing Add: 59 Brook Rd Pittsford NY 14534

PERRY, REGENIA ALFREDA
ART HISTORIAN
b Virgilina, Va, Mar 30, 41. Study: Va State Col, BS, 61; Case Western Reserve Univ, Va Mus Fine Arts Out of State fel, 61-62, MA, 62; Univ Pa, 63-64, PhD(art hist), 66; Yale Univ, 70-71; additional study at Case Western Reserve Univ, Cleveland, Ohio. Teaching: Asst prof art hist, Howard Univ, 65-66; asst prof art hist, Ind State Univ, Terre Haute, 66-67; prof art hist, Va Commonwealth Univ, 67- Pos: Spec res asst, Cleveland Mus Art, 64-65; vis scholar, Piedmont Univ Ctr, Winston-Salem, 71-72. Awards: Danforth Found Post-Doctoral Fel, 70-71. Mem: Col Art Asn Am; Am Asn Mus; Soc Archit Historians; Am Asn Univ Prof. Publ: Auth, A History of Afro-American Art 1619-1976, 78; auth, James Van Derzee—photographer, 73. Mailing Add: 513 N Adams St Richmond VA 23220

PERRY, RICHARD C
ART DEALER, COLLECTOR
b Atlanta, Ga, June 15, 40. Pos: Dir, Merrill Chase Galleries, Oak Brook, Ill, 70- Specialty: Fifteenth through 20th century graphic art works. Collection: Chagall, Dali, Delacroix, Durer, Legrand, Manet, Picasso, Rembrandt, Renoir, Toulouse-Lautrec, Villon & Whistler, plus many others. Mailing Add: c/o Merrill Chase Gallery 89 Oak Brook Ctr Oak Brook IL 60521

PERRY, WILLIAM M
CARTOONIST
b Chicago, Ill, Sept 26, 05. Study: Art Inst Chicago; Chicago Acad Fine Arts. Pos: Asst to Carl Ed on cartoon Harold Teen & Frank King on cartoon Gasoline Alley; cartoonist & auth, Ned Handy, 46-51 & Sunday cartoon, Gasoline Alley, 50-75. Mem: Nat Cartoonists Soc. Mailing Add: 1311 Lancaster Dr Orlando FL 32806

PERSHING, LOUISE
PAINTER, SCULPTOR
b Pittsburgh, Pa. Study: Pa Acad Fine Arts; Carnegie-Mellon Univ; Univ Pittsburgh; Hans Hoffman. Work: Gulf Oil Corp, Alcoa Aluminum Corp, Jones & Laughlin Steel Corp & Westinghouse Corp, Pittsburgh; Univ WVa. Exhib: Carnegie Int, 37 & 50; Painting in the US, Carnegie Inst Int, 43-49; one-man shows, Westinghouse Corp, 65 & Gulf Oil Corp, 66, Pittsburgh; Mus Art, Carnegie Inst Int, Pittsburgh, 74. Awards: Twelve awards, Assoc Artists Pittsburgh, 30-72; Artist of the Year, Pittsburgh CofC, 66; Nat Soc Arts & Lett Award of Merit, 69. Style & Technique: Non-welded precision construction, satin finish minimal. Media: Oil; Stainless & Cor-ten Steel, Brass & Aluminum. Dealer: Gallery 407 407 Craig St Pittsburgh PA 15213. Mailing Add: 916 College Ave Pittsburgh PA 15232

PERSKY, ROBERT S
GALLERY DIRECTOR, ART DEALER
b Jersey City, NY, Jan 5, 30. Study: NY Univ, 49; Harvard Law Sch, JD, 52. Pos: Dir, Images...A Gallery of Contemp Photog Art, 76- Specialty: Centemporary Color photography. Mailing Add: 11 E 57th St New York NY 10022

PESNER, CAROLE MANISHIN
ART DEALER
b Boston, Mass, Aug 5, 37. Study: Ecole du Louvre, Inst d'Art et d'Archit, Paris, 58; Smith Col, Northampton, Mass, BA, 59. Pos: Mgr, Kraushaar Galleries, New York, 59- Specialty: 20th century American art. Publ: Auth & co-auth, Kraushaar Gallery Publ & Catalogs. Mailing Add: Kraushaar Galleries 1055 Madison Ave New York NY 10028

PETER, FRIEDRICH GUNTHER
CALLIGRAPHER, EDUCATOR
b Dresden, Ger, Feb 23, 33. Study: Hochschule fuer Bildende Kuenste, W Berlin, Ger, 50-56; Meisterschueler Dipl in lettering & graphic design, 56-57. Comn: Festival banners, Vancouver Int Festival, BC, 64; Definitive series, Can postage stamps prospective invitational design competition, Can Post Off, 70. Exhib: Spectrum Can 76, Olympics, Montreal, 76. Exhibitions Designed: 26 Letters (traveling exhib), Fine Arts Gallery, Univ BC, Vancouver. Teaching: Instr graphic design, Vancouver Sch of Art, BC, 59- Pos: Chmn graphic design, Vancouver Sch of Art, BC, 76- Awards: Winner, Int Typeface Design Competition, Visual Graphics, 66; Second Prize, Int Typeface Design Competition, Letraset Corp, 72. Mem: Royal Can Acad; Graphic Designers of Can. Style & Technique: Calligraphic and typeface design and graphic design. Publ: Contribr, Top symbols and trademarks of the world, Ricci, Milan, 70; auth & ed, Idea Mag, No 110, Yoshinobu Kawasaki, 72; auth & ed, Novum education Vancouver School of Art, Novum/Gebrauchsgraphik Mag, 3/75; contribr (calligraphy), Im Aufwind, Oncken, Ger, 77; contribr (calligraphy), Searching for You, Harper & Row, 78. Mailing Add: 193 N St James Rd North Vancouver BC V7N 1L1 Can

PETER, GEORGE
PAINTER, INSTRUCTOR
b New York, NY. Study: Brooklyn Mus Art Sch, with Reuben Tam, Abraham Rattner & Gabor Peterdi. Work: Butler Inst Am Art, Ohio; Ga Mus Art; Norfolk Mus Art & Sci, Va; Telfair Acad Arts & Sci, Ga; Univ Mass. Comn: Paintings, Sea Fare of the Agean Restaurant, 63-75, Broadway Maintenance, 68, Winslow Construct Corp, 75 & HBSA Indust, Inc, 65-75, New York. Exhib: Am Embassy, Athens, Greece; 6th & 7th Ann Print, Brooklyn Mus, NY; Berkshire Mus, Mass; New York World's Fair, 65; Artists Equity Asn, Union Carbide Corp Bldg, 74. Teaching: Teacher contemp painting, Westchester Art Workshop, White Plains, NY, 69-; lectr & demonstr contemp painting, many cols & schs. Mem: Artists Equity Asn, New York: Mamaroneck Artist Guild, NY. Style & Technique: Lyrical, colorfields of nature and meditative painting using brush and knife; sometimes impressionistic semi-abstract. Media: Oil, Acrylic. Mailing Add: 8 Kingwood Rd Scarsdale NY 10583

PETERDI, GABOR F
PAINTER, PRINTMAKER
b Pestujhely, Hungary, Sept 17, 15; US citizen. Study: Hungarian Acad, Budapest; Acad Julien, Paris; Atelier 17, Paris, with Hayter. Work: Whitney Mus Am Art, Mus Mod Art & Metrop Mus Art, New York; Art Inst Chicago; Boston Mus Fine Arts & over 150 mus in the US & abroad. Exhib: Retrospectives, Brooklyn Mus, 59, Cleveland Mus, 62, Corcoran Gallery Art & Yale Univ Art Gallery, 64 & Honolulu Acad Arts, 68; over 100 one-man shows & 22 retrospectives. Teaching: Instr, Brooklyn Mus Art Sch, 48-52; assoc prof, Hunter Col, 52-59; prof art, Yale Univ, 60- Awards: Prix du Rome, 30; Mus Western Art, Tokyo, 64; Guggenheim Fel, 64-65. Bibliog: V Johnson (auth), Graphic Work 1934-69, Touchstone, 69. Mem: Silvermine Guild Artists (vpres, 65-); Florentine Acad Design; Nat Drawing Soc. Media: Oil, Intaglio. Publ: Auth, Printmaking, Macmillan, 59; auth, Great Prints of the World, 69, Macmillan; auth, Printmaking, Encycl Britannica. Dealer: Grace Borgenicht Gallery 1018 Madison Ave New York NY 10021. Mailing Add: 108 Highland Ave Rowayton CT 06853

PETERS, CARL W
PAINTER
b Rochester, NY, Nov 14, 97. Study: Rochester Inst Technol; Nat Acad Summer Sch, Woodstock, NY; also with John F Carlson. Work: Many in pub collections. Comn: Evolution of Contemporary Commerce in Rochester (mural), Genessee Valley Trust, Rochester, 30; From Painting Man to Modern Lines (mural), Madison High Sch, Rochester, US Govt, 37; Settling of Genessee Valley (mural), West High Sch, Rochester, US Govt, 38; mural at Charlotte High Sch, US Govt, 40; Tribute to Devotion (mural), Rochester Acad Med, 41. Exhib: Nat Acad Design, New York; Pa Acad Fine Arts, Philadelphia; Corcoran Gallery Art, Washington, DC; Art Inst Chicago; Am Watercolor Soc, New York. Teaching: Prof life class, Univ Rochester; instr pvt sch. Awards: Fairchild Gift, Univ Rochester, 24; First, Second & Third Hallgarten Prizes, Nat Acad Design, 26, 28 & 32; Gold Medal, Rockport Art Asn, 71; plus many others. Mem: Am Watercolor Soc; Rockport Art Asn; Rochester Art Club; Acad Artists; Genessee Group. Style & Technique: Expressionism. Media: Oil, Watercolor. Mailing Add: 208 Jefferson Ave Fairport NY 14450

PETERS, LARRY DEAN
CURATOR, GALLERY DIRECTOR
b Manhattan, Kans, July 15, 38. Study: Washburn Univ, BFA, 62; Southern Ill Univ, MFA, 65, under pottery & sculptor, Nicholas Vergette. Work: Kabul, Afghanistan Embassy; Singapore Embassy. Exhib: 16th Mid-Am Exhib, William Rockhill Nelson Gallery, Kansas City, Mo, 66. Collections Arranged: Artists of the American West, 74, Topeka Crafts Exhib I & II, 77 & 78, Recent Acquisitions, 78, Ukiyo-E, Pictures of the Floating World (The Japanese Woodblock Print), 78, Gallery Fine Arts, Topeka Pub Libr. Teaching: Instr pottery, Washburn Univ of Topeka Night Sch, Kans, 69-70. Pos: Readers adv, Dept of Fine Arts, Topeka Pub Libr, 65-73 & gallery dir, Gallery of Fine Arts, 73- Mem: Am Asn Mus; Mountain Plain Mus Conf; Kans Mus Asn; Kans Art Comn (art adv panel mem); Kans Artist Craftsmen Asn (sec, 69-71; pres, 71-73); Topeka Arts Comn (bd mem). Style & Technique: Work in stoneware in a traditional manner producing mostly utilitarian pots; collage with torn papers. Media: Pottery. Mailing Add: Topeka Pub Libr 1515 W Tenth St Topeka KS 66604

PETERSEN, ROLAND CONRAD
PAINTER, PRINTMAKER
b Endelave, Denmark, Mar 31, 26; US citizen. Study: Univ Calif, Berkeley, AB, 49 & MA, 50; San Francisco Art Inst, 51; Calif Col Arts & Crafts, summer 54; Atelier 17, Paris, 50, 63 & 70, with Stanley W Hayter; Islington Studio, London, 77. Work: Mus Mod Art & Whitney Mus Am Art, New York; Philadelphia Mus Art, Pa; Nat Collection Fine Arts, Washington, DC; Univ Reading, Eng. Comn: Dams of the West (portfolio of 25 color prints), US Dept Interior, Bur Reclamation, Washington, DC, 70. Exhib: Illinois Biennial, Urbana, 61-69; Carnegie Inst Int, Pittsburgh, 64; 25th Ann Exhib Contemp Art, Art Inst Chicago, 65; American Painting, Va Mus Fine Arts, Richmond, 66-70; Trois Graveurs et Un Sculpteur, Ctr Cult Am, Paris, 71; one-man shows, E B Crocker Art Gallery, Sacramento, Calif, 65, Adele Bednarz Gallery, Los Angeles, 66-76, De Young Mem Mus, San Francisco, 68, La Jolla Mus, Calif, 71, Phoenix Art Mus, Ariz, 72, Santa Barbara Mus, Calif, 73, Davis Art Ctr, 76, ACG, Sacramento, 77 & Univ Reading, Eng, 77; Nat Gallery, Washington, DC, 72; plus many one-man exhibs. Teaching: Instr painting, Wash State Univ, 52-56; prof painting & printmaking, Univ Calif, Davis, 56-; instr printmaking, Univ Calif, Berkeley, summer 65. Pos: Mem educ process, Col Lett & Sci, Univ Calif, Davis, 65, mem exec comt, 65-66. Awards: Guggenheim Fel, 63; appointee, Inst Creative Arts, Univ Calif, 67 & 70; Fulbright Travel Award, 70. Bibliog: Michael Benedikt (auth), rev in Art News, 67; James Mellow (auth), rev in Art Int, 67; William Wilson (auth), rev in Los Angeles Times, 76. plus others. Mem: Intercontinental Biog Asn; Calif Soc Etchers; San Francisco Art Mus. Style & Technique: Painting: Figures in space in oil & acrylic; printing: photo viscosity etching. Dealer: Staempfli Gallery 47 E 77th St New York NY 10021; Bednarz Galleries 902 N La Cienega Blvd Los Angeles CA 90069. Mailing Add: Art Dept Univ Calif Davis CA 95616

PETERSEN, WILL
PRINTMAKER, ART WRITER
b Chicago, Ill, Dec 9, 28. Study: Mich State Univ, BA, 51, MA, 52; Calif Col Arts & Crafts, MFA, 56; calligraphy with Tahara, Japan, 54; study of Noh with Takashi Kawamura, Kyoto, Japan, 57-65. Work: Dept Prints & Drawings, Chicago Art Inst; Victoria & Albert Mus, London, Eng; Achenbach Found for Graphic Arts, Calif Palace of the Legion of Hon, San Francisco; Baltimore Mus of Art; Bibliot Nat, Paris. Comn: Lithographs for bk covers, N Atlantic Press, Vt, 73-74; lithographs (four ed), Lakeside Studios, Mich, 75-76. Exhib: Fourth Int Biennial Color Lithography, Cincinnati Art Mus, Ohio, 56; Ten Yrs of Am Prints, Brooklyn Mus Art, NY, 56; Fourth Int Bordhighera Biennale, Italy, 57; Gravures Americaines d'Aujourd'hui, Paris, 57; 15th, 16th & 17th Kyoto Art Exhib, Japan, 63-65; Int Soc Plastic & AV Art Int, Seoul, Korea, 67; Brit Int Print Biennial, Bradford Art Mus, Yorkshire, Eng, 70. Teaching: Instr printmaking, Ohio State Univ, 65-69; assoc prof printmaking, Creative Arts Ctr, WVa Univ, 70-77. Pos: Founder & pres, Bay Printmakers Soc, Oakland, Calif, 55-57; master printer, Lakeside Studios, Mich, 69-70; dir & master printer, Plucked Chicken Press, Morgantown, WVa, 77- Awards: Best-of-the-Yr, Kyoto Fine Arts Mus, Mainichi Newspapers, 63; Suda Prize, Kyoto Art Exhib, Kyoto Fine Arts Mus, 65; Hon Mention, Okla Print Ann, Okla Art Ctr, 76. Bibliog: Nancy Wilson Rose (auth), The World of Zen, Random House, 60; Cid Corman (auth), Foreword, In: Gist of Origin, Grossman, New York, 76; James Hinz (ed), Will Petersen, Swarthmore Col, 76. Style & Technique: Lithography, noted for whole-stone multi-colored prints developed in 1955-57; drawing. Media: Stone Lithography. Publ: Auth, Stone Garden, Evergreen Rev, Grove Press, Vol 1 (1957); transl, Akutagawa's A Fool's Life, Mushinsha, 70; auth, The Mask, Asphodel, 74; auth, Kazuraki, Asphodel, 75; transl, Zeami's Noh: Yashima, Mushinsha, 77. Dealer: Quincunx Assocs 190 Chestnut St Morgantown WV 26505. Mailing Add: Plucked Chicken Press PO Box 160 Morgantown WV 26505

PETERSON, A E S
PAINTER
b Northampton, Mass, June 30, 08. Study: Herman Itchkawich, Providence, RI & C Gordon Harris, Lincoln; plus others. Work: Nat Shawmut Bank Boston; Grant Capitol Mgt Corp, Providence; RI Hosp Trust Co; Tillinghast-Stiles Co, East Providence; RI Group Health Asn, Providence. Exhib: Am Watercolor Soc, Nat Acad Design Gallery, New York, 68-72 & 75; Audubon Artists, 69-75 & 77; Butler Inst Am Art, Youngstown, Ohio, 70; Nat Arts Club, New York, 71-75; Rocky Mountain Nat Watermedia Exhib, Foothills Art Ctr, Golden, Colo, 74; Painters & Sculptors Soc, 75; Allied Artists of Am, 76; Nat Asn of Women Artists, 76-78; Nat Soc Painters in Casein & Acrylic, 77. Pos: Treas, Providence Watercolor Club, 62-70, rec secy, 71-; chmn traveling exhib, Painters & Sculptors Soc NJ, 71-, chmn awards, 74-76, vpres watercolor, 77. Awards: Naomi Lorne Mem Medal for Old Bard, Nat Soc Painters Casein, 68; Gold Medal for Cabanas, Catharine Lorillard Wolf Art Club, 71, Kathleen Grumbacher Medal for Urban Renewal, 73; Medal of Honor for Urban Renewal, Painters & Sculptors Soc NJ, 73. Bibliog: R Stevens (auth), Nobody home, La Rev Mod, 11/1/65; Ralph Fabri (auth), Old bard, Syndicate Mag, 6/69 & Cabanas, Today's Art Mag, 5/72. Mem: Am Watercolor Soc; Nat Soc Painters Casein & Acrylic (dir, 70-); Allied Artists Am; Nat Asn Women Artists; Knickerbocker Artists of New York. Style & Technique: Objective based on abstract pattern and design. Media: Watercolor, Casein, Graphics. Mailing Add: 27 Holbrook Ave Rumford East Providence RI 02916

PETERSON, CHESTER G
GRAPHIC DESIGNER
b Bridgeton, NJ, Apr 27, 22. Study: Philadelphia Mus Col Art, graphic design; also with Anna Reeves. Pos: Art dir, Cowan Printing & Adv, Bridgeton, NJ, 40-62; exec art dir, Wyble Adv, Millville, NJ, 62-68; vpres creative serv, Franklin Mint, Franklin Center, Pa, 68- Mem: Art Dirs Club, Philadelphia Jr Exec Club Philadelphia (recording secy); Artists Guild. Style & Technique: Strong communicating graphic design, using fine typography, illustration, photography and various printing techniques creatively. Mailing Add: 12 Linden St Bridgeton NJ 08302

PETERSON, HAROLD PATRICK
ART LIBRARIAN, ART EDITOR
b Chicago, Ill, Aug 27, 35. Study: Harvard Col, AB; Univ Wis, MA. Pos: Art librn, Minneapolis Inst of Arts, 72-, ed, 73- Mem: Art Libr Soc NAm; Col Art Asn; Midwest Art Hist Asn. Interest: Decorative arts, history of printing, illustration of books. Publ: Ed, Picasso, Braque, Leger: Masterpieces from Swiss Collections, 75, Charles Biederman: A Retrospective, 76, I Wear the Morning Star, 76 & James Tissot: Catalogue Raisonné of His Prints, 78, Minneapolis Inst Arts; ed, Chinese Jades: Archaic & Modern, Tuttle, 77. Mailing Add: Minneapolis Inst of Arts Minneapolis MN 55404

PETERSON, JOHN DOUGLAS
ART ADMINISTRATOR, DESIGNER
b Peshtigo, Wis, July 9, 39. Study: Univ Wis, 58; Layton Sch Art, cert indust design, BFA, 62; Cranbrook Acad Art, 62-64, MFA, 66; Oakland Univ, 64-65. Exhib: Made of Plastic, Bloomfield Art Asn, 70; Detroit Artists Mkt, 71; James Yaw Gallery, 71; Bloomfield Art Asn, 71. Collections Arranged: Dr & Mrs Hilbert De Lawter-African Collection, 67; Miava Grottel Retrospective-Ceramics, 67; Wallace Mitchell Retrospective-Painting, 71; Sam Richardson Sculpture, 73; Michigan Survey Competition, Painting & Drawing, 75. Teaching: Instr exhib design, Cranbrook Acad Art, 70-72. Pos: Pres, Romaine Gallery, 64-65; asst dir, Cranbrook Acad Art/Mus, 68-70, assoc dir, 70-71, dean students, Acad, 72-74, dir mus, 71-77; pres, VCI Inc, 77-; dir, Lakeview Ctr for the Arts & Sci, 77- Mem: Arts Coun Triangle; Cranbrook Acad Art Alumni Asn (bd mem, 69-70, vpres, 71-72); Midwest Mus Asn; Am Asn Mus; Art Mus Develop Asn; Advocates for the Arts; Am Asn Mus, Mich Mus Asn; Detroit Focus: Art & the City (adv bd, 74-75). Mailing Add: Lakeview Mus of Arts & Sci 1125 W Lake Ave Peoria IL 61603

PETERSON, LARRY D
PAINTER, INSTRUCTOR
b Holdrege, Nebr, Jan 1, 35. Study: Kearney State Col, BA, 58; Northern Colo Univ, MA, 62; Univ Kans, EdD, 75. Work: Univ Minn; The Gallery, Kearney, Nebr; 280 works in pvt

collections. Comn: Watercolor, ATO Fraternity, Kearney State Col, 67; acrylic & oil paintings, First Methodist Church, Kearney, 72; watercolor paintings, Kearney State Bank, 77. Exhib: 26th Nat Watercolor Exhib, Jackson, Miss, 67; 5th Nat Art Exhib, New Orleans, La, 69; 34th Ann, Sioux City, Iowa, 72; 13th Midwest Biennial, 74 & Nebraska '75 Exhib, Joslyn Art Mus, 75, Omaha; 12th Ann, Asn Nebr Art Clubs, Grand Island, Nebr, 76; Ann Am Nat Miniature Exhib, Laramie, Wyo, 77. Teaching: Instr art, North Platte Pub Schs, 58-65; instr art, North Platte Col, 66-67; prof art, Kearney State Col, 67-; grad asst, Univ Kans, Lawrence, 70-71. Awards: Nebr Art Teachers Asn Distinguished Serv Award, 69; Award of Excellence, Nat Art Exhib, Rock Springs, 71; Outstanding Educators of Am Award, 73; Award, 12th Ann, Asn Nebr Art Clubs, Grand Island, 76; Award, Midwest Landscape Exhib, Elder Gallery, Nebr Wesleyan Univ, Lincoln, 77. Bibliog: Nancy Kalis (auth), one-man rev, Art Rev, Des Moines, Iowa, 68; Rêva Remy (auth), one-man rev in Rev Mod Art, Paris, 68 & 72. Mem: Nat Art Educ Asn; Nebr Art Teachers Asn (past pres); Asn Nebr Art Clubs (past pres); Kappa Pi (past pres, Beta Beta Chap); Nat Art Fraternity. Style & Technique: Color field painter; studying the land and painting from the environment. Media: Watercolor, Acrylic. Publ: Contribr, Art in action, Nat Art Publ, 62-64; co-auth, Nebraska art guide K-6, Elem Art Curric, State Nebr, 66. Dealer: Warehouse Gallery, 720 W Oklahoma Grand Island NE 68801; Haymarket Art Gallery 119 S Ninth St Lincoln NE 68508. Mailing Add: 4 Seminole Lane Kearney NE 68847

PETERSON, ROGER TORY
ILLUSTRATOR, WRITER
b Jamestown, NY, Aug 28, 08. Study: Art Students League; Nat Acad Design; Hon Doctoral Degrees from Franklin & Marshall Col, Ohio State Univ, Fairfield Univ, Allegheny Col, Wesleyan Univ & Colby Col. Work: New Britain Mus of Am Art, Conn; Am Mus of Natural Hist, New York; Calif Acad of Arts & Sci, San Francisco; Carnegie Mus of Natural Hist, Pittsburgh, Pa; Metrop Mus of Art, New York. Exhib: Animal in Art, Royal Ont Mus, Toronto, Can, 75; Northwood Inst, Midland, Mich, 76; Bird Art Exhib, Leigh Yawkey Woodson Art Mus, Wausau, Wis, 76 & 77; Birds of Prey, Glenbow Inst, Calgary, Alta, Can, 77; plus others. Teaching: Instr art & sci, Rivers Sch, Brookline, Mass, 31-34. Pos: Art ed, Audubon Mag, 34-43; Audubon Screen Tour lectr, 46-; art dir, Nat Wildlife Fedn, 46-75; ed, Houghton Mifflin Co, Am Naturalist Series, 65-; spec consult, Nat Audubon Soc, 70-; roving reporter, Int Wildlife Mag, 70; mem, Galapagos Int Sci Proj, 64; Operation Deepfreeze, 65. Awards: Gold Medal, World Wildlife Fund, 72; Golden Key Award, Outstanding Teacher, Am Asn Sch Admin; The Explorer's Medal, Explorer's Club, 74. Bibliog: Jerry Bowles (auth), Artist profile: Roger Tory Peterson, Acquire, 76; Sevlin/Naismith (auth), The world of Roger Tory Peterson, Times Bks, 77; John Diffily (auth), A field guide to Roger Tory Peterson, Am Artist, 77. Mem: Soc Animal Artists; Soc Wildlife Artists, Eng (vpres); Nat Audubon Soc (bd dirs, 58-60, 65-67 & 68-70); Am Ornithologists Union (1st vpres); Int Comt Bird Protection (chmn, 65-70). Publ: Illusr, Birds of South Carolina, 49, Birds of Newfoundland, 51, Arizona and its Bird Life, 52, Birds of Nova Scotia, 61, Birds of Colorado, 65 & Birds of New York State, 73; plus others. Dealer: Mill Pond Press Inc 204 S Nassau St Venice FL 33595. Mailing Add: Neck Rd Old Lyme CT 06371

PETERSON, THALIA GOUMA
See Gouma-Peterson, Thalia

PETHEO, BELA FRANCIS
PAINTER, PRINTMAKER
b Budapest, Hungary, May 14, 34; US citizen. Study: Univ Budapest, MA, 56; Acad Fine Arts, Vienna, 57-59, with A P Guetersloh; Univ Vienna, 58-69; Univ Chicago, MFA, 63. Work: Hungarian State Mus Fine Arts, Budapest; Kunstmus, Bern, Switz; Univ Minn Permanent Collection, Minneapolis; Carleton Col Permanent Collection, Northfield, Minn; plus others. Comn: Kindliche Untugenden (mural), Asn Austrian Boyscouts, Vienna, 58; The History of Handwriting (exhib panel), Noble & Noble Publ for Hall of Educ, New York World's Fair, 64; plus others. Exhib: Hamline Univ, 66; Coffman Gallery, Univ Minn, 68; Moorhead State Col, 69; Biennale Wis Printmakers, 71; Duluth: A Painterly Essay, Tweed Mus Art, Minn, 75; plus others. Teaching: Instr art, Univ Northern Iowa, 64-66; assoc prof art & artist in residence, St John's Univ, 66- Awards: Belobende Anerkennung, Acad Fine Arts, Vienna, 58; graphic prize, Univ Chicago, 62. Bibliog: Arturo Carlo Quintavalle (auth), Bela Petheo, Univ Parma & St John's Univ Res Coun Publ, 67; plus others. Mem: Col Art Asn Am. Style & Technique: Anti-reductivist, impressionistic color, expressionistic vision in all-media portraits, landscapes, etc. Media: Lithography. Publ: Auth, Rembrandt's pupils in the Museum of Fine Arts in Budapest, Szabad Muveszet, 6/56; auth, Polymer-coated lithographic transfer paper, In: Five artists—their printmaking methods, Artists Proof, 68; auth, The college art gallery, Art J, summer 71; auth, Manuscript illuminations and the modern stained glass painter, in stained glass, winter 75. Mailing Add: St John's Univ Collegeville MN 56321

PETLIN, IRVING
PAINTER
b Chicago, Ill, Dec 17, 34. Study: Art Inst of Chicago, BFA, 52-56; Yale Univ, MFA, with Josef Albers, 59. Work: Art Inst of Chicago; Des Moines Art Ctr; Mus Mod Art, New York; Mus d'Art Mod, Paris, France. Exhib: Art Inst of Chicago, 53, 56 & 72; Mus d'Art Mod, Paris, 61-66; Chicago Imagist Art, Mus Contemp Art, Chicago, 72; Whitney Mus Am Art, New York, 73; Retrospective, Palais des Beaux-Arts, Brussels, Belg, 65; Neuberger Mus, State Univ NY Col, Purchase, 78; Arts Club of Chicago, 78. Teaching: Instr, Univ Calif, Los Angeles, 63-66; vis prof, Columbia Univ, New York, 78. Awards: Ryerson Fel, 56; Copley Found Grant, 61; Guggenheim Found Fel, 71. Style & Technique: Surrealism, new figuration. Media: Oil on Canvas; Pastel on Paper. Dealer: Odyssia Gallery 41 E 57th St New York NY 10022; Rebecca Cooper Gallery 2130 P St NW Washington DC 20037. Mailing Add: 267 W 11th St New York NY 10014

PETRIE, FERDINAND RALPH
PAINTER, ILLUSTRATOR
b Hackensack, NJ, Sept 17, 25. Study: Parsons Sch Design, New York, cert advert, 49; Art Students League, with Frank Reilly; Famous Artists Course Illus, cert, 59. Work: Nat Collection Fine Art, Smithsonian Inst, Washington, DC; Indianapolis Mus Art; J F Kennedy Libr, Boston; US Navy Combat Art Gallery, Washington, DC. Exhib: One-man exhib, Audubon Naturalists Soc, 70; Allied Artists Am, Nat Acad Design Gallery, New York, 71-77; Am Artists Prof League Grant Nat, New York, 71-77; Am Watercolor Soc Travel Exhib, 73, 75, 76 & 77; White House Loan Exhib from Smithsonian Inst, Washington, DC, 73-75. Teaching: Instr painting & drawing, Fairleigh Dickinson Univ, Rutherford, 69-70; pvt instr watercolor, 72-; instr, DuCret Sch Art, 75- Pos: Illusr, J Gans Assoc Studio, New York, 50-69. Awards: Salmagundi Club Awards, 70-75; Grand Nat Award, Am Artists Prof League, 71-74; US Navy Gold Medal for Watercolor, 74. Mem: NJ Watercolor Soc; Allied Artists Am; Salmagundi Club; Rockport Art Asn; Am Watercolor Soc. Style & Technique: Traditional transparent w/c, realistic. Media: Watercolor, Oil. Publ: Illusr, New York Life Ins Calendar, 70, 72, 74 & 79; illusr, Reader's Digest covers, 77 & 78; Pallette talk, Grumbacher Mag, 75; illusr, Salvation Army, 75. Dealer: Petrie Gallery 22 Broadway Rockport MA 01966; Grand Central Galleries New York NY 10017. Mailing Add: 51 Vreeland Ave Rutherford NJ 07070

PETRIE, SYLVIA SPENCER
PRINTMAKER, PAINTER
b Wooster, Ohio, June 15, 31. Study: Col Wooster, BA; State Univ Iowa, with Mauricio Lasansky & Eugene Ludens; Univ RI. Work: Graphics Soc, Hollis, NH; Art Ctr Mus, Wooster Col; Gilbert Stuart Birthplace, Saundertown, RI; Fantle's, Sioux Falls, SDak; Wayne Gallery, Providence, RI. Exhib: 4th Midwest Biennial, Joslyn Art Mus, Omaha, Nebr, 56; Mo Valley Exhib Oil Painting, Mulvane Art Mus, Topeka, Kans, 56; 9th Nat Print Exhib, Silvermine Guild, New Canaan, Conn, 72; Images on Paper, Springfield Art Asn, Ill, 73; 64th & 66th Am Annuals, Art Asn Newport, RI, 75 & 77; 16th Bradley Nat Print & Drawing Exhib, Peoria, Ill, 77; plus others. Pos: Vis artist, Title III Prog, Coventry Elem Schs, RI, 75-77. Awards: Netta Strain Scott Prize Art, Wooster Col, 53; First Prize & Purchase Award, Fantle's, 56; First Prize Graphics, Westerly Art Festival, 75; plus many others. Bibliog: Frank Kempe (auth), Harry & his Juniper tree, NDevon J, Eng, 5/74; Karen D Mensel (auth), Sylvia Petrie at Artists Guild, Anyart J, 11/75; Elizabeth Findley (auth), Petrie prints and pastels depend on point of view, Eve Bull, Providence, 10/15/77. Mem: Cambridge Art Asn; Graphics Soc; Artists Guild & Gallery; Art Asn of Newport; South County Art Asn. Style & Technique: Landscapes; figurescapes and interiors, with emphasis on light and form. Media: Intaglio, Collagraph; Oil, Pastel. Publ: Illusr, From under the Hill of Night, Vanderbilt Univ, 69; illusr, The Idol, Biscuit City Press, 73. Dealer: Artists Guild & Gallery Rte 1 Charlestown RI 02908. Mailing Add: 66 Dendron Rd Peacedale RI 02879

PETRO, JOSEPH (VICTOR), JR
PAINTER, ILLUSTRATOR
b Lexington, Ky, Nov 4, 32. Study: Transylvania Col, with Victor Hammer; grad sch, Cincinnati Med Sch, art as appl to med. Work: Paintings in pvt collections throughout US & Europe; bronze sculpture in Hermitage Mus, Leningrad, USSR. Comn: Covers, Family Weekly Mag, NY; Brown & Bigelow calendars; 32 horse paintings, Keeneland Collection, Keeneland Racing Asn, Lexington, Ky; 28 portraits of pres of Transylvania Col, 1794-, Transylvania Col; series of paintings of all Triple Crown winners for Oaklawn Park Racetrack, 73-77. Pos: Publ, series ltd number collector prints, 54-69; consult, Spindletop Res, Inc, Lexington, 65-68; head, Dept Appl Art, Loyola Univ of Chicago, Rome Ctr, Italy, 69-77; vis prof art, John Cabot Int Col, Rome, Italy, 75-76; cult adv, US Info Serv, Am Embassy, Rome, Italy, 73-77. Mem: Am Fedn Arts. Publ: Illusr, var publ including Thoroughbred Rec, Nat Geog, Holiday, Better Homes & Gardens & others. Mailing Add: 357 Henry Clay Blvd Lexington KY 40502

PETROCHUK, KONSTANTIN
PHOTOGRAPHER, FILM MAKER
b Wurzach, WGer, Apr 30, 47; US citizen. Study: Kent State Univ, BFA, with Richard Myers, MA. Exhib: Sinking Creek Film Festival, Vanderbilt Univ, 74; Ann Arbor Film Festival, Mich, 75; Kenyon Film Festival, Gambier, Ohio, 75; Butler Inst Am Art Photo Show, Youngstown, Ohio, 75; Three Rivers Photo Show, Pittsburgh, 75; Cineprobe, Mus of Mod Art, New York, 77; Contemp Media Study Ctr, Dayton, Ohio, 78. Teaching: Instr photog, Akron Art Inst, Ohio, 73; asst film making, Kent State Univ, 73-74; arts curric coordr, Upward Bound, US Dept Health, Educ & Welfare, 75. Pos: Graphic artist & stationary camera supvr, Halbert's Inc, Bath, Ohio, 72-73; art dir, Human Issue Mag, Kent, 72-73; asst cur, Blossom-Kent Art Prog, Kent State Univ, 75- Style & Technique: Information oriented presentation of concrete facts and images, but through an experimental format. Mailing Add: 437 Lake St Kent OH 44240

PETTET, WILLIAM
PAINTER
b Wittier, Calif, Oct 10, 42. Study: Chouinard Art Inst, Los Angeles. Work: Whitney Mus Am Art, New York; Mus Mod Art, New York. Exhib: Nicholas Wilder Gallery, Los Angeles, 66; Whitney Mus Am Art, New York, 67 & 73; Corcoran Mus Art Biennial, 69; Aldrich Mus Art, 69; Recent Acquisitions, 70 & 60s & 70s, 74, Mus Mod Art, New York; one-man shows, David Whitney Gallery, New York, 70, Willard Gallery, New York, 75 & Suzanne Mathews Gallery, San Antonio, Tex, 78; Spray, Santa Barbara Mus Art, Calif, 71; Art of the 70s, Seattle Art Mus, Wash, 72; New in the 70s, Austin Art Mus, Tex, 77. Teaching: Instr painting, Skowhegen Sch Paintings & Sculpture, summer 72; fac mem mentor prog, Empire State Col, 77. Awards: Tamarind Fel, 70. Style & Technique: Color abstract paintings. Media: Liquitex. Dealer: Willard Gallery 29 E 72nd St New York NY 10021. Mailing Add: 31 Des Brosses St New York NY 10013

PETTIBONE, JOHN WOLCOTT
ART ADMINISTRATOR, GRAPHIC ARTIST
b Springfield, Ohio, Jan 30, 42. Study: Wittenberg Univ, 62-63; Cleveland Inst Art, 63-65, Ford grant, 64. Work: Am Red Cross, Washington, DC; Town of Rockport, Mass. Exhib: Rockport Art Asn, 71-; Am Fortnight Exhibition, Hong Kong, 73. Teaching: Instr drawing, Lakewood Pub Schs, Ohio, 59; instr drawing, Springfield Art Asn, Ohio, 61-63; instr drawing, Rockport Pub Schs, 73- Mem: Rockport Art Asn (asst cur, 69-74, cur, 74-, bd mem, 71-); Arms & Armour Soc, London; Medieval Acad Am; Co Mil Historians, Washington, DC. Style & Technique: Figures, landscapes and portraits. Media: Conte Crayon, Silverpoint. Collection: Arms and armor dating from 14th century. Dealer: Rockport Art Asn 12 Main St Rockport MA 01966. Mailing Add: PO Box 145 Rockport MA 01966

PETTIBONE, RICHARD H
PAINTER
b Los Angeles, Calif, Jan 5, 38. Study: Pasadena City Col, AA, 59; Otis Art Inst, MFA, 62. Work: Israel Mus, Jerusalem; Lowe Art Ctr, Syracuse, NY; De Mennil Found, Houston, Tex; Rose Art Mus, Brandeis Univ, Waltham, Mass. Exhib: Small Images, Chicago Art Inst, 75; Dorothy & Herbert Vogel Collection, Inst Contemp Art, Univ Pa, Philadelphia, 75; Painting & Sculpture in Calif, Mus Mod Art, San Francisco, 76; Miniature, Calif State Univ, Los Angeles, 77; Small Objects, Whitney Mus Downtown, New York, 77; Art About Art, Whitney Mus Am Art, New York, 78; one-man shows, Ferus Gallery, Los Angeles, 65, Castelli Gallery, New York, 69, O K Harris, New York, 70-76; Morgan Gallery, Kansas City, 75 & Max Protetch Gallery, Washington, DC, 76. Style & Technique: Small paintings using various techniques. Media: Oil on Canvas; Silkscreen on Canvas. Dealer: O K Harris 383 W Broadway New York NY 10012. Mailing Add: Star Route Charlotteville NY 12036

PETTY, JOHN L, JR
MUSEUM DIRECTOR, CONSERVATOR
b 1939. Study: Bob Jones Univ, BA, 62; Univ Ariz, 62-66. Work: Kress Collection; Gallager Collection Int Contemp Art; Pfeiffer Collection Am Painting; Oliver James Collection Am Art; Woodruff Collection Contemp Prints. Collections Arranged: (All with catalogs) Thomas

Hart Benton, 62; Edward Hooper Retrospective, 63, Yankee Painter-Winslow Homer Retrospective, 63, American Painting 1765-1963, 64, The Bird in Art, 64-65, Henry Moore-Retrospective, 65, Charles Burchfield-His Golden Year, 65-66 & Walt Kuhn, 66. Pos: Cur, Univ Ariz Art Gallery, 62-66; actg dir & cur, Wichita Art Mus, 66-67; dir, Washington Co Mus Fine Arts, Hagerstown, Md, 67-70; dir, Bob Jones Univ Art Gallery, 70-; developed lab for restoration & conserv, Galleries Fine Arts, Ind. Mailing Add: Greenville Co Art Mus 420 College St Greenville SC 29601

PEZZATI, PIETRO
PAINTER
b Boston, Mass, Sept 18, 02. Study: Child-Walker Sch Art; also with Charles Hopkinson; in Europe. Work: Med Sch & Bus Sch, Harvard Univ; Sch Med & Sch Educ, Univ Pa; Mass Gen Hosp; Yale Sch Med; Mass Hist Soc; plus many others. Exhib: Exhibited regionally and nat in group and one-man shows. Teaching: Instr, schs and pvt classes; demonstr technique and slide lect hist of portraiture, pvt groups. Mailing Add: c/o Fenway Studios 30 Ipswich St Boston MA 02215

PFAHL, CHARLES ANTON, III
PAINTER
b Akron, Ohio, May 15, 46. Study: With Robert Brackman, Madison, Conn, John Koch, New York & Jack Richard, Cuyahoga Falls, Ohio. Exhib: Allied Artist Ann, Nat Acad Design, New York, 69-71, Am Watercolor Ann, 70 & 71; Audubon Artist Ann, 70-72; Butler Inst Am Art Ann, Youngstown, Ohio, 72-74; Three Centuries of American Nude, New York Cult Ctr, Minneapolis Inst Arts, Sarah Blaffer Campbell Gallery at Univ Houston, 75. Awards: Salmagundi Club Junius Allen Award, 71 & 72; Stacey Grant, 72; Inst Arts & Lett Grant, 73; plus others. Media: Pastel, Oil. Mailing Add: c/o Harbor Gallery 43 Main St Cold Spring Harbor NY 11724

PFEIFER, BODO
PAINTER, SCULPTOR
b Dusseldorf, Ger, July 17, 36; Can citizen. Study: Ecole Beaux Artes, Montreal; Acad Fine Arts, Hamburg, Ger; Vancouver Sch Art, BC, dipl. Work: Vancouver Art Gallery; Nat Gallery, Ottawa, Ont; Art Gallery Ont, Toronto; Montreal Mus Fine Art, PQ; Can Coun, Ottawa, Ont. Comn: Mural, Dept Transp, Ottawa, Vancouver Int Airport, 68; mural, McCarter Nairne & Partners, Architects for Moore's Off Bldg, Vancouver, 68. Exhib: Canada 101, Edinburgh Int Festival, 68; Survey 68, Montreal Mus Fine Art, 68; Can Artist, Art Gallery Ont, 68; The New Art of Vancouver, Newport Harbour Art Mus, 7th Biennial Exhib, Nat Gallery Can, Ottawa, 68; The New Art of Vancouver, Newport Harbour Art Mus, 69. Teaching: Sessional instr painting & drawing, Univ Calgary, 71- Awards: Can Coun Grants, 66-71; Can Group Painters Award in Painting, 67; Award in Painting, Survey 68, Montreal Mus Fine Art, 68. Bibliog: W Townsend (auth), Canadian art today, Studio Int, 70; Artists of Pacific Canada, Nat Film Bd Can, 71. Mailing Add: Dept Art Univ Calgary Calgary AB T2N 1N4 Can

PFEIFER, MARCUSE
ART DEALER, GALLERY OWNER
b Little Rock, Ark, Nov 4, 36. Study: Sarah Lawrence Col, AB, 58. Collections Arranged: Gravure, 74, American Indian Photographs from the 19th & early 20th century, 74, Cyanotype, 75 & Catalogue 1 for Robert Schoelkopf Gallery (auth), 75, Robert Schoelkopf Gallery. Pos: Asst to dir, New Sch Art Ctr, New York, 66-70; dir photog art, Robert Schoelkopf Gallery, New York, 70-76; gallery owner, Marcuse Pfeifer Gallery, 76- Specialty: Photography. Mailing Add: 825 Madison Ave New York NY 10021

PFRIEM, BERNARD
PAINTER
b Cleveland, Ohio, Sept 7, 16. Study: John Huntington Polytech Inst, 34-36; Cleveland Inst Art, 36-40; Europ study, 50-52. Work: Mus Mod Art; Chase Manhattan Bank, NY; Brooklyn Mus, NY; Columbia Banking, Savings & Loan Asn, Rochester, NY; Metrop Mus, New York; plus others. Comn: Murals, Guerrero & Mexico City, Mex; plus many portraits. Exhib: Six shows, Iolas Gallery, NY, 49-63; Whitney Mus Am Art, 52 & 65; retrospective, Cleveland Inst Art, 63; Richard Feigen Gallery, Chicago, 67; Am Drawing Soc, 70; Cleveland Inst Art, 73; Pa State Univ, 74; Carnegie Inst; also in France, Ger & Italy; plus others. Teaching: Instr drawing & painting, Peoples Art Ctr, Mus Mod Art, 46-51; instr drawing, Cooper Union Sch Art & Archit; instr, Silvermine Col Art, New Canaan, Conn; instr, Sarah Lawrence Col, 69- Pos: Dir, studio arts sessions in Southern France for Sarah Lawrence Col. Awards: Mary Ranney Traveling Scholar, Western Reserve Univ; Copley Award Painting, 59; Prize Drawing, Norfolk Mus Arts & Sci; plus many others. Bibliog: Patrick Waldberg (auth), Bernard Pfriem (monogr), William & Noma Copley Found, 61 & Main et marvielles, Mercure, France, 61; Patricia Allen Dreyfus (auth), The inward journey (monogr), Am Artist, 9/72. Mailing Add: 84710 Lacoste Vancluse France

PHARR, MR & MRS WALTER NELSON
COLLECTORS
Mr Pharr, b Greenwood, Miss, Nov 9, 06; Mrs Pharr, b Detroit, Mich, Apr 1, 23. Study: Mr Pharr, Washington & Lee Univ; Mrs Pharr, Garland Jr Col, Boston. Collection: International modern art; marine paintings including eighteen by J E Butterworth, others by R Salmon & T Birch; plus others. Mailing Add: 154 E 66th St New York NY 10021

PHELAN, LINN LOVEJOY
DESIGNER
b Rochester, NY, Aug 25, 06. Study: Rochester Inst Technol, dipl, 28; Ohio State Univ, BFA(ceramic art), 32; Alfred Univ, MS(educ), 55. Exhib: Rochester Mem Art Gallery, 28-58; Everson Mus, Syracuse, 32-50; Albright-Knox Mus, Buffalo, 51; New York State Craftsman, Ithaca Col, 54-75; NY State Fair, Syracuse, 60-75. Teaching: Instr pottery, Sch Am Craftsman, 44-50; instr art, Alfred-Almond Cent Sch, 50-67; lectr art, State Univ NY Col Ceramics, Alfred Univ, 67-72. Pos: Owner & operator, Linnwood Pottery, 50-; mgr fair, York State Craftsmen, Inc, 57-59; exec comt, NY State Art Teachers, Albany, 58-61, pres, 60-61; mus chmn, Almond Hist Soc, 65-, pres, 78- Awards: NY State Fair Awards, 75. Style & Technique: Scrifitto and brush design. Media: Ceramics. Mailing Add: 114 S Main St Almond NY 14804

PHELPS, NAN DEE
PAINTER, PHOTOGRAPHER
b London, Ky. Study: Self-taught; scholar to Cincinnati Art Mus, Ohio. Work: The Henry Ford Collection, Dearborn, Mich; CofC, Pulaski, Va; also in pvt collections. Comn: The Shepherd and Sheep, Orphanage, Trinidad Island, 65; 20 murals, comn by churches, Hamilton, Ohio, Middletown, Ohio, New Miami, Ohio & Toledo, Ohio; Tenn; numerous paintings in Peru, SAm. Exhib: All-American Fine Art Show, Cincinnati, Ohio; Cincinnati Art Mus, 42-56; Lynn Kottler Galleries, New York, 75. Awards: First Place, Ford Motor Co, 60; First Place mag cover, Kiwanis Club, Cincinnati, 60; Greater Hamilton Art Club Award. Bibliog: Della Hicks (auth), Never, never land. Media: Oil. Publ: Auth, Self-taught artist, Ford Times News, 58. Mailing Add: 1721 Green Wood Ave Hamilton OH 45011

PHELPS, ROSEMARIE BECK
See Beck, Rosemarie

PHILBRICK, MARGARET ELDER
PRINTMAKER, PAINTER
b Northampton, Mass, July 4, 14. Study: Mass Col Art, grad; De Cordova Mus Workshop, with Donald Stoltenberg. Work: Libr of Cong, Washington, DC; Wiggin Collection, Boston Pub Libr; Nat Bezalel Mus, Jerusalem; First Nat Bank, Boston; New Brit Mus, Conn. Exhib: US Info Agency Serv Exhib to Far East, 58-59; 2nd Int Miniature Print Exhib, Pratt Graphic Art Ctr, New York, 66; Boston Printmakers 23rd Nat Exhib, De Cordova Mus, Lincoln, Mass, 71; Soc Am Graphic Artists 51st Nat, Kennedy Galleries, New York, 71; retrospective, Ainsworth Gallery, Boston, 72; 40 Yr Retrospective Exhib of Graphics, Westenhook Gallery, Sheffield, Mass. Awards: Alice Standish Buel Mem Purchase Award, Soc Am Graphic Artists, 71; John Taylor Arms Mem Prize, Nat Acad Design, 72; Ralph Fabri Award, Nat Acad of Design, 77. Mem: Boston Printmakers (exec bd, 50-78); Boston Watercolor Soc (exec bd, 75-77; Soc Am Graphic Artists; Nat Acad Design; Am Color Print Soc. Style & Technique: Mixed media and watercolors mostly abstract; collographs abstract; etchings and serigraphs representational. Media: Intaglio. Publ: Illusr, On Gardening, 64 & In Praise of Vegetables, 66, Scribners; illusr, Natural Flower Arrangements, Doubleday, 72; illusr, West Dedham and Westwood 300 years, 72; illusr, Sheffield: Frontier Town, 76. Dealer: Ainsworth Gallery 42 Bromfield St Boston MA 02170; Westenhook Gallery Sheffield MA 01257. Mailing Add: Sheffield MA 01257

PHILIPP, ROBERT
PAINTER
b New York, NY, Feb 2, 95. Study: Art Students League, with DuMond & Bridgman, 10-14; Nat Acad Design, with Volk & Maynard, 14-17. Work: Whitney Mus Am Art; Brooklyn Mus; Mus Fine Arts Houston; Corcoran Gallery Art; Norton Gallery Art; plus many others. Exhib: Exhibited nationally. Teaching: Vis prof, Univ Ill, 40; instr, High Mus Art, 46; Instr, Art Students League; instr, Nat Acad Design. Awards: Prizes, Nat Acad Design, 22, 47 & 51; Bronze Medal, Allied Artists Am, 58; W C Osborne Award, Am Watercolor Soc, 67; plus others. Mem: Academician Nat Acad Design; Lotos Club; Banjamin Franklin fel Royal Soc Art London. Mailing Add: 881 Seventh Ave New York NY 10019

PHILLIPS, BERTRAND D
PAINTER, PHOTOGRAPHER
b Chicago, Ill, Nov 19, 38. Study: Art Inst Chicago, with Paul Wieghardt; Leroy Neiman, BFA; Northwestern Univ, MFA. Governors State Univ, Park Forest South, Ill; Du Sable Mus African Am Hist, Chicago. Exhib: Black & White, Kovler Gallery, Chicago, 69; Black Experience, Bergman Gallery, Univ Chicago, 71; Existence Black, Southern Ill Univ, 72; Black Art Expressions, Ill State Univ, 73; Directions in Afro-American Art, Herbert F Johnson Mus Art, Cornell Univ, 74; Dulin Gallery of Art, Knoxville, Tenn, 77; Second St Gallery, Charlottesville, Va, 77; Eastern Mich Univ, Ypsilanti, Mich, 77; one-man shows, Governors State Univ, 77, Valparaiso Univ, Ind, 77 & The Darkroom, Chicago, 78. Teaching: Instr drawing & painting, Elmhurst Col, 70-72; asst prof drawing & painting, Northwestern Univ, 72- Awards: George D Brown Foreign Traveling Fel, Art Inst Chicago, 61. Bibliog: Elton Fax (auth), Black Artists of the New Generation, Dodd Mead & Co, New York, 77. Style & Technique: Representational and abstracted figurative forms of social themes. Mailing Add: 6617 S Perry Chicago IL 60621

PHILLIPS, BONNIE
ART DEALER
b Salt Lake City, Utah, July 8, 42. Study: Univ Utah, BA. Work: Salt Lake Art Ctr, Utah; Utah Mus Fine Arts, Salt Lake City; Braithwaite Gallery, Southern Utah State Col, Cedar City. Exhib: Intermountain Biennial, Salt Lake Art Ctr, 66-77. Pos: Co-owner, Phillips Gallery, Salt Lake City. Style & Technique: Abstract and semi-abstract watercolor, gouache and ink and landscapes of the region. Media: Watercolor, Gouache. Mailing Add: Phillips Gallery 444 E Second South Salt Lake City UT 84111

PHILLIPS, DONNA-LEE
PHOTOGRAPHER, WRITER
b Winthrop, Mass, Nov 2, 41. Study: Cooper Union, New York, BFA, 68; Pratt Inst, Brooklyn, MFA, 72. Work: Portland Mus of Fine Art, Maine; William Hayes Fogg Mus of Art, Harvard Univ, Cambridge, Mass. Exhib: One-person shows, Soho Photo, New York, 72 & M H de Young Mem Mus, San Francisco, 77; Capricorn Asunder, San Francisco Art Comn, 72 & 76; Portland Mus of Fine Art, 76; Photography & Language, LaMamelle Art Ctr, San Francisco, 76; Univ Nev 1st Ann, Reno, 76; The Landscape co-cur, Santa Rose Jr Col, Calif, 77; Young Contemp Photographers, William Hayes Fogg Mus of Art, 77. Collections Arranged: Photoerotica (auth, catalogue; co-cur), Camerawork Gallery, 77. Teaching: Instr photog, Univ Calif Exten, San Francisco, 75-, Hayward State Col, 75- & Sonoma State Col, 75-; Facilitator feminist art, Calif Col Arts & Crafts, Oakland, 78- Pos: Mgr & designer, Camerawork NSF Press, 76- Awards: Nat Endowment for the Arts Photographers grant, 73. Bibliog: KQED-TV, Donna-Lee Phillips, Images, 75. Style & Technique: Conceptual photography, utilizing autobiographical/fictional material, photographs and writing. Media: Photographic imagery, words. Publ: Designer, Photography & Language, 76 & ed, Eros & Photography, 77, Camerawork/NFS Press. Mailing Add: 1360 Howard St San Francisco CA 94103

PHILLIPS, GIFFORD
COLLECTOR, WRITER
b Washington, DC, June 30, 18. Study: Stanford Univ, 36-38; Yale Univ, BA, 42. Mem: Mus Mod Art, New York (trustee, 66-); Phillips Collection (trustee); Pasadena Art Mus (trustee, 67-); Rothko Found, New York (mem bd trustees, 76-); Mus Mod Art Int Coun (bd dirs); Los Angeles Co Mus Art Contemp Art Coun. Collection: Contemporary American painting and sculpture. Publ: Auth, Arts in a democratic society, 66; auth, articles in Art News, Artforum & Art in Am. Mailing Add: 11777 San Vicente Blvd Suite 507 Los Angeles CA 90049

PHILLIPS, GORDON DALE
PAINTER, SCULPTOR
b Boone, NC, Sept 9, 27. Study: Corcoran Sch Art. Exhib: Franklin Mint, Pa, 73-74. Awards: Gold Medals for Distinguished Western Art, Franklin Mint, 73 & 74. Style & Technique: Realistic Western Americana. Media: Oil, Watercolor; Dealer: Kennedy Galleries Inc 40 W 57th St New York NY 10019. Mailing Add: 1830 Tree View Ct Crofton MD 21114

PHILLIPS, IRVING W
CARTOONIST, ILLUSTRATOR
b Wilton, Wis, Nov 29, 05. Study: Chicago Acad Fine Arts. Comn: Stage play adaptations, One Foot in Heaven, Gown of Glory, Mother was a Bachelor & Rumple, Alvin Theatre, New York, 55; plus others. Exhib: Nat Cartoonist Soc; New York World's Fair; Smithsonian Inst Permanent Collection; one-man shows, Comedy in Art, Ariz State Univ & El Prado Gallery, Sedona, Ariz; plus var pvt collections. Pos: Cartoon humor ed, Esquire Mag, 37-39; cartoon staff, Chicago Sun-Times Syndicate, 40-52; motion picture assignments with Warner Bros, RKO, Charles Rodgers Prod & United Artists; auth & illusr, syndicated strip appearing int in 180 papers in 22 countries, The strange world of Mr Mum; instr cartooning & humor writing, Phoenix Col, currently. Awards: Int First Prize & Cup, Salone dell'Umorismo of Bordighera, Italy, 69. Mem: Writers Guild Am; Dramatists Guild; Nat Cartoonists Soc; Mag Cartoonists Guild; Newspaper Cartoon Coun; plus others. Publ: Auth & illusr, The strange world of Mr Mum, 65; auth, The twin witches of fingle fu, 69; auth, No comment by Mr Mum, Popular Libr, 71; auth & co-auth, 260 TV scripts; contribr, scripts & animation to ABC-TV children's prog, Curiosity Shop; plus many others. Mailing Add: 2807 E Sylvia St Phoenix AZ 85032

PHILLIPS, JAMES
ART HISTORIAN, PAINTER
b Black River Falls, Wis, Aug 11, 29. Study: Layton Sch Art, Milwaukee, Wis; Univ Wis-Madison, BS; Art Students League; Acad de Grande Chaumiere; Ecole dy Louvre, Paris; Univ Tex, Austin, MA, MFA & PhD. Work: Art Inst Chicago; Whitney Mus Am Art, New York. Exhib: Forty Artists Under Forty, Fulbright Painters (nationwide showings) & Young America, Whitney Mus Am Art, New York; one-man show, G Gallery, New York, 62. Teaching: Instr art hist, Kearney State Univ, Nebr, 66-68; instr art hist, Univ Tex, Austin, 68- Awards: Fulbright Prize Award, US State Dept, 56-57; Louis Comfort Tiffany Award, Tiffany Found, 57-58; Neysa McMein Purchase Award, Whitney Mus Am Art, 60. Mem: Col Art Asn; Am Archaeol Soc. Style & Technique: Magic realist. Media: Egg Tempera; Oil. Res: Roman and late antique art, emphasis on architecture. Publ: Contribr, Temoin de France, Appleton, 66. Mailing Add: 909A Kirschner Pl Austin TX 98758

PHILLIPS, JOHN GOLDSMITH
MUSEUM CURATOR
b Glens Falls, NY, Jan 22, 07. Study: Harvard Univ, AB. Teaching: Lectr var aspects Europ art & new installations, Metrop Mus Art, New York. Pos: Chmn emer Western Europ arts, Metrop Mus Art, 71- Awards: Guggenheim Fel, 57. Publ: Auth, Early Florentine designers and engravers, Metrop Mus Art, 55; auth, China-trade porcelain, 56. Mailing Add: 431 Brazilian Ave Palm Beach FL 33480

PHILLIPS, LAUGHLIN
MUSEUM DIRECTOR
b Washington, DC, Oct 20, 24. Study: Yale Univ, 42-43; Univ Chicago, MA(philos), 49. Pos: Ed in chief, Washingtonian Mag; pres & trustee, Phillips Collection, Washington, DC, 67-, dir, 72- Mailing Add: 1600 21st St Washington DC 20009

PHILLIPS, MARJORIE
MUSEUM DIRECTOR, PAINTER
b Bourbon, Ind, Oct 25, 94. Study: Art Students League; additional study with Kenneth Hayes Miller & Boardman Robinson. Work: Whitney Mus Am Art, New York; Corcoran Gallery Art, Washington, DC; Santa Barbara Mus, Calif; Yale Univ Art Gallery; Phillips Collection, Washington, DC; Mus Fine Arts, Boston. Exhib: Exhibition of American Painting, Tate Gallery, London, 46; Carnegie Inst Int, Pittsburgh, several yrs; one-woman shows, Calif Palace of Legion of Honor, San Francisco, 59, Edward Root Art Ctr, Munson-Williams-Proctor Inst, Utica, NY, 65 & retrospective, Marlborough Galleries, London, 73; Franz Bader Gallery, Washington, DC, 77; Phillips Collection Exhib, 78; Cosmos Club, 78. Collections Arranged: Seymour Lipton's Sculpture, 64; Giacomotti Sculpture and Painting, 65; Alexander Calder Sculpture, 67; Contemporary Sculpture, 68; Cezanne Exhib (with Art Inst Chicago & Boston Mus Fine Arts), to celebrate 50th Anniversary of Phillips Collection opening, 71; Forty Paintings by Washington, DC, Artists, 71-72; plus others. Pos: Assoc dir, Phillips Collection, 25-66, dir, 66-72, dir emer & trustee, 72- Awards: Award of Merit, Pa Mus Sch Art, 59; DFA(hon), Smith Col, 72. Mem: Am Fedn Arts. Media: Oil. Publ: Auth, Duncan Phillips and his Collection, Atlantic Mo Press, Little, 71. Mailing Add: 2101 Foxhall Rd NW Washington DC 20007

PHILLIPS, MATT
PAINTER
b New York, NY. Study: Univ Chicago, MA; Stanford Univ; Barnes Found. Work: Metrop Mus Art; Nat Gallery Art; Philadelphia Mus Art; Whitney Mus; Nat Collection Fine Art, New York Pub Libr. Exhib: Retrospective, Baltimore Mus of Art, 61-75; Princeton Gallery Fine Art, 71; Smithsonian Inst Traveling Exhib, 72; William Zierler Gallery, New York, 72-73; Retrospective, Phillips Collection, Washington, DC, 76-77; Middendorf/Lane, Washington, DC, 78; Donald Morris Gallery, Birmingham, Mich; plus others. Teaching: Head dept art, Bard Col, 64- Style & Technique: Oil color hand printed monotypes; paintings: watercolors. Publ: Auth, Maurice Prendergast: the monotypes (catalog), 67 & Milton Avery: works on paper (catalog), 71, Bard Col; auth, The monotype today, Artist's Proof, 69; The monotype: an edition of one, Smithsonian Inst Traveling Exhib, 72. Dealer: Marilyn Pearl 29 W 57th St New York NY 10019. Mailing Add: Bard Col Annandale-on-Hudson NY 12504

PHILLIPS, MELITA AHL
SCULPTOR, PAINTER
b Newark, NJ, May 20, 04. Study: Parsons Sch Design, cert, 24; Art Students League; also with Howard Giles, Felicie Waldo Howell & Henry Mitchell. Work: Arden Hosp, Goshen, NY; Wilmington Trust Co, Del; Cecil Co Libr, Elkton, Md; Harford Co Libr, Belair, Md; Miami Univ. Comn: Portrait head (sculpture), of dir, YWCA, Newark, Del, 70; stained glass window, Cecil Co Libr, 74 & Lion (bronze) Sculpture Mem, 78. Exhib: Ann Exhib, Catharine Lorillard Wolfe Art Club, Nat Acad Design, 70 & Ann Exhib, Nat Arts Club, New York, 74; Ann Md Exhib, Acad Arts, Easton, 71; Ann Exhib, Hudson Valley Art Asn, Westchester, NY; mem show, Lever House, New York, 75. Pos: Ed format & design & managing ed, Del Med J, 59-72. Awards: Nat First Place Award Format Design & Ed, Med J; First Place & Best Show, Cecil Alliance Arts, 72; Hudson Valley Art Asn Award Winning Mem, 74. Mem: Nat League Am Pen Women; Hudson Valley Art Asn; Nat Arts Club, New York. Style & Technique: Realistic; watercolors, loose and airy; oils, soft and broad; pastels, sketchy. Media: Stone, Bronze, Terra Cotta. Dealer: George S B Scarlett Gallery Rd 3 Kennett Square PA 19348. Mailing Add: Whiteoaks RD 3 Leeds Elkton MD 21921

PIATEK, FRANCIS JOHN
PAINTER
b Chicago, Ill, Dec 9, 44. Study: Sch Art Inst Chicago, BFA & MFA. Work: Art Inst Chicago. Comn: Mural, Main State Bank Chicago, 72. Exhib: Whitney Mus Am Art Ann Exhib Contemp Am Painting, 68; one-man shows, Hyde Park Art Ctr, 69, Phyllis Kind Gallery, 72, Merrimac Col, 74 & NAME Gallery, Chicago, 75. Teaching: Instr painting, Art Inst Chicago, 70-71 & 75-; instr painting, Washington Univ, St Louis, 73-74. Awards: Art Inst Traveling Fel, Francis Ryerson, 67; Pauline Potter Palmer Award, 68 & John G Curtis Prize, 69, Chicago & Vicinity Shows. Style & Technique: From organic spatial abstraction to direct symbolic images. Media: Oil, Acrylic. Mailing Add: 3925 N Troy St Chicago IL 60618

PICARD, LIL
PAINTER, SCULPTOR
b Landau, Ger; US citizen. Study: Col Strassbourg, Alsace-Loraine; study in Vienna, Austria & Berlin, Ger; Art Students League, with Jevza Modell. Work: Schniewind Collection, Nevege, Ger; Hahn Collection, Cologne, Ger. Exhib: Parnass Gallery, Wuppethal, Ger, 62; Insel Gallery, Hamburg, Ger, 63; Smolin Gallery, New York, 65; Kunsthalle, Baden-Baden, Ger; Stedelijk Mus, Holland; plus others. Pos: Art critic, Kunstwerk, Baden-Baden & Die Welt, Hamburg. Interest: Self performances in personal realism style. Publ: Contrib ed, Inter/View. Mailing Add: 40 E Ninth St New York NY 10003

PICCILLO, JOSEPH
PAINTER, EDUCATOR
b Buffalo, NY, 1937. Study: State Univ NY Col Buffalo, MFA, 64. Work: Mus Mod Art, New York; Brooklyn Mus; Southern Ill Univ, Carbondale; Butler Inst Am Art, Youngstown, Ohio; Minn Mus Art, Minneapolis. Exhib: One-man show, Albright-Knox Art Gallery, Buffalo, 69; Smithsonian Inst Traveling Drawing Exhib, 71. Teaching: Instr art, State Univ NY Col Buffalo, currently. Pos: Consult, NY State Coun Arts, 75- Awards: Childe Hassam Purchase Award, Am Acad Arts & Lett, 68; Fels, State Univ NY, 68, 69 & 72. Bibliog: Diane Cochrane (auth), J Piccillo's game structures, Am Artist, 12/73. Style & Technique: Large drawings on canvas. Publ: Illusr, covers, Poverty in America, 5/17/68 & Black vs Jew-A tragic confrontation, 1/31/69, Time Mag. Dealer: Oscar Krasner Gallery Inc 1043 Madison Ave New York NY 10021. Mailing Add: 296 Bryant St Buffalo NY 14222

PICCOLO, THOMAS FRANK
SCULPTOR, JEWELER
b Bridgeport, Conn, June 3, 45. Study: NTex Univ; Tex Tech Univ; El Centro Col; Univ Tex, Dallas, BA(summa cum laude), 77; E Tex State Univ. Comn: Bronze-wood combinations, Fryburger Collection, San Antonio, Tex, 75; Brookhaven Country Club, Dallas, 76. Exhib: NTex Regional Painting & Sculpture, Richardson, 74; one-man shows, Gargoyle Gallery, Aspen, Colo, 74, San Angelo State Univ, 75 & Contemporary Gallery, Dallas, 75; France-Louisianne Festival, New Orleans, 75. Teaching: Prof sculpture, El Centro Col, 73-; prof, Community Serv Prog, Dallas, 74-; jeweler workshops at var univs. Awards: Richardson Bank First Sculpture Award, NTex Regional, 74. Bibliog: USA Info Serv (auth), Film on Artists, France-Louisianne Festival, 75; article in Tex Mo, 12/76; Janet Kutner (auth), article in Art News, 4/77. Mem: Artists Equity Asn; Tex Soc Sculptors; Tex Wood-Carvers Guild. Style & Technique: Abstract figurative wood sculpture; body sculpture in silver. Media: Wood, Stone; Silver, Gold. Publ: Auth, Wood and metal flow in modern sculpture, San Angelo Standard Times, 75. Dealer: Ralph Kahn c/o Contemp Gallery The Quadrangel-Routh St Dallas TX 75221. Mailing Add: 6410 Dykes Way Dallas TX 75230

PICHER, CLAUDE
ART ADMINISTRATOR, PAINTER
b Quebec City, Que, May 30, 27. Study: Que Fine Arts Sch, 45-46; New Sch Social Res, New York, 48, with Julian Levi; Ecole du Louvre, Paris, 48-49, with Jean Cassou; Ecole Nat Superieure des Beaux-Arts de Paris, with Demeter Galanis. Work: Nat Gallery Can, Ottawa; Art Gallery Ont, Toronto; Lord Beaverbrook Art Gallery, Fredericton, NB; Agnes Etherington Art Gallery, Kingston, Ont. Comn: Mural of Old Que, Hall of the Claridge, Quebec City, 67. Exhib: Montreal Mus Fine Arts, 58 & 64; 2nd Int Biennial, Mus Mod Art, Paris, France, 61; Lord Beaverbrook Art Gallery, 62; Que Mus, Quebec City, 67. Pos: Eastern rep, Nat Gallery of Can, 58-61; assoc dir, Que Mus, 63-64. Awards: Jessie Dow Found Award, 73rd Spring Exhib, Montreal Mus Fine Arts, 56; Acquisition Prize, Nat Gallery of Can, Govt of Can, 57 & Lord Beaverbrook Art Gallery, Can Art Coun, 62. Bibliog: Robert Fulford (auth), Twenty-four young Canadian artists, Can Art Mag, 61; Guy Viau (auth), La peinture au Canada-Francais, Ministere des Affaires Culturelles, 64; Guy Robert (auth), La peinture au Quebec depuis 1940, Ed La Press, 73. Mem: Royal Can Acad Arts. Style & Technique: Completely figurative oil painting with brush or palette knife; landscapes, portraits and still life. Media: Oil. Interest: Art of the past until 1920; totally uninterested in contemporary art, like Op, Pop, Minimal, etc. Dealer: Walter Klinkhoff Gallery 1200 Sherbrooke St W Montreal PQ Can. Mailing Add: St-Leandre RR 8 Matane County PQ G0J 2V0 Can

PICK, JOHN
ART ADMINISTRATOR
b West Bend, Wis, Sept 18, 11. Study: Univ Notre Dame, BA, 33; Univ Wis, MA, 34 & PhD, 38; grad study at Harvard Univ & Oxford Univ. Work: Milwaukee Art Ctr; Marquette Univ Art Collection. Collections Arranged: Marquette Univ Art Collection (with catalog & suppl). Teaching: Fulbright lectr, Royal Univ Malta, 55-56; vis prof, Cambridge Univ, Eng, 76 & Oxford Univ, Eng, 77. Pos: Chmn, Univ Comt Fine Arts, Marquette Univ, 51-75; cult attaché, Embassy of Malta, Washington, DC, 68- Mem: Am Asn Univ Prof; Mod Lang Asn Am; Eng-Speaking Union; fel Royal Soc Arts, London. Res: Brochures on icons, Spanish colonial art and others. Publ: Auth, Gerard Manley Hopkins: Priest and Poet, 42 & A Hopkins Reader, 52, Oxford Univ Press; Hopkins—the Windhover, Merrill, 68. Mailing Add: Le Redan Madliena Malta

PICKEN, GEORGE
PAINTER, PRINTMAKER
b New York, NY, Oct 26, 98. Study: Art Students League, 24; also study in Europe. Work: Corcoran Gallery Art; Lowe Art Ctr, Syracuse Univ; Lowe Art Gallery, Miami Univ; Hudson River Mus; Whitney Mus Am Art; plus many others. Comn: Murals, US Post Off, Edward & Hudson Falls, NY & Chardon, Ohio. Exhib: Corcoran Gallery Art, 41, 43, 45 & 61; Whitney Mus Am Art, 42-46 & 60; Va Mus Fine Arts, 42, 44 & 46; Pa Acad Fine Arts, 44-46; Carnegie Inst, 44-46; plus many other group & one-man shows. Teaching: Instr art, Cooper Union Art Sch, 43-64; asst prof painting & dept rep, Sch Painting & Sculpture, Columbia Univ, 43-64; spec asst prof fine arts, Hofstra Univ, 65-66; vis prof painting, Kansas City Art Inst, 65-66; vis prof painting, Univ Hartford, 67-68; instr painting, Lenox Sch Boys, Mass, 67-68. Awards: Prize, Corcoran Gallery Art, 43. Mem: Fedn Mod Painters & Sculptors; Soc Am Graphic Artists; Am Asn Univ Prof. Mailing Add: Church St Tyringham MA 01264

PICKENS, ALTON
PAINTER, INSTRUCTOR
b Seattle, Wash, Jan 19, 17. Study: Reed Col. Work: Mus Mod Art. Teaching: Prof art, Vassar Col, 56- Style & Technique: Expressionist. Mailing Add: Dept Art Vassar Col Poughkeepsie NY 12601

PICKENS, VINTON LIDDELL
PAINTER
b Charlotte, NC. Study: Corcoran Art Sch, with Eugene Weisz, Washington, DC; Am Univ, with Ben L Summerford. Work: Butler Inst Am Art, Youngstown, Ohio; Watkins Gallery, Washington, DC; Miami Mus Mod Art, Fla; Univ Maine; Art-in-the-Embassies Prog, State Dept. Exhib: Corcoran Biennial; Soc Washington Artists; Va Artists Biennial, Richmond; one-man shows, Chase Gallery, New York & Franz Bader Gallery, Washington, DC. Mem: Touchstone Gallery, Washington, DC; Artists Equity Asn. Style & Technique: Painting: semi-abstract, recognizable subject matter; drawing: realistic subjects imaginatively combined. Publ: Auth & illusr, Paint an Elephant, Atlantic, 58; auth, Serendipity. Mailing Add: Janelia Farm Ashburn VA 22011

PICKFORD, ROLLIN, JR
PAINTER
b Fresno, Calif. Study: Calif State Univ; Stanford Univ, BA; also with Alexander Nepote, Ralph DuCasse, James Weeks & Joseph Mugnaini. Work: Springfield Art Mus, Mo; State of Calif Collection, Sacramento; Ford Motor Co, Dearborn, Mich; City of Santa Paula, Calif; Monterey Peninsula Mus Art. Exhib: All-California Exhib, Laguna Beach, Calif, 60; Watercolor USA, Springfield, Mo, 62, 65 & 66; Mainstreams Marietta, Ohio, 68; Austrian-Am Exchange Exhib, Linz, Salzburg & Vienna, Austria, 72; Taiwan-Am Exchange Exhib, 73; Royal Watercolor Soc, London-WCoast Watercolor Soc Exchange Exhib, 75-76. Teaching: Instr art, Fresno State Col, 48-62. Pos: Pres, Fresno Art League, 46-47. Awards: Best of Show, All-California Exhib, 60; First Prize & Purchase Award, Watercolor USA, 62; First Prize & Purchase Award, Calif State Fair, 63. Mem: West Coast Watercolor Soc; Carmel Art Asn; Fresno Arts Ctr; Old Bergen Art Guild. Style & Technique: From abstract expressionism to impressionism and realism. Media: Watercolor, Oil, Acrylic. Publ: Illusr, stories by William Saroyan, Lincoln-Mercury Times & Ford Times, 50's; auth, A philosophical approach to watercolor, Am Artist, 69. Mailing Add: 1839 Van Ness Fresno CA 93721

PICKHARDT, CARL
PAINTER, PRINTMAKER
b Westwood, Mass, May 28, 08. Study: Harvard Univ, AB, 31; study with Harold Zimmerman, 30-35. Work: Mus Mod Art, New York; Mus Fine Arts, Boston; Newark Art Mus, NJ; Libr Cong, Washington, DC; Brooklyn Art Mus, NY. Exhib: Int Biennial of Color Lithography, 51; Carnegie Inst Int, 52; Int Exhib, Japan, 52; Am Drawing Biennial, Norfolk, Va, 66; Pa Acad Fine Arts, Philadelphia, 68. Teaching: Instr printmaking, Worcester Mus Art Sch, 49-50; instr printmaking, Art Students League, 51; instr painting, Fitchburg Art Mus, 51-62. Awards: Schope Prize, Nat Acad Design, 42. Bibliog: Parker Tyler (auth), Carl Pickhardt, Horizon, 72. Style & Technique: Abstractions; paintings in irregular shapes. Mailing Add: 66 Forest St Sherborn MA 01770

PIENE, OTTO
SCULPTOR, PAINTER
b Laasphe, Westphalia, Ger, Apr 18, 28. Study: Blocherer Art Sch & Acad of Fine Arts, Munich, 48-50; Dusseldorf Art Acad, WGer, 50-53; Univ Cologne, WGer, 53-57. Work: Albright-Knox Art Gallery, Buffalo, NY; Mus Mod Art, New York; Carnegie Inst Int Mus Art, Pittsburgh, Pa; Nat Gallery of Can, Ottawa, Ont; Stedelijk Mus, Amsterdam, Holland. Comn: Olympic Rainbow, Munich, 72. Exhib: Vision in Motion, Hessenhuis, Antwerp, Belg, 59; Festival d'Art d'Avantgarde, Paris, 60; The Movement Movement, Stedelijk Mus, 61; Carnegie Inst Int, 61; Sixteen German Artists, Corcoran Gallery of Art, Washington, DC, 62; Light & Movement, Kunstverein, Rheinland & Westfalen, Dusseldorf, 65; Mus am Ostwall, Dortmund, WGer retrospect, 67; Light Sculpture, Cleveland Mus Art, Ohio, 68; Inflatible Sculpture, Jewish Mus, New York & Witte Mem Mus, San Antonio, Tex, 69; Kinetics, Hayward Gallery, London, 70; 35th Bienniale of Venice, Italy, 70; Earth, Air, Fire, Water: Elements of Art, Mus Fine Arts, Boston, Mass, 71; Graphic Bienniale, Tokyo, Japan, 72; Westphalian Art, Westfalisches Landsmuseum, Munster, Ger, 73; one-man shows, Mus Schloss Morsbroich, Leverkusen, WGer, 62, Westfalisches Landsmuseum, Munster, Ger, 68, Trumbull Col, Yale Univ, New Haven, Conn, 69, Centro de Arte y Communicacion, Buenos Aires, Art, 72 & Kolnischer Kunstverein, Cologne, 73. Teaching: Vis prof art, Univ Pa, Philadelphia, 64; resident fel, Ctr for Adv Visual Studies, Mass Inst Technol, 68-70; prof environmental art, Sch of Archit & Planning, Mass Inst Technol, 72. Pos: Co-founder, Group Zero, Dusseldorf, WGer, 57, co-publr, Zero Mag, 58; dir, Ctr for Adv Visual Studies, Mass Inst Technol, Cambridge. Awards: Konrad von Soest Prize, Munster, 68; Tamarind Fel, Los Angeles, Calif, 69; Prize, Tokyo Graphics Biennale, Mus Mod Art, Tokyo, Japan, 72. Bibliog: Fuergen Wissmann (auth), Otto Piene, Recklinghausen, WGer, 76; Dietrich Mahlow, et al (auth), Otto Piene—Werkverzeichnis der Druckgrafik 1960-76, Karlsruhe, WGer, 77; Lawrence Alloway (auth), Otto Piene, St Gallen, Switz, 78. Style & Technique: Kinetic & iflatible sculpture, using air currents, gases, light; very large scale. Publ: Auth, Sky art: a notebook for a book, Artscanada, 6/69; auth, More Sky, Cambridge, Mass, 73. Mailing Add: c/o Mass Inst Technol 40 Massachusetts Ave Cambridge MA 02139

PIERCE, DANNY P
SCULPTOR, PRINTMAKER
Study: Schouinard Inst Art, Los Angeles; Am Art Sch, New York; Brooklyn Mus Art Sch; Univ Alaska. Work: Mus Mod Art, New York; Libr Cong; Nat Libr, Paris; Nat Mus Sweden, Stockholm; Huntington Libr, San Marino, Calif. Comn: Eskimo scene panels, Univ Alaska, 62, abstract design in concrete for cafeteria bldg, 63. Exhib: Traveling Exhib Prints, Europe, Eurasia, 59-62; Northwest Printmakers Int, Seattle Art Mus, 68; Washington Art, Worlds Fair, Osaka, Japan, 70; Edge of the Sea, Bradley Gallery, Milwaukee, 73, one-man show, Small Bronzes, 74. Teaching: Assoc prof art, Univ Wis-Milwaukee, 65- Pos: Artist in residence, Univ Alaska, 59-63. Awards: Green Memorial Award for Best Oil, Conn Acad Art, 49; Purchase Award, Libr Cong, 52, 53 & 58; Northwest Printmakers International Award, Seattle Art Mus, 68. Style & Technique: Contemporary approach to realism. Publ: Auth & illusr, Little No Name, 59, The Bear That Woke Too Soon, 64, Little Ezukvuk, 65, Washington's Dilemma-Sackcloth and Butternut, 73, Edge of the Sea, 74 & Cattle Drive 76, 77, pvt publ. Dealer: Cushing Gallery 2723 Fairmount Dallas TX 75201; Jean Seth's Canyon Rd Art Gallery 710 Canyon Rd Santa Fe NM 87501. Mailing Add: 3547 N Murray Ave Milwaukee WI 53211

PIERCE, DELILAH W
PAINTER, EDUCATOR
b Washington, DC, Mar 3, 04. Study: DC Teachers Col, dipl; Howard Univ, BS; Columbia Univ, MA; also with Lois Jones, Céline Tabary, Ralph Pearson, James Lesene Wells & Jack Perlmutter. Work: Howard Univ Gallery Art & DC Teachers Col, Washington, DC; Barnett-Aden Gallery Collection; Anacostia Mus, Smithsonian Affil. Comn: Portrait of Dr Eugene A Clark, comn by family for Eugene A Clarke Pub Sch, Washington, DC, 69. Exhib: Atlanta Univ Art Show, 52 & 53; Area Show, 57-59 & Travel Exhib, 60-61, Corcoran Gallery Art; Baltimore Gallery Art Area Show, 59; Smith-Mason Gallery Nat Exhib, 71; Trenton Mus, 72; Am Embassy, Dar Es Salaam, Tanzania, Africa, 73-75; Univ of Pa Mus, 74; Howard Univ Gallery, 76; Afro-Am Hist & Cult Mus, Philadelphia, Pa, 76; FESTAC, Lagos, Nigeria, 77; Frick Fine Arts Mus, Univ of Pittsburgh, 77. Teaching: Instr art, sec pub schs, Washington, DC, 25-52; instr art & art educ, DC Teachers Col, 52-56, prof art & art educ, 56-69, vis prof art educ, 70-71; vis prof art educ, Howard Univ Sch Educ, 64-67. Awards: Agnes Meyer Summer Fel, 62; award for achievement in field of art & art educ, Phi Delta Kappa, 63; mus donor prog purchase award, Am Fedn Art, 64; Smith-Mason Achievement & Serv Award. Bibliog: Cedric Dover (auth), American Negro art, NY Graphic Soc, 60; J E Atkinson (auth), Black dimensions in contemporary American art, Ca ation Co, 71; New Directions, Howard Univ Mag, 4/76. Mem: Soc Washington Artists (treas, 69-); Artist Equity Asn (third vpres); Washington Watercolor Asn; Nat Conf Artists (nat treas, 73-); DC Art Asn. Style & Technique: Not seeking realism nor abstraction; rather, ordered patterns, shapes, space and color relations expressed in the simplest form. Media: Oil, Acrylic. Publ: Auth, Can art serve as a balance wheel in education?, Educ Arts Asn J, 49; auth, The significance of art experiences in the education of the Negro, J Negro Life & Hist. Dealer: Smith-Mason Gallery 1207 Rhode Island Ave NW Washington DC 20005. Mailing Add: 1753 Verbena St NW Washington DC 20012

PIERCE, DIANE (DIANE PIERCE HUXTABLE)
PAINTER, ILLUSTRATOR
b Lakewood, Ohio, Mar 6, 39. Study: Cleveland Inst Art, Ohio, dipl, 61; Western Reserve Univ, BA, 62. Work: Ward Found Mus, Salisbury, Md; Heard Mus, McKinney, Tex. Comn: Christmas card, Nat Audubon Soc, New York, 77 & Nat Wild Turkey Fedn, 77; warbler calendar, Nat Wildlife Fedn, 79. Exhib: One-person show, Cornell Lab of Ornithology, 73; Int Exhib Wildbird Artists, Woodson Art Mus, Wausau, Wis, 76 & 77; Wildfowl Art Exhib, Ward Found, 76 & 77; Soc Animal Artists Mem Show, New York, 76-78; Midwest Wildlife Art Show, Kansas City, Mo, 76-78; Tidewater Inn Waterfowl Festival, Easton, Md, 77. Bibliog: Stalking birds with pen & brush, Explorer Mag, Cleveland Mus Natural Hist, 78. Mem: Sco Animal Artists; Ward Found. Style & Technique: Bird paintings; watercolor portraits with transparent and/or opaque; birds in landscapes. Media: Watercolor, Oil. Publ: Contribr, The Living Bird, Cornell Univ Lab of Ornithology, 72-78; contribr, Audubon Mag, 75; illusr, An Introduction to Ornithology, Macmillan, 75; contribr (cover), Ducks Unlimited Mag, 77; contribr (illus), Children's Sci Mag, 77. Mailing Add: c/o Edge of the Wild King Mem Hwy Mentor OH 44060

PIERCE, ELIZABETH R
PAINTER
b Brooklyn, NY. Study: Art Students League, with John Groth, John Stewart Curry & Anne Goldthwaite; Art League Long Island, NY, with Edgar A Whitney; Columbia Univ Exten. Work: Children's room, Jamaica Pub Libr, NY. Exhib: Nat Asn Women Artists Ann, Nat Acad Design Galleries; Nova Scotia Soc Artists, Halifax; Nat Mus, Washington, DC; Yarmouth Art Soc, NS; Royal Bank of Can, Yarmouth, NS. Teaching: Instr adult educ oil painting, Nova Scotia Dept Educ, Yarmouth, 59-67. Mem: Nat Asn Women Artists; life mem Art Students League; Yarmouth Art Soc. Media: Oil. Mailing Add: RR 1 Yarmouth NS B5A 4A5 Can

PIERCE, J MICHAEL
PRINTMAKER, INSTRUCTOR
b Sullivan, Ind, May 18, 43. Study: Columbus Col of Art & Design, Ohio; Art Inst of Chicago, BFA; Pratt Inst New York, MFA. Work: Philadelphia Mus of Art; Baltimore Mus of Art; Art Inst of Chicago; Libr of Cong; Nat Collection of Fine Arts, Washington, DC. Exhib: Libr of Cong; Philadelphia Mus of Art; Baltimore Mus of Art; Nat Collection of Fine Arts, Washington, DC; Seattle Art Mus, Wash; Columbus Gallery of Fine Arts, Ohio; Cleveland Mus of Art, Ohio; Scand Traveling Exhib. Teaching: Instr painting, Univ Va, Charlottesville, 68-72; assoc prof printmaking, Montgomery Col, Md, 69-; instr drawing, Montgomery Co Adult Educ, 70-72. Mem: Soc Washington Printmakers (pres, 76-); Col Art Asn. Style & Technique: Color drawing and paintings on handmade and cast paper; lithography drawings on paper. Mailing Add: 208 Forest Ave Rockville MD 20850

PIERCE, JAMES SMITH
ART HISTORIAN, SCULPTOR
b Brooklyn, NY, Apr 26, 30. Study: Oberlin Col, AB, 52; Harvard Univ, PhD, 62. Exhib: One-man shows, Rasdall Gallery, Univ Ky, 74, Noyes Gallery, Antioch Col, Yellow Springs, Ohio, 75, Edna Carlsten Gallery, Univ Wis-Stevens Point, 75, Pensacola Art Ctr, 75, Tenn Fine Arts Ctr, Nashville, 75, Tex Tech Univ Mus, 75, Ball State Univ Art Gallery, 75, Univ Okla Mus Art, 75, Univ Gallery of Fine Art, Ohio State Univ, 76, Mercer Univ Art Gallery, Ga, 76, Univ SDak Art Gallery, 76, Univ S Miss Art Gallery, 76, Memphis State Univ Art Gallery, 76, Creighton Univ Gallery, Omaha, 76, Western Ill Univ Mus/Gallery, Macomb, Ill, 76, West Liberty State Col Art Gallery, WVa, 77, Ashland Col Gallery, Ohio, 77, Haas Gallery of Art, Bloomsburg State Col, Pa, 77, Koenig Art Gallery, Concordia Col, Seward, Nebr, 77, Hardin-Simmons Univ Gallery, Abilene, Tex, 77, Lindenwood Cols Art Gallery, St Charles, Mo, 77, Univ Tenn at Chattanooga Art Gallery, 77 & Barnhart Gallery, Univ Ky, 78; Art Gallery, Southwest Tex State Univ, 74; Lee Hall Gallery, Col Archit, Clemson Univ, SC, 75; Univ Ky Art Galleries, 75, 76 & 77 twice; Georgetown Col Art Gallery, Georgetown, Ky, 76; Hirshhorn Mus, Smithsonian Inst, Washington, DC, 77-78; La Jolla Mus of Contemp Art, Calif, 78; Seattle Art Mus, Wash, 78. Collections Arranged: Gerald Ferstman (with catalog), Ctr Contemp Art, Univ Ky, 70, Jim Campbell (with catalog), 70, Deborah Frederick (with catalog), 71, David Middlebrook (with catalog), 71 & Recent Early American, 73, Sacred Symmetry: Ancient Earthworks of the Ohio Valley (with catalog), Univ Art Gallery, 73. Teaching: From asst prof to assoc prof art hist, Case Western Reserve Univ, 59-69; prof art hist, Univ Ky, 69-, chmn dept art, 69-73. Pos: Dir, Ctr Contemp Art, Univ Ky, 70-71. Awards: America the Beautiful Fund Grant, 72; Best Images and Fantasy Award, Nat Film Soc, 73; Nat Endowment for the Humanities independent study fel, 76. Bibliog: Pratt farm turf maze, Art Int, XX, 4-5, 4-5/76; John Beardsley (auth), Probing the earth: contemporary land projects, Hirshhorn Mus, Smithsonian Inst, Washington, DC, 77. Mem: Col Art Asn; Soc Archit Historians. Style & Technique: Basic Earthforms. Media: Earth, Rock. Res: Relation of past to the present. Publ: Auth, Visual and auditory space in baroque Rome, J Aesthetics & Art Criticism, 59; auth, Architectural drawings and the intent of the architect, Art J, 67; auth, Contemplating parallax, Art Int, Vol 12, No 7; auth, From Abacus to Zeus:

A Handbook of Art History, Prentice-Hall, 68; auth, Paul Klee and Primitive Art, Garland, 75. Mailing Add: Dept of Art Univ of Ky Lexington KY 40506

PIERCE, PATRICIA JOBE
ART DEALER, WRITER
b Seattle, Wash, May 18, 43. Study: Univ Conn, 64; Boston Univ Sch Fine & Appl Arts, BFA, 65. Pos: Pres, Pierce Galleries, Inc, Hingham, Mass, 66- Mem: Archives Am Art; Appraisers Asn Am; Frick Art Ref Libr; patron Brockton Mus Art; Mus Fine Arts, Boston. Res: Edmund Charles Tarbell and the Boston School of painting; John Joseph Enneking and the lives of Boston painters; surrealism and the current work of Samuel Rose. Specialty: 18th to 20th century American painting, specializing in American impressionism; supports and promotes Boston living painters and their work; agent for Samuel Rose and Arnold Carl Savrann. Collection: 19th century American impressionists, W Metcalf, E C Tarbell, William Paxton, J J Enneking and Twachtman; wildlife by A C Savrann; surreal paintings by Samuel Rose. Publ: Co-auth, John Joseph Enneking, American Impressionist Painter, 72; auth, William S Barrett (1854-1927) and His Sea, 73; auth, Charles Courtney Curran, Realist, 74; auth, Edmund C Tarbell and the Boston School, 76; auth, The Ten, Rumford Press, 77. Mailing Add: c/o Pierce Galleries Inc 721 Main St Rte 228 Hingham MA 02043

PIEROTTI, JOHN
CARTOONIST
b New York, NY. Study: Art Students League; Cooper Union; Mechanics Inst. Work: Collection of All Works, Syracuse Univ; Wayne State Univ; Univ Wis. Exhib: Man and this World, Montreal, Can; Yugoslavia; Metrop Mus Art, New York. Awards: Six Silurian Awards for best ed cartoon, 65-72; Page One Award for best sports cartoon, 65-68; Page One Awards for best ed cartoon, 68-73; Best Ed Cartoonist Award, Nat Cartoonists Soc, 75. Mem: Nat Cartoonists Soc (pres, 57-59); Artists & Writers. Publ: Illusr, sports & ed cartoonist, New York Post, currently. Mailing Add: 2004 Ocean Ave Brigantine NJ 08203

PIERRE-NOEL, VERGNIAUD
DESIGNER
b Port-au-Prince, Haiti, Aug 2, 10; US citizen. Study: Cent Sch Damien, Univ Haiti, dipl; Columbia Univ, cert; Casa de Moneda, Buenos Aires, cert. Work: Nat Mus Haiti, Port-au-Prince; Am Mus Nat Hist, New York; UN, New York; Pan Am Health Organ, Washington, DC; Wingspread Collection, Racine, Wis. Comn: Insects of Haiti, Serv Tech Damien, 33; Caribbean Cong commemorative stamp designs, Govt Haiti, 40; bicentennial commemorative stamp designs 1749-1949, Haiti Postal Admin, 49; UN Commemorative stamp design, New York, 65; WHO commemorative poster design, Washington, DC, 68. Exhib: Am Mus Natural Hist Staff Artists Exhib, New York, 36; Mil Club Haiti, Port-au-Prince, 40; Women Club Arg, Buenos Aires, 48; Nat Asn Indust Artists, Washington, DC, 65; Washington Tech Inst, DC, 68. Pos: Graphic designer, Dept Educ, Haiti, 30-34, Am Mus Natural Hist, 35-40, Haiti Postal Admin, 40-54 & Pan Am Health Orgn, 56-75. Awards: Gold Medal Award for Bicentennial of City of Port-au-Prince, 49; First Award for UN Postage Stamp Design, 65; First Award, Nat Asn Indust Artists, 65. Bibliog: Verniaud Pierre-Noel, Cent Life Ins Fla Calendar, 61. Albert F Kunze (auth), V Pierre-Noel, creator of stamp designs for Haiti, Linn's Weekly Stamp News, 10/52; Belmont Faries (auth), Philatelic news, Washington Star, 2/62. Mem: Mus Mod Art, New York; Indust Graphics Int; Washington Tech Inst Advert Design (adv comt). Style & Technique: Allegoric, symbolic. Media: Pen & Ink, Airbrush. Publ: Contribr illus, Am Mus Natural Hist, New York, 31, Entom Soc Am, 31, Haiti Postal Admin, 40, UN Postal Admin, 65 & Pan Am Health Orgn, 75. Mailing Add: 4706 17th St NW Washington DC 20011

PIGOTT, MARJORIE
PAINTER
b Yokohama, Japan; Can citizen. Study: Master Artists of Nanga Sch Art, Japan, 12 yrs, teachers dipl. Work: London Art Gallery & Mus, Ont; Univ Western Ont; Atlantic Inst Educ, Halifax, NS; Confedn Art Gallery, Charlottetown, PEI; Nat Gallery Can, Ottawa; plus others. Exhib: 11 Can Soc Painters Watercolour Ann, 61-74; 4th Biennial Exhib, Nat Gallery Can, 61; 10 Ont Soc Artists Ann, 63-74; Art Galleries, Hamilton, London & Montreal, 67-74; Royal Can Acad, 70; plus others. Awards: Sumi-ye Soc Am Award for Northern Woods, 67; Hamilton Spectator Award for Liquid Rhythm 4, Can Soc Painters Watercolour. Mem: Can Soc Painters Watercolour; Ont Soc Artists; Royal Can Acad Arts. Style & Technique: Semi-abstract wet-into-wet pure watercolor. Publ: Ltd ed, Roberts Gallery, Toronto, 78. Dealer: Roberts Gallery 641 Yonge St Toronto ON Can. Mailing Add: Apt 1503 77 St Clair Ave E Toronto ON M4T 1M5 Can

PIJANOWSKI, EUGENE M
METALWORKER, INSTRUCTOR
b Detroit, Mich, Oct 5, 38. Study: Wayne State Univ, BFA, 65, MA, 67; Cranbrook Acad of Art, Bloomfield Hills, Mich, 67-69; Tokyo Univ of Art, Japan, 69-71. Work: Kalamazoo Inst of Art, Mich; Ga State Univ Art Gallery, Atlanta; Worshipful Co of Goldsmiths Hall, London, Eng; Tex Tech Univ Art Gallery, Lubbock. Exhib: Int Jewelry Show, Munich, WGer, 73-75 & 77; Work by Eight Am Metalsmiths & Jewelers (traveling exhib), Aberdeen Art Gallery & Richard DeMarco Gallery, Edinburgh, Scotland & Sheffield Polytech Sch Art & Design, Eng, 74; Goldsmith (competition/exhib), Renwick Gallery, Smithsonian Inst, Washington, DC & Minn Mus of Art, St Paul, 74; Masterworks of the 70's: Jewelers & Weavers, Albright-Knox Art Gallery, Buffalo, NY, 74; Six Am Jewelers, Electrum Gallery, London, Eng, 76; Bicentennial Metal Exhib, US Embassy, Bucharest, Romania, 76; Contemp Jewelry, Design Ctr, Cult Complex, Manila, Philippines, 77. Teaching: Instr metalwork, jewelry & crafts design, San Diego State Univ, Calif, 72-73; lectr Japanese metalworking, many workshops throughout the US, 73-77; assoc prof metalwork, jewelry & three-dimensional design, Purdue Univ, West Lafayette, Ind, 73- Pos: Designer & manufacturer, Gene Ltd, Yokohama, Japan, 70-72. Awards: Purchase Prizes (2), Int Ital Jewelry Exhib, Milan, 71; Award, Profiles in Jewelry, USA, Tex Tech Univ, 73; Ind Artist-Craftsman Award, Objects & Crafts 1975, Indianapolis Mus of Art, 75. Bibliog: Donald J Wilcox (auth), Body Jewelry: International Perspectives, Henry Regenry Co, 73; Jackie Bims (auth), Six contemporary American jewelers, Crafts (Eng), 9-10/76; C E Licka (auth), The 1977 metalsmith exhibit: a historical critique, Goldsmith J, 8/77. Mem: World Crafts Coun; Soc NAm Goldsmiths; Am Crafts Coun; Ind Artist-craftsman. Style & Technique: Geometric/organic graphic imagery incorporated with metals of various colors and utilizing the inlay and coloring porcesses of Japanese metalwork. Media: Metal and silk, Ikat preferred. Publ: Contribr, Donald J Wilcox, auth, Body Jewelry: International Perspective, Regenry Co, 73; contribr, Marcia Chamberlain, auth, Metal Jewelry Techniques, Watson-Guptill, 76; co-auth, Lamination of nonferrous metals by diffusion: adaptations of the traditional Japanese technique of Mokume-Gane, Goldsmiths J, 1977. Mailing Add: 615 Kossuth St Lafayette IN 47905

PIJANOWSKI, HIROKO SATO
METALWORKER, INSTRUCTOR
b Tokyo, Japan, Jan 1, 42. Study: Rikkyo Univ, BA, 64; Calif State Univ, Northridge, 65-66; Cranbrook Acad of Art, Bloomfield Hills, Mich, MFA, 68. Work: Crocker Art Gallery, Sacramento, Calif; Worshipful Co of Goldsmiths Hall, London, Eng; Tex Tech Univ Art Gallery, Lubbock. Exhib: Nat Sterling Design, Mus Contemp Crafts, New York, 69; Int Jewelry Show, Munich, WGer, 73-75 & 77; Work by Eight Am Metalsmiths & Jewelers (traveling exhib), Aberdeen Art Callery & Richard DeMarco Gallery, Edinburgh, Scotland & Sheffield Polytech Sch Art & Design, Eng, 74; Goldsmith (competition & exhib), Renwick Gallery, Smithsonian Inst, Washington, DC, 74; Hist of Silver & Goldsmithing in Am, The Lowe Art Mus, Coral Gables, Fla, 75; Six Am Jewelers, Electrum Gallery, London, Eng, 76; Contemp Jewelry, Design Ctr, Cult Complex, Manila, Philippines, 77. Teaching: Lectr, workshops on Japanese metalworking, 74-77. Pos: Designer & manufacturer, Gene Ltd, Yokohama, Japan, 70-72; designer & manufacturer, Hiro Ltd, Lafayette, Ind, 73- Awards: Fourth Prize, Sterling Silver Design Competition, New York, 68; Cash Award, Profiles in US Jewelry, Tex Tech Univ, 73 & 77; Cash Award, Objects & Crafts 1975, Indianapolis Mus of Art, Ind, 75. Bibliog: Donald J Wilcox, (auth), Body Jewelry: International Perspectives, Henry Regenry Co, 73; article in gold & silver, Ger, 75. Mem: Soc NAm Goldsmiths; Japan Jewelry Designer Asn; Am Crafts Coun; World Crafts Coun; Ind Artist-Craftsman. Style & Technique: Geometric/organic graphic imagery incorporated with metals of various colors and utilizing inlay and coloring processes of Japanese metalwork; lamination of metal (Mokume Gane). Media: Metal, gemstone and silk and cotton (Ikat) fabric. Publ: Contribr, Donald J Wilcox, auth, Body Jewelry: International perspectives, Henry Regenry Co, 73; contribr, Marcia Chamberlain, auth, Metal Jewelry Techniques, Watson-Guptill, 76; co-auth, Lamination of nonferrous metals by diffusion: adaptations of the traditional Japanese technique of Mokuna-Gane, Goldsmiths J, 77. Mailing Add: 615 Kossuth St Lafayette IN 47905

PIKE, JOHN
ILLUSTRATOR, PAINTER
b Boston, Mass, June 30, 11. Study: Hawthorne Sch Art, 28-31; also with Richard Miller. Comn: Paintings, USAF Hist Found, France, Ger, Greenland, Ecuador, Colombia, Panama & others; advert for Lederle Labs, Alcoa, Standard Oil & Falstaff; plus others. Exhib: Grand Cent Art Gallery; St Petersburg Art Club, Fla; Oklahoma City Mus Conserv Art; Great Plains Mus, Lawton, Okla & San Diego Fine Arts Festival, 60-61; also over 50 one-man shows plus others. Teaching: Instr, John Pike Watercolor Sch, Woodstock, NY, summers. Awards: Salmagundi Black & White Prizes, 41; Am Watercolor Soc Award, 42; William A Paton Prize, Art Students League, 76; plus others. Mem: Academician Nat Acad Design; Am Watercolor Soc; Soc Illusr; Salmagundi Club; Woodstock Art Asn; plus others. Publ: Contribr, illus & covers in Colliers, Reader's Digest, Life, Fortune & True Mags. Mailing Add: PO Box 428 Woodstock NY 12498

PILAVIN, SELMA F
PATRON
b Providence, RI, Sept 20, 08. Pos: Bd dirs, Mus Art, RI Sch of Design, 68-; trustee, RI Sch of Design, 74- Awards: Providence Art Club Medal, Providence Art Club, 71. Bibliog: The Albert Pilavin Collection: Twentieth Century, Am Art, Vol I, 69, Vol II, 73; article in The Connoisseur, 2/70. Mem: Providence Art Club. Interest: 20th Century American. Mailing Add: 601 Elmgrove Ave Providence RI 02906

PILGRIM, JAMES F
CURATOR, ART HISTORIAN
b Richmond, Ind, Feb 19, 41. Collections Arranged: American Impressionist Paintings, Corcoran Gallery, 68; John Storrs Retrospective, 69; Robert Morris (co-auth, catalog), 69; Alexander Liberman (co-auth, catalog), 70. The Vincent Melzac Collection, 70; Paintings from the Metrop, 71; Treasured Masterpieces from the Metrop Mus, Loan to Japan, summer 72. Teaching: Asst prof mus studies, George Washington Univ, 70-71. Pos: Cur Am art, Corcoran Gallery Art, 68-70, chief cur, 70-71; assoc cur Am painting, Metrop Mus Art, 71, asst cur in chief, 71-74, deputy vdir curatorial affairs, 74- Awards: Ford Found Fel Mus Training, NY Univ, 64-66; Clawson Mills Fel, Metrop Mus Art, 67-68. Mem: Am Inst Conserv; Col Art Asn; Am Asn Mus. Res: Late 19th & 20th century art. Publ: Contribr, J William Middendorf Collection (catalog), 67; auth, Recent Paintings of Leon Berkowitz, 68; auth, H Marc Moyens Collection (catalog), 70. Mailing Add: Metrop Mus Art Fifth Ave & 82nd St New York NY 10028

PILLIN, POLIA
PAINTER, CERAMIST
b Czenstochowa, Poland, Sept 1, 09; US citizen. Study: Jewish People's Inst, Chicago; Studio of Todros Geller, Chicago. Work: Long Beach Mus, Calif; Syracuse Mus Art, NY; Otis Art Inst, Los Angeles, Calif; Dallas Art Mus, Tex; Univ Maine. Exhib: Art Inst of Chicago; San Francisco Art Mus; Pa Acad Fine Arts; Butler Inst Am Art, Youngstown, Ohio; Los Angeles Art Mus; Seattle Art Mus, Wash; de Young Art Mus, San Francisco; Syracuse Art Mus, NY; Landau Gallery, Los Angeles; Feingarten Galleries, Los Angeles; Adele Bednarz Galleries, Los Angeles; Wichita Art Asn, Kans; Portland Art Mus, Ore; Scripps Col, La Jolla, Calif; Cincinnati Art Mus, Ohio. Awards: Los Angeles Co Art Inst, 48; Syracuse Mus, 51 & 53; Calif State Fair, 55, 57 & 60. Bibliog: Dennis Burns (auth), Like a Jewel (film), 72; Dale Wilson Smith (auth), The American Artist, Paintings on Clay, 55; articles in Los Angeles Times Home Sect. Mem: Nat Watercolor Soc. Style & Technique: Painting in watercolor and oil; abstract and figurative, expressionist in style, strongly delineated and structural; lyric in content. Media: Oil on Paper; Ceramic Painting; Decoration on Fired, Glazed Clay. Dealer: Richard Challis c/o Challis Galleries 1390 S Coast Hwy Laguna Beach CA 92652. Mailing Add: 4913 Melrose Ave Los Angeles CA 90029

PILSK, ADELE INEZ
ART ADMINISTRATOR
b Nashville, Tenn, Jan 21, 37. Study: Peabody Col, MA; Richmond Art Ctr, Calif; Univ Mo, BJ; also with leading ceramists in country. Teaching: Instr ceramics, Sarratt Crafts Ctr, Vanderbilt Univ, 77; instr clay, Metrop Pub Sch, Davidson Co, 77. Pos: Crafts res & educ coordr, Tenn Arts Coun, 77- Mem: Am Crafts Coun; Tenn Artists-Craftsmen's Asn (student vpres, 76, regional vpres, 77); Cumberland Valley Artist-Craftsmen's Asn (pres, 78); Gualala Arts, Calif; Int Guild Craft Journalists, Authors & Photogr. Style & Technique: Hand built & wheel thrown clayworks and architectural commissions. Publ: Auth, Kai Walters: eccelesiastical fibers, 77, A tribute: Mary Frances Davidson, 78 & Jimmie Benedict, 78, Fiberarts; auth, Jan Havens: a profile, Ceramics Mo, (in press). Mailing Add: 1244 Mary Helen Dr Nashville TN 37220

PINARDI, ENRICO VITTORIO
SCULPTOR, PAINTER
b Cambridge, Mass, Feb 11, 34. Study: Apprentice with Pelligrini & Cascieri, five yrs; Boston Archit Ctr; Sch Mus Fine Arts, Boston; Mass Col Art, BS(educ); RI Sch Design, MFA. Work: Worcester Art Mus, De Cordova Mus, Lincoln & Boston Inst Contemp Art, Mass; Chase Manhattan Bank, New York. Exhib: New England Art Part IV Sculpture, 64 & Surrealism, 70, De Cordova Mus; 21 Sculptors & Painters, Boston Univ, 64; New England Art Today, Northeastern Univ, 65; 10 Sculptors, Nashua, NH, 68. Teaching: Instr sculpture, Worcester Art Mus Sch, 63-67; assoc prof, RI Col, 74. Media: Wood. Dealer: Sidney Kanegis Gallery 244 Newbury Boston MA 02116. Mailing Add: 87 Child Hyde Park MA 02136

PINCKNEY, STANLEY
PAINTER, TAPESTRY ARTIST
b Boston, Mass, Sept 30, 40. Study: Famous Artist Sch, Westport, Conn, 57-61; Mus Sch Fine Arts, Boston, Mass. Work: Nat Ctr African-Am Art, Roxbury, Mass; Mus Dynamique, Dakar, Senegal, W Africa; Palace de l'Pres, Dakar. Comn: Jewelry (one necklace, two bracelets), comn by Ellen Mayer, Concord, Mass, 72; wood sculpture, Ester Anderson, Boston Mus Fine Arts, 74; tapestry (45in x 72in), Cortland Bennett, Mus Sch Fine Arts, Boston, 75; tapestry (45in x 80in), comn by Harold Pinckney, Lynn, Mass, 76. Exhib: Pinckney & Hagins, Rose Art Mus, Brandeis Univ, Waltham, Mass, 69, Concourse Gallery, 72 & New Boston City Hall, 72; Arts-Contemp of Senegal, Mus Dynamique, Dakar, 70 & Univ Stockholm, Sweden, 70; Osubamba, Boston Ctr for the Arts, 76 & Cyclorama Gallery, Boston, 76; A Century of the Mus Sch, Boston Mus Fine Arts, 77; New Beginnings, Master Artists-in-Residency, New Boston City Hall, 77. Collections Arranged: Twelve Black Artists, Rose Art Mus, Brandeis Univ, 69; Osubamba (auth, catalogue), Boston Ctr for the Arts, 76 & Cyclorama Gallery, Boston, 76; A Century of the Museum School (auth, catalogue), Boston Mus Fine Arts, 77. Teaching: Instr African & traditional arts, Mus Sch Fine Art, Boston, 72- Pos: Mem, African-Am Artists-in-Residency Prog, Northeastern Univ, Boston, 77- Awards: 19th Albert H Whitin Fel, Ann Traveling Fel Competition, Boston Mus Fine Arts, 69; Ford Found Fac Enrichment-Artist Grant, Mus Sch Fine Art, 78. Bibliog: Kay Bourne (auth), Textile designs, Bay State Banner, 75; Dick Sauer (auth), Commentary-art, Craft Horizons, 76; article in Boston Mus Fine Arts Centennial Catalogue, 76. Style & Technique: Tapestries, monumental watercolors. Collection: Traditional African art, sculpture and musical instruments, jewelry. Mailing Add: c/o Designs Unlimited 832 Parker St Boston MA 02119

PINCUS-WITTEN, ROBERT A
ART HISTORIAN, WRITER
b New York, NY, Apr 5, 35. Study: Cooper Union, Emil Schweinburg grant, 56; Univ Chicago, dept fel, 56-63, MA & PhD; Univ Paris exchange fel, Sorbonne, 63-64. Teaching: Prof art hist, Queens Col, City Univ of New York; prof art hist, Grad Ctr, City Univ NY. Pos: Assoc ed, Arts Mag. Res: Symbolism; the history of contemporary art. Publ: Auth, Les Salons de la Rose/Croix, Picadilly Gallery (London), 68; auth, Against order: poetical sources of chance art, In: Against Order, Chance and Art, Inst Contemp Art, Univ Pa, 70; auth, Occult Symbolism in France, Garland Press, New York, 76; auth, On target—symbolist roots of American abstraction, Arts Mag, 4/76; auth, Post-Minimalism—American Art of the Decade, London Press, New York, 77; auth, The Seventies, A View of a Decade, 1967-1977, Mus of Contemp Art, Chicago, 77; auth, The Furniture Paradigm, Improbable Furniture, Inst of Contemp Art, Philadelphia, 77. Mailing Add: Dept of Art Queens Col Flushing NY 11367

PINDELL, HOWARDENA DOREEN
PAINTER, CURATOR
b Philadelphia, PA, Apr 14, 43. Study: Boston Univ Sch Fine & Applied Arts, BFA, 65; Cumminton Sch Arts, 63; Sch Art & Archit, Yale Univ, MFA, 67. Work: Mus Modern Art, New York; Fogg Art Mus, Harvard Univ; Whitney Mus Am Art, New York; Roy R Neuberger Mus, Purchase, NY; Chase Manhattan Bank, New York & Tokyo. Exhib: Young Am Artists, Mus Mod Art, Stockholm & five European Mus, 73; New Am Graphic Art, Fogg Art Mus, Cambridge, Mass, 73; Painting & Sculpture Today, Indianapolis Mus, Ind & Taft Mus, Cincinnati, 74; Five Americans in Paris, Gerald Piltzer Gallery, Paris, 75; 9th Paris Biennale, Mus Mod Art, Paris, 75; H Pindell: Video Drawings, Sonja Heine Onstad Found, Oslo, Norway, 76; Vassar Col Art Gallery, 77. Collections Arranged: Pop Art Prints, Drawings and Multiples, 70, California Prints, 72 & tour, 73, Projects: Chuck Close and Liliana Porter, 73, Published in Germany (co-dir), 74, Printed, Cut, Folded and Torn, 74, Felix Vallotton (co-dir), 74, Points of View, 75, Projects: John Walker, 75, Projects: Mary Miss and Charles Simonds, 76, Narrative Prints, 76 & Abstraction-Creation, 77, Mus Mod Art, New York. Pos: Exhib asst, Mus Mod Art, New York, 67-69, cur asst, 69-71 & asst cur, prints & illus books, 71-77, assoc cur, 77- Awards: Painting Award, Nat Endowment for Arts, 72-73. Bibliog: Gordon Hazlett (auth), California, Arts Mag, 10/74; Marina Urbach (auth), Paris Biennale, 9th catalog, Paris, 9/75; Françoise Eliet, Five Americans in Paris, Art Press, Paris, 4/75; Carter Radcliff (auth), The paint thickens, Artforum, summer 76. Style & Technique: Works on paper using numbers, grids or points of color. Media: Paper, Pen & Ink; Canvas, Acrylic. Res: 20th Century prints. Publ: Auth, Mary Quinn Sullivan, Notable American Women, Harvard Univ, 72; auth, California Prints, Arts Mag, New York, 5/72; auth, Ed Ruscha: Words, Print Collectors Newsletter, 1/73; auth, Robert Rauschenberg: Link, Mus Mod Art, 10/75; auth, Alan Shields: Tales of Brave Ulysses, 1/75 & Artists' Periodicals: Alternative Space, 9/77, Print Collector's Newsletter. Mailing Add: 322 Seventh Ave New York NY 10001

PINEDA, MARIANNA (MARIANNA PINEDA TOVISH)
SCULPTOR
b Evanston, Ill, May 10, 25. Study: Cranbrook Acad Art, 42, with Carl Milles; Bennington Col, 42-43, with Moselsio; Univ Calif, Berkeley, 43-45, with R Puccinelli; Columbia Univ, 45-46, with Maldarelli; also with Ossip Zadkene, Paris, 49-50. Work: Walker Art Ctr, Minneapolis; Mus Fine Arts, Boston; Munson-Williams-Proctor Inst, Utica, NY; Addison Gallery Am Art, Andover, Mass; Radcliffe Col, Mass. Comn: Medallion for Jan Veen Mem Libr, Boston Conserv Music; Mem relief, Newton Col, Mass; bronze group for East Boston Housing Proj. Exhib: Metrop Mus Art, New York, 51; Whitney Mus Am Art Ann, New York, 54-59; Minneapolis Art Inst, 54; DeCordova Mus, Mass, 54, 63, 64, 66 & 72; Denver Art Mus, 55; Univ Ill, 57; Mus of the Legion of Honor, San Francisco, 57; Art Inst Chicago, 57 & 61; Inst of Contemp Art, Boston, 58; Boston Mus of Fine Arts, 60; Carnegie Inst Int, Pittsburgh, 60; Mus Mod Art, New York, 60; Dallas Mus of Fine Arts, 61; Los Angeles Co Mus, 76. Teaching: Instr sculpture, Boston Col, 75- Awards: Mather Prize for sculpture, Art Inst Chicago, 57; Grand Prize, Boston Arts Festival, 60; Radcliffe Inst Independent Study Scholar, 62-64. Mem: Artists Equity Asn; Sculptors Guild; Boston Visual Artists Union. Style & Technique: Figure is used as symbol. Media: All Sculpture Media; Drawing. Publ: Contrib & illusr, Art in Am, 2/55 & Audience Mag, winter 60. Dealer: Alpha Gallery 121 Newbury St Boston MA 02116. Mailing Add: 164 Rawson Rd Brookline MA 02146

PINES, NED L
COLLECTOR
b Malden, Mass, Dec 10, 05. Collection: Modern art. Mailing Add: 355 Lexington Ave New York NY 10017

PINKERTON, CLAYTON (DAVID)
PAINTER
b San Francisco, Calif, Mar 6, 31. Study: Calif Col Arts & Crafts, BAEd & MFA; Harwood Found, Univ NMex. Work: De Young Mus & Calif Palace Legion of Honor, San Francisco; Ill Bell Tel, Chicago. Exhib: Recent Paintings USA: The Figure, Mus Mod Art, New York, 63; one-man shows, San Francisco Mus Art, Calif, 67, Esther Robles Gallery, Los Angeles, 68 & Arleigh Gallery, San Francisco, 70; Contemp Am Painting & Sculpture, Univ Ill, 67 & 69; Human Concern, Whitney Mus Am Art, New York; Three Centuries of American Painting, Calif Palace Legion of Honor, 71; First Soap Box Derby, San Francisco Mus Art, 75. Teaching: Prof fine arts, Calif Col Arts & Crafts, 60-; dir col internship prog, Richmond Art Ctr. Awards: Fulbright Scholar, 57-58; James Phelan Award, 57 & 61. Bibliog: Joan Mondale (auth), Politics in art, Lerner, 77. Mailing Add: PO Box 97 Point Sta Richmond CA 94807

PINKNEY, HELEN LOUISE
ART ADMINISTRATOR, ART HISTORIAN
b Decatur, Ill. Study: Dayton Art Inst Sch, grad. Collections Arranged: The Camera, the Paper and I, collection of photographs by Jane Reece, 52; The Wonderful World of Photography, Jane Reece Mem Exhib, 63; Oriental & Europ Textiles Exhib, 72; Am Indian Textiles & Baskets, 73. Pos: Registr of collections, Dayton Art Inst, 36-45, cur, 45-59, librn, 45-, assoc cur textiles, 59- Mem: Am Asn Mus; Spec Libr Asn, Mus Div. Res: Extensive research on Jane Reece Photographic Collection; general research as curator on collections, including textiles; bibliographic research as librarian for museum and school. Publ: Auth, articles and catalogues on Jane Reece Collection in Dayton Art Inst Bulletin, 52 & 63. Mailing Add: 37 Stoddard Ave Dayton OH 45405

PINKOWSKI, EMILY JOAN
PAINTER
b Chicago, Ill. Study: Mundelein Col, scholar; Univ Chicago, PhB; Am Acad Art, com art cert. Johnson & Johnson Co; work comn by City of Chicago for publ of The New Chicago Plan, Dept Planning & Develop. Exhib: Butler Inst Am Art, Youngstown, Ohio, 69-72; New Horizons in Art, Ill Competition, Chicago, 70-75; Women '71, Northern Ill Univ, DeKalb, 71; Chicago & Vicinity Show, Art Inst Chicago, 73; 27th Ill Exhib, Ill State Mus, Springfield, 74; Painting & Sculpture Today, Indianapolis Mus of Art, 76. Awards: Second Prize, New Horizons in Art, Ill Competition, North Shore Art League, 71; Second Prize, Styka Show, Am Coun Polish Cult Clubs, 71; Borg-Warner Purchase Award, 72; $1000 Arthur A Baer Mem Award, Beverly Art Ctr, Ill, 77. Mem: Deerfield Sculpture Garden (mem, Deerfield Bicentennial Sculpture Comt, 76-); Artemisia Gallery (charter mem); Womens' Coop Gallery; Chicago Artists Coalition; San Francisco Womens Art Ctr. Style & Technique: Handpainting and/or airbrush in acrylics on canvas or hand-shaped wood. Mailing Add: 3085 Blackthorn Rd Riverwoods IL 60015

PINSKY, ALFRED
PAINTER, EDUCATOR
b Montreal, PQ, Mar 31, 21. Study: Montreal Mus Fine Arts; also with Anne Savage. Exhib: Can Soc Graphic Art; Can Group Painters; Montreal Mus Fine Arts. Teaching: Prof fine arts, Concordia Univ, currently. Pos: Former chmn dept fine arts, Sir George Williams Univ; auth, critical rev of exhibs, CBC, Montreal. Awards: Montreal Mus Fine Arts Scholar, 38-39. Mailing Add: Dept Fine Arts Concordia Univ Montreal PQ H3G 1M8 Can

PINTO, ANGELO RAPHAEL
PAINTER, ETCHER
b Casal Velino, Italy, Sept 27, 08; US citizen. Study: Pa Mus & Sch of Indust Arts, Philadelphia; Barnes Found, Merion, Pa, with scholars to study & paint in Europe, 31, 32, 33. Work: Barnes Found; Acad Fine Arts, Philadelphia; Metrop Mus Art, New York Publ Libr, New York; Libr of Cong, Washington, DC. Comn: Ballets & costumes, Philadelphia Ballet Co, 37. Exhib: One-man shows, Bignou Gallery, Paris, France, 33, Valentine Gallery, New York, 34, Mellon Galleries, Philadelphia, 35, Makler Gallery, Philadelphia, 60, Medici II Gallery, Miami, Fla, 70 & 74. Teaching: Fac mem of Barnes Found, 35- Awards: First Prize American Painters, Four Arts Club, Miami Beach, 38; Hon Mention, Print Club, Philadelphia. Bibliog: Helen McCloy (auth), Art of Pinto Brothers, Parnassus, 35. Mem: Art Alliance, Philadelphia; United Scenic Artists, New York. Dealer: Medici Gallery 1052 Kane Concourse Bay Harbor Islands FL 33154; Makler Gallery 1716 Locust St Philadelphia PA 19103. Mailing Add: 28 W 69th St New York NY 10023

PINTO, BIAGIO
PAINTER
b Philadelphia, Pa, Oct 6, 11. Study: Graphic Sketch Club, Philadelphia; Sch Indust Arts, Philadelphia; Barnes Found, Merion, Pa; also study in Italy & France. Work: Barnes Found; Dallas Contemp Mus Art, Tex; Pa Acad Fine Arts, Philadelphia; Mus Art, Eugene, Ore; Philadelphia Mus Art. Comn: Posters, USAF, Washington, DC, 43 & Pa Opera Co, Philadelphia, 73. Exhib: Whitney Mus Art, New York; Chicago Art Inst; Del Art Mus, Wilmington; Mus of Mod Art, Miami, Fla; Metrop Mus, New York, NY; Tweed Mus, Duluth, Minn; William Penn Mem Mus, Harrisburg, Pa; Lakeview Ctr for the Arts & Sci, Peoria, Ill; Allentown Mus, Pa; Pa Acad Fine Arts; Corcoran Gallery Art, Washington, DC; Detroit Inst Art, Mich; also one-man shows in Philadelphia, New York & Paris. Teaching: Instr painting, Philadelphia Col Art, 62-72 & Main Line Ctr Art, Haverford, Pa, 64-72. Awards: European Fels, Albert C Barnes Found, 31 & 32; John A Lee Cult Award, City of Philadelphia, 62; Philadelphia Sketch Club Medal. Bibliog: Albert C Barnes (auth), The Art in Painting, Harcourt Brace, 37; Valerie Seward (auth), Art as I see it, Lancaster Mag, 57; Irine Patai (auth), Encounters, Life of Jacques Lipchitz, Funk & Wagnalls, 61. Mem: Artists Equity Asn (dir, Philadelphia Chap, 65-66); Friends of Barnes Found; Philadelphia Art Alliance (juror, 66-72); Fla Artists Group; Philadelphia Print Club. Media: Oil. Publ: Illusr, Town & Country, New York, Harper's Bazaar, New York & Holiday Mag, New York. Dealer: Benjamin Mangel Gallery 202 Bala Ave Bala-Cynwyd PA 19004. Mailing Add: 1645 S Gulf Blvd Manasota Key Englewood FL 33533

PINTO, JAMES
PAINTER, SCULPTOR
b Bijelina, Yugoslavia, Apr 24, 07; US citizen. Study: Univ Zagreb, Yugoslavia; Chouinard Art Inst, Los Angeles; mural painting with David Alfaro Siqueiros; also with Jean Charlot. Work: Witte Mem Mus, San Antonio, Tex; Mus Contemp Art, Belgrad, Yugoslavia; Berg Art Ctr, Concordia Col, Moorehead, Minn; Mala Umetnicka Galeria, Sarajevo, Yugoslavia; Univ Art Gallery, Univ NMex, Albuquerque; Kresge Found, Detroit, Mich; Hirshhorn Collection;

plus numerous others. Comn: Co-worker with Rico Lebrun on Genesis Mural, Pomona Col, Calif, 60; outdoor sculpture mural, Nell Fernandez Harris, San Miguel, 68; indoor mural, Hotel Inst Allende, 70. Exhib: American Painting Today, Metrop Mus Art, New York, 52; 15th Ann Contemp Art, Art Inst Chicago, 55; Instituto Nacional Bellas Artes, Mexico City, 58; 62nd Ann Western Artists, Denver Art Mus, 62; 1st Anual de Escultura, Museo Arte Moderno, 71-72; Nat Acad of Sci, Washington, DC, 76. Teaching: Dean fac, Inst Allende, 50- Awards: First Prize, 1st Nat Vet Exhib, Santa Monica, Calif, 47; First Prize, Nat Univ Mex & US Embassy, Mexico City, 49; Purchase Prize, Life-Day Exhib Contemp Art, Fargo NDak, 57. Bibliog: Felipe Cossio del Pomar (auth), Critica de arte de baudelaire a malraux, Fondo de Cultura Economica, 56; Brooks (auth), Painting and Understanding of Abstract Art, 64 & Baldwin (auth), Contemporary Sculpture Techniques, 67, Reinhold. Media: Acrylic, Bronze. Dealer: Galeria de Arte Misrachi, Genova 20 Mexico DF. Mailing Add: Apdo Postal 12 San Miguel de Allende Gto Mexico

PINZARRONE, PAUL
PAINTER
b Grand Rapids, Mich, Nov 19, 51. Study: Univ Ill, BFA(painting), 73. Work: Butler Inst Am Art, Youngstown, Ohio; Ill State Mus, Springfield; Kemper Ins Co, Chicago; Schiss, Hardin & Waite, Chicago; Union League, Chicago. Exhib: 13th Midwest Biennial, Joslyn Mus, Omaha, Nebr, 74; New Horizons in Art, Chicago, 75; 28th Ill Exhib, Springfield, 75; 39th & 40th Midyear Exhibs, Butler Inst, 75 & 76; Mainstreams 75-, Marietta Int, Ohio, 75. Teaching: Instr art, Rock Valley Col, Rockford, Ill, 75-76, Rockford Col, 76 & Rock Valley Col, 78. Awards: Purchase Prize, Container Corp Am, 73; First Prize, New Orleans Int, 75; First Prize, Ill State Fair Prof, 75. Style & Technique: Spray-paint on reverse of acrylic sheet. Dealer: Art Independent Gallery Lake Geneva WI; Gloria Luria Gallery Miami FL. Mailing Add: 103 Paris Ave Rockford IL 61107

PIRKL, JAMES JOSEPH
DESIGNER, EDUCATOR
b Nyack, NY, Dec 27, 30. Study: Pratt Inst, cert adv design, 51 & BID, 58; Wayne State Univ; Syracuse Univ. Teaching: Instr, Ctr for Creative Studies, Detroit, Mich, 63-65; asst prof indust design, dept of design, Syracuse Univ, 65-68, assoc prof, 69-73 & prof, 74- Pos: Jr designer, General Motors Design staff, 58-59, designer, 59-60, sr designer, 61-64 & asst chief designer, 64-65; principal, James J Pirkl/Design, Cazenovia, NY, 65- Mem: Indust Designers Soc Am (mem bd dirs, 77-, vchmn, Cent NY Chap, 75-76 & chmn, 77-); Human Factors Soc; Am Asn Univ Prof. Publ: Co-ed, State of the Art and Science of Design, 71. Mailing Add: Meadow Hill Rd Cazenovia NY 13035

PISANI, JOSEPH
DESIGNER, PAINTER
b New Rochelle, NY, Oct 1, 38. Study: San Francisco Art Inst; Calif Col Arts & Crafts, with George Post, Richard Diebenkorn, Nathan Oliveira & Ralph Borge, BFA. Work: Dept of Defense, The Pentagon, Arlington, Va; Calif Col Arts & Crafts Gallery, Oakland; Hq Dept of the Army, Pentagon. Comn: Mondovi Tomb, Caesar Mondavi Family, St Helina, Calif, 62; History of the Army Mural, Gen Lenard, The Pentagon, 62; General Marshall Mem Corridor, Secy of the Army, Pentagon, 75; Army Bicentennial Murals, Secy of Defense, 75-76; Gen Pershing mural, Gen Yerks, Ft Myer, Va, 77-78. Exhib: Armu Wide Art Exhib, The Pentagon, 63, 65; Corcoran Washington Area Show, 69; Artist Equity Group Shows, Washington, DC, 72, 73; Va Beach Art Shows, 73, 75. Pos: Chief graphic arts, Chief of Staff (Personnel), Pentagon, 67-73, graphic designer, Dept of Defense, 73-75, US Army art dir, Hq, 75- Awards: Outstanding Achievement in Art, Bank of Am, 61; Scholar to Study Fine Arts, Scholastic Mag, 62; First Prize for Painting, Art League of Va, 70; plus many other awards. Bibliog: Article in Washingtonian, 1/73. Mem: Art League of Va; League of Reston Artist; Art Guild of Woodbridge, Va. Style & Technique: Personal expressive realism. Media: Watercolor; Printmaking. Publ: Illusr, ARFICA, 69; illusr, The Executive, 70; illusr, Joint Munitions Effectiveness Manual, 74; illusr, The Pentagon, 75; plus others. Dealer: The Artist Studio 718 Pine St Herndon VA 22070; T T Nieh 3147 Juniper Lane Falls Church VA 22044. Mailing Add: 2658 Quincy Adams Dr Herndon VA 22070

PISANO, RONALD GEORGE
ART HISTORIAN, CURATOR
b New York, NY, Dec 19, 48. Study: Adelphi Univ, Garden City, NY, BA; Univ Del. Collections Arranged: Students of William Merritt Chase for the Heckscher Mus & the Parrish Art Mus; Intimate Realists, Baruch Col, City Univ New York; Ethel Paxson: Paintings & Drawings of Brazil, 1916-1920, Marbella Gallery, New York; Reynolds Beal, Hammer Galleries, New York; G Ruger Donoho, The Parrish Art Mus & Hirschl & Adler Galleries, New York; The Art of the Director: Eva Gatling, The Mus at Stony Brook; William Merritt Chase, A Benefit Exhib for the Parrish Art Mus, M Knoedler & Co, New York. Pos: Dir exhib, Baruch Col, New York, 74-76; consult cur of Am art, Heckscher Mus, Huntington, NY, 75-77; guest cur, Mus of Stony Brook, NY, 77; assoc cur, Parrish Art Mus, Southampton, NY, 77. Awards: A Conger Goodyear Award, Adelphi Univ, 71; Stebbins Family Res Grant, Heckscher Mus, 72-73. Mem: Col Art Asn. Res: Late 19th and early 20th century American art; William Merritt Chase; artists of Long Island. Publ: Auth, The teaching career of William Merritt Chase, Am Artist, 76; auth, William Merritt Chase, Am Art Rev, 76; auth, O Brisil Visto Por Ethel Paxson de 1916 a 1921, US Info Serv, 77; auth, Catalog of the Heckscher Museum, Part I: American Art, Heckscher Mus, 78. Mailing Add: 353 Riverside Dr 4-A New York NY 10025

PITCHER, JOHN CHARLES
PAINTER
b Kalamazoo, Mich, Aug 6, 49. Work: Anchorage Hist & Fine Arts Mus, Alaska. Exhib: Charles & Emma Frye Art Mus, Seattle, Wash, 75; Artique Ltd Fine Art Gallery, Anchorage, Alaska, 76 & 77; Cooper Ornithological Soc, Idaho State Univ, Pocatello, 77; Nat Audubon Western Regional Conf, Asilomar, Calif, 78. Bibliog: Richard T Appleton (auth), John Pitcher Seeks Perfection, Alaska Mag, 10/74. Style & Technique: Representational, painting birds & flora; opaque dry brush technique. Media: Watercolor; Gouache; Etching. Collection: Four series of limited edition lithographic reproduction wildlife (bird) prints. Dealer: Artique Ltd Fine Art Gallery 314 G St Anchorage AK 99503. Mailing Add: 2839 Teleguana Anchorage AK 99503

PITZ, MOLLY WOOD
PAINTER
b Ambler, Pa, May 12, 13. Study: Philadelphia Mus Sch Indust Art. Work: Pa State Univ; also in pvt collections. Exhib: Philadelphia Watercolor Club, 39-45 & 63; Woodmere Art Gallery, 43-46 & 48-52; William Jeanes Mem Libr, 48-55 & 59-69; Philadelphia Mus Col Art, 59; Philadelphia Art Alliance, 65; plus others. Awards: Hartford Found Fel, 64. Mem: Philadelphia Art Alliance; Philadelphia Watercolor Club; Bryn Mawr Art Ctr, Art Teachers Workshop; Allen Lane Art Ctr; Philadelphia Mus Sch Art Alumni Asn. Mailing Add: 3 Cornelia Pl Philadelphia PA 19118

PIZITZ, SILVIA
COLLECTOR, PATRON
b Birmingham, Ala. Study: Painting with George Elmer Browne, Europe; Cornell Univ; Columbia Univ; Nat Acad Sch Fine Arts; Grand Cent Art Sch; Univ Munich & Art Sch. Collections Arranged: New York Painter (assembled, arranged & cataloged), Marlborough Gallery, 67. Pos: Assoc chmn, Cornell Friends of Mus. Interest: Started collections at New York University and University of Alabama in Birmingham; made donations to Museum of Modern Art, New York, New York University, Cornell University, New York and Birmingham Museum of Art, Alabama. Collection: Neoplastic, constructivist, minimal. Mailing Add: 45 E 72nd St New York NY 10021

PLACE, BRADLEY EUGENE
EDUCATOR
b Rule, Tex, Nov 4, 20. Study: Tex A&M Univ, 38-40; NTex Univ, with Carlos Merida & Ivan Johnson, BS, 42. Teaching: From asst prof to prof lettering & typography, Univ Tulsa, 47-68, chmn dept art, 64- Pos: Consult & art dir community develop proj, Int US Jr CofC; mem art selection comt, Bank of Okla & Williams Co, Tulsa; mem, Mayor's Art Comn, Tulsa; Mem gov link comt, Prison Art Prog, 70-; mem visual arts adv panel, Okla Arts & Humanities Coun, 72-; mem selection comt, Art for Pub Places, Tulsa, 75- Awards: Brad Trust Scholar, 73. Bibliog: Jenk Jones, Jr (auth), Honor roll for May, Tulsa Tribune, 71; Connie Cronley (auth), Profile of a teacher of artists, Tulsa, 6/14/73; Myrna Smart (auth), Dilemma of penal reform, Arts & Humanities Coun Tulsa & KTEW-TV, 5/74. Mem: Tulsa Advert Fedn; Tulsa Art Dir Club (exec bd, 70-75 & 77 pres, 74-75); Tulsa Arts & Humanities (mem bd, Chmn Mayor's Arts Comn, 77). Mailing Add: 2156 S Fulton Pl Tulsa OK 74114

PLACZEK, ADOLF KURT
ART LIBRARIAN, ART HISTORIAN
b Vienna, Austria, Mar 9, 13; US citizen. Study: Univ Vienna, 31-38; Inst of Art History, 34-38; Sch Libr Serv, Columbia Univ, 41-42. Teaching: Adj prof archit hist, Columbia Univ, 65- Pos: Asst librn, Avery Archit & Fine Arts Libr, Columbia Univ, 48-60, librn, 60- Mem: Soc Archit Hist (secy, 63-67, dir, 68-72, 2nd vpres, 74-76, 1st vpres, 76-78). Res: Eighteenth century European and nineteenth century American architecture. Publ: Ed, Avery Index to Architectural Periodicals, 63 & Catalog of the Avery Architectural Library, 68, G K Hall Press; contribr, Palladio, The Four Books of Architecture, Dover Press, 65; co-auth, Piranesi, Drawings & Etchings, Sackler Found, 75; contribr, Hitchcock, American Architectural Books, DaCapo Press, 76. Mailing Add: 176 W 87th St New York NY 10024

PLAGENS, PETER
PAINTER, EDUCATOR
b Dayton, Ohio, Mar 1, 41. Study: Univ Southern Calif, BFA, 62; Syracuse Univ, MFA, 64. Exhib: 24 Young Los Angeles Artists, Los Angeles Co Mus Art, 71; Continuing Abstraction, Whitney Mus, NY, 74; Betty Gold Gallery, Los Angeles, 74; John Doyle Gallery, Paris, 75; Nancy Hoffman Gallery, NY, 75; plus other group & solo shows, 63- Teaching: Assoc prof art, Calif State Univ, Northridge. Pos: Cur, Long Beach Mus, Calif, 65-66; assoc ed, Artforum. Style & Technique: Abstract. Publ: Ecology of evil, 12/72, Peter and the pressure cooker, 6/74 & None dare call it BoHo, 9/75, Artforum; Soft touch of hard edge, LAICA J, 4/75; Sunshine Muse: Contemporary Art on the West Coast, Praeger Publ, 75. Mailing Add: c/o Nancy Hoffman Gallery 429 W Broadway New York NY 10012

PLAMONDON, MARIUS GERALD
SCULPTOR, CRAFTSMAN
b Quebec, PQ, July 21, 19. Study: Ecoles Beaux-Arts, Quebec; also in France & Italy. Comn: Stone carvings, stained glass, numerous churches, univ bldgs, hotels & hosps. Exhib: Exhibited nationally & int. Pos: Pres, Ecoles Beaux Arts, Quebec; pres, Soc Sculptors Can, 59-61; vpres, Int Asn Plastic Arts, UNESCO. Awards: Scholar to Europe, 38-40; Royal Soc Fel, 55-56. Mem: Sculptors Soc Can; Stained Glass Asn Am; Royal Can Acad Arts. Mailing Add: 1871 Sheppard Ave Quebec PQ G1S 1L1 Can

PLATH, IONA
DESIGNER, WRITER
b Dodge Center, Minn, May 24, 07. Study: Westmoreland Col; Art Students League; Art Inst Chicago. Teaching: Instr art & design, 30-; instr handweaving, 65- Pos: Free lance designer, 47- Style & Technique: Creative weaving based on traditional techniques. Publ: Auth & illusr, Decorative Arts of Sweden, Scribner's, 48 & Dover, 65; auth & illusr, Hand Weaving, 64 & The Craft of Handweaving, 72, Scribner's. Mailing Add: 17 Mountain View Ave Woodstock NY 12498

PLATUS, LIBBY
FIBRE SCULPTOR, LECTURER
b Los Angeles, Calif. Study: Univ Calif, Los Angeles, BA. Comn: Fibre sculpture wall, Irvine Co's Big Canyon Country Club, Newport Beach, Calif; fibre sculpture ceiling environment, Holiday Inn Airport Lakes, Miami; fibre sculpture wall hangings, McCulloch Properties, Silver Lakes Resort Hotel, Victorville, Calif, Sheraton Nat Hotel, Arlington, Va, Security Pac Bank, South Pasadena, Calif, Blue Cross of Southern Calif, Woodland Hills, Calif & Discovery Bay, Hawaii; plus others. Exhib: Richmond Designer Craftsmen, Calif, 71; Calif Crafts VIII, E B Crocker Gallery, 73; Laguna Beach Mus Art, 73; Riverside Art Ctr, Calif, 74; Calif State Univ, Fullerton, 74; Calif Design 76, Los Angeles, 76; Fiberworks Int Exhib, Cleveland Mus of Art; plus others. Teaching: Guest speaker archit fibre sculpture, Handweaver's Guild Am, Pittsburgh, 76; leader workshop archit fibre sculpture, Carnegie-Mellon Univ, 76; guest lectr, Honolulu Acad of Art, 77; guest panelist, Art/Archit Handweaver's Guild of Am Colo Conf, 78; leader workshop marketing fiber art, Colo State Univ, 78; lectr, Arrowmont, Tenn, 78; lectr, Am Crafts Coun SE Region Conf, Berea, Ky, 78; lectr, Am Soc Interior Designers, 78; US deleg, World Craft Conf, Kyoto, Japan, 78. Awards: Winner, Tex Christian Univ Nat Invitational Competition for Fiberwork Comn. Bibliog: Dona Z Meilach (auth), Soft Sculpture, Crown, 74; article in Craft Horizons, 12/74; Ellen Appel (auth), An Introduction to Fiber Art, Childton, 78; plus others. Mem: Am Crafts Coun; Artists Equity; Calif Design; Handweaver's Guild Am; Southern Calif Designer-Crafts. Media: Fibres, Leather. Publ: Contribr, Shuttle, Spindle & Dyepot, fall 75 & spring 77. Mailing Add: 1359 Holmby Ave Los Angeles CA 90024

PLAUT, JAMES S
ART ADMINISTRATOR, WRITER
b Cincinnati, Ohio, Feb 1, 12. Study: Harvard Univ, AB, 33, AM, 35. Collections Arranged: In charge of all exhib planning, US Pavilion, Brussels World's Fair, 58, New York World's Fair, 64, Montreal, 67 & Osaka, 70; First World Crafts Exhib, Ont Sci Ctr, Toronto, 74. Teaching: Lectr hist art, Harvard Univ, 34-35, 37-38; lectr hist art, New Eng Conserv Music, 38-39. Pos: Asst cur paintings, Mus Fine Arts, Boston, 35-39; dir, Inst Contemp Art, Boston, 39-56; vpres, Old Sturbridge Village, Mass, 59-62; secy gen, World Crafts Coun, 67-76; adv, NJ State Mus & Pac Northwest Arts Ctr; pres, Aid to Artisans Inc, 76-; planning consult,

New York Pub Libr, 76-; mem vis comt, Prog in Artisanry, Boston Univ, 75- Awards: Off, Royal Order St Olav, Norway, 50; Comdr, Royal Order of Leopold, Belg Govt, 58; hon DFA, Wheaton Col, 74. Mem: Art Vis Comt of Wheaton Col (chmn); MacDowell Colony; Coun Arts, Mass Inst Technol. Publ: Auth, Oskar Kokoschka, 48; auth, Steuben glass, 48, 51 & 72; auth, Assignment in Israel, 60; In Praise of Hands (with Octavio Paz), 74. Mailing Add: 64 Fairgreen Pl Chestnut Hill MA 02167

PLAVCAN, JOSEPH MICHAEL
PAINTER, SCULPTOR
b Braddock, Pa. Study: Pa Acad Fine Arts, cert; Univ Pittsburgh, MA; also with George Ericson & Daniel Garber. Work: Butler Inst Am Art, Youngstown, Ohio; IBM Corp, New York; Allstate Ins Collection Am Paintings, Chicago; Wayne State Univ; Gannon Learning Ctr, Erie, Pa. Comn: Mural, Church of the Nativity, Lorain, Ohio, 60; sculpture, Kennedy Mem, Erie Lyndora & Sharon, Pa, 68; sculpture, Bishop Gannon Mem, Sharon, Pa, 69; sculpture, Bishop McManaman Mem, Oil City, Pa, 69; decoration, St Barnabas House, Northeast, Pa, 75. Exhib: Carnegie Inst, Pittsburgh, 30; Corcoran Biennial, Washington, DC, 51; Pa Acad Fine Arts, 52; Nat Acad Design, 52; one-man show, Butler Inst Am Art, 75. Teaching: Instr art, pvt classes, 31-71; instr art, Sch Dist, City of Erie, Pa, 32-71; instr art, US Vet Admin, 46-60. Awards: Soc Washington Artists, 29, Corcoran Gallery Art, 31 & Butler Inst Am Art, 44. Style & Technique: Realism to hard edge semi-abstract with brilliant color developed in prismatic sequences. Media: Acrylic, Oil; Clay. Dealer: Capricorn Galleries 8004 Norfolk Ave Bethesda MD 20014. Mailing Add: 232 Gridley Ave Erie PA 16508

PLEASANTS, FREDERICK R
COLLECTOR, PATRON
b Upper Montclair, NJ, Nov 30, 06. Study: Princeton Univ, BS; Harvard Univ, MA. Teaching: Lectr, Ariz State Mus, 60-64. Pos: Cur, Brooklyn Mus, 50-58; cur, Ariz State Mus, 58-64. Res: Primitive art, problems of anthropology in relation to museums in America. Collection: Primitive art of Africa, Oceania and pre-Columbian America. Mailing Add: 2100 E Adams Tucson AZ 85719

PLEISSNER, OGDEN MINTON
PAINTER
b Brooklyn, NY, Apr 29, 05. Study: Brooklyn Friends Sch; Art Students League. Work: Metrop Mus Art, New York; Nat Collection Fine Arts, Washington, DC; Philadelphia Mus, Pa; Brooklyn Mus; Toledo Mus Art, Ohio. Exhib: Carnegie Inst Int, Pittsburgh; Art Inst Chicago; Nat Acad Design & Am Watercolor Soc, New York; American Art, Metrop Mus Art. Pos: Mem fine arts comn, Nat Collection Fine Arts; dir & trustee, Louis C Tiffany Found; trustee, Shelburne Mus. Awards: Joseph Pennell Medal, Philadelphia Watercolor Club, 54; Gold Medal, Am Watercolor Soc, 56; Altman Prize, Nat Acad Design, 59. Bibliog: Alexander Eliot (auth), American painting; Norman Kent (auth), articles in Am Artist. Mem: Nat Acad Design (vpres); Am Watercolor Soc; Century Asn; Philadelphia Watercolor Club; Royal Soc Arts. Dealer: Hirschl & Adler 21 E 67th St New York NY 10021. Mailing Add: Box 513 Manchester VT 05254

PLETCHER, GERRY
PAINTER, PRINTMAKER
b State College, Pa. Study: Edinboro State Col, BS(art educ); Pa State Univ, MA; also with Montenegro, Carol Summers, Harold Altman, Nelson Sandgren & Shobaken. Work: Evansville Mus Arts & Sci, Ind; Fisk Univ, Tenn; Jacksonville State Univ, Ala; Watkins Art Inst, Tenn Arts Comn, Tenn Botanical Gardens & Art Mus at Cheekwood, and others. Exhib: 31st Southeastern Competition & Exhib, Gallery Contemp Art, Winston-Salem, NC, 69; Cent South Art Exhib, Nashville, 69, 70 & 71; Graphics USA 1970, Nat Art Exhib, Dubuque, Iowa, 70; Ark Nat Art Exhib, Ark State Univ, 70; Nat Acad Design 145th Ann, New York, 70; plus others. Teaching: Instr printmaking, Univ Tenn, Nashville, 68- Awards: Graphics Purchase Award, 22nd Ann Mid-States Art Exhib, Evansville Mus Arts & Sci, 69; seven Purchase Prizes, Tenn Arts Comn, 72; Purchase Award, 13th Ann Tenn All-State, 73. Bibliog: Sweimal drei, Aufbau, 3/19/71; Artists USA, 1972-73; Am Printmakers, 74. Style & Technique: Free, powerful and timeless. Media: Etchings, Woodcuts, Acrylic, Oil. Dealer: Gallery III 122 Stadium Dr Hendersonville TN 37075. Mailing Add: 605 Brook Hollow Rd Nashville TN 37205

PLOCHMANN, CAROLYN GASSAN
PAINTER
b Toledo, Ohio, May 4, 26. Study: Toledo Mus Art Sch Design, 43-47; Univ Toledo, BA, 47; State Univ Iowa, MFA, 49; with Alfeo Faggi, 50; Southern Ill Univ, 51-52. Work: Selden Rodman Collection, Oakland, NJ; Evansville Mus Arts & Sci, Ind; Fleishmann Found Collection, Cincinnati, Ohio; Butler Inst Am Art, Youngstown, Ohio; plus others. Comn: Mural, North Side Old Nat Bank, Evansville, 53. Exhib: One-man shows, Witte Mus, San Antonio, Tex, 68 & Toledo Mus Art, 68; 164th Prints & Drawings Ann, Pa Acad Fine Arts, Philadelphia, 69; 52nd Ann Mem Exhib, Philadelphia Watercolor Club, 69; Woodstock Artists Asn 50th Ann, NY, 69. Teaching: Supvr art, Allyn Training Sch, Southern Ill Univ, Carbondale, 49-50. Awards: George W Stevens Fel, Toledo Mus Art, 47-49; Tupperware Art Fund First Award, 53; Emily Lowe Found Competition Award, 58. Bibliog: Louise Bruner (auth), Art notes, Toledo Blade, 10/10/65; Donald Key (auth), rev in Milwaukee J, 6/18/69. Mem: Silvermine Guild Artists; Woodstock Art Asn; Philadelphia Watercolor Club; Toledo Fedn Art Socs. Media: Oil, Acrylic, Graphics. Publ: Auth, University Portrait: Nine Paintings by Carolyn Gassan Plochmann, Southern Ill Univ Press, 59; auth, bk rev in The Egyptian; auth, cover article in Prize-winning graphics, 66. Dealer: Kennedy Galleries 40 W 57th St New York NY 10019. Mailing Add: Rte 1 Carbondale IL 62901

PLOUS, PHYLLIS
CURATOR
b Green Bay, Wis, Dec 13, 25. Study: Univ Wis, with Oskar Hagen & James Watrous, BA, 47; Univ London; Univ Calif, Santa Barbara. Collections Arranged: Ralph A Blakelock Retrospective (with catalog), 69; Charles Demuth Retrospective (with catalog), 71; Sculpture-20's & 30's (with catalog), 72; 19 Sculptors of the 40's (with catalog), 73; Five American Painters (with catalog), 74; Four from the East/Four from the West, 74. Pos: Asst to dir, Santa Barbara Mus Art, 54-55; asst to dir, Art Galleries, Univ Calif, Santa Barbara, 63-72, cur exhibs, 72- Mem: Col Art Asn Am. Mailing Add: 375 Toro Canyon Rd Carpinteria CA 93013

PLUMMER, JOHN H
ART ADMINISTRATOR, EDUCATOR
b Rochester, Minn, Dec 15, 19. Study: Carleton Col, AB; Columbia Univ, PhD. Teaching: Instr & lectr, Columbia Univ, instr, Barnard Col, 52-56, vis prof, Univ, 61; vis lectr, Harvd Univ, 63; adj prof, Columbia Univ, 64- Pos: Res assoc, Pierpont Morgan Libr, New York, 55-56, cur mediaeval & renaissance mss, 56-66, res fel for art, 66- Res: Mediaeval and modern art. Publ: Auth, Liturgical Manuscripts, 64 & The Glazier Collection of Illuminated manuscripts, 68, Pierpont Morgan; auth, The Hours of Catherine of Cleves, Pierpont Morgan, Boston Bk & Braziller, 66. Mailing Add: 453 N Western Hwy Blauvelt NY 10913

PLUNKETT, EDWARD MILTON
PAINTER, LECTURER
b Highland Park, Mich, Mar 13, 22. Study: Art Inst Chicago, BArt Educ, 46; Inst Fine Arts, NY Univ. Work: Metrop Mus Art, New York. Exhib: One-man show, David Herbert Gallery, New York, 59, Devorah Sherman Gallery, Chicago, 61, Baruch Col, 69, Graham Gallery, 71 & Hokin Gallery, Chicago, 75. Teaching: Lectr art hist, City Col New York, 54-66; lectr art hist, John Jay Col, 61-66. Mem: Col Art Asn Am; Artists Equity Asn. Style & Technique: Satirical illustrations and collages dealing with silent film period from 1910-1925. Media: Mixed Media, Acrylic, Collage. Mailing Add: 303 E 76th St New York NY 10021

PNEUMAN, MILDRED Y
PAINTER
b Oskaloosa, Iowa, Sept 15, 99. Study: Univ Colo, BA & BEd, 21 & MFA, 47. Work: Univ Colo Mus; Univ Colo Fac Club; PEO Mem Libr, Des Moines, Iowa. Exhib: Hoosier Salon Asn, Marshall Fields, Chicago, 28-40; Am Color Print Soc; Colo State Fairs, 65-68; Denver Metrop, 69; Northern Colo Exhibs, Boulder Art Asn, 70. Teaching: Instr art, Los Angeles Pub Schs, 21-23; instr art, Gary Pub Schs, 23-25. Pos: Mem bd, Boulder Pub Libr Art Gallery, 67-70. Awards: Tri Kappa Prizes, 35-36; Colo State Fair Awards, 44. Mem: Boulder Artists Guild (pres, 69-70); Boulder Art Asn; Rossmoor Art Asn (vpres, 74-75); Soc Western Artists. Style & Technique: Realist, special interest in mountain forms and clouds. Collection: 130 prints, woodcuts, lithographs, etchings, serigraphs and others, from the United States, Europe and Asia. Publ: Auth, A study of the mountain form in painting, Univ Colo, 47. Mailing Add: 1380 Running Springs Rd Apt 4 Walnut Creek CA 94595

PODUSKA, T F
LECTURER, PAINTER
b Cedar Falls, Iowa, Dec 6, 25. Study: Univ Northern Iowa, BA(art educ). Work: Denver Art Mus, Contemp Collection, Polumbus Corp, Amaco Security Life Bldg, Central Bank & Trust & Mountain Bell, Denver, Colo. Exhib: Am Watercolor Soc Ann, New York, 74-77; Colo Gov Mansion, 74; Spree 75, Colo; two-woman show, Amory Show, Golden, Colo, 75; Northeastern Jr Col, Sterling, 75; Mainstreams 76, Marietta, Ohio, 76; Nat Acad of Design, New York, NY, 77; Midwest Landscape Exhib, Lincoln, Nebr, 77; Brass Cheque Gallery, Denver, Colo, 77. Teaching: Bus skills workshops, 75. Pos: Juror, Southeastern Colo Regional Show, 73, Foothills Art Ctr, 73 & Gilpin Co Arts Asn, 75; lectr, consult & proj asst, Colo Coun Arts & Humanities, 73; trustee, Denver Art Mus, 77-78. Awards: Colo Governor's Award for Arts & Humanities, 77; Merit Award, Nat Acad of Design, 77. Mem: Denver Art Mus (exec bd vol, 2nd vpres, 75-76, pub rels chmn, 74-75); Artists Equity Asn (nat regional rep, 73-74, nat ed bd, 78); Greater Denver Coun Arts & Humanities (bd mem, 72-75); Am Asn Mus. Style & Technique: Space colorist; energy and force fundamental to paintings, producing a vastness and harmony in movement. Media: Water Media, Paper. Publ: Co-auth, Insuring the artist's work, Am Artist Bus Lett, suppl, 74; co-auth, Business Practices for Artists, Artists Equity Asn, 75. Mailing Add: 13587 W 22nd Pl Golden CO 80401

POGUE, STEPHANIE ELAINE
PRINTMAKER, EDUCATOR
b Shelby, NC, Sept 27, 44. Study: Howard Univ, Washington, DC, BFA; Cranbrook Acad of Art, Bloomfield Hills, Mich, MFA; also with Prof James A Porter, Mavis Pusey & George Baer. Work: Whitney Mus of Am Art, New York; Tenn Mus Collection, Nashville; Ark Art Ctr, Little Rock; Univ NDak, Grand Forks. Comn: Color etching (ed of 200), Studio 22, Inc, Chicago, 69; color etching (ed of 100), Studio Mus in Harlem, New York, 76; color etching (ed of 75; included in portfolio of several artists), The Printmaking Workshop, New York, 78. Exhib: One-person shows, Xavier Univ, New Orleans, 71, Va State Univ, Petersburg, 74, Ala A&M State Univ, Normal, 74 & Cinque Gallery, New York, 77; two-person shows, Pogue & Puryear, Fisk Univ, Nashville, 72, Hooks & Pogue, Ga Southern Univ, Statesboro, 76; 12th NDak Ann Nat Print & Drawing Exhib, Grand Forks, 67; 10th Nat Exhib of Prints & Drawings, Okla Art Ctr, Oklahoma City, 68; Nat Print Exhib, 37th Potsdam Festival of the Arts, State Univ NY, Potsdam, 68; Black Artists in Am, Whitney Mus of Am Art, New York, 71; Prof Artists for Young Artists, Metrop Mus of Art, New York, 75; 9th Ann Prints, Drawings & Crafts Exhib, Ark Art Ctr, Little Rock, 76; Tenn Bicentennial Art Exhib, Tenn Arts Comn, Tenn State Mus, Nashville, 76; Migraciones: Una Exhibicion de Artistas Graficos Afro-Americanos, El Museo de Arte Moderna la Tertulia, Cali, Colombia, 76. Teaching: Assoc prof graphics, Fisk Univ, 68- Awards: Purchase Award, 12th NDak Ann Nat Print & Drawing Exhib, Univ NDak, 67; Major Print Award, 8th Ann Prints, Drawings & Crafts Exhib, Ark Art Ctr, 75; Purchase Award, Tenn Bicentennial Art Exhib, Tenn State Mus, 76. Mem: Tenn Art League. Style & Technique: Semi-abstract landscapes and figurative compositions. Media: Color viscosity etching; intaglio. Mailing Add: 1809 Morena St Apt B3 Nashville TN 37208

POHL, LOUIS G
PAINTER, PRINTMAKER
b Cincinnati, Ohio, Sept 14, 15. Study: Cincinnati Art Acad. Work: Cincinnati Mus Asn; Honolulu Acad Art. Exhib: Butler Inst Am Art, 39 & 44; Art of Cincinnati, 40-42; one-man shows, Cincinnati Mus Asn, Contemp Art Ctr, 61 & Honolulu Acad Art; plus others. Teaching: Instr, Univ Hawaii, 53-56; instr, Honolulu Sch Art; instr drawing, painting & illus, Honolulu Acad Art. Pos: Cartoonist, daily cartoon School Daze, Honolulu Advertizer. Awards: Four prizes, Honolulu Acad Art, 47-57; McInerny Found Grant, 54-55; Printmaker of the Year, 65; plus others. Mem: Hawaii Painters & Sculptors League; Honolulu Printmakers. Mailing Add: 3507 Nuuanu Pali Dr Honolulu HI 96187

POINDEXTER, ELINOR FULLER
ART DEALER
b Montreal, Can; US citizen. Pos: Dir, Poindexter Gallery. Mem: Art Dealers Asn Am. Specialty: Contemporary painting and sculpture, especially American. Collection: Contemporary works. Mailing Add: 1160 Fifth Ave New York NY 10029

POINIER, ARTHUR BEST
CARTOONIST
b Oak Park, Ill, Feb 9, 11. Study: Ohio Wesleyan Univ, AB, LHD, 55; Drake Univ, 34. Pos: Sports cartoonist, Columbus Dispatch, Ohio, 29-32; cartoonist, Des Moines Register & Tribune, Iowa, 34-36; cartoonist comic strip, Jitter, 36-43; polit cartoonist, Detroit Free Press, 40-51 & Detroit News, 51-76; with Bell-McClure Syndicate & with United Features Syndicate, 50- Mem: Asn Am Ed Cartoonists (past pres). Mailing Add: 5470 Miller Rd Ann Arbor MI 48103

POLAN, LINCOLN M
COLLECTOR
b Wheeling, WVa, Feb 12, 09. Study: NY Univ; Univ Va; Ohio State Univ. Pos: Mem bd dirs, Huntington Galleries, WVa. Mem: Mus of Mod Art; Metrop Mus Art. Collection: Line and wash drawings by Rodin; drawings by French impressionists; American paintings, predominantly of the Ash Can School; Renaissance portraits of men; Renaissance prints and engravings. Collections exhibited at Huntington Galleries Art Museum, Charleston Art Gallery, University of West Virginia Art Museum, Museum of Fine Arts, Houston, Texas and Phoenix Art Museum, Arizona. Mailing Add: 2 Prospect Dr Huntington WV 25701

POLAN, NANCY MOORE
PAINTER
b Newark, Ohio. Study: Marshall Univ, AB; Huntington Galleries: Fletcher Martin, Hilton Leech, Paul Puzinas & Robert Friemark; Al Schmidt, Fla. Work: Huntington Galleries; OVAR Mus, Portugal. Exhib: Am Watercolor Soc, 61, 66, 72 & 74 & Framed Travel Exhib, 72-73; Nat Arts Club, New York, 62-78; Joan Miro Graphics, Barcelona, 70 & Travel Exhib, 70-71; 21st Contemp Art, La Scala, Florence, Italy, 71; one-woman show, New York World's Fair, 65; plus many other group & one-woman shows. Pos: Mem Art Comn Int Platform Asn, 68-75; hon vpres, Centro Studi e Scambi Internazionali, Rome, Italy, 78; fel, Intercontinental Biog Asn, 75. Awards: Ralph & Elizabeth C Norton Mem Award, 3rd Nat Jury Show Am Art, Chautauqua, NY, 60; Nat Arts Club Watercolor Award, Ann Artist Mem Exhib, 62, 63, 64 & 69; Bronze Medal, 71, Acad Laurel Medal & Dipl, 74 & Gold Medal, 76, Centro Studi e Scambi Internazionali, Rome, Italy. Mem: Nat Arts Club; assoc Allied Artists Am; Pen & Brush Soc; assoc Am Watercolor Soc; Am Fedn Arts; Acad Internazionali Leonardo da Vinci. Style & Technique: Oil and water media, realism and lineo impressionism, flowers and missiles. Media: Watercolor, Acrylic. Publ: Contribr, cover, La ReVue Moderne, 61 & 66; Talent Mag Int Platform Asn, 77; spec issue, WVa Hillbilly, 73. Mailing Add: 2 Prospect Dr Huntington WV 25701

POLESKIE, STEPHEN FRANCIS
PAINTER, PRINTMAKER
b Pringle, Pa, June 3, 38. Study: Wilkes Col, BA(econ), 59; New Sch Social Res, 61. Work: Whitney Mus Art, Metrop Mus Art & Mus Mod Art, New York; Walker Art Ctr, Minneapolis, Minn; Ft Worth Art Ctr, Tex. Comn: Seven ed silk-screen prints, Assoc Am Artists, 65-72; Seagansett-Patchogue (ed silk-screen prints), Int Graphic Arts Soc, 72. Exhib: Contemporary American Printmakers, S London Mus, Eng, 67; Word & Image-Posters and Typography (1879-1967), Mus Mod Art, New York, 68; Recent Acquisitions: Prints and Drawings, Metrop Mus Art, 69; Oversize Prints, Whitney Mus Am Art, 71; Primera Bienal Americana de Artes Graficas, Mus Tertulia, Carton Colombia, SAm, 71. Teaching: Assoc prof silk-screen & drawing, Cornell Univ, 68-; vis prof, Univ Calif, Berkeley, 76. Bibliog: Work reproduced in The Art of the Print, H Abrams, 76. Style & Technique: Have been using a Pitts special airplane built and flown by me to make smoke drawings in the sky. Dealer: Louis K Meisel Gallery 141 Prince St New York NY 10022; Smith-Andersen Gallery 200 Homer St Palo Alto CA 94301. Mailing Add: 306 Stone Quarry Rd Ithaca NY 14850

POLIMENAKOS, CARMON
ART ADMINISTRATOR
b Mo, June 27, 39. Study: Southwest Mo State Col, BS in Educ. Pos: Art dir, Mod Classics, New York, 72-76; cur-partner Valentino Galleries, New York, 73-76; consult-art importer, Novoexport, Moscow, 75-76; cur, Anat Mus & bus dir, Dept of Anat, Col of Med, Univ of Ill, Chicago, 76- Specialty: Contemporary works, painting, graphics, sculpture. Publ: Contribr med illustrations, Lowen Zaneveld (auth), endocrinology text, Little & Brown Co. Mailing Add: 1630 W Estes No 304 Chicago IL 60626

POLK, FRANK FREDRICK
SCULPTOR
b Louisville, Ky, Sept 1, 08. Study: With Hughlette Wheeler, George Phippen & J R Williams. Work: Colorado Springs Fine Arts Ctr; John Ascuaga's Nuggett, Sparks, Nev & pvt collection Ezra Brooks. Exhib: Cowboy Artists Am Ann Show, Cowboy Hall Fame, Oklahoma City, 68-72 & Phoenix Art Mus, Ariz, 73-75; Matthews traveling exhib to eastern mus & galleries, including the Kennedy Gallery, New York, 71. Awards: Golden Spur Award, Bronze, Nat Rodeo Cowboy's Asn, 68; Silver Medal, George Phippen Mem Ann Art Show, Prescott, Ariz, 76. Bibliog: Anne Grose (auth), Cowpoke sculptor, Quarter Horse J, 1/68; Patricia Broder (auth), Bronzes of the American West, Abrams, 74; Ten Years with the Cowboy Artists of America, Northland Press, 76. Mem: Cowboy Artists Am. Style & Technique: Precise authenticity and detail of cowboy art from 1918 to the present day western life. Dealer: Texas Trails Gallery 247 S Broadway San Antonio TX 78205; Linda McAdoo Gallery 7155 Main St Scottsdale AZ 85251. Mailing Add: Box 126 Mayer AZ 86333

POLLACK, PETER
PHOTOGRAPHER, WRITER
b Wing, NDak, Mar 21, 11. Study: Art Inst Chicago; Inst Design, Chicago. Work: (Photographs) Art Inst Chicago; Worcester Art Mus; Whitney Mus Am Art. Pos: Cur photog, Art Inst Chicago, 45-57; dir, Am Fedn Arts, 62-64; hon cur photog, Worcester Art Mus, 64-; dir art, W J Sloane, New York, 65-70; dir photog, Harry N Abrams, Inc, 70-; ed, series of facsimile editions publ by Amphoto Press, 71- Publ: Auth, Understanding Primitive Art (Sula's Zoo), 68; auth, The Picture History of Photography, rev ed, 70. Mailing Add: 1001 Bayou Pl Sarasota FL 33579

POLLACK, REGINALD MURRAY
PAINTER, WRITER
b Middle Village, NY, July 29, 24. Study: Apprentice to Moses Soyer, 41; study with Wallace Harrison, 46-47; Acad Grande Chaumiere, Paris, 48-52. Work: Whitney Mus Am Art & Mus Mod Art, New York; Brooklyn Mus, NY; Collection de l'Etat, France; Tel Aviv Mus, Jerusalem Mus & Haifa Mus, Israel; plus many other pub & pvt collections. Comn: Peace (greeting card), Jewish Mus, New York, 61; painting for Great Thoughts of Western Man series, Container Corp Am, 64; cover for State of NY Dir, Bell Tel Co, 68-69; Chinese animal destiny calendar, Colgate-Palmolive Co, 72; Jacob's Dream (103 ft painting), Washington Cathedral, 74. Exhib: 35 one-man shows, 12 at Peridot Gallery, New York, 49-69 & Hall Gallery, Miami Beach, 72; Mixed Emotions, Long Beach Mus, Calif, 69; The Artist Collects, Lytton Art Ctr, Los Angeles, 69; plus many other group shows. Teaching: Vis critic art, Yale Univ, 62-63; instr art, Cooper Union, 63-64; staff mem, Human Rels Training Ctr, Univ Calif, Los Angeles, at Lake Arrowhead, 66; pvt art classes, 67-69; instr, Quaker Half-Way House, Los Angeles, 68. Awards: Prix Othon Friesz-V, Paris, 56; Prix des Peintres Etrangers - Laureate, Paris, 58; Ingram-Merrill Found Grants in painting, 64 & 70-71. Style & Technique: Transcendental idea, human condition symbolic with religious motifs; sometimes deeply introspective and psychological in approach, with Baroque styling; classically trained in the French tradition and feels the base of everything is in the spontaneity, the drawing and the traces of the human touch. Media: Laser light, oil and multimedia. Publ: Auth & illusr, The Magician and the Child, Atheneum, 71; illusr, Ctr for Dem Insts Mag, 3/72; auth, To artists with love & Brancusi's sculpture versus his home, Art News; illusr, Sounds Freedomring, Martin, Holt-Rinehart & Winston; illusr, Ted Knight (auth), Oedipus, 73. Mailing Add: 205 River Bend Rd Great Falls VA 22066

POLLAK, THERESA
EDUCATOR, PAINTER
b Richmond, Va, Aug 13, 99. Study: Richmond Art Club; Westhampton Col, Univ Richmond, BS; Art Students League; Fogg Mus, Harvard Univ, Carnegie fel; Steiger Paint Group, Edgartown, Mass; with Hans Hofmann, Provincetown, Mass; Univ Richmond, hon DFA, 73. Work: Va Commonwealth Univ, Richmond; Va Mus Fine Arts, Richmond; Chrysler Mus Norfolk, Va; Univ Va, Charlottesville; Washington & Lee Univ, Lexington, Va. Exhib: 12th Biennial Exhib Contemp Am Painting, Corcoran Gallery Art, Washington, DC, 30; 1st Biennial Contemp Am Painting, Whitney Mus Am Art, New York, 32; New Eng Soc Contemp Art, Boston Mus Fine Arts, 33; Oakland Art Gallery, Calif, 41, 42 & 43; Butler Art Inst, Youngstown, Ohio, 47; Univ Ga, 58; Fredericksburg Gallery of Mod Art, 64; 20th Century Gallery, Williamsburg, Va, 64; 19th Irene Leache Mem Regional Painting Exhib, Chrysler Mus Norfolk, 68; Virginia Artists 1971, Va Mus Fine Arts, Richmond, 71; one-person show, Scott-McKennis Fine Art, Richmond, Va, 77. Teaching: Instr drawing & painting, Va Commonwealth Univ, 28-35, prof drawing & painting, 35-69, emer prof, 69-, fac chmn, 42-50; instr drawing & painting, Westhampton Col, Univ Richmond, 30-35. Awards: Cert Distinction, Va Mus Fine Arts, 71; Theresa Pollak Bldg of Fine Arts, Va Commonwealth Univ, 71; First Laureate Award, preeminent in art, Va Cult Laureate Ctr, 77. Mem: Richmond Artists Asn; Art Students League; Va Mus Fine Arts; Valentine Mus, Richmond. Style & Technique: Semi-abstract expressionist direction; free handling of media, but with strong underlying formal structure. Media: Oil; Miscellaneous Media. Publ: Contribr, art criticisms in Richmond Newsleader & Richmond Times Dispatch, 31-49; auth, An Art School-Some Reminiscences, Va Commonwealth Univ, 69. Mailing Add: 3912 Stuart Ave Richmond VA 23221

POLLAND, DONALD JACK
SCULPTOR
b Los Angeles, Calif, May 24, 32. Work: Whitney Gallery Western Art, Buffalo Bill Hist Ctr, Cody, Wyo; C M Russell Mus, Great Falls, Mont; Favell Mus Western Art & Artifacts, Klamath Falls, Ore; Mont Hist Soc Mus, Helena. Comn: Three Am Indian sculptures & three cowboy sculptures, Lance Corp, Boston, 74; four western sculptures, Am Express Corp, 75. Exhib: Three-man show, Troy's Cowboy Art Gallery, Scottsdale, Ariz, 72; retrospective, R W Norton Mus, Shreveport, La, 74; C M Russell Mus, Great Falls, Mont, 71; Rancho Calif Art Show, Temecula, 72; George Phippen Mem Art Exhib, Prescott, Ariz, 75. Pos: Art dir, Control Dynamics, North Hollywood, Calif, 62-63; free lance illusr, Space Age Indust, 64-68. Awards: Best of Show & Second Place in Sculpture, Rancho Calif Art Comt, 72; Gold Medal for First Place in Sculpture, George Phippen Mem Art Show, 75. Bibliog: R W Norton (auth), The Old West in Miniature, R W Norton Art Found, 74; Patricia J Broder (auth), Bronzes of the American West, Harry N Abrams, Inc, 75; Fielding L Greaves (auth), Old West in Miniature, Southwest Art Mag, 75. Mem: George Phippen Mem Art Found (co-founder & vpres). Style & Technique: Classical realism in a miniature scale of wildlife and American western historical subjects; wax modeling for lost-wax metal sculpture. Mailing Add: PO Box 609 Prescott AZ 86301

POLLARD, DONALD PENCE
DESIGNER, PAINTER
b Bronxville, NY, Sept 13, 24. Study: Pvt study with Harriet Lumis; RI Sch Design, BFA; Brown Univ. Work: Eisenhower Mus; Kennedy Collection; Govt of Can, Ottawa, Ont; also in pvt collections in the US, Europe, Asia & the Far East. Comn: Design of the Great Ring of Canada (with Alexander Seidel); other comns as assigned by Steuben Glass. Exhib: Conn Nat Acad, 42; all major Steuben Exhibs, 53-; Phillips Mall Ann, 72. Pos: Sr designer, Steuben Glass, 50- Media: Crystal, Oil. Mailing Add: Steuben Glass 715 Fifth Ave New York NY 10022

POLLARO, PAUL
PAINTER
b Brooklyn, NY. Study: Flatiron Sch Art, New York; Art Students League. Work: Finch Col Mus; Notre Dame Univ; Manhattanville Col; Wagner Col; MacDowell Colony Collection, Peterborough, NH. Exhib: 159th Ann, Pa Acad Fine Arts, Philadelphia, 64; Am Acad Arts & Lett, 66 & 72; Nat Inst Arts & Lett, 69 & 72, Artists of the 20th Century, Gallery Mod Art, 70 & Artists at Work, Finch Col Mus, 71, New York. Teaching: Instr painting, New Sch Social Res, 64-69; asst prof painting, Wagner Col, 69-76; vis artist, Notre Dame Univ, summers 65 & 67. Awards: Second Prize, Jersey City Mus, 62; MacDowell Colony Fels, 66, 68 & 71; Tiffany Found Grant, 67. Mailing Add: c/o Babcock Galleries 805 Madison Ave New York NY 10021

POLLOCK, MERLIN F
PAINTER
b Manitowoc, Wis, Jan 3, 05. Study: Art Inst Chicago, BFA & MFA; Ecole Beaux Arts, Paris; Sch Fine Arts, Fontainebleau, France. Work: Syracuse Univ; Munson-Williams-Proctor Inst, Utica; Everson Mus, Syracuse; State Univ NY Col Environ Sci & Forestry, Syracuse. Comn: Steel (fresco), Tildon Tech High Sch, Chicago; mural, O'Fallon Ill Post Off, comn by US Treas Dept. Exhib: Flint Mich Inst Art, 57; Wesleyan Univ, Lincoln, Nebr, 58; Rocky Mountain Nat Art Exhib, Utah State Univ, Logan, 58; 125 Years of New York State Painting & Sculpture, NY State Fair, 66; one-man shows, Mich State Univ, East Lansing, 59, Everson Mus, Syracuse, 66, Lubin House, New York, NY, 70 & Lowe Art Ctr, Syracuse Univ, 71. Teaching: Instr mural painting, fresco & drawing, Art Inst Chicago, 35-43; prof painting, Syracuse Univ, 46-71. Pos: Supvr mural painting, Ill Art Proj, Works Proj Admin, 40-43; chmn grad prog, Sch Art, Syracuse Univ, 47-71, actg dean, Sch Art, 60-61, 67-68 & 69-70. Awards: James Nelson Raymond Fel, Art Inst Chicago, 30; Syracuse Ann, Everson Mus, 50, 60, 64 & 66; Finger Lakes Ann, Rochester Mem Mus, 56-58 & 60. Media: Acrylic, Watercolor, Oil, Fresco. Mailing Add: 120 Wellwood Dr Fayetteville NY 13066

POLONSKY, ARTHUR
PAINTER, EDUCATOR
b Lynn, Mass, June 6, 25. Study: Boston Mus Sch, with Karl Zerbe, 43-48, dipl (with highest honors), 48; Europ traveling fel, 48-50. Work: Fogg Mus, Harvard Univ, Cambridge; Mus Fine Arts, Boston; Addison Gallery Am Art, Andover; Brandeis Univ, Waltham; Stedelijk Mus, Amsterdam, Holland. Comn: Portrait of Dr William Dameshek, Tufts-New Eng Med Ctr, Boston, 66; Stone with the Angel (portfolio of ten original lithographs), Impressions Workshop, Inc, Boston, 69; portrait of Dr Sidney Farber, Harvard Med Sch for Boston Children's Hosp, 71. Exhib: Salon des Jeunes Peintres, Paris, 49; Art Today-50, Metrop Mus Art, New York, 50; Exhib Am Art, Stedelijk Mus, Amsterdam, Holland, 50; Carnegie Inst Int Expos, Pittsburgh, 51; Chateau des Rohans, Strasbourg, 58; eleven one-man exhibs in

Boston, New York & Washington, 51-75. Teaching: Instr painting, Boston Mus Sch, 50-60; asst prof painting, drawing & design, Brandeis Univ, 54-65; assoc prof painting, drawing & design, Boston Univ, Sch for the Arts, 65- Pos: Founding mem & dir, Artists' Equity Asn, 48-67; mem, Boston Visual Artists' Union, 73- Awards: Tiffany Found Grant for painting, 51-52; First Prize, Boston Arts Festival, 54; Purchase Award, Drawings '74, Wheaton Nat Exhib, Wheaton Col, 74. Bibliog: Article on young artists in Life Mag, 12/48; reviews of exhibs in Art News, Arts Mag, New York Times, Time Mag, New Yorker Mag & others, 48-65; microfilm records of papers, letters, reviews and tape recorded interviews in Archives Am Art, Smithsonian Inst, 72. Dealer: Shore Gallery 8 Newbury St Boston MA 02116; Mickelson Gallery 707 G St NW Washington DC 20001. Mailing Add: 364 Cabot St Newtonville MA 02160

POLSKY, CYNTHIA
ARTIST, ART ADMINISTRATOR
b New York, NY, Feb 16, 39. Study: Art Students League; New Sch Social Res; Marymount Manhattan Col, BA. Work: Corcoran Gallery Am Art, Washington, DC; Israel Mus, Jerusalem; Allentown Art Mus, Pa; Ulrich Mus of Art, Wichita, Kans; Fogg Art Mus, Cambridge, Mass; Guild Hall, East Hampton, NY; American Embassy, London, Eng. Exhib: One-woman shows, Benson Gallery, Bridgehampton, Long Island, NY, 68, Comara Gallery, Los Angeles, 69, Artisan Gallery, Houston, Tex, 70, Palm Springs Desert Mus, 72-73 & Crispo Gallery, New York, 73 & 74; Watercolor Exhib, Comara Gallery, 72; Ulrich Mus of Art, Wichita, Kans, 77. Pos: Artist-in-residence, St Mary's Col, St Mary's City, Md, 74; gov, Brooklyn Mus, NY; trustee, Storm King Art Ctr, Mountainville, NY. Bibliog: Judith Denham (auth), article in Art Week, 73; Alfred Frankenstein (auth), article in San Francisco Chronicle, 73. Style & Technique: Color abstraction. Media: Acrylic, Watercolor. Dealer: Andrew Crispo Gallery 41 E 57th St New York NY 10022. Mailing Add: 50 E 79th St New York NY 10021

POLZER, JOSEPH
ART HISTORIAN
b Vienna, Austria, May 7, 29; US citizen. Study: Univ Iowa, BA(art), 50, MA(art hist), 52; Inst Fine Arts, NY Univ, PhD(art hist), 63. Teaching: Instr, Univ Kans, 57-58; lectr, Univ Buffalo, 58-62, from asst prof to prof, Univ Louisville, 62-73; prof art & head dept, Queen's Univ, Kinston, 73- Res: Late Rome, Renaissance. Publ: Auth, articles in Late Antique & Renaissance Art. Mailing Add: Dept of Art Queen's Univ Kingston ON Can

POMERANTZ, LOUIS
ART CONSERVATOR, LECTURER
b Brooklyn, NY, Sept 26, 19. Study: Art Students League; Acad Julian; Rijksmuseum, Amsterdam, Holland, with H H Mertens; Worcester Art Mus, with G Stout; Brooklyn Mus, with C & S Keck; Cent Lab of Belg Mus. Collections Arranged: Know What You See, Univ Chicago, Ill Arts Coun, 70-72 & Found of the Am Inst for Conserv, Smithsonian Inst, 76-79; Learning to See, Univ Iowa Mus Art, 77. Pos: Conservator, Dept of Paintings & Sculpture, Art Inst of Chicago, 56-61; consult conserv, Milwaukee Art Ctr, Wis, 58-76, Nat Gallery of Can, Ottawa, Ont, 61, George F Harding Mus, Chicago, 65-68, Iowa Mus of Art, Iowa City, 73- & StateHist Soc of Iowa, 73-74; vol, Comt to Rescue Italian Art, 66; consult, UN Develop Prog in Israel, Israel Mus, Jerusalem, UNESCO, 68, Mus Contemp Art, Chicago, 76, Minn Hist Soc, 76 & SITES, Smithsonian Inst, Washington, DC, 77. Mem: Fel Int Inst for Conserv of Hist & Artistic Works; fel Am Inst for Conserv; Int Inst for Conserv-Am Group (founding mem; secy-treas, 59-61; treas, 62-63; vchmn, 64-65; chmn, 66-68); Am Asn Mus; Midwest Mus Conf. Publ: Auth, Is Your Contemporary Painting More Temporary Than You Think?, Int Bk Co, 62; auth, Know What You See—The Examination of Paintings by Photo-Optical Techniques, Univ Chicago & Ill Arts Coun, 70; auth, Preventive Care of Paintings: What to Do About It, Midwest Mus Conf, 71; co-auth, Conservators advise artists, Col Art Asn J, 77; contribr, Mus News, Bull of Am Group & Am Inst for Conserv Bull. Mailing Add: 1424 Elinor Pl Evanston IL 60201

POMEROY, JAMES CALWELL, JR
PERFORMANCE ARTIST, SCULPTOR
b Reading, Pa, Mar 21, 45. Study: Univ Mont; Univ Tex, Austin, BFA, 68; Ariz State Univ; Univ Calif, Berkeley, MFA, 72. Work: Univ Calif Art Mus, Berkeley; Mildura Art Ctr, Australia. Comn: Edition of Unique Binders, Soc Encouragement Comtemp Art, San Francisco Mus Mod Art, 73; Lightweight Phantoms (stereoscopic installation), The Exploratorium, San Francisco, 76. Exhib: The Metal Experience, Oakland Mus, Calif, 71; Young Bay Area Sculptors, San Francisco Art Mus, 71; Bay Area Underground, Univ Calif Art Mus, Berkeley, 72; W Coast 72, E B Crocker Art Gallery, Sacramento, 72; Contemp Am Painting & Sculpture 1974, Krannert Art Mus, Univ Ill, Champaign, 74; Visual Verbal, Univ Calif Art Galleries, Santa Barbara, 75; DFW/SFO Exchange, Ft Worth Art Mus & San Francisco Mus Mod Art, 75-76; Biennial of Sydney, Gallery of New S Wales, Australia, 76. Collections Arranged: Rushmore—Another Look (auth, catalog), San Francisco Art Inst, 76; 77-78 SFAI Annual (auth, catalog), Ft Mason, San Francisco, 77; Country Muse and other performances and exhibitions, 80 Langton St, San Francisco, 75- Teaching: Lectr painting, drawing, design & photog, Calif State Univ, San Jose, 74-76, lectr painting & drawing, Sacramento, 75 & lectr interdisiplinary art, San Francisco, 75. Pos: Mem artists comt, San Francisco Art Inst, 72-, trustee, 75-77, vchmn artists comt, 76-77, chmn sculpture, 77-; mem, 80 Langton St, San Francisco, 75-, vpres, 75-76; artist-in-residence, Exploratorium, San Francisco, 76-77. Awards: Eisner Prize, Univ Calif, Berkeley, 71; Nat Endowment for Arts Visual Arts Fel, 75. Bibliog: Cecile McCann (auth), Pomeroy, Remsing: Form-process, Artweek, 6/74; David Clark (auth), Jim Pomeroy's visual & musical structures, Artweek, 5/75; Carter Ratcliff (auth), Report from San Francisco, Art in Am, 5/77. Media: Performance, stereo photog, mechanical music, rubber stamps and text works. Res: Stereography, 75-77; comprehensive survey of Mt Rushmore, 76, and alternative spaces, 77-78. Specialty: A nonprofit, nonstatic oriented space for performance and exhibition. Publ: Contribr, Wordworks II, Jessica Jacobs, San Jose, 75; contribr, Work, Steve Davis, San Francisco, 75; contribr, Art for binary vision, and/or, Seattle, 77. Dealer: Hansen-Fuller 228 Grant St San Francisco CA 94108. Mailing Add: PO Box 6145 San Francisco CA 94101

PONCE DE LEON, MICHAEL
PRINTMAKER, PAINTER
b Miami, Fla, July 4, 22. Study: Univ Mex, BA; Art Students League; Nat Acad Design; Brooklyn Mus Art Sch; also in Europe. Work: Mus Mod Art & Metrop Mus Art, New York; Nat Gallery Art & Smithsonian Inst, Washington, DC; Brooklyn Mus; plus others. Comn: Many print editions, 60-; ten prints, US State Dept, 66; glass sculpture, Steuben Glass, 71. Exhib: Mus Arte Mod, Paris; Victoria & Albert Mus, London; Venice Bienale, 70; Mus Mod Art & Metrop Mus, New York; Smithsonian Inst, Washington, DC; plus others. Teaching: Instr printmaking, Hunter Col, 59-66; prof, NY Univ, 77 & Pratt Inst, 78; instr printmaking, Art Students League, 78- Pos: Int Cult Exchange, US State Dept, teaching, lect & travel, Yugoslavia, 65, India & Pakistan, 67-68 & Spain, 71. Awards: More than 60 medals & awards, incl Tiffany Found Grants, 54 & 55; Fulbright Grants, 56 & 57; Guggenheim Found Grant, 67. Bibliog: J Ross & C Romano (auth), The Complete Printmaker, Macmillan, 72; J Heller (auth), Prints, Holt, 72; G Peterdi (auth), Printmaking, Macmillan, 72; F Eichenberg (auth), The Art of the Print, Abrams, 77; D Saff, Printmaking History and Process, Holt, Rinehart & Winston, 78. Mem: Soc Am Graphic Artists (treas, 68); Asn Am Univ Prof. Style & Technique: Avant garde metal-collage-intaglio consisting of metal Shapes & objects, inked, fitted and printed on one-inch handmade paper, by a hydraulic press. Publ: Contribr, Experiments in three dimensions, Art in Am, 68; auth, The collage intaglio, 72; The collage-intaglios of Michael Ponce de Leon, Am Artist, 8/74. Dealer: Jane Haslem Gallery 2121 P St NW Washington DC 20036. Mailing Add: 463 West St New York NY 10014

POND, CLAYTON
PAINTER, PRINTMAKER
b Long Island, NY, June 10, 41. Study: Carnegie Inst Technol, BFA, 64; Pratt Inst, MFA, 66. Work: Nat Collection Fine Arts, Washington, DC; Mus Mod Art, New York; Boston Mus Fine Arts; Philadelphia Mus Art; Art Inst Chicago. Exhib: Whitney Mus Am Art Ann, New York, 67; one-man exhibs, paintings, Martha Jackson Gallery, New York, 68 & 72 & paintings & prints, De Cordova Mus, Lincoln, Mass, 72; Int Exhib Colored Graphics, Mus Mod Art, Paris, 70; US Pavilion, Osaka World's Fair, 70; New Am Prints (traveling exhib), US Info Agency, Vienna, 71; City Mus & Art Gallery, Hong Kong, 72; 23rd Libr Cong Exhib, Nat Collection Fine Arts, Smithsonian Inst, 73; plus others. Teaching: Instr photog & printmaking, C W Post Col, Long Island Univ, 66-68; adj instr serigraphy, Sch Visual Arts, New York, 68-70; guest lectr, Univ Wis-Madison, spring 72. Awards: State Dept Grant, Smithsonian Inst Int Art Prog & Abby Gray Found, 67; Boston Mus Purchase Award, Boston Printmakers 20th Ann, 68; Color Print USA Purchase Award, WTex Mus, 69; plus others. Bibliog: Richard S Field (auth), Silkscreen, the media medium, Art News Mag, 1/72; Jules Heller (auth), Printmaking Today, Holt, Rinehart & Winston, 72; Marshall B Davidson (auth), Artists' America, Am Heritage, 73. Mem: Am Color Print Soc; Print Coun Am; Boston Printmakers; Philadelphia Print Club. Dealer: Martha Jackson Gallery 521 W 57th St New York NY 10019. Mailing Add: 130 Greene St New York NY 10012

POOL, NELDA LEE
ART APPRAISER, ART DEALER
b Gorman, Tex, July 3, 41. Study: Tarleton State Col, AA, 61; N Tex State Univ, BFA, 63; Tex Tech Univ, Lubbock, grad study, 65 & San Miguel de Allende Art Inst, Mex, 65. Work: Delgado Mus of Art, New Orleans, La; El Paso Mus of Art, Tex. Comn: Portrait of late Sam Jones, Supt Rising Star Pub Sch, comn by Student Coun, 66; designed terrazo marble floors, Sweetwater High Sch, Tex, comn by Balfour Co, 67 & Student Ctr, Tarleton State Univ, Stephenville, Tex, comn by Student Coun, 68. Exhib: Artist of SE in Tex, Delgado Mus of Art, New Orleans, La, 64; Tex Fine Arts Asn Travelling Exhib, 64-67; Int Designer/Craftsmen Exhib, El Paso Mus, Tex, 65; Tex Watercolor Soc Exhib, Elizabeth Ney Mus, San Antonio, Tex, 67. Collections Arranged: President Carter's Inaugural Reception Exhibition, The Capitol, Washington, DC, 77. Teaching: Chairperson art dept, Ector High Sch, Odessa, Tex, 63-68. Pos: Partner, Pandoras, 68-69 & owner-operator, Nelda Lee's Painting & Jewelry, Odessa, 69- Awards: First Place/Sculpture, Artist of the SE in Tex, Delgado Mus of Art, 64; First Place/Design, Int Designer/Craftsmen Exhib, 65; First Place/Mixed-Media, Tex Fine Arts Exhib, 65. Bibliog: Rita Darden (auth), Young Odessan becomes fine arts appraiser, Odessa Am, 11/72; Helen Callaway (auth), Warm glimpses of a vanishing America, SW Scene Mag, 72; Scheryl Vannoy (auth), Texas art dealer stages exhibition at Capitol, San Angelo Standard Times, 77. Mem: Am Soc of Appraisers; Nat Soc of Lit & Arts. Specialty: Eighteenth—twentieth century English and American masters. Publ: Auth, History of Art in Odessa, Texas, Permian Basin Hist Ann, 69; co-auth, Painter of a vanishing America, SW Art, 74. Mailing Add: 2610 E 21st St PO Box 6385 Odessa TX 79762

POOLE, RICHARD ELLIOTT
PAINTER, INSTRUCTOR
b Pasadena, Calif, Feb 26, 31. Study: Otis Art Inst, Calif State Univ, Los Angeles, BA, MA(painting), 58. Exhib: Nat Watercolor Soc Ann, Los Angeles Art Mus, San Francisco De Young Mus & San Francisco Palace of Legion of Honor, 64-73; US Embassy Sweden Invitational, 72; 5th Ann Watercolor West, 73; one-man shows, Heritage Gallery, Los Angeles, 70, 71 & 73 & Mittwoch Gallery, Bonn, Ger, 74, plus others. Teaching: Instr painting & drawing, Pasadena City Schs, 60- Awards: Uecker Award, Ann Pasadena Art Mus, 63; Katharine Steale Dan Award, Pasadena Art Mus, 64. Mem: Los Angeles Art Asn; Nat Watercolor Soc. Style & Technique: Landscapes and figurative paintings. Media: Oil, Watercolor, Acrylic. Dealer: Heritage Gallery 667 N La Cienega Blvd Los Angeles CA 90069; Mittwoch Galerie 53 Bonn Busch Strasse 61 Germany. Mailing Add: 1211 Beverwil Dr Los Angeles CA 90035

POONS, LARRY
PAINTER
b Tokyo, Japan, Oct 1, 37. Study: Boston Mus Fine Arts Sch, 58. Work: Mus Mod Art; Albright-Knox Art Gallery; Stedelijk Mus, Holland; Woodward Found, Washington, DC. Exhib: Art Inst Chicago, 66; Corcoran Gallery Art, 67; Carnegie Inst, 67; Documenta IV, Kassel, Ger, 68; Whitney Mus Am Art Ann, 68 & 72 & Whitney Biennial, 73; Albright-Knox Art Gallery, Buffalo, NY, 68 & 70; Pasadena Art Mus, Calif, 69; plus many others. Teaching: Vis fac, NY Studio Sch, 67. Bibliog: Lawrence Alloway (auth), Systemic Painting, Guggenheim Mus, 66; Gregory Battcock (ed), Minimal Art: A Critical Anthology, Dutton, 68; E C Goosen (auth), The Art of the Real USA 1948-1968, Mus Mod Art, 68; plus others. Publ: Auth, The Structure of Color, 71. Dealer: M Knoedler & Co Inc 21 E 70th St New York NY 10021. Mailing Add: 831 Broadway New York NY 10003

POOR, ANNE
PAINTER
b New York, NY, Jan 2, 18. Study: Bennington Col; Art Students League, with Alexander Brook, William Zorach & Yasuo Kuniyoshi; Acad Julian, Paris, painting with Jean Lurcat & Abraham Rattner; also asst for in fresco to Henry Varnum Poor. Work: Whitney Mus Am Art; Brooklyn Mus; Art Inst Chicago; Wichita Mus; Des Moines Art Ctr. Comn: Murals, Pub Works Admin, 37; murals in true fresco, comn by Nathaniel Saltonstall, Wellfleet, Mass, 51-52, Skowhegan Sch Painting & Sculpture, 54, South Solon Free Meeting House, Maine, 57 & Mr & Mrs Robert Graham, Stamford, Conn, 58. Exhib: Artists for Victory, Metrop Mus Art, 42; Am Brit Art Ctr, New York, 44, 45 & 48; Maynard Walker Gallery, New York, 50; five shows, Graham Gallery, New York, 57-71; plus others. Teaching: Mem fac painting & dir, Skowhegan Sch Painting & Sculpture, 47-61, gov & trustee, 63- Awards: Edwin Austin Abbey Mem Fel for Mural Painting, 48 & First Prize for Landscape Painting, 70, Nat Acad Design; Nat Inst Arts & Lett Grant in Art, 57. Bibliog: Alan Gussow (auth), A sense of place, Friends of Earth, Sat Rev Press, 72. Mem: Artists Equity Asn. Media: Oil, Watercolor. Publ: Illusr, Greece, Viking Press, 64. Dealer: Graham Gallery 1014 Madison Ave New York NY 10021. Mailing Add: 92 S Mountain Rd New York NY 10956

POOR, ROBERT JOHN
ART HISTORIAN
b Rockport, Ill, July 10, 31. Study: Boston Univ, BA, 53 & MA, 57; Univ Chicago, with Ludwig Bachhofer, PhD(art hist), 61. Collections Arranged: Art of India (exhib catalog), 69 & Far Eastern Art in Minnesota Collections (exhib catalog), 70, Univ Minn Gallery; Hanga, The Modern Japanese Print (exhib catalog), Minn Mus Art, St Paul, 72. Teaching: Asst prof Asian art, Dartmouth Col, 61-65; assoc prof Asian art, Univ Minn, Minneapolis, 65- Pos: Consult Asian art, Minneapolis Inst Art; cur Asian art, Minn Mus Art, St Paul. Res: Chinese bronzes. Publ: Auth, Notes on the Sung archaeological catalogs, 65 & auth, Some remarkable examples of I-Hsing ware, 66-67, Arch of Chinese Art Soc Am; auth, Ancient Chinese Bronzes, Inter-Cult Arts Press, 68; auth, Evolution of a secular vesseltype, 68 & On the Mo-tzu-Yu, 70, Oriental Art. Mailing Add: Dept Art Hist Univ Minn Minneapolis MN 55455

POPE, ANNEMARIE HENLE
ART ADMINISTRATOR
b Dortmund, Ger; US citizen. Study: Heidelberg Univ, PhD, 32; Radcliffe Col, Harvard Univ, exchange fel, 33-34. Pos: Asst dir, Portland Art Mus, Ore, 41-42; dir in charge exhibs, Am Fedn Arts, 47-51; chief traveling exhibs, Smithsonian Inst, 51-64; pres, Int Exhibs Found, 65- Awards: Royal Swedish Order of Polar Star, 57; Chevalier des Arts et des Lettres; Order of Merit, First Class, Ger, 64. Mem: Am Asn Mus; Washington Friends of Am Mus Bath, Eng (chmn); Am Fedn Arts; Master Drawings Asn; Drawing Soc; plus others. Publ: Auth, acknowledgments for catalogues publ by Int Exhibs Found in connection with traveling exhibs. Mailing Add: Int Exhibs Found 1729 H St NW Washington DC 20006

POPE, JOHN ALEXANDER
HISTORIAN, MUSEUM DIRECTOR
b Detroit, Mich, Aug 4, 06. Study: Yale Col, BA, 30; Harvard Univ, MA, 40, PhD, 55. Teaching: Lectr Chinese art, Columbia Univ, 41-43; res prof Oriental art, Univ Mich, 62-71; lectr, US, Europe & Far East. Pos: Assoc in res, Freer Gallery Art, Washington, DC, 43-46, asst dir, 46-62, dir, 62-71, dir emer, 71- Mem: Am Oriental Soc; Oriental Ceramic Soc, London; Asn Asian Studies; Asia Soc; Japan Soc. Publ: Auth, Fourteenth century blue & white: a group of Chinese porcelains in the Topkapu Sarayi Müzesi, Istanbul, Freer Gallery Art Occasional Papers, Vol 2, No 1; auth, Chinese porcelains from the Ardebil Shrine, Freer Gallery Art, 56; sr co-auth, Freer Chinese bronzes, Freer Gallery Art Oriental Studies, Vol 1, No 7; contribr, Harvard J Asiatic Studies; co-auth, Porcelains in the Frick Collection, New York, 74; plus others, including contributions to over 20 publ in the US, Japan, Taiwan & Borneo. Mailing Add: c/o Freer Gallery Art Washington DC 20560

POPE, MARY ANN IRWIN
PAINTER
b Louisville, Ky, Mar 8, 32. Study: Art Ctr, Louisville; Univ Louisville; Cooper Union. Work: Nat Collection Fine Art, Washington, DC; Mint Mus, Charlotte, NC; Huntsville Mus of Art. Exhib: Mid-South, Brooks Art Gallery, Memphis, Tenn, 71-74; 38th Ann Nat Exhib Miniature Artists, Washington, DC, 71; Piedmont Painting & Sculpture Exhib, Mint Mus, Charlotte, NC, 72 & 73; Artrain, Southeast Tour, 74; Calif Nat Watercolor Show, Laguna Beach Mus, 74 & Palos Altos Mus, Calif, 75. Teaching: Instr painting, Art Ctr, 59; instr painting, Huntsville Art League, Ala, 66-, dir adult classes, 67-; part-time instr, Univ Ala in Huntsville. Awards: Shaw Warehouse Award, 32nd Nat Watercolor Exhib, 72; Mint Mus Purchase Award, Piedmont Painting & Sculpture Exhib, 72; Birmingham Jury Show, 73. Mem: Huntsville Art League & Mus Asn; Ala Watercolor Soc; Calif Nat Watercolor Soc; Ala Art League. Style & Technique: Fairly realistic; subject matter used in unusual context or juxtaposition. Media: Acrylic, Watercolor. Mailing Add: 1705 Greenwyche Rd SE Huntsville AL 35801

POPE, RICHARD CORAINE
PAINTER, DESIGNER
b Spokane, Wash, Aug 5, 28. Study: Univ Louisville, BA & MA; Cincinnati Art Acad, with Noel Martin. Exhib: Work has been widely exhibited in regional shows. Teaching: Instr graphic design, Univ Louisville, 65-66; assoc prof graphic design, Univ Ala, Huntsville, 66- Pos: Art dir, Staples Advert, Louisville, 57-64. Mem: Huntsville Art League & Mus Asn. Media: Opaque Watercolor; Calligraphy, Serigraphy. Mailing Add: 1705 Greenwyche Rd SE Huntsville AL 35801

POPESCU, CARA
SCULPTOR, PAINTER
b Munich, Bavaria, Ger; Can citizen. Study: Fine Arts Acad, Acad di Belle Arti, Florence, Italy; Fine Art Acad, Berlin, Ger; Fine Art Acad, Stuttgart, Ger, with painter, Willi Baumeister & sculpture masterclass with Otto Baum; L'Ecole des Beaux-Arts, Montreal, Que, with printmaker, A Dumouchel. Work: Cult Ctr Montreal-Verdun, Que; Gallery Hellhof, Frankfurt, WGer; Bell Tel Co of Can, Toronto; Bank of Commerce, Montreal; plus pvt collections in US, Brazil, WGer & Can. Comn: Fifteen Stations of the Cross, St Rock Church, Montreal, 68. Exhib: L'Assoc Sculpteurs du Que, Gallerie L'Etable, Mus des Beaux-Arts, Montreal & Mus du Que, Park des Champs, 63; Expo 67, Comitee Consultatif, Ger Pavilion, 67; Ctr Cult de la Prov Que, Montreal, 68; Asn Sculptors of Que & Preserv, 69, St Jean, Que & 70, Montreal; one-person shows, Ctr Cult, Montreal-Verdun, 68, Gallery Hembus-Hellhof, Frankfurt, WGer, 73-74 & Gallery Danielli, Toronto, Ont, 76-77; Three Sculptors Exhib in Goethe Inst, Toronto, 78, Montreal, 78 & Ottawa, 78; plus others. Teaching: Prof perception & three-dimensions for painters, L'Univ du Que, Montreal, 69-71. Bibliog: Cara Popescu, Frankfurt Allgemeine, 73; James Purdie (auth), Cara Popescu, Globe & Mail, Toronto, 76; J Ahlvik (auth), Her art...Toronto Mirror, 77. Mem: Ont Soc Artists; Visual Arts Ont; Sculptor's Soc Can (exec mem, 78); Sculptor's Soc WGer; Soc des Sculpteurs du Que (exec mem, 65-70). Style & Technique: Abstract and semi-abstract; painting, printmaking and sculpture. Media: Stone; Bronze; Aluminum; Concrete. Publ: Co-auth, Sculptures in Expo: seen by sculptor, Cara Popescu, Karusell-Montreal CFMB Radio, Que, 67. Dealer: Dominion Gallery of Can Montreal PQ Can; MacDowell Gallery Toronto ON Can. Mailing Add: One Woodland Heights Toronto ON M6S 2W3 Can

POPINSKY, ARNOLD DAVE
SCULPTOR, CERAMIST
b Bronx, NY, Aug 21, 30. Study: Albright Art Sch, State Univ NY, Buffalo, BS; Univ Wis-Madison, MS; Alfred Univ. Comn: Metal sculpture, Wright Art Ctr, Beloit, Wis, 64; 3 cast iron plaques, 64 & aluminum sculpture, 68, Beloit Col, Wis. Exhib: Colt & Popinsky, Wright Art Ctr, Beloit, Wis, 67; one-man shows, Lang Art Ctr, Claremont, Calif, 69, Univ WFla, Pensacola, 73 & Fishey Whale Gallery, Milwaukee, Wis, 75; Wis Designer-Craftsman, Milwaukee Art Ctr, 73. Teaching: Prof sculpture & ceramics, Beloit Col, Wis, 57-76. Pos: Artist-in-residence, Inst Artes Plasticas, Univ Guadalajara, Mex, 64-65; vis sculptor, Scripps Col & Claremont Grad Sch, Calif, 68-69; artist-in-residence, Univ WFla, Pensacola, 72-73; owner, Clarksville Pottery, Austin, Tex. Mem: Col Art Asn; Am Craft Coun; Austin Contemp Visual Arts Asn (mem bd dirs, 78); Rock Prairie Arts Coun. Style & Technique: Metal & ceramic sculptures, non-representational & fluidly organized geometric shapes. Media: Clay; Metal. Mailing Add: 1004 Eason Austin TX 78703

POPPELMAN, RAYMOND JAMES
ART DEALER, COLLECTOR
b Marvin, SDak, Mar 6, 07. Study: Univ Md, BA(bus admin, econ); self-taugh vis Libr Cong, Washington, DC & art mus throughout the world. Pos: Artists' rep for descendant artists of Grandma Moses family, including Forrest K Moses (son), Betty Moses (grand-daughter) & Thomas E Moses (great-grandson), 68-73;, agt for Richard Luney & Betty Moses, currently. Specialty: Primitives and wildlife. Collection: Primitives of the Grandma Moses family; Indian art by Fritz Scholder; African animals by Richard Luney; various others. Mailing Add: River Gate Village No 40 3940 Algonquin Dr Las Vegas NV 89109

PORTANOVA, JOSEPH DOMENICO
PORTRAIT SCULPTOR, DESIGNER
b Boston, Mass, May 16, 09. Study: With Cyrus E Dallin. Work: Dr Lee de Forest (sculpture), Smithsonian Inst, Washington, DC; Dr Robert A Millikan (sculpture), Calif Inst Technol, Pasadena; Dr Fabien Sevitzky (sculpture), Dade Co Auditorium, Miami, Fla; Richard Bard (sculpture), Lake Bard, Ventura Co, Calif; J B (Cap) Haralson (sculpture), Amateur Athletic Union, Indianapolis, Ind. Comn: Dr Charles LeRoy Lowman (sculpture), Orthopaedic Hosp, Los Angeles, 62; Leo M Harvey (sculpture), Harvey Aluminum Co, Torrance, Calif, 62; twelve bas-relief tablets, Los Angeles Mem Coliseum, 63-: John E Longden (bust), 66, William Shoemaker (bust), 71 & Joe Hernandez (bust), 74, Santa Anita Park, Arcadia, Calif. Exhib: Los Angeles Co Mus Art, 58; Laguna Beach Art Asn, Calif, 60; Calif Art Club, Los Angeles, 62; Calif State Fair, Sacramento, 63; Nat Acad Design, New York, 64. Pos: VPres design, Hoffman Electronics Corp, 44-65; dir design, Teledyne-Packard Bell, 65-74. Awards: First Prize, Laguna Beach Art Asn, 60; First Prize, Calif Art Club, 62; Gold Medal, Calif State Fair, 63. Bibliog: Clay & bronze, Saturday Night, 1/39; Janice Lovoos (auth), The portrait sculpture of Joseph Portanova, Am Artist, 1/65. Mem: Calif Art Club (second vpres & bd dirs, 63); fel Am Inst Fine Arts (vpres, 64). Style & Technique: Traditional portraiture. Media: Bronze. Mailing Add: 72-571 Jamie Way Rancho Mirage CA 92270

PORTER, ALBERT WRIGHT
EDUCATOR, PAINTER
b Brooklyn, NY, Nov 25, 23. Study: Ecole Des Beaux-Arts, Paris; Chouinard Art Inst; Univ of Calif, Los Angeles, BA; Calif State Univ, Los Angeles, MA; Otis Art Inst. Work: Los Angeles City Art Comn; Utah State Univ. Exhib: Arts of Southern Calif, Long Beach Art Mus, 66; Nat Watercolor Soc, Laguna Beach, Calif, 69; Southern Calif Expo, Del Mar, 72; Watercolor West, Riverside Art Mus, Calif, 74; Nat Watercolor Soc, Northridge, Calif, 77. Teaching: Prof art, Calif State Univ, Fullerton, 71- Pos: Art Supervisor, Los Angeles City Schs, 58-71. Awards: Cash Award, Nat Watercolor Soc, Del Mar Col, 72. Mem: Nat Watercolor Soc (1st vpres, 77); Watercolor West; Calif Art Educ Asn; Los Angeles Art Asn; Orange Co Art Asn. Style & Technique: Inventive watercolors using wet into wet and glazing techniques, imaginative drawings. Media: Watercolor, Pen & Ink. Publ: Auth, Shape and Form: Design Elements, 74, auth, Pattern: A Design Principle, 75 & auth, The Art of Sketching, 77, Davis Publ. Mailing Add: 8554 Day St Sunland CA 91040

PORTER, (EDWIN) DAVID
PAINTER, SCULPTOR
b Chicago, Ill, May 18, 12. Study: Whitney Mus Am Art; Miami Mus Mod Art; Chyrsler Art Mus; Norfolk Mus Arts & Sci; Parish Art Mus, Southampton; plus many others. Exhib: Ninth Street Exhib, New York, 51; Editions in Plastic, Jewish Mus, New York, 69; Outdoor Sculpture, Artists of the Region, Guild Hall, NY, 70; Artists at Dartmouth Retrospective, City Hall, Boston, 71; Artists of Sufolk County, Part V, New Directions, Heckscher Mus, Huntington, NY, 71; one-man shows, Am Inst of Architects, NY Chap, 69 & Guild Hall, East Hampton, 70; plus many others. Teaching: Artist in residence, Dartmouth Col, 64-65; artist in residence, Cooper Union, 67-68; lectr art, Corcoran Gallery Art, Washington, DC, 68 & 69; instr painting, Guild Hall, East Hampton, 75-78; lectr painting techniques, Wainscoth, NY, 76. Awards: Gold Medal of Pres Gronchi of Italy, Sassoferrato, Italy, 61; Beaux Arts Award in Painting, Beaux Arts Club, 69; Nat Inst Arts & Lett Grant, 70; plus many others. Bibliog: Today's living, New York Herald Tribune, 56; The Making of a Construction (TV film interview), Voice Am, 57; maj articles on work publ in newspapers in Norway & Sweden, 60. Publ: Auth, Why I ran away, Am Weekly, 7/10/60. Mailing Add: Wainscott NY 11975

PORTER, ELIOT FURNESS
PHOTOGRAPHER, WRITER
b Winnetka, Ill, Dec 6, 01. Study: Harvard Univ, BS, 24; Harvard Med Sch, MD, 29; Colby Col, Hon DFA, 69. Work: Metrop Mus Art & Mus Mod Art, New York; George Eastman House, Rochester, NY; Worcester Mus Art, Mass; New Orleans Mus Art; plus many pvt collections. Comn: In Wildness is the Preservation of the World (book), Sierra Club, 62; Forever Wild-The Adirondacks (book), Harper & Row, 66; Appalachian Wilderness (book), 69 & Birds of North America (book), 72, E P Dutton; photo-murals, Independent Life Ins Bldg, Jacksonville, 75. Exhib: An American Place, New York, 39; The Seasons, George Eastman House, 60; The Photographer & the American Landscape, Mus Mod Art, New York, 63; M H De Young Mem Mus, San Francisco, 65; Traveling Retrospective, Univ Art Mus, Albuquerque, NMex, 73. Awards: Silver Plaque, Wild Life Photography, Country Life Int Exhib, 50; Am Acad Arts & Sci Fel, 71. Mem: Advocates for the Arts; Friends of Photog. Style & Technique: Wild life and nature photography and dye-transfer printing. Media: Color Photography; Nature Writing. Publ: Auth, Summer Island, 66 & auth, Galapagos, the Flow of Wildness, 68, Sierra Club; co-auth, Down the Colorado, 69, co-auth, The Tree Where Man was Born, a Personal Experience, 72 & auth, Birds of North America, 72, Dutton. Mailing Add: Rte 4 Box 33 Santa Fe NM 87501

PORTER, ELMER JOHNSON
PAINTER, EDUCATOR
b Richmond, Ind, May 5, 07. Study: Art Inst Chicago, BAE; Ohio State Univ, MA; Earlham Col; Univ Cincinnati; Univ Colo; Butler Univ; San Carlos Univ, Guatemala. Exhib: Hoosier Salon, Chicago; Art League, Columbus, Ohio; Art Asn Richmond, Ind; also in Cincinnati & New York. Teaching: Instr art, McKinley High Sch, Cedar Rapids, Iowa, 30-37; instr art, Hughes High Sch, Cincinnati, 38-46; prof art, Ind State Univ, Terre Haute, 46-73, emer prof, 73- Pos: Jury mem, US Vet Admin Bicentennial Art Exhib, Washington, DC, 7/76. Awards: Appl Arts Prize, Indianapolis Art Asn, 29; Watercolor Award, Art League, Columbus, 38; Bonsib Purchase Prize, Hoosier Salon, 39. Mem: Art Educ Asn Ind (pres, 52-53, secy-treas, 54-67); Kappa Pi (int secy, 70-); Nat Art Educ Asn; Am Soc Bookplate Collectors & Designers; Pen & Brush Club. Media: Watercolor. Publ: Auth, Bookplates of Ernest Haskel, Bookplate Ann, 51. Mailing Add: 3115 Margaret Ave Terre Haute IN 47802

PORTER, J ERWIN
PAINTER
b Medina, NY, Jan 13, 03. Study: Rochester Inst Technol. Work: Marine Midland Bank; Monroe Co Savings Bank; Rochester Savings Bank; New Paltz Savings Bank; Charles Rand Penny Found; plus others. Comn: Paintings depicting Bicentennial events surrounding restoration of Ft Stanwix, comn by Oneida Co Savings Bank of Rome, NY, 77. Exhib: Four shows, Am Watercolor Soc, 61-68; Nat Acad Design, 63 & 65; six shows, Allied Artists Am, 63-77; one-man show, Smithsonian Inst, 67; Nat Arts Club Ann, 67-70; plus others. Awards: Rochester Art Club Awards, 64, 65, 68 & 69; Widmer Wine Co Award, Mem Art Gallery Finger Lakes Exhib, 68. Bibliog: Article in Am Artist, 6/66. Mem: Fel Rochester Mus & Sci Ctr; Am Watercolor Soc; Allied Artists Am; Pastel Soc of Am. Mailing Add: 116 El Pinon Green Valley AZ 85614

PORTER, LILIANA
INSTRUCTOR, PRINTMAKER
b Buenos Aires, Arg, Oct 6, 41; Arg citizen. Study: Sch of Fine Arts, Buenos Aires; printmaking, Iberoamerican Univ & La Ciudadela, Mexico City & Pratt Graphic Art Ctr, New York. Work: Mus of Mod Art, New York; Mus of Fine Arts, Philadelphia; Museo de Bellas Artes, Caracas, Venezuela & Santiago, Chile; La Bibliot Nat, Paris. Exhib: Int Biennial of Prints, Tokyo, 68, 70 & 74; Int Print Biennial, Krakow, Poland, 68-74; Museo de Bellas Artes, Caracas, 69; Museo de Bellas Artes, Santiago, 69; Info, Mus of Mod Art, New York, 70; Bks Made by Artist (traveling show), US, 72; Proj Ser, Mus of Mod Art, New York, 73; Museo de Arte Moderno, Bogota, Colombia, 74; Biennial of Paris, 75. Teaching: Instr etching, New York Graphic Workshop, 65-68; instr art tutorials, State Univ NY, Old Westbury, 75-76; instr graphics, Lucca, Italy, summers, 75-77. Pos: Co-dir, Studio Camniteer-Porter, 77- Awards: Drawing Award, Biennial of Cali, 73; Park Sq Gallery Award, Fourth Brit Int Print Bienniale, 74. Bibliog: James Collins (auth), articles in Artforum, 73 & Arts Mag, 5/77. Style & Technique: Study of visual disparity between reality and its image, through photography, photoetching, etching, drawing, silkscreen, collage. Media: Silkscreen, Etching. Publ: Contribr, Wrinkle, 68, Nail, 73 & String, 73, New York Graphic Workshop. Mailing Add: 3 Sheridan Sq 2J New York NY 10014

PORTER, PRISCILLA MANNING
CRAFTSMAN, INSTRUCTOR
b Baltimore, Md, Feb 1, 17. Study: Bennington Col, BA, 40. Work: Bowl in Collection of Pottery Sch, Faenza, Italy; fused glass sculpture, New Brit Mus, Conn; fused glass animal, Permanent Collection of Corning Mus Glass, NY. Comn: Fused glass cross, St John's Episcopal Church, Washington, Conn, 62; fused weed-ash cross, Emmanuel Episcopal Church, Baltimore, 63; Noah's Ark (fused glass epoxied to plate glass panels), NShore Unitarian Soc, Plandome, Long Island, 71; fused glass altar piece, Our Lady of Perpetual Help R C Church, Washington, Conn, 75; 12 fused glass panels, Taft Sch Libr, Watertown, Conn, 77. Exhib: San Jose State Col Glass Exhib, 64; Craftsmen of the Eastern States, sponsored by Smithsonian Inst, 66. Teaching: Instr ceramics, Dept of Educ, Mus Mod Art, New York, 52-61. Awards: Cert of Merit, Artist-Craftsmen New York, 68. Mem: Soc Conn Craftsmen; Artist-Craftsmen New York. Publ: Auth, Heat fusion of glass, Stained Glass, spring-summer 74. Mailing Add: Plumb Hill Rd Washington CT 06793

PORTMANN, FRIEDA BERTHA ANNE
PAINTER, SCULPTOR
b Tacoma, Wash. Study: With Fernand Leger, Glenn Lukens, Clifford Still, Norman Lewis Rice, Peter Camfferman, Edward Du Penn, Julius Heller, Hayter, Lasansky & H Matsumoto. Work: Univ Southern Calif, Los Angeles; Art Inst Chicago; Calif Col Fine Arts, Oakland; plus many in pvt collections. Comn: Sacajewea (wooden garden sculpture), Seattle; Beer & Skittles (mural), pvt home, Seattle; Pioneer Teacher (oil), Pioneer Asn, Seattle; Lily Madonna (ceramics), Garden, Cath Sch, Seattle; numerous portraits in oil. Exhib: Prints, Boston Mus Arts; Paintings, Prints, Sculpture & Crafts, Seattle Art Mus; Sculpture, Denver Mus Art; Painting & Print, Oakland Mus Art; Paintings, Argent Gallery, New York. Teaching: Art dir, Walla Walla Pub Schs, Wash; instr art & orchestra, Aberdeen Pub Schs, Wash; instr jr & high sch art, Seattle Pub Schs. Mem: Northwest Printmakers (pres); Women Painters Wash (secy). Media: Leather, Weaving, Ceramics. Mailing Add: 6221 Greenwood N Seattle WA 98103

POSEN, STEPHEN
PAINTER
b St Louis, Mo, Sept 27, 39. Study: Washington Univ, BFA, Milliken traveling scholar, 64-65; Fulbright grant, Italy, 64-66; Yale Univ, MFA. Work: Va Mus Fine Arts; Chase Manhattan Collection. Exhib: Highlight of the 1971 Season, Aldrich Mus Contemp Art, Ridgefield, Conn, 71; The New Realsits, Chicago Mus Contemp Art, 71; Relativating Realism, Stedelijk Van Abbe Mus, Eindhoven, Holland, 72; Whitney Mus Am Art Ann, New York, 72; Documenta 5, Kassel, WGer, 72. Teaching: Instr drawing, Cooper Union. Bibliog: David Shirey (auth), Downtown art scene, 4/3/71 & John Canaday (auth), Whitney annual, 2/6/72, New York Times; Ivan Karp (auth), Rent is the only reality, Arts Mag, 1/72. Mailing Add: c/o Robert Miller Gallery 724 Fifth Ave New York NY 10019

POSES, MR & MRS JACK I
COLLECTORS
Mr Poses, b Russia, Dec 28, 99; US citizen; Mrs Poses, b New York, NY, June 5, 08. Study: Mr Poses, NY Univ, BCS, 23 & MBA, 24; Brandeis Univ, LLD, 68; Mrs Poses, Hunter Col, BA, 27; Bryn Mawr Col, Susan B Anthony Fel (grad work in social econ), 28; Sch Law, NY Univ, LLB, 30. Pos: Mr Poses, vchmn, New York Bd Higher Educ, 63-; mem bd trustees, mem educ & budget comts, founder Poses Inst Fine Arts & chmn coun fine arts, Brandeis Univ; founder, Einstein Med Sch; Mrs Poses, mem & secy, NYC Charter Rev Comn, 61; mem bd visitors, Grad Ctr, City Univ New York, 77-78; practicing attorney, New York, currently. Awards: Mr Poses, Chevalier, Legion of Honor, 58; Citation Distinguished & Exceptional Serv to City New York, Mayor Lindsay, 67; plus others. Interest: Established numerous scholarships at many leading universities, as well as devoting active support to major art museums. Collection: French and American. Mailing Add: 1107 Fifth Ave New York NY 10028

POSEY, ERNEST NOEL
PAINTER, INSTRUCTOR
b New Orleans, La, 1937. Study: Tulane Univ, Art Ctr Col; La State Univ, BFA. Work: San Francisco Mus Art; Santa Barbara Mus Art; New Orleans Mus of Art; San Jose Mus of Art; Achenbach Found; Chase Manhattan Bank; J Walter Thompson Co; plus numerous pvt collections. Exhib: New Orleans Mus Artist Annuals, 59-62; Brata Gallery, New York, 62; Alonzo Gallery, New York, 66; Gertrude Kasle Gallery, Detroit, 66; Nat Collection Fine Arts, 66-68; Nat Inst Arts & Lett, 67, 70 & 72; Calif Now, 68; Contemp Am Painting & Sculpture, Krannert Art Mus, Champaign, Ill, 69; Looking West, Joslyn Art Mus, 70; San Francisco Inst Centennial Exhib, 71; New Accessions, San Francisco Mus Art, 73; Esther Robles Gallery, Los Angeles, 73; Ala Story Collection, Santa Barbara Mus of Art, 73; Surface & Image, Walnut Creek Art Ctr, 76; Simonne Stern Gallery, New Orleans, 76, 77 & 78; Crocker Mus Ann, Sacramento, 77; Achenbach Found, Calif Palace of the Legion of Hon, 77; solo exhibs, Henri Gallery, Washington, DC, 66, Van der Voort Gallery, San Francisco, 68, Glade Gallery, New Orleans, 70, Esther Bear Gallery, Santa Barbara, 71, Calif Palace of the Legion of Hon, 71, William Sawyer Gallery, San Francisco, 71, Bank of Am Plaza, San Francisco, 73, San Francisco Acad of Art, 75, Source Gallery, San Francisco, 76, San Jose Mus of Art, Calif, 77, Bank of Am Concourse, San Francisco, 77, Nuage Gallery, Los Angeles, 78, Walnut Creek Civic Arts Gallery, 78 & Los Robles Gallery, Palo Alto, Calif, 78; plus others. Teaching: Instr painting & design, San Francisco Acad Art, 72- Mailing Add: 1253 Pacific Ave San Francisco CA 94109

POSEY, LESLIE THOMAS
SCULPTOR, INSTRUCTOR
b Harshaw, Wis, Jan 20, 00. Study: Wis Sch Fine & Appl Arts, with Ferd Koenig, 19-23; Pa Acad Fine Art, scholar, 23, with Albert Laessle; Art Inst Chicago, 24, with Albin Polasek, 29-30. Work: Manatee Art League, Bradenton, Fla; Contemp Arts Gallery, Pinellas Park, Fla; Longboat Key Art Ctr, Fla. Comn: Beethoven (limestone), Dr O Seivert, Wildwood Park, Wis, 33; decorative cast stone, Church of the Redeemer, Sarasota, Fla, 52; garden figure in cast stone, Nat Coun Garden Clubs, Athens, Ga, 54; Kellogg portrait (stone), Dept Fire Control, Oneco, Fla, 58; Terry portrait (bronze), Longboat Key Art Ctr, 70. Exhib: Wis Sculptors & Painters, 23 & Lincoln Int, 30, Milwaukee Art Inst; Am Artists Exhib, Art Inst Chicago, 30; Hoosier Salon, Marshall Fields Gallery, Chicago, 30; Fla Int, Lake Land, 50. Teaching: Dir sculpture, Posey Sch Sculpture, 37-; instr sculpture, Manatee Art League, Bradenton, Fla, 52-61; instr sculpture, Longboat Key Art Ctr, 61-71. Pos: Sculptor, Am Terra-Cotta Co, Chicago, 25-26; head sculpture & design, Indianapolis Terra-Cotta Co, Ind, 26-29. Awards: Medal & Award, Milwaukee Art Inst, 23; First Prize, Hoosier Salon, Katherine Barker Hickox, 30; First Prize, Sarasota Art Asn, Fla Fedn Art, 40. Mem: Longboat Key Art Ctr; Sarasota Art Asn (dir, 71-73). Style & Technique: Traditional; realism; direct and indirect carving. Media: Stone. Mailing Add: 401 N Tuttle Ave Sarasota FL 33580

POSNER, DONALD
ART HISTORIAN
b New York, NY, Aug 30, 31. Study: Queens Col, AB, 56; Harvard Univ, AM, 57; NY Univ, PhD, 62. Teaching: Instr art hist, Queens Col, 57; asst prof art hist, Columbia Univ, 61-62; prof art hist, NY Univ Inst Fine Arts, 62- Pos: Art historian in residence, Am Acad Rome, 68-69; ed-in-chief, Art Bull, 68-71. Awards: Phi Beta Kappa Award, 56; Rome Prize Fel, Am Acad Rome, 59-61; C R Morey Bk Award, 72. Mem: Col Art Asn Am (dir, 70-74); Société d'Etudes XVIIIe siècle; Am Soc Eighteenth Century Studies. Res: Italian painting of 16th through 18th century; French painting of 18th century. Publ: Auth, Annibale Carracci, 71; auth, Caravaggio's homo-erotic early works, Art Quart, 71; co-auth, 17th & 18th Century Art, 72; auth, Watteau's Lady at her Toilet, 73; auth, Jacques Callot and the dances called Sfessania, Art Bull, 77. Mailing Add: NY Univ Inst Fine Arts 1 E 78th St New York NY 10021

POSNER, JUDITH L
ART DEALER, COLLECTOR
b Milwaukee, Wis, Sept 22, 41. Study: Univ Wis, BA(fine arts). Pos: Dir & pres, Judith L Posner & Assocs, Inc, currently. Specialty: 19th and 20th century American and European painting, sculpture and graphics. Mailing Add: 152 W Wisconsin Ave Milwaukee WI 53203

POSNER, RICHARD PERRY
GLASS ARTIST, LECTURER
b Los Angeles, Calif, Aug 16, 48. Study: Calif State Univ, Chico, BA; Calif Col of Arts & Crafts, MFA; Pilchuck Glass Sch; Penland Sch of Crafts. Work: Exploratorium Mus, San Francisco. Comn: Leaded glass window (84 sq ft), Exploratorium Mus, Palace of Fine Arts, San Francisco, 78. Exhib: Scripps Col Ann, Claremont, Calif, 76; Calif Design XII, Los Angeles, 76; Corning Mus of Glass, Corning Glass Ctr, NY, 76; Wight Gallery, Univ Calif, Los Angeles, 76; Renwick Gallery, Smithsonian Inst, Washington, DC, 77; Mus of Contemp Crafts, New York, 78. Teaching: Instr glass, Calif Col of Arts & Crafts, summers 75 & 76; lectr glass, Dept of Art, Univ Calif, Los Angeles, 76-77. Pos: Artist-in-residence, Exploratorium Mus, 78- Awards: Univ res grant, Univ Calif, Los Angeles, 76-77; Nat Endowment for the Arts Craftsman Fel, 77-78; Fulbright Travel Grant—Sweden, 78. Mem: Los Angeles Inst of Contemp Art; Glass Art Soc. Style & Technique: The flat glass canvas is viewed as both a portrait and a window through which to travel. Media: Flat glass; molten glass. Publ: Auth, The Picture Window, Chanie Bros Press, 76; contribr, Otto Rigan, auth, New Glass, Simon & Schuster, 76. Mailing Add: 979 North Point Apt B San Francisco CA 94109

POST, ANNE B
SCULPTOR, GRAPHIC ARTIST
b St Louis, Mo. Study: Bennington Col, BA(fine arts); study with Simon Moselsio, Stephen Hirsch & Edwin Park; study in Europe. Work: Israel Mus, Jerusalem; Norfolk Mus, Va; Art Dept Mus, Wellesley Col; Dept Fine Arts Mus, Univ Chicago; Dept Visual Art Mus, Bennington Col. Exhib: Toledo Mus Art; St Louis Mus Art; Contemp Art Exhib, New York World's Fair; NY Univ; Cooper Union Mus & Gallery; Univ NJ Mus; J B Neumann Gallery, New York. Teaching: Drawing & sculpture, Army Hosps, WVa, Tex, Mo & Settlement House, St Louis, 42-46. Bibliog: Günter Klotz (auth), Zcichnunsen und skulpturen der Anne Post, Klotz-Makowckie, 65; Sculpture-Anne Post, art in Norfolk Mus publ; Sculpture of Anne Post, art in Am Home. Mem: Metrop Mus Art; Smithsonian Inst. Media: Wood, Stone. Mailing Add: 29 Washington Sq W New York NY 10011

POST, GEORGE (BOOTH)
PAINTER, EDUCATOR
b Oakland, Calif, Sept 29, 06. Study: Calif Sch Fine Arts. Work: San Francisco Mus Art; Seattle Art Mus; Calif Palace of Legion of Honor; San Diego Fine Arts Soc; Metrop Mus Art; plus many others. Exhib: Metrop Mus Art; San Francisco Mus Art; DeYoung Mem Mus; Seattle Art Mus; San Diego Fine Arts Gallery; plus many others. Teaching: Instr, Stanford Univ, 40; prof fine arts, Calif Col Arts & Crafts, 47-73; instr, San Jose Col, 51-52; class workshops conducted in Spain, 74, Oaxaca & Taxco, Mex, 75, Albuquerque, NMex, 75, 76 & 77, Salt Lake City, Utah, 76, Aspen, Colo, 76, Sorrento, 76, Little Rock, Ark, 77 & San Miguel, Mex, 78. Awards: Prizes, Mother Lode Exhib, 55, 58 & 60; Third Award, Ann Lodi Grape Festival, 59; Purchase Awards, Watercolor USA, Springfield Mus Art, Mo, 66 & Jack London Square Art Festival, 68; Second Award, Oakland Art Asn, 66; HallxofxJustice, Third Award, Hall of Justice, 70, Hon Mention, 72, First Award, Zellerbach Show, 75, Second Awards, Ann Shows, 76 & 77, SWA; plus others. Mem: Am Watercolor Soc; San Francisco Art Asn; Calif Nat Watercolor Soc; Int Inst Arts & Lett; WCoast Watercolor Soc. Publ: Contribr illus in Fortune, Calif Arts & Archit, Art Digest, Am Artist & Ford Times Mags. Mailing Add: 327 Cumberland St San Francisco CA 94114

POSTIGLIONE, COREY M
ART DEALER, EDUCATOR
b Chicago, Ill, July 25, 43. Study: Univ Ill, Circle Campus, BFA; also with Martin Hurtig & Roland Ginzel. Exhib: One-man shows, Evanston Art Ctr, Ill, 72, Mayer Kaplan Ctr, Skokie, Ill, 73 & Jan Cicero Gallery, Evanston, Ill, 76; New Talent Show, Richard Gray Gallery, Chicago, 74; Ill State Mus Bicentennial Show, Springfield, 76; Cool Abstraction, Richard Gray Gallery, Chicago, 76; Ferrari, Marks & Postiglione, Jan Cicero Gallery, Chicago, 77. Teaching: Instr painting, Evanston Art Ctr, Ill, 71-; instr painting, Ill Inst of Technol, Chicago, 75- Pos: Contribr ed, New Art Examiner, New Art Asn, 75-76 & illusr the little artist cartoon, 75-76; asst dir, Jan Cicero Gallery, Chicago, 77- Bibliog: Alan G Artner (auth), Cool abstraction, Chicago Tribune, 76; Jane Allen (auth), One Person Show Jan Cicero Gallery, New Art Examiner, New Art Asn, 76; Franz Schultz (auth), Jan Cicero Group Show, Chicago Daily News, 77. Style & Technique: Painting, modular shaped canvases; drawing, large scale, emphasis on interlay of shape and line. Media: (Painting) Acrylic on Canvas; (Drawing) Dry Media, Pencil, Charcoal, Pastel in Combination. Publ: Auth, Interview with five abstract painters, New Art Examiner, 76. Dealer: Jan Cicero 433 N Clark St Chicago IL 60610. Mailing Add: 4041 N Keystone Apt GC Chicago IL 60641

POTTER, (GEORGE) KENNETH
PAINTER, DESIGNER
b Bakersfield, Calif, Feb 26, 26. Study: Acad Art, San Francisco, 47 & 48; Acad Frochot, Paris, with Metzinger, 50-52; Inst Statale dei Belli Arte, Florence, Italy, summer 51; study in Sicily, 53; San Francisco State Univ, BA, 74. Work: City of San Francisco Art Comn, 58; Univ San Francisco Collection, 65; hist mural (ink & acrylic on canvas), Corte Madera Town Hall, 66; Fed Housing & Urban Development, Regional Off, San Francisco, 69; Col Marin, Kentfield, Calif, 72. Comn: Murals (acrylic on canvas), Macy's, Stockton, 65; two murals (ink & acrylic on canvas), Regional Off Moore Bus Forms, Oakland, 69; Hale Mem Stained Glass Dome, Soc Calif Pioneers, San Francisco Civic Ctr, 74. Exhib: Phelan Awards Competition, San Francisco Mus Art, 49; 94th & 107th Ann Am Watercolor Soc, New York, 61 & 74; A City Buys Art, Calif Palace of Legion of Honor, San Francisco, 63; Watercolor USA, Springfield Art Mus, Mo, 73 & 74. Teaching: Instr watercolor, Civic Art Ctr, Walnut Creek, Calif, 68-70; instr watercolor, Acad Art, San Francisco, 70; instr watercolor, San Francisco State Univ, 74 & 75. Pos: Art dir, McCann-Erikson Inc Advert, Rio de Janeiro, 54-55; art dir, Johnson & Lewis Advert, San Francisco, 57; art dir, Michelson Advert, Palo Alto, Calif, 59-60; artist demonstr, Grumbacher, Inc, New York. Awards: Non-purchase Award for Watercolor, Calif State Fair & Expos, 58 & 72; First Award for Watercolor, Delta Ann, Antioch, Calif, 69; First Award Watercolor, Alameda Co Fair Statewide Competition, 74. Bibliog: Harold Rogers (auth), Color out of the West, Christian Sci Monitor, 2/26/49; Mabel Greene (auth), I began to draw, then to talk, San Francisco News-Editorial, 11/13/52; Milton Goldring (auth), O pintor Americano Kenneth Potter, Correio da Manha, Rio de Janeiro, 6/2/55. Mem: West Coast Watercolor Soc (pres, 68-70); East Bay Artists Asn (vpres, 70). Style & Technique: Restructuring interrelationships of design elements in various materials; humanist values; finding organic objective solutions, which are unique to each situation. Media: Watercolor, Oil, Acrylic. Publ: Contribr, Golden Gate Bridge, 5/27/62, A walk in Chinatown, 6/10/62 & A walk in the art world, 9/29/63, Bonanza, San Francisco Chronicle; contribr, Mission San Antonio, Calif Automobile Asn, 9/67; contribr, Marin portfolio, Image Mag, 10/67. Mailing Add: 105 Sonora Way Corte Madera CA 94925

POTTER, TED
PAINTER, ART ADMINISTRATOR
b Springhill, Kans, Dec 6, 33. Study: Univ Kans; Univ Calif Grad Sch, Berkeley; Calif Col Arts & Crafts, MFA, 62. Work: Salem Col, Winston-Salem, NC; NC Nat Bank, Charlotte; Arts Coun Winston-Salem; Glide Found, San Francisco; Calif Col Arts & Crafts. Pos: Dir art, Glide Found, 65-67; dir, Southeastern Ctr Contemp Art, Winston-Salem, 68- Mem: NC State Arts Soc (adv coun, 69-72); Nat Endowment for the Arts (individual artist fel panel, Visual Arts Div, 71-72); NC State Arts Coun (bd mem). Mailing Add: Southeastern Ctr Contemp Art 750 Marguerite Dr Winston-Salem NC 27106

POTTS, DON
SCULPTOR, EDUCATOR
b San Francisco, Calif, Oct 5, 36. Study: San Jose State Col, BA, 36, MA, 65; Univ Iowa, 63. Work: Univ Iowa, Iowa City; Joslyn Art Mus, Omaha; La Jolla Mus Art, Calif; Pasadena Art Mus, Calif; San Francisco Mus Art; plus others. Exhib: One-man shows, Denver Art Mus, 72, Walker Art Ctr, Minneapolis, 72, Whitney Mus Am Art, New York, 72, Univ Art Mus, Univ Calif, Berkeley, 73, Mus Contemp Art, Chicago, 73 & Garden of the Literarizchez Colloquim & Gallery Andre, West Berlin, Ger, 76; Mus of Mod Art, New York, 69; Univ Art Mus, Univ Calif, Berkeley, 70; San Francisco Mus of Mod Art, Calif, 71 & 76; Inst of Contemp Art, Boston, Mass, 74; Stadtische Kunsthalle Dusseldorf, Ger, 76; Documenta, Kasel, Ger, 77; Stedelijk Mus, Amsterdam, 78; plus many other group & one-man shows. Teaching: Instr, San Jose State Univ. Awards: Nat Endowment Arts Fel Grant, 70; Lewis Comfort Tiffany Found Grant, 73-74; Berliner Kunztler Prog, Deutzcher Acad Auztanzchdient, Buro Berlin, Ger, 75- Mailing Add: c/o Hansen Fuller Gallery 228 Grant Ave San Francisco CA 94108

POTVIN, DANIEL
PAINTER, GLASS BLOWER
b Metabetchoan, PQ, Apr 20, 46. Study: Ecole des Beaux-Arts de Quebec, Fine Arts Dipl; Fac des Sci Educ, Univ Laval, Quebec, degree in plastic arts, 72. Comn: Stained glass window comn by Mr & Mrs Paul Nadeau, 73. Exhib: One-man show, Marie Reine de Clerge Seminary, 70; St Jerome Musical Camp, Kovinck Pavilion, Univ Laval, 72; Polyvante de l'Ancienne, Lorette, 74; Montreal Royal Ctr Art, 75. Collections Arranged: The Enchanted Forest, Mus du Quebec, 74; In the Country of Lines and Colors, travel tour, Educ Serv, 75. Teaching: Teacher plastic arts, Polyvalante de l'Ancienne, Lorette, 72-74. Pos: Cult agent, Mus de Quebec, 74. Mem: Asn des Createurs Quebec. Style & Technique: Oil, watercolor, leaded stained glass windows. Publ: Illusr, poster design, Mus du Quebec, 74. Mailing Add: 500 Blvd Pie XI Val St Michel PQ G0A 4T0 Can

POUCHER, ELIZABETH MORRIS
SCULPTOR
b Yonker, NY. Study: Vassar Col, AB; NY Univ; Columbia Univ; Art Students League; Alexander Archipenko; Acad Grande Chaumiere, Paris, France; Ecole Animalier, Paris; also with Andre L'Hote. Work: Nat Portrait Gallery, Smithsonian Inst, Washington, DC; Taylor Art Gallery, Vassar Col, Poughkeepsie, NY; Mus City New York; plus many pvt collections. Comn: Many portraits for pvt commissions, 70-72. Exhib: Bronxville Ann, NY, 68-; Hudson Valley Art Asn, White Plains, NY, 68, 76 & 77; Pen & Brush, New York, 68, 75, 76 & 77; Allied Artists Am, New York, 68, 75 & 77; Nat Sculpture Soc Exhibs, 68, 75, 76 & 77. Awards: Silver Medal for Sculpture, Pen & Brush, 70, Bronze Medal for Sculpture, 73, Gold Medal for Sculpture, 76 & Drawing Prize, Graphics & Drawing Exhib, 77; Honorable Mention, Hudson Valley Art Asn, 70, Mrs John Newington Award for Sculpture, 75; First Prize for Sculpture, Bronxville Ann, NY, 71 & 73. Mem: Nat Sculpture Soc; Allied Artists Am; Pen & Brush (bd dirs, 69-72); Hudson Valley Art Asn. Style & Technique: Middle of the road representative. Mailing Add: 9 Brooklands Bronxville NY 10708

POULOS, BASILIOS NICHOLAS
PAINTER, EDUCATOR
b Columbia, SC, Dec 15, 41. Study: Atlanta Sch Art, BFA; Tulane Univ, MFA; Univ SC. Work: Am Tel & Tel, New York; Chase Manhattan Bank, New York; Greenville Co Mus, SC; Tulane Univ, New Orleans, La; United Va Bankshares, Richmond. Exhib: One-man exhibs, High Mus Art, Atlanta, Ga, 65, Columbia Mus Art, SC, 67 & Simonne Stern Gallery, New Orleans, La, 73, 74 & 76; Aldrich Mus Contemp Art, Ridgefield, Conn, 74; Watson de Nagy & Co, Houston, Tex, 75 & 76; 35th Biennial, Corcoran Gallery Art, Washington, DC, 77. Teaching: Vis assoc prof painting, Rice Univ, 75-77; mem fac art hist, New Sch for Social Res, NY, 77- Awards: Fine Arts Found Grant, Atlanta, Ga, 65; French Govt Grant, 65-66; Guggenheim Found Fel, 73-74. Bibliog: Mimi Crossley (auth), Poulos at Watson De Nagy, Art in Am, 77. Media: Acrylic on Canvas. Dealer: Watson de Nagy 2106 Berthea Houston TX 77006. Mailing Add: 310 E Ninth Houston TX 77007

POUNIAN, ALBERT KACHOUNI
PAINTER, EDUCATOR
b Chicago, Ill, Mar 7, 24. Study: Art Inst of Chicago, BFA, 48 & MFA, 49. Work: Borg-Warner Corp, Chicago; Ill Bell Tel, Chicago; Harper Col, Palatine, Ill; Barat Col, Lake Forest, Ill. Exhib: Chicago & Vicinity, Art Inst of Chicago; Ringling Mus, Sarasota, Fla; Northwest Territory, Springfield, Ill; Violence in Contemp Am Art, Mus Contemp Art, Chicago, 68. Teaching: Instr, painting & drawing, Art Inst of Chicago, 48-56; lectr art hist, Lake Forest Col, 50-65; prof painting & drawing, Barat Col Lake Forest, 49- & chmn art dept, 70-74; Fulbright-Hays Exchange Prof, Sch Fine Arts, Ulster Col, Northern Ireland Polytechnic, Belfast, Northern Ireland. Pos: Consult & contribr, Am Educ Encycl; coordr, Nat Upward Bound Exhib, Off Econ Opportunity, 66 & consult, 67-68. Mem: Am Asn Univ Prof. Style & Technique: Representational, abstraction. Media: Acrylic, Pen & Ink. Publ: Auth, many art in Am Educ Encycl. Mailing Add: 46 N Washington Circle Lake Forest IL 60045

POUSETTE-DART, RICHARD
PAINTER
b St Paul, Minn, June 8, 16. Study: Bard Col, hon DHL, 65. Work: Mus Mod Art; Whitney Mus Art; Addison Gallery Am Art, Andover, Mass; Albright-Knox Art Gallery; Nat Collection Fine Arts, Washington, DC; plus many others. Exhib: Abstract Painting & Sculpture in America, 44 & Traveling Exhibs, 69 & 71, Mus Mod Art, New York; The New Decade, 55 & Retrospective Exhib, 63 & 74, Whitney Mus Am Art, New York; New York School Exhibition, Los Angeles Mus Fine Arts; Documenta 2, Kassel, WGer, 59; Walker Art Ctr, Minneapolis, 60; Mus Mod Art, 61 & 69; Corcoran Gallery Art, Washington, DC, 64; American Abstract Expressionists & Imagists, Solomon Guggenheim Mus, 61; Wadsworth Atheneum, Hartford, Conn, 62; Nat Gallery, Washington, DC, 73; plus many other group & one-man shows. Teaching: Lectr, Boston Mus Sch Fine Arts, 59; instr painting, New Sch Social Res, 59-61; instr advan paintings, Sch Visual Arts, New York, 65; lectr, Minneapolis Inst Fine Arts, 65; guest critic, Columbia Univ, 68; instr painting, Sarah Lawrence Col, 71 & 73. Awards: Second Prize, Corcoran Gallery Biennale, 64; Comstock Prize, Art Inst Chicago, 65; Nat Arts Coun Award, 66; plus many others. Bibliog: Richard Pousette-Dart: transcendental expressionist, 61, Lawrence Campbell (auth), Pousette-Dart: circles and cycles, 63 & Charlotte Willard (auth), Yankee Vedanta, 67, Art News; plus many others. Dealer: Andrew Crispo 41 E 57th St New York NY 10022. Mailing Add: 286 Haverstraw Rd Suffern NY 10901

POWELL, EARL ALEXANDER, III
CURATOR, ART HISTORIAN
b Spartanburg, SC, Oct 24, 43. Study: Williams Col, BA, 66; Harvard Univ, MA, 70, PhD, 74. Teaching: Asst prof Am art, Univ Tex, Austin, 74-76. Pos: Cur Michener Collection, Univ Tex, Austin, 74-76; mus cur & asst to asst dir, Nat Gallery of Art, Washington, DC, 76- Mem: Col Art Asn. Res: English influences in the art of Thomas Cole. Publ: Co-auth, American Art at Harvard (catalog), 72; co-auth, Selections from the Michener Collection, 75; auth, articles on Am art in Arts Mag. Mailing Add: 1324 34th St NW Washington DC 20007

POWELL, LESLIE (JOSEPH)
PAINTER, DESIGNER
b Minneapolis, Kans, Mar 16, 06. Study: Okla Univ, 22-23; Chicago Acad Fine Arts, 24-25; Art Students League, fall 27; Columbia Univ, BFA, 52 & MFA, 54. Work: Brooklyn Mus Art; Newark Mus Art, NJ; Univ Ga Mus Art; Mus NMex Gallery Art, Santa Fe; Okla Art Ctr; plus others. Comn: Power (with Boyd Cruise), Industry, Communication & others, Samuel L Peters H S Commerce, New Orleans, La, 30 & 31; Town & Country (painting), Security Bank & Trust Co, Lawton, Okla, 48. Exhib: Okla Art Ctr, Oklahoma City; Philbrook Mus Art, Tulsa; one-man shows, Charles Morgan Gallery, New York, 38 & 39; Norlyst Gallery, 57 & Bodley Gallery, 60, New York; plus many other group & one-man shows. Teaching: Instr art, Ft Sill I&E Ctr, Okla, 26; instr design & painting, Arts & Crafts Club, New Orleans, 26; instr merchandising, Tulane Univ Sch Archit, 29-30. Pos: Designer, Richard Hudnut Co, 27-47; free lance designer, var firms, 27- Awards: Blanche Benjamin Award for best La Landscape, 31. Mem: Artists Equity Asn; Audubon Soc. Media: Oil, Watercolor, Pastel. Res: Chinese art. Interest: Modern art-abstract interpretations of classical and modern music; ballet paintings. Publ: Auth, revs in Villager, 67-69, Village Voice, 74- Dealer: Art for Industry 663 Fifth Ave New York NY 10022. Mailing Add: 39 1/2 Washington Sq S New York NY 10012

POWER, MARK
PHOTOGRAPHER, CRITIC
b Washington, DC, Mar 6, 37. Study: Bowdoin Col; Art Ctr Sch. Work: Pasadena Mus Art, Calif; Libr Cong, Washington, DC; Corcoran Gallery of Art, Washington, DC; Smithsonian Inst, Washington, DC; Polaroid Corp, Cambridge, Mass. Exhib: One-man shows, Recent Work, 70, Recent Work, 74, Corcoran Gallery, Washington, DC, 70 & 74 & Rita Hayworth series, Diane Brown Gallery, Washington, DC, 77; Mexican Photographs, Jefferson Place Gallery, Washington, DC, 74; Six Washington Artists, Iowa City Mus, Iowa, 75; 13 Virginia Photogrs, Eric Shindler Gallery, Richmond, 75. Teaching: Asst prof photog, Corcoran Sch Art, Washington, DC, 70- Pos: Photog critic, Washington Post, 74-75. Awards: Grant in Aid Fel, Washington Gallery Mod Art Fund, 70-72; Materials Grant, Polaroid Corp, 72-75. Bibliog: Andrea Cohen (auth), Washington photography, Washingtonian Mag, 72; David Tannous (auth), Art in America, 12/77-1/78. Style & Technique: Straight photography. Publ: Photographs, Camera Mag, Switz, 67, 69, 74 & 78; photographs, Creative Camera, Eng, 70; photogr, Glooskap's Children, 71; photogr, When Gloucester was Gloucester, 72; auth, introd, George Krause-1, 72; auth, introd, Nancy Rexroth, Iowa, 77. Mailing Add: c/o Corcoran Sch Art 17th & NY Ave NW Washington DC 20006

POZZATTI, RUDY O
PRINTMAKER, PAINTER
b Telluride, Colo, Jan 14, 25. Study: Univ Colo, BFA & MFA; Hon LHD, Univ Colo, 73; also with Wendell H Black, Max Beckman & Ben Shahn. Work: Mus Mod Art, New York; Libr Cong, Washington, DC; Art Inst Chicago, Ill; Sheldon Mem Art Gallery, Lincoln, Nebr; Cleveland Mus Art, Ohio. Comn: Spec Print Eds, Cleveland Print Club, Cleveland Mus Art, 54; Int Graphic Arts Soc, New York, 58-61 & 63; Conrad Hilton Hotel, New York, 61; Clairol, Inc, comn for New York World's Fair, 63; Ferdinand Roten Galleries, Baltimore, Md, 67 & 68. Exhib: Work of Rudy Pozzatti, Cleveland Mus Art, 55; Young Americans, Whitney Mus Am Arts, New York, 61; Stampe di Due Mondi: Prints of Two Worlds, Tyler Sch Art, Rome, Italy, 67; 20 Year Retrospective, Sheldon Mem Art Gallery, Univ Nebr, 69; Artists Abroad, Inst Int Educ, Am Fedn Arts, New York, 69. Teaching: Asst prof printmaking & painting, Univ Nebr, 50-56; prof printmaking, Ind Univ, 56-72, distinguished prof, 72- Awards: Guggenheim Fel, 63-64; George Norlin Silver Medal, Assoc Alumni of Univ Colo, 72. Bibliog: Norman Geske (auth), Rudy Pozzatti; American Printmaker, Univ Kans, 71; Richard Taylor (auth), Pozzatti (film), Artists in America, NETV, 71; Nancy Carroll (auth), A visit with Rudy Pozzatti, North Shore Art League, 72. Mem: Soc Am Graphic Artists; Boston Printmakers; Col Art Asn, New York (bd dirs). Style & Technique: Figurative. Media: All Media. Dealer: Jane Haslem Gallery 2121 P St NW Washington DC 20007; Weyhe Gallery 794 Lexington Ave New York NY 10021. Mailing Add: 117 S Meadowbrook Ave Bloomington IN 47401

POZZI, LUCIO
PAINTER
b Milano, Italy, Nov 29, 35; US citizen. Study: Sculpture with Michael Noble. Teaching: Asst prof art & art hist, Cooper Union, 69-75; vis prof art, Princeton Univ, 75. Style & Technique: Paint and performances. Res: Modern movement. Publ: Auth, five stories, 75 & an instructional manual. Dealer: John Weber Gallery 420 W Broadway New York NY 10012. Mailing Add: 142 Greene St New York NY 10012

PRACZUKOWSKI, EDWARD LEON
PAINTER, EDUCATOR
b Norwich, Conn, May 25, 30. Study: Norwich Art Sch, fine arts dipl, 50; Sch Mus Boston, cert with hons in painting, 56, Clarrisa Bartlett travel fel & grad cert, 59; Tufts Univ, BS(art educ), 58; Cranbrook Acad, MFA, 65. Exhib: Am Drawing Biennial, Mus Arts & Sci, Norfolk, Va, 65 & 67; Drawing USA, St Paul Art Ctr, Minn, 66 & 69; Nat Drawing & Small Sculpture Show, Ball State Univ, 67; Nat Polymer Exhib, EMich Univ, 67 & 68; 11th Ann Nat Drawing Exhib, Oklahoma Art Ctr, 69. Teaching: Assoc prof drawing & painting, Univ Wash, 65- Awards: First Prize Painting, Int Arts Festival, Detroit, 65; MacDowell Colony Grants, 66 & 69; Purchase Award, 5th Ann Drawing & Sculpture Exhib, Western Wash State Col, 68. Mem: Edward MacDowell Colony, New York; Allied Artists, Seattle, Wash. Style & Technique: Theme of macromicrocism of the universe. Media: Acrylic. Mailing Add: 5707 26th St NE Seattle WA 98105

PRAEGER, FREDERICK A
COLLECTOR, PUBLISHER
b Vienna, Austria, Sept 16, 15; US citizen. Study: Univ Vienna. Teaching: Adj prof, Grad Sch Librarianship, Univ Denver, Colo. Pos: Pres, Frederick A Praeger, Publ, New York, 50-68; chmn, Phaidon Publ, Ltd, London, 67-68; gen mgr, Ed Praeger, Munich, 69-74; pres, Westview Press, 75- Collection: Contemporary art. Mailing Add: Westview Press 5500 Central Ave Boulder CO 80301

PRAGER, DAVID A
COLLECTOR
b Long Branch, NJ, July 25, 13. Study: Columbia Univ, BA & LLD; also with Jack Tworkov. Pos: Asst secy, Friends of Whitney Mus Am Art, New York, 59-63, secy, 63-67; mem acquisitions comt, Whitney Mus Am Art, 60-61, 67-68 & 70-71; bd trustees, Am Fedn Arts, 67-, treas, 69-76; treas, Munic Art Soc, 67-69, bd dirs, 69-, pres, 72-74, vpres, 74- Mem: Century Asn. Collection: Contemporary American painting. Mailing Add: 14 E 90th St New York NY 10028

PRAKAPAS, EUGENE JOSEPH
ART DEALER
b Lowell, Mass, July 29, 32. Study: Yale Univ, BA, 53; Oxford Univ, Eng (Balliol), MA, 59. Pos: Dir, Prakapas Gallery, New York. Specialty: Photography of the 19th and 20th century; 20th century American art, with speical emphasis on the 20's and 30's. Mailing Add: 19 E 71st St New York NY 10021

PRAMUK, EDWARD RICHARD
PAINTER, EDUCATOR
b Akron, Ohio, Feb 14, 36. Study: Kent State Univ, BFA, MA; Queens Col, grad study; Akron Art Inst; also with John Ferren, James Brooks & Louis Finkelstein. Work: New Orleans Mus Art; Kent State Univ. Comn: Paintings, James Talcott Inc, New York, 74. Exhib: One-man shows, La State Univ, Baton Rouge, 68, 71, New Orleans Mus Art, 74; Galerie Simonne Stern, New Orleans, 71, 74; 7th Nat Drawing & Sculpture Show, Corpus Christi, Tex, 73; New Orleans Mus Art Biennial, 73; Westbeth Gallery, New York, 75; Pelham-Von Stoffler Gallery, Houston, Tex, 78; Edinboro State Univ, Edinboro, NY, 78. Teaching: Prof art, La State Univ, 64- Awards: Award, La Prof Artists, Baton Rouge, 71; Purchase Award, 7th Nat Drawing & Sculpture Show, 73; Purchase Award 1974, New Orleans Mus Art. Style & Technique: Geometric abstraction. Media: Acrylic. Mailing Add: 1152 Aberdeen Ave Baton Rouge LA 70808

PRANGE, SALLY BOWEN
CERAMIC ARTIST
b Valparaiso, Ind, Aug 11, 27. Study: Univ Mich, Ann Arbor, BA; workshops with Paul Soldner, Karen Karnes, Warren McKenzie, Don Reitz & Michael Cardew. Work: Victoria & Albert Mus, London, Eng; William Hayes Ackland Mem Art Ctr, Univ NC, Chapel Hill; NC Mus of Art, Raleigh; J Patrick Lannan Found Contemp Art, Palm Beach, Fla; Wachovia Bank, Charlotte, NC. Exhib: Ann Ceramic & Sculpture Show, Butler Inst Am Art, Youngstown, Ohio, 67-68 & 71; Ann Craftsmen, Southeastern Ctr Contemp Art, Winston-Salem, NC, 74, 76 & 77; Marietta Col Crafts Nat, Ohio, 75; one-woman show, DuPont Gallery, Washington & Lee Univ, Lexington, Va, 75; 34th Exhib Int Ceramics, Faenza, Italy, 76; Women in Art, Southeastern Ctr Contemp Art, Winston-Salem, NC, 76; Two Artists, Fayetteville Mus of Art, NC, 76 & NC Mus of Art, Raleigh, 76 & 77; Ceramic Conjunction 1977, Long Beach Mus of Art, Calif, 77. Teaching: Instr ceramic pottery, independent group lessons, 57-64 & night classes, Evening College Univ NC, Chapel Hill, 65-66. Mem: Piedmont Crafts, Inc; Am Crafts Coun; World Crafts Coun; Carolina Designer Craftsmen; Nat Coun Educ Ceramic Art. Style & Technique: High-fired porcelain reduction with matt crystal glazes; art pottery and color fusion with gold lustre; functional pottery; some stoneware and porcelain sculpture. Mailing Add: 1804 Rolling Rd Chapel Hill NC 27514

PRATT, DALLAS
PATRON, COLLECTOR
b New York, NY, Aug 21, 14. Study: Yale Univ, BA; Columbia Univ, MD. Pos: Ed, Columbia Libr Columns, 51-; co-founder & trustee, Am Mus Britain, 59-; ed, Am in Britain, 63-64; founder, John Judkyn Mem, Bath, Eng, 64- Collection: Renaissance maps and manuscripts. Publ: Auth, Discovery of a world-early maps of America, Antiques Mag, 12/69 & 1/70; auth, Angel-motors, Columbia Libr Columns, 5/72; auth, The Best Books, Col Libr Columns, 5/74. Mailing Add: 228 E 49th St New York NY 10017

PRATT, FRANCES (FRANCES ELIZABETH USUI)
PAINTER, ILLUSTRATOR
b Glen Ridge, NJ, May 25, 13. Study: New York Sch Appl Design for Women; Art Students League, with Richard Lahey; Hans Hofmann Sch Art. Work: Brooklyn Mus, NY; Va Mus Fine Arts, Richmond. Exhib: Denver Art Mus Ann, 42; Addison Gallery, 45; Cleveland Mus Art, 47; Brooklyn Mus Watercolor Int, 47, 49 & 51; Corcoran Gallery Art Biennial, 49. Collections Arranged: Ancient Mexico in Miniature, Am Fedn Arts, 64-66; Guerrero, Stone Sculpture from the State of Guerrero, Mex, Finch Col Mus Art, 65. Teaching: Instr painting, Ballard Sch New York, 42-59; instr painting, Parsons Sch Design, 48-51. Pos: Owner-dir, Frances Pratt, Inc, Gallery. Awards: Anne Payne Robertson Prize, 46 & Prize for Oil, 50, Nat Asn Women Artists Ann; Audubon Prize for Crayon Mixed Media, Audubon Artists Ann, 52. Res: Pre-classic cultures of Mexico (1500 BC-200 AD). Specialty: Antiquities; decorative arts, sculpture and painting of the 20th century. Collection: Paintings, prints, Japanese tea bowls. Publ: Co-auth, Encaustic, Methods & Materials, 49; illusr, Mezcala Stone Sculpture: the Human Figure, Mus Primitive Art, 67; illusr, Chalcacingo, 71 & 260 illus for Ceramic Figures of Ancient Mexico, 78, Akad Druck—U Verlagsanstalt, Graz, Austria; illusr, Paleolithic & Megalithic Traits in the Olmec Tradition of Mexico, Inst Canarium, Hallein, Austria, 72; illusr, Olmec hieroglyphic writing, Archaeology, 73; illusr, The Aztel treasure house, Harper's, 77. Mailing Add: 33 W 12th St New York NY 10011

PRATT, MARY FRANCES
PAINTER
b Fredericton, NB, Can, Mar 15, 35. Study: Mount Allison Univ, Sackville, NB, studied with Alex Colville & Lawren Harris, Jr. Work: Nat Gallery Can, Ottawa, Ont; NB Mus, St John, NB; Mem Univ, St John's, NF; Univ NB, Fredericton; Confederation Centre, Charlottetown, PEI. Exhib: Atlantic Awards Exhib, Dalhousie Univ, Halifax, NS, 61; Mary Pratt: A Partial Retrospective, traveling show to eight centres in eastern Can, 73; Mary Pratt: Paintings & Drawings, traveling show, from Vancouver to St John's 75; SCAN, Vancouver Art Gallery, BC, 74; 9 out of 10 A Survey of Can Art, Art Gallery, Hamilton, Ont, 74; The Acute Image in Can Art, Ownes Art Gallery, Mt Allison Univ, Sackville, NB, 74; Towards a New Reality, Art Gallery Ont, Toronto, 75; Some Can Women Artists, Nat Gallery Can, Ottawa, Ont, 75; Rothman's Realist Show, int traveling show, 76-77. Pos: Dir art prog, Fredericton Recreation Comn, 55-57; instr exten dept, Mem Univ, NF, 61-63; mem staff, Art in the Sch, CBC TV Series, St John's, NF, 68-70; lectr & vis artist, Nat Gallery Can, Dalhousie Univ & Mt Allison Univ, 74-77. Bibliog: Bob Smith (producer, feature prog), Take 30, 70 & The Pratts of Newfoundland, 73, CBC-TV; Harry Bruce (auth), The fine art of familiarity, Can Mag, 11/75. Mem: Royal Can Acad Art. Style & Technique: Photo realist, working from slides in oil paintings; prints and drawings done from life. Media: Graphite for drawing; silkscreen and lithography for prints. Dealer: Aggregation Gallery 83 Front St East Toronto On Can M5E 1B8. Mailing Add: Box 87 Mt Carmel NF A0B 2M0 Can

PRATT, VERNON GAITHER
PAINTER, EDUCATOR
b Durham, NC, Dec 9, 40. Study: Phillips Acad, Andover, Mass; Duke Univ; Univ NC; San Francisco Art Inst with James Weeks & Richard Diebenkorn, BFA, 62, MFA, 64. Work: Duke Univ Mus of Art; San Francisco Art Asn; R J Reynolds World Hq, Winston-Salem, NC. Exhib: Patrons of the James River Juried Ann, Newport News, Va; Piedmont Painting Anns, Mint Mus of Art, Charlotte, NC; Southeastern Ctr for Contemp Art, Winston-Salem, 70, 73 & 77; Art on Paper, Weatherspoon Gallery, Greensboro, NC, 72; O K Harris Gallery, New York, 73; DeGestlo Gallery, Hamburg, Ger, 73; Basel Int Art Fair, Switz, 73; Award Winners, NC Mus of Art, Raleigh, 74; New Orleans Mus, La, 77. Collections Arranged: Real Cool-Cool Real, Duke Univ Mus of Art, 73. Teaching: Asst prof art, Duke Univ, 64- Awards: Nealie Sullivan Award for Drawing, San Francisco Art Inst, 62; First Purchase Award, NC Mus of Art, NC Art Soc, 72. Style & Technique: Minimal-logical, nonobjective, paintings and relief. Media: Acrylic/oil on linen/canvas; wood. Mailing Add: 416 W Markham Ave Durham NC 27701

PRDY, DONALD R
PAINTER
b Conn, Apr 10, 24. Study: Univ Conn, BA; Boston Univ, MA. Work: New Britain Mus; Colby Col; Chase Manhattan Bank Collection; Univ Kans; Chrysler Mus. Exhib: USA Int Show; Silvermine Guild Artists; Audubon Artists; Allied Artists Am. Awards: Gold Medal, Allied Artists Am; First Prize, Silvermine Guild Artists; Jane Peterson Award, Audubon Artists. Bibliog: F Whitaker (auth), article in Am Artist. Mem: Am Fedn Arts; Allied Artists Am; Silvermine Guild Artists. Media: Oil. Collection: American and Barbizon. Dealer: Schoneberg Galleries 823 Madison Ave New York NY 10021. Mailing Add: 163 Westport Rd Wilton CT 06897

PREBLE, MICHAEL ANDREW
ART ADMINISTRATOR, EDUCATOR
b Tampa, Fla, July 27, 47. Study: Cornell Univ, BA(art hist); Calif State Univ, Dominguez Hills, MA(art hist & mus studies). Collections Arranged: Realism: Points of View, 76, Media: Paper, 77 & Reflections on Mass Culture, 78, Mt San Antonio Col, Walnut, Calif; William Baziotes Retrospective Exhibition, (auth, catalog introd), Newport Harbor Art Mus, Newport Beach, Calif, 78. Pos: Dir, Art Gallery, Mt San Antonio Col, Walnut, Calif, 74- Res: Museum studies; Surrealism and Biomorphism in America; mass culture. Mailing Add: Mt San Antonio Col 1100 N Grand Ave Walnut CA 91789

PREIS, ALFRED
ART ADMINISTRATOR, ARCHITECT
b Vienna, Austria, Feb 2, 11; US citizen. Study: Vienna Inst Technol, Archit. Work: USS Ariz Mem, Pearl Harbor, Hawaii; Honolulu Zoo Entrance Bldg; First United Methodist Church, Honolulu; Laupahoehoe High & Elementary Sch, Hawaii; Wahiawa Intermediate Sch, Oahu. Pos: Designer, Dahl & Conrad, 39-41; designer, Hart Wood, 42-43; principal archit, Alfred Preis, FAIA, 43-63; state planning coordr, Dept Planning & Econ Develop, 63-66; exec dir, State Found Cult & the Arts, 66- Awards: Am Church Archit Award, 56; Honor Awards,

Am Inst Archit, Hawaii, 52-63. Mem: Fel Am Inst Archit (pres, Hawaii Br, 51). Mailing Add: State Found Cult & Arts 250 S King St Rm 310 Honolulu HI 96813

PREISSLER, AUDREY
PAINTER
b New York, NY, Oct 31, 32. Study: Primarily self-taught. Work: Truman Libr, Independence, Mo; Kiplinger Collection, Washington, DC; Ford Motor Co, Dearborn, Mich; AMTRAK, Washington, DC; Ford Theatre, Washington, DC; Am Tel & Tel Exec Hq. Comn: Festivals (paintings in book form), UNICEF, New York, 60; paintings for traveling art show, Ford Motor Co, 70; AMTRAK Americana East portfolio, US Govt, 76-77. Exhib: Nat Watercolor Show, Smithsonian Inst, Washington, DC, 70; one-woman show, UN Bldg, New York, 66, Inter-Am Bank Gallery, Washington, DC, 68. Bibliog: Free-wheeling way/water painting, Grumbacher Mag, Issue 33, 77; Audrey Preissler, article in Art Voices/S Mag, 1-2/78. Style & Technique: Personal expressionism, figurative; vested with subtle humor, luminous color; humanistic art of social concern; open brushwork, sensitive almost calligraphic draftsmanship or line; colorful, inventive and imposing. Media: Watercolor and Acrylic on Board, Wood, Paper and Cloth. Mailing Add: c/o Albatross Gallery 1492 Washington St Harpers Ferry WV 25425

PREKOP, MARTIN DENNIS
SCULPTOR, EDUCATOR
b Toledo, Ohio, July 2, 40. Study: Cleveland Inst Art; Cranbrook Acad Art, MFA; RI Sch Design, MFA; Slade Sch Art, London, Eng. Exhib: Roof Works, Mus Contemp Art, 72; Four Illinois Photographers, Art Inst Chicago, 74 & Chicago Area Artists, 75; one-man shows, Photographs, Yale Univ, 75 & Name Gallery, Chicago, 75. Teaching: Asst prof & grad prog chmn painting, sculpture & photog, Art Inst Chicago, 66-, chmn Freshman Found, 70-73 & chmn grad div, 73- Awards: Fulbright Fel, US State Dept, 65. Bibliog: Jan Vendermark (auth), Roof Works Rev, Art Forum, 72. Style & Technique: Sculpture, photographic installation usually in wood or related media. Mailing Add: 4050 W Cortland Chicago IL 60639

PRENT, MARK
ENVIRONMENTAL ARTIST, SCULPTOR
b Montreal, PQ, Can, Dec 23, 47. Study: Sir George Williams Univ, Montreal, 66-70, BFA, 70, study with John Ivor Smith. Work: Art Gallery of Ont, Toronto; Art Bank of Can; Sir George Williams Art Galleries. Exhib: Survey 70, Mus of Fine Arts, Montreal, 70; Winnipeg Biennial, Winnipeg Art Gallery, Can, 70; Royal Can Acad Traveling Show, Mus of Fine Arts, Montreal & Confederation Art Gallery & Mus, Charlottetown, Can, 71; Realism: Emulsion & Omission, Agnes Etherington Art Gallery, Kingston, Ont & Art Gallery of the Univ of Guelph, Ont, 72; Diversity Can East, Edmonton Gallery, Can, 72; 8th Biennale de Paris, Nat Mus of Mod Art, France, 73; Rebecca Cooper Gallery, Washington, DC, 74; Isaacs Gallery at the Owens Art Gallery, Mt Allison Univ, Sackville, NB, 74; one-man shows, Wiseman Gallery, Sir George Williams Univ, Montreal, 71, Art Gallery of York Univ, Toronto, 74, Akadamie der Kunste, Berlin, WGer, 75-76, Kunsthalle Nürnburg, WGer, 76, Stedelijk Mus, Amsterdam, Holland, 78 & Mus of Contemp Art, Montreal, 78. Awards: Guggenheim Mem Found Fel, 77; Can Coun Sr Arts Award, 78-79; Victor M Lynch-Staunton Award, 78. Bibliog: Michael Greenwood (auth), Mark Prent, Artscanada, Toronto, spring 72; Werner Rhode (auth), Mark Prent's macabre manipulation, Mag Kunst, Mainz, 75; Karl Ruhrberg (auth), Mark Prent und das Skandalose, Mark Prent: Extended Realism (catalog), Akadamie der Kunste, Berlin, 75. Mem: Can Artists Representatives. Style & Technique: Enclosed environments which require viewer participation; extended realism, environmental sculpture use of body-casts. Media: Polyester Resin, Fiberglass and Mixed Media. Dealer: Isaacs Gallery 832 Yonge St Toronto ON M4W 2H1 Can. Mailing Add: 2955 Edouard-Montpetit Apt 6 Montreal PQ H3T 1K3 Can

PRENTICE, DAVID RAMAGE
PAINTER, DESIGNER
b Hartford, Conn, Dec 22, 43. Study: Hartford Art Sch. Work: Wadsworth Atheneum, Hartford; Yale Univ, New Haven, Conn; Mus Mod Art, New York; Nat Gallery, Washington, DC; Aldrich Mus, Ridgefield, Conn. Exhib: One-man shows, Teuscher Gallery, 66, Sonnabend Gallery, 70 & Livingstone-Learmonth Gallery, 75, New York; Other Ideas, Detroit Inst Fine Arts, Mich, 69; Prospect, Dusseldorf, Ger, 69; Whitney Mus Am Art Ann, New York, 70. Teaching: Guest instr painting, Hartford Art Sch, Univ Hartford, fall 70. Media: Acrylic. Mailing Add: 654 Broadway New York NY 10012

PRESCOTT, KENNETH WADE
EDUCATOR, WRITER
b Jackson, Mich, Aug 9, 20. Study: Western Mich Univ, BS; Univ Del, EdM; Univ Mich, MA & PhD. Collections Arranged: Ben Shahn Retrospective Exhib, Nat Mus Mod Art, Tokyo & other Japanese mus (with catalog), 70. Teaching: Instr changing perspectives in the humanities, Temple Univ, 60-70; prof art & chmn dept, Univ Tex, Austin, 74- Pos: Dir, Kansas City Mus, Mo, 54-58; managing dir, Acad Nat Sci, Philadelphia, 58-63; dir, NJ State Mus, Trenton, 63-71; prog officer, Div Arts & Humanities, Ford Found, New York, 71-74; mem ed bd, Am Art J, 76- Mem: Tex Asn of Schs of Art (mem bd, 76-); Am Color Print Soc (hon vpres, 68-71); Col Art Asn Am; Nat Coun Art Adminr (mem bd, 77-80); Am Fedn Arts. Res: Preparation of catalog resumes on contemporary American artists. Collection: Works of contemporary American artists. Publ: Co-auth, Domjan the Woodcutter, 66; contribr, Ben Shahn (1898-1969), Nov 6-27 (catalog), Kennedy Galleries, New York, 71; auth, Dorothea Greenbaum, Retrospective, 1927-72 (catalog), 72; auth, The Complete Graphic Works of Ben Shahn, 73; auth, Social Realism and the religious aspects of the world of Ben Shahn, Vatican Mus, Italy, summer 76; auth, catalog, Ben Shahn: a retrospective, 76-77. Mailing Add: Dept of Art Univ of Tex Austin TX 78712

PRESS, NANCY NEUMANN
CURATOR, EDUCATOR
b Los Angeles, Calif, Mar 18, 40. Study: Mills Col, Oakland, Calif, 57-61, BA(art), painting with Ralph DuCasse; San Francisco State Univ, 64-66, MA(art, sculpture). Exhib: 1st Ann Calif Craftsmen's Exhib, Oakland Art Mus, 61; Contemp Craftsmen of the Far West, Mus of Contemp Crafts, New York, 61; San Francisco Art Inst Ann Exhib, San Francisco Mus of Art, 65. Exhibitions Arranged: The Handwrought Object: 1776-1976 (auth, catalog), 7/10-8/22/76 & Landscape: New Views (auth, catalog), 1/17-3/5/78, Herbert F Johnson Mus of Art. Pos: Cur crafts & coordr educ, Herbert F Johnson Mus of Art, 72- Mem: Am Crafts Coun; NY State Craftsmen, Inc; Northeast Mus Conf; Nat Art Educ Asn. Mailing Add: Herbert F Johnson Mus of Art Cornell Univ Ithaca NY 14853

PRESTINI, JAMES LIBERO
SCULPTOR, DESIGNER
b Waterford, Conn, Jan 13, 08. Study: Yale Univ, BS, 30, Sch Educ, 32; Univ Stockholm, 38, with Carl Malmsten; Inst Design, Chicago, 39, with L Moholy-Nagy; also study in Italy, 53-56. Work: Mus Mod Art & Metrop Mus Art, New York; Art Inst Chicago; Nat Collection Fine Arts, Smithsonian Inst, Washington, DC; San Francisco Mus Art. Comn: Aluminum sculpture, R S Reynolds Mem Sculpture Award, Richmond, Va, 72. Exhib: James Prestini, Sculpture from Structural Steel Elements, San Francisco Mus Art, 69; James Prestini, Art Inst Chicago, 69; Excellence: Art from the University, Univ Calif, Berkeley, 70; International Collection of 20th Century Design, Mus Mod Art, New York, 72; Twentieth Century Accessions 1967-1974, Metrop Mus Art, New York, 74. Teaching: Instr design, Lake Forest Acad, 33-42; instr design, Inst Design, Chicago, 39-46; & 52-53; assoc prof design, NTex State Univ, 42-43; prof design, Univ Calif, Berkeley, 56-, res prof, Creative Arts Inst, 67-68 & Bauhaus-Archiv, WBerlin, 77. Awards: Guggenheim Fel for Sculpture, 72-73; Award for Excellence in Fine Art in Steel, Am Iron & Steel Inst, New York, 71; Univ Calif Berkeley Award, 75. Bibliog: Edgar Kaufmann (auth), Prestini's art in wood, Pantheon, 50; Gerald Nordland (auth), James Prestini, sculpture from structural steel elements, San Francisco Mus Art, 69; George Staempfli (auth), James Prestini, recent sculpture, Staempfli Gallery, 71 & 74. Mem: Life fel Metrop Mus Art. Style & Technique: Dynamics of my sculpture is the interaction between the positive, negative, and virtual spaces; and the reflections of the environment. Media: Steel, Aluminum, Wood. Publ: Co-auth, The Place of Scientific Research in Design, 48; co-auth, Research in Low-cost Seating for Homes, 48; co-auth, Survey on Construction Materials Demonstration & Training Center, 51; auth, Survey of Italian Furniture Industry (Milan), 54; auth, Proposed policy statement on architectural research for the College of Architecture of the University of California, Berkeley, 58. Dealer: Staempfli Gallery 47 E 77th St New York NY 10021. Mailing Add: 2324 Blake St Berkeley CA 94704

PRESTON, MALCOLM H
CRITIC, PAINTER
b West New York, NJ, May 25, 19. Study: Univ Wis, BA; Columbia Univ, MA & PhD. Work: Hofstra Univ Collection; Dayton Art Inst; Portland Mus. Exhib: ACA Gallery; Hansa Gallery; SAG Gallery; Harbor Gallery; Eggleston Gallery; Kendall Gallery. Teaching: Asst instr fine arts, New Sch Social Res, 40-41; instr fine arts, Adelphi Univ, 47-48; prof fine arts, Hofstra Univ, 49-74. Pos: Dir, Inst Arts, Hofstra Univ, 60-64; art critic, Newsday, 68-; art critic, Boston Herald Traveler, 70-72. Awards: Joe & Emily Lowe Found Educ Res Grant, 50; Ford Found Grant, 56 & 57; Shell Oil Res Grant, 64. Media: Oil. Publ: Contribr, Christian Sci Monitor, Boston Globe & other mag & newspapers; writer, producer & principal performer, Arts Around Us & American Art Today (Ford Found-sponsored nat educ television series), 55-56. Mailing Add: Box 182 Truro MA 02666

PRESTOPINO, GREGORIO
PAINTER
b New York, NY, June 29, 07. Study: Nat Acad Design. Work: Whitney Mus Am Art, New York; Walker Art Ctr, Minneapolis, Minn; Joseph H Hirshhorn Collection, Washington, DC; Art Inst Chicago; NJ State Mus, Trenton. Comn: Mosaic, comn by Dr Rebecca Notterman, Prof Bldg, Princeton. Exhib: Whitney Mus Am Art Am Painting Ann, 45; Mus Mod Art, New York; Pa Acad Fine Arts, Philadelphia; Corcoran Gallery Art, Washington, DC; Phillips Acad, Andover, Mass. Teaching: Instr painting, Brooklyn Mus Sch, 46-51; artist in residence, Mich State Univ, 60. Awards: Nat Inst Arts & Lett Grant, 61; B Altman Figure Painting Award, 72 & William A Paton Prize, 77, Nat Acad Design; Emily Goldsmith Award, Am Watercolor Soc, 77. Bibliog: J Hubley (auth), Harlem Wednesday (film), Storyboard, Inc, 56; J G Smith (auth), Watercolors of Gregorio Prestopino, Am Artist, 10/57. Mem: MacDowell Colony (dir, 71); academician Nat Acad Design. Media: Oil, Watercolor. Dealer: Midtown Galleries Inc 11 E 57th St New York NY 10003. Mailing Add: Roosevelt NJ 08555

PRETSCH, JOHN EDWARD
CARTOONIST, ILLUSTRATOR
b Philadelphia, Pa, Apr 14, 25. Pos: Sun supplement artist, news artist & promotional layout artist, Philadelphia Eve Bull, formerly, news artist, 66-; advert layout artist, Sears Roebuck & Co, formerly. Publ: Illusr, Five Years, Five Countries, Five Campaigns with the 141st Infantry Regiment, 45; illusr cartoons in Colliers, Sat Eve Post & Philadelphia Eve Bull. Mailing Add: 4337 H St Philadelphia PA 19124

PREUSS, ROGER
PAINTER, WRITER
b Waterville, Minn, Jan 29, 22. Study: Minneapolis Col Art & Design, BFA. Work: Nat Wildlife Gallery, Washington, DC; Mont Hist Soc Mus, Helena; Smithsonian Hall Philately, Washington, DC; Mont State Univ Inabnit Collection, Missoula; US Fed Bldg & Minn State Capitol, St Paul; also in Europ pub collections. Comn: 1949-50 Fed Duck Stamp Design, US Dept Interior, Washington, DC, 48; 16 painting wildlife series, Shedd-Brown Collection, Minneapolis, 50; 150 paintings of wildlife, Thos D Murphy Co, Red Oak, Iowa, 54; 12 paintings (Minn Today), Greater Minneapolis C of C, 68; 72 paintings, The Haas Corp, Sleepy Eye, Minn, 73. Exhib: Contemp Bird Painting Biennial, Joslyn Art Mus, Omaha, Nebr, 48; Minneapolis Inst of Arts, 49; Demarest Mem Mus, Hackensack, NJ, 52; Minn Hist Soc Mus, St Paul, 52; NAm Wildlife Art Expos, Minneapolis Auditorium, 52; Am Swed Inst, Minneapolis, 53; Nat Wildlife Art Exhib, Milwaukee Pub Mus, 54; Minn Natural Hist Mus, Minneapolis, 56; Mont Hist Soc Mus, Helena, 64; Inst Contemp Arts, London, 68; Harris Fine Arts Ctr, Brigham Young Univ, Provo, 69; Animal Artists, Grand Cent Art Galleries, New York, NY, 72; one-man exhib, US Bicentennial Exhib, Le Sueur Co Hist Soc Mus, Elysian, Minn, 76. Teaching: Sem lectr wildlife painting, Minneapolis Col Art. Awards: Fed Duck Stamp Design Award, US Fish & Wildlife Serv, 49; Audubon Soc Art Award, 59; named US Bicentennial Wildlife Artist, Am Heritage Asn, 76. Bibliog: Marion McKinley (auth), Roger Preuss-artist, SDak Conserv Digest, 1/70; Sam Macalus (auth), Roger Preuss: master painter and active wildlifer, Water, Woods & Wildlife, 1/74; Alan LeWin (auth), Roger Preuss: Pigments in the wild, Northliner Mag, 7/77; Your BFA: Care and Maintenance (film), Union Independent Cols of Art, 77. Mem: Soc Animal Artists; fel Int Inst Arts; Minn Artists Asn (dir & vpres, 53-56); Am Artists Prof League; fel Explorers Club, New York, NY. Style & Technique: Traditional realism, with emphasis on anatomical accuracy and special fidelity to detail of natural habitat, mood, and setting correlated to the specific nature subject. Media: Oil, Watercolor. Publ: Auth & illusr, The official wildlife of America calendar, 55-; auth & illusr, Outdoor Horizons, 57; auth & illusr, American game birds, 64; illusr, Twilight over the wilderness, 71; contribr/illusr, Nat Wildlife, Country Gentleman, The Farmer, Western Can Outdoors, Colliers, Sports Afield, Today's Art & many other nat periodicals & ltd ed prints. Dealer: Wildlife of America Gallery Box 556-WA Minneapolis MN 55440. Mailing Add: 2224 Grand Ave Minneapolis MN 55405

PREUSSER, ROBERT ORMEROD
PAINTER, EDUCATOR
b Houston, Tex, Nov 13, 19. Study: Pvt study with McNeill Davidson, Houston, 30-39; Inst Design, Chicago, 39-40 & 41-42; Newcomb Sch Art, Tulane Univ, 40-41; Art Ctr Sch, Los Angeles, 46-47. Work: Mus Fine Arts, Houston; Contemp Arts Mus, Houston, Witte Mem Mus, San Antonio, Tex; Tex Christian Univ, Ft Worth; Addison Gallery Am Art, Andover, Mass. Exhib: Directions in American Painting, Carnegie Inst, Pittsburgh, 41; Int Watercolor

Exhib, Art Inst of Chicago, 42, Abstract & Surrealist American Exhib, 47 & Am Artists Ann, 51; Fifth Biennial Contemp American Exhib, 46; Contemp American Artists Ann, 46 & 47; Gulf-Caribbean Exhib, Houston Mus of Fine Arts Circulating Exhib, 56-57; Survey of American Painting, Am Fedn Arts Circulating Exhib, 57-58; Texas Painting & Sculpture—the 20th Century, Owens Arts Ctr Circulating Exhib, Dallas, 71-72. Teaching: Instr painting, Houston Mus Fine Arts Sch, 47-54; instr painting, Univ Houston, 51-54; prof visual design, Mass Inst Technol, 54-; instr drawing, Harvard Univ Grad Sch Design, 55-56. Pos: Art ed, Tex Cancer Bull, 48-50; co-dir, Contemp Arts Mus, Houston, 49-51; stage set designer, Tex Stage, Houston, 50-51; assoc cur educ, Mus Fine Arts, Houston, 52-54; dir educ, Ctr Advan Visual Studies, Mass Inst Technol, 74-; co-ed, Leonardo, 74- Awards: Purchase Prize, 16th Ann Houston Artists Exhib, Mus Fine Arts, Houston, 40; Contemp Arts Mus Purchase Prize, 27th Ann Houston Artists Exhib, 52. Bibliog: Ralph M Pearson (auth), Chap 3, In: The Modern Renaissance in American Art, Harper & Row, 54; Vision in engineering (interview), Int Sci & Technol, 10/65. Style & Technique: Abstract. Media: Mixed Media. Publ: Auth, Visual education for science & engineering students, In: Education of Vision, Braziller, 65, Fr & Ger ed, 67; auth, Art & the engineer, Mech Eng, 12/67; auth, Relation of art to science and technology: an educational experiment at MIT, Leonardo, Vol 6, No 3, 73; auth, Revitalizing art & humanizing technology: an educational challenge, Impact, Vol 24, No 1, 74; auth, Coloured illumination and the environment, in: Colour for Architecture, Studio Vista, 76. Dealer: Joan Peterson Gallery 561 Boylston St Boston MA 02116. Mailing Add: 2 Willard St Ct Cambridge MA 02138

PREZAMENT, JOSEPH
PAINTER
b Winnipeg, Man, Jan 3, 23. Study: Winnipeg Sch Art; Montreal Mus Fine Arts; Ecole des Beaux Arts. Exhib: Royal Can Acad, Montreal Mus Fine Arts, 67; Burnaby Art Soc, BC, 67; Can Painters & Engravers, Toronto, 68; Can Soc Graphic Artists, Toronto, 68; Canadian Printmakers Showcase, Toronto, 69. Mem: Can Soc Graphic Artists. Media: Oil. Dealer: West-End Art Gallery 1358 Greene Ave Montreal PQ Can. Mailing Add: 2284 Regent Ave Montreal PQ H4A 2R1 Can

PRIBBLE, EASTON
PAINTER, INSTRUCTOR
b Falmouth, Ky, July 31, 17. Study: Univ Cincinnati. Work: Whitney Mus Am Art, New York; Munson-Williams-Proctor Inst, Utica; Joseph Hirshhorn Collection, Washington, DC; Parrish Mus, Southampton, NY; Utica Col, NY. Comn: Painted wood relief mural, Munson-Williams-Proctor Inst Sch Art, 61; painted wood relief mural, Oneida Co Off Bldg, NY, 69. Exhib: Whitney Ann Am Painting, Whitney Mus Am Art, 50, 54 & 55; Univ Nebr Ann, Lincoln, 56; Everson Mus, Syracuse, 63; Retrospective Exhib, Munson-Williams-Proctor Inst Mus of Art, 76. Teaching: Instr painting, Munson-Williams-Proctor Inst Sch Art, 57-; instr hist art, Utica Col, 60-73. Awards: Painting Award, Everson Mus, 60 & 64; Painting Award, Munson-Williams-Proctor Inst, 63. Media: Oil, Acrylic, Pastel. Publ: Contribr, Contemporary American culture, Chicago Rev, 54; contribr, New talent in America, Art in Am, 56. Mailing Add: Munson-Williams-Proctor Inst 310 Genesee St Utica NY 13502

PRICE, ANNE KIRKENDALL
ART CRITIC
b Birch Tree, Mo, June 14, 22. Study: Univ Mo, Columbia, BJ; Univ Ga, Athens, art seminars; Southern Regional Educ Bd workshop for art critics. Pos: Art critic, Morning Advocate, Baton Rouge, La, 60- Awards: Award for Arts Coverage, La Coun Music & Performing Art, 74; Communicator of the Yr Award, Pub Relations Soc of La, 78. Mem: Capitol Corresp (pres, 68); Baton Rouge Arts Coun. Mailing Add: 4780 Newcomb Dr Baton Rouge LA 70808

PRICE, GEORGE
CARTOONIST
b Coytesville, NJ, June 9, 01. Pos: Cartoonist & bk illusr. Publ: Contribr, cartoons in New Yorker Mag, 26-; auth & illusr, We Buy Old Gold, 52 & George Price's Characters, 55; auth & illusr, My Dear Five Hundred Friends, S&S, 63; auth & illusr, People Zoo, 71. Mailing Add: 81 Westervelt Ave Tenafly NJ 07670

PRICE, KENNETH
PRINTMAKER, SCULPTOR
b Los Angeles, Calif, 1935. Study: Univ Calif; Otis Art Inst; Chouinard Art Inst; Univ Southern Calif, BFA, 56; State Univ NY Albany, MFA, 58. Work: Los Angeles Co Mus Art. Exhib: Fifty California Artists, San Francisco Mus Art, 62; New American Sculpture, Pasadena Art Mus, 64; two-man shows, 66 & American Sculpture of the Sixties, 67, Los Angeles Co Mus Art; Ten from Los Angeles, Seattle Art Mus, 66; one-man show, 69 & ann group show, 72, Whitney Mus Am Art; Ft Worth Art Mus, Tex, 69; Pasadena Art Mus, Calif, 69; Int Biennial Prints, Nat Mus Mod Art, Tokyo, Japan, 70; Eleven Los Angeles Artists, Hayward Gallery, London, Eng, 71; Mus Mod Art, New York, 71; West Coast USA, Kolnischer Kunstverein, Cologne, WGer, 72; Philadelphia Mus Art, 72; plus many other group & one-man shows. Awards: Tamarind Fel, 68-69. Bibliog: Thomas Hess (auth), Art, New York Mag, 12/74; Judith Tannenbaum (auth), Kenneth Price—Willard, Arts Mag, 2/75; Kenneth Price at Willard, Art in Am, 5-6/75. Dealer: Willard Gallery 29 E 72nd St New York NY 10021. Mailing Add: Box 1356 Taos NM 87571

PRICE, LESLIE KENNETH
PAINTER, EDUCATOR
b New York, NY. Study: Sch Visual Arts, NY, 63-64; Pratt Inst, with James Gahagan, Ernest Briggs, G Laderman, BFA, 69; Mills Col, Oakland, Calif, MFA, 71. Work: Oakland Mus, Calif; Johnson Publ Co, Chicago. Exhib: Oakland Mus, 70; Blacks USA, New York Cult Ctr, 73; New Directions in Afro-Am Art, Cornell Univ, Ithaca, NY, 74; Berkeley Art Ctr, Calif, 76; San Jose Mus, Calif, 76; Studio Mus in Harlem, NY, 77. Teaching: Assoc prof painting, Humboldt State Univ, Arcata, Calif, 72- Awards: Painting Award, Pratt Inst, 68; Award of Merit, Calif Palace of the Legion of Honor, 73; Howorarium, Cornell Univ, 74. Bibliog: Alfred Frankenstein (auth), article in San Francisco Chronicle, 11/77. Mem: Nat Conf of Artists. Style & Technique: Form in space, light in color; acrylics, glazings. Media: Acrylic, Graphite (Painting). Publ: Contribr, Black Artists on Art, Vol II, Contemporary Crafts, 72; contribr, Existance Black, Southern Ill Univ, 72; contribr, Directions in Afro-American Art, Cornell Univ, 74. Mailing Add: 3414 Fernway Arcata CA 95521

PRICE, MICHAEL BENJAMIN
SCULPTOR
b Chicago, Ill, Oct 21, 40. Study: Univ Ill, Urbana-Champaign, with Frank Gallo, 62-64, AB(math), 63, MA(math), 64; Tulane Univ, MFA(sculpture). Work: Art Gallery Mus, Mobile, Ala; Hamline Univ Gallery; Gov Mansion, St Paul. Exhib: One-man shows, Vincent Price Gallery, Chicago, 69 & Krasner Gallery, New York, 73-74 & 76-77; Encounter V, Minn Mus Art, St Paul, 71; Living American Artists and the Figure, Mus Art, Pa State Univ, University Park, 74; Esculturas, Maison Bernard, Caracas, Venezuela, 75; Copper & Graphite, Friends Gallery, Minneapolis Inst of Art, 78. Teaching: Instr sculpture, Univ Ala, Huntsville, 66; assoc prof sculpture, drawing & art hist, Hamline Univ, 70- Awards: Purchase Prize, Gulf Coast Art Exhib, 68. Style & Technique: Clay modeling; figurative sculpture. Media: Cast Bronze. Dealer: Oscar Krasner c/o Krasner Gallery 1043 Madison Ave New York NY 10021. Mailing Add: 1302 Englewood St St Paul MN 55104

PRICE, ROSALIE PETTUS
PAINTER
b Birmingham, Ala. Study: Birmingham-Southern Col, AB; Univ Ala, MA. Work: Birmingham Mus Art; Springfield Art Mus, Mo; Spain Ctr Collection, Univ Ala, Birmingham; Birmingham Trust Nat Bank; SCent Bell Tel Co, Birmingham. Exhib: Southern States Art League, High Mus of Art, Atlanta, Ga, 43 & 46; Calif Water Color Soc Ann, 45, 46, 47 & 48; Watercolor Soc of Ala & Birmingham Art Asn, 45-77; Am Watercolor Soc, New York, 47 & 74; Delgado Mus of Art, New Orleans & Art Asn of New Orleans, 47 & 48; Southeastern Ann, 47 & 48; Watercolor & Print Exhib, Pa Acad of the Fine Arts, 48; Watercolor USA, Art Mus, Springfield, Mo, 68, 71 & 72; 35th Ann Midyear Show, Butler Inst of Am Art, Youngstown, Ohio, 70; Nat Watercolor Soc Ann, 70; Ann Nat Drawing & Small Sculpture Show, Del Mar Col, Corpus Christi, Tex, 71, 73 & 77; Ann Drawing & Small Sculpture Show, Ball State Univ, Muncie, Ind, 72 & 74; one-man shows, Birmingham Mus of Art, 66 & 73. Teaching: Instr drawing & watercolor, Birmingham Mus Art, 67-70; instr art appreciation, color & design, Samford Univ, 69-70. Awards: Little House on Linden Purchase Award, Birmingham Art Asn, 68; W Alden Brown Mem Prize, Nat Soc Painters in Casein, 70; Purchase Award, Watercolor USA, 72. Bibliog: Martin Hames (interviewer), The implacable abstraction of objects, Ala Educ TV, 1/13/72. Mem: Nat Watercolor Soc; Watercolor Soc Ala (secy, 48-49); La Watercolor Soc; Birmingham Art Asn (pres, 47-49); Nat Soc Painters Casein & Acrylic. Style & Technique: Lyrical abstractions of symbolic imagery; various techniques. Media: Acrylic, Oil, Ink. Mailing Add: 300 Windsor Dr Birmingham AL 35209

PRICE, VINCENT
COLLECTOR, ART DEALER
b St Louis, Mo, May 27, 11. Study: Yale Univ, BA, 33; Univ London, 34-35; Ohio Wesleyan, hon LLD; Calif Col Arts & Crafts, hon DFA; Columbia Col, hon DFA. Pos: Founder, Mod Inst Art, 45; former pres, Univ Calif, Los Angeles Art Coun; dir, Vincent Price Art Gallery; former mem bd, Archives Am Art; mem, Whitney Mus Friends Am Art; mem, US Indian Arts & Crafts Bd; former mem fine arts comt, White House; bd dir, Ctr Arts of Indian Affairs; adv comt, Friends of Art, Univ Southern Calif; art consult, Sears Roebuck & Co. Mem: Royal Soc Art; Indian Arts & Crafts Bd, Dept Interior (chmn, 68-72). Publ: Auth, Vincent Price on art, syndicated column, Chicago Tribune, 3 yrs; auth, many articles on art in nat mags & newspapers; auth, I Like What I Know, The Book of Joe & Treasury of American Art; co-ed (with Ferdinand V Delacroix), Drawings of Delacroix; plus others. Mailing Add: 315 S Beverly Dr Beverly Hills CA 90212

PRIDE, JOY
PAINTER, WRITER
b Lexington, Ky. Study: Univ Ky, BA & MA; Barnes Found, Merion, Pa; Art Students League; New Sch Social Res; Scand Acad; Acad Julian; Acad Andre L'Hote, Paris; also with Stuart Davis. Work: Home of Henry Clay-Ashland, Senate Off Bldg, Washington DC; Lexington Pub Schs. Comn: Hist Ky Landmarks, Ky Schs. Exhib: Speed Mus Regional, Louisville, Ky, 30; Nat Asn Women Artists Ann, 45-60; Pen & Brush, 45-66; one-man shows, Lexington, 35, Los Angeles, 45 & Newburyport, Mass, 72. Teaching: Head dept of Art, Barmore Sch, New York; head dept art, Murray State Teachers Col; instr art, Univ KY. Pos: Art dir gen publ, Christian Sci Publ Soc; art dir-prod ed, McCormack Mathers Publ Co; sr art ed, Macmillan Co. Awards: Hon Mention, Nat Asn Women Artists; Pen & Brush; Cape Cod Art Asn. Style & Technique: A combination of simplified, abstracted representation in high key color. Media: Oil, Graphics, Tempera. Res: Influences other than painting traditions on modern schools of painting. Publ: Auth, Sing of America, Crowell; auth, America Sings, Hansen; designer, Story of American Freedom & designer, World Hist, Macmillan; designer, The Bible in Story and Song (children's bk & rec), Christian Sci Publ Soc. Mailing Add: 74 Pilot Dr Box 438 South Dennis MA 02660

PRIEBE, KARL
PAINTER
b Milwaukee, Wis, July 1, 14. Work: Va Mus Fine Arts, Richmond; Barnes Found, Merion, Pa; Milwaukee Art Inst; Fisk Univ; plus many others. Exhib: One-man shows, Perls Gallery, New York, Hammer Gallery, New York, Shima Mura Gallery, Tokyo, Waterman Gallery, Paris & Palace of Legion of Honor, San Francisco; plus many other group & one-man shows. Awards: Madison Salon Award, Milwaukee Art Inst Award, Int Watercolor Show Award, Chicago Art Inst. Bibliog: Articles in Life Mag & Art Digest. Media: Casein. Mailing Add: 5419 N 35th St Milwaukee WI 53209

PRIEST, HARTWELL WYSE
PAINTER, PRINTMAKER
b Brantford, Ont, Jan 1, 01; US citizen. Study: Smith Col, 24; Paris-Atelier, with Andre L'Hote; also with Hans Hofmann, New York. Work: Etching, Libr of Cong, Washington, DC; etching, Newark Pub Libr, NJ; lithograph, Norton Gallery, West Palm Beach, Fla; print, Smith Col Art Mus Pvt Collection; Univ Maine; Hunt Botanical Libr, Richmond Mus Fine Art; plus others. Comn: Murals, Children's Ward, Univ Va Hosp, Charlottesville, 55; flowers & woodland scene for ann report, Hunt Botanical Libr, Pittsburgh, 71. Exhib: Nat Asn Women Artists Ann, 44-; Soc Am Graphic Artists Ann, 56-; Artistes Feminins, Exhib Les Services Americans d'Information, Ostende & Brussels, Berne, 56; Audubon Artists, New York, 68; Nat Asn Women Artists Foreign Exhib, Palazzo Vechio, Florence, Italy, 72; plus others. Pos: Pres, Summit Art Asn, NJ, 45-46; mem bd, 2nd St Gallery, 77 & assoc mem, McGaffey Art Ctr. Awards: Medal of Honor, 53, Alice S Buell Mem Award for Graphics, 70, John Carl Georgi Mem Award, 73 & Janet E Turmer Mem Award for Graphics, 75, Nat Asn Women Artists; Pen & Brush Award, 73; Edna Stauffer Mem Prize for Etching, 77. Mem: Nat Asn Women Artists (mem jury, 55, exten comt, 73-75); Richmond Mus of Fine Arts (mem, Loan-Own Gallery); Soc Am Graphic Artists; Washington Printmakers; Pen & Brush. Mailing Add: 41 Old Farm Rd Charlottesville VA 22901

PRIEST, T
PAINTER, PRINTMAKER
b Worcester, Mass, Jan 20, 28. Study: Worcester Art Mus Sch, Mass, 47-48 & eve classes; Quinsigamond Community Col, Worcester, 72 & 73; Univ Mass, Amherst, BFA(painting), 75, MFA(painting), 77. Work: Worcester Art Mus, Mass; Aldrich Mus Contemp Art, Ridgefield, Conn; DeCordova Mus, Lincoln, Mass; Bundy Art Ctr, Waitsfield, Vt; Mead Paper Corp Collection, New York. Comn: Mosaic mural, St Mary's Church, Shrewsbury, Mass, 62; three color serigraph, Worcester Art Mus, 77. Exhib: Watergate, Galerie Borjeson, Malmö, Sweden (traveling), 74; 20th Ann Drawing & Small Sculpture, Ball State Univ, 74;

Six New Eng Artists, Worcester Art Mus, Mass, 74; New Eng Women, DeCrodova Mus, Lincoln, 75; Painting Invitational, Brockton Art Ctr, Mass, 75; one-person show, Drawings, Worcester Art Mus, Mass, 76. Teaching: Instr color form design, Worcester Art Mus Sch, 70- Pos: Color integrated sem, Hampshire Col, Amherst, Mass, 75. Awards: Purchase Award, Mead Paper Corp, 66; Kinnicutt Travel Award, Worcester Art Mus, 74. Bibliog: Nina Kaiden & Bartlett hayes (auth), Artist and Advocate, Renaissance, 67. Mem: Boston Visual Artists Union; Col Art Asn. Style & Technique: Hard-edge painter, works deal with color and light, are sometimes optical in effect. Media: Acrylic and Oil on Canvas; Silk Screen Printing. Dealer: Clark Gallery Lincoln MA 01773; Ethel Putterman Gallery Orleans MA 02653. Mailing Add: 5 Pratt St Worcester MA 01609

PRINCE, ARNOLD
SCULPTOR, EDUCATOR
b Basseterre, West Indies, Apr 17, 25. Study: Brit Coun with John Harrison, Jose DeGreeft, William Zorach, John Hovvannes; Art Students League. Work: First Vest Pocket Park, New York; Art Students League. Comn: Concrete sculpture, City North Adams, Mass, 68; gate post sculpture, Spruces Residential Park, 72; concrete sculpture, comn by Robert Potrin, Stamford, Vt, 73. Exhib: St Marks on the Bowery, 64; Sculptors Guild Exhib, 69-; Slide Show Collection of Afro-Am Artists, Univ Ala, 71; Boston Pub Libr, 73; one-man show, RI Sch Design, 75. Teaching: Dir sculpture educ, Fed Govt Poverty Proj Harlem, HARYOU, 64-67; adj prof sculpture, North Adams State Col, 70-72; asst prof fine arts & sculpture, RI Sch Design, 72- Bibliog: Article in Village Voice, 12/65; article in NAdams Transcript, 66-71. Mem: Sculptors Guild NY. Style & Technique: Direct carving in wood and stone; large scale; not too much preplan, mostly follow the block. Media: Wood, Stone, Concrete. Dealer: Sculptors Guild Inc 75 Rockefeller Plaza New York NY 10020. Mailing Add: 2 College St Providence RI 02903

PRINCE, RICHARD EDMUND
SCULPTOR, EDUCATOR
b Comox, BC, Apr 6, 49. Study: Univ BC, BA(art hist), 71 & study, 72-73; Emma Lake Artists Workshop, Sask, with Ron Kitaj, 70. Work: Nat Gallery Can, Ottawa; Vancouver Art Gallery, BC; Govt of BC, Victoria Art Collection; Univ BC; Vancouver Art Collection, Can. Exhib: Two-man show, Directions 72, Vancouver Art Gallery, 72; Pacific Vibrations, Vancouver Art Gallery, 73; one-man show, Woodlore and Other Romances, Anna Leonowen's Gallery, Halifax, NS, 74; Nine out of Ten: Contemporary Can Art, Art Gallery Hamilton, Ont, 74-75; Landscape Abbreviations, Art Gallery Victoria, BC, 74-75. Teaching: Instr sculpture, Vancouver Community Col, BC, 74-75; instr fine arts & sculpture, Univ BC, 75- Awards: Bursary Award, Can Coun, Govt of Can, 72-73; Art Vancouver for 74 Award, City of Vancouver, 74; Can Coun Arts Grant, Govt of Can, 75. Bibliog: Avis Lang Rosenberg (auth), Richard Prince, Artscanada, 2/73; Alex Mogelon (auth), Art in Boxes, Van Nostrand, New York, 74. Style & Technique: Small or medium scale constructions; some kinetic and electronic involvement; landscape subject matter. Media: Wood, Metal; Plastic, Electronic. Dealer: Equinox Galleries Penthouse 1525 W Eighth Ave Vancouver BC Can. Mailing Add: 8849 Oak St Vancouver BC V6P 4B5 Can

PRINGLE, BURT EVINS
GRAPHIC ARTIST, AQUARELLIST
b Savannah, Ga, Feb 11, 29. Work: Hall of Fame Portraits, Gator Bowl, Jacksonville & Jacksonville Art Mus, Fla. Comn: Murals, USA, Stuttgart, Ger, 53; Migratory Bird Treaty Commemorative Postage Stamp, 66 & VI Commemorative Postage Stamp, 67, US Post Off. Exhib: Jacksonville Arts Festival, 61-64; one-man show, Norton Gallery & Sch Art, West Palm Beach, Fla, 68. Pos: Display dir, Retail stores, 45- Awards: Soc l'Exploition Brussels World's Fair, 58; one Bronze & two Gold Medals, Display World Mag, 58-59; 18 Honorariums, UN Postal Admin, 66-75. Bibliog: A Beltramo (auth), Il Collezionista, Italy, 68. Mem: Am Fedn Arts; Fla Watercolor Soc; St Augustine Art Asn. Style & Technique: Realistic. Media: Watercolor, Gouaches. Mailing Add: 1722 Paine Ave Jacksonville FL 32211

PRINS, (J) WARNER
PAINTER, ILLUSTRATOR
b Amsterdam, Holland, July 24, 01. Work: Metrop Mus Art; Jewish Mus, NY; Munson-Williams-Proctor Inst, Utica. Comn: Ceramic murals, pub bldg, NY & Int Hotel, Airport, New York. Exhib: One-man shows, Carlebach Gallery, 50, Archit League, 52, The Contemporaries, 53 & Juster Gallery, 59, NY. Mem: Artists Equity Asn. Publ: Illusr, An old faith in the new world; illusr, Phedre, 68; illusr, Haggadah, A S Barnes, 69. Mailing Add: 888 Park Ave New York NY 10021

PRITZLAFF, MR & MRS JOHN, JR
COLLECTORS
Mr Pritzlaff, b Milwaukee, Wis, May 10, 25; Mrs Pritzlaff, b St Louis, Mo. Study: Mr Pritzlaff, Princeton Univ, BA, 49; Mrs Pritzlaff, Briarcliff Col. Pos: Mr Pritzlaff, US Ambassador to Malta, 69-72; Ariz State Sen, 75-; mem bd dirs, Heard Mus, Phoenix, Ariz, 76-77; Mrs Pritzlaff, pres, bd dirs, Phoenix Art Mus. Mailing Add: 4954 E Rockridge Rd Phoenix AZ 85018

PROCHOWNIK, WALTER A
LECTURER, PAINTER
b Buffalo, NY, Dec 12, 23. Study: Art Inst of Buffalo; Art Students League. Work: Albright-Knox Art Gallery, Buffalo, NY; Norfolk Mus Arts & Sci, Va; Minn Mus Arts, St Paul; Burchfield Ctr, State Univ NY, Buffalo; Ball State Univ Art Gallery, Muncie, Ind. Comn: You the People (mural), Co of Erie, Rath Off Bldg, Buffalo, 74. Exhib: One-man shows, Member's Gallery, Albright-Knox Art Gallery, Buffalo, 64, Col of Wooster, Ohio, 66, Chautauqua Art Asn Gallery, NY, 68 & Burchfield Ctr, Buffalo, 75; Smithsonian travel tour, 68-69. Teaching: Lectr art, Millard Fillmore Col, State Univ NY, Buffalo, 63- Awards: First Oil Award, Chautauqua Art Asn, 58; Purchase Prize, Drawings USA, 63 & 66; Perkin-Elmer Corp Award, Silvermine Guild, 69. Mem: Patteran Artists. Style & Technique: Abstract paintings with close fusion of colors, creating atmospheric space. Media: Oil; Mixed. Dealer: More-Rubin Gallery 460 Franklin St Buffalo NY 14201. Mailing Add: 1885 Hertel Ave Buffalo NY 14214

PROCTER, BURT
PAINTER
b Gloucester, Mass, June 24, 01. Study: Chicago Art Inst; Otis Art Inst, Los Angeles; Chouinard Art Inst, Los Angeles; Grand Central Sch Art, New York, with Harold Von Schmidt, Pruett Carter & Lawrence Murphy. Work: Mus Navajo Ceremonial Art, Santa Fe, NMex; Univ Northern Ariz, Flagstaff; Palm Springs Mus, Calif; plus pvt collections of Barry Goldwater, Phoenix, Ariz & Harrison Eitlejorg, Indianapolis, Ind. Comn: Spec oil paintings, comn by Dr Robert Sukman, Edmond, Okla, 71, Lee Hobbs, Wichita, Kans, 73, Theodore Mollring, Jackson, Wyo, 74, Harry E Hanley, Dundee, Ill, 75 & Melvin Warren, Clifton, Tex, 75. Exhib: Western Show, Grand Cent Galleries, New York, 74 & 75; Nat Acad Design, New York; One-man shows, Red Ridge Mus, Oklahoma City, 72, Wichita Art Asn, 73 & Southwest Mus, Los Angeles, 74. Teaching: Instr pvt classes in oil painting, 47-62. Awards: Isabel Steinchneider Mem Award, Hudson Valley Art Asn, New York, 70; Margaret Fernald Dole Mem Award, Hudson Valley Art Asn, 72; Samuel James Campbell Cash Award, Grand Cent, NY, 73. Mem: Laguna Beach Art Asn; Hudson Valley Art Asn; Grand Central Art Galleries. Style & Technique: Representational, based on composition and design; impressionistic and broad rather than photographic with true values and drawing. Media: Oils. Mailing Add: 402 Goldenrod Corona del Mar CA 92625

PROCTOR, GIFFORD MACGREGOR
SCULPTOR, DESIGNER
b New York, NY, Feb 5, 12. Study: Yale Univ, BFA; Am Acad in Rome, Prix de Rome fel, 35; apprentice to a Phimister Proctor (father); study & travel abroad, 5 yrs. Comn: Four heroic granite eagles, US Govt, Fed Off Bldg, New Orleans, La, 40; first spec serv force mem, Helena, Mont, 48; two portrait statues, comn by State of Ore, Nat Capitol Bldg, Washington, DC, 53; relief globe of moon, Washington Plaza Hotel, Seattle, 59; many medals, portrait busts, garden & decorative sculpture. Teaching: Artist in residence, Beloit Col, 40-42. Pos: Asst to pres, Chandler Cudlipp Assts NY, NY Interior Planning & Design, 58-65; coordr planning & design, Student Union, San Fernando Valley State Col, Northridge, Calif, 69- Bibliog: Clement Morro (auth), The Valley Forge Washington, La Rev Mod, 38; sci ed (auth), Want to Buy a Moon?, Life Mag, 11/30/62. Mem: Nat Sculpture Soc. Media: Bronze. Mailing Add: 9 Pearce Mitchell Pl Stanford CA 94305

PROHASKA, RAY
PAINTER, ILLUSTRATOR
b Muo, Yugoslavia, Feb 5, 01; US citizen. Study: Calif Sch Fine Art, San Francisco. Work: Butler Inst Am Art, Youngstown, Ohio; Krannert Art Gallery, Univ Ill, Champaign; Guild Hall, East Hampton, NY; Int Tel & Tel Co, New York; New Britain Mus, Conn. Exhib: Va Mus Biennial, Richmond, 65-69; NC Mus Art, 71; Benson Gallery, Bridgehampton, NY; Southampton Col, NY; Guild Hall, East Hampton, NY. Teaching: Instr illus, Art Students League, 61-62; artist in residence, Washington & Lee Univ, 64-69; artist in residence, Wake Forest Univ, 69- Awards: Gold Medal for Painting, 63, One-man Show Award, 63 & Hall of Fame & Soc Medal of Honor, 72, Guild Hall; Childe Hassam Fund Award, Am Acad Arts & Lett, 72; Marjorie Peabody Waite Award, Nat Inst Arts & Lett, 74; plus many others. Mem: Soc Illusr (pres, 59-60). Style & Technique: Lyrical abstraction; monoprint; silk screen printing and drawing. Publ: Illusr, Eddie-no-name, 63; illusr, Who's Afraid, 63; auth, A Basic Course in Design—Introduction to Drawing & Painting, 71. Mailing Add: Box 726 Bridgehampton NY 11932

PROKOPOFF, STEPHEN STEPHEN
MUSEUM DIRECTOR, ART HISTORIAN
b Chicago, Ill, Dec 29, 29. Study: Univ Calif, Berkeley, BA & MA; NY Univ, PhD. Exhibitions Arranged: Romantic Minimalism, 67; Spirit of the Comics, 68; Highway, 69; Two Generations of Color Painting, 70; Against Order, 71; White on White, 72; Post-Mondrian Abstraction in America, 73; Logic of Vision, 74; Made In Chicago, 75; plus many others. Teaching: Robert B Mayor prof art hist, Univ Chicago, 75- Pos: Dir, Hathorn Gallery, Skidmore Col, 66-67, Inst Contemp Art, Univ Pa, 67-71 & Mus Contemp Art, Chicago, 71-77, Inst Contemp Art, Boston, 78- Mem: Am Asn Mus Dirs; Am Asn Mus; Col Art Asn Am. Publ: Co-auth, 19th Century Architecture of Saratoga Springs, NY, 72. Mailing Add: 955 Boylston St Boston MA 02115

PROSS, LESTER FRED
EDUCATOR, PAINTER
b Bristol, Conn, Aug 14, 24. Study: Oberlin Col, BA, 45, MA, 46; Ohio Univ, with Ben Shahn, summer 52; Skowhegan Sch Painting & Sculpture, summer 53; also with Simon, Zorach, Levine, Hebald & Bocour; Univ of Colo Kyoto Sem, Japan, 75-76; study of painting with Kono Shuson. Exhib: Midstates Ann, Evansville, 64; Face of Kentucky I & II Traveling Exhib, 68-70; Appalachian Corridors II Traveling Exhib, 70-71; Morehead State Univ, 73; Ky Bicentennial, 74. Teaching: Prof art, Berea Col, 46-, chmn dept, 50-; Fulbright lectr painting & art hist, Univ Panjab, 57-58; vis assoc prof art educ & hist, Union Col, summer 61; vis prof art, Am Univ Cairo, 67-68. Pos: Pres, Ky Art Educ Asn, 55; chmn adv bd, Appalachian Mus, Berea Col, 69-; bd dirs, Doris Ulmann Found. Awards: Haskell Traveling Fel, Oberlin Col, 57-58. Mem: Col Art Asn Am; Mid-Am Col Art Asn; Ky Guild Artists & Craftsmen (pres, 61-63); Asn Asian Studies; Asia Soc. Media: Oil, Watercolor, Acrylic. Publ: Illusr, Mountain Life & Work. Mailing Add: 1287 CPO Berea KY 40404

PROVDER, CARL
PAINTER, INSTRUCTOR
b Brooklyn, NY, Feb 7, 33. Study: Pratt Inst, BFA; Columbia Univ, MA, prof dipl; Inst Allende, MFA; Educ Alliance Art Sch; Art Students League; NY Univ; Acad Belli Arti, Perugia; also with Samuel Adler. Exhib: 147th Ann Exhib, Nat Acad Design, New York, 72; 73rd Ann, Nat Arts Club, 72; one-man shows, Hist Mus, East Meadow, NY, 72, Paideia Gallery, Los Angeles, 76, Riverside Mus, Calif, 76 & Coast Village Gallery, Santa Barbara, Calif, 77; Contemp Artists Brooklyn, Brooklyn Mus, 72; Painters & Sculptors Soc, Jersey City Mus, NJ, 72; Garelicks Gallery, Scottsdale, Ariz, 76 & 77. Teaching: Instr fine arts, Bd Educ, New York, 64-73; instr fine arts, San Diego Community Col, 74- Awards: First Prize/Mixed Media, Southern Calif Expo, Del Mar, 77; Purchase Award, Small Image Art Show, San Diego, 78. Bibliog: H G L (auth), Carl Povder, 3/25/71 & Dorothy Hall (auth), Provder at Gallery 84, 1/13/72, Park East; Malcolm Preston (auth), Unbridled intuition, Newsday, 5/17/72. Mem: Artists Equity Asn; Col Art Asn Am; San Diego Art Guild; Art Inst San Diego; La Jolla Mus Contemp Art. Style & Technique: Lyrical abstraction; semi-abstract figure and landscape forms in oil and mixed media. Mailing Add: 1416 Elva Terr Encinitas CA 92024

PROWN, JULES DAVID
ART HISTORIAN
b Freehold, NJ, Mar 14, 30. Study: Lafayette Col, AB, 51; Harvard Univ, AM(fine arts), 53; Univ Del, AM(early Am cult), 56; Harvard Univ, PhD(fine arts), 61. Collections Arranged: John Singleton Copley (auth, catalogue; travelling exhib), 65-66 & American Art from Alumni Collections, 68, Yale Univ Art Gallery. Teaching: Teaching fel art hist, Harvard Univ, Cambridge, Mass, 56-57; from instr art hist to prof art hist, 61- Pos: Asst to dir, William Hayes Fogg Art Mus, Harvard Univ, 59-61; cur, Garvan & Related Collections of Am Art, Yale Univ, New Haven, 63-68; dir, Yale Brit Art Ctr, New Haven, 68-76. Awards: Edward R Bacon Art Scholar, Harvard Univ, 58-59; Guggenheim Fel, 64-65; Blanche Elizabeth MacLeish Billings Award, Yale Univ, 66. Mem: Am Asn of Mus; Am Soc for 18th Century Studies (exec bd mem, 73-76); Col Art Asn (bd dir, ?5-); Whitney Mus of Am Art, New York (bd dir, 75-); Nat Humanities Inst (mem exec Bd, 75-). Res: American and English art; John Singleton Copley; Benjamin West. Publ: Auth, John Singleton Copley, 2 vols, Harvard Univ

Press, 66; co-auth, The visual arts in higher education, Col Art Asn, 66; auth, American Painting from Its Beginnings to the Armory Show, Skira, 69; auth, The architecture of the Yale Center for British Art, Yale Ctr for Brit Art, 77. Mailing Add: Dept of Art Hist Yale Univ Box 2009 New Haven CT 06520

PRUITT, A KELLY
PAINTER, SCULPTOR
b Waxahachie, Tex, Feb 9, 24. Work: Mus NMex, Santa Fe; Diamond M Mus, Snyder, Tex. Comn: The Plainsman (bronze), Frank Phillips Col, Borger, Tex, 67. Exhib: Guest Artist, Tex State Fair, Dallas, 69; 19th Ann Tucson Festival Exhib, Tucson Art Ctr, Ariz, 69; one-man exhib, Okla Mus Art, Red Ridge, Oklahoma City, 72. Bibliog: A Lamp Out of The West, Chyka Carey Prod, 64; Jane Pattie (auth), A Kelly Pruitt: cowboy with a paint brush, Cattleman Mag, 66; Ed Ainsworth (auth), The Cowboy in Art, World, 68. Style & Technique: Western art completely creative without use of models, photos or scenes. Media: Oil, Bronze. Publ: Illusr, The Cattleman, 66 & 68; illusr, The Paint Horse J, 67; illusr & auth article, In: The Paint Horse J, 67; auth, Wild Red from Presidio, Part I, 75. Mailing Add: c/o Cross Galleries 3629 W Seventh St Ft Worth TX 76107

PRUITT, LYNN
SCULPTOR, GALLERY DIRECTOR
b Washington, DC, May 24, 37. Work: Marlboro Hall, Prince George Com Col, Largo, Md. Comn: Sculptured canvas wall relief, Naval Acad, Annapolis, Md, 76. Exhib: Corcoran Gallery Art, Washington, DC, 65 & 72; Md Regional, Baltimore Mus, 66, 67, 70 & 74; Group demonstration of welded steel sculpture and exhibition for the Dept of Transportation, Smithsonian Inst, Washington, DC, 69; Studio Gallery, Washington, DC, 70 & 76; Art Barn, Washington, DC, 70, 74 & 78; one-person shows Montgomery Col, Rockville, Md, 74; Washington Womens Arts Ctr, Washington, DC, 75-77; Talking of Michelangelo Gallery, Washington, DC, 75; Maryland Artists Today, East Coast Univ Tour, Baltimore Mus, 75 & 76; Towson State Col, Baltimore, Md, 76; Md Col Art, Silver Spring, 76; Blind Sculpture, Md Nat Capitol Park & Planning Comn, Kenilworth, 77; Nat Audubon Soc, Chevy Chase, Md, 77. Teaching: Instr basic art, Jewish Community Ctr, Rockville, Md, 74- Pos: Juror, Prince George's Community Col, 72-75, Nat Inst Health, 73-75, Md Col Art, 76 & Scholastic Art Awards, Washington, DC, Md & Va, 77-78; Dir & consult, Holden Gallery, Inc, Kensington, Md, 76- Awards: First in Painting, 68, 69 & 70, Best in Show, 68, 69 & 70 & First in Sculpture, 70, 71, 73 & 74, Nat Inst Health, Bethesda, Md. Bibliog: Washington Artists, Artist Equity Asn, 62 & 72; US Dept Housing & Urban Develop, 75. Mem: Washington Womens Arts Ctr; Am Crafts Coun. Style & Technique: Sculpture; mixed media, plaster, steel, wood, leather, plexiglass and others. Media: Sculpture, plaster. Mailing Add: 303 Nimitz Ave Rockville MD 20851

PO-TSU-NU
See Montoya, Geronima Cruz

PUCCINELLI, RAIMONDO
SCULPTOR, GRAPHIC ARTIST
b San Francisco, Calif, May 5, 04. Study: Calif Sch Fine Arts, San Francisco; Rudolph Schaeffer Sch Design, San Francisco; apprentice to woodcarvers, stone cutters & masters of plaster; Univ Calif, Berkeley. Work: Edgard Varese (granite portrait), Columbia Univ Music Libr, New York; Mother & Child (porphyry), Fresno Mall, Calif; Hans Rothe (bronze portrait), Stadt Theatre Mus, Schleswig, Ger; Bison (diorite), City of San Francisco Hosp; bronze figure, Duke Univ, NC; Musee Moderne, Ceret, France; Schiller Nat Mus, Marbach, Ger; Städtische Galerie, Würzburg; Kulturgeschichtlich Mus, Osnabrück, Ger; Bocholt Mus, Ger; Jugenberg Mus, Gemen, Ger; Stedelijk Mus, Zutphen, Neth; Hirshhorn Mus, Smithsonian Inst, Washington, DC; Israel Mus, Jerusalem Music Ctr. Comn: Panther (polished diorite), Salinas Col, Calif, 40; Polar Bear (polished marble), Mills Col, Oakland, Calif, 41; Bear (dioite), Univ Calif, Berkeley, 44; Franciscan Saints, 57-58, bronze doors, 58 & St Bernadette & Virgin (terra-cotta), 58, House of Theology, Franciscan Monastery, Centerville, Ohio; Cross (bronze), St Andrew's Church, Mayo, Md, 60. Exhib: Twenty Contemporary Sculptors, Grand Cent Galleries, New York, 46; Contemporary American Sculpture, Whitney Mus Am Art, New York, 48 & 49; Sculpture Exhib, Nat Inst Arts & Lett, New York, 53, 55 & 57; Bienniale Int del Bronzetto, Padova, Italy, 67; Modern Sculpture, Corcoran Gallery Art, Washington, DC, 62; one-man exhibs (74-78), Duke Univ Mus of Art, Durham, NC, Kunsthaus der Stadt Bocholt, Ger, Kulturring Kaufbeuren, Ger; Schloss Nordkirchen, Ger; Kunstgeschichtliche Mus, Osnabrück, Ger, Kreishaus in Steinfurt, Ger, Städtische Galerie Würzburg, Cult Inst, Cologne, Ger, Stedelijk Mus, Zutphen, Neth, Nieuw Kunsthuis, Doetinchem, Neth, Kasteel d'Erp, Maasbree, Neth, Slot Mus, Zeist, Neth, Handwerksmuseum, Münster, Ger, Cube Gallery, Tokyo, Japan, Galleria Il Castello, Milano, Italy & Galleria San Benedetto, Brescia, Italy, plus other one-man exhibs in US, Latin Am & Europe. Teaching: Instr sculpture & drawing, Mills Col, 38-47; prof sculpture & drawing, Univ Calif, Berkeley, 42-47; asst prof sculpture & drawing, Univ NC, Chapel Hill, 47-48; instr design & art hist, Queens Col, New York, 48-51; dean sculpture & drawing, Rinehart Sch Sculpture, Peabody Inst & Md Inst Col Art, 58-60; prof sculpture, Int Univ Arts, Florence. Pos: Cult envoy for Latin Am, US Dept State, 56. Awards: Sculpture Prize, San Francisco Mus Art, 37 & 38; Sculpture Award, Los Angeles Co Mus Art, 39; Medaglio d'Oro for Il Fiorino, Palazzo Strozzi, Florence, Italy, 66. Bibliog: Wanda Svevo (auth), Puccinelli & his sculpture, Habitat Mag, 58; Carra & Cavallo (auth), Puccinelli, Il Castello, 71; Italo Sesti (auth), Raimondo Puccinelli—scultore del visibile, Scenâ Illustrata, 71; William S Heckscher (auth), Puccinelli, Duke Univ, 74; Selhorst & Modlmayr (auths), Raimondo Puccinelli, Kulturamt, Ger, 76; Erwin Birnmayer (auth), Graphische Kunst—Puccinelli, Ed Curt Visel, Ger, 78. Mem: Hon mem Florentine Acad. Publ: Auth, Bronze sculpture, Arts & Archit, 39; auth, Sculpture, a visual language, Architects' Report, winter 61; auth, We Think with Entire Being, Duke Univ. Mailing Add: Piazza Donatello 18 Florence Italy

PUCHALSKI, GREGORY JOHN
CORRESPONDENCE ARTIST, PHOTOGRAPHER
b Buffalo, NY, Aug 24, 48. Study: Univ Buffalo, BFA; also with Donald Blumberg. Work: Rose Mus, Calgary, Alta. Exhib: Int Cyclopeida Plan & Occurances, Anderson Gallery, Richmond, Va, 73; 1st Ann Toronto Correspondence & Junk Art Exhib, 1234567 Gallery, Toronto, 74; Secrets of the Universe Revealed by Artist, Oval House Gallery, London, Eng, 74; Galeria Sztuhimdh, Krakow, Poland, 75; Pictorial History of the World, Kemper Gallery, Kansas City, Kans, 75; one-man shows, Eastern Mont Col, 77 & Hallwalls, Buffalo, NY, 77. Pos: Artist, Turner Advert, Atlanta, Ga, 73-74; ed, 491 Mag, 73- Bibliog: Karen Wantuck (auth), Dadadadadadadadada, Creative Loafing, 3/74. Style & Technique: Dada-surrealism with influence of photo realist. Media: Oil, Collage, Photography. Publ: Contribr, Quoz Mag, Mod Correspondence, Fix Mag & West Bay Dadist, 74-75. Mailing Add: 120 Geary St Buffalo NY 14210

PUCKER, BERNARD H
ART DEALER
b Kansas City, Mo, Oct 19, 37. Study: Columbia Univ, BA, 59; Hebrew Univ, Jerusalem, 60; Brandeis Univ, MA, 66. Pos: Dir, Pucker Safrai Gallery, Boston. Specialty: Contemporary artists; Chagall graphics; Israeli artists; New England artists; fantastic realist painters; Eskimo and African bronzes, by David Aronson & Kieff. Mailing Add: 171 Newbury St Boston MA 02116

PUFAHL, JOHN K
EDUCATOR, PRINTMAKER
b Urbana, Ill, Nov 6, 42. Study: Ill Wesleyan Univ, BFA(hon), 65; Northern Ill Univ, MA & MFA, studied with David F Driesbach, 67; San Francisco State Col, Printmaking and the Photo Image, Symp, 74. Work: Univ Wis, Platteville; Art Gallery of Windsor, Ont; Bd Educ, Windsor, Ont. Exhib: Chicago & Vicinity Exhib, Art Inst Chicago, 66; 162nd Ann Exhib, Philadelphia Acad Fine Arts, 67; 10th Ann Calgary Graphics Exhib, Alta, Can, 70; Can Graphics, Toronto & London, Ont, 70; Can Print Exhib, Windsor, Ont, 74; Calgary Int Drawing Exhib, Alta, 74; Imprint 76 (in conjunction with Olympic Games), Montreal, Que, 76; Fourth Biennale Int de l'Image, Epinal & Paris, France, 77 & 78. Collections Arranged: Can Printmakers, Art Gallery of Toronto, Ont, 70; Imprint 76, Art Gallery Ont, 76-77. Teaching: Asst instr intaglio, Ill Wesleyan Univ, Bloomington, 64-65; assoc prof intaglio & drawing, Univ Windsor, Ont, 67- Pos: Juror, Litho USA, Erie, Pa, 69; exec mem, Can Soc Graphic Arts, 74; consult, Sault Col printmaking facilities, Ont, 74; pres, Pufahl & Krassov Ltd, Press Manufacturers, 74-; juror, Comn Proj, Essex Co Civic & Educ Centre, Ont, 75; adv, Imprint 76, Can Soc Graphic Arts, 76; actg dir, Sch Fine Arts, Univ Windsor, Ont, 76-77; artist-in-residence, Sch of Art, Yeovil Col, Somerset, Eng, 78. Awards: Can Coun grant, Adaptation of Stainless Steel to Intaglio Printmaking, 77. Mem: Can Univ Art Asn; Print & Drawing Coun Can; Printmakers Coun, London, Eng. Style & Technique: Nature-centered, somewhat surrealistic. Media: Color intaglio with photo-transfer; air brush and ink drawing. Publ: Contribr, Canadian print workshops, Art Mag, 77. Mailing Add: 1111 Garden Ct Dr Windsor ON N8S 2S1 Can

PULIDO, GUILLERMO AGUILAR
SCULPTOR, VIDEO ARTIST
b Guadalajara, Jalisco, Mex, Feb 15, 20. Study: Univ of Calif, Berkeley, study with Willard Rosenquist, 70-72 & MA(fine arts), 77; San Francisco Art Inst, BFA, 72-75. Work: Ctr for Art & Commun, Buenos Aires, Argentina; Nac Sch of Commun, Mexico City; Southwest Chicano Arts Ctr, Houston, Tex. Comn: Multi-media installation, Ctr for Contemp Music, Mills Col, Oakland, Calif, 74; multi-media, San Francisco Art Inst Invitational Comt, 75; mural (video Images; with Daniel Galvez), San Francisco Art Comn, Valencia Gardens, San Francisco, 75. Exhib: Calif Ceramic and Glass, Oakland Mus, Calif, 74; Invitational, San Francisco Art Inst, 75; Space Vs Space, Museo Ex-Convento de la Carmen, dept de Bellas Artes, Guadelajara, Mex, 76; Tribal Art, Anthology Film Arch, New York, 77; Nac Sch of Comn, Mexico City, 77; Video Exhib, Fundacion Miro, Barcelona, Spain, 77; The Fifth Sun, Univ of Calif at Berkeley Art Mus, 77; Santa Barbara Mus of Art, Univ of Calif, 78; Roots and New Visions, Nat Hispanic Show, Fondo del Sol, 78. Collections Arranged: Documents and Video of Disabled Artist, San Francisco Art Inst, 75; Monuments for a Sacred Space, C N Gorman Mus, Univ of Calif, Davis, 77. Teaching: Artist-in-Residence, Alvorado Art Project, San Francisco, Unified Sch District, 74-75; Dir film/video, Southwest Chicano Arts Ctr, Houston, 77. Pos: Film Res, Pacific Film Archive, Univ of Calif, Berkeley, 70-72; visual artist, San Francisco Art Comn, 75; producer, Independent, Peru, 75-76. Awards: Best of Festival, Video Festival, San Francisco Art Festival, 74; Harry Lloyd Ford Prize, Univ of Calif, 77; Travel Grant, Monuments for a Sacred Space, Tinker Found, 77. Style & Technique: Environmental anthropological and socialogical studies using photo documentary and audio-visual techniques; multi-media with emphasis on film, video and audio enviroments, including performance or sculptural works. Mailing Add: 3518 Polk Houston TX 77003

PULITZER, MR & MRS JOSEPH, JR
COLLECTORS
Mr Pulitzer, b St Louis, Mo, May 13, 13. Study: Mr Pulitzer, Harvard Univ, AB, 36. Pos: Mrs Pulitzer, art historian & former cur, St Louis Art Mus. Collection: 19th and 20th century paintings, sculptures and drawings. Mailing Add: 9501 Clayton Rd St Louis MO 63124

PULOS, ARTHUR JON
INDUSTRIAL DESIGNER, DESIGN EDUCATOR
b Vandergrift, Pa, Feb 3, 17. Study: Carnegie Inst Technol, BFA, 39; Univ Ore, MFA, 43. Work: Walker Art Ctr, Minn; Newark Mus Fine Arts, NJ; Detroit Inst Art, Mich; Mus Mod Art, New York; Utrecht Mus Decorative Arts, Holland. Comn: Altar pewter, Univ Ill Chapel, 52; ecclesiastical cross & candlesticks, First Presbyterian Church, Champaign, Ill, 53; sterling flatware, Fraser Co, New York, 63; plus jewelry & silverware for pvt comn, 40- Exhib: Brussels World Fair, 60; Metrop Mus, 66; Smithsonian Inst, 66; Louvre, Paris, 66; US Info Agency Exhib, 66. Teaching: Prof indust design, Univ Ill, 46-55; prof indust design & chmn dept, Syracuse Univ, 55- Pos: Pres, Pulos Design Assoc, Inc, 58- Awards: Award for Ceramics, Pittsburgh Art Asn, 39; Award for Flatware, Wichita Art Asn, 48; Award for Hollow Ware, Chicago Art Inst, 52. Mem: Fel Indust Designers Soc Am (pres, 73-, chmn bd, 75-); Int Coun of Soc of Indust Design (vpres for prof affairs, 77-). Publ: Auth, Industrial Design Careers, 70 & 78; auth, Post-materialism, Indust Designers Soc Am J, 71; auth, Design for a humane technology, Am Iron & Steel Indust, 72; auth, The universal object, Indust Design Mag, 73; auth, Contact-Selling Design Services, 75; auth, History of Design in America, Nat Endowment Arts, 76; auth, articles on design in Am & foreign design publ. Mailing Add: 1939 E Genesee St Syracuse NY 13210

PUNIA, CONSTANCE EDITH
PAINTER
b Brooklyn, NY. Study: Brooklyn Mus Art Sch; oil with Edwin Dickinson & Yonia Fain; oil and sumi-e with Murray Hantman. Exhib: Fine Arts Festival, Parrish Art Mus, Southampton, NY, 67 & 68; Asn Belgo-Hispanique Int Festival Art, Chartier Mus, Brussels, Belg, 73 & Paris, France, 74 & 75; Les Surindependants, Paris, 75; Grand Prix Humanitaire de France, Paris, 75; Des Artistes Francais, Grand Palais, Paris, France, 76 & 77; Sun Yat Sen Ctr of Asian Studies at St John's Univ, Jamaica, NY, 76; Nat A Arts Club, New York, NY, 77. Awards: Palmes d'Or Medal, Asn Belgo-Hispanique, 73 & 74; Silver Medal & Laureate of Honor, Grand Prix Humanitaire de France, 75; Bronze Medal, Akad Raymond Duncan, 75; Order of Merit Medal, Acad of Sci & Human Rels, Dominican Repub. Mem: Des Artistes Francais; Nat League Am Pen Women; Sumi-E Soc Am; Asn Belgo-Hispanique; Les Surindependants; Guild Creative Art, Shrewsbury, NJ. Style & Technique: Non-objective, close values and intensities. Media: Oil, Sumi-e. Dealer: Galeries Raymond Duncan 31 Rue de Seine Paris France Mailing Add: 215 Adams St Brooklyn NY 11201

PURSER, STUART ROBERT
PAINTER, EDUCATOR
b Stamps, Ark, Feb 8, 07. Study: La Col, BA, 28; Art Inst Chicago, BFA, 32, MFA, 33; Ohio State Univ, 44; also with Boris Anisfeld, 30-33. Work: Nat Gallery, Melbourne, Australia; High Mus Art, Atlanta, Ga; Hunter Gallery Art, Chattanooga, Tenn; Univ Miss. Comn: Post Office mural, US Treas Dept, Gretna, La, 38 & Ferriday, La, 41, Forty-Eight State Mural for Post Office, Leeland, Miss, 39, Bankhead Memorial Mural for Post Office, Carrolton, Ala, 40. Exhib: Nat Oil Exhib, Art Inst Chicago, 38, Nat Watercolor Ann Exhib, 41; Pa Acad Ann, Philadelphia, 38-40; 1st Ann Oil Exhib, Metrop Mus, New York, 50; Am Drawing Ann, Norfolk Mus, Va, 61-63. Teaching: Instr art, Wash State Univ, 34-35; prof art & chmn dept, La Col, 35-45; prof art, Art Inst Chicago, summers 36-37; prof art & chmn dept, Univ Chattanooga, 45-49; prof art & chmn dept, Univ Miss, 49-51; chmn dept art, Univ Fla, 51-56, prof art, 51-; vis prof art, Univ Calif, Northridge, 58 & 61; prof art, Cent Wash State Col, summer 61; head, Idyllwild Found, Univ Southern Calif, summer 62; prof art, Eastern Wash State Col, summers 65-67. Awards: First Award, Delgado Mus, New Orleans, 42-44; Southeastern Annual First Award, High Mus Art, 60; First Award, Ocala Arts Festival, 68. Mem: Southeastern Col Arts Asn (pres, 45); Southeastern Arts Asn (pres, 53); Nat Art Educ Asn (mem coun, 53-55). Style & Technique: Semi-Abstract. Media: Oil. Publ: Auth, Applehead, 74; auth & illusr, Jesse J Aaron-Sculptor, 75; auth, Drawing Handbook, 75. Mailing Add: 2210 NW Second Ave Gainesville FL 32603

PURYEAR, MARTIN
SCULPTOR
b Washington, DC, May 23, 41. Study: Cath Univ Am, BA; Royal Acad Art, Stockholm; Yale Sch Art & Archit, MFA. Work: Nat Collection Fine Arts, Washington, DC; Guggenheim Mus, New York. Comn: Large-scale wooden sculpture, Artpark, Lewiston, NY, 77. Exhib: One-man shows, Henry 2 Gallery, Washington, DC, 73 & Corcoran Gallery, Washington, DC, 77; Young Am Artists: 1978 Exxon Nat Exhib, Guggenheim Mus, 78. Teaching: Asst prof sculpture, Fisk Univ, Nashville, Tenn, 71-73, Univ Md, College Park, 74- Bibliog: David Bourdon, Martin Puryear at Henry 2, 1-2/74 & David Tannous, Martin Puryear at the Corcoran Gallery, 5-6/78, Art in Am. Style & Technique: Hewn and constructed sculpture. Media: Wood, Related Materials. Dealer: Protetch-McIntosh Gallery 2151 P St NW Washington DC 20037. Mailing Add: 2606 Myrtle Ave NE Washington DC 20018

PUSEY, MAVIS
PAINTER, PRINTMAKER
b Jamaica, WI. Study: Art Students League with Will Barnet, Harry Sternberg, 61-65; Printmaking Workshop with Robert Blackburn, 69-72; Birgit Schold Printmaking Workshop, London, 67-68; New Sch for Social Res, New York, 74 & 76. Work: Mus Mod Art; Chemical Bank, NY; First Nat Bank Chicago; Tougaloo Col, Miss; Citibank, New York; First Nat Bank of Chicago; New York Pub Libr; Cleveland State Univ. Exhib: Art Students League New York, 63; E Weyhe Inc, New York, 65; Brand Libr of Arts & Music, Calif, 65; Far Gallery, New York, 66; UCLA Art Gallery Presentation traveling exhib, 66-67; Curwen Gallery, London, 68; Whitney Mus, New York, 71; Staten Island Mus, NY, 75; Queensborough Col, New York, 75; Lehman Col, Bronx, NY, 75; Int Woman's Arts Festival/Int Woman's Yr, Woman's Int Art Ctr, New York, 75-76; Bankers Trust Club, NY, 76; Am Drawing Competition, Portsmouth Community Arts Ctr, Va, 76; New Sch for Social Res Fac Show, 76; Duffy-Gibbs Gallery, Soho, New York, 77; Huntington Art Ctr 21st Nat Print Traveling Exhib, 77; Somerset Co Col Traveling Exhib, 77; Newark Art Libr Traveling Exhib, 77; Bergen Community Mus Traveling Exhib, 77; Fla Int Univ North Miami Campus Traveling Exhib, 77; Tamiami Campus Fine Arts Gallery Traveling Exhib, 77; one-woman exhibs, Galerie Louis Soulanges, Paris, 68, Marist Col, Poughkeepsie, NY, 75, Stony Brook Union Gallery, NY, 75, Grimaldis Gallery, Baltimore, Md, 77 & Rainbow Art Found, New York, 77. Teaching: Guest artist, Pa Acad Fine Arts, 72-75; instr painting, New Sch Social Res, 73-; asst prof painting, State Univ NY Stony Brook, 74-77; instr, Rutgers State Univ, NJ. Awards: Louis Comfort Tiffany Found Grant, 72 & Purchase Award, 74; Award, Staten Island Mus, 75; Award, Int Woman's Yr, 76; plus others. Bibliog: Prints by American Negro artists, Cult Exchange Ctr, Los Angeles, Calif, 66; Carrefour Newspaper, Paris, 67; Studio Int J Mod Art, London, 67; Linda Blandford (auth), Four 1970s successes, Quee Mag, London, 68; New York Times, 74; and others. Style & Technique: Abstract, geometric. Media: Oil. Mailing Add: 116 W 21st St New York NY10011

PUTNAM, MRS JOHN B
COLLECTOR
b Cleveland, Ohio, June 19, 03. Mem: Art Collectors Club. Collection: Paintings and modern art. Mailing Add: 12817 Lake Shore Blvd Cleveland OH 44108

PUTNAM, MARION WALTON
See Walton, Marion

PUTNAM, WALLACE (BRADSTREET)
PAINTER, WRITER
b West Newton, Mass, Apr 16, 99. Study: Art schs, Boston. Work: Mus Mod Art, New York; Yale Univ Societe Anonyme Collection; Brooklyn Mus Collection; Southern Ill Univ; Roy Nenberger Collection. Exhib: Int Exhib Mod Art, Societe Anonyme, Brooklyn Mus, 26; Fantastic Art, Dada, Surrealism, Mus Mod Art, New York, 36. Media: Oil. Publ: Auth & illusr, Manhattan Manners, 35; auth & illusr, Miracle Enough, 68; Moby Dick Seen Again, 75. Mailing Add: Baptist Church Rd Yorktown Heights NY 10598

PUTTERMAN, FLORENCE GRACE
PAINTER
b Brooklyn, NY, Apr 14, 27. Study: NY Univ, BS; Bucknell Univ; Pa State Univ. Work: Bucknell Univ, Lewisburg, Pa; Lycoming Col, Williamsport, Pa. Exhib: Ga State Print Ann, Atlanta, 72 & 73; Mainstreams 74, Marietta Col, Ohio; Potsdam Print Ann, NY, 74; Philadelphia Print Club, 74; Ball State Drawing Ann, Muncie, Ind, 75; Everson Mus, Syracuse, NY, 76; Soc Am Graphics Artists, 77; Libr Cong Biennial Print Exhib, Nat Collection Fine Arts, Washington, DC, 77; Washington Co Mus Fine Arts, Hagerstown, Md, 78. Teaching: Artist in residence, Fed Title III Prog, 67-68 & 69-70; instr, Lycoming Col. Pos: Founder & pres, Arts Unlimited, Selinsgrove, Pa, 65-; cur, Milton Shoe Co Print Collection, Pa, 70-; bd dirs, Fetherston Mus, Lewisburg, Pa, 75- Awards: Best in Show Award, Everhart Mus, Scranton, Pa, 68; Purchase Awards, Appalachian Corridors, Charleston, WVa, 75 & Arena 75, Binghamton, NY; John Kellam Award, Silvermine Guild, New Canaan, Conn, 77. Mem: Am Fedn Arts; Hunterdon Co Art Ctr; Art Alliance Cent Pa; Mid-State Artists (treas, 70). Style & Technique: Printmaker working in etching, lithography and experimental technique; also painter and potter. Mailing Add: 101 Charles Ave Selinsgrove PA 17870

PYLYSHENKO, WOLODYMYR WALTER
See Mirko

Q

QUANDT, ELIZABETH (ELIZABETH QUANDT BARR)
PRINTMAKER
b Oxfordshire, Eng, July 13, 22; US citizen. Study: San Francisco Art Inst, BFA, MFA. Work: New York Pub Libr; Stanford Univ Art Mus; Libr of Cong; Achenbach Found & Transamerica Corp, San Francisco; Atlantic Richfield Corp, Los Angeles. Comn: Edition of 20 Prints, City of San Francisco, 74. Exhib: Five Printmakers, San Francisco Mus Art, 71; Calif in Print, Van Straaten Gallery, Chicago, 74; one-woman exhib, Monoprint Drawings, Achenbach Found, Calif Palace of the Legion of Honor, San Francisco, 75; Nat Acad of Design, 76 & 77; World Print Competition, 77; WCoast Prints, Impressions Press, Boston, 77; Philadelphia Print Club, 77. Teaching: Instr printmaking, Santa Rosa Jr Col, Calif, 70- Mem: Calif Soc Printmakers. Style & Technique: Etching, drawing both black and white and color. Dealer: Smith Andersen Gallery 200 Homer St Palo Alto CA 94301; Gimpel-Weitzenhoffer Inc 1040 Madison Ave New York NY 10021. Mailing Add: 920 McDonald Ave Santa Rosa CA 95404

QUAT, HELEN S
PRINTMAKER, PAINTER
b Brooklyn, NY, Oct 2, 18. Study: Skidmore Col; Columbia Univ; Art Students League; also with Raphael Soyer, Joseph Solman, Leo Manso, Ruth Leaf & Krishna Reddy; Empire State Col, State Univ NY, grad. Work: Univ Mass, Amherst; NJ State Mus, Trenton; Nassau Community Col. Exhib: Pratt Graphics Ctr 3rd Int Miniature Print Exhib, 68; 164th Ann, Pa Acad Fine Arts, 69; Int Exhib Women Artists, Ont & France, 69; State Univ NY Potsdam 10th Print Ann, 69-70; Nat Exhib Prints & Drawings, Okla Art Ctr, 69-72; Brooklyn Mus. Teaching: Teacher, Huntington Twp Art League. Awards: Vadley Art Co Award for Graphics, Catharine Lorillard Wolfe Art Club, 67; Purchase Prize, Hunterdon Art Ctr, NJ, 70; Mr & Mrs Benjamin Ganeles Prize, Nat Asn Women Artists, 71. Mem: Nat Asn Women Artists; Soc of Am Graphic Artists; Women in the Arts; Prof Artists Guild; fel MacDowell Colony; Graphic Eye Gallery. Style & Technique: Etchings based on natural rock forms and skyscapes; principles of color viscosity are used on multi-level aquatinted plates combined with smaller intaglio plates. Dealer: Alonzo Gallery 30 W 57th St New York NY 10019. Mailing Add: 16 Elliot Rd Great Neck NY 11021

QUAYTMAN, HARVEY
PAINTER
b Far Rockaway, NY, Apr 20, 37. Study: Syracuse Univ; Tufts Univ; Boston Mus Fine Arts Sch, BFA. Work: Pasadena Art Mus; Whitney Mus Am Art; Fogg Art Mus; Houston Mus Fine Arts; Mus Mod & Experimental Arts, Santiago, Chile; Carnegie Inst of Technol, Pittsburgh, Pa; Power Gallery of Contemp Art, Sydney, Australia; plus others. Exhib: Inst Contemp Art, Houston, 67 & 73; Whitney Mus Am Art Ann, 69 & 72 & Structure of Color, Whitney Mus Am Art, 70; L'art Vivant aux Etats Unis, Fondation Maeght, St Paul de Vence, France, 70; Young Am Artists, Gent of Te Radhus, Charlottenborg, Denmark, 73; Painting Endures, Inst Contemp Art, Boston, 75; 14 Abstract Painters, Univ Calif, Los Angeles, 75; New Painting in New York, Univ of Tex, Austin, 77; one-man shows, Paula Cooper Gallery, New York, 69 & 71, Onnasch Gallery, Cologne, Ger, 71, Mikro Gallery, Berlin, Ger, 72, Cunningham Ward Gallery, New York, 74 & David McKee Gallery, New York, 75, 77 & 78. Teaching: Former instr, Boston Mus Fine Arts Sch, Middlebury Col, Essex Col Art, Colchester, Eng & Sch Visual Arts, New York; instr, Cooper Union. Awards: J W Paige Traveling Fel, Boston Mus Fine Arts, 60-61; CAPS Awards, 72 & 75. Mailing Add: c/o David McKee Inc 140 E 63rd St New York NY 10021

QUEST, CHARLES FRANCIS
PAINTER, EDUCATOR
b Troy, NY, June 6, 04. Study: Wash Univ Sch Fine Arts, St Louis, Mo, 24-29; advan study in Paris, 29; summer study, Spain, France & Eng, 60. Work: Brit Mus, London; Victoria & Albert Mus, London; Greenville Co Mus of Art, Greenville, SC; Bibliot Nat, Paris; Mus Mod Art & Metrop Mus Art, New York; plus many others in mus & pvt collections throughout world. Comn: Altar painting, St Mary's Church, Helena, Ark, 34; baptistry murals, St Michael & St George Episcopal Church, St Louis, Mo, 34; altar painting, Trinity Episcopal Church, St Louis, 35; altar painting, Old Cathedral, St Louis, 59-60. Exhib: Les Peintres Graveurs Actuels Aux Etats-Uni, Bibliot Nat, Paris, 51; Am Watercolor, Drawings & Prints Exhib, Metrop Mus Art, New York, 52; Art in the Embassies Prog, Dept of State, Washington, DC, 67; 53rd Exhib, Soc Am Graphic Artists, New York, 75; plus many group & one-man exhibs in mus & galleries throughout world. Teaching: Instr art, St Louis Pub Schs, Mo, 29-44; prof art, Wash Univ Sch Fine Arts, 44-71, emer prof, 71- Awards: Purchase Prizes, 3rd Ann Nat Print Exhib, Brooklyn Mus, 49; Nat Print Exhib, Libr of Cong, 52 & 51st Ann Print Exhib, Soc Am Graphic Artists, 71; plus many others. Bibliog: Article in St Louis Post Dispatch, 60; demonstr printmaking, 68 & demonstr figure drawing, 68, Art in St Louis, KMOX-TV, St Louis. Mem: St Louis Artists Guild; Soc Am Graphic Artists, New York. Media: Oil; Printmaking Media. Dealer: Hampton III Gallery Taylors SC 29678. Mailing Add: 200 Hillswick Rd Tryon NC 28782

QUEST, DOROTHY (JOHNSON)
PORTRAIT PAINTER
b St Louis, Mo, Feb 28, 09. Study: Wash Univ Sch Fine Arts, St Louis, Mo, 28-33; study in Europe, 29; Columbia Univ, summer 37. Work: Wash Univ Olin Libr, St Louis Univ Med Sch & Eden Seminary, St Louis, Mo; Univ Eastern Ill, Charleston; Washington & Lee Univ, Va. Comn: Portrait of Capt James B Eads, Mo Athletic Club, 54; portraits of twelve men, Dodge Mem Hall, Boston, 57; Mrs Clay Jordan, Mem Home, St Louis, 63; John Lilly, Pres, St Louis Co Nat Bank, 63; portrait of Pierre Laclede, Pierre Laclede Bldg, St Louis, 64; portrait of Dr R C Grier, former pres of Erskine Col, 78; plus over 650 other portraits, 31- Exhib: St Louis City Art Mus Ann; St Louis Artists Guild Ann; one-man show, Tryon Fine Arts Ctr, NC, 72. Teaching: Instr art, Community Sch, St Louis, 36-38; head art dept, Acad Sacred Heart, St Louis, 39-41; head art dept, Maryville Col, St Louis, 44-45; instr art, Tryon Fine Arts Ctr, 71- Pos: Lectr painting, St Louis City Art Mus, radio sta KMOX & KSD, pvt clubs, churches & schs. Bibliog: Eloise Lang (auth), article in St Louis Post Dispatch, 65; Walter Orthwein (auth), article, 67 & Lynn Hawkins (auth), article, 69, In: St Louis Globe Democrat. Mem: Tryon Painters & Sculptors, Inc (chmn exhibs out-of-town artists, 70-); Spartanburg Art Asn. Media: Oil. Dealer: Tryon Painters & Sculptors, Inc Melrose Ave Tryon NC 28782; Hampton III Gallery Taylors SC 29678. Mailing Add: 200 Hillswick Rd Tryon NC 28782

QUICK, BIRNEY MACNABB
PAINTER, INSTRUCTOR
b Proctor, Minn, Nov 9, 12. Study: Vesper L George Sch, Boston; Minneapolis Col Art Design; Louis Comfort Tiffany fel & Chaloner fel, 38. Work: Minneapolis Inst Art; Univ Minn Art Gallery; Gen Mills Collection; Int Multifood Corp Collection; Northwestern Nat Life Collection. Comn: Oil on canvas, Med Arts Bldg, Duluth, Minn, 46, Minn Mutual Life Ins Co, St Paul, 58, Minn Fed Savings Loan, St Paul, 60, Grand Marais St Bank, Minn, 68 & St John's Catholic Church, Grand Marais, 72. Exhib: Am Painters & Sculptors Show, Art Inst Chicago; Minn Biennial, Minneapolis Art Inst; Independent Artist's Show, Boston; one-man shows, Walker Art Ctr & Minneapolis Art Inst; Tweed Gallery, Univ Minn, Duluth. Teaching: Prof painting, Minneapolis Sch Art, 46-77, emer prof, 77- Pos: Dir studies abroad, Am Cols Art, 70-71. Awards: Biennial Award in Drawing, Minneapolis Art Inst, 60. Style & Technique: Mystical realist. Media: Oil, Watercolor. Mailing Add: 4537 Dupont Ave S Minneapolis MN 55409

QUIGLEY, MICHAEL ALLEN
ART ADMINISTRATOR
b Buffalo, NY, Oct 28, 50. Study: Univ Pa, BA(art hist), 71. Exhibitions Arranged: Joan Jonas/Stage Sets, Inst of Contemp Art, Univ Pa, 76. Pos: Mus asst, Nat Collection of Fine Arts, Smithsonian Inst, Washington, DC, summer 1971; curatorial asst, Inst of Contemp Art, Univ Pa, 71-75, asst dir, 75- Mailing Add: Inst of Contemp Art Univ Pa 34th & Walnut Sts Philadelphia PA 19104

QUINN, BRIAN GRANT
SCULPTOR
b Wahoo, Nebr, Oct 21, 50. Study: Nebr Wesleyan Univ, with Maynard Whitney, BAE; Ariz State Univ, with Ben Goo, MFA. Work: Weber State Col, Odgen, Utah; Nebr Wesleyan Univ, Lincoln, Nebr; also numerous private collections. Exhib: Marietta Col Crafts Nat, Grover M Hermann Fine Arts Ctr, Ohio, 74; 18th Nat Art Round-Up, Las Vegas Art Mus, Nev, 75; Mainstreams, 75 & 8th Ann Int Competitive Exhib for Painting & Sculpture, Marietta Col; 21st Mother Lode Int Color Slide Exhib, Auburn, Calif, 75; 21st & 22nd Ann Drawing & Small Sculpture Shows, Ball State Univ, Muncie, Ind, 75 & 76; 18th Ann Nat Exhib, Fall River, Mass, 76; Small Sculpture & Drawing Show, Elder Gallery, Nebr Wesleyan Univ, Lincoln, 76; seven in seventy-seven, Scottsdale Ctr for the Arts, Scottsdale, Ariz, 77; First Ann Jewelry/Small Sculpture Invitational Exhib, Weber State Col, Ogden, Utah, 77; First Ann Wood in Art Exhib, Ariz State Univ Art Collections, Tempe, Ariz, 77; one-man exhib, Fun & Games, Colorado Women's Col, Denver, Colo, 77; plus others. Pos: Preparator, Phoenix Art Mus, 75; asst to Fritz Scholder, 75-; vis staff instr desiger & drawing, Glendale Community Col, 76- Awards: Artist-in-Residence, Nat Endowment for the Art, 75-76; Fred Wells Purchase Award, Small Sculpture and Drawing Exhib, Nebr Wesleyan Univ, 76; Am Art Heritage Cash Award, First Arizona Wood in Art Exhibition, Ariz State Univ Art Collections, 77. Bibliog: Suzanne Muchnic (auth), Textile, jewelry and sculpture invitational, Artweek, 4/9/77; Ragina Taum Cooke (auth), Artlook, Southwest Art, 7/77; James Mills (auth), Quinn works express beauty, lyricism yet remain lighthearted, Roundup, Denver Post, 10/9/77; plus others. Mem: Southern Asn of Sculptors. Style & Technique: Abstract wood, metal, stone and mixed media sculpture; extensive use of polychrome surfaces and found objects. Dealer: Gallery of Contemp Art 2 Ledout St Taos NM. Mailing Add: 2925 E St Johns Rd Phoenix AZ 85032

QUINN, HENRIETTA REIST
COLLECTOR
b Lancaster, Pa, Dec 11, 18. Study: Edgewood Park Jr Col. Collection: American primitive paintings; eighteenth century porcelain; eighteenth century miniature memoribilia; eighteenth century American and English furniture. Mailing Add: Rollings Meadows Cornwall PA 17016

QUINN, NOEL JOSEPH
PAINTER, INSTRUCTOR
b Pawtucket, RI, Dec 25, 15. Study: RI Sch Design, grad, 36, fel, Paris; Parsons Sch Fine & Appl Arts, Paris & Italy, cert dipl; Ecole Beaux Arts; also with Andre L'hote & Andre Cassandre; Nat Gallery & Kaiser Frederick Mus, Berlin, Ger. Work: Butler Art Inst, Youngstown, Ohio; Air Force Acad, Denver; Pentagon, Libr of Cong & House of Rep, Washington, DC; Calif State Agr Collection, Sacramento; Los Angeles Turf Club, Santa Anita Park, Arcadia, Calif. Comn: Thoroughbred Racing (portfolio of paintings), Los Angeles Turf Club, 60. Exhib: American Paintings & Prints, Metrop Mus Art, New York, 52; Hallmark Int Show, Wildenstein Galleries, New York, 53; Southwest Watercolor Soc Show, Southern Methodist Univ, Dallas, 69; one-man show, Yoseido Gallery, Tokyo, 55; plus many others. Teaching: Instr watercolor, Otis Art Inst, 53-75; guest instr, Palo Verdes Art Ctr, 76-77. Awards: Hallmark Int Award, 52; Cert of Esteem for work in Korea & Japan, Secy Defense Charles E Wilson, 55; Watercolor USA Award, Springfield Art Mus, 64. Bibliog: Norman Kent (auth), 100 American Watercolorists, Watson-Guptill, 69. Mem: Nat Watercolor Soc; Soc Motion Picture illusr (pres, 65-68); fel Int Inst Arts & Lett. Media: Watercolor. Interest: Part of each year devoted to educating the blind in terms of their sight; creator of new language of symbols for color and value in bas-relief; paintings reproduced in the language overlay provide the pertinent clues which enable them to complete the picture. Publ: Auth, article in Am Artist Mag, 5/63; auth, Scene, Southwestern Watercolor Soc Mag. Mailing Add: 3946 San Rafael Ave Los Angeles CA 90065

QUINN, RAYMOND JOHN
ILLUSTRATOR, PAINTER
b Ridgefield Park, NJ, July 17, 38. Study: Parson's Sch of Design, study with Alan Gussow & Mario Raffo, New York. Work: Central Fla Mus, Orlando; Dartmouth Col Mus, Hanover, NH. Comn: Diorama, Staten Island Inst of Arts & Sci, 64, Philadelphia Zoo, 65 & Am Mus of Nat Hist, New York, 70; exhibits, New England Aquarium, Boston, 74-76 & NH Audubon Soc, Concord, 77. Exhib: Soc of Animal Artists, New York, 66-77; Whale Art, Mus of Sci, Boston, 71; Whales in Art, Central Fla Mus, Orlando, 71; Fine Arts in NH, Holderness, 76; Wildlife Art Show, Aspen, Colo, 76; Fine Alliance Whale Symposium, Columbia Univ, New York, 78. Teaching: Instr painting, Manchester Inst Arts & Sci, 74 75. Pos: Artists & preparetor, Acad of Nat Sci, Philadelphia, Pa, 65-68; chief, exhibs, Squam Lakes Sci Ctr, NH, 65-73. Awards: Best in Show, Art in NH, Squam Lakes Bd of Trade, 76. Bibliog: Peter L Ames (auth), John R Quinn, Fla Audubon Soc, 68; NH Network, Let There Be Beasties, Durham, NH, 77. Mem: Soc of Animal Artists, New York. Style & Technique: Primarily in acrylics, producing nature art in the realism school; also write and illustrate books. Media: Acrylic, Fiberglas, Scratchboard, Etching. Publ: Auth-illusr, The Winter Woods, Devin-Adair, 76; auth-illusr, Nature's World Records, Walker Co, 76; auth-illusr, Nature's Signs & Secrets, Walker Co, 77; auth-illusr, The Summer Woodlands, Devin-Adair, 78. Dealer: The Schoolhouse Gallery Periwinkle Way Sanibel FL 33957. Mailing Add: 3 Langdon St Plymouth NH 03264

QUINN, SANDI (CASSANDRASU DHOOGE-QUINN VACHON)
INSTRUCTOR, CALLIGRAPHER
b Moline, Ill, Mar 4, 41. Study: Scholar, Chicago Art Inst; Mus Fine Arts Sch, Boston, AA. Work: Mus Fine Arts, Boston, Mass; De Cordova Mus, Lincoln, Mass; Danforth Mus, Framingham, Mass; Colonade Hotel, Boston, Mass; Cambridge Ctr for Adult Educ, Mass; Brattle House, Cambridge, Mass. Comn: Outdoor Christmas plaques for ann display on Boston Common, comn by Kevin White, Mayor's Off of Cult Affairs, 72; Reverend Meek Tribute, Old South Church, Boston, Mass, 73, comn by Archbishop Meideros, Boston Off, 74; Tribute for Billboards, comn by Kevin White for Donnelly & Sons, 75; Personal Quote, comn by Senator Edward Kennedy, Boston Off, 77. Exhib: One-woman shows, Boston Ctr for Adult Educ, Mass, 72, 74, 75 & 77, Advert Club Greater Boston, Mass, 73 & Atlantic Mo Bldg, Boston, Mass, 74; Soc Scribes & Illuminators, Middlesex, Eng, 77. Teaching: Instr calligraphy, Cambridge Ctr for Adult Educ, Mass & Boston Ctr for Adult Educ, 71-, De Cordova Mus, Lincoln, Mass, 72-75, Danforth Mus, Framingham, Mass, 75- & Emmanuel Col, Brookline, Mass, 77-; founder & co-dir, Sch of Calligraphy, Boston, Mass, 75- Bibliog: Bill Fripp (auth), She proves calligraphy alive & well, Globe, 72; Bob Garret (auth), Writing beautiful, Herald, 73; Virginia Bohlin (auth), Today's living, Herald, 74; Paul Vander Voort (auth), The renaissance woman, Signs of the Times, 71. Media: Pen and Ink, 24K Gold and Acrylics. Publ: Auth, Catalogue of Calligraphy, 77. Mailing Add: 499 E Broadway South Boston MA 02127

QUINN, WILLIAM
PAINTER
b St Louis, Mo, Sept 5, 29. Study: Washington Univ, BFA, study with Paul Burlin & Carl Holty; Univ Ill, MFA, 57. Work: Butler Inst of Am Art, Youngstown, Ohio; Brooks Mem Art Gallery, Memphis, Tenn; Nelson-Atkins Gallery, Kansas City, Mo; St Louis Art Mus; Weatherspoon Art Gallery, Univ NC. Exhib: Philadelphia Print Soc; Mulvane Art Ctr, Topeka, Kans; Univ Mo, Columbia; St Louis Art Mus; Mexican-Am Cult Inst, Mexico City; plus many others. Exhib: Schweig Gallery, St Louis; Eastern Mich Univ, Ypsilanti; Painters Gallery, St Louis; Southwest Mo State Col, Springfield; Terry Moore Gallery, St Louis. Teaching: Prof painting & drawing, Washington Univ, 58- Awards: Thirty-six awards in regional museums and galleries. Style & Technique: Palette knife abstracts. Media: Oil and acrylic. Publ: Illusr, George Mylonas, auth, The Rise & Fall of the Mycenaean States, Washington Univ Press, 66. Dealer: Schweig Gallery, Maryland Plaza St Louis MO 63108. Mailing Add: Sch of Fine Arts Washington Univ St Louis MO 63130

QUINSAC, ANNIE-PAULE
ART HISTORIAN, WRITER
b Bouches du Rhone, France, Aug 2, 45. Study: Univ Montpellier, 59 61; Paris, DES, 63; Sorbonne, Paris, PhD, 68. Exhibitions Arranged: Ottocento Painting in American Collections (with catalog), NY Cult Ctr, Columbia Mus Arts & Mass Inst Technol, 72-73; Exhib Segantini: Japan 1978, Japan, 78. Teaching: Prof art history, Univ SC, 70- Pos: Mitarbeiter, Inst Kunstwissenshaft, Zurich, 74-75. Awards: Mellon Fel, Univ Pittsburgh, 69-70. Mem: Nat Soc Lit & Arts; Col Art Asn Am; Arte Lombarda Milan; Soc Amis de Segantini. Res: 19th century Italian studies. Publ: Auth, Peinture Divisionniste Italienne: Origines et premiers developpements, Klincksieck, 72; auth, Catalogue raisonne of Giovanni Segantini, Swiss Inst Art Res, 79. Mailing Add: 3119 Heyward St Columbia SC 29208

QUIRARTE, JACINTO
ART HISTORIAN, EDUCATOR
b Jerome, Ariz, Aug 17, 31. Study: San Francisco State Col, BA, 54, MA, 58, sec teaching credential, 58; Nat Univ of Mex, PhD, 64. Teaching: Art teacher, Colegio Americano, Mexico City, 59-61; asst to Alberto Ruz Lhuillier, Seminario de Cultura Maya, Nat Univ of Mex, 61-62; dean of men & prof hist of Pre-Columbian art, Univ of the Americas, 62-64; dir cult affairs, Centro Venezolano Americano, Caracas, 64-66; vis prof hist of art & archit of Pre-Columbian Mex, Cent Univ Caracas, 66 & hist of contemp art of Latin Am & Pre-Columbian art, Yale Univ, New Haven, Conn, 67; prof hist of Pre-Columbian, Colonial & contemp art of Mex & Guatemala, Univ of Tex, Austin, 67-72; dean, Col of Fine & Applied Arts, Univ of Tex, San Antonio, 72-; vis prof hist of Pre-Columbian art of Mesoamerica & Colonial art of Latin Am, Univ of NMex, 71. Pos: Bd mem & vpres, San Antonio Arts Coun, 73-77; mem visual arts & humanities panel, Tex Com on the Arts & Humanities, 76-; mem, Nat Humanities Fac & Tex Alliance for the Arts; consult, Tex Educ Agency; adv bd, Harvard J on Chicano Affairs, El Centro Cultural y Museo del Barrio, Albuquerque, Mex, Mus, San Francisco & La Luz Mag, Denver. Mem: Mid-Am Col Art Asn; Soc for Am Archaeol; Int Cong of Americanists; Int Cong of the Hist of Art; Int Cong of Ethnology & Anthrop. Publ: Auth, El estilo artístico de Izapa, Cuadernos de Historia del Arte, No 3, Instituto de Investigaciones Estéticas, Universidad Nacional Autonoma de Mexico, 73; auth, Izapan style art-a study of its form and meaning, Studies in Pre-Columbian Art & Archaeology, No 10, Dumbarton Oaks, Trustees for Harvard Univ, Washington, DC, 73; auth, Mexican American Artists, 73 & Maya Vase, (in prep), forthcoming, Univ of Tex Press, Austin. Mailing Add: Off of the Dean Col of Fine & Applied Arts Univ of Tex San Antonio TX 78285

QUIRK, THOMAS CHARLES, JR
PAINTER, EDUCATOR
b Pittsburgh, Pa, Dec 31, 22. Study: Edinboro State Col, BS, 48; Univ Pittsburgh, MEd, 64. Work: Butler Inst Am Art, Youngstown, Ohio; Chatham Col, Pittsburgh; Pittsburgh Pub Schs; Millersville State Col, Pa; Rutgers Univ, Camden, NJ. Exhib: Pa Acad Fine Arts Ann, Philadelphia, 69; Nat Acad Design Ann, New York, 74; Am Drawing Biennial XXIV, Norfolk, Va, 71; Drawing & Small Sculpture Ann, Ball State Univ, 71; Philadelphia Watercolor Club Ann, 74 & 75; Philadelphia Watercolor Club, 76; Ann Nat Soc of Painters in Casein & Acrylic, New York, 76 & 77. Teaching: Asst prof painting & drawing, Kutztown State Col, 66- Pos: Artist in residence, Everhart Mus, Scranton, Pa, 72- Awards: Prizes, Drawing Ann, Ball State Univ, 71 & Millersville State Col Watercolor Show, 76; Dawson Mem Prize, Philadelphia Watercolor Club, 74. Mem: Soc Painters in Casein & Acrylic; Philadelphia Watercolor Club. Style & Technique: Surrealist, egg tempera technique. Media: Watercolor, Acrylic & Oil. Mailing Add: 310 E Main St Kutztown PA 19530

QUISGARD, LIZ WHITNEY
PAINTER, SCULPTOR
b Philadelphia, Pa, Oct 23, 29. Study: Md Inst Col Art, dipl, 49, BFA(summa cum laude), 66; also with Morris Louis, 57-60; Rinehart Sch Sculpture, MFA, 66. Work: Univ Ariz Ghallager Mem Collection, Tucson; Lever House, New York; Univ Baltimore, Md; Johns Hopkins Univ; Hampton Sch, Towson, Md; plus many pvt collections. Comn: Mural painting, William Fell Sch, Baltimore, Md, 78. Exhib: Corcoran Biennial Am Painting, Corcoran Gallery Art, Washington, DC, 63; Univ Colo Show, 63; Am Painting & Sculpture Ann, Pa Acad Fine Arts, Philadelphia, 64; Art Inst Chicago Ann, 65; Baltimore Mus Traveling Show,

78; one-man shows, Jefferson Place Gallery, Washington, DC, 61, Emmerich Gallery, New York, 62, Univ Md, 69, Gallery 707, Los Angeles, 74, South Houston Gallery, New York, 74, Arts & Sci Ctr, Nashua, NH, 75, Gannon Col, Eric, Pa, 78 & Mechanic Gallery, Baltimore, Md, 78; plus many others. Teaching: Instr painting & design, Baltimore Hebrew Congregation, 62-; instr painting & color theory, Md Inst, Baltimore, 65-; lectr design, Goucher Col, 66-69; lectr art hist, Univ Md, Catonsville, 69-70; instr painting, Baltimore Jewish Community Ctr, 74. Pos: Theatre designer, Goucher Col, Theatre Hopkins & Ctr Stage, Baltimore, 66-; art critic, Baltimore Sun, 69 & 70; area reviewer, Craft Horizons Mag, 69- Awards: Artists Prize, Baltimore Mus Regional Exhib, 58; Rinehart Fel, Md Inst, 64-66; Best in Show, Loyola Col, 66. Bibliog: B Rose (auth), rev in Art Int, 11/62; rev in Arts Mag, 11/62 & Art News, 11/62. Style & Technique: Wall-sized paintings and environmental sculpture groupings. Publ: Auth, Baltimore's top twelve, Baltimore Mag, 5/69; auth & illusr, An artist's travel log (series of three articles), Baltimore News Am, 71. Mailing Add: 321 Rossiter Ave Baltimore MD 21212

R

RABB, MR & MRS IRVING W
COLLECTORS
Study: Mr Rabb, Harvard Univ, AB, Harvard Bus Sch; Mrs Rabb, Smith Col, AB; Radcliffe Col, AM. Collection: Twentieth century sculpture, including Henry Moore, Giacometti, Maillot, Arp, Lipshitz, Calder, Dubuffet, Nevelson and Laurens; twentieth century drawings and collages, with emphasis on Cubism and sculpture drawings. Mailing Add: 1010 Memorial Dr Cambridge MA 02138

RABIN, BERNARD
ART RESTORER
b New York, NY, Nov 1, 16. Study: Newark Art Sch; New Sch Social Res; Brooklyn Mus, with Sheldon & Caroline Keck; also restoration at the Uffizi, Florence, Italy. Work: Restoration Works, Montclair Art Mus, Princeton Univ Art Mus, Carnegie-Mellon Mus, NJ Hist Soc & in pvt collections. Comn: Restoration of Monet's Water Lilies, Mus Mod Art, New York, 59. Teaching: Lectr, Int Conf Conservators, Lisbon, 10/72. Pos: Official restorer, Princeton Univ Art Mus & Norton Simon Art Mus, Pasadena, Calif; head Am restorers, Comt Rescue Ital Art, 67. Mem: Am Asn Mus; fel Int Inst Conserv. Publ: Auth, articles in J Int Inst Conserv, 59-70. Mailing Add: 38 Halsey St Newark NJ 07102

RABINOVICH, RAQUEL
PAINTER, SCULPTOR
b Buenos Aires, Arg, Mar 30, 29. Study: Univ Cordoba, Arg; Univ Edinburgh; Atelier Andre LHote, Paris. Work: Mus Mod Art, Buenos Aires; Genaro Perez Mus, Cordoba; Fondo Nac Art, Buenos Aires. Comn: Homage to R C Murphy (glass outdoor monumental sculpture). Exhib: Primer Salon Artistas Jovenes Latin Am, Mus Art Mod, Arg, 65; New Directions (Artists of Suffolk Co), Hecksher Mus, Huntington, NY, 71; Benson Gallery, Bridgehampton, NY, 73; Hecksher Mus, Huntington, NY, 74; Susan Caldwell Gallery, New York, 75; Am Abstract Artists Exhib, 77; plus others. Awards: Salon Parques Nac Prize, 63; Fondo Nac Art Fel, 64. Bibliog: M Preston (auth), Raquel Rabinovich, Newsday, New York, 72; D Bayon (auth), Aventura Plastica de Hispanoamerica, 74; John Gruen (auth), article in Soho Weekly News, 75; plus others. Dealer: Susan Caldwell Gallery 383 West Broadway New York NY 10012. Mailing Add: 81 Leonard St New York NY 10013

RABINOVITCH, WILLIAM AVRUM
PAINTER
b New London, Conn, Sept 16, 36. Study: Worcester Polytech Inst, BSME; Boston Mus Sch Fine Arts; San Francisco Art Inst, MFA; Whitney Mus, independent study prog, 73. Work: Monterey Peninsula Col, Calif; Monterey Conf Ctr, Calif; Fairmont Hotel, San Francisco. Exhib: One-man shows, Monterey Peninsula Mus Art, 65, Am Embassy & Asn Cult Hisp Norteamericano, 68, Large Paints, Monterey Jazz Festival, 71 & Rabinovitch & Guerra Gallery, New York, 75 & 76; Whitney Counterweight, Soho Gallery, New York, 77. Pos: Dir, Rabinovitch & Guerra Gallery, New York; proj dir, Whitney Counterweight, Soho Gallery, New York & Whitney Mus Biennial, 77. Awards: First Prize, Monterey Peninsula Mus Art & Monterey Jazz Festival, 65 & First Prize, Monterey Co Fair, 70; grant, Nat Endowment Arts, 77. Style & Technique: Expressionistic with strong color representing a complex combination of personal images. Media: Oil, Acrylic, Watercolor, Sculpture. Dealer: Rabinovitch & Guerra Gallery 74 Grand St New York NY 10013. Mailing Add: 33 Crosby St Apt 14 New York NY 10013

RABINOWITCH, DAVID
SCULPTOR
b Toronto, Ont, Mar 6, 43. Study: Univ Western Ont, BA, 65; self-taught. Work: Nat Gallery Can; Art Gallery Ont, Toronto; Mus of Mod Art, New York; Hauselandes Mus, Krefeld; Stattesmuseum, Stuttgart, WGer; Wall-Laff Richartz Mus, Cologne; Berkeley Mus, Calif. Comn: Sculpture, Proj 74, Cologne, WGer, 74; plaster installations, Clocktower, New York & PS 1, New York, 76; elliptical sculpture, Bruckner Festival, Lirz, Austria, 77; sculpture, Documenta VI, Kassel, WGer, 77. Exhib: Carmen Lamanna Gallery, Toronto, 71; Helman Gallery, St Louis, 71, Rolfricke Gallery, Cologne, 72; Bykert Gallery, New York, 73; Toselli Gallery, Milan, 74; Rooms, PS 1, New York, NY, 76; Bienniale de Paris, Mus of Mod Art, Paris, France, 77; Recent Acquisitions, Mus of Mod Art, 77; Documenta VI, Kassel, WGer, 77; Sculpture, Münster, WGer, 77; Four Sculptors, Art Gallery of Ont, Toronto, 78; one-man shows, Mus Wiesbaden, 75 & Clocktower, New York, 76. Collections Arranged: Dorothy & Herbert Vögel Traveling Collection Exhib; Henry Levison Collection, York Univ, Toronto. Teaching: Instr sculpture, Yale Univ, 74-75. Awards: Can Coun Sr Award, 73 & Sr Grant, 77; NY State Coun Arts Award, 74; Guggenheim Fel, 75. Bibliog: Kenneth Baker (auth), David Rabinowitch, Arts Mag, 74; Walter Klepac (auth), David Rabinowitch, Artscanada & David Rabinowitch, Parachute Mag, 76; Rolf Gilbert (auth), David Rabinowitch, Artforum; Thomas Lawson (auth), David Rabinowitch, Arts Mag, 77. Mem: Life academician Royal Can Acad of Art. Dealer: Carmen Lamanna 840 Yonge St Toronto ON Can. Mailing Add: 110 Catherine St S Hamilton ON Can

RABINOWITCH, ROYDEN LESLIE
SCULPTOR
b Toronto, Ont, Mar 6, 43. Study: Self taught. Work: Nat Gallery Can, Ottawa; Aldrich Mus, Conn. Exhib: Heart of London, Nat Gallery Can, 69 & New Sculpture at Stratford, 71; New Direction in Sculpture, Ont Art Gallery, 70; Pilote Gallery Lausanne, Switz, 71; Contemp Art Today, 74; plus one-man shows. Teaching: Chmn admin, Ont Col Art, 73-74. Awards: Can Coun Arts Bursary, 71 & 72 & Sr Arts Grant, 75. Bibliog: Ken Baker (auth), article in Arts in Am, 71; Barry Lord (auth), article in Arts Int, 72; Roald Narguard (auth), article in Artscanada, 73. Style & Technique: Constructivist; steel fabrication. Media: Steel. Dealer: Sable-Castelli Toronto ON Can. Mailing Add: PO Box 210 New York NY 10013

RABKIN, LEO
PAINTER, SCULPTOR
b Cincinnati, Ohio, July 21, 19. Study: Univ Cincinnati; NY Univ; also with Iglehart, Tony Smith & Baziotes. Work: Mus Mod Art, Whitney Mus Am Art & Guggenheim Mus, New York; NC Mus Art, Raleigh; Neuberger Mus, NY; plus others. Exhib: Seven Painting & Sculpture Biennials, 59-69 & Drawings & Watercolor, 74 & 75, Whitney Mus Am Art; Light/Motion/Space, Walker Art Ctr, Minneapolis, 67; A Plastic Presence, San Francisco Mus Art, Milwaukee Art Ctr & Jewish Mus, 70; Retrospective, Storm King Art Ctr, Mountainville, NY, 70; Am Acad Arts & Lett, 72; 10th St Show, two Soho galleries, New York, NY, 77; Retrospective, Allentown Art Mus, Pa, 78; one-man show, Truman Gallery, New York, NY, 78. Awards: Ford Found Award for Watercolor, 61; First Prize for Watercolor, Silvermine Guild Artists, 61; popular award for sculpture, First Ann Westchester, 67. Mem: Am Abstr Artists (pres, 64-); US Comn Int Asn Art (secy, 68-70); Fine Arts Fedn New York (mem bd dirs, 70-). Media: Watercolor; Box Constructions. Collection: Whirligigs; Shaker furniture; American primitive sculpture (articulated figures). Publ: Ed, American Abstract Artists, 1936-1966, 66. Mailing Add: 218 W 20th St New York NY 10011

RABOW, ROSE
ART DEALER, COLLECTOR
b Salt Lake City, Utah. Pos: Dir, Rose Rabow Galleries. Specialty: Contemporary master artists of West Coast; strong individual styles, mostly linking Eastern and Western vision. Mailing Add: 2130 Leavenworth San Francisco CA 94133

RABUT, PAUL
ILLUSTRATOR, PAINTER
b New York, NY, Apr 6, 14. Study: City Col New York; Nat Acad Design; Art Students League; also with Jules Gottlieb, Harvey Dunn & Lewis Daniel. Work: USA Med Mus, Washington, DC; US Postal Serv Collection; Gen Elec Collection. Comn: Designed 6 cent Natural Hist Commemorative US Postage Stamp, Haida Ceremonial Canoe, 5/6/70 & 11 cent Airmail Commemorative US Postage Stamp, City of Refuge, Nat Park Serv, 4/3/72. Exhib: Soc Illusr, 41-72; Art Dirs Club, 42-53; Art Inst Chicago, 43; Nat Acad Design, 50; State Dept Traveling Exhib Advert Art, Europe & SAm, 52-53; plus others. Teaching: Lectr illus, photog, primitive arts of Africa & Northwest Coast & South Seas. Pos: Consult primitive art, galleries & collectors; art dir & stylist animated films, Fed Aeronaut Admin, US Army, US Navy & Fr Govt. Awards: Medal, Nat Acad Design, 32; Prizes, Art Dirs Club, 42, 43, 46 & 51. Mem: Soc Illusr; Westport Artists. Collection: Primitive art, especially Africa, oceanic, pre-Columbian America & American Indian. Publ: Auth & illusr, Paul Rabut visits the tall timber, True Mag, 49; auth & illusr, My life as a head hunter, Argosy Mag, 53; illusr, leading nat mags. Mailing Add: 104 Easton Rd Westport CT 06880

RACHEL, VAUGHAN
PHOTOGRAPHER, WRITER
b Oakland, Calif, May 15, 33. Study: Colby Jr Col, NH, AA, 53; Hans Hofmann Sch Fine Arts with Hans Hofmann, 54; Calif Inst of Arts, Valencia, BFA, 73 & MFA, 75. Exhib: Photographs by Women About Women, Baldwin St Gallery, Ont, Can, 72; Exposures: Photography & Its Extensions, Womanspace, Los Angeles, 73; Woman & the Printing Arts, Woman's Bldg, Los Angeles, 75; Some Los Angeles Photographers, Grossmont Col Art Gallery, El Cajon, Calif, 75; Breadth of Vision, Fashion Inst of Technol, New York, 75; one-woman show, Home Ground, Calif Inst of Arts, Valencia, 75. Pos: Slide coordr, Libr, Calif Inst of Arts, Valencia, 71-; consult, Visual Resources, Inc, New York, 75- Bibliog: Brian van Der Horst (auth), Cool, Man, Cool, Village Voice, New York, 12/23/74. Mem: Womanspace, Los Angeles (bd dirs); Women's Caucus For Art, CAA, Washington, DC (adv bd); Los Angeles Inst Contemp Art, 74. Style & Technique: Photojournalism. Publ: Auth, Thirteen Stories, 74; contribr, Anonymous Was A Woman, 74; contribr, Journal, LAICA, 2/75; contribr, Art: A Woman's Sensibility, 75. Mailing Add: 1225 Linda Rosa Ave Los Angeles CA 90041

RACHELSKI, FLORIAN W
PAINTER, SCULPTOR
b Poland; US citizen. Study: Ecole Nat Beaux Arts, Paris. Comn: Monument of Christ, St Mary's Church, Paris, 53; monument of the Madonna, St Trinity Church, Osining, NY, 59. Exhib: Salon Nat Beaux Arts, Salon des Artistes Francais & Salon d'Hiver, Paris; Nat Acad Design & Nat Sculpture Soc, New York. Awards: Bronze Medal, 55 & Silver Medal, 56, Salon des Artistes Francais; Prix Bingguely le Jeune, Winter Salon, Paris, 58. Mem: Syndicat Nat des Artistes Createur Prof, 53; fel Nat Sculpture Soc. Media: Wood, Stone, Bronze, Marble. Publ: Auth, articles in J l'Amateur d'Art, La Rev Mod, Masgue et Visages, Nat Sculpture Rev & Le Livre D'Or Sculpture. Mailing Add: 206 E Ninth St New York NY 10003

RACINE, ALBERT BATISTE
WOODCARVER
b Browning, Mont, Apr 19, 07. Study: Studied with Winol Reiss, Edward E Hale, Adrian Vision & Karl Hutig. Work: John F Kennedy Gallery, Washington, DC; Univ of E Ger; Mus of the Plains Indian; also in pvt collections of Clayton Mercer, Washington & Gary Hopkins, NY. Comn: The Lord's Last Supper, Methodist Church, Browning, Mont, 38; Transition of Blackfeet Indians, Blackfeet Tribe, Browning, 58; Scout & Wagons, comn by Jim Starry, Alaska, 74; Custer's Last Stand, comn by Diana Howden, Springfield, Ore, 76; Buffalo Chase, comn by Robert Stefko, 77. Exhib: Blackfeet and Western Art Gallery, 67-73; Mus of the Plains Indians, 74; Historical Mus and Gallery of Benton Co, Prosser, Wash, 75; Mont Historical Mus, Helena, Mont, 65. Awards: Best of Show & First Place, Ann Art Exhib, Reeds Port, Ore, 75; Honorable Mention, Lost Dutchman Art Exhib, 78, Apache Junction, Ariz, 78. Bibliog: Maxine Snodgrass (auth), Indian Artists of America, Univ Press, Okla, 67; Dale Burke (auth), New Interpretations, Western Life Publ Inc, 68; Jim Ludwig (auth), Blackfeet of the Plains (doc movie), 70. Style & Technique: Woodcarving, pen & ink. Media: Woodcarving. Interest: Preservation of Western and Indian history. Publ: Auth of articles in New York Times, 69, Hungry Horse News, 68, Montana Historical Mag, 70, Los Angeles Times, 70. Dealer: Inez Racine 3405 S Tomahawk Rd Apache Junction AZ 85220. Mailing Add: Box 16 Babb MT 59411

RACITI, CHERIE
PAINTER, SCULPTOR
b Chicago, Ill, June 17, 42. Study: Univ Ill, Urbana, 60-61; Memphis Acad Arts, Tenn, 63-65; San Francisco State Univ, BA, 68. Work: San Francisco Mus of Mod Art, Calif; plus pvt collections. Exhib: One-woman exhibs, Univ Calif Art Mus, Berkeley, 72 & Nicholas Wilder

Gallery, Los Angeles, 75; Six Painters, San Francisco Art Inst, 73; Univ Nev, Las Vegas, 75; Whitney Mus Am Art Biennial, New York, 75; one-person show, Adaline Kent Award Exhib, San Francisco Art Inst, 77. Bibliog: Lynn Hershman (auth), Resin painters, Artweek, 9/23/72; Claudia King (auth), 5 Women Artists in Las Vegas, Univ Nev, 3/75; Phillip Linhares (auth), interview, Currant, 4-5/75. Mem: San Francisco Art Inst Artist Comt. Style & Technique: Abstract structural paintings using industrial fabrics and plastic resins. Media: Acrylic Polymer; Spunbonded Polypropylene. Dealer: Nicholas Wilder Gallery 8225 1/2 Santa Monica Blvd Los Angeles CA 90046. Mailing Add: 636 Fourth St San Francisco CA 94107

RACZ, ANDRE
PAINTER, PRINTMAKER
b Cluj, Romania, Nov 21, 16; US citizen. Study: Univ Bucharest, BA, 35. Work: Mus Mod Art, Whitney Mus Am Art & New York Pub Libr, New York; Libr of Cong, Washington, DC; Bibliot Nat, Paris. Exhib: 50 Yrs Am Art, Mus Mod Art, Paris, London, Belgrade & Barcelona, 55; Retrospective, Mus de Bellas Artes, Santiago, Chile, 57; 1st Biennial Relig Art, Salzburg, Austria, 58; Int Watercolor Biennial, Brooklyn Mus, 61; Nat Inst Arts & Lett, New York, 68; 50 Yrs American Printmaking, Mus Mod Art, 74; Surrealism & Am Art 1931-1947, Rutgers Univ, 77; 50th Anniversary Retrospective, Atelier 17, Univ Wis, 77. Teaching: Prof painting, Columbia Univ, 51-, prof painting & chmn div painting & sculpture, 64-73 & 75-77. Awards: Guggenheim Fel Printmaking, 56; Fulbright Res Scholar, Chile, 57; Ford Found Fel, 62. Bibliog: Carmen Valle (auth), Poets on painters & sculptors, Tiger's Eye, 49; Rosamel del Valle (auth), Una tarde con el pintor Andre Racz, Nacion, 49; Antonio Romera (auth), Andre Racz pintor y grabador, Ed Pacifico, 50. Mem: Soc Am Graphic Artists; Am Asn Univ Prof. Publ: Auth, The Reign of Claws, 45, XII Prophets of Aleijadinho, 47, Via Crucis, 48, Mother & Child, 49 & Canciones Negras, 53. Mailing Add: PO Box 43 Demarest NJ 07627

RADIN, DAN
PAINTER
b New York, NY, May 12, 29. Study: Queens Col; Cranbrook Acad Art, BFA & MFA. Work: Cranbrook Mus, Bloomfield Hills, Mich; Detroit Inst Arts, Mich; Butler Inst Am Art, Youngstown, Ohio; Lowe Gallery, Univ Miami, Coral Gables, Fla. Exhib: Butler Inst Am Art 26th Ann, 61; Painting Part II, 63 & Landscape II, 71, De Cordova Mus; Am Acad Ann, Rome, 64; Contemp Surv, J B Speed Mus, Louisville, Ky, 66; The Figure Today, Slater Mus, Norwich, Conn, 77. Teaching: Instr painting, Swain Sch Design, New Bedford, Mass, 64-71; instr painting & drawing, Univ Conn, 72; instr drawing, RI Sch Design, 72. Awards: Louis Comfort Tiffany Found Awards in Painting, 62 & 64; Second Purchase Award, Lowe Gallery, 63. Media: Oil, Acrylic. Mailing Add: Rte 1 Norwich CT 06360

RADOCZY, ALBERT
PAINTER
b Stamford, Conn, Oct 24, 14. Study: Parsons Sch Design; Cooper Union, grad. Work: Brooklyn Mus, NY; Ball State Teachers Col, Ind; Lyman Allyn Mus, Conn; Sloan-Kettering Mem. Comn: Tapestry murals, Allegheny Col, Meadville, Pa, 66. Exhib: NJ State Mus Ann, Trenton, 61; Whitney Mus Am Art Ann, New York, 62; Brooklyn Mus Nat Print Exhib, NY, 62; Mus Mod Art Lending Collection, 65; Bergen Community Mus, 73; The Figure in Drawing, Univ of Bridgeport, 77. Teaching: Lectr drawing, Cooper Union, 50-55; prof design, City Col New York, 55- Awards: Purchase Award, Ball State Teachers Col, 59. Style & Technique: Human symbols in spontaneous line techniques. Media: Oil. Mailing Add: 61 Cedar St Cresskill NJ 07626

RADULOVIC, SAVO
PAINTER, CRAFTSMAN
b Montenegro, Yugoslavia, Jan 27, 11; US citizen. Study: St Louis Sch Fine Arts, Wash Univ, 30-32; Fogg Mus Art, Harvard Univ, Carnegie fel, 37; Acad Belle Arte, Rome, Italy, Fulbright fel, 49-50. Work: City Art Mus St Louis; Univ Ariz; Hist Sect, War Dept, Pentagon, Washington, DC; Col William & Mary, Williamsburg, Va; Mus Mod Art, Miami Beach, Fla; also in pvt collections US & abroad. Exhib: Nat Acad Design; Pa Acad Fine Arts; Whitney Mus Am Art; City Art Mus St Louis; Philadelphia Mus Art; plus many others. Pos: Owner & dir, Artists Little Gallery, New York, 46-75. Awards: Purchase Prize, City Art Mus St Louis, 41. Mem: Artists Equity Asn. Mailing Add: 750 Lexington Ave New York NY 10022

RAE, EDWIN C
ART HISTORIAN
b New Canaan, Conn, Aug 31, 11. Study: Harvard Col, BA, 33, Harvard Univ, MA, 34, PhD, 43. Teaching: Instr hist art, Brown Univ, 38-39; instr hist art, Univ Ill, Urbana, 39-42, prof hist art, 47- Awards: Legion Honneur Scholars & Res Grants. Mem: Soc Archit Historians (asst ed jour, 41); Col Art Asn Am; Archaeol Inst Am; Royal Soc Antiquaries Ireland. Res: Gothic architecture and sculpture, particularly in Ireland. Publ: Auth, The education of the artist, Art J, 61; auth, The sculpture of the cloister of Jerpoint Abbey, 66 & Irish sepulchral monuments of the later Middle Ages, 70-71, J Royal Soc Antiquaries Ireland; auth, The rice monument in Waterford Cathedral, Royal Irish Acad Proc, 70. Mailing Add: Fine Arts Bldg Univ of Ill Champaign IL 61820

RAFFAEL, JOSEPH
PAINTER
b Brooklyn, NY, Feb 22, 33. Study: Cooper Union Art Sch, cert; Yale Univ, BFA. Work: Metrop Mus Art, New York; San Francisco Mus Art, Los Angeles Co Art Mus & Univ Art Mus, Univ Calif, Berkeley; Art Inst Chicago, Ill. Exhib: Human Concern, Personal Torment, Whitney Mus Am Art, New York, 70; American Painting (organized by Peter Selz), Richmond Art Mus, Va, 70; Darmstadt Biennial, Ger, 70; 70th Am Exhib, Art Inst Chicago, 72, 74 & 76; Tokyo Biennial Figure Art, 74 & Bicentennial Exhib, Dept Interior, originating at Corcoran Gallery Art, 76-77 & 78; one-man exhibs, Arco Ctr for Visual Arts, Los Angeles, Calif, 77, Mus of Fine Arts, St Petersburg, Fla, 77, Calif Yrs 1969-78 (with catalogue), San Francisco Mus of Mod Art, 78, Des Moines Art Ctr, Iowa, 78, Joslyn Art Mus, Nebr, 78, Newport Harbor Art Mus, Newport Beach, Calif, 78 & Denver Art Mus, Colo, 78. Teaching: Instr art, Sch Visual Arts, 66-69; assoc prof art, Univ Calif, Berkeley, 69; prof art, Sacramento State Univ, 69-73. Awards: Fulbright Award, 58-60; L C Tiffany Found Fel, 60; First Prize, Tokyo Biennial Figure Art, 74; First Prize & Purchase Award, Oakland Mus, Calif, 75. Bibliog: Grace Glueck (auth), O to be born under Pisces, New York Times, 1/69; Gloria Smith (auth), The Eyes Have It: Joseph Raffael (film), NBC-TV, 72; Wm S Wilson (auth), The paintings of Jos Raffael, Studio Int, 5/74. Media: Oil. Dealer: Nancy Hoffman Gallery 429 W Broadway New York NY 10012. Mailing Add: PO Box 210 San Geronimo CA 94963

RAFFAEL, JUDITH K
PAINTER, STAINED GLASS ARTIST
b Los Angeles, Calif, June 24, 37. Study: Los Angeles Art Inst; San Francisco Art Inst. Work: Los Angeles Co Mus & Security Pacific Bank, Los Angeles; Oakland Mus, Calif. Comn: Stained Glass, (20ft x 30ft), Northbrae Community Church, 59; stained glass (55ft x 35ft), Holy Name of Jesus Christ, 63; stained glass (100ft x 13ft), Salvation Army, 72; Portrait of Dean of Law Sch, Stanford Univ, 77. Exhib: North, South, East, West & Middle, Moore Col of Art, Philadelphia, Pratt Graphics Ctr, New York, Corcoran Gallery of Art, Washington, DC & Ft Worth Art Mus, Tex, 75; Other Work, San Francisco Mus of Art, 76; Recent Acquisitions, Oakland Mus, 77; one-woman show, Four Quilts By 70 Women, Berkeley, 72-73. Teaching: Instr theatre design & stained glass, Bennington Col, 66-69; instr theatre design, Actors Workshop, San Francisco, 60-64. Pos: Staff designer, Actors Workshop, 60-64 & Cummings Stained Glass Studio, 63-65; designer, Bennington Col, 66-69. Awards: L C Tiffany, Stained Glass, 66. Bibliog: Otto Regan (auth), New Glass, San Francisco Book Co, 77; Giacopetti (auth), Native Funk and Flash, Scrimshaw Press, 74 & Craze for Quilts, Life Mag, 5/5/72. Style & Technique: Watercolor, acrylic, photography, stained glass, quiltmaking. Media: Watercolor. Dealer: Roy Boyd Gallery 233 E Ontario St Chicago IL 60611. Mailing Add: PO Box 210 San Geronimo CA 94963

RAFFEL, ALVIN ROBERT
PAINTER, INSTRUCTOR
b Dayton, Ohio, Dec 25, 05. Study: Chicago Acad Fine Arts; Art Inst Chicago, with F DeForest Schook. Work: Dayton Art Inst; Canton Art Mus, Ohio. Comn: Seascape (oil), George E Morris, Chicago, 33; portrait of A H Allen, comn by Mrs A H Allen, Chicago, 34; portrait of Karl Koeker, Dayton, Ohio, 35; portrait of S H McCoy, Springfield High Sch, Ohio, 56; landscape (oil), Widow's Home, Dayton, 58. Exhib: Ohio Ann, Dayton Art Inst, 45; Cincinnati Ann, Cincinnati Art Mus, 45; Portrait of America, New York, 46; Carnegie Ann, Pittsburgh, 46-48; Provincetown Arts Festival, Mass, 58. Teaching: Prof painting & life drawing, Sch of Dayton Art Inst, 46- Awards: First Purchase Prize for Fellaheen, Dayton Art Inst, 45; Award for Holiday on the Ice, Mrs G S Weng, 48; Award for The Lesser Light to Rule the Night, Jefferson Patterson, 51. Mem: Am Asn Univ Prof; Dayton Soc Painters & Sculptors. Style & Technique: American representational using brush and palette-knife technique. Media: Oil, Watercolor. Publ: Auth, Art, Exponent, 61. Mailing Add: 6720 Mad River Rd Dayton OH 45459

RAFSKY, JESSICA C
COLLECTOR
b New York NY, Sept 18, 24. Study: George Washington Univ; NY Univ. Mem: Assoc Guggenheim Mus; sustaining mem Mus Mod Art; assoc Metrop Mus Art; assoc Am Fedn Arts; plus others. Interest: Benefactor of Foundation Maeght and friend of Tate Gallery, British Mus, London, Eng. Collection: Contemporary art. Mailing Add: 200 E 62nd St New York NY 10021

RAGGIO, OLGA
ART ADMINISTRATOR, CURATOR
Study: Liceo E O Visconti, Rome, BA(with hon), 44; Lycee Chateaubriand, Rome, Baccalaureat I, 45; Vatican Libr, dipl, 47; Sch of Art Hist & Archaeol & Sch of Mod Lang, Univ of Rome, PhD(cum laude), 49; Inst of Fine Arts, New York, grad study, 51-52. Exhibitions Arranged: Renaissance Sculpture from Northern Italy, 72, Patterns of Collecting: Selected Acquisitions 1965-75 (co-auth & ed, catalog), 75, The Fire & the Talent: a presentation of French Terracottas, 76, Bernini: A Bacchanal Group, 77 & Highlights from the Untermyer Collection, 77-78, Metrop Mus of Art, New York. Teaching: Adj asst prof fine arts, Inst of Fine Arts, New York Univ, 64-67, adj assoc prof fine arts, 67-68, adj prof fine arts, 68- Pos: Jr res fel, Metrop Mus of Art, New York, 50-52, curatorial asst, Dept of European Sculpture & Decorative Arts, 52-54, asst cur, 54-63, assoc res cur, 63-68, cur, 68-71, chmn, Dept of European Sculpture & Decorative Arts, 71- Publ: Auth, El Patio de Velez Blanco—Un monumento senero del Renacimiento, Murcia, Publ de la Univ de Murcia, 68; auth, Problemes belliphontains, La Revue de l'Art, Vol 23, 74; co-auth with T Hoving and others, The Chase, The Capture: Collecting at Metropolitan, New York, 76; ed, Notable Acquisitions, 1965-75, Metrop Mus of Art, New York, 76; auth, Sculpture in the Grand Manner: Two Groups by Anguier & Monnot, Apollo, 11/77. Mailing Add: c/o Dept of Europ Sculpture & Decorative Arts Metrop Mus of Art Fifth Ave at 82nd St New York NY 10028

RAGLAND, BOB
PAINTER, LECTURER
b Cleveland, Ohio, Dec 11, 38. Study: Rocky Mountain Sch Art, Denver, Colo; study with Phil Steele. Work: Denver Pub Libr; Karamu House, Cleveland; Irving St Ctr, Cult Arts Prog, Denver. Comn: Logo, Merto State Col Black Student Union, 74; art print, Big Sisters of Colo, 75. Exhib: Metrop Fine Art Show, Denver Mus Fine Art, 66; 16th Ann Drawing Exhib, Dallas Mus Fine Art, Traveling Exhib, 67; one-man show, Cleveland State Univ, 68; Art in Embassies Abroad, US State Dept, 73; 7th Ann Drawing Exhib, Del Mar Col, Corpus Christi, Tex, 73. Teaching: Instr painting & drawing, Denver Pub Libr, 69-71 & Eastside Action Ctr, Denver, 69-71; artist-in-residence, Model Cities Cult Arts Ctr Workshop, 71-73. Pos: Chmn, Arts & Humanities Comt, 68-69; founding fac mem, Auraria Campus, Community Col, Denver, 70-72; lectr Afro-American art of the 60's & 70's. Bibliog: Duncan Pollock (auth), Sophisticated graffitti mural project, 12/72 & Pat Agnew (auth), Bob Ragland an artist who happens to be Black, 9/74, Southwest Art Mag; Art of Bob Ragland, article in Empire Mag, 6/21/74. Mem: Colo Black Umbrella. Style & Technique: Landscapes and figures in traditional manner; watercolor, conte crayon, charcoal, acrylic and welded metal sculptures. Collection: Traditional renderings of the figure and landscape in all mediums. Dealer: Helen Mason Smith/Mason Gallery Art 1207 Rhode Island Ave NW Washington DC 20002. Mailing Add: 1723 E 25th Ave Denver CO 80205

RAGLAND, JACK WHITNEY
PAINTER, PRINTMAKER
b El Monte, Calif, Feb 25, 38. Study: Ariz State Univ, BA & MA, with Dr Harry Wood, Arthur Jacobson & Ben Goo; Univ Calif, Los Angeles, with Dr Lester Longman, Sam Amato & William Brice; Akad Angewandte Kunst; Akad Bildenden Künste; Graphische Bundes-Lehrund Versuchsanstalt, Vienna. Work: Albertina Mus, Vienna, Austria; Phoenix Art Mus, Ariz; Graphische Bundes-Lehr-und Versuchsanstalt, Vienna; Kunsthaus, Basel, Switz; Los Angeles Co Mus, Calif. Exhib: Ariz Ann Exhib, Phoenix, 61; Tucson Southwest Exhib, Ariz, 61; Exhib Nat Recognized Artists, Seattle, 63 & Ft Lauderdale, Fla, 64 & 65; Iowa Ann Exhib, Des Moines, 70 & 72; Artists Fedn Traveling Exhib, Eight Midwest States, 75; plus many one-man shows. Teaching: Grad asst drawing & painting, Univ Calif, Los Angeles, 61-64; instr drawing & painting, Ariz State Univ, summer 63; assoc prof drawing, printmaking & painting, Simpson Col, 64-76. Awards: Grand Purchase Prize, Ariz Ann, Phoenix Art Mus, 61; Painting Selected as One of Top Representational Paintings in USA, Allied Publ, 62. Bibliog: Applause, NY Mag of Arts, 11/3/71; New woman, Fla Mag, 11-12/74. Mem: Col Art Asn; Mid-Am Col Art Asn. Style & Technique: Realist tradition in both paintings and prints, using both local and symbolic color. Media: Acrylic; Serigraphy. Publ: Auth, Works of Wilhelm Jarushka, Graphische Bundes-Lehr-und-Versuchsanstalt Mag, 71. Mailing Add: 1005 Ann Parkway Indianola IA 50125

RAHILL, MARGARET FISH
CURATOR, ART CRITIC
b Milwaukee, Wis, Feb 21, 19. Study: Univ Wis, Milwaukee. Collections Arranged: Karl Priebe Retrospective (with catalog), 68, Marc Chagall Painting and Prints from Milwaukee Collections (with catalog), 70, Eskimo Sculptures and Stone Prints from Baffin Island, Canada (with catalog), 70, Wisconsin Art of the 1920's and 1930's (with catalog), 75 & American Plains Indians, Paintings and Drawings (with catalog), 76, Charles Allis Library. Pos: Art ed & critic, Milwaukee Sentinal, contribr reviewer, Milwaukee Art J & art critic, Wis Archit, 46-61; pub relations, Milwaukee Art Ctr, 69; pub relations & exhibs, Layton Sch of Art, 62-68; cur, Charles Allis Library, 68- Awards: Four Milwaukee Press Club Ann Awards for articles on art, museums, art education, 55-60; Milwaukee Art Comn Award for Excellence, 76; Milwaukee Pub Libr Bookfellows Award for Creative Exhibs and Programming, 76. Mem: Hon mem Wis Painters & Sculptors Inc; hon mem Wis Designer-Craftsman Inc; Wis Women in Art. Res: American 19th century landscapists; Wisconsin art and artists. Publ: Auth, Richard Lorenz, Milwaukee Art Ctr, 65. Mailing Add: 2633 N Hackett Ave E Milwaukee WI 53211

RAHJA, VIRGINIA HELGA
PAINTER, ART ADMINISTRATOR
b Aurora, Minn, Apr 21, 21. Study: Hamline Univ, BA, 44; Sch Assoc Arts, DFA, 66. Exhib: Many exhibs & ann, Walker Art Ctr, Minn Art Inst, St Paul Gallery, Minn State Fair & Hamline Galleries. Teaching: Assoc prof painting, Hamline Univ, 43-48 & dir, Hamline Galleries, 45-48; prof painting, Sch Assoc Arts, St Paul, 48-65, dean, 48-73, dir, 73-, pres, 75- Pos: Asst supt fine arts, Minn State Fair, 44-48. Mem: Nat Asn Interior Designers; Am Asn Univ Women; Midwest Col Art Conf. Style & Technique: Abstract and non-objective. Media: Oil. Mailing Add: 360 S Lexington Pkwy St Paul MN 55105

RAIN, CHARLES (WHEDON)
PAINTER
b Knoxville, Tenn, Dec 27, 11. Study: Art Inst Chicago, 31-33; pvt study in Berlin, Vienna & Paris, 33-34. Work: Springfield Mus Fine Arts; Univ Ill; Ariz State Univ, Tempe; DeBeers Mus, Johannesburg, SAfrica; Va Mus Fine Arts. Exhib: Springfield Mus Fine Arts, 47 & 63; five shows, Univ Ill, 49-57; Los Angeles Mus Art, 51 & 56; Denver Art Mus, 57; Albright-Knox Art Gallery, Buffalo, 61; plus many others. Awards: Purchase Prizes, Springfield Mus Fine Arts, Mass, 47 & Univ Ill, 50. Style & Technique: Underpainting and glazing in oil on gesso panels. Dealer: FAR Gallery 746 Madison Ave New York NY 10021. Mailing Add: 10 Mitchell Pl New York NY 10017

RAINEY, FROELICH GLADSTONE
ART ADMINISTRATOR, WRITER
b Black River Falls, Wis, June 18, 07. Study: Univ Chicago, PhB, 29; Am Sch in France, 30; Yale Univ, PhD, 35. Teaching: Asst prof anthrop, Univ PR, 35; prof anthrop, Univ Alaska, 35-42; prof anthrop, Univ Pa, 47- Pos: Asst in anthrop, Peabody Mus, Yale Univ, 31-35; anthrop res in WI, 33-35; dir, Univ Mus, Univ Pa, 47-77, dir Appl Sci Ctr for Archaeol, 60-, archaeol res in Italy, 61-, supvr archaeol res, Univ Mus expeds all over the world. Awards: Grants for Res, Am Mus Natural Hist, 34-42; Comdr, Order of Merit, Ital Repub. Mem: Am Asn Mus (pres, 61-63, exec comt, 63-); Int Coun Mus; Mus Coun Philadelphia; Soc Am Archaeol; Soc Pa Archaeol; plus others. Publ: Auth, Archaeology, 70, Dating the past, 71 & Archaeology, 72, In: Encycl Britannica Yearbk Sci & the Future; auth, The Ipiutak Culture. Excavations at Point Hope, Alaska, Addison-Wesley, 71; auth, Looting of archaeological sites, Sci Yr. Mailing Add: Univ Pa Mus 33rd & Spruce Sts Philadelphia PA 19104

RAINEY, JOHN WATTS
PAINTER, COLLECTOR
b Denver, Colo, Feb 9, 48. Study: Minneapolis Col Art & Design, BFA; Ateliers '63, Haarlem, Holland; Calif Col Arts & Crafts, MFA. Exhib: Metrop Show, 74 & All-Colo Show, 75, Denver Art Mus; one-man shows, William Kastan Gallery, Denver, 74 & Metrop State Col, 75; Colo Women's Col, 74. Pos: Media consult, Colo Dept Educ, Denver, 74- Style & Technique: Realist, objects, people and landscapes. Media: Acrylic, Watercolor, Pencil. Collection: Print collection includes Maxfield Parrish, John Clem Clarke, William Wiley, Philip Pearstein, and Scott McIntire. Mailing Add: 1208 S Vine St Denver CO 80210

RAKOCY, WILLIAM (JOSEPH)
PAINTER
b Youngstown, Ohio, Apr 14, 24. Study: Butler Inst Am Art, with Clyde Singer, 39-41; Am Acad Art, 44; Kansas City Art Inst, with Ross Braught, Ed Lanning & Bruce Mitchell, MFA, 51. Work: Mural, US Naval Training Sta, Great Lakes, Ill; mural, YMCA, Youngstown; watercolor, Butler Inst Am Art, Youngstown; drawings & prints, El Paso Mus Art, Tex. Comn: Mural, Woodrow Wilson High Sch, Youngstown, 46; four murals (with Robert Sonoga & Chet Kwiecinski), McSorleys Colonial Rest, Pittsburgh, Pa, 55; three murals, YMCA, Youngstown; three murals, Mesa Inn, El Paso, Tex, 75; six dioramas, Cavalry Mus, El Paso, Tex, 78. Exhib: Butler Inst Am Art Ann, 55. Teaching: Instr painting & drawing, Mohn Sch Art, 54-56; asst prof painting & drawing, Col Artesia, 66-67, assoc prof painting & drawing, 67-71. Pos: Installation cur, Wilderness Park Mus, 77. Awards: Art Travel Grant to Study in Italy, Ital Businessmen, Kansas City, Mo, 53; First Award in Watercolor, Butler Inst Am Art, 56. Mem: Kansas City Area Artists Asn; El Paso Art Asn; Mogollon Artists Asn (pres); Western Asn Art Schs & Univ Mus; El Paso Hist Soc. Style & Technique: Nature as a point of departure for interesting color, shape and design. Media: Oil, Watercolor, Acrylic. Interest: Promoter of art auctions to assist artists via sales and scholarships. Publ: Auth, Sketches on Mogollon, 64; auth, A Western Portfolio, 65; auth, Art reporter, El Paso, Texas, 72; auth, Sketches & Observations, 72; auth, Art look, South West Gallery Mag; auth, Mogollon Diary. Mailing Add: 4210 Emory Way El Paso TX 79925

RAKOVAN, LAWRENCE FRANCIS
PRINTMAKER, PAINTER
b Eleria, Ohio, Oct 26, 39. Study: Detroit Soc Arts & Crafts; Wayne State Univ, BS; RI Sch Design, MA. Work: Brooklyn Mus, NY; Bowdoin Col Mus Art, Brunswick, Maine; Calif Col Arts & Crafts, Oakland; Portland Mus Art, Maine; Univ Maine, Orono. Comn: 14 Stations of the Cross & exterior monumental cross with stoneware reliefs of The Four Evangelists, St Charles Borromeo Church, Brunswick, Maine, 75. Exhib: Grad show, RI Sch Design, Carr House, Providence, 69; 5 Young Painters, Providence, 69-70; 21 paintings & prints, Rotunda, Union Theol Sem, 72; two-man show, St Peter's Ctr, New York, 73; Maine 75, Bowdoin Col, 75; Sculpture in Wood, Maine Festival of Arts, Bowdoin Col, 77; two-man exhib, Benbow Gallery, Newport, RI, 77; one-man show, Treat Gallery, Bates Col, 76. Teaching: Assoc prof painting & printmaking, Univ Maine, Portland-Gorham, 67- Awards: State of Maine Res Grant, 73. Mem: Col Art Asn Am; Skowhegan Sch Painting & Sculpture; Colby Col Mus; Smithsonian Inst. Style & Technique: Work from nature in oil paint, stone lithography and stoneware. Media: Oil, Stone Lithography. Dealer: Benbow Gallery Newport RI 02840. Mailing Add: Mere Point Rd 5 Brunswick ME 04011

RALEIGH, HENRY PATRICK
PAINTER, WRITER
b New York, NY, Feb 5, 31. Study: Pratt Inst, BS, 56 & MS, 59; New York Univ, PhD, 63. Exhib: Ten Artists Under Thirty, Riverside Mus, New York, 64; Artists of the Mid-Hudson Valley, Albany Inst of Art, NY, 70-75. Teaching: Chmn art dept, Pratt Inst Art Sch, 61-68; prof film hist, art criticism & aesthet, State Univ NY, New Paltz, 68-, co-dean fac fine & performing art, 71-73 & chmn studio art & art hist, 68-74. Awards: Travel Grant, 7th Int Am Coun Learned Soc, Cong, Rumania, 72. Mem: Am Soc Aesthet. Style & Technique: Realism, traditional technique. Media: Oils. Res: Application of value study to examinations of contemporary art and art criticism. Publ: Auth, Value and artistic alternative, J Aesthet & Art Criticism, 69; auth, Art as communicable knowledge, J Aesthet Educ, 71; auth, Exhaustion thresholds of painting, Bucknell Rev, 72; auth, Revival of aesthetic symbolism, 74 & Aesthethic of chance, 75, J Aesthet & Art Criticism. Mailing Add: State Univ NY New Paltz NY 12561

RALEY, MR & MRS ROBERT L
COLLECTORS
Mr Raley, b Baltimore, Md, Aug 22, 24. Study: Mr Raley, Univ Pa, MArch, with Louis Kahn; Univ Del, MA(early Am studies). Pos: Mr Raley, Mem bd dir, Del Art Mus; mem Am art comt, Philadelphia Mus Art; state adv, Nat Trust for Historic Preservation. Mem: Am Inst Architects; Am Asn Mus (mem trustees comt). Collection: Twentieth century European and American paintings and drawings and contemporary sculpture. Mailing Add: 800 Center Mill Rd Greenville DE 19807

RALSTON, JAMES KENNETH
PAINTER, ILLUSTRATOR
b Choteau, Mont, Mar 31, 96. Study: Art Inst Chicago; Rocky Mt Col, Hon DFA, 71. Work: Jefferson Nat Expansion Mem, St Louis, Mo; Custer Battlefield Nat Monument, Mont; Mont Hist Soc Mus & Galleries, Helena; Buffalo Bill Hist Ctr, Whitney Gallery Western Art, Cody, Wyo; Western Heritage Mus Treasures of West Collection, Billings, Mont. Comn: Murals, The Crossing, Jordan Hotel, Glendive, Mont, 52 & Billings Munic Airport, Logan Field, 58; paintings, After the Battle, Treasures of West Collection, 55, Into the Unknown, Jefferson Nat Expansion Monument, 64 & The Return, First Westside Nat Bank, Great Falls, Mont, 71. Exhib: Gainsborough Gallery, Calgary, Alta, 59; Charles M Russell Gallery, Great Falls, 62 & 71; Mont Hist Soc, 64; Galeries Lafayette, Paris, 66; Yellowstone Art Ctr, Billings, 67 & 71. Bibliog: Michael Kennedy (auth), Man who avoids footprints of CMR, Mont Mag Western Hist, 61; R W Fenwick (auth), J K Ralston & his art, Empire Mag, 67; Ed Ainsworth (auth), The Cowboy in Art, Bk World Publ, 68; James Graff (producer), The Old West of J K Ralston (doc film), Rendezvous 75, Mont Hist Soc, 76. Mem: Mont Inst Arts; Billings Arts Asn; Yellowstone Art Ctr (chmn ann art auction). Media: Oil, Ink, Watercolor. Publ: Auth & illusr, Rhymes of a Cowboy, Rimrock Publ, 69. Mailing Add: 2103 Alderson Ave Billings MT 59102

RAMANAUSKAS, DALIA IRENA
PAINTER, DRAFTSMAN
b Kaunas, Lithuania, Jan 10, 36; US citizen. Study: Southern Conn Col, BS(art educ). Work: Del Art Mus, Wilmington; Minn Mus Art; Smithsonian Inst, Washington, DC; Va Mus, Richmond; New Britain Mus Am Art, Conn. Comn: Sepia drawing, Rebekah Harkness Kean Dance Theater, New York, 64. Exhib: Objects & ... 8 Women Realists, Art Gallery, Univ Mass, Amherst, 73; Painting and Sculpture Today, Indianapolis Mus, 74; Work on Paper, Weatherspoon Art Gallery, Univ NC, 74; Realism, Ulrich Mus Art, Wichita, 75; Drawings by Four Artists, DM Gallery, London, 75; Art 77, Root Art Ctr, Hamilton Col, Clinton, NY; Am Drawing 1927-1977, Minn Mus of Art, St Paul. Awards: Am Drawing 20th Ann Purchase Award, Norfolk Mus Arts & Sci, 63. Bibliog: Rev in Artforum, 4/74; M L D'Otrange Mastai (auth), Illusionism in Art, Abaris, 76. Style & Technique: Pen drawings and paintings. Media: Color Inks, Watercolor. Dealer: O K Harris 383 W Broadway New York NY 10012. Mailing Add: PO Box 264 Main St Ivoryton CT 06442

RAMBERG, CHRISTINA (CHRISTINA RAMBERG HANSON)
PAINTER
b Camp Campbell, Ky, Aug 21, 46. Study: Art Inst Chicago, BFA, 68. Exhib: Famous Artists, 69 & Chicago Imagist Art, 72, Mus Contemp Art, Chicago; Spirit of the Comic in the 50's & 60's, Univ Pa, Philadelphia, 69; False Image II, Hyde Park Art Ctr, Chicago, 69; Whitney Ann, Whitney Mus Am Art, New York, 72 & 73. Teaching: Vis artist-instr painting, Univ Colo, Boulder, 72. Media: Acrylic. Dealer: Phyllis Kind Gallery 226 E Ontario St Chicago IL 60611. Mailing Add: 709 W Buena Chicago IL 60613

RAMIREZ, GABRIEL
PAINTER
b Medida, Yucatan, Mex, Jan 4, 38. Exhib: Mus Fine Arts, St Petersburg, Fla, 74; Mus Arts & Sci, Ft Worth, Tex, 73; Galeria Arvil, Mex, 75; Mus de Arte Contemporaneo, de Bogota, Colombia, 76; Inst Panameno de Arte Panama, 76; plus others. Awards: XI Premio Int de Dibuix Joan Miro, Barcelona, Spain, 72. Bibliog: Jomi Garcia Ascot (auth), Presentation, 65; Alfonso de Neuvillate (auth), Pintura Actual, Artes de Mex, 66; Gustavo Sainz (auth), Gabriel Ramirez, Siete, 73. Media: Oil & Acrylic on Canvas. Mailing Add: c/o Arvil SA Hamburgo 241 Mexico 6 DF Mexico

RAMIREZ, JOEL TITO
PAINTER, ILLUSTRATOR
b Albuquerque, NMex, June 3, 23. Study: Univ NMex, with Randall Davey, Kenneth M Adams & Ralph Douglass; also with Enrique Montenegro & Raymond Jonson. Work: Mus NMex, Santa Fe; Univ Albuquerque; NMex State Univ; Galerie de Paris et Madrid, Spain, Nice, France & New York. Comn: La Hacienda, Ford Motor Co, Dearborn, Mich, 73; Keep New Mexico Beautiful, Kennecott Copper Corp, 74; En Dios Confiamos, El Valle State Bank, Albuquerque, 74; Color slides of paintings, Samuel H Kress Found, Univ Ala, 74. Exhib: War with Japan, 47; Fiesta Show, Mus NMex, 62; Art Intimates, Galerie de Paris, New York, 65. Teaching: Teacher oil painting, Ramirez Art Studio, 65-73. Pos: First vpres, NMex Art League, 58-59. Awards: Devocion, Rodeo de Sante Fe, Paul F Rutledge, 59; Anitiqua, Fine Arts Mus, Santa Fe, James T Forrest, 62; Los Trampas, Fiesta Show, Bernique Longley, 63. Bibliog: Jacinto Quirate (auth), Southwest Artists, Exxon Oil Co, 73 & Mexican-American Artists, Univ Tex, Austin, 74; Frank Duane (auth), Pilgrims to the West, KLRN-TV, San Antonio, Tex, 73. Style & Technique: Romantic, overlapping, transparent planes, brass comb technique. Publ: Contribr, After Cortez, 73; illusr, Juan Diego and the Virgin of Guadalupe, 75; illusr, St Bernadette of Lourdes, 75. Dealer: Langells 3600 Fourth St NW Albuquerque NM 87107. Mailing Add: 10305 Santa Paula NE Albuquerque NM 87111

RAMIREZ-VAZQUEZ, PEDRO
DESIGNER, ARCHITECT
b Mexico, Apr 16, 19. Study: Nat Univ Mexico, Archit Degree. Comn: Nat Mus of Anthrop, Mexican Govt, 64; Aztec Soccer Stadium, Asoc de Football, Mexico, 65; Artistic & Graphic Design, Games of the 19th Olympiad, Mexican Govt, 68; Sculpture La Paz Ausente, Daum & Cie, Paris, France, 74; Basilica of Guadalupe, Mexico, 76. Exhib: Sculptures in Lead Glass, Galeria Mer-Kup, Mexico, 75. Collections Arranged: Mexican Exhib, Brussels World Fair, Belg, 58; 2000 Years of Costa Rican Treasures, Mus of Anthrop, Mexico, 75; Exhib of Negro African Art, Mus of Anthrop, Mexico, 75. Teaching: Prof town planning, Sch of Archit, Nat Univ Mexico, 42-59. Pos: Gen mgr, Admin Comt of Fed Prog of Sch Construction, Mexico, 58-64; pres organizing comt, Games of the 19th Olympiad, Mexico, 66-70; pres, Metrop Univ, Mexico, 74-75; secy, Human Settlements & Pub Works of Mexican Govt, 77- Awards: Grand Prize for design of the Prefabricated Rural Sch, XII Triennial of Milan; Grand Prize, 8th Biennial of Art Exhib, Sao Paulo, Nat Mus of Anthrop, 65; Special Prize, Excellence in Design, Indust Design Soc of Am, 69. Bibliog: Medicine National School, L'Archit d'Aujourd'hui, 55; Raymond Lifchez (auth), Archit Record, Nat Mus of Anthrop, 69; Encyclopedia Britannica, Nat. Mus. of Anthrop. 1976. Mem: Am Inst of Archit; Acad of Arts of the Mexican Repub; Int Coun of Mus of Mod Art, New York; Indust Designers Soc of Am; Royal Soc of Arts, London. Style & Technique: (Architecture) Integration of spaces built to the landscape using materials found in region where construction is being built; (design and sculptures in lead glass) perspective and cuttings represent main elements. Publ: Auth, 4000 Years of Mexican Architecture, Libreros Mexicanos, 56; contribr (prologue), Henri Stierlin, auth, Mayan Architecture, Geneva, 63; co-auth, The National Museum of Anthropology, Helvetica Press, 68. Dealer: Cristal Art Londres 161 Local 41 Mexico DF Mexico 20. Mailing Add: Ave de las Fuentes 170 Mexico DF Mexico 20

RAMOS, MELVIN JOHN
PAINTER, EDUCATOR
b Sacramento, Calif, July 24, 35. Study: Sacramento Jr Col, 54, with Wayne Thiebaud; San Jose State Col, 55; Sacramento State Col, 55-58 & MA. Work: Mus Mod Art, New York; Neue Galerie, Aachen, Ger; Oakland Art Mus & San Francisco Art Mus, Calif; Univ Mus, Potsdam, NY. Comn: Paintings, Time Inc, New York, 68 & Syracuse Univ, NY, 70. Exhib: Pop Art USA, Oakland Mus & Six More, Los Angeles Co Mus, Calif, 63; Human Concern, Personal Torment, Whitney Mus Am Art, New York & Pop Art Revisited, Hayward Gallery, London, 69; Looking West, Joslyn Art Mus, Omaha, Nebr, 70; Am Pop Art, Whitney Mus Am Art, 74; Krannert Mus, Univ Ill, Champaign, 74; Cornell Univ, Ithaca, NY, 74; Retrospective, Kaiser Wilhelm Mus, Krefeld, WGer, 75; plus others. Teaching: Assoc prof painting, Calif State Univ, Hayward, 66- Bibliog: Honey Truewoman (auth), Realism in drag, Artsmag, 2/74; John Perreault (auth), Classic pop revisited, Art in Am, 3-4/74; Liz Claridge (auth), Mel Ramos, Mathews Miller Dunbar, London, 75. Media: Oil. Publ: Contribr, History of Modern Art, 69, Erotic Art 2, 70, Art Now/New Age, 71, The High Art of Cooking & Art as Image & Idea, 72. Dealer: Calle Moragrega 38 Horta de San Juan Spain; Louis K Meisel Gallery 141 Prince St New York NY 10012. Mailing Add: 5941 Ocean View Dr Oakland CA 94618

RAMOS-PRIDA, FERNANDO
PAINTER
b Mexico DF, Mex, Jan 2, 37. Study: Sch Painting & Sculpture, La Esmeralda, 55-56; Univ Sch Painting & Sculpture, San Carlos, 56. Work: Mus Mod Art, Mexico City. Exhib: Biennale de Jeunes Artistes, Paris, 65; Chef d'Oeuvres d'Art Mexicain Traveling Exhib, Europe; Mex Collective Exhib, Expo '67, Montreal; Fifteen of Mexico's Artists, Phoenix Art Mus, 73-74; Jennes peintres Mexicains, Galerie St Germain, Paris, France, 77; one-man shows, Mus of Mod Art, Mexico City, Mex, 71 & 75 & Galería de Arte Mexicano, Mexico City, Mex, 72, 74 & 77, as well as numerous earlier one-man shows in Mexico City & the US. Awards: Confrontacion 66 First Prize, Nat Inst Fine Arts, Mexico City, 66. Bibliog: Alfonso de Neuvillate (auth), Pintura actual, Artes de Mexico, 66; Image of Mexico, Tex Quart, Univ Tex, 69. Style & Technique: Color etchings. Media: Oil on Canvas; Acrylic on Paper or Canvas. Dealer: Galeria de Arte Mexicano Milan 18 Mexico 6 DF Mexico. Mailing Add: Hortensias 112 Colonia Florida Mexico 20 DF Mexico

RAMSAUER, JOSEPH FRANCIS
PAINTER, ART ADMINISTRATOR
b Chicago, Ill, Aug 12, 43. Study: Southern Ill Univ, Carbondale, BA, 67, MFA, 69; also with David Slivka. Work: Univ Galleries, Southern Ill Univ. Comn: Jr Theatre Show Wagon, Davenport Park Bd, Iowa, 71; Saukenuk Indian Mem, Ill State Bicentennial Comn, Black Hawk Col, Ill, 76. Exhib: Mid-Am Two, City Art Mus of St Louis, 69; 19th Mid-South Biennial, Brooks Mem Art Gallery, Memphis, 75; 4th Ann Nat, Cascade Gallery, Seattle Center, Wash, 75; Washington & Jefferson Nat, Washington & Jefferson Col, Washington, Pa, 76; Am Painters in Paris, Paris Convention Ctr, France, 76; Ann Seven State Competition, Univ Wis, Platteville, 77; 41st Nat Ann Midyear Show, Butler Inst of Am Art, Youngstown, Ohio, 77; 69th Ann Jury Exhib, Birmingham Mus of Art, Ala, 77. Collections Arranged: Spectrum Invitational, Davenport Munic Gallery, Iowa, 72; Black Hawk Col & Ill Cent Col Art Fac Exhib, 74. Teaching: Chmn art dept, Black Hawk Col, 69- Awards: Second Place, 14th Mid-Miss Ann, Quad-Cities Times, 76; Best of Show, Ann Seven State Competition, 77; First Place in Acrylic Division & The Judges Award, Pilot Club of Golden Sands Int Fine Arts Exhibit. Mem: Col Art Asn; Mid-Am Art Asn. Style & Technique: Surrealistic paintings in hard edge, flat color with billboard collage. Media: Acrylic collage. Mailing Add: 2411 46th St Moline IL 61265

RAMSTEAD, EDWARD OLIVER, JR
PAINTER, ILLUSTRATOR
b Petersburg, Alaska, Apr 8, 30. Study: Eastern Washington Col, with Francis Coelho; Univ Wash; Calif State Univ Los Angeles, with John Cornish & Jim Fuller. Exhib: Los Angeles & Vicinity, 58; Technical Illustration, Huntsville, Ala, 68; Timae, Los Angeles, 71; Int Graphics Inst, Baltimore, 74. Pos: Conceptual design, General Dynamics, Pomona, Calif, 59-75. Awards: Gold Medal, Huntsville, 68; First Award, Cherry Valley; Best of Show, Int Graphics Inst, 74. Mem: Los Angeles Soc Illus. Media: Watercolors, Acrylics, Inks, Oils. Publ: Contribr, Janes Fighting Ships, 71, Time Mag, 73, Marine Eng Mag, 74 & Proceedings Mag, 75; illusr, Iranian postage stamp, 75. Mailing Add: No 19 Alder Walk Mt Baldy CA 91759

RANALLI, DANIEL
PHOTOGRAPHER, ART ADMINISTRATOR
b New Haven, Conn, Oct 17, 46. Study: Clark Univ, Worcester, Mass, BA, 68; Boston Univ, Mass, MA, 71; Mass Inst of Technol, photog with Minor White. Work: Polaroid Europa Collection, Amsterdam; Franklin Furnace Archives, New York; Pub Art Inst, Kyoto, Japan. Comn: Stage set projections, James Cunningham & Acme Dance Co, New York, 78. Exhib: Inst of Contemp Art, Boston, 71; N E Artists Under 36, De Cordova Mus, 76; New Photographics/77, Washington State Col, 77; Photograms, Chicago Gallery of Photog, 77; one-man shows, Mass Inst of Technol Photog Gallery, 77; Foto Gallery, New York, 78; Carl Siembab Gallery, Boston, 78. Teaching: Instr photog & art, Bryant & Stratton Jr Col, 68-71; prog adv photog & art, Campus-Free Col, Boston & DC, 73-75; Dir Artists-in-Residence, Mass Arts & Humanities Foundation, 75- Awards: Juror, Boston Inst of Cont Art, Urban Spaces Grant, 77. Bibliog: Robert Taylor (auth), Artists Worth Meeting, Boston Sunday Globe, 6/2/76; Jessica Alonso (auth), Expressions of Finesse, The Boston Globe, 4/26/77; Candida Finkel (auth), Light Lines, Afterimage, Rochester, NY, 6/77. Mem: Mass Alliance for Art Educ (bd of trustees 76-); Nat Endowment for Arts (adv comt for Artists in Schs/dance, 77); Boston Visual Artists Union (vpres, 77-). Style & Technique: Photographer primarily camera-less (e.g. photogram), abstract work; artist's books. Publ: Auth, Trail Pouch, Right Hemisphere, 77; contribr, Panopticon, Panopticon Gallery, 77; co-auth, Darkroom Dynamics, Curtin & London, 78; contribr, Patron's Choice, Mus Calender, De Cordova Mus, 77. Dealer: Marcuse Pfeiffer Gallery 825 Madison Ave New York NY; Carl Siembab 162 Newbury St Boston MA. Mailing Add: 76 Sumner St Newton MA 02159

RAND, PAUL
PAINTER, DESIGNER
b New York, NY, Aug 15, 14. Study: Pratt Inst; Art Students League, with George Grosz; Parsons Sch Design. Work: Mus Mod Art; Libr of Cong, Washington, DC. Exhib: One-man shows, Composing Room, 47, Am Inst Graphic Arts Gallery, 58 & IBM Gallery, 71; Brooklyn Mus, 72; many shows, Art Dirs Club New York. Teaching: Instr design, Cooper Union, 42; instr graphic design, Pratt Inst, 46-47; prof graphic design, Yale Univ, 56-69 & 74- Pos: Art dir, Esquire Apparel Arts, 37-41; art dir, Weintraub Advert Agency, 41-54; design consult, IBM Corp & Westinghouse Elec Corp, 56- Awards: Citation, Philadelphia Col Art, 62; Gold Medal, Am Inst Graphic Arts, 66; Art Dirs Hall of Fame, 72. Bibliog: Georgine Oeri (auth), Paul Rand, Graphis Mag, 47; Y Kamekura (auth), The work of Paul Rand, Zokeisha, Tokyo & Knopf, NY, 59; article in Am Artist, 70. Mem: Art Dirs Club New York; Am Inst Graphic Arts; Alliance Graphique Int, Paris; Benjamin Franklin fel, Royal Soc Arts & Sci, London. Publ: Auth, Thoughts on design, Wittenborn, 47 & Van Nostrand Reinhold, 70; auth, Black in the Visual Arts, Harvard Univ, 49; illusr, I Know a Lot of Things, 56, Sparkle & Spin, 57, Little 1, 62 & Listen, Listen, 70, Harcourt; auth, The Trademarks of Paul Rand, Wittenborn, 60. Mailing Add: 87 Goodhill Rd Weston CT 06880

RANDALL, (LILLIAN) PAULA
SCULPTOR, DESIGNER
b Plato, Minn, Dec 21, 95. Study: Minneapolis Inst Arts; Univ Southern Calif; Otis Art Inst, Los Angeles. Work: Western Div, Nat Audubon Soc, Sacramento, Calif; Off Tournament Roses, Pasadena, Calif. Exhib: All Calif Exhib, Laguna Beach Art Mus, Calif, 64; Univ Taiwan, Formosa, 64; Brandeis Univ Exhib, Granada Hills, Calif, 67; Form & the Inner Eye Tactile Show, Calif State Univ, Los Angeles & Pierce Col, San Fernando, Calif, 72; 22-Nation Bicentennial Show, Galerie Int, New York, NY, 76; one-person shows, Galerie Vallombreuse, Biarritz, France, 75 & Pacificulture Asian Art Mus, Pasadena, Calif, 77. Teaching: Pvt sculpture classes, 69-; instr sculpture, Pasadena Sch Fine Arts, 70. Awards: Laguna Beach Art Mus Award, All Calif Show, 64; Spec Achievement Award, All Calif Exhib, Indio, 66; Pasadena Soc Artists Spec Award, 71. Bibliog: Louise Bouett (auth), An approach to understanding art: Paula Randall, Daily News; Carla Tomaso (auth), Ageless art: the inner circuits of Paula Randall, Pasadena Guardian, 75; Meet this lady sculptor, Senior World, San Diego, 7/75. Mem: Pasadena Soc Artists (secy-treas publicity, 62-72); Laguna Beach Art Mus; Los Angeles Co Art Gallery. Style & Technique: Stylized, contemporary impressionist. Media: Wood, Stone, Plastics, Welded Metals. Mailing Add: 441 Ramona Ave Sierra Madre CA 91024

RANDALL, RICHARD HARDING, JR
GALLERY DIRECTOR, ART HISTORIAN
b Baltimore, Md, Jan 31, 26. Study: Princeton Univ, AB(archit); Harvard Univ, MA(fine arts). Collections Arranged: American Furniture in the MFA (with catalog), Mus Fine Arts, Boston, 64; reinstallation of the entire collection of the Walters Art Gallery, 74. Pos: Assoc cur, Cloisters, Metrop Mus Art, New York, 53-59; asst cur, Mus Fine Arts, Boston, Mass, 59-64; asst dir, Walters Art Gallery, Baltimore, 64-65, dir, 65- Mem: Am Mus Dirs Asn. Res: American furniture, medieval art, arms and armour. Publ: Auth, Bestiary of the Cloisters, 59. Mailing Add: 301 Kendall Rd Baltimore MD 21210

RANDALL, RUTH HUNIE
DESIGNER
b Dayton, Ohio, Sept 30, 96. Study: Cleveland Art Inst, design & art educ; Syracuse Univ, BFA & MFA; State Univ NY Col Ceramics, Alfred Univ; Kunstgewerbe Schule, Vienna; also with Ruth Reeves & Ivan Mestrovic. Work: Everson Mus, Syracuse, NY; Walker Art Mus, Youngstown, Ohio; San Antonio Mus, Tex; Syracuse Univ. Comn: Ceramic sculpture relief, Exterior Br Libr, Syracuse Bd Educ Bldg Comt, 60. Exhib: World's Fairs, San Francisco & New York; Paris Decorative Arts; Nat Ceramic Exhibs, 30-62. Teaching: Prof design & crafts, Syracuse Univ Sch Art, 30-62. Awards: Second Prize Awards, Nat Ceramic Show, 30, 36 & 56; First Prize for Ceramic Sculpture, Rochester Mus, NY, 62. Bibliog: Article on personal ceramic collection, Syracuse Mus Bull, 60. Mem: Southwest Fla Craft Guild; NY State Craftsmen (bd dirs, 58-60); Syracuse Ceramic Guild (pres, 56). Media: Ceramics. Collection: Japanese Mingei ceramics and Peruvian ceramics for Syracuse University Art School Collection. Publ: Illusr ceramics page, Craft Horizons, 39 & 73; auth, Ceramic Sculpture, Watson Guptill, 46. Dealer: Gallery DeLeon Ft Myers FL 33900. Mailing Add: 334 NE La Salle Rd Port Charlotte FL 33952

RANDALL, THEODORE A
SCULPTOR, EDUCATOR
b Indianapolis, Ind, Oct 18, 14. Study: Yale Univ, BFA, 38; State Univ NY Col Ceramics, Alfred Univ, MFA, 49. Comn: Pottery, Syracuse Mus Fine Arts & St Stephens Church, Albany, NY. Teaching: Lectr motives & meaning in art & ceramics today; instr, State Univ NY Col Ceramics, Alfred Univ, 52-53, asst prof, 53-56, head div art, 56-73, prof ceramics, 60- Awards: Prizes, Albright Art Gallery, Smithsonian Inst & York State Craftsmen; plus others. Mem: Fel Am Ceramic Soc; fel Acad Int Ceramics; fel Nat Coun Educ for Ceramic Arts (past pres); fel Nat Asn Schs Art (pres); State Univ NY Coun Art Dept Chmn. Publ: Auth, Notions about the usefulness of pottery, Pottery Quart, 61; auth articles in Am Ceramic Soc J & Bull, Ceramic Age, Ceramic Indust & Ceramics Monthly. Mailing Add: Box 774 Alfred NY 14802

RANDELL, RICHARD K
SCULPTOR
b Minneapolis, Minn, 1929. Work: Minneapolis Art Inst; Minn Mus Art, St Paul; Univ Minn; St Paul Gallery; Walker Art Ctr, Minneapolis. Exhib: Walker Art Ctr Biennial, 56, 58, 62 & 66; Ohio State Univ, 66; Univ Ill, 67; American Sculpture of the Sixties, Los Angeles Co Mus Art, 67; Southern Ill Univ, 67; plus many others. Teaching: Instr, Hamline Univ, 54-61; instr, Macalester Col, 61; instr, Univ Minn, 61-65; instr, Sacramento State Col, 66. Awards:

Purchase Prizes, Walker Art Ctr Biennial, 56, 62 & 66; First Prize & Purchase Prize, 57 & Hon Mention, 59, Minneapolis Art Inst; Purchase Prize, St Paul Art Gallery, 61. Bibliog: Maurice Tuchman (auth), American Sculpture of the Sixties, Los Angeles Co Mus Art, 67. Mailing Add: c/o B J Randell 954 Wagon Wheel Trail St Paul MN 55120

RANES, CHRIS
PAINTER, PRINTMAKER
b Warsaw, Poland; US citizen. Study: Pratt Inst, New York, Art Cert; Univ Santa Clara, BA & MA. Work: Smithsonian Inst, Washington, DC; Pratt Inst, Brooklyn, NY; Triton Mus Art, Santa Clara, Calif; de Saisset Mus, Santa Clara Univ, Calif. Comn: Eldorado Country Club, Palm Desert, Calif, 60; Riviera Hotel, Palm Springs, Calif, 62. Exhib: Palm Springs Desert Mus, Calif, 65-68; Am Pen Women, Smithsonian Inst, Washington, DC, 66; La Jolla Mus Contemp Art, Calif, 66-68; de Saisset Gallery & Mus, Santa Clara Univ, Calif, 69-71; Laguna Gloria Art Mus, Austin, Tex, 73; Syntex Gallery, Palo Alto, Calif, 76-77; Oakland Mus, Calif, 76; one-person shows, Triton Mus Art, Santa Clara, Calif, 76-77 & de Saisset Gallery & Mus, Santa Clara Univ, Calif, 78. Teaching: Lectr painting & graphic printmaking, Univ Santa Clara, Calif, 68-73, lectr French, 72-73. Pos: Textile designer & stylist, Riverdale Fabrics, Blanc Studios, New York, 51-55. Awards: Second Prize, Calif State Competition, 66 & Nat Award of Merit, Nat Biennial, 66, Nat League of Am Pen Women. Bibliog: Janet Kutner (auth), Scene in art, Dallas News, 9/72; Roberta Loach (auth), Chris Ranes Stanford exhibition, Visual Dialog, Spring 76; H J Weeks (auth), Tell paintings, San Jose Mercury, 1/77. Mem: San Francisco Women Artists (chmn, Artist's Coun, 76-); Ctr for the Visual Arts, Oakland, Calif; Richmond Art Ctr. Style & Technique: Three styles combined into an individual expression, abstract expressionistic, hard-edge and elements of surrealism. Media: Oil on canvas; etchings on zinc, limited editions of twenty. Mailing Add: 3973 Bibbits Dr Palo Alto CA 94303

RANKIN, DON
PAINTER
b Dec 9, 42. Study: Famous Artists' Sch; also with Bill Yeager; Samford Univ, BA(fine art & psychol). Work: Numerous collections in Southeast & New Eng states. Comn: Birmingham Centennial Seal, 69; Birmingham Centennial Commemorative Coins, Arlington Shrine, 70, Univ Ala Med Complex, 71 & Birmingham-Jefferson Civic Ctr, 71. Exhib: Ala Watercolor Soc, 67-71; Birmingham Art Asn Ann, 68 & Ala Centennial Show, 71, Birmingham Mus Art; Southeast Tour of Artrain (selected exhibitor for Ala), 74; First Ann Juried Exhib, Southern Watercolor Soc, Cheekwood, Tenn, 77; Second Ann Juried Exhib, Southern Watercolor Soc, Columbus Mus Arts & Sci, 78; one-man show, Birmingham Mus Art, 74; plus other group & one-man shows. Teaching: Instr techniques of watercolor & drawing, Birmingham Mus Art Educ Coun. Mem: Ala Watercolor Soc (past vpres, bd dirs); charter mem La Watercolor Soc (reporter-at-large); Southern Watercolor Soc (co-founder, active mem & vpres). Style & Technique: Representational approach to transparent watercolor basing all color on the use of the primary system of colors in conjunction with multiple washes to produce color and form. Media: Watercolor. Mailing Add: 2475 Regent Lane Birmingham AL 35226

RANKINE, V V
SCULPTOR, PAINTER
b Boston, Mass. Study: Amedee Ozenfant Sch, New York; Black Mt Col, with Alberts & De Kooning. Work: Nat Collection Fine Arts, Washington, DC; Corcoran Gallery Art, Washington, DC; Oklahoma City Mus; Indianapolis Mus Art, Woodward Found, Washington, DC. Comn: Altar painting, Robert Owen Shrine, New Harmony, Ind, 65. Exhib: Six shows, Jefferson Pl Gallery, Washington, DC, 63-72; Betty Parsons Gallery, New York, 66-78; 30th Corcoran Biennial, Washington, DC, 67-68; Four Americans, Axiom Gallery, London, Eng, 68; Painting & Sculpture Today, Indianapolis Mus, 65; one-person show, Fraser's Stable Gallery, Washington, DC, 78. Teaching: Dir art dept, Madeira Sch, Greenway, Va, 67-70; artist in residence, Inst Man & Sci, Rensselaer, NY, summer 68; instr humanities art, Hunter Col High Sch, New York, 70-71. Awards: Painting Prize, Corcoran Gallery Ann Exhib, 55. Bibliog: Leslie Judd Ahlander (auth), article, 11/64 & Legrace Benson (auth), article, 12/69, Art Int; Lawrence Campbell (auth), article in Art News, 3/69. Style & Technique: Hard edged, purist. Media: Plexiglas; Acrylic on Wood. Dealer: Betty Parsons Gallery 24 W 57th St New York NY 10019. Mailing Add: 3524 Williamsburg Ln Washington DC 20008

RANNIT, ALEKSIS
ART HISTORIAN
b Kallaste, Estonia, Oct 14, 14. Study: Tartu State Univ, dipl art hist; Columbia Univ, MS. Teaching: Prof art hist, Ecole Superieure Arts et Metiers, Freiburg, Ger, 46-50; prof art hist, res assoc & cur Slavic & E Europ collections, Yale Univ, currently. Pos: Chief cur prints & rare bks, Lithuanian Nat Libr, Kaunas, 41-44; sci secy, Div Fine Arts, Fr High Comn, Ger, 50-53; art ref librn & cataloger prints, Art & Archit Div, New York Pub Libr, 53 & 61. Awards: Olsen Found Fel Res & Writing on Coptic Art & Symbolism, 55. Mem: Int Asn Art Critics; Int Pen Clubs, London (exec comt); Asn Ger Art Historians; Estonian Lit Soc (pres); academician Acad Int Sci & Lett, Paris; plus others. Publ: Auth, Eduard Wiiralt (monogr), 43 & 46 & V K Jonynas (monogr), 47; auth, M K Ciurlionis (monogr), UNESCO, 49; auth, Honegger, Swis Purist Artist (monogr), 71; contribr, Brockhaus Encycl & Schweizer Lexicon; plus others. Mailing Add: Yale Univ Box 1603A New Haven CT 06520

RANSOM, HENRY CLEVELAND, JR
PAINTER
b Chattanooga, Tenn, Aug 19, 42. Study: Univ Ga, BFA, 64, MFA, 72. Work: Montgomery Mus of Fine Art, Ala; Mint Mus of Art, Charlotte, NC; Hunter Mus of Art, Chattanooga, TN. Exhib: Artists in Ga III, High Mus of Art, Atlanta, Ga, 74; Ann Realists Invitational, Southeastern Ctr for Contemp Art, Winston-Salem, NC, 75; 1975 Art Acquisition Nat, Univ Tex, Arlington; 53rd Ann Exhib, Shreveport Art Guild, La, 75; 38th Ann Exhib, Soc of the Four Arts, Palm Beach, Fla, 76; one-man shows, Mint Mus of Art, 76, Hunter Mus of Art, Chattanooga, 76 & Montgomery Mus of Fine Art, 76. Awards: Purchase Award, Mint Mus of Art Ann, NC Nat Bank, 73; Atwater Kent Award, 39th Ann Exhib, Soc of the Four Arts, Palm Beach Fla, 77; Purchase Award, Mint Mus of Art Biennial, 77. Style & Technique: Make paintings as absolutely accurate visual recordings as possible and refuse to record an intellectual fact unverified by visual perception. Media: Oil painting. Publ: Contribr, Ga Rev, Univ Ga Press, 76. Dealer: Far Gallery 22 E 80th St New York NY 10028. Mailing Add: PO Box 25 Good Hope GA 30641

RANSON, NANCY SUSSMAN
PAINTER, SERIGRAPHER
b New York, NY, Sept 13, 05. Study: Pratt Inst Sch Art & Design, BFA; Art Students League; Brooklyn Mus Art Sch; also with Alexander Brook; Robert Laurent & Jean Charlot. Work: Fogg Mus Art, Harvard Univ, Cambridge, Mass; Butler Inst of Am Art, Youngstown, Ohio; Archives of Am Art, Smithsonian Inst, Washington, DC; Mus City of New York; Philadelphia Free Libr, Pa; Nat Art Gallery, Sydney, Australia; Nat Mus Mod Art, New Delhi, India. Exhib: Am Watercolor Soc, 40, 42 & 43; Critics Choice Show, Grand Cent Galleries, New York, 46; Brooklyn Mus, 50, 54 & 56; Whitney Mus Am Art, New York, 51; Nat Exhib Contemp Artists US, Pomona, Calif, 56; Nat Art Gallery of New South Wales, Sydney, Australia, 56; Pa Acad Fine Arts, 57; Color Prints of Americas, NJ State Mus, 70; solo shows, George Binet Gallery, New York, 48-50, Brooklyn Pub Libr Main Br, 51 & Univ of Maine, Orono, 64. Awards: Medal of Honor in Graphics, Nat Asn Women Artists, 56; MacDowell Found Fel, 64; First Prize in Graphics, Am Soc Contemp Artists, 70. Mem: New York Soc Women Artists (vpres, 68-69); Am Soc Contemp Artists (pres, 69-71, mem permanent bd, 71-); Nat Asn Women Artists (chmn foreign exhibs, 63-67, chmn admis, 69-71, chmn nominations, 75-77 & mem adv bd, 77-80); Audubon Artists (dir graphics, 70-73 & 75-78); Am Color Print Soc. Style & Technique: Themes are generally temples, archaeological sites and other areas around the world in abstract or semi-representational with emphasis on design and color. Media: Oil, Acrylic; Serigraphy. Mailing Add: 1299 Ocean Ave Brooklyn NY 11230

RAPAPORT, MARJORIE O'BRIEN
See O'Brien, Marjorie

RAPP, EBBA (EBBA RAPP MCLAUCHLAN)
SCULPTOR, PAINTER
b Seattle, Wash. Study: Grad Cornish Sch, teaching cert; Univ Wash, with Alexander Archipenko & Paul Bonifas; Archie Bray Found, Helena, Mont, with Rudy Autio. Work: Seattle Art Mus & Frye Mus, Seattle; Capitol Bldg, Olympia, Wash; Seattle Pub Libr, Magnolia Dr; Univ Wash Law Bldg. Comn: Oil portraits, Prof Rudolph Nottelmann, 60 & Prof Gordon Gose, 63, for Univ Wash Law Sch, Miss Nellie Cornish, founder of Cornish Sch; Gov Rosellini, State of Wash, 69; 7 1/2 ft stoneware bas relief, Holy Trinity Lutheran Church, Mercer Island, 70; 6 ft cast stone fountain, Joshua Green, Jr, Seattle, 71. Exhib: One-man shows, Seattle Art Mus, Frye Mus, Seattle, Capitol Mus, Univ Puget Sound & Robles Art Gllery, Los Angeles, 48; American Painting Today, Grand Rapids Art Gallery, Mich, 61; Century 21 World's Fair, Seattle, 62; Denver Art Mus, 64 & 66; Henry Gallery, Univ Wash, 72. Teaching: Instr ceramic sculpture, Cornish Sch, Seattle, 40-42 & Edison Tech Sch, Seattle, 50-52. Awards: First Award, Women Painters of Washington, Musica Art Found, 44 & Frye Art Mus, 58; First Award, Bellevue Fair Asn, 55; Drawing Award, Seattle Art Mus. Bibliog: Architectural Craftsmen of the Northwest, 61. Media: Cast Stone & Bronze, Clay; Acrylic, Oil. Mailing Add: 2808 Tenth Ave E Seattle WA 98102

RAPP, LOIS
PAINTER
Study: Philadelphia Col Art, dipl teacher's training & cert illus, 25-29; also with Earl Horter. Work: Woodmere Art Gallery, Philadelphia; Valley Forge Mem Chapel, Pa; Gwynedd-Mercy Col, Gwynedd Valley, Pa; Norristown Pub Libr, Pa; Montgomery Hosp, Norristown. Exhib: Am Drawing Ann XV, Norfolk, Va, 57; Am Watercolor Soc 91st Ann, New York, 58; Regional Exhib, Philadelphia Mus Art, 59; Philadelphia Watercolor Club, 71; Woodmere Art Gallery, 72. Teaching: Instr art, Mater Misericordiae Acad, Merion, Pa, 33-45; instr art, Collegeville Trappe Pub Schs, Pa, 35-48; instr art, Conshocken Art League, Pa, 35-37. Awards: Gold Medal for Along the Schuylkill River, Lansdale Art League, 52; Awards for Meeting House Interior, 60 & Falls of the Potomac, 63, Woodmere Art Gallery. Mem: Am Watercolor Soc; Woodmere Art Gallery (exhib comt, 65-69); Philadelphia Watercolor Club (bd dirs, 68-70). Media: Watercolor, Oil, Pastel. Mailing Add: 116 Haws Ave Norristown PA 19401

RAPPIN, ADRIAN
PAINTER
b New York, NY, Jan 20, 34. Study: Acad Fine Arts, Rome; Brandeis Univ, BA; Art Acad Cincinnati; Art Students League. Work: Staten Island Mus, New York; Gibbes Gallery, Charleston Mus, SC; Lincoln Univ, Oxford, Pa; Randolph Macon Col, Lynchburg, Va; Kellogg Found, Battle Creek, Mich; plus others. Exhib: Allied Artists Am, Nat Acad Design Galleries, 61-77; Audubon Artists, 74-77; one-man exhibs, Barzansky Gallery, 64, 66 & 69; 50 Am Artists, New York, 65-69; UNICEF Int, Monaco, 65-67; Kalamazoo, Mich, 70; plus others. Mem: Allied Artists Am; 50 Am Artists; Intercontinental Artists; Am Artists Prof League. Style & Technique: City scenes, figures, portraits, landscapes. Media: Oil on Canvas & Masonite. Publ: Reproductions painting, Christmas Fund, New York Times, 67-70, Songs of Our Times, Hansen, 73 & The Bookshelf for Boys & Girls, Univ Soc Press, 73-74; plus others. Mailing Add: 14 W 68th St New York NY 10023

RASCOE, STEPHEN THOMAS
PAINTER, EDUCATOR
b Uvalde, Tex, May 8, 24. Study: Univ Tex, Austin; Art Inst Chicago, BFA & MFA. Work: Houston Mus Fine Arts, Tex; Dallas Mus Fine Arts; Southern Methodist Univ, Dallas; Ford Motor Co, Dearborn, Mich; Ling-Temco-Vought Res Ctr, Grand Prairie, Tex. Comn: Rancho Seco Land & Cattle Co, Corpus Christi, Tex, 67; Tex Instruments Corp, Dallas, 67; Arlington Bank & Trust Co, Tex, 69; First Nat Bank, 69 & Lakewood Bank, 71, Dallas; mural, Jarvis Putty & Jarvis, Dallas, 76. Exhib: Longview Ann, Tex, 57-72; Artists West of the Mississippi, Denver, 67; San Antonio Hemisphere, Tex, 68. Teaching: Assoc prof art, Univ Tex, Arlington, 64- Pos: Pres, S Tex Art League, 60-61; pres, Arlington Art Asn, Tex, 67-68. Awards: Houston Mus Fine Arts Purchase Award, Tex Show, 56; First Prize, Tex Painting & Sculpture Show, Dallas Mus, 57; D D Feldman Award, 58. Mem: Dallas Art Asn; Ft Worth Art Asn; Mus S Tex, Corpus Christi. Media: Oil. Dealer: Mary Nye Contemporary Art 5906 Norway Rd Dallas TX 75230. Mailing Add: 2002 Westview Terr Arlington TX 76013

RASKINS, ELLEN
ILLUSTRATOR, DESIGNER
b Milwaukee, Wis. Study: Univ of Wis, Madison. Exhib: 50 Yrs of Graphic Arts in Am, Am Inst of Graphic Arts, 66; Biennale of Illus, Bratislava, Czech, 69; Biennale of Applied Graphic Arts, Brno, Czech, 72;

RASMUSSEN, ANTON JESSE
PAINTER, ART ADMINISTRATOR
b Salt Lake City, Utah, Nov 12, 42. Study: Univ Utah, BFA, 67, MFA, 74. Work: Utah Mus of Fine Arts, Salt Lake City, Eccles Health Sci Libr, Univ Utah, Salt Lake City; Davis Co Libr, Farmington, Utah. Comn: Oil painting (10ft x 16ft), Davis Co Libr, Bountiful, Utah, 76 & three panels (3 1/2ft x 7ft), Clearfield, Utah, 77. Exhib: Weber State Col, Ogden, Utah, 75; Utah Painting 75, Utah Mus of Fine Arts, Salt Lake City, 75; one-man exhibs, Davis Co Libr, S Davis Br, Bountiful, Utah, 76, N Davis Br, Clearfield, Utah, 76 & Eccles Health Sci Libr, Univ Utah, Salt Lake City, 76; Two Utah Artists, Boise State Univ, Idaho, 77. Teaching: Adj asst prof painting & drawing, Univ Utah, Salt Lake City, 74- Pos: Dir, Bountiful Art Ctr, Univ Utah Exten, Bountiful, 74-; asst dir, Prog for Higher Educ, Davis Co/Univ Utah, Bountiful, 75- Bibliog: Claudia Sisemore (producer, Color film), Anton J Rasmussen—painter of abstractions from nature, pvt publ, 77. Style & Technique: Organic abstractions from

nature; science, microscopic world and aerial landscapes; nature studies concept; universality of nature. Media: Oil on Masonite or canvas with special processes to develop organic forms. Mailing Add: 100 N Main North Salt Lake UT 84054

RASMUSSEN, KEITH ERIC
PRINTMAKER, INSTRUCTOR
b Madelia, Minn, July 29, 42. Study: Minneapolis Col of Art & Design, BFA, 66; Pa State Univ, MFA, 70. Work: Minneapolis Inst of Arts, Minn; High Mus of Art, Atlanta, Ga; Brooklyn Mus, NY; Inst of Man & Sci, Rennsaelerville, NY; Atlanta Br, Int Bus Machines Corp, Ga. Exhib: One-man show, Minneapolis Inst of Arts, 72; Ga Artists Exhib, High Mus of Art, 74; Davidson Nat Print & Drawing Exhib, NC, 75; Watercolor USA, Springfield Art Mus, Mo, 75-77; 20th Printmakers Exhib, Brooklyn Mus, 76; Boston Printmakers Exhib, Delgado Mus, Boston, Mass, 77; Bradley Nat Printmaking Exhib, Bradley Univ, Peoria, Ill, 77; NJ State Mus Printmakers Exhib, Clinton, 77. Teaching: Fac mem printmaking & drawing, Atlanta Col of Art, Ga, 72- Pos: Cur, Art Ctr Gallery, Univ Wis-Stout, Menominee, 70-72; mem, Atlanta Arts Festival Bd, 77-80. Style & Technique: Representational prints. Media: Lithography, drawing, watercolor. Mailing Add: 1015 Rosedale Rd Atlanta GA 30306

RASMUSSEN, ROBERT NORMAN
See Redd Ekks

RATCLIFF, CARTER
ART CRITIC, WRITER
b Seattle, Wash, Aug 20, 41. Study: Univ Chicago, BA, 63. Teaching: Workshop dir, Poetry Proj, St Mark's Church, New York, 69-70; instr art hist & art criticism, Sch Visual Arts, 71- Pos: Ed assoc, Art News, 69-72; adv ed, Art Int, 70-75; contribr, Britannica Encycl Am Art, 73; contrib ed, Art in Am, 77- Awards: Poets Found Grant, 69; Nat Endowment Arts fels, 72 & 78; Guggenheim Mem Found fel, 76. Res: History of American art criticism. Publ: Auth, Deseo: Rafael Ferrer, 73; auth, Alex Katz, 73; auth, Art Criticism: Other Minds, Other Eyes (6 parts), 74-75; auth, Willem de Kooning, 75; auth, Alexander Liberman, 78. Mailing Add: 67 E 11th St New York NY 10003

RATH, HILDEGARD
PAINTER, LECTURER
b Freudenstadt, Württemberg, Ger, Mar 22, 09; US citizen. Study: Atelier House, Stuttgart, Ger, with Adolf Senglaub; Kunstgewerbe Sch, Stuttgart; Akad Bildenden Kunste, Berlin, Ger; also with Otto Manigk, Berlin. Work: Wurttembergische Kultministerium, Stuttgart; Metrop Mus Art, New York; New York Pub Libr; Brooklyn Mus, NY; Libr of Cong, Washington, DC; over 800 works in mus & pvt collections. Comn: Oil paintings, portraits & landscapes, comn by Willi Eiselen, Ulm, Donau, Ger, 32; portraits, landscapes & still lifes, comn by Walter Freudenberg, Baden, Ger, 46; Triplets, comn by Mrs Sig Buchmeyer, Paris, 48; Mrs Siegtraut Gauss-Glock, Wurttemberg, Ger, 54; Madonna, comn by Klaus Heuck, Frankfurt, Ger, 59. Exhib: Weissenhof Ausstellung Stuttgart Int, 27; Allied Artists Am, Nat Acad Design Galleries, New York, 51; Artists Equity Bldg Fund Exhib, Whitney Mus Am Art, 51; Artists Equity Asn, 52; 15th Nat Print Exhib, Libr of Cong, 57; murals, traveling exhibs, throughout US, 57, 77, 78 & 79. Teaching: Dir painting, Europ Sch Fine Art, 49-54; lectr hist art, Great Neck Pub Schs, 61-62; lectr serigraphy, NShore Art Ctr, 61-62. Awards: Dr Blaicher Award, 27; Grumbacher Award, 52; Prix de Paris, 63; Cert Merit for Distinguished Serv to the Community, Cambridge, Eng, 76. Bibliog: Hennemann-Bayer (auth), Zur Ausstellung, Schwarzwalder Bote Stuttgart, 59; Dannecker (auth), Von werker, Stuttgarter Nachrichten, 59; P H Buhner (auth), Hildegard Rath im Kunsthaus Schaller, Stuttgarter Zeitung, 59. Mem: Int Platform Asn; Wurttembergischer Kunstverein, Stuttgart; Southern Vt Art Asn; Nat Asn of Adult Educators; Nat Soc of Mural Painters; Knickerbocker Artists; Artists Equity Asn NY. Media: Oil, Pastel, Watercolor. Publ: Auth articles in Art Digest, 52, Schwarzwald Zeitung, 59 & Am Artist, 63; contribr, Enciclopedia Int Degli Artisti, 70-71. Dealer: Weintraub Gallery 992 Madison Ave New York NY 10021. Mailing Add: PO Box 298 Manchester Center VT 05255

RATHBONE, PERRY TOWNSEND
MUSEUM DIRECTOR
b Germantown, Pa, July 3, 11. Study: Harvard Col, AB, 33, Harvard Univ, 33-34; Wash Univ, Hon DFA, 58; Northeastern Univ, Hon DHL, 60; Bates Col, Hon DFA, 64; Suffolk Univ, Hon DHL, 69; Williams Col, Hon DHL, 70; Boston Col, Hon DFA, 70. Pos: Cur, Detroit Inst Art, 36-40; secy & dir masterpieces of art, New York World's Fair, 39; dir, City Art Mus St Louis, 40-55; dir, Boston Mus Fine Arts, 55-72; mem, Mayor of Boston's Art Adv Comt, 69-; dir, Christie's USA, 73-; chmn bd, Metrop Boston Art Ctr; trustee, New Eng Conserv Music, Inst Contemp Art, Boston & Boston Art Festival; vchmn comt to visit fine arts dept, Harvard Univ; trustee, RI Sch Design & Int Exhibs Found, Washington, DC; mem fine arts vis comt, RI Sch Design; mem vis comt art & archeol, Dept Fine Arts, Wash Univ; mem art adv comt, Chase Manhattan Bank, New York; trustee, Am Fedn Arts. Awards: Chevalier, Legion of Honor. Mem: Am Asn Mus (vpres, 60-, mem coun); Asn Art Mus Dirs (pres, 59-60 & 69-70); Benjamin Franklin fel Royal Soc Arts, London. Publ: Auth, Max Beckmann, 48, Mississippi Panorama, 49, Westward the Way, 54, Lee Gatch, 60 & Handbook for the Forsyth Wickes Collection, 68; contribr art mags & mus bull. Mailing Add: 151 Coolidge Hill Cambridge MA 02138

RATKAI, GEORGE
PAINTER, SCULPTOR
b Budapest, Hungary, Dec 24, 07. Work: Tel-Aviv Mus, Israel; Abbott Labs Collection; Univ Ill; Butler Inst Am Art; Univ Nebr; plus many others. Exhib: Audubon Artists, 55-65; Provincetown Art Asn, 56-64; Relig Art Exhib, Univ Nebr, 65; Manfield State Col, Pa, 65; Bass Mus Art, Miami, 65; plus many others. Awards: Prize, Art of Dem Living, 51; Gold Medals, 53 & 65 & Mem Medal, 56, Audubon Artists; Childe Hassam Award, 59. Mem: Artists Equity Asn; Audubon Artists; fel Int Inst Arts & Lett; Am Fedn Arts; Nat Soc Painters in Casein; plus others. Mailing Add: 350 W 57th St New York NY 10019

RATZENBERGER, KATHARINE M
ART LIBRARIAN
b Baltimore, Md, Jan 17, 50. Study: Univ Del, BA(art hist), 72; Ind Univ, MLS, 74; George Washington Univ. Pos: Ref librn, Libr of Nat Collection of Fine Arts & the Nat Portrait Gallery, Smithsonian Inst, 74- Mem: Art Libr Soc/NAm (national Chmn, 1978; chmn, D.C. chap, 75-76). Res: Historiography of American Portraiture. Mailing Add: NCFA/NPG Library Smithsonian Inst Washington DC 20560

RAUCH, JOHN G
COLLECTOR, PATRON
b Indianapolis, Ind, July 16, 90. Study: Harvard Col, AB, 11, Harvard Law Sch, 11-12; Butler Univ, Hon LLD, 68. Pos: Trustee, Art Asn Indianapolis, 40-62, pres bd trustees, 62-; chmn bd trustees, Ind Hist Soc, 50- Mailing Add: 3050 N Meridian St Indianapolis IN 46208

RAUL ESPARZA S (RAUL ESPARZA SANCHEZ)
MURALIST, SCULPTOR
b Torreon, Mex, Nov 29, 23. Study: With Horacio Renteria & Arnold C Taylor. Work: City Santa Fe Springs Neighborhood Ctr & Libr, Calif. Comn: Murals, History of the Laguna, Int Bank of North, 57; History of Trade and Commerce, Sch of Com & Admin, Univ Coahuila, 65 & History of Medicine, Sch Med, 70; Religious Theme, Sacred Heart of Mary Church, Torreon, 72; History of Mexico and Mankind, Calif Mus Sci & Indust, 75. Exhib: Venustiano Carranza Sch, 57; Inst Mex Norteamericano, Monterrey, Nuevo Leon, 62, Guadalajara, Morelia, 63 & Mexico City, 65. Teaching: Artist clay modeling, Calif Mus Sci & Indust, 73-75, artist & instr, 73-; artist, paints, Community Ctr South El Monte, Calif, 73-75. Awards: First Place, Sequia, 57; Hon Mention, La Periferia de la Ciudad, 69. Bibliog: Rosa Turon (auth), Raul Esparza, El Siglo de Torreon, Coahuila, 63; Jose S Valdez (auth), El Dia y Otros de Mexico, 73; Nicolas Avila (auth), Raul Esparza, La Opinion, Los Angeles, 75. Media: Clay; Acrylics. Mailing Add: Calif Mus Sci & Indust 700 State Dr Los Angeles CA 90037

RAUSCHENBERG, ROBERT
PAINTER
b Port Arthur, Tex, Oct 22, 25. Study: Kansas City Art Inst & Sch Design, 46-47; Acad Julian, Paris, 47; Black Mt Col, with Josef Albers, 48-49; Art Students League, with Vaclav Vytlacil & Morris Kantor, 49-50. Work: Albright-Knox Art Gallery; Whitney Mus Am Art; White Mus, Cornell Univ; Tate Gallery, London; Mus Mod Art, New York; Goucher Col; also in many pvt collections. Exhib: Dada, Surrealism & Their Heritage, Mus Mod Art, 68; Directions I: Options, Milwaukee Art Ctr, 68; Arts Coun Gt Brit, 68; Whitney Mus Am Art Ann, 69, 70 & 73; Guggenheim Mus, 72; Retrospective 1976-1978 Bicentennial Exhib (travelling show), Nat Collection Fine Arts, Smithsonian Inst, Washington, DC; plus many other group & one-man shows, US & abroad. Awards: Winner, Venice Biennale, 64; Awards, Corcoran Biennial Contemp Am Painters, 65 & Art Inst Chicago, 66; plus others. Bibliog: Dore Ashton (auth), The Unknown Shore, Little, 62; Tracy Atkinson (auth), Directions I: Options 1968, Milwaukee Art Ctr, 68; Gregory Battcock (ed), Minimal Art: a Critical Anthology, Dutton, 68; plus many others. Mailing Add: c/o Leo Castelli Gallery 420 W Broadway New York NY 10012

RAUTBORD, DOROTHY H
COLLECTOR, PATRON
b Winamac, Ind, Aug 13, 06. Study: Univ Ill; self-taught. Pos: Pres bd, Norton Gallery Mus of Art, Palm Beach, Fla; bd mem, Contemp Art Mus, Chicago West; Oriental comt, Chicago Art Inst. Mem: Arts Club, Chicago. Collection: Post impressionism. Mailing Add: 44 Cocoanut Row Palm Beach FL 33480

RAVE, GEORGIA
PAINTER, EDUCATOR
b Mt Vernon, NY, June 3, 36. Study: Hunter Col, BFA, 57 & MA, 66. Teaching: Instr drawing & art educ, Hunter Col, New York, 66-70; lectr drawing & art educ, Newark State Col, Union, NJ, 72-73; lectr drawing, painting & art educ, Manhattanville Col, Purchase, NY, 73- Pos: Dir grad prog art educ, Hunter Col, 67-70; coordr MAT in art, Manhattanville Col, Purchase, NY, 75- Awards: City Univ Fac Res Grant, City Univ New York, 68; Shuster Grant, Hunter Col, 69. Mem: Inst for the Study of Art in Educ; Univ Coun for Art Educ. Style & Technique: Flat, amorphic forms on circular canvas. Media: Acrylic, Ink; Canvas, Graphite. Mailing Add: c/o Westbeth Gallery 463 West St New York NY 10014

RAVEL, DANA B
ART DEALER
b Portland, Ore, July 19, 43. Pos: Owner, Galerie Ravel, Fine Original Graphics, Austin, Tex. Mem: Austin Contemp Visual Arts Asn (bd of dirs, 77-). Specialty: Regional, national, international prints, multiple sculpture. Mailing Add: c/o Galerie Ravel Fine Original Graphics 1210 W Fifth Austin TX 78703

RAVEN, ARLENE
WRITER, ART CRITIC
b Baltimore, Md, July 12, 44. Study: Hood Col, BA; Univ Madrid; Md Inst Col Art; George Washington Univ, MFA; Johns Hopkins Univ, NDEA, Kress & Gilman fels, 69-73, MA; Int Col, PhD, 75. Teaching: Tutor, Int Col, 74- Pos: Co-founder, Ctr Feminist Art Hist Studies, 73-; vpres, Women's Community Inc, Los Angeles, 73-; co-founder & dir, Woman's Bldg, Los Angeles, 73-; ed, Chrysalis Mag, 76- Awards: Calif Arts Comn Grant, 75. Bibliog: Shirley Koploy (auth), Art: the woman's building, MS Mag, 10/74; Focus, KNBC-TV, 74; Femal imagery, MS Mag, 5/75. Mem: Col Art Asn Am; Women's Caucus Art (bd dirs, 74-). Res: Washington color school; theoretical perspective on women's art; abstract expressionist men's and women's art; Georgia O'Keeffe and Romaine Brooks. Publ: Auth, Happy Birthday America, Georgia O'Keefe, Interview with Kate Millett & Interview with Judy Chicago, Chrysalis Mag, 77-78; auth, Through the peephole, Lesbian Sensibility in Art, No. 4, 78; plus others. Mailing Add: PO Box 54335 Los Angeles CA 90054

RAWLINSON, JONLANE FREDERICK
PAINTER, INSTRUCTOR
b Memphis, Tenn, Feb 12, 40. Study: Memphis State Univ, 58-59; Memphis Acad Arts, BFA, 63; Syracuse Univ, MFA, 75. Work: Parthenon, Nashville, Tenn; Watkins Collection of Tenn Art; Fall Creek Falls Collection of Tenn Art; Memphis Acad Art Collection. Comn: Mississippi River Bridge (painting), Young Republican Party, US House of Rep, 73; paintings of farm, Pin Oak Farms, Versailles, Ky, 75. Exhib: Mid-South Exhib, Memphis, 71; Tenn All-State Competition, 71-73; Cent South Exhib, Nashville, 72-73; Tenn Watercolor Soc, 72-75; Watercolor USA, Springfield, Mo, 75. Teaching: Graphic art instr, Univ Tenn, 65-75; instr art, Memphis Acad Arts, 72-; vis prof, EArk Community Col, Forrest City, 75. Awards: Second Purchase Prize for Mixed Media, Tenn All-State Competition, 71; Art Dirs Club Memphis First Prize, Art South, 72; First Award & Gold Medal of Merit, Tenn Watercolor Soc, 75. Mem: Tenn Watercolor Soc (vpres, 75). Style & Technique: Semi-abstract landscapes, mostly inner city; collage. Media: Watercolor. Mailing Add: 420 Garland St Memphis TN 38104

RAY, DEBORAH
PAINTER, ILLUSTRATOR
b Philadelphia, Pa, Aug 31, 40. Study: Philadelphia Col of Art; Pa Acad of Fine Arts, 58-62; Univ Pa, Albert C Barnes Found, 62-64. Work: Drexel Univ, Philadelphia, Pa; Libr of Cong, Washington, DC; Univ Minn, Minneapolis; Free Libr of Philadelphia; Montgomery Co Col, Center Square, Pa. Comn: Graphic murals, Chase Manhattan Bank, 69. Exhib: Pa Acad of Fine Arts Bienniel, 67 & 69; Nat Drawing Exhib, Ball State Univ, 73; Philadelphia Artists, Philadelphia Mus of Art, 73 & 74; Hibiya Libr, Am Libr Asn, Tokoyo, 75; 110th Exhib of

Am Watercolor Soc, Nat Acad of Design, New York, 77; American Women in Fine Arts, Moore Col of Art, Philadelphia, 77; Mus of Philadelphia Civic Ctr, 78; also many one-woman shows, 67-77. Awards: Louis Comfort Tiffany Found Grant, 68; Jr League Award, Earth Arts 73, Mus Philadelphia Civic Ctr, 73; Am Inst of Graphic Arts Award for Illustration, 76. Bibliog: McCann & Richard (auth), Child's First Books, H H Wilson Co, 73; Eleanor Eby (auth), Children's corner, Philadelphia Inquirer, 75; Paul West (auth), Children's books, New York Times, 77. Mem: Artists Equity Asn (mem bd dir, 77-79); Women's Caucus for Art; Muse-Coop Gallery of the Philadelphia Women's Caucus for Art (mem bd dir, 77-79). Style & Technique: Landscape paintings in acrylic and watercolor, which reflects my interest in living functional form and the unity of natural things. Media: Acrylic on Canvas, Watercolor/Pencil, Mixed. Publ: Auth & illusr, Abdul Abul-Bul Amir & Ivan Skavinsky Skavar, Macrae Smith, 69; illusr, The Winter Picnic, 70, Frog, Frog, Frog, 71 & The Train, 72, Pantheon; illusr, I Have a Sister, My Sister is Deaf, Harper & Row, 77. Mailing Add: 223 E Gowen Ave Philadelphia PA 19119

RAY, JIM
MUSEUM DIRECTOR
b Hayti, Mo, Sept 16, 24. Study: Univ Mo, Columbia, BS. Collections Arranged: Drawing America—1973 (with catalog); Architecture of St Joseph (with catalog); Engraving America 1974 (with catalog). Pos: Dir, Albrecht Art Mus, St Joseph, Mo, 73- Mem: Am Asn Mus; Mo Mus Assocs. Publ: Auth, The Stained Glass Windows of St Joseph, 76; auth, Drawing Missouri, 1976, 76. Mailing Add: 2706 Union St St Joseph MO 64506

RAY, ROBERT ARTHUR
SCULPTOR, ARCHITECT
b Pittsburgh, Pa, Aug 27, 34. Study: Pa State Univ, BArchit, 60; Art Inst Chicago, MFA, 72. Work: Am Tel & Tel; Standard Oil of Ind. Comn: Light, sound performance, Univ Wis, 67-69. Exhib: Sculpture: The Chicago Style, Univ of Chicago, 73; 26th Ill State Mus, Springfield, 73; one-man shows, Welna Gallery, 73 & Sculpture for Public Places, Aquinas Col, Grand Rapids, Mich, 75; Sculpture for a New Era, Midwest Bicentennial, Chicago, 75. Teaching: Asst prof sculpture, Univ Wis, Green Bay, 65-71; asst prof sculpture, De Paul Univ, Chicago, 73- Pos: Regist archit, many states; consult, Univ Wis Exten, 67-68; consult vchancellor, campus develop, Univ Wis, Green Bay, 68-69; consult designer, Two Rivers, Wis, 68-69. Awards: Scarab, Nat Archit Hon Soc, 59. Bibliog: Dan Curry (auth), Heavy Duty Metal Man, 16mm film, 75. Mem: Col Art Asn. Style & Technique: Large scale, formal pieces. Media: Welded Steel; Aluminum. Publ: Auth, A Study of the Wasmuth Monograph, Frank Lloyd Wright; Ausgefuehrhte Bauten und Entwuerfe, Berlin 1910, 1966. Dealer: Richard Friedman 114 W Kinzie St Chicago IL 60610. Mailing Add: 1682 N Ada St Chicago IL 60622

RAY, ROBERT (DONALD)
PAINTER, SCULPTOR
b Denver, Colo, Oct 2, 24. Study: Univ Southern Calif, BFA(cum laude); Centro Estudios Universitarios, Mexico City, MA(magna cum laude). Work: Baltimore Mus Art, Md; Brooklyn Mus Art, NY; Denver Art Mus, Colo; Mus NMex, Santa Fe; Columbia Mus Art, SC. Exhib: Denver Art Mus, 53-; Colorado Springs Fine Arts Ctr, Colo, 55-; 13th Nat Exhib Prints, Libr Cong, Washington, DC, 55; Mus NMex, Santa Fe, 56-; New Talent, USA, Am Fedn Arts, New York, 56; Mid-Am Ann, Nelson Gallery-Atkins Mus, Kansas City, Mo, 57, 58 & 59; Contemp Am Paintings & Sculpture, Univ Ill, Urbana, 57 & 59; 1st Provincetown Arts Festival, Chrysler Art Mus, Mass, 58; Roswell Mus & Art Ctr, 59 & 62; Taos Now, San Diego Mus Fine Arts, Calif, 60; Art & The Atom, Calif Palace of Legion of Honor, 65; The West—80 Contemporaries, Univ Ariz Art Gallery, Tucson, 67; one-man show, Mus NMex, Santa Fe, 59 & 67 & Colorado Springs Fine Arts Ctr, Colo, 68; Three Cultures—Three Dimensions, 69 & Southwestern Artists Biennial, 70, Mus NMex; 73rd Ann Exhib Western Art, Denver Art Mus, 71. Awards: Purchase Award, Ball State Teachers Col, 59; First Prize for Sculpture, Mus NMex, 69; Graphics Award, Taos Art Asn, NMex, 72. Bibliog: Fels (auth), Compression & expansion in the works of Blackburn & Ray, 72; Harmsen (auth), Harmsen's Western Americana, Northland, 72. Mem: Taos Art Asn. Style & Technique: Abstract. Dealer: Mission Gallery Taos NM 87571. Mailing Add: 115 Los Cordovas Rte Taos NM 87571

RAYBON, PHARES HENDERSON
PAINTER, EDUCATOR
b Randolph, Ala, Sept 10, 14. Study: Wash Sch Art, cert; Univ Ala, BFA, MA; Univ Okla. Exhib: Int Painting Exhib, Tampa, Fla, 52; Ann Delta Show, Little Rock, Ark, 67; one-man shows, Ark Festival Arts, Little Rock, 68 & Ouachita Baptist Univ, 71. Teaching: Asst prof painting, Miss Col, 50-51; prof painting, Ouachita Baptist Univ, 51- Awards: First Award in Commercial Design, Ala State Fair,49, First Award in Wood Engraving, 49; Grumbacher Award Merit, 52. Style & Technique: Landscapes and cityscapes with painting knife techniques. Media: Oil Mailing Add: 1520 Pine Manor Dr Arkadelphia AR 71923

RAYBURN, BRYAN B
ART ADMINISTRATOR
b Stonewall, Okla, June 30, 31. Study: Univ Okla, BBA, 53. Pos: Dep dir, Nat Cowboy Hall Fame & Western Heritage Ctr, 69- Mem: Nat Acad Western Art (trustee & mem exec comt). Mailing Add: 6000 Indian Hill Rd Edmond OK 73034

RAYDON, ALEXANDER R
ART DEALER, COLLECTOR
Study: Tech Univ Munich, grad engr. Pos: Dir, Raydon Gallery. Mem: Am Asn of Mus; Int Coun of Mus. Res: American art of the nineteenth and early twentieth centuries. Specialty: Paintings, sculpture, prints and drawings from the Renaissance to the present, with emphasis on the nineteenth and early twentieth centuries. Publ: Ed, America's Vanishing Resource, 70, America the Beautiful, 71, Americans Abroad, 72 & Charles Burchfield—Master Doodler, 72; Am Scene—Am Artists Abroad, 75-77 & Masters in European Portraiture, 76, spec Bicentennial traveling exhibs. Mailing Add: 1091 Madison Ave New York NY 10028

RAYEN, JAMES WILSON
PAINTER, EDUCATOR
b Youngstown, Ohio, Apr 9, 35. Study: Yale Univ, BA, BFA & MFA; with Josef Albers, Seawell Sillman & Rico Lebrun. Work: Addison Gallery Am Art, Andover, Mass; Yale Univ, New Haven, Conn; Wellesley Col, Mass; First Nat Bank, Boston. Exhib: One-man shows, Durlacher Brothers Gallery, New York, 66 & Eleanor Rigelhaupt Gallery, Boston, 68; Young New Eng Painters, Ringling Mus, Sarasota, Fla, 69; Landscape II, De Cordova Mus, Lincoln, Mass, 71; 10 Year Retrospective, Brockton Art Ctr, Mass, 73; Recent & Revised, Wellesley Col Mus, 78. Teaching: Assoc prof, Wellesley Col, 61- Awards: Ital Govt Grant in Painting, 59-60; Ford Found Grant in the Humanities, 69-70; Wellesley Col Fac Grant, summer 75. Mem: Boston Visual Artists Union. Style & Technique: Invented landscape images based upon trees and water, beginning with direct observation and progressing toward the reconstruction which memory affords and various media demand. Media: Acrylic. Mailing Add: Box 219 Wellesley MA 02181

RAYNER, ADA (ADA RAYNER HENSCHE)
PAINTER
b London, Eng, Feb 9, 01; US citizen. Study: Grand Cent Art Sch, New York, with Wayman Adams, 27-29; Art Students League, with Ivan Olinsky, 30; Cape Sch Art, with Henry Hensche, 32-36. Work: Grand Cent Art Gallery, New York; Walter Chrysler Mus, Norfolk, Va; Ft Wayne Mus; Paper Mill Playhouse, NJ; plus pvt collections. Exhib: New York Watercolor Exhib; Provincetown Art Asn, 35-; Okla Asn Conservative Artists; Copely Soc Boston, 67-68; Miniature Painters Washington, 71-72. Awards: Founders Second Place for Best Painting, Miniature Painters, 73. Style & Technique: Landscape; flowers; still life; impressionistic. Media: Oil, Watercolor. Mailing Add: Conwell St Provincetown MA 02657

REALE, NICHOLAS ALBERT
PAINTER, INSTRUCTOR
b Irvington, NJ, Mar 20, 22. Study: Pratt Inst; Art Students League; New Sch of Social Res, New York; Workshop Sch of Design, New York. Work: Nat Acad of Design, New York; Newark Mus, NJ; Univ of Ariz; Jersey City Mus; Morgan Guarrantee & Trust Co, New York. Exhib: Metrop Mus of Art, New York; New York Worlds Fair, 65; Everhart Mus, Scranton, Pa, 67; Pa Acad of Fine Arts, Philadelphia, 68; Montclair Mus, NJ, 69; Butler Inst of Am Art, Youngstown, Ohio, 72; Frye Mus, Seattle, Wash, 75; NJ State Mus, 75; Nat Acad of Design, New York, 78. Teaching: Instr graphic design, Newark Sch of Fine & Indust Art, 67; instr painting, Summit Art Ctr, NJ, 69- Awards: High Winds Award, Am Watercolor Soc Nat, 76; Assoc Mems Award, Allied Artist Nat, New York, 77; Sadie & Max Tessler Award, Audubon Artist Nat, New York, 78. Mem: Am Watercolor Soc; Allied Artist of Am; Audubon Artist; Assoc Artist of NJ; Nat Casein Soc. Media: Watercolor, Oil, Acrylic. Dealer: c/o George Dembo Gallery Nine 9 Passaic Ave Chatham NJ 07928. Mailing Add: 81 Wilder St Hillside NJ 07205

REARDON, MARY A
PAINTER
b Quincy, Mass. Study: Radcliffe Col, AB; Yale Univ Sch Fine Arts, BFA; also with Eugene Savage, Jean Charlot & David Siqueiros; New Eng Sch Law, Hon LHD, 74. Work: Mural drawings, De Cordova Mus, Lincoln, Mass; Radcliffe Col, Cambridge, Mass. Comn: Mosaic chapel, Our Lady of Guadalupe, 65 & mosaic ceilings, Last Judgment & Creation, Nat Shrine Immaculate Conception, Washington, DC, 72; Formation of a Priest (fresco), St John's Sem, Brighton, Mass; altarpiece & figures, Baltimore Cathedral, Md, 67; altar painting, St Mary of Nativity, Scituate, Mass, 75; Chapel of the Patrons, St Mary's Cathedral, San Francisco, Calif; plus many portraits. Exhib: 1st & 2nd Int Exhibs Relig Art, Trieste, Italy, 61 & 66; 7th Centennial Exhib, Basilica St Anthony, Padua, Italy, 63; one-man exhib, Trieste, 71; additional exhibs in Boston, New York & Richmond, Va. Teaching: Instr adult educ, Boston Mus Fine Arts; assoc prof studio courses, Emmanuel Col, Boston, 51-70. Pos: Mem ladies comt, Boston Mus Fine Arts; design consult, San Francisco Cathedral, 74- Awards: President's Medal, 2nd Int Exhib Relig Art, 66. Mem: Nat Soc Mural Painters; Cambridge Art Asn; Harvard Club of Boston; NShore Arts Asn; Copley Soc. Media: Oil, Watercolor. Publ: Co-auth, Pope Pius XII—Rock of Peace; illusr, Snow Treasure, They Came from Scotland, Bird in Hand & Grenfell. Mailing Add: 12 Martin's Lane Hingham MA 02043

REBBECK, LESTER JAMES, JR
PAINTER, SCULPTOR
b Chicago, Ill, June 25, 29. Study: Art Inst Chicago & Univ Chicago, hist with K Blackshear, BAEd, MAEd, 59; also painting with Wieghardt, drawing with Isoble McKinnon. Comn: Paintings & prints, comn by William Fischer, 69. Exhib: Creative Galleries, 54; Concordia Teachers Col, 56; Boston Soc Independent Artists, 56; Sculptors Gallery, St Louis, 67; Ball State Teachers Col, 75. Teaching: Asst prof art appreciation & painting, Harper Col, 67-71. Pos: Gallery dir, Countryside Art Gallery, Arlington Heights, Ill, 63-68; gallery dir, Chicago Soc of Artists Gallery, 67-68. Awards: GI Show Medal Award, Art Inst Chicago, 53; First Place Oils, McHenry Art Fair, 60, Best of Show, 62. Bibliog: Dona Z Meilach (auth), Creating Art from Anything, Reilly & Lee, 68. Mem: Col Art Asn Am. Style & Technique: Figure, Landscape, still life; work is organic & abstract in form. Media: Oil on Canvas; Wood Sculpture. Mailing Add: 222 N Yale Arlington Heights IL 60005

REBECK, STEVEN AUGUSTUS
SCULPTOR
b Cleveland, Ohio, May 25, 91. Study: With Carl Bitter; Cleveland Sch Art, with Carl Heber. Comn: Shakespeare (bust in stone), for garden, Cleveland; Soldiers Mem, Alliance, Ohio; Spanish War Veteran (bronze); Lincoln (bronze); sphinx statue, Masonic Temple, St Louis, Mo. Awards: Awards & medals for portraits & busts, Cleveland Mus Art, 23. Mem: Nat Sculpture Soc. Interest: Portraits and memorial tablets. Mailing Add: 13800 Superior Rd Cleveland OH 44112

REBER, MICK
SCULPTOR, PAINTER
b St George, Utah, June 6, 42. Study: Brigham Young Univ, BFA & MFA; independent studies in San Francisco, Chicago, Montreal & New York. Work: NMex Jr Col Art Mus, Hobbs; Nev State Bank, Las Vegas. Comn: Brigham Young Univ, Provo, Utah, 68; paintings, 20th Century Fox, 73; sculptural park, City of Las Vegas, Nev, 78; sculptural playground, Clark Co Sch Dist, Las Vegas, 78. Exhib: Nat Sculpture Traveling Exhib, NC, 73; Four Corners Biennial, Phoenix Art Mus, Ariz, 73; Mainstreams Exhib, Marietta Col, Ohio, 74; four-man show, Exhibiting Artists Fedn, Vt (traveling to eastern states), 75; Western State Art Found Traveling Exhib, San Francisco Mus of Mod Art, Denver Art Mus & Seattle Art Mus, 78; one-man shows, Brigham Young Univ, 68 & 72, NMex Jr Col, 73, J K M Olsen, San Francisco, 73, Western States Col, Colo, 74, Tameron-Durango, Ft Lewis Col, Colo, 76, Recent Paintings & Sculptures, NMex Civic Ctr, 77 & Main Gallery World Hq of Bank of Am, San Francisco, 78. Teaching: Prof advan painting & sculpture, Ft Lewis Col, Durango, Colo, 68-76; vis lectr recent sculpture, Univ Utah, 11/76. Awards: Painting Award, Springville Nat, Springville Mus of Art, Utah, 70; First Cash Award, Four Corners Biennial, Phoenix Art Mus, 73; Selected for Nat Traveling Exhib, Exhibiting Artists Fedn, 74. Bibliog: H Lester Cooke (auth), A Biennial of Painting & Sculpture (catalog), 73; Cassy Cohen (auth), Mick Reber, Nevadan, 7/11/76; Paul Abe (auth), ...And Then There's Mick Reber, NMex Daily Times, 77. Style & Technique: Human form within the environment evoking content as it relates to the subconscious; contemporary; air brush and hard edge painting; Laminated wood, bronze and steel sculpture. Media: Acrylic on Canvas; Laminated Wood. Publ: Contribr, Dr R L Cantor, auth, American Sculpture in the Seventies. Dealer: Mary Lynn 8625 W El Campo Grande Lone Mountain Las Vegas NV 89108. Mailing Add: 8625 W El Campo Grande Las Vegas NV 89108

REBERT, JO LIEFELD
PAINTER, LECTURER
b Detroit, Mich, Sept 30, 15. Study: Detroit Soc Arts & Crafts, grad; Detroit Inst Musical Art, artists dipl; also with Joseph Canzanni. Work: Eastland Bank, Anaheim, Calif; Great Western Savings & Loan, Los Angeles; Mus Belles Artes, Mexico City; Calif State Fair Collection; Brentwood Savings & Loan, Hollywood, Calif; plus others. Exhib: Watercolor USA; Nat Watercolor Soc; Calif State Fair; one-man matted traveling shows, US Univs, 70, 71, 74 & 75; one-man shows, Brand Art Ctr, Glendale, 71, Inst Mexicano, Mexico City, 70 & Paris Am Acad, France, 75; plus many others. Teaching: Instr painting, Downey Mus Art Sch, Calif, 60-69; instr painting, Chouinard Art Inst, Los Angeles, 66-67; instr painting, Univ Southern Calif, 72-73; pvt art classes & lectr throughout USA. Pos: Juror, Nat Watercolor Soc, Calif State Fair, Watercolor USA & others. Awards: Eight awards, Nat Watercolor Soc, 58-73; Awards, Calif State Fair, 66-71 & Watercolor USA, 71. Bibliog: Edward Reep (auth), Content of Watercolor, 70; Gerald Brommer (auth), Watercolor, 73; plus others. Mem: Nat Watercolor Soc (treas & historian, 64-67); WCoast Watercolor Soc; Women Painters West. Style & Technique: Vibrant linear style watercolors, each with different elements dictated by a long distillation process. Publ: Auth, Handbook on Copper Enameling, Ceramics Monthly Mag, 55; auth, Toward Inventive Painting, 74 & See & Hear How Painting is Visual Music, 75. Mailing Add: 2960 Glenmanor Pl Los Angeles CA 90039

REBOLI, JOSEPH JOHN
PAINTER, ILLUSTRATOR
b Port Jefferson, NY, Sept 25, 45. Study: Paier Sch Art, New Haven, Conn. Work: New Haven Paint & Clay Club; Awixa Pond Art Asn, Bay Shore, NY. Exhib: Conn Classic Art Exhib, Trumbull, Conn, 64; Nat Benedictine Art Awards, New York, 65; 23rd New Eng Exhib of Painting & Sculpture, Silvermine, Conn, 72; Suffolk Mus, Stony Brook, NY, 74; Christopher Gallery, New York, 77; Ann Long Island Exhib, Heckscher Mus, 77; Gallery North, Setauket, NY, 78. Awards: Best in Show, Conn Classic Art Exhib, 64; William Browning Award, 26th New Eng Exhib of Painting & Sculpture, 75; Best in Show, Smithtown Twp Arts Coun Long Island Exhib, 76. Media: Oil. Publ: Illusr, Guideposts Mag, 11/71; illusr, Ralston's Ring, Ballentine, 71; illusr, Good Housekeeping Mag, 7/72 & 9/72; illusr, Clothes Mag, 5/72. Dealer: Christopher Gallery 766 Madison Ave New York NY 10021. Mailing Add: 87 Cedar St Stony Brook NY 11790

RECANATI, DINA
SCULPTOR
b Cairo, Egypt. Study: Art Students League, with Jose de Creft, 59-62. Work: Israel Mus, Jerusalem; Tel Aviv Mus; President's Garden Collection, Jerusalem; Ben Gurion Airport, Tel Aviv. Comn: Gate (bronze), Ministry of Transportation, Israel, 74 & Gates (spec bronze ed), Am-Israel Cult Found, New York, 76. Exhib: Nat Arts Club, New York, 61-62; Silvermine Guild of Artists, Conn, 62-65; Jersey City Mus, NJ, 63; Claude Bernard Gallery, Paris, 66-67; Gordon Gallery, Tel Aviv, 70-75; Queens Co Art Cult Ctr, NY, 73; Jewish Mus, New York, 75; Delson Richter Galleries Auspices, Washington, DC, 77; Danforth Mus, Boston, Mass, 77; Padua Biennale, Italy, 77. Bibliog: Paul Waldo Schwartz (auth), Scrooge in style in Paris, New York Times, 65; Zvi Sas (auth), Sculptor of powerful temperament, L'Info, 70; Emanuel Bar Kadma (auth), Yediot Ahronot, The source of inspiration, ancient Eqypt, 77. Style & Technique: Architectural forms, monumental outdoor environments, textured gates, columns, walls and indoor free standing bronze sculptures. Publ: Contribr, The Artist's Notebook, Gordon Galleries, Israel, 75. Dealer: E P Gurewitsch Works of Art 55 E 74th St New York, NY 10021. Mailing Add: 944 Fifth Ave New York NY 10021

RECCHIA, RICHARD (HENRY)
SCULPTOR
b Quincy, Mass. Study: Boston Art Mus Sch Art; also study in France & Italy. Work: Bas reliefs on bldg, Boston Art Mus & replica, J B Speed Mus, Louisville, Ky; Brookgreen Gardens Mus, SC. Comn: Bas reliefs, Gov Curtis Guild, Boston Common, 16, Sam Walter Foss, Brown Univ, 16 & Phi Beta Kappa, Harvard Univ, 17; Gov Oliver Ames Mem, Northeaston, Mass, 21; Gov John Stark Equestrian Statue, State of NH, Manchester, 48. Exhib: Int Expos, Bologna, Italy, 31; Nat Acad Design Ann, New York; Corcoran Gallery Art, Washington, DC; Nat Sculpture Soc Ann, New York; New York World's Fair, 42. Pos: Founder, Boston Soc Sculptors. Awards: Gold Cross & Medal of Honor, Int Expos, Bologna, 31; Watrous Gold Medal, Nat Acad Design, 42; Lindsay Morris Mem Prize for Bas Relief, Nat Sculpture Soc, 49. Bibliog: Richard Recchia creates heroic size equestrian, Am Art, 6/50; Meara (auth), A garden where statues grow, NShore Mag, 68; Stickler (auth), Stark hold symbol of freedom high, NH Sun News, 9/27/70. Mem: Nat Acad Design; Nat Sculpture Soc. Style & Technique: Traditional and contemporary; one of the first American sculptors to do abstract work. Media: Bronze, Marble. Publ: Illusr, Down to Earth, 64. Mailing Add: 6 Summer Rockport MA 01966

REDBIRD
See Cochran, George McKee

REDD, RICHARD JAMES
PAINTER
b Toledo, Ohio, Oct 22, 31. Study: Toledo Mus Sch; Univ Toledo, BEd, 53; Univ Iowa, MFA, 58, study with Eugene Ludins & Mauricio Lasansky. Work: Allentown Art Mus, Pa; Lehigh Univ, Bethlehem, Pa; Philip & Muriel Berman Collection, Allentown; Louis Dieruff Mem Collection, Allentown; Kutztown State Col, Pa. Exhib: One-man shows, Allentown Art Mus, 61, Kutztown State Col, 68, Moravian Col, Bethlehem, Pa, 71 & Kemmerer Mus, Bethlehem, 72; Earth Art, Civic Ctr Mus, Philadelphia, 73. Teaching: Prof art & art hist, Lehigh Univ, 58-; chmn dept fine art, 70-77. Awards: Garth Howland Award, Lehigh Art Alliance, 63 & 75; Second Prize, Reading Mus Regional; First Award, Lehigh Art Alliance, 64. Mem: Lehigh Art Alliance (bd dir, 72-75, pres, 76-78); Col Art Asn. Style & Technique: Encaustic painting in hot wax on wood panels; organic fantasy; earth subjects, intaglio printmaking. Mailing Add: RD 3 Stonesthrow Rd Bethlehem PA 18015

REDD EKKS (ROBERT NORMAN RASMUSSEN)
SCULPTOR, CERAMIST
b Islo, Norway, Feb 11, 37. Study: San Francisco Art Inst, BFA, 59; Calif Col Arts & Crafts, MFA, 70. Exhib: Ceramic show, Univ Calif, Santa Barbara, 73, Mix, San Francisco Mus Art, 73, Ceramic Sculpture, San Francisco Art Inst, 74, ceramic conjunction, Brant Libr, Burbank, 75 & Sculpture Show, Col of Marin, San Rafael, 75, Calif. Teaching: Instr ceramics, San Francisco Art Inst, 71-; instr ceramics, Univ Wis-Madison, summer, 75. Style & Technique: Ceramic sculpture. Mailing Add: c/o San Francisco Art Inst 800 Chestnut St San Francisco CA 94133

REDDING, STEVE
ART DEALER, COLLECTOR
b Marshall, Tex. Pos: Dir, S/R Gallery, Los Angeles. Specialty: Works on paper, 19th and 20th century masters; selected contemporary American artists. Collection: West Coast artists & works by Chagall, Nolde, Miro, Taulouse-Lautrec, and others. Mailing Add: 8400 de Longpre Ave Los Angeles CA 90069

REDDINGTON, CHARLES LEONARD
PAINTER, GALLERY DIRECTOR
b Chicago, Ill, Mar 22, 29. Study: Art Inst Chicago, dipl, 54, BFA, 58, with Paul Wieghardt; Southern Ill Univ, MFA, 70. Work: Commonwealth Govt Collection, Canberra, Australia; Art Gallery NSW, Sydney; Nat Gallery Victoria, Melbourne; Western Australian Art Gallery, Perth; Southern Ill Univ, Carbondale. Comn: Harold Mertz Pub Collection, New York, 63; Four Color Lithographs, Nat Gallery Victoria, Melbourne, 64. Exhib: Australian Painting Today, 64; Young Contemporaries of Australia, Japan, 65; Travel Exhib of Art, Ind, 71; one-man show, Swope Art Gallery, Terre Haute, Ind, 73; Nat Drawing, USA, 75. Teaching: Lectr drawing & painting, NSW Univ, Sydney, 63-66; assoc prof painting, Ind State Univ, Terre Haute, 70- Pos: Dir, Turman Gallery, Ind State Univ, Terre Haute, 75- Awards: Willis Painting Award, H O Willis Corp, Inc, Sydney, 65; Louis Comfort Tiffany Grant, 70; Works on Paper Prize, Indianapolis Mus, 72. Bibliog: Daniel Thomas (auth), Australian Prints, Art Gallery, NSW, 65; Robert Hughes (auth), Art in Australia, Pelican Books, 70; James Gleeson (auth), Modern Painters, Landsdowne Press, 71. Mem: Col Art Conf; Art Inst Chicago Alumnae; Int Inst Conserv Historic & Artistic Works. Style & Technique: Figurative fantasy; heavy modeling. Media: Acrylic; Oil. Dealer: Gallery A 21 Gipps St Paddington NSW Sydney Australia. Mailing Add: 504 Hulman St Terre Haute IN 47802

REDDIX, ROSCOE CHESTER
PAINTER, EDUCATOR
b New Orleans, La, Nov 15, 33. Study: Southern Univ, BA; Univ New Orleans; Ind Univ, Bloomington, MS(art educ); Univ Southern Miss; also with Dr Eddie Jordan & Dr Arthur Britt. Comn: Portrait of William G Brown & logo design, Dr Emmitt Bashful, Southwestern Athletic Conf; slide set of works, Univ South Ala; plastic painting, Southern Univ New Orleans. Exhib: Expo 72, La Artist Exhib, Ill State Univ; NJ State Mus; Black Artist, Ind Univ; one-man shows, Ala State Univ & Southern Univ New Orleans. Teaching: Instr art, Shreveport, La & New Orleans, La; asst prof art, Southern Univ New Orleans, 74- Pos: Chmn, Shreveport Local Artist, 70-71. Awards: Hon Mention, Echos of Africa, Nat Show. Bibliog: Samella S Lewis & Ruth Waddy (auth), Black Artist on Art, Contemp Crafts; Alberta Collier (auth), A critique of one-man show, New Orleans Times Picayune, 5/30/72. Mem: Nat Conf Artist (state dir, 73); Col Art Asn; Creative Artists Alliance New Orleans. Style & Technique: Social realism in the direction of expressionism; symbology of a proud people; plastic resins in a hard edge semiabstract. Media: Oil. Publ: Contribr, Black Artist on Art, Vol 2, 71. Mailing Add: 1330 Cambronne St New Orleans LA 70118

REDDY, KRISHNA N
PRINTMAKER, SCULPTOR
b Chittoor, Andhra State, India, July 15, 25. Study: Int Univ at Santiniketan, India, dipl(fine arts), 47; Univ of London, Slade Sch of Fine Arts, cert(fine arts), 52; Academie Grande Chaumiere, Paris, cert(fine arts), sculpture with Zadkine, 55; Atelier 17, Int Ctr for Gravure, Paris, 55; Academie DiBelle Arti DiBrera, Milan, cert(fine arts), sculpture with Marino Marini, 57. Work: Mus of Mod Art, New York & Paris; Libr of Cong, Nat Galleries & Smithsonian Inst, Washington, DC. Comn: Monumental sculpture in marble, Int Schulpture Symposium, St Margarethan, Austria, 62 & Montreal, 64. Exhib: Ann Int Print Show, Philadelphia Art Club, Seattle, Portland & Cincinnati Art Mus, 54; La Gravure Francaise Contemporaine, Bibliotheque Royale de Bruxelles, 64; Gravures Contemporaines, Bibliotheque Nat de Paris, 73; Invitational Prints, Univ of Massachusetts Art Gallery, 74; 50 Yrs of Atelier 17, Elvehjem Art Ctr, Univ of Wis, 77; Brooklyn Mus of Art, 78; one-man shows, Acad of Fine Arts, New Delhi, 73, Madison Art Ctr, 73, Assoc Am Artists, New York, 74, Univ of Calif Gallery, Santa Cruz, 75 & Galerie Vivant, Tokyo, 78. Teaching: Prof & co-dir printmaking, Atelier 17, Int Ctr for Graphics, Paris, 57-76; co-ordinator & assoc prof printmaking, Dept of Art & Art Educ, New York Univ, 77- Pos: Dir, Art Dept, Col of Fine Arts, Kalakshetra, Madras, 47-49. Awards: Padma Shree, awarded by the Pres of India, 72; Chosen to make a print for portfolio, 33 Contemporary Masters, to be presented to Nobel Prize winners, Hommage Aux Prix Nobel, Sweden, 74. Bibliog: S W Hayter (auth), About Prints, 64 & New Ways of Gravure, 66, Oxford Univ Press, London; Gabor Peterdi (auth), Printmaking, Macmillan Co, New York, 71; Contemporary Indian Art Series, Krishna Reddy, Fine Arts Coun of New Delhi, India, 74. Style & Technique: Special methods developed by the artist for sculpture in stone, wood and bronze and printmaking. Media: Engraving; Etching; Stone Carving. Dealer: Assoc Am Artists 663 Fifth Ave New York NY 10022. Mailing Add: 80 Wooster St New York NY 10012

REDINGER, WALTER FRED
SCULPTOR
b Wallacetown, Ont, Jan 6, 42. Study: Beal-Spec Art, London, Ont; Meinsinger Sch Art, Detroit; Ont Col Art, Toronto. Work: Nat Art Gallery, Ottawa; Art Gallery Ont, Toronto; Can Coun, Ottawa; Univ Western Ont; Univ Sask. Comn: Caucasian totems (set of 5), Rothman's, Stratford, 72; caucasian totems (set of 4), Samuel Bronfman, Can Jewish Cong, 73; Xabis (monument, 6 units), Ct House, London, Ont, 74; Montagne (monument), Pinetree Develop, Toronto, 75; Umbria (monuments, 3 units), Univ Guelph, 75. Exhib: Survey, Montreal Mus Fine Arts, 68; Galerie du France, Paris, 69; Plastic Presence, Jewish Mus New York, Milwaukee Art Ctr, 70; Venice Biennale, 72; Owens Art Gallery, Mt Allison, NB, 75. Awards: Sculpture Prize, Montreal Mus, 69; Can Coun Jr Awards, 68-71, Sr Awards, 73-74. Bibliog: Robert Arn (auth), Rebirth of humanism, Arts Can, 74; Document Venice Biennale (film), Educ TV Toronto, 74; film, Can Broadcasting Co, 74. Mem: Royal Can Acad Arts. Media: Fiberglass, Steel. Dealer: Isaacs Gallery 832 Yonge St Toronto ON Can. Mailing Add: Rte 3 West Lorne ON N0L 2P0 Can

RED STAR, KEVIN FRANCIS
PAINTER, ILLUSTRATOR
b Crow Reservation, Mont, Oct 9, 43. Study: Inst Am Indian Arts, with James A McGrath & Fritz Scholder; San Francisco Art Inst; Mont State Univ, Bozeman; Eastern Mont Col, Billings. Work: Ctr for Arts of Indian Am, Washington, DC; Plains Indian Mus, Browning, Mont. Comn: Mixed media mural on canvas, Crow Tribe, Sun Lodge Motel Complex, 74; mixed media mural, Adult Educ Prog, Crow Reservation, 74. Exhib: Scottsdale Nat Indian Art Exhib, Ariz, 65; Heard Mus Exhib, Phoenix, Ariz, 66; Spring Art Exhib: San Francisco Art Inst, 70; Ann Contemp Indian Art Exhib, 75; one-man shows, Sun Spirits Gallery, Santa Fe, NMex & Copper Village Gallery, Anaconda, Mont, 75. Teaching: Teacher art, Boys Club, Billings, summer 71 & 72; asst teacher art, Lodge Grass High Sch, Mont, 73-74; art instr adult educ, Crow Reservation, Crow Agency, 73-74. Awards: Gov's Trophy, Ariz Art Coun, 65. Bibliog: Kevin Red Star, article in Southwest Art Mag, Houston, Tex, 10/75. Mem:

Yellowstone Art Asn; Bighorn Art Asn; Crow, Northern Cheyenne Fine Arts Alliance (chmn); Santa Fe Door Studios. Style & Technique: Acrylics or mixed media on paper & canvas; collages, textures, colors, lines, space; North American Indian theme; oil on canvas. Dealer: Treasure State Gallery 1214 Fourth Ave N Great Falls MT 59401. Mailing Add: PO Box 337 Lodge Grass MT 59050

REDSTONE, LOUIS GORDON
ARCHITECT, ART WRITER
b Grodno, Poland, Mar 16, 03, US citizen. Study: Univ of Mich, BS(archit), 29; Cranbrook Acad of Art, MArch & Urban Design, 48. Comn: Brick mural, Jewish Community Ctr, West Bloomfield, Mich, 75 & First Federal Savings & Loan of Detroit, Operations Ctr, Troy, Mich, 76; Tapestries (woven in Mex by Mr Delgado), Manufacturers Bank & 333 W Fort Off Bldg, Detroit, Mich, 78. Exhib: Ann Mich Artists Water Color Exhib, Detroit, 28 & 42; The Levant Fair, Israeli Artists Inst Exhib, Tel Aviv, Israel, 34; Watercolor USA, 69; Mich Watercolor Soc, 72. Bibliog: William Tall (auth), L G R: Minor Miracles in Watercolors, 11/22/69 & Marsha Miro (auth), Art in Architecture, 2/22/77, Detroit Free Press; Joy Hakanson (auth), Louis G Redstone: Fighting His Own War on Ugliness, Detroit News, 72. Mem: Archives of Am Art: Detroit Inst of Art, Founders Soc & Friends of Mod Art; patron Mich Foundation for the Arts, 77 (bd mem, 78); Mich Gov Spec Comn on Art in State Bldgs. Style & Technique: Abstract approach using liquid watercolors. Media: Watercolor. Interest: Support of Michigan Society of Ceramic Artists. Collection: Pre-Columbian Art, Aztec, Inca. Publ: Auth, Art in Architecture, McGraw-Hill, 68; contribr, Art in Architecture, Am Inst of Archit J, 5/68; auth, New Dimensions in Shopping Centers and Stores, McGraw-Hill Bk Co, 73; contribr, Art in Public Places in the US, Bowling Green Univ, 75; auth, The New Downtowns, McGraw-Hill Bk Co, 76. Dealer: Les Arwin c/o Arwin Galleries 222 W Grand River Detroit MI 48226. Mailing Add: 19303 Appoline Detroit MI 48235

REECE, MAYNARD
PAINTER, ILLUSTRATOR
b Arnolds Park, Iowa, Apr 26, 20. Work: Cent Nat Bank, Des Moines, Iowa; Iowa Des Moines Nat Bank. Comn: Designs for postage stamps, Govt of Bermuda, 65; First Iowa Duck Stamp, State Conserv Comn, 72; Marshlander Mallards, Ducks Unlimited Inc, 73; Canada Geese & Mallards, Winnebego Indust; Canada Geese, Remington Arms, Bridgeport, Conn, 76. Exhib: Various mus throughout the US & Can. Awards: Five Time Winner, Fed Duck Stamp Competition; Cert Merit & Award Distinctive Merit, Art Dirs Club New York. Bibliog: George Harrison (auth), Iowa artist Maynard Reese: bringing art out of the blind, Acquire, 77; Diane Milobar (auth), Maynard Reese: wildlife artist, The Iowan, 77; Bob Strohm (auth), First, you've gotta know wildlife, Nat Wildlife Mag, 77. Mem: Grand Cent Art Galleries New York; Izaak Walton League (hon pres, 74-75); Soc of Animal Artists; Nat Audubon Soc; Outdoor Writers Asn Am (past bd mem). Style & Technique: Realism of natural history material. Media: Oil, Watercolor; Stone Lithography. Publ: Illusr, Life, Outdoor Life, Sports Afield, Sports Illus, Ducks Unlimited, Nat Wildlife & Sat Eve Post; auth & illusr, Fish & Fishing, Meredith, 63; illusr, Waterfowl in Iowa & Iowa Fish & Fishing, Iowa Conserv Comn. Dealer: Mill Pond Press Inc 201 S Nassau St Venice FL 33595. Mailing Add: 5315 Robertson Dr Des Moines IA 50312

REED, DAVID FREDRICK
PAINTER
b San Diego, Calif, Jan 20, 46. Study: Reed Col, BA; New York Studio Sch; Skowhegan Sch Painting & Sculpture. Work: Roswell Mus & Art Ctr, NMex: Musee Nat d'Art Moderne, Centre George Pompidou, Paris; Reed Col, Portland, Ore; New York Studio Sch, New York. Exhib: Cunningham Ward Exhib, New York, 74; 4th Ann Contemporary Reflections, Aldrich Mus Contemp Art, Ridgefield, Conn, 75; Whitney Mus Biennial Contemp Am Art, New York, 75; Student Choice Sch of Art, Yale Univ, New Haven, Conn, 76; Max Protetch Gallery, New York, 77; Nancy Lurie Gallery, Chicago, Ill, 77; one-man show, Susan Caldwell, Inc, New York, 75. Awards: Rockefeller Found Grant, 66; Roswell Mus & Art Ctr Grant, 69. Bibliog: Jeremy Gilbert-Rolfe (auth), rev in Artforum, 6/74; Peter Schjeldahl (auth), David Reed at Susan Caldwell, Art in Am, 7-8/75; Sharon Gold (auth), David Reed at Max Protetch, Artforum, summer 77. Media: Oil with Wax, Acrylic on Canvas. Publ: Auth, On jumping, spring 75, auth, On intermediate cases, spring 75 & co-auth, Painters, spring 75, Art-Rite. Dealer: Max Protetch Gallery 21 W 58th St New York NY 10019. Mailing Add: 315 Broadway New York NY 10007

REED, DOEL
PAINTER
b Logansport, Ind, May 21, 94. Study: Art Acad Cincinnati, with L H Meaken, James R Hopkins & H H Wessel. Work: Bibliot Nat, Paris; Victoria & Albert Mus, London; Metrop Mus Art, New York; Rosenwald Collection, Philadelphia; Pa Acad Fine Arts, Philadelphia. Comn: Six murals, Okla State Off Bldg, Oklahoma City, 41. Exhib: Many ann, Nat Acad Design, Audubon Artists, Allied Artists Am, Soc Am Graphic Artists & Nat Soc Painters Casein. Teaching: Prof art & chmn dept, Okla State Univ, 24-59. Awards: Gold Medal of Honor, 51 & John Taylor Arms Mem Medal, 54, Audubon Artists; Samuel Morse Medal, Nat Acad Design, 65. Bibliog: Doel Reed makes an aquatint, Mus NMex Press, 65. Mem: Nat Acad Design; Allied Artists Am; Audubon Artists; Soc Am Graphic Artists; Nat Soc Painters Casein. Style & Technique: Traditional. Media: Graphics. Dealer: Mission Gallery Taos NM 87571; Cremer Gallery 8575 E 31st Pl Tulsa OK 74145. Mailing Add: Box 1244 Taos NM 87571

REED, HAL
PAINTER, SCULPTOR
b Frederick, Okla, Feb 22, 21. Study: Trade Tech Col Los Angeles; Art Ctr Col Design; Art League San Francisco; also with Nicolai Fechin. Work: State of Calif Gov Off, Sacramento; Los Angeles City Hall Permanent Collection; plus other pub & pvt collections. Comn: Robert Fulton Medal, 71 & Charles A Lindbergh Medal, 75, Nat Commemorative Soc, Lansdowne, Pa; Eleanor Roosevelt Medal, Soc Commemorative Femmes Celebres, 71; Atomic Age Medal, Soc Medalists, 71; Ethan Alan Medal, Am Bicentennial Commemorative, Springfield, Pa; Thomas Paine Bust, Los Angeles, Calif. Exhib: Nat Open, Miniature Painters, Sculptors & Gravesr Soc, Washington, DC, 72; Nat Open, Miniature Art Soc NJ, 72; Am Artists Prof League, New York, 72; Calif State Fair, Sacramento, 72; Olive Hyde Art Ctr 2nd Ann, Fremont, Calif, 72; plus many others. Teaching: Instr color, compos, anat, perspective & advan painting, Art League Los Angeles, 65- Pos: Founder, Art League Los Angeles, 65- Awards: First Award in Sculpture, Portrait, Seascape & Graphics, San Fernando Art Guild, 69; First in Sculpture & McLeod Award, Miniature Painters, Sculpture Soc, Washington, 72; First in Sculpture & Purchase Award, Miniature Art Soc NJ, 72. Mem: Coun Traditional Artists Soc (pres, 71-72); fel Am Artists Prof League; fel Am Inst Fine Arts; Valley Artists Guild, Los Angeles (pres, 58-); Calif Art Club. Media: Oil, Acrylic; Bronze. Publ: Auth, How to Compose Pictures & Achieve Color Harmony, Walter Foster Publ, 69- Mailing Add: 20914 Pilar Rd Woodland Hills CA 91364

REED, HAROLD
ART DEALER
b Newark, NJ, Jan 11, 37. Study: Stanford Univ, BA; Art Students League. Pos, Dir, Harold Reed Gallery, New York. Mailing Add: Harold Reed Gallery 120 E 78th St New York NY 10021

REED, JESSE FLOYD
PAINTER, PRINTMAKER
b Belington, WVa, July 25, 20. Study: Grand Cent Sch Art, 39-42; Art Students League, 45-47; Davis & Elkins Col, BA; WVa Univ, MA(hist). Work: Huntington Galleries, WVa; Charleston Art Gallery, WVa; Rosenberg Libr, Galveston, Tex. Exhib: Print Show, Brooklyn Mus, 49; Libr Cong, 55; Print Club Albany Ann; Soc Washington Printmakers Ann; Boston Printmakers Ann. Teaching: Prof art & hist, Davis & Elkins Col, 49- Awards: Artist of the Year, Print Club Albany, 68, Purchase Award, 74; Purchase Award, Morgantown Art Asn, 75; Merit Award & Purchase Award, Charleston Art Gallery, WVa, 75. Mem: Salmagundi Club; Boston Printmakers; Soc Washington Printmakers; Print Club Albany. Style & Technique: Romantic realistic interpretations of people and places from around the world. Media: Watercolor; Aquatint Etching. Mailing Add: PO Box 650 Elkins WV 26241

REED, MICHAEL ARTHUR
ART WRITER, ART EDITOR
b South Bend, Ind, May 5, 47. Study: Kalamazoo Col, BA(Eng). Pos: Contribr, Southwestern Art, Austin, Tex, 76-; co-ed designer, Artspace Mag, Albuquerque, 76- Res: The history of modern ceramics in mainstream art; interviews with major contemporary ceramists. Publ: Auth, History of Fine Art Printmaking in the Southwest (3 parts), Southwestern Art, 76; auth, Tamarind Institute (2 part series), Artspace, 76; auth, Roger Sweet (mongr), Artspace, 78. Mailing Add: Box 4547 Albuquerque NM 87106

REED, PAUL ALLEN
PAINTER, INSTRUCTOR
b Washington, DC, Mar 28, 19. Study: San Diego State Col; Corcoran Sch Art. Work: In 40 pub collections, including: San Francisco Mus of Art; Everson Mus of Art, Syracuse, NY; Corcoran Gallery Art & Nat Collection Fine Arts, Washington, DC; Detroit Inst Art; Walker Art Ctr, Minneapolis; Albright-Knox Art Gallery, Buffalo, NY. Exhib: 25th Ann Soc Am Art, Art Inst Chicago, 65; Washington Color Painters, Washington, DC, Tex, Calif, Mass & Minn, 65-66; 250 Yrs American Art, Corcoran Gallery Art, 66; Jackson Pollock to the Present, Steinberg Gallery, Wash Univ, St Louis, 69; Inaugural Exhib, Wadsworth Atheneum, Hartford, Conn, 69; Washington 20 Yrs, Baltimore Mus Art, 70; one-man exhib, Phoenix Art Mus, 77. Teaching: Instr painting, Art League Northern Va, 71-74; asst prof & coordr first yr prog, Corcoran Sch Art, 71- Bibliog: Barbara Rose (auth), The primacy of color 5/64 & Legrace Benson (auth), The Washington scene, 69, Art Int; Walter Hopps (auth), The Vincent Melzac Collection, Corcoran Gallery Art, 71. Media: Acrylic, Unprimed Canvas. Mailing Add: 3541 N Utah St Arlington VA 22207

REED, WALT ARNOLD
ART HISTORIAN, WRITER
b Big Spring, Tex, July 21, 17. Study: Pratt Inst; Phoenix Art Inst; also with Franklin Booth. Comn: Designer US postage stamp series, 50 state flags, US Postal Serv, 76. Teaching: Art instr, Famous Artists Sch, Westport, Conn, 57-66, asst to dir, 66-72. Pos: Art dir, CARE, New York, 52-55; ed, North Light Publ, Westport, 72- Awards: Wrangler Award Best Western Art Book,at Cowboy Hall Fame & Western Heritage Ctr, 72. Mem: Westport Artists; New York Soc Illusr; Westport-Weston Arts Coun; Sanford Low Mem Collection Am Illus, New Brit Mus Am Art (mem adv comt). Res: American illustrations, 1880 to the present. Publ: Auth, The Illustrator in America 1900-1960's, Reinhold, 65; auth, Harold Von Schmidt Draws and Paints the Old West, Northland, 72; auth, John Clymer, Northland, 76; auth, The Figure: An Artist's Approach to Drawing and Construction, North Light, 76. Mailing Add: 7 Belaire Dr Westport CT 06880

REEP, EDWARD ARNOLD
PAINTER, EDUCATOR
b Brooklyn, NY, May 10, 18. Study: Art Ctr Col Design, cert, 41; also with E J Bisttram, Stanley Reckless & Willard Nash. Work: Los Angeles Co Mus, Calif; 66 works, US War Dept, Pentagon; Grunwald Graphic Arts Collection, Univ Calif, Los Angeles; Lytton Collection, Los Angeles; State of Calif Collection, Sacramento. Comn: Three panels of early conquests in Calif, SAm & US (with Gordon Mellor), USA Private's Club, Ft Ord, Calif, 41; Painter's Impression of International Airports (10 pages in full color), Life Mag, 6/56; Impressions of the Berlin Wall, Ger, US Govt, 71. Exhib: Whitney Mus Am Art Ann, New York, 46-48; Los Angeles Co Mus Ann, 46-60; Corcoran Gallery Art Biennial, Washington, DC, 49; Nat Acad Design, New York; Nat Gallery Art, Washington, DC. Teaching: Instr painting & drawing, Art Ctr Col Design, Los Angeles, 46-50; instr painting & drawing & chmn, Dept Painting, Chouinard Art Inst, Los Angeles, 50-69; prof painting, artist in residence, E Carolina Univ, 70- Pos: Coord art chmn, Los Angeles City Art Festival Exhibs, 51. Awards: First Purchase Prize for Watercolor, Los Angeles Co Mus, 51; First Prize in Oil Painting, Los Angeles All City Ann, 63; Nat Endowment Arts Grant, 75. Bibliog: Niece (auth), Art, an approach, William C Brown, 59; Schaad (auth), Realm of Contemporary Still-life, 62 & Mugnaini (auth), Drawing, a Search for Form, 65, Van Nostrand Reinhold. Mem: Nat Watercolor Soc (pres, 51-52). Media: Oil, Watercolor. Publ: Auth, The Content of Watercolor, Van Nostrand Reinhold, 69. Mailing Add: 201 Poplar Dr Greenville NC 27834

REES, JOSEPH F
SCULPTOR
b 1946. Study: Calif Col Arts & Crafts, scholar, 71-73, BFA, 71, MFA, 73. Work: Oakland Mus, Calif. Exhib: Calif Expo 71; SFAI Centennial Celebration, De Young Exhib, San Jose, 71; Grad Show, Kaiser Ctr, 72; 3rd Ann Regional Arts Competition, San Jose, 72; Coop Gallery, Las Vegas, 72; New Mus Mod Art Gallery, Oakland, 73; Univ Calif, San Jose, 75; Acad Art Col, San Francisco, 75; one-man show, Berkeley Art Ctr, Calif, 75; plus others. Teaching: Instr, Calif Col Arts & Crafts, Oakland, 73; instr, Acad Art Col, San Francisco, 73, chmn sculpture dept, 74-76; guest lectr, Univ Calif, Stanislaus, 73, San Francisco Art Inst, 74 & Calif Col Arts & Crafts, 75; instr, Univ Calif, Hayward, 76. Pos: Dir, New Mus Mod Art, Oakland. Awards: Third Place, Calif Expo 71. Mailing Add: 743 47th St Oakland CA 94609

REESE, PEARL HARDAWAY
See Hardaway, Pearl

REESE, THOMAS FORD
ART HISTORIAN, EDUCATOR
b New Orleans, La, Oct 9, 43. Study: Facultad de Filosofia y Letras, Univ de Madrid, 63-64; Tulane Univ, BA, 65; Yale Univ, MA, 69, PhD, 73. Teaching: Asst prof art hist, Univ Tex,

Austin, 70-76, assoc prof art hist, 76- Awards: John Simon Guggenheim fel, 76-77; Acad corresp, Real Acad de Bellas Artes de San Fernando, Madrid, 77. Mem: Soc Archit Hist; Am Soc Spanish & Portuguese Art Hist Studies (exec secy, 75-76). Res: History of the arts of Spain and Portugal; Latin American Colonial Art; European architecture since 1400. Publ: Co-ed, Newsletter of the Am Soc Hispanic Art Hist Studies, 74-76; auth, The Architecture of Ventura Rodriguez, New York, 76. Mailing Add: 1408 Northwood Rd Austin TX 78703

REESE, WILLIAM FOSTER
PAINTER
b Pierre, SDak, July 10, 38. Study: Wash State Univ; Orange Coast Col; Los Angeles Trade Tech Sch; Art Ctr Sch Design, Los Angeles. Work: Frye Art Mus, Seattle, Wash. Comn: Painting, Walter Lommell Hosp, Woodburn, Ore, 72; paintings, St Francis Hotel, San Francisco, 72. Exhib: Two-man show, Frye Art Mus, 72; Allied Artists of Am Show, Nat Acad Galleries, New York, 74; 50th & 51st Ann Nat, Springville Mus Art, Utah, 74-75; Rocky Mountain Nat, Golden, Colo, 75, 76 & 77; Am Watercolor Soc Show, 76; Pastel Soc Show, 76-77; NAWA Show, Cowboy Hall of Fame, Oklahoma City, 77; one-man show, Frye Art Mus, 77. Awards: West Coast Oil Show Childe Hassam Award, Frye Mus, 67, Puget Sound Exhib Leon Augustine Hermitte Award, 75 & 77; House of Heydenryk Award, Nat Arts Club, 77; Best of Show, Mus of Great Plains, 78. Bibliog: Lila Schade (auth), William F Reese, Southland Artist Mag, 10/65; Ed Hearn (auth), Bill Reese, View Northwest, 6/74; John Manson (auth), Artist of the Rockies, 76. Mem: Puget Sound Group Northwest Painters (secy, 70-71, treas, 71-72); Northwest Watercolor Soc; assoc Allied Artists Am; Whiskey Painters Am; Pastel Soc of Am; Soc of Animal Artists. Style & Technique: Figurative; objective. Media: Oil, Watercolor, Pastel. Mailing Add: 15511 SE 44th Ct Bellevue WA 98006

REEVES, JAMES FRANKLIN
ART HISTORIAN, COLLECTOR
b Huntsville, Ala, July 4, 46. Study: Univ Ala, Huntsville, BA(art hist), 72; Vanderbilt Univ, Nashville, Tenn, MA(art hist), 75. Collections Arranged: Gilbert Gaul, (with catalog), Tenn Fine Arts Ctr, Nashville & Huntsville Mus Art, 75. Pos: Asst, P L Hay House Mus, Macon, Ga, 66-67; asst to dir, 73-75, cur Huntsville Mus Art, 75- Mem: Col Art Asn Am; Southeastern Col Art Conf; Kappa Pi (pres local chapter, 71-72). Res: Gilbert Gaul, 1855-1919; Huntsville architecture, 1820-1975. Collection: 19th and 20th century American paintings; 18th and 19th century American decorative arts; 19th century European paintings; Oriental porcelains and sculpture. Mailing Add: 2005 Kildare St Huntsville AL 35811

REEVES, JOHN ALEXANDER
PHOTOGRAPHER
b Burlington, Ont, Can, Apr 24, 38. Study: Sir George Williams Art Sch, Montreal, 56-57; Ont Col Art, Toronto, 57-61, AOCA. Work: Nat Film Bd Can, Ottawa. Exhib: Call Them Canadians (traveling exhib), 67, NW Territories Centennial Exhib (traveling exhib), 69 & Spec Summer Exhib, Conf Ctr Ottawa, 78, Nat Film Bd Can; 10th Biennale Fedn Int de l'Art Photog, Bordeaux, France, 68; one-man show, Deja Vue Gallery, Toronto, 77. Awards: Am Inst Graphic Arts Award, 63 & 68; Award of Merit, Art Dir Club, Toronto, 72. Bibliog: Charles Oberdorf (auth), article in Camera Can Mag, 11/72 & 6/77; Gary Michael Dault (art critic), Toronto Star, 6/77. Mem: Royal Can Acad Art. Style & Technique: Photo-journalist. Publ: Auth, John Fillion—Thoughts About my Sculpture, Martlet Press, 68. Dealer: Deja Vue Gallery 122 Scollard St Toronto ON Can. Mailing Add: 11 Yorkville Ave Toronto ON M4W 1L3 Can

REFREGIER, ANTON
PAINTER
b Moscow, Russia, Mar 20, 05; US citizen. Study: RI Sch Design, 20-25; also with Hans Hoffman, Munich, Ger, 27. Work: Mus Art, Univ Wyo; Corcoran Gallery & Smithsonian Inst, Washington, DC; St Laurence Univ, Canton, NY. Comn: Glass constructions, Burlington Mills, New York; murals, Gracie Square Hosp Lobby, New York, Metrop Hosp Psychiat Addition Lobby, New York, 70, Syracuse Univ, Mayo Clin & Univ Ky Med Ctr; mosaic mural, 1199 Hosp Workers Union, 70; paintings, US Dept Interior, Grand Coulee Dam, 71. Exhib: Moscow Mus Fine Arts, Leningrad, 66; ACA Gallery; Whitney Mus Am Art; Carnegie Inst; Retrospective Exhib, Bailey Mus, Charlottesville, Va, 77; NY State Exhib of WPA Artists, Gray Gallery, NY Univ, 77; Exhib of New York WPA Artists Inc, Parsons Inst, NY, 77; plus many others nat & int. Teaching: Vis instr, Univ Ark, 52; vis instr, Cleveland Sch Fine Arts; assoc prof, Bard Col, 62-64. Pos: Artist-correspondent, Fortune Mag, UN Original Conf, San Francisco. Awards: Hallmark Competition, 53; Salmagundi Club Prize, Nat Acad of Design, 77; mural grant, NY State Coun on the Arts, 78. Bibliog: Incl in BBC film on US Fed art patronage, 78. Mem: Artists Equity Asn; Nat Soc Mural Painters; Nat Acad Design. Style & Technique: Art forms in architecture using tapestry, mosaic, glass and ceramic, choosing materials in relation to the function of the area. Publ: Auth, Natural Figure Drawing, 49, An Artist's Journey, 65 & We Make Our Tomorrow, 65; contribr, Fortune, What's New & other mags. Mailing Add: Glasco Turnpike Rte 1 Box 345 Woodstock NY 12498

RÉGAT, JEAN JACQUES
SCULPTOR, MURALIST
b Paris, France, Sept 12, 45. Study: Univ Alaska, BA; Soc Beaux Arts, France. Work: Alaska State Mus, Juneau; Kinsey Collection, Los Angeles; Earth Resource Collection, Sheik Said, Emirate of Abu Dabi; Fairbanks North Star Borough Libr; Kobuk Valley Jade Co, Aleyaska. Exhib: One-man show, Artique Gallery, Anchorage, 72-77; Alaska State Mus, Juneau; Heritage Northwest Gallery, Juneau, 73-74; House of Wood, Fairbanks, 74-78; Erdon Gallery, Houston, Tex; Rendezvous Gallery, Anchorage. Bibliog: Maureen Blewett (staffwriter), Regat Complete Herioc Panels, Anchorage Daily Times, 74; Jeanne Montague (ed), Alaskan Toten Poles, Anchorage Daily News, 2/13/71; Judy Shuler (auth), Jacques & Mary Régat, Alaska J, autumn 77. Style & Technique: Hand carved, impressionistic, cubism, realism, abstract, native Northwest Coast designing. Media: Stone, Wood. Dealer: Rendezvous Gallery 414 K St Anchorage AK 99501; House of Wood 529 Fourth Fairbanks AK 99701. Mailing Add: c/o Regat Studio 518 Pearl Dr Anchorage AK 99502

REGAT, MARY E
SCULPTOR, MURALIST
b Duluth, Minn, Nov 12, 43. Study: Univ Alaska. Work: Anchorage Fine Arts Mus, Alaska; Post Oak Towers Bldg, Alaska Interstate Corp, Houston, Tex; Soroptimist Plazza, Anchorage; RCA-Alascom, Anchorage; Larry Carr Collection, Anchorage. Exhib: All Alaska Juried Art Show, Anchorage; one-woman shows, Color Ctr Gallery, 70 & 71 & Artique Gallery, 72-77; Alaska State Mus, Juneau, 73; House of Wood, Fairbanks, 74-78; Rendezvous Gallery; plus others. Awards: Sculpture Award, Design I, 71; Purchase Award, Anchorage Fine Arts Mus, 71. Bibliog: Voula Crouch (auth), Carving a canoe, Alaska Sportsman, 71 & Sam—sculpture in soapstone, Alaska J, winter 72. Mem: Alaska Artist Guild; Anchorage Fine Arts Mus Asn. Style & Technique: Impressionism; cubism; realism; hand carving; native Northwest Coast totem designing. Media: Stone, Wood; Oil, Acrylic. Dealer: Rendezvous Gallery 414 K St Anchorage AK 99501; House of Wood 529 Fourth Fairbanks AK 99701. Mailing Add: Regat Sculpture Studio 518 Pearl Dr Anchorage AK 99502

REGENSTEINER, ELSE (FRIEDSAM)
DESIGNER
b Munich, Ger, Apr 21, 06; US citizen. Study: Univ Munich; Inst Design, Chicago; Black Mountain Col, with Moholy-Nagy, Marli Ehrman & Anni & Josef Albers. Work: Cooper Union Mus, New York; Art Inst Chicago; Ill State Univ; Univ Houston. Exhib: Designer-Craftsmen USA, circulated by Smithsonian Inst, 53; Designer-Craftsmen Ill, Ill State Mus, Springfield, 66; Decorative Arts Nat, Wichita, Kans, 70; Textiles for Collectors, Art Inst Chicago, 71; Fabrications, Cranbrook Acad Art, 72; Am Crafts, Philadelphia Mus of Art, 77. Teaching: Instr weaving, Hull House, Chicago, 41-45; instr weaving, Inst Design, Chicago, 42-46; prof weaving, Art Inst Chicago, 45-71; workshops & lect throughout US, Can & Greece, 71-; consult, Am Farm Sch, Thessaloniki, Greece, 72- Pos: Ed bd, The Working Craftsman, Northbrook, Ill. Awards: First Prize for Drapery & Upholstery, Int Textile Exhib, Univ NC, 46; five Citations of Merit, Am Inst Interior Design, 47, 48 & 51; Hon Mention, State Mus Art, Springfield, 66. Mem: Am Crafts Coun (fel, Collegium of Craftsmen, 76); Handweavers Guild Am (bd dirs, 71-78). Style & Technique: Loom controlled as well as off loom techniques for wallhangings and three dimensional textile constructions. Publ: Contribr, Weaving in Illinois, Directions 1970, Ill Art Educ Asn, 70; auth articles in Handweaver & Craftsman, 65 & 69; auth, The Art of Weaving, 70 & auth, Weaver's Study Course, Ideas & Techniques, 75, Van Nostrand Reinhold; auth articles in Shuttle, Spindle & Dyepot, 71, 72, 73 & 74. Mailing Add: 1416 E 55th St Chicago IL 60615

REGINATO, PETER
SCULPTOR
b Dallas, Tex, Aug 19, 45. Study: San Francisco Art Inst, 63-66. Work: Allen Ctr, Houston, Tex; Houston Mus of Fine Arts; Storm King Art Ctr, Mountainville, NY; Chase Manhattan Bank, New York, NY; Great Southwest Atlanta Corp, Ga. Comn: High Plains Drifter (large sculpture), Allen Ctr, Houston, Tex, 73; Outdoor Sculpture Exhib (sculpture), Rutgers State Univ, Camden, NJ, 78. Exhib: One-man shows, Tibor de Nagy Gallery, New York, 71, 73, 74, 75 & 77, Watson de Nagy & Co, Houston, Tex, 73, 74, 76 & 78, B R Kornblatt Gallery, Baltimore, Md, 76, Diane Brown Gallery, Washington, DC, 78; Park Place Invitational, New York, 67; Whitney Mus of Am Art Biennial, 70; Highlights of the Season, Aldrich Mus, Ridgefield, Conn, 71; Indianapolis Mus of Art Ann, 72; Univ of RI, Providence, 73; Sculpture in the Park, North Jersey Cult Coun, 74; Modern Sculpture in Houston Collections, 74 & Geometry: A Summer Exhibition, Mus Fine Arts, Houston; Sculpture Now, Gallery Ariadne, New York, 75; The Condition of Sculpture, Hayward Gallery, London, Eng, 75; plus others. Teaching: Adj lectr sculpture, Hunter Col, 71- Awards: John Simon Guggenheim Mem Found fel, 76. Bibliog: John Canaday (auth), rev in New York Times, 2/17/73; Phyllis Tuchman (auth), rev in Art News, 6/75; Jeanne Siegel (auth), rev in Art in Am, 6/75; Moria Hodgson (auth), After the Monument, Soho News, 4/75; Hilton Kramer (auth), rev in New York Times, 3/18/78; plus others. Style & Technique: Welded steel. Media: Steel. Dealer: Tibor de Nagy Gallery 29 W 57th St New York NY 10019; Watson de Nagy & Co Houston TX. Mailing Add: 60 Greene St New York NY 10012

REHBERGER, GUSTAV
PAINTER, DRAFTSMAN
b Riedlingsdorf, Austria, Oct 20, 10; US citizen. Study: Art Inst Chicago, scholar; Art Instr Schs, Minneapolis, scholar. Work: Lyman Allyn Mus, New London, Conn; St Johns Univ, NY; Sports Hall, Peking, China; numerous pvt collections in US, Can, Mex, Europe, Saudi Arabia & China. Exhib: One-man shows, Soc of Illusrs, New York, 57 & 65, Wickersham Gallery, New York, 71 & Jacques Seligman Gallery, New York, 77. Teaching: Instr & lectr, Art Students League, 72- Awards: Prizes, Audubon Artists, 49 & 66; Awards, Art Directors Club of New York, 54 & 55; Award, Allied Artists of Am, 74; Award, Pastel Soc of Am, 76. Style & Technique: Representational with a powerful imagination; known as a volcanic expressionist. Mailing Add: Studio 1206 Carnegie Hall New York NY 10019

REIBACK, EARL M
SCULPTOR, PAINTER
b New York, NY, May 30, 43. Study: Lehigh Univ, BA & BS(eng physics); Mass Inst Technol, MS(nuclear eng). Work: Whitney Mus Am Art, New York; Philadelphia Mus Art; Milwaukee Art Ctr; New Orleans Mus Art; Wichita Art Mus, Kans. Exhib: Light & Motion Show, Worcester Art Mus, Mass, 67; Milwaukee Art Ctr, Wis, 67; Experiments in Light & Technology, Brooklyn Mus, NY, 68; one-man shows, Chapman Kelley Gallery, Dallas, Tex, 69, Electric Gallery, Toronto, Ont, 71 & 76, Waddell Gallery, New York, 72 & 73 & Colibri Gallery, San Juan, PR, 74; Bienal de Arte, Coltejer Medellin, Colombia, SAm, 71; US Info Serv Exhib, 15 Europ & Middle Eastern countries, 71-73; Metrop Mus Art, New York; Philadelphia Mus Art; Albright-Knox Art Gallery, Buffalo, NY; Mus Contemp Art, Chicago; New Orleans Mus Art, La; Long Beach Mus Contemp Art, Calif; Aldrich Mus Contemp Art, Ridgefield, Conn; Mus d'Art Contemporain, Montreal, Que; Am Ctr, Beirut, Lebanon; US Cult Ctr, Tel Aviv, Israel; Fine Arts Gallery, Ankara, Turkey; plus many others. Bibliog: Articles in Time, Fortune & House & Garden; color plates in Encycl Britannica Ann, 71. Style & Technique: Lumia, kinetic light, light projections. Publ: Auth articles in House & Garden, 1/69 & Electronics Age, spring 70. Mailing Add: 20 E Ninth St New York NY 10003

REIBEL, BERTRAM
SCULPTOR, GRAPHIC ARTIST
b New York, NY, June 14, 01. Study: Art Inst Chicago; also with Alexander Archipenko. Exhib: Metrop Mus Art & Nat Acad Design, New York; Pa Acad Fine Arts, Philadelphia; Northwest Printmakers; Libr of Cong, Washington, DC; plus many others, incl one-man shows at Univ d'El Salvador, San Salvador, Korean Design Ctr, Seoul & Merrick Art Gallery, New Brighton, Pa. Pos: Chmn, Young Designers' Competitions. Mem: Artists Equity Asn; Asn Int Arts Plastiques. Media: Wood, Bronze, Stone. Mailing Add: 1127 Hardscrabble Rd Chappaqua NY 10514

REICH, NATHANIEL E
PAINTER
b Brooklyn, NY. Study: Art Students League; Pratt Inst; Brooklyn Inst Arts & Sci. Work: Huntington Hartford Collection, Gallery Mod Art, New York; Joe & Emily Lowe Mus, Univ Miami; Washington Co Mus Fine Arts, Hagerstown, Md; Evansville Mus Arts & Sci, Ind; New York Heart Asn; plus others. Exhib: 8th Serv Command Competition USA, 44; 4th Har Zion Temple Art Show, Philadelphia, 66; Prospect Park Centennial, 66; Mus Mod Art, Paris, 70; Boston Inst Fine Arts, 71. Awards: St Gaudens Medal, 23; First Prize, Eighth Serv Command Competition, USA, 44. Mem: Artists Equity Asn. Style & Technique: Surrealist period replaced by assemblage and oils. Media: Oil. Mailing Add: 1620 Ave I Brooklyn NY 11230

REICH, SHELDON
ART HISTORIAN
b Brooklyn, NY, Sept 5, 31. Study: Univ of Miami, BA, 54; New York Univ, MA, 57; Univ of Iowa, PhD, 66. Pos: Prof of art hist, Univ of Ariz, Tucson, 60-68; dept head of art hist, Univ of Cincinnati, 68-72; prof of art hist, Univ Ariz, 72- Mem: Col Art Assoc; Am Asn of Univ Prof; Mid-Am Col Art Asn. Res: Specialize in early 20th century American painting. Publ: Auth, John Marin: A Stylist Analysis and a Catalogue Raisonne, Univ Ariz, 70; auth, A H Maurer, Smithsonian, 73; auth, Isabel Bishop, Univ Ariz, 74; auth, Graphic Styles of the American Eight, Univ Utah, 76. Mailing Add: 710 N Alamo Ave Tucson AZ 85711

REICHEK, JESSE
PRINTMAKER, PAINTER
b Brooklyn, NY, Aug 16, 16. Study: Inst Design, Chicago, 41-42; Acad Julian, Paris, 47-51. Work: Amon Carter Mus Western Art, Ft Worth, Tex; Art Inst Chicago; Bibliot Nat, Paris; Los Angeles Co Mus Art, Los Angeles; Mus Mod Art, New York; plus many others. Exhib: Mus Mod Art, 62, 65 & 69; one-man shows, Am Cult Ctr, Florence, Italy, 64 & Univ NMex Mus, 66; retrospective, Univ Southern Calif Art Mus, 67; San Francisco Mus Art, 69; plus many other group & one-man shows. Teaching: Assoc prof design, Univ Calif, Berkeley, 58-60, prof, 60-; artist in residence, Tamarind Lithography Workshop, Los Angeles, 66; res prof, Creative Arts Inst, Univ Calif, 66-67. Awards: Co-partic, Graham Found Grant, 62; Res Travel Grant, Creative Arts Inst, Univ Calif, summer 63; Tamarind Fel, 66. Publ: Auth, Jesse Reichek-Dessins, Ed Cahiers Art, Paris, 60; auth, La Montee de la Nuit, 61 & Fontis, 61, P A Benoit, Alex; auth, Etcetera, New Directions, 65; auth, The Architect & the City, Mass Inst Technol, 66; plus many others. Dealer: Betty Parsons Gallery 24 W 57th St New York NY 10019. Mailing Add: 5925 Red Hill Rd Petaluma CA 94953

REICHERT, DONALD KARL
PAINTER, EDUCATOR
b Libau, Man, Jan 11, 32. Study: Univ Man Sch Art, with Robert A Nelson & George Swinton & BFA, 56; Inst Allende, Mex, with James Pinto; Emma Lake Artist's Workshops, with Jules Olitzki, Stepan Wolpe, Lawrence Alloway, John Cage & Frank Stella. Work: Nat Gallery Can; Art Gallery Ont; Winnipeg Art Gallery; Mt Allison Univ; Montreal Mus Fine Arts. Exhib: Winnipeg Show Nat Biennial; Montreal Spring Show Nat; Nat Gallery Biennial; Visua '67, Nat Exhib; Midwest Painters. Teaching: Artist in residence, Univ NB, 61-62; asst prof painting, Univ Man Sch Art, 64- Awards: Bursary, 62 & Sr Nat Award, 67, Can Coun. Mem: Royal Can Acad Arts. Media: Acrylic, Oil, Ink. Mailing Add: 228 Glenwood Crescent Winnipeg MB R2L 1J9 Can

REICHERT, DONALD O
PAINTER, MUSEUM DIRECTOR
b Chicago, Ill, Nov 10, 12. Study: Am Int Col; with Emmy Zweybruck, Paval Tchelitchew & Owen Smith; Attingham, Nat Trust, England. Work: Mus Fine Arts, Springfield, Mass; Pittsfield Mus Art, Mass; Smith Col, Northampton, Mass; Fitchburg Mus Art, Mass; Olsen Found, Leete's Island, Conn. Collections Arranged: Maxfield Parrish Retrospect, 66; David Bumbeck, 66; Otto & Gertrud Natzler, 70; Weston Priory Porcelain, 72; American Indian Basketry, 75. Pos: Asst dir, Yale Univ, 51-54; asst dir, Olsen Found, Leetes Island, 54-55; cur, George Walter Vincent Smith Art Mus, Springfield, Mass, 55-70, dir, 70-77; retired. Awards: Barstow Award; Springfield Art League Award; Fitchburg Award. Mem: Am Asn Mus. Media: Watercolor, Collage. Publ: Co-auth, Maxfield Parrish Retrospect, 66; co-auth, The George Walter Vincent & Belle Townsley Smith Collection of Islamic Rugs, 71; auth of catalogues current with most mus exhibs. Mailing Add: 32 Park One Ct West Springfield MA 01087

REICHMAN, FRED (THOMAS)
PAINTER
b Bellingham, Wash, Jan 28, 25. Study: Univ Calif, Berkeley, BA(cum laude) & MA; San Francisco Art Inst. Work: San Francisco Mus Art, Oakland Mus Art Div, Santa Barbara Mus Art & Univ Art Mus, Berkeley, Calif; Edwin A Ulrich Mus Art, Wichita, Kans; plus others. Comn: Murals, Stanford Univ Med Sch, Palo Alto, Calif, 61 & San Francisco Art Festival, Civic Ctr, 68. Exhib: Calif Palace of Legion of Honor, San Francisco, 60; Rose Rabow Galleries, San Francisco, 58-76; 50 Calif Artists, Whitney Mus Am Art, New York, 62; one-man exhibs, San Francisco Mus Art, 56 & 69 & Santa Barbara Mus Art, 74; Expo 70, Osaka, Japan, 70; 7 Bay Area Artists, Oakland Mus, 71; Benson Gallery, Bridgehampton, NY, 66 & 72. Teaching: Instr art, Univ Calif Exten, San Francisco, 66- Awards: Artist's Coun Prize, San Francisco Art Asn Ann, 54; Purchase Award, San Francisco Art Festival, 64; Award of Merit, Art Festival City & Co San Francisco, 68. Bibliog: Judy Stone (auth), interview, San Francisco Chronicle, 10/15/63; Mimi Jacobs (auth), interview in Pac Sun, 1/16/75. Media: Oil, Acrylic. Dealer: Gallery Paule Anglim 710 Montgomery San Francisco CA 94111. Mailing Add: 1235 Stanyan St San Francisco CA 94117

REID, CHARLES
ART WRITER, PAINTER
b Cambridge, NY, Aug 12, 36. Study: S Kent Sch; Univ of Vt; Art Students League, study with Frank Reiley. Work: Yellowstone Art Ctr, Billings, Mont; Brigham Young Univ, Salt Lake City, Utah, Smith Col Mus, South Hampton, Mass. Comn: US Postage Stamp to Commemorate Family Planning, US Postal Dept. Exhib: Nat Acad of Design, Am Watercolor Soc & Am Inst of Arts & Letters, New York. Awards: First Altman Figure Award, 72 & Second Altman Figure Award, 74, Nat Acad of Design, New York; Childe Hassam Purchase Awards, Am Acad of Arts & Letters, 76 & 77. Mem: Assoc Nat Acad of Design. Style & Technique: Realism. Media: Watercolor; Oil. Publ: Auth & illusr, Figure Painting in Watercolor, 72, Portrait Painting in Watercolor, 73 & Flower Painting in Oil, 76, Watson-Guptil; co-auth, Six Artists Paint a Portrait, 74. Dealer: Far Gallery Two E 80th St New York NY. Mailing Add: Box 113 Greens Farms CT 06436

REID, ROBERT DENNIS
PAINTER, INSTRUCTOR
b Atlanta, Ga, 1924. Study: Clark Col, 41-43; Art Inst Chicago, 43-46; Parson Sch Design, New York, 48-50. Work: Myers Col, Birmingham, Ala; Univ Notre Dame, South Bend, Ind; Cornell Univ, Ithaca, NY; Montclair Art Mus, NJ; Mus et Galerie des Beaux-Arts, Bordeaux, France. Exhib: US Info Serv Tour, Paris, Brest, Vannes & Tours, 71; Black Artists: Two Generations, 71 & Recent Acquisitions, 71, Newark Mus; Black Artists Am, Whitney Mus Am Art, 71; Artists Postcards, Drawing Ctr, New York & Smithsonian Inst-sponsored tour, 78-79; one-man shows, Alonzo Gallery, 72, Leslie Rankow Gallery, New York, 74-75 & Lenore Gray Gallery, Providence, RI, 77; plus many other group & one-man shows. Teaching: Asst prof drawing, RI Sch Design, 70-; instr painting, State Univ NY Col Purchase, summer 75; vis instr, Parsons Sch of Design, New York, 77 & Drew Univ, Madison, NJ, 78. Awards: Childe Hassam Purchase Award, Am Acad Arts & Lett, 69. Media: Oil. Dealer: Elaine Benson Gallery Bridgehampton Long Island NY; Fairweather-Hardin Gallery 101 E Ontario St Chicago IL 60611. Mailing Add: 233 Lafayette St New York NY 10012

REID, (WILLIAM) RICHARD
PAINTER
b Regina, Sask, Apr 3, 30. Study: Univ Man Sch Art, BFA; Inst Allende, Mex; also with Oskar Kokoschka. Exhib: London, Eng, 60-63; Paris, France, 63; one-man shows, Griffiths Gallery, Vancouver, 68, Albert White Gallery, Toronto, 68, Pandora's Box Gallery, Victoria, 68 & Univ BC Fine Arts Gallery, 74; plus many others. Teaching: Instr painting & printmaking, Univ BC. Awards: Can Coun Awards, 63-64 & 67. Mailing Add: 268 River Rd Richmond BC V7C 1A1 Can

REIDER, DAVID H
DESIGNER, PHOTOGRAPHER
b Portsmouth, Ohio, Apr 6, 16. Study: Univ Buffalo; Cleveland Sch Art. Work: Milwaukee Art Inst, Wis; Mus Saarbrucken, Ger. Exhib: Milwaukee Art Inst; Albion Col; Univ Mich; Saarbrucken, Ger; Am Fedn Arts Exhib, 59-61. Teaching: Lectr design, Buffalo State Teachers Col, 42; instr design, Univ Buffalo, 42-46; head dept design, Albright Art Sch, 42-47; asst prof design, Univ Mich, Ann Arbor, 47-54, assoc prof, 55-59, prof, 59- Mem: Am Asn Univ Prof; Mus Mod Art (comt art educ); Soc Photog Educ. Publ: Contribr to numerous archit & indust publ. Mailing Add: Sch of Art Univ of Mich Ann Arbor MI 48104

REIF, RUBIN
PAINTER, EDUCATOR
b Warsaw, Poland, Aug 10, 10. Study: Cooper Union Art Sch; Art Students League; Hans Hofmann Sch Fine Arts; Acad Fine Arts, Florence, Italy. Work: Ohio Univ; Art Students League; Cooper Union Collection; Ark Indust Develop Comn; also in many pvt collections. Exhib: Am Fedn Arts Traveling Exhib, 48-49 & 67-69; Cincinnati Mus Asn; Ark Art Ctr, Little Rock, 60, 61 & 67-69; Springfield Art Mus, Mo, 67-69; Okla Art Ctr, 67-69; plus many other group & one-man shows. Teaching: Assoc prof art, Univ Ark, Fayetteville, currently. Awards: Prizes, Ohio State Fair, 52, Ark Festival Arts, 62 & 63 & Okla Ann, 64; plus many others. Style & Technique: Original, but based on religious or myth. Mailing Add: Dept of Art Univ of Ark Fayetteville AR 72701

REIFF, ROBERT FRANK
ART HISTORIAN, PAINTER
b Rochester, NY, Jan 23, 18. Study: Univ Rochester, AB, 41; Colorado Springs Fine Arts Ctr, 42, with Boardman Robinson & Adolf Dehn; Columbia Univ, MA, 50, PhD, 60; also with Hans Hofmann, 51. Work: Rochester Mem Art Gallery; Pasadena Art Inst; Middlebury Col; Allen Mem Art Gallery, Oberlin, Ohio. Exhib: Rochester Mem Art Gallery, 36-69; Albright-Knox Art Gallery, Buffalo, 52; Walker Art Ctr, 57; Berkshire Art Asn, 58; Stratton Mountain Summer Exhib, Vt, 71; Johnson Gallery, Middlebury, Vt, 78. Teaching: Instr sculpture, Muhlenberg Col, 47-49; instr sculpture & design, Oberlin Col, 50-55; asst prof humanities, Univ Chicago, 55-56; asst prof art hist, St Cloud State Col, Minn, 56-57; prof art hist & chmn art dept, Middlebury Col, 58- Pos: Trustee, Sheldon Mus, Middlebury, Vt, 60- Awards: Rochester Mem Art Gallery, 41, 45, 58 & 62; Walker Art Ctr, 52; Award for Before Processing, Albright-Knox Art Gallery, 56. Mem: Col Art Asn Am; Am Asn Univ Prof. Media: Oil, Acrylic, Watercolor. Res: Late painting of Arshile Gorky; modern art; nineteenth century European and Far Eastern art. Publ: Auth, Indian Miniatures: The Rajput Painters, Tuttle, 59 & Renoir, McGraw, 68; contribr, McGraw-Hill Dict Art, 69 & Encycl World Art, Vol 14, 70; auth articles in Col Art J, winter 70-71 & winter 71-72; auth, Arshile Gorky's Art From 1943-1948, Garland, 77. Mailing Add: 20 Gorham Lane Middlebury VT 05753

REILING, SUSAN WALLACE
CURATOR, ART HISTORIAN
b Denver, Colo, Aug 2, 40. Study: Moore Inst of Art, Philadelphia, BFA(interior design), 62; Univ Miami, MA(art hist & museology), 72, DA(Europ hist), 77. Collections Arranged: Religious Masks from Indonesia, Antique Europ Fans, 71, Two Centuries of Oriental Art in the Deering Collection, 72, 17th & 18th Century SAm Colonial Religious Sculpture, 72 & Antique Costumes, 73, Vizcaya Mus & Gardens, Miami, Fla. Teaching: Guest lectr interior design & decorative arts, Miami-Dade Community Col, 74-, coordr mus intern prog, Museology, 75- Pos: Cur decorative arts, Vizcaya Mus & Gardens, 71-76, cur of the collections, 76- Mem: Am Asn Mus; Int Inst for Conserv of Hist & Artistic Works; Am Inst for Conserv of Hist & Artist Works; Am Soc of Interior Designers; Comité Int de Photogrammetrie Architecturale. Res: Conservation methods; European decorative arts, architecture and landscape architecture, archaeology; cultural anthropology. Publ: Auth, The Restoration of a 17th century mantelpiece, Proj Quart, 75; auth, Vizcaya, Compass Mag, 75; auth, Vizcaya Mus & Gardens (official mus bk), Fla Natural Color, 76. Mailing Add: 100 Prospect Dr Miami FL 33133

REILLEY, PATRICK RICHARD
ART DEALER, APPRAISER
b San Francisco, Calif, Sept 16, 50. Study: Rockwell Col; Calif State Univ, Chico. Pos: Asst dir, Arts & Crafts Gallery, Chico, 67-70; asst dir, Kotzbeck Gallery, San Francisco, 70-72; dir & owner, Marquoit Galleries, 72- Bibliog: F Herbert Hoover (auth), Hoover's Guide to Galleries: San Francisco, Camaro, 74. Mem: Am Soc Appraisers. Specialty: Contemporary art, all media except crafts; primarily new West Coast artists. Mailing Add: c/o Marquoit Galleries 40 Gold St San Francisco CA 94133

REILLY, RICHARD
ART CRITIC
b New York, NY, Mar 13, 26. Pos: Art critic, San Diego Union. Mailing Add: PO Box 1530 La Jolla CA 92037

REIMANN, WILLIAM P
SCULPTOR, EDUCATOR
b Minneapolis, Minn, Nov 29, 35. Study: Yale Univ, BA, 57, BFA, 59, MFA, 61; with Josef Albers, Rico Lebrun, Robert M Engman, James Rosati, Gilbert Franklin, Seymour Lipton, Gabor Peterdi, Neil Welliver & Bernard Chaet. Work: Mus Mod Art, Whitney Mus Am Art & Rockefeller Univ, New York; Boston Mus Fine Arts. Comn: Sculpture, Yale Univ Dept Art & Archit, 64; suspended sculptures, Endo Labs, Garden City, NY, 65 & Rockefeller Univ, 70-71; courtyard sculpture, Harvard Col Observ, Cambridge, Mass, 72; sculpture, Transformation of a Rectangle, Revere Copper & Brass Corp, New York. Exhib: Structured Sculpture, Galerie Chalette, New York, 61-68; Sculpture Ann, 64-65 & Young Americans, 65, Whitney Mus Am Art; Int Exhib Contemp Painting & Sculpture, Carnegie Inst, Pittsburgh, 67-68; one-man show, Sculpture & Drawings, State Univ NY, 75. Teaching: Asst prof art, Old Dom Col, 61-64; lectr visual & environ studies, Harvard Univ, 64-, actg coordr studies, Carpenter Ctr Visual Arts, spring 71, sr preceptor visual & environ studies, 75- Media: Plexiglas, Stainless Steel, Pencil. Dealer: Galerie Chalette 9 E 88th St New York NY 10028; Art Resources 405 Avondale Houston TX 77006. Mailing Add: Gerry's Landing Cambridge MA 02138

REINDORF, SAMUEL
PAINTER
b Warsaw, Poland, Sept 1, 14; US citizen. Study: Cent Tech Sch, Toronto; Am Artists Sch, New York, scholar, with Saul Wilson Nahum Tschacbasov & Saul Baizerman. Work: Fairfield Mus, Conn; Toronto Art Gallery, Ont; Riverside Mus & Hall of Art, New York; Tygeson Gallery, Toronto. Exhib: Toronto Art Gallery, 34-38; Riverside Mus, 39-40; New York World's Fair, 63-65; Butler Inst Am Art, 63-65; 26th Ann Exhib Contemp Am Painting, Palm Beach, 64; Palace of Fine Art, Guadalajara, Mex; plus 25 one-man shows in US, Can & Mex. Awards: First Prize, 26th Exhib Contemp Am Painting, 64; Hon Mention for Clown, Conn Acad Fine Art, 68. Bibliog: Emily Genauer (auth), article in Herald Tribune, 63; Lotta Dempsey (auth), article in Toronto Daily Star, 66; Richard Day (auth), article in Bridgeport Post, 70; articles in El Informador, Guadalajara, 2/76, El Ocidental, Guadalajara, 2/76 & Times-Picayune, New Orleans, La, 11/76. Mem: Artists Equity Asn. Style & Technique: In drawings, watercolors style is Oriental in influence; paintings style between impressionistic and semi abstract. Media: Oil, Pastel, Watercolor. Publ: Auth articles in Art News, 64, Toronto Star, 65, Toronto Globe & Mail, 66, Excelsior, Mexico City, 67 & Dallas Morning News, 67. Dealer: Collector's Gallery New Orleans LA; Veerhoff Gallery Washington DC. Mailing Add: Apartado 285 San Miguel de Allende Guanajuato Mexico

REINER, MR & MRS JULES
COLLECTORS, PATRONS
Mr Reiner, b New York, NY, Mar 3, 18. Study: Mr Reiner, St Johns Univ, LLB; Mrs Reiner, NY Univ, BA. Mem: Friends Whitney Mus Am Art; assoc Guggenheim Mus; Mus Mod Art (contribr); Metrop Mus Art; Friends Hofstra Univ Mus. Collection: Late nineteenth century art; twentieth century art. Mailing Add: 295 Madison Ave New York NY 10017

REINHARDT, SIEGFRIED GERHARD
PAINTER, DESIGNER
b Eydkuhnen, Ger, July 31, 25; US citizen. Study: Wash Univ, AB. Work: Am Acad Arts & Lett; City Art Mus St Louis; Concordia Teachers Col; Southern Ill Univ; Whitney Mus Am Art; plus many others. Comn: Murals, Rand McNally, Skokie, Ill, Edison Bros Shoe Co, St Louis, Teamsters Local 88 Med Bldg & Nooter Corp, St Louis. Exhib: 14 shows, City Art Mus St Louis, 43-61; Whitney Mus Am Art, 51-55 & 60; Cincinnati Art Ctr, 55, 58 & 61; Pa Acad Fine Arts, 60-61; plus many others group & one-man shows. Teaching: Lectr, pvt groups, TV & radio; instr painting & drawing, Wash Univ, 55-70. Pos: Designer & executor stained glass windows, Emil Frei, Inc, 48-; painting Man of Sorrows, weekly TV show, 55, 57 & 58. Awards: Six Awards, St Louis Art Guild, 51-58; Awards, Cincinnati Contemp Art Ctr, 58 & Int Exhib Sacred Art, Trieste, Italy, 61; plus many others. Bibliog: Nathaniel Pousette-Dart (ed), American Painting Today, Hastings, 56; Lee Nordness (ed), Art: USA: Now, C J Bucher, 62. Mem: St Louis Art Guild. Dealer: Midtown Galleries 11 E 57th St New York NY 10022; Albrecht Gallery of Art 2818 Frederick Blvd St Joseph MO 64506. Mailing Add: 635 Craig Woods Dr Kirkwood MO 63122

REINHART, MARGARET EMILY
PAINTER
b De Pere, Wis, May 19, 08. Study: Fontbonne Col, AB; Univ of Mo, MA; studied with Jean Charlot, Walter Quirt, Boris Margo, Ben Cunningham, Gaell Lindstrom, four summers of European study. Work: Green Bay Wis Pub Sch Collection; Avila Col Collection. Comn: Calligraphic design for Pope Pius XII, comn by Bishop Edwin O'Hara, 49; calligraphic design for Bishop Marling, comn by Kansas City Diocesan Confraternity, 50; fresco mural, O'Shaughnessy Hall, work with Jean Charlot, comn by Notre Dame, 55; Stations of the Cross in metal, comn by S Dallavis, Foyle Chapel, Kansas City, 64. Exhib: Jr League of Voters, Kansas City, Mo, 68 & 69; Am Assoc of Univ Women, Kansas City, 74; one-woman shows, Neville Art Mus, Green Bay, 47, Blue Springs City Hall, Mo, 75. Collections Arranged: Women Religious of the Congregration of St Joseph at Avila Col, 70; Faculty of Cols, Kansas City Regional Coun for Higher Educ, 75. Teaching: Instr painting/design, St Teresa Acad, Kansas City, 45-50; asst prof painting/art hist-humanities, 50-65 & prof painting/art educ, Avila Col, 65-67; art inst, Vita Int Col Tour, Europe, 68 & 69. Pos: Art supervisor, St Louis & St Joseph parochial schs, 38-39; chmn dept fine arts, Avila Col, 63-64, coordr art, 69-76, artist-in-residence painting, 76- Awards: Medal of Honor, Pres Dallavis, Avila Col, 63; Grant for Study in New York, Kansas City Regional Coun for Higher Educ, 70; Service Award, Dean Richard Scott, Avila Col, 75. Mem: Nat Art Educ Assoc, 60-78. Style & Technique: Expressive style with metaphorical content. Media: Oil Painting, Watercolor (Aquarelle). Mailing Add: Avila Col 11901 Wornall Rd Kansas City MO 64145

REINSEL, WALTER N
PAINTER
b Reading, Pa, Aug 11, 05. Study: Pa Acad Fine Arts, with Arthur Carles; also with Andre L'Hote, Paris & Mirmande, France. Work: Philadelphia Mus Art; Reading Pub Mus, Pa; Woodmere Art Gallery, Philadelphia; Container Corp, Chicago, Ill; Oil, Capehart Farnsworth. Exhib: Many ann, Pa Acad Fine Arts, 38-60 & one-man show, 48; Philadelphia Watercolor Club Ann, 50-75; Am Watercolor Soc, 58-62; Audubon Artists; also 13 one-man shows. Pos: Art dir & supvr, N W Ayer & Son, 30-65. Awards: Harrison Morris Prize, Pa Acad Fine Arts Fel, 53-57; Philadelphia Sketch Club Medals, 52, 66 & 75; Philadelphia Watercolor Club Medal & Award, 67 & T Oakley Mem Prize, 68. Mem: Artists Equity Asn, Philadelphia Chap; Philadelphia Watercolor Club; Pa Acad Fine Arts; Philadelphia Art Alliance. Style & Technique: Semi-abstract emitional reaction and development of natural forms. Media: Watercolor, Oil, Acrylic. Mailing Add: 2219 Rittenhouse Sq Philadelphia PA 19103

REISMAN, PHILIP
PAINTER, ILLUSTRATOR
b Warsaw, Poland, July 18, 04; US citizen. Study: Art Students League, illus & compos with Wallace Morgan, life drawing with George Bridgeman; also etching & compos with Harry Wickey. Work: Bibliot Nat, Paris; Syracuse Univ Collection; Bates Col; Wadsworth Atheneum, Hartford, Conn; Hirschhorn Mus, Washington, DC; Norfolk Mus, Va. Comn: Mural, Bellevue Psychiat Hosp, New York, 38. Exhib: Mural Show, Mus Mod Art, New York, 32; Whitney Mus Am Art, New York; Nat Acad Design, 56; Art USA, 59; Pa Acad Fine Arts, Philadelphia. Teaching: Instr art, Workshop Sch, New York, 54-56; instr art, Five Towns Arts Found, 68-70; instr art, Educ Alliance, New York, 71- Awards: Mickiewitz Centennial Comt Prize, 55; Joseph Isidor Gold Medal, Nat Acad Design, 56; Childe Hassam Purchse Prize, 68. Bibliog: Lincoln Kirstein (auth), Philip Reisman, Hound & Horn, 33; Henry Goodman (auth), Philip Reisman, AD, 41; illustrations reproduced by Life, 41. Mem: Artists Equity Asn New York (vpres, pres). Style & Technique: Directly on a soft Japanese paper, usually Kochi for watercolors; oil on Belgian linen, with brush and paint knife for printing. Publ: Illusr, Anna Karenina, Vols I & II, 40 & Crime and Punishment, 44, Random. Dealer: Harbor Gallery 43 Main St Cold Spring Harbor NY 11724 Mailing Add: 4 W 18th St New York NY 10011

REITZENSTEIN, REINHARD
ENVIRONMENTAL ARTIST
b Uelzen, Ger, May 27, 49; Can citizen. Study: Ont Col Art. Work: Nat Gallery Can. Exhib: Young Contemporaries, 75; New Landscapes, Nat Gallery Can, 74; A Response to the Environment, Rutgers Univ, 75; Landscape Canada Traveling Exhib, Art Gallery Ont & Edmonton, 76; 17 Can Artists: A Protean View, Vancouver Art Gallery, 76; 03 23 03, Nat Gallery of Can, 77; Carmen Lamanna Gallery, Bologne Art Fair, Italy, 77; one-man shows, Carmen Lamanna Gallery, Toronto, Can, 75, 76 & 77 & London Art Gallery, Ont. Teaching: Toured with work through parts of Ontario, exhibiting, teaching & demonstrating work, 71 & 72. Awards: Can Coun Proj Cost Grants, 74 & 76-77; Ont Arts Coun Individual Artist Grants, 75 & 76-77. Bibliog: Walter Klepak (auth), Reinhard Reitzenstein, Queen Street Mag, 75; Joyce Zemans (auth), Reinhard Reitzenstein, Arts Can, 77; Beth Learn (auth), Reinhard Reitzenstein, Queen Street Mag, 77. Style & Technique: Aspects and characteristics of myself and of both the natural and human environments. Media: Mixed. natural environment such as wind, light, sound, and growth. Media: Publ: Auth, Natural Areas Divisions Charter, 75. Dealer: Carmen Lamanna Gallery 840 Yonge St Toronto ON Can. Mailing Add: RR 1 MacDonald's Corners ON K0G 1M0 Can

RELIS, SANDY
PAINTER, SCULPTOR
b New York, NY, Apr 27, 31. Study: Art Students League, scholar, with Corbino, Marsh & Brown; Brooklyn Mus Sch Art, scholar, with Max Bechmann & Baziotes; New Sch Social Res, scholar, with Egas & Prestipino; Philadelphia Mus Sch Art, scholar, with Matta. Exhib: One-man shows, Ataliar Gallery, 54, Gallery En Bas, 58, Neiman Gallery, 63 & Newton Free Libr, Mass, 65; one-man exhib, Holocaust Haggadah, Second Story Spring St Soc, 75 & 76 & Yeshiva Univ Mus, 76. Teaching: Instr children's summer prog, Guggenheim Mus, 73; lectr, Teachers Col, Columbia Univ, 74. Pos: Pres, Found Community Artists, 73; ed, Art Workers News, 73-74. Style & Technique: Expressionist in painting, construction and assemblage. Dealer: Noho Gallery 542 La Guardia Pl New York NY 10021. Mailing Add: 48 W 22nd St New York NY 10010

REMBERT, VIRGINIA PITTS
ART HISTORIAN
b Birmingham, Ala, Nov 15, 21. Study: Univ Montevallo, BA, 42; Columbia Univ, MA, 44, univ traveling fel, 67, Am Asn Univ Women fel, 67, PhD, 70; Univ Wis, MA, 59. Work: NC State Mus, Raleigh. Exhib: Ala State Exhib, Birmingham, 43; NC State Exhib, Raleigh, 48 & 49; Ala Watercolor Soc, Birmingham, 62. Teaching: Instr art, Beloit Col, 53-55; asst prof art hist, Mass Col Art, 56-60; from asst prof to prof art & chmn dept, Birmingham Southern Col, 60-73; prof art & chmn dept, Univ Ala, Birmingham, 74-75; Donaghey Distinguished prof art & art hist, Univ Ark, Little Rock, 75- Pos: Pres, Ala Watercolor Soc, 62-63; pres, Birmingham Art Asn, 70-71. Awards: Silver Bowl Award, Birmingham Area Chamber of Com, 70. Mem: Col Art Asn; Southeastern Col Art Asn (bd dirs, 74-76, pres, 77-78). Res: Mondrian's life, work and influence in America; Gorky, Newman, Baber and Bosch. Publ: Column, Birmingham News, 66-73; articles in Mass Col Art Alumni Bull, 58, Southeastern Col Art Asn Rev, 68-78; Birmingham Mus Art Anniversary Bull, 72 & Birmingham Art Asn Newslett, 72-74; auth, article in Arts Mag, 78. Mailing Add: 12060 Southridge Rd Little Rock AR 72212

REMBSKI, STANISLAV
PAINTER, WRITER
b Sochaczew, Poland. Study: Technol Inst, Warsaw, Poland; Ecole Beaux Arts, Paris; Royal Acad Fine Arts, Berlin, Ger. Work: President Woodrow Wilson, Woodrow Wilson House, Washington, DC; President Franklin D Roosevelt, F D R Mem Libr, Hyde Park, NY; Lawrence Cardinal Shehan, Archbishop's House, Baltimore; Fleet Adm William D Leahy, Hist Soc, Madison, Wis; Leon Dabo, Nat Acad Design, New York. Comn: Conversion of William Duke of Acquitaine, Trustees of St Barnard's Sch, Gladstone, NJ, 31; I Am the Life, Mem Episcopal Church, 62. Exhib: One-man shows, Dudensing Galleries, New York, 27, Carnegie Hall Gallery, New York, 34, Arthur U Newton Galleries, New York, 35, Baltimore Mus Art, 47; Baltimore Inst Art, Md, 50. Pos: Vis critic, Md Inst Art, 52-55. Mem: Salmagundi Club; Allied Artists Am; Nat Soc Mural Painters; Am Artists Prof League; Charcoal Club, Baltimore. Media: Oil, Crayon, Pencil. Publ: Auth, Mysticism in Art, Leonardo da Vinci Forum, 36; auth, Freedom, New Age, 72. Mailing Add: 1404 Park Ave Baltimore MD 21217

REMENICK, SEYMOUR
PAINTER
b Detroit, Mich, Apr 3, 23. Study: Tyler Sch Fine Arts, 40-42; Hans Hofmann Sch, 46-48. Work: Philadelphia Mus; Pa Acad Fine Arts; RI Sch Design; Phoenix Art Mus; Dallas Mus Contemp Art. Exhib: Am Painting, Rome, Italy, 55; Four Young Americans, RI Sch Design, 56; 11 Contemp Am Painters, Paris, France, 56; Art Inst Chicago Ann, 61; Drawing Show, Philadelphia Mus, 65. Awards: Louis Comfort Tiffany Found Grant, 55; Benjamin Altman Landscpae Prize, Nat Acad Design, 60; Hallmark Purchase Award, 60. Media: Oil. Dealer: Pearl Fox Gallery 103 Windsor Ave Melrose Park PA 19126. Mailing Add: 1836 Pine St Philadelphia PA 19103

REMINGTON, DEBORAH WILLIAMS
PAINTER
b Haddonfield, NJ, June 25, 35. Study: San Francisco Art Inst, BFA, 57; studies in Asia, 57-59. Work: Whitney Mus Am Art, New York; Mus Boymans von Beuningen, Rotterdam, Holland; Centre d'Art et de Cult George Pompidou, Paris; San Francisco Mus Art; Toledo Mus Art. Exhib: One-person shows, Bykert Gallery, New York, 67, 69, 72 & 74, Galerie Darthea Speyer, Paris, 68, 71 & 73, Hamilton Gallery, New York, 77 & Portland Ctr for the Visual Arts, Ore, 77; L'Art Vivant Americain, Fondation Maeght, St Paul de Vence, France, 70; Whitney Mus Ann Exhib, 72; 71st Am Exhib, Art Inst Chicago, 74; Image, Color, and Form, Toledo Mus Art, 75; Painting Endures, Inst Contemp Art, Boston, 75. Awards: Fel, Tamarind Inst, Albuquerque, 73. Bibliog: R C Kenedy (auth), Deborah Remington, Art Int, summer 74; Donald Miller (auth), Deborah Remington's Portraits of Objects in Space, Art News, 10/75; Corinne Robins (auth), Deborah Remington, Paintings without answers, Arts Mag, 4/77. Media: Oil on Canvas. Mailing Add: 309 W Broadway New York NY 10013

REMSEN, JOHN EVERETT, II
ART CONSULTANT, PAINTER
b Glen Cove, NY, Apr 21, 39. Study: Pratt Inst, BFA, NY Univ, MA(art educ); drawing with Richard Linder, painting with Stephen Greene; graphic workshops with Jacob Landau, Fritz Eichenberg & Walter Rogalski. Work: Pratt Inst, Brooklyn, NY. Exhib: Guild Hall, East Hampton, NY; City Center Galleries, New York, 60; IBM Galleries, New York, 61; Paumanok Galleries, East Norwich, NY, 63; Parish Art Mus, Southampton, NY, 68, 69 & 71; one-man exhibs, Suffolk Community Col, Selden, NY, 66 & State Univ at Stony Brook, NY, 77-78. Pos: Dir, Crane Korchin Galleries, Manhasset, NY, 70-72; mgr, Eileen Kulick

Gallery, New York, 74; dir, Viridian Gallery, New York, 74-76; consult, Jerry Brewster Gallery, New York, 76. Specialty: Nineteenth-twentieth century American painting and graphic arts. Mailing Add: 77 Main St Box 803 Setauket NY 11733

REMSING, (JOSEPH) GARY
PAINTER, SCULPTOR
b Spokane, Wash, Sept 18, 46. Study: San Jose State Univ, BA & MA. Work: De Saisset Mus, Univ Santa Clara; Oakland Mus. Exhib: One-man exhibs, De Saisset Mus, 69 & 74, Atherton Gallery, Menlo Park, Calif, 70 & 72, William Sawyer Gallery, San Francisco, 71, 73 & 74 & Gerard John Hayes Gallery, Los Angeles, 72; Selection of Young Contemp Calif Artists, 69 & 70; Looking West 1970, Joslyn Art Mus, Omaha, 70; plus others. Teaching: Instr, Modesto Jr Col, 71- Awards: Award, Walnut Creek Civic Arts Ctr Gallery, 69; Award, Maryville Col (Tenn), 70; Award, Calif Arts Comn, 70. Bibliog: Articles in San Francisco Chronicle, 9/8/69 & 5/7/71; articles in Artforum, 11/69; articles in Art Wk, 5/71, 4/72 & 6/74; plus others. Dealer: William Sawyer Gallery 3043 Clay St San Francisco CA 94115. Mailing Add: 1418 Oakwood Dr Modesto CA 95350

RENICK, CHARLES COOLEY
SCULPTOR, EDUCATOR
b Williamsburg, Va, Apr 29, 25. Study: Va Commonwealth Univ, BFA & MFA. Teaching: Prof sculpture, Va Commonwealth Univ, 53- Mailing Add: PO Box 74 Bumpass VA 23024 Richmond VA PO Box 74 Bumpass VA 23024

RENK, MERRY
DESIGNER, SCULPTOR
b Trenton, NJ, July 8, 21. Study: Sch Indust Arts, Trenton, NJ; Inst Design, Chicago. Work: San Francisco State Col Libr; San Francisco Art Comn; Univ Wis; Oakland Mus Art, Calif. Comn: Wedding crown, Johnson's Wax Collection, Objects USA, 70. Exhib: One-woman show, Nordness Galleries, New York, 70, De Young Mem Mus, San Francisco, 71 & Mus Hist & Technol, Smithsonian Inst, 71-72; Objects USA Traveling Exhib, US & Europe, 70-72. Awards: San Francisco Art Comn Awards, 54 & 59; San Francisco Women Artists Award, 65. Bibliog: Uchida (auth), Jewelry by Merry Renk, Crafts Horizons, 11 & 12/61; C McCann (auth), Three fine craftsmen, Artweek, 2/71; A Fried (auth), article in San Francisco Examr, 3/71. Mem: Metal Arts Guild (pres, 53). Style & Technique: Contemporary constructions; plique-a-jour enamel; metamorphic organic symbols. Dealer: Nordness Galleries 237 E 75th St New York NY 10021. Mailing Add: 17 Saturn St San Francisco CA 94114

RENNELS, FREDERIC M
SCULPTOR
b Sioux City, Iowa, June 4, 42. Study: Eastern Ill Univ, BS, 64; Stanford Univ, summer grad sculpture study, 67-68; Cranbrook Acad Art, MFA, 71. Comn: Large scale outdoor sculpture, Iowa State Univ, 75. Exhib: One-man shows, Spectrum Gallery, New York, 72, Razor Gallery, New York, 74 & De Pauw Univ, Chicago, 76; Multiples USA, Kalamazoo, Mich, 71; Detroit Art Inst, 74; Chicago Art Inst, 75; Art in Pub Places Exhib, Cheney Mus, Spokane, Wash, 77; plus others. Awards: Cranbrook Acad Founders Award, 70; Multiple USA Award, 70. Style & Technique: Contemp abstract sculptures of varying scales. Media: Mixed. Mailing Add: c/o Art Dept Univ of Puget Sound Tacoma WA 98416

RENNER, ERIC
PAINTER, PHOTOGRAPHER
b Philadelphia, Pa, Nov 6, 41. Study: Cranbrook Acad of Art, MFA; Univ Cincinnati, BS; study with John Wood, D M Yeary, Laurie Klingensmith. Work: Mus of Mod Art, New York; Nat Gallery of Canada, Ottawa; Mus of Mod Art, Mexico City; Museo de Arte de Sao Paulo, Brazil; Visual Studies Workshop, New York. Exhib: Nat Gallery of Canada, 71, 73 & 75; Museo de Arte de Sao Paulo, Brazil, 75 & one-man show, 78; one-man show, Mus of Mod Art, Mexico City, 71. Awards: Nat Endowment for the Arts, Artist in the School, 76. Media: Pinhole Photography, Watercolor with Neutral Glue. Publ: Co-auth, Primitive Systems for Recycling Human Waste, Subsistance Press, 69; auth, From the Stars, the Sun, and the Air for Laurie, 75 & auth, The Horsefetter, 77, Visual Studies Workshop Dealer: Visual Studies Workshop 31 Prince St Rochester NY 14607. Mailing Add: Star Rte Box 42 Ojo Caliente NM 87549

RENNICK, DAN
PAINTED CONSTRUCTIONS, PAINTER
b July 3, 05; US citizen. Study: NY Univ, BA; New Sch Social Res, with Henry Pearson and Licio Isolani. Work: Musee Carnavalet, Paris; Indianapolis Mus of Art; Munson-Williams-Proctor Inst, Utica; also incl in 96 pvt collections. Pos: Mag design consult; formerly vpres & ed, Hearst Mag, New York, retired. Mem: Artists Equity Asn of NY; Allied Artists Am. Style & Technique: Painted constructions; shadow boxes; shaped masonite. Media: Mixed Media, Acrylic. Mailing Add: 1415 Glenwood Rd Brooklyn NY 11230

RENNIE, HELEN (SEWELL)
PAINTER, DESIGNER
b Cambridge, Md. Study: Corcoran Sch Art, hon student; Nat Acad Design; also with Charles W Hawthorne, Provincetown. Work: Phillips Gallery Collections, Washington, DC; C Law Watkins Collection, Am Univ; US Dept Com, Washington, DC; US Dept State, Washington, DC; Clarendon Trust Co, Arlington, Va. Comn: Mural design, Roosevelt High Sch, Washington, DC, Pub Works Art Proj, 33-34. Exhib: Exhib, Mus Mod Art, New York, 46, Recent Drawings USA, 56; Corcoran Gallery Art Biennial, Washington, DC, 59; Baltimore Mus Regional, 64; Washington Artists, Phillips Gallery, 71-72; one-person shows, Baltimore Mus of Art, Phillips Gallery, Washington, DC, Univ PR, San Juan & Franz Bader Gallery, Washington, DC. Teaching: Instr drawing & painting, Phillips Gallery Sch; instr drawing & painting, Art League Washington. Pos: Artist-designer, War Food Admin, Washington, DC, 40-45; art dir, US Navy Dept, Washington, DC, 48-51; visual info off, US Off Price Stabilization, Washington, DC, 51-53. Awards: Five awards from various donors, Soc Washington Artists, 48-71; Baltimore Mus Regional, 59 & 60. Mem: Soc Washington Artists (vpres); Women in the Visual Arts. Media: Oil, Acrylic. Dealer: Franz Bader Gallery 2124 Pennsylvania Ave NW Washington DC 20037. Mailing Add: 1306 30th St NW Washington DC 20007

RENOUF, EDDA
PAINTER, PRINTMAKER
b Mexico City, Mex, June 17, 43; US citizen. Study: Sarah Lawrence Col, Bronxville, NY, BA, 65; Acadamie Julian, Paris, 63-64; Sorbonne, Paris, 63-64; Institut D'Art Et D'Archeologie, Paris, 63-64; Art Students League, New York, 67-68; Sch of Arts, Columbia Univ, MFA, 71. Work: Mus of Mod Art, New York; Whitney Mus of Am Art, New York; Philadelphia Mus of Art, Pa; Musee De Grenoble, Grenoble, France; Ctr George Pompidou, Paris, France. Exhib: Actualite d'un Bilan, Yvon Lambert, Paris, 72; Recent Acquisitions, Mus of Mod Art, New York, 73; Eighth Paris Biennial, Musee D'Art Moderne, Paris, 73; Prospekt, Dusseldorf Art Mus, Ger, 73; Fundamental Painting, Stedelijk Mus, Amsterdam, Holland, 75; Dorothy & Herbert Vogel Collection, Inst of Contemp Art, Philadelphia, 75; Prints: Bochner, Lewitt, Mangold, Marden, Martin, Renouf, Rockburne & Ryman, Art Gallery of Ont, Toronto, Can, 76; Extraordinary Women, Mus of Mod Art, New York, 77; Matrix 36, Wadsworth Atheneum, Hartford, Conn, 78; Contemp Drawing/New York, Univ Calif Santa Barbara, 78. Awards: Gurgundfund (Fel to Paris), Mus of Fine Arts Exhib, Columbia Univ, New York, 71-72. Bibliog: Hayden Herrera (auth), Edda Renouf at Julian Pretto, Art in Am, 1/77; Margaret Betz (auth), New Editions, Art News, 9/77; Henry Martin (auth), In Milan Spring, Art Int, 5/75. Mem: Mus of Mod Art, New York; New Mus, New York. Style & Technique: Abstract, reduced compositions removing threads from linen canvas and applying acrylic paint; use chalk in drawings. Media: Acrylic, Linen Canvas, Pastel Chalk, Paper. Publ: Auth, Lines, Flash Art Edition, 74; auth, Lines and Non-Lines, Lapp Princess Press Ltd, New York, 77. Dealer: Blum-Helman Gallery 13 E 75th St New York NY 10021; Yvon Lambert Gallery 5 Rue Grenier-St-Lazare 75003 Paris France. Mailing Add: 20 W 30th St New York NY 10001

RENOUF, EDWARD PECHMANN
PAINTER, SCULPTOR
b Hsiku, China, Nov 23, 06; US citizen. Study: Phillips Andover Acad, 24; Harvard Univ, 28; Columbia Univ, 36-40; also drawing & painting with Carlos Merida, Mex, 41. Comn: Steel sculpture, Horace Mann Sch, Riverdale, NY, 65, mural painting, 67. Exhib: Whitney Mus Am Art Sculpture Ann, 60 & 64; three-man show, Zabriskie Gallery, New York, 60; Conn Acad Show, Wadsworth Atheneum, Hartford, 61; Pa Acad Fine Arts 161st Ann, Philadelphia, 66; plus others. Teaching: Vis artist painting, Akad Bildenden Kunste, Munich, Ger, 70. Awards: Honorable Mention, Conn Acad, 61; Second Prize for Sculpture, Sharon Creative Arts Found, 64. Bibliog: John Canaday (auth), Art: an image is created, 1/5/60, Brian O' Doherty (auth), article, 3/31/62 & Stuart Preston (auth), article, 2/27/65, New York Times; plus others. Mem: Sculptors Guild; Fedn Mod Painters & Sculptors. Style & Technique: Calligraphic abstraction; abstract and figurative. Media: Acrylic, Oil, Gouache; Graphite; Wax; Steel. Publ: Contribr, Dyn, Mex, 42. Dealer: Allan Stone Gallery 48 E 86th St New York NY 10028. Mailing Add: East St Washington CT 06793

RENSCH, ROSLYN (ROSLYN MARIA ERBES)
ART HISTORIAN, WRITER
b Detroit, Mich. Study: Northwestern Univ, BM & MM; Univ Ill, MA(art hist); Univ Wis-Madison, PhD(art hist), 64. Teaching: Lectr art hist & humanities & chmn div humanities, Nat Col Educ, 62-65; prof art hist & humanities, Ind State Univ, 65-76. Mem: Col Art Asn Am; Midwest Art Hist Soc; Int Ctr Medieval Art. Res: Pre-Romanesque stone carving in the British Isles; representations of the harp in art monuments; American landscape painting. Publ: Auth, Harp, its History, Technique & Repertoire, Praeger, 69; auth, Development of the medieval harp: A re-examination of the evidence of the Utrecht Psalter and its progeny, Gesta, Vol 11, No 2; auth, Harp carvings on the Irish crosses, Am Harp J, winter 74; auth, Landscape painting in America to c 1900 (Turman Gallery catalog), Ind State Univ, 75. Mailing Add: 701 Delaware Ave Terre Haute IN 47804

REOPEL, JOYCE
DRAFTSMAN
b Worcester, Mass, Jan 21, 38. Study: Ruskin Sch Drawing & Fine Arts, Oxford Univ; Yale-Norfolk Art Sch, fel; Worcester Mus Art Sch, grad; Radcliffe Inst, scholar. Work: Ohio State Univ; Fogg Art Mus, Cambridge, Mass; Pa Acad Fine Arts, Philadelphia; Addison Gallery Am Art, Andover, Mass; Univ Mass, Amherst; plus others. Exhib: Boston Arts Festival; Nat Inst Arts & Lett; Worcester Mus Art; De Cordova & Dana Mus, Lincoln. Mass; Victoria & Albert Mus, London, Eng; plus others. Awards: Nat Inst Arts & Lett; Wheaton Col Award for Res; Ford Found Grant. Style & Technique: Figurative; humanist. Mailing Add: c/o Forum Gallery 1018 Madison Ave New York NY 10021

REPLINGER, DOT (DOROTHY THIELE)
WEAVER, DESIGNER
b Chicago, Ill, Jan 30, 24. Study: Sch Art Inst Chicago, BA(Ed), study with Carolyn Howlett & Else Regensteiner. Work: Amerinvesco, Chicago; Caterpillar Int, Peoria, Ill; Haskins & Sells, Stand Oil Bldg, Chicago. Comn: Ark curtain, Sinai Temple, Champaign, Ill, 76; wall piece, Friends of Champaign Pub Libr, Ill, 78. Exhib: Craft Multiples, Renwick Gallery, Smithsonian, Washington, DC, 75; Marietta Crafts Nat, Ohio, 75 & 77; Miss River Crafts Show, Brooks Mem Art Gallery, Memphis, Tenn, 76; Mid-States Craft Exhib, Evansville Mus Arts, Ind, 77; Clay & Fiber—15 Viewpoints, Wustum Mus Fine Arts, Racine, Wis, 78. Awards: Craftsmen's Fel, Nat Endowment for the Arts, 76-77; Creativity Award, Miss River Craft Show, 76; Purchase Award, Mid-States Craft Exhib, Evansville, Ind, 77. Mem: Am Crafts Coun (state rep, 70-76); Handweavers Guild Am; Midwest Weavers Cong. Media: Fiber. Mailing Add: 4 Burnett Circle Urbana IL 61801

RESEK, KATE FRANCES
PAINTER
b Cleveland, Ohio. Study: Univ Wis, Madison, BS(fine arts); Columbia Univ, MFA with Stephen Green & Adja Yunckers, 69. Work: Aldrich Mus of Contemp Art, Ridgefield, Conn; Neuberger Mus, Purchase, NY; Housatonic Mus, Bridgeport, Conn; Col of Med of NJ, Newark; Columbia Univ. Exhib: One-man shows, Soho 20, New York, 74 & 76, Noyes, Van Cline & Davenport, New York, 77 & Bertha Urdang Gallery, New York, 77; Contemp Reflections 1974-1975, Aldrich Mus of Contemp Art, 75; 40th Ann Show, Butler Inst of Am Art, Youngstown, Ohio, 76; New Acquisitions, Neuberger Mus, 76; New Acquisitions, Aldrich Mus of Contemp Art, 78. Teaching: Instr drawing/painting, Fairleigh Dickinson Univ, Teaneck, NJ, 73-74; instr drawing/painting, State Univ NY, Purchase, 75-76. Awards: Silver Hill Award/Painting, 71 & Inez Leon Greenberg Award/Drawing, 71, Silvermine 22nd New Eng Exhib. Bibliog: Lawrence Alloway (auth), Women Artists of the 70's, Metrop Mus of Art, 4/76; Ellen Lubell (auth), Kate Resek, Arts Mag, 12/76; Janice Glander-Bandyk (auth), Kate Resek, Arts Mag, 4/77. Mem: Women's Caucus of Art; Women in the Arts; Col Art Asn. Style & Technique: Large paintings using crushed pastels and acrylic stain; drawings using pastels; abstract. Media: Pastel and acrylic. Mailing Add: 152 Crescent Ave Leonia NJ 07605

RESIKA, PAUL
PAINTER
b New York, NY, Aug 15, 28. Study: With S Wilson, 40-44 & Hans Hofmann, 45-47, New York; also in Venice & Rome, 50-54. Work: Indianapolis Mus Art; Colby Col; Chase Manhattan Bank; Sheldon Mem Gallery, Univ Nebr-Lincoln; Joseph H Hirshhorn Collection, Washington, DC; Sara Roby Found; Mus Contemp Art, Bordighera, Italy. Exhib: One-man exhibs, George Dix Gallery, New York, 48, Peridot-Washburn Gallery, New York, 64-73 & Graham Gallery, New York, 76; Nat Acad Design, New York, 61 & 72; Am Landscape, Smithsonian Inst, Washington, DC, 68; Hassam Exhib, Am Acad Arts & Lett, 69-71 & 73, Award Exhib, 75; Calton Gallery, New York, 75; Art of Pastel, Graham Gallery,

New York, 77. Teaching: Adj prof painting & drawing, Cooper Union, 66-; instr painting, Art Students League, 68-69; instr, Skowhegan Sch Painting, 73; instr Grad Sch, Univ Pa, 74. Pos: Artist in residence, Dartmouth Col, 72. Awards: Louis Comfort Tiffany Found Grant, 59; Ingram Merrill Prize, 69; Hassam Purchase Prize, Am Acad Arts & Lett, 71 & Award, 77. Bibliog: Claire Nicholas White (auth), Resika's...mountains, Art News, 4/67; Mimi Shorr (auth), Passions in balance, Am Artist, 12/72; article, Art in Am, 7-8/76; also numerous reviews & articles in New York Times, Time, Arts, Art News, Art Int, Am Artist. Mem: Assoc mem Nat Acad of Design. Dealer: Graham Gallery 1014 Madison Ave New York NY 10021. Mailing Add: 114 E 84th St New York NY 10028

RESNICK, MARCIA AYLENE
PHOTOGRAPHER, CONCEPTUAL ARTIST
b New York, NY, Nov 21, 50. Study: NY UNiv, 67-69; Cooper Union, BFA, 72; Calif Inst Arts, MFA, 73. Work: Mus Mod Art, New York; Metrop Mus Art, New York; George Eastman House, Int Mus Photog; Contemp Arts Mus, Houston; San Francisco Mus. Exhib: Transparency 72, Exten Ctr Gallery, Univ Calif, San Francisco, 72; Variety Show II, Humboldt State Univ, 74; Photography Unlimited, Harvard Fogg Mus, 74; Extended Document, George Eastman House, Rochester, 75; Women of Photography, San Francisco Mus & Traveling Show, 75. Teaching: Instr photog, Queens Col, New York, Cooper Union, New York & Int Ctr of Photog. Awards: Nat Endowment Arts Photography grants, 75 & 78; Creative Artists Pub Serv Prog grant, 77. Bibliog: Pop up people, Time-Life Yearbk, 74; Layered eye, Camera 35 Mag, 7/74; Peter Frank (auth), Picture books, Soho Weekly News, 7/17/75. Style & Technique: Photographs manipulated with pencil or paint to make a specific art statement. Publ: Auth, Landscape, 75; auth, See, 75; auth, Tahitian Eve, 75; auth, Re-visions, 78; auth, Landscape-Loftscape, 78. Dealer: Light Gallery 1018 Madison Ave New York NY 10002. Mailing Add: 530 Canal St New York NY 10013

RESNICK, MILTON
PAINTER
b Bratslav, Russia, Jan 8, 17; US citizen. Study: Paris & New York. Work: Calif Mus Fine Arts, Berkeley; Mus Mod Art & Whitney Mus Am Art, New York; Wadsworth Atheneum; Wake Forest Col, Winston-Salem, NC; also many others including pvt collections. Exhib: One man show, De Young Mem Mus, San Francisco, 55; four shows, Whitney Mus Am Art, 57-67 & Whitney Biennial, 73; San Francisco Mus Art, 63; Univ Tex Art Mus, 64 & 68; Jewish Mus, NY, 67; Mus Mod Art, New York, 69; Univ Calif, Santa Barbara, 74; plus many other group & one-man shows. Teaching: Instr, Pratt Inst, Brooklyn; vis lectr & critic, var schs, RI, Yale Summer Sch, Wagner Col & Silvermine; vis prof, Univ Calif, Berkeley, 55-56; instr, NY Univ, 64-; vis lectr & critic, NY Studio Sch, 65-; vis prof, Univ Wis-Madison, 66-67. Dealer: Max Hutchinson Gallery 138 Greene St New York NY 10012. Mailing Add: 80 Forsyth St New York NY 10002

RETZER, HOWARD EARL
COLLECTOR, PAINTER
b Rochester, Pa, Jan 31, 25. Study: Geneva Col, Pa; Univ Colo, BA; Temple Univ Sch of Med, MD; study for five years with Pawel A Kontny. Exhib: Fur Rendevous, Anchorage, Alaska, 75; Zang Mus, Denver, Colo, 77-78. Bibliog: John Jellico (auth), Howard Retzer, Southwestern Art, 77. Style & Technique: Landscapes, especially the West and Alaska done on marble dust and linen. Media: Oil with Palette Knife & Brush; Mixed Media with Watercolor and Pastel. Collection: Many works of Kontny, as well as Fechin, Frank Hoffman, Timmermans, Frank Tenny Johnson & others. Dealer: O'Briens Art Emporium 7122 Stetson Dr Scottsdale AZ 85251. Mailing Add: 5800 S Elati Littleton CO 80120

REUTER, LAUREL J
GALLERY DIRECTOR, LECTURER
b Devils Lake, NDak, Oct 17, 43. Study: Univ NDak, MA, 74. Collections Arranged: American Women Artists (with catalog), 73; Kenneth Patchen (with catalog), 74; Indian Images (with catalog), 76; John Ihle Retrospective (with catalog), 76; Jiri Anderle (with catalog), 77; and numerous others. Pos: Founder & dir, Univ Art Gallery, Univ NDak, 70- Awards: Mus Internship Fel, Minneapolis Inst Arts, 72; Nat Endowment Arts Mus Prof Fel, 73. Mem: Am Asn Mus. Mailing Add: 321 Princeton St Grand Forks ND 58201

REVINGTON, GEORGE D, III
COLLECTOR
Collection: Modern American painting and sculpture, exhibited at the American Federation of Arts, Museum of Modern Art and at various galleries and art shows. Mailing Add: 1211 Ravinia Rd West Lafayette IN 47906

REVOR, REMY
DESIGNER, EDUCATOR
b Chippewa Falls, Wis, Sept 17, 14. Study: Mt Mary Col, BA; Sch Art Inst Chicago, BFA & MFA. Work: Milwaukee Art Ctr; St Paul Art Ctr, Minn; Mus Tex Tech Univ; Objects USA, Johnson Collection Contemp Crafts. Exhib: Wis Designer Craftsmen Ann, 53-72; Mus Contemp Crafts, New York, 62, 63 & 66-68; Wichita Art Asn, 64; Chicago Pub Libr, 64 & 74. Teaching: Assoc prof textile design, Mt Mary Col, 52-70, prof, 70-; instr textile design, Arrowmont Sch Arts & Crafts, Gatlinburg, Tenn, summers 69-78; vis lectr, Univ Tenn, Knoxville, 73-74. Awards: Louis Comfort Tiffany Found Award for Textiles, 62; Am Inst Architects Gold Medal Award for Craftsmanship, 67; Fulbright Award for Res Textile Design, Finland, 69-70. Mem: Wis Designer Craftsmen (publ chmn, 66-68); Col Art Asn Am. Style & Technique: Silk screen textiles suitable for wall hangings, clothing; bold pattern, vivid color; batiks. Mailing Add: Mt Mary Col Milwaukee WI 53222

REWALD, JOHN
ART HISTORIAN, EDUCATOR
b Berlin, Ger, May 12, 12; US citizen. Study: Univ Hamburg, 31; Univ Frankfurt am Main, 31-32; Sorbonne, PhD, 36. Teaching: Lectr on visits with artists in Europe & forgeries of modern art; vis prof, Princeton Univ, 61; prof art hist, Univ Chicago, 64-71; prof art hist, Grad Ctr, City Univ New York, 71- Pos: Cur pvt collection, John Hay Whitney; assoc, Mus Mod Art, 43- Awards: Prix Charles Blanc, Acad Francaise, 41; Knight, Legion of Honor, 54. Publ: Auth, The History of Impressionism, 46, 55, 61, & 73 & Post-Impressionism—from Van Gogh to Gauguin, 56 & 62, Mus Mod Art; auth bks on Cezanne, Bonnard, Pissarro, Seurat, Manzu, Degas & Maillol; ed, Cezanne, Gauguin, Pissarro Letters; plus many others. Mailing Add: 1075 Park Ave New York NY 10028

REY, H A
ILLUSTRATOR, WRITER
b Hamburg, Ger, Sept 16, 98; US citizen. Study: Univ Munich; Univ Hamburg. Work: Kerlan Collection; Univ Southern Miss; Univ Ore. Mem: Am Craftsmans Coun. Media: Gouache, India Ink, Crayon. Publ: Numerous illustrated children's books, Harper, 41-62; also Curious George series & others, Houghton, 41-66; illusr, The Stars: A New Way to See Them & The Constellations, Hougton-Mifflin. Mailing Add: 14 Hilliard St Cambridge MA 02138

REYNAL, JEANNE
MOSAIC ARTIST
b White Plains, NY, Apr 1, 03. Study: Atelier, Paris, France, apprentice with Boris Anrep, 30-38. Work: Ford Found, White Plains; Mus Mod Art, New York; Walker Art Ctr, Minneapolis; Whitney Mus Am Art; Rockefeller Univ; plus many others. Comn: Ford Found Prog Adult Educ, White Plains, 59; Our Lady of Florida, Palm Beach, 62; Cliff House, Avon, Conn, 62; Nebr State Capitol, Lincoln, 65 & 66; SS Joachim & Ann Church, Queens Village, NY, 67; plus many others. Exhib: Loeb Student Ctr, NY Univ, 61; PVI Gallery, New York, 64; San Francisco Mus Art Traveling Exhib, Lincoln, Nebr, Amarillo, Tex, Boston & Montreal, 64; Betty Parsons Gallery, 71; Newport Art Asn, RI, 71; Craft Horizons, 71 & 76; Bodley Gallery, New York, 76; plus many others. Awards: Emmanuel Walter Fund Purchase Prize for Yuba (mosaic), San Francisco Art Asn, 45. Bibliog: Hans Unger (auth), Practical Mosaic, 65; Barbara Poses Kafka (auth), Art & architecture, Craft Horizons, 1-2/68; Paul Falkenberg (producer & ed), Mosaics: the Work of Jeanne Reynal (film), 68. Mailing Add: 240 W 11th St New York NY 10014

REYNARD, CAROLYN COLE
PAINTER, INSTRUCTOR
b Wichita, Kans, Aug 6, 34. Study: Wichita State Univ, BFA; Ohio Univ, MFA. Work: Wichita State Univ. Exhib: Air Capitol Annual, Wichita Art Mus, Kans, 56; Exhibition 80, Huntington Galleries, WVa, 57-59; Santa Barbara Art Mus, Calif, 60; Artists of Santa Barbara, Faulkner Gallery, Santa Barbara, 60-62; Artists of Central New York, Munson-Williams-Proctor Inst Mus Art, Utica, NY, 64-65 & 67. Teaching: Instr art, Ohio Univ, 58-59; asst prof art, State Univ NY Col Oswego, 63-69; instr art, Wappingers Cent Sch Dist, NY, 69- Mem: NY State Art Teachers Asn; Dutchess Co Art Asn. Style & Technique: Organic abstraction of natural forms; transparent glazes. Media: Acrylic. Publ: Auth, I can't draw, 71 & auth, Getting it all together, 74, Sch Arts. Mailing Add: 104 College Ave Poughkeepsie NY 12603

REYNOLDS, JAMES ELWOOD
PAINTER
b Taft, Calif, Nov 9, 26. Study: Kann Inst Art, Beverly Hills, Calif; Sch Allied Arts, Glendale, Calif. Work: Phoenix Art Mus, Ariz; Cowboy Hall Fame, Oklahoma City; Mus Southwest, Midland, Tex. Comn: Design gold & silver medals for Cowboy Artists Am 8th Ann Exhib & future competition, Cowboy Artists Am & Franklin Mint, 73; painting used by Marlboro for spec Christmas advert, Philip Morris Co, 74. Exhib: Cowboy Hall Fame, Oklahoma City, 69-73; Ann Cowboy Artists Am Show, Phoenix Art Mus, 73-75. Awards: Gold Medal First Prize, Cowboy Hall Fame, 71; Most Outstanding Western Painter, 74-75; Artist of the Yr, Tucson Festival of Arts, Ariz, 77; plus others. Mem: Cowboy Artists Am (secy, 72-73, vpres, 74-75, pres, 75-76); Western Art Asn, Phoenix; Phoenix Art Mus; Ariz Artists in Action. Style & Technique: Broad realism. Media: Oil. Publ: Contribr, Cowboy in Art, 68; contribr, West & Walter Bimson, Univ Ariz, 71; contribr, American cowboy in life & legend, Nat Geographic, 72; contribr, Renaissance of Western Art, Franklin Mint, 74; contribr, Western Painting Today, Watson-Guptill, 75. Mailing Add: Star Rte 1 Box 213 Sedona AZ 86336

REYNOLDS, JOSEPH GARDINER
DESIGNER
b Wickford, RI, Apr 9, 86. Study: RI Sch Design. Work: Stained glass windows, Washington Cathedral; Mem Chapel & Am Church, Paris, France; Wellesley Mem Chapel, Mass; St George's Sch Chapel, Newport, RI. Exhib: US Pavilion, Paris; Mus Fine Arts, New York; Providence Art Club. Mem: Medieval Acad. Media: Stained Glass. Res: Medieval cathedrals; medieval stained glass. Mailing Add: 296 Payson Rd Belmont MA 02178

REYNOLDS, NANCY DU PONT
SCULPTOR
b Greenville, Del, Dec 28, 19. Comn: Lucite carving on copper bases, Stevenson Ctr Natural Sci, Vanderbilt Univ; lucite carving for meditation chapel, Lutheran Towers Bldg, Wilmington, Del; lucite carving, Goldsborough Off Bldg, Wilmington; lucite carvings, Wilmington Trust Co; bronze statue of a child, Children's Bur, Wilmington; bronze fountain, Longwood Gardens, Kennett Square, Pa. Exhib: Corcoran Gallery Art, Washington, DC; Nat Acad Design, New York; Del Art Mus, Wilmington; one-man shows, Rehoboth Art League, Del & Caldwell's, Wilmington; Lever House, New York; Metrop Mus of Art, New York; Goldsborough Gallery, NC. Mem: Nat League Am Pen Women (Diamond State Br); Burr Artists; Del Art Mus; Rehoboth Art League; Catharine Lorillard Wolfe Art Club. Media: Bronze, Lucite. Mailing Add: Foxwood Old Kennett Rd Greenville DE 19807

REYNOLDS, RALPH WILLIAM
EDUCATOR, PAINTER
b Albany, Wis, Nov 10, 05. Study: Art Inst Chicago, 25-27 & 31; Beloit Col, BA, 38; State Univ Iowa, MA, 39; also with Grant Wood, Jean Charlot, Eliot O'Hara, Charles Burchfield, William Thon, Clarence Carter & Millard Sheets. Work: Indiana Univ Pa; Westminster Col (Pa); One Hundred Friends Pittsburgh Art; Univ Club, Pittsburgh; Univ Pittsburgh, Johnstown; also many pub schs, banks & indust concerns in western Pa. Comn: Many portraits, Pa, 42- Exhib: Pittsburgh Watercolor Soc, Arts & Crafts Ctr, 51-72; Am Watercolor Soc, Nat Acad Design Galleries, 59; Am Artists Prof League's Grand Nat, Lever House, New York, 72 & 73; one-man shows, Univ Club Pittsburgh & Westminster Col, 68; plus many others. Teaching: Student instr art, Beloit Col, 33-38; head dept art, SDak State Univ, 40-41; prof art, Indiana Univ Pa, 41-71, emer prof, 72- Pos: Com artist, var studios, Chicago & Cleveland, 27-33. Awards: Awards, Ann Allied Artists Johnstown, Pa, 51-72; 5 Ida Smith Mem Awards & First Prize, Pittsburgh Watercolor Soc, 51-63; Purchase Awards, Penelec & US Bank Shows, 60-76; plus over 70 others. Mem: Indiana Art Asn, Pa (pres, 42); Allied Artists Johnstown, Pa; Pittsburgh Watercolor Soc (vpres, 52); Assoc Artists Pittsburgh; fel Am Artists Prof League (vpres, Pa Chap, 74 & 75, pres, 76 & 77). Style & Technique: Realistic, with a variety of approaches in both broad and detailed techniques. Media: Watercolor. Dealer: Arts & Crafts Ctr Fifth & Shady Ave Pittsburgh PA 15232. Mailing Add: 363 S Third St Indiana PA 15701

REYNOLDS, RICHARD (HENRY)
SCULPTOR, PAINTER
b New York, NY, May 16, 13. Study: San Bernardino Valley Col, AA, 33, Univ Calif, Berkeley, BA, 36, cert, 39; Univ Calif, Los Angeles, SS, 39; Mills Col, with Moholy-Nagy, SS, 40; Univ of the Pac, MA, 42; Rudolph Schaefer Sch; Ore State Univ, Shell grant; Morningside Col, Sioux City, Iowa, Hon DFA, 76. Comn: Steel Viking symbol, Edison High Sch, Stockton, Calif, 64; metal Bengal tiger, Class of 1950, Univ of the Pac, 65; cast stone buffalo, Manteca Union High Sch, Calif, 65; bronze relief, New Wing Stockton Rec Bldg, 66; President's Medallion Morningside Col, 76. Exhib: Northern Calif Arts Painting Open,

Sacramento, 70; Da Vinci Int, New York Coliseum, 70; Post-Sabbatical Exhib, Stockton Fine Arts Gallery, 72; Stockton Art League 25th Ann Exhib, Haggin Galleries, 74; Santa Cruz Art League's 45th Statewide Ann Exhib, 75; plus others. Teaching: Instr art & asst chmn div arts & lett, Stockton Col, 39-48; prof art, Univ of the Pac, 48-, chmn dept art, 48-73; guest prof art educ, Univ Idaho, summer 54; guest lectr, Alaska Methodist Univ, 62. Second Prize for Painting, San Joaquin Co Fair & Exposition, 72; Blue Ribbons, Stockton Art League 25th Ann Exhib, 74; First Prize/Sculpture, San Joaquin Co Fair & Expo Art Exhib, 76; plus others. Mem: Life fel Int Inst Arts & Lett; Pac Arts Asn (ed, Journalette & pres, Northern Calif Sect, 51-52); Nat Art Educ Asn (chmn nat mem comt, 52-53); Outstanding Educators of Am; hon mem Stockton Art League (pres, 52-53); Nat Soc Lit & Arts. Style & Technique: Contemporary sculpture; experimental and semi-representational painting. Media: Stone, Wood; Acrylic, Mixed Media. Publ: Contribr, Arts & Archit, 1/48; auth, A plea for wider distribution of art values, Col Art J, winter 51-52; auth, A buffalo sculpture for a California high school, Am Artist, 1/66; auth, Auto paint art, Design, spring 73; contribr poster design, Pythian Mag, Fall 1974; plus others. Dealer: Stockton Fine Arts Gallery 2310 Pacific Ave Stockton CA 95207. Mailing Add: 1656 W Longview Ave Stockton CA 95207

REYNOLDS, ROBERT
PAINTER, EDUCATOR
b San Luis Obispo, Calif, Mar 7, 36. Study: Art Ctr Col of Design, Los Angeles, Calif, BPA; Calif Polytech State Univ, San Luis Obispo, MA; also with Lorser Fettelson, Harry Carmean, Robert Clark, Arne Nybak & Joe Henninger. Work: City of Stockton, Calif; Spec Collections, Chancellor's Off, Calif State Univ & Col System. Comn: Paintings, Queen Mary Liner, Long Beach, Calif, 67; bicentennial coin, 71 & bicentennial off seal, 71, City of San Luis Obispo, Calif; off co seal, Co of San Luis Obispo, 74; painting & limited print, Calif Polytech State Univ, 76. Exhib: One-man shows, Red Door Art Gallery, Morro Bay, Calif, 69-76 & Flair Gallery, Stockton, Calif, 76-78; Watercolor West, Orange Co, Calif, 73; Int Wildlife Art Show, Mzuri Found, Reno & San Francisco, 74-76 & Safari Club Int, Las Vegas, Nev, 75-78; one-man retrospective art exhib, Art Ctr, San Luis Obispo, Calif, 75; traveling exhib, Ford Motor Co, Dearborn, Mich, 77-78; Cunningham Art Mus Watercolor Exhib, Bakersfield, Calif, 78. Teaching: Prof art, drawing & painting, Dept Art, Calif Polytech State Univ, 64-; art instr drawing & painting, Evening Div, Cuesta Community Col, 72-76; instr watercolor, artist-in-residence, Stockton City, Calif, 76- Pos: Past pres, Art Asn, San Luis Obispo, Calif, 68-69; mem design & review bd, City of San Luis Obispo, 68-73; mem bd of trustees, San Luis Obispo Art Ctr, 69-78; founding mem, Cent Coast Watercolor Soc, Calif, 77- Awards: First Place Award in Watercolor, Flower Festival, City of Lompoc, Calif, 71; Best of Show Award, Art Festival, City of Pismo Beach, Calif, 70, Purchase Award, Art Exhib, Fair Bd Asn, Paso Robles, 72. Bibliog: Alice Landell (auth), Robert Reynolds, WestArt Newspaper, 73; James Hayes (auth), A retrospective, Telegam-Tribune, 74; Laurie A Robins (auth), Robert Reynolds within, Cable TV Guide, 76. Mem: Allied Art, Cambria, Calif; Artist's Equity. Style & Technique: Subjects that deal with landscape, the human figure and wildlife, representational with a stong emphasis on design. Media: Watercolor, Acrylic; Printmaking. Publ: Illusr, VEP Productions, Calif Polytech State Univ, 64-74; illusr, Vocational Report, Vocational Div State of Calif, 67; contribr, WestCoast Graphics, WestArt, 70; illusr, Disappearing windmill, 74 & California Mendocino Coast, 77, Ford Times, Ford Motor Co. Dealer: Bill Todd 3146 Polk Way Stockton CA 95209. Mailing Add: 77 Verde Dr San Luis Obispo CA 93401

REYNOLDS, VALRAE
CURATOR
b San Francisco, Calif, Dec 18, 44. Study: Univ Calif, Davis, BA, 66; New York Univ, MA, 68, cert mus training, 69. Collections Arranged: Temple Sculpture of Indian Asia, 71-72, Islamic Carpets: Flat Weaves, 72, Tibet, A Lost World, 73 & Silk, Tea and Porcelain, Trade Goods from the Orient, 75-76, Newark Mus. Pos: Ford Fel arms & armor dept, Metrop Mus of Art, New York, Fall 1968; Ford Fel Islamic ceramics, Asian Art Mus, San Francisco, Spring 1969; asst cur Oriental collection, Newark Mus, 69-70, cur Oriental collection, 70- Awards: Nat Endowment for Humanities grant for film production, Tibet, A Lost World, 73-74. Mem: Comt for S Asian Art; Asia Soc; Japan Soc; China Inst in Am (mem art comt, 76-); Tibet Soc. Res: Arts of Tibet, India and Himalayas; Islamic interaction with China. Publ: Auth, Islamic Ceramics, 70, Temple Sculpture of India, SE Asia and Nepal, 70 & Journey to Tibet, 72, The Museum & Tibetan Art in the Newark Mus, 9/73, Arts of Asia; ed Tibet, A Living Tradition, Tibetan J, Libr of Tibetan Works & Arch, 76. Mailing Add: Newark Mus 43 Washington St Newark NJ 07101

RHOADS, EUGENIA ECKFORD
PAINTER
b Dyesburg, Tenn, Jan 9, 01. Study: Miss Univ Women, AB, 23; Columbia Univ, MA, 24; Am Beaux Art Sch, Fontainbleau, summer 32; also with Robert Brackman, Francis Speight, Walter Stuemig, Helen Sawyer & Henry Pitz. Work: Del Art Mus, Wilmington; Miss Univ Women Art Collection; Univ Del Art Collection; Du Pont Co Collection, Wilmington & Atlanta; Wilmington Trust Co. Exhib: Brooks Mem Art Gallery, Memphis, Tenn, 55; Nat Collection, Smithsonian Inst, Washington, DC, 56-58; Birmingham Art Mus, Ala, 62; Allied Art, Nat Acad, 66; Am Watercolor Soc, 67. Teaching: Instr art & design, NC Col Women, 24-26; instr art educ, Univ NC, summers 29 & 30; dir, Tower Hill Sch, Wilmington, 27-35. Pos: Mem adv comn, Rohoboth Art League, Del, 36-; chmn educ coun, Wilmington Art Mus, 40-48; mem visual arts coun, Del State Arts Coun, 69- Awards: Trio Award, Birmingham Mus Art, 62; Breath of Spring Award, Nat League Am Pen Women, 63; Best in Show Founders Award for Reflections, Rehoboth Art League, 73; plus others. Mem: Nat League Am Pen Women (pres, Diamond State Br, 54); Wilmington Soc Fine Arts (secy bd, 69-); Philadelphia Art Alliance; Allied Artists Am; Am Watercolor Soc. Media: Watercolor, Oil. Publ: Auth, Wonder Windows, Dutton, 31. Dealer: Warehouse Gallery Arden DE 19803. Mailing Add: 108 School Rd Wilmington DE 19803

RHODEN, JOHN W
SCULPTOR
b Birmingham, Ala, 1918. Study: With Richmond Barthe, 38; Columbia Univ Sch Painting & Sculpture, with Oronzio Maldarelli, Hugo Robus & William Zorach. Work: Stockholm Mus; Carl Milles Collection; Heinz Collection, Pittsburgh; Steinberg Colletion, St Louis, Mo; Del Mus; plus many others. Comn: Zodiacal structure and curved wall (metals & jewel glass), Sheraton Hotel, Philadelphia, 57; Monumental Bronze, Harlem Hosp, 66; Monumental Abstraction, Metrop Hosp, 68; Clifton Sr High Sch, Baltimore, 71; Monumental Bronze, Bellevue Hosp, New York, 75; IS 223, Queens, NY, 75; Monumental Sculpture, Afro-Am Mus, Philadelphia, Pa, 76. Exhib: Metrop Mus Art; Audubon Ann; Pa Acad Fine Arts; Nat Acad Design; Am Acad Arts; plus many others. Pos: Specialist, US Dept State Tour Iceland, Europe & NAfrica, 55-56; mem artist deleg, US Dept State Tour USSR, Poland & Yugoslavia, 59 & Asia, 60; consult, Seni-Rupa Inst Teknol, Bandung, Indonesia, 62. Awards: Rockefeller Grant, 59; Medal Pro Sculptura Egregia, Howard Univ, 61; Guggenheim Fel, 61; plus others. Mem: Life mem Munic Art Soc; Am Soc Contemp Artists. Media: Stone, Bronze. Mailing Add: 23 Cranberry St Brooklyn NY 11201

RHODES, JAMES MELVIN
GLASS BLOWER, SCULPTOR
b Gorman, Tex, Dec 1, 38. Study: Univ Wis, Mechanical eng; Univ Hawaii, BA. Work: State Found on Cult & the Arts, Hawaii. Comn: Glass mural, comn by Thomas Dunn, Hilo, Hawaii, 77. Exhib: Honolulu Acad Art, Hawaii, 72; two-man shows, The Foundry, Honolulu, Hawaii, 72 & 74, Metes & Bounds, Sausalito, Calif, 74, Hand & Eye, Honolulu, 74, Downtown Gallery, Honolulu, Hawaii, 77. Teaching: Instr arts & crafts, Schofield Arts & Crafts, Wahiawa, Hawaii, 70-74; instr off hand glass blowing, The Foundry, Honolulu, Hawaii, 70-74. Pos: Chmn, Easter Art Festival, Hawaii, 76; vpres, Big Island Artists Guild, Hawaii, 76. Awards: Am Fac Award, Hawaii Craftsmen Show, 73; Campus Ctr Bd Award, Univ Hawaii Show, Univ Hawaii, 74. Mem: Big Island Artists Guild. Style & Technique: Flat glass and off hand blown glass. Media: Blown glass. Dealer: Downtown Gallery 125 Merchant St Honolulu HI 96813. Mailing Add: Box 1131 Keaau HI 96749

RHODES, REILLY PATRICK
ART MUSEUM DIRECTOR
b Bloomington, Ill, Mar 28, 41. Study: Kansas City Art Inst, BFA, 66; Wichita State Univ, MFA, 68; Sterling Inst, Boston, art gallery mgt, 69; Syracuse Univ, mus mgt, 70; Univ Mo-Columbia, pub rels, 70. Pos: Dir, Albrecht Gallery, St Joseph, Mo, 68-71; dir, Canton Art Inst, Ohio, 71-73; dir, Charles W Bowers Mem Mus, Santa Ana, Calif, 73- Awards: Macy's Ann Exhib Award, 65. Mem: Int Coun Mus; Am Asn Mus; Western Asn Art Mus; Am Fedn Arts; Art Mus Develop Dirs Asn. Publ: Auth, Public Relations Catalogue, Albrecht Gallery; auth introd to var catalogs, including L E Shafer Bronzes, An Exhibition of Sculpture & Drawings by O V Shaffer, Moses Soyer: A Selection of Paintings 1960-1970, The Art of Irving Ramsey Wiles (1861-1948) & All Ohio (Canton Art Inst Ann). Mailing Add: Charles W Bowers Mem Mus 2002 N Main St Santa Ana CA 92706

RHYNE, CHARLES SYLVANUS
ART HISTORIAN, GALLERY DIRECTOR
b Philadelphia, Pa, Mar 29, 32. Study: Wittenberg Col, AB, 54; Univ Chicago, MA, 56, advan study, 56-60; Fulbright fels, Courtauld Inst, Univ London, 62-64. Collections Arranged: David Reed: Recent Paintings, 11/75, Andrew Leicester: Earth Drawings, 9/76 & Lee Kelly: Outdoor Pub Sculpture in the Northwest, 10/76, Reed Col Art Gallery. Teaching: Instr art hist & humantities, Reed Col, 60-62, asst prof art hist, 62-66, assoc prof art hist, 66-; vis teacher art hist, Mus Art Sch, Portland, 74-75. Pos: Chief reader, Advan Placement Prog, Art Hist of Art Educ Testing Serv, Princeton, NJ, 70-75; bd dirs, Portland Ctr for the Visual Arts, 73-; dir art gallery, Reed Col, 74-; mem long-range planning comt, Portland Art Mus, 75- Awards: Sr Fel, Humanities Res Inst, Reed Col, 67-68; Younger Humanities Fel, Nat Endowment for Humanities, 72-73; Resident fel, Yale Ctr for Brit Art, 78. Mem: Col Art Asn (mem nominating comt, 70; mem art preservation comt, 77); Soc of Archit Historians; Soc of Indust Archaeol. Res: English romantic landscape painting, especially John Constable (preparing catalogue raisonne); architecture of bridges. Publ: Auth, Fresh light on John Constable, Apollo, 68; contribr, Advanced Placement Art, Col Entrance Exam Bd, 70; auth, Review of Plowden, bridges: the spans of North America, Soc of Indust Archit Newsletter, 74. Mailing Add: Reed Col Portland OR 97202

RIBAK, LOUIS
PAINTER
b Russia, Dec 3, 02; US citizen. Study: Pa Acad Fine Arts; Art Students League. Work: Whitney Mus, New York; El Paso Mus, Tex; Mus Fine Arts, Santa Fe, NMex; Brooklyn Mus; Springfield Art Mus, Mo. Exhib: El Paso Mus, 69; Watercolor USA, Springfield Art Mus, 70; retrospective, Mus Fine Arts, Santa Fe, 75. Teaching: Founder, teacher art & dir, Taos Valley Art Sch, 47-53. Awards: First Prize, El Paso Mus, 69; Taos Art Asn First Prize, Stables Gallery, 69 & 71; Watercolor USA Award, 70. Bibliog: Salpeter (auth), article in Esquire, 42; Mary Fuller (auth), article, 73 & Barbara Merrick (auth), article, 75, Southwest Art Mag. Style & Technique: Abstract. Media: Acrylic, Oil. Mailing Add: Box 891 Taos NM 87571

RICARDO, CLIFFORD
See Joseph, Cliff

RICCI, JERRI
PAINTER
b Perth Amboy, NJ. Study: New York Sch Appl Design for Women, 35; Art Students League, with Scott Williams, George Bridgman, Mahonri Young & others, 35-38. Work: Fairleigh Dickinson Col; Parrish Mus, Southampton, NY; Am Acad Arts & Lett; Butler Art Inst, Clark Univ; Addison Gallery Am Art, Andover, Mass; plus others. Exhib: Toledo Mus Art; Pa Acad Fine Arts; Art Inst Chicago; Dayton Art Inst; Addison Gallery Am Art; plus others. Awards: Silver Medal, Catharine Lorillard Wolfe Art Club, 54; Clara Obrig Award, Nat Acad Design; Gold Medal, Audubon Artists, 55; plus many others. Mem: Am Watercolor Soc; Allied Artists Am; assoc Nat Acad Design; Philadelphia Watercolor Club; Audubon Artists; plus others. Mailing Add: 1 Atlantic Ave Rockport MA 01966

RICE, ANTHONY HOPKINS
SCULPTOR, PAINTER
b Angeles Pampanga, Philippine Islands, July 21, 48. Study: Va Commonwealth Univ, Richmond, BFA, 70; Univ NC, Chapel Hill, MFA, 72. Work: High Mus Art, Atlanta, Ga. Comn: Outdoor environmental sculpture, Wright State Univ, Dayton, Ohio, 74. Exhib: New Sculpture, Washington, Baltimore, Richmond, Corcoran Gallery, Washington, DC, 70; Translucent and Transparent Art, St Petersburg Mus Art, Fla, 71; one-man show, Cochise Col, Douglas, Ariz, 73; Ga Artists Show, High Mus Art, 74; Nat Sculpture '75 Traveling Exhib, Huntsville Mus Art, Ala, 75. Teaching: Asst prof art, Wesleyan Col, Macon, Ga, 72- Awards: Honorable Mention, El Paso Mus Art, 74. Bibliog: Frances Taylor (auth), review in Ceramics Monthly, 74. Mem: Col Art Asn; Am Asn Univ Prof; Southeastern Col Art Asn; Southern Asn Sculptors; Popular Cult Asn South. Media: Steel, Wood. Dealer: Taylor-Thill Gallery Inc 3726 Fairfax Dallas TX 75209. Mailing Add: 4132 Laura Ann Pl Macon GA 31204

RICE, DAN
PAINTER
b Long Beach, Calif, June 17, 26. Study: Univ Calif, Los Angeles; Black Mountain Col, BA; Univ Calif, Berkeley; Mass Inst Technol, MA(arch); also with DeKooning, Kline, Shahn, Motherwell, Stamos, Tworkov, Guston, Albers, Bolotowski & Rothko. Work: Wadsworth Atheneum, Hartford, Conn; Albright-Knox Art Gallery, Buffalo, NY; Mus Mod Art, New York; Princeton Univ Mus, NJ; Dillard Univ Mus, New Orleans. Teaching: Instr painting & drawing, Black Mountain Col, NC, 56-57; instr painting, Art Students League, 68-69; vis prof painting, State Univ NY Buffalo, summer 70; instr life drawing, Univ Conn, 71-72. Pos: Consult, Franz Kline Estate, New York, 63-; cataloguer, Works of Mark Rothko, New York, 69-70. Awards: Longview Found Grant, 62. Bibliog: Jonathan Williams (auth), Dan Rice, painter, Art Int Mag, 60. Media: Oil. Publ: Illusr, The Disolving Fabric, 55; illusr, All That

is Lovely in Men, 56; illusr, The Dutiful Son, 60; illusr, Corrosive Sublimate, 71; illusr, The Plum Poems, 72. Mailing Add: c/o Catherine Viviano Gallery 250 E 65th St New York NY 10022

RICE, HAROLD RANDOLPH
EDUCATOR, WRITER
b Salineville, Ohio, May 22, 12. Study: Univ Cincinnati, BSAA & BS(art educ), 34, MEd, 42; Columbia Univ, Arthur Wesley Dow scholar, 43-44, EdD, 44; Moore Col Art, hon LHD, 63. Teaching: Art supvr, Wyoming Pub Schs, Ohio, 34-42; adj instr, Univ Cincinnati, 40-42; teaching fel, Columbia Univ, 42-44; head dept art, Univ Ala, 44-46; dean, Moore Inst Art, 46-62, first pres, 51-62; pres & dean, Moore Col Art, 62-63; dean, Col Design, Archit & Art, Univ Cincinnati, 63-72, prof design, art & educ, 72- Pos: Contrib art ed, Jr Arts & Activities, 37-46; chmn comt on art, Ohio Elem Educ Policies Comt, 40-42; chmn arts & skills corps, Am Red Cross, Ala, 44-46; dir, Philadelphia Art Alliance, 47-63; nat scholar juror, Scholastic Arts Awards, nine yrs, 49-75, nat jury chmn, ann, 74-; adv art ed, Bk Knowledge, 50-63; mem bd dirs, Contemp Arts Ctr, 64-69, mem adv bd, 69-72. Mem: Fel & life mem Nat Asn Schs Art (secy, 50-55, pres, 55-57); life mem Eastern Arts Asn (vpres, 56-58, pres, 58-60); Nat Art Educ Asn (coun mem, 60-63); hon mem Cincinnati Art Club; Int Coun Fine Arts Deans; plus others. Publ: Auth, numerous articles for prof mag & jour, 29- Mailing Add: 640 Evening Star Lane Cincinnati OH 45220

RICE, JAMES WILLIAM, JR
ILLUSTRATOR, SCULPTOR
b Coleman Co, Tex, Feb 10, 34. Study: Univ Tex, Austin, BFA, MEd, with Charles Umland, John Guerin & Michael Frary. Comn: Mural, 68 & sculpture, 68, Camp Moore Mus, Tangipahoa, La; sculpture, Hammond State Sch, La, 74; mural & paintings, Citizens Nat Bank, Hammond, La, 75. Teaching: Asst prof art, Southeastern La Univ, Hammond, 64-67 & 70-75 & La State Univ, Baton Rouge, 68-69. Style & Technique: Illustration: realistic, story-telling, detailed and humorous; Sculpture: realistic, figurative. Media: Pen & Ink, Watercolor, Acrylic; Wax, Clay. Publ: Auth & illusr, Gaston the Green Nosed Alligator, 74 & Lyn and the Fuzzy, 75, Pelican; auth & illusr, Prairie Christmas, Shoal Creek, 77; auth & illusr, Gaston Goes to Mardi Gras, 77 & Gaston Goes to Texas, 78, Pelican. Mailing Add: Box 227 Hamilton TX 76531

RICE, NORMAN LEWIS
PAINTER, EDUCATOR
b Aurora, Ill, July 22, 05. Study: Univ Ill, BA, 26; Art Inst Chicago, 26-30; Otis Art Inst, DFA, 67. Teaching: Instr drawing & design, Art Inst Chicago, 28-43; prof painting, Syracuse Univ, 46-54; prof painting & hist art, Carnegie-Mellon Univ, 54-73. Pos: From asst dean to dean, Art Inst Chicago, 30-43; dir, Sch Art, Syracuse Univ, 46-54; dean, Col Fine Arts, Carnegie-Mellon Univ, 54-72, emer dean, 72- Mem: Fel Nat Asn Schs Art; fel Am Coun Arts in Educ; plus others. Mailing Add: 222 Carnegie Pl Pittsburgh PA 15208

RICE, PHILIP SOMERSET
PAINTER, EDUCATOR
b Mobile, Ala, July 3, 44. Study: Mid Tenn State Univ, BS(art), 67; Pratt Contemp Printmaking Ctr, with Jurgen Fischer, 67; Southern Ill Univ, Carbondale, MFA, 71. Work: Rose Hulman Inst Technol, Terre Haute, Ind; univ galleries, Southern Ill Univ, Carbondale; Mid Tenn State Univ Galleries, Murfreesboro. Comn: Historical oil painting, Murfreesboro CofC, 66. Exhib: Print in America, Peabody Mus, Nashville, Tenn, 66; Wabash Valley Ann, Terre Haute, 71; Chapel Hill Nat Printmakers, NC, 71; Brooks Goldsmith's Ann, Memphis, Tenn, 72; Quincy Art Ann, Ill, 72. Teaching: Dir art, Isaac Litton Jr High, Nashville, 67-70; asst instr art, Pratt Contemp Printmaking Ctr, 67; instr drawing & painting, Southern Ill Univ, Carbondale, 70-71; instr, Springfield Art Asn, 71-74; asst prof art, Sangamon State Univ, 73-74; asst prof art, Murray State Univ, 74- Pos: Exec dir, Springfield Art Asn, 71-72. Bibliog: Parisian Arts Int Mem: Col Art Asn Am; Am Fedn Arts. Style & Technique: Photo realists of blow-up images in geometric spaces; figurative. Media: Oil, Acrylic. Mailing Add: 402 S Eighth Murray KY 42071

RICE, SHELLEY ENID
ART CRITIC, ART HISTORIAN
b Bronx, NY, Aug 20, 50. Study: Smith Col, 68-69; State Univ NY, Stony Brook, BA (summa cum laude with hons), 72, with Lawrence Alloway; Inst Fine Arts, NY Univ, MA, with R Rosenblum & R Goldwater; Princeton Univ, two yrs with Sam Hunter and Peter Bunnell. Teaching: Instr art hist, Brooklyn Col, NY, 72-77; instr art hist & photog criticism, Sch of Visual Arts, New York, 75- Pos: Contrib ed, Photog mag, 75-; mem bd dirs, Franklin Furnace Arch, 76-; photog criticism ed, Village Voice, 77. Awards: Danforth Found Fel, 72-76. Mem: Soc Photog Educ; Col Art Asn; Visual Studies Workshop, Rochester. Res: Historical and contemporary photography. Publ: Auth, Irving Penn at the Modern, Art in Am, 75; auth, Women, photographs and criticism, Photograph, 76; auth, Duane Michal's real dreams (reprint from Voice), Afterimage, 76; auth, The daybooks of Edward Weston, Art J, 76-77; auth, Caught in a stopgap of stop-time (on M Lesy), Voice, 77. Mailing Add: 255 W 12th St New York NY 10014

RICH, FRANCES L
SCULPTOR, DRAFTSMAN
b Spokane, Wash, Jan 8, 10. Study: Smith Col, BA, 31; sculpture with Malvina Hoffman & frescoes with Angel Zarraga, Paris, France, 33-35; Beaux Art Acad; Boston Mus Sch, 35-36, with Alexander Iacovleff; Cranbrook Acad Art, 37-40, sculpture with Carl Milles; Claremont Col, 46, with Millard Sheets; Columbia Univ, 47. Work: Palm Springs Desert Mus, Calif; Santa Catalina Sch, Monterey, Calif; also pvt collection of Father Edward Boyle, Holy Trinity Church, Bremerton, Wash; Bronze Portrait Head, Virgil Thomson, Thomson Rm, NY Univ. Comn: Bronze bas relief Nunc Dimittis, comn by Mr & Mrs James Coonan for St Peters Episcopal Church, Redwood City, Calif, 55; bronze Our Lady of Combermere, Madonna House, Ont, 56; bronze bust of Katharine Hepburn, Am Shakespeare Festival Theatre, Stratford, Conn, 60; bronze St Francis of Assisi, St Margarets Episcopal Church, Palm Desert, 70 & Pierce Col, Athens, Greece, 71; Christ of the Sacred Heart, St Sebastian's Church, West Los Angeles, 74; bronze plaque honoring Dr Mario Gonzalez Ulloa, 77; 15 bronze flying birds, Aviary Hall, Living Desert Mus, Palm Desert, Calif, 78; bronze of St Francis of Assisi, Smith Col, Northampton, Mass, 78; plus others. Exhib: One-man shows, Santa Barbara Mus Art, 52, Calif Palace Legion of Hon, 55, Palm Springs Desert Mus, 69 & 77; Calif Relig Artists, De Young Mem, 52; Lenten Exhib Liturgical Arts, Denver Art Mus, 55. Bibliog: Articles in Liturgical Arts Quart; Sculpture of Frances Rich, 69; Sculpture of Frances Rich, Manzanita Press, 74; plus others. Mem: Archit League New York; Alumna Cranbrook Acad Art. Style & Technique: Simplified realism with own personal style. Media: Bronze. Mailing Add: PO Box 213 Palm Desert CA 92260

RICH, GARRY LORENCE
PAINTER
b Newton Co, Mo, Nov 11, 43. Style & Technique: Kansas City Art Inst, BFA; NY Univ, MA. Work: Whitney Mus Am Art, New York, NY; Aldrich Mus Contemp Art, Ridgefield, Conn; Phoenix Art Mus, Ariz; Nelson Gallery Art, Kansas City, Mo; Miami Art Ctr, Fla. Exhib: Whitney Mus Am Art Ann, 71; Highlights of the Season, Aldrich Mus Contemp Art, Ridgefield, 71; one-man shows, Max Hutchinson Gallery, New York, 71-72 & 74, Henri Gallery, Washington, DC, 72 & Gallery A, Sydney, Australia, 72. Teaching: Asst prof painting, NY Univ, 65-71; asst prof painting, Hofstra Univ, 71-72; asst prof painting, Bard Col, 72- Awards: Max Beckman fel, Brooklyn Mus, 66; Nat Coun Arts Nat Endowment, 67 & 74; Anderson fel, NY Univ, 68. Bibliog: Domingo (auth), Color abstractionism, 12/70 & Bowling (auth), Color & recent painting, 72, Arts Mag; Ratcliff (auth), Young New York painters, Art News, 70. Dealer: Max Hutchinson Gallery 127 Green St New York NY 10013. Mailing Add: 167 Crosby St New York NY 10012

RICHARD, BETTI
SCULPTOR
b New York, NY, Mar 16, 16. Study: Art Students League; also with Paul Manship. Work: Phoenix Art Mus, Ariz; San Joachin Pioneer Mus & Haggin Art Galleries, Stockton, Calif; Melick Libr, Eureka Col, Ill; Rosary Hill Col, Buffalo, NY; Metrop Opera House, New York. Comn: St Francis statue, St Francis of Assisi Church, New York, 57; marble statue of Our Lady, House Theol, Centerville, Ohio, 58; St John Baptiste de la Salle, St John Vianney Sem, East Aurora, NY, 63; busts of Mozart & Wagner, Metrop Opera, New York, 63 & 70, bust of Sir Rudolf Bing & eleven portrait medals of composers; Cardinal Gibbons Mem, Baltimore, Md, 67; statue of St Francis, Our Lady of Angels Convent, Aston, Pa; statue of St Francis, St Francis Interfaith Ctr of Auraria Higher Educ Complex, Denver, Colo. Exhib: Allied Artists Ann, 42-71; Nat Acad Design Ann, 44-71; Nat Sculpture Soc Ann, 47-72; Third Int Exhib, Philadelphia Mus, Pa, 49; Fall Exhib Kuenstlerhaus, Vienna, 54. Awards: Barnett Prize, Nat Acad Design, 47; Gold Medal for Sculpture, Allied Artists Am, 56; John Gregory Award, Nat Sculpture Soc, 60. Bibliog: Jacques Schnier (auth), Sculpture in modern America, Univ Calif, 49; Norman Kent (auth), Sculpture of Betti Richard, Am Artist Mag. Mem: Fel Nat Sculpture Soc (secy, 71-); Archit League New York (vpres sculpture, 61-63); Allied Artists Am; Audubon Artists. Media: Bronze, Stone, Wood and Cast Stone. Mailing Add: 131 E 66th St New York NY 10021

RICHARD, GEORGE MAIRET
MUSEUM DIRECTOR
b Hoquiam, Wash, Mar 25, 23. Study: Univ Wis, BA, 47, MA(political sci), 65; First AAC Seminar for State Arts Coun Exec, Columbia Univ, 66. Pos: Dir, Wis Arts Found & Coun, Milwaukee, 65-69; dir, Wustum Mus Fine Arts, Racine, 70- Mem: Am Asn Mus; Wis Fedn Mus. Res: Public administration and roles of governing boards. Publ: Auth, The Beginnings of Art Education in Milwaukee 1880-1920, 61; auth, Relations Between Staff and Board in a Public/Private Museum, 73. Mailing Add: Wustum Mus Fine Arts 2519 Northwestern Ave Racine WI 53404

RICHARD, JACK
PAINTER, GALLERY DIRECTOR
b Akron, Ohio, Mar 7, 22. Study: Chicago Prof Sch Art scholar; Univ Ohio, Athens; Kent Univ; Akron Univ; also with R Brackman, A Bohrod, Y Kunioshi, P Sample, J Carroll & many others. Work: Canton Art Inst, Ohio; Umbaugh Pole Bldg Collection, Ravenna, Ohio; Woodrum Ins Collection, Stow, Ohio. Comn: President & Mrs Eisenhower (by permission), Tupperware Int, Orlando, Fla; mural, Central Christian Church Kettering, Dayton, Valley Savings & Loan, Cuyahoga Falls, First United Church of Christ, Akron & Marcel's Supper Club, Cuyahoga Falls, Ohio. Exhib: Retrospective, Ambassador Col, Pasadena, 70; City Ctr Gallery, New York; Fifty Am Artists, Gallerie Int & Salmagundi Club, New York; Butler Inst Am Art Nat, Youngstown, Ohio. Teaching: Instr painting & design Cuyahoga Valley Art Ctr, Cuyahoga Falls, 53-63; instr painting & design, Almond Tea Galleries, Cuyahoga Falls, 63-; instr, Woman's City Club, Akron, Ohio, 60- Pos: Dir, Cuyahoga Valley Art Ctr, 53-63; dir, Almond Tea Galleries, 63-; illusr, Stevens-Gross Studios, Chicago. Awards: Purchase Award & Second Award Painting, Canton Art Inst; Best in Show Award, Akron Art Inst, 48; Huntington Hartford Fel, Huntington Hartford Found, 58. Bibliog: Five Rotos, Beacon J, Knight Newspapers; York; M M (auth), Jack Richard Al Lavoro, Il Pungold Verde, Italy, 74. Mem: Artists, Ohio; Ohio Arts & Crafts Guild; Cuyahoga Valley Art Ctr, Ohio; Tri-County Art Soc, Ohio. Style & Technique: All major mediums from magic realism through non-objective abstract. Media: Oils, Acrylics; Pastels, Watercolors. Interest: Assisting in training of young artists and rehabilitation use of arts. Collection: R Brackman, L Grell, R Skemp, G Eluegren, D Cornwell, Ball, Japanese Prints, A Loomis. Publ: Illusr, Staley J, Ind, 43-45; illusr, The Helm Mag; illusr, Ohio Edison Ann Report, 60; illusr, Ohio Story, TV prog, Ohio Bell Tel. Mailing Add: c/o Almond Tea Galleries 2250 Front St Cuyahoga Falls OH 44221

RICHARD, PAUL
ART CRITIC
b Chicago, Ill, Nov, 22, 39. Study: Harvard Col, BA, 61; Univ Pa Grad Sch Fine Arts. Pos: Art critic, Washington Post, DC, 68- Mailing Add: 1150 15th St NW Washington DC 20071

RICHARDS, BILL
PAINTER, EDUCATOR
b Grantsville, WVa, July 15, 36. Study: Ohio Univ, with Dwight Mutchler, BFA; Ind Univ, with Leon Golub & James McGarrell, MFA; Skowhegan Sch Painting & Sculpture. Work: Philadelphia Mus Art; Brooklyn Mus; NJ State Mus Art, Trenton; Miami Dade Jr Col; Dechert, Price & Rhodes, Philadelphia. Exhib: Friends Collect 20th Century, Philadelphia Mus Art, 67; Pa Acad Fine Arts Ann, 68; Made in Philadelphia 2, Inst Contemp Art, 74; Whitney Mus Am Art Biennial, 75; one-man show, Marian Locks Gallery, Philadelphia, 75. Teaching: Assoc prof painting & drawing, Moore Col Art, 67- Bibliog: Paul Richard (auth), rev in Washington Post, 11/73; Susan Heineman (auth), rev in Artforum, 1/75; Victoria Donohoe (auth), rev in Philadelphia Inquirer, 5/75. Style & Technique: Abstract process. Media: Oil on Canvas. Dealer: Olympia Galleries Ltd 230 S 22nd St Philadelphia PA 19103. Mailing Add: 40 W 24th St New York NY 10010

RICHARDS, JEANNE HERRON
ETCHER, PAINTER
b Aurora, Ill. Study: Univ Iowa, with Mauricio Lasansky, BFA, 52, MFA, 54; Atelier 17, Fulbright grant, 54-55, with Stanley William Hayter. Work: Lessing J Rosenwald Collection, Nat Gallery Art; Prints & Photographs, Libr Cong, Washington, DC; Nat Collection Fine Arts, Washington, DC; Sheldon Mem Art Galleries, Univ Nebr-Lincoln; British Mus, London, Eng. Exhib: Five Libr Cong Pennell Exhibs Prints, 47-61; Mid-Am Exhib, Nelson-Atkins Gallery, Kansas City, Mo, 52, 54-55, 58, 61 & 63; Contemp Prints, Drawings & Watercolors, Metrop Mus of Art, New York, 52; NW Printmakers, Seattle Art Mus, Wash,

53 & 61; All Prize Print Show, Dallas Mus Fine Arts, Tex, 55; Bay Printmakers, Oakland Mus Art, Calif, 56-59; Boston Printmakers, Boston Mus Fine Arts, 56-57, 59 & 61; Prints From Brooklyn Mus Nat, Am Fedn Arts US Tour, 56; Intaglio Prints USA, US Info Agency Tour SAm, 59; Nat Print & Drawing, Dulin Gallery of Art, Knoxville, Tenn, 68; one-man show, Univ Ill, Champaign, 69; Sheldon Mem Art Galleries, Univ Nebr, Lincoln, 70; 19th Area Exhib, Corcoran Gallery Art, Washington, DC, 74; plus others. Teaching: Asst instr drawing, Univ Iowa, 55-56; asst prof prints & drawing, Univ Nebr-Lincoln, 57-63. Awards: Purchase Award, Corcoran Gallery Art, 57; Purchase Award, Print Club Albany 13th Nat, 69; SW Printmakers Purchase Prize to Philadelphia Mus of Art in hon of Carl Zigrosser, 76. Mem: Soc Washington Printmakers, DC; Print Club Albany. Style & Technique: Figurative, formal, geometric. Dealer: Gallery 4 110 S Pitt Alexandria VA 22314. Mailing Add: 1711 N Cliff St Alexandria VA 22301

RICHARDS, KARL FREDERICK
EDUCATOR, PAINTER
b Youngstown, Ohio, June 14, 20. Study: Cleveland Inst Art, dipl, 44; Western Reserve Univ, BSEd, 44; State Univ Iowa, MA, 47; Ohio State Univ, PhD, 56. Teaching: Asst prof art, Bowling Green State Univ, 47-56; prof art & chmn dept, Tex Christian Univ, 56-71; prof art & chmn dept, Ark State Univ, 71- Mailing Add: PO Box RR State University AR 72467

RICHARDS, LEE
EDUCATOR, JEWELER
b Colby, Kans, June 3, 32. Study: Kansas State Teachers Col, with Mary Kretsinger, BS(educ), 54; NMex State Univ, MA(sculpture), 67; Univ Kans, with Carlyle Smith, EdD, 75. Work: In many pvt collections. Exhib: 17th Ann Int Designer/Craftsmen, El Paso, 67; Neches River Festival Art Show, Beaumont, Tex, 68; 19th Ann Art Exhib, Beaumont, 69; 17th Ann Designer/Craftsmen, Lawrence, Kans, 71; Crafts Biennial, Mus NMex, Santa Fe, 74. Teaching: Instr art educ & jewelry, Lamar State Col, 67-70; prof jewelry, Haskell Indian Jr Col, Lawrence, 71-72; assoc prof art educ & jewelry, NMex State Univ, 72- Pos: Art dir, Agr Exten Serv, Baton Rouge, La, 59-61; art supvr, Govt Proj Upward Bound, El Paso, Tex, 66. Mem: Nat Art Educ Asn; Am Crafts Coun; NMex Designer/Craftsman; NMex Art Educ Asn. Style & Technique: Fabrication, rational design using fusing and other textural effects. Media: Metal, Semi-Precious Stones. Publ: Auth & illusr, Make Good Visuals, 60. Dealer: El Studio Carolyn Lutheran Old Mesilla NM 88001. Mailing Add: Dept of Art NMex State Univ Las Cruces NM 88003

RICHARDS, TALLY
ART DEALER, ART WRITER
b Clarkston, Ga. Collections Arranged: Fritz Scholder (first exhib in commercial NMex gallery), 71, Fritz Scholder (auth, catalog), 73, Sculpture by Jerome Kirk (auth, catalog), 73, Fritz Scholder-Indians & Landscapes (auth, catalog), 75 & Larry Bell in Taos-One Fracture from the Iceberg, 75, Tally Richards Gallery of Contemp Art, Taos, NMex. Pos: Owner/dir, Tally Richards Gallery of Contemp Art, 69- Specialty: Contemporary art being produced, with the exception of sculpture by Jerome Kirk, by artists living in New Mexico. Publ: Auth, Contemporary vs Traditional, SW Art Gallery Mag, 72; auth, Scholder, Dartmouth: Renewed Commitments, SW Art Mag, 74; auth, Larry Bell, 75; auth, Indian in Paris, Am Indian Art Mag, 77. Mailing Add: PO Box 1734 2 Ledoux St Taos NM 87571

RICHARDS, WALTER DUBOIS
PAINTER, PRINTMAKER
b Penfield, Ohio, Sept 18, 07. Study: Cleveland Sch Art, grad, 30. Work: Cleveland Mus Art; Whitney Mus Am Art, New York; New Britain Mus Am Art, Conn; USAF Art Collection, Dayton, Ohio; Johnson Mus, Tex. Comn: Vietnam (paintings), USAF, 66; Beautification of America (stamp design), in honor of Mrs Lyndon Johnson, comn by US Postal Serv, 69 & Am Trees (block of four stamps), 78; 100th Anniversary National Park Service (stamp design), Cape Hatteras, US Postal Serv, 72. Exhib: Int Watercolor Exhib, Art Inst Chicago, 38; 12th Biennial, Brooklyn Mus Art, 43; Royal Soc Painters in Watercolor, London, 62; Am Prints Around the World, various nations, 63; 200 Years of Watercolor Painting, Metrop Mus Art, New York, 66. Teaching: Instr pvt classes drawing & watercolor, 68- Pos: Illusr, Tranquillini Studios, Cleveland, 31-36; illusr, Charles E Cooper Studios, New York, 36-50. Awards: First Lithography, May Show, Cleveland Mus Art, 35-38; Lily Saportas Award, Am Watercolor Soc, 62; First Graphics, Hudson Valley Art Asn, 75. Bibliog: Fred Whitaker (auth), Walter illustrator, Am Artist Mag, 3/58; Howard Munce (auth), One artist: one subject: endless variations, N Light Mag, 11/12/72; Susan E Meyer (auth), On location with the Fairfield Watercolor Group, Am Artist, 7/72. Mem: Am Watercolor Soc (recording secy, 60-61, vpres, 62-70); assoc Nat Acad Design; Conn Watercolor Soc; Soc Illusr; Fairfield Watercolor Group (pres, 48-). Style & Technique: Graphic, realistic. Media: Watercolor; Lithography. Publ: Illusr, Divided South searches its soul, 56 & The age of psychology in the US, 57, Life Mag; illusr, Readers Digest, Colliers, Am Legion & Fortune Mag; auth, 200 Years of American Illustration, NY Hist Soc Mus, 77. Mailing Add: PO Box 1134 87 Oak St New Canaan CT 06840

RICHARDSON, BRENDA
MUSEUM CURATOR, WRITER
b Howell, Mich, July 15, 42. Study: Univ Mich, Ann Arbor, BA, 64; Univ Calif, Berkeley, MA, 66. Collections Arranged: Eighties, Univ Art Mus, Berkeley, 70, William T Wiley (with catalog), 71, Eight New York Painters, 72, Terry Fox (with catalog), 73, Joan Brown (with catalog), 74 & Stephen A Davis, Howard Fried, Steven J Kaltenbach, 74; Fourteen Artists, Baltimore Mus Art, 75, Andy Warhol, 75; Mel Bochner (with catalog), 76; Frank Stella Black Paintings (with catalog), 76; plus many others. Pos: Cur exhib, Univ Art Mus, Berkeley, 66-72, asst curatorial dir, 72-74; cur painting & sculpture, Baltimore Mus Art, Md, 75-77, asst dir for art, 77- Awards: Distinguished Alumni Lectureship, Univ Calif, Berkeley, 73. Publ: Auth, Howard Fried: Paradox of approach-avoidance, summer 71 & Nancy Graves: a new way of seeing, 4/72, Arts Mag; plus many others. Mailing Add: 4300 N Charles Baltimore MD 21218

RICHARDSON, CONSTANCE (COLEMAN)
PAINTER
b Indianapolis, Ind, Jan 18, 05. Study: Pa Acad Fine Arts. Work: Indianapolis Mus Art; Detroit Inst Arts; Santa Barbara Mus Art; John D Rockefeller III Collection; Columbus Gallery Fine Arts; Pa Acad Fine Arts, Philadelphia. Comn: This Land is Ours (painting), Omaha Nat Bank, 66. Exhib: Am Painting Today, Metrop Mus Art, New York, 50; Am Landscape, A Changing Frontier, Nat Collection Fine Arts, Washington, DC, 66; Fifty Artists from Fifty States Circulating Exhib, Am Fedn Arts, 67-68; Am Paintings of Ports & Harbors, 1774-1968, Jacksonville-Norfolk, 69; Remnants of Things Past, Jacksonville-St Petersburg, 71. Bibliog: Louise Bruner (auth), Constance Richardson, Am Artist, 1/61; Alan Gussow (auth), A sense of place: the artist & the American land, Sat Rev, 71. Media: Oil. Dealer: Kennedy Galleries 20 E 56th St New York NY 10022. Mailing Add: 285 Locust St Philadelphia PA 19106

RICHARDSON, EDGAR PRESTON
ART HISTORIAN
b Glens Falls, NY, Dec 2, 02. Study: Univ Pa; Williams Col; Pa Acad Fine Arts. Pos: Ed, Art Quart, 38-64; dir, Detroit Inst Arts, 45-62; dir, H F du Pont Winterthur Mus, 62-66; chmn, Smithsonian Art Comn, 63-66; pres, Pa Acad Fine Arts, 68-70. Mem: Arch Am Art (dir); Am Philos Soc; Hist Soc Pa (vpres); Nat Portrait Gallery Comn; Am Antiquarian Soc. Publ: Auth, The Way of Western Art, 39 & 67; auth, American Romantic Painting, 44; auth, Washington Allston, 48 & 67; auth, Painting in America—the Story of 450 Years, 56 & 65; auth, A Short History of Painting in America, 63. Mailing Add: 285 Locust St Philadelphia PA 19106

RICHARDSON, FRANK, JR
MURALIST
b Baltimore, Md, Jan 14, 50. Study: Community Col of Baltimore, AA; Md Inst Col Art, BFA; Towson State Col; Riverside Art Ctr with Jacob Laurence, Romare Bearden. Work: ILE-IFE Mus Afro-American Cult, Philadelphia; ThirdWorld Mus, 111 & Assoc, Baltimore; Merabash Mus, Inc, Willingboro, NJ; Old Slave Mart Mus, Charleston, SC; Nat Ctr Afro-American Artists, Inc, Dorchester, Mass. Comn: Mural for film Amazing Grace, 74; mural, Enoch Pratt Free Libr, Baltimore, 74; Black Art (murals), FAN: Baltimore Arts Tower, 74; Amen America, (murals with Berkeley S Thompson), Asn Black Arts/East, Nat Endowment for the Arts, 75. Exhib: 1st & 2nd Wide-Regional, Black Art Show, Baltimore; Black Mural Painter, Inst Art Ctr, Lima, Peru, 75; Mural Painter, Univ Pretoria, Repub South Africa, 75. Collections Arranged: An Evening With the Links, 74; Awards Extravaganza 74. Teaching: Dir graphics, Sinai Druid Camp, Baltimore, 71-72; dir, Mus Prep Sch, 72-; instr printing, Career Opportunities Inc, Baltimore, 71- Awards: Best Black Art Work in Show, Black Cult Endowment, INC, 69; Children's Hour Prog, Md Art Coun, 74; ThirdWorld Prep Sch, Nat Endowment Arts, 75. Bibliog: Averil Jordan-Kadis (auth), Colorful Mural, Baltimore Sun, 67; Priscilla Coger (auth), Mr Richardson's Beautiful Wall, Baltimore Afro-American, 72; James Kelmartin (auth), Museum Unit to Expand, News American, 75. Mem: Asn of Black Arts/East. Style & Technique: Realistically black & white graphically illustrated, expressionistic, cubistic form. Media: Paint. Mailing Add: 552 Baker St Baltimore MD 21217

RICHARDSON, GRETCHEN (MRS RONALD FREELANDER)
SCULPTOR
b Detroit, Mich. Study: Wellesley Col, BA; Acad Julian, Paris, France; Art Students League, with William Zorach & Jose de Creeft. Work: Work in numerous pvt collections. Exhib: Int Arts Club, London, Eng; Pa Acad Fine Arts, Audubon Artists & Knickerbocker Artists, Lever House, New York; plus several one-man shows. Awards: I A R Wylie Prize, Nat Asn Women Artists, 52, Amelia Peabody Prize, 55 & Mary Kellner Mem Prize, 59 & 72; Award, Knickerbocker Artists, 70. Mem: Audubon Artists (sculpture jury, 71); Nat Asn Women Artists (exec comt, 52-55, sculpture jury, 69-71 & 77-79); Artists Equity Asn New York. Style & Technique: Stone carving, semi-abstract of human and animal forms. Media: Stone, Marble. Dealer: Bodley Gallery 1063 Madison Ave New York NY 10028. Mailing Add: 530 Park Ave New York NY 10021

RICHARDSON, JAMES LEWIS
EDUCATOR, PRINTMAKER
b Monett, Mo, Oct 8, 27. Study: Southwest Mo State Univ, BS, 52 & BS(educ), 54; Univ Ark, MEd, 62; Wichita State Univ, MFA, 70. Work: Spiva Art Ctr, Joplin, Mo; Hunter Col, New York; Wichita State Univ, Kans; Univ Mo, Rolla; Univ Ark, Fayetteville. Exhib: One-man show, Marymount Col, Salina, Kans; Watercolor USA, Springfield, Mo, 65; 10-State Regional, Springfield, Mo, 62, 71 & 72; Delta Print & Drawing, Little Rock, Ark, 70-71; Nat Touring Show, Kans Printmakers, 71. Teaching: Prof printmaking, Southwest Mo State Univ, 61- & head art dept, 74- Awards: First Place, Mo Col Fac, State of Mo, 69; Third Place, Delta Print & Drawing, Ark Arts Ctr, 73. Mem: Nat Art Educ Asn; Mo State Teachers Art Educ Asn (district pres, 60-61). Style & Technique: Expressionist, printmaking. Media: Intaglio; Zinc, Copper & Collograph. Publ: Illusr, album cover and poster, world premiere opera Everyman, print also used by Southwest Mo State Univ Dept Music for Pub Broadcasting TV, 75. Mailing Add: Rte 10 Box 448 Springfield MO 65803

RICHARDSON, PHYLLIS A
ART ADMINISTRATOR, PAINTER
b Red Wing, Minn, May 15, 41. Study: Luther Col (Iowa), BA; Univ Minn, MA; Univ Ore; also with Chico de Silva, Brazil. Comn: Many pvt comns. Exhib: One-man show, Shades of the Past, Mus Art, Univ Ore, 74; Under 35 Invitational, Portland Art Mus, 74; Grand Galleria Nat Art Show, Seattle, 75; Ga Nat Show, 75; One Hundred Eighteen Art Gallery, Minneapolis, 75. Teaching: Sec teacher art, Columbia Heights, Minn, 69-71, art curric coordr, 71-73; asst prof art, Ore Col Educ, 73-76. Pos: Supt art, State of Ore, 74- Awards: Foreign Artist Award, Ministeria de Cultura, Brazil, 69. Mem: Artists Equity Asn; Portland Art Mus; Arts Ore Asn; Nat Art Educ Asn. Style & Technique: Stains on raw canvas with various color fields. Media: Acrylic, Mixed Media. Mailing Add: c/o Gallery 118 1007 Harmon Pl Minneapolis MN 55403

RICHARDSON, SAM
PAINTER, EDUCATOR
b Oakland, Calif, July 19, 34. Study: Calif Col Arts & Crafts, BA, 56 & MFA, 60. Work: Ft Worth Mus Art, Tex; Whitney Mus Am Art, New York; Milwaukee Mus Art; Univ Wis; Univ Sydney, Australia. Exhib: Paints Behind the Painters, Calif Palace of Legion of Honor, San Francisco, 67; Ill Biennial, Univ Ill, 67; Plastic as Plastic, 63 & Creative Casting, 73, Mus Contemp Crafts, New York; New Methods & Materials, Mus Mod Art, New York, 69; Reed Col Exhib, Ore, 69; Whitney Mus Am Art, 68-69; San Francisco Art Inst, 71; Mus Contemp Arts, Chicago, 71-72; Stanford Univ, Calif, 72; Vassar Col, 72; Rutgers Univ, 75; plus many other group & one-man shows. Teaching: Instr art, Oakland City Col, 60-61; art dir, Mus Contemp Crafts, New York, 61-63; asst prof art, San Jose State Univ, 63-66, assoc prof art, 67-72, prof art, 72- Dealer: Martha Jackson Gallery 521 W 57th St New York NY 10019; Hansen Fuller Gallery 228 Grant Ave San Francisco CA 94108. Mailing Add: 4121 Sequoyah Rd Oakland CA 94605

RICHENBURG, ROBERT BARTLETT
PAINTER, SCULPTOR
b Boston, Mass, July 14, 17. Style & Technique: George Washington Univ; Boston Univ; Corcoran Sch Art; Art Students League; Ozenfant Sch Art; Hans Hofmann Sch Fine Art. Work: Chrysler Mus Art; Aldrich Mus Contemp Art, Ridgefield, Conn; Berkeley Mus Art, Univ Calif; Whitney Mus Am Art; Mus Mod Art, New York; plus many others. Exhib: One-man shows, Tibor De Nagy Gallery, 59-64; Santa Barbara Mus Art, 61, Dayton Art Inst, 62 & Cornell Univ, Ithaca, NY, 64; Am Fedn Arts Traveling Exhibs, 60-61, 64-65 & 68-69; Mus Mod Art, New York, 61 & 63-64; Whitney Mus Am Art Painting Ann, 61, 64 & 68, Sculpture Ann, 68; Retrospective, Dana Arts Ctr, Colgate Univ, 70 & Ithaca Col Mus Art, 71; plus many other one-man & group shows. Teaching: Instr art, Pratt Inst; instr art, Cooper

Union; instr art, NY Univ; assoc prof art, Cornell Univ, 64-67; assoc prof art, grad adv art dept, fac coun mem & chmn self-study comt, Hunter Col, 67-70; Aruba Res Ctr, City Univ Prog, 70; prof art, Ithaca Col, 70- Mem: Am Asn Univ Prof; Col Art Asn Am; life mem Art Students League. Style & Technique: Style continuously evolves using many techniques and materials. Mailing Add: 121 E Remington Rd Ithaca NY 14850

RICHMAN, ROBERT M
ART ADMINISTRATOR, WRITER
b Connersville, Ind, Dec 22, 14. Study: Western Mich Univ, AB(Eng) & AB(hist); Univ Mich, AM. Collections Arranged: Arranged over 100 exhibits of recent work by contemporary artists from Europe, Asia and the Americas. Teaching: Instr, Univ Mich, 38-45; prof, Adelphi Col, 45-47; lectr philos art, Nat Gallery Art, Phillips Gallery & Libr Cong. Pos: Founder & pres, Inst Contemp Arts, Washington, DC, 47, trustee, mem exec comt & bd trustees, 47-; lit & art ed, New Repub Mag, 51-54; mem, President's Fine Arts Comt, 56-, chmn, 60-; mem, Washington Festival, 57-, dir, 58; mem, Am Nat Theatre & Acad, 58-; trustee, Nat Cult Ctr, 59-; trustee, Opera Soc Washington, 59-; trustee, Meridian House Found, 60-; trustee, Arena Stage, Washington Drama Soc, 60-; consult arts, Dept State, 61; trustee, Ctr Arts of Indian Am, 65- Awards: Hopwood Awards, 42-44; Cosmos Club Award, 55; Comdr Brit Empire, 59. Mem: Am Asn Mus Dirs; Am Asn Mus; fel Inst Arts & Lett; Col Art Asn Am; Artists Equity Asn; plus others. Publ: Publ, The Potter's Portfolio, 50; ed, The Arts at Mid-Century, 54; auth, Nature in the Modern Arts; contribr, New Repub & Kenyon Rev; plus others. Mailing Add: 3102 R St NW Washington DC 20007

RICHMOND, FREDERICK W
COLLECTOR, PATRON
b Boston, Mass, Nov 15, 23. Study: Harvard Univ, 42-43; Boston Univ, AB, 45; Pratt Inst, LLD. Pos: Chmn bd, Carnegie Hall Corp, 61; mem, NY State Coun Arts; chmn, New York Comt Young Audiences; co-chmn, Mayor's Comt Scholastic Achievement; bd mem, New York Studio Sch; (D) US Rep, House of Representatives, Washington, DC. Collection: Modern art. Mailing Add: 43 Pierpont St Brooklyn NY 11201

RICHMOND, LAWRENCE
COLLECTOR
b Hollis, NY, Oct 30, 09. Study: Dartmouth Col, AB. Pos: Trustee, Provincetown Art Asn & Mus (till 77, Provincetown Art Asn), 74, 75, 76 & 77, vpres, 77 & pres-elect, 78; pres, Provincetown Symphony Soc, 68-69. Collection: Primarily modern American painting and sculpture; African sculpture. Mailing Add: 7 Woodcrest Rd Great Neck NY 11024

RICHTER, HANK
PAINTER, SCULPTOR
b Cleveland, Ohio, Oct 10, 28. Study: Philadelphia Mus Sch of Art. Work: Heard Mus, Phoenix, Ariz; DeGrazia-Gonzales Cult Ctr & Mus, Casa Grande, Ariz; Valley Nat Bank Collection, Phoenix; First Nat Bank Collection, Tucson, Ariz; Read Mullan's Gallery of Western Art, Ariz State Univ. Comn: Corp Sculpture, Anchor Life, Elizabeth, NJ, 68; Fountain sculptures, Ariz Children's Colony, Randolph, 69; Green Pastures Rayetta (bronze sculpture of Champion Brown Swiss Cow), St John's Dairy, Glendale, Ariz, 77; Ted DeGrazia portrait (ltd edition pewter bas-relief plate) & Tracks Across America (series of six ltd edition pewter bas-relief sculptures), comn by Richard Smith, Century Reproductions, Inc, Wilmington, Mass, 77. Exhib: The West in Bronze, Phoenix Art Mus, 71; The West & Walter Bimson, Univ Ariz Mus Art, Tucson, 72; Mountain Oyster Invitational Show, Tucson, 74-77; Charles M Russell Invitational Art Auction, Great Falls, Mont, 76; First Ann San Dimas Am Indian & Cowboy Artists Soc Show, Calif, 77. Teaching: Student instr anat, Philadelphia Mus Sch Art, 49-50; instr creative design, Kachina Sch Art, Phoenix, 54-56; instr pvt classes, currently. Awards: Gold Medal, Atlanta Film Festival, 69; Golden Eagle, CINE/USA, 69. Bibliog: The West & Walter Bimson, Univ Ariz Press, 72; Pat Broder (auth), Bronzes of the American West, Abrams, 75; Lil Rhodes (auth), A man and his art, Southwest Art, 78. Mem: Am Indian & Cowboy Artists Soc; Western Art Assoc. Style & Technique: Traditional style depicting historical and contemporary western subject matter. Media: (Sculpture) Bronze and Pewter; (Painting) Oil and Acrylic. Dealer: Jack DeCoursey c/o Mary Livingston's Gallery 2 1211 N Broadway Santa Ana CA 92701; Richard Smith c/o Century Reproductions Inc 1612 W Geneva Tempe AZ 85282. Mailing Add: 219 W Montebello Phoenix AZ 85013

RICKEY, GEORGE W
SCULPTOR
b South Bend, Ind, June 6, 07. Study: Trinity Col, Scotland; Balliol Col, Oxford Univ, BA & MA, 41; Ruskin Sch Drawing, Oxford Univ; Acad Andre L'Hote & Acad Mod, Paris; Hon DFA, Knox Col, 70, Union Col, 73 & Ind Univ, Bloomington, 74. Work: Albright-Knox Art Gallery, Buffalo, NY; Joseph H Hirshhorn Mus & Sculpture Garden, Washington, DC; Mus Boymans-van Beuningen, Rotterdam, Neth; Universitätsbauamt Ulm, Ger; Physikzentrum, New Univ, Kiel, Ger; Mus Mod Art, New York; Neue Nationalgalerie, Berlin, Ger. Comn: Kinetic sculpture, Kunsthalle, Hamburg, Ger, 63, Rijksmuseum Kroller-Muller, Otterlo, Neth, 65, Nordpark, Dusseldorf, Ger, 65 & Nat Collection Fine Arts, Washington, DC, 67; Ft Worth City Hall, Tex, 74; comn for Prince Jonah Kalanianaole Bldg, Honolulu, Hawaii, 75. Exhib: Sculpture from Twenty Nations, Guggenheim Mus, New York, 67; Plus by Minus, Albright-Knox Art Gallery, 68; Int Sculptors' Symp, Osaka, Japan, 69; George Rickey Retrospective, 51-71, Univ Calif Los Angeles Art Coun, 71-72; Kestner Gesellschaft, Hannover, Ger, 73; Fordham Univ Plaza, Lincoln Ctr, New York, 75; Kunsthalle Bielefeld, Ger, 76; Städel Mus, Frankfurt, Ger, 77; Hammerskjold Plaza, New York, NY, 77. Awards: Nat Fine Arts Honor Award, Am Inst Architects, 72. Bibliog: Engineer of movement, Time Mag, 11/4/66; Peter Riedl (auth), George Rickey: kinetische objekte, Philipp Reclam J, Stuttgart, 70; Nan Rosenthal (auth), George Rickey, Abrams, New York, 77. Mem: Nat Inst Arts & Lett. Media: Stainless Steel. Publ: Auth, Constructivism: Origins & Evolution, Braziller, 67. Mailing Add: East Chatham NY 12060

RIDLEY, GREGORY D, JR
PAINTER, SCULPTOR
b Smyrna, Tenn, July 18, 25. Study: Fisk Univ, 45-48, with Aaron Douglas; Univ Louisville, Ky, with Ulfret Wilke; Tenn State Univ, BS, 51. Work: Fisk Univ; Winston-Salem State Teacher's Col, NC; Tenn State Univ; Carver Savings Bank, New York; McDonald's Restaurants, New York. Comn: Directed mural, Harlem Hosp Ctr, 70; St Jaquims, Queens, NY, 71; McDonald's Restaurant, Harlem, 73-74. Exhib: Fisk Univ Show, Pa, Ky & Tenn, 66-75; South Cent Show, Nashville, Tenn, 67-71; Amstad II, 75. Teaching: Asst prof art, Ala State Col, 51-58, Grambling Col, 58-62, Elizabeth City State, 62-64, Tenn State Univ, 66-71 & 75-78 & Fisk Univ, 66-71; adj in art, Brooklyn Col, 66-75, Lehman Col, summers 71-74 & Medgar Evers Col, summers 71-75. Pos: Cult coordr, Harlem Backstreet Youth Inc, 67. Awards: Six Prizes, Atlanta Univ Ann, 51-65; Gettysburg First Prize Gold Medal, Am Soc Vet, 65. Bibliog: TV documentaries, WTOL, Toledo, Ohio, 62 & WLAC, Nashville, 70; Cedric Dover (auth), American Negro Art. Mem: Nat Conf Artist (vchmn, 62); Am Asn Univ Prof; Nat Educ Asn. Style & Technique: Sculpture in stone and wood; repousse in metal. Res: Great Battles of the Civil War. Collection: 216 other artists work including African masks. Publ: Contribr, Great Negroes Past and Present, 65, Decision for Destiny, 74 & Amstad II, 75; auth, Two Centuries of Black American Art, Driskell, 77. Mailing Add: 1106 28th Ave N Nashville TN 37208

RIDLON, JAMES A
SCULPTOR, EDUCATOR
b Nyack, NY, July 11, 34. Study: Syracuse Univ, BA, 57, MFA, 65; San Francisco State Col, 58-59. Work: Munson-Williams-Proctor Inst, Utica, NY; Julliard Sch, New York; Rochester Mem Gallery, NY; Everson Mus, Syracuse, NY; State Legislature Bldg, Albany, NY. Comn: Sculptured mural, C & U Broadcasting, 58; Bert Bell Mem Trophy, Long Island Athletic Club, 68; assemblage, Merchants Nat Bank Bldg, Rochester, 71. Exhib: One-man shows, Wells Col, 71 & Schuman Gallery, Rochester, 71; Graphics 71, Nat Print & Drawing Exhib, Western NMex Univ, 71; New Paintings, Everson Mus Art, 74; one-man retrospective, Logan Alexander Ctr Creative Arts, Concord Col, 75; Lubin House Gallery, New York, 77; Herbert F Johnson Mus, Cornell Univ, Ithaca, NY, 77; Two Rivers Gallery, Binghamton, NY, 77; plus others. Teaching: Asst sculpture, San Francisco State Col, 58; lectr art educ, Syracuse Univ, 65-67, assoc prof sculpture & synaesthetic educ, 68-74, prof sculpture & synaesthetic educ, 74- Pos: Dir, NY State Summer Sch Arts Sch of Visual Arts. Awards: Purchase Prize, 32nd Ann Exhib, Munson-Williams-Proctor Inst, 68; Graphics 1969 Award, NY State Fair, 69; First Prize in Sculpture, 10th Ann Westchester Art Soc Exhib, 70. Mem: Nat Art Educ Asn; NY State Art Teachers Asn; Assoc Artists Syracuse; Cooperstown Art Asn. Style & Technique: Abstract; collage. Publ: Contribr, Synaesthetic Education, Syracuse Univ, 71; auth, Synaesthetic education as a basis for symbolic expression, Humanities J, 5/73. Dealer: Oxford Gallery 267 Oxford Rochester NY 14607; Alan Brown Gallery 60 E Hartsdale Ave Hartsdale NY 10530. Mailing Add: Fire House 20 401 Elliott St Syracuse NY 13204

RIEGEL, MICHAEL BYRON
METALSMITH
b Hannibal, Mo, Nov 21, 46. Study: Eastern Ill Univ, Charleston, BSEd, 68, MA, 72; Southern Ill Univ, Carbondale, MFA, 74, study with Brent Kington. Work: Ark Art Ctr, Little Rock; Ill State Mus, Springfield. Exhib: 2nd Biennial Lake Superior Nat Craft Exhib, Tweed Mus of Art, Univ Minn, Duluth, 72; 7th Biennial Beaux Arts Designer Craftsmen Exhib, Columbus Gallery of Fine Arts, Ohio, 73; Miss River Craft Exhib, Brooks Mem Art Gallery, Memphis, Tenn, 73 & 75; Baroque 74, Forms in Metal, 75 & Homage to the Bag, 75, Mus of Contemp Crafts, New York; Craft Multiples, Renwick Gallery, Smithsonian Inst, Washington, DC, 75; Goldsmiths, Phoenix Art Mus, Ariz, 77. Teaching: Instr design & 2-D design, Southeast Mo State Univ, Cape Girardeau, 75 & instr metalsmithing, 76; instr art metals & drawing, Calif State Univ, Sacramento, 76- Awards: Exhib Award, Goldsmiths, Renwick Gallery, 74, Design in Steel Award Prog, 74-75, Steel Indust, 75 & Miss River Craft Show, Brooks Mem Art Gallery, 76. Mem: Artists Blacksmiths Asn of NAm; Calif Blacksmiths Asn. Style & Technique: Figurative steel objects; chiseling and other blacksmithing techniques. Media: Steel. Mailing Add: c/o Dept of Art Calif State Univ 6000 J St Sacramento CA 95819

RIES, MARTIN
PAINTER, ART HISTORIAN
b Washington, DC, Dec 26, 26. Study: Corcoran Gallery Art, 40-44; Am Univ, with Jack Tworkov & Leo Steppat, BA, 50; Hunter Col, MA, 68, with Leo Steinberg, William Rubin, Ad Reinhardt & E C Goossen. Work: Pace Univ Mus; Riverside Mus Collection, Rose Art Mus, Brandeis Univ; Inst Cult Hisp, Madrid, Spain. Exhib: Corcoran Gallery Art, 52; Inst Cult Hisp, Univ Madrid, 55; Mus Mod Art, 56; Paul Gallery, Tokyo, Japan, 68; Verfeil, France, 73; plus others. Teaching: Instr medieval art hist, Marymount Col, 59; instr mod art hist, Hunter Col, 63-67; assoc prof hist art, drawing & painting, Long Island Univ, 68. Pos: Asst dir pub rels, Nat Cong Comt, 51; asst dir, Hudson River Mus, Yonkers, NY, 57-67; adv, Westchester Cult Ctr, 65-67; contrib ed, Arts Mag. Awards: Honorable Mention, 52nd Nat Soc Arts & Lett Award, Corcoran Gallery Art; Critics Choice, Whyte Gallery, 57. Style & Technique: Poetic, mystic and pagan; concerned with present day malaise, contemporary esthetics and life, as well as social and political themes. Res: Minotaur in Western art, from ancient Greek myth to contemporary art. Publ: Auth, Elusive Goya, New Repub, 57; auth, monthly articles, Hundon River Mus Bull, 57-67; auth, Endowments for great society, Art Voices Mag, 65 & New Art, 66. Mailing Add: 36 Livingston Rd Scarsdale NY 10583

RIESLAND, ALANA KATHLEEN CORDY-COLLINS
See Cordy-Collins, Alana

RIESS, LORE
PAINTER, PRINTMAKER
b Berlin, Ger; US citizen. Study: Art Acad, Contempora (Bauhaus Sch), Berlin; Sumi Drawing & Calligraphy, Tokyo; Art Students League. Work: Corcoran Gallery Art, Washington, DC; Israel Mus, Jerusalem; Tel-Aviv Mus, Israel; US Embassy, Tokyo; Rutgers Univ, NJ. Comn: Ed of etchings, Mickelson Gallery, Washington, DC, 71. Exhib: One-man shows, Nihon Bashi Gallery, Tokyo, 65, Nat Asn Women Artists, 69, Painters & Sculptors Soc Nat, Old Jaffa Nora Gallery, Israel, 70, Painters & Sculptors Soc Nat, 71 & Int Miniature Print Exhib, 71. Awards: William McNulty Merit Award, Art Students League, 64; M J Kaplan Prize, Nat Asn Women Artists, 69; Gallery of Graphic Art Award, Int Miniature Print Exhib, 71. Bibliog: T Ichinose (auth), Colorful abstract oils by Lore Riess, Mainichi Daily News, 65; articles in Art News, 5/66, Washington Post, 1/67 & Jerusalem Post, 7/70 & 3/71. Media: Oil. Dealer: Alonzo Gallery 30 W 57th St New York NY 10019. Add: One Lincoln Plaza New York NY 10023

RIFKIN, DR & MRS HAROLD
COLLECTORS
Collection: American art of the early twentieth century. Mailing Add: 35 E 75th St New York NY 10021

RIFKIND, ROBERT GORE
COLLECTOR
b Beverly Hills, Calif, July 12, 28. Study: Univ Calif, Los Angeles, AB, 50; Harvard Univ, LLB, 54. Collections Arranged: German Expressionist Art, The Robert Gore Rifkind Collection of prints, drawings, illustrated books, periodicals and posters, Frederick S Wight Art Galleries, Univ Calif, Los Angeles, Mar-Apr, 77, New Orleans Mus of Art, La, June-Aug, 78, Busch-Reisinger Mus, Harvard Univ, Cambridge, Mass, Nov 78-Jan 79; Milwaukee Art Inst, Wis, Mar-Apr, 79 & St Louis Art Mus, Mo, Nov-Dec, 79. Collection: Approximately 6,000 German Expressionist graphic works; German Expressionist Art History Library consisting of approximately 4,500 volumes, including periodicals and catalogues. Publ: Contribr, O P Reed, Jr, auth, German Expressionist Art, The Robert Gore Rifkind Collection, Prints, Drawings, Illustrated Books, Periodicals, Posters, A Wofsy Fine Arts, 77. Mailing Add: 9454 Wilshire Blvd Beverly Hills CA 90212

RIGBY, IDA KATHERINE
ART HISTORIAN
b Los Angeles, Calif, May 10, 44. Study: Stanford Univ, BA(hist & philos), MA(educ); Ecole des Beaux Arts, Tours, France; Univ Calif, Berkeley, MA, PhD(art hist), 74. Teaching: Asst prof mod art hist, Univ Montana, Missoula, spring 1972; instr mod art hist, Newcomb Col, Tulane Univ, New Orleans, 72-74; asst prof mod art hist, Univ Victoria, BC, 74-76; asst prof mod art & archit, San Diego State Univ, 76- Awards: Kress Found Grant; Grant, Deutscher Akademischer Austauschdienst, Bonn. Mem: Col Art Asn; Art Historians of Southern Calif; Univ Art Asn of Can. Res: German Expressionism; German Romanticism; and the relationship between the two in the area of landscape painting; German Expressionist artists and politics; politics of opposition and official collaboration in Germany during the 1930's. Publ: Auth, The Role of Titles, In: Friedrich Hundertwasser, Univ Calif, Berkeley Press, 69; auth, The iconography of Nazi art, Vol 6 (Nov, 1973); auth, Karl Hofer: paradise lost, Vol 7 (Apr, 1974), SECAC Rev & Newsletter; auth, Karl Hofer, Garland Publ, 76; auth, The Expressionist Artist and Revolution, 1918-1922 & Entartete Kunst, 1933-1938, In: German Expressionist Art: The Robert Gore Rifkind Collection, Univ Calif, Los Angeles Press, 77. Mailing Add: Dept of Art San Diego State Univ San Diego CA 92182

RIGG, MARGARET RUTH
PAINTER, CALLIGRAPHER
b Pittsburgh, Pa, Dec 14, 29. Study: Carnegie-Mellon Univ, 45-49; Fla State Univ, BA, 51; Scarrett Col; Presby Sch, MA, 55; George Peabody Col; Chicago Art Inst, 65; painting with Edmund Lewandowski & Florence Kawa; design & theory with Mathias Goeritz; Chinese calligraphy with Tsutomu Yoshida, Kim Hahn & Tennyson Chang; Eng calligraphy with Sister Corita Kent & Jan Steward. Work: Tenn Collection, Smithsonian Inst; Emillle Mus, Seoul, Korea; Turku Univ Mus, Finland; NH Mus, Manchester; Korea Fulbright House, Seoul. Comn: Stained glass windows, Mexico City Nat Cathedral, 61; stained glass window, communion table, lecturn & celtic cross, Univ NC, Chapel Hill, 61; calligraphy mural, Experiment House, Vere, Jamaica; calligraphy letterhead & gates to campus, Eckerd Col, 72. Exhib: Man's Disorder, God's Design, Univ Ill, 52 & Krannert Art Mus, Univ Nebr-Lincoln, 61; Am Artists, Am Cult Ctr, Seoul, 73; Bicentennial Art, Mus Fine Arts, St Petersburg, Fla, 75-76; Ringling Mus Art Arch, Sarasota, Fla; plus others. Teaching: Artist in residence, Fla Presby Col, 65-67; prof visual art, Eckerd Col, 67- Pos: Staff artist, Bd Publ, Fla State Univ, 51-53; art ed, Motive Mag, 54-65; owner-publr, Possum Press. Awards: Fulbright-Hays Sr Res Grant in Chinese Calligraphy, Korea, 72. Bibliog: Meinke & Hodgell (auth), Very Seldom Animals, 69, 2nd ed, 77 & Survivor's Box, Vol 1, 75, Barbara Chaulk (auth), Poems & Why, 75 & Amos Wilder (auth), The Web, 78, Possum Press. Mem: Int Soc Women Calligraphers; COSMEP; Soc Italic Handwriting; Nashville Artist Guild (pres, 63-64); Fla Artist Group, Inc; Soc Art Dir. Brush calligraphy on Oriental paper; construction painting. Media: Quill & Ink, Brush & Chinese Ink. Dealer: Joan Hodgell c/o Contemp Gallery 110 First Ave NE St Petersburg FL 33701. Mailing Add: 4260 Narvarez Way S St Petersburg FL 33712

RIGSBY, JOHN DAVID
PAINTER, ART ADMINISTRATOR
b Tallassee, Ala, Oct 10, 34. Study: Univ Ala, BFA & MS(urban studies); Southern Conn State Col; Columbia Univ, with Leon Goldin. Work: Telfair Acad Arts & Sci, Savannah, Ga; Univ Ala Gallery Collection; Beaufort Mus, SC; US Embassy, Tunis, Tunisia; Brit Coun, Tunis. Comn: Sculpture, Mobil Art Ctr, Ala, 63. Exhib: One-man shows, Delgado Mus, New Orleans, 64, Galerie Munic, Tunis, 67, Telfair Acad, 69 & Columbia Mus, SC, 71; Am Artists Tunisia, US Info Serv, 66; Guild SC Artists Ann, 71; Springs Mills, 73; two-man show, Sch Art & Archit, Yale Univ, 73 & Alabama Bag, Washington, DC, 75; plus others. Teaching: Nat Endowment Arts artist in residence, Beaufort Pub Sch Syst, SC, 70-73. Pos: Consult art, Ctr Urban Educ, New York, 68-69; dir Vol Community Serv Prog, Action Bridgeport Community Develop, Conn, 68-69; nat coordr visual arts educ prog, Nat Endowment Arts, 74- Awards: Merit Award, Artists of Southeast & Tex, Delgado Mus, 63; Merit Award, Guild SC Artists Exhib, 71; Springs Mills Traveling Exhib Award, 72. Bibliog: Al Wardi (auth), Dans le tournoi de l'art avec John David Rigsby, L'Action, 2/29/67; Gaynor Pearson (auth), The one room school now has wheels, Conn Educ, 2/68; Oliver & Sisk (auth), Artist in residence—a first for South Carolina, SC Educ J, winter 71. Mem: Guild SC Artists; Nat Art Educ Asn; Col Art Asn Am; Nat Soc Lit & Arts. Style & Technique: Abstract painterly assemblage. Media: Oil, Acrylic. Res: Design of cultural enrichment programs as a basis for community participation; relationship of public arts legislation to the process of artists in schools programs. Mailing Add: c/o 641 Gallery 641 Indiana Ave Washington DC 20004

RILEY, ART (ARTHUR IRWIN)
PAINTER, PHOTOGRAPHER
b Boston, Mass, Sept 14, 11. Study: Art Ctr Sch Los Angeles. Exhib: Am Watercolor Soc, New York; Calif Watercolor Soc, Los Angeles Co Mus Art; Springfield Art Mus, Mo; Youngstown Art Mus, Ohio; one-man show, Pacific Grove Art Mus, Calif. Pos: Artist, MGM Studios, 5 yrs; artist, Walt Disney Studios, 37-65. Awards: Am Watercolor Soc Award; Laguna Beach Art Asn Award; Butler Inst Am Art Award; plus others. Mem: Acad Motion Picture Arts & Sci; Am Watercolor Soc. Style & Technique: Direct painting on location. Publ: Auth & illusr, article in Am Artist Mag; contribr, Sat Eve Post, Ariz Hwys, Ford Times, Life Mag & others. Dealer: Pebble Beach California Gallery Pebble Beach CA 93953; The Palette Carmel CA 93921. Mailing Add: 608 N First St Burbank CA 91502

RILEY, BERNARD JOSEPH
PAINTER
b Bridgeport, Conn, Mar 27, 15. Study: Self-taught & study with Nelson Gordy, James Dougherty. Work: Metrop Mus Mus of Art, New York; Mus of Art, Science & Industry, Bridgeport, Conn; Corcoran Gallery, Washington, DC; Municipal Court Bldg, Washington, DC; Sacred Heart Univ, Bridgeport, Conn. Comn: Life of St Aloysius Gonzaga (7 1/2ft x 28ft), Fairfield Univ, 59; processional (gold leaf, 5 1/2ft x 12ft), comn by Dr Harold Wesley, Stamford, Conn, 70; Medici (6ft x 9ft), St Vincents Medical Ctr, 77; History of Bridgeport (14ft x 40ft), Conn Comn of the Arts, Bridgeport Pub Libr, 76. Exhib: Pa Acad of Fine Arts, Philadelphia, 46, 52 & 58; New England Regional Silvermine Artist, New Cannan, 51-56; Silvermine Guild of Artist, 55-75; Nat Acad of Design Ann, New York, 56, 67 & 68; Detroit Inst Fine Art, 58; Wooster Sch, Danbury, 64; New York Worlds Fair, 64-65; Carlson Foundation Exhib, Bridgeport Univ, 67; Fairfield Library, 68; New York Hilton Gallery, 68; NC Mus of Art, 68; Am Acad of Arts & Lett, New York, 75; Housatonic Community Col, 76. Awards: Americana, Silvermine Regional, 53 & Maganini; Three Carl J Blenner Awards, New Haven Paint & Clay, Blenner Foundation. Bibliog: Audio staff of the Burroughs Library (auth & publ), Story of the History of the Bridgeport Mural, 76. Mem: Silvermine Guild of Artists (bd of trustees), 58-; Conn Acad of Fine Art; Paint & Clay Club; 3rd Stream Art Asn. Style & Technique: Multiple figures in line and form. Media: Oil and/or Acrylic. Dealer: Silvermine Guild of Artist 1037 Silvermine Rd New Cannan CT 06840. Mailing Add: 295 Figlar Ave Fairfield CT 06430

RILEY, CHAPIN
COLLECTOR
Mem: Art Collectors Club. Collection: Modern painting and sculpture. Mailing Add: 9 Plastic St Worcester MA 01604

RILEY, GERALD PATRICK
CRAFTSMAN, SCULPTOR
b Oklahoma City, Okla, Sept 6, 41. Study: Univ Okla, BFA, 64, MA(art educ), 71. Work: Ark Arts Ctr, Little Rock; Contemp Arts Found, Oklahoma City; Okla State Art Collection, Oklahoma City; Fred Jones Mem Art Ctr, Univ Okla. Comn: Body sculpture and set design for ballet, Firebird, presented by Oklahoma City Ballet Soc, 74-75. Exhib: 5th Ann Okla Designer Craftsman Exhib, Mus Art, Univ Okla, 72, Mask, Fred Jones Mem Art Ctr, 74; Three Craftsmen, Ark State Univ, 73; Exhib Am Craftsmen, Fairtree Gallery Contemp Crafts, New York, 73; Plummage, Elements Gallery of Contemp Crafts, Greenwich, Conn, 74; plus others. Teaching: Instr gen art, Okla Art Ctr, 66-71; instr art & chmn dept, John Marshall High Sch, Oklahoma City, 68-75; pvt instr, 75- Pos: Educ dir, Okla Art Ctr, 67-69; dir creative educ lab, Oklahoma City Arts Coun, 71-72. Awards: Jewelry Award, Okla Designer Craftsman, 70 & 71; Purchase Award, Ark Arts Ctr, 71. Bibliog: Exhibitions, Craft Horizons, 3-4/69, 1-2/70 & 11-12/71. Mem: Nat Art Educ Asn (states assembly, 67-71); Okla Art Educ Asn (pres, 69-71); Oklahoma City Art Educ Asn (pres, 67-68); Am Crafts Coun; Okla Designer Craftsman Asn (vpres, 69-71). Style & Technique: Constructed sculptures made of found objects woven into shapes. Media: Constructed Objects, Assorted Fibers; Leather, Metal. Mailing Add: c/o Okla Art Ctr 3113 Pershing Blvd Fair Park-Plaza Cir Oklahoma City OK 73107

RILEY, ROY JOHN
PAINTER, DESIGNER
b Independence, Kans, Apr 19, 03. Study: Calif Arts & Crafts; Detroit Art Sch; Huettles Art Sch, Chicago; Univ Tulsa, with Franz Vanderlachen; also with Merlin Enabnet. Comn: Mural, Travel & Transport Bldg, Chicago World's Fair, 33. Exhib: Assoc Artists Philbrook, Tulsa, Okla; Ruskin Club, Tulsa; Verdigris Valley Art Exhib, Independence, Kans; Scottsdale Artist League, Ariz; two one-man shows, Philbrook Art Gallery, Tulsa. Pos: Demonstr, Artist in Action Shows, Philbrook Art Gallery, Art Asns in Bartlesville, Okla, Ft Smith, Ark, civic group in Scottsdale, Ariz & univs. Awards: Philbrook Art Gallery, 45, Ruskin Club, 45 & Scottsdale Artist League, 69. Style & Technique: Sculpture compositions in primitive art; light plastics representative of stone. Media: Oil. Dealer: Fisher Gallery 1081 N Palm Canyon Dr Palm Springs CA 92263. Mailing Add: 140 W Granada Rd Phoenix AZ 85003

RIMMER, DAVID MCLELLAN
FILM ARTIST
b Vancouver, BC, Jan 20, 42. Study: Univ BC, BA. Work: Nat Gallery Can, Ottawa; Mus Mod Art, New York; Vancouver Art Gallery; Donnel Br, New York Pub Libr; Cinemateque Canadienne, Montreal. Comn: Films, Can Coun Arts, Ottawa, 69, 71 & 73. Exhib: One-man film show, Mus Mod Art, New York, 71; Am Film Festival, New York, 72; Form & Structure in Recent Film, Vancouver Art Gallery, 72; Canada Trajectoires '73, Mus Mod Art, Paris, 73; London Independent & Avant-Guard Film Festival, Eng, 73. Teaching: Instr film, Simon Fraser Univ, 69; instr film, Univ BC, 73-; instr film, Vancouver Sch Art, 75- Awards: Award of Merit, Yale Film Festival, 68; Best British Columbia Film & Best Editing Award, Vancouver Int Film Festival, 69; First Prize in Experimental Category, 14th Ann Am Film Festival, 72. Bibliog: Gene Youngblood (auth), The new Canadian cinema: images from the age of paradox, Arts Can Mag, 4/70; Kristina Nordstrom (auth), The films of David Rimmer, Village Voice, New York, 4/72; Roger Greenspun (auth), Quick—who are David Rimmer and James Herbert, New York Times, 10/8/72. Style & Technique: Structural, personal, conceptual films. Media: Movie Film. Dealer: Canadian Filmmakers Dist Ctr 67 Portland St Toronto ON Can. Mailing Add: 358 Powell St Vancouver BC V6A 1G4 Can

RINEHART, MICHAEL
ART LIBRARIAN, EDITOR
b Maimi, Fla, Dec 27, 34. Study: Harvard Univ, BA, 56; Courtauld Inst, Univ London, 57-59. Teaching: Lectr Italian Renaissance art, WillwimsxColWilliams Col, Williamstown, Mass, 67- Pos: Librn, Clark Art Inst, Williamstown. Mem: Col Art Asn. Publ: Auth, Fifty Years of Beresoniana (catalog), Valdonega, Verona, 62; ed B Berenson, Italian Pictures of the Renaissance, Florentine School, London, 63; auth, A Drawing by Vasari for the Studio of Francesca I, Burlington Mag, 64; auth, Practical Support on an International Basis for the Bibliography of Art History, CNRS, Paris, 69. Mailing Add: c/o Clark Art Inst Williamstown MA 01267

RING, EDWARD ALFRED
ART PUBLISHER, COLLECTOR
b New York, NY. Collections Arranged: Focus on Light, NJ State Mus, Trenton, 67. Pos: Owner, Carter Gallery, formerly; mem, NJ State Coun Arts, 67-, chmn, 71-; partner, Artnews. Mem: Am Fedn Arts; Metrop Mus Art; Mus Mod Art; Los Angeles Mus Art. Mailing Add: RR 1 Box 303 Titusville NJ 08560

RINGGOLD, FAITH
PAINTER, SCULPTOR
b New York, NY, Oct 8, 34. Study: City Col New York, BS, 55, MA, 59; also with Robert Gwathney. Work: Chase Manhattan Bank, New York. Comn: For the Womens House (mural), Women House Detention, Rikers Island, NY, 71. Exhib: Memorial for MLK, Mus Mod Art, New York, 68; American Women Artists, Kunsthaus, Hamburg, Ger, 72; Women Choose Women, New York Cult Ctr, 73; Faith Ringgold, Retrospect, Univ Art Gallery, Rutgers Univ, 73; Jubilee, Boston Mus, 75; 2nd World Black & African Festival Arts & Cult, Lagos, Nigeria, 77; one-person show, Douglass Col, Rutgers Univ, New Brunswick, NJ, 78. Teaching: Artist lecturer African crafts, Bank Street Col, New York, 70-; artist lectr Black art, Wagner Col, 70-; artist lectr African arts, Mus Natural Hist, New York, 73- Awards: Creative Artists Pub Serv Prog Grant, 71; Am Asn Univ Women Artists fel, 8 76. Bibliog: Mel Tapley (auth), Harlem the show, 12/27/75 & About the arts, 6/5/76, Amsterdam News; Lucy Lippard (auth), Faith Ringgold—Flying her own flag, MS Mag, 7/76. Style & Technique: Soft sculptural and painting environment. Media: Mixed. Publ: Co-auth, What's more important to me is art for people, Arts Mag, Sept-Oct/70; contribr, Black art, what is it?, Art Gallery Guide, 4/70; auth, An open show in every museum, 4/72, The Gedok show, fall 73 & Documenta, summer 73, Feminist Art J. Mailing Add: 345 W 145th St New York NY 10031

RINHART, GEORGE R
ART DEALER, COLLECTOR
b Neptune, NJ, Sept 2, 44. Study: Fla State Univ; study of hist of photog with Walker Evans, Philippe Halsman & Todd Webb. Teaching: Sem on hist of photog, Univ of NMex, Albuquerque, fall 75; sem hist of 19th & 20th century photog, Univ of Ga, Athens, summer

77. Pos: Mem bd of dirs, Photog Hist Soc of NY, 71-; chmn bd, Hastings Galleries Ltd; pres, Underwood & Underwood News Photos Inc; pres & owner, Rinhart Galleries Inc, New York. Bibliog: Articles in New York Times, Popular photog, Camera 35 (spec issue), Preview Mag, Antique Trader & Bus Wk. Mem: Honorable Order of Ky Colonels, 77- Res: History of stereographs of the world, extensive research in history of 19th and 20th century photography and individual photographers (some 6000); Civil War Period; Lincoln and Lincolniana expert; American presidency expert. Specialty: Paintings, drawings, photographs, post cards, Americana. Collection: American presidency; Lincolniana, Lincoln Collection. Mailing Add: Rinhart Galleries Inc 710 Park Ave New York NY 10021

RIPPEY, CLAYTON
PAINTER, EDUCATOR
b La Grande, Ore, Apr 24, 23. Study: Northwestern Univ; Stanford Univ, BA & MA, with Daniel Mendelowitz, Ray Faulkner & Anton Refrigier; San Jose State Col, with George Post; Inst Allende, Mex, with James Pinto & Fred Samuelson. Work: Cunningham Mus, Bakersfield, Calif; Dance Mag Hq, New York; Wakayama Castle, Japan. Comn: Pylon design & mural, Bakersfield Col, Calif, 58; two murals, Valley Plaza Mall, Bakersfield, 67; three-dimensional mural, Tenneco Corp Hq, Bakersfield, 69; mural, Bakersfield Californian Publ Hq, 75; mural, Nat Martinize Corp, 77; plus others. Exhib: Lucian Labaudt Gallery, San Francisco, 55; Cunningham Mem Mus, Bakersfield, 58, 61 & 66; Circulo de Belles Artes, Palma, Spain, 60; Pioneer & Haggen Mus, Stockton, Calif, 64; Port Townsend Art Ctr (festival guest exhibitor), Wash, 65; plus over 40 one-man shows. Teaching: Prof painting, Bakersfield Col, 49-, chmn dept, 68-72; prof painting, Maui Community Col, Univ Hawaii, 67-68. Pos: Dir exhibs, Cunningham Mus, Bakersfield, 54-55; dir exhibs, Bakersfield Col Gallery, 61-62. Awards: 13 Awards, Traveling Show, Kern Co, 60; Best of Show, Kern Co Fair Asn, 63, 65 & 67; Best of Show, Taft Art Asn, 72. Mem: Hon life mem Taft Art Asn; Bakersfield Art Asn (vpres, 54); Calif Art Educ Asn. Dealer: Gallery Yves Jaubert 75 Farbour St Honore Paris France; Dealer: Cezanne Gallery Int PO Box 2354 Bakersfield CA 93303. Mailing Add: 4017 Eton Bakersfield CA 93306

RIPPON, RUTH MARGARET
CERAMIST, EDUCATOR
b Sacramento, Calif, Jan 12, 27. Study: Calif Col Arts & Crafts, BA(educ), 47 & MFA, 51, with Antonio Prieto; San Francisco Sch Fine Arts, scholar, with Joan J Pearson. Work: Crocker Art Mus, Sacramento; Prieto Mem Collection, Mills Col, Oakland; Chico State Univ; Calif Expos & Fair, Sacramento; Artists Contemp Gallery, Sacramento. Comn: Relief tile garden wall, Ralph Jones, landscape archit, Piedmont, Calif, 57; relief tile garden wall, Calif Expos by Grant Duggins, 58; Nativity Creche, Crocker Art Mus, Sacramento, 72. Exhib: Nat & int shows, Everson Mus, Syracuse, NY; Wichita Decorative Arts, Kans; Calif Crafts, Oakland Nat Tour, US Info Serv, 60; one-person shows, Artists Contemp Gallery, Sacramento, 67, 69, 72 & 74, Univ Pac, Stockton, Calif, 76 & Univ Rochester, NY, 76; Calif Crafts, Sacramento; 20-Yr Retrospective, Crocker Art Mus, Sacramento, 71; Oakland Mus, 74; Calif State Univ, 75; Crocker Kingsley Retrospective, Sacramento, 75; plus others. Teaching: Crafts dir, Presidio of San Francisco, 54-56; prof ceramics, Calif State Univ, Sacramento, 56- Awards: Many Purchase Awards, Calif State Fair & Expos, Sacramento, 48-66; Presidents Wives Series, San Francisco Potters Asn, DeYoung Mus, 69-70. Bibliog: Oppi Untracht (auth), Ruth Rippon, Sgraffito Through Glaze, 57 & Fred Ball (auth), Ruth Rippon Retrospective, 71, Ceramics Monthly Mag; Ruth Holland (auth), Rippon Retrospective, Creative Arts League 71 Catalog, 71. Mem: Creative Arts League Sacramento; Asn San Francisco Potters; Am Crafts Coun; Crocker Art Gallery Asn. Style & Technique: Wheel thrown pottery and sculpture; coil and slab constructions with emphasis on textural surfaces, sgraffito, incised, perforated. Media: Stoneware, Porcelain Clay; Watercolor, Pencil. Mailing Add: 57 Sandburg Dr Sacramento CA 95819

RIPPON, TOM MICHAEL
SCULPTOR
b Sacramento, Calif, Apr 1, 54. Study: Univ Calif, Davis, with Bob Arneson, 71-75. Work: Antonio Preito Collection, Mills Col; Hokoku Shinbun, Kanazawa-Shi, Japan; Univ Nev; Cent Iowa Art Asn, Fisher Community Ctr, Marshalltown. Exhib: Decade of Ceramic Art, San Francisco Mus, 73; Sensible Cup Traveling Exhib, Kanazawa-Shi, 73-; Evanston Ceramic Invitational, Evanston Art Ctr, Ill, 74; one-man show, Quay Gallery, San Francisco, 75; Clay USA, Fendrick Gallery, Washington, DC, 75. Awards: Kingsley Art Award, Crocker Art Gallery, Sacramento, 72; Purchase Award, Univ Nev, 73; Nat Endowment Arts Artists Fel, 74. Bibliog: Cecil McCann (auth), rev in Artweek, 3/75; rev in Craft Horizons, 7/75. Media: Clay. Collection: West Coast artists; naives. Mailing Add: Box 646 Port Orford OR 97465

RIPPS, RODNEY
PAINTER
b New York, NY. Study: York Col, BA; Hunter Col, MA. Exhib: Critics Choice, Munson-Williams-Proctor Inst, Utica, NY, 77; Painting 75, 76, 77, Contemporary Arts Ctr, Cincinnati, Ohio, 77; one-man shows, Nancy Lurie Gallery, Chicago, 77, Brooke Alexander Gallery, New York, 77 & 78 & Galerie Daniel Templon, Paris, 78; plus many others. Teaching: Instr painting, Brooklyn Mus Art Sch, 74-76. Pos: Vis artist, Art Inst Chicago, 77 & Ill State Univ, Bloomington, 78. Bibliog: Carter Ratcliff (auth), The Paint Thickens, Artforum, summer 76; David Rush (auth), Paintings with a Sculptural Character, Artweek (cover), 10/76; Ken Wahl (auth), The Paintings of Rodney Ripps, Flash Art (cover), 4/78. Style & Technique: Paintings that project off the wall; thickly painted. Mailing Add: 315 Broadway New York NY 10007

RISELING, ROBERT LOWELL
EDUCATOR, PAINTER
b Sioux City, Iowa, June 5, 41. Study: Univ Northern Iowa, BA, 63, MA, 66; State Univ Iowa, 64; Univ Wis-Madison, MFA, 72. Work: Memphis Acad of Art, Tenn; State Tenn, Nashville; Augustana Col, Rock Island, Ill; Rochester Art Ctr, Minn; Univ Northern Iowa, Cedar Falls. Exhib: Environment/COW, John Michael Kohler Arts Ctr, Sheboygan, Wis, 69; Images '71, Anoka-Ramsey State Jr Col, 71; State Col Fac Exhib, Minn Mus Art, St Paul, 74; Rochester Open, Rochester Art Ctr, 74; 17th Ann Delta, Ark Arts Ctr, Little Rock, 74. Teaching: Instr art, Monticello, Iowa, 63-65; grad asst, Dept Art, Univ Northern Iowa, 65-66; asst dir & resident artist, 66-67, dir art, Rochester Art Ctr, 67; instr, 67-71; teaching asst, Dept Art, Univ Wis, 71-72; asst prof, Dept Art, St Cloud State Univ, 72-74; asst prof, Memphis Acad Arts, Tenn, 74- Awards: Purchase Award, Minn Printmakers, 70; First Award Painting, 8th Ann, Waterloo, 71; Second Award Painting, 40th Ann Arrowhead, Tweed Gallery, Duluth, Minn, 73. Style & Technique: Color field; ambiguous form. Media: Oil, Dye. Mailing Add: 1273 N Parkway Memphis TN 38104

RISHEL, JOSEPH JOHN, JR
CURATOR
b Clifton Springs, NY, May 15, 40. Study: Hobart Col, BA, 62; Univ Chicago, MA, 65. Pos: Cur, European painting before 1900 & John G Johnson Collection, Philadelphia Mus Art, 71- Mailing Add: Philadelphia Mus Art Franklin Pkwy at 26th St Philadelphia PA 19101

RISHELL, ROBERT CLIFFORD
PAINTER, SCULPTOR
b Oakland, Calif, Feb 14, 17. Study: Calif Col Arts & Crafts, three scholars, BFA & MFA; Univ Calif, teaching credential; and with Xavier Martinez, Hamilton Wolf & Maurice Logan. Work: West Point Mus, NY; Nat Cowboy Hall of Fame & Am Heritage Ctr, Oklahoma City, Okla; Eitlejorge Collection, Indianapolis Mus, Ind; Calif State Capitol Bldg, Sacramento; Desert Mus, Palm Springs, Calif. Comn: Murals, AFL-CIO Labor Temple, Oakland, 48, Transamerica Bldg, Oakland, 60, D W Nicholsen Hq, San Leandro, Calif, 64, Title Ins Bldg, Oakland, 65; desert & coastal diorama, Oakland Mus, 68. Exhib: Soc Western Artists, DeYoung Mus, San Francisco, 49-71; Springville Nat Show, Utah, 55; Springfield Nat Show, Mass, 60; Nat Acad Western Art, Nat Cowboy Hall of Fame, 73-75; Kansas City Soc Western Art Show, Kansas City, Mo, 74. Teaching: Teacher portrait, San Leandro Unified Sch Dist, 53-73, teacher landscape, 53- Pos: Prof artist, Bohemian Club, San Francisco, 68-; mem, Oakland Arts Coun, 75- Awards: Russell Award & Pop Award, Soc Western Artists, 64, Best of Show & Pop Award, 71; Silver Medal Sculpture, Kansas City Soc Western Art, 74. Bibliog: Ainsworth (auth), Cowboy in Art, World, 68; Greaves (auth), Master of light, Southwest Art, 73; Hassrick (auth), Western Painting Today, Watson-Guptill, 75. Mem: Soc Western Artists (bd, 52-56); Nat Acad Western Art; Oakland Mus Comn (chmn, 75-). Style & Technique: Painting with a feeling for inner light and atmosphere. Media: Acrylic, Oil; Bronze. Publ: Contribr, Palm Springs Life, 69-73, Ariz Highways, 73-74, Southwest Art, 73, Persimmon Hill, 73 & Am Artist. Mailing Add: 10 Stantonville Ct Oakland CA 94619

RISING, DOROTHY MILNE
PAINTER, ILLUSTRATOR
b Tacoma, Wash, Sept 13, 95. Study: Pratt Inst, dipl, 16; Cleveland Sch Art, with Henry Keller, 20; Univ Wash, BA, 32, MFA, 33. Work: Seattle Art Mus; Frye Art Mus, Seattle; Pac Nat Bank Washington, Tacoma; Three Grumbacher Collections; Lakeside Sch. Exhib: Northwest Ann, Art Mus Pavilion, 69, Northwest Watercolor Soc, 69 & 77; West Coast Oil Exhib, Frye Art Mus, 69, Puget Sound Area Exhib, 71; Pac Northwest Art Ann, Erb Mem Art Gallery, Eugene, Ore, 72; plus others. Teaching: Instr art, Univ Puget Sound, 16-17; instr & supvr art, Western Wash Col, 17-19; instr art, Seattle High Schs, 33-66. Awards: Music & Art Found First Prize, Henry Gallery, 50; Nat League Am Pen Women Best Watercolor in Show, Smithsonian Inst, 55; Women Painters Award, 75; plus others. Bibliog: Around the world through an artist's eyes, Pen Woman, 67; Edna Daw (auth), A word about Dorothy Rising, Age of Achievement, 71. Mem: Fel Royal Soc Art, London; Nat League Am Pen Women (pres, Seattle Br, 70-72); Women Painters Wash (pres, 49); Northwest Watercolor Soc; President's Forum. Style & Technique: Sketches from nature subjects for creative paintings. Media: Oil, Watercolor. Publ: Auth & illusr, Contemporary versus academic art, Town Crier, 34; auth, The silver Bible, Christian Sci Monitor, 64; auth & illusr, December events in many lands, 12/74, Seeing Sweden past and present, 3/75 & Journey behind the Iron Curtain, 5/75, Age of Achievement; plus many others. Mailing Add: 5033 17th Ave NE Seattle WA 98105

RISLEY, JOHN HOLLISTER
SCULPTOR, EDUCATOR
b Brookline, Mass, Sept 20, 19. Study: Amherst Col, BA(cum laude); R I Sch Design, BFA; Cranbrook Acad Art, MFA. Work: Wesleyan Univ; Fred Olsen Found, Conn; Hartford Jewish Community Ctr, Conn; Rose Art Gallery, Brandeis Univ. Comn: Wood & metal relief, IBM Hq, New York, 65; wrought iron relief, Cleveland Garden Ctr, Ohio, 66; copper relief, Nat Bank, Quarryville, Pa, 71; wood & metal sculptures, Brookside Elementary Sch, Waterville, Maine, 70; bronze sculpture, Univ Maine, Portland, 70. Teaching: Prof sculpture, Wesleyan Univ, 54-, chmn dept of art, 68- Awards: First Prize for Furniture, US Designer Craftsman, 53; Drakenfield Prize, 18th Ceramic Ann, 54; New Haven Arts Festival Sculpture Prize, 66. Mailing Add: 30 Maple Shade Rd Middletown CT 06457

RISS, MURRAY
PHOTOGRAPHER, EDUCATOR
b Poland, Feb 6, 40; US citizen. Study: City Univ New York, BA; Cooper Union Sch Art; RI Sch Design, MFA, with Harry Callahan. Work: Mus Mod Art, New York; Bibliotheque Nat, Paris; Art Inst Chicago; Nat Gallery Art, Can; New Orleans Mus Fine Arts. Comn: Photograph Reelfoot Lake, State of Tenn, 72. Exhib: Vision and Expression, Int Mus Photog, George Eastman House, Rochester, NY, 68, Contemporary Photographers VII (traveling exhib); Mus Mod Art, New York, 70-71; New Orleans Biennale, La, 75; one-man shows, Minneapolis Mus Fine Art, 71, traveling show, Visual Studies Workshop, New York, 76-78; Southern Artist (worldwide traveling exhib), US Info Agency, 76. Teaching: Assoc prof photog, Memphis Acad Art, 68- Pos: Vis sr lectr, Univ Haifa, Israel, 75-76. Bibliog: William Parker (auth), Introduction to my portfolio, Ctr Photog Studies, 75. Publ: Illusr, Sleep Book, Harper & Row, 74. Mailing Add: 1328 Carr Ave Memphis TN 38104

RITCHIE, ANDREW C
ART ADMINISTRATOR, ART HISTORIAN
b Bellshill, Scotland, Sept 18, 07; US citizen. Study: Univ Pittsburgh, BA & MA; Univ London, PhD; Yale Univ, hon MA. Teaching: Lectr art & res asst, Frick Collection, New York, 35-42; vis lectr art, NY Univ, 36-40; lectr Brit art, Fr & Span Post-Renaissance painting & mod art; vis Clark prof art hist, Williams Col, 71-73. Pos: Dir, Albright-Knox Art Gallery, Buffalo, 42-49; dir dept painting & sculpture, Mus Mod Art, New York, 49-57; dir, Yale Univ Art Gallery, New Haven, Conn, 57-70, emer dir, 70- Awards: Decorated Cross Legion of Honor, France, 46; Order of Orange Nassau, Netherlands, 48; Off Cross of Order of Merit, Fed Repub Ger, 57. Mem: Col Art Asn Am; Asn Am Mus Dir. Publ: Auth, English Painters, Hogarth to Constable, 42; auth, Abstract Painting & Sculpture in America, 51 & Arno, 70; auth, Sculpture of the Twentieth Century, 52; auth, Edouard Vuillard, 54 & Arno, 70; co-auth, Selected Paintings & Sculpture from the Yale University Art Gallery, Yale Univ, 72; plus many others. Mailing Add: RFD Canaan CT 06018

RITCHIE, WILLIAM
PRINTMAKER, VIDEO ARTIST
b Yakima, Wash, Dec 24, 41. Study: Cent Wash State Col, BA, 64; San Jose State Col, MA, 66; studied with Rolf Nesch, Norway, 69; intern Nat Ctr for Experiments in Television, 74. Work: Philadelphia Mus Art, Pa; US Info Agency, Japan; Kobe Mus, Japan; Univ Calgary, Can; Seattle Pub Libr, Wash. Comn: Mural, Cent Wash State Col Libr, 63; print, Henry Gallery Asn, Seattle, Wash, 70; Bumbershoot 77 (sculpture), City of Seattle, Wash, 77. Exhib: Nat Drawing Exhib, San Francisco Mus Art, Calif, 69; Int Print Exhib, Seattle Art Mus, Wash, 70; Nat Art Exhib, San Francisco Art Inst Centennial, Calif Palace of the Legion of Honor, 71; Nat Print Exhib, Libr of Cong, Washington, DC, 71; British Int Print Biennale, Bradford Galleries, Eng, 72; Second NWest Film & Video Exhib, Portland Art Mus, Ore, 74; 30 Yrs of Am Printmaking, Brooklyn Mus Art, NY, 76; Boston Printmakers 29th Nat, De

Cordova Mus, Lincoln, Mass, 77. Teaching: Prof printmaking, Univ Wash, Seattle, 66- Awards: Stuart M Egnal Purchase Prize, Philadelphia Print Club, 69; First Prize, NWest Film & Video Festival, Portland Art Mus, Ore, 73; Nat Endowment for the Arts Fel, 74. Bibliog: Korot & Schneider (co-auth), Video Art, Harcourt, Brace, Jovanovitch, 76; F Eichenberg (auth), The Art of the Print, Harry N Abrams, 76; Victor Ancona (auth), Bill Ritchie: video in the Northwest, Videography Mag, Vol 12, Number 6. Mem: Seattle Asn for Media Artists (secy-treas, 74-77). Style & Technique: Surreal and lyrical, suggestion of intellectualism; all graphic media used, traditional and contemporary alike. Media: All print media; improvisational ensemble in video. Mailing Add: 360 Halladay Seattle WA 98109

RITTER, RICHARD QUINTIN
GLASS BLOWER
b Mich, Oct 25, 40. Study: Art Sch of the Soc of Arts & Crafts, grad cert(crafts). Work: Corning Mus Bicentenial Collection, NY; Mint Mus, Charlotte, NC: Univ of Ill Mus Collection; Zanesville Art Mus Collection; Detroit Metrop Art Mus Collection. Exhib: Corning Mus Bicentenial Exhib, NY, 76; Contemp Art Glass, Bergstrom Art Ctr, Neenah, Wis, 76; Nat Crafts Exhib, Krannert Art Mus, Ill, 76; Hist & Am Glass, La State Univ, 76; Third Nat Glass Invitational, Univ of Wis, Madison, 76; New Am Glass: Focus WVa, Huntington, WVa, 76; 12 Nat Craftmen, Lee Hall Gallery, Clemson, SC, 77; Int Paperweight Exhib, Habatat Gallery, Mich, 77. Teaching: Instr glassblowing & metalcraft, Bloomfield Art Assoc, Birmingham, Mich, 69-72 & glassblowing, Penland Sch of Crafts, NC, 74-77. Awards: Purchase Prize, Gift to Cabinet of W Ger, Dow Chemical, 73, Gift to Soviet Union, Gov of NC, 74 & NC Glass, Hanes Found, 76. Mem: Glass Art Soc. Style & Technique: Off hand glassblowing, work with colored glass rods to construct portrait murrinis. Media: Glass; Metal. Mailing Add: Rte 1 Box 213 Cass City MI 48726

RIVARD, J BERNARD
PAINTER
b South Bend, Ind, May 5, 30. Study: Chicago Acad Fine Arts; Univ Fla, BS. Work: El Paso Mus Art, Tex; Hammond Pub Libr, Ind. Exhib: El Paso Sun Carnival Nat Exhib, 64, 65 & 67; NMex State Fair Prof Exhib, Albuquerque, var times, 67-74; one-man show, NMex Arts Comn, Santa Fe, 68 & Roswell, NM, 76; NMex Arts Comn, 73. Pos: Mem bd dirs, NMex Arts & Crafts Fair, Albuquerque, 70-71; adv, Albuquerque Pub Sch Art Career Educ Adv Bd, 74-75. Awards: Second Prize, El Paso Sun Carnival Nat Exhib, 65; First Prize, NMex State Fair Prof Exhib, 71 & 72. Mem: Artists Equity Asn (prog chmn, Albuquerque Chap, 72-73, pres, 75-76, finance comt, 75-76). Style & Technique: Objective, oil, color etchings, transparent & opaque acrylic and ink with acrylic. Publ: Auth, article in SW Art Mag, 3/76. Dealer: High Plateau Gallery 1715 San Pedro NE Albuquerque NM 87110. Mailing Add: 1701 Ridgecrest Dr SE Albuquerque NM 87108

RIVARD, NANCY J
CURATOR, ART HISTORIAN
b Saginaw, Mich. Study: Oakland Univ, Mich, BA(studio art), 69; Wayne State Univ, Mich, MA(art hist), 73; Attingham Summer Inst, England, 77. Collections Arranged: Heritage & Horizon: American Painting 1776-1976 (with catalogue), Detroit Inst of Art, 76 & Daniel Chester French; An American Sculptor, 77. Pos: Asst cur Am art, Detroit Inst of Arts, 72-76 & cur Am art, 77- Mem: Decorative Art Chap of the Soc of Archit Hist. Res: Late 19th and early 20th century painting and sculpture with a particular emphasis on turn-of-the-century Beaux-Art, and Arts and Crafts Movements. Publ: Contribr, American Paintings Acquired During the Last Decade, 77 & auth, Curatorial Notes on the Collection: Cotopaxi, Detroit Inst of Arts Bull, 78. Mailing Add: The Detroit Inst of Arts 5200 Woodward Ave Detroit MI 48202

RIVERA, FRANK
PAINTER
b Cleveland, Ohio, Aug 28, 39. Study: Yale Univ Grad Sch Fine Arts, BFA, 62, study with Alex Katz & Jack Tworkov; Univ Pa, MFA, 67, study with Pi Dorazio, Savelli, Helen Frankenthaler & Ludwig Sander. Exhib: Ann Am Painting & Sculpture, Pa Acad Fine Arts, 68; NJ State Mus Painting & Sculpture Ann, 72; Univ Rochester Gallery Art, 72; Susan Caldwell Gallery, New York, 74; 1975 Biennial Exhib Am Art, Whitney Mus Am Art, 75. Teaching: Assoc prof painting & chairperson art dept, Mercer Col, Trenton, NJ, 67- Awards: Nat Endowment Humanities Grant for Study & Travel in France, 72-73. Bibliog: Elizabeth Stevens (auth), Review Whitney Biennial, This Week Mag, Trenton Times, 3/23/75. Style & Technique: Abstract. Media: Acrylic on Canvas. Mailing Add: 118 Forsyth St New York NY 10002

RIVERON, ENRIQUE
PAINTER, SCULPTOR
b Cienfuegos, Las Villas, Cuba, Jan 31, 04; US citizen. Study: Acad Villate, Havana, Cuba; Acad San Fernando, Madrid, Spain; La Colarouse & Grand Chaumiere, Paris, France; travel scholar from Cuba, Spain, France, Italy & Belgium. Work: Fine Arts Mus, Havana, Cuba; Wichita Art Mus, Kans; Lowe Art Mus, Coral Gables, Fla; Miami Mus Mod Art, Fla. Comn: Murals, La Conga Restaurant, Hollywood, Calif, 38, J Lewins residence, Wichita, Kans, 46 & murals (with Antonio Gattorno), Restaurant Capri, Wichita, Kans, 54. Exhib: One-man shows, Asn Paris Amerique Latin, France, 26, Galeria Sud Americana, New York, 57 & Retrospective Paintings, Wichita Art Mus, Kans, 58; 1970 Hortt Winners, Mus of Arts, Ft Lauderdale, Fla, 71; 200 Years Cuban Paintings, Miami Art Ctr, 72. Teaching: Instr cartooning, Wichita Art Asn, Kans, 49-53; instr painting, Wichita Univ, Kans, 58-59. Pos: Founder & dir, Index Gallery, Wichita, Kans, 58-60; Arger Gallery, Coral Gables, Fla, 60-61 & Gala (group Latin-American artists), 69- Awards: Sculpture Award, Sculptors of Fla, Miami, 70; Sculpture Award, Ft Lauderdale, Fla, Mus of Arts, 70; Painting Award, 3rd Ann Pan-Am, Miami, 72. Bibliog: Dore Ashton (auth), Art criticism, NY Times, 4/13/57; Carroll E Hogan (auth), Catalog Preface, Dir Wichita Art Mus, Kans, 5/58; J Gomez-Sicre (auth), Catalog Preface, Dir Visual Arts, Orgn Am States, Washington, DC, 74. Style & Technique: Geometric & hard-edge in acrylic on canvas; welded sculpture in steel and iron. Publ: Illus & cartoons, New Yorker, NY Times, Modern Screen & Cine Mundial, New York, 27-50; contribr, Creating art from anything, 68. Mailing Add: 1726 Espanola Dr Miami FL 33133

RIVERS, LARRY
PAINTER
b New York, NY, 1923. Study: Hans Hofmann Sch Fine Arts, 47-48; NY Univ. Work: Brooklyn Mus; Corcoran Gallery Art; Kansas City Art Inst; Metrop Mus Art; Minneapolis Inst Art; plus many others including pvt collections. Comn: Outdoor billboard, First New York Film Festival, 63. Exhib: Nine shows, Whitney Mus Am Art, 54-64; Pa Acad Fine Arts, 63; retrospective exhib, Jewish Mus, NY, 65, Rose Art Mus, Brandeis Univ, 65 & Art Inst Chicago, 70; Two Decades Am Painting (traveling exhib to Japan, India & Australia), Mus Mod Art, New York, 66; Marlborough Gallery, 68; Gotham Gallery, 68; Documenta, Kassel, WGer, 68; Va Mus Fine Art, Richmond, 70; plus many other group & one-man shows. Teaching: Artist in residence, Slade Sch Fine Arts, London, 64; Md Inst Col Art. Awards: Corcoran Gallery Art Award, 54. Bibliog: William Gaunt (auth), The Observer's Book of Modern Art From Impressionism to the Present Day, Frederick Warne & Co Ltd, London, 64; Lucy R Lippard (auth), Pop Art, Praeger, 66; Sam Hunter (auth), Larry Rivers (monogr), Abrams, 70; plus many others. Publ: Illusr, When the Sun Tries to Go On. Dealer: Marlborough Gallery Inc 41 E 57th St New York NY 10022. Mailing Add: 92 Little Plains Rd Southampton NY 11968

RIVOLI, MARIO
ILLUSTRATOR, PAINTER
b New York, NY, Jan 31, 43. Study: Sch Visual Art, with instr Bob Peak. Work: Mus of Contemp Crafts, New York; Smithsonian Inst, Washington, DC; Philadelphia Mus of Art, Pa. Comn: 27ft Art Deco Mural, Stromberg's Penthouse Restaurant, 76; Decoration of House Organ, Carnegie Hall Cinema, Denver, Colo, 77; Portrait of Simon Deavalier, comn by Pres of Haiti, 78. Exhib: Soc of Illusrs Show, 69; Kerlan Collection for Bk Illus, 70; Denim Show, Smithsonian Inst, 77; Show of Wearable Art, Philadelphia Mus of Art, 77-78; Homage to the Bag, Mus of Contemp Crafts, 77. Teaching: Instr bk jacket design, Dell Publ, New York, 76. Pos: Consult bk design, E P Dutton, New York, 75-76; theatre designer, Harry M Koutoukas; graphic & set designs, Sch for Garqoyles, Sawayder Theatre, 76-77 & 77-78. Awards: Illus of 69, Soc of Illusrs, 69; Album award, Ace Lieberman/John Rielly, RCA Records, 74; Special merit, Washington Square Outdoor Art Exhib, 76. Bibliog: Connie Bogen (auth), Golden Hands, Cosmopolitan mag, 75; Jim Mills (auth), Mario Rivoli, Daly News, 77; Julie Schafler (auth), Mario Rivoli, Soho News, 78. Style & Technique: Mixed media; assemblage. Media: Graphite Lead, Pen & Ink; Magic Markers. Publ: Illusr, Song for Clowns, Atheneum, 65 & Do Tigers Bite Kings, 68, Antheneum; illusr, Best Foot Forward, E P Dutton, 70; auth, Incomplete Book of Slease, Slim and Supersition, pvt publ, 76. Dealer: Julie Artisan Gallery 687 Madison Ave New York NY 10021. Mailing Add: 1220 Marion St Denver CO 80218

RIZK, ROMANOS
PAINTER, INSTRUCTOR
b Providence, RI, Aug 12, 27. Study: Vesper George Sch Art, Boston, Mass; Butera Sch Art, Boston; Cape Sch Art, Provincetown, Mass, with Henry Hensche. Work: Mus Fine Arts, Mobile, Ala; Inter-Am Publ, New York; Ford Motor Co, Detroit; pvt collection of Shah Mohammed Reza Pahlavi, Iran. Exhib: Cape Cod Art Asn Invitational, Hyannis, Mass, 63, 65 & 72; one-man shows, Shore Galleries, Boston, 64-70, Bristol Art Mus, RI, 70 & Arwin Galleries, Detroit, 72 & 75; Provincetown Art Asn Invitational, 71 & 72. Teaching: Pvt instr, 62- Pos: Mem gov bd, Fine Arts Work Ctr, Provincetown, 68-70, mem adv comt, 70- Awards: First Prize, Falmouth Artists' Guild, 65; First Prize, Cape Cod Art Asn, 65, 68 & 71; First Prize, Artists' Asn Nantucket, 66. Mem: Provincetown Art Asn (trustee, 67-73, hon vpres, 74-). Style & Technique: Non-objective, abstract expressionism; free, spontaneous, painterly, using a wide variety of textures. Media: Acrylic, Oil. Publ: Print ed painting, Int Art Publ Co, 70. Dealer: Arwin Galleries 222 Grand River W Detroit MI 48226. Mailing Add: 8 Kiley Ct Provincetown MA 02657

ROACH, RUTH S
JEWELER, DESIGNER
b Chisholm, Minn, May 20, 13. Study: Univ Northern Iowa, Cedar Falls, with Robert von Neumann. Work: Mus of Contemp Crafts, New York; Rochester Mem Gallery of Art, NY; Huntington Galleries, WVa; Brooks Mem Gallery of Art, Memphis, Tenn; Sheldon Mem Gallery of Art, Lincoln, Nebr. Exhib: One-person shows, Des Moines Art Ctr, Iowa, 54, Minneapolis Inst of Art, Minn, 63 & Sheldon Mem Gallery of Art, Lincoln, 69; Am Jewelry & Related Objects, Huntington Galleries, WVa, 55; Fiber-Clay-Metal, St Paul Gallery & Sch of Art, Minn, 55 & 62; Craftsmanship in a Changing World, Mus of Contemp Crafts, New York, 56; Midwest Designer Craftsmen, Art Inst of Chicago, 57 & Joslyn Mus of Art, Omaha, Nebr, 59; Designer Craftsmen USA, Mus of Contemp Crafts, New York, 60; Am Jewelry Today, Everhart Mus of Art, Scranton, Pa, 63; Art of Personal Adornment, 66 & Objects USA (traveling exhib), 69-74, Mus of Contemp Crafts, New York. Teaching: Vis artist jewelry & metal, Univ Northern Iowa, Cedar Falls, summers 1961-68, Des Moines Art Ctr, Iowa, 62 & Wartburg Col, Waverly, Iowa, 67. Awards: Purchase Award, Am Jewelry & Related Objects, Mem Gallery of Art, Rochester, NY, 57 & Mississippi River Craft Show, Brooks Mem Art Gallery, Memphis, Tenn, 63; First Prize, Nat Am Jewelry Today, Everhart Mus of Art, Scranton, 63. Style & Technique: Contemporary, fabricated precious metals. Media: Gems. Publ: Contribr, Creative Jewelry, Art in Am, 59; contribr, Murray Bovin, auth, Jewelry Making for Schools, Tradesmen & Craftsmen, Athena Art, 67; contribr, Design Quart, Walker Art Ctr, Minneapolis, 60; contribr, Oppi Untracht, auth, Metal Techniques for Craftsmen, Doubleday, 68; contribr, Lee Nordness, auth, Objects USA, Viking, 70. Mailing Add: 3737 Fountainhead Lane Naples FL 33940

ROBB, CHARLES (CHARLES ROBERT BUSH)
PAINTER
b Toronto, Ont, Can, June 28, 38. Study: Ont Col Art, AOCA, 59, with Jock MacDonald, John Alfson & Carl Schaefer. Work: Can Coun Art Bank, Ottawa. Exhib: Can Group of Painters, Norman Mackenzie Art Gallery, Regina, Sask, 60; Royal Can Acad Arts (traveling exhib), 61 & 62; 4th Biennial Can Art, Ottawa, Ont, 61; Creative Arts Prog, Univ Colo, Denver, 63; one-man shows, Andre Emmerich, New York, 63, David Mirvish Gallery, Toronto, 64, Nightingale Gallery, Toronto, 70 & Pollock Gallery, Toronto, 77 & 78; Galleria Odysia, Rome, Italy, 64-65; 6th Biennial Can Art, Ottawa, 65; three-man show, Agnes Etherington Art Centre, Queens Univ, Kingston, Ont, 77; Art for Bus Sake, Art Gallery Ont, Toronto, 75. Bibliog: Michael Fried (auth), Toronto Letter, Art Int, 63; D Adlow (auth), Stripes by Robb, Christian Sci Monitor, 64; Kay Woods (auth), Charles Robb, Arts Canada, 77. Style & Technique: Abstract expressionism; color field. Media: Acrylic on Canvas; Casein on Paper. Dealer: Pollock Gallery 122 Scollard St Toronto ON M5R 1G2 Can. Mailing Add: 121 Nymark Ave 104 Willowdale ON M2J 2H3 Can

ROBB, DAVID M
EDUCATOR, ART HISTORIAN
b Tak Hing Chau, China, Sept 19, 03; US citizen. Study: Oberlin Col, AB, 26, AM, 27; Carnegie Found fel fine arts, 27-30; Princeton Univ, AM, 31, MFA, 35, Inst Advan Study fel, 38-39, PhD, 41. Teaching: Assoc prof hist art, Colgate Univ, 30-35; assoc prof hist art, Univ Minn, 35-39; prof hist art, Univ Pa, 39-74; retired. Awards: Fulbright Fel; Guggenheim Fel. Mem: Col Art Asn Am (pres, 60-62); Soc Archit Historians; Philadelphia Art Alliance. Res: Medieval art. Publ: Co-auth, Art in the Western World, 35 & 62; auth, Harper History of Painting, 52; auth, Art of the Illuminated Manuscript, 73. Mailing Add: 506 Narberth Ave Merion Station PA 19066

ROBB, PEGGY HIGHT
PAINTER
b Gallup, NMex, Sept 14, 24. Study: Univ NMex, BFA & MA, with Raymond Jonson & Kenneth Adams; Art Students League. Work: Univ NMex, Albuquerque. Comn: Stained glass window & portraits, Christian Ctr, Albuquerque, 75. Exhib: NMex Biennial, Santa Fe,

58-63; NMex State Fair, Albuquerque, 59 & 63; Southwestern Fiesta, Santa Fe, 66; Sun Carnival Art Exhib, El Paso, Tex, 71. Awards: First Prize, NMex State Fair, 59 & 63; Hon Mention, NMex Biennial, Santa Fe, 61. Mem: Fel of Christian Artists in Media & Entertainment. Style & Technique: Semi-abstract to non-objective, portraiture, landscapes. Media: Oil, Acrylic. Mailing Add: 7200 Rio Grande Blvd NW Albuquerque NM 87107

ROBB, MR & MRS SIDNEY R
COLLECTORS
Mr Robb, b Boston, Mass, Oct 20, 00. Study: Mr Robb, Harvard Univ, Hon MA, 62, Tufts Univ, Hon LLD, 61, Boston Col, Hon LHD, 64, Suffolk Univ, Hon DCS, 66. Pos: Mr Robb, Trustee, Boston Mus Fine Arts. Awards: Mr Robb, Hon Alumni, Hebrew Univ Jerusalem, 65. Collection: Impressionists, primarily Degas, Pissarro, Vuillard, Mary Cassatt, Bonnard and Moore; sculptures—Degas, Maillol, Lehmbruck and Moore. Mailing Add: 65 Commonwealth Ave Boston MA 02116

ROBBIN, ANTHONY STUART
PAINTER
b Washington, DC, Nov 24, 43. Study: Columbia Col, BA; Yale Univ Sch Art, BFA & MFA. Work: Addison Gallery Am Art, Andover, Mass; Whitney Mus Am Art. Exhib: Bykert Gallery, New York, 71; Paley & Lowe Inc, New York, 72; Ann, Whitney Mus Am Art, 72, one-man show, 75. Media: Acrylic. Publ: Auth, Smithson sites & non sites, Art News, 69; auth, Two ocean projects, 69 & auth, A protein sensibility, 71, Arts Mag; auth, Hutchison ecological art, Art Int, 70; auth, Visual paradox & 4-D geometry, Tracts Mag, 75. Mailing Add: 423 Broome St New York NY 10013

ROBBINS, DANIEL J
ART HISTORIAN, MUSEUM DIRECTOR
b New York, NY, Jan 15, 33. Study: Univ Chicago, BA; Yale Univ, MA; NY Univ Inst Fine Arts, PhD; Univ Paris. Collections Arranged: Cezanne & Structure, Guggenheim Mus Art, 63, Albert Gleizes Retrospective, 64-65; Contemp Wall Sculpture, Am Fedn Arts, 63-64, Decade of New Talent, 64 65. Teaching: Instr, Ind Univ, 55; prof, Brown Univ, 65-71; lectr, Harvard Univ, 71-75; vis prof, Dartmouth Col, 75-76 & Yale Univ, 77; Clark prof, Williams Col, 78- Pos: Cur, Nat Gallery Art, Washington, DC, 59-60; cur, Guggenheim Mus Art, 61-64; dir, Mus Art, RI Sch Design, 64-71; dir, Fogg Art Mus, Harvard Univ, 71- Awards: French Govt Fel, Paris, 58; Nat Endowment Humanities Sr Fel, 76; Guggenheim Fel, 78-79. Mem: Am Fedn Arts (trustee). Publ: Auth, Painting Between the Wars, 65; auth, Joaquin Torres Garcia, Guggenheim Mus, 71; auth, Jacques Villon, Fogg Mus, 76; auth, Folk Sculpture Without Folk, Brooklyn Mus, 76; contribr, Art J, Art France, Art Int, Art News, Apollo, Studio Int. Mailing Add: Farcevol Farm Braintree VT 05060

ROBBINS, EUGENIA S
ART WRITER, ART EDITOR
b New York, NY, Apr 22, 35. Study: Smith Col, BA. Pos: Art ed, George Braziller Inc, 60-64; bk ed, Art in Am, 64-67; news ed, Art J, Col Art Asn of Am, 67 & Col Art Asn Newsletter, 76- Res: Persian art and architecture; modern art and architecture; Art books. Publ: Auth & co-auth, articles in Studio Int, Art in Am, NY Post; auth, Art, Collier's Yr Bk; auth, regular column in Art J & rev in Art in Am & Art J; ed, Pope, Persian Architecture, SC Welsh & M Dickson, The Houghton Shahnameh. Mailing Add: RR 2 Path Rd Randolph VT 05060

ROBBINS, FRANK
CARTOONIST, ILLUSTRATOR
b Boston, Mass, Sept 9, 17. Study: Boston Mus Fine Arts Sch; Nat Acad Design. Comn: Portrait, Polyclinic Hosp, NY. Exhib: Whitney Mus Am Art, 56; Corcoran Gallery Art, 57 & 58; Toledo Mus Art, 57 & 58; Nat Acad Design, 57 & 58; Audubon Artists, 57 & 58; plus others. Pos: Auth & illusr comic strip, Scorch Smith, 39-44; auth & illusr comic strip, Johnny Hazard, King Features Syndicate, currently. Awards: Prize, Nat Acad Design, 36. Mem: Nat Cartoonists Soc. Publ: Contribr, Life, Look, Cosmopolitan & other nat mags. Mailing Add: c/o Nat Cartoonists Soc Tel 9 Evony Ct Brooklyn NY 11229

ROBBINS, HULDA D
PAINTER, PRINTMAKER
b Atlanta, Ga, Oct 19, 10. Study: Pa Mus Sch Indust Art, Philadelphia; Prussian Acad, Berlin, with Ludwig Bartning; Barnes Found, Merion, Pa. Work: Metrop Mus Art, New York; Victoria & Albert Mus, London, Eng; Bibliot Nat, Paris; Art Mus Ont; Smithsonian Inst, Washington, DC. Exhib: Portrait of America, New York & Tour, 45-46; Current Am Prints, Carnegie Inst, Pittsburgh, 48; Nat Print Ann, Brooklyn Mus & Tour, 48-49; Nat Exhib Prints, Libr Cong, Washington, DC, 56; US Info Agency Print Exhib Europ Tour, 72- Teaching: Instr basic & advan serigraphy, Nat Serigraph Soc Sch, 54-60; instr creative painting, Atlantic Co Jewish Community Ctr, Margate, NJ, 60-67. Awards: Purchase Award, Prints For Children, Mus Mod Art, 41; Paintings By Printmakers Award, Nat Serigraph Soc, 47, Babette S Kornblith Purchase Prize, 49. Mem: Print Club; Graphic Soc; Am Color Print Soc. Style & Technique: Abstract-figurative; neo-expressionist. Media: Oil. Mailing Add: 16 S Buffalo Ave Ventnor NJ 08406

ROBBINS, WARREN M
MUSEUM DIRECTOR, EDUCATOR
b Worcester, Mass, Sept 4, 23. Study: Univ NH, BA(eng), 45; Univ Mich, MA(hist), 49. Collections Arranged: Traditional African Art from the Peabody Museum, 66; The Heritage of African Art, 67; Edward Mitchell Bannister, 67; Ben Shahn on Human Rights, 68; The Art of Henry O Tanner (with catalog), 69; The Language of African Art (with catalog), 70; African Art—The De Havenon Collection, 71; African Art in Washington Collections, 72; Tribute to Africa— the Photography and the Collection of Elliot Elisofon, 74; African Textiles & Traditional Dress, 75; The Art of Zaire, 76; The Art of Sierra Leone, 76; Religious & Secular Art of Ethiopia, 76-77; The Sculptor's Eye, Chaim Gross Collection, 76; The Traditional Art of the Nigerian Peoples, 77. Teaching: Lectr African art, Mus African Art, Washington, DC, 64-; lectr infleunce of African sculpture on mod western art, mus & univs in US, 68- Pos: Founder/dir, Mus African Art, 64- Bibliog: John Coppola (auth), Teaching Museum, Topic Mag, 12/76; Barbaralee Diamondstein (auth), Light from the Dark Continent, CBS TV, 3/77; Katherine Kuh (auth), An educational explosion; The Museum of African Art, Sat Rev, 5/77. Mem: Asn of Art Mus Dirs; DC Comn on the Arts & Humanities; Am Asn Mus; Libr of Cong (Arts Adv Comt); Duke Ellington Sch of the Arts (bd dirs). Res: Influence of African sculpture on modern western art. Publ: Auth, African Art in American Collections, 66 & The Impact of African Sculpture on Modern Western Art, Praeger; contribr, Art in Society, Vol 5, No 3; auth, Traditional American Values in a World of Hostilities, Adult Educ, 75; auth, African Art in America, Vista, 75. Mailing Add: 530 Sixth St SE Washington DC 20003

ROBERDS, GENE ALLEN
PRINTMAKER, SCULPTOR
b Cole Camp, Mo, May 4, 35. Study: Eastern Ill State Col, BS, 57; Univ Ill, MFA, 61. Work: Jacksonville Art Mus, Fla; Jacksonville Jr Col Gallery; Carver Orgn, Evansville, Ind. Comn: Vignette for stock cert, Dayton Corp, Minneapolis, 67. Exhib: Minnesota Artists, Walker Art Ctr, 66; Art of Two Cities, New York, 66; Nat Invitational Print Show, San Diego, 71. Teaching: Instr printmaking, Murray State Col, 61-64; asst prof printmaking, Minneapolis Sch Art, 64-68; asst prof printmaking, Jacksonville Univ, 68-71. Pos: Co-owner & artist, Cain and Roberds Studios, 70- Mem: Intercontinental Biog Asn. Style & Technique: Linear figure drawing, sculpture, etching and engraving of a representational surrealist nature. Publ: Illusr, Minn Rev, 66; illusr, The Metaphysical Giraffe, 67. Mailing Add: RFD 1 Box 71-F St Augustine FL 32084

ROBERSON, SAMUEL ARNDT
ARCHITECTURAL HISTORIAN, EDUCATOR
b Honolulu, Hawaii, May 5 39. Study: Williams Col, BA, 61, MA, 63; Salzburg-Klessheim Sch, cert, 65; Yale Univ, PhD, 74. Collections Arranged: American Paintings from a Private Long Meadow Collection, Amherst Col, 71; Five College Modern Architecture, Amherst Col, 72. Teaching: Instr art hist, Williams Col, Williamstown, Mass, 61-63 & Yale Univ, New Haven, Conn, 64-66; instr art hist, Princeton Univ, 66-68 & Amherst Col, Mass, 69-72; asst prof art hist, Herron Sch of Art, 72-76, assoc prof art hist, 76-; vis assoc prof art hist, Ind Univ, Bloomington, 76. Pos: Chmn art hist, Herron Sch of Art, 72-; consult, Eye of Thomas Jefferson, Nat Gallery of Art, Bicentennial Exhib, Washington, DC, 74-76; acad coordr (Nat Endowment for the Humanities learning mus prog), Indianapolis Mus of Art, 76- Mem: Soc of Archit Historians; Col Art Asn; Soc Archit Historians Great Brit; Mid-Am Col Art Asn. Res: Eighteenth and nineteenth century American architecture and landscape gardening. Publ: Auth, The Technical Creation of the Greek Slave, 65 & co-auth, The Greek Slave, 65; Newark Mus; contribr, Praeger Encyclopedia of Art, Praeger Publ, 71. Mailing Add: Herron Sch of Art 1701 N Pennsylvania Indianapolis IN 46202

ROBERSON, WILLIAM
WEAVER
b Ripley, Miss, Feb 15, 39; Study: Memphis State Univ; Memphis Acad Arts, BFA; Ind Univ. Work: Ark Art Ctr, Little Rock; Tenn Craft Collection, Craft Mus, Nashville; 1st Nat Bank, Orlando, Fla; Memphis Acad Arts; Falls Creek State Park, Tenn. Comn: Tapestries, comn by Lausanne Sch, Memphis, 70, Jewish Community Ctr, Memphis, 71, Holiday Inns of Am, Aberdeer, Tex, 73, Opreyland Hotel, Nashville, Tenn & First Fed Savings, Ft Myers, Fla. Exhib: Miss River Craft Show, Brook's Mus, Memphis, 65, 67 & 69; Young Americans, Mus Contemp Crafts, New York, 69; Piedmont Craft Exhib, Sneed Mus, Charlotte, NC, 70; Miss Arts Festival, Jackson, 71; Southeastern Craftmen Show, San Antonio, Tex, 72. Teaching: Assoc prof fiber design, Memphis Acad Arts, 69- Awards: Tenn Craftmen's Show, Tenn Artist Craftsmen Asn, 65; Alumni Traveling Fel, Memphis Acad Arts, 68; Piedmont Craft Show, Sneed Mus, 70. Mem: Am Craftsman Coun; Memphis Guild of Handloom Weavers; Tenn Artist Craftsmen's Asn (vpres, 73); Friends of Penland Asn; Am Guild Handloom Weavers. Style & Technique: Contemporary tapestry executed in the traditional tapestry techniques. Mailing Add: 694 N Trezevant St Memphis TN 38112

ROBERT, HENRY FLOOD, JR
MUSEUM DIRECTOR
b El Dorado, Ark, Feb 26, 43. Study: Palomar Col, AA, 66; Ariz State Univ, BFA, 70, MFA, 73; Harvard Univ, dipl (arts admin), 77. Collections Arranged: Zelda Sayre Fitzgerald Retrospective, 74, Marathon Art by Three Artists, 75, Corporate Collections in Montgomery, 76, George Verdak: Eras of the Dance, 76-77 & Art, Inc: Corporate Collections in The United States, 78, Montgomery Mus of Fine Arts, Ala. Pos: Dir, Mem Union Gallery, Ariz State Univ, Tempe, 69-70, asst dir, Univ Art Mus, 70-72; asst dir, Loch Haven Art Ctr, Orlando, Fla, 73-74; dir, Montgomery Mus of Fine Arts, 74- Mem: Am Asn of Mus; Int Conf of Mus. Publ: Auth, Paolo Soleri: Arcology and the Future of Man, 75, contribr, Venetian Drawings from the Collection of Janos Scholz, 76, The Throne of the Third Heaven of the Nations Millenium General Assembly, 77 & Anne Goldthwaite: 1869-1944, 77 & auth, Walter Gauknek Retrospective, 78, Montgomery Mus of Fine Arts. Mailing Add: 440 S McDonough St Montgomery AL 36104

ROBERTS, CLYDE HARRY
PAINTER, INSTRUCTOR
b Sandusky, Ohio, June 12, 23. Study: Cleveland Inst Art, dipl, 46; Columbia Univ, MA, 49; also with John Pike, Robert Brackman & Edgar Whitney. Work: Washington Co Mus Fine Arts, Hagerstown, Md; Ford Times Gallery, Dearborn, Mich. Exhib: Many exhibs, Baltimore Watercolor Open, Cumberland Valley Exhib, Miss Art Asn Open & Cleveland Mus May Show. Teaching: Instr painting, Washington Co Mus Art, 49-70, dir, Sch, 68-70; instr painting, Hagerstown Jr Col, 57-; supvr art, Washington Co Bd Educ, 68- Awards: First Award, Miss Art Asn, 50; Popular Prize, Cumberland Valley Artists, 71; Artists Members Award, Baltimore Watercolor Club, 71 & 74. Bibliog: Jerome Palms (auth), article in Ford Times Mag, 58; G Horn (auth), article in Art Today, 68. Mem: Baltimore Watercolor Club; Md Art Asn (secy, 62-64); Nat Art Educ Asn; Washington Co Arts Coun; Washington Watercolor Soc. Style & Technique: Realistic transparent watercolor landscapes. Publ: Illusr, Ford Times Mag, 58; contribr, Sch Arts, 68; contribr, Artists News Unlimited, 71; contribr, Nat Geog Sch Ed, 73. Dealer: Hill Top House Harpers Ferry WV 25425; Benjamen's Art Gallery Hagerstown MD 21740. Mailing Add: 219 N Colonial Dr Hagerstown MD 21740

ROBERTS, COLETTE (JACQUELINE)
ART CRITIC, ART ADMINISTRATOR
b Paris, France, Sept 16, 10; US citizen. Study: Sorbonne, MA; Acad Ranson, with Roger Bissiere, 25-31; Ecole Louvre, 28-37; Inst Art & Archeol, with Henri Focillon. Exhib: Exhibited extensively throughout France. Collections Arranged: Organized exchange cult exhibs, sponsored by Am & Fr Embassies. Teaching: The road to mod art summer lect series, Coun Int Educ Exchange, 51-; instr, Queens Col, NY, 60; instr, NY Univ, 60, adj asst prof art hist, 68- Pos: Directed & organized meet the artist prog, NY Univ; gallery dir, Nat Asn Women Artists, New York, 47-49; secy to cur Far Eastern art, Metrop Mus Art, 50-51; dir, Grand Cent Mod Gallery, NY, 52-68; assoc dir, Sachs Gallery, New York, 68- Awards: Palmes Academiques, 60; MacDowell Colony Fel, 60. Specialty: Modern American art. Publ: Auth, Mark Tobey, 60, Louise Nevelson, Sculptor, 64 & Pocket Museum, 64; contribr art ed, In: Fr-Am, 53- Mailing Add: c/o A M Sachs Gallery 29 W 57th St New York NY 10019

ROBERTS, DONALD
EDUCATOR, PRINTMAKER
b Wolfeboro, NH, Nov 24, 23. Study: Vesper George Sch of Art, Boston, cert; RI Sch of Design, Providence, BFA; Ohio Univ, Athens, MFA. Work: Cleveland Mus of Art; Tate Gallery, London; Rosenwald Collection, Los Angeles; Seattle Mus, Wash; Libr of Cong, Washington, DC. Exhib: Columbus Gallery, Ohio, 56; Dayton Art Inst, Ohio, 60 & 65; 36th

NW Int, Seattle, Wash, 64; 1st-3rd Lithography Ann, Tallahassee, Fla, 64-67; The Print Club, Philadelphia, 68; Contemp Am Prints, Krannert Mus, Champaign-Urbana, Ill, 70; Huntington Galleries, WVa, 71; All-Ohio Painting & Sculpture Biennial, Dayton Art Inst, 74. Teaching: Prof printmaking, drawing & painting, Ohio Univ, Athens, 53- Awards: Tamarind Lithography Grant, 62; Purchase Award, 9th Ann Paint of the Yr, Mead Corp, 63; Pennypacker Award, 4th Ann Soc Am Graphic Artists, 65. Bibliog: William Sargent (auth), American Printmakers, Ashland Oil Corp, 76. Style & Technique: Lithographs, assemblages; Formica constructions usually geometric; collages. Mailing Add: 330 Frum Rd Athens OH 45701

ROBERTS, GILROY
SCULPTOR
b Mar 11, 05; US citizen. Study: Frankford High Sch Eve Art Class, Philadelphia; Corcoran Gallery Art Sch; also with John R Sinnock & Heinz Warneke. Work: US Mint, Philadelphia; Smithsonian Inst, Washington, DC; Franklin Mint, Franklin Center, Pa. Comn: Portrait of Anthony Drexel, Drexel Univ, 38; Kennedy half dollar, US Mint, 63; portrait of Albert Einstein, Inst Advan Study, Princeton; portrait of David Sarnoff, RCA Corp; portrait of Ernie Pyle, Scripps Howard News Alliance. Exhib: Pa Acad Fine Arts, Philadelphia, 36-37; Corcoran Gallery Art, Washington, DC, 42; Nat Sculpture Soc, New York; Madrid, Spain, 51; Rome, Italy, 61. Pos: Picture engraver, Bur Engraving & Painting, Washington, DC, 38-44; chief sculptor & engraver, US Mint, Philadelphia, 48-64; chmn & chief sculptor, Franklin Mint, 64- Awards: Honorable Mention, Nat Sculptors Soc, 51; Gold Medal & Citation, Int Exhib Coins & Medals, Madrid, Spain, 51; Gold Medal, Numismatic Asn, 51. Bibliog: Willard Garvin (auth), The suburb that has its own mint, Sunday Bull Mag, 1/51; Thomas Baker (auth), The creation of the Kennedy half dollar, Coin Asn Mag, 6/72. Mem: Fel Nat Sculpture Soc; Franklin Inst; Rittenhouse Astron Soc; Philadelphia Sketch Club. Style & Technique: Coins, medals and plaques. Publ: Auth, Birth of a dime design, 10/67 & auth, Creating designs in circles, 5/68, Coins Mag. Mailing Add: 67 Llangollen Lane Newtown Square PA 19073

ROBERTS, HELENE EMYLOU
ART LIBRARIAN
b Seattle, Wash, Mar 23, 31. Study: Univ Wash, BA, 53, MA, 57, MLS, 61. Pos: Art Librn, Dartmouth Col, Hanover, NH, 63-66 & slide librn, 68-70; cur visual collections, Harvard Univ, 70- Mem: Art Libr Soc NAm; Spec Libr; Res Soc for Victorian Per (treas, 70-75); Victorian Per Newsletter (adv ed, 75-78). Res: Dante Gabriel Rossetti; Victorian Art; 18th and 19th century art periodicals; images of women in art; 19th century art criticism. Interest: Victorian Art; art criticism; iconogrpahy (especially of women's images). Publ: Auth, American Art Periodicals of the 19th Century, Univ Rochester, 63; auth, British Art Periodicals of the 18th and 19th Century, Victorian Per Newsletter, 7/70; auth, Marriage, Redundancy or Sin, In: Suffer & Be Still, Ind Univ, 72; auth, The Dream World of Dante Gabriel Rossetti, Victorian Studies, 6/74; auth, Trains of fascinating & endless imagry: associationist art criticism before 1850, Victorian Per Newsletter, 77. Mailing Add: c/o Fogg Art Mus Harvard Univ Cambridge MA 02138

ROBERTS, LUCILLE D (MALKIA)
PAINTER, EDUCATOR
b Washington, DC. Study: Howard Univ; Univ Mich, AM; NY Univ; Acad Grande Chaumiere, Paris; Univ Ghana; also with Jose Gutierriez, Mexico City, Mex. Work: Atlanta Univ Collection; WVa State Col Collection; Jefferson Community Col, Water Town, NY. Exhib: Nat Exhib Black Artists, Smith-Mason Gallery, Washington, DC, 71; Black Artists Exhib, Afro-Am Cult Ctr, Cleveland State Univ, 72; one-man shows, Porter Gallery, Howard Univ, 71 & Col Mus, Hampton Inst, 72. Teaching: Asst prof art, DC Teachers Col, Washington, 65-; vis assoc prof African & Afro-Am art, State Univ NY Col Oswego, 70-71. Awards: First Prize, Mem Show, 65 & Evening Star Award, 66, Soc Washington Artists; James A Porter Award, Cleveland State Univ, 72. Bibliog: Lewis (auth) & Wadday (auth), Black Artists on Art, 69; J Edwin Atkinson (auth), Black Dimensions in Contemporary Art, Carnation Co, 70. Mem: Nat Conf Artists; Black Acad Arts & Lett; Soc Washington Artists; DC Art Asn. Media: Oil, Acrylic. Mailing Add: 2445 Lyttonsville Rd 1116 Silver Spring MD 20910

ROBERTS, PERCIVAL R
ART ADMINISTRATOR, PAINTER
b Wilmington, Del, Nov 2, 35. Study: Univ Del, BA, 57 & MA, 62; Haystack Mt Sch Art, Maine, summer 57; Ill State Univ, EdD, 68; L'Libre Universite Asie, LittD. Work: Univ Del; Ill State Univ; Clarion State Col; Delaware Poetry Ctr; Bloomsburg State Col. Exhib: US Fine Arts Registry, New York, 67; one-man show, Nat Design Ctr, 68; Susquehanna Univ, Selinsgrove, Pa; Haas Gallery of Art, Bloomsburg State Col, Pa, 69; Mansfield State Col, 70; Lycoming Col, 72; Hazel Sanford Gallery, Clarion State Col, 74; Am Painters in Paris, 76. Teaching: Instr drawing & painting, Univ Del, part-time, 60-64; lectr art, Ill State Univ, 65-68; prof art educ, art hist & visual aesthetics, Bloomsburg State Col, 68-; prof psychology art, Univ Scranton, part-time, 72- Pos: Chmn, Art Comn, State of Del, 62-65; pres, Del Art Educ Soc, 63-65; dir, Broadway Gallery Art, Ill, 67-68; bd dirs, MidState Artists Asn, 68-; chmn, Higher Educ Div, Eastern Region Nat Art Educ Asn, 71-74; consult var col; comt mem & judge, Pa, 71, Visual Arts Adv Panel, Pa Coun on the Arts, 75- & other nat & regional jury assignments. Awards: SHIP Award, Nat Art Educ Asn, 65; First Artist in residence, William Penn Mem Mus, 71; Distinguished Teaching Award, Commonwealth Pa, 75 & 76. Bibliog: William Wantling (auth), Its the Celtic Revival, Vidette, Ill State Univ, 68; Glenn Canouse (auth), He Makes Poetry...Art...Time, Press-Enterprise, 6/74; Valery O'Connell (auth), A true artist resorts to expression in two modes, Art News, Summer 68. Mem: MidState Artists Asn; Pa Art Educ Asn; Nat Art Educ Asn. Style & Technique: Contemporary cultural imagery produced with hard-edge acrylics. Res: Research into areas of aesthetics and synesthesia as a component of the aesthetic experience. Publ: Auth, Word Echoes, Accad Leonardo da Vinci, Rome, 66; auth, Out, Out, Brief Candle, Prairie Press, 68; auth, Landscape Painters of Pennsylvania, 70 & auth, Alice Neel: Portraits, 72, BSC; auth, Centaurian Flight, 69 & Red Sky in the Morning, 74, Mitre Press, London. Mailing Add: Dept of Art Bloomsburg State Col Bloomsburg PA 17815

ROBERTS, PRISCILLA WARREN
PAINTER
b Glen Ridge, NJ, June 13, 16. Study: Art Students League; Nat Acad Design. Work: Metrop Mus Art, New York; Dallas Mus Fine Arts; Walker Art Ctr, Minneapolis; Butler Inst Am Art, Youngstown, Ohio; IBM Collection, New York. Exhib: Carnegie Inst Int, Pittsburgh, 50; Nat Acad Design, New York, 69; Corcoran Gallery Art, Washington, DC; Univ Ill, Urbana; Allied Artists, New York. Awards: Hallgarten Prizes & Proctor Portrait Prize, Nat Acad Design, 47; Third Prize, Carnegie Inst Int, 50. Mem: Nat Acad Design; hon mem Catharine Lorillard Wolfe Asn. Style & Technique: Realistic. Media: Oil on Panel. Publ: Contribr, Pictures, painter, and you-Ray Bethers. Dealer: Grand Central Galleries 40 Vanderbilt Ave New York NY 10017. Mailing Add: Box 281 Wilton CT 06897

ROBERTS, THOMAS (KIETH)
PAINTER
b Toronto, Ont, Dec 22, 09. Study: Cent Tech Sch, Toronto; Ont Col Art, Toronto. Work: Ford Motor Co; Rio-Algom; Seagrams; plus collections of many other Can co & insts. Exhib: Many ann, Royal Acad Arts, Montreal & Toronto, Montreal Mus Fine Arts & Ont Soc Artists, Toronto, 29-; plus one-man shows in Montreal, Toronto, Halifax & Vancouver, Can. Awards: Ralph Clarke Stone Award, 49. Mem: Royal Can Acad; Ont Soc Artists. Style & Technique: Outdoor representational. Media: Oil, Watercolor, Acrylic. Dealer: Eaton's Fine Art Galleries Yonge & College Sts Toronto ON Can. Mailing Add: 1312 Stavebank Rd Port Credit ON L5G 2V2 Can

ROBERTS, WILLIAM EDWARD
PAINTER, EDUCATOR
b Cleveland, Ohio, July 1, 41. Study: Kent State Univ, BFA, 68, MA, 71; Cornell Univ, studied lithography with Arnold Singer, 73. Work: Everson Mus of Art, Syracuse, NY; Kent State Univ, Ohio; State univ NY col Potsdam; Marine Midland Bank, Erie, Pa; Wells Col, Aurora, NY. Exhib: Midyear show, Akron Art Inst, Ohio, 68; Ohio Artists & Craftsmen, Massilon Mus, Ohio, 69; one-man shows, Canton Art Inst, Ohio, 71, Everson Mus of Art, Syracuse, 74 & Schenectady Mus, NY, 76; Midyear Show, Butler Inst Am Art, Youngstown, Ohio, 73; Nat Drawing & Small Sculpture Show, Ball State Univ, Muncie, Ind, 73; NY Exhib, Munson-Williams-Proctor Inst, Utica, NY, 75. Teaching: Assoc prof painting, Wells Col, Aurora, NY, 71-; instr painting, Auburn Prison, NY, 75-77. Awards: Purchase Award, State Univ NY Col Potsdam, State of Ny, 73; Purchase Award, Erie, Pa Ann, Marine Midland Bank, 73. Bibliog: Jolly Schram (auth), Primitive painting, Daily Record, Roswell, NMex, 73; Ann Hartranft (auth), Everson has a winner, Syracuse Post Standard, NY, 74; Eileen Watkins (auth), Black & white, Star Ledger, Newark, NJ, 75. Mem: Col Art Asn; Am Asn Univ Prof. Style & Technique: Painting and drawing; hard edge, personal, surreal. Media: Acrylic on canvas. Mailing Add: Aurora NY 13026

ROBERTS, (WILLIAM) GOODRIDGE
PAINTER
b Barbados, BWI, Sept 24, 04. Study: Beaux-Arts, Montreal, 24-26; Art Students League, 27-29; Univ NB, LLD, 60. Work: Nat Gallery Can; Montreal Mus Fine Arts; Vancouver Art Gallery; Winnipeg Art Gallery; Bezalel Mus, Israel; plus many others. Comn: Painting of Quebec landscape presented to Queen Elizabeth by Royal Can Air Force Asn, 54. Exhib: Carnegie Inst, 52 & 55; Valencia Int, 55; Mexico City, 58; Brussels, Belg, 58; Tate Gallery, London, 64; plus many other group & one-man shows. Teaching: Vis fel, Univ NB, 59-60. Pos: Off war artist, RCAF, 43-45. Awards: Prizes, Montreal Mus Fine Arts, 48 & 56 & Winnipeg Art Gallery, 57; Glazebrook Award, 59; plus many others. Mem: Can Group Painters; Can Soc Graphic Art; Can Soc Painters in Water Colour; Contemp Arts Soc, Montreal; plus others. Mailing Add: 355 Lansdowne Ave Montreal PQ H3Z 2L5 Can

ROBERTS, WILLIAM GRIFFITH
PAINTER
b Nelson, BC, July 25, 21. Study: Vancouver Sch Art; Ont Col Art. Work: Nat Gallery Can, Ottawa; Ont Art Gallery, Toronto; Hamilton Art Gallery; USCG, Gov Island, NY; NC Nat Bank Corp. Comn: St Lawrence Seaway Dam (painting), Cornwall, Ont, Eng Electric Co, London, 57; Early Toronto Schools (mural), Bd of Educ, Toronto, 60; Early History St Lawrence River, Upper Canada Village, Cornwall, Ont, 66; Early Houses of Hamilton, McNab House Mus, Ont, 66; Toronto Stock Exchange, Loewen, Ondaatje McCutcheon & Co, Ltd, 74. Exhib: The Winnipeg Show, 57-58; Montreal Spring Show, 59; Ottawa Nat Gallery, 59-60. Awards: Winnipeg Prize, Winnipeg Art Gallery; Can Soc Painters in Watercolor, Winnipeg Art Gallery; Forester Award, Ont Soc Artists. Style & Technique: Realist. Media: Watercolor, Oil, Acrylic. Dealer: Far Gallery 22 E 80th St New York NY 10021. Mailing Add: RR 3 Ayton ON Can

ROBERTSON, CHARLES J
ART ADMINISTRATOR
b Houston, Tex, Sept 12, 34. Study: Univ Va, BA, 56; Harvard Univ, MA, 58; Courtauld Inst, Univ London, 60; George Washington Univ, JD, 64. Pos: Assoc dir, NC Mus Art, 75-77; assoc adminr, Nat Collection Fine Arts, 77- Mem: Am Asn Mus; Col Art Asn Am; Soc Archit Historians; Victorian Soc Am. Mailing Add: Nat Collection Fine Arts Smithsonian Inst Washington DC 20560

ROBERTSON, D HALL
PAINTER
b Washington, DC, Aug 12, 18. Study: Corcoran Sch Art, Washington; Art Students League. Comn: Mural, US Govt Post Off, Miss, 40. Exhib: Two biennials, Corcoran Gallery Art, 39-45, one-man show, 46; Carnegie Inst Print Exhib, 51; Libr Cong, Washington, DC, 51; Rochester Mem Art Gallery, NY, 51; Best American Art During Last Five Years, Metrop Mus Art, New York, 52; Pa Acad Fine Arts, 54. Teaching: Instr oil painting, US Army, Pentagon, Washington, DC, 69-73. Pos: Art dir, US Army Hq Mil Dist, Washington, DC, 54-73. Awards: First Prize in Oils, Northern Va Fair, 59, First Prize in Watercolors, 69; $1000 Prize for Bicentennial mural, Richmond, Va, 76. Mem: Am Fedn Arts. Style & Technique: Traditional style with smooth technique. Media: Oil, Watercolor. Mailing Add: 723 Barkley Dr Fredericksburg VA 22401

ROBERTSON, JOAN ELIZABETH (JOAN ELIZABETH MITCHELL)
CURATOR, DRAFTSMAN
b Washington, DC, June 11, 42. Study: Bucknell Univ, Lewisburg, Pa, BAArt, 64; Univ Iowa, MA(printmaking), 67, study with Mauricio Lasansky. Work: Kemper Ins Companies art collection, Long Grove, Ill. Collections Arranged: Kemper Ins Companies art collection, brochure preparation & monthly exhibs, 73- Teaching: Instr linocuts & etching, Suburban Fine Arts Ctr, Highland Park, Ill, 70-71. Pos: Art Cur, Kemper Ins Companies, Long Grove, Ill, 73- Bibliog: Gladys Riskind (auth), Entering into the Kemper Picture...by Acquisition, Chicago Tribune, 7/74; Carole Stodder (auth), A Day's Work—Fine Art at Kemper, Chicago New Art Examiner, Summer, 74; Ron Seely (auth), She Brings Art to Company Wall, Libertyville Independent Register, 9/76. Style & Technique: Tightly realistic, using colored pencils on Bristol for fullest intensity. Media: Colored Pencil Drawings; Intaglio Printing. Specialty: Primarily contemporary Chicago and Midwest artists working in most media, including fiber work. Publ: Auth, Kemper Art Collection, Kemper Ins Mag, Kemper, 73; contribr, Invest in Art? Maybe if..., Pioneer Press, 77. Mailing Add: Rt 3 Box 611-C 831 Corona Dr Lake Villa IL 60046

ROBERTSON, NANCY ELIZABETH
See Dillow, Nancy E

ROBINS, CORINNE
ART CRITIC, WRITER
b New York, NY, July 31, 34. Study: Walden Sch; NY Univ; New Sch Social Res. Teaching: Lectr Am art, US Info Serv, Brazil, 6-wks, 72; lectr New York art world & the young artist, Cooper Union, 74; Women Critics Panel, Sch Visual Arts, 75; lectr Drawing Now, Jamaica Art Ctr, 76; Critics Works in Progress, AIR Gallery, 76; lectr art hist, criticism & social change, Pratt Inst, 77. Art, Prince St, 75. Pos: Asst managing ed, Madmoiselle Mag, 57-59; cur exhib, Soho Ctr for Visual Artists, 76; contrib ed, Arts Mag, 76- Publ: Auth, Nancy Spero: political artist of poetry and the nightmare, Feminist Art J, spring, 75; auth, Deborah Remington: cool fire, Arts Mag, 10/75; auth, Michelle Stuart: the mapping of myth & time, Arts Mag, 12/76; auth, Organization of Independent Artists, Arts Mag, 11/77; auth, Artists in residence—AIR Gallery, Womanart, Winter 1977. Mailing Add: 83 Wooster St New York NY 10012

ROBINSON, C DAVID
ARCHITECT, COLLECTOR
b New York, NY, June 12, 36. Study: Princeton Univ, NJ, BA(art, magna cum laude), 57; Sch of Archit, Univ Calif, Berkeley (high honors), 61-62; Grad Sch Fine Arts, Univ Pa, BArch, 65. Pos: Co-owner, Robinson & Mills, Architecture & Planning, currently. Mem: Int Coun Mus Mod Art; Western Asn Art Mus (vis spec, 73-78); San Francisco Art Inst (trustee, chmn bd, 76-); DeYoung Mus, San Francisco; San Francisco Mus Art (trustee). Collection: Contemporary, New York School 1960's & 1970's and West Coast. Mailing Add: 1005 Sansome St San Francisco CA 94111

ROBINSON, CHARLES K
ART ADMINISTRATOR, WRITER
b Miami, Fla, Sept 29, 35. Pos: Vpres, Halfpenny Playhouse, Kearny, NJ, 63-; exec dir, Hudson Co Cult Coun, NJ, 66-71; mem adv bd, NJ Music & Arts Mag, 69-73; dir, Jersey City Awake (cult prog), NJ, 71-75; mem theatre adv panel, NY State Coun on the Arts, 74-; pres, The Jerz Co (touring theatrical troupe), Kearny, NJ, 74-; producer touring theatrical shows, Jerz—A Musical Salute to the State of New Jersey, 74-, Tarheel—A Musical Salute to the State of North Carolina, 76- & One for Good Measure—The Musical Metric Show, 77-; mem arts comt, NJ State Hist Comn, 75- & Edison Centennial Comt, 77-; dir, Div Cult & Heritage Affairs, Dept Health & Soc Serv, Hudson Co, Jersey City, NJ, 75-; pres, NJ Coalition for Arts & Humanities, 76-; mem, Arts in Educ Adv Bd, NJ State Dept Educ, 77- Bibliog: A H Reiss (auth), Arts prove key resource to troubled city, Arts Mgt Newsletter, 3-4/74; Jeffrey Stoll (auth), Hudson cultural council works to counter county's image as a wasteland, NY Times 12/75; Grace Glueck (auth), Hudson's savior of culture, NY Times, 2/76; Bruce Chadwick (auth), Council asks cue to culture needs, New York Daily News, 8/17/76. Mem: Asn Col, Univ & Community Arts Adminrs; Am Coun Arts. Mailing Add: Hudson Co Div Cult & Heritage Affairs 595 Newark Ave Jersey City NJ 07306

ROBINSON, CHARLOTTE
PAINTER, PRINTMAKER
b San Antonio, Tex. Study: Art Students League, New York, 48; New York Univ, 49; Corcoran Art Sch, 51. KMus Espanol de Arts Contemporaneo, Madrid, Spain; The New Sch for Social Res, New York; Am Tel & Tel, New York & Chicago; Caldwell Col, NJ; Inland Steel, Washington, DC. Exhib: Mus Espanol de Arts Contemporaneo, Madrid, Spain, 61; Chrysler Mus, Norfolk, Va, 65; 2nd Int Contemp Art Fair, Paris, France, 75; The Bronx Mus, New York, 76; The Mint Mus, Charlotte, NC, 77; Collectors Choice, Sheldon Swope Gallery, Terre Haute, Ind, 77; From the Ctr (traveling show), originating in Washington Women's Art Ctr, Washington, DC, 77. Collections Arranged: Jennie Lee's Night, Torpedo Factory Art Ctr, Alexandria, Va, 75; One to One, Eight Artists & Eight Cur, Washington Women's Ctr, Washington, DC, 76; Artists Co, Nine From Washington, DC, Nat Endowment for the Arts & Humanities mus traveling show, 77. Teaching: Instr painting, Torpedo Factory Art Ctr, Art League, Alexandria, Va, 67-75; instr drawing, Smithsonian Assoc Prog, Washington, DC, 76-; instr art world sem, Washington Women's Art Ctr, Washington, DC, 76- Pos: Co-dir workshops, Washington Women's Art Ctr, Washington, DC, 75-76, dir exhib & mem bd, 76-78; trustee, Bronx Mus, New York, 76-77. Awards: Scholar, Student Exhib, Corcoran Art Sch, Washington, DC, 51; First Prize Painting, Worldwide Air Force Exhib, Pentagon, Washington, DC, 56 & Marshal Award Show, Art League, Alexandria, Va, 70. Bibliog: Sanchez Camargo (auth), Charlotte Robinson Painter, El Alcazar, Madrid, Spain, 63; Pat Krebs (auth), Can you tell artist's sex by a painting, Charlotte Observer, NC, 77; Jo Ann Lewis (auth), Monumental & magnificient fun, Washington Post, DC, 11/19/77. Mem: Artists Equity, Washington, DC. Style & Technique: Landscape related abstract stained paintings, silk screens and lithographs; drawings, self-portraits and satirical animal drawing. Media: Painting and drawing. Dealer: Fendrick Gallery 3059 M St Washington DC 20007. Mailing Add: 6324 Crosswoods Dr Falls Church VA 22044

ROBINSON, FRANKLIN W
ART ADMINISTRATOR, ART HISTORIAN
b Providence, RI, May 21, 39. Study: Harvard Univ, BA, 61, MA, 63, PhD, 70. Teaching: Asst prof art hist, Dartmouth Col, 69-75; assoc prof art hist, dir grad prog hist art & dir mus art, Williams Col, 75- Mem: Col Art Asn; Am Asn Mus; Print Club Mus Fine Arts. Res: Baroque Art; prints and drawings. Publ: Auth, Dutch Drawings from the Abrams Collection, 69; auth, 100 Master Drawings from New England Private Collections, 72; auth, Gabriel Metsu, 75; auth, Dutch Life in the Golden Century, 75; auth, Seventeenth Century Dutch Drawings from American Collections, 77. Mailing Add: Williams Col Williamstown MA 01267

ROBINSON, GROVE
EDUCATOR, PAINTER
b Asheville, NC, May 17, 35. Study: Mars Hill Col, Assoc in Arts Cert, 55; Univ NC, Chapel Hill, 55-56; painting with Kenneth Ness, sculpture with Robert Howard, art hist with Clemens Sommer; Yale-Norfolk Summer Art Sch, 57, printmaking with Rudy Pozzatti; Columbia Univ, BFA, 58, MFA, 60, painting with John Heliker & Edwin Dickenson, printmaking with Hans Mueller, art hist with Meyer Schapiro; Fulbright Fel to France, 58-59. Work: NC Mus Art, Raleigh; Carroll Reece Mus, E Tenn State Univ. Comn: Murals, Union Univ, Jackson, Tenn, 75, 78. Exhib: Award Winners Show, NC Mus of Art, 56 & 61; Atlanta Art Mus, group juried show, 56; James Gallery Invitational, New York, 59; NC Artists Ann, NC Mus of Art, 60 & 65; 8th Ann Piedmont Craft Exhib, Mint Mus, Charlotte, NC, 71; 18th Biennial Mid-South Exhib, Brooks Art Gallery, Memphis, Tenn, 73; Four Tenn Artists, Univ of Ga, Athens, 74; Painters in Tenn Univs, Middle Tenn State Univ, Murphreesboro, 77; one-man show, East Tenn State Univ, 64. Teaching: Instr, Meredith Col, Raleigh, 65-71; chmn & assoc prof dept of art, Union Univ, Jackson, Tenn, 71- Pos: Vpres for visual arts, Jackson Art Coun, Tenn, 72-74; crafts adv panel, Tenn Arts Comn, 72-76. Awards: Purchase Award, 19th NC Artists Ann, NC Mus of Art, 56. Bibliog: M Beth (auth), 28th NC Artists Ann Art Review, Veritas Corp Inc, 66; Acquisitions from NC Anns 1946-1966 (catalog), N Mus of Art, 67; W C Burton (auth), Mixed Bag, Greensboro Daily News, 69. Style & Technique: Intermedia. Media: Acrylic Painting, Printmaking. Publ: Illusr, Union Univ Forum, Union Univ, 77. Mailing Add: 17 Laure Lane Jackson TN 38301

ROBINSON, JAY THURSTON
PAINTER
b Detroit, Mich, Aug 1, 15. Study: Yale Col, BA; Cranbrook Acad Art, MFA. Work: Cranbrook Mus, Bloomfield Hills, Mich; Detroit Inst Art; Houston Mus Fine Arts; J B Speed Mus, Louisville, Ky; Philbrook Art Ctr, Tulsa. Exhib: Audubon Artists, New York; Carnegie Inst Int, Pittsburgh; Corcoran Gallery Art Biennial, Washington, DC; Nat Acad Design, New York; Pa Acad Fine Arts, Philadelphia. Awards: Louis Comfort Tiffany Found Fel, 49; seven Childe Hassam Fund Purchase Awards, Am Acad Arts & Lett. Mem: Artists Equity Asn New York; Westchester Art Soc. Style & Technique: Non-objective; semi-abstract on human themes; portraits; style is linear, rhythmic, with varied shapes, using all painting media; also fired enamel on copper; acids on copper with gold leaf. Mailing Add: 60 Church St Pleasantville NY 10570

ROBINSON, MARGOT (MARGOT STEIGMAN)
PAINTER, SCULPTOR
b New York, NY. Study: Art Students League, with Harry Sternberg, 47; Robert Blackburn's Creative Workshop, 49-55; painting with John Von Wicht, 53-55; Gerard Koch Studio, Paris, 68; Donald Mavros Studio, New York, 71-72. Work: Am Express Co, Main Off, New York; Data Processing Co, Boston & Chicago Off. Exhib: Brooklyn Mus Nat Print Ann, New York; Soc of Am Graphic Artists Print Ann, New York; Pa Acad of Fine Arts, Philadelphia; Cincinnati Mus Color Lithography Biennial, Ohio; Riverside Mus, New York; Whitney Mus of Am Art, New York; Brooklyn Mus Community Exhib, New York. Pos: Dir, Creative Graphic Workshop, New York, 52-54; registr, Nat Acad Sch of Fine Arts, New York, 55-57; vpres, Noho Gallery, New York, 76-77 & secy, 77-78. Mem: Women in the Arts. Style & Technique: Figurative, landscape and figurative in the prints, emphasis on still life in early paintings; now abstract figurative, oil and acrylic; scdlpture in wax, plaster and clay for bronzes; wood and stone carvings; graphic media. Media: Mixed Media. Dealer: Noho Gallery 542 La Guardia Pl New York NY. Mailing Add: 141 Joralemon St Brooklyn NY 11201

ROBINSON, MARY ANN
ART ADMINISTRATOR, EDUCATOR
b McPherson, Kans, Sept 24, 23. Study: Kans State Univ, BS, 45; McCormick Theological Sem, MA, 55; Wichita State Univ, MA, 72; studied under Maude Ellsworth, Jan Lundgren, Robert Kisskaden, Robert Wood & James Pike. Exhib: Kans Biennial Art Exhib, Birger Sandzen Mem Gallery, Lindsborg, Kans, 72; Kans Ann Watercolor Exhib, Wichita Art Asn, 73; Am Contemp Arts & Crafts, Fla, 73; Kans Watercolor Soc Mem Show, Art Ctr Gallery, Hays, Kans, 77; Birger Sandzen Mem Gallery, 77. Teaching: Assoc prof art educ & art hist & chmn dept art, McPherson Col, Kans, 63- Pos: Supvr art in pub sch, McPherson, Kans, 47-49; dir, Friendship Hall Gallery, McPherson Col, Kans, 63- Mem: Kans Watercolor Soc (bd mem, 77-79); Kans Art Educ Asn; Nat Art Educ Asn; McPherson Arts Coun. Style & Technique: Landscapes, florals; abstract impressionistic. Media: Watercolor and acrylic. Mailing Add: 601 S Walnut McPherson KS 67460

ROBINSON, ROBERT DOKE
PAINTER, EDUCATOR
b Kansas City, Kans, Nov 11, 22. Study: Minneapolis Sch Art; Walker Art Ctr Sch; Univ Minn, with S Chatwood Burton, BA, BS & MA; Okla State Univ, with Ivan Doseff & Schaefer-Simmern, cert. Work: Chaffee Art Mus, Rutland, Vt; Lawrence Recreation Ctr, Rutland. Exhib: SVt Art Ctr, Manchester, 61. Teaching: Lectr art & the community & art educ, art clubs, gallery groups, high schs & cols; asst prof art & chmn dept, Castleton State Col, 60- Pos: Owner & pres, R D Robinson Advert Co, 51-58; art dir, Grubb-Clealand Advert Agency; pres, Mid-Vt Artists, 63-65. Mem: Delta Phi Delta; Nat Art Educ Asn; Grand Marais, Minn Art Ctr. Style & Technique: Representational. Media: Oil, Watercolor. Publ: Contribr illus, nat & int mod med publ & others. Mailing Add: Dept of Art Castleton State Col Castleton VT 05735

ROBINSON, SALLY W
PAINTER, PRINTMAKER
b Detrot, Mich, Nov 2, 24. Study: Bennington Col, BA; Wayne State Univ, MA & MFA; Cranbrook Acad Art; also with Hans Hofmann, Paul Feeley, Karl Knaths & Leon Kroll. Work: Chase Manhattan Bank, New York; Detroit Inst Arts; plus pvt collections. Exhib: Two-man show, Univ Mich, 73; one-man shows, Klein Vogel Gallery, Royal Oak, Mich, 74, Bertha Urdang Gallery, New York, 75 & Arnold Klein Gallery, 77; Asset Gallery, London, Eng, 75; Toledo Mus, Winston Traveling Show; Zella 9 Gallery, London, Eng. Teaching: Instr silk screen, Wayne State Univ, 73-74. Awards: Second Prize, Bloomfield Art Asn, 72; Second Prize, Soc Women Painters, 74 & First Prize, 75. Mem: Friends Mod Art; Founders Soc; Detroit Artists Market (bd dirs); Soc Women Painters (pres); Bloomfield Art Asn (bd dirs). Style & Technique: Cliche-Verre, a new printmaking technique using film, Kodak dyes, photosensitive paper and dye transfer. Publ: Contribr, Mich Art J, 76. Dealer: Klein-Vogel Gallery 4520 N Woodward Royal Oak MI 48053; Rina Gallery E 74th St & Madison New York NY 10021. Mailing Add: 572 Linden Rd Birmingham MI 48009

ROBINSON, THOMAS
ART DEALER, COLLECTOR
b Ft Worth, Tex, Feb 9, 38. Study: Tex Christian Univ; Tex Wesleyan Col. Pos: Dir, Robinson Galleries, Inc, 69- Bibliog: Article in SW Art Gallery Mag, 6/71. Specialty: Art of the nineteenth and twentieth centuries in America; American sculpture, paintings and graphics. Mailing Add: Robinson Galleries Inc 1100 Bissonnet Houston TX 77005

ROBINSON, WAHNETA THERESA
CURATOR, ART HISTORIAN
b Adrian, Mich. Study: Long Beach City Col, AA; Long Beach State Univ, BA & MA; Univ Calif, Los Angeles, with Dr E Maurice Bloch. Collections Arranged: Nineteenth Century American Landscape Painting (with catalog), 66; Seven Decades of Design (with catalog), 67; African Art, 68; Alexander Calder's Gouaches (with catalog), 70; American Portraits—Old & New, 71; Masuo Ikeda—Prints (with catalog), 71; Hans Burkhardt—Retrospect, 72; William Gropper—Paintings & Graphics, 72; The American Personality—The Artist-Illustrator of Life in the United States, 1860-1930 (contribr, catalogue), Grunwald Ctr for Graphic Arts, Univ Calif, Los Angeles, 76. Pos: Cur, Long Beach Mus Art, Calif, 66-74; retired. Mem: Col Art Asn Am; Art Historians Southern Calif; Am Asn Univ Women. Res: Essential historical data gathered about artists and art works for exhibition, publication and lectures. Mailing Add: Villa Serra 10870 N Stelling Rd Apt 31-I Cupertino CA 95014

ROBISON, ANDREW
MUSEUM CURATOR, WRITER
b Memphis, Tenn, May 23, 40. Study: Princeton Univ, AB & PhD; Oxford Univ, MA; Fulbright Res Scholar, India. Collections Arranged: Giovanni Battista Piranesi & Picasso Prints, 70, Princeton Univ; diverse print & drawing exhib, Nat Gallery of Art, 74- Pos: Cur prints & drawings, Nat Gallery Art, 74- Mem: Grolier Club, NY; Col Art Asn; Print Coun Am (pres, 75-). Res: 18th century Italian graphic art; origins of etching. Collection: Prints and 18th century Italian illustrated books. Publ: Auth, Vedute di Roma of Giovanni Battista Piranesi, 70; auth, Disasters of War, 73; auth, Albrizzi-Piazzetta Tasso, 74; auth, Religious Experience, 75; auth, Paper in Prints, 77. Mailing Add: Dept of Graphic Arts Nat Gallery of Art Washington DC 20565

ROBISON, JOAN SETTLE
ART LIBRARIAN
b Baltimore, Md, Aug 27, 49. Study: Towson State Univ, BS art educ & Painting, 71; Univ Md, grad study, 77- Pos: Asst librn, Baltimore Mus of Art, Md, 74-75, librn, 75- Mem: Art Libr Soc NAm, Col Art Asn. Interest: Twentieth century American art. Mailing Add: 402 Pleasant Hill Dr Owings Mills MD 21117

ROBLES, ESTHER WAGGONER
ART DEALER, COLLECTOR
b Sacramento, Calif. Study: Cumnock Sch Girls & Sch Expression, Los Angeles; Univ Calif, Los Angeles; Univ Paris; toured art monuments in Europe. Pos: Adv, Fed Arts Proj, Calif Arts Comn; founding mem & vpres, Southern Calif Art Dealers Asn, 70-72; hon mem art adv panel, Comn Internal Revenue, 70-72; organizer & vpres, Art Sponsors, Inc; ed, The Lively Art; appraiser of 20th century art; co-owner & dir exhibs, Esther Robles Gallery, 72- Mem: Founding mem Grunwald Soc; Univ Calif, Los Angeles Alumni Asn. Specialty: Twentieth century and vanguard painting and sculpture. Collection: American & European artists; works of Claire Falkenstein, R Cremean, William Scott, Allen Davie and others. Mailing Add: 12947 San Vicente Blvd Los Angeles CA 90049

ROBLES, JULIAN
PAINTER, SCULPTOR
b Bronx, NY, June 24, 33. Study: Nat Acad Art & Design, with Robert Phillip; Art Students League, with Sidney Dickinson. Work: NMex State Fair Gallery, Albuquerque; Diamond M Mus, Snyder, Tex. Comn: Portraits, Haruke Fujita, wife of Consul Gen Japan, 67, Adm Edward O McDonnell, Lincoln Family, Oyster Bay, Long Island, 68, Ernestine Evans, Secy State NMex, 69, Margaret Jamison, Santa Fe, NMex, 70 & Jean & Merle Rosenbaum, Santa Fe, 71. Exhib: NMex State Fair Art Exhib, Albuquerque, 71. Awards: First Award-Purchase Prize, NMex State Fair, 71; Second Prize for Pastels, NMex Fine Art Award, 72. Res: Researching and recording authentic western Indian life and ceremonials. Mailing Add: PO Box 1845 Taos NM 87571

ROBY, SARA (MARY BARNES)
COLLECTOR, PATRON
b Pittsburgh, Pa. Study: Pa Acad Fine Arts; Art Students League, with Kenneth Hayes Miller & Reginald Marsh. Exhib: Sara Roby Found Collection, Whitney Mus Am Art, 59; US Tour, leading mus Am, 60-62; Latin Am Tour, 13 countries, US Info Agency, 62-63; Am Fedn Arts Circulating Exhib, US & Can, 66-68. Interest: Encourage young American artists through the purchase and exhibition of their work. Collection: American artists from Hopper and Marsh to young contemporaries in all medias except prints with special emphasis on the elements of form and craftsmanship. Publ: The Collection of the Sara Roby Foundation, 66; Realism and Surrealism in American Art from the Sara Roby Foundation Collection, 71 & Americans: Individualists at Work from the Sara Roby Foundation Collection, 72, Am Fedn Arts. Mailing Add: 55 E 72nd St New York NY 10021

ROCH, ERNST
DESIGNER, GRAPHIC ARTIST
b Osijek, Yugoslavia, Dec 8, 28; Can citizen. Study: State Sch Appl Arts, Graz, Austria. Exhib: Design Collaborative with Rolf Harder, Montreal, 70, Biennale Venice, 72, Zagreb & Belgrade, 73, Braunschweig & Oldenburg, 74; Nat Libr, Ottawa, Ont, 77. Awards: Numerous awards from Am Inst Graphic Arts, Art Dir Club, Montreal & Toronto & Asn Graphic Designers Can; Most Beautiful Books of the World Leipzig, 75. Bibliog: John Gibson (auth), Ernst Roch, Printing Rev, 6/61; Hans Kuh (auth), Design Collaborative, Gebrauchsgraphik, Munich, 6/70; Allan Harrison & Hans Neuburg (auth), Graphic Designs by Rolf Harder & Ernst Roch, Montreal, 77. Mem: Royal Can Acad Arts; Alliance Graphique Int; Am Inst Graphic Arts; Int Inst Typographic Arts; Soc Graphic Designers Can. Publ: Ed, Arts of the Eskimo: Prints, 74. Mailing Add: PO Box 1056 Sta B Montreal PQ H3B 3K5 Can

ROCKBURNE, DOROTHEA
SCULPTOR
b Verdun, PQ. Study: Black Mountain Col, BA. Work: Mus Mod Art, New York; Walker Art Ctr, Minneapolis. Exhib: One-man shows, Bykert Gallery, New York, 70, 72 & 73 & Sonnabend Gallery, Paris, 71; exhib, Mus Mod Art, New York, 71, Eight Contemp Artists, 74; Documenta 5, Kassel, WGer, 72. Awards: Guggenheim Fel, 72-73. Bibliog: Robert Pincus-Witten (auth), article in Artforum, 2/71; Gregoire Muller (auth), Materialith painterlines, Arts Mag, 10/71; cover photo & three articles, Artforum, 4/72. Mailing Add: c/o John Weber Gallery 420 W Broadway New York NY 10013

ROCKEFELLER, MR & MRS DAVID
COLLECTORS
Mr Rockefeller, b New York, NY, June 12, 15. Study: Mr Rockefeller, Harvard Univ, BS, 36; Univ Chicago, PhD, 40; Columbia Univ, LLD, 54, Bowdoin Col, 58, Jewish Theol Sem, 58, Williams Col, 66, Wagner Col, 67, Harvard Univ, 69, Pace Col, 70. Pos: Trustee & chmn bd trustees, Mus Mod Art, New York. Collection: Paintings, modern art. Mailing Add: 146 E 65th St New York NY 10021

ROCKEFELLER, JOHN DAVISON, III
COLLECTOR, PATRON
b New York, NY, Mar 21, 06. Study: Princeton Univ, BS, 29. Pos: Bd mem, Am Mus Natural Hist, 33-55; dir, Lincoln Ctr Performing Arts, Inc, chmn, 61-70, hon chmn, 70-; emer trustee, Princeton Univ, 67- Mem: Asia Soc (pres & trustee, 56-64, chmn, 64-74); Am Asn Mus; life mem Brooklyn Mus & Metrop Mus Art; corp mem Mus Mod Art; Mus Primitive Art; plus others. Collection: Emphasis on American and Asian art. Mailing Add: 30 Rockefeller Plaza New York NY 10020

ROCKEFELLER, MRS LAURANCE S
COLLECTOR
Collection: Paintings & modern art. Mailing Add: 834 Fifth Ave New York NY 10021

ROCKEFELLER, NELSON ALDRICH
COLLECTOR, PATRON
b Bar Harbor, Maine, July 8, 08. Study: Dartmouth Col, AB, 30. Pos: Trustee, Mus Mod Art, 32-75, pres, 39-41 & 46-53, chmn, 57-58; founder, tre & pres, Mus Primitive Art, 54-; hon trustee, Metrop Mus Art. Mem: Am Asn Mus; Asia Soc; Assocs Guggenheim Mus; life mem Col Art Asn Am; Coun Nat Mus France. Collection: Emphasis on primitive and modern art. Mailing Add: 30 Rockefeller Plaza Rm 5600 New York NY 10020

ROCKLIN, RAYMOND
SCULPTOR, LECTURER
b Moodus, Conn, Aug 18, 22. Study: Educ Alliance, New York, with Abbo Ostrovsky; Cooper Union Art Sch, with Milton Hebald & John Havannes. Work: Whitney Mus Am Art, New York; Provincetown Mus Art, Mass; Temple Israel, St Louis; Skowhegan Sch Painting & Sculpture. Comn: Wall brass, comn by Mrs Beskind, New York, 62 & Mrs Nina Waller, Baltimore, 63. Exhib: Young Americans, Whitney Mus Am Art, 56; Oakland Art Mus, 59; Gallerina Tiberina, Rome, 59; Univ Calif, Berkeley, 60; Claude Bernard Gallery, Paris, 60. Teaching: Guest artist, Am Univ, 56; asst prof art, Univ Calif, Berkeley, 59-60; guest artist, Ball State Teachers Col, summer 64. Awards: Cooper Union Art Sch scholar to Skowhegan Sch Painting & Sculpture, 51; Fulbright grant, Italy, 52-53; Yaddo Found Fel, 56. Bibliog: M Seuphor (auth), Raymond Rocklin, The Sculpture of this Century, 61; F Hazan (auth), article in Dictionary of Modern Sculpture. Mem: Sculptors Guild; Am Abstract Artists; Fedn Mod Painters & Sculptors. Media: Bronze, Steel, Wood. Dealer: Sculptors Guild 10 E 53rd St New York NY 10022. Mailing Add: 232B Watch Hill Rd Peekskill NY 10566

ROCKMORE, NOEL
PAINTER
b New York, NY. Exhib: Cleveland Mus Art; Isaac Delgado Mus Art, New Orleans; Butler Inst Am Art, Youngstown, Ohio; Whitney Mus Am Art, Mus Mod Art & Metrop Mus Art, New York; Pa Acad Fine Arts, Philadelphia; plus one-man shows. Awards: Hallgarten Prize, 56 & 57 & Wallace Truman Prize, 59, Nat Acad Design; Tiffany Found Fels, 56 & 63; Ford Found & Am Fedn Arts Grant, 64; plus others. Publ: Auth, Preservation Hall Portraits, 68. Mailing Add: 638 Royal St New Orleans LA 70130

ROCKWELL, NORMAN
ILLUSTRATOR
b New York, NY, Feb 3, 94. Study: Art Students League; Univ Vt, DFA, 49; Middlebury Col, HHD, 54; Univ Mass, DFA, 61; also with George Bridgeman & Thomas Fogarty. Work: Metrop Mus Art, New York. Mem: Soc Illusr. Publ: Auth, Norman Rockwell, Illustrator, 46; auth, Norman Rockwell: My Adventures as an Illustrator, 59; auth, The Norman Rockwell Album, 61; auth, Norman Rockwell, Artist and Illustrator, 70; contribr, Sat Eve Post & Look Mag; plus others. Mailing Add: Stockbridge MA 01262

ROCKWELL, PETER BARSTOW
SCULPTOR, LECTURER
b New Rochelle, NY, Sept 16, 36. Study: Haverford Col, BA, 58; Pa Acad Fine Arts, 58-61, J Henry Shiedt traveling fel, 61; Scuola del Marmo, Carrara, Italy, 62; also study with Wallace Kelly. Work: Nat Portrait Gallery, Washington, DC; New Britain Mus Am Art, Conn. Comn: Monument with Norman Rockwell, Cathedral in the Pines, Rindge, NH, 66; commemorative statue, St Paul's Am Church, Rome, 70; gargoyles, Washington Cathedral, Washington, DC, 75; Wolf Mem Statue, Fairmont Park, Philadelphia, 78. Exhib: Jewelry by Contemp Painters & Sculptors, Mus Mod Art, New York, 67-68; V Biennale Della Sculpture, Carrara, 69; Am Artists in Rome, US Info Serv, Italy, 68, 71 & 73; one-man shows, Mickelson Gallery, Washington, Byck Gallery, Louisville, Ky, plus others. Teaching: Lectr stone technol, Int Ctr Conserv, Rome, 74-; instr sculpture & art hist, St Stephen's Sch, Rome, Italy; lectr art hist, Nat Trust for Hist Preserv Spec Tours, 75. Bibliog: Ken Wlaschin (auth), Peter Rockwell: the Cellino of the circus world, Italviews, 65. Style & Technique: Direct carving, marble and limestone; lost wax castings in bronze; bronze fountains. Res: Stone working technology. Dealer: Mickelson Gallery 707 G St NW Washington DC 20001. Mailing Add: Via L Manara 51 Rome Italy

RODA (RHODA LILLIAN SABLOW)
DESIGNER, PAINTER
b Port Chester, NY, Nov 26, 26. Study: Univ Wis; Rochester Inst Technol; Art Students League; also with Frank Vincent DuMont & Frank Reilly. Work: Needle Arts Gallery, Birmingham, Mich. Comn: Cranbrook 50th Anniversary (needlepoint rug), Cranbrook Acad, Bloomfield Hills, Mich, 73; needlepoint designs of main altar area & furniture, Christ Episcopal Church, Detroit, Mich, 75. Exhib: Allied Artists Am, Nat Acad, New York, 69; Ahda Artzt Gallery, New York, 70; Needle Arts Gallery, Birmingham, Mich, 71, 74 & 76; Lever House, New York, 77. Bibliog: Lesley Umans (auth), Encaustic painting, Reporter Dispatch, AP, 7/70 & Creative stitchery, Women's Wear Daily, 8/71; Lillian Braun (auth), 3-D needlepoint, int, Detroit Free Press, 10/74. Style & Technique: Figurative in oil/encaustic media; palette knife and hot-element technique, oversize fruits and vegetables in acrylic media; needlepoint design, fast drying oil media. Mailing Add: Rural Dr Scarsdale NY 10583

RODE, MEREDITH EAGON
PRINTMAKER, EDUCATOR
b Delaware, Ohio, Mar 27, 28. Study: Corcoran Sch of Art, 55-58; George Washington Univ, BA, 58; Art Students League of New York (scholar), study with George Grosz & Harry Sternberg, 59; Univ of Md, MFA, 74. Exhib: Baltimore Mus of Art, Md, 77; Utah Mus of Fine Arts, Salt Lake City, 77; Works on Paper, Blaffer Gallery, Univ of Houston, Tex, 77; Printmakers Guild of Annapolis Exhib, Hopkins Univ, Baltimore, Md, 77; Los Angeles Women's Art Ctr, 77; On Paper-Four Artists, Prince George's Col, Largo, Md, 78. Teaching: Instr studio art, Corcoran Sch of Art, 62-68; assoc prof studio art, Univ of the District of Columbia, 68- Pos: Chmn(actg), Federal City Col, Washington, DC, 71-72; vpres (Nat), Women's Caucus for Art, 75-76. Mem: Soc of Washington Printmakers; Women's Caucus for Art (vpres, 75-76); Southeastern Graphics Coun; Col Art Asn. Media: Lithography; Drawing; Graphite. Publ: Auth, Articles in Art J, Col Art Asn, 75. Dealer: Plum Gallery 3762 Howard Ave Kensington MD. Mailing Add: 7319 Baltimore Ave Takoma Park MD 20012

RODGERS, JACK A
ART ADMINISTRATOR
b Littlefield, Tex, Oct 5, 38. Study: Tex Tech Univ, BA(advert & design); Univ Tex Southwestern Med Sch, Dallas, MMA. Teaching: Asst prof & deputy chmn dept med commun, Univ Tex Med Sch, San Antonio, 67-75. Pos: Supvr med illus, Univ Tex Med Br,

Galveston, Tex, 64-66; exec dir, San Antonio Art Inst, Tex, 76- Awards: Nat Eaton Award, Nat Student Am Med Asn; First Place, Dept Neurol Exhib, Univ Tex Med Br, Galveston, Tex & Dept Surgery Exhib, Tex Med Asn. Mailing Add: San Antonio Art Inst PO Box 6092 San Antonio TX 78209

RODMAN, RUTH M
PRINTMAKER
b Boston, Mass, Apr 13, 28. Study: Mass Sch of Art; Sch of the Mus of Fine Arts, Boston, with Karl Zerbe; De Cordova Mus, Lincoln, Mass, with Stoltenberg. Work: New York Pub Libr; Boston Pub Libr, Mass; De Cordova Mus; Brockton Art Ctr, Mass; Minneapolis Inst of Art, Minn. Comn: Prints for all pvt rooms & eight pub spaces, St Elizabeth's Hosp, Boston, 77, lobby, Mt Sinai Hosp, Miami, Fla, Citibank, New York, Royal Crown Corp, Atlanta, Ga & Bank of Am, San Francisco, Calif. Exhib: De Cordova Mus, Lincoln, Mass, 73-77; Ann Nat Boston Printmaker Exhib; Silvermine Guild of Artists Nat Print Exhib, Conn, 74; Worcester Mus, Mass, 74-75; one-person show, Brockton Art Ctr, Mass, 75; Boston Visual Artist Union; Boston Ctr for the Arts. Awards: Purchase Prizes, Boston Printmakers, Rose Art Mus, Brandeis Univ, 73 & De Cordova Mus, 74 & 76; Nat Print Show, Silvermine Nat Print Exhib. Bibliog: J Silverman (auth), feature article, Boston Sunday Globe & Wayland-Weston Town Crier, 75; Carol LeBrun Danikian (auth), review in Christian Sci Monitor, 11/76; Corporations—the new medicis, Newsweek Mag, 11/76. Mem: Boston Printmakers; Boston Visual Artists Union; Nat Asn Am Penwomen. Style & Technique: (Collagraphs) abstract landscapes and colorful reflections; (Lithographs) with texture; both combined. Publ: Illusr, Collagraph Printmaking, Watson-Guptill, 75 & A Time for Living, Dutton, 75. Dealer: Adi Gallery 530 McAllister St San Francisco CA 94102; AAA Gallery 663 Fifth Ave New York NY 10022 Mailing Add: 16 Linn Lane Wayland MA 01778

RODMAN, SELDEN
WRITER, COLLECTOR
b New York, NY, Feb 19, 09. Study: Yale Univ, 31. Pos: Art comnr, State NJ, 64-65. Interest: Initiated and directed tempera murals by eight self-taught artists in Cathedral St Trinite, Port-au-Prince, Haiti, 49-51; comn three murals by Seymour Leichman and sculpture by James Kearns, 60-68. Collection: Contemporary figurative painting and sculpture; collection has been widely shown in the United States and Mexico, and has been catalogued by Vanderbilt University and by San Carlos Academy, Mexico. Publ: Auth, Conversations with Artists, 57; auth, The Insiders, 59; auth, The Miracle of Haitian Art, 74; auth, Tongues of Fallen Angels, 74; auth, The Brazil Traveler, 75; auth, Genius in the Backlands, 77; plus others. Mailing Add: 659 Valley Rd Oakland NJ 07436

RODRIGUE, GEORGE G
PAINTER
b New Iberia, La, Mar 13, 44. Study: Univ Southwestern La; Art Ctr Col Design, Los Angeles. Work: Art Ctr Southwestern La, Lafayette; New Orleans Mus Art; Coun Develop Fr in La, Lafayette. Comn: Painting for Prime Minister PQ, comn by Gov McKeithen, 69; Acadian Heritage for City Hall, comn by Mayor Kenneth Bowen, Lafayette, 72. Exhib: 1971 Artists of Southeast & Tex Biennial, Isaac Delgado Mus, New Orleans, 71; New Orleans Cult Ctr, 73; Watergate Mus Tour, Malmo, Sweden, 74; La Salon, Grand Palais des Champs-Elysees, Paris, 74 & 75. Awards: Hon Mention, Soc Fr Artists, 74; Tommasso Champanello Award, Int Acad Arts & Sci, Rome, 70. Bibliog: Rodrigue-Cajun Painter, Oxmore House, 76. Mem: Soc Fr Artists. Style & Technique: Bayou surrealist; Cajun primitive. Media: Oil Publ: Illusr, Discovery Mag, autumn 73. Mailing Add: 1206 Jefferson Lafayette LA 70501

RODRIGUEZ, JOE BASTIDA
ART DIRECTOR, PAINTER
b Houston, Tex, Mar 27, 49. Exhib: Dale Gas, Contemp Arts Mus, Houston, Tex, 77; Ancient Roots New Visions (nat tour exhib of nine major mus), 77-79. Teaching: Art dir, Asn Advan Mexican Americans, 73-76. Pos: Dir, SW Chicano Arts Ctr-Chicano Art Gallery, 76- Awards: Michael Angelo Award, Dominican Col, 71 & 72. Bibliog: James Conlon & James Kennedy (auth), Ethnic American Art Slide Library, Univ South Ala, 74-75. Mem: Cult Arts Coun of Houston (bd dir, 77-). Style & Technique: Abstract surrealist. Media: Watercolor. Mailing Add: 109 Frawley Houston TX 77009

RODRIGUEZ, OSCAR
PAINTER, SCULPTOR
b Mexico, DF, Mex, May 14, 43. Study: La Esmeralda, Nat Sch Painting & Sculpture, Inst Fine Arts, Mexico, DF, 65-67; Benito Juarez Univ, Engraving Workshop, Oaxaca, Mex, 72; Pratt Graphic Ctr, New York, 72. Work: Eliot Felt Ballet Found, New York; Simon Fraser Univ, Vancouver, Can; Mus Casa de Los Once Patios, Patzcuaro, Michoacan, Mex; La Casa del Lago Cult Difusion Ctr, Nat Univ Mex, Mexico, DF; Benito Juarez Univ. Exhib: One-man shows, La Casa del Lago Cult Difusion Ctr, 68, Galeria Jack Misrachi, Mexico, DF, 70, Palacio Clavijero, Morelia, Michoacan, 71, Polyforum Cult Siquieros, Mexico, DF, 73 & Galeria de Arte Danilo Ongay, Mexico, DF, 75 & 76; Primera Bienal de Arte de Morelia, Michoacan, 74; Salon Nac de Artes Plasticas, Seccion Beinal de Grafico, Inst Fine Arts, Mexico City, 77; Arte Actual de IberoAmerica, Inst Cult Hispanica, Madrid, Spain, 77. Pos: Organizer, Galeria Movil, truck converted to gallery circulating through city, Govt Mexico City, 73; organizer, Muestra de Arte Grafico, Collective Print Exhib, Nat Co Light & Power, Mexico, DF, 74; organizer, Mex Art: A View of the Seventies, Rotterdam, Holland, 76. Bibliog: Margarita Nelken (auth), Oscar Rodriguez, 2/2/67 & Enrique Gual (auth), Propositos y Rilicarios, 2/12/67, Newspaper Excelsior, Mexico, DF; Alfonso de Neuvillate y Oritz (auth), Oscar Rodriguez: Las Fueras y Comercio, 10/76. Mem: Salon de la Plastica Mex. Style & Technique: Interpretation of the human figure as an abstract form with metaphysic connotations; acrylic dry brush; watercolor with abrasion of paper; oil; all graphic techniques; carved sculpture in brute wood, often tree trunks, with inlays of cast aluminum; illuminated acrylic sculptures & tapestries. Publ: Contribr (scene & costume design; films), Divinas Palabras, Mex, 77 & A Fuego Lento, Mex, 78. Dealer: Galeria de Arte Misrachi Genova 20 Mexico 6 DF Mexico. Mailing Add: Edificio Condesa Calle Matehuala Entrada H Dept 2 Mexico 11 DF Mexico

RODRIGUEZ, RALPH NOEL
CURATOR, PAINTER
b Houston, Tex, Dec 27, 52. Study: Univ of Tex, Austin, BFA, 76. Pos: Cur, Southwest Chicano Art Gallery, Asn for the Advancement of Mex Am, 77- Mailing Add: 105 Ishmeal Houston TX 77076

RODRIGUEZ, VERNEDA
See McLean, Roddy

RODRIGUEZ LUNA, ANTONIO
See Luna

RODRIGUEZ-MORALES, LUIS MANUEL
ART ADMINISTRATOR, EDUCATOR
b Santurce, PR, Jan 12, 25. Study: Univ PR, BA(hist), 46; Cath Univ Am, 47-48. Teaching: Prof hist, Univ PR, 48. Pos: Dir off cult activities, Govt San Juan, PR; dir, Gen Arch PR, San Juan, 58-73; pres, Ateneo Puertorriqueno, San Juan, 65-66; asst dir, Inst Puerto Rican Cult, 72-73, dir, 73- Awards: Premio Manuel A Perea, Govt PR, 68. Publ: Auth, Consideraciones en torno a la Edicion de Actas Capitulares, 52; co-auth, Actas Capitulares de San Juan Bautista de Puerto Rico, 3 vols, 49, 50 & 54; auth, Ciudad de San Juan a mediados del Siglo XVIII vista a traves de sus Actas Capitulares; auth, Essays and Other Conferences, 62; Language and Other Themes, 68. Mailing Add: Inst of Puerto Rican Cult Box 4184 San Juan PR 00905

ROEBLING, MARY G
COLLECTOR, PATRON
b Collingswood, NJ, July 29, 05. Mem: Am Art Asn; Arch Am Art; Philadelphia Print Club; NJ Cult Ctr Adv Coun (first chmn); Metrop Mus Art. Collection: Paintings, sculpture, fine porcelain and glass. Mailing Add: Lafayette House 777 W State St Trenton NJ 08618

ROESCH, KURT (FERDINAND)
PAINTER
b Berlin, Ger, Sept 12, 05; US citizen. Study: Acad Art, Berlin. Work: Mus Mod Art, New York; Albright-Knox Art Gallery, Buffalo; Metrop Mus Art, New York; Currier Gallery, Manchester, NH; Univ Nebr. Exhib: Carnegie Inst, 41-58; Documenta, Kassel, Ger, 55; one-man shows, Curt Valentin Gallery, 49-53; Currier Gallery, 55. Pos: Emer mem fac, Sarah Lawrence Col. Mem: NH Art Asn. Mailing Add: Richards Lane New Canaan CT 06840

ROESLER, NORBERT LEONHARD HUGO
COLLECTOR
b Plankenberg, Austria, Aug 8, 01; US citizen. Mem: Drawing Soc; fel Pierpont Morgan Libr. Collection: Drawings by Dutch, French, Italian, English and others. Mailing Add: 785 Park Ave New York NY 10021

ROEVER, JOAN MARILYN
ILLUSTRATOR CHILDREN'S BOOKS, DIORAMIST
b Philadelphia, Pa, Dec 13, 35. Study: Philadelphia Mus Col of Art. Work: State Mus, Jackson, Miss; Cameron Co Libr, La. Mem: Soc of Animal Artists, New York. Style & Technique: Wildlife artist; detailed realism, paintings of all animal and plant species. Media: (Painting) Acrylic; (Dioramas) Oil. Publ: Auth-illusr, The Mustangs, 72, The North American Eagles, 73, The Brown Pelican, 74, Wolves, 75 & Whales in Danger, 76, Steck-Vaughn. Mailing Add: 251 14th St S Cocoa Beach FL 32931

ROGALSKI, WALTER
PRINTMAKER, LECTURER
b Glen Cove, NY, Apr 10, 23. Study: Brooklyn Mus Sch, with Xavier Gonzalez, Arthur Osver, C Seide & Gabor Peterdi, 47-51. Work: Mus Mod Art; Brooklyn Mus; Cleveland Mus Art; Fogg Mus Art; Seattle Art Mus; plus many others. Exhib: Six shows, Brooklyn Mus, 51-68; Soc Am Graphic Artists, 66 & 69; Cincinnati Mus Asn, 68; Am Fedn Arts Traveling Exhib, 69; Nat Print Exhib, Potsdam, NY, 69; plus many others. Teaching: Lectr etching, engraving, lithography & photo silkscreening; prof graphic art, Grad Sch Art & Design, Pratt Inst. Awards: Prizes, De Cordova & Dana Mus, 61 & Yale Gallery Fine Arts, 61; Purchase Prize, Assoc Am Artists, 66; plus others. Mem: Soc Am Graphic Artists. Publ: Auth, Prints & Drawings by Walter R Rogalski (catalog), Print Club Cleveland & Cleveland Mus Art, 54; contribr, Artists Proof Mag. Mailing Add: Dept of Printmaking Pratt Inst Brooklyn NY 11205

ROGERS, BARBARA JOAN
PAINTER
b Newcomerstown, Ohio, Apr 28, 37. Study: Ohio State Univ, BSc; Univ Calif, Berkeley, MA. Work: San Francisco Mus Mod Art; Oakland Art Mus, Calif. Exhib: New Realist Painters, Univ Calif, Davis, 69; West Coast 70, Biennial, Crocker Art Gallery, Sacramento, Calif, 70; Twelve Painters and the Human Figure, Santa Barbara Mus of Art, Calif, 73; one-woman exhib, San Francisco Mus Mod Art, 73; Contemp Am Painting & Sculpture, Krannert Art Mus, Univ Ill, Champaign, 74; 71st Am Exhib, Art Inst of Chicago, 74; Six Painters, Six Attitudes, Oakland Mus, 75; plus others. Teaching: Vis lectr drawing & painting, Univ Calif, Berkeley, 72-73; vis artist painting & grad sem, Univ Wash, Seattle, 75; vis artist painting & drawing, San Francisco Art Inst, 75-76. Awards: Eisner Prize, Univ Calif, Berkeley, 63. Bibliog: P D French (auth), Summer 68 & 1/70, Artforum; Jerome Tarshis (auth), Art News, 11/73. Style & Technique: Realist, figurative. Media: Airbrushed acrylic paint on paper or canvas; graphite on paper. Dealer: Hansen Fuller Gallery 228 Grant Ave San Francisco CA 94108. Mailing Add: 6389 Colby St Oakland CA 94618

ROGERS, CHARLES B
PAINTER, MUSEUM DIRECTOR
b Great Bend, Kans, Jan 27, 11. Study: Nat Acad Design; Tiffany Found; Bethany Col, BFA; Calif Col Arts & Crafts, MFA; with Dong Kingman; Jay Connaway Sch Art. Work: Libr of Cong Pennell Collection, Washington, DC; Metrop Mus Art Arms Collection, New York; Inst Mex Norteamericanos, Mexico City; Philadelphia Mus Art; Boston Pub Libr. Comn: Mural, US Govt Post Off, Council Grove, Kans, 40; Smoky Valley Landscape, Citizens Bank Mem, Ellsworth, Kans, 69; Splitter Farm, comn by Dr Stan Splitter, Oakland, Calif, 71; Autumn in Kansas, C L Clark Law Off, Salina, Kans, 72. Exhib: One-man exhibs, US Nat Mus, Smithsonian Inst, Washington, DC, Inst Mex Norteamericanos, Mexico City, Munic Tower Galleries, Los Angeles,Galleries de Arte, Monterrey, Mex & Inst Technol, Rochester, NY; plus many other group & one-man shows. Collections Arranged: The Great West-Paintings & Prints by Charles B Rogers; Paintings of the Southwest by Peter Hurd, Bethany College. Teaching: Head sch art, Bethany Col, 47-53; head sch art, Kans Wesleyan Univ, 66-67. Pos: Mgr & asst dir, Huntington Hartford Found, 54-66; dir, Rogers House Mus-Gallery, 67- Awards: Over 130 art awards including, Am Inst Fine Arts & Mikami Award. Bibliog: Ed Smith (auth), Charles B Rogers—Artist, Kans State Publ, 68; Art Professor Charles B Rogers, Kans State Univ, 69. Mem: Soc Am Graphic Artists; Carmel Art Asn, Calif; Prairie Watercolor Painters; Kans Fedn Art (bd mem, 71-). Style & Technique: Broadly poetic realism in Oriental sumi; egg emulsion and emulsified oil techniques. Specialty: Paintings and prints of the great West. Publ: Auth, Painting the American West, Artists Mag, London; auth, Charles B Rogers pleads for the spirit in art, Am Artist Mag, 8/63; auth, Heart of art, Art & Artists, 65; auth, Quill of the Kansan, pvt publ, 70; auth, Images of the American West, Celestial Arts. Mailing Add: Rogers House Mus-Gallery Snake Row Ellsworth KS 67439

ROGERS, JOHN
PAINTER, LECTURER
b Brooklyn, NY, Dec 9, 06. Study: Art Students League. Exhib: Am Watercolor Soc, 41-72; Brooklyn Mus Int, 46; Watercolor USA, Springfield, Mo, 62; Watercolor Soc, London, 65; Nat Acad Design, 70. Teaching: Instr watercolors, Garden City Adult Sch, 55-70; instr watercolor, Elmont Adult Prog, 57-70. Pos: Artist, New York Times, 28-30; artist & illusr, New York Post, 50-55. Awards: Am Watercolor Soc Silver Medal, 42; First Prize in Watercolor, Salmagundi Club, 70; Gold Medal, Am Artists Prof League. Bibliog: Norman Kent (auth), John Rogers watercolorist, Am Artist, 48. Mem: Am Watercolor Soc (exhib chmn, 68); Am Artists Prof League; Salmagundi Club; Art League Nassau Co (pres, 66); Art Students League. Media: Watercolor. Publ: Auth, articles in Am Artist, 48, Design Mag, 51, Artist's Mag, London, 52 & Watercolor Simplified, 65. Dealer: Garden City Gallery 923 Franklin Ave Garden City NY 11530. Mailing Add: 2107 Renfrew Ave Elmont NY 11003

ROGERS, JOHN H
SCULPTOR, EDUCATOR
b Walton, Ky, Dec 20, 21. Study: Eastern Ky Univ; Tyler Sch Art, Temple Univ, BFA & MFA. Work: Ala Archives, Montgomery; Marine Corps Combat Art Collection, Marine Corps Mus, Washington, DC; Auburn Univ, Ala; Dept Defense, Pentagon, Washington, DC. Comn: Bust of Gen H M Smith USMC, Ala Archives, Montgomery, 69; mem plaque of Lt Gen J A Chaisson, USMC, 75. Exhib: Minneapolis Womens Club Ann Print Show, Minn, 66; Armed Forces of US as Seen by the Contemporary Artist, Smithsonian Inst, Washington, 68; Artists in Vietnam, Smithsonian Traveling Exhib Serv, 68-70; Atlanta Col Art Fac Exhib, High Mus Art, Ga, 72; Inaugural Exhib, USMC Hist Ctr, Washington, DC, 77. Teaching: Sr sem humanities, Atlanta Col Art, 70-71; prof fine arts & sr symp, Univ NDak, 73- Pos: Acad dean, Minneapolis Col Art & Design, 64-68; asst head, Marine Corps Combat Art Prog, Washington, 68-69, head, 69-70; dean, Atlanta Col Art, Ga, 70-73; dean col fine arts, Univ NDak, 73- Awards: Mem Award, Minneapolis Womens Club, 66. Mem: Nat Asn Schs Art (deleg, 71-72, div V, 73-); NDak Alliance for Arts Educ; NDak Coun Arts & Humanities; Int Coun Fine Arts Deans (deleg, 73-77). Style & Technique: Figurative images in cast metals; constructivist pieces in wood. Publ: Ed, Directory of Arts Resources in the State of North Dakota, 77. Mailing Add: 2919 Chestnut St Grand Forks ND 58201

ROGERS, LEO M
COLLECTOR
b Boston, Mass, Dec 24, 02. Study: Columbia Col, BA, 23; Columbia Univ, ChE, 25. Collection: Cezanne, Manet, Degas, Soutine, Modigliani, Sisley, Signac, Roualt, Vuillard, Picasso, Pascin, Lautrec, Cassat, Renoir, Pisarro, Van Gogh, Morisot, Daumier, Brach, Homer & Ryder. Mailing Add: 601 Longboat Club Rd 201S Longboat Key FL 33548

ROGERS, MILLARD FOSTER, JR
MUSEUM DIRECTOR, ART HISTORIAN
b Texarkana, Tex, Aug 27, 32. Study: Mich State Univ, BA(hon), 54; Univ Mich, MA, 58; Victoria & Albert Mus, London, 59, with John Pope-Hennessy. Collections Arranged: New Eng Glass Co, 1818-1880, Toledo Mus Art, 63; Indian Miniature Painting, Univ Wis, 71, Canadian Landscapes, 73. Teaching: Prof art hist dept, Univ Wis-Madison, 67-74. Pos: Asst to dir, Toledo Mus Art, Ohio, 59-63, cur Am art, 64-67; dir, Elvehjem Art Ctr, Univ Wis-Madison, 67-74; dir, Cincinnati Art Mus, 74- Awards: Gosline Fel, Toledo Mus Art, 58-59. Mem: Asn Art Mus Dirs; Am Asn Mus. Res: Junius Brutus Stearns, 1815-1885; 19th century American Bozzetti. Publ: Auth, La pintura Espanola en el Museo de Arte de Toledo, Goya, 8/62; auth, The salutation of Beatrice by Dante Gabriel Rossetti, Connoisseur, 7/63; auth, Benjamin West and the caliph: two paintings for Fonthill Abbey, Apollo, 6/66; auth, Nydia, popular Victorian image, Antiques, 3/70; auth, Randolph Rogers, American Sculptor in Rome, Univ Mass, 71. Mailing Add: Cincinnati Art Mus Eden Park Cincinnati OH 45202

ROGERS, MIRIAM
ASSEMBLAGE ARTIST
b San Rafael, Calif, Mar 9, 00. Work: Brockton Art Ctr; pvt collections of Alfonso Ossorio, East Hampton, Dr Albert Schweitzer, Africa, Cardinal Richard Cushing, Boston, Queen Frederika, Greece, Jacques Cousteau, Monaco, plus others. Exhib: Cape Cod Arts Ctr, Hyannis, 62 & 73; Van Diemen-Lilienfeld Galleries, New York, 68; Brockton Art Mus, 69; Copley Soc, Boston; Roger Lussier Gallery, Boston; plus others. Pos: Artist in residence, Boston Mus Fine Arts, Fogg Art Mus, Brockton Art Ctr & Falmouth Artists Guild. Bibliog: Article in Lapidary Digest. Style & Technique: Abstract wall hangings and table tops. Media: Shells, Stones, Pebbles. Mailing Add: 71 Williston Rd Brookline MA 02146

ROGERS, OTTO DONALD
PAINTER, EDUCATOR
b Kerrobert, Sask, Nov 19, 35. Study: Sask Teacher's Col, cert, 53; Univ Wis, BSc(art educ), 58, MA(fine art), 59. Work: Nat Gallery Can, Ottawa; Montreal Mus Fine Arts; Nat Mus Iceland, Reykjavik; Fredericton Art Gallery, NB; Windsor Art Gallery, Ont. Comn: Sculpture in steel (with George Kerr, architect), Prince Albert Regional Libr, 65. Exhib: Biennial, Nat Gallery Can, 66, Royal Can Acad Art Exhib, 70; Directors Choice Exhib, sponsored by Can Coun, Confedn Art Gallery & Mus, Charlottetown, PEI, 68; Art in Saskatchewan, Waddington Fine Arts Gallery, Montreal, 69; Art Bank Can Exhib, Mendel Gallery, Saskatoon, 72. Teaching: Prof painting, Univ Sask, 59-, head dept art, 73- Pos: Mem acquisitions comt, Mendel Gallery, 72-73. Awards: Sr Award for Study in Europe, 67-68. Bibliog: R Harper (auth), History of Canadian Painting, 66; W Townshend (auth), Canadian art today, Studio Int, 70; C McConnell (auth), Otto Rogers, Arts Can, 71. Mem: Royal Can Acad Art. Media: Acrylic. Mailing Add: Dept of Art Univ Sask Saskatoon SK S7N 0W0 Can

ROGERS, P J
PRINTMAKER, GRAPHICS
b Rochester, NY, June 13, 25. Study: Wells Col, BA; Univ Buffalo; Acad Fine Arts, Vienna; Art Students League; also with Victor Hammer, Lazlo Szabo & Robert Brackman. Work: Wayne Tech Col; Tulsa Civic Ctr, Okla; Univ Akron; Akron Gen Hosp; Salem YWCA. Comn: Portrait comns, Buffalo, Akron, Los Angeles & Hudson, Ohio, 52-72; murals for Hall of Man, Buffalo Mus Sci, 53-55; portrait of founder, Novatny Elec Co, Akron, 67; poster for opening of new theater, Akron Weathervane Theater, 70; portrait of Dr D J Guzzetta, pres of Univ Akron, 75. Exhib: Big Bend Nat, Tallahassee, Fla, 68; Akron Art Inst May Show, 69; 34th Ohio Artists & Craftsmen Show, Massillon Mus, Ohio, 70; Canton Art Inst Ann All Ohio Fall Show, 70 & 71; Cleveland May Show, 73, 76 & 77; plus others. Teaching: Instr painting, Buffalo Mus Sci, 55; instr arts & crafts, Univ Akron Spec Progs, 58. Pos: Art preparator, Buffalo Mus Sci, 52-55. Awards: Honor Award, Ohio Print Show, Cuyahoga Valley Art Inst, 69; Second Prize, Salem Art Show, Ohio, 74; Top Graphic Cash Award, Cleveland Mus Art, 76. Bibliog: Stevens (auth), Aux Etats-Unis, expositions diverses, P J Rogers, La Rev Mod. Mem: New Orgn Visual Arts, Cleveland; Women's Art League Akron (corresp secy, 68-); Graphics Soc, Hollis, NH. Style & Technique: Plates are designed, etched or cut and printed by artist; large format with new realism, usually establishes mood with eastern influence. Dealer: Akron Art Inst 69 E Market Akron OH 44308; Downtown Gallery 262 Crystal Ct Minneapolis MN 55402. Mailing Add: 954 Hereford Dr Akron OH 44303

ROGERS, PETER WILFRID
PAINTER
b London, Eng, Aug 24, 33. Study: St Martins Sch Art, London, Eng. Work: Bristol Art Gallery, Eng; Roswell Mus, NMex; Macnider Mus, Mason City, Iowa; Mus of Southwest, Midland, Tex. Comn: Mural, Tex State Archives & Libr, Austin, 64; 48 paintings & drawings of Alaska, Atlantic Richfield Co, New York, 70-71; mural, Tex Tech Mus, 74. Exhib: Royal Soc Brit Artists, 57-59; one-man shows, Tooth's, London, 66, Fairmount Gallery, Dallas, 69, Artium Orbis, Santa Fe, 71, 72, Grace Cathedral, San Francisco, 73 & Janus Gallery, Santa Fe, 75; Heard Mus, Phoenix, Ariz, 75; plus others. Style & Technique: Semi-abstract, often of mystical import; academic realism for much commissioned work, generally landscape. Publ: Auth & illusr, The Quest. Dealer: Janus Gallery 116 1/2 E Palace Ave Santa Fe NM 87501. Mailing Add: 301 E Berger Santa Fe NM 87501

ROGOVIN, HOWARD SAND
PAINTER
b Ashville, NC, Feb 22, 27. Study: Northwestern Univ, BS; Art Students League, with Kantor & Grosz; Univ Colo, MFA. Teaching: Vis artist, Kansas City Art Inst, Mo, 68-69; assoc prof drawing, Univ Iowa, 69-72. Awards: Yaddo, 60; Nat Coun Arts, 69; Old Gold Medal, Univ Iowa, 70. Dealer: Babcock Gallery 805 Madison Ave New York NY 10021. Mailing Add: 1428 Lexington Ave New York NY 10028

ROGOVIN, MARK
MURALIST, EDUCATOR
b Buffalo, NY, July 31, 46. Study: Spec study in Mexico, with Elizabeth Catlett Mora, Jose Chavez Morado & David Alfaro Siqueiros, 65-68; RI Sch of Design, Providence, BFA, 68; Art Inst of Chicago, MFA, 70. Comn: Outdoor mural (18ft x 89ft), side of Am Nat Bank, comn by Rockford Evening Cosmopolitan Club, Ill, 75; indoor mural (8ft x 24ft), Col of DuPage, Glen Ellyn, Ill, 75; outdoor mural (10ft x 100ft), comn by several neighborhood orgn on Chicago's West Side, 76. Exhib: Murals for the People, Mus of Contemp Art, Chicago, 71; Street Art—Pub Murals in the USA (Bicentennial traveling exhib), Amerika-Haus, W Berlin, 76; Mural Art USA (traveling exhib), Maison de la Cult Andre Malraux, Reims, 77. Teaching: Sch prog artist, Urban Gateways, Chicago, 73-; artist-in-residence murals, Col of DuPage, Glen Ellyn, Ill, Spring 1975 & Univ Nebr, Omaha, 77 & Univ Nebr, Lincoln, 78. Pos: Dir & co-founder, Pub Art Workshop, 72- Bibliog: Hermann Kopp (auth), Kunstler der demokratischen Offentlichkeit, Tendenzen, Fed Repub of Ger, 7/74; Macarlo Matus (auth), Mark Rogovin, muralista Norteamericano, El Dia, Mexico City, 2/76; Victoria Petrilli (auth), Waking up Chicago's Walls, World Mag, 5/77. Mem: United Scenic Artists Local; Chicago Artists Coalition; Nat Murals Network. Style & Technique: Realistic expressionist with dynamic perspective. Media: Acrylics. Publ: Co-auth, Mural Manual, Beacon Press, 75 & Silhouette Murals, Pub Art Workshop, 76. Mailing Add: 5623 W Madison St Chicago IL 60644

ROHLFING, CHRISTIAN
ART ADMINISTRATOR, CURATOR
b Philadelphia, Pa, Nov 14, 16. Study: Univ Chicago. Pos: Bd dirs & adv bd, Four Winds Mus Theatre; adminstr & cur collections, Cooper-Hewitt Mus Design, New York, currently. Mailing Add: 343 E 30th St New York NY 10016

ROHM, ROBERT
SCULPTOR
b Cincinnati, Ohio, Feb 6, 34. Study: Pratt Inst, BID, 56; Cranbrook Acad Art, Bloomfield Hills, Mich, MFA, 60. Work: Mus Mod Art, New York; Kunsthalle, Zurich, Switz; Finch Col Mus, New York; Columbus Gallery Fine Art; Allen Art Mus, Oberlin Col. Exhib: Sculpture Ann, Whitney Mus Am Art, 62, 64, 70 & 73, Anti-illusion: Procedures/Materials, 69; Soft Art, NJ State Mus, Trenton, 69; 557,087, Seattle Art Mus Pavilion, Wash, 69; Painting & Sculpture Today, Indianapolis Mus Art, Ind, 70; Works Mostly on Paper, Va Mus Art, Richmond, 70; 955,000, Vancouver Art Mus, BC, 70; one-man exhib, O K Harris, Works of Art, New York, 70, 72, 73, 75 & 77; US Sect, Triennial, New Delhi, India, 71; Recent Abstract Art, Fogg Mus, Cambridge, Mass, 71; two-man show, Boston Mus Fine Art, 74; Contemp Selections, Art Mus STex, Corpus Christi, 75; Bicentennial Collection, Inst Contemp Art, Boston, 75. Teaching: Instr sculpture, Columbus Col Art & Design, 56-59; instr sculpture, Pratt Inst, 60-65; prof sculpture, Univ RI, 65- Awards: Guggenheim Found Fel, 64; Nat Endowment Arts Award, 74; Artpark, Lewiston, NY, 77; plus others. Bibliog: Ralph Pomeroy (auth), An interview with Robert Rohm, Artforum, 4/70, Robert Rohm, Arts Can, 4/70 & Moving things, Art & Artists, 11/74; plus others. Style & Technique: Constructions using basic and common building materials in a direct and blunt manner. Dealer: OK Harris Works of Art 383 W Broadway New York NY 10012. Mailing Add: 26 Lake St Wakefield RI 02879

ROHRER, WARREN
PAINTER, INSTRUCTOR
b Lancaster, Pa, Dec 4, 27. Study: Eastern Mennonite Col, BA; Madison Col, BS; Pa State Univ; Pa Acad Fine Arts. Work: Philadelphia Mus Art; Pa Acad Fine Arts; Del Art Mus; Univ Del; Allentown Art Mus, Pa; Dickinson Col. Comn: Commemorative Woodcut, Eastern Mennonite Col, Harrisonburg, Va, 61. Exhib: Pittsburgh Int, Carnegie Inst Fine Arts, 55; 154th & 163rd Ann, Pa Acad Fine Arts, Philadelphia, 59 & 68; one-man shows, Makler Gallery, Philadelphia, 63, 65, 67, 69 & 71, Marian Locks Gallery, Philadelphia, 74, 76 & 78 & Lamagna Gallery, New York, 76; A Sense of Place: The American Artist & the Land, Joslyn Art Mus, Omaha, 73; Delaware Water Gap, Corcoran Gallery Art, Washington, DC, 75; Philadelphia: Three Centuries of Am Art, Philadelphia Mus Art, 76; Philadelphia Houston Exchange, Inst Contemp Art, Philadelphia, 76; Susan Caldwell Gallery, New York, 77; plus many one-man shows. Teaching: Instr painting, Philadelphia Col Art, 67- Pos: Gubernatorial appt, Pa Coun on the Arts, 76. Awards: Prizes, Del Art Mus, 58 & 65; Hon Mention, Pa Acad Fine Arts, 59. Style & Technique: Landscape ideas (light, sky, field & water), with layered brushwork. Media: Oil, Pastel. Dealer: Marian Locks Gallery 1524 Walnut St Philadelphia PA 19102. Mailing Add: RD 1 Box 410 Christiana PA 17509

ROJO, VICENTE
PAINTER
b Barcelona, Spain, Mar 15, 32. Work: Mus Mod Art, Mex; Banco Cedulas Hipotecarias SA, Mex; Casa de las Americas, Havanna, Cuba; Biblioteca Luis Arango, Bogota, Colombia; Banco Nac de Mex. Comn: Portfolio of five lithographs, Lublin Inc, New York, 69. Exhib: 2nd Biennial De Jovenes, Paris, 61; Mexico: The New Generation Traveling Exhib, US, 66; Expo '67, Montreal, PQ, 67; 1st Triennial India, New Delhi, 68; Contemporary Mexican Painting, Mus Mod Art, Tokyo, 74; plus others. Bibliog: J J Gurrola (producer), Rojo (film), 66 & J Garcia Ponce (auth), Vicente Rojo, 71, Nat Univ Mex; Octavio Paz (auth), Discos

visuales, Ediciones Era, 68. Style & Technique: Abstract geometric. Media: Acrylic, Oil. Dealer: Galeria Juan Martin Amberes 17 Mexico DF Mexico. Mailing Add: Dulce Olivia 57 Mexico DF Mexico

ROJTMAN, MRS MARC B
COLLECTOR
Pos: Bd gov, New York Cult Ctr; fel, Morgan Libr; pres, Rojtman Found Inc. Mem: Art Collectors Club; Drawing Soc; fel in perpetuity Metrop Mus Art; Inst Fine Arts, NY Univ (mem bd adv); Cooper Hewitt Mus, Smithsonian Inst (mem adv coun). Collection: Paintings, prints, drawings. Mailing Add: 22 E 64th St New York NY 10021

ROLAND, ARTHUR
PAINTER, EDUCATOR
b Detroit, Mich, Aug 23, 35. Study: Mezinger Art Sch, Detroit; Wayne State Univ; Studio 21 Art Sch, Detroit; also with LeRoy Foster. Work: Merabash Art Mus, New Egypt, NJ; Howard Univ; Johnson Publications, Chicago. Comn: Wall of Pride (mural)(with Harold Neal, John Lockhart, Robin Harper, James Mathis, Henry King & James Malone), Grace Episcopal Church, Detroit, 68; portrait, Barry Gordy Family (oil), 70; Black Family (oil), Chaney Elem Sch, Detroit, 73; Logo, Taurus Prod, Atlanta, Ga, 73. Exhib: Detroit Inst Arts, 68; one-man show, Forest Hills Learning Resource Ctr, Toronto, 70; Carnegie Inst, Pittsburgh, 71; NJ State Art Mus, Trenton, 71; Indiana Univ, Bloomington, 74. Teaching: Teacher youth in art, Harlem Gallery Square, Detroit, summer 69; teacher advan painting, Your Heritage House Detroit, 70-74; teacher creativity on the move, United Community Serv, Detroit, summer 74 & 75. Pos: Art dir, Outlook Mag, Detroit, 69; chmn art comt, Harlem Gallery Square, 72; art dir, Detroit Expo 1974, 74; art dir creativity on the move, United Community Serv, 74-75. Awards: Art Festival First Prize, United Auto Workers, 68; Push Expo 72 First Prize, Rev Jessie Jackson, 72; Art Festival First Prize, Harlem Gallery Square, 73.. Bibliog: The Johnson Publication Company's art collection, Ebony Mag, 12/73; Culture can be such fun, too, Detroit Free Press, 8/74; This barber is an artist too, Detroit News, 8/74. Mem: Concerned Citizens Comt; Detroit Bicentennial Art Comt; Seasonal Activities Creative Knowledge (bd mem, 75). Style & Technique: Realistic painter of people's expressions and reactions to their cultural environment. Media: Oil, Charcoal. Publ: Illusr, Ancient Africa: History, Nations, Empires & People, 69. Mailing Add: 4614 Woodward Ave Detroit MI 48201

ROLLER, MARION BENDER
SCULPTOR, PAINTER
b Boston, Mass. Study: Vesper George Sch Art, dipl; Art Students League, with John Hovannes; Greenwich House, with Lu Duble; Queens Col, BA; also watercolors with Edgar Whitney. Comn: Head of child, Nassau Ctr Emotionally Disturbed Children, Woodbury, NY, 68; plus many other pvt comn. Exhib: Allied Artists Am, 59-74 & 77; Nat Acad Design, New York, 62-69 & 77; Am Artists Prof League, 65, 66 & 68; Nat Sculpture Soc, New York, 69-; Audubon Artists, 73; Reflections: Images of Am (toured Eastern Europe), US Info Agency, 76-78; Fine Arts Fedn, New York, 77-; Nat Arts Club Gala Exhib for Award Winners, 78; plus others. Teaching: Instr art, Fashion Inst Technol, 67; instr, Traphagen Sch. Awards: Mrs John Newington Award, Am Artists Prof League, 65, Archer Milton Huntington Award, 68; Knickerbocker Artists Prize for Sculpture, 66; Gold Medal, Pen & Brush, 71, Honorable Mention for Sculpture & Watercolor, 75, Brush Award for Etching, 75 & First Hon Mention in Watercolor; plus others. Bibliog: G Kramer (auth), Profile, Hudson Register Star, 65. Mem: Nat Sculpture Soc; Allied Artists Am (asst corresp secy, 66-); Pen & Brush (co-chmn, 67-); Catharine Lorillard Wolfe Art Club; Hudson Valley Art Asn. Media: Terra-Cotta, Bronze; Watercolor. Mailing Add: 1 W 67th St New York NY 10023

ROLLINS, JO LUTZ
ART DEALER, PAINTER
b Sherburn, Minn, July 21, 1896. Study: Cornell Col; Univ Minn, BA & MA; Minneapolis Sch Art; Corcoran Art Sch; and with Cameron Booth, BJO Nordfeldt, Edmund Kinsinger & Hans Hofmann, Munich. Work: Minneapolis Art Inst. Teaching: From instr to prof studio art, Univ Minn, 28-65. Pos: Dir, West Lake Gallery, Minneapolis. Awards: Rockefeller Found Grant, Univ Grad Sch, 50; Grad Sch Grants, Univ Minn, 50-65. Mem: Artists Equity; Minn Artists Asn (pres, 63-66). Specialty: Women's cooperative, painting, sculpture, prints. Dealer: West Lake Gallery 1612 W Lake St Minneapolis MN 55408. Mailing Add: 3406 Humboldt Ave S Minneapolis MN 55408

ROLLMAN-SHAY, ED & CHARLOTTE
PAINTERS, PRINTMAKERS
Ed, b Boston, Mass, Nov 12, 47; Charlotte, b Harrisburg, Ill, Oct 15, 47. Study: Both, Murray State Univ, Ky, BFA, 69; Univ Ill, Champaign, MFA, 71. Most work collaborative. Work: Minn Mus of Art, St Paul; Univ NDak, Grand Forks; Dulin Gallery of Art, Knoxville, Tenn; Bradley Univ, Peoria, Ill; Calif Col of Arts & Crafts, San Francisco. Comn: Oil Planetarium (10ft x 25ft), Ponderosa Collection, Dayton, Ohio, 74; wall graphic (11ft x 250ft), Skate Away, Muncie, Ind, 77; billboard (10ft x 25ft), Indianapolis Art League, Ind, 78. Exhib: 74th Chicago Artists & Vicinity Show, Chicago Art Inst, 73; World Print Competition, Calif Col of Arts & Crafts, San Francisco, 73; Works On Twinrocker Handmade Paper, Ind Mus of Art, Indianapolis, 75; Crimes of Passion, Univ Ky, Lexington, 77; Rutgers Nat Drawing 77, Camden Col of Arts & Sci, NJ, 77. Collections Arranged: Rollman-Shay, Not In New York Gallery, Cincinnati, Ohio, 74 & 76, Krannert Gallery, Univ Evansville, Ind, 74, Nancy Lurie Gallery, Chicago, Ill, 76, Ball State Univ Art Gallery, Muncie, Ind, 76. Awards: Purchase Awards, 55th Soc Am Graphic Artists Nat Print Exhib, New York, 77 & Drawings & Prints 77, Miami Univ, Oxford, Ohio, 77; Bronstein Purchase Award, 1977 Mid-States Exhib, Evansville Mus of Art, Ind, 77. Bibliog: Ellen Brown (auth), Ed & Charlotte Rollman-Shay, Art In Am, 3-4/76; Lynn Karn (auth), Ed & Charlotte Rollman-Shay, New Art Examiner, 1/77; Franz Schulze (auth), Illinois Artists, Chicago Daily News, 1/23/77. Style & Technique: Representational. Media: Oil, Watercolor. . Dealer: Nancy Lurie Gallery 1632 N LaSalle Chicago IL 60614; Kathryn Markel Gallery 50 W 57th St New York NY 10019. Mailing Add: 617 N Dicks St Muncie IN 47303

ROLLY, RONALD JOSEPH
ART DEALER
b Waterbury, Conn, Dec 31, 37. Pos: Dir, Rolly-Michaux Galleries, Boston & New York. Specialty: 19th and 20th century masters and contemporaries; paintings, sculpture and graphics. Mailing Add: c/o Rolly-Michaux Galleries 290 Dartmouth St Boston MA 02116

ROLOFF, JOHN SCOTT
CERAMIST, SCULPTOR
b Portland, Ore, Sept 20, 47. Study: Univ Calif, Davis, with Bob Arneson, William Wiley, Roy DeForest & Wayne Thiebaud, BA; Calif State Univ, Humboldt, MA. Work: Calif State Univ, Fullerton, 76; Univ NC Mus, 77; Lang Art Gallery, Scripps Col, Claremont, Calif, 77; Mus Mod Art, San Francisco, 77; Herbert F Johnson Mus, Cornell Univ, Ithaca, NY, 78. Exhib: Coffee, Tea & Other Cups, Mus Contemp Crafts, New York, 70; Ceramic Invitational, San Francisco Art Inst, 74; Clay Images, Calif State Univ, Los Angeles, 74; Clay USA, Fendrick Gallery, Washington, DC, 75; Whitney Mus Am Art, Biennial, New York, 75. Teaching: Instr ceramics, San Francisco Art Inst, 73-74; asst prof ceramics, Univ Ky, 74- Awards: Calif, Ceramics & Glass, Oakland Mus, 74; Craftsmens Fel, Nat Endowment for the Arts, 77. Bibliog: Cecile McCann (auth), Ceramic sculpture, Art Week, 3/74; Sean Licka (auth), A prima facie clay sampler (part II), Currant Mag, 10/75. Style & Technique: Ceramic sculpture; personal mythology related to landscape, ships, organic processes and metaphor. Dealer: Lester Gallery PO Box 485 Inverness CA 94837. Mailing Add: PO Box 1275 Lexington KY 40590

ROMAN, SHIRLEY
PRINTMAKER
b New York, NY. Study: Am Artists Sch; Brooklyn Mus Sch; Queens Col; also with Gregorio Prestopino, Raphael Soyer, Ruth Leaf & Agnes Mills. Work: De Cordova Mus, Lincoln, Mass; Hunterdon Art Ctr, NJ; Nassau Community Col, Garden City, NY; Queens Col, Flushing, NY; Libr Cong, Washington, DC. Exhib: Philadelphia Print Club, 69-74; Nat Acad Design, 70; Okla Printmakers Soc, 73; Silvermine Guild, 73; Honolulu Inst Art, 74. Awards: Eric & Vita Schwartz Prize, Nat Asn Women Artists, 71; Windsor Newton Artists Award, Nat Arts Club, 72; Purchase Prize, Boston Printmakers 25th Ann, 73. Mem: Philadelphia Print Club; Nat Asn Women Artists; Audubon Artists; Jamaica Arts Mobilization. Style & Technique: Intaglio. Mailing Add: c/o Bermond Art Ltd 3000 Marcus Ave Lake Success NY 11040

ROMANO, CLARE CAMILLE
PRINTMAKER, PAINTER
b Palisade, NJ. Study: Cooper Union Sch Art, 39-43; Ecole Beaux-Arts, Fontainebleau, France, 49; Inst Statale Arte, Florence, Italy, Fulbright Grant, 58-59. Work: Mus Mod Art, Whitney Mus Am Art & Metrop Mus Art, New York; Libr of Cong & Nat Collection Fine Arts, Washington, DC. Comn: Tapestry, Mfrs Hanover Bank, New York, 69. Exhib: American Prints, South London Art Gallery, Eng, 67; Cincinnati Mus Art Print Exhib, 68; 1st Biennial Am Graphic Art, Colombia, SAm, 71; 2nd Triennial Int Exhib Woodcuts, Ugo Carpi Mus, Italy, 72; American Prints, US Info Agency, Australian Nat Mus, Canberra, 72. Teaching: Instr printmaking, New Sch Social Res, 60-73; adj assoc prof printmaking, Pratt Graphic Arts Ctr, 63-; assoc prof printmaking, Pratt Inst, 64- Awards: Louis Comfort Tiffany Grant, 52; Fulbright Grant, 58; Citation for Prof Achievement, Cooper Union Sch Art, 66. Bibliog: Pat Gilmour (auth), Modern prints, Studio Vista, London, 70; Jules Heller (auth), Printmaking Today, Holt, Rinehart & Winston, 72; Fritz Eichenberg (auth), The Art of the Print, Abrams, 77. Mem: Soc Am Graphic Artists (pres, 70-72); Print Club Philadelphia; Mod Painters & Sculptors; assoc Nat Acad Design. Publ: Co-illusr, Spoon River Anthology, 63; co-illusr, Leaves of Grass, 64; auth, Artist's Proof, 64 & 66; auth, American Encyclopedia, 71; co-auth, The Complete Printmaker, 72. Dealer: Assoc Am Artists 663 Fifth Ave New York NY 10022. Mailing Add: Sch Art & Design Pratt Inst New York NY 11205

ROMANO, EMANUEL GLICEN
PAINTER, ILLUSTRATOR
b Rome, Italy, Sept 23, 97. Study: In Switz; also with Enrico Glicenstein. Work: Univ Art Mus, Univ Tex, Austin; Fogg Mus Art; Metrop Mus Art, New York; Detroit Inst Art; Mus Ville Paris; plus others. Comn: Mural, Klondike Bldg, Welfare Island, NY; portraits in many pvt collections. Exhib: Whitney Mus Am Art; City Col New York; Ft Worth Art Asn; one-man shows, Greenville Mus Art, SC, 62 & Haifa Mus & Tel-Aviv Mus, Israel; plus many others. Teaching: Lectr mural painting in ancient and modern times. Mem: Artists League Am. Publ: Contribr drawings, in The Waste Land, The Hollow Men, Waiting for Godot, Beckett, Rhinoceros & Ionesco; plus many others. Mailing Add: 163 E 74th St New York NY 10021

ROMANO, JAIME (LUIS)
PAINTER
b Santurce, PR, May 10, 42. Study: Univ PR, BA(humanitis), 66; Am Univ, MA, 69. Work: Mus Bellas Artes, Ponce, PR; Ateneo Puertorriqueno, San Juan, PR; Inst Cult Puertorriquena, San Juan; Mus Antropologia y Arte, Univ PR, Rio Piedras; C Law Watkins Mem Collection, Am Univ, Washington, DC. Exhib: Certamen Navidad Ateneo Puertorriqueno, San Juan, 66-68 & 71; David Lloyd Kreeger Award Exhib, Washington, 69; Expos Panamericana Artes Graficas, Cali, Colombia, 70; Primera & Segunda Bienal Grabado Latinoamericano, San Juan, 70 & 72. Teaching: Instr advan drawing & painting, Univ PR, Rio Piedras, 69-71, acad adv, 70-71. Pos: Vpres, Fondo Becas Artes Plasticas, Inc, San Juan, 70- Awards: First Prize in Painting, Soc Amigos de Cristobal Ruiz, 67; First Prize in Painting, David Lloyd Kreeger Award Exhib, 68; First Prize in Painting, Certamen Ateneo Puertorriqueno, 68. Bibliog: Ernesto Alvarez (auth), Jaime Romano, Artes Graficas, 66; Antonio Molina (auth), Lo ultimo de Romano, El Mundo, 68; The seven minutes, San Juan Star, 10/15/72; plus one other. Media: Acrylic. Publ: Auth, Ernesto Alvarez, 66; auth, Art in Puerto Rico-Boom or Bust?, 71; auth, On Criticism, Critics & Criteria, 72. Mailing Add: c/o Galeria Santiago 207 Calle del Cristo San Juan PR 00901

ROMANO, SALVATORE MICHAEL
SCULPTOR, PAINTER
b Cliffside Park, NJ, Sept 12, 25. Study: Art Students League, with Jon Corbino; Acad Grande Chaumiere, Paris, with Edouard Georges & Ehrl Kerkam. Work: Chase Manhattan Bank, New York. Exhib: Primary Structures, Jewish Mus, New York, 66; one-man shows, A M Sachs Gallery, New York, 68, Max Hutchinson Gallery, New York, 71, 73 & 75 & Sculpture Now Gallery, New York; Highlights of the Season, 68-69, Aldrich Mus Contemp Art, Ridgefield, Conn, 69; Monumenta, A Biennial Exhib Outdoor Sculpture, Newport, RI, 74; Wave Hill Sculpture Garden Exhib, New York, 77. Teaching: Adj instr sculpture, Cooper Union Sch Arts & Archit, 68-70; lectr painting & sculpture, Lehman Col, 69-71, asst prof, 72-; lectr kinetic sculpture, US Info Serv, Brazil, 72. Bibliog: John Canaday (auth), article, 3/73 & John Russell (auth), article, 3/17/74, New York Lawrence Alloway (auth), Salvatore Romano's sculpture, Arts Mag, 10/77; Donald B Kuspit (auth), rev in Art in Am, 1-2/78; plus others. Style & Technique: Symmetrical forms which develop self-contradiction through a movement due to flotation. Media: Plastics, Wood, Metal, Water. Publ: Auth, article in, Lehman Col Art News Lett, 71. Dealer: Max Hutchinson Gallery 127 Greene St New York NY 10012. Mailing Add: 83 Wooster St New York NY 10017

ROMANO, UMBERTO ROBERTO
PAINTER, SCULPTOR
b Naples, Italy, Feb 26, 06; US citizen. Study: Nat Acad Design, New York, 21-26; Tiffany Found, summer 25; Am Acad Rome, 26-27. Work: Nat Collection Fine Arts, Washington, DC; Whitney Mus Am Art; Roosevelt Libr, Hyde Park, NY; Corcoran Gallery, Washington, DC; Smith Mus, Springfield, Mass. Comn: Mural, Three Centuries of New England History, Springfield Post Off, 38; portrait of Sara Delano Roosevelt, March of Dimes, Hyde Park Libr,

42; mosaic mural, After Chaos Came Order, Munic Ct House, New York, 61; Pupil Learns from Past & Looks Toward the Future, PS 234, Brooklyn, 64; Mother and Child (stained glass window), Allen Stevenson Sch, New York, 67. Exhib: Carnegie Inst Int, Pittsburgh, 33-49; one-man shows, Worcester Art Mus, Mass, 35 & Galerie Andre Weil, Paris, 49; Oriental Fragment, US Govt Traveling Show, Orient, 50-52; Fragment—Man Weeps, US Govt Traveling Relig Show, Italy, Fr, Spain & Ger, 58-61. Teaching: Instr painting & sculpture & dir, Worcester Art Mus Sch, 33-40; pvt instr, Gloucester, Mass, 33-60, New York & Chatham, Mass, 50- Pos: First vpres, Int Asn Plastic Arts, 65-; first vpres, Nat Acad Design, 65-; dir, Abbey Found, 66-; pres, Audubon Artists, 71-72. Awards: Pulitzer Prize, Columbia Univ, 26; Carnegie Award, Nat Acad Design, 54; Gold Medal of Honor, Century Asn, 69. Bibliog: Edward Alden Jewell (auth), Romano portrays horrors of war, New York Times, 44; Harry Salpeter (auth), Renaissance of Umberto Romano, Esquire, 45; Richard Merrifield (auth), Umberto Romano, Yankee Mag, 52. Mem: Century Asn (exhib comt, 70-); Rockport Art Asn; Nat Mural Soc (dir, 62-); Provincetown Art Asn; Castle Hill Found (dir, 50-58). Media: Oil, Acrylic; Bronze, Marble. Publ: Contribr, American Art Today, Nat Art Soc, 39; illusr, Dante's the Divine Comedy, 46 & contribr, Best of Art, 48, Doubleday; contribr, Contemporary American Painting, Univ Ill, 49; contribr, Expressionism in Art, Liveright, 58. Dealer: Wellfleet Art Gallery Cape Cod MA 02650; ACA Gallery 25 E 73rd St New York NY 10021. Mailing Add: 162 E 83rd St New York NY 10028

ROMANO, VINCENT W
See Nirvanno, Comet

ROMANS, VAN ANTHONY
SCULPTOR/DESIGNER, GALLERY DIRECTOR
b Baltimore, Md, Jan 13, 44. Study: Univ Calif, Fullerton, BA(art design), studied with Dextra Frankel; Univ Southern Calif, MFA, PhD in progress, studied 3-D arts & mus design with Lee Chesney. Work: Claremont Grad Sch Gallery, Calif; Univ Southern Calif, Los Angeles; Calif State Univ, Fullerton; Orange Coast Col, Costa Mesa, Calif. Comn: Westcliff Shopping Ctr (designed), comn by Richard Marowitz, 76; Courtyard Shopping Ctr (designed), comn by Jerry Stout, 77. Exhib: One-man shows, Laguna Mus Art, Laguna Beach, Calif, 70, Oakland Mus Art, Calif, 71, Univ Southern Calif, Los Angeles, 72 & others; Six Promising Young Sculptors, Claremont Cols, Calif, 73; Environments/Spaces, Orange Coast Col, 75; Spaces, Pac Design Ctr, Calif, 76. Collections Arranged: Thonet & Thereafter, show of chair hist incl Bauhaus (auth, catalogue), Japanese Sword Show, collection from collectors & Los Angeles Co Art Mus, Western Indian Show—Dau Naningha & Persian Rug Show (designed exhib), 57 rugs from cols & collections, Orange Coast Col Art Gallery. Teaching: Prof design & exhib design/visual promotion, Orange Coast Col, Costa Mesa, Calif, 73-; asst prof design, Univ Southern Calif, Los Angeles, 73- Pos: Dir display prog, Orange Coast Col, Costa Mesa, Calif, 73-, dir galleries & dir interior design, 75-; mem, Orange Co Art Alliance, Calif, 77; lectr, Newport Harbor Art Mus, Newport Beach, Calif; mem educ comt, Bowers Mus, Santa Ana, Calif; consult for fairs & exhibs, Orange Co, Calif. Awards: Most Outstanding Educator, Orange Coast Col, 75. Bibliog: Wilson (auth), Sculpture, 74. Mem: Am Soc Interior Designers. Style & Technique: Design is the basis; scale usually large. Media: Metal and light non-welding techniques as bolts and screws are used. Mailing Add: Dir Orange Coast Col Art Gallery 2701 Fairview Rd Costa Mesa CA 92626

ROME, HAROLD
COLLECTOR, PAINTER
b Hartford, Conn, May 27, 08. Study: Yale Univ, BA, 29, Yale Law Sch, 28-30, Yale Sch Archit, BFA, 34. Exhib: One-man paintings & songs, Marble Arch Gallery, New York, 64; one-man show paintings, Bodley Gallery, New York, 70. Pos: Composer & writer. Mem: Dramatists Guild. Collection: African sculpture; large collection of West African heddle-pulleys. Publ: Composer, Fanny, 54, Destry Rides Again, 59, I Can Get It for You Wholesale, 62, Zulu & the Zayda, 65, Scarlett (mus adaptation, Gone with the Wind), Imperial Theatre, Tokyo, 70; plus many others. Mailing Add: c/o Chappell & Co 810 Seventh Ave New York NY 10019

ROMELING, W B
PAINTER
b Schenectady, NY, Feb 26, 09. Study: Pratt Inst, Brooklyn; Syracuse Univ; Sch Fine Arts; also with Ogden Pleissner. Work: Schenectady Mus; Cooperstown Art Asn. Exhib: Central New York, Munson-Williams-Proctor Inst, Utica, NY, 62; Invitational Watercolor Show, Sharon, Conn, 67-68; one-man show, Bennington Gallery, Vt, 70-71, Muggleton Gallery, Auburn, NY, 70-71 & Munson-Williams-Proctor Sch Art, 77; Cooperstown Ann, NY, 70-71; Retrospective, Muggleton Gallery, 77. Teaching: Instr art, Owen D Young Sch, Van Hornesville, NY, 43-69. Awards: Purchase Prize, Schenectady Mus, 63; First Prize for Still Life, Cooperstown Art Asn, 66, Godley Watercolor Award, 70. Mem: Cooperstown Art Asn (pres, 70-72); Southern Vt Artists. Style & Technique: Transparent watercolor in fresh, traditional technique. Publ: Contribr (watercolor), Am Artist Mag, 12/77. Dealer: Richard Comins, RD 2 Duck Trap Lincolnville ME 04847; Robert Muggleton 7 Williams St Auburn NY 13021. Mailing Add: Box 53 Van Hornesville NY 13475

ROMERO, MIKE
PAINTER, COLLECTOR
b Santa Clara Pueblo, NMex, Sept 6, 50. Study: Inst Am Indian Arts, with John Cortez Kindred & Allan Houser. Work: Inst Am Indian Arts Gallery, Santa Fe, NMex. Comn: Murals, Inst Am Indian Arts, 72. Exhib: Scottsdale Nat Indian Art Show, Ariz, 72; Mus NMex, Santa Fe, 73; New Directions, Contemp Indian Arts Exhib, Ft Worth, Tex, 74; The Best of Ten Retrospective, Inst Am Indian Arts, 74. Awards: Spec Award Graphics, Scottsdale Nat Indian Arts, 72; First Place in Murals, Inst Am Indian Arts, 74; Hon Mention Pencil Drawing, Tanner's Indian Arts Show, 75. Bibliog: Inst Am Indian Arts Alumni Exhib, Amon Carter Mus Western Art Publ, 73. Style & Technique: Contemporary Indian art, personal style. Media: Acrylics, Pencils. Collection: North American Indians, painting, pottery, sculpture & artifacts. Publ: Contribr, Southwest Art Mag, 74. Mailing Add: Lonewolf Studio PO Box 98 Espanola NM 87532

ROMEU, JOOST A
CONCEPTUAL ARTIST
b Bremerhaven, Ger, Jan 16, 48; US citizen. Study: Drexel Univ, BS. Work: Kansas City Art Inst; MTL Gallery, Belg. Exhib: Deurle, Belg, 73; Projekt '74, Koln, Ger; Diskussies Omtrent Joost A Romeu, Univ Antwerp, Belg, 75; Idea Warehouse, New York, 75. Bibliog: Foote (auth), The apotheosis of the crummy space, Artforum; J L Mackie (auth), The Directon of Causation; Merleau Ponty (auth), Primacy of Perception. Style & Technique: Plagnacism (plagiaristic, analysis, criticism). Publ: Art after philosophy, 73; auth & illusr, ONCE1, ONCE2,...., ONCE24. Mailing Add: 38 White St New York NY 10013

ROMOSER, RUTH AMELIA
PAINTER, SCULPTOR
b Baltimore, Md, Apt 26, 16. Study: Baltimore Art Inst, grad; sculpture with Xavier Corbera, Barcelona, Spain; Robert Motherwell Workshop; graphics with Joseph Ruffo. Work: Miami Mus Mod Art, Fla; Lowe Mus, Univ Miami; Miami Herald; Nat Cardiac Hosp, Miami; Int Gallery, Baltimore, Md. Comn: Two paintings for 12 productions, Actors Studio M, Coral Gables, Fla, 63-64. Exhib: Ringling Southeast Nat Art Show, Sarasota, Fla, 61-63; Nat Drawing Exhib, Cheltenham, Pa, 64; Four Arts Plaza Nat, Palm Beach, 66; Hortt Mem Regional, Ft Lauderdale Mus Arts, 66; one-man show, Nat Design Ctr, New York, 67; Jacksonville Mus, Fla; Norton Gallery, Palm Beach, Fla; Fla Int Univ, Miami; Fla Atlantic Univ, Boca Raton; Fla Southern Col, Lakeland. Awards: Eighth Ann Hortt Mem Award, Fort Lauderdale Mus Arts, 67; Design Derby Award, Designers-Decorators Guild, 69; Artspo 70, Coral Gables, 70. Bibliog: Nellie Bower (auth), Arriving at a style, Miami Daily News, 65; Bernard Davis (auth), Romoser Foreward (catalog), Miami Mus Mod Art, 68; Doris Reno (auth), Lively arts, Miami Herald, 69. Mem: Blue Dome Art Fel; Women's Caucus of Art; Fla Artists Group; Lowe Mus; Miami Art Ctr. Style & Technique: Mixed media collage, using brush, knife or air brush. Media: Oil, Acrylic. Publ: Ed, All Florida Artist in the House Mag, 63; auth, rev in Art News Mag, 67. Mailing Add: 8025 SW 64th St Miami FL 33143

ROMPPANEN, EION ANTTI
See Eino

RONALD, WILLIAM
PAINTER
b Stratford, Ont, Aug 13, 26; US citizen. Study: Ont Col Art, hon grad, 51. Work: Mus Mod Art, Guggenheim Mus & Whitney Mus Am Art, New York; Nat Gallery Can, Ottawa, Ont; Carnegie Inst, Pittsburgh, Pa; among others. Comn: Acrylic mural, Nat Art Ctr, Ottawa, 70. Exhib: Carnegie Int, 58; Brussels World's Fair & traveling exhib, 58; Sao Paulo Biennale, Mus Arte Mod, 59; Whitney Mus Am Art Ann, 59; Can Biennial, Nat Gallery Can, 68; plus many one-man shows, 54-72. Pos: Host of TV show on arts, Can Broadcasting Corp, Toronto, Ont, 66-67. Awards: Hallmark Corp Art Award for Watercolor, 52; Nat Award, Can Sect, Int Guggenheim Awards, 56; Award, Second Biennial Exhib Can Painting, Nat Gallery Can, 57. Bibliog: David Ralston & Hugo McPherson (auth), Ronald Chapel in Toronto Harbour, Can Art, 4/66; William Cameron (auth), Portrait of the artist as a violently honest man, Macleans Mag, 2/71; From crisis to crisis with William Ronald, Sat Night, 7-8/75. Mailing Add: 392 Brunswick Ave Toronto ON Can

RONEY, HAROLD ARTHUR
PAINTER, LECTURER
b Sullivan, Ill, Nov 7, 99. Study: Chicago Acad Art; Art Inst Chicago; also with Harry Leith-Ross, John Folinsbee & George A Aldrich. Work: Sullivan Pub Libr, Ill; Witte Mem Mus; Austin Pub Libr, Tex; South Bend Pub Sch, Ind; Southwest Tex State Univ; plus others. Exhib: River Square Gallery, San Antonio, 71; Coppini Acad Fine Arts, San Antonio, 71; plus many others. Teaching: Instr oil landscape, Froman Sch Art, Cloudcroft, NMex, 58- Media: Oil. Mailing Add: RR 8 Box 294-B San Antonio TX 78229

ROSATI, JAMES
SCULPTOR, EDUCATOR
b Washington, Pa, June 9, 12. Work: Yale Gallery Fine Arts; NY Univ; Whitney Mus Am Art; Albright-Knox Art Gallery, Buffalo, NY; Hirshhorn Mus, Washington, DC; also in many pvt collections. Comn: Sculpture, St John's Abbey, Collegeville, Md. Exhib: Six shows, Whitney Mus Am Art Ann, 52-66; Int Coun Mus Mod Art Exhib, France, Ger & Scandinavia, 65-66; Flint Inst, 66; Colby Col, 67; Mus Contemp Crafts Traveling Exhib, 67-68; plus many other group & one-man shows. Teaching: Instr, Pratt Inst & Cooper Union, NY; vis critic sculpture, Hopkins Art Ctr, Dartmouth Col, spring 63; adj assoc prof sculpture, Yale Univ, 64- Awards: Logan Medal & Prize, Art Inst Chicago, 62; Carborundum Major Abrasive Mkt Award, 63; Guggenheim Fel, 64; plus others. Bibliog: Michel Seuphor (auth), The Sculpture of This Century, Dictionary of Modern Sculpture, A Zwemmer Ltd, London, 59; Jean Selz (auth), Modern Sculpture, Braziller, 63; Herbert Read (auth), A Concise History of Modern Sculpture, Praeger, 64. Dealer: Marlborough Gallery 41 E 57th St New York NY 10028. Mailing Add: 252 W 14th St New York NY 10011

ROSE, BARBARA E
ART HISTORIAN, ART WRITER
b Washington, DC, June 11, 37. Study: Smith Col; Barnard Col, BA; Sorbonne, Paris; Columbia Univ, MA, MPhil. Teaching: Prof art Hist, Sarah Lawrence Col, 66-70; vis lectr art hist, Yale Univ, 70. Pos: Contrib ed, Art Int, 63-65, Art in Am & Artforum, 65-72 & Arts Mag, 78. Awards: Fulbright Fel, 61-62; Distinguished Art Criticism Award, Col Art Asn, 66 & 69. Mem: PEN Club; Asn Int Contemp Artists. Interest: Modern and American art. Publ: Auth, Helen Frankenthaler, Abrams, 70; auth, Claes Oldenburg, Mus Mod Art, New York, 72; co-auth, Pavilion-Experiments in Art & Technology, Dutton, 74; auth, American Art Since 1900, Praeger, 76; co-auth, American Painting, Skira, 77. Mailing Add: 117 E 57th St New York NY 10022

ROSE, BERNICE BEREND
CURATOR
b Miami Beach, Fla. Study: Hunter Col, BA, study with Robert Motherwell, William Baziotes & Ray Parker; The Inst of Fine Arts, New York Univ, MA. Collections Arranged: Jackson Pollack: Works on Paper, 69, A Salute to Alexander Calder (auth, catalog), 69, Surrealism (auth, catalog), 70, Drawing Now (auth, catalog), 76 & Jean Arp, 77, Mus of Mod Art, New York. Pos: Cur, Mus of Mod Art, New York, 65- Publ: Auth, Jackson Pollock: Works on Paper & co-auth, Sol Lewitt, Mus of Mod Art, New York. Mailing Add: c/o Mus of Mod Art 11 W 53 St New York NY 10019

ROSE, HERMAN
PAINTER, PRINTMAKER
b Brooklyn, NY, Nov 6, 09. Study: Nat Acad Design, 27-29. Work: Mus Mod Art; Whitney Mus Am Art; Univ Tex; Univ Calif; Smithsonian Inst Print Collection; also in many pvt collections. Exhib: Mus Mod Art, 48 & 52; six shows, Whitney Mus Am Art, 48-58; Pa Acad Fine Arts, 52; ACA Gallery, 55 & 56; one-man show, Forum Gallery, NY, 62. Teaching: Instr, Brooklyn Col, 49-51 & 58-61; instr, New Sch Social Res, 54-55 & 63-; instr, Hofstra Col, 59-60; artist in residence, Univ Va, 66. Awards: Yaddo Found Fel, 55; Longview Award, 60 & 61; Altman Prize, Art Students League, 76. Media: Graphics. Dealer: Zabriskie Gallery 29 W 57th St New York NY 10019. Mailing Add: 463 West New York NY 10014

ROSE, LEATRICE
PAINTER, INSTRUCTOR
b New York, NY. Study: Cooper Union, 45; Art Students League, 46; Hans Hofmann Sch, 47. Exhib: Artists Ann, Whitney Mus of Am Art, 50; Pa Acad of Fine Arts Ann, 66; Recent

Still Life, Mus of Art, RI Sch of Design, 66; Women Choose Women, New York Cult Ctr, 73; Nat Acad of Design Ann, 74-76; Whitney Mus of Am Art, Downtown, 78; one-woman shows, Zabriskie Gallery, 65, Landmark Gallery, 74 & Tibor de Nagy Gallery, 76. Teaching: Instr painting, New York State Univ Stony Brook, 74-75 & Sch of Visual Art, New York 77. Awards: New York State Creative Artists Pub Serv Grant, 74; Am Asn of Univ Women Grant, 76-77; Nat Endowment for the Arts Grant, 77. Bibliog: John Ashbery (auth), Dash, Dodd & Rose, Art in Am, 3/74; April Kingsley (auth), The Lugano review, Art Int, 3/20/74; Lawrence Alloway (auth), Art, The Nation, 10/25/75. Style & Technique: Oil painting, interiors and figures. Dealer: Tibor de Nagy Gallery 29 W 57th St New York NY 10019. Mailing Add: 463 West St New York NY 10014

ROSE, MARY ANNE
PAINTER, ART ADMINISTRATOR
b San Francisco, Calif, Aug 10, 49. Study: Univ of Calif, Santa Cruz, AB, 70; Univ of Calif, Berkeley, MA, 72, MFA, 73. Exhib: San Francisco Mus of Mod Art, 73; Univ Art Mus, Berkeley, 73; Market St Program, Pasadena Mus of Mod Art, 73; 18 Bay Area Artists, Los Angeles Inst of Contemp Art, 76; San Francisco Mus of Mod Art, 77; 18 Bay Area Artists, Univ Art Mus, Berkeley, 77; Mike Roddy, Mary Anne Rose, Athol McBean Gallery, San Francisco Art Inst, 78. Pos: Security Supervisor, Univ Art Mus, Berkeley, 74- Awards: Purchase Prize, San Francisco Art Festival, Home Savings & Loan, 72; Eisner Award in the Creative Arts, Univ of Calif, Berkeley, 72; Resident, Cite Int des Arts, Paris, 78- Mem: San Francisco Art Inst (artist trustee, 73-). Style & Technique: Paintings, drawings (process and idea oriented): abstract Media: Acrylic on Canvas, Traditional Graphic Media. Mailing Add: 1045 17th St San Francisco CA 94107

ROSE, PETER HENRY
ART DEALER
b New York, NY, Feb 25, 35. Study: Hamilton Col, BA; Univ Pa, MA; Columbia Univ; Ecole Superieure, Univ Paris. Pos: Co-owner, Peter Rose Gallery. Mem: Arts & Bus Coun New York. Specialty: 20th century contemporary American art. Mailing Add: Peter Rose Gallery 340 E 52nd St New York NY 10022

ROSE, ROSLYN
PRINTMAKER, INSTRUCTOR
b Irvington, NJ, May 26, 29. Study: Rutgers Univ; Pratt Graphic Ctr; Skidmore Col, BS. Work: NJ State Mus, Trenton; McAllen Int Mus, Tex; Upsala Col, East Orange, NJ; Rosenberg Libr, Galveston, Tex; Citibank of New York, Moscow, Russia. Comn: Etchings, New York Graphic Soc, Ltd, Greenwich, Conn, 70-; Etchings, Editions Scaglione, Southfield, Mich, 76-77. Exhib: Wadsworth Atheneum, Hartford, Conn, 65 & 75; Audubon Ann, New York, 66-70 & 75; Nat Print Show, Hunterdon Art Ctr, Clinton, NJ, 66-76; Birmingham Mus of the Arts, Ala, 67; NJ State Mus, Trenton, 67, 69 & 71; Portland Mus, Ore, 68; Seattle Art Mus, Wash, 68; Women in the Arts, Florence, Italy, 72; Newark Mus, NJ, 74; The Print Club, Philadelphia, 75. Collections Arranged: Liberated Printmakers (traveling exhib), NJ Coun on the Arts, 72. Teaching: Instr printmaking, Newark Mus, 72- Awards: Best-in-Show, Tri-State Exhib, Summit Art Ctr, NJ, 69, 71 & 75; Graphic Award, Rochester Int Religious, Coun of Churches & Synagogues, 70; Memorial Graphic Prize, Nat Asn Women Artists, Georgi & Mock, 77. Bibliog: J H Newman & L S Newman (auths), Plastics for the Craftsman, Crown, 72; Thelma R Newman (auth), Innovative Printmaking, Crown, 77. Mem: Artists Equity of NJ (mem exec bd, 71-75); Nat Asn of Women Artists; Assoc Artists of NJ; Printmaking Coun of NJ. Style & Technique: Interpretations of natural images using color abstractly and shapes realistically. Media: Etching and screen printing. Publ: Auth, Outline of Printmaking, NJ Coun on the Arts, 72. Dealer: Assoc Artists of America 663 Fifth Ave New York NY 10022. Mailing Add: 457 Baldwin Rd Maplewood NJ 07040

ROSE, SAMUEL
PAINTER
b Cleveland, Ohio, Sept 17, 41. Study: Cape Cod Sch Art, Provincetown, with Henry Henche; Cooper Sch & Kent State Univ; Boston Atelier, with R H Ives Gammell; also with Basil Kalashnifoff, Cleveland. Work: Maryhill Mus Art & St Ignatius Church, Washington, DC. Comn: Many incl Maharaj Ji, Mrs F Lee Bailey, Patricia Barlow & Patricia Pierce. Exhib: Nat Acad, New York, 68; Nat Arts Club, New York, 69; Copley Art Soc & Concord Art Asn, 71; Jordan Marsh, Boston, 72-73; one-man show, Concord Art Asn, 75; among others. Teaching: Pvt art classes. Awards: Julius Hallgarten Gold Medal, Nat Acad, 68; First Prize, Nat Arts Club, 69 & Copley Art Soc & Concord Art Asn, 63, 67 & 69; Greenshields Grant, Montreal, 63-70. Mem: Copley Soc; Salmagundi Club; Guild Boston Artists; Concord Art Asn; Am Artists Prof League. Style & Technique: Murals, portraits, imaginary canvases. Media: Oil. Mailing Add: c/o Pierce Galleries Inc 721 Main St Hingham MA 02043

ROSE, THOMAS ALBERT
SCULPTOR
b Washington, DC, Oct 15, 42. Study: Univ Wis-Madison, 60-62; Univ Ill, Urbana, BFA, 65; Univ Calif, Berkeley, MA, 67, study grant to Univ Lund, 67-68. Work: Univ NMex Mus, Albuquerque; Libr Cong, Washington, DC; Metromedia Collection Los Angeles, Calif, John Bolles, San Francisco, Calif; San Francisco Art Comn; plus others. Exhib: Sculpture, Plastics West Coast, Hanson Gallery, San Francisco, 67; Walker Art Ctr, Minneapolis, 74; Sculptor as Draughsman, JPL Fine Arts London, Eng; Small Objects, Downtown Whitney, New York; one-man shows, The Clocktower & Truman Gallery, New York. plus others. Teaching: Asst to Bertil Lundberg, lithography, A B F Sch, Malmo, Sweden, 67-68; instr sculpture, Univ Calif, Berkeley, 68-69; instr sculpture & graphics, NMex State Univ, 69-72; instr sculpture, Univ Minn, Minneapolis, 72- Awards: Nat Endowment Arts vis artist grant & State Arts Comn Grant, NMex State Univ, 72-73; Kresge Found Grant, 72-73; plus others. Media: Plastic, Porcelain. Dealer: Truman Gallery New York NY; Hanson-Cowles Gallery 331 Second Ave N Minneapolis MN 55041. Mailing Add: 4210 Harriet Ave S Minneapolis MN 55409

ROSE, TIMOTHY G
ART ADMINISTRATOR, MUSEUM DIRECTOR
b Salt Lake City, Utah, Dec 29, 44. Study: Shimer Col, Mt Carroll, Ill, 62-63; San Francisco Art Inst, 69; Brigham Young Univ, BA, 77. Collections Arranged: Annual Quilt & Fiber Show, 77, Utah Valley Sculptors, 77, Annual National Show, 78 & regional one-man shows, 77-78, Springville Mus Art, Utah. Teaching: Instr oil painting, Springville Mus; teaching asst art appreciation, Brigham Young Univ. Pos: Dir, Springville Mus Art, 77-; secy-treas, Utah Mus Asn, 77-78; adv comt mem, Utah State Div Fine Arts Mus Outreach Prog. Mem: Am Asn Mus; Utah Mus Asn. Mailing Add: 789 S 400 East Springville UT 84663

ROSEBERG, CARL ANDERSSON
SCULPTOR, ART HISTORIAN
b Vinton, Iowa, Sept 26, 16. Study: Univ Iowa, BFA, 39, MFA, 47; Cranbrook Acad Arts, summers 47 & 48; Univ Va, summer 64; Univ Mysore, summer 65; Tyler Sch Art, summer 67. Work: Springfield Art Mus, Mo; Chrysler Mus, Norfolk, Va; Va Mus Fine Arts, Richmond; Thalimers, Richmond; Univ Iowa. Comn: Bronze hwy markers, Rockingham Co Citizens Comt, Va, 55; William & Mary Medallion, Marshall-Wythe Sch Law, Col William & Mary, 67, Col William & Mary Medallion, 68 & Donald W Davis Commemorative Plaque, Life Sci Bldg, 70, William G Guy Commemorative Plaque, Rogers Hall, 75. Exhib: One-man show, Norfolk Mus Arts & Sci, 63, 12 Va Sculptors, 70; Am Art Today, New York World's Fair, 64; Va Sculptors Traveling Exhib, 70-72; Tidewater Col Fac Exhib, Chrysler Mus, 72. Teaching: Instr, Col William & Mary, 47-52, asst prof fine arts, 52-57, assoc prof, 57-66, prof & Heritage fel, 66- Awards: Fulbright Fel, India; Award of Honor, Va Chap Am Inst Architects, 68; Thomas Jefferson Award, Robert McConnell Found, 71; plus others. Mem: Asian Soc; Am Asn Mus; Audubon Artists; Twentieth Century Gallery (mem bd); Tidewater Artists. Res: Art of India. Publ: Illusr, Little Red Riding Hood & Big Bad Wolf, 53; illusr roll titles for The Colonial Naturalist (film), 64. Mailing Add: 110 Hickory Signpost Rd Williamsburg VA 23185

ROSEN, BEVERLY DORIS
PAINTER, EDUCATOR
b Boston, Mass. Study: Simmons Col, BS; Univ Colo; Univ Denver, MA. Work: Knight Pub Sch, Denver; Colorado Springs Fine Arts Ctr, Colo; Univ Colo, Denver; Johns Manville Collection; Univ Denver. Comn: Painting, New Eng Life, Salt Lake City, 70; two outside murals, Colo Agency, State Mutual Am, Denver, 73, two inside paintings, 73. Exhib: 73rd Western Ann, Denver Art Mus, 71; 12th Midwest Biennial Exhib, Joslyn Art Mus, Omaha, Nebr, 71; Colo Ann, Denver Art Mus, 72-78; 50th Ann Nat Exhib, Springville Mus Art, Utah, 74; 6th Biennial Exhib, Salt Lake Art Ctr, 74; Southwest Biennial, Mus Fine Arts, Santa Fe, NMex, 74; Ten Take Ten, Colorado Springs Fine Arts Ctr, 77. Teaching: Assoc prof painting, Univ Denver, 64- Pos: Dir, Univ Denver Gallery, 75. Awards: Purchase Prize, Gallery Fine Arts Ctr, 70; Monied Prize, Gilpin Co Art Asn, Central City, Colo, 70; Nat Educ Asn Grant & Colo Coun Grant for Gallery Exhib, Univ Devner Gallery, 75. Mem: Artists Equity Asn; Colo Art Educ Asn; Colo Artists Asn Exhib; Denver Art Mus. Style & Technique: Accent on color and a surface that suggests paint scarred by time. Media: Acrylic on Paper & Canvas. Mailing Add: 2830 E Cedar Ave Denver CO 80209

ROSEN, HY(MAN) (JOSEPH)
CARTOONIST
b Albany, NY, Feb 10, 23. Study: Art Inst Chicago; Art Students League; State Univ NY Albany; Stanford Univ, fel. Teaching: Instr cartooning, State Univ NY Albany, currently. Pos: Ed cartoonist, Albany Times-Union, 45; ed cartoonist, Hearst Newspapers. Awards: Top Award, Freedom Found, Valley Forge, Pa, 50, 55 & 60; Top Award, Nat Conf Christians & Jews, 62. Mem: Asn Am Ed Cartoonists (pres, 72). Style & Technique: Brush and ink on grafix paper; caricature; personalities in the news. Media: Ink. Mailing Add: Times-Union Albany-Shaker Rd Albany NY 12201

ROSEN, ISRAEL
COLLECTOR
b Baltimore, Md, Dec 28, 11. Study: Johns Hopkins Univ, AB, 31; Univ Md Sch Med, MD, 35. Mem: Baltimore Mus Art (accessions comt contemp art, 61-67, comt spec funds & develop, 70-, bd trustees, 72-); Univ Calif Art Mus, Berkeley (nat comt, 70-). Collection: Modern art, with special emphasis on abstract expressionism, including works by Pollock, de Kooning, Still, Kline, Rothko, Baziotes, Tobey, Rauschenberg, as well as works by twentieth century European artist artists such as Picasso, Mondrian, Kandinsky, Klee, Leger & Gris. Publ: Auth, Toward a definition of abstract expressionism, Baltimore Mus News, 59; auth, Edward Joseph Gallagher, III Memorial Collection, Baltimore Mus Art, 64 & Metrop Mus Art, 65. Mailing Add: 1 E University Pkwy Baltimore MD 21218

ROSEN, JAMES MAHLON
PAINTER, ART HISTORIAN
b Detroit, Mich, Dec 3, 33. Study: Cooper Union, with Franz Klein, Ludwig Sander, Leo Manso & Paul Zucker; Wayne State Univ, with Ernst Scheyer, BA; Cranbrook Acad Art, with Zoltan Sepeshy, MFA. Work: Mus Mod Art, New York; Whitney Mus Am Art, New York; Newark Art Mus, NJ; Univ Ore Art Mus, Eugene; Joslyn Art Mus, Omaha, Nebr. Exhib: Color Field 1890-1970, Albright-Knox Art Gallery, Buffalo, NY, 71; one-man show, Mus Mod Art Penthouse Show, 73 & Betty Parsons Gallery, New York, 74; Drawings USA, Minn Mus Art, 73; A Sense of Place, Joslyn Mus, 73. Teaching: Instr studio, Wayne State Univ, 61-63; asst prof studio & art hist, Univ Hawaii, 65-67; instr art hist, Santa Rosa Jr Col, 67- Awards: Huntington Hartford Found Fel Painting, 63; Yaddo Found Fel Painting, 68 & 72; Nat Endowment Fel, 72-73. Bibliog: Jean Charlot (auth), Art criticism, Honolulu Star Bull, 66; Alfred Frankenstein (auth), Perception traps, San Francisco Chronicle, 70; John Canaday (auth), art criticism column, New York Times, 74. Style & Technique: Oil and wax-oil emulsion with brush and roller; watercolor with brush and roller. Media: Oil, Watercolor. Res: Perception and structuring in 15th and 16th century Italian art and architecture. Publ: Auth, Notes From a Painter's Journal, 60; auth, Qualities of Camouflaging, 70. Dealer: Betty Parsons Gallery 24 W 57th St New York NY 10019; Annex Gallery 604 College Ave Santa Rosa CA 95404. Mailing Add: Dept of Art Santa Rosa Jr Col Santa Rosa CA 95401

ROSENBERG, ALEX JACOB
PUBLISHER, EDITOR
b New York, NY, May 25 19. Study: Philadelphia Mus of Art, Albright Col. Exhib: An Am Portrait 1776-1976 (original print & multiple sculpture portfolio) traveling to Santa Barbara Mus of Art, Calif, Carpenter Ctr for the Visual Arts, Harvard Univ, Cambridge, Mass, Okla Art Ctr, Oklahoma City, Birmingham Mus of Art, Ala, San Diego Gallery of Fine Arts, Calif, Rose Art Mus, Brandeis Univ, Waltham, Mass, Hunter Art Mus, Chattanooga, Tenn, Phoenix Art Mus, Ariz, Johns Hopkins Univ, Baltimore, Md, Mint Mus of Art, Charlotte, NY & Everson Art Mus, Syracuse, NY, plus many other mus, 76-77. Pos: Dir & bd mem, Artists' Rights Today, Inc, 76-; publr & ed-in-chief, Transworld Art Corp, New York, 73- Awards: Spec Prize for Publ, 7th Int Triennial of Colored Graphic Prints, Kunstgesellschaft, Grenchen, Switz, 76. Publ: Ed, The 12 Tribes of Israel—Dali, 73, The Prophets—R Rubin, 73, Homage to Tobey, 74, Our Unfinished Revolution—Calder, 76 & An American Portrait 1776-1976, 76, Transworld Art. Mailing Add: 600 Fifth Ave New York NY 10020

ROSENBERG, BERNARD
ART PUBLISHER, BOOK DEALER
b New York, NY, Aug 2, 38. Study: City Col of New York, cert advert. Pos: Owner, Olana Gallery, Bronx, 71- Res: American art. Specialty: Issues catalogues quarterly of books and exhibition catalogues on American art from Colonial period to present. Publ: Auth, Olana's Guide to American Artists, A Contribution Toward a Bibliography, Olana Gallery, 2/78. Mailing Add: PO Box 325 Bronx NY 10471

ROSENBERG, CAROLE HALSBAND
ART EDITOR, ART DEALER
b New York, NY, Nov 16, 36. Study: Hunter Col, Brooklyn Col, BA; Yeshiva Univ; NY Univ. Collections Arranged: An Am Portrait 1776-1976 (traveling exhib of original prints portfolio; ed, catalogue), 76; Mark Tobey Retrospective (ed, catalogue), 77 & Yaacov Agam (ed, catalogue), 77. Pos: Art ed, Transworld Art Corp, 74-; dir, Original Graphics, New York; mem bd, Artists' Rights Today, Inc, 76- Awards: Spec Prize for Publ, Seventh Int Triennial of Colored Graphic Prints, Grenchen, Switz, 76. Specialty: Contemporary painting, sculpture, prints and multiples. Collection: Contemporary painting, sculpture, prints and multiples. Mailing Add: 600 Fifth Ave New York NY 10020

ROSENBERG, CHARLES MICHAEL
WRITER, ART HISTORIAN
b Chicago, Ill, Aug 3, 45. Study: Swarthmore Col, BA; Univ Mich, Ann Arbor, MA & PhD. Teaching: Asst prof art hist, State Univ NY, Brockport, 73- Awards: Kress Found Art Hist Fel, 71-73; State Univ NY Res Fel & Grant, 75; Nat Endowment for the Humanities Summer Stipend, 77. Mem: Col Art Asn Am; NCent Sect of Renaissance Soc Am. Res: Italian Renaissance art and culture. Publ: Auth, Drawing by Mathias Zundt, Engraving by Hans Sebald Beham, & A 17th Century Tankard, 71; auth, Some New Documents Concerning Donatello's Unexecuted Monument to Borso d'Este in Modena, 73; auth, Notes on the Borsian Addition to the Palazzo Schifanoia, 73; auth, Per il bene di...nostra cipta: Borso d'Este & the Certosa of Ferrara, 76; auth, Francesco Del Cossa's Letter Reconsidered, 78. Mailing Add: Dept of Art State Univ NY Brockport NY 14420

ROSENBERG, HAROLD
WRITER, EDUCATOR
b New York, NY, Feb 2, 06. Study: City Col New York, 23-24; Brooklyn Law Sch, LLB; St Lawrence Univ, 27; Lake Forest Col, LittD, 68; Md Inst, Col Art, DFA, 70; Parsons Sch of Fine Arts, DFA, 76. Teaching: Regents lectr, Univ Calif, 62; lectr, Christian Gauss Sem, Princeton Univ, 63; lectr, Baldwin Sem, Oberlin Col; vis prof, Univ Southern Ill, 66; prof art & mem comt social thought, Univ Chicago, 67- Pos: Art ed, Am Guide Series, 38-40; art critic, New Yorker, 67- Awards: Frank Jewett Mather Award, Col Art Asn, 64; Citation, Univ Calif, Berkeley, 70; Morton Dauwen Zabel Award, Am Acad Arts & Lett, 76. Mem: Int Asn Art Critics; Am Acad Arts & Sci. Publ: Auth, Artworks and Packages, 69 & The De-definition of Art, 72, Horizon; auth, Act and the Actor, World, 71; contribr, Art News & Art News Ann; auth, Art on the Edge, Macmillan, 75 & Willem De Kooning, Abrams, 75; plus many others. Mailing Add: New Yorker Mag 25 W 43rd St New York NY 10036

ROSENBERG, JAKOB
WRITER
b Berlin, Ger, Sept 5, 93. Study: Univ Bern; Univ Zurich; Univ Frankfurt-am-Main; Univ Munich, PhD, 22; Harvard Univ, hon MA, 42, hon DA, 61. Teaching: Resident fel & lectr, Harvard Univ, 37-39, assoc prof, 40-47, prof fine arts, 48-64, emer prof, 64-; Robert Sterling Clark prof, Williams Col, 64-65; sr fel, Nat Gallery, Washington, DC, 66-67. Pos: Cur prints, Fogg Mus Art, Harvard Univ, 39. Mem: Col Art Asn Am; fel Am Acad Arts & Sci; hon fel Pierpont Morgan Libr. Publ: Auth, Great Draughtsmen from Pisanello to Picasso, Harvard Univ, 59; auth, Zeichnungen Cranachs, 60; auth, Rembrandt, Life and Work, Phaidon, 64; auth, On Quality in Art, Princeton Univ, 67; co-auth, Dutch Art and Architecture, Penguin, 72; plus many others. Mailing Add: 19 Bellevue Rd Arlington MA 02174

ROSENBLATT, ADOLPH
PAINTER, SCULPTOR
b New Haven, Conn, Feb 23, 33. Study: Sch Design, Yale Univ, BFA, 56, with Albers, Brooks & Marca-Relli. Work: Libr Cong, Washington, DC. Exhib: Riverside Mus, New York, 62; Dorsky Gallery, 63, 64 & 72; Schoelkopf Gallery, New York, 66 & 68; Hyde Park Art Ctr, Chicago, 73; Tower Gallery, South Hampton, 75; Performing Arts Ctr, Milwaukee, Wis, 78; Razor Gallery, New York, 78; plus others. Awards: Great Lakes Film Festival Award, 76. Style & Technique: Polychrome environmental sculptures of clay; films animating sculpture and paintings. Publ: Auth, Book of Lithographs, Peter Deitsch Gallery, New York, 71; producer, dir & ed, Underpass (film), 74; producer, dir & ed, Daydream Diner (film), 75. Mailing Add: 4211 N Maryland Milwaukee WI 53211

ROSENBLATT, SUZANNE MARIS
PAINTER, DRAFTSMAN
b Hackensack, NJ, July 2, 37. Study: Oberlin Col, Ohio, BA, 59; Cent Sch Arts & Crafts, London, 57-58; Cooper Union, 60; Art Students League, 61-63. Work: City Ctr, New York; Libr Performing Arts, Dance Film Col, Lincoln Center, NY. Comn: Courtroom drawings, WISN-TV, Milwaukee, 73-77 & Milwaukee's Pub TV, 74. Exhib: One-woman shows, Bradley Gallery, Milwaukee, 71, Wustum Mus, Racine, 72, Oshkosh Pub Mus, Wis, 72 & New York Center Gallery, 76; Ft Wayne Mus Art, Ind, 76; Performing Arts Ctr, Milwaukee, Wis, 76-78. Awards: Hon Mention, Media Am, Seattle, Wash, 75. Bibliog: Dean Jensen (auth), Personal vision of circus magic, Milwaukee Sentinel, 71; Donald Key (auth), Show of painted people shadowed by circus, Milwaukee J, 71. Mem: Wis Women in Arts; Artists of Midwest; Nat Art Workers Community. Style & Technique: Movement and fantasy quality of dance. Media: Acrylic on Wood & Paper; Ink & Brush on Paper. Publ: Illusr, Jumping rope, 70 & Quiet ethnics, 71, Insight, Milwaukee J; producer, dir & ed, Animated film paintings & drawings of dancers, Dance Film Festival, New York, 75 & Philadelphia Art Alliance, 76; auth & illusr, Everyone is Going Somewhere, Macmillan Co, 76. Mailing Add: 4211 N Maryland Milwaukee WI 53211

ROSENBLUM, JAY
PAINTER
b New York, NY, Oct 12, 33. Study: Pratt Inst, with Richard Lindner; Bard Col, with Louis Schanker, BA, 55; Cranbrook Acad Art, with Fred Mitchell, MFA, 56. Work: Larry Aldrich Mus Contemp Art, Ridgefield, Conn; Whitney Mus Am Art, New York; Albright-Knox Mus Lending Serv, Buffalo; 180 Beacon St Collection, Cambridge, Mass. Comn: Painting, comn by Larry Aldrich, Phoenix, Ariz, 71. Exhib: Festival of Two Worlds, Spoleto, Italy, 56; Detroit Inst Art, 56; Highlights of 1970 Season, Aldrich Mus, 70; one-man shows, A M Sachs Gallery, 70 & Blue Parrot Gallery, New York, 72; Recent Prints USA, New York Cult Ctr, 72. Teaching: Instr painting, Dalton Sch, NY, 63-; instr painting, 92nd St YMHA, New York, 65-; adj lectr painting, Queensboro Community Col, 69-; adj lectr painting, Lehman Col, 71- Awards: Carlos Lopez Mem Prize in Painting, Detroit Inst Art, 56; Painter of Year, 1970, Larry Aldrich, 70; City Walls Inc Grant, 72. Bibliog: Cindy Nemser (auth), rev in Arts Mag, 10/70; Carter Ratcliff (auth), rev in Art Int, 2/71; Ward Jackson (auth), Art now: New York, 71. Media: Acrylic. Dealer: Allan Stone Gallery 48 E 86th St New York NY 10028; Blue Parrot Print Gallery 1057 Madison Ave New York NY 10028. Mailing Add: 502 E 11th St New York NY 10009

ROSENBLUM, ROBERT
ART HISTORIAN
b New York, NY, July 24, 27. Study: Queens Col, BA; Yale Univ, MA; NY Univ, PhD. Teaching: Instr hist art, Univ Mich, 55-56; assoc prof hist art, Princeton Univ, 56-66; prof hist art, NY Univ, 67- Res: Modern art, 1760 to the present. Publ: Auth, Cubism and Twentieth Century Art, 60; auth, Transformations in Late Eighteenth Century Art, 67; auth, Ingres, 67; auth, Frank Stella, 70; auth, Modern Painting and the Northern Romantic Tradition: Friedrich to Rothko, 75. Mailing Add: 1 E 78th St New York NY 10021

ROSENBLUM, SADIE SKOLETSKY
PAINTER, SCULPTOR
b Odessa, Russia, Feb 12, 99; US citizen. Study: Art Students League; New Sch Social Res; also with Raphael Soyer, Kunioshr, Ben-Zion & Samuel Adler. Work: Philadelphia Mus Art; Ohio Univ; El Paso Mus Art; Brandeis Univ Mus; Lowe Art Mus, Univ Miami; plus many others. Exhib: Mus Mod Art, New York; Corcoran Gallery Art, Washington, DC; one-man shows, Mus Arts, Ft Lauderdale, Fla, 62 & 65, Lowe Art Mus, Univ Miami, 64 & Columbia Mus, SC, 72; plus many others. Pos: Assoc mem adv bd, Peabody Col. Media: Oil. Mailing Add: Apt 12 F 5750 Collins Ave Miami Beach FL 33140

ROSENBORG, RALPH M
PAINTER
b Brooklyn, NY, June 9, 13. Study: Sch Art League, NY; Am Mus Natural Hist. Work: Mus Mod Art; Guggenheim Mus; Phillips Collection, Washington, DC; Metrop Mus Art; Cleveland Art Mus; plus many others. Exhib: More than 300 group exhibs, 34-; 53 one-man shows, New York & other prin cities in US, 35- Teaching: Instr art, Brooklyn Mus, 36-38; instr, Ox-Bow Summer Sch, Saugatuck, Mich, 49. Awards: Purchase Award, Am Acad Arts & Lett, 60. Mem: Fedn Mod Painters & Sculptors. Mailing Add: 165 Lexington Ave New York NY 10016

ROSENFELD, RICHARD JOEL
ART DEALER
b Philadelphia, Pa, May 31, 40. Study: Pratt Inst, New York, MFA, 64; Univ Pa, Philadelphia & Pa Acad Fine Art (coordinated prog), BFA, 62. Teaching: Instr painting & art hist, Perkiomen Sch, Pennsburg, Pa, 63-65. Pos: Mgr, Artists Galleries, Cheltenham, Pa, 67-72; Co-dir, Longman Gallery, Pa, 72-75; dir-owner, Rosenfeld Gallery, Philadelphia, Pa, 76-; bd dirs, Fel of Pa Acad Fine Arts. Bibliog: Susan Perloff (auth), Article in Pa Gazette, 6/77. Specialty: Contemporary art, all media including crafts. Mailing Add: Rosenfeld Gallery 113 Arch St Philadelphia PA 19006

ROSENHOUSE, IRWIN JACOB
PRINTMAKER, ILLUSTRATOR
b Chicago, Ill, Mar 1, 24. Study: Cooper Union, cert, 50. Work: Metrop Mus Art; Cooper Union Mus; New York Pub Libr Graphics Collection; Everhart Mus, Pa; Brooklyn Col. Exhib: Am Fedn Arts; Libr Cong; Mus Mod Art, New York; Pa Acad Fine Arts; Boston Printmakers. Teaching: Instr drawing, painting & graphics, Mus Mod Art Educ Ctr, 68-70; instr graphics, Brooklyn Col, 72; adj prof art, Nassau Community Col, 73- Pos: Resident artist, Huntington Hartford Found, 59 & 61; owner & operator, Rosenhouse Gallery, New York, 63-71; free lance designer & illusr, 72. Awards: Award for Graphics, Louis Comfort Tiffany Found. Style & Technique: Figurative, modern romantic based on loose drawing technique. Media: Graphics. Publ: Illusr, What Kind of Feet Does a Bear Have, Bobbs, 63; illusr, Have You Seen Trees, Young-Scott, 67. Dealer: Rosenhouse Gallery 33 Greenwich Ave New York NY 10014. Mailing Add: 256 Mott St New York NY 10012

ROSEN-QUERALT, JANN
SCULPTOR, DESIGNER
b Detroit, Mich, Nov 28, 51. Study: Apprenticeship with Grau-Garriga, Barcelona, Spain, 72-73; Handweavers Guild of Am, Cranbrook, Mich, with Barbara Shawcroft, 72; Syracuse Univ, NY, BFA, 74; Cranbrook Acad of Art, Bloomfield Hills, Mich, MFA, 76. Comn: Dance costumes, Power Center of the Performing Arts, Ann Arbor, Mich, 72; sculpture (steel rods, wool and cotton panels), comn by Juanjo Ponce, Barcelona, 73; tapestry (wool, jute, synthetic fibers), comn by Dr & Mrs Norman Goldston, Shaker Heights, Ohio, 74; children's environment (proj coordr; stretch fabric structures), Your Heritage House, Detroit, Mich, 76; Flight Rythms dance set (laminated wood & polyester panels), comn by Amy Zell Ellsworth, Dancentral, Cambridge, Mass, 77. Exhib: Threads & Lints, Lowe Art Ctr, Syracuse Univ, NY, 72; Honor Show, Lubin House, New York, 72; Fabrics & Fibers, Geneva Mus, NY, 74; Fingerlakes Exhib, Mem Art Gallery, Rochester, NY, 74; Birmingham/Bloomfield Art Asn Fac Show, Birmingham, Mich, 75 & 77; Summer Show, Cranbrook Acad of Art Mus, Bloomfield Hills, 75 & 76; Beaux Arts Designer/Craftsman 75, Columbus Gallery of Fine Arts, Ohio, 75; Fiber Structures, Mus of Art, Carnegie Inst Int, 76; Int Woman's Art Festival Slide Exhib, Ford Found, New York, 76; Art of Basketry, Florence Duhl Gallery, New York, 77; Protofibers, Lowe Art Gallery, Syracuse, 77; Womanworks 77, Union Gallery, Ann Arbor, Mich, 77; 18th Ann Mid-Mich Exhib, Midland Ctr for the Arts, Mich, 77. Collections Arranged: Linear Perspectives, Henry Ford Community Col, Dearborn, Mich, 78. Teaching: Instr weaving & textiles, Henry Ford Community Col, Dearborn, 77-; instr sculptural weaving & primitive weaving, Ctr For Creative Studies, Detroit, 77- Pos: Designer & artist, 72- Awards: Old Mill Yarn Award, Fiber Structures, Mus of Art, Carnegie Inst Int, Pittsburgh, 76. Bibliog: Patricia Smith (auth), Birmingham/Bloomfield art association exhibits originals, Birmingham Eccentric, 6/75; Sue Higgenbarth (auth), Airiness of summer, Oakland Press, 6/76; Lisa Hammel (auth), 16 artists put all of their crafts in 60 baskets, New York Times, 2/77. Style & Technique: Sculpture juxtaposing linear elements and planes with space resulting in sense experiences. Media: Cotton, wool, jute, paper, elastics and synthetics with such metals as steel, brass, aluminum in rods, wires, bars and sheets. Publ: Auth, The Two-Fold Nature of Things, Cranbrook Acad of Art, 76; contribr (catalogue), Fiber Structures, Van Nostrand Reinhold Co, 76; contribr, Protofibers—A Loan Exhibition of Works of Art in Fibrous Materials, Lowe Art Gallery, Syracuse Univ, 77. Mailing Add: 14081 Winchester Oak Park MI 48237

ROSENQUIST, JAMES
PAINTER
b Grand Forks, NDak, Nov 29, 33. Study: Univ Minn, Minneapolis, scholar, 48, study with Cameron Booth; Art Students League, 54-55; Aspen Inst of Humanist Studies, Colo, Eastern philo & hist, 65. Work: Art Gallery of Ont, Toronto; Stedelijk Mus, Amsterdam; Kaiser Wilhelm Mus, Krefeld, Ger; Mus Mod Art, New York; Musee Nat d'art Moderne, Paris. Exhib: New Realists, Sidney Janis Gallery, New York, 62; Six Painters & the Object, Solomon R Guggenheim Mus, New York, 63; Mixed-Media, 63 & Kid Stuff, 71, Albright-Knox Art Gallery, Buffalo, NY; Americans 1963, Around the Automobile, 65 The 1960s, 67 & Works from Change, 74, Mus Mod Art, New York; Am Pop Art, Stedelijk Mus, Amsterdam, 64; Salon du Mai, Paris, 64; Sound, Light, Silence, William Rockhill Nelson Gallery of Art, Kansas City, Mo, 66; 9th Biennial of Sao Paulo, Brazil, 67; Ann, 67 & Am

Pop Art, 74, Whitney Mus of Am Art, New Yrok; Documenta IV, Kassel, WGer, 68; New York: The Second Breakthrough, 1959-1964, Univ Calif, Irvine, 69; Prints by Four New York Painters, 69 & New York Painting & Sculpture: 1940-1970, 69-70, Metrop Mus of Art, New York; Am Painting, Va Mus of Fine Art, Richmond, 70; Art & Technol, Los Angeles Co Mus of Art, Los Angeles, 71; Am Drawing: 1970-1973, Yale Univ, 73; Am Art—Third Quarter Century, Seattle Art Mus, Wash, 73; one-man shows, Moderna Museet, Stockholm, Sweden, 65 & 66, Museo d'Arte Moderna, Turin, Italy, 65, Kunstverein Baden-Baden, WGer, 66, Kunsthalle Bern, Switz, 66, Louisiana Mus, Humblebaek, Denmark, 66, Stedelijk Mus, Amsterdam, 66 & 73, Mus des Arts Decoratifs, Paris, 67, Nat Gallery of Can, Ottawa, 68, Metrop Mus of Art, New York, 68, Wallraf-Richartz Mus & Kunsthalle, Cologne, WGer, 72, Whitney Mus of Am Art, New York, 72, Mus of Contemp Art, Chicago, 72 & Portland Art Ctr, Ore, 73. Teaching: Vis lectr, Yale Univ, New Haven, Conn, 64. Pos: Commercial display artist, Gen Outdoor Advert Co, 52-54 & Bonwit Teller & Tiffany & Co, New York, 59. Awards: Torcuato di Tella Int Prize, Buenos Aires, 65. Bibliog: J Siegel (auth), An Interview with James Rosenquist, Artforum, New York, 6/72; J Loring (auth), Prints: James Ro Rosenquist's Horse Blinders, Artmagazine, New York, 2/73; P Tuchman (auth), Pop: interview with James Rosenquist, Art News, New York, 5/74. Style & Technique: Very large format; graphic realism. Media: Oil on Canvas. Dealer: Leo Castelli Gallery 420 W Broadway New York NY 10012. Mailing Add: 1724 E Seventh Ave Ybor City Tampa FL 33605

ROSENQUIT, BERNARD
PAINTER, PRINTMAKER
b Hotin, Roumania, Dec 26, 23; US citizen. Study: Inst Art & Archeol, Paris; Fontainebleau Sch Fine Arts, France; Brooklyn Mus Sch Fine Art; Atelier 17, New York; Art Students League. Work: Metrop Mus Art, New York; Brooklyn Mus Fine Art; Victoria & Albert Mus, London, Eng; Smithsonian Inst, Washington, DC; New York Pub Libr Print Collection; plus others. Exhib: Honolulu Acad Fine Arts; Boston Mus Fine Arts; Mus Mod Art, New York; Newark Mus Art, NJ; seven one-man shows, Roko Gallery, New York, 51-71; plus others. Awards: Fulbright Grant Painting, Paris, 58; Louis Comfort Tiffany Found Grant Printmaking, 59. Mem: Artists Equity Asn New York; life mem Art Students League. Media: Oil, Gouache, Wood. Dealer: Roko Gallery 90 E Tenth St New York NY 10003. Mailing Add: 87 Barrow St New York NY 10014

ROSENTHAL, MRS ALAN H
COLLECTOR
Collection: Ethnographica. Mailing Add: 169 E 69th St New York NY 10021

ROSENTHAL, GERTRUDE
ART HISTORIAN, ART ADMINISTRATOR
b Mayen, Ger, May 19, 03; US citizen. Study: Univ Pairs, 25-26; Univ Cologne & Univ Bonn, with A E Brinckmann, PhD(magna cum laude), 32; Goucher Col, hon LHD, 68; Md Inst Baltimore Col Art, hon DFA, 68. Collections Arranged: Bacchiacca & His Friends, Baltimore Mus Art, 60, Four Paris Painters—Manet, Degas, Morisot & Mary Cassatt (with catalog), 62; Nineteen Hundred Fourteen (with catalog), 64; From El Greco To Pollock, Early & Late Works by American & European Artists (with catalog), 68; Cone Collection, Mary Frick Jacobs Collection, Daingerfield Collection & Wurtzburger Primitive Art Collection. Teaching: Vis prof, Johns Hopkins Univ, 48-50, vis lectr, 52-53. Pos: Res asst, Courtauld Inst, Univ London, 39-40; art librn, Goucher Col, 40-45; from cur to chief cur, Baltimore Mus Art, 45-69, emer chief cur, 69-, res specialist, 75-; ed, Baltimore Mus News, 59-63; consult, Western Col Honolulu Acad Arts, 72- Awards: Nat Found Arts Res Grant Am & Ger Romantic Nineteenth Century Painting, 68; Studies in Honor of G Rosenthal, 68 & 72; Nat Endowment for the Arts Grant, 76-78. Mem: Am Asn Mus; Col Art Asn Am; Mus Mod Art; Walters Art Gallery; Baltimore Mus Art. Res: European and American art from the 16th century to 1965. Publ: Auth, articles on Gauguin, 52, Matisse, 56 & German Expressionism, 57, Baltimore Mus News; ed, Biennale Venezia 1960, Stati Uniti d'America, 60; ed, Annual II, Studies on Thomas Cole, Baltimore Mus Art, 68; ed, J Honolulu Acad Arts, Vol 1, No 1, 74 & Vol 3 No 3. Mailing Add: 3925 Beech Ave Baltimore MD 21211

ROSENTHAL, GLORIA M
PAINTER
b Brooklyn, NY, May 24, 28. Study: Com Art Training, Archit Design, Univ Cincinnati; Post Col; Artist in Am Sch; Queen's Col; Provincetown Workshop; Nassau Community Col; Pratt Graphic Ctr; pvt & independent study. Work: Bankers Trust, New York; Sperry Gyroscope, Lake Success, NY; Weaver Schs, Milwaukee, Wis; Lutz Jr Mus, Manchester, Conn; Col Town, Inc, New York. Exhib: Audubon Artists; Nat Asn Women Artists; Nat Acad Design, 70-75; Silvermine Regional, Silvermine, Conn, 72; one-man show, Saratoga Performing Art Ctr, NY, 72; Palazzo Vecchio, Florence, Italy, 72; Winners of the Past Ten Years, Brooklyn Mus, 75. Pos: Artist in residence, Gloria Rosenthal Gallery, Rocky Neck Art Colony, Mass, 72- Awards: Grumbacher Award, Audubon Artists, Nat Acad Design, 70; Charles H Woodbury Award, Nat Asn Women Artists, 72 & Medal of Honor, 75. Mem: Nat Asn Women Artists; Rocky Neck Art Colony, (vpres, 73); Syosset Players (vpres, 66, pres, 67). Style & Technique: Lyrical abstractions; semiabstractions; origin of life. Media: Oil, Collage. Mailing Add: 43 Miller Blvd Syosset NY 11791

ROSENTHAL, JOHN W
SLIDE MAKER, PHOTOGRAPHER OF ART
b Munich, Ger, Mar 25, 28; US citizen. Study: Univ of Chicago, BA(liberal arts). Teaching: Helped photograph the collections & taught photogrs at the Art Inst of Chicago & Mus of Contemp Art, 70-77. Pos: Commercial photogr, Koopman-Neumer, Chicago, Ill, 55-65; owner-dir, Rosenthal Art Slides, Chicago, 60- Bibliog: N De Laurier (auth), Slide Buyer's Guide, Col Art Asn, 76. Media: Slide Maker; Photographer. Specialty: Extensive collections of High quality slides pertaining to art and art history. Publ: Auth, Rosenthal Art Slides, 74 & Vol II, 78, pvt publ. Mailing Add: 5456 S Ridgewood Court Chicago IL 60615

ROSENTHAL, RACHEL
SCULPTOR
b Paris, France, Nov 9, 26; US citizen. Study: New Sch Social Res, New York; Sorbonne, Paris; also with Hans Hofmann, Karl Knaths, William S Hayter & John Mason. Exhib: Rental Gallery, Los Angeles Co Mus, 72; Ceramic Int, Calgary, Can, 73; Ceramic Conjunction, Glendale, Calif, 73 & 75; one-woman show, Woman's Bldg Los Angeles, Grandview Gallery, 74; 1st Ann Calif Sculpture Exhib, Calif State Univ, Northridge, 74. Teaching: Instr art mkt, Joan of Art Sem, Calif, 72-74. Pos: Founding mem bd dir, Womanspace, Los Angeles, 72-74, co-chmn, 73-74. Awards: Gold Medal Art, High Sch Mus & Art, New York, 45. Bibliog: Nancy Youdelman (auth), Sculptures by Rosenthal, Artweek, 74. Mem: Los Angeles Co Mus Art; Artists Equity Asn; Los Angeles Inst Contemp Art; Artists Econ Action; Am Crafts Coun. Style & Technique: Abstract sculpture, hand-built clay, coil method; collage using xerographic photos and other objects. Media: Stoneware, Raku. Publ: Illusr, Pearl Hunter, Schuman, 52; auth, Coiled sculpture, Ceramics Monthly, 74; auth, article in Los Angeles Inst Contemp Art J, 75. Mailing Add: 6041 Calvin Ave Tarzana CA 91356

ROSENTHAL, SEYMOUR JOSEPH
PAINTER, LITHOGRAPHER
b New York, NY, Aug 14, 21. Work: Metrop Mus Art, New York; Indianapolis Mus Art; Suffolk Mus, Stony Brook, NY; Technion Bldg, Haifa, Israel; Harry S Truman Libr, Independence, Mo. Comn: Drawings of children, New York Bd Educ, 57; painting of Moses, Borough Pres, Queens, NY, 62; Pfizer Pharmaceutical; Park Davis. Exhib: Civil Rights Art Show, Brooklyn Mus, 62; one-man shows, Herzl Inst, 64, Suffolk Mus, 68 & ACA Gallery, New York, 69; Major Drawings of 19th & 20th Century Exhib, Gallery Mod Art, New York, 64-65, Art Dealers Choice Exhib, 67; Indianapolis Mus Art, 72. Bibliog: Edwin Newman (auth), feature on Today Show, NBC TV, 70; Alfred Werner (auth), feature on Directions, ABC TV, 71. Mem: Artists Equity Asn; Comt Arts & Lit in Jewish Life, Jewish Fedn Philanthropies & United Jewish Appeal. Style & Technique: Impressionism from real life. Media: Watercolor, Oil, Tempera. Publ: Illusr, Parke Davis Med J, 56; illusr, Scope, 56; contribr, Commonweal, Vol 90, No 15. Dealer: Associated American Artists 663 Fifth Ave New York NY 10022; ACA Gallery 25 E 73rd St New York NY 10021. Mailing Add: 161-08 Jewel Ave Flushing NY 11365

ROSENTHAL, STEPHEN
PAINTER
b Richmond, Va, May 28, 35. Study: Art Students League, with Edwin Dickinson; Tyler Sch Fine Arts, Philadelphia, with Boris Blai & BFA, 60. Work: Arts Club Chicago; Yale Univ Art Gallery, New Haven, Conn; Art Fund, New York. Exhib: Am Acad Arts & Lett, New York, 63; Amon Carter Mus, Ft Worth, Tex, 64; Int Watercolor Biennial, Brooklyn Mus, NY, 65; Herron Inst, Indianapolis, Ind, 67; Pa Acad Fine Arts Biennial Exhib, Philadelphia, 67. Teaching: Instr design, Cooper Union, New York, 66-67; lectr painting, Univ NC, Greensboro, 71-72. Pos: Bk reviewer, Arts Mag, New York, 71-72. Awards: Mason Lord Prize, Baltimore Mus Art, 67. Bibliog: Raymond Charmet (auth), Un jeune Americain, Arts, 66; Leach Levy (auth), The drawn line in painting, Parker St 470, 71. Media: Tempera. Dealer: 55 Mercer 55 Mercer St New York NY 10013. Mailing Add: c/o John Weber Gallery 420 W Broadway New York NY 10012

ROSENTHAL, TONY (BERNARD)
SCULPTOR
b Highland Park, Ill, Aug 9, 14. Study: Univ Mich, BFA, 36; Cranbrook Acad Art. Work: Mus Mod Art, New York; Whitney Mus Am Art; Middlehiem Mus, Antwerp, Belg; Israel Mus, Jerusalem; Albright-Knox Art Gallery, Buffalo. Comn: Cube, Alamo, New York, 66; Large Cube, Univ Mich, Ann Arbor, 68; Bronze Disk, Rondo, New York Pub Libr, 69; Sun Disk, Financial Ctr Pac, Honolulu, Hawaii, 71; Police Plaza Sculpture, New York, 74. Exhib: Nine Whitney Mus Am Art Ann, 53-72; Third Bienal, Sao Paulo, Brazil, 55; Recent Sculpture USA, Mus Mod Art, 59; Biennale, Middleheim Mus, 71; Am Painting & Sculpture 1948-1969, Krannert Art Mus, Univ Ill, Champaign, 71; Aldrich Mus Contemp Arts, Ridgefield, Conn, 73; Stanford Mus, Calif, 76; Guild Hall, East Hampton, NY, 76; Meadowbrook Art Gallery, Oakland Univ, Rochester, Minn, 76; plus many one-man exhibs. Awards: Ford Found Purchase Prize, Krannert Art Mus, 63; Outstanding Achievement Award, Univ Mich, 67; First Prize, Iron & Steel Inst, 75. Bibliog: Bernard Rosenthal, Life, 52; Gibson Danes (auth), Bernard Rosenthal, Art Int, 68; Sam Hunter (auth), Rosenthal: sculptures, 68. Dealer: M Knoedler 21 E 70th St New York NY 10021. Mailing Add: 173 E 73rd St New York NY 10021

ROSENWALD, BARBARA K
COLLECTOR
b Norfolk, Va, July 30, 24. Study: Boston Mus Sch Fine Arts; Fogg Mus, Harvard Univ; Stella Elkins Tyler Sch Fine Arts; also in Paris, France & Florence, Italy. Collection: Modern Italian art, including works by Afro, Campigli, Moscha; French modern art, including works by Pignon and others. Mailing Add: Box 496 Rushland Bucks County PA 18956

ROSENWALD, LESSING JULIUS
COLLECTOR, PATRON
b Chicago, Ill, Feb 10, 91. Study: Cornell Univ; Univ Pa, Hon DHL; Lincoln Univ, Hon DHL; Jefferson Med Col, Hon LLD. Pos: Hon mem bd gov, Philadelphia Mus Art; former trustee, Free Libr Philadelphia; trustee, Rosenbach Found, Philadelphia; assoc, Blake Trust, London; trustee & benefactor, Nat Gallery Art; benefactor, Libr of Cong, Washington, DC; hon mem, Inst Advan Study, Philadelphia Mus Art. Awards: Philadelphia Award, Artists Equity Asn, 61; Distinguished Achievement Award, Philadelphia Art Alliance, 63. Mem: Grolier Club, NY; Benjamin Franklin fel Royal Soc Arts, Eng; Print Coun Am. Collection: Prints, drawings, miniatures and rare illustrated books, including, Fior di Virtu 1491 and The Nineteenth Book. Mailing Add: 1146 Fox Chase Rd Jenkintown PA 19046

ROSENZWEIG, DAPHNE LANGE
ART HISTORIAN, COLLECTOR
b Evanston, Ill, July 7, 41. Study: Mt Holyoke Col, AB; Columbia Univ, MA & PhD; Univ Wis; Corcoran Sch Art; Nat Taiwan Univ, spec scholar. Collections Arranged: Art of the Orient: Eighth Century to the Present, Univ NMex, 72. Teaching: Lectr Oriental art, Univ NMex, Albuquerque, 69-73; asst prof Oriental art, Oberlin Col, 73- Awards: Fulbright Fel, Repub China, 67-69; Columbia Univ Grant, 69; Mary E Wooley Fel, 70. Mem: Midwest Art Historians Soc; Asn Asian Studies; Asia House; China Inst. Res: Painting the Ch'ing Dynasty of China, with emphasis on court painting. Collection: Chinese paintings, Oriental ceramics; modern Japanese prints. Publ: Auth, Landscape Painting by Haiao Yun-ts'ung, Allen Art Mus Bull, 2/74; auth, Court painting and the K'ang-hsi Emperor, Ch'ing Shih Wen t'i, 12/75; auth, Court painting of the K'ang-hsi era: the socioeconomic aspects, Monumenta Serica, 75. Mailing Add: Dept of Art Oberlin Col Oberlin OH 44074

ROSENZWEIG, PHYLLIS D
CURATORIAL ASSISTANT
b Brooklyn, NY, Dec 27, 43. Study: Hunter Col, City Univ New York, BA, 64; Inst Fine Arts, New York, 65-69. Collections Arranged: The Thomas Eakins Collection (auth, catalog), Hirshhorn Mus & Sculpture Garden, Smithsonian Inst, Washington, DC, 77. Pos: Curatorial asst, Hirshhorn Mus & Sculpture Garden, 71- Res: Concentration on permanent collection of Hirshhorn Museum; contribution to catalogues of permanent collection and bicentennial exhibition; specialty is 19th and 20th century art. Mailing Add: Hirshhorn Mus & Sculpture Garden Smithsonian Inst Washington DC 20560

ROSKILL, MARK WENTWORTH
ART HISTORIAN, ART CRITIC
b London, Eng, Nov 10, 33. Study: Trinity Col (Eng), BA, 56, MA, 61; Harvard Univ, MA, 57; Courtauld Inst, Univ London, 57; Princeton Univ, MFA & PhD, 61. Teaching: Instr & asst, Princeton Univ, 59-61; from instr to asst prof, Harvard Univ, 61-68; assoc prof, Univ Mass, Amherst, 68-73, prof, 73- Awards: Am Coun Learned Socs Fel, 65-66 & 74-75. Mem: Col Art Asn Am. Res: 19th and 20th century art; criticism; methodology of art history. Publ:

Ed, The Letters of Vincent Van Gogh, 63; auth, Dolce's Aretino and Venetian Art Theory of the Cinquecento, 68; auth, Van Gogh, Gauguin and the Impressionist Circle, 70; contribr, Atlantic Brief Lives, 71; auth, What is Art History, 75; plus others. Mailing Add: Dept of Art Univ of Mass Amherst MA 01002

ROSLER, MARTHA ROSE
VIDEO ARTIST, ART CRITIC
b Brooklyn, NY, July 29, 43. Study: Brooklyn Mus Art Sch; Brooklyn Col, BA; Univ Calif, San Diego, MFA. Work: Alexander Mackie Col for Advan Studies; Contemp Arts Mus, Houston, Tex; Centro de Arte y Communicación, Buenos Aires, Arg; Long Beach Mus Art, Calif. Exhib: Impact Art-Video Art 74, Lausanne & Brussels, 74-75; 2nd Int Encounter on Video, Paris, 75; 3rd Int Encounter on Video, Ferrara, Italy, 75; 4th Int Encounter on Video, Buenos Aires, 75; Southland Video Anthology, Long Beach, San Francisco & New York, 75; San Francisco Mus Art, 75; one-person shows, Long Beach Mus Art, Calif, 77 & Whitney Mus Am Art, New York, 77; Social Criticism & Practise, San Francisco Art Inst, 77; Contemp Arts Mus, Houston, 77-78, Am Narrative & Story Art, 1967-1977 (traveling exhib), 77-78; Artwords/Bookworks (traveling exhib), Los Angeles Inst Contemp Art, 78. Teaching: Instr, San Diego State Univ, 75-76 & Univ Calif San Diego, 75-78; instr photog, Orange Coast Col, Costa Mesa, 77-; instr film, photog & media, Univ Calif, Irvine, 78- Awards: Nat Endowment for Arts Fel, 75-77. Style & Technique: Representation and interrogation of common cultural preoccupations and images, usally embedded in a narrative. Media: Images & Texts. Res: Meaning of art images and objects and their placement in a cultural context. Publ: Auth, Lee Friedlander's guarded strategies, Artforum, 75; auth, Immigrating & auth, McTowersMaid, mail distrib, 75 & New-Found Career, 78, J Los Angeles Inst Contemp Art; auth, Under the Rug, Fox, 76; auth, Lee Friedlander's Guarded Strategies, 75 & Private and the Public: feminist art in Southern California, 77, Artforum, 76; auth, Private & the public: feminist art in Southern California, Artforum, 77; auth, Tijuana Maid, mail distrib & Heresies, 77. Mailing Add: 851 San Dieguito Dr Encinitas CA 92024

ROSOFSKY, SEYMOUR
PAINTER, PRINTMAKER
b Chicago, Ill, Aug 4, 24. Study: Art Inst Chicago, BFA, 49, MFA, 50. Work: Mus Mod Art, New York; Art Inst Chicago; Los Angeles Co Mus; Brooklyn Mus; Pasadena Mus. Exhib: Mythology in our Time, Bologna, Italy, 66; Fantasy & Figure, Am Fedn Arts Touring Exhib, 68-69; Human Concern & Personal Torment, Whitney Mus Am Art, 69; Chemin de la Creation, France, 70; Tamarind Touring Exhib, US & SAm, 70; plus many one-man shows in US & Europe. Teaching: Prof art, City Cols Chicago, 53- Awards: Guggenheim Fel, 62-64; Tamarind Fel, 68; Cassandra Found Award, 73; plus others. Mem: Alumni Asn Art Inst Chicago. Media: Oil, Watercolor; Lithography, Etching. Dealer: Galerie du Dragon Rue du Dragon 19 Paris France; Hank Baum Gallery Three Embarcadero Ctr San Francisco CA 94111. Mailing Add: 859 Fullerton Chicago IL 60614

ROSS, ALEXANDER
PAINTER
b Dunfermline, Scotland, Oct 28, 08; US citizen. Study: Carnegie Inst Technol, with Robert Lepper; Boston Col, hon MA. Work: New Britain Mus, Conn; Waterbury Mus, Conn; US Air Force Collection, Denver, Colo; Am Acad Design, New York; Mormon Church, Salt Lake City, Utah. Comn: Portrait of Pres John F Kennedy, comn by Romaine Pearson Publ Inc, New York, 71; paintings, Phoenix Arthritis Ctr, Ariz, 74; stained-glass doors, St Peter's Church, Danbury, Conn, 77; plus many portrait comns, by pvt individuals & major Am publ. Exhib: Am Watercolor Soc, Royal Soc Painters, London, 66; 200 Years Watercolor, Metrop Mus Art, New York, 67; 18th Ann New Eng Exhib, Silvermine Guild, Conn, 68; Landscape One, De Cordova Mus, Lincoln, Mass, 70; Spring Rebirth, SNew Eng Invitational, Fairfield Univ, Conn, 70; 200 Yrs Am Illus, NY Hist Soc, New York, 77; Royal Soc Painters, London, Eng; Smithsonian Inst, Washington, DC; Wadsworth Atheneum, Hartford, Conn; Tenn Ctr for the Arts, Nashville; plus others. Teaching: Lectr creative painting, Cath Univ Am, summer 54. Pos: Mem art comt, Fairfield Univ, 69-; adv bd, Soc Medallists, 76- Awards: First Prize Popular Opinion Award, Los Angeles Co Fair, 60; Thomas Saxe Found Award, New Canaan Ann, 67; Adolf & Cedar Obrig Award, Nat Acad Design, 72. Bibliog: Robert Ulrich Godsoe (auth), Alex Ross: reluctant prophet, Esquire, 48; Charles Daugherty (auth), Six Artists Paint A Landscape, N Light Publ, 75. Mem: Nat Acad Design; Conn Acad Fine Arts; Am Watercolor Soc (dir, 75-77); Silvermine Guild Artists; Conn Watercolor Soc. Style & Technique: Modern impressionism, with freely executed techniques. Media: Oil, Watercolor, Acrylic. Publ: Illusr, covers, Good Housekeeping, 42-54, Sat Eve Post, 43-50, Cosmopolitan, 44-60, Ladies Home J, 45-60 & McCalls, 45-60; auth, How I use watercolor, Am Artist, 62; auth, New Directions in Watercolor (film), Electrographic Corp, 71. Dealer: Joe Demers 5 Harbour House Harbourtown Hilton Head Island SC 29928; Thompson Gallery 2020 N Central Ave Phoenix AZ 85004. Mailing Add: 8 Hawthorn Trail Ridgefield CT 06877

ROSS, BEATRICE BROOK
PAINTER
b New York, NY. Study: Brooklyn Mus Art Sch, with Ruben Tam; Sch Chinese Brushwork, scholar, study with Wang Chi Yuan; also with Leo Manso. Work: Ford Productions, Toronto, Can; Textured Prod, New York; pvt collection of D H Northington, New York, W Thornton, New York, Laura Ford, Ontario, Can, Hideo Hikawa, Tokyo, Japan, plus others. Comn: Two paintings, Muller, Jordan & Herricks Advert Agency, New York, 71. Exhib: Silvermine Guild Artists, New Canaan, Conn, 68 & 70; Audubon Artists, New York, 68 & 70; Guild Hall Mus, Easthampton, NY, 69-72; Nat Arts Club, New York, 70; Four Contemp Artists, Suffolk Mus, Stony Brook, NY, 71; C W Post Col, 76; two-person show, St John's Univ, 76; Port Washington Libr, New York, 77. Awards: Benjamin Altman Landscape Prize, Nat Acad Design, 68; Second Prize Oil, Heckscher Mus, 70; McDowell Colony Fel, 75; plus others. Bibliog: Malcolm Preston (auth), article in Newsday, 72. Mem: Prof Artists Guild (vpres admis, 73-75; exec vpres, 75); Artists Equity; Easthampton Guild; Women in the Arts. Style & Technique: Transcendental abstractions; brush technique. Media: Oil, Collage. Dealer: RAA Gallery 527 Madison Ave New York NY 11753. Mailing Add: 19 Briar Ln Jericho NY 11753

ROSS, CHARLES
SCULPTOR
b Philadelphia, Pa, Dec 17, 37. Study: Univ Calif, AB, 60, MA, 62. Work: Whitney Mus Am Art; Univ Art Gallery, Berkeley, Calif; Univ Pa, Philadelphia; Indianapolis Mus Art; Nelson Art Gallery, Kansas City, Mo. Exhib: New Alchemy, Elements, Systems & Forces, Art Gallery of Ont, Toronto, 69; Whitney Mus Am Art Sculpture Ann, 69; Elements of Art, Mus Fine Arts, Boston, 71; Fire, Air, Earth, Water, Univ Wis, 74; Painting & Sculpture Today, Indianapolis Mus Art, 74; one-man shows, La Jolla Mus Contemp Art, Calif, Inst Contemp Art, Philadelphia & Mus Contemp Art, Chicago, 76-77, John Weber Gallery, 77 & Susan Caldwell Gallery, 77, New York & Mass Inst Technol, Cambridge, 78; Maps: Their Sci & Their Art, Mus Natural Hist, New York, 77; Probing the Earth: Contemp Land Proj, Hirshhorn Mus, Washington, DC, 77; Cult & Customs, US Customs House, New York, 77; Drawings for Outdoor Sculpture: 1946-1977, Weber Gallery, 77. Teaching: Instr, Univ Calif, 65; instr, Sch Visual Arts, New York, 67, 70 & 71; instr, Herbert Lehman Col, 68; vis prof arch, Univ Utah, 72 & 73, artist in residence, 74. Pos: Dir, Solar Ctr, Las Vegas, NMex. Awards: Am Inst Graphic Arts Award, 76. Bibliog: David Shapiro & Lindsay Stamm (auth), Charles Ross, Arts Mag, 6/77; Sunlight Convergence/Solar Burn, Co-Evolution Quart, winter 77; Donald Kuspit (auth), Light's measure, Art in Am, 3-4/78. Style & Technique: Large prisms, solar spectrums and astronomical works dealing with the core and contexts of light energy; images drawn by light itself; art as a point of contact with the universe energy system. Publ: Auth, Sunlight Convergence/Solar Burn, Univ Utah Press, 76. Dealer: John Weber Gallery 420 W Broadway New York NY 10012. Mailing Add: 383 W Broadway New York NY 10012

ROSS, CONRAD HAROLD
PRINTMAKER, EDUCATOR
b Chicago, Ill, Apr 26, 31. Study: Univ Ill, BFA, 53; Univ Chicago, 54; Univ Iowa, MFA, 59. Work: Libr Cong, Washington, DC; Springfield Art Mus, Mo; Norfolk Mus Arts & Sci, Va; Dallas Mus Fine Arts, Tex; Macon Mus Arts & Sci, Ga. Exhib: The Henderson Series—Prints, Drawings Constructions, Birmingham-Southern Art Gallery, Ala, 71; 7th Dulin Nat Print & Drawing Competition, Knoxville, Tenn, 71; Monotypes—A Survey Exhibit, Pratt Graphics Ctr Gallery, New York, 72; 1973 Artists Biennial, New Orleans Mus Art, La; Annual Color Print USA, Tex Tech Univ, Lubbock, 73 & 74. Teaching: Instr drawing, design, lettering & art appreciation, La Polytech Inst, 61-63; asst prof drawing & printmaking, Auburn Univ, 63-; vis lectr drawing & printmaking, Kans Univ, 68. Awards: Louis Comfort Tiffany Found Grant printmaking, 60; Auburn Univ Res Grant-in-Aid, 65-67; Purchase Award, LaGrange Nat II, Prints and Drawings, Ga, 75. Mem: Ala Art League (treas, 75-78); Col Art Asn Am; Nat Art Workers Community; Southeastern Graphics Coun. collagraph/collage, intaglio printmaking. Publ: Contribr, Artists' proof the annual of prints and printmaking, 70. Mailing Add: 447 Wrights Mill Rd Auburn AL 36830

ROSS, DAVID ANTHONY
CURATOR, LECTURER
b New York, NY, Apr 26, 49. Study: Syracuse Univ, BS, 71. Collections Arranged: Traveling exhib, Circuit: A Video Invitational (survey of video art, 68-72), 72-74; Southland Video Anthology (survey of video art in Southern Calif, 68-75, with catalog), Long Beach Mus Art, 75. Teaching: Lectr video art, Grad Sch, Univ Calif, San Diego, 74- Pos: Asst dir, Everson Mus Art, Syracuse, 71-72, cur video arts, 71-74; dep dir TV & film, Long Beach Mus Art, 74-77; chief cur, Univ Art Mus, Univ Calif, Berkeley, 77- Awards: JDR 3rd Found Res Study Grant, 74. Mem: Am Asn Mus; Advocates for Arts. Res: Relationship between development of new art and context that supports art in American society and development of new support structures. Publ: Co-auth, Douglas Davis: Videotapes, Manifestos, Drawings and Objects, 72; co-auth, Frank Gillette: Video Process & Metaprocess, 73; co-auth, Nam June Paik: Videa & Videology, 74; co-auth, Peter Campus: Video Works, 74; auth, Southland Video Anthology, 75 & 76-77. Mailing Add: Univ Art Mus Berkeley 2626 Bancroft Way Berkeley CA 94704

ROSS, DOUGLAS ALLAN
SCULPTOR, INSTRUCTOR
b Los Angeles, Calif, Jan 23, 37. Study: Carleton Col, BA, 59; Minneapolis Col of Art & Design, 59-61; Univ Minn, MFA, 65. Work: Northrup Gallery, Univ Minn, Minneapolis, Muhlenberg Col, Allentown, Pa; Ill State Univ, Normal. Exhib: Biennial of Painting & Sculpture, 62, Invitation 1963 & Drawings in Minn, 65, Walker Art Ctr, Minneapolis; Minn Artists Biennial, Minneapolis Inst of Art, 63; Mid-Am I, William Rockhill Nelson Gallery of Art, Kansas City, Mo & St Louis Art Mus, Mo, 68; Third Invitational, Northern Contemp Galleries (traveling exhib), Northern Counties, Eng, 69; Invitational Sculpture, Ill State Ctr for the Visual Arts, 74; 19th Ann Exhib of Prints & Drawings, Okla Art Ctr, Oklahoma City, 77. Collections Arranged: First Great Plains sculpture Exhib, Sheldon Mem Art Gallery, Lincoln, Nebr, 75; Drawings by Sculptors, SW Mo State Univ, 75 & Syracuse Univ, NY, 76; Second Ann Great Plains Sculpture Exhib, Sheldon Mem Art Gallery, 76; Nebr Alumni, Nebr Mus of Fine Arts, 76. Teaching: Asst prof sculpture/drawing, Univ Nebr, Lincoln, 66-69; lectr grade II sculpture, Manchester Polytech, Eng, 69-70; assoc prof sculpture/drawing, Univ Nebr, 70- Awards: Second Prize, 3rd Minn Artist's Biennial, Minneapolis, 63; Measuregraph Award, Mid-Am I, William Rockhill Nelson Gallery of Art, Addressograph/Multigraph, 68; Purchase Award, One-man Show, Muhlenberg Col, 76. Mem: Mid-Am Col Art Asn (prog dir & exhib dir, 75-76). Style & Technique: Abstract. Media: Mixed. Mailing Add: 1933 B St Lincoln NE 68502

ROSS, FRED (JOSEPH)
PAINTER, INSTRUCTOR
b St John, NB, May 12, 27. Study: St John Voc Sch; Pa Acad Fine Arts, with Ben Kamihira; also with Pablo O'Higgins, Mex. Work: Can Coun Art Bank, Ottawa, Ont; Winnipeg Art Gallery, Man; NB Mus, St John. Comn: Mural, NB Tourist Bur, St John, 58; mural, Prince of Wales Col, Charlottetown, PEI, 61; mural, NB Govt Centennial Bldg, 67. Exhib: One-man shows, Walter Klinkhoff Gallery, Montreal, 69, 71 & 75, Galerie Dresdnere, Toronto, 73, 76 & 77; Nat Gallery Ann Exhib, 53, 58 & 66; Royal Can Acad Ann Exhib, 58, 59, 61 & 70; 8th Ann, Montreal Mus, 65 & Survey Exhib, 68. Teaching: Instr drawing, Exten Dept, Univ NB, Fredericton, 70-77; instr painting, summer workshop, Sunbury Shores, St Andrews, NB, 70-77; instr painting, summer workshop, Mt Allison Univ, Sackville, NB, 73-77. Pos: Mem bd dir, Sunbury Shores Arts & Nature Ctr, 75- Awards: O'Keefe Art Award, 50; Price Fine Arts Award, Price Kraft & Paperboard Corp, 70; Short Term Grant, Can Coun, 73 & 76. Bibliog: Painting a Province, Nat Film Bd, 62; Paul Duval (auth), Four Decades, 74 & High Realism, 75, Clark Irwin Co. Style & Technique: Realistic figurative paintings in tempera on canvas, drawings in ink and pastel, landscapes in tempera. Dealer: Galerie Dresdnere 130 Bloor St W Toronto ON Can. Mailing Add: 3 Goodrich St St John NB E2K 4A5 Can

ROSS, JAMES MATTHEW
EDUCATOR, PAINTER
b Ann Arbor, Mich, Sept 8, 31. Study: Univ Mich, AB; Cranbrook Acad Art, MFA; Rockham Sch Grad Studies, Ann Arbor; Accad Belle Arti, Rome. Work: Butler Inst Am Art; Cranbrook Mus Art; Wustum Mus, Racine, Wis; Madison Art Ctr, Wis; Detroit Inst Art. Exhib: Michigan Artists, 51-60 & 63; Detroit Inst Art & Pa Acad Fine Arts, 59-60; Walker Art Ctr, 59-60; Wis Painters & Sculptors Ann, Milwaukee Art Ctr, 63-65; Univ Wis-Whitewater, 65; plus others. Teaching: Asst prof art, Univ Wis-Platteville, 62- Awards: Fulbright Grant Painting to Italy, 60 & 61; Prizes, Wis Painters & Sculptors, 63 & Mich Fine Arts Exhib, 64; plus others. Mem: Col Art Asn Am; Wis Painters & Sculptors Soc; Am Asn Univ Prof. Mailing Add: Dept of Art Univ of Wis-Platteville Platteville WI 53818

ROSS, JANICE KOENIG
PAINTER
b Harrisburg, Pa. Study: Pa State Univ, BA; Univ Ill, MFA. Exhib: Dixie Ann, Montgomery Mus Fine Arts, Ala, 71 & 72; Hunter Gallery Ann, Chattanooga, 72; Chattahoochie Valley

Ann Nat Painting & Sculpture Exhib, La Grange, Ga, 72 & 73; Piedmont Ann Crafts Exhib, Mint Mus, Charlotte, NC, 73; Ann Exhib, Springfield Art Mus, Mo, 74; one-person shows, George Washington Carver Mus, Tuskegee Institute, Ala, 76, Telfair Peet Gallery, Auburn Univ, & Univ NAla, Florence, 78; Cent S Exhib, The Parthenon, Nashville, Tenn, 76; Piedmont Graphic Exhib, Greenville Co Mus, Greenville, SC, 76; Nat Drawing & Sculpture Show, Kutztown State Col, Pa, 77. Teaching: Assoc prof basic art, Tuskegee Inst, Ala, 68- Mem: Col Art Asn; Women's Caucus for Art; Nat Art Worker's Community; Ala Art League (chmn artists welfare comt); African Craftsmen in Am, Inc (Ala coordr, 71-72 & 74-75). Media: Oil, Graphic Media. Publ: Auth, MFA Survey, Col Art Asn, fall 78. Mailing Add: 447 Wrights's Mill Rd Auburn AL 36830

ROSS, JOHN T
PRINTMAKER, EDUCATOR
b New York, NY, Sept 25, 21. Study: Cooper Union Art Sch, BFA, with Morris Kantor & Will Barnet; New Sch Social Res, with Antonio Frasconi & Louis Schanker; Columbia Univ, 53. Work: Nat Collection Fine Arts, Washington, DC; Hirshhorn Collection; Metrop Mus Art, New York; Libr Cong, Washington, DC; Cincinnati Art Mus. Comn: Ed prints, Hilton Hotel, 63, Assoc Am Artists, 64, 66 & 72, Philadelphia Print Club, 67, NY State Coun Arts, 67 & Int Poetry Forum, 68. Exhib: 2nd Int Color Print Exhib, Grenchen, Switz, 61; Int Biennale Gravure, Cracow, Poland, 68; Prize-winning Am Prints, Pratt Graphic Art Ctr, New York, 68; Nat Acad Fine Arts, Amsterdam, Neth, 68; Biennial Print Exhib, Calif State Col, Long Beach, 69; plus many group & one-man shows. Teaching: Instr printmaking, New Sch Social Res, 57-; instr printmaking, Pratt Graphic Ctr, 63-; prof art, Manhattanville Col, 64-; demonstr & lectr, US Info Agency Exhib, Romania & Yugoslavia, 64-66. Pos: Dir, Art Ctr Northern NJ, 66-67; pres, US Comt-Int Asn Art, 67-69. Awards: Louis Comfort Tiffany Found Grant printmaking, 54; Purchase Prize for 100 Prints of the Year, AAA Gallery, 63; citation for prof achievement, Cooper Union Art Sch, 66. Bibliog: Articles in Am Artist, 52, Artists Proof, 64 & Art in Am, 65. Mem: Soc Am Graphic Artists (pres, 61-65, exec coun, 65-); assoc Nat Acad Design; Boston Printmakers; Philadelphia Print Club; Am Color Print Soc. Publ: Illusr, many bks; co-auth, The Complete Printmaker, Macmillan, 72. Dealer: Assoc Am Artists 663 Fifth Ave New York NY 10022. Mailing Add: 110 Davison Pl Englewood NJ 07631

ROSS, KENNETH
ART ADMINISTRATOR
b El Paso, Tex, Aug 1, 10. Study: Pasadena Jr Col; Chouinard Art Inst; Art Ctr Sch Los Angeles; Nat Acad, Florence, Italy; Acad Grande Chaumiere, Paris; Euston Rd Sch Drawing & Painting, London. Teaching: Lectr hist art & art appreciation, Univ Southern Calif. Pos: Dir, Pasadena Art Inst, Calif; dir, Mod Inst Art, Beverly Hills, Calif; art critic, Pasadena Star News & Los Angeles Daily News, Calif; dir, Los Angeles Munic Arts Dept, (Art Gallery, Watts Tower Art Ctr, Jr Arts Ctr, Bur Music & Cult Heritage Bd), 50- Mem: Jr Arts Ctr Los Angeles (bd trustees); Munic Art Assoc, Los Angeles; Alliance Calif State Arts Coun (bd trustees); Comt Simon Rodia's Tower Watts (bd trustees); Craft & Folk Art Mus (bd trustees). Mailing Add: Municipal Arts Dept Rm 1500 City Hall Los Angeles CA 90012

ROSS, MARVIN CHAUNCEY
MUSEUM CURATOR, ART HISTORIAN
b Moriches, NY, Nov 21, 04. Study: Harvard Univ, AB & AM; NY Univ; Univ Berlin; Centro de Estudios Historicos, Madrid, Spain. Collections Arranged: Early Christian & Byzantine Art, Walters Art Gallery, Baltimore, Md, 47; Raoul Dufy, Los Angeles Co Mus Art, Calif, 53. Pos: Cur medieval art, Walters Art Gallery, Baltimore, 34-52; chief cur art, Los Angeles Co Mus Art, 52-55; cur, Hillwood (art collection of Mrs Merriweather Post), Smithsonian Inst, Washington, DC, 59- Mem: Am Asn Mus; Archaeol Inst Am; Am Ceramic Circle; English Ceramic Circle. Publ: Ed, The west of Alfred Jacob Miller, 51 & 67; ed, George Catlin, last rambles with the Indians, 59; auth, catalogue of the Byzantine antiquities in Dumbarton Oaks Collection, 62 & 65; auth, The art of Karl Faberge and his contemporaries, 65; auth, Russian porcelains: Merriweather Post Collection, 68. Mailing Add: 2230 California St NW Washington DC 20008

ROSSE, MARYVONNE
SCULPTOR
b Palo Alto, Calif, Mar 4, 17. Study: Acad Fine Arts, The Hague, Neth, dipl. Work: Mus Holland, Mich. Comn: Plaques, J Bos, Neth, 38; medals, Koninklyk Begeer, Neth, 38; portraits, D Tutein Noltenius, Neth, 42; garden ornaments, Nederlandshe Olie Fabriek, Delft, Neth, 46; commercial prototypes, D G Williams Inc, Brooklyn, 48-66. Exhib: Pulchri Studios, The Hague, 36-47; New York World's Fair, 39; Pen & Brush Club, 67-72; Catharine Lorillard Wolfe Art Club, 67-72; Nat Sculpture Soc, 71-72. Collections Arranged: Catharine Lorillard Wolfe Art Club, Nat Acad Gallery; Nat Arts Club. Teaching: Instr sculpture, Rockland Found, Nyack, NY, 47; instr art, King Coit Theatre Sch Children, New York, 47-48. Pos: Sculpture, D G Williams, Brooklyn, NY, 48-66; ed news lett, Catharine Lorillard Wolfe Art Club, 68-72. Awards: Hon Mention, Catharine Lorillard Wolfe Art Club, Nat Acad, 70; Pen & Brush Solo Exhib Award, 71; Gold Medal, Catharine Lorillard Wolfe Art Club Ann, 72. Mem: Nat Sculpture Soc; Pen & Brush Club (sculpture chmn, 69-); Burr Artists (historian, 68-); Catharine Lorillard Wolfe Art Club (bd mem & sculpture chmn, 69-). Media: Clay, Plaster, Wood, Bronze. Mailing Add: 431 Buena Vista Rd New City NY 10956

ROSSEN, SUSAN F
ART HISTORIAN, ART EDITOR
Study: Smith Col, AB(art hist), 63; Univ of Mich, Wayne State Univ, MA(art hist), 71. Teaching: Lectr 19th century art, Univ of Detroit, 71. Pos: Asst cur of educ, Detroit Inst of Arts, 64-68, assoc cur European art, 71-72, sr ed & coordr of publ, Detroit Inst of Arts Bull, 72- Awards: Art Libr Soc of NAm Award for Best Art Book of 1977 (Henri Matisse Paper Cut-Outs), 77. Mem: Am Asn of Mus; Mus Publ of Am; Women's Caucus for Art, Col Art Asn. Res: Nineteenth and twentieth century art and women artists. Publ: Ed, The Twilight of the Medici: Late Baroque Art in Florence 1670-1743, Detroit Inst of Arts, 74; ed, French Painting 1776-1830, Detroit Inst of Arts & Metrop Mus of Art, 75; ed, Arts and Crafts in Detroit 1900-1976, Detroit Inst of Arts, 76; ed, Henri Matisse Paper Cut-Outs, St Louis Art Mus & Detroit Inst of Arts, 77. Mailing Add: 5200 Woodward Ave Detroit MI 48202

ROSSI, BARBARA
PAINTER, PRINTMAKER
b Chicago, Ill. Study: Art Inst Chicago, MFA. Work: Art Inst Chicago; Baltimore Mus Art; Mus des 20, Jahrhunderts, Vienna. Exhib: XII Bienal de Sao Paulo, Made in Chicago, 73, traveling 73-74, Nat Collection Fine Arts, Washington, DC, 74 & Mus Contemp Art, Chicago, 75; American Drawings, 1963-1973 & Bienal Exhib, 75, Whitney Mus Am Art, New York; Beispiel Eisenstadt IV Exhib, 74; one-woman show, Phyllis Kind Gallery, Chicago, 75. Teaching: Vis artist, Art Inst Chicago, 71- Awards: Nat Endowment for Arts Artist's Fel, 73; Mr & Mrs Frank Armstrong Prize, 74th Artists of Chicago & Vicinity Exhib, Art Inst Chicago, 73. Bibliog: Franz Schulze (auth), Fantastic Images, Chicago Art Since 1945, Follett, 72. Mailing Add: c/o Phyllis Kind Gallery 226 E Ontario Chicago IL 60611

ROSSMAN, RUTH SCHARFF
PAINTER, INSTRUCTOR
b Brooklyn, NY. Study: Cleveland Inst Art; Case-Western Reserve Univ, BS; Kahn Inst Art; Univ Calif, Los Angeles; also with Sueo Serisawa & Rico Lebrun. Work: Pa Acad Fine Arts; Univ Redlands; Nat Watercolor Soc; Brandeis Inst; Ahmanson Collection, Calif; plus others. Exhib: Denver Mus Art Ann, 58, 59 & 62; Los Angeles Co Mus Art, Los Angeles; San Francisco Mus Art, 60; Ringling Mus Art, Sarasota, Fla, 60; Detroit Inst Art; Pa Acad Fine Arts, 60 & 65; Watercolor USA; Laguna Beach Mus Art, 60, 67, 72 & 74; Recent Paintings USA: Figure, Mus Mod Art, New York, 61; one-woman shows, Heritage Gallery, Los Angeles, 63 & 66 & Canton Community Ctr, Ohio, 67; Marymount Col; Long Beach Mus Art, Calif, 63; Butler Mus Am Art, Youngstown, Ohio, 64 & 69; Washington & Jefferson Col, 69; Chico State Col, Calif, 72; Mt St Mary's Col, 75; Palm Springs Desert Mus, Calif, 76; plus others. Teaching: Teacher art, Pub Sch Syst, Canton; teacher art, Canton Art Inst & Arts & Crafts Ctr, Los Angeles. Awards: Purchase Award, Pa Acad Fine Arts, 65; All-City Ann Purchase Awards, Los Angeles, 65 & 69; Rocky Mountain Nat, 77; plus others. Bibliog: Emily Genauer, article in New York Herald Tribune, 5/61; Fidel A Danielli (art critic), article in Artforum, 7/63 & 6/66; William Wilson & Henry Seldis (art critics), article in Los Angeles Times, 63 & 6/66. Mem: Nat Watercolor Soc (secy, 73-74, 1st vpres, 74-75, pres, 75-76). Style & Technique: Form of expressionism which evokes an emotional response in the viewer. Media: Acrylic, Oil. Mailing Add: 401 Cascada Way Los Angeles CA 90049

ROSTAND, MICHEL
PAINTER
b Sadagore-Nice, Austria; Aug 9, 95; Can citizen. Study: Art Sch Nice; Univ Vienna, LLD. Work: Mus Granby & in pvt collections of Queen Elizabeth II, Former President Eisenhower; Former VPres Rockefeller. Exhib: Mus Fine Arts, Paris, 48-50; Mus Fine Arts, Montreal, 53; Guggenheim Mus, New York, 62-63; Rembrandt Gallery, New York, 65; Dominion Gallery, Montreal, 73-74. Awards: Miniature Soc Washington, DC, 66, 71 & 75; Miniature Soc NJ, 75. Bibliog: Paul Gladu (auth), article in Le Petit J, 59; article in Rev Mod des Arts, Paris, 59 & 68; Jean Claude Leblond (auth), article in Rev: Vie des Arts, Montreal, 74. Mem: Montreal Mus Fine Arts; Soc Prof Artists, Montreal; Miniature Soc Washington, DC; Miniature Soc NJ. Style & Technique: Impressionistic with brush and knife. Media: Oil, Ink, Chalk. Dealer: Dominion Gallery 1438 W Sherbrooke Montreal PQ Can. Mailing Add: 4050 Chemin de la cote Ste Catherine Montreal PQ G0A 3M0 Can

ROSTER, FRED HOWARD
SCULPTOR, EDUCATOR
b Palo Alto, Calif, June 27, 44. Study: Gavilan Col, AA; San Jose State Col, BA & MA; Univ Hawaii, MFA & with Herbert H Sanders. Work: Honolulu Acad Art, Hawaii; State Found Cult & Arts, Honolulu; Contemp Arts Ctr Hawaii; Hawaii State Dept Educ; Hawaii Loa Col, Kailua. Comn: Ceramic sculptural pots, Flora Pacifica, Honolulu, 70; stained glass mural, Vladimir Ossipoff Corp for Hilo, Hawaii, 71; carved doors, United Church Christ, Honolulu, 74; sand cast mural, Ft Derussy, 75. Exhib: San Francisco Potters Asn Ann, DeYoung Mus, 68; Design Ten, Calif, 68; Artists of Hawaii Ann, Honolulu Acad Art, 69-72; Hawaii Craftsmen's Ann, Honolulu, 69-72; one-man show, Contemp Arts Ctr Hawaii, 72. Teaching: Instr ceramics, San Jose State Col, 68-69; asst prof sculpture, Univ Hawaii, 69-, chmn dept, 72- Awards: Elizabeth Moses Award, San Francisco Potter's Asn, 68; Sculptural Grant Award, Windward Artists Guild, 71; Hawaii Craftsman Award, 74. Mem: Honolulu Acad Art. Style & Technique: Figurative abstractions. Media: Bronze, Wood, Plastic, Clay. Mailing Add: c/o Downtown Gallery Ltd 125 Merchant St Honolulu HI 96813

ROSTER, LAILA BERGS
GALLERY DIRECTOR, ART CRITIC
b Dresden, Ger, Dec 12, 44; US citizen. Study: San Mateo Col, AA, 64; San Jose State Univ, BA, 67; Honolulu Acad Art, with Rudy Pozzatti. Work: State Found Cult & Arts, Honolulu. Exhib: Honolulu Printmakers Ann, 71-75; Hawaii Craftsmen Ann, 72-73; Windward Artists Guild Ann, 73-75; Foundry Invitation, 73-75; Artists Hawaii, Honolulu Acad Arts, 74. Exhibitons Arranged: Hawaiian Missionary Stamps, 75; Eric Yanagi Photo Essay, 75; Yousuf Karsh, Men Who Make Our World, 75; Recent Sculpture, Charles Watson, 75; Terry Tarrant Sculpture, 75; Art Out of Context, 75; Drawings by Seven Women, 75; 6 by 6 Ceramics, 75. Teaching: Teacher drawing, Honolulu Acad Arts, 69-, teacher painting, 73- Pos: Dir, Lytton Ctr Visual Arts, Palo Alto, Calif, 67-69; art critic, Star Bull, 74-; dir, Contemporary Arts Ctr Hawaii, 75- Mem: Hawaii Craftsmen (secy, 71, 72, vpres, 73-75); Hawaii Painters & Sculptors League; Honolulu Printmakers (vpres, 74); Honolulu Acad Arts. Style & Technique: Semi-realistic, semi-expressionistic. Media: Acrylic, Drawing. Specialty: Contemporary art. Publ: Contribr, Currant Mag, 75- Mailing Add: c/o Gima's Art Gallery Ala Moana Ctr Honolulu HI 96814

ROSTON, ARNOLD
ARTIST, EDUCATOR
b Racine, Wis, June 29, 18. Study: City Col New York, 35-37; Nat Acad Design, 37-39; New Sch Social Res, 39-40, with Alexey Brodovitch; Harvard Univ Grad Sch Design, 75. Work: Metrop Mus Art & Mus Mod Art, New York; New York Pub Libr Print Collection; Vatican Collection, Rome; Libr Cong, Washington, DC. Comn: Copper mural wall, Great Publ Works, Great Neck Pub Libr, NY, 71; arch graphics, Bonded Serv Co, Mex, Australia, New York and other cities around world, 67- Exhib: New York World's Fair; Pa Acad Fine Arts, Philadelphia; Brooklyn Mus Art Ann Instructors Show; Cooper Union Art Sch 90th Yr Instructors Show, Cooper-Hewitt Mus, NY; Nat Ann Exhibs Advert & Ed Art, New York. Teaching: Instr graphic design, Cooper Union, 46-53; instr graphic design, Brooklyn Mus Art Sch, 54-55; instr graphic design, Pratt Inst, 54-55. Pos: Asst art dir, New York Times, 40; visual info specialist, US Off Emergency Mgt, 41-43; creative dir, RKO-MBS, 44-56; art group head, Grey Advert Agency, 56-58; pres, Roston & Co, Great Neck, NY, 59-; art adv bd, New York Community Col, 72-75; dean grad prog media, Ctr Understanding Media, New Sch Social Res, 75- Awards: Yaddo Found Resident Fel, 38; Hemispherical Poster Awards, Mus Mod Art, 40-41; Art Dirs Gold Medal, Nat Exhib Advert & Ed Art, 54, plus others. Mem: Art Dirs Club (secy, 71-73); Art Dirs Scholar Fund (pres, 62-); Assoc Coun Arts; Sch Art League of New York Bd Educ (trustee, 69-, secy, 73-75). Interest: Works of master artists donated to Whitney Museum of American Art, Hofstra University, Joseph and Emily Lowe Museum, National Portrait Gallery of the Smithsonian and others. Collection: Master drawings, from Penni, Turner and Zuccaro to Ben Shahn, Warhol and Kuniyoshi; prints from Pissarro, Matisse and Picasso to Castellon, Teichman and Steinberg. Mailing Add: 75 Horatio St New York NY 10014

ROSZAK, THEODORE
PAINTER, SCULPTOR
b Poland, May 1, 07; US citizen. Study: Art Inst Chicago, 22-29; Univ Chicago; Univ Ill; Columbia Univ. Work: Mus Mod Art, New York; Whitney Mus Am Art; Yale Gallery Art, New Haven, Conn; Pa Acad Fine Arts; plus others. Comn: Spire & Bell Tower, Mass Inst Technol, Cambridge, 56; US Embassy Eagle, London, 60; Invocation V, Maremont Bldg, Chicago, 62; Flight, New York World's Fair, 64; Sentinel, Pub Health Lab, New York, 68. Exhib: Whitney Mus Am Art Retrospective, 56; Tate Gallery, London, 59; US Nat Exhib, Moscow, USSR, 59; Venice Biennale, 60; Guggenheim Int, New York, 64; plus others. Teaching: Prof sculpture, Sarah Lawrence Col, 40-56; vis critic, Columbia Univ, 70-72. Awards: Frank G Logan Medal for sculpture, 47 & 51 & Campagna Award, 62, Art Inst Chicago; George G Widener Gold Medal, Pa Acad Fine Arts, 56. Bibliog: Peter Selz (auth), Theodore Roszak, Mus Mod Art, 59; Michel Conil Lacolste (auth), Theodore Roszak, Dict Mod Sculpture, 60; H H Arnason (auth), Theodore Roszak, Sculptor, Art Am, 61. Mem: Drawing Soc (adv coun, 72); Louis Comfort Tiffany Found (trustee, 64-); Skowhegan Sch Painting & Sculpture (mem bd gov, 60-); Nat Inst Arts & Lett (vpres, 70). Style & Technique: Forms and ideas derived from nature and the man made world, two and three dimensional. Publ: Auth & illusr, In pursuit of an image, 55. Dealer: Pierre Matisse Art Gallery 41 E 57th St New York NY 10021. Mailing Add: One St Lukes Pl New York NY 10014

ROTAN, WALTER
SCULPTOR
b Baltimore, Md, Mar 29, 12. Study: Md Inst; Pa Acad Fine Arts; also with Albert Laessie. Work: Pa Acad Fine Arts; Brookgreen Gardens, SC. Exhib: Nat Acad Design; Pa Acad Fine Arts; Art Inst Chicago; Philadelphia Mus Art; Carnegie Inst; plus many others. Teaching: Head art dept, Taft Sch, Watertown, Conn, 38-53. Awards: Cresson Traveling Scholar, 33 & Prize, 46, Pa Acad Fine Arts; four Prizes, Nat Acad Design, 36-45; Prize, Allied Artists Am, 56; plus others. Mem: Fel Nat Sculpture Soc; Audubon Artists; fel Pa Acad Fine Arts. Mailing Add: 45 Christopher St New York NY 10014

ROTENBERG, HAROLD
PAINTER
b Attleboro, Mass, July 12, 05. Study: Mus Fine Arts, Boston; Harvard Summer Sch; Acad Grande Chaumiere, Paris; Bezalel Art Sch, Jerusalem; also with Charles Hawthorne, Provincetown, Mass. Exhib: Rockport Art Asn, Mass, 40-72; Safad, Israel, 42-72; Vose Art Gallery, Boston, 52-62; Babcock Gallery, New York, 55-60; Soc des Artistes Independants, Paris, 62-72. Teaching: Instr drawing, Sch Practical Art, Boston, 29-37; instr drawing, Boston Mus Fine Arts, 29-40. Pos: Dir art, Hecht House, Boston, 30-52. Mem: Artists Equity Asn; Rockport Art Asn; Soc Artistes Independants, Paris; Israel Artists Asn. Media: Oil. Mailing Add: 200 E 62nd St New York NY 10021

ROTH, DAVID
PAINTER
b New York, NY, June 7, 42. Study: Ill Inst Technol, study with Harry Callahan & Aaron Siskind. Work: Albright-Knox Gallery, Buffalo; Ball State Univ, Ind; Mus Contemp Art, Tehran, Iran; Philadelphia Mus Art; Rockefeller Inst, New York. Exhib: 32nd Ann for Soc Contemp Art, Art Inst Chicago, 72; Painting or Sculpture?, Newark Mus, 72; 8th Nat Print Exhib, Brooklyn Mus, 72; Small Works-Selections from Richard Brown Baker Collection, Mus Art RI Sch Design, 73; Contemp Am Artist, Cleveland Mus Art, 74; Painting & Sculpture Today, Indianapolis Mus Art, 74 & 76. Bibliog: Marcia Hafif (auth), A fusion of real & pictorial space, Arts Mag, 3/72; Tom Hinson (auth), Contemporary American Artists, Cleveland Mus Art, 73; Carter Ratcliff (auth), NY Leter, Art Int, summer 73. Style & Technique: Programs in string. Media: Liquitex (Acrylic) on string. Dealer: Robert Elkon Gallery 1063 Madison Ave New York NY 10028. Mailing Add: Box 45 Mt Kisco NY 10549

ROTH, FRANK
PAINTER
b Boston, Mass, Feb 22, 36. Study: Cooper Union, 54; Hofmann Sch, 55. Work: Albright-Knox Art Gallery, Buffalo, NY; Whitney Mus Am Art; Santa Barbara Mus Art, Calif; Baltimore Mus Art; Walker Art Ctr, Minneapolis; plus many others. Exhib: Midland Group, Nottingham, Eng, 66; Ulster Mus, Belfast, Ireland; Art in Embassies, 69; Philadelphia Art Alliance, 69; Toledo Mus Art, 69; Va Mus Fine Arts, Richmond, 70; Indianapolis Mus Art, Ind, 70; Amherst Col, 72; Contemp Am Painting, Lehigh Univ, 72; plus many other group & one-man shows. Teaching: Instr painting, State Univ Iowa, summer 64; instr painting & drawing, Sch Visual Arts, NY, 63-; Ford Found artist in residence, Univ RI, 66; instr, Univ Calif, Berkeley, 68; instr, Univ Calif, Irvine, 71. Awards: Ford Found Purchase Award, 62; Guggenheim Fel, 64; Minister Foreign Affairs Award, Int Exhib Young Artists, Tokyo, Japan, 67; plus others. Bibliog: William H Gerdts, Jr (auth), Painting & Sculpture in New Jersey, Van Nostrand-Reinhold, 64. Mailing Add: c/o Martha Jackson Gallery 521 W 57th St New York NY 10019

ROTH, JAMES BUFORD
ART CONSULTANT
b Moniteau Co, Mo, May 11, 10. Study: Kansas City Art Inst, with Ernest Lawson & Ross Braught; Fogg Mus, Harvard Univ, Carnegie grantee. Comn: Rearidos, Grace & Holy Trinity Church, Kansas City, Mo, 39 & Rockhurst Col Chapel, Kansas City, 40. Teaching: Lectr painting tech, Kansas City Art Inst, 40-49; lectr painting tech, Univ Kans, 50-74; lectr painting tech, Univ Mo, 50-74; lectr painting tech, Am Asn Mus Workshops, 70 & 72. Pos: Art conservator & restorer, William Rockhill Nelson Gallery Art, 33-74; art conservator & restorer, Atkins Mus Fine Arts, 38-74, retired; consult. Awards: Bronze Medal for painting, Midwestern Exhib, Kansas City Art Inst, 32; First Prize, Sweepstakes, Kansas City Art Inst. Mem: Fel Int Inst Conserv Artistic Hist Works; Am Inst Conserv. Res: Transfer techniques for paintings; in-painting restorations using plastics as media. Publ: Co-auth, Separation of two layers of Chinese wall painting, 52; auth, Wax relining, Am Asn Mus Bull, Notes on transfer technique, Expos Painting Conserv, 62, Conservation of paintings, Mus Roundup & Unique painting technique of George Caleb Bingham, Int Inst Conserv, 71. Mailing Add: Rte 1 Box 121 Osage Beach MO 65065

ROTHMAN, SIDNEY
GALLERY DIRECTOR, ART CRITIC
b US, May 7, 18. Study: Brooklyn Col; Columbia Univ, BA(lang & art hist); New York Sch Archit Design. Collections Arranged: New Jersey Artists Show, 68; South American Collection, 69; Yugoslavian Printmakers, 72; Collection of European Prints, Fordham Univ, 72. Teaching: Lectr art, Women's Club Island, Beach Haven, NJ, 67-68; lectr art, Deborah Hosp, Browns Mills, NJ, 69; lectr art, Long Beach Found, Loveladies, NJ, 71. Pos: Art dealer, Philadelphia area, 46-66; gallery dir, Barnegat Light, 58-; assessor of paintings, Long Beach Found Arts & Sci, 71-72. Bibliog: Dorothy Grafly (auth), articles in Art in Am, 53 & Art Focus, 11/72; Miriam Bush (auth), article in Asbury Park Press, 6/8/75; article in Philadelphia Inquirer, 8/3/75. Mem: Long Beach Found Arts & Sci (bd dirs); Ocean Co Cult & Heritage Comn, NJ; Artists Equity Asn. Res: Spanish art of time of Velasquez thru Ribera. Specialty: Showing only living artists of all mediums, sponsoring foreign contemporary artists. Publ: Auth, Articles in Beach Haven Times, 67-71; contribr, Arts of Asia, Hong Kong, 71. Mailing Add: 21st on Central Ave Barnegat Light NJ 08006

ROTHOLZ, RINA
PRINTMAKER
b Israel; US citizen. Study: Pratt Graphic Arts Ctr, New York; Brooklyn Mus Art Sch, NY. Work: Boston Mus Fine Arts; Rose Art Mus, Brandeis Univ; Mus Mod Art, New York; Israel Mus, Jerusalem; Albright-Knox Art Gallery, Buffalo, NY; plus many other pub & pvt collections. Comn: Ed of 50 prints, 69 & ed of 200 prints, Commentary Libr Collection of Art Treasure; Blue Disc (greeting card design), UNICEF, 72; 36 ingots (reprod by Franklin Mint), Judaic Heritage Soc, 73-78. Exhib: One-man shows, Pucker/Safrai Gallery, Boston, 72, 74 & 77 & Port Washington Libr, New York, 75; De Cordova Mus, Lincoln, Mass, 71; Audubon Artists, 62-75; Boston Printmakers Ann & Traveling Shows, 67-78; New Direction in American Printmaking, 68 & 69; Nat Acad, New York, 74; Queens Mus, NY, 74; Potsdam Print Exhib, State Univ NY Col, Purchase, 76; plus many other group & one-man shows. Teaching: Lectr & demonstrations, Bd Coop Educ Serv, Scholars in Residence Prog, Nassau Co, NY. Awards: First Prize for Graphics, Port Washington Ann, 70; Purchase Prize, Nassau Community Graphic Exhib, 72 & 73; Prize in Graphics, Nat Asn Women Artists, 72 & 74. Mem: Boston Printmakers; Graphic Arts Coun NY; Nat Asn Women Artists; Prof Artists Guild. Res: Discovered process of Tuilegraphy, which is the carving of vinyl asbestos tiles while they are still warm, then printing the tiles as intaglio plates to achieve a variety of textures, shapes, and high reliefs. Publ: Auth, Tuilegraphy, Artist's Proof, Vol 7. Mailing Add: 42 Shepherd Lane Roslyn Heights NY 11577

ROTHSCHILD, AMALIE (ROSENFELD)
SCULPTOR, PAINTER
b Baltimore, Md, Jan 1, 16. Study: Md Inst Col Art, dipl; New York Sch Fine & Appl Art; and with Herman Maril. Work: Corcoran Gallery Art & Phillips Collection, Washington, DC; Martenet Collection, Baltimore Mus Art; Peale Mus, Baltimore; Honolulu Acad of Arts. Comn: Design for needlepoint ark curtain, Baltimore Hebrew Congregation, 51; mural, Town House Motor Hotel, Baltimore, 60; design for needlepoint wall hanging, Sun Life Ins Co Am, Baltimore, 66; design for aggregate archit panels, Martin Luther King, Jr Elementary Sch, Baltimore, 69; design for needlepoint wall hanging, Walters Art Gallery, Baltimore, 74. Exhib: Synagogue Art Today, Jewish Mus, New York, 52; Living Today, Corcoran Gallery Art, 58, Three Artists from Washington & Baltimore, 59; solo exhib, Baltimore Mus Art, 71 & Celebration for the Artists, Nat Acad Sci, 75. Teaching: Instr painting, Metrop Sch Art, Baltimore, 56-59; lectr fine arts, Goucher Col, 60-68. Pos: Pres, Artists Union Baltimore, 48-50; organizer & chmn, Baltimore Outdoor Art Festival, 52-57; chmn, Artists' Comt, Baltimore Mus Art, 56-58; Baltimore Mus of Art (bd trustees, 77-). Awards: Prize for Painting, Baltimore Mus Art, 50, Prize for Work in Any Medium, 54; Award for Painting, Corcoran Gallery Art, 57. Bibliog: Peter Blake (auth), An American Synagogue for Today & Tomorrow, Union Am Hebrew Congregations, 54; Theodore L Low (auth), Man the maker, WMAR-TV & Walters Art Gallery, Baltimore, 60; Lincoln F Johnson, Jr (auth), Amalie Rothschild: drawings, Goucher Col, 68. Mem: Artists Equity Asn. Style & Technique: Geometric constructions of metal and diverse materials joined mechanically; hard-edge painting. Media: Metal, Wood, Acrylic. Dealer: B R Kornblatt 326 N Charles St Baltimore MD 21201. Mailing Add: 2909 Woodvalley Dr Baltimore MD 21208

ROTHSCHILD, JUDITH
PAINTER
b New York, NY. Study: Fieldston Sch, with Victor D'Amico & Alex Brook; Art Students League, with Reginald Marsh; Cranbrook Acad Art; Wellesley Col, BA(art hist); study with Hans Hofmann; Atelier 17, with Hayter. Work: Guggenheim Mus, New York; Fogg Art Mus, Harvard Univ, Cambridge, Mass; City Art Gallery, Auckland, New Zealand; First Nat Bank Chicago, Chicago & New York; Roy R Neuberger Collection, New York. Exhib: One-man shows, Rose Fried Gallery, 58, La Boetie Gallery, 68 & Lee Ault Gallery, 75 & 77, New York, Annely Juda Gallery, London, Eng, 75-76, Neuburger Mus, State Univ NY Col, Purchase, 77 & Williams Col Mus, Williamstown, Mass, 78; The Non-Objective World, Annely Juda Gallery, London, Galleria Milan, Milan & Liatowich Gallery, Basle, 73-74. Teaching: Artist in residence in painting, Univ Syracuse, 70-71; guest artist painting, Pratt Univ, summer 74 & RI Sch Design, summers 75, 76 & 77. Pos: Staff consult, Fine Arts Work Ctr of Provincetown, 71-; corres ed, Leonardo Mag, Europe, 71- Mem: Am Abstract Artists (pres); Am Fedn Arts (exec comt & bd trustees); New York Studio Sch (bd trsutees). Style & Technique: Painted reliefs, a collaging of painted papers and canvas on board to give thin, low relief effect; abstract, based on nature. Media: Oil, Collage; Silk Screen. Mailing Add: 1110 Park Ave New York NY 10028

ROTHSCHILD, LINCOLN
SCULPTOR, WRITER
b New York, NY, Aug 9, 02. Study: Columbia Univ, AB, 23, AM, 33; NY Univ Inst Fine Arts; Art Students League, with Kenneth Hayes Miller, Boardman Robinson & Allen Tucker. Work: Wood carving, Mother & Child, Whitney Mus Am Art. Teaching: Instr art hist, Columbia Univ, 25-35; asst prof art hist & chmn dept art, Adelphi Col, 46-50; lectr art hist, City Col New York, 64-68. Pos: Dir, New York Unit Index Am Design, 37-40; nat exec dir, Artists Equity Asn, 51-57; ed, Pragmatist in Art, 64- Awards: First Prize for sculpture, Village Art Ctr, 49. Mem: Col Art Asn Am; Am Soc Aesthetics; life mem Art Students League; Am Artists Cong. Style & Technique: Non-academic realism; direct carving. Media: Wood. Res: Interpretation of style; American art. Publ: Auth, Sculpture Through the Ages, 42; auth, Style in art, 60; To Keep Art Alive, (the effort of) Kenneth Hayes Miller, American Painter 1876-1956, 74; Forms and their meaning in Western Art, 76. Mailing Add: 63 Livingston Ave Dobbs Ferry NY 10522

ROTTERDAM, PAUL Z
PAINTER
b Austria, Feb 12, 39; US citizen. Study: Acad & Univ Vienna. Work: Graphische Sammlung Albertina, Vienna, Austria; Busch-Reisinger Mus, Cambridge, Mass; Neue Galeries am Landesmuseum Joanneum, Graz, Austria; MIT Collection, Cambridge; Guggenheim Mus, New York. Exhib: 4th Biennial, Paris, 65; 8th Biennial, Tokyo, 65; Whitney Biennial Am Art, 75; Acquisitions, Guggenheim Mus, 75; Susan Caldwell Gallery, New York, 75; Mus de l'Abbaye St Croix, Les Sables d'Olonne, France, 76; Mus de Nice, France, 77; Birmingham Mus Art, Ala, 77. Teaching: Lectr painting, Harvard Univ, 68- & Cooper Union Sch Art, 74-75. Style & Technique: Introspective abstraction. Dealer: Susan Caldwell 388 W Broadway New York NY 10012 Mailing Add: 115 W Broadway New York NY 10013

ROUKES, NICHOLAS M
KINETIC ARTIST, WRITER
b San Jose, Calif, Nov 22, 25. Study: San Jose State Col, Calif; Fresno State Col, BA, 49; Stanford Univ, MA, 51. Work: Can Coun Art Bank, Ottawa. Comn: Kinetic Light, Provincial Judges Court; 30 foot column, Calgary, Alta, 74. Teaching: Prof art educ & sculpture, Univ Calgary, Alta, 66- Media: Plastics; Kinetic Art. Res: New media for art, plastics, new art technology. Publ: Auth, Painting with acrylics, 65; auth, Sculpture in Plastics, 68; auth, Crafts in Plastics, 70; auth, Plastics for Kinetic Art, 74. Mailing Add: Dept of Art Univ of Calgary Calgary AB T2N 1N4 Can

ROUSE, JOHN R
CURATOR, COLLECTOR
b Cunningham, Kans. Study: Bethel Col, BA. Pos: Dir-cur, Wichita Art Asn, 72- Mem: Am Asn Mus; Am Crafts Coun; Kans Mus Asn; Mountain Plains Mus Asn. Collection: Old Staffordshire figures. Mailing Add: 1400 N Woodlawn Wichita KS 67208

ROUSSEAU-VERMETTE, MARIETTE
TAPESTRY ARTIST
b Trois Pistoles, PQ, Aug 29, 26. Study: Ecole Beaux Arts, Quebec, 48; Liebes Studio; Oakland Col Arts & Crafts, Calif. Work: Galerie Nat Can, Ottawa; Mus Quebec; many Can embassies; Univ Vancouver Arts Fac Hall; Vancouver Art Gallery. Comn: Theater stage curtains, Govt Nat Art Ctr Performing Art, 65 & J F Kennedy Ctr, Washington, DC, 71; tapestries, Macmillan Bloedel Hall, Vancouver, 68, Hall of Justice Perce, 68 & Hall of the Toronto Star, 71-72. Exhib: Biennales, Lausanne, Switz, 62, 65, 69, 71 & 76; Quebec & Ont Contemp Painters Centennial Exhib, 65; 300 Yrs Art, Nat Gallery Can, 67; Mus Mod Art, New York, 69; Mus Beaux Arts, Montreal, 61; Que Art Gallery, 72; Winnipeg Art Gallery, 76. Teaching: Prof tapestry, Ctr Art Ste-Adele, PQ, 52-56; prof tapestry, Ctr Art Laval, PQ, 70-; Banff Sch of Art, Alta & Sheridan Sch of Arts & Crafts, Mississauga, Ont, summers. Pos: Dir, Can Conf of Arts, 58-75; dir, Can Craft Coun, 74-75; dir, Royal Can Acad, 74-75. Awards: First Prize, PQ Art Contest, 57; Can Art Coun Traveling Bursary, 67; Cult Inst Rome, Italy Bursary, 72-73. Bibliog: Andre Kuenzi (auth), La Nouvelle Tapisserie, Bonvent, 73; Constantine Larsen (auth), Beyond Craft, The Art Fabric, 73; Madeleine Jarry (auth), La Tapisserie, Off du Livre, 74. Mem: Assoc Can Royal Acad (dir, 74-75); Asn Artistes Prof; World Craft Coun; Montreal Mus Fine Art. Style & Technique: Own technique developed on a basse-lisse, lowm, materiel used, very textured wool. Collection: Canadian paintings, sculptures and tapestries; graphic art; Polish tapestries, icons and paintings. Dealer: Gallery Paule Anglim 710 Montgomery St San Francisco CA 94111; Grace Borgenicht Gallery 1018 Madison Ave New York NY 10002. Mailing Add: 373 Rue Morin Ste-Adele PQ J0R 1L0 Can

ROUSSEL, CLAUDE PATRICE
SCULPTOR, INSTRUCTOR
b Edmundston, NB, July 6, 30. Study: Ecole Beaux-Arts, Montreal, PQ, 50-56; Can Coun sr traveling fel, Europe, 61. Work: Smithsonian Inst, Washington, DC; NB Mus, St John; Confedn Art Gallery, Charlottetown, P E I; Univ Moncton, NB; Mt Allison Univ, Sackville, NB. Comn: Mural, Frederickton Airport, NB, 64; mural, NB Centennial Bldg, 66; monument, fishermen, Escuminac, NB, 69; exterior sculpture & interior mural, Univ Moncton Nursing Pavillion, 71; archit sculpture for City Hall, City of St John, 72; plus 20 other archit projs. Exhib: Survey 69, Montreal Mus Fine Arts, 69; Confedn Art Gallery, 70; Air & Space Mus, Smithsonian Inst, 71; Man and His World, Montreal, 71; Owens Art Gallery, 75. Teaching: Instr art, Edmundston Pub Schs, 56-59; instr art, Univ Moncton, 63- Pos: Asst cur, Beaverbrook Art Gallery, Frederickton, 59-61. Awards: Allied Arts Medal, Royal Archit Soc Can, 64; St John City Hall Sculpture Competition, City of St John, 72; Winner of Sailing Olympics Sculpture Competition, Kingston, Ont. Bibliog: Painting a province, Nat Film Bd, 60; J Villon (auth), L'art en acadie, Rev Liberte, 70; E Michel (auth), Reseau soleil, C B C, 71; plus others. Mem: Can Artist Representation (Moncton rep, 72); Can Coun. Style & Technique: Expresses the poetry, the aspirations and problems of region. Media: Wood, Stone, Steel. Mailing Add: 905 Amirault Dieppe Moncton NB Can

ROVETTI, PAUL F
MUSEUM DIRECTOR
b New Haven, Conn, Jan 29, 39. Study: Columbia Univ, BA, 61; Cooperstown Grad Prog, MA, 66. Pos: Dir, Mattatuck Mus, Waterbury, Conn, 66-69; dir, William Benton Mus of Art, Univ Conn, Storrs, 69- Awards: Scriven Found Fel, 65-66; Nat Endowment Arts Mus Prof Fel, 73. Mem: Am Asn Mus; New Eng Conf, An Asn Mus (Conn rep, 69-); Int Coun Mus. Res: Nineteenth century American painting; nineteenth century American folk art. Publ: Auth, Dwight W Tryon: A Retrospective Exhibition (catalog), Univ Conn Mus Art, 71; co-auth, The American Earls (catalog with Harold Spencer), 72 & auth, Nineteenth Century Folk Painting: Our Spirited National Heritage, 73, William Benton Mus Art. Mailing Add: William Benton Mus of Art Bldg U-140 Storrs CT 06268

ROWAN, C PATRICK
SCULPTOR, EDUCATOR
b Milwaukee, Wis, Jan 7, 37. Study: Univ Wis-Madison, BS(archit), 62; Univ Wis-Milwaukee, BFA, 69, MS(painting), 70; Univ Fla, Gainesville, MFA(sculpture), 71. Work: Springfield Art Mus, Mo; Joslyn Art Mus, Omaha, Nebr. Comn: Outdoor sculpture, Univ Wis-Milwaukee, 73; exterior sculpture, Univ Fla, 73; exterior sculpture, Univ Nebr-Lincoln, 74; sculpture & drawing, Weeping Water Hist Mus, Nebr, 76; interior sculpture, Niobrara Community Civic Ctr, Nebr, 76. Exhib: One-man exhib, Hastings Col Fine Arts Galleries, Nebr, 73, Sheldon Mem Art Gallery, Univ Nebr-Lincoln, 76, Univ Nebr Fine Arts Galleries, Omaha, 76, Kearney State Col Art Gallery, Nebr, 76 & Millersville State Col Galleries, Pa, 77; Springfield Ann Competitive Exhib, Mo, 76; Northwestern Biennial II, Brookings, SDak, 76; 37th Ann Competition, Sioux City Art Ctr, Iowa, 76; Arena 77 Best of Show Spec Exhib, Binghamton, NY, 77. Collections Arranged: Wichita Art Mus Sculpture Exhib, Kans, 74; Nat Drawing Exhib, Southern Ill Univ, 75; Nat Sculpture 75 Touring Exhib, Huntsville, Ala, 75-76; Ward-Hasse Galleries Ann Exhib, New York, 76-77. Teaching: Asst prof drawing, painting & design, Univ Nebr-Lincoln, 71-76, assoc prof drawing, design & sculpture, 76- Pos: Art dir, All-State Fine Arts, Univ Nebr-Lincoln, 74-, design coordr, Dept of Art, 76- Awards: Purchase Award, Sioux City Ann, Sioux City Art Ctr, Iowa, 71; Best of Show, Arena 75 Exhib, Binghamton, NY, 75; Purchase Award, Great Plains Landscape Sculpture, Univ Nebr-Omaha, 76. Bibliog: J G Y Campbell (auth), Weeping Water, Nebr, Univ Nebr, Press, 76. Mem: Nat Col Art Asn; Mid-Am Col Art Asn; Am Studies Col Asn; Southern Asn of Sculptors, Inc; Am Mus of Natural Hist. Style & Technique: Primitive—integration and representation of art, archaeology and anthropology. Media: Wood, stone, canvas, bones, paint, metal and found objects. Res: Study of the integration of art, archaeology and anthropology in primitive cultures. Publ: Auth, Cybernetics and the Visual Arts, Univ Fla, 71. Mailing Add: Dept of Art Univ Nebr Lincoln NE 68588

ROWAN, DENNIS MICHAEL
PRINTMAKER, EDUCATOR
b Milwaukee, Wis, Jan 6, 38. Study: Univ Wis, BS, 62; Univ Ill, MFA, 64. Work: Art Inst Chicago; Boston Mus Fine Arts; Seattle Art Mus, Wash; Okla Art Ctr, Oklahoma City; Honolulu Acad Arts, Hawaii. Exhib: Boston Mus Fine Arts, 61, 64-65, 68-69 & 70; Milwaukee Art Ctr, 60, 61 & 62; Boston Printmakers Exhib, 61-72; Pasadena Art Mus, Calif, 62; Smithsonian Inst, Washington, DC, 62; Walker Art Ctr, Minneapolis, 62; Chicago Art Inst, 62 & 66; Pa Acad Fine Arts, 63; Albany Inst Hist & Art, 63; Seattle Art Mus, Wash, 63-65, 67, 70 & 71; six shows, Northwest Printmakers Int Exhib, Seattle, 63-71; Nat Acad Design 140th Ann, 65; William Rockhill Nelson Gallery Art, Kansas City, 68; City Art Mus, St Louis, Mo, 68; Okla Art Ctr, 68, 70 & 72; Int Print Biennale, Krakow, Poland, 68 & 74; 22nd Int Printmaking Biennale, Buenos Aires, Arg, 70; 2nd Int Printmaking Biennale, Buenos Aires, Arg, 70; Brit Int Print Biennale, Bradford, Yorkshire, Eng, 70, 72 & 74; De Cordova Mus, Lincoln, Mass, 71; 22nd Prints Nat, Libr Cong, Washington, DC, 71; Miami Art Ctr, 73; Brooklyn Mus, NY, 73; Calif Palace of Legion of Honor, San Francisco, 73; Vienna Graphics Biennale, Austria, 73; US Nat Mus, Washington, DC, 74; Kansas City Art Inst, 75; 3rd Biennale Int de l'Image, Epinal, France, 75. Teaching: Prof art, Univ Ill, Urbana-Champaign, 64-, assoc, Ctr Advan Study, 71- Awards: Purchase Award, 2nd Biennale Int Gravure, Cracow, Poland, 68; Yorkshire Arts Asn Purchase Prize, Brit Int Print Biennale, 70; Juror's Prize, Graphikbiennale Wien, Europahaus, Vienna, Austria, 72. Style & Technique: Surrealist; intaglio. Publ: Contribr, Prize-winning graphics, Vol 3, 65 & Vol 4, 66; contribr, John Ross & Clare Romano, auth, Complete Printmaker, Free Press, New York & Collier-Macmillan Ltd, Toronto, 72; contribr, Walter Chamberlin, auth, Etching & Engraving, Thames & Hudson, London, 72 & Viking Press, New York, 73. Mailing Add: 143 Fine Arts Bldg Univ Ill Champaign IL 61820

ROWAN, FRANCES PHYSIOC
PAINTER, PRINTMAKER
b Ossining, NY. Study: Randolph-Macon Woman's Col, 29-30; Cooper Union, cert, 36; also graphics with Harry Sternberg & woodcuts with Carol Summers. Work: Randolph-Macon Woman's Col, Lynchburg, Va; Freeport High Sch, NY. Exhib: Brooklyn Mus 11th Nat Print Show, 58; Audubon Artists, 58 & 59; Am Fedn Arts Traveling Show, 58-59; Knickerbocker Artists, 61; Silvermine Guild Artists 6th Nat Print Show, 66. Teaching: Instr drawing & painting, Country Art Gallery, Westbury, NY, 55-66; instr drawing & painting, Five Towns Music & Art Found, 70-72; instr drawing, still life & figure, Longboat Key Art Ctr, 77- Awards: First Prizes, Malverne Artists, 52 & Hofstra Univ, 57; Sam Flax Award, Knickerbocker Artists, 61. Mem: Prof Artists Guild; Silvermine Guild Artists. Style & Technique: Subject matter as a jumping off place, simplifying, balancing light and dark patterns and creating in experimentation. Media: Graphics. Mailing Add: 601 Broadway Box 453 Longboat Key FL 33548

ROWAN, HERMAN
PAINTER, EDUCATOR
b New York, NY, July 20, 23. Study: Cooper Union; San Francisco State Col; Kans State Col, BS; State Univ Iowa, MA & MFA. Work: Walker Art Ctr, Minneapolis; Brooklyn Mus, NY; Univ Notre Dame, South Bend, Ind; Columbus Mus, Ohio; San Diego Gallery Fine Arts, Calif. Exhib: Art USA, New York, 60; San Francisco Mus Nat Ann, 63; Southwest Ann, Houston Mus, 63; Walker Art Ctr Exhib, 65; Box-Top Art, Tour NZ Galleries, 71-72. Teaching: Prof painting, Univ Minn, Minneapolis, 63- Awards: Lyman Award, Albright Gallery, 59; Purchase Prize, San Diego Gallery Fine Arts, 63; hon mention, Calif Western Univ, 63. Style & Technique: Neo-expressionist. Media: Oil. Mailing Add: Univ Minn Minneapolis MN 55455

ROWE, CHARLES ALFRED
PAINTER, DESIGNER
b Great Falls, Mont, Feb 7, 34. Study: Mont State Univ, 52-53; Southern Methodist Univ, 56-57; Univ Chicago, 57-58; Art Inst Chicago, BFA, 60; Tyler Sch Art, Philadelphia, MFA, 68; also with John Rogers Cox, Boris Margo & Max Brill. Work: Univ Del; Sidney Mickelson Collection, Washington, DC; Great Falls Pub Schs. Comn: Designed a coord arts coun symbol & related printed materials for Mont Arts Coun, Missoula, 73; designed numerous fabrics for major accounts for Galleon Fabrics, Inc, New York, 74- Exhib: One-man shows, Mickelson Gallery, Washington, DC, 70 & 74, C M Russell Mus, Great Falls, Mont, 73 & Pleiades Gallery, New York, 77; Butler Inst Art Mid-Year Show, Youngstown, Ohio, 73; Ball State Univ Nat Drawing & Small Sculpture Show, 74; Am Painters in Paris, France, 76-77. Teaching: Prof drawing & painting, Univ Del, 64- Pos: Graphic package designer, Am Can Co, Bellwood, Ill, 60-62; graphic designer, Abrams-Bannister Engraving, Inc, Greenville, SC, 62-64; artist in residence, Nat Endowment Arts & Humanities, 72-73. Awards: Drawing of Distinction, Mead Painting of the Year Exhib, Atlanta, Ga, 64; Southeastern Art Exhib Third Prize, Atlanta Mus, 64. Bibliog: Artist in residence, Mont Arts, Vol 25, No 1; Artist employs original method and style, Great Falls Tribune, 10/72; Mary Hemple (auth), Charles Rowe, the creator of a new art form, Del Today Mag, 1/73. Style & Technique: Surrealism which tends toward a metaphysical visual image; Western and wildlife paintings; fabric illustrations vary in imagery and style depending on fashion trends. Mailing Add: 133 Aronimink Dr Chapel Hill Newark DE 19711

ROWE, REGINALD M
PAINTER, SCULPTOR
b New York, NY, Dec 8, 20. Study: Princeton Univ, BA, 44; Art Students League, with Louis Bosa, 46-47; Inst Allende, Univ Guanajuato, 58-59, MFA, 59. Comn: Mural & outdoor sculpture, Hemisfair 1968, San Antonio, Tex, 68. Exhib: Artists of the Southeast & Texas, Isaac Delgado Mus Art, New Orleans, La, 71; two-man show, Witte Mus, San Antonio, 68; one-man shows, Wellons Gallery, 52, 53 & 56, Bianchini Gallery, 60 & Ruth White Gallery, 64 & 70, New York, Watson/de Nagy Gallery, Houston, 76, Marion Koogler McNay Mus, San Antonio, Tex, 77 & Tex Christian Univ, Ft Worth, Tex, 78; Tibor De Nagy Gallery, Houston, 74; Univ NFla, 75. Teaching: Teaching: Painting drawing & design, San Antonio Art Inst, 64- Pos: Chmn exhibs, Witte Mus, 65-67; vis artist, Univ NFla, 75. Awards: San Miguel Allende, 60. Bibliog: Ernest Hemingway (auth), catalog statement for first New York show, 52; reviews in Arts, Art News, Pictures on Exhib, Times, Tribune & Art Int, 52-70. Dealer: Watson/de Nagy Gallery 1106 Berthea Houston TX 77006. Mailing Add: 219 W Gramercy San Antonio TX 78212

ROWELL, MARGIT
ART HISTORIAN
b New Haven, Conn, Nov 2, 37. Study: Inst Art Archeologie, MA; Univ Paris, PhD. Exhibitions Arranged: Piet Mondrian Retrospective Exhib, 71; Miro, Magnetic Fields (with catalog), 72; Jean Dubuffet, Retrospective (with catalog), 73; Frantisek Kupka, Retrospective (with catalog), 75. Teaching: Instr art hist, Sch Visual Arts, 69-72; instr contemp art, New Sch Social Res, 74. Pos, Cur spec exhib, Solomon R Guggenheim Mus, 73- Awards: Frank Jewett Mather Award, Col Art Asn Am, 72; Guggenheim Found Grant, 76; Nat Endowment

Arts Grant Mus Prof, 76. Mem: Int Asn Art Critics; Am Asn Mus; Int Coun Mus. Res: 20th century European art and aesthetics. Publ: Auth, Joan Miro, Abrams, 71; auth, La Peinture le geste, l'action, Klincksieck, Paris, 72. Mailing Add: 16 Greene St New York NY 10013

ROWLAND, ELDEN HART
PAINTER
b Cincinnati, Ohio, May 31, 15. Study: Cincinnati Art Acad; Cent Acad Commercial Art, Cincinnati; San Antonio Art Inst, Tex; also Jerry Farnsworth, Cape Cod & Robert Brackman, Conn. Work: Joe & Emily Lowe Gallery, Coral Gables, Fla; New Col, Sarasota; Stetson Univ, Deland; Spring Hill Col, Mobile, Ala; Berkshire Art Asn, Pittsfield, Mass. Comn: Mural paintings, Monsanto Chem, Springfield, 55. Exhib: Soc Four Arts, Palm Beach, Fla, 60; Lowe Gallery Mem Ann, 62; Cooperstown Ann, 71; Greater Schenectady Ann, NY, 71; Berkshire Art Asn Ann, 71. Teaching: Instr painting, Hilton Leech Art Sch, Sarasota. Awards: First Purchase Awards, Joe & Emily Lowe Art Gallery, 62, Spring Hill Col, 63 & Berkshire Art Asn, 71. Mem: Fla Artist Group; Sarasota Art Asn; Schenectady Art Mus; Ringling Mus Art. Style & Technique: Abstract and non-objective paintings in acrylic and collage. Publ: Auth, Painters' sutra, 72. Dealer: Gail Hinchen Gallery 56 Jean Rd Manchester CT 06040. Mailing Add: 5453 Avenida del Mare Sarasota FL 33581

ROYCE, RICHARD BENJAMIN
MASTER PRINTER, PRINTMAKER
b New York, NY, Aug 18, 41. Study: Univ Wis, BS & MA; Atelier 17, with William Stanley Hayter, Paris; Beaux-Arts, Paris. Work: State Hist Soc, Madison. Wis; Bibliot Nat, Paris. Comn: Modern Head (form schneider & printer of Roy Lichtenstein's woodcut), Germini Ltd, Los Angeles, 70; printer & publ of Etchings for Raphael Soyer, Claire Falkenstein & Joyce Treman. Exhib: Walker Biennial, Minn, 64; Salon de Mai, Paris, 66; Salon de L'Automne, Paris, 66; Salon de Jeune Sculptors, 67; Nat Print Show, Long Beach, Calif, 69. Teaching: Asst printmaking, Atelier 17, Paris, 66-67; instr printmaking, Univ Southern Calif, 67-69. Pos: Master printer & dir, Atelier Royce, West Los Angeles, 74- Awards: Justin Dart Award, Univ Southern Calif, 69. Bibliog: John Coplans (ed), article, In: Roy Lichtenstein: Graphics, Reliefs & Sculpture, 1969-70, Univ Calif, Irvine, 70; Edith Weiss (auth), Richard Royce, master printmaker Bel-Air Scene, 5/28/75; Betje Howell (auth), Artist to printmaker: a commitment to self, Los Angeles Herald Examr, 6/1/75. Mem: Los Angeles Printmakers Soc; Los Angeles Co Mus Print Coun; Los Angeles Inst Contemp Art; Artists Equity; Los Angeles Co Mus. Style & Technique: Etching and engraving, subjective and objective. Media: Printmaking, Sculpture. Publ: Illusr, Paris Rev, 67. Mailing Add: c/o Atelier Royce 2231 Carmelina Ave W Los Angeles CA 90064

ROYSHER, HUDSON (BRISBINE)
DESIGNER, ART ADMINISTRATOR
b Cleveland, Ohio, Nov 21, 11. Study: Cleveland Art Inst, grad dipl, 34; Western Reserve Univ, MS, 34; Univ Southern Calif, MFA, 48. Work: Univ Buffalo, NY; Univ Southern Calif, Los Angeles; Syracuse Univ, NY; Calif State Univ, Los Angeles; Bethune-Cookman Col, Daytona Beach, Fla. Exhib: US State Dept Traveling Exhib, 50-52; Eleven Southern Californians, De Young Mem Mus, San Francisco, Calif, 52; Smithsonian Inst Traveling Exhib, 53-55; Designer Craftsmen of the West Traveling Exhib, 57; Masters of Contemporary American Crafts Exhib, Brooklyn Mus, 61. Teaching: Asst prof indust design, Univ Southern Calif, 39-42; head div indust design, Chouinard Art Inst, 45-50; prof art, Calif State Univ, Los Angeles, 50-70, chmn dept art, 70- Awards: Spec award for continued excellence, Cleveland Mus Art, 40 & 46; outstanding prof award, 66 & outstanding educator award, 72, trustees of Calif State Univ & Cols. Bibliog: A welded steel education, Design Mag, 1/51; H E Winter (auth), Three American silversmiths, Amerika, 5/53; Churches and temples, Progressive Archit, 10/56. Mem: Indust Designers Soc Am; Am Asn Univ Prof (chap pres); Southern Calif Designer Craftsmen; Am Craftsman's Coun; Asn Calif State Univ Prof (chap pres, 63-65 & 71-72). Style & Technique: Exclusively ceremonial and ecclesiastical appointments in gold, silver, bronze, marble, enamel and accessory materials. Mailing Add: 1784 S Santa Anita Ave Arcadia CA 91006

ROZMAN, JOSEPH JOHN
PAINTER, PRINTMAKER
b Milwaukee, Wis, Dec 26, 44. Study: Univ Wis, Milwaukee, BFA(with honors); MFA. Work: Milwaukee Art Ctr, Wis; De Cordova Mus, Lincoln, Mass; Southwest Tex State Col; Univ Wis, Milwaukee; Wis State Univ-Stevens Point; plus others. Comn: Complete ed of etchings for membership drive, Milwaukee Art Ctr, 69; Award Emblem Design, Lakefront Festival of Arts, Milwaukee Art Ctr, 73 & 77. Exhib: Young Printmakers Nat, Herron Mus of Art, Indianapolis, 67; 19th, 20th & 21st Boston Printmakers Nat, Boston Mus Fine Arts, 67-69; Nat Print & Drawing Exhib, Okla Art Ctr, Oklahoma City, 67-68 & 72; Int NW Printmakers Exhib, Seattle Art Mus & Portland Art Ctr, 68 & 69; 3rd, 4th & 5th Pratt Int Miniature Print Traveling Exhib, NY, 68, 71 & 75; Colorprint USA, WTex Mus, 69 & 71; Printmaking-Wis Ed, Milwaukee Art Ctr, 72; Small Environments, Southern Ill Univ, Carbondale & Madison Art Ctr, 72; 20 Am Printmakers, State Univ NY Col Oneonta, 72; one-man show, Milwaukee Art Ctr, 73; The Collagraph—A Survey, Pratt Graphics Ctr, New York, 75; Wis Dir, Inaugural Exhib of New Milwaukee Art Ctr, 75; Artists/Toys Exhib, Milwaukee Art Ctr, 77; plus others. Teaching: Instr printmaking, Milwaukee Art Ctr, 68-76; instr printmaking & painting, Carthage Col, 69-72; vis lectr art, Univ Wis, Parkside, 70-71; instr printmaking & design, Layton Sch Art & Design, 73-74; asst prof printmaking, painting & film, Mt Mary Col (Wis), 75- Awards: Mr & Mrs Frank G Logan Medal & Prize, Art Inst Chicago, 66; Purchase Award, 23rd Nat Boston Printmakers Exhib, De Cordova Mus, 71; Main Award, Watercolor Wis, Wustum Mus of Fine Arts, 77. Bibliog: James Auer (auth), They call him the Wizard of Roz, Milwaukee J, 3/11/73; Genene Grimm (auth), Joe Rozman: The busiest boy on the block, Art Scene Mag, 2/69; Chris Kohlmann (auth), Milwaukee's fantastic imagery, Midwest Art, 4/74. Mem: Boston Printmakers. Graphics Soc; Wis Painters & Sculptors. Style & Technique: 3-D constructed watercolored fantasy paintings; heavily embossed etchings; collage animated films. Mailing Add: 4419 Lindermann Ave Racine WI 53405

ROZZI, (JAMES A)
PAINTER, SCULPTOR
b Pittsburgh, Pa, Jan 22, 21. Work: State Capitol, Carson City, Nev; Favell Mus, Klamath Falls, Ore; Elks Lodge, Las Vegas; State Bicentennial Comt, Nev. Comn: Mural, Valley of Fire State Park Visitors Ctr, Nev, 68. Exhib: US Army Nat Art Exhib, Dallas, Tex, 45; Heldorado Western Art Show, Las Vegas, 69-75; Death Valley Western Art Show, Calif, 70-75; Nev Bicentennial Calendar Competition, 75; George Phippen Mem Art Show, Prescott, Ariz, 75. Teaching: Teacher adult educ, San Bernardino Valley Col, Calif, 49-60; teacher drawing, Las Vegas Art League, 67-69. Pos: Pres, Arts & Crafts Guild, Las Vegas, 63-65. Awards: First Place Purchase Awards, Elks Lodge, Las Vegas, 69, 73 & 74; First Place Trophy for Oils, Death Valley 49'ers, 71; Third Place Medal, George Phippen Mem Comt, 75. Bibliog: Ray Chesson (staff writer), article in, Rev J, 71; Florine Lawlor (staff writer), article in, Las Vegas Sun Newspaper, 71. Mem: Nat Cowboy Hall Fame; Nat Soc Lit & Arts. Media: Oil, Watercolor; Bronze. Interest: Western Americana subjects. Publ: Illusr, Loma Linda Med Col Handbook, 51; illusr, San Bernardino Valley Col Handbook, 58; auth, Screen Process Mag, 58; illusr, Las Vegas Jazz Festival Mag, 63; illusr, True West Mag, 71. Mailing Add: 1041 Franklin Ave Las Vegas NV 89104

RUBEN, LEONARD
DESIGNER, EDUCATOR
b St Paul, Minn, June 3, 21. Study: Pratt Inst, cert, 48, BFA, 50; Columbia Univ, MA, 61; NY Univ, PhD, 70. Work: Designers Register, Nat Endowment Arts, Washington, DC; Mus Art Sci & Indust, Bridgeport, Conn; Young & Rubicam, NY. Exhib: Clio Awards, New York, 69-74; Am Inst Graphic Arts, 73; Int Broadcasters Award, Hollywood, 73; Int Film & TV Festival, New York, 73-75; Designers Register, Nat Endowment Arts, Washington, DC, 74-75. Teaching: Assoc prof art & advert, Univ Tex, Austin, 71- Pos: Art dir, Young & Rubicam, New York, 51-60; creative dir, Lake, Spiro, Shurman, Memphis, Tenn, 68-69; pres, Ruben & Ruben, Austin, Tex, 72- Awards: Communication Graphics First Award, Am Inst Graphic Arts, 73; Golden Spike, First Place, Int Broadcasting Award, 73; Silver Medal, Int Film & TV Festival, 73-75. Mem: Am Inst Graphic Arts, New York; Dallas-Ft Worth Soc Visual Communications. Style & Technique: Designer for TV, humor, simplicity; for print, strength, concept, type excitement. Media: TV, Film & Video Tape. Publ: Designer, Augustus Vincent Tack, 72; designer, Color Forum, 72; designer, The Twenties, 73. Mailing Add: Rte 7 Box 722 C Austin TX 78703

RUBEN, RICHARDS
PAINTER, EDUCATOR
b Los Angeles, Calif, Nov 29, 25. Study: Chouinard Art Inst. Work: Wooster Mus, Mass; Brooklyn Mus, NY; Los Angeles Co Mus Art; Corcoran Gallery Art, Washington, DC; Pasadena Art Mus, Calif. Exhib: Pittsburgh Int, 55; Sao Paulo 111rd Biennial, Brazil, 55; 1st Paris Biennial, France, 59; Whitney Mus Am Art, 62-63 & 64; Arte de America y Espana, Madrid, Spain, 63; San Francisco Mus Art, Calif, 71; one-man exhib, Johnson Mus, Cornell Univ. Teaching: Asst prof drawing & painting, Pomona Col, 58-62; asst prof drawing & painting, NY Univ, 63-; instr drawing & painting, Pratt Inst, 67-71. Awards: First Prize for oil, San Francisco Mus Art, 53; Tiffany Grant, 54; Tamarind Fel, 61. Mailing Add: 85 Mercer St New York NY 10012

RUBENSTEIN, LEWIS W
PAINTER, PRINTMAKER
b Buffalo, NY, Dec 15, 08. Study: Harvard Univ, AB, traveling fel, Europe; also with Leger & Ozenfant, Paris, frescoes with Rico Lebrun & lithography with Emil Ganso, Rome; plastic painting media with Jose Gutierez & sumi with Keigetsu, Tokyo. Work: Ford Found, New York; Am Univ, Washington, DC; Vassar Col Art Gallery, Poughkeepsie, NY; US Info Agency; Addison Gallery Am Art. Comn: Frescoes, Busch-Reisinger Mus, Cambridge, Mass, 37; murals, Post Off, US Sect Fine Arts, Wareham, Mass, 40 & Jewish Ctr, Buffalo, 50; four paintings, Marine Midland Nat Bank, Poughkeepsie, 65. Exhib: Whitney Mus Am Art, 38, Nat Acad Design, 46, 52, 56 & 63, New York; Vassar Col Art Gallery, 40-74, retrospective, 74; Libr Cong, Washington, DC, 52-60; Soc Am Graphic Artists, New York, 52-77; Am Watercolor Soc, New York, 55 & 64; Retrospective, Schenectady Mus, NY, 75. Teaching: Instr fresco painting, Boston Mus Sch Art, 37-38; prof painting, Vassar Col, 39-74; instr fresco painting, Univ Buffalo, summer 41. Awards: Am Artists Group & Knobloch Prizes, Soc Am Graphic Artists, 52 & 54; Fulbright Grant, Japan, 57-58; Fairfield Award, Silvermine Guild Artists, 59. Bibliog: Guillermo Rivas (auth), Lewis Rubenstein, Mex Life, 8/51; Erica Beckh Rubenstein (auth), Lewis Rubenstein's Time Painting, Vassar Alumnae Mag, 5/57; Masao Ishizawa (auth), Rubenstein and his sumi painting, Hoshun, Japan, 2/25/59. Mem: Soc Am Graphic Artists. Style & Technique: Time painting (originated by Lewis Rubenstein), continuous scroll paintings seen moving through special viewing frames. Publ: Auth, Fresco painting today, Am Scholar, 35; Time Painting (film), 56-57 & Ceremony for a New Planet (film), 72, Vassar Col; illusr, Foreign Serv J, 58-66; co-auth, Psalm 104 (film), Weston Woods Studios, 70. Mailing Add: 153 College Ave Poughkeepsie NY 12603

RUBIN, ARNOLD GARY
ART HISTORIAN
b Richmond, Va, July 24, 37. Study: Rensselaer Polytech Inst, 55-60, BArch; Ind Univ, Bloomington, MA(art hist), 64, PhD(art hist), 69. Collections Arranged: Sculpture of Black Africa: Paul Tishman Collection (with catalog), Los Angeles Co Mus Art, 68; Yoruba Sculpture in Los Angeles Collections (with catalog), Pomona Col, Claremont, Calif, 69; Sculptor's Eye: The African Art Collection of Mr & Mrs Chiam Gross, Mus African Art, Washington, DC. Teaching: Assoc prof art of Africa, Oceania & Native Am, Univ Calif, Los Angeles, 67- Awards: Foreign Area Fel Prog Dissertation Res Grant, Am Coun Learned Socs/Social Sci Res Coun, Ford Found, 64-66; Fulbright-Hays African Area Studies Ctr Fac Res Grant, Dept Health, Educ & Welfare, 69-70. Mem: Col Art Asn Am. Res: Art of Africa, Oceania, Native America, especially the Benue River Valley of Northern Nigeria. Publ: Auth, Bronzes of the Middle Benue, WAfrican J Archaeol, 73 & Accumulation: Power & display in African sculpture, 75, Art Forum. Mailing Add: Dept of Art Dickson Art Ctr Univ of Calif Los Angeles CA 90024

RUBIN, DONALD VINCENT
SCULPTOR
b New York, NY, July 10, 37. Exhib: Central South Exhib, The Parthenon, Nashville, 73, 74; Death Valley Art Exhib, Calif, 74-77; George Phippen Mem Western Art Show, Prescott, Ariz, 75; Salmagundi Club Graphics & Sculpture Exhib, New York, 75-78; 1st Ann Exhib, Nat Acad Design, New York, 76; Bicentennial Art Exhib, Los Angeles Mus Sci & Indust, 76; one-man shows, Brass Door Galleries, Houston, 77, Hunter Gallery, San Francisco, 77 & Indian Paint Brush, Vail, Colo, 77. Awards: Richman Award for Distinguished Sculptures, Salmagundi Club, 75, 76 & 77. Bibliog: Ralph Perrill (auth), Capturing the freedom and toughness of the Old West, SW Art Mag, 9/77. Mem: Am Artists Prof League; Soc Animal Artists; Salmagundi Club. Style & Technique: Realistic Western Americana. Media: Bronze. Dealer: Hunter Gallery 278 Post St San Francisco CA 94108; Kennedy Galleries 40 W 57th St New York NY 10019. Mailing Add: 305 Meadowbrook Dr Huntsville AL 35803

RUBIN, IRWIN
PAINTER, DESIGNER
b Brooklyn, NY, July 26, 30. Study: Brooklyn Mus Sch Art; Cooper Union Art Sch; Yale Univ, BFA & MFA. Exhib: Fla State Univ, 60; Baltimore Mus Art, 60; Bertha Schaefer Gallery, NY, 60-63; Stable Gallery, NY, 64; Byron Gallery, 65; plus others. Teaching: Instr drawing & color design, Univ Tex, 55; asst prof, Fla State Univ, 56-58; instr, Pratt Inst, Brooklyn, 64-; assoc prof art Cooper Union Art Sch, 67- Pos: Art dir, McGraw-Hill Bk Co, New York, 58-63; art dir, Harcourt Brace Jovanovich, Inc, New York, 71- Publ: Auth, Permanency in collage, Arts Mag, 57. Mailing Add: 126 Lincoln Pl Brooklyn NY 11217

RUBIN, LAWRENCE
ART DEALER, COLLECTOR
b New York, NY, Feb 22, 33. Study: Brown Univ; Columbia Univ, BA; Univ Paris. Pos: Dir, Knoedler Contemp Art, New York. Specialty: Painters Stella, Motherwell, Poons, Louis, Bannard, Olitski, Holland, Sander and Dzubas; sculptors Caro, Arman and Scott. Collection: Contemporary painting and sculpture. Mailing Add: 118 E 61st St New York NY 10021

RUBIN, WILLIAM
ART CURATOR, ART HISTORIAN
b New York, NY, Aug 11, 27. Study: Columbia Univ, AB, MA & PhD; Univ Paris. Exhibitions Arranged: Dada, Surrealism & Their Heritage, 68, New Am Painting & Sculpture, 69, Stella, 70, Picasso, 72 & Miro, 73, in the Collection of Mus Mod Art, The Paintings of Gerald Murphy, 74, Anthony Caro, 75, Andre Masson, 76 & Cezanne: The Late Work, 77 (with catalogs). Teaching: Prof art hist, Sarah Lawrence Col, 52-67; prof art hist, City Univ New York Grad Div, 60-68; adj prof art hist, NY Univ Inst Fine Arts, 68- Pos: Am art ed, Art Int Mag, 59-64; chief cur painting & sculpture, Mus Mod Art, New York, 68-73, dir painting & sculpture, 73- Publ: Auth, Modern sacred art and the Church of Assy, 61, Dada and surrealist art, 69; plus others. Mailing Add: Museum of Modern Art 11 W 53rd St New York NY 10019

RUBINS, DAVID KRESZ
SCULPTOR
b Minneapolis, Minn, Sept 5, 02. Study: Beaux Arts Inst Design, New York; Ecole Beaux Arts & Acad Julian, Paris, asst to James E Fraser. Work: Minneapolis Inst Art, Minn; Ind Univ, Bloomington; Indianapolis Mus Art, Ind. Comn: Figure on Steps, Arch Bldg, Washington, DC, 33; work in Riley Hosp, Indianapolis, 36-72; Lilly Monument, Crown Hill Cemetery, Indianapolis, 61; Lincoln Monument, State Off Bldg Plaza, Indianapolis, 64. Exhib: Archit League, New York, 33; Nat Acad Design, New York, 33; Ind Artists Ann, Indianapolis, 36-70; Am Sculpture Today, Metrop Mus Art, 51. Teaching: From instr to prof sculpture & anat, Herron Sch Art, Indianapolis, 35- & sculptor-in-residence. Awards: Fel Am Acad Rome, 28; Nat Inst Arts & Lett Grant sculpture, 54. Style & Technique: Idealistic realism. Publ: Auth, The Human Figure—an Anatomy for Artists, Viking Press, 53. Mailing Add: 3923 La Salle Ct Indianapolis IN 46205

RUBINSTEIN, SUSAN R
PHOTOGRAPHER
b New York, NY, May 17, 46. Study: Brooklyn Mus Art Sch; Am Univ, BA(fine arts & graphic design); Art Ctr Col of Design, Los Angeles, Calif, photog with Todd Walker. Work: Denver Mus of Art, Colo; Bibliot Nat de Paris, France; Exchange Nat Bank of Chicago; Mus of Art & Hist, Fribourg, Switz; Het Sterckhof Mus, Antwerp, Belg. Exhib: Ironic Reality, San Jose Mus of Art, Calif, 74-75; White Plains Pub Libr, NY, 75; Am Ctr, Stockholm, Sweden, 75; Le Mus Francais de la Photog, Bieures, France, 76; NY State Artists Series, Herbert F Johnson Mus of Art, Ithaca, 77; Landscape in Photog, Prakapas Gallery, New York, 77; Art in Pub Spaces, Orgn Independent Artists, New York, 77. Teaching: Workshop on photog exploration of reality and illusion, Marymount Manhattan Col, New York, 78. Bibliog: John Hunter (auth), Ironic Reality, Art Week, 1/75; Jacques J Halber (auth), Brief vit Belge, Foto, 3/77; Arthur Secunda (auth), article in Visual Dialogue, winter 77-78. Mem: Soc Photog Educators. Style & Technique: Interplay of reality and illusion. Media: Light. Dealer: Susan Spiritus Gallery 3336 Via Lido Newport Beach CA 92663. Mailing Add: 463 West St D816 New York NY 10014

RUBLE, RONALD L
PRINTMAKER, PAINTER
b St Louis, Mo, Aug 15, 35. Work: Metrop Mus & Art Ctr, Miami, Fla; Henderson Mus, Univ Colo, Boulder; Theodore Lyman Wright Art Ctr, Beloit Col, Fine Arts Ctr, Viterbo Col, La Crosse, Oshkosh Pub Mus, Wis. Exhib: Mach 1, 2nd Int Graphics Biennial, Metrop Mus, Miami, 2nd NH Int Graphics Ann, Arts & Sci Ctr, Nashua, 3rd Hawaii Nat Print Exhib, Honolulu Acad Arts, 3rd Nat Print Exhib, Otis Art Inst, Los Angeles, 15th Nat Print Exhib, Bradley Univ, Peoria, Ill, 75. Awards: Hon Mention, Silvermine Guild Artists, 74; Purchase Award, Univ Colo, 74; Purchase Award, Dee & Dan Rowlands, Metrop Mus & Art Ctr, Miami, 75. Mem: The Graphic Soc, Hollis, NH; assoc mem Soc Am Graphic Artists. Style & Technique: Figurative landscapes and interiors; etching and lithography; painting, tempera technique. Media: Etching, Lithography; Acrylic, Watercolor. Mailing Add: c/o New Morning Gallery 3 1/2 Kitchen Pl Asheville NC 28803

RUDA, EDWIN
PAINTER
b New York, NY, May 15, 22. Study: Columbia Univ, MA, 49; Sch Painting & Sculpture, Mexico City, 49-51; Univ Ill, MFA, 56. Work: State of NY Collection, Albany Mall; Indianapolis Mus Art, Ind; Dallas Mus Fine Art, Tex; Nat Gallery of Australia, Canberra; Mass Inst Technol, Cambridge. Exhib: Smithsonian Traveling Exhib, Latin Am, 66; Systemic Painting, Guggenheim Mus, 66 & Whitney Mus Am Art Painting Ann, 69, New York; Two Generations of Color Painting, Inst Contemp Art, Philadelphia, 70; Gallery A, Sydney, Australia, 71; Painting & Sculpture Today, Indianapolis, Ind; Paintings on Paper, Aldrich Mus Contemp Art, Ridgefield, Conn; 73 Biennial, Whitney Mus Am Art, New York; Contemp Am Painting & Sculpture, Krannert Art Mus, Univ Ill, Urbana, 74; 10th Anniversary Exhib 1964-1974, Aldrich Mus Contemp Art, 74; Baltimore Mus, 75, Drawing Show, 76; Benefit Exhib for Udine, Italy, NY Univ, 76; one-man show, Max Hutchinson Gallery, New York, 77. Teaching: Instr painting, Univ Tex, Austin, 56-59; instr painting, Sch Visual Arts, New York, 67-71. Pos: Co-founder, Park Pl Gallery Art Res. Bibliog: Carter Ratcliff (auth), Striped for action, Artnews, 2/72; Dore Ashton (auth), New York Commentary, Studio Int, 2/70; Peter Schjeldahl (auth), In and out of step in Soho, New York Times, 10/73. Publ: Auth, Park Place 1963-67: some informal notes in retrospect, Art Mag, 67; auth, Jack Krueger: frontiers of zero, Artforum, 4/68. Mailing Add: c/o Max Hutchinson Gallery 138 Greene St New York NY 10012

RUDDLEY, JOHN
ART ADMINISTRATOR, PAINTER
b New York, NY, Oct 29, 12. Study: Cooper Union Sch Art & Archit, with Tully Filmus, Ernest Fiene & Paul Feeley; DaVinci Sch Art; Columbia Univ, BS(hist art); Columbia Univ, MA(art educ). Work: Corcoran Sch Art, Washington, DC; Arts Club Washington. Exhib: Corcoran Gallery Art, Washington, DC, 63; Arts Club Washington, 63; Corcoran Sch Art, 63-64; Avant Gallery, Alexandria, Va, 64; Columbia Univ Gallery, New York, 65. Teaching: Prof design & painting, Corcoran Sch Art, 62-64; prof hist art, Lab Inst Design, New York, 64-69; prof painting, Pace Col, Pleasantville, NY, 70-71. Pos: Dean & head, Corcoran Sch Art, 62-65; supvr art, Westchester Co, White Plains, NY, 65-; dir, Westchester Art Workshop, 65-; trustee, Hammond Mus, North Salem, NY, 69-; bd govs, Cooper Union, New York, 69- Mem: Am Soc Aesthetics; Arts Club Washington; Inst Study Art; Int Soc Educ Art; Nat Art Educ Asn. Style & Technique: Personal concepts of form and color to compositionally express in contemporary style man's interaction with his environment. Media: Acrylic, Oil, Watercolor. Publ: Auth, Series of book reviews, Nat Art Educ Asn J, 64-72. Mailing Add: 97-40 62nd Ave Rego Park New York NY 11374

RUDQUIST, JERRY JACOB
PAINTER, INSTRUCTOR
b Fargo, NDak, June 13, 34. Study: Minneapolis Col Art & Design, BFA, 56; Cranbrook Acad Art, MFA, 58. Work: Walker Art Ctr & Univ Minn Gallery, Minneapolis; Minneapolis Inst Arts; St Cloud State Col & Anoka Ramsey State Jr Col, Minn. Exhib: Walker Art Ctr, Minneapolis, 58, 60, 62, 65 & 77; Minneapolis Art Inst, 59, 61, 63, 65 & 75; Minn Portfolio (traveling exhib, Middle East & Europe), St Paul Gallery, 60; Denver Art Mus, Colo, 63; Joslyn Mus Art, Omaha, Nebr, 64, 68 & 70; Art Across America, Mead Nat Painting Exhib, Columbus, Ohio, 65; Birmingham Mus Art, Ala, 66; Art in the Embassies Prog, US State Dept, 68-71; New Art from the Twin Cities, Chicago, 70; Drei Amerikaner aus dem Mittleren Western, Mannheimer Symposion der Kunste, WGer, 72; one-man exhibs, Walker Art Ctr, Minneapolis, 63 & Minneapolis Inst Arts, 64, 71 & 75; Colo 1st Nat Print & Drawing Competition, 74; Rutgers Nat Drawing Exhib, 75; Emporia State Univ, 78. Teaching: Prof art, Macalester Col, 58-; vis lectr & critic art, Boston Univ, summer 69. Awards: Spec Donor & Purchase Award, Walker Art Ctr, 62; Purchase Award, Minneapolis Inst Arts, 65; Purchase Award, World Print Competition, San Francisco, 73. Bibliog: Dan Paris (auth), Rudquist (film), produced by Minneapolis Inst Arts, Macalester Col & Minn State Arts Coun, 71; Samuel Sachs II (auth), Jerry Rudquist: recent works, Minneapolis Inst Arts, 71. Media: Oil. Dealer: Suzanne Kohn Gallery 1690 Grand Ave St Paul MN 55105. Mailing Add: 2322 Seabury Ave S Minneapolis MN 55406

RUDY, CHARLES
SCULPTOR
b York, Pa, Nov 14, 04. Study: Pa Acad Fine Arts, Philadelphia. Work: Pa Mus Fine Arts; Brookgreen Gardens, Georgetown, SC; Philadelphia Mus, Pa; Metrop Mus Art, New York; Carnegie Inst, Pittsburgh, Pa. Comn: US Post Off, Bronx, NY, 39; US Govt Bldg, 39; five stone figures (with Roy Larson), Va Polytech Inst, Blacksburg, 54; sculpture (with Willard Hahn), Lehigh Co Ct House, 64; bronze gates (with Edward Green), William Penn Hist Mus, Harrisburg, Pa, 64. Exhib: Pa Acad Fine Arts, Philadelphia, 28-68; Whitney Mus Am Art, 36-53, Metrop Mus Art, 50 & Nat Acad Design, 50-71, New York; Art Inst Chicago, 39-52. Teaching: Head dept sculpture, Cooper Union, 31-41; instr sculpture, Pa Acad Fine Arts, 50-52. Pos: Mem Art Comn Pa, 49-72. Awards: Guggenheim Found Fel, 42; Gold Medal, Nat Sculpture Soc, 73; Hall of Fame, York, Pa, 77. Bibliog: Scrap sculpture welding, Life, 12/20/43. Mem: Nat Acad Design; Nat Sculpture Soc; Pa Acad Fine Arts. Media: Bronze, Wood, Terra Cotta. Publ: Auth, Challenge to form, Mag Art, 40. Mailing Add: PO Box 106 Ottsville PA 18942

RUELLAN, ANDREE
PAINTER
b New York, NY, Apr 6, 05. Study: Art Students League, scholar, 20-22; Maurice Sterne Sch, Rome, scholar, 22-23; Acad Suedoise, Paris, with Per Krogh & Charles Dufresne. Work: Oils, Fogg Mus, Harvard Univ; Metrop Mus Art, New York; Phillips Mem Gallery, Washington, DC & Columbia Mus Art, SC; drawings, Whitney Mus Am Art, New York. Comn: Murals, Post Off, Emporia, Va, 40 & Lawrenceville, Ga, 41. Exhib: Carnegie Inst Int, 30-50; 10 ann, Whitney Mus Am Art; Grantees Exhib, Am Acad Arts & Lett, 45; Am Painting Today, Metrop Mus Art, 50; Storm King Art Ctr Retrospective, 66; Artists for Victory, Metrop Mus Art, New York; Pa Acad Fine Arts Ann; Detroit Mus; Mus City New York; Art Inst Chicago; Corcoran Gallery, Washington, DC; Springfield Mus Art, Mass; Libr Cong, Washington, DC; Va Mus Fine Arts, Richmond; Heckscher Mus, New York; Retrospective, Lehigh Univ; one-person show, Woodstock Art Acad, 77. Teaching: Vis artist, Pa State Univ, summer 57. Awards: Am Acad Arts & Lett Grant, 45; Pennell Mem Medal, Philadelphia Watercolor Club, 45, Dawson Medal, 50; Guggenheim Found Fel, 50-51. Bibliog: Harry Salpeter (auth), About Andree Ruellan, Coronet, 12/38; Ernest Watson (auth), Andree Ruellan, Am Artist, 10/43; Arthur Zaidenburg (auth), The Art of the Artist, Crown, 51. Mem: Woostock Artists Asn; Art Students League; Philadelphia Watercolor Club. Media: Oil, Gouache, Graphics. Dealer: Kraushaar Galleries 1055 Madison Ave New York NY 10028. Mailing Add: Shady NY 12479

RUFFING, ANNE ELIZABETH
PAINTER
b Brooklyn, NY. Study: Cornell Univ, BS; Drexel Inst Technol; also studied with John Pike. Work: Metrop Mus Art, New York; Brooklyn Mus, NY; Libr of Cong; Charles Warren Ctr, Harvard Univ, Cambridge, Mass; Libr of Nat Collection of Fine Arts, Smithsonian Inst, Washington, DC; plus many others. Comn: Four Wildlife Drawings, Johnston Hist Mus, North Brunswick, NJ, 76; four hist landmark lithographs, NY State Senate, comn by City of Kingston, NY, 76. Exhib: 14th Ann Exhib Painting & Sculpture, Berkshire Mus, Mass, 65; Cooperstown Ann Nat Art Exhib, Cooperstown Mus, NY, 69; Int Women's Arts Festival, World Trade Ctr, New York, 75-76; Rocky Mountain Nat Watermedia Exhib, Golden, Colo, 76; 25th Ann Exhib Painting & Sculpture, Berkshire Mus, 76; one-woman shows, Art in Industry, Int Bus Machines Corp, New York, 66 & A E Ruffing Exhib, Hall of Fame, Goshen, NY, 71. Awards: First Place, Watercolor, Eric Sloane Day Exhib, Eric Sloane, 74; Int Women's Year Award, Int Women's Arts Festival, D Gillespie, 76. Bibliog: Bruce Henry Davis (auth), Introducing the art of A E R, 1/77, Memories of Childhood, 2/77 & Glimpses of yesterday, 7/77, Collector's News, Am Masters Found. Style & Technique: Representational landscapes, children and wildlife. Media: Watercolor, pen and ink. Publ: Illusr, Ideals Old Fashioned Issue (title page plus two others), Ideals, 75. Mailing Add: Box 125 Bloomington NY 12411

RUFFO, JOSEPH MARTIN
PRINTMAKER, DESIGNER
b Norwich, Conn, Dec 6, 41. Study: Pratt Inst; Cranbrook Acad Art. Work: Brooks Mem Art Gallery, Memphis, Tenn, Ark Art Ctr, Little Rock; Mus Mod Art, Salvador, Brazil; Memphis Acad Arts, Tenn; Miss Art Asn, Jackson. Exhib: 48th Ann Print Exhib, Soc Am Graphic Artists, New York, 67; 12th Ann Mid South Exhib, Memphis, 67; 10th Dixie Ann, Montgomery Mus Art, 69; Nat Print & Drawing Exhib, Miss Art Asn, 69; Miami Art Ctr Mem Exhib, 71. Teaching: Instr art, Memphis Acad Arts, 64-68; instr art, Fla Mem Col, 69-77; asst prof art & chmn dept, Barry Col, 69-74, chmn div fine arts, 74-77. Awards: Fulbright Grant, Brazil, 63; Best in Show, 12th Ann Mid South Exhib, 67, Purchase Prize, 10th Dixie Ann Prints & Drawings, 68. Style & Technique: Representational etchings silkscreen and lithography combinations. Mailing Add: 2500 Iowa St Cedar Falls IA 50613

RUGGLES, JOANNE BEAULE
PRINTMAKER, EDUCATOR
b New York, NY, May 19, 46. Study: Akron State Univ; Ohio State Univ, BFA(painting) & MFA(painting, printmaking & photography). Work: Ohio State Univ, Columbus; Calif

Polytech State Univ, San Luis Obispo. Exhib: Refocus, Univ Iowa, 70; Akron Inst Ann, 70; 48th Ann Spring Show, Erie Art Ctr, 70; Ann All Ohio Show, Canton Art Inst, 71-72 & 77; 7th Ann Print Exhib, Brand Libr Art Gallery, 77; 21st Ann Print Exhib, Hunterdon Art Ctr, 77; 11th Nat Print & Drawing Competition, Dulin Gallery of Art, 77; 20th Nat Print & Drawing Competition, Okla Art Ctr, 78; one-woman shows, Ohio State Univ, 70 & Canton Art Inst, 77. Teaching: Lectr drawing & painting, Ohio State Univ, 70-71 & Allan Hancock Col, 71-76; lectr drawing & printmaking, Calif Polytech State Univ, 73- Pos: Mem bd dir, Neighborhood Arts Agency, San Luis Obispo, Calif, 76- Mem: Calif Soc of Printmakers; Artists Equity Asn. Style & Technique: Serigraphs and intaglio prints involving photographic processes, figure and landscape drawings in mixed media. Publ: Co-auth, Darkroom Graphics: Creative Photographic Techniques for Photographers and Artists, Amphoto, 75; contribr, Encyclopedia of PhotograPhotography, Amphoto/Eastman Kodak, 78. Mailing Add: 151 Hathway Ave San Luis Obispo CA 93401

RUGOLO, LAWRENCE
SCREENPRINTER, EDUCATOR
b Milwaukee, Wis, Oct 2, 31. Study: Univ Wis-Milwaukee, BA(art & art educ), 54; Univ Iowa, MFA, 59. Work: Albrecht Art Mus, St Joseph, Mo; Springfield Art Mus, Mo; State Univ NY Col, Potsdam; Univ Ark, Little Rock; State Hist Soc Mo, Columbia; plus others. Exhib: 5th & 9th Nat Print Exhibs, Silvermine Guild of Artists, New Canaan, Conn, 64 & 72; Northwest Printmakers 38th, 40th & 41st Int Exhibs, Seattle, Wash, 67, 69 & 70; Colorprint: USA, Nat Print Exhib, Tex Tech Univ, Lubbock, 71 & 74; 6th Exhib, Tulsa Arts Coun, Okla, 73; one-man show, Albrecht Art Mus, 75; plus many others. Teaching: Assoc prof screenprinting & design, Univ Mo-Columbia, 68-73, prof, screenprinting & design, 73, chmn art dept, 73-76. Awards: Two Purchase Awards, 5th Ann Art Exhib, Tulsa Arts Coun, 72; Purchase Award, Potsdam Prints, State Univ NY, 72 & 74; Purchase Award, 44th Ann Exhib, Springfield Art Mus, 74. Mem: Nat & Midwest Col Art Asns. Style & Technique: Fusion of geometric patterns with life forms; richly textured surfaces set off against bold flat areas; muted colors. Mailing Add: 415 Parkade Blvd Columbia MO 65201

RUIZ, NATHAN CHARLES
See Shiner, Nate

RUMFORD, BEATRIX TYSON
ART ADMINISTRATOR
b Baltimore, Md, June 16, 39. Study: Wellesley Col, 58-62; State Univ NY Oneonta & NY State Hist Asn Cooperstown, 64-65; Bath Summer Sch, Courtauld Inst, Univ London travel course, 69; Nat Trust Summer Sch, Attingham Park, Shropshire, Eng & study tour, Oslo, Norway, 70. Collections Arranged: The Beardsley Limner, 72-73; Folk Art in America: A Living Tradition, 74-76; plus organize five major exhibs on American Folk Art Ann. Pos: Art res ed, D C Heath & Co, Boston, 62-64; res assoc, Chicago Hist Soc, Ill, 66-67; from asst cur to assoc cur, Colonial Williamsburg, Va, 67-71; from assoc dir to dir, Abby Aldrich Rockefeller Folk Art Collection, 71- Mem: NY State Hist Asn (trustee, 75-); Furnishings Comt, Exec Mansion, Richmond, Va; Bermuda Nat Trust (consult, 73-); Antique Collectors Guild, Richmond, Va (exec coun, 74). Res: Role of death as reflected in the art and folkways of the Northeast in the 18th and 19th centuries. Publ: Samuel Kirk & Son, American Silver Craftsmen Since 1815 (exhib catalog), 66; auth, The household accessories at Colonial Williamsburg, 69 & Nonacademic English painting, 74, Antiques; auth, What is American Folk Art?, 74; Folk art, In: World Bk Encycl, 75. Mailing Add: Tayloe House 110 E Nicholson St Williamsburg VA 23185

RUMSEY, DAVID MACIVER
ENVIRONMENTAL ARTIST, COLLECTOR
b New York, NY, Apr 29, 44. Study: Yale Univ, BA, 66, BFA & MFA, 69. Exhib: Spaces, Mus Mod Art, New York, 70; Work for New Spaces, Walker Art Mus, Minneapolis, 71; Pulsa & Television Sensoriums, Automation House, 71; Pulsa, Philadelphia Mus Fine Arts, 71; Calif Inst Arts, 72. Teaching: Lectr art, Yale Univ, 68-72; vis artist, Calif Inst Arts, 70-73. Pos: Mem Pulsa Group; Am Soc for Eastern Arts & Ctr for World Music (assoc dir, 73-75). Style & Technique: Environmental art, using television, film, electronics, light and sound. Interest: Life-involved large scale speculative sculpture, San Francisco, 75- Mailing Add: 1830 Page St San Francisco CA 94117

RUPPERSBERG, ALLEN RAWSON
CONCEPTUAL ARTIST
b Cleveland, Ohio, Jan 5, 44. Study: Chouinard Art Inst, BFA. Work: Los Angeles Co Mus Art, Los Angeles; Guggenheim Mus, New York; Pasadena Mus Mod Art; Stedelijk Mus, Amsterdam, Holland. Exhib: Live in Your Head/When Attitudes Become Form, Kunsthalle Berne, Switz, 69; one-man shows, Pasadena Mus Mod Art, 70, Stedelijk Mus, 73 & Mus Mod Art, New York, 77; Whitney Ann Exhib, Contemp Am Sculpture, Whitney Mus, 70; Documenta 5, Mus Fridericianum, Kassel, Ger, 72; The Mod Era, San Francisco Mus Mod Art, 76; Ft Worth Art Mus, Tex, 77; Nine Artists: Theodoron Awards, Guggenheim Mus, 77; Am Narrative/Story Art, Contemp Arts Mus, Houston, 77. Awards: Theodoron Award, Guggenheim Mus; Nat Endowment for the Arts, 76. Bibliog: Helene Winer (auth), Scenarios/documents/images II, Art Am, 5-6/73; Peter Plagens (auth), Wilde about Harry, Artforum, 4/75. Mailing Add: 1314 Second St Santa Monica CA 90401

RUSCHA, EDWARD JOSEPH
PAINTER, FILMMAKER
b Omaha, Nebr, Dec 16, 37. Study: Chouinard Art Inst. Work: Mus Mod Art & Whitney Mus Am Art, New York; Los Angeles Co Mus Art; Joseph Hirshhorn Collection, Washington, DC; Oakland Mus Art, Calif. Exhib: Drawings USA, Minn Mus Art, St Paul, 71; Continuing Surrealism, La Jolla Mus Art, Calif, 71; Top Boxed Art, Ill State Univ, Normal, 71; 11 Los Angeles Artists, Hayward Gallery, London, 71; Art Systems, Centro Arte Y Comunication, Buenos Aires, Arg, 71; Albright-Knox Art Gallery, Buffalo, NY, 76; Stedelijk Mus, Amsterdam, Holland, 76; Ace Gallery, Los Angeles, 77; Ft Worth Art Mus, Tex, 77; plus many other group & one-man shows. Teaching: Lectr painting, Univ Calif, Los Angeles, 69-70. Bibliog: Joyce Haber (auth), article in Los Angeles Times, 5/19/71; Rosalind Kraus (auth), rev in Artforum, 5/71; Reyner Banham (auth), A London-Los Angeles love affair, West, 6/6/71; plus many others. Publ: Auth, On the sunset strip, 66, Thirty-four parking lots, 67, Royal road test, 67, Business cards, 68 & Nine swimming pools, 68, Heavy Indust Publ; plus many others. Mailing Add: 1024 3/4 N Western Ave Hollywood CA 90029

RUSH, ANDREW
PRINTMAKER, PAINTER
b Mich, Sept 24, 31. Study: Univ Ill, BFA(hons), 53; Univ Iowa, MFA, 58; Fulbright fel, Florence, Italy, 58-59. Work: Uffizi Mus, Florence, Italy; Brooklyn Mus, NY; Libr of Cong, Washington, DC; Dallas Mus, Tex; Seattle Mus, Wash. Comn: Law Prints (portfolio of three offset lithographs), Lawyers Publ Co, 68 & 74; mem bd ed etching, Asn Am Artists, New York, 68 & 73; ed etchings, Tucson Art Ctr, 71. Exhib: USIS Traveling Exhib to Europe & Latin Am, 60-65; Graphic Art USA, Am prints to Soviet Union, 63; Brooklyn Mus Biennial, 64; 50 American Printmakers, Am Pavilion, New York Worlds Fair, 64-65; Intag 71, 30 Printmakers, San Fernando State Univ, 71. Teaching: Assoc prof art, Univ Ariz, 59-69; vis artist in residence, Ohio State Univ, 70. Awards: Seattle Mus Int Printmakers Award, 63; Purchase Award, Brooklyn Mus Biennial, 64. Bibliog: Andrew Rush, Southwest Art Gallery Mag, 3/72. Style & Technique: Intaglio printmaker, watercolorist. Dealer: Assoc Am Artists 663 Fifth Ave New York NY 10022; ADI 530 McAllister San Francisco CA 94102. Mailing Add: PO Box E Oracle AZ 85623

RUSH, JON N
SCULPTOR, EDUCATOR
b Atlanta, Ga, Sept 24, 35. Study: Sch of Art Inst Chicago, 53-55; Cranbrook Acad Art, Bloomfield Hills, Mich, BFA, MFA, with Tex Schiwetz. Work: Columbus Gallery Fine Art, Ohio; Univ Mich, Ann Arbor. Comn: Sculpture, Summerset Mall, Troy, Mich, 70. Exhib: Hong Kong Int Competition, China, 62; one-man show, Columbus Gallery Fine Art, 62; Bundy Art Gallery, Waitsfield, Vt, 63; Mich Artists, Detroit Inst Fine Art, Mich, 66; Mich Sculptors, Eastern Mich Univ, Ypsilanti, 71; All Mich Artists, Flint Art Inst, 74; Sculpture Inside & Out, Univ Mich, Ann Arbor, 75; Fifteen Mich Sculptors, City of Lansing, Mich, 76. Teaching: Prof sculpture, Univ Mich, 62- Awards: Detroit Foundry Prize, Mich Artists Show, Detroit Sculpture Foundry, 66; Award for Sculpture, Columbus Sculpture & Drawing Show, Ohio, 62 & All Mich Artists, Flint Inst Art, 72; Tiffany Found Grant for Sculpture, 70. Style & Technique: Geometric fabricated Steel and bronze. Media: Stainless Steel, Cor-Ten Steel. Mailing Add: 7930 Fifth St Dexter MI 48130

RUSKIN, LEWIS J
COLLECTOR, PATRON
b London, Eng, July 30, 05. Study: Ariz State Univ, hon LLD, 68. Pos: Chmn, Ariz Comn Arts & Humanities, 67- Awards: Hon Fel, Phoenix Art Mus. Interest: Donated Renaissance and Baroque paintings to the Phoenix Art Museum and Renaissance, Baroque and Barbizon paintings and sculpture to Arizona State University Gallery. Collection: 16th, 17th and 18th century paintings. Mailing Add: 5800 E Foothill Dr N Paradise Valley AZ 85253

RUSKIN, LYNNE
See Caimite

RUSSELL, (GEORGE) GORDON
PAINTER
b Altoona, Pa, July 15, 32. Study: Pa State Univ, with Hobson Pittman; Pa Acad Fine Arts, with Walter Stuempfig; Barnes Found. Work: Pa Acad Fine Arts, Philadelphia; Fogg Art Mus, Harvard Univ; Mus Fine Arts, Bowdoin Col, Maine; Krannert Art Mus, Univ Ill, Urbana; New York Hosp Collection, NY. Exhib: Pa Acad Fine Arts Ann & Fel Ann; Contemporary Paintings, Yale Univ Art Gallery, 62; one-man shows, Durlacher Bros, New York, 57-67, Ft Worth Art Ctr, Tex, 62 & Larcada Gallery, New York, 69 & 71. Awards: Lewis S Ware Mem, 53, J Henry Schiedt Mem, 54 & Toppan Prize, 54, Pa Acad Fine Arts. Mem: Fel Pa Acad Fine Arts. Style & Technique: Realist, working primarily in oils and gouache. Dealer: Larcada Gallery 23 E 67th St New York NY 10021. Mailing Add: 117 E Caroline Ave Altoona PA 16602

RUSSELL, HELEN DIANE
ART HISTORIAN
b Kansas City, Mo, Apr 8, 36. Study: Vassar Col, AB; Radcliffe Grad Sch; Johns Hopkins Univ, PhD. Collections Arranged: Protest and Social Comment in Prints, 70; Kathe Kollwitz, 71; Rare Etchings by Giovanni Battista & Giovanni Domenico Tiepolo, 72 (with catalogs); Jacques Callot, Prints and Related Drawings, 75; Europ Countryside: 16th & 17th century prints. Teaching: Prof lectr 15th-17th century Europ painting & graphic arts, Am Univ, Washington, DC, 66-72. Pos: Asst to chief, Smithsonian Inst Traveling Exhib Serv, Washington, 60-61; mus cur, Nat Gallery Art, Washington, 64-70, asst cur graphic arts, 70-76, cur French Prints, 76- Awards: Woodrow Wilson Nat Fel, 58-59; Samuel H Kress Fel, 73. Mem: Col Art Asn Am; Women's Caucus for Art (adv bd, 77-); Print Coun Am. Res: Prints and drawings of the 16th through 18th centuries. Publ: Auth, A museum worker speaks, Washington Print Club Newslett, 72; auth, Aldo Rizzi, The etchings of the Tiepolos (rev), Print Collectors Newslett, 72; auth, Heinemann drawings at the Pierpont Morgan Library (rev), Master Drawings, 73; auth, Francoise Viatte, Dessins de Stefano della Bella, Art Bull, 77. Mailing Add: Nat Gallery Art Washington DC 20565

RUSSELL, JOHN LAUREL
ART DEALER, COLLECTOR
b Cochrane, Ont, Aug 14, 16. Study: Russell Sch Art, Toronto, 37-38. Pos: Owner, Beaver Hall, Gananoque, Ont. Mem: Fel Royal Soc Arts; fel Royal Geog Soc; Can Guild Crafts (dir); Can Antique Dealer's Asn (dir); life gov Montreal Numis & Hist Soc. Specialty: General antiques. Collection: Early Canadian painting of the 18th and 19th centuries. Mailing Add: Beaver Hall Gananoque ON K7G 2W7 Can

RUSSELL, PHILIP C
PAINTER, INSTRUCTOR
b Tulsa, Okla, July 9, 33. Study: Colo Springs Fine Arts Ctr, study with V Vytlacil; Univ Iowa, study with M Lasansky; Univ Calif, Berkeley, study with R Motherwell, W Kahn, MA. Work: Philbrook Art Ctr, Tulsa; Wichita Mus Art; Dallas Mus Fine Arts; Palace of the Legion of Honor, San Francisco; Butler Inst Am Art, Youngstown, Ohio. Exhib: US Info Serv (traveling exhib), S Am, 57-59; Drawings, Dallas Mus Fine Arts, 58-59; Mid Am Ann Exhib, Nelson Gallery, Kansas City, Mo, 58; Philadelphia Mus Art, 58; Calif Soc of Etchers, 44th Ann Nat Exhib, 59; Area Gallery, New York, 61 & 63; New York World's Fair, 63-64. Collections Arranged: 10th Street Days-Co-ops of the 50's, Noho Gallery & Landmark Gallery, Dec/Jan 77. Teaching: Instr drawing, Univ Okla, 57-58; instr composition, Philadelphia Col Art, 62-63; instr art/art hist, Edgemont Sch, Scarsdale, NY, 69- Pos: Coodr arts, Edgemont Schs, Scarsdale, 71- Awards: Purchase Awards, Drawing and Prints, Dallas Mus, 58 & 59, Calif Soc of Etchers, Legion of Honor, San Francisco, 59 & Am Graphic Arts, Wichita Art Assoc, 59. Bibliog: John Canaday (auth), Art: Street of Strugglers, 12/14/61 & Goodbye Forever, A Sad Farewell to 10th Street, 5/9/63, New York Times; Joellen Bard (auth), 10th Street Days, Educ Art & Serv, Inc, 12/77. Style & Technique: Landscapes in oil, abstract expressionist style, brush and spatula. Media: Oil Painting; Intaglio. Mailing Add: 145 W 79th St 16A New York NY 10024

RUSSELL, ROBERT PRICE
EDUCATOR, PAINTER
b Rochelle, Ill, June 23, 39. Study: Kansas City Art Inst, Mo, BFA, 61; Southern Ill Univ, Carbondale, MFA, 63. Work: El Paso Mus of Art, Tex; Roswell Mus and Art Ctr, NMex; Springfield Art Mus, Mo; Wustum Mus of Fine Arts, Racine, Wis; Mobil Oil, NY. Exhib: The 15th Ann Eight State Exhib, Okla Art Ctr, Oklahoma City, 73; Selected Painters Exhib,

Mulvane Art Ctr, Washburn Univ, Topeka, Kans, 74; Accessions/1976-77, Springfield Art Mus, Mo, 77; one-man shows, Univ Art Mus, Univ Okla, Norman, 73, Tex Christian Univ, Ft Worth, 73, Roswell Mus and Art Ctr, NMex, 75, Humboldt State Univ, Arcata, Calif, 75 & Southwest Mo State Univ, Springfield, 75. Teaching: Instr art, Univ Wis-Stevens Point, 63-66; assoc prof art, Pittsburgh State Univ, Kans, 67- Pos: Artist-in-residence, Area arts prog, Wis, 66-67, Hanover Col, Ind, 73, Roswell Mus and Art Ctr, NMex, 74-75 & Buena Vista Col, Iowa, 76. Awards: Purchase Awards, Second Nat Exhib Prints and Drawings, Dickinson State Col, 69, 15th Ann Nat Sun Carnival Art Exhib, El Paso Mus of Art, Tex, 70 & 46th Ann Exhib, Springfield Art Mus, 76. Style & Technique: Non-objective. Media: Acrylic Polymer. Dealer: Douglas Drake Gallery 4500 State Line Kansas City KS 66103. Mailing Add: 1901 S Elm Pittsburg KS 66762

RUSSELL, SHIRLEY XIMENA (HOPPER)
PAINTER
b Del Rey, Calif, May 16, 86. Study: Stanford Univ, AB, 07; San Jose State, dipl; Sch Fine Arts, Oakland; San Francisco Sch Fine Arts; Univ Hawaii; also with Andre Lhote, Umberto Romano, Hans Hofmann, Rico Le Brun, Serisawa & Norman Ives. Work: Honolulu Acad Arts; State Found Cult & Arts, Capitol Bldg, Honolulu; Castle & Cooke Art Collection; Tokyo Nat Mus Art; Lawrence Rockefeller Collection. Comn: Portraits, Leslie B Hicks, Hawaiian Elec Co, Honolulu & Chief Justices Perry & Kemp, Bar Asn Honolulu; also pvt comns. Exhib: Mus Fine Arts, Los Angeles, 37; Palace Legion of Honor, San Francisco, 46; one-woman shows, Honolulu Acad Arts, Contemp Art Gallery, 67 & Downtown Gallery, 75, Honolulu. Teaching: Instr Calif high schs, 08-18; instr art McKinley High Sch, Honolulu, 23-46; instr, Univ Hawaii, summers 30-39; instr, Honolulu Acad Arts, 54-55. Pos: Secy, Asn Honolulu Artists, 39-41, pres, 41-42. Awards: Grand Prize for Paukahana, 33 & First Prize for still life, 46, Honolulu Acad Arts; Grand Prize for US Mail, Territorial Fair, Honolulu, 53; plus many others. Bibliog: Meg Torbert & Kenneth Kingrey (auth), Art in Hawaii, Design Quart, Walker Art Ctr, 60; Saga of the Sandwich Islands, 68; Francis Haar & Prithwick Neogy (auths), Artists of Hawaii, Univ Hawaii Press, 74. Mem: Painters & Sculptors League; Honolulu Acad Arts. Style & Technique: Realistic, impressionistic with stress on interaction of color and organization, semi-abstract. Media: Oil. Dealer: Downtown Gallery 125 Richards St Honolulu HI 96813. Mailing Add: 4220 Puu Panini Ave Honolulu HI 96816

RUSSIN, ROBERT I
SCULPTOR, EDUCATOR
b New York, NY, Aug 26, 14. Study: City Univ New York, BA & MA; Beaux Arts Inst Design. Work: Colorado Springs Fine Arts Ctr; Palm Springs Desert Mus, Calif; Pomona Col, Claremont, Calif; Galleria d'Arte Mod, Santo Domingo, Dominican Repub; Brookhaven Nat Labs, NY. Comn: Family group marble sculpture, Menorah Med Ctr, Kansas City, 74; two Bicentennial bronze figures, State Wyo, Cheyenne, 76; Juan Pablo Duarte (marble monument), Dominican Repub, 77; bronze group, Lobby of Nat Theater, Santo Domingo, 77; Am Family Group (marble Bicentennial), Dominican Repub, 78; plus many others. Exhib: Pa Acad Fine Arts Sculpture Biennial, Philadelphia, 66; one-man shows, Tucson Art Ctr, Ariz, 66, Colorado Springs Fine Arts Ctr, 67, Palm Springs Desert Mus, 70, Magnes Mus, Berkeley, Calif, 70, Galleria d'Arte Mod, Santo Domingo, 76-77 & Fine Arts Mus, Univ Wyo, 77. Teaching: Instr sculpture, Cooper Union Art Inst, 44-47; prof sculpture, Univ Wyo, 47- Awards: Lincoln Sesquicentennial Medal, US Cong, 59; Charles G B Steele Sculpture Award, Pa Acad Fine Arts, 66; Order of Duarte, Sanchez & Mella, by Pres Joachim Balaguer, Dominican Repub, 77. Bibliog: Rebecca Northen (auth), Robert Russin, sculptor to Wyoming, Western Farm Life, 9/50; O A Sealy (auth), Russin's metal magic, 2/56 & F K Frame (auth), Russin's Lincoln, 2/65, Empire Mag; Tom Francis (auth), Robert Russin, Wyoming sculptor, Am Artist, 1/60. Mem: Nat Sculpture Soc; Sculptors Guild. Style & Technique: Bronze and marble figurative sculpture. Publ: Contribr, A new sculptural medium, Col Art J, 56, The Lincoln monument on the Lincoln highway, Lincoln Herald, 61 & A university bronze foundry, Am Artist, 63. Dealer: Heritage Gallery 718 N La Cienega Blvd Los Angeles CA 90069. Mailing Add: 716 Ivinson Ave Laramie WY 82070

RUSSO, ALEXANDER PETER
PAINTER, EDUCATOR
b Atlantic City, NJ, June 11, 22. Study: Pratt Inst, 40-42; Swarthmore Col, 47; Bard Col, summer 47; Guggenheim fel, 48-50; Breevort-Eickenmeyer fel, Columbia Univ, 50-52, BFA, 52; Fulbright grant, Acad Fine Arts, Rome, 52-54; Univ Buffalo, 55. Work: Albright-Knox Gallery, Buffalo, NY; Corcoran Gallery Art, Washington, DC; Nat Collection Fine Arts, Washington, DC; Fed Ins Deposit Corp, Washington; Acad Arts & Lett, New York. Comn: Encaustic mural, Telesio Interlandi, Capo San Andrea, Sicily, 53; var design comns, Doubleday Publ Co, Dutton Publ, Birge Co & Cohn Hall Marx, 56-60; acrylic painting series, US Navy Dept, 64; acrylic mural, Dr Martin Cherkasky, NY, 70; Vet Mem sculpture, Frederick, Md, 75. Exhib: Carnegie Nat, Pittsburgh, 46; Int Exhib, Bordighera, Italy, 53 & 54; Four Am Artists Exhib, Biblioteca, Rome, 54; Albright-Knox Gallery Regional, Buffalo, NY, 56; Corcoran Biennials, Washington, DC; plus many one-man shows. Teaching: Assoc prof painting & drawing, Corcoran Sch Art, 61-70, chmn fac & painting dept, 66-69; prof art & chmn dept, Hood Col, 71- Pos: Combat artist, US Navy Dept, Washington, 42-46; actg art dir, Sewell, Thompson, Caire Advert, New Orleans, 48-49; free-lance artist & designer, var agencies & orgns, New York, 58-60; guest lectr art, Roanoke & Hollins Cols, Univ Southern Ill, Miss Art Asn, plus others. Bibliog: Carl Fortes (auth), Tape on aesthetics and teaching methods of Alexander Russo, Boston Univ, 68; Anne M Jonas (auth), Focus on: Alexander Russo, The Art Scene, 70/71. Mem: Col Art Asn; Arts Club Washington (chmn exhibs, 70-71); Artists Equity; Soc Washington Artists; Edward McDowell Colony. Style & Technique: Figurative, symbolic, abstract in contemporary techniques. Media: Acrylic, Oil. Publ: Illusr, To All Hands, an Amphibious Adventure, 44 & illusr, Many a Watchful Night, 45, McGraw; auth, The Italian experience, Inst Int Educ, 53. Dealer: Frank Rehn Galleries 60th & Madison Ave New York NY 10010. Mailing Add: Hood Col Frederick MD 21701

RUSSO, KATHLEEN L
ART HISTORIAN
b Shrewsbury, Mass, Jan 14, 47. Study: Univ Miami, BA, MA; Fla State Univ, PhD(art hist), Study Ctr, Florence, Italy with Fred Licht; Harvard Univ. Teaching: Asst prof art hist, Fla Atlantic Univ, 73- Res: Italian Baroque and European Rococo, 19th century, in Europe and America. Mailing Add: Dept of Art Fla Atlantic Univ Boca Raton FL 33431

RUST, DAVID E
ART HISTORIAN, COLLECTOR
b Bloomington, Ill. Study: Harvard Col, BA; NY Univ Inst Fine Arts, MA, 63. Collections Arranged: English Drawings & Watercolors, 62; Old Master Drawings from Chatsworth, 69; Nathan Cummings Collection, 70; Francois Boucher....100 Drawings (auth, catacatalogue), 73; French Paintings from the Ailsa Mellon Bruce Collection (auth, catalogue), 78. Pos: Cur Fr Painting, Nat Gallery Art, Washington, DC, 61- Collection: Paintings and drawings, mostly European sixteenth-eighteenth century, some nineteenth century; American nineteenth century and some contemporary. Publ: Auth, Twentieth Century Paintings & Sculpture of the French School in the Chester Dale Collection, 65; auth, Eighteenth & Nineteenth Century Paintings & Sculpture of the French School in the Chester Dale Collection, 65; auth, The drawings of Vincenzo Tamagni da San Gimignano, Report & Studies Hist Art, 68. Mailing Add: Nat Gallery Art Washington DC 20565

RUST, EDWIN C
SCULPTOR, ART ADMINISTRATOR
b Hammonton, Calif, Dec 5, 10. Study: Cornell Univ; Yale Univ, BFA; also with Archipenko & Milles. Work: US Ct House, Washington, DC; Univ Tenn Ctr Health Serv; Ouachita Baptist Univ, Arkadelphia, Ark; Cook Convention Ctr, Memphis; Memphis Acad Arts, Tenn. Exhib: Whitney Mus Am Art, New York, 40; Carnegie Inst Int, Pittsburgh, 40; Philadelphia Mus Art, 40 & 49; Mus Mod Art, New York, 42; Brooks Mem Mus, 50 & 52. Teaching: Assoc prof sculpture, Col William & Mary, 36-43, head fine arts dept, 39-43. Pos: Dir, Memphis Acad Arts, 49-75, emer dir, 75- Mailing Add: 3725 Waynoka Ave Memphis TN 38111

RUSTVOLD, KATHERINE JO
ART DEALER, GALLERY DIRECTOR
b Grand Forks, NDak, Jan 24, 50. Collections Arranged: Jackson Pollock's Psychoanalytic Drawings, 5/76; Am Wildlife Painting, 1/77; Equestrian Exhib, 10/77. Pos: Exec dir, Petersen Galleries, Beverly Hills, Calif, 77-; fine arts consult, Biltmore Galleries, Los Angeles, 77- Mem: Art Dealers Asn Southern Calif, Inc. Specialty: Nineteenth and twentieth century American art, with emphasis on Western and wildlife art. Mailing Add: Petersen Galleries 9433 Wilshire Blvd Beverly Hills CA 90212

RUTA, PETER PAUL
PAINTER, EDITOR
b Dresden, Ger, Feb 7, 18; US citizen. Study: Art Students League, with Morris Kantor & Jean Charlot, 38-42 & 45-46; Acad Fine Arts Venice, 47-49, degree; Acad Venice, with Guido Cadorin, 48. Work: Uffizi Gallery, Florence, Italy; Univ Southern Ill. Exhib: One-man shows, Stonington Gallery, Conn, 60, Angeleski Gallery, 62, Hacker Gallery, 62, Surebaja Gallery, 67 & Graham Gallery, 72, New York. Awards: First Prize, Westchester Art Soc, 65. Style & Technique: Landscapes and still lifes in a contemporary representational style. Media: Oil. Publ: Ed, Arts Mag, 68-71; ed, Int Art Exhibs, 69. Dealer: Larcada Gallery 23 E 67th St New York NY 10021. Mailing Add: 463 West St New York NY 10014

RUTHERFORD, ERICA
PAINTER
b Edinburgh, Scotland, Feb 1, 23. Study: Royal Acad Dramatic Art; Slade Sch Fine Art, theatre design with I V Pulunin; Academia, Florence, theatre design with Vangetti. Work: Corcoran Gallery, Washington, DC; Indianapolis Mus; Mus Contemp Art, Madrid, Spain; Arts Coun Gt Brit; Confederation Art Ctr Mus, PEI. Comn: Puppets, Telegoons, BBC Film Ser; theatre designs, Eng. Exhib: Leicester Galleries, London, Eng, 59-64; one-man shows, Indianapolis Mus, 69, Pollock Gallery, Toronto, Ont, 75 & New Directions Gallery, St Louis, Mo, 76; Landscape Abbreviations, Victoria Art Gallery, 74; Through the Looking Glass, Ont Gallery Art, 75; Gallery Pascal, Toronto, Ont, 77; Byck Gallery, Louisville, Ky; Burnaby Nat, BC. Teaching: Vis assoc prof painting & drawing, Univ WVa, 69-71; assoc prof painting, Univ Mo-Columbia, 71-; vis artist, Fanshawe Col, London, Ont; teacher art, Sheridan Col, Oakville, Ont, Guelph Univ, Ont, 76-77. Awards: Best of Show Award, J B Speed Mus Regional Biannual, 69; Hon Mention, Brooks Mem Gallery, Memphis, Tenn, 72; Colorprint USA Purchase Award, Tex Tech Univ, 74. Mem: Col Art Asn Am. Style & Technique: Abstract figuration. Media: Acrylic, Screenprint. Mailing Add: c/o Pollock Galleries 356 Dundas St W Toronto ON Can

RUTHLING, FORD
PAINTER
b Santa Fe, NMex, Apr 23, 33. Study: With Randall Davey, largely self taught. Work: Mus NMex; Wichita Falls Fine Art Mus; Univ Utah Collection. Comn: US Pueblo Pottery Postage Stamp (4 thirteen cent stamps), 77; plus others. Exhib: Nelson Atkins Mus; Mus NMex; Oklahoma City Mus Fine Art; Dallas Mus Fine Art; Wichita Falls Mus Fine Art. Media: Oil, Graphics. Mailing Add: 313 E Berger St Santa Fe NM 87501

RUTHVEN, JOHN ALDRICH
PAINTER, LECTURER
b Cincinnati, Ohio, Nov 12, 24. Study: Cincinnati Art Acad; Cent Acad Com Art; DHumL, Miami Univ, Ohio & St Francis Col, Loretto, Pa. Work: Hermitage Mus, Leningrad, Russia; Armstrong Space Mus, Wapakoneta, Ohio; Ruthven Conf Ctr, Middletown, Ohio; Smithsonian Inst, Washington, DC; Cincinnati Natural Hist Mus. Comn: Cardinals for Gov Conf, State Ohio, Columbus, 68, Eagle to the Moon, 69; Colonial Williamsburg Ser, Va, 70-75; Cardinal, USSR, 70; Miami Indian, Miami Univ, 74. Exhib: Delta Queen Art Exhib, Cincinnati, 68; Topflight Exhib, Abercrombie & Fitch, Chicago, 69; Ducks Unlimited, Hilton Head, SC, 72; Ohio State Fair, Columbus, 74; White House Reception, 76; Leigh-Yawkey-Woodson Mus, Wausau, Wis, 76 & 77; Wildlife Festival, Easton, Md, 77. Pos: Mem bd dir, Cincinnati Nature Ctr, 69-; trustee, Cincinnati Natural Hist Mus, 75-; trustee, Ducks Unlimited, 75- Awards: Sachs Fine Art Award, Cincinnati Art Acad, 69; Printing Industry Am Award, 70-77; Ohioana Career Medal, Martha Kinne Cooper Ohioana Libr, 75. Bibliog: Jerry Bowles (auth), John Ruthven, Acquire Mag, 73; Cincinnati Art, Town & Country, 75; Dan Johnston (auth), John Ruthven, Artist, pvt publ, 75. Mem: Soc Animal Artists New York. Style & Technique: Realistic wildlife and Indians. Media: Opaque Watercolor. Publ: Co-auth, Topflight, 69; auth, Carolina Paraquet, Audubon Mag, 72; also auth, Regal Series Prints, 68-75, North American Series Prints, 69-75 & Aquatint Series Prints, 71-75, Wildlife Int Publ. Mailing Add: Rte 1 Box 35-A Georgetown OH 45121

RUTLAND, EMILY EDITH
PAINTER
b Lee Co, Tex. Work: Centennial Mus, Corpus Christi, Tex; Corpus Christi Mus; Dallas Mus, Tex; Tex Tech Univ. Exhib: Tex Fine Arts Exhib, Austin, 65; Corpus Christi Art Found, 68; Tex A&I Univ, 71 & 72; Univ Corpus Christi, 73; one-woman exhib, Dos Caminos Art Gallery, Kingsville, 74; First Presby Church, Kingsville, Tex, 77. Mem: SW Watercolor Soc; Tex Fine Arts Asn; STex Art League; Art Found Corpus Christi; Art Community Ctr. Media: Oil, Acrylic. Mailing Add: 615 W Nettie Kingsville TX 78363

RUTSCH, ALEXANDER
PAINTER, SCULPTOR
b Austria. Study: Acad Fine Art, Belgrade, Yugoslavia; Vienna, Austria; govt study grant, Paris. Work: Albertina Graphic Art Collection, Austria; Austrian Gallery, Belvedere, Vienna; Munic Mus, Vienna; Mus Mod Art, Paris; Mus Liege, Belg. Exhib: Int Sculptors, Mus Rodin, Paris, 62-63; one-man show, Galerie Vendome, Brussels, Belg, 65; Int Exhib, Grand Palais de Champs Elyses, Paris, 66; Avanti Galleries, 74 & Harkness House Gallery, 75, New York. Awards: Silver Medal of Arts, Sci & Lett & Bronze Medal for art, City of Paris, 58; First Prize

(three portraits of Picasso), Salon Artistique Int de Sceaux, 54. Bibliog: Jean Desville (producer), The world of Rutsch (film), 64; Carlton Lake (auth), In quest of Dali, Putnams, 69; Roger Seiler (auth), Inner eye of Alexander Rutsch (film), produced by IBM, 72. Mailing Add: 222 Highbrook Ave Pelham NY 10803

RUVOLO, FELIX EMMANUELE
PAINTER, EDUCATOR
b New York, NY, Apr 28, 12. Study: In Catania, Sicily. Work: Krannert Art Mus, Univ Ill, Urbana; Art Inst Chicago; Walker Art Ctr, Minneapolis; Oakland Mus, Calif; Univ Calif Mus Fine Arts, Berkeley. Comn: Colored lithograph, Collectors Press, 67. Exhib: Abstract & Surrealist Art in America, Mus Mod Art, New York, 51; 60 Americans—1960, Walker Art Ctr, 60; American Drawing, Moore Col Art Gallery, Philadelphia, 68; Drawings 1969, Ithaca Col Art Gallery, NY, 69; American Drawing & Sculpture, 1948-1969, Krannert Art Mus, 71. Teaching: Prof art, Art Inst Chicago, 44-48; prof art, Univ Calif, Berkeley, 50-; prof art, Univ Southern Calif, summer 63. Awards: San Francisco Mus Art Award, 64; Hall of Justice Competition Award, San Francisco Art Comn, 67; Grants, Univ Calif Inst Creative Arts, 64 & 71. Bibliog: K Kuli (auth), Felix Ruvolo, Mag Art, 47 & Painters who teach, Pictorial Living, 59; N Pousette Dart (auth), American Painting Today, Hastings, 57. Mailing Add: 78 Strathmoor Dr Berkeley CA 94705

RUZICKA, RUDOLPH
ILLUSTRATOR, DESIGNER
b Bohemia, June 29, 83. Study: Art Inst Chicago; NY Sch Art. Work: Print Collections of Metrop Mus Art, New York, Libr of Cong, Washington, DC, Art Inst Chicago & Newark Mus, NJ; plus others. Pos: Illusr bks, 15- Awards: Alice McFadden Brinton Prize, Philadelphia Print Club, 24; Bronze Medal, Sesquicentennial Expos, Philadelphia, 26; Gold Medal, Am Inst Graphic Arts, 35. Mem: Academician Nat Acad Design; fel Am Acad Arts & Sci; Colonial Soc Mass; hon mem Soc Printers Boston; Mass Hist Soc. Publ: Auth, Thomas Bewick, Engraver, 43; Studies in Type Design. Mailing Add: PO Box 376 Hanover NH 03755

RYDEN, KENNETH GLENN
SCULPTOR
b Chicago, Ill, May 16, 45. Study: Univ Wis, Superior, BFA; Univ Kans, Lawrence, MFA; study with Bernard Frazer, Eldon Tefft & Victor Timmerman. Work: Grover Hermann Fine Arts Ctr, Marietta, Ohio; Swope Art Gallery, Terre Haute, Ind; Southern Ill Univ Art Collection, Edwardsville; Wabash Col Art Collection, Crawfordsville, Ind. Comn: Delyte Morris Mem, Southern Ill Univ at Edwardsville, 76 & John Rendleman Mem, 76. Exhib: 16th, 17th & 18th Kans Designer Craftsman Exhibs, Spooner Mus, Lawrence, 69, 71 & 72; 11th Midwest Biennial, Joslyn Art Mus, Omaha, Nebr, 70; 40th, 41st, 42nd & 46th Ann Exhib, Springfield Art Mus, Mo, 70-76; Mainstreams 73, Grover M Hermann Fine Arts Ctr, Marietta, Ohio, 73; Mid-States Arts Exhib, Evansville Mus Arts & Sci, 73 & 76; 30th & 33th Ann Wabash Valley Exhib, Sheldon Swope Art Gallery, Ind, 74 & 77; New Horizons Show North Shore Art League, Chicago, 75. Teaching: Instr sculpture, Univ Mo, Columbia, 70-73; asst prof sculpture, Southern Ill Univ, Edwardsville, 73- Awards: Purchase Award, Mainstreams 73, Grover M Hermann Fine Arts Ctr, 73; Top Purchase Award, 33rd Ann Wabash Valley Sheldon Swope Art Gallery, 77; Cash Award, St Louis Artists' Guild, 77. Mem: Nat Col Art Asn; Southern Sculptors Asn; Nat Sculpture Ctr. Style & Technique: Contemporary figurative and non-figurative work with emphasis on light and a synthesis of physical and psychic aspects of life. Media: Cast and fabricated metal; materials for light control. Dealer: Prairie House Gallery 213 S Sixth St Springfield IL 62701. Mailing Add: 129 Springer Ave Edwardsville IL 62025

RYDER, MAHLER BESSINGER
PAINTER, ILLUSTRATOR
b Columbus, Ohio, July 7, 37. Study: Columbus Col of Art & Design, 55-58; Art Students League, 66-68, with Theodore Stamos; Sch of Visual Art, 67-68, with Edwin Gorey; RI Sch of Design, Provincetown Workshop, Mass, 77, with Victor Candell & Leo Manso. Work: E J Arnold Collection, Wis Univ, Superior; Col of Art & Design, Columbus, Ohio; RI Hosp Trust, Providence; Nat Ctr Afro-Am Artists, Boston, Mass. Comn: Mural for night club interior, US Army Baumholder, Ger, 62-63; Edward M Bannister (grave restoration), comn by RI State Coun for the Arts, Textron Inc, 75; A study of Am Revolution RI Black Regiment, RI State Bicentennial Comn, 75. Exhib: Am Artist in Uniform & US Military Artists, Bonn Gov & US Foreign Serv, US & Europe, 62; one-man exhib, Frankfurt Am Playhouse, Ger, 62-63; Eight by Eight, Riverside Mus, NY, 67; New Voices: 15 New York Artists, Am Greeting Cards Gallery, New York, 68; 30 Contemp Black Artists (traveling exhib), Minneapolis Inst of Arts, Minn, 68-70; Afro-Am Artists, 1800-1969, Mus of the Philadelphia Civic Ctr, Pa, 69; Drawing Soc Regional Exhib, Addison Gallery of Am Art, Andover, Mass, 70; Afro Am Artists New York & Boston, Mus of Fine Arts, Boston, 70; Contemp Black Artists in Am, Whitney Mus of Am Art, New York, 71; The New Humanists, Grace Gallery, New York City Community Col of the City Univ of New York, Brooklyn, 73; Blacks: USA: 1973, New York Cult Ctr, 73; one-man exhib, Whitney Mus of Am Art, 73 & Lenore Gray Gallery, Providence, RI, 75; Source Detroit & Canadian Heritage: Black Input, Gallery Seven, Detroit, Mich, 75 & 76; Nat Endowment Awards Exhib, Newport, RI, 76; Art from Black Perspectives, Detroit Bank & Trust, 78; two-man show, Two Afro-Am Artists (Mahler Bessinger Ryder & Romere Bearden), Nat Ctr for Afro-Am Art, 77. Teaching: Instr children's sculpture, Sompsec, Bd of Educ, New York, 66-67; instr illus & drawing, Art Students League, Ford Foundation Prog, summer 68; instr painting & drawing, New Sch of Social Res, New York, summer 69; asst prof illus & drawing, RI Sch of Design, 69- Pos: Exec secy protempore, Comt to establish Studio Mus in Harlem, New York, 66-67 & Black Emergency Cult Coalition, 69-70; dir, Afro-Am Art Ctr, Bd of Educ, Providence, RI, 71-72 & Fantasy World for Children, Providence Pub Libr, 72-73; mem exec bd, RI Vol Lawyers for the Art, 78. Awards: Painting & Sculpture Award, Art Students League, Ford Found, 64-66; RI State Coun for the Arts Proj Award, 72, 75 & 78; Nat Endowment for the Arts Award for work on Fragmentary Images & Symbolic Dialogue, 73. Bibliog: Robert Doty (auth), Contemporary Black Artists in America, Dodd Mead, 71; Neal & Di Gregorio (auths), Practically Speaking, Nat Libr J, 72; Barry Schwartz (auth), The New Humanism: Art in Time of Change, Praeger, 74. Mem: Black Emergency Cult Coalition; Arts RI (trustee, 71-72); RI Arts in Educ (task force comt, 72); Talented & Gifted Children RI Task Force Comt, 77; MacDowell Colony (residence, 72-73; fel, 72-). Style & Technique: Collage on paper, mixed media; Xerox; photo silk screen; found materials. Media: Collage. Publ: Auth, Eight by Eight (catalog), Riverside Mus, 67; illusr, Arts in Society, Univ Wis, 72-74; contribr & illusr, RI State Libr Booklet, 72; contribr, The New Humanism: Art in Time of Change, Praeger, 74; illusr & contribr, Any Art J, RI State Coun for the Art, 77. Dealer: Suzette Schochet Gallery Brick Market Place Newport RI 02840; Gallery Seven Fisher Bldg Studio 315 Detroit MI. Mailing Add: c/o RI Sch of Design 2 College St Providence RI 02906

RYERSON, MARGERY AUSTEN
PAINTER, ETCHER
b Morristown, NJ. Study: Vassar Col, AB; Art Students League, with Robert Henri; also with Charles Hawthorne, Provincetown, Mass. Work: Oil portrait, Vassar Col Gallery, Poughkeepsie; Fr Mus, Seattle, Wash; etchings, Metrop Mus Art, New York; oil portrait, Philbrook Art Ctr, Tulsa, Okla; etching, Bibliot Nat, Paris. Exhib: Allied Artists Am, New York, 71 & 77; NJ Watercolor Soc, Morristown, 71; Am Watercolor Soc, 72 & 76; Nat Acad Design & Audubon Artists, 72 & 74, New York. Pos: Corresp secy, Audubon Artists, 58-59; rec secy, Soc Am Graphic Artists; vpres, Allied Artists Am, 52-53. Awards: Maynard Prize, Nat Acad Design, 59; Hook Prize, Am Watercolor Soc, 62; Silver Medal, Nat Arts Club, 71. Bibliog: E Hobson (auth), An artist and a child, Foster's Daily Democrat, Dover, NH, 8/15/70; Ralph Fabri (auth), Today's art, 3/25/75; Charles Morralli (auth), article in Am Artist, 1/10/76. Mem: Nat Acad Design; life mem Am Watercolor Soc; life mem Allied Artists Am; NJ Watercolor Soc; Nat Arts Club. Style & Technique: Broad, strong conservative work, much of it painted with a knife. Media: Watercolor, Oil. Publ: Ed, Robert Harris, auth, The art spirit, 23 & Hawthorne on painting, 36; illusr, Winkie boo, 48; contribr, The artist, 60; contribr, Am Artist. Dealer: Grand Central Art Galleries 43rd St & Madison Ave New York NY 10017; Chapellier Galleries 815 Park Ave New York NY 10021. Mailing Add: 15 Gramercy Park S New York NY 10003

RYMAN, ROBERT
PAINTER
b Nashville, Tenn, May 30, 30. Study: Tenn Polytech Inst, 48-49; George Peabody Col, 49-50. Work: Mus Mod Art, New York; Milwaukee Art Ctr, Wis; Wadsworth Atheneum, Hartford, Conn; Stedelijk Mus, Amsterdam, Neth; Basel Art Mus, Switz. Exhib: One-man shows, Robert Ryman, 72, Guggenheim Mus, New York, Stedelijk Mus, 74, Palais Des Beaux-Arts, Brussels, 74 & Kunsthalle, Basel, Switz, 75; Whitechapel Art Gallery, London, 77. Bibliog: Barbara M Reise (auth), Robert Ryman, Studio Int, 2/74, 3/74 & Data, Vol 4, No 11; Phyllis Tuchman (auth), An interview with Robert Ryman, Artforum, 5/71. Dealer: John Weber Gallery 420 W Broadway New York NY 10012; Konrad Fischer Dusseldorf Germany. Mailing Add: 637 Greenwich St New York NY 10014

S

SAALBURG, ALLEN RUSSEL
PAINTER, PRINTMAKER
b Rochelle, Ill, June 25, 1899. Study: Art Students League. Work: Paintings, US Air Force Hist Art Collection, Washington, DC & Whitney Mus, Juliana Force Collection, New York; prints, Philadelphia Mus Art & Bucks Co Hist Soc, Doylestown, Pa. Comn: Murals, Arsenal & five park dept bldgs, New York, 36, Pa RR, Steamship Line & USS Constitution, 38 & New York World's Fair Sci Bldg, 39; movie sets, Green Pastures & Two Bouquets, Marc Connolly, Hollywood, Calif, 38; fullscale mural of Clairol Bldg, New York World's Fair, 64. Exhib: Decorative Panels Exhib, Bernheim Jeune Gallery, Paris, 27-30; Kraushaar Gallery, several 37-75, Whitney Mus, 38, Bodley Gallery, New York, 73 & 74. Bibliog: Robert V Godsoe (auth), article, Esquire Mag; Robert Blattner (auth), article, Am Artist Mag, 58. Media: Oil, Gouache. Dealer: Bodley Gallery 1063 Madison Ave New York NY 10028. Mailing Add: Canal Press Frenchtown NJ 08825

SAAR, BETYE
ASSEMBLAGE & COLLAGE ARTIST
b Los Angeles, Calif, July 30, 26. Study: Univ Calif, Los Angeles, BA; Univ Southern Calif; Long Beach State Col; San Fernando Valley State Col. Work: Univ Mass, Amherst; Wellington Evest Collection, Boston; Golden State Mutual Life Ins Collection, Los Angeles; Los Angeles Co Mus Art; Univ Calif Mus, Berkeley. Exhib: Sculpture Ann, 70 & Contemporary Black Artists in America, 71, Whitney Mus Am Art, New York; Black Artist Exhib, Los Angeles Co Mus Art, 72; one-woman exhibs, Calif State Univ, Los Angeles, 73, Whitney Mus Am Art, 75 & Jan Baum/Iris Silverman Gallery, Los Angeles, 77; Painting/Sculpture in Calif: Mod Era, San Francisco Mus Mod Art, 76 & Smithsonian Inst, Washington, DC, 77; San Francisco Mus Mod Art, 77. Teaching: Vis artist, Calif State Univ, Hayward, fall 71; prof art, Calif State Univ, Northridge, 73-75 & Otis Art Inst, 76- Pos: Costume designer, Inner City Cult Ctr, Los Angeles, 68-71. Awards: Purchase Award, Calif State Col, Los Angeles, 72; Purchase Award, Downy Mus Art, 72; Nat Endowment Arts Award, 74. Bibliog: Cindy Nemser, Conversation with Bettye Saar, Feminist Art J, winter 75-76; Channing D Johnson, Betye Saar's Hoodoo World of Art, Essence, 3/76; Spirit Catcher: The Art of Betye Saar, The Originals: Women in Art series, WNET-PBS, New York. Style & Technique: Mixed media, small intimate boxes and windows; materials combined with paint and graphics. Publ: Auth, Handbook, 67. Mailing Add: 8074 Willow Glen Rd Los Angeles CA 90046

SAARI, PETER H
PAINTER, SCULPTOR
b New York, NY, Feb 15, 51. Study: Sch of Visual Arts, 69-70; C W Post Col, 70-74, BFA; Tyler Sch of Art, Rome, Italy, 72-73, study with Stephen Greene; Yale Sch of Art, 74-76, MFA, study with William Bailey & Al Held. Work: Hirshhorn Mus, Washington, DC. Exhib: Abstraction: Alive & Well, State Univ, Potsdam, NY, 75; Report from Soho, Grey Art Gallery, New YorkUniv, 75; Rothmans Int Realist Exhib (traveling), Ont, Can, 76-78; This is Today: An Exhib of Works by Living Artists, Root Art Ctr, Hamilton Col, Clinton, NY, 77; Artists Look at Art, Helen Foresman Spencer Mus, Univ of Kans, Lawrence, 78; one-man shows, Lamagna Gallery, New York, 75 & 76, O K Harris Gallery, New York, 77 & 78. Teaching: Asst instr advan painting, Yale Sch of Art, New Haven, Conn, 75-76; guest lectr, St Lawrence Univ, 78. Awards: Yale Fel, 74-76. Bibliog: Alan Moore (auth), Reviews, Art Forum, Vol 12, No 10 (1974); John R Clark (auth), Peter Saari's new paintings, Artsmagazine, Vol 50, No 6 (1976); Gregory Battcock (auth), Why Art, E P Dutton, New York, 77. Style & Technique: Acrylic and plaster on irregular shaped canvases, resemble fragments of ancient wall painting, painted architectural ornamentation. Dealer: Ivan Karp 383 W Broadway New York NY. Mailing Add: 73 Warren St New York NY 10007

SAARINEN, LILIAN
SCULPTOR
b New York, NY, Apr 17, 12. Study: Art Students League, with Alexander Archipenko, 28; study with Hans Warneke, 34-36; with Albert Stewart; Cranbrook Acad Art, with Carl Milles, 36-40. Work: IBM Collection; Addison Mus Gallery, Andover, Mass; Fogg Art Mus, Harvard Univ. Comn: Sculpture for Fenton Civic Ctr, Saarinen, Saarinen & Assocs, 38 & for Crow Island Sch, 65; sculpture for Toffennetti Restaurant, Skidmore, Owings & Merrill,

Chicago, 48; eagle for Detroit Fed Reserve Bank, Leineweber Yamasaki & Hellmuth, Detroit, 52; bronze portrait, comn by Prof B F Skinner, 65. Exhib: World's Fair, 39; Los Angeles Co Art Fair, 44; Boston Arts Festival, 54-60; Beverly Farms Regional Art Exhib, Mass, 63; St Gaudens Hist Park, Cornish, NH, 75. Teaching: Instr lang of clay, Pratt Inst, Brooklyn, 59-60, Mus Fine Arts, Boston, 63-64 & Mass Inst Technol, 63-67. Awards: Jefferson Nat Expansion Mem Competition Award for Sculpture Gateway to the West, 48; Walter B Ford Prize for Eagle, 54; Beverly Farms Regional Art Exhib Award for Portrait Edwin O'Connor, 61. Bibliog: Clay sculpture, Arts & Archit, 9/42; Emily Genauer (auth), Super sculpture, This Week Mag, Detroit News, 9/54; Mabel Colgate (auth), Visit with L Saarinen, Boston Globe, 5/7/70. Mem: Cambridge Art Asn; St Gaudens Nat Hist Park (trustee, 73-75); Fine Arts Work Ctr Provincetown (hon trustee, 69-). Media: Terra Cotta, Metal. Publ: Auth & illusr, Who Am I?, Reynal & Hitchcock, 46; design for eagle used on book jackets, Americans, 63 & Short Chronology of American History, 63. Mailing Add: 224 Brattle St Cambridge MA 02138

SABATELLA, JOSEPH JOHN
ART ADMINISTRATOR, PAINTER
b Chicago, Ill, May 5, 31. Study: Univ of Ill, BFA(painting & graphics), 54; Univ of Ill, MFA(painting & graphics), 58. Comn: Acrylic painting on masonite (4ft x 48ft), Campus cafeteria, Univ of Fla, Gainesville, 64. Exhib: Isaac Delgado Mus of Art, New Orleans, LA, 57; Hunterdon Print Society, Nat Print Show, 57; Libr of Congress, Washington, DC, 57; Society of four Arts, West Palm Beach Fla, 63; Atlantic Artist Show, Clemson Col, SC, 64; one-man shows, Atelier Chapman Kelley, Dallas, Tex, 64 & Visual Arts Comt of the Jacksonville Coun of the Arts, Fla, 69. Teaching: Prof drawing & design, Univ of Fla, Gainesville, 59-66. Pos: Mgr, Elenhank Designers Inc, Riverside Ill, 58-59; asst Dean, Col of Archit & Fine Arts, Univ of Fla, 66-75; dean, Col of Fine Arts, Univ of Fla, 75- Awards: First Award, Arts Festival Six, City of Jacksonville, Fla, 63. Mem: Int Coun of Fine Arts Deans; Fine Arts Comn, representing the Nat Asn of Land Grant Cols and Univ, Washington, DC. Style & Technique: Abstract expressionist, representational. Media: Oil on Canvas. Mailing Add: 2510 N W 30th Terrace Gainesville FL 32605

SABATINI, RAPHAEL
PAINTER, EDUCATOR
b Philadelphia, Pa, Nov 26, 98. Study: Pa Acad Fine Arts, Cresson traveling scholarships; also with Arthur B Carles, Fernand Leger, Antoine Bourdelle & Constentin Brancusi. Work: Philadelphia Mus Art; Pa Acad Fine Arts, Philadelphia; Sturgis R Ingersoll Collection, Pennlyn, Pa. Comn: Frieze for Fine Art Bldg, Sesquecentennial, Philadelphia, 26; Mother Mary Drexel Chapel, Langhorn, Pa, 29; NW Ayer Bldg, Philadelphia, 28. Exhib: Sesquecentennial, Philadelphia, 26; Golden Gate Expos, San Francisco; Pa Acad Fine Art Ann. Teaching: Prof painting & sculpture, Tyler Sch Art, Temple Univ, 36-66, prof emer, 66- Pos: Comnr, Philadelphia Art Comn, 65-68; consult, Fine Art Comn, Redevelop Auth, Philadelphia, 71- Awards: Limback Found Award for distinguished teaching, 62; Percy Owens Mem Award for distinguished Pa artist, 63; 400th Anniversary of Michelangelo Award, Am Inst Ital Cult, 64. Mem: Artists Equity Asn; Philadelphia Art Alliance; Philadelphia Art Mus; fel Pa Acad Fine Arts. Style & Technique: Color and form to express concepts. Publ: Auth, Sculpture processes, Prothman Baldwin, 57. Mailing Add: 7318 Oak Lane Rd Melrose Park PA 19126

SABELIS, HUIBERT
COLLECTOR, PAINTER
b Wageningen-Gelderland, Neth, Feb 28, 42; Can citizen. Study: Tech Sch Art, Neth, with Bloothoofd, 57-60; Art Instr Schs Inc, Minneapolis, 64; Lino printmaking with Henk Krijger, 73. Work: Royal Ont Mus, Toronto; Philippine Nat Mus, Manila; UNESCO of Japan, Tokyo; Cownasville Art Ctr, Que; HRH Prince Bernard of the Neth. Exhib: One-man shows, Philippine Nat Mus, 72, Manila Hilton Art Gallery, 73, Richmond Arts Ctr, BC, 73, Galerie Heritage, Toronto, 74; Isetan Gallery, Tokyo, 74. Bibliog: Ian Trowell (auth), Netherlands artist, Art Mag, 74; article in Holland Herald Mag, 74; Fortunato Gerrado (auth), Philippine Themes, Philippine Can Trade Guide, 75. Style & Technique: Figro-fantasism using acrylics applied with sable brushes and soft colors mixed with compatible bright colors. Media: Acrylic on Canvas, India Ink. Collection: Work by Ladislav Guderna, Sengig, Appel and many Czech and Canadian art works. Dealer: Dr Igor Kuchinsky 118A Yorkville Ave Toronto ON Can. Mailing Add: 309 Kristin Grove Mississauga ON L5A 3E7 Can

SABINE, JULIA
ART LIBRARIAN
b Chicago, Ill, Feb 4, 05. Study: Cornell Univ, BA; Yale Univ; Inst Art & Archaeol, Paris; Univ Chicago, PhD. Teaching: Vis instr, Univ Ky & Rutgers Univ, formerly. Pos: Supvr art & music librn, Newark Pub Libr, formerly. Mailing Add: 1416 Genessee St Utica NY 13502

SABLOW, RHODA LILLIAN
See Roda

SABO, BETTY JEAN
PAINTER, ART DEALER
b Kansas City, Mo, Sept 15, 28. Study: Univ NMex; also with Randall Davey, Carl von Hassler, Charles Reynolds & Al Merrill. Comn: Baldequino (mural), designed wrought iron & line etchings on windows, St Bernadettes Cath Church, Albuquerque, 61; painted windows, Ascension Church, Pojoaque, NMex, 63; 15 paintings for children murals, pediatrics ward, St Joseph's Hosp, 66. Exhib: NMex State Mus Bicentennial, Santa Fe, 68; Albuquerque I, Albuquerque Mus, 68; Ariz-NMex Regional Exhib, Phoenix, Ariz, 70-71; Catharine Lorillard Wolfe Exhib, Nat Acad, NY, 71 & Nat Arts Club, NY, 72-73. Pos: Standards chmn, NMex Arts & Crafts Fair Bd, 67-68; dir, Naciemiento Art Competition, Nacimiento Mining Co, 72; mem, Old Town Archit Rev Bd, Albuquerque, 73-; co-owner, Galeria del Sol. Awards: Grand Award, NMex State Fair Prof, 68 & First Prize Oils, 70; Purchase Award, Regional Art Exhib, Phoenix, 70. Bibliog: James Newton (auth), Chili, not chicken soup, Phoenix Gazette, 73; Flo Wilks (auth), The colorful way of the land, SW Art, 12/77. Mem: Catharine Lorillard Wolfe Art Club; Artists Equity Asn, Albuquerque; NMex Art League; Am Artists Prof League. Style & Technique: Realistic landscapes mostly applied with delicate knife technique with brushed on detail. Media: Oil. Specialty: Regional arts and crafts; cooperative gallery. Dealer: Galeria del Sol 206 1/2 San Felipe NW Albuquerque NM 87102. Mailing Add: 705 Parkland Circle SE Albuquerque NM 87108

SACHS, A M
ART DEALER, COLLECTOR
b New York, NY. Study: Univ Mich, Ann Arbor, BA. Pos: Dir, A M Sachs Gallery. Mem: Art Dealers Asn Am. Specialty: Contemporary American painters. Collection: Attilio Salemme, John Ferren; contemporary American painters including Power Byothe, Daniel Brustlein, Bert Carpenter, John Gundelfinger, Stephen Lorber, Stephen Pace & Jullian Denby. Mailing Add: 29 W 57th St New York NY 10019

SACHS, SAMUEL, II
ART HISTORIAN, MUSEUM DIRECTOR
b New York, NY, Nov 30, 35. Study: Harvard Univ, AB(cum laude); NY Univ Inst Fine Arts, AM. Collections Arranged: Chinese Art from the Collection of His Majesty, The King of Sweden, 67; The Past Rediscovered, XIX Century French Painting 1800-1900, 69 & Fakes and Forgeries, 73 (with catalog). Teaching: Lectr art hist, Univ Mich, Ann Arbor, 62-63; lectr art hist, Minneapolis Inst Arts, 64- Pos: Asst prints & drawings, Minneapolis Inst Arts, 58-60, chief cur, 64-73, dir, 73-; asst dir, Univ Mich Mus Art, 62-64. Mem: Am Asn Mus; Am Fedn Arts (exhib comt); Col Art Asn Am; Asn Art Mus Dir; Int Coun of Mus. Res: Fakes and forgeries; American 19th and 20th century painting. Publ: Auth, Reconstructing the whirlwind of 26th St, Art News, 2/63; auth, Drawings and watercolors of Thomas Moran, In: Thomas Moran (catalog), Univ Calif, Riverside, 63; auth, American paintings at the Minneapolis Institute of Arts, 71; auth, Art forges ahead, Auction Mag, 1/72. Mailing Add: 2400 Third Ave S Minneapolis MN 55404

SACHSE, JANICE R
PAINTER, PRINTMAKER
b New Orleans, La, May 6, 08. Study: La State Univ, with Conrad Albrizio; Newcomb Col, Tulane Univ, New Orleans. Work: New Orleans Mus Art; Anglo Am Mus & Alexandria Libr Collection, La State Univ; Bell Tel Co, Birmingham, Ala; Fidelity Nat Bank, Baton Rouge, La. Exhib: Work Selected From La Boetie Gallery, New York for New York World's Fair, 65; Volkfest Exhib from New Orleans Galleries, Berlin, Ger, 68; Nat Invitational Art on Paper, Weatherspoon Gallery, Univ NC, 68; 11th Midwest Biennial, Joslyn Art Mus, Omaha, Nebr, 70; Sally Jackson Gallery, Hong Kong, 70; one-person show, La State Univ Union Art Gallery, 72; plus others. Pos: Adv coun, New Orleans Mus Art, 77- Awards: Ten juried prizes including purchase prize for govt bldg, Centroplex, Baton Rouge, La, 77. Dealer: Sandra Zahn Oreck Gallery & Sculpture Studio 717 Dante New Orleans LA 70118. Mailing Add: 370 S Lakeshore Dr Baton Rouge LA 70808

SACKLARIAN, STEPHEN
PAINTER, SCULPTOR
b Varna, Bulgaria, Nov 25, 99; US citizen. Study: Fleisher Mem Art Sch; Philadelphia Col of Art; Pa Acad of Fine Arts; Wharton Sch, Univ Pa; also studied sculpture with Paul Manship. Work: Smithsonian Inst, Washington, DC; Philadelphia Mus of Art, Pa; Norton Simon Mus of Art, Pasadena, Calif; Everson Mus of Art, Syracuse, NY; Denver Mus of Art, Colo; plus 40 other museums. Comn: Wood sculpture, Furman Family Trust, Washington, DC, 68; painting, Int Sci Meeting on Aging, Bulgarian Govt, Sophia, 77. Exhib: Notre Dame Art Gallery, Ind, 75; Greenville Mus of Art, SC, 76; Everson Mus of Art, Syracuse, 76-77; one-man shows, Fla Gulf Coast Art Ctr, Clearwater, 76, Moravian Col, Bethlehem, Pa, 76 & Washington, DC, 76. Teaching: Artist-in-residence painting, Univ Notre Dame, Ind, 75; guest lectr art, Moravian Col, Bethlehem, Pa, 75-76. Awards: Achievement in Art, Bulgarian Govt, 76. Style & Technique: Abstract expressionism; highly constructive colorist; very imaginative; strongly emotional and sexual. Media: Acrylic on canvas; wood sculpture. Mailing Add: c/o Dr A F Furman 12308 Loch Carron Cir Washington DC 20022

SADEK, GEORGE
EDUCATOR, DESIGNER
b Czech, Oct 12, 28; US citizen. Study: Hunter Col; City Univ New York, BA; Ind Univ, MFA. Work: Mus Mod Art, New York; Libr of Cong, Washington, DC; Morgan Libr. Exhib: Type Dir Club New York, 69; Am Inst Graphic Arts, 70; Typomondus, Frankfurt, Ger, 71. Teaching: From instr to asst prof graphic design, Ind Univ, 60-66; prof graphic design, Cooper Union, 66-, chmn dept art, 66-68. Pos: Dean Sch Art, Cooper Union, 68- Bibliog: Articles in Am Inst Graphic Arts J, 68 & Print, 70. Mem: Nat Asn Schs Art (bd mem, 68-71); Am Inst Graphic Arts (bd mem, 69-72); Col Art Asn (vpres, 74-76, pres, 76-78). Mailing Add: Cooper Union Sch Art Cooper Sq New York NY 10003

SADIK, MARVIN SHERWOOD
GALLERY DIRECTOR, ART HISTORIAN
b Springfield, Mass, June 27, 32. Study: Harvard Univ, AB, 54, AM, 61. Collections Arranged: Painting in British India, 63; The Portrayal of the Negro in American Painting, 64; Salton Collection of Renaissance & Baroque Medals & Plaquettes, 65; As Maine Goes, 66; Winslow Homer at Prout's Neck, 66; The Drawings of Hyman Bloom (with catalog), 68; Edith Halpert & the Downtown Gallery (with catalog), 68; Paintings of Charles Hawthorne (with catalog), 68; Portrait Reliefs of Augustus St Gaudens, 69; Life Portraits of John Quincy Adams (with catalog), 70; Black Presence in the Era of the American Revolution, 73; Christian Gullager: Portrait Painter to Federal America (with catalog), 76. Pos: Curatorial asst, Worcester Art Mus, Mass, 55-57; cur & dir, Bowdoin Col Mus Art, 61-67; dir, Univ Conn Mus Art, 67-69; dir, Nat Portrait Gallery, Smithsonian Inst, 69- Awards: Knight of Dannebrog, Denmark. Mem: Asn Art Mus Dirs; Colonial Soc Mass; Am Antiquarian Soc; Century Asn; Col Art Asn Am (coun, 75-). Res: Monograph and catalog raisonne on Gilbert Stuart in progress. Publ: Auth, Colonial & federal portraits at Bowdoin Col, 66. Mailing Add: Nat Portrait Gallery F St & Eighth St NW Washington DC 20560

SAFER, JOHN
SCULPTOR
b Washington, DC, Sept 6, 22. Work: Baltimore Mus Art, Md; Corcoran Gallery Art, Washington, DC; New York Cult Ctr; Philadelphia Mus Art, Pa; San Francisco Mus Art. Exhib: One-man shows, Pyramid Gallery, Washington, DC, 70, Westmoreland Co Mus, Greensburg, Pa, 71, Valley House Gallery, 71, US Embassy, London, 72; Findlay Galleries, 74 & 78 & High Mus, Atlanta, Ga, 78. Bibliog: Gerald Nordland (auth), John Safer and the light fantastic, Art Gallery Mag, 2/72; article in Harvard Law Sch Bull, winter 77; Doug Lewis (auth), article in Arts Mag, 78. Dealer: David Findlay Galleries Inc 984 Madison Ave New York NY 10021. Mailing Add: 10401 Grosvenor Lane Rockville MD 20852

SAFF, DONALD JAY
PRINTMAKER, ART ADMINISTRATOR
b New York, NY, Dec 12, 37. Study: Queens Col, City Univ NY, BA, 59; Columbia Univ, MA, 60; Pratt Inst, MFA, 62; Teachers Col, Columbia Univ, EdD, 64; Pratt Graphic Art Workshop, 59-62. Work: Mus of Mod Art, New York; Metrop Mus of Art, New York; William Hayes Fogg Art Mus, Harvard Univ, Cambridge, Mass; Nat Gallery of Art, Washington, DC; Philadelphia Mus of Art. Comn: 200 Prints, 67, 200 Prints, 68 & 125 Prints, 71, Int Graphic Arts Soc. Exhib: Smithsonian Inst, 61; Jacksonville Art Mus, Fla, 66; 15th Ann Print Show, Brooklyn Mus, 66; Ringling Mus of Art, Sarasota, Fla, 66; Boston Printmakers, Mus of Fine Arts, Boston, 66; Art on Paper, Univ NC, 68; group show, 69 & 20th Nat Print Exhib, Brooklyn Mus, 76. Teaching: Instr printmaking & design, Teachers Col, Columbia Univ, summers 65 & 66; assoc prof printmaking & design, Univ S Fla, Tampa, 65-67. Pos: Chmn visual arts dept, Univ S Fla, Tampa, 67-71, dir, Graphicstudio, 68-76, dean, Col of Fine Arts, 71-; consult ed, Art Jour, co-dir, Pyramid Arts Ltd, Tampa, Fla. Awards: Fulbright Grant, Italy, 64-65; Patrick Gavin Mem Prize, Boston Printmaking Asn, 66; Grant

Proj, Dir, Univ S Fla, Nat Endowment for the Arts, 73-77. Bibliog: Article in New York Herald Tribune, 12/65; John Canaday (auth), article in New York Times, 10/68; article in Print Collector's Newsletter, 7-8/72. Mem: Nat Coun of Art Adminrs (mem bd dirs, 73-75); Int Coun of Fine Arts Deans; Col Art Asn. Media: Prints and drawing. Publ: Co-auth, Images of Destruction: Monsu Desiderio and Jacques Callot, Queens Col, 64; auth, Modern Masters of Intaglio, Queens Col, 64; co-auth, Printmaking History and Technique, Holt, Rinehart & Winston, Fall 1977. Mailing Add: 514 Riverhills Dr Temple Terrace FL 33617

SAFFORD, ARTHUR R
LECTURER, PAINTER
b Boston, Mass, Nov 5, 00. Study: Alandale Sch Art, Boston, 22-26; Mass Sch Art, 27-37; Calvin Coolidge Col, BA, 44, MA(philos art), 48. Comn: Portraits Dr Chesley York, Pres, Portia Law Sch, Boston, 50, Francis Ierardi, Int Braille Press, 60, Dr Beaumont Herman, Pres West Mass Univ, 65 & Hon Daniel T O'Connell, Boston Bar Asn, Superior Court House, 70. Exhib: Jordan Marsh Ann; Manchester Arts Invitational, 48-50; Eastern States Expos, 60; Springfield Acad Arts, 61; Am Artists Prof League, 68. Teaching: Prof appreciation art, Calvin Coolidge Col, 46-48; instr oil & watercolor, Boston Univ, 48-56. Awards: Award, Gloucester Story, NShore Arts Asn, 55; Award, Fishing Gear, Jordan Marsh Ann, 58; Award, Figure Painting, Springfield Acad Arts, 61. Bibliog: Earl J Dias (auth), Hub art expert, New Bedford Standard Times, 50; Jera Elwell (auth), Arthur Safford the artist, NShore Town Talk, 70; A J Philpot (auth), Safford's paintings, Boston Globe, 44. Mem: NShore Arts Asn (pres, 58-62); Am Artists Prof League. Style & Technique: Realistic and impressionistic works in all mediums, portraits, landscapes, seascapes, fanciful. Media: Oil, Watercolor. Mailing Add: 3 Rock Neck Ave East Gloucester MA 01930

SAFFORD, RUTH PERKINS
PAINTER
b Boston, Mass. Study: Mass Col Art, BS; also with Henry B Snell. Work: Farnsworth Mus, Rockland, Maine; Va Mus Fine Arts, Richmond; Mint Mus, Charlotte, NC; Navy Hist Mus, Washington, DC; Ball Mus, Muncie, Ind. Comn: Portraits of interiors, Nat Cathedral, Mt Vernon, Lee Mansion, Hyde Park & Gunstor Hall; plus many others. Exhib: Critics Choice, Cincinnati; New England Contemporary Art; Am Watercolor Soc; Corcoran Gallery Art; Mellon Found Traveling Exhib, three yrs. Teaching: Instr art, Harvard Sch Educ. Mem: Am & Washington Watercolor Socs; N Art Asn; Northern Art Asn; assoc Smithsonian Inst. Media: Watercolor. Publ: Auth article in Am Artist. Mailing Add: c/o Guild Boston Artists 162 Newbury Boston MA 02116

SAGE, BILL B
CERAMIST, EDUCATOR
b Rapid City, SDak. Study: Black Hills State Univ, Spearfish, SDak, BS(art educ); Mont State Univ, Bozeman, MAA(sculpture); Mills Col, Oakland, Calif, MFA(ceramics & sculpture). Work: Crocker Art Gallery, Sacramento, Calif; Mills Col, Oakland, Calif; Archie Bray Found, Helena, Mont; Utah State Art Mus, Logan; Univ Utah, Salt Lake City. Comn: Welded steel sculpture, Robert DeWeese, Bozeman, Mont, 63; bronze sculpture, Walter Treadwell, Oakland, Calif, 65; ceramic wall sculpture, Reinhardt House, Mills Col, 65; ceramic sculpture, Murphy Favre, Inc, Spokane, Wash, 74. Exhib: 23rd & 24th Ceramic Nat, Everson Mus of Art, Syracuse, NY, 64 & 66; NW Craftsmen USA 66, Mus of Contemp Crafts, New York, 66; Folk Art Exchange Exhib, Prefecture of Hyogo, Japan, 68; Calif Crafts 6th Biennial Pac Dimensions, Crocker Art Gallery, Sacramento, 69; 21st-24th & 28th Spokane Ann Art Exhib, Cheney Cowles Mem Mus, Wash, 69-72 & 76; Ceramics/NW, Russell Gallery, Great Falls, Mont, 70; 1st-6th Ceramics W Ann, Art Gallery, Utah State Univ, Logan, 72-77; NW Am Crafts Coun Award Winner's Exhib, Mus of Am Crafts, New York, 73. Teaching: Instr arts & crafts, jr & sr high sch, Billings, Mont, 56-63; Assoc prof ceramics, Eastern Wash Univ, Cheney, 65- Pos: Chmn interim, Eastern Wash State Col, Cheney, summer 1968; Mem art comt, Cheney Cowles Mem Mus, Spokane, 70-73, vpres, 71-72; Wash representative, Am Craft Com, 74- Awards: Nat Merit Award, NW Craftsmen USA 66, Am Crafts Coun, New York, 66; Jury Award, Ceramics/NW, Russell Gallery, Great Falls, 70; First Place Award, Verbal/Visual Exhib, Mont Inst of the Arts, 76. Bibliog: LaDonna Fehlberg (auth), photograph & article in Mont Inst of the Arts J, Fall 1976. Mem: Archie Bray Found; Contemp Crafts Asn, Portland, Ore; NW Designer Craftsmen; Mont Inst of the Arts (vpres & pres branch, 60-62); Am Crafts Coun (state rep, 74-); Wash Art Asn, vpres, 67-68, pres, 69-70). Style & Technique: (Sculpture) Lost wax bronze casting, fabricated steel; (Ceramics) slab building and combination of ceramics and other materials. Media: Ceramic and ceramic combined with Plexiglas. Publ: Auth, Pottery, photography, poetry, Mont Inst of the Arts Quart, 67; auth, A potter's graffiti, Mont Arts, 67; contribr (photo), Ceramics Mo, 9/69 & 10/70. Mailing Add: Rt 2 Box 142 Cheney WA 99004

SAHLSTRAND, JAMES MICHAEL
PHOTOGRAPHER, EDUCATOR
b Minneapolis, Minn, May 4, 36. Study: Univ Minn, BA, MFA. Comn: Photographs SE Wash, Walla Walla Community Col, 76-77 & photographs E Wash, Eastern Wash Univ & Turnbull Game Reserve Res Sta, 77, Wash State Arts Comn. Exhib: Young Photogr (traveling exhib), 68-70; Be-ing without Clothes, Mass Inst Technol, 70; Photo-Media, Mus Contemp Crafts, New York, 71; San Francisco Mus of Art, 72; Synthetic Color, Univ Southern Ill, 74. Teaching: Assoc prof photog, Cent Wash Univ, Ellensburg, 65- Pos: Conceived & dir, New Photographics, ann exhib photographically related work, 71-; pres, Roslyn Arts, 72- Mem: Soc Photog Educ. Style & Technique: Photographic. Media: Color, multiple image. Collection: Vintage prints by Edward Weston, Brett Weston and portraits of Edward Weston. Mailing Add: Rte 4 Box 279 Ellensburg WA 98926

SAHLSTRAND, MARGARET AHRENS
PRINTMAKER, CRAFTSMAN
b Saint Louis, Mo, Oct 1, 39. Study: Lindenwood, Col, Saint Charles, Mo, 61; Univ of Iowa, Iowa City, MFA, printmaking with Mauricio Lasansky, 64. Work: Kobe Mus of Fine Arts, Hygo Prefecture Mus Collection, Japan; Okla Art Ctr, Oklahoma City; Wash State Printmakers Collection, Evergreen State Col, Olympia; Rainier Bank, Seattle, Wash. Comn: Ed cast paper prints, Weyerhaeuser Co, Launching Ceremony & N Pacific Paper Co, 76; cast paper mural (4ft x 6ft), Jr & Sr High Sch, Lacrosse, Wash, 77; cast paper mural (4ft x 8ft), Cottonwood Elem Sch, Silverdale, Wash, 77; four cast paper prints, Environmental Protection Agency, San Francisco, 77; three cast paper prints, Wash State Arts comn, Turnbull Res Station, Cheney, Wash, 77. Exhib: Int Trienniale of Colored Graphics, Kunstverein, Grenchen, Switz, 67; Int Miniature Print Exhib, Pratt Graphics Ctr, New York, 68; Seven from Wash, Printmaking Today, Hygo Prefecture, Japan-Wash Shington Sister State Exchange, 70; Ann Drawing and Small Sculpture Exhib, Del Mar Col, Corpus Christi Tex, 72-74 & 76; Nat Experimental Printmaking Show, Tusculum Col, Greenville, Tenn; Northwest Crafts Exhib, Henry Gallery, Seattle, 75 & 77; 1st Editions Graphics Competition, Oregon Arts Comn, Salem Ore, 76; World Print Competition, San Francisco Mus of Art, 77; one-man show, Cast Paperworks, Slocumb Gallery, E Tenn State Univ, Johnson City, 77; Paper as Medium, SITES, Smithsonian Inst, Washington, DC, 78-; Cast Paper, Pratt Graphics Ctr, New York, 78; Paper, Dayton Art Inst, Ohio, 78. Teaching: Assoc prof printmaking & drawing, Cent Wash Univ, Ellensburg, 65- Awards: Cannon Prize, Printmaking, Nat Acad of Design, New York, 66; Flax Award, Int Miniautre Print Exhib, Flax Art Materials, 68; Purchase Award, Statewide Services, Univ of Oregon, Eugene, 75. Mem: Am Crafts Coun, New York; Fiberworks, Berkeley, Calif; Contemp Crafts Asn, Portland, Ore. Style & Technique: Both drawing and cast paper subjects are everyday life using garments, plant forms native to the area and personal experiences in a realistic manner. Media: Printmaking, Cast Paper; Drawing. Dealer: Source Gallery 1099 Folsom San Francisco CA 94103; White Whale Gallery 7811 Pioneer Way Gig Harbor WA 98335. Mailing Add: Rte 4 Box 279 Ellensburg WA 98926

SAHRBECK, EVERETT WILLIAM
PAINTER
b East Orange, NJ, Nov 4, 10. Study: NY Univ. Work: De Cordova Mus, Lincoln, Mass; Montclair Art Mus; Newark Art Mus; Overlook Hosp, Summit, NJ; First Nat Bank Boston. Exhib: Am Watercolor Soc Ann, 54-72; Montclair Art Mus Statewide Ann, 55-67; Royal Soc Painters Watercolors, London, 63; Landscape I, De Cordova Mus, 70. Pos: Art dir, Reach, McClinton & Co, 34-68. Awards: Am Watercolor Soc Ann Prize, 61; Silver Medal of Honor, NJ Watercolor Soc, 70; Cape Cod Art Asn Watercolor Prize, 71, 72, 74, 76 & 77. Mem: Am Watercolor Soc; NJ Watercolor Soc (pres); Cape Cod Art Asn (pres, 71-72). Style & Technique: Fluid, strong design. Media: Pastel, Watercolor, Acrylic. Dealer: New England Gallery Chatham MA 02633. Mailing Add: Box 401 South Harwich MA 02661

SAIDENBERG, DANIEL
ART DEALER
b Winnipeg, Man, Oct 12, 06. Study: Julliard Sch Music. Pos: Pres, Saidenberg Gallery. Specialty: 20th century European and American masters. Mailing Add: 1018 Madison Ave New York NY 10021

SAIDENBERG, ELEANORE B
ART DEALER, COLLECTOR
b Chicago, Ill, Apr 7, 11. Pos: Owner & dir, Saidenberg Gallery Inc, New York. Mem: Art Dealers Asn Am (bd mem, 65-70). Specialty: Picasso, Leger, Klee, Masson, Gris, Braque & others. Collection: Picasso and School of Paris; Klee, Kandinsky, Feininger. Publ: Auth, Pablo Picasso Paintings, 57, Picasso Exhibition, 67-68, Fernand Leger-Gouaches, Watercolors, Drawings, 68, Paul Klee-a Retrospective Exhibition, 69 & Picasso-Recent Works on Paper-1967-1970, 70, (all catalogs). Mailing Add: Saidenberg Gallery Inc 1018 Madison Ave New York NY 10021

ST AMAND, JOSEPH
PAINTER
b New York, NY, Nov 10, 25. Study: Univ Calif, Berkeley; Calif Sch Fine Art, San Francisco. Work: Cathedral Sch, Kristiansand, Norway. Exhib: San Francisco Mus Art 75th Ann, 57; Palace Legion of Honor Winter Exhib, Calif, 60-64; Carnegie Inst Int, Pittsburgh, 64; Univ Calif, Santa Cruz, 69. Media: Oil. Mailing Add: 953 Kansas St San Francisco CA 94107

ST CLAIR, MICHAEL
ART DEALER
b Bradford, Pa, May 28, 12. Study: Kansas City Art Inst, Vanderslice scholar, with Thomas Hart Benton; Art Students League, with George Grosz; Colorado Springs Fine Arts Ctr, scholar, with Boardman Robinson. Exhib: One-man exhib, Okla Art Ctr, Oklahoma City. Teaching: Instr drawing & painting, Okla Art Ctr Sch. Pos: Dir, Babcock Galleries, New York, 59- Mem: Art Dealers Asn Am. Specialty: 19th and 20th century American paintings. Mailing Add: 20 E 67th St New York NY 10021

ST FLORIAN, FRIEDRICH GARTLER
EDUCATOR, DESIGNER
b Graz, Austria, Dec 21, 32; US citizen. Study: Tech Univ Graz, dipl archit, 58; Ecole Nat Superiure d'Archit, Brussels, Belg, 55-56; Atelier, with Victor Bourgeois; Columbia Univ, March, 62. Work: Mus Mod Art, New York; Mass Inst Technol, Cambridge. Exhib: Nat Inst Architects, Rome, Italy, 67; Changing Form in Archit, 14th Trinnale, Milano, Italy, 68; one-man shows, Mod Museet, Stockholm, 69, Hayden Gallery, Mass Inst Technol, 73 & Mus Art, Univ Tex, 76; Inst Contemp Art, London, Eng, 73; Archit Studies & Proj, Mus Mod Art, New York, 75; RI Sch Design Mus Art, 77. Teaching: From asst to assoc prof design, RI Sch Design, 63-77, chmn archit div, 77- Awards: Fulbright Fel, 61-62; Ctr for Advan Visual Studies Fel, Mass Inst Technol, 71-77; Nat Endowment for the Arts Awards, 73-74 & 76-77. Mem: Am Inst Architects. Style & Technique: Exploration of holography in architecture. Publ: Auth, On my imaginary architecture, Leonardo, 77. Mailing Add: 43 Barnes St Providence RI 02906

ST JOHN, BRUCE
ART ADMINISTRATOR, ART HISTORIAN
b Brooklyn, NY, Jan 10, 16. Study: Middlebury Col, AB, 38; Columbia Univ, 40; NY Univ, 46; Neth Inst Art Hist Sem, 64. Collections Arranged: The Independents of 1910, 60; The Life and Times of John Sloan, 61; The Calder Family, 61; Jerome Myers, 66. Pos: Dir, Mint Mus Art, 50-55; cur, Delaware Art Mus, 55-57, dir, 57-73. Res: John Sloan and the Eight. Publ: Ed, John Sloan's New York Scene 1906-1913, Harper & Row, 65; auth, John Sloan, Praeger, 71; auth, John Sloan in Philadelphia 1888-1904, Am Art J, 71. Mailing Add: Rushmore Rd Stormville NY 12582

ST JOHN, JOHN MILTON
PAINTER, MURALIST
b Oak Park, Ill, Apr 30, 11. Study: Univ Ky, AB; Syracuse Univ, MS; with Eliot O'Hara, Dong Kingman & Jerry Farnsworth; also with Jose Gutierrez, Mex. Work: Mus Art, Tel Aviv, Israel; Mus Art, Ponce, PR; Palacio de Bellas Artes, Lima, Peru; Palacio Nacional, Cartagena, Colombia; Syracuse Univ, NY. Comn: Epochs of Florida History (first exterior monumental mural on a pub bldg in US), City of Coral Gables, 55; Science of Highways (four murals), Ky State Off Bldg, Frankfort, 59; We, the People (two murals), Ky State Off Bldg, Louisville, 60; Landmarks of the Twenties, City Hall, Coral Gables; Man's Quest (exterior mural), Christiansen Family, Coral Gables. Exhib: Southeastern Regional, High Mus Art, Atlanta, 53; Mid-Am, Evansville Mus, Ind, 62; SCoast Ann, Ringling Mus, Sarasota, Fla, 63; one-man show, Dominico-Am Inst Cult, Santo Domingo, Republico Dominicano, 68. Pos: Dir, Old Mill Gallery. Bibliog: Piero Sanavio (auth), John St John, La Casa del Arte, San Juan, PR, 62. Style & Technique: Abstract realism, oil with painting knife. Media: Oil for easel paintings, vinyl for exterior murals. Mailing Add: Old Mill Gallery 486 First St Solvang CA 93463

ST JOHN, TERRY N
PAINTER, CURATOR
b Sacramento, Calif, Dec 24, 34. Study: Univ Calif, Berkeley, AB; San Francisco Art Inst, spec study with James Weeks; Calif Col Arts & Crafts, Oakland, MFA. Exhib: James D Phelan Award Show, Calif Palace of Legion of Honor, 65; Lucien Lubaudt Gallery, San Francisco, 65; Three, Col Notre Dame, Belmont, 73; Painted Landscape, Lester Gallery, Inverness, Calif, 75; one-man show, Crown Col, Univ Calif, Santa Cruz, 75. Pos: Assoc cur, Oakland Mus, 69- Bibliog: Thomas Albright (auth), rev in San Francisco Chronicle, 2/12/75. Style & Technique: Still lifes, landscapes. Media: Oil on Canvas. Publ: Auth, Society of Six (catalog), Oakland Mus, 72; auth, Louis Siegriest: a painter's topography, Currant Mag, 75. Mailing Add: 2736 Shasta Rd Berkeley CA 93308

ST MAUR, KIRK (KIRK SEYMOUR MCREYNOLDS)
SCULPTOR, EDUCATOR
b Quincy, Ill, July 7, 49. Study: Studied watercolor with F Morrison; Quincy Col; Univ Minn; Carleton Col, BA, 72, studied with R Jacobson, Academia di Belle Arti, Florence, Italy, 72-75, studied with S Loffredo, O Gallo, Buoninsegii, studied anat with Harkevitch; asst to R Puccinelli, Univ Int de Belle Arte, 73 & 74; Villa Schifanoia, Florence, MA, studied with E Manfrini; Simi Studio, Florence, 74-77. Comn: Series of drawings of bulls, Am Chianina Asn, 73; oil mural of old bridge, The Abbey, Quincy, Ill, 76; Heroic bronze of St Michael, Church of Buriano, Quarrata, Italy, 76; oil mural, comn by Dr William McReynolds, Quincy, Ill, 76. Exhib: Anthology of the Art of Kirk McReynolds, Quincy Art Ctr, Ill, 74; The Great Collective, Centro di Arte, Florence, Italy, 75; Foreign Artists in Tuscany, Torre dir Bellosguardo, Italy, 76; one-man show, Drawings, & Paintings & Sculpture of St Maur, Perseo Gallery, Florence, Italy, 77; Paintings & Sculpture of St Maur, The Abbey, Quincy, Ill, 77. Teaching: Prof sculpture, Gonzaga Univ Italian Prog, 77- Bibliog: Art Critic (auth), Kirk McReynolds, La Nazione, Florence, Italy, 77; Mario Bucci (auth), Kirk McReynolds, Sansoni Editrice, Florence, Italy, 77. Mem: Am Fedn of the Arts. Style & Technique: Classical draftsman; naturalistic figure sculpture in bronze, teracotta and marble; landscapes in oils. Media: Clay and bronze. Dealer: Venable-Neslage Galleries 1742 Connecticut Ave SW Washington DC 20009; The John Pence Gallery 550 Sutter St San Francisco CA 94108. Mailing Add: PO Box 158 Payson IL 62360

ST TAMARA
PAINTER, PRINTMAKER
b Navahradak, Byelorussia; US citizen. Study: Western Col, Oxford, Ohio, BA; Columbia Univ, MFA, studied with John Heliker; Art Students League, Studied with Seong Moy. Work: UNICEF, United Nations, New York; New York Pub Libr, New York; Woodbridge Free Pub Libr, NJ; Columbia Univ, New York; Fine Arts Mus, Asbury Park, NJ. Comn: Four Icons, Byelorussian Church, Cleveland, Ohio; Woodcut portrait of Dr Francisak Sharyna, comn by Dr V Kipel, New York Pub Libr, 68. Exhib: Young Printmakers 1967 (traveling show), The Herron Sch of Art, Indianapolis, Ind, 67; 37th Nat Art Exhib, Cooperstown, New York, 72; Davidson Nat Print & Drawing Competition, NC, 73; First New Hampshire Graphics Ann, Nashua, 73; 2nd Miami Graphics Biennial Int Exhib, Fla, 75; 3rd Hawaii Nat Print Exhib, Honolulu, 75; 15th Ann Artists Salon, The Okla Mus of Art, Oklahoma City, 76; 28th Nat Exhib of Contemporary Realism in Art, Mus of Fine Arts, Springfield, Mass, 77. Awards: Gold Medal, 75th Open Exhib, Nat Acad of Design, Catharine Lorillard Wolfe Art Club, Inc, 71; Purchase Prize, Nat Exhib of Medium & Small Prints, The Print Club of Albany, 75; Graphics Award, 15th Ann Artists Salon, The Oklahoma Mus of Art, 76. Bibliog: Pat Hipp (auth), Woods Enhance Her Art, Asbury Park Press, 3/13/77; Zina Stankievic, Let's Get Acquainted with an Artist, Byelarus, 77. Mem: Metrop Mus & Art Ctr; Hunterdon Art Ctr; Printmaking Coun of NJ; Catherine Lorillard Wolfe Art Club, Inc; The Print Club of Albany. Style & Technique: Landscapes in oil, free interpretation of nature's moods and impressions, semi-abstract; Etchings; studies of wildlife in representational style. Media: Oil and Etching. Publ: Auth & illusr, Asian Crafts, Lion Press, 70; illusr, Biography of a Polar Bear, G P Putnam's Sons, 72, Come Visit A Prairie Dog Town, Harcourt Brace Jovanovich, 76, Animal Games, Holiday House, 76 & Save That Raccoon, Harcourt Brace Jovanovich, 78. Mailing Add: 235 Hockhockson Rd PO Box 97B Tinton Falls NJ 07724

SAITO, SEIJI
SCULPTOR
b Utsunomiya, Japan, 1933. Study: Warabi Art Studio, Saitama Prefecture; Tokyo Univ Art, BFA(sculpture) & MFA(stone carving); Brooklyn Mus Art Sch, scholar, 8 yrs; stone carving with Kametaro Akashi & granite carving with Odillio Beggi. Work: Looking Back (bronze), Expansion (bronze), Muse (life size marble), Pensive (life size bronze) & Mother & Child (alabaster), Pepsico Co, Purchase NY; Mother & Child (life size granite), Methodist Hosp of Brooklyn, NY; Lea (life size bronze), Isaac Delgado Mus Art, New Orleans; Mother & Child (alabaster relief), Non-Ferros Int Corp, New York; Young Girl (marble), The Toyo Trust & Banking Co, Ltd, New York. Exhib: Ann Exhib of Nat Sculpture Soc, NY, 70-75; Ann Exhib of Nat Acad Design, New York; two-man show, Warner Commun Bldg, Rockefeller Plaza, New York; Japanese Artists of Brooklyn, Brooklyn Mus, NY; Azuma Gallery, New York, 75; plus many others. Teaching: Instr sculpture, Brooklyn Mus Art, summer 74. Pos: Awards jury for sculpture, Ann Exhib Audubon Artists, 73; mem sculpture panel for fel, Creative Artists Pub Serv Prog, 75. Awards: Outstanding Prize, Ann Art Festival Exhib, Tochigikaikan Gallery, Japan, 58; Cert of Merit, Ann Exhib of Nat Acad Design, New York, 73. Mem: Nat Sculpture Soc. Media: Stone, Bronze, Wood. Mailing Add: 925 Union St Apt 1G Brooklyn NY 11215

SAKAI, KAZUYA
PAINTER, ART EDITOR
b Buenos Aires, Arg, Oct 1, 27. Study: Univ Waseda, Japan, BA(lit), 52. Work: Univ Tex Art Mus, Austin; Inst Contemp Art, Boston; Mus Mod Art, Mex; Nat Mus Fine Arts, Buenos Aires, Arg; Nat Mus Mod Art, Japan. Comn: Murals, Pacifico Inc & Corrientes Mall, Buenos Aires, 59; ceiling, La Moderna Mall, Buenos Aires, 60. Exhib: Expos Universal de Bruselas, 58; Bienal de Sao Paulo, 61 & 62; Latin Am, New Departures, Inst Contemp Art, Boston, 61; Bienal de Venecia, 62 & 64; Mus Mod Art, Paris, 63; Guggenheim Mus, 64; Nat Mus Fine Arts, Buenos Aires, 65; The Emergent Decade, Cornell Univ & Guggenheim Mus, 66; Mus Mod Art, Rio de Janiero, 67; Mus Mod Art, Mexico City, 76; Univ Tex Mus, Austin, 77. Teaching: Vis prof painting, Univ Iowa, 72-74 & Univ Tex, Austin, 77. Pos: Art dir, ed art column & ed in chief, Plural Mag, Mex, 73-76. Awards: First Prize & Nat Prize in Painting, Pipino y Marquez Found, 60; First Prize, Salon de Pintura Actura, Buenos Aires, 61; First Prize, Brussel's World Fair, 68. Bibliog: Thomas Messer (auth), Emergent decade, Cornell Univ & Guggenheim Mus, 66; Romero Brest (auth), Art Today, Penguin, 69; Damian Bryon (auth), Aventura Plastica Latinoamericano, Foudode Cult Economica, 75. Style & Technique: Abstract geometric. Media: Acrylic on Canvas with Air Brushes. Publ: Auth, Hawaiian, Japanese Sculpture, 60 & Japanese Primitive Sculpture, 69, Ed Mundo Nuevo, Buenos Aires; auth, Noh Theatre of Japan, Ed Bellas Artes, 68, The Tale of Ugetsu, Ed Era, 72 & Korin, Madero, Mex, 75. Dealer: Galeria Juan Martin Amberes 17 Mexico 6 DF Mexico. Mailing Add: Anatole France 71-401 Mexico DF Mexico

SAKAOKA, YASUE
SCULPTOR, INSTRUCTOR
b Himaji-City, Japan, Nov 12, 33. Study: Reed Col; Portland Mus Art Sch, BA; Univ Ore, MFA; Rinehart Inst Sculpture, 63-65; also with Fredrick Litman, Michel Russo, Manuel Izquierdo & Jan Zach. Work: Parkside Gardens, Baltimore, Md; Jasper Park, Ore; Verlane, Lutherville, Md. Comn: Four concrete panels, Lane Co Recreation Comn, Albany, Ore, 63; two totem sculptures, Welsh Construct Co, Baltimore, 65; play sculptures, Hollygrove Camp Broadnax, Va, 70-71; play sculptures in concrete, South Hill City Coun, Va, 70- Exhib: Northwest Inst Sculpture Ann, 62 & 63; Rinehart Inst Ann, Baltimore, 64 & 65; Int Gallery Exhib, Baltimore, 65; Southern Asn Sculptors, Inc Ann Traveling Exhib, 70-71; Galerie Int Exhib, NY, 71-73. Teaching: Instr, Univ Ore Exten Div, 61-63; instr sculpture, Md Inst Eve Sch, Baltimore, 63-65; asst prof art, St Paul's Col, Lawrenceville, Va, 65-77; instr sculpture, Music & Arts Camp, Long Lake, NY, 73; instr, Mansfield State Col, 78. Pos: Dir arts & crafts prog, YW-YMHA Summer Camp, East Orange, NJ, 72. Awards: Comn Awards, Jr CofC, Albany, Ore, 60, Welsh Construct Co, 63 & South Hill City Coun, 70. Mem: Col Art Asn Am; Nat Art Educ Asn; Va Art Educ Asn; Southern Asn Sculptors Inc. Style & Technique: Abstractly, getting inspiration directly from materials and shapes to test what sculptures present to viewers; appearances of mass in space. Media: Bronze, Marble, Steel. Dealer: Eric Shindler Gallery 2305 E Broad St Richmond VA 23220. Mailing Add: PO Box 84 Mansfield PA 16933

SALAMONE, GLADYS L
PAINTER
b New York, NY. Work: US Army War Col, Carlisle, Pa; Lobo Arts Theater, Albuquerque; Kirtland AFB Officers Club, NMex; Albuquerque Nat Bank; Bank of NMex. Exhib: Ouray Co Art Asn, Colo, 68-74; Denver Art Mus, 69; Lawton, Okla Art Coun Int Art Show, 70-73; Nat Art Show, Pikes Peak Art Asn, Colo, 70-74; Okla Mus Art, 75. Awards: Best of Show, NMex Art League, 70; First Prize in watercolor, Montrose Art League, 72; First Prize in graphics, NMex Art League, 74; plus others. Mem: Am Artists Prof League; NMex Art League; Nor Este Art Asn. Style & Technique: Realism with brush and palette knife. Media: Oil. Mailing Add: 8301 Pickard Ave NE Albuquerque NM 87110

SALAZAR, JUAN
PAINTER, DESIGNER
b Mexico City, Mex, Apr 11, 34. Study: Inst Politecnico Nac; Escuela Pintura y Escultura Inst Nac Bellas Artes, with Carlos Orozco Romero. Comn: Engravings, Carton y Papel, S A, Mexico City, 71. Exhib: One-man shows, Galeria Arte Mex, Mexico City, 69, Agra Gallery, Washington, DC & Mus Nac Arte Mod, Mexico City, 72; 10th Anniversary Friends of Mex Art Show, Phoenix Art Mus, 73; Galeria Arte Mex, Mexico City, 77. Bibliog: Toby Joysmith (auth), The gallery goer: Mexico & purist Paris, The News, Mexico City, 77. Style & Technique: Abstraction and nature. Media: Oil. Dealer: Galeria de Arte Mexicano Milan 18 Mexico City Mex. Mailing Add: Madrid 209/3 Mexico City 21 DF Mexico

SALDIVAR, JAIME
PAINTER
b Mex, Dec 26, 23. Work: Mus Mod Art, Mexico City; Pres House los Finos Mex. Comn: Zocalo, Count Mariguy Hourlon; Villa, Pres Diaz Ordaz; Suave Patria, Pres Echeverria; Cathedral, Manuel Marron Collection. Exhib: Mischrachi Gallery, 65 & 69; Arte Naif Hispanamericano, Madrid, 67; Naif Triennial, Bratislava, Czech, 68; Retahlos de Poetos, Castle of Chapultepec, 71. Res: Art naif. Publ: Auth, Naif Painters, 70; auth, 400 Years of Plastic Arts in Mexico, 71. Mailing Add: c/o Mischrachi Gallery Genova Mexico DF Mexico

SALEMME, ANTONIO
PAINTER, SCULPTOR
b Gaeta, Italy, Nov 2, 92; US citizen. Study: Eric Pape Art Sch, Boston Mus Fine Arts Sch with George L Noyes; study tour of Spain & France with R R Goodell of Simmons Col; sculpture in Rome (patron William A Read of New York). Work: Metrop Mus Art, Columbia Univ; Newark Mus, NJ; Syracuse Mus, NY; Man Centennial Ctr, Winnipeg. Comn: Henry Ittleson, comn by Ittelson family, CIT Bldg, New York, 57; Gen Dwight D Eisenhower, Columbia Univ Alumni, 65; Dr Josiah Trent, comn by Dr & Mrs James Semans, Duke Univ Med Ctr, 75; bronze portraits of Pres John F Kennedy, Kennedy Mem Libr & Gen Dwight D Eisenhower, 77. Exhib: Gen Int Exhib, Salon des Tuileries, Paris, France, 32, 34, 35; Gen Int Exhib, Salon d'Automne, Paris, France, 33-34; Gen Nat, Pa Acad Fine Arts, 30-50; Art in Am, Metrop Mus Art, 50; Blossom-Kent 3rd Ann Sculpture Exhib, Kent State Univ, 70. Teaching: Instr sculpture, Nat Inst Archit Educ, 20-23; instr sculpture, Roerich Mus Sch Art, New York, 20-23; Spence Sch, New York, 37-38. Pos: Dir, Manhattan Art Proj of WPA for Mural Painting, New York, 34-35. Awards: Hon Mention Sculpture, Pa Acad Fine Arts, 30 & Art Inst Chicago, 31; Guggenheim Fel, 32 & 35. Mem: Hon life mem Nat Inst Archit Educ. Media: Oil, Watercolor; Terra Cotta, Bronze. Mailing Add: RD 4 Box 473 Easton PA 18042

SALEMME, LUCIA (AUTORINO)
PAINTER, WRITER
b New York, NY, Sept 23, 19. Study: Art Students League, 38. Work: Whitney Mus Am Art; Nat Gallery Art, Washington, DC; Ital Embassy; New York Pub Libr Print Collection. Comn: Mosaic mural, Mayer & Whittlesey, New York, 58; many portraits, 59-72; art restoration, Art Students League Painting Collection, New York, 72 & Manhattan House murals, 77. Exhib: One-woman exhibs, Duveen-Graham Gallery, 56, Loeb Student Ctr, NY Univ, 62, Grand Cent Mod Gallery, 64, Dorsky Gallery, 65, William Zierler Gallery, New York, 72 & 74, Fair Lawn Pub Libr, NJ, 76, Cape Split Place Gallery, Maine, 77 & Barbara Fiedler Gallery, Washington, DC, 78; plus many other group exhibs. Teaching: Instr, People's Art Ctr, Mus Mod Art, 57-61; asst prof painting & drawing, NY Univ, 59-70; instr painting & drawing, Art Students League, 70- Awards: Solomon R Guggenheim Found Scholar, 42; MacDowell Colony Fel, 62. Style & Technique: Oil on canvas, semi-abstract. Media: Watercolor, Ink. Publ: Auth, Color Exercises for the Painter, 70 & Compositional Exercises for the Painter, 73, Watson-Guptill. Dealer: William Zierler Gallery 360 E 72nd St New York NY 10021; Barbara Fiedler Gallery 1621 21st St NW Washington DC 20009. Mailing Add: 112 W 21st St New York NY 10011

SALEMME, MARTHA
PAINTER
b Geneva, Ill, Aug 30, 12. Study: With Antonio Salemme. Work: New York Hosp. Exhib: One-woman exhibs, New York, Paris & Sweden, 48, 63 & 74-76; Hudson River Mus, Yonkers, NY, 58; Jersey City Mus, 59 & 61; Int Platform Asn Exhib, Washington, DC, 69-71, 73, 75 & 77; plus other group exhibs. Mem: Int Platform Asn. Mailing Add: RD 4 Easton PA 18042

SALERNO, CHARLES
SCULPTOR, EDUCATOR
b Brooklyn, NY, Aug 21, 16. Study: Art Students League; Acad Grande Chaumiere, Paris; Escuela Pintura Y Escultura, Mexico City; State Univ NY, teaching cert. Work: Mus Art RI Sch Design; Ariz State Univ Collection Am Art; Atlanta Art Asn, Ga; Wadsworth Atheneum, Hartford, Conn; Grand Rapids Art Mus, Mich. Exhib: Carvers, Modelers, Welders, Mus Mod Art, 50; Am Pavilion, Brussels Fair, Belg, 58; New York World's Fair, 64; one-man shows, Weyhe Gallery, New York; retrospective, Sculpture Ctr, NY, 75. Teaching: Asst prof sculpture, City Col New York, 64-74 & Nat Acad Design, 78- Awards: Louis Comfort Tiffany Found Fel sculpture, 48; Purchase Prize, Staten Island Mus, 59; Margaret Hirsch-Levine Prize in sculpture, Audubon Artists Ann, 71. Bibliog: Frances Christoph (auth), Salerno sculpture, Weyhe Gallery, 65. Mem: Audubon Artists (dir sculpture); Nat Acad Design; Sculptors Guild; Nat Sculpture Soc. Style & Technique: Figurative direct carvings of humans and animals welded to glyptic possibilities of marble, onyx, alabaster, etc. Media: Stone. Dealer: Weyhe Gallery 794 Lexington Ave New York NY 10021. Mailing Add: 269 Little Clove Rd Staten Island NY 10301

SALINAS, BARUJ
PAINTER, GRAPHIC ARTIST
b Havana, Cuba, July 6, 35; US citizen. Study: Kent State Univ, BArch. Work: Inst Nac Bellas Artes, Mexico City; Beit Uri Mus, Kineret, Israel; Inst Int Educ, New York; Miami Mus Mod Art & Ft Lauderdale Mus Arts, Fla; plus others. Exhib: One-man shows, Palacio Bellas Artes, Mex, 71, Galeria Misrachi, Mex, 74, Harmon Gallery, Fla, 75, Galeria Pecanins, Barcelona, 75 & EditArt, Geneva, Switz, 75. Awards: Best transparent watercolor, Tex Watercolor Soc, 64; best watercolor, 10th Hortt Mem Ann, 68; Cintas Found Competition Grant, 70 & 71. Bibliog: Wifredo Fernandez (auth), Baruj Salinas su mundo pictorico, Ed Punto Cardinal, 71; Merle De Kuper (auth), Twenty-eight artists in Mexico, Ed Montauriol, 72. Style & Technique: Abstract, based on feeling of space and atmosphere; using brushes, pouring, spattering with surface of canvas flat on working area. Media: Acrylic, Misc Media. Publ: Illusr, Calendario del hombre Descalzo, 70; Resumen A I P, 71; Narradores Cubanos de Hoy, 75. Dealer: Harmon Gallery 1258 Third St S Naples FL 33940. Mailing Add: 2740 SW 92nd Ave Miami FL 33165

SALLA, SALVATORE
PAINTER, INSTRUCTOR
b Khosrovabad, Iran, Aug 3, 03; US citizen. Study: Fribourg Col, Switz; Royal Univ Galata, Constantinople, BA(archit); also with Chevalier Leonardo de Mango. Work: Springfield Mus, Ill; Grant's Mem Auditorium, Northlake, Ill; Acad Magical Arts, Hollywood, Calif; Niavaran Imp Palace, Tehran, Iran. Comn: Multum in Parvo (mural), Encycl Britannica, Chicago, 36; GI Heroes of Bataan, Vet Park Admin, Maywood, Ill, 49 & Last Mission (mural), Northlake, Ill, 60. Exhib: 33rd & 37th Ann Exhib, Artists of Chicago & Vicinity, Art Inst Chicago, 29 & 33; NShore Art Asn, Gloucester, Mass, 47-48; Combined Ins Art Gallery, Chicago, 66-68; La Jolla Art Asn, Calif, 73. Teaching: Life class educator constructive anat, drawing & painting, Am Acad Fine Arts, Chicago, 48-67. Pos: Official portrait painter, Chicago Civic Opera Co, 29-32. Bibliog: George Johnstone (auth), Salvatore Salla, Tops, 5/65; Malcolm L Karam (auth), Who's who in Assyrian art, Assyrian Star, 6/71; William W Larsen (auth), Salvatore Salla, Genii, 10-12/74. Mem: Fine Arts Soc of San Diego; La Jolla Art Asn. Style & Technique: Conservative expressionist; pastose-palette knife technique. Media: Oil, Watercolor. Publ: Contribr, Look at the Art Institute, 58. Mailing Add: 2420 Dulzura Ave San Diego CA 92104

SALMOIRAGHI, FRANK
PHOTOGRAPHER, INSTRUCTOR
b Herrin, Ill, Apr 27, 42. Study: Southern Ill Univ, BS, 65; Ohio Univ, MFA, 68. Work: Int Mus Photog, George Eastman House; Nat Mus Can. Exhib: Young Photographers, Univ NMex, 68; Vision & Expression, George Eastman House, 68-69; Serial & Modular Imagery, Purdue Univ, 69; one-man shows, Southern Ill Univ, 64 & A Presence Beyond Reality, Honolulu Art Acad, 71. Teaching: Teaching asst photog, Ohio Univ, 66-68; instr photog, Univ Hawaii, 68-71. Pos: Free-lance photogr. Awards: Intramural Res Grant, 68-70 & Honorarium to Document Vis Artists Tony Smith & Harold Tovish, 69-70, Univ Hawaii. Publ: Illusr, Popular Photog Ann; illusr, Young Photographers (catalog), Univ NMex, 68; illusr, Contemporary Photographers: Vision & Expression (catalog), George Eastman House, 68; illusr, Nude in the window, Camera Mag, 71. Mailing Add: c/o The Foundry 899 Waimann St Honolulu HI 96813

SALMON, DONNA ELAINE
ILLUSTRATOR
b Los Angeles, Calif, Feb 23, 35. Study: Univ of Denver Sch of Art. Exhib: Univ of Denver, 55; Univ of Northern Colo, 64. Teaching: Pvt instr for painting, 70-74. Pos: Free lance illusr, Salmon Studios, Calif, 60-; scientific Bks, McGraw-Hill, Harcourt-Brace & Freeman Publ. Awards: Book Design Illus Award for Symmetry, Freeman Pub, 72. Style & Technique: Visual realism and accuracy; pen and ink, acrylic and wash and air brush. Media: Pen, Ink; Acrylic. Publ: Illusr, The Psychology of Consciousness, Freeman Publ Co, 72 & Harcourt Brace, 76; illusr, Biochemistry/Stryer, 75, illusr & contribr, Chemistry/Linus Pauling, 75, illusr, An Indroduction to Genetic Analysis, 76 & The Handbook of Scientific Photography, 77, Freeman Publ Co. Mailing Add: PO Box 712 Vallejo CA 94590

SALMON, LARRY
CURATOR
b Winfield, Kans, May 5, 45. Study: Univ Kans, BA, 67; Harvard Univ, AM, 68. Pos: Curatorial asst, City Art Mus, St Louis, Mo, summer 68; asst cur textiles, Mus Fine Arts, Boston, 68-69, actg cur textiles, 69-71, cur textiles, 71- Mem: Am Asn Mus; Ctr Int Etude Textiles Anciens; Costume Soc Am; Int Coun of Mus (costume comt). Mailing Add: Museum of Fine Arts Boston MA 02115

SALMON, RAYMOND MERLE
CARTOONIST, EDUCATOR
b Akron, Colo, Sept 6, 31. Study: Mesa Col; Univ of Denver; Chicago Acad of Fine Arts; Univ of Colo; Calif Col of Arts and Crafts; San Francisco State Univ; Colorado Springs Fine Arts Ctr; Univ of Northern Colo, BA & MA(fine arts). Exhib: Univ of Denver Art Mus, 55; Colorado Springs F A Ctr, 61; Tacoma Art Mus, Wash, 64; State Univ Mo, 65; Master Cartoonists Exhib, Parke-Bernet, New York, 71. Teaching: Chmn fine arts, 66-74, John F Kennedy Univ, Calif & dean, Col of Fine Arts. Pos: Free lance graphic artist, Salmon Studios, Calif, 60-; art educ, John F Kennedy Univ, 66-74; art educ/commercial dept, Solano Community Col, 71-; cartoonist, assoc with Morrie Turner Wee Pals Comic Strip, 74- Mem: Nat Cartoonists Soc, New York; Northern Calif Cartoon and Humor Assoc. Style & Technique: Graphic illus, cartoonist, watercolor and acrylic painter & printmaker. Media: Pen and Ink; Color Wash. Publ: Cartoons in Saturday Review, FM and the Fine Arts Mag & Writer's Digest. Mailing Add: PO Box 712 Vallejo CA 94590

SALOMON, LAWRENCE
SCULPTOR, EDUCATOR
b Chicago, Ill, July 18, 40. Study: Art Inst of Chicago; Univ of Ill, BFA; Univ of Chicago, grad study(art hist). Exhib: Chicago Bienniel, 68 & Critic Choice, 69, Art Inst of Chicago; Playboy Invitational, Lake Geneva, Wis, 69; Kinetic Sculpture, Alonzo Gallery, New York, 69; Lyman Wright Art Ctr, Beloit, Wis, 70; The Five: Pub Works, The Univ of Chicago, 71; Art for Pub Places, Dept of Housing & Urban Develop Nat Competition, 73; Cool Abstraction, Richard Gray Gallery, Chicago, 76; one-man show, Planespace, Jan Cicero Gallery, 77; Romantic Structures: Abstract Art in Chicago (traveling exhib), Univ of Mo & Kans, 78. Teaching: Assoc prof fine art, Univ of Ill, Chicago Circle, 65- Awards: Art in Pub Places, Nat Competition, Dept of Housing & Urban Develop, 73. Bibliog: Amy Goldin (auth), Greasy Kid Stuff, Art Gallery Mag, 73; Chicago Art, articles in Art in Am, 77; C L Morrison, Chicago Dialectics, Art News, 2/78. Mem: The Five; Participating Artists of Chicago (secy, 68-70), Art for Pub Places (bd of dir, 78-). Style & Technique: Monumental Public Abstraction. Media: Metal. Dealer: Jan Cicero Gallery 433 N Clark Chicago IL. Mailing Add: 2116 N Bissell Chicago IL 60614

SALT, JOHN
PAINTER
b Birmingham, Eng, 1937. Study: Birmingham Col of Art, Eng; Slade Sch of Fine Arts, London. Exhib: Am Painting and Sculpture Today, 70; Am Painting 1970, Virginia Mus of Art, Richmond; Radical Realism, Mus of Contemp Art, Chicago, 71; VII Biennale de Paris, Parc Floral, Paris, 71; Die Metamorphose des Dinges, Palais des Beaux-Arts, Brussels, 71; Relativerend Realisme, Stedelijk van Abbemuseum, Eindhoven, Netherlands, 72; Sharp-Forcus Realism, Sidney Janis Gallery, New York, 72; Verkehrskultur, Westfalische Kunstverein, Munster, W Ger, 72; one-man show, Univ of Birmingham, Eng, 66. Teaching: Instr, various Cols of Art, Eng, 60-67 & Maryland Col of Art, Baltimore, 67-68. Bibliog: Grace Glueck (auth), New York Gallery Notes, Art in Am, New York, 11-12/70; J Patrick Marandel (auth), New York Letter, Art Int, Lugano, 1/71; Juergen Weichardt (auth), Neue Landschaft, Magazin Kunst, Mainz, 1, 72. Style & Technique: Sharp focus realism. Media: Oil on Canvas. Mailing Add: c/o O K Harris Gallery 465 W Broadway New York NY 10013

SALTER, JOHN RANDALL
SCULPTOR, PAINTER
b Boston, Mass, Apr 16, 98. Study: Art Inst Chicago, BFA; Univ Iowa, MA & MFA. Work: Northern Ariz Univ, Flagstaff; Menninger Clin, Topeka, Kans; var Roman Cath Churches; Univ Iowa, Iowa City. Comn: Paintings, archit design, sculpture, tiles & stained glass, Church of the Epiphany, Flagstaff, 63; woodblock wall mural, St Pius Church, Flagstaff, 69. Exhib: Allied Artists Painting Nat, Nat Acad Design Galleries, 66; Watercolor Biennial, Phoenix Art Mus, 69; Collectors Choice, Northern Ariz Univ, 70; Prints Exhib, Fedn Rocky Mountain States, 71; All Indian Artists, Heard Mus, Phoenix, 74; Nat Am Indian Exhib, Pine Ridge, SDak, 77; Nat Contemp Indian Art, Turtle Mountain Gallery, Philadelphia; one-man show, Verde Valley Art Asn, Jerome, Ariz. Teaching: Assoc prof art, Northern Ariz Univ, 46-66; vis prof art, Inst Allende, San Miguel Allende, Mex, 73-74. Awards: First Prize watercolor, Nat Indian Art Show, Pine Ridge, SDak, 73. Bibliog: Bugatti (auth), entry in Encycl Internazionale Degli Artisti, 71. Style & Technique: Do not exploit materials for themselves alone, but correlate what I am trying to express with the materials I am working with. Media: Oil, Watercolor, Acrylic; Stone. Publ: Auth, A Comparison of Three Fertility Figures, Univ Iowa Press, 54. Dealer: Turtle Mountain Gallery 220 Locust St Philadelphia PA 19106; Gallery Three 3819 N Third St Phoenix AZ 85012. Mailing Add: 11137 N Palmeras Dr Sun City AZ 85373

SALTER, RICHARD MACKINTIRE
PAINTER, PHOTOGRAPHER
b Iowa City, Iowa, May 7, 40. Study: Northern Ariz Univ, BA, 64; Univ Guanajuato, Inst Allende, Mex, MFA, 68. Work: Arthur Adams Western Collection, Beloit, Wis; Red Cloud Indian Sch, Pine Ridge, SDak; Phoenix Indian Sch, Ariz; Univ Wis, Green Bay; Northern Ariz Univ. Comn: Com Design, US Borax Co, Boron, Calif, 65-66; Photography, Orput & Orput, Architects, Rockford, Ill, 71. Exhib: Inst Allende, Mex, 66; Rockford & Vicinity, Burpee Art Mus, Ill, 69-77; one-man shows, Rockford Col, 74, Univ Wis, Green Bay, 77 & Concordia Col, Milwaukee, Wis, 77; Red Cloud Indian Art Show, Pine Ridge, SDak, 74-77; 50th Ann Exhib, Springville Art Mus, Utah, 75; Marion Locks Gallery, Philadelphia, 77. Teaching: Instr painting, Stanislaus State Col, 68; instr creative photog, Univ Wis-Green Bay, 73. Bibliog: Platt Cline (auth), NAU Show, Ariz Daily Sun, 73; Barbara Manger (auth), Salter Exhib, Mid-West Art Mag, 74 & 77. Mem: Rockford Art Asn; Wis Painters & Sculptors Asn; Col Art Asn Am. Style & Technique: Abstract and figurative, dealing with contemporary American Indian themes and images. Media: Acrylic. Dealer: Gallery A Taos NM 87571; Collector's Gallery Milwaukee Art Ctr Milwaukee WI. Mailing Add: Rte 1 Box 524 AA Lake Geneva WI 53147

SALTMARCHE, KENNETH CHARLES
PAINTER, ART ADMINISTRATOR
b Cardiff, Wales, Sept 29, 20; Can citizen. Study: Ont Col Art, Toronto, assoc, 46; Art Students League, with Julian Levi. Work: Art Gallery Hamilton, Ont; London Art Mus, Ont; Govt Ont, Toronto. Collections Arranged: Some Canadians in Spain, 65; William G R Hind: Confederation Painter in Canada, 67; Things: Still Life Painting 17th to 20th Century, 70. Pos: Dir, Art Gallery Windsor, 46-; art critic, Windsor Star, 47- Mem: Ont Asn Art Galleries (pres, 68-69); Can Art Mus Dirs Orgn (secy, 62-64); Can Mus Asn. Mailing Add: 995 Chilver Rd Windsor ON Can

SALTONSTALL, ELIZABETH
PAINTER
b Chestnut Hill, Mass, July 26, 00. Study: Sch Mus Fine Arts, Boston, dipl; also painting with Andre L'Hote, Paris & lithography with Stow Wengenroth. Work: Libr Cong, Boston Mus Fine Arts; Boston Pub Libr; Yale Univ Art Gallery; Bixler Mus, Colby Col, Maine. Exhib: Libr Cong, Washington, DC, 42, 44, 45 & 49; Carnegie Inst Graphics, 46, 47 & 50; Boston Printmakers, 58, 67 & 69; Audubon Artists Ann, 60, 67 & 69; Print Club Albany, 71. Teaching: Instr painting, Winsor Sch, Boston, 23-28; instr painting, Milton Acad, Mass, 28-65. Mem: Artists Equity Asn; Audubon Artists; Nat Asn Women Artists; Pen & Brush Club; Boston Printmakers. Style & Technique: Representational or semi-abstract in oils and acrylics; lithography, representational. Mailing Add: 231 Chestnut Hill Rd Chestnut Hill MA 02167

SALTZMAN, MARVIN
PAINTER, PRINTMAKER
b Chicago, Ill, June 16, 31. Study: Art Inst Chicago, 54-56; Univ Southern Calif, BFA, MFA, 56-59. Work: Nat Collection, Washington, DC; Univ Calif, Berkeley Art Mus; Ackland Art Mus, Chapel Hill, NC; Univ Southern Calif, Los Angeles; Portland Mus Art, Ore. Exhib: Los Angeles Artists & Vicinity Ann, Los Angeles Co Mus, 57-59; Pasadena Mus Nat Print

Festival, Calif, 58; Ball State Ann, 59, 61, 66 & 67; Artists of Ore Painting & Sculpture Ann, 64-65; Northwest Printmakers, Seattle, Wash, 66-67. Teaching: Vis lectr printmaking, Univ Southern Calif, 66-67; prof painting & studio chmn, Univ NC, Chapel Hill, 67-74, chmn fine arts div, 76-, Pogue Fel, 78-79. Media: Oil; Intaglio. Mailing Add: 717 Emory Dr Chapel Hill NC 27514

SALTZMAN, WILLIAM
PAINTER, DESIGNER
b Minneapolis, Minn, July 9, 16. Study: Univ Minn, BS, 40. Work: Mayo Clin, Rochester, Minn; Minneapolis Inst Art; Walker Art Ctr, Minneapolis; Joslyn Mus, Omaha, Nebr; plus others. Comn: Ten Commandments, Eternal Light (welded sculpture & candelabra), B'nai Abraham Synagogue, St Louis Park, Minneapolis, 65; stained glass windows & meditation chapel, Univ Minn Hosps, Minneapolis, 65; copper relief sculptures, Univ Nebr Law Sch Bldg, Lincoln & First Nat Bank, Sioux Falls, SDak, 75; plus others. Exhib: Abstract and Surrealist American Art, 58th Ann Exhib Am Paintings & Sculpture, Art Inst Chicago, 48; 13th Ann Watercolor Exhib, San Francisco Art Asn, San Francisco Mus Art, 49; Ann Exhib Contemp Am Painting, Whitney Mus Am Art, New York, 52; 1952 Pittsburgh Int Exhib Contemp Painting, Carnegie Inst Int, 52; 5th Midwest Biennial Exhib, Joslyn Art Mus, 58; one-man show, Philbrook Mus, Tulsa, Okla, 72; Watercolor USA, Springfield Mus, Mo, 77; Sculpture, Coast to Coast Stores Hq, Edina, Minn, 78; plus others. Teaching: Instr painting & drawing, Exten Div, Univ Minn, asst & actg dir, Univ Minn Gallery, Minneapolis, 46-48; guest instr, St Olaf Col, 51-54; vis prof, Univ Nebr, Lincoln, spring 64; assoc prof art, Macalester Col, 66-74, prof art, 74- Pos: Supvr art, Fairmont Pub Schs, Minn; camouflage adv, USA Engrs, 42-46; mem gov comt, Minn State Art Soc, 46-50; resident artist & dir, Rochester Art Ctr, 48-64; juror, many exhibs, Iowa, Wis & Minn, 48- Awards: Best in Painting Award, 48th Ann Minn State Fair, St Paul, 59; Guild for Relig Arch Award, 73; AIA Assoc Art Award, 73; plus others. Mem: Nat Soc Mural Painters & Sculptors. Style & Technique: Semi-abstract expression of visual energy. Dealer: Suzanne Kohn Gallery 1690 Grand Ave St Paul MN 55105. Mailing Add: 5140 Lyndale Ave S Minneapolis MN 55419

SALZMAN, RICK
VIDEO ARTIST, SCULPTOR
b New Brunswick, NJ, Sept 11, 43. Study: Fla State Univ, with Karl Zerbe & Arthur Deschasis, AB; Syracuse Univ, MFA; George Washington Univ. Work: Chrysler Mus Art, Provincetown, Mass; World Trade Ctr Bldg, New York; Norton Gallery Art, West Palm Beach, Fla; Fairlawn Pub Libr, NJ; Drury Col, Springfield, Mo. Exhib: One-man shows, Spectrum Gallery, 72 & Razor Gallery, 74, New York; Nat Sculpture, traveling to selected mus, US, 73-74; Pa Sculpture, Philadelphia, 73; 3rd Int Encounter on Video, France, Italy & Arg, 75. Bibliog: John Canaday (auth), article in New York Times, 3/73; Gordon Brown & Nancy Murray (auths), article in Arts Mag, 4/73. Mem: Col Art Asn Am; Artist's Equity Asn; Soc Plastic Engrs. Style & Technique: Personal and group performance in video and photography; color and light in plastics. Mailing Add: c/o Razor Gallery 464 W Broadway New York NY 10012

SAMARAS, LUCAS
SCULPTOR
b Kastoria, Greece, Sept 14, 36; US citizen. Study: Rutgers Univ, BA, 59, with Alan Kaprow; Columbia Univ, 59-62, with Meyer Schapiro. Work: Metrop Mus Art, Whitney Mus Am Art & Mus Mod Art, New York; Albright-Knox Art Gallery, Buffalo, NY; Los Angeles Co Mus Art; Walker Art Ctr, Minneapolis; City Art Mus, St Louis. Exhib: Art Inst Chicago, 67 & 74; The Obsessive Image, Inst Contemp Art, London, 68; Dada, Surrealism & Their Heritage, Mus Mod Art, New York, 68; Documenta, Kassel, Ger, 68 & 72; Retrospective, Mus Contemp Arts, Chicago, 71 & Whitney Mus Am Art Ann, 72; Whitney Mus Am Art, 74; Art Inst Chicago, 74; Mus Contemp Art, Chicago, 75; plus others. Bibliog: Barbara Schwartz (auth), An interview with Lucas Samaras, Craft Horizons, 12/72; Kim Levin (auth), Eros, Samaras & recent art, 12/72 & Jeffrey Hoffeld (auth), Lucas Samaras: the new pastels, 3/75, Artsmag; Sam Hunter (auth), American Art of the Twentieth Century, 73; plus others. Mailing Add: 52 W 71st St New York NY 10023

SAMBURG, GRACE (BLANCHE)
PAINTER, LITHOGRAPHER
b New York, NY. Study: Art Students League, painting with Morris Kantor & Raphael Soyer; New Sch for Social Res, stage design & lighting; Contemp Art Gallery Graphic Workshop, with Michael Ponce de Leon; also with Philip Guston. Work: Slide Collection, Mus Fine Arts, Boston. Exhib: One-woman shows, Interart Gallery & Green Mountain Gallery, New York, 73 & Women in the Arts Found, New York, 76; Silvermine Guild of Artists Ann, New Canaan, Conn, 59; ACA Gallery, New York, 61-63; Works on Paper, Brooklyn Mus, New York, 75; Fairleigh Dickinson Univ, NJ, 75; Artists Choice (traveling exhib), State Univ NY, Binghamton, 76; Chatham Col, Pittsburgh, Pa, 76; Randolph-Macon Women's Col, Lynchburg, Va, 77; Va Polytechnic Inst & State Univ, Blacksburg, 77. Bibliog: Lawrence Campbell (auth), rev in Art News, 9/73; Gordon Brown (auth), rev in Arts Mag, 11/73; Lucy Lippard (auth), From the Center, Feminist Essays on Women's Art, Dutton, 76. Mem: Women in the Arts. Style & Technique: Figurative paintings of the urban environment, interior and exterior; glaze technique frequently employed. Media: Oil on Canvas. Publ: Contribr, Arts Mag, 67; contribr, Art News, 67. Dealer: Gloria Cortella Inc 41 E 57th St New York NY 10022. Mailing Add: 3 Rutherford Pl New York NY 10003

SAMERJAN, GEORGE E
DESIGNER, PAINTER
b Boston, Mass, May 12, 15. Study: Art Ctr Col, grad, 38; Chouinard Art Inst, 33; Otis Art Inst, 40-41; also with Alexander Brook & Willard Nash. Work: San Diego Fine Arts Soc; Fla Southern Col; Abbott Labs; Ford Motor Co Collection; Cole of Calif, Los Angeles; plus others. Comn: Designed Arctic Commemorative Stamp, 59, Adlai Stevenson Mem Stamp, 65 & Erie Canal Sesquicentennial Stamp, 67, US Post Off Dept; SC Tricentennial, 70. Exhib: Nat Acad Design; Pa Acad Fine Arts, Philadelphia; Denver Art Mus; Corcoran Gallery Art, Washington, DC; Liege Belg & Paris, France; plus others. Teaching: Lectr, Introduction to the Graphic Arts & adj asst prof, NY Univ. Pos: Doc artist, USAF in the Arctic & elsewhere; chmn, Soc Illusrs Sem, 62-63. Awards: Art Dirs Club Philadelphia & Calif Watercolor Soc Awards; Am Watercolor Soc Award, Oakland Art Gallery; plus others. Mem: Am Watercolor Soc; Audubon Artists. Mailing Add: Cantitoe St Katonah NY 10536

SAMPLINER, MR & MRS PAUL H
COLLECTORS
Collection: French impressionist paintings. Mailing Add: 150 Central Park S New York NY 10019

SAMSTAG, GORDON
PAINTER, SCULPTOR
b New York, NY, June 21, 06. Study: Nat Acad Design Sch; Art Students League; also schs in Paris. Work: Toledo Mus, Ohio; Santa Barbara Mus; Aldridge Collection, Australia. Comn: Paintings, Reidsville, NC Post Off & Scarsdale, NY Post Off; 23D Collage, Diamond Christensen, Adelaide. Exhib: Pa Acad Fine Arts; Corcoran Gallery Art, 58; Carnegie Int, 59; Contemp Art Soc Interstate, Hobart Tas, Melbourne & Sydney, 67-70. Teaching: Dir, Am Art Sch, New York, 51-61; sr lectr fine art, painting & sculpture, South Australian Sch Art, 61-71. Awards: Clarke Prize, Nat Acad Design, 49; Lippincott Prize, Pa Acad Fine Arts, 50; Woodville Critics Prize, 68. Mem: Nat Acad Design; Contemp Art Soc (pres, 68); Royal South Australian Soc Art; Burnside Painting Group (pres, 64). Publ: Ed, Bull Australian Soc Educ Through Art, 68, Contemp Art Soc Quart, 69 & Collection, Elliot Aldridge, 70. Mailing Add: 14 Bayview Crescent Beaumont South Australia

SAMUELS, GERALD
PAINTER, SCULPTOR
b Brooklyn, NY, Nov 14, 27. Study: Long Island Univ; City Col New York; NY Univ; Pratt Inst; also with Moses Soyer, Phillip Evergood, Hand Hoffman. Work: Mass Inst Technol; San Francisco Mus. Exhib: One-man shows, Drawing & Sculpture, Molesworth Gallery, New York, 69, Painting, River Run Gallery, Martha's Vineyard, 74 & Painting, Landmark Gallery, New York, 75; Paintings, Maine Coast Artist, 74. Teaching: Asst prof painting, sculpture, drawing & painting, Brooklyn Col, 70- Style & Technique: Expressionist. Mailing Add: 799 Greenwich St New York NY 10014

SAMUELS, HAROLD & PEGGY
ART HISTORIANS, ART DEALERS
Harold, b Brooklyn, NY, July 9, 17; Peggy, b Brooklyn, NY, Nov 27, 22. Study: Harold, Ohio Univ, BA(art hist), MA; Harvard Univ, LLB; Art Students League; also with Stuart Davis & Wayne Davis; Peggy, NY Univ, BS, 44. Pos: Both presently writers, art dealers, antiquarian book dealers as Harold & Peggy Samuels; Peggy was an ed Woman's Day, 45-48; both have lectured on how to buy a painting, restoring paintings, how to buy western painting, buying paintings for investment and other subjects pertaining to art. Res: Maintain data on 2000 artists of American West before 1950; biographer and preparer of catalog raisonne for Frederic Remington. Specialty: Paintings of the American and Canadian West before 1950, including illustrations. Interest: Peggy, Biographical data pertaining to American artists of the first third of the 20th century. Publ: Co-auth, Illustrated Biographical Encyclopedia of Artists of the American West, Doubleday, 76; Harold, auth, The Life of Frederic Remington & Catalog Raisonne of the Paintings of Frederic Remington (in press); co-auth, The Collected Writings of Frederic Remington, Doubleday, 78. Mailing Add: Box 465 Locust Valley NY 11560

SAMUELS, JOHN STOCKWELL, 3D
COLLECTOR, PATRON
b Galveston, Tex, Sept 15, 33. Study: Tex A & M Univ, BA(econ & eng), 54 & MS(econ), 54; Harvard Univ, BL, 60. Collection: American and French paintings and decorative arts. Mailing Add: 25 Broadway New York NY 10004

SAMUELSON, FRED BINDER
PAINTER, INSTRUCTOR
b Harvey, Ill, Nov 29, 25. Study: Sch Art Inst Chicago, BFA, 51 & MFA, 53; Univ Chicago, 46-53. Work: Denver Art Mus, Colo; Witte Mus, San Antonio, Tex; Ohio Univ, Athens; Tex Fine Arts Asn, Laguna Gloria Mus, Austin. Comn: Acrylic mural, Hemisfair 68, San Antonio. Exhib: 60th Ann Exhib Western Art, Denver Art Mus, 54; 20th Ann Tex Painting & Sculpture Exhib, Dallas Mus Fine Art, 58; Southwest Am Art Ann, Okla Art Ctr, 60; Segundo Festival Pictorico Acapulco, 64; 53rd Tex Fine Arts Asn Ann, 64. Teaching: Instr painting & drawing, Inst Allende, San Miguel de Allende, Mex, 55-63, head grad studies & painting, 65-; chmn fac, San Antonio Art Inst, 63-64. Bibliog: Leonard Brooks (auth), Oil Painting Traditional and New, 59 & Wash Drawings, 61, Van Nostrand Reinhold; interview, Time-Life, 65. Style & Technique: Abstractions with reference to physical things. Media: Acrylic. Dealer: Four Winds Gallery Kalamazoo MI 49001. Mailing Add: Apartado Postal 70 San Miguel de Allende Mexico

SANBORN, HERBERT J
LITHOGRAPHER, PAINTER
b Worcester, Mass, Oct 28, 07. Study: Nat Acad Design, Pulitzer traveling fel, 29; Teachers Col, Columbia Univ; Univ Chicago. Work: Libr Cong; Nat Collection Fine Arts, Smithsonian Inst; Hunterdon Co Art Ctr. Exhib: 10th Biennial Nat Print Exhib, Print Club Albany, 63; Jacksonville Coun Arts Festival, 64; Print Club Philadelphia Mem Exhib, 64; Va Artists, Va Mus Art, 65; Corcoran Gallery Art Area Ann, 65. Pos: Dir, Davenport Munic Art Gallery, 33-35; dir mus, Oglebay Inst, Wheeling, WVa, 36-42; exhibs officer, Libr Cong, Washington, DC, 46-76. Awards: Third Prize, 3rd Ann Va Printmakers, Univ Va, 62; Purchase Prize, Hunterdon Co Art Ctr, 64. Mem: Washington Chap Am Inst Graphic Arts (pres, 71); Print Club Philadelphia; Inter-Soc Color Coun; Soc Washington Printmakers; Artists Equity Asn. Publ: Auth, Hill towns of Spain (lithographs), 30; auth, Modern art influences on printing design, 56. Mailing Add: 3541 Forest Dr Alexandria VA 22302

SANCHEZ, CAROL LEE
PAINTER
b Albuquerque, NMex, Jan 13, 34. Study: Radford Sch, El Paso, with Carillo P Gonzales; Univ NMex, with Lez Haas, Walter Kuhlman & Kenneth Adams, 60-63. Comn: Portrait (charcoal), comn by Maurice Bonney, Albuquerque, 61; portrait (charcoal & conte), comn by N D Patterson, SAfrica, 64; landscape (oil), comn by Hon E Lee Francis, Cubero, NMex, 66; portrait (conte), comn by Philip Rose, Vt, 68; landscape with Am Indian symbols (oil), Native Am Studies, San Francisco State Univ, 76. Exhib: San Francisco Art Festival, 67 & 72; one-person shows, San Francisco Art Festival, 73-77 & Frederic Burk Found, 78; Nat Am Cult Symposium, Univ Calif, Berkeley, 76; Ethnic Studies Fac Show, San Francisco State Univ, 77. Teaching: Instr 2-dimensional design, Heliotrope, San Francisco, 68-70; instr painting & drawing, Fire Mountain Inst, San Francisco, 74-; lectr Native Am studies dept, San Francisco State Univ, 76-78; lectr world studies dept, San Francisco Art Inst, spring 78. Pos: Bd dirs, Casa Fondo de Recursos Cult, San Francisco, 71-; dir, Bay Area Poets Coalition, San Francisco, 73-74; Bay area coordr, Poetry in the Schs, 74-; co-dir, Intersection Gallery, 75-; state coordr, Calif Poets in the Sch, 76-78. Bibliog: Paul de Barros (auth), The poetry scene, Calif Living, San Francisco Examr. Mem: Artists Equity; Galeria de la Raza (secy, 73); Casa Hispana de Bellas Artes. Style & Technique: Portraits, landscapes, combining realism and symbolism; hardedge; abstract expressionism. Media: Conte, Charcoal, Oil. Publ: Contribr, Cosmos Mag, 70 & Second Coming Mag, 74; ed & illusr, Poets Gallery Mag, 74; auth, Conversations from the Nightmare, 75; auth, Message Bringer Woman, Taurean Horn, 77. Mailing Add: 32 Collingwood San Francisco CA 94114

SANCHEZ, EMILIO
PAINTER
b Nuevitas, Cuba, June 10, 21; US citizen. Study: Art Students League. Work: Metrop Mus Art & Mus Mod Art, New York; Brooklyn Mus, NY; Philadelphia Mus Art; Albright-Knox Mus, Buffalo, NY. Exhib: Colteser Bienal, Medellin, Colombia; Bienal 1 & 2, San Juan, PR; Pa Acad Fine Arts; Am Color Print Ann. Pos: Dir, Coe Kerr Gallery, Inc, New York. Awards: Eyre Medal, Pa Acad Fine Arts, 69; David Kapan Purchase Award, Am Color Print Soc, 70. Mailing Add: c/o Assoc Am Artists 663 Fifth Ave New York NY 10022

SANCHEZ, RAUL ESPARZA
See Raul Espara S

SANCHEZ, THORVALD
PAINTER
b Havana, Cuba, June 11, 33; US citizen. Work: Milwaukee Art Ctr, Wis. Exhib: Pintura Cubana, Caracas, Venezuela, 72; 15th Ann Hortt Competition, Ft Lauderdale, Fla, 73; 35th Ann Exhib, Soc Four Arts, Palm Beach, Fla, 73; East Coast Painters, Longboat Key Art Ctr, Sarasota, Fla, 74; Fla Artists, Norton Mus, West Palm Beach, 75. Awards: Best of Show Award, Fla Gulf Coast 9th Show, High Mus Art, Atlanta, Ga, 74. Bibliog: Georgia Dupuis (auth), Transition theme of Sanchez work, Palm Beach Post, 74. Mem: Fla Artist Group. Style & Technique: Hard-edge; flat color-no brushstroke technique. Media: Acrylic, Collage. Dealer: Center Gallery 327 Acacia Rd West Palm Beach FL 33401. Mailing Add: 146 Seminole Ave Palm Beach FL 33480

SANDBACK, FREDERICK LANE
SCULPTOR
b Bronxville, NY, Aug 29, 43. Study: Yale Univ, BA, 62-66, Sch Art & Archit, 66-69, BFA & MFA. Work: Mus Mod Art & Whitney Mus Am Art, New York; Nat Gallery Can, Ottawa, Ont; Kunsthalle Basel, Switz; Kaiser Wilhelm Mus, Krefeld, Ger. Exhib: One-man shows, Kunsthalle, Berne, Switz, 73; Folkwang Mus, Essen, WGer, 74 & Hessisches Landesmuseum, Darmstadt, 75; Sculpture Ann, Whitney Mus Am Art, 68; When Attitudes Become Form, Kunsthalle Bern, 69; Mus Mod Art, 69; Inst Contemp Art, Univ Pa, 69; Actualite d'un Bilan, Galerie Yuon Lambert, Paris, 72. Bibliog: Peter Hutchinson (auth), Perception of illusion: object & environment, Arts Mag, 4/68; Paul Wember (auth), Frederick Lane Sandback, Mus Hauslange, Krefeld, 69; Hermann Kern (auth), Fred Sandback, Kunstaum München, 75. Style & Technique: Three dimensional colored line situations. Media: Painted or Dyed Yard & Cord. Publ: Auth, 16 Variationen von 2 Diagonalen Linien, 72; auth, 16 Variationen von 2 Horizontalen Linien, 73. Mailing Add: c/o John Weber Gallery 420 W Broadway New York NY 10012

SANDBERG, HANNAH
PAINTER, EDUCATOR
b Safed, Upper Galilee, Israel, Aug 12, 04; US citizen. Comn: Ktubah (ceremonial marriage contract), Temple Emmanuel, Toronto, Ont, 74. Exhib: John J Myers Gallery, New York, 63; Zacks Gallery, Stong Col, York Univ, 75 & 78; one-woman shows, Lynn Kottler Galleries, New York, 56, New York Pub Libr, Hudson Park Br, 57, Living Art Gallery of the Educ Alliance, New York, 61, John J Myers Gallery, New York, 64, East Side Gallery, New York, 64 & 67, The Jewish Mus, Theological Seminary of Am, New York, 67, Zacks Gallery, Stong Col, York Univ, 71 & 74 & Hart House Art Gallery, Univ Toronto, 76. Teaching: Lectr 20th century painting, Yeshiva Univ, New York, 58-61; assoc fel painting, Stong Col, York Univ, Toronto, 70- Pos: Artist in residence, Stong Col, York Univ, Toronto, 75- Awards: Int Women's Year Grant, Genesis, Ont Arts Coun, 75. Style & Technique: Using strikingly brilliant colours and fluid shapes, paintings are luminous symbolic abstractions of Biblical themes, usually incorporating Hebrew calligraphy; expressionistic landscapes in a variety of media. Media: Painting, Acrylic-Liquitex; Gouache. Mailing Add: 11 Catford Rd Downsview ON M3J 1P9 Can

SANDE, RHODA
ART DEALER
b Staten Island, NY. Study: Pratt Inst & Parsons Sch of Design. Pos: Owner & dir, Rhoda Sande Gallery, New York. Specialty: Twentieth Century American and Mexican paintings, drawings, and sculpture. Collection: Picasso, Valtat, antique Persian calligraphy. Mailing Add: 61 E 57th St New York NY 10022

SANDECKI, ALBERT EDWARD
PAINTER, INSTRUCTOR
b Camden, NJ, Oct 10, 35. Study: Pa Acad Fine Arts, 53-59. Work: McNay Art Inst, Tex; Lubbock Mus, Tex; Corcoran Gallery Art, Washington, DC; Albright-Knox Mus, Buffalo, NY; plus many others in pvt collections. Exhib: Audubon Artists, 57; Pa Acad Fine Arts Ann, 57-60; Nat Acad Design Ann, 58; Wadsworth Atheneum Ann, 60; Philadelphia Watercolor Soc, 60-67; plus many other group & one-man shows. Teaching: Instr portraiture & still life, Sanski Art Ctr, 59- Bibliog: Edith De Shazo (auth), article in Courier-Post; John Cannady (auth), article in New York Times. Mem: Fel Pa Acad Fine Arts. Media: Watercolor, Oil. Interest: Conservator of paintings. Mailing Add: 50 Tanner St Haddonfield NJ 08033

SANDER, DENNIS JAY
ARCHITECT, DESIGNER
b Pittsburgh, Pa, Apr 30, 41. Study: Carnegie Mellon Univ, 55-59; Univ Pa, MA(magna cum laude), 63, Chandler scholar, BArch, 65, Grand Prix, Scheneck-Woodman fel, with Louis I Kahn & MArch(with distinction). Work: Whitney Mus Am Art; Ft Wayne Mus Fine Arts; Indianapolis Mus Fine Arts. Comn: Vet Stadium, City Philadelphia, 66-67; master plans, Bronx Zoo & NY Aquarium & Bldgs, 68-69; South Dearborn High Sch, 71; Alpha Rehabilitation Ctr, Alpha Ctr, Inc, Delaware City, Ind, 72. Exhib: Progressive Archit 19th Ann Design Awards, 72; Yale Math Bldg Competition, City Thousand Oaks, Calif, 70; Niagara Falls Conv Ctr, 73; Landscape of Man Exhib, Indianapolis, Mus Fine Arts, 73; one-man show, Ft Wayne Mus Fine Arts, 74. Teaching: Asst prof archit, Ball State Univ, 70-73 & Ohio State Univ, 73- Pos: Prin, Dennis J Sander AIA & Assoc, 68-; dir design, Morris Ketchum & Assoc, 69-70; chief consult archit, City Columbus Ohio Dept Develop, 73-74. Awards: First Design Award, Progressive Archit 19th Ann Awards, 73; Hon Mention, Niagara Falls Conv Ctr Nat Competition, 73. Bibliog: Ray Hughey (auth), With an eye for tomorrow, Citizen Jour, Columbus, 74. Mem: Corp Mem, Am Inst Archit; Asn Collegiate Sch Archit; Archit Soc Ohio, Pa & Ind; Nat Coun Archit Registr Bds. Res: Solar design in architectural design; environmental design criteria; schools and institutional buildings; social order influences on design; urban futurism. Collection: Modern art; young artists including, Ray Fried, Shiela Fried, Ann Schaller & writer, Henry Miller. Mailing Add: 5401 Riverforest Rd Dublin OH 43107

SANDERS, ANDREW DOMINICK
PAINTER, INSTRUCTOR
b Erie, Pa, Dec 22, 18. Study: Philadelphia Mus Sch Art, dipl, 42. Exhib: Butler Inst Am Art Anns, Youngstown, Ohio, 53, 54, 55, 64, 72 & 74; Nat Acad Design 146th, 147th & 149th Anns, New York, 71, 72 & 74; Audubon Artists 30th-33rd Anns, Nat Acad Design Galleries, 72-75; Mainstreams 72 & 73, 5th & 6th Ann, Marietta Col, Ohio. Teaching: Instr drawing, painting & art hist, Ringling Sch Art, Sarasota, Fla, 49-59; instr drawing & painting, Columbus Col Art & Design, 60-63; dir drawing & painting, Art Sch, Erie, 64- Awards: Edward C Roberts Award, Conn Acad Fine Arts, 73; Cert Merit, Nat Acad Design & Painters & Sculptors Soc NJ, 74. Bibliog: Joan Tomcho (auth), article in Am Artist, 9/75. Mem: Audubon Artists. Media: Oil. Publ: Auth, Murray Stern: social surrealist, Am Artist, 2/77. Mailing Add: Art School 18 N Park Row Erie PA 16501

SANDERS, JOOP A
PAINTER
b Amsterdam, Holland, Oct 6, 22; US citizen. Study: Art Students League, with George Grosz; also with De Kooning. Work: Stedelijke Mus, Amsterdam; Munic Mus, The Hague; Belzalel Mus, Jerusalem; Dillard Univ. Exhib: Ninth St Show, 51; Stable Shows, 52-55; one-man retrospective, Stedelijke Mus, 60; Carnegie Int, 60; Options, Mus Contemp Art, Chicago, 68. Teaching: Vis lectr, Carnegie Inst Technol, spring 65; prof painting, State Univ NY Col New Paltz, 66-, res found awards, 71-72; vis lectr, Univ Calif, Berkeley, spring 68. Awards: Longview Found Fel, 60-61. Media: Oil, Acrylic, Watercolor. Mailing Add: White Lands Rd 118A Stone Ridge NY 12484

SANDERSON, CHARLES HOWARD
PAINTER, INSTRUCTOR
b Hamilton, Kans, Mar 6, 25. Study: Kans State Univ; Emporia State Univ, Kans; Wichita State Univ, BS(art educ) & post-grad study; Ft Hays State Univ, Kans, MS(art educ). Work: Okla Art Ctr, Oklahoma City; Wichita Art Mus, Kans; Springfield Art Mus, Mo; Hockaday Ctr for the Arts, Kalispell, Mont; Birger Sandzen Mem Gallery, Lindsborg, Kans; plus others. Exhib: Mid-Am Ann, Nelson Gallery, Kansas City, Mo, 53-60; Okla Printmakers Soc Nat Print & Drawing Exhib, Okla Art Ctr, Oklahoma City, 60; Midwest Biennial, Joslyn Art Mus, Omaha, Nebr, 62-64; Watercolor USA, Springfield Art Mus, Mo, 62-75; one-man show, Wichita Art Mus, Kans, 65; Sanderson-Booty Exhib, Galerie Monti-Carlo, Charleroi, Belg, 72; Am Painters in Paris, France, 76; Charles M Russell Art Mus Art Auction, Great Falls, Mont, 77. Collections Arranged: Group Two—Invitational Kans Exhib, Century II Concert Hall Foyer, Wichita, 73-75. Teaching: Instr art, Kans Pub Schs, 51-78; instr painting, Wichita Art Asn, Kans, 58-71; instr teaching methods, Friends Univ, Wichita, 68-74; lectr & instr, Kans Art Educators Workshop, Wichita, 72-75; instr watercolor, Wichita State Univ Continuing Educ, 75- Awards: Purchase awards, Air Capitol Ann, Wichita Art Mus, 56-58; Kans Watercolor Soc Ann Exhib, 70-73, 75 & 76. Bibliog: Dorothy Woods Belden (auth), Creative Kansan, Kans Mag, spring 1974; Larry Hatteberg (auth), Channel Ten Mag Feature, Channel Ten Television, 76; Watercolor, Acrylic, Sculpture & Demonstration (four educ videotapes), Wichita Bd of Educ, 77. Mem: Kans Watercolor Soc (founder, 69 & pres, 71-72); Wichita Artists Guild; Whiskey Painters of Am; Kans Art Educ Asn. Style & Technique: Landscape, flora and building in changing styles of geometric, realistic, abstract and non-objective. Media: Watercolor, acrylic. Mailing Add: 902 Waddington Wichita KS 67212

SANDERSON, RAYMOND PHILLIPS
SCULPTOR
b Bowling Green, Mo, July 9, 08. Study: Art Inst Chicago; Kansas City Art Inst; also with Raoul Josset, Chicago, Ill. Work: Ariz State Univ Art Collection, Tempe; Symphony Hall, Phoenix Civic Plaza & Heard Mus, Ariz; Glendale Community Col, Ariz; Bust of Earl Halliburton at Duncan Airport, Okla. Comn: Miners Monument, Emergency Relief Admin, Bisbee, Ariz, 33; Three Ships, US Maritime Comn, 43; sculpture, 17 Valley Nat Banks, Ariz, 49-73; War Mem, Univ Ariz, Tucson, 50; Nikki Song Peters Mem, Scottsdale Fine Arts Comn, Ariz, 69. Exhib: Phillips Sanderson-40 Year Retrospective, Ariz State Univ, 73. Teaching: Assoc prof sculpture, Ariz State Col, 47-50. Style & Technique: Semi-abstract, nonobjective. Media: Wood, Bronze. Dealer: Thompson Gallery 3625 Bishop Lane Scottsdale AZ 85251. Mailing Add: 8002 E Granada Rd Scottsdale AZ 85257

SANDERSON, ROBERT WRIGHT
ART DEALER
b New Albany, Ind, Jan 28, 20. Study: Col William & Mary, BA. Pos: Dir, Bruce Gallery. Mem: Brooks Art Gallery, Memphis (trustee); Memphis Acad Art (trustee). Specialty: Contemporary art. Collection: Ships of the American Navies of the Revolutionary War. Mailing Add: c/o Bruce Gallery 4646 Poplar Ave Memphis TN 38117

SANDESON, WILLIAM SEYMOUR
CARTOONIST
b Mound City, Ill, Dec 16, 13. Study: Chicago Acad Fine Arts, 31-32. Pos: Free-lance cartoonist for nat mags, 32-37; ed cartoonist, New Orleans Item-Tribune, 37-41; cartoonist, picture ed & art dir, St Louis Star-Times, 41-51, daily cartoon feature, Sketching Up with the News, Star-Times; ed cartoonist, Ft Wayne News-Sentinel, Ind, 51- Awards: Honor Medal, 52, 53 & 56 & Distinguished Serv Award, 71-73, Freedoms Found; George Washington Honor Medal, 54, 55 & 57-60; Ind Sch Bell Award, 67; plus others. Mem: Nat Cartoonists Soc; Am Asn Ed Cartoonists; Cong Club; Ft Wayne Press (pres, 65). Mailing Add: 119 W Sherwood Terr Ft Wayne IN 46802

SANDGREN, ERNEST NELSON
PAINTER, EDUCATOR
b Dauphin, Man, Dec 17, 17. Study: Univ Ore, BA & MFA; Univ Michoacan, Mex; Chicago Inst Design. Work: Portland Art Mus, Ore; Am Embassy Collection; Victoria & Albert Mus, London. Comn: Murals in Eugene, Ore, State Univ Libr, Corvallis & Portland, Ore. Exhib: Denver Art Mus; Santa Barbara Mus Art; Brooklyn Mus, NY; also nat tours; Am Cult Ctr, Paris, Turin & Bordighera, Italy & Johannesburg, SAfrica; 46 USA Printmakers, New Forms Gallery, Athens, Greece, 64. Teaching: Instr art, Univ Ore, 47; prof art, Ore State Univ, 48-; guest printmaker instr, Pa State Univ, summer 66; guest printmaker instr, Cent Ore Col, summers 70-72. Pos: Exped artist, Am Quintana Roo Mex Exped, 65 & 66; exped artist, CEDAM Exped to Durango, Mex, 70. Awards: Northwest Painting Exhib, Spokane, Wash, 57; M H De Young Mem Mus, 58; Yaddo Fel, 61; plus others. Mem: Ore Artists Alliance; Portland Art Mus. Publ: Co-auth, A Search for Visual Relationships & Northwest Four & Two (color art films). Mailing Add: Art Dept Ore State Univ Corvallis OR 97331

SANDGROUND, MARK BERNARD, SR
COLLECTOR, PATRON
b Boston, Mass, June 6, 32. Study: Univ Mich, BA, 52; Univ Va, LLB, 55 & JD, 71. Teaching: Prof humanities & cooking, Free Col Belgravia, Lower Sch, 65-66. Pos: Pres, La Nicoise; dir, Hal Landers Art Trust Ltd. Awards: La Chaine des Les Robsier Chevalier, 71; Klip & Klop

Gold Medal, 72. Bibliog: D Kane (auth), Killer Kock and the White Princess, McGraw, 72; The Gypsie princess (film), 72. Mem: Friends of Corcoran Gallery Art (bd dir, 67-, pres, 68-70); Pyramid Gallery (bd dir, 71-). Res: Graphic works of Jose Louis Cuevas. Collection: Cuevas, Rico Lebrun, Lowell Nesbitt & Anne Truitt. Publ: Auth, Collected letters from unknown artists, 1846-1871, privately publ, 52; auth, Erotica from the Falls Church Collection, 72. Mailing Add: 1025 Connecticut Ave NW Apt 911 Washington DC 20036

SANDLER, BARBARA
PAINTER
b New York, NY, Sept 14, 43. Study: Art Students League, George Bridgeman scholar, 63, also with Edwin Dickenson & Robert Beverly Hale. Work: Mus Mod Art, New York; Chicago Art Inst; Joseph Hirshhorn Mus, Washington, DC; Chase Manhattan Bank; Bicentennial Comt, Smithsonian Inst. Comn: Poster & lithograph for Bicentennial, Spec Proj Group, Chicago, 75; posters, Circle in the Square Theatre, New York, 77-78; var record covers for Columbia & Verve Records. Exhib: Aspects of Realism, Bernard Danenberg Gallery, New York, 72; one-person shows, Danenberg Gallery, 73, Gimpel Weitzenhoffer Gallery, New York, 75, First Woman's Bank, New York, 75 & Newman Southern Gallery, Conn, 78; Gimpel Weistzenhoffer Gallery, New York, 74; Contemporary American Painting, Lehigh Univ, 75. Awards: Elizabeth T Greenshields Mem Found Grant, 74. Bibliog: Articles in Best Bets Mag, New York, 2/75 & Archit Digest, 2/76. Media: Oil on Canvas; Graphite on Paper. Publ: Illusr, The Long View, Knopf, 74; illusr, Indian Oratorio, Ballantine Bks, 75; contribr, Super Realism, Dutton, 75. Dealer: Gimpel Weitzenhoffer Ltd 1040 Madison Ave New York NY 10021. Mailing Add: 10 W 23rd St New York NY 10010

SANDLER, IRVING HARRY
ART HISTORIAN, EDUCATOR
b New York, NY, July 22, 25. Study: Temple Univ, BA, 48; Univ Pa, MA, 50. Teaching: Instr art hist, NY Univ, 60-71; instr art hist, State Univ NY Col Purchase, 71- Pos: Art critic, Art News, 56-62; art critic, New York Post, 60-65; vis critic, State Univ NY, 69-70; contrib ed, Art Am, 72. Awards: Tona Shepherd Fund Grant Travel in Ger & Austria; Guggenheim Found Fel, 65. Bibliog: Jay Jacobs (auth), Of myths and men, Art Am, 3-4/70; Rosalind Constable (auth), The myth of the myth-makers, Washington Post Bk World, 11/29/70; Gesture-makers and colourfieldsmen, Times Lit Suppl, 6/8/71. Mem: Int Asn Art Critics (pres, 70-); Col Art Asn Am; Inst Study Art Educ (pres bd dirs, mem comt visual arts). Res: American art since 1930. Publ: Auth, The triumph of American painting, a history of abstract expressism, 70; ed, Alex Katz, 71; ed, Art Criticism and Art Education, 72; contribr, Contemporary Art: 1942-1972: Collection of the Albright-Knox Gallery, 73; contribr, The Hirshhorn Museum and Sculpture Garden, 74; plus others. Mailing Add: 100 Bleecker St New York NY 10012

SANDOL, MAYNARD
PAINTER
b Newark, NJ, 1930. Study: Newark State Col, 52; also with Robert Motherwell. Work: Newark Mus Art; Wadsworth Atheneum, Hartford, Conn; Princeton Univ, NJ; Finch Col Mus, New York; Joseph Hirshhorn Collection, Washington, DC; also pvt collections. Exhib: Corcoran Gallery of Art, Washington, DC; Mus Mod Art & Am Greetings Gallery, New York; NJ Pavilion, New York World's Fair; NJ State Mus, Trenton; plus others. Bibliog: William H Gerdts, Jr (auth), Paintings and Sculpture in New Jersey, Van Nostrand, 64. Style & Technique: Visionary painter of life. Media: Oil, Acrylic, Watercolor. Mailing Add: Bunn St Box 364 RR 2 Califon NJ 07830

SANGIAMO, ALBERT
EDUCATOR, PAINTER
b Brooklyn, NY. Study: Brooklyn Col, AB; Yale Univ, BFA & MFA. Work: Baltimore Mus, Md; St Paul Art Ctr, Minn. Exhib: One-man shows, Baltimore Mus, 69, Towson State Col, 71, Decker Art Gallery, Md, 75 & Md Ats Coun Traveling Show, 75; Smithsonian Traveling Exhib Am Drawing, 65. Teaching: Teacher painting & drawing, Md Inst Col Art, 61-, chmn found dept, 61-73, chmn dept fine arts, 73- Awards: Grand Prize, Baltimore Mus, 59; Purchase Prizes, St Paul Arts Ctr, 64; Hon Mention, Am Drawing Ann Norfolk Mus, 66. Style & Technique: Trees and realist portraits. Media: Synthetic Charcoal, Acrylic. Mailing Add: 1715 Bolton St Baltimore MD 21217

SANGUINETTI, EUGENE F
ART ADMINISTRATOR, LECTURER
b Yuma, Ariz, May 12, 17. Study: Univ Santa Clara, BA, 39; Univ Ariz, 60-62. Collections Arranged: Selected Drawings from the Collection of Edward Jacobson, 70; Drawings by Living Americans, Objects from Buddhist Cultures & Etching Renaissance in France: 1850-1880, 71 (with catalog); Drawings by New York Artists (with catalog), Prehistoric Utah Petroglyphs & Pictographs & Ron Resch and the Computer, 72; Abraham Walkowitz Retrospective (with catalog), 74; plus other retrospectives & one-man exhibs. Teaching: Lectr art hist, Univ Ariz, 62-64; adj prof art, Univ Utah, 67- Pos: Dir, Tucson Mus & Art Ctr, Ariz, 64-67; dir, Utah Mus Fine Arts, Univ Utah, Salt Lake City, 67-; judge art shows, Colo, Utah & Idaho, 68-72, Bellevue & Seattle, Wash, 75. Mem: Asn Am Mus; Western Asn Art Mus; Col Art Asn Am; Asn Archit Historians; Am Fedn Arts. Res: American art of the first half of the 20th century. Specialty: Paintings, tapestries and furniture from American and European periods, Oriental material, Egyptian and Cyprist antiquities; French and English objects and decoration. Publ: Contribr, Alexander H Wyant Retrospective, 68, John Marin Drawings Retrospective, 69, Alex Katz Retrospective, 71; Social concern and the worker: French prints from 1830-1910, 73. Mailing Add: 101 Arts & Archit Ctr Univ of Utah Salt Lake City UT 84112

SANKOWSKY, ITZHAK
PAINTER, SCULPTOR
b Kishinew, Romania, Mar 9, 08; US citizen. Study: Acad Fine Arts & Univ Florence, Italy; Univ Pa, MA(math); and with Arthur B Carles, Jr. Work: Philadelphia Mus Art; Jewish Mus Art, New York; Mus Tel Aviv; Harrisburg Mus Art; also in pvt collection of Milton Shapp. Comn: Stained glass windows & mem plaques, Har-Zion Temple, Philadelphia, 60-66; candelabra, Philadelphia Psychiat Hosp, 62; stained glass windows, Levine Mem Chapel, Philadelphia, 63-64; sculpture bas-relief, Home for Jewish Aged, Philadelphia, 64-65; illus for book, Jewish Publ Soc, Philadelphia, 67. Exhib: One-man shows, Arts & Crafts, Pittsburgh, 52, Philadelphia Art Alliance, 56-68, Agra Gallery, Washington, DC, 65 & Franklin & Marshall Col, 67; Philadelphia Acad Fine Arts, Int Watercolor Show, Chicago, 40-69; plus others. Teaching: Instr painting & sculpture, Philadelphia Mus Art, 48-, Allens Lane Art Ctr, Philadelphia, 48-51 & Main Line Ctr Art, Philadelphia, 50-53. Awards: Within the Ghetto Walls, YM-YWHA, Philadelphia, 51; Purchase Prize for Print, Burr Gallery Nat Exhib, 58-59. Mem: Philadelphia Print Club; Artists Equity Asn; Am Color Print Soc; Philadelphia Art Alliance. Style & Technique: Cold wax painting; sculpture in wood, wax & styrofoam; prints-woodcut, Plexiglas engraving. Publ: Auth, Art in Israel, Jewish Frontier, New York, 35; auth, Art in Israel, Bull Har-Zion Temple, Philadelphia, 65; auth, Always time for art, suppl to the Jewish Exponent, Philadelphia, 73. Dealer: Caroly Siegel Gallery 50 Parkview Rd Cheltenham PA 19012. Mailing Add: 217 Upland Rd Merion PA 19066

SANTLOFER, JONATHAN
PAINTER
b New York, NY, Apr 26, 46. Study: Boston Univ, BFA; Pratt Inst, MFA, studied painting with George McNeil. Work: Norton Simon Inc; Inst of Contemp Art, Tokyo, Japan. Exhib: 40 Years of Am Collage, Buecker & Harpsichord, New York, 76; Six Artists, 112 Greene St, New York, 76; Contemp Reflections, The Aldrich Mus of Contemp Art, Conn, 76; New Work/New York, The New Mus, NY, 77; one-man exhibs, Drawings, Inst of Contemp Art, Tokyo, 77, Drawings, The Jersey City Mus, NJ, 77 & Paintings, Franklin & Marshall Col, Pa, 78. Teaching: Instr art hist/studio, Jersey City State Col, NJ, 74-; instr contemp art, The New Sch, New York, 76- Awards: Skowhegan Scholar, Summer Painting Grant, Skowhegan Sch of Painting & Sculpture, Maine, 66. Bibliog: Marcia Tucker (auth), New Work/New York, The New Mus Catalogue, 77; Terukata Fujieda (auth), Flatness, Graphication, Tokyo, 77. Media: Oil; Pencil. Mailing Add: 814 Jefferson St Hoboken NJ 07030

SAPHIRE, LAWRENCE M
ART WRITER
b Brooklyn, NY, Jan 12, 31. Study: Yale Univ, BA, 52, writing with Robert Penn Warren; Yale Sch of Fine Arts, 51-53; Univ Paris I at Sorbonne, two dipl. Pos: Dir, Blue Moon Gallery, New York; writer & ed, Blue Moon Press, Yorktown Heights, NY. Res: Modern prints, particularly Léger, André Masson. Specialty: Modern European painting, sculpture, graphics, original print publications in books and albums. Publ: Auth & ed, Sea Bird Saga (including Wallace Putnam lithographs), Blue Moon Gallery, 66; auth, Poems (including André Masson etchings), Ed de la Lune Bleue, 74; auth (catalogues), André Masson/Second Surrealist Period, 75 & The Genius of André Masson, 76 & auth, Fernand Léger/Complete Graphic Work, 78, Blue Moon Press. Mailing Add: 9 E 84th St New York NY 10028

SAPIEN, DARRYL RUDOLPH
PERFORMANCE ARTIST
b Los Angeles, Calif, Mar 12, 50. Study: Fullerton Col, AA, 71; San Francisco Art Inst, BA, 72, MA, 76. Work: Univ Art Mus, Univ Calif, Berkeley; San Francisco Mus Mod Art. Comn: This is Not A Test (participation performance), Soc for Encouragement of Contemp Art, San Francisco, 76. Exhib: Tricycle: Contemp Recreation (performance), Mus Conceptual Art, San Francisco, 75; Splitting the Axis (performance), Univ Art Mus, Univ Calif, Berkeley, 75; Within the Nucleus(performance), San Francisco Mus Mod Art, 76; Painting & Sculpture in Calif: The Mod Era, San Francisco Mus Mod Art, 76; Gallery of the Nat Collection of Fine Arts, Washington, DC, 77; The Principle of the Arch (performance), PS 1, New York 77; A Bridge Can Also Be a Work of Art (performance), Arte Fiera di Bologna, Italy, 77. Awards: Nat Endowment for the Arts Award, 73; Louise Riskin Award, Video Pavillion, San Francisco Art Festivel, 75. Bibliog: Jack Burnham (auth), Contemporary ritual, Arts Mag, 73; Robert McDonald (auth), The total art of Darryl Sapien, Artweek, 75; William Kleb (auth), Art performance San Francisco, Performing Arts J, 77. Style & Technique: Live events which are a combination of sculpture, theater and dance occurring indoors or outdoors in combination with closed circuit video and sound systems; also deeply involved in creating and exhibiting drawings. Media: Live performance with closed circuit video systems and sound systems, multiple media, et al. Publ: Auth, Splitting the axis & Video art and the ultimate cliche, La Mamelle, 76; contribr, Other Sources (catalog), San Francisco Art Inst, 76; contribr, Oggi in California, Data, 77. Dealer: Galerie Paule Anglim 710 Montgomery St San Francisco CA 94111. Mailing Add: 725 Tehama St San Francisco CA 94103

SARET, ALAN DANIEL
SCULPTOR
b New York, NY, Dec 25, 44. Study: Cornell Univ, BArch, with Peter Kahn & Alan Atwell; Hunter Col, with Robert Morris. Work: Mus of Mod Art, New York; Whitney Mus, New York; Los Angeles Co Mus of Art, Los Angeles, Calif; Detroit Inst of the Art; Art Gallery of Ont. Exhib: When Attitudes Become Form, Bern Kunsthalle, 69; Whitney Ann, 69 & Whitney Biannual, 77, Whitney Mus of Am Art, New York; Recent Acquisitions, Mus of Mod Art, New York, 75-76. Pos: Revelator, ALAEL, 74- Awards: Guggenheim Fel, 69. Bibliog: Emily Wasserman (auth), Alan Saret's studio exhib, 3/70 & Alan Saret: A synthesis, 5/70, Artforum; Jonathan Crary (auth), Alan Saret, Arts, 9/77. Style & Technique: Experimental techniques with flexible materials, multiple pencil drawings, watercolors in realistic mode, casting, machining and all standard construction techniques for architectural works. Publ: Auth, The Ghosthouse, ALAEL, 76. Mailing Add: c/o Stephen Reichard Inc 87 Franklin St New York NY 10013

SARFF, WALTER
PAINTER, DESIGNER
b Pekin, Ill, Oct 29, 05. Study: Sch Mod Photog, New York, grad, 49; Sch Portrait & Commercial Photog, New York; also with Alexey Brodovitch & Adolph Fassbender; Nat Acad Art, Chicago, traveling scholar, 31, grad; Grand Cent Sch Art, New York; Art Students League; Woodstock Sch Painting, NY; also with Hubert Ropp, Chicago & Yasuo Kuniyoshi, New York. Work: Collections of George Hillenbrand, M Owen Page & Anna Carolan. Exhib: Springfield Art Mus, Mass; Worcester Art Mus, Mass; Denver Art Mus, Colo; San Francisco Art Mus; Seattle Art Mus; plus many others. Teaching: Instr & asst registr, Nat Acad Art, Chicago, 29-31; pvt instr, 31-42. Pos: Dir, Sawkill Gallery, Woodstock; chmn exec bd, Woodstock Artists Asn, 39 & juror; exec secy, Ulster Co Artists Union; pres, Sarff-Zumpano, Inc. Mem: Am Soc Mag Photogr; Artists Equity Asn; Art Students League; hon mem Hypo Club; Mus Mod Art; plus others. Publ: Contribr, Am Ann Photog, cover, Am Photog, Art Photog, Cath Digest & Charm; plus others. Mailing Add: 78 Morningside Ave Yonkers NY 10703

SARGENT, MARGARET HOLLAND
PAINTER, DESIGNER
Study: Univ Calif, Los Angeles, 45-47; Tokyo, Japan, 56; with, Herbert Abrams, NY, 59-61 & Marcos Blahove, Fairfax, Va, 69; Art Students League, with John Sanden, 74. Comn: Portrait of President Gerald Ford, Time, Inc; portrait of Terry Meeuwsen, Miss America, 73; portrait of Diana Pohlam, First Woman Chaplain, USN Proc Cover; portraits of Pres Jimmy Carter & Tennessee Williams, playwright; Nacal Comdr Alexander M Haig. Exhib: One-man shows, Turkish Am Asn, Ankara, 63, Frye Art Mus, 71, Woodside Gallery, Seattle, 72 & Excelsior Club, NY, 74-75; plus many others. Pos: USN combat artist, Nacal. Mem: Salmagundi Club. Awards: Painter & Painting of Year, Most Popular Painting, Painters Club, NY; H M Salmagundi Award; Nacal Award Outstanding Achievement in Oil Painting, 77; plus others. Style & Technique: Realistic proportions and colors; direct painting on linen or textured ground on Masonite. Mailing Add: 2750 Glendower Ave Los Angeles CA 90027

SARGENT, RICHARD
PAINTER, CURATOR
b St Louis, Mo, 1932. Study: Univ Southern Calif, BFA & MFA. Comn: Mural, Audio Workshop, New York, 58; painting on environmental electricity, Int Sci & Technol Mag, 63. Exhib: One-man shows, Los Angeles City Limits, Los Angeles City Hall, 55, Nonagon Gallery, New York, 61 & Heads, Berkeley Art Ctr, 68; Drawing & Small Sculpture, Ball State Teachers Col, 57, 58 & 62; West Coast Graphic Design, Am Inst Graphic Arts, 74. Collections Arranged: David Anderson Sculpture, 72; Karen Breschi, Larry Fuente Sculpture, 73; Berkeley City Limits, 73; Water Works, 75; John Battenberg, Sculpture: Flesh Sex Death Hate Skin Love, 75; Fiber Space, 75; Joseph Rees, Neon-Argon, 75. Pos: Cur, Long Beach Mus Art, 64-65; counr, Calif Sch Blind, 66-69; cur, Berkeley Art Ctr, 69- Style & Technique: Black calligraphic brush strokes on white ground; gestalt-expressionist imagery. Media: Acrylic on Masonite; India Ink on Paper; 35mm Color Slides; Offset Lithography. Publ: Illusr, New York Times, 59, Western J Surgery, Obstet & Gyn, 59, Africa Today, 61 & 62; illusr, Poems Read in the Spirit of Peace & Gladness, 66; illusr, San Francisco Earthquake, 68. Mailing Add: 2316 McGee Ave Berkeley CA 94703

SARKISIAN, PAUL
PAINTER
b Chicago, Ill, Aug 18, 28. Study: Art Inst Chicago; Otis Art Inst, Los Angeles; Mex City Col. Work: Pasadena Art Mus, Calif; Corcoran Gallery Art, Washington, DC; Santa Barbara Mus, Calif; Chicago Art Inst; Hirshhorn Mus, Washington, DC. Exhib: One-man exhib, Pasadena Art Mus, 68, Corcoran Gallery Art, 69, Santa Barbara Mus, 70 & Mus Contemp Art, Chicago, 72; Documenta, Ger, 72. Teaching: Vis prof painting, Univ Calif, Los Angeles, 70; vis prof painting, Univ Ore, Eugene, 71; vis prof painting, Univ S Fla, Tampa, 72. Style & Technique: Realism. Media: Air Brush. Mailing Add: Cerrillos NM 87010

SARNOFF, ARTHUR SARON
PAINTER
b Brooklyn, NY, Dec 30, 12. Study: Indust Sch Art; Grand Cent Sch Art; also with Harvey Dunne. Work: Bass Mus; Springfield Mus; Parrish Mus; Hartford Mus; Grand Cent Galleries & Nat Art Mus Sport, New York. Comn: Fine art prints, Arthur Kaplan Co, Donald Art Co & Cataldi Fine Prints; portraits of Pres Kennedy, Bob Hope and many notables. Exhib: Int Art Galleries; Continental Art Galleries; Sports in Action, Grand Cent Art Galleries; Nat Acad Art; Allied Art Show; plus others. Awards: Outdoor advert award, Art Dirs Club; Art League of Nassau Award. Mem: Soc Illusrs; Allied Artists Am. Style & Technique: Painter: all media; illustrator: graphic artist. Media: Oil, Acrylic. Mailing Add: c/o Grant Central Galleries 40 Vanderbilt Ave New York NY 10017

SARNOFF, LOLO
SCULPTOR, COLLECTOR
b Frankfurt am Main, Ger, Jan 9, 16; US citizen. Study: Reimann Art Sch, Berlin, Ger, grad, 36. Work: Nat Acad Sci, Washington, DC; Nat Air & Space Mus, Washington, DC; Kennedy Ctr, Washington, DC; Corning Glass Ctr, Corning, NY. Comn: Light sculptures, US Embassy, New Delhi, 70 & Sofia; flame, Kennedy Ctr, 71. Exhib: One-person shows, Agra Gallery, Washington, DC, 68, Corning Mus Glass, NY, 70 & Franz Bader Gallery, Washington, DC, 76; two-person shows, Gallery Two, Woodstock, Vt, 69 & Gallery Marc, Washington, DC, 71; Hood Col, Frederick, Md, 72; Int Kunstnesse, Basel, Switz, 71; Gallery Two, Woodstock, 74 & 76; The Athenaeum, Alexandria, Va, 75; Art Barn, Washington, DC, 76; Washington Int Art Fair, 76; Franz Bader Gallery, 76; Womanart, New York, 77; Nat Women's Pen Club Art Show, Washington, DC, 77; Gallery von Bartha, Basel, 78. Mem: Nat League Am Pen Women; Artists Equity Asn. Media: Acrylic, Fiberoptics. Collection: 20th century drawings, paintings and sculptures; 18th century Fayence; 18th century porcelain. Dealer: Franz Bader Gallery 2124 Pennsylvania Ave Washington DC 20037; Gallery von Bartha Austrasse 126 Basel Switz. Mailing Add: 7507 Hampden Lane Bethesda MD 20014

SARNOFF, ROBERT W
COLLECTOR
b New York, NY, July 2, 18. Pos: Trustee, John F Kennedy Libr Corp; chmn bd, Bus Comt for Arts. Collection: Contemporary art. Mailing Add: 350 Park Ave New York NY 10022

SARSONY, ROBERT
PAINTER, PRINTMAKER
b Easton, Pa, Jan 1, 38. Work: Butler Inst Am Art, Youngstown, Ohio; Ga Mus Art, Athens; Joslyn Art Mus, Omaha, Nebr; Sara Roby Found, New York; Univ Kans Mus Art, Lawrence; plus others. Exhib: Allied Artist Show, New York, 63-65; one-man shows, Capricorn Galleries, Bethesda, Md, 67-71; Mainstream 71, Marietta Col, Ohio, 71; Three Young Realists, ACA Galleries, New York, 71; New Jersey Contemporary Masters, Heritage Arts, South Orange, 71-72; plus others. Bibliog: John S Le Maire (auth), Robert Sarsony, NJ Bus Mag, 69; George Albert Perret (auth), Robert Sarsony—painter, Heritage Arts, 71. Media: Oil, Watercolor; Graphics. Dealer: Christopher Gallery 766 Madison Ave New York NY 10021. Mailing Add: 60 Gristmill Rd Randolph NJ 07801

SARVIS, ALVA TAYLOR
PRINTMAKER
b Nanking, China, Nov 27, 24; US citizen. Study: Univ Calif, Berkeley; Calif Col Arts & Crafts, BFA; Univ NMex, MA. Work: US Info Agency, Beirut, New Delhi; Wachovia Bank Collection, Asheville, NC; Lewis Col, Lockport, Ill; US Steel/Ryan Homes, Pittsburgh; Huntsville Mus Art, Ala. Exhib: 156th Pa Acad Ann Exhib, 61; 5th Okla Printmakers Nat, 63; 5th Ann Mercyhurst Nat, 65; 162nd Pa Acad Ann, 67; 1st NH Int Graphics Ann, 74. Teaching: Instr gen studio, Univ NDak, 60-63; asst prof gen studio, San Diego State Col, 63-65; assoc prof printmaking, Va Polytech Inst, 70- Awards: Huntington Hartford Found Fel in Residence, Los Angeles, 65; Alice McFadden Eyre Medal, 162nd Pa Acad Ann Exhib, 67; Third Prize, 4th Gtr New Orleans Nat, 74. Mem: SE Col Art Conf. Style & Technique: Intaglio; literary overtones. Media: Etching. Publ: Co-auth, Gesso Block for printmaking, Sch Arts, 12/69; co-auth, Computer modulated drawing, SE Col Art Conf, 74; Prints of William Blake, SE Graphics Coun, 75; auth, Lithography on your etching press, Sch Arts, 75. Mailing Add: 110 Orchard View Lane Blacksburg VA 24060

SASAKI, TOMIYO
PAINTER, VIDEO ARTIST
b Vernon, BC, Can, Dec 21, 43. Study: Alta Col of Art, Calgary; San Francisco Art Inst, BFA, 67; Calif Col of Arts & Crafts, Oakland, MA, 69. Work: Nat Gallery of Art, Ottawa, Can; Can Coun, Ottawa; New York City Hospital; Synapse, Syracuse, NY; Chattau Gua-Cattaraugus Libr, Jamestown, NY. Exhib: Montreal Mus of Art, Can, 70; Ont Gallery of Art, Toronto, Can, 70; Nat Gallery of Art, Ottawa, 72; Aldrich Mus of Art, Ridgefield, Conn, 74; Contemp Mus of Art, Chicago, 74; Painting Exhib, Mus of Mod Art, New York, 77; two-person show, Bard Col of Art Gallery, Hudson on Avon, NY, 76; one-man shows, 55 Mercer Gallery, New York, 74 & Rutgers Univ Art Gallery, NJ, 76. Teaching: Artist-in-residence video, Media Studies, Buffalo, NY, 76. Awards: Sr Arts Grant (sculpture & filmmaking), Can Coun, 74; Video Grants Creative Artists Pub Serv, New York, 76 & Can Coun, 76. Bibliog: Barry Lord (auth), Realism, Arts Can, 70; Ann Wooster Sargent (auth), Video, Soho News & Ithaca News, 77. Mem: Artists Equity. Style & Technique: Repeated actions and transformations. Media: Painting; Video. Mailing Add: 118 Forsyth St New York NY 10002

SASSONE, MARCO
PAINTER
b Florence, Italy, July 27, 42. Study: Ist Galileo Galilei, Florence; Acad Fine Arts, with Silvio Loffredo, Florence. Work: Los Angeles Co Mus Art; Nat Art Gallery, Wellington, NZ; Galleria d'Arte Int, Florence; Hunt-Wesson (subsid Norton Simon, Inc); Newport Harbor Art Mus, Calif. Comn: California (poster/exhib), Galleria d'Arte Int, 73; Air California (mag cover), Urbanus Commun Corp, South Laguna, Calif, 74; Orange Co Illustrated (mag cover), Orange Co Illus, Newport Beach, Calif, 73-74; Only in Laguna (bk cover), Hardy House Publ, Newport Beach, 75; auction poster, KCET-TV, Los Angeles, 77 & 78. Exhib: Watercolor USA, Springfield Art Mus, Mo, 72; Contemporary Italian Artist, Nat Art Gallery, Wellington, NZ, 73; Grand Nat Competition, Am Artist Prof League, New York, 73-75; Maxwell Galleries, Ltd, San Francisco, 74; one-man shows, Galleria d'Arte Int, plus 12 more in US, 68-75, Galleria Arte Int, Florence, Italy, 73, Bernard Galleries, Walnut Creek, Calif, 76, Wally Findlay Galleries, Beverly Hills, Calif, 77 & Chicago, 78; Nat Acad Design, New York, 77. Pos: Lectr-guest artist, Bowers Mus, Santa Ana, Calif, 70, Lakewood Artist Guild, Calif, 71 & San Fernando Valley Art Club, Calif, 73. Awards: Spec Recognition in Commemorative Exhib of Great Flood of Florence, Lo Sprone Gallery, 67; First Prize, LaMirada Ann, Calif, 74; First Prize, Calif Int Artist of the Year Competion, Huntington Beach, 74. Bibliog: Phyllis Barton (auth), Sassone, Arti Grafiche Il Torchio, Florence, Italy, 10/73; Festival of Arts Featured Artist, KOCE-TV, Huntington Beach, Calif, 7/74; John Wilson (producer), I Am an Artist Sassone, Fine Arts Films Inc, 76. Mem: Am Artists Prof League, New York. Style & Technique: Contemporary landscapes and marinescapes, children. Media: Oil, Original Serigraphs. Publ: Contribr, Gambit, pub TV mag of KCET, Los Angeles, 73-75; illusr, Air California Mag, Urbanus Commun Corp, South Laguna, Calif, 11/71. Mailing Add: 1414 Mar Vista Way Laguna Beach CA 92651

SATO, MASAAKI
PAINTER, PRINTMAKER
b Kofu, Japan, Feb 28, 41. Study: Kofu Saito Fine Arts Inst, Japan; Heatherley Sch Fine Arts, London, Eng; Brooklyn Mus Art Sch, NY; Pratt Inst. Work: Aldrich Mus Contemp Art, Ridgefield, Conn; Mus Honolulu Acad Art; Minn Mus Art, Minneapolis; ETenn State Univ. Exhib: One-man shows, Drian Gallery, London, 69, Wenger Gallery, San Francisco, 73, Brooklyn Mus Little Gallery, 73, Renaissance Gallery, New York, 74, Atelier Gallery, Kofu City, Japan, 76, Slocumb Gallery, ETenn State Univ, 76, Soho Ctr for Visual Arts, New York, 76 & Edward Williams Col, NJ, 77. Bibliog: Richard Walker (auth), Gallery reviews, Art Rev, 8/31/68; Arthur Bloomfield (auth), An artist of many styles, San Francisco Examiner, 9/24/73; Malcolm Preston (auth), Westbeth Connection, Newsday, 7/31/75. Mem: Contemp Artists Orgn; Am Soc Contemp Artists. Media: Acrylic, Oil; Serigraphy. Dealer: Nobe Gallery 250 W 57th St New York NY 10019; Wenger Galleries 5721 La Jolla Blvd La Jolla CA 92037. Mailing Add: Studio D-1001 463 West St New York NY 10014

SATO, TADASHI
PAINTER, SCULPTOR
b Maui, Hawaii, Feb 6, 23. Study: Honolulu Sch Art; Brooklyn Mus Art Sch; New Sch Social Res, New York, with Davis; also with Ralston Crawford, Stuart Davis, John Ferren & Wilson Stamper. Work: Albright-Knox Art Gallery, Buffalo, NY; Guggenheim Mus & Whitney Mus Am Art, New York; Honolulu Acad Arts, Hawaii; Univ Art Gallery, Tucson, Ariz. Comn: Oil mural, Maui War Mem Gym, Wailuka, Hawaii, 62; concrete relief wall, State Libr, Kahului, Maui, 63; two oil murals, State Libr, Aina Haina, Oahu, Hawaii, 65; mosaic floor design, Hawaii State Capitol Bldg, Honolulu, 69; mosaic mural, West Maui Mem Gym, Maui, 72. Exhib: 52 Young Painters of America, Guggenheim Mus, 54; Pacific Heritage Exhibit, Los Angeles, Calif, 63; Four Contemporary Painters, McRoberts & Tunnard Ltd, London, 64; White House Festival of Arts, White House, Washington, DC, 65; American Paintings in Berlin Art Festival, Ger, 67. Awards: John Hay Whitney Found Opportunity Fel, 53; McInerny Found Honolulu Community Fel, 55; Best Painting in Show, Honolulu Acad Arts, 57. Mem: Hui No Eau, Kahului, Maui (bd dirs, 72); Lahaina Art Soc, Maui; Hawaii Painters & Sculptors League. Media: Oil. Mailing Add: PO Box 476 Lahaina Maui HI 96761

SATORSKY, CYRIL
PRINTMAKER, ILLUSTRATOR
b London, Eng. Study: Leeds Col Art, nat dipl design; Royal Col Art, Royal scholar, traveling scholar, res scholar, ARCA & first class hon degree. Work: Cincinnati Art Mus; Wooster Col; Essex Community Col. Exhib: Philadelphia Print Club Ann; Rental Gallery, Baltimore Mus, 70; Sixth Dulin Nat Print Show, Knoxville, Tenn, 70; one-man show, Gallery Four, Alexandria, Va, 74. Teaching: Prof illus & printmaking, Md Inst Col Art, 65- Pos: Adv to univ publ, Univ Tex, Austin, 62-65. Mem: Philadelphia Print Club. Publ: Auth & illusr, A pride of Rabbis, Aquarius, 70; illusr, Frenchman & the Seven Deadly Sins, Scribners, 71; illusr, Sir Gawain & the Green Knight, Limited Ed Club, 72. Dealer: Ferdinand Roten 123 W Mulberry St Baltimore MD 21201. Mailing Add: 4014 Roland Ave Baltimore MD 21211

SATTERFIELD, JOHN EDWARD
JEWELER, EDUCATOR
b Clearwater, Fla, Sept 14, 31. Study: Univ Fla, BDesign; Univ Kans, MFA; study with Hëkki Seppa, Stanley Lechtzin & Earl Krentzin. Work: Soc NAm Goldsmiths Collection, Minn Mus Art; Mint Mus, Charlotte, NC; Gilchrist Mills, NC. Exhib: Am Jewelry Today, Scranton, Pa, 68; Richmond Biennial Crafts Exhib, Va, 73; Southeastern Crafts Invitational, Greenville Co Art Mus, SC, 75; Goldsmith 1974, Renwick Gallery, Washington, DC, 74; Am Jewelry Invitational, Soc NAm Goldsmiths, Atlanta, Ga, 75 & Soc NAm Goldsmiths, Seattle, Wash, 77; Nine NC Jewelers, Western Carolina Univ, 77. Teaching: Assoc prof design & metal, ECarolina Univ, 67-, assoc prof art, Univ Abroad Prog, Univ Nac Heredia, Costa Rica, CentAm, 75. Pos: Art dir, Advertising Design Studio, Clearwater, Fla, 57-63; Peace Corps Vol arts & crafts develop, Peru, SAm, 63-65. Awards: Award, Kans Designer Craftsmen Exhib, Lawrence, 66; Purchase Award, Goldsmith 1974, Renwick Gallery, 74; Mus Purchase, Mint Mus Art, 78. Bibliog: American Craftsmen, John Satterfield (film), Cinemasonics, Inc, 74; article in Goldsmith J, Vol 3 (Aug, 1977). Mem: Am Crafts Coun; Soc NAm Goldsmiths; Carolina Designer Craftsmen (standards jury); Piedmont Craftsmen (standards jury). Style & Technique: Silver and gold casting, fabrication and electroforming. Media: Metal. Mailing Add: Rte 1 Box 34 Greenville NC 27834

SÄTTY, WILFRIED
GRAPHIC ARTIST, FILM MAKER
b Bremen, WGer, Apr 12, 39; Ger citizen. Study: Design in Ger; mostly self-taught. Work: Mus Mod Art, New York; San Francisco Mus Art; Nat Mus Art, Belgrade, Yugoslavia; Nat Mus, Warsaw, Poland; Kristiandsand Art Asn, Norway. Comn: Calif for McCarthy (poster), McCarthy Campaign Hq, San Francisco, 68, Satirical Theatre Group (poster), Committee, 68, exhib poster, Berkeley Gallery, 70, poster insert, Earth Mag, 72, Rolling Stones Concert poster, (with David Singer), comn by Bill Graham, 73. Exhib: Second Joint Show, Moore Gallery, San Francisco, 68, Time Zone Data, Berkeley Gallery, 70, one-man show, Goethe Ctr, 71 & Claire Wiles Gallery, 73-74, Dr Reidar Wennesland Art Collection, 71. Teaching: Pvt art classes, 70; lectr imagination vs media, San Francisco State Univ, 74; lectr media & poster art, San Francisco Mus Art, 74. Awards: Bk Show Award Winner, Am Inst Graphic Arts, 76-77. Bibliog: Segment in doc film on Calif, RIA (Ital TV Rome), 71; Media: Black Magic of Am (color film), ROTF (Fr Nat TV), 72; Cosmic Bicycle (animated color film), Bonanza Films, San Francisco, 72. Style & Technique: Litho-offset printing, montage, drawing, film making and fabric design. Res: Electronic visual language expert as it pertains to sub-conscious phenomenon. Publ: Illusr, Bk World (Sun suppl, Washington Post), 73-75; auth, Cosmic Bicycle, 71 & Time Zone, 73, Straight Arrow Books; illusr, Annotated Dracula, 75 & The Illustrated Edgar Allan Poe, C N Potter. Mailing Add: 2143 Powell St San Francisco CA 94133

SATURENSKY, RUTH
See Colorado, Charlotte

SAUCY, CLAUDE GERALD
PAINTER, EDUCATOR
b Thayngen, Switz, Nov 24, 29. Study: Kunstgewerbe Schule, Zurich; Univ Zurich. Work: Mus Mod Art, New York; Wadsworth Atheneum, Hartford, Conn. Exhib: Invitational Artist, New Haven Art Festival, Conn, 69; Invitational Artists, Sharon Creative Arts Found, Conn, 70. Teaching: Chmn dept art & art hist, Kent Sch, 66- Awards: Hon Mention, New Haven Festival Art, 67; Art Prize, Sharon Creative Arts Found, 69. Bibliog: H Steiner (auth), Claude Saucy, Schaffhauser-Nachrichten, 10/65. Media: Graphics. Dealer: FAR Gallery 746 Madison Ave New York NY 10021. Mailing Add: Rte 1 Box 155-D Kent OH 06757

SAUL, PETER
PAINTER
b San Francisco, Calif, Aug 16, 34. Study: Stanford Univ; Calif Sch Fine Arts, 50-52; Wash Univ, BFA, 56, with Fred Conway. Work: Art Inst Chicago; Whitney Mus Am Art, New York; Mus Mod Art, New York; Univ Mass. Exhib: One-man exhibs, San Francisco Art Inst, Reed Col & Calif Col Arts & Crafts, 68, Mus St Etinne, France, 71 & Calif State Univ, Sacramento, 73; Mus Mod Art, New York, 68; Univ Okla, 68; Univ Ill, 69; Whitney Mus Am Art, 69; Corcoran Gallery Art, Washington, DC, 71; Art Inst Chicago, 72; Lerner-Heller Gallery, New York, 73; Krannert Art Mus, Univ Ill, Urbana, 74; Painting & Sculpture Today, Indianapolis Mus Art, Ind & Taft Mus, Ohio, 74; plus others. Awards: New Talent Award, Art in Am Mag, 62; William & Norma Copley Found Grant, 62. Dealer: Allan Frumkin Gallery 620 N Michigan Ave Chicago IL 60611. Mailing Add: 383 Lovell St Mill Valley CA 94941

SAULS, FREDERICK INABINETTE
SCULPTOR, PAINTER
b Seattle, Wash, Mar 22, 34. Study: Stanford Univ, BA; Calif Col Arts & Crafts, MFA Prog; Univ Calif, MA. Work: Mus Mod Art, Skopje, Yugoslavia; Ithaca Mus Art, Cornell Univ, NY; Univ Calif Mus; Picker Art Gallery, Colgate Univ, Hamilton, NY; Univ Minn Mus Art. Exhib: San Francisco Mus Mod Art Ann, Calif, 60-63; Paris Biennale, Paris Mus Mod Art, 64; Sauls Sculpture, Univ Ky Mus, 66; Sauls Graphics, Univ Minn Mus, 67; UNESCO Int traveling exhib mod art, 68. Teaching: Assoc sculpture, Univ Calif, Berkeley, 63-64; vis artist sculpture, Univ Ky, 65-67; asst prof sculpture, Univ Minn, 68. Awards: Grand Prize, Am Sculptors, Paris Mus Mod Art, France, 63; Harry Lord Ford Grad Prize, Univ Calif, 65. Style & Technique: Bronze and aluminum sculpture; paintings, graphics. Mailing Add: 2270 N Beachwood Dr Apt One Hollywood CA 90068

SAUNDERS, AULUS WARD
PAINTER, EDUCATOR
b Perry, Mo, Sept 22, 04. Study: Westminster Col (Mo), BA; St Louis Sch Fine Arts; Wash Univ, MA; Univ Iowa, PhD; also with Charles Cagle. Work: State Univ NY Col Oswego; Mo Hist Soc; plus pvt collections. Exhib: Midwestern Ann Art Exhib, Kansas City Art Inst, 35; 30th & 31st Ann Exhib Paintings Am Artists, St Louis City Art Mus, 36 & 37; 18th Ann Exhib Artists Cent NY, Munson-Williams-Proctor Inst, Utica, NY, 55; one-man shows, Denison Univ, 51 & State Univ NY A&T Col, Morrisville, 67. Teaching: Prof art, State Univ NY Col Oswego, 37-70, chmn dept, 37-68, prof emer, 74-; vis prof, Southern Ill Univ, Carbondale, summer 49; vis prof, Pa State Univ, University Park, summers 50-52. Style & Technique: Romantic and semi-abstract realist. Media: Watercolor, Acrylic, Oil. Res: Psychology of art, especially genesis and stability of art talent in children. Publ: Auth, The stability of artistic aptitude, Psychol Monogr, 36; auth, Feeling and form, Sch Arts, 10/70. Mailing Add: 165 E Third St Oswego NY 13126

SAUNDERS, EDITH DARIEL CHASE
PAINTER, INSTRUCTOR
b Waterville, Me, Mar 19, 22. Study: Univ NC, Greensboro, with Robert Partin, Boris Margo, Gilbert Carpenter also with Fredric Taubes, Wally Turner, Kenneth Bates, Barclay Shieks, David Lund, Philip Moose, Peter Ostuni, Leo Manso; John Brady Sch of Art, Blowing Rock, NC; Madam Sun To-Ze Hsu, Formosa; Anna Maria D'Annuzio, Florence, Italy; Leroy Nieman, New York. Work: Wachovia Bank; Reynolds Tobacco; NC Mus of Art, South Port; Hunt Mfg Co Collection; Westminster Presbyterian Church, Knoxville, Tenn. Comn: Acrylic, oil, paster & charcoal portraits, 55-78. Exhib: NC Mus of Art, Raleigh; Damon Gallery, Washington, DC; Gallery of Contemp Art, Winston-Salem, NC; Spring Maid Art Exhib, Lancaster, SC; Madison Gallery, New York; Island Gallery, Manteo, NC; Contemp Graphic Artists (traveling exhib); Weatherspoon Art Gallery, Greensboro; Regional Gallery, Boone, NC; Assoc Artists of NC. Collections Arranged: Arts Coun Gallery, 57, 62, 64, 65, 77 & Southeastern Art Festival, Winston-Salem; Arts & Sci Mus & Herman Art Gallery, Statesville, NC; Tarboro Public Library, NC; Contemporary Graphic Artists (nat traveling exhib); Regional Gallery, Boone, NC; Hickory Mus of Art, NC; Greenville Art Gallery, NC. Teaching: Instr painting, Arts & Crafts Asn, 55-73 & Creative Arts, Winston-Salem, 75-78. Pos: Art chmn-coordr, Winston-Salem Women's Club, 60-61; oriental painting instr, Guilford Tech Inst, Jamestown, NC, 73; columnist, Edy and Art (weekly), The Suburbanite, 74-76 & 77-78. Awards: Purchase Prizes, Northwest Art Exhib, Lowe's Collection, Lowe's Co, 62 & Southport Art Festival, City of Southport, NC, 63; Hunt Mfg Purchase Award, Watercolor Soc of NC, 75. Bibliog: Wilkes Art Guild (auth & publisher), NC Artists and Craftsmen, 60; William S Powell (auth), North Carolina Lives, Historical Record Asn, 62; Am Biographical Inst (auth & publisher), Personalities of the South American Biographical Institute, 77. Mem: Assoc Artists of Winston-Salem (sec, 58 & pres, 62); Watercolor Soc of NC (nominating chmn bd of dir, 74). Style & Technique: Acrylic-surrealism, abstract, impressionistic and portraits; oil portraits and flowers; ink oriental style flowers and non-objective. Media: Acrylic on Canvas, Rice Paper; Ink-Calligraphy loosley painted on Rice Paper. Dealer: Creative Arts/Stratford Oaks 514 S Stratford Rd Winston-Salem NC 27103. Mailing Add: 2250 Hilltop Dr Winston-Salem NC 27106

SAUNDERS, J BOYD
PRINTMAKER, EDUCATOR
b Memphis, Tenn, June 12, 37. Study: Memphis State Univ, BS; Univ Miss, MFA; Bottega Arte Grafica, Florence, Italy. Work: Denison Univ Print Collection, Ohio; Columbia Mus Art Print Collection, SC; SC State Collection, Columbia; Bottega Arte Grafica Collection; Univ Ariz Print Collection, Tucson. Comn: Mixed media altar panel, Guess Chapel, Univ Church, Oxford, Miss, 62; mem portrait comn, Tipoff Club, Columbia, SC, 69; oil mural, Univ House, Univ SC, 72. Exhib: Soc Washington Printmakers 24th Nat, Smithsonian Inst, Washington, DC, 62; 1st Int Printmaker's Exhib, Gallerie Bottega & Arte Grafica, Florence, 67; 34th Graphic Arts & Drawing Nat, Wichita, Kans, 69; 5th Dulin Print & Drawing Competition Nat, Knoxville, Tenn, 70; 15th NDak Print & Drawing Ann, Grand Forks, 72. Teaching: Instr art, Univ Miss, 61-62; instr art, Southwest Tex State Col, 62-65; assoc prof art, Univ SC, 65- Pos: Staff artist, Dan Kilgo & Assocs, Tuscaloosa, Ala, 59-60; designer-illusr, Chaparral Press, Kyle, Tex, 63-65; art purchasing comt, SC Collection, Columbia, 69-70; steering comt mem, Fiesta '72, Columbia, 72. Awards: Third Prize, 6th Ann Mid-South Exhib Paintings, Prints & Drawings, Memphis, Tenn, 61; Grand Prize, Guild Columbia Artists, 71; Purchase Prize, 15th NDak Ann Print & Drawing Competition, 72. Bibliog: Jack Morris (auth), Boyd Saunders, printmaker, Contemp Artists SC, 69; Harriet Door (auth), Two forceful exhibitions, Charlotte Observer, NC, 72; Adger Brown (auth), Boyd Saunders/vital forces, State-Rec, Columbia, 72. Mem: Print Coun Am; Guild SC Artists (adv bd, 56); Columbia Art Asn; Southeastern Graphics Soc (pres); Am Asn Univ Prof. Style & Technique: Semi-realistic, independent and varied. Media: Graphic. Publ: Illusr, Bosque Territory: A History of an Agrarian Community, 64; illusr, Lyndon Baines Johnson: the Formative Years, 65; auth, A summer's printmaking in Florence. Art Educ J, 68. Dealer: Hubris Press Columbia SC 29210. Mailing Add: Dept of Art Univ of SC Columbia SC 29208

SAUNDERS, RAYMOND JENNINGS
PAINTER, EDUCATOR
b Pittsburgh, Pa, Oct 28, 34. Study: Pa Acad Fine Arts, nat scholastic scholar, 53-57; Univ Pa, nat scholastic scholar; Carnegie Inst Technol, BFA, 60; Calif Col Arts & Crafts, MFA, 61. Work: Mus Mod Art, New York; Whitney Mus Am Art, Andover Collection Am Art; Pa Acad Fine Arts; Nat Inst Arts & Lett. Exhib: Mus Mod Art, 71; one-man shows, San Francisco Mus Art, 71, Providence Mus Art, 72 & RI Sch Design, 72; Mus Fine Arts, Boston, 70; Whitney Mus Am Art Ann, 72; Pa Acad Fine Arts, 72; Oakland Art Mus, Calif, 74; plus others. Teaching: Prof painting, Calif State Univ, Hayward, 68-; vis critic, RI Sch Design, 68, vis artist, 72; vis artist, Yale Univ, 72. Pos: Nat consult urban affairs, Volt Tech Serv, New York, 68-; art consult, Dept Black Studies, Univ Calif, Berkeley, 69-; mem Afro-Am Acquisitions Comt, Univ Art Mus, Berkeley, 71- Awards: Thomas Eakins Prize, Pa Acad Fine Arts, 55; Award, Nat Inst Arts & Lett, 63; Prix de Rome, Am Acad Rome, 64-66. Bibliog: Bearden & McHolty (auth), The Painter's Mind, Crown, 69. Mem: Fel Am Acad Rome. Publ: Auth, Black is a color, privately publ, 68. Dealer: Terry Dintenfass Gallery 18 E 67th St New York NY 10021. Mailing Add: 6007 Rock Ridge Blvd Oakland CA 94618

SAVAGE, NAOMI
PHOTOGRAPHER
b NJ, June 25, 27. Study: Bennington Col; and with Man Ray. Work: Mus Mod Art, New York; Fogg Mus, Boston; NJ State Mus; Univs of Kans, Ill & Princeton. Comn: 8 x 50 ft wall of photo engravings, LBJ Presidential Libr, Austin, Tex, 72; 60 tennis photographs, Youth Tennis Found, Princeton, NJ, 73-74. Exhib: Always the Young Stranger, Mus Mod Art, New York, 53; Photography as Printmaking, Mus Mod Art, 68; Two Generations of Photographs-Man Ray & Naomi Savage, NJ State Mus, 68; Light & Lens-Methods of Photography, Hudson River Mus, Yonkers, NY, 73; Women of Photography, San Francisco Mus Art, 75. Awards: Photography, Cassandra Found, 70; Photography, Nat Endowment for Arts, 71. Bibliog: Peggy Lewis (auth), Two Generations of Photographs—Man Ray & Naomi Savage, NJ State Mus, 68; Julia Scully, Everchanging faces of Naomi Savage, Mod Photography, 1/70. Style & Technique: Photo engravings, inkless photo intaglio prints, photo collage; portraits, masks, Versailles, dental and ophthalmological equipment, paper and plastic objects and tennis. Dealer: Witkin Gallery 41 E 57th St New York NY 10022. Mailing Add: 41 Drakes Corner Rd Princeton NJ 08540

SAVAGE, ROGER
PAINTER, PRINTMAKER
b Windsor, Ont, Sept 25, 41. Study: Mt Allison Univ, Sackville, NB, Can, BFA, 63; study with Alex Colville, Lawren Harris, Jr & E B Pulford. Work: Univ Waterloo Collection, Ont; City of Wolfsburg Collection, WGer; Can Coun Art Bank, Ottawa, Ont; NS Art Bank, Halifax; Glenbow-Alberta Inst, Calgary, Alta. Exhib: 3rd Brit Int Print Biennale, Bradford, UK, 72; 10th Biennale of Graphic Art, Ljubljana, Yugoslavia, 73; 3rd Int Grafik Biennale, Frechen, WGer, 74; 2nd Norsk Int Grafikk Biennale, Fredrikstad, Norway, 74; 8th Print Biennial, Burnaby, BC, 75. Pos: Juror, Can Coun Art Bank, 73. Awards: Can Coun Travel Grant, 70; Award of Recognition, 74 & Prof Artists Award, 75, Prov of NS. Bibliog: Julia Healy (auth), Roger Savage's Art, 4th Estate, Halifax, 3/21/74; Karl Mackeeman (auth), Printmaker seeks recognition, Atlantic Advocate, 1/75; Don Curley (auth), Silk & Color (film), Univ of the Air, TV Series, 75. Mem: Can Artists Representation (rep to nat coun, 74-75; NS chmn, 75); Eye Level Co-op Gallery (chmn, 74-75). Style & Technique: Realism. Media: Serigraphy; Gouache, Acrylic. Publ: Contribr, Canadian Artists in Exhibition, 74 & 75. Dealer: Zwickers Art Gallery 5415 Doyle St Halifax NS Can. Mailing Add: RR 1 Liverpool NS B0T 1K0 Can

SAVAS, JO-ANN (MRS GEORGE T SAVAS)
PAINTER, INSTRUCTOR
b Opelika, Ala, Jan 30, 34. Study: Auburn Univ, Alpha Delta Pi scholar, BS(art educ). Exhib: Nat Acad Galleries, New York; New York World's Fair; Chateau de la Napole, Cannes, France; Southern Contemporaries Collection of Sears-Roebuck; Int Women's Show, Nat Women's Watercolor Exhib; plus 49 major one-man shows & other exhibs. Teaching: Pvt art instr, Huntsville. Pos: Tech illusr, Army Ballistic Missile Agency, Redstone Arsenal, Ala, 57-58; brochure designer, Huntsville Symphony Orchestra, 72-; dir art dept, Madison Acad, Huntsville, Ala, 74-77. Mem: Huntsville Art League & Mus Asn (first pres); Nat Asn Women Artists. Style & Technique: Creative painting in many styles and in all media; art is characterized by variety and originality. Media: Watercolor, Oil, Acrylic. Mailing Add: 3506 Mae Dr SE Huntsville AL 35801

SAVELLI, ANGELO
PAINTER, SCULPTOR
b Pizzo Calabria, Italy, Oct 30, 11. Study: Liceo Artistico, Rome, Italy; Acad di Belle Arti, Rome. Work: Mus Mod Art, New York; Galleria Naz d'Arte Mod, Rome; Philadelphia Mus Art; Nat Collection Fine Arts, Smithsonian Inst, Washington, DC; also pvt collection of Nelson Rockefeller. Comn: Fresco painting Boimond Chapel, comn by Mr Boimond, Sora, Italy, 35; outdoor work, comn by Mayor Alexander, Lincoln Sq, Syracuse, NY, 72. Exhib: Galleria del Naviglio, Milan, Italy, 53; Castelli Gallery, New York, 58; Ctr d'Art Italien, Paris, 58; Corcoran Art Gallery, Washington, DC, 59; XXXII Int Biennale, Venice, 64; Everson Mus, Syracuse, NY, 72; Tweed Mus Art, Duluth, Minn, 73; Hutchinson Gallery, New York, 78; Parsons-Dreyfuss Gallery, New York, 78. Teaching: Asst prof drawing, Liceo Artistico, Rome, Italy, 40-43, 48-54; asst prof painting, Univ Pa, 60-69; vis artist painting, Cornell Univ, 74- Awards: Fel Paris France, Minister Naz Educ, 48; Grand Price per Lincisione, XXXII Venice Biennale, 64. Mailing Add: c/o Max Hutchinson Gallery 127 Greene St New York NY 10012

SAVITT, SAM
PAINTER, ILLUSTRATOR
b Wilkes-Barre, Pa. Study: Pratt Inst; Art Students League; drawing with Paul Brown, painting with Howard Trafton & John Vickery & sculpture with Seymour Lipton. Work: St Lawrence Univ, Canton, NY; plus pvt collections including William Randolph Hearst, Jr, Raymond Firestone & August Busch. Exhib: New York Racing Asn, Jamaica, New York, 66; Concourse Gallery, Boston, Mass, 69; Int Sports Core, Oak Brook, Ill, 75; West Returns, Grand Cent Gallery, New York, 78. Teaching: Guest lectr horses in art, 55- Pos: Official artist, US Equestrian Team, 60- Awards: Jr Bk Award, Boys Clubs of Am, 58. Bibliog: Anthony Amaral (auth), About cowboys and broncos, Ariz Hwy, 5/70; Nancy Boyce (auth), Sam Savitt speaks, Horse Play, 4/74; Annette Cummings (auth), Profile, Lead Line, 3/78. Mem: Soc Illusr; Graphic Artists Guild; Authors Guild. Style & Technique: Horses and horse-related subjects in pencil, oil, ink, gouache, casein, watercolor and combined mediums. Publ: Auth & illusr, Midnight, Dutton, 58; auth & illusr, Rodeo: Cowboys, Bulls & Broncos, 63 & America's Horses, 65, Doubleday; auth & illusr, Eqestrian Olympic Sketchbook, Barnes, 68; auth & illusr, Sam Savitt Horse Charts, Black Horse Press, 63-75. Dealer: Arthur Ackermann & Son Inc 50 E 57th St New York NY 10022. Mailing Add: North Salem NY 10560

SAVITZ, FRIEDA (FRIEDA SAVITZ LADEN)
PAINTER, EDUCATOR
b New York, NY, Dec 3, 31. Study: NY Univ, BS, MA, with Hale Woodruff, William Biazotes & Chiam Koppleman; Univ Wis; Cooper Union, with Robert Gwathmey; Columbia Univ, with John Heliker; Hans Hofmann Sch Scholar, New York & Provincetown, Mass. Work: Chrysler Mus, Provincetown, Mass; Hudson River Mus, Yonkers, NY; Am Tel & Tel Co; Pall Mall Collection. Exhib: Smithsonian Inst, Washington, DC, 56; Nat Gallery Art, Washington, DC, 56; Chrysler Mus, Provincetown, Mass, 58; Art USA, New York, 59-60; Brooklyn Mus, NY, 75 & 76; Ford Found Int Traveling Exhib, 75-76; Hudson River Mus, Yonkers, NY, 76; Int Women's Exhib, Copenhagen, Denmark, 76; World Print Exhib, San Francisco Mus Mod Art, 77; one-person shows, Hudson River Mus, 73 & Ariz State Univ, Tempe, 78. Teaching: Art instr compos, painting & drawing, Summit Art Ctr, NJ, 74-; classes in own studio, New York, 74- Awards: Ford Found Int Women's Award, 75. Mem: Artist equity; Women in the Arts; Southern Vt Art Asn; Graphic Soc. Style & Technique: Internal landscapes, abstracted, expressionistic impressions of the world without and the world within. Media: Oil, Pastel. Dealer: Union Art Galleries 349 Geary St San Francisco CA 94109; Hansen Galleries 70-72 Wooster St New York NY 10012. Mailing Add: 109 W Clarkstown Rd New City NY 10956

SAVOY, CHYRL LENORE
SCULPTOR, EDUCATOR
b New Orleans, La, May 23, 44. Study: La State Univ, BA(art); Acad Fine Arts, Florence, with Gallo & Berti; diploma di Profitto, Universita degli Studi di Firenze, Florence; Wayne State Univ, MFA(sculpture). Work: Our Lady Bayous Convent, Abbeville, La; Couvent St Dominique de la Gloire de Dieu, Maison Mere des Dominicaines, Flavigny, France; Our Lady Star of the Sea, Cameron, La; Cath Church, SAfrica; Herrod Jr High Sch Libr, Abbeville. Comn: Renovation & redesigning of chapel, Dominican Rural Missionaries, Abbeville, 72; St John the Baptist (sculpture design), Our Lady Star of the Sea, Cameron, La, 73; monumental sculpture, Rural Dominican Missionaries, Abbeville, La, 74. Exhib: 58th Exhib Mich Artists, Detroit Inst Arts Mus, 71; Artist's Biennial Exhib of Artists of Southwest & Tex, New Orleans Mus Art, 71; 14th Ann Delta Art Exhib, Ark Art Ctr, Little Rock, 71; one-man show, New Orleans Mus Art, La, 72; 7th Ann Nat Drawing & Small Sculpture Show, Del Mar Col, Corpus Christi, Tex, 73; Am Painters in Paris, Palais des Congres, Paris, 75-76; Appalachian Nat Drawing Competition, Appalachian State Univ, Boone, NC, 76; Beaumont Art League Sculpture Show, Brown Scurlock Gallery, Tex, 78. Teaching: Grad student asst sculpture, Wayne State Univ, summer 70; asst prof fine arts, La State Univ, Shreveport, 73-77. Awards: Purchase Award, New Orleans Mus Art, 71; hon mentions, 13th Ann Piedmont Painting & Sculpture Exhib, 73; Samuel Wiener Sculpture Award, 51st Regional Exhib, 73. Style & Technique: Contemporary direct carving and assemblage of carved pieces; contemporary sculpture in direct and cast metal. Media: Wood, Metal. Mailing Add: 1009 Poinciana Ave Mamou LA 70554

SAWADA, IKUNE
PAINTER
b Japan, Aug 30, 36. Study: Kyoto Art Univ, BFA. Work: Seattle Art Mus; Art Gallery Gtr Victoria, BC; Brooklyn Col; Art Univ Kyoto. Comn: Mural, Puget Sound Mutual Savings Bank, Seattle, 75; King Co Bldg, Seattle, Wash, 76. Exhib: Ann Exhib Northwest Artists, Seattle Art Mus, 71-75; Wash State Artmobile Exhib, 72; Ann Puget Sound Area Exhib, Charles & Emma Frye Art Mus, Seattle, 72 & 75; Nat Art Competition, Springfield Art Mus, Utah, 75; Asian Artist Exhib, Western Wash State Col Mus, 75. Teaching: Teacher art & art hist, Pub High Sch, Japan, 60-65. Awards: Lulu Fairbanks Award, Found Int Understanding Through Students, 70; Second Place Award, Fed Way Arts Festival, Washington, 72; Honorable Mention Award, Ann Exhib Northwest Artists, Seattle Art Mus, 74. Bibliog: Natsuhiko Tsutsumi (auth), People in Seattle, Katei-Zenka, 75. Style & Technique: Realism with a feeling of abstract; built up texture creating many colors showing through other colors. Media: Oil, Watercolor. Dealer: Francine Seders Gallery 6701 Greenwood Ave N Seattle WA 98103. Mailing Add: 2129 47th Ave SW Seattle WA 98116

SAWAI, NOBORU
PRINTMAKER, EDUCATOR
b Takamatsu, Japan, Feb 18, 31; US citizen. Study: Augsburg Col, Minneapolis, BA, 66; Univ Minn, MFA, 69; Yoshida Hanga Acad, Tokyo, woodcut printmaking with Toshi Yoshida, 70. Work: Nat Gallery Can, Ottawa; Glenbow Mus, Calgary, Alta; Edmonton Art Gallery, Alta; Winnipeg Art Gallery, Man. Comn: Sculpture, Trinity Lutheran Congregation, Minneapolis, 67. Exhib: 38th Ann Exhib, Japan Printmakers Asn, Tokyo, 70; Can Nat Exhib, Toronto, 73; 1st Ann Nat Print Exhib, Los Angeles, 73; 2nd NH Int Graphics Ann, 74; 11th Int Biennial Graphic Art, Ljubljana, Yugoslavia, 75. Teaching: Instr printmaking, drawing & art hist, Berea Col, Ky, 70-71; asst prof printmaking, Univ Calgary, 71- Awards: Manisphere Award, Manisphere 10th Ann Show, 73; Purchase Award, London Mus, Ont, 74; Edition Award, Art Gallery of Brant, Brantford, Ont, 75. Bibliog: Dennis Elliot (auth), 12th Annual Calgary Graphic Show, Arts Can Mag, 72; Ruth Weisberg (auth), Prints of wit and humor, W Coast Art Works, 5/4/74; Rino Boccaccini (auth), Noboru Sawai, Voce di Ferrara, 9/21/74. Style & Technique: Combined techniques of traditional Japanese woodcuts and European copper etching. Media: Woodcuts, Etching; Watercolor. Dealer: Mido Gallery 936 Main St Vancouver BC Can. Mailing Add: Dept of Art Univ Calgary Calgary A3 T2N 1N4 Can

SAWYER, ALAN R
ART CONSULTANT
b Wakefield, Mass, June 18, 19. Study: Bates Col, BS, 41; Boston Mus Fine Arts Sch; Boston Univ, 47-48; Harvard Univ, MA(art hist), 49; Bates Col, Hon DFA, 69. Collections Arranged: Designer-Craftsmen USA, 54, Design in Scandinavia, 56, coordr of Midwest Designer-Craftsmen Exhib, 57 & installation of all primtive art exhibs, 52-59, Art Inst Chicago; installation of rug & textile exhibs, Textile Mus, 59-71; cur, Master Craftsmen of Ancient Peru Exhib, Guggenheim Mus, 65-69. Teaching: Instr art dept, Tex Women's Univ, 49-52; group discussion leader, Looking at Modern Art, Ford Found, Art Inst Chicago, 55-57; lectr, Pub Lect Prog, Univ Chicago-Art Inst Chicago, 59; adj prof art & archaeol, Columbia Univ, 68-69; lectr, Smithsonian Assocs, 71-73; prof art, Univ BC, 75- Pos: Cur primitive art, Tex Woman's Univ, 49-52; asst to cur decorative arts, Art Inst Chicago, 52-54, asst cur decorative arts in charge Early Americana & pre-Columbian art, 54-56, assoc cur in charge primitive art, 56-58, cur primitive art, 58-59; dir, Textile Mus, 59-71; dir, Park Forest Art Ctr; mem, Univ Pa Archeol Exped to Bolivia, 55; leader of Textile Mus Archaeol Exped to Peru, 60; leader, Brooklyn Mus Study Tour to Peru, 65; independent art consult, 71-74. Mem: Archaeol Inst Am; Soc Am Archaeol; Inst Andean Studies. Publ: Auth, Handbook of the Nathan Cummings Collection of Ancient Peruvian Art, 54 & Animal Sculpture in Pre-Columbian Art, 57, Art Inst Chicago; auth, A group of early Nasca sculptures in the Whyte Collection, Archaeol Mag, 62; auth, Ancient Peruvian Ceramics, Metrop Mus Art, 66; auth, Ancient Peruvian Art, 68; plus numerous other articles & catalogs on Peruvian art. Mailing Add: Dept Fine Arts Univ Brit Columbia Vancouver BC V6T 1W5 Can

SAWYER, CHARLES HENRY
MUSEUM DIRECTOR
b Andover, Mass, Oct 20, 06. Study: Yale Univ, AB; Harvard Law Sch & Harvard Grad Sch; Amherst Col, hon LHD; Univ NH, hon DFA; Clark Univ, hon LHD. Teaching: Prof hist art, Sch Archit & Design, Yale Univ, 47-56; prof mus practice & hist art, Univ Mich, Ann Arbor, 57-75. Pos: Dir, Addison Gallery Am Art, Andover, Mass, 30-40, mem art comt, 40-; dir, Worcester Mus Art, Mass, 40-47; mem Mass Art Comn, 43-45; trustee, Corning Mus Glass, 50-76; mem Smithsonian Art Comn, 54-; dir, Univ Mich Mus Art, 57-72; mem art gallery coun, Univ Notre Dame, 72- Mem: Am Asn Mus; Asn Art Mus Dirs; Col Art Asn Am; Am Antiquarian Soc; Am Acad Arts & Sci. Publ: Auth, Art education in English public schools, 37; auth, Report of committee on visual arts at Harvard, 54-55; auth, Integration in the arts, 57 & The college art department and the work of art, 65, Col Art J; contribr, var art mags. Mailing Add: 2 Highland Lane Ann Arbor MI 48104

SAWYER, HELEN (HELEN SAWYER FARNSWORTH)
PAINTER, WRITER
b Washington, DC. Study: Masters Sch, Dobbs Ferry; Nat Acad Design Sch, with Charles Hawthorne. Work: Whitney Mus Am Art; Pa Acad Fine Arts; Toledo Mus; Atlanta Mus; Indianapolis Mus. Comn: Paintings, Blue Ridge Spring, Chesapeake & Ohio RR, New York, First Nat City Bank & Circus Parade, G Lister Carlyle. Exhib: Carnegie Nat & Int, Pittsburgh; Am Painting Today, Metrop Mus Art; Century of Progress, Chicago; San Francisco World's Fair; New York World's Fair; plus one-man shows throughout US & abroad. Awards: Award for The Bareback Rider, Ringling Mus; First Hon Mention for Trees by the Turn, Art Inst Chicago; First Prize for landscape & still life, Atlanta Mus. Bibliog: Ernest Watson (auth), Helen Sawyer, Am Artist. Mem: Nat Acad Design; Fla Artists Group; Audubon Artists; Nat Asn Women Painters & Sculptors. Style & Technique: Color, light, feeling. Media: Oil, Watercolor. Res: Material on life and work in Syracuse University Archives and Archives of American Art. Publ: Auth, Paintings in oils on paper, Am Artists; auth, Living Among the Modern Primitives, Scribner. Dealer: Frank Oehlschlaeger Gallery 28 Blvd of the Presidents St Armands Key Sarasota FL 33578. Mailing Add: 3842 Flamingo Sarasota FL 33581

SAWYER, WILLIAM
ART DEALER, COLLECTOR
b Lindsay, Okla, Feb 16, 20. Pos: Dir, William Sawyer Gallery, San Francisco, Calif. Specialty: Contemporary American painting, sculpture and graphics. Collection: Contemporary American and Mexican paintings, sculpture and graphics. Mailing Add: 3045 Clay St San Francisco CA 94109

SAXE, HENRY
SCULPTOR
b Montreal, Que, Sept 24, 37. Study: Ecole Des Beaux Arts, Montreal. Work: Nat Gallery of Can; Montreal Mus of Fine Arts; Musee Art Contemporain, Montreal; Art Gallery of Ont; Can Coun Art Bank. Exhib: The Bienale De Jeune Peinture de Paris, Musee Art Moderne, 68; Can Art d'Aujourdhul, Paris, Rome, Bruxelles, Lausanne, 68; Third Int Pioneers Exhib, Lausanne, Paris, 71; Boucherville, Montreal, Toronto, London, Nat Gallery, Can, 73; Owens Art Gallery, Sackville, NB, 76; Agnes Etherington Art Ctr, Queens Univ, 74; two-man shows, Baxter & Saxe, Eastern Circuit, Nat Gallery, Can, 68; Ron Martin & Henry Saxe, Venice Bienale & Ctr for Inter Am Activities, 78; one-man show, Henry Saxe, Dunlap Libr, Univ of Manitoba, 76. Awards: Can Coun Grants, 67-69 & 71 & Sr Awards, 73 & 77. Mailing Add: PO Box 143 Tamworth ON K0K 3G0 Can

SAXON, CHARLES DAVID
CARTOONIST, ILLUSTRATOR
b New York, NY, Nov 13, 20. Study: Columbia Univ, BA; Hamilton Col, LHD. Work: Brooklyn Mus, NY; Libr of Cong; Columbia Univ. Awards: Gold Medal, Art Dirs Club New York, 62; Spec Award for TV Cartoon, Venice Film Festival, 65. Bibliog: Jack Dillon (auth), article, Graphis, 71. Media: Pencil, Ink. Publ: Auth & illusr, Oh, Happy, Happy, Happy!, 59-60; contribr, New Yorker Anthologies; contribr, Great Cartoons of the World, 69-71; auth & illusr, One Man's Fancy, 77. Mailing Add: 228 Weed St New Canaan CT 06840

SAYRE, ELEANOR AXSON
CURATOR
b Philadelphia, Pa, Mar 26, 16. Study: Bryn Mawr Col, AB, 38; Harvard Univ, 38-40. Collections Arranged: Rembrandt: Experimental Etcher, in collaboration with Morgan

Library; Albrecht Duerer: Master Printmaker; Goya. Teaching: Intermittent seminars in prints through Harvard Univ & Radcliffe Col for students of five cols. Pos: Asst in exhibs, Yale Univ Art Gallery, 40-41; gallery asst, Lyman Allyn Mus, New London, Conn, 42; asst dept educ, RI Sch Design Mus, 42-45; from asst cur to cur prints & drawings, Mus Fine Arts, Boston, 45- Awards: Lazo de Dama of the Order of Isabel la Católica, 75. Mem: Keepers Pub Collections Graphic Art (int adv comt); Real Academia de Bellas Artes de San Fernando; Hispanic Soc Am. Publ: Auth, A Christmas book, 66; co-auth, Rembrandt: experimental etcher, 69; auth, Late caprichos of Goya, 71; co-auth, Duerer: master printmaker, 72; auth, The Changing Image: Prints by Francisco Goya, 74. Mailing Add: Dept of Prints & Drawings Museum Fine Arts Boston MA 02115

SAZEGAR, MORTEZA
PAINTER
b Teheran, Iran, Nov 11, 33; US citizen. Study: Univ Tex, El Paso, BA, 55 & BS, 56; Baylor Univ Col Med, 56-57; Cornell Univ, 58-59. Work: Whitney Mus Am Art, New York; San Francisco Mus Art; Corcoran Gallery Art, Washington, DC; Prudential Ins Co, Newark, NJ; Int Minerals & Chem Corp, Chicago. Exhib: One-man shows, Poindexter Gallery, New York, 64-77; Art Inst Chicago, 65; Whitney Mus Am Art Ann, 69-70; Cleveland Mus Art, 72; Corcoran Gallery Art, 73. Bibliog: Donald B Goodall (auth), Color Forum, Univ Tex Art Mus, 72; Gene Baro (auth), The Way of Color, Corcoran Gallery Art, 73. Style & Technique: Abstract painting with emphasis on color and formal order. Media: Acrylic. Dealer: Poindexter Gallery 24 E 84th St New York NY 10028. Mailing Add: RR 1 Cochranville PA 19330

SCALA, JOSEPH (A)
SCULPTOR, EDUCATOR
b Queens, NY, Feb 20, 40. Study: C W Post Col, BS(math), 62; Cornell Univ, MFA(sculpture), 71. Work: Metrop Mus Art, New York, Herbert Johnson Mus, Ithaca, NY; Battelle Mem Inst, Acad Contemp Problems, Columbus, Ohio. Comn: Laser sculpture (with Dr Howard Moraff), Andrew Dickson White Mus, Ithaca, NY, 70; Sound/Light Sculpture (with Dr Milford Kime), Rochester Jr League, 70; Cybernetic Fountain, Cornell Univ Physics Dept, 72. Exhib: Some More Beginnings, Brooklyn Mus, NY, 68; Mirrors, Motors, Motion, Albright-Knox Gallery, Buffalo, NY, 70; one-person one-piece show, Everson Mus, Syracuse, NY, 72; two-person show, Ward-Nasse Gallery, New York, 75; Can Comput Show Art Exhib, Toronto, Ont, 75. Teaching: Instr multi-media, Cornell Univ, summers 70 & 71; assoc prof art & eng comput graphics, Syracuse Univ, 71- Pos: Pres & founder, Collaborations in Art, Sci & Technol, Inc (CAST), 69-; interim dir, Lowe Art Gallery, Syracuse Univ, chairperson museuology prog, Syracuse Univ. Awards: Winner Young Sculptors Competition, Sculptors Guild, New York, 69; Grants for CAST, New York State Coun Arts, 70-75. Bibliog: Milford Kime (auth), Laser art, Laser Focus, 73; article in HUD Nat Community Art Competition Publ, 74. Style & Technique: Aesthetic exploration of light and computer graphics in 2 and 3 dimensions. Mailing Add: 960 Westcott St Syracuse NY 13210

SCALISE, NICHOLAS PETER
PAINTER
b Meriden, Conn, June 4, 32. Study: Horace C Wilcox Tech Sch, Meriden; Paier Sch Art, New Haven, Conn. Work: Meriden World War II Mem Hosp, Meriden. Exhib: Nat Acad Design, New York, 66; Nat Art League, New York, 69; Butler Inst Am Art, Youngstown, Ohio, 69; Nat Soc Painters in Casein, New York, 70; Wadsworth Atheneum, Hartford, Conn, 72; Silvermine Exhib, Conn, 77; New Eng in Winter Watercolor Exhib, De Cordova Mus, Lincoln, Mass, 77 & 78. Teaching: Instr drawing & painting, Famous Artists Sch, Westport, Conn, 56-69. Awards: Lucien Schimpf Award, Springfield Acad Artist, Mass, 69; Patron's Award, Nat Soc Painters in Casein, New York, 69; Charles R Miller Award, Springfield Acad Artist, 73. Mem: Springfield Acad Artist; Meriden Arts & Crafts, Conn; Conn Acad Fine Arts, Hartford. Style & Technique: Figure, landscape, floral, realistic, impressionistic, brushwork, some palette knife. Media: Oil, Watercolor. Dealer: Manuel Baker c/o IFA Galleries Inc 2023 Connecticut Ave Washington DC 20008. Mailing Add: 59 Susan Lane Meriden CT 06450

SCANGA, ITALO
SCULPTOR, EDUCATOR
b Lago, Italy, June 6, 32; US citizen. Study: Mich State Univ, BA & MA. Work: Metrop Mus Art, New York; Fogg Mus, Cambridge, Mass; Philadelphia Mus Art; Mus Art, RI Sch Design, Providence; Pa Acad Fine Arts, Philadelphia. Exhib: Whitney Mus Am Art Sculpture Ann, New York, 70; Mus Mod Art, New York, 71; Mus Contemp Art, Chicago, 71; Corcoran Gallery Art, Washington, DC, 71; one-man show, Whitney Mus Am Art, New York, 72; Tony Alessandra, New York, 75 & 77; Henry Gallery, Washington, DC, 75; Casat Gallery, La Jolla, Calif, 77. Teaching: Asst prof sculpture, RI Sch Design, 64-66; assoc prof sculpture, Tyler Sch Art, Philadelphia, 67-; vis assoc prof visual arts, Univ Calif, San Diego, 76-77. Awards: Best in Show, 48th Ann Wis Painters & Sculptors Show, 62; Howard Found Grant, Brown Univ, 70; Cassandra Found Grant, 72. Bibliog: Willoughby Sharp (auth), Pythagoras & Christ, Avalanche Mag, 71; Pat Stewart (auth), article in Art in Am, 75; Eric Cammeron (auth), article in Artforum, 77; plus others. Style & Technique: Narrative. Media: Mixed Media. Dealer: Tony Alessandra 39 W 67th St New York NY 10023; Charles Casat Gallery 5721 La Jolla Blvd La Jolla CA 92037. Mailing Add: 1359 71st Ave Philadelphia PA 19126

SCARBROUGH, CLEVE KNOX, JR
MUSEUM DIRECTOR, ART HISTORIAN
b Florence, Ala, July 17, 39. Study: Univ NAla, BS, 62; Univ Iowa, MA, 67. Collections Arranged: Pre-Columbian Art of the Americas, 70, Graphics by Four Modern Swiss Sculptors, circulated by Smithsonian Traveling Serv, 72- & Completed Charlotte Museum of History, 76, Mint Mus Art, Charlotte, NC. Teaching: Grad asst, Univ Iowa, 64-67; asst prof art hist, Univ Tenn, Knoxville, 67-69. Pos: Dir, Mint Mus Art, 69-76; mem, Charlotte Mecklenburg Bicentennial Comt, 75-76; dir, High Mus Art, 76-; mem visual arts adv panel, Tenn Arts Comn, 76, chmn comt, 77, rev comt, Art in Pub Places, 78. Mem: Southeastern Mus Conf (bd mem, 76-77); Col Art Asn; Am Asn Mus; NC Mus Coun (bd mem, 70-75, pres, 76). Publ: Ed, North Carolinians Collect, 71; ed, Graphics by Four Modern Swiss Sculptors, 72. Mailing Add: Hunter Mus Art 10 Bluff View Chattanooga TN 37403

SCARPITTA, SALVATORE
SCULPTOR
b New York, NY, 1919. Study: Study in Italy, 36-59. Work: Stedelijk Mus, Amsterdam, Holland; Albright-Knox Art Gallery, Buffalo, NY; Los Angeles Co Mus Art; Mus Mod Art, New York; Tel-Aviv Mus, Israel. Exhib: Corcoran Gallery Art, Washington, DC, 63; 1st Salon Int Galeries Pilotes, Mus Cantonal Beaux-Arts, Lausanne, Switz, 63; one-man exhib, Royaux Mus, Brussels, Belg, 64; Md Inst, 64; Art Inst Chicago, 64; Univ Ill, 65; Inst Contemp Art, Univ Pa, 70; Hofstra Univ, 71; 3rd Quadriennial, Rome, Italy, 72; plus others. Teaching: Vis critic, Md Inst, Col Art, 66- Bibliog: Harriet Janis & Rudi Blesh (auth), Collage, Personalities—Concepts—Techniques, Chilton, 62; Allen S Weller (auth), The Joys & Sorrows of Recent American Art, Univ Ill, 68; B H Friedman (auth), The ivory tower, Art News, 4/69. Dealer: Leo Castelli Gallery 4 E 77th St New York NY 10021. Mailing Add: Dept of Fine Art Md Inst Col Art Baltimore MD 21217

SCHAB, MARGO POLLINS
ART DEALER
b Cincinnati, Ohio, Aug 4, 45. Pos: Pres, Margo Pollins Schab, New York. Specialty: Important prints, drawings and paintings of the 19th and 20th century. Mailing Add: 1000 Park Ave New York NY 10028

SCHABACKER, BETTY BARCHET
PAINTER, LECTURER
b Baltimore, Md, Aug 14, 25. Study: Conn Col Women; Marian Carey Art Asn, Newport, RI; Coronado Sch Art, Calif, with Monty Lewis; also with Gerd & Irene Koch, Ojai, Calif. Work: B K Smith Gallery, Lake Erie Col, Painesville, Ohio; First Nat Bank Pa, Erie; Western Union, New York; McGraw Edison, Columbia, Mo; Erie Zoo, Pa. Exhib: Mus Mod Art, Paris, 61-63; Butler Inst Am Art Ann, 64-77; Chautauqua Exhib Am Art, 66-74; Audubon Artists, 67-78; 14 one-person shows, Nat Acad Design. Pos: Artist in residence, Lake Erie Col, 71. Awards: Grumbacher Award, Providence Art Club, RI, 59; Nancy Hubbard Lance Award, Lake Erie Col, 71; First Toastmaster, Ann Fine Art Series, 73. Mem: Nat Watercolor Soc; Northwestern Pa Artists Asn; Audubon Artists; Artists Equity Asn; Los Angeles Art Asn. Style & Technique: Start with an image in mind and a reason behind painting; method is cut, fit, stain, refit and paste, working directly to keep work fresh and spontaneous. Media: Watercolor, Cloth Collage. Dealer: The Inn Gallery Clymer NY 14724. Mailing Add: 540 Wilkins Rd Erie PA 16505

SCHACHTER, JUSTINE RANSON
GRAPHIC ARTIST, ILLUSTRATOR
b Brooklyn, NY, Dec 18, 27. Study: Tyler Sch Fine Arts, Temple Univ, scholar; Brooklyn Mus Art Sch, with John Bindrum, Milton Hebald & John Ferren; Art Students League, with Will Barnett. Work: Bellmore Pub Libr, NY; Island Trees Pub Libr, Levittown, NY; Wantagh High Sch, NY. Comn: Poster, NY State Parent-Teacher Asn, 70-73. Exhib: One-man show, Ruth White Gallery, 61; Nat Asn Women Artists Traveling Graphics Show, US & Europe, 69-70; Am Soc Contemp Artists, New York, 69-77. Teaching: Artist in residence, Community Arts Prog, Wantagh High Sch, 72 & Syosset High Sch, 74. Pos: Dir graphic arts, Audio-Visual Educ TV, Mineola Pub Sch, 64-65; exec dir, Art Forms Creative Ctr, 71-73. Awards: Award for graphics, Brooklyn Soc Artists Ann, 49; awards for mixed media, Nassau Co Off Cult Develop, 70 & Am Soc Contemp Artists, 71 & 75. Bibliog: Elyse Sommer (auth), Rock and Stone Craft, Crown, 72. Mem: Am Soc Contemp Artists (chmn admis, 68-71); Nat Asn Women Artists; Artists Equity Asn; Int Asn Arts. Style & Technique: Fine line pen and ink drawings on paper and stone. Publ: Illusr, Long Island Free Press, 70-71; illusr, Make a glad sound, Consort Music, Inc, 74; illusr, You can play a recorder, Music minus one, 74; illusr, Treasury of Stories, Waldman, 78. Mailing Add: 14 Trumpet Lane Levittown NY 11756

SCHACTMAN, BARRY ROBERT
PAINTER, EDUCATOR
b Newark, NJ, May 10, 30. Study: Univ of Miami; Art Students League; Rutgers Univ; Tyler Sch of Art of Temple Univ; Yale Univ Sch of Art, BFA, 58, MFA, 60, study with Joseh Albers & Rico Lebrun. Work: Yale Univ Art Mus, New Haven, Conn; St Louis Univ, Mo; Mus of Isreal, Jerusalem; Minn Mus of Art, St Paul; Weatherspoon Art Gallery, Univ of NC, Greensboro. Exhib: Drawings from 17 States, Drawing Soc Regional Exhib, Houston Mus of Fine Arts, Tex, 65; Drawings USA, Nat Traveling Exhib, St Paul Art Ctr, Minn, 66-68; Mid-Am I Exhib, Nelson Gallery of Art, Kansas City & City Art Mus, St Louis, Mo, 68; Drawing Soc MidWest Regional Exhib, Indianapolis Mus of Art, Ind, 70; Drawing Soc Nat Traveling Exhib, Am Fedn of Arts, 70-72; Drawing USA (nat traveling exhib), Minn Mus of Art, St Paul, 71-73; Nat Invitational Drawing Exhib, Mitchell Gallery, Southern Ill Univ, Carbondale, 75; Drawing Mo 1976, Bicentennial Invitational Exhib (traveling exhib), Albrecht Art Mus, St Joseph, Mo, 76. Teaching: Instr drawing & design, Univ of Tex, Austin, 59-61; prof drawing & painting, Washington Univ, St Louis, Mo, 61-; vis artist drawing, Portland Sch of Art, Maine, summer 74 & Ark Art Ctr, Little Rock, 77. Pos: Assoc dean, Sch Fine Arts, Washington Univ, St Louis, Mo, 77- Awards: Purchase Prize, Drawing USA, Minn Mus of Art, St Paul, 71; plus others. Bibliog: Bernard Chaet (auth), The Art of Drawing, Holt, Rinehart and Winston Inc, NY, 70 & 78; The Drawing Soc Nat Exhib, Am Fedn of Arts, NY, 70; Drawings in St Paul from the Permanent Collection, Minn Mus of Art, St Paul, 71. Style & Technique: Figurative painter and draughtsman. Media: Pen and Ink, Charcoal; Oil. Mailing Add: 437 E Glendale Rd St Louis MO 63119

SCHAEFER, CARL FELLMAN
PAINTER
b Hanover, Ont, Apr 30, 03. Study: Ont Col Art, Toronto, with J E H MacDonald & Arthur Lismer; Cent Sch Arts & Crafts, London; fel, Ont Col Art, 76; Univ Waterloo, Ont, hon DLett, 76. Work: Nat Gallery Can; Art Gallery Ont; Art Gallery Hamilton; Art Gallery London; Va Mus Fine Arts, Richmond. Comn: Ser of paintings on prod, Can Packers, Ltd, Toronto, 42. Exhib: Coronation Exhib George VI, London, 37; Century of Can Art, Tate Gallery, London, 38; 18th Int Art Inst Chicago, 39; 11th Int, Brooklyn Mus, 41; 1st Biennial, Sao Paulo Mus Arte Mod, 51; Retrospective 1926-1969, Sir George Williams Univ, Montreal, 69-70; Aviation Paintings, Can War Mus, Ottawa, 72; Can Paintings to People's Repub of China, 75; Can Paintings in the Thirties, Nat Gallery Can, 75; Ont Community Collects, Art Gallery Ont, Toronto, 75; Retrospective 1932-1967, Robert McLaughlin Gallery, Oshawa, 76; Can Paintings in Univ Toronto, Art Gallery Ont, 77-78. Teaching: Instr painting, Cent Tech Sch, Toronto, 30-40; dir art, Hart House, Univ Toronto, 34-40; instr & dir painting, Ont Col Art, 48-55, emer chmn dept drawing & painting, 68- Pos: Off war artist, Europ Theatre Opers & Iceland, RCAF, 43-46. Awards: Queen's Coronation Medal, Elizabeth II, 53 & Can Silver Jubilee Medal, 52-77 & 78; Can Centennial Medal, Dom Can, 67. Bibliog: Donald W Buchanan (auth), The Growth of Canadian Painting, Collins, 50; J Russell Harper (auth), Painting in Canada, a History, Univ Toronto Press, 66; Can Artists Series (monogr), Carl Schaefer, Gage Publ, 77. Mem: Can Soc Graphic Art; Can Soc Painters Watercolour; fel Royal Soc Arts; Royal Can Acad Arts; life fel Int Inst Arts & Lett. Media: Watercolor, Egg Tempera. Publ: Auth, Iceland, Atlantis on the Arctic Circle, Can Art Mag, 46. Dealer: Roberts Gallery 641 Yonge St Toronto ON Can. Mailing Add: 157 St Clements Ave Toronto ON M4R 1H1 Can

SCHAEFER, RONALD H
PRINTMAKER, EDUCATOR
b Milwaukee, Wis, June 2, 39. Study: Univ Wis-Milwaukee, BS(art), 62; Univ Wis-Madison, MS(art), 63, MFA, 64. Work: Joslyn Mus, Omaha, Nebr; Tampa Pub Libr; First Nat Bank Minneapolis; plus four cols & univs. Exhib: Five Okla Printmakers Ann, 64-72; three Boston Printmakers Ann, 65-67; 12th & 19th Ball State Univ Drawing & Small Sculpture Ann, 66

& 73; Miami Biennial Print, 73; NH Int Ann, 73; plus other int exhibs. Teaching: Prof printmaking & chmn dept, Univ NDak, 65- Awards: 25 Printmakers Nat Invitational Purchase Award, Minot State Col, 71; Graphic Chem & Ink Co Award, First NH Print Int, 73; Purchase Award, Los Angeles, Print Exhib, 73. Mem: Print Club. Style & Technique: Intaglio and relief etching; fantasy landscape. Mailing Add: 119 Conklin Ave Grand Forks ND 58201

SCHAFER, ALICE PAULINE
PRINTMAKER
b Albany, NY, Feb 11, 99. Study: Albany Sch Fine Arts, grad(cum laude). Work: Metrop Mus Art; Southern Vt Art Ctr, Manchester, Vt; New York Pub Libr; Hunt Bot Libr, Carnegie-Mellon Univ, Pittsburgh; Butler Inst Am Art, Youngstown, Ohio. Comn: Etchings, facade, Nat Commercial Bank & Trust, Albany, 50 & Doll Lady, Print Club Albany, 61. Exhib: 3rd Nat Buffalo Printmakers, NY, 40; 123rd Ann, Nat Acad Design, New York, 49; Royal Soc, Exchange, London, 54; Soc Am Graphic Artists 51st Ann, New York, 71; Nat Asn Women Artists 83rd Ann, 72. Awards: Alice Standist Buell Mem Award, Pen & Brush Club, 65; Gold Medal, Am Artists Prof League, 66; John Taylor Arms Mem Prize, Print Club Albany, 68. Mem: Print Club Albany (pres, 50); Catharine Lorillard Wolfe Art Club; Soc Am Graphic Artists; Nat Asn Women Artists; Miniature Painters, Sculptors & Gravers Soc Washington, DC. Media: Wood, Linoleum. Collection: Contemporary printmakers. Mailing Add: 33 Hawthorne Ave Albany NY 12203

SCHAFFER, ROSE
PAINTER, LECTURER
b Newark, NJ. Study: Art Students League, 35-40, with George Bridgeman & Ivan Oninsky; also with Bernard Karfiol, Sol Wilson, Seong Moy & Antonio Frasconi. Work: Smithsonian Inst, Washington, DC; Norfolk Mus Arts & Sci, Va; Springfield Mus Art, Mass; State NJ Cult Ctr; J F Kennedy Libr. Exhib: Nat Acad Design, New York; Boston Mus Art, Mass; Delgado Mus, New Orleans; Brooklyn Mus, NY; Philadelphia Print Club, Pa. Teaching: Lectr mod art, adult schs & other orgn; conductor of art tours. Awards: Terry Nat Award, Miami Beach, Fla, 55; Seton Hall Univ Award, 56; Two Purchase Prizes, Art for Overlook, 55-60; plus others. Mem: Nat Asn Women Artists; Nat Fedn Arts; Princeton Art Asn; Artists Equity Asn; Print Coun NJ. Style & Technique: Semi-abstract; representational. Media: Woodcut, Lithograph, Acrylic, Oil. Mailing Add: 119A Old Nassau Rd Jamesburg NJ 08831

SCHAFFNER, J LURAY
See Luray, J

SCHAFFNER, RUTH S
ART DEALER
b Mannheim, Ger; US citizen. Study: Itten Art Sch, Berlin; Sorbonne, Paris; New Sch of Soc Research, New York; Clarence White Sch of Photog, New York. Pos: Owner, Ruth Schaffer's Gallery, Santa Barbara, 73, Los Angeles, 74- Mem: Art Dealers Assoc of Southern Calif. Specialty: Avante-garde and contemporary paintings and sculpture. Mailing Add: 8406 Melrose Ave Los Angeles CA 90069

SCHANG, FREDERICK, JR
COLLECTOR
b New York, NY, Dec 15, 93. Study: Columbia Univ, BLit, 15. Pos: Pres, Columbia Artists Mgt, 49-60. Awards: Ritter of Dannebrog, Govt Denmark; Order of Vasa, Govt Sweden. Collection: Works of Paul Klee; collection shown at Minn Mus Art, Soc Four Arts, Palm Beach & var cols & mus. Interest: Collection of visiting cards donated to Columbia University (600 items), and Metropolitan Museum of Art, New York (50 items) in 1977. Publ: Auth, Visiting Cards of Celebrities, F Hazen, Paris, 71 & Visiting Cards of Violinists, Southeastern Printing Co, 75; auth, Visiting Cards of Prima Donnas, Vantage, 77. Mailing Add: 200 Mac Farlane Dr Delray Beach FL 33444

SCHANKER, LOUIS
PRINTMAKER, PAINTER
b New York, NY, July 20, 03. Study: Art Students League; Cooper Union Art Sch; Educ Alliance; also abroad. Work: Brooklyn Mus, NY; Metrop Mus Art, Whitney Mus Am Art & Mus Mod Art, New York; Philadelphia Mus Art; Art Inst Chicago; plus others. Exhib: Solomon R Guggenheim Mus, New York; San Francisco Mus Art; Libr Cong, Washington, DC; Victoria & Albert Mus, London; Bertha Schaefer Gallery, 73; plus many other group & one-man shows. Teaching: Instr art, New Sch Social Res, 40-60; assoc prof art, Bard Col, 49-64, prof emer, 64-; Univ Colo, 53; Univ Minn, 59. Awards: Brooklyn Mus Award, 47; Yaddo Fel, 58; Univ Ill Award, 58; plus others. Bibliog: S W Hayter (auth), About Prints, Oxford Univ Press, 62. Mem: Fedn Mod Painters & Sculptors; Sculptors Guild. Media: Acrylic on Plexiglas; Collages. Publ: Auth, Line-form-color, 44; illusr, book of prints, Brooklyn Mus, 74. Mailing Add: Box 359 Stamford CT 06904

SCHAPIRO, MEYER
EDUCATOR, ART HISTORIAN
b Shavly, Russia, Sept 23, 04; US citizen. Study: Columbia Univ, AB, MA & PhD. Teaching: Prof hist art, Columbia Univ, 28- Res: Early Christian, medieval and modern art. Mailing Add: Columbia Univ New York NY 10014

SCHAPIRO, MIRIAM
PAINTER
b Toronto, Ont, Nov 15, 23; US citizen. Study: Univ Iowa, BA, 45, MA, 46, MFA, 49. Work: Whitney Mus Am Art & Mus Mod Art, New York; Stanford Univ, Palo Alto, Calif; Allen Mem Art Mus; Oberlin Hirshhorn Mus. Exhib: Carnegie Int, 58; eight one-woman shows, Andre Emmerich Gallery, New York, 58-73 & Comsky Gallery, Los Angeles, 74; Toward a New Abstraction, Jewish Mus, 63; Mus Mod Art, New York, 67; Paul Brach & Miriam Schapiro—Double Retrospective, Newport Harbor Art Mus, 69; Womanhouse, A Collab Proj, Los Angeles, 72; Teacher, Parsons Sch Design, Univ Calif, San Diego, 67-71; co-originator The Shrine, The Computer and The Dollhouse, retrospective, Univ Calif, San Diego, 75. Teaching: Co-originator feminist art prog, Calif Inst Arts, 72-75. Awards: Ford Found Tamarind Fel, 64; Nat Endowment for the Arts, 76. Bibliog: Nancy Marmor (auth), Miriam Schapiro at Comsky, Art in Am, 74; Dorothy Seiberling (auth), Lacy fare, New York Mag, 7/76; Daniels Ruddick (auth), Working It Out, Pantheon, 77; plus others. Publ: Auth, The education of women as artists, project womanhouse, Col Art J, summer 72; co-auth, Womanhouse (catalog), 72; ed, Anonymous Was a Woman, 74 & Art: A Woman's Sensibility, 75, Feminist Art Prog, Cal-Arts; auth, Women and the Creative Process, Univ Man, 74. Dealer: Andre Emmerich Gallery 41 E 57th St New York NY 10021. Mailing Add: 393 W Broadway New York NY 10012

SCHAR, STUART
ART ADMINISTRATOR
b Chicago, Ill, Aug 27, 39. Study: Univ Chicago, BFA, 63, MFA, 64, PhD (arts admin), 67. Comn: Painting for Frank Lloyd Wright house, Brookfield, Ill, 73; lithograph for Lyons Twp High Sch, City of LaGrange, Ill, 74; painting for Aurora Pub Libr, City of Aurora, Ill, 75. Exhib: Field Mus of Chicago, 60; Art Inst of Chicago, 60-64, 70 & 74; Midway Studios, Chicago, 64-65 & 72; Lexington Studios, Chicago, 64-65, 75-76; Printmaking 1969, Northern Ariz Univ, Flagstaff, 69; John Hancock Ctr, Chicago, 73; Columbus Gallery of Fine Arts, Ohio, 76; Oberlin Col, Ohio, 77; Western Art League Asn, 77. Teaching: Asst prof rendering & drafting, Chicago Tech Col, 64, asst prof design & graphics, 65; asst prof art, Univ Ill, Chicago Circle, 66-70, assoc prof urban sci, 70-75; prof art, Kent State Univ, 75- Pos: Res assoc higher educ, NCent Asn Cols & Sec Schs, 65, asst to exec secy, 66; admin asst to chmn art dept, Univ Ill, Chicago Circle, 66-69, actg chmn art dept, 69; artist-in-residence, Joliet Art League, Ill, 70-72; Dir sch of art, Kent State Univ, 75-, co-dir, Blossom Kent Art, Music & Theatre summer progs, 75-, dir, James A Michener Mus, Univ Galleries, Eells Outdoor Gallery & Jack Lord Purchase Collections, 75- Awards: Best of Show, Midway Studios, 72, Gen Motors Purchase Award, Art Inst of Chicago, 74; Best of Show, Western Art League Asn, 77. Mem: Col Art Asn; Am Asn Univ Prof; Am Inst Planners. Publ: Co-auth, Guide for the Evaluation of Institutions of Higher Education, NCent Asn Cols & Sec Schs, 66; auth, The education of an art student, Tallyrand, Vol 3 (1970); co-auth, A Self Study Report: The University of Illinois at Chicago Circle, Univ Ill, 71. Mailing Add: 2760 Sandy Lake Rd Ravenna OH 44266

SCHARF, WILLIAM
PAINTER
b Media, Pa, Feb 22, 27. Study: Samuel Fleisher Mem Art Sch, Philadelphia, Pa; Pa Acad of the Fine Arts, Philadelphia; The Barnes Foundation, Merion, Pa. Work: Rockefeller Univ, New York; Neuberger Mus, Purchase, NY; Boston Inst of Contemp Art, Ma; Chase Manhattan Bank, New York; Winston-Salem Mus of Art, NC, plus others. Exhib: Pa Acad Anns, Philadelphia, 47; Inst of Contemp Art, Boston, 51; Univ Ill Ann, 62; Aldrich Mus, Ridgefield, Conn, 63; Brandeis Univ, Waltham, Mass, 63; San Francisco Art Inst, 70; The Neuberger Mus, Purchase, NY, 76; The High Mus, Atlanta, Ga, 78. Mailing Add: 75 Central Park W New York NY 10023

SCHARFF, CONSTANCE KRAMER
PRINTMAKER, PAINTER
b New York, NY. Study: Brooklyn Mus Art Sch, grad; also with Adja Jounkers & Abraham Rattner. Work: Brooklyn Mus, NY; Philadelphia Mus Art; Israel Mus, Jerusalem; Smithsonian Inst Archives; Butler Inst Am Art, Youngstown, Ohio. Comn: Ed prints, Contemp Arts Asn, NY, 56 & 60 & Am Asn Contemp Arts, 68. Exhib: Libr Cong, Washington, DC, 54, 55 & 63; Silvermine Guild, 65; Potsdam Nat Print Show, 66; Soc Am Graphic Artists, 72-75; Award Winners Show, Community Church, NY, 74. Pos: Juror, All NJ State Show, 71; invited juror of select Audubon Artists, 74, chmn print jury, 73-74 & 77-78. Awards: Medal of Honor, Nat Asn Women Artists, 68; Grumbacher Award, Nat Asn Women Artists, 73; Edna Stauffer Award, Audubon Artists, 73. Mem: Soc Am Graphic Artists; Nat Soc Painters Casein & Acrylic (rec secy, 67-); Audubon Artists; Nat Asn Women Artists (watercolor & print juries, 60-); Washington Printmakers. Style & Technique: Printing woodcuts, using collage, collograph, acetate, velour papers to interpret impressions. Dealer: Discovery Art Galleries 1191 Valley Rd Clifton NJ 07013. Mailing Add: 115 Jaffrey St Brooklyn NY 11235

SCHARY, EMANUEL
PAINTER
b Feb 27, 24; US citizen. Study: Carnegie Inst Technol Sch Fine Arts; Art Students League; Pratt Graphics Ctr; and with Edwin Dickenson, Howard Trafton, Frank Reilly, Ivan Olinsky, Robert Hale & Jurgen Fischer. Work: Nat Fine Art Collection, Smithsonian Inst, Washington, DC; Brooklyn Mus; Israel Mus, Jerusalem; Vatican Mus, Rome, Italy; Mus of Haifa, Israel. Comn: New York World's Fair Pavilion, Weizmann Inst Sci, 64-65; large painting, West Hempstead Community Ctr, NY; numerous litho ed for var group collectors. Exhib: One-man shows, Tel-Aviv, Israel, 68 & Kean Col, NJ, 73; Brooklyn Mus, 70; New York, Assoc Am Artists, 74; Kansas City Country Club Plaza, 74; Guild Gallery, New York, 78. Awards: Kiwanis Travel Award in Graphics, NY, 68; First Prize for Painting, New Rochelle, NY, 70; Medallion, Long Branch, NJ, 71. Bibliog: Michael Patterson (auth), Elmont artist...master, New York Sunday News, 4/5/70; Ann Shapiro (auth), New York artist comes to Kansas City, Kansas City Chronicle, 9/74; Rusty Hoffland (auth), Art show '75, NSide News, Atlanta, Ga, 2/6/75. Mem: Life mem Art Students League; Univ Mich Artists & Craftsmens Guild. Style & Technique: Designed realism; human form in relationship to his environment. Media: Acrylic, Graphics. Dealer: Guild Gallery 1145 Madison Ave New York NY 10028; Assoc Am Artists 663 Fifth Ave New York NY 10022. Mailing Add: 536 Kirkby Rd Elmont NY 11003

SCHARY, SAUL
ILLUSTRATOR, PAINTER
b Newark, NJ, Nov 3, 04. Study: Pa Acad Fine Arts; Grand Chaumiere, Paris; copying at the Louvre. Work: Pa Acad Collection, Philadelphia; Ferdinand Howald Collection, Columbus, Ohio. Comn: Rape of Sabine Women, Ben Mardens Riviera, Ft Lee, NJ, 34. Exhib: Carnegie Inst Int; Whitney Mus; Chicago World's Fair, 39; Calif Palace of Legion of Honor, San Francisco; Pa Mus Fine Arts; illus for Alice in Wonderland exhibited throughout the country; plus many one-man shows. Awards: Prize for Illus for Bullfinch Age of Fable. Bibliog: Articles in Scribners, Art Digest & Parnassus. Mem: Artists Equity Asn; Royal Soc Art. Style & Technique: Renaissance structure allied to color. Media: Oil, Watercolor. Mailing Add: 56 W Tenth St New York NY 10011

SCHARY, SUSAN
PAINTER
b Philadelphia, Pa, Aug 7, 36. Study: Tyler Sch, Temple Univ, BFA (hons); also with Vladamir Shatolov. Work: Temple Univ, Thomas Paine Ctr, Villanova Univ, Cent High Sch & City Hall, Philadelphia. Exhib: Florence Art Gallery, Italy, 65; 100 Distinguished Philadelphia Artists, 67; one-woman shows, Philadelphia, 64 & 67 & Los Angeles, 71, 72 & Louis Newman Galleries, 77; Printmakers Exhib, Mus Sci & Indust, Los Angeles & Japan, 75. Teaching: Instr, Harcum Jr Col, Bryn Mawr, Pa, 60-62; instr painting & drawing, Fleisher Art Mem, 66-68. Awards: Gimble Awards, 47-50; hon mention, Fidelity Bank Ann, 58; Dean's Prize, Tyler Sch, 58. Mem: Artists Equity Asn. Style & Technique: Figurative, surrealistic strong Chiara-scuro technique. Media: Oil, Lithography. Mailing Add: 228 St Albans Ave South Pasadena CA 91030

SCHEIBE, FRED KARL
PAINTER, CURATOR
b Kiel, WGer, Dec 2, 11; US citizen. Study: Clark Univ, BA, 38; Univ Pa, MA, 41; Univ Cincinnati, PhD, 54. Work: First Man on the Moon, Eisenhower Mus, Abilene, Kans; Galaxy, Nelson D Rockefeller Collection, New York; Mexico, A Poem, Langenheim Mem Libr, Greenville, Pa; Starry Night, Hartwick Col Art Collection, Oneonta, NY; Univ Maine Art Collection. Comn: Industry is King (mural, 75ft x 33ft), CofC, Abingdon, VA, 63. Exhib: One-man shows, Stuttgart, WGer, 63, Yager Mus, Hartwick Col, 70 & Exhib of Idioplasmic Precipitates, Two Rivers Gallery, Robinson Ctr, NY, 71; Idioplasmic Precipitates, Die Galerie, Munich, WGer, 71; Bicentennial Exhib, Washington, DC, 76. Pos: Cur, Stucki-Scheibe Art Mus, 78- Bibliog: Frank Perretta (auth), Idioplasmic precipitates, Oneonta Star, 3/25/67. Mem: Cooperstown Art Asn. Media: Enamel. Interest: Idioplasmic precipitates; developed secret enamel formula which produces vividly colored paintings. Mailing Add: PO Box 808 Farmington ME 04938

SCHEIN, EUGENIE
PAINTER, PRINTMAKER
US citizen. Study: Hunter Col, BA; Columbia Univ, MA; Martha Graham Sch Dance; Nat Univ Mex. Work: Carvell Mus, La; Ga Mus Art, Athens; Lowe Art Mus, Coral Gables, Fla; Miami Mus Mod Art, Fla. Exhib: Int Watercolors, Brooklyn Mus; Cincinnati Mus; Riverside Mus, New York; Soc Four Arts, Palm Beach; Fla Artists Asn; Lowe Mus, Univ Miami, Coral Gables, Fla; Hollywood Art & Cult Ctr, Fla; plus others. Teaching: Instr mod dance, Hunter Col, 26-52; instr mod dance, Univ Miami, 56-60. Mem: Lowe Art Mus; Miami Mus Mod Art; Artists Equity Asn (vpres, 72-). Style & Technique: Semi-abstract using the human figure in movement. Media: Oil, Acrylic, Watercolor. Mailing Add: 1070 Stillwater Dr Miami Beach FL 33141

SCHELLIN, ROBERT WILLIAM
PAINTER, EDUCATOR
b Akron, Ohio, July 28, 10. Study: Univ Wis-Milwaukee, BA, 33; with Hans Hofmann, New York, 39-40; Univ Wis-Madison, MA, 48. Work: Milwaukee Art Ctr; Madison Art Asn; Univ Wis-Milwaukee; Kenosha Pub Mus, Wis. Exhib: US Info Agency Am Crafts Exhib, Europe, 61-62; Wis Craftsmen, Smithsonian Inst, Washington, DC, 62, Four Ceramists, Tweed Gallery, Duluth, Minn, 63; Wisconsin Art, 1850 to Today, Milwaukee Art Ctr, 63, Commemorative Exhib Wis Art, 64; one-man retrospective, Univ Wis-Milwaukee, 75. Teaching: Instr painting, Milwaukee State Col, 45-51; prof ceramics, Univ Wis-Milwaukee, 51-75, emer prof, 75- Pos: Mem Milwaukee Art Comn, 62-70, chmn, 68-70. Awards: Silver Medal, Milwaukee Art Inst, 33; Design Excellence Award, Milwaukee Art Ctr, 57, First Award for Ceramics, 62. Mem: Wis Painters & Sculptors; Wis Designer Craftsmen; Am Craftsmen Coun. Media: Acrylic, Clay. Mailing Add: 3335 N Bartlett Ave Milwaukee WI 53211

SCHELLSTEDE, RICHARD LEE
ART DEALER
b Tulsa, Okla, Apr 3, 48. Study: Northeastern Okla State Univ, BA(bus mgt, tourism promotion). Collections Arranged: Five State Area Artists Fine Art Shows, Northeastern Okla State Univ, 75; Five State Artists, Green Country Art Assoc, Afton, Okla, 72-74; American Artists, Green Country Art Assoc, Tulsa, Okla, 67-77; Invitational to America's Outstanding Artists, Int Petroleum Exhib, 76; one-man & small group shows, Green Country Art Ctr, Tulsa, Okla, 74-78. Pos: Dir & exec vpres, Green Country Art Ctr, Tulsa, Okla, 75- Mem: Green Country Art Assoc (vpres). Specialty: Original paintings, oils, watercolors, acrylics and graphics by outstanding artists through the world. Mailing Add: c/o Green Country Art Ctr 1825 E 15th Tulsa OK 74104

SCHEPIS, ANTHONY JOSEPH
EDUCATOR, PAINTER
b Cleveland, Ohio, Mar 6, 27. Study: Cooper Sch of Art, dipl; Cleveland Inst of Art, cert; Kent State Univ, MA. Work: Akron Art Inst, Ohio; Massillon Mus of Art, Ohio; Butler Inst of Am Art, Youngstown, Ohio. Exhib: Nat Mid-Year Show, Butler Inst of Am Art, 55-74; May Show, 73-78 & Artists of the Western Reserve, 65, Cleveland Mus of Art; 47th All-Ohio Exhib, Akron Art Inst, 70; All-Ohio Exhib, Canton Art Inst, 71 & 77; Nova Park Ctr Invitational, 76; Cleveland/Toronto 78 Exhib, Harbourfront Gallery, Toronto, 78. Teaching: Instr life drawing & painting, Cooper Sch of Art, Cleveland, Ohio, 58-; instr life drawing & advanced painting, Cleveland Inst of Art, Ohio, 75- Pos: Chmn dept of Fine Art, Cooper Sch of Art, Cleveland, 76- Awards: Edwin C Shaw Purchase Award, 47th All-Ohio Exhib, Akron Art Inst, 70; Purchase Award, 5th Regional Exhib, Massillon Mus of Art, 71; Purchase Award, Nat Mid-Year Show, Butler Inst of Am Art, 74. Mem: New Organization of the Visual Arts, Cleveland. Style & Technique: Illusionistic, hyper-realism. Media: Oil Painting, Silk Screen Printing. Mailing Add: 34720 Sherwood Dr Solon OH 44139

SCHERER, HERBERT GROVER
ART LIBRARIAN, ART HISTORIAN
b Brooklyn, NY, May 16, 30. Study: Western Reserve Univ, BA(art), 53, MA(art hist), 60, MLS, 63. Teaching: Instr art hist & methodology, Univ Minn, Minneapolis, 66- Pos: Art librn, Syracuse Univ, 63-66 & Univ Minn, Minneapolis, 66- Awards: Res Grants from Kress Found, Am Philos Soc & Univ Minn, 67. Mem: Charter mem Art Libr NAm; Col Art Asn Am; ArtBibliog Mod (adv bd). Publ: Program of the thirty-nine ceiling paintings of the Jesuit Church of St Ignatius in Antwerp, painted by P P Rubens in 1620, Am Philos Soc Yearbk, 68; Minneapolis art deco extravaganza, Arts Mag, summer 71. Mailing Add: Art Libr 12 Walter Libr Univ of Minn Minneapolis MN 55455

SCHERPEREEL, RICHARD CHARLES
EDUCATOR, PAINTER
b Mishawaka, Ind, Dec 1, 31. Study: Univ Notre Dame, BFA & MFA; McMurry Col, MEd; George Peabody Col for Teachers, EdD. Comn: S Tex totems, Tex A&I Univ, Kingsville, 75. Exhib: Mid States Artist Exhib, 66-68; Found Exhib, Art Mus S Tex, 70-74; Del Mar Nat Drawing & Small Sculpture Exhib, 71; Tex Fine Arts Asn, 72-74. Teaching: Teacher art, Irving Pub Schs, Tex, 59-60 & Elkhart, Ind, 60-63; prof & chmn dept art, Bloomsburg State Col, Pa, 64-68 & Tex A&I Univ, 68- Mem: Nat Coun Art Adminr (bd dirs, 72-, secy-treas, 72-); Art Mus S Tex (bd mem, 74-75); Tex Fine Arts Asn (bd dirs, 71-74); S Tex Art League (pres, 72-73); Coastal Bend Art Educ Asn (pres, 73-74). Mailing Add: Dept of Art Tex A&I Univ Kingsville TX 78363

SCHERR, MARY ANN
GOLDSMITH, DESIGNER
b Akron, Ohio. Study: Cleveland Inst of Art, Ohio, study with Kenneth Bates; Univ of Akron; Kent State Univ; Akron Art Inst. Work: Smithsonian Inst, Washington, DC; Mus of Contemp Crafts, New York; Akron Art Inst Mus; Massilon Mus of Art. Comn: Stainless steel jewelry, US Steel Corp, Pittsburgh, Pa, 63; David (ring), comn for the Duke of Windsor, Consolidated Foods Corp, New York, 68; Intuition (sculpture), James A Michener Collection, Kent State Gallery, 74; four aluminum sculptures, Aluminum Corp of Am, Pittsburgh, 75; Signature V Jewelry Collection, Reed & Barton, Silversmiths, Taunton, Mass, 77. Exhib: The Goldsmith, Renwick Gallery, Smithsonian Inst, Washington, DC & Mus Contemp Crafts, New York, 74; Technol & the Artist, Nat Endowment for the Arts Touring Exhib, 74; Portable World, Seattle World's Fair, Wash, 74; Contemp Crafts of the Americas-Int, Smithsonian Inst, 75; Hist of Silver & Gold Smithing in Am, Lowe Mus, Coral Gables, Fla, 76; Scherr/Harper, Am Goldsmiths, Goldsmith Hall, London, Eng, 78; Craft: Art & Religion, Vatican, Rome, Italy, 78; one-woman shows, Scherr Jewelry, Art Inst of Chicago, 66 & Following Sea Gallery, Honolulu, Hawaii, 77. Teaching: Assoc prof jewelry & metals, Kent State Univ, Ohio, 50-; instr graphics, illus & design, Akron Art Inst, 54-65; assoc prof design, Univ of Akron, Ohio, 64-65. Pos: Graphics designer, Burton-Brown Advert Agency, Chicago, 45; automobile designer, Ford Motor Co, Detroit, Mich, 46-47; bk illusr, Saalfield Publ Co, Akron, 50-53; dress designer, Stern-Made Manufacturer, Boston, 56; sculptor/designer products, Alliance for Progress/US Gov, New York & Scherr & McDermont Design, Inc, 66-69. Awards: Silver Metal-Int, Jablonic, Prague, Czech, 74; Honor Award, NAm Goldsmiths, Phoenix Mus of Art, Ariz, 77; Outstanding Contrib to the Arts, Ohio Arts Coun, 78. Bibliog: Oppi Utracht (auth), Metal Techniques, Doubleday, 68; Body-Monitoring, Electronic Jewelry, article in Fortune Mag, 12/73; Joseph Ordos (auth), Goldsmiths (doc film), Univ of Minn, 75. Mem: Soc of NAm Goldsmiths (bd of dirs, 76-78); Am Crafts Coun; World Crafts Coun (sponsor); hon mem Ohio Designer/Craftsmen. Style & Technique: Special interest in functional jewelry, devices which monitor body; strong design forms; general research with techniques. Media: Jewelry; Graphic Design. Publ: Contribr, Metal Jewelry Techniques Step be Step Jewelry, Golden Press, 68; contribr, Metal Alloys & Patinas for Casting, Kent State Univ Press, 75; contribr, Penland Book of Jewelry Making, Bobbs-Merill Co, 75; contribr, The Great Gadget Catalog, Grosett & Dunlap, 76; illusr, We Jews, Hawthorne Bks, 78. Mailing Add: 521 B East 85th St New York NY 10028

SCHEU, LEONARD
PAINTER, LECTURER
b San Francisco, Calif, Fab 19, 04. Study: Calif Sch Fine Arts, San Francisco; Art Students League, drawing with George Bridgeman. Work: Ford Motor Co Collection, Dearborn Mus, Mich. Comn: Calif Motherlode & Jacksonville, Ore, Ford Motor Co. Exhib: US Naval Acad, Annapolis, Md, 65; Butler Inst Am Art, Youngstown, Ohio, 68; Holyoke Mus, Mass, 69; Erie Pub Mus, Pa, 70; Anchorage Fine Arts Mus, 71; Nat Drawing Exhib, Del Mar Col, Corpus Christi, Tex; Drawing & Small Sculpture Exhib, Ball State Univ; Purdue Univ, Ind; Univ Wis; Memphis Univ, Tenn; Nat Orange Show, San Bernardino, Calif. Teaching: Instr painting & drawing, Whittier Sch Syst, Calif, 61-70; prof art, Banff Sch Fine Arts, Univ Alta, 62-65; instr painting, drawing & art hist, Orange Coast Col, 62-67. Pos: Juror, local & nat exhibs, 53- Awards: Honorable Mention, Laguna Beach Art Asn. Bibliog: M Jackson (auth), article in Laguna Beach Post, 55; Margaret Paige (auth), article in SCoast News, 64; article in St Vincent, Latrobe, Pa, 66. Mem: Laguna Beach Art Asn (mem bd, 56-, pres, 56-57, exhib chmn, 56-58); Calif Nat Watercolor Soc; Nat Soc Painters Casein (bd mem, 56-59). Style & Technique: Realism, landscape; transparent and opaque color. Media: Watercolor, Oil. Publ: Illusr, Good ghost towns never die, Lincoln Mercury Times, 54; illusr, Saga of Cinnabar, New Almaden, 54 & Gold rush town that took its time, 61, Ford Times. Dealer: William D Gorman 43 W 33rd St Bayonne NJ 07002. Mailing Add: 309 Agate St Laguna Beach CA 92651

SCHEYER, ERNST
ART HISTORIAN, LECTURER
b Breslau, Ger, July 3, 00; US citizen. Study: Univ Freiburg, Ger, Dr rer pol, 22; Univ Cologne, Ger, PhD(hist art), 26. Collections Arranged: Art at Time of Goethe, Detroit Inst Arts, 50. Teaching: Prof art hist, Wayne State Univ, Detroit, 38-71. Pos: Cur asst, Mus Appl Arts, Cologne, 26-29; cur, Mus Appl Arts, Breslau, 29-33; hon res fel, Detroit Inst Arts, 36- Awards: Bronze Plaque, Mich Acad Sci, Arts & Lett, 66; Georg Dehio Prize for Art Hist, Künstlergilde, Esslingen, Ger, 70; Order of Merit First Class, Ger Fed Rep, 74. Mem: Life mem Thomas Mann Arch; Gerhart Hauptmann Gesellschaft; Eichendorff Gesellschaft. Res: Interrelation of art and literature; Northern European art of the 17th and 20th centuries. Publ: Auth, Lyonel Feininger, Wayne State Univ, 64 & Circle of Henry Adams, 70; auth, Mary Wigman-O Schlemmer/Dance Perspectives, New York, 70. Mailing Add: 201 Kirby Ave Detroit MI 48202

SCHIEFERDECKER, IVAN E
PRINTMAKER
b Keokuk, Iowa, Apr 14, 35. Study: Univ Ill, BFA; Univ Iowa, MFA. Work: Colorado Springs Art Ctr; Ohio Univ; Dulin Art Gallery, Knoxville, Tenn; Springfield Art Mus, Mo; Montgomery Art Mus, Ala. Exhib: Pa Acad Fine Arts Ann Prints & Drawings, 65; Potsdam Ann Print Exhib, 69; Color Print USA, 70; Dulin Nat Print & Drawing Competition, 70; Nat Print Show, Cent Wash State Col, 75; J B Speed Art Mus, Louisville, Ky, 77. Teaching: Assoc prof printmaking, Western Ky Univ, 64- Mem: Col Art Asn. Mailing Add: Col Heights Sta PO Box 33 Bowling Green KY 42101

SCHIETINGER, JAMES FREDERICK
SCULPTOR, PHOTOGRAPHER
b Baltimore, Md, Sept 27, 46. Study: Fla Presby Col, 64-66; Fla Atlantic Univ, 67; Univ SFla, BA, 68, MFA, 71. Work: Univ SFla; Norton Gallery Art, West Palm Beach. Exhib: 25th Ceramic Nat, Everson Mus, Syracuse, 69; New Photographics, Cent Wash State Col, 71; Photo-Media Show, Mus Contemp Crafts, New York, 71; Light and Lens: Methods of Photography, Hudson River Mus, NY, 73; Images-Dimensional, Moveable, Transferable, Akron Art Inst, 73. Teaching: Instr art hist, Fla Atlantic Univ, 71; instr ceramics, Univ SFla, 71-72; instr art, Miami-Dade Community Col, Miami, 72-73. Awards: Winter Park Art Show First Prize in Sculpture, 70; Technol & Artist-Craftsman Symposium Award, Octagon Art Ctr, 73; Las Olas Art Festival Best in Show, Ft Lauderdale, 75. Mem: Am Crafts Coun; Craft Prof Vt. Style & Technique: Photographic images on clay surfaces using underglazes and overglazes. Media: Clay. Mailing Add: RFD 2 Box 52 B Ludlow VT 05149

SCHIFF, JEAN
DRAFTSMAN, VIDEO ARTIST
b Keokuk, Iowa, Oct 20, 29. Study: Chicago Art Inst, 49-52; Washburn Univ, 57-60; Univ Kans, 61-63; Col San Mateo, 63-64; Univ Denver, BFA, 66; Univ Colo, Boulder, MFA, 70. Work: St Paul Fine Art Ctr, Minn; Wichita Art Asn; Bucknell Univ; Francis McCray Gallery, Western NMex Univ; Mulvane Art Ctr, Washburn Univ. Comn: Illustration, Scott Printing Co, Denver, 75. Exhib: Norfolk Mus Arts & Sci Am Drawing Biennial, circulated by Smithsonian Inst, 69; Southwest Fine Arts Biennial, Mus NMex, Santa Fe, 72; 14 Women, Univ NDak, Grand Forks, 73; Joslyn Mus Exchange Exhib, Omaha, 73; Auraria Lives, United Bank Ctr, Denver, 75; Aspen Arts Festival, Colo, 77; Colo State Univ, Ft Collins, 78; plus others. Teaching: Instr drawing, Univ Colo, Denver, summer 70; instr drawing, Metrop State Col, 70-71, assoc prof, 71-; instr drawing, Temple Buell Col, 70-71; instr drawing, Denver Community Col, 71; instr video workshops, Univ Colo, Colorado Springs, 75, Colo

State Univ, Ft Collins, 77 & Red Deer Col, Alta, Can, 77. Awards: Grad Fel, Univ Colo, Boulder, 70; Purchase Award, Stanislaus State Col, 72. Mem: Col Art Asn Am; Asn Independent Film & Video Makers, Inc; Denver Art Mus. Style & Technique: Figurative, graphic, detailed and conceptually oriented; multi-media environment, working with the simulation of movement in drawing via audio and light and extending the meaning of image through the implication of time. Media: Colored Pencil, Electronic Media. Dealer: William Kastan Rm 306 2865 S Colorado Blvd Denver CO 80207. Mailing Add: 945 S Downing Denver CO 80209

SCHIFF, LONNY
PAINTER, ART RESTORER
Study: Univ Ill, BA(hons), 53; Worcester Art Mus Sch, fine arts cert, 64; Impressions Workshop, etching study, 65. Work: Brockton Art Ctr, Mass; Brockton Hosp; Hosp Asn, Burlington, Mass; Res Consult, Framingham, Mass; Wellesley Off Park; plus others. Comn: Complete restoration of oils by Enneking, A C Goodwin, Cargelliere, and others, 67; restoration painting, Longfellow's Wayside Inn, 68; wall graphics designer, Framingham Union Hosp, 76- plus others. Exhib: One-woman shows, Cape Cod Art Asn, 72, Spectrum Gallery, Brewster, Mass, 72-75, Brandeis Univ, 73, Copley Soc of Boston, 73 & 78, Brockton Art Ctr, 74, Attleboro Mus, 75; Holyoke Mus, Mass, 75; Va Mus Fine Arts, Richmond, 75; Shore Galleries, Boston, 75; Harvard Univ, 76-77; Hallway Gallery, Georgetown, DC, 77; plus others. Teaching: Instr oil painting, Adult Classes, Worcester Art Mus, 63-67; instr art appreciation & techniques, Sudbury Art Asn, 68-69; instr printmaking workshop, Charles River Art Ctr, 68, lectr & demonstrator, 69- Pos: Co-chmn hist res & visual arts displays, Framingham 275th Anniversary, 75. Awards: First Prize for Graphics & Larry Newman Prize in Oils, Cape Cod Art Asn, 71 & 75; Copley Soc First Prize, 77 & 78; Best in Show, Nat League Am Pen Women, 76; plus others. Mem: Nat Asn Women Artists; Cambridge Art Asn (former dir); Int Inst Conservators Art, London, Eng; Boston Watercolor Soc; Nat Slide Libr, Palm Beach. Style & Technique: Depict imaginary visions in brilliant colors; transforms animals, birds and fish into compositions that have been influenced by gentle surrealists like Klee and Miro to make the unseen and unconscious visual and exciting with washes and veils of color. Media: Watercolor, Graphic, Pastel. Res: Lost old masters; conservation. Dealer: Hallway Gallery 3235 P St NW Georgetown DC 20007. Mailing Add: Box 2156 Framingham Centre MA 01701

SCHILLER, BEATRICE
PAINTER, GRAPHIC ARTIST
b Chicago, Ill. Study: Inst Design; Ill Inst Technol; Art Inst Chicago; also with Richard Florsheim, Jack Kearney, Herbert Davidson; Kwak Wai Lau & Stanley Mitruk. Work: Standard Oil Bldg, Chicago; Excel Packing Co, Wichita, Kans. Exhib: Nat Exhib Small Paintings, Purdue Univ, West Lafayette, 64; 17th Ann Nat Exhib Realistic Art, Mus Fine Arts, Springfield, Mass, 66; Art Inst Chicago Art Rental & Sales Gallery, 66-; Butler Inst Am Art, Youngstown, Ohio, 67; New Horizons in Sculpture & Painting, Chicago, 70; plus others. Awards: Honorable Mention, Munic Art League Chicago, 71; Honorable Mention, Chicago Soc Artists, 74; Honorable Mention, Munic Art League, 74; plus others. Mem: Chicago Soc Artists; Ill Inst Technol (alumni); Arts Club of Chicago; Art Inst Chicago Art Rental & Sales Gallery; NShore Art League; plus others. Media: Watercolor, Graphic, Acrylic. Dealer: Art Rental & Sales Gallery Art Inst of Chicago Michigan Ave & Adams St Chicago IL 60603. Mailing Add: 3150 N Lake Shore Dr Chicago IL 60657

SCHIMANSKY, DONYA DOBRILA
ART LIBRARIAN, ART HISTORIAN
b Yugoslavia; US citizen. Study: Univ Belgrade, Yugoslavia, BA & MA(art hist); Univ Cologna, WGer, study with Prof Hans Kaufmann; Univ Hamburg, completed courses towards PhD, medieval art with Prof Wolfgang Schöne; City Univ New York, MLS. Pos: Asst to the chmn, The Cloisters, New York, 69-73; asst chief librn, Metrop Mus of Art Libr, 73-76, mus librn, 76- Mem: Int Ctr of Medieval Art (secy, 69-74; adv bd, 74-); Spec Libr Asn, New York (secy/treas, 78-); Art Libr Soc NAm (chmn var com, 75-). Res: As art historian, research on wall painting in Byzantine art; as art librarian, research on classification of art books. Publ: Auth, The study of medieval ecclesiastical costume, 71 & On stained glass, 72, Metrop Mus of Art Bull; auth, The Metropolitan Museum of Art Library Classification System: how it works, Art Libr Soc Newsletter, 76; auth, Art in Prague, Stone Press, New York, (in prep). Mailing Add: c/o Metrop Mus of Art Fifth Ave & 82nd St New York NY 10028

SCHIMMEL, NORBERT
COLLECTOR
b Sept 2, 04; US citizen. Pos: Trustee, Am Archaeol Inst; mem vis comt, Fine Arts Dept, Harvard Univ & Fogg Art Mus; mem vis comt, Egyptian, Near Eastern & Greek & Roman art, Metrop Mus Art, New York. Collection: Ancient art, especially Etruscan, Egyptian, Greek, Near Eastern and Iranian; works exhibited at Metropolitan Museum of Art, 59 and Fogg Art Museum, 64. Publ: Auth, Herbert Hoffmann. Mailing Add: 25 E 83rd New York NY 10028

SCHIMMEL, WILLIAM BERRY
PAINTER, LECTURER
b Olean, NY, July 21, 06. Study: Rutgers Univ, BLitt; Nat Acad Design; also with Gerry Pierce & Roy Mason. Work: Phoenix Fine Art Mus, Ariz; Cincinnati Mus Fine Art, Ohio; Univ Mus, Univ NC; Phoenix Pub Libr; Nat Casualty Life Ins Bldg, Phoenix. Exhib: Nat Acad Ann Watercolor Exhib, three yrs; Am Watercolor Soc Exhibs, eight yrs; Butler Inst Am Art, Youngstown, Ohio. Teaching: Instr watercolor & oil, Seattle Art Asn, Wash, Ft Worth Pub Sch Syst, Tex, Sch Mines, Brainerd, Minn, Flagstaff Art Asn, Ariz, Tucson Watercolor Guild & Phoenix Art Mus, Ariz, also pvt classes in Denver & Estes Park, Colo, Jackson, Wyo, Prescott & Phoenix, Ariz. Pos: Art dir, Benton & Bowles, New York, 35-38. Awards: Am Watercolor Soc Emily Goldsmith Award, 70; eight Valley Nat Bank Purchase Awards, Ariz State Fair. Mem: Am Watercolor Soc; Am Artists Prof League; Nat Arts Club New York; Int Inst Arts & Lett. Media: Watercolor, Oil. Publ: Auth, Watercolor, the Happy Medium, Macmillan, 58. Dealer: Linda McAdoo Gallery 7155 Main St Scottsdale AZ 85251. Mailing Add: 7625 E Camelback 248B Scottsdale AZ 85251

SCHIRA, CYNTHIA JONES
WEAVER
b Pittsfield, Mass, June 1, 34. Study: Rhode Island Sch of Design, BFA, 56; L'ecole D'Art Decoratif, Aubusson, France, 56-57; Univ of Kans, MFA, 67. Work: Mus Bellerive, Zurich, Switz; Chicago Art Inst, Ill; Columbia Mus of Art, SC; Joslyn Art Mus, Omaha, Nebr; Northern Ill Univ Student Art Collection. Comn: Wall hangings (5ft x 12ft), City Fed Savings & Loan, Audubon, NJ, 74 (10ft x 10ft), Commercial Bank of Japan, Los Angeles, 75 (8ft x 17ft), Iron Blosam Lodge, Snowbird, Utah, 75 (4ft x 32ft), Galleria Bank, Houston, Tex, 76 & (6ft x 24ft), Am Cyanamid, Wayne, NJ, 77. Exhib: Forms in Fibers, Chicago Art Inst, 70, 6th & 8th Int Tapestry Bienniale, Lausanne, Switzerland, 73 & 77; The Dyer's Art, Mus of Contemporary Crafts, New York, 76; Fiber Structures, Carnegie-Mellon Mus, Pittsburgh, Pa, 76; Textiles-Past & Prologue, Greenville Co Mus of Art, SC, 76; Art in Crafts, Bronx Mus, New York, 78. Teaching: Asst prof of Textile design, Univ of Kans, Lawrence, 76- Awards: Textron Fel, 56-57; Louis Comfort Tiffany Award, 66-67; Nat Endowment for the Arts Craftsman's Fel, 74-75. Mem: Am Crafts Coun. Style & Technique: Wall hangings of woven brocade and woven aluminum reliefs. Mailing Add: 1700 New Hampshire St Lawrence KS 66044

SCHLAGETER, ROBERT WILLIAM
ART ADMINISTRATOR
b Streator, Ill, May 10, 25. Study: Univ Ill, BA & MFA; Univ Heidelberg, cert; Univ Chicago; Harvard Univ. Collections Arranged: Fifty Years of American Art (1900-1950), 68; Age of Dunlap; Art of the Early Republic Exhibition. Teaching: Asst prof art hist, Univ Tenn, Knoxville, 52-58. Pos: Dir, Mint Mus Art, Charlotte, NC, 58-66; assoc dir, Downtown Gallery, New York, 67; assoc dir, Ackland Art Ctr, Univ NC, Chapel Hill, 67- Mailing Add: Ackland Art Ctr Univ of NC Chapel Hill NC 27514

SCHLAIKJER, JES (WILHELM)
PAINTER, ILLUSTRATOR
b New York, NY, Sept 22, 97. Study: Ecole des Beaux Arts, Lyons, France; Art Inst Chicago; also with Forsberg, Cornwell, Dunn & Henri. Work: Ranger Collection, US Naval Acad; War Dept; Nat Hq ARC; Army Med Ctr; Dept of State; also in pvt collections. Awards: First & Second Hallgarten Prizes, 26 & 32; First Altman Prize, 28. Mem: Nat Acad Design; Grand Cent Art Gallery; Artists Guild. Publ: Contribr & illusr, Woman's Home Companion, Am Mag, Collier's, Redbook Mag, Am Legion Monthly & others; also inspiration series Army posters, World War II. Mailing Add: 4526 Verplanck Pl NW Washington DC 20016

SCHLAM, MURRAY J
SCULPTOR
b Tyczyn, Austria, May 7, 11; US citizen. Style & Technique: Langfuhr Univ, Free City Danzig; Archipenko Art Sch; NY Univ, with Prof Ross; Art Students League, with Robert Brackman. Work: Fordham Univ, Lincoln Ctr, New York; Einstein Med Col, Bronx, NY; Mus Bat-Yam, Israel; Univ Miami, Fla; St Francis Hosp, Miami. Comn: Dr Bela Schick, Einstein Med Col, 59; Heman Muehlstein, Muehlstein Plastic Co, New York, 60; Dr Leo Michel, Grossinger Country Club, NY, 62; Rocky Marciano, pvt collection, 64; Leo Lowenstein, Fordham Univ, Lincoln Ctr, 68. Exhib: Int Art Exchange, New York Armory, 50; Attran Gallery, New York, 60; Art in Masonry, Lewis State Theater, New York, 62; Madison Ave Gallery, New York, 75; Gillary Gallery, Jericho, NY, 75; one-man show, Nat Mus Fine Arts, Santiago, Chile, 77. Teaching: Asst dir sculpture, Art Life Sch, New York, 53-57; instr drawing, City Col New York, 61-63; instr sculpture, Albert Pels Art Sch, New York, 64-66. Pos: Art dir, Grossinger Hotel, 53-67; art dir, Second Masonic Dist, 62-64. Awards: Gold Medal, Second Masonic Dist, New York, 62. Mem: Fel Royal Soc Art, London; Vet Art Asn, New York. Style & Technique: Modern, welding with special texture. Media: Bronze. Mailing Add: 25 Chateau Dr Dix Hills NY 11746

SCHLANGER, JEFF
SCULPTOR
b New York, NY, 37. Study: Swarthmore Col, BA; Cranbrook Acad of Art, study with Maija Grotell. Work: Sheldon Mem Art Gallery, Univ Nebr, Lincoln; Mus of Contemp Crafts, New York. Exhib: Objects: USA, Johnson Wax Collection traveling in USA, Europe & Japan, 69-74; 27th Nat Ceramic Exhib, Everson Mus, Syracuse, NY, 72; Contemp Ceramic Art, Kyoto Mus of Mod Art, Tokyo, Japan, 72; Total Cup, Kanazawa City, Tokyo, Kyoto, Japan, 73; Contemp Crafts of the Americas: 75, Ft Collins, Colo, 75; The Object as Poet, Renwick Gallery, Smithsonian Inst, Washington, DC & Mus of Contemp Crafts, New York, 77; one-man show, Estadio CHILE, State Col of Ceramics, Alfred, NY, 78. Teaching: Instr ceramics, Hunter Col, 75 & Pratt Inst Grad Sch, 77. Awards: Tiffany Found Scholar, 67; Craftsmen's Fel, Nat Endowment for the Arts, 73. Media: Clay, Wood. Publ: Auth, Maija Grotell, Craft Horizons, 11/69. Mailing Add: 556 Stratton Rd New Rochelle NY 10804

SCHLEMM, BETTY LOU
PAINTER
b Jersey City, NJ, Jan 13, 34. Study: Phoenix Sch Design, New York, scholar; Nat Acad Design, New York, scholar. Work: USN; also in many pvt collections. Exhib: Am Watercolor Soc; Butler Inst Am Art; Nat Acad Design; Allied Artists Am; Audubon Artists. Awards: Silver Medal, Am Watercolor Soc, 64; Gold Medal, Hudson Valley Art Asn, 65; Robert Lehman Travel Grant, Washington Sq Outdoor Art Exhib, 67. Bibliog: Article in Christian Sci Monitor, 67; 100 Watercolor Techniques, Watson-Guptill, 69. Mem: Am Watercolor Soc; Allied Artists Am (secy, 64-65); Rockport Art Asn (mem bd, 70-); Boston Watercolor Soc (vpres, 76-); NJ Watercolor Soc. Style & Technique: Free brush work; impressionistic. Media: Transparent Watercolor. Publ: Auth, Watercolor page, Am Artist, 64 & 76; auth, Painting With Light, Watson-Guptill, 78. Dealer: Guild of Boston Artists 162 Newbury St Boston MA 02116; Grand Central Art Galleries 40 Vanderbilt Ave New York NY 10017. Mailing Add: Caleb's Lane Rockport MA 01966

SCHLEMOWITZ, ABRAM
SCULPTOR
b New York, NY, July 19, 11. Study: Beaux-Arts Inst Design, 28-33; Art Students League, 34; Nat Acad Design, 35-39. Work: Chrysler Mus, Provincetown, Mass; Univ Calif, Berkeley. Exhib: One-man shows, Howard Wise Gallery, 61 & 62; Collaboration: Artist & Architect, Mus Contemp Crafts, 62; 12 New York Sculptors, Riverside Mus, 62; Humanists of the 60's, New Sch Social Res, 63; Art in Embassies Traveling Exhib, Mus Mod Art, circulated internationally, 63-64; Retrospective 1960-1977, Kingsborough Col, City Univ New York, 77; plus others. Teaching: Instr, Contemp Art Ctr, YMHA, New York, 36-39; instr, Pratt Inst, 62-63; lectr, Univ Calif, Berkeley, 63-64; lectr, Univ Ky, 65; prof, Univ Wis, 65-67; Distinguished lectr, Kingsborough Col, City Univ New York, 70- Pos: Organizing chmn, New Sculpture Group, 57-58. Awards: Guggenheim Fel, 63; Longview Found, 60. Style & Technique: Bronze casting; enamel on steel. Mailing Add: 139 W 22nd St New York NY 10011

SCHLEY, EVANDER DUER (VAN)
CONCEPTUAL ARTIST, PHOTOGRAPHER
b Montreal, PQ, Apr 21, 41; US citizen. Work: Place and Process (film), in collections of Ft Worth Art Ctr, Miami-Dade Col & Boston Mus Fine Arts. Exhib: Software, Jewish Mus, New York, 70; Information, Mus Mod Art, New York, 70; one-man show, Everson Mus, Syracuse, 73; Project 74, Kunstverein, Cologne, Ger, 74; Video Show, Arts Coun Gt Brit, London Serpentine Gallery, 75; plus others. Teaching: Lectr art & archit, Univ Calif, Santa Barbara, 72. Awards: Avalanche Mag Art Award, 72. Bibliog: Billy Adler (auth), In the Midnight Hour (videotape), GBF, Inc, 69; article in Ramparts Mag, 73; Willoughby Sharp Videoviews Van Schley, Elecric Arts Intermix, New York, 74. Media: Videotape, Film. Publ: Auth, Signs, 72;

contribr, Avalanche Mag, 73; auth, World Run, Flash Art, 74; contribr, Art Press, 74; contribr, Los Angeles Inst Contemp Art J, 75. Mailing Add: Box 309 Topanga CA 90290

SCHLICHER, KARL THEODORE
PAINTER, EDUCATOR
b Terre Haute, Ind, May 14, 05. Study: Univ Wis, BS & MS; Colt Sch Art; Art Inst Chicago; Univ Chicago; Ohio State Univ, PhD; also with Reynolds, Giesbert, Coats, Hopkins, Grimes & others. Work: Portraits in pvt collections. Exhib: Art of the Southwest, 56; Lufkin Art League; Nacogdoches Fair; Fac Exhibs, Stephen F Austin State Univ & one-man retrospective, 75. Teaching: Prof art, Stephen F Austin State Univ, 48-, head dept art, 48-65. Pos: Ed & publ, Trends in Art Educ, 51-56. Mem: Col Art Asn Am; Tex Fine Arts Asn; Tex Art Educ Asn (pres, 56-58); Royal Soc Arts; Nat Art Educ Asn; plus others. Style & Technique: Traditional; portraits, figures and landscapes. Media: Oil, Pastel, Charcoal. Publ: Contribr, Tex Outlook, Western Arts Asn Res Bull & Tex Trends in Art Educ. Mailing Add: Dept of Art Stephen F Austin State Univ Nacogdoches TX 75961

SCHLIEFER, STAFFORD LERRIG
PAINTER, LECTURER
b Kingston, Jamaica, WI, Jan 29, 39; Jamaican & US citizen. Study: Self-taught. Work: Nat Mus of Jamaica, Kingston; Papal Collection of the Vatican, Italy; Nat Trust Comn of Jamaica; Olympia Int Gallery, Kingston; Bank of Jamaica, Kingston. Comn: Portrait, comn by Adolph R Bernstein, Chicago, 70; mural, comn by Sinclair T Brody, Jamaica, 72. Exhib: 2nd Biennial of Int Art, Medellin, Columbia, 70; Three Decades of Jamaican Painting, Commonwealth Inst Art Gallery, London, 71; Ann Nat Exhib of Painting (Jamaican), Kingston, 71; 1st Biennial de Sao Paulo, Brazil, 71; World Black & African Festival of Arts & Cult, 75 & 77. Teaching: Guest lectr Caribbean art in humanities, Mohave Community Col, Kingman, Ariz, 74-75, instr art, 75- Awards: Cert of Merit, Jamaica Festival Comn, 69 & 71; High Commendation, Inst of Jamaica, 71. Bibliog: Ignacy Eker (auth), In the melting pot, Jamaica Daily Gleaner, 71; Bobby Ghishays (auth), Art News (TV prog), Jamaica Broadcasting Co TV, 71; Mason Carrol (auth), Desert scenery inspires artist Stafford Schliefer, Mohave Co Miner, Ariz, 74 & 75. Mem: Contemp Jamaican Artists Asn. Style & Technique: Abstract open-field landscapes and figurative compositions in oils and watercolor; palette knife, brush; mixed media and collages. Dealer: Brockman Gallery Production 4334 Degnan Blvd PO Box 43608 Los Angeles CA 90008. Mailing Add: 1055 Gardencrest Dr Kingman AZ 86401

SCHLOSBERG, CARL MARTIN
ART DEALER
b Los Angeles, Calif, Feb 5, 36. Style & Technique: Univ Calif, Los Angeles, BS, 58. Pos: Dir, Carl Schlosberg Fine Arts, 72- Mem: Graphic Arts coun, Los Angeles Co Mus; Univ Calif, Los Angeles Art Coun; Los Angeles Inst Contemp Art; Nat Soc Lit & Arts; Artists Equity Asn. Specialty: Contemporary paintings, graphics, tapestry, sculpture; publisher of Lee Waisler editions; 20th century master prints. Mailing Add: 15447 Valley Vista Blvd Sherman Oaks CA 91403

SCHLOSS, ARLEEN P (ARLEEN P KELLY)
MULTI MEDIA ARTIST, PAINTER
b Brooklyn, NY, Dec 12, 43. Study: Parsons Sch Design, cert; New York Univ, BA; Art Students League. Work: Aldrich Mus of Contemp Art, Ridgefield, Conn; Am Tel & Tel Longlines, NJ. Exhib: Tenth Anniv Exhib, Aldrich Mus, Conn, 74; Contemporary Reflections, 1971-74 (traveling show), Am Fed of the Arts, 75-77; Artists Books USA, Allen Mem Art Mus, Oberlin Col, 79; one-woman show, Diagrams, Rush Rhees Gallery, Rochester Univ, 75. Collections Arranged: 10 New York Women Artists (with catalog), State Univ NY, Albany, 72; Abstraction-Alive and Well (with catalog), Brainerd Hall, State Univ NY, Potsdam, 75; Contemporary Reflections 1971-74 (with catalog), Am Federation of the Arts, 75-77. Teaching: Artist-in-residence art & music, New York public schs, 67-75; guest lectr art, Rochester Univ, 75. Bibliog: Robert Palmer (auth), Music: Kitchen Sink, New York Times, 10/13/77; Jill Dunbar (auth), Avant-Garde-The Other End, The Villager, 12/8/77. Style & Technique: Mixed media, combine voice as an instrument with wall sculptures, both visual and musical. Media: Audio & Visual Materials. Publ: Contribr, Weaving: A Handbook of The Fibre Arts, Holt, Rinehart & Winston, 78. Mailing Add: 330 Broome St New York NY 10002

SCHLOSS, EDITH
PAINTER, ART CRITIC
US citizen. Study: Art Students League. Exhib: Assemblage, Mus Mod Art, New York, 61; Women in Art, Stamford Mus, Conn, 72; one-woman shows, Il Segno, Rome, 68 & 74, Green Mountain Gallery, 70, 72 & 74, Am Acad Rome, 71 & Ingber Gallery, 74, 75 & 77. Pos: Ed assoc, Art News, 55-61; art critic for Italy, Int Herald Tribune, Paris, France; corresp to Italy, The Nation, New York. Bibliog: James Mellon (auth), The private sensibility of Edith Schloss, 3/25/72 & Hilton Kramer (auth), 3/16/74 & 3/25/72, New York Times; Allen Ellenzweig (auth), article in Arts Mag, 3/77; Charles North (auth), article in Art in Am, 6/77; plus others. Style & Technique: Post abstract expressionist. Media: Oil, Watercolor, Assemblage. Publ: Auth & illusr, Seven Dogs Walk in Rome or More, Prove Dieci, Rome, 74. Dealer: Ingber Gallery 3 E 78th St New York NY 10021; Galleria Il Segno Via Capole le Case Rome Italy. Mailing Add: Via Della Vetrina 18 Rome Italy

SCHLUMP, JOHN OTTO
EDUCATOR, PRINTMAKER
b Monroe, Mich, Oct 5, 33. Study: Wittenberg Univ, BS & BFA, study with Ralston Thompson; Mich State Univ, MA, study with James McConnell; Univ of Toled; Univ of Calgary, study with Toshida Yoshida & Sadao Watanabe. Work: British Mus, London, Eng; Libr of Congress, Washington, DC; Cleveland Mus of Art, Ohio. Comn: Silkscreen, The Eye Corp, Chicago, Ill, 72; two silkscreen ed, 72-75 & four silkscreen ed, 78, Lakeside Studio, Mich; large silkscreen (8ft), Continental Cablevision Corp, Springfield, Ohio, 76; 50 ft wall mural, Ohio Arts Coun, Mus Walls, Springfield. Exhib: All-Ohio Printmakers Exhib, Dayton (5 locations), 66; Small Sculpture & Drawing Exhib, Ball State, 66; Lutheran Brotherhood Exhib, Minneapolis, Minn, 72; Lakeside Traveling Exhib (50 states), 70-78; Lakeside Exhib, Univ of Mo, 77; Cincinnati Art Mus Exhib, Ohio; Columbus Art League Exhib, Ohio. Teaching: Art instr printmaking, Frostburg State Col, Md, 59-61; prof printmaking & mod art, Wittenberg Univ, Springfield, Ohio, 61- Pos: Art supervision, Delta Pub Schs, Ohio, 56-59, instr & chmn of dept, Frostburg State Col, 59-61; chmn art dept, Wittenberg Univ, Springfield, 61- Awards: Nat Defense Grant (guidance & counseling), Fed Gov, 59; Int Dimensions Grant, Wittenberg Univ, 75-76; Res & Creativity Grant, Luthern Church in Am. Mem: Nat Art Asn; Springfield Art Asn (bd of dir, 71-77); Nat Art Educ Asn; Ohio Art Educ Asn (pres, 64-65); Mid-Ohio Col Art Asn. Style & Technique: Silkscreen, abstract (figurative), hard edge. Media: Printmaking; Silkscreen; Drawing. Res: Hanga, Japanese relief printmaking, public school, arts & crafts techniques. Publ: Auth, Arts & Crafts Techniques, 78. Dealer: The Lakeside Studio 150 S Lakeside Rd Lakeside MI 19116. Mailing Add: 2810 Skylark Rd Springfield OH 45502

SCHLUP, ELAINE SMITHA
DESIGNER, JEWELER
b Chicago, Ill, Jan 19, 30. Study: Drake Univ, Des Moines, Iowa, BFA, 66, MFA, 68, with Condon Kuhl; Calif State Univ, Long Beach, advan study with Dieter Muller Stach; Gemological Inst Am. Exhib: Calif Crafts Pac Dimension VI Biennial, Sacramento, 68; Nat Relig Art & Archit, Los Angeles, 71; Metal Experience Show, Oakland Mus Art, Calif, 71; 10th & 11th Ann Purchase Prize Competition, Riverside, Calif, 72-73; Goldsmith '75, Nat Endowment Arts, Atlanta, Ga, 75. Teaching: Instr jewelry & art hist, Edmonds Community Col, Lynnwood, Wash, 69-70; instr jewelry, Seattle Pac Col, Wash, 69-70; instr jewelry, Barnsdall Art & Craft Ctr, Los Angeles, 71-75. Awards: Hon Mention, All Media Show, Laguna Beach Art Mus, Calif, 71. Bibliog: Beverly Johnson (auth), Imagery from nature, Home Mag, Los Angeles Times, 4/74; Judith Olson (auth), Opportunity Golden, Daily Pilot, Costa Mesa, Calif, 9/9/76; Elaine Schlup (auth), Reflections in a Goldsmith's Eye, Orange Co Illus, 12/77. Mem: Retail Jewelers Am; Calif Jewelers Asn; Am Gem Soc; Southern Calif Designer-Crafts. Style & Technique: Elegant body adornment inspired by the sea and barnacles, in particular; repousse, chased, forged, cast, reticulated & electroformed gold & silver. Media: Diamonds, Gems. Mailing Add: 301 Marine Balboa Island CA 92662

SCHMALZ, CARL (NELSON, JR)
PAINTER, EDUCATOR
b Ann Arbor, Mich, Dec 26, 26. Study: Eliot O'Hara Watercolor Sch, summers 43 & 44; Harvard Univ, AB, 48, MA, 49, PhD, 58. Work: Walker Art Mus, Brunswick, Maine; Jones & Laughlin Steel Corp, Cleveland, Ohio; Diners Club Am; Blue Cross-Blue Shield; Hampshire Col; plus others. Exhib: Colby Col Invitational, 58; Portland Summer Art Festival, 58 & 59; Am Watercolor Soc, 66, 68 & 70; Watercolor USA, Springfield, Mo, 70; Wichita Centennial Nat Art Exhib, Kans, 70; Wall of Fame Bicentennial Exhib, Baltimore Watercolor Soc, 76; plus others. Teaching: Asst prof art hist & assoc dir, Bowdoin Col, 53-62; prof art hist, Amherst Col, 62-; dir pvt watercolor workshops, Kennebunkport, Maine, 71-; lectr/demonstr. Pos: Vpres & mem bd dirs, Portland Mus Art, 57-62; art consult, O'Hara Picture Trust, 69- Awards: First Prize for Watercolor, Cambridge Art Asn Ann, 47; First Prize for Traditional Watercolor, Virginia Beach Boardwalk Show, 65; Southern Mo Trust Purchase Award, Watercolor USA, 70. Mem: Col Art Asn; Acad Artists Asn; Berkshire Art Asn. Style & Technique: Representational landscape. Media: Watercolor, Serigraph. Publ: Contribr, A staining and transparent palette, In: Watercolor Portraiture, Putnam, 49; auth, The watercolor page, 2/72 & Eliot O'Hara, great teacher of watercolor, 3/72, Am Artist Mag; auth, Watercolor Lessons from Eliot O'Hara, Watson-Guptill, 74; auth, Watercolor Your Way, Watson-Guptill, 78; plus others. Dealer: Foster Harmon c/o Harmon Gallery 1258 Third St S Naples FL 33940. Mailing Add: 40 Arnold Rd Amherst MA 01002

SCHMANDT-BESSERAT, DENISE
ART HISTORIAN, ARCHAEOLOGIST
b Ay-Champagne, France, Aug 10, 33. Study: Ecole du Louvre, Paris, dipl, 65. Collections Arranged: Permanent exhib, Near Eastern Collections (with catalog), Peabody Mus, Harvard Univ, 68; The Legacy of Sumer, the First Civilization (with catalog & children's catalog), 75 & Ancient Persia—The Art of an Empire, 78, Univ Tex Art Mus. Teaching: Asst prof Paleolithic art & ancient Near East, Univ Tex, Austin, 72- Awards: Radcliffe Fel, Radcliffe Inst, Cambridge, Mass, 69-71; Nat Endowment for the Arts Grant, 74-75 & 77-78. Mem: Archaeol Inst Am (pres, Cent Tex Chap, 74-76); fel Radcliffe Inst; Am Oriental Studies; fel Am Anthropological Asn. Res: Research fel, Peabody Mus, Harvard Univ, 69-71; field experience, Harvard Survey of Kerman, South-eastern Iran, 67, Canadian expedition to Ganj-Dareh Tepe, Kermanshah, Iran, 71 & Univ Tex expedition to Israel, 75. Publ: Ed, The Legacy of Sumer, Bibliot Mesopotamica, Vol 4, 76 & Immortal Egypt, 78, Undena Publ; auth, An Archaic recording system and the origin of writing, Syro-Mesopotamian Studies, Vol 1 (1977); auth, The earliest uses of clay in Syria, Expedition, Vol 19 (1977); auth, The earliest uses of clay in Anatolia, Anatolian Studies, Vol 27 (1978). Mailing Add: 11 Hull Circle Austin TX 78746

SCHMECKEBIER, LAURENCE E
ART HISTORIAN, SCULPTOR
b Chicago Heights, Ill, Mar 1, 06. Study: Univ Wis, BA, 27; Univ Marburg, 27-28; Sorbonne, 28; Univ Munich, PhD, 30. Work: Syracuse Univ Collection. Exhib: Cleveland Mus Ann May Show, 49-54; Rochester Mem Mus Finger Lakes Exhib, 55-57; Regional Artists Exhib, Everson Mus, Syracuse, 56, 57, 59 & 60; Cent NY Artists, 56, 58 & 59; Corning Glass Ctr Ann May Show, Munson-Williams Proctor Inst, Utica, NY, 70. Teaching: Asst prof art hist, Univ Wis-Madison, 31-38; prof fine arts & chmn dept, Univ Minn, Minneapolis, 38-46; prof art hist & dir, Cleveland Inst Art, 46-54; prof fine arts & dean, Syracuse Univ, 54-71, emer prof, 71- Awards: Cert of Merit, May Show, Cleveland Mus Art, 49-51; George L Herdle Award, Rochester Mem Mus, 55; First Prize for Sculpture, Chautauqua Art Asn Exhib, 56. Mem: Col Art Asn Am; Appraisers Asn Am. Res: Italian Renaissance painting; modern Mexican art; contemporary American art. Publ: Auth, Italian Renaissance Painting, 38; auth, Modern Mexican Art, 39; auth, John Steuart Curry's Pageant of America, 43; auth, Art in Red Wing, 46; auth, Ivan Mestrovic, Sculptor and Patriot, 59. Mailing Add: RD 1 Lyme NH 03768

SCHMID, RICHARD ALAN
PAINTER
b Chicago, Ill, Oct 5, 34. Study: Am Acad Art, Chicago, 52-55, with William Mosby. Exhib: Invitational Drawing Exhib, Otis Art Inst, Los Angeles, 66; 33rd Ann, Butler Inst Am Art, Youngstown, Ohio, 68; 23rd Ann Drawing Biennial, Norfolk Mus Arts & Sci, 69; 164th Ann, Pa Acad Fine Arts, Philadelphia, 69; Am Watercolor Soc Ann, Nat Acad Design Galleries, New York, 70-71; plus many one-man shows throughout US, 58-72. Awards: Jane Peterson Prize, Allied Artists Am, 67; Gold Medal of Honor, Am Watercolor Soc, 71, Gold Medal of Honor for Marianne, Am Artist, 72; plus others. Style & Technique: Realism. Media: Oil, Watercolor. Publ: Auth, Richard Schmid Paints the Figure, 73 & auth, Richard Schmid Paints Landscapes, 75, Watson-Guptill. Dealer: Talisman Gallery Bartlesville OK 74003; Voltaires Gallery Rt 7 New Milford CT 06776. Mailing Add: Spring Lake Rd Sherman CT 06784

SCHMIDT, ARNOLD ALFRED
PAINTER, SCULPTOR
b Plainfield, NJ, Jan 9, 30. Study: Art Students League, 49-50; Cooper Union, cert, 56; Hunter Col, BA & MA, 65; also with Hannes Beckmann, Neil Welliver & Tony Smith. Work: Mus Mod Art; Rose Art Inst, Brandeis Univ; Newark Mus; Fairleigh Dickinson Univ; Stedelijk Mus, Schiedam, Netherlands. Exhib: The Responsive Eye, Mus Mod Art, 65, Optical Art, 66 & Recent Acquisitions, 66; Op Art and Others, Newark Mus, 67; Form and Color, Stedelijk Mus, 67; American Paintings of the Nineteen Sixties, Currier Mus Art, 72; plus others. Bibliog: Alfred Barr (auth), What is Modern Art, Mus Mod Art, 67; Ray Faulkner & Edwin Ilegfeld (auth), Art Today, Holt, Reinhart & Winston, 69. Media: Acrylic. Mailing Add: 505 La Guardia Pl New York NY 10012

SCHMIDT, FREDERICK LEE
PAINTER, EDUCATOR
b Hays, Kans, Dec 11, 37. Study: Univ Northern Colo, BA; Univ Iowa, with Eugene Ludins & Stuart Edie, MFA; also with Joe Patrick & Howard Rogovin. Work: Northwestern Col (Iowa); Sioux City Art Ctr, Iowa; Worthen Bank, Little Rock, Ark; Univ Iowa; First & Merchants Bank, Richmond, Va. Exhib: Sioux City 32nd Ann, 69; Des Moines State Capitol, Iowa, 69; Benedicta Arts Ctr 2nd Drawing Exhib, St Joseph, Mo, 71; 34th Semi-Ann Southeastern Exhib, Winston-Salem, NC, 72; 13th Ann Southeast Painting, Charlotte, NC, 73; Little Rock Arts & Design Fair, 77; plus others. Teaching: Asst prof art, Northwestern Col (Iowa), 68-70; asst prof art, Western Carolina Univ, 70-72; asst prof art, Va Polytech Inst & State Univ, 72-76; instr, Ark State Univ & Ark Arts Ctr, 76-77. Awards: Northwestern Col Summer Grant, 69; Helene Wurlitzer Found Grant, 72; Purchase Awards, Roanoke Area Artists Show, 74 & Little Rock Arts & Design Fair, 77. Mem: Nat Col Art Asn. Style & Technique: Figurative. Media: Acrylic, Oil, Watercolor. Mailing Add: 217 W 20th Apt C Little Rock AR 72206

SCHMIDT, HARVEY LESTER
ILLUSTRATOR, WRITER
b Dallas, Tex, Sept 12, 29. Study: Univ Tex, BFA, 52. Pos: Graphic artist on staff NBC-TV, 55-58; free lance artist, 58- Awards: Gold Medal, NY Soc Illusr, 59, 60 & 63; Composer Award for Fantasticks, 61; Outstanding Country-Western Song Award, 70. Mem: Am Soc Compos, Auth & Publ. Publ: Contribr illus, Life, Look, Esquire, Fortune, Sports Illus, The Lamp, Harpers' Bazaar & Seventeen Mags; co-auth, The In & Out Book, 59; illusr, The Mighty Ones, 59; co-auth, The Worry Book, 62. Compos: 110 in the Shade, 63; painter & composer, A Texas Romance, 1909 (art film), 64; I Do, I Do, 66; Celebration, 69; Colette, 70. Mailing Add: 313 W 74th St New York NY 10023

SCHMIDT, JULIUS
SCULPTOR
b Stamford, Conn, June 2, 23. Study: Okla Agr & Mech Col; Cranbrook Acad Art, BFA & MFA; with Ossip Zadkine, Paris, France, 53; Acad Belle Arti, Florence, Italy, 54. Work: Mus Mod Art, New York; Art Inst Chicago; Albright-Knox Art Gallery, Buffalo; Princeton Mus Art; Whitney Mus Am Art, New York. Exhib: Sixteen Americans, Mus Mod Art, New York, 59; The Hirshhorn Collection, Guggenheim Mus, New York, 62; 7th Biennial, Sao Paulo, Brazil, 63; Sculpture in the Open Air, Battersea Park, London, Eng, 63; Biennial, Middleheim, Belg, 71. Teaching: Chmn dept sculpture, Kansas City Art Inst, 54-59; vis artist sculpture, RI Sch Design, 59-60; vis artist sculpture, Univ Calif, Berkeley, 61-62; chmn dept sculpture, Cranbrook Acad Art, 62-70; head dept sculpture, Univ Iowa, 70- Bibliog: H Read (auth), Concise History of Modern Sculpture, Praeger, 64; Redstone (auth), Art in Architecture, McGraw, 68. Media: Bronze, Iron. Mailing Add: Sch of Art Univ of Iowa Iowa City IA 52242

SCHMIDT, KATHERINE (KATHERINE SCHMIDT SHUBERT)
PAINTER
b Xenia, Ohio, Aug 15, 98. Study: Art Students League; study mus in Europe, 25-28. Work: Whitney Mus Am Art; Metrop Mus Art; Mus Mod Art; Newark Mus; Santa Barbara Mus Art. Exhib: Daniel Gallery; Downtown Gallery; Issacson Gallery; Durlacher Gallery; Zabriskie Gallery. Bibliog: E Halpert (auth), Director Downtown Gallery; B Burroughs (auth), article in Aris Mag. Style & Technique: Realist; underpaint on light transparent grey ground with white lead and transparent light undertones. Media: Oil, Pencil, Conte. Dealer: Zabriskie Gallery 29 W 57th St New York NY 10019. Mailing Add: Taylors Lane Little Compton RI 02837

SCHMIDT, MARY MORRIS
ART LIBRARIAN
b Minneapolis, Minn, June 23, 26. Study: Univ Minn, BA, 47, MS(libr sci), 54 & MA(art hist), 55; Univ Paris, Fulbright Fel, 56-57. Pos: Art Librn, Univ Minn, Minneapolis, 53-55; cataloger-reference librn, Metrop Mus of Art, New York, 57-58; indexer, 58-65 & ed, 65-69, Art Index, H W Wilson Co, Bronx, NY; fine arts librn, Columbia Univ, New York, 69-77; librn, Marquand Libr, Princeton Univ, NJ, 77- Mem: Art Libr Soc of NAm (chmn New York chap awards comt, 72; mem publ awards comt, 73; chmn New York chap, 76); Col Art Asn of Am. Interest: Romantic book illustration. Mailing Add: Marquand Libr Princeton Univ Princeton NJ 08512

SCHMIDT, RANDALL BERNARD
SCULPTOR, EDUCATOR
b Ft Dodge, Iowa, Oct 2, 42. Study: Hamline Univ, BA; Univ NMex, MA. Work: Univ NMex Art Mus, Albuquerque; Univ Art Collections, Ariz State Univ, Tempe; Col Art Collection, Ariz Western Col, Yuma; Univ Art Collections, Pac Lutheran Univ, Tacoma, Wash; Yuma Fine Arts Asn. Exhib: Nat Crafts Exhib, Univ NMex Art Mus, 68; 25th Ceramics Nat, Everson Mus Art, Syracuse, NY, 68-70; Media 68 & Media 72, Civic Arts Gallery, Walnut Creek, Calif, 68-72; Southwest Crafts '70, Am Crafts Coun, Los Angeles, 70; Crafts 72, Richmond Art Ctr, Calif, 72. Teaching: Asst prof ceramics, Ariz State Univ, 68-75, assoc prof ceramics, 75-; guest artist, Pac Lutheran Univ, summer 71. Awards: Best of Show, 1st Ann Art Exhib, Phoenix Jewish Community Ctr, 68; Award, Media 68, Civic Arts Gallery, 68; Award, Four Corner Painting & Sculpture Biennial, Phoenix Art Mus, Ariz, 71; plus others. Mem: Ariz Designer-Craftsmen; Nat Coun Educ for Ceramic Arts. Media: Ceramics, Vinyl. Res: Exploration of expanded vinyl as a sculptural material. Publ: Contribr, Teaching Secondary School Art, W Brown Co, 71. Mailing Add: 834 W 12th St Tempe AZ 85281

SCHMIDT, STEPHEN
MUSEUM DIRECTOR
b New York, NY, Dec 11, 25. Study: Mohawk Col; Univ NMex, BA. Pos: Dir, Fort Concho Preservation & Mus, on leave; regional mus coordr & develop officer, Nat Mus Kenya, 2 yrs. Mem: Am Asn Mus; Mountain-Plains Mus Conf; Am Asn State & Local Hist; Nat Trust Hist Preserv; Co Mil Historians; plus others. Mailing Add: Ft Concho Preservation & Mus 716 Burges St San Angelo TX 76901

SCHMITT, MARILYN LOW
ART HISTORIAN
b Chicago, Ill, May 24, 39. Study: Lawrence Univ, Wis, BA, 60; Univ of Calif, Berkeley, MA, 62; Seminar, Bibliotheque royale, Brussels, 62; Yale Univ, PhD, 72. Teaching: Vis lectureships, Univ of Nebr, 63, Univ of Colo, 75 & Southern Methodist Univ, 77; instr, Dickinson Col, Carlisle, Pa, 64-66; asst prof art hist, Southern Conn State Col, New Haven, 70-75 & Univ of Miami, 75- Awards: Woodrow Wilson Fel, 60-61; Am Asn of Univ Women Fel, 68-69; Phi Beta Kappa. Mem: Col Art Asn of Am; Int Ctr of Medieval Art; Women's Caucus for Art; Soc of Archit Hist; Mediaeval Acad of Am. Res: Romanesque sculpture in France. Publ: Auth, Bellerophon and the Chimaera in Archaic Greek Art, Am J of Archeol, 66; translr, Paris through the Ages, Braziller, 68; auth, rev, Architectura, 75; auth, The carved gable of Beaulieu-les-Loches, Gesta, 75; auth, rev, Art Bull, 77; auth, Alice Neel, Arts Mag, 78. Mailing Add: Art Dept Univ of Miami Coral Gables FL 33124

SCHMUTZHART, BERTHOLD JOSEF
SCULPTOR, EDUCATOR
b Salzburg, Austria, Aug 17, 28; US citizen. Study: Acad Appl Art, Vienna, Austria; masterclass for ceramics & sculpture. Work: Mr & Mrs Hirshhorn Collection; Fredericksburg Gallery Mod Art, Va. Comn: Christ (wood), St James Church, Washington, DC, 62, Christ (bronze), 64; bacchus fountain, Fredericksburg Gallery, 67; Christ (steel), St Clements Church, Inkster, Mich, 68, processional cross (bronze), 71; cross (guilded wood), Church of Reformation, Washington, DC, 74. Exhib: Southern Sculpture, Little Rock, Ark, 66 & Louisville, Ky, 68; Washington Artists, Massilon Mus, Ohio, 69; Twenty Washington Artists, Nat Collection Fine Arts, Washington, DC, 70; Art Barn, US Dept Interior, Washington, DC, 71; Int Monetary Fund Exhib, Washington, DC, 75. Teaching: Assoc prof sculpture & & chmn sculpture dept, Corcoran Sch Art, Washington, DC, 63- Awards: First Prize, Washington Religious Arts Soc, 60; First Prize, Southern Sculpture, 66; First Prize Silver Medal, Audubon Soc, 71. Bibliog: Off Econ Opportunity (auth), A Face for the Future (film), Booker Assocs, Reston, Va, 65; Tools for Learning (film), Kingsbury Ctr, Washington, DC, 71. Mem: Am Asn Univ Prof; Guild Religious Archit; Artist's Equity Asn (pres, Washington, DC Chap, 73). Media: Wood, Steel, Bronze. Dealer: Franz Bader Gallery 2124 Pennsylvania Ave Washington DC 20037. Mailing Add: 1011 E Capitol St Washington DC 20003

SCHMUTZHART, SLAITHONG CHENGTRAKUL
INSTRUCTOR, SCULPTOR
b Bangkok, Thailand, Jan 1, 34; US citizen. Study: Corcoran Sch of Art, Washington, DC, dipl sculpture, 68, dipl ceramics, 70; Univ of DC, BA(fine arts), 77. Comn: Polychromed wood altar relief (8ft x 10ft), Sr Citizens Home, Inkster, Mich; polychromed wood relief (6ft x 10ft), comn by Dr Morton Ehudin for dental off, Oxon Hill, Md, 77; Corten steel standing figure (8ft), comn by Mr & Mrs Leon Baer, Alexandria, Va, 77; polychromed wood relief (7ft x 10ft), comn by James Ellison, Capitol Hill, Washington, DC, 77. Exhib: Husband & Wife Show, Gallery of the Int Monetary Fund, Washington, DC, 65; Nat Collection of Fine Arts, Washington, DC, 68; Columbia Mus of Art, SC; Macon Mus of Arts & Sci, Ga; Gibbes Art Gallery, Charleston, SC, 71-77; Birmingham Mus of Art, Ala; Dulin Gallery, Knoxville, Tenn; Columbus Mus, Ga; Brooks Mem Art Gallery, Memphis, Tenn; Corcoran Gallery, Washington, DC, 75; Phillips Gallery, Washington, DC, 76; one-man show, Franz Bader Gallery, Washington, DC, 77. Teaching: Asst instr sculpture, Off of Economic Opportunity, Job Corps, 65-66; instr art, Lab Sch, Kingsbury Ctr, Washington, DC, 68-71; instr sculpture, Smithsonian Inst, 78- Awards: Ford Found Scholar in Sculpture, 66. Bibliog: Sarah B Conroy (auth), Living in style, Washington Post, 2/71; Benjamin Forgey (auth), Washingtons Artists, Sunday Star, 12/71; Anne Ogden (auth), New Ways with Stained glass, House Beautiful, 8/73. Mem: Artists Equity Asn. Style & Technique: Abstract figurative welded steel (Corten), polychromed wooden relief panels showing flora, fauna and other living things. Media: Welded Steel, Woodcarving. Dealer: Franz Badger Gallery Washington DC. Mailing Add: 1011 E Capitol St Washington DC 20003

SCHNACKENBERG, ROY
PAINTER, SCULPTOR
b Chicago, Ill, Jan 14, 34. Work: Whitney Mus Am Art, New York; Art Inst Chicago. Exhib: Whitney Recent Acquisitions Show, 67 & Whitney Ann, 67-69; New American Realists, Göteberg, Sweden, 70; Beyond Illustration, The Art of Playboy (world tour), 71-; Recent Acquisitions Show, Art Inst Chicago, 71; Dept Interior Bicentennial Exhib, Corcoran Gallery, Washington, DC. Awards: Copley Found Award, 67. Mailing Add: 50 E Scott Rd Barrington IL 60010

SCHNEEBAUM, TOBIAS
PAINTER
b New York, NY, Apr 25, 21. Study: Work Prog Admin, 35-36; City Col New York, BA, 42; Brooklyn Mus Art Sch, with R Tamayo, 46 & A Osver, 47. Work: Mus Estado, Guadalajara, Mex; Mus Nat, Cuzco, Peru. Exhib: Smithsonian Inst, Washington, DC, 55; Peridot Gallery, 55-70; Univ Nebr, 63; Art Inst Chicago, 64; Univ Colo, 65. Teaching: Instr painting, Ajijic Sch Art, Mex, 47-49. Awards: Yaddo Fel, 53 & 55; Fulbright Fel, 55 & 56; Firefly Fund Award, 75. Style & Technique: Impressionistic. Media: Oil. Publ: Illusr, The Girl in the Abstract Bed, 54; illusr, Jungle Journey, 59; auth, Keep the River on Your Right, Grove Press, 69. Dealer: Peridot-Washburn Gallery 820 Madison Ave New York NY 10021. Mailing Add: 463 West St New York NY 10014

SCHNEEMANN, CAROLEE
FILMMAKER, PERFORMANCE ARTIST, WRITER
b Fox Chase, Pa, Oct 12, 39. Study: Univ Ill, Urbana, MFA; Bard Col, Annandale-on-Hudson, New York, MA; Columbia Univ Sch of Painting & Sculpture, New York; New Sch for Social Res, New York; Universidad de Puebla, Mexico. Work: Mus of Contemp Art, Chicago; Erotica Archives Mus, Yugoslavia; also in pvt collections of Robert Rauschenberg, Fla, Billy Kulver, NJ, Arman, Paris & Claes Oldenburg, New York. Exhib: Music Box Music, New Sch for Social Res, New York, 64; Snug Harbor, Avant Garde Festival, Staten Island, New York, 67; Drawings for Happenings, Mus of Côntemp Art, Chicago, 68; Happenings and Fluxus, Kolnischer Kunstverein, Cologne, WGer, 71; Schlagt-Auf (Ein Gestalt), Fluxfestival, Forum Theatre, Berlin, 71; Film Retrospective, Calif State Univ, San Francisco, 74; Up to and including her limits, Univ Art Mus, Berkeley, Calif & Anthology Film Archives, New York, 74. Teaching: Instr art, Univ Ill, Chicago, 61-62. Pos: Founder-dir, Kinetic Theatre, New York, 63-68; artist-in-residence, Colby Col, Maine, 68; artist-in-residence, Dartington Col, Totnes, Devon, England, 72; founder-mem, Int-Local group, New York, 76. Awards: Performance Grant, Benedict Arnold Found, New York, 64; New York State Coun on the Arts Grant, 68 & 74 & Creative Artists Pub Serv Grant, 78; Nat Endowment for the Arts Grant, Washington, DC, 74 & 77. Bibliog: P Hutchinson (auth), Dance Without Movement, Art & Artists, London, 1/69; Caroline Tisdall (auth), Arts-Microcosms, The Guardian, London, 4/71; V Glassner (auth), Interviews with Three Filmmakers, Time Out, London, 3/72. Publ: Auth, Kenneth Anger's Scorpio Rising, Film Culture No 32, New York, 64; auth, Division and Rubble, Manipulation, New York, 10/67; auth, Love Paint Ritual, Technicians of the Sacred, New York, 69; auth, Bananna Hands, Plays for Children to Direct, London, 70; auth, Free From Recollections of New York, Nat Film Theatre Expanded Film Cinema J, London, 11/70; auth, More Than Meat Joy (complete performance works & selected writings), Documentext, 78. Mailing Add: 114 W 29th St New York NY 10001

SCHNEIDER, IRA
VIDEO ARTIST, LECTURER
b New York, NY, Mar 2, 39. Study: Brown Univ, AB, 60; Univ Wis, MA, 64. Work: Mus Mod Art Film Arch, New York; Donnell Film Libr, New York; Anthology Film Arch, New York; Long Beach Mus Art, Calif. Comn: Wipe Cycle (video installation, with Frank Gillette), Howard Wise Gallery, New York, 69; Manhattan is an Island (video installation),

74 & Video 75 (video installation), 75, The Kitchen, New York. Exhib: Videotape (circuit), Los Angeles Co Mus, Los Angeles, 73; Video Art, Inst Contemp Art, Philadelphia, 75; Videotape, 13th Biennial, Sao Paulo, Brazil, 76; Manhattan is an Island (video installation), Whitney Mus Am Art, New York, 77; Proj XIII (videotape), Mus Mod Art, New York, 77. Teaching: Vis lectr video art, Univ Calif, San Diego, 76-77 & 78. Pos: Ed, Radical Software, Raindance Mag, 70-74; pres, Raindance Found, New York, 72- Awards: Film Contest Award, Philharmonic Hall, Lincoln Ctr, New York, Nat Student Asn, 67; Nat Endowment Arts Individual Artist Fel, 76; Guggenheim Found Fel, 77. Bibliog: Gene Youngblood (auth), Expanded Cinema, Dutton, 70; David Antin (auth), Aspects of the video medium?, Artforum, 76; Russell Conor (auth), Panorama—video gallery, WNET Pub Broadcasting System, 77. Style & Technique: Conceptual collages of sound and picture recorded inthe video medium and presented either as single-channel TV programs or multichannel installations. Media: Video. Publ: Contribr, Guerillo Television, Holt Rhinehart & Winston, 71; Co-ed with Beryl Korot, Video Art, Hartcourt Brace Jovanovich, 76. Dealer: Electronic Art Intermix 84 Fifth Ave New York NY 10011. Mailing Add: 51 Fifth Ave New York NY 10003

SCHNEIDER, JO ANNE
PAINTER
b Lima, Ohio, Dec 4, 19. Study: Sch Fine Arts, Syracuse Univ. Work: Butler Inst Am Art, Youngstown, Ohio; Syracuse Univ; Allentown Mus, Pa; St Lawrence Univ; Neuberger Mus, Purchase, NY. Exhib: Corcoran Gallery Art; Whitney Mus Am Art Ann; 50 Years of American Art, Am Fedn Art, 64; Childe Hassam Fund Exhib, Am Acad Arts & Lett, 71; plus one-man exhibs, 54- Awards: First Prize, Guild Hall, 67; Marion K Haldenstein Mem Prize, Nat Asn Women Artists, 70; Stanley Grumbacher Mem Award, Audubon Artists, 72. Style & Technique: Realistic style with mystical overtones, which give an animist quality to everyday objects. Media: Oil. Dealer: Frank Rehn Gallery 655 Madison Ave New York NY 10021. Mailing Add: 35 E 75th St New York NY 10021

SCHNEIDER, JULIE (SAECKER)
PAINTER
b Seattle, Wash, Mar 7, 44. Study: Univ Wis, Madison, BS(art;honors); Univ Wis, MFA(painting, two-dimensional), 76. Work: Minn Mus of Art, St Paul; Algur Meadows Mus, Shreveport, La; Rutgers Univ, Camden, NJ; State Univ NY Col, Potsdam; Univ NDak, Minot. Exhib: Drawings USA/75 Nat Exhib (traveling show), 75 & Drawings USA/77 Nat Exhib (traveling show), 77, Minn Mus of Art, St Paul; Nat Drawing Exhib, Potsdam, NY, 75 & 77; 65th Ann Exhib of Contemp Am Art, Art Asn of Newport, RI, 76; Am Drawings 1976, Tidewater Art Coun & Portsmouth Community Art Ctr, Va, 76; Smithsonian Travel Exhib, 76; Davidson Nat Print & Drawing Competition, NC, 76; Appalachian Nat Drawing Competition, Boone, NC, 76; Bradley Print & Drawing Competition , Bradley Univ, Peoria, Ill, 77. Awards: Purchase Awards, Am Drawings 1976, 76, Rutgers Nat Drawing 77, Rutgers Univ, 77 & Drawings USA/77, Minn Mus of Art, St Paul, 77. Style & Technique: Figurative drawings, neo-realism. Media: Graphite, silverpoint and gouache. Dealer: Fairweather-Hardin Galleries 101 E Ontario Chicago IL 60611. Mailing Add: 41 Hoxsey St Williamstown MA 01267

SCHNEIDER, LISA DAWN
ART DEALER, ART CRITIC
b Brookline, Mass, Nov 16, 54. Study: Boston Mus of Fine Arts Sch, Mass; Decordiva Mus; Syracuse Univ, Visual & Performing Arts Sch; Finch Col; Arts Sch League; Marymount Col, BA(fine arts). Pos: Asst dir, Galerie Denise/Rene, 76-77, co-dir, O'Rourke Gallery, 8-12/77, art critic & art ed, Women's Week, 11/77- & 2/78- & dir, Robert Freidus Gallery, New York, 1/78- Mem: Patron, Brooklyn Mus. Specialty: Contemporary painting, prints, photography and sculpture. Collection: Contemporary prints, drawings and photography. Mailing Add: 135 E 54th St New York NY 10022

SCHNEIDER, NOEL
SCULPTOR
b New York, NY, July 31, 20. Study: Art Students League, with William Zorach; City Univ New York. Comn: Willner Memorial Bas Relief, Bergen Co YMHA, 64. Exhib: One-man show, Bosshart Art Mus, NJ State Col, 62; Stamford Mus Nat, Conn, 68; one-man slide show, City Univ New York, 69; two-man show, Meet Sculptor Ser, Sculpture Ctr, New York, 69; 28th Ann Nat Exhib Painters & Sculptors, Jersey City Mus, 69; Salmagundi Club, 70; Nat Arts Club, 74; Brooklyn Mus, NY, 76 & 77. Awards: First Prize for Sculpture, Lever House, 68; Gold Medal for Sculpture, Salmagundi Club, 70; First Prize for Sculpture, Nat Arts Club, 74. Bibliog: Feature in New York Sunday News, 4/22/56; interview in New York World Telegram & Sun, 2/21/62; article in New Writers, 9/74. Mem: Am Vet Soc Artists (vpres). Style & Technique: Carvings and constructions in wood, stone stained glass and metal, ranging from intense expressionism to satirical abstraction. Media: Welded Metal, Wood. Dealer: Sculpture Center 167 E 69th St New York NY 10021. Mailing Add: 124 Oxford St Manhattan Beach Brooklyn NY 11235

SCHNEIDERMAN, DOROTHY
ART DEALER
b New York, NY, Apr 11, 19. Pos: Dir, Harbor Gallery, 65- Specialty: Contemporary American realists. Mailing Add: 43 Main St Cold Spring Harbor NY 11724

SCHNEIER, DONNA FRANCES
ART DEALER
b St Louis, Mo, Mar 30, 38. Study: Brandeis Univ, BA;,NY Univ, MFA. Pos: Pres, Gallery 6M, New York, 66-73; pres, Donna Schneier Inc, New York, 73- Mem: New York Hist Soc; Visual Studies Workshop, New York; Soc for Photog Educ. Specialty: Photography. Mailing Add: 251 E 71st St New York NY 10021

SCHNESSEL, S MICHAEL
ART WRITER, ART DEALER
b Hof, WGer, Apr 7, 47; US citizen. Study: Community Col of Baltimore, AA, 66; Syracuse Univ, BA, 68. Pos: Dir, The Exhumation, currently. Res: Created the first in-depth studies of two important 20th century illustrators, Louis Icart and Jessie Willcox Smith. Specialty: The Exhumation specializes in posters from 1875 to 1940; Art Nouveau and Art Deco graphics. Publ: Auth, A Collector's Guide to Louis Icart, The Exhumation, 73; auth, Icart, Clarkson Potter, 76; auth, Jessie Willcox Smith, Thomas Y Crowell, 77. Mailing Add: PO Box 2057 Princeton NJ 08540

SCHNIER, JACQUES
SCULPTOR
b Dec 25, 98; US citizen. Study: Stanford Univ, AB(civil eng); Univ Calif, MA; Calif Sch Fine Arts, San Francisco. Work: Oakland Art Mus, Calif; Legion of Honor Mus, San Francisco; Santa Barbara Mus Art; Honolulu Acad Art; San Francisco Mus Art. Comn: US Half Dollar, commemorating San Francisco-Oakland Bay Bridge, 36; archit relief, Berkeley High Sch, Calif, 39; carved acrylic sculpture, Calif Col Arts & Crafts Founders Centennial Award for Neil Armstrong, 72; sculpture, San Francisco Med Ctr, 75; Elizebeth S Fine Mem, Temple Emanu-El, San Francisco, 75; plus others. Exhib: 3rd Sculpture Int, Philadelphia Mus, 49; 3rd Traveling Biennial, Santa Barbara Mus Art, Calif, 59; one-man shows, Sculpture, Stanford Univ Mus, 62, Sculpture, Santa Barbara Mus Art, 63, Bronze Sculpture, Ryder Gallery, Univ Calif, Berkeley, 65, Transparency and Reflection, Judah Magnes Mus, Berkeley, 71 & Refractions and Reflections, Willis Gallery, San Francisco, 75 & 77. Teaching: Instr sculpture, Calif Col Arts & Crafts, Oakland, 35-36; from lectr to prof sculpture, Univ Calif, Berkeley, 36-66. Pos: Chmn adv bd, Nat Sculpture Ctr, Univ Kans, 61-77; mem adv bd, Int Sculpture Symp, Eugene, Ore, 71-74. Awards: First Sculpture Prize & Gold Medal, Oakland Art Mus, 48; Inst Creative Arts Fel, Univ Calif, Berkeley, 63, Berkeley Citation, 70. Bibliog: Yvonne Greer Thiel (auth), Artists and People, Philos Libr, 59; Irving Stone (ed), There was Light, Doubleday, 70; Thelma Newman (auth), Plastics as Sculpture, Chilton, 74; plus others. Style & Technique: Non-figurative; form and content are inseparable; refraction and reflection of light passing through crystal acrylic is key feature. Media: Acrylic, Bronze. Publ: Auth, The Tibetan Lamaist ritual: Chod, Int J Psychoanal, Vol 37, No 6; auth, Reinforced polyester plastic and acrylic color for sculpture, 68 & Reflection and transparency in carved acrylic sculpture, 70, Proc Nat Sculpture Conf; auth, The cubic element in my sculpture, 69 & Transparency and reflection as entities in sculpture of carved acrylic resin, 72, Leonardo. Mailing Add: 4081 Happy Valley Rd Lafayette CA 94549

SCHNITTMANN, SASCHA S
SCULPTOR
b New York, NY, Sept 1, 13. Study: Cooper Union Art Sch; Nat Acad Design; Beaux Arts Inst Design; Ecole Beaux Artes, Paris; also study with Olympio Brindisi, George Grey Barnard, Attilio Piccirilli, Charles Keck, Robert Aitken, Alexandre Sambougnac, Ceasare Stea, Gaetano Cecere & others. Work: Pan-Am Soc; Am Mus Natural Hist; Dayton Art Inst; Kansas City Art Inst; Moscow State Univ, Russia; plus many others. Comn: Am Legion Monument, St Louis; aluminum figures for War Mem Stadium, Little Rock, Ark; Martin Luther King, Jr (heroic mem portrait bust four times life size), 68; fountain figures, Henry Ford Centennial Libr, Dearborn, Mich & Darsa Fountain, St Louis; Elvis Presley Monument (25ft bronze on top of 10ft granite plinth), comn by Las Vegas Hilton Hotel, 78-; also many busts, mem & monuments including busts & portraits of notable persons throughout the world. Exhib: St Louis Art Guild, 42; City Art Mus St Louis, 42; Seattle Art Mus, Wash, 42; Whitney Mus Am Art, New York, 43; Chicago Art Club, 43; plus others. Pos: Dir & cur, Triton Mus Art, formerly. Awards: Soc Independent Artists, 42; City Art Mus St Louis, 42; Art Inst Chicago, 43; plus many others. Bibliog: Sculptor Schnittmann gives church valuable bronzes, San Jose Mercury, 12/16/71; Leonard Neft (auth), St Joseph's celebration, The Mercury, 3/19/71; Bust of Martin Luther King unveiled at Grace Cathedral, Voice of the People, 2/26/72. Mem: Life fel Russian Sculpture Soc; Am Acad Sculptors; hon life mem Ecole Beaux Arts, Paris; Soc Independent Artists; Am Inst Archit Sculptors; plus many others. Media: Marble, Bronze. Publ: Auth & illusr, Anatomy & Dissection for Artists, 39; auth & illusr, Plastic Histology, 40; contribr to archit mags. Mailing Add: 915 Commercial St San Jose CA 95112

SCHNITZER, ARLENE DIRECTOR
ART DEALER, COLLECTOR
b Salem, Ore, Jan 10, 29. Study: Univ Wash, Seattle, 47-48; Portland Art Mus Sch, 59-61; studied with Michele Russo. Pos: Dir, Fountain Gallery of Art, Portland, Ore; Exec comt, ArtQuake, City of Portland, 78; appointed Oregon Govt Ethics Comn, 78- Mem: Portland Ctr for Visual Arts (trustee; exec comt); Arts & Crafts Soc (trustee); Cult Res Comm, CofC; Artists Equity. Specialty: Featuring the most noted artists of the Northwest; also sculpture, paintings, prints & pottery. Collection: Primarily most noted artists of the Northwest; largest collection outside of a museum of works by C S Price, including carvings. Mailing Add: 117 NW 21st Ave Portland OR 97209

SCHNORE, MARY LOUISE
See Owens, Mary

SCHNORRENBERG, JOHN MARTIN
ART HISTORIAN, ART ADMINISTRATOR
b New York, NY, Dec 1, 31. Study: Univ NC, Chapel Hill, AB(Phi Beta Kappa), 49-52, MA, 53; Princeton Univ, MFA, 57, PhD, 64. Teaching: Instr of art hist, Columbia Univ, New York, 58-59; asst & assoc prof of art hist, Univ of NC, Chapel Hill, 59-76; chmn & prof of art, Univ Ala, Birmingham, 76- Awards: Tanner Award for Excellence in Teaching, Univ NC, Chapel Hill, 66; Nat Endowment for Humanities, Jr Fel, 67-68. Mem: Col Art Asn; Mediaeval Acad of Am; Soc of Archit Historians; Archeol Inst of Am; Southeastern Col of Art Conf (ed, Review, 66-70; pres, 75-76). Res: Late gothic architecture, gothic survival, modern architecture. Publ: Ed & contribr, A Medieval Treasury From Southeastern Collections, Ackland Art Ctr, 71; ed, Catalogue of Collection... of Ackland art Center, Chapel Hill, 71. Mailing Add: 3824 11th Ave South Birmingham AL 35222

SCHNURR-COLFLESH, E
PAINTER
b Sandusky, Ohio, July 21, 32. Study: Cleveland Inst Art, BFA. Work: Mus Fine Arts, St Petersburg, Fla. Exhib: Recent Paintings USA: The Figure, Mus Mod Art, New York, 62; Pa Acad Fine Arts, Philadelphia, 66; one-man shows, Caravan House Gallery, New York, 72 & Roko Gallery, New York, 77; Butler Inst Am Art, Youngstown, Ohio, 75; Sons and Others, Women Artists See Men, Queens Mus, Flushing, NY, 75; Am Acad Arts & Lett Hassam Purchase Exhib, New York, 76; plus others. Awards: Childe Hassam Purchase, 76. Style & Technique: Figurative. Media: Watercolor on Paper; Oil on Canvas. Mailing Add. 507 W 111th St New York NY 10025

SCHOELER, PAUL JEAN RENE
ARCHITECT
b Toronto, Ont, Oct 29, 23. Study: McGill Univ, BArch, grad study, 3 yrs town planning. Comn: Juvenile Court, City of Ottawa, 60; Expo 67, Can Pavilion, Govt of Can, 67; off bldg, Pub Serv Alliance of Can, 67; Garneau High Sch, Carleton Bd of Educ, 71; Charlebois High Sch, Ottawa Bd of Educ, 72. Exhib: Milan Triennale, Italy, 64; Expo 67, Montreal, 67; Design Ctr, Montreal, 68; traveling exhib, Royal Can Acad, 70. Pos: Co-owner, Schoeler & Heaton Architects, Ottawa, 58- Awards: Juvenile Court Competition, City of Ottawa, 60; Week End House Gold Medal, Milan Triennale, 64. Bibliog: J Folch-Ribas (auth), Au dela des formalismes, 71 & M Tremblay-Gillon (auth), Sortir de l'orniere, Vie des Arts, 73; Stig Harvor (auth), Charlebois Building, Can Architect, 1/73. Mem: Ont Asn Architects; Order of Quebec Architects; Royal Archit Inst Can; Royal Can Acad Arts. Mailing Add: 148 Bank St Ottawa ON K1P 5N8 Can

SCHOELKOPF, ROBERT J, JR
ART DEALER
b New York, NY, Nov 9, 27. Study: Yale Col, BA. Pos: Dir & owner, Robert Schoelkopf Gallery. Mem: Art Dealers Asn Am. Specialty: 19th and 20th century American painting, sculpture and photography. Mailing Add: 825 Madison Ave New York NY 10021

SCHOEN, MR & MRS ARTHUR BOYER
COLLECTORS
Mr Schoen, b Pittsburgh, Pa, Apr 17, 23; Mrs Schoen, b New York, NY, Sept 27, 15. Study: Mr Schoen, Princeton Univ, BA. Mrs Schoen, Columbia Univ; Grand Cent Sch Art, New York. Pos: Mr Schoen, bd adv, Ocean Learning Inst, West Palm Beach, Fla. Mem: Parrish Art Mus (Mrs Schoen, pres, 70-76, trustee); Metrop Mus Art; Mus City New York; Mrs Schoen, York Club (past pres). Collection: Paintings: 18th century Lowestoft (Chinese export); 10th and 12th century Persian pottery; 18th century English and American furniture; archaeological artifacts. Mailing Add: 17 E 89th St New York NY 10028

SCHOENER, ALLON
ART CONSULTANT
b Cleveland, Ohio, Jan 1, 26. Study: Yale Univ, BA, 46, MA, 49; Courtauld Inst Art, Univ London, 47-48. Collections Arranged: Lower East Side: Portal to American Life, Jewish Mus, 66, Word From Jerusalem, 72; Erie Canal: 1817-1967, NY State Coun Arts, 67; Harlem on My Mind, Metrop Mus Art, 69. Pos: Asst dir, Jewish Mus, 66-67; visual arts prog dir, NY State Coun Arts, 67-72; consult traveling exhib, Smithsonian Inst, Washington, DC & Jewish Mus, New York; consult multiple exhib prog, Libr of Cong, Washington, DC. Publ: Ed, Portal to America, Holt, Rinehart & Winston, 67; ed, Harlem on My Mind, Random, 69. Mailing Add: Grafton VT 05146

SCHOENER, JASON
PAINTER, EDUCATOR
b Cleveland, Ohio, May 17, 19. Study: Cleveland Inst Art, dipl; Western Reserve Univ, BS; Art Students League; Columbia Univ, MA. Work: Cleveland Mus Art; Whitney Mus Am Art, New York; Calif Palace Legion of Honor, San Francisco; Columbus Gallery Fine Art; Munson-Williams-Proctor Inst, Utica, NY. Exhib: San Francisco Mus Art Painting Ann, 53-65; one-man shows, Midtown Galleries, New York, 59-, Lehigh Univ, 65, Cleveland Inst Art, 68, Richard DeMarco Gallery, Edinburgh, Scotland, 73 & St Mary's Col, Md, 75; Brooklyn Mus Int Watercolor Exhibs, 59 & 61; Pa Acad Fine Arts Watercolor Ann, 59-69; Calif Palace Legion of Honor Winter Invitationals, 68 & 70; Landscape I & II, De Cordova Mus, 70 & 71; Wichita Art Asn, Kans, 75; Kalamazoo Art Inst, Mich, 75; Expressions From Maine, Hobe Sound Galleries, Fla, 76; 76 Maine Artists, Maine State Mus, 76; 41st Ann Butler Art Inst Am Art, Youngstown, Ohio, 77. Teaching: Instr, Munson-Williams-Proctor Inst, 49-53; assoc prof, Calif Col Arts & Crafts, Oakland, 53-61, dir pub rels & spec serv, 53-55, chmn dept fine arts, 55-70, dir, Eve Col, 55-69, prof, 61-, dir, Div Fine Arts, 70-78, dean advanced studies, 78-; vis lectr, Mills Col, 62-63; vis prof, Athens Technol Inst, Greece, 64-65. Awards: Award, Calif State Fair, 58; Award, Maine Art Gallery, 61; Childe Hassam Award, Am Acad Arts & Lett, 78. Mem: Art Students League; Am Asn Univ Prof. Media: Oil, Watercolor, Gouache. Publ: Contribr, Art patronage in Greece, Art J, winter 66-67. Dealer: Midtown Galleries 11 E 57th St New York NY 10022; Gumps Gallery 250 Post St San Francisco CA 94118. Mailing Add: 74 Ross Circle Oakland CA 94618

SCHOENHERR, JOHN CARL
ILLUSTRATOR, PAINTER
b New York, NY, July 5, 35. Study: Art Students League; Pratt Inst, BFA, study with Will Barnet & William A Smith. Work: Nat Park Serv; US Air Force. Exhib: Brandywine Mus, Chadds Ford, Pa, 73; Soc Illusr, New York, 64-68, 71 & 75; Contemp Am Illusr of Childrens Bks, Rutgers Univ, NY, 74; Royal Ont Mus, Toronto, Can, 75; one-man show, New York Zoological Soc, 78. Bibliog: Kingman, Foster & Lontoft (auths), Illustrators of Childrens Books 1957-1966, Horn Bk Inc, 68; Diana Klemin (auth), The Illustrated Book, Clarkson N Potter Publ, 70; Contemporary American Illustrators of Childrens Books, Rutgers Univ, 74. Mem: Soc of Illusr; Illusr Guild; Soc Animal Artists; Rutgers Adv Coun on Childrens Lit. Style & Technique: Subjective realism, utilizing traditional techniques and patinated éclaboussage. Media: Polymer Monochrome Dry Brush, Egg Tempra, Polymer Tempera, Oil. Publ: Illusr, Rascal, E P Dutton, 63; auth & illusr, The Barn, Atlantic Mo Press, 68; illusr, Julie of the Wolves, Harper & Row, 72; illusr, A Bat is Born, Doubleday, 77; illusr, Dune, Berkeley, 78. Mailing Add: RD 2 Box 260 Stockton NJ 08559

SCHOLDER, FRITZ
PAINTER, PRINTMAKER
b Breckenridge, Minn, Oct 6, 37. Study: Univ Kans; Wis State Univ; Sacramento City Col, with Wayne Thiebaud; Sacramento State Univ, BA; Univ Ariz, MFA. Work: Brooklyn Mus; Houston Mus Fine Arts; Phoenix Art Mus; San Diego Gallery Fine Art; Dallas Mus Fine Art. Exhib: Winter Invitational, Palace Legion of Honor, San Francisco, 61; Am Indian Art, Edinburgh Art Festival & Berlin Festival, 66; Indian Painting, Mus Bellas Artes, Buenos Aires & Bibliot Nac, Chile, 67; Two Am Painters, Nat Collection Fine Art, Smithsonian Inst, 72; Two American Painters, Madrid, Berlin, Bucharest, Belgrade, Ankara, Athens & London, Dept Interior Bicentennial Exhib, Corcoran Gallery, Washington, DC, San Francisco Mus Art, plus others, 76-77; 10th Int Biennial Prints, Nat Mus Mod Art, Tokyo & Kyoto, Japan, 76-77; one-man show, Oakland Art Mus, Calif, 77; Saginaw Art Mus, Mich, 77. Pos: Artist in residence, Dartmouth Col, 73. Awards: Opportunity Fel, John Hay Whitney Found, 62-63; Grand Prize, Biennial Am Indian Arts, Washington, DC, 67; Am Acad Arts & Lett Award in Painting, New York, 77. Bibliog: J J Brody (auth), Indian Painters and White Patrons, Univ NMex, 71; C Adams (auth), Fritz Scholder Lithographs, New York Graphic Soc, 75; films, Three Indian Artists, 72 & Fritz Scholder, Pub Broadcasting Serv, 76; plus others. Publ: Auth, Ten Indians (ed of etchings), El Dorado Press, 75. Dealer: Elaine Horwitch Galleries 4200 N Marshall Way Scottsdale AZ 85251; Cordier & Ekstrom 980 Madison Ave New York NY 10021. Mailing Add: 118 Cattle Track Rd Scottsdale AZ 85253

SCHOLDER, LAURENCE
PRINTMAKER, EDUCATOR
b Brooklyn, NY, Nov 23, 42. Study: Carnegie Inst Technol, BFA; Univ Iowa, MA. Work: Ft Worth Art Ctr, Tex; Houston Mus Fine Arts; Okla Art Ctr, Oklahoma City; Brooklyn Mus, NY; Dallas Mus Fine Arts, Tex. Exhib: American Graphic Workshops '68, Cincinnati Art Mus, 68; Multiples USA, Western Mich Univ, Kalamazoo, 70; Midwest Biennial, Joslyn Art Mus, Omaha, Nebr, 70 & 72; Seattle Print Int, Seattle Art Mus, 71; Libr of Cong 22nd Print Nat, Washington, DC, 71. Teaching: Asst prof printmaking, Southern Methodist Univ, 68-73, assoc prof printmaking, 73- Pos: Artist's rep, Bd Trustees, Dallas Mus Fine Art, 71-72. Awards: Purchase Awards, Young Printmakers, Herron Art Inst, 67 & Print & Drawing Nat, Okla Art Ctr, 68; Merit Award, Southwest Graphics, San Antonio, 72; Nat Endowment for the Arts Printmaker's Fel, 75. Media: Intaglio. Dealer: Delahunty Gallery 2611 Cedar Springs Dallas TX 75201. Mailing Add: 3109 Drexel Dr Dallas TX 75205

SCHOLZ, JANOS
COLLECTOR, ART HISTORIAN
b Sopron, Hungary, Dec 20, 03. Study: Royal Hungarian Col Agr, Dipl Ing; Royal Hungarian Conserv Music, dipl. Teaching: Adj prof art hist, Columbia Univ, 65; sr fel, NY Univ. Res: Italian drawings. Collection: Drawings by the Old Italian Masters; porcelain; fayences; carpets. Publ: Auth, articles and books on Italian drawings. Mailing Add: 863 Park Ave New York NY 10021

SCHON, NANCY QUINT
SCULPTOR, INSTRUCTOR
b Boston, Mass, Sept 24, 28. Study: Boston Univ, AA, 48; spec instr under Edna Hibel, 52; Boston Mus Sch (hons in sculpture), study with F Allen & Peter Abate, 53; Tufts Univ, BA(sociology), 53; Boston Mus Sch, Teaching Fel, 55; Kansas City Art Inst, study with Julius Schmidt, 57; courses at Univ Calif Los Angeles, Mass Inst of Technol, Harvard & Boston Art Inst. Work: Easter Seal Collection, NJ; Ford Alliance Competition, New York; Pvt collection of Sen Harrison Williams, Washington, DC. Comn: Bronze, Am Speech and Hearing Assoc, Washington, DC, 66; bronze, Easter Seal Collection, NJ, 73. Exhib: Univ of NH, 75; Addison Gallery, Andover, Mass, 75; Wellesley Col Mus, 76; New Rochelle Art Asn, NY, 76; Boston Mus of Fine Arts, 77; Springfield Mus of Art, Ohio, 77; Galerie de Tours, San Francisco, Calif, 77; G W Vincent Smith Mus, 77; Regis Col, 77; Fine Boston Area Artist, Concourse Art Gallery, Boston, 78; one-women shows, Newton Free Libr, Mass, 76, Faculty Hall, Mass Inst of Technol, Cambridge, Mass, 77, Prestige Gallery, Peabody Ctr, Mass, 75 & 77, Pierce Galleries Inc, Hingham, Mass, 78 & Bristol Mus, RI, 78. Teaching: Instr sculpture, Boston Psychopathic Hospital, 49-51; pvt sculpture classes for adults & children, 59-; founder sculpture & arts, Jewish Community Ctr, Kansas City, Mo, 57-59. Pos: Gov's task force, Accessibility of the Arts (gov's comm), Boston Mass, 72-74; Gov's Coun on Arts & Humanities, Boston, Mass, 72-75; Newton Cultural Affairs Comn, 73-76. Awards: Carroll Ctr for the Blind Mem Award, Mass, 71; Good Samaritan Award, Easter Seal/Sculpture Competition, 73; First Place, Sculpture Competition, Ford Alliance, NY, 74. Bibliog: David Freudberg (auth), Nancy Schon Sculpturess, WGBH Radio, Boston, 3/23/77; Katharine Childes Jones, Nancy Schon Sculptures, Tech Talk, 5/15/77; Edward Cooper (auth), Interview with Nancy Schon, WBUR Radio, Boston, 6/26/77. Mem: New Eng Sculpture Asn (pres/secy, 51); Galerie Refusee, Kansas City, Mo (pres, 55); Cambridge Art Asn; Boston Visual Arts Coun; Springfield Art League. Style & Technique: Sculpture created in traditional wax and bronze technique; various patinas used including bronze brown, black, gold & silver. Media: Bronze. Dealer: Pierce Galleries Inc 721 Main St Rte 228 Hingham MA 02043. Mailing Add: 291 Otis St West Newton MA 02165

SCHONBERGER, FRED
PAINTER, SCULPTOR
b Arnhem, Holland, Dec 16, 30; Can citizen. Study: Kunst Nyverheid, Arnhem, with Jacob Van Arnhem & Hoff; Uffizi, Florence, Italy, with Kroller Muller. Work: Queens Univ (Ont); Reyerson Inst, Toronto, Ont; plus others. Comn: Mural, Holy Name Parish, Kirkland Lake, Ont, 59; cement fondu sculpture, County Court House, Kingston, 68; mural, Rene Turgeon, Ottawa, 72. Exhib: Lady Dunn Int Exhib, Beaver Brook Gallery, Fredericton, 61; Kingston Art Asn Ann Spring Exhib, 63-68; Expos Provinciale Quebec, 64; Nine Kingston Artists, Can Art Coun, 67-68; two-man show, Agnes Etherington Art Ctr, Queens Univ (Ont), 68 & 75. Teaching: Instr drawing, painting & sculpture, Ont Dept Educ, Community Prog Br, Ont, 62-71; instr drawing, painting & sculpture, Queens Univ (Ont), 63-70. Pos: Pres, Kingston Artists Workshop, 63-65; chmn & exec mem, Gallery Asn & Comt for Children's Art, 66-69; dir, Gallery Schonberger, presently. Awards: Grand Prix for Mars-1964 & Fourth Prize for Love, Concours Nat Art Quebec, 64. Mem: Soc Can Artists; Can Artists Representatives (rep, Kingston Chap, 72-). Style & Technique: Magic realism and surrealism. Media: Oil, Tempera, Fibreglass. Dealer: Gilhooly Galleries Billings Bridge Ottawa ON Can. Mailing Add: Gallery Schonberger 326 King St E Kingston ON K7L 3B4 Can

SCHONWALTER, JEAN FRANCES
PAINTER, INSTRUCTOR
b Philadelphia, Pa. Study: Moore Col Art, scholar, BFA; Pa Acad Fine Arts, grad fel. Work: Philadelphia Mus Art; NJ State Mus, Trenton; Brooklyn Mus, NY; Slater Mus, Norwich, Conn; New York Pub Libr. Comn: Two paintings of Temple B'nai Jeshurun, NJ, 59. Exhib: Libr of Cong, Washington, DC; NJ State Mus Exhibs; Boston Mus Exhibs; Butler Inst Am Art, Youngstown, Ohio; Nat Acad Design, New York. Teaching: Instr life painting, Newark Sch Fine & Indust Art, NJ, 69- Awards: Pennypacker Prize for Graphics, Soc Am Graphic Artists, 66; Purchase Prize, NJ State Mus, 67; First Prize & Medal of Honor for Graphics, Nat Asn Women Artists, 71. Bibliog: Dona Meilach (auth), Direct Metal Sculpture, Crown, 58; E F Singer (auth), Meet the artist—Jean Schonwalter, Suburban Life, 70. Mem: Artists Equity Asn NJ; Soc Am Graphic Artists; Assoc Artists NJ; Nat Asn Women Artists. Style & Technique: Figurative; expressionist. Media: Oil; Bronze. Dealer: Randall Galleries 823 Madison Ave New York NY 10021. Mailing Add: 27 Deaville Dr Parsippany NJ 07054

SCHOOLER, LEE
COLLECTOR
b Chicago, Ill, June 15, 23. Study: Roosevelt Univ, BA, 46; Mundelein Col, hon LHD, 72. Mem: Am Fedn Arts; Mus Mod Art, New York; Art Inst Chicago; Mus Contemp Art, Chicago (trustee). Collection: Contemporary painting and sculpture; pre-Columbian sculpture; antique Oriental rugs. Mailing Add: 43 E Elm St Chicago IL 60611

SCHOOLEY, ELMER WAYNE
PAINTER, EDUCATOR
b Lawrence, Kans, Feb 20, 16. Study: Univ Colo, BFA, 38; State Univ Iowa, MA, 41. Work: Mus Mod Art, New York; Hallmark Collection, Kansas City; Mus NMex, Santa Fe; Roswell Mus, NMex; Metrop Mus Art, New York. Comn: Fresco (with Gussie Du Jardin), Las Vegas, NMex Hosp, 50. Exhib: Houston Southwestern Exhib, 62; Kansas City Mid-Am Exhib, 64; Tucson Festival Art Exhib, 64; Eight State Exhib, Oklahoma City, 68; Biennial Southwestern Exhib, Santa Fe, 72. Teaching: Asst prof, NMex Western Univ, 46-47; prof arts & crafts, NMex Highlands Univ, 47-77; artist-in-residence, Roswell Mus, NMex, 77-78. Awards: Purchase Prize, Ford Found, 62; Prizes, Southwest Biennial, Santa Fe, 70, 72 & 74; Honorable Mention, Kansas City Hallmark Purchase, 64. Style & Technique: Landscape. Media: Oil. Mailing Add: PO Box 5 Montezuma NM 87731

SCHOONOVER, MARGARET LEFRANC
See Lefranc, Margaret

SCHORGL, THOMAS BARRY
CURATOR, PRINTMAKER
b St Louis, Mo, Mar 1, 50. Study: Univ Iowa, BFA, 73, MA(drawing), 74; Miami Univ, Ohio, 75-76; study with James Lechay, Mauricio Lasansky, Robert Wolfe, Atelier Garrigue & Dadi Wirz. Work: Sch Art, Univ Iowa; Miami Univ Print Collection, Oxford, Ohio. Exhib: Miami

Univ, 76; Miami Printmakers Europ Ctr Luxemburg, 76; Miami Univ Alumni Show, Grinnel Col, Iowa, 77. Teaching: Teaching asst drawing, Univ Iowa, 73-74; teaching asst prints & drawing, Miami Univ Ohio, 75-76. Pos: Cur, Art Ctr Inc, South Bend, 77- Media: Printmaking & Painting. Res: Eighteenth, nineteenth & twentieth century prints and painting. Publ: Co-auth, 20th Century American Masters, Art Ctr catalog, 77. Mailing Add: 1246 1/2 E Jefferson Blvd South Bend IN 46617

SCHORR, JUSTIN
PAINTER, EDUCATOR
b New York, NY, June 10, 28. Study: City Col New York, BSS, 50; Columbia Univ Teachers Col, EdD, 62. Work: Butler Inst Am Art, Youngstown, Ohio; Waldemar Res Found; Lock Haven State Col. Exhib: Brooklyn Mus, 58; Nat Acad Design, New York, 59; Pa Acad Fine Arts, Philadelphia, 63; Butler Inst Am Art, 64. Teaching: Prof painting, Columbia Univ Teachers Col, 62- Media: Oil. Publ: Auth, Aspects of Art, Barnes, 67; auth, Toward the Transformation of Art, Fairleigh Dickenson Univ, 74. Mailing Add: 106 Morningside Dr New York NY 10027

SCHRAG, KARL
PAINTER
b Karslruhe, Ger, Dec 7, 12; US citizen. Study: Ecole Beaux Arts, Geneva & Paris; Acad Ranson, Paris; Art Students League, with Lucien Simon, Roger Bissiere, Harry Sternberg & S W Hayter. Work: Nat Gallery Art; Metrop Mus Art; Mus Mod Art; Whitney Mus Am Art; Art Inst Chicago; plus many others. Exhib: Several one-man shows, Kraushaar Galleries, New York, 47-; Mod Art in US, Tate Gallery, London & other Europ mus, 56; Am Fedn Arts one-man exhib, Brooklyn Mus & Tour, 62; Whitney Mus Am Art Painting Ann, 65; Retrospective Exhib Prints, Nat Collection Fine Arts, Washington, DC, 72. Teaching: Dir etching, Atelier 17, New York, 50-51; instr printmaking, Brooklyn Col, 53-54; instr drawing & printmaking, Cooper Union, 54-68. Awards: Purchase Awards, Brooklyn Mus Print Ann, 47 & 50; Cert of Merit for Best Exhib US, 4th Int Exhib Contemp Art, New Delhi, India, 62; Am Acad Arts & Lett Grant, 66. Bibliog: John Gordon (auth), Karl Schrag, Am Fedn Arts, 60; US Info Agency staff (auth), Printmakers USA (film), Sidney Stiber Prod, 61; Una E Johnson (auth), Karl Schrag, A Catalogue Raisonne of the Graphic Works, 1939-1970, Sch Art, Syracuse Univ, 71. Mem: Soc Am Graphic Artists; Artists Equity Asn; Art Students League. Style & Technique: Color offers wealth of expression; interrelated lines or brush strokes are like the melody to this color orchestration. Media: Oil, Gouache, Graphic. Publ: Auth, Some Thoughts on Art, Cable, 58; auth, Happiness and torment of printmaking, Artist's Proof, 66; auth, The artist alone versus the artist in the workshop, New Univ Thought, autumn, 67; auth, Light & darkness in contemporary printmaking, Print Rev, 7/77. Dealer: Kraushaar Galleries 1055 Madison Ave New York NY 10028; Associated American Artists 663 Fifth Ave New York NY 10022. Mailing Add: 127 E 95th St New York NY 10028

SCHRAMM, JAMES SIEGMUND
COLLECTOR, PATRON
b Burlington, Iowa, Feb 4, 04. Study: Coe Col, hon LLD, 54; Amherst Col, hon LHD, 61; Grinnell Col, hon DFA, 72. Pos: Pres & trustee, Des Moines Art Ctr, 42-; trustee, Chicago Mus Contemp Art, 69-70; hon chmn, Amherst Col Asn Art, 71- Awards: Distinguished Serv Award, Univ Iowa, 71. Mem: Am Fedn Arts (exec comt, 42-, pres, 56-58); Whitney Mus Am Art Friends; Guggenheim Mus Friends. Interest: Supporting art departments in colleges and universities; encouraging American contemporary artists. Collection: American painting and sculpture from the thirties; some European, Japanese and American prints; African sculpture. Mailing Add: 2700 S Main St Burlington IA 52601

SCHRECK, MICHAEL HENRY
PAINTER, SCULPTOR
b Austria; US citizen. Study: Art Students League, with T vonDraeger. Work: Ft Lauderdale Mus; Heckscher Mus, New York; Metrop Mus, Miami; Mus Fine Arts, Lausanne, Switz; Tel Aviv Mus & Mus Mod Art, Haifa, Israel. Comn: Masada Monument, Hollywood, Fla; Exhib: Mus Fine Arts, Montreal, 53-56; Jersey City Mus, 59; one-man show, Selected Artist Gallery, New York, 61; Mus Mod Art, Paris, 64; Gallery LaCloche, Paris, 64. Bibliog: J J Levecque (auth), article in La Galerie des Arts, 3/65; Alfred Werner (auth), Michael Schreck Sculpture, Univ Miami, 75; plus others. Mem: Life fel Royal Soc Arts, London; Am Fedn Arts; Smithsonian Inst; Artists Equity Asn. Style & Technique: Painting expressionist to abstract sculpture; organic to abstract forms in bronze, marble and onyx. Dealer: Gloria Luria Gallery 1128 Kane Concourse Bay Harbor Islands FL 33154; Dominion Gallery 1438 Sherbrooke St W Montreal PQ Can. Mailing Add: 3111 N Ocean Dr Hollywood FL 33019

SCHRECKENGOST, VIKTOR
DESIGNER, SCULPTOR
b Sebring, Ohio, June 26, 06. Study: Cleveland Sch Art, 25-29; Univ Vienna, Austria, 29-30. Work: Cleveland Mus Am Art; Metrop Mus Art; Whitney Mus Am Art; Memphis Mus Art; also in pvt collections. Comn: Designer K K Culver Air Trophy, Oberlin Mem Tablet; sculpture for bird bldg, Cleveland Zoo, Pachyderm Bldg, 50; Cleveland Hopkins Airport, 56. Exhib: Major mus in US; also Century Progress, Chicago, San Francisco & New York World's Fair, Paris Expos. Teaching: Instr, Cleveland Sch Art, 30-, head dept indust design, 36-; instr, Case Western Reserve Univ, formerly. Pos: Former art dir, Salem China Co, Sebring Pottery Co, Am Limoges China Co, Sebring; art dir, Murray, Ohio Mfg Co, Cleveland Holophane Co, Inc, Newark; now head designer Murray Ohio Mfg Co, Nashville; consult designer, Harris-Intertype Corp & divs; designer, Am Artists Group, Inc, New York; mem fine arts adv comt, Cleveland Planning Comn, 61- Awards: Spec & First Award, Cleveland Mus Art, 55; Gold Medal Fine Arts, Am Inst Architect, 58; Visual Arts Award, Women's City Club Cleveland, 73. Style & Technique: Glass designer. Mem: Fel Int Inst Arts & Lett; Cleveland Soc Artists; NY Archit League; Indust Designers Soc Am (past nat vpres & dir); Am Watercolor Soc; plus others. Publ: Auth articles in var publs. Mailing Add: 2265 Stillman Rd Cleveland Heights OH 44118

SCHREIBER, EILEEN SHER
PAINTER, LECTURER
b Denver, Colo. Study: Univ Utah, 42-45; NY Univ Exten, 66-68; Montclair State Col, 75-77. Work: Morris Mus Arts & Sci, Morristown, NJ; Am Tel & Tel Co; RCA; Int Bus Machines; Champion Int Paper; also in collection of Sen Harrison Williams, NJ. Comn: Painting on NJ beach area, Broad Nat Bank, Newark, 70; Wolfgang Rapp Architects, Elkins Park, Pa, 72. Exhib: NJ Mus in Trenton, 69 & 73; Am Watercolor Soc Nat, Nat Acad Galleries, New York; Audubon Artists, New York; Pallazzo Vecchio, Florence, Italy; Va State Mus, 75; plus others. Teaching: Lectr collage. Awards: Nat Asn Women Artists, 70; Best in Show Cash Award, Short Hills State Show, 76; Purchase Award, Tri-State Exhib, Somerset Co Col, 77; plus others. Bibliog: D Bainbridge (auth), Commentaries on artists, NJ Music & Art Mag, 4/68; M Lenson (auth), rev in Newark Eve News, 4/70; article in Newark Star Ledger, 6/74. Mem: Nat Asn Women Artists (watercolor jury, 70-72, chmn, 73-); Artists Equity Asn; Nat Painters & Sculptors Soc; Hunterdon Art Asn; Summit Art Asn. Style & Technique: Landscape collage under glass; acrylic hard edge landscape, modern, semi-abstract, contemporary. Media: Collage, Collograph Print, Acrylic, Watercolor. Dealer: Lillian Kornbluth 7-21 Fair Lawn Ave Fair Lawn NJ 07410; Sidney Rothman The Gallery Barnegat Light NJ 08006. Mailing Add: 22 Powell Dr West Orange NJ 07052

SCHREIBER, MARTIN
SCULPTOR, PAINTER
b Berlin, Ger, Nov 8, 23; US citizen. Study: Art Students League; Brooklyn Mus Art Sch; also with Ruben Tam. Work: Nassau Community Col; Contemp Arts Ctr, Cincinnati, Ohio; Mary Washington Col, Univ Va; Corcoran Mus, Washington, DC. Exhib: 3rd Ann Op Art Festival, East Hampton Gallery, New York, 66; Op Art and Its Antecedents, Am Fedn Arts Traveling Exhib, 67; Silvermine Ann; Gallery MacKay, Montreal, 68; one-man show, Spectrum Gallery, New York, 71. Awards: First Prize in Acrylic, Silvermine, Conn, 65. Mem: Art Dirs Club NY. Style & Technique: Graduated optical bands of color out of central core; hard edge. Media: Chrome Plated Steel; Acrylic. Dealer: Razor Gallery 464 W Broadway New York NY 10029. Mailing Add: 1578 Pea Pond Rd North Bellmore NY 11710

SCHREYER, GRETA L
PAINTER, LECTURER
b Vienna, Austria, July 28, 23; US citizen. Study: Acad Arts, Vienna; Columbia Univ, with Seong Moy; Art Students League; Pratt Inst; also with Moses Soyer & Fred Taubes. Work: Mus Ha'aretz, Tel Aviv, Israel; Jersey City State Col; New Sch Social Res, New York; Pasadena Mus, Calif; Mus Art & Sci, Norfolk, Va; plus others. Exhib: Four shows, New Sch Art Ctr, New York, 60-68; Knickerbocker Artists, New York; one-man shows, St Olaf Col, 66 & Panama Art Asn, Fla, 67; Roko Gallery, New York, 72; plus other one-man shows. Teaching: Guest lectr, Brandeis Univ, 67-68; guest lectr, Women Comt, Westbury Chap, 68-69; guest lectr, Mus Mod Art, Metrop Mus Art, Whitney Mus Am Art & Guggenheim Mus, New York, 69- Awards: Grumbacher Awards, 56 & 69. Mem: Am Fedn Arts; Artists Equity Asn New York. Media: Oil, Watercolor, Lithography. Dealer: Roko Gallery 90 E Tenth St New York NY 10003. Mailing Add: 54 W 74th St New York NY 10023

SCHRUT, SHERRY
PAINTER, PRINTMAKER
b Detroit, Mich, Apr 27, 28. Study: Wayne State Univ, Detroit, BA (art), 50; post grad work at Long Beach State Col, Calif & Univ Calif, Los Angeles; in Mich, studied with Cyril Miles, Jane Betsey Welling & Sarkis Sarkisian; in Calif, studied with Robert Frame & June Schwarcz. Work: Security Pac Nat Bank, Palm Desert, Calif; Cedars-Sinai Med Ctr, Thalians Bldg, Los Angeles; Int Cult Ctr for Youth, Jerusalem, Israel; Suicide Prevention Ctr, Los Angeles; Atlantic Richfield Co, Los Angeles. Comn: Brochure & Bk Design, Southern Calif Psychoanalytic Inst, Beverly Hills, Calif, 71 & 74; relief intaglio etching, Dr Judd & Katherine Marmor, Los Angeles; collagraph intaglio relief print, State Sen Alan Sieroty, Los Angeles, 76; watercolor-collage painting, Eudorah Moore, Calif Design, Pasadena, 77; enamel cloisonne locket, Cyril Miles, Huntington Woods, Mich, 77. Exhib: 39th, 42nd & 43rd Ann Painting Exhib, Detroit Inst of Art, Mich, 48, 51 & 52; Long Beach Ann Painting Exhib, Long Beach Mus of Art, Calif, 53; 24th Nat Ceramic Exhib, Everson Mus of Art, Syracuse, NY, 68; Painting Exhib, Downey Mus of Art, Calif, 68; Crafts Exhib, Craft & Folk Art Mus, Los Angeles, 71; one-woman show of enamels, Brand Libr & Art Ctr, Glendale, Calif, 72; Collage & Assemblage in Southern Calif, Los Angeles Inst Contemp Art, Century City, 75; 1st Int Exhib of Enamels, Laguna Beach Mus of Art, 76; Works on Paper, Newport Harbor Art Mus, Calif, 77; one-woman show of enamels, Galeria Del Sol, Santa Barbara, CA, 76. Collection: Hatikvah, the Hope, 4th Int Traveling Print show, Jewish Community Ctr, Los Angeles, 73. Teaching: Instr mixed media workshop for teachers, Mich Fedn Teachers, Detroit, 50; workshop instr cloisonne enameling, Craft & Folk Art Mus, Los Angeles, 73-74. Awards: Second Prize, Painting, Wayne State Univ, Detroit, 51; Second Prize, Watercolor, Long Beach Mus of Art, 53; First Prize, enamel, Westwood Ctr for the Arts, Calif, 68. Bibliog: Barbara Probstein (auth), The fiery art, Home Mag, Los Angeles Times, 73 & Cloisonne enameling, Sch Arts Mag, Davis Publ, 1/75; W F Alexander, auth, Cloisonne extraordinaire, California contemporary artists, In: Cloisonne & Related Arts, Wallace-Homestead Bk Co, 77. Mem: Southern Calif Designer-Crafts, Inc (treas, 75-78); Enamel Guild/West (mem bd, 77); Am Crafts Coun; World Crafts Coun; Calif Design. Style & Technique: Nonobjective forms incorporating watercolor, collage acrylic and cloisonne enamel with contemporary approach to a traditional technique. Media: Painting, enameling, printmaking. Publ: Contribr, Donna Meilach & Lee Snow, co-auth, Creative Stitchery, Crown Publ, 70; contribr, Porcelain Enamel, Historical, Contemporary, Industrial and Artistic, San Diego Univ Press, 76; contribr, Henry Cote, auth, Enameling for Secondary Schools, Lawrence Univ Press, RI, 76; contribr, Crafts, 1976, Southern Calif Designer-Crafts, Inc, 76; contribr, The Center Mag, Ctr for Democratic Insts, Santa Barbara, Calif, 78. Dealer: Lonny Gans Gallery 9353 W Third St Beverly Hills CA 90210. Mailing Add: 911 Honeywood Rd Los Angeles CA 90049

SCHUCKER, CHARLES
PAINTER
b Gap, Pa, Jan 19, 08. Study: Md Inst Fine & Mech Arts, grad, 34; traveling scholar, Europe, 35. Work: Whitney Mus Am Art; Brooklyn Mus; Newark Mus Asn; New Brit Mus Am Art; Howard Wise Collection; plus others. Exhib: Art Inst Chicago, 41, 42, 54 & 59; one-man shows, Whitney Mus Am Art, New York, 71, Max Hutchinson Gallery, New York, 72, 74 & 78, Katonah Gallery, 77 & Aaron Gallery, Washington, DC, 78; Carnegie Inst Int, Pittsburgh, 49; Metrop Mus Art, New York, 59; Walker Art Ctr, Minneapolis, 50; Whitney Mus Am Art, 52-57, 59, 63 & 73; San Francisco Mus Art, Calif, 55; Brooklyn Mus Biannual, NY, 56; Amherst Col, Mass, 72; plus many others. Teaching: Instr art, City Col New York; instr art, NY Univ; prof art, Pratt Inst, 56-75, emer prof, 75- Pos: Mem Fed Art Proj, Works Prog Admin, 38-42. Awards: Guggenheim Found Fel; Nat Inst Arts & Lett. Style & Technique: Stain painting using poured oil paints, achieves abstract imagery conveying unmistakable aura and feel of landscape. Dealer: Max Hutchinson Gallery 138 Greene St New York NY 10012. Mailing Add: Studio 33 Middagh St Brooklyn Heights NY 11201

SCHUELER, JON R
PAINTER, LECTURER
b Milwaukee, Wis, Sept 12, 16. Study: Univ Wis, BA(econ), 38, MA(Eng lit), 40; Calif Sch Fine Arts, 48-51, with David Park, Elmer Bischoff, Richard Diebenkorn, Hassel Smith, Clyfford Still & Clay Spohn. Work: Ford Found; Coty Mus, Maine; Corinthian Broadcasting Co; Whitney Mus Am Art, New York; Union Carbide Corp Collection. Comn: Lithographs, New York Hilton Hotel, 62. Exhib: Whitney Mus Am Art; Corcoran Gallery Art, Washington, DC; Walker Art Ctr, Minneapolis; Md Inst; Cornell Univ; Richard de Marco Gallery, Edinburgh, Scotland; Edinburgh 73; Cleveland Mus, Ohio; Landmark Gallery, New York; plus others. Teaching: Lectr painting, Yale Univ Summer Sch Art & Md Inst, Col Art Asn Am & others. Bibliog: John I H Baur (auth), Nature in Abstraction, Macmillan, 58; B H Friedman (ed), School of New York, Grove Press, 59; Lloyd Goodrich & John I H Baur (auth), American Art of Our Century, Whitney Mus Am Art, 61. Media: Oil, Watercolor.

Publ: Contribr, Letter on the Sky, It Is Mag. Dealer: Ben Heller 121 E 73rd St New York NY 10021. Mailing Add: 80 Wig Hill Rd Chester CT 06412

SCHULER, MELVIN ALBERT
SCULPTOR, PAINTER
b San Francisco, Calif, Apr 29, 24. Study: Calif Col Arts & Crafts, BAEd, 46, MFA, 47; Danish Royal Acad Fine Arts, Copenhagen, 55-56. Work: Nat Collection Fine Arts, Smithsonian Inst, Washington, DC; Hirshhorn Mus & Sculpture Garden, Washington, DC; Storm King Art Ctr, Mountainville, NY; Portland Mus Art, Ore; La Jolla Mus Contemp Art, Calif. Comn: Three black walnut sculptures (10ft), Santa Rosa City Hall, Calif, 68; sculpture (copper over redwood), Medford City Hall, Ore, 73; sculpture (11ft copper over redwood), Eureka Redevelop Agency, Calif, 75; wall sculpture (5ft round), Ore State Capitol, Salem, 76; sculpture (8ft copper over redwood), Tri-Met Mall, Portland, 77. Exhib: Univ Nev, Reno, 66; E B Crocker Gallery, Sacramento, 65; Richmond Art Mus, Calif, 68; Hirshhorn La Quinta Collection, Palm Springs, Calif, 68; La Jolla Mus Contemp Art, Calif, 71; Portland Mus Art, Ore, 73 & 76; Henry Gallery, Univ Wash, Seattle, 75; Wash State Univ, Pullman, 75; Univ Ore Mus Art, Eugene, 76; Spokane Sculpture Invitational, Wash, 77; Palo Alto Outdoor Sculpture Exhib, Calif, 77; Palm Springs Desert Mus, Calif, 78. Teaching: Prof art, Humboldt State Univ, Arcata, 47-77. Style & Technique: Five to eight foot carved wood non-figuarative sculpture; copper-covered, carved redwood, black walnut or Oregon myrtle. Media: Watercolor; Wood. Dealer: Ankrum Gallery 657 N La Cienega Blvd Los Angeles CA 90069; James Willis Gallery 109 Geary St San Francisco CA 94108. Mailing Add: PO Box 612 Arcata CA 95521

SCHULHOF, MR & MRS RUDOLPH B
COLLECTORS
Collection: Modern art since 1945. Mailing Add: Dock Lane Kings Point NY 11024

SCHULLER, GRETE
SCULPTOR
b Vienna, Austria; US citizen. Study: Vienna Lyzeum; Vienna Kunstakademie; Art Students League, sculpture with W Zorach; Sculpture Ctr, New York. Work: Norfolk Mus Arts & Sci, Va; Mus Natural Hist, New York; Mus Sci, Boston. Exhib: Acad Arts & Lett, 55; Univ Notre Dame, 59; Detroit Inst Arts, 59-60; Pa Acad Fine Arts, Philadelphia, 59-60; 150 Years American Art, New Westbury Garden, NY, 60; plus many others. Awards: Pauline Law Prize, Allied Artists Am, 72; Roman Bronze Foundry Prize, Nat Sculpture Soc, Lever House, 73, Bronze Medal, 75; Goldie Paley Prize, Nat Asn Women Artists, 75; plus others. Mem: Fel Nat Sculpture Soc; Allied Artists Am; Audubon Artists; Sculptors League; Nat Asn Women Artists. Style & Technique: Simplified animal forms; direct carving. Media: Stone. Publ: Auth, The form is in the fieldstone, Nat Sculpture Rev, fall 71. Dealer: Clay Gallery 1162 Madison Ave New York NY 10028. Mailing Add: 8 Barstow Rd Apt 7G Great Neck NY 11021

SCHULMAN, JACOB
COLLECTOR
b New York, NY, July 2, 15. Study: Sch Educ, NY Univ, BS. Collection: Contemporary painters and sculptors with emphasis on Jewish or Biblical themes, including works by Baskin, Bloom, Levine, Rattner, Shahn, Weber and Zorach. Mailing Add: 117 First Ave Gloversville NY 12078

SCHULTE, MR & MRS ARTHUR D
COLLECTORS
Mr Schulte, b New York, NY, 1906. Study: Mr Schulte, Yale Univ; Mrs Schulte, Hunter Col, Columbia Univ, NY Univ. Collection: French, American, Italian and Greek paintings and sculpture. Mailing Add: 810 Fifth Ave New York NY 10021

SCHULTHESS, AMALIA
SCULPTOR, PAINTER
b Switz; US citizen. Study: Kantonsschule Trogen, Switz, grad; Kunstgewerbeschule, Zurich, Switz. Work: Santa Barbara Mus Art; La Jolla Art Ctr; Long Beach Mus Art. Exhib: Mostra Internazionale Del Marmo, Carrara, Italy, 72; Salon de Mai, France, 75; Salon de la Jeune Sculpture, France, 75; Scultori e Artigiani in un Centro Storico, Pietrasanta, Italy, 75. Style & Technique: Sculpture in wood, bronze, aluminum, glass, marble and a variety of stones. Dealer: Rose Rabow Galleries 2130 Leavenworth St San Francisco CA 94133. Mailing Add: 11a via C Castracani 55042 Forte dei Marmi Lucca Italy

SCHULTZ, CAROLINE REEL
PAINTER, LECTURER
b Evansville, Ind. Study: Art Ctr Col Design, Los Angeles, 58; Univ Ill-Urbana, 60-62; Wellfleet Sch, with W Kennedy, 60; Art Mart Sch, Martha's Vineyard; European Sch, Mallorca, Spain, 61; also with Nichola Ziroli & Billy M Jackson. Work: Mt Kenya Safari Club, EAfrica; Pavillon, Scottsdale, Ariz; New Masters, Carmel, Calif; Bruners Fine Art, Santa Rosa, Calif. Comn: Wildlife (screen), comn by John Batten, III, Twin Disc Corp, Racine, Wis, 75. Exhib: One-women shows, San Diego Art Inst, Balboa Park, Calif, EAfrican Wild Life Asn Gallery, Nairobi, Kenya, La Jolla Art Asst, Calif; Game Coin, San Antonio, 75; Shikar Safari Club 75, San Diego Zoo, 75; Safari Int, Las Vegas, 76; Abercrombie & Fitch, San Francisco, 76. Teaching: Lectr animal anat & Africa through the eyes of an artist. Pos: US art dir, EAfrican Wild Life Soc, 75. Awards: Purchase Award, Comedians Classic, 72; three Awards, Palm Springs Festival Arts & Music, 71 & 72; Lenten Art Festival, San Diego, 72; plus many others. Mem: San Diego Art Inst; La Jolla Art Asn; Desert Art Ctr, Palm Springs, Calif. Mailing Add: 5361 Balboa Ave San Diego CA 92117

SCHULTZ, DOUGLAS GEORGE
CURATOR
b Oakland, Calif, Oct 3, 47. Study: Univ Calif, Berkeley, BA, MA. Collections Arranged: Duayne Hatchett: Recent Paintings and Sculpture (auth, catalogue), 74, Recent Photographs by Russell Drisch (auth, catalogue), 76, Antoni Tapies: Thirty-Three Years of His Work, 77 & In Western New York (co-auth, catalogue), 77, Albright-Knox Art Gallery. Teaching: Adj prof mus studies, State Univ NY, Buffalo, 75- Pos: Curatorial intern, Albright-Knox Art Gallery, 72, asst cur, 73-75, assoc cur, 75-76, cur, 77-; mem professional adv comt, Arts Develop Servs, Buffalo, NY. Mailing Add: 1285 Elmwood Ave Buffalo NY 14222

SCHULTZ, HAROLD A
PAINTER, EDUCATOR
b Grafton, Wis, Jan 6, 07. Study: Layton Sch Art; Northwestern Univ, BS & MA. Exhib: Art Inst Chicago; Chicago Soc Artists; Brooklyn Mus; Ferargil Gallery. Teaching: Lectr, American Art Today; head dept art, Francis W Parker Sch, Chicago, 32-40; prof art & design, Univ Ill, 40-75, emer prof, 75- Style & Technique: Loose handling of rich color and free forms used as personal interpretation of subject matter—prairie farmlands, fishing villages and harbors. Publ: Co-auth, Art in the Elementary School, 48. Mailing Add: 2017 Burlison Dr Urbana IL 61801

SCHULTZ, ROGER D
PAINTER, SCULPTOR
b Troy, Ohio, Nov 17, 40. Study: Univ Cincinnati, BS. Work: Fine Arts Mus NMex, Santa Fe; Fine Arts Collection, Univ Cincinnati; First Nat Bank Ariz, Phoenix; Westinghouse Corp, Norman, Okla; Ansul Co, Marinette, Wis. Comn: Sphere sculpture, Bank N Mex, Albuquerque, 69; sculpture, First Northern Savings & Loan Asn, Santa Fe, 70; adobe residence, Dr & Mrs Robert M Zone, Santa Fe, 71; sculpture, Horizon Country Club, Belen, NMex, 72. Exhib: NMex Biennial, 67, 69 & 71 & Southwest Biennial, 68 & 72; Fine Arts Mus NMex; Sesquicentennial Fine Arts Exhib, Univ Cincinnati, 68; 11th & 12th Midwest Biennials, Joslyn Art Mus, Omaha, Nebr, 70 & 72; Mainstreams '72, Marietta Col, Ohio, 72. Awards: Alfred Morang Competition First Place Award, 67; Univ Cincinnati Purchase Award, 68; Major Award & Purchase Award, Fine Arts Mus NMex, 71. Media: Acrylic; Copper, Bronze. Dealer: Janus Gallery 116 1/2 E Palace Ave Santa Fe NM 87501 Mailing Add: PO Box 4574 Santa Fe NM 87502

SCHULZ, CHARLES MONROE
CARTOONIST
b Minneapolis, Minn, Nov 25, 22. Study: Anderson Col, Hon LHD, 63. Pos: Cartoonist, St Paul Pioneer Press & Sat Eve Post, 48-49; created syndicated comic strip Peanuts, 50- Awards: Outstanding Cartoonists of the Year, Nat Cartoonists Soc, 55; Outstanding Humorist of the Year, Yale Univ, 57; Emmy Award for CBS Cartoon Spec, 66; plus others. Publ: Auth & illusr, Love is Walking Hand in Hand, 65, A Charlie Brown Christmas, 65, You Need Help, Charlie Brown, 66, Charlie Brown's All-stars, 66 & You've Had It, Charlie Brown, 69; plus more than 100 others. Mailing Add: c/o Fawcett World 1515 Broadway New York NY 10036

SCHULZ, CORNELIA
PAINTER
b Pasadena, Calif, Oct 21, 36. Study: Los Angeles Co Art Inst, 56-58; San Francisco Art Inst, BFA, 60, MFA, 62. Exhib: Contemp Calif Sculpture, Oakland Art Mus, Kaiser Ctr, 63; Univ Art Mus, Univ Calif, Berkeley, 72; Mills Col Art Gallery, Oakland, Calif, 74; Hansen-Fuller Gallery, San Francisco, 75; North, East, West, South & Middle, Contemp Am Drawings, Moore Col Art, Philadelphia, 75. Teaching: Instr art, Calif Col Arts & Crafts, Oakland, 72-73; lectr art, Univ Calif, Davis, 73-75, asst prof art, 75- Awards: Soc Encouragement of Contemp Art Grant, 75. Style & Technique: Free versus contrasting formal shape. Media: Enamel Paint on Canvas. Dealer: Hansen-Fuller Gallery 228 Grant Ave San Francisco CA 94108. Mailing Add: 466 Cascade Dr Fairfax CA 94108

SCHULZ, KEN
PAINTER, LECTURER
b Racine, Wis, Jan 19, 20. Study: Layton Sch Art, Milwaukee; also with Gerhard C F Miller. Comn: Many pvt comns. Exhib: Ann Am Watercolor Soc, NY; Ann Allied Artists Am, NY; Ann Knickerbocker Artists, NY; Ann Audubon Artists, Inc, NY; Ann Nat Acad Design, NY. Teaching: Pvt art classes & watercolor workshops, Arrowmont Sch, Gatlinburg, 66- Pos: Artist-owner, Ken Schulz Gallery, Gatlinburg, Tenn, 66- Awards: Best of Show, Circa 1964, Wustom Mus Fine Arts, Wis; Kathrine M Howe Mem Prize, Knickerbocker Artists, 72. Bibliog: Karen Tansel (auth), article in Racine J Times, 72; Flo Gullockson (auth), Knoxville News-Sentinel, 75; Deborah Walther (auth), article in Decor Mag, 12/77. Mem: Am Watercolor Soc; Salmagundi Club; Allied Artists of Am; Audubon Artists; Knickerbocker Artists. Style & Technique: Landscapes, seascapes, Americana scenes, wildlife; realism technique. Media: Watercolor, Egg Tempera. Mailing Add: PO Box 396 Gatlinburg TN 37738

SCHULZ, WILLIAM GALLAGHER
SCULPTOR, PAINTER
b St Charles, Mo, Mar 25, 20. Study: St Louis Sch Fine Arts; Washington Univ, with Max Beckman, Fred Conway, Philip Guston, BFA, 48; Escuela de Pintura, Univ Michoacan, Mex, 49-53; Md Inst, Baltimore, MFA, 62. Work: Schutzverband Bildender Kunstler, Frankfurt, Ger; De Barndesteed, Vriji Acad, Amsterdam, Holland; Kunstverein, Erlangen, Ger. Exhib: Good Design Show, Mus Mod Art, New York, 50; Junge Amerikanische Kunstler, Ger, 58; St Paul Ceramic, Minn, 64; Northwest Ceramics, Seattle, Wash, 65; Sen Mike Mansfield Mont Artists Exhib, Washington, DC, 67. Teaching: Instr drawing & watercolor, Washington Univ, 48-49; instr weaving, Escuela de Pintura, Univ Michoacan, 50-53; asst prof ceramics, Eastern Mont Col, Billings, 62-67. Pos: Arts & crafts dir, USAREUR, Ger & Austria, 53-59; off handicrafts adv, Amman & Jerusalem, Jordan, 59-60; handicrafts expert, UNDP, Gilbert, Ellice, Solomon, New Hebrides, Fiji, Samoa & New Guinea Islands, 67-74; consult, UN Develop Adv Team, Suva, Fiji Islands, 73. Awards: Rinehart Fel, Md Inst, Baltimore, 62. Mem: Artists Equity Asn, Inc. Style & Technique: Intimate sized Neo-expressionist bronze sculpture dealing with primal concepts of feeling, touching and seeing. Media: Bronze, Ceramics. Publ: Auth, various UN reports. Dealer: New West 2935 C Louisiana NE Albuquerque NM 87110. Mailing Add: 1603 SE Salmon Portland OR 97214

SCHULZE, FRANZ
EDUCATOR, ART CRITIC
b Uniontown, Pa, Jan 30, 27. Study: Northwestern Univ, 43; Univ Chicago, PhB, 45; Art Inst Chicago, BFA, 49, MFA, 50; Acad Fine Arts, Munich. Teaching: Instr, Purdue Univ, 50-52; prof, Lake Forest Col, 52-74, Hollender prof art, 74- Pos: Art critic, Chicago Daily News, 62-; contrib ed, Art News, 75-; contrib ed, Inland Architect, 75- Awards: Ford Found Critics Fel, 64; Harbison Award, Danford Found, 71; Graham Found Advan Fine Arts Fel, 71. Mem: Col Art Asn Am; Arch Am Art; Am Asn Univ Prof; Louis Corinth Mem Found. Res: Art and architecture in the Midwest, especially Chicago. Publ: Auth, Art, Architecture and Civilization, 68; auth, Fantastic Images: Chicago Art Since 1945, 72; auth, 100 Years of Architecture in Chicago, 76. Mailing Add: Dept of Art Lake Forest Col Lake Forest IL 60045

SCHULZE, JOHN H
PHOTOGRAPHER, EDUCATOR
b Scottsbluff, Nebr, June 7, 15. Study: Kans State Teachers Col, BS; Univ Iowa, MFA. Work: Nihon Univ, Tokyo; Haydon Gallery, Mass Inst Technol; Univ Ala; Oakland Mus. Comn: Photog mural, Sci Bldg, Univ Northern Iowa, 71. Exhib: American Photography: The Sixties, Sheldon Mem Art Gallery, Nebr, 66; Photography in Fine Arts V, Metrop Mus Art, 67; Photography USA, De Cordova Mus, 68; Focus Gallery, San Francisco, 68; Exposure Gallery, New York, 73; plus others. Teaching: Prof photog, Sch Art, Univ Iowa, 48-, res prof, 68-69; artist in residence, Washburn Univ, 72; artist in residence, Northwest Mo State Col, 72. Bibliog: Elusive Shadow (film), Univ Iowa Camera, 65. Mem: Soc Photog Educ (chmn, 70); Col Art Asn Am; Mid Am Col Art Asn. Style & Technique: Straight print plus photomontage or assemblage. Publ: Contribr, London Times (educ suppl), 64; contribr,

Camera Int, 65; contribr, Contemp Photographer, 67; contribr, Aperture, 69; contribr, Photog Ann, 69. Mailing Add: 5 Forest Glen Iowa City IA 52240

SCHULZE, PAUL
DESIGNER
b New York, NY, Feb 7, 34. Study: Parsons Sch Design, cert; NY Univ, BS(indust design), 60. Comn: Crystal cross, Steuben Glass, St Clement's Episcopal Church, New York. Exhib: Studies in Crystal 1966, Steuben Glass, NY, 65, Islands in Crystal, 66. Teaching: Instr eng drawing & three dimensional design, Parsons Sch Design, 62-70. Pos: Off interior design, Bus Equip Sales Co, New York, 60-61; designer, Steuben Glass, 61-69, asst dir design, 69-70, dir design, 70- Awards: Student Competition Award, Am Soc Indust Designers, 59. Mem: Guild for Organic Environment; Nat Alumni Coun Parsons Sch Design. Media: Glass, Mixed Media. Publ: Illusr, Organics, Steendrukkerij & Co, Holland, 61; illusr, articles in Indust Design & Progressive Archit. Mailing Add: Lindley Rd RD 2 Corning NY 14830

SCHUMACHER, HERBERT CHARLES
CERAMIST, EDUCATOR
b Wichita, Kans, Jan 21, 32. Study: Kans Univ, BFA, pottery with J Sheldon Carey, MFA & EdD. Work: Mus Int Folk Art, Santa Fe, NMex; Libr Gallery, Utah State Univ, Logan. Exhib: Young Americans-1962, Mus Contemp Crafts, New York, 62; Wichita Nat Decorative Arts & Ceramics Exhib, 62, 64 & 65; 20th Ann Scripps Col Exhib, Claremont, Calif, 64; Ceramic Arts, USA, 1966, Int Mineral & Chem Corp, Skokie, Ill, 66; Ceramics West, Logan, Utah, 72, 73 & 74. Teaching: Prof ceramics, Univ Northern Colo, Greeley, 63- Awards: Cash Award in Crafts, Mus of NMex, 67; Merit Award in Crafts, Am Craftsmen's Coun, 69; Purchase Award, Colo State Univ, 70. Mem: Nat Coun on Educ in Ceramic Arts. Style & Technique: Primarily on the potter's wheel exploring a variety of forms in stoneware clay; recognized expert on stoneware glazes. Media: Stoneware Clay. Publ: Auth, Planning, Constructing & Operating the Chalk Creek Pottery, Nat Coun on Educ in Ceramic Arts, 71. Mailing Add: 2541 17th Ave Greeley CO 80631

SCHUMAN, ROBERT CONRAD
PAINTER, WEAVER
b Baldwin, NY, July 12, 23. Study: NY Univ, 48; Columbia Univ, 48; Pratt Inst Art Sch, BFA, 50; Univ Hawaii, MEd, 59; pvt study with Robert Brackman & Jean Charlot. Exhib: Easter Art Exhib, Honolulu, 63 & 65; Libr Hawaii, Honolulu, 65; Hui Noeau, Maui, 65 & 68; Waldorf Astoria Art Gallery, NY, 66; Wall Hangings, Tapestries and Woven Rugs, Lahaina Art Soc, 73; plus others. Teaching: Instr art, Baldwin, NY, 48-50; instr, Nanakuli, Oahu, 51, Eleele Kauai, 51-57; art supvr, Univ Hawaii, 58-64; instr art, Honolohua, Maui, 65; art instr & chmn dept, Baldwin High Sch, Maui, 66-67; instr art, Lahainaluna High Sch, 68- Pos: Judge, Children's Art Show, Honolulu Acad Arts, 57; dir, State Art Week, 59; producer & dir documentary film, Lahainaluna, 75. Awards: Prize, Hui Noeau, 64; Prize, Maui Co Fair, 64. Mem: Nat Art Educ Asn; Hawaii Educ Asn; Hawaii Arts Coun; Hui Noeau (bd dirs); Pacific Art Asn; plus others. Style & Technique: Abstract impressionist painting; emphasis on use of native material in weaving. Publ: Contribr, prof art jour. Mailing Add: Box 470-C RR 1 Honokeana Lahaina HI 96761

SCHUMSKY, FELICIE ROBERTA
ART PUBLISHER
b New York, NY, June 14, 40. Study: New York Univ. Pos: Pres, Felicie Inc, New York, 65- & FKH Editions, New York, 74-75. Specialty: Publish works by Wayland Moore, Edward Sokol, Russ Elliott, Mildred Barrett, Jean Jansem, and others. Mailing Add: 141 E 56th St New York NY

SCHUSELKA, ELFI
PRINTMAKER, SCULPTOR
b Vienna, Austria, Feb 13, 40. Study: Art hist & theatre, Univ Vienna; Acad Arts, Vienna; photog, Graphic & Experimental Inst, Vienna; studied with Oskar Kokoschka, Sch of Vision, Salzburg, Austria; Art Students League, New York; Pratt Graphics Ctr, New York. Work: Albertina, Vienna, Austria; Amon Carter Mus Western Art, Ft Worth, Tex; Bibliot Nat, Paris, France; Nat Mus Hist, Taipei, Taiwan; Mus Mod Art, New York. Exhib: Int Print Biennale, Cracow, Poland, 70 & 76; Brooklyn Mus Print Exhib, NY, 70 & 76; Int Exhib Graphic Art, Ljubljana, Yugoslavia, 75; Int Print Biennale, Fredrikstad, Norway, 76 & 78; Int Exhib Graphic Art, Frechen, Ger, 76; Int Biennale Biella, Italy, 76; Invitational one-man show wallsculptures, 55 Mercer, New York, 77; plus others. Teaching: Instr printmaking, Sch Visual Arts, New York, 70-73; instr art, Pratt/Phoenix Sch of Design, New York, 74. Awards: Purchase Award, SAGA Print Exhib, 71; Pratt Graphics Ann Print Exhib, 70 & 72; NJ Ann Nat, 70. Bibliog: Fritz Eichenberg (auth), New talent, Artist Proof, 70; Gene Baro (auth), 30 Years of American Printmaking, Brooklyn Mus, NY, 76; Jill Dunbar, Shattered sculpture, The Villager, 10/77. Mem: Artist Equity of NY; Soc Am Graphic Artists (mem coun, 76 & 77). Style & Technique: (Sculpture) Mixed media, plaster, rope, wire, clothes and paint; (Prints) partly photographic mixing lithograph and silkscreen. Dealer: Pace Gallery 32 E 57th St New York NY 10022; Truman Gallery 38 E 57th St New York NY 10022. Mailing Add: 133 Eldridge St New York NY 10002

SCHUSTER, CITA FLETCHER (SARAH E)
ART DEALER, APPRAISER
b El Paso, Tex, Sept 12, 29. Study: Vassar Col, AB, 50; Univ Tex, El Paso, with David Deming; Univ Calif, Los Angeles, Am Soc Appraisers sem fine arts. Exhib: Motorola Regional, El Paso, 60; Int Designer Craftsmen, El Paso Mus Art, 73; La Watercolor Soc 5th Int, Baton Rouge, 74; one-man exhib, Univ Tex, El Paso, 75; Int Woman's Art Slide Festival, 76; 19th Ann Sun Carnival Nat, El Paso Mus Art, Tex, 76-77. Pos: Owner-dir, Two-Twenty-Two Gallery, El Paso, 63- Bibliog: Betty Chamberlain (auth), Professional page, Am Artist, 11/74. Mem: Appraisers Asn Am; Valuors Consortium, Houston; assoc Am Soc Appraisers; La Watercolor Soc. Media: Watercolor, Acrylic. Specialty: Contemporary American art. Mailing Add: 6109 Pinehurst El Paso TX 79912

SCHUSTER, EUGENE IVAN
ART DEALER, ART HISTORIAN
b St Louis, Mo, Dec 8, 36. Study: Wayne State Univ, BA & MA; Univ Mich, Ann Arbor, 59-62; Univ London, Warburg Inst, Fulbright scholar with E H Gombrich & Courtauld Inst, 62-65; London Sch Econ, 62-65. Teaching: Lectr art hist, Wayne State Univ, 59-62; lectr art hist, Eastern Mich Univ, 60; lectr art hist, Rackham Exten, Univ Mich, 61; lectr art hist, Nat Gallery, London, 62-65. Pos: Dir, London Arts Gallery; owner, Nanny's Soup Kettle Inc, Dearborn. Awards: Louis La Med Prize for outstanding masters thesis on topic of Jewish cultural concern. Mem: Founders Soc, Detroit Inst Arts; Detroit Art Dealers Asn; Appraisers Asn Am. Res: Quattrocento in Florence, especially formative changes caused by humanistic studies and leading to the Renaissance. Specialty: Old and modern master graphics; western painting and sculpture from the 15th to the 20th centuries. Publ: Auth, Les peintres maudits: a study of the cultural relationship of the Jewish artists of Paris, 60; auth, Sir Charles Locke Eastlake, Plymouth Art Mus, Eng. Mailing Add: 321 Fisher Bldg Detroit MI 48202

SCHUTTE, THOMAS FREDERICK
ART ADMINISTRATOR
b Rochester, NY, Dec 19, 35. Study: Valparaiso Univ, Ind, AB, 57; Ind Univ, Bloomington, MBA, 58; Univ Colo, Boulder, DBA, 63. Pos: Asst dean, Wharton Sch, Univ Pa, Philadelphia, 73-75; pres, Philadelphia Col of Art, 75-; dir, Union of Independent Cols of Art, 75-; organizer, East Coast Art Cols Consortium, 76; chmn & moderator, Indust Design Sem, Design & the Corp, New York, 77. Interest: American 18th and 19th century decorative arts; corporate design management. Publ: Auth, Is the antiques dealer aware of his economic position in the market place?, 1-5/63 & A salesmanship model for the antiques dealer, 4/64, Antiques Dealer; ed, An Uneasy Coalition: Design & Corporate America, Univ Pa, 75. Mailing Add: 405 Mulberry Lane Haverford PA 19041

SCHUTZ, ESTELLE
PAINTER, PRINTMAKER
b New York, NY, Oct 10, 07. Study: Cooper Union, cert; Pratt Graphic Ctr. Work: Philadelphia Mus of Art; Brooklyn Mus, NY; McAllen Int Mus, Tex. Exhib: Brooklyn Mus, NY; Pa Acad Fine Arts, Philadelphia; Philadelphia Mus of Art; Heckscher Mus, Huntington, NY; McAllen Int Mus; Audubon Artists Ann, Nat Acad Design, New York; Silvermine Ann, Silvermine Guild of Artists, New Canaan, Conn; Nat Asn Women Artists Ann, New York; Nat Print Exhib, Soc Am Graphic Artists Ann, New York & Tokyo; Boston Printmakers Exhib, Mass; one-woman shows, Kans State Univ, Manhattan; Western Mich Univ, Kalamazoo, Fla State Univ, Tallahassee & Hofstra Univ, Hempstead, NY. Awards: John Taylor Arms Award/Printmaking, Audubon Ann, New York; Burndy Corp Award/Painting, Silvermine Ann, New Canaan, Conn; John Carl Georgio/Walter Giger Mem Award/Printmaking, Nat Asn Women Artists Ann, New York. Mem: Soc Am Graphic Artists; Nat Asn Women Artists; Prof Artists Guild. Style & Technique: Abstract painting; embossed intaglio printmaking. Media: Acrylics for painting; etching for printmaking. Mailing Add: 19 Gilbert Rd Great Neck NY 11024

SCHUTZ, PRESCOTT DIETRICH
ART DEALER
b New York, NY, Feb 19, 48. Study: Sorbonne, École du Louvre, Paris; Columbia Univ, BA(art hist). Pos: Dir contemp art, Hirschl & Adler Galleries, 73- Mem: Drawing Ctr, New York. Specialty: American art; contemporary American realism. Mailing Add: c/o Hirschl & Adler Galleries 21 E 70th St New York NY 10021

SCHWAB, ELOISA (MRS A H RODRIGUEZ)
PAINTER
b Habana, Cuba, July 4, 94; US citizen. Study: Acad Julien, Paris; Art Students League, with Bridgman & Miller. Work: Hickory Mus, NC; NJ Mus, Paterson; Arnot Art Mus, Elmira, NY; Art Students League; Mus City of New York; plus others. Exhib: Pa Acad Fine Arts; Paterson Art League; Fair Lawn Art Asn; Composers, Authors, Artists of Am; Burr Artists; plus many one-man shows. Awards: State Show Award, Paterson, NJ; Award, Gotham Painters; First Prize, Fair Lawn Art Asn Outdoor Show. Mem: Burr Artists (corresp secy, 70-); Gotham Painters (corresp secy); Fair Lawn Art Asn; life mem Art Students League. Style & Technique: Contemporary. Media: Watercolor, Casein, Oil. Mailing Add: 15-26B Plaza Rd Fair Lawn NJ 07410

SCHWABACHER, ETHEL K
PAINTER, ART CRITIC
b New York, NY, May 20, 03. Study: With Max Weber, 28; in Europe, 28-33; with Arshile Gorky, 35-36. Work: Whitney Mus Am Art, New York; Albright-Knox Gallery, Buffalo; Rockefeller Univ; Syracuse Univ; Wichita State Univ. Exhib: Whitney Mus Am Art Ann, 52-65; Mexico City Biennale, 60; Walker Art Ctr, 60; Carnegie Inst Int, 61; Brooklyn Mus Watercolor Int, 61-62; Abstract Expressionism: First & Second Generation, 72; plus many others. Style & Technique: Post-abstract expressionist. Media: Acrylic, Pastel, Watercolor. Publ: Auth, Arshile Gorky, Whitney Mus Am Art & Macmillan, 57 & Arte Visivi, Rome, 62; auth, John Ford, Nadelstein Press, 74. Mailing Add: 1192 Park Ave New York NY 10028

SCHWACHA, GEORGE
PAINTER
b Newark, NJ, Oct 2, 08. Study: With Arthur W Woelfle & John Grabach. Work: Albany Inst Hist & Art; Mint Mus Art; Elisabet Ney Mus; Am Watercolor Soc; New Haven Paint & Clay Club; plus many others. Exhib: Corcoran Gallery Art; Currier Gallery Art; Denver Art Mus; Elgin Acad Art; Delgado Mus Art; plus many others. Awards: Award, Meriden Arts & Crafts, 52; Award, Fla Southern Col, 52; Gold Medal, Audubon Artists, 61; plus others. Style & Technique: Realistic. Mailing Add: 273 Glenwood Ave Bloomfield NJ 07003

SCHWALB, SUSAN
GRAPHIC ARTIST, PAINTER
b New York, NY, Feb 26, 44. Study: Carnegie-Mellon Univ, Pittsburgh, Pa, BFA, 65. Work: Pilathea Art Mus of Mod Art, Ont; MacDowell Colony, Peterborough, NH; Carnegie-Mellon Univ. Exhib: All Media Show, Westmoreland Co Mus, Greenburgh, Pa, 64; Works on Paper, Brooklyn Mus, 75; Drawings, Hansen Galleries, New York, 75; Paper, Fabric, Glass, Just Above Midtown Gallery, New York, 77; Women Artists 78, City Univ New York Grad Ctr, New York, 78; 1st Int Drawing Exhib, Bronx Mus, NY, 78; Women Working in Art, Franklin & Marshall Col, Lancaster, Pa, 78; solo shows, Watercolor Drawings, Open Mind Gallery, New York, 74 & Orchid Series, Rutgers Univ, New Brunswick & Newark, NJ, 77. Pos: Art dir, Aphra, Literary Mag, 74-75 & Women Artist News, 75-77. Awards: Fel, Va Ctr for Creative Arts, 73 & MacDowell Colony, 74 & 75; Comt for the Visual Arts Grant, New York, 77. Bibliog: Joan Marter (auth), Women Artists, Arts Mag, 2/78 & Susan Schwalb, Womenart, winter 77-78. Mem: Artists Equity of New York; Coalition of Women's Art Orgn (exec comt, 77-78); Women's Caucus for Art (steering comt mem, NY Chap); Women in the Arts Found. Style & Technique: Silverpoint and other metalpoint drawings, ink and watercolor. Media: Landscapes in Pencil & Intercolor; Floral Images in Silverpoint. Publ: Illusr, Illustrated Issue of Aphra, 73; contribr, Crafting with Plastics, Chilton Bk Co, 75; contribr, Women Artist News, Mid-March Assoc, 75-77; auth, Notes From Houston, Womanart, 78. Mailing Add: 233 E 21st St New York NY 10010

SCHWALBACH, MARY JO
PAINTER, SCULPTOR
b Milwaukee, Wis, July 8, 39. Study: Pine Manor Jr Col, AA; Univ Wis, BS; NY Univ Inst Fine Arts; Sch Visual Arts; also in Paris & Rome. Work: Univ Calif Mus, Berkeley; Jazz Mus, New York; Kellogg State Bank, Green Bay, Wis; Am City Bank, Menomonee Falls, Wis; Kimberly State Bank, Wis. Comn: Sculpture, 1st Fed Savings & Loan, Menomonee Falls, 69; three hockey sculptures, Philadelphia Flyers, The Spectrum, Philadelphia, 70; sculpture of

Mario Andretti, Clipper Mag, New York, 72; sculpture, Computer TV Gulf & Western Bldg, New York, 72; Am Baseball Asn, 72. Exhib: One-man shows, Rhoda Sande Gallery, New York, 69, West Bend Mus Fine Arts, Wis, 69 & Dannenberg, New York, 72; retrospective, Bergstrom Mus, Neenah, Wis, 70; Beyond Realism, Upstairs Gallery, East Hampton, NY, 72. Teaching: Asst instr printmaking, Mus Mod Art Sch, New York, 65. Pos: Mem staff, Mus Mod Art, 62-67. Bibliog: S Walton (auth), Mary Jo Schwalbach-sports artist, Sporting News, 71; article in Clipper Mag, 8/72; S Fischler (auth), Mary Jo Schwalbach-sports action, Sports Hockey, 72. Media: Mixed Media. Publ: Illusr, Down Beat, 65-72 & Prestige Record Jackets, 66-69; art reproduced in New Yorker, 70. Mailing Add: 14 E 80th St New York NY 10021

SCHWANDNER, KATHLEEN M
ART DEALER, COLLECTOR
b Jeanette, Pa, Sept 13, 47. Study: Chaffey Col; El Camino Col; Orange Coast Col; pvt study with art marketing consult, Calvin J Goodman. Collections Arranged: Bank of Am, Southern Calif Br Off, 77-78; Mattel Inc, Hawthorne, Calif, 77-78; McDonald Enterprises, Thousand Oaks, Calif, 77; Daylin Corp, Los Angeles, Calif, 77. Pos: Art consult to corp collectors, Los Angeles, 76-; coordr for NAm Gallery Artists Festival, Tucson, Ariz, 75- Specialty: Institutional art emphasizing wall paintings, original prints, fiber work and batiks. Collection: Contemporary paintings and oritinal prints, figurative and oriental. Mailing Add: 8153 Billowvista Dr Playa del Rey CA 90291

SCHWARCZ, JUNE THERESE
CRAFTSMAN
b Denver, Colo, June 10, 18. Study: Univ Colo, 36-38; Univ Chicago, 38-39; Pratt Inst, 39-41; Inst Design, Chicago, with Moholy Nagy. Work: Lannan Found, Palm Beach, Fla; Johnson Wax Collection; Minn Mus Art, St Paul; Oakland Art Mus, Calif; Mus Contemp Craft, New York. Comn: Enameled bowl with technique demonstration bowls, Mus Contemp Crafts, 58; three piece panel, Cent Nat Bank, Enid, Okla, 62. Exhib: New Talent USA, Art in Am, 60; one-man show, Mus Contemp Crafts, 65; Objects USA, Johnson Wax Collection & Exhib, 69; one-man shows, Mus Bellerive (Kunstgewerbermuseum), Zurich, Switz, 71, Schmuckmuseum, Pforzheim, Ger, 72 & Mus Contemp Crafts, New York; two-man show, de Young Mus, San Francisco. Awards: Ceramic Nat Purchase Award, Everson Mus, Syracuse, 60; First Calif Craftsmen's Biennial, Oakland Mus, 61; Goldsmith 70, Minn Mus Art, 70. Bibliog: Uchida (auth), June Schwarcz, 9/59 & Ventura (auth), June Schwarcz: electroforming, 11/65, Crafts Horizons; Nordress (auth), Objects: USA, Viking, 70. Mem: Am Crafts Coun. Style & Technique: Transparent enamel over copper that has been worked by etching, engraving or electroplating. Media: Enamel. Publ: Contribr, Craftmen's World, 59 & Research in Crafts, 61, Am Crafts Coun; auth, The arts turn to plating, J Electroplaters Soc, 11/67. Mailing Add: 18 Wray Ave Sausalito CA 94965

SCHWARTZ, AUBREY E
PRINTMAKER
b New York, NY, Jan 13, 28. Study: Art Students League; Brooklyn Mus Art Sch. Work: Nat Gallery Art, Washington, DC; Brooklyn Mus Art; Philadelphia Mus Art; Libr Cong, Washington, DC; Art Inst Chicago. Comn: Ed lithographs, Predatory Birds, Gehenna Press, 58, Midget & Dwarf, Tamarind Workshop, 60 & Bestiary, Kanthos Press, 61; ed etchings, Mothers & Children, New York, 59 & Wildflowers, New York, 66. Exhib: Young Am Whitney Mus Am Art, 57; Print Coun Am Show, 57; one-man show, Grippi Gallery, New York, 58; Art USA, New York Coliseum, 59; Contemp Graphic Art, US State Dept, 59. Awards: Guggenheim Found Fel Creative Printmaking, 58-60; Tamarind Fel Creative Lithography, 60; First Prize for Graphic Art, Boston Arts Festival, 60. Bibliog: Carl Zigrosser (auth), catalog, Print Coun Am, 59; Allan Fern (auth), catalog, US State Dept, 61. Mailing Add: Harpur College State Univ NY Binghamton NY 13901

SCHWARTZ, BARBARA ANN
PAINTER, WRITER
b Philadelphia, Pa, Aug 23, 48. Study: Carnegie-Mellon Univ, BFA, 70. Exhib: Marion Locks Gallery, Philadelphia, 72; Brooklyn Mus, NY, 74; Whitney Biennial Exhib Contemp Am Art, 75; Artists Space, New York, 75; John Doyle Gallery, Chicago, 75; Artpark, Lewiston, NY, 76; Willard Gallery, New York, 76 & 78; Art in Pub Spaces, New York, 77. Teaching: Instr drawing, Brooklyn Mus Art Sch, 74-75; instr drawing & sculpture, Sch Visual Arts, New York. Bibliog: Jeanne Siege (auth), rev in Art Am, 75 & Arts Mag, 1/77; rev in Art in Am, 75, SoHo News, New York Mag, Arts Mag & Artforum, 76. Style & Technique: Casein on hydrocal/plaster over wire mesh screen; paintings often have a relief quality. Publ: Ed, Art News, 71-72; auth, Young New York artists, 72 & auth, New York sculpture (column), 72-75, Craft Horizons; auth, SoHo, an interview with a neighborhood, Bolaffi Arte, 74. Mailing Add: 90 Prince St 3rd Floor New York NY 10012

SCHWARTZ, CARL E
PAINTER, INSTRUCTOR
b Detroit, Mich, Sept 21, 35. Study: Art Inst Chicago, BFA; Univ Chicago, BFA. Work: Art Inst Chicago; Libr Cong, Washington, DC; Dayton Art Inst; Brit Mus; Brooklyn Mus Art. Exhib: Ann Exhib Mich Artists, Detroit Art Inst, 55, 65 & 69; Butler Inst Am Art Nat, 63-65; Art Across Am Traveling Exhib, Columbus Gallery Fine Arts, 65-67; Am Painting Exhib, Smithsonian Inst, Washington, DC & Tour, 72; 18th Nat Print Exhib, Brooklyn Mus, 72-73; Calif Palace of Legion of Honor, San Francisco, 73; Eight State Painting Exhib, J B Speed Mus Art, 75; Boston Printmakers 76; one-man show, Ill State Mus, 77; plus others. Teaching: Instr figure painting & drawing, NShore Art League, 58-; instr figure painting & drawing, Suburban Fine Arts Ctr, 60-71 & 73- Awards: Purchase Awards, J B Speed Mus Art, 73, Ill State Mus, 74 & Dickinson State Univ, 76. Bibliog: Allan Davidson (auth), article in Art League News, 67; Thomas Carbol (auth), The Printmaker in Illinois, Ill Art Educ Asn, 72. Mem: Arts Club Am; Artists Guild Chicago; Contemp Art Mus Chicago; NShore Art League; Art Inst Chicago. Media: Acrylic. Publ: Illusr, Playboy, 65 & 67; auth, article in NShore Art League News, 69. Mailing Add: 4228 N Hazel Chicago IL 60613

SCHWARTZ, EUGENE M
COLLECTOR, PATRON
b Butte, Mont, Mar 18, 27. Study: New Sch Social Res; NY Univ; Columbia Univ; Univ Wash. Pos: Acquisitions comt, Whitney Mus Am Art, 67-68 & 68-69. Collection: Contemporary American art since World War II, chiefly of the sixties: parts of the collection shown as a group at Jewish Museum, Everson Museum of Art and the Albany Institute of History and Art. Mailing Add: 1160 Park Ave New York NY 10028

SCHWARTZ, HENRY
PAINTER, INSTRUCTOR
b Winthrop, Mass, Oct 27, 27. Study: Sch Mus Fine Arts, Boston, traveling fel & dipl, 53; Akad Bildendedunst, Salzburg, Austria, with Oskar, Kokoschka, dipl. Work: Mus Fine Arts, Boston; Wheaton Col, Mass. Exhib: Boston Arts Festivals, 54-58; five one-man shows, Boris Mirski Gallery, 56-68; Carnegie Inst Int, 61; Harvard Univ, 75. Teaching: Instr painting, Sch Mus Fine Arts, 56- Style & Technique: Surrealist-expressionist. Media: Oil. Publ: Illusr, filmstrip, United Churches of Christ, 61; illusr, Boston Mag, 64-65. Mailing Add: 8 Garrison St Boston MA 02116

SCHWARTZ, MARVIN D
ART HISTORIAN
b New York, NY, Feb 15, 26. Study: City Col New York, BS, 46; Inst Fine Arts, NY Univ, 47-51; Univ Del, MA, 54. Teaching: Lectr, City Col New York, 48-51, 56-64; lectr, State Univ NY Col Purchase, 69- Pos: Jr cur, Detroit Inst Arts, 51-52; cur decorative arts & indust design lab, Brooklyn Mus, 54-68, ed publ, 59-60; adv dept design, Sears, Roebuck & Co, 64-72; lectr & consult, Metrop Mus Art, 68-; trustee, Jerome Levy Found; NY ed, Antique Monthly, 74- Awards: Recipient Stipend, Belg-Am Educ Found. Mem: Soc Archit Historians; Col Art Asn Am; fel H F DuPont Winterthur Mus. Publ: Auth, weekly antiques column, New York Times, 66-72; auth, Collectors Guide to Antique American Ceramics; auth, Collectors Guide to Antique American Glass; auth, Collectors Guide to American Clocks, 75; auth, Collectors Guide to American Silver, 75; plus many others. Mailing Add: Off Pub Educ Metrop Mus of Art New York NY 10028

SCHWARTZ, SING-SI
PHOTOGRAPHER
b New York, NY, Oct 20, 54. Study: New Sch for Social Res, advan photo printing with George Tice; psychol portraiture with Phillippe Halsman, 73; Rochester Inst Technol, AAS, 75. Comn: Photograph, Burma Airline & posters, Burma Govt, 71; photograph, Vt Bi-Centennial Comn, 75. Exhib: One-man shows, Pen & Brush Club, New York, 77, Rochester Inst Technol, NY, 77, Dawson Gristmill Gallery, Vt, 77 & Portchester Libr, NY, 78. Pos: Mem staff, Villager Newspaper, New York, 68-74; photogr/correspondent, Cosmorama Pictorial, Hong Kong, 70- Awards: Elected as one of 100 outstanding Chinese abroad for accomplishments in photography, Chinese Govt, Taiwan, 71-77. Bibliog: Beautiful girls of Hong Kong seen through the eyes of photographer Sing-Si Schwartz, Ming-Pao Weekly, Hong Kong, 8/15/71. Mem: Nat Arts Club; Am Soc Mag Photogr; Overseas Press Club. Publ: Photogr, Creating with Card Weaving, Crown Publ Inc, 73; contribr, photographs in Am Artist Mag, 74 & 78; photogr, The How and Why of Chinese Painting, Van Nostrand, 74; contribr, 40 American Watercolorists & How They Work, Watson-Guptill, 77; photogr, Joan Whitney Payson Gallery of Art, Westbrook Col, Maine, 77. Mailing Add: Nat Arts Club 15 Gramercy Park S New York NY 10003

SCHWARTZ, THERESE
PAINTER, WRITER
b New York, NY. Study: Corcoran Sch Art, Washington, DC; Am Univ; Brooklyn Mus Art Sch. Work: Corcoran Gallery Art; Howard Univ; Fred C Olsen Found; Ciba-Geigy Corp; Barnet Aden Collection. Comn: Traveling Watercolor Show, Howard Univ under Cong grant, Southern univs & mus, 53-54. Exhib: Phillips Mem Gallery, 54; Mus Art Mod, Paris, 56; Univ NC, 69; Stanford Mus, Conn, 72; Suffolk Co Mus, 72; plus others. Teaching: Instr fine arts, Fairleigh Dickinson Univ, currently. Pos: Ed, New York Element, 68-72; contrib ed, Feminist Art J; mem bd dirs, Princeton Arts J. Awards: Second Prize for Oils, Corcoran Gallery Art Regional Show, 52; New Talent USA Award, Art Am, 62; Women Artists Year Three, Mabel Smith Douglass Libr, Rutgers Univ, 73. Bibliog: S Zimmerman (auth), The unencumbered icon, 9/66 & G Brown (auth), Reviews, 9/69, Arts Mag; P Scheldjahl, New York, Art Int, 10/69. Style & Technique: Abstract, with areas of pure color. Publ: Auth, var articles, New York Element, 68-72; auth, Plastic Sculpture and Collage, Hearthside, 69; auth, The political scene, column in Arts Mag, 70-71; auth, The politicalization of the avant-garde (ser), Art in Am, 11/71, 3/72 & 3/73. Dealer: Landmark Gallery 469 Broome St New York NY 10013. Mailing Add: Apt 9A 161 W 75th St New York NY 10023

SCHWARTZ, WILLIAM S
PAINTER, LITHOGRAPHER
b Russia; US citizen. Study: Vilna Art Sch, Russia, 08-12; Art Inst Chicago, with hons, 15-17. Work: Art Inst Chicago & Springfield Mus, Ill; Joslyn Mus, Omaha, Nebr; Montclair Mus, NJ; Santa Barbara Mus, Calif; Libr Cong, Washington, DC. Comn: Chicago World's Fair, 33; Eldorado Post Off, Ill, 37; River Boat & Bridge, Fairfield Post Off, Ill, 37; Nurse Home in Cook Co, Chicago. Exhib: Three one-man shows, Art Inst Chicago; plus many traveling exhib. Awards: Marshall Fuller Prize, 27, M V Kohmstam Prize, 28 & John C Schafer Prize, 30, Art Inst Chicago. Bibliog: Manuel Chapman (auth), A Study, L M Stein Publ; Walter Blair (auth), article in Southwest Rev; Leo Katz (auth), Understanding Modern Art, Delphin Soc. articles in Chicago Tribune & other newspapers & periodicals. Mem: Alumni Art Inst Chicago; Philadelphia Watercolor Club. Style & Technique: Representational and abstract creative. Media: Watercolor, Oil. Mailing Add: 880 N Lake Shore Dr 18B Chicago IL 60611

SCHWARTZBAUM, PAUL MARTIN
CONSERVATOR
b Albany, NY, July 30, 46. Study: City Col New York, 63-67, BS, 67; NY Univ, Inst Fine Arts, 67-72, MA, 72, cert conserv, 72; Courtauld Inst, Technol Dept, intern, 70-71; Inst Royal du Patrimonie Artistique, 71-72, cert conserv, 72. Pos: Paintings conservator, Henry Francis du Pont Winterthur Mus, Del, 72- Mem: Int Inst Conserv Hist & Artistic Works; Am Inst Conserv Hist & Artistic Works; Int Coun Mus; Am Asn Mus; Washington Regional Conserv Guild. Publ: Auth, Conservation of a Late Gothic Chair Stall, 70. Mailing Add: Henry Francis du Pont Winterthur Mus Winterthur DE 19735

SCHWARZ, FELIX CONRAD
PAINTER, EDUCATOR
b New York, NY, Apr 13, 06. Study: Corcoran Sch Art; George Washington Univ; Columbia Univ; also study in Eng, France, Belg, Italy, Holland & Switz. Work: George Washington Univ. Comn: Many portraits for pvt comns. Exhib: One-man shows, Birmingham Mus Art, 68, Montgomery Mus Fine Arts, 68, Spring Hill Col, 69, Thor Gallery, Louisville, Ky, 69 & Sheridan Gallery, St Petersburg, 75; plus many others. Teaching: Prof fine arts at the State Univs of Va, NC, Minn & Wis over a period of 40 yrs; lectr hist & art appreciation, Inst of Lifetime Learning. Pos: Former ed, Advanced Sch Digest. Bibliog: Rev articles in La Rev Mod, Art News, New York Times, New York Herald Tribune & others. Media: Oil. Mailing Add: 1500 North Dakota Ave NE St Petersburg FL 33703

SCHWARZ, GLADYS
PAINTER
b New York, NY. Study: Art Students League, with George Grosz; Pratt Graphic Workshop; Blackburn Graphic Workshop. Work: Collectors Am Art; plus several pvt collections. Comn: Series of rehearsal drawings for Broadway plays comn by producers, Raisin in the Sun, 58-59 & The Sign in Sidney Brusteins Window, 64. Exhib: Butler Inst Am Art, Youngstown, Ohio, 69; one-woman shows, Ella Lerner Gallery, New York, 70, Damon Runyon-Winchell Gallery, New York, 75, Heritage Gallery, Los Angeles & Palm Springs Mus, Calif, 78; 13th Ann Nat Print & Drawing Exhib, Okla Art Inst, 71; Graphic Nat Print & Drawing Exhib,

West NMex, 71. Teaching: Pvt instr oil, watercolor & drawing classes, New York, 58-68; instr watercolor & drawing, Craft Students League, New York, 60-68. Awards: Hon Mention, 5th Ann Nat Print Exhib, Springfield, Mass, 72. Mem: Life mem Art Students League. Style & Technique: Prismatic realistic oils and watercolors; drawing and etching. Dealer: Heritage Gallery 718 N La Cienega Blvd Los Angeles CA 90069. Mailing Add: 444 Central Park W New York NY 10025

SCHWARZ, KURT L
ART DEALER, ART HISTORIAN
b Vienna, Austria, Apr 5, 09; US citizen. Study: Inst for Art Hist, Univ Vienna, PhD. Pos: Owner, Kurt L Schwarz & Martha M Schwarz—Antiquarian & Art Books, 47- Mem: Antiquarian Booksellers Asn of Am (chap chmn, 63-65); Antiquarian Booksellers Asn Int, Eng; Art Libr Soc NAm. Specialty: Rare books on the arts, prints. Mailing Add: 738 S Bristol Ave Los Angeles CA 90049

SCHWARZ, MYRTLE COOPER
DESIGNER, MOSAIC ARTIST
b Breckenridge Co, Ky, Dec 10, 00. Study: Western Ky State Univ, AB; Col William & Mary, MA; Columbia Univ, MA & EdD. Exhib: One-man shows, Col William & Mary, Phillips Univ, Okla State Univ, Monticello Col & Univ Wis; Art Club & Art Ctr, St Petersburg, Fla; Sheridan Gallery, St Petersburg; Gulf Coast Art Ctr, Clearwater, Fla. plus numerous nat & regional shows. Teaching: Instr, Exten Serv, Univ Ky; prof educ, Col William & Mary; prin high sch & supt schs, Va & Ky; prof art educ & dir, Community Ctr, Phillips Univ; prof educ & dir art educ, Okla State Univ; vis prof, Monticello Col; prof Eng, Wis State Univ; instr creative crafts, Continuing Educ, Inst for Lifetime Learning. Pos: Chmn math & pres art sect, Va Educ Asn; mem comt, Seven Coop Univs Teacher Training; chmn Lang Arts Develop, Va State Curriculum; mem comt, Prof Standards & Develop, Nat Educ Asn; dir, Community Art Ctr, Enid, Okla. Mem: Enid Artists League; Univ Women's Serv Club; Nat Art Educ Asn (chmn Div Higher Educ & Teacher Training). Style & Technique: Mosaic murals, some pictorial and some abstract, designed with ceramic tile and stained glass, satirically interpreting the political and social scene. Media: Stained Glass, Ceramics. Publ: Auth, articles in Va J Educ, In Ky & Okla J Educ. Mailing Add: 1500 North Dakota Ave NE St Petersburg FL 33703

SCHWEDLER, WM A
PAINTER
b Chicago, Ill, Mar 22, 42. Study: Art Inst Chicago, BFA, 64; Pratt Inst, MFA, 66. Work: Art Inst Chicago; Philadelphia Mus; Whitney Mus; Hirshhorn Mus, Washington, DC; Mass Inst Technol. Exhib: Toward a New Metaphysics, Allan Frumkin Gallery, New York, 70; one-man shows, Pyramid Gallery, Washington, DC, 70, Kornblee Gallery, New York, 72; Phyllis Kind Gallery, Chicago, 73 & Andrew Crispo Gallery, New York, 75. Awards: James Nelson Raymond Traveling Fel, Art Inst Chicago, 64. Bibliog: John Perreault (auth), William Schwedler, Pa State Univ, 69; James Speyer (auth), William Schwedler, Pyramid Gallery, 70. Dealer: Pyramid Gallery 2121 P St NW Washington DC 20037. Mailing Add: 52 White St New York NY 10013

SCHWEISS, RUTH KELLER
SCULPTOR, DESIGNER
US citizen. Study: Wash Univ, St Louis, fine arts cert; Cranbrook Art Acad, Bloomfield Hills, Mich, three yr int fel, sculpture with Carl Milles. Work: Cranbrook Art Mus; plus many pvt collections. Comn: Life size garden sculpture, comn by Lawrence Roos, St Louis, 65; bear for pool garden, comn by J A Baer, II, St Louis, 70; Blachette (six ft bronze), Founder Monument, St Charles, Mo, 72; Children in the Rain, Ger Coun, Hamm, Ger, 73; Sons of Founders (bronze reliefs), Stix, Baer & Fuller, St Louis, 75. Exhib: Nat Acad Design, New York, 43; Detroit Art Mus Regional Show, Mich, 43; Pacific Show, Hawaiian Art Mus, Honolulu, 44; Int Art Show, Rotunda Gallery, London, 73; Ars Longa Gallery, Houston, 74. Awards: Mus Purchase Prize, Cranbrook Art Mus, 42; Ruth Renfrow Sculpture Prize, St Louis Art Mus, 45; Thalinger Sculpture Prize, St Louis Artists Guild, 50. Bibliog: Blanchett, Garden sculpture & other articles, St Louis Post Dispatch & Globe Dem, 55-75; Ruth Keller Schweiss, Gonterman Assoc, 65; The World of Ruth Keller Schweiss (film), Rick Noel, 74. Mem: Acad Prof Artists (exec secy, 68-75); Nat Soc Arts & Lett (corresp secy, 69-71, treas, 75-); Media Nine; St Louis Artists Guild (secy & mem bd, 65-67). Style & Technique: Impressionist; direct carving and direct modeling in metal epoxies; fired clay portraits. Media: Bronze Castings of Limited Editions from Any Carved or Modeled Medium. Mailing Add: 4 Daniel Rd St Louis MO 63124

SCHWEITZER, GERTRUDE
PAINTER, SCULPTOR
b New York, NY. Study: Pratt Inst; Nat Acad Design, New York; Acad Julian, Paris. Work: Metrop Mus Art, New York; Art Inst Chicago; Toledo Mus Art; Brooklyn Mus; Whitney Mus Am Art, New York; plus many others. Exhib: One-man exhibs, Norton Gallery Art, West Palm Beach, 47 & 66, Galerie Charpentier, Paris, 48, 54 & 61, Hanover Gallery, London, 53, Philadelphia Art Alliance, 69 & Hokin Gallery, Palm Beach, 71; plus many others. Pos: Chmn arts & skill corps, Am Red Cross, 42-45. Awards: Am Watercolor Soc Medal, 34; Soc Four Arts Awards in Watercolor, 48 & 59 & Awards in Oils, 50 & 51; NJ State Exhib First Prize as Best Woman Painter, Montclair Art Mus, 52; plus many others. Bibliog: Rene Barotte (auth), G Schweitzer, Peintures et Dessins, Ed Chene, Paris, 65. Mem: Nat Acad Design; Audubon Artists; Am Artists Prof League; Am Watercolor Soc. Mailing Add: Stone Hill Farm Colts Neck NJ 07722

SCHWEITZER, M R
ART DEALER, COLLECTOR
b Sept 7, 11. Pos: Owner, M R Schweitzer Galleries. Mem: Charter mem, Am Soc Appraisers. Res: American painting by little-known masters, 1830-1930. Specialty: American painting, 1830-1930; European painting, 16th to 19th centuries. Collection: American 20th century and English 19th century; Catalan, Spanish and Italian 17th century. Mailing Add: 958 Madison Ave New York NY 10021

SCHWEIZER, PAUL DOUGLAS
ART HISTORIAN, CURATOR
b Brooklyn, NY, Nov 26, 46. Study: Marietta Col, Ohio, BA, 68, Univ Del, MA, 74, PhD candidate, 76. Collections Arranged: Avant-Garde Painting & Sculpture in America: 1910-25 (collab effort; co-auth, catalogue), Del Art Mus, spring 75; A Catalogue of the Choptank Collection, Middletown, Del, 75. Teaching: Instr art hist, Univ Del, Wilmington, 76; instr art hist, St Lawrence Univ, 77-78, asst prof fine arts, 78- Pos: Consult, Choptank Collection, Middletown, Del, 76-; consult, The Art Searcher, Gloucester, Mass, 77-; cur collections, St Lawrence Univ, Canton, NY, 77-78. Awards: Unidel Fel, Univ Del, 72-76. Mem: Col Art Asn; Victorian Soc in Am (exec comt, Wilmington Chap); St Lawrence Co Hist Soc; Mid-Am Col Art Asn; Down Jersey Marine Hist Soc. Res: John Constable and his influence in America; Edward Moran and American marine painting; American academic painting of the late 19th century. Publ: Auth, Genteel taste at the National Academy of Design, Am Art Rev, 75; auth, John Constable and the Rainbow, Studies in Art Hist, Univ Md, 76; auth, Stieglitz material given to St Lawrence University, Bull of Friends of Owen B Young Libr, 78. Mailing Add: Dept of Fine Arts St Lawrence Univ Canton NY 13617

SCHWIDDER, ERNST CARL
SCULPTOR, DESIGNER
b St Louis, Mo, Nov 9, 31. Study: Univ Wash, BA, 53 & MFA, 55. Comn: Stone sculpture & carved wood furniture, St John Lutheran Church, Westfield, Mass, 64; wood sculpture & carved wood furniture, Faith Lutheran Church, Detroit, Mich, 67, St Joseph Cath Church, Chicago, 72 & St Matthew Lutheran Church, Portland, Ore, 75; cast concrete sculpture, Tower, Demaray Hall, Seattle Pac Univ, 68; bronze sculpture & stone furniture, Our Savior Lutheran Church, Everett, Wash, 69; wood sculpture, Hope Lutheran Church, Bradenton, Fla, 74. Exhib: Eight Washington Artists, Portland Art Mus, 55; Mus Mod Art Int Biennial, Sao Paulo, Brazil, 55; Pacific Coast Art, San Francisco Mus Art, 56; Artists West of the Mississippi, Colorado Springs Art Ctr, 57; Cult Exchange Expos, Moscow, USSR, 59. Teaching: Chmn sculpture & design, Valparaiso Univ, Ind, 58-61 & Seattle Pac Univ, 63-67; chmn sculpture & design, Pac Lutheran Univ, Tacoma, 67-, prof, 75- Pos: Consult designer, Charles Edward Stade & Assocs, Park Ridge, Ill, 61- Style & Technique: Figurative, yet strongly allegorical in content. Media: Wood, Fabricated & Cast Metal, Cast Concrete, Stone. Mailing Add: Box 520 Steilacoom WA 98388

SCHWIEGER, C ROBERT
PRINTMAKER, EDUCATOR
b Scottsbluff, Nebr, Dec 5, 36. Study: Nebr Western Col, AA; Chadron State Col, BFA(educ); Univ Northern Colo, MA; Univ Denver, MFA. Work: Ohio State Univ; Univ Dallas; WTex Mus, Lubbock; Univ Calif, San Diego. Comn: Gilded gold and mixed media on glass mural, Univ Northern Colo, 66. Exhib: 12th Midwest Biennial, Joslyn Art Mus, Omaha, 72; 1st Miami Graphics Biennial, Miami Art Ctr, 73; Drawing Exhib, State Univ NY Col Potsdam, 73 & 75; 35th Exhib Contemp Art, Soc Four Arts, Palm Beach, 74; New Photographics/75, Cent Wash State Col, 75; plus others. Teaching: Assoc prof & chmn div art, Minot State Col, 67- Awards: Purchase Award, Western NMex Univ, 71; Northwest Printmakers Int Jury Commendation, Seattle Art Mus, 71; 16th Nat Print & Drawing Exhib Jury Commendation, Okla Art Ctr, 74. Mem: Col Art Asn Am. Publ: Contribr, Col Educ Rec, 6/69. Mailing Add: 706 25th St NW Minot ND 58701

SCHWIERING, CONRAD
PAINTER
b Boulder, Colo, Aug 8, 16. Study: Univ Wyo, BA; Art Students League; Grand Cent Sch Art, New York; Am Mus Nat Hist, New York; study with Bert Phillips, Taos, NMex, Charles S Chapman, New York & George B Bridgman, New York. Work: Nat Cowboy Hall of Fame, Oklahoma City; Whitney Gallery Western Art, Cody, Wyo; Long Beach Art Mus, Calif; Wyo State Mus, Cheyenne; Mont Hist Soc, Helena. Exhib: Allied Artists Am, New York, 54; Whitney Gallery Western Art, Cody, 64 & 70; Springville Nat Ann Art Exhib, Utah, 66; Nat Acad Western Art, Nat Cowboy Hall of Fame, 72-77; Kansas City Soc Western Art, Mo, 74. Teaching: Instr fine art, Univ Wyo, Laramie, 49; instr mountain landscape, Teton Artists Asn, Jackson Hole, 57-64. Awards: Medal Honor, Grand Cent Sch Art, 41; Best of Show, Springville Nat Art Show, 66. Bibliog: Robert Wakefield (auth), Schwiering & the West, North Plains Press, Aberdeen, SDak, 73; Jack Rosenthal (auth), Conrad Schwiering-Mountain Painter, TV documentary, Harriscope Broadcasting Corp, Los Angeles, 73; Dean Krakel, II (auth), Painter of the Tetons, Persimmon Hill Mag, Nat Cowboy Hall of Fame & Western Heritage, Oklahoma City. Mem: Soc Western Artists; Nat Acad Western Art; Am Inst Fine Art. Style & Technique: Impressionist with emphasis on study of moods and light a la prima. Media: Oil. Publ: Contribr, Cowboy in Art, 68; contribr, Western Painting Today, 75. Dealer: Grand Cent Art Galleries Madison Ave & E 43rd St New York NY 10017; Trailside Galleries 7330 Scottsdale Mall Scottsdale AZ 85251. Mailing Add: Star Rte Box 223 Jackson Hole WY 83001

SCHWINGER, SYLVIA
ART DEALER, PAINTER
b Passaic, NJ. Work: Temple Beth Abraham, New York. Exhib: NJ Miniature Soc, Nutley, 74; Westfield Art Exhib, Union, NJ, 75. Collections Arranged: Art on Paper, 74, Wonderful World of Art, 75, Japanese Woodblock Prints & Etchings, 75, American, European and Israeli Contemporary Art, 75, Bicentennial—An American Portrait, 76, Etchings by American Artists, 76 & Focus on Women, 77, Nutley Art Gallery, Ltd. Pos: Dir, Nutley Art Gallery, Ltd, 73- Mem: Bloomfield Art League (ed, newsletter, 75). Style & Technique: Realistic landscapes and portraits; primitives; religious wall hanging. Media: Oil and acrylic; Wool. Specialty: Contemporary limited edition graphics; master prints; Judaica. Collection: Master prints and sculptures of contemporary artists; Louis Icart drypoint etchings. Mailing Add: c/o Nutley Art Gallery Ltd 509 Franklin Ave Nutley NJ 07110

SCOTT, ARDEN
SCULPTOR
b Port Chester, NY, Oct 21, 38. Comn: Nassau Co Mus Fine Arts, NY, 77. Exhib: Drawing in Space-19 American Sculptors, Katonah Gallery, New York, 72; Whitney Mus Biennial, 73; Front & Center, NY Sculpture, Wayne, NJ, 74; one-person show, 112 Green Gallery, NY, 74; O K Harris Gallery, New York, 75; Outdoor Sculpture, Merriewold West, 76; Forms in Focus, Coop City Gallery, 77. Teaching: Prof sculpture, Bard Col, 75- & Parsons Sch Design, 78. Bibliog: Marcia Tucker (auth), Making it big, MS Mag, 4/74. Style & Technique: Large scale sculpture. Media: Wood. Dealer: O K Harris Gallery 340 W Broadway New York NY 10013. Mailing Add: 73 Leonard St New York NY 10013

SCOTT, CAMPBELL
PRINTMAKER, SCULPTOR
b Milngavie, Scotland, Oct 5, 30; Can citizen. Study: Studied with S W Hayter in Paris; Glasgow Sch Art, Scotland; five yr apprenticeship with a woodcarver, Scotland. Work: British Mus, London, Eng; Bibliot Nat, Paris, France; Scottish Nat Gallery Mod Art; Montreal Mus Art, Can; Victoria & Albert Mus, London, Eng. Comn: Bronze sculpture, Pub Libr, Niagara Falls, Can; wood sculpture, Pub Libr, St Catharines, Can. Exhib: 1st Biennial Int Graphics, Krakow, Poland, 66; FAAP Gravura, Sao Paulo, Brazil, 68; 1st British Int Print Biennale, Gt Brit, 69; Traveling Exhib, Nat Gallery Can, Ottawa, 69; 4th Am Biennial Engraving, Santiago, Chile, 70; Exhib Can Graphics, Can Embassy, Washington, DC, 71 & Pratt Inst, New York, 71. Mem: Can Graphic Arts Soc. Style & Technique: Woodcuts; etchings; engravings; sculpture; modern jewelry. Mailing Add: 89 Byron Niagara on the Lake ON L0S 1J0 Can

SCOTT, CURTIS S
CERAMIST, EDUCATOR
b San Diego, Calif, July 25, 46. Study: Tex Tech Univ, BFA; Tex Christian Univ, MFA. Work: Ark Art Ctr, Little Rock. Exhib: Southwestern Crafts Biennial, Mus NMex, Santa Fe, 71 & 77; 15th Delta Exhib, Ark Art Ctr, 72; 19th & 20th Ann Drawing & Sculpture Show, Ball State Univ, 73 & 74; Drawings 74 Nat Exhib, Watson Gallery, Wheaton Col, Mass, 74; Ariz Nat Exhib Crafts, Scottsdale Ctr for the Arts, 76; one-man shows, Frontroom Craft Gallery, Dallas, Tex, 76, Nice Things, Austin, 76 & Okla Art Ctr, Oklahoma City, 77. Teaching: Teaching asst drawing, Tex Christian Univ, 69-71; asst prof ceramics & drawing, Amarillo Col, 71-77. Awards: Grand Prize Painting, 14th Delta Exhib, Ark Art Ctr, 71; Pottery Award, 15th Tex Crafts Exhib, Dallas Mus Fine Arts, 71; Pottery Purchase, Southwestern Crafts Biennial, Mus NMex, 71 & 77. Mem: Am Crafts Coun. Style & Technique: Wheelthrown Raku pottery. Media: Ceramics, Drawing. Publ: Contribr, Surface treatments for Raku, Ceramics Mo, 78. Dealer: Southwest Craft Ctr Gallery 420 Paseo Dr La Villita San Antonio TX 78205; Okla Art Ctr Sales Gallery 3113 Gen Pershing Blvd Oklahoma City OK 73107. Mailing Add: 33 Misti Lane Rt 1 Driftwood TX 78619

SCOTT, DAVID WINFIELD
ART ADMINISTRATOR
b Fall River, Mass, July 10, 16. Study: Art Students League; Harvard Col, AB; Claremont Grad Sch, MA & MFA; Univ Calif, Berkeley, PhD. Pos: From lectr art to prof, Scripps Col, 46-63; dir, Nat Collection Fine Arts, Washington, DC, 64-69; consult, Nat Gallery Art, Washington, DC, 69- Mailing Add: 3016 Cortland Pl NW Washington DC 20008

SCOTT, HENRY (EDWARDS), JR
PAINTER, EDUCATOR
b Cambridge, Mass, Aug 22, 00. Study: Harvard Univ, Sachs fel, 25, Bacon art scholar, 26-28, BA & MA; Art Students League; also with Edward Forbes, Italy. Work: Fogg Art Mus, Cambridge; Univ Kans Med Ctr & Univ Mo, Kansas City; Amherst Col; Regency House, Kansas City. Comn: Originated & directed stage production of Giotto's Frescoes of the Nativity, Pittsburgh, 32-33, Amherst Col, 35-; stage designs for Amherst Masquers, 35-36; stage designs for Univ Kansas City Playhouse, 49-50; also many portraits. Exhib: Amherst Col, 41; Springfield, Mass, 42; Boston & Cambridge, Mass, 47; four shows, Martha's Vineyard, 47-63; Kansas City, Mo, 50-69; plus others. Collections Arranged: Eight exhibs yearly, Univ Mo-Kansas City, 48-65. Teaching: Lectr & asst head tutor, Div Fine Arts, Harvard Univ & Radcliffe Col, 23-26; instr art, Univ Rochester, 28-29; asst prof art, Univ Pittsburgh, 29-34; assoc prof art, Amherst Col, 35-43; assoc prof art, Univ Mo-Kansas City, 47-59, chmn dept art, 47-64, prof, 59-70, emer prof, 70 Pos: Asst to dir, Mem Art Gallery, Univ Rochester, 28-29; cur art, Amherst Col, 38-43; mem, Munic Art Comn, Kansas City, Mo, 54-69. Awards: Prize, Rochester Art Asn, 28. Mem: Col Art Asn Am; Am Asn Univ Prof. Style & Technique: Representational; some abstractions. Media: Watercolor, Oil. Publ: Auth, Historical Outline of the Fine Arts, 36. Mailing Add: South Rd Chilmark MA 02535

SCOTT, JOHN TARRELL
EDUCATOR, SCULPTOR, PRINTMAKER
b New Orleans, La, June 30, 40. Study: Xavier Univ La, BA, 62; Mich State Univ, MFA, 65. Work: Johnson Publ Co, Chicago, Ill; Golden State Mutual Life Insurance Co, Los Angeles, Calif. Comn: Relief wall sculpture, Civic Ctr, Naples Co, Fla, 60-61; bronze pieta (3/4 life-size), Edgewood United Church, Lansing, Mich, 64; Madonna & St Joseph (life-size steel), St Angela Marici Church, Metaire, La, 68; life-size steel figure, Mt Carmel High Sch, New Orleans, 76. Exhib: Young Am, New Orleans, La, 59; two-person show, Orleans Gallery, New Orleans, 66; Drawing Exhib, La State Univ, New Orleans, 66; Black Am Artists Nat, Ill Bell Tel Co, Chicago, 70; Fiske Univ, Nashville, Tenn, 73; The Classic Revival, Ill Bell Tel Co, 75; Migrations, Colombia, SAm, 76; Mitchell Mus, Mt Vernon, Ill, 76. Teaching: Prof printmaking & sculpture & chmn art dept, Xavier Univ of La, New Orleans, 65- Pos: Mem environmental design adv bd, City of New Orleans, 74-; co-host, Nat/Int Sculpture Conf, New Orleans, 75. Mem: Creative Artists Alliance of New Orleans. Style & Technique: Figurative/abstraction dealing with the condition of man. Media: Lithograph, Etching for Print; Bronze, Steel for Sculpture. Mailing Add: Dept of Art Xavier Univ of La Palmetto & Pine Sts New Orleans LA 70125

SCOTT, JONATHAN
PAINTER
b Bath, Eng, Oct 30, 14. Study: Heatherly Sch, London; Mauritz Heymann Sch, Munich; The Accad, Florence. Work: Pasadena Art Mus, Calif; Santa Fe, NMex; Lindsay Art Asn, Calif; San Marino High Sch, Calif; G G de Silva Collection, Los Angeles. Comn: Paintings, USN Art Prog, 63-64; also portrait comns. Exhib: New Eng Art Club, London, 38; Los Angeles Mus; Frye Mus, Seattle; McNay Mus, San Antonio, 62; Southwest Fine Arts Biennial, Santa Fe, NMex, 74; Santa Barbara Mus, Calif; Occidental Col, Los Angeles, 76; Butler Inst Am Art, Youngstown, Ohio; Ringling Mus, Sarasota, Fla; Mus Maritime, Paris, France; Kramer Gallery, Los Angeles; Stables Gallery, Taos, NMex; plus others. Teaching: Instr drawing & painting, Univ Southern Calif, 46; instr drawing & painting, Pasadena Art Mus, 47-48; instr drawing & painting, Riverside Art Asn, 62-63. Awards: Awards, Calif Watercolor Soc, 55, Laguna Beach Art Asn, 61 & NMex Watercolor Soc, 74. Mem: Nat Watercolor Soc (pres, 60); Taos Art Asn (art comt & mem bd, 72). Style & Technique: Semi-abstract birds, animals and human figures. Media: Oil, Watercolor. Dealer: Stables Gallery Taos NM 87571. Mailing Add: PO Box 1154 Taos NM 87571

SCOTT, MARIAN (DALE)
PAINTER
b Montreal, Que, June 26, 06. Study: Montreal Art Asn, 17-20, scholar; Monument Nat, 18-20, with Dionnet; Ecole Beaux Arts, Montreal, 23-25; Slade Sch, London. Work: Nat Gallery Can, Ottawa; McGill Univ Art Collection, Montreal; Montreal Mus Fine Arts; Mus Quebec; Dept External Affairs, Ottawa, Mus Art Contemporain, Montreal. Comn: Oils, Endocrinology, Dr Hans Selye, McGill Univ, 43 & Tree of Life, Mrs Paul Sise, Montreal Gen Hosp Chapel, 58. Exhib: New York World's Fair, 39; Panorama, Peinture du Quebec, Mus Art Contemporain, 40-66; Biennale, Sao Paulo, Brazil, 51-53; 50 Years of Canadian Painting, Nat Gallery Can; Expos Createurs Quebec, 71. Teaching: Instr painting, St George's Sch, Montreal, 37-39; instr painting, Montreal Mus Fine Arts, 42-45. Awards: First Prize for Painting, Can Group Painters, 66; Purchase Award, Thomas More Inst, Montreal, 67; Baxter Purchase Award, Ont Soc Artists. Mem: Royal Can Acad Arts. Media: Acrylic. Mailing Add: 451 Clarke Ave Montreal PQ H3Y 3C5 Can

SCOTT, SAM
PAINTER, INSTRUCTOR
b Chicago, Ill, Apr 7, 40. Study: Univ Mich, BFA; Md Inst Col Art, MFA; also with Grace Hartigan, David Hare, Joseph Goto, Zubel Kachadoorian. Work: NMex Fine Arts Mus, Santa Fe; Roswell Mus Fine Arts, NMex. Comn: Mural painting, Westinghouse Elec Corp Bldg, Norman, Okla, 72; mural, Jelco Corp Bldg, Minneapolis, Minn, 72. Exhib: Corcoran Mus Ann, Washington, DC, 67; 73rd Western Ann, Denver Art Mus, 71; Richard Demarco Edinburgh Festival Show, Scotland, 73; one-man show, Mus NMex, Santa Fe, 74; Biennial Contemp Am Art, Whitney Mus Am Art, New York, 75. Teaching: Instr painting, Md Inst Col Art, 67-69; instr painting, St Johns Col, Santa Fe, 71- Awards: Walters Fine Arts Mus Traveling Grant, Baltimore, 67; Weatherhead Found Purchase Prize, Cleveland, Ohio, 70; NMex Arts Comn Prize, 73. Bibliog: V G Kirby (auth), Sam Scott, another universe, Southwest Gallery Mag, 72; Arthur Sussman (auth), Paintings of Sam Scott, The aesthetic end, KOAT TV, Albuquerque, 5/19/74. Style & Technique: Lyric expressionist. Media: Oil on Canvas. Publ: Contribr, NMex Mag, 71. Dealer: Tibor de Nagy Gallery 1106 Berthea Houston TX 77006. Mailing Add: 149 Mesa Verde St Santa Fe NM 87501

SCOTT, WALTER
PAINTER, ARCHITECT
b Pittsburgh, Pa, May 24, 19. Study: Carnegie Inst Technol, BArch, 41, with Sam Rosenberg, Kindred McCleary & Camille Grapin. Exhib: New Rochelle Art Asn, NY, 65; Westchester Art Soc Open, White Plains, NY, 66-68; New Eng Exhib, Silvermine Guild of Artists, New Canaan, Conn, 65-76; Nat Soc of Painters in Casein & Acrylic Ann, New York, 72-78; NJ Painters & Sculptors Soc Ann, Nat Arts Club, New York, 76; Hudson River Open, Hudson River Mus, Yonkers, NY, 76-77; one-man shows, Mamaronek Artists Guild, NY, 72 & Briarcliff Col, NY, 75. Pos: Architect, Harrison & Abramovitz, Architects, New York, 48- Awards: John Kellam, 66, Roy Johnson, 69, Silvermine Guild Award, 72 & Koenig Art, 74, New Eng Exhib, Silvermine Guild; Hyplar Award, Nat Soc Painters Casein & Acrylic Ann, Grumbacher, 72; Geigy Award, Hudson River Mus Open, Geigy Chemical Co, 67. Mem: Silvermine Guild of Artists (exhib comt, 72-73); Nat Soc Painters Casein & Acrylic (bd dir, 77-78); Hudson River Contemp Artists; Artists Equity Asn; Am Inst of Architects. Style & Technique: Abstract to distilled representational painting. Media: Acrylic, Oil, Watercolor. Dealer: Silvermine Guild of Artists New Canaan CT 06840. Mailing Add: 266 Pennsylvania Ave Crestwood NY 10707

SCOTT-GIBSON, HERBERT NATHANIEL
ART ADMINISTRATOR, EDUCATOR
b Danville, Ill, Mar 13, 28. Study: Univ Ill, BS(music educ); Boston Univ, MFA. Pos: Mus educator-in-charge, Metrop Mus of Art Community Prog, 77- Mem: Brooklyn Mus (gov); Brooklyn Inst of Art & Sci (trustee); Brooklyn Arts & Cult Asn (dir, bd mem). Mailing Add: Metrop Mus of Art New York NY 10028

SCRIVER, ROBERT MACFIE (BOB)
SCULPTOR
b Browning, Mont, Aug 15, 14. Study: Carroll Col, Helena, Mont, hon PhD(art), 76. Work: Glenbow Found, Calgary, Alta; Whitney Gallery Western Art, Cody, Wyo; Mont Hist Soc, Helena; Cowboy Hall Fame, Oklahoma City; Panhandle Plains Mus, Canyon, Tex. Comn: Over life size statue of bison, Great Falls High Sch, Mont, 67; Bill Linderman (heroic statue), Rodeo Cowboy Asn for Cowboy Hall of Fame, Oklahoma City, 68; Rustler (statue), C M Russell High Sch, Great Falls, 68; plus many others. Exhib: Soc Animal Artists, New York, 61; Audubon Artists, New York, 64; Nat Acad Design, New York, 64; Acad Artists, Springfield, Mass, 64; Int Art Guild, D'Palais de la Scala, Monte Carlo, Monaco, 67; Acad Western Art, Cowboy Hall of Fame, Oklahoma City, 73; Allied Art Ctr, Calgary, Alta, 73; one-man show, Stremmel Galleries at Security N Bank, Reno, Nev, 75; Nat Sculpture Soc Bronze, Tex, 75; Rodeo in Bronze Series, Wells Fargo Bank, San Francisco, 76; Grand Central Art Gallery, New York, 76; plus many one-man shows. Awards: Gold Medals, Cowboy Hall of Fame, 69-71, Silver Medal, 72; Silver Medal, Nat Acad Western Art, 73; plus others. Bibliog: Article in Am Artist Mag, 63; article in La Rev Mod, 64; article in Mont Hist Soc. Mem: Salmagundi Club; Nat Sculpture Soc; Cowboy Artists Am; academician Nat Acad Western Art. Style & Technique: Realistic. Media: Bronze. Publ: Auth, An Honest Try, 75. Mailing Add: Box 172 Browning MT 59417

SCULLY, VINCENT
ART HISTORIAN, EDUCATOR
b New Haven, Conn, Aug 21, 20. Study: Yale Univ, BA, 40, MA, 47, PhD, 49. Teaching: Asst, Yale Univ, 47-48, instr, 49-52, Morse fel, 51, asst prof, 52-56, assoc prof, 56-61, prof, 61-66, Col John Trumbull prof hist art, 66- Awards: Howard Found Fel, Sicily, 56; Bollingen Fel, Greece & Turkey, 57-58; Nat Humanities Found Sr Fel, 72-73; plus others. Mem: Col Art Asn Am; Soc Archit Historians; Conn Bldg Cong; Conn Acad Arts & Sci. Publ: Auth, The Shingle Style and the Stick Style, Yale Univ, 55 & 71; auth, Modern Architecture, 61 & 74 & Louis I Kahn, 62, Braziller; auth, The Earth, the Temple and the Gods, Yale Univ, 62 & Praeger, 69; auth, American Architecture and Urbanism, Praeger, 69; auth, Pueblo Mountain Village Dance, Viking, 75; plus others. Mailing Add: 389 St Ronan St New Haven CT 06511

SCURIS, STEPHANIE
SCULPTOR, EDUCATOR
b Lacedaemonos, Greece, Jan 20, 31. Study: Sch Art & Archit, Yale Univ, BFA & MFA, with Josef Albers. Work: Jewish Community Ctr, Baltimore, West View Ctr, Baltimore. Comn: Sculpture, Bankers Trust Co, New York; lobby sculpture, Cinema I & II, New York. Exhib: New Haven Art Festival, 58-59; Art: USA Traveling Exhib, 58 & 60; Mus Mod Art, New York, 62; Whitney Mus Am Art, New York, 64; plus others. Teaching: Instr sculpture, Md Inst Art, 61- Awards: Winterwitz Award, Prize for Outstanding Work & Alumni Award, Yale Univ; Peabody Award, 61-62; Rinehart Fel, 61-64. Mailing Add: Md Inst of Art 116 W Lanvale St Baltimore MD 21217

SEABOURN, BERT DAIL
PAINTER, ILLUSTRATOR
b Iraan, Tex, July 9, 31. Study: Oklahoma City Univ, cert in art; Famous Artists Schs, Westport, Conn, cert in art; Okla Cent State Univ. Work: Okla Art Ctr, Oklahoma City; Five Civilized Tribes Mus, Muskogee, Okla; Heard Mus, Phoenix; Vatican Mus Mod Religious Art, Italy; Pac Northwest Indian Ctr, Gonzaga Univ. Exhib: Kans Printmakers Nat, Wichita, 61; Contemp Am Art Ann, Oklahoma City, 64; Int Petrol Art Exhib, Tulsa, Okla, 66; Ctr Arts of Indian Am, Washington, DC, 68; Eight State Painting & Sculpture Ann, Oklahoma City, 71. Pos: Artist & journalist, USN, 51-55; art dir & artist, Okla Gas & Elec Co, Oklahoma City, 55- Awards: Grand Award, Five Civilized Tribes Mus, 73; Grand Award, Red Cloud Indian Ann, 74; Special Award, Scottsdale Ann, 75. Mem: Artists of Okla, Inc (pres, 69); Art Dirs Club Oklahoma City (pres, 70); Okla Art Guild (pres, 70); Southwest Watercolor Asn; Okla City Advert Club. Style & Technique: Very loose, depicting symbolism in exploring Indian legends and folklore. Media: Watercolor, Acrylic. Publ: Auth & illusr, Indian Gallery, 72. Mailing Add: 6105 Covington Lane Oklahoma City OK 73132

SEACE, BARRY WILLIAM
PRINTMAKER, EDUCATOR
b Harrisburg, Pa, Oct 10, 46. Study: Kutztown State Col, with Frederick Keller, BS(art educ), 68; Univ Tenn, with Byron McKeeby, MFA(printmaking), 72. Work: Montgomery Mus Fine Art, Ala; Northern Ill Univ Ctr Gallery, DeKalb; Tenn State Mus, Nashville; Libr Cong Print Collection, Washington, DC; Calif Col Arts & Crafts, San Francisco. Exhib: Colorprint USA, Lubbock, Tex, 71, 73, 74; Boston Printmakers 25th Anniversary Exhib, 73; New Orleans Int Exhib, 74; Nat Drawing Exhib, Southern Ill Univ, DeKalb, 75; Springfield 56th Nat Exhib, Mus Fine Art, Mass, 75; one-man show, Montreal Mus Fine Arts, Que, 76. Teaching: Teaching asst drawing, Univ Tenn, Knoxville, 70-72; asst prof printmaking, Mt Holyoke Col, 72- Awards: Purchase Award, 4th Ann Nat Graphics Exhib, DeKalb, 71; Purchase Award, 8th Ann Nat Print & Drawing Competition, Dulin Gallery, 73; Merit Award, Springfield 56th Nat, Mus Fine Art, Mass, 75. Mem: Col Art Asn Am; Graphics Soc, Hollis, NH; Springfield Art League; Friends of Art, Mt Holyoke Col. Style & Technique: Experimental printmaking, hand drawn imagery as well as video manipulated images that are translated into photo intaglio or photo serigraphy. Media: Intaglio, Relief, Lithography, Screen Printing. Dealer: Ferdinand Roten Galleries Inc 123 W Mulberry St Baltimore MD 21201. Mailing Add: 5 Stanton Ave South Hadley MA 01075

SEAMAN, DRAKE F
PAINTER
US citizen. Study: Kachina Art Sch, 59-63, with Jay Datus; also murals with Ray Strong, 70. Comn: Landscape mural, Seventh Day Adventist Church, Santa Barbara, Calif. Exhib: Palace Arts & Sci, San Francisco, 70; Santa Barbara Mus Art, 70; O'Brien's Art Emporium, Scottsdale, Ariz, 70-71; Troys Cowboy Art Gallery, Scottsdale, 71-72; Jamison Gallery, Tucson, Ariz, 72; El Prado Gallery, Sedona, Ariz, 74-78; Am Painters in Paris, France, 75; plus others. Teaching: Instr landscape, Brooks Fine Arts Ctr, Santa Barbara, 69-70. Bibliog: Bob Austin (auth), Reflections on Oil, Austin Gallery, 70; article in SW Art, 4/76. Media: Oil. Publ: Auth (autobiog), Modern Veterinary Practice, 74 & Animal Cavalcade, 74. Mailing Add: PO Box 23 Williams AZ 86046

SEAMES, CLARANN
PAINTER, ILLUSTRATOR
b Buffalo, NY. Study: Albright Art Sch, cert(with honors); Univ Buffalo, BFA(with honors); Syracuse Univ, MFA; also with Charles Burchfield. Work: Albright/Knox Gallery, Buffalo, NY; Munson-Williams-Proctor Inst, Utica, NY; Utica Col; Syracuse Univ; Gallery on the Park, Troy. Comn: Oil painting, comn by Irving Kirshenbaum, New York, 64, Mrs J M Navel, Buffalo, 68, Daryll Badore, Syracuse, 69 & Karen Sakol, Boston, 75; ink portrait, comn by Mrs Gordon MacArther, Eden, NY, 75. Exhib: Cooperstown Nat, NY, 75; Western NY Regional Exhib, Albright-Knox Gallery; Cent NY Artists Ann, Munson-Williams-Proctor Inst; Young Am Gallery, St Louis, Mo; Robertson Mem Ann, Binghamton. Teaching: Instr painting, Albright Art Sch, 55-58; instr figure drawing, Univ Buffalo, 55-59; prof fashion illusr, Syracuse Univ, 61- Pos: Head fashion illusr, L L Berger, Buffalo, NY, 55-59; all art advertising, Casual MS, 61-70; art dir, Syracuse Mag, 63-65. Bibliog: Art rev in Buffalo Eve News & Courier, Syracuse Herald J & many others. Style & Technique: Presentational; non-representational. Media: Pencil, Ink, Wash, Oil, Acrylic. Mailing Add: 101 Janet Dr Syracuse NY 13224

SEARLES, CHARLES ROBERT
PAINTER
b Philadelphia, Pa, July 11, 37. Study: Fleisher Art Mem, Philadelphia; Pa Acad Fine Arts, Philadelphia. Work: Mus Nat Ctr Afro-Am Artist, Mass; Howard Univ; First Pa Bank, Philadelphia; Herbert A Allen Co, New York. Comn: Mural, Ile, Ife Afro-Am Mus, Philadelphia, 73. Exhib: Contemporary Black Artist in America, Whitney Mus Am Art, New York, 71; All Phases Due II, Studio Mus, New York, 71; one-man show, Bryn Mawr Col, 72; Direction in Afro-American Art, Herbert F Johnson Mus, Ithaca, NY, 74; one-man show, Howard Univ, 74; plus others. Teaching: Lectr drawing, Philadelphia Mus Art, summer 70; instr art, Model Cities Cult Arts, 70-74; instr, Philadelphia Col Art, 73- Awards: Drake Press Award, Pa Acad Fine Arts, 70, Cresson Traveling Scholar, 71 & Ware Traveling Awards, 73; Quaker Storage Co Prize, 73; Howard Univ Achievement in the Arts, for development of Pan-African visual arts expression. Style & Technique: Two dimensional design; stron color and representational images. strong Media: Acrylic, Watercolor. Mailing Add: 4834 Cedar Ave Philadelphia PA 19143

SEARLES, STEPHEN
SCULPTOR
b Leonia, NJ. Study: Art Students League, with George Bridgman, Frank V DuMond & Reginald Marsh; Grand Cent Sch Art, New York, with Georg Lober & Harvey Dunn; Gloucester with Emile Gruppé; also with Gelin, Fontainebleau, France. Comn: Our Lady of Good Voyage statue, Church of Our Lady of Good Voyage, Gloucester, Mass; Whaler & other sculptures made of Gloucester fishermen; Athletes in Action sculpture for African Hall, Am Mus Natural Hist, New York; plus many portrait busts in bronze of well-known artists. Exhib: Sculpture Exhibs, Grassy Gallery, Biarritz, France, 46, Palace of Fontainebleau, France, 49, Guild of Boston Artists, 72 & Rockport Art Asn, 72. Teaching: Instr drawing & sculpture, Biarritz Am Univ, 45-46; instr life drawing & sculpture, Newark Sch Fine & Indust Art, 50-53; instr life drawing, Vesper George Sch Art, Boston, 62- Awards: Sculpture Awards, Salmagundi Club, 52, Acad Artists Asn, Springfield Mus Art, 65 & 69 & Am Artists Prof League, 76 & 77. Mem: Nat Sculpture Soc; Am Artists Prof League; Am Vet Soc Artists; Nat Arts Club; life mem Art Students League. Style & Technique: Representational. Media: Bronze, Stone. Dealer: Guild of Boston Artists 162 Newbury St Boston MA 02116. Mailing Add: 30 Ipswich St Boston MA 02215

SEAWELL, THOMAS ROBERT
PRINTMAKER, PAINTER
b Baltimore, Md, Mar 17, 36. Study: Washington Univ, BFA, 58; Tex Christian Univ, MFA, 60. Work: Pushkin Mus, Moscow; Brit Mus, London; Libr Cong, Washington, DC; Mem Art Gallery, Rochester, NY; Brooklyn Mus, NY. Exhib: Prints & Posters from USA, seven mus in Israel, 69; Boston Printmakers Nat Exhibs, 70-77; Prints USA 1974, UP Gallery, Univ Pittsburgh; 2nd NH Int Graphics Ann, Nashua, 74; 2nd Miami Graphics Biennial, Metrop Mus & Art Ctr, 75; 30 Yrs of Am Printmaking Including 20th Nat Print Exhib, Brooklyn Mus, 76. Teaching: Prof drawing & printmaking, State Univ NY Col Oswego, 63- Awards: State Univ NY Res Found Printmaking Fels, 67, 70 & 74. Bibliog: Lewis Turco (auth), The Inhabitant (poem collection based on prints by Thomas Seawell), Despa Press, 70; American Printmakers 74, Graphics Group, Arcadia, Calif, 74. Mem: Boston Printmakers; Graphics Soc; Soc NJ Painters & Sculptors; Soc Am Graphic Artists; Philadelphia Watercolor Club. Style & Technique: Screen printer; etcher. Dealer: Pace Editions 32 E 57th St New York NY 10010; Pace Editions 115 E 23rd St New York NY 10010. Mailing Add: 199 Conway Terr Oswego NY 13126

SECKEL, PAUL BERNHARD
PAINTER, PRINTMAKER
b Osnabrueck, Ger, July 18, 18; US citizen. Study: London Cent Sch Arts & Crafts; Univ Buffalo, BFA; Yale Univ, MFA. Exhib: Recent Drawings, USA, Mus Mod Art, New York, 56; Drawings by Invitation, Flint Inst Art, 57; Exhib of Paintings Eligible for Purchase, Am Acad Arts & Lett, 63; Audubon Artists Ann. Awards: Emily Lowe Award, 63. Mem: Westchester Art Asn. Style & Technique: Expressionism abstracted from naturalistic reality. Media: Acrylic, Oil. Publ: Auth, How to Make Original Color Lithographs—A Manual for Professional Artists, 70. Dealer: Wiener Gallery 963 Madison Ave New York NY 10021. Mailing Add: 12 Van Etten Blvd New Rochelle NY 10804

SECKLER, DOROTHY GEES
ART CRITIC, PAINTER
b Baltimore, Md, July 9, 10. Study: Teachers Col, Columbia Univ, BS(art educ); Md Inst Art, dipl traveling scholar, 31; NY Univ; also in Europe. Work: Mus Mod Art, New York. Teaching: Lectr mod art; lectr, Mus Mod Art, 45-49; part-time instr, NY Univ, 47-52; lectr & instr, City Col New York, 57-60; lectr & instr, Pratt Inst, 60-61. Pos: Assoc ed, Art News & Art News Ann, 50-55; gallery ed, Art in Am, 55-61, contrib ed, 61-68; spec contribr fine arts, MD (Med News Mag), 57-73. Awards: Am Fedn Arts Award for Art Criticism, 54. Bibliog: Archives Am Art, Smithsonian Inst, Washington, DC. Publ: Co-auth, The questioning public, Mus Mod Art Bull, 49; co-auth mod art sect, Famous Artist's Course, 53; co-auth, Figure Drawing Comes to Life, 57; contribr, Encycl World Art, 59; auth (catalogue), Provincetown Painters, Everson Mus, Syracuse, NY, 77. contribr numerous articles, Arts, Art in Am & Art News; also rev on exhibs & monogr. Mailing Add: 64 Sagamore Rd Bronxville NY 10708

SECUNDA, (HOLLAND) ARTHUR
PAINTER, COLLAGE ARTIST
b Jersey City, NJ, Nov 12, 27. Study: NY Univ; Art Students League; Acad Grande Chaumiere; Acad Julian; with Zadkine & L'hote, Paris, 48-50; Inst Meschini, Rome; also study in Mex. Work: Smithsonian Inst, Washington, DC; Nat Collection Fine Arts, Washington, DC; Mus Mod Art, New York; Art Inst Chicago; Brooklyn Mus; plus many others in US, Sweden, Belg & Switz. Exhib: One-man shows, La Jolla Art Mus, Calif, 66, Galerie Richard Foncke, Gent, Belg, 68, Konstsalongen Kavaletten, Uppsala, Sweden, 71, Galerie Leger, Malmo, Sweden & Arras Gallery, New York, 75; plus many others. Awards: Tamarind Fel, Calif, 70 & NMex, 72. Style & Technique: Combining the color of California with the geometry of New York; torn and assembled colored paper form exotic collages both illusionistic and symbolic. Dealer: Arras Gallery 29 W 57th St New York NY 10019. Mailing Add: PO Box 6363 Beverly Hills CA 90212

SEDERS, FRANCINE LAVINAL
ART DEALER
b Paris, France, Dec 12, 32, US citizen. Study: Univ Paris Law Sch, MLaws; Univ Wash, MCS. Pos: Mgr, Otto Seligman Gallery, Seattle, Wash, 65-66, mgr-owner, 66-70; mgr-owner, Francine Seders Gallery, Seattle, 70- Specialty: Contemporary paintings, sculpture and graphics. Mailing Add: 6701 Greenwood Ave N Seattle WA 98103

SEEMAN, HELENE ZUCKER
ART LIBRARIAN, ART DEALER
b New York, NY, Apr 20, 50. Study: Boston Univ, BA; Queens Col, NY, MLS. Collections Arranged: Realism, Hathorn Gallery, Skidmore Col, Saratoga Springs, NY, 74; Lowe Art Mus, Fla, 75; Photorealism Traveling Exhibition, NZ mus, 75-76; Audrey Flack, Univ Bridgeport, Conn, 75; Look Again, Taft Mus, Cincinnati, Ohio, 76; Joyce Stillman Myers, Tolarno Galleries, Melbourne, Australia, 76; Rothmans of Pall Mall Traveling Exhibition, 77-78; New Realism, Jacksonville Mus, Fla, 77; Off the Beaten Path, Brainerd Gallery, State Univ NY Col, Potsdam, 77; Whitney Mus Am Art, New York, 78. Pos: Asst dir, Louis K Meisel Gallery, New York, 73- Mem: Art Libr Soc NAm. Interest: Organization, research and published documentation of artists and special exhibitions. Mailing Add: 12416 84 Rd 6B Kew Gardens NY 11415

SEERY, JOHN
PAINTER
Work: Art Inst Chicago; Whitney Mus Am Art, New York; Boston Mus Fine Arts; Cincinnati Mus Contemp Art; RI Sch Design Mus. Exhib: Andre Emmerich Gallery, 70 & 72; Spoleto Art Festival, Italy; 2 Generations of Lola Field Painting, Univ Pa, 70; Indianapolis Mus Art, 72; Contemp Graphics from the Museum's Collections, RI Sch Design Mus, 73; Pratt Inst Gallery, New York, 74; Toledo Mus Art, Ohio, 75; NY Univ, 76; 10 Americans, Australia; one-man shows, New York & Chicago. Bibliog: Sdzeleahl (auth), From creative plumbing to lyrical abstraction, New York Times, 70; Marandel (auth), La nouvelle peinture abstraction Americaine, Opus (Fr), 71; Ratcliff (auth), Painterly vs painted, Art News J, 72. Dealer: Andre Emmerich Gallery 41 E 57th St New York NY 10022. Mailing Add: 73 Leonard St New York NY 10013

SEGAL, GEORGE
SCULPTOR
b New York, NY, Nov 26, 24. Study: NY Univ, BS(art educ), 50; Rutgers Univ, MFA, 63. Work: Mus Mod Art, New York; Mus Mod Art, Stockholm, Sweden; Art Gallery Ont, Toronto; Nat Gallery Can, Ottawa, Ont; Art Inst Chicago; plus others. Exhib: Whitney Mus Am Art, Ann, 60, 64 & 68, exhib, 65, 70 & 72; Mus Contemp Art, Chicago, 68 & 71-72; Documenta, Kassel, WGer, 68; Vancouver Art Gallery, BC, 69; Haywood Gallery, London, 69; Galerie Speyer, Paris, 69; Expo 70, Osaka, Japan; Walker Art Ctr, Minneapolis, 70-71; NJ State Mus, Trenton, 71; Art Inst Chicago, 71; Munson-Williams-Proctor Inst, Utica, NY, 72; Detroit Inst Art, 73; plus many other group & one-man shows. Teaching: NJ High Schs, 57-63. Awards: Walter K Gutman Found Award, 62; First Prize, Art Inst Chicago, 66. Bibliog: George Segal, Artsmag, 12/74; Ellen Zeiffer (auth), George Segal: sculptural environments, Am Artist, 1/75; Robert Pincus Witten (auth), Reviews: George Segal, Artforum, 1/75; plus others. Dealer: Sidney Janis Gallery 6 W 57th St New York NY 10019. Mailing Add: Davidsons Mill Rd South Brunswick NJ 08901

SEGALOVE, ILENE JUDY
VIDEO ARTIST, PHOTOGRAPHER
b Los Angeles, Calif, Nov 24, 50. Study: Univ Calif, Santa Barbara, BFA; Loyola Univ, MA(commun arts). Exhib: 1975 Biennial Exhib, Whitney Mus; Video Show, Serpentine Gallery, Eng, 75; Artists Choice, Los Angeles Co Mus Art, 75; Southland Video, Long Beach Mus Mod Art, 75; Documentary Tapes, Mus Mod Art, New York, 75; Whitney Biennial, New York, 75 & 77; Los Angeles Inst Contemp Art, Calif, 76; Long Beach Mus Art, Calif, 77; one-person show, Univ Calif, Irvine, 78. Teaching: Instr inter-media, Otis Art Inst, Los Angeles, 75- Awards: Nat Endowment for the Arts in Video, 76. Style & Technique: Journalistic conceptual photography; typography. Media: Color Video, Photography,

Sculpture. Publ: Ed, Radical Software, 72; co-auth, West Mag of Los Angeles Times & New West Mag. Mailing Add: 838 Bay St Santa Monica CA 90405

SEGGER, MARTIN JOSEPH
ART HISTORIAN, MUSEUM DIRECTOR
b Ipswich, Eng, Nov 22, 46; Can citizen. Study: Univ Victoria, BA, 69, with Alan Gowans, dipl educ, 70; Warburg Inst, Univ London, with E H Gombrich, MPhil, 73. Collections Arranged: Arts of the Forgotten Pioneers (with catalog), Maltwood Mus, 71; Samuel Maclure-Architect, BC Prov Mus, 74, House Beautiful, an Exhibit of Decorative Arts 1860-1920 (with catalog), 75. Teaching: Lectr art hist, Univ Victoria, BC, 71- Pos: Dir, Maltwood Mus, Victoria, 71-; consult mus training, BC Prov Mus, Victoria, 74-77; adv bd, Brit Columbia Heritage, 77-, dir trust, 78- Awards: Rackham Found Res Grant, Univ Mich, 71. Mem: Am Soc Archit Historians; Can Mus Asn (nat exec mem, 75-77); Victorian Soc, UK; Heritage Can; Nat Trust, UK. Publ: Auth, Victoria-An Architectural History, 75; auth, Area Heritage Preservation Report-City of Victoria, 75; ed, Canadian Antiques Collector, BC Issue, 75. Mailing Add: 1035 Sutlej St Victoria BC V8V 2V9 Can

SEGY, LADISLAS
ART DEALER, COLLECTOR
b Budapest, Hungary, Feb 10, 04; US citizen. Study: Cent State Univ, hon DLitt, 53. Collections Arranged: Circulating Exhib African Sculpture, throughout US, 49- Teaching: Lectr, African Sculpture & Its Background & African Sculpture & Mod Art, US. Pos: Dir & owner, Segy Gallery. Specialty: African sculpture. Collection: African art; French and American modern painting and sculpture; Peruvian textiles; Mexican Mascala sculptures; prehistoric axes. Publ: Auth, African Sculpture, 58 & Masks of Black Africa, 75, Dover; auth, African Sculpture Speaks, Da Capo, 4th ed, 75; over 50 papers in scholarly mag in eight countries; plus others. Mailing Add: 50 W 57th St New York NY 10019

SEIDE, CHARLES
PAINTER, EDUCATOR
b Brooklyn, NY, May 14, 15. Study: Nat Acad Design, 32-37, with Leon Kroll. Work: Fogg Mus Art, Cambridge, Mass. Exhib: Paintings of Year, Pepsi-Cola Co, 46 & 48; Nat Acad Design, 51 & 57; Pa Acad Fine Arts, 52; Art USA, 58. Teaching: Instr painting & mat tech, Brooklyn Mus Art Sch, 46-62; prof art, Cooper Union, 50-, dir, Eve Sch, 66-68, head dept art, 68-70, head dept painting, 70-71; instr painting, Silvermine Col Art, 66-67. Pos: Nat dir, Artists Equity Asn, 53-54; vpres, Brooklyn Soc Artists, 53-55. Awards: Prize for Painting, Pepsi-Cola Co, 46, Regional Fel, 48; Graphics Prize, Brooklyn Soc Artists, 57. Bibliog: Dorothy Seckler (auth), Changing means to new ends, Art News, 52; Vincent Longo (auth), Studio talk, Arts Mag, 5/56. Mem: Am Asn Univ Prof. Media: Oil, Acrylic. Publ: Contribr, Encaustic, Materials and Methods, 49; contribr, Diameter, 51; illusr, Brooklyn Heights Press, 53. Mailing Add: 1 Washington Sq Village New York NY 10012

SEIDEL, ALEXANDER CARL-VICTOR
PAINTER, DESIGNER
b Milda, Thuringia, Ger, Aug 22, 97; US citizen. Study: Royal Sch of Applied Art, Munich, with Julius Diez; art studies in Rome, Italy, 22-27; English Acad, Rome. Comn: Murals & drawings, Hall of Biology of Man, Synoptic Bird Hall & Alcove of Extinct Birds, Am Mus Natural Hist, 43-61; illusr child's bk of wild birds, 55 & bk about water mammals, 60, Maxton Publ Inc, New York; engraving designs for Steuben Glass, 63-76. Pos: Staff artist, Am Mus of Natural Hist, New York, 43-61. Awards: Gold Medal Award, contrib to the arts internationally & for his own love of humanity as depicted in his masterpiece designs for Steuben Glass, Nat Soc Arts & Lett, NJ Chap, 75. Mailing Add: 816 Third Pl Plainfield NJ 07060

SEIDLER, DORIS
PAINTER, PRINTMAKER
b London, Eng. Study: Atelier 17, New York, with Stanley William Hayter. Work: Libr Cong, Washington, DC; Smithsonian Inst, Washington, DC; Philadelphia Mus Art; Brooklyn Mus; Seattle Mus Art. Exhib: Brooklyn Mus Bi-Ann; Vancouver Int Print Exhib; 1st & 2nd Hawaii Nat Print Exhib, Honolulu Acad Arts; Pa Acad Fine Arts, Philadelphia; Soc Am Graphic Artists, Kennedy Gallery, 71; Jewish Mus, New York; Atelier 17, Brooklyn Mus, 78. Awards: MacDowell Artists Colony Fel, 66 & 75; Purchase Award, Brooklyn Mus, 68; Medal for Creative Graphics, Audubon Artists, 72. Mem: Soc Am Graphic Artists (rec secy, 64-71). Publ: Auth, articles in Artist Proof. Dealer: Assoc Am Artists Gallery 663 Fifth Ave New York NY 10019; Roko Gallery 90 E Tenth St New York NY 10003. Mailing Add: 14 Stoner Ave Great Neck NY 11021

SEKIMACHI, KAY
WEAVER, INSTRUCTOR
b San Francisco, Calif, Sept 30, 26. Study: Calif Col Arts & Crafts, with Trude Guermonprez; Haystack Mountain Sch of Crafts, with Jack Lenor Larsen. Work: Bonaventure Hotel, Los Angeles, Calif; Matthews Ctr, Ariz State Univ, Tempe; Mus Contemp Crafts, New York; Smithsonian Inst, Washington, DC; The Royal Scottish Mus, Edinburgh. Comn: Rm Dividers, Japan Air Lines Lounge, Terminal Bldg, San Francisco Int Airport. Exhib: Mod Am Wall Hangings, Victoria & Albert Mus, London, 62; Wall Hangings, Mus Mod Art, New York, 68; Woven Structures, Camden Arts Ctr, London, Eng, 72; 6th Biennale Int de la Tapisserie, Lausanne, Switz, 73; Govett-Brewster Art Gallery, New Plymouth, NZ, 74; 2nd Int Exhib of Miniature Textiles, Brit Crafts Ctr, London, Eng, 76; Fiberworks: Americas & Japan, Nat Mus Mod Art, Kyoto, Japan, 77. Teaching: Instr weaving, Adult Div, San Francisco Community Col, 65-; workshop instr, US & Hawaii. Awards: Textile Award, Fiber/Clay & Metal, St Paul, Minn, 53; Designer/Craftsman USA Award, Brooklyn Mus, NY, 53; Nat Endowment Arts Craftmen's Fel, 74. Bibliog: Lee Nordness (auth), Objects, USA, Viking, 70; Jack L Larsen & Mildred Constantine (co-auth), Beyond Craft: The Art Fabric, Van Nostrand, Reinhold, 73; Irene Waller (auth), Textile Sculpture, Studio Vista, London, 77. Mem: Am Crafts Coun. Dealer: Allrich Gallery 2 Embarcadero Ctr San Francisco CA 94111. Mailing Add: 2147 Oregon St Berkeley CA 94705

SEKULA, ALLAN
VIDEO ARTIST, ART CRITIC
b Erie, Pa. Study: Univ Calif, San Diego, BA(visual arts), 72 & MFA(visual arts), 74. Exhib: Artists' Videotapes, Palais des Beaux Arts, Brussels, 75; two-person exhib, The Kitchen, New York, 75; Southland Video Anthology, Long Beach Mus Art, Calif, 75; Narrative in Contemporary Art, Univ Guelph, 75; Fantastic Autobiography, Los Angeles Inst Contemp Art, 76. Teaching: Guest lectr, Grossmont Col, 75; lectr & instr doc art, photog, Univ Calif, San Diego, 75- Style & Technique: Photographic and text narrative; video narrative. Media: Photography, Video. Res: Socio-semiotics of the photographic image. Publ: Auth, Aerospace folktales, J Los Angeles Inst Contemp Art, 12/74; auth, On the invention of photographic meaning, 1/75, Galella, book review, 4/75 & The instrumental image: Steichen at war, 12/75, Artforum. Mailing Add: 230 Birmingham Dr 6 Cardiff CA 92007

SELCHOW, ROGER HOFFMAN
PAINTER, SCULPTOR
b Greenwich, Conn, Feb 13, 11. Study: Grand Cent Sch Art, New York; Columbia Univ; also with Dong Kingman; Acad dela Grande Chaumiere, Paris, France; also with Andre Lhote & Fernand Leger, Paris; Inst Statale d'Arte, Florence, Italy. Work: Mus des Beaux-Arts, Liege, Belg; Wadsworth Atheneum, Hartford, Conn; NY Univ Art Collection, New York; Brooklyn Mus, NY; Metrop Mus of Art, New York; plus others; Exhib: Collage Exhib, Galerie Arnaud, Paris, 55; Int Collage Exhib, Rose Fried Gallery, New York, 56; one-man shows, Ind State Col Gallery, Terre Haute, 57 & APIAW, Salle de l'Emulation, Liege, Belg, 58; Groupe Espace de Paris, Vaison-la-Romaine, France, 59; Vingt-Ans d'APIAW, Mus des Beaux Arts, Liege, Belg, 65; Selchow Retrospective, Bruce Mus, Greenwich, Conn, 69. Pos: Dir, Atelier du Vieux Vaison, Vaison-la-Romaine, France, 53-60. Awards: Two First Place Medals, Grand Cent Sch Art, 33; First Prize, Greenwich Soc Artists, 54. Bibliog: Robert Vrinat (auth), Portrait d'Artiste—Selchow, Acualite Artistique Paris, 4/53; Gilbert Chaboud (auth), Un Americain Vaisonnais: Selchow, Le Meridionale-La France Orange, 3/55; Denys Chevalier (auth), Selchow—Peintures Recentes (catalog), Galerie de l'Univ, Paris, 63. Style & Technique: Evolution from geometric abstraction to a free contemporary realism; oils of palette-knife textures under transparent glazes; also watercolors, ink drawing, assemblages, wire and glass sculptural forms. Media: Oil, watercolor. Dealer: Raydon Gallery 1091 Madison Ave New York NY 10028; Helene Trosky Yarmouth Rd Purchase NY 10577. Mailing Add: 65 Sherbrooke St E Apt 1403 Montreal PQ H2X 1C4 Can

SELETZ, EMIL
SCULPTOR
b Chicago, Ill, Feb 12, 09. Study: Short training periods with Jo Davidson & George Gray Barnard. Comn: Dr Robert Gordon Sproul (bronze bust), Univ of Calif; Einstein (heroic bronze), Albert Einstein Col of Med, New York; Sir William Osler (bronze), Temple Med Sch, Philadelphia; Heroic Bust of Lincoln, San Jose Court House, Calif & Law Sch, Philadelphia; Franklin Roosevelt (heroic bust), President L B Johnson Libr, Tex. Exhib: Ann Exhib, Artists of the SW, 50-70; Ann Exhib, Painters & Sculptors Club, 52-68; Calif Art Club, 55-68; Show Case 21, 62-77; one-man shows, Beverly Hills Women's Club, 67; Univ Southern Calif, 68. Awards: Gold Medal, Artist of the SW, 52 & 68; First in Sculpture, Painters & Sculptors Club of Calif, 70; First in Sculpture, Show Case 21, 76. Mem: Show Case 21, Calif Art Club; Artists of the SW (pres, 60-67); Painters & Sculptors Club Calif. Style & Technique: Tradition portrait sculptor. Media: Bronze. Mailing Add: 9201 Sunset Blvd Los Angeles CA 90069

SELEY, JASON
SCULPTOR
b Newark, NJ, May 20, 19. Study: Cornell Univ, AB, 40; Art Students League, with Ossip Zadkine; Ecole Nat Superieur des Beaux Arts, Atelier Gaumond. Work: Mus Mod Art, New York; Whitney Mus Am Art, New York; Nat Gallery, Ottawa, Can; NJ State Mus, Trenton; Univ Mus, Univ Calif, Berkeley. Comn: Taliesmen (bronze abstract), Casper Col, Wyo, 69-70. Exhib: The Art of Assemblage, Mus Mod Art, New York, 61, Americans 1963, 63; Festival of Two Worlds, Spoleto, Italy, 62; Sculpture in the Open Air, Battersea Park, London, Eng, 63; Documenta III, Kassel, Ger, 64. Teaching: Assoc prof sculpture, Hofstra Univ, 53-65; assoc prof sculpture, NY Univ, 65-67; prof sculpture & chmn dept art, Cornell Univ, 68- Pos: Artist in residence, Deutscher Akademischer Austauschienst, Berlin, 70-71. Awards: US State Dept & US Off Educ Maintenance & Travel Grant, Haiti, 47-49; Fulbright Scholar for France, Inst Int Educ, 49-50. Bibliog: Herbert Read (auth), A Concise History of Modern Sculpture, Praeger, 65. Mem: Col Art Asn Am. Style & Technique: Sculpture with automobile bumpers. Mailing Add: 209 Hudson St Ithaca NY 14850

SELIG, J DANIEL
MUSEUM DIRECTOR, CURATOR
b Philadelphia, Pa, Apr 12, 38. Study: Univ Pa, BA, 59; Harvard Univ, MA, 60; Yale Univ, MA, 62. Collections Arranged: John Quidor: Painter of American Legend (co-auth, catalogue), Wichita Art Mus, 73; The Lyric Landscape of Leonid (auth, catalogue), 74, Graphic Art of Bernard Kohn, 74 & Colonial Spanish Art of the Americas (co-auth, catalogue), 75, Reading Pub Mus, Pa; Architecture on Paper, AIA Gallery, Philadelphia, 74. Teaching: Asst prof art hist, Univ Notre Dame, South Bend, Ind, 69-71; vis lectr art hist, Univ Ill, Chicago, 71-72. Pos: Lectr, Div of Educ, Boston Mus of Fine Arts, Mass, 62-67; cur & asst to dir, Wichita Art Mus, Kans, 72-73; dir, Reading Pub Mus, Pa, 73-76; dir, Trenton City Mus, 77- Awards: Nat Endowment for the Arts grant, 73. Mem: Am Asn of Mus; NE Mus Conf (chmn small mus comt, 74-77). Publ: Auth, Traditional Boston architecture, Cult Resources of Boston, 65; auth, A voice for small museums, Museologist, 76; auth, The Reading Museum—The American Collection, Am Art Rev, Jan-Feb & Mar-Apr, 74; auth, The Reality of Realism: Hopper's Sunlight on Brownstones, Wichita Art Mus Bull, winter 73; auth, Architecture on Paper (catalogue), Reading Pub Mus, 73. Mailing Add: c/o Trenton City Mus 10 Capitol St Trenton NJ 08608

SELIG, MR & MRS MANFRED
COLLECTORS, PATRONS
Collection: Old and modern paintings; graphic art. Mailing Add: Empire Children's Wear Co 88 Vine St Seattle WA 98121

SELIGER, CHARLES
PAINTER, DESIGNER
b New York, NY, June 3, 26. Work: Mus Mod Art & Whitney Mus Am Art, New York; Seattle Mus Art, Wash; Addison Mus Art, Andover, Mass; Munson-Williams-Proctor Inst, Utica, NY. Exhib: Abstract & Surrealist American Art, Art Inst Chicago, 47 & 65th Am Exhib, 62; Abstract Art in America, Mus Mod Art, New York, 51; Art of Organic Forms, Smithsonian Inst, Washington, DC, 68; Miniaturen '70 Int, Galerie 66 h g Krupp, Hofheim, Ger, 70; one-man show, Andrew Crispo Gallery, New York, 74; 20th Century Am Painting & Sculpture, 75 & 77 & 20th Century Am Masters, Andrew Crispo Gallery, New York; Art 77: A Selection of Works by Contemp Artists from New York Galleries, 77 & This is Today: An Exhib of Works by Living Artists, 77, Root Art Ctr, Hamilton Col, Clinton, NY; Albright-Knox Art Gallery, Buffalo, NY, 77-78. Teaching: Instr painting, Mt Vernon Art Ctr, NY, 50-53. Pos: Vpres design, Commercial Decal Inc, Mt Vernon, 60- Style & Technique: Small scale, delicate, linear paintings pertaining to nature and forms of the natural world; done on unstretched canvas carefully prepared for fine detail and subtle color. Media: Oil, Acrylic. Dealer: Andrew Crispo Gallery 41 E 57th St New York NY 10022. Mailing Add: 10 Lenox Ave Mt Vernon NY 10552

SELIGMAN, THOMAS KNOWLES
CURATOR, ART ADMINISTRATOR
b Santa Barbara, Calif, Jan 1, 44. Study: Stanford Univ, BA, 65; Acad of Art Col, San Francisco, BFA, 67; Sch of Visual Arts, New York, MFA, 68. Collections Arranged: Eskimo Art from the Toronto-Dominion Bank, 72, Man and Animals in Pre-Columbian

Mesoamerica, 73, Australian Aboriginal Art from the Louis Allen Collection, 74, African and Ancient Mexican Art—The Loran Collection (co-auth, catalog), 74-75, Fire, Earth and Water—Sculpture from the Land Collection of Mesoamerican Art (ed, catalog), exhib travelled to Honolulu Acad of Arts & Seattle Art Mus, 75 & Masterpieces of Primitive Art from the Museum of Primitive Art in New York, 77, San Francisco Mus Fine Arts. Teaching: Asst prof African art hist, Cuttington Col, Liberia, Africa, 69-71. Pos: Dir, Africana Mus, Liberia, Africa, 69-71; deputy dir educ & exhibs, Fine Arts Mus of San Francisco, 72- Awards: Aid to Mus Prof Award, Nat Endowment for the Arts, 75. Mem: African Studies Asn; Am Anthrop Asn; Am Asn Mus; Friends of Ethnic Arts (dir, 74-). Res: African aesthetics; art in context in Liberia, Sierra Leone and Ivory Coast. Publ: Auth, African art at the M H de Young Memorial Museum, African Arts, Univ Calif, Los Angeles, Vol 7 (4); auth, Educational use of an anthropology collection in an art museum, Curator, fall 74; auth, An indigenous concept of fakes—authentic African art?, African Arts, Univ Calif, Los Angeles, Vol 9 (3). Mailing Add: Fine Arts Mus of San Francisco Golden Gate Park San Francisco CA 94118

SELIGMANN, HERBERT J
ART WRITER
b New York, NY Nov 13, 91. Study: Harvard Col, BA (cum laude), 12. Pos: Commentator, Georgia O'Keeffe (film), TV Pub Broadcasting System, 77. Publ: Ed, Letters of John Marin, An Am Place, 31; auth, Essays on John Marin, Marsden Hartley, 55, auth, The Zorachs of Robinhood Cove, 58 & auth, Vincent Hartgen, 60, Down East Mag; auth, Alfred Stieglitz Talking, Yale Univ Libr, 66. Mailing Add: 10 E 70th St New York NY 10022

SELLA, ALVIN CONRAD
PAINTER, EDUCATOR
b Union City, NJ, Aug 30, 19. Study: Yale Univ Sch Art; Art Students League, with Brackman & Bridgman; Columbia Univ, with Machau; Col Fine Arts, Syracuse Univ; Univ NMex; also in Mex. Work: Bristol Iron & Steel Co; Collectors of Am Art; Sullins Col. Exhib: Am Fedn Arts Traveling Exhib, 61-62; one-man exhibs, Centenary Col, Lauren Rogers Mus Art, Laurel, Miss, Munic Art Gallery, Jackson, Miss & Birmingham Mus Art, Ala, 69 & Dick Jemison Gallery, Birmingham, 76; Birmingham Mus Art, 76, Watercolor Soc Ala, 76; plus many others. Teaching: Head dept art, Sullins Col, 48-61; prof art, Univ Ala, 61-; vis prof, Spring Workshops, Miss Art Colony, 62-64; vis prof, Shreveport Art Colony, 64-68; artist in residence, Summer Sch Arts, Univ SC, 68. Awards: First Award, 54th Ann Miss Exhib; Third Prize, 7th Mobile Art Exhib, 72; 32nd Ann Watercolor Exhib First & Second Prize, Birmingham Mus Art, 72. Mem: Art Students League; Am Asn Univ Prof; Col Art Asn Am; fel Int Inst Arts & Lett. Mailing Add: Dept of Art Univ of Ala University AL 35486

SELLERS, CHARLES COLEMAN
ART HISTORIAN
b Overbrook, Pa, Mar 16, 03. Study: Haverford Col, BA, 25; Harvard Univ, MA, 26. Teaching: Instr Am art, Dickinson Col, 50-56; librn, Waldron Phoenix Belknap Jr, Res Libr Am Painting, 56-59. Awards: Bancroft Prize, Columbia Univ, 70. Publ: Auth, Portraits and Miniatures by C W Peale, 52; ed, American Colonial Painting, 59; auth, Benjamin Franklin in Portraiture, 62; auth, Charles Willson Peale with Patron and Populace, 69; auth, Patience Wright, American Artist & Spy in George III's, London, 76. Mailing Add: 161 W Louther St Carlisle PA 17013

SELLERS, JOHN LEWIS
EDUCATOR, DESIGNER
b Alexander City, Ala, Aug 28, 34. Study: Auburn Univ, BAA; Peabody Col, MA; also with Maltby Sykes for printmaking & Harry Lowe for painting. Collections Arranged: Emil Ruder (retrospective exhib of works of the man who developed the Swiss Grid Systems & Int System of Design; auth, catalog), Lubin House Gallery, New York 72. Teaching: Head advert design dept & head independent study degree progs, MFA advert design, Col Visual & Performing Arts, Syracuse Univ, 73- Pos: Art dir, Motive Mag, Nashville, Tenn, 65-67; assoc creative designer, McDonald & Saussy Agency, Inc, Nashville, 65-68; partner & creative dir, Les Hart Agency, Inc, Nashville, 68-70. Awards: Magazine of the Year Award Runner Up, Mag Publ Asn, Mag Ed Asn & Columbia Univ Sch Journalism, 67; Best US Travel Brochure, Int Asn Travel Agents, 68. Bibliog: Don Barron (auth), Syracuse U: Preparation for the big world, Art Direction, 10/76; Jo Yanow (auth), John Sellers: The professional as educator, Graphics Today, Spring, 77; Paul Palange (auth), A teacher first, Syracuse Alumni Mag, Fall 77. Mem: Art Dirs Club New York, Inc (chmn int educators conf, 76). Res: Currently interviewing outstanding designers for textbook, Concept in Advertising. Mailing Add: 117 Circle Rd Syracuse NY 13210

SELLERS, WILLIAM FREEMAN
SCULPTOR, EDUCATOR
b Bay City, Mich, June 1, 29. Study: Univ Mich, BArch, 54, MFA, 62. Work: Suspension, Six Cubes & Converging Cubes, Mem Art Gallery, Rochester, NY. Comn: Four Squares (painted steel), Student Asn, NY State Univ Col Cortland, 69. Exhib: Sculpture & Prints Ann, Whitney Mus Am Art, New York, 66, Contemp Am Sculpture Ann, 68; Plus by Minus: Today's Half-Century, Albright-Knox Art Gallery, Buffalo, 68; American Sculpture of the Sixties, Grand Rapids Art Mus, Mich, 69; Painting and Sculpture Today, Indianapolis Mus Art, 70; plus others. Teaching: Instr design, Rochester Inst Technol, 62-65; asst prof sculpture, Univ Rochester, 66-70; asst prof art, Lehman Col, 70-, chmn dept art, 75-77. Awards: Jurors' Show Award, Mem Art Gallery, 66. Style & Technique: Geometrically determined form. Media: Metal, Wood. Dealer: Max Hutchinson Gallery 138 Greene St New York NY 10012. Mailing Add: Salt Point Turnpike Salt Point NY 12578

SELLIN, DAVID
ART HISTORIAN, CURATOR
b Philadelphia, Pa, Apr 13, 30. Study: Skölds Atelier, Stockholm, Sweden, 46-47; Univ Pa, BA(phi beta kappa), 52; Royal Acad Art, Stockholm, painting, 52-53; Univ Pa, MA, 56, PhD, 68; Univ Rome, Italy, 56-57; Univ Cologne, 67-68. Collections Arranged: Eakins Collection, Philadelphia Mus Art, 61; African Art and the School of Paris, Colgate Univ Art Ctr, 66; James Wines, 66, David Jacobs, Jack Massey, Eric Ryan, Franklin Drake, Minnie Evans, Jacqueline Gourevilch, plus others; Fred and Florence Olsen Collection, James Lord Collection, Davison Art Ctr, Wesleyan, 70-72; American Art in the Making (circulated to nine mus, auth catalog), Smithsonian Inst, 76; 1876 Exhibition (consult), Smithsonian Inst, 75; Eakins, MacDowell and Kenton (consult & auth catalog), Northcross, Roanoke, Va, 77. Teaching: Assoc prof art hist, Colgate Univ, Hamilton, NY, 63-67 & Wesleyan Univ, Middletown, Conn, 68-72; guest prof art hist, Newcomb Col, Tulane Univ, New Orleans, 67-68. Pos: Asst cur, Philadelphia Mus Art, 58-60; dir schs, Pa Acad Fine Arts, 60-62; gallery dir, Colgate Univ, 63-67 & Wesleyan Univ, 70-72; cur, Off Archit, US Capitol, Washington, DC, 76- Awards: King Gustav V Fel, 52; Fulbright-Hays Fel, Rome, 56; Smithsonian Inst Fel, 72. Mem: Victorian Soc Am; Columbia Hist Soc; Soc Am Historians. Res: North Italian art circa 1400 and the international Gothic style; 19th century American art and its sources. Publ: Auth, Michelino da Besozzo, Univ Pa, 68; auth, Essays on: Centennial Sculpture, Remington, Fremiet, in Sculpture of a City, Walker, 74; auth, The First Pose: Eakins, Roberts, and a Century of...Nudes, Norton, 76; auth, Thomas Eakins' Gross Clinic, Norton (in prep). Mailing Add: 1834 16th St NW Washington DC 20009

SELONKE, IRENE A
PAINTER
b Chicago, Ill. Study: Art Inst Chicago; Kansas City Art Inst; also with Joseph Fleck, Taos, NMex & Olga Dormandi, Paris. France. Work: Ralph Foster Mus, Point Lookout, Mo; Gill Studios, Olatha, Kans; Johnson Co Nat Bank, Prairie Village, Kans; Golden Ox, Washington, DC; Mo State Hist Soc; plus others. Comn: Tron furs, Sylvan Tron, Kansas City, 60; hist mural, comn by Mr & Mrs Dave Lorenz, Platt Woods, Mo, 66. Exhib: Coun Am Artists, Lever House, New York, 64; Nat League Am Pen Women Biennial State Show, St Louis, Mo, 65; Nat League Am Pen Women Nat Exhib, Salt Palace, Salt Lake City, 69; All Western Art Exhib, Ellensberg, Wash, 73; WTex Watercolor Exhib, Lubbock, 75; Best of Show Exhib, Topeka, Kans, 76; Ann Exhib, C M Russell Mus, 75-78; plus others. Pos: Illusr, Workbasket Mag & Workbench Mag, Kansas City, 59-61. Awards: Awards, Nat League Am Pen Women, 62-69; Awards, Greater Kansas City Art Asn, 62-68; Pikes Peak Nat Award, 72. Mem: Nat League Am Pen Women (state art chmn, 71-72). Media: Watercolor. Dealer: Sportsman's Gallery Crown Ctr Kansas City MO. Mailing Add: 3318 W 95th St Leawood KS 66206

SELTZER, PHYLLIS
PRINTMAKER, PAINTER
b Detroit, Mich, May 17, 28. Study: Univ Iowa, BFA & MFA; Lasansky's Workshop, sr study hist of technol, with M Kranzberg. Work: Brooklyn Art Mus; Cleveland Mus Art; Minn Mus Art, Minneapolis; Nat Gallery Art, Ottawa, Ont; Butler Mus, Youngstown, Ohio. Comn: Bicentennial print, Cleveland Area Arts Coun, 75; ed of 25, Exodus print, Cleveland Health Dept. Exhib: Davidson Nat Print & Drawing 1973; Cleveland Mus Art May Show, 73 & 74; 19th Nat Print Exhib, Brooklyn Mus, 74; Focus, Mich Artists, Detroit Art Inst, 74; AAA, New Talent in Printmaking, New York, 75; one-person show, Conley Gallery, Akron, Ohio, 77; two-person show, Mansfield Art Gallery, Ohio, 77. Teaching: Lectr art hist & printmaking, Lake Erie Col, Painesville, Ohio, 70-72; lectr art fund, Cleveland State Univ, 71- Pos: Coordr fine arts, Cleveland Col, Case Western Reserve Univ, 66-70; interior designer, Dalton, Van Dijk, Johnson, Cleveland, 72-74. Awards: Tiffany Fel, 52; Painting Award, Walker Mus, 61; Purchase Award, Brooklyn Mus 19th Nat, 75. Bibliog: Elizabeth McClelland (auth), article in WCLV Guide, Cleveland, 73; Dorothy Hall (auth), Art & artists, Park East, New York, 5/29/75; Helen Cullinan (auth), Prints at JCU, Plain Dealer, Cleveland, 6/75. Mem: New Orgn Visual Arts (secy, 73, vpres, 74); Am Soc Aesthet. Style & Technique: Realistic, literary; new technologies in printmaking; air brush acrylic painting. Media: Ozalid, Silkscreen; Acrylic on Canvas. Mailing Add: 11225 Harborview Dr Cleveland OH 44102

SELVIG, FORREST HALL
ART HISTORIAN, WRITER
b Tacoma, Wash, Jan 3, 24. Study: Harvard Col, AB, 49; Univ Calif, Berkeley, 53-56. Collections Arranged: Selections From Richard Brown Baker Collection, 60; The Nabis, 61; Pavel Tchelitchew, 64; Jean Helion, 65; Charles Demuth (with catalog), 68; plus others. Pos: Asst dir, Minneapolis Art Inst, Minn, 61-63; asst dir, Gallery Mod Art, New York, 63-65; dir, Akron Art Inst, 66-68; ed, New York Graphic Soc, Greenwich, Conn, 68-71. Bibliog: Ben Shahn Talks with Forrest Selvig, Archiv Am Art J, Vol 17 (1977). Mem: Am Asn Mus. Res: Late 19th century French painting, especially the Nabis and the Symbolists. Publ: Auth, The Nabis and Their Circle, 62; auth, American Collections, 63; auth, Review of the Whitney Sculpture Annual, 69; ed, 19th Century Landscape Painting, 71. Mailing Add: Via Capodistria 7 00198 Rome Italy

SELWITZ, RUTH F
PAINTER, PRINTMAKER
b Pittsburgh, Pa, July 4, 33. Study: Carnegie Inst Technol; Art Inst Pittsburgh; Samuel Rosenberg's Workshop for Prof Artists. Work: Butler Inst Am Art, Youngstown, Ohio; Springfield Art Mus, Mo; Westmoreland Co Mus Art, Greensburg, Pa; Mellon Nat Bank, Pittsburgh; WQED TV, Pittsburgh. Exhib: Assoc Artists Annuals, Carnegie Mus, Pittsburgh, 61-78; Mellon Nat Bank, 62; Butler Inst Art Nat Mid-Yr Show, Youngstown, Ohio, 63, 64, 65, 66 & 67; Pittsburgh Playhouse, 66; Chataqua Nat Jury Shows, NY, 66, 67 & 68; Watercolor USA, Springfield Art Mus, Mo, 67; ALCOA Invitational, 68; Appalacian Corridors Exhib, Charleston, WVa, 68; Westmoreland Co Mus Art, Greensburg, Pa, 68-77; Pittsburgh Plan Art, 71, 72 & 76; Panoras Gallery, New York, 73. Awards: Purchase Prize, Midyear Nat Show, Butler Inst Am Art, 64; Patrons Fund Prize, Assoc Artists Pittsburgh, 65 & 67; First Prize, Watercolor USA, Springfield Art Mus, 67. Bibliog: Margie Carlin (auth), Abstract color form in area artist's work, Pittsburgh Press, 1/73; Donald Miller (auth), Three woman art show winds down, Pittsburgh Post-Gazette, 5/75; Helen Kaiser (auth), Spray art makes splash in Monroeville, Pittsburgh Press, 11/76. Mem: Assoc Artists Pittsburgh; Pittsburgh Watercolor Soc; Pittsburgh Plan Art; Soc Sculptors; Pittsburgh Print Group. Style & Technique: Spray gun for irridescent effects; abstract; close color values. Media: Acrylic on Canvas; Serigraphs. Dealer: Pittsburgh Plan for Art 407 S Craig St Pittsburgh PA 15213. Mailing Add: 1169 Princeton Rd Monroeville PA 15146

SELZ, PETER H
ART HISTORIAN
b Munich, Ger, Mar 27, 19. Study: Univ Chicago, fel, 46-49, MA & PhD; Univ Paris, Fulbright Award, 49-50; Calif Col Arts & Crafts, hon DFA, 67. Exhibitions Arranged: Directions In Kinetic Sculpture (with catalog), 65; Funk (with catalog), 67; Richard Lindner, 69; Pol Bury, 70; Excellence, 70; Harold Paris (with catalog), 72; Ferdinand Hodler (with catalog), 72; plus many earlier exhibs arranged at Pomona Col, Mus Mod Art, New York & Univ Art Mus, Berkeley. Teaching: Asst prof art hist, Inst Design, Univ Chicago, 53-54; prof art hist, Univ Calif, Berkeley, 65- Pos: Head art educ prog, Inst Design, Ill Inst Technol, 53-55; chmn dept art & dir art gallery, Pomona Col, 55-58; cur painting & sculpture exhibs, Mus Mod Art, 58-65; dir, Univ Art Mus, Univ Calif, Berkeley, 65-73; ed, Art Am; mem consult comt, Art Quart. Awards: Belg-Am Educ Found Fel, 53; Order of Merit, Fed Ger Repub, 63; Sr Fel, Nat Endowment Humanities, 72; plus others. Mem: Col Art Asn Am (dir, 59-68). Publ: Auth, Alberto Giacomatti, 65; auth, Sam Francis, 75; contribr, Art Bull, Art News, Art J, Arts, Arts & Archit, Sch Arts, Penrose Ann & Encycl Britannica; co-auth, The American Presidency in Political Cartoons: 1776-1976, Peregrine Smith, 76; plus many others. Mailing Add: Dept of Art Hist Univ of Calif Berkeley CA 94720

SEMAK, MICHAEL
PHOTOGRAPHER, EDUCATOR
b Welland, Ont, Jan 9, 34. Study: Ryerson Polytech Inst, Toronto, cert archit technol, 59. Work: Nat Gallery Can, Pub Arch, Ottawa; George Eastman House, Rochester, NY; Mus Mod Art, New York. Comn: Photographing Canada, Nat Film Bd, Ottawa, 64, 66, 67, 72

& 74; Photographing Tunisia, Nat Geog Soc, Washington, DC, 67; Photographing WVa, Time-Life Bks, New York, 68; Photographing Italy, Can Coun, Ottawa, 71; Photographing USSR, York Univ, Toronto, 75. Exhib: Ghana Image 4, Nat Film Bd, Ottawa, 69; Ghetto, New Sch Social Res, New York, 70; Mixed Subjects, Image Gallery, New York, 71; Italy 1971, Il Diaframma Gallery, Milan, 73; Mixed Subjects, Deja Vue Gallery, Toronto, 75. Teaching: Lectr photog, Visual Arts Dept, Fac Fine Arts, York Univ, Toronto, 71-73, asst prof, 73- Pos: Toronto chmn interarts, Canada-USSR Asn, 73- Awards: Gold Medal for Photog Excellence for Ghana Show, Nat Film Bd, 69; Award of Excellence in Photo-Jour, Pravda Newspaper, Moscow, 70 & 72; Excellence Int Fedn Photog Arts Dipl, Switz, 72. Bibliog: Don Long (auth), Tell a story, Can Photo Ann, 75. Mem: Royal Can Acad Art. Style & Technique: Black and white, avilable light, small camera photography. Publ: Ed, Master of the Leica, Leica Fotografie, 69; ed, Concerned photographer, Popular Photog, 70; Semak portfolio, Creative Camera, 70 & 73, Camera Can, 71 & Nuova Fotografia, 73; co-auth, Michael Semak monograph, Impressions Mag, 74. Mailing Add: 1796 Spruce Hill Rd Pickering ON L1V 1S4 Can

SEMANS, JAMES HUSTEAD
PATRON
b Uniontown, Pa, May 30, 10. Study: Princeton Univ, AB; Johns Hopkins Univ, MD. Pos: Chmn bd trustees, NC Sch Arts, 64-; bd mem, Mary Duke Biddle Found. Publ: Auth, Siena-Six Summers of Music, 74. Mailing Add: 1415 Bivins St Durham NC 27707

SEMMEL, JOAN
PAINTER
b New York, NY, Oct 19, 32. Study: Cooper Union, dipl, 52; Art Students League, with Morris Kantor, 58-59; Pratt Inst, BFA, 63, MFA, 72. Work: Mus Mod Art, Seccion Contemporaneo, Barcelona, Spain; Mus Plastic Arts, Montevideo, Uruguay; Mus Contemp Art, Ibiza, Spain, Pratt Inst & Alan Stone Collection, New York. Exhib: Salon de Mayo, Barcelona, Spain, 65; Concurso Nac, Madrid, 67-69; Contemporary Reflections, Larry Aldrich Mus, Ridgefield, Conn, 74; Sons & Others, Queens Mus, New York, 75; two-person show, Soho Visual Arts Ctr (Larry Aldrich Mus), 75; one-person shows, Lerner-Heller Gallery, New York, 75, 77 & 78 & Pelham von Stoffler Gallery, Houston, Tex, 77; Nothing But Nudes, Downtown Whitney, New York, 77; Contemp Women: Consiousness & Content (cur), Brooklyn Mus, 77. Awards: Off Educ EPDA Fel, 70-72; Creative Artists Pub Serv Prog Award, NY State Coun on Arts, 75-76. Bibliog: Joan Semmel (videotape), Queens Col Art Doc, 74; Dorothy Sieberling (auth), The female view of erotica, New York Mag, 2/11/74; Lawrence Alloway (auth), article in The Nation, 5/24/75. Mem: Women in the Arts; Womens Ad Hoc Comt. Style & Technique: Powerful figurative forms, expressionistic in color, occupying a deep perspective space within highly realistic format. Media: Oil. Publ: Co-auth & ed, A New Eros, Hacker Art Bks, 76. Dealer: Lerner-Heller Gallery 789 Madison Ave New York NY 10021. Mailing Add: 109 Spring St New York NY 10012

SENDAK, MAURICE BERNARD
WRITER, ILLUSTRATOR
b Brooklyn, NY, June 10, 28. Study: Art Students League, 49-51. Exhib: One-man show, Gallery Sch, Visual Arts, New York, 64; Ashmolean Mus, Oxford, Eng, 75. Pos: Writer, illusr children's bks, 51- Awards: Caldecott Award for Where the Wild Things Are, 63; Hans Christian Andersen Illusr Award (first American), 70. Publ: Auth & illusr, In the Night Kitchen, 70; illusr, The Animal Family, 65; auth & illusr, In the Night Kitchen Coloring Book, 71, Pictures By Maurice Sendak, 71 & The Juniper Tree & Other Tales from Grimm, 73; plus many others. Mailing Add: 200 Chestnut Hill Rd Ridgefield CT 06877

SENIOR, DOROTHY ELIZABETH
PAINTER
b Willimantic, Conn. Study: Converse Art Sch, Norwich Free Acad, Conn; Chestnut Hill Art Sch; with Walter Olin Green; also with Herman Itchkawich, RI & Helen Van Wyk, Mass; plus others. Work: Admiral Inn, Cumberland, RI. Comn: Designer sand & sea sketches, stationery. Exhib: Rockport Art Asn, Mass, 69; Acad Artists Asn, Mus Fine Arts, Springfield, Mass, 69; Nat Arts Club, New York, 71; Nat Soc Painters in Casein & Acrylic, New York, 71 & Traveling Exhibs; Pen & Brush, New York, 72; New Eng Group-Old Bergen Art Guild of Bayonne, NJ Nat Travel Exhib; exhibs in leading mus, libr & univ in the USA. Awards: Slater Mus, Pawtucket, RI, 65; Nat Arts Club, NY, 67; Pen & Brush, NY: 72. Mem: Nat Arts Club; Nat Soc Painters in Casein & Acrylic; Pen & Brush; Am Artists Prof League; Acad Artists Asn. Style & Technique: Defined in practice, good technique is the ability to employ a medium and materials, with sufficient skill to achieve a predetermined, expressive effect; realistic style. Media: Oil, Pastel. Mailing Add: 20 Garden Dr Lincoln RI 02865

SENNEMA, DAVID C
ART ADMINISTRATOR, EDUCATOR
b Grand Rapids, Mich, July 6, 34. Study: Albion Col, Mich, BA, 56. Teaching: Prof, arts adminr & dir community arts mgt, Sangamon State Univ, Springfield, Ill, 73-76. Pos: Exec dir, SC Arts Comn, Columbia, 67-70; asst dir, Fed/State Prog Nat Endowment Arts, Washington, DC, 71-73, consult; dir, SC Mus Comn, 76- Mem: Am Asn Mus; Am Asn State & Local Hist; Carolina Coliseum Adv Comt (chmn). Publ: Auth, Building a Foundation for Community Arts Activity, 74; auth, Euphoria State Arts Agency - A Simulation, 74. Mailing Add: SC Mus Comn PO Box 11296 Columbia SC 29211

SEPLOWIN, CHARLES JOSEPH
SCULPTOR
b New York, NY, July 19, 45. Style & Technique: Univ NH, BA(arts); RI Sch Design, MFA(sculpture). Exhib: Warren Benedict Gallery, 74; Aldrich Mus, 75; Flint Inst Art, 75; Grand Rapids Mus Art, 75. Teaching: Instr sculpture, Guggenheim Mus Prog, New York, 71-74; instr sculpture, Montclair State Col, 74- Bibliog: Barbara Schwartz (auth), article in Craft Horizons, 8/74; Martin Ries (auth), article in Arts Mag, 9/74. Mailing Add: 463 West St New York NY 10014

SEPPÄ, HEIKKI MARKUS
GOLDSMITH, SILVERSMITH, EDUCATOR
b Säkkijärvi, Finland, Mar 3, 27; US citizen. Study: Golsmith Sch of Helsinki, Cent Sch of Indust Arts, Finland, Master Silversmith Status, 63; Georg Jensen Silversmiths, Copenhagen, Denmark, 48-49; Cranbrook Acad of Art, Mich, 60-61. Work: Evansville Mus Sci & Art, Ind; Steinberg Gallery Art, Wash Univ, St Louis, Mo; Tex Tech Univ, Lubbock; State Univ, El Paso, Tex; Univ Ill, Normal. Comn: Over 200 pvt collections, St Louis area patrons, 65-78; The Search, W G Elliot Soc of Wash Univ, 69. Exhib: Goldsmith 74, Renwick Gallery, Smithsonian Inst, Washington, DC, 74; Seppa & Neschnle, City Art Mus, St Louis, 74-75; Forms in Metal, Mus Contemp Crafts, New York, 75; Reprice, Mus of Cranbrook Acad Art, Bloomfield Hills, Mich, 75; Lowe Art Mus, Univ Miami, Coral Gables, Fla, 75; Krannert Art Mus, Univ Ill, Champaign, 76; The Metalsmith, Phoenix Art Mus, Ariz, 77; 3-Exhib, Burnaby Art Gallery, BC, 77. Teaching: Assoc prof metalsmithing, Wash Univ, St Louis, 65- Awards: Craftsman Fel, Nat Endowment for the Arts, 75; dipl for lifetime work in profession, Precious Metal Indust League of Finland. Bibliog: John Cione (auth), Jewelry Making by Penland Craftsman, Rutledge Bks, Penland Sch of Crafts, 75; Joseph Ordos (producer), Three American Goldsmiths (film), Univ Minn, 76; Izabel Blase (auth), He made his toy's, Goldsmith J, Soc NAm Goldsmiths, 77. Mem: Soc NAm Goldsmiths (mem comt, 70-). Style & Technique: Reticulation on gold and silver; shell structures technique. Media: Gold, Silver, Base Metals. Publ: Auth, Form Emphasis for Metalsmiths, Kent State Univ Press, 78. Mailing Add: 8 Price Ct St Louis MO 63132

SERAPHIN, JOSEPH ANTHONY
ART DEALER, PUBLISHER
b Philadelphia, Pa, May 8, 45. Pos: Art dealer, Olympia Galleries, Ltd, Currently. Specialty: American Abstract School; German Expressionism; Surrealism. Publ: Publ, Olympia Galleries Collection of Thomas Eakins' Photographs, Larry Rivers—Paintings 53-73, Bill Richards—Paintings, Olympia Galleries, Ltd. Mailing Add: Olympia Galleries Ltd 117 W Charlton St Savannah GA 31401

SERGER, HELEN
ART DEALER
b Skoczow, Poland, Feb 1, 01; US citizen. Mem: Art Dealers Asn Am. Specialty: Paintings, drawings and graphics by German and Austrian expressionists; 20th century masters; Dada, Bauhaus and surrealist artists. Mailing Add: 9 E 82nd St New York NY 10028

SERISAWA, IKUO
ART DEALER
US citizen. Study: Art Inst Chicago, 43-47. Pos: Owner & dir, I Serisawa Gallery. Specialty: Contemporary paintings and graphics; also antique Oriental prints and modern Oriental graphics. Mailing Add: 485 W Ave 43 Los Angeles CA 90065

SERISAWA, SUEO
PAINTER
b Yokohama, Japan, Apr 10, 10; US citizen. Study: Study with Yoichi Serisawa (father) & George Barker; Otis Art Inst. Work: Metrop Mus Art, New York; Los Angeles Co Mus Art; Santa Barbara Mus Art; Smithsonian Inst, Washington, DC; San Diego Fine Arts Gallery. Exhib: Carnegie Inst Int, Pittsburgh, 52; Tokyo Int, Japan, 52; Sao Paulo Biennale, Brazil, 55; Whitney Mus Am Art, New York, 60; Pacific Heritage, US State Dept, Berlin, Ger, 65; plus others. Teaching: Instr painting, Kann Inst Art, 48-51; instr painting, Scripps Col, 49-50 & Univ Southern Calif, Idyllwild Campus, 75- Awards: Carol H Beck Gold Medal, Pa Acad Fine Arts, 47; Purchase Award, Metrop Mus Art, 50; Purchase Award, Los Angeles Co Mus, 50, 56 & 57. Bibliog: Arthur Millier (auth), Inner development of artist, Am Artist, 50; Ed Biberman (auth), 20 Artists (film), Los Angeles Mus & Univ Calif, Los Angeles, 70; Joe Mugnaini (auth), Oil Painting Techniques and Materials, 69 & Logics of Drawing, 73, Reinholt; plus others. Style & Technique: Universal humanism. Media: Sumi Ink, Woodcut, Oil. Dealer: I Serisawa Gallery 8320 Melrose Ave Los Angeles CA 90069. Mailing Add: 3033 Warren Lane Costa Mesa CA 92626

SERNIAK, REGINA
PAINTER, WRITER
b Passaic, NJ. Study: Cooper Union; Hunter Col, (art hist). Work: Columbia Mus of Art, SC; Greenville Co Mus, SC; Comune de Urbino, Italy; Aldrich Mus of Contemp Art, Ridgefield, Conn. Exhib: Collegeo Raffaello, Urbino, Italy, 73; Art Exhib, Beth Elohim, New York, 74; ACA Gallery, New York, 74; Contemp Reflections, Aldrich Mus of Contemp Art, 76; Soho Ctr for Visual Artists, New York, 77. Teaching: Instr painting & drawing, NY Univ, New York, 76- Pos: Designer scenery & costumes, Paterson Lyric Opera Theatre, NJ, 65-74; promotion for art & antiques, Channel 13 TV Sta, New York, 76. Awards: First Prize/Painting, Ann John Roebling Exhib, John Roebling Found, 60. Bibliog: Notable Americans, Hist Preserv Am, 76. Style & Technique: Paintings are created through a build-up of overlays of transparent images, producing multiple depth layers and tension with the surface of the canvas. Media: Acrylic. Publ: Auth, The Golden Handbook of Collectibles, Western Publ, 76; auth, American Woodworking Tools, E P Dutton, 77. Mailing Add: 31 E Seventh St New York NY 10003

SERRA, RICHARD
SCULPTOR
b San Francisco, Calif, 1939. Study: Univ Calif, Berkeley; Univ Calif, Santa Barbara, BA; Yale Univ, BA & MFA. Exhib: Stedelijk Mus, Amsterdam, Holland, 69; Kunsthalle, Bern, Switz, 69; Solomon R Guggenheim Mus, New York, 69; Pasadena Art Mus, 70; Whitney Mus Am Art, New York, 72; plus many others. Mailing Add: PO Box 645 Canal St Sta New York NY 10013

SERRA, RUDY
SCULPTOR
b San Francisco, Calif, Apr 9, 48. Study: City Col San Francisco, AA; San Francisco State Col, BA; Univ Calif, Berkeley, MA & MFA. Exhib: Serra, Wall, Zecher, San Francisco Art Inst, 73; Deborah Butterfield & Rudy Serra, Univ Art Mus, Berkeley, 74; Public Sculpture, the Urban Environment, Oakland Mus, 74; 1975 Whitney Biennial, New York, 75; Introduction, Hansen Fuller Gallery, San Francisco, 75; one-man shows, Chico State Col, Calif, 75 & Calif Gallery, San Francisco, 76; Los Angeles Inst Contemp Art, 76; San Francisco Art Inst, 76; Univ Art Mus, Berkeley, 77; San Francisco Mus Art, 77; Nelson Gallery, Univ Calif, Davis, 78. Teaching: Vis asst prof sculpture, Calif State Univ, Chico, 75; asst prof, Am River Col, Sacramento, 76- Awards: Nat Endowment for the Arts Grant in Sculpture, 76. Bibliog: Roberta Smith (auth), Biennial review, Artforum, 5/75; Amy Goldin (auth), The new Whitney Biennial, Art in Am, 5-6/75; Judith Dunham (auth), Introduction 75, Artweek, 7/75. Style & Technique: Structural, tension, space containment. Media: Wood, Steel. Mailing Add: 1045 17th St San Francisco CA 94110

SERRA-BADUE, DANIEL
PAINTER, EDUCATOR
b Santiago de Cuba, Sept 8, 14. Study: Escuela Munic Bellas Artes, Santiago de Cuba, 24-26; Borrell-Nicolau & Luis Muntane, Escuela Bellas Artes, Barcelona, 32-36; Art Students League, Nat Acad Design & Columbia Univ, 38-40; Escuela Nac Bellas Artes, Havana, 43; Pratt Inst Graphic Art Ctr, New York, 64; Art Critics Workshop, Am Fedn Arts, 67. Work: Museo Municipal, Santiago de Cuba; Museo Nac, La Habana; Butler Inst Am Art, Youngstown, Ohio; New York Pub Libr; Metrop Mus Art, New York; plus others. Exhib: Int Exhib Graphics, Univ Conn Mus Art, 71; Columbia Mus Art, SC, 72; Am Soc Contemp Artists Ann, New York, 74; Ibizagrafica/76, Bienal de Ibiza, Museo de Arte Contemp, Ibiza, 76; Six Cuban Painters Working in New York, Ctr Inter-Am Relations, New York, 75; 149th Ann Exhib, Royal Scottish Acad, Edinburgh, 75; 55th Nat Print Exhib, Soc Am Graphic Artists, AAA Gallery, New York, 77; plus others. Teaching: Prof artistic anat & perspective,

Sch Plastic Arts, Santiago de Cuba, 45-60; instr art, Univ Oriente, Cuba, summers 48 & 50; prof design, Sch Journalism, Santiago de Cuba, 54-59; prof still life painting, Nat Sch Fine Arts, Havana, 60-62; lectr painting, Columbia Univ, 62-63; instr drawing & painting, Brooklyn Mus Art Sch, 62-; asst prof art hist, St Peter's Col (NJ), 67-70, chmn dept, 67-77, assoc prof, 70-77, prof, 77- Pos: Asst dir cult, Ministry Educ, Havana, 59-60. Awards: John Simon Guggenheim Mem Found Fel, 38 & 39; Oscar B Cintas Found Fel, 63 & 64; First Prize in Painting, Am Soc Contemp Artists, 74; plus others. Bibliog: Al Brunelle (auth), Daniel Serra-Badue, Art News, 2/73; Rafael Santos Torroella (auth), Serra-Badue, El Noticiero Universal, Barcelona, 6/5/73; Alberto del Castillo (auth), Daniel Serra-Badue, Goya, Madrid, 7-8/73; plus many others. Mem: Am Soc Contemp Artists; Col Art Asn Am; Printmaking Coun NJ; Soc Archit Historians; Artists Equity New York; plus others. Style & Technique: Surrealism, expressing the elusive ambiguity of the message through very assertive techniques. Publ: Auth, weekly articles in Diario de la Marina, Havana, 46-47; auth, weekly articles in Diario de Cuba, Santiago de Cuba, 57-58; auth, The Plastics Arts in Santiago de Cuba; plus others. Mailing Add: Dept of Fine Arts St Peter's Col Jersey City NJ 07306

SERWAZI, ALBERT B
PAINTER
b Philadelphia, Pa, Aug 20, 05. Study: Pa Acad Fine Arts. Work: Pa Acad Fine Arts; Corcoran Gallery Art, Washington, DC; Whitney Mus Am Art, NY; Allentown Art Mus, Pa; Wichita State Univ. Exhib: Ann, Pa Acad Fine Arts, 34-64; Painting in the United States, Carnegie Inst, 39-45; Artist for Victory, Metrop Mus Art, 43; Ann, Nat Acad Design, 47, 52, 58 & 70-75. Awards: J Henry Scheidt Memorial Prize Oil, Pa Acad Fine Arts, 41; Gold Medal, Philadelphia Sketch Club, 44. Mem: Academician Nat Acad Design; fel Pa Acad Fine Arts; Chester Co Art Asn, Pa; Del Art Mus; Philadelphia Watercolor Club. Style & Technique: Representational; still life; landscape and seascape. Media: Oil, Watercolor. Mailing Add: 3725 Gradyville Rd Newtown Square PA 19073

SETTERBERG, CARL GEORG
PAINTER, ILLUSTRATOR
b Las Animas, Colo. Study: Art Inst Chicago; Am Acad Fine Arts. Work: McChord AFB, Washington, DC; Air Force Acad, Colorado Springs; Columbus Mus, Ga; De Beers Collection; Soc Illusr. Comn: 14 doc paintings, USAF; portraits, Air Force Acad. Exhib: Am Watercolor Soc, 42-72; Allied Artists Am, 48-71; Nat Acad Design, 48-71; Royal Acad, 60; Western Art Asn, Phoenix Art Mus, 71. Pos: Illusr, McCalls, Colliers, Womans Home Companion, Am, Red Bk & others. Awards: Ranger Fund Award, Nat Acad Design, 58; Watercolor USA Award, Am Watercolor Soc, 67, William Church Osborne Award, 69; plus others. Bibliog: Norman Kent (auth), Watercolor Techniques, Watson-Guptill, 68; Ralph Fabri (auth), American Watercolor Society, 69. Mem: Nat Acad Design; Am Watercolor Soc; Audubon Artists; Salmagundi Club; Soc Illusr (vpres). Media: Oil, Watercolor. Publ: Auth, Treatise, Am Artist, 61. Mailing Add: Samarkand Villa 28 2663 Tallant Rd Santa Barbara CA 93105

SEVERINO, DOMINICK ALEXANDER
EDUCATOR, ART ADMINISTRATOR
b Boston, Mass, Sept 14, 14. Study: Mass Sch Art, BS; Boston Univ, EdM; Harvard Univ, EdD. Teaching: Instr art, RI Col Educ, 39-43; prof art, Univ Wis, 52-55. Pos: Asst dean art & design, RI Sch Design, 47-48; chmn dept art, Bradford Durfee Tech Inst, 48-52; dir fine & appl art, Ohio State Univ, 55-57, assoc dean, Col Educ, 57-, exec comt, Comn on Interprof Educ; exec comt, Ohio Fac Senate, State of Ohio Univ. Mem: Col Art Asn Am; Nat Art Educ Asn; Am Fedn Art; Asn Sch Adminr; Nat Educ Asn. Mailing Add: 6215 Olentangy River Rd Worthington OH 43085

SEVY, BARBARA SNETSINGER
ART LIBRARIAN
b Montpelier, Vt, June 4, 26. Study: Univ Vt, BS; Drexel Univ, MSLS. Pos: Librn, Philadelphia Mus Art, 68- Mem: Art Libr Soc NAm; Am Libr Asn (chmn art sect, 74); Spec Libr Asn (secy mus div, 68-69). Mailing Add: 26th St & Benjamin Franklin Pkwy Philadelphia PA 19101

SEWARDS, MICHELE BOURQUE
LITHOGRAPHER, CRAFTSMAN
b St Louis, Mo, Aug 15, 44. Study: NY State Col Ceramic Design, Alfred Univ, pottery with Val Cushing, printmaking with John Wood, BFA, 66; Univ NMex, lithography with Garo Z Antreasian, MA, 72. Work: Tamarind Inst Lithography & Art Mus, Univ NMex, Albuquerque; Roswell Mus & Art Ctr, NMex; Univ Iowa Mus Art, Iowa City; Grunewald Ctr for Graphic Arts, UCLA. Exhib: Ann Purchase Show, Univ NMex Art Mus, 74 & 75; Southwest Fine Arts Biennial, Mus NMex, Santa Fe, 74; NMex Fine Arts Biennial, Mus NMex, 75; Miami Graphics Biennial, 75; one-person shows of lithographs, Hill's Gallery, Santa Fe, 75 & Roswell Mus & Art Ctr, 74; 12 Contemp Artists Working in NMex, Univ NMex Art Mus, Albuquerque, 76; NW Int Small Format Print Exhib, Seattle, Wash, 76; Contemp Issues: Works on Paper by Women, Woman's Bldg, Los Angeles, 77; Made in NMex, Mus NMex, Santa Fe, 77. Awards: Artist in Residence Grant in lithography, Roswell Mus, 73-74; Guest Artist, Tamarind Inst of Lithography, 74; CETA Grant in Lithography, NMex Arts Comn, 77-78. Mem: Graphics Soc. Media: Stone, Clay, Cloth. Publ: Contribr, Roswell Mus Quart, Vol 22 (winter, 1970); contribr, Fervent Valley, 71 & Tamarind Inst Report, 12/74; contribr, Robert Lloyd, post, homage, image, 76. Dealer: Ed Hill 4141 Pinnacle St Suite 114 El Paso TX 79902; Hills Gallery Contemp Art 110 W San Francisco Santa Fe NM 87501. Mailing Add: PO Box 578 Placitas NM 87043

SEWELL, JACK VINCENT
MUSEUM CURATOR
b Dearborn, Mo, June 11, 23. Study: St Joseph Jr Col, Mo, 41-43; City Col New York, 43-44; Univ Chicago, MFA, 50; Harvard Univ, 51-53. Collections Arranged: Complete reinstallation of Oriental Collections, Art Inst Chicago, 58. Teaching: Lectr, Indian & Far Eastern Art, The Arts of China, Strength in Delicacy—A Study of Archaic Chinese Bronzes & Sculpture of Gandhara. Pos: Mem staff, Oriental dept, Art Inst Chicago, 50-56, assoc cur Oriental art, 56-58, cur, 58- Mem: Far Eastern Ceramic Group; Japan-Am Soc Chicago (dir & vpres); The Cliff Dwellers; Arts Club Chicago. Publ: Contribr, Archaeol & Chicago Art Inst Quart. Mailing Add: 1350 N Lake Shore Dr Chicago IL 60610

SEXAUER, DONALD RICHARD
PRINTMAKER, EDUCATOR
b Erie, Pa. Study: Col William & Mary; Edinboro State Col, BS; Kent State Univ, MA. Work: Butler Inst Am Art, Youngstown, Ohio; New York Pub Libr; Mint Mus Art, Charlotte, NC; Montgomery Mus Fine Arts, Ala; Franklin Mint, Pa; plus others. Comn: Print eds, Woman, Assoc Am Artists, Int Graphic Art Soc, 66, To Fly, To Fly, 66; Vietnam Fragments (folio), Off, Chief Mil Hist, Washington, DC, 71; Mecklenburg Bicentennial Comn (folio). Exhib: Soc Am Graphic Artists, 64-; New Talent In Printmaking, New York, 66; 140th Ann, Nat Acad Design, 66; San Diego Print Exhib, 71; 16th Hunterdon Nat, Clinton, NJ, 72. Teaching: Prof printmaking, Sch Art, E Carolina Univ, 60- Awards: Print Prize, Nat Acad Design 140th Ann, 66; Purchase Awards, Piedmont Print Ann, Mint Mus, 69-74; Purchase Award, Bradley Print Show, Peoria. Mem: Soc Am Graphic Artists; Acad Artists Asn. Style & Technique: Figurative imagery, primarily intaglio, both black and white and multi-color. Publ: Illusr, Red clay reader number 5, Southern Lit Rev, 68. Dealer: Foliograph Tyson's Corner Ctr McLean VA 22101. Mailing Add: 109 Greenbriar Dr Greenville NC 27834

SEYFFERT, RICHARD LEOPOLD
PAINTER, INSTRUCTOR
b Philadelphia, Pa, Aug 11, 15. Study: Nat Acad Design Sch, with Leon Kroll, Gifford Beal & father, Leopold Seyffert. Work: Pentagon; Rutgers Univ; Overseas Press Club; USAF Acad; Nat Arts Club. Comn: Portraits of Gov John Stelle, Ill, W K Kellogg, Miss Fanny Hurst, Charles J Biddle, Edward R Murrow, W C Whitney, W H Auden & Richard Rogers. Exhib: Nat Acad Design Ann, 63; Century Asn Ann, 65; Allied Artists Am Ann, 69; Hudson Valley Art Asn Ann, 74. Teaching: Instr painting, Art Students League, 70- Awards: Century Portrait Prize, Century Asn Art Comn, 65; Frank Reilly Mem Award, Allied Artists Am, 69; Newington Award, Hudson Valley Art Asn, 74. Mem: Nat Arts Club (gov, 65-); Allied Artists Am; Artists Fel (trustee, 75-); Hudson Valley Art Asn. Style & Technique: Realistic interpretive portraits, still life and landscapes. Media: Oil, Pastel. Dealer: Portraits Inc 41 E 57th St New York NY 10022. Mailing Add: 15 Gramercy Park New York NY 10003

SEYFRIED, JOHN LOUIS
SCULPTOR
b St Louis, Mo, Sept 26, 30. Study: Wash Univ, BFA, 58; Syracuse Univ; Cranbrook Acad Art, MFA, 62. Work: Albreit Mus; Charleston Art Gallery; Tenn Arts Comn. Comn: Heroic fountain group, Chase Park Plaza, St Louis, Mo, 63-64; wall mural, Fred Seidel, New York, 66; five welded reliefs, Self Mem Hosp, Greenville, SC, 67; heroic mem & wall relief, Prof Photo Am, Des Plaines, Ill, 68-69; River (heroic fountain), Mid-Am Mall, Memphis, Tenn, 75-76; plus others. Exhib: Mich Show, Detroit, 61-62; Mo Show, St Louis, 62-64; Drawings Int, Detroit, 64; Mid-South Show, Memphis, 66, 68, 70 & 72; New Media Sculpture Show, Atlanta, Ga, 69; plus others. Teaching: Instr sculpture & ceramics, Webster Col, St Louis, 62-63; asst prof art, Meramec Community Col, Kirkwood, Mo, 63-64; assoc prof sculpture, Memphis Acad Arts, Tenn, 65- Pos: Exec dir, People's Art Ctr, 62-63. Dealer: New Bertha Schaefer Gallery 57th St New York NY 10022. Mailing Add: 1495 Harbert Ave Memphis TN 38104

SEYLE, ROBERT HARLEY
SCULPTOR, DESIGNER
b National City, Calif, Oct 9, 37. Study: La Sierra Col, Riverside, Calif; Otis Art Inst, Los Angeles, BFA, MFA. Work: Storm King Art Mus, Corning, NY; Palm Springs Desert Mus, Calif; Beneficial Ins Group, Los Angeles; Metro Media Studios, Hollywood, Calif. Comn: Nail sculpture 11, Henry J Ittleson, Jr, Palm Springs, 67; nail sculpture 50, Vallejo Dr Seventh-day Adventist Church, Glendale, Calif, 69; nail sculpture 89, Julian Brody, Des Moines, Iowa, 72; nail sculpture 110, Dr Alonzo Proctor, Lodi, Calif, 74; nail sculpture 125, Steve Chase of Arthur Elrod Interiors, Palm Springs, 75. Exhib: Contemp Am Painting & Sculpture, Univ Ill, Urbana, 67; Calif Design Ten, Pasadena Art Mus, 68; Calif Expos, Sacramento, 68; one-man show, Palm Springs Desert Mus, 74; group show, Calif State Capitol Bldg, Sacramento, 75. Bibliog: Janice Lovoos & Felice Paramore (auths), Modern Mosaic Techniques, Watson-Guptill; Ray Faulkner & Edwin Ziegfeld (auths), Art Today, Holt, Rinehart & Winston Inc; Bernard Morris (auth), California people, Eyewitness News, ABC-TV, 74. Style & Technique: Flat panels of wood, cut & chiseled to shape with the surface covered with a design of nails driven into the wood. Mailing Add: 5047 Greenleaf Dr Riverside CA 92505

SEYLER, DAVID W
SCULPTOR, EDUCATOR
Study: Art Acad Cincinnati, dipl; Art Inst Chicago; Univ Chicago, BFA; Univ Wis, MFA. Work: Syracuse Univ, NY; Univ Chicago; Cincinnati Art Mus; Sheldon Art Gallery, Lincoln, Nebr. Comn: Mural, USN Great Lakes Training Sta, 43; stained glass & altar, Holy Trinity Episcopal Church, Lincoln, 62-72; mural, KOLN-TV, Lincoln, 68-69; designer & sculptor, Nebr State Centennial Medal & Univ Nebr Centennial Medal. Teaching: Prof sculpture & head crafts dept, Univ Nebr, Lincoln, 48- Awards: Woods Found Travel Grant, Italy, 59-60; Univ Nebr Found Grant, Eng, 71-72. Bibliog: Warren E Cox (auth), Pottery & Porcelain & Herbert Peck (auth), The Book of Rookwood Pottery, Crown; Paul Evans (auth), American Art Pottery, Scribner, 75; Kovel (auth), Collector's Guide to American Art Pottery, Crown, 76. Mem: Nebr Arts Coun; Nebr Craft Coun; Nebr Art Asn; Col Art Asn Am; fel Int Soc Arts & Lett. Media: Stone, Ceramic, Bronze, Fibre. Dealer: Sharon Gallery & Lakewood Arts Studio Lincoln NE 68508. Mailing Add: 3434 S 28th St Lincoln NE 68502

SEYMOUR, CATRYNA TEN EYCK
See Ten Eyck, Catryna

SEYMOUR, RACHEL
COLLECTOR, PATRON
b Philadelphia, Pa, Mar 28, 37. Study: Univ Pa, BA(hist art). Collection: Primarily living Philadelphia painters and watercolorists. Mailing Add: 1213 Waverly Walkway Philadelphia PA 19147

SHACKELFORD, SHELBY
PAINTER
b Halifax, Va, Sept 27, 99. Study: Md Inst Art, Baltimore, with Marguerite & William Zorach, Othon Friesz & Fernand Leger, grad. Work: Baltimore Mus Art; New York Pub Libr; Morgan State Col; Western Md Col; Int Bank Chicago; manuscripts and originals of published drawings in archives of library at Univ Ore. Exhib: Corcoran Gallery, Washington, DC, 65; Eastern Show Regional, 68; Notre Dame Col, 72; Jewish Community Ctr, Baltimore, 72; Fells Point Gallery, 75; Cherry Stone Gallery, 76 & 77; plus many Md Regional Shows. Teaching: Head dept art, St Timothy's Sch, Stevenson, Md, 44-62; instr painting, Baltimore Mus Art, 50-65. Pos: Trustee, Baltimore Mus Art, 71-77, mem 20th century accession comt, 68- Awards: First Prize for Painting, Baltimore Mus Art, 59 & Purchase Prizes, 50-54; Prize for Drawing, Eastern Art Asn; Prize, Jewish Community Ctr. Media: Casein, Soot. Publ: Auth & illusr, Now for Creatures, 34; auth & illusr, Electric Eel Calling, 40. Mailing Add: 300 Northfield Pl Baltimore MD 21210

SHADBOLT, JACK LEONARD
PAINTER
b Shoeburyness, Eng, Feb 4, 09. Study: Euston Rd Group, London, Eng; Andre L'Hote, Paris; Art Students League. Work: Art Gallery Toronto, Ont; Nat Gallery Can; Montreal Mus Fine

Arts; Seattle Art Mus, Wash; Vancouver Art Gallery; plus others. Comn: Murals, Edmonton Int Airport & Charlottetown Mem Ctr; other comn in pvt collections. Exhib: Can Traveling Exhibs; Sao Paulo, Brazil; Caracas, Venezuela; Carnegie Inst; Seattle World's Fair, 62; Retrospective, Vancouver Art Gallery, 78; plus others. Teaching: Head drawing & painting sect, Vancouver Sch Art. Publ: Auth articles on contemp art problems in Can. Dealer: Bau-Xi Gallery 1876 W First Ave Vancouver BC Can. Mailing Add: 5121 Harborview Rd N Burnaby BC V5B 1C9 Can

SHADDLE, ALICE
SCULPTOR, PAINTER
b Hinsdale, Ill, Dec 21, 28. Study: Oberlin Col; Univ Chicago, Ill; Sch of Art Inst Chicago, BFA & MFA. Work: Smithsonian Inst, Washington, DC. Comn: Portrait of Franz Liszt (three-dimensional collage), Mercury Rec Mfg Co, 66. Exhib: Made With Paper, 67 & Chicago Needs Famous Artists, 69, Mus Contemp Art, Chicago; Soc for Contemp Art, 69, Exhib by Artist in Chicago & Vicinity, 75 & Vision, 76, Art Inst Chicago; Indianapolis Mus Art, Ind, 76; 26th Ill Invitational, Ill State Mus, Springfield, 76; Nat Drawing Show, Kohler Arts Ctr, Sheboygan, Wis, 76. Teaching: Instr printmaking & drawing, Roosevelt Univ, Chicago, 64-66; childrens painting teacher, Hyde Park Ctr, Chicago, 55-78; childrens painting teacher, Triangle Art Ctr, Chicago, 78- Awards: Logan Medal, 75th Exhib by Artist of Chicago & Vicinity, Art Inst Chicago, 75. Bibliog: Meilach & Ten Hoor (auth), Collage & Assemblage, Crown, 73; C L Morrison (auth, rev), Artforum, 76. Mem: Artemisia Gallery & Fund (treas, 77-78); Hyde Park Art Ctr (scholar chmn). Style & Technique: Laminated paper sculptures, collage reliefs and painted collages. Media: Paper, Latex, Heavy Wrapping Paper; Oil & Canvas, Watercolor on Foiled Paper. Publ: Contribr, Art: Choosing & Expressing, Benefic Press, 77. Dealer: Artemisia Gallery 9 W Hubbard Chicago IL 60610. Mailing Add: 4858 S Kenwood Chicago IL 60615

SHADRACH, JEAN H
PAINTER, ART DEALER
b La Junta, Colo. Study: Univ NMex; Sumie, Okinawa; Constatine & Roman Chatov Studio, Atlanta, Ga; Alaska Methodist Univ; Anchorage Community Col. Work: Anchorage Fine Arts Mus; Alyeska Pipeline Co, Anchorage; Jewelmont, Inc, Minneapolis; Standard Oil of Calif; Murray, Kraft & Rockney; also in pvt collection of Sen Ted Stevens, Washington, DC. Exhib: All Alaska Art Exhib, Anchorage, 68-72; Northwestern Watercolor Soc Ann, Seattle, 70; Design I, Anchorage, 71; Artists of Alaska Traveling Show, US, 71-; Frye Mus, Seattle; plus others. Pos: Co-owner, Artique, Ltd, Fine Art Gallery, Anchorage, 71- Awards: Best of Show, Elmendorf AFB, 69; Drawing Award, All Alaska Art Exhib, 70; Governor's Award, Alaska, 70. Mem: Alaska Artist Guild (pres, 70-71); Artists Equity Asn. Style & Technique: Impressionistic, with palette knife; tries to capture essence of subject. Media: Acrylic. Specialty: Alaskan artists work. Publ: Auth, Okinawa Sketchbook, 62. Dealer: Artique Ltd 314 G St Anchorage AK 99501. Mailing Add: 3530 Fordham Dr Anchorage AK 99504

SHAHLY, JEHAN
PAINTER
b Detroit, Mich, Dec 12, 28. Study: Mich State Univ, BA; Art Students League; New Sch Social Res. Work: San Francisco Mus Art; Univ Southern Ill; Univ Mass; Geigy Collection; Bradford Jr Col. Exhib: Tanager Gallery, New York, 60; Bleecker Gallery, New York, 62; Grand Central Mods Gallery, New York, 62 & 63; Six Painters, Kansas City Mus, 63; one-woman show, Green Mountain Gallery, New York, 73. Awards: Purchase Prize, San Francisco Mus Art, 56; Purchase Prize, Wichita Mus, Kans, 57. Bibliog: Brian O'Doherty (auth), review in New York Times, 62; Lawrence Campbell (auth), review in Art News Mag, 11/73; April Kinsley (auth), review in Art Int, 1/74. Style & Technique: Expressionistic rendering of a literal style of both figures and landscapes. Media: Oil. Dealer: Green Mountain Gallery 135 Greene St New York NY 10012. Mailing Add: 799 Greenwich St New York NY 10014

SHALIT, MITZI (MILDRED M SHALIT)
ART CONSULTANT, ART DEALER
b New York, NY, Apr 5, 23. Study: Pratt Inst, Brooklyn, NY; Art Students League; Fleisher Art Mem, Philadelphia, Pa. Pos: Pvt dealer & art consult specializing in corp art collections and cataloging of same. Mailing Add: 41 Conshochocken State Rd 302 Bala Cynwyd PA 19004

SHALKOP, ROBERT LEROY
MUSEUM DIRECTOR, ART HISTORIAN
b Milford, Conn, July 30, 22. Study: Maryville Col, Tenn, 40-42; Univ Chicago, 46-50, MA, 49; Sorbonne, Univ Paris, 51-52. Collections Arranged: Arroyo Hondo, the Folk Art of a New Mexican Village (with catalog); Reflections of Spain: a Comparative View of Spanish Colonial Sculpture (with catalog), 68; Reflections of Spain II: Spanish Colonial Painting (with catalog), 69; 100 Years of Painting in the Pike's Peak Region (with catalog); Russian Orthodox Art in Alaska (with catalog), 73; Sydney Laurence, an Alaskan Impressionist (with catalog), 75; Eustace Ziegler (with catalog), 77. Pos: Dir, Rahr Civic Ctr, Manitowoc, Wis, 53-56; dir, Everhart Mus, Scranton, Pa, 56-62; dir, Brooks Mem Art Gallery, Memphis, Tenn, 62-64; assoc dir, Colorado Springs Fine Arts Ctr & cur, Taylor Mus, 64-71; dir, Anchorage Hist & Fine Arts Mus, 72- Mem: Asn Art Mus Dirs; Am Asn Mus; Western Asn Art Mus (regional rep, 74-). Publ: Auth, Wooden Saints, the Santos of New Mexico, 67. Mailing Add: Anchorage Hist & Fine Arts Mus 121 W Seventh Ave Anchorage AK 99501

SHAMAN, SANFORD SIVITZ
GALLERY DIRECTOR, CURATOR
b Pittsburgh, Pa, July 11, 46. Study: Ohio Univ, Athens, BFA, 68; State Univ NY Binghamton, 70-71; Villa Schifanoia Grad Sch Fine Arts, Florence, Italy, MFA, 74. Collections Arranged: Harris K Prior Memorial Exhibition (cataloged), Mem Art Gallery, Rochester, NY, 76. Pos: Cur, Huntington Galleries, WVa, 74-75; asst cur, Mem Art Gallery, Rochester, NY, 75-77; dir, Gallery of Art, Univ Northern Iowa, Cedar Falls, 77-, cataloger, Permanent Collection, 77- Awards: Villa Schifanoia Grad Sch Fine Arts Scholar, Florence, 72; Am Asn Mus Scholar, Curatorship Sem, 76. Mem: Iowa Mus Asn. Publ: Contribr, Annual Report, Memorial Art Gallery of the University of Rochester, Mem Art Gallery, 76. Mailing Add: Univ Northern Iowa Gallery of Art Cedar Falls IA 50613

SHANE, FREDERICK E
PAINTER, EDUCATOR
b Feb 2, 06; US citizen. Study: Kansas City Art Inst, 23-24; also with Randall Davey, Santa Fe, NMex, 24; Braodmoor Art Acad, summers 25 & 26. Work: City Art Mus, St Louis, Mo; Mus Art & Archaeol, Univ Mo-Columbia; Springfield Mus Art, Mo; State Univ NY Col, Oswego; IBM Corp Collection; plus many others. Comn: Paintings of Army Medicine, War Dept, Abbott Collection, Washington, DC; Portrait of James M Wood, Stephens Col; mural, US Post Off, Eldon, Mo; Scruggs-Vandervoort-Barney Collection, Univ Mo; Jefferson City Jr Col. Exhib: Art Inst Chicago; Corcoran Gallery Art, Washington, DC; Pa Acad Fine Arts, Philadelphia; Carnegie Inst Int, Pittsburgh; New York World's Fair, 39-40 & 64-65; Watercolor USA, 76; plus many others. Teaching: Prof art, Univ Mo, 38-71, chmn dept, 58-67, emer prof fine arts, 71- Pos: Artist corresp, Army Med Corps, 44. Awards: Second Painting Prize, Davenport Mus Art, Iowa, 50; Popular Painting Prize, Columbia Art League, 60; Byler Award for Achievement in Art & Teaching, 71; plus many others. Bibliog: Archives Am Art, Smithsonian Inst, Washington, DC. Media: Oil, Casein. Publ: Auth, Fred Shane Drawings, Univ Mo. Mailing Add: 633 N Foothill Rd Beverly Hills CA 90210

SHANGRAW, CLARENCE FRANK
ART HISTORIAN, CURATOR
b Burlington, Vt, Aug 9, 35. Study: Inst Far Eastern Lang, Yale Univ, cert; Univ Calif, Berkeley, AB(with high honors), MA(Oriental lang & lit). Collections Arranged: Avery Brundage Collection of Asian Art Permanent Collection, 65-; Chinese Treasures from the Avery Brundage Collection, 69; Paintings from the Abe Collection, Osaka, 70; Chinese Gold, Silver & White Porcelain from the Carl Kempe Collection, 71; Ancient Indonesian Art of the Central & Eastern Japanese Periods, 71; Hans Popper Collection of Oriental Art, 73; Rarities of the Musee Guimet: Asian Art from a French Museum, winter 75; Exhibition of Archeological Finds of the People's Republic of China, summer 75. Pos: Res asst, De Young Mus, San Francisco, 65-66, asst cur, 66-67; cur, Asian Art Mus, San Francisco, 69-71, sr cur, 72- Mem: Col Art Asn Am; Asn Asian Studies; Oriental Ceramics Soc, London; Am Asn Mus. Res: Early Chinese ceramics, prehistoric to the Han; Chinese Buddhist sculpture; archaeology in China. Publ: Contribr, Selection '68; contribr, The Avery Brundage Collection: Chinese, Korean & Japanese Sculpture, 74; auth, Early painted pottery from Northwest China in the Avery Brundage Collection, Archaeology, 75; auth, Forme und Farbe: a review, Artibus Asiae, 75; auth, The beginnings of China's painted pottery traditions, Occasional Papers, Los Angeles Mus Art, 75. Mailing Add: Asian Art Mus Golden Gate Park San Francisco CA 94118

SHANGRAW, SYLVIA CHEN
ART HISTORIAN, CURATOR
b Honolulu, Hawaii, Feb 18, 37. Study: Mt Holyoke Col, South Hadley, Mass, BA(cum laude), 58; Univ Calif, Berkeley, MA(Oriental lang & lit), 65, PhC, 67. Collections Arranged: A Flower from Every Meadow, Indian Miniatures Collection, 73; Visions of Tantric Buddhism (with catalog), 74. Pos: Asst cur, Ctr of Asian Art & Culture, San Francisco, 67-69; cur, Asian Art Mus of San Francisco, 69- Res: Chinese art, especially ceramics, bronzes & paintings; Ch'ing dynasty aesthetics. Publ: Contribr, Chinese, Japanese & Korean Sculptures in the Avery Brundage Collection, 74. Mailing Add: Asian Art Mus San Francisco Golden Gate Park San Francisco CA 94118

SHANKS, BRUCE MCKINLEY
EDITORIAL CARTOONIST
b Buffalo, NY, Jan 29, 08. Work: Dept Justice & Supreme Ct Off, Washington, DC. Exhib: Var schs, banks, cols. Pos: Ed cartoonist, Buffalo Eve News, currently. Awards: Pulitzer Prize, 58; Grand Award, Nat Safety Coun, 61; Cartoon Citation, All-Am Conf Combat Communism, Washington, DC, 64; plus others. Publ: Cartoons in New York Times, Newsweek, US News & World Report, Time & others. Mailing Add: 250 NE 20th St Apt 217 Boca Raton FL 33431

SHANNONHOUSE, SANDRA LYNNE
SCULPTURE, CERAMIST
b Petaluma, Calif, May 19, 47. Study: Univ Calif, Davis, BS, 69, MFA, 73, with Robert Arneson. Work: Utah Mus Fine Arts, Salt Lake City. Exhib: Statements, Oakland Mus Art, Calif, 73; A Decade of Ceramic Art 1962-1972, San Francisco Mus Mod Art, Calif, 73; R Joseph Monson Collection, Seattle Mus Art, Wash, 74; Rising Stars, Carborundum Mus, Niagara Falls, NY, 75; one-man shows, Quay Gallery, San Francisco, 75 & 78; Birthday Show, Mus Contemp Crafts, New York, 76; Calif Clay I & II, Braunstein/Quay Gallery, New York, 76 & 77; An Exhib of Bay Area Ceramics, Fine Arts Mus, San Francisco, 77. Teaching: Lectr form in theatre, Univ Calif, Davis, 74; instr ceramics & drawings, Am River Col, Sacramento, Calif, 75-76; guest artist, Otis Art Inst, Los Angeles, Calif, 76-78; artist-in-residence ceramics, Oxbow Summer Sch of Art, Saugatuck, Mich, 76. Bibliog: Suzanne Foley (auth), A Decade of Ceramic Art, San Francisco Mus Art, 72; Sandy Ballatore (auth), The California clay rush, Art in Am, 76. Style & Technique: Hand built clay forms sometimes combined with other materials. Media: Clay; Mixed-Media. Dealer: Ruth Braunstein c/o Quay Gallery 560 Sutter San Francisco CA. Mailing Add: 110 East E St Benicia CA 94510

SHAPERO, ESTHER GELLER
See Geller, Esther

SHAPIRO, BABE
PAINTER
b Irvington, NJ, May 4, 37. Study: NJ State Teachers Col, Newark, BS; Hunter Col, with Robert Motherwell, MA. Work: Kresge Art Ctr, Mich State Univ; Newark Mus; Andrew Dickson White Mus, Cornell Univ; Albright-Knox Art Gallery, Buffalo; Corcoran Gallery Art, Washington, DC. Exhib: Biennial Exhib Contemp Am Painting, Univ Ill, 63; New York World's Fair, 65; Cincinnati Art Mus, 66; Indianapolis Mus Art, 70; New Museum Acquisitions, Colorado Springs Fine Arts Mus, 72; plus others. Pos: Ford Found artist in residence, Quincy Art Club, Ill, 66; dir & artist in residence, Grad Sch Painting, Md Inst Col Art, Baltimore, currently. Awards: Newark Mus Triennial Purchase Prize Award, 58 & 61; First Prize in Painting, Monmouth Col (NJ), 63. Style & Technique: Perceptual abstractions, built into volumes and planes from stripes arranged in systemic, regularly ordered values from light to dark. Media: Acrylic. Dealer: A M Sachs Gallery 29 W 57th St New York NY 10019; Gertrude Kasle Gallery 310 Fisher Bldg Detroit MI 48202. Mailing Add: 31 Walker St New York NY 10013

SHAPIRO, DAISY VIERTEL
COLLECTOR, PATRON
b New York, NY, July 8, 92. Study: Painting with Louise Pollet & Alex Redein. Mem: Solomon R Guggenheim Mus; Archit Am Art; fel Morgan Libr; Am Fedn Arts; Mus City of New York; plus others. Collection: Contemporary American painting and sculpture; donations of many works of art to museums and colleges including Dartmouth College. Mailing Add: 200 East End Ave New York NY 10028

SHAPIRO, DAVID
PAINTER
b New York, NY, June 26, 44. Study: Skowhegan Sch, Maine, 65; Pratt Inst, BFA, 66; Ind Univ, Bloomington, MFA, 68. Work: Ind Univ Art Mus, Bloomington; San Francisco Mus Art, Calif; Guggenheim Mus, New York; Westinghouse Corp, Pittsburgh; Krege Art Ctr, Mich State Univ, Lansing. Exhib: Gertrude Kasle Gallery, Detroit, 70 & 73; Poindexter

Gallery, New York, 71, 73, 74 & 77; William Sawyer Gallery, San Francisco, 73; Alexander Milliken Gallery, New York, 78; Roy Boyd Gallery, Chicago, 78. Teaching: Instr, Pratt Inst, 69-71; vis artist, Barnard Col, 72; guest artist, Kansas City Art Inst, 73; instr, Parsons Sch Design, 74- Dealer: Alexander Milliken Gallery 141 Prince St New York NY 10012. Mailing Add: 315 Riverside Dr New York NY 10025

SHAPIRO, DAVID
PAINTER, ART HISTORIAN
b New York, NY, Aug 28, 16. Study: Educ Alliance Art Sch, 33-35; Am Artists Sch, 36-39. Work: Metrop Mus Art, New York; Brooklyn Mus, NY; Philadelphia Mus Art; Springfield Mus Fine Art, Mass; Libr Cong, Washington, DC. Comn: Black & white intaglios, Assoc Am Artists Gallery, New York, 70-75; color lithographs, Litografie Int, Milan, Italy, 70; stained glass windows, Garden Jewish Ctr, Flushing, NY, 70; black & white intaglio, Ferdinand Roten Galleries, 77. Exhib: Pa Acad Ann, Philadelphia, 47; Whitney Ann, New York, 52; Brooklyn Mus Print Ann, 53; Libr Cong Print Ann, 53; Corcoran Biennial, Washington, DC, 59. Teaching: Instr studio art, Smith Col, 46-47; asst prof studio art & art hist, Univ BC, 47-49; prof studio art & art hist, Hofstra Univ, Hempstead, NY, 61- Pos: Art ed, Hofstra Rev, Hofstra Univ, 65-70. Awards: Fulbright Fel, 51-53; Purchase Awards, Brooklyn Mus Print Ann, 46, Libr Cong Print Ann, 50 & Mus Fine Arts, Springfield, Mass, 57. Mem: Soc Am Graphic Artists (pres, 68-70, exec coun, 70-); Col Art Asn Am. Style & Technique: Recognizable imagery in all media used, expressionistic. Res: American art with emphasis on art of the 30's. Publ: Auth, Stanley William Hayter, expression of the unconscious (catalog essay), 4/70; contribr, 19th century American painting, New York Hist Soc Quart, 1/72; auth, Social Realism: Art as a Weapon, Frederick Ungar Publ Co, 73; contribr, Searth for an American image, Am Art Rev, 5-6/74; contribr, Abstract expressionism: the politics of apolitical painting, Prospects, 77. Dealer: Assoc Am Artists Gallery 663 Fifth Ave New York NY 10022; Van Straaten Gallery 646 N Michigan Ave Chicago IL 60611. Mailing Add: 124 Susquehanna Ave Great Neck NY 11021

SHAPIRO, FRANK D
EDUCATOR, PAINTER
b New York, NY, July 28, 14. Study: City Col Ny, BSS, MS(educ), 35; Nat Acad of Design, 32-35. Comn: Mural, Wash NJ Post Off, Sect of Fine Arts of Fed Govt, 41. Exhib: Corcoran Gallery, Washington, DC, 42; Syracuse Mus, NY, 42; Detroit Mus, Mich, 42; Norfolk Mus, Va, 67: Albright-Knox Art Gallery, Buffalo, NY, 67; Art Gallery, State Univ NY, Albany, 69; Nat Arts Club, New York, 77. Teaching: Chmn fine arts dept, Fashion Inst Technol, State Univ NY, 58- Awards: Steers Prize, City Col NY, 34; Runner-Up Award, St Louis Post Off Mural Competition, Fine Arts Sect of Fed Govt, 40. Media: Watercolor. Mailing Add: 67-44A 190 Lane Fresh Meadows New York NY 11365

SHAPIRO, IRVING
PAINTER, INSTRUCTOR
b Chicago, Ill, Mar 28, 27. Study: Art Inst Chicago; Chicago Acad Fine Art; Am Acad Art, Chicago. Work: Univ Vt; Columbus Mus Art, Ga; Lakeview Mus Art, Peoria, Ill; Ill State Mus, Springfield; Macon Mus Art, Ga. Exhib: Am Watercolor Soc Ann, Nat Acad Design Gallery, 58-72; Union League Club Chicago, 55, 57 & 59; Butler Inst Am Art, Youngstown, Ohio, 62; Art Inst Chicago Sales & Rental Galleries, 66-68. Teaching: Instr watercolors, Am Acad Art, 45-, dir, 71- Awards: First Watercolor Awards, Union League Club Chicago, 55 & 57; Ranger Award, Am Watercolor Soc, 58; Ill State Mus Purchase Award, 66-67. Mem: Am Watercolor Soc; Artists Guild Chicago. Media: Watercolor. Publ: Auth & illusr article in Am Artist Mag, 59; contribr, 100 Watercolor Techniques, 70, Acrylic Watercolor, 71 & Palette Talks, 72. Dealer: Blair Galleries Santa Fe NM 87501; Mongerson Gallery 620 N Michigan Ave Chicago IL 60611. Mailing Add: 3330 Maple Leaf Dr Glenview IL 60025

SHAPIRO, JOEL (ELIAS)
SCULPTOR
b New York, NY, Sept 27, 41. Study: NY Univ, BA & MA. Work: Fogg Art Mus; Mus Mod Art, New York; Whitney Mus Am Art, New York; Weatherspoon Art Gallery, Univ NC; Panza di Biumo, Milano. Exhib: Anti-Illusion: Procedure/Material, 69, Sculpture Ann, 70 & American Drawings: 1963-1973, Whitney Mus Am Art; Hanging/Leaning, Emily Lowe Gallery, Hofstra Univ, Long Island, NY, 70; one-man shows, Paula Cooper Gallery, New York, 70, 72, 74, 76 & 77, Clocktower, New York, 73, Galleria Salvatore Ala, Milano, 74, Garage Art, Ltd, London, 75, Walter Kelly Gallery, Chicago, 75, Mus Contemp Art, Chicago, 76 & Albright-Knox Art Gallery, Buffalo, NY, 77; Works on Paper, Soc Contemp Art 31st Ann, 74 & 71st Am Exhib, 74, Art Inst Chicago; Critical Perspectives in Am Art, Univ Mass, Amherst & Venice Biennale, 76; Int Tendencies, Venice Biennale, 76; Sydney Biennale, Australia, 76; Whitney Biennale, New York, 77; Documenta 6, Kassel, WGer, 77. Bibliog: Marcia Tucker & James Monte (auth), Anti-illusion: procedure/material, Whitney Mus Am Art, 69; Robert Pincus-Witten (auth), New York, 5/70, Roberta P Smith (auth), article, 6/73, Jeremy Gilbert-Rolfe (auth), Joel Shapiro: works in progress, 12/73 & Carter Ratcliff (auth), cover article, 4/76, Artforum. Mailing Add: c/o Paula Cooper 155 Wooster St New York NY 10012

SHAPIRO-LIEB, VERED
See Lieb, Vered

SHAPLEY, FERN RUSK
CURATOR, WRITER
b Mahomet, Ill, Sept 20, 90. Study: Univ Mo, AB, AM, PhD, AED; Bryn Mawr Col. Pos: Asst art & archaeol, Univ Mo, 16-17, asst prof art, 25; res asst, Nat Gallery Art, 43-47, cur paintings, 47-56, asst chief cur, 56-60, cur res, Samuel H Kress Found, 60-71. Awards: Fel, Bryn Mawr Col; European Fel, 15; Fel, Univ Mo, 15-16. Publ: Auth, George Caleb Bingham, the Missouri Artist, 17; auth, European Paintings from the Gulbenkian Collection, 50; auth, Paintings from the Samuel H Kress Collection; Italian Schools, XIII-XV Century, 66, XV-XVI Century, 68 & XVI-XVIII Century, 73; co-auth, Comparisons in Art, 57; contribr, Gazette Beaux Arts, Art Quart, Art in Am, Am J Archaeol and others. Mailing Add: Nat Gallery Art Constitution Ave at Sixth St NW Washington DC 20565

SHAPLEY, JOHN
ART HISTORIAN
b Mo, Aug 7, 90. Study: Univ Mo, AB; Princeton Univ, MA; Univ Vienna, PhD. Teaching: Asst prof art, Brown Univ, 19-24; prof art, NY Univ, 24-29; prof art, Univ Chicago, 29-39; prof art, Cath Univ Am, 52-60; prof art, Univ Baghdad, 60-63; prof art, Howard Univ, 63-70; prof art, George Washington Univ, 72-75. Awards: Carnegie Corp Medal; Decoration, Shah of Iran, 60. Publ: Translr, W Worringer, auth, Form Problems of the Gothic, 18; ed, Art Bull, 21-39; ed bd, Survey of Persian Art, 33-; co-auth, Comparisons in Art, Praeger, 57; contribr, var serials in Art Bull, Archeol & others. Mailing Add: 326 A St SE Washington DC 20003

SHAPSHAK, RENE
SCULPTOR
b Paris, France; US citizen. Study: Ecole des Beaux Arts, Paris; Ecole des Beaux Arts, Bruxelles; Art Sch, London, Eng. Work: Philathea Col Mus Mod Art, London, Ont; Butler Inst Am Art, Youngstown, Ohio; Munic Mus, Paris; Cecil Rhodes Mus, Bishop-Stortford, Eng; Pinakotheki, Athens, Greece; plus many others. Comn: Marble bas-relief, 42 & granite bas-relief, 42, New Gen Post Off, Capetown, SAfrica; metal sculptures, SAfrican Broadcasting Corp, 50 & munition factory, Pretoria, 54; fountain, City of New York, 72; plus many others. Exhib: One-man exhib, UN, 55; Palais des Beaux Arts, Paris, 55; Whitney Mus Am Art, New York, 56; Mus Art Mod, Paris, 71-72; Willimantic State Col, Conn; plus others. Pos: Dir, Rene Shapshak Mus Mod Art, London, Ont, Canada. Awards: Eloy Alfaro Medal, Panama, 65; Knight of Malta & St John of Jerusalem, 71; Comdr, Order of St Dennis of Zante, Greece, 75. Mem: Am Fedn Arts; Fr Art Theatre; Syndicate African Artists (patron); fel Royal Soc Arts; fel Nat Soc Lit & Arts. Style & Technique: Modern contemporary abstract sculpture. Mailing Add: 163 W 23rd St New York NY 10011

SHARF, FREDERIC ALAN
ART HISTORIAN, COLLECTOR
b Boston, Mass, Aug 13, 34. Study: Phillips Acad, Andover, Mass, grad, 52; Harvard Col, BA, 56, Harvard Univ, MA, 57. Collections Arranged: Essex County Artists, 1865-1910, 71 & John W Mansfield, An American Artist Rediscovered, 77, The Essex Inst, Salem, Mass. Mem: Arch Am Art (trustee). Res: Boston artists, 1840-1890. Interest: Catalogued the papers of J W Mansfield given to the Archives of American Art. Collection: Boston artists, 1840-1890. Publ: Various articles in Art Quart, Antiques Mag, Old Time New Eng & Essex Inst Hist Quart, 58- Mailing Add: 155 Heath St Chestnut Hill MA 02167

SHARITS, PAUL JEFFREY
FILM ARTIST, EDUCATOR
b Denver, Colo, Feb 7, 43. Study: Univ Denver, BFA(painting), 64; Ind Univ, MFA(visual design), 66. Work: Mus Mod Art, New York & Paris; Wallraf-Richartz Mus, Cologne, Ger; Albright-Knox Art Gallery, Buffalo, NY; Ga Mus Art, Athens; Anthology Film Arch, New York. Comn: 4-screen film environment, Contemp Arts Mus, Houston, 71; 4-screen film environment, Artpark, State of NY, Lewiston, 75. Exhib: One-man shows, 4-screen film piece, Sound Strip/Film Strip, 72 & 3-screen film piece, Synchronousoundtracks, 74, Bykert Gallery, New York, 2-screen Damaged Film Loop, Galerie Ricke, Cologne, 74 & exhib, 77, two 4-screen pieces, Albright-Knox Art Gallery, Buffalo, 76 & Galerie Ricke, Cologne, 77; Projected Images, Walker Art Ctr, Minneapolis, 74; Edinburgh Film Festival, Scotland, 76; Structural Film Retrospective, Nat Film Theatre, London, 76; Hist of the Am Avant-Garde Cinema, Mus Mod Art, New York, 76; Open to New Ideas: A Collection of New Art for Jimmy Carter, Ga Mus Art, Univ Ga, Athens, 76; Documenta 6, Kassel, WGer; Illusion & Reality (traveling exhib), Australia, 77; Film Retrospective, Centre Nat d'Art et de Cult Georges-Pompidou, Paris, 77; plus many others. Teaching: Instr film, Md Art Inst, Baltimore, 67-70; asst prof film, Antioch Col, Yellow Springs, Ohio, 70-73 & State Univ NY, Buffalo, 73- Awards: Individual Film Artist Award, Nat Endowment Arts, 74; Film Making Grant, Creative Artists Pub Serv Prog, New York, 75; Bicentennial Film Proj Grant, Nat Endowment for the Arts & NY State Coun on the Arts, 76. Bibliog: Regina Cornwell (auth), Sharits: Object & illusion, 9/71 & Rosalind Krauss (auth), Sharits: stop time, 4/73, Artforum; Annette Michelson (auth), Sharits & the critique of illusionism, Projected Images, 74. Mem: Col Art Asn Am (co-chmn comt on film, 75-). Style & Technique: Structural analyses of the material bases of cinema in a manner critical of its conventional illusionism; emphasis on perceptual realities. Media: Film. Publ: Auth, Red, blue, Godard, Film Quart, summer 66; auth, Notes on film, Film Cult, summer 69; auth, Words per page, Afterimage, Cambridge, Eng, fall 72; auth, Blank deflections: golden cinema, Film Cult, winter-spring 70; co-auth, Eight interviews/statements, Art in Am, 7-8/75. Dealer: Droll-Kolbert Gallery 724 Fifth Ave New York NY 10019; Galerie Ricke Friesenplatz 23 Cologne WGer. Mailing Add: Ctr for Media Study State Univ NY Buffalo NY 14261

SHARK, HERMAN R
MASTER PRINTER, PRINTMAKER
b Devils Lake, NDak, June 10, 46. Study: Univ Wis, Madison, BS(art), 68; Univ NMex, Albuquerque, MA, 70, with Garo Antreasian & Clinton Adams. Work: Univ Wis, Milwaukee; Fla State Univ, Tallahassee; Bradford Art Gallery, Yorkshire, Eng; Nat Collection of Fine Arts, Washington, DC; Univ NMex, Albuquerque. Exhib: US Pavilion, 35th Venice Biennale, Italy, 70; Venice 35, Rome & Smithsonian Inst, Washington, DC, 71; Bradford Biennale, 72. Collections Arranged: Shark's Lithography Ltd: The First Two Years, St Charles on Wazee, Denver, Colo. Teaching: Instr lithography, 35th Venice Biennale, 70; lectr lithography, Slade Sch Fine Art, Univ Col, London, Eng, 71-75. Pos: Printer fel, Tamarind Lithography Workshop, Los Angeles, 69; sr printer, Ed Alecto, London, Eng, 70-72; master printer, Petersburg Press, London, 72-74; dir & master printer, Shark's Lithography Ltd, Boulder, 76- Bibliog: Clinton Adams (ed), Three New Lithography Workshops, Tamarind Tech Papers, 4/76; Calvin Goodman (auth), Master printers & print, Am Artist, 10/76; Sally Sprout (auth), Bud Shark, master printmaker, Ocular Quart, fall 77. Publ: Auth, Graphics column, Studio Int, Vol 183 (6 issues; 1973). Mailing Add: 2886 Bluff St Boulder CO 80302

SHARP, ANNE
PAINTER, PRINTMAKER
b Red Bank, NJ, Nov 1, 43. Study: Pratt Inst, Brooklyn, NY, BFA, 65, with Richard Lindner; Brooklyn Col, MFA, with Lee Bontecou. Work: Smithsonian Inst, Nat Air & Space Mus, Washington, DC; Albright-Knox Art Gallery, Buffalo, NY; Contemp Gallery, Dallas, Tex; Int Mus of Erotic Art, San Francisco, Calif; Philip Morris, Inc, New York. Exhib: Encuentros, Int Art Exhib, Pamplona, Spain, 72; Int Mus of Erotic Art, San Francisco, 72-75; Community Gallery, Brooklyn Mus, 73; Ten Downtown Travels, Arnot Art Mus, Elmira, NY, 75; Yr of the Woman, Bronx Mus, NY, 75; MOMA Bookstore, Mus Mod Art, New York, 75-76; 40 Yrs of Am Collage, Buecker & Harpsichords, New York, 76; Ten Yrs Ten Downtown, Proj Studios One, Queens, NY, 77; Women Artists 78, Grad Ctr of City Univ of New York; one-person shows, Pace Ed, New York, 74, Katonah Gallery, NY, 74 & Contemp Gallery, Dallas, Tex, 75; plus others. Awards: Teaching fel, Artist's Show, Brooklyn, NY, 72; artist sponsor, Great Lakes Col Asn Apprenticeship Prog, 73-76; resident artist, Artist Open House, Va Ctr for Creative Art, 75. Bibliog: Emily Genauer (auth), Art & the artist, New York Post, 74; Peter Frank (auth), Prints, Art News, 2/75; Grace Glueck (auth), They create a new art scene, New York Sunday Times, 5/75. Mem: Women's Caucus on Art; Col Art Asn Am. Style & Technique: Planetary landscapes, postcard collages, painting, collage & silkscreen prints. Media: Watercolor; Three-Dimensional Wall Pieces; Mixed-Media Drawing. Publ: Auth, Ten Downtown, 74 & Philadelphic censorship, 74, Artworkers News, New York; contribr, Women Artists in America II, Univ Tenn, 75; illusr, Terminal Placebos, 75 & Planting Beeches, 75, New Rivers Press, New York. Mailing Add: Waverly Mews 23 Waverly Pl 3H New York NY 10003

SHARP, HAROLD
ILLUSTRATOR
b New York, NY, Mar 2, 19. Study: Nat Acad Design, 37-41; Columbia Univ, BA; Hunter Col, MA. Awards: Ashton Award, Hunter Col. Media: Watercolor, Ink. Publ: Illusr, L W Frolich Agency, New York Times, Gray Agency, J Am Med Asn & Physician Publ; cartoons publ in Sat Rev in Lit, Esquire, NY Times & Ladies Home J. Mailing Add: 3973 Saxon Ave New York NY 10463

SHARP, WILLOUGHBY
ART ADMINISTRATOR, VIDEO ARTIST
b New York, NY, Jan 23, 36. Study: Brown Univ, BA; Univ Paris; Univ Lausanne; Columbia Univ, MA. Work: Mus Mod Art, New York; Boston Mus Fine Arts; Mus Conceptual Art, San Francisco; plus others. Exhib: Information, Mus Mod Art, New York, 70; Earth, Air, Fire, Water: Elements of Art, Boston Mus Fine Art, 71; Encuentros, Pamplona, Spain, 72; Circuit: A Video Invitational, Everson Mus Art, Syracuse, NY, Henry Gallery, Univ Wash, Cranbrook Acad, Bloomfield & Los Angeles Co Mus, plus others, 73-74; Kunst Bleibt Kunst: Project, 74, Cologne, Ger, 74. Pos: Dir, Kineticism Press, 68-; pres, Avalanche Video, 70-; vpres, Ctr New Art Activities, Inc, 74- Awards: Rockefeller Found Grant, 71; Kaplan Fund Grant, 71; Nat Endowment Arts Grant, 72. Bibliog: Robert E Dallos (auth), Sculpture, New York Times, 8/30/67; Anthony Bannon (auth), Sharp puts himself into his art literally, Buffalo Eve News, 3/17/75; Douglas David (auth), Art, Newsweek, 7/21/75. Style & Technique: Video performance. Dealer: Electronic Arts Intermix Inc 84 Fifth Ave New York NY 10011. Mailing Add: Ctr New Art Activities Inc 93 Grand St New York NY 10013

SHARPE, DAVID FLEMMING
PAINTER, PRINTMAKER
b Owensboro, Ky, June 7, 44. Study: Art Inst of Chicago, BFA, 66, MFA, 68. Work: Art Inst of Chicago; Everson Mus, Syracuse, NY; Okla Art Ctr, Oklahoma City; Owens-Corning Corp Collections; Am Tel & Tel Collection. Exhib: Artists Under 30, 68, Soc of Contemp Art, 69 & 71, Recent Acquisitions, 70 & Distinguished Alumni 1945 to Present, 76, Art Inst of Chicago; Chicago Painting in the 1960s (touring major mus of Can), 71-72; Outside City Limits (touring NY state), 77-78; Masterpieces of Chicago Art, Chicago Cult Ctr, 77; Soho Ctr for Visual Arts, New York, 77; New Work-New York (traveling USA & Europe), 77-78; Larry Aldridge Mus Contemp Art, Ridgefield, Conn, 78. Style & Technique: Oil on canvas. Media: Oil Painting, Drawing, Watercolor. Dealer: Sonia Zaks 620 N Michigan Ave Chicago IL 60611. Mailing Add: 114 W Houston New York NY 10012

SHATALOW, VLADIMIR MIHAILOVICH
PAINTER
b Belgorod, Russia, July 20, 17; US citizen. Study: Inst Art, Kharkov, 34-36 & Inst Art, Kiev, USSR, 38-41. Work: Nat Acad of Design, New York; Mint Mus of Art, Charlotte, NC; Woodmere Art Gallery, Philadelphia; Sun Co Collection, Radnor, Pa; Moore Col of Art, Philadelphia. Exhib: Butler Inst Am Art, Youngstown, Ohio, 68; Watercolor Show, Pa Acad Fine Arts, Philadelphia, 69; Am Watercolor Soc Ann, New York, 70; Wichita Centennial Watercolor Competition, Kans, 71; Watercolor USA Nat, Springfield, Mo, 72; Marietta Col, Ohio. Awards: Gold Medal of Honor for Oil Painting, Allied Am Artists, New York, 65; Gold Medal for Watercolor, Nat Art Club, New York, 68; Audubon Artists Medal of Hon, New York, 73 & 78. Mem: Allied Am Artists; Artists Equity Asn; Audubon Artists; Philadelphia Watercolor Club; Am Watercolor Soc. Media: Oil, Tempera, Acrylic. Mailing Add: 2104 Poplar St Philadelphia PA 19130

SHATTER, SUSAN LOUISE
PAINTER
b New York, NY, Jan 17, 43. Study: Pratt Inst, BFA, 65; Skowhegan Sch Painting & Sculpture, summer 65; Boston Univ, MFA, 72. Work: Boston Mus of Fine Arts; Univ Utah Mus, Salt Lake City; Chase Manhattan Bank, New York; Philadelphia Mus of Art; Fed Reserve Bank of Boston. Comn: Colorado River in Utah (4ft x 8ft painting), Am 1976, US Dept Interior, 75; Panorama of Manhattan Island (3 1/2ft x 12 1/2ft), Am Tel & Tel Co, New York, 77. Exhib: New Talent Knoedler Gallery, New York, 71; one-woman shows, Fischbach Gallery, New York, 73, 75 & 78; A Sense of Place (traveling shows), 74; Boston Watercolor Today, Mus of Fine Arts, Boston, 76; America 1976 (traveling shows), Corcoran Gallery of Art, Washington, DC, 77. Teaching: Vis artist, Univ Pa, Philadelphia, 74-75; mem fac painting, Skowhegan Sch Painting, Maine, summer 77. Awards: Mass Coun Arts & Humanities Award, 74; Radcliffe Inst Fel, Boston, 75; Ingram-Merrill Found Grand, New York, 76. Bibliog: John Perreault (auth), Light rays caught and bent, Village Voice, 10/72; Hilton Kramer (auth), Review of Fischbach Show, New York Times, 12/73; Kay Larsen (auth), Review of Fischbach Show, Art News, 9/76. Style & Technique: Large panoramic landscapes and cityscapes, architecturally structured and loosely painted. Media: Watercolor; Acrylic. Dealer: Fischbach Gallery 29 W 57th St New York NY 10019. Mailing Add: 86 South St Boston MA 02111

SHAW, COURTNEY ANN
ART LIBRARIAN, ART HISTORIAN
b Hagerstown, Md, Feb 10, 46. Study: Univ Wis-Madison, BA; Case Western Res Univ, MSLS; Ariz State Univ. Teaching: Teacher art hist, Lake Placid, NY. Pos: Asst librn, Yavapai Jr Col, Prescott, Ariz; art librn, Ariz State Univ; head fine arts libr, Lake Placid Sch Art; art librn & expert, Medieval & Renaissance tapestries studies, Univ Md. Mem: Art Libr Soc; Medieval Acad of Am, Washington, DC; Conservation Guild; Art Libr Soc NAm (co-chmn, DC, Va & Md Chap). Mailing Add: Art-Sociology Bldg Univ of Md College Park MD 20742

SHAW, DONALD EDWARD
PAINTER, SCULPTOR
b Boston, Mass, Aug 24, 34. Study: Boston Mus Sch Fine Arts. Exhib: Inst Aragon, Guadalajara, Mex & Univ Guadalajara, 68; David Gallery, Houston, 72; Vorpal Gallery, San Francisco, 71; Gallery Mod Art, Taos, 71 & 72; The Small Store, Houston, Tex, 73 & 74; Houston Pub Libr, Tex, 74; Group Exhib, Blaffer Gallery, Univ of Houston, Tex, 74 & 75; Art Mus of STex, Corpus Christi, 75; Robinson Gallery, Houston, Tex, 76; Videotape: Sky Drawings, Tex Gallery, Houston, 76; Inauguration, San Angelo State Univ Mus, Tex, 76; Tex 30, Nave Mus, Victoria, Tex, 77; Kornblatt Gallery, Baltimore, Md, 77; one-man show, Moody Gallery, Houston, Tex, 78; plus many others. Bibliog: Ann Holmes (auth), Fantastic artists, Southwest Art Gallery Mag, 2/72; N Laliberte & A Mogelon (auths), Art in Boxes, Van Nostrand, Reinhold Co, 74. Awards: Travel grant to Arg, Casa De'Arg, 77. Media: Mixed Media. Publ: Contribr, Logo, Agencia Noticias Mex, 69 & cover illus, Southwest Art Gallery Mag, 72. Dealer: Moody Gallery Houston TX. Mailing Add: c/o Moody Gallery 2015J W Gray Houston TX 77019

SHAW, ELSIE BABBITT
SCULPTOR, PAINTER
b Charlotte, NC, Dec 6, 29. Study: Salem Acad, 48; Mt Vernon Jr Col, 49; Rollins Col, BA, 51; study with Jerry Farnsworth, 60, Hilton Leech, 60 & Syd Solomon, 65. Work: Mint Mus Art, Charlotte; Greenville Mus Art, SC; Tyler Mus Art, Tex; Am Nat Bank, Chattanooga, Tenn; Univ NC. Comn: Citrus Grove (11 & 1/2 ft copper & bronze), comn by Frank Hubbard, Orlando & Art Sources, Jacksonville, for Citrus Club, Orlando, Fla, 73; Fruit Picker (copper & bronze), John Chisholm Law Off, New Smyrna Beach, Fla, 75. Exhib: Nat Acad Design, New York, 63, 67 & 71; Isaac Delgado, New Orleans, La, 64; Southeastern Ann, Atlanta, Ga, 64-65; Butler Inst Art, Youngstown, Ohio, 66-68; Allied Artists Am, New York, 66 & 67. Teaching: Artist in residence basic & metal sculpture, Maitland Art Ctr, Fla, summer 75. Awards: Piedmont Purchase Award, Mint Mus Art, Charlotte, NC, 64; Mr & Mrs R E Holley Award, Arts Nat, Tyler Mus Art, Tex, 69; Salmagundi Club Prize, Nat Acad Design, 71. Bibliog: Mary Lou Norwood (auth), Exploring Florida waterways in a houseboat, Am Artist Mag, 4/69; TV documentary, Sound on Art & Artists, Channel 24 TV, Orlando, 73; Dona Z Meilach (auth), Small Environments, Box Art, Crown Publ, Inc, New York, 75. Style & Technique: Figurative realist; sprayed enamel paintings finished with oils; direct welded and brazed scrap copper tubing and sheet copper, decorated and shaped with bronze welding rod via oxygen-acetylene. Dealer: Art Sources Gulf Life Tower Jacksonville FL 32207; Galleries Int Winter Park FL 32789. Mailing Add: PO Box 1060 DeLand FL 32720

SHAW, ERNEST CARL
SCULPTOR
b New York, NY, Apr 17, 42. Work: Aldrich Mus Contemp Art, Ridgefield, Conn; Bradley Collection, Milwaukee, Wis; also in collection of Nelson Rockefeller, NY. Exhib: Storm King Art Ctr, Mountainville, NY, 77; Contemp Reflections, Aldrich Mus Contemp Art, 77; Hamilton Gallery of Contemp Art, New York, 77; Sculpture & Painting, Indianapolis Mus Art, Ind, 78; one-man outdoor shows, Milwaukee Ctr for Performing Arts, 77, Poughkeepsie Main Mall, 77, Tanglewood Festival, summer 78 & Storm King Art Ctr, 78; one-man shows, Sculpture Now, New York, 78; three-man show, Hamilton Gallery Contemp Art, 78. Style & Technique: Steel; large scale. Dealer: Max Hutchinson c/o Sculpture Now Greene St New York NY. Mailing Add: 2 Wawarsing Rd New Paltz NY 12561

SHAW, (GEORGE) KENDALL
PAINTER, INSTRUCTOR
b New Orleans, La, Mar 30, 24. Study: Ga Inst Technol, 44-46; Tulane Univ, BS, 49, MFA, 59; La State Univ, 50; New Sch Social Res, 50-52; Brooklyn Mus Art Sch, 53; also with Edward Corbett, Ralston Crawford, Stuart Davis, O Louis Guglielmi, George Rickey & Mark Rothko. Work: Albright-Knox Art Gallery, Buffalo, NY; Mus Contemp Art, Nagaoka, Japan; NY Univ; Tulane Univ, New Orleans; Chase Manhattan Bank, NY. Exhib: Four one-man exhibs, Tibor de Nagy Gallery, New York, 64-68 & addtional one-man exhibs, John Bernard Myers Gallery, New York, 72 & Alessandra Gallery, New York, 77; Contemporary Painting, Mus Contemp Art, Nagaoka, 65; Modular Painting, Albright-Knox Art Gallery, 70; Sets for The First Reader by Gertrude Stein, Mus Mod Art & Metrop Mus Art, New York, 70-71. Teaching: Instr painting, Parsons Sch Design, 66-; instr painting, Brooklyn Mus Art Sch, 69-Mem: Col Art Asn Am. Mailing Add: 725 Union St Brooklyn NY 11215

SHAW, HARRY HUTCHISON
PAINTER
b Savannah, Ohio, Oct 4, 97. Study: Univ Mich; Cleveland Sch Art; Pa Acad Fine Arts; Russ Moffet Sch, Provincetown; Ohio State Univ, BFA & MA; Nat Univ Mex; Stanford Univ. Work: Smithsonian Inst, Washington, DC; Mod Mus Art, Mexico City; Lord Neuffield Found, London, Eng; US Embassy, Mexico City; Columbia Art Mus, SC. Comn: Akron YWCA, 29; Women's League Chapel, Univ Mich, Ann Arbor, 30; Pub Libr, Lafayette, La. Exhib: Inst Mex-Am Cult Rels, Mexico City, 64-68; Inst Cult Rels, Guadalajara & Monterrey, Mex, 68; Mus Art, Columbia, SC, 70; Butler Inst Am Art, Youngstown, Ohio; Pa Acad Fine Arts, Philadelphia; plus many others, incl exhibs in Paris, London & Torremolinos, Spain. Teaching: Instr, Miami Univ, 25-26; instr painting, Art Mus Sch, Clearwater, Fla, 41-42; assoc prof art, Univ Southwestern La, 42-59. Pos: Head dept art, Marietta Col, 36; dir summer sch, Ohio Sch Painting, 36-38. Bibliog: Conroy Maddox (auth), article in Arts Rev, London, 62. Mem: Cent Stud E Scambi Int, Rome; Longboat Key Art Asn. Style & Technique: Creative semi abstract painting. Media: Oil, Acrylic, Watercolor. Dealer: Hobe Sound Gallery Hobe Sound FL 33455. Mailing Add: 501 Sloop Lane Sarasota FL 33577

SHAW, RENATA VITZTHUM
ART LIBRARIAN
b Mänttä, Finland, July 21, 26; US citizen. Study: Univ Chicago, MA(art hist), 49; Univ Helsinki, Finland, MPhil(art hist), 51; Ecole de Louvre, Paris, dipl (museology), 52; Catholic Univ Am, MS(libr sci), 62. Pos: Reference librn art, Prints & Photog Div, Libr of Congress, Washington, DC, 62-67, supervisory librn art, 67-71, bibliog specialist art, 71-; chmn, Washington Art Libr Resources Comt, 77- Mem: Art Librn NAm; Spec Libr Asn (chmn picture div, 74-75 & div cabinet, 77-78; mem bd dirs, 77-). Res: Art bibliography; collection development; visual librarianship; organization of visual collections. Interest: Development of a research collection in the field of art history encompassing all periods, present holdings 260,859 volumes. Publ: Auth, Picture searching (bibliog), Spec Libr, 73; auth, Handbook of Latin American Studies: Book Annotations, Univ Fla, 74; auth, Quarterly Journal of the Library of Congress: Essays, Libr of Cong, 75; auth, Encyclopedia of Library & Information Science, Marcel Dekker, 77. Mailing Add: 4850 Langdrum Lane Chevy Chase MD 20015

SHAW, RICHARD BLAKE
SCULPTOR
b Hollywood, Calif, Sept 12, 41. Study: Orange Coast Col, 61-63; San Francisco Art Inst, BFA, 65; Alfred Univ, 65; Univ Calif, Davis, MA, 68. Work: Oakland Mus, Calif; San Francisco Mus; Nat Mus Art, Tokyo; Johnson's Wax Collection; US Info Agency. Exhib: One-man shows, Dilexi Gallery, San Francisco, 68, San Francisco Mus Art, 73, Quay Gallery, 70, 71, 73 & 76 & E G Gallery, Kansas City, Mo, 74; Objects USA, Johnson's Wax Collection, 69; Whitney Mus Am Art Sculpture Ann, New York, 70; Contemporary American Ceramic Mus Mod Art, Kyoto & Tokyo, Japan, 71-72; International Ceramics, 1972, Victoria & Albert Mus, London, 72; Am Crafts—a Contemp View, Mus of Contemp Art, Chicago, 76; The Object as Poet, Renwick Gallery, Smithsonian Inst, Washington, DC, 76; Painting & Sculpture in Calif—the Mod Era, Nat Collection of Fine Arts, Washington, DC, 77; The Chosen Object: Europ & Am Still Life, Joslyn Art Mus, Omaha, Nebr, 77. Teaching: Chmn ceramics dept, San Francisco Art Inst, 65-; mem fac, Univ Wis-Madison, summer 71. Awards: Agnus Brandenstein Fel, 64-65; Nat Endowment Arts, 70- & crafts grant, 74. Bibliog: Articles in Arts Int, 5&6/66, Objects USA, Viking Press, 69 & Arts Can, summer 71; Daniel Rhodes (auth), Clay & Glazes for the Potter. Mem: Order Golden Brush; Int Soc Ceramists. Media: Ceramics, Mixed Media. Dealer: Ruth Braunstein c/o Quay

Gallery 560 Sutter St San Francisco CA 94102. Mailing Add: 231 Frustuck Ave Fairfax CA 94930

SHEAD, S RAY
PAINTER, PRINTMAKER
b Cartersville, Ga, Nov 27, 38. Study: Atlanta Art Inst, BFA, 60; Art Ctr Col Design, BPA, 63; Ga State Univ; Inst Allende, Mex; also with John Rodgers & Loser Fiedelson, Los Angeles. Work: Columbus Mus, Ga; Montgomery Mus, Ala; Opelika Art League, Ala; Atlanta High Mus, Ga; Southwest Ga Art Mus, Albany. Comn: Painting, Chrysler Corp, Atlanta, 60; sculpture, Dibco-Wayne Corp, Atlanta, 68; painting, Callaway Gardens, Ga, 70. Exhib: Dixie Ann, Montgomery, Ala, 60; 6th Ann Callaway Gardens Exhib, Ga, 69; 49th Shreveport Art Exhib, La, 70; Ga Artists Exhib I & II, Atlanta, 71-72; SC Artists, 74. Teaching: Assoc prof art & head dept, LaGrange Col, 68-73; head dept art, Presby Col, 73- Pos: Art dir, Compton Advert, New York, 63-67; art dir, Marschalk Co, Atlanta, 67; head, Visual Communications Art Dept, DeKalb Col, Decatur, Ga, currently. Awards: 2nd Dixie Ann Award, 60; Southern Contemp Award, 69; 6th Ann Columbus Exhib Award, 70. Mem: Col Art Asn Am. Media: Acrylic, Epoxy. Dealer: Beverly Singlee Atlanta GA 30034; Ann Jacobs Gallery 17 S Rhodes Ctr NW Atlanta GA 30309. Mailing Add: 2933 Cocklebor Trail Decatur GA 30034

SHEAKS, BARCLAY
PAINTER
b East Chicago, Ind. Study: Va Commonwealth Univ, BFA; Col William & Mary, teaching cert. Work: Va Mus Fine Arts, Richmond; Butler Inst Am Art, Youngstown, Ohio; Columbia Mus Fine Arts, SC; Mobile Mus, Ala; Chrysler Mus, Norfolk, Va; Mariners Mus, Newport News, Va. Comn: Portrait of USS Am, USN, 64; portrait of USS Enterprise, comn by off of ship, 65; portrait of USS John F Kennedy, City of Newport News, 69; painting series, Exec Suite, Tenneco Corp, Newport News Shipyard, 72; space paintings, NASA, Langley Res Ctr, Hampton, Va; 120ft painting depicting surface of Mars, US Bicentennial Expo on Sci & Technol, Kennedy Space Ctr, 76; plus others. Exhib: Nat Drawing Biennial (drawing selected for Smithsonian Inst Nat Traveling Exhib), Norfolk Mus, Va, 65; Butler Inst Am Art Mid Year Show Am Painting, 65, 66 & 67; 99 Exhibition, Am Watercolor Soc, Nat Acad Design, New York, 66; Juried Art Exhib, Corcoran Gallery Art, Washington, DC, 67; Ten Top Realists SE, Gallery Contemp Art, Winston-Salem, NC, 69-70. Teaching: Head art dept, Newport News Pub Schs, 49-69; assoc prof art, Va Wesleyan Col, 69- Pos: Art consult, Hunt Mfg Co, Philadelphia, 65; lectr, Va Mus, Richmond, 70; artist in residence, Richmond Humanities Ctr, 71. Bibliog: Russel Woody (auth), chap, In: Painting in Synthetic Media & Complete Guide to Polymer Paintings, Van Nostrand Reinhold. Mem: Tidewater Artists Asn; Salmagundi Club. Style & Technique: Thin applications of acrylic paint in styles ranging from loose romantic realism to hard edge super realism. Media: Acrylic, Polymer. Publ: Auth, Painting with Acrylics from Start to Finish, 72 & Drawing and Painting the Natural Environment, Davis, Mass, 74; auth, Painting with Oils, Davis. Dealer: Chester Smith Seaside Art Gallery Nags Head NC 27959. Mailing Add: 51 Hopkins St Newport News VA 23601

SHECHTMAN, GEORGE HENOCH
ART DEALER
b Paterson, NJ, Dec 8, 41. Study: Rutgers Univ, BA(art hist), 64. Pos: Dir, Christopher Gallery, New York. Specialty: Contemporary American paintings. Mailing Add: c/o Christopher Gallery 766 Madison Ave New York NY 10021

SHECTER, MARK
PAINTER
b Baltimore, Md, Apr 18, 43. Study: Philadelphia Col of Fine Arts; Boston Univ; Leicester Col; Am Univ, Washington, DC; Univ Miami, Coral Gables, Fla, BA. Work: Corcoran Mus of Art, Washington, DC; Lowe Mus of Art, Univ Miami, Fla; Rose Mus of Art, Brandeis Univ, Boston; Jewish Theological Seminary Mus, Cincinnati, Ohio; Hagerstown Mus of Fine Art, Md. Comn: Adam (monumental 8ft figure), Beth Tfiloh Synagogue, Baltimore, 68; Moses, Jewish Mus, Baltimore, 68; Art in Embassies Prog, US State Dept, 70: Dr Soloman Schechter, Theological Seminary, New York, 74; Colorama (yellow still life), Jewish Community Ctr, Baltimore, 77. Exhib: Chrysler Mus of Art at Norfolk, Va, 68; Int Art Exhib, Coloseum, New York, 69; Johns Hopkins Univ Art Exhib, Baltimore, 70; Am Painters in Paris Exhib, Vendome Art Gallery, France, 75. Awards: Honorable Mention, NY Int Art Show, 69. Style & Technique: Contemporary realism. Dealer: Globe Gallery 1727 N Charles St Baltimore MD 21201; George Gallery 7 E 14th St New York NY 10003. Mailing Add: 1800 N Charles St Baltimore MD 21201

SHECTER, PEARL S
PAINTER
b New York, NY, Dec 17, 10. Study: Hunter Col, BFA; Columbia Univ, MFA; Hans Hofmann Sch Painting; Archipenko Sch Art, New York; New Bauhaus Sch Design, with Moholy-Nagy; Acad Grande Chaumiere, Paris. Work: NY Univ; John F Kennedy Libr; Miami Univ, Ohio; Int Rels Found, New York; also in many pvt collections. Exhib: Walker Art Ctr, Minn, 63; Carnegie Endowment Ctr, New York, 63; Lehigh Univ, Allentown, Pa, 67; Mfs Hanover Trust Bank, 70 & 71; Union Carbide Gallery, New York, 72, 75 & 78. Teaching: Lectr studio courses, NY Univ, 58-69; instr studio courses, Newton-Harvard Creative Art Ctr, 63. Pos: Art dir, Elisabeth Irwin High Sch, 75. Awards: Carnegie Found Grant, 50; Gold Medal, Patronato Scholastico Arti, Italy, 63. Bibliog: Artists New York (tape), Voice of Am, 72. Mem: Int Asn Art Bull UNESCO; Artists New York (pres, 72-75); NY Soc Women Artists (secy); Nat Soc Lit & Art. Style & Technique: Paintings with colle letters have a mysticism and spirituality. Media: Acrylic, Gold Leaf, Collage. Publ: Contribr, Art News, Art Digest & Art Now, 63-70. Mailing Add: 60 E Ninth St New York NY 10003

SHEEHAN, EVELYN
PAINTER
b Hymera, Ind, Dec 27, 19. Study: Scripps Col, with Jean Ames; also study with Phil Dike & Rex Brandt. Work: Lytton Collection, Los Angeles; Calif Bank, San Francisco; Mus Art, Univ Ore, Eugene; Tacoma Bank, Wash; Automatic Sales Co, Portland, Ore. Exhib: 144th Ann Exhib, Nat Acad Design, New York, 69; Spokane Ann Art Exhib, Cheney-Cowles Mus Art, Wash, 69; Watercolor USA, Springfield Art Mus, Mo, 70; 32nd Ann Northwest Exhib, Seattle Art Mus, Wash, 71; Dimensional Construction Exhib, Portland Contemp Craft Gallery, 77; Exhib of Paintings, Governor's Ceremonial Chambers, Salem, 77; one-man show, Mus Art, Univ Ore, Eugene, 71. Awards: Top Cash Award, Nat Soc Painters in Casein, 67; Lytton Purchase Award, Watercolor USA, 67; Mo Award, 32nd Ann Nat Watercolor Soc, 71. Mem: Nat Soc Painters in Casein; Nat Watercolor Soc; Portland Art Asn. Style & Technique: Non-objective and loosely representational, with the human form the main theme. Media: Water-Based Media for Painting; Collage. Mailing Add: 3935 SW Corbett Ave Portland OR 97201

SHEEHE, LILLIAN CAROLYN
PAINTER
b Conemaugh, Pa, Oct 16, 15. Study: Indiana Univ Pa, BS(art); ceramics & sculpture with Sheldone Grumbling, majolica with Hugh Geise & painting & sculpture with George Ream. Work: Court of Gabrielle (serigraph), David Glosser Libr; Trees at Christmastime in California (serigraph), Flood Mus; 130 glass-fired paintings & sagged bottle collection, C of C, Johnstown, Pa. Comn: Golf mural, J Cover, Johnstown, Pa, 44; designed & printed Christmas cards, Pa Rehab Ctr & Bur Voc Rehab, 59-71; emblem design, Lee Hosp Rehab Med Dept, 66; landscape mosaic, Mrs Lyn Hoffman, 70; art calendar, Allied Artists Am, 71. Exhib: All Allied Artists Shows, 36-; Pittsylvania Ceramic Guild All-Pa Competition, 64-71; Three Rivers Arts Festival, 65 & 66; Allied Artists Graphic Arts Show, 70; Sheraton '75. Teaching: Art supvr, East Conemaugh Schs, 36-42; instr art & world hist, Westmont High Sch, 44-45 & 53-54; instr art & art supvr, Ferndale-Dale Grade & High Schs, 55-59; instr arts & crafts, Pa Voc Rehab Ctr, 59-75. Pos: Designer & coordr, Around About Now in Johnstown, 71-72; designer & coordr, Around The County, 75. Awards: Purchase Award, 61 & Allied Artists Best of Show, 70, US Bank Show; Phoebe Jerema Award, Pittsylvania Ceramic Guild, 71; David Glosser Libr Craft Award, 73. Bibliog: Art Exhibit (two TV shows on glass work), George Mengelson, Producer, 69; article, Johnstown Tribune-Democrat, 7/76; Catholic Register, Altoona, Pa, 5/76. Mem: Allied Artists (mem bd for many yrs, pres, 70-72); Pittsylvania Ceramic Guild; Area Arts Coun (pres, 75-77); Arts Assocs; Cult Affairs Comt (coordr spec events publ, chmn, 75-78). Style & Technique: Contemporary-modern; original technique of studied and applied glass tolerances to unique fired-glass art. Media: Fired Glass, Oil, Copper Enameling. Res: Experimented twenty-years on uses of fired glass and its combinations for pictorial work. Collection: Eighty photogravures on satin, circa 1885. Publ: Auth & illusr, Allied Artists Fall Show Catalog (plus cover design), 58; auth, Useless to useful, Leather Craftsman Mag, 61; auth & illusr, Antiquity in a day, Ceramics Arts & Crafts, 64; auth & illusr, Textbook on Photo—Tinting—Color—Oils, Bur Voc Rehab, 65; auth, I Dreamed in Glass, Antique Trader, 7/77; plus others. Mailing Add: 1333 Christopher St Johnstown PA 15905

SHEETS, MILLARD OWEN
DESIGNER, PAINTER
b Pomona, Calif, June 24, 07. Study: Chouinard Art Inst, 28; Otis Art Inst, Hon MFA, 63; Univ Notre Dame, Hon LLD, 64. Work: Metrop Mus Art & Whitney Mus Art, New York; Art Inst Chicago; Los Angeles Mus Art; San Francisco Mus Art; plus many others. Comn: Libr tower granite mosaic, Univ Notre Dame, South Bend, Ind; mosaic dome & chapel, Nat Shrine, Washington, DC; mosaic facade, Detroit Pub Libr; mural, Rainbow Tower, Hilton Hotel, Honolulu; two large murals, Los Angeles City Hall E, Los Angeles; numerous banks & savings & loan bldgs & murals in Calif & Tex. Exhib: Albright-Knox Art Gallery, Buffalo, NY; Art Inst Chicago; Va Mus Fine Arts, Richmond; Sao Paulo, Brazil; Arthur Tooth Galleries, London, Eng; plus many others. Teaching: Chouinard Art Inst, 28-35; prof art, Scripps Col, 31-, head dept art, 32-55; dir, Otis Art Inst, 55-62. Pos: Artist, Life Mag, Burma-India Front, 43-44; US State Dept Specialist Prog to Turkey & Russia, 60-61; trustee, Scripps Col, 66-; trustee, Calif Inst Arts, 68-76; trustee, Art Ctr Sch of Design. Awards: Prizes, Art Inst Chicago, Nat Watercolor Soc & Philadelphia Watercolor Soc; plus many others. Mem: Nat Acad Design; Nat Watercolor Soc; Am Watercolor Soc; Econ Round Table, Los Angeles; Bohemian Club. Mailing Add: Box 150 Barking Rocks Gualala CA 95445

SHELDON, OLGA N (MRS A B SHELDON)
PATRON, COLLECTOR
b Lexington, Nebr, Aug 25, 97. Awards: Distinguished Nebraskan Award, Nebr Soc Washington, DC, 71. Collection: Works of Robert Henri; American art; works on loan or donated to Sheldon Memorial Art Gallery, University of Nebraska, Lincoln; Philip Johnson Building donated by family. Mailing Add: PO Box 158 Lexington NE 68850

SHELTON, GILBERT KEY
CARTOONIST, ILLUSTRATOR
b Dallas, Tex, May 31, 40. Study: Univ of Tex, BA, 61. Exhib: The Phonus Balonus, Corcoran Gallery, Washington, DC, 69; Comix Mus of Contemp Art, Chicago, 72. Pos: Ed-in-chief, Rip Off Press, San Francisco, 72- Bibliog: Jacob Brackman (auth), The International Comix Conspiracy, Playboy Mag, 70; Harvey Kurtzman (auth), @&%$#!! or, takin' the lid off the id, Esquire Mag, 6/71. Style & Technique: Pen, brush and ink. Publ: Auth & illusr, The Collected Freak Brothers, 71 & Further Adventures of the Fabulous Furry Freak Brothers, 72, co-auth & co-illusr, The Adventures of Fat Freddy's Cat, 77, The Fabulous Furry Freak Brothers in Grass Roots, 77 & Throughly Ripped with the Fabulous Furry Freak Brothers, 78, Rip Off Press. Dealer: Simon Lowinsky Gallery 228 Grant Ave San Francisco CA 94108. Mailing Add: 1250 17th St San Francisco CA 94107

SHELTON, ROBERT LEE
DESIGNER, EDUCATOR
b Memphis, Tenn, Apr 8, 39. Study: Memphis State Univ, BFA; Univ Ala, MA. Work: Columbus Mus Art, Ga; Montgomery Mus Fine Art, Ala; SCent Bell, Regional Off, Birmingham, Ala; First Nat Bank, Montgomery, Ala; Ambassadors Off, Fed Repub Ger. Exhib: Nat Small Painting Biennial, Purdue Univ, 66; Nat Black & White Prints, Kans State Univ, 66; Mid-South Ann, Memphis, Tenn, 69; Hunter Gallery Ann, Chattanooga, Tenn, 69; Graphics USA, Dubuque, Iowa, 70. Teaching: Asst prof drawing & design, Auburn Univ, Ala, 64-68; assoc prof printmaking & design, Birmingham-Southern Col, Ala, 68- Pos: Vpres, Ala Art League, 69-71. Awards: First Prize, Macon Mus, 68; First Purchase Award, Columbus Mus Art, 69 & 72; First Purchase Award, Montgomery Mus Art, 70. Bibliog: Martin Hames (auth), Robert Shelton, 1975 Birmingham Festival of Arts Bull, 3/75. Mem: Birmingham Art Asn (bd mem, 74-75); Tenn Valley Art Asn. Style & Technique: Drawings, prints, paintings in partial figurative and geometric forms. Media: Crayon, Oil, Assemblage. Publ: Auth, Contemporary printmaking in the US, Birmingham Festival Bull, 73. Dealer: Courtyard Gallery 2800 Sixth Ave S Birmingham AL 35208. Mailing Add: 1209 Greensboro Rd Birmingham AL 35208

SHENG, SHAO FANG
PAINTER, CRAFTSMAN
b Tientsin, China, Sept 13, 18; US citizen. Study: Painting with Old Master of Peking; Taliesin East & West, artist with Frank Lloyd Wright; Fla Southern Col; Marietta Col. Work: Norfolk Mus Arts & Sci; Zanesville Art Inst, Ohio. Comn: Paintings & frescoes, Chinese Govt, 45; paintings, comn by Frank Lloyd Wright, 48-49; mural & five paintings, comn by Herbert Randall, 59; paintings, comn by Noah Gang, 68; paintings, Charleston Nat Bank, 71; plus others. Exhib: Fla Southern Col, Lakeland, 50; one-man show, Art Inst Chicago, 50; Am Fedn Arts Traveling Exhib, US, 51; Mountain State Arts & Craft Fair, Cedar Lake, Ripley, WVa, 66-76; Contemp Art Gallery, Palm Beach, 68-69. Teaching: Instr painting, Fla Southern Col, 48-49; instr painting & Chinese lang, Chautauqua Inst, 55-78; instr painting & jewelry, Parkersburg Community Col, 72-78. Pos: Res painter, Acad Sinic, Manking, China, 42-44. Awards: First Prize for Yin-Yang, The Creative & Receptive, Appalachian Corridors, 68;

First Prize for Dream of Rockhound (oil), Chautauqua Art Gallery, 69; First Prize for Facet 3D (sculpture), Allied Artists WVa, 71; plus others. Mem: Int Platform Asn; Nat Soc Arts & Lett; Ohio Arts & Crafts Guild; WVa Artists & Craftsmen Guild; Allied Artists WVa. Style & Technique: Traditional Chinese watercolor; oil and watercolor for contemporary paintings; ceramics; silver, gold, brass, bronze, gemstone jewelry; enamelling. Mailing Add: Rte 1 Williamstown WV 26187

SHEON, AARON
ART HISTORIAN
b Toledo, Ohio, Oct 7, 37. Study: Univ Mich, AB, MA, 60; Inst d'Art et d'Archeolgie, Paris, 62; Princeton Univ, MFA, PhD, 66. Pos: Assoc prof, Univ Pittsburgh, Pa, 66. Awards: Wilson Fel, Princeton Univ, 62; Ford Found Grant, Univ Pittsburgh, 67; Bowman Fac Award, Univ Pittsburgh, 76. Mem: Col Art Asn; Soc Fr Art Hist. Res: French 19th and 20th century art history; art and scientific thought; educational role of the museum. Publ: Auth, Gosman Collection, Univ Pittsburgh, 69; auth, French Art & Science, Art Quart, 71; auth, Discovery of graffiti, Art J, 76; auth, Multistable perception in romantic caricatures, Studies in Romanticism, 77; auth, Monticelli (exhib catalogue), Pittsburgh Mus Art, 78. Mailing Add: Dept of Fine Arts Univ Pittsburgh Pittsburgh PA 15260

SHEPARD, LEWIS ALBERT
ART DEALER, ART HISTORIAN
b East Orange, NJ, May 24, 45. Study: Rutgers Univ, New Brunswick, BA, 67; Ind Univ, Bloomington, MA, 70. Collections Arranged: Cowboys, Indians, Trappers & Traders (with catalogue), Mead Art Gallery, Amherst Col, 73 & Am Painters of the Arctic (with catalogue), 75. Teaching: Asst instr mod art, Ind Univ, Bloomington, 69-70; instr Am art, Amherst Col, 73-76. Pos: Trainee catalogue & dept head, Sotheby Parke Bernet, New York, 70-72; cur, Mead Art Gallery, Amherst Col, 72-77; proprietor, dealer & appraiser, pvt pract, Worcester, Mass, 77- Mem: Col Art Asn. Res: American 19th and 20th century painting; Western Americana; Arctic exploration; arts and crafts movement. Specialty: American and European 19th and 20th century art. Collection: American drawings 1830-1930. Publ: Auth, Willard Metcalf Exhibition—a Review, Am Art Rev, 77; auth, American Art at Amherst College—a Summary Catalogue, Amherst Col, 78. Mailing Add: 2 Congress St Worcester MA 01609

SHEPHERD, DOROTHY G (MRS ERNST PAYER)
MUSEUM CURATOR
b Wellend, Ont, Aug 15, 16. Study: Univ Mich, AB & MA; Inst Fine Arts, NY Univ. Teaching: Lect, Islamic Art & Archit, Art & Archit of Spain, Islamic & Medieval Textiles & Art of the Ancient Near East; adj prof hist art, Case Western Reserve Univ, currently. Pos: Monuments officer, Monuments & Fine Arts Sect, SHAEF, Berlin, 45-47; cur textiles & Near Eastern art, Cleveland Mus Art, 54- Mem: Col Art Asn Am; Archaeol Soc Am; Am Res Ctr in Egypt; Centre Int Etudes Textiles Anciens, Middle East Inst; Am Soc Aesthet. Publ: Contribr to Arts Orientalis & Cleveland Mus Art Bull. Mailing Add: Cleveland Mus Art 11150 East Blvd Cleveland OH 44106

SHEPPARD, CARL DUNKLE
ART HISTORIAN
b Washington, DC, Jan 11, 16. Study: Amherst Col, BA; Harvard Univ, MA, 42, PhD, 47. Teaching: Instr, Univ Mich, Ann Arbor, 46-49; from asst prof to prof, Univ Calif, Los Angeles, 50-64; prof art hist & chmn dept, Univ Minn, Minneapolis, 64-75. Awards: Fulbright Res Grant, Italy, 56-57; Del Amo Found Grant, Spain, 57; McMillan Travel Grant, Italy, 68. Mem: Col Art Asn Am (mem bd dirs, 70-); Soc Archit Historians; Int Ctr Medieval Art (pres & treas); Medieval Acad; Int Cong Art Historians. Publ: Auth, introd & chapters 7, 8 & 11, Looking at Modern Painting, Norton, 62; auth, Subtleties of Lombard marble sculpture of the VIIth & VIIIth centuries, Gazette Beaux Arts, 64; auth, Carbon 14 dating & Santa Sophia, Dumbarton Oaks Papers, Istanbul, 65; auth, Byzantine carved marble slabs, Art Bull, 3/69; auth, Classicism in Tuscan Romanesque sculpture, Gesta, 77. Mailing Add: Dept of Art Hist 108 Jones Hall Univ of Minn Minneapolis MN 55455

SHEPPARD, JOHN CRAIG
PAINTER, EDUCATOR
b Lawton, Okla, July 22, 13. Study: Univ Okla, BFA(painting), 37, BFA(sculpture), 38; Univ Nev, Reno, Hon DFA, 74; also in Norway, France & Mex. Work: Mus Art Mod, Paris; Brooklyn Mus, NY; El Paso Mus Art; Gilcrease Mus Art, Tulsa, Okla; Mus Great Plains, Lawton. Comn: Murals, Bus Admin Bldg, Univ Okla, Norman, 41, Student Union Bldg, Mont State Univ, Bozeman, 42, Will Rogers Theater, Tulsa, 46 & in pvt homes, Okla, Nev, Kans & Tex; Arthur Orvis Portrait, Univ Nev, Reno, 68. Exhib: Mus Art, Bergen, Norway, 56; De Young Mus Art, San Francisco, 58; Salon Art Libre & Mus Beaux Arts, Paris, 62; Brooklyn Mus, 63; Watercolor USA, Springfield Art Mus, 68. Teaching: Instr sculpture & painting, Mont State Univ, 40-42; chmn dept art, Univ Nev, Reno, 47-71, emer prof, 74-; guest lectr Indian art, Univ Oslo, 55-56. Pos: Dir prod illus, Douglas Aircraft Co, Tulsa, 42-46. Awards: Bronze Medal, Denver Art Mus, 41; Silver Medal, Kansas City Midwest Ann, 44; Purchase Prize, Mus Art Mod, Paris, 62. Bibliog: Green Peyton (auth), America's Heartland: The Southwest, Univ Okla, 48; Robert Laxalt (auth), Nevada, Coward, 70. Mem: Am Asn Univ Prof; Pac Art Asn (regional rep, 50-); Western Asn Mus Dirs (regional dir, 48-65); Nev State Arts Coun (chmn, 62); Nev Art Gallery (bd dirs, 50-62). Style & Technique: Representational, Western action landscapes. Media: Watercolor, Oil. Publ: Illusr, Horses of the Conquest, 49 & Life & Death of an Oilman, 51, Univ Okla; co-auth & illusr, Landmarks on the Emigrant Trail, 71 & illusr, Centennial Portfolio, 74, Univ Nev, Reno. Mailing Add: 1000 Primrose St Reno NV 89509

SHEPPARD, JOSEPH SHERLY
PAINTER, SCULPTOR
b Owings Mills, Md, Dec 20, 30. Study: Md Inst Art, cert fine art; also with Jacques Maroger. Work: Baltimore Mus Art; Butler Inst Am Art, Youngstown, Ohio; Davenport Munic Art Gallery, Iowa; Univ Ariz Mus; Norfolk Mus Arts & Sci, Va. Comn: Portrait of Pres Hawkins, Towson State Col, Md, 67; Discovery of Scurvy, Pub Health Hosp, Baltimore, 68; Battle of Ft McHenry, Equitable Trust Co, Baltimore, 69; Christ Crowned with Thorns, Lutheran High Sch, Baltimore Co, 70; seven hist murals, Baltimore Police Dept, 70-71. Exhib: Allied Artists Nat, 56 & 59; Realists, Laguna Beach, 64; Regional, Butler Inst Am Art Nat, 67 & one-man show, 72; Baltimore Mus Art Regional, 71; Westmoreland Co Mus, Greenburg, Pa, 72; one-man show, Galerie de Tours, San Francisco, Calif. Teaching: Instr oil painting, Dickinson Col, 55-57; instr oil painting, Md Inst Art, 63- Awards: Emily Lowe Prize, Allied Artists, 56; Guggenheim Found Fel, 57-58; Purchase Prize, Butler Inst Am Art, 67. Mem: Allied Artists Am. Style & Technique: Representational. Media: Oil. Publ: Auth, Anatomy, 75 & auth, The Female Figure, 75, Watson-Guptill. Dealer: Grand Central Galleries 40 Vanderbilt Ave New York NY 10017; IFA Gallery 2623 Connecticut Ave NW Washington DC 20008. Mailing Add: c/o Galerie de Tours 559 Sutter St San Francisco CA 94102

SHEPPARD, LUVON
ART ADMINISTRATOR, EDUCATOR
b Sanford, Fla, Aug 15, 40. Study: Rochester Inst Technol, BFA, 69, MST, 70; also illus & printmaking with Norman Bate. Work: Mem Art Gallery, Univ Rochester; Forum East Gallery, Monroe Co Community Col. Comn: Large ethnic paintings, Baden St Settlement House & Black Studies Dept, State Univ NY Col Brockport, 73; mural, YWCA, Rochester, 71. Exhib: Rochester Finger Lakes Exhib, Mem Art Gallery, 69, 70 & 75; one-man show, Monroe Community Col, Rochester, 73; two-man show, Langston Hughes Ctr, Buffalo, 74. Collections Arranged: Allofus Art Workshop Fac Show, Nazareth Art Ctr, 74; Soul In 3, Mem Art Gallery, 4/74; Exposure 4, Mem Art Gallery, 2/75. Teaching: Dir & instr, Action for a Better Community Sidewalk Art Studios, Rochester, 68-69; dir & instr painting, Allofus Art Workshop, Univ Rochester, 71-; instr photo-design, Rochester Inst Technol, 72- Pos: Coordr Neighborhood Serv, Mem Art Gallery, Univ Rochester, 70- Awards: Best of Show (First Place), Rochester Curb Stone, 69-70; First Place Watercolor, Hammondsport Art Show, 71 & First Place Painting 72. Bibliog: James DeVinney (auth), Evolution of moment (videotape), on pub TV, 71; Marie Linton (auth), Black artist profile, About Time Mag, 73; Sally Walsh (auth), Luvon Sheppard-profile, Rochester Democrat & Chronicle, 75. Mem: Rochester Print Club; Monroe Co Arts Coun (bd of dir, chmn Individual Artists Prog, 73); Allofus Art Group (founder & chmn, 71). Style & Technique: Expressionistic naturalism based on the theater of involvement using Mylar. Media: Watercolor, Oil. Publ: Contribr, Scene News Mag, Monroe Co Arts Coun, 70; contribr, About Time Mag, 73; auth, article in Mus News Mag, 74. Mailing Add: c/o Mem Art Gallery 490 University Ave Rochester NY 14607

SHERBELL, RHODA
SCULPTOR, COLLECTOR
b Brooklyn, NY. Study: Art Students League, with William Zorach; Brooklyn Mus Art Sch, with Hugo Robies; study in Italy & France. Work: The Dancers, Okla Mus Art, Oklahoma City; The Flying Acrobats, Colby Col Art Mus, Waterville, Maine; Sculpture Garden, Stony Brook Mus, NY. Comn: Marguerite & William Zorach Bronze, Nat Arts Collection, Smithsonian Inst, Washington, DC, 64; bronzes of Aaron Copland & Yogi Berra, Montclair Art Mus; Casey Stengel, Country Art Gallery Long Island, Baseball Hall of Fame, Cooperstown, NY; Yogi Berra, comn by Percy Uris. Exhib: Pa Acad Fine Arts & Detroit Inst Art, 60; Am Acad Arts & Lett, 60; Brooklyn Mus Art Award Winners, 65; Nat Acad Design & Heckscher Mus Show, 67; Retrospective Sculpture & Drawing Show, Huntington Hartford Gallery, New York, 70; Retrospective Sculpture, Nat Art Mus of Sport, 77. Pos: Mem bd adv, Nat Art Mus of Sport; dir sculpture, Allied Artists; dir pub rels, Audubon Artists; asst to dir, Emily Lowe Gallery, Hofstra Univ. Awards: Am Acad Arts & Lett & Nat Inst Arts & Lett Grant, 60; Ford Found Purchase Award, 65; Louis Comfort Tiffany Found Grant, 66; Awards (two), Mainstream 77, Allied Artists Am, 77. Bibliog: The artist & the sportsman, Nat Art Mus Sport, 68; Alfredo Valente (auth), Rhoda Sherbell sculpture, New York Cult Ctr & Fairleigh Dickinson, 70; Woman in Bronze, educ television spec, Channel 21. Mem: Allied Artists Am; Audubon Artists; New York Soc Women Artists; Catharine Lorillard Wolfe Art Club. Style & Technique: Contemporary realism, modeling in clay and bronze. Media: Bronze. Collection: Contemporary American realistic work, including M Soyer, W Zorach, Marguerite Zorach, Mervin Honig, Harry Sternberg, John Koch, Agostine, H Jackson, Margit Beck and others. Dealer: Frank Rehn Inc 655 Madison Ave New York NY 10021. Mailing Add: 64 Jane Ct Westbury NY 11590

SHERE, CHARLES EVERETT
ART CRITIC
b Berkeley, Calif, Aug 20, 35. Study: Univ Calif, Berkeley, AB(hons), 61. Pos: Writer & producer art-oriented TV progs, KQED-TV, San Francisco, 67-75; writer rev & essays, Oakland Tribune, 73- Res: Extensive personal research into art of the early 20th century, especially Marcel Duchamp, and current California art. Publ: Auth, article on Vancouver painters, Arts Can, 12/75; auth, New Deal Art in California (catalogue essay), Univ Santa Clara, 76. Mailing Add: 1824 Curtis St Berkeley CA 94702

SHERIDAN, HELEN ADLER
ART LIBRARIAN
b Kansas City, Mo, Oct 3, 37. Study: Ohio State Univ; Univ Kans, BA; Univ Calif Los Angeles, MA; Western Mich Univ, MLS. Teaching: Instr arts of the 20th century, Western Mich Univ, 66-75. Pos: Head librn, Kalamazoo Inst Arts, Mich, 75- Mem: Col Art Asn; Art Libr Soc NAm (vchmn, Mich Chap, 76-77 & chmn, 77-78). Res: Regionalist artists and western Michigan area artists. Interest: American arts of the 20th century, especially regionalist art; documentation of local artists; problems in art librarianship. Mailing Add: 314 S Park St Kalamazoo MI 49006

SHERKER, MICHAEL Z
PAINTER, EDUCATOR
b New York, NY, Nov 9, 36. Study: Brooklyn Col, BA; Univ Mich, MFA; Columbia Univ, PhD. Work: Univ NC; Columbia Univ; Sfaad Mus, Israel; Newark Airport, Port Authority NY. Comn: Mem to Jewish Martyr, Polish Relief Workers Comt, 73; murals in St Gregorius Major, Roman Catholic Church, New York. Exhib: One-man shows, Soho Gallery, Newton Gallery, Village Gallery, Winter Gallery, Atran House Gallery, Raven Gallery, Artists' Market, Downtown Gallery & Allied Arts Ctr; plus many group exhibs. Teaching: Instr painting & drawing, Cent Carolina Univ, 64-66; prof painting & drawing, City Univ New York, 66- Awards: Cent Carolina Univ Fac Res Grant-In-Aid, 65. Mem: Col Art Asn; Brooklyn Mus Community Gallery (bd mem, 75-76). Style & Technique: Direct painting, monotypes. Media: Oil, Watercolor, Gouache, Nu-Pastel. Dealer: Soho Gallery 98 Prince St New York NY 10012. Mailing Add: 395 12th St Brooklyn NY 11215

SHERMAN, CLAIRE RICHTER
ART HISTORIAN, EDUCATOR
b Boston, Mass, Feb 11, 30. Study: Radcliffe Col, BA, 51; Univ Mich, with Marvin J Eisenberg, MA, 58; Johns Hopkins Univ, with Adolf Katzenellenbogen, PhD, 64. Teaching: Instr art hist, Univ Mich, 58-59; lectr art hist, Am Univ, 66-72; vis assoc prof of art, McIntire Dept of Art, Univ of Va, 76. Awards: Fulbright Scholar, 51-52; Am Asn Univ Women Fel, 62; Grant in Aid, Am Coun Learned Socs, 75. Mem: Col Art Asn Am; Southeastern Medieval Asn; Women's Caucus for Art. Res: Illustrations of Aristotle's Ethics & Politics in 14th & 15th century manuscripts; women scholars in the arts. Publ: Auth, The Portraits of Charles V of France (1338-80), 69; auth, Representations of Charles V of France as a wise ruler, 71; auth, The Queen in Charles V's Coronation Book, Viator, Medieval & Renaissance Studies, 8 (1977); auth, Some visual definitions of the illustrations of Aristotle's Nichomachean Ethics and Politics in the French translation of Nicole Oresme, Art Bull, 59 (1977). Mailing Add: 4516 Que Lane NW Washington DC 20007

SHERMAN, LENORE (WALTON)
PAINTER, LECTURER
b New York, NY, May 11, 20. Study: With Leon Franks, Hayward Veal, Orrin A White & Sergei Bongart, watercolor with James Couper Wright & portrait with Eignar Hansen. Work: San Diego Law Libr; Chateaubriand Restaurant, San Diego; var banks. Exhib: San Diego Art Inst 18th Ann, 71; Mission Valley Expos Art, Calif, 67; Rancho Calif, 70-71; Southern Calif Expos, Del Mar, Calif, 70-72; Calif Fed Women's Club Fine Arts Festival, 71. Teaching: Instr oil painting, Del Gardens Art Asn, San Diego, spring 72; instr oil painting, Foothills Art Asn, La Mesa, Calif, summer 72; lectr var seminars. Awards: First Award for Oils, San Diego Landmarks Theme, Southern Calif Expos, 70; First Award for California Landmarks & Second Award for Still Life, Calif Fedn Clubs Fine Arts Festival, 71; Purchase Award, San Diego Art Inst 18th Ann, 71. Bibliog: Ed Ainsworth (auth), The Cowboy in Art, World Publ, 68; articles in San Diego Union, 60-72. Mem: San Diego Art Inst. Style & Technique: Impressionist realist, primarily in oils. Publ: Auth, Creative Painting, 75 & Paint More Successfully, 78, Foster Art Serv. Mailing Add: 6217 Winona Ave San Diego CA 92120

SHERMAN, SARAI
PAINTER, DESIGNER
b Philadelphia, Pa. Study: Tyler Sch Art, Temple Univ, BFA, BS(educ); Barnes Found; Univ Iowa, MFA. Work: Whitney Mus Am Art & Mus Mod Art, New York; Hirshhorn Collection, Smithsonian Inst, Washington, DC; Uffizi Gallery Print Collection, Florence, Italy; Tel Aviv Mus, Israel. Exhib: Recent Painting USA: The Figure, Mus Mod Art, New York, int tour, 62-63; Premio Marzotto, Milan, Paris, Hamburg, London & Belgrade, 67-68; Venice Biennial, Int Graphics: USA, Italy, 72; one-man show, Forum Gallery, 74; Childe Hassam Acquisition Fund, 75. Awards: Award for Painting, Nat Inst Arts & Lett, 64; Europ Community Prize, Premio Marzotto, 67; Ann Painting Award, Repub of San Marino, 75. Bibliog: Bryant (auth) & Venturoli (auth), Painting of Sarai Sherman (monogr), Galleria Penelope, Rome, 63; Pastorino (auth), Pittura come vita, Documenta Film, Rome, 68; Bernari (auth), Folk rock, blues, flower children, Ed Grafica Romero, 69. Style & Technique: Imagery, iconography which deal with condition of man; technique reinforces this concept. Media: Oil, Graphics. Dealer: Forum Gallery 1018 Madison Ave New York NY 10028. Mailing Add: 17 W Ninth St New York NY 10011

SHERMAN, Z CHARLOTTE
PAINTER
b Los Angeles, Calif, June 18, 24. Study: Univ Calif, Los Angeles; Kann Art Inst; Otis Art Inst, three scholars. Work: Munic Art Gallery, Los Angeles; Palm Springs Mus, Calif; Glass Container Corp Am; Winthrop Rockefeller Found, Ark; Hillel Found, Los Angeles. Exhib: Sao Paulo Biennial, 61; Heritage Gallery, Los Angeles, 63-77; D'Allesio Gallery, New York, 65 & 66; Grand Prix Int de Deauville, Paris, 72; Prix de Rome Palais des Beaux Artes, Rome, 73; Palm Springs Mus, 77. Awards: Phelan Found Award, 61; Pasadena Mus Ann Award, 61; All City Exhib Award, Barnsdale, Los Angeles, 63 & 65. Bibliog: Joseph Mugnaini (auth), Oil painting techniques, Van Nostrand, 63; Bertrand Sorlot (auth), article in La Rev Mod, Paris, 74. Mem: Nat Watercolor Soc. Style & Technique: Abstract, utilizing linear quality combined with tonal structure of strong design in bold, thickly painted light and dark patterns. Media: Oil. Dealer: Heritage Gallery 718 N La Cienega Blvd Los Angeles CA 90069. Mailing Add: 1300 Chautauqua Blvd Pacific Palisades CA 90272

SHERROD, PHILIP LAWRENCE
PAINTER
b Pauls Valley, Okla, Oct 12, 35. Study: Okla State Univ, BS, 57, BA(etching, pottery & drawing), 59; Art Students League, Am Fed Arts & Lett Scholar, 60. Work: Tulane Univ Mus, Women's Col, New Orleans, La; Everhart Mus, Scranton, Pa; Almsford House, Anderson Fine Arts Ctr, Ind. Exhib: Nat Acad of Design, New York, 66; Gallery 9, Chatham, NJ, 67; Childe Hassam Exhib, Am Acad of Arts & Lett, New York, 67, 69, 70, 71, 73 & 74; Leonard Hutton Gallery, New York, 68; Jacques Seligmann Gallery, New York, 68; La Boetie Gallery, New York, 68; Carroll Reese Mus, ETenn Univ, Johnson City, 68; East Rockaway Art Exhib, Hewlett, Long Island, NY, 69; three-man exhib, Cancer Int, New York, 69; Nightengale Gallery, Toronto, Ont, 69; Y Women's Div Art Exhib, Green Lane, Union, NJ, 73-76 & 78; two-man show, Allan Stone Gallery, New York, 73; Humanist Ctr, New York, 73 & 74; Grace Gallery, New York City Community Col, Brookl 73; Morristown Pub Libr, NJ, 74; Nat Acad of Design Invitational, 75; Allan Stone Gallery, New York, 75; Portrait Painting 1970-1975, Allan Frumkin Gallery, New York, 75; Am Acad of Arts & Lett Invitational Award Show, 75 & 76; Friends of the Fac, Lady-Cliff Col Tower Art Gallery, Highland Falls, NY, 75; Werbin Gallery, New York, 75; Works on Paper, Monique Knowlton Gallery, New York, 76; Allied Artists 63rd Ann, Nat Acad Design, New York, 76; Portraits, Boston Univ, Mass, 76; Am Drawings, Nat Drawing Competition, Portsmouth, 76; Figure Drawings Invitational Show, Bridgeport, Conn, 76; Figurative Alliance Talk Panel, New York, 76; Still Life Drawing Show, Boston Univ, 76-77; Am Acad in Rome, 7 New York, 77; Instructors Show, Summit Art Ctr, NJ, 77; All Street Painters, March Gallery, New York; Symbolism and Fig in Art, Talk Panel, Union, NJ, 78; 20 Painters Pai Bayonne, Bayonne Jewish Ctr, NJ, 78; one-man shows, Selected Artists Gallery, New York, 68, Sonraed Galleries, New York, 71, Artemis E Gallery, New York, 72, Pace Col, New York, 72, Paul Kessler Gallery, Provincetown, Mass, 73-76, Gallery 100, Princeton, NJ, 75 & Allan Stone Gallery, New York, 76 & 78. Teaching: Instr color & design, Okla State Univ, 59; instr painting, Taos, NMex, 59-62; asst painting, Art Students League, New York, 64; instr, Morristown Art Asn, NJ, 73-74; instr, Summit Art Ctr, NJ, 77-78. Awards: First Awards in Etching, Pottery & Drawing, Okla State Univ, 59; Fedn of Arts & Lett Scholar, 63; Childe Hassam Purchase Awards, Am Acad Arts & Lett, 67, 69 & 74. Bibliog: Barry Schwartz (auth), Arts in Society (Humanist Alternative), Univ Wis, 4/73 & New Humanism: Art in a Time of Change, Praeger, 74; David L Shirey (auth), article in New York Times, 2/71. Style & Technique: Self expressionist; bold, raw, intense color; from people, landscapes and still lifes to large symbolic works of personal imagery. Media: Oil, Etching. Dealer: Allan Stone Gallery 48 E 86th St New York NY 10028. Mailing Add: 41 W 24th St New York NY 10010

SHERRY, WILLIAM GRANT
PAINTER, SCULPTOR
b Amagansett, NY, Dec 7, 14. Study: Acad Julian, Paris, cert, with Pierre Jerome; Heatherly Sch Art, London, with Ian McNab. Work: Farnsworth Mus, Rockland, Maine; Zellerbach Collection, San Francisco; Wintersteen Collection, Philadelphia; Mod Mus Art, Ft Lauderdale, Fla; Am Embassy, Pakistan; Parliament Bldg, Can; Springfield Mus Fine Art, Mass. Exhib: De Young Mus, San Francisco; Colby Col, Maine; Ringling Mus, Sarasota, Fla, 49; Boston Arts Festival, 56; Art USA, Madison Square Garden, New York, 58. Teaching: Chief instr painting & art dir, Fla Gulf Coast Art Ctr, Beleair, Fla, 57-64; art instr, Hamilton AFB, Ignacio, Calif, 65-67. Awards: Laguna Beach Festival Arts, Nat Painting Contest, 51; Mr & Mrs Chauncey A Steiger Purchase Prize, Springfield Mus, 57. Style & Technique: Traditional style and impression acrylic lay in-oil paint finish. Media: Oil, Wax. Dealer: Shreve of Centigrade Post & Grant Ave San Francisco CA. Mailing Add: 51 Park Terr Mill Valley CA 94941

SHERWOOD, A (FRANCES ANN CRANE)
SCULPTOR, DESIGNER
b Birmingham, Ala, Sept 12, 32. Study: Univ Fla; Hampton Inst; Wesley Col; Del State Col; Univ Philippines; Okaloosa Walton Col, Niceville, Fla; Univ W Fla, Pensacola. Work: Lilliputian Found, Washington, DC; Acad Art, Easton, Md; USN; USAF; Mobile Art Gallery, Ala. Comn: Oil paintings, Phillips Sch, Hampton, Va, 66, Col & Mrs W O Brimberry, 67 & Mrs Lenora Whitmire Blackburn, 74-75. Exhib: Norfolk Mus, Va, 66 & 67; Va Mus Fine Arts, Richmond, 67; Audubon Soc, Washington, DC, 69; Royal Art Gallery, Manila, Philippines, 72; Meat Packers Gallery, Pensacola, 74; Bicentennial Show, US Embassy, Manila, Philippines, 76. Teaching: Instr art, Pope AFB, NC, 61-63; instr art, Alexander Graham Bell Jr High Sch, Fayetteville, NC, 62-63; instr art, Max Bruner Jr High Sch, Ft Walton, Fla, 74-75; instr art, Dept of Defense, PI, 76-78. Pos: TV art illusr, Univ Fla Agr Educ Dept, 58-60; art illusr, Spec Serv, Pope AFB, 61-63; art illusr, Mag O'Club, Langley AFB, 63-65. Awards: Atlantic City Nat Art Show, NJ, 68 & 69; Mobile Art Fair, Ala, 73 & 74; Billy Bowlegs Art Festival, Ft Walton Beach, Fla, 73, 74 & 75. Bibliog: S Sternberger (auth), Art is where she finds it, Eve J, Del, 70; Sharon Demarko (auth), Finding art wherever she looks, Pensacola News J, 73; Capt Karen Miller (auth), article in Ladycom Mag, 8/75. Style & Technique: Sculptures are created by welding antique American metal into fine art forms; graphics are of delicate fine lines. Collection: Pre-Columbian pottery; Central American stone ware; Chinese celadon; Sung, Ming and Ching porcelain; brass from Asia; ethnic artifacts of the Philippines. Publ: Illusr, Flavet News, Gainesville, Fla, 58-60; illusr var bulletins, Gainesville, Fla, 58-60; illusr, Agr News & Univ Fla, 59. Mailing Add: 6665 W Sixth Ave Hialeah FL 33012

SHERWOOD, RICHARD E
PATRON, COLLECTOR
b Los Angeles, Calif, July 24, 28. Study: Yale Univ, BA; Harvard Univ, LLB. Pos: Trustee, Los Angeles Co Mus Art, 65-, pres, 74-; pres, Partnership for the Arts in Calif, Inc, 75-; mem, Overseers Comt to Visit the Harvard Art Mus, 75- Mailing Add: 611 W Sixth St Suite 3600 Los Angeles CA 90017

SHESTACK, ALAN
MUSEUM DIRECTOR, ART HISTORIAN
b New York, NY, June 23, 38. Study: Wesleyan Univ, Middletown, Conn, BA; Harvard Univ, Cambridge, Mass, MA. Collections Arranged: Master E S (with catalog), Philadelphia Mus Art, 67; Fifteenth-century Engravings (with catalog), Nat Gallery Art, Washington, DC, 67-68; Graphic Art of the Danube School (with catalog), Yale Art Gallery, St Louis Art Mus, Philadelphia Mus Art, 68-69. Teaching: Adj prof hist art, Yale Univ, 71- Pos: Mus cur graphic art, Nat Gallery, 65-67; cur prints & drawing, Yale Univ Art Gallery, New Haven, Conn, 68-71, dir, 71- Mem: Col Art Asn Am (bd dirs, 73-76); Am Asn Mus; Art Mus Dirs; Print Coun Am. Res: Fifteenth century printmaking in Europe; German art of 15th and 16th centuries. Publ: Auth, The Complete Engravings of Martin Schongauer, 68 & Master LCz & Master WB, 71. Mailing Add: Box 2006 Yale Sta New Haven CT 06520

SHIBLEY, GERTRUDE
PAINTER
b Brooklyn, NY. Study: Brooklyn Col, BA; with Francis Criss, 42; Hans Hofmann Sch Fine Arts, 52-53. Work: Wichita State Univ Mus Collection, Kans; Philadelphia Mus Fine Arts Rental Collection; Univ Ala, Birmingham. Exhib: World's Fair, New York, 40; Nat Asn Women Painters, Nat Acad Design Gallery, 51-52; Prizewinners Village Art Ctr, Whitney Mus Am Art, New York, 54; Art USA, New York, 58; Southampton Col, 71; New York WPA Artists, Then & Now, Parsons Sch of Design, 77; Tenth St Days—the Co-ops of the 50s, New York, 77; plus others. Teaching: Instr painting, Halloran Hosp, Staten Island, 42-44; instr painting, Ruth Ettinger Sch, New York, 55-56. Pos: Ceramist, Design Technics, 44-48. Awards: Prize for One-man Show, Village Art Ctr, 49; Hon Mention, Terry Art Award, Miami, Fla, 52. Mem: Guild Hall. Style & Technique: Abstract forms in flat planes of strong colors done in the acrylic medium set up a interplay of shapes. Media: Oil. Dealer: Phoenix Gallery 30 W 57th St New York NY 10019. Mailing Add: 351 W 24th St New York NY 10011

SHIELDS, ALAN J
DESIGNER, PAINTER
b Lost Springs, Kans, Feb 4, 44. Study: Kans State Univ. Work: Mus Mod Art, Whitney Mus Am Art & Guggenheim Mus, New York; Akron Art Inst, Ohio; Hirshhorn Mus, Washington, DC. Exhib: One-man shows, Univ RI, 73, Madison Art Ctr, Wis, 73 & Univ Kans, 75; Retrospective, Mus Contemp Art, Chicago, 73 & Contemp Arts Mus, Houston, 73; Whitney Mus Am Art, 69 & 72; Inst Contemp Art, Univ Pa, 70 & 72; Art Inst Chicago, 70, 72 & 73; Corcoran Gallery Art, Washington, DC, 71; Guggenheim Mus, New York, 71; Documenta, Kassel, WGer, 72; NY Cult Ctr, 73; Seattle Art Mus, Wash, 73; Paris Biennial, 73; Mus Mod Art, New York, 74; Mus St Etienne, France, 75. Awards: Guggenheim Fel, 73. Bibliog: Emily Wasserman (auth), Talking to Alan Shields, Artforum, 2/71; Diane Kelder (auth), Things with printmaking techniques, Art in Am, 5/73; Howardena Pindell (auth), Tales of brave Ulysses, Print Collectors Newslett, 1/75. Dealer: Paula Cooper 155 Wooster St New York NY 10012. Mailing Add: PO Box 1554 Shelter Island NY 11964

SHIKLER, AARON
PAINTER
b Brooklyn, NY, Mar 18, 22. Study: Tyler Sch Fine Arts, Temple Univ, BFA, BSEd & MFA; Barnes Found; Hans Hofmann Sch. Work: Metrop Mus Art, New York; Mint Mus Art, Charlotte, NC; Parrish Mus Art, Southampton, NY; Nat Acad Design; Montclair Art Mus, NJ. Comn: Portraits of President & Mrs John F Kennedy for White House. Exhib: New Britain Mus Art, Conn, 64; Gallery Mod Art, New York, 65; Nat Acad Design, 65; Brooklyn Mus, 71; Calif Palace of Legion of Honor, San Francisco, 71; plus others. Awards: Ranger Award, 59; Proctor Prize, Nat Acad Design, 59 & 60 & Benjamin Figure Prize, 76; Thomas B Clarke Prize, 61; US Dept State traveling grant, 76; plus others. Bibliog: Shikler & Levine, Brooklyn Mus, 4/71; articles in Am Artist, 9/71 & Current Biog, 12/71. Mem: Nat Acad Design; Century Asn. Publ: Contribr two chaps, In: Pastel Painting, 68. Dealer: Davis & Long Co 746 Madison Ave New York NY 10021. Mailing Add: 44 W 77th St New York NY 10024

SHIMIZU, YOSHIAKI
ART HISTORIAN, EDUCATOR
b Tokyo, Japan, Feb 27, 36. Study: Harvard Col, BA, 63; Univ Kans, MA, 68; Princeton Univ, MFA, 71, PhD, 74. Teaching: Asst prof art & archaeol, Princeton Univ, NJ, 73-75; asst prof oriental art, Univ Calif, Berkeley, 75- Res: Primarily in Japanese art of the medieval period with reference to Chinese art. Publ: Auth, Japanese Painting from Joe D Price Collection, Univ Kans Mus Art, 68; contribr, Traditions of Japanese Art, Fogg Art Mus, Harvard Univ, 70; auth, Reconstruction Problems of Kokawa-dera Engi (in Japanese), Ars Buddhica, Mainichi Press, Tokyo, 72; co-auth, Japanese Ink Paintings, Princeton Univ Press, 76. Mailing Add: 1786 Spruce Berkeley CA 94709

SHIMODA, OSAMU
SCULPTOR, PAINTER
b Manchuria, June 4, 24. Study: St Paul Univ, Tokyo; Acad Grande Chaumiere, Paris. Work: St Paul Univ, Tokyo; Syracuse Mus; Nat Mus Mod Art, Tokyo. Comn: Murals, Hawaii CofC & Indust, 59. Exhib: Granite Gallery, New York, 66; Nat Mus Mod Art Ann, Tokyo, 67; Suzanne Kohen Gallery, Minneapolis, 70; Bertha Schaefer Gallery, 70; Sculptors Guild, 71 & 72. Mem: Sculptors Guild. Media: Iron. Dealer: New Bertha Schaefer Gallery 983 Park Ave New York NY 10022. Mailing Add: 12 Whitewell Pl Brooklyn NY 11215

SHIMOMURA, ROGER YUTAKA
PAINTER, EDUCATOR
b Seattle, Wash, June 26, 39. Study: Univ Wash, BA(graphic design), 61; Cornish Sch of Allied Arts (illus), 64; Stanford Univ, summer painting workshop, 67; Cornell Univ, summer workshop, 68; Syracuse Univ, MFA(painting), 69. Work: Kemper Insurance, Chicago, Ill; Metrop Mus & Art Ctr, Miami, Fla; Ill Bell Tel Co, Chicago; Sonesta Int Hotel Corp, Key Biscayne, Fla; McCroy Corp, New York. Comn: Tryptych (72in x 144in), Seattle Opera House, Wash, 77. Exhib: One-man exhib, Kansas City Art Inst, Mo, 75; Polly Friedlander Gallery, Seattle, 75-76; Frannel Gallery, Tokyo, Japan, 76; Gallery Heian, Kyoto, Japan, 76; Pyramid Galleries Ltd, Washington, DC, 76; Tacoma Art Mus, Wash, 77; Morgan Gallery, Kansas City, Kans, 77; Dobrick Gallery, Chicago, 77; plus others. Teaching: Asst instr painting & drawing, Univ Wash, Seattle, 65-66 & Syracuse Univ, NY, 67-69; prof art, Univ Kans, Lawrence, 69- Awards: Japan Found Grant, 75; Nat Endowment for the Arts Grant, 77; five Gen Res Grants, Univ Kans; plus numerous others. Bibliog: Harold Haydon (auth), An unexpected sensation, Chicago Sun-Times, 5/17/74; JoAnn Lewis (auth), The American ethic, Washington Post, 6/3/76; David L Shirley (auth), Twitting the Samurai style, New York Sunday Times, 11/23/76. Mem: Col Art Asn. Style & Technique: Handpainted. Media: Acrylic on Canvas. Dealer: Dobrick Gallery 161 E Erie Chicago IL 60611; Pyramid Galleries Ltd 2121 P St NW Washington DC 20037. Mailing Add: 1019 Delaware Lawrence KS 66044

SHINER, NATE
PAINTER, EDUCATOR
b Vallejo, Calif, Mar 13, 44. Study: Napa Col, AA; Sacramento State Col, BA & MA. Exhib: San Francisco Art Inst Centennial, San Francisco Mus Art, Calif, 71; Contemporary Painting in America, Whitney Mus Am Art, New York, 72, Biennial Exhib Contemp Am Art, 73 & Extraordinary Realities, 74; Sacramento Sampler, Oakland Art Mus, Calif; Davidson Nat Print & Drawing Competition, 76; Artists Biennial, New Orleans Mus of Art, 77. Teaching: Instr drawing, Sacramento State Col, 70-71; instr drawing & painting, Sacramento City Col, 71-73; instr drawing & painting, Univ Fla, 73- Style & Technique: Narrative. Media: Acrylic. Mailing Add: 3433 NW First Ct Gainesville FL 32607

SHIPLEY, JAMES R
EDUCATOR, DESIGNER
b Marion, Ohio, Dec 26, 10. Study: Cleveland Inst Art, dipl, 35, with Viktor Schreckengost; Western Reserve Univ, BS, 36; Univ Southern Calif; Inst Design, Chicago; Univ Ill, AM, 48. Exhib: May Show, Cleveland Mus Art, 35; Mich Artists Ann, Detroit Inst Art, 37. Teaching: Prof art, Dept Art & Design, Univ Ill, Champaign, 39-, head dept, 55-77; instr prod design, Inst Design, Chicago, summer 48; acad dir design, Advan Studies for Designers, Inst Contemp Art, Boston, summer 58. Pos: Commercial artist, J H Maish Advert Agency, Marion, Ohio, 29-31; designer, Gen Motors Corp, Detroit, 36-38; free lance designer & art dir, var Midwestern Firms, 44-; consult, State of Ind Comn for Higher Educ, 76. Awards: Univ Ill Res Bd Grant Visual Pollution, 70-72. Mem: Fel Nat Asn Schs Art (vpres, 60-61, pres, 61-63, chmn accreditation comt, 66-69); Midwest Col Art Asn (vpres, 60-61, pres, 61-62); Indust Designer Soc Am (educ comt, 65-70); Ill Arts Coun (adv panel visual arts, 70-74). Publ: Auth, Programs in art in the state universities, Print, 1-2/60; auth, Interior Design, Small Homes Coun, rev ed, 69; co-auth, The new artist, In: Contemporary American Painting & Sculpture, 1969, Univ Ill, 69; contribr, Graduate Education in the Humanities & the Arts, State Ill Bd Higher Educ, 70. Mailing Add: Dept of Art & Design Univ of Ill Champaign IL 61820

SHIPLEY, ROGER DOUGLAS
SCULPTOR, EDUCATOR
b Cleveland Heights, Ohio, Dec 27, 41. Study: Am Sch at Fontainebleau, France, cert painting, with Monsieur Goetz, 62; Otterbein Col, Westerville, Ohio, BA, 64; Cleveland Inst of Art, 64-65, painting with Louis Bosa & sculpture with Willliam McVey; Cranbrook Acad of Art, Bloomfield Hills, Mich, MFA, 67. Work: State of WVa Art & Humanities Coun, Charleston; Kalamazoo Inst of Arts, Mich; Cranbrook Acad of Art; Lock Haven State Col, Pa; Otterbein Col, Westerville, Ohio. Exhib: Ann Exhib of Mich Artists, Detroit Inst of Art, 66; 31st Ann Mid-Year Show, Butler Inst of Am Art, Youngstown, Ohio, 66; May Shows, Cleveland Mus of Art, 67-77; Appalachian Corridors Exhib 1 & 3, Charleston, WVa, 68 & 72; A Plastic Presence, Jewish Mus of Art, New York, Milwaukee Art Ctr, Wis & San Francisco Mus of Art, 69-70; Transparent & Translucent Art, Mus of Fine Arts, St Petersburg, Fla & Jacksonville Art Mus, Fla, 71; one-man shows, William Penn Mem Mus, Harrisburg, Pa, 71, Bucknell Univ, Lewisburg, Pa, 75 & Lock Haven State Col, Pa, 76; Soft & Light Exhib, Taft Mus, Cincinnati, Ohio, 73; 11th Ann Nat Drawing & Small Sculpture Show, Delmar Col, Corpus Christi, Tex, 77; 30th Ann Ohio Ceramic, Sculpture & Crafts Show, Butler Inst of Am Art, Youngstown, Ohio, 78. Teaching: Assoc prof painting, drawing, printmaking & two-dimensional design & chmn art dept, Lycoming Col, 67- Pos: Vpres, Greater Williamsport Community Arts Coun, 77- Awards: Cash Prize, 13th Ann Drawing & Small Sculpture Show, Ball State Univ, Muncie, Ind, 67; Special Mention, 50th & 52nd May Shows, Cleveland Mus of Art, 68 & 71; Achievement Award, Appalachian Corridors Exhib 3, WVa Arts & Humanities Coun, 72. Bibliog: Joy Hakanson (auth), Freedom and doubt in art, Detroit News Mag, 8/67; Thomas Willis (auth), Bringing the art of plastics into focus, Chicago Tribune, 2/70; Owen Findsen (auth), The brightness of lesser lights, Cincinnati Enquirer, 10/73. Mem: Bald Eagle Art League. Style & Technique: Conceptual—primary forms enclosing colored and mirrored Plexiglass shapes; moving components sometimes incorporated. Media: Plexiglass, mirror and transparent colored sheet, stencil-cut silkscreen printing of the interior motifs of sculptures; Dealer: Henri Gallery 1500 21st St NW Washington DC 20036; Langman Gallery Inc 218 Old York Rd Jenkintown, PA 19046. Mailing Add: 3000 Inwood Rd Williamsport PA 17701

SHIPPEN, ZOË (ZOË SHIPPEN VARNUM)
PAINTER
b Boston, Mass, Nov 12, 02. Study: Detroit Sch Fine Arts; Boston Mus Sch; Mary C Wheeler Sch, Providence, RI; Ecole des Beaux Arts Americaine, Fontainbleau, France; Kunst Acadamie, Vienna, Austria; Art Students League. Work: Parrish Mus, Southampton, NY. Comn: Many portraits including the two children of the late President John F Kennedy. Exhib: Washington Gallery, Miami Beach, Fla, 44-47; Worth Ave Gallery, Palm Beach, Fla, 44-61; Arthur U Newton Gallery, New York, 46; El Lyceum, Havana, Cuba, 47; James Hunt Barker Gallery, Palm Beach, 73. Style & Technique: Portraits of children, mostly heads. Media: Pastel, Oil. Dealer: Portraits Inc 41 E 57th St New York NY 10022; James Hunt Barker Galleries 345 Worth Ave Palm Beach FL 33480. Mailing Add: 220 Fairview Rd Palm Beach FL 33480

SHIR, LILLIAN
See Shuff, Lily

SHOEMAKER, PETER
PAINTER, EDUCATOR
b Newport, RI, Jan 9, 20. Study: Calif Sch Fine Arts, San Francisco, cert, with Clyfford Still, Clay Spohn & Elmer Bischoff, 47-50; Univ Calif, Berkeley, BA, 51. Work: Calif Palace of Legion of Honor, San Francisco; Richmond Art Ctr, Calif; Oakland Mus, Calif. Exhib: Corcoran Biennial, Washington, DC, 57; Pacemakers, Contemp Arts Mus, Houston, 57; Carnegie Int, Pittsburgh, 58; Painters Behind Painters, Calif Palace of Legion of Honor, 67; Closing Show, Bolles Gallery, San Francisco, 75; Crocker-Kingsley Ann, Sacramento, Calif, 77. Teaching: Assoc prof painting, Calif Col Arts & Crafts, Oakland, 60- Bibliog: Mary Fuller (auth), Was there a San Francisco school?, Artforum, 1/71. Mem: San Francisco Art Inst. Style & Technique: Content oriented abstract impressionist. Dealer: Ctr for the Visual Arts 1333 Broadway Oakland CA 94612. Mailing Add: 622 Panoramic Way Berkeley CA 94704

SHOEMAKER, VAUGHN
EDITORIAL CARTOONIST, PAINTER
b Chicago, Ill, Aug 11, 02. Study: Chicago Art Inst; Chicago Acad Fine Arts, Ill. Work: Huntington Libr, San Marino, Calif; Syracuse Univ, NY; Wheaton Col, Ill. Exhib: Obrien Galleries, Chicago, 35 & 36; Marshall Field Galleries, Chicago, 38. Teaching: Instr ed cartooning, Chicago Acad Fine Arts, 27-42; instr ed cartooning, Studio Sch Art, Chicago, 43-45. Pos: Cartoonist, Chicago Daily News, 22-25, chief ed cartoonist, 25-52; ed cartoonist, New York Herald Tribune, 56-61; chief ed cartoonist, Chicago Am-Chicago Today, 61-72. Awards: Pulitzer Prizes, Columbia Univ, 38 & 47; Headliners Award, Atlantic City, 43. Bibliog: Gerald W Johnson (auth), The Lines are Drawn, Lippincott, 58. Mem: Hon mem Palette & Chisel Acad Fine Arts, Chicago; hon mem Ridge Art Asn, Chicago. Publ: Auth, '38 A D, '39 A D, '40 A D, '41-42 A D, '43-44 A D & '45-46 A D; plus others. Mailing Add: Drawer V Carmel CA 93921

SHOKLER, HARRY
PAINTER, SERIGRAPHER
b Cincinnati, Ohio, Apr 25, 96. Study: Cincinnati Art Acad; Pa Sch Fine Arts, summer; New York Sch Fine & Appl Arts; Colorossi, Paris. Work: Metrop Mus Art, New York; Philadelphia Mus Art; Carnegie Inst, Pa; Libr of Cong, Washington, DC; Syracuse Mus, NY. Exhib: Paris Salon, 28; Nat Acad Design, New York; Pa Acad Fine Arts, Philadelphia; Southern Vt Artists; Dayton Art Inst; plus over 50 one-man shows. Teaching: Lectr serigraphy, Princeton Univ, Columbia Univ & others, 41-45; instr oil painting, Southern Vt Artists. Awards: Award for Pigeon Cove, Chaffee Art Mus, 69; Award for Tunisian Coffee House, Albany Print Biennial; Award for West River in March, Miller Art Ctr. Mem: Southern Vt Artists (art comt & trustee, 75); Miller Art Ctr; Chaffee Art Mus; Chester Art Guild; West River Artists. Media: Oil. Publ: Auth, Artists Manual for Silk Screen Printmaking. Dealer: Grand Cent Art Galleries 40 Vanderbilt Ave New York NY 10017. Mailing Add: Londonderry VT 05148

SHOOK, GEORG
PAINTER
b Miss, May 24, 32. Study: Univ Fla; Ringling Inst Art, Sarasota, Fla; with Bernard Robinson, Orlando, Fla. Work: Ellen J Martin & THB Dunnegan Collections, Springfield, Mo; City of Springfield Collection & Watercolor USA Collection, Springfield Art Mus; Lloyd O Angell Collection, Golden, Colo; Nat Bank of Com; Artists Registry, Brooks Mem Art Gallery, Memphis, Tenn. Exhib: 9th-13th Tenn All-State Artists Ann, Nashville, 69-73; 14th-18th Mid-South Ann, Brooks Art Gallery, Memphis, 69-73; Watercolor USA, Springfield Art Mus, 70-73; Cent South Ann, Parthenon Galleries, Nashville, 70-73; 105th, 106th, 109th & 110th Ann Am Watercolor Soc, New York, 72, 73, 76 & 77; plus others. Pos: Art dir, Memphis Publ Co, 61- Awards: Four consecutive Purchase Awards, Watercolor USA, Springfield, Mo; six consecutive Awards, Tenn Watercolor Soc; CFS Award, Am Watercolor Soc, New York. Bibliog: Watercolor page, Am Artist Mag, 4/73; Articles in Todays Art Mag, 11/73 & Southwest Art Mag, 9/74, 1/75, 4/75 & 5/75; cover & feature article, North Light Mag, 7/77; Forty Artists and How They Work, Watson-Guptill Bks, 77; cover & feature article, Art Voices S Mag, 3/78. Mem: Art Dirs Club, Memphis (pres, 70-72); Memphis Watercolor Soc (co-founder & dir, 69-); Tenn Watercolor Soc (pres, 71-72); Southern Watercolor Soc (pres, 77-78); Artist's Registry, Brooks Mem Art Gallery. Style & Technique: Realism in the traditional sense; technique is controlled dry brush with wash overtones. Media: Watercolor. Mailing Add: 1239 Cherrydale Cove Memphis TN 38111

SHOOTER, TOM
PAINTER
b Williamsport, Pa, Aug 18, 41. Study: Lycoming Col, 59-61; Sch Mus Fine Arts, Boston, cert, 65 & grad cert, 66; with Jan Cox, Boston, 66; Tufts Univ, BFA, 71. Work: Tufts Univ Collection; Sch Mus Fine Arts Collection, Boston; Spaulding & Sly Corp Collection, Boston; Tufts New Eng Med Ctr Collection, Boston; Commercial Union Assurance Co Collection, Boston. Exhib: Stretched, Unstretched & Folded, Boston City Hall, ICA & Sunne Savage Gallery, 72; Works on Paper, Fogg Mus, Harvard Univ, 74; Corporations Collect, De Cordova Mus, Lincoln, Mass, 74; Painting Invitational, Brockton Art Ctr, Mass, 75; Painted in Boston, Inst Contemp Art, 75; Sunne Savage Gallery, Boston, 76 & Drawings, 77; Boston 78, Brockton Art Ctr, 78. Teaching: Instr painting, Sch Mus Fine Arts, Boston, 65-66; instr painting, Tufts Univ in Italy, Naples, 68-69; instr painting & drawing, Cambridge Ctr Adult Educ, 70-78; instr painting, Sch Mus Fine Arts, Boston, 76-77. Awards: 34th James William Paige Fel, Boston Mus Fine Arts, 66; Nat Endowment for Arts & Humanities Grant, 66. Bibliog: Carl Belz (auth), Circuit artist at State House, Art in Am, 2/74 & Painted in Boston, Inst Contemp Art, 75; Kay Larson (auth), Boston, identity crisis, Art News & The flowering of Boston art, 2/75; Jane Holtz-Kay (auth), rev in Art News, 2/76 & On view in Boston, Art News, summer 76. Mem: Boston Visual Artist Union. Style & Technique: Abstract oil on canvas, mixed media collage and drawing. Dealer: Sunne Savage Gallery 105 Newbury St Boston MA 02116. Mailing Add: 270 Congress St Boston MA 02110

SHOR, BERNICE ABRAMOWITZ
ART EDITOR
b Newark, NJ, July 11, 45. Study: Conn Col, BA. Pos: Ed, Art Now Gallery Guide, 74- Mailing Add: Art Now 144 N 14th St Kenilworth NJ 07033

SHORE, MARY
PAINTER
b Philadelphia, Pa, Mar 19, 12. Study: Cooper Union Art Sch, scholar; Art Inst Chicago. Work: Addison Gallery Am Art, Andover, Mass; Fitchburg Art Mus, Mass; Baltimore Art Mus. Exhib: One-man shows, Norlyst Gallery, New York, 49, Lyceum, Havana, Cuba, 50, De Cordova Mus, Lincoln, Mass, 56 & 57, Boris Mirski Gallery, Boston, 60 & 64, Philadelphia Art Alliance, 63 & 65, Fitchburg Art Mus, 65, Hilliard Gallery, Martha's Vineyard, Mass, 71, Pingree Sch Gallery, Hamilton, Mass, 72, Stockbridge Sch Gallery, 72 & Horizon Gallery, 75 & 77; Traveling Assemblage Exhib, Mus Mod Art, US & Can, 63; Montserrat Gallery, Beverly, Mass, 77. Awards: Blanche E Colman Art Found Award, 66. Mem: Artists Equity Asn (past pres New Eng Chap & nat dir). Style & Technique: Semi-abstract. Mailing Add: Way Rd Gloucester MA 01930

SHORE, RICHARD PAUL
SCULPTOR
b Jersey City, NJ, Aug 27, 43. Study: Marietta Col, BA, 66; New Sch Social Res, New York, 66-67. Work: Storm King Art Ctr Mus Art, Mountainville, NY; Aldrich Mus Contemp Art, Ridgefield, Conn; Broadway Bank & Trust Co, Paterson, NJ; Newark Airport; Tenafly Pub Sch Syst, NJ; plus others. Exhib: Sculpture in the Park Van Saun Park, Paramus, NJ; Bergen Community Mus Art, Paramus, 72; World Trade Ctr, New York; Kornbluth Gallery, 72-74; Aldrich Mus Contemp Art; plus others. Teaching: Guest lectr aesthet, Caldwell Col, 70-71; mem fac, Art Ctr Northern NJ, 72- Awards: Saks Award, Westchester Art Soc, 71; Ellen A Ross Mem Prize, 71 & Painters & Sculptors Soc Prize, 72, Jersey City Mus Nat Exhib; plus others. Mem: Mod Arts Guild; Painters & Sculptors Soc NJ. Dealer: Alonzo Gallery 26 E 63rd St New York NY 10021; Kornbluth Gallery 7-21 Fair Lawn Ave Fair Lawn NJ 07410. Mailing Add: 130 Glenbrook Pkwy 6C Englewood NJ 07631

SHORES, (JAMES) FRANKLIN
PAINTER
b Hampton, Va, Nov 9, 42. Study: Pa Acad Fine Arts. Work: Pa Acad Fine Arts, Philadelphia; Camden Pub Libr, Maine. Exhib: Pa Acad Fine Arts Ann, 67 & 69; Philadelphia Watercolor Club Exhibs, 68- Pos: Instr art, Pa Acad Fine Arts, 65- Awards: Cresson Europ Traveling Scholar & Eakins Figure Painting Prize, Pa Acad Fine Arts, 64. Mem: Philadelphia Watercolor Club (pres). Media: Watercolor, Oil. Mailing Add: 612 S Ninth St Philadelphia PA 19147

SHORTER, EDWARD SWIFT
PAINTER, COLLECTOR
b Columbus, Ga, July 2, 02. Study: Mercer Univ, AB & LLD; Corcoran Sch Art; Fontainbleu, Paris, with Andre L'Hote, Wayman Adams & Hugh Breckenridge; Boston Mus Sch Art. Work: Corcoran Gallery Art; Atlanta Art Asn; Ft Hays, Kans; Wesleyan Col & Mercer Univ, Macon, Ga. Comn: Portrait, Mercer Univ; paintings, Housing Authority Columbus, Tift Col & St Francis Hosp. Exhib: Pa Acad Fine Arts; Corcoran Gallery Art; Southern States Art League; Soc Washington Artists; Southeastern Art Ann. Collections Arranged: Am Traditionalists of Twentieth Century; Special Exhibition Old Master Drawings & Graphics; Contemporary Exhibition Georgia Artists. Pos: Actg dir, Columbus Mus Arts & Crafts, 53-55, dir, 55-68, emer dir, 68-; pres, Asn Ga Artists, 55-57. Awards: Gari Melcher Award, Artists Fel; Algenon Sydney Sullivan Award, Mercer Univ. Mem: Am Asn Mus; Artists Equity Asn; Am Artists Prof League; Salmagundi Club; Soc Washington Artists. Media: Oil. Collection: American paintings; European porcelains; Oriental ivories and rugs. Mailing Add: PO Box 1374 Columbus GA 31906

SHOSTAK, EDWIN BENNETT
SCULPTOR
b New York, NY, Aug 23, 41. Study: Ohio Univ, 59-60; Cooper Union, 60-61. Work: Phillip Johnson Collection, New Canaan, Conn. Exhib: New Eyes, Walter Chrysler Mus of Art, Provincetown, Mass, 63; Bykert Gallery, New York, 65; Am Exhib of Am Sculpture, Whitney Mus of Am Art, New York, 70 & Biennial, 73; Group Show, Holly Solomon Gallery, New York, 75, Summer Group Show, 76 & Sculptors' Drawings, 76; 76 Jefferson St, Mus of Mod Art, New York, 75; Selections for New & Old Collections, Art Mus of STex, Corpus Christi, 76; Six Artists, The Gallery, William Patterson Col, Wayne, NJ, 76; Art Gallery, State Univ at Potsdam, NY, 77; Non-Collectible Art from the Collection of Horace & Holly Solomon, Sarah Lawrence Col, Bronxville, NY, 77; Patterning & Decoration, Mus of the Am Found for the Arts, Miami, Fla, 77; Patterning & Decoration, Alexandre Monet, Brussels, Belg, 77; one-man shows, Fischbach Gallery, New York, 71 & 73, Sch Visual Arts, 74 & Holly Solomon Gallery, 75. Awards: Guggenheim Fel, 74-75. Bibliog: Robert Hughes (auth), In search of the new, pursuit of the old, Time Mag, 1/71; Barbara Rose (auth), New York Mag, 6/73; Michael Andre (auth), rev in Art News, 12/75; Gerrit Henry (auth), rev in Art in Am, 1/76 & Views from the studio, Art News, 5/76; Lil Picard (auth), rev in Kunstforum, 76; plus numerous others. Style & Technique: Construction, using various building materials. Media: Wood, Metals. Dealer: Hollis Solcman 444 E 57th St New York NY 10022. Mailing Add: 5 W 21st St New York NY 10010

SHOULBERG, HARRY
PAINTER
b Philadelphia, Pa, Oct 25, 03. Study: Am Artists Sch; also with Carl Holty & Sol Wilson. Work: Metrop Mus Art, New York; Carnegie Inst, Pittsburgh; Norfolk Mus Arts & Sci, Va; Denver Mus, Colo; Butler Inst Am Art. Exhib: American Oil Painting, Corcoran Gallery Art, Washington, DC, 41; Print & Watercolor Exhib, Pa Acad Fine Arts, Philadelphia, 46; Libr of Cong Print Exhib, Washington, DC, 47; Audubon Artists 28th Ann, New York, 70; Nat Acad Design 146th Ann, New York, 71; League of Present Day Artists, New York, 75; Nat Soc of Painters in Casein & Acrylic at the Nat Acad of Design, New York, 76 & 77; Harbor Gallery, Cold Spring Harbor, NY, 76; Summit Gallery, New York, 77. Awards: Emily Lowe Award, 56; Kapp Award, Silvermine Guild, 57; M J Kaplan Mem Award, Am Soc Contemp Artists, 66. Bibliog: H Shokler (auth), Artists manual for silk screen printmaking, 46 & A Reese (auth), American prize prints of the 20th century, 49, Am Artists Group. Mem: Audubon Artists; Am Soc Contemp Artists; NJ Soc Painters & Sculptors; Artists Equity Asn; Nat Soc Painters Casein & Acrylic. Style & Technique: Romantic expressionism; heavy impasto painting. Media: Oil. Dealer: Harbor Gallery 43 Main St Cold Spring Harbor NY 11724. Mailing Add: 112-114 W 14th St New York NY 10011

SHOWELL, KENNETH L
PAINTER
b Huron, SDak, Oct 22, 39. Study: Kansas City Art Inst, BFA, 63; Ind Univ, MFA, 65. Work: Art Inst Chicago; Whitney Mus Am Art, New York; Michener Collection, Univ Tex, Austin; Akron Mus, Ohio. Exhib: Whitney Mus Am Art Ann, 67-69; Highlights of the 1969-1970 Art Season, Aldrich Mus, Ridgefield, Conn; Lyrical Abstraction, Whitney Mus Am Art, New York, 71; Spray, Santa Barbara Mus Art, 71; Painting & Sculpture Today 1972, Indianapolis Mus Art, Ind, 72. Bibliog: R Pincus-Witten (auth), New York, Artforum, 1/70; C Ratcliff (auth), The new informalists, 2/70 & J Weissman (auth), Showdown in Soho, 11/74, Art News. Media: Acrylic, Oil. Mailing Add: 11 Lispenard St New York NY 10013

SHRADY, FREDERICK C
SCULPTOR
b Eastview, NY, Oct 22, 07. Study: Oxford Univ; Art Students League; painting with Yashuti Takaka, Paris; study in Florence, Italy. Work: Metrop Mus Art, New York; Holy Cross Col; Fordham Univ, New York, NY; Vatican Mus, Vatican State; pvt collection of Pope Paul. Comn: Descent from the Cross (16 ft painting), St Stephen's Cathedral, Vienna, 46; bronze doors, Basilica of the Annunciation, Nazareth, Holy Land, 69; Sea Battle (15 ft bronze fountain), comn by Charles Englehard, Boca Grande, Fla, 70; Dionysis & Appolo (12 ft bronze), Univ Bridgeport, Conn, 74; St Eliza Seton Shrine, St Patrick's Cathedral, New York, 75. Awards: Legion of Honor & Palme D'Acadamie, 37, French Govt; Hon DFA, Holy Cross Col, 69. Media: Bronze or Metal Fabrication. Dealer: Weintraub Gallery 992 Madison Ave New York NY 10021. Mailing Add: Maple Rd Monroe CT 06468

SHUBERT, KATHERINE SCHMIDT
See Schmidt, Katherine

SHUBIN, MORRIS JACK
PAINTER, LECTURER
b Mansfield, Wash, Feb 25, 20. Work: Laguna Beach Mus Art, Calif; Utah State Univ, Logan; Las Vegas Art Mus, Nev; Rio Hondo Col, Whittier, Calif; City of La Mirada, Calif. Exhib: Nat Watercolor Soc Ann, 66-; Watercolor USA, Springfield Art Mus, Mo, 68-; Am Watercolor Soc Ann, New York, 69-; Nat Watercolor Competition, Wichita, Kans, 70. Teaching: Guest artist watercolor painting, Asilomar Workshops, Pacific Grove, Calif, 73-76; conducted, Watercolor Workshops, Tucson, San Antonio, Las Vegas & Mexico, 74-75. Bibliog: Gerald Brommer (auth), Transparent Watercolor, Davis, 73. Mem: Am Watercolor Soc; Nat Watercolor Soc (treas, 70-72, vpres, 72-73); WCoast Watercolor Soc; Pasadena Soc Artists; Laguna Beach Art Mus. Style & Technique: Contemporary. Media: Watercolor, Ink Wash, Mixed Media. Publ: Auth, Watercolor page, Am Artists, 8/74. Mailing Add: 313 N 12th St Montebello CA 90640

SHUCK, KENNETH MENAUGH
MUSEUM DIRECTOR, PAINTER
b Harrodsburg, Ky, May 21, 21. Study: Ohio State Univ, BS(art educ) & MA(art hist); Univ Chile, Inst Int Educ scholar, 50. Exhib: Denver Art Mus Ann; Watercolor USA & 10 State Regional, Springfield, Mo. Collections Arranged: 10 State Regional Exhib, 51-75; Watercolor USA, 61-75. Pos: Dir, Springfield Art Mus, Mo, 51-76; dir, Fine Arts Dept, Mo State Fair, 67-71; arts consult, painter (watercolor) & craftsman, 51- Mem: Midwest Mus Conf (pres, 63); Mo State Coun Arts (chmn visual arts, 66-68); Am Asn Mus; Am Fedn Arts. Media: Watercolor, Acrylic. Mailing Add: 938 E Elm Springfield MO 65806

SHUFF, LILY (LILLIAN SHIR)
PAINTER, ENGRAVER
b New York, NY. Study: Hunter Col, BA & MA; Columbia Univ; Brooklyn Acad Fine Art; Art Students League, with Morris Kantor; also with Adja Junkers & Jerry Farnsworth. Work: Metrop Mus Art, New York; Libr of Cong, Washington, DC; Yale Univ Art Gallery, New Haven, Conn; Butler Inst Am Art, Youngstown, Ohio; Bezalel Nat Mus, Jerusalem; plus 33 other nat mus collections. Exhib: Ten Years of American Prints 1947-1956, Brooklyn Mus, NY, 56; Munic Mus Art, Uneo Park, Tokyo, 60; Mus Nac Bellas Artes, Buenos Aires, 63; Royal Scottish Acad, Edinburgh, Scotland, 63; Int Cult Ctr, New Delhi, India, 66. Awards: Thirty-five awards, including: Gold Medal of Honor for Watercolor, NJ Mus, 56 & 62; Awards, Nat Casein Soc, 63, 65, 66, 67, 73, 76 & 77; Winsor & Newton Prize for Oil, Am Soc Contemp Artists, 66, 68 & 70; Elizabeth Rungius Fulda Prize for Oil, Nat Asn Women Artists, 69, 70, 76 & 77; plus many others. Bibliog: Article in Think, 59; Alfred Khouri Collection, Norfolk Mus, 63; Archives of American Art, Smithsonian Inst, Washington, DC. Mem: Nat Asn Women Artists (chmn mem jury, 56-58 & 64-66, bd dirs, 58-67); Nat Soc Painters Casein (rec secy, 57-64 & 70-77); New York Soc Women Artists (bd gov, 56-71); Audubon Artists (graphics dir, 70-72); NJ Painters & Sculptors (admis jury, 71). Style & Technique: Abstract romanticism. Media: Oil, Watercolor. Interest: Slides of paintings circulated in universities and colleges in US by Georgia Museum of Fine Art, Athens. Publ: Contribr, Art Collector's Almanac, 65; contribr, Today's Art, 70, 74 & 77; contribr, How to Paint a Prize Winner, 70. Dealer: East Side Gallery 307 E 37th St New York NY 10016. Mailing Add: 155 W 68th St New York NY 10023

SHULL, CARL EDWIN
PAINTER, EDUCATOR
b Greenup, Ill, Dec 8, 12. Study: Eastern Ill Univ, BA(educ), 39; Peabody Col, MA, 40; Chicago Art Inst, advan work, 40-42; Ohio State Univ, PhD, 54. Work: Canton Art Inst, Ohio; Sheldon Swope Art Gallery, Terre Haute, Ind; Lakeview Ctr Arts & Sci, Ill; Eastern Ill Univ collection; Evansville Mus Arts & Sci, Ind. Comn: Murals, US Navy, South Pac Area, 44-45; Space Flight, pvt comn, Terre Haute, Ind, 71; Sports in Art (35 paintings on sports), Field House, Lakeland Col, Mattoon, Ill, 74. Exhib: One-man shows, Univ Mo-Columbia, 46, Univ Ill, 62, Evansville Mus Arts & Sci, 71 & Univ Wis, Platteville, 74; Ohio Watercolor Soc, Ohio Art Mus, Columbus, 53; Mid Year Am Painting Exhib, Butler Inst Am Art, Youngstown, Ohio, 53 & 63; Interior Valley Show, Cincinnati Art Mus, Ohio, 55; Int Serigraph Soc, New York, 56; Nat Painting Show, Sheldon Swope Art Gallery, Terre Haute, Ind, 67. Teaching: Instr arts & crafts, Univ Mo, 46-47; prof painting & drawing, Eastern Ill Univ, Charleston, 47- Pos: Commercial artist, Graham & Hugent Studios, Chicago, Ill, 41-42. Awards: Purchase Awards, Wabash Valley Exhib, Sheldon Swope Art Gallery, Terre Haute, Ind, 68 & 71, Mississippi Valley Show, Lakeview Ctr Arts & Sci, Peoria, Ill, 68 & Tri State Exhib, Evansville Mus Art & Sci, Ind, 71. Bibliog: Robert Wisemen (auth), Approaches in Life Drawing (film), Eastern Ill Univ, 70; Howard Wooden (auth), Television Film on Shull's Painting, Sta WTHI, Terre Haute, Ind, 71; Willis Waltman (auth), Shull's Life Class Relates Work to Other Art Areas, Eastern Ill Univ, 77. Style & Technique: Expressionist in various techniques. Media: Oil and water based paints. Interest: Personal library of approximately 1000 books on the arts and related subjects. Publ: Auth-illusr, Techniques in Life Drawing, 74, Elements in Landscape Painting, 74, Heads, Heads, Heads, 75, Lore and Design of Nature's Harvest, 76 & Lore and Legend of Birds in Design, 77, Eastern Ill Univ. Mailing Add: RR4 Charleston IL 61920

SHUMACKER, ELIZABETH WIGHT
PAINTER, INSTRUCTOR
b Chattanooga, Tenn, Sept 25, 12. Study: Univ Chattanooga, BA, postgrad work in painting & graphics; spec drawing classes, Hunter Mus, Chattanooga, Tenn. Work: High Mus Art, Atlanta, Ga; Brooks MemGallery, Memphis, Tenn; Inst Cult Mexicano-Norteamericano, Guadalajara, Mex; Hunter Mus, Chattanooga; Tenn Arts Comn. Exhib: Numerous exhibs & two one-men shows, Hunter Mus Art, Tenn, 48-76; High Mus, Atlanta, 53-58 & 61; Butler

Inst Am Art, Youngstown, Ohio, 55 & 62; Brooks Mem Art Gallery, Memphis, Tenn, 56-69; Smithsonian Inst, Washington, DC, 60; Springfield Art Mus, Mo, 62; one-man shows in six Mex cities. Teaching: Instr beginning, intermediate & advan painting, Hunter Gallery Art, Chattanooga, Tenn, 55-75; Vis instr advan painting, Univ Chattanooga, spring 69 & Univ Tenn, Chattanooga, 75. Awards: First Prize Water Color, Southeastern Ann, Atlanta, 75 & Mid-South Exhib, Brooks Mem Gallery, Memphis, Tenn, 57; First Prize & Best in Show, 2nd Nat Small Painting Exhib, Gallery North, Mt Clemens, Mich, 74. Mem: Tenn Water Color Soc. Style & Technique: Water colors; oils; polymers; collages in semi-abstract style, covering landscapes, figures and still lives. Media: Polymer; collage. Mailing Add: 1400 Riverview Rd Chattanooga TN 37405

SHUNNEY, ANDREW
PAINTER
b Attleboro, Mass, Mar 12, 21. Study: RI Sch Design; Art Students League; also with Diego Rivera, Mex. Work: Art in Embassies prog, State Dept, Washington, DC; Kenneth Taylor Gallery, Nantucket, Mass; Buehrle Collection, Zurich, Switz; Salon Automne, Paris, France; Countess Guy de Toulouse-Lautrec Collection. Style & Technique: Post impressionist. Media: Oil, Acrylic, Gouache. Mailing Add: 154 Main St Nantucket MA 02554

SHUTE, BEN E
PAINTER
b Altoona, Wis, July 13, 05. Study: Art Inst Chicago; Chicago Acad Fine Arts. Work: High Mus Art, Atlanta; Columbus Mus Arts & Crafts, Ga; Ga Inst Technol, Atlanta; Emory Univ, Atlanta; Mus Art, Columbia, SC; plus others. Exhib: Calif Palace of Legion of Honor, San Francisco; Pasadena Art Inst; Butler Inst Am Art, Youngstown, Ohio; Telfair Acad Art; Brooklyn Mus; plus others. Teaching: Lectr contemp Am painting; instr art, Atlanta Art Inst, 28-43, head fine arts dept, 43-70. Pos: Chmn, Southeastern Ann Exhib, 16 yrs; mem bd Ga Art Asn. Awards: Atlanta Watercolor Club, 60; Mead Paper Co Award, 61; Southeastern Ann, 61; plus others. Mem: Asn Ga Artists; Nat Soc Painters in Casein. Mailing Add: 1002 Cardova Dr NE Atlanta GA 30324

SHUTE, ROBERTA E
SCULPTOR, PAINTER
b Saskatoon, Sask. Study: Corcoran Mus Art Sch, 49-52; Am Univ, 52-53; study with Hans Hofmann, 53. Comn: Environmental sculpture (with Maxine Cable), Noche Crist, engrs. & technicians, Allied Chem, New York, 70; happening for Summers in the Park Prog, Nat Park Serv, Washington, DC, 72. Exhib: One-woman shows, Studio St Germain-des-Pres, Paris, 61, Spectrum Gallery, Soho, NY, 68, 71 & 73 & Gallery Ten Ltd, Washington, DC, 75 & 77; Norfolk Mus, 51 & 56; Baltimore Mus, 53; Pa Acad, 54; Art: USA Nat, New York, 58. Teaching: Painting, Corcoran Mus Sch, 51-52; guest lectr plastic sculpture, Am Univ, 72; sculpture, Glen Echo Creative Educ Prog, 73. Awards: Nathan Goodman Estate Award, 51; Second Prize, Washington Soc Artists, 62; First Prize, Art & Religion, 63. Mem: Artists Equity Asn. Style & Technique: Abstract sculpture in plastic, primarily free formed. Dealer: Gallery Ten Ltd 1519 Connecticut Ave NW Washington DC 20036. Mailing Add: 3536 Edmunds St NW Washington DC 20007

SHUTT, KEN
SCULPTOR, PAINTER
b Long Beach, Calif, Dec 12, 28. Study: Pasadena City Col, AA(art), Chouinard Sch Fine Arts, Los Angeles; Art Ctr Sch, Los Angeles. Work: Honolulu Advert News Bldg, Oahu; Hawaii State Capitol, Oahu; Univ Hawaii, Oahu; Hawaii State Off Bldgs, Oahu & Hawaii; Laupahoehoe Sch, Hawaii. Comn: Sculptures, Challenge of the Sea, Sea Life Park, Makapuu, Oahu, 64, Birds in Flight, Am Savings & Loan, Honolulu, 68, Sky Sailor, Hawaii Air Acad, Honolulu Airport, 73, Sails, Harbor Lights Condominium, Kahalui, Maui, 74 & Polynesian Sails, Maui Surf Hotel, Kaanapali, Maui, 74. Exhib: Artists of Hawaii Ann Show, Honolulu Acad Arts, 64, 66 & 71; Artists of Honolulu Exchange Show, Toronto, Can, 74; Honolulu Munic Off Bldg Int Competition, 75. Awards: First Place Sculpture Award, Los Angeles Asn Art Guild, 60; Entrance to City Fountain Design Competition Award, City of Manhattan Beach, Calif, 62. Mem: Hawaii Painters & Sculptors League; Hawaii Coun for the Arts. Style & Technique: Sculpture by addition, light in feeling, open involvement with space, cantilevered asymmetrical compositions. Media: Epoxy Resin & Wood; Watercolor. Mailing Add: PO Box 1124 Haneohe HI 96744

SIBERELL, ANNE HICKS
PRINTMAKER, ILLUSTRATOR
b Los Angeles, Calif. Study: Univ Calif, 2 yrs; Chouinard Art Inst, 3 yrs, BFA; Silvermine Col Art, New Canaan, Conn, painting with John Wheat & Richard Lytle; Rowayton Art Ctr, Conn, printmaking with Antonio Frasconi; Col San Mateo, Calif, etching. Work: Kerlan Collection, Walter Libr, Univ Minn, Minneapolis; Col San Mateo Collection; Silvermine Col Art; Bankers Trust Collection, San Francisco; Westport City Schs Collection, Conn. Comn: Ed 100 woodcuts, Silvermine Guild Art, Silvermine Col Art, 66. Exhib: Traveling Print Exhib, 67; Phelan Awards, Palace of Legion of Hon, 69; Graphic Artist, San Francisco Art Festival, 74; Nat Exp Printmakers Show, Tusculum Col, Greenville, Tenn, 75; Mandeville Art Gallery, Univ San Diego, 77; Burlingame Civic Arts Coun, Calif, 77; one-artist shows, Print Rm, John Bolles Gallery, San Francisco, 72 & Bakersfield Col Art Gallery, 77; plus numerous others. Teaching: Art for Children, Silvermine Col Art, 66-68 & Martin Luther King Jr Ctr, San Mateo, 68-70; woodblock printmaking, San Mateo Adult Educ, 70, illus children's lit, 74-75 & teaching, 76-78; guest lectr, Bakersfield Col, Calif, 77. Pos: Asst art ed, Walt Disney Prods, Inc, 56-59; ed filmstrip prep from children's lit, Weston Woods Studios, Conn, 60. Awards: Award for Color Woodcut, Conn Mus Show, Hartford, 68; First Award, City of Burlingame Sponsored competition, 73; Rounce & Coffin Award for Bk Design & Illus, 73. Bibliog: Design without Clients, Fortune Mag, 75; TV interview, Festival of the Arts, San Carlos, Calif, 75; plus other articles. Mem: Los Angeles Printmaking Soc; Calif Soc Printmakers; Appeltree Etchers, Inc (bd dirs, 72-74). Style & Technique: Embossing using elements of collage or assemblage; woodcut and color etching; experimental techniques in papermaking and in printmaking materials, including metals and plastics. Media: Oil Based Paint and Ink; Collage and Metals. Publ: Illusr, Walt Disney Mag, 56-59; co-auth, Rainbow Over All, 67, Lamb, Said the Lion, I Am Here, 71, Who Found America?, 73 & Feast of Thanksgiving, 74. Dealer: Zara Gallery 553 Pacific St San Francisco CA 94133. Mailing Add: 1041 La Cuesta Rd Hillsborough CA 94010

SIBLEY, CHARLES KENNETH
PAINTER, EDUCATOR
b Huntington, WVa, Dec 20, 21. Study: Ohio State Univ, BS; Art Inst Chicago; Columbia Univ, MA; State Univ Iowa, MFA. Work: Metrop Mus Art, New York; NC Mus, Raleigh; Va Mus, Richmond; Rochester Mem Mus, NY; Harvard Univ, Cambridge, Mass. Comn: Panels, USS Kennedy, 71; Va Landscape (oil), Gov Mansion, Richmond, 72; mural, Old Dom Univ Libr, Norfolk, Va, 77. Exhib: Carnegie Int, Pittsburgh, 57; Whitney Mus Am Art Bi-Ann, New York, 57-59; Nat Soc Arts & Lett, 59; Nat Acad Design, 61; 50 Artists—50 States, Am Fedn Arts, 68. Teaching: Instr painting & design, Duke Univ, 50-51 & Tex State Univ, 52-54; prof painting & design, Old Dom Univ, 55-, chmn dept, 55-70. Pos: Mem bd dirs, Norfolk Va Children's Art Ctr; mem, Va State Fine Arts Comn, 77- Awards: Louis Comfort Tiffany Grant, 55; Stern Medal, Nat Acad Design, 61; Irene Leache Mem First Prize, Norfolk Mus, 71. Media: Oil, Acrylic, Watercolor. Mailing Add: 108 London Blvd Portsmouth VA 23704

SICKBERT, JO
PAINTER
b Independence, Mo, Oct 27, 31. Study: Univ Kans. Work: Albrecht Art Mus, St Joseph, Mo. Exhib: One-artist exhibs, Albrecht Art Mus, 74, Folk Art Show, Philbrook Art Ctr, Tulsa, Okla, 75, Chicago Tribune Bicentennial Show, 75 & Jack O'Grady Galleries, Chicago, 76 & 78. Awards: Best of Show & Top Nat Award, Am Pen Women, 71; Winner, Saturday Eve Post Cover Contest, 74; Cert of Excellence, Chicago 76, 76. Style & Technique: American primitive. Media: Acrylic. Dealer: Jack O'Grady Galleries 333 N Michigan Ave Chicago IL 60601. Mailing Add: 10316 Beverly Overland Park KS 66207

SICKMAN, JESSALEE BANE
PAINTER, INSTRUCTOR
b Denver, Colo, Aug 17, 05. Study: Univ Colo; Goucher Col; Corcoran Sch Art, Washington, DC; also with Richard Lahey & Eugen Weisz. Work: Corcoran Gallery Art. Comn: Portrait, comn by Mr Pach, Cleveland, Ohio, 51; Pigeons, comn by Mrs Bruton, Alexandria, Va, 55; Figure Study, comn by Mrs Woods, San Diego, Calif, 71. Exhib: One-man Watercolor Show, Pub Libr, Washington, DC, 42; Corcoran Gallery Art Biennial Exhibs, 42-50; Colony Club, Washington, DC, 58 & 62; Soc Washington Artists, Smithsonian Inst, 68 & Arts Club. Teaching: Instr still life, Warrentown Country Sch, Va, 40; instr life portrait, Corcoran Sch Art, 40-63; instr portrait & still life, Sickman Studios, Washington, DC, 64- Awards: Landscape Award, Corcoran Sch Art, 37; Alice Barney Mem Portrait Award, 38. Mem: Artists Equity Asn; Soc Washington Artists. Style & Technique: Abstract, semi abstract, and realism. Media: Oil. Mailing Add: 1215 Eye St NW Washington DC 20015

SICKMAN, LAURENCE CHALFANT STEVENS
ART ADMINISTRATOR, ART HISTORIAN
b Denver, Colo, Aug 27, 06. Study: Harvard Univ, AB(cum laude), 30, Harvard-Yenching fel China Peking, 30-35, resident fel, Fogg Art Mus, 37-39; Rockhurst Col, Hon DFA, 72; Baker Univ, Baldwin, Kans, LHD, 73; Mo Univ, Hon DLit, 74; Kansas City Art Inst, Hon DFA, 75; Columbia Univ, LHD, 77. Teaching: Lectr hist art, Univ Kans, 70-; lectr hist art, Univ Mo-Kansas City, 70-77. Pos: Cur Oriental art, Nelson Gallery Art, Kansas City, Mo, 35-45, from vdir to dir, 46-77, ed, Arch Asian Art, 66-74, emer dir & consult to trustees, Nelson Gallery, 77- Awards: Knight Order of the Pole Star, H M King of Sweden, 68; Charles Lang Freer Medal (for Distinguished Contribution to the Knowledge and Understanding of Oriental Civilizations as Reflected in their Arts), 73. Mem: Asn Art Mus Dirs (pres, 64); Am Asn Mus (coun mem, 63-69); Col Art Asn Am (bd dirs, 63-68); Chinese Art Soc Am (bd gov, 48-, ed, Arch, 48-66); Am Coun Learned Socs (comt Far Eastern Studies, 48-53). Res: Far Eastern art, especially Chinese paintings and sculpture. Publ: Ed, The university prints, Oriental Art, Series O, Early Chinese Art, 38; co-auth, The art & architecture of China, Pelican History of Art, 56; ed & contribr, Chinese Calligraphy & Painting in the Collection of John M Crawford, Jr, 62. Mailing Add: Nelson Gallery Atkins Mus 4525 Oak St Kansas City MO 64111

SIDEN, FRANKLIN
ART DEALER, LECTURER
b Highland Park, Mich, Nov 16, 22. Study: Soc Arts & Crafts, 32-36; Meinzinger Art Sch, 40; Univ Ill, BS, 47; Wayne State Univ, MA(art hist), 77. Teaching: Instr mod art, Bloomfield Birmingham Art Asn, 74 & 76-77; instr mod art & collecting prints, Univ Courses in Adult Educ, 78. Pos: Owner, Franklin Siden Gallery, Detroit, Mich, 64-72 & West Bloomfield, Mich, 72- Bibliog: Six Detroit dealers who are serving a growing art market, The Art Gallery, 66. Mem: Founders Soc, Detroit Inst Arts; Friends of Mod Art, Detroit Inst Arts; Mus Mod Art, New York; Cranbrook Acad Arts, Bloomfield Hills; Arts Coun Triangle. Specialty: Modern and contemporary paintings, sculptures and prints. Mailing Add: Franklin Siden Gallery 6024 Brook Lane West Bloomfield MI 48033

SIDEN, HARRIET FIELD
ART LIBRARIAN, COLLECTOR
b Detroit, Mich, Jan 27, 31. Study: Univ Mich, BA(art hist), 52; Wayne State Univ, MSLS, 75. Pos: Art librn, D'Arcy, MacManus & Masius, Bloomfield Hills, 75- Mem: Art Librn Soc NAm; Theatre Libr Asn; Spec Libr Asn. Interest: Art in relation to business and advertising. Collection: Contemporary paintings, sculpture and graphics. Mailing Add: c/o D'Arcy MacManus & Masius Woodward at Long Lake Bloomfield Hills MI 48013

SIDENIUS, W CHRISTIAN
DESIGNER, LIGHT ARTIST
b Hackensack, NJ, Sept 15, 23. Study: Stevens Inst Technol (mech eng); Lumia with Thomas Wilfred. Work: Walker Art Mus. Comn: Lumia instruments comn by A Metcalf, NY, 66, F Hunter, 68, G Volodin, 69, O Vandeveen, 70 & D Evans, Conn, 70. Exhib: Lights in Orbit, H Wise, NY; New Haven Festival, Slade Ely, New Haven & Booth Libr, Newtown, Conn. Pos: Dir, Lumia the Theatre of Light, 65-75; repair & maintain Wilfred Lumia Suite, Mus Mod Art. Bibliog: T D Jones (auth), Art of Light & Color, 72 & S Kranz (auth), Science & Technology in Art, 74, Van Nostrand Reinhold; R Farrel (auth). Lumia Film, privately publ, 74. Style & Technique: A theatre performance of all possible light art, especially Lumia. Media: Light projection art mainly in own theatre. Mailing Add: Rte 34 Sandy Hook CT 06482

SIDER, DENO
PAINTER, SCULPTOR
b Norwich, Conn, Mar 2, 26. Study: Norwich Acad, dipl; also with Leon Franks. Work: Mattatuck Mus, Conn. Comn: Map of US & decor, Aldo, Hollywood, 56; side panels & fish murals (mixed media), Aquarium, Tarzana, 66. Exhib: Int Madonna Festival, Los Angeles, 58-61 & 63-64; Calif State Show, Sacramento, 62 & 66; Los Angeles Co Art Show, Los Angeles, 66; Hollywood Bowl Art Festival, Los Angeles, 68-69; Gallery Tour, distrib by Ira Roberts. Teaching: Instr art & oils & owner, Sider Art Sch, Hollywood, 54-64; instr art & oils, Leedes Art Sch, Encino, Calif, 64- Pos: Partner, Leedes Art Gallery, 64-71, owner, 71- Awards: Madonna Festival Award, Methodist Church, Los Angeles, 63 & 64; Hollywood Bowl Best of Show, 68 & 69; Tuaca Purchase Award, 70. Mem: Life mem San Fernando Valley Art Club; Calif Art Club; Valley Artist Guild; Burbank Art Asn. Style & Technique: Impressionism. Media: Oil, Clay, Ink, Charcoal. Specialty: French academic impressionist sculpture and paintings. Collection: Leon Franks; Egyptian 18th Dynasty art; G McGregor; T'sung Dynasty scrolls. Publ: Illusr, Epicurean Mag, 69-70; illusr & ed, Prospector News, 71-; illus & supv, Polygems, 77- Mailing Add: 19319 Van Owen Reseda CA 91335

SIDERIS, ALEXANDER
PAINTER
b Skopelos, Greece, Feb 21, 98. Study: Art Students League; Acad Julian, Paris; also with George Bridgman & Pierre Laurence. Work: Wesleyan Col, Macon, Ga; Greek Church, Philadelphia; murals, Church of the Annunciation, Pensacola, Fla; Byzantine mural, Greek Cathedral, New York; Church of Holy Trinity, Salt Lake City, Utah; 42 paintings on permanent display, Island of Skopelos, Greece; plus others. Exhib: Barbizon Gallery, 54; Nat Arts Club, 55; Knickerbocker Artists, 59-61; one-man show, Hellenic Am Union Gallery, Athens, Greece, 68; six shows, Newton Gallery; plus other group & one-man shows. Awards: Prize, Am Artists Prof League, 53; Award, Nat Arts Club, 61; Gold Medal Prize, 64 & Hon Mention for Oil, 70, Knickerbocker Artists. Mem: Am Artists Prof League (vpres NY Chap, 56-58). Style & Technique: Impressionistic in the academic style. Mailing Add: 116 Pinehurst Ave New York NY 10033

SIEBER, ROY
EDUCATOR, CURATOR
b Shawano, Wis, Apr 28, 23. Study: New Sch Social Res, BA, 49; Univ Iowa, MA, 51, PhD, 57. Teaching: Lect, African Art to cols, Peace Corps & others; from instr to asst prof art hist, Univ Iowa, 50-62; mem fac, Ind Univ, 62-64, prof art hist, 64-74, Rudy Prof fine arts, 74-, chmn fine arts dept, 67-70; vis prof, Univ Ghana, 64 & 67; vis prof, Univ Ife, Nigeria, 71; Benedict Distinguished Vis Prof, Carleton Col, 76-77. Pos: Mem foreign area fel prog, Africa Screening Comt, 59-63; cur primitive art, Ind Univ Fine Arts Mus, 62-; mem primitive art adv comt, Metrop Mus Art; mem joint comt Africa, Am Coun Learned Socs-Social Sci Res Coun, 62-70; trustee, Mus African Art. Awards: African-Am Univ Grant, 64; Ind Univ Int Studies Grant, 64 & 67; Nat Endowment for Humanities Sr Fel, 70-71; plus others. Mem: Royal Anthrop Inst; African Studies Asn (chmn arts & humanities comt, 63); Col Art Asn Am; Am Asn Univ Prof; Midwest Art Asn (secy, 63). Res: African art. Publ: Auth, Sculpture of Northern Nigeria, Mus Primitive Art, NY, 61; co-auth, Sculpture of Black Africa, Los Angeles Co Mus Art, 68; auth, African Textiles & Decorative Arts, Mus Mod Art, NY, 72; plus numerous articles & symp. Mailing Add: 114 Glenwood Ave E Bloomington IN 47401

SIEBNER, HERBERT (VOM SIEBENSTEIN)
PAINTER, MURALIST
b Stettin, Ger, Apr 16, 25; Can citizen. Study: Atelier Max Richter, Stettin, 41-43; Berlin Acad, under Carl Hofer, with Kaus & Schumacher, 46-49. Work: Seattle Art Mus; Confedn Art Mus, PEI; Nat Gallery Ottawa; City of West Berlin; Vancouver Art Gallery. Comn: Sgraffito, Crown House, Victoria, BC, 60; sgraffito-encaustic, Univ Victoria, 65; planetary hist, Mus Victoria, 68; life-frieze, Govt BC, 75. Exhib: World's Fair Expos, Brussels, 57, Seattle, 62; Int Graphic Expos, Lugano, Switz, 58, Lubljana, Yugoslavia, 59; Can Biennial, Ottawa, 58 & 62; Int Triennial of Xylographia, Carpy, Italy, 69; Int Graphic Exhib, Spain, 71, Italy, 72. Teaching: Vis prof painting, Univ Wash, 63 & Univ BC, 64; lectr painting, Univ Victoria, 67 & 69. Awards: Reid Award Graphic, Royal Ont Mus, Toronto, 56; Sculpture, BC, 57; Painting, Seattle Art Mus, 57; Can Coun Sr Grant, 62; Guest of Hon, Berlin Acad, 63; Hon Citizen, City of Victoria, BC, 73. Bibliog: Anthony Emery (auth), Art of Herbert Siebner, Can Art Mag, 58; Robin Skelton (auth), The man & the vision, Malahat Rev, Univ BC, 71; Creative Canada, Univ Toronto, 72. Mem: Union Prof Artists, Ger; Can Group Painters; Soc BC Artists; Royal Can Acad; The Limners. Style & Technique: Figurative; expressionistic; symbolic. Media: Sgraffito, Acrylic & Lithography. Publ: Illusr, Inscriptions, 67 & Muse Book, 72; auth, Colour, Line & Form, 70. Mailing Add: 270 Meadow Brook Rd Victoria BC V8X 3X3 Can

SIEG, ROBERT LAWRENCE
SCULPTOR, ENAMELIST
b Cement, Okla. Study: Cent State Univ, Okla, BA, 63; Inst Allende, Univ de Guanajuato, MFA, 68. Work: Ark Arts Ctr, Little Rock; Okla Art Ctr, Oklahoma City; Mus Art, Univ Okla, Norman; Okla Arts & Humanities Coun Collection, Oklahoma City. Exhib: Past Jurors Invitational, Okla Art Ctr, 69; Small Environments, Madison Art Ctr, Wis & Southern Ill Univ, 72; Eight-State Exhib of Painting & Sculpture, Okla Art Ctr, 73; Okla State Art Mus, 73; Mus of Art, Univ of Okla, 77; Goddard Arts Ctr, Okla, 78; Inter-D Exhib, McAllen Int Mus, Tex; Midwest Biennial Joslyn Art Mus, Omaha, Nebr; Monroe Ann, Masur Mus of Art, La; Delta Art Exhib, Ark Art Ctr. Teaching: Asst prof art, ECent Okla State Univ, 66-77. Awards: Sculpture Award, 15th Mid-Am, Nelson Gallery Art, Kansas City, 65; Inter-Am Craft Alliance Award, McAllen Int Mus, Tex, 70; AAC Purchase Awards, Toys Designed by Artists, Ark Art Ctr, 74. Bibliog: B J Smith (auth), Features artist, Cimarron Rev, 4/73. Mem: Okla Designer Craftsman. Style & Technique: Sculpture of relief and dimensional construction. Media: Wood, Metal. Mailing Add: 1017 E Central Blvd Ada OK 74820

SIEGEL, ADRIAN
PHOTOGRAPHER, PAINTER
b New York, NY, July 17, 98. Work: Philadelphia Mus Art; Mus Mod Art, New York. Comn: Circulating exhibs, Musicians at Work & People & Art, Philadelphia Mus Art. Exhib: Three Photographers, Philadelphia Mus Art; Six Photographers, Mus Mod Art, 49; Pa Acad Fine Arts Ann, Philadelphia; Pepsi Cola Show, Metrop Mus Art, New York; Artists Equity Exhib, Civic Ctr, Philadelphia, 72. Pos: Official photogr, Philadelphia Orch, 37. Awards: Gold Medal, Art Dirs Club, New York, 49. Bibliog: Orchestra man looks at the world's great musicians, Life, 43; Charles D Sigsbee (auth), Idol moments in the orchestra, Sun Mag, 52; A lens among the strings, High Fidelity Mag, 55. Mem: Philadelphia Art Alliance; Artists Equity Asn; fel Royal Soc Art, London; Philadelphia Print Club; Pa Acad Fine Arts. Publ: Auth, Concerto for Camera, Philadelphia Orchestra Asn. Mailing Add: 1907 Pine St Philadelphia PA 19103

SIEGEL, IRENE
PAINTER
b Chicago, Ill. Study: Northwestern Univ, BS; Univ Chicago; Ill Inst Technol Inst Design, Moholy-Nagy scholar, 54, MS. Work: Art Inst Chicago; Mus Mod Art, New York; Los Angeles Co Mus; World Bank, Washington, DC; Pasadena Mus, Calif. Exhib: Drawing Soc Show, Mus Fine Arts, Houston, Tex, 65; Form & Fantasy, Am Fedn Art, 69; Tamarind Prints, Mus Mod Art, 69; Soc Contemp Art, Art Inst Chicago, 71; Relativerend Realisme, Van Abbemuseum, Eindhoven, Holland, 72. Awards: Mr & Mrs Frank Logan Prize, 66; Tamarind Fel, Ford Found, 67. Bibliog: William S Lieberman (auth), Homage to Lithography, Mus Mod Art, 69; Garo Antreasian (auth), The Tamarind Book of Lithography, Abrams, 71, Franz Schulze (auth), Fantastic Images, Follett, 72. Publ: Illusr, Barnyard Epithets & Other Obscenities, 70. Mailing Add: 421 Roslyn Pl Chicago IL 60614

SIEGEL, (LEO) DINK
ILLUSTRATOR
b Birmingham, Ala. Study: Nat Acad Design; Art Students League; Am Sch Art; also with Robert Brackman. Mem: Soc Illusr. Media: Watercolor, Ink. Publ: Illusr, Redbook, Cosmopolitan, Sat Eve Post, Field & Stream Mag, Good Housekeeping, New Yorker & Playboy. Mailing Add: 100 W 57th St New York NY 10019

SIEGRIEST, LUNDY
PAINTER
b Oakland, Calif, Apr 4, 25. Study: Calif Col Arts & Crafts, Oakland, cert. Work: Whitney Mus Am Art, New York; Denver Art Mus, Colo; Libr of Cong, Washington, DC; Santa Barbara Mus, Calif; Oakland Mus. Exhib: 3rd Biennale Sao Paulo, Brazil, 55; Carnegie Inst Int, Pittsburgh, 55; Young Americans Under 35, 58 & Contemporary American Painting, 60, Whitney Mus Am Art; 17 American Painters, Brussels World's Fair, 58. Teaching: Instr painting, Acad Art, San Francisco, 51-64; instr painting, Jr Ctr Art, Oakland, 53-71; instr painting, Civic Arts, Walnut Creek, Calif, 64. Awards: Albert M Bender Grant, 52; Purchase Awards, Calif Palace of Legion of Honor, 52 & Santa Barbara Mus, 55. Bibliog: New talent, art USA, Art in Am, 57; Contemporary American Painting, Univ Ill, 63. Media: Oil, Mixed Media. Dealer: Gumps Gallery 250 Post St San Francisco CA 94133. Mailing Add: 479 Cavour St Oakland CA 94618

SIEVAN, MAURICE
PAINTER
b Ukraine, Russia, Dec 7, 98; US citizen. Study: Nat Acad Design, New York, with Leon Kroll & Charles Hawthorne; Art Students League; also with Andre L'Hote, Paris. Work: Mus Mod Art, New York; Brooklyn Mus, NY; Baltimore Mus, Md; Butler Inst Am Art, Youngstown, Ohio; Hirshhorn Mus, Washington, DC. Exhib: Salon Automne, Paris, 31; Art Inst of Chicago, 41; Brooklyn Mus Int Watercolor Exhibs, 41, 53 & 58; Artists for Victory, Metrop Mus Art, New York, 42; Painting USA, Carnegie Inst Fine Arts, Pittsburgh, 43, 44 & 45; Romantic Painting Am, 43, Recent Drawings, 56 & New Acquisitions, 64-65, Mus Mod Art; Wadsworth Atheneum, 44; Va Mus, 44; Pa Acad, 44 & 46; Corcoran Mus, 45; Mortimer Brandt Gallery, New York, 45; Passedoit Gallery, New York, 55 & 57; Retrospective, Mint Mus, Charlotte, NC, 55; Andrew Dickson White Mus of Art, Cornell Univ, 61; Albert Landry Gallery, New York, 61 & 63; Holland Goldowsky Gallery, Chicago, 61; HCE Gallery, Provincetown, Mass, 61; Retrospective, Queens Mus, Flushing, NY, 74. Teaching: Instr art, Summit Art Asn, 40-50; instr art, Queens Col, Flushing, NY, 46-68. Awards: Newhouse Mem Award, Audubon Artists, 46; NY State Coun Arts Funded Retrospective Exhib, Queens Mus, New York; Mark Rothko Found Grant, 73. Bibliog: Lawrence Campbell (auth), Maurice Sievan, Art News, 5/55; Ivan Karp (auth), Seven paintings by Sievan, Barone Gallery, 1/60; Hilton Kramer (auth), Sievan paints a lyric Queens landscape, New York Times, 3/74. Mem: Woodstock Art Asn; Fedn Mod Painters & Sculptors (all comts); Col Art Asn Am; Artists Equity Asn. Media: Oil, Watercolor, Pastel. Mailing Add: 924 West End Ave New York NY 10025

SIGEL, BARRY CHAIM
PAINTER
b Baltimore, Md, Sept 22, 43. Study: Md Inst Art; Acad Art, New Haven; with Mrs Francis, North Truro, Mass; also with A G Giovanni, Giorzinko, Sicily. Work: Union Plumbers Am Hall, Pasadena; Mural on The Red Truck, Head of the Meadow, Cape Cod, Mass; Harvey House Rest, Baltimore; Grand Canyon Hist Mus, Ariz; Royal Mus, Bombay, India. Comn: Portraiture & bust, Richard Lyttle, New Haven, Conn, 68; mural, Pierre's Beauty Salon, New York, 69; watercolor, Mr & Mrs Dilly McKenzie, Cape Cod, Mass, 69; outdoor sign, Right-on Church of Good Vibes, Mesa, Wyo, 70; collage (with Ann Kutti), Layed Back'n Mello Rest Home, San Francisco, 72; Mystical Glow with Buffalo (oil), pvt collector, New York, NY. Exhib: Baltimore Mus Art, 65 & 66; Datza Mabot Gallery, Pecarino, Sicily, 67; Grand Prix de Still Life, Ostend, Belg, 68; Greenwich Village Outdoor Show, 69; Green Mountain Art Gallery, New York, 71 & one-man show, 77; La Galleria 641, Washington, DC, 75; Davidson Nat Print & Drawing Competition, 76; Art on Canvasboard, Univ SC, 77. Teaching: Critic painting, Scungia Acad, Sicily, 69; Introd to Advan Conceptual Art, Educ Alliance, 76; instr Feminine Carpentry, YWCA, Brooklyn, NY, 77. Awards: Louis Waitsman Prize, Baltimore Arts Asn, 66; Chalk Championship New York, 71. Bibliog: N P Clark (auth), article in Baltimore News Post, 66; Tworkov (auth), You call these Paintings?, NH Hist Mag, 68. Mem: Charcoal Club Baltimore. Media: Oil, Acrylic, Watercolor, Feathers, Sand. Dealer: Green Mountain Art Gallery 135 Greene St New York NY 10012. Mailing Add: 463 West Apt 327 New York NY 10014

SIGOLOFF, VIOLET BRUCE
ART DEALER, PAINTER
b Huntington, WVa. Study: Trinity Univ, with Phillip Wilson. Work: Paintings & portraits in pvt collections, US & Mex. Exhib: San Antonio Art League, 64-70; one-woman show, St Marys Univ, San Antonio, 66; Southwestern Fine Arts Exhib, Univ Tex, 67; Trinity Univ, 68. Pos: Owner & dir, Wonderland Gallery, 66-, owner & dir, Wonderland Art Sch, 69-72; owner, Sigoloff Gallery, 72- Awards: Watercolor & Miniature Award, Composers, Authors & Artists Exhib, New York, 65; San Antonio's Outstanding Woman in Art, San Antonio Express & Eve News, 67. Mem: Tex Fine Arts Asn; San Antonio Art League. Style & Technique: Palette knife, realism, portraits. Media: Oil. Specialty: Fine art, contemporary and antique paintings. Mailing Add: 8410 Tiffany Dr San Antonio TX 78230

SIGRIN, MICHAEL E
ART ADMINISTRATOR, MUSEUM DIRECTOR
b New York, NY, July 29, 44. Study: Pa State Univ, BA; New Sch of Social Res, New York; Univ Iowa, MFA. Work: Mus Mod Art, New York; Univ Iowa, Iowa City; Farleigh-Dickinson Univ, NJ. Exhib: Exposure Gallery, New York, 73 & 74; Farleigh-Dickinson Univ, 74; Univ Iowa, 76. Teaching: Instr photog, Farleigh-Dickinson Univ, 72-74. Pos: Dir, Exposure Gallery, New York, 70-74; dir, Cent Iowa Art Asn, 77- Mem: Soc Photog Educ; Col Art Asn. Media: Photography, Film. Mailing Add: c/o Central Iowa Art Asn 709 S Center Marshalltown IA 50158

SIHVONEN, OLI
PAINTER
b Brooklyn, NY, Jan 31, 21. Study: Art Students League; Black Mt Col, NC; with Josef Albers & Buckminster Fuller. Work: Mus Mod Art & Whitney Mus Am Art, New York; Corcoran Gallery Art, Washington, DC; Dallas Mus Fine Arts; Art Inst Chicago. Comn: Lobby wall painting, State Agency Bldg, S Mall, Albany, NY, 68; painting, Northwestern Univ, Evanston, Ill, 69. Exhib: Geometric Abstraction in America, 62 & Whitney Ann, 63, 65 & 67, Whitney Mus Am Art; The Responsive Eye, Mus Mod Art, New York, 65; 30th Biennial Am Painting, Corcoran Gallery Art, 67; Plus X Minus Today's Half Century, Albright-Knox, Buffalo, NY, 68. Awards: Nat Coun Arts Award, 67; Purchase Award, Corcoran Biennial, 67. Media: Acrylic, Oil. Mailing Add: 245 Grand St New York NY 10002

SILBER, MAURICE
PAINTER, ILLUSTRATOR
b Brooklyn, NY, Apr 12, 22. Study: Cooper Union; Pratt Inst, indust design with Donald Dohner; study with Ed Whitney, Robert E Wood, Tom Hill & John Pike. Work: USAF Art Collection & USN Combat Art Collection, Washington, DC; Air Force Mus, Pease AFB, NH. Comn: Philadelphia Naval Shipyard, NACAL Assignment, 72-74; Eglin AFB, USAF, Fla, 72; San Antonio, Tex, USAF, 73; US Dept Interior, Nat Park Serv, 75. Exhib: Salmagundi Club, New York, 71-75; Am Artists Prof League, NY, 73-74; Illusrs Am, Port Washington, NY, 74; Hudson Valley Art Asn, White Plains, NY, 75; Soc Illusrs, New York, 75. Pos: Painter jury of awards, Washington Sq Outdoor Art Show, 72-75 & Salmagundi Club, 73. Awards: First Prize & Spec Award, Westinghouse, New York World's Fair, 39; plus others. Bibliog: Air Force Art, Bolling Beam, Morkap Pub Co, 10/73; Air Force Art, Seacoast Flyer, Star Press, Maine, 9/74; AFSA, US Air Force, Impressions at Eglin, 12/74. Mem: Salmagundi Club (chmn admis); Soc Illusrs; Nat Art League; Artists Fel; Am Artists Prof League. Style & Technique: Watercolor and pen and ink; graphics; felt pen markers. Publ: Auth & illusr, The Water Color Page, Am Artist, 6/72. Mailing Add: 183-07 69th Ave Fresh Meadows NY 11365

SILBER, ZAVEL
See Zavel

SILBERFELD, KAY
CONSERVATOR
b New York, NY, July 31, 34. Study: Sarah Lawrence Col, BA, 56; apprenticeship in painti g concerv with Richard D Buck, Dir, Intermus Conserv Asn, Oberlin, Ohio, 60-62. Pos: Asst conservator paintings, Baltimore Mus of Art, Md, 62-72; conservator of paintings, Nat Gallery of Art, Washington, DC, 72- Mem: Am Inst for Conserv; Int Inst for Conserv; Washington Conserv Guild. Publ: Auth, Art conservation, Sarah Lawrence Alumnae Mag, Spring, 63; auth, The lost paintings of Thomas Cole: examination and treatment, Mus News, Am Asn Mus, 3/65; auth, Examination and treatment of Rembrandt's Portrait of Titus, Ann IV, Baltimore Mus, 68. Mailing Add: Nat Gallery of Art Washington DC 20565

SILBERMAN, ARTHUR
ART LIBRARY DIRECTOR, LECTURER
b Antwerp, Belgium, Jan 8, 29; US citizen. Collections Arranged: From Pictographs to Jerome Tiger (traveling educ exhib), 68-72, American Indian Painting (traveling educ exhib), 72-75, 100 Years of Native American Painting, 78, Okla Mus of Art, Oklahoma City. Pos: Dir, Native Am Painting Ref Libr, Oklahoma City, 75-; hon cur, Native Am painting, Okla Hist Soc Mus, Oklahoma City, 76-; guest cur, Okla Mus of Art, Oklahoma City, 78; consult, Okla Television Authority, 78. Res: All phases of history and development of Native American painting; oral history tapes, slide reference library collection, archival material. Interest: To increase the appreciation of Native American painting by making reference material available to educators, writers, publishers and museums; to increase public awareness through lectures, publications and exhibits. Publ: Auth, Tiger, 71 & Early Kiowa Art, 73, Okla Today Mag, State of Okla; auth, Animals in Indian Art (sound slides), State of Okla Dept of Libr, 73; auth, 100 Years of Native American Painting, Okla Mus of Art, 78. Mailing Add: Box 32434 Oklahoma City OK 73123

SILBERSTEIN-STORFER, MURIEL ROSOFF
INSTRUCTOR, PAINTER
b Brooklyn, NY. Study: Carnegie Inst Technol, BFA; Philadelphia Mus Art, with Hobson Pitman; Inst Mod Art, with Victor D'Amico, Donald Stacy & Jane Bland. Comn: Prog drawings, Philadelphia Symphony Orch Children's Concerts, 49; murals & other projs, Mt Sinai Hosp & Philadelphia Psychiat Hosp. Exhib: Jewish Community Ctr Group Show, 71-72; Pacem in Terris Gallery, New York, 76-77; one-woman shows, Panoras Gallery, New York, 72, Pacem in Terris Gallery, New York, 75 & Gallery 84, 78. Teaching: Instr art, Inst Mod Art, Mus Mod Art, New York, 63; guest lectr art educ, var cols & community groups, New York, 67-; instr, Int Playgroups Art Workshops, New York, 70-; instr, Staten Island Community Col, 70-; instr parent-child classes, Metrop Mus Art; instr, Napeague Inst Art. Pos: Assoc tech dir & scene designer, Pittsburgh Playhouse, 44-46; interior display designer, var Pittsburgh Dept Stores, 46-47; art educ consult, Staten Island Ment Health Schs, Head Start, Staten Island Community Col & others. Awards: Woman of Achievement, Staten Island Advan, 67; Achievement Award, Lambda Kappa Mu Sorority. Mem: New York Art Comn (comnr, 70-); Metrop Mus Art (trustee, 71-77 & emer trustee, 77-); Staten Island Coun Arts; Art Comn of the City of New York (pres); Snug Harbor Cult Ctr (trustee); Napeague Inst Art (trustee). Style & Technique: Found materials mounted on canvas, combined with paint. Media: Assemblage, Collage. Res: Art education; community arts projects. Publ: Contribr, Art Caravan; auth, pamphlet for parent-child workshops, Metrop Mus of Art, New York. Mailing Add: 427 E 74th St New York NY 10021

SILINS, JANIS
PAINTER
b Riga, Latvia, June 1, 96; US citizen. Study: Univ Moscow; Riga Univ, MA & PhD; Univ Stockholm; Univ Marburg; Art Sch Ilya Mashkov, Moscow; Art Sch Kazan. Work: Univ Art Collection, Riga; Art Mus Jelgava, Latvia. Exhib: One-man shows, Würzburg, Ger, 46 & Yonkers, NY, 68 & 69; Exhib Artists in Exile, Stuttgart, Ger, 48; Ringling Mus Art, Sarasota, 63; Latvian Exhib Arts & Crafts, Boston, 64; Latvian Artist Group New York, 67. Collections Arranged: Hugh Gowan Miller Collection Paintings, Norfolk Mus, Va, 55; Arts of Norway, Morse Art Gallery, Winter Park, Fla & Tour, 58; plus many others. Teaching: Instr art hist, Riga Univ & Latvian Acad Art, 31-44; instr art hist, Univ Würzburg, 46-51; instr art hist, Rollins Col, 56-63. Pos: Dir art mus, Riga Univ, 41-44; art consult, Norfolk Mus, 55-; exec dir, Morse Gallery Art, 56-60. Awards: Order of Three Stars, Govt Latvia, 36; Kriskian Baron Award, Riga Univ, 37. Bibliog: J Kadilis (auth), Janis Silins, Cels, 46; L Liberts (auth), Janis Silins, 46 & A Annus (auth), Seeking for beauty & truth, 66, Laiks; plus others. Mem: Latvian Artist Group New York; Sarasota Art Asn; Orlando Art Asn (mem bd, 62); Asn Artists, Sadarbs, Riga (secy, 24-38); Am Asn Univ Prof. Style & Technique: Expressive realism. Media: Oil, Watercolor. Res: Basic problems of art philosophy, especially ontology of art; principles of modern art; Latvian art. Publ: Auth, Michelangelo, 31; auth, Karlis Zale, His Monumental Sculpture, 38 & 43; auth, Laudolf Liberts, Painter & Stage Designer, 42; auth, Janis Gailis, a Latvian Landscape Painter, 48; Images & Ideas, 64. Mailing Add: 1258 Chestnut St Roselle NJ 07203

SILKOTCH, MARY ELLEN
PAINTER
b New York, NY, Sept 12, 11. Study: Van Emburgh Sch Art; also with Jonas Lie, Sigismund Ivanowski & Dudley Gloyne, summers. Work: In pvt collections. Exhib: Nat Acad Women Artists; Montclair Art Mus, NJ; Am Artists Prof League; Atlantic City Art Ctr; Irvington Mus & Art Asn; plus others. Teaching: Instr art, Van Emburgh Sch, Plainfield, 44-64; instr art, Adult Educ, Dunellen, NJ, 48-57; instr art, Bound Brook Adult Educ, 50-57; instr art, North Plainfield, 51-54. Pos: Vpres, Academic Artists, 67-; vpres, Trailside Mus Arts Ctr NJ. Awards: Prizes, Am Artists Prof League, Plainfield Art Asn & East Orange, NJ; plus others. Mem: Nat Asn Women Artists; Plainfield Art Asn (pres, 52-60); Am Artists Prof League (pres, NJ Chap, 69-71); Artists Equity Asn; Westfield Art Asn. Style & Technique: Traditional. Mailing Add: 341 Hazelwood Pl Piscataway NJ 08854

SILLS, THOMAS ALBERT
PAINTER
b Castalia, NC, Aug 20, 14. Work: Whitney Mus Am Art, Metrop Mus Art, Mus Mod Art & Chase Manhattan Collection, New York; Sheldon Mem Gallery, Lincoln, Nebr; plus many others. Exhib: Wilson Col, Chambersberg, Pa, 68; Student Ctr Art Gallery, Brooklyn Col, NY, 69; New American Painting & Sculpture, The First Generation, Mus Mod Art, New York, 69; Afro-Am Artists Exhib, Mus Philadelphia Civic Ctr, Pa, 69; Mt Holyoke Col, South Hadley, Mass, 69; plus other group & one-man exhibs. Awards: William & Norma Copley Found Award, 57. Mailing Add: 240 W 11th St New York NY 10014

SILVER, PAT
DRAFTSMAN, ART DEALER
b San Francisco, Calif, June 6, 22. Work: Town of Los Altos Hills & City of Menlo Park, Calif. Comn: Illus for poetry bk, St Mary's Col Press, Winona, Wis, 73. Exhib: 5th & 8th Ann Hortt Mem Exhib, 63 & 66, 3rd Ann Drawing Exhib, 67, Ft Lauderdale Mus Art, Fla; Helen Euphrat De Anza Col Graphics Regional Exhib, Cupertino, Calif, 72; 5th Ann Pastel Exhib, Pastel Soc Am, Nat Arts Club, Gramercy Park, NY, 77. Pos: Owner of artists coop gallery, Viewpoints Art Gallery, Los Altos, 73- Awards: First Award Drawing, 37th Ann, Fla Fedn Art, 63; Cert Award, Graphics Arts Awards Competition, Printing Indust Am, 74; First Award, Soc Western Artists, 76. Mem: Pastel Soc Am; San Francisco Women Artists; Soc Western Artists; Palo Alto Art Club. Style & Technique: Drawings representational; prints and paintings impressionistic; figural. Media: Charcoal, Pastel; Etching, Drypoint. Mailing Add: 14440 de Bell Rd Los Altos Hills CA 94022

SILVER, THOMAS C
SCULPTOR, EDUCATOR
b Salem, Ore, May 27, 42. Study: San Francisco Art Inst, 60-61, with Joan Brown; Calif State Col, Long Beach, BA 66; Univ Kans, MFA, with Elden Tefft. Work: De Witt Gallery, Hope Col, Holland, Mich; Anderson Gallery, Richmond, Va; Va Mus of Fine Arts, Richmond. Exhib: Traveling Exhib of the Americas, Oakland Mus, Calif, 63-65 & 65-67; A, Craftsmen Coun, Mus West, 65; New Sculpture, Corcoran Gallery of Art, Washington, DC, 70; Traveling Sculpture Exhib, Va Mus of Fine Arts, 71-73; Henri Gallery, Washington, DC, 71; Va Mus of Fine Arts, 72; May Show, Cleveland Mus of Art, Ohio, 72-77; Contemp Relig Imagery in Am Art, Ringling Mus of Art, Sarasota, Fla, 74. Teaching: Instr sculpture, Va Commonwealth Univ, 65-72; assoc prof sculpture, Cleveland State Univ, Ohio, 72- Awards: Century 21 Ctr Merit Award, 63; three First Prizes & Honorable Mention, 14th Ann Kans Designers & Craftsmen Exhib, 67; Cert of Distinction, Va Artists Show, Va Mus of Fine Arts, 69 & 71. Bibliog: Alan R Meisec (auth), Exhibitions, Craft Horizon, 63; La Mar Harrington (auth), First annual Western Craft Council, Craft Horizon, 64; L Judd Ahlander (auth), Contemporary Religious Imagery in American Art (catalog), Ringling Mus of Art, 74. Style & Technique: Assemblage; drawing; performance. Media: Bronze. Mailing Add: 3270 Hyde Park Cleveland Heights OH 44118

SILVERBERG, ELLEN RUTH
ART DEALER
b New York, NY, Mar 7, 47. Study: Art Students League; Cooper Union, BFA, 67. Pos: Owner-dir, Art Gallery Studio 53 Ltd, New York. Specialty: Contemporary limited edition graphics and oils, specializing in Simbari, Jan Balet, Norman Rockwell, Boulanger & Folon. Mailing Add: 424 Park Ave New York NY 10022

SILVERMAN, BURTON PHILIP
PAINTER, ILLUSTRATOR
b Brooklyn, NY, June 11, 28. Study: Pratt Inst; Art Students League, 46-49; Columbia Univ, BA, 49. Work: Brooklyn Mus; Philadelphia Mus Art; Anchorage Mus Art, Alaska; New Britain Mus Am Art, Conn; Parrish Mus Art, Southampton, NY. Exhib: Pa Acad Art Ann, Philadelphia, 49; Butler Inst Am Art Ann, Ohio, 54-70, 71, 74 & 76; Nat Acad Design, New York, 64-78; San Diego Arts Festival, Calif, 66; Childe Hassam Exhib, Am Inst Arts & Lett, New York, 67, 74 & 76; NY Hist Soc, 76; Pa State Mus of Art, 76; Portsmouth Mus of Art, WVa, 76; Drawing Invitational, San Diego, Calif, 77. Teaching: Instr drawing & painting, Sch Visual Arts, New York, 64-67. Awards: Henry W Ranger Purchase Prize, 65, Benjamin Altman Figure Prize, 69 & others, 61, 66 & 67, Nat Acad Design; Dillard Collection Purchase Prize, Art on Paper, Univ NC, 66. Bibliog: Fredrick Whitaker (auth), Four realists, 10/64 & Elizabeth Case (auth), Burton Silverman captures the moment, 6/71, Am Artist Mag; Joseph Singer (auth), How to Paint Portraits in Pastel, Watson-Guptill, 72. Mem: Academician Nat Acad Design. Style & Technique: Realist with links to traditional realism of past; classicism with impressionist overtones; techniques characterized by simple, straightforward brush strokes. Media: Oil, Watercolor, Pastel. Publ: Co-auth, A new look at the eight, Art News, 2/58; auth, Homage to Thomas Eakins, 67 & Art for Pablo Picasso's Sake, 68, Book World; auth, A Portfolio of Drawings, 68; auth, Painting People, Watson-Guptill, 77. Dealer: FAR Gallery 22 E 80th St New York NY 10021. Mailing Add: 324 W 71st St New York NY 10023

SILVERMAN, DAVID FREDERICK
SCULPTOR, EDUCATOR
b Bronx, NY, June 28, 48. Study: State Univ NY, New Paltz, BA(art educ); Rutgers Univ, New Brunswick, NJ, studied with Hui, Ka Kwong; Alfred Univ, NY, MFA(ceramics), with Dan Rhodes, Bob Turner, Val Cushing & Ted Randall. Exhib: 31st Int Competition Contemp Artistic Ceramics, Faenza, Italy, 73; three-man traveling show, Decalcomania, Univ Rochester, Alfred Univ & Ohio State Univ, 74-75; 3rd Biennial Lake Superior Int Craft Exhib, Univ Minn, Duluth, 75; 27th Ohio Ceramic & Sculptural Ann, Butler Inst Am Art, Youngstown, Ohio, 75-77; one-man shows, Hand of Man Gallery, Bedford Hills, NY, 73, Adelphi Univ, NY, 78 & Parkersburg Art Ctr, WVa, 78. Teaching: Instr ceramic sculpture, Alfred Univ, 73-74; instr ceramics, Ohio Univ, Athens, 74- Awards: 14th Ann Winterpark Art Festival, 73, Craft Fair Ithaca, NY State Craftsman, 74 & 27th Ohio Ceramic & Sculpture Ann, Butler Inst Am Art, 75. Bibliog: John Kenny (auth), The Complete Book of Pottery Making. Mem: Am Crafts Coun; NY State Craftsmen; Nat Coun Educ for Ceramic Arts. Style & Technique: Ceramic hand building, porcelain, lowfire, overglaze, decal & unglazed surface decoration. Media: Clay; Fibers. Publ: Contribr, Ceramics Monthly, 72-75 & Craft Horizons, 72-73. Mailing Add: 21 Home St Athens OH 45701

SILVERMAN, RONALD H
EDUCATOR, WRITER
Study: Univ Calif, Los Angeles, BA, 52; Los Angeles State Col, MA, 55; Stanford Univ, EdD, 62. Teaching: Prof art, Calif State Univ, Los Angeles, 55- Publ: Auth, Spectrum of Music,

Macmillan, 74; auth, Goals and roles in art education of children, In: The Arts, Human Development and Education, McCutchan, 76; auth, A comprehensive model for teaching art, In: Report of the NAEA Commission on Art Education, Nat Art Educ Asn, 77. Mailing Add: Art Dept Calif State Univ Los Angeles CA 90032

SILVERMAN, SHERLEY C
PAINTER, SCULPTOR
b Maywood, Ill, Jan 20, 09. Study: Univ Ill; Chicago Acad Fine Arts; Frederick Grant; worked in Pietrasanta, Italy, 63-65; also with John Kearney & Ralph Bormacher. Work: B'nai B'rith Exhib Hall, Washington, DC; also in many nat & int collections, as well as in numerous pvt collections, notably that of Mr & Mrs Harold Green, Palm Springs, Calif. Comn: Welded steel sculpture, comn by Hon Philip Klutznick; Ode to Eleanor (painting), comn by Mrs Nelson Hartstone, Palm Beach; Mother & Child, comn by Mr & Mrs Richard Tucker. Exhib: Patronat Premi Int, DiBuix Joan Miro, Barcelona, Spain; UNESCO; Int Biennale Della Regioni, Italy; Tournoi Int Des Beaux Arts, France; Int Contemp Exhib, Rome, Italy; among many others. Teaching: Pvt art classes, 60- Pos: Hon past pres, Mid-Am Art Asn, Chicago, 68-70. Awards: Gold Medal f Recognition & Bronze Plaque, La Scala Gallery, Florence, Italy; Int Medal of Honor, Int Centro Studi E Scambi; Honoris Causa Silver Medal, Acad Int, Tommaso, Campanella. Mem: US Commite Int Centro Studi E Scambi; Int Arts Guild (comdr); Acad Int Leonardo Da Vinci; Acad Int, Tommaso, Campanella. Style & Technique: Impressionism. Mailing Add: 9240 W Bay Harbor Dr Bay Harbor Islands FL 33154

SILVIA, JUDITH HEIDLER RICHARDSON
ART DEALER, MUSEUM DIRECTOR
b Newport, RI, Feb 4, 42. Study: Swarthmore Col; Bennington Col, BA; Sorbonne Univ Paris, Ecole des Lettres. Pos: Asst dir, Pace Gallery, New York, 66-69; dir, Sonnabend Gallery, New York, 69-74; dir, Multiples Inc, New York, 74-75; exec dir, Art Asn & Mus of Newport, RI, 75- Specialty: Twentieth century. Mailing Add: c/o Art Asn & Mus of Newport 76 Bellevue Ave Newport RI 02840

SIME, JOHN
ART ADMINISTRATOR
b Milford Haven, Wales, Nov 5, 25. Study: Trinity Col, Cambridge Univ, MA. Pos: Dir, Artist's Workshop, Hockley Valley Sch, New Sch Art, 62-70; exec dir, Three Schs Art, Toronto, Ont, 70- Awards: Can Coun Travel Grant, 68 & 72. Bibliog: Vera Frenkel (auth), The new school of art: insight-explosions, Arts Can, 10/68. Mem: Toronto Arts Coun. Mailing Add: 296 Brunswick Ave Toronto ON Can

SIMEL, ELAINE
PRINTMAKER, PAINTER
b New York, NY. Study: High Sch Music & Art, New York; Black Mountain Col, NC; Syracuse Univ, NY, BFA; studied with Josef Albers, Robert Motherwell, Harry Sternberg & Ruth Leaf. Work: De Cordova & Dana Mus, Lincoln, Mass; Publ Clearing House, Port Washington, NY. Exhib: Colorprint USA, Tex, 75; 3rd Ann US Int Graphics, Lehigh Univ, Pa & Art Now, Inc doc of same in traveling ser, 75; Huntington Twp Art League Heckscher Mus, NY, 77; Soc Am Graphic Artists, Am Art Asn Gallery, New York, 77; Boston Printmakers 29th Nat Exhib, De Cordova & Dana Mus, 77; Audubon Artists 35th Ann Exhib, Nat Acad Galleries, New York, 77; plus many others. Pos: Dir, Graphic Eye Gallery, Port Washington, NY, 74- Awards: John Carl Georgi Mem Prize, Nat Asn Women Artists, 76. Bibliog: Malcolm Preston (auth article), Newsday, 4/75; David Shirey (auth), Artistic Cooperation, NY Times, 3/76; Malcolm Preston (auth), Art rev/etchings of life, Newsday, 7/77. Mem: Nat Asn Women Artists; Graphic Arts Coun NY; Soc of Am Graphic Artists. Style & Technique: Color double intaglio etchings drawn from nature and the human form; patterns, shapes and designs are integral parts of work. Media: Etchings; drawings; oil paintings. Publ: Contribr, Ruth Leaf, auth, Printmaking Techniques, Watsun-Guptill, 76. Dealer: Bermond Art Ltd 3000 Marcus Ave Lake Success NY 11040. Mailing Add: 17 Bengeyfield Dr East Williston NY 11596

SIMKIN, PHILLIPS M
SCULPTOR
b Philadelphia, Pa, Jan 19, 44. Study: Tyler Art Sch, Temple Univ, BFA; Cornell Univ, MFA; Univ Pa, post grad fel. Comn: Sculpture, Pub Ctr for Collection & Dissemination of Secrets (with Peter Voetsch), Inst Contemp Art, Univ Pa, 73; Displacement Proj I (with Doris Olafson), Inst Contemp Art, Boston, 74; Displacement Proj II (with Doris Olafson), Philadelphia Mus Art, 74; Artpark (with Tom Farmer), Lewiston State Arts Park, NY, 75. Exhib: One-man shows, Univ Md Art Gallery, College Park, 72 & Marian Locks Gallery, Philadelphia, 76-77; Made in Philadelphia-in Urban Sites, 73; Displacement Proj II-a Public Event, Philadelphia, 74; Commodity Exchange, Human Puzzle, Lewiston, NY, 75; Choices, Inst Art & Urban Resources, PS1, NY, 76; Project Looking Glass, Three Centuries of Am Art exhib, Philadelphia Mus of Art, 76; Proj—Is There Anything Else You Want to Tell Me?, Brooklyn Mus, 77; solo proj, Pa Acad of Fine Arts, Philadelphia, 78. Teaching: Asst prof studio fine arts, York Col, City Univ New York, 73-; adj asst prof studio fine arts, Moore Col Art, Philadelphia, 73-; artist-in-residence, Brooklyn Mus, 77. Pos: Pres, Experiential Systs Inc, Philadelphia, 68-; art dir, Earthweek Inc, Philadelphia, 71-73; co-dir (with John Formicola), The Luncheonette Inc Artist Ctr, Philadelphia, 75. Awards: Serv Grant, L M Johnson Found, Grand Forks, NDak, 71-76; Short Term Activities Grant, Nat Endowment Arts, Washington, DC, 73, Artist Fel, 75-76; Creative Artists Pub Serv Sculpture Grant, New York, 76. Bibliog: J Withers (auth), Phillips Simkin, The List, 3rd ed, Independent Curators Inc, 78. Style & Technique: Experientialist; events, occurrences and formats. Dealer: Marian Locks Gallery 1524 Walnut St Philadelphia PA 19105. Mailing Add: 137 Waverly Pl New York NY 10014

SIMMONS, CLEDA MARIE
PAINTER
b Douglas, Wyo, June 24, 27. Study: Univ NMex, Albuquerque, with Ralph Douglas & Raymond Jonson; studied seven yrs in Madrid, Spain. Work: Ateneo de Belles Artes, Madrid; Pan Am Gallery, San Antonio, Tex. Exhib: USIS Traveling Show, Mus Mod Art, Paris & Madrid, 53; one-woman shows, Ateneo de Belles Artes, 54 & Roswell Art Mus, NMex, 61; two-woman show, Jonson Gallery, Univ NMex, 56; Detroit Art Inst, 64; Denver Mus, 70; EQUUS, Denver, Colo, 77. Pos: Graphic artist, ESA Women Int, Loveland, Colo, 69-70, art ed, 70-73, art dir, 73-77, ed Jonquil Mag, assoc ed & art dir, 77- Awards: Purchase Award, Ateneo de Belles Artes, Madrid, Spain, 54. Bibliog: Mary Hagen (auth), The challenge of art, Southwest Art Mag, 1/77. Mem: Int Soc Artists (area rep, 77-). Style & Technique: Predominately expressionist using collage techniques with papers, acrylic, ink, pencil and other media. Media: Acrylic on Hardboard or Canvas, Mixed Media including Paper, Pen and Pencil on Canvas or Illustration Board. Publ: Illusr, Our Government, 69; co-auth, Art of Editorship, ESA Women Int, 72; illusr, Beneath the Peaks, ESA Women Int, 73; illusr, This is Loveland, League of Women Voters, 76. Dealer: Hugo Anderson Gift Gallery 526 N Cleveland Loveland CO 80537. Mailing Add: 468 W Third Loveland CO 80537

SIMON, BERNARD
SCULPTOR, INSTRUCTOR
b Russia, Jan 6, 96. Study: Educ Alliance & Art Workshop, New York. Work: Slater Mem Mus, Norwich, Conn; Norfolk Mus Arts & Sci, Va; Fogg Mus, Boston; Hirshhorn Collection; also in pvt collections. Exhib: Audubon Artists; Silvermine Guild Art; Boston Arts Festival Provincetown Group; Hyannis Art Asn; plus others. Teaching: Instr, Mus Mod Art, New York; instr, New Sch Social Res; instr, Bayonne Art Ctr. Awards: Prizes, Knickerbocker Artists, Audubon Artists & NJ Soc Painters & Sculptors; plus others. Mem: Silvermine Guild Arts; Brooklyn Soc Artists; Knickerbocker Artists; Provincetown Art Asn; Cape Cod Art Asn. Style & Technique: Direct carving. Media: Marble, Wood. Mailing Add: 490 West End Ave New York NY 10024

SIMON, ELLEN R
DESIGNER, STAINED GLASS ARTIST
b Toronto, Ont, Apr 15, 16. Study: Ont Col Art; Art Students League; New Sch Social Res; also with Joep Nicolas & Yvonne Williams. Work: Albertina Collection, Vienna; New York Pub Libr; Brooklyn Mus, NY; Nat Gallery Can; Art Gallery Ont. Comn: Stained glass windows in many churches & synagogues in Can; Sidney Hillman Mem Window, Hastings-on-Hudson, NY; Church of St Michael & All Angels, Toronto, 60-67; windows for Holy Family Narthex, Princeton Univ Chapel, 66; Adlai Stevenson Mem Window; plus others. Exhib: Nat Gallery Can; Philadelphia Mus Art; Smithsonian Inst; Mus Contemp Crafts, New York; Shaw-Rimmington Gallery, Toronto; plus others. Teaching: Instr stained glass, Riverside Church Arts & Crafts Prog, NY, 65-76. Awards: Best in Category, Pen & Brush, 74. Style & Technique: Painted and unpainted windows and panels in antique glass; neo-figurative and semi-abstract, incorporating meaning. Publ: Auth & illusr, The Critter Book, 40; illusr, Inga of Porcupine Mine, 42, Americans All, 44 & Music in Early Childhood, 52. Mailing Add: 23 Boswell Ave Toronto ON M5R 1M5 Can

SIMON, HELENE
SCULPTOR
b Bagdad, Iraq; US citizen. Study: Bedford Col, London; Am Univ, Beirut, Lebanon; Islamic Art with Mary Devonshire, Cairo, Egypt; painting with Anthony Toney & Jacob Lawrence; New Sch, sculpture with Lorrie Goulet. Work: Phoenix Art Mus, Ariz; Jewish Mus, New York; Hirshhorn Mus, Washington, DC; NY Univ Art Collection, New York; Fordham Univ Art Collection, Bronx; also in pvt collections, Paris, London, Teheran, Iran & Milan, Italy. Exhib: One-man shows, Bodley Gallery, New York, 71 & 73, Fordham Univ, 75; Sculptors 9, Caravan House, New York, 71; Stable Gallery, Scottsdale, Ariz, 73. Bibliog: Andrea Mikotajuk (auth), In the galleries, 12/71 & 1/72 & Gordon Brown (auth), In the galleries, 12/73, Arts Mag; article in Fordham Univ Publ, 75. Style & Technique: Semi-abstract. Media: Marble, Bronze. Mailing Add: 200 E 74th St New York NY 10021

SIMON, HERBERT BERNHEIMER
SCULPTOR, EDUCATOR
b Nashville, Tenn, Sept 20, 27. Study: Brooklyn Mus Art Sch; Hans Hofmann Studio, NY; Colorado Springs Fine Art Ctr; Hunter Col, study with Robert Motherwell; NY Univ, BA & MA, study with Philip Guston. Work: Everhart Mus, Scranton, Pa. Comn: Two Modules, free-standing sculpture, Coal St Park, Wilkes-Barre, Pa, 77; Facets, aluminum relief, Wilkes Col, Wilkes-Barre, Pa, 77. Exhib: Drawings USA, Mus Mod Art, New York, 55; Susquehanna Regional, Roberson Ctr Arts, Binghamton, NY, 71; Regional Exhib, William Penn Mus, Harrisburg, Pa, 72; 13th Ann Exhib, Allentown, Pa, 76; Regional Exhib, Everhart Mus, Scranton, Pa, 76; one-man shows, Phoenix Gallery, NY, 64 & 66 & Sordoni Art Gallery, Wilkes-Barre, Pa, 74. Teaching: Instr painting & drawing, Sch Design, NC State Col, Raleigh, 56-58; asst prof sculpture & 3-D design, Wilkes Col, Wilkes-Barre, Pa, 69- Awards: Fel, MacDowell Colony, Peterborough, NH, 63. Style & Technique: Geometric, modular constructions of welded steel and aluminum. Media: Welding. Mailing Add: 25 E Center St Shavertown PA 18708

SIMON, HOWARD
ILLUSTRATOR, PAINTER
b New York, NY, July 22, 03. Study: Nat Acad Design, New York; Acad Julian, Paris. Work: Metrop Mus Art; New York Pub Libr Print Collection; Mills Col Print Collection, Calif; Brooks Mem, Memphis; Univ Ore Libr; plus others. Comn: Portfolio of 12 wood engravings for genessis eng on wood text, 77. Exhib: 50 Prints of Yr; 50 Bks of Yr; Victoria & Albert Mus, London; one-man show, Smithsonian Inst; Art Ctr, New York; plus others. Teaching: Adj assoc prof painting & drawing, NY Univ-Sch Visual Arts, 45-65; head, Art Dept, Barlow Sch, Amenia, NY, currently. 45-65. Media: Watercolor, Oil; Wood. Publ: Illusr many bks, 26-; auth, Cabin on a Ridge, Follett, 69; illusr, William Keyser (auth), Day of the Week, Harvey House Publ, New York, 77. Mailing Add: Dept of Art Barlow Sch Amenia NY 12501

SIMON, JEWEL WOODARD
PAINTER, SCULPTOR
b Houston, Tex, July 28, 11. Study: Atlanta Univ, AB(summa cum laude), 31, painting with Hale Woodruff, 46; pvt study with B L Hellman, 34; sculpture with Alice Dunbar, 47; Atlanta Col Art, BFA, 67; Art Instr Inc, cert grad, 62. Work: Educ Dept, Ringling Mus, Sarasota, Fla; Atlanta Univ Gallery; Du Sable Mus, Chicago; Carver Mus, Tuskegee, Ala; Kiah Mus, Savannah, Ga; Slide collections distributed by Univ S Ala, Mobile to Nat Arch, Carnegie Inst & 52 cols & univs in US & Can. Comn: Portrait of E Luther Brookes, Alpha Phi Alpha Fraternity, Clark Col, Atlanta, 61; portrait of pres of Va Mutual Ins Co, comn by G L Townes, Richmond, 65; cover design & stage backdrop, Climbing Jacobs Ladder, United Methodist Church Centennial, Dallas, 68; portrait of Frankie Adams, Atlanta Sch Social Work, 70; oil landscapes, cover design, The Vision, Atlanta Life Ins Co, Atlanta, Memphis & Dallas, 73; plus others. Exhib: Houston Fine Art Mus, 57; The Negro in American Art Touring Show, Univ Calif, Los Angeles Art Galleries, 66-67; Experiment in Friendship, Moscow, Leningrad, Prague & tour, 66-67; Art: USA, New York, 58; New York World's Fair, 67; Handshake Gallery, 76; Peachtree Ctr Gallery, 77; Grandview Gallery, 77; one-woman shows, Jewish Community Ctr, 68 & 71, EOA Youth Ctr, Miami, 69, Jackson State Col, 70, Clark Col, 73 & Carver Mus, Tuskegee, Ala, 74. Collections Arranged: South Eastern, 50, End of Year Show, 64-67, Show of Georgia Artists, 71 & Highlights of Atlanta University Collection Touring Show, 73, High Mus Art, Atlanta. Pos: Lectr, Carver Mus, Tuskegee, Stillman Col, Tuscaloosa, Emory Univ & Ga Inst Technol, Atlanta; career consult, High Schs & Elem Schs. Awards: Eight Purchase Awards & five Hon Mentions, Atlanta Univ, 49-68; Bronze Woman of the Year in Fine Art, Iota Phi Lambda Sorority, 50; Distinguished Contrib in Art, Atlanta Univ Alumni Asn, 66; James Weldon Johnson Award, Atlanta Br, WAACP, 77. Bibliog: Samella S Lewis & Ruth C Waddy (auths), Black Artists on Art, 69; Marion Brown (auth), The Negro in the Fine Arts, Negro Heritage Libr, Vol 2, 70; Women Artists in America, II, Art Dept, Univ Tenn, Chattanooga. Mem: Nat Conf Artists (nat treas, 58-73); Graphic Soc; Black Artists Atlanta (treas, 73-75); Ga Arts Coun; High Mus Collectors. Style & Technique: Realistic landscapes and portraits; sculpture in plaster and limestone; abstract paintings in acrylics; prints in many styles. Media: Oil on Linen Canvas, Watercolor; Lithographs. Publ:

Contribr, Prints by American Negro Artists, Cult Exchange Ctr, 64, Black Dimensions in Art, Carnation Co, 70 & American Printmakers, Graphic Group, Arcadia, Calif, 74. Mailing Add: 67 Ashby St SW Atlanta GA 30314

SIMON, LEONARD RONALD
ART ADMINISTRATOR, ART WRITER
b Norristown, Pa, Dec 9, 36. Study: Ohio State Univ. Collections Arranged: Two Centuries of Black American Art (co-auth, catalogue), 75. Teaching: Instr Black Am art, Univ Calif, Riverside, 76-77. Pos: Registr, Stanford Mus, 65-69; deputy dir, Calif Arts Coun, 76- Mem: Col Art Asn. Publ: Auth, The American presence of the Black artist, Am Art Rev, 76; auth, The sound of people, Arts in Soc, Vol 12 (1). Mailing Add: 360 S Mills Ave Claremont CA 91711

SIMON, NORTON
COLLECTOR
b Portland, Ore, Feb 5, 07. Pos: Chmn, mem & trustee, Norton Simon Mus Art, Pasadena, currently. Collection: Paintings. Mailing Add: 3440 Wilshire Blvd Los Angeles CA 90010

SIMON, RITA
See Atirnomis

SIMON, SIDNEY
SCULPTOR, PAINTER
b Pittsburgh, Pa, May 21, 17. Study: Carnegie Inst Technol; Pa Acad Fine Arts, Emlen Cresson fel, 40 & Edwin Austin Abbey fel, 40-41, BFA, with George Harding; Univ Pa, BA; Barnes Found. Work: Metrop Mus Art, New York; Arch-Hist Div, US War Dept, Washington, DC; Am Embassy, Paris; Cornell Univ Med Ctr, Kramer Col, Ithaca, NY; Colby Col, Waterville, Maine. Comn: Crucifix & St John, Our Lady of Angels, Glenmont, NY; bronze grill, State Univ NY Downstate Med Ctr Entrance Hall; wall design, Walt Whitman High Sch, Yonkers, NY; The Circus (mobile), Woodland House, Hartford, Conn; entrance sculpture, 747 Bldg, New York, 72. Exhib: Pa Acad Fine Arts Ann, 48-52 & 62-72; Am Painting, Metrop Mus Art, 50; nine shows, Whitney Mus Am Art Ann, 50-62; Mus Mod Art Assemblage Exhib, 62; L'Aquarelle Contemporaine aux Etats Units, State Dept, 63. Teaching: Instr drawing, New Sch Social Res; instr & founding dir, Skowhegan Sch Painting & Sculpture, Maine, 45-58 & 75-76; instr painting, Brooklyn Mus Sch; vis prof, Salzburg Sem Am Studies, 71; instr, Art Students League, 73- Pos: Artist in residence, Am Acad Rome, Italy, 69-70; vis sculptor, Sarah Lawrence Col, 71-72; mem, New York City Art Comn, 75- Bibliog: Robert Rice (auth), Sidney Simon, Motel on Mountain, 60; Richard McLanathan (auth), Sidney Simon, Grippi Gallery, 75; Barbara Kafka (auth), article in Craft Horizon, 67. Mem: Artists Equity Asn; Archit League; Skowhegan Sch Painting & Sculpture; Provincetown Art Asn; Sculpture's Guild (vpres). Style & Technique: Humanistic. Media: Wood, Stone, Bronze. Mailing Add: 95 Bedford St New York NY 10014

SIMONDS, CHARLES FREDERICK
SCULPTOR, ARCHITECT
b New York, NY, Nov 14, 45. Study: Univ Calif, Berkeley, BA, 67; Rutgers Univ, Douglass Col, New Brunswick, NJ, MFA, 67. Work: Mus Mod Art, New York; Mass Inst Technol, Cambridge; Centre Georges Pompidou, Paris; Allen Mem Art Mus, Oberlin, Ohio; Ctr Nat d'Art Contemp, Ctr Beaubourg, Paris. Comn: Dwellings, over 150 works constructed in the streets of New York for an imaginary civilization of little people migrating through the city, 70-; Project Uphill-La Placita (park playlot sculpture), Lower East Side Coalition for Human Housing, 74; full scale Dwellings, 74 & Growth House, 75, Art Park. Exhib: Biennial of Paris, 73 & 75; Whitney Biennial, 74 & 76; Interventions in the landscape, Mass Inst Technol, 74; one-man shows, Ctr Beaubourg, Paris, 75 & Mus Mod Art, 76; Small Scale in Contemp Art, Art Inst Chicago, 75; Vassar Col Art Gallery, 75. Pos: Mem bd, Lower East Side Coalition for Human Housing, 74- Awards: Artist in Residence Grant, 74 & Young Artists Grant, Nat Endowment for the Arts, 74-75. Bibliog: Eds, Vernacular myth, Artrite, spring 74; Dale McConathy (auth), Keeping time, Reinhardt, Smithson, Simonds Arts Can, 6/75. Publ: Auth, Microcosm to macrocosm, 2/74 & auth, Three peoples, 75, Art Forum. Mailing Add: 138 Prince St New York NY 10012

SIMONEAU, EVERETT HUBERT
ILLUSTRATOR, PAINTER
b Portland, Maine, Dec 16, 22. Study: Portland Sch Fine & Appl Art, Portland, cert; also marine painting with Alexander Bower. Work: Over 450 pvt collectors world-wide. Exhib: One-man show, Portland Mus Art, 48; Young Artist Under 25, Jacques Scligman Galleries, New York, 48; Jordan Marsh Spring Art Shows, Boston, 56-73; Eastern States Art Exhib, Springfield, Mass, 60; Maine Arts Festival, Augusta, 63, 64 & 65. Pos: Supvry illusr, Portsmouth Naval Shipyard, Kittery, Maine, 61-; owner, Gallery-E Simoneau, Ogunquit, Maine, 61- Awards: 2nd Ann Purchase Prize, WCSH-TV, Portland, 67; First Prize Ribbon, 11th & 12th Ann York Art Asn, 67 & 68. Mem: Ogunquit Art Asn, Maine; York Art Asn, Maine (pres, 60 & 61, vpres, 62 & 63); Barn Gallery Assocs, Ogunquit. Style & Technique: Traditional marines in oil with knives; personal vertical style of subjects in casein with knives; multi-faces in special acrylic technique; traditional watercolors. Media: Oil, Casein. Publ: Illusr, Numerous training aid books, ship's information books, technical manuals, artist's conceptions, for US Naval Shipyard, 56- Mailing Add: 32 Lindsay Rd York Village ME 03909

SIMONI, JOHN PETER
PAINTER, EDUCATOR
b Denver, Colo, Apr 12, 11. Study: Colo State Col Educ, BA & MA; Nat Univ Mex; Kansas City Art Inst, with Thomas Hart Benton; Univ Colo, with Max Beckmann; Ohio State Univ, PhD; Mass Inst Technol; also in Trentino, Italy. Work: Colo Friends of Art Collection. Comn: Reliefs, sculpture, murals, Southwest-Citizens Fed Savings & Loan Asn, Wichita, Kans State Bank, Newton, Fine Arts Ctr Theatre, Univ Wichita, East Heights Methodist Church & Citizens Nat Bank, Emporia, Kans; mural paintings, The Kerr McGee Ctr, Oklahoma City, Okla, 75, The Mid-Kans Savings & Loan Bank of Wichita, 76, Reading & Bates Petroleum Ctr of Tulsa, Okla, 76 & Sheplers of Wichita, Kans, 76; plus others. Exhib: Mulvane Mus Art; Wichita Art Mus; Colo State Univ; Birger Sandzen Mem Gallery, Lindsborg, Kans; Univ Wichita. Collections Arranged: Organized Elsie Allen Art Gallery & assembled the Allen Collection of Paintings, Baker Univ; arranged & catalogued the Bloomfield Collection of Paintings, Univ Wichita, 56. Teaching: Lectr art educ today, Ital Renaissance, art in relig & others; head dept art, Baker Univ, 37-55; prof art, Univ Wichita, 55-57, chmn dept art, 57-63; prof art, Wichita State Univ, 64- Pos: Gallery dir, Baker Univ, 37-55; dir univ galleries, Univ Wichita, 57-63; designer, John Coultis Interiors, 57-76; color consult, Western Lithograph Co, Wichita, Kans & Houston, Tex, 61-63; co-dir univ gallery, Wichita State Univ, 64-67. Awards: Trentino Prize, Italy, 28; Carter Prize, Denver, 31; Knight Officer, Order of Merit, Repub of Italy, 66. Mem: Am Soc Aesthet; Col Art Asn Am; Kans Fedn Art; Southwestern Col Art Conf (pres, 62-64); fel Int Inst Arts & Lett; Warren Hall Coutts III Mem Art Gallery, El Dorado, Kans (mem bd trustees, 77-); plus others. Publ: Weekly art column for Wichita Eagle; monthly art column, The Baldwin Ledger, 65-68; writer on art, Estes Park Trail Gazette, 60-; columnist, Art in the Bluestream, El Dorado Times, 76- Mailing Add: PO Box 1154 Estes Park CO 80517

SIMONT, MARC
ILLUSTRATOR
b Paris, France, Nov 23, 15; US citizen. Study: Acad Ranson; Nat Acad Design; also with Andre Lhote. Awards: Caldecott Medal, Am Libr Asn, 57. Bibliog: Elizabeth Lansing (auth), biog paper, In: Caldecott Medal Books, Horn Bk, 57. Mem: Author's League. Publ: Illusr, The Happy Day, 49, The Thirteen Clocks, 51 & A Tree is Nice, 57; auth & illusr, The Lovely Summer, 52 & A Child's Eye View of the World, 72. Mailing Add: Town St West Cornwall CT 06796

SIMPER, FREDERICK
PAINTER
b Mishawaka, Ind, July 31, 14. Study: Self-taught. Work: Detroit Inst Arts; South Bend Art Mus, Ind; US Embassies Collection. Exhib: Detroit Inst Arts, 38-68; Art Inst Chicago, 48; Watercolor USA, Springfield, Mo, 65; Butler Inst Art, Youngstown, Ohio; Pa Acad Fine Arts, Philadelphia. Teaching: Instr watercolor, Soc Arts & Crafts, Detroit, 48-51; instr watercolor, Bloomfield Art Asn, Birmingham, Mich, 68-70. Pos: Art dir, D'Arcy, Macmanus Int, 49- Awards: Detroit Inst Arts Founders Soc Award, 42; Baltimore Sun Award for Black & White Drawing, 45; Mich Watercolor Soc Award, 72. Mem: Mich Watercolor Soc. Style & Technique: Personal realism in freely executed moods of nature; scenes, vegetation, birds. Media: Watercolor. Dealer: Arwin Galleries 222 Grand River W Detroit MI 48226. Mailing Add: 3075 Spring Ct West Bloomfield MI 48033

SIMPKINS, HENRY JOHN
PAINTER, ILLUSTRATOR
b Winnipeg, Man, Jan 16, 06. Study: Winnipeg Sch Art, with Frans Johnson; also with Lemoine Fitzgerald & Jessie Dow. Comn: Mural (oil), Trans Can Tel Co, Expo 67. Exhib: Can Nat Gallery Traveling Exhib, 37; Royal Can Acad Art, 58; one-man shows, Klinkhoff Gallery, Montreal, 69 & Wallack Gallery, Ottawa, 70 & 72; Father & Son Exhib, Meinhard Galleries, Houston, Tex, 77. Pos: Illusr, Brigden's Ltd, Winnipeg, 25-28; illusr, Rice Studio, New York, 28-29; illusr, Rapid Grip & Battens, Montreal, 30-58. Awards: First Prize for Watercolor, Jessie Dow, 32 & 34. Mem: Assoc mem Royal Can Acad Arts. Media: Watercolor, Oil. Dealer: Klinkhoff Galleries 1200 Sherbrooke St W Montreal PQ Can; Wallack Galleries 202 Bank St Ottawa ON Can. Mailing Add: 313 Pine Beach Blvd Dorval PQ H9S 2W2 Can

SIMPSON, DAVID
PAINTER, EDUCATOR
b Pasadena, Calif, Jan 20, 28. Study: Calif Sch Fine Arts, with Clifford Still & others, BFA, 56; San Francisco State Col, MA, 58. Work: San Francisco Mus Art; Oakland Art Mus, Calif; Mus Mod Art, New York; Philadelphia Mus Art; Baltimore Mus Art. Exhib: Carnegie Inst Int, Pittsburgh, 61 & 64; Americans 1963, Mus Mod Art, New York, 63; Calif Painters & Sculptors: The Mod Era, San Francisco & Washington, DC, 76; plus others. Teaching: Prof art, Univ Calif, Berkeley, 65- Style & Technique: Abstract-formalist. Media: Acrylic. Dealer: John Berggruen Gallery 228 Grant Ave San Francisco CA 94111. Mailing Add: 565 Vistamont Berkeley CA 94708

SIMPSON, LEE
PAINTER
b Cisco, Tex, Oct 9, 23. Study: Columbia Univ, with Arnold Leondar; also with Louise Nevelson & Elaine DeKooning, New York. Work: Couse Mus, Taos, NMex; Johnson-Everheart Collection, Miami Beach, Fla; State Nat Bank, El Paso, Tex; Whirlpool Corp, Benton Harbor, Mich; UN Plaza, New York. Comn: Mural, Perryton Nat Bank, Tex, 69. Exhib: Spec Group Show, Panhandle-Plains Hist Mus, Canyon, Tex, 69; 9th & 10th Ann Awards Show, Taos Art Asn, 71 & 72; Southwest Fine Arts Biennial, Mus NMex, Santa Fe, 72; one-man show, WTex State Univ, Canyon, 68. Teaching: Guest lectr oil painting, WTex State Univ, 69; guest instr oil painting, Amarillo Jr Col, 69-70. Pos: Owner & instr oil painting, Simpson Gallery & Studio, Amarillo, 62-70. Awards: Juror's Citation Award, State Citation Show, Tex Fine Arts Asn, 68 & 69; First Award, 9th Ann Awards Show, Taos Art Asn, 72. Mem: Taos Art Asn. Media: Oil. Dealer: Gallery A PO Box 1221 E Kit Carson St Taos NM 87571. Mailing Add: PO Box 1209 Taos NM 87571

SIMPSON, MARILYN JEAN
PAINTER, INSTRUCTOR
b Birmingham, Ala, Aug 24, 29. Study: Univ Ala; Art Students League; Inst Allende, San Miguel Allende, Mex; Madison Art Sch, Conn; with Robert Brackman; Am Univ Avignon, France; Rome & Florence, Italy. Exhib: Nat Arts Club, Gramercy Park; Grand Nat Exhib, NY; Am Arts Prof League; Kottler Gallery; Smithsonian Inst, Washington, DC. Teaching: Dir & instr, Acad Fine Arts, Ft Walton Beach, Fla. Awards: Am Artists Prof League & Nat Arts Club. Mem: Am Artists Prof League. Media: Pastel, Oil. Mailing Add: Acad Fine Arts 24 Ft Walton Square Ft Walton Beach FL 32548

SIMPSON, MERTON D
PAINTER, ART DEALER
b Charleston, SC, Sept 20, 28. Study: NY Univ; Cooper Union Art Sch, with Robert Motherwell & Baziotes; also with William Halsey. Work: James J Sweeney Collection, Guggenheim Mus; Howard Univ, Washington, DC; Scott Field Mus, Chicago; Atlanta Univ; Gibbs Art Gallery. Exhib: Guggenheim Mus & Metrop Mus Art, New York; Brooklyn Mus, NY; Nat Gallery, Paris; Nat Mus Japan. Pos: Owner, Merton D Simpson Gallery, New York. Awards: Red Cross Exchange Exhib Award, Tokyo & Paris, 50; Awards, Atlanta Univ, 50, 51 & 56 & Oakland Art Mus, 52. Specialty: Primitive art, especially African. Mailing Add: 1063 Madison Ave New York NY 10028

SIMPSON, TOMMY HALL
PAINTER, SCULPTOR
b Elgin, Ill, Aug 12, 39. Study: Northern Ill Univ, BS; Univ London, student exchange grant, 61; Cranbrook Acad Fine Arts, MFA(painting). Work: Fairtree Fine Crafts Inst, Santa Barbara, Calif; Wadsworth Atheneum, Hartford, Conn; Playboy, Inc, Chicago; Hirschorn Collection, Greenwich, Conn. Comn: Ceramic mural, Holiday Inn, Inc, Elgin, 68; carved wooden panel & wall, J Walter Thompson Advert Agency, New York, 71; painted & carved clock, Wadsworth Atheneum, Hartford, 73. Exhib: Fantasy Furniture, 66, The Bed, 67 & Baroque Art, 74, Mus Contemp Crafts, New York; one-man shows, Thomas Simpson, Cranbrook Galleries, Bloomfield Hills, Mich, 68 & Gloria Christmas, Art Inst Chicago, 68-69; Objects USA, Johnson Wax Traveling Exhib, US & Europe, 69; Fantasy & Figure, Renwick Gallery, Smithsonian Inst, Washington, DC, 74. Teaching: Grad asst painting, Cranbrook

Acad Art, 63-64; instr painting, Univ Ill, Chicago Circle, 69-70; instr drawing & wood working, Univ Hartford, West Hartford, Conn, 70-72. Pos: Artist in residence, Fairtree Inst Fine Crafts, 73-74. Awards: Nat Endowment Arts Grant, 74. Mem: Am Craft Coun; NY State Craftsmen. Style & Technique: Abstracted whimsy in paintings and in objects; oil, gouache or acrylic painting on carved wood, paper or canvas; sculpture in wood and metal. Publ: Auth, Fantasy Furniture, 68 & If I Had a Kite, 73. Mailing Add: 123 Byram Shore Rd Greenwich CT 06830

SIMPSON, WILLIAM KELLY
ART HISTORIAN, EDUCATOR
b New York, NY, Jan 3, 28. Study: Yale Univ, BA, 47, MA, 48, PhD, 54; Ecole Practique Hautes Etudes, Paris. Collections Arranged: The Pennsylvania-Yale Expedition to Nubia, Peabody Mus, Yale Univ, New Haven, Conn, 63; Recent Accessions in Egyptian & Ancient Near Eastern Art & The Horace L Mayer Collection, 72, Mus Fine Arts, Boston; also Metrop Mus, New York & Univ Pa Mus, Philadelphia. Teaching: Prof Egyptol, Yale Univ, 56-; vis prof Egyptol, Univ Pa. Pos: Cur Egyptian art, Mus Fine Arts, Boston, 70- Awards: Guggenheim Found Fel, 65. Mem: Archaeol Inst Am; Am Oriental Soc; Am Res Ctr in Egypt; Egypt Explor Soc; Soc Francaise Egyptologie. Res: Art, history, and literature of ancient Egypt. Publ: Auth, Papyrus Reisner I-Records of a Building Project, 63; auth, Papyrus Reisner II-Accounts of the Dockyard Workshop, 65; auth, Papyrus Reisner III-Records of a Building Project in the Early Twelfth Dynasty, 69; co-auth, The Ancient Near East: A History, 71; co-auth, The Literature of Ancient Egypt, 72; auth, The Mastaba of Queen Mersyankh III, 74. Mailing Add: Katonah's Wood Rd Katonah NY 10536

SIMS, AGNES
PAINTER, SCULPTOR
b Rosemont, Pa, Oct 14, 10. Study: Philadelphia Sch Design for Women; Pa Acad Fine Arts. Work: Mus NMex; Colorado Springs Fine Arts Ctr; Denver Art Mus. Comn: Mural, NMex Petroglyphs, Mutual Bldg & Loan, 70. Exhib: One-man show, Mus NMex; Colorado Springs Fine Arts Ctr; Santa Barbara Mus Art, Calif; Walker Art Ctr, Minneapolis; Exhib of Wall Hangings Based on Southwest Indian Petroglyphs for US Info Serv at US Embassy, London, Eng, 64; plus others. Collections Arranged: Exhib of Reproductions of Southwest Indian Petroglyphs, Brooklyn Mus, 53 & Mus L'Homme, Paris, 54. Awards: Am Philos Soc Grant for Res & Rec Southwest Indian Petroglyphs, 49; Neosho Grant, 52; Ingram Merrill Found Grant, 60. Mem: Hon assoc Archaeol, Sch Am Res; Artists Equity Asn. Publ: Auth & illusr, San Cristobal Petroglyphs, 50. Mailing Add: 600 Canyon Rd Santa Fe NM 87501

SIMS, PATTERSON
CURATOR
b Nov 17, 47. Study: Chestnut Hill Acad, Philadelphia, Pa; Darrow Sch, New Lebanon, NY; Trinity Col, Hartford, Conn; New Sch for Social Res, New York, BA. Collections Arranged: Seven Decades of MacDowell Colony Artists, James Yu Gallery, 76; On Canvas, 76, 30 Years of American Art, 77, Whitney Biennial Exhibition, 77, American Art 1900-1950, 77, Selections from the Promised Gift of Mrs Percy Uris, 77 & American Art 1920-1945, 77-78, Whitney Mus Am Art, New York; American Art 1900-1950, Seattle Art Mus, 77; School of Visual Arts 1977 End of the Year Show, 77. Teaching: Part-time instr, Sch Continuing Educ, NY Univ. Pos: Mem adv bd, Fabric Workshop, Philadelphia, Pa, Inst of Contemp Art, Boston & The New Gallery, Cleveland, Ohio; asst dir, O K Harris Works of Art, New York, 69-76; assoc cur permanent collection, Whitney Mus Am Art, 76- Publ: Auth, Alan Shields, Moore Col Art, Pa; auth, Fifty Years of American Art, Seattle Art Mus; auth, Whitney Review 1976-77, Whitney Mus Am Art. Mailing Add: c/o Whitney Mus Am Art 945 Madison Ave at 75th St New York NY 10021

SIMSON, BEVLYN A
PAINTER, PRINTMAKER
b Columbus, Ohio, Sept 9, 17. Study: Ohio State Univ, BFA & MFA; mus in Europe & Japan. Work: Chase-Manhattan Bank, New York; Kresge Collection, Detroit; Columbus Gallery Fine Arts; J B Speed Mus, Louisville, Ky; Tyler Mus, Tex; plus others. Comn: Eleven paintings, Lobby, Ohio State Nisonger Ctr Mentally Retarded; three-panel paintings, First Investment Co & Raymond Lapin, Fed Nat Mortgage Asn, Washington, DC. Exhib: Salon 1969, Soc L'Ecole Francais Salles d'Expos la ville Paris, 69; 2nd Biennial Cincinnati Art Mus, 70; one-person shows, J B Speed Mus, 70, Bodley Gallery, New York, 70 & 74 & Capital Univ, Columbus, Ohio, 77; Palais Beaux-Arts, Rome, Italy, 72; 23rd Grant Prix Int de Peinture de Deauville, France, 72; 37th Nat Painting Show, Butler Inst Am Art, Youngstown, Ohio, 73; 16th Nat Show, Chautauqua Asn, New York, 73; Contemp Prints for Collectors, Columbus Gallery Fine Arts, 74 & 75; 2nd Int Art Exhib (US rep), Paramaribe, Suriname, 74; Ohio Women Artists: Past & Present, Butler Inst Am Art, 76; plus others. Awards: Columbus Gallery Fine Arts Painting Award, 69, 71 & 73; Grand Prix Int, Deauville, France, 72; Nat Community Art Competition, Washington, DC, 73. Bibliog: L Soretsky (auth), rev in Arts Mag & Arts Digest, New York, 2/71; Jacqueline Hall (auth), Bevlyn Simson displays works internationally, Columbus Dispatch, 4/9/75; Mary Bridgman (auth), Bevlyn Simson rhymes colors & shapes, Columbus Dispatch, 12/11/77. Mem: Nat League Am Pen Women; Nat Soc Lit & Arts; Am Fedn Arts; Bexley Area Art Guild; Columbus Art League (treas & past pres). Style & Technique: Neo-geometric, multi-panel and shaped, acrylic paintings using airbrush; prints include lithographs, silkscreen and relief prints. Publ: Auth, Prints & Poetry, 69. Dealer: Bodley Gallery 1063 Madison Ave New York NY 10021; Collector's Showroom Inc 325 N Wells St Chicago IL 60611. Mailing Add: 289 S Roosevelt Ave Columbus OH 43209

SINAIKO, ARLIE
SCULPTOR, COLLECTOR
b Kapule, Russia, Oct 1, 02; US citizen. Study: Univ Wis, BS; Northwestern Univ, MD; Art Inst Chicago; Sculpture Ctr, New York; Art Students League; Atelier, with Archipenko, Lassaw & Harkavy. Work: Harry Lynde Bradley Collection, Milwaukee; Ringling Mus, Sarasota, Fla; Phoenix Art Mus, Ariz; Witte Mem Mus, San Antonio, Tex; Delgado Mus, New Orleans; plus many others. Exhib: Pa Acad Fine Arts; Detroit Inst Art; Riverside Mus, NY; Art USA, 1959; Provincetown Art Asn, Mass. Pos: Chmn art comn, Int Synagogue, NY. Awards: Purchase Prize, Pa Acad Fine Arts, 61; Hon Mention for Sculpture, Audubon Artists, 68; Kellner Award for Sculpture, Am Soc Contemp Artists, 71. Mem: Am Soc Contemp Artists (exec comt, 67); Artists Equity Asn; Audubon Artists (exec comt, 72); Provincetown Art Asn; Sculptors League. Collection: Renoir sculpture, Klee drawing; also work of Derain, Dufy, Fujita and many contemporary artists and many lithographs and etchings of Picasso, Braque, Matisse, Roualt and Miro; early American primitive painters. Mailing Add: 115 Central Park W New York NY 10023

SINGER, ARTHUR B
ILLUSTRATOR, PAINTER
b Manhattan, NY, Dec 4, 17. Study: Cooper Union Art Sch, cert, studied painting & design with, Mr & Mrs Wallace Harrison, painting with Guy Pene Dubois & painting & illus with Lewis Daniel & Howard Willard; Art Students League. Work: Buckingham Palace, London, Eng. Comn: Birds of Fla (map), Nat Geographic Soc, 73; Oceanic Birds of Antartica, 73, Parrots, 74 & Cranes of the World, 78, Audubon Soc Mag; Madagascar's Birds, Defenders of Wildlife, 75. Exhib: One-man shows, Head & Horns Mus, NY Zoo Soc, 42 & 70, Lab of Ornithology, Cornell Univ, Ithaca, NY, 73 & Wichita Art Asn, Kans, 74; The Bird in Art, Univ Ariz Art Gallery, Tucson, 65 & Ark Arts Ctr, Little Rock, 65; Nature in Art, Newark Mus, NJ, 72; Audubon Artists, Graham Gallery, New York, 73; Animals in Art, Royal Ont Mus, Toronto, 75. Awards: First Recipient of Augustus St Gaudens Medal, Cooper Union, 62. Bibliog: Dick Kirkpatrick (auth), National Wildlife visits Arthur Singer, Nat Wildlife Mag, 12-1/70; Barbara Delatiner (auth), Art that's all in the family, New York Times, 7/77; Oliver L Austin Jr (auth), Arthur Singer, The Fla Naturalist, 7/66. Mem: Soc Animal Artists; Cornell Lab of Ornithology; Am Ornithologists Union; Linnaran Soc of New York. Style & Technique: Work is realistic with knowledge of design; related to Oriental and Audubon in a a way of depiction. Media: Watercolor, Oil, Acrylic. Collection: Japanese prints of artists like Hirshige, Holsusic and Utamsio; Southwest Indian pottery, Peruvian weaving, African sculpture, Audubon's Elephant folio prints and Fine old bird books. Publ: Auth & illusr, Birds of the World, 61 & A Guide to Field Identification Birds of North American, 66, Golden Press; illusr, Zoo Animals, Golden Press, 67; illusr, The Hamlyn Guide to Birds of Britain and Europe, Hamlyn Publ, 70; illusr, The Life of the Hummingbird, Crown Publ, 73. Mailing Add: 30 Hightop Lane Jericho NY 11753

SINGER, CLYDE J
PAINTER
b Malvern, Ohio, Oct 20, 08. Study: Columbus Art Sch, Ohio; Art Students League, with Kenneth Hayes Miller, John Steuart Curry & Thomas Hart Benton. Work: Pa Acad Fine Arts, Philadelphia; Columbus Gallery Fine Arts, Ohio; Thomas Gilcrease Inst Hist & Art, Tulsa, Okla; Butler Inst Am Art, Youngstown, Ohio; Canton Art Inst, Ohio. Comn: Skaters (mural), Post Off, New Concord, Ohio, 40. Exhib: Over 40 exhibs in maj mus, 35-58, incl Carnegie Mus Int, Pittsburgh, Pa, 36-39; Corcoran Gallery Art Biennial, Washington, DC, 37; Golden Gate Int Expos, San Francisco, 39; Whitney Mus Am Art Painting & Sculpture Biennial, 41; Artists for Victory, Rockefeller Ctr, New York, 45. Pos: Art critic, Vindicator, Youngstown, 40-; asst dir, Butler Inst Am Art, 40- Awards: Norman Wait Harris Silver Medal, Art Inst Chicago, 35; First Hallgarten Prize, Nat Acad Design, 38; Pagasus Award, Ohioana Libr Asn, 72. Bibliog: Roger Bonham (auth), Clyde Singer; Ohio painter, Am Artist, 2/69; Paul Chew (auth), Singer Retrospective 1932-1972, Westmoreland Co Mus Art, 3/72. Style & Technique: Figurative, street genre in a realist manner. Media: Oil. Mailing Add: 210 Forest Park Dr Youngstown OH 44512

SINGER, ESTHER FORMAN
PAINTER, ART CRITIC
b New York, NY. Study: Art Students League, 40-41; Temple Univ, 41-44; NY Univ, 47-49; New Sch Social Res, 68-70. Work: NJ State Mus, Trenton; Finch Mus Contemp Art, New York; Hudson River Mus, Yonkers, NY; Seton Hall Univ Collection, South Orange, NJ; Newark Mus, NJ; Bloomfield Col Mus Collection. Exhib: Kenosha Pub Mus, Wis, 70; Ft Hood Spec Serv, 74; Women Artists, Newark Pub Libr, 75; Brandeis Univ, 77; Lever House, New York, NY, 77; NJ State Mus, Trenton, 77; 1978 Invitational, Morris Mus, 78; plus numerous other group & one-man shows. Pos: Guest panelist, Art Forms, WOR-TV, 67-68; ed, Jewish Standard Newspaper, 70-71, Am Artist Mag, 72- & Worraii Press, 74- judge, Menlo Park Outdoor-Indoor Art Show, 71; adv, Art Exhibs Coun, NJ, 71-72; judge, Art Exhibs Coun Art Show, 72; art ed, Newark News Newspaper, 72-74. Awards: Nat Design Ctr Award for Contemp Art, 66; First Prize for Oils, Roseland Festival Art, 66, 67 & 68 & Summit Art Ctr-Collage, 68. Bibliog: Smith (auth), Feature story & cover photo, NJ Music & Art Mag, 10/65; Nancye Kallis (auth), rev in Art Rev Mag, 4/66; Carlette Winslow (auth), article in NJ Suburban Life Mag, 3/70. Mem: Artists Equity Asn NY; Artists Equity Asn NJ; Nat Soc Painters & Sculptors; Miniature Artists Asn NJ; Nat Soc Lit & Arts. Style & Technique: Abstract, contemporary. Media: Oil, Acrylic, Mixed Media. Dealer: Gallery 52 52 S Orange Ave South Orange NJ 07079; Hait Gallery Maplewood NJ 07040. Mailing Add: 70 Glenview Rd South Orange NJ 07079

SING HOO (SING HOO YUEN)
SCULPTOR, PAINTER
b Canton, China, May 15, 08; Can citizen. Study: Toronto Col Art; Ont Col Art, assoc, with A Barnes & Emmannual Hahn; Slade Sch, Univ London, with Turner. Work: London Mus, Eng; Nat Gallery Ottawa, Ont; Royal Ont Mus, Toronto. Comn: Sun Dial & bronze figures of daughter & gardener, Parks, Toronto. Exhib: Ont Soc Artists, 32-68; Can Nat Exhib, 32-68; Royal Can Acad Art, 36-72; Sculptor's Soc Can, 40-67. Teaching: Lectr Oriental & Western art, Chinese Sch, 36-40. Pos: Asst, Paleont Dept, Royal Ont Mus, 34-40. Mem: Royal Can Acad Arts. Media: Bronze, Marble, Wood, Clay, Wax. Mailing Add: 139 Livingstone Ave Toronto ON M6E 2L9 Can

SINGLETARY, ROBERT EUGENE
GRAPHIC ARTIST, MURALIST
b Bloomington, Ill, Dec 4, 45. Study: Ill State Univ, with Walter Bock & Harold Boyd; Corcoran Gallery Art, Washington, DC. Work: Philadelphia Mus Art; State Dept, Washington, DC; Univ Ark, Little Rock; Philip Morris, Inc, Richmond, Va. Exhib: 4th Biennial of Drawings USA, St Paul, Minn, 69; Nat Drawing Exhib, San Francisco Mus, 70; Drawing Soc Nat Exhib, Corcoran Gallery Art, 70; one-man show, Fendrick Gallery, Washington, DC, 72. Awards: Purchase Award, Philadelphia Mus Art, 70. Bibliog: Drawing Society's 1970 National Exhibition, Am Fedn Art, 70; Cornelia Noland (auth), The Singletary style, Washingtonian, 8/71; Joanna Eagle (auth), Washington, DC, Art Gallery Mag, 4/72. Media: Graphite Lead. Dealer: Fendrick Gallery 3059 M St Washington DC 20007. Mailing Add: 300 S Fairfax St Alexandria VA 22314

SINGLETON, ROBERT ELLISON
PAINTER, PRINTMAKER
b Jacksonville, NC, Dec 13, 37. Study: Col William & Mary; Richmond Prof Inst; also with Teresa Pollock. Work: Mint Mus Art, Charlotte, NC; Loch Haven Art Ctr, Orlando, Fla; Fla Gas, Orlando; Twentieth Century Gallery, Williamsburg, Va; Archit Designers Inc, Dallas, Tex. Comn: Murals & paintings, Sentinel Star Co, Orlando, 68 & 71; paintings, Koger Properties, San Antonio, Tex, Jacksonville & Orlando, 69 & 71; paintings, George Barley Inc, 70-72; painting, Tupperware Int, Orlando, 72; paintings, Bank E Orange, Orlando, 72. Exhib: One-man shows, Mus Arts & Sci, Daytona Beach, Fla, 68, Coconut Grove Playhouse Gallery, Miami, Fla, 69, Ludwig Katzenstein Gallery, Baltimore, 70 & Loch Haven Art Ctr, Orlando, 70; Piedmont Graphics Competition, Mint Mus Art, Charlotte, 71 & 72; John F Kennedy Ctr, Washington, DC, 76; Hunter Mus, Chattanooga, Tenn, 77. Teaching: Instr painting, Loch Haven Art Ctr, Orlando, 68- lect & sem critiques throughout Southwestern states, 68-Pos: Cur exhibs, Jamestown Festival Park, Va, 62-63. Awards: First Place, Int Winter Park Sidewalk Art Festival, 67-69; MacDowell Colony Grant, 70-72. Bibliog: Articles in Am Artists; filmed documentary, WFIA-TV, Tampa, 71; series of interviews (video-tape),

WMFE-TV, Orlando, 72-73; 20 Landscape Painters and How They Work, Watson-Guptill, 77. Dealer: Gallery Int 401-B Park Ave N Winter Park FL 32789; Vorpal Galleries 465 W Broadway New York NY 10012. Mailing Add: PO Box 117 Clayton GA 30525

SINNARD, ELAINE (JANICE)
PAINTER, SCULPTOR
b Ft Collins, Colo, Feb 14, 26. Study: Art Students League, 48-49, with Reginald Marsh; NY Univ, 51, with Samuel Adler; also with Robert D Kaufmann, 51; Sculpture Ctr, 55, with Dorothea Denslow; Acad Grande Chaumiere, Paris, 56; also with Betty Dodson, 60. Comn: Five wall hangings (with Mrs Cris Darlington, Marlin Studios), Scandinavian Airline, New York, 61; three oil paintings, Basker Bldg Corp 5660, Miami Beach, Fla, 70. Exhib: City Ctr Gallery, New York, 54; Riverside Mus 8th Ann, New York, 55; 1st Ann Metrop Young Artists, Nat Arts Club, New York, 58; one-woman shows, Ward Eggleston Galleries, New York, 59 & Fairleigh Dickinson Univ, NJ, 60. Bibliog: Article in Art News, 54; James E Duffy (auth), article in World Telegram, 59; Fran Hepperle (auth), article in Times Herald Rec, 72. Style & Technique: Sfumato technique. Media: Oil. Dealer: Lord & Taylor Art Gallery Fifth & 39th St New York NY 10016. Mailing Add: Box 304 New Hampton NY 10958

SINSABAUGH, ART
PHOTOGRAPHER, EDUCATOR
b Irvington, NJ, Oct 31, 24. Study: Ill Inst Technol Inst Design, BS, with Moholy-Nagy & Harry Callahan, MS, with Aaron Siskind. Work: Mus Mod Art, New York; Art Inst Chicago; George Eastman House, Rochester, NY; Exchange Nat Bank, Chicago; Smithsonian Inst, Washington, DC. Comn: The Quality of Life (photo essay), Chicago Planning Comn, First City Plan of Chicago, 61-63; Midwest Landscape No 34 (photog mural), Univ Ill Med Ctr, Chicago, 65. Exhib: Abstract Photography, Am Fedn Arts, New York, 55; The Photographer & the American Landscape, Mus Mod Art, New York, 63; one-man show, Art Inst Chicago, 63 & Gallery 500d, Chicago, 65; Photography USA, De Cordova Mus, Lincoln, Mass, 68. Teaching: Instr photog, Ill Inst Technol Inst Design, 49-58; prof art & head of photog prog, Univ Ill, Champaign, 58- Awards: Arts in Am Mag Award, New Talent, USA Award Show, 62; Guggenheim Fel, 69; Assoc, Univ Ill Ctr Advan Studies, Champaign, 72; photogr fel, Nat Endowment Arts, 76. Bibliog: Gene Thornton (auth), Two tales of one city, New York Times, 3/22/70; Great print makers of today, Life Libr of Photog, 70; Allen Porter (auth), Sinsabaugh, Camera, Switz, 6/72. Mem: Founding mem Soc Photog Educ. Publ: Co-auth, 6 Mid-Am chants/11 Midwest photographs, 64; contribr, Portfolio of works, Tri Quart, winter 65; contribr, Portfolio of works & cover, New Lett, spring 72. Mailing Add: 132 Fine Arts Bldg Univ of Ill Champaign IL 61820

SINTON, NELL (WALTER)
PAINTER
b San Francisco, Calif. Study: San Francisco Art Inst, with Maurice Sterne; Inst Creative & Artistic Develop. Work: San Francisco Mus Art; Oakland Mus Art, Calif; Chase Manhattan Bank, New York; Am Tel & Tel Co, NJ; Univ Calif Mus, Berkeley. Exhib: San Francisco Mus Art, 57, 63 & 70; Stanford Res Inst, Palo Alto, Calif, 58; Staempfli Gallery, New York, 60; Am Acad Arts & Lett, New York, 67; Univ Calif, Berkeley, 72; plus others. Teaching: Instr drawing, San Francisco Art Inst, 70-71; symp, Mt Holyoke Col, Mass, 76; artist-in-residence, La State Univ, 77 & Univ of Ill, Urbana, 78. Pos: Artist mem, San Francisco Art Comn, City & Co, 58-63. Awards: San Francisco Art Inst Award, De Young Mus, 56; Oakland Mus Art Awards, 58 & 61. Bibliog: M Tapie (auth), Morphologie autre, 60; F Martin (auth), Review San Francisco, Art Int, 63 & Artforum, 63 & 67. Mem: San Francisco Art Inst (trustee, 66-73). Style & Technique: Figurative. Media: Acrylic, Watercolor and Pastel on Paper and Canvas. Publ: Auth, rev in Clear Creek Mag, 70 & 71. Dealer: Braunstein-Quay Gallery 560 Sutter St San Francisco CA 94108. Mailing Add: 1020 Francisco St San Francisco CA 94109

SIPE, GARY ROBERT
ART LIBRARIAN
b Indianapolis, Ind, Sept 15, 50. Study: L'Universita di Bologna, 71-72; Ind Univ, BA(art hist), 73 & MLS, 75. Pos: Libr dir, Atlanta Col of Art, 77- Mem: Art Libr Soc of NAm. Interest: Twentieth century and contemporary art. Publ: Auth, Recent art publications of note, 77, Bibliography of artists' books, 77 & Recent publications of galleries and museums on the Southeast, 77, Contemp Art/SE. Mailing Add: 35 Lombardy Way 608 Atlanta GA 30309

SIPIORA, LEONARD PAUL
MUSEUM DIRECTOR, WRITER
b Lawrence, Mass, Sept 1, 34. Study: Vanderbilt Univ; Univ Mich, Ann Arbor, AB(cum laude), 55, MA, 56. Collections Arranged: Ann Nat Sun Carnival Exhib; Biennial, Int Designer Craftsmen; W S Horton Retrospective, 70; Tom Lea Retrospective, 71; Walter Griffin Retrospective, 71. Pos: Co-founder & pres, El Paso Arts Coun, 69-70, dir, 71-; bd mem, Tex Mus Conf & pres, 77-79; mem chmn, Mountain-Plains Mus Conf (vpres, 77-78); Tex Comt on the Humanities & Pub Policy (mem bd). Mem: Kappa Pi; Am Asn Mus; Am Fedn Arts; Am Platform Asn; Nat Soc Arts & Lett (first vpres, El Paso Chap). Collection: American paintings and graphics. Publ: Auth, The Universality of Tom Lea (catalog), 71; auth, A community oriented art museum, Southwest Gallery Art Mag, 71; auth foreword, Biography of John Enneking, 72. Mailing Add: 1211 Montana St El Paso TX 79902

SIRENA (CONTESSA ANTONIA MASTROCRISTINO FANARA)
PAINTER, COLLECTOR
b White Plains, NY. Work: Mus Mod Art, Rome, Italy; Mus Castello Sforzesco, Milano, Italy; Mus Campidoglio, Rome; Regione Fruili Venezia Giulia, Regione Siciliana; Regione Sarda. Comn: Paintings for Federico Fellini, Frankie Laine, Gina Lollobrigida, Vittorio de Sica, The Vatican & Pope Paul XI. Exhib: One-woman shows, Van Diemen-Lillienfield Galleries, New York, 66, Gallerie Andre Weil, Paris, 68, Mike Douglas TV Show Exhib, 68, Palazzo delle Esposizioni, Comune di Roma, Rome, 69 & State Gallery in Teatro Massimo, Palermo, Sicily, 70; C W Post Gallery, 77; plus many others. Teaching: Lectr art, cols & orgns, internationally, 70- Pos: Dir, Sirena Art Galleries, Long Island, NY, 63-; lect & exhib of Esoteric art, Int Festival Esoteric Sci, NY, 75. Awards: First Int Prize Gold Cup, Quadriennale of Europe, 67; Dame of Grand Cross Award, Order of St Constantine, 68; Gold Medal of Pres of Senate, Mayor of Rome, 72; Gold Medal Award, Accad of Paestum; plus many others. Bibliog: Aurelio Prete (auth), Sirena, ERS, Rome, 66; Guilio Bolaffi (auth), Bolaffi on modern art, Torino, Italy, 70 & 72; Giovanni Quattrucci (auth), Sirena, Europe Ed, 72. Mem: Accad of Paestum; Accad dei 500; Accad Tiberina; Int Comt Cult, Rome; Metrop Mus Art. Style & Technique: Transexpressionism; marbleized oil gold. Publ: Illusr & auth, autobiography, MPH Publ, 76. Mailing Add: 1035 Fifth Ave New York NY 10028

SIRUGO, SALVATORE
PAINTER
b Pozzallo, Italy; US citizen. Study: Art Students League, 48-49; Brooklyn Mus Art Sch, NY, 50-51. Work: Pace Col, New York; Southern Ill Univ, Carbondale; Dillard Univ, New Orleans, La; Ciba-Geigy Corp, Harrison, NY. Exhib: Whitney Mus Am Art Ann, New York, 52; Pa Acad Fine Arts Ann, Philadelphia, 53; Art USA, New York, 58; Provincetown Arts Festival, Mass, 58; Tenth St Days—The Co-ops of the 50s, New York, 77; one-man exhibs, Camino Gallery, 59, Tanager Gallery, 61, K Gallery, 63, Great Jones Gallery, 66 & Landmark Gallery, 76. Awards: Emily Lowe Award, 51; Woodstock Found Award, Woodstock Artists Asn, 52; Longview Found Award, 62. Bibliog: F W McDarrah (auth), The Artist's World in Pictures, Dutton, 61; Natalie Edgar (auth), The private worlds of Sal Sirugo, Art News, 11/66; Corinne Robins (auth), Sal Sirugo, Arts, 1/77. Mem: Life mem Art Students League (bd control, 61); Artists' Club. Media: Acrylic, Casein. Mailing Add: 321 W 24th St New York NY 10011

SISLER, REBECCA
SCULPTOR, ART ADMINISTRATOR
b Mt Forest, Ont, Oct 16, 32. Study: Ont Col of Art; Royal Danish Acad Fine Arts. Work: Art Gallery of Ont, Toronto; Hamilton Teacher's Col, Ont; Peel Art Gallery; Univ Guelph. Comn: Stone fountain group, Centennial Park, St Thomas, Ont, 76; peace mem, Town of Markham, 67; The Knight (stone figure), comn by pvt donor for Peel Art Gallery, Brampton, 74; wooden cross, St Paul's Cathedral, London, Ont, 77. Exhib: Royal Can Acad; Art Gallery of Ont, Toronto; Nat Gallery of Can, Ottawa, Ont; Artist's Choice, Can Nat Exhib, 68; Ont Soc Artists 100 Yrs, Art Gallery of Ont, 72; Toronto-Dominion Sculpture Exhib, Toronto-Dominion Ctr, Toronto, 72; Ann Show of Ont Soc Artists & Sculptors, Soc of Can, Art Gallery of Ont. Pos: Educ dir, McMichael Can Collection, 69-70; dir, Sisler Gallery, 74-77; exec dir, Royal Can Acad of Arts, 78- Awards: Sculpture Award, Art Gallery of Toronto, Can Coun, 58 & Can Nat Exhib Artist's Choice, 68. Bibliog: Pearl McCarthy (auth), Art & artists, 58, Kay Kritzwiser (auth), Sisleri an industrious sculptor, 64 & Art, 73, Globe & Mail, Toronto. Mem: Royal Can Acad Arts (coun, 76-77); Sculptor's Soc of Can; Ont Soc of Artists. Style & Technique: Simplified forms in wood, stone & bronze, usually semi-abstract figures. Publ: Auth, The Girls, A Biography of Frances Loring & Florence Wyle, Clarke-Irwin, 72; auth, Frances Loring, Monograph & Florence Wyle, Monograph, Dundurn Press, 77. Mailing Add: 60 Birch Ave Toronto ON M4V 1C8 Can

SISSON, JACQUELINE D
LIBRARIAN, WRITER
b Oxford, Ohio, July 3, 25. Study: Ohio State Univ, BA. Collections Arranged: Chardin: his paintings & engravings (with catalog), Columbus Gallery Fine Arts, 65. Teaching: Instr libr res methodology, Ohio State Univ, 63-69, asst prof, 69-74, assoc prof, 74-, librn, 59-63, head dept fine arts libr, 63- Awards: Spec Libr Asn Prof Award, 76. Mem: Am Libr Asn (bd dirs, col & res librs, 73, chmn art subsect, 72-73); Art Res Libr Ohio (organizer & coordr, 69-); Art Libraries Soc NAm; Col Art Asn; Int Ctr Medieval Art. Res: Cooperative systems for libraries, collection development, indexing, book reviews. Publ: Auth, Cooperative Systems Between Art Libraries, 69; auth, Index to A Venturis Storia dell 'Arte Italiana, 2 vols, 75; auth, Cooperation among art libraries, Libr Trends, 1/75; contribr, Arlo Union List of Serials, 75; auth, Case history of the compilation of a large cumulative index, The Indexer, 10/77. Mailing Add: 1813 N High St Columbus OH 43210

SISSON, LAURENCE P
PAINTER
b Boston, Mass, Apr 27, 28. Study: Worcester Mus Sch, grad, 49; Yale Univ, summer sch, scholar, 48-49. Work: Mus Fine Arts, Boston; Portland Mus, Maine; Dartmouth Col; DeCordova Mus, Mass; Worcester Mus, Mass. Comn: Four murals, Boston Five Cent Saving Bank Br Offs, 55-67; mural, Worcester Polytech Inst, 66; mural, Carrick Agency, Whitinsville, Mass, 72. Exhib: Hallmark Int Exhib, 49; Ill Art Festival, 51; Am Watercolor Soc, 55-60; one-man shows, Gallery Mod Art, New York, 69 & Brockton Art Ctr, Mass, 72. Teaching: Teacher & dir, Portland Art Mus Sch, Maine, 54-58. Pos: Corporator, Worcester Art Mus, 72- Awards: Fourth Am Prize, Hallmark Int Show, 49; First Prize, Boston Arts Festival, 56 & 64 & Boston Watercolor Soc, 57. Bibliog: Maine Harvesters of the Sea (film), Film Group, 69; W Caldwell (auth), The man and the artist, Down E Mag, 68. Style & Technique: Avant-garde romantic landscape surrealist. Media: Oil, Watercolor. Publ: Auth, Along Time River, 75. Dealer: Hobe Sound Galleries Rte A1A Hobe Sound FL 33455; Shore Gallery Eight Newbury St Boston MA 02116. Mailing Add: 170 W Brookline St Boston MA 02118 West Southport ME 170 W Brookline St Boston MA 02118

SISTER ADELE
PHOTOGRAPHER, EDUCATOR
b New Bedford, Mass, Dec 4, 15. Study: Carnegie-Mellon Univ; Univ Hawaii; Univ Southern Calif, BS & MS; Univ Calif, Berkeley, PhD; study with Ansel Adams, Wynn Bullock, Imogen Cunningham & Jerry Uelsmann. Work: Bibliot Nat, Paris, France; Libr of Cong, Washington, DC; Oakland Art Mus, Calif; San Francisco Gen Hosp Med Ctr, Calif; Standard Oil of Ind, Chicago. Comn: Wall murals (color photomontage), Harrah's of Tahoe, Nev, 76; color photomontages, Occidental Life, Los Angeles, Calif, 77. Exhib: One-person shows, Look Again, Monterey Mus Art, Calif, 71, Color Composites, Galleria Villa Schifanoia, Florence, Italy, 74, Suor Adele, OP, Galleria, Il Diaframma, Milan, Italy, 74, Haiku Photography: Color Photomontage as an Art Form, Calif Mus, Los Angeles, 75, Counterpoint, Focus Gallery, San Francisco, 75 & Photo Colormontage, San Jose Mus Art, Calif, 77; Friends of Photog Show, Carmel, Calif, 73 & 75; First Light, Humboldt State Univ, Arcata, Calif, 75 & Seven Calif Photogr, San Francisco Art Comn Gallery, Calif, 76. Teaching: Asst prof Eng, Calif State Univ, Fresno, 40-50; assoc prof humanities & photog, Dominican Col of San Rafael, 51-74. Pos: Artist in residence, Dominican Col of San Rafael, 74- Bibliog: Jean Leroy (auth), Les songes de Soeur Adele, Photo-Rev, Paris, 12/73; Joan Murray (auth), Multiple Imagery, Artweek, 3/75; Ada Garfinkel (auth), Nun's Montages Stunning, Independent-J, San Rafael, 12/77. Mem: San Francisco Women Artists; Soc for Photog Educ; Friends of Photog, Carmel. Style & Technique: Realistic, surreal and abstract elements. Media: Color photomontage. Dealer: Louis Newman Galleries Bonaventure Hotel 404 S Figueroa St Los Angeles CA 90071. Mailing Add: Dominican Col 1520 Grand Ave San Rafael CA 94901

SISTER THOMASITA (MARY THOMASITA FESSLER)
SCULPTOR, EDUCATOR
b Milwaukee, Wis, Feb 23, 12. Study: St Mary's Acad; Univ Wis-Milwaukee, BE; Art Inst Chicago, BFA & MFA. Comn: Two wood mosaic murals, Marquette Univ Mem Libr; mahogany carved sanctuary crucifix, outdoor stone sculpture, rectory crucifix & wood mosaic stations of the cross for the Sisters' Chapel, St Cyprian's Church, River Grove, Ill; stained glass windows, St Xavier's Hosp, Dubuque, Iowa; plus many others for homes, schs, churches & pub bldgs. Exhib: New York, Washington, DC, Dayton, Ohio, Seattle, Wash, Chicago & many others. Teaching: St Anthony's High Sch, Sterling, Colo; St Mary's Acad, Milwaukee; chmn art dept, Cardinal Stritch Col, 47-; also summer sessions at Cath Univ Am, Univ Notre Dame, St Martin's Col, Maryhurst Col, Holy Name Col & Marquette Univ; also world-wide lect on liturgical art; summer art study tour dir to all parts of the world. Pos: Mem Am deleg, 1st Int Cong Cath Artists, Rome, 50; Milwaukee Art Ctr Exhib Comt, 50-; bd mem, Milwaukee Children's Arts Prog, 52-; US rep, 4th Int Assembly Int Soc Educ through Art,

Montreal, PQ, 63; Gov Coun on Arts, 63-; adv bd Arts & Activities Mag; adv bd, Wis Montessori Soc, 63- Awards: Friends of Art Award, 64; Quota Club Women of Achievement Award, 64; Theta Sigma Phi Award to Do'ers of the 70's, 70; plus others. Bibliog: Articles in Liturgical Arts, J Arts & Lett, Cath Art Quart & many others. Mem: Liturgical Arts Asn; Col Art Asn Am; Nat Art Educ Asn; Int Soc for Educ through Art; Wis Arts Comn. Style & Technique: Oil and oil collage. Publ: Auth, articles in New World, Everyday Art, Cath Trends in Art Educ, Salesianum & Sch Arts; plus many others. Mailing Add: Studio San Damiano Milwaukee WI 53217

SISTI, ANTHONY J (TONY)
COLLECTOR, PAINTER
b New York, NY, Apr 21, 01. Study: Albright Art Sch, Buffalo; Royal Acad, Florence, Italy; Dr degree, with Falice Carena; Acad Julian, Paris, France; Royal Acad, Munich. Comn: Portrait, Hon Frank A Sedita, Mayor of Buffalo, Fedn Ital Socs of Buffalo, 70. Exhib: One-man & group exhibs, Mus Mod Art, Mus of City of New York & Riverside Mus, New York; one-man show, Carl Battaglia Gallery Ltd, New York, 78; Calif Palace of Legion of Honor, San Francisco; Howard Univ, Washington, DC; Albright-Knox Art Gallery; plus others. Pos: Chmn, First Allentown Exhib, 56; pres, Patteran Soc, 57; chmn, Civic Art Festival, Buffalo, 65. Awards: Prize, Patteran Soc, 43; Prize, Western NY Exhib, Buffalo, 47; Prize, Buffalo Soc Artists, 47; plus others. Collection: Old masters, impressionists, modern art. Mailing Add: 469 Franklin St Buffalo NY 14203

SITTON, JOHN M
PAINTER, LECTURER
b Forsyth, Ga, Jan 9, 07. Study: Yale Univ, BFA, 29; Am Acad Rome, fel painting, 29-32; with Eugene Savage & Barry Faulkner. Work: Addison Gallery Am Art, Andover, Mass; Mint Mus, Charlotte, NC; Lubbock Art Mus, Tex. Comn: Mural painting, Bd Room, Fed Res Bldg, Atlanta, Ga, 37; mural, Riverside Mem Chapel, New York, 38; murals residence of Judge E Stephen Blair, Deerfield Beach, Fla, 74. Exhib: One-man exhib, Grand Cent Art Galleries, New York, 33, High Art Mus, Atlanta, 39, Light House Gallery, Tequesta, Fla, 71 & Parker Playhouse, Ft Lauderdale, Fla, 71; American Painters in Paris, 76; plus others. Teaching: Instr art anat, NY Univ, 32; instr watercolor, Columbia Univ, 36-37; asst prof painting & art hist, Cornell Univ, 40-44. Pos: Dir, Finch Summer Sch Painting, 38; dir life drawing, NY Sch Appl Design Women, 38-41. Awards: Prix di Rome, Am Acad Rome, 29; Nat Mural Competition, Riverside Mem Chapel, 38; First Award Portraiture (oil), Broward Art Guild, Ft Lauderdale, 75; Water Color Prize, Fla Tri-Co Award Ann Exhib, 78. Mem: Life mem Century Asn; life mem Allied Artists Am; Alumni Asn Am Acad Rome; Boca Raton Art Ctr; Artist Equity Asn. Style & Technique: Representational impressionistic. Media: Oil, Watercolor. Publ: Auth, An adventure in painting, 38 & Painting of my silk decorations, 38, Art Instr Mag. Mailing Add: 1241 SE 14th St Deerfield Beach FL 33441

SIVARD, ROBERT PAUL
PAINTER
b New York, NY, Dec 7, 14. Study: Pratt Inst; Nat Acad Design; Acad Julien, Paris. Work: NJ State Mus Art; Gibbs Art Gallery, Charleston, SC; Libr of Cong, Washington, DC. Comn: Murals (with Frank Schwartz), Ore State Capitol, 39; commemorative postage stamp, The American Woman, 60. Exhib: Mus Art Mod, Paris, 54; US Embassy, Paris, 55 & 71; Carnegie Int, 57; Galerie Charpentier, 59; Philadelphia Mus, 60; Dallas Mus, 65. Collections Arranged: US Nat Exhib, Moscow, 59; Off US Exhibs, Sao Paulo Bienales, 59, 61, 63 & 65 & Venice Bienales, 62 & 64. Pos: Dir visual & art serv, US Embassy, Paris, 50-55; chief exhibs div, US Info Agency, 58-65, agency art dir, 66-75. Awards: Thomas B Clarke Award for Painting, Nat Acad Design, 58; Gold Medal, Art Dirs Club, 58; Butler Mus Purchase Prize, 70. Bibliog: Articles in Time Mag, 4/18/55 & 5/12/69, Medicine de France, No 222, 71, Chicago Tribune Mag, 6/2/74 & Smithsonian Mag, 12/76. Style & Technique: Genre paintings, historical portraits, shopfronts. Media: Casein. Dealer: Midtown Gallery 11 E 57th St New York NY 10022. Mailing Add: 3013 Dumbarton Ave NW Washington DC 20007

SJOLSETH, MINN SOLVEIG
PAINTER, PRINTMAKER
b Todalen, Norway; Can citizen. Study: Regina Sch Fine Arts, Sask, with Kenneth Locheed; Nasjonal Galleriet, Oslo, Norway. Work: Frye Art Mus, Seattle, Wash; Ketchican Mus, Alaska; Riveredge Found, Calgary, Alta; City Hall, Prince George, BC; BC House, London, Eng; plus others. Exhib: One-woman shows, City Mus, Vancouver, 59, Haida, Reflections of Lapland, Frye Art Mus, Seattle, 70 & 75, Native Studies of BC, BC House, London, Eng, 66, Prince George Art Galleries, BC, 75 & Indigenous People of the Northern Hemisphere, Kristiansund N Kunstforening, Norway, 78; Vancouver and the Sea, Maritime Mus, Vancouver, BC, 60-61; BC Artist Exhib, Art Gallery of Greater Victoria, 61; BC Ann Exhib, Vancouver Art Gallery, 65. Collections Arranged: Vancouver Pub Libr, 70 & 77; Can Broadcasting Co, Television slide & talk show, 75; Channel 8, BC Television slide & talk show, 75; Kittimaat Mus, BC, 76; Prince Rupert Mus, 77; BC Television slide & talk show, 76. Bibliog: J Hooper (auth), Artists in Haida-Gwai, The Beaver, Hudsons Bay Co, 69; Anthony Carter (auth), From history's locker, Indian Heritage, 75; Arne Grimstad (auth), Landet er ditt, Luther Forlag, 77. Style & Technique: Brush and pallette knife paintings. Media: Charcoal, pastel, oil, egg tempera, watercolor. Mailing Add: 3581 W 26th Ave Vancouver BC V6S 1N8 Can

SKALAGARD, HANS
MARINE PAINTER, LECTURER
b Skuø, Faroe Islands, Europe, Feb 7, 24; nat US. Study: Royal Acad Art, Copenhagen; with marine artist Anton Otto Fisher, New York. Work: Constitution, Dudley Knox Libr & War of 1812 Constitution & Guerriere, Hermann Hall, Naval Post Grad Sch, Monterey, Calif; Casco, Reid Hall, Robert Louis Stevenson Sch, Pebble Beach, Calif; Frigate Ship United States, Salvation Army Hq & Savannah US Frigate, Allen Knight Maritime Mus, Monterey; pen & ink drawing, Calif Palace of the Legion of Honor, San Francisco. Comn: Olivebank Deck View, comn by Dr Wm Rustad, Sea Cliff, San Francisco, 68; USN BB Maine, comn by Hal Whitten, Dean Witter & Assoc, San Mateo, Calif, 73; Bear USCG Steam Barque, comn by Lt Ken Holloman, Carmel, 74; Anna Maerske, comn by Capt Olsen, Port Capt Maersk Line, San Francisco, 75; Point Lobos, Moonlight Seas, comn by Maj Gen & Mrs Collier Ross, Presidio, Monterey, 75. Exhib: Calif Palace of the Legion of Honor, 60; Lucein Labaudt Art Gallery, San Francisco, 60; Robert Louis Stevenson Sch, 67, 68 & 69; Galerie De Tours, San Francisco, 72; Gallerie Vallombreuse, Biarritz, France, 75. Pos: Dir, Skaalegaard's Square-Rigger Art Gallery, Carmel, 66-; Calif hist librn, Mayo Hayes O'Donnel Libr, Monterey Hist & Art Asn, 72 & 73; dir bd, Allen Knight Maritime Mus, 72-76; cult dir, Sons of Norway, Monterey, 74-76. Awards: Ribbon for Pen and Ink, Am Artists Exhib, Eugene, Ore, 63; Silver Medal & Hon Dipl, 70; Gold Medal & Title Master Painter, Tommaso Campanella Acad Arts, Lett & Sci, Rome, 72. Bibliog: Mary Howard (auth), Exhibit of sailing ships at sea intrigues Hans Skaalegaard's audience, Lindsey Gazette, 10/14/62; Dan Wyant (auth), Artist brings back majesty of ships under sail, Eugene Register-Guard, Ore, 9/1/63; Judith A Eisner (auth), Carmel closeup, Pine Cone, Carmel, 9/14/72. Style & Technique: Drawings in pencil, pen and ink; paintings in watercolors, oils on canvas, in very refined, authentic and technically accurate manner. Mailing Add: Los Cortes Bldg PO Box 6611 Carmel CA 93921

SKELLEY, ROBERT CHARLES
EDUCATOR, PRINTMAKER
b Bellevue, Ohio, Jan 15, 34. Study: Ind Univ, AB & MFA. Work: Libr of Cong, Washington, DC; Mint Mus, Charlotte, NC; Montgomery Mus Art, Ala; Springfield Col, Mass; Southern Ill Univ, Carbondale. Exhib: Dixie Ann Graphic Exhib, Montgomery Mus Art; Boston Printmakers, Mass; Mint Mus Ann Graphics; Libr of Cong Print Ann; American Graphics, Col of Pac, Stockton, Calif. Teaching: Assoc prof graphic design, Univ Fla, Gainesville, 61- Awards: Dixie Ann Best in Show Purchase, Montgomery Mus Art; Boston Printmakers Hon Mention, Boston Mus Art; Libr of Cong Purchase Award. Bibliog: Graphic rev in La Rev Mod, 1/65 & Art Rev Mag, 4/66; Norman Kent (auth), Robert Skelley wood cuts, Am Artist Mag, 1/71; Lanny Sommesse (auth), Robert Skelley Woodcuts, Novum Gebrauchs Graphik, 10/76. Mem: Soc Am Graphic Artists; Southern Graphic Artist Circle. Style & Technique: Lineal social abstract realism; extra delicate fine line wood block prints. Mailing Add: Dept of Art Univ Fla Gainesville FL 32607

SKELLY, BARBARA JEAN
DESIGNER, ENAMELIST, METALSMITH
b Springfield, Mass, Apr 2, 43. Study: Boston Univ, BFA, 65; Univ Wash, MFA, 73, with Ruth Penington, Ramona Solberg & John Marshall. Work: St Michael & All Angels Episcopal Church, Issaquah, Wash. Comn: Fourteen Stations of the Cross (enamel plaques), St Michael & All Angels Episcopal Church, Issaquah, 77-; numerous jewelry comn for individuals. Exhib: Goldsmith '74, Renwick Gallery, Smithsonian Inst, Washington, DC, 74; Goldsmith '74 (traveling exhib), Minn Mus of Art, St Paul, 74-76; useful Objects by NW Craftsmen, Contemp Crafts, Portland, Ore, 76; Goldsmith '76, Phoenix Art Mus, Ariz, 76 & Henry Art Gallery, Seattle, Wash, 77; 41st Int Eucharistic Cong Exhib Liturgical Arts, Civic Ctr, Philadelphia, 76; NW Silversmiths & Jewelers, Mod Art Pavilion, Seattle Art Mus, 76; Crafts Exhib, Bellevue Art Mus, Wash, 77. Awards: Two First Awards, Biennial Crafts Show, Bainbridge Arts & Crafts, Wash, 74; Fashion Group Award, NW Crafts Exhib, 75. Bibliog: Beverly Bauer (auth), Portland, Craft Horizons, 2/77. Mem: Am Crafts Coun; World Crafts Coun; Soc NAm Goldsmiths; NW Designer Craftsmen. Style & Technique: Work is mainly in cloisonne and plique-a-jour enamel, fabricated jewelry and metalwork. Media: Silver, Gold, Enamel. Mailing Add: 22075 SE 61st Issaquah WA 98027

SKELTON, ROBIN
ART WRITER, COLLAGE ARTIST
b Easington, E Yorkshire, Eng, Oct 12, 25; Can citizen. Study: Univ Leeds, MA, 51. Work: Univ Victoria, BC; Art Gallery of Greater Victoria, BC. Mem: Limners Soc of Artists (vpres). Style & Technique: Collage and soapstone carvings. Media: Paper, Stone. Res: Contemporary art. Interest: Contemporary Canadian. Collection: Contemporary Canadian. Publ: Auth, The art of Mel Ramos, 68, Sculpture as metaphor, 69 & Carlos Mensa, pararealist, 73, Malahat Rev; auth, Pop Art, Art Int, 69; auth, Carl Morris, Encore, 78. Mailing Add: 1255 Victoria Ave Victoria BC V8S 4P3 Can

SKEMP, ROBERT OLIVER
PAINTER
b Scotdale, Pa, Aug 22, 10. Study: Art Students League, with Thomas Hart Benton, George Bridgman, Frank Dumond & Robert Laurent; Grand Cent Sch Art; in France & Spain; also with George Luks. Work: Rayburn Bldg, Washington, DC; US Coast Guard, Washington, DC; R J Reynolds Tobacco Co, Winston-Salem, NC; Ackland Gallery, Univ NC, Chapel Hill; Springfield Art Mus, Ill. Comn: Man's Search for Happiness, Church of Jesus Christ of Latter-Day Saints, World's Fair, New York, 64 & Osaka, 69; portraits, Gen Armistead Maupin for Order of the Cincinnatti, Washington, DC, 74, Mrs Charles Scribner, III, New York, 74, Chief Judge Howard A Stevens for Court of Appeals, 75 & Bishop Thom Blair for Christ Church Cathedral, St Louis, Mo, 75; plus others. Exhib: Ann Exhib Advert Art, 49-63; Art: USA, New York, 64. Awards: Gold Medal, 51, two Gold Medals, 52 & Second & Third Places, 53, Art Dirs Club Chicago. Bibliog: Howard Munce (auth), Portrait painting, Northlight Mag, winter 70. Style & Technique: Academic-free impressionism. Media: Oil. Dealer: Portraits Inc 41 E 57th St New York NY 10022; Grand Cent Art Gallery 40 Vanderbilt Ave New York NY 10017. Mailing Add: 32 Hyde Lane Westport CT 06880

SKINNER, ELSA KELLS
ILLUSTRATOR, PAINTER
b Syracuse, NY. Study: Syracuse Univ, BFA; Univ NMex, with Randall Davey & Kenneth Adams; also with Rex Brant, Milford Zornes, Robert E Wood, Jr, Bud Biggs & George Post. Work: Old Mine at Golden, Albuquerque City Hall, NMex; Seminole Child, Bernalillo Co Health Bldg, Albuquerque; Out Cerrillos Way, NMex Bank & Trust Co, Hobbs; War Dance, Miccosukee Indian Learning Ctr, Fla. Comn: Oil portrait of Onate, NMex Hist Soc, NMex State Univ, Las Cruces. Exhib: Nat Asn Am Pen Women Nat, Smithsonian Inst, Washington, DC, 60; Mus NMex Biennial, Santa Fe, 63; Southwestern Regional, Oklahoma City, 64; El Paso Sun Carnival Nat, Tex, 67; Albuquerque I, Mus of Albuquerque, NMex, 69; Watercolor Oklahoma, Oklahoma City Mus, 75. Pos: Painter & designer, Charles Hall, New York, 32-33; free lance bookjacket designer, Thomas Nelson & Sons, 34-35; designer, Decorative Utilities Corp, Newark, NJ, 34-40; free lance illusr & designer, Berland Printing Co, New York, 35-39. Awards: The Humming-bird, First Prize Watercolor, 62 & Gold and Brown, First Prize Mixed & The Creatures, First Prize Acrylic, 67, NMex State Fair; Old Mine at Golden, First Purchase Award, City of Albuquerque, 68. Mem: Southwestern Watercolor Soc; NMex Art League. Style & Technique: Traditional and abstract style; watercolor-wet in wet; oil-free brush technique, also calligraphic. Media: Watercolor. Dealer: NMex Art League's Ken Roberts Gallery 3401 Juan Tabo Blvd Albuquerque NM. Mailing Add: 2245 Inez Dr Albuquerque NM 87110

SKINNER, ORIN ENSIGN
DESIGNER
b Sweden Valley, Pa, Nov 5, 92. Study: Rochester Atheneum Art Sch, NY, grad, 15, with Herman J Butler; also res in France & Eng, 23-25. Comn: Stained glass windows, Princeton Univ Chapel, 30, St John the Divine Cathedral, New York, 32, Heinz Mem Chapel, Univ Pittsburgh, 38, St Patrick's Cathedral, New York, 56 & Grace Cathedral, San Francisco, 66. Pos: Designer, Charles A Baker, Rochester, 12-16; designer, R Toland Wright, Cleveland, 17-19; mgr, treas & pres, Charles J Connick Assocs, 20-; ed, Stained Glass, 30-48. Awards: Master Craftsman, Boston Soc Arts & Crafts, 40. Mem: Fel Int Inst Arts & Lett; fel Stained Glass Asn Am (pres, 48-49). Media: Stained Glass. Res: Restoration of Great Western Rose Window of Rheims Cathedral. Publ: Contribr, Am Architect, 27, Liturgical Arts, 37, Am Fabricks, 50 & Holy Cross Mag, 67. Mailing Add: 37 Walden St Newtonville MA 02160

SKLAR, DOROTHY
PAINTER
b New York, NY. Study: Univ Calif, Los Angeles, BE; Chouinard Art Ctr Sch, Los Angeles; also with S Macdonald Wright & Millard Sheets. Work: Los Angeles Munic Art Comn, Los Angeles City Hall; Baptist Univ, Shawnee, Okla; Westside Jewish Community Ctr, Los Angeles. Exhib: Pa Acad Fine Arts, 53, 54 & 57; Los Angeles Co Mus Art, 55; Butler Inst Am Art, Youngstown, Ohio, 63-68; Frye Mus, Seattle, Wash, 66; Calif State Fair, Sacramento, 66; Nat Soc Painters in Casein & Acrylic, 77. Teaching: Instr art, Santa Monica City Schs, 43. Awards: Award in Oil, Laguna Art Asn, 60; Ida M Holiday Mem Award, Nat Asn Women Artists, 60; Childe Hassam Award, Frye Mus, 66. Mem: Nat Watercolor Soc (treas, 61, vpres, 62); Artists Equity Asn (treas, Southern Calif Chap, 51); Nat Soc Painters Casein; Nat Asn Women Artists; Laguna Beach Art Asn; Artists for Econ Action (vpres, 77-). Media: Watercolor, Acrylic. Mailing Add: 6612 Colgate Los Angeles CA 90048

SKLAR-WEINSTEIN, ARLENE (JOYCE)
PAINTER, PRINTMAKER
b Detroit, Mich, Oct 25, 31. Study: Parsons Sch Design; Mus Mod Art, New York, scholar & with Bernard Pfreim; Albright Art Sch; NY Univ, with Hale Woodruff, BA, 52, MS(art educ), 55; Pratt Graphics Ctr, with Andrew Stasik; Ctr for Understanding Media, film making, 74. Work: Mus Mod Art, New York; New York Pub Libr Permanent Print Collection; Grace Gallery, New York City Community Col, Brooklyn; Hudson River Mus Permanent Collection, Yonkers, NY; Mfrs Hanover Trust Co, Mount Vernon, NY. Exhib: Regional graphics, Albright-Knox Gallery, Buffalo, NY, 52; The Visionaires, East Hampton Galleries, New York, 68; Yonkers Art Asn Regional, Hudson River Mus, 70 & 71; Nat Asn Women Artists Nat, Lever House, New York, 72; one-man shows, Evolutions, Hudson River Mus, 71 & West Broadway Gallery, 72, 73 & 75. Teaching: Chmn dept art for jr high sch, Plainedge Schs, Farmingdale, NY, 53-56; instr art & dir art sch, YM-YWHA, Inwood-Washington Heights, NY, 56-58; coord-instr art workshops, H Hastings Creative Arts Coun, NY, 62-68. Pos: Visual arts coordr, Coun Arts Westchester, White Plains, NY, 69-70; art specialist, Hillside Sch, Hastings-on-Hudson, NY, 73- Awards: Geigy Award for Painting, Ciba-Geigy Corp, 69; First Prize, Hudson River Mus Regional, Yonkers Art Asn, 71; Print Competition Award, Gestetner Corp, 71. Bibliog: Masters & Houston (auth), Psychedelic Art, Grove, 68; H H Arnason (auth), History of Modern Art, Abrams, 69. Mem: Yonkers Art Asn, Hudson River Mus (pres, 70-72); Women in Art (rotating leadership, 72); Nat Asn Women Artists. Media: Acrylic. Dealer: West Broadway Gallery 431 W Broadway New York NY 10013. Mailing Add: 18 Harvard Lane Hastings-on-Hudson NY 10706

SKOLLE, JOHN
PAINTER, WRITER
b Plauen, Ger, Feb 7, 03; US citizen. Study: Acad Fine Arts & Univ, Leipzig, Ger; Art Students League; Hiler Col, Santa Fe, NMex, BFA. Work: Mus Fine Arts, Santa Fe; Jonson Gallery, Univ NMex, Albuquerque; Mus Fine Arts, Dallas. Comn: Bk & newspaper illus, Lutetia Press, Paris, 38-40; bar & dining room murals, Camelback Inn, Phoenix, Ariz, 49; mural, comn by Loomis Bowes, architect, 50. Exhib: Carnegie Inst, Pittsburgh, 46 & 47; Fine Arts Ctr, Colorado Springs, 47 & 48; Mus Fine Arts, Dallas, 47 & 60; Mus Fine Arts, Santa Fe, 51 & 52; Jonson Gallery, 63, 69 & 72. Teaching: Head art dept, Brownmoor Sch Girls, Phoenix, 46-52; assoc dir drawing & painting, Art Ctr Sch, Albuquerque, 62-68. Awards: First Prize for Colorado Farm, Denver Art Mus, 30; Silver Medal for Sargasso Sea, Calif Palace of Legion of Honor, San Francisco, 46; Helene Wurlitzer Found Fel, Taos, NMex, 60. Bibliog: Peyton Boswell, Jr (auth), Santa Fe Fiesta Exhibition, Art Digest, NY, 9/48; Ruth Morgan (auth), The art of John Skolle, Southwest Rev, 49; W L Trimble (auth), John Skolle Exhibit at Jonson Gallery, New Mexico, Cult News, 11/69. Style & Technique: Well-defined representational; abstract imaginative. Media: Pen & Ink, Wash; Oil, Acrylic. Publ: Auth, The Outline of Imagination, Southwest Rev, Dallas, 53; auth, The Blue Men, Hudson Rev, NY, 55; auth, Azalai, Harper, NY, 55; auth, The Lady of the Casa, Rydal Press, NMex, 61; auth, Aden & the Cisterns of Taweela, South Arabia, Mus NMex, 63; auth, bk to incl intimate biog references to famous Europ painters, writers & composers, in preparation. Mailing Add: c/o Jonson Gallery Univ of NMex 1909 Las Lomas Rd Albuquerque NM 87106

SKOLNICK, ARNOLD
PAINTER, GRAPHIC ARTIST
b Brooklyn, NY, Feb 25, 37. Study: Pratt Inst, BFA, study with Jack Tworkov; Art Students League, Ford Found scholar, 69-70, study with Edwin Dickinson. Exhib: Images of Concern Photog Show, Neikrug Gallery, 72, one-man show, Rated X, 73. Teaching: Instr design & content, NY Univ, 72 & Ctr for Photog, New York, 74-75. Pos: Art ed, New Renaissance Mag, currently. Mem: Life mem Art Students League. Style & Technique: Combination of real and surreal; life force; totems of life; the life strugg the mysteries and secrets of life. Media: Oil on Linen; Charcoal on Paper; Pen & Ink on Paper. Publ: Illusr, Story of Music for Young People, Pantheon Bks, 68; designer, Five British Sculptors Work & Talk, Grossman, 68; designer, Calder an Autobiography with Pictures, Random House, 70; designer, Out of the Silence, Amon Carter Mus, 73, Holt, Reinhart Winston, 74. Mailing Add: 211 W 20th St New York NY 10011

SLACK, DEE
PAINTER
b Salisbury, Md, Apr 5, 46. Study: Md Inst Col Art, BFA. Comn: Portrait of Robert Gordon comn by Mr & Mrs Gordon, Scranton, Pa, 72; tropical seascape, comn by Mr & Mrs A Kaupinis, Houston, Tex; painting of Honor and her cat George, comn by Honor Moore, New York, 73; ceramic sculpture of Fred the Cat, comn by Kathryn Walker, New York, 74; poster for the firm, The Merlin Group, comn by Sandra Manley, New York. Exhib: Painterly Realism, travel show, Am Fedn Arts, 70-72; Multi-Media, 71 & Drawing Each Other, 71, Brooklyn Mus, NY; one-woman shows, Green Mountain Gallery, New York, 72, 74 & 75 & Fells Point Gallery, Baltimore, 76; Sons & Others-Women Artists See Men, Queens Mus, Gallery Asn of NY, 75. Style & Technique: Representational; thick fluid handling of paint with some areas described by bare linen; animals, people, land & city scapes. Media: Oil on Raw Linen. Dealer: Green Mountain Gallery 135 Greene St New York NY 10012. Mailing Add: 114 Mercer St New York NY 10012

SLADE, ROY
PAINTER, GALLERY DIRECTOR
b Cardiff, Wales, July 14, 33. Study: Cardiff Col Art, NDD, 54; Univ Wales, ATD, 54. Work: Arts Coun Gt Brit; Contemp Art Soc; Nuffield Found; Westinghouse Corp; Brit Overseas Airways Corp. Exhib: Contemp Painting, Nat Mus Wales, 53-60; Art in Alliance, Washington, DC, 68; one-man shows, Jefferson Pl Gallery, Washington, DC, 68, 70 & 72; Washington Art, State Univ NY Col, Potsdam & State Univ NY, Albany, 71; Nat Print Club, Nat Col Fine Art, Washington, DC, 72; plus others. Teaching: Sr lectr post-grad studies, Leeds Col Art, Eng, 64-69; prof painting, Corcoran Sch Art, Washington, DC, 67-68, dean, 70-77, dir, Gallery, 72-; pres, Cranbrook Acad of Art, Bloomfield Hills, Mich, 77- Pos: Vis, Boston Sch of Mus Fine Art, 70-; mem, DC Comn Arts, 72-; lectr, numerous univs & schs; bd dirs, Nat Asn Schs of Art, 73-74; Mus & Visual Arts Panel, Nat Endowment for Arts, 74-; bd dirs, Artists for Environ Found, 74- Awards: Fulbright-Hays Scholar, 67; Welsh Soc of Philadelphia Award. Mem: Nat Soc of Lit & Arts. Publ: Auth, Up the American Vanishing Point, 11/68 & Report from Washington, 1/72; Studio Int; auth, A new cultural centre, Yorkshire Post, 2/69; auth, Artist in America, Contemp Rev, 5/69. Dealer: Pyramid Galleries Ltd Washington DC. Mailing Add: c/o Cranbrook Acad of Art 500 Lone Pine Rd Bloomfield Hills MI 48013 of Art New York Ave & 17th St NW Washington DC 20006

SLATE, JOSEPH FRANK
PAINTER, WRITER
b Holliday's Cove, WVa, Jan 19, 28. Study: Univ Wash, BA, 51; printmaking, Tokyo, Japan, 57; Yale Univ Sch Art & Archit, Alumni fel & BFA, 60; additional study with Josef Albers; study of sumi-e painting, Kyoto, Japan, 75. Work: Drawings, Yale Univ; Poems & Prints (bk), Newberry Collection of Rare Bks, Univ Chicago. Exhib: 12th Nat Print Show, Brooklyn Mus, 60; Pioneer Gallery, Cooperstown, NY, 61; Artist in Residence Exhib, Milton Col, Univ Wis, 63; Whitney Mus, New York, 74; Cent Ohio Watercolor Soc, Schumacher Gallery, Columbus, 75; Hopkins Hall Gallery, Columbus, Ohio, 76. Teaching: Chmn dept, Kenyon Col, 64-72, prof art, 62-, chmn fine arts div, 67-69. Pos: Consult, studies on aesthet & perception, Yale Univ Dept Psychol, 60-65; mem exec comt, Kress Found Consortium Art Hist, 65-69; consult, Nat Endowment for the Arts, 77- Awards: Yale Alumni Fel, 60; Painting Award, Ohio Expo, 62; Outstanding Educator of Am, 73. Mem: Mid-Ohio Cols Art Asn (pres, 64-65); Col Art Asn Am; Mid-Am Col Art Asn. Publ: Auth, Those Old Italians, 62 & Respect, 64, New Yorker; auth, This Heavy Folk Thing, Kenyon Rev, 69; auth, So Hard to Look At, Contempora, 70; contribr, The Art of Drawing, 72; co-auth, Poems & Prints, Pothanger Press, 74. Dealer: Accent House 405 N Main Mount Vernon OH 43050; Merton Boyo Gallery Columbus OH. Mailing Add: Box 417 Gambier OH 43022

SLATER, GARY LEE
SCULPTOR
b Montevideo, Minn, Oct 27, 47. Study: Univ Minn, BFA, 70; Ariz State Univ, MFA, 73. Work: Tucson Mus of Art, Ariz; Univ Minn, Minneapolis; Phoenix Community Col, Ariz; City of Phoenix, Ariz; Bowers Mus, Santa Ana, Calif. Comn: Right Angle Variation (9ft), comn by Norman Levitt for Scottsdale, Ariz, 75; Devil Wind (11ft), Missouri Medical Bldg, Phoenix, Ariz, 75; Meta X 20ft inside sculpture), Sentry Ctr Insurance Hq Scottsdale, Ariz, 76; Evolution (10ft), Southern Desert Medical Bldg, Tempe, Ariz, 76. Exhib: 7th & 11th Ann Nat Drawing & Sculpture Show, Corpus Christi, Tex, 73 & 77; two-man show, Corten Steel: Contemp Sculpture, Bowers Mus, Santa Ana, Calif, 74; 9th-11th SW Invitational, Yuma, Ariz, 74-77; SW Fine Arts Biennial, Santa Fe, NMex, 76; Summer Outdoor Sculpture Exhib, Palo Alto, Calif, 77. Awards: Nat Endowment for the Arts grant, 73-74; Purchase Awards, 9th Ann Drawing & Sculpture Show, Del Mar Col, Corpus Christi, Tex, 75 & Ariz Outlook 76, Tucson Mus of Art, 76. Style & Technique: Contemporary; objective. Media: Metal. Dealer: Elaine Horwitch Gallery 4200 N Marshall Way Scottsdale AZ 85251. Mailing Add: 2037 W Camino Cir Mesa AZ 85201

SLATER, VAN E
PRINTMAKER, EDUCATOR
b Magnolia, Kans, June 14, 37. Study: Univ Calif, Los Angeles, BA & MA. Work: Oakland Mus, Calif; in pvt collection of Bill Cosby; plus many other pub & pvt collections. Exhib: Oakland Mus; Emerald Gallery, Diplomat Hotel, Hollywood Beach, Fla; Long Beach Mus, Calif; Carnegie Inst, Pittsburgh; plus many others. Collections Arranged: Community Art Exhibition, 73; Elementary Schools of Compton, Calif, 73; Dr Samella Lewis Art Exhibition & Lecture, 73; Art West Associated, Inc Art Exhibition, 74; Bernie Casey Art Exhibition & Lecture, 74; plus many others. Teaching: Assoc prof art, Compton Col, Calif, 66-; drawing instr, Santa Monica City Col, 65-66; drawing instr, Los Angeles City Col, 69-70; lectr, many orgns; nat art consult. . Awards: Hale Woodruff Award, Carnegie Inst, Pittsburgh, 72; Watts Festival Purchase Award, Calif, 72; plus others. Bibliog: Ruth G Waddy & Dr Samella Lewis (auth), Black Artists on Art, Vol II, 69-70; Collecting, arranging & coordinating a great exhibition, Los Angeles Sentinel Newspaper, 10/73; article in Metrop Gazette Newspaper, Compton, Calif, 10/4/73; plus others. Mem: Charter mem Int Soc Artists. Res: Afro-American and American art. Publ: Printmaking: Four Artists (film), Four Media, Babette Eddelston, 68; auth, Local Black Artists of Southern California, 69, 70 & 71; Black Art Black Artists (film), Univ Calif Exten, Los Angeles, 71; auth, Black Artists of Southern California, 72. Mailing Add: Compton Community Col 1111 E Artesia Blvd Compton CA 90221

SLATKES, LEONARD JOSEPH
ART HISTORIAN
b Hartford, Conn, Jan 11, 30. Study: Syracuse Univ, 48-52, BFA, 52; Oberlin Col, 52-54, MA, 54; Inst Fine Arts, NY Univ, 56-58; Columbia Univ, 58-60; Univ Utrecht, Fulbright Fels, US Educ Found, 60-62, PhD, 62. Teaching: Asst prof art hist, Univ Chicago, 62-64 & Univ Pittsburgh, 64-66; assoc prof art hist, Queens Col, City Univ New York, 66- Awards: Grant-in-Aid, Am Coun Learned Soc, 66; Research Grant, City Univ New York, 69. Mem: Col Art Asn. Res: Northern Renaissance art; Northern mannerism; Italian and Northern Baroque art; history of graphic arts. Publ: Auth, Dirck van Baburen: A Dutch Artist in Utrecht and Rome, 65; auth, Hendrick Terbrugghen in America, 65-66; auth articles in Oud-Holland, Master Drawings, Art Quart, plus others. Mailing Add: Dept of Art Queens Col Flushing NY 11367 New York NY Dept of Art Queens Col Flushing NY 11367

SLAUGHTER, LURLINE EDDY
PAINTER
b Heidelberg, Miss, June 19, 19. Study: Miss State Col Women, Columbus, grad; Miss Art Colony Workshops, with Alvin Sella, Fred Mitchell, Ida Kohlmeyer, Howard Goodson, Frank Engel, Andrew Bucci, Alex Russo & Bob Gelinas; also with Marie Hull & Malcolm Norwood. Work: Pine Bluff Arts Ctr, Ark; Miss State Col Women; Univ of the South, Sewanee, Tenn; Miss State Univ, Starkville. Exhib: Six Nat Oil Painting Exhibs, Jackson, Miss, 60-69; Hunter Gallery Ann, Chattanooga, Tenn, 65; Cent South Ann, Parthenon Mus, Nashville, Tenn, 66; Masur Mus Ann, Monroe, La, 66; Fine Arts Registry, Brooks Mem Mus, Memphis, Tenn, 70; one-man shows, NY, Miss, Tenn & Ark. Awards: Outstanding Artist Award, Fine Arts Registry, 66; Best in Show Awards, Holiday Arts Festival, McComb, Miss, 67 & 75 & Miss Art Colony, 74. Mem: Miss Art Colony (bd dirs, 65-). Style & Technique: Large forms in warm vivid colors glazed in darker shades to produce a translucence. Media: Acrylic, Oil. Mailing Add: Seldom Seen Plantation Silver City MS 39166

SLAVIN, ARLENE
PAINTER
b New York, NY, Oct 26, 42. Study: Cooper Union, BFA; Pratt Inst, MFA. Exhib: Whitney Biennial Contemp Art, 73; Am Drawings 1967-1973, Whitney Mus; Women Choose Women, New York Cult Ctr, 73; one-woman shows, Janie C Lee Gallery, Tex, 73, Fischbach Gallery, 73 & 74 & Brooke Alexander Gallery, 76; Painting & Sculpture Today, Cincinnati Contemp

Art Ctr, 74. Teaching: Instr painting, Hofstra Univ, Long Island, NY, 71-72, Pratt Inst, 74 & Skowhegen Art Sch, Maine, 75 & 76; vis critic, Grad Sch, Univ Pa, 77. Awards: Printmaking grant, Nat Endowment for the Arts, 77. Style & Technique: Color overlays and color line drawings of birds. Media: Mixed Media, Hand-Colored Prints, Silkscreens. Dealer: Pam Adler Gallery 50 W 57th St New York NY. Mailing Add: 119 E 18th St New York NY 10003

SLAVIN, NEAL
PHOTOGRAPHER
b New York, NY, Aug 19, 41. Study: Scholar, Lincoln, Col, Oxford Univ, Eng, 61; Cooper Union, BFA, 63. Work: Mus of Mod Art, New York; Metrop Mus of Art, New York; Int Mus Photog, George Eastman House, Rochester, NY; Univ Md, Baltimore; Wadsworth Atheneum, Hartford, Conn; Stedelijk Mus, Amsterdam, Holland. Exhib: One-man shows, Nat Mus of Ancient Art, Lisbon, Portugal, 68, Royal Ont Mus, Toronto, 71, Photokina, Cologne, WGer, 76, Oakland Mus, Calif, 76, Matrix, Wadsworth Atheneum, 76 & Ctr for Creative Photog, Univ Ariz, Tucson, 76; Basel Art Fair, Switz, 76; Dusseldorf Art Fair, WGer, 76; Rooms, Mus of Mod Art, New York, 76; Contemp Am Photographs, Frederick S Wight Gallery, Univ Calif, Los Angeles, 76; Galerie Zabriskie, Paris, France, 77; Castelli Graphics Gallery, New York, 77; Dokumenta, Kassel, WGer, 77. Pos: Lectr, Cooper Union Forum, New York, 75, Colliquium on the Collection & Preserv of Color Photographs, Int Mus Photog, Rochester, NY, 75, Int Ctr of Photog, New York, 77, Univ Calif, Los Angeles, 77, San Francisco Mus of Art, 77, Henry Art Gallery, Univ Wash, Seattle, 77 & Wadsworth Atheneum, Hartford, Conn, 77. Awards: Fulbright Fel Photog, Portugal, 68; Nat Endowment for Arts Grant, 72; Creative Artist Pub Serv Prog Award, 77. Bibliog: Amerika 76, D U Mag, Denmark, 1/76; The ten toughest photographs of 1975, Esquire, 2/76; New frontiers in color, Newsweek, 4/76. Publ: Auth, Portugal, Lustrom Press, 71; auth, When Two or More Are Gathered Together, Farras, Strauss & Giroux, New York, 76; auth, articles in many mag. Mailing Add: 62 Greene St New York NY 10012

SLAVIT, ANN L
SCULPTOR, PAINTER
b Binghamton, NY, May 7, 48. Study: Mus Sch Fine Arts, Boston, 69-70, with Jan Cox & T Lux Feininger; Tufts Univ, BFA, grad study, 77; Rutgers Univ, New Brunswick, NJ. Comn: Environmental pneumatic sculpture, Mus Contemp Crafts, New York, 78. Exhib: Media Show, Sch of Mus Fine Arts, Boston, 70; New Talent Show, Alan Stone Gallery, New York, 76; Light Erotica, Boston Artists Market, 76; Women on Women, George W V Smith Mus, Springfield, Mass, 77; From Painting to Sculpture, Boston Visual Artists Union, 77; Mixed-Meida, Univ Mass, Boston, 78; Cohen Arts Ctr Gallery, Medford, Mass, 78. Teaching: Instr sculpture, Boston Mus Sch, Tufts Univ, 77- Pos: Artist-in-residence, Watertown W Jr High, 76, Cambridge Arts Ctr & Martin Luther King Sch, currently. Awards: Hon Mention, Boit Show & Dana Pond Award First Prize in Painting, Boston Mus Sch, 69; Grants for Sculpture & Artist-in-residence, Mass Arts & Humanities Found, 77 & 78. Bibliog: Martin Fishkin (auth), Critic's choice, Boston Globe, 77; Pamela Allara (auth), The great legs, New Boston Rev, 78. Mem: Boston Visual Artists Union (gallery selection comt, 77); Mass Arts & Humanities Coun; Cambridge Arts Coun. Style & Technique: Monumental indoor and outdoor pneumatic environmental soft sculpture. Media: Sculpture; Painting. Mailing Add: 49 Sherborn St Arlington MA 02174

SLAWINSKI, JOSEPH
MURALIST, CONSERVATOR
b Warsaw, Poland, Nov 27, 05; US citizen. Study: With S Kalinowski & W Drapiewski, Poland; Munic Sch Dec Arts & Painting, Warsaw, dipl; Acad Fine Arts, Warsaw, dipl; also studied in Italy, France, Belg & Holland. Comn: Ten hist paintings (4 1/2ft x 10ft, sgraffito), Resurrection Mausoleum, Chicago, Ill, 67; Baptism of Mieszko (4 1/2ft x 7ft, hist copper), St Joseph's Cathedral, Cath Diocese of Buffalo, NY, 66; Cantacle to the Sun (sgraffito, 10ft x 6ft), Daemen Col, Snyder, NY, 68; Commodore Perry (sgraffito alfresco mural, 24 1/2ft x 9ft), Buffalo Bd of Educ, W Hertel Mid Sch, Buffalo, NY, 69; Peace (sgraffito mural, 22ft x 7 1/2ft), Barnabite Fathers, Our Lady of Fatima Basilica, 75. Exhib: Nat Mus, Warsaw, 54. Teaching: Prof mural techniques & conserv of works of art, Munic Sch Dec Arts & Painting & Acad Fine Arts, Warsaw, 37-47. Pos: Owner, Niagara Falls Gallery & Studio Sgraffito. Awards: Monetary Award, Nat Mus, Warsaw, 56; Polonia Restituta for Artistic Work & Lect, Poland, 46. Style & Technique: Mural techniques such as sgraffito, tempera, encaustic, stained glass, alfresco, mosaic, metal art; conservation of works of art. Media: Sgraffito; Alfresco-Tempera. Res: Special study of Geiotto's fresco technique in Assisi, Italy. Specialty: Mural art; sketches, drawings, work cartoons adapted to specific mural techniques; examples of mural techniques. Mailing Add: 125 Buffalo Ave Niagara Falls NY 14303

SLEIGH, SYLVIA
PAINTER, INSTRUCTOR
b Llandudno, Wales. Study: Brighton Sch Art, Eng. Exhib: One-artist shows, Bennington Col, Vt, 63, Soho 20 Gallery, 73, Fine Arts Ctr, Univ RI, Kingston, 74 & AIR Gallery, 74; Tokyo Int Biennial: New Image in Painting, 74. Teaching: Instr life painting, New Sch, 73- Pos: Selection Comt, Women Choose Women, New York Cult Ctr, 73. Bibliog: John Russell (auth), Sylvia Sleigh, Lerner-Heller Gallery, New York, 72; Linda Nochlin (auth), Some women realists, Arts, 74; John Perreault (auth), Male nudes, Village Voice, New York, 10/18/73. Mem: AIR Gallery. Style & Technique: Realist. Media: Oil on Canvas. Publ: Contribr, Anonymous was a Woman, 74 & Art: A Woman's Sensibility, 75, Feminist Art Prog, Calif Inst of the Arts. Dealer: AIR Gallery 97 Wooster St New York NY 10012. Mailing Add: 330 W 20th St New York NY 10011

SLES, STEVEN LAWRENCE
PAINTER, POET
b Jersey City, NJ, June 16, 40. Study: Inst Allende, Mex; Bard Col; Univ Madrid; Swarthmore Col; Art Students League; also with Hans Hofmann & Sol Wilson. Work: HRH Princess Anne, Buckingham Palace, Eng; Bertrand Russell House, Sussex, Eng; Mus Fine Arts & Munic Mus, Valencia, Spain. Exhib: FAR Gallery, New York; Provincetown Art Asn, Mass; Jersey City Mus; Petchburi Gallery, Bangkok, Thailand; Galeria Toison, Madrid, Spain; plus others. Pos: Pres & dir, Sles Art Corp Worldwide, Tucson; mem, Worldwide Asn Mouth & Foot-painting Artists, Inc, Vaduz, Lichtenstein. Awards: Purchase Prize, Pearson Gallery, Swarthmore Col, 62; Charles T Bainbridge Award, Jersey City, 70; First & Second Prizes, Kenny Inst Int Mus Art Show, Minn, 71; plus others. Bibliog: Articles in Elizabeth Daily J, 4-9/64; Agramunt (auth), article in Avanzada, Madrid, 9/70; Sheer Determination (film), Vereinigung Der Mund und Fussmalenden Kunstler in Aller Welt Gallery, 64-71; plus others. Mem: Fel Royal Soc Arts; Int Arts Guild; Nat Soc Lit & Arts; dipl mem Vereinigung Mund und Fussmalenden Kunstler in Aller Welt, Lichtenstein. Style & Technique: Figurative, semi-abstract and abstract; oniric and goyesque-real portraits depicting poverty, anxiety, war; monumental to miniatures; many imaginative landscapes. Media: Oil, Graphic Ink, Glass. Publ: Auth, Ahora Que Te Has Ido, Poesia Espanola, Madrid, 70; auth, Amor, Rio Que Estas Dormido, Poesia de Venezuela, Caracas, 70; auth, Mujer en la Oscuridad del Dia, Azor, Barcelona, Spain, 70; auth, Three poetries, Arbol de Fuego, Caracas, 70; auth, El Guerrero y la Guerra de la Vida, Mensaje, Lerida, Spain, 70; others in France & US, 72 & 75. Mailing Add: 5371 E Fourth St Tucson AZ 85711

SLETTEHAUGH, THOMAS CHESTER
PAINTER, EDUCATOR
b Minneapolis, Minn, May 8, 25. Study: Univ Minn, BS, 49, MEd, 50, with Walter Quint, Peter Lupori, Malcolm Myers & John Rood; Pa State Univ, DEd, 56, with Viktor Lowenfeld & Kenneth Beittel; spec study, Williams Col, Univ SC, Univ Ga & Syracuse Univ. Work: Bucharest Univ, Romania; Cult Ctr, Budapest, Hungary; Cortland Gallery, State Univ NY Col Cortland. Comn: Symbol of Excellence, comn by admin, Miss State Col Women, 70; Miss State Col Women Crest for Apollo 14, comn by Alumni Asn, 71. Exhib: Carnegie Mus Regional, Pittsburgh, 70; one-man show prints, Outer Space Concepts, Kunstforum Gallery, Garmisch-Park, WGer, 71 & Grape Leaf—Variations, Bucharest Univ, 72; Burtrand Russell Centenary, Nottingham, Eng, 73; Heidelberg Univ Gallery, 75; Nature Variations, Cambridge Univ, Eng & Centro de Altos Estudios, Madrid, Spain, 76; Serigraph Techniques, Nat Gallery, Budapest, Hungary, 77. Collections Arranged: Max Klager—Printmaker (etchings & silkscreen), Heidelberg Univ, WGer. Teaching: Prof art, Frostburg State Col, 62-68; prof fine arts, Miss State Col Women, 68-70; assoc prof grad studies art educ, Univ Minn, 70-; vis art scholar, Cambridge Univ, Eng, Leicester Polytech, Eng, London Univ, Eng, Heidelberg Univ, WGer, Ctr of Cult & Pedagogy, Zagreb, Yugoslavia, Pedagogical Inst, Budapest, Hungary, Friendship House, Moscow, USSR, Leningrad Peace Comt, Leningrad, USSR & Art Sch, Vienna, Austria, 76-77. Pos: Cur art, Frostburg State Col, 62-68; coun mem, Md Arts Coun, 66-68; gallery dir, Miss State Col Women, 68-70; coun mem, Miss Coun Arts, 68-70; coun mem, Minn Art Educators, 71-72; secy, US Soc for Educ through Art, INSEA/UNESCO. Awards: Intercultural Art of Hungary & America Award, Off Int Progs, Univ Minn, 71; Psychoaesthetics Develop Award, Col Educ, Univ Minn, 71. Bibliog: Hans Stumbauer (auth), Art education in Austria, Art Sch Linz, 71; Paul Cornel Chitic (auth), articles in Tribune & Art Rev, Bucharest, Romania, 72. Mem: Int Soc Educ in Art; Int Soc Aesthet; Int Soc Art Hist; Int Soc Empirical Aesthet; Int Union Architects. Res: Creative intellect of artists and perceptive development of the individual. Publ: Auth, Difference in reactions of children in various levels of development to three-dimensional abstract forms, 74 & Art education for the golden agers and the creative use of leisure time, 75, Int Soc Educ in Art; auth, Art education beyond creative activities, 74 & Training free-lance art educators, 75, Nat Art Educ Asn; auth, Psychoaesthetics-the creative intellect, Int Union Architects, 75; auth, The analysis & synthesis of psychoaesthetics, Cambridge Univ, 75. Mailing Add: 135 Wulling Hall Univ of Minn Minneapolis MN 55455

SLIDER, DORLA DEAN
PAINTER
b Tampa, Fla, Sept 9, 29. Study: Study with Walter Emerson Baum, 40-48. Work: Hartford Ins Group, Conn; Marietta Col, Ohio; Del Art Mus; Reading Art Mus, Pa; Allentown Art Mus, Pa; Plymouth Meeting Mall Asn, Pa; Philco Corp, Pa. Exhib: Am Watercolor Soc, Nat Acad Design, New York, 67/77; Allied Artists of Am, Nat Acad Design, 67-77; Pa Acad Fine Arts, Philadelphia, 69; Audubon Artists, Nat Acad Design, 72-78; William Penn Mus, Harrisburg, Pa, 75; Watercolor USA, Springfield, Ohio; Butler Inst of Am Art, Ohio. Awards: Gold Medal, Catharine Lorillard Wolfe Art Club, Nat Acad Design, New York, 70; Award of Excellence, Mainstreams Int, Ohio, 71; Herb Olsen Award, Am Watercolor Soc, New York, 72; Gold Medal, Knickerbocker Artists New York, 77. Bibliog: Henry C Pitz (auth), Brandywine Tradition, Houghton Mifflin Co, Boston, 69; articles in Brandywine Bugle, Trade Mag, Pa, 71-74. Mem: Am Watercolor Soc; Philadelphia Watercolor Club; Nat Soc Painters in Casein & Acrylic; Knickerbocker Artists; Artists Equity Asn. Style & Technique: Landscapes in watercolor, oil, acrylic, ink and pencil. Dealer: Chadds Ford Gallery Inc Rte 1 & 100 Chadds Ford PA 19317. Mailing Add: 1387 Kutz Dr Pottstown PA 19464

SLIVKA, DAVID
SCULPTOR
b Chicago, Ill. Study: Calif Sch Fine Arts. Work: Univ Tex Mus, Austin; Walker Art Ctr, Minneapolis; Univ of Pa, Philadelphia; Baltimore Mus; Everson Mus, Syracuse, NY; Neuberger Mus, Purchase, NY; Brooklyn Mus, NY; Stuttgart Mus, Ger. Exhib: Mus of Mod Art, 62; Hirshhorn Collection Modern Sculpture, Guggenheim Mus, 62-63; Univ Tex Mus, 66; Mus of Fine Arts, Boston, 68; Selections from Chase Manhattan Bank Collection, 71; Albright-Knox Art Gallery, Buffalo, NY, 74; one-man shows, Southern Ill Univ, Carbondale, 68, Everson Mus, Syracuse, NY, 74 & Univ of Pa, Philadelphia, 75. Teaching: Prof sculpture, Univ Mass, Amherst, 64-67; artist in residence, Southern Ill Univ, Carbondale, 67-68; Queens Col, NY, 71-73; prof, Pa Acad of Fine Arts, Philadelphia, 73-78. Awards: Brandeis Univ Creative Arts Award for Am Sculpture, 62; Louis Comfort Tiffany Award-Sculpture, 77. Bibliog: Harvey Arnason (auth), Modern Sculpture from the Joseph Hirshhorn Collection, Guggenheim Mus, 62; Georgine Oeri (auth), The sculpture of David Slivka, Quadrum, 63; Harold Rosenberg (auth), The anxious object, Illus, 65. Media: Bronze, Wood, Marble. Mailing Add: Box 537 Chelsea Sta New York NY 10011

SLIVKA, ROSE
ART EDITOR
Pos: Ed-in-chief & writer, Craft Horizons. Mailing Add: 44 W 53rd St New York NY 10019

SLOAN, JEANETTE PASIN
PAINTER, PRINTMAKER
b Chicago, Ill, Mar 18, 46. Study: Marymount Col, Tarrytown, NY, BFA, 67; Art Inst of Chicago; Univ Chicago, MFA, 69, with Joshua Taylor & Max Kahn. Work: Nat Col Fine Arts, Smithsonian Inst, Washington, DC; Cleveland Mus Fine Arts; Chase Manhattan Bank, New York; Am Tel & Tel Collection, Chicago; Ill State Mus, Springfield. Exhib: Northeastern Ill Univ, Chicago, 75; Nat Drawing Competition, Cheney Cowles Mem Mus, Spokane, Wash, 75; Artemisia Invitational, Name Gallery & ARC Gallery, Chicago, 76; New Horizons, North Shore Art League, Chicago, 76; Ill Invitational, Ill State Mus, 76; Galesburg Civic Art Ctr, Ill, 76; Univ Club, Chicago, 76; Jeanette Pasin Sloan-G W Einstein & Co, New York, 77; Gallery Artists, van Straaten Gallery, Chicago, 77; 16th Bradley Nat Drawing & Print Show, Peoria, Ill, 77; Seven Artists—Contemp Drawings, Cleveland Mus Art, 78; Jesse Besser Mus, Canton, Ohio, 78; Hapatat Gallery, Dearborn, Mich, 78; Hackley Art Mus, Muskegon, Mich, 78; Madison Art Ctr, Wis, 78. Awards: Purchase Award, Ill State Mus, 76; Purchase Award, New Horizons, George S May Int, 76; Galex Award, 11th Ann Galex Competition, Galesburg Civic Art Ctr, Ill, 77. Bibliog: Gerrit Henry (auth), rev in Art News, 1/78. Style & Technique: Realism; acrylic paintings and colored pencil drawings; lithography. Mailing Add: c/o G W Einstein 243 E 82nd St New York NY 10028

SLOAN, LOUIS BAYNARD
PAINTER, CONSERVATOR
b Philadelphia, Pa, June 28, 32. Study: Pa Acad Fine Arts, Philadelphia. Work: Philadelphia Mus Art; Pa Acad Fine Arts; Rutgers Univ, Camden, NJ; Children's Hosp Philadelphia.

Exhib: Pa Acad Fine Arts Fel Ann Exhib, 56-64, Ann Exhib, 61-64; Nat Acad Design, New York; A Black Perspective on Art, Black Enterprise Mag, New York, 65; Earth Art II, Prof Arts of the Delaware Valley, 65. Teaching: Instr painting, Pa Acad Fine Art, 60- Pos: Asst conservator painting, Philadelphia Mus Art, 62- Awards: Cresson Traveling Scholar, Pa Acad Fine Arts, 56 & Sesnan Gold Medal, 62; Louis Comfort Tiffany Grant, Tiffany Found, NY, 61 & 62; Guggenheim Fel, 64. Mem: Pa Acad Fine Arts Fel (vpres, 65-). Style & Technique: Magic realist. Media: Oil. Mailing Add: 5124 Chester Ave Philadelphia PA 19143

SLOAN, RICHARD
PAINTER, ILLUSTRATOR
b Chicago, Ill, Dec 11, 35. Study: Am Acad of Art, Chicago, Ill; Famous Artists Sch, Westport, Conn. Work: R W Norton Gallery, Shreveport, La; Smithsonian Inst, Washington, DC; Denver Mus Natural Hist, Colo; Miss State Wildlife Mus, Jackson; Ga Mus Sci & Indust, Atlanta. Comn: Fifty paintings of birds of NAm, Griggsville Wild Bird Soc of Ill, 67-77. Exhib: Soc of Animal Artists, Abercrombie & Fitch, New York, 69; Three Centuries of Am Wildlife Art, Gallier Hall, New Orleans, La, 73; Soc of Animal Artists, Gen Electric Gallery, Fairfield, Conn, 77, Sportsman's Edge Ltd, New York, & Owens Gallery, Oklahoma City, Okla, 78; one-man shows, The Birds of Falconry, Abercrombie & Fitch, Chicago, 65 & NAm Birds, La State Exhib Mus, Shreveport, 70. Pos: Staff artist, Lincoln Park Zoo, Chicago, 62-65. Bibliog: Joan Hunter (auth), Mosquitoes, Martins & Art, The Living Museum, Ill State Mus, 72; Mary Martin (auth), Three Centuries...Wildlife, La Conservationist, La Wildlife & Fish, 74; Andy Barton (auth), Richard Sloan Wildlife Painter, Channel 12, CBS-TV, 75. Mem: Soc of Animal Artists, New York; Int Soc of Artists, New York. Style & Technique: Realist. Media: Acrylic on Gesso Panel. Publ: Illusr (cover painting), The Fla Naturalist, Fla Audubon Soc, 69; illusr (cover painting), La Conservationist, La Wildlife & Fish Comn, 74; illusr, Wings Upon the Heavens, Ideals Publ Co, 76; illusr, Nat Wildlife, Nat Wildlife Fed, 76; illusr (cover painting), Turkey Call, Nat Wild Turkey Fedn, 78. Dealer: Taylor Clark Inc 2623 Government St Baton Rouge LA 70806. Mailing Add: PO Box 9039 Shreveport LA 71109

SLOAN, ROBERT SMULLYAN
PAINTER, ART DEALER
b New York, NY, Dec 5, 15. Study: City Col New York, AB, 36; Inst Fine Arts, NY Univ, 37-39. Work: IBM Collection; Bradford Jr Col, Haverhill, Mass; White Art Mus, Ithaca, NY. Comn: Many covers & spec features, Time, Coronet & Colliers, 41-50; posters, Russian War Relief, 43 & Doing All You Can, Brother, US Treas, 43. Exhib: Carnegie Inst, 48; Corcoran Biennial, 49; Portraits of Year, Portraits, Inc, 49; Am Watercolor Soc Exhib, Nat Acad Design Gallery, 56; one-man shows, Leger Galleries, White Plains, NY, 55, Herbert F Johnson Mus, Cornell Univ, 74 & Capricorn Galleries, Bethesda, Md, 75. Pos: Independent art dealer. Awards: Citation for Distinguished Serv, US Treas, 43; Watercolor Div Award, Nat Soldier Art Show, USA, 45. Bibliog: George Wiswell (auth), Discovery of a Copley portrait, Am Heritage Mag, 60. Mem: Appraisers Asn Am; Mamaroneck Artists Guild (pres, 54). Style & Technique: Genre and landscape; naturalistic; Old Master oil technique. Media: Oil. Specialty: American and European painting. Publ: Illusr, Army Educ Prog & other mags. Mailing Add: 1412 Arlington St Mamaroneck NY 10543

SLOANE, ERIC
ILLUSTRATOR, WRITER
b New York, NY, Feb 27, 10. Study: Art Students League; Sch Fine Arts, Yale Univ, 29; New York Sch Fine & Applied Art, 35. Work: Sloane Mus of Early Am Tools, Kent, Conn. Comn: Designed & executed Willett's Mem, Am Mus Natural Hist; murals, Int Silver Co, Meriden, Conn, Morton Salt Co, Chicago & Wings Club, New York; two murals, Nat Air & Space Mus, Washington, DC; plus others. Collections Arranged: Donor, Eric Sloane Mus Early Am Tools, Kent, Conn. Awards: Gold Medal, Hudson Valley Art Asn, 64; Freedom Found Award, 65; Gold Medal, Nat Acad Design. Mem: Nat Acad Design; Salmagundi Club; Dutch Treat Club; Wings Club; Lotos Club. Publ: Auth, Skies and the Artist, 51; auth, Return to Taos, 60; auth, Museum of Early American Tools, 64; auth, Reverence for Wood, 65; auth, Remember America, 71; plus many others. Mailing Add: Weather Hill Cornwall Bridge CT 06754

SLOANE, JOSEPH CURTIS
ART HISTORIAN
b Pottstown, Pa, Aug 8, 09. Study: Princeton Univ, AB, 31, MFA, 34, Hodder fel, 48, PhD, 49. Teaching: Instr art hist, Princeton Univ, 35-37; asst prof art hist & chmn dept art, Rutgers Univ, 37-38; from assoc prof art hist to prof & chmn dept art, Bryn Mawr Col, 38-58; prof art hist & chmn dept art, Univ NC, Chapel Hill, 58-78, dir, William Hayes Ackland Art Ctr. Pos: Chmn, NC Art Comn, 75-78; retired. Awards: Fulbright Sr Res Grant, 52; Alumni Distinguished Prof, Univ NC, 63; NC Award (Arts), 76. Mem: Col Art Asn Am (past pres); NC Art Soc (past pres); Asn Art Mus Dirs; Am Coun Arts Educ (past pres). Res: 19th and 20th century art, especially painting. Publ: Auth, French Painting Between the Past & the Present, Princeton Univ, 51; auth, Paul Marc Joseph Chenavard, Univ NC, 62; auth, The American Situation, Univ NC Publ, 76; auth, articles in Art Bull, Art Quart, Gazette Beaux-Arts, Art J & others. Mailing Add: 407 Morgan Creek Rd Chapel Hill NC 27514

SLOANE, PATRICIA HERMINE
PAINTER
b New York, NY, Nov 21, 34. Study: Dayton Art Inst, 47-49, scholar, 49; RI Sch Design, scholar, 53-54, BFA, 55; Ohio Univ Grad Col, scholar, 55-56; Nat Acad Design, 56-58; Hunter Col, MA, 68; also with Hans Hofmann; NY Univ, PhD, 72. Work: Mus Mod Art Lending Collection, New York; Andrew Dickson White Mus, Cornell Univ; Univ Notre Dame, Ind. Comn: Bk jacket design & bk design for New York City publ. Exhib: Riverdale YMHA, 64; Emanu-el Midtown YMHA, 64; Chelsea Exhib, St Peter's Episcopal Church, 64; one-man show, Grand Cent Moderns, 68; Fordham Univ; Univ RI, 68; plus others. Teaching: Instr introd to fine arts, Ohio Univ, 56; instr arts & crafts, Jewish Community Ctr, Providence, RI; instr, Scarsdale Studio Workshop, 65-; instr, Univ RI, Trenton Jr Col & others; gallery lectr, Whitney Mus Am Art; asst prof, City Univ New York, 70- Awards: Nat Endowment for the Humanities summer stipend, 73; Guggenheim Found fel, 74. Mem: Col Art Asn Am; Am Soc Aesthet. Publ: Contribr drawings in Village Voice; auth critical articles in East (newspaper of the arts); auth, Color: Basic Principles and New Directions, Reinhold, 68. Mailing Add: 79 Mercer St New York NY 10012

SLOANE, PHYLLIS LESTER
PAINTER, PRINTMAKER
b Worcester, Mass. Study: Carnegie-Mellon Univ, BFA. Work: Cleveland Mus of Art, Ohio; Philadelphia Mus of Art, Pa; Case Western Reserv Univ, Cleveland; Murray State Univ, Ky; Hunterdon Art Ctr, Clinton, NJ. Comn: Mural in tiles, Park Synagogue, Cleveland, 65; five panel mural, The Temple, Cleveland, 64; Mural (on bldg side), Cleveland Area Arts Coun, Am Inst of Architects & NOVA, 74; mural, Suburban Hosp, Cleveland, 74-; ed of print La Nue, Univ Print Club, Cleveland, 77. Exhib: 47th Ann Exhib, Akron Art Inst, Ohio, 70; Ohio Women Artists: Past & Present, Butler Inst of Am Art, Youngstown, 76; Ann May Show, Cleveland Mus of Art, 77; 19th Nat Print & Drawing Exhib, Okla Art Ctr, Oklahoma City, 77; 21st Nat Print Exhib, Hunterdon Art Ctr, Clinton, NJ, 77; two-person show, Images, Mansfield Art Ctr, Ohio, 77; Print Club Ann, Philadelphia, 77; one-person show, Col of Wooster Art Mus, Ohio, 78. Awards: Spec Mention/Graphics, Ann May Show, Cleveland Mus of Art, 73; Marsh Purchase Award, 21st Nat Print Show, Hunterdon Art Ctr, 77; Hankins Mem Prize, Philadelphia Print Club Ann Exhib, 77. Mem: New Orgn for Visual Arts (bd trustees, 73-). Style & Technique: Figurative prints and paintings. Media: Acrylic; Silkscreen and Etching. Dealer: New Gallery 11427 Bellflower Rd Cleveland OH 44106. Mailing Add: 2558 Fairmount Blvd Cleveland OH 44106

SLONE, SANDI
PAINTER, INSTRUCTOR
b Boston, Mass, Oct 1, 39. Study: Wheaton Col, 57-59; Sch of Mus Fine Arts, Boston, 70-73; Wellesley Col, BA, 74. Exhib: Corcoran Biennial, 77; New Acquisitions, Young American Painters, Boston Mus Fine Arts, 77; Boston Mus Fine Arts Bicentennial, 77; New Abstract Painters, Edmonton Art Gallery, Alta, 77; one-person show, Inst Contemp Art, Boston, 77. Teaching: Instr painting, Sch of Mus Fine Arts, Boston, 71-; instr painting, Boston Col, 73-76 & Brandeis Univ, 76-77. Bibliog: Kenworth Moffett (auth), Sandi Slone: recent paintings, Inst Contemp Art, Boston, 77; Paul Richards (auth), Corcoran Biennial, Washington Post, 2/77; Carter Ratcliffe (auth), New York roundup, Art Int, 7-8/77. Style & Technique: Abstract painter. Media: Acrylic on Cotton Duck. Dealer: Acquauella Contemp Art 18 E 79th St New York NY 10021; Harcus Krakow 7 Newbury St Boston MA 02116. Mailing Add: 30 Bowker St Brookline MA 02146

SLORP, JOHN STEPHEN
CALLIGRAPHER, INSTRUCTOR
b Hartford, Conn, Dec 5, 36. Study: Calif Col of Arts & Crafts, Oakland, BFA, 63 & MFA, 65; Univ NDak, 64. Teaching: Instr calligraphy, Md Inst Col of Art, 65-; summer instr two-dimensional design, Emma Lake, Univ Sask, Can, 66, 68 & 70. Pos: Chmn found dept, Md Inst Col of Art, 73-; mem comt advan placement, Studio Art, Col Entrance Exam Bd, Princeton, NJ, 76-77. Style & Technique: Calligraphy, concrete poetry. Mailing Add: Md Inst 1300 Mt Royal Ave Baltimore MD 21217

SLOSHBERG, LEAH PHYFER
MUSEUM DIRECTOR
b New Albany, Miss, Feb 21, 37. Study: Miss State Col Women, BFA; Tulane Univ La, MA. Collections Arranged: Burgoyne Diller Retrospective, 66; Focus on Light, 67; Ben Shahn Retrospective, 69. Pos: Cur arts, NJ State Mus, Trenton, asst dir, 69-71, dir, 71- Mem: Am Asn Mus. Mailing Add: New Jersey State Mus 205 W State St Trenton NJ 08625

SLOTNICK, MORTIMER H
PAINTER
b New York, NY, Nov 7, 20. Study: City Col New York; Columbia Univ. Work: In pvt collections of Mrs Harry S Truman, Mrs Cordell Hull and others; Nat Collection of Fine Arts, Smithsonian Inst, Washington, DC; Johnson Art Mus, Cornell Univ. Exhib: Whitney Mus Am Art, Riverside Mus, Hudson River Mus, New York Pub Libr, Nat Acad Design, New York, plus others. Teaching: Prof art & art educ, City Col New York; supvr arts & humanities, City Sch Dist, New Rochelle, NY; lectr art educ, Col New Rochelle. Mem: Allied Artists Am; Am Artists Prof League; Am Vet Soc Artists. Style & Technique: Traditionalist-painter in the realist-impressionist technique. Publ: Works publ by Am Artists Group, Donald Art Co, Bernard Picture Co & Scafa-Tornabene Art Publ. Mailing Add: 43 Amherst Dr New Rochelle NY 10804

SLUSKY, JOSEPH
SCULPTOR, INSTRUCTOR
b Philadelphia, Pa, June 7, 42. Study: Univ Calif, Berkeley, BArch, MA(art), study with James Prestini, Ibram Lassaw, James Melchert, Wilfred Zogbaum, Sidney Gordin, Harold Paris, Richard O'Hanlon, William King & Robert Hudson. Work: Hayward Area Festival of the Arts, Calif. Comn: Sculpture for front of bldg, McCue, Boone, Tomsick, Archit, San Francisco, 70; sculpture for foyer, comn by Mortimer Fleishhacker, San Francisco, 73; sculpture for interior, comn by Al Goldhaggen, Oakland, Calif, 75. Exhib: 400th Ann Michelangelo Exhib & Competition, Calif Palace of Legion of Honor, San Francisco, 65; Three Am Artists, Skanska, Konstmuseum, Lund, Sweden, 68; Wham Traveling Show, San Francisco Bay Area Exhib, Asn Western Mus, 75-; Contemp Sculpture by Northern Calif Artists, Civic Ctr Plaza, Richmond, Calif, 75; Bay Area Artists Exhib/Sale, Oakland Mus, Calif, 77; Contemp Sculpture by Berkeley Artists, City Hall Lawn, Berkeley, Calif, 77; Variations on the Sculptural Idea, Ctr for the Visual Arts, Oakland, Calif, 77; Five Berkeley Artists, Ohlone Col, Fremont, Calif, 78; one-man shows, Sculpture & Drawings, DeSaisset Art Gallery & Mus, Santa Clara, Calif, 75, Mills Col, Oakland, 76 & Richmond Art Ctr, Richmond, Calif, 76. Teaching: Lectr sculpture, Univ Calif, Berkeley, 69-71 & summer 73; instr sculpture, San Jose City Col, Calif, 72-; instr sculpture & drawing, Ohlone Col, Fremont, Calif, 72- Awards: Eisner Award for Creative Achievement, Univ Calif, Berkeley, 66; Purchase Award, Hayward Festival of the Arts, 75. Bibliog: Miriam Dungan Cross (auth), Clean art show comes to Berkeley, Oakland Tribune, 69; Judith Dunham (auth), Slusky-Simonds at Berkeley Art Center, Ark Week, 73; Alfred Frankenstein (auth), Comedies in scrap metal, San Francisco Chronicle, 74; Dwight Johnson (auth), First show project a remarkable display of beauty, Palo Alto Times, Calif, 74; Paul Allman (auth), A Richmond visit by Art Who?, Berkeley Gazette, 76; Thomas Albright (auth), Large sculpture exhibition in an adequate space, San Francisco Chronicle, 77; Judith Dunham (auth), Visibility for Bay Area sculpture, Artweek, 77; Ruud van der Veer (auth), Sculptors at Ohlone, Oakland Tribune, 78. Style & Technique: Welded metal non-representational sculpture with filler containing polyester resin applied over the surface, then spray painted with automotive acrylic lacquer paints. Media: Metal; Pen & Ink, Colored Pencils. Publ: Contribr, Anybody want a half-ton work of art, Daily Rev Newspaper, Hayward, 75. Mailing Add: 2324 Blake St Apt 3 Berkeley CA 94704

SLUSSER, JAMES BERNARD
ART DEALER, KINETIC ARTIST
b Detroit, Mich, Jan 24, 52. Study: Int Art Inst; Soc Arts & Crafts; also with Peggy Lovisa Everts. Work: Actypi Collection, Athens, Greece; Forner Collection, Buenos Aires, Arg; Levy Collection, Lausanne, Switz; Vasarely Collection, Annet-Sur-Marne, France; Everts Collection, Detroit. Exhib: One-man show, Arts Extended Gallery, Detroit, 71; Bertrand Russell Peace Show, Eng, 72; Plymouth House Galleries, Mich, 73; Detroit Women's City Club, 73; Detroit Inst Arts, 73. Teaching: Artist in residence, St Gabriels Conservatory, Detroit, 73-74. Pos: Art dir, Morgan Travel art series; dir, Slusser Gallery, Detroit, currently. Bibliog: Logan Wise (auth), Art Nailed Down, Logan Wise Publ, 73. Mem: Detroit Inst Arts; Art Promotionals of Mich; St Gabriels Conservatory. Style & Technique: Op art. Media: Serigraph, Etching; Oil, Acrylic. Specialty: Paintings, graphics, pottery and original jewelry.

Publ: Illusr, cover Beacon W High Sch Publ, 71; contribr, Art in Am, 74. Mailing Add: 16129 Mack Detroit MI 48224

SMALL, AMY GANS
SCULPTOR, INSTRUCTOR
b New York, NY. Study: Hartford Art Sch, 8 yrs; Art Students League, with Zorack; New Sch Social Res, with Seymour Lipton; Nat Park Col, Forest Glen, Md; Sculpture Ctr, New York; Cent Cult, Inst Nat Bellas Artes, Mexico City, Mex, 71-72; also with Lothar J Kestenbaum & many others. Work: Selected Artists Gallery, New York; also in pvt collections. Comn: Head of Ann Buckman (clay & cast stone), comn by Dr Moses Buckman, Westchester, NY, 50; stone figures for sculpture garden, comn by Evan Frankel, Easthampton, NY, 61; plus others. Exhib: Woodstock Presentation Show, NY, 50; Woodstock Art Asn, 25 yrs; one-man shows, Krasner Gallery, New York, 58 & 59 & Selected Artists Gallery, New York, 61 & 68; Easthampton Guild Shows, 61, 67 & 68; plus many others. Teaching: Instr sculpture, Lighthouse Sch for the Blind, New York, 60-61; head sculpture sect, Woodstock Sch Art, 69-71; head pvt sch, Easthampton & Woodstock, 69-72; instr sculpture, Univ Poughkeepsie, 70-71. Awards: Best in Show, Westchester Arts & Crafts Guild Show; Presentation Show Award, Woodstock Artists Asn, 48. Bibliog: Zaidenberg (auth), Anyone Can Sculpt, Harper & Row, 52 & New & Classic Sculpture Methods, World, 72; Howard DeVree & Stuart Preston (auth), articles in New York Times, 61; plus others. Mem: Woodstock Art Asn (mem bd); Artists Equity Asn New York (bd mem). Media: Wood, Stone, Metal. Dealer: Am Leonard Gallery Tinker St Woodstock NY 12498; Selected Artists Gallery 655 Madison Ave & 60th St New York NY 10021. Mailing Add: Box 307 Plochmann Ln Woodstock NY 12498

SMART, MARY-LEIGH
COLLECTOR, PATRON
b Springfield, Ill, Feb 27, 17. Study: Oxford Univ, dipl Extra Mural Delegacy, 35; Wellesley Col, BA, 37; Columbia Univ, MA, 39; also with Bernard Karfiol, 38-39. Mem: Barn Gallery Assocs, Ogunquit, Maine (founding secy & prog dir, 58-69, pres, 69-70, hon dir, 70-); Inst Contemp Art, Boston (corporator, 65-73); De Cordova Mus, Lincoln, Mass (acquisitions comt, 66-); Strawbery Banke, Portsmouth, NH (overseer, 71-74); founding mem Univ Art Galleries, Univ NH (bd adv, 73-, vpres & mem bd overseers, 75-); Maine Coast Artists, Rockport (mem adv bd, 75-). Interest: Contemporary art and organizations promoting it; publisher of two works of conceptual art by Christopher C Cook. Collection: 20th century New England painting and sculpture; American, European and Asian contemporary graphics. Publ: Ed & auth, Hamilton Easter Field Art Foundation Collection (catalogue), 66; ed, Art: Ogunquit, A National Exhibition of Artists Who Have Worked in Ogunquit (catalogue), 67; auth, Barn Gallery Assocs in Action, 69 & The Barn Gallery, 70. Mailing Add: Surf Point York ME 03909

SMART, WINI
PAINTER, ART DEALER
b Neptune, NJ, Mar 17, 32. Study: Philadelphia Mus Col of Art; Fleisher Art Mem, Philadelphia; Art Students League. Work: Northeast Harbor Libr, Maine; Boro Hall, Red Bank, NJ, Town Hall, Dover Twp, Toms River, NJ; Point Pleasant Beach Libr, NJ. Comn: Battle of Monmouth (mural), NJ Nat Gas Co, Freehold, 64; hist mural, NJ Nat Gas Co, Red Bank, 65; two hist murals, First Nat Bank, Toms River, 68; mural & bas-relief, First Presby Church, Freehold, 70; hist mural, Boro of Freehold, 75. Exhib: NJ Artists Triennial Exhib, Newark Mus, 64; NJ Watercolor Soc Ann, Monmouth Mus, 68, 72, 74 & 75; Knickerbocker Artist Ann, Nat Arts Club, New York, 73, 74, 75 & 76; Franklin Mint Marine Art Competition, 74; Nat Acad of Design, New York, 75; one-artist show, Union League, Philadelphia, 76. Pos: Dir, Smart Studio, Northeast Harbor. Awards: Winsor & Newton Award, NJ Watercolor Soc, 68 & 75; Purchase Awards, Monmouth Art Festival, Red Bank, 66 & 68; Best in Show, Freehold Art Soc Ann, 74 & 75. Mem: Manasquan River Group of Artists, Spring Lake, NJ (pres, 54-56); Freehold Art Soc (pres, 60-62, 68-70); Catherine Lorillard Wolfe Art Club, New York; Guild of Art, Shrewsbury, NJ; NJ Watercolor Soc. Style & Technique: Traditional transparent watercolors of marine and landscapes. Media: Watercolor, Oil. Specialty: Watercolors of Maine. Publ: Illusr, Early History of Toms River & Dover Township, 67 & Cooks & Artists, 58. Dealer: Left Bank Gallery St Simon Island GA; Windsor Gallery Miami FL. Mailing Add: 28 Fairview Ave Bricktown NJ 08723

SMIGOCKI, STEPHEN VINCENT
PRINTMAKER, GRAPHIC ARTIST
b Washington, DC, Nov 20, 42. Study: Univ Md, BA(fine arts), 64, MA(drawing), 68; summer work at Univ S Fla, Tampa; Fla State Univ, PhD (art education) painting with Karl Zerbe. Work: Ringling Mus, Sarasota, Fla; Huntington Gallery, WVa; WVa Sci & Cult Complex, Charleston, WVa. Exhib: Official Festival of States Competition, St Petersburg, Fla, 70; Dallas Summer Arts Festival Nat Competition, Tex, 71; Biennial I Six State Painting Competition, Va Commonwealth Univ, 73; Drawings 74 Nat Exhib, Wheaton Col, Norton, Mass, 74; Thirteen State Regional Exhib, Appalachian Corridors, Charleston, WVa, 75. Teaching: Instr art, Fairmont State Col, WVa, 72- Pos: Graphic artist, Univ Md Ctr of Adult Educ, 64-66. Awards: Purchase Awards, Huntington Galleries Exhib 280, WVa, 72 & Appalachian Corridors, 75. Media: Graphic media, Watercolor. Dealer: Louis Andre/Wolfe St Gallery 420 S Washington Alexandria VA 22314. Mailing Add: 35 Park Dr Fairmont WV 26554

SMITH, ALBERT
COMIC ARTIST, ART EDITOR
b Brooklyn, NY, Mar 21, 02. Pos: Artist, ed, Syndicate Dept, New York World, 20-30; comic artist, United Features Syndicate, 30-32; ghost artist, writer several well-known comic strips, 32-; artist, Bell Syndicate, 32-; artist, Mutt & Jeff Comic Strip, 32-; head, Smith Serv, 50, feature ed, Smith Serv Div, Am Press Asn; writer, comic artist, Rural Delivery, Remember When, 50-; artist, Life in the Suburbs, Cicero's Cat. Mem: Nat Cartoonists Soc (pres); Am Newspaper Comic Coun, Inc. Mailing Add: c/o McNaught Syndicate 60 E 42nd St New York NY 10017

SMITH, ALBERT E
PAINTER
b San Francisco, Calif. Exhib: One-man shows, De Saiset Gallery, Univ of Santa Clara, 71 & Calif State Univ, Hayward, City of San Jose Mus, Calif, 72; one-man show, Calif State Univ, Hayward, 73; 1st Painting Exhib, Cult Ctr, City of Palo Alto, Calif, 73; Univ Calif Exten Gallery, San Francisco, 74; Off the Stretcher Show, Col Marin, 75; plus many other group & one-man shows. Pos: Owner, Atherton Gallery, Menlo Park, Calif. Specialty: American and English artists. Mailing Add: 1616 El Camino Real Menlo Park CA 94025

SMITH, ALEXIS (PATRICIA ANNE)
CONCEPTUAL ARTIST
b Los Angeles, Calif, Aug 24, 49. Study: Univ Calif, Irvine, 66-70, BA(art), 70; study with Robert Irwin & Ed Moses. Exhib: Lowe, Munger, Smith, Wilson, Los Angeles Co Mus Art, 72; Southern California Attitudes, Pasadena Mus Mod Art, Calif, 72; Both Kinds, Berkeley Art Mus, Calif, 75; Four Los Angeles Artists, Corcoran Gallery Am Art, Washington, DC, 75; Whitney Biennial, Whitney Mus Am Art, New York, 75; Via Los Angeles, Portland Ctr Visual Arts, Ore, 76; Autobiographical Fantasies, Los Angeles Inst of Contemp Art, Calif, 76; Paris Biennale, France, 77; Am Narrative/Story Art, Contemp Art Mus, Houston, Tex, 77; solo exhibs, Riko Mizuno Gallery, 74, Whitney Mus of Am Art, 75, Long Beach Mus of Art, 75, Nicholas Wilder Gallery, 77 & Holly Solomon Gallery, 77. Awards: New Talent Award, Contemp Arts Coun, Los Angeles Co Mus Art, 74; Nat Endowment Arts fel grant, 76-77. Bibliog: Jane Livingston (auth), Ms LA: 3 women in the city of angels, Art in Am, 73; Peter Plagens (auth), rev in Artforum, 74; John Russell (auth), Whitney finds this land is its land, New York Times, 75; Nancy Marmer (auth), Alexis Smith: the narrative act, Artforum, 12/76; staff, Alexis Smith: Scheherezade the storyteller, Flash Art, 11-12/77. Style & Technique: Serial collages with narrative text; environments containing objects. Media: Paper Collage, Drawing. Publ: Contribr centerfold, Avalanche, fall 75; auth, Alone (bk), 77. Dealer: Nicholas Wilder Gallery 225 1/2 Santa Monica Blvd Los Angeles CA 90046; Holly Solomon Gallery 392 W Broadway New York NY 10012. Mailing Add: 1709 Lincoln Blvd Venice CA 90291

SMITH, ALFRED JAMES, JR
PAINTER, SCULPTOR
b Montclair, NJ, July 9, 48. Study: Boston Univ, BFA, 70 & MFA, 72 with John Wilson & David Aronson. Work: Howard Univ, Washington, DC; Univ DC; Harvard Univ, Cambridge, Mass; Studio Mus, Harlem, NY; Nat Ctr of Afro-Am Artists, Dorchester, Mass. Comn: Wall mural, Boston Univ Afro-Am Ctr, 70; wall mural, Northeastern Univ African-Am Inst, Boston, 71; floor painting, Highland Park Free Sch for Children, comn by City of Boston, 72; painting, Afro-Cultural House, Univ Mass, 72; sculpture/musical instrument, Ethnic Music Ctr, Howard Univ, 76. Exhib: Twelve Black Artists from Boston, Rose Mu, Brandeis Univ, 69; Fourteen Black Artists from Boston, Studio Mus, Harlem, 69; Afro-Am Artists/Boston & New York, Boston Mus of Fine Arts, 70; Directions in Afro-Am Art, Herbert F Johnson Mus, Cornell Univ, 74; 19th Ann Area Competition, Corcoran Gallery of Art, Washington, DC, 74; Jubilee, Boston Mus of Fine Arts, 75; one-man shows, Celebration of Life, Howard Univ, 75 & Procession Series, Studio Mus, Harlem, 76; FESTAC 2nd World Festival of Arts & Culture, Lagos, Nigeria, 77. Teaching: Assoc prof painting, drawing & sculpture, Howard Univ, 72- Awards: Art Award, Boston Univ, 67, 68 & 70; Better Spaces Award, City of Boston Comn for Sculptors, 72; Craftsmen's Grant, Nat Endowment for the Arts, 75. Bibliog: Ida Lewis (auth), Review of Boston Museum Show, Essence, 70; Benny Andrews (auth), The arts (art work featured), Encore, 8/76; featured artworks & cover photo, Black Art, Black Collegian, 6/77. Mem: Nat Conf Artists. Style & Technique: Figure painter, wood carver (sculpture, furniture & musical instruments). Media: (Painting) Oil and Ink Wash; (Sculpture) Wood. r Mailing Add: 5300 Kansas Ave NW Washington DC 20011

SMITH, ALVIN
PAINTER, EDUCATOR
b Gary, Ind, Nov 27, 33. Study: State Univ Iowa, BA, 55; Kansas City Art Inst, 57; Univ Ill, AM, 60; Teachers Col, Columbia Univ, Heft Scholar, 67-69. Work: Atlanta Univ; Dayton Mus, Ohio; Teachers Col, Columbia Univ; Kerlan Collection, Univ Minn; Mt Holyoke Col. Exhib: Childe Hassam Exhib, Am Acad Arts & Lett, 68; Allusions, Community Gallery, Brooklyn Mus, 70; Eight Afro-Am Artists, Rath Mus, Geneva, Switz, 71; Irish Exhib Living Art, Dublin, Ireland, 72; Young American Artists, Gentofte Kunstvenner, Copenhagen, Denmark, 72. Teaching: Lectr art educ, Queens Col (NY). Pos: Art corresp, Art Int, 72. Awards: Painting Purchase Award, Dayton Mus, 62 & 72; Dow Painting Award, Columbia Univ; Creative Artists Pub Serv Grant, Cult Coun Found, NY State Coun Arts, 72. Bibliog: Peter Schjeldahl (auth), A triumph rather than a threat, New York Times, 4/27/69; Barbara Rose (auth), article in Art in Am, 9/10/70; Jean-Luc Daval (auth), article in Art Int, 10/20/71. Mem: Brooklyn Mus (adv comt, Community Gallery, 69-); Inst Soc Educ Through Art; Nat Art Educ Asn. Media: Mixed Media. Res: Fine art by Afro-Americans: 1945-1970. Publ: Illusr, Shadow of a Bull, 65; illusr, cover, Art Int, summer 71. Mailing Add: 1885 Seventh Ave New York NY 10026

SMITH, ARTHUR HALL
PAINTER, ART EDUCATOR
b Norfolk, Va, Mar 23, 29. Study: Ill Wesleyan Univ, BFA, 51; Ecole Beaux-Arts, Paris, Fulbright fel, 51; Atelier 17, Paris, 52, with S W Hayter; grad study, Univ Wash, 55; also with Mark Tobey, Seattle, Wash, 55-57. Work: Chrysler Mus, Norfolk; Corcoran Gallery Art, Washington, DC; Phillips Collection, Washington, DC; Baltimore Mus Art, Md; Seattle Art Mus. Comn: Centennial murals, Mem Ctr, Ill Wesleyan Univ, Bloomington, 50; Mammals in World Art, Mammal Hall, US Mus Natural Hist, Smithsonian Inst, Washington, DC, 58; Truckee Storage Triptych, Bur Water Reclamation, US Dept Interior, Washington, DC, 72. Exhib: 7th Ann Va-NC Painting, Norfolk Mus Arts, 49; Va Artists Ann, Va Mus Fine Arts, Richmond, 51; Huit Americains de Paris, Ctr Cult Am, Paris, France, 64; The American Artist and Water Reclamation, Nat Gallery Art, Washington, DC, 72; 25 Yr Retrospective, Exhib Hall, Cathedral St John the Divine, New York, NY & Dimock Gallery, Washington, DC, 76; Grafik aus den USA, Bawag Found, Vienna, Austria, 76; one-man shows, Washington Artists Series, Corcoran Gallery Art, 61 & Editions of One, Fine Arts Pavilion, Montgomery Jr Col, Takoma Park, Md, 77. Teaching: Asst prof painting, George Washington Univ, 74- Awards: Merwin Medal for Painting, Bloomington Art Asn, 48; Painting Prize, 15th Area Exhib, Corcoran Gallery Art, 62. Bibliog: Benjamin Forgey (auth), article, Art News, 4/76. Media: Oil, Acrylic, Ink. Publ: Auth, Introductory essay, Mark Tobey Exhib, St Alban's Sch, Washington, DC, 59; auth, Introduction to the Drawings of Kevin MacDonald Exhib, Phillips Collection, Washington, DC, 77. Dealer: Franz Bader Gallery 2124 Pennsylvania Ave NW Washington DC 20037. Mailing Add: Apt 23 2131 Florida Ave NW Washington DC 20008

SMITH, B J
MUSEUM DIRECTOR, INSTRUCTOR
b Beaver, Okla, Aug 22, 31. Study: Okla State Univ, Stillwater, BFA, 55; Univ Okla, Norman, MFA, 59. Work: Joslyn Art Mus, Omaha, Nebr; Okla Art Ctr, Oklahoma City; Mus of Art, Univ Okla, Norman; State Collection of Okla Artists & craftsmen, Oklahoma City. Exhib: Young Painters, Kans State Art Asn, Manhattan, 58; Okla Artists Ann, Philbrook Art Ctr, Tulsa, 58, 64-68 & 73; Ann Eight State Exhib, 63, 64, 68, 70 & 74, 13 Artists You Should Collect, 65, Okla Art Ctr, Oklahoma City; 9th Midwest Biennial, Joslyn Art Mus, Omaha, 66; Springfield Ann, Springfield Art Mus, Mo, 66, 70 & 71; Okla in Washington, John F Kennedy Ctr for the Performing Arts, Washington, DC, 76. Teaching: Asst prof drawing, color & design, Okla State Univ, 65- Pos: Asst to dir, Okla Art Ctr, Oklahoma City, 61-65; dir, Gardiner Art Gallery, Okla State Univ, 65- Awards: Purchase Awards, 9th Midwest Biennial, Joslyn Art Mus, Omaha, 66, Okla Biennial, Okla Art Ctr, Oklahoma City, 67 &

Okla Artists Ann, Philbrook Art Ctr, Tulsa, 68. Style & Technique: Hard-edge and stylized landscapes and color compositions. Media: Acrylic on masonite. Mailing Add: 2132 W Sunset Dr Stillwater OK 74074

SMITH, BARBARA TURNER
INSTRUCTOR, VIDEO ARTIST
b Pasadena, Calif, July 6, 31. Study: Pomona Col, BA, 53; Chouinard Art Inst, 65; workshops with Alex Hay, 68 & Steve Paxton, 69; Univ Calif, Irvine, MFA, 71, with Bob Irwin, Larry Bell & Emerson Woelfer. Work: Newport Harbor Art Mus, Newport Beach, Calif. Exhib: People Who Should Be Seen, Los Angeles Co Art Mus, Los Angeles, 65; New Art From Orange Co & Bks from Southern Calif, Newport Harbor Art Mus, 72; Survivors 72, Henry Gallery, Univ Wash, 72; 21 Artists, Visible-Invisible, 72 & 1st, 2nd & 5th Southland Video Anthology, Long Beach Mus of Art; Mus of Drawers, Herbert Distel Gallery, Bern, Switz, 73; All Night Sculptures, Mus of Conceptual Art, San Francisco, 73; Performance Conf, Womanspace & Woman's Bldg, 73, 75 & 77; Retrospective (auth, catalogue), Univ Calif, San Diego, 74; Irvine Milieu, La Jolla Mus of Contemp Art, Calif, 75. Teaching: Fac fel art, Univ Redlands, Calif, 75-; vis performance artist, Univ Calif, San Diego, 77. Pos: Co-founder, F-Space Gallery, Santa Ana, Calif, 70-72; founding mem, Grandview I & II Gallery, Los Angeles, 73-75; organizer, New Dimensions in Sci series, Los Angeles Inst of Contemp Art, 75; comt mem, Performance & Video, Los Angeles Inst of Contemp Art, 77- Awards: Nat Endowment for the Arts individual Artist & Grant, 74. Bibliog: Melinda Wortz (auth), Art is magic, Artweek, 74; G S Lischka,(ed), die Lowin, Switz, 12/75; Nancy Buchanan (auth), Barbara Smith: Communication/Communion, In: George Miller, ed, The Portrait Rev, Vol V, 76. Style & Technique: Performance art with a spiritual or ritual quality. Media: Body and Video. Publ: Auth, Rope, privately publ, 71; auth, Burden case tried, dismissed, Artweek, 73; auth, Women in industry, Los Angeles Inst of Contemp Art J, 74; contribr, Buddha mind performance, In: Tom Marioni, ed, Vision, Crown, 75; auth, Rachel Rosenthal performs Charm, Artweek, 2/77. Mailing Add: 1127 E Del Mar Pasadena CA 91106

SMITH, BEN
PRINTMAKER
b Atlanta, Ga, Mar 18, 41. Study: Atlanta Sch Art, prof artists cert, 64, BFA, 67; Tulane Univ, MFA, 70. Work: Art in the Embassies Prog, Washington, DC; Brooklyn Mus, NY; Delgado Mus, New Orleans; Tenn Fine Arts Ctr, Cheekwood-Nashville; Weiss Cinemas, throughout the South. Exhib: One-man shows, Bienville Gallery, New Orleans, 70, 72 & 74, Tenn Fine Arts Ctr, 72; Washington Printmakers 25th Exhib, Nat Mus, Washington, DC, 64; III Bienal Int del Deporte en las Bellas Artes, Mus do Atarazanas, Barcelona, Spain, 71; Image South, Jane Haslem Gallery, Washington, DC, 73. Style & Technique: Oganic minimalist built around an arabesque form system using the figure as a point of departure. Media: Woodcut. Mailing Add: c/o Image South Gallery 1931 Peachtree Rd NE Atlanta GA 30309

SMITH, MRS BERTRAM
COLLECTOR, PATRON
b Dallas, Tex. Study: New York Inst Fine Arts. Pos: Patron, trustee, mem painting & sculpture acquisitions comt & secy int coun, Mus Mod Art. Collection: Post-impressionist, School of Paris paintings, drawings and sculpture. Mailing Add: 907 Fifth Ave New York NY 10021

SMITH, BRADFORD LEAMAN
SCULPTOR, JEWELER
b Los Angeles, Calif, July 8, 40. Study: Chicago Art Inst, cert, 63; independent work & study, Florence, Italy, 63-64. Comn: Carved walnut & mahogany door, Dianus, Inc, Oakland, Calif, 66; carved black walnut door, Vorpal Gallery, San Francisco, 69; cast stone relief mural, The Shoe Box, De Vargas Mall, Santa Fe, NMex, 73; sculpture-cast-fabricated rubber & environ sculpture-rubber, steel, plastic, electronic components, Inst Regional Educ, Santa Fe, 75. Exhib: Zellerbach Mem Sculpture Exhib, Palace of The Legion of Honor, San Francisco, 65; 41st Ann Northern Calif Artist, Crocker Mus, Sacramento, 66; Metal Exp Show, Oakland Mus, 70; Southwest Crafts Biennial, Int Folk Art Mus, Santa Fe, 74, 75 & 76; Contemp Crafts of The Americas, Colo State Univ, 75; A Survey of Contemp New Mexican Sculpture, Mus of Fine Arts, Santa Fe, 76; The Armory Show, Armory for the Arts, Santa Fe, NMex, 77. Pos: Prosthetic worker, 68-69; designer, Gargoles W, 76-77. Awards: Anna Louise Raymond traveling fel sculpture, Chicago Art Inst, 63; Us Govt Award for develop of new prod method of lower limb prothesis, Oak Knoll Naval Hosp, 69. Bibliog: Nilda Fernandez Getty (auth), Contemporary Crafts of the Americas; 1975, Regnery, 75; article, Amotea Mag, Albuquerque, NMex, Vol 2, No 15 (1976); article, Artifact Mag, Santa Fe Armory for the Arts, NMex, Vol 1, No 2 (1977). Style & Technique: Figurative, expressionistic, surreal images in cast and fabricated metal and rubber. Media: Cast Bronze; Cast & Fabricated Rubber. Publ: Designer & illusr, Your Chance to Live-Student Manual, 72 & Your Chance to Live-Teachers Guide, Defense Civil Preparedness Agency; designer & illusr, 30 Designs for Commercial Production Sculpture, 74 & 6 Bicentennial Designs for Commemorative Production Sculpture, 75, Gargoles West, Santa Fe. Mailing Add: 1351 Pacheco St Santa Fe NM 87501

SMITH, CECIL ALDEN
PAINTER, ILLUSTRATOR
b Salt Lake City, Utah, Feb 12, 10. Study: Univ Utah, art major, 29-30; Brigham Young Univ, art Major, 34-35; pvt study with Jack Sears, 28-32; pvt study with John Carroll, Max Weber & Yasuo Kuniyoshi, 41-42. Work: Corcoran Gallery Art, Washington, DC; Am Index of Design, Washington, DC; Denver Art Mus, Colo; Boise Art Mus, Idaho; Peggy & Harold Samuels traveling collection, Locust Valley, NY. Comn: 9ft x 12ft painted mural, State Bur Mines, Boise, Idaho, 31; four painted murals (two 90ft x 18ft & two 45ft x 18ft), Brigham Young Univ, Provo, Utah, 66-67; 9ft x 12ft painted mural, Utah Idaho Sugar Co, Salt Lake City, Utah, 68; two 12ft x 18ft painted murals, Veltex Corp, Utah & Tex, 69-70. Exhib: Utah State Art Collection & Permanent Exhib, Capitol Bldg, Salt Lake City, Utah, 30; Denver Art Mus, Colo, 36-37; Corcoran Gallery Art, Washington, DC, 37; Expos in the Louvre, Paris, France, 37; Boise Mus Art, Idaho, 39; Las Vegas Art League, Nev, 57; Springville Art Mus, Utah, 66-67; Western Heritage Art Fair, Littleton, Colo, 76 & 77. Teaching: Instr anat & life drawing, Art Ctr, Salt Lake City, Utah, 37-38. Pos: Scenic artist, Old Salt Lake Theatre, Utah, 28-29; book illusr, Caxton Printers, 40-50; art dir, Agnew Advert Agency, Lewiston, Idaho, 59-60; asst art dir, Brigham Young Univ Motion Picture Dept, Provo, Utah, 66-71. Awards: Western Award, Paris Expos, France, US Govt, 37; Bronze Medal, 76 & Gold Medal, 77, Western Heritage Art Fair, Chuck Tayman, Pres, 77. Bibliog: M V Weedon (auth), Western artist Cecil Smith-last of the rare breed, Western Horseman, 77; Dave Oliveria (auth), Cecil Smith-Last of the rare breed, Daily Interlake, Kalispell, Mont, 77 & A rare breed of artist, SW Art Mag, 2/78. Style & Technique: Well designed realism after the manner of Vermeer and other old Flemish masters; series of thin washes and under coatings with brushes. Media: Oil, Egg Tempera and Mixed Media. Publ: Auth & illusr, Ride 'em Cowboy, Newspaper Enterprises of Am, 37-38; illusr, Forged in Strong Fires, Hoogles and Alexander, Singing Sails and others, Caston Printers, 40-50; illusr, Story illus for Blue Book, McCalls Corp, 41; illusr, numerous covers and inside spreads, Western Horseman, 52-77; illusr, Bullets West, Lancer Publ, 71. Dealer: Art Serv Assoc Box 325 Somers MT 59932. Mailing Add: 1485 Montana 208 Somers MT 59932

SMITH, CHARLES (WILLIAM)
PAINTER
b Lofton, Va, June 22, 93. Study: Corcoran Sch Art, Washington, DC; Yale Univ, cert in art. Work: Mus Mod Art, New York; Rosenwald Collection, Nat Mus, Washington, DC; Guggenheim Mus, New York; Seattle Art Mus: Yale Univ, New Haven, Conn. Comn: Mosaics for pub schs & banks. Exhib: Over forty one-man shows in mus, galleries, cols & univs throughout USA. Teaching: Instr graphic art & painting, Bennington Col, Vt, 38-46; prof painting, Univ Va, 46-63, chmn dept art, 47-63. Bibliog: Schniewind (auth), Abstractions, Charles Smith, Johnson, 39; O'Neal (auth), Prints & paintings, 58; Charles Smith, Univ Va. Media: Oil, Acrylic. Publ: Auth, Linoleum Block Printing, 25; auth, Old Va in Block Prints, 29; auth, Old Charleston, 33; auth, Experiments in Relief Print Making, 54; auth, My Zoological Garden (portfolio block paintings), 56. Mailing Add: 211 Fourth St Charlottesville VA 22901

SMITH, DAVID LOEFFLER
PAINTER, EDUCATOR
b New York, NY, May 1, 28. Study: Bard Col, BA; Cranbrook Acad Art, MFA; also with Hans Hofmann & Raphael Soyer. Exhib: Carnegie Inst, 60 & 61; Seligman Gallery, New York; one-man shows, First St Gallery, New York, 72, 73, 76 & 77. Teaching: Dean & dir, Swain Sch Design, New Bedford, Mass; actg chmn dept art, Chatham Col. Awards: Henry Posner Prize, Carnegie Inst, 61. Media: Oil. Publ: Auth, articles in Am Artist, 59-62, Antiques Mag, 11/67, Arts Mag, 3/68 & Art & Artists, 1/70 & 5/71. Dealer: First St Gallery 118 Prince St New York NY 10012. Mailing Add: 122 Hawthorn St New Bedford MA 02740

SMITH, DOLPH
PAINTER, EDUCATOR
b Memphis, Tenn, July 26, 33. Study: Memphis State Univ; Memphis Acad Arts, BFA, 60. Work: Ark State Univ, Jonesboro; Brooks Mem Art Gallery, Memphis, Tenn; Southwestern at Memphis; Tenn Arts Comn, State of Tenn, Nashville; NC Nat Bank, Charlotte. Comn: Paintings for various locations nationwide, Holiday Inns Am, 65-72; painting for Tenn Exec Mansion Christmas Card, comn by Gov & Mrs Winfield Dunn, 71; painting for Sen Albert Gore, Democratic Party, Shelby Co, Tenn, 71. Exhib: Watercolor USA, Springfield, Mo, 65; Am Watercolor Soc, New York, 66; Bryant Gallery, New Orleans, La, 68; Northwest Jr Col, Miss, 68; Ark State Univ, Jonesboro, 69; Invitational (one of four Mid-South artists chosen to celebrate Memphis sesquicentennial with an exhib), Brooks Mem Art Gallery, 69; Vanderbilt Univ Fac Club, Nashville, Tenn, 70; Memphis Acad of Arts, Tenn, 72 & 77; one-man shows, Brooks Mem Art Gallery, 65, Charles Bowers Mem Mus, Santa Ana, Calif, 67 & Cheekwood, Nashville, Tenn, 73. Teaching: Asst prof painting & drawing, Memphis Acad Arts, 64-; vis instr painting, Southwestern Col, 66-68. Pos: Art dir, Ward Archer Assoc, Memphis, 64-67. Awards: First Prize for Watercolor, Mid-South Exhib, Brooks Mem Art Gallery, 64 & Grand Award (cash prize), 76; Purchase Prize, Tenn Bicentennial Art Competition, 76. Bibliog: Jo Potter (auth), The Real World of Dolph Smith, WKNO TV, 65; William Thomas (auth), Dolph Smith's Mid-South, Mid-South Mag, 2/9/69. Media: Watercolor. Publ: Illusr, Delta Rev Mag, 10/67, 11-12/69 & fall 70; illusr, Mid-South Mag, 12/71. Dealer: Memphis Academy of Arts Overton Park Memphis TN 38104. Mailing Add: 1458 Vinton Memphis TN 38104

SMITH, DONALD C
EDUCATOR, PAINTER
b Dexter, Mo, July 10, 35. Study: Univ Mo, BA & MA; Santa Reparata Graphic Art Ctr, Florence, Italy; also painting with, Fred Conway & printmaking with Maricio Lasansky. Work: Am Broadcasting Corp; Spiva Art Ctr, Joplin, Mo; Santa Reparata Stamperia d'Arte Grafica, Florence. Exhib: City Art Mus of St Louis, Mo, 58 & 60; RI Arts Ann, 66-67; Allan Stone Gallery, New York, 71-72 & 76; Providence Art Club Drawing Exhib, RI, 74; Davidson Nat Print & Drawing Competition, 75; Boston Printmakers Ann, 75; one-man shows, SW Mo State Col, Springfield, 63, NW Mo State Univ, Maryville, 63, RI Col, Providence, 69 & Wheelock Col, Boston, 71. Teaching: Prof painting, drawing & printmaking, RI Col, 64- Pos: Dir, Spiva Art Ctr, Joplin, Mo, 60-64. Awards: Univ Fel, Univ Mo, 58. Style & Technique: Representational. Media: Oil, Etching. Dealer: Allan Stone Gallery 86th St New York NY. Mailing Add: 132 Pine Hill Ave Johnston RI 02919

SMITH, DONALD EUGENE
ART ADMINISTRATOR, EDUCATOR
b Birmingham, Ala, Dec 6, 35. Study: Northern Ill Univ, BS in Educ, 58, MS in Educ, 61; Claremont Grad Sch, Calif, MFA, 65; Fla State Univ, PhD, 74; Acad Julien, Paris; Rome, Italy; Pasadena Art Mus, Calif. Work: Pasadena Art Mus; Riverside Art Ctr & Mus, Calif; Claremont Cols, Calif. Comn: Copper mural (8ft x 11ft), Dr Ruth Maier, Saarbrucken, WGer, 71. Exhib: Art Rental Gallery, Los Angeles Co Mus of Art, Los Angeles, 68; Southern Calif State Art Exhib, 68; US Int Univ, Eng, 69; KERA Pub Television 1977 Art Exhib, Dallas, Tex, 77. Collections Arranged: 1901-1976 Tex Woman's Univ Alumnal Exhib, Denton. Teaching: Prof graphics, printmaking & drawing, Tex Woman's Univ, 75-, prof art educ res methods, 75- Pos: Dean of students & instr, Calif Inst of the Arts, Los Angeles, 65-68; chmn fine arts dept, Schiller Col, Ger 68-69; regional dir admis, Europe, US Int Univ, Eng, 69-72; vis assoc prof art, Calif State Univ, Sacramento, 74-75; chmn art dept, Tex Woman's Univ, 75- Mem: Nat Art Educ Asn; Col Art Asn; Tex Asn of Schs of Art; Int Asn for Educ through Art. Style & Technique: Intaglio; laminated zinc. Media: Drypoint and Embossing. Collection: European and American prints. Mailing Add: 1002 Burning Tree Pkwy Denton TX 76201

SMITH, ELIZABETH JEAN
ART LIBRARIAN
b Indiana, Pa, Apr 25, 30. Study: Va Commonwealth Univ, BFA, 52; Rutgers Univ, MLS, 61. Exhib: Va Show, Va Mus of Art, Richmond, 53. Pos: Asst art librn, Smith Col, Northampton, Mass, 61-64; arts & Archit librn, Pa State Univ, University Park, 64- Mem: Art Libr Soc NAm, Col Art Asn. Res: Pennsylvania farmhouses, early 19th century of Georgian derivation. Mailing Add: E409 Pattee Libr Pa State Univ University Park PA 16802

SMITH, EMILY GUTHRIE
PAINTER
b Ft Worth, Tex, July 8, 09. Study: Tex Woman's Univ; Art Students League; Univ Okla; also with Mitchell Jamieson & Frederic Taubes. Work: Ft Worth Art Mus; Dallas Mus Fine Arts, Tex; WTex Mus Fine Arts, Lubbock; Univ Tex, Arlington; Longview Mus Fine Arts, Tex. Exhib: Tex Pavilion, Hemisfair, San Antonio, 68; Am Watercolor Soc, New York; one-man retrospective, Ft Worth Art Mus; one-man show, 20th Century Texas Painters, Wichita Falls Mus Fine Arts; Pastel Soc of Am, 76 & 77; Mainstreams 77, Marietta, Ohio, 77. Teaching:

Instr portrait painting, mosaics & drawing, Ft Worth Art Ctr Mus, 55-70; instr, Taos, NMex & Las Vegas, NMex, summers 60-69. Awards: Tex Ann Award, Dallas Mus Fine Arts, 63; Top Award, Tarrant Co Ann, Ft Worth Art Mus, 65; First Award, Longview Invitational, Jr Serv League, 68. Mem: Ft Worth Art Mus; Pastel Soc of Am; Dallas Mus Fine Arts. Style & Technique: Realistic impressionistic full of light. Media: Pastel, Oil, Mosaic, Murals. Collection: Contemporary painting. Dealer: L & L Gallery 1107 N Fourth Longview TX 75601; Moulton Galleries 501 Garrison Ave Ft Smith AR 72913. Mailing Add: 408 Crestwood Dr Ft Worth TX 76107

SMITH, ERNEST JOHN
ARCHITECT, DESIGNER
b Winnipeg, Man, Dec 17, 19. Study: Univ Man, BArch(with honors) & winner Can Gold Medal, RAIC, 44; Mass Inst Technol, fel, 46, MArch, 47; Banff Sch Advan Mgt. Work: Nat Gallery Ottawa Royal Can Acad Collection; Sch Archit, Univ Man. Comn: Can Embassy Bldg, Govt Can, Warsaw, Poland, 62; Centennial Centre, Centennial Bd, Winnipeg, Man, 65; Lombard Place Complex, Winnipeg, 68; Winnipeg Sq Develop, Trizec Corp, Winnipeg, 74. Exhib: Residence, East Kildonan, Man, 61; Sch Archit, Univ Man, 61; Man Asn Archit, Winnipeg & Montreal, 68; Kiwanis Ctr Deaf, Winnipeg, 75. Teaching: Sr design critic, Univ Man, 3 yrs. Awards: Honrable Mention, Residence, East Kildonan, Man, Massey Medals Archit Competition, 61 & Exhib, Sch Archit, Univ Man, 61; Honorable Mention, Pan-Am Swimming Pool, Man Asn Archit, 68. Bibliog: George Derksen (auth), Smith Carter Parkin prepares for the future, Man Bus J, 6/70; Deanna Waters (auth), Interview with the professionals, Opportunity, 74. Mem: Fel Royal Archit Inst Can (dean, 72-75); Academician Royal Can Acad Arts (mem coun, 74); Man Asn Archit (pres, 53-54, 58-61, mem exec comt, 49-54); Ont Asn Archit; Nat Joint Comt Construction Materials (chmn, 63-65). Publ: Contribr, Can Archit. Mailing Add: 1190 Waverly St Winnipeg MB Can

SMITH, FRANK ANTHONY
PAINTER
b Salt Lake City, Utah, Aug 4, 39. Study: Univ Utah, BFA, 62, MFA, 64. Work: Univ Utah Mus Fine Art; Utah State Univ; Salt Lake Art Ctr. Comn: Buffalo dance piece, Repertory Dance Theatre, 66, Diamond dance piece (with Linda C Smith), 71; stimuli sensory environ for children, Salt Lake Art Ctr, 70; mural, Univ Utah Biol Bldg, 72. Exhib: Drawings USA, 63; three-man show, Mickelson Gallery, Washington, DC, 65; Artists West of the Mississippi, 67; 73rd Western Ann, Denver, 72; Realist Painting 12 Viewpoints, 72. Teaching: Assoc prof painting & drawing, Univ Utah, 68- Awards: San Francisco Art Dirs Gold Medal, 64; Purchase Award, 3rd Intermountain Biennial, 68. Style & Technique: Airbrush acrylic paint on canvas with stencils. Media: Acrylic. Dealer: Nancy Hoffman Gallery 429 W Broadway New York NY 10013. Mailing Add: Dept of Art Univ of Utah Salt Lake City UT 84112

SMITH, GEORGE W
SCULPTOR, EDUCATOR
b Buffalo, NY, Apr 21, 41. Study: San Francisco Art Inst, BFA; Hunter Col, City Univ New York, with Tony Smith, MA. Work: Newark Mus, NJ; Everson Mus Art, Syracuse, NY; collection of Reese Palley, New York. Comn: 22nd ann theme sculpture, City & Co Art Comn, San Francisco, 68; sculptures, San Jose Br, Nat Asn Advan Colored People, in connection with Olympics in Mex, 68. Exhib: One-man show, Reese Palley Gallery, New York, 70; Contemp Am Black Artists, Hudson River Mus, Yonkers, NY, 70; Whitney Mus Am Art Sculpture Ann, 70-71; Black Artists-Two Generations, Newark Mus, 71; one-man show, Everson Mus Art, Syracuse, 72. Teaching: Asst prof sculpture, State Univ NY Buffalo, 72-73, vis prof sculpture & drawing, 74- Awards: John Simon Guggenheim Mem Found Fel in Sculpture, 71-72. Bibliog: S S Lewis (auth), Black Artists on Art, Vol II, Contemp Crafts, Inc, Calif, 71. Media: Steel, Bronze. Mailing Add: c/o Reese Palley Gallery 93 Prince St New York NY 10012

SMITH, GORD
SCULPTOR, PAINTER
b Montreal, PQ, Oct 8, 37. Study: Sir George Williams Univ. Work: Nat Gallery Can; Montreal Mus Fine Art; Mus Art Contemporaine Montreal; Sir George Williams Univ; McGill Univ; plus others. Comn: Bronze relief, Waterloo Trust Co, Kitchener, 63; steel screen, Can Pavilion, Expo '67; stainless steel relief, Int Nickel Co Can, Toronto, 67; bronze sculpture, Can Embassy, Bonn, Ger, 68; stainless steel split circle, Confedn Ctr, PEI, 72; plus others. Exhib: Six shows, Waddington Galleries, Montreal, 59-69; Three Canadians Exhibition, Art Gallery Toronto, 61-62; Montreal Mus Fine Art, 62; Can Outdoor Sculpture Competition, Nat Gallery Can, 61-64; Isaacs Gallery, Toronto, 63; plus others. Teaching: Assoc prof sculpture, Univ Victoria. Awards: First Prize, Nat Fedn Can Univs, 57; First Prize, Beth Tzedec Art Exhib, Toronto, 68; Nat Design Coun Chmns Award, 70; plus others. Bibliog: Gordon Burwash (auth), Focus (film), Nat Film Bd Can, 63; Anita Aarons (auth), article in Royal Archit Inst Can Allied Arts Catalogue, 66. Mem: Royal Can Acad Art; Que Sculptor's Asn. Publ: Contribr, The Can Architect, 62; contribr, Can Art Mag, 64; contribr, Ecole Montreal, 64; contribr, Symp Que, 65; co-auth, Gord Smith, Sculptor (monogr), Que Sculptor's Asn, 72. Dealer: Waddington Galleries 1456 Sherbrooke St W Montreal PQ Can. Mailing Add: 1302 Morrison Dr Ottawa ON K2H 7L9 Can

SMITH, GORDON
PAINTER
b Brighton, Eng, June 18, 19. Study: Winnipeg Sch Art; Vancouver Sch Art; Calif Sch Fine Arts; Harvard Univ Summer Sch; Simon Fraser Univ, LLD, 74. Work: Nat Gallery Can; Mus Mod Art, New York; Victoria & Albert Mus, London; Albright-Knox Art Mus, Buffalo, NY; Art Gallery Ont; plus others. Exhib: Can Exhib, Warsaw, Poland, 62; Can Biennial, 63; Seattle World's Fair, 63; New Design Gallery, Vancouver, BC, 64; Graphic Biennials, Yugoslavia, Ger, Norway & New York; one-man shows, Toronto, Montreal, New York & Vancouver. Teaching: Assoc prof art, Univ BC, formerly. Awards: Can Biennial, 56; Can Coun Sr Fel for Study Abroad, 60-61. Mem: BC Soc Art; Can Soc Painter-Etchers & Engravers; assoc Royal Can Acad Arts; Can Group Painters. Media: Acrylic on Canvas, Graphic Media. Mailing Add: 5030 The Byway West Vancouver BC V7W 1L7 Can

SMITH, GORDON MACKINTOSH
MUSEUM DIRECTOR
b Reading, Pa, June 21, 06. Study: Williams Col, BA, 29; Grad Sch Arts & Sci, Harvard Univ, 29-31; in Europe, 31-32; D'Youville Col, hon LittD, 63. Pos: Cur, Berks Co Hist Soc, 35-36; asst regional dir, New Eng Fed Art Proj, Works Prog Admin, 36-41; proj specialist, Off Strategic Serv, Washington, DC, 44-46; dir, Currier Gallery Art, 46-55; dir, Albright-Knox Art Gallery, Buffalo, NY, 55-73, emer dir, 73- Mem: Benjamin Franklin fel, Royal Soc Arts, London; Am Fedn Arts; Asn Art Mus Dirs; Col Art Asn Am; Intermuseum Conserv Asn. Mailing Add: 61 Oakland Pl Buffalo NY 14222

SMITH, GRIFFIN (MARY-GRIFFIN SMITH HOEVELER)
ART CRITIC
b Augusta, Ga, Apr 23, 30. Study: Wellesley Col, AB(art hist), 51; Harvard-Fogg Mus, with Sydney J Freedberg; Univ Florence. Teaching: Lectr museology, Univ Miami, 68-69; vis prof art hist, Miami-Dade Community Col, 70-71. Pos: Registrar-cur, Lowe Mus, Univ Miami, 65-69; art ed & critic, Miami Herald, 69-77; US corresp, Art News, New York, 74- Publ: Auth, 33 Miami artists, 11/71 & Portrait of the black arts, Haiti, 8/72, Tropic Mag. Mailing Add: 1317 Alhambra Circle Coral Gables FL 33134

SMITH, HASSEL W, JR
PAINTER
b Sturgis, Mich, Apr 24, 15. Study: Northwestern Univ, BS; Calif Sch Fine Arts, with Maurice Sterne. Work: Tate Gallery, London; Albright-Knox Art Gallery, Buffalo, NY; Corcoran Gallery Art, Washington, DC; Whitney Mus Am Art, New York; San Francisco Mus Art; plus others. Exhib: Retrospectives, Pasadena Art Mus, 61 & San Francisco State Col, 64; Painters of the Southwest Traveling Exhib, 62; John Moore's Ann, Liverpool, Eng, 63; one-man show, Santa Barbara Mus Art, 69; plus many others. Teaching: Instr, Calif Sch Fine Arts, 45-48; instr, San Francisco State Col, 46-47; instr, Univ Ore, 48-49; instr, Calif Sch Fine Arts, 49-52; instr, Presidio Hill Elem Sch, San Francisco, 52-55; lectr, Univ Calif, Berkeley, 63-64, 64-65 & 77-78 & San Francisco Art Inst, 78; prof & artist in residence, Art Dept, Univ Calif Los Angeles, 65-66; prin lectr painting, Polytech Fac Art & Design, Bristol, Eng, 66-77; artist in residence, Univ Calif, Davis, 73 & 76; vis lectr, Cardiff Col of Art, Wales, 73- Awards: Abraham Rosenberg Fel, 41-42. Mailing Add: 19 Ashgrove Rd Bristol England

SMITH, HELEN M
ILLUSTRATOR, PAINTER
b Canton, Ohio, Oct 19, 17. Study: Univ Melbourne, Australia, 42-43; Wash Univ, BFA, 53, MA, 58; Art Instr, Inc, cert; St Louis Univ. Exhib: St Louis Artists Guild; Ann Mo Exhib; Liturgical Art, Seattle; Cath Art Exhib, Calif; Springfield Art Mus, Mo; plus others. Teaching: Instr art, Villa Duchesne, St Louis, 53-56; instr art & head art dept, Maryville Col, 58-60; asst prof art & archaeol, 60-68, dir art dept, 60-61, dir art & archaeol depts, 61-68; lectr, Harvard Univ & Oriental Inst Archaeol, Yale Univ, 60; asst prof art hist & dir instr graphics, Southern Ill Univ, 68. Pos: Med illusr, St Louis Univ Med Ctr, 61-65; dir med illus, Dept Ophthal, Wash Univ, 64-68; consult, Am Col Radiol, 64- Awards: Ruth Kelso Renfrow Art Club Award, 55; First, Second & Third Prizes, Soc Tech Writers & Publ Exhib. Mem: St Louis Artists Guild; Archaeol Soc Am; Oriental Archaeol Soc; fel Int Inst Arts & Lett; Ill Art Educ Asn. Publ: Illusr, Aghios Kosmos, 59; illusr many med jour & bks. Mailing Add: 11447 Clayton Rd St Louis MO 63131

SMITH, HENRY HOLMES
PHOTOGRAPHER, EDUCATOR
b Bloomington, Ill, Oct 23, 09. Study: Ill State Univ; Art Inst Chicago; Ohio State Univ; New Bauhaus, Chicago Sch Design; Ind Univ; also with L Moholy-Nagy, Gyorgy Kepes, Hin Bredendieck, Alexander Archipenko. Work: Mus Mod Art, New York; Eastman House, Rochester, NY; Mus Fine Arts, St Petersburg, Fla; Univ Nebr Mus Art, Lincoln; Art Inst Chicago Mus. Exhib: Abstract Photography, Mus Mod Art, New York, 51, Sense of Abstraction, 60; Photography at Mid-Century, Eastman House, 59, Twentieth Century Photographers, 66; Photographers Choice, Art Gallery, Ind Univ, Bloomington, 59, 50th Anniversary, Mus Art, 73; plus others. Teaching: Instr photog, New Bauhuas, Chicago, 37-38; prof photog, Ind Univ, Bloomington, 47-77, emer prof, 77- Mem: Found mem Soc Photog Educ (vchmn, 63-67, mem bd dirs, 63-73). Res: Esthetics of photography. Publ: Auth, New figures in a classic tradition, In: Aaron Siskind Photographer, 65; auth, Photography in our time, In: Photographers on Photography, 66; auth, Traumas of fair women, In: Women & Other Visions, 75; auth, Across Atlantic & out of woods, In: Photographys of Moholy-Nagy, 75; auth, Models for critics, In: Photographic History, 75; plus others. Dealer: The Gallery N Grant St Bloomington IN 47401. Mailing Add: PO Box 3741 Incline Village NV 89450

SMITH, HOWARD ROSS
MUSEUM CURATOR
b Los Angeles, Calif, Aug 21, 10. Study: Univ Calif, MA; Calif Col Arts & Crafts; and with Eugen Neuhaus. Teaching: Head dept art, Univ Maine, 42-49. Pos: Cur, Calif Palace of Legion of Honor, 51-55; from asst dir to assoc dir, 55-70; Retired. Mailing Add: Apt 1901 1400 Geary Blvd San Francisco CA 94109

SMITH, JAMES MORTON
MUSEUM DIRECTOR, HISTORIAN
b Bernie, Mo, May 28, 19. Study: Southern Ill Univ, BEd, 41; Univ Okla, MA, 46; Cornell Univ, PhD, 51. Teaching: Prof hist, Cornell Univ, 66-70; prof hist, Univ Del, 76- Pos: Ed, Inst Early Am Hist & Cult, 55-66; dir, State Hist Soc Wis, 70-76; dir, Winterthur Mus, 76- Mem: Asn Art Mus Dirs; Am Hist Asn; Orgn Am Historians. Res: Early American history and culture. Mailing Add: Winterthur Mus Winterthur DE 19735

SMITH, JO-AN
DESIGNER, JEWELER
b Eugene, Ore, Apr 8, 33. Study: Univ Wash, 50-52, with Spencer Moseley; Ind Univ, 65, with Leopoldo Castedo; pvt studies in Buenos Aires, Arg, 66; also with Carlos Minero, San Salvador, El Salvador, 67; Univ Tex, El Paso, BA, 71, with Wiltz, Harrison; NMEx State Univ, MA, 75, with Lee Richards & Trinidad Lopez. Work: Tex A&M Univ; NMEx State Univ; Smithsonian Inst, Washington, DC; plus others. Comn: Seedpod I (enamel-silver), comn by John Richardson, San Francisco, Calif, 73; geometric (sterling), comn by Joan Maley, Ger, 74; gold bands, comn by Dr & Mrs Gregory Maltby, Las Cruces, NMex, 74; Rhythm Solo II (sterling), comn by Elizabeth Gillette, University Park, NMex, 75; sterling box, Fred Vickers, Las Cruces, 75. Exhib: Sterling Silver Design Competition, Sterling Silversmiths Guild of Am, New York, 74; 39th Ann Nat Arts & Crafts Competition, Cooperstown, NY, 74; El Paso's 18th Nat Sun Carnival Art Exhib, Tex, 75; Int Competition & Festival of Enamels & Glass, San Diego, 75; Biennale Int l'Art de l'email, Limoges, France, 75; Ariz Nat Exhib, Scottsdale, 76; Int Festival of Enamels, Laguna Beach, 76; The Metalsmith, Phoenix Art Mus, Ariz & Henry Gallery, Univ Wash, Seattle, 76-77; Update: Body Ornament, Am Craft Coun, Winston-Salem, NC, 77; Marietta Col Craft Nat, Ohio, 77; Am Goldsmith Now, St Louis, Mo, 78. Teaching: Grad asst jewelry & three-dimensional design, NMex State Univ, 74-75; workshop instr jewelry, enameling, hist & design of jewelry & silversmithing, 75 & lectr jewelry & two-dimensional design, 76-78. Pos: Custom designer, Glenn Cutter Jewelers, Las Cruces, NMex, 75- Awards: Second Place Purchase Prize in Crafts, Llano Estacado Art Asn, 74; First Place in Show, Las Cruces Chap, NMex Designer Craftsmen, 74; Hon Mention, The Metalsmith, Phoenix & Seattle, 76-77. Mem: Soc NAm Goldsmiths; Dona Ana Arts Coun (bd mem, applied design); Las Cruces Designer-Craftsmen; Enamel Guild: W; Am Crafts Coun. Style & Technique: Contemporary metalwork, cloisonne & champleve. Media: Silver, Gold, Enamel. Publ: Contribr, Bead J, Craftsman's Gallery, Design, Golddust, Goldsmith's J & Working Craftsman. Dealer: Glenn Cutter Jewelers 1400 El Paseo Las Cruces NM 88001;

Dallas Fine Arts Mus Shop Fair Park Dallas TX 75210. Mailing Add: Box 1681 Las Cruces NM 88001

SMITH, JOHN BERTIE
EDUCATOR, PAINTER
b Lamesa, Tex, June 5, 08. Study: Baylor Univ, AB, 29; Univ Chicago, AM, 31; Columbia Univ, EdD, 46. Work: Arroyo Hondo (watercolor), Denver Art Mus. Exhib: Denver Art Mus Ann, 38-42; Artists West of Miss, Colorado Springs Fine Arts Ctr, Colo, 45; Southeastern Art Ann, Atlanta, Ga, 47; one-man show, Mobile Art Ctr, Ala, 48; Tex Watercolor Soc, San Antonio, 55; Europ Landscapes, Baylor Art Mus, 77. Teaching: Chmn dept art, Adams State Col, 31-39; chmn dept art, Univ Wyo, 39-45; chmn dept art, Univ Ala, 45-49; dean, Kansas City Art Inst, 49-54; chmn dept art, Hardin-Simmons Univ, 54-60; chmn dept art, Baylor Univ, 60-, chmn fine arts coun, 72- Pos: Pres, Southeastern Arts Asn, 49-50; pres, Midwestern Col Art Conf, 54-55; pres, Tex Fine Arts Asn, 58-59. Mem: Am Asn Univ Prof; Col Art Asn Am; Tex Art Educ Asn (pres, 69-71); Tex Asn Art Schs. Style & Technique: Expression in design of landscape images. Media: Watercolor. Mailing Add: 2109 Charboneau Dr Waco TX 76710

SMITH, JOHN IVOR
SCULPTOR, EDUCATOR
b London, Eng, Jan 28, 27; Can citizen. Study: McGill Univ, BSc, 48; Montreal Mus Fine Arts; study with Arthur Lismer, Jacques de Tonnancour & Eldon Grier. Work: Art Gallery Ont, Toronto; Provincial Mus Que, Quebec City; Winnipeg Art Gallery, Manitoba; London Pub Art Mus, Ont; Edmonton Art Gallery, Alta. Comn: 20' Fiberglas chimeric figure, Expo '67, Montreal, 67; 9' Fiberglas female figure, Can Govt Exhib Comn, Ottawa, 67. Exhib: Nat Outdoor Sculpture Show, Ottawa, Ont, 60; Can Sculpture, Dorothy Cameron Gallery, Toronto, Ont, 64; Sculpture '67, City Hall, Nat Gallery Can, Toronto, 67; Expo '67, Montreal, 67; Can Sculpture, Rodin Gallery, Pairs, France, 70. Teaching: Assoc prof sculpture, Concordia Univ, Montreal, 66- Awards: First Prizes, Winnipeg Art Gallery, 59-61; Grand Centennial Award, Montreal Mus Fine Arts, 60; Senior Art Awards, Can Coun, 67, 69 & 73. Mem: Royal Can Acad. Style & Technique: Figurative; cast in Fiberglas reinforced resin from clay or plaster original. Media: Epoxy or Polyester Resin, Automotive Enamels. Dealer: Isaacs Gallery 832 Yonge St Toronto ON Can. Mailing Add: 727 Rue Principale Piedmont PQ J0R 1K0 Can

SMITH, JOSEPH ANTHONY
PAINTER, ILLUSTRATOR
b Bellefonte, Pa, Sept 5, 36. Study: Pa State Univ, with Hobson Pittman, 55-57 & 60; Pratt Inst, BFA. Work: Pa Acad Fine Arts, Philadelphia; Bloomsburg State Col, Pa; Rutgers Univ. Exhib: Pa Acad Fine Arts, 61, 67 & 69; 4th Collectors Choice Exhib, City Mus St Louis, Mo, 62; one-man exhib paintings, drawings & sculpture, Staten Island Inst Arts & Sci, 66; Nat Acad Arts & Lett, New York, 68; Am Drawings: The Last Decade, Katonah Gallery, New York, 71; Bethel Gallery, Conn, 78; plus others. Teaching: Assoc prof fine art, Pratt Inst, 61-; asst prof fine art, Pa State Univ, University Park, summers 69-73. Pos: Design consult, Brooks Bros, 70-75; exhib designer & consult, Staten Island Inst Arts & Sci, 70-75; mem bd dirs, Staten Island Coun Arts, 71-76. Awards: Mary S Litt Award for Watercolor, 100th Ann Am Watercolor Soc, 67; Hon Mention, Pa Acad Fine Arts Bi-Ann Exhib Watercolors, Prints & Drawings, 67; First Prize Juror's Choice, 3rd Ann Arts Festival, Pa State Univ, University Park, 71. Mem: Am Fedn Arts; Soc Illustrators. Style & Technique: Highly detailed renderings of figures, animals, landscapes, etc, which include irrational or dreamlike elements. Media: Pencil, Wax. Publ: Illusr, Sierra Club Survival Songbook, 71; illusr, David Johnson Passed Through Here, 71; illusr, Harper's Mag, New Times, Newsweek & Time Mag. Mailing Add: RFD 4 Rte 39 New Fairfield CT 06810

SMITH, JUSTIN V
COLLECTOR
b Minneapolis, Minn, Oct 25, 03. Study: Princeton Univ, AB, 25. Pos: Mem bd dirs, Walker Art Ctr, Minneapolis. Collection: Painting and sculpture of the 20th century. Mailing Add: 1121 Hennepin Ave Minneapolis MN 55403

SMITH, KEITH A
PHOTOGRAPHER, PRINTMAKER
b Tipton, Ind, May 20, 38. Study: Sch of Art Inst Chicago, BAE, with Aatis Lillstrom, Ken Josephson, Vera Berdich & Sonia Sheridan; Inst Design, Ill Inst Technol, MS(photog), with Aaron Siskind, Arthur Siegel & Misch Kohn. Work: Mus Mod Art, New York; Art Inst of Chicago; Int Mus Photog, George Eastman House, Rochester, NY; Nat Gallery of Can, Ottawa, Ont. Exhib: One-man shows, Art Inst of Chicago, 68, Visual Studies Workshop, 70 & 75, Int Mus of Photog, George Eastman House, 70, Light Gallery, New York, 71, 74 & 76, Lichtropfen, Agen, WGer, 76, Vision Gallery, Boston, 77 & Chicago Ctr for Contemp Photog, 78; two-person show, Mus Mod Art, New York, 74; Teaching: Instr photog, Univ Calif, Los Angeles, 70; instr photog generative systems, Sch of Art Inst Chicago, 71-74; coordr of printmaking, Visula Studies Workshop, Rochester, 74- Awards: Guggenheim Fel in Photog, 72. Media: Photography with Etching; Etching with Photoetching. Publ: Contribr, Vision & Expression, Horizon Press, 68, Time/Life Bks on Photog, 72, Combattimento Per 'Un Immagine, Amici Dell'ane Contemporanea, 73 & Light & Lens, Method of Photography, Morgan & Morgan, 74; auth, When I Was Two, Visual Studies Workshop, 77. Dealer: Light Gallery 728 Fifth Ave New York NY 10019. Mailing Add: c/o Visual Studies Workshop 31 Prince St Rochester NY 14620

SMITH, KENT ALVIN
SCULPTOR
b White Earth Indian Reservation, Minn, Dec 23, 43. Study: Univ Minn, Minneapolis, BA(sculpture), 71, MFA(sculpture), 75, study with Katherine Nash. Work: Fed Reserve Bank, Minneapolis; General Mills, Inc, Minneapolis; Bemidji State Univ, Minn; Univ Galleries, Univ Minn, Minneapolis. Comn: Outdoor sculpture, Portfolio Management Corp, Minneapolis, 75. Exhib: Minn '74, Rochester Art Ctr; Bois Fort Gallery, Ely, Minn, 74 & 75; Ojibwe Exhib, Bemidji State Univ & Minn State Hist Soc, St Paul, 74 & 75; Flatland Sculpture, Drake Univ, Des Moines, Iowa, 75; Drawing Show, Univ Minn, 75. Teaching: Artist in residence, Bemidji State Univ, 74-75, instr contemp Am Indian sculpture & painting, 74- Pos: Res asst, Ceramic Shell, Univ Minn, 68-69; sculpture asst to Katherine Nash, Minneapolis, 68-69; gallery technician, Univ Minn Galleries, 69-73. Bibliog: Gerald Vizenor (auth), The Everlasting Sky, Collier/Macmillan, 70; Brian Anderson (auth), The present: is there Indian art, Minneapolis Tribune, 10/22/72; Don Morrison (auth), Ojibwe art 1974, Minneapolis Star, 6/74. Mem: Col Art Asn; Ojibwe Art Asn. Style & Technique: Constructions and reliefs integrating cubist/constructivist and traditional American Indian art traditions. Media: Cast Metal, Wood. Dealer: Art Lending Gallery 430 Oak Grove Minneapolis MN 55403. Mailing Add: Dept of Art Bemidji State Univ Bemidji MN 56601

SMITH, LAWRENCE BEALL
PAINTER, ILLUSTRATOR
b Washington, DC, Oct 2, 09. Study: Art Inst Chicago, Univ Chicago, PhB, 31; with Ernest Thurn, Gloucester, Mass; also with Charles Hopkinson & Harold Zimmerman, Boston. Work: Fogg Mus, Cambridge, Mass; Sheldon Swope Art Gallery, Terre Haute, Ind; Metrop Mus, New York; Wichita Art Mus, Kans; Norfolk Mus, Va; Univ Chicago; Va Univ Col; Colby Col, Maine; Univ of Mo; Brandeis Univ, New York; Harvard Univ; John Herron Art Inst, Indianapolis; Addison Gallery, Andover, Mass; Libr of Cong, Washington, DC. Comn: Normandy Invasion, Abbott Labs, Washington, DC, 44; Paintings of Mo, Scruggs-Vandervort-Barney, Univ Mo, 46; portraits of Robert Hutchins, Univ Chicago, 52 & Harold Swift, 60 & Charles Merrill, Jr, Boston, 65. Exhib: Carnegie Inst, Pittsburgh, 41; Whitney Mus, New York, 60; Norfolk Mus Drawing Biennial, 67; Nat Acad Design Ann, New York, 74 & 75. Pos: Mem adv bd, Katonah Gallery, NY, 54-75. Awards: Phi Beta Kappa, Univ of Chicago, 31; Cert of Excellence, Am Inst Graphic Arts, 53; Purchase Prize, Norfolk Mus, 67. Bibliog: Harry Salperer (auth), The shorthand caricaturist, Esquire Mag, 42. Style & Technique: Figurative and elements of humor. Media: Painting, Oil; Graphics, Lithography; Sculpture, Stone. Publ: Illusr, Robin Hood, Grossett, 54; illusr, Girls Are Silly by Ogden Nash, Watts, 62; illusr, Tom Jones by Henry Fielding, Bk of Month Club, 64; illusr, Washington Square by Henry James, 71 & Age of Innocence by Edith Wharton, 73, Ltd Ed Club. Dealer: Assoc Am Artists 663 Fifth Ave New York NY 10021. Mailing Add: Rte 121 Cross River NY 10518

SMITH, LAWSON WENTWORTH
SCULPTOR, EDUCATOR
b Havana, Cuba, Apr 20, 47; US citizen. Study: Okla State Univ, BFA, 70; Univ Nebr, MFA, 74. Work: Sioux City Art Mus, Iowa; Ctr for Visual Arts Gallery, Ill State Univ, Bloomington & Normal; Ball State Univ Art Gallery, Muncie, Ind. Exhib: Potsdam Nat Drawing Exhib, NY, 73; Friends of Contemp Arts Exhib, Denver, Colo, 73; Nebr Artists, 73 & Midwest Biennial, 74, Joslyn Mus, Omaha; Ctr for Visual Arts Sculpture Exhib, Ill State Univ, 75; Great Plains Sculpture Exhib, Sheldon Art Mus, Lincoln, nebr, 75; Eight State Exhib, Okla Art Ctr, 76; Davidson Nat Print & Drawing Exhib, Middletown, Conn, 76; Ball State Univ Nat Exhib, 76; Cooperstown Art Asn Nat Exhib, NY, 77; one-man shows, Contemp Arts Found, Oklahoma City, 71, Henri Gallery, Washington, DC, 76 & 77 & McClung Mus, Univ Tenn, Knoxville, 78. Teaching: Instr sculpture, Wichita State Univ, Kans, 74-75; asst prof studio art, Syracuse Univ, NY, 76- Awards: Sculpture Awards, 35th Ann Exhib, Sioux City Art Ctr, Iowa, 73 & Art Inc Ann Exhib, Great Bend, Kans, 76; Purchase Award, Ball State Univ, Muncie, Ind, 76. Style & Technique: Assemblage with found and handmade objects. Media: Wood, Silk. Dealer. Henri Gallery 21st & P St NW Washington DC 20036. Mailing Add: 111 Euclid Dr Fayetteville NY 13066

SMITH, LEON POLK
PAINTER, SCULPTOR
b Chickasha, Okla, May 20, 06. Study: ECent State Col, BA, 34; Columbia Univ, MA, 38. Work: Guggenheim Mus; Metrop Mus Art; Mus Mod Art; Mus Bellas Artes, Caracas; Cleveland Mus. Exhib: Construction Geometry in Painting, New York, 60; one-man shows, Mus Bellas Artes, 62 & Galeria Muller, Stuttgart, Ger, 64; New Shapes of Color, Stedelijk Mus, Amsterdam, 66; retrospect, San Francisco Mus & Rose Mus, 68; Paris-New York, Musée Nat d'Art Mod, Georges Pompidou (Beaubourg), Paris, France. Teaching: Lectr, Brandeis Univ, 68; resident artist, Univ Calif, Davis, 72. Awards: Grants, Longview Found, 56, Nat Coun Arts, 67 & Tamarind, 68; plus others. Dealer: Denise Rene Galeries, New York, Paris & Dusseldorf. Mailing Add: Box 386 Shoreham NY 11786

SMITH, LYN WALL
ART WRITER, PAINTER
b Cadott, Wis, Aug 25, 09. Study: Univ Minn, BS; Utah Art Ctr. Exhib: Nat Orange Show, San Bernardino, Calif, 74; Santa Paula Ann, Calif, 74-77; Women Painters of the West, Calif State Polytechnic Univ, Pomona, 76 & Brand Art Ctr, Glendale, Calif, 77; Pasadena Festival of the Arts, Calif, 77. Bibliog: Herm Boodman (auth), Page one: stage & screen, Radio Sta KNOB, Santa Ana, Calif, 5/77; Robert Cahn (auth), Reference, Libr J, 2/1/78. Mem: Los Angeles Art Asn; Women Painters of the West (bd mem, 77 & 78); Burbank Art Asn (ed, 73-76; pres, 76-78). Style & Technique: All subjects in oil, watercolor, modern innovative application with a brayer. Media: Acrylic used as Watercolor on Aqueous Paper. Publ: Co-auth, Dictionary of Art & Artists in Southern California Before 1930, Dustin Publ, Los Angeles, 75; co-auth, Index to Reproductions of American Paintings, Scarecrow Press, NJ, 77. Dealer: Joseph Moure Galleries 935 Mountain St Glendale CA 92102. Mailing Add: 11336 Camarillo St North Hollywood CA 91602

SMITH, MOISHE
PRINTMAKER
b Chicago, Ill, Jan 10, 29. Study: New Sch Social Res, BA, 50; Univ Iowa, with Lasansky, MFA, 53; Skowhegan Sch Painting & Sculpture; Acad Florence; also with Giorgio Morandi. Work: Mus Boymans, Beuningen, Rotterdam; Kestner Mus, Hannover; Galleria Degli Uffizi, Florence; Metrop Mus Art, New York; Nat Gallery Art, Washington, DC. Exhib: Sao Paulo Int, Brazil, 55; Print Coun Am Traveling Exhib, 59 & 62; Int Prints, Cincinnati Mus, Ohio, 62; Salon de Mai, Paris, 65; Libr Cong, 69, 71 & 73. Teaching: Vis artist printmaking, Univ Wis, 66-67; vis artist printmaking, Ohio State Univ, spring 71; vis artist, Univ Iowa, autumn 71; assoc prof, Univ Wis-Parkside, 72-77; prof, Utah State Univ, Logan, 77- Awards: Four Seasons Res Grant, Southern Ill Univ, 57; Fulbright Fel, 59-61; Guggenheim Found Fel, 67. Mem: Boston Printmakers; Print Club; Nat Acad of Design; Soc Am Graphic Artists. Style & Technique: Realistic. Media: Intaglio. Mailing Add: Dept of Art Utah State Univ Logan UT 84322

SMITH, OLIVER
PAINTER
b Lynn, Mass, Oct 1, 96. Study: RI Sch Design; and with Charles Hawthorn, Provincetown, Mass. Work: Univ Fla, Gainesville; Remington Rand Corp. Comn: Stained glass, Princeton Univ Chapel, Temple Emanu-El, New York, Wittenberg Univ, Springfield, Ohio, Mellon Cathedral, Pittsburgh, Pa & Nazareth Hosp Chapel, Philadelphia. Exhib: Am Watercolor Soc; Audubon Artists; Philadelphia Watercolor Club; Smithsonian Inst, Washington, DC; Rockport Art Asn, Mass. Awards: Gulf Coast Art Ctr Award; Rockport Art Asn Award; St Petersburg Art Club Award, Fla. Mem: Salmagundi Club; Rockport Art Asn; St Petersburg Art Club; Clearwater Art Asn; Gulf Coast Art Ctr. Media: Watercolor. Res: Stained glass windows; glass blowing by hand. Mailing Add: 223 Shore Dr Ozona FL 33560

SMITH, PAUL J
MUSEUM DIRECTOR
b Sept 8, 31. Study: Art Inst Buffalo; Sch for Am Craftsmen. Collections Arranged: Both nat & int collections assembled. Teaching: Mem of bd of visitors, Sch of Artisanry, Boston Univ, Mass. Pos: Vpres, Louis Comfort Tiffany Found; mem bd trustees, Haystack Mountain Sch

Crafts, Deer Isle, Maine; adv int dept, Am Crafts Coun; mem bd, Opportunity Resources of Arts, Inc; dir, Mus Contemp Crafts, currently. Mailing Add: Mus of Contemp Crafts 29 W 53rd St New York NY 10019

SMITH, PAUL ROLAND
PAINTER, EDUCATOR
b Colony, Kans, Sept 12, 16. Study: Pittsburg State Col, BS; Univ Iowa, MFA. Work: Des Moines Art Ctr, Iowa; Wright Mus, Beloit, Wis; Univ Iowa, Iowa City; Sioux City Art Ctr, Iowa; St Cloud Mus, St Cloud State Col, Minn. Exhib: One-man shows, Assoc Am Artists Gallery, New York, 54 & Krasner Gallery, New York, 73, 74, 75, 76 & 77. Teaching: Prof painting & drawing, Univ Northern Iowa, 51-65; prof painting & drawing & chmn dept art, Hamline Univ, 65-75. Pos: Mem bd dirs, Minn Mus Art, 71- Awards: First Awards, Des Moines Art Ctr, 57, Minn Centennial State Fair, 58 & Sioux City Art Ctr, 59. Mem: Artists Equity Asn (pres, 64-67); Midwest Col Art Asn (prog dir, 69); Col Art Asn Am; Walker Art Ctr; Minn State Arts Coun (chmn visual arts, 71-). Style & Technique: Figurative. Media: Oil and Watercolor on Canvas and Paper. Publ: Auth, Adult Nursery Rhymes, Waverly Publ, 72. Mailing Add: Box 352 Nisswa MN 56468

SMITH, R HARMER
PAINTER, ETCHER
b Jersey City, NJ, July 27, 06. Study: Sch Fine & Appl Art, Pratt Inst, cert archit; Sch Fine Arts, Yale Univ, BFA; Art Students League. Work: USN Art Collection, Washington, DC; Jersey City Pub Libr; Staten Island Inst of Arts & Sci Mus; Old Bergen Church, Jersey City; Madison Pub Libr, NJ. Exhib: Am Watercolor Soc; Archit League; Jersey City Mus Asn; Madison Pub Libr, NJ. Awards: Trustees' Prize for Upstream, Jersey City Mus Asn, 53; Jersey J Medal for Snug Berth, 61; Patrons' Prize for From the Bridge, Hudson Artists, 67. Bibliog: Fred H Scherff (auth), R Harmer Smith, Pencil Points, 10/37. Mem: Jersey City Mus Asn (gov); hon mem Hudson Artists; NJ Watercolor Soc; Salmagundi Club. Style & Technique: Direct expression. Media: Watercolor. Publ: Auth & illusr, Pencil sketches by R Harmer Smith, Pencil Points, 7/31; contribr, reproductions in, Pencil Points & Am Artist, 30-40. Mailing Add: 44 Hamilton St Madison NJ 07940

SMITH, RALPH ALEXANDER
WRITER, EDUCATOR
b Ellwood City, Pa, June 12, 29. Study: Columbia Univ, AB, Teachers Col, MA & EdD. Teaching: Instr art hist & art educ, Kent State Univ, 59-61; asst prof art hist & art educ & chmn dept art, Wis State Univ-Oshkosh, 61-63; asst prof art hist & art educ, State Univ NY Col New Paltz, 63-64; asst prof aesthet educ, Univ Ill, Urbana, 64-67, assoc prof, 67-71, prof, 71- Awards: First Barkan Mem Award. Mem: Am Soc Aesthet; Philos Educ Soc; Nat Art Educ Asn; Inst Study Art in Educ; World Future Soc. Res: Theoretical foundations of aesthetic and humanistic education. Publ: Ed, Aesthetics and criticism in art education, Rand, 66, auth, Aesthetic education: a role for the humanities program, Teachers Col Rec, 1/68; ed, Aesthetic concepts and education, 70 & Aesthetics and problems of education, 71, Univ Ill Press; Regaining Educational Leadership, Wiley, 75. Mailing Add: 228B Educ Univ of Ill Urbana IL 61801

SMITH, RAY WINFIELD
COLLECTOR, ART HISTORIAN
b Marlboro, NH, June 4, 97. Pos: Ed consult, J Glass Studies; chmn, Int Comt Ancient Glass. Res: Technological research with Brookhaven National Laboratory on ancient glass. Collection: Ancient glass; medieval furniture, rugs and paintings. Publ: Auth, Glass from the ancient world, 57; many radio & TV interviews; TV prog, Nefertiti & the Computer, BBC, 3/20/71. Mailing Add: 3710 Lake St Houston TX 77006

SMITH, ROBERT ALAN
PAINTER, INSTRUCTOR
b Pasadena, Calif. Study: Chouinard Art Inst, Los Angeles, 46; Inst Allende, San Miguel de Allende, Mex, 48; painting with David Alfaro Siqueiros, Mex; Chouinard Art Inst, 53. Work: Libr of Cong, Washington, DC; Nat Collection, Smithsonian Inst, Washington, DC; Metrop Mus Art, New York; Philadelphia Mus, Pa; Pasadena Art Mus, Calif. Exhib: Ann Print Exhib, Libr of Cong, 59 & 60; 50 American Printmakers, De Cordova Mus, Mass, 61; Santa Barbara Mus Art, Calif, 64; American Art Today, New York World's Fair, 65; White House, Washington, DC, 67. Teaching: Instr painting, Calif Inst Arts, Los Angeles, 65; instr, Ventura Col, 65- Awards: Purchase Awards, Libr of Cong, 60 & Pasadena Art Mus, 62; James D Phelan Award for Calif Painters, 61. Bibliog: Langsner (auth), Art news from Los Angeles, Art News Mag, 2/59 & 2/60 & Los Angeles letter, Art Int, 3/62; Seldis (auth), Art, Los Angeles Times, 10/61. Mem: Western Serigraph Inst. Interest: Paintings of the Holy Spirit. Publ: Contribr, Western Serigraph Inst Bull, 61 & Ventura Fine Arts Mag, 62; illusr, Long Ago Elf, 68 & Crocodiles Have Big Teeth All Day, 70, Follett. Mailing Add: PO Box 6351 Ventura CA 93003

SMITH, ROBERT LEWIS
MUSEUM DIRECTOR, EDUCATOR
b Salem, Ohio, Aug 5, 40. Study: Univ Southern Calif; Univ Calif, Los Angeles, BA, 63, MFA, 66. Exhibitions Arranged: Three Photographers—Bullock, Sommer, Teske, 68; Three Photographers—Curran, Heinecken, Parker, 69; California Ceramics, 70; P Lodato, 70; Sand Work—Schroeder, Zehr, 71; Jud Fine, 72; Anderson, L Dill, Card, Lodato, 73. Teaching: Assoc prof exhib & design, Calif State Univ, Northridge, 66- Pos: Gallery dir, Calif State Univ, Northridge, 66-70; gallery dir, Brand Lib Art Ctr, Glendale, Calif, 70-73; dir/founder, Los Angeles Inst Contemp Art, 74- Bibliog: Michael Auping (auth), Interview with Bob Smith, La Mamelle, Berkeley, Calif, 75. Publ: Auth & designer numerous exhib catalogs. Mailing Add: 2020 S Robertson Blvd Los Angeles CA 90034

SMITH, ROSS RANSOM WILLIAMS
ART DEALER, COLLECTOR
b Baltimore, Md, Dec 6, 41. Study: Columbia Univ; Univ Copenhagen, MA(philos). Pos: Regional mgr, Ferdinand Roten Galleries, 76-77; dir, Platemark Press, 77- Mem: Southern Graphics Coun. Specialty: Contemporary American graphics, specializing in artists working in the Southeastern United States. Collection: Durer, Rembrandt and contemporary fantastic realism. Mailing Add: 213 Elizabeth St Atlanta GA 30307

SMITH, SAM
PAINTER, EDUCATOR
b Thorndale, Tex, Feb 11, 18. Study: With Randall Davey, Jack Levine, Ben Turner & Carl von Hassler. Work: War Dept Hist Properties Sect; Santa Fe Mus; Univ NMex; NMex State Fair Collection; Panhandle Mus Fine Art. Comn: Mural, Camp Barkley, Tex, War Dept, 42; paintings, Infantry Weapons, Camp Barkley, 42. Exhib: One-man show, Corcoran Gallery Art, Washington, DC, 48; Santa Fe Mus Fine Art, NMex, 49; Botts Mus Art, Albuquerque, NMex, 64; Panhandle-Plains Hist Mus, Canyon, Tex, 64; Roswell Mus Art, NMex, 65. Teaching: Prof art, Univ NMex, 56- Awards: Questa, NMex Purchase Prize, 62 & First Prize for Watercolor, 62, NMex State Fair; First Prize for Watercolor, Ouray Alpine Show, Colo, 64. Bibliog: Robert Ruark (auth), Sam Smith, artist, Assoc Press, 48. Mem: Life mem NMex Art League; Artists Equity Asn (pres). Media: Watercolor, Oil. Dealer: Gallery del Sol Old Town Rd Albuquerque NM 87104. Mailing Add: 213 Utah NE Albuquerque NM 87108

SMITH, SHERRY
WEAVER, EDUCATOR
b Chicago, Ill, Mar 21, 43. Study: Stanford Univ, Calif, BA, 65; Cranbrook Acad Art, Bloomfield Hills, Mich, MFA, 67. Work: Art Inst Chicago; Hackley Art Mus, Muskegon, Mich, Am Tel & Tel Co; Borg Warner Corp; Colorado Springs Fine Arts Ctr, Colo. Comn: Wall hangings, Detroit Plaza Hotel, 77, Fed Bldg, Ann Arbor, 78 & Du Page Co Hosp, Ill, 78. Exhib: Mus Mod Art, New York, 69; Biennale of Tapestry, Lausanne, Switz, 71-77; Denver Art Mus, Colo, 72; Three-Dimensional Fibers, Govett-Brewster Art Gallery, New Plymouth, NZ, 74; Am Crafts 76, Mus Contemp Art, Chicago, 76; Fiberworks, Cleveland Mus Art, Ohio, 77; one-person show, Hadler Gallery, New York, 78. Teaching: Instr weaving & textile design, Colo State Univ, Ft Collins, 71-75; asst prof weaving & textile design, Univ Mich, Ann Arbor, 75- Bibliog: Larson & Constantine, Beyond Crafts, The Art Fabric, Van Nostrand, 75; Kuenzi (auth), La nouvelle tapisserie, Bonvent, 75; Waller (auth), Textile sculptures, Studio Vista, 77. Style & Technique: Weave and work with hand-plaited webbing. Dealer: Jacques Baruch Gallery 900 N Michigan Ave Chicago IL 60611; Hadler Galleries 35 E 20th St New York NY 10003. Mailing Add: 1733 Jackson Ave Ann Arbor MI 48103

SMITH, SHIRLANN
PAINTER
b Wichita, Kans. Study: Kans State Univ, BFA; Provincetown Workshop Art Sch, Mass; Art Students League. Work: Whitney Mus Am Art, New York; Berkeley Univ Art Mus; Aldrich Mus Contemp Art, Ridgefield, Conn; Phoenix Art Mus, Ariz; Everson Mus, Syracuse, NY; Chase Manhattan Bank, New York. Exhib: American Painting 1970, Va Mus, Richmond; Lyrical Abstraction, Aldrich Mus Contemp Art, 70; Recent Acquisitions & Lyrical Abstraction, Whitney Mus Am Art, New York, 71; New Accessions USA, Colorado Springs Fine Art Ctr, 72; From the Museum Collection Art by Women, Berkeley Univ Art Mus, 73; Abstract Works from Collection, Ulrich Mus, Wichita, Kans, 75; Auditorium Installation Exhib, Everson Mus, Syracuse, NY, 76-77. Awards: Grumbacher Artists Mat Co Award for Mixed Media, New Eng Exhib, Silvermine, 67. Bibliog: Lawrence Campbell (auth), photo rev in, Art News, 2/73; April Kingsley (auth), photo rev in, Art Int, 3/73. Mailing Add: 141 Wooster St New York NY 10012

SMITH, SUSAN CARLTON
ILLUSTRATOR, PAINTER
b Athens, Ga, June 30, 23. Study: Self-taught; Univ Ga, Athens, BS(zool), MFA(drama); Univ Va & Univ Ga, grad work in zoo & botany. Work: Ga Mus Art & Univ Ga, Athens; Duke Univ Mus Art; Trent Collection, Duke Univ Med Ctr Libr, Durham; Health Affairs Libr, Univ NC. Comn: Watercolor portrait of Venus Flytrap wildflower, Hunt Botanical Libr, Carnegie-Mellon Univ, Pittsburgh, Pa; ser of native Va wildflowers in watercolor, Univ Va Biological Sta, Mountain Lake; watercolor portraits of wildflowers poisonous to animals, comn by veterinarian, Sch Med, Univ Ga, Athens; Phallus impudicans (watercolor of mushroom), Duke Univ Mus Art, Durham, NC; original hand puppets, comn by Ga State Dept of Educ. Exhib: Southeastern Art Exhib, Atlanta Mus Art, Ga, 51; Nature Sculptures & Watercolors, Carnegie Libr, Atlanta, 52-53; Watercolor Miniatures, Brooklyn Pub Libr, NY, 53; Ga Mus Art, Univ Ga, Athens, 58-67; Nature Sculptures & Watercolor Miniatures, Ga Mus Art, 58-67; 2nd Int Exhib of 20th Century Botanical Art & Illus, Hunt Botanical Libr, 68-69; NC Wildlife Artists Show, State Mus Natural Hist, Raleigh, 69; Plants in Art, 500 Yrs of Botanical Art (traveling exhib), Hunt Inst for Botanical Doc, Carnegie-Mellon Univ, 69; 11th Int Botanical Cong Botanical Art Exhib, Seattle, Wash, 69; Nature Interpretations: Watercolors & Sculptures, Duke Univ Mus Art, 71-; Int Exhib of Botanical Art, Johannesburgh, SAfrica, 73; Boston Mus Sci, Mass, 74; NC Botanical Garden, 76; Int Mycological Cong, Fla, 77; Traveling Exhib of NC Artists, 78; Arch, Raleigh, NC, 75, Callaway Gardens, Pine Mount, Ga, 76 & Univ Ga Botanical Gardens, Athens, 77. Pos: Sci illusr, US Pub Health Communicable Disease Ctr, Atlanta, 51-52; free lance biological illusr, Athens, Ga & Durham, NC, 53-; illusr, Archaeol Dept, Univ Ga, Athens, 53-54, costumer, speech & drama dept, 55-65, bilogical illusr, Sci Ctr, 64-66; asst cur, Trent Collection, Med Ctr Libr, Duke Univ, 67-; free lance botanical illusr, Dept of Botany, Duke Univ & Univ NC, Chapel Hill, 67- Awards: Best Children's Bk Illus for Ladybug, Ladybug, Am Inst Graphic Arts, 69; Printing Indust of Am Award for Illus for Hey Bug! & Other Poems About Little Things, 72. Bibliog: Lucile McMasters (auth), Art in nature, Atlanta J-Constitution Mag, 50; Meg McGriff (auth), Watercolors & nature sculptures, Athens Banner Herald, 77; Ann Commire (auth), Susan Carlton Smith, something about the author, Gale Res Co, Vol 12, 77. Style & Technique: Imaginative watercolor nature studies in exact one-to-one scale or in miniature formats; sculptures from natural objects; pen & ink drawings. Media: Watercolor; Natural Materials. Publ: Illusr, Plant Variation & Classification, Wadsworth, 67; illusr, Wildflowers of North Carolina, Univ NC Press, 68; illusr & contribr, Ladybug, Ladybug, 69 & illusr, Hey Bug! & Other Poems About Little Things, 72, Am Heritage Press, New York; illusr, A Child's Book of Flowers, Doubleday Publ Co, 76. Dealer: Paul R Reynolds 12 E 41st St New York NY 10017. Mailing Add: Duke Univ Med Ctr Libr Durham NC 27710

SMITH, THELMA DEGOEDE
PAINTER, TEACHER
b Los Angeles, Calif, May 5, 15. Study: Calif State Univ, Los Angeles, BA(with hons); Calif State Univ, Fullerton, MA. Work: Long Beach Mus Art, Calif; Downey Mus Art, Calif; Ill State Univ; Nat Orange Show Hq, San Bernardino, Calif; Hunt Foods Inc Collection, Fullerton. Exhib: All Calif Purchase Prize Exhib, Laguna Beach Mus Art, 69-71; Calif Hawaii Regional, San Diego Mus Art Fine Arts Gallery, 71, 72 & 74; one-woman show, Loma Linda Univ, 71 & Palos Verdes Mus Art, 74; All Calif Exhib, Palos Verdes Mus Art, 73-74; American Painters in Paris, New Conv Ctr, 76. Teaching: Instr oil painting, N Orange Co Community Col Dist, Fullerton, 67- Awards: Best of Show, First Award & Purchase Prize, 13th Ann Art Unlimited, Downey Mus Art, 70; Purchase Award, 16th All Calif Competition, Laguna Beach Mus Art, 70; First Purchase Prize, Nat Orange Show, San Bernardino, 71 & 74. Bibliog: TV interview & presentation of paintings, Channel 10, Brea, Calif, 73. Mem: Los Angeles Art Asn; Orange Co Art Asn (dir, 70-75); Laguna Beach Art Asn. Style & Technique: Minimal geometric airbrush paintings utilizing an illusion of luminosity. Media: Acrylic. Mailing Add: 2916 Hillcrest Ave Orange CA 92667

SMITH, TONY
SCULPTOR
b South Orange, NJ, 1912. Study: Art Students League, 34-35; New Bauhaus, Chicago, archit study, 37-38; archit apprentice of Frank Lloyd Wright, 38-40. Work: Mus Mod Art, New York; Corcoran Gallery Art, Washington, DC; Wadsworth Atheneum, Hartford, Conn; NJ State Mus, Trenton; Detroit Inst Art, Mich. Exhib: Wadsworth Atheneum, Hartford, Conn,

64, 67 & 74; Jewish Mus, New York, 67; Philadelphia Inst Contemp Art, 67; Documenta, Kassel, WGer, 68; one-man shows, Univ Hawaii, Honolulu, 69, Newark Mus, NJ, 70, Montclair Art Mus, NJ, 70, Princeton Univ Art Mus, 70, NJ State Mus, 71, Mus Mod Art, 72 & Univ Md, 74; Whitney Mus Am Art Ann, 70-73; Contemp Arts Ctr, Cincinnati, 70; Univ Nebr, 70; Metrop Mus Art, New York, 70; Expo 70, Osaka, Japan; 11th Int Biennial Outdoor Sculpture Exhib, Antwerp, Belg, 71; Nat Welfare Rights Benefit Show, Washington, DC, 71; Los Angeles Co Mus Art, Los Angeles, 71; San Francisco Mus Art, 71; Seattle Art Mus Pavilion, Wash, 73; Cleveland Mus Art, 74; Painting & Sculpture Today 1974, Indianapolis Mus Art, Ind & Contemp Arts Ctr, Cincinnati, 74; Art Inst Chicago, 74; Walker Art Ctr, Minneapolis, 74; New Orleans Mus Art, La, 76; Meadow Brook Art Gallery, Oakland Univ, Rochester, Mich, 77; plus others. Mailing Add: c/o Fourcade Droll Inc 36 E 75th St New York NY 10021

SMITH, VICTOR JOACHIM
PAINTER, EDUCATOR
b Grand Island, Nebr, Apr 3, 29. Study: Chouinard Art Inst, Los Angeles; Calif State Univ, Long Beach, BA, MA. Work: San Francisco Mus Art, Calif; Long Beach Mus Art; Newport Harbor Art Mus, Newport Beach, Calif; Laguna Beach Mus Art, Calif; La Jolla Mus Contemp Art, Calif; plus others. Exhib: Gutai Int Festival of Art, Osaka, Japan, 60; Mus Mod Art, Turin, Italy, 62; Morphologie Autre (traveling exhib), France, Italy, Ger & Spain, 62-63; Mus-Manifeste (traveling exhib), Austria, WGer & Italy, 64-65; Galleria d'Arte Cortina, Milan, Italy, 69; one-man shows, Long Beach Mus Art, 60, Santa Barbara Mus Art, Calif, 62, Pasadena Art Mus, Calif, 63, Los Angeles Munic Art Gallery, 68, Los Angeles Co Mus Art, Los Angeles, 72 & Newport Harbor Art Mus, 75; plus others. Teaching: Prof drawing & painting, Calif State Univ, Fullerton, 62- Pos: Chmn art dept, Calif State Univ, 76-77, vchmn art dept, 77- Awards: Over fifty awards for painting in Calif. Bibliog: Michele Tapie (auth), Morphologie autre, Int Inst of Aesthetic Res, Turin, 60; article in Artforum, Vol 1 (1962); Allan S Weller (auth), Contemporary American painting & sculpture, Univ Ill Press, 67. Style & Technique: Abstract, symbolic landscape. Media: Mixed-Media. Publ: Auth, Morris Graves, 63 & The Pacific Coast invitational, 63, Artforum. Mailing Add: Dept of Art Calif State Univ Fullerton CA 92634

SMITH, VINCENT D
PAINTER
b Brooklyn, NY, Dec 12, 29. Study: Art Students League New York with Reginald Marsh, 53; Brooklyn Mus, NY, 54-56; Skowhegan Sch Painting & Sculpture, Maine, studied with Sidney Simon & Ben Shann, 55; Bub Blackburn Printmaking Workshop, New York, with Krisna Reddy & Bob Cale, 71. Work: Mus Mod Art, New York; Columbus Gallery Fine Art, Ohio; Newark Mus Asn, NJ; Brooklyn Mus, NY; Univ Va Art Mus, Charlottesville. Comn: Four Murals on Canvas, Boys & Girls High Sch, Brooklyn Bd Educ, New York, 76. Exhib: Fifteen Under Forty, Hall of Springs, Mus, Saratoga, NY, 70; Afro-Am Artist New York & Boston, Boston, Mass, 70; Contemp Black Am Artist, Whitney Mus Am Art, New York; Ill Bell Tel Travel Show, Chicago, 71-72; Freedom Ways, Hudson River Mus, Yonkers, NY, 71; Two Generations, Newark Mus, NJ, 71; People & Places, Whitney Mus Downtown, New York, 74; 4th Ann Black Esthetics Exhib, Mus of Sci & Indust, Chicago, 74; 150th Ann Exhib, Nat Acad Design, New York, 75; one-man shows, Paa Ya Paa Gallery, Nairobi, Kenya, 73, Chemchemi Creative Arts Ctr, Arusha, Tanzonia, 73, Kibo Art Gallery, Mt Kilimanjaro, Tanzonia, 73, Reading Pub Mus, Pa, 74, Portland Art Mus, Maine, 74 & Erie Art Ctr, Pa, 77. Teaching: Instr painting & printmaking, Whitney Mus Am Art, New York, 67-76. Awards: Nat Endowment Arts Travel Grant, 73; Childe Hassam Fund Purchase Award, Am Acad Arts & Letters, 73-74; Thomas B Clarke Award, 149th Ann Exhib, Nat Acad Design, 74. Bibliog: Dorathy Gloster (auth), Art in the Black American Community, African Progress Mag, 72; John Canady (auth), Vincent Smith: expressive style, NY Times, 73; Mel Taple (auth), Painters images like ringside at creation, Amsterdam News, New York, 73. Style & Technique: African American expressionistic style with oil painting sand; African masks, ritual figures and landscape with Black experience motif. Media: Painting and Printmaking. Publ: Contribr, J Edward Atkinson, ed, Black Dimensions in Contemporary American Art, New Amsterdam Libr, 71; contribr, Romare Bearden & Harry Henderson, co-auth, Six Black Masters, Doubleday, 72; contribr, Atticia Book, Custom Commun Systs, 73; contribr, Theresa Cederholm, auth, Afro-American Artists: A Bio-Bibliographical Directory, Boston Pub Libr, 73; illusr, Folklore Stories from Africa, Garrard Publ, 75. Mailing Add: 264 E Broadway New York NY 10002

SMITH, WILLIAM ARTHUR
PAINTER, PRINTMAKER
b Toledo, Ohio, Apr 19, 18. Study: Keane's Art Sch, Toledo; Art Students League; Grand Cent Art Sch, New York; Ecole Beaux Arts, Paris; Acad Grande Chaumiere, Paris; Univ Toledo, MA. Work: Metrop Mus Art, New York; Los Angeles Co Mus, Calif; Libr Cong, Washington, DC; Nat Acad Design, New York. Comn: Mural of hist Md, State of Md, Md House, Aberdeen, 68; design of ten postage stamps, US Postal Serv. Exhib: Contemp Arts US, Los Angeles, 56; 200 Yrs Watercolor Painting Am, Metrop Mus Art, 66-67; 27 one-man exhibs, major cities Europe, Asia & US. Teaching: Lectr, var univs & art schs, Europe, Asia & US. Awards: Nat Acad Design Awards, 49 & 51; Nat Acad Design Prize for Oil Painting, Adolf & Clara Obrig, 51; Two Grand Prizes & Gold Medals, Am Watercolor Soc, 56 & 65. Mem: Nat Acad Design (mem coun & rec secy, 54-55, mem coun, 76-); Am Watercolor Soc (pres, 56-57, hon pres, 57-); Int Asn Art (exec comt, 63-69, vpres, 66-69, pres, US Comt, 70-, int pres, 73-76 & hon pres for life, 76-); Audubon Artists; Nat Soc Mural Painters. Style & Technique: Figurative. Media: Oil, Watercolor; Lithography, Intaglio. Publ: Auth & illusr, Art behind the iron curtain, 2/60 & Changing art of the Orient, 8/65, Harpers Bazaar; auth, Ben Shahn, In: Ben Shahn, Osaka Shiritsu Bijutsukan-Mainichi Shimbun, Japan, 70. Mailing Add: Windy Bush Rd Pineville PA 18946

SMITHER, EDWARD MURRAY
ART DEALER
b Huntsville, Tex, July 23, 37. Study: Sam Houston State Univ, BS, 58; Dallas Mus Fine Arts Sch, drawing; Dallas Mus Contemp Art, with Douglas MacAgy. Pos: Asst dir, Atelier Chapman Kelley, Dallas, 64-70; dir, Cranfill Gallery, Dallas, 70-72; owner & dir, Smither Gallery, Dallas, 72-74 & Delahunty Inc Gallery, Dallas, 74-75. Mem: Dallas Mus Fine Arts; Ft Worth Art Mus. Specialty: Contemporary painting, graphics and sculpture by artists living in Texas and Southwest. Publ: Co-auth, George White, 74. Mailing Add: 2611 Cedar Springs Dallas TX 75201

SMITH-GORDON, NANNETTE
ART DEALER
b England, July 17, 34. Pos: Dir, Apollo Print Shop, Brooklyn Heights, NY, 68-70; asst dir, Horizon Gallery, New York, 70-74; dir, Landmark Gallery, New York, 75- Specialty: Abstract-expressionists. Mailing Add: c/o Landmark Gallery 469 Broome St New York NY 10013

SMONGESKI, JOSEPH LEON
PAINTER, DESIGNER
b Two Rivers, Wis, Feb 6, 14. Study: Art Inst Chicago; Univ Chicago; Univ Wis-Madison. Work: St Ann's, Wollaston, Mass; Boston Mus Fine Arts; Thomas Mann Publ Libr, Two Rivers; Copley Soc, Boston; Chicago Art Inst. Exhib: Art Inst Chicago, 39; Layton Art Ctr, Milwaukee, 39; Copley Soc Boston, Boston Mus Fine Arts, 58 & 71-75; Parrish Mus, Long Island, NY, 64; S Shore Art Ctr, Cohasset, Mass, 64, 65 & 66. Teaching: Instr painting, S Shore Art Ctr; instr painting, Milton Adult Educ Ctr, Mass. Pos: Color consult, Western Publ Co, New York, 41-46; designer, D C Heath & Co, Boston, 46-65; art dir, D C Heath & Raytheon, Lexington, Mass, 65- Awards: New Eng Book Show Award, Bookbuilders of Boston, 73. Bibliog: Articles in Quincy Patriot Ledger, 74, Boston Globe, 74-75. Mem: Copley Soc of Boston (jury comt); Milton Art Asn (jury comt); Bookbuilders of Boston. Style & Technique: Figurative painting based on color structure of Paul Cezanne. Media: Watercolor, Oil. Dealer: Farr Gallery 22 E 80th St New York NY 10021. Mailing Add: 42 Brook Wollaston MA 02170 Quincy MA 42 Brook Wollaston MA 02170

SMYTH, CRAIG HUGH
ART ADMINISTRATOR, ART HISTORIAN
b New York, NY, July 28, 15. Teaching: Lectr, Frick Collection, New York, 46-50; from asst prof to prof, Inst Fine Arts, NY Univ, 50-, actg dir & actg head dept fine arts, 51-53, dir & head grad dept fine arts, 53-; prof fine arts, Harvard Univ, 73- Pos: Res asst & sr mus aide, Nat Gallery Art, Washington, DC, 41-42; dir, Harvard Univ Ctr for Ital Renaissance Studies, Florence, 73- Mem: Col Art Asn Am (dir, 53-57, secy, 56); Comite Int Hist Art (alt US mem, 70-); US Nat Comt Hist Art; Metrop Mus Art (hon trustee, 68-). Res: 16th century Italian painting and drawing; 16th century Italian architecture. Publ: Auth, Mannerism & Maniera, 63; auth, Sunken courts of the Villa Giula & the Villa Imperiale, In: Essays in Memory of Karl Lehmann, 63; co-auth, Michelangelo & St Peter's—I: the attic as originally built on the south hemicycle, Burlington Mag, 69; auth, Bronzino as draughtsman, 71; co-auth, Michelangelo & St Peter's—II: Observations on the interior of the Apses, a model of the Apse vault, and related drawings, Römisches Jahrbuch Für Kunstgeschichte, 75. Mailing Add: Villa I Tatti Via di Vincigliata 26 Florence Italy

SMYTH, DAVID RICHARD
SCULPTOR
b Washington, DC, Dec 2, 43. Study: Corcoran Sch Art, Washington, DC, 62-64; Art Inst Chicago, BFA, 67, MFA, 69. Work: Whitney Mus Am Art, New York; also in collections of James Speyers, Art Inst Chicago; Whitney Halsted, Chicago & Ronald Feldman, New York. Comn: Relief painting, Blue Cross-Blue Shield, C F Murphy Archit, Chicago, 69. Exhib: Allan Franklin Gallery, Chicago & New York, 68 & 70; Painting & Sculpture Biennial, Art Inst of Chicago, 69, Alumni Painting & Sculpture, Sch, 77 & Drawings of the Seventies, 77; Contemp Am Painting & Sculpture, Univ Ill, Urbana, 69; Inst Contemp Art, Univ Pa, 70; Whitney Mus Am Art, New York, 72; Ronald Feldman Fine Arts, Inc, New York, 72; Mus of Contemp Art, Chicago, 72; Prints, Brooklyn Mus, 74; one-man exhibs, Whitney Mus, New York, 72 & Berry Col, Mt Berry, Ga, 75; plus numerous other group and one-man exhibs. Awards: George D Brown Traveling Fel, Art Inst Chicago, 69 & Richard Rice Jenkins Award, 70; Tamarind Inst Fel, Albuquerque, NMex, 72. Bibliog: Articles & reviews in Art News, 70, 74, 11/75 & 4/76, Arts Mag, 2/71, 11/73, 6/74, 9/74, 10/74 & 11/75, Artforum, 1/69 & 1-2/72 & others. Mailing Add: c/o Ronald Feldman Fine Arts Inc 33 E 74th St New York NY 10021

SMYTH, ED
ILLUSTRATOR, PAINTER
b New York, NY, May 21, 16. Study: Pratt Inst; Columbia Univ with Mario Cooper; Wash Univ with Gustav Goetsch & Fred Carpenter. Work: Vesuvius Crucible Co, Pittsburgh, Pa. Exhib: Wyo State Art Mus, Cheyenne, 75; Royal Watercolor Soc, Nat Cowboy Hall of Fame, Oklahoma City, 76; Wyo Image, State Capitol, Cheyenne, 77. Pos: Artist/photogr/writer, Ralston Purina Co, St Louis, Mo, 46-70; asst dir, Bradford Brinton Mem, Big Horn, Wyo, 75-; freelance art & photog, writing, 70- Awards: Silver Medals, Ann Shows, St Louis Art Dir Club, 60-61; First Award/Film, Nat Agr Advert & Marketing Asn, 68; Best of Show, Wyo Artists Asn, 74. Bibliog: Archie L Nash (auth), Ed Smyth, artist with brush & camera, Western Horseman Mag, 9/67; Jack Rice (auth), Artist with camera is drawn to horses, St Louis Post-Dispatch Mag, 10/67; Sandy Teague (auth), Ed Smyth, rodeo artist, Rodeo Sports News Suppl, (in press). Mem: Wyo Artists' Asn. Style & Technique: Realistic portrayal of today's western scene; cowboys, horses and Indians. Media: Watercolor, Pen & Ink, Conte. Publ: Auth & illusr, Born to buck, Western Horseman, 10/67; auth & illusr, Hooked by the wily trout, 9/72 & illusr, Murchison's moose, Fall 1974, Saturday Evening Post; auth & illusr, Big Horn art bonanza—Bradford Brinton Mem, Art West, Fall 1977. Mailing Add: The Line Camp Box 308 Story WY 82842

SNEED, PATRICIA M
ART DEALER, COLLECTOR
b Spencer, Iowa, Oct 24, 22. Study: Drake Univ, 40-42; Univ Cincinnati, 45-46. Collections Arranged: Fifty Artists for Fifty States (nat art exhib), 65-; Art in Other Media, 70. Pos: Pres & bd trustees, Burpee Art Mus; owner & dir, Sneed Gallery, 35 & 58-; mem art adv panel, State of Ill, 66- Mem: Am Fedn Arts. Specialty: Contemporary American art. Collection: Contemporary American art. Publ: Auth, Show Me a Picture (children's art appreciation prog). Mailing Add: 2024 Harlem Blvd Rockford IL 61103

SNELGROVE, WALTER H
PAINTER
b Seattle, Wash, Mar 22, 24. Study: Univ Wash; Calif Sch Fine Arts, with Hassel Smith, Antonio Sotamayor & James Weeks; Univ Calif, Berkeley, BA & MA, with James McCray & M O'Hagan. Work: Whitney Mus Am Art, New York; Oakland Mus, Calif; Colorado Springs Fine Arts Ctr, Colo; Calif Palace of Legion of Honor; Stanford Univ. Exhib: Carnegie Int, Pittsburgh; Art Inst Chicago; Albright-Knox Art Gallery, Buffalo, NY; Whitney Mus Am Art, 62-63; Denver Art Mus, Colo, 64; Carnegie Inst Int, 64; Va Mus Fine Arts, Richmond; retrospective, Foothill Col, 67; plus others. Teaching: Instr, Univ Calif, 51-53. Awards: Prizes, Oakland Mus, 62; San Francisco Mus Art, 63; Kelham Mem Awards, Calif Palace of Legion of Honor; plus others. Mem: San Francisco Art Asn. Mailing Add: 2966 Adeline St Berkeley CA 94703

SNELSON, KENNETH D
SCULPTOR
b Pendleton, Ore, June 29, 27. Work: Whitney Mus Am Art, New York; Mus Mod Art, New York; Milwaukee Art Ctr; Kröller Müller Mus, Otterloo, Holland; Staedelijk Mus, Amsterdam, Holland; City of Iowa City; City of Baltimore City; Joseph H Hirshhorn Mus; Storm King Art Ctr. Comn: Tower of Light Pavillion, New York World's Fair, 64; Japan Iron & Steel Fedn, Expo '70, Osaka, Japan, 70. Exhib: Sculpture of the Sixties, Los Angeles Co Mus, Calif, 67; Five Monumental Sculptures, Kröller Müller Mus, 69; Int Sculpture Symp,

Osaka, Japan, 69; Kunsthalle Düsseldorf, Ger, 70; Snelson Sculpture Exhib, Hannover Kunstuerein, Hannover, Ger, 71; Wilhelm Lehmbruck Mus, Duisburg, Ger; one-man exhib, Berlin Nationalgalerie, 77. Media: Steel. Publ: Auth, A design for the atom, Indust Design, 2/63; auth, Continuous Tension, Discontinuous Compression Structures, 65 & A Model for Atomic Forms, 66, US Patent Off. Mailing Add: 140 Sullivan St New York NY 10012

SNIDOW, GORDON E
PAINTER, SCULPTOR
b Paris, Mo, Sept 30, 36. Study: Art Ctr Col Design, BA. Work: Nat Cowboy Hall Fame, Oklahoma City; Phoenix Mus, Ariz; Gilcrease Mus, Tulsa, Okla; Mont Hist Soc, Helena; W B Davis Mus, Duncan, Okla. Exhib: Cowboy Artist Am Ann Exhib, Nat Cowboy Hall Fame & Phoenix Art Mus, 65-75; two-man show, Nat Coboy ll Fame, 70; one-man show, C M Russell Gallery, Mont Hist Soc, 73. Awards: Silver Medal for Drawing, Cowboy Artist Am Exhib, 69 & 73, Gold Medal for Sculpture, 73, Silver Medal for Watercolor, 74, Gold Medals for Watercolor & Mixed Media, 75, Silver Medal for Mixed Media, 76 & Best of Show & Gold Medal for Mixed Media, 77. Bibliog: Meigs (auth), The Cowboy in American Prints, Sage Swallow, 72; Broder (auth), Bronzes of the American West, Abrams, 74; Hassrick (auth), American Painting Today, Watson-Guptill, 75. Mem: Cowboy Artist Am (secy-treas, 67-68, vpres, 68-69, pres, 70-71). Style & Technique: Realistic contemporary Western subjects in oils, watercolor, charcoal; sculpture and lithography. Publ: Contribr, Persimmon Hill, 70; auth, Gordon Snidow, Chronicler of the Contemporary West, 73. Mailing Add: PO Box 2496 Ruidoso NM 88345

SNODGRASS, JEANNE OWENS (MRS M EUGENE KING)
MUSEOLOGIST, ART HISTORIAN
b Muskogee, Okla, Sept 12, 27. Study: Art Instr, Inc; Northeastern State Col; Okla Univ. Collections Arranged: 214 exhibs of Indian art & artifacts, Philbrook Art Ctr, 55-68; Am Indian Artists Nat Competition Ann, Philbrook Art Ctr, 55-68. Teaching: Lectr, American Indian painting. Pos: Asst to dir & cur Am Indian Art, Philbrook Art Ctr, 55-68; admin asst to pres, Educ Dimensions, Inc, 69-71; registr, Gilcrease Mus, 73-; assoc, Am Indian Affairs & mem Arts & Crafts Adv Comt; juror, many nat & regional Indian Art Exhibs. Awards: Outstanding Contrib to Indian Art Award, US Dept Interior, 67. Mem: Okla Mus Asn (secy); Ethno-Hist Asn; Tulsa Hist Soc. Publ: Auth, American Indian Paintings, 64; ed, American Indian Basketry, 64; auth, American Indian Painters: a biographical directory, Heye Found, 68. Mailing Add: 1027 E 41st Apt 15 Tulsa OK 74105

SNOW, CYNTHIA REEVES
PAINTER, EDUCATOR
b Laurel Springs, NC, Oct 2, 07. Study: Univ NC, Greensboro, AB; Peabody Col, Nashville, Tenn, MA; NY Univ; Univ Minn; Walter Art Ctr. Work: Thaw (oil), New Britain Mus Am Art, Conn; watercolor, Benton Mus Art, Storrs, Conn; watercolor, Eastern Conn Col, Willimantic. Exhib. Gallery on the Green, Canton, Conn, 71; Sharon Arts Festival, Conn, 71; Slater Mem Mus, Norwich, Conn, 71; Nat Conf-Aesthet, Fairfield Univ, 73; Eastern Connecticut Artists, Slater Mem Mus, 73; plus many other group & one-man shows, incl 13 of the latter in New Eng area. Teaching: Instr, Fla State Univ, Tallahassee, 40-47; prof, Univ Conn, Storrs, 48- Awards: Music Inn Gallery Award for Desert Form (watercolor), 66; Sharon Fine Arts Ctr Water Color Prize for Lyric in Red, 72; Water Color Prize for Landscape Theme-9b, New Eng Ann, Mystic, Conn, 73; John Slade Ely Award, Nat Soc Women Artists, 74; First Prize, Conn Water Color Soc, 77; plus others. Mem: Conn Watercolor Soc; Springfield Art League; Nat Soc Women Painters; Mystic Art Asn; Conn Acad Fine Arts. Media: Watercolor, Oil. Mailing Add: PO Box 13663 Del Mar CA 92014 of Art Univ of Conn Storrs CT 06268

SNOW, JOHN
PRINTMAKER, PAINTER
b Vancouver, BC, Dec 12, 11. Work: Victoria & Albert Mus, London, Eng; Nat Gallery Can; Univ Toronto; Can Coun. Exhib: Premiere Expos Bienale Int Gravure, Tokyo & Osaka, Japan, 57; 5th Int Biennial Color Lithography, Cincinnati, 58; Royal Acad Arts, London, 63; Cardiff Commonwealth Arts Festival, Cardiff & Brit Isles, 65; Salon Beaux Arts, Paris, 69. Awards: C W Jeffrey's Award, Can Soc Graphic Art, 61; Jessie Dow Award, Montreal Mus Fine Arts, 62. Mem: Can Soc Graphic Art; assoc Royal Can Acad Arts. Mailing Add: 915 18th Ave SW Calgary AB T2T 0H2 Can

SNOW, LEE ERLIN
DESIGNER, INSTRUCTOR
b Buffalo, NY, Jan 2, 24. Study: Univ Buffalo, BA(sociol & psychol), 47; Otis Art Inst, worked toward MFA, scholar with Joseph Young in mosaics; Univ Calif, Los Angeles, with Neda Al-Hilali. Work: Skirball Mus, Los Angeles; Halls Crown Ctr, Kansas City. Comn: Mosaic portrait of Bess Hawes, Folk Music Classes of Univ Calif, Los Angeles; stitcheries, comn by Dr William Kramer, Los Angeles; painting-water color, comn by Dr & Mrs M Wexler, Beverly Hills; necklace, comn by Betty Sheinbaum, Brentwood; painting-oil, comn by Joyce Block, Japan. Exhib: Calif Design X, Pasadena Mus, 68; Southern Calif Designer Craftsmen, Laguna Mus Art, 73; Ball State Univ, 73; Fairtree Gallery, New York, 73; Southern Calif Designer Crafts, Brand Libr Art Gallery, 78; Art Rental Gallery, Los Angeles Co Mus of Art, 76, 77 & 78; Juried Show, Southern Calif Designer-Crafts, Brand Libr Art Gallery, 78; solo shows, Southwest Craft Ctr Gallery, San Antonio, 75, Front Rm, Dallas, Tex, 76 & Galeria del Sol, Santa Barbara, Calif, 76. Teaching: Instr multimedia fibre, Barnsdall Arts & Crafts Ctr, Los Angeles, 72-76; workshop leader non-loom weaving, World Crafts Conf, Toronto, Ont, 74; instr multimedia fibre, Los Angeles Co Mus Art, Los Angeles, 75. Pos: Monthly pub serv radio, Starship Earth, KHJ Radio, interviewing prominent people in visual arts. Awards: Scholar Award Mosaics, with Dr Joseph L Young, Los Angeles, 60; Award for Study, Westwood Art Asn, 63 & Third Prize for Painting. Bibliog: Dorothy Bartlett (auth), You gotta have art, Westart, Bud Pisarek Publ, 11/73; 1/2 hr film interview, Theta Cable TV, Los Angeles, 73; Lois McAfee (auth), Oh, what a tangled web, Sun-Tel, San Bernardino, 1/75. Mem: Southern Calif Designer-Crafts (vchmn, 70-71, 75-76; bd mem, 74-75; chmn, 77-78); chmn, 77-78); Westwood Art Asn (first vchmn, 69-70); Los Angeles Art Asn; Am Crafts Coun; Southern Calif Weavers Guild. Style & Technique: Innovative free form nonrepresentational design in bright reds or earth tones; super representational in oil. super representational oils. Crochet; Oil. Tapestry; Sculptural Crochet. Res: Teaching innovations and frequent usage of material in contemporary crafts. Publ: Contribr, Creating Art from Anything, 68, co-auth, Creative Stitchery, 70, co-auth, Weaving Off-Loom, 73 & contribr, Creating Art from Fibers and Fabrics, 74, Regnery; contribr, How to Create Your Own Designs, Doubleday, 75. Mailing Add: 430 S Burnside Ave Apt 11-L Los Angeles CA 90036

SNOW, MICHAEL
PAINTER, FILM MAKER
b Toronto, Ont, Dec 10, 29. Study: Ont Col Art, Toronto. Work: Mus Mod Art & Anthology Film Arch, New York; Art Gallery Toronto; Montreal Mus Fine Arts; Nat Gallery Can. Exhib: Gallery Mod Art & Whitney Mus Am Art, New York; Carnegie Inst, Pittsburgh; Mus Mod Art, New York; Isaacs Gallery, New York & Toronto; represented Can, Venice Bienale, Italy, 70; plus many others. Awards: Grand Prize, 4th Int Exp Film Festival, Brussels, Belg, 68; Guggenheim Fel, 72. Mem: Royal Can Acad Arts. Dealer: Isaacs Gallery 832 Yonge St Toronto ON Can. Mailing Add: 137 Summerhill Ave Toronto ON M4T 1B1 Can

SNOW, VIVIAN DOUGLAS
PAINTER, EDUCATOR
b Salt Lake City, Utah, Mar 31, 27. Study: Univ Utah, 43-46; Columbia Univ, 46-47; Am Art Sch, 46-47; Cranbrook Acad Arts, BFA, 49, MFA, 50; Fulbright grant, Acad Fine Arts, Rome, 50-51. Work: Cranbrook Acad Art Mus; Mus Mod Art; Utah Inst Fine Arts; Miles Lab Collection; Bank of Las Vegas, Nev; plus others. Comn: Murals, Salt Lake City Pub Libr, Grad Sch of Social Work, Univ of Utah & Iron Blossom, Snowbird, Utah. Exhib: Denver Art Mus, 56, 57 & 71; Colorado Springs Fine Arts Ctr, 57 & 65; one-man shows, Feingarten Gallery, New York, 61, Los Angeles, 62, 64, 66 & 67 & Salt Lake Art Ctr, 63; Nat Inst of Arts & Lett, 75; Fiedler Gallery, Washington, DC, 77; plus many other group & one-man shows. Teaching: Instr, Flint Inst Art, Mich, 50; guest instr, Stanford Univ, summer 52; instr, Wayne State Univ, 52-54; mem fac, Univ Utah, 54-, prof art, 59-, chmn dept, 65-71. Mailing Add: 125 S 1300 East Salt Lake City UT 84102

SNYDER, BARRY
ART DEALER, COLLECTOR
b Newark, NJ, Jan 5, 29. Study: Tyler Sch Fine Art, Temple Univ. Pos: Dir, Princeton Gallery Fine Art, Princeton, NJ, 69- Specialty: Quality works of fine art, including works by important American contemporary artists. Collection: Private collection includes contemporary, Africa, Precolumbian and American Primitive. Mailing Add: 162 Nassau St Second Level Princeton NJ 08540

SNYDER, JAMES WILBERT (WILB)
PAINTER
b Philadelphia, Pa. Study: Univ Pa Sch Fine Arts, BFA; NY Univ, MA, PhD; Cambridge Univ; Am Univ Beirut; and with Elliot O'Hara. Work: Pvt collections throughout US. Exhib: One-man & group shows in Philadelphia, Cape Cod, NJ & Southwest Fla. Teaching: Instr social sci, Univ Pa, NY Univ & Athens Col, Greece; analyst, Exec Agency, US Fed Govt, Washington, DC. Awards: Var Blue Ribbons & Hon Mentions in Shows & Exhibs. Mem: Sanibel-Captiva Art League (mem bd); Art Coun Southwest Fla; Soc NAm Artists. Media: Watercolor. Mailing Add: Gulf Dr Sanibel FL 33957

SNYDER, JOAN
PAINTER
b New Brunswick, NJ, Apr 16, 40. Study: Rutgers Univ, MFA. Work: Allan Mus, Oberlin Col, Ohio; Whitney Mus Am Art, New York; Dallas Mus of Fine Arts, Tex. Exhib: American Drawings 1963-1973, Whitney Mus Am Art, New York, Whitney Biennial, 73; New York Avant-Garde, Saidye Bronfman Ctr, Montreal, 73; 14 Abstract Painters, Frederick S Wight Art Gallery, Univ Calif, Los Angeles, 75; Corcoran Biennial, Washington, DC, 75; Neuberger Mus, Purchase, NY, 78; Hamilton Gallery of Contemp Art, 78. Teaching: Instr, Princeton Univ. Bibliog: Marcia Tucker (auth), Anatomy of a stroke; recent paintings by Joan Snyder, Artforum, 5/19/71; Lawrence Alloway (auth), article in, Nation, 6/73; Douglas Davis (auth), Art without limits, Newsweek, 12/24/73. Media: Oil, Acrylic. Dealer: Patricia Hamilton Gallery of Contemp Art 20 W 57th St New York NY. Mailing Add: PO Box 295 Martins Creek PA 18063

SNYDER, KIM LAWRENCE
CURATOR, PAINTER
b Ft Washakie, Wyo, June 5, 42. Study: Cent Wyo Col, Riverton, AA, 70; Idaho State Univ, BA, 74; Univ Idaho, MFA, 76. Work: Mus of the Plains Indian, Browning, Mont; Cent Wyo Col, Riverton; Shoshone Indian Ctr, Ft Washakie. Exhib: Cent Wyo Col, 70; Transition Art Gallery, Pocatello, Idaho, 73; Columbia Basin Col, Pasco, Wash, 75; one-man show, Paintings & Sculpture by Kim Snyder, Mus of the Plains Indian, 75; Univ Art Gallery, Moscow, Idaho, 76; Idaho State Capitol, Boise, 76. Collections Arranged: Chippewa-Cree Crafts, 76-77, Paintings by Frank Day (ed, catalogue), 77, Metalwork by Gail Larson (ed, catalogue), 77, Fashions by Jewel Gilham (ed, catalogue), 77, Shoshone Arts & Crafts (ed, Catalogue), 77 & Indian Tipi Exhib, 77, Mus of the Plains Indian. Teaching: Instr painting, Univ Idaho, Moscow, 75-76. Pos: Mus cur, Idaho State Hist Mus, 76- Awards: First Prize Sculpture, Wind River Artists Nat Exhib, Wind River Valley Artist Guild, 75. Bibliog: Norma Ashbee (auth), Today in Montana, KRTV, Great Falls, Mont, 77; George Horse Capture (auth), Indian Country, KFBB-TV, Great Falls, 77; Allen Bell (auth), Rocky Mountain Mix, KUID-TV, Moscow, Idaho, 76. Mem: Wind River Valley Artists Guild. Style & Technique: Indian surrealism; oil, acrylic and acrylic lacquer paintings using airbrush technique. Media: Acrylic, Acrylic Lacquer. Publ: Contribr, Paintings and Sculpture by Kim Snyder, Artcraft Printers, 75. Mailing Add: 1560 W Wright St Boise ID 83705

SNYDER, PATRICIA STEGMAN
See Stegman, Patricia

SNYDER, SEYMOUR
ILLUSTRATOR, INSTRUCTOR
b Newark, NJ, Aug 11, 97. Study: Pa Acad Fine Arts; Grand Cent Sch Art; Art Students League; Newark Sch Art, NJ. Comn: Advert & promotional work, var nat co. Exhib: Lynn Kottler Gallery, 68; Am Artists Prof League, New York, 69; Nat Arts Club, New York, 70. Teaching: Instr com art & lectr art hist, High Sch Art & Design & New York Adult Educ Prog, 62-69; instr illus & design, Pels Sch Art, New York, 70-74 & NY Inst Technol, 75- Awards: Watercolor Prize, Salmagundi Club, 69. Mem: Life mem Art Students League; Am Artists Prof League; Artists Equity Asn. Publ: Illusr, McCalls, House & Gardens, Better Homes & Gardens, Successful Farming & Am Home; illusr, var calendars. Mailing Add: 315 E 68th St New York NY 10021

SNYDER, TONI GOESSLER
GOLDSMITH, PRINTMAKER
b Heidenheim, Ger, Nov 19, 42. Study: Peace Col, Raleigh, NC; Goldschmiede Schule & Kunst-und Werkschule, Pforzheim, Ger; also with Prof Ullrich. Work: Ga State Univ; also in pvt collection of Helen Drutt & Kenneth Helfaund, Philadelphia. Comn: Brooch-pendant, Inst Contemp Art, Univ Pa, 75; The Monstrance, 41st Int Eucharistic Cong for Official Presentation to His Holiness Pope Paul VI, 77. Exhib: Univ NMex Mus Art, 73; De Cordova Mus, Lincoln, Mass, 75; The Goldsmith, Renwick Gallery, Smithsonian Inst, Washington, DC, 75; The Collector, Mus Contemp Crafts, New York, 76; Metalsmith Art, John M Kohler Art Ctr, Sheboygan, Wis, 76; Philadelphia Mus Art, 76; Ga State Univ, 77; Design Ctr of the Philippines, Manila, 77. Collections Arranged: Opals (traveling show); Technology and Artist-Craftsman, 73-75, Kenneth Helfand (touring exhib), 74. Teaching: Instr metal & design, Moore Col Art, Philadelphia, 75-76; asst prof metal & design, Philadelphia Col Art,

76. Mem: Soc NAm Goldsmiths; Am Craft Coun. Style & Technique: Fabrication technique in goldsmithing; classical traditional and contemporary style. Media: Gold, Silver; Intaglio; Watercolor. Publ: Contribr, Harry Hollandes Plastic Jewelry, Watson-Guptill, 75; auth, European jeweler, Goldschmiedezeitung, 76 & Gold und Silver Mag, 78. Dealer: Helen Drutt Gallery 1624 Spruce St Philadelphia Pa 19103. Mailing Add: Box 304 Audubon PA 19407

SNYDER, WILLIAM B
PAINTER, INSTRUCTOR
b San Francisco, Calif, Sept 26, 26. Study: Chouinard's Art Inst, 43; San Francisco State Col; Stanford Univ, fel, 61-62. Work: City Fairfield, Calif; City Chico, Calif; Haggin Mus, Stockton, Calif; Joe & Elsie Erdelac Found, Cleveland; Richmond Art Ctr, Calif. Exhib: Art: USA 58, New York, 58; Church Art USA: 58, Grace Cathedral, San Francisco, 58; 4th & 5th Winter Invitational, Palace Legion Honor, San Francisco, 63 & 64; Phelan Award Biennial DeYoung Mus, 65; Downtown Dog Show, San Francisco MOMA, 78; Collector's Exhib, Oakland Art Mus, 78; one-man shows, Haggin Mus, Stockton, Calif, 58, Pac Art Ctr, Univ of Pac, Stockton, Calif, 59, Crocker Art Gallery, Sacramento, Calif, 59, Col of Notre Dame, Belmont, 73, Wooster Col, Ohio, 74, Sacramento State Univ, Calif, 77 & Capricorn Gallery, San Francisco, 78. Teaching: Instr drawing, Stanford Univ, 61-62; instr art, Foothills Jr Col, 62-63; instr drawing & painting, Lancy Col, 64- Pos: Set illusr, MGM Picture Studio, Culver City, Calif, 46-47. Awards: First Prize, San Joaquin Valley Regional Fall Arts Festival, Stockton Art League, Calif, 58; Purchase Award, Chico Savings & Loan, 66; Purchase Award, Fairfield Art Comn, 74. Bibliog: Tom Albright (auth), $5,000: Study for nightwatch, Art Gallery Mag, 3/73 & Interview: William Snyder, Currant Art Mag, 8/75; Ralph Pomery, Triumph of Disneyanity, Art & Artists, London, 8/74. Mem: San Geronimo Artists Protective & Abalone Asn. Style & Technique: Neo-Baroque anecdotal realism. Media: Oil on Canvas, Watercolor. Publ: Illusr, Monterey Advocate, Penadero, 66-68. Dealer: Zara Gallery 553 Pacific San Francisco CA 94133. Mailing Add: PO Box 106 Woodacre CA 94973

SOBY, JAMES THRALL
WRITER, CRITIC
b Hartford, Conn, Dec 14, 06. Study: Williams Col, 24-26, Hon LHD, 62. Pos: Asst dir, Mus Mod Art, 43, dir painting & sculpture, 43-45, trustee, 43-61, hon chmn comt on mus collections, mem exec & prog comt, vpres, 68-; art critic, Sat Rev Lit, 46-57; actg ed, Mag of Art, 50-51, chmn ed bd, 51-52. Awards: Star of Solidarity, Ital Govt. Publ: Auth, Modern art & the New Past, 57, Juan Gris, 58, Joan Miro, 59, Ben Shahn; Ten Paintings, 63 & Magritte, 65; plus many earlier publ; contribr articles & criticism, leading art publ. Mailing Add: 262 Brushy Ridge Rd New Canaan CT 06840

SOFFER, SASSON
SCULPTOR
b Baghdad, Iraq, June 1, 25; US citizen. Study: Brooklyn Col, 50-54, with Mark Rothko & others. Work: Whitney Mus Am Art, New York; Indianapolis Mus Fine Art; Albright-Knox Gallery, Buffalo; Rockefeller Inst, New York; Butler Inst Am Art, Youngstown, Ohio. Exhib: Whitney Mus Am Art, New York; Carnegie Inst Int, Pittsburgh; Yale Univ Art Gallery; Harvard Univ; one-man shows, Betty Parsons Gallery, New York, 61-63, Corpus Christi Mus, Tex, 64, Portland Mus, Maine, 66, Montclair State Col, NJ, 74 & Battery Park, New York, 75 & 76. plus others. Pos: Ford Found artist in residence, Portland Mus, 66. Awards: Ford Found Purchase Award, Whitney Mus Am Art, 62; Purchase Award, North Jersey Cult Coun, 74. Style & Technique: Abstract. Mailing Add: 78 Grand St New York NY 10013

SOKOL, DAVID MARTIN
ART HISTORIAN, ART ADMINISTRATOR
b New York, NY, Nov 3, 42. Study: Hunter Col, AB, 63; Inst for Fine Arts, NY Univ, MA, 66, PhD, 70. Teaching: Instr art hist, Kingsborough Community Col, Brooklyn, NY, 66-68; asst prof art hist, Western Ill Univ, Macomb, 68-71; assoc prof art & archit hist, Univ Ill, Chicago, 71- Pos: Chmn acquisitions comt, Frank L Wright Home & Studio Found, 75-77. Mem: Col Art Asn (placement comt, 77); Am Studies Asn (nat coun, 76-78); Am Asn Univ Prof (comt T, 75-). Res: American painting and decorative arts, relations between American and European. Publ: Auth, John Quider: Painter of American Legend, Wichita Art Mus, 73; auth, American Architecture & Art, 76 & American Decorative Arts & Old World Influences, 78, Gale; co-auth, History of American Art, Abrams, (in prep). Mailing Add: 330 S Taylor Ave Oak Park IL 60302

SOKOLE, MIRON
PAINTER, EDUCATOR
b Odessa, Russia; US citizen. Study: Cooper Union, cert; Nat Acad Art, with Ivan Olinsky. Work: Butler Inst Am Art, Youngstown, Ohio; Mus Tel Aviv, Israel; Univ Minn, Minneapolis; IBM Collection; Upjohn Collection; US State Dept. Exhib: Metrop Mus, 42, 44 & 52; Carnegie Inst, 43, 44, 45 & 49; Int Expos, Mus Art Mod, Paris, 46; Dayton Art Inst, 53; Watercolors Show, Whitney Mus Am Art, New York, 53 & 54; Dallas Mus, 56; Memphis Mus, 56; Cincinnati Art Mus, 58; Corcoran Gallery Art Biennial, Washington, DC, 58; Collectors Gallery, 63 & 68; 21st Ann, Norfolk Mus, Va, 65; Fashion Inst of Technol, 71; Woodstock Art Asn, 73; WPA Then & Now Show, 77; plus others. Teaching: Instr painting & drawing, Am Artists Sch, New York, 38-41; resident artist, Kansas City Art Inst, Mo, 47-51; prof art, Fashion Inst Technol, New York, 62- Pos: Free lance stage designer, 35-38; stage & indust designer, 42-46. Bibliog: Salpeter (auth), Miron Sokole, Esquire, 9/45; A Guskin (auth), Painting in USA, 54; Martha Cheney (auth), Modern art in America, Tudor. Mem: Woodstock Artists Asn; Exp Art & Technol; Artists Equity Asn (nat dir, 52). Style & Technique: Nonobjective. Media: Oil, Acrylic. Dealer: Art Collectors Place 51 E 73rd St New York NY 10021. Mailing Add: 250 W 22nd St New York NY 10011

SOKOLOWSKI, LINDA ROBINSON
PRINTMAKER, PAINTER
b Utica, NY, May 20, 43. Study: RI Sch of Design, BFA(painting), 65; State Univ NY, Potsdam; Univ Iowa, MA, 70 & MFA, 71, with Mauricio Lasansky & James Lechay. Work: State Univ NY, Potsdam; Stout State Univ, Menomonie, Wis. Exhib: Davidson Nat Print & Drawing Competition, 74; Nat Print & Drawing Competition, Mt Holyoke, 74; Mauricio Lasansky & Printmakers of the Iowa Workshop Tradition, Miami Univ, Ohio, 76; Ball State Univ Drawing & Small Sculpture Nat Exhib, Muncie, Ind, 77; Int Miniature Print Competition, Pratt Graphic Ctr, 77; one-man shows, The Bathers, Kraushaar Galleries, New York, 76; The Graphic Works 1972-1977, State Univ NY Binghamton, 78. Teaching: Instr-assoc prof art, State Univ NY, Binghamton, 71- Style & Technique: Figurative drawings and etchings; landscapes, all in oil wash and multi-media with collage. Publ: Auth, The Original Prints and Restrikes from the Plates of Kaethe Kollwitz, Univ Iowa Press, 70; illusr, Boundary 2, a journal of post-modern literature, State Univ NY, Binghamton, fall 76. Dealer: Antoinette Kraushaar c/o Kraushaar Galleries 1055 Madison Ave New York NY 10028. Mailing Add: RFD 1 Box 194 Swan Lake NY 12783

SOLBERG, MORTEN EDWARD
PAINTER
b Cleveland, Ohio, Nov 8, 35. Study: Cleveland Inst Art. Work: Nat Gallery Art, Washington, DC; Cleveland Mus Art; Am Bicentennial Gallery, Huntington Beach, Calif. Comn: Painting of hist fountain, Marriott Hotels, Newport Beach, Calif, 75; painting of hist settings, Irvine Co, Newport Beach, 75. Exhib: Nat Acad Design, New York, 66 & 76; Watercolor USA, Springfield, Mo, 67; Soc Painters in Casein & Acrylic, New York, 67; Am Watercolor Soc, New York, 68, 74, 75 & 76; Nat Watercolor Soc, Los Angeles, 70-75. Pos: Art dir, Am Greeting Corp, Cleveland, 58-68; art dir, Buzza Cardoza Corp, Anaheim, Calif, 68-71; pres, Calif Graphics, Design Studio, Orange, 71-73. Awards: Paul B Remey Mem Award, Am Watercolor Soc, 68, High Winds Medal, 74 & Winsor & Newton Award, 75. Bibliog: Angie McCance (auth), Morten Solberg, Artist, Register, 74; Janell Gregg (auth), Contributing artist, Orange Co Illus, 75; article in Southwest Art, 5/76; Ray Merchant (auth), article in Am Artist Mag, 10/76. Mem: Nat Watercolor Soc (ad hoc bd mem, 74, first vpres, 75). Style & Technique: Contemporary impressionism, interpreting the subject to a point of subtle abstraction. Media: Watercolor; Acrylic. Dealer: Carson Gallery Denver CO. Mailing Add: Box 1317 Running Springs CA 92382

SOLDNER, PAUL EDMUND
SCULPTOR, CERAMIST
b Summerfield, Ill, Apr 24, 21. Study: Bluffton Col, BA; Univ Colo, MA; County Art Inst, Los Angeles, MFA. Work: Nat Mus Mod Art, Kyoto, Japan, Japan; San Francisco Mus Art; Oakland Art Mus, Calif; Emerson Mus, Syracuse, NY; Smithsonian Mus, Washington, DC; Syracuse Mus, NY. Comn: Ceramic mural, Home Savings & Loan Asn Los Angeles, 56; 40 large planters, Scripps Col, 61; three major pieces, Objects USA for circulating exhib, US & Europe, Johnson Wax Collection, 69. Exhib: Ostend Int Exhib, Belg, 59; Ceramic Int, Prague, Czech, 62; Triennali, Venice, Italy, 64; Contemporary Ceramic Art, Nat Mus Mod Art, Kyoto, Japan, 71; Int Ceramics, Victoria & Albert Mus, London, Eng, 72; World Craft Exhib, Toronto, Can, 74; Masters in Ceramic Art, Everson Mus, Syracuse, NY, 75; and others. Teaching: Prof ceramics, Scripps Col & Claremont Grad Sch, Calif, 55-66 & 70-; vis prof ceramics, Univ Colo, Boulder, 66-67; prof ceramics, Univ Iowa, 67-68. Pos: Exhib dir, Nat Ceramics Invitational, Scripps Col, 57-; adv vol, Int Tech Assistance, 65-; mem steering comt, Int Sch Ceramics, Rome, 65-; dir US sect, World Crafts Coun, 71-74; prog chmn, Nat Craft Conf, Ft Collins Colo, summer 73; dir, Ctr for the Hand Sch, Anderson Ranch, Snowmass, Colo, 73-75. Awards: Louis Comfort Tiffany Found Grant, 66 & 72; Purchase Award, Victoria & Albert Mus, 72; Gov Award Arts & Humanities, Colo, 75; Craftsmen's Fel Grant, Nat Endowment for the Arts, 76. Bibliog: Robert Fulton (auth), Earth & Fire (film), Image Resources, Film Libr, 72; Joan Campbell (auth), Paul Soldner, Pottery in Australia, 71; Daniel Wilson (auth), With These Hands, ABC-TV, Johnson Wax Sponsor, 71; John W Conrad (auth), Contemporary Ceramics, Prentice-Hall, 77; Donald Campbell (auth), Using the Potter's Wheel, Van Nostrand Reinhold, 77; and others. Mem: Am Craft Coun (5 state craftsman-trustee, 71-74, fel, Collegium of Craftsmen of US, 77); Nat Coun Educ Ceramic Arts (panelist). Style & Technique: Originated new aesthetic movement in media of clay non-utilitarian associated with contemporary American Raku. Media: Clay. Mailing Add: PO Box 90 Aspen CO 81611

SOLERI, PAOLO
ARCHITECT-ENVIRONMENTAL PLANNER, SCULPTOR
b Torino, Italy, 1919. Study: Polytech Torino, Frank Lloyd Wright fel. Work: Mus Mod Art, New York. Comn: II Donnone (sculpture), Phoenix Civic Ctr, Ariz, 72. Exhib: Corcoran Gallery Art, Washington, DC, 70; Whitney Mus Am Art, New York, 70; Mus Contemp Art, Chicago, 70; Nat Conf Ctr, Ottawa, Can, 71; Univ Art Mus, Berkeley, Calif, 71; Two Suns Arcology Exhib, Xerox Corp-sponsored, 76; plus others. Awards: Graham Found, 62; Guggenheim Found, 64 & 67. Publ: Auth, Arcology: The City in the Image of Man, 69 & The Sketchbooks of Paolo Soleri, 71, Mass Inst Technol; auth, The Bridge Between Matter & Spirit is Matter Becoming Spirit, Doubleday, 73. Mailing Add: Cosanti Found 6433 Doubletree Rd Scottsdale AZ 85253

SOLINGER, DAVID M
COLLECTOR, PATRON
Pos: Mem bd trustees, Am Fedn Arts, 54-; pres, Whitney Mus Am Art, 66-73, chmn, 73-77, hon pres, 77-; chmn mus coun, Cornell Univ. Collection: 20th century paintings and sculpture. Mailing Add: 250 Park Ave New York NY 10017

SOLLEY, THOMAS TREAT
MUSEUM DIRECTOR
b New York, NY, Sept 4, 24. Study: Yale Univ, BA, 50; Ind Univ, MA, 66. Collections Arranged: The American Scene, 1900-1970, 70; Noguchi & Richey & Smith, 70; Hungarian Art, The Twentieth Century Avant-Garde, 72. Pos: Archit proj engr, Eli Lilly Co, Indianapolis, 51-61; pvt architect, Indianapolis, 61-64; asst dir, Art Mus, Ind Univ, Bloomington, 68-71, dir, 71- Mem: Childrens Mus Indianapolis (adv trustee); Asn of Art Mus Dirs. Mailing Add: Art Mus Ind Univ Bloomington IN 47401

SOLMAN, JOSEPH
PAINTER, EDUCATOR
b Vitebsk, Russia, Jan 25, 09; US citizen. Study: Nat Acad Design, New York, 26-29; Art Students League, 29-30. Work: Whitney Mus Am Art, New York; Phillips Gallery, Washington, DC; Fogg Mus, Cambridge, Mass; Butler Inst Am Art, Youngstown, Ohio; Los Angeles Co Mus. Exhib: ACA Galleries, New York, NY, 50-; Whitney Mus Am Art Ann, 52, 53 & 55; Int Asn Plastic Arts Europ Traveling Show Am Art, 56; 2nd Expos Contemp Art, Inst Brasil-Estados Unidos, Rio de Janeiro, 60. Teaching: Instr oil painting, Mus Mod Art, 52-54; instr oil painting, New Sch Social Res, 64-66; instr oil painting, City Col New York, 67- Pos: Ed & co-ed, Art Front Mag, 37-39. Awards: Nat Inst Arts & Lett Award for Painting, 61; Isaac N Maynard Prize for Portrait, 69 & Saltus Gold Medal for Merit, 71, Nat Acad Design. Bibliog: D Seckler (auth), Solman paints a picture, Art News, summer 51; S Burrey (auth), Joseph Solman: the growth of conviction, Arts, 10/55; Una E Johnson (auth introd), The Monotypes of Joseph Solman, Da Capo Press, 77. Mem: Fedn Mod Painters & Sculptors (pres, 65-67, vpres, 67-). Media: Oil, Gouache. Publ: Auth, Joseph Solman, Crown, 66. Dealer: ACA Galleries 25 E 73rd St New York NY 10021. Mailing Add: 19 Beachcroft Rd Gloucester MA 01930

SOLMSSEN, PETER
ART ADMINISTRATOR
b Berlin, Ger, Nov 1, 31; US citizen. Study: Harvard Col, AB, 52; Univ Pa Law Sch, JD, 59. Exhib: One-man photog exhib, Mus Art, Sao Paulo, Brazil, 70. Pos: US cult attache, Sao Paulo, 67-70; adv on the Arts, US Dept State, 74- Publ: Auth & illusr, Sao Paulo, 70. Mailing Add: Advisor on the Arts Dept of State (CU/ARTS) Washington DC 20520

SOLODKIN, JUDITH
PRINTMAKER, EDUCATOR
b New York, NY, Apr 7, 45. Study: Brooklyn Col, BA, 65; Columbia Univ, MFA, 67; Fulbright Hays scholar alternate, France, 66-67; Prix de Rome alternate, Italy, 66-67; Tamarind Inst, Ford Found grant, 72-74, Tamarind Master Printer, 74. Work: Art Mus, Univ NMex; Tamarind Inst Collection, NMex; Pratt Graphics Ctr Collection New York; Printmaking Workshop Collection, New York. Exhib: Dallas Mus Fine Arts, 72; James Yu Gallery, New York, 75; Printmakers 12, Salena Art Gallery, Long Island Univ, Brooklyn, NY, 77; Printmakers 12, Atlantic Gallery, Brooklyn, NY, 77; one-person shows, Roots of Creativity series, Douglass Col, Rutgers Univ & Elizabeth Pub Libr, NJ, 76, Cartouche Lithographs, Razor Gallery, 77 & SOLO Press, SOLO Show, Nobe Gallery, 78. Teaching: Instr lithography, Univ Ind, Bloomington, 74-; instr lithography, Pratt Graphics Ctr, 74-, Sch Visual Arts, 75- & Douglass Col, Rutgers Univ, 77-78. Pos: Master printer, Petersburg Press & Solo Press, 74-; partic artist, Great Lakes Col Asn Apprenticeship Prog, 76 & 78 & Parsons-New Sch Apprenticeship Prog, 77; proprietor & master printer, SOLO Press, 78. Awards: Louis Comfort Tiffany grant to SOLO Press Apprenticeship Prog, 77. Media: Lithography, Intaglio, Woodcut, Photo Process, Silkscreen. Dealer: Kathryn Markel Fine Arts; Ellen Sragow Ltd. Mailing Add: 201 Eighth Ave New York NY 10011

SOLOMON, BERNARD ALAN
PRINTMAKER, EDUCATOR
b Chicago, Ill, June 21, 46. Study: Art Inst of Chicago, with Raymond Martin & Adrian Troy, BFA, 68; Inst of Design, Ill Inst Technol, with Misch Kohn, MSVD, 70. Work: Nat Collection of Fine Arts, Washington, DC; ICS/D, US State Dept, Kingston, Jamaica; New York Pub Libr Print & Drawing Collection; Huntsville Mus Art, Ala; Greenville Co Mus Art, SC. Comn: Playboy Mag, Art Paul, art dir, Chicago, 69; Bicentennial Ser, Everitt Williams, pres, Sea Island Bank, Statesboro, Ga, 76; Poster Poems Grant (in collab with poet Charles Levendosky), Ga Coun for Arts & Nat Endowment for Arts, 75. Exhib: NW Printmakers Int, Seattle, Wash, 68; Colorprint USA, Lubbock, Tex, 72; one-man show, Klutznick Exhib Hall, B'nai B'rith Nat Hq, Washington, DC, 73; Southeastern Printmakers Cullowhee, NC, 75; 3rd Int US Graphics Ann Traveling Exhib, Hollis, NH, 75; 12th-14th Ann Piedmont Graphics Exhib, Greenville, SC, 75-77; Old Master & Contemp Prints, 75, Huntsville, Ala, 77; Int Nuch Kunst Ausstellung, Leipzig, EGer, 77. Teaching: Instr printmaking, Mercyhurst Col, Erie, Pa, 69-71; asst prof printmaking, Ga Southern Col, Statesboro, 71- Awards: Gov's Award in the Arts, State of Ga, 75. Bibliog: Wood engraver keeps alive a nearly lost art, Black Star & Assoc Press, 74; Claude Felton (auth), Reviving a lost art form, Atlanta Jour-Constitution, 74; Rochelle Ratner (auth), Toward a definition of collaboration, Soho News, 77. Mem: Southeastern Graphics Coun (secy-treas, 72-74); Southeastern Col Arts Conf (mem rev bd); Int Graphics Soc. Style & Technique: Figurative expressionist; printmaker, predominantly relief, either woodcut or wood engraving. Media: Wood Engraving/Etching. Publ: Illusr, The Zaddick Christ, Attic Press, 74; illusr, Charles Levendosky, auth, small town America, 74, illusr, Yevgeny Yevtuchenko, auth, Babi Yar, 74 & auth & illusr, Modes of Death, 75, Boxwood Press; auth, When is a print not a print, Savannah Mag, 77. Dealer: John C Sirica 3609 Norton Pl NW Washington DC 20016 Mailing Add: 33 N East St Statesboro GA 30458

SOLOMON, DANIEL
PAINTER
b Topeka, Kans, July 13, 45. Study: Univ Ore, BSc. Comn: Outdoor mural, Benson & Hedges Tobacco Co, 71. Exhib: Can Artists, Art Gallery Ont, 68; Survey 69, Montreal Mus Fine Arts, 69; one-man shows, Isaacs Gallery, 70, 71, 73 & 74 & Mirvish Gallery, 77. Teaching: Instr painting, Ont Col Art, Toronto, 70- Awards: Can Coun Bursary for Painting, 70, 72 & 75. Bibliog: L Lippard (auth), rev, 2/69 & M Greenwood (auth), rev, 8-9/71, Arts Mag; also rev, Arts Mag, 6/70. Media: Acrylic. Mailing Add: c/o David Mirvish Gallery 596 Markham St Toronto ON M6G 2L8 Can

SOLOMON, DAVID
PAINTER, DESIGNER
b Los Angeles, Calif, Sept 16, 43. Study: Art Ctr Col Design, Los Angeles, BS(indust design, with distinction); study with Peter Egeli. Comn: Painting of ship, comn by crew, USS Orlick, 70; symbol for Laguna Beach, CofC, 73; painting of tug boat, Foss Tug Boat Co, Seattle, Wash, 75; painting of Port of Seattle, Port of Seattle, 75. Exhib: Laguna Beach Mus Art, Calif, 75; Watercolor West, Riverside, Calif, 75; Chicano Artists Exhib, Gov Mansion, Sacramento, Calif, 75; Am Watercolor Soc Ann, New York, 75; Nat Watercolor Soc, Los Angeles, 75; Allied Artists Nat Acad, New York, 77; Solomon Logan Gallery, Laguna Beach, Calif, 77. Teaching: Instr watercolor, Santa Ana Col, Calif. Pos: Consult archit design, R B Brout Assocs, North Hollywood, Calif, 66-; consult conceptual design, Arthur Valdes, Newport Beach, Calif, 73-; consult exhib design, Watash Group, Altamonte Springs, Fla, 74-; dir cult arts adv bd, Calif Partners of the Americas, Orange Co, 75- Awards: Alice Granberry Walters Best Realistic Oil Painting Award, Virginia Beach Ann, 70; Best in Show-Realistic Category, Fiesta de Artes, La Mirada, 73 & 74; First Award of Excellence, Occidental Life Ins, Cinco de Mayo Fiesta, 74; Purchase Award, Tex Fine Arts Asn, 76; Purchase Award, Nat Watercolor Soc, 76 & Representational Award, 77. Mem: Laguna Beach Mus Art; Festival Arts; Showcase 21; Rockport Art Asn; Nat Watercolor Soc. Style & Technique: Representational transparent watercolors. Dealer: Solomon Logan Gallery 422 S Coast Hwy Laguna Beach CA 92651. Mailing Add: 3174 Bonn Laguna Beach CA 92651

SOLOMON, GERALD
ART DEALER
b May 31, 34. Pos: Pres-dir, Solomon & Co Fine Art, New York. Specialty: 20th century American and European paintings, graphics, drawing and sculpture. Mailing Add: c/o Solomon & Co Fine Art 959 Madison Ave New York NY 10021

SOLOMON, HOLLY
ART DEALER, COLLECTOR
b Fairfield, Conn. Study: Vassar Col; Sarah Lawrence Col, BA. Teaching: Instr art hist, Fashion Inst Am, 73-75. Pos: Dir, Holly Solomon Gallery, Inc, New York. Awards: Award for Film, Edinborough Film Festival, 73. Bibliog: Andy Worhol (auth), 50 Best Friends, 65. Specialty: Avant garde American. Collection: Pop art, conceptual art, story art, earth art, body art and performing art. Mailing Add: 392 W Broadway New York NY 10012

SOLOMON, HYDE
PAINTER
b May 3, 11; US citizen. Study: Art Students League. Work: Whitney Mus Am Art, New York; Wadsworth Atheneum, Hartford, Conn; Munson-Williams-Proctor Inst, Utica, NY; Art Mus Princeton Univ, NJ; Univ Calif Mus, Berkeley; Mus of Fine Arts, Santa Fe, NMex; Area Arts Found, Amarillo, Tex; Susan Morse Hilles Collection, Dartmouth Col; Boston Mus of Fine Arts; Univ of Va, Charlottesville; Telfair Acad of Fine Arts, Savannah, Ga; Brandeis Univ Mus, Mass; plus others in corp collections. Exhib: Talent 1950, Kootz Gallery, New York; Nebr Univ Ann, 56, 58 & 60; Corcoran Gallery Biennials, Washington, DC, 57 & 59; Va Mus of Fine Arts, Richmond; Carnegie Inst Int, Pittsburgh, 57-59; 60 American Painters, Walker Art Ctr, Minneapolis, 60; Nature in Abstraction, Whitney Mus Am Art, New York, 60; 157th Ann, Pa Acad Fine Arts, 62; Five Am Painters, Knoedler Gallery, New York, NY, 63; Autumn Invitational, Roswell Mus, NMex, 77; 156th & 157th Painting Annuals, Nat Acad of Design, New York, NY, 77 & 78. Pos: Artist in residence, Princeton Univ, 59-62. Awards: Mus Purchase Award, Gloria Vanderbilt, 57; Childe Hassam Fund Purchase Award, Acad Arts & Lett, 70; Mark Rothko Found Grant. Bibliog: Thomas B Hess (auth), US painting: some recent directions, Art News Ann, 56; Martica Sawin (auth), Profile of Hyde Solomon, Arts Mag, 11/58. Media: Oil. Dealer: Poindexter Gallery 24 E 84th St New York NY 10028. Mailing Add: PO Box 2538 Taos NM 87571

SOLOMON, RICHARD H
ART PUBLISHER, PRINT DEALER, COLLECTOR
b Boston, Mass, May 12, 34. Study: Harvard Col, AB, 56; Harvard Bus Sch, MBA, 58. Pos: Pres, Pace Editions Inc/Pace Primitive & Ancient Art, New York. Specialty: Contemporary graphics (prints, multiples, tapestries, posters), African, Oceanic and American Indian art. Collection: Contemporary art and Primitive art. Mailing Add: c/o Pace Primitive & Ancient Art Pace Editions Inc 32 E 57th St New York NY 10022

SOLOMON, RUTH B
ART ADMINISTRATOR
b New York, NY, June 8, 21. Study: Hofstra Univ, BS, 67, fel, 67-68, MA, 68. Collections Arranged: Artists of Suffolk County Exhibitions, Heckscher Mus, Huntington, NY, 70-75, Windows and Doors, 72, Mistaken Identity, 73 & The Drama of the Sea, 75 (all with catalogs). Pos: Asst dir, Heckscher Mus, 68- Mem: Am Asn Mus; Int Coun Mus; Long Island Mus Asn (chmn, 78). Res: Artists of Suffolk County Register; active biographical and slide file of approximately five hundred eastern Long Island artists. Publ: Auth, Teachers Guide to Heckscher Museum Collection, 68; auth, Exhibition Catalogues, Heckscher Mus, 70- Mailing Add: 37 Highwood Rd East Norwich NY 11732

SOLOMON, MR & MRS SIDNEY L
COLLECTORS
Mr Solomon b Salem, Mass, Feb 21, 02; Mrs Solomon b Boston, Mass, May 15, 09. Study: Mr Solomon, Harvard Col, Harvard Univ Bus Sch; Mrs Solomon, Radcliffe Col, AB; Simmons Col, BS. Collection: Sculpture of the twentieth century to contemporary, including Giacometti, Lipschitz, Marini, Nevelson, Dubuffet, Arp, Chadwick, Calder, Schmidt, Doris Cassar & Trova; painting collection includes Sargent, Vuillard, Tomayo, Leger, Giacometti, Monet and Matta; drawings of Maillol, Archipenko, Degas, Lachaise & many others; watercolors of Nolde & Marini; also a collection of pop art. Mailing Add: 834 Fifth Ave New York NY 10021

SOLOMON, SYD
PAINTER, INSTRUCTOR
b Uniontown, Pa, July 12, 17. Study: Art Inst Chicago, 35; Ecole de Beaux Arts, Paris, 45. Work: Whitney Mus Am Art & Solomon R Guggenheim Mus, New York; Philadelphia Mus Art, Wadsworth Atheneum, Hartford, Conn; Joseph H Hirshhorn Mus, Washington, DC; among others. Exhib: Nat & int exhibs incl, Univ Ill, Corcoran, Biennial, Whitney Mus, Corcoran Gallery Art, Washington, DC; Guggenheim Mus; Art Inst Chicago, Nat Acad, New York; Retrospective, Ringling Mus, Sarasota, Fla, 74; plus many others. Teaching: Prof art, New Col, Sarasota, Fla, 66-69; dir painting classes, Ringling Mus Art, 52-55, Univ Ill, 68 & Roberson Ctr Art, 69. Pos: Camouflage designer, Engrs Bd, Washington, DC, 42; dir fac, Famous Artists Sch, 53-73. Awards: Ford Found Purchase Award, 65; Int Hallmark Exhib Award, New York; Silvermine Guild Award; plus others. Mem: Nat Soc Lit & Arts. Style & Technique: Abstract paintings in oil and acrylic combines with subject references to natural phenomena. Dealer: Saidenberg Gallery 1037 Madison Ave New York NY 10021; Art Sources 2101 Gulf Life Tower Jacksonville FL 32207. Mailing Add: 9210 Blind Pass Rd Sarasota FL 33581

SOLOWAY, RETA
PAINTER, LECTURER
b Washington, DC, June 10, 11. Study: Corcoran Sch Art, 22-27; Parsons, 28-30; Philadelphia Mus Sch Art, 31-35; Philadelphia Graphic Sketch, 35-36; Nat Acad Sch, 69; New Sch Social Res, 71; Sarah Lawrence Col, 75; Hofstra Univ, 76-77; and with Umberto Romano, Thornton Oakley, Henry Pitz, Joseph Stefanelli, Eric Isenburger & Mario Cooper. Work: Gregory Mus, Hicksville, NY. Comn: Portraits, Maj Gen Arthur Gaines, Denver, Colo, 70 & Dean Emer Charles Smythe, Pennington Prep Sch, 71. Exhib: Nat Art League, 65-75; Malverne Artists Long Island, 65-75; Allied Artists Am, 69-75; Catharine Lorillard Wolfe Art Club, 75. Teaching: Demonstr, Nat Acad, 66-75 & 77, Nat Arts Club, 73-77, Malverne Libr, 70- & IPA Nat Conv, Washington, DC, 72- Pos: Art adv & trustee, Gregory Mus. Awards: Best in Show, Gregory Mus Inc, 71; First in Oil, Long Beach Open Spring Exhib, 71; First in Oil, Malverne Artists 28th Open Exhib, 72-74. Mem: Allied Artists Am (adv, 69-72, corresp secy, 73-78); Artists Equity Asn NY; Nat Soc Painters in Casein & Acrylic (dir, Soc & treas, Pen & Brush Club); Catharine Lorillard Wolfe Art Club; Am Artists Prof League. Media: Oil, Watercolor. Publ: Contribr, Portrait in Occupational Therapy, 46 & Portrait of the World, 65. Dealer: Whit Gallery Ltd 351 E 61st St New York NY 10021. Mailing Add: 145 Lexington Ave Franklin Square NY 11010

SOLTESZ, FRANK JOSEPH
PAINTER
b Derry, Pa, June 14, 12. Study: Art Inst Pittsburgh, scholar, oil painting with Samuel Rosenberg; Carnegie Inst Technol, scholar; also with Charles Kinghan. Work: Frye Mus, Seattle, Wash. Comn: Paintings, The Fine Am Art Calendar, 74-75; painting, Graymoor Friars, 75. Exhib: Assoc Artists Exhib, Pittsburgh, 39; Am Watercolor Soc, New York, 62-75; Hudson Valley Art Asn, White Plains, NY, 62-75; Acad Artists, Springfield, Mass, 63-75; Am Artists Prof League, New York, 69-75. Teaching: Pvt classes in watercolor, Ridgefield, Conn, 64. Awards: Gold Medal of Honor, Hudson Valley Art Asn, 65; Gold Medal of Honor, Am Artists Prof League, 68 & 72. Mem: Am Watercolor Soc; Am Artists Prof League; Hudson Valley Art Asn (dir, 67-72); Acad Artists Asn (coun mem, 71-); Providence Art Club. Style & Technique: Realistic style in watercolor, oil, gouache, pen and ink, acrylic; portraits in charcoal and watercolor. Mailing Add: Rising Sun Trail Sherman CT 06784

SOLWAY, CARL E
ART DEALER
b Chicago, Ill, Jan 12, 35. Pos: Dir, Carl Solway Gallery, Cincinnati & New York. Mem: Art Dealers Asn Am. Specialty: 20th century American and European painting, sculpture and graphics; urban environment and wall projects; Eye Editions, publisher of graphic works by John Cage, Buckminster Fuller, Richard Hamilton & Nancy Graves. Mailing Add: 314 W Fourth St Cincinnati OH 45202

SOMERS, H
PAINTER
b Zweibruecken, Ger, May 28, 22; US citizen. Study: Dookie Col, Australia; City Col New York, cert; Art Students League; Brisbane Art Ctr, Australia; also with Joseph Schwartz & S Greene. Work: Dookie Libr, Victoria, Australia; Stadtmuseum Zweibruecken, Ger; Hollywood Art Mus, Fla; Metrop Mus & Art Ctr, Miami Fla; Jewish Mus, New York, NY; among others. Exhib: One-man shows, Galerie Felix Vercel, New York, 70-75 & Hilde Gerst Gallery, Palm Beach, Fla, 73-74; French Cult Charge D'Affairs Exhib, Washington, DC, 74; 19th & 20th Century Masters of Impressionism, Trosby Galleries, Palm Beach, 73-75; Carel Gallery, Miami Beach, Fla, 74-78; Hollywood Art Mus, Fla, 76; Mayer Gallery, Ft Lauderdale, 77; Richard Thompson Gallery, San Francisco, Calif, 78; also in Tokyo, Paris, Caracas, Johannesburg, Bruxelles, Montreal, Munich & others. Bibliog: Charles Z Offin (auth), H Somers, 70, 71 & 72 & Beatrice Dain (auth), H Somers, 3/74, Pictures on Exhibit; Lawrence Dame (auth), Somers the Impressionist, Palm Beach Post, 1/73. Mem: Am Artists Prof League. Style & Technique: Modern impressionism; pointillist palette knife technique. Media: Oil on Canvas, Graphic. Publ: The Art of Collecting, 63. Dealer: Hilde Gerst 681 Madison Ave New York NY 10021. Mailing Add: 5118 Adams St Hollywood FL 33021

SOMERVILLE, ROMAINE STEC
CURATOR, ART ADMINISTRATOR
b Scranton, Pa, May 24, 30. Study: Marymount Col, BA, 51; Columbia Univ, MA, 53; Yale Univ, 58-60. Collections Arranged: The Peale Collection of the Maryland Historical Society, 75 & Life in Maryland in the 18th Century, Bicentennial Exhib, 76, Md Hist Soc. Teaching: Lectr art hist, Marywood Col, Scranton, Pa, 54-58; lectr Am decorative arts, Johns Hopkins Univ Evening Sch, 78- Pos: Bd mem, Baltimore Heritage, Inc, 68-, Baltimore City Comt, Md Hist Trust, 71- & Soc for Preserv of Md Antiq, 75-77; asst dir/chief cur, Md Hist Soc, presently. Res: Nineteenth century American architecture, decorative arts and painting. Publ: Co-auth, Four Generations of Commissions: The Peale Collection of the Maryland Historical Society, 75 & contribr, Maryland Heritage, Five Baltimore Institutions Celebrate the American Bicentennial, 76, Md Hist Soc; auth, A Peale exhibition at the Maryland Historical Society, 76 & Furniture at the Maryland Historical Society, 76, Antiques Mag. Mailing Add: 118 W Lafayette Ave Baltimore MD 21217

SOMMER, FRANK H
ART LIBRARIAN, ART WRITER
b Newark, NJ, July 30, 22. Study: Yale Col; Yale Grad Sch; Corpus Christi Col of Cambridge Univ; Art Students League. Work: Yale Univ Art Gallery; Peabody Mus, Yale Univ; Brooklyn Mus, NY; Mus of Mod Art, New York; Wintherthur Mus, Del. Collections Arranged: Pennsylvanian German Folk Art, 62 & Recent Accessions, Winterthur Libr, 63-78, Winterthur Mus. Teaching: Teaching asst, Yale Univ, 46-48; from instr to prof anthrop & art hist, Univ Del, 48- Pos, Coordr, Winterthur Prog, Univ Del, 51-53; keeper of folk art, Winterthur Mus, 58-63; hd of librs, Winterthur Mus, 63- Awards: Henry Fel, Cambridge Univ, 47-48. Mem: Col Art Asn; Art Libr Soc NAm; Grolier Club. Res: Design books, trade catalogues, architectural books; Anglo-American classicism and United States folk art. Collection: Emblem books, 18th century intellectual history. Publ: Co-auth, Northwest Argentine Archeology, 48 & Excavations, 49, Yale Univ; auth, Triumph of Neptune, Warburg, 61; auth, Thomas Jefferson's First Plan, Friends of Independence Hall Nat Park, 76; auth, Metamorphoses of Britannia, Yale Univ, 76. Mailing Add: c/o Winterthur Mus Winterthur DE 19735

SOMMER, FREDERICK
PAINTER, PHOTOGRAPHER, LANDSCAPE ARCHITECT
b Angri, Italy, Sept 7, 05; US citizen. Study: Cornell Univ, Ithaca, NY, MA(landscape archit), 27. Work: Ctr for Creative Photog, Univ of Ariz, Tucson. Exhib: Realism in Photog, 49 & Picture Puzzles (with Man Ray, Clarence John Laughlin & Robert Cumming), 75, Mus of Mod Art, New York; one-man shows, Watercolors, Increase Robinson Gallery, Chicago, 34, Photogs, Santa Barbara Mus of Art, 46, Photogs & Drawings, Egan Gallery, New York, 49, Photogs, Paintings & Drawings, Inst of Design, Ill Inst of Technol, Chicago, 57, Art Inst of Chicago, 63, Drawings & Objects, Washington Gallery of Mod Art, DC & Pasadena Art Mus, 65, Philadelphia Col of Art, Pa, 68 & Light Gallery, New York, 72. Pos: Coordr, Fine Arts Studies, Prescott Col, Ariz, 66-71. Bibliog: Cynthia Jaffee McCabe (auth), The Golden Door, Artist-Immigrants of America, 1876-1976, Hirshhorn Mus & Sculpture Garden, Smithsonian Inst, Washington, DC, 76. Publ: Auth, The Poetic Logic of Art & Aesthetics, 72. Mailing Add: c/o Mountain Club Prescott AZ 86301

SOMMER, WASSILY
PAINTER, EDUCATOR
b St Petersburg, Russia, Jan 2, 12; US citizen. Study: Munich Art Mus, Ger; spec study with painter Oskar Kokoschka, Austria; Philadelphia Mus Sch; Pa Acad Fine Arts. Work: Anchorage Hist & Fine Arts Mus; Alaska State Mus, Juneau; Alaska Methodist Univ; Anchorage Community Col; Consortium Libr, Anchorage. Comn: Portrait of Ora D Clark, Anchorage Women's Club, Clark Jr High Sch, 63; two murals (Alaska motif), Leo Daly & Assocs, Seattle for Elmendorf AFB Officer's Club, Anchorage, 66. Exhib: One-man shows, Anchorage Hist & Fine Arts Mus, 68, 71 & 78, Art Inc Gallery, Anchorage, 78 & Rodevous Gallery, Anchorage, 78; 22nd & 23rd Spokane Ann Art Exhib, Cheney Cowles Mus, 69 & 70; 12th Ann Wash State Art Exhib, Wenatchee, 71; five-man shows, Mel Koehler Gallery, Seattle, 72; Grand Galleria Third Ann Nat Art Competition, Seattle, 74; Contemp Art from Alaska, Smithsonian Inst, Washington, DC, 78. Teaching: Prof art, Univ Alaska, Anchorage, 67- Awards: Thomas Eakins Award in Painting, Pa Acad Fine Arts, 59; Best of Show, Alaska Centennial Exhib, Alaska State Mus, Juneau, 67; plus many others. Mem: Fel Pa Acad Fine Arts; hon life mem Alaska Artists Guild. Style & Technique: Modern semiabstract style; acrylic and oil painting techniques. Media: Acrylic, Oil. Mailing Add: 2744 E 20th Ave Anchorage AK 99504

SOMMERBURG, MIRIAM
PAINTER, SCULPTOR
b Hamburg, Ger; US citizen. Study: Sculpture with Richard Luksch, Ger & design with Freidrich Adler, Ger. Work: Metrop Mus Art, New York; Butler Inst Am Art, Youngstown, Ohio; Springfield Mus, Mo; B'nai B'rith Mus; Norfolk Mus, Va. Exhib: Brooklyn Mus, NY, 51-54; Whitney Mus, NY, 51-54; Ger Acad of Fine Arts, Berlin, 54; Pa Acad, Philadelphia, 54 & 66; Burlington Gallery, London, Eng, 55; Stedelijk Mus, Amsterdam, Neth, 56; Mus of Mod Art, Rio de Janeiro, 63; Museo de Belles Artes, Buenos Aires, Arg, 63; Edinburgh, Scotland, 63, Birmingham, Eng, 64, Mus Cognac, Cannes, France, 65-66, New Delhi, Bombay & Calcutta, India, 65-66 & Palazzo Vecchio, Florence & Pompeiian Pavilo, Naples, Italy, 72; Palace of Fine Arts, Mexico City, Mex, 72; Am Drawings, Portsmouth, Va, 76; plus many others. Pos: Life fel, Intercontinental Biog Asn, Eng, 72- Awards: First, Second & Third Prizes for Sculpture & Graphics, Village Art Ctr, 46-60; Award, Creative Gallery, 51; Award, Fla S Col, 52; Award, Knickerbocker Art Gallery, 54; Awards, Am Soc of Contemp Artists, 58, 62 & 64; Awards (two), Design in Hardwood, Chicago, 59; Award, Silvermine Guild, 59; Mem Award for Sculpture, Nat Asn Women Artists, 61; Medal for Creative Sculpture, Audubon Artists, 66 & Award for Sculpture, 78; Int Women's Yr Award, 75-76. Bibliog: Articles in, La Rev Mod, Paris, 66-74 & Hermitage Mag, 66, M Elliott Bevlin (ed), article in, Design Through Discovery, Holt, 70; Joseph L Young (auth), Mosaics; among others. Mem: Audubon Artists (sculpture jury, 68); Am Asn Contemp Artists; Nat Asn Women Artists (sculpture jury, 62-65, graphics jury, 66-69); Print Coun Am; Artists Equity. Style & Technique: Semi-abstract expressionist. Media: Wood, Stone, Stained Glass, Mosaic in the Round. Mailing Add: c/o Westbeth-Artists Housing Apt G227 463 West St New York NY 10014

SOMMERS, JOHN SHERMAN
LITHOGRAPHER, EDUCATOR
b Cassopolis, Mich, May 31, 27. Study: Albion Col, BA, 52, postgrad, 66-68; Univ NMex, 68, 70-72; Tamarind Lithography Workshop printer fel, 68-69, cert Tamarind Master Printer, 69. Work: Tamarind Collection, Univ NMex; Amon Carter Mus Western Art; Mus Mod Art, New York; Grunwald Graphic Arts Found, Univ Calif, Los Angeles; Pasadena Art Mus. Exhib: Group & one-man shows, 23rd Nat Print Exhib, Washington, DC, 73; Southwestern Fine Arts Biennial, Santa Fe, NMex, 73-75; Univ Dallas Graphics Invitational, Irving, Tex, 74; 2nd Miami Graphics Biennial, Fla, 75; 20, Colorado-New Mexico Invitational, Colorado Springs Fine Arts Ctr, 75. Teaching: Lectr in art, Univ NMex, 75-; lithography workshops, Tamarind Inst, Univ NMex, 74-75 & Calif, Ariz, Mich, Ind & Ill, 74-75. Pos: Studio mgr, Tamarind Inst, Univ NMex, 70-75 & tech dir, 75- Awards: Purchase Prize, Northern Ill Univ, 68; Cash Award-First, NMex State Univ, 75. Media: Lithography, Watercolor. Publ: Co-auth, Dessin a la pointe, lithographic line engraving, No 1 & auth, Acrylic reversal, No 2, co-auth, Gum arabic: is there an alternative, No 4, Tamarind Tech Papers; co-ed, Graphics Mag, spring, 75. Dealer: Mission Gallery Taos NM 87571. Mailing Add: 8414 San Juan Rd NE Albuquerque NM 87108

SONDAY, MILTON FRANKLIN, JR
CURATOR
b Hamburg, Pa, Dec 18, 39. Study: Wyomissing Inst of Fine Arts, Pa, 55-61; Carnegie-Mellon Univ, Pittsburgh, Pa, 57-61, BFA(painting & design), 61; Penland Sch of Crafts, NC, summer 66; E Tenn State Univ (Penland Sch), summer 67; US Dept Agr Grad Sch, Washington, DC, fall 67; The Textile Mus (seminar), 67: The New Sch, New York, 68; Ctr Int d'Etude des Textiles Anciens, Lyon, France, 9/69. Exhib: Student Exhib, Carnegie Inst of Technol, 57-61; Reading Pub Mus & Art Gallery, Pa, 63; Gallery of Mod Art, Fredricksburg, Va, 63; Acting cur of Textiles, Cooper-Hewitt Mus of Design, Smithsonian Mus, New York, 68-; asst cur of textiles, Cooper Union Mus, New York, 67-68; mus asst & staff artist, The Textile Mus, Washington, DC, 62-65, keeper of rugs, 65-67. Awards: New York Home Fashion League Art Award, 72. Mem: Ctr Int d'Etudes des Textiles Anciens, Lyon, France. Publ: Illusr, Horsemen in Tapestry Roundels Found in Egypt, The Textile Mus J, 63; illusr, Principles of Textile Conservation Science, The Textile Mus J, 63-64; illusr, Tiahuanaco Tapestry Design, The Textile Mus J, 63; auth, Counterchange & New Color, Handweaver and Craftsman, summer, 69; co-auth, with N Kajitani, A Type of Mughal Sash, J of The Textile Mus, 70 & A Second Type of Mughal Sash, 71. Mailing Add: c/o Cooper-Hewitt Mus 9 E 90th St New York NY 10028

SONENBERG, JACK
PAINTER
b Toronto, Ont, Dec 28, 25; US citizen. Study: Ont Col Art, Toronto; NY Univ; Washington Univ, BFA. Work: Guggenheim Mus, New York; Whitney Mus Am Art, New York; Metrop Mus Art, New York; Nat Gallery Can, Ottawa. Exhib: Whitney Mus Am Art Painting Ann, 67; Whitney Mus Am Art Biennial, 73; Cut Folded & Torn, Mus Mud Art, 74; Painting & Sculpture Today, Indianapolis Mus Contemp Art Ctr, 74; Small Scale in Contemp Art, Chicago Art Inst, 75. Teaching: Instr painting & printmaking, Pratt Inst, 68- Pos: Ford Found & Am Fedn Arts Artist in resident grant, Hampton Inst, 66. Awards: First Prize for Painting, 13th New Eng Ann, 62; NY State Coun CAPS Grant, 73; Guggenheim Found Grant, 73. Media: Wood, Canvas, Metal. Dealer: Brooke Alexander 328 E 78th St New York NY 10021; Fischbach Gallery 29 W 57th St New York NY 10010. Mailing Add: 217 E 23rd St New York NY 10010

SONFIST, ALAN
PAINTER
b New York, NY, May 26, 46. Study: Pratt Inst; Hunter Col, MA. Work: Mus Mod Art, New York; Boston Mus Fine Art; Oberlin Art Mus, Ohio; Wallarf-Richartz Mus, Köln, Ger; Power Inst, Sydney, Australia. Exhib: One-man shows, Reese Palley, New York, 70, Landscapes 72, Paley and Lowe, New York, Autobiography of Alan Sonfist, Johnson Mus, Ithaca, NY, Leaves, Autobiography, Thelen Galerie, Köln, Ger, 75, Alan Sonfist Autobiography, Neue Galerie, Aachen, Ger, 75; Boston Element Show, Mus Fine Arts, 71; Stedelijk Mus, Holland, 71; Nature of Things, Harcus Karkow, Boston, 71; Autobiography, Boston Mus of Fine Art, Mass, 77. Teaching: Vis prof, Pa Col Art, Philadelphia, 73-74. Bibliog: Gracie Gleuck (auth), Nature artist, NY Times, 11/70; Cindy Nemser (auth), Sonfist-phenomenist, Art in Am, 3/71; Benthall (auth), Sonfist & Hacue, Studio Int, 6/71; R Horvitz (auth), Nature as artifact, Artforum, 10/73. Mailing Add: 833 Broadway New York NY 10003

SONNEMAN, EVE
PHOTOGRAPHER, FILMMAKER
b Chicago, Ill, Jan 14, 46. Study: Univ Ill, Urbana-Champaign, BFA, 67; Univ NMex, Albuquerque, MA, 69. Work: Mus Mod Art, New York; Mus Fine Arts, Houston; Art Inst Chicago; Minneapolis Inst Art; Menil Found, Houston. Exhib: One-man shows, Art Resources Ctr, Whitney Mus, New York, 73, Tex Gallery, Houston, 74, 75 & 77, Galerie Farideh Cadot, Paris, France, 77 & Castelli Gallery, New York, 77 & 78; Light Gallery, New York, 73 & 75; Bykert Gallery, New York, 74 & 75; From the Vogel Collection, Inst Contemp Art, Philadelphia, 75; Paris Biennale, France, 77; Documenta VI, Kassel, Ger, 77; plus many others. Teaching: Vis artist photog, Rice Univ, 71-72; vis instr photog, Sch Visual Arts, New York, 75-; vis instr art, Cooper Union Col Art & Architecture, 75- Awards: Photography grants, Nat Endowment Arts, 71-72 & 78. Bibliog: Seibundo Shinkosha (auth), Photographers in New York, Japan, 73; Jeremy Gilbert-Rolfe (auth), Review of Bykert exhibition, Artforum, 2/74; Group Portrait: 3 New York Photographers (film), Cable Arts, NY State Coun Arts, 75; Real Time, Printed Matter Press, New York, NY; Carter Ratcliff (auth), rev in Art in Am, Vol 65, No 6. Style & Technique: Color and black and white sequence photographs exploring the perception of time. Publ: Contribr photog, Is America Used Up, Grossman, 73. Dealer: Castelli Gallery 4 E 77th St New York NY 10021. Mailing Add: 98 Bowery New York NY 10013

SONNENBERG, MR & MRS BENJAMIN
COLLECTORS
Collection: Ancient art, ethnographica. Mailing Add: 19 Gramercy Park New York NY 10003

SONNENBERG, FRANCES
SCULPTOR, INSTRUCTOR
b Brooklyn, NY. Study: With Prof Alfred Van Loen. Comn: Five ft carved acrylic sculpture, Aquarius, Fla, 75. Exhib: Audubon Artists, Nat Acad Gallery, New York, 73 & 74; Nat Sculpture Soc, Lever House, New York, 74; Nat Asn Women Artists, Nat Acad Gallery, 75; one-woman shows, Stephan Gallery, New York, Buyways Gallery, Fla, Shelter Rock Gallery, NY, Cedar Crest Col, Pa & Adelphi Univ, NY. Teaching: Sculpture Classes in own studio, 72- Mem: Nat Asn Women Artists; NY Soc Women Artists (secy, 73-74, rec secy, 74-); Metrop Painters & Sculptors (rec secy, 73-, secy, 74-); Am Soc Contemp Artists; Artist Craftsman. Style & Technique: Carves directly into acrylic; also innovative in combining color; abstract & figurative. Mailing Add: Rockhill Rd Roslyn Heights NY 11577

SONNENSCHEIN, HUGO
PATRON, ART HISTORIAN
b Chicago, Ill, Feb 22, 17. Study: Swarthmore Col; Lake Forest Col, BA; Univ Va, LLB & JD; John Marshall Law Sch, Chicago, LLM. Pos: Ed, Chicago Bar Rec, 50-66; trustee, Lake Forest Col, 69-; mem comt libr, Art Inst Chicago, 73- Mem: Gov life mem Art Inst Chicago; Mus Mod Art; Soc Contemp Art; Asn Art Historians. Res: Prints and drawings; legal art. Interest: Donor, Sonnenschein Collection to Lake Forest Col, Lake Forest Acad & Univ Mich. Mailing Add: 115 S La Salle St Chicago IL 60603

SONNIER, KEITH
ENVIRONMENTAL ARTIST, VIDEO ARTIST
b Mamou, La, 1941. Study: Univ Southwestern La, Lafayette, 59-63, BA, 63; France, 63-64; Rutgers Univ, New Brunswick, NJ, 64-66, MFA, 66. Exhib: Eccentric Abstraction, Fischbach Gallery, New York, 66; When Attitudes Become Form (traveling Europe), Kunsthalle, Berne, Switz, 69; Tokyo Biennale (toured Japan), Metrop Art Gallery, 70; Prospect 71, Projection, Kunsthalle, Dusseldorf, 71; Documenta 5, Kassel, Ger, 72; Contemporanea, Parcheggio Borghese, Rome, 73; Projekt 74, Kunsthalle, Cologne, 74; one-man shows, Douglass Col, New Brunswick, NJ, 66, Stedelijk van Abbemuseum, Eindhoven, Neth, 70 & Mus of Mod Art, New York, 71. Awards: Guggenheim Fel, New York, 74. Bibliog: David Antin (auth), Eccentric Abstraction, 11/66 & Robert Pincus-Witten (auth), Keith Sonnier: Video and film as color field, 5/72, Artforum, New York; Lucy Lippart (auth), On Erotic Art, Hudson Review, New York, spring 67. Style & Technique: Mixed media sculpture and environment, film and videotape. Publ: Auth, Object-Situation-Object 1969-70, Cologne, 72. Mailing Add: c/o Leo Castelli Gallery E 77th St New York NY 10021

SORBY, J RICHARD
PAINTER, EDUCATOR
b Duluth, Minn, Dec 21, 11. Study: Univ Minn; Univ Northern Colo, AB, 37, MA, 51; Art Inst Chicago; Univ of the Am; Univ Calif, Los Angeles, with John Ferren; Univ Colo, with Jimmy Ernst. Work: William Rockhill Nelson Gallery, Kansas City, Mo; Denver Art Mus, Colo; Oakland Art Mus; Whitney Mus, New York; Pa Acad of Fine Arts, Philadelphia; Walker Art Ctr, Minneapolis; de Saisset Gallery, Santa Clara, Calif; Richmond Mus of Art, Calif; Crown Col, Univ Calif, Santa Cruz; Art Ctr, San Luis Obispo, Calif; Joslyn Mem Mus Art, Omaha, Nebr; Brigham Young Univ; Rural Electrification Admin, Washington, DC. Comn: Spaulding Mem, Papantla (pyroxylin), Univ Northern Colo, Greeley, 58. Exhib: Denver Art Mus Ann Western Artists, 40-59; Nat Watercolor Competition, Nat Gallery Art, Washington, DC, 41; 1st & 2nd Ann Rocky Mountain Nat, Utah State Univ, 57 & 58; Northern Calif Artists Ann, Crocker Art Gallery, Sacramento, 61-68; Mid-Am Ann Exhibs, Nelson Gallery Art, Kansas City, Mo. Teaching: Instr art, Univ Nebr, Lincoln, 40-42; assoc prof painting, Sch Art, Univ Denver, 47-59; prof painting & design, Calif State Univ, San Jose, 59-72, emer prof, 72- Awards: First Award & Purchase for Crown of Light, 4th Biennial 10 State Exhib, Joslyn Mem Mus, 56; First Prize for Passing Shadows (acrylic collage), Univ Santa Clara Sullivan-Hickson Fund, 66; First Award & Purchase for Mountain Stream, 27 Ann, Cedar City, Utah, 67. Bibliog: Arneil (auth), Work of Richard Sorby, Empire Mag, Denver Post, 11/58; M L Stribling (auth), Painting in found materials, 71. Mem: East Bay Artists Asn (vpres, 67-68); Group 21 (vpres, 72). Style & Technique: Poetry of painting—evocative generalization of mood or feeling inspired by some aspect of nature. Media: Acrylic, Watercolor, Mixed Media. Publ: Illusr, Lincoln-Mercury Times, 54, Ford Times, 56 & Empire Mag, Denver Post, 58. Dealer: Copenhagen Galleri Hamlet Sq Solvang CA 93463. Mailing Add: Morningsun Studio Glen Haven CO 80532

SOREFF, HELEN
PAINTER
b New York, NY. Study: Atlanta Art Inst, BFA; Art Students League; NY Univ; C W Post Col, Long Island Univ, MA, 76. Comn: Painting, Big Thing Show, Seattle Wash Art Comt, 69; painting, Inter-Disciplinary Jour, Queens Col, NY, 72. Exhib: Corcoran Mus Lending Libr, Washington, DC, 64-66; Albright-Knox Mus, Buffalo, NY, 65-66; Seattle Art Mus, 69; Women Choose Women, New York Cult Ctr, 72; New York City Invitational, John Weber Gallery, 75; Hal Bromm Gallery, New York, NY, 76; Marianne Deson Gallery, Chicago, Ill, 77; one-woman shows, Mercer Gallery, 77 & Bertha Urdang Gallery, New York, 77. Teaching: Instr basic art, Univ Wash, Seattle, 69; lectr contemp art, Spec Progs, Hofstra Univ, Hempstead, NY, 71-72. Pos: Organizer, C W Post Women in the Arts Exhib, 8/72; cur, New Drawings, Women's Interart Ctr, 11/74. Awards: High Mus of Art Scholar, Atlanta, 50; Beaux Arts Scholar, Atlanta Art Inst, 52; Grand Concours, Art Students League, 53. Bibliog: Axel Hecht (auth), Four Westbeth artists, Paik, Colette, Haacke, Soreff, Der Stern Mag, Hamburg, Ger; John Gruen (auth), SoHo News Art Ed, 4/75. Mem: Women in the Arts, New York. Style & Technique: Minimal conceptual linear abstractions. Media: Acrylic. Dealer: Kathryn Markel Gallery 50 W 57th St New York NY; Bertha Urdang Gallery 23 E 74th St New York NY. Mailing Add: 79 Mercer St New York NY 10012

SOREL, EDWARD
ILLUSTRATOR, WRITER
b New York, NY, Mar 26, 29. Study: High Sch Music & Art, dipl, 47; Cooper Union, dipl, 51. Exhib: One-man shows, Graham Gallery, New York, 73 & New Sch Social Res, 74; Push Pin Style, Mus des Arts Decoratifs, Paris, 70; Univ Ky, 75. Pos: Co-founder, Push-Pin Studios, New York, 53-56; art dir, CBS Promotion Art, New York, 56-57; syndicated cartoonist, King Features, 69-71; contribr, Atlantic Mag, 69-; contrib ed, New York Mag, 72-; cartoonist, Village Voice, 74- Awards: New York Herald Tribune Book Award for Illustration, 62; St Gauden's Medal, Cooper Union, 73. Bibliog: Carlos C Drake (auth), Edward Sorel, Graphis, No 105, 63; Jerome Snyder (auth), Edward Sorel, Graphis, No 154, 71-72. Mem: Am Inst Graphic Arts; Illusr Guild; Alliance Graphique. Style & Technique: Satirical cartoons & drawings. Media: Pen & Ink, Watercolor. Publ: Illusr, Gwendolyn the Miracle Hen, 63; illusr, Word People, 70; illusr, Magical Storybook, 72; auth & illusr, Moon Missing, 72; auth & illusr, Making the World Safe for Hypocrisy, 72. Mailing Add: Rte 301 Carmel NY 10512

SORELL, VICTOR ALEXANDER
ART HISTORIAN, ART ADMINISTRATOR
b Mexico City, Mex, Oct 31, 44; Can citizen. Study: Shimer Col, with Andrew Armstrong, BA; Univ Chicago, with Joshua C Taylor and John Rewald, MA. Collections Arranged: Mexposición I (with catalog in Eng & Span), A Montgomery Ward Gallery, Univ Ill, Chicago Circle, 75, II: Photographic Images of the Mex Revolution by Agustín Víctor Casasola, A Montgomery Ward Gallery, Univ Ill, Chicago Circle, 76 & III: Woman as Creator, Subject & Theme in Art, Cult Ctr, Chicago Pub Libr, 78. Teaching: Chmn art dept, Chicago State Univ, 69- Pos: Co-ed, Abrazo (Embrace) J, 76-; prog adminr, Park Forest Art Ctr, 78. Awards: Fac Scholar, Int Design Conf, Aspen, 75; Fac Scholar, Inst Bilingual Educ, Educ Prof Develop Act, 75; co-recipient grant, Ill Humanities Coun, 76. Mem: Am Studies Asn (chmn local chap mem comt, 75-76); Col Art Asn Am (chmn mural movement sessions & host comt mem, 1976 Conf); el Movimiento Artistíco Chicano (vchmn, MARCH, 75-77); Am & Brit Soc Aesthet. Res: Documentary investigation of modern (1900-present) Canadian and US mural art. Publ: Made in Chicago (transl), 12th Sao Paulo Bienal, 73; auth, Leopoldo Mendez (catalog), 75; auth, Latin American muralists in Chicago, Revista Chicano—Riqueña, Ind Univ-Northwest, 75; co-reviewer articles in American studies sect, Am Quart, 69-73; transl, José David Alfaro Siqueiros (auth), Como Se Pinto un Mural (How to Paint a Mural), 78. Mailing Add: 10601 S Parkside Ave Apt 3B Chicago Ridge IL 60415

SORGE, WALTER
PAINTER, PRINTMAKER
b Forestberg, Alta, Can, Oct 25, 31. Study: Univ Calif, Los Angeles, BA, 54, MA, 55; Columbia Univ, New York, EDD, 64; also with Stanley William Hayter, Paris, France, 61-62 & 68. Work: Victoria & Albert Mus, London, Eng; J B Speed Mus, Louisville, Ky; Sheldon Swope Art Gallery, Terre Haute, Ind; Evansville Mus of Arts & Sci, Ind. Exhib: One-manshows, Vancouver Art Gallery, Can, 55, J B Speed Mus, Louisville, Ky, 69, Inst Mex NAm de Relationes Cult, Mexico City, 71; Sheldon Swope Art Gallery, Terre Haute, Ind, 71, Am Embassies, Ankara, Izmir & Istanbul, Turkey, 74-75; 2nd Can Biennial, 57 & Canadian Watercolors, Drawings & Prints, 66, Nat Gallery of Can; Smithsonian Inst Traveling Exhib, Washington, DC, 67. Pos: Chmn dept painting, drawing & printmaking, Ky Southern Col, 64-69 & Hardin-Simmons Univ, Tex, 69-70; chmn dept, Eastern Ill Univ, Charleston, 70-75, prof painting, drawing & printmaking, 75-; exchange prof, Portsmouth Polytech Inst, EnG, 77. Awards: C W Jefferys Award, 26th Ann Exhib, Can Soc of Graphic Art, 59; Jr League Purchase Award, Mid-States Art Exhib, Evansville Mus of Arts & Sci, Ind, 67; Helen Van Aken Purchase Award, 5th Ann Gulf Coast Exhib, Mobile Art Gallery, 70. Style & Technique: Landscape and figurative work in watercolor and mixed media; printmaking, copper and steel color intaglio. Media: Watercolor, Mixed Media; Metal Plate Color Intaglio. Mailing Add: 715 Lincoln Charleston IL 61920

SORIANO, JUAN
PAINTER, SCULPTOR
b Guadalajara, Jalisco, Mex, Aug 18, 20. Work: Mus de Arte Mod, Mex; Banco de Cedulas Hipotecarias, SA, Mex; Coleccion de Lomas Verdes, SA, Mex; Salon de la Plastica de Mex; Inst Nac de bellas artes, Mex. Exhib: Mexico: The New Generation, Univ Tex, Austin, 66; Expo 67, Mex & Montreal, 67; Palace of Fine Arts, 69; Juan Soriano, Painting 1942-1969, Inst Nac Bellas Artes, 69; Contemp Mex Painting, Mus Mod Art, Japan, 74. Awards: Premio de Adquisicion, Salon de la Plastica de Mex. Bibliog: Cardoza Y Aragon (auth), Pintura Actual, 64 & Damian Bayon (auth), Aventura Plastica, 74, Fondo de Cult Economica. Style & Technique: Figurative with an oneiric tradition. Media: Oil, Pastel; Ceramic, Bronze. Dealer: Galeria de Arte Mexicano Milan 18 Mexico 6 DF Mexico. Mailing Add: c/o Galeria Juan Martin Amberes 17 Mexico DF Mexico

SOROKA, MARGERY
PAINTER
b New York, NY, May 30, 20. Study: Hunter Col; Art Students League; with Edgar A Whitney & Rex Brandt. Work: Va State Col; Northland State Jr Col, Thief River Falls, Minn; E R Squibb Sci Info Libr, New Brunswick, NJ; Forbes, Inc, New York; Old Queens Gallery, Highland Park, NJ. Exhib: Am Watercolor Soc, var times, 64-78; Watercolor USA, 68; Audubon Artists, 68-78. Pos: Art Dir, Planned Parenthood Fedn of Am, Inc, New York, 73- Awards: Lena Newcastle Award, Am Watercolor Soc, 68; Winsor Newton Award, Nat Arts Club, 68; Salmagundi Art Club Award, 74. Bibliog: L E Levick (auth), Review, New York J-Am, 66. Mem: Am Watercolor Soc; Knickerbocker Artists; Salmagundi Art Club; Whiskey Painters Am. Style & Technique: Abstract-] Expressionist. Media: Watercolors. Publ: Contribr, The Artist's Sketchbook by Rex Brandt, 67; contribr, The Watercolor Page, Am Artist Mag, 2/71. Mailing Add: 200 E 16th St New York NY 10003

SOROKIN, MAXINE ANN
PAINTER, EDUCATOR
b Brooklyn, NY, Dec 15, 48. Study: Kingsborough Community Col, AA, 67; Brooklyn Col, BA (cum laude), 70, MFA, with Philip Pearlstein, Jimmy Ernst, Robert Wolff & Samuel Gelber, 72. Comn: Window & Portal Paintings, Congregation of Kehillath Jacobs Synagogue, Newton, Mass, 73. Exhib: New York figurative Painting Show, First St Gallery, 71; two-person traveling exhib, Austrian Inst, New York, 72; Invitational, Newton city Hall, Mass, 73-76; Meetinghouse Gallery, Boston, 73; Boston Visual Artists Union, 74 & 75. Teaching: Teaching fel & grad asst painting, Brooklyn Col, 71-72; lectr art, Univ Mass, Boston, 72-73; instr art, Art Inst of Boston, 73- Awards: Eisler Award Painting Excellence, City Univ New York, 70. Bibliog: Lise Taylor (producer), Woman 76, WBZ Television, 76. Mem: Boston Visual Artists Union (mem materials comt, 75-77); West Roxbury Artists Asn (exhib chmn, 76-77, vpres, 77-78); West Roxbury Hist Soc (mem res comt, 75-); Victorian Soc. Style & Technique: Figurative realist. Media: Oil; Pen and Ink. Dealer: Crieger Art Assocs 801 Water Street Framingham MA 01701. Mailing Add: 61 Perham St West Roxbury MA 02132

SOSNOWITZ, HENRY ABRAM
COLLECTOR, PATRON
b Warsaw, Poland, July 13, 40; US citizen. Study: Lublin Univs, Warsaw, BA; also with Henryk Sienkiewicz. Work: Sosnowitz collection of artist Kenneth Hari in Vatican, Rome, Trenton State Mus, NJ, Lincoln Ctr Libr & Mus Collection, Sport Mus & Metrop Mus Art, New York. Interest: American art, to create a renaissance in the US. Collection: Artists Donald Delue, Kenneth Hari, G'Miglio, J A Whistler, Mary Cassett, F Leyendecker. Mailing Add: Box 243 Keasbey NJ 08832

SOULT, JAMES THOMAS
CURATOR, GRAPHIC ARTIST
b Beloit, Wis, Mar 12, 35. Study: Col San Mateo; Hayward State Univ, with Mel Ramos, BA; San Jose State Univ, also with Al Barela, MA. Work: Richmond Art Ctr, Calif; City of Fremont, Calif; Alameda Co Art Comn, Alameda. Exhib: New York Int, NY Coliseum, New York, 70; Washington & Jefferson 4th Nat Painting Show, Ball State Univ, 72; Trading Co,

Univ Calif, San Francisco, 74; one-man show, Xergo Gallery, Oakland, Calif, 74. Collections Arranged: Richmond Area Artists, 73; Battenberg-Beaseley Sculpture Exhib, 74; Artes Plasticas de Mexico (with catalog under NEA grant), 74-75. Teaching: Instr drawing, Ohlone Col, Fremont, Calif, 70-73. Pos: Activ coordr, Olive Hyde Art Ctr, Fremont, 68-72; cur, Richmond Art Ctr, Calif, 72- Awards: Cal-Expo, State of Calif, Sacramento, 71; 10th Ann Benedictine Awards, Julius Wiles & Sons Inc, 72; Zellerbach Gallery Exhib, KQED-TV, 73. Bibliog: 3 Bay Area artists on KQED-TV, 73; Dona Meilach (auth), Soft Sculpture, Crown, 74; Thomas Albright (auth), The Trading Company San Francisco Chronicle, 75. Mem: Western Asn Art Mus; Am Asn Mus. Style & Technique: Drawing media on canvas and/or paper; abstracted natural forms relating to flesh contrasted with hard geometrical forms. Media: Colored Pencil & Other Media on Paper; Silverpoint on Canvas. Dealer: ADI Gallery 530 McAllister St San Francisco CA 94102; Contemp Royale 1509 W Seventh Ave Vancouver BC Can. Mailing Add: 1025 Parkside Dr Richmond CA 94803

SOUZA, PAUL MARCIEL
PAINTER, INSTRUCTOR
b Honomu, Hawaii, Jan 16, 18. Study: Honolulu Acad Arts; Univ Hawaii; Art Ctr Col Design. Work: Lytton Savings & Loan, Canoga Park, Calif; Pac Savings & Loan, Downey, Calif; Univ Hawaii; Ahmanson Collection, Los Angeles. Comn: Exterior ceramic mural, Long Beach Harbor Admin Bldg; paintings for Gunsmoke (TV prog), Columbia Broadcasting Syst. Exhib: One-man shows, Comara Gallery, Los Angeles, 62, Emerson Gallery, Encino, Calif, 65, Challis Galleries, Laguna Beach, Calif, 74, Goteborg, Sweden, 75; Am Watercolor Soc, New York. Teaching: Instr painting & drawing, Art Ctr Col Design, Los Angeles, 46- Awards: John Singer Sargent Mem Award in Watercolor, Springfield Art Mus, 63; Sanders Purchase Award, 70 & Ahmanson Award, 73, Nat Watercolor Soc. Bibliog: Henry J Seldis, Souza creates refreshing debut, Los Angeles Times Calendar, 7/29/62. Mem: Am Watercolor Soc; Nat Watercolor Soc (vpres, 64-65 & 70-71). Style & Technique: Combined realism and abstraction. Media: Watercolor, Oil. Mailing Add: 2828 Oak Point Dr Hollywood CA 90068

SOVARY, LILLY
PAINTER, DESIGNER
b Sovar, Hungary; US citizen. Study: Calif State Univ, San Francisco, with Alexander Nepote; Calif State Univ, San Jose, with Dr Tansey; Univ Idaho, with John Davis & Ray Obermyer. Work: Collections of own paintings, sculptured driftwoods and collages being held in its entirety for presentation at some future date. Exhib: San Francisco Univ Art Dept Exhib, 53-54, Univ Idaho Archit & Art Dept, 56-59 & 81st Ann Painting Exhib, San Francisco Mus Art, 62; plus many other viewings. Teaching: Guest lectr, Univ Idaho, 56-59 & organic art & lang arts, Calif Col Arts & Crafts, 71 & Langley-Porter Clin, 73. Bibliog: Dana Atchley & William Farley (auths), Sovary: The Contemporary Artist (film), Calif Col Arts & Crafts & Dana Atchley's Space Atlas & Notebook, 72-73. Media: Watercolor, Casein, Oil, Crayon & Driftwood. Res: Comparison of contemporary architectural styles. Publ: Contribr, miscellaneous excerpts and poems in: Assembling, Assemblying Press, 71. Mailing Add: 1276 Second Ave San Francisco CA 94122

SOVIAK, HARRY
PAINTER, INSTRUCTOR
b Lorain, Ohio, May 25, 35. Study: Bowling Green State Univ, Ohio; Cranbrook Acad of Art, Bloomfield Hills, Mich, BFA, MFA with Fred Mitchell & Zoltan Sepeshy. Work: Philadelphia Mus of Art; Ill Bell Telephone Co, Chicago; NJ State Mus, Trenton; New York Univ, Continental Bank, Philadelphia. Exhib: Albright-Knox Art Gallery, Buffalo, NY, 63; San Francisco Mus of Art, 65; De Cordova Mus, Lincoln, Mass, 65; Mus of Mod Art, New York, 66; Finch Col Mus of Art, New York, 67; Philadelphia Mus of Art, 70; Whitney Mus of Am Art, New York, 70; NJ State Mus, Trenton, 70; one-man shows, Richard Feigen Gallery, New York, 64, 67 & 70 & Marion Locks Gallery, Philadelphia, 70, 73 & 76. Teaching: Prof painting/drawing, Philadelphia Col of Art, Philadelphia, 63- Awards: Buenos Aires Convention Fel, 58-59. Bibliog: J Patrice Marandel (auth), Harry Soviak, Art Int, 11/70. Style & Technique: Representational still life. Media: Watercolor, Oil. Dealer: Marian Locks Gallery 1524 Walnut St Philadelphia Pa 19102. Mailing Add: 181 St John's Pl Brooklyn NY 11217

SOWERS, MIRIAM R
PAINTER, WRITER
b Bluffton, Ohio, Oct 4, 22. Study: Miami Univ; Art Inst Chicago; Univ NMex. Work: Tex A&I Univ; Goldwaters Dept Store; Mus of NMex Art Gallery; Lovelace Clin, Albuquerque; New York World's Fair; Nat Arch, Washington, DC. Comn: Many comn portraits; stained glass mural-painting. Exhib: Dayton Art Inst, Ohio; Butler Inst Am Art; Akron Art Inst; Santa Fe Mus Biennial; Ohio State Fair; Roswell Mus, NMex; Sun Carnival, El Paso; Fiesta Show, Tucson, Ariz; Canton Ohio Art Inst; Ohio Tri-State Show; IPA Nat, Washington, DC; All-Albuquerque Show, NMex; Jonson Gallery, Univ NMex; Am Painters in Paris (for the Bicentennial), France; one-man show, Am Bible Soc Gallery, New York; plus other group & one-man shows. Pos: Owner, Symbol Gallery Art, 61- Awards: Prizes, Toledo Mus Art, Ouray Colo Nat & NMex State Fair; plus others. Bibliog: Mary Carroll Nelson (auth), article in, Southwest Art Mag; articles in Albuquerque J & Tribune & The Santa Fe New Mexican. Mem: Delta Phi Delta. Style & Technique: Oils transparently paletted with accents of glazed metallic leafs; strong design and powerful morale. Specialty: Oils on gold leaf; silver and copper; symbolism of man and nature. Publ: Auth, Parables from Paradise, Branden Press. Mailing Add: 2049 S Plaza NW Albuquerque NM 87104

SOYER, ISAAC
PAINTER, INSTRUCTOR
b Russia, Apr 20, 02; US citizen. Study: Nat Acad Design; Cooper Union; also in Paris, France & Madrid, Spain. Work: Employment Agency, Whitney Mus Am Art, New York; Portrait of My Father, Brooklyn Mus; Rebecca, Albright-Knox Mus, Buffalo; The Art Beauty Shoppe, Dallas Mus Fine Arts; Cafeteria, Brooks Mem Gallery, Memphis, Tenn. Exhib: Mus Mod Art, New York; Art Inst Chicago; Pa Acad Fine Arts, Philadelphia; Corcoran Gallery Art, Washington, DC; New York World's Fair. Teaching: Instr painting & drawing, Educ Alliance Art Sch, New York; instr painting & drawing, New Sch Social Res; instr painting & drawing, Art Students League, 69- Awards: First Prize, Western NY Exhib, 44; First Prize for Landscape, Audubon Artists Exhib, 45. Bibliog: John H Bauer (auth), Revolution and Tradition in American Art, 51; L Goodrich & J Bauer (auth), American Art of Our Century, 61; Edmund Feldman (auth), Varieties of Visual Experience, Abrams, 72. Media: Oil. Mailing Add: 122 E 61st St New York NY 10021

SOYER, RAPHAEL
PAINTER
b Russia, Dec 25, 99; US citizen. Study: Cooper Union; Nat Acad Design; Art Students League. Work: Metrop Mus Art, New York; Whitney Mus Am Art, New York; Mus Mod Art, New York; Addison Mus Art, Andover, Mass; Philadelphia Mus Art, Pa. Exhib: Carnegie Inst Int, Pittsburgh; Whitney Mus Am Art; Calif Palace Legion of Honor, San Francisco; Pa Mus Fine Arts; Art Inst Chicago; Nat Collection of Fine Arts, Washington, DC, 77. Teaching: Instr painting, Art Students League; instr painting, Am Art Sch; instr painting, New Sch Social Res. Bibliog: Lloyd Goodrich (auth), Raphael Soyer, Praeger, 67; Sylvan Cole (auth), 50 Years of Printmaking, Da Capo, 67; Lloyd Goodrich (auth), Raphael Soyer, Abrams, 72; plus others. Mem: Nat Acad Design; Am Acad Arts & Lett. Media: Oil, Graphic. Publ: Auth & illusr, A Painter's Pilgrimmage, 62; auth & illusr, Homage to Thomas Eakins, 66; auth & illusr, Self Revealment, 69; auth, Diary of an Artist, New Repub Bk Co, 77. Dealer: Forum Gallery 1018 Madison Ave New York NY 10021. Mailing Add: 88 Central Park W New York NY 10023

SPAETH, ELOISE O'MARA
COLLECTOR, WRITER
b Decatur, Ill, June 19, 04. Study: Millikin Univ. Pos: Trustee, Dayton Art Inst, 38-44, dir, Mod Gallery, 40-44; trustee, Am Fedn Arts, 45-, chmn exten serv, 47-59; trustee, Guild Hall Mus, 50-, chmn acquisitions comt, 62-; trustee & vpres, Arch Am Art, 59, chmn, currently; chmn, East Div Arch, 59; mem, Smithsonian Inst Fine Art Comn. Mem: Am Asn Mus; Col Art Asn Am; Art Collectors Club. Collection: Contemporary religious art; antiquities; contemporary American and European art. Publ: Auth, American Art Museums and Galleries, 60, 66 & 69; auth, Collecting Art, 68; contribr to art & relig publ. Mailing Add: 65 E 76th St New York NY 10021

SPAFFORD, MICHAEL CHARLES
EDUCATOR, PAINTER
b Palm Springs, Calif, Nov 6, 35. Study: Pomona Co, BA, 59; Harvard Univ, MA(art hist), 60. Work: Seattle Art Mus, Wash; Galeria de Inst Mexicano-Norte Americano, Mexico City; Undergrad Libr, Univ Wash. Exhib: Art Across America, Knoedler Gallery, New York (travel), 65-67; Drawing Society 1970, Am Fedn Arts, New York (travel), 70-71; 73rd Western Ann Invitational, Denver Art Mus, 71; Art of the Pacific Northwest from 1930s to the Present, Smithsonian Inst, 75; one-man show, Labors of Hercules & Other Works, Utah Mus Fine Arts, 75. Teaching: Instr painting, Mexico City Col, 61-62; assoc prof painting-drawing, Univ Wash, 63- Awards: Louis Comfort Tiffany Found Grant Painting, 66; Prix de Rome, Am Acad Rome, 67-69. Mem: The Artists Group, Seattle (pres, 73-74). Style & Technique: Figurative expressionism. Media: Oil on Canvas. Dealer: Francine Seders Gallery 6701 Greenwood Ave N Seattle WA 98103. Mailing Add: 2418 E Interlaken Blvd Seattle WA 98112

SPAGNOLO, KATHLEEN MARY
PRINTMAKER, ILLUSTRATOR
b London, Eng, Sept 12, 19. Study: Bromley Art Sch; Royal scholar & Princess of Wales scholar to Royal Col Art, London, 39-42; Sch Design, with E W Tristram; Am Univ, with Robert Gates & Krishna Reddy. Work: Dept of Interior, Washington, DC; Univ Va, Charlottesville; George Washington Univ; Libr Cong, Washington, DC. Comn: Rendering (bench), Index Am Design, Nat Gallery Art, Washington, DC, 69. Exhib: Corcoran Gallery Art, Washington, DC, 62; Philadelphia Print Club, 63; Silvermine Guild Artists, 63; Soc Washington Printmakers, 69-75. Mem: Soc Washington Printmakers; Washington Watercolor Asn; Washington Print Club; Artist's Equity Asn. Media: Graphics. Dealer: Emerson Gallery McLean VA 22101. Mailing Add: 7401 Recard Lane Alexandria VA 22307

SPAMPINATO, CLEMENTE
SCULPTOR
b Italy, Jan 10, 12; US citizen. Study: Acad Fine Arts, Rome, Italy; Fr Acad Nude, Rome; Sch of Governatorate, Rome; Royal Sch of the Medal, Rome. Work: Nat Mus Sport, New Madison Square Garden, New York; Rockwell Gallery Western Art, Corning, NY; Isaac Delgado Mus Art, New Orleans, La; Notre Dame Univ, Ind; Okla Art Ctr, Oklahoma City. Comn: Soccer trophy, Int Competition, Ital Govt, 40; Navy Goat (bronze statue), Comt Class 1915, US Naval Acad, Annapolis, Md, 57; several archit reliefs, Bd Educ & Dept Pub works, New York, 57-72; three different bronze statues of Columbus, Huntington, NY, 64, Mineola, NY, 65 & Bridgeport, Conn, 71; two lime-stone has reliefs, Brooklyn Heights Br Libr, NY, 60; plus others. Exhib: Sport Sculpture Nat, Rome, 40-48; Allied Artists Am, New York, 46-51; Am Artists Prof Art League, New York, 51; Nat Sculpture Soc, New York, 52-72; Nat Acad Design, New York, 64-72; plus others. Awards: First Prize, Nat Competition Sport Figure, Rome, 39; First Prize, Nat Competition Ski Trophy Olympic Games, Rome, 40; Gold Medal, Grand Award Munic Art League, Chicago, 70. Mem: Fel Nat Sculpture Soc; Circolo Artistico Int; Int Fine Arts Coun; Int Am Inst. Media: Bronze, Marble. Dealer: Campanile Galleries Inc 200 S Michigan Ave Chicago IL 60604. Mailing Add: 36 Littleworth Ln Sea Cliff NY 11579

SPANDORF, LILY GABRIELLA
PAINTER
Study: Acad Arts, Vienna, grad. Work: Smithsonian Inst & Libr Cong, Washington, DC; Washington Co Mus Fine Arts, Hagerstown, Md; Munic Mus, Rome, Italy; White House, Washington, DC. Comn: Paintings, presented as gifts of State to Princess Margaret, Pres of Korea, Chung Hoo Park & former pres of Iceland, Asgeir Asgeirsson by President Lyndon B Johnson; designed US postage stamp for Christmas, 63, Post Off Dept. Exhib: Washington Watercolor Asn Nat, 61-67; Am Drawing Ann & Smithsonian Travel Exhib, Norfolk Mus, Va, 63; Metrop Art Exhib, Smithsonian Inst, 63-66; one-man shows, Agra Gallery & Bodley Gallery, New York; plus others; exhibited widely, Europe, Eng, Italy & US. Pos: Contrib artist, var Washington, DC newspapers & other publ. Awards: Numerous awards, Italy, Eng & US. Mem: Washington Press Club; Artist's Equity Asn; Washington Watercolor Asn. Style & Technique: Modern impressionism; loose washes of color lated defined with line; free and spontaneous with fine use of brush and pen. Media: Gouache, Watercolor, Mixed Media. Mailing Add: 1603 19th ST NW Washington DC 20009

SPARK, VICTOR DAVID
ART DEALER
b Brooklyn, NY, May 16, 98. Study: NY Univ, BS, 21. Pos: Dir, Victor D Spark Art Gallery. Specialty: American and foreign paintings, drawings and other works of art; appraisals of fine art. Mailing Add: 1000 Park Ave New York NY 10028

SPARKS, JOHN EDWIN
PRINTMAKER, INSTRUCTOR
b Washington, DC, Sept 14, 42. Study: Richmond Prof Inst; Yale-Norfolk Summer Sch Art & Music; Md Inst Col Art, BFA; Univ Ill, Urbana, MFA. Work: Libr of Cong, Washington, DC. Exhib: 36th Int Exhib, Northwest Printmakers, Seattle, 65; Libr of Cong Print Exhib, Washington, DC, 66; 47th Exhib, Soc Am Graphic Artists, New York, 66; 3rd Print Show, Eastern Mich Univ, Ypsilanti, 70; 10th Nat Print Exhib, Silvermine Guild Artists, Conn, 74. Teaching: Instr lithography & intaglio, Md Inst Col Art, 66-, chmn, Printmaking Dept; instr intaglio & lithography, Lake Placid Summer Workshop, 71-75; instr intaglio, NS Col of Art & Design, 77. Pos: Cataloger, George A Lucas Print Collection, Union of Independent Cols

Art, 69; dir first restrike ed, Rodolphe Bresdin's etching Flight into Egypt, 70; art adv, Md Arts Coun, 70-71. Awards: Printmaking Grant, Louis Comfort Tiffany Found, 67. Media: Intaglio, Lithography. Mailing Add: 2942 Guilford Ave Baltimore MD 21218

SPAULDING, WARREN DAN
PAINTER, LECTURER
b Boston, Mass, Oct 7, 16. Study: Mass Sch Art, cert painting, 37; Sch Fine Art, Yale Univ, Alice K English fel foreign travel & study, 49, BFA & MFA. Work: Univ Maine, Orono; Joslyn Art Mus, Omaha; US Sect Fine Arts, Marine Hosp, Carville, La; Branford Col, Yale Univ; St Louis Artists Guild, Mo. Exhib: Cincinnati Art Mus Am Art Ann, 40; Am Watercolors, Nat Gallery Art, Washington, DC, 40; Pa Acad Fine Arts Painting & Sculpture Ann, 51 & 54; Midwest Biennial, Joslyn Art Mus, 56 & 58; Maine Art Gallery Ann, 61-77; one-man show, Parsonage Gallery, Durham, NH, 77. Teaching: Instr painting, Sch Fine Arts, Yale Univ, 49-50; art dir, Taft Sch, Watertown, Conn, 50-51; prof compos, Sch Fine Arts, Washington Univ, 51-61; instr art, Farnsworth Art Mus, 73-74. Awards: Nat Watercolor Competition Purchase Award, US Sect Fine Art, 40; First Prize for Oil & Sculpture Exhib, St Louis Artists Guild, 51; Purchase Prize, Midwest Biennial, Joslyn Art Mus, 58. Mem: Maine Art Gallery; Waldoboro Gallery. Style & Technique: Designed naturalism; non-objective abstraction; assemblage. Media: All Media. Mailing Add: South Thomaston ME 04858

SPAVENTA, GEORGE
SCULPTOR
b New York, NY, Feb 22, 18. Study: Leonardo da Vinci Art Sch; Beaux Art Inst Design; Acad Grande Chaumiere, Paris, France. Work: Univ Calif, Berkeley; Mass Inst Technol, Cambridge. Exhib: Carnegie Inst, 49-50; Mus Mod Art, New York, Traveling Exhib, US, 64-65, Paris & other Europ cities, 65-66. Teaching: Instr sculpture, New York Studio Sch; instr sculpture, Skowhegan Sch Painting & Sculpture, 68; instr sculpture, Md Inst Art, 69. Dealer: Poindexter Gallery 24 E 84th St New York NY 10028. Mailing Add: 463 West St New York NY 10014

SPEAR, RICHARD EDMUND
EDUCATOR, MUSEUM DIRECTOR
b Michigan City, Ind, Feb 3, 40. Study: Univ Chicago, BA(art hist); Princeton Univ, MFA(art hist) & PhD(art hist). Teaching: Prof Baroque art, Oberlin Col, 64- Pos: Dir, Allen Mem Art Mus, Oberlin Col, 72-; pres, Intermuseum Conserv Asn, 75-77. Awards: Premio Daria Borghese gold medal, Rome, 72. Mem: Asn of Art Mus Dirs; Col Art Asn. Res: Seventeenth century painting. Publ: Auth, Caravaggio and his followers, Cleveland Mus of Art, 71 & Harper & Row, rev ed, 75; auth, Renaissance and Baroque paintings from the Sciarra and Fiano Collections, Pa State Press & Ugo Bozzi, Rome, 72. Mailing Add: Allen Mem Art Mus Oberlin Col Oberlin OH 44074

SPECTOR, NAOMI
ART DEALER, WRITER
b Lynn, Mass, Mar 6, 39. Study: Brandeis Univ, BA, 60; NY Univ, MA, 66. Pos: Asst dir, Byron Gallery, New York, 63-64; mgr, Fischbach Gallery, New York, 67-70; dir, John Weber Gallery, New York, 73- Res: Contemporary art. Specialty: Minimal-conceptual. Publ: Auth, Stephen Antonakos: Pillows, Catalogue for Contemp Art Ctr, Houston, 71; auth, Stephen Antonakos: Six Neons, Catalogue for NY State Coun Arts, 73; auth, Robert Ryman, Catalogue for Stedelijk Mus Show, Amsterdam, 74; auth, Robert Mangold: Essential Painting, Catalogue for La Jolla Mus Contemp Art, 74; auth, Dorothea Rockburne, Essay for Catalogue for Contemp Art Ctr, Cincinnati, 75; auth, Dorothea Rockburne: New Color Work, Essay for Catalogue, John Weber Gallery, New York, 76; auth, Robert Ryman: Six Aquatints, The Print Collector's Newsletter, 3-4/77; auth, Robert Ryman, Catalogue for Whitechapel Art Gallery, London, Eng, 77. Mailing Add: 435 W Broadway New York NY 10012

SPEED, (ULYSSES) GRANT
SCULPTOR
b San Angelo, Tex, Jan 6, 30. Study: Brigham Young Univ, BS; also with Soloman Aranda. Work: Whitney Mus, Cody, Wyo; Diamond M Mus, Snyder, Tex; Devonian Found, Calgary, Alta; Repub Nat Bank, Dallas. Comn: Sculpture, Brigham Young Univ Animal Sci Dept, 75-76, 76-77 & 77-78. Exhib: Nat Cowboy Hall Fame & Western Heritage Ctr, Cowboy Artists Am, 66-72; Ann Preview Exhib, Tex Art Gallery, 71-78; Phoenix Art Mus, 73-75; two-man show, Tex Art Gallery, Dallas, 75; Spec Exhib, Whitney Mus, Cody, 75. Awards: Todd Whatley Mem Award, Rodeo Cowboy Asn, 66; Achievement Award Art, Brigham Young Univ Animal Sci Dept, 72; Purchase Award, Men's Art Coun Phoenix, 73; Gold Medal Award/Sculpture, Cowboy Artist's of Am Ann, 76. Bibliog: Article in Am Artist, 68; Ed Ainsworth (auth), Cowboy in Art, World, 68; Pat Broder (auth), Bronzes of the American West, Abrams, 74. Mem: Cowboy Artists Am (pres, 72-73, bd dirs, 73-74 & 76-78). Style & Technique: Loose realism. Media: Bronze. Publ: Auth, Hooked on cowboyin', Western Horseman, 70. Dealer: Tex Art Gallery 1408 Main St Dallas TX 75202; Main Trail Galleries Jackson WY 83001. Mailing Add: 139 S 400 East Lindon UT 84062

SPEERS, TERYL TOWNSEND
PAINTER, EDUCATOR
b Coronado, Calif, May 9, 38. Study: Ray Froman Sch Art, Univ Tex, study with Millard Sheets, Chen Chi, Charles Reid, Edgar Whitney & Carl Molno. Work: Foothills Art Ctr, Golden, Colo; US Navy. Comn: Painting, Admiral Townsend, US Bristol County, 68; painting, Grumman Int corp offices, 76. Exhib: Nat Acad Design Ann, New York, 75; Am Watercolor Soc Ann, New York, 75; Mus Albuquerque Western Fedn Group Show, 75; Watercolor Soc Group Show, Brimingham Mus Art, Ala, 76; Western Fedn Group Show, Tucson Mus Art, Ariz, 76; Butler Inst Am Art Mid-Yr Ann, Youngstown, Ohio, 77; Watercolor USA Ann, Springfield, Ill, 77; Checkwood Art Ctr, Southern Watercolor Soc Group Show, Tenn, 77; one-man show, Stephen F Austin State Univ, Tex, 78. Teaching: Instr water media painting, Canary Hill Galleries, Houston, Tex, 74-77, Tex Art Supply, Inc, Houston, 75-77 & pvt studio, Houston, 78- Pos: Art experience facilitator, Tex Inst Child Psychiat, 75-76; adv, Houston Chamber of Com Cult Comt, 77- Awards: Century Award of Merit, Rocky Mt Nat Exhib, 74, Art Asn Award, 77; Director's Award, Southern Watercolor Ann Exhib, 77. Bibliog: Pat Lasher (auth), Seeing the ordinary in a special way, Southwest Art Mag, 9/77; Naomi Brotherton (auth), Spotlight on the artist, The Scene, Southwestern Watercolor Soc, 1/78. Mem: Watercolor Art Soc, Houston (vpres, 74-75, pres, 75-76); Southwestern Watercolor Soc (vpres, Houston Chap, 74); Southern Watercolor Soc; Art League Houston; Ala Watercolor Soc. Style & Technique: Landscape, floral and figure in watermedia, using vibrant color and strong value pattern. Media: Watermedia; Pencil Dealer: Gallery Worth Ave 155 Worth Ave Palm Beach FL 33480; Adele M Fine Art 3317 McKinney Ave Suite 102 Dallas TX 75204. Mailing Add: 4710 Morningside Houston TX 77005

SPEIGHT, FRANCIS
PAINTER, EDUCATOR
b Windsor, NC, Sept 11, 96. Study: Wake Forest Col, DHL; Corcoran Gallery Art; Pa Acad Fine Arts; Col of the Holy Cross, DFA, 64. Work: NC Mus Art; Toronto Gallery Art; Pa Acad Fine Arts; Rochester Mem Gallery; Butler Inst Am Art; plus many others. Exhib: Retrospective, NC Mus Art, Raleigh, 61 & Pa State Univ, 74; Teaching: Instr, Pa Acad Fine Arts, 26-61; prof art & artist in residence, ECarolina Univ, 61-76, emer prof, 76-; instr, Pa Acad Fine Arts, summers, 30- Awards: Percy Owens Award, Pa Acad Fine Arts, 61; Prize, Pa Nat Exhib, Ligonier Valley, 61; Gold Medal for Achievement in Art, State of NC, 64; plus many others. Mem: Nat Acad Design; Nat Inst Arts & Lett; NC Art Soc (adv bd). Mailing Add: 508 E Ninth St Greenville NC 27834

SPEIGHT, SARAH BLAKESLEE
See Blakeslee, Sarah

SPEISER, STUART M
COLLECTOR, PATRON
b New York, NY, June 4, 23. Exhib: Stuart M Speiser Collection of Photorealism, shown at 20 museums, including, Addison Gallery Am Art, Andover, Mass, 74, Allentown Art Mus, Pa, 74, Witte Mem Mus, San Antonio, Tex, 74, Brooks Mem Mus, Memphis, Tenn, 75 & Krannert Mus, Champaign, Ill, 75. Bibliog: Judy Beardsall (auth), Stuart M Speiser Photo-Realist Collection, Art Gallery Mag, 10/73; Phyllis Derfner (auth), New York letter, Art Int Lugano Rev, 11/73; Gregory Battcock (auth), New York, Art & Artists, London, 3/74. Interest: Promoting new art movements and pioneering in law as it pertains to artists, in capacity as an attorney. Collection: Photorealism. Mailing Add: 200 Park Ave New York NY 10017

SPELMAN, JILL SULLIVAN
PAINTER
b Chicago, Ill, Feb 17, 37. Study: Hilton Leech Art Sch, Sarasota, Fla, 55-57; and with Paul Ninas, New Orleans, 56-58. Work: Univ Mass, Amherst. Exhib: Three-man shows, Sarasota Art Asn, Fla, 58 & Landscape of the Mind, Phoenix Gallery, New York, 71; Watercolor USA, Springfield Art Mus, Mo, 67; Mainstreams '70, Marietta Col, Ohio, 70; Salon 72, Ward Nasse Gallery, New York, 72; one-man shows, Phoenix Gallery, New York, 73, 75 & 77 & Ward-Nasse Gallery, New York, 77. Teaching: Lectr, Ringling Mus Art, Sarasota, 58-60. Pos: Pres, Phoenix Coop Gallery, 72-74. Awards: Sarasota Art Asn First Prize, Art Student Exhib, 57; Hamel Prize, Sarasota Art Asn Ann, 58; Grumbacher Oil Prize, Knickerbocker Artists Ann, 70. Mem: Asn Artist-Run Galleries (ad hoc comt, 74, steering comt, 75, assoc ed, Artists Review Art, 77-78). Media: Landscape based abstraction using a pouring technique. Media: Acrylic. Dealer: Rhodd Sande Gallery 61 E 57th St New York NY. Mailing Add: 22 W 96th St New York NY 10025

SPENCE, ANDY
PAINTER
b Bryn Mawr, Pa, Oct 4, 47. Study: Tyler Sch Art, Temple Univ, Philadelphia, BFA, 69; Univ Calif, Santa Barbara, MFA, 71. Exhib: One-man exhib, Nicholas Wilder Gallery, Los Angeles, 74 & 76; 24 From Los Angeles, Los Angeles Munic Art Gallery, 74; Biennial of Contemp Art, Whitney Mus of Am Art, New York, 75; Charles Casat Gallery, La Jolla, 76; Four Californians, La Jolla Mus of Contemp Art, 77; 100plus Current Directions in Southern California Art, Los Angeles Inst Contemp Art, 77; Abstract Painting: A Selected Exhibition, Long Beach City Col Art Gallery, 77. Bibliog: Reviews of one-man exhib in Art Walk, William Wilson (auth), Los Angeles Times, 4/25/74 & 4/9/76; Review of Whitney Ann, Tom Hess (auth), New York Mag, 4/75; Andrew Spence: Avoiding Gravity Plays, David Rush (auth), Artweek, 9/25/76; Six Approaches to Formalist Abstraction, Timothy App (auth), Artweek, 3/5/77; Four Abstractionists—Krebs, Spence, Therrien & Georgesco, Suzanne Muchnic (auth), Artweek, 5/26/77. Style & Technique: Abstract painting. Media: Rhoplex/Oil Paint on Canvas or Wood. Dealer: Nicholas Wilder Gallery 8225 1/2 Santa Monica Blvd Los Angeles CA 90046; Charles Casat Gallery, 5721 La Jolla Blvd La Jolla CA 92037 Mailing Add: 64 N Moore St 3E New York NY 10013

SPENCE, ROBERT
ART HISTORIAN
b Greensboro, Md, Aug 20, 25. Study: Univ Md, College Park, BA & MA; Univ Wis-Madison, PhD; also study with John Summerson & Anthony Blunt. Teaching: Prof Am & mod art hist, Univ Pittsburgh, 62-66; prof Am & mod art hist, Univ Nebr, Lincoln, 66-, chmn dept art, 70-74. Pos: Mem bd trustees, Nebr Art Asn, 70; mem, Comt Arts Coun, Lincoln, 68. Mem: Col Art Asn Am; Nat Coun Art Adminr; Soc Archit Hist. Res: American authors and the visual arts; art in Nebraska. Publ: Auth, Daniel H Burnham and the Renaissance in American Architecture, 60; co-auth, Kress Study Collection of Italian Renaissance Art at University of Wisconsin, 61; auth, Leonard Baskin: the Artist as Counter-Decadent, 63; auth, Misch Kohn: a Critical Study of His Printmaking, 65; co-auth, The Etchings of J Alden Weir, 68. Mailing Add: Dept of Art Univ Nebr Lincoln NE 68588

SPENCER, ELEANOR PATTERSON
WRITER, ART HISTORIAN
b Northampton, Mass. Study: Smith Col, BA & MA; Radcliffe Col, PhD; Goucher Col, LHD, 67. Teaching: Prof hist art, Goucher Col, 30-62. Pos: Trustee, Walters Art Gallery, Baltimore, 62; trustee, Baltimore Mus Art, 62; trustee, Peale Mus, Baltimore, 62. Awards: Sachs fel, Harvard Univ, 28; Fulbright fel, 62. Mem: Col Art Asn Am. Res: Illuminated manuscripts of the fifteenth century in France. Publ: Auth, articles in, Scriptorium, 63, 65 & 69; auth, articles in, Burlington Mag, 65, 66 & 77. Mailing Add: 7 rue Fustel de Coulanges 75005 Paris France

SPENCER, HAROLD EDWIN
ART HISTORIAN, PAINTER
b Corning, NY, Oct 1, 20. Study: Art Students League, 41-42; Univ of Calif, BA(highest honors in art), 48 & James Phelan scholar, MA, 49; Harvard Univ (summer scholar), 58, Fac of Arts & Sci Fel, 60-61 & Frank Knox Fel, 64, PhD, 68. Exhib: Mo Exhib, St Louis Art Mus, 52, 55, 59 & 61; Ann Drawing and Print Exhib, San Francisco Art Mus, 55-56; Washington Printmakers Soc, Smithsonian Inst, Washington, DC, 57 & 62; Conn Acad of Art Ann, Wadsworth Atheneum, Hartford, Conn, 76. Pos: Chmn art dept, Blackburn Col, Carlinville, Ill, 49-62; assoc prof, Occidental Col, Los Angeles, Calif, 62-68, chmn art dept, 63-68; assoc prof, Univ Conn, Storrs, 68-69, prof, 69-, assoc dept head, 77- Awards: Purchase Award, New York State Exhib, Syracuse Mus Art, 41; Ruth Kelso Renfrow Prize, 17th Mo Exhib, St Louis Art Mus, 59; Jr League Prize, 18th Mo Exhib, St Louis Art Mus, 61. Bibliog: Alfred Frankenstein (auth), Review: The Lively Arts, San Francisco Chronicle, 55; Review of one-man show, Constance Perkins (auth), Thorne Hall Gallery, Los Angeles, Art Forum, 63; Review of Readings in Art Hist, Roberta Capers (auth), Art Bulletin, 71. Mem: Col Art Asn; Am Soc for Aesthetics; Am Asn Profs; Conn Acad of Arts & Sci. Style & Technique:

Figurative imagery. Media: Oil; Monotype. Res: Nineteenth Century European Painting and American Art. Publ: Auth, The Brisbane Portraits, J Royal Australian Hist Soc, 66; ed, Readings in Art History (two vols), Scribner's, 69 & 76; auth, The American Earls (introd to catalog), William Benton Mus Art, 72; auth, The Image Maker: Man and His Art, Scribner's, 75; auth, Criehaven: A Bellows Pastoral, William Benton Mus Art, Bulletin, 77. Mailing Add: RR 1 Box 56 Ashford CT 06278

SPENCER, JOHN R
ART HISTORIAN, ART ADMINISTRATOR
b Moline, Ill, Sept 20, 23. Study: Grinnell Col, BA, 47, hon DFA, 72; Yale Univ, MA, 51, PhD, 53; also with Charles Seymour, Jr. Teaching: Instr & asst prof art, Yale Univ, 52-58; assoc prof art & actg chmn dept, Univ Fla, 58-62; prof hist art, Oberlin Col, 62-72. Pos: Dir mus, Oberlin Col, 62-72; dir mus prog, Nat Endowment Arts, 72- Mem: Col Art Asn Am (secy, 67, vpres, 71); Am Asn Mus; Asn Art Mus Dir; Instituto per la Storia dell'arte lombarda; Am Fedn Arts. Res: 15th century Italian art, with emphasis on painting and theoretical writings. Publ: Auth, L B Alberti, on painting, 55 & 67; auth, Filarete's treatise on architecture, 65. Mailing Add: Nat Endowment for the Arts 2401 E St NW Washington DC 20506

SPERAKIS, NICHOLAS GEORGE
PAINTER, PRINTMAKER
b New York, NY, June 8, 43. Study: Pratt Inst, scholar, fall 60; Nat Acad Design Sch Fine Art, New York, scholar, painting with Louis Boucie, 60-61; Art Students League, scholar, painting with Joseph Hirsch, Charles Alsom, Edwin Dickenson, Will Barnet & Harry Sternberg & graphics with Harry Sternberg, 61-63; Pratt Graphic Art Ctr, scholar, printmaking with Sid Hammer, Clair Romano & Ed Casserella. Work: Brooklyn Mus Print Collection, NY; Philadelphia MusFine Art Print Collection, Pa; Chrysler Mus Permanent Collection, Provincetown, Mass; Norfolk Mus Arts & Sci, Va; 42nd St Pub Libr, New York. Comn: Portraits, Johnethan Charnolble, Collection of Carla Rueban, Mari Galleri NY, s, Larchmont, 66, Dr John Courins, Maplewood, NJ, 66, Marvin Bolotzky, New York, 67, Chaim Gross, New York, 69 & George Viener, Redding, Pa, 71. Exhib: Three Brooklyn Mus Biennials, 64, 66 & 70; 100 Prints From Pratt Graphic Art Ctr, Jewish Mus, New York, summer 64; New Acquisitions, Chrysler Mus, Provincetown, Mass, 64 & 65, New Acquisitions, Norfolk Mus Arts & Sci, 65. Teaching: Instr painting & graphics, Art Sch Educ Alliance, 68-69; instr graphics, 92nd St YMHA, New York, 70-71; instr graphics, Brooklyn Mus Art Sch, 71-72. Awards: Purchase Prize, Mercyhurst Col Paint Ann, 64; Lawrence & Hinda Rosenthal fel, Am Acad Arts & Lett & Nat Inst Arts & Lett, 69; J S Guggenheim Mem Found fel graphics, 70. Bibliog: Robert Henkes (auth), The crucifixion as depicted by contemporary artists, Nazarine Col, 72; Barry Shwarts (auth), 20th century humanist art, Praeger, 73; Una Johnson (auth), American printmaking, Brooklyn Mus, (in prep). Mem: Fedn Am Art; Artists Equity Asn; Rhino Horn Orgn Humanist Art. Style & Technique: Symbolic, religious figures, portraits. Interest: Pre-Colombian art, African art, Roman-Catalan frescoes, 11th-14th centuries, Spanish & Florentine Old Masters. Dealer: Paul Kessler Gallery 108 Commercial St Provincetown MA 02657. Mailing Add: 153 Centre St Rm 102 New York NY 10013

SPERO, NANCY
PAINTER
b Cleveland, Ohio, Aug, 24, 26. Study: Art Inst Chicago, BFA, 49; Atelier Andre L'Hote; Ecole des Beaux Arts, 49-50. Work: Mass Inst Technol; Judson Mem Church, New York; First Nat Bank, Chicago. Exhib: Huit Americains de Paris, Am Cult Ctr, Paris, 64; Collage of Indignation II, New York Cult Ctr, 71 & Women Choose Women, 73; American Women Artist Show, Gedok-Kunsthaus, Hamburg, WGer, 72; In Her Own Image, Philadelphia Mus Art, 74; Words at Liberty, Mus of Contemp Art, Chicago, 77; Contemp Issues, Univ Houston, 77, Univ Utah, 77 & Woman's Bldg, Los Angeles, 77; one-woman shows, Galerie Breteau, Paris, 62, 65 & 68, Univ Calif, San Diego, 71, Woman's Ctr, Williams Col, 74, AIR Gallery, New York, 73, 74 & 76, Herter Gallery, Univ Mass, Amherst, 77 & Marianne Deson Gallery, Chicago, 77. Awards: NY State Coun for the Arts CAPS fel, 76-77; Nat Endowment Arts grant, 77-78. Bibliog: The Art of Nancy Spero, film by Patsy Scala, 72; Corinne Robins (auth), Nancy Spero: Political artist of poetry and nightmare, Feminist Art J, spring 75 & Nancy Spero, Arts Mag, 11/76; Lucy Lippard (auth), From the Center, E P Dutton & Co Inc, New York, 76; Lawrence Alloway (auth), Art, The Nation, 9/25/76. Alloway (auth), Art, The Nation, 4/2/73; Corinne Robins (auth), Nancy Spero: political artist of poetry and the nightmare, Feminist Art J, spring 75; Donald Kuspit (auth), Art in Am, 7-8/75. Style & Technique: Juxtaposition of collaged painted images with printed slogans and political documentation on paper glued to form extended sequences. Media: Collage on Paper. Publ: Auth, The Whitney Museum and women, Art Gallery Mag, 1/71; contribr, Women's speakout, NY Element, 2-3/72; co-ed, Rip-off file, Ad Hoc Comt Women Artists, 73; contribr, Art: a woman's sensibility, Calif Inst Fine Arts, 75. Dealer: AIR Gallery 97 Wooster St New York NY 10012. Mailing Add: 530 La Guardia Pl New York NY 10012

SPERRY, ROBERT
CERAMIST, FILM MAKER
b Bushnell, Ill, Mar 12, 27. Study: Univ Sask, BA, 50; Art Inst Chicago, BFA, 54; Univ Wash, MFA, 55. Work: Smithsonian Inst, Washington, DC; Everson Art Mus, Syracuse; Henry Gallery, Univ Wash; Joe & Emile Lowe Art Mus, Coral Gables, Fla; Univ Ore Mus Art. Exhib: Ceramic Nat, Syracuse, 54-64; Young Americans, New York, 55-56; Int Ceramic Exhib, Ostend, Belg, 59; 3rd Int Exhib Contemp Ceramics, Prague, 62; Am Studio Potter, Victoria & Albert Mus, Eng, 66. Teaching: Prof ceramics, Univ Wash, 55- Awards: Tiffany Grant, 57; Ctr Asian Arts Award, 63; Japan Soc Award, 66. Style & Technique: Wheel thrown stoneware pottery. Media: Clay. Publ: Auth, The Village Potters of Onda (film), 66; auth, Profiles Cast Long Shadows (film), 68. Mailing Add: 1404 E Lynn Seattle WA 98112

SPEYER, A JAMES
CURATOR
b Pittsburgh, Pa. Study: Carnegie Inst Technol, BS; Chelsea Polytechnique, London, Eng; Sorbonne; Ill Inst Technol, with Mies van der Rohe, MA. Collections Arranged: Am Bi-Ann, Twentieth Century Sculpture Exhib, Art Inst Chicago, 67, Mies van der Rohe Retrospective, 68. Teaching: Instr advan archit, Ill Inst Technol, 46-61; vis prof archit, Nat Univ Athens, 57-60; instr mod art, Ford Found Sem, Art Inst Chicago. Pos: Pvt architect, 46-57; Chicago corresp, Art News Mag, 55-57; cur contemp art, Art Inst Chicago, 61- Mailing Add: Art Inst of Chicago Michigan Ave & Adams St Chicago IL 60603

SPEYER, NORA
PAINTER
b Pittsburgh, Pa. Study: Tyler Sch Fine Art, Philadelphia. Work: Union Carbide; Ciba-Geigy Corp; Univ Ill Mus; First Nat Bank, Chicago; also pvt collection of David Rockefeller. Exhib: One-woman shows, Darthea Speyer Gallery, Stable Gallery, Poindexter Gallery, Landmark Gallery; Pittsburgh Int. Bibliog: April Kingsley (auth), article in Art Int; Budd Hopkins (auth), article in Art News; A woman's sensibility, Art Mag. Style & Technique: Heavy use of paint, build up slowly; a special approach of build up and glazing. Media: Oil. Dealer: Landmark Gallery Inc 469 Broome St New York NY 10013. Mailing Add: 178 Prince St New York NY 10012

SPICKETT, RONALD JOHN, (SR)
PAINTER, INSTRUCTOR
b Regina, Sask, Apr 11, 26. Study: Alta Col Art, Calgary, dipl; Ont Col Art, Toronto; Inst Allende Mex, scholar, 55. Work: Nat Gallery Ottawa; Dept External Affairs, Can Govt; London Art Gallery, Ont; Art Gallery Toronto; Edmonton Art Gallery. Comn: Sculpture, Med Arts Bldg, Calgary, 60; sculpture, Bank of Montreal, Edmonton, 62; mural painting, Bowlen Bldg, Govt Alta, Calgary, 68-69. Exhib: Environment, Calgary, touring shows, 61-77; Nat Gallery Can Biennial; Mem Univ Gallery, Nfld, 70; Banff Festival Arts, Alta, 71. Teaching: Instr painting & drawing, Univ Calgary, 69- Awards: Can Coun Award, Govt Can, 63, 69 & 76. Bibliog: Articles in Can Art & 300 Yrs of Can Art. Mem: Royal Can Acad Art. Media: Oil. Mailing Add: 3427 Elbow Dr Calgary AB T2T 0H2 Can

SPIEGEL, SAM
COLLECTOR
b Austria, Nov 11, 04. Study: Univ Vienna. Mem: Art Collectors Club. Collection: Modern impressionist art. Mailing Add: 475 Park Ave New York NY 10022

SPIER, PETER EDWARD
ILLUSTRATOR, WRITER
b Amsterdam, Neth, June 6, 27; nat US. Study: Ryks Acad Voor Beeldende Kunsten, Amsterdam, 45-47. Pos: Jr ed, Elsevier's Weekly, Amsterdam, 50-51 & Elsevier Publ Co, Houston, 52; free-lance auth, illusr, New York, 52-; speaker & lectr, schs & libr. Awards: Runner-up for Caldecott Medal, 60 & winner, Caldecott Medal, 78; Boston Globe Award, 67; Christopher Award, 70 & 78; NY Times Award, 77. Publ: Auth & illusr, Fast-Slow, High-Low, 72, Crash! Bang! Boom!, 72, The Star-Spangled Banner, 73, Tin Lizzie, 76, Noah's Ark, 77, Oh, Were They Ever Happy!, 78 & Bored, Nothing to Do, 78; illusr, over 150 bks; contribr illus, many nat mags. Mailing Add: Wardencliff Rd Shoreham NY 11786

SPINK, FRANK HENRY, JR
WRITER, PAINTER
b Chicago, Ill, Sept 23, 35. Study: Univ Ill, Urbana, BArch, 58; Univ Wash, MUP, 64. Work: Chung Cheng Art Gallery, St John's Univ, Jamaica, NY. Exhib: Jack London Square, Oakland, Calif, 65; Fremont Fall Art Fair, Calif, 66; Soc Western Artists, DeYoung Mus, San Francisco, 67; Palace Fine Arts Dedication Festival, San Francisco, 67; 12th, 13th & 14th Ann Sumie Soc, New York, 75, 76 & 77. Pos: Pres, Fremont Art Asn, 66-67; dir of publ, Urban Land Inst, 72- Awards: Summer Sketch Prize, Univ Ill, 55; Hon Mention, 14th Ann Sumi Soc, New York, 77. Mem: Sumie Soc Am. Style & Technique: Watercolor landscapes, Chinese watercolor; abstract in acrylic-collage. Res: Adaptive reuse of existing building for the National Trust for Historic Preservation. Publ: Auth, Project Reference File, 71-; illusr, Residential Streets, Objectives, Principles & Design Considerations, 74; ed, Community Builders Handbook Series, 75; contribr, Storm Water Management-Objectives, Principles & Design Considerations, 73; contribr, Shopping Center Development Handbook, 77; contribr, Residential Development Handbook, 78. Mailing Add: 5158 Piedmont Pl Annandale VA 22003

SPITZ, BARBARA S
PRINTMAKER
b Chicago, Ill, Jan 8, 26. Study: Art Inst Chicago; RI Sch Design; Brown Univ, AB. Work: Art Inst Chicago; Philadelphia Mus of Art; Smart Gallery, Univ of Chicago; De Cordova Mus, Lincoln, Mass; Okla Art Ctr, Oklahoma City. Comn: First Ill Print Comn Prog, 73. Exhib: Art Inst Chicago 71st Ann, 68; Soc Am Graphic Artists 51st Ann, Kennedy Galleries, New York, 71; Smithsonian Traveling Exhibs, 73 & 74; Libr Cong & Nat Collection Fine Arts, 73 & 74; Tokyo Cent Mus, 77; Nat Acad of Design, New York, 77; Pratt Graphic Ctr, New York, 77. Awards: Munic Art League Prize, Art Inst 71st Ann, 68; Purchase Awards, Boston Printmakers 23rd, 24th & 27th Ann, De Cordova Mus, 71, 72 & 75; Purchase Award, Okla Art Ctr 14th Ann, 72; Childe Hassam Purchase Award, Am Acad of Arts & Lett, 73; First Prize Ill Regional Print Show, 77; Stuart M Egnal Prize, Int Biennial Print Exhib, Print Club, Philadelphia, 77. Bibliog: Articles in Printmaker in Illinois, Ill Educ Asn, 72, Illinois Printmakers I Proj, Ill Arts Coun, 74 & others. Mem: Artist Equity Asn; Chicago Soc Artists; Arts Club Chicago; Boston Printmakers. Style & Technique: Combination of traditional methods of etching, engraving and aquatint with contemporary innovations, such as power tools and photoengraving. Media: Intaglio. Dealer: Van Straaten Gallery 646 N Michigan Ave Chicago IL 60611. Mailing Add: 150 Indian Tree Dr Highland Park IL 60035

SPITZER, FRANCES R
COLLECTOR
b New York, NY, Mar 31, 18. Study: Syracuse Univ, BS. Collection: French impressionists; contemporary American art; oils by Monet, Modigliani, Redon, Feininger, Picasso & Boudin; sculptures by Giacomette, Moore & Lipschitz. Mailing Add: 200 E 66th St New York NY 10021

SPOHN, CLAY (EDGAR)
PAINTER, INSTRUCTOR
b San Francisco, Calif, Nov 24, 98. Study: Berkeley Sch Arts & Crafts, 11-12; Calif Sch Fine Arts, San Francisco, 12-21; Univ Calif, Berkeley, 19-21; Art Students League, 22-24; Acad Mod, Paris, France, with Othon Friesz, 26; also mus in Italy & France, 27. Work: San Francisco Mus Art; Oakland Mus, Calif; Univ Ore Mus, Eugene; plus work in pvt collections. Comn: Copper Repousse, Fed Arts Projs, Volunteer Fire Dept, Carmel, Calif, 37; Copper Repousse, Fed Art Projs, Contra Costa Valley Community Ctr, Calif, 38; Egg Tempera Mural Painting, Fed Art Projs, Union High Sch, Los Gatos, Calif, 39. Exhib: Art of Our Times, San Francisco Mus Fine Arts, 45; 1st & 2nd Spring Ann Int Exhib, Calif Palace of Legion of Honor, San Francisco, 45 & 48; Am Abstract Artists 13th Ann, Riverside Mus, New York, 49; Contemp Am Painting & Sculpture Exhib, Univ Ill, Urbana, 53; Clay Spohn Retrospective, Oakland Mus, Calif, 74. Teaching: Instr painting, Calif Sch Fine Arts, San Francisco, 45-50; vis lectr painting, Mt Holyoke Col, Mass, spring 58; instr painting & drawing, Sch Visual Arts, New York, 64-69. Awards: Two San Francisco Art Asn Artists Fund Prizes, San Francisco Mus Art, 39 & 45; Albert M Bender Grant Award, San Francisco, 44; 66th Ann Exhib of Painting & Sculpture Anonymous Donor Award, San Francisco Mus Art, 46. Bibliog: Mary Fuller (auth), Clay Spohn, Art in Am Mag, New York, No 6, 63; Mary Fuller McChesney (auth), A Period of Exploration-San Francisco 1945-1950, Art Dept, Oakland Mus, 73; Peter Plagens (auth), Sunshine Muse, Praeger Publ, New York, 74. Style & Technique: Subjective individualist, painting and objects. Media: Oil on Canvas, Acrylic on Canvas. Mailing Add: 245 Grand St New York NY 10002

SPONENBURGH, MARK
ART HISTORIAN, SCULPTOR
b Cadillac, Mich, June 15, 16. Study: Cranbrook Acad Art, scholar, 40; Wayne Univ; Ecole Beaux-Arts, Paris, France; Univ London; Univ Cairo. Work: Detroit Inst Art; Portland Art Mus; Univ Ore; Mus Mod Art, Egypt; Pakistan; plus others. Exhib: Pa Acad Fine Arts; Durand-Ruel & Paris Salon, France; Inst Fine Arts Cairo; Nat Gallery, Pakistan; 29 one-man exhibs, sculpture; plus others. Collections Arranged: Sculpture Pacific Northwest, Univ Ore, 55; 2000 Years Horse & Rider in Arts of Pakistan, 59 & Folk Arts of Swat, 61, Nat Col Arts, Pakistan; CRIA, Corvallis Arts Coun, 67- Teaching: Assoc prof, Univ Ore, 46-56; vis prof, Royal Col Arts, 56-57; prof & prin, Nat Col Arts, Pakistan, 58-61; prof, Ore State Univ, 61- Pos: Consult, Nat Col of Art, Pakistan, Moukhtar Mus, Cairo, Egypt & Marine Sci Ctr, Newport, Ore. Awards: Tiffany Found fel, 41; Fulbright Found fel, 51-53; Purchase Prizes, Detroit Art Inst & Portland Art Mus; plus others. Mem: Col Art Asn Am; Northwest Inst Sculpture; Royal Soc of Antiquaries; Mus Asn Gt Brit. Style & Technique: Direct carving Media: Wood, Stone. Publ: Contribr, Arts Quart, J Inst Egypte, Rev Caire, Near E Bull & J Near E Studies; plus others. Mailing Add: Dept of Art Ore State Univ Corvallis OR 97331

SPONGBERG, GRACE
PAINTER, PHOTOGRAPHER
b Chicago, Ill, Apr 25. 06. Study: Art Inst Chicago. Work: Horace Mann Sch, Chicago; Bennett Sch, Chicago; Byford Sch, Chicago; Mus Vaxco, Sweden. Exhib: Pa Acad Fine Arts; Art Inst Chicago; Joslyn Art Mus; Chicago Soc Art; Riverside Mus; plus others. Mem: Chicago Soc Art. Style & Technique: Direct and recognizable colors, but not photographic. Media: Watercolor. Mailing Add: 909 N Rush St Chicago IL 60611

SPRAGUE, MARK ANDERSON
PAINTER, EDUCATOR
b Champaign, Ill, Jan 5, 20. Study: Univ Ill, BFA, 46, MFA, 49. Work: Ill State Univ Mus, Bloomington. Comn: Painting for Great Ideas of Western Man, Container Corp Am, Chicago, Ill. Exhib: Am Fedn Arts Circulating Exhib, Washington, DC, 49; Art Inst Chicago 60th Am Ann, 51; Western Art Ann, Denver, Colo, 51-52; Corcoran Gallery Art Biennial, Washington, DC, 51-53; Nat Acad Design Ann, New York, 58-62. Teaching: Prof art, Univ Ill, Champaign, 46- Style & Technique: Abstract expressionist; direct painting technique. Media: Oil, Polymer, Collage. Mailing Add: 912 Devonshire Dr Champaign IL 61820

SPRAGUE, NANCY KUNZMAN
SCULPTOR
b New York, NY, Sept 27, 40. Study: RI Sch Design; Univ Pa, BFA; Tyler Sch Art, Temple Univ; Univ Kans; Univ Iowa, MA & MFA. Work: Tenn Sculpture '71, Tenn Arts Comn, Fairleigh Dickinson Univ. Comn: Bronze sculpture, Friends of Elvis Presley, 71. Exhib: 16th Ann Drawing & Small Sculpture, Ball State Univ, 70; Mid S Art Exhib, Brooks Mem Art Gallery, Memphis, 71; 24th Ann Iowa Artists Exhib, Des Moines Art Ctr, 72; Goldsmith Civic Ctr Sculpture Show, Memphis, Tenn, 73; Mainstreams 74, Marietta Col, Ohio. Mem: Col Art Asn Am. Style & Technique: Abstract. Media: Cast Bronze, Welded Steel. Dealer: Ruth White Gallery 401 E 74th St New York NY 10021. Mailing Add: Windham Way Rte 3 Iowa City IA 52240

SPRANG, ELIZABETH LEWIS
PAINTER, LITHOGRAPHER
b Capitol View, Md. Study: Univ Calif, Los Angeles, 3 yrs; studied painting with F Tolles Chamberlain, lithography with Lynton Kistler & Richard Haines, Calif; studied American & Meso-American art & symbolism with Jose Arguelles & Tibetan thangka painting with Glen Eddy, Naropa Inst, Colo. Exhib: Pasadena Soc Artists, 47-55 & San Gabriel Valley Artists, Pasadena Art Inst, 48-55, Los Angeles Co Mus, Los Angeles, 50, Libr Cong Ann Print Show, 52-55, Oakland Art Mus, Calif, 53, Calif State Fair, Sacramento, 53-55, Pa Acad of Fine Arts, 55 & Northwest Printmakers Ann, Seattle Art Mus, 55 (all under name of Elizabeth Lewis); one-woman show (as Elizabeth Sprang), Heard Mus, Phoenix, Ariz, 66. Awards: First Prize for Prints, 29th Ann Pasadena Soc Artists. Mem: Artists Equity Asn, Santa Fe Chap (treas, 73-74). Style & Technique: 3D process invented by self for interpretations of prehistoric Indian petroglyphs; semi-abstract mystical landscapes and designs in oils, inspired by faraway places like Antarctica and Ladakh, Colorado River Basin. Media: (Prints) Lithography; (Painting) 3D Mixed Media and Oil. Publ: Illusr, Conspicuous California Plants, San Pasqual Press, 38; auth & illusr, Art, beauty and country life in Utah, Dialogue Mag, 70; auth & illusr, Goodbye River, Mojave Books, 78. Dealer: Los Llanos Gallery 72 E San Francisco St Santa Fe NM 87501. Mailing Add: 904 Bishops Lodge Rd Santa Fe NM 87501

SPRINGER, LYNN ELISE
CURATOR
b San Diego, Calif, Apr 9, 43. Study: Washington Univ, BA(art hist), 65, museology, 67; Winterthur Mus/Univ Del, Summer Inst, 69; Attingham Park/Brit Nat Trust Summer Sch, Eng Country House, 70-71, 73 & 75. Pos: Asst cur decorative arts, St Louis Art Mus, 72-74, assoc cur Am & Europ decorative arts, 75-76, cur Am & Europ decorative arts, 77- Mem: Fel Am Friends of Attingham; Decorative Arts Chap, Soc of Archit Historians (secy); Nat Trust for Hist Preserv; Victorian Soc in Am; Am Ceramic Circle. Publ: Auth, A collection of Biblical pictures, Antiques, 72; auth exhib catalogue, The Rediscovered work of William J Hinchey, 74 & co-auth exhib catalogue, Currents of Expansion: Painting in the Midwest, 1820-1940, 77, St Louis Art Mus. Mailing Add: St Louis Art Mus Forest Park St Louis MO 63110

SPROAT, CHRISTOPHER TOWNSEND
SCULPTOR
b Boston, Mass, Sept 23, 45. Study: Skowhegan Sch Painting & Sculpture; Boston Univ; Boston Mus Sch Fine Arts, also with George Aarons. Exhib: One man shows, Inst Contemp Art, Boston, 70 & Neon Sculpture, Brockton Art Ctr, Mass, 73; Elements of Art, Mus Fine Arts, Boston, 71-72 & Rohm/Sproat, 74; Whitney Mus Am Art Biennial, New York, 73; Hayden Gallery, Mass Inst of Technol, Cambridge, Mass. Awards: Blanche E Colman Award, 72; Mass Arts & Humanities Found Fel, 75; Nat Endowment for Arts Grant, 75-76. Bibliog: Kenneth Baker (auth), Sproat & Samaras, Boston Rev Arts, 4/72; Carl Belz (auth), Deliberating with color, drawing with light, Art in Am, 5-6/72. Mem: Inst Contemp Art. Style & Technique: Sculpture with electrical materials and light. Dealer: Harkus Krakow Rosen Sonnabend Gallery 7 Newbury St Boston MA 02116. Mailing Add: 34 Farnsworth St Boston MA 02210

SPROUL, ANN STEPHENSON
PAINTER
b DeWitt, Mo, Aug 9, 07. Study: Cent Mo State Univ; also with William B Schimmel, Ariz, John Pike & Edgar Whitney, New York & John Pellew, Conn. Work: Pvt gälleries in Chile, Switzerland, Czechoslovakia, England & Canada. Comn: Mural of Frontier Town, Silver Spur Saloon & Restaurant, Cave Creek; Christmas card designs, comn by Mr & Mrs Dow Patterson, Phoenix, 73-74 & Cave Creek Community Schs, 74; illus Christmas letter, comn by Armstrong Congoleum, Cecil Armstrong, Carefree, Ariz, 74. Exhib: Plaza Art Fair, Kansas City. Mo, 63-69; Gtr Kansas City Art Asn, Kansas City Mus, 64; Ararat Temple Beaux Arts, Ararat Temple Auditorium, Kansas City, 64; one-man show, Am Asn Univ Women, Sophian Plaza, Kansas City, 65; Discovery of Art Mag Exhib, Kansas City, 68. Teaching: High Sch teacher art & art supvr, Carrollton Pub Schs, Mo, 59-69; teacher watercolor, Community Sch, Cave Creek, 74- Pos: Owner & demonstr watercolor & brush tech, Washboard Watercolor Gallery, Frontier Town, Cave Creek, 72- Awards: First in Watercolor, Gtr Kansas City Art Asn, 64 & Mo Div, Nat League Am Pen Women, 65; Publisher's Award, Discovery of Arts Mag, 68. Bibliog: Article in Ariz Desert Foothills, Mesa, Ariz, 75; Watercolor Techniques by Ann Sproul (film of tech demonstrations for schs), Outdoor Pictures, Anacortes, Wash, 75. Mem: Nat League Am Pen Women. Style & Technique: Free and swift technique in watercolor landscape with flat sable brush; developed new technique for snow-capped peaks and bringing mountains down into fog. Media: Watercolor, Pencil. Publ: Auth, The Art of Poster Making, Kappa Delta Pi Scroll, 28; illusr, Of Time & Space (poems), 74. Mailing Add: 5924 E Carriage Dr PO Box 93 Cave Creek AZ 85331

SPROUT, FRANCIS ALLEN
PAINTER, EDUCATOR
b Tucson, Ariz, Mar 5, 40. Study: Univ Ariz, BFA; Univ Calif, San Diego, MFA. Work: Univ Calif Exten Off, La Jolla; Johnson Publ Co, Chicago; Johns-Manville Corp, Atlanta, Ga; also pvt collection of Frederick Mayer, Denver. Comn: Cover design, Jour Umoja, Univ Colo, Boulder, 75. Exhib: Los Angeles 1972: a Panorama of Black Artists, Los Angeles Co Mus Art, 72; Emerging Southern California Artists, Pollock Gallery, Art Mus, Southern Methodist Univ, Dallas, 72; 74th Western Ann, 73 & 2nd & 3rd All-Colo, 74-75, Denver Art Mus; Colo-Nebr Exchange, Joslyn Mus Art, Omaha, 73. Teaching: Asst prof painting, Univ Denver, 72-75; instr Afro-Am art hist, Univ Colo, 74-77. Awards: San Diego Fel in Visual Arts, Univ Calif, 70-71; Ford Found Advan Study Fel, New York, 71-72. Bibliog: Lenore Goldberg (auth), A Black panorama, Artweek, 2/26 Rena Andrews (auth), The fine arts, Roundup Sect, Denver Post, 12/31/73. Mem: Artists Equity Asn; Nat Conf Artists; Col Art Asn Am; I-25 Artists Alliance, Colo. Style & Technique: Geometric abstractions in acrylic paint with various metal additives. Mailing Add: c/o McIntyre 2652 S Jackson Denver CO 80210

SPRUCE, EVERETT FRANKLIN
PAINTER, PRINTMAKER
b Faulkner Co, Ark, Dec 25, 08. Study: Dallas Art Inst, 25-29; pvt study with Olin H Travis & Thomas M Stell. Work: Mus Fine Arts Houston; Mus Mod Art, New York; Calif Palace of Legion of Honor, San Francisco; Mus Fine Arts Rio de Janeiro, Brazil; Nelson Gallery, Kansas City, Mo; Metrop Mus, New York; Whitney Mus of Am Art, New York; Dallas Mus of Fine Arts, Tex; Walker Art Ctr, Minneapolis, Minn; McNay Art Inst & Witte Mus, San Antonio, Tex; Pa Acad, Philadelphia; Baltimore Mus of Art, Md; plus many others. Exhib: Carnegie Inst, Pittsburgh; Corcoran Gallery Art, Washington, DC; Brussels, Belg & Bordhighera, Italy; Ford Found Retrospective, circulated nationally by Am Fedn Arts; Pan-Am Union, Washington, DC; Dallas Mus Fine Arts; plus others. Teaching: Instr, Dallas Mus Sch, 36-40; instr art, Univ Tex, Austin, 40-44, asst prof, 44-47, chmn dept art, 48-50, prof art & mem grad fac, 54-74, emer prof, 75- Pos: Gallery asst, Dallas Mus Fine Arts, 31-34, registrar, 35, asst dir, 35-40. Awards: Bordighera, Italy, 54; D D Feldman Award, Tex State Fair, 55; Dallas Mus Fine Arts Prize, 55; plus others. Bibliog: John I H Baur (auth), Revolution and Tradition in Modern American Art, Harvard Univ, 59; John Leeper (auth), Everett Spruce, Am Fedn Arts, 59; Portfolio of Paintings, Vol I, In: Blaffer Series, Univ Tex. Mailing Add: 15 Peak Rd Austin TX 78746

SPRUYT, E LEE
PAINTER, PRINTMAKER
b Lisbon, Port, Feb 10, 31; US citizen. Study: Apprentice (at 14) to Pachita Crespi; Pratt Inst Night Sch; Art Students League; RI Sch Design; Carnegie Inst Technol, three yrs, scholar; Ateneum Sch, Finland; study with Roger Anliker, Robert Rabinowitz & Samuel Rosenberg. Work: In Europe & US. Comn: Three pen & ink drawings, Metrop Opera Bd Rm, 73; three pen & ink drawings, Opera News Yearbk for 74-75 season, 74; 250 edition signed prints, Metrop Opera 90th Anniversary Poster, 75. Exhib: Six one-man shows, 65-78; Archit League, New York, 70 & 72; traveling exhib, 60 drawings & gouaches, Portrait of the Old Met, Mus Performing Arts, Lincoln Ctr, 72-73; Tribute to Rudolph Bing, Robert Tobin Foundation, Marion Koogler McNay Art Inst, San Antonio, Tex, 73; John F Kennedy Ctr for Performing Arts, Texico Grant, Washington, DC, 74; Art in Embassies Prog, Washington, DC, with work in Bolivia, Uruguay, Jordan, Paris, Quebec, Equador, Belgium & State Dept, Washington, DC. Teaching: Instr drawing, Carnegie-Mellon Univ; instr art, Boys Club, RI. Bibliog: Ten drawings in Show Mag, 2/70 & 3/70; article in NY Times, 10/72, Metrop Opera Prog, 11/72 & American Artist, 9/73. Media: Oil, Gouache & Encaustic. Mailing Add: 419 E 91st St New York NY 10028

SPURGEON, SARAH (EDNA M)
PAINTER, EDUCATOR
b Harlan, Iowa, Oct 30, 03. Study: Univ Iowa, BA & MA; Harvard Univ; Grand Cent Sch Art; also with Grant Wood, Paul Sachs & others. Work: Iowa Mem Union, Iowa City; Seattle Art Mus, Wash; Ginkgo Mus, Vantage, Wash; Henry Gallery, Univ Wash, Seattle. Comn: Mural, Univ Experimental Sch, Iowa City. Exhib: Kansas City Art Inst; Joslyn Mus; Des Moines Art Salon; Seattle Art Mus; Gumps, San Francisco; plus others. Teaching: Assoc prof art, Cent Wash Univ, 39-42, 44-71, emer prof, 71- Awards: Carnegie Fel, 29-30; Prizes, Iowa Art Salon, 30 & 31; Prizes, Univ Iowa, 31; Sarah Spurgeon Art Gallery, Randal Art Bldg, Cent Wash Univ, dedicated 77. Mem: Nat Educ Asn; Am Asn Univ Prof; Wash Educ Asn; Women Painters Wash. Publ: Contribr, Design & Childhood Educ Mag. Mailing Add: 204 E Ninth St Ellensburg WA 98926

SPURGIN, JOHN EDWIN
ART ADMINISTRATOR, PAINTER
b Indianapolis, Ind, Dec 17, 32. Study: Ind State Univ, VA, MA; Mich State Univ with Angelo Ippolito; Univ Cincinnati, MFA with Robert Knipschild. Work: Mich Educ Asn, East Lansing; Hubbard Milling Co, Mankato, Minn, Bemidji State Univ, Minn; Southwest State Univ, Marshall, Minn; Univ Cincinnati, Ohio. Exhib: DeWaters Art Inst, Flint, Mich, 62, 64 & 65; Kresge Art Ctr, Mich State Univ, 64; 13th Ann Invitational, Univ Mich, Ann Arbor, 65; Biennial of Painting & Sculpture, Walker Art Ctr, Minneapolis, 66; Okla Art Ctr, Oklahoma City, 67; Minn Artists' Biennial, Minneapolis Inst of Arts, 67; Wichita Nat Print Exhib, Kans, 67 & 69; Int Festival of the Arts, Man, Can, 69; Minn Mus, St Paul, 70; Miami Univ, Oxford, Ohio, 72; NE La Univ, Monroe, 74; one-man shows, Univ Wis, Marshfield, 75 & Southwest State Univ, Marshall, 77. Collections Arranged: American National Bank Collection Exhibition, St Paul, Minn, 74. Teaching: Instr art educ, Flint Inst of Art, Mich, 60-64; prof design, painting & printmaking, Mankato State Univ, 65-, chmn art dept, 75- Pos:

Gallery dir, Gallery Five Hundred, Fine Arts, Inc, Mankato, 69-72 & Nichols Gallery, Mankato State Univ, 73-75. Awards: First Prize/Painting, Rochester Area Artists, Rochester Art Ctr, Minn, 66; Best-in-Show, Southern Minn Art Exhib, Mankato Free Press, 67 & 72; Minn State Individual Artists Grant, 77-78. Mem: Col Art Asn; Mid-Am Col Art Asn. Style & Technique: Painting and printmaking of land-form subjects in an abstract style. Media: Acrylic polymer painting, serigraphy and mixed-media. Mailing Add: 2629 E Main St Mankato MN 56001

SPURLOCK, WILLIAM HENRY, II
GALLERY DIRECTOR, ART HISTORIAN
b Chicago, Ill, Oct 23, 45. Study: Trinity Univ, San Antonio, Tex, BA; Univ NMex, Albuquerque, MA; Union Grad Sch, PhD. Collections Arranged: Robert Irwin, Wright State Univ Art Gallery, 74, Room for Wright State, Stephen Antonakos Neon Sculpture (with catalog), 75, Projection Art (with catalog), 75, Patrick Ireland, 75, Richard Nonas, Lucas Samaras, 76; plus others. Teaching: Asst dir educ in art hist & admin, Des Moines Art Ctr, Iowa, 72-74; asst prof arts admin & art hist, Wright State Univ, Dayton, Ohio, 74- Pos: Dir, Art Gallery, Wright State Univ, 74- Mem: Am Asn Mus; Col Art Asn; Western Asn Art Mus; Int Coun of Mus; Am Fedn Arts. Res: Contemporary art forms, environmental arts. Publ: Auth, Vito Acconci: Middle of the World, 76; auth, Barry Le Va, Accumulated Vision: Extended Boundaries, 77; auth, John Willenbecher: Common Place Books, 77; auth, Cecile Abish, 78; auth, Richard Fisher, Current Charts: Chosen Lands, 78; auth, Federal Art Patronage in the State of New Mexico: 1933-1943 (catalog), Mus NMex, (in press); auth, numerous articles & essays on contemp art & artists. Mailing Add: Fine Arts Gallery Wright State Univ Dayton OH 45435

SQUADRA, JOHN
PAINTER, INSTRUCTOR
b New York, NY, June 25, 32. Study: RI Sch Design, BFA, 53. Comn: Mural for travel off, Maddox & Starbuck, Ltd, New York, 69; mural, Robert Shapiro Designs, Wilton, Conn, 74; theater poster, Hartmann Theatre, Stamford, Conn, 75. Exhib: 21st Ann Norwich Art Asn, Converse Art Gallery, Conn, 64; Ind Artists, Herron Mus, Indianapolis, 67; 7th Ann Art Festival, Nature Ctr, Westport, Conn, 74; 21st Ann Exhib, Berkshire Mus, Pittsfield, Mass, 75; Artist's Showcase, Mus of Art, Bridgeport, Conn, 78. Teaching: Teacher oils, acrylics, watercolor & mem bd dirs, Rowayton Arts Ctr, Conn, 74- Awards: Top Ten, Irene Leache Mem, Norfolk Mus, Va, 55; Second Prize All Mem Award Show, Rowayton Arts Ctr, 77; Third Prize, Darien Art Show, 77. Bibliog: Carlye Burrows (auth), Six new shows, New York Herald Tribune, 53; John Squadra—artist (TV show), Norfolk, Va TV, 55. Mem: Rowayton Arts Ctr. Style & Technique: Surrealist. Media: Oil, Acrylic. Publ: Illusr, Songs From Silences, 75. Dealer: B E L Gallery Westport CT. Mailing Add: 151 Highland Ave Rowayton CT 06853

SQUIER, JACK LESLIE
SCULPTOR, EDUCATOR
b Feb 27, 27; US citizen. Study: Ind Univ, BS, 50; Cornell Univ, MFA, 52. Work: Mus Mod Art & Whitney Mus Am Art, New York; Hirshhorn Mus, Washington, DC; Everson Mus, Syracuse, NY; Johnson Mus, Cornell Univ; Stanford Univ Mus. Comn: Disc (fiber glass & aluminum leaf sculpture), Ithaca Col, 68. Exhib: Carnegie Int, Pittsburgh; Brussels World's Fair; Recent Sculpture USA, Mus Mod Art; 30 Americans Under 35, 57 & many ann, Whitney Mus Am Art. Teaching: Prof sculpture, Cornell Univ, 58- Bibliog: William Lipke (auth), Disc, by Jack Squier, Cornell Univ, 68. Mem: Int Asn Art (dep vpres, 72-); Sculptors Guild. Style & Technique: Realistic portraits of full female figure in small scale. Media: Resin, Fiber Glass, Bronze. Mailing Add: 211 Berkshire Rd Ithaca NY 14850

SQUIRES, GERALD LEOPOLD
PAINTER, EDUCATOR
b Nfld, Can, Nov 17, 37. Study: Danforth Tech, Toronto; Ont Col Art, Toronto; mainly self-taught. Work: Breakwater Bk Publ Co, Nfld; Montreal Mus Fine Arts; Mem Univ Nfld; Univ Toronto; Saidye & Samuel Bronfman Collection, Montreal. Comn: Can Permanent Trust, St John's, Nfld, 72; Dept Pub Works, Paradise, Nfld, 77; painting, comn by Can Cath Conf Asn for New Can Sunday Mass Bk, Ottawa, 76. Exhib: Ont Soc Artist, 65; Western Ont Ann, 66; Montreal Mus Fine Arts, 67; Painters in Nfld, 68-71; Studies in Steel, Atlantic Prov Art Circuit, 74, Black Expo, 75 & Boatman Series (traveling exhib), 76-78, Mem Univ Art Gallery; 50 Can Drawings (traveling exhib), 77; plus others. Teaching: Instr art, Mem Univ Nfld, 70-73, exten artist in residence, 72. Awards: First & Second Prize, Great Northern AUK Workshop Conceptual Partic Painting & Sculpture, Nfld Arts & Lett Competition, 72. Bibliog: Kat Kritzweiser (auth), From a modern squires an old monk's dream, Globe & Mail Toronto; Robert Percival (auth), Sculpture Review, Art Mag, 75; Peter Bell (auth), The visual arts in Newfoundland, Arts Atlantic, Vol 1 (fall, 77). Mem: Great Northern AUK Workshop; founding mem Oshawa Art Gallery. Media: Acrylic, Steel. Dealer: Ron Mason Mt Scio Rd St John's NF Can; George Ruckus c/o Picture Loan Gallery 3 Charles St W Toronto ON Can. Mailing Add: Ferryland NF A0A 2H0 Can

SQUIRES, NORMA-JEAN
SCULPTOR, PAINTER
b Toronto, Ont; US citizen. Study: Art Students League; Cooper Univ, cert, 61; also spec studies with James Rosati, sculptor. Work: Sterling Forest Gardens, Long Island, NY; Galeria Vandres, Madrid, Spain; Warner Brothers, Burbank, Calif. Exhib: One-woman shows, Hudson River Mus, Yonkers, NY, 66, East Hampton Gallery, New York, 69 & Kieran Gallery, Riverside, Calif, 74; Affect-Effect, La Jolla Mus Art, Calif, 69; Recent Trends in American Art, Westmoreland Co Mus Art, Greensburg, Pa, 69; 4x4 plus 4x8, Newport Harbor Mus, 75; Many Arts of Sci, Calif Inst of Technol, Pasadena, 76; plus others. Teaching: Instr sculpture, Lucinda Art Sch, Tenafly, NJ, 67-69. Awards: Sarah Cooper Hewitt Award for the Advan of Sci & Art, Cooper Union, 61. Bibliog: Shirley Fischler (auth), newspaper profile in, Toronto Daily Star, 4/68; Burton Wasserman (auth), Modern painting—the movements, the artists, their work, Davis Publ, 70. Style & Technique: Kinetic geometrical forms moving in an open-ended space. Media: Wood, Aluminum, Mirrors, Motors. Dealer: David Stuart Los Angeles CA. Mailing Add: 2764 Woodwardia Dr Los Angeles CA 90024

STACHELBERG, MRS CHARLES G
COLLECTOR, PATRON
b New York, NY. Study: Columbia Univ Exten; NY Univ. Collection: Late 19th and 20th century art. Mailing Add: 169 E 69th St New York NY 10021

STACK, FRANK HUNTINGTON
PAINTER, PRINTMAKER
b Houston, Tex, Oct 31, 37. Study: Univ Tex, Austin, BFA; Art Inst Chicago; Univ Wyo, Laramie, MFA; Acad Grande Chaumiere, Paris. Work: Minneapolis Inst of Art, Minn; Sheldon Mem Gallery, Univ of Nebr; Madison Art Ctr, Wis; Ga Mus of Art, Athens; Kalamazoo Art Inst, Mich. Exhib: Ten Missouri Painters, 69, Mo State Coun Arts tour show, 69; Living Am Artists & the Figure, Pa State Univ Art Mus, 74; one-man shows, Paintings by Frank Stack, Jewish Community Ctr, Kansas City, Mo, 73 & Etchings by Frank Stack, US Info Serv, US Embassy, Turkey. Teaching: Instr, asst prof, assoc prof & prof art, Univ Mo-Columbia, 63- Pos: Asst fine arts ed, Houston Chronicle, Tex, 59-60. Awards: Summer Res Fel, 68 & 74 & Foreign Study Grant, 70, Univ Mo Res Coun. Bibliog: Etchings by Frank Stack, Sunday Clothes, winter 72; Donald Hoffman (auth), Artists at the Center, Kansas City Star, 7/29/73; Sidney Larson (auth), Etchings and Lithographs by Frank Stack, Singing Wind Publ, 76; exhib catalog, Watercolors by Frank Stack, Mo Arts Coun, 77. Mem: Col Art Asn Am. Media: Oil Painting, Watercolor; Etching, Lithography. Publ: Contribr, Motive Mag, 58, 69 & 70; co-auth, A selection of etchings by John Sloan, Univ Mo, 68; auth, A metal plate sketchbook, Am Artist, 10/75; illusr, Hog Killin' Time & Other Poems, Trilobite Press, 75; illusr, Duplicate Keys—Poems by Jon Bracker, Thorpe Springs Press, Berkeley, 78. Dealer: The Lakeside Studio 150 S Lakeshore Rd Lakeside MI 49116; Assoc Am Artists 663 Fifth Ave New York NY 10022. Mailing Add: 409 Thilly Ave Columbia MO 65201

STACK, GAEL Z
EDUCATOR, PAINTER
b Chicago, Ill, Apr 28, 41. Study: Univ Ill, Champaign, BFA; Southern Ill Univ, MFA. Work: Mus of Fine Art, Houston. Exhib: 16th Ann Nat Exhib Prints & Drawings, Okla Art Ctr, Oklahoma City, 74; Univ St Thomas, Houston, 74; Houston Area Show, 74-76; Woman: Art, Houston, 77; one-man shows, Graphics Gallery, San Francisco, 74, Meredith Long Gallery, Houston, 75-77 & Corpus Christi Mus, Tex, 77; 19th Ann Delta Exhib, 76; New Acquisitions: Works on Paper, Mus of Fine Arts, Houston, 76. Teaching: Instr, Univ Wis, La Crosse, 72-73; asst prof, Univ Houston, 74- Awards: Honorable Mention, 19th Ann Delta Exhib, 76. Dealer: Meredith Long & Co 2323 San Felipe Houston TX 77098. Mailing Add: 2015 W Main Houston TX 77098

STACKS, WILLIAM LEON
PAINTER, ART RESTORER
b Charlotte, NC, Apr 25, 28. Study: With Alice Steadman, W Lester Stevens & William J Potter. Work: Mariner's Mus, Norfolk, Va; NC Nat Bank, Charlotte; Greenville Art Ctr, NC; Goldsboro Art Ctr, NC; NY State Mus; plus numerous other corporate & pvt collections. Comn: Restoration comns, pvt & corporate collections, govt bldgs & univs, incl Davidson Col, Wofford Col, Univ SC, Univ NC, Wake Forest Univ, Clemson Univ & Winthrop Col. Exhib: Nat Soc Painters in Casein & Acrylic, New York, 72; Washington Soc Miniature Painters, 71-74; NJ Soc Miniature Painters, 72-73; Allied Artists of Am, 72-73; Am Artists Prof League, 73-74; Nat Arts Club; plus other group shows & 80 one-man shows. Collections Arranged: (Assisted) Elliott Daingerfield Retrospective (with catalog), Mint Mus, Charlotte & NC State Mus, Raleigh, 71. Pos: Bd mem, NC Arts Coun, 72- Awards: Eight Hon Mentions in Numerous Travel Shows; President's Scroll Honor, Nat Arts Club, 75; Third Founders Award, Washington Soc Miniature Painters, 77; D Wu Ject-Key Mem Award, Salmagundi Club, 77. Mem: Allied Artists Am; Salmagundi Club; Nat Arts Club; Am Artists Prof League; NJ Soc Miniature Painters. Style & Technique: Academic impressionist. Dealer: Annex Gallery 132 N College St Charlotte NC 28202; Connoisseur Gallery Bernardsville NJ 07924. Mailing Add: PO Box 1573 Morganton NC 28655

STACY, DONALD L
PAINTER, EDUCATOR
b West Paterson, NJ, Sept 3, 25. Study: Newark Sch Fine Art; Art Students League; Univ Paris Sch Art & Archeol; Univ Aix-Marseille; Pratt Graphic Art Ctr; New Sch Social Res. Work: Print Dept, Mus Mod Art; Birla Acad Art, Calcutta. Comn: Three decorative wall panels, US Plywood. Exhib: Documenta II, Kassel, Ger; Kyoto Gallery, Japan; Grenchen, Switz; Philadelphia Print Club; Knoedlers, York; George Wittenborn, Art Books, New York. Teaching: Mem fac, Dept Art, Inst Mod Art, Mus Mod Art, 57-69, Dept Art, Sch Visual Arts, New York, 69-70 & Dept Art, New Sch Social Res, 67- Pos: Mem bd ed, Main Currents in Mod Thought & Fields within Fields. Awards: Fulbright Grant, 53-55. Mem: Am Inst for Conserv of Hist & Artistic Works; Engadiner Kollegium, Zurich. Style & Technique: Protohuman images found within a field of all over texture. Media: Acrylic, Oil. Publ: Contribr, articles in: The Nat Encycl, 69; auth, The Runaway Dot: a Concept Book for Children, Bobbs, 69; contribr, articles in: Main Currents in Mod Thought, 69-74; contribr, Emergent Man, Gordon & Breach, 73; auth, Experiments in Art, Scholastic, 75. Mailing Add: 17 E 16th St New York NY 10003

STADLER, ALBERT
PAINTER
b New York, NY, Aug 12, 23. Study: Univ Pa; Univ Fla. Exhib: Corcoran Gallery Art, Washington, DC; Dayton Art Inst, Ohio; Los Angeles Co Mus Art, Calif; Walker Art Ctr, Minneapolis, Minn; Art Gallery Toronto, Ont; 20th Nat Print Exhib, Brooklyn Mus, NY, 77; plus many others. Media: Acrylic. Interest: Color, in all its changing hues, chroma's and lights. Dealer: Poindexter Gallery 24 E 84th St New York NY 10028. Mailing Add: 1568 Second Ave New York NY 10028

STAEMPFLI, GEORGE W
ART DEALER, PAINTER
b Bern, Switz, Dec 6, 10; US citizen. Study: Univ Erlangen, PhD, 35. Exhib: One-man shows, M Knoedler & Co, New York, 41 & 47. Pos: Cur, Mus Fine Arts, Houston, Tex, 55-57; coordr fine arts, Am Pavilion, Brussels Expo, 57-58; pres, Staempfli Gallery, 69- Specialty: Contemporary European and American painting and sculpture. Mailing Add: 47 E 77th St New York NY 10021

STAFFEL, RUDOLF HARRY
CERAMIST, INSTRUCTOR
b San Antonio, Tex, June 15, 11. Study: Chicago Art Inst, Ill; Escuela Para Maestros, San Juan Teotihuacan, Mex; pvt study with Jose Arpa & Xavier Gonzalez, San Antonio. Work: Mus of Contemp Crafts, New York; Philadelphia Mus Art; Smithsonian Inst, Washington, DC; Dartmouth Col Galleries & Collections, Hopkins Ctr, Hanover, NH; Everson Mus, Syracuse, NY. Exhib: Porcelain by Rudolf Staffel, Mus Contemp Crafts, NY, 66; Craftsman 1966, Mus Contemp Crafts, New York, 66; Twenty-Five Years of Art in Clay USA, Lang Art Gallery, Scripps Col, 69; Objects USA, Johnson Collection Exhib, Smithsonian Inst, Washington, DC, 69; Ceramics 70 Plus Woven Forms, Everson Mus Art, Syracuse, NY, 70; Thirty Ceramists USA, Victoria & Albert Mus, London, Eng, 72; Contemp Clay—Ten Approaches, Dartmouth Col Galleries, Hanover, 76; 300 Years of American Art, Philadelphia Mus Art, 76; Tureens 1976, Campbell Mus, Camden, NJ, 76; one-man show, Helen Drutt Gallery, Philadelphia, 76. Teaching: Prof ceramics, Tyler Sch Art, Temple Univ, 40- Pos: Exec comt, Temple Univ Chap, Am Asn Univ Prof, 74-77. Awards: Lindbach Award, Excellence in Teaching, Temple Univ, 66; Merit Award, Ceramic Arts—USA—1966, Int Mineral and Chemicals Corp, 66; Craftsman Fel, Nat Endowment for the Arts, Washington, DC, 77. Bibliog: Richard B Petterson (auth), Ceramic Art in America, Prof Publ Inc, 69; Roger D Bonham (auth), Full Cover, Ceramic Monthly, 2/75; Robert & Paula

Winokur (auth), The Light of Rudolf Staffel, Craft Horizons, 4/77. Mem: Nat Coun for Educ Ceramic Arts; Am Asn Col Prof. Style & Technique: Wheel thrown and handbuilt translucent procelain. Media: Ceramic Clay. Dealer: Helen Drutt Gallery 1625 Spruce St Philadelphia PA 19103. Mailing Add: 104 W Mermaid Ln Philadelphia PA 19118

STAHL, BEN (ALBERT)
PAINTER, ILLUSTRATOR
b Chicago, Ill, Sept 7, 10. Work: New Britain Mus Am Art; Albion Col; Adelphi Col; Duke Univ. Comn: 14 stations of cross for Cath Bible & Cath Press, Chicago, 55. Exhib: Art Inst Chicago; Nat Acad Design; Audubon Mus; Bridgeport Univ, 69; Ft Lauderdale, Fla, 70; plus others. Teaching: Mem founding fac, Art Inst Chicago, 41, Am Acad Art, Chicago, 42 & Famous Artists Schs, Westport, Conn, 49- Pos: Mem bd adv, Am Art Found; founder & vpres, Mus of the Cross, Sarasota, Fla, 65- Awards: Saltus Gold Medal, Nat Acad Design, 49; Art Dirs Club, Chicago, 49; Art Dirs Clubs, New York, 52; plus others. Mem: Soc Illustrators; Westport Artists (co-founder); Sarasota Art Asn (vpres, 53); Am Artists Prof League; Int Platform Asn. Publ: Auth & illusr, Blackbeard's Ghost, 65; illusr, Gone With the Wind (anniversary ed); auth & illusr, The Secret of Red Skull, Houghton Mifflin, 71; illusr, Sat Eve Post & other nat mag. Mailing Add: Apdo 421 GTO San Miguel de Allende Mexico

STALEY, ALLEN
ART HISTORIAN
b St Louis, Mo, June 4, 35. Study: Princeton Univ, BA, 57; Yale Univ, MA, 60, PhD, 65. Teaching: Lectr, Frick Collection, New York, 62-65; assoc prof, Columbia Univ, 69- Pos: Asst cur, Philadelphia Mus Art, 65-68. Res: English painting. Publ: Co-auth, Victorian Artists in England (catalog), 65; co-auth, Romantic Art in Britain (catalog), 68; ed, From Realism to Symbolism: Whistler and His World (catalog), 71; Pre-Raphaelite Landscape, 73. Mailing Add: 1 W 72nd St New York NY 10023

STALLWITZ, CAROLYN
PAINTER, PHOTOGRAPHER
b Abilene, Tex, Apr 27, 36. Study: WTex State Univ, with Clarence Kincaid, Jr, BS(art); also with Emilio Caballero, Stefan Kramer & Lee Simpson. Work: Pioneer Natural Gas Co, Amarillo, Tex; Ark Art Ctr Gallery, Little Rock; Amarillo Art Ctr Shop. Exhib: Southwestern Watercolor Soc Exhib, 69; Tex Watercolor Soc, 70; Wichita Centennial Nat Art Exhib, 70; Best of Southwest, 71; Amarillo Fine Art Asn Citation Show, 73; Denver Audubon Wildlife Art Show, 77. Teaching: Instr drawing, Amarillo Art Ctr, 73-74, instr watercolor, 74- Mem: Moore Co Arts Asn (pres, 69-70); Tex Arts Alliance; Amarillo Fine Art Asn; Tex Fine Art Asn; Tex Watercolor Soc. Style & Technique: Wildlife and western realism, with emphasis on birds and wild flowers. Media: Watercolor, Pencil. Dealer: Hughes Home Beautiful 2740 Duniven Circle Amarillo TX 79109. Mailing Add: Box 1225 Dumas TX 79029

STAMATS, PETER OWEN
COLLECTOR, PATRON
b Cedar Rapids, Iowa, July 20, 29. Study: Dartmouth Col, BA, 51. Pos: Mem, Iowa State Arts Coun, 66-70. Mem: Am Fedn Arts; Cedar Rapids Art Asn (dir, 58-, pres, 59-60). Interest: Support of Cedar Rapids Art Ctr. Collection: 15th century to 20th century prints. Mailing Add: 427 Sixth Ave SE Cedar Rapids IA 52406

STAMATY, STANLEY
CARTOONIST, ILLUSTRATOR
b Dayton, Ohio, May 21, 16. Study: Cincinnati Art Acad. Comn: Poster for Fire Prev Week, Am Ins Asn. Exhib: Int Salon Humor Ann, Montreal, 69-; Parke Bernet Gallery, New York; M H deYoung Mem Mus Cartoon Exhib; Metrop Mus Art Cartoon Exhib; one-man show, Brookdale Col, 74. Pos: Mem adv bd, Guild Creative Art, 65- Mem: Nat Cartoonists Soc; Cartoonists Guild (chmn mem comt, 72-73); Monmouth Arts Found. Style & Technique: Black and white cartoon style. Media: Ink, Watercolor, Acrylic, Mixed Media. Collection: Best Cartoons of the Year; Best of the Best Cartoons; Ford Times Collection of American Art. Publ: Work publ by Am Bk Co, McGraw-Hill, W H Sadlier Inc, Fairchild Bks & Visuals, Bankers Mag, Sat Rev & New York Times. Mailing Add: PO Box 75 Elberon NJ 07740

STAMM, GEOFFREY EATON
ART ADMINISTRATOR, ART HISTORIAN
b Washington, DC, July 30, 43. Study: Univ Paris, CPLF cert, 64; Hamilton Col, AB, 65; Am Univ, Washington, DC; Corcoran Sch of Art, Washington, DC; Inst of Art Admin, Harvard Univ, cert, 74. Pos: Coordr spec proj, Indian Arts & Crafts Bd, Washington, DC, 69-74; asst to gen mgr, 74-; mem, Fed Interagency Crafts Comt, Washington, DC, 76- Mem: Am Crafts Coun; World Crafts Coun; NAm Craft Adminr; Am Asn of Mus; Int Coun of Mus. Res: Twentieth century American Indian, Eskimo and Aleut fine arts and handcrafts. Publ: Contribr & illusr, Institute of American Indian Arts, 68, illusr, Future directions in Native American art, 73 & ed, Protection for Native American artists and Craftsmen, 74, US Dept of Interior; illusr, Encouraging American craftsmen, US Dept of Commerce, 71; contribr, Authentic Indian Jewelry, Gro-Pub, 75. Mailing Add: 2475 Virginia Ave NW Washington DC 20037

STAMM, JOHN DAVIES
COLLECTOR
b Milwaukee, Wis, May 2, 14. Study: NY Univ, BS. Collection: Modern American paintings; lithographs by Lautrec, as well as books, catalogs, magazines and papers pertaining to him. Publ: Auth, Lautrec Posters & Lithographs (exhib catalog), Milwaukee Art Inst, 65; auth, introd, Philip Evergood Exhibition (catalog). Mailing Add: 120 E 95th St New York NY 10028

STAMM, TED
PAINTER, ARTIST
b Brooklyn, NY, Aug 30, 44. Study: Hofstra Univ, BFA, 67. Work: Aldrich Mus, Ridgefield, Conn; Phoenix Mus, Ariz. Exhib: Contemp Reflections 1971-72, Aldrich Mus; Int Art Fair, Cologne, WGer; Five from Soho, Rose Art Mus, Waltham, Mass; Herrick-Brutten Collection, The Clocktower, New York, 75; Soho & Downtown Manhattan, Akademie der Kunste, Berlin, Ger, 76; Selections from Soho-Berlin, La Mus Mod Art, Humlebaek, Denmark; Documenta-6, Kassel, WGer, 77; A Painting Show, Project Studios 1, Long Island City, NY, 77; Book Objects, Albright-Knox Art Gallery, Buffalo, NY; Selections from the Collection, Aldrich Mus, Ridgefield, Conn, 78; Artists Books-USA, Dalhousie Art Gallery, NS, 78; one-man shows, Artists Space, New York, 75, Galerie December, Dusseldorf, Ger, 75, Studio la Citta, Verona, Italy, 76 & Hal Bromm Gallery, New York, 77. Teaching: Instr contemp art, Brooklyn Mus Art Sch, 71-77; adj prof painting & drawing, C W Post Ctr, Long Island Univ, Greenvale, 77; adj prof hist contemp art, Jersey City State Col, 77. Pos: Guest lectr, Hofstra Univ, 71 & 75 & Praff Inst, Brooklyn, 76. Bibliog: Lucio Pozzi (auth), Adesso la Pittura Dipinge la Pittura, Bolaffiarte, 5/74; Yvonne Friedrichs (auth), Ted Stamm—das Bild als Objekt, Rheinische Post, Dusseldorf, 11/75; Edit Deak (auth), Ted Stamm, Hal Bromm Gallery, Artforum, 2/78. Mem: Cf (a collaborative publ group), New York. Style & Technique: Structural. Media: Painting; Installations; Book Works; Street Works. Publ: Contribr, Special Execution Tags, Art-Rite 4, 73 & Statement Regarding Artists Books, Art-Rite 14, 76. Dealer: Hal Bromm Gallery 90 W Broadway New York NY 10012. Mailing Add: 101 Wooster St New York NY 10012

STAMOS, THEODOROS (S)
PAINTER
b New York, NY, Dec 31, 22. Study: Am Artists Sch. Work: Mus Mod Art, New York; Metrop Mus Art, New York; Whitney Mus Am Art, New York; Univ Calif Mus, Berkeley; NJ State Mus, Trenton. Comn: Oil mural, SS Arg, Moore McCormack Lines, 46, tapestry, New York, 71. Exhib: Documenta, Kassel, Ger; New Am Painting, Paris, Zurich, New York, London, Madrid & others; Abstr Expressionists & Imagists, Guggenheim Mus, New York; Dada, Surrealism & Their Inheritors, Mus Mod Art; Corcoran Gallery Art, Washington, DC; Whitney Mus Am Art, New York; Metrop Mus Art, New York; Santa Barbara Mus, 70; Charles E Slatkin Gallery, New York, 72; Joslyn Art Mus, Omaha, Nebr, 73. Teaching: Instr art, Art Students League; lectr art, Columbia Univ; prof art, Brandeis Univ. Awards: Brandies Univ Creative Arts Award, Tiffany Found Fel; Nat Arts Grant. Bibliog: K Sawyer (auth), Stamos, Mus Poche Paris, 60; R Pomeroy (auth), Theodoros Stamos, Abrams, 73. Mem: Life fel Metrop Mus Art. Publ: Illusr, Sorrows of Cold Stone, Dodd. Mailing Add: c/o Marlborough Gallery 40 W 57th St New York NY 10019

STAMPER, WILLSON YOUNG
PAINTER
b New York, NY, Jan 5, 12. Study: Art Students League; Cincinnati Art Acad; US Navy Photog Sch; US Navy Advanced Motion Picture Sch; also pvt study with Kimon Nicolaides & Rico Lebrun. Work: Mus Mod Art, New York; Cincinnati Art Mus; Cincinnati Mod Art Soc; Honolulu Acad Arts; Advertiser Art Found, Honolulu. Comn: Two Ceramic Murals, Int Airport, Honolulu, 75; Portrait of Famous Chanter, State Found for Cult & Arts, Honolulu, 75. Exhib: One-man shows, Cincinnati Art Mus, 37, Honolulu Acad Art, 46, 50 & 54; San Francisco Worlds Fair, 39; Albright Art Gallery, Buffalo, 51; Carnegie Inst Int, Pittsburgh, 52. Teaching: Instr drawing & painting, Cincinnati Art Acad, 37-43; dir, Sch of Honolulu Acad Arts, 45-62. Pos: Conservator of art, Cincinnati Art Mus & Taft Mus, 36-43; conservator art, Honolulu Acad Art, 45-62. Awards: First Prize Artist of Greater Cincinnati, Cincinnati Art Mus, 42; Purchase Award, Watamull Found, 45, 48, 49 & 58; First Prize Honolulu Ann, Honolulu Acad Arts, 47-49 & 52, 55. Bibliog: Article in Le Revue Mod des Arts et de Lavie, 6/49; Madge Tennent (auth), Miracle in art, Paradise of Pac Mag, 58; Art in Hawaii, House Beautiful Mag, 58; biog, interviews & reproductions in Artists of Hawaii, Vol 1, State Found Cult & the Arts, Univ Press of Hawaii, 74. Mem: Hawaii Painter & Sculptors League; Int Inst Conservation Hist & Artistic Works. Style & Technique: Non-objective and o'e; varied technique. Media: Oil, Watercolor. Publ: Contribr, George B Bridgeman's One Hundred Best Heads, Bridgeman Publ, 33; contribr, K Nicolaides' Natural Way to Draw, Houghton Mifflin, 41; illusr & co-auth, Cultural Considerations for Planning in Micronesia, Trust Territory Planning, US State Dept, 68. Dealer: Downtown Gallery Fort St Honolulu HI 96813. Mailing Add: 224 N Kalaheo Ave Kailua HI 96734

STAMPFLE, FELICE
ART CURATOR, WRITER
b Kansas City, Mo, July 25, 12. Study: Washington Univ, AB & AM; Radcliffe Col. Pos: Cur drawings & prints, Pierpont Morgan Libr, 45-; ed, Master Drawings, 63- Res: Drawings, especially 18th century Italian. Publ: Auth, var articles, reviews & exhib catalogs. Mailing Add: 450 E 63rd St New York NY 10021

STANCZAK, JULIAN
PAINTER, INSTRUCTOR
b Borownica, Poland, Nov 5, 28; US citizen. Study: Uganda, Africa & London, Eng; Cleveland Inst Art, BFA, 54; Yale Univ, with Albers & Marca-Relli, MFA, 56. Work: Dayton Art Inst, Ohio; Albright-Knox Art Gallery, Buffalo; Larry Aldrich Mus, Ridgefield, Conn; Des Moines Art Ctr, Iowa; Libr Cong, Washington, DC; plus others. Exhib: One-man shows, Kent State Univ & Dartmouth Col, 68; Albright-Knox Art Gallery, 68; Univ Ill, 69; Herron Mus Art, Indianapolis, Ind, 69; plus others. Teaching: Instr, Art Acad Cincinnati, 57-64; instr painting & drawing, Cleveland Inst Art, 64-; artist in residence, Dartmouth Col, 68. Awards: Cleveland Fine Arts Award, 70; Outstanding Educ Am, 70; Ohio Arts Coun Award, 72. Bibliog: George Rickey (auth), Constructivism: Origins and Evolution, Braziller, 67; Udo Kultermann (auth), Neue Formen des Bildes, Verlag Ernst Wasmuth, Tubingen, 69; Kenneth F Bates (auth), Basic Design, World Publ, 70; plus many others. Mem: Am Abstract Artists; Am Int Platform Asn. Res: Pioneer in optical art. Dealer: Martha Jackson Gallery 32 E 69th St New York NY 10021. Mailing Add: 6229 Cabrini Ln Seven Hills OH 44131

STANDEN, EDITH APPLETON
ART HISTORIAN
b Halifax, NS, Feb 21, 05; US citizen. Study: Oxford Univ, BA. Pos: Art secy, Joseph Widener Collection, Elkins Park, Pa, 29-42; assoc cur, Metrop Mus Art, New York, 49-70, cur consult, 70- Mem: Col Art Asn Am. Res: European post-medieval tapestries. Publ: Auth, var articles in Metrop Mus Bull, Metrop Mus J & Art Bull, and others, 51-77; co-auth, Art treasures of the Metropolitan, 52 & Decorative art from the Samuel H Kress Collection, 64. Mailing Add: Metrop Mus of Art Fifth Ave & 82nd St New York NY 10028

STANFORTH, MELVIN SIDNEY
EDUCATOR, PRINTMAKER
b Tuscaloosa, Ala, Sept 22, 37. Study: Univ Ala, BFA; Wayne State Univ, MFA. Work: Weatherspoon Gallery, Univ NC, Greensboro; NC Nat Bank Corp Hq, Charlotte. Exhib: Davidson Nat Print & Drawing Exhib, Davidson Col, 73; Piedmont Graphics Ann, Winston-Salem, NC, 73, 75 & 76; Regional Painting Exhib, 73-76 & Regional Drawing & Prints Exhib, 73-77, Southeastern Ctr Contemp Arts, Winston-Salem, NC; Ball State Univ Nat Drawing Exhib, Muncie, Ind, 74; Potsdam Nat Drawing Exhib, NY, 75. Teaching: Prof drawing & design, E Carolina Univ, Greenville, NC, 69- Awards: Second Purchase Award, NC Artists Exhib, NC Arts Coun, 71; Purchase Awards, Regional Painting Exhib, 73 & Regional Drawing & Prints Exhib, 73, Southeastern Ctr Contemp Arts, Winston-Salem, NC. Style & Technique: Contemporary. Media: Lithography. Mailing Add: 2205 E Fifth St Greenville NC 27834

STANKARD, PAUL JOSEPH
CRAFTSMAN, GLASS ARTIST
b N Attleboro, Mass, Apr 7, 43. Study: Salem Tech Inst. Work: Smithsonian Inst, Washington, DC; Corning Mus Glass, NY; John Nelson Bergstrom Mus, Neenah, Wis; NJ State Mus, Trenton; Wheaton Hist Mus, Millville, NJ. Comn: Floral glass paperweights, comn by Smithsonian Inst, Washington, DC, 77. Exhib: NJ State Mus, Trenton, 72; Glass Art, John Nelson Bergstrom Mus, Neenah, 76; Pa Hort Soc, Philadelphia, 77; Gloucester Co

Col, Sewell, NJ, 78; Corning Mus Glass, NY, 78; Wheaton Hist Mus, Millville, NJ, 78. Bibliog: David Brodie (auth), Orchid Paperweights of Glass Artist, Paul Stankard, Am Orchid Soc Bull, 77; Mark Forrest (auth), Feature prog, Channel 3 TV, Philadelphia, Pa, 78. Mem: Am Paperweight Guild (dir, 77-). Style & Technique: Developing the illusions of botanical accuracy in glass. Media: Glass. Dealer: George Kamm 2479 Lincoln Hwy E Lancaster PA 17602. Mailing Add: 618 W Landing Rd Mantua NJ 08051

STANKIEWICZ, RICHARD PETER
SCULPTOR, EDUCATOR
b Philadelphia, Pa, Oct 18, 22. Study: With Hans Hofmann, Fernand Leger & Ossip Zadkine. Work: Beaubourg Collection, Paris, France; Whitney Mus Am Art, New York; Mus Mod Art, New York; Mus Mod Art, Stockholm; Guggenheim Mus, New York; Albright-Knox Mus, Buffalo. Exhib: Venice Biennale, 58; Pittsburgh Int, Carnegie Inst, 58-61; Bienal, Sao Paulo, 61; Four Americans, Mod Mus, Stockholm, 62; Nat Gallery Victoria, Melbourne. Teaching: Prof art, State Univ NY Albany, 67-; vis artist, Amherst Col, 70-71. Awards: Brandeis Univ & Nat Coun Arts Awards. Media: Metals. Dealer: Zabriskie Gallery 29 W 57th St New York NY 10019. Mailing Add: Star Rte Huntington MA 01050

STANLEY, BOB
PAINTER
b Yonkers, NY, Jan 3, 32. Study: Ogelthorpe Univ, BA; Columbia Univ; Art Students League; Brooklyn Mus Art Sch, Max Beckman painting scholar, 55 & 56. Work: Whitney Mus Am Art, New York; Milwaukee Art Ctr, Wis; Washington Univ Mus, St Louis; Fogg Art Mus, Cambridge, Mass; Minneapolis Mus of Art, Minn; Univ of Houston Art Ctr, Tex; Metrop Mus Art, New York. Exhib: Whitney Mus Am Art Painting Ann, 67, 69 & 72 & 73 Biennial; Documenta 4, Kassel, Ger, 68; Obsessive Image, Inst Contemp Arts, London, Eng, 68; Monumental Art, Contemp Arts Ctr, Cincinnati, Ohio, 71; Three Centuries of the American Nude, NY Cult Ctr, 75; two-man show (with Bart Wasserman), PS1, Long Island City, NJ, 77; one-man shows, New York Cult Ctr, 74 & Union Gallery, La State Univ, Baton Rouge, 76. Awards: Cassandra Found Award, 69. Bibliog: Christgau (auth), Big paintings, Cheetah Mag, 68; Honnef (auth), Mythen des alltags-transzendiert, Gegenverkehr, Aachen, 69; Gassiot-Talabot (auth), Robert Stanley, Opus Int, 12/71-1/72; Taylor (auth), Bob Stanley, Art Int, 9/74; Colin Naylor & Genesis P Orridge (co-ed), Contemporary Artists, St James Press, London, Eng, 77; Carter Ratcliff (auth), Bob Stanley & Bart Wasserman at PS1, Art in Am, 1-2/78. Media: Oil, Acrylic, Crayon. Mailing Add: 3 Crosby St New York NY 10013

STAPLETON, JOSEPH F
INSTRUCTOR, PAINTER
b Brooklyn, NY, Mar 20, 21. Study: St John's Univ, Brooklyn, NY, BS(summa cum laude); Brooklyn Col; Columbia Univ; Art Students League, with Vytlacil, Dumond, Kantor, Olitsley, Herty & Barnet. Work: Birla Inst, Calcutta, India; Art Students League; Pratt Inst, New York. Exhib: Am Painting Today, Metrop Mus Art, New York, 50; Ann Invitational, Pa Acad Art, Philadelphia, 52; one-man shows, Hofstra Col, Long Island, 56 & Charles Egan Gallery, New York, 63-64; Ten-Yr Retrospective Avant Garde Gallery, New York, 57. Teaching: Instr painting, Metrop Mus Art, New York, 57-59; instr painting & drawing, Pratt Inst, 70-; instr painting & drawing, Art Students League, New York, 73- Bibliog: Russell Arnold (auth), Portfolio of drawings—Joseph Stapleton, Crucible, Atlantic Christian Col, fall 68. Style & Technique: Beginning as a portrait painter, work has evolved over the years to an abstract style combining elements of Oriental and Western art. Media: Oils; Ink. Publ: Auth & illusr, Leaflets in Japanese for psychological warfare, US Govt, 44-45; illusr, Who Wrote the Classics?, John Day Co, 68. Mailing Add: 24 E 20th St New York NY 10003

STAPP, RAY VERYL
EDUCATOR, PAINTER
b Norton, Kans, July 10, 13. Study: Bethany Col, Lindsborg, Kans, with Birger Sandzen, BFA; Kansas City Art Inst, with Thomas Hart Benton; Art Students League, with Dumond, Reilly & Trafton; Teachers Col, Columbia Univ, with Ziegfield, MA; Pa State Univ, with Lowenfeld, EdD. Work: Painting, Lowenfeld Mem Collection, Pa State Univ. Exhib: Nat Craft & Ceramics Show, Wichita Art Asn, Kans, 57; Erie Art Asn, Pa, 60; 18th Ann Area Show, Peoria, Ill, 69. Teaching: From instr to asst prof design & art educ, Bethany Col, 49-56; from asst prof to assoc prof art, Edinboro State Col, 57-64; from assoc prof to prof design & art educ, Eastern Ill Univ, 64- Pos: Engraver & lithographer, Hallmark Card Co, 37-39; advert artist, Armstrong Cork Co, 48-49; prod illusr, Boeing Airplane Co, 56-57. Mem: Nat Art Educ Asn; Western Arts; Ill Art Educ Asn (coun mem, 69-70). Media: Oil. Res: Relationships of measures of creativity, general intelligence and memory; extension of research used as criteria for evaluating children in grades 4-8. Publ: Auth, You can mix your own glazes, 58 & Planning an art lesson, 67, Arts & Activities; auth, Lettering can be easy, Sch Arts, 72; auth, Evaluation of one humanities course, Humanities J, 75; auth, Some things to think about, Arts & Activities, 77. Mailing Add: 42 Circle Dr Charleston IL 61920

STAPP, WILLIAM F
CURATOR
b McKinney, Tex, Mar 2, 45. Study: Tulane Univ, BA, 67; Univ Pa, MA, 70; Goddard Col, MA, 77; Princeton Univ, with Peter Bunnell. Collections Arranged: Survey of the Photographic Collection, Princeton Univ, 74-76. Teaching: Mus teacher mus collections, Philadelphia Mus of Art, 71-76; instr hist photog, Moore Col of Art, Philadelphia, 75-76 & Philadelphia Col of Art, 75-76. Pos: Res asst, Princeton Univ Art Mus, 75-76; cur, Nat Portrait Gallery, 76- Mem: Soc for Photog Educ; Photog Hist Soc of NY. Res: History of photography; 19th century and portrait photography. Publ: Auth, Early attempts to improve the daguerreotype, Image, 76; contribr, Philadelphia: Three Centuries of American Art, Philadelphia Mus of Art, 76. Mailing Add: Nat Portrait Gallery Eighth & F Sts NW Washington DC 20007

STAPRANS, RAIMONDS
PAINTER, SCULPTOR
b Riga, Latvia, Oct 13, 26; US citizen. Study: Sch Art, Esslinger, Stuttgart, 46; Univ Wash, BA, 52; Univ Calif, MA, 55; also with Archipenko. Work: Calif Palace Legion of Honor, San Francisco; Oakland Mus, Calif; Santa Barbara Mus, Calif; Los Angeles Co Mus; Phoenix Art Mus. Exhib: Portland Art Mus, Ore, 56 & 57; Oakland Art Mus, 57; Palace Legion of Honor Winter Invitational, 57, 59 & 60; Litton Industs, 62; Am Acad Arts & Lett, New York, 70; plus many one-man shows, in US, Can & Europe. Bibliog: California Canvas (film), KRON, San Francisco, 66; Artists Eye (film), Motion Media, 67. Media: Oil; Plastic. Dealer: Maxwell Galleries 551 Sutter San Francisco CA 94102. Mailing Add: 2052 20th St San Francisco CA 94107

STARK, BRUCE GUNSTEN
CARTOONIST
b Queens, NY, Feb 17, 33. Study: Sch Visual Arts, New York, 55-58. Work: Everett Dirksen Libr; L B Johnson Libr; Baseball Hall of Fame; Cooperstown, NY; Basketball Hall of Fame, Mass. Exhib: One-man shows, Art Inst Pittsburgh, 68, Univ Kutztown, Pa, 70 & NY Bank for Savings, New York, 71; Nat Art Mus Sport, New York, 71. Pos: Artist, cartoonist, New York Daily News, 61- Awards: Third, Fourth & Sixth Prize, Int Salon de Caricatures, Montreal, 66, 68 & 69; Nat Cartoonist Soc Reuben Category Awards for Sports, 66 & Spec Features, 68; Page One Award for Best Sports Cartoon, 70 & 73 & New York, 71; Original cartoons requested by Presidents Nixon & Johnson; first color cartoon appearing on front page, New York Daily News. Mailing Add: 161 Chestnut St Emerson NJ 07630

STARK, GEORGE KING
EDUCATOR, SCULPTOR
b Schenectady, NY, June 14, 23. Study: State Univ NY Col Buffalo, BS(art educ); Teachers Col, Columbia Univ, MA; State Univ NY Buffalo, EdD; and with Dorothy Denslow. Work: IBM Collection; Lowe Art Mus, Univ Miami, Fla; Am Art Clay Co; State Univ NY Col Buffalo; State Univ NY Col Oswego; also in pvt collections. Comn: Sculptured light fixtures, Savoy Hilton Hotel, New York, 59; space modulator, Sheraton-Palace Hotel, San Francisco, 60; divider screen, Park-Sheraton Hotel, New York, 60; wall relief sculpture, Prudential Steamship Lines, New York, 61; sculptured fountain, comn by Robert E Maytag, Newton, Iowa, 71. Exhib: 17th & 19th Ceramic Nat, 52 & 56 & Ceramic Int Exhib, 58, Syracuse Mus Fine Arts; Western NY Ann, Albright-Knox Gallery, Buffalo, 57 & 60; one-man show, Lowe Art Mus, 67. Teaching: Prof art, State Univ NY Col Oswego, 64- Awards: Shared First Prize for Ceramic Sculpture, 19th Ceramic Nat, 56; Am Inst Architects Sculpture Award, Albright-Knox Gallery, 57 & 60. Res: Analysis of artist-teacher's statements on their creativity. Publ: Auth, Silent images, 11/63 & Mass communication and faculty/student dialogue, 4/69, Art Educ J; auth, On sculpture, Sch Arts, 3/64; auth, Games theory in education, Sch & Soc, fall 67; auth, Think stream, S & W, fall & winter 69-70. Mailing Add: 229 E Seventh St Oswego NY 13126

STARK, MELVILLE F
PAINTER, EDUCATOR
b Honesdale, Pa, Sept 29, 03. Study: East Stroudsburg State Col; Univ Pa, MS; Mus Col Fine Arts, Philadelphia; Syracuse Univ, with Cullan Yates & W E Baum; also in Eng & France. Work: In 22 US Embassies; Lehigh Co Ct House, Allentown, Pa; Allentown City Hall; Reading Art Mus, Pa; plus many others. Exhib: Am Watercolor Soc; Pa Acad Fine Arts; Nat Soc Painters Casein; Mus Fine Arts, Springfield, Mass; Allied Artists Exhib, Butler Art Inst; Philadelphia Watercolor Club. Teaching: Head dept painting, Baum Art Sch Allentown Art Mus, 31-62, dir, Sch, 56-62; head dept painting, Cedar Crest Col, 40-55; head dept art hist, Muhlenberg Col, 55-60. Pos: Dir, Allentown Art Mus, 54-60. Awards: First Myers Mem Award, Nat Soc Painters Casein; first Prize for Landscape, Manatee Art League, Brandenton, Fla; Hon Mention, Mus Fine Arts, Springfield; First Prize, Sarasota Art Asn; First Prize, Longboat Key Art Asn. Mem: Mus Fine Arts, Springfield; Rockport Art Asn; NShore Art Asn; Sarasota Art Asn; Salmagundi Club. Media: Oil, Watercolor, Pastel, Acrylic. Mailing Add: RD 1 Zionsville PA 18092

STARK, RON
PHOTOGRAPHER
b Sidney, NY, June 27, 44. Study: Univ Denver; NY State Univ, BA. Work: Baltimore Mus Art, Md; Smithsonian Inst, Washington, DC. Comn: Walt Disney movie stills, comn by M Goldfarb, Denver, Colo, 65; photo exhib, comn by L Hager, Woodland Mus, Cooperstown, NY, 67 & 68; photo exhib, NY State Univ, 68. Exhib: Baltimore Mus Art, 70; Mass Inst Technol Gallery, Boston, 71; one-man shows, Studio Gallery, Washington, DC, Graphiks Biennale, Vienna, Austria, 72 & San Francisco Mus Art, 74; Corcoran Gallery Art, 72; Phillips Collection, Washington, DC, 73. Teaching: Student lectr commun, Univ Denver, 62-64; student lectr photog, film & TV, State Univ NY, 66-68; instr photog, Smithsonian Inst, 69- Awards: Va Mus Grant, 74; Int Inst Educ Travel Grant, 74. Style & Technique: Nudes; pigment on watercolor paper. Dealer: Middendorf Gallery Washington DC. Mailing Add: 6048 1/2 Ramshorn Pl McLean VA 22101

STARK, SHIRLEY
SCULPTOR
b New York, NY, May 27, 27. Study: Univ Detroit; Wayne State Univ. Work: Mus of NMex, Santa Fe, NMex; Children's Mus, Detroit; Wurlitzer Found, Taos, NMex. Comn: Works listed from Ritual Ser with Tomas Garcia, Sudario (basalt), Mem to Milford Greer, painter, comn by Lou Criss, Ranchos de Taos, NMex, 72, Sun-Rite (basalt), 73 & Shakti (basalt), 74, comn by William Bomar, Taos. Exhib: Ohio Ceramic & Sculpture Show, Butler Inst Am Art, Youngstown, Ohio, 62 & 68; Southern Sculpture: 67, Traveling Exhib to Ten Mus in US, 67; 14th Drawing & Small Sculpture Show, Ball State Univ Gallery, 68; 1974 Fall Invitational, Roswell Mus; guest exhibitor, 65th Ann Exhib, Mus Art, Carnegie Inst, 75. Pos: Formal asst to Dimitri Hadzi, Ore Int Sculpture Symp, Eugene, 74. Awards: Sculpture Fel, MacDowell Colony, Peterborough, NH, 68; Sculpture Grant, Wurlitzer Found, Taos, 69, 71 & 74; Vis Andrew Mellon Prof Sculpture, Carnegie-Mellon Univ, 75. Bibliog: Shirley Stark (monogr), Draco Trust, Draco Found, Independence, Calif, 73; Gwen Finkel Chanzit (auth), The Midland Collection, Midland Fed Savings, Denver, 73; Leaonead Pack Bailey (auth), Broadside Authors & Artists, Broadside, 74. Mem: Artists Equity; Int Asn Art; UNESCO; Taos Art Asn. Style & Technique: Cutting stone with pneumatic equipment. Publ: Illusr, Broadside No 23, May, 1968, In: At Bay (poetry), Broadside, 68. Mailing Add: c/o The Arwin Galleries 222 Grand River W Detroit MI 48226

STARKS, ELLIOTT ROLAND
ART ADMINISTRATOR, EDUCATOR
b Madison, Wis, Feb 24, 22. Study: Univ Wis-Madison, BS, 43, MS, 46. Collections Arranged: Wis Union Collection Original Art, 51-; Frank Lloyd Wright, 55; Alexander Calder Exhib, 56; Leo Steppat Mem Sculpture Exhib, 67. Teaching: Instr art, Amphitheater Sch, Tucson, Ariz, 46-47; instr art, Thomas Sch, Tucson, 48-50; asst prof social educ & dir, Wis Union, Univ Wis-Madison, 51-74; retired. Mem: Madison Art Asn; Elvehjem Art Ctr; Wis Arts Coun; Int Asn Col Unions. Publ: Auth, Arts and Crafts in the College Union, 62. Mailing Add: 3509 Gregory St Madison WI 53711

STARRS, MILDRED
PAINTER
b Brooklyn, NY. Study: Maxwell Training Sch Teachers; Pratt Inst; NY Univ, with J Haney, cert. Work: Meadowbrook Hosp, Long Island; John F Kennedy Bldg Art Gallery; George Washington Univ Law Sch, Washington, DC; Nat Gallery Sports, New York. Comn: Toni, Lauri, Dr & Mrs Alfred Lapin, NY; Terri, Mr & Mrs Richard Wheeler, NY; Jennifer, Mr & Mrs Victor Borod, Miami, Fla; Summer & Winter (two), comn by Mr & Mrs Michael McCormack, NY; Hollywood, comn by Mrs Frederick Paulsen, NY; Sta Basket & Home, comn by Mr & Mrs Dick Waters, Conn; Dogwood, comn by Mr & Mrs John Robinson, NY; Arrangement in White Vase, comn by Mrs Harry Schroeder, Fla. Exhib: One-man shows, Barbizon Gallery, New York, 65-67 & George Washington Univ, 66; Acad Artists Asn, Springfield Mus, Mass, 65-72; Catharine Lorillard Wolfe Art Club, Nat Gallery, 67; Hudson

Valley Art Asn, Co Ctr, White Plains, NY, 69-77; Allied Artists Am, Nat Gallery, New York, 71 & 76; Am Watercolor Soc, Nat Gallery, New York, 77; Am Artists Prof League, Grand Cent Gallery, New York, 77. Teaching: Instr art, Bd Educ, New York, 27-61, chmn art, 46-61. Awards: First Prize, St Luke Art Guild, 63 & 64; Best in Show, Catharine Lorillard Wolfe Art Club, 67; Spec Awards, Nat Art League, 70 & 77; Gold Medal & Best Watercolor in Show, Nat Art Club, 76. Mem: Am Artists Prof League (treas, 67- & vpres); Int Soc of Artists; Nat Art League (vpres, 62-75); Catharine Lorillard Wolfe Art Club (mem bd dirs & treas, 66-72); Hudson Valley Art Asn; Acad Artists Asn. Media: Watercolor. Mailing Add: 301 Park Lane Douglaston NY 11363

STARS, WILLIAM KENNETH
EDUCATOR, MUSEUM DIRECTOR
b DePauw, Ind, Mar 13, 21. Study: Duke Univ, BA(philos), 48; Dept Art, Univ NC, MA(art hist), 50; Dept Art Educ, NY Univ, grad study, 54-67. Exhib: Nat Collegiate Press Cartooning, 48; Ala Water Color Soc, 53-66; NC Mus Art, 53-66; High Mus, 53-66; Loeb Student Ctr, 53-66. Collections Arranged: All collections of the Duke Univ Mus Art. Teaching: Instr sculpture, drawing, Durham High Sch, Duke Univ, 50-66; asst prof art educ, ceramics, Duke Univ, 69-75, assoc prof, 75-, dir arts & crafts workshop, 69- Pos: Conservator & restorer, Duke Univ Mus Art, 67-73, actg dir, 73-74, dir, 74- Awards: Nat Collegiate Press Cartooning Award, 48; Outstanding Prof, Duke Univ, 66. Mem: Int Inst Conserv; Southeastern Col Art Conf; Nat Art Educ Asn; Am Asn Univ Prof. Style & Technique: Abstract painting. Media: Egg Tempera. Publ: Auth, Richard Miller (catalog), Duke Univ Art Dept, 67; auth, DeGrazia of Arizona (catalog), auth, Raimondo Puccinelli (catalog), 74 & auth, Italian Paintings from the Mary & Harry L Dalton Collection, 74, Duke Univ Mus Art; auth, Patented Inventions. Mailing Add: 1916 Glendale Ave Durham NC 27701

STASACK, EDWARD ARMEN
PAINTER, PRINTMAKER
b Chicago, Ill, Oct 1, 29. Study: Univ Ill, BFA & MFA. Work: Libr Cong, Washington, DC; Honolulu Acad Arts, Hawaii; Philadelphia Mus Art, Pa; Boston Pub Libr, Mass; Achenbach Found Collection, San Francisco; Calif Palace of Legion of Honor. Comn: Precast concrete murals, City of Honolulu, Fort St Mall, 68, Chart House Restaurant, Honolulu, 69, Honolulu Community Col, 72 & Petroglyph Environment, Maui Mall, Kahului, 73. Exhib: Carnegie Inst Int, Pittsburgh, Pa, 65; Buenos Aires Print Biennial, Arg, 70; Krakow Print Biennial, Poland, 70; one-man shows, Downtown Gallery, New York, 65, Downtown Gallery, Honolulu, 73, Am Embassy, Istanbul & US Consulate, Izmir, Turkey, 76, Am Cult Ctr, Bucharest, Romania, 76 & Honolulu Acad of Arts, Hawaii, 76. Teaching: Prof art & chmn dept, Univ Hawaii, 69-72. Awards: Tiffany Found Fels, 58 & 62; Rockefeller Found Fel, 59; MacDowall Colony Found Fels, 71 & 75; Award, Exhib of Last Days of Capt Cook, Hawaii State & US Bicentennial Comn, 76. Bibliog: George Tahara (auth), Drawing-Painting-Stasack (film), 67; Neogy & Haar (auth), Artists of Hawaii, 74. Mem: Soc Am Graphic Artists; Honolulu Printmakers (pres, 59-61); Hawaii Painters & Sculptors; Boston Printmakers. Style & Technique: Expressionist-surrealist. Media: Acrylic, Oil; Intaglio. Publ: Auth, Hawaiian petroglyphs, Malamalama Mag, 67; auth, reviews, Honolulu Star-Bull, 68 & 74; co-auth, Hawaiian petroglyphs, Bishop Mus, 70. Mailing Add: 2560 Campus Rd Honolulu HI 96822

STASIK, ANDREW J
PRINTMAKER, GALLERY DIRECTOR
b New Brunswick, NJ, Mar 16, 32. Study: NY Univ; Columbia Univ, BFA, 54; Univ Iowa; Ohio Univ, MFA, 56. Work: Mus Fine Arts, Budapest, Hungary; Nat Mus, Krakow, Poland; Metrop Mus Art, New York; Nat Collection Fine Arts, Washington, DC; Libr of Cong, Washington, DC; plus many others. Exhib: Int Biennale Graphics, Krakow, Poland, 66, 68, 70 & 72; Int Expos Original Drawings; Rijeka, Yugoslavia, 68; Prints/Multiples, Univ Wash, 70; 4th Am Biennale Santiago, Chile, 70; plus many other group & one-man shows in Austria, Norway, Yugoslavia, Porto Alegre, Romania, PR, Poland, Can, Sweden, Japan, New York, Pa & Ohio. Teaching: Asst prof printmaking, Pratt Inst. Pos: Vis critic printmaking, Yale Univ; ed, Print Rev; dir, Pratt Graphics Ctr. Awards: Purchase Award, Okla Art Ctr, 12th Ann Nat Exhib Prints & Drawings, 70; Purchase Prize, Multiples Exhib, Western Mich Univ, 70; President's Award in Graphics, Audubon Artists Ann, 70; plus many others. Publ: Auth & illusr, Prints & poems (folio), 63; ed, Printmaking in Eastern Europe, Abrams, 71. Mailing Add: Pratt Graphics Ctr 831 Broadway New York NY 10003

STATMAN, JAN B
PAINTER, INSTRUCTOR
b New York, NY. Study: Hunter Col, with William Baziotes, Bernard Klonis & Richard Lippold, AB; and with Saul Berliner. Work: Mus Mod Art Alto Aragon, Huesca, Spain; Civic Mus Contemp Art, Sasso Ferrato, Italy; Longview Bank & Trust Co, Tex; McGregor Electronics, Tex; plus others. Exhib: 13th Ann Nat Sun Carnival Art Exhib, El Paso Mus Art, Tex, 71; 4th Gtr New Orleans Nat Exhib, 74; 20th Century Women in Tex Art, LaGuna Gloria Art Mus, Austin, 74; Tri-States Exhibs, Beaumont Art League, Brown & Surlock Gallery, Beaumont, Tex, 76; The Barn—Vanishing Am Landmark, Springfield Mus of Art, Springfield, Mo & Civic Fine Arts Asn, Sioux Falls, SDak, 77; one-artist shows, Barnwell Art Ctr, Shreveport, La & Longview Mus & Arts Ctr, Tex, 75 & Legends of the Mother Goddess, Kilgore Col, Tex, 77; plus other group & one-artist shows. Teaching: Instr painting, Longview Mus & Arts Ctr, Tex, 72-; instr pvt workshops. Awards: First Prize Painting, 33rd Ann Cedar City Nat Art Exhib, Utah, 73; Best of Show & First Prize Oil & Acrylic Painting, 3rd Ann NMex Art League Small Painting Exhib, 73; Merit Award, 16th Ann Exhib, Longview Mus & Arts Ctr, 74; plus others. Bibliog: Faye Hagood (auth), If you are an artist you don't have to look like one, Longview News, 69; Lovinia Green (auth), Kifro interview, Feminine point of view, Longview Post, 73; Ruthe Winegarten (auth), A New York Yankee in Longview Texas, Equal Times, Dallas, Tex, 76. Mem: Tex Fine Arts Asn; ETex Fine Arts Asn; Tex Press Women; Nat Fedn Press Women. Media: Acrylic, Oil, Watercolor; Serigraphy. Publ: Auth, Art Notes (weekly column), Longview News, 65-70; auth, Artists World (weekly column), Our Longview Post, 70-77. Mailing Add: 27 Country Pl Longview TX 75601

STAVEN, LELAND CARROLL
EDUCATOR, PAINTER
b Milwaukee, Wis, Dec 17, 33. Study: Univ Wis-Milwaukee, BFA, 56; Layton Sch Art, grad work, 57; Calif Col Arts & Crafts, MFA, 60; Ill Inst Technol, postgrad work, 63. Work: Univ Ga Art Mus; Ga Tech Univ Art Gallery; South DeKalb Col; LaGrange Col. Exhib: 18th Southeastern Ann Exhib, Atlanta, Ga, 63; Contemp Southern Art Exhib, 64; 1st Cent S Exhib, Nashville, Tenn, 66; 1st Ann Greater Birmingham Arts Alliance Exhib, Ala, 75; 2nd Ann Nat Dogwood Festival Art Show, Atlanta, 75. Teaching: Chmn dept painting, drawing & printmaking, Berry Col, 60-68 & Mercer Univ Atlanta, 68-69; assoc prof painting, drawing & printmaking & cur, Dalton Galleries, Agnes Scott Col, 70- Pos: Vchmn, Ga Comn on Arts, Atlanta, 67-72. Awards: Purchase Awards, Asn Ga Artists, 61 & Fourth Ann Callaway Gardens Art Exhib, 67; Achievement Award, Appalachian Corridors: Exhib I, 68. Mem: Southeastern Col Art Conf. Style & Technique: Interiors with parapsychological phenomena represented on shaped canvas triptychs. Media: Acrylic, Oil. Dealer: Ann Jacob Gallery Peachtree Ctr 231 Peachtree St NE Atlanta GA 30303. Mailing Add: 1553 Springbrook Dr Decatur GA 30033

STEAD, REXFORD ARTHUR
ART ADMINISTRATOR, ART HISTORIAN
b Recife, Pernambuco, Brazil, Jan 24, 23; US citizen. Study: Brown Univ; Asia Inst, MA; also with Arthur Upham Pope & Robert von Heine-Geldern. Collections Arranged: Pre-Hispanic Art of Mexico, 65; Cocle Ceramics, 66; Art of Ancient Iran, 66; Sculpture of Ancient WMex, 70; Art of Black Africa, 73; Age of the Pharaohs, 74; Two Centuries of Black Am Art, 76; Heeramaneck Collection of Ancient Near Eastern & Cent Asian Art, 77-78. Pos: Dir, Mus Fine Arts, St Petersburg, Fla, 62-67 & Hon Trustee, 68-; dep dir, Los Angeles Co Mus Art, 67- Mem: Am Asn Mus; Calif Confederation of the Arts; Nat Schs Alumni Coun. Res: Ancient art with emphasis on pre-Islamic Iran, also Safavid period court carpets. Publ: Contribr, A Survey of Persian Art, A U Pope Mem Vol, 72; auth, The Ardabil Carpets, 74; contribr to many journ, mus catalogs, reports & others, 50- Mailing Add: Los Angeles Co Mus of Art 5905 Wilshire Blvd Los Angeles CA 90036

STEADMAN, DAVID WILTON
ART HISTORIAN, GALLERY DIRECTOR
b Honolulu, Hawaii, Oct 24, 36. Study: Harvard Col, BA(magna cum laude), 60; Harvard Univ, MAT, 61; Univ Calif, Berkeley, MA(art hist), 66; Princeton Univ, PhD, 74. Collections Arranged: P P Rubens before 1620 (with catalog), Princeton Art Mus, 71; Selections from the Norton Simon, Inc Mus Art (with catalog), 73; Graphic Art of Francisco Goya (with catalog), Galleries of Claremont Cols, 75, 18th Century Drawing from California Collections (with catalog), 76 & Works on Paper 1900-1960 from Southern Calif Collections (with catalog), 77. Teaching: Asst prof 17th & 18th centuries art, Pomona Col, 74- Pos: Lectr, Frick Collection, New York, 70-71; asst dir, Art Mus, Princeton Univ, 71-72, actg dir, 72-73, assoc dir, 73; dir, Galleries of Claremont Cols, 74-; res cur, Norton Simon Mus, Pasadena, Calif, 77- Awards: Nat Defense Educ Act fel, 66-69; Chester Dale Fel, Nat Gallery Art, 69-70. Mem: Western Asn Art Mus; Col Art Asn. Res: 17th and 18th century drawings. Mailing Add: Pomona Col Claremont CA 91711

STEBBINS, THEODORE ELLIS, JR
ART HISTORIAN, ART ADMINISTRATOR
b New York, NY, Aug 11, 38. Study: Yale Univ, BA, 60; Harvard Univ Law Sch, JD, 64, Harvard Univ, PhD, 71. Collections Arranged: Luminous Landscape, Fogg Art Mus, 66; Martin Johnson Heade, Whitney Mus Am Art, 69; New Haven Scene, New Haven Colony Hist Soc, 70; Richard Brown Baker Collects, Yale Univ, 75; Am Landscapes at the Wadsworth Atheneum, Hudson River Sch, 76; Am Master Drawings, Whitney Mus, 76. Teaching: Instr hist art, Smith Col, 67; asst prof hist art, Yale Univ, 69-75, Morse fel, 72, assoc prof, 75-77. Pos: Assoc cur, Garvan Collections, Yale Univ Art Gallery, 68-77, cur Am painting & sculpture, 71-77; cur Am painting, Mus of Fine Arts, Boston, Mass, 77- Awards: Chester Dale Fel, Nat Gallery Art, Washington, DC, 66. Mem: Col Art Asn Am; Am Fedn Arts. Res: American landscape painting of the nineteenth century; history of American drawings and watercolors. Collection: Nineteenth and 20th century American art. Publ: Auth, Thomas Cole at Crawford Notch, Nat Gallery Art, 68; auth, Martin Johnson Heade, Whitney Mus Am Art, 69; auth, American Landscape: Some new acquisitions at Yale, Yale Univ Art Gallery Bull, autumn 71; auth, Life and Works of Martin Johnson Heade, Yale Univ, 75; auth, American Master Drawings and Watercolors: Works on Paper from Colonial Times to Present, Harper & Row, 76. Mailing Add: Mus of Fine Arts Boston MA 02115

STECKEL, ANITA
PAINTER, COLLAGE ARTIST
b New York, NY. Study: Cooper Union, two yrs; with Edwin Dickenson, two yrs. Exhib: One-woman shows, New York, NY, 61-77; Self Portraits, 65 & Landscapes, 67, Sch of Visual Arts, New York; Human Concern—Personal Torment, Whitney Mus Am Art, New York, 69; Westbeth Graphics, Palace of Fine Arts, Mexico City, 72 & Chung-Hsing Mus, China, 73; The Eye of Woman, Hobart Col & Smith Col, 74; Contemp Reflections, Aldrich Mus Contemp Art, Ridgefield, Conn, 74; Point of View—19 Women, Portland Mus of Art, Maine, 74; Am Fedn of Arts Traveling Show, ten mus nationwide, 75-77; The Year of the Woman—Reprise, Bronx Mus of Arts, NY, 76; 40 Yrs of Am Collage, St Peter's Col, NJ, 76; two-person show, Soho Ctr, New York, 76; Contemp Women, Brooklyn Mus, NY, 77. Teaching: Instr fine arts, Sch of Visual Arts, 74- Bibliog: Found woman artist, Ms Mag, 73; Erotic art by women, New York Mag, 74; The feminist fantasy of Anita Steckel, Chrysalis Mag, 77. Style & Technique: Collage, painting and drawing on found art photographs, merging fantasy and reality. Media: Collage, drawing and painting and various combinations of the three. Publ: Auth, Women artists fight Puritanism and censorship, Village Voice, 73 & Sarah Lawrence Col, 74; contribr, Women's sexual imagery, Heresies, Vol 1 (1977). Mailing Add: Box 1099A 463 West St New York NY 10014

STECZYNSKI, JOHN MYRON
EDUCATOR, PAINTER
b Chicago, Ill, June 22, 36. Study: Art Inst Chicago; Craft Ctr, Worcester, Mass; Univ Notre Dame, BFA, 58; Yale Univ, Woodrow Wilson fel, 58, MFA, 61; Acad Fine Arts, Polish Govt grant, 60, Warsaw; and with Umberto Romano. Comn: Wood relief panels, Ursuline Provincialate, Kirkwood, Mo, 57-58; wood sculpture, Moreau Sem, Notre Dame, Ind, 58; dossals for Easter, 71, Christmas, 71, Lent, 73 & Penticost, 75, Univ Lutheran Church, Cambridge, Mass; slide show, Lincoln Summer Day Camp, Mass, 74; drawing, Newton Col, 75. Exhib: One-man shows, Warsaw, Poland & Worcester Art Mus, 61; fac-student exhibs, Newton Col, 69-75; New England Landscape, de Cordova Mus, Lincoln, Mass, 72; Fiberworks, Boston City Hall, 75; plus others. Teaching: Prof art, Worcester Art Mus Sch, 61-64; instr art hist, Boston Mus Fine Arts Sch, 64-67 & Tufts in Italy, Naples, 67-68; asst prof & chmn dept art, Newton Col of the Sacred Heart, 68-75; lectr. Awards: Polish Arts Club Chicago Prize, 59; Chopin Fine Arts Club Award, Butler Inst Am Art, 61; Hon Mention, Northeastern Regional Exhib Contemp Craftsmen, 63. Style & Technique: Figurative. Media: Pen & Ink; Miscellaneous Media. Mailing Add: Sunnyside Lane RFD 2 Lincoln MA 01773

STEEL, RHYS CAPARN
See Caparn, Rhys

STEELE, BENJAMIN CHARLES
PAINTER, EDUCATOR
b Roundup, Mont, Nov 17, 17. Study: Cleveland Inst Art, dipl; Kent State Univ, BS; Denver Univ, MA; Univ Ore; Ill State Univ; Mont State Univ. Comn: Arts of the West (mural), Denver Univ; Indoor and Outdoor Sports (mural), Eastern Mont Col. Exhib: Greater Southeastern, Meade Paper Co Show, Atlanta, Ga, 57; Atlanta Watercolor Soc, Ga, 59; Univ Mont Regional, 68; Fedn Rocky Mt States, 68; one-man shows in all major US cities, World War II Drawings & Paintings of POW's. Teaching: Art teacher, New London, Ohio High Sch, 51-52; crafts dir, Fort Riley, Kans, 53-54; staff crafts dir, Mil District Wash, 54-56 & Fort

MacPherson, Ga, 54-59; prof art & head dept, Eastern Mont Col, Billings, 59- Awards: First Prize Design, Drawing & Painting, Cleveland Inst Art, 47 & Second Prize, 50; Second Prize, Atlanta Watercolor Soc Show, 57. Bibliog: Dorothy Larsen (auth), Man of gentle fiber & Nancy Olson (auth), Briefly biographical, Mont Arts Mag; also feature art in Washington Post, Altanta Const, Kansas City Star & many others. Mem: Nat Art Educ Asn; Mont Art Educ Asn (br treas); Billins Art Asn (dir); Mont Inst Arts; Yellowstone Art Ctr (past pres bd). Style & Technique: Transparent watercolor landscapes; semi-abstract and realistic oil paintings, brush and palette knife; pen and ink drawings; egg tempera murals. Publ: Auth, Craft Directors Handbook, 55; illusr, Code of the US fighting man, Army Digest, 66; illusr, cover design, Mont Arts, 73; illusr, cover designs, Horizons O'er the Musselshell & Along the Zimmerman Trail, 74. Mailing Add: 2425 Cascade Ave Billings MT 59102

STEELE, EMILY
SCULPTOR, GLASS ARTIST
b Springfield, Mo, Apr 23, 39. Study: Hartt Conserv, Hartford, Conn, 53-54; Mannes Conserv, New York, 54-56, violin study with Vladimir Grafmann; Oberlin Conserv, Ohio, 56, violin study; Oberlin Col, 57-60, BA. Work: Strobech-Reiss & Co, Dearborn, Chicago; Financial Mgt Corp, Burbank, Calif; Harriet Febland's Advan Painter's Workshop, New York; Bob Hammerschmidt & Assocs, Los Angeles; Alflex Corp, Gardena, Calif. Comn: Glass-steel murals, Good Samaritan Hosp, Corvallis, Ore, 75; glass-steel sculptures, Henry Kwee, Singapore, Malaysia, 75 & Rainier Nat Bank, Seattle, 77. Exhib: Glass Art Exhib, White Gallery, Portland State Univ, 74; Ore Artists, Portland Art Mus, 74 & 77; Ore Artists, Horner Art Mus, Ore State Univ, 74 & 77; Contemp Ore Artists, Coos Art Mus, 75; 40 Ore Artists Commemorative Exhib Timberline, Mt Hood, Ore, 77; Contemp Stained Glass Art, Pac Design Ctr, Los Angeles, 78; solo exhibs, Ankrum Gallery, Los Angeles, 74, 77 & 78 & Fountain Gallery Art, Portland, 74 & 78. Awards: Finalist, Glass Sculpture Competition, Glass Mag, San Francisco, 77 & Finalist Archit Glass Competition, 77. Bibliog: Royal Col Art (auth), American Glass Artists—Slides Presented, London, Eng, 76; Fred Abrams (auth), Glass—1976, Glass Mag, 76; Jan Baross (auth), Emily Steele, Channel 6, Portland & Channel 9, Eugene, Ore, 76. Style & Technique: Three-dimensional free-standing molded glass and steel sculpture. Media: Glass and Steel Sculpture and Murals. Interest: Invention of new glass and steel sculpture technique. Mailing Add: Joan Ankrum & Bill Challee c/o Ankrum Gallery 657 N La Cienega Blvd Los Angeles CA 90069

STEELE, LISA
VIDEO ARTIST
b Kansas City, Mo, Sept 22, 47; Study: Univ Mo, Kansas City, 65-68. Work: Art Gallery of Ont, Toronto; The Kitchen, New York; Western Front, Vancouver, BC. Exhib: Can Trajectoires, 73, Musee d'Art Moderne de la Ville de Paris, France, 73; Toronto Video Artists, Everson Mus of Art, Syracuse, 74; Videoscape, Art Gallery of Ont, Toronto, 74; Video Art, Inst of Contemp Art, Philadelphia, Contemp Arts Ctr, Cincinnati & Mus of Contemp Art, Chicago, 75; A Response to the Environment, Rutgers Univ Art Gallery, New Brunswick, NJ, 75; Video Int, Aarhus Mus of Art, Denmark, 76; Videotapes, Mus of Mod Art, New York, 77; Southland Video Anthology, Part 4, Long Beach Mus of Art, Calif, 77. Pos: Video coordr, A Space Gallery, Toronto, 72-74. Bibliog: Peggy Gale (auth), Lisa Steele: looking very closely, Parachute, Montreal, 1-3/76; Eric Cameron (auth), Structural Videotape in Canada, In: Ira Schneider (ed), Video Art, Harcourt, Brace & Jovanovich, 76; Peggy Gale, Video art in Canada: four worlds, Studio Int, London, 5-6/76. Style & Technique: Personal narrative videotapes. Media: Videotape. Mailing Add: c/o Art Metropole 24, Yonge St 3rd Floor Toronto ON M5B 1N8 Can

STEEN, RONALD EARL
MUSEUM DIRECTOR, INSTRUCTOR
b Chicago, Ill, Apr 4, 40. Study: Calif State Univ, Los Angeles, BA(Am studies), 68, BA(art hist), 74, MA(art hist), 75. Collections Arranged: Recollections of Past Times I, II, III, 76, A Treasury of Historical Prints, 76, Beyond the Garden Wall, Los Angeles Print Soc, 4th National Competition, 77, Hollywood-The Matrix, 77 & Donna Marie Schuster, A Retrospect, 77, Downey Mus of Art. Teaching: Instr mod & Renaissance art, Citrus Community Col, 75-; instr mod & Am art and art hist, Glendale Community Col, 76- Pos: Cur & exhib coordr, Monterey Park Art Coun, 75-76; ed, Orlando Gallery Art Newsletter, 75-; exec dir & cur, Downey Mus of Art, 76-; mem, Los Angeles Art Educ Comn, 77- Bibliog: Stewart Alsop II (auth), Ron Steen's heritage: the genes show their strength, Guardian J of News, 6/76; New Director for Downey Museum, SE News, 7/76; Peyton Canary (auth), Museum chief fosters art appreciation, Los Angeles Times, 8/76. Mem: Pasadena Art Mus Men's Comt. Res: The Dutch genre master Jan Steen, a contemporary of Rembrandt; Los Angeles artists of the 20's & 30's. Specialty: Collection of Southern California artists since 1956. Publ: Auth, David Hammons (catalogue), Calif State Col, Los Angeles, 74; auth, reviews on Jean Edlestein, 12/74, Sabato Fiorello, 3/75, Joyce Wisdom, 5/75 & Gloriane Harris & Stephen Seemayer, 9/75, Art Week; auth, review on Claude Kent, Calif State Univ Times, 2/75. Mailing Add: 10419 S Rives Ave Downey CA 90241

STEFAN, ROSS
PAINTER
b Milwaukee, Wis, June 13, 34. Study: Primarily self-taught; collab with Dan Muller, Milwaukee, Dale Nichols, Antigua, Guatemala & Frederic Whitaker, La Jolla, Calif. Work: Ford Motor Co; Milwaukee Jour; Harmsen's Western Americana, Denver; Gilcrease Inst Am Hist & Art, Tulsa; Amerind Found, Dragoon, Ariz; Up With People Traveling Collection of Art; also represented nationally in private collections. Exhib: One-man shows, Raymond Burr Galleries, Beverly Hills, Calif, 60, Panhandle Plains Hist Mus, Canyon, Tex, 67 & Wollheim's Rosequist Galleries, Tucson, 70-78; Our Western Heritage, Univ Ariz, 62; Harmsen's Western Americana, Colo State Univ, 73; Western Legacy, United Bank of Denver, 73; among many others. Awards: Artist of the Yr, Tucson Festival Soc Award, 78. Bibliog: Joseph Stacey (auth), Praised be the man named Ross Stefan, Arizona Highways, 71 & Through Indian country with Ross Stefan, 75; Frederic Whitaker (auth), Ross Stefan: the development of a prodigy, Am Artist, 9/73; Royal B Hassrick (auth), article in Western Painting Today, Watson-Guptill, 75; Sen Barry Goldwater (auth), Ross Stefan 1975, Wollheims' Rosequist Galleries; John K Goodman (auth), Ross Stefan, Northland Press, 77. Mem: Grand Cent Art Galleries, Inc, New York. Style & Technique: Impressionism. Media: Oil on Canvas. Interest: Painter of the Southwest as it is today; since 1948, Southern Arizona, Navajo & Hopi country, the Rio Grande North to Santa Fe & Taos, New Mexico. Mailing Add: c/o Wollheims' Rosequist Galleries 2843 N Campbell Ave Tucson AZ 85719

STEFANELLI, JOSEPH J
PAINTER
b Philadelphia, Pa, Mar 20, 21. Study: Philadelphia Mus Col Art, 38-40; Pa Acad Fine Arts, 40-41; New Sch Social Res, New York, 49-50; Art Students League, 50-51; Hans Hofmann Sch Painting, New York, 51-52. Work: Whitney Mus Am Art; Walker Art Ctr, Norfolk Art Mus; Baltimore Mus; NY Univ; plus others. Comn: Mural (10ft x 40ft), comn by Brooklyn Bd Educ, PS 308 Elem Sch, 77. Exhib: Whitney Mus Am Art; Mus Mod Art, New York; Pa Acad Fine Arts; Walker Art Ctr, Minneapolis; Corcoran Gallery Art; Carnegie Inst Int; Art Inst Chicago; one-man shows, Westbeth Galleries, 71 & New Sch Social Res, 72; plus others. Teaching: Instr, Univ Calif, Berkeley, summers 60 & 63; vis critic, Cornell Univ; artist in residence, Princeton Univ, 63-66; vis critic, Univ Ark; instr, Columbia Univ, 66-; instr, New Sch Social Res, 66- Awards: Fulbright Award for Rome, 58-59; Am Res Ctr Egypt Fel, 66-67; NY State Coun Arts Award, 71; plus others. Mailing Add: 463 West St New York NY 10014

STEFANOTTY, ROBERT ALAN
ART ADMINISTRATOR
b Arlington, NJ, Feb 1, 47. Study: Bowland Col, Univ Lancaster, Eng, AB(with hons), aesthet with Prof Sibley; Bryn Mawr Grad Sch. Pos: Owner-dir, Stefanotty Gallery Ltd, New York, 73-75; pres, Stefanotty Transactions Co, Baden, Switz, 75-; trustee, Bronx Mus Arts, 75- Mailing Add: 2109 Broadway New York NY 10023

STEFFLER, ALVA W
EDUCATOR, CURATOR
b Philadelphia, Pa, June 22, 34. Study: Pa Art Acad; Ind Univ, MAT; Northern Ill Univ. Teaching: Asst prof art hist, painting & sculpture, Grace Col, Winona Lake, Ind, 67-69; assoc prof studio & art hist, Wheaton Col, Ill, 69- Pos: Coordr of creative arts major, Grace Col, Winona Lake, 68-69; cur & dir Am art collection, Wheaton Col, Ill, 71- Res: American art history and museology. Mailing Add: 318 E Madison Wheaton IL 60187

STEG, J L
PRINTMAKER
b Alexandria, Va. Study: Rochester Inst Technol, 3 yr cert; State Univ Iowa, BFA & MFA. Work: Libr Cong, Washington, DC; Smithsonian Nat Collection, Washington, DC; Brooklyn Mus, NY; Mus Mod Art, New York; Fogg Mus, Cambridge, Mass. Exhib: Eight Am Intaglio Printmakers, Ger, 65; Graphic Arts USA to Russia, 66; Prints of Two Worlds, Rome & Philadelphia, 66; Big Prints, USA, State Univ NY Col New Palts, 68; one-man shows, Weyhe Gallery, 45 & Assoc Am Artists, 64, New York; USIS Cult Ctr, Ankara, Turkey, 75. Teaching: Instr drawing & painting, Cornell Univ, 49-51; prof drawing & printing, Tulane Univ La, 51- Awards: Charles Lea Prize, Philadelphia Print Club, 50-64; Purchase Prize, Eighth Int Print & Drawing Exhib, Lugano, 64; Purchase Prizes, State Univ NY Col Potsdam Print Exhib, 64-68. Mem: Am Color Print Soc. Publ: Auth, article in, Artists Proof, 66. Dealer: Assoc Am Artists 663 Fifth Ave New York NY 10022. Mailing Add: Newcomb Col Dept of Art Tulane Univ New Orleans LA 70118

STEGALL, JAMES PARK
PAINTER, INSTRUCTOR
b Wichita Falls, Tex, Feb 8, 42. Study: Pa Acad Fine Arts, Philadelphia; restoration of painting with Marilyn Roswell Weidner; also with Walter Stuempfif & Ben Kamihira, Spain. Exhib: Nat Acad Design, New York, 56-64; Pa Acad Fine Arts Ann, 63-65; Pittsburgh Nat, 65; Tarrant Co Ann, Ft Worth, Tex, 68. Teaching: Instr art, Ft Worth Art Ctr Mus, 68- Awards: Cresson Mem Award, Pa Acad Fine Arts, 64, Fel, 65; First Purchase Award, Pittsburgh Nat, 65; First Prize, Tarrant Co Ann, 69. Mem: Fel Pa Acad Fine Arts. Style & Technique: Realist, interested in play of light, rich color, softened by glazes. Media: Oil. Mailing Add: c/o Carlin Galleries 710 Montgomery Ft Worth TX 76107

STEGEMAN, CHARLES
PAINTER, EDUCATOR
b Ede, Netherlands, June 5, 24; Can citizen. Study: Acad Beeldende Kunst, The Hague; Acad Royale Beaux Arts, Brussels; Inst Nat Superieur Beaux-Arts, Antwerp. Work: Nat Gallery Can; Ont Art Gallery; Vancouver Art Gallery; Art Gallery Gtr Victoria; Univ BC. Exhib: Western Art Circuit, Western Can, 52-53; Toronto Art Gallery, 61; Winnipeg Biannual, 61; Montreal Mus Fine Arts, 62; Chicago Centennial Exhib, Ill, 63. Teaching: Prof painting, Art Inst Chicago, 62-69; prof painting & chmn dept, Haverford Col, 69- Media: Oil, Acrylic. Mailing Add: 1930 Lafayette Rd Gladwyne PA 19035

STEGMAN, PATRICIA (PATRICIA STEGMAN SNYDER)
PAINTER
b San Antonio, Tex, Nov 27, 29. Study: Kansas City Univ, Mo, 48-49; Kansas City Art Inst, Mo, BFA, 52; Art Students League, study with Reginald Marsh, Will Barnet, Vaclav Vytlacil & Morris Kantor, 54-57. Work: Numerous pvt collections. Exhib: Brata Gallery, New York, NY, 61 & 62; Expatriates, River Quay Gallery, Kansas City, Mo, 74; Life Drawings, Atlantic Gallery, Brooklyn, NY, 77; Tenth St Now, Landmark Gallery, New York, NY, 77; Tenth St Days—Retrospective of Art of the 50s, Fourteen Sculptors Gallery, New York, 77; one-artist shows, Brata Gallery, New York, 61 & 63 & Atlantic Gallery, Brooklyn, NY, 75 & 76. Teaching: Teacher children's classes painting & drawing, Kansas City Art Inst, 52. Pos: Scenic artist/designer, Circle Repertory Co, New York, 74 & Big Apple Theatre Co, Brooklyn, 74 & 75; staff writer, Artists Review Art, New York, NY, 76- Mem: Art Students League. Style & Technique: Strong, bold, expressionistic. Media: Oil; Etching, Lithography. Dealer: Artists Space 155 Wooster St New York NY 10012. Mailing Add: 245 Dean St Brooklyn NY 11217

STEIG, WILLIAM
CARTOONIST, SCULPTOR
b New York, NY, Nov 14, 07. Study: City Col New York, 23-25; Nat Acad Design, 25-29. Work: Wood sculpture, RI Mus Art & Smith Col; paintings, Brooklyn Mus. Exhib: One-man exhib, Downtown Gallery, New York, 39; Smith Col, 40; plus others. Awards: Caldecott Medal, 70; William Allen White Award, 75; Christopher Award for Dominic, 73. Media: Wood. Publ: Auth & illusr, The Real Thief, 73, Dominic, 72, Abel's Island, 76, The Amazing Bone, 76 & Caleb & Kate, 77; contribr, New Yorker & other leading mags. Mailing Add: RD 1 Box KH2 Kent CT 06757

STEIGER, FREDERIC
PAINTER
b Solwutz, Rumania; Can citizen. Study: Self taught. Work: Contemporary Art Western Hemisphere, Int Bus Machine Corp; Hallmark Collection Can Art, Toronto; Toronto Pub Libr; Mem Univ Nfld. Comn: Portraits of speakers & prime ministers including Premier J R Smallwood of Nfld, 51 & Premier William G Davis of Ont, 76; painting for Imperial Oil Bldg, St John's, Nfld: Hallmark Cards, 62-74; painting, Lt Col Keiller MacKay, former Lt Gov Ont, 65. Exhib: Eaton Fine Art Gallery, Toronto, 73-74; Can Opera Festival, O'Keefe Centre Gallery, Toronto, 74; Royal Can Acad; Ont Soc Artists. Teaching: Teacher, Summer Sch Teachers, Woodstock, Ont & pvt studio. Awards: Bronze Medal for Courage; Contemporary Art of Western Hemisphere, IBM Corp. Bibliog: Articles in La Rev Mod, Paris & Oesterreichische Kunst, Vienna. Style & Technique: Abstract and semi-abstract; knife technique. Media: Oil. Mailing Add: 406 Bloor St E Toronto ON Can

STEIGMAN, MARGOT
See Robinson, Margot

STEIN, CLAIRE A
ART ADMINISTRATOR
b New York, NY, Sept 19, 23. Study: Art Students League; Adelphi Col, BA; sculpture with Robert Cronbach. Collections Arranged: Nat Sculpture Soc Ann, 68-78; North Shore Community Art Ctr Exhib, 60s. Pos: Bd dir, North Shore Community Art Ctr, 57-62. Mem: Nat Sculpture Soc (exec dir, 67-). Publ: Contribr, Nat Sculpture Rev, fall 73, winter 74 & 75 & spring 75; contribr sculpture suppl, Grolier Encyclopedia, 70-73. Mailing Add: c/o Nat Sculpture Soc 777 Third Ave New York NY 10017

STEIN, FRITZ HENRY
ART DEALER
b New York, NY, July 25, 32. Study: Univ RI, BA; New York Sch Interior Design; also with Harve Stein & Murray Kupferman. Pos: Art dir, G Fox Co, Hartford, Conn, 55-60; co-owner, Constitution Galleries, West Hartford, Conn & Gloucester, Mass, 60-63; interior designer, Silberman's of Norwich, Conn, 63-71; owner, Stone Ledge Studio Art Galleries, Noank, Conn, 71- Mem: Lyman Allyn Mus, New London, Conn; Slater Mem Mus, Norwich; Mystic Art Asn, Mystic, Conn. Specialty: 18th and 19th century collectors' gallery; also dealer for many fine artists' estates. Mailing Add: Box 237 59 High St Noank CT 06340

STEIN, HARVE
PAINTER, RESTORER
b Chicago, Ill, Apr 23, 04. Study: Art Inst Chicago, 22-26; Julian Acad, Paris, France, 27; Art Students League, 30-33; and with Harvey Dunn. Work: US State Dept; Univ Minn; Brown Univ; Pub Arch, Toronto; Montclair Art Mus, NJ; plus others. Exhib: Nat Watercolor Exhibs throughout US. Teaching: Instr painting, Conn Col, 46, 47 & 51; instr, New London Art Students League, 48-59; Mitchell Col, summer sessions, 55-56; emer prof fine art, RI Sch Design. Pos: Restorer, Stone Ledge Studio Art Galleries, Noank, Conn, 63- Awards: Providence Watercolor Club Award, 56; New Haven Paint & Clay Club, 57; Providence Art Club, 63; plus others. Mem: Hon life mem Soc Illustrators; Am Watercolor Soc; Audubon Artists; Artists Fel; Appraisers Asn Am; plus others. Media: Watercolor. Publ: Illusr, many bks; contribr, nat mags; auth, Illustrator explains, Am Artist Mag, 58. Mailing Add: PO Box 237 Noank CT 06340

STEIN, ROGER BREED
ART HISTORIAN, EDUCATOR
b Orange, NJ, Mar 29, 32. Study: Harvard Univ, AB, 54, AM, 58, PhD(hist Am civilization), 60. Collections Arranged: Guest cur, The View & the Vision (with catalog), Henry Art Gallery, Univ Washington, 68, Seascape & the American Imagination (with catalog), Whitney Mus of Am Art, New York, 75. Teaching: Assoc prof Eng & Am art hist, Univ Wash, Seattle, 67-70; assoc prof Eng & Am art hist, State Univ NY, Binghamton, 70- Awards: Prize in Humanities, Am Acad Arts & Sci, 60; Guggenheim Fel, 68-69; Fulbright lectr, 76-77; Smithsonian Fel, Nat Collection of Fine Arts, 77-78. Mem: Am Studies Asn; Orgn of Am Historians; Mod Lang Asn; Col Art Asn Am. Publ: Auth, John Ruskin & American Aesthetic Thought, 1840-1900, 67; auth, Introduction, American Naval Prints, Int Exhibs Found, Washington, DC, 76-77; auth, Structure as meaning: towards a cultural interpretation of American painting, Am Art Rev. III (1976); auth, Copley's Watson and the Shark and aesthetics in the 1770's, Discoveries & Considerations, State Univ NY Press, 76. Mailing Add: Dept of Eng State Univ NY Binghamton NY 13901

STEIN, RONALD JAY
SCULPTOR
b New York, NY, Sept 15, 30. Study: Cooper Union, cert fine art, with Will Barnet; Yale Univ, with Joseph Albers, BFA; Rutgers Univ, MFA. Work: Carnegie Inst, Pittsburgh, Pa; Guggenheim Mus, New York; Tenn Fine Arts Ctr, Nashville; Wadsworth Atheneum, Hartford, Conn; Loch Haven Art Ctr, Fla. Comn: Mosaic murals (with Lee Krasner Pollock), Uris Bros, New York, 58; plaster sculpture, Playboy Mag. Exhib: Carnegie Int, 57; Inst Contemp Art, Boston, 58; Art Inst Chicago Int, 60; one-man show, Marlborough Gallery, London, Eng, 67; Art in the Mirror, Mus Mod Art, New York, 70. Style & Technique: Modern. Media: Plastic; All Media. Dealer: Marlborough Gallery 41 E 57th St New York NY 10022. Mailing Add: 76 E 79th St New York NY 10021

STEIN, WALTER
PAINTER, SCULPTOR
b New York, NY, Nov 30, 24. Study: Art Students League; Cooper Union; NY Univ; New Sch Social Res; Acad Belle Arti, Florence. Work: Phillips Collection, Washington, DC; Indianapolis Mus Art; Fogg Art Mus, Cambridge, Mass; Mus Mod Art, New York; Metrop Mus Art, New York. Teaching: Instr painting, Scarsdale Art Ctr, NY, 68-69; instr drawing, Cooper Union, 69-70; instr painting, Five Towns Art Ctr, NY, 70-71. Media: Oil, Watercolor; Aluminum, Plastic. Publ: Ed & illusr, Common Botany, 53; illusr, Histoires Naturelles, Harvard Univ, 60; ed & illusr, Tichborne's Elegy, 68. Mailing Add: 103 Reade New York NY 10013

STEINBERG, SAUL
CARTOONIST
b Ramnicul-Sarat, Bucharest, Rumania, June 15, 14, US citizen. Study: Univ of Bucharest, sociology and psychology, 32; Univ of Milan, archit, 32. Work: Mus of Mod Art, New York; Metrop Mus Art, New York; Albright-Knox Art Gallery, Buffalo, NY; Fogg Mus, Harvard Univ, Cambridge, Mass; Victoria & Albert Mus, London. Comn: Mural, Terrace Plaza Hotel, Cincinnati, Ohio, 48. Exhib: Fourteen Americans, Mus Mod Art, New York, 46; Art Inst, Chicago, 49; Inst Contemp Arts, London, 52; Roy & Marie Neuberger Collection (traveling), Whitney Mus, New York, 55; Brussels World's Fair, 58; Salon du Mai, Paris, 66; Carnegie Inst Technol, Pittsburgh, Pa, 70; Found Maeght, L'Art Vivant, 70; one-man shows, Stedelijk Mus, Amsterdam, 53, Arts Club, Chicago, 53, Kunsthalle, Basel, 54, Inst of Contemp Arts, London, 57, Kunsthalle, Hamburg, 68 & Kunstverein, Cologne (traveling, W Ger & Austria), 74; retrospective, Kolnischer Kunstverein, Cologne, Ger, 74-75. Pos: Cartoons, Bertoldo, Milan, 36-39; staff, New Yorker, 41- 24 Bibliog: John Ashbery (auth), Saul The Stamp of Genius, Art News, New York, 11/69 & Saul Steinberg: Calligraphy, Art News Ann, New York, 70; Grace Glueck (auth), The Artist Speaks: Saul Steinberg, Art in Am, New York, 11-12/70. Style & Technique: Satirical cartoons. Publ: Illusr, Cartoons published in Sombra, Brazil, Cascabel, Argentina & Settebello, Italy; auth, All in Line, The Art of Living & The Passport, New York, 45; auth, Steinberg Dessins, Paris, 55; co-auth (with Inge Morath), Anti-Photographer Masks, In: Creative Camera, London, 2/69. Dealer: Sidney Janis Gallery 6 W 57 St New York NY 10019. Mailing Add: c/o The New Yorker 25 W 43rd St New York NY 10036

STEINER, JULIA BOURNE
COLLECTOR, PATRON
b Savannah, Ga. Study: Miss Nina Pape Pvt Sch, Savannah, Ga; Univ Ga, MA; Columbia Univ. Mem: Eleanor Gay Lee Found (first vpres, 77-79); Artists, Authors & Composers (first vpres, 77-79). Interest: All the arts and contribute considerably in donations and purchases. Collection: Paintings of the well known master painters and hand painted china and glass. Mailing Add: 2 Tudor City Pl New York NY 10017

STEINER, MICHAEL
SCULPTOR
b New York, NY, 1945. Work: Storm King Art Ctr; Boston Mus Fine Arts; Mus Mod Art. Exhib: Light Show, Inst Contemp Art, Philadelphia, 64; Larry Aldrich Mus, Ridgefield, Conn, 68; Minimal Art, Gemeentemuseum, The Hague, Holland, 68; Eight American Sculptors, Pioneer Ct, Chicago, 68; Norman MacKenzie Art Gallery, Univ Sask, Regina, 70; Whitney Mus Am Art, 70 & 72; Akron Art Inst, 71; Edmonton Art Gallery, Alta, 72; Mus d'Art Contemporain, Montreal, 73; Nat Inst Arts & Lett, 75; plus others. Teaching: Instr, Emma Lake Workshop, Univ Sask, Regina, 69; vis artist, Cranbrook Art Inst, Bloomfield Heights, Mich, 69. Awards: Guggenheim Award, 71. Bibliog: Terry Fenton (auth), article in Art Int, 70. Media: Steel, Aluminum, Brass. Mailing Add: 704 Broadway New York NY 10003

STEINER, PAUL
WRITER
b Ger; US citizen. Study: NY Univ, BS. Pos: Assoc ed, Esquire, Inc, 47-52; feature writer-columnist, NAm Newspaper Alliance, Women's News Serv, 60-; pop scene serv, syndicated rev of mus exhibs, Metrop Mus Art, Mus Mod Art, Whitney Mus Art, Guggenheim Mus, Contemp Crafts Mus, Asia House Gallery & Am Folk Art Mus, 67-78. Pos: Contrib ed, Nat Jeweller, 76, 77 & 78; columnist, Murray Hill News, 77-; corresp, NY Post, 77-78. Awards: Columnist Award, 69 & Press Award, 70, Beaux Arts Soc NY. Res: Writes and lectures on art, artists, art collection, how to start collecting, buying at auction, avoiding fakes, buying graphics; exclusive interviews with major artists, Chagall, Dali, Calder, Wyeth, Warhol, Will Barnett, Jose de Creeft, etc. Publ: Auth, Picasso, NAm Newspaper Alliance, 71 & 72; auth, Costume Institute, Metrop Mus Art, New York Times, 73; auth, George Segal, Mel Ramos, Paul Wunderlich, Frank Gallo, Allen Jones, Reg Butler, Rauschenberg, Masson, De Ruth, Nino d'Onofrio, Gem Mag, 74, 75, 76, 77 & 78; auth, Rube Goldberg, Abe Rattner, Sanguino, DeCreeft, Sports Orbit, syndicated, 74; auth, Henry Straeter, Abel Mag, 74. Mailing Add: 161 W 54th St New York NY 10019

STEINFELS, MELVILLE P
PAINTER, DESIGNER
b Salt Lake City, Utah, Nov 3, 10. Study: Art Inst Chicago; Chicago Sch Design. Work: Murals (buon fresco, fresco secco, mosaic, ceramic tile), Church of the Epiphany, Chicago, Loyola Univ, Chicago, Our Lady of Sorrows Church, Farmington, Mich, Newman Club, Ann Arbor, Mich, St Mary Magdalen Church, Melvindale, Mich & many others. Comn: Murals, All Saints Mausoleum, Des Plaines, Ill, Resurrection Mausoleum, Justice, Ill & Queen of Heaven Mausoleum, Hillside, Ill. Teaching: Resident artist, Siena Heights Col, 45-50; instr drawing, painting & design. Mailing Add: 332 Talcott Pl Park Ridge IL 60068

STEINHOUSE, TOBIE (THELMA)
PAINTER, PRINTMAKER
b Montreal, PQ. Study: Sir George Williams Univ; Art Students League, with Morris Kantor & Harry Sternberg, 46-47; Ecole Beaux-Arts, Paris; Atelier 17, Paris, France, with W S Hayter, 61-62. Work: Nat Gallery Can, Ottawa; Montreal Mus Fine Arts, PQ; Confederation Art Gallery, Charlottetown, PEI; Ministry of External Affairs of Can, Moscow Embassy, USSR; McMichael Conserv Collection, Kleinburg, Ont. Comn: Songes et Lumiere (portfolio of eight color engravings), Graphic Guild Montreal, Reverberations (portfolio of color engravings), 70, The Edge of Day, 71, Songes et Lumiere, 72; editions publ incl Seuil de Printemps, 73, Les Voix du Rêve, 74, Rêves en Pleine Lumière, 74, Marécages, 75, Vienne Avril, 75, Orientale, 75, Into My Green World, 76, Ladder to the Sun, 76, Late Afternoon, 76, Secret of Old Trees, 76, Les Filets—Crépuscule, 76, Paysage—La Rue, 77, Le Ciel Intérieur, 77, Les Nuages Passent, 77 & Green World (album of six plates), 77. Exhib: One-man show, Galerie Lara Vincy, France, 57; Montreal Mus Fine Arts, 59 & 63; 2nd Int Biennial Engraving, Santiago, Chile, 65; 1st & 3rd Brit Int Print Biennial, Bradford, Eng, 68 & 72; 9th Int Biennial Art, Menton, France, 72; plus others. Pos: Judge, Can Soc Graphic Art & Soc Can Painter-Etchers & Engravers Exhib, 70. Awards: Sterling Trust Award, Soc Can Painter-Etchers & Engravers, 63; Jessie Dow First Prize Award, Montreal Mus Fine Arts, 63; Govt Can Centennial Medal of Honor, 67; plus others. Bibliog: Guy Viau (auth), La Peinture Moderne au Canada Francais, Ministere Affaires Cult, PQ, 64; Guy Robert (auth), Ecole de Montreal, Collection Artistes Can, 65; V Nixon (auth), Tobie Steinhouse-artist, Vie des Arts Mag, summer 72; plus others. Mem: Royal Can Acad Arts; Can Group Painters (pres, 66-68); L'Atelier Libre Recherches Graphique; Soc Can Painter-Etchers & Engravers; Can Soc Graphic Art; plus others. Dealer: La Guilde Graphique 4677 St Denis St Montreal PQ H2J 2L5 Can; Galerie Les Deux B St Antoine-sur-Richelieu PQ Can. Mailing Add: 208 Côte St Antoine Rd Montreal PQ H3Y 2J3 Can

STEINKE, BETTINA
PAINTER
b Biddeford, Maine, June 25, 13. Study: Fawcett Art Inst, Newark, NJ; Cooper Union, New York; Phoenix Art Inst, New York. Work: Nat Cowboy Hall of Fame & Western Heritage, Oklahoma City; Ft Worth Mus, Tex; Gilcrease Mus, Tulsa, Okla; Philbrook Mus, Tulsa; also in pvt collections in US & abroad. Exhib: One-man shows, Well Known Personalities, Philbrook Mus, 54, Eskimo, Winnipeg, 56, Portraits Around US, Oklahoma City, 68 & Palm Springs Desert Mus, 78; Watercolor Show, Curacao, Neth, 47; two-man show, O'Brien's Art Emporium, Scottsdale, Ariz, 75. Awards: Silver Medal for Drawing, Nat Acad Western Art, 74. Bibliog: Fred Whitaker (auth), Painter of people, Am Artist, 1/71; plus many others. Mem: Soc Illusr; Nat Acad Western Art. Style & Technique: Representational, direct, alla prima. Media: Oil. Publ: Illusr, NBC Symphony Orch, 37; illusr, articles in, Lamp, 50-53; also illusr for var mags & bks. Mailing Add: c/o Blair Galleries Ltd PO Box 2342 Santa Fe NM 87501

STEINMETZ, GRACE ERNST TITUS
PAINTER, LECTURER
b Lancaster, Pa. Study: Pa Acad Fine Arts; Barnes Found; Millersville State Col, BS; Univ Pa, MS. Work: Univ Southern Fla, Lakeland; Franklin & Marshall Col; Elizabethtown Col, Pa; Millersville State Col, Pa; Lancaster Co Art Asn, Pa. Exhib: Am Watercolor Soc, 68; Painters & Sculptors Soc NJ, 69; Knickerbocker Soc, 70; Moore Col Art, 70; Nat Soc Painters Casein & Acrylic, 72; Audubon Artists, 78. Teaching: Assoc prof art hist, Elizabethtown Col, 64-65; adj prof oil painting, 69 & 73-74. Awards: Best of Show, Lancaster Co Art Asn, 67 & 75; Award for Nontraditional Watercolor, Painters & Sculptors Soc NJ, 68; Grumbacher

First Prize, Nat Soc Painters Casein & Acrylic, 69. Mem: Nat Soc Painters Casein & Acrylic; Echo Valley Art Group; fel Royal Soc Arts. Style & Technique: Exploration of light and textural emphasis in landscape and figurative expression. Media: Oil, Watercolor, Casein, Acrylic. Mailing Add: Box 340 RD 7 Manheim PA 17545

STEIR, PAT
PAINTER
b Newark, NJ, 1938. Study: Boston Univ, 60; Pratt Inst, 62. Work: Whitney Mus Am Art, New York; Ciba-Geigy Corp, New York. Exhib: Drawings, Mus Mod Art, New York, 64; Landscapes, Mus Mod Art, New York, 72; Paintings on Paper, Larry Aldrich Mus Contemp Art, Ridgefield, Conn, 72; Drawing Exhib, Corcoran Gallery, Washington, DC, 72; Annual, Whitney Mus Am Art, 72; American Drawings, 1963-1973, Whitney Mus Am Art, New York, 73; Mus Mod Art, 73; Recent Acquisitions, Whitney Mus Am Art, 73; Biennial Exhib, Contemp Am Art, Whitney Mus Am Art, 73 & 77; Women Choose Women, New York Cult Ctr, 73; 28 Painters of the New York Avant-Garde, 74, Saidye Bronfman Centre, Montreal, 74; Recent Am Drawings (traveling), Am Fedn Arts, 75; Painting and Sculpture Today 1976, Indianapolis Mus Art; American Artists 76—A Celebration, Marion Koogler McNay Art Inst, San Antonio, Tex, 87; Private Notations: Artist's Sketchbooks II, Philadelphia Col Art, 76; Drawings of the 70's, Art Inst Chicago, 77; one-woman show, Douglas Col, Rutgers Univ, New Brunswick, NJ, 72; Corcoran Gallery Art, Washington, DC, 73; Ball State Univ, Muncie, Ind, 73; Univ Md, 76; White Gallery, Portland State Univ, Ore, 76. Awards: Nat Endowment for the Arts, 74. Bibliog: Jonathan Crary (auth), Pat Steir, Arts Mag, 6/76; Michael Andre (auth), Pat Steir, Art News, spec prints ed, 9/76; Paul Brach (auth), Pat Steir (rev), Artforum, 10/76. Mailing Add: c/o Droll/Kolbert Gallery Inc 724 Fifth Ave New York NY 10019

STELL, H KENYON
EDUCATOR, PAINTER
b Adams, NY, Jan 22, 10. Study: Syracuse Univ, BFA(illus) & cert art educ; NY Univ, MA(educ admin); Syracuse Univ, doctoral study. Work: Marine Midland Bank, Cortland, NY. Exhib: Nassau-Suffolk Art League, Garden City, NY, 46; Assoc Artists Syracuse, Mus Fine Art, 48; State Univ Art Faculties Exhib, 54-56. Teaching: Art supvr, Toaz Jr High Sch & Huntington High Sch, Huntington, NY, 39-47; prof art & chmn dept, State Univ NY Col Cortland, 47-66, prof art hist, 66-74, emer prof, 74-; vis prof art, Univ Maine, Orono, summer 51. Pos: Chmn art, State Univ NY Col Fac Asn, 50; dir, Art Show, 51 & mem art adv comt, NY State Fair, Syracuse; pres, Cortland Col Chap, Am Asn Univ Prof, 52 & dir & organizer, Art in Western Europe, study abroad prog, summer 63, State Univ NY Col Cortland; juror art exhibs, Roberson Mem Show, Buffalo Soc Artists, 62-70; consult, Marine Bank Art Collection, 69. Awards: 15 Yr Citation, Nat Art Educ Asn, 60; Mace Bearer, State Univ NY Col Cortland Commencement, 74. Mem: Nat Art Educ Asn. Style & Technique: Expressionistic; expressive realism. Media: Acrylic, Oil, Woodcut. Res: John Trumbull. Mailing Add: Apt E-434 921 Spanish Circle Delray Beach FL 33444

STELLA, FRANK
PAINTER
b Malden, Mass, May, 1936. Study: Phillips Acad, with Patrick Morgan; Princeton Univ, with William Seitz & Stephen Greene. Work: Mus Mod Art; Whitney Mus Am Art; Pasadena Art Mus; Albright-Knox Art Gallery, Buffalo, NY; Walker Art Ctr, Minneapolis, Minn; plus many others. Exhib: Corcoran Gallery Art, Washington, DC, 67; Int Biennial Exhib Painting, Tokyo, Japan, 67; Documenta IV, Kassel, Ger, 68; The Art of the Real, Mus Mod Art, 68, Retrospective, 70; Philadelphia Mus Art, 68; Whitney Mus Am Art Ann, 69 & 72; Mus Mod Art, New York, 69-70; Mus Contemp Arts, Chicago, 70; Contemp Arts Ctr, Cincinnati, 70; Carnegie Inst Int, 71; Whitney Mus Am Art, 71; High Mus, Atlanta, Ga, 72; Art Mus STex, Corpus Christi, 72; Mus Fine Arts, Houston, 74; Univ Miami, 74; Va Mus Fine Art, Richmond, 74; Walker Art Ctr, Minneapolis, 74; plus many others. Awards: First Prize, Int Biennial Exhib Paintings, Tokyo, 67. Bibliog: Lawrence Alloway (auth), Systemic Painting, Guggenheim Mus, 66; Oto Bihalji-Merin (auth), Adventures of Modern Art, Abrams, 66; Gregory Battcock (ed), Minimal Art: A Critical Anthology, Dutton, 68; plus many others. Dealer: Lawrence Rubin Gallery 49 W 57th St New York NY 10019. Mailing Add: 17 Jones St New York NY 10013

STELLINGS, ALEXA
ART DEALER
b New York, NY, Aug 5, 48. Study: Cornell Univ, 66-67; Columbia Univ, BA(art hist; summa cum laude), 72. Pos: Asst dir, Pyramid Galleries, Washington, DC, 73-74; dir graphics dept, Gimpel & Weitzenhoffer, Ltd, 74- Specialty: Contemporary art. Mailing Add: c/o Gimpel & Weitzenhoffer 1040 Madison Ave New York NY 10021

STELZER, MICHAEL NORMAN
SCULPTOR
b Brooklyn, NY, Jan 6, 38. Study: Pratt Inst, 56; Art Students League, 60-62; Nat Acad Sch Fine Arts, Edward Mooney traveling scholar, 66 & Nat Sculpture Soc Joseph Nicolosi grant, 67; and with Nathaniel Choate, 64, Michael Lantz, 64-67 & Donald DeLue, 68 & 69. Comn: 12 ft relief, Worchester Polytech Inst, 64. Exhib: Am Artists Prof League Grand Nat, 63, 76 & 77; Nat Arts Club, 63-64; Nat Acad Design, 64-67, 70-71 & 74-77; Allied Artists Am, 67 & 71-77; Nat Sculpture Soc Ann Exhib, 68-77. Teaching: Instr sculpture, pvt classes, Brooklyn Heights, NY, 68- Awards: Helen Foster Barnett Prize, Nat Acad Design, 66; Gold Medal, Hudson Valley Art Asn, 76; Gold Medal, Grand Nat Exhib, Am Artists Pro Prof League, 76. Bibliog: Article in, Pen & Brush, 66; Opportunities offered the young sculptor, 67 & Interpreting the human figure, 68, Nat Sculpture Rev. Mem: Nat Sculpture Soc; Salmagundi Club; Allied Artists Am; Nat Art League. Style & Technique: Representational; fluid modeling of the figure and naturalistic portraiture. Mailing Add: 8 Everit St Brooklyn NY 11201

STEMELOS, ELECTRA GEORGIA MOUSMOULES
PAINTER, INSTRUCTOR
b Jersey City, NJ. Study: Corcoran Mus Sch, study with Aurelius Battaglia & Heinz Warneke, 43-45; Nat Art Sch, 45-48; Magda Sch Design, Am Univ, Washington, DC, 46; work with Margaret Cramer, 61-63; Univ Mich, study with Guy Palazola, 64; Ctr Creative Studies, 65-68; Wayne State Univ, BA(painting), 70; Eastern Mich Univ, MFA(watercolor), 76. Work: Nat Watercolor Soc, Calif; Northwest Br, YWCA, Detroit; State Farm Ins Co, Dearborn, Mich; Brown, Lund & Fitzgerald, Washington, DC; Eastern Ill Univ. Comn: Hardedge acrylic, Northwest Br, YWCA, Detroit, 70. Exhib: Rocky Mountain Nat Watermedia Exhib, Golden, Colo, 75, 76 & 77; Mus Tex Tech Univ, WTex Watercolor Asn, 75-76; 109th Ann, Am Watercolor Soc Exhib, New York, 76; Third Ann, Nat Pastel Show, New York, 76; Butler Inst Am Art, Youngstown, Ohio, 76; Source Detroit, Cranbrook Art Mus, Birmingham, Mich, 76; Watercolor USA 77, Springfield Art Mus, 77; Nat Watercolor Soc, Fine Arts Gallery, Calif State Univ, Northridge, 77. Teaching: Instr drawing & painting, Nat Art Sch, Washington, DC, 45-48; instr drawing & painting, Northwest Br, YWCA, Detroit, 68-72; instr watercolor, Ann Arbor Asn, Mich, 77- Pos: Chmn, Friends of the Barn, Livonia, Mich, 73-; mem, Livonia Arts Comn, 74-76. Awards: Hon Mentions, 28th & 29th Ann, Mich Watercolor Soc, 74 & 75, Purchase Award, 30th Ann, 76; Purchase Award, 7 for 76, Eastern Ill Univ, 76; Purchase Award, 57th Ann, Nat Watercolor Soc, 77. Mem: Nat Watercolor Soc, Calif; Mich Watercolor Soc (chmn, Detroit, 77-79, pres & records secy/historian); Mid-W Watercolor Soc; Birmingham-Bloomfield Art Asn; Ann Arbor Art Asn. Style & Technique: Magic realism using plants in watercolors; hardedge in acrylics; impressionistic in oil pastels. Media: Watercolor, Acrylic, Pencil, Pastel, Camera. Publ: Auth, Bibliography of Georgia O'Keefe, J Nat Art Educ Asn, 76; illusr, 24 drawings, The Tree House, Ann Arbor, 76. Dealer: ADI Gallery 530 McAllister St San Francisco 94102; Habitat Gallery 1820 N Telegraph Rd Dearborn MI 48128. Mailing Add: 4450 Fenton Rd Hartland MI 48029

STENBERY, ALGOT
PAINTER
b Cambridge, Mass, Apr 24, 02. Study: Hartford Art Sch, with Albertus Jones; Boston Mus Art Sch, with Frederick Bosley; Art Students League, with Kimon Nicolaides. Work: Metrop Mus Art, New York; G R Dick Collection; Edith Wetmore Collection. Comn: Mural, Work Proj Admin, Harlem Housing Proj Social Rm, 34 & Post Off, Wayne, Mich, 38; mural tiles, Chrysler Bldg, New York, 36; mural for Liner Bremen grand staircase, 68. Exhib: World's Fair, 35; Long Island Art Asn, 61; Am Watercolor Soc, 66; Nat Soc Casein Painters, 70; Salmagundi Club, 70. Teaching: Instr drawing & painting, Cooper Union, 33-40; instr drawing & painting, Am Artists Sch, 40-42. Media: Gouache, Oil. Mailing Add: 144 Bleecker St New York NY 10012

STEPHANY, JAROMIR
PHOTOGRAPHER, EDUCATOR
b Rochester, NY, Mar 23, 30. Study: Rochester Inst Technol, AAS, 56, with Ralph Hattersley, Miner White & B Newhall, BFA, 58; Ind Univ, with Henry Holems Smith, MFA, 60. Work: Int Mus Photog, George Eastman House; Univ Md, Baltimore Co, Libr Spec Collection. Exhib: Mus Mod Art, New York, 60; nat traveling exhib, Univ Fla, 60-61; Smithsonian Inst, Washington, DC, 69; Md Coun Arts, 71-72; Baltimore Mus Art, 70; one-man shows, Foto Gallery, New York, 75, Univ Md, Baltimore Co, 75, Dundalk CC, Md, 77 & Mus Without Walls, Md, 75-76; Addison Gallery Am Art, 75; plus others. Teaching: Assoc prof, Dept Visual Arts, Univ Md, Baltimore Co, 72-; lectr hist photog, Md Inst Col Art, 66-77; vis prof hist photog, Univ Del, 76. Pos: Series writer, Developing Image, Extended Learning Inst, Channel 53-TV, Va. Mem: Soc Photog Educ (chmn & ed newsletter, Mid-Atlantic Region). Style & Technique: Photography in sequence form. Mailing Add: 786 Creekview Rd Severna Park MD 21146

STEPHEN, FRANCIS B
JEWELER, INSTRUCTOR
b Dublin, Tex, Mar 7, 16. Study: Fine Art Ctr, Colorado Springs, Colo; Univ Okla, MFA, study with Jean Charlot & Robert von Neumann. Work: Witte Mem Mus, San Antonio, Tex; Okla Art Ctr; Hallmark Collection, Mo. Exhib: 2nd Regional Crafts Exhib, Witte Mem Mus, San Antonio, 58; The Patron Church, Mus Contemp Crafts, New York, 61; 11th Mid-Am Exhib, Nelson Gallery, Kansas City, Mo, 61; Craft Exhib, Dallas Mus Fine Arts, 71-74 & 78; South Central States Crafts Exhib, Denver Art Mus, Colo, 73; Contemporary Crafts of The Americas, Denver Art Mus, 74; Lake Superior Int Crafts Exhib, Tweed Mus Art, Univ Minn, Duluth, 74-75; The Metalsmith, Phoenix Art Mus, Ariz, 77; Houston Designer/Craftsmen Exhib, Sarah Campbell Blaffer Gallery, Univ Houston, Tex, 77. Teaching: Asst prof jewelry & sculpture, North Tex State Univ, Denton, 64-67; prof jewelry, Tex Tech Univ, Lubbock, 67- Awards: Swarovski Award, Great Designs in Jewelry, Swarovski & Co, 67; Grand Award, 15th Tex Crafts Exhib, 71; Purchase Award, Miniature Works, Tex Tech Mus Art, 75. Mem: Soc of NAm Goldsmiths (assoc). Style & Technique: Jewelry: Figurative using metals and other materials, sculpture: Figurative and kinetic, using bronze, clay and other metals and materials. Dealer: Ralph Kohn Contemp Gallery 2425 Cedar Springs Dallas TX 75201 Mailing Add: 4610 29th Lubbock TX 79410

STEPHENS, CURTIS
DESIGNER, PHOTOGRAPHER
b Athens, Ga, Dec 13, 32. Study: Univ Ga, MFA. Work: Objects USA, Johnson's Wax Collection; Ill State Mus, Springfield. Exhib: Designed for Production, Mus Contemp Crafts, 64; Objects USA, Johnson's Wax Collection, Smithsonian Inst, 69; 24th & 25th Ill Exhib, Ill State Mus, 71 & 72. Teaching: Asst prof art, LaGrange Col, 61-63; asst prof art, Univ Northern Mich, 66-68; assoc prof art & design, Univ Ill, Champaign-Urbana, 68-, asst head dept, 75- Pos: Designer, Callaway Mills, LaGrange, Ga, 63-66; photogr, 1960 Pandora (Popular Photog Award-winning Univ of Ga yearbk). Bibliog: Lee Nordness (auth), Objects: USA, Viking Press, 70; Jay Hartley Newman & Lee Scott Newman (auth), Plastics for the Craftsman, Crown, 72. Media: Plastics. Mailing Add: Dept of Art & Design Univ of Ill Champaign IL 61820

STEPHENS, RICHARD ALAN
ART ADMINISTRATOR, PAINTER
b San Francisco, Calif, Apr 13, 25. Study: Menlo Col, AA; Stanford Univ, BA, MA. Work: Alfred Marion Collection. Teaching: Prof art hist & advert, Acad Art Col, 51-54, pres, 51- Mem: Nat Asn Trade & Tech Schs (pub rels officer); Soc Communicative Arts. Style & Technique: Realistic. Media: Oil, Watercolor. Mailing Add: 625 Sutter San Francisco CA 94102

STEPHENS, WILLIAM BLAKELY
EDUCATOR, PAINTER
b Corpus Christi, Tex, June 8, 30. Study: Univ Tex, BFA, 56, with Hiram Williams, MEd, 57, MFA, 66; Univ Fla, EdD, 72. Exhib: 23rd Ann Tex Painting & Sculpture, Dallas Mus Fine Arts, 61; 4th Ann Southwest States Exhib, Roswell, NMex, 62; Art on Paper, Weatherspoon Gallery, Greensboro, NC, 67; Appalachian Corridors Exhib, Charleston, WVa, 68; Super Graphics, Brooks Mem Art Mus, Memphis, Tenn, 74. Teaching: Asst occup ther, Univ Fla, 70-71; assoc prof art educ, Memphis State Univ, 72-76; assoc prof & chmn, Dept of Art, Tex Eastern Univ, 76- Pos: Coordr art educ, Univ Ky, 64-66; art ed, New Voices in Educ, 71-72. Mem: Life mem Tex Fine Arts Asn; Asn Teacher Educators (nat comt, 75-76); Nat & Tenn Art Educ Asns. Style & Technique: Painting of modern pictures in a modern manner. Media: Acrylic Paint. Res: Artists' personality types. Publ: Auth, Blue Ridge Studies, Fac Publ, Appalachian State Univ, 5/69; auth, On creativity and teaching: talk with Hiram Williams, Art J, summer 71; auth, Relationship between selected personality characteristics..., Studies in Art Educ, spring 73; auth, University art departments and academies of art: the relation of artists' psychological types to their specialties and interests, Bull of Res in Psychological Type, summer 77. Dealer: Regional Gallery of Art PO Box 17 Boone NC 28607. Mailing Add: Dept of Art Tex Eastern Univ Tyler TX 75701

STEPHENSON, JOHN H
SCULPTOR, EDUCATOR
b Waterloo, Iowa, Oct 27, 29. Study: Univ Northern Iowa, BA; Cranbrook Acad Art, MFA. Work: Int Mus Ceramics Faenza, Italy; Everson Mus, Syracuse, NY; Portland Art Mus, Ore; Parrish Art Mus, South Hampton, NY; St Paul Art Ctr, Minn. Comn: The Wall (ceramic mural), Arbor A, Int Mkt, Ann Arbor, Mich, 71; Champion No 3 (sculpture), Mich Mall, Battle Creek, Mich, 76. Exhib: Fiber, Clay & Metal, St Paul Art Ctr, 64; Concorso Int Della Ceramica Arte, Faenza, 65; Objects USA, Smithsonian Inst, Washington, DC, 70; Focus, Detroit Inst Art, Mich, 75; 4th Mich Artist Biennial, Mich State Univ, 75; 1977 Ceramic Conjunction, Long Beach Mus of Art, Calif, 77; Contemp Ceramic Sculpture, Univ of NC, Chapel Hill, 77; Mich Sculpture 77, Macomb Community Col, 77; City of East Lansing Bicentennial Sculpture Exhib, Mich, 76; one-man show, Gallery 7, Fisher Bldg, Detroit, Mich, 78. Teaching: Instr ceramics, Cleveland Inst Art, 58-59; prof ceramics, Univ Mich, Ann Arbor, 59- Awards: Rackham Res Grants, Japan, 62 & Mixed Media, Univ Mich, 69; Medaglia Oro Della Citta Faenza, 65. Style & Technique: Welded corten steel or aluminum with porcelain or fired clay involvement. Dealer: Gallery 7 Fisher Bldg Detroit MI 48202. Mailing Add: 4380 Waters Rd Ann Arbor MI 48103

STEPHENSON, SUSANNE G
CERAMIST
b Canton, Ohio, Nov 5 35. Study: Carnegie-Mellon Univ, BFA; Cranbrook Acad of Fine Art, Bloomfield Hills, Mich, MFA. Work: Mus of Contemp Crafts, New York; Butler Inst of Am Art, Youngstown, Ohio; Univ Mich Mus of Art, Ann Arbor; Columbus Gallery of Fine Arts, Ohio; State Col NY Fredonia. Comn: Ceramic Planters, Burroughs Corp, Detroit, Mich, 70, Grosse Pointe Br, Nat Bank of Detroit, 72 & Harper Hosp, Detroit, 72; Liturgical Vessels, Lutheran Chapel, Eastern Mich Univ, Ypsilanti, 72. Exhib: Tamaya Dept Store Gallery, Fuyuoka, Japan, 63; 7th Fiber, Clay & Metal Show, St Paul, Minn, 64; Art USA, 2nd Nat Exhib, Univ Northern Ill, DeKalb, 64; 23rd Concorso Int della Ceramic d'Arte, Faenza, Italy, 65; Nat Ceramic Exhib, Everson Mus of Art, Syracuse, NY, 66, 68 & 70; Mich Artist Craftsmen Show, Detroit Inst of Arts, Mich, 66, 69 & 72; Porcelain, 4th Ann Exhib, Grossman Gallery, Univ Wis-Whitewater, 72; Centennial Exhib of Ceramics, John Michael Kohler Arts Ctr, Sheboygan, Wis, 73, one-woman shows, Soup Tureens 1976, Campbell Mus of Campbell Soup Co, Camden, NJ, 76, Midland Ctr for the Arts, Mich, 76 & Birmingham Gallery, Mich, 76; 10th Biennial Craft Exhib, El Paso Designer Craftsmen, El Paso Mus of Art, Tex, 77; Works in Fiber, Metal, Clay by Women, Bronx Mus, NY, 78. Teaching: Instr ceramics, Univ Mich, Ann Arbor, 60-61; prof ceramics, Eastern Mich Univ, 63- Awards: Artisan's Award for collection of Univ Mich Mus of Art, Mich Designer Craftsmen Exhib, Detroit Inst of Art, Artisan's, Ann Arbor, 69; Best in Ceramics, Beaux Arts Designer Craftsmen Exhib, Columbus, Ohio, J C Penney Co, 73; Ceramic Award, Beaux Arts Designer Craftsmen Exhib, Columbus, Ohio, Rockwell Int, 76. Mem: Am Craftsmen's Coun; Mich Potters Asn; Nat Coun Educ for Ceramic Arts; Am Asn Univ Prof. Style & Technique: Work is in porcelain and stoneware, mainly with container forms, colored clay slips, unglazed lusters and some thrown and hand-built nonfunctional sculptured forms. Publ: Contrib, Polly Rottenberg, auth, The Complete Book of Ceramic Art, Crown Publ, 72; contribr, Leon I Nigrosh, auth, Claywork, Davis Publ, Mass, 65; contribr, Thomas Shafer, auth, Pottery Decoration, Watson-Guptill, 76; contribr, Hildegard Storr-Beitz, auth, Ornaments and Surfaces, Aus dem Hause, Verlagsanstalt, Dortmund, Ger, 76; contribr, Julie Hall, auth, Tradition & Change, E P Dutton, 77. Dealer: Detroit Gallery of Contemp Crafts 301 Fisher Bldg Detroit MI 48202. Mailing Add: 4380 Waters Rd Detroit MI 48103

STERN, MR & MRS ARTHUR LEWIS
COLLECTORS
b Mr Stern, Rochester, NY, Apr 11, 11; Mrs Stern, New York, NY, Apr 21, 13. Study: Mr Stern, Yale Univ, BA; Harvard Law Sch, JD; Mrs Stern, Goucher Col, BA; Rochester Inst Technol. Pos: Mr Stern, mem bd dirs, Mem Art Gallery, Rochester, 60-, pres, 67-69; Mrs Stern, chmn art selection comt, Mem Art Gallery, 64- Mem: Am Fedn Art; Mus Mod Art. Collection: Modern painting and sculpture; Greek, Asian and European artifacts. Mailing Add: 14 Elmwood Hill Ln Rochester NY 14610

STERN, GERD JACOB
SCULPTOR, KINETIC ARTIST
b Saarbrucken, Ger, Oct 12, 28; US citizen. Study: Black Mountain Col, with M C Richards. Work: Los Angeles Co Mus, Los Angeles; Museo de Arte Contemperaneo, Caracas, Venezuela. Comn: Contact Is The Only Love, San Francisco Mus Art, 62; Resurrection (kinetic sculpture), Immaculate Heart Col, Los Angeles, 62; Money Talks (kinetic sculpture), Coin Amusement Co, Los Angeles, 63; Over (kinetic poem sculpture), comn by Judith McBean, for Oakland Mus Art, Calif, 64; Fanflashtic—Environment, NY State Coun of Arts, 76. Exhib: Contact Is The Only Love, Holland, 67; Walker Art Ctr, Minneapolis, Minn, 68; Abbemuseu, Eindhoven, Neth, 68; Imagimotion, Whitney Mus Am Art, New York, 68; Fanflashtic, Mus Mod Art, New York, 68; Lower East Side (audio-visual environment), Jewish Mus, New York, 69; Contemplation Environment, Contemp Crafts Mus, New York, 71; Television Broadcast, Boston & Mus Mod Art, New York, 76 & 77. Collections Arranged: Arte de Videom Museo de Arte Contemperaneo, Caracas, Venezuela, 75. Teaching: Assoc in multi-media educ, Harvard Grad Sch Educ, Cambridge, Mass, 67-69; vis prof multi-media, Univ Calif, Santa Cruz, 71-72. Pos: Panel mem, NY State Coun on Art, 72-76; trustee, Am the Beautiful Fund, Washington, DC, 72-; pres, Intermedia Systs Corp, 72- Bibliog: R Kostelanetz (auth), The Theatre of Mixed Means, Viking Press, 68; Douglas Davis (auth), Art and the Future, Praeger, 73; S Kranz (auth), Science and Technology in the Arts, Van Nostrand, Reinhold, 76. Mem: Boston Visual Artists' Union; Independent Asn of Video & Film Makers; Canyon Film Coop; Filmmakers' Coop; Multi-Image Asn. Style & Technique: Poetic collage of words and images. Media: Kinetic Sculpture, Video & Multi-Media. Publ: Auth, Media, Information, and Then?, State Univ Albany, 75; auth, Funding of Television Arts—Open Circuits, Mass Inst Technol Press, 77; auth, Flip-Flop, IDCA, 76. Dealer: David Stuart Gallery 748 N La Cienega Blvd Los Angeles CA 90069 Mailing Add: 12 Boston Ave Medford MA 02155

STERN, H PETER
COLLECTOR
Study: Harvard Univ, AB(magna cum laude), 50; Columbia Univ, MA, 52; Yale Univ Law Sch, LLB, 54. Pos: Pres, Ralph E Ogden Found, Mountainville, NY; trustee, Vassar Col, Hudson Valley Philharmonic Soc, Nat Temple Hill Asn, Vail's Gate, NY, 64-71 & Old Mus Village of Smith's Cove, Monroe, NY, 67-71; vchmn, Int Fund Monuments, New York; vchmn, Mid-Hudson Pattern for Prog, 68-; pres & mem bd trustees, Storm King Art Ctr. Collection: Contemporary paintings, graphics and sculpture. Mailing Add: Taylor Rd Mountainville NY 10953

STERN, IRENE MONAT
PAINTER
b Nov 20, 32; US citizen. Study: New Sch Social Res; classes at Mus Mod Art & Whitney Mus; mainly self-taught. Work: Nat Collection of Fine Arts, Smithsonian, Gen Elec World Hq, Joseph H Hirshhorn Mus, First Nat City Bank, Int Off; plus others. Comn: Am Broadcasting Co Western Hq; Atlantic Richfield Collection; Pac Mutual Life Ins Co Exec Hq; Dr Wallace Baer, Rand Corp; Welton Becket, architect. Exhib: Esther Robles Gallery, Los Angeles, 73; Color-73, Brand Mus & Libr; Am Acad Arts & Lett, 74; Downtown Gallery, Honolulu, 74; Source Gallery, San Francisco, 75; plus others. Bibliog: Educ Lect Ser, Metrop Mus Art; articles in Life Mag, 4/24/72, Interiors, 74 & Artweek, 5/31/75. Style & Technique: Large Style & Technique: Large-scale luminous lyrical abstractions; broad translucent veils and deltas of warm earthy color. Media: Acrylics on Canvas. Mailing Add: PO Box 1972 Santa Monica CA 90406

STERN, JAN PETER
SCULPTOR
b Nov 14, 26; US citizen. Study: Syracuse Univ Col Fine Arts, BID; New Sch Social Res. Work: Nat Collection Smithsonian Inst, Capitol Mall, Washington, DC; Pasadena Art Mus; Joseph H Hirshhorn Mus; Univ Mich Inst Sci & Technol; Atlantic Richfield Collection; plus others. Comn: Monumental sculptures, Prudential Ctr, Boston, 66, Maritime Plaza, Golden Gateway Ctr, San Francisco, 67, Alcoa Hq, Chicago, 68, Cardinal Spellman Retreat House, New York, 69 & Los Angeles City Hall Mall, 72. Exhib: Phoenix Art Mus, 67; Mus Contemp Art, 68; St Louis Art Mus, 68; San Francisco Mus Art, 70; Marlborough Gallery, New York, 70; plus other group & one-man shows. Bibliog: Monumental sculpture show, Artforum, 2/68; Louis Redstone (auth), Art in Architecture, 68 & Garrett Eckbo (auth), Landscape We See, 69, McGraw, documented by Nat Educ TV; plus others. Style & Technique: Fusion of lyric and geometric forms. Media: Highly Polished Stainless Steel, Metals. Mailing Add: PO Box 1972 Santa Monica CA 90406

STERN, JEAN
ART HISTORIAN, CONSULTANT
b Casablanca, Morocco, Mar 28, 46; US citizen. Study: Calif State Univ, San Diego, MA(art hist), 72; Univ Calif, Los Angeles, Am art with F Maurice Bloch, Pre-Hispanic art with H B Nicholson, Clement Meighan, 74. Teaching: Instr art hist, San Diego Mesa Col, 76-77. Pos: Consult in Pre-Hispanic Art, Fine Arts Gallery of San Diego, 76; cur, Petersen Art Galleries, Beverly Hills, Calif, 76- Mem: Appraisers Asn Am. Res: Early 20th century American art; Pre-Hispanic art (Iconography of Western Mexico). Publ: Co-auth, Pre-Hispanic Art: Jules Berman Collection, Fine Arts Gallery, San Diego, 73; auth, Historical Implication of Roman Coins, Fine Arts Gallery, 75; auth, Robert Henri & the 1915 San Diego Exposition, Am Art Rev, 9-10/75; ed, The Cross & The Sword: Art of the Spanish Southwest (exhib catalog), Fine Arts Gallery of San Diego, 76; co-ed, Pre-Hispanic Art History, Peek Publ, Palo Alto, Calif, 77. Mailing Add: 4533 Colbath Ave No 14 Sherman Oaks CA 91423

STERN, LEONARD B
ART DEALER, COLLECTOR
b New York, NY, 38. Study: NY Univ, BS; Columbia Univ, MBA. Pos: Founding bd mem, Studio Mus in Harlem, 70-74; treas, James Van derZee Inst, 74-76; treas, Aurora Music Found, 74-76; pres, Leonard B Stern, presently. Specialty: Contemporary American artists. Mailing Add: 274 Madison Ave New York NY 10019

STERN, LOUIS
ART DEALER, APPRAISER
b Jan 7, 45; US citizen. Study: Calif State Univ, Northridge, BA. Pos: Dir, Wally Findlay Galleries, Beverly Hills, Calif. Mem: Los Angeles County Mus Art (graphic arts coun). Specialty: 19th and 20th century American and European, American illustration, California painters. Mailing Add: 4455 Ventura Canyon Sherman Oaks CA 91423

STERNBERG, HARRY
PAINTER, GRAPHIC ARTIST
b New York, NY, July 9, 04. Study: Art Students League; and graphics with Harry Wickey. Work: Mus Mod Art & Metrop Mus Art, New York; Whitney Mus; H de Young Mem Mus; Syracuse Univ Mus; Thorne Mus, Keene State Col; Libr of Cong, Washington, DC; New York Pub Libr; Univ of Minn; Brooklyn Mus of Art; Addison Gallery of Am Art; Cleveland Mus of Art; Univ of Nebr; Art Students League; Fogg Mus, Boston; Victoria & Albert Mus, London; Bibliot Nat, Paris. Comn: Murals, US Treas Dept, Sellersville, Pa, 36 & Chicago, Ill, 38. Exhib: Whitney Mus Am Art Ann, New York, 48-50; Am Acad Arts & Lett, New York, 72; Retrospective Graphics Exhib, Wichita State Univ, 76; one-man show (paintings), ACA Gallery, 75. Teaching: Instr painting & graphics, Art Students League, 34-68; instr graphics, New Sch Social Res, 42-45; head dept art, Idyllwild Sch Music & Art, Univ Southern Calif, 59-69. Awards: J S Guggenheim Mem Found Fel, 63; Purchase Award, Am Acad Arts & Lett, 72. Style & Technique: Expressionistic; primarily direct painting with over glazes. Media: Acrylic; Metalplate. Publ: Auth, Silk screen color printing & Modern methods and materials of etching, McGraw; auth, Composition, Woodcut & Abstract-realist Drawing, Pitman; director & producer, The Many Worlds of Art (film); auth, Catalogue de raissoné Sternberg Graphics, Wichita State Univ, 76. Dealer: ACA Gallery 25 E 73rd St New York NY 10021. Mailing Add: 1606 Conway Dr Escondido CA 92025

STERNE, DAHLI
PAINTER, SCULPTOR
b Stettin, Ger, Jan 3, 01; US citizen. Study: Kaiserin Auguste Victoria Acad, BA; and with Albert Pels, Ludolf Liberts & Josef Shilhavy, US. Work: Oklahoma City Art Ctr; Evanston Mus Art; Fla Southern Col; Seton Hall Univ; Gracie Mansion, New York; plus others. Exhib: Nat Arts Club, 53-58; Allied Artists Am, 55; 50 Am Artists, 55-58; Col Mt St Vincent, New York; Allied Artists Am; plus others. Pos: Art dir, Nat Coun Jewish Women. Awards: Citation, Okla Art Asn, 54; Award, Am Artists Prof League, 55; Gold Medal, Ogunquit Art Ctr, 57. Mem: Am Artists Prof League; Catharine Lorillard Wolfe Art Club; Artists Equity Asn; 50 Am Artists; Nat Soc Arts & Lett (vpres, 71-72). Media: Oil Mailing Add: 315 W 70th St New York NY 10023

STERNE, HEDDA
PAINTER
b Bucharest, Romania, Aug 4, 16; US citizen. Study: Pvt study in Paris, Bucharest & Vienna. Work: Univ Ill; Metrop Mus Art; Mus Mod Art; Univ Nebr; Art Inst Chicago; plus many others. Exhib: Painting & Sculpture Today, Art Asn Indianapolis, 65-66; Flint Inst Invitational, 66-67; The Visual Assault, Univ Ga, 67-68 & Barnard Col, 68; Phillips Collection, Westmoreland Mus, 69; Lee Ault & Co, New York, 75; Retrospective Show, Montclair Mus of Art, 77; plus many others. Teaching: Instr art hist, Carbondale Col, 64; conducted workshop for art teachers, NY State Coun Arts, 68. Awards: Fulbright Fel to Venice, 63; First Prize, Art Inst Newport Ann, 67; Tamarind Fel, 67; Childe Hassam

Purchasing Award, Acad of Arts & Lett; plus others. Bibliog: Robert Motherwell & Reinhardt (ed), Modern Artists in America, Wittenborn, 51; Nathaniel Pousette-Dart (ed), American Painting Today, Hastings, 56; Herbert Read (auth), The Quest and the Quarry, Rome-New York Art Found Inc, 61; plus others. Style & Technique: Abstract. Mailing Add: c/o Betty Parsons Gallery 24 W 57th St New York NY 10019

STEVANOV, ZORAN
PAINTER, SCULPTOR
b Novi Sad, Yugoslavia, June 25, 45; US citizen. Study: Fla Atlantic Univ, Boca Raton, BA, 66-68; Wichita State Univ, Kans, MFA, 68-70. Work: Wichita State Univ; Kansas State Teachers Col, Emporia; Ft Hays Kansas State Col, Hays. Comn: Sculpture fountain, State of Kansas, Emporia State Col Libr, 71-73. Exhib: Nat Exhib of Drawing & Sculpture, Muncie, Ind, 67; Nat Ann Exhib, Monroe, La, 71; Kans Biennial Art Exhib, Lindsborg, 72; Eight State Ann Exhib, Oklahoma City, 74; three-man show, Lynn Kottler Gallery, New York, 75. Teaching: Instr sculpture & design, Kans State Teachers Col, 70-73; assoc prof design, Ft Hays Kans State Col, 73- Awards: Second Prize Ann State Exhib, Fort Lauderdale, Fla, 67; First Prize Ann State Exhib, Hollywood, Fla, 68; Third Prize Nat Art Exhib, Winter Park, Fla, 68. Mem: Col Art Asn. Dealer: Paula Insel Gallery 987 Third Ave New York NY 10022. Mailing Add: 1208 Donald Hays KS 67601

STEVENS, EDWARD JOHN, JR
PAINTER, EDUCATOR
b Jersey City, NJ, Feb 4, 23. Study: NJ State Teachers Col, Newark, BA, 43; Columbia Univ Teachers Col, MA, 44, Art Exten, 44-47, with Henry Varnum Poor & George Picken. Work: Whitney Mus Am Art, New York; NJ State Mus, Trenton; Art Inst Chicago, Ill; Pa Acad Fine Arts; Honolulu Acad Arts, Hawaii. Exhib: 22 one-man exhibs, Weyhe Gallery, New York, 44-77; Whitney Mus Am Art Ann, 54; Brooklyn Mus Int Watercolor Exhib, 55; Pa Acad Fine Arts Ann, 63; Newark Mus NJ Triennial, 64. Teaching: Instr painting, Newark Sch Fine & Indust Art, 47-59, coord dir, 59- Awards: Artist of Yr, Hudson Artists, 54; Bronze Medal, NJ Tercentenary, 64; Henry Ward Ranger Fund Purchase Award, Nat Acad Design, 68. Mem: Philadelphia Watercolor Club; Audubon Artists. Media: Gouache. Dealer: E Weyhe 794 Lexington Ave New York NY 10021. Mailing Add: 621 Palisade Ave Jersey City NJ 07307

STEVENS, ELISABETH GOSS
WRITER, ART CRITIC
b Rome, NY, Aug 11, 29. Study: Wellesley Col, BA, 51; Columbia Univ, MA(high hons), 56. Pos: Ed assoc, Art News, 64-65; art critic, Washington Post, 65; free lance art critic & writer, 65-; columnist, The Gallery, Wall St J, 69-71; Sunday art columnist, Trenton Times, 74-77. Awards: Nat Endowment Arts Art Critic's Fel, 73-74. Publ: Auth, The graphics boom (ser), Wall St J, 1-2/71; auth, The urban museum crisis (sr), Washington Post, 6-7/72; contribr, Black Arts Ctr Mus News, 3/75; auth, Howard Russell Butler (exhib catalog), E R Squibb & Sons, 77. Mailing Add: 289 Carter Rd RD 2 Princeton NJ 08540

STEVENS, MARJORIE
PAINTER
b Terre Haute, Ind, Mar 8, 02. Study: Largely self-taught; instr from George Post & Dong Kingman; Univ Calif Exten; Acad Advert Arts. Exhib: Calif State Fair, every year since 52; one-woman shows, De Young Mem Mus, San Francisco, 55, Emma Frye Mus, Seattle, 60 & Rosicrucian Mus, San Jose, Calif, 77; Am Watercolor Soc, 63, 65, 66, 69, 74 & 75; West Coast Watercolor Soc, all shows since 63. Teaching: Watercolor classes, Daly City Adult Classes, Calif, 67 & 68; watercolor painting, pvt classes, 75. Awards: Irma Rittigstein Mem, Soc Western Artists, 66 & Klumpkey Mem, 68; Larry Quackenbush Mem, Am Watercolor Soc, 70; Jade for Asilomar Award for Best Watercolor, Soc of Western Artists, 77. Bibliog: Frederick Whitaker (auth), Watercolor in California, Mag Am Artists, 5/68. Mem: Am Watercolor Soc; Soc Western Artists (bd dirs, 56-74, bd trustees, 70-75); charter mem West Coast Watercolor Soc. Style & Technique: Conservative; representational; impressionist. Media: Watercolor, Transparent and Opaque; Collage. Mailing Add: 1550 Haight St San Francisco CA 94117

STEVENS, MAY
PAINTER
b Boston, Mass, June 9, 24. Study: Mass Col Art, BFA, 46; Art Students League, 48; Acad Julian, Paris, 48; Work: Whitney Mus Am Art; Washington Univ; Brooklyn Mus; Herbert F Johnson Mus, Cornell Univ; Wichita State Univ Art Mus. Exhib: Nat Inst Arts & Lett, 69; Recent Acquisitions & Women Artists From Permanent Collection, Whitney Mus Am Art, 70; Am Women Artists, Hamburg, Ger, 72; Women Choose Women, New York Cult Ctr, 73; Johnson Mus, Cornell Univ, 73; Everson Mus, Syracuse, NY, 76; plus many others. Teaching: Instr painting, Sch Visual Arts, 62-; adj lectr art, Queens Col (NY), 64-75; vis artist, Cornell Univ, 73. Awards: Childe Hassam Purchase Awards, Nat Inst Arts & Lett, 68 & 69; MacDowell Colony fels, 70-73; Creative Artists Pub Serv Grant, 74. Bibliog: Linda Nochlin (auth), Some women realists: Part I, Arts, 2/74; Barry Schwartz (auth), New Humanism: Art in a Time of Change, Praeger, 74; Lucy R Lippard (auth), From the Center: Feminist Essays on Women's Art, Dutton, 76; among others. Mem: Artists Equity Asn; Col Art Asn. Style & Technique: Satirical images in large simple forms with bold use of red, white, cobalt and ultramarine; political; quasi-pop. Media: Oil, Acrylic. Publ: Auth, Sara Ruddick & Pamela Daniels, ed, Working It Out, Pantheon, 77. Mailing Add: 97 Wooster St New York NY 10012

STEVENS, NELSON L
PAINTER, EDUCATOR
b Brooklyn, NY, Apr 26, 38. Study: Ohio Univ, BFA, 62; Kent State Univ, 69. Comn: Work to Unify African People, United Community Construct Worker, Roxbury, Mass, 73; I am a Black Woman, Univ Year for Action, Springfield, Mass, 74; United Community, Ctr Exp Educ & M Jackson, Springfield, 75. Exhib: Afri-Cobra I, II & III & Afri-Cobra 77, Philadelphia, Pa; one-man show, Studio Mus in Harlem, NY; Levels & Degrees, Fisk Univ, Nashville, Tenn; FESTAC'77, Lagos, Nigeria & Janet Carter Gallery, New York, NY, 77. Teaching: Teacher, Cleveland Pub Sch Syst, 62-66 & Cleveland Mus Art, 66-68; asst prof art, Northern Ill Univ, DeKalb, 69-72; assoc prof art, Dept Afro-Am Studies, Univ Mass, Amherst, 72- Awards: Many community awards for mural programs. Mem: Col Art Asn Am; Nat Conf Artists; Afri-Cobra. Style & Technique: Rhythm energy. Media: Acrylic, Acrylic Spray; Color Pencil. Publ: Illusr, The Cry of My People, Archie Shepp Album, ABC Dunhill, 72; illusr, There is a Trumpet in My Soul, Archie Shepp Album, Artista, 75; illusr cover, Mass Rev, Univ Mass; contribr, 1000 silk screen posters of Uhuru head; illusr, Sweet Earth Flying, Marion Brown Album; illusr, Hoo Doo Bone Series, 77; illusr, In the Bell of the Horn Series, 78. Mailing Add: Dept of Art Univ Mass Amherst MA 01002

STEVENS, RICHARD CLIVE
PAINTER, ILLUSTRATOR
b Springfield, Mass, Jan 4, 17. Work: Springfield Mus Fine Arts, Mass; Wistariahurst Mus, Holyoke, Mass. Exhib: Hudson Valley Art Asn 42nd Ann Exhib, White Plains, NY, 70; Mem Spring Exhib, Copley Soc, Boston, 70; one-man exhib, Rand Mus, Westfield Athenaeum, Westfield, Mass, 73; Springfield Art League 55th Nat Exhib, Walter Vincent Smith Mus, 74; Acad Artists Asn 26th Ann Nat Exhib Art, Mus Fine Arts, Springfield, 75. Awards: Muriel Alvord Award, Acad Artists Asn Nat Exhib, 65; Best Watercolor in Show, West Springfield Art Festival, 74; Best Watercolor in Show, Agawam Art Festival, 75. Mem: Acad Artists Asn (pres, 74 & 75); Springfield Art League. Style & Technique: Landscapes in realistic style. Media: Watercolor, Pencil. Mailing Add: 463 Ridge Rd Wilbraham MA 01095

STEVENS, WALTER HOLLIS
PAINTER, EDUCATOR
b Mineola, NY, Aug 5, 27. Study: Drake Univ, BFA, 51; Univ Ill, Urbana, MFA, 55. Work: Birmingham Mus Art, Ala; Ark Art Ctr, Little Rock; Mint Mus Art, Charlotte, NC; Okla Art Ctr, Oklahoma City; Tenn Fine Arts Ctr, Nashville. Exhib: One-man shows, Contemp Arts, Inc, New York, 60 & 64; Contemporary Arts, Traveling Exhib to SAm, 60 & 65; Mid-South Exhib, Brooks Mem Art Gallery, Memphis, Tenn, 62-66, 69 & 71; Seven Delta Exhibs, Ark Art Ctr, 61-70; five Watercolor USA Exhibs, Springfield Mo, 68-76. Teaching: Prof painting, Univ Tenn, Knoxville, 57- Awards: First Purchase Awards, Ala Watercolor Nat, Birmingham Mus, 57 & 60; First Purchase Award, Cent South Exhib, Nashville, 66; Watercolor USA Purchase Award, Springfield, Mo, 75. Bibliog: New talent issue, Art in Am, 57; Robert Schlageter (auth), Walter H Stevens, Mint Mus, 59. Mem: Tenn Watercolor Soc; Knoxville Watercolor Soc. Style & Technique: Nature-oriented abstract expressionism. Media: Watercolor, Acrylic, Oil. Dealer: Rechenbach's Gallery 5214 Homberg Dr NW Knoxville TN 37919. Mailing Add: 2305 Woodson Dr Knoxville TN 37920

STEVENS, WILLIAM ANSEL, SR
PAINTER, ILLUSTRATOR
b Akron, Ohio, Sept 6, 19. Study: Kent State Univ; NMex State Univ; also with E Ladislaw Novotny, Fredric Taubes, Gerry Pierce, Kenneth Barrack & Ramon Froman. Work: US Naval Air Station Corpus Christi, Tex Hist Collection; White Sands Missile Range, NMex; US Forest Serv; White Sands Nat Monument; CofC, Alamogordo. Comn: Various oil portraits & landscapes in the US & Ger. Exhib: Otero Co Fair, NMex, 62-73; US Forest Serv White Sands Art Exhib, 63-67, 70 & 71; NMex State Fair, Albuquerque, 65; Llano Estacado Art Exhib, Hobbs, NMex, 67-68; Sun Carnival Art Exhib, El Paso, Tex, 68-69. Pos: Owner, Art Enterprises, Alamogordo, 60-; ed & illusr, Mgt Digest, 74-75. Awards: Grand Champion Art Award, Otero Co Fair, Alamagordo CofC, 62; Grand Champion Art Award, US Forest Serv, White Sands, NMex, 64 & 71; First Place Art Award, CofC Banquet, Alamogordo, 71. Bibliog: B Schwartz (auth), Sun dial, El Paso Times Sunday Mag, 5/75; J Baldwin (auth), article in art sect, Alamogordo Daily News; E White (auth), article in art sect, Missile Ranger, White Sands Missile Range, Dept Defense Publ. Mem: NMex Desert Arts League (pres, 69-70). Style & Technique: Realistic style depicting individual oil technique; various moods of the Southwestern United States. Media: Oil, Pen & Ink. Publ: Illusr, Capabilities of the White Sands Complex, 75. Mailing Add: 1416 Taft Ave Alamogordo NM 88310

STEVENSON, A BROCKIE
PAINTER
b Montgomery Co, Pa, Sept 24, 19. Study: Pa Acad Fine Arts, Philadelphia; Barnes Found, Merion, Pa; Skowhegan Sch Painting & Sculpture, Maine. Work: Corcoran Gallery Art & Nat Collection Fine Arts, Washington, DC; Pa Acad Fine Arts; State Univ NY Potsdam; Woodward Found, Washington, DC. Exhib: Washington Art, State Univ NY Potsdam & Albany, 71; Eight Washington Artists, Columbia Mus Art, SC, 71; Pyramid Galleries, Washington, DC, 73; Our Land, Our Sky, Our Water, Spokane World's Fair, 74; retrospective, Northern Va Community Col, Annandale, 74; one-man show, Fendrick Gallery, Washington, DC, 78. Teaching: Instr compos, Sch Fine Arts, Washington Univ, 60-62; assoc prof design, Corcoran Sch Art, Washington, DC, 65-, chmn dept painting & drawing, 72- Pos: War artist corresp, European Theater Opers Southern Base Sect, USA, Eng, 43-44 & Off Chief Eng, France, 44-45. Bibliog: Lincoln Kirstein (auth), Am battle art, 1588-1944, Mag Art, 5/44; Benjamin Forgey (auth), rev in, Washington Star-News, 5/15/74; Jo Ann Lewis (auth), Mod art crowd, Washingtonian, 5/75; among others. Style & Technique: Abstracted hard-edge realism, generally with geometric shapes and flat colors. Media: Acrylic. Dealer: Fendrick Gallery 3059 M St Washington DC 20007. Mailing Add: Corcoran Sch of Art 17th & New York Ave NW Washington DC 20006

STEVENSON, BRANSON GRAVES
PAINTER, PRINTMAKER
b Franklin Co, Ga, Apr 5, 01. Study: Inst Nac, Panama; Col Great Falls, Mont; and with Margarite Wildenhain, Bernard Leach & Shoji Hamada. Work: Mont Inst Arts, Helena; C M Russell Gallery, Great Falls, Mont; Mont Hist Soc, Helena; Univ Ore, Eugene. Comn: Fresco mural, Great Falls, 45; Story of Paper (glass mural), Great Falls Pub Libr, 68; doc TV film, Jr League Great Falls, 71; 138 proofs of lithographs, First Nat Bank, Great Falls, 71-72. Exhib: Retrospective, Russell Gallery, 70; one-man show, Yellowstone Art Ctr, Billings, Mont, 72; Mont Hist Soc, 72; Northern Mont Col, 72; Ore Arts Comn, Eugene, 72. Teaching: Lectr humanities, Col Great Falls, 63- Pos: Founder, dir, secy & trustee, Archie Bray Found, Helena, 51- Awards: Purchase Prize for Rhubarb (lithograph), Univ Ore; Awards for Emulsion Wax Watercolors, Etching, Drawings & Lithographs, Mont State Fair. Bibliog: Kathleen Cronin (auth), article in, Mobil World, 71; Ray Steele (auth), Branson G Stevenson, the man & his works, KRTV, 72. Mem: C M Russell Mus (dir, 53-); life mem Mont Hist Soc & Art Gallery; life mem & fel Mont Inst Arts. Media: Graphics. Collection: Etchings and graphics, including etchings by Goya, Rembrandt and Seymore Haden, sculpture by C M Russell and painting by Florencio Molino Campos. Publ: Contribr, Craft Horizons, Ceramic Indust, Mont Arts & others. Dealer: Import Depot Great Falls MT 59401; Russell Mus Great Falls, MT 59401. Mailing Add: 715 Fourth Ave N Great Falls MT 59401

STEVENSON, HAROLD
PAINTER
b Idabel, Okla, Mar 11, 29. Study: Univ Okla, Norman; Univ Mex, Mexico City; Art Students League, New York. Work: Whitney Mus, New York. Exhib: Piccola Biennale, Venice, 62; Ann Exhib, Whitney Mus, New York, 62; Pop Art, Palais des Beaux-Arts, Brussels, 65; Erotic Art 66, Sidney Janis Gallery, New York, 66; The Obsessive Image, Inst Contemp Arts, London, 68; Prospect 68, Dusseldorf, 68; Pop Art, Iolas Gallery, New York, 72; Galleria La Medusa, Rome, 73; one-man shows: Okla Art Ctr & Univ Okla, Oklahoma City, 49; Iolas Gallery, New York, 74. Teaching: Artist-in-residence, Austin Col, Sherman, Tex. Bibliog: Andy Warhol (auth), Harold film, New York, 64; Lucy Lippard (auth), Pop Art, New York, 66. Dealer: Galerie Iris Clert 3 rue Duphot Paris 75001 France; Alexander Iolas Gallery 15 E 55th St New York NY 10022. Mailing Add: 302 S East Adams Idabel OK 74745

STEWARD, DONN HORATIO
PRINTMAKER, MASTER PRINTER
b Moose Jaw, Sask, Can, Nov 26, 21; US citizen. Study: Univ Iowa, Iowa City, BA, 42, MA, 48, study with Mauricio Lasansky; Fulbright scholar, Ecole des Beaux-Arts, Paris, 52-53; Tamarind Litho Inst, printer fel, Los Angeles, 65-66. Work: (Printmaker) Brooklyn Mus; British Fine Arts Coun, London; Des Moines Art Ctr, Iowa; Northwest Printmakers, Seattle, Wash; San Francisco Mus Art; (Master Printer), Mus Mod Art, Metrop Mus Art, Whitney Mus Art & Brooklyn Mus Art, New York; Univ Iowa Mus Art. Exhib: (Printmaker) Northwest Printmakers Ann Int, Seattle, 48-57; Des Moines Art Ctr, 49-54; Brooklyn Mus Nat Print Ann, 51, 53 & 54; Artists of Suffolk Co, Part VI, Prints, Heckscher Mus, Huntington, NY, 72 & Donn Steward, Master Printer, 75. (Master Printer) Prints by 4 New York Painters, Frankenthaler, Motherwell, Newman & Johns, Metrop Mus Art, 70; A la Pintura, Motherwell, Alberti, Metrop Mus Art & Univ Iowa Mus Art, 72. Teaching: Instr printmaking, Univ Iowa, 48-54; asst prof printmaking, Fla State Univ, Tallahassee, 54-57; vis lectr printmaking, Washington Univ, St Louis, Mo, 57-58. Pos: Printer's asst, Mauricio Lasansky, Iowa City, 47-52; master printer, Universal Ltd Art Ed, West Islip, NY, 66-74; master printer-publ, Donn H Steward, Halesite, NY, 74- Bibliog: Diane Kelder (auth), Tradition and craftsmanship in modern prints, Art News, 1/72 & Motherwell's A la pintura, Art in Am, 9-10/72; Amei Wallach (auth), Donn Steward, Printer, Sun Newsday, Long Island, 2/9/75; Richard S Field (auth), Recent American Etching (catalogue), Nat Collection of Fine Arts, Washington, DC, 10/75. Mem: Am Crafts Coun; Graphic Soc. Style & Technique: Abstract expression; also use of found half-tone plates as part of images; all styles as master printer. Media: Intaglio. Publ: Contribr, The Genesis of a Book, Robert Motherwell's A la pintura, catalog, Metrop Mus Art, New York, 72. Mailing Add: One Noyes Lane Apt 7 Halesite NY 11743

STEWART, ALBERT T
SCULPTOR
b Kensington, Eng, Apr 9, 00. Study: Beaux-Arts Inst Design; Art Students League; also with Paul Manship. Work: Metrop Mus Art; Fogg Mus Art; Reading Mus Art. Comn: Tablets, panels, figures, doors & fountains, Seamen's Mem, NY, Buffalo City Hall, NY, St Paul City Hall & Court House, St Bartholomew's Church, NY & Am Battle Monument, Thiacourt, France; plus many others. Awards: Prize, Nat Acad Design, 31, Citation, 55, Prize, Pasadena Art Inst, 48; Prize, Chaffey Art Asn, 51; plus others. Mem: Nat Sculpture Soc; Am Mus Natural Hist; academician Nat Acad Design. Mailing Add: 4215 Via Padova Claremont CA 91711

STEWART, ARTHUR
PAINTER
b Marion, Ala, July 29, 15. Study: Auburn Univ; Art Inst Chicago; and with Kelly Fitzpatrick. Work: Birmingham Mus Art, Ala; Montgomery Mus Art, Ala; Norfolk Mus Arts & Sci, Va; Atlanta Art Asn, Ga; also in collection of Queen Elizabeth II, Eng. Comn: Four murals (with Kelly Fitzpatrick), Bank of Tallassee, Ala. Exhib: Art in War Traveling Exhib, Life Mag, 41-42; four Southeastern Ann, 49-59; Norfolk Mus Arts & Sci Traveling Exhib, 64; Ala Watercolor Soc, 69-70; Am Watercolor Soc. Teaching: Instr drawing, Birmingham Mus Art; pvt instr. Pos: Chmn Beaux Arts Ball, Birmingham Mus Art, 59, mem bd, 65-66. Awards: Purchase Award for Spanish Bouquet, Norfolk Mus Arts & Sci, 64; Award for Early Light, Meade Co, 64; Harriete Murray Award for Rosalie, Birmingham Centennial Exhib, 72; plus others. Bibliog: Alfred Frankfurter (auth), Parisian scenes, San Francisco Chronicle, 49; Richard Howard (auth), Arthur Stewart florals, Crescenzi Gallery, 67. Mem: Birmingham Art Asn (vpres, 65-66); Ala Watercolor Soc (pres, 65-67); Ala Art League; Ala Art Asn. Style & Technique: Romantic realist. Media: Watercolor, Oil, Acrylic. Dealer: Elizabeth Agee 1915 11th Ave S Birmingham AL 35205. Mailing Add: 2969 Pump House Rd Birmingham AL 35243

STEWART, CHARLES CARL
PAINTER, SCULPTOR
b Toledo, Ohio, May 23, 22. Study: Toledo Art Mus, 45; Art Students League, 45-48; Taos Valley Art Sch, NMex, 47. Exhib: One-man shows, Stables Gallery, Taos, 56-58, 61, 65, 68 & 70, Philbrook Art Ctr, 58, Santa Fe Mus, 59, Studio Gallery, Topeka, 60 & Gallery A, Taos, 61-68; plus many other group & one-man shows. Teaching: Teacher painting & sculpture, Taos Art Asn, 54 & Philbrook Art Ctr, Tulsa, Okla, 60. Pos: Proprietor, Stewart Gallery, Inc, Taos, 70- Awards: Collectors Choice No 5, Denver Art Mus, 59; 1st Ann Southwest American Painter Exhib, Oklahoma City Art Ctr, 59; Stage Sets, The Play is the Thing, Taos Little Theatre, 68. Mailing Add: Box 554 Taos NM 87571

STEWART, DOROTHY S
PAINTER
b Brooklyn, NY. Study: Art Students League; Nat Acad Sch Fine Art, New York; NY Univ; and with Edgar Whitney, Paul Puzinas & others. Work: Gregory Mus, Hicksville, NY; Mercy Hosp, Rockville Centre, NY. Comn: In pvt collections. Exhib: Allied Artists Am 56-61st Ann, 69-77; Catharine Lorillard Wolfe Art Club 68-78th Ann, 65-77; & Am Watercolor Soc 105th Ann, 72, all at Nat Acad Galleries; Salmagundi Club, 74-77; Women in Art, Hammond Mus, 74; New Brit Mus of Am Art, 77. Teaching: Instr art, Malverne Sr High Sch, NY, 65-66. Awards: First Prize Oil Painting, Gregory Mus, 72; Ivy Larric Kevlin Prize, Kent Art Asn, 74; Washington Sq Outdoor Art Exhib Scholar, 74; Salmagundi Club Prize, 76; plus others. Mem: Catharine Lorillard Wolfe Art Club (dir, 70, 2nd vpres, 71-74); Allied Artists Am (chmn pub rels comt, 72-77); Am Artists Prof League; Kent Art Asn (pres, 77-78); life mem Art Students League; among others. Style & Technique: Realist traditional and contemporary oil and watermedia techniques. Publ: Contribr, Prize-winning art book 7, Allied Publ, Inc, Ft Lauderdale, Fla, 67. Mailing Add: 14 Club Dr Candlewood Trails New Milford CT 06776

STEWART, JACK
PAINTER, EDUCATOR
b Atlanta, Ga, Jan 27, 26. Study: With Steffen Thomas, Atlanta; Yale Univ Sch Fine Arts, BFA; Columbia Univ Sch Archit; NY Univ, MA. Work: Yale Univ Art Gallery; Columbia, SC Mus Fine Arts; Greenville Mus, SC. Comn: Mural on facade of Versailles Hotel, Miami Beach, Fla, 55; six mosaic murals on SS Santa Paula, Grace Lines, 57; mural on facade of Hotel Aruba Caribbean, Netherlands Antilles, 58; two mosaic murals in Pub Sch 28, Manhattan, NY, 58; stained glass for off of Cinerama, Inc, New York, 60. Exhib: Pa Acad Fine Arts, Philadelphia, 53; New York City Ctr Show, 56; Inform & Interpret, Nat Fedn Arts Nat Traveling Show, 65-66; Grippi & Wadell Gallery, 63-64; Col Raffaello, Urbino, Italy, 73; NY Univ, 75; Woods Gerry Gallery, Providence, RI, 76. Teaching: Lectr art & archit, New Sch Social Res, 53-58; instr design, Pratt Inst, 55-61; lectr drawing & painting, Columbia Univ, 67-76; instr drawing & painting, Cooper Union Sch Art & Archit, 60-71, assoc prof & chmn dept, 71-74; instr graphics & drawing, Queens Col (NY), 74-76; instr painting & drawing, NY Univ, 74-76; provost & vpres acad affairs, RI Sch of Design, 76-77. Mem: Am Asn Univ Prof; Nat Soc Lit & Arts; Yale Club. Style & Technique: Acrylic paintings exploring spatial polarities between photo images and gestural abstraction; invented epoxy laminated stained glass technique, 57. Publ: Contribr, Mosaic Art Today, 59; ed, Modern Mosaic Techniques, Watson Guptill, 67; auth, short articles on drawing & mosaic, In: Jefferson Encycl, World, 69; contribr, Art of Mosaic, 69. Mailing Add: 31 E Seventh St New York NY 10003

STEWART, JARVIS ANTHONY
EDUCATOR, PAINTER
b Maryville, Mo, Dec 28, 14. Study: St Joseph Jr Col, 32-33; Phillips Univ, BFA, 42, with E J McFarland; Ohio State Univ, MA, 47, PhD, 51; also with Ernest Thurn, Pablo O'Higgins, Felipe Cossio & Hoyt Sherman. Work: Columbus Gallery Fine Arts, Ohio; Otterbein Col, Westerville, Ohio; Phillips Univ, Enid, Okla. Teaching: Instr design, Phillips Univ, 42-43; prof design & art hist, Ohio Wesleyan Univ, 43- Pos: Asst for murals, Am Hotels Corp, Robidoux Hotel, St Joseph, Mo, 39-40. Res: Craftsmen of the Mexican Bajio; sociology of art. Mailing Add: 61 Westgate Dr Delaware OH 43015

STEWART, JOHN LINCOLN
EDUCATOR, WRITER
b Alton, Ill, Jan 24, 17. Study: Denison Univ, AB, 38; Ohio State Univ, MA, 39, PhD, 47; Denison Univ, hon DA, 64. Teaching: From asst prof to prof, Dartmouth Col, 49-54; prof Am lit & provost, John Muir Col, Univ Calif, San Diego, 64- Pos: Assoc dir, Hopkins Art Ctr, Dartmouth Col, 62-64; dir, Mandeville Ctr for Arts, Univ Calif, San Diego, 75-76. Awards: Howard Found fel, 53-54; Dartmouth fac fel, 62-63. Res: Contemporary American and British literatures. Publ: Auth, John Crowe Ransom, Univ Minn, 62; auth, Burden of Time, the Fugitives and Agrarians, Princeton Univ, 65; co-auth, Horizons Circled, Univ Calif, 74; plus others. Mailing Add: John Muir Col Univ of Calif at San Diego La Jolla CA 92037

STEWART, JOHN P
PRINTMAKER, PAINTER
b Ft Leavenworth, Kans, Mar 11, 45. Study: Univ Colo, with Roland Reiss & Wendel Black, BFA, 67; Univ Calif, Santa Barbara, MFA, 69. Work: Corcoran Gallery Art, Washington, DC; Whitney Mus Am Art, New York; Ponce Mus, PR; New Orleans Mus of Art, La; Santa Barbara Mus Art, Calif. Exhib: Recent Acquisitions, Whitney Mus, New York, 72; Five American Artists, Multitude Gallery, Paris, France, 72; Pyramid Gallery, Washington, DC, 72, 74, 76 & 78; Drawings, Cincinnati Art Mus, Ohio, 74; Gimpel/Weitzenhoffer, New York, 75; Contemp Art Ctr, Cincinnati, Ohio, 76; Galeria de Las Americas, San Juan, PR, 76; and others. Teaching: Asst prof, Univ Cincinnati, 73- Style & Technique: Realist. Dealer: Pyramid Gallery 2121 P St NW Washington DC 20037. Mailing Add: Dept of Fine Arts Univ of Cincinnati Cincinnati OH 45221

STEWART, LIZBETH MCNETT
SCULPTOR, CERAMIST
b Philadelphia, Pa, Dec 22, 48. Study: Moore Col Arts, BFA(ceramics), 71. Work: Lannan Found, Palm Beach, Fla; Campbell Mus, Camden, NJ. Comn: Award of Excellence, Moore Col Art, Philadelphia, 77. Exhib: Clay, Whitney Mus Am Art, New York, 74; Soup Tureens 1976, Nat Invitational, Campbell Mus, Camden, NJ, 76; Philadelphia, Three Centuries of American Art, Philadelphia Art Mus, 76; Exhib of Liturgical Arts, 41st Int Eucharistic Cong, Philadelphia Civic Ctr, 76; Am Crafts 77, Philadelphia Mus Art, 77; Am Art 77, Helen Drutt Gallery, Philadelphia, 77; Clay, Fiber Metal, Bronx Mus, 78. Awards: Traveling Fel, Moore Col Art, 70; Purchase Award, Permanent Collection, Campbell Mus, 76; Craftsman Fellowship Grant, Nat Endowment for Arts, 76. Bibliog: David Honks (auth), Philadelphia: 3 Centuries of Am Art, Philadelphia Mus Art, 76; Professional Women (doc film), Channel Six, Philadelphia, 76. Style & Technique: Hand-built porcelain images glazed and decorated with lustres; ceramic figures often combined with structured fibre applique. Dealer: Helen Drutt 1625 Spruce St Philadelphia PA 19103. Mailing Add: 2013 Walnut St Philadelphia PA 19103

STEWART, NORMAN (WILLIAM)
PRINTMAKER, INSTRUCTOR
b Detroit, Mich, Mar 31, 47. Study: Univ Mich, BFA, 69, MA, 72, studied with Sewell Sillman, 75-77; Cranbrook Acad of Art, MFA, 77, with Tamarind master printer Irwin Hollander; Rochester Inst Technol, 77. Work: Cranbrook Art Mus, Cranbrook Acad of Art, Bloomfield Hills, Mich; Flint Inst of Art, Mich; Sch of Art, Univ Mich, Ann Arbor; plus numerous corp collections. Comn: Print ed, Adat Shalom Synagogue, Farmington Hills, Mich, 73 & Mich Coun for the Arts & Flint Schs, 73; fabric design, Bassett Furniture Co, Bassett, Va, 74; print ed, Pub Broadcasting Serv, WTVS, Detroit, 75. Exhib: Exhib for Mich artists, Detroit Inst of Arts, 70, 71 & 77; 61st & 62nd Ann Exhib of Conn Acad of Fine Arts, Wadsworth Atheneum, Hartford, Conn, 71 & 72; 8th Ann Conn Acad of Fine Arts & Conn Watercolor Combined Exhib, New Britain Mus of Am Art, Conn, 72; one-man show, Xochipilli Gallery, Rochester, Mich, 75; Mich Invitational, Midland Ctr for the Arts, 76; Cranbrook Art Mus, Cranbrook Acad of Art, 76 & 77; 11th Dulin Nat Print & Drawing Competition, Dulin Gallery of Art, Knoxville, Tenn, 77; 25th Nat Exhib of Prints (traveling exhib), Smithsonian Inst & Nat Collection of Fine Arts, Washington, DC, 77-79. Teaching: Guest lectr, Flint Inst of Art, 73, Sch of Art, Univ Mich, 74 & Parsons Sch of Design, New York, 77. Pos: Chmn dept design & fine arts, Bloomfield Hills Lahser High Sch, 69-; art curric developer, US Off of Educ & Educ Systems for the Seventies, 69; art prog evaluator, NCent Accreditation Asn, 71; mem, Scholastic Art Awards Adv Bd, SE Mich, 74- Mem: Col Art Asn Am; Mich Art Educ Asn (treas, 73-75); Nat Art Educ Asn; Mich Educ Asn; Nat Educ Asn. Style & Technique: Works deal with printed surfaces which evolve from extensive color layering in matrix formations, screen process printing and wax drawing. Media: Screen process Printing, Drawing and Painting. Mailing Add: 5571 Wing Lake Rd Birmingham MI 58010

STEWART, PATRICIA KAYE
ART CRITIC, ART ADMINISTRATOR
b El Paso, Tex, Oct 26, 47. Study: Univ Pa, BA; Columbia Univ. Collections Arranged: Comix, Mus Contemp Art, Chicago, Ill, 72 & arrangements, selections & cataloging all exhibs, 72-74. Pos: Cur, Mus Contemp Art, Chicago, 72-74; art critic, 75- Publ: Auth, Comix, 72. Mailing Add: 2204 Rittenhouse St Philadelphia PA 19104

STEWART, ROBERT GORDON
CURATOR, ART HISTORIAN
b Baltimore, Md, Mar 5, 31. Study: Univ Pa, BFA, 54. Collections Arranged: Nucleus for a National Collection, 1st Exhib Nat Portrait Gallery, Smithsonian Inst, 65, Recent Acquisitions, 66; National Gallery of 19th Century Distinguished Americans (with catalog), 69; Henry Benbridge (with catalog), 71. Teaching: Vis lectr museology, George Washington Univ, 67-70. Pos: Architect & cur, Jefferson Barracks Hist Park, St Louis, Mo, 58-61; dir properties, Nat Trust Hist Preservation, 61-64; cur collection, Nat Portrait Gallery, Smithsonian Inst, 64- Res: American portraiture from 18th century to present. Publ: Contribr, In the Minds and the Hearts of the People, 74; contribr, The Dye is Now Cast, 75; contribr,

Abroad in America, 76. Mailing Add: 3901 Cathedral Ave NW No 304 Washington DC 20016

STEWART, WILLIAM
PAINTER
b Waco, Tex, Aug 18, 38. Study: Univ Tex, BFA, 60, MFA, 62. Work: Fordham Univ, Bronx, NY; Fairleigh Dickinson Univ, Madison, NJ. Exhib: Drawing Exhib, Univ NC, 66; Newark Mus, NJ, 71; Biennale de Paris, France, 71; Nat Endowment and NY State Coun on the Arts Grant Exhib, Thomas Moore Chapel, Fordham Univ, 76; one-man shows, O K Harris Gallery, New York, 69, Rudolf Zwirner Gallery, Cologne, Ger, 70 & Pergola Gallery, San Miguel de Allende, 78. Teaching: Instr painting & drawing, Instituto Allende, San Miguel de Allende, Guanajuato, Mex, 77- Pos: Asst dir educ dept & instr, San Francisco Mus Art, Calif, 63-64; art instr, Fairleigh Dickinson Univ, 68-70 & City Col New York, 71-72; instr educ dept, Newark Mus, 73-74. Bibliog: Colin Naylor (ed), Contemporary Artists, St James Press Ltd, London, Eng, 77. Mem: Col Art Asn of Am. Style & Technique: A figurative painter working from nature in a painterly direction. Media: Oil, Watercolor Pastel. Dealer: Tatistcheff & Co Inc 35 E 35th St New York NY 10016. Mailing Add: 2905 Lakeshore Dr Waco TX 76708

STICKER, ROBERT EDWARD
PAINTER
b Jersey City, NJ, Dec 26, 22. Study: Art Students League, with Frank Reilly. Work: V] esuvius Crucible Co, Pittsburgh; IBM Corp, Union Carbide Corp, Am Tel & Tel, New York. Exhib: Franklin Mint Marine Compettition, 74. Pos: Mem bd control, Art Students I eague, 59- Awards: Gold Medal, Franklin Mint Nat Marine Competition, 74. Mem: Hudson Valley Art Asn; Am Artists Prof League. Style & Technique: Realistic marine art, preferably of a historical nature. Media: Oil. Publ: Famous small boat voyages, 69-72 & Classical work boats of America, 73- (ser of paintings), Yachting Mag. Dealer: Grand Central Art Galleries New York NY; Doll & Richards Boston MA. Mailing Add: 136 David St Staten Island NY 10308

STIEBEL, ERIC
ART DEALER
b Frankfurt, Ger, July 22, 11; US citizen. Study: Univ Frankfurt, 29-30; Univ Munich, 30-31; Univ Berlin, 31-32. Pos: Pres, Rosenberg & Stiebel, currently. Mem: Nat Antique & Art Dealers Asn Am; Art & Antique Dealers League Am; Art Dealers Asn Am; Int Confedn Dealer in Works Art; Syndicat Nat des Antiquaires. Specialty: Old master paintings and drawings; important French 18th century furniture; Renaissance bronzes. Mailing Add: 32 E 57th St New York NY 10022

STIEBEL, GERALD GUSTAVE
ART DEALER
b New York, NY, Sept 28, 44. Study: C W Post Col, BA, 65; Study Ctr Fine & Decorative Arts, London, cert, 66; Columbia Univ, MA, 67. Collections Arranged: Grand Gallery Exhib, Metrop Mus Art, 74-75. Pos: Treas, Rosenberg & Stiebel, Inc, 68-71, vpres, 71- Mem: Syndicat Nat des Antiquaires; Int Confedn Dealers in Works Art; Art Dealers Asn Am; Art & Antique Dealers League Am; Nat Antique & Art Dealers Asn Am (secy, 71-73, vpres, 73-77, pres, 77-). Specialty: Old master paintings and drawings; important French 18th century furniture; Renaissance bronzes. Publ: Auth, Article in The Designer Mag, 72. Mailing Add: 32 E 57th St New York NY 10022

STIEBEL, PENELOPE HUNTER
See Hunter-Stiebel, Penelope

STIEGELMEYER, NORMAN EARL
PAINTER, SCULPTOR
b Denver, Colo, Oct 28, 37. Study: San Francisco Art Inst, BFA & MFA; Acad of Art, Nuremburg, Ger. Work: San Francisco Mus of Mod Art; Oakland Mus of Art, Calif; City of San Francisco. Exhib: One-man shows, Richmond Art Ctr, Calif, 66, Quay Gallery, 67, San Francisco Art Inst, 68, Calif Palace of the Legion of Honor Mus, 69 & Phoenix Gallery, 74, San Francisco; Whitney Painting Ann, 68 & Human Concern & Personal Torment, 69, Whitney Mus of Am Art, New York; Just Yesterday, San Francisco Mus of Art, 69; West Coast Artists (touring show), Fla State Mus, 69; Recent Acquisitions, Oakland Mus of Art, 75; Painting & Sculpture in Calif—The Mod Era, San Francisco Mus of Art & Nat Collection of Fine Arts, Washington, DC, 77; Bay Area Update, Huntsville Mus of Art, Ala, 77. Teaching: Prof drawing & painting, Univ Calif Extension, San Francisco; prof drawing & painting, Diablo Valley Col, Pleasant Hill, 75- Pos: Guest cur, San Francisco Art Festival, 68-69, San Francisco Art Inst Art Gallery, 71 & Walnut Creek Art Ctr, 75. Awards: Painting Award, San Francisco Art Inst, James J Schwabacher, 64; Fulbright Scholar & Ger Govt Acad Exchange Serv Grant, W Ger, 65; One-Man Mus Show Award, Calif Palace of Legion of Honor Mus, 69. Bibliog: Fred Martin (auth), one-man show reviews, Art Int, 66; Palmer French (auth), California reviews, Artforum, 69; Carter Ratcliff (auth), Art in California, Art in Am, 77. Mem: Walnut Creek Art Ctr (mem exhib comt, 76-). Style & Technique: Surrealist—visionary images and metaphysical symbolism in a figurative context; also transparent Plexiglas boxes with symbolic images. Media: Acrylic, Oil and Plexiglas; Mixed Media Sculpture. Publ: Auth, Omnibus-Exstasis-et-Celestialis (111 line drawings), 70 & The SilverBook of Drawings, 71, Cumberland Press. Dealer: Gallery Rebecca Cooper 2130 P St NW Washington DC 20037. Mailing Add: 146 Oakvale Rd Walnut Creek CA 94596

STILL, CLYFFORD
PAINTER
b Grandin, NDak, Nov 30, 04. Study: Spokane Univ, BA, 33; Wash State Col, MA. Work: Baltimore Mus Art; Albright-Knox Art Gallery, Buffalo, NY; Mus Mod Art; Phillips Collection, Washington, DC; Whitney Mus Am Art; plus others. Exhib: One-man shows, San Francisco Mus Art, 43 & 76 & Univ Pa, 64; Fifteen Americans Traveling Exhib, Mus Mod Art, 52, The New American Painting, circulating Europe, 58-59 & The New American Painting and Sculpture, 69; retrospective, Albright-Knox Art Gallery, 59; Documenta II, Kassel, Ger, 59; Mus Mod Art, New York, 69; plus others. Teaching: Mem fac, Wash State Col, 33-41, Yaddo, 34-35, Richmond Prof Inst, Col William & Mary, 43-45, Calif Sch Fine Arts, 46-50; originated Subject of the Artist, New York, 47-48, Brooklyn Col, 52, Hunter Col, 52 & Univ Pa, 62. Style & Technique: Abstract. Mailing Add: PO Box 337 New Windsor MD 21776

STILLMAN, E CLARK
COLLECTOR
b Eureka, Utah, Oct 24, 07. Study: Univ Mich, AB & AM. Res: African sculpture; medieval and modern book illumination and illustration. Collection: Traditional Congolese sculpture; manuscript and printed Books of Hours. Mailing Add: 24 Gramercy Park New York NY 10003

STINSKI, GERALD PAUL
PAINTER, COLLECTOR
b Menasha, Wis, June 15, 29. Work: Pvt & corporate collections. Comn: Del Monte Foods, Gallo Wineries, Consolidated Foods (Nathan Cummings Collection), plus others. Exhib: Southeastern Regional, Atlanta, Ga; Tidewater Art Asn, Norfolk, Va. Bibliog: Haddad's Fine Art Reproductions, 72. Style & Technique: Trompe l'oeil. Collection: 16th century drawings, including Raphael; pre-Columbian sculpture, Etruscan and early Christian santos. Dealer: Zantman Galleries PO Box 5818 Carmel-by-the-Sea CA 93921; Conacher Galleries 134 Maiden Lane San Francisco CA 94108 Mailing Add: 65 Manzanita Rd Fairfax CA 94930

STIPE, WILLIAM S
PAINTER
b 1916. Study: Univ Iowa, BA & MA, 36; Mus Sch, Boston, with Karl Zerbe, 40; Inst Design, Chicago, 47. Work: Springfield Art Mus, Mo; Ohio Univ, Athens; Northern Trust Co, Chicago; Int Minerals & Chem Corp, Skokie, Ill; Kans State Univ. Comn: Wall painting, Evanston CofC, Davis L Bus Stop, 71. Exhib: Denver Art Mus, Colo; Mus Fine Arts, Boston, Mass; Butler Inst Am Art, Youngstown, Ohio; Columbia Mus Art, SC; one-man shows, Culver-Stockton Col, Canton, Mo & Ill Arts Coun Gallery, Chicago, 72; plus many other group & one-man shows. Teaching: Mem fac, Northwestern Univ, 48. Awards: Second Prize, Washington, DC Watercolor Club, 49; Pauline Palmer Second Prize, 59th Ann Chicago Show, Art Inst, 56; First Prize for Painting, Old Orchard Art Fair, Skokie, Ill, 70. Interest: Experimentation with copy machine art. Mailing Add: 1216 W Jarvis Chicago IL 60626

STITT, SUSAN (MARGARET)
MUSEUM DIRECTOR
b East Liverpool, Ohio, Jan 24, 42. Study: Col William & Mary, AB; Univ Pa, MA. Pos: Asst to dir, Hist Soc Pa; dir, Mus Albemarle; adminr, Mus Early Southern Decorative Arts; asst to dir, Brooklyn Mus; proj dir surv placement & training, Old Sturbridge Village, Mass; dir, Mus at Stony Brook, currently. Mem: Int Coun Mus; Am Asn Mus (mem coun); Long Island Mus Asn; Am Asn State & Local Hist; Opportunity Resources Arts (bd dirs); NY State Coun Arts (mus aid advisor). Publ: Auth, The will of Stephen Charlton & Hungars Parish, Va Mag Hist & Biog, 7/69; auth, Museum of Early Southern Decorative Arts, 70; auth, The Museum Labor Market, 74; auth, Today's labor practices, the search for equaltiy, Mus News, 9-10/75. Mailing Add: Mus at Stony Brook Stony Brook NY 11790

STODDARD, DONNA MELISSA
EDUCATOR, GALLERY DIRECTOR
b St Petersburg, Fla, July 1, 16. Study: Fla Southern Col, BS, 37; Pittsburgh Art Inst; Pa State Col, MEd, 42; New York Sch Interior Design, 53; Univ Tampa, 59; Univ Fla, 60; Philathea Col, hon LHD, 68. Collections Arranged: Directed Fla Int Art Exhib, 52; organized & installed permanent contemp art collection, Fla Southern Col. Pos: Coordr dept art, Fla Southern Col, 40-, dir, Melvin Gallery, currently; WEDU TV Co Art Chmn Art Auction, 68-69. Awards: Am Cult Award, 52; Grumbacher Award, 53; Miami Women's Club Gold Medal, 53; plus others. Mem: Am Asn Univ Women; Col Art Asn Am; fel Royal Soc Art, London; Am Asn Univ Prof; Kappa Pi (vpres); plus others. Publ: Contribr, Design Mag. Mailing Add: Dept of Art Fla Southern Col Lakeland FL 33802

STODDARD, WHITNEY SNOW
ART HISTORIAN
b Greenfield, Mass, Mar 25, 13. Study: Williams Col, BA, 35; Harvard Univ, MA, 38, PhD, 41, with Koehler, Post & Sachs. Teaching: Instr art, Williams Col, 38-43, asst prof, 43-49, assoc prof, 49-54, prof, 54-, chmn dept, 69- Awards: Fulbright Advan Res Grant, 54. Mem: Col Art Asn Am; Soc Archit Historians; Medieval Acad Am; Int Ctr Medieval Art (vpres, 72). Res: Provencal Romanesque sculpture. Publ: Auth, The West Portals of Saint-Denis and Chartres, Harvard Univ, 52; auth, Adventure in Architecture, Building the New St Johns, 58; auth, Monastery and Cathedral in France, 68 & The Facade of Saint Gilles du Gard, 72, Wesleyan Univ. Mailing Add: Williams Col Williamstown MA 01267

STOESSEL, HENRY KURT
PAINTER, DESIGNER
b Chemnitz, Ger, Apr 17, 09; US citizen. Study: Chicago Art Inst, 25-28; Ray Schs, Chicago, 25-27; Grand Central Sch Art, New York, 28-30; New Sch Soc Res, 38-39; also with Eric Pape, 30-31. Work: USAF Mus Collection (20 paintings), Washington, DC; US Pentagon Traveling Shows. Comn: Artist Corresp, USAF, S Vietnam, 66. Exhib: Guest show, Woodstock Artist Asn, 50; 2nd Ann Nat Soc of Painters in Casein, 56; 47th Ann Hudson Valley Art Asn Exhib, 75. Teaching: Pvt classes. Pos: Art dir, Arnold Hoffman Studios, New York, 31-38; owner & pres, Stoessel Studios, Inc, New York, 38- & Stoessel Graphics, Inc, New York, 60- Awards: Salmagundi Prize, 74; plus 61 graphic design awards. Bibliog: G Byrnes (auth), Complete Guide to Drawing, Illustrating & Painting, Simon & Shuster, 48. Mem: Am Artists Prof League; Salmagundi Club (Jury of Awards, 74-75); Soc of Illusrs (chmn, Warwick Students projects, 62-64; chmn, membership, 66); Long Beach Art Asn. Style & Technique: Lyric expressionist. Media: Oil-Acrylic. Mailing Add: 116 Pinehurst Ave New York NY 10033

STOFFLET, MARY
ART CRITIC, ART HISTORIAN
b Long Branch, NJ, Dec 23, 42. Study: Skidmore Col, BA, 64; New York Univ, MA, 69; Rockefeller/Nat Endowment for the Arts fel in mus educ, M H de Young Mem Mus, San Francisco, 75-76. Collections Arranged: International Rubber Stamp Art Exhibition, La Mamelle Arts Ctr, San Francisco, 76; Cityscapes, Fine Arts Mus of San Francisco, Downtown Ctr, 77. Teaching: Instr art hist, Oakland Mus, Calif, 77; lectr art hist, San Francisco State Univ, 77. Pos: Newsletter ed, Western Asn of Art Mus, Oakland, 74-77; contrib ed, Artweek, 74-; assoc ed, La Mamelle, 75-77, contrib ed, 77-; contrib ed, Visual Dialog, 75- & Feminist Art J, 75-77; ed, Front, 76-; coordr intern prog, M H de Young Mem Mus, 77- Mem: Col Art Asn; Art Libr Soc of NAm; Bay Area Lawyers for the Arts (bd mem); Assoc Art Publrs (bd mem); Women's Caucus for Art. Publ: Auth & ed, Three Bay Area Artists (catalogue), Univ Calif, Riverside, 76. Mailing Add: PO Box 14397 San Francisco CA 94114

STOIANOVICH, MARCELLE
PAINTER
Study: Col d'Art Applique a'Industrie, Paris, France. Work: Work in pvt collections. Comn: Posters for Am Christmas Fund, Paris; book jacket designs for Doubleday & Co; hand-made jewelry. Exhib: Salon des Artistes Francais, Paris, France; Maison Francaise, Columbia Univ, New York; Assoc Am Artists, New York; American Club, Athens & Macedonian Ctr, Salonika, Greece; Venable Gallery, Washington, DC; plus many others. Awards: Hon Mention for Watercolor, Beaux-Arts, Paris, 50; Hon Mention, Soc Artistique de Clichy, Paris, 52; Selected Film Credits, Festival Am Films, Deauville, France, 75. Bibliog: Lithographies

ed by Rombaldi, Paris, France, Collier Art Co, Perspective Et de Vaduz, Angeli Ed. Media: Watercolor. Mailing Add: 9 Rue Campagne Premiere Paris 14 France

STOKES, THOMAS PHELPS
PAINTER
b New York, NY, Mar 15, 34. Exhib: Collectors Exhib, Cleveland Mus, 64; Members Gallery, Albright-Knox Art Gallery, Buffalo, 66; Phillips Collection, Washington, DC, 69; Gift of Time, Mus NMex, Santa Fe, 70; Univ Art Gallery, Va Polytech Inst & State Univ, 71; Avco Ctr for Visual Art, 77; Ruth Schaftner Gallery, Los Angeles, Calif; plus others. Bibliog: John Canaday (auth), rev in New York Times, 5/4/68 & 9/27/69; Anita Feldman (auth), Thomas Stokes, summer 68 & rev, fall 69, Arts Mag; C Ratcliff (auth), article in Art Int, 11/69. Media: Oil. Mailing Add: c/o Betty Parsons Gallery 24 W 57th St New York NY 10019

STOKSTAD, MARILYN
ART HISTORIAN, EDUCATOR
b Lansing, Mich, Feb 16, 29. Study: Carleton Col, BA, 50; Mich State Univ, MA, 53; Univ Mich, PhD, 57. Teaching: Prof hist art, Univ Kans, 58-, chmn dept, 61-72, dir, Mus Art, 61-67, assoc dean, Col Arts & Sci, 72- Pos: Res cur medieval art, Nelson Gallery, Kansas City, 69- Awards: Fulbright Fel, 51-52; Am Asn Univ Women Award, 54-55; Nat Endowment Humanities Fel, 67-68. Mem: Col Art Asn Am (bd dirs, 71-74, secy, 74-); Midwest Col Art Conf (pres, 64-65); Int Ctr Medieval Art (bd dirs, 72-); Am Asn Univ Prof (nat coun, 72-); Soc Archit Historians; plus others. Res: Medieval art; art of the British Isles and Scandinavia; Spanish art. Publ: Auth, Renaissance art outside Italy, Art Horizons, 68; auth, Three apostles from Vich, Bull Nelson Gallery, 70; ed, Hortus Imaginum: Studies in Western Art, Humanistic Series 45, Univ Kans, 74; plus others. Mailing Add: 2020 W Ninth St Lawrence KS 66044

STOLL, MRS BERRY VINCENT
COLLECTOR
b Louisville, Ky, Feb 2, 06. Study: Bryn Mawr Col; Louisville Art Sch. Pos: Vpres, J B Speed Art Mus, Louisville. Collection: Paintings and antiques. Mailing Add: 3905 Lime Kiln Ln Louisville KY 40222

STOLL, VIVIAN CAMPBELL
See Campbell, Vivian

STOLLER, JOHN CHAPMAN
ART DEALER
b Minneapolis, Minn, Feb 7, 40. Study: Univ Minn, degree in art hist. Pos: Owner, John C Stoller & Co, presently. Specialty: Contemporary American and European paintings, drawings, sculpture and graphics. Mailing Add: John C Stoller & Co Dayton's 700 on the Mall Minneapolis MN 55402

STOLOFF, CAROLYN
PAINTER
b New York, NY. Study: Univ Ill; Columbia Univ, BA; Art Students League; Atelier 17; with Xavier Gonzalez, Eric Isenburger & Hans Hofmann. Exhib: Whitney Mus Am Art; Pa Acad Fine Arts; Audubon Artists; Nat Asn Women Artists; NJ Soc Painters & Sculptors; one-person shows, Dabin Gallery, Manhattanville Col (two shows) & others, New York, NY. plus many others. Teaching: Instr painting & drawing, Manhattanville Col, formerly, chmn dept art, 58-63, lectr, art & Eng, until 74. Awards: Silver Anniversary Medal, Audubon Artists, 67, Hon Mention, 72. Publ: Auth, Stepping Out, Unicorn Press, 71; auth, Dying to Survive, Doubleday & Co, 73; auth, In the Red Meadow, New Rivers Press, 73; auth, Lighter-Than-Night Verse, Red Hill Publ, 77. Mailing Add: 24 W Eighth St New York NY 10011

STOLOFF, IRMA
SCULPTOR
b New York, NY. Study: Art Students League, with Alexander Stirling Calder, Boardman Robinson, Howard Giles, Yasuo Kuniyoshi & Alexander Archipenko. Work: Butler Inst Am Art, Youngstown, Ohio; Rose Art Mus, Brandeis Univ; Norfolk Mus, Va. Comn: Portraits, bas-reliefs & figure compositions, pub & pvt comns. Exhib: Allied Artists Am, Nat Acad Design Galleries, 66, New York Soc Women Artists, 70, Audubon Artists, 72 & Nat Asn Women Artists, 72; Nat Arts Club Ann, 69; plus others. Teaching: Pvt instr. Awards: Barstow Prize for Sculpture, Nat Asn Women Artists, 53; Excalibur Award for Sculpture, Catharine Lorillard Wolfe Art Club, 69; Mr & Mrs Michael J Solomone Prize for Sculpture, Audubon Artists, 71. Bibliog: Datos biograficos de Irma Stoloff, Espacios, Mexico City, 11/53; Irma Stoloff y la escultura abstracta, La Presna, 11/53; Cornelia Justice (auth), The artists outpouring, Ledger Star, 68; plus others. Mem: Audubon Artists (exec bd, 65-70); Nat Asn Women Artists (sculpture jury, 52-74 & 77-79, finance comt, 65-66, prog comt, 70); Silvermine Guild Artists; New York Soc Women Artists (exhib comt, 66); Artists Equity Asn. Mailing Add: 46 E 91st St New York NY 10028

STOLOW, NATHAN
ART CONSERVATOR, LECTURER
b Montreal, Que, May 4, 28. Study: McGill Univ, Montreal, BS, 49; Univ Toronto, MA, 52; Courtauld Inst Art, Univ London, PhD, 56. Exhib Arranged: Progress in Conservation, Gallery of Can (circulated to 16 mus and galleries across Can), 72-74. Teaching: Lectr art conserv, Univ Ottawa, Can, 76-78 & Ctr for Restoration & Museology, Mex, 78- Pos: Dir & sci consult, Nat Conserv Res Lab, Nat Gallery of Can, 57-72; dir, Can Conserv Inst, Nat Mus Can, Ottawa, 72-76; spec adv, Nat Mus Can, Ottawa, 76- Awards: Can Centennial Medal, Recognition of Conserv Contribs, Govt Can, 78. Mem: Int Coun of Mus (coordr comt for conserv, 58-, mem exec coun, 72-74); fel Am Inst Conserv; Int Inst for Conserv, London (coun mem, 72-78). Res: Consultant on conservation of works of art and collections; expert on art materials; scientific research on old masters. Publ: Auth, Controlled Environment for Works of Art in Transit, UNESCO, Rome Ctr, 66; auth, The Canadian Art Fraud Case, Can Art, 64; auth, Conservation of the Contemporary, Arts Can, 69; co-auth, On Picture Varnishes and Their Solvents, Case Western Reserve Univ & Oberlin Col, 71; ed, Progress in Conservation (catalog), Nat Gallery of Can, 72. Mailing Add: PO Box 2542 Sta D Ottawa ON K1P 5W6 Can

STOLTENBERG, DONALD HUGO
PAINTER, PRINTMAKER
b Milwaukee, Wis, Oct 15, 27. Study: Inst Design, Ill Inst Technol, BS(visual design). Work: Boston Mus Fine Art; Addison Gallery Am Art, Andover, Mass; De Cordova Mus, Lincoln, Mass; Portland Mus Art. Exhib: Venice Observed, Fogg Mus, Cambridge, Mass, 56; Boston Arts Festival, 56-61; Corcoran Gallery Art Exhib, Washington, DC, 63; Landscape, De Cordova Mus, 71; Am Art Exhib, Art Inst Chicago; Mass Open, Worcester Art Mus, 77. Teaching: Instr painting & printmaking, De Cordova Mus Sch; vis critic, RI Sch Design. Awards: Grand Prize, Boston Arts Festival, 57, First Prize in Painting, 59; First Purchase Prize, Portland Mus Arts Festival. Mem: Boston Printmakers (mem bd, 71-); Boston Watercolor Soc. Publ: Auth, Collagraph Printmaking, Davis, 75. Mailing Add: 947 Satucket Rd RD 1 Brewster MA 02631

STOMPS, WALTER E, JR
PAINTER, EDUCATOR
b Hamilton, Ohio, July 13, 29. Study: Miami Univ, BFA; Art Inst Chicago, with Boris Anisfeld, Paul Weighardt, Isabelle MacKinnon & Edgar Pillet, MFA; Syracuse Univ. Work: Cleveland Mus Art; Dayton Art Inst; Miami Univ. Comn: Ctr City Murals Proj, Nat Endowment Arts, Dayton, 72; Gen Motors (Frigidaire), Dayton; Bicentennial Poster Proj, Dayton. Exhib: Everson Mus Painting Exhib, Syracuse, NY, 63; Ohio Painting & Sculpture Exhib, Dayton, 66; Nat Drawing & Sculpture Exhib, Muncie, Ind, 67; Ohio Print & Drawing Exhib, Dayton, 68; Cincinnati Invitational, 72; Mid-States Exhib, Evansville, Ind, 77; Cent S Exhib, Nashville, Tenn, 77. Teaching: Instr painting & drawing, Western Ky Univ, 75- Awards: James Nelson Raymond Award, Art Inst Chicago, 59; Ohio Painting & Sculpture Exhib Purchase Award, Dayton Art Inst, 66, Ohio Print & Drawing Exhib Purchase Award, 68. Style & Technique: Colorfield painter. Media: Acrylic. Publ: Illusr, Dayton USA, 72. Mailing Add: 624 Lynwood Dr Bowling Green KY 42101

STONE, ALEX BENJAMIN
ART DEALER, COLLECTOR
b Sczuczyn, Poland, Mar 14, 22. Study: St John's Univ; Kans State Univ, DVM; Stanford Univ Med Sch. Pos: Mem bd dir, Friends Art, Davenport, Iowa, 71- Mem: Am Fedn Art; Mus Mod Art; Davenport Art Mus (acquisitions comt). Specialty: 19th century American landscapists; contemporary American and European prints. Collection: Eclectic—15th century Venetians to 20th century surrealists. Mailing Add: 4520 Fourth Ave Moline IL 61265

STONE, GWEN
PAINTER, PRINTMAKER
b New York, NY, Feb 1, 13. Study: Col of Marin, Kentfield, Calif; San Francisco Art Inst, Calif; Univ Calif, Berkeley, teaching cert; also with Walt Kuhlman. Work: San Francisco Art Comn Civic Ctr; Monterey Peninsula Mus of Art, Calif; Clorox Corp, Oakland, Calif; Bank of Am World Hq, San Francisco; Int Bus Machines Corp, Palo Alto, Calif. Exhib: San Francisco Mus of Mod Art Ann, 59; Okla Nat Drawing & Watercolor Exhib, Okla Art Ctr, Oklahoma City, 65; one-person shows, Calif Palace of the Legion of Honor, San Francisco, 66 & 67, E B Crocker Art Gallery, Sacramento, Calif, 68 & San Jose Mus of Art, Calif, 76; Art in the Sixties, Univ Austin, Tex, 74; Works on Paper by Women Nat, Woman's Bldg, Los Angeles, Calif, 77. Teaching: Instr life drawing, Col of Marin, Kentfield, 67-69, instr design, 67-70, instr collage & assemblage, 75-77. Pos: Guest instr, Mendocino Art Ctr, Calif, summer 1970. Awards: Purchase Awards, San Francisco Art Festival, San Francisco Art Comn, 65, Nat Print Exhib, Col of Siskiyous, Weed, Calif, 75 & Painting & Print Exhib, Palo Alto Civic Ctr, Calif, 75. Bibliog: E M Polley (auth), East Bay, 65 & Marilyn Hagberg (auth), San Diego, 65, Artforum; Lynn Grant (auth), review in Visual Dialog, Vol 2 (1976). Mem: Ctr for Visual Arts, Oakland, Calif; Calif Soc of Printmakers, Berkeley, Style & Technique: Personal explorations in space and shapes: painting, prints, collages and soft sculpture. Media: Acrylic; Silkscreen; Fabric. Publ: Auth, Conversation with Robert Arneson, 76, Eleanor Bender talks with Gwen Stone, 76, Women Artists: Realities, 77 & Conversation with Wayne Thiebaud, 77, Visual Dialog. Mailing Add: Box L Suisun CA 94585

STONE, JOHN LEWIS, JR
PAINTER
b Presidio, Tex, Nov 24, 37. Study: Ft Worth Mus Fine Arts; Tex Christian Univ; Univ Tex, Arlington; Pa Acad Fine Arts. Work: Pvt collections of individuals & corporations. Exhib: 34th & 35th Ann, Miniature Painters, Sculptors & Gravers Soc, Washington, DC; Heritage Hall Mus, Ft Worth, 71; one-man show, Cross Gallery, 71 & 72; Snyder Mus Fine Art, 71; Longview Invitationals, 71 & 72. Teaching: Instr watercolor workshop, Tex Christian Univ. Awards: 34th Ann Borjorne' Egli Award & 35th Ann Elizabeth Curtis Award, Miniature Painters, Sculptors & Gravers Soc; First Prize in Drawing, Heritage Hall Mus, 70; Beggs Award for Watercolor, Snyder Mus Fine Art, 71. Media: Watercolor, Oil, Tempera. Mailing Add: c/o Gross Galleries 3629 W Seventh St Ft Worth TX 76107

STONE, SYLVIA
SCULPTOR
b Toronto, Ont; US citizen. Study: Pvt study in Can; Art Students League. Work: Walker Art Ctr, Minneapolis; Whitney Mus Am Art, New York; Hartford Atheneum, Conn; Xerox Corp, New York; Larry Aldrich Mus, Ridgefield, Conn. Comn: Sunrise Mall, comn by Tankoos-Muss Corp, New York, 73. Exhib: One-woman shows, Tibor de Nagy Gallery, 67-69, Andre Emmerich Gallery, 72, 75 & 77 & Bennington Col, 77; 14 Sculptors—Industrial Edge, Walker Art Ctr, Minneapolis, 69; Whitney Mus Am Art Sculpture Ann, New York, 69, 71 & 73; Plastic Presence, Jewish Mus, Milwaukee Art Ctr & San Francisco, 70; 200 Yrs Am Sculpture, Whitney Mus Am Art, New York, 75; Hayward Gallery, London, Eng, 75; 3rd Biennalle Small Sculpture, Budapest, Hungary, 75; plus others. Awards: Creative Artist Pub Serv Award, NY State, 71; Nat Endowment for the Arts, 76. Bibliog: M Friedman (auth), Sylvia Stone: industrial edge, Art Int, 70; Irv Sandler (auth), Sylvia Stone at Emmerich, Art in Am, 72 & Sylvia Stone's Egyptian Gardens, Arts Mag, 4/77; Corrinne Robbins, The edges of illusions, Art Spectrum, 75. Media: Plexiglas. Dealer: Andre Emmerich Gallery 41 E 57th St New York NY 10022. Mailing Add: 435 W Broadway New York NY 10013

STONE, WILLARD
DESIGNER, SCULPTOR
b Oktaha, Okla, Feb 29, 16. Study: Bacone Col, Muskogee, Okla; spec studies under Acee Blue Eagle and Woodrow Crumbo. Work: Gilcrease Mus, Tulsa, Okla; Nat Cowboy Hall of Fame, Oklahoma City; Okla State Univ; Okla Hist Bldg, Oklahoma City. Comn: Sequoyah the Teacher, 65 & Alice Brown Davis (chief of the Seminoles), 67, Okla Hist Soc; bust of Henry Bellmon, Gov Okla, 66; The Good Earth (mural), pvt collection, 71; Chiefs of the Five Civilized Tribes, Five Civilized Tribes Mus, currently. Exhib: One-man shows, Kennedy Galleries, New York, Gilcrease Mus, Tulsa, Philbrook Art Ctr, Tulsa, El Paso Mus Art, Tex & Tex Tech Univ. Pos: Artist in residence, Thomas Gilcrease Mus, 46-49; pattern maker designer, Ernest Ornamental Iron Works, 48-50; tool designer, die maker, Douglas Aircraft, 50-59. Awards: Waite Phillips Trophy Grand Award, Philbrook Art Ctr, 72; Grand Award, Five Civilized Tribes Mus, 73 & Masters Grand Award, 74. Mem: Gilcrease Mus; Nat Cowboy Hall of Fame; Five Civilized Tribes Mus; Green Country Artists Asn; Ozark Arts-Crafts Asn. Media: Sculpture in Wood & Bronze. Res: Bronze busts of old Indian chiefs, years 1800-1860. Mailing Add: Star Rte E Box 6 Locust Grove OK 74352

STONEBARGER, VIRGINIA
PAINTER, INSTRUCTOR
b Ann Arbor, Mich, Mar 9, 26. Study: Antioch Col, BA, 50; Colorado Springs Fine Arts Ctr, 50-51; Art Students League, 51-52; Hans Hofmann Sch, 54; NY Univ, 54 & 56; Univ Wis-Milwaukee, MS, 72. Exhib: Univ Minn, 54; Art: USA, 58; Univ Wis, 59; Milwaukee Art Ctr, 59-61; one-woman shows, Lakeland Col, 69 & Univ Wis, 71; plus many others. Teaching: Instr art, Univ Lake Sch, Hartland, Wis, 59-62; instr art, Waukesha Co Tech Inst, 70-72; instr, Milwaukee Area Tech Col, Com Art Inst, 73-77. Awards: Prize, Watertown, Wis, 58; Prize, Milwaukee Art Ctr, 60; Danforth Found Fel, 69; plus others. Mem: Wis Women in the Arts. Mailing Add: 2443 N Cramer Milwaukee WI 53211

STONEHAM, JOHN
ART LIBRARIAN
b Eng, Oct 1, 29; US citizen. Teaching: Teacher litt, Md Inst. Pos: Co-ed, The Lively Arts, Baltimore, 59-61; head librn, Md Inst, 65- Mem: Worst Verse Conspiracy of Baltimore (co-founder); Art Libr Soc NAm. Res: Bad verse, military costume, curiosa, fox-hunting, Chaucer, Malory and graffiti. Publ: Auth, bk reviews in Baltimore Sun, 54-67. Mailing Add: Md Inst Col of Art 1400 Cathedral St Baltimore MD 21201

STONER, JOYCE HILL
CONSERVATOR, ART EDITOR
b Washington, DC, Oct 9, 46. Study: Col William & Mary, BA(fine arts; summa cum laude); NY Univ, Inst Fine Arts, Conserv Ctr, MA(fine arts) & dipl conserv, spec grad study with Bernard Rabin. Work: Paintings (conservation treatments), Freer Gallery of Art, Smithsonian Inst, Washington, DC, Winterthur Mus, Del, Va Mus Fine Arts, Richmond, Colonial Williamsburg, Del Art Mus, Wilmington; murals (in consult with Susanne P Sack), New York Pub Libr. Exhibitions Arranged: Know What You See, a traveling exhib organized by Louis Pomerantz, Found Am Inst Conserv & Smithsonian Inst Traveling Exhib Serv, 76; Flaking, Foxing and Fine Works, conserv exhib, Del Art Mus, 77. Teaching: Assoc prof intro art conserv, Va Commonwealth Univ, 75-76; asst prof paintings conserv, Univ Del, 76- Pos: Managing ed, Art & Archaeol Tech Abstracts, 69-; consult conserv paintings, Freer Gallery Art, 75-76; exec dir, Found Am Inst Conserv, 75-; paintings conservator, Winterthur Mus, Del, 76- Mem: Phi Beta Kappa; assoc mem, Int Inst Conserv Historic & Artistic Works; fel Am Inst Conserv Historic & Artistic Works; Found Am Inst Conserv (exec dir, 75-); Fac Energy Conserv Workshops, Am Asn Mus; Int Coun Mus. Res: History of art conservation in America. Publ: Auth, The Use of Computers in Museums, Int Inst for Conserv—Am Group Tech Papers, 68-70; co-auth, Linseed Oil—Metal Acetylacetonate Systems, II Fungicidal Studies on Canvas Supports, J Paint Technol, 12/75; auth, An Oral History Archive, Mus News, 77; ed, Annotated Bibliography of the Care of Collections During an Energy Crisis, Am Asn Mus Energy Workshop Planning Comt, 78; auth, Pioneers in American Museums—George L Stout, Mus News, 78. Mailing Add: Winterthur Mus Winterthur DE 19735

STONES, MARGARET ALISON
ART HISTORIAN
b England, Mar 11, 42. Study: Univ London, BA(French & German), 64, PhD(hist of art), 70. Teaching: Assoc prof Medieval art, Univ Minn, 69-; vis prof Medieval art, Univ Reading, 75. Mem: Medieval Acad Am; Brit Archaeol Asn; Int Arthurian Soc; Int Ctr Medieval Art. Res: Manuscript illumination. Publ: Contribr, Secular Manuscript Illumination in France, Medieval Manuscripts, Univ NC, 76; contribr, Sacred and Profane Art: Secular and Liturgical Book—Illumination in the Thirteenth Century, The Epic in Medieval Soc, Tubingen, 77; contribr, The Earliest illustrated prose Lancelot MS.?, Reading Medieval Studies III, 77; auth, The Minnesota Vincent of Beauvais from Cambron, James Ford Bell Libr, Univ Minn, 77; co-auth, Medieval Illumination, Glass and Sculpture in Minnesota Collections (catalogue), Univ Minn, 78. Mailing Add: Dept of Art Hist Univ of Minn Minneapolis MN 55455

STORER, INEZ MARY
PAINTER, ART DEALER
b Santa Monica, Calif, Oct 11, 33. Study: Univ Calif, Berkeley, 54-55; San Francisco Art Inst with Nathan Oliviera, 55; Los Angeles Art Ctr with Lorser Feitleson, 56; Dominican Col, BA, 70; San Francisco State Univ, MA, 71. Work: Oakland Art Mus, Calif; Dallas Art Mus; United Gas & Pipeline, Houston; Container Corp of Am; Ammex Corp, Ga. Exhib: One-man shows, Reno Mus of Art, Nev, 65, Mills Col, Oakland, 74; Re: Vision Gallery, Los Angeles, 76 & San Francisco Mus Mod Art, 78; Painting & Sculpture Ann, Richmond Art Ctr, Calif, 66; San Francisco Women Artists Ann, San Francisco Mus of Mod Art, 68; Interstices, Cranbrook Acad of Art Mus, Bloomfield Hills, Mich, 75, Flint Inst of Arts, Mich, 75 & San Jose Mus of Art, Calif, 75; Inst for Int Printmaking, Rice Univ, Houston, 76; Women on Paper, Harry Anderson Collection, Palo Alto, Calif, 76; San Francisco Art Mus, 77; San Francisco Art Inst Ann 1977; Bay Area Artists Exhib, Oakland Art Mus, 77. Teaching: Prof painting, Col of Marin, Kentfield, 69-; lectr, San Francisco State Univ, 70-72; prof painting, Calif State Col, Sonoma, 76- & Univ Calif, Santa Cruz, 76. Pos: Dir, Lester Gallery of Contemp Art, 73-; invited artist, Int Inst for Experimental Printmaking, San Francisco, 75- Bibliog: Roberta Loach (critic/ed), Visual Dialogue, Winter 1976 & Greece, 77, Art Mag. Mem: San Francisco Art Dealers Asn (mem bd dirs, 75-). Style & Technique: Collage, assemblage, enamel on Plexiglass imagery. Media: Small Scupture; Collage/Assemblage. Publ: Illusr, Laura N Baker (auth), O Children of the Wind and Pines, Lippincott, 67; illusr, Floating Island: Collection of Poetry, Michael Sikes, 77. Dealer: Smith Anderson 200 Homer St Palo Alto CA 94301 Mailing Add: PO Box 117 Inverness CA 94937

STORM, HOWARD
PAINTER
b Newton, Mass, Oct 26, 46. Study: Denison Univ; J Ferguson Stained Glass Studio, Weston, Mass, apprenticeship; San Francisco Art Inst, BFA, 69; Univ Calif, Berkeley, MA, 70, MFA, 72. Work: Roswell Mus, NMex; Denison Univ; Mt St Joseph Col (Ohio); Ky Arts Comn, Frankfort; Baylor Univ. Exhib: One-man shows, San Francisco Art Inst, 69, Roswell Mus, 71, Berkeley Mus, 72 & Baylor Univ, 73; Huntington Galleries, 72-74; Univ Cincinnati, 74; Cincinnati Art Mus, 75; plus others. Teaching: Asst prof painting, Northern Ky State Col, 72- Pos: Artist in residence grant, Roswell Mus, 71-72. Awards: Eisner Prize, Univ Calif, Berkeley, 72; Purchase Award, Preview '73; Purchase Award, Huntington Galleries. Mem: Col Art Asn Am; Mid-west Art Asn. Style & Technique: Painted wood sculpture. Media: Acrylic. Mailing Add: 247 Licking Pike Alexandria KY 41001

STORM, LARUE
PAINTER, SCULPTOR
b Pittsburgh, Pa. Study: Univ Miami, AB & MA; Art Students League, Woodstock; also printmaking with Calvaert Brun, Paris & study in Los Angeles & Mich. Work: Lowe Mus, Coral Gables, Fla; Columbia Mus Art, Ga; Norton Gallery Art, West Palm Beach, Fla. Exhib: Corcoran Gallery Art Biennial, Washington, DC, 57; Butler Inst Am Art, Youngstown, Ohio, 58-60; Miami Six, El Paso Mus, 65; Fla Creates, var mus Fla, 71-; one-man show, Lowe Mus Art, Norton Gallery Art & Columbia Mus Art; plus others. Teaching: Instr drawing & design, Univ Miami, 67- Media: Graphic. Publ: Auth, Jose Guadalupe Posada: Guerrilla Fighter of the Throwaways, Carrell, 70. Mailing Add: 3737 Justison Rd Coconut Grove Miami FL 33133

STORM, MARK (KENNEDY)
PAINTER, ILLUSTRATOR
b Valdez, Alaska, Sept 4, 11. Study: Univ Tex Archit Sch, 30-34. Work: Old Court House Mus, Lincoln, NMex; Tex Ranger Mus, Waco, Tex. Comn: Oil painting, Int Ropes Ltd, London, 69; murals, Mus Nat Sci, Houston, 70; oil painting, Houston Livestock Show & Rodeo, 73; oil paintings, Melacres Charolais Ranch, Chapel Hill, Tex, 74 & Pearce Indust Inc, Houston, 77. Exhib: 1st Ann Tex Cowboy Artists Asn Show, Salado, Tex, 73; 2nd Ann Tex Cowboy Artists Asn Show, Snyder, 74; When You Say Cowboy, Amarillo Art Ctr, Tex, 74; Tex Cowboy Artists', Phippen-O'Brien Gallery, Scottsdale, Ariz, 74; Tex Cowboy Artists, Stamford Art Found, Tex, 74; Ann Tex Cowboy Artists, Amarillo, 75 & 76, Snyder, 77. Pos: Art classification, Rotary Club of Houston, 61-; Western artist, Houston C of C, 73- Awards: Best of Show, Ann Tex Cowboy Artists Show, 76, Best of Show Runner-up, 77. Bibliog: Jim Scarbrough (auth), Mark Storm, Quarter Horse J, 71; Leon Hale (auth), Cowboy artist..., Houston Post, 74. Mem: Tex Cowboy Artists Asn (chmn bd dir, 73, pres, 75-76). Style & Technique: Representative. Media: Oil, Pen and Ink, Acrylic, Gouache. Publ: Illusr, Picture Tales from Mexico, 41; illusr, Marsmen in Burma, 49; illusr, Texas Brags, 50; auth & illusr, Gruyo of the Flying H, 56; contribr, XIT—The American Cowboy, Oxmoor. Dealer: Gallery at Shoal Creek 1500 W 34th St Austin TX 78731. Mailing Add: 2322 University Blvd Houston TX 77005

STORY, WILLIAM EASTON
PAINTER, GALLERY DIRECTOR
b Valley City, NDak, Feb 13, 25. Study: Art Inst Chicago, BFA; Ball State Teachers Col, MA; also with Stanley William Hayter. Work: Butler Inst Am Art, Youngstown, Ohio; Ball State Univ Art Gallery. Exhib: Whitney Mus Am Art Ann, 57; Corcoran Gallery 25th Biennial, Washington, DC, 57; Cincinnati Art Mus 2nd Interior Valley Competition, 58; Artistas Brasileiros E Am, Mus Art Mos, Sao Paulo, Brazil, 60; Collages by American Artists, Ball State Univ Art Gallery, 72. Teaching: Asst prof art & supvr art gallery, Ball State Univ, 56-66. Pos: Asst dir, Am Mus in Brit, Bath, Eng, 66-68; dir, Parrish Art Mus, Southampton, 68-69; dir, Ella Sharp Mus, Jackson, Mich, 69-72; dir, Ball State Univ Art Gallery, 72- Mem: Am Asn Mus; Midwest Mus Asn; Asn Ind Mus. Publ: Contribr, America in Britain, 67 & 68. Mailing Add: Art Gallery Ball State Univ Muncie IN 47306

STOUT, GEORGE LESLIE
ART CONSULT
b Winterset, Iowa, Oct 5, 97. Study: Univ Iowa, BA, 21; Harvard Univ, AM, 29; Clark Univ, hon LittD, 55. Pos: Head conserv, Fogg Art Mus, Harvard Univ, 29-47; dir, Worcester Art Mus, 47-54; dir, Isabella Stewart Gardner Mus, Boston, 55-70. Publ: Co-auth, Painting Materials, Van Nostrand Reinhold, 42; auth, The Care of Pictures, Columbia Univ, 48 & Dover, 75; auth, Treasures of the Isabella Stewart Gardner Museum, Crown, 69. Mailing Add: 350 Sharon Park Dr C-23 Menlo Park CA 94025

STOUT, MYRON STEDMAN
PAINTER
b Denton, Tex, Dec 5, 08. Work: Brooklyn Mus; Carnegie Mus, Pittsburgh; Guggenheim Mus, New York; Mus Mod Art, New York; Whitney Mus, New York. Exhib: Whitney Mus Am Art, 58; Mus Mod Art, 59; Jewish Mus, 63; Guggenheim Mus, 64-65; Corcoran Biennial, 69. Dealer: Richard Bellamy 1078 Madison Ave New York NY 10028. Mailing Add: 4 Brewster St Provincetown MA 02657

STOUT, RICHARD GORDON
PAINTER
b Beaumont, Tex, Aug 21, 34. Study: Cincinnati Art Acad, 52-53; Sch Art Inst Chicago, BFA, 57; Univ Tex, MFA, 69. Work: Mus Fine Arts, Houston; Dallas Mus Fine Arts; Marion Koogler McNay Art Inst, San Antonio; Rice Univ; Univ Houston. Comn: Mural, Tex Fine Arts Asn for Hemisfair, now in libr lobby, Univ Houston, 68. Exhib: Momentium Mid Continental Exhib, Chicago, 56-57; 2nd Int Triennial Oriental Colored Graphic, Basel, Switz, 61; One Hundred Contemporary American Draftsmen, Univ Mich, 63; Marion Koogler McNay Art Inst, 64 & 71; Contemporary Arts Mus, Houston, 75; plus others. Teaching: Instr painting, Mus Fine Arts, Houston, 58-67; assoc prof drawing & painting, Univ Houston, 67- Awards: Longview Purchase Prize, Jr Serv League, 65 & 72; Tex Fine Arts Asn Awards, 66 & 71; Houston Area Exhib First Prize, Blaffer Gallery, Univ Houston, 75; plus others. Mem: Mus Fine Arts, Houston (adv bd, 73-). Style & Technique: Non-figurative, evokative imagery, close color, somewhat geometric. Media: Acrylic. Dealer: Houston Galleries 2323 San Felipe Houston TX 77019. Mailing Add: 1213 Bonnie Brae Houston TX 77006

STOVALL, LUTHER MCKINLEY (LOU)
PRINTMAKER
b Athens, Ga, Jan 1, 37. Study: RI Sch Design; Howard Univ, BFA. Work: Nat Collection Fine Arts, Smithsonian Inst, Washington, DC; Ringling Mus; Corcoran Gallery Art; Washington Post Co. Comn: Poster, Peace Corps, Washington, DC, 70; poster, Houston Mus Fine Arts, 70; posters, Corcoran Gallery Art, Washington, DC, 70 & 71; Bikes Have Equal Rights (poster), DC Dept Motor Vehicles, Washington Ecol Ctr, 70-72; print, Equal Employment Opportunity Comn Portfolio, Washington, DC, 73; A Sense of Amity, comn by AFL-CIO, 76. Exhib: Prints & Posters, Corcoran Gallery Art, Du Pont Ctr, Washington, DC, 69-71; Johns Hopkins Ctr Advan Inst Study, Washington, DC, 70-71; Atlantic Christian Col, NC, 72; Traveling Exhib Prints & Posters, Baltimore Mus Art, Md, 72-73; two-man show (with Sam Gilliam), Fendrick Gallery, Washington, DC, 74; 'Tis Mindful of Sweetness, Fendrick Gallery, Washington, DC, 77. Teaching: Master printmaking & silkscreen, Workshop, Corcoran Gallery Art, 69-72. Pos: Dir, Workshop, Inc, 68- Awards: Stern Grant, 68-72; Individual Artist Grant, 72 & Workshop Grant, 72-76, Nat Endowment Arts. Bibliog: Jay Jacobs (auth), We have to like the way you look, Art Gallery, 3/70; Paul Richard (auth), The community art spirit, 3/73 & Art & energy, 11/13/74, Washington Post. Style & Technique: Expanding the possibilities of the silkscreen medium through use of stains, glazes, soft paper and new techniques in stenciling. Mailing Add: Workshop Inc 3145 Newark St NW Washington DC 20008

STOWMAN, ANNETTE BURR
PAINTER
b Paris, France, Jan 21, 09; US citizen. Study: Vassar Col, AB, 29; Art Students League, 56-58. Work: Hickory Art Mus, NC; Greenville Mus Art, SC; Tamahassee DAR Sch, SC; Riveredge Found Collection, Can. Exhib: New York City Ctr Gallery, 61; Nat Artists Club Exhib, 62; (olorama Gallery, New York World's Fair, 65; Volusia Co, Fla Regional Show, 68; Metrop Mus, 78; Goldsboro Art Mus, NC, 78. Teaching: Instr art, Daytona Community

Col Div Continuing Educ, 70- Awards: Hon Mention, Nat Artists Club, 62; Equal Award, Volusie Co Art Show, 68; First Prize, Daytona Art League, 71, Second Prize, 74; Artists Choice, New Smyrna Beach Artists Workshop, 72; Second Prize, New Smyrna Beach Art Fiesta, 72. Mem: Burr Artists; life mem Art Students League; New Smyrna Beach Artists Workshop; Daytona Art League; artist mem Nat League Am Pen Women. Style & Technique: Neo-impressionist landscapes in oil, broadly treated; expressionist acrylics. Media: Oil. Dealer: Burr Artists 15 Gramercy Park S New York NY 10003. Mailing Add: PO Box 278 Edgewater FL 32032

STRAIGHT, MICHAEL
COLLECTOR
b Southampton, NY, Sept 1, 16. Study: Cambridge Univ, MA. Collection: 15th, 16th and 17th century French and Italian paintings. Mailing Add: 3077 N St NW Washington DC 20007

STRAIGHT, ROBERT LARRY
PAINTER, EDUCATOR
b Halstead, Kans, Apr 19, 46. Study: Cranbrook Acad Art, MFA, study with George Ortman; Calif State Univ at Long Beach. Work: Downey Mus Art, Calif; State Univ Col, Potsdam, NY; City of Hartford, Conn. Exhib: Mich Artist Show, Detroit Inst Art, 70; Ga Artist Show, High Mus Art, Atlanta, 72; Contemporary Reflections, Aldrich Mus Contemp Art, Ridgefield, Conn, 75; Hunter Mus, Chattanooga, Tenn, 76; Tenn State Univ, Johnson City, 76; Russell Sage Col, Troy, NY, 76; Works on Paper, Kutztown State Col, Pa, 76; 27th Ann New Eng Exhib, The Silverman Guild, New Canaan, Conn, 77; one-man shows, Conn Col, New London, 74, Greater Reston Arts Ctr, 75 & Univ Del, Newark, 78. Teaching: Instr art, Spelman Col, Atlanta, Ga, 71-72; asst prof painting, Conn Col, New London, 72- Awards: Purchase Prize, Potsdam Nat Drawing Exhib, 75; artist-in-residence, Yaddo, Saratoga Springs, NY, 76. Mem: Col Art Asn. Style & Technique: Abstract paintings and reliefs using a variety of textures and materials. Media: Painting and Drawing. Mailing Add: 107 Nameaug Ave New London CT 06320

STRALEM, DONALD S
COLLECTOR, PATRON
b Port Washington, NY. Study: Harvard Univ, 24; Cambridge Univ, 25. Pos: Pres, Palm Springs Desert Mus, Calif. Mem: Fogg Art Mus (overseers comt). Collection: Impressionists, naifs. Mailing Add: 941 Park Ave New York NY 10028

STRASEN, BARBARA ELAINE
PAINTER, ENVIRONMENTAL ARTIST
b Brooklyn, NY, Aug 12, 42. Study: Yale Univ Sch Art, scholar, with Alex Katz, Bernard Chaet, summer 62; Carnegie-Mellon Univ, with Robert Lepper & Roger Anliker, BFA, 63; Univ Calif, Berkeley, Hassel Smith, Elmer Bischoff & Earl Loran, MA, 64. Exhib: One-woman shows, Dilexi Gallery, San Francisco, 68 & Louis K Meisel Gallery, New York, 75; Invitational Show, AIR Gallery, New York, 73; one-woman retrospective of 3-D paintings, San Jose State Univ, 75; Biennial Contemp Art, Whitney Mus Am Art, New York, 75; Parsons-Dreyfuss Gallery, New York, 77; Munic Art Gallery, Los Angeles, Calif, 78; plus many others. Teaching: Instr visual arts, Southwestern Col (Calif), 71-73; asst prof visual arts, Univ Calif, San Diego, 73-78. Pos: Mem performance group, Nine Women Artists, San Diego, 71-72. Awards: Individual Artists Fel, Nat Endowment Arts, 75-76; Creative Arts Grant, Regents of Univ of Calif, 76; res proj grants, Univ Calif, San Diego, 76 & 77. Bibliog: Noel Frackman (auth), rev in Arts Mag, 6/75; David Bourdon (auth), rev of show at Parsons-Dreyfuss Gallery, Village Voice, 6/13/77. Style & Technique: Representational painting, using painting and cutout shapes, photography and some video, in three parallel thinking modes, to develop narrative imagery. Media: Acrylic. Publ: Auth, Immigrants, J Los Angeles Inst Contemp Arts, 2/75. Dealer: Parsons-Dreyfuss Gallery 54 W 57th St New York NY 10019. Mailing Add: 930 Agate St San Diego CA 92109

STRATER, HENRY
PAINTER
b Louisville, Ky, Jan 21, 96. Study: Acad Julien, Paris; Art Students League; Pa Acad Fine Arts, with Arthur Carles & Charles Grafly; Acad San Fernando; Acad Grande Chaumiere, Paris; Ecole M Denis, with Edouard Vuillard; also with Ignacio Zuloaga, Spain. Work: Philadelphia Mus Art; Art Mus Princeton Univ; Detroit Inst Arts; City Art Mus St Louis; Butler Inst Am Art, Youngstown, Ohio. Exhib: Salon Automne, Paris, 22; Whitney Studio Club Portrait Exhib, 26; Brooklyn Mus Watercolor Ann, 26; Corcoran Gallery Art Biennial, Washington, DC, 32; IBM Gallery Sci & Art, Golden Gate Expos, San Francisco, 39-40. Pos: Trustee, Mus Art Ogunquit, Maine, 52- Awards: Second Prize, Golden Gate Expos, IBM Fine Arts Collection, 39; Third Prize for Oil, Soc Four Arts, 47; First Prize for Drawing, Norton Gallery Art, 60. Bibliog: Sarah Lansdell (auth), An adventure in color, Courier-J Sun Illus Mag, 65; Betty Chamberlain (auth), Henry Strater: form and adventure through color, Am Artists, 5/72; Henry Strater (film), Jane Morrison Prod, 75; plus others. Mem: Ogunquit Art Asn (pres, 46-48); The Players, New York; Arts Club, Louisville; Soc Four Arts; Palm Beach Art Inst. Style & Technique: New realism; luminous color based on bold contrasts and subtle gradations; versatile in subject matter. Media: Oil. Publ: Illusr, 14 Cantos, Ezra Pound, Three Mts Press, Paris, 23; contribr, Living American Art, 35-37; auth, 24 Drawings by Henry Strater, Anthoenson, 58; ed, Henry Strater, 62; ed, Henry Strater, New Paintings, Frank Rehn Gallery, 67. Dealer: Frank Rehn Gallery 655 Madison Ave New York NY 10021. Mailing Add: Shore Rd Ogunquit ME 03907

STRATTON, DOROTHY (MRS WILLIAM A KING)
PAINTER, PRINTMAKER
b Worcester, Mass. Study: Pratt Inst, cert, 42; Brooklyn Mus Sch, 42-43; Univ Calif, with Rico Lebrun, 56-57; Univ Calif, Los Angeles, 61; Univ Calif, San Diego, 66-67. Work: Long Beach Mus Art; Tunisian Ministry Cult Affairs, Tunis; Los Angeles Munic Art Collection, City Hall; Art in Embassies, Dept of State, Washington, DC; Southwestern Col (Calif). Exhib: One-woman shows, Pasadena Art Mus, 59, La Jolla Mus Art, 62 & Tunisian Comt Cult Coop US Info Serv, Tunis, 65; Art in Embassies Prog, 18 countries, 65-79; Calif Soc Printmakers Nat, Richmond Art Ctr, 72; Univ San Diego, 73. Pos: Miniature set decorator, Paramount Pictures, George Pal Prod, 45-47; gallery receptionist & ed publicity, Munic Art Dept, Los Angeles, 52-61; registr & mem secy, La Jolla Mus Art, 64-65, vol art ref libr, 66-74; mem, Contemp Art Comt, Fine Arts Soc, San Diego, 72-79. Awards: Twenty-six. Mem: Artists Equity Asn (publicity comt, 46-50); Fine Arts Gallery of San Diego; La Jolla Mus of Contemp Art; Los Angeles Co Mus of Art; life mem Westwood Art Asn (pres, 56-57); Arts Coun, Univ Calif, Los Angeles (fine arts comt rep, 57-62). Style & Technique: Stems from nature and living forces in our environment; from representational to abstraction, with a personal idiom. Mailing Add: 7820 Roseland Dr PO Box 2151 La Jolla CA 92038

STRAUSER, STERLING BOYD
PAINTER
b Bloomsburg, Pa, Aug 15, 07. Study: Bloomsburg State Col, with George Keller, BA. Work: Cheekwood Mus, Nashville, Tenn; Everhart Mus, Scranton, Pa; Lehigh Univ; Vanderbilt Univ; E Stroudsburg State Col. Exhib: Art: USA, 58, New York, 58; Sports & Recreation Panorama, Munic Art Gallery, Davenport, Iowa, 59; one-man show, Lehigh Univ, 61, Lyzon Gallery, Nashville, 65- & William Penn Mus, Harrisburg, Pa, 73. Awards: Top Award Regional Art Exhib, Everhart Mus, 58. Bibliog: Lee Nordness (auth), The great momentalist, 6/58 & David Burliuk (auth), American momentalist, 6/61, Color & Rhyme. Style & Technique: Romantic expressionist using floating oil technique with heavy impasto. Media: Oil. Publ: Illusr, Mademoiselle, 6/56. Dealer: Lyzon Gallery 411 Thompson Lane Nashville TN 37211. Mailing Add: 150 Analomink St East Stroudsburg PA 18301

STRAUTMANIS, EDVINS
PAINTER, SCULPTOR
b Liepaja, Latvia, Oct 27, 33. Study: Art Inst of Chicago, 52-56, dipl; Univ Chicago, 58-59. Work: Gov's State Univ, Park Forest South, Ill; Chase Manhattan Bank, New York; HMH Publ Co, Chicago. Comn: Steel outdoor sculpture (16ft x 18ft x 24ft), Lewis Manilow, 69, now owned by Gov's State Univ, 76. Exhib: Soc for Contemp Art, Art Inst of Chicago, 65, 66 & 70; Sculpture Ann, Whitney Mus of Am Art, New York, 68; Painting: Off the Wall, Des Moines Art Ctr, Iowa, 68; Contemp Am Painting & Sculpture, Krannert Art Mus, Champaign, Ill, 69; Painting & Sculpture Today, Indianapolis Mus of Art, 70 & 74 & Contemp Art Ctr & Taft Mus, Cincinnati, 74. Bibliog: Dennis Adrian (auth), Art panorama, Chicago Daily News, 3/73; Whee Kim (auth), Definition of pictorial space, Arts Mag, 4/74. Style & Technique: Painting large formats, acrylic and oil; sculpture, steel and wood. Dealer: Allan Stone Gallery 48 E 86th St New York NY 10028. Mailing Add: 69 Green St New York NY 10012

STRAWBRIDGE, EDWARD R
PAINTER
b Nov 22, 03; US citizen. Study: Grad of Pa Mus & Sch of Indust Art; Chester Springs; Cape Cod Sch Art. Exhib: Pa Acad Fine Arts; NJ State Mus, Trenton; Harrisburg State Mus, Pa; Oakland Art Gallery, Calif; Nat Acad Design, New York; John Herron Art Inst, Indianapolis, Ind; one-man shows: Palace of Legion of Honor, San Francisco & Philadelphia Art Alliance. Mem: Philadelphia Water Color Club; Am Water Color Soc; Philadelphia Sketch Club; Soc of Western Artists. Mailing Add: 800 Longfield Rd Erdenheim PA 19118

STRAWN, MELVIN NICHOLAS
PAINTER, SCULPTOR
b Boise, Idaho, Aug 5, 29. Study: Chouinard Art Inst; Los Angeles Co Art Inst; Jepson Art Inst; Calif Col Arts & Crafts, BFA & MFA. Work: Oakland Art Mus; Antioch Col; Colo State Univ. Comn: Environ design (sculpture), Ottawa Col, Kans, 72. Exhib: Colo State Univ Centennial Exhib, 70; Cedar City Nat, Utah, 72; I-25 Artists Alliance, Colorado Springs Fine Arts Ctr, 72; plus others. Teaching: Instr art, Midwestern Univ, Mich State Univ, Antioch Col & Univ Denver, 56-72; chmn dept art, Antioch Col, 66-69; dir, Sch Art, Univ Denver, 69- Awards: First Purchase Award, Colo State Univ Centennial, 70. Mem: I-25 Artists Alliance; Col Art Asn Am. Media: Oil. Mailing Add: 7 S Lane Cherry Hills Village CO 80110

STREET, JOHN MICHAEL
PAINTER
b Toronto, Ont, Sept 14, 42. Study: Ont Col Art. Work: McLaughlin Art Gallery, Oshawa, Ont; Ont Inst Studies Educ, Toronto; Can Art Bank, Ottawa; Toronto-Dom Bank; Edward F Albee Found; plus others. Exhib: Int Exhib Graphics, Montreal Mus Fine Art, 71; one-man shows, Shaw-Rimmington Gallery, Toronto, 72, Galerie Gilles Gheerbrant, Montreal, 74 & Loranger Gallery, Toronto, 78; 9 out of 10, Art Gallery of Hamilton, 74; group show, Aames Gallery, New York, 74; plus many others. Pos: Layout & design artist, 61-71. Awards: Purchase Award, Ont Soc Artists 100th Ann Open Exhib, 72. Style & Technique: Mixed media work in printing, drawing and painting. Media: Printing; Drawing, Painting. Dealer: Loranger Gallery 180 Bloor St W Toronto ON Can. Mailing Add: 2072 Jeanne-Mance Montreal PQ H2X 2J5 Can

STREETER, TAL
SCULPTOR
b Oklahoma City, Okla, Aug 1, 34. Study: Univ Kans, BFA & MFA; Colorado Springs Fine Arts Ctr, with Robert Motherwell; Colo Col; with Seymour Lipton, 3 yrs. Work: Mus Mod Art, New York; San Francisco Mus Art; Wadsworth Atheneum, Hartford, Conn; Nat Collection Fine Arts, Smithsonian Inst, Washington, DC; Smith Col Mus Art. Comn: Ark Art Ctr, Little Rock; Gt Southwest Park, High Mus Art, Mem Arts Ctr, Atlanta, Ga; Sculpture in Environment, New York City Parks Dept; Hong-Ik Univ, Seoul, Korea. Exhib: American Sculpture, Sheldon Mem Art Gallery, Lincoln, 70; Painting & Sculpture Today, Indianapolis Mus Art, 70; Cool Art & Highlights of the Season, Larry Aldrich Mus, Ridgefield, Conn, 70; Red Line in the Sky: Tal Streeter's Kites, Univ Kans Mus Art, 72; Outdoor Sculptors Indoors, Storm King Art Ctr, Mountainville, NY, 72 & 74; Eight Am Artists, Am Cult Ctr, Seoul, Korea, 73; Hudson River Mus, New York, 74. Teaching: Vis artist, Fairleigh Dickinson Univ, Madison Campus, 62; vis artist in residence, Dartmouth Col, 63; vis artist, Univ NC, Greensboro, 70 & 72-73; Fulbright prof, Seoul, Korea, 71; vis lectr, US Info Serv, Japan, 72; adj prof, Queen's Col, 73; adj prof, State Univ NY Col Purchase, 74- Awards: State Univ NY Int Studies Grant, Japan, 69. Bibliog: Joseph Love (auth), Dolmens in the Vast Field of a Domed Sky, Minami Gallery, Tokyo, 71; G A Ruda (auth), Kitesmanship: Tal Streeter, Craft Horizons, 74; Donald Ritchie (auth), Kite crazy, Natural Hist, 75; plus others. Style & Technique: Metaphysics in search of form. Media: Steel, Paper. Publ: Auth, Seymour Lipton, the Sculptor's Way, 61 & Kite: Red Line in the Sky, 72, Univ Kans Mus Art; auth, Red Line to the Sky: Notebook for a Contemporary Monument, Space Design, 71; auth, The Art of the Japanese Kite, Weatherhill/Lippincott, 74. Dealer: A M Sachs Gallery 29 W 57th St New York NY 10019; Lippincott Large-Scale Sculpture 400 Sackett Point Rd North Haven CT 06473. Mailing Add: Old Verbank Sch Millbrook NY 12545

STREETMAN, JOHN WILLIAM, III
ART ADMINISTRATOR
b Marion, NC, Jan 19, 41. Study: Western Carolina Univ, AB(Eng, theatre hist, criticism); Oxford Univ Lincoln Col, cert Shakespeare studies. Collections Arranged: Indonesia, Jewel of the East Indies, 71; Two American Realists: William Bailey and DeWitt Hardy (under grant from New York Times Media Publ), 73 & 74. Pos: Founding dir, Jewett Creative Arts Ctr, South Berwick, Maine, 66-70; exec dir, Polk Pub Mus, Lakeland, Fla, 70-75; dir, Mus Arts & Sci, Evansville, Ind, 75- Mem: Fla Art Mus Dirs Asn; Fla League Arts (bd dirs & trustee); Am Asn Mus; Midwestern Mus Conf. Mailing Add: 411 SE Riverside Dr Evansville IN 47713

STREETT, TYLDEN WESTCOTT
SCULPTOR, EDUCATOR
b Baltimore, Md, Nov 28, 22. Study: Johns Hopkins Univ; St John's Col; Md Inst Col Art, with Sidney Waugh & Cecil Howard, BFA & MFA; also asst to Lee Lawrie. Comn: Archit sculpture, Kirk in the Hills, Bloomfield Hills, Mich, 57; archit sculpture (with Lee Lawrie) West Point, NY, 58; archit sculpture, Cathedral, Washington, DC, 59; archit sculpture, Roland Park Presby Church, Washington, DC, 59; archit sculpture, Kuwait Embassy, Washington, DC, 65. Exhib: Corcoran Gallery Art, Washington, DC, 60; Baltimore Mus Art, 69. Teaching: Instr sculpture, Md Inst Col Art, Baltimore, 59-, dir, Grad Studies, 66-; instr sculpture, Jewish Community Ctr, Baltimore, 63-65. Awards: Rinehart Traveling Fel, 53; Louis Comfort Tiffany Found Award, 56; John Gregory Award, 62. Mem: Nat Sculpture Soc; Artists Equity Asn. Style & Technique: Figurative. Publ: Auth, Plaster Casting Using a Waste Mold (film), 70. Dealer: Phoenix Galleries 5 W Chase St Baltimore MD 21201. Mailing Add: 4622 Keswick Rd Baltimore MD 21210

STREL, DONALD O
MUSEUM DIRECTOR
b San Francisco, Calif, Sept 24, 34. Study: San Francisco State Col, BA(design), MA(creative arts). Collections Arranged: Scholder & Gorman, 73; African Art, 74; Agnes Martin Serigraphs, 74; Watercolor NMex, 74; Louis Ribak Retrospective, 75; Patterns & Fields, 75; Visions From Another World, 75; Landscape Painting in NMex, 75. Teaching: Instr, San Francisco State Col, 66-67; asst prof art, Northern Ill Univ, 67-72; dir art workshops, Colo Projs & instr art, Young Artists Studios, Sch Art Inst Chicago, 68-70. Pos: Juror, Taos Ann, 72, Southern Colo Ann, 73, Mus Southwest, 74, Mus Albuquerque, 74 & Pac Northwest Ann, 77; dir, Mus Fine Arts, Santa Fe, 72- Mem: Am Mus Asn. Mailing Add: Mus Fine Arts Santa Fe NM 87501

STRICKLAND, ALLEN
PAINTER
b Washington, DC. Study: Corcoran Art Sch; also with Bourgonier & Morriset, Paris. Exhib: Salon des Artistes Francaises; Nat League Am Pen Women; one-man shows, 66 & 75, Two-man show, 73; Beaux Arts, Daytona Beach, Fla, 75. Awards: Lillian Gittner Award for Portraits, Daytona Beach Art League, 73-74; First Prize, Beaux Arts, Daytona Beach, 75; plus many others. Bibliog: Article in Daytona Beach Sun News Jour, 7/19/70. Mem: Daytona Beach Art League; Nat League Am Pen Women; Beaux Arts of Daytona Beach; St Augustine Art Asn. Style & Technique: Representational, impressionistic, portraits. Media: Oil. Mailing Add: 487 John Anderson Ormond Beach FL 32014

STRICKLAND, THOMAS J
PAINTER
b Keyport, NJ, Dec 28, 32. Study: Newark Sch Fine & Indust Arts, NJ; Am Art Sch & Nat Acad Fine Arts, New York, with Robert Philipp. Work: Elliott Mus, Stuart, Fla; Hollywood Art Mus, Fla; St Hugh Catholic Church; St Vincent Col. Exhib: Metrop Young Artists 1st Ann, Nat Arts Club, 58, Am Artists Prof League, 58 & 61; Butler Inst Am Art Fine Arts Festival, Youngstown, Ohio, 63; 7th Grand Prix Int Peinture Cote d'Azur, Cannes, France, 71; Hollywood Art Mus, Fla, 72 & 75; Cape Coral Nat Art Show, Fla, 73; Martin Co Hist Soc, Elliott Mus, Fla, 74; Am Painters in Paris, 75; plus others. Awards: Digby Chandler Prize, Knickerbocker Artists Exhib, 65; First Prize, Hollywood Arts & Crafts Guild Ann Mems Art Exhib, 72; First Prize, Hollywood Art Mus Ann Regional Show, Fla, 73; Charles Hawthorne Mem Award, Nat Arts Club, 77; plus others. Bibliog: Ann D Browne (auth), Personality of the month, Directions, 12/73; Lawrence T Mahoney (auth), The 2703 faces of Tom Strickland, Tropic, 8/15/76. Mem: Grove House, Miami; Miami Art Ctr; Miami Palette Club; Pastel Soc of Am; Nat Soc Lit & Arts. Style & Technique: Romantic and impressionistic; mostly of women; stressing color, light on form and drawing. Media: Oil, Pastel. Publ: Auth, A painting demonstration by Thomas J Strickland, Directions, 5/74 & 7/74; auth, The impressionistic pastels of Thomas J Strickland, Today's Art, 5/76, Painting self-portraits, 7/76 & How Thomas Strickland paints a still life, 3/77. Mailing Add: 2598 Taluga Dr Miami FL 33133

STRIDER, MARJORIE VIRGINIA
SCULPTOR
b Guthrie, Okla. Study: Kansas City Art Inst, Mo; Okla Univ, BFA. Work: Albright-Knox Mus, Buffalo, NY; Univ of Colo Mus, Boulder; Wadsworth Atheneum, Hartford, Conn; Larry Aldrich Mus, Conn, NY Univ, New York; Des Moines Art Ctr, Iowa; Hirshhorn Mus, Washington, DC; plus others. Exhib: One-woman shows, Hoffman Gallery, New York, 73 & 74, The Clocktower, New York, NY, 77 & City Univ Grad Ctr, New York, NY, 77; Whitney Sculpture Ann, Whitney Mus Am Art, New York, 70; PS1, Queens, NY, 77-78; plus others. Teaching: Prof sculpture, Sch Visual Arts, New York, 68-; prof sculpture, Univ Iowa, summer 70; prof sculpture, Univ Ga, summer 72; also lectr var univ & col throughout US. Awards: McDowell Colony Fel, 73; Longview Found Grant, 73; Nat Endowment Arts Grant, 74. Bibliog: L Lippard (auth), chap, In: Conceptual Art, 72 & Michael Kirby (auth), The New Theatre, 74, Dutton; M Compton (auth), chap, In: Movements of Modern Art, Hamlyn, 70; Gregory Battcock (auth), Super Realism, Dutton, 75; plus others. Style & Technique: Realistic painted sculpture and wall reliefs; very detailed. Media: Plastic, Bronze. Publ: Auth, Moving out-moving up, Art News, 1/71; auth, Radical scale, Art & Artists, 1/72; illusr & contribr, Modern American Painting & Sculpture, Abrams, 72. Dealer: Nancy Hoffman 429 W Broadway New York NY 10012. Mailing Add: 7 Worth St New York NY 10013

STRINGER, MARY EVELYN
EDUCATOR, ART HISTORIAN
b Huntsville, Mo, July 31, 21. Study: Univ Mo, AB; Univ NC, AM; Harvard Univ, univ traveling fel, 66-67, with Ernst Kitzinger, PhD, 73. Teaching: Prof art, Miss Univ Women, 47- Awards: Fulbright Scholar, 55-56; Danforth Found Grant, 59-60 & 64-65. Mem: Col Art Asn Am; Medieval Acad; Int Ctr Medieval Art; Southeastern Col Art Conf; Nat Orgn Women. Publ: Auth, Review of Andrew Martindale, Gothic Art, 69; auth, Composite nativity-adoration of English medieval alabasters, NC Mus Art Bull, 70. Mailing Add: Box 1109 College Station Columbus MS 39701

STRISIK, PAUL
PAINTER
b Brooklyn, NY, Apr 21, 18. Study: Art Students League, with Frank Vincent Dumond. Work: Parrish Mus Art, Southampton, NY; Percy H Whitney Mus, Fairhope, Ala; Mattatuck Mus, Conn; Utah State Univ; Union Carbide & Chem Collection. Exhib: Am Watercolor Soc Ann; Nat Acad Design Am; Allied Artists Am Ann; plus other nat shows. Awards: Bronze Medal of Honor, Nat Arts Club, 70; Best in Show, Am Artists Prof League Grant Nat, 72; Obrig Prize, Nat Acad Design, 72; plus many others. Mem: Rockport Art Asn (pres, 68-72); assoc Nat Acad Design; Am Watercolor Soc; Allied Artists Am; Knickerbocker Artists. Media: Oil, Watercolor, Acrylic. Publ: Auth, Watercolor page, Am Artists, 4/70. Mailing Add: 123 Marmion Way Rockport MA 01966

STROMBOTNE, JAMES
PAINTER
b Watertown, SDak, 1934. Study: Pomona Col, BA; Claremont Grad Sch, MFA. Work: Whitney Mus Am Art; Mus Mod Art, New York; Cleveland Art Mus; Amon Carter Mus Western Art; Santa Barbara Mus; plus many others. Exhib: One-man shows, Redlands Univ & Univ Calif, Riverside, 60, Pasadena Art Mus & Nexus Gallery, La Jolla, Calif, 61, Bertha Schaefer Gallery, New York, 66, 68 & 73, Mt San Antonio Col, Calif, 67, San Jose State Col, Calif, 68 & 77, Richard Capper Gallery, San Francisco, 68 & 71, Santa Barbara Mus Art, Calif, 71, Jodi Scully Gallery, Los Angeles, 72 & 74, James Willis Gallery, San Francisco, 73 & 77 & Int Mus of Erotic Art, San Francisco, 75; Whitney Mus Am Art, 60-63; Carnegie Inst Int, 64; Am Fedn Arts, 64; New Sch Social Res, NY, 64 & 68; Corcoran Gallery Art, 67; Painting & Sculpture in Calif: The Mod Era, Nat Gallery, Washington, DC & San Francisco Mus Mod Art, Calif; plus many others. Teaching: Mem, Inst Creative Arts, Univ Calif, 65-66. Awards: Honnold Traveling Fel, Pomona Col, 56; Guggenheim Fel, 62-63; Tamarind Lithography Workshop Fel, 68; plus others. Mailing Add: 31555 First Ave South Laguna CA 92677

STRONG, CHARLES RALPH
PAINTER, EDUCATOR
b Greeley, Colo, Dec 25, 38. Study: Coronado Sch Fine Art, 57; San Francisco Art Inst, BFA, 62, MFA, 63; also with Elmer Bischoff, Jack Jefferson, Frank Lobdell & James Weeks. Work: De Saisset Art Gallery, Univ Santa Clara; Oakland Mus, Calif; San Francisco Art Inst. Exhib: One-artist shows, Chief Joseph Series, Crown Col, Univ Calif, Santa Cruz, 72, James Willis Gallery, San Francisco, 73, Somona State Col, 73, Smith-Andersen Galleries, Palo Alto, 72 & 75 & San Francisco, 76 & James Willis Gallery, San Francisco, 76; Calif Works of Paper 1950-1971, Univ Art Mus, Berkeley, 72; three-artist show, Painted Images, Oakland Mus, 71; Linda Farris Gallery, Seattle, 74; Eastern Wash Hist Soc Traveling Exhib, Western US & Can, 74-76; Works on/of Paper, Zara Gallery, San Francisco, 77; Smith-Andersen Gallery, Palo Alto, 78; plus others. Teaching: Instr painting & drawing, San Francisco State Col, 65-68; lectr painting & drawing, Stanford Univ, summers 70, 71 & 74; assoc prof art, Col Notre Dame (Calif), 70-, gallery dir, 76- Awards: Fulbright Fel to Eng, 64. Bibliog: Work in The Paper Revolution, Am Artist, 8/77; Jules Heller (auth), Paper—the white art, 78; article, Visual Dialogue Mag, 78. Style & Technique: Large, painterly, non-objective; uses simple, sometimes geometric, shapes; since 76, paintings in the papermaking process. Dealer: Smith-Andersen Gallery 200 Homer Ave Palo Alto CA 94301. Mailing Add: Star Rte Box 79 Redwood City CA 94062

STRONGHILOS, CAROL
PAINTER
b New York, NY. Study: Hunter Col, MA; Art Students League; Brooklyn Mus Art Sch, study with Reuben Tam. Exhib: NJ State Mus, 72; Monmouth Col, 72; Brooklyn Mus, 74; Larry Aldrich Mus, 75; Women in the Arts, 76 & 77; Newark Mus, 77; Art in Pub Bldg, NY Orgn of Independent Artists, World Trade Ctr, 77; Women 78, Women's Caucus for the Arts, City Univ New York, 78; one-woman shows, Brooklyn Mus, 71 & Whitney Mus, 75. Teaching: Instr painting, Brooklyn Mus Art Sch, 71-77 & Brooklyn House of Detention, 74-77; instr painting & drawing, Five Towns Music & Art Ctr, 74-76. Pos: Founder, NY Feminist Art Inst, New York; consult, Am the Beautiful Fund, 76-77. Awards: Fac & Alumni First Prize, Brooklyn Mus, 70. Mem: Women in the Arts; Woman's Caucus for Art, Col Art Asn. Style & Technique: Large abstract color and texturized paintings concerned with movement and energy, applied by squeezing paint on canvas. Media: Acrylic. Mailing Add: 15 Laight St New York NY 10013

STROTHER, JOSEPH WILLIS
ART ADMINISTRATOR, PAINTER
b New Orleans, La, Dec 14, 33. Study: La Col, BA; Univ Ga, MA & EdD. Work: Chattahooche Art Asn Collection; Ga Mus of Art; NC Nat Bank Collection; Wachovia Bank State Collection; Ga Mus; Dillard Collection, Weatherspoon Gallery, Univ NC, Greensboro. Exhib: Mead Painting of Year, Atlanta, 61; four shows, Nat Art on Paper, Greensboro, 64-69; NC Artist Ann, 71-74; Ga Artist Ann, 72-74; Tex Ann, 74. Teaching: Art supvr, Marietta City Schs, Ga, 57-61; instr art, Montgomery Co, Md, 61-64; instr art, Univ NC, Greensboro, 64-66; assoc prof art, Univ Ga, 66-76; prof of art & dir, Sch of Art/Archit, La Tech Univ, 76- Awards: Purchase Award, Chattahooche Art Asn, 69; Award, Ocala Jr Col, 69; Purchase Award, NC Sch Ment Health Exten, Chapel Hill, 71. Mem: Nat Art Educ Asn; Col Art Asn Am. Media: Acrylic. Mailing Add: Sch of Art/Archit La Tech Univ Ruston LA 71272

STROTHER, VIRGINIA VAUGHN
PAINTER
b Ft Worth, Tex, July 19, 20. Study: Tex Christian Univ, BFA (with hons) & Spec Div Courses printmaking; watercolor with Barse Miller. Work: Tex Fine Arts Asn Permanent Collection, Austin; Univ Tex, Arlington; Sci Dept, Tex Christian Univ; Woman's Club Ft Worth Permanent Collection; plus many others. Exhib: Nat Invitational Art Exhib, Cedar City, Utah, 72-74; Tex Fine Arts Asn Nat Ann, Laguna Gloria Mus, Austin, 72 & 75; Delta Seven State Exhib, Ark Art Ctr, Little Rock, 72; El Paso Mus Nat Exhibs, 72 & 76; Eight State Exhib Painting & Sculpture, Okla Art Ctr, Oklahoma City, 74; Monroe Nat Ann, Masur Mus Art, La, 73; plus seven one-man exhibs. Teaching: Dir preparatory workshop art, Tex Christian Univ, 50-54. Awards: Citations & Travel Awards, Tex Fine Arts Asn, 69, 70 & 72; Award of Merit, NMex Art League, Albuquerque, 71; Award, Ft Worth Art Mus, 73. Mem: Ft Worth Art Mus; Tex Watercolor Soc; Tex Fine Arts Asn (state adv bd, 68-75); NMex Art League; Nat League Am Pen Women (pres, Ft Worth Br, 70-72). Style & Technique: Abstract design paintings in oil and acrylic; subjective watercolors. Dealer: Contemp Fine Arts Gallery 2425 Cedar Springs Dallas TX 75201. Mailing Add: 4109 Shannon Dr Ft Worth TX 76116

STROUD, PETER ANTHONY
PAINTER, EDUCATOR
b London, Eng, May 23, 21. Study: Teacher Training Col, London Univ, Central Hammersmith Schs Art, 48-53. Work: Tate Gallery, London; Guggenheim Mus, New York; Los Angeles Co Mus; Detroit Inst Fine Arts; Pasadena Art Mus. Comn: Mural, Int Union Archit Congress Bldg, London, 61; mural, State Sch Leverkusen, Ger, 63; mural, Mfrs Hanover Trust Co, New York, 69. Exhib: Carnegie Inst Int, Pittsburgh, 61 & 64; Guggenheim Mus Int, 64; The Responsive Eye, Mus Mod Art, New York, 65; European Painters Today, Jewish Mus, New York, 68; Mus Mod Art, Oxford, Eng, 69; Nat Gallery of Victoria, Melbourne, Australia, 70; Univ Calif, Santa Barbara, 70; Ulster Mus, Belfast, Northern Ireland, 71; Finch Col, New York, 72; plus others. Teaching: Prof visual studies, Bennington Col, 63-68; prof painting, Grad Sch, Rutgers Univ, New Brunswick, 68- Awards: Pasadena Mus Fel, 64. Bibliog: Lawrence Alloway (auth), catalog intro, Int Contemp Art, London, 61; Dore Ashton (auth), Peter Stroud's relief-paintings, Studio Int, 66; John Coplans (auth), Interview with Peter Stroud, Artforum, 66. Media: Acrylic. Mailing Add: 311 Church St New York NY 10013

STRUCKUS, THERESA KHOURY
See Priest, T

STRUPPECK, JULES
SCULPTOR, EDUCATOR
b Grangeville, La, May 29, 15. Study: Univ Okla, BFA; La State Univ, MA. Exhib: Am Fedn Arts Traveling Exhib, 41; Bertha Schaefer Gallery, 53; Whitney Mus Am Art, 54; Archit League, 54; San Francisco Mus Art, 66. Teaching: Prof sculpture, Newcomb Col, Tulane Univ La, presently. Awards: Prizes, Gallery Art, Miami, Bertha Schaefer Gallery & Marine Hosp, New Orleans, La; plus others. Publ: Auth, The Creation of Sculpture, Holt, Reinhart & Winston, 52; contribr, Design Mag. Mailing Add: Dept of Art Newcomb Col Tulane Univ New Orleans LA 70118

STUART, DAVID
ART DEALER
b Scotland, SDak. Study: Otis Art Inst, Los Angeles. Pos: Dir, David Stuart Galleries. Mem: Art Dealers Asn Am. Specialty: Contemporary painting and sculpture; pre-Columbian and African arts. Mailing Add: 748 N La Cienega Blvd Penthouse Los Angeles CA 90069

STUART, DONALD ALEXANDER
DESIGNER/CRAFTSMAN, INSTRUCTOR
b Toronto, Ont, Aug 25, 44. Study: Ont Col Art, AOCA, with Helen Francis Gregor; Tapestry Workshop with Mariette Rousseau-Vermette; Plastic Workshop with Harry Hollinger. Comn: Four murals, Centennial Comn, Mississauga, Ont, 67; two tapestries, Blessed Sacrament Church, Chatham, Ont, 76; Royal Medallion (tapestry), Royal Bank of Can, Toronto, 77; sterling silver coffee serv, Royal Philatelic Soc, Int Conf, Toronto, 78; plus many other tapestries & jewelry, pvt comns, 69-78. Exhib: World Silver Fair, Mex, 74; Contemporary Crafts of the Americas, Ft Collins, Colo, Washington, DC & tour with Smithsonian Inst, 75-77; Fibre Structures, Carnegie Inst Mus Art, 76; Contemp Ont Crafts, Agnes Etherington Gallery, Kingston, 76; 100 Years, The Evolution of the Ontario College of Art, Art Gallery of Ont, 76-77; Lake Superior 77, Duluth, Minn, 77. Teaching: Teaching master weaving, jewelry & design, Georgian Col, Barrie, Ont, 72- Pos: Mgr, Weaving indust in Pangnirting Buffin Island, for Eskimo women, 69-72. Awards: Hon Mention, Contemp Crafts of the Americas, 75; Best Contemp Design Award, 76 & Award of Excellence, Ont Crafts Exhib, 76, Ont Crafts Coun. Bibliog: J Purdie (auth), At the Galleries, Globe & Mail, Toronto, 76; D Piper (auth), Donald Stuart, Can Interiors, McLean & Hunter, 76; B Dingman (auth), Donald Stuart, Craftsman, Ont Crafts Coun, 77. Mem: Ont Crafts Coun (dir, 74-); Craft Collab (pres, 77-); Metal Arts Guild; Can Crafts Coun; Am Crafts Coun. Style & Technique: Tapestry, traditional knots and weaves, but strong use of colour and textures in abstract way; jewelry, inlay techniques. Media: Tapestry, Jewelry. Publ: Contribr, Canada Crafts, Clark & Irwin, 74; contribr, The wonderful world of crafts, Toronto Star, 76; contribr, Donald Stuart's international distinction, Craftsnews, Ont Crafts Coun, 76; contribr, The OCA Revisited Canada Crafts, Page Publ, 77; auth, Teaching contracts, Craftsnews, 77. Dealer: Scott Hunter Fibre Art Group 35 Hess St South Hamilton ON L8P 3N2 Can; Art Gallery of Ont Grange Park Toronto ON M5T 1G4 Can. Mailing Add: 4 Maple Crescent RR3 Barrie ON L4M 4S5 Can

STUART, JOSEPH MARTIN
PAINTER, MUSEUM DIRECTOR
b Seminole, Okla, Nov 9, 32. Study: Univ NMex, BFA, 59, MA, 62. Work: Art Mus, Univ NMex, Albuquerque; Melick Libr Collection, Eureka Col; Salt Lake Art Ctr, Salt Lake City; Col of Idaho, Caldwell; Sioux City Art Ctr, Iowa. Comn: Mural, Donald B Anderson, Roswell, NMex, 61. Exhib: Two-man shows, Mus Art, Univ Ore, 63 & Jonson Gallery, Univ NMex, Albuquerque, 69; Northwest Artists 50th & 52nd Ann, Seattle Art Mus, 64 & 66; Midwest Biennial, Joslyn Art Mus, Omaha; Drawings USA, Minn Mus of Art, St Paul, 77; Nat Drawings, Rutgers Univ, Camden, NJ, 77; one-man show, Northern State Col, 75; plus others. Collections Arranged: Jannis Spyropoulos: Paintings, Roswell Mus & Art Ctr, NMex, 62; Edward Kienholz: Sculpture, Boise Gallery Art, Idaho, 67; Lure of the West, Salt Lake Art Ctr, 71; Art of South Dakota, SDak Mem Art Ctr, Brookings, 74 & The Calligraphic Statement, 77. Teaching: Lectr art, Univ Utah, 69; assoc prof art hist, SDak State Univ, 71- Pos: Cur, Mus Art, Univ Ore, 62-63; dir, Boise Gallery Art, 64-68; dir, Salt Lake Art Ctr, 68-71; dir, SDak Mem Art Ctr, 71-; dir res proj, Surv Art in SDak, State & Nat Endowment Arts Grant, 72-74. Awards: First Prize in Painting, Cheney Cowles Mem Mus, Spokane, 65; Salt Lake Art Ctr Purchase Award, 67; Purchase Award, Sioux City Art Ctr, 73. Mem: Am Soc Archit Historians; SDak Mem Art Ctr; Am Asn Mus; Artists Equity Asn; SDak Mus Asn. Media: Acrylic. Publ: Auth, Nature in abstract-expressionism, Roswell Mus Bull, 60; auth, The need for art education in the public schools, Pac Art Asn Rev, 62; auth, An interview with Billy Apple, Boise Art Asn Bull, 66; auth, Stimuli, Utah Archit, fall 69; auth, Index of South Dakota Artists, SDak State Univ, 74; auth, Architecture of Harold Spitznagel, 75 & Palmer Eide Retrospective, 77, SDak Mem Art Ctr, Brookings. Mailing Add: 719 Eighth St Brookings SD 57006

STUART, KENNETH JAMES
ART DIRECTOR
b Milwaukee, Wis. Study: Pa Acad Fine Arts, with Arthur B Carles; also in Paris, France. Work: Hitler, Libr Cong, Washington, DC. Teaching: Head dept illus, Moore Col Art, Philadelphia, 39-44, bd managers, 44-56. Pos: Mag & bk illusr & painter, 44; art ed, Sat Eve Post, Philadelphia, 44-62; art dir, Reader's Digest, New York, 62-77, developmental work, 77- Awards: Salmagundi Gold Medal, 60; Typographic Excellence Award, Type Dir Club New York, 62; Show Award for Outstanding Work in Mag Illus, Soc Illustrators, 66; plus many others. Mem: Salmagundi Club. Style & Technique: Magazine and book design; illustrations in watercolor. Mailing Add: 295 Ridgefield Rd Wilton CT 06897

STUART, MICHELLE
PAINTER, SCULPTOR
b Los Angeles, Calif, Feb 10, 19. Study: Chouinard Art Inst, Los Angeles; apprenticed to Diego Rivera, Mex; New Sch Social Res. Work: Allen Mem Art Mus, Oberlin Col; Aldrich Mus Contemp Art, Ridgefield, Conn; Power Inst Mus, Sydney, Australia; Mus Art, Univ NMex; Landesmuseum, Graz, Austria. Exhib: Works on Paper, Mus Mod Art, New York, 74; one-woman shows, Max Hutchinson Gallery, 74 & 75; Fine Art Ctr, Oneonta State Univ, NY, 75, Gallery Fine Art, State Univ NY Col, Stony Brook, 76 & PS 1, New York, 76; Painting and Sculpture Today, Indianapolis Mus Art & Taft Mus, Cincinnati, 75; Edinburgh Arts, Scotland, 75; Power Inst Mus, Sydney, Australia, 75; Art Gallery of New S Wales, Sydney, 75; Grey Gallery Art, NY Univ, 75; Fine Arts Ctr Gallery, State Univ NY Col, Potsdam, 75; Soho Ctr for Visual Arts, New York, 76; Mus Mod Art, 76; plus others. Teaching: Instr painting, Sch Visual Arts, New York, 75; instr advan painting, Pratt Sch Art & Design, 75; instr perception, State Univ NY Col Old Westbury, 75-76. Awards: Nat Endowment for Arts Fel for Individual Artists, 74; NY State Creative Artists Pub Serv Grant, 75; Guggenheim Mem Found Fel, 75. Bibliog: Lawrence Alloway (auth), Michelle Stuart; a fabric of significations, Artforum, 74; Edit DeAk (auth), Michelle Stuart, Art Rite, 74; Lawrence Alloway (auth), Michelle Stuart (catalog monogr), State Univ NY Col Oneonta, 75. Style & Technique: Large paintings and drawings in a reductive style, made by indenting and polishing. Media: Rocks; Soil Pigment; Graphite. Publ: Illusr, In, On, Or, About the Premises, Cape-Goliard, London, 68. Dealer: Max Hutchinson Gallery 138 Greene St New York NY 10012. Mailing Add: 152 Wooster St New York NY 10012

STUART, SIGNE NELSON
See Nelson, Signe

STUBBS, ROBERT
ART ADMINISTRATOR
b London, Eng, Jan 29, 24; US citizen. Pos: Adminr, Pa Acad Fine Arts, Philadelphia, 69- Mailing Add: Pa Acad Fine Arts Broad & Cherry Sts Philadelphia PA 19102

STUCKI, MARGARET ELIZABETH
PAINTER, WRITER
b West New York, NJ, Jan 9, 28; US & Swiss citizen. Study: Barnard Col, BA, 49; Art Students League, with Robert Brackman & Reginald Marsh; Columbia Univ Teachers Col, MA, 59; NY Univ, ABD, 62; Freedom Univ, PhD, 75. Work: Yager Mus, Hartwick Col, Oneonta, NY; Lutheran Church of the Atonement, Oneonta; Univ Cincinnati; Bethune-Cookman Art Mus. Comn: Portrait of Mr Tobler, Pres, Stein-Tobler, Union City, NJ, 52; portraits of three past pres, Mich Technol Univ, 69-75; eight ft by twelve ft Oneonta Madonna Triptych, Hartwick Rev, 70; 12ft by 12ft Cape Canaveral Mermaid Triptych, Bird's Meadow Publ Co, Inc, 74. Exhib: Scholastic Mag Contest, Carnegie Inst, 46; Am Artists Prof League NJ Exhib, 63 & Grand Nat, New York, NY, 72; Wichita Art Asn, 67; Swiss Ctr Art Gallery, New York, NY, 75. Teaching: Asst prof drawing & painting, Hartwick Col, NY, 62-71; prof painting & hist of art, Shelton Col, Cape Canaveral, 71-74; prof hist of art, Rollins Col, Patrick AFB, Fla, 71-75; prof painting, Brevard Community Cocoa, Fla. Pos: Assoc ed, Hartwick Rev, Oneonta, NY, 68-71; art ed, Christian Educator, art consult, Am Kidney Fund, 75-; art columnist, New Am Rev, 77- Awards: First Nat Prize Category for Pastel, Collier's Mag Award, 46; Col Ctr of Finger Lakes Res Grant, 67. Bibliog: Tom Butler (auth), Artistic odd couple, Sunrise, Today, Gannett Fla Corp, 8/5/73; E M Root (auth), We Believe, Am Opinion, 11/73; Pat Phillips (auth), Art & politics linked, Star-Advocate, 3/7/74; John Rozmital (auth), Corrupted art, Am Mercury, summer 75. Mem: Am Artists Prof League; Am Asn Univ Women. Style & Technique: Impressionistic approach to traditional realism. Media: Oil, Acrylic, Pastel, Charcoal, Graphics. Res: Philosophy or metaphysics of art, aesthetics. Publ: Auth, The Revolutionary Mission of Modern Art or CRUD & Other Essays on Art, 73; auth, War on Light: The Destruction of the Image of God in Man Through Modern Art, 75. Mailing Add: 17 Court St Farmington ME 04938

STULER, JACK
PHOTOGRAPHER, EDUCATOR
b Homestead, Pa, Aug 30, 32. Study: Phoenix Col, 57; Ariz State Univ, BA, 60, with Van Deren Coke, 61, MFA, 63; workshop with Ansel Adams, 66. Work: George Eastman House, Rochester, NY; Gen Aniline Films, New York; Univ Collections, Ariz State Univ, Tempe; Yuma Art Ctr, Ariz; Phoenix Col. Exhib: Three Photographers, George Eastman House, 63, Photog 63/Int Exhib, 63; Photog In Twentieth Century, Nat Gallery Can, 67; Am Photog: The Sixties, Sheldon Mem Art Gallery, Univ Nebr, Lincoln, 66; Photog USA, De Cordova Mus, Lincoln, Mass, 68; Celebrations, Hayden Gallery, Mass Inst Technol, 74; Ariz Arts Showcase, John F Kennedy Ctr for the Performing Arts, Washington, DC, 74; First Light (nat competition), Focus Gallery, San Francisco, Calif, 75; one-man show, Univ of Ore, Eugene, 76. Teaching: Asst prof photog art, Ariz State Univ, 66-72, assoc prof, 73-75, prof, 75- Awards: First Award Biennial Photog, Phoenix Art Mus, 67; 3rd Southwestern Art Invitational Best of Show, Yuma Fine Arts Asn, 68; Summer Fel, Ariz State Univ, 68. Bibliog: Nathan Lyons (auth), The younger generation, Art Am, 12/63. Mem: Soc Photog Educ; Inst Cult Exchange Through Photog (mem adv bd, 66-). Publ: Contribr, Photography in the twentieth century, Horizon, 67; contribr, Photog Ann, 69; contribr, Being without clothes, Aperture, 15:3, 70; contribr, Camera, Lucerne, Switz, 11/71. Mailing Add: 1109 E Fairmont Tempe AZ 85282

STULL, JEAN HIMROD
PAINTER, INSTRUCTOR
b Waterford, Pa, Jan 30, 29. Study: Edinboro State Col, BS(art educ); Pa State Univ, University Park, grad study. Work: Mus Fine Arts, Springfield, Mass; Frye Mus, Seattle; First Nat Bank of Pa, Erie; Edinboro State Col; Midwestern Intermediate Unit III Traveling Collection, Pa; plus others. Exhib: Midyear Show, Butler Inst Am Art, Youngstown, Ohio, 62, 66 & 68; Nat Acad Design, New York, 66 & 68; Audubon Artists, New York, 66 & 68; Watercolor USA, Springfield, Mo, 66-68 & 75; Watercolors, Prints & Drawings, Pa Acad Fine Arts, Philadelphia, 69; plus many others. Teaching: Teacher art Bessemer Sch Dist, Pa, 49-51 & Ft LeBoeuf Sch Dist, Waterford, 56- Awards: Lena Newcastle Mem Award, Am Watercolor Soc, 66; Awards of Excellence, Mainstreams, Marietta Col, 70 & 74; Foothills Art Ctr Award, 74; Rocky Mountain Nat Watermedia Award, 75; Crow Purchase Award, San Deigo Watercolor Soc Nat, 77; plus numerous others. Bibliog: Meyer (auth), Forty Watercolorists and How They Work, Watson-Guptill, 76. Mem: Am Watercolor Soc; Northwestern Pa Artists Asn. Style & Technique: Expressionist. Media: Watercolor. Publ: Auth & illusr, untitled weekly column in Erie Dispatch, 56; contribr & illusr, The Sandpiper, 56-74; auth & illusr, untitled weekly column in Erie Times-News, 57 & 58; auth & illusr, Finding birds on Presque Isle, 65; auth, The watercolor page, Am Artist, 1/75. Mailing Add: Benson Rd RD 2 Waterford PA 16441

STULL, ROBERT J
SCULPTOR, ART ADMINISTRATOR
b Springfield, Ohio, Nov 4, 35. Study: Ohio State Univ, BS, 62, MA, 63; New York Univ Japanese Language Sch, 64-65; Fulbright Res Scholar Ceramics, Japan, 65-67. Work: Smithsonian Inst, Washington, DC; Kyoto Col of Fine Arts, Japan. Comn: Ceramic sculpture, First Nat Bank, Chicago, 69, Martin Luther King Libr, Columbus, Ohio, 72, SAI Archit & Assoc, Boston, 73 & Gallery Seven, Detroit, Mich, 77; mural painting, St John's Parrish Ctr, Columbus, Ohio, 75. Exhib: Brooklyn Mus, NY, 66; 1st Biennale Int of Ceramic Art, Vaiiauris, France, 68; Everson Mus, Syracuse, NY, 68; Ind Univ Mus, Bloomington, 69; Mus of Contemp Crafts, New York, 70; Detroit Inst of Art, 71; Musee D'Art Moderne, Paris, France, 72; L'Domo et L'Arte, Milan, Italy, 73. Teaching: Assoc prof ceramics, Univ of Mich, 68-72; prof ceramics & visual commun, Ohio State Univ, 72- Pos: Founder & gen partner, JDS Assoc, Columbus, 74-; chmn, Dept of Art, Ohio State Univ, 75- Awards: Outstanding Achievement Award, African Studies Ctr, Univ of Mich, 75; Virginia Kiah Award, Nat Conf of Artists, 78. Bibliog: Cover, Ceramics Mo Mag, 65; Four Artists, Ind Univ Press, 69; Lee Nordness (auth), Objects USA, Viking Press, 70. Mem: Col Art Asn; Nat Conf of Artists (bd of dirs, 76-); Kuumba Theatre, Chicago (chmn, bd of dirs). Style & Technique: Monumental ceramic sculptures with lusters and high color glazes; large field oriented paintings. Media:

Ceramic; Acrylic. Collection: African art; Japanese, Chinese and Korean ceramics. Publ: Prod/dir, seven television tapes for the Nat Guard Bureau, Washington, DC, 77. Dealer: Gallery Seven/Charles McGee Gallery Fisher Bldg Detroit MI. Mailing Add: 2287 Brookwood Rd Columbus OH 43209

STURGEON, JOHN FLOYD
VIDEO ARTIST
b Springfield, Ill, Jan 6, 46. Study: Yale Univ, Yale-Norfolk fel, 67; Univ Ill, BFA, 68; Cornell Univ, MFA, 70. Work: Otis Art Inst, Los Angeles; Long Beach Mus Art; Cornell Univ; Nat Gallery Victoria, Melbourne, Australia; Vancouver Sch Art, BC. Exhib: Biennial Contemp Am Art, Whitney Mus, New York, 75; Video Show, Art Coun Gt Brit, Serpentine Gallery, London, 75; Southland Video Anthology, Long Beach Mus Art, 75 & 76; Eight from Los Angeles, San Francisco Art Inst, 75; Site, San Francisco, Calif, 76; Int Festival of Video, Aarhus Mus Art, Denmark, 76; San Francisco Mus Mod Art, 76; 76 Biennale of Sydney, Art Gallery New South Wales, Australia, 76; Los Angeles Louver Gallery, Venice, Calif, 77; Calif Mus Sci & Indust, Los Angeles, 77; one-man show, Long Beach Mus Art, Calif, 78. Awards: Individual Fel Grant, Nat Endowment Art, 75. Bibliog: David James (auth), Dwelling oar, 73 & Richard Lorber (auth), X & translate, 74, Art & Cinema; Schneider/Korot, ed, Video Art, Harcourt, Brace & Jovanovich. Style & Technique: Conceptual, poetic. Media: Video Tape. Mailing Add: 11 Dudley Ave Venice CA 90291

STURGEON, MARY C
ART HISTORIAN, ARCHAEOLOGIST
b Los Angeles, Calif, Dec 6, 43. Study: Univ Minn, BA(summa cum laude), 65; Bryn Mawr Col, MA, 68, PhD(class archaeol & Greek), 71; Am Sch Class Studies in Athens, residence, 68-70 & 70-71. Teaching: Asst prof Greek & Roman Art, Oberlin Col, 72-77; assoc prof Greek art, Univ NC, Chapel Hill, 77- Mem: Archaeol Inst Am (chmn fellowship comt, 78); Col Art Asn; Am Sch Class Studies in Athens (managing comt). Res: Greek sculpture. Publ: Auth, A New Group of Sculptures from Ancient Cornith, Hesperia, 75; auth, A Hellenistic Lion-Bull Group in Oberlin, Allen Mem Art Mus Bull, 75; auth, A Bronze Statuette of Herakles, Allen Mem Art Mus Bull, 76; auth, The Reliefs of the Theatre of Dionysos in Athens, Am J Archaeol, 77; auth, Corinth IX 2: Sculpture, The Reliefs from the Theater, Princeton-Am Sch, 77. Mailing Add: Dept of Art Ackland 003A Univ of NC Chapel Hill NC 27514

STURMAN, EUGENE
PAINTER, SCULPTOR
b New York, NY, Jan 28, 45. Study: Alfred Univ, BA, 67; Univ NMex, MA, 69; Tamarind Lithograph Workshop, 70. Work: Metro Media Studios, Hollywood, Calif; Warner Bros Records, Universal City, Calif. Exhib: LA Six 74, Los Angeles Co Mus, 74; 24 from Los Angeles, Barnsdall Munic Gallery, Los Angeles, 74; Basle Art Fair, Switz, 74 & 75; Whitney Mus Am Art Biennial, 75. Teaching: Instr printmaking, Long Beach State Univ, 72-74; lectr printmaking, painting & drawing, Univ Calif, Los Angeles, 74- Awards: Michael Levins Award, Alfred Univ, 66; New Talent Award, Los Angeles Co Mus, 74; Nat Endowment Arts Grant, 75. Style & Technique: Oxides on metal. Media: Copper, Lead, Steel. Dealer: Cirrus Gallery 708 N Manhattan Pl Los Angeles CA 90005. Mailing Add: 1108 W Washington Blvd Venice CA 90291

STURTEVANT, ELAINE F
PAINTER, FILMMAKER
b Lakewood, Ohio. Study: Univ of Zürich, Switz; Chicago Art Inst; Art Students League; Univ Iowa, BA; Columbia Univ, New York, MA. Work: Stedelijk Mus, Amsterdam; Moderna Museet, Stockholm; Everson Mus, Syracuse, NY; Musée Nat d'Art Moderne, Paris. Exhib: The Mirror of Art, Mus Mod Art, 66; New York, Philadelphia Mus Contemp Art, 66; Salon De Mai, 69; one-man shows, Bianchini Gallery, New York, 65; Gallerie J, Paris, 66; Galerie Claude Givaudan, Paris, 69 & 70; Reese Palley Gallery, New York, 71, Onnasch Gallery, New York, 74 & Everson Mus, Syracuse, NY, 73. Bibliog: Yoshiaki Tono (auth), Sturtevant, Modern Art, Tokyo, Japan, 65; D Davis (auth), Country Art and City Art, Newsweek, 3/74; J Bell (ed), Contemporary Artist, St Martin Press, London, 78. Media: Oil; Film. Mailing Add: 1 W 67th St New York NY 10023

STUSSY, JAN
PAINTER, EDUCATOR
b Benton Co, Mo, Aug 13, 21. Study: Univ Calif, Los Angeles, AB, 44; Univ Southern Calif, MFA, 53; also with Stanton MacDonald-Wright, 44-72. Work: Bird Catcher, San Francisco Mus Art; Hurt Bird, Los Angeles Mus Art; Kims' Decision, Mus Mod Art, New York; Family of Acrobats, Santa Barbara Mus Art; Female Gesture, Fine Arts Gallery, Univ NMex. Comn: Painting on Masonite, Container Corp Am, New York, 66; painting, Automatic Retailers Am, Los Angeles, 66; silk screen, Metromedia, Los Angeles, 72. Exhib: Galeria Schneider, Rome, Italy, 59; The Human Figure, Mus Mod Art, 62; Ann Nat Exhib, Krannert Art Mus, Ill, 65; Int Exchange Exhib, Munic Gallery, Oslo, Norway, 74. Teaching: Prof painting & drawing, Univ Calif, Los Angeles, 46- Awards: Critics Award for Best One-Man Show of Year, Newspaper Critics, Santiago, Chile, 68; Univ Calif, Los Angeles Fine Arts Coun Award, 70; Tamarind Inst Artist Invitational Award, 70. Bibliog: A house stamped with its owner talents, Living for Young Homemakers, 6/54; Mayo Mohs (auth), Man in a box, Time, 10/6/67; Leslie Wenger (auth), Man is a devout acrobat, Currant, Vol I Number I, 4-5/75. Mem: Los Angeles Printmakers Soc; Westwood Inst for the Arts. Style & Technique: Paintings, prints, drawings, photographs. Media: Oil, Acrylic. Publ: Auth, Equipment for landscape painting, Am Artist, 2/51; auth, Will you be on our jury?, Am Artist, 1/52. Mailing Add: 12444 Rochedale Lane Los Angeles CA 90049

STUSSY, MAXINE KIM
SCULPTOR
b Los Angeles, Calif, Nov 11, 23. Study: Univ Southern Calif, art scholar, 43; Univ Calif, Los Angeles, AB, 47; also res & pvt study in Rome (Brunifoundry), France, Eng, Ger, 59 & 63. Comn: Bob Hope Award Trophy, Bob Hope Athletic Award Comn, 60; Bob Hope New Talent Award, Universal Studios, 61; Wall Sculptures in Wood, Neuropsychiatric Hosp Lobby, Univ Calif, Los Angeles, 68; Wood Sculpture, St Martin of Tours Church, Brentwood, 72. Exhib: Los Angeles Co Mus, Los Angeles, 54, 58, 59, 61; Art USA, Madison Sq Garden, New York, 58; Galleria Schneider, Rome, Italy, 59; Denver Art Mus, 60; 25 Calif Women of Art, Lytton Ctr of Visual Arts, Los Angeles, 68; plus others. Awards: First Prize, Sculpture, Bronze, Los Angeles Co Art Mus, 61. Bibliog: Bea Miller (auth), The anatomy of an artist, Home Mag, Los Angeles Times, 70; Beverly Edna Johnson (auth), Sculptures evolved from wood, Home Mag, Los Angeles Times, 75; Kathleen Reinoehl (auth), The many faces of Maxine Kim Stussy, Am Artist Mag, 7/75. Style & Technique: Abstract sculpture, based on human & animal forms. Media: Laminated or Carved Wood, Metal; Bronze, Concrete, Fired Clay. Dealer: Pavilion Gallery 7150 Main St Scottsdale AZ. Mailing Add: 12444 Rochedale Lane W Los Angeles CA 90049

SUAREZ, MAGDALENA FRIMKESS
PAINTER, SCULPTOR
b Venezuela, July 22, 29. Study: Escuela de Artes Plasticas, Caracas, 43-45; Cath Univ Chile, with Sewell Sillman, 58-61; also with Norman Calberg & Paul Harris. Exhib: Venezuela Ann Salon, 44; Chilean Ann Salon, 53; one-man show, Brazilian Inst Cult, Chile, 61; Fridmen Galerie, Encinco, Calif, 73; Fred Mayer Collection Ceramics, Claremont, Calif, 74. Bibliog: Sculptora de suspenso, Elite, Venezuela, 62. Publ: Contribr, Craft Horizon, 12/73. Mailing Add: 1137 Cabrillo Ave Venice CA 90291 Los Angeles CA 1137 Cabrillo Ave Venice CA 90291

SUBA, SUSANNE
PAINTER, ILLUSTRATOR
b Budapest, Hungary. Study: Pratt Inst, grad. Work: Metrop Mus Art, New York; Brooklyn Mus, NY; Art Inst Chicago; Mus City of New York; Kalamazoo Inst Art, Mich. Exhib: Ansdell Gallery, London, Eng; Hammer Gallery, New York; Kalamazoo Inst Art; Art Inst Chicago; Mus Mod Art, New York. Awards: Awards, Am Inst Graphic Art, Art Dirs Club New York & Art Dirs Club Chicago. Mailing Add: 1019 Third Ave New York NY 10021

SUBLETT, CARL C
PAINTER, EDUCATOR
b Johnson Co, Ky, Feb 4, 19. Study: Western Ky Univ; Univ Study Ctr, Florence, Italy; Univ Tenn. Work: Dulin Gallery Art, Knoxville, Tenn; Hunter Gallery Art, Chattanooga, Tenn; Mint Mus, Charlotte, NC; Stephens Col, Springfield, Mo; Tenn Arts Comn, Nashville, Tenn. Exhib: Southeastern Art Ann, Atlanta, Ga; Paintings of Yr, Atlanta; New Painters of South, Birmingham, Ala; Watercolor USA, Springfield, Mo, 64-72; Am Watercolor Soc, New York, 72. Teaching: Former assoc prof art, Univ Tenn. Awards: Rudolph Lesch Award, Am Watercolor Soc, 72; Purchase Award, Am Collection, Hunter Gallery Art, 72; Purchase Award, Collection Tenn Art League & Parthenon, Nashville, 72. Mem: Dulin Gallery Art (adv bd, 71-); Knoxville Watercolor Soc; Tenn Watercolorists; Mus Mod Art; Port Clyde Arts & Crafts Soc, Maine. Media: Watercolor, Oil, Acrylic. Publ: Contribr, Artist and Advocates, Mead Corp; contribr, Nat Drawing Soc. Mailing Add: c/o Collectors Gallery 2401 Abbott Martin Rd Nashville TN 37215

SUDLOW, ROBERT N
PAINTER, EDUCATOR
b Holton, Kans, Feb 25, 20. Study: Univ Kans, BFA; Univ Calif, Berkeley; Calif Col Arts & Crafts, Oakland, MFA; Acad Grande Chaumiere, Paris; Acad Andre L'Hote, Paris. Work: City Art Mus, St Louis, Mo; Mulvane Art Ctr, Washburn Univ; Joslyn Art Mus, Omaha; Stephens Col; Baker Univ. Exhib: One-man shows, Albrecht Art Mus, St Joseph, Mo, 77, Nelson Art Mus, Kansas City, Mo, 77, Mulvane Art Ctr, Topeka, Kans, Univ of Kans, Lawrence, 77, Hampton II Gallery, Taylor, SC, 7E7 Gallery, Lawrence, Kans, 77 & Beauchamp Gallery, Topeka, Kans, 77; A Sense of Place, Am Landscape Painting Traveling Exhib, 74; Summer Invitational, Nelson Art Mus, 74-75; Com State Bank, Topeka, Kans, 75; Muchnic Art Ctr, Atchison, Kans, 75; plus others. Teaching: Prof painting & sculpture, Univ Kans, 47-; Watkins fac fel, 58; instr drawing & painting, Spiva Art Ctr, 71. Awards: Governors Artist, 75; Octoberfest Regional Award, 77. Style & Technique: Landscape. Media: Oil, Watercolor. Dealer: Johnson Welsh Gallery 5911 Main St Kansas City MO 64113; Gump's San Francisco CA. Mailing Add: 1416 W Seventh Lawrence KS 66044

SUFI (AHMAD ANTUNG)
SCULPTOR, CRAFTSMAN
b Palembang, Indonesia, Sept 7, 30. Study: Craft Students League; New Sch Social Res, scholar, 66; Educ Alliance; Haystack Mountain Sch Arts & Crafts. Work: Pvt collections of Dr Edna S Levine, Dr Walter Krauss, George L Sherry, Gloria Furman & Lucile Gaston; plus many other pvt collections. Comn: Loft bed & interior design, comn by Buck Clark, New York, 68; mural-window (Plexiglas), comn by Teannie Clark, New York, 71; Oetra Banda Restaurant, New York; and pvt comn by Susan Grand, New York & Dolores Urove, Brooklyn. Exhib: Int Art Exhib, Minneapolis/St Paul, 72; American Craft Coun Gallery, New York, 73; Brooklyn Mus, 73; Yonkers Mus, NY, 74; Silvermine Guild, Conn, 74; plus others. Awards: Second Prize, Brooklyn Heights Promenade Art Show, 71; Best in Sculpture, Artist-Craftsmen New York Ann Show, 72 & 74. Bibliog: Article, 67 & Dinki Di (auth), article, 72, In: UN Secretarial News; Corine Coleman (auth), articles in Phoenix Newspaper, 72; Dido Smith (auth), article in Craft Horizon, 72 & 74. Mem: Heights-Hills Artists Coop; Artist-Craftsmen New York; Artists Equity Asn; Sculptors Guild. Style & Technique: Works are non-representational in the traditional sense, concerned with manifestation of being and the expression of total whole by the most economical means of plastic literacy called gestaltive dynamism; space is primary material; simplicity of material crystalizes form. Media: Bronze, Concrete, Glass. Mailing Add: Rte 169 Brooklyn CT 06234

SUGARMAN, GEORGE
SCULPTOR, PAINTER
b New York, NY, May 11, 12. Study: City Col New York, BA; Atelier Zadkine, Paris, 51. Work: Walker Art Ctr, Minneapolis; Kunstmuseum, Zurich, Switz; Mus Mod Art, New York; Whitney Mus Am Art, New York; Chicago Art Inst. Comn: Metal sculptures, Xerox Data Systs, El Segundo, Calif, 69, Empire State Mall, 70, First Nat Bank, St Paul, Minn, 71, Fed Courthouse, Baltimore, 75-77 & Miami Int Airport, Fla, 77. Exhib: Whitney Mus Am Art Sculpture Ann, 60-; Carnegie Inst Int, Pittsburgh, 61; Sao Paulo Biennal, Brazil, 63; Sculpture of the Sixties, Los Angeles Co Mus Art, 67; Int Pavilion, Venice Biennal, 69; Retrospective, Stedlijk Mus, Amsterdam, Holland, 69-70; 200 Yrs Am Sculpture, Whitney Mus Am Art, New York, 76; plus others. Teaching: Assoc prof sculpture, Hunter Col, 60-70; vis prof sculpture, Grad Sch Art & Archit, Yale Univ, 67-68. Awards: Second Prize for Sculpture, Pittsburgh Int, 61-62; Longview Found Grants, 61-63; Nat Art Coun Award, 66. Bibliog: Barbara Rose (auth), American Art Since 1950, 67; I Sandler (auth), Sugarman-Sculptural Complex, First Nat Bank St Paul, 71; Sam Hunter (auth), American Art of the 20th Century, 72; plus others. Media: Metal; Acrylic. Dealer: Robert Miller 724 Madison Ave New York NY 10021. Mailing Add: 21 Bond St New York NY 10012

SUGIMOTO, HENRY Y
PAINTER
US citizen. Study: Calif Col Arts & Crafts, BFA; Calif Sch Fine Arts; Acad Colarossi, Paris. Work: Mus Crecy, France; Calif Palace Legion of Honor, San Francisco; Hendrix Col Fine Art Mus, Ark; Wakayama Mod Art Mus, Japan; Univ Ark Art Mus. Comn: NY Japanese Consulate General's Residence, 73; murals, Lobby, Wakayama City Hall, Japan, 77. Exhib: Salon Automne, Paris, 31; Rine Art Exhib, San Francisco World Expos, 39; US Exhib, Mod World Exhib, Tokyo, Japan, 50; Salon Artistes Francais, Paris, 63; Months of Waiting, Doc Painting Traveling Exhib, 72; one-man exhib, Interchurch Ctr Gallery, 78. Teaching: Instr art, Denson High Sch, Ark, 43-44. Pos: Art consult, War Relocation Authority, 43-45. Awards: Art Concour Award, Found Western Art, 37; Recognition Medal, San Francisco World's Fair, 39; Recognition Plaque for Months of Waiting Los Angeles Co Bd Supervisors,

72. Bibliog: New America, Life & War Relocation Authority, 46. Mem: Washington Printmaker Soc; Nika-Kai Art Asn, Tokyo. Media: Oil, Watercolor, Wood. Res: Documentary painting of the War Relocation Centers of Japanese during World War II. Publ: Illusr, Songs for the Land of Dawn, 49; illusr, Toshio and Tama, 49; illusr, New Friends for Susan, 51; contribr, Beauty Behind Barbed Wire, 52; contribr, Nisei, 69. Dealer: Wiener Gallery 963 Madison Ave New York NY 10021. Mailing Add: 600 W 146th St New York NY 10031

SULLINS, ROBERT M
PAINTER, EDUCATOR
b Los Angeles, Calif, Aug 31, 26. Study: Univ Wyo, 46-47; Univ Ill, 47-48; Univ Wyo, BA(art), 50, MA(art), 58; Fulbright fel, 59-60; Inst Allende, San Miguel Allende, Mex, MFA, 66. Work: Norfolk Mus Arts & Sci, Va; Northern Ill Univ, DeKalb; Civic Ctr, Scottsdale, Ariz; Inst Int Educ, New York. Comn: Crucifixion (mural), St Joseph's Cath Church, Rawlins, Wyo, 61; Upstatescape (painting), State Univ NY, Col Oswego, 66; mural, The Flame Room, Rawlins, 67; Kinetic machine, Mirrors, Motors & Motion Show, Rochester Mus, NY, 70. Exhib: One-man shows, Jason Gallery New York, 66, Aspect/Aegis Gallery, New York, 68, Univ Wyo, 75, Univ Utah, 75, Las Vegas Art Mus, 76 & Civic Ctr, Scottsdale, Ariz, 76; Childe Hassam Exhib, Am Acad Arts & Lett, 69; Kinetic Art Show, Albright- Knox Art Gallery, Buffalo, NY, 70; Am Drawing Biennial, XXIV, Norfolk Mus Arts & Sci, 71; Xerox Show, Rochester, NY. Teaching: Prof art, State Univ NY, Col Oswego, 60- Pos: Supvr art, Pub Schs Rawlins, Wyo, 55-59. Awards: Robert Ahl Mem grant, 60; State of NY Res Fel, 71. Style & Technique: Drawing. Media: Acrylics, Polyester Resins. Dealer: Abe-Rothstein-Horizon Galleries 10345 W Olympic Blvd Los Angeles CA 90064 & 43 Glendale Rd Newton Ctr MA 02159. Mailing Add: 51 E Eighth St Oswego NY 13126

SULLIVAN, JIM
PAINTER
b Providence, RI, Apr 1, 39. Study: RI Sch Design, Providence, Fulbright scholar & BFA, 61; Stanford Univ, 62-63. Work: Whitney Mus Am Art, New York; Worcester Art Mus, Mass; Albany State Mus. Exhib: Whitney Mus Am Art Ann, 67, 69 & 72; Lyrical Abstraction, Larry Aldrich Mus, Conn & Whitney Mus Am Art, 70-71; Beautiful Painting, Columbus Gallery Fine Arts, Ohio, 71; Small Works Group Show, Mus Mod Art, New York, 71; Ind Mus Art, Indianapolis, 72. Teaching: Assoc prof painting, Bard Col, 65- Awards: Guggenheim Found Grant, 72. Bibliog: David Shirey (auth), art rev in New York Times, 10/23/71; Peter Schjeldahl (auth), rev with reprod in Art in Am, 2/72; Carter Ratcliff (auth), rev with reprod in Art Spectrum, 2/75; plus others. Dealer: Willard Gallery 29 E 72nd St New York NY. Mailing Add: 59 Wooster St New York NY 10013

SULLIVAN, MAX WILLIAM
ART ADMINISTRATOR
b Fremont, Mich, Sept 27, 09. Study: Western Mich Univ, AB, 32; Harvard Univ, AM, 41; Providence Col, hon LLD, 50. Teaching: Instr, Cranbrook Sch, 33-35; instr arts & crafts, Middlesex Sch, Concord, Mass, 35-38; head art dept, Groton Sch, Mass, 38-42; consult art educ, Harvard Sch Educ, 40-42; dir educ, RI Sch Design, 44-45. Pos: Dir Exhib New Eng handicrafts, Worcester Mus Art, 42-43; consult, Metrop Mus Art, 43-44; dean sch, RI Sch Design, 45-47, pres corp, 47-55; dir, Portland Art Mus, Portland Art Asn & Mus Art Sch, 56-61, secy bd trustees, 57-60; dir, Everson Mus Art, Syracuse, NY, 61-71; prog dir, Kimbell Art Mus, Ft Worth, Tex, 71-74, dir admin serv, 74-76; dir, Univ Art Gallery, Univ of Tex at Arlington, 76- Mem: Am Inst Architects; Ft Worth Club; Am Asn Mus; Harvard Club; Int Ctr Arts, Boston (trustee & pres, 74-). Res: Contemporary architecture and contemporary sculpture; classical studies, especially Magna Graecia & Central Italy. Publ: Auth & ed, Contemporary New England Handicrafts, Worcester Art Mus, Mass, 43; contribr & ed, Calligraphy: The Golden Age & Its Modern Revival, Portland Art Mus, 58; contribr, Everson Dedication Portfolio, 69 & American Ship Portraits & Marine Painting, 70, Everson Mus; contribr, Catalogue of the Collection, Kimbell Art Mus, 72. Mailing Add: Ridgleawood One 4500 Westridge Ave Ft Worth TX 76116

SULLIVAN, RUTH WILKINS
ART HISTORIAN, CURATOR
b Boston, Mass, Nov 20, 26. Study: Wellesley Col, AB. Collections Arranged: Chinese Export Porcelain, 65; American Painting from 1830 (with catalog), 65; Some Recent Images in American Painting, 68; Chinese Art from the Cloud Wampler Collection (with catalog), 68; American Ship Portraits & Marine Painting (with catalog), 70. Pos: Registr, Everson Mus Art, 60-62, ed publ, 63-70, cur collections, 66-70; consult, Mus Am China Trade, 71; cur educ, Kimbell Art Mus, 71- Awards: Woman of Achievement in Arts, Post Stand, 68. Mem: Col Art Asn Am; Archaeol Inst of Am. Res: Chinese gold and silver from the T'ang Dynasty; Chinese export silver for the Anglo-American market; classical studies, particularly Western Greek foundations of Sicily and Magna Graecia. Collection: American silver of the Colonial period. Publ: Auth, What is an art museum?, 68; co-auth, Chinese Export Silver: 1785-1885, 75; contribr to Kimbell Catalogue of the Collection; plus others. Mailing Add: Ridgleawood One 4500 Westridge Ave Ft Worth TX 76116

SULTAN, ALTOON
PAINTER
b Brooklyn, NY, Sept 29, 48. Study: Brooklyn Col, BA, 69, MFA, 71, study with Phillip Pearlstein; Boston Univ at Tanglewood, 69; Skowhegan Sch Painting & Sculpture, study with Gabriel Laderman, 70. Work: NJ State Mus, Trenton; Metromedia Collection, New York; Madison Fine Arts Ctr, Wis. Exhib: Contemp Figure: The New Realism, Suffolk Mus, Stony Brook, NY, 71; Sons and Others: Women Artists see Men, Queens Mus, New York, 75; Portrait Painting, 1970-1975, Frumkin Gallery, New York, 75; American Painterly Realism, Univ Mo, Kansas City, 77; Brooklyn Col Art Dept, Past & Present 1942-1977, Davis & Long Gallery, New York, 77; Artists Salute Skowhegan, Kennedy Gallery, New York, 77; one-woman show, Marlborough Gallery, 77. Awards: MacDowell Colony Fel, 72 & 74; Yaddo Fel, 75 & 76. Style & Technique: Figurative painter; architectural motifs. Media: Oil; Gouache. Dealer: Marlborough Gallery 40 W 57th St New York NY 10019. Mailing Add: 131 Allen St New York NY 10002

SUMM, HELMUT
PAINTER, EDUCATOR
b Hamburg, Ger, Mar 10, 08; US citizen. Study: Univ Wis, grad, 30; Marquette Univ, MEd, 46; also with Umberto Romano, Carl Peters & Robert Von Neumann. Work: Milwaukee Art Ctr Collection; Milwaukee J Gallery Wis Art; Univ Wis-Green Bay Contemp Art Collection; Lakeland Col Collection Wis Art; Gimbel's Airscapes, Milwaukee. Comn: Mural, St John's Lutheran Sch, Glendale, Wis, 56; mural, Home for Aged Lutherans, Milwaukee, 57; oil painting, Cudahy YMCA, Wis. Exhib: Soc Am Etchers Nat Acad Design Galleries, 48; Univ Okla Nat, 50; Am Watercolor Soc Traveling Exhib, 60; Milwaukee Art Ctr Friends of Art, 64-; Wis Watercolor Soc, 74; Retrospective Exhib, Fine Arts Galleries, Univ Wis, Milwaukee, 78. Teaching: Instr art, Milwaukee Pub Schs, 31-48; dir dept art, Univ Wis-Milwaukee Exten, 48-56, prof art & art educ, Univ Wis-Milwaukee & Exten, 56- Awards: Award for Oil Painting, Am Inst Architects, 63; Purchase Award for Oil, Beloit & Vicinity Exhib, 64; Watercolor Award, Wis Salon, 65. Bibliog: Don Key (auth), Review of Theodore's Gallery, 65 & Violet Dewey (auth), What's new in art, 67, Milwaukee J; reproduction in Wis Beautiful, 67. Mem: Wis Watercolor Soc (coordr, Silver Anniversary Exhib, 78); Wis Painters & Sculptors (pres, 63); Delta Phi Delta. Style & Technique: Moods gained by expressionistic treatment of color and shape patterns, blurring against sharp accents; searching for non-obvious oneness of visual statement. Media: Oil, Watercolor, Graphics. Publ: Auth, University of Wisconsin Extension Art Programs, WTMJ. Dealer: Friends of Art Milwaukee Art Ctr 750 N Lincoln Memorial Dr Milwaukee WI 53202. Mailing Add: 6183 N Lake Dr Milwaukee WI 53217

SUMMER, (EMILY) EUGENIA
PAINTER, SCULPTOR
b Newton, Miss, June 13, 23. Study: Miss State Col Women, BS; Columbia Univ, MA; Art Inst Chicago; Calif Col Arts & Crafts; Penland Sch Crafts, NC; Seattle Univ. Work: Miss Art Asn, Munic Art Gallery, Jackson; First Nat Bank Collection, Jackson; Nat Bank Commerce Collection, Columbus, Miss; First Nat Bank, Laurel, Miss; Sears Roebuck Collection, Laurel. Exhib: Am Fedn Arts Circulating Exhib, 61-62; Art in Embassies Prog, US State Dept, Rio de Janeiro, Brazil, 66-67; Mid-South Exhibs, Brooks Mem Art Gallery, Memphis, Tenn; Eighth Decade: Painters Choice, Ga Col Milledgeville, 71; 5th Greater New Orleans Int Art Exhib, 75. Teaching: Assoc prof art, Miss State Col Women, 50- Awards: Dumas Milner Purchase Award, Nat Watercolor Exhib, Jackson, 62, Jurors Award, 68; First Prize in Watercolor Painting, Mid-South Exhib, Brooks Gallery, 65; Miss State Col Women Grants for Studying & Producing Works in Plastics. Mem: Col Art Asn Am; Miss Art Asn; Am Crafts Coun; Southeastern Col Art Conf; Kappa Pi. Style & Technique: Abstractionist in acrylic painting; landscapist in watercolor using wet in wet technique. Mailing Add: 915 Fifth Ave S Columbus MS 39701

SUMMERFORD, BEN LONG
PAINTER, EDUCATOR
b Montgomery, Ala, Feb 3, 24. Study: Am Univ, BA & MA; Ecole Beaux-Arts, Paris; also with Karl Knaths & Jack Tworkov. Work: Corcoran Gallery Art, Washington, DC; Phillips Gallery, Washington, DC; Fort Wayne Mus Art, Ind; Nat Collection Fine Arts, Washington, DC. Exhib: Fulbright Painters, Whitney Mus Am Art, 59; one-man shows, Jefferson Pl Gallery, Washington, DC, 64 & 67 & Franz Bader Gallery, 75. Teaching: Prof painting, Am Univ, 50-, chmn dept art, 57- Awards: Fulbright Fel, France, 49-50. Style & Technique: Visual art with interest in light, still life and interiors. Media: Oil. Mailing Add: 10216 Brown's Mill Rd Vienna VA 22180

SUMMERS, CAROL
PRINTMAKER
b Kingston, NY, Dec 26, 25. Study: Bard Col, BA, 51. Work: Brooklyn Mus, NY; Metrop Mus Art, New York; Mus Mod Art, New York; Victoria & Albert Mus, London; Bibliot Nat, Paris. Exhib: One-person shows, Mus Mod Art, 64-66, AAA Gallery, New York, 67 & Bard Col, 68; Retrospective, San Francisco Mus Art, Calif, 67; 20th Nat Print Exhib, Brooklyn Mus, 77; plus others. Awards: Ital Govt Grant, Italy, 55; Louis Comfort Tiffany Found Fels, 55 & 61; Guggenheim Found Fel, 59. Mem: Print Coun Am (artist adv bd); Print Club Philadelphia. Style & Technique: Large simple landscape; elements saturated color; technique usually similar to rubbings. Media: Wood. Mailing Add: c/o ADI Gallery 530 McAllister St San Francisco CA 94102

SUMMERS, ROBERT
PAINTER, SCULPTOR
b Cleburne, Tex, Aug 13, 40. Work: Frost Nat Bank, San Antonio, Tex; Hale Trailer Co, Sherman, Tex; Inn of the Golden West, Odessa, Tex; Bosque Co Bank, Meridian, Tex; Gallery of Original Western Art, Stephenville, Tex. Comn: Acrylic tempera painting, comn by Mrs Melvin A Bearup, Tucson; 15 courthouses of Permian Basin, comn by George Abell, Midland, Tex. Exhib: Am Artists Prof League, Lever House, New York; Tex Fine Arts Regional, Ft Worth Art Ctr, Tex; Tex Fine Arts State Show, Austin; Old Cowboys Reunion & Rodeo, Stamford, Tex; Midland West '75, Tex; Tex Rangers Hall of Fame, Tex Asn Prof Artists, 76. Awards: Gold Medal Award, Franklin Mint, Franklin Center, Pa, 73; Juror's Choice Award, Tex Fine Arts Exhib, Austin; Official Tex Bicentennial Artist, 75-76, Tex Legis & Gov of Tex. Bibliog: Randall Benham (auth), article in Tex Parade Mag, 74; Jon McConal (contrib ed), Ft Worth Star Telegram; Helen Callaway (auth), Southwest Scene, Dallas Morning News. Mem: Tex Asn Prof Artists (first pres, 73-74); Tex Watercolor Asn; Am Artists Prof League. Style & Technique: Egg and acrylic tempera, oil, watercolor, pastel; bronze sculpting. Media: Acrylic Tempera Painting; Bronzes. Mailing Add: Box 150 Glen Rose TX 76043

SUMMY, ANNE TUNIS
PAINTER
b Baltimore, Md. Study: Pa Acad Fine Arts; Inst Allende, Mex. Work: William Penn Mem Mus Contemp Collection, Harrisburg; Franklin & Marshall Col. Comn: Portrait, Armstrong Cork Co, Lancaster, Pa, 69. Exhib: Butler Inst Am Art Midyear Show, Youngstown, Ohio, 68; Pa Acad Fine Arts Fel Shows, 69-70; one-man show, William Penn Mem Mus, 71; Soc Four Arts, 74; Md Biennial, Baltimore Mus Art, 74. Awards: Newman Medal, Nat Soc Painters in Casein & Acrylics, 68, Lorne Medal, 69; Landscape Painters Pa Purchase Award, Bloomsburg Col, 70; Blue Ribbon, Cape Coral Nat, Fla, 74; Hon Mention, 13th Maj Fla Artists, Harman Gallery, Naples, Fla, 76; First Harman Award, Fla Artists Group, 77. Bibliog: Articles in La Rev Mod, 1/70. Style & Technique: Three dimensional cut paper constructions; abstract. Media: Acrylic. Dealer: Naples Art Gallery 275 Broad Ave S Naples FL 33940. Mailing Add: 2885 Gulf Shore Blvd N Naples FL 33940

SUNDBERG, CARL GUSTAVE
ENAMELIST, ART DIRECTOR
b Erie, Pa, June 23, 28. Study: Albright Art Sch, Univ Buffalo, grad; study with Joseph Plaucan, Virginia Cuthbert, Albert Blaustien, Letterio Calipia & Robert Bruce. Work: Butler Inst Am Art, Youngstown, Ohio; Tyler Mus Art, Tex; Erie Pub Mus; Erie Pub Libr; Union Bank Erie; Albright-Knox Rental Art Gallery. Comn: Porcelain coat of arms, Episcopal Diocese of Erie, 68; six porcelain panels (mod motif with coins), Union Bank, Erie, 69; three porcelain enamel panels, Gannon Resource Ctr, Erie, 73; three enclosure set (Plexiglas-enamel), St Vincent Hosp, Erie, 74. Exhib: One-man show, Chautauqua, 70; Chautauqua Nat Jury Shows, NY, 67-77; Midyear Shows, Butler Inst Am Art, Youngstown, 68 & 70-77; Washington & Jefferson Col Nat Exhib, 69, 72 & 74; Miss Nat Arts Festival, 70; Audubon Artists, New York, 71; two-man show, Thiel Col, Greenville, Pa, 77. Teaching: Instr painting, Erie Art Ctr, 64- Pos: Art dir, Erie Ceramic Arts Co, 53-; dir, Galerie 8, Erie, 67-74. Awards: Purchase Prize, Butler Inst Am Art Mid Year Show, 70; Purchase Prize, Tyler Mus Art 7th Nat Exhib, 70; Prize for Non-Traditional, Chautauqua Exhib, 72 & 76. Bibliog:

Clyde Singer (auth), article in Youngstown Vindicator, 6/28/70; Ada C Tanner (auth), article in Chautauqua Daily, 8/17/70; Peggy Krider (auth), Art Demonstration (film), Villa Maria Col, 70. Mem: Erie Art Ctr (pres, 67-69); Erie Arts Coun (vpres, 70-71); Albright-Knox Art Gallery, Chautauqua Art Asn; Northwestern Pa Artist Asn (co-dir). Style & Technique: Abstract constructivist with lines and dots with frequent religious connotation. Media: Porcelain, Enamel, Graphic. Mailing Add: 5518 Bondy Dr Erie PA 16509

SUNDBERG, WILDA (REGELMAN)
PAINTER
b Erie, Pa, Oct 5, 30. Study: Albright Art Sch, Univ Buffalo, 49-51; Gannon Col, 64-66; also with Joseph Plavcan, Al Blaustein & Virginia Cuthbert. Work: Thiel Col, Greenville, Pa; Erie Pub Libr. Comn: Illustrate pvt homes, 70-72. Exhib: Catharine Lorillard Wolfe Art Club, Nat Acad Design, New York, 70; Muse Art Gallery, Springfield Art Mus, Mo, 71; Albright Knox Mem Gallery, Buffalo, 71; Erie Spring Show, 71-; Ann Watercolor Exhib, Mus of Tex Tech Univ, Lubbock, 75; two-man show, Thiel Col, Pa, 77; one-woman shows, Gannon Col, 76 & Waterford Community Ctr, Pa, 76; plus others. Teaching: Pvt instr, Erie, 64-66; instr art, Erie Art Ctr, 64-72. Pos: Fashion illusr, Erie Dry Goods, 51-55. Awards: Chautauqua Nat Watercolor Award, Chautauqua Art Asn, 70; Third Award for Watercolor, Edinboro Summer Gallery, Pa, 70, First Prize for Watercolor, 75. Bibliog: Peggy Krider (auth), Watercolor Demonstration (film), Villa Maria Col, 70; Ada Tanner (auth), article in Chautauqua News, NY, 70; Meg Loncharic (auth), Women in the arts, Erie Times, 70. Mem: Erie Art Ctr (bd dirs, 71-72); Albright Knox Art Gallery; Chautauqua Art Asn; Northwestern Pa Artist Asn (mem bd); Artists Equity, Philadelphia Chap, Pa; Erie Arts Coun. Media: Transparent Watercolor. Mailing Add: 5518 Bondy Dr Erie PA 16509

SUNDERLAND, ELIZABETH READ
ART HISTORIAN
b Ann Arbor, Mich, June 12, 10. Study: Univ Mich, AB; Univ Munich, Ger; Harvard Univ, AM & PhD. Teaching: Instr fine art, Duke Univ, 39-42; asst prof fine art, Wheaton Col (Mass), 42-43; asst prof fine art, Duke Univ, 43-51, assoc prof, 51-71, prof hist art, 71- Awards: Guggenheim Found Fel, 52-53; Duke Univ Endowment Res Grant, Italy, 65-66. Mem: Soc Archit Historians (dir); Mediaeval Acad Am (councillor); hon mem Soc Amis Arts Charlieu; hon mem La Diana; Acad Macon; plus others. Res: Medieval architecture of the 8th through 11th centuries. Publ: Auth, Charlieu a l'Epoque Medievale, Lyon, 71; contribr, J Soc Archit Historians, Art Bull, Speculum, La Diana, J Archit Inst Japan & others. Mailing Add: Dept of Art East Duke Bldg Duke Univ Durham NC 27708

SUNDERLAND, NITA KATHLEEN
EDUCATOR, SCULPTOR
b Olney, Ill, Nov 9, 27. Study: Duke Univ; Bradley Univ, BFA & MA. Comn: Archit sculpture, Bradley Univ Bookstore, 64, monumental sculpture, Williams Hall Mall, 67; archit sculpture, St John's Cath Church, Woodhull, Ill, 69; monument bronze sculpture, City Beautiful Comt, City Peoria, Fulton Street Mall, 75. Exhib: Eastern Mich Univ Sculpture Exhib, 64; one-man show, Lakeview Ctr Arts & Sci, 65; one-man show, Gilman Galleries, 65 & group exhib, Art for Archit, 68; Ill State Mus Exhib, Ill Artists, 66. Teaching: Prof sculpture, Bradley Univ, 56- Style & Technique: Figurative; carving and casting. Media: Stone, Wood; Bronze, Aluminum. Dealer: Gilman Galleries 103 E Oak St Chicago IL 60611. Mailing Add: Grosenbach Hill Rd Rte 1 Washington IL 61571

SUNKEL, ROBERT CLEVELAND
ART HISTORIAN, ART ADMINISTRATOR
b Clarksville, Tex, Jan 19, 33. Study: Kilgore Col, Tex, AA; Tex Christian Univ, BFA & MFA; Herron Sch Art, Ind Univ; Temple Univ; Northern Ill Univ. Teaching: Instr art, Henderson State Col, 58-60; instr art, Northwest Mo State Univ, 60-63, actg chmn dept, 63-71, asst prof, 71-74, assoc prof & cur, Percival DeLuce Mem Collection, 74-76, chmn, Dept of Art & cur, DeLuce Mem Collection, 76- Pos: Cur, Percival De Luce Mem Collection, Northwest Mo State Univ, 71- Mem: Soc Archit Historians; Am Asn Univ Prof; Col Art Asn Am; Mid-Am Col Art Conf; Midwest Art Hist Soc. Res: English Baroque and Palladian architecture, particularly the work of Wren, Gibbs and Hawksmoor. Mailing Add: PO Box 75 Maryville MO 64468

SURREY, MILT
PAINTER
b New York, NY, Mar 18, 22. Work: Cincinnati Art Mus; Columbia Mus Art, SC; Detroit Inst Arts; Evansville Mus Art, Ind; Miami Mus Mod Art. Exhib: Soc Four Arts, Palm Beach, 69; Nat Arts Club, New York, 69; Cape Coral Nat Art Show, 70; George Walter Vincent Smith Art Mus, Springfield, Mass, 70; Parrish Art Mus, Southampton, NY, 70. Awards: John Knecht Mem Award, Berwick Arts Festival, 69; Third Place Award, Garden Valley Nat Art Show, 69; Second Place Award, Roslyn Art Show, 70. Media: Oil. Mailing Add: 201 Montrose Rd Westbury NY 11590

SURREY, PHILIP HENRY
PAINTER
b Calgary, Alta, Oct 8, 10. Study: Winnipeg Sch Art, with LeMoine FitzGerald; Vancouver Sch Art, with Frederick Varley & Jock Macdonald; Art Students League, with Alexander Abels. Work: Nat Gallery Can, Ottawa; Montreal Mus Fine Arts; Mus Quebec, Quebec City; Art Gallery Hamilton, Ont; Art Gallery Winnipeg, Man; plus others. Exhib: Hamilton Art Gallery Winter Exhibs, 58-71; 25 Quebec Painters, Montreal Mus Fine Arts, 61; Master Can Painters & Sculptors, London, 63; one-man retrospective, Peintre Dans La Ville, Mus Art Contemp, Montreal, 71 & Ctr Cult Can, Paris, 72. Teaching: Former instr drawing, Concordia Univ. Awards: First Prize, Montreal Spring Show, 53; Second Prize, Winnipeg Show, 60. Bibliog: J De Roussan (auth), Le peintre des reflets de la ville, Vie Arts, 63 & Philip Surrey, Ed Lidec, Montreal, 68; Paul Duval (auth), Four Decades, Clarke, Irwin, Toronto; plus others. Media: Acrylic, Oil, Pastel. Dealer: Galerie Gilles Corbeil 2165 Crescent St Montreal PQ Can; Theodore Waddington Galleries 1456 Sherbrooke W Montreal PQ Can. Mailing Add: 478 Grosvenor Ave Montreal PQ H3Y 2S4 Can

SUSSMAN, ARTHUR
PAINTER
b Brooklyn, NY, Mar 30, 27. Study: Syracuse Univ, BFA; Brooklyn Mus Sch Art. Work: NMex Mus Fine Art, Santa Fe; Okla Art Ctr. Exhib: One-man shows, Inst Cult Rels, Mexico City, Mex, 61, Malaga, Spain, 63, Miami Mus Mod Art, 64, Artists House, Haifa, Israel, 64, Bernard Black Gallery, NY, 65, Jonson Gallery, Univ NMex, 77 & Newman Fine Arts, Scottsdale, Ariz, 78; plus many others. Teaching: Artist in residence, Univ Albuquerque, formerly. Pos: Art & film ed, KOAT TV, Albuquerque, currently; courtroom sketch artist, currently. Awards: Oriental Studies Found Grant, 62. Mem: Nat Mural Painters Soc. Style & Technique: Color dyes and pencil sketches for courtroom trial work; nationally known for Old Testament interpretations. Media: Oil, Mixed Media. Dealer: Newman Fine Arts 4224 N Craftsman Ct Scottsdale AZ. Mailing Add: 10309 Santa Paula Ave NE Albuquerque NM 87111

SUSSMAN, BONNIE K
ART DEALER, COLLECTOR
b Minneapolis, Minn. Study: Univ Minn, BS. Pos: Dir-owner, Peter M David Gallery, Minneapolis, 70- Bibliog: Don Morrison (auth), articles in Minneapolis Star, 70-77; Mike Steele (auth), articles in Minneapolis Tribune, 6/73; Charles Ohlenkamp (auth), article, Minneapolis Mag, 11/77; Janet Koplos (auth), articles, Minneapolis Star, 77-78; William R Hegeman (auth), articles, Minneapolis Tribune, 1/78. Mem: Metrop Art Dealers Asn, Twin Cities of Minnesota (founder & mem). Specialty: Contemporary prints, drawings, watercolor, photography; artists' books; handmade paper. Collection: Sculpture and paintings. Mailing Add: 430 Oak Grove St No 101 Minneapolis MN 55403

SUSSMAN, ELISABETH SACKS
CURATOR
b Baltimore, Md, July 16, 39. Study: Simmons Col, BS, 60; Boston Univ, MA(art hist), 64, grad work, 75- Collections Arranged: Roots of the San Francisco Bay Region Domestic Architectural Tradition, Univ Art Mus, Berkeley, 72; Frontier America, Mus Fine Arts, Boston, 75; Al Held—Paintings & Drawings 1973-1978 (auth catalogue), Inst Contemp Art, Boston, 78. Teaching: Museology, Tufts Univ, 75-77. Pos: Spec asst, Mus Fine Arts, Boston, 72-75; cur, Inst Contemp Art, Boston, 76- Mem: New Eng Coun, Am Asn Mus. Publ: Co-auth, San Francisco's shingle-style architects: Fitting a house to the land, Sat Rev, 72; co-auth, Building with nature: Roots of the San Francisco Bay Tradition, Peregrin-Smith, 74; contribr, Frontier America: The Far West, Mus Fine Arts, Boston, 75. Mailing Add: 45 Crescent St Cambridge MA 02138

SUTER, SHERWOOD EUGENE
EDUCATOR, PAINTER
b Bluffton, Ohio, Sept 22, 28. Study: Western Mich Univ, BS(art), 50; Columbia Univ, MFA & Fine Arts Educ, 56. Work: Abilene Savings Asn, Tex; First State Bank, Abilene. Exhib: State-wide Show of Paintings, Abilene Fine Arts Mus, Kendall Art Mus, San Angelo, Tex, Women's Art Forum, Wichita Falls & Howard Payne Col, Brownwood, 70-71; one-man show, Abilene Chamber of Commerce, 76. Collections Arranged: American Watercolor Society Annual Show, McMurry Col, Abilene. Teaching: Assoc prof & chmn art dept, McMurry Col, 57-; painting teacher, Evening Classes, YWCA, 74- & Abilene Fine Arts Mus, 74- Awards: Top Award/Watercolor, 70 & Top Award/Oil, 71, Abilene Fine Arts Mus, Abilene Savings Asn. Style & Technique: Abstract and non-objective oils; watercolors are more representational. Media: Watercolor; Oil. Mailing Add: 802 Mulberry Abilene TX 79601

SUTHERLAND, MARYLOU
ART LIBRARIAN
b Kalamazoo, Mich, Jan 6, 48. Study: Occidental Col, 66-68; Univ Calif, Berkeley, 68-70, BA(art hist); Univ Mich, 71-72, MLS. Pos: Art librn, Phoenix Pub Libr. Mem: Art Libr Soc NAm; Art Libr Soc Ariz (secy/treas, 76-77 & 77-78). Interest: Contemporary West Coast and Southwestern art. Mailing Add: 12 E McDowell Rd Phoenix AZ 85004

SUTHERLAND, SANDY
PAINTER,
b Cincinnati, Ohio, Apr 10, 02. Study: Art Students League; Mech Inst, NY. Work: Nat Arts Club. Exhib: Metrop Mus Art Exhib Am Watercolors, 52; Am Watercolor Soc, 70; Allied Artists Am, 71; Grand Cent Art Galleries, 72; Nat Arts Club, 72. Awards: Am Watercolor Soc Prize for Non-Mem, 51; Hoe Medal for Free Hand Drawing, Mech Inst, 55; First Award of Merit for Painting, Kenneth Taylor Gallery, 58. Mem: Allied Artists Am (dir); Am Watercolor Soc (rec secy, treas); Grand Cent Art Gallery; life mem Art Students League; Nat Arts Club. Media: Oil, Watercolor. Publ: Auth, Figure sketching in watercolor, 63 & Painting in oil on paper, 68, Am Artist. Mailing Add: 6740 Gulfport Blvd St Petersburg FL 33707

SUTTMAN, PAUL
SCULPTOR
b NMex, July 16, 33. Study: Univ NMex, BFA, 55; Cranbrook Acad Art, MFA, 57. Work: Joseph H Hirshhorn Mus, Washington, DC; Mus Mod Art, New York; Art Mus, Macomb Col, Mich; Kalamazoo Art Ctr; Roswell Art Ctr. Comn: Two figures, Eastland Shopping Ctr, Detroit, 65; figure, Martha Cooke Bldg, Univ Mich, 68. Exhib: Sculpture From Hirshhorn Collection, Guggenheim Mus, 62; Sculptors From Midwest, John Herron Inst, 63; Biennale Sculpture Contemp, Rodin Mus, Paris, 68 & 70; US Info Serv Traveling Exhib, Istanbul & Ankara, Turkey, 72; After Surrealism, Metaphors & Similies, Ringling Art Mus, Sarasota, Fla, 72; Los Angeles Mus, 77; Jodi Scurry Gallery, 77; Mus of Albuquerque, 78. Teaching: Instr sculpture, Univ Mich, Ann Arbor, 58-62; artist in residence, Dartmouth Col, spring 73; vis prof art, Univ NMex, 76- Awards: Rackham Found Res Grant, Italy, 60; Fulbright Fel Paris, Inst Int Educ, 63; Prix de Rome Fel, Am Acad Rome, 65-68. Bibliog: The Bronze Man, Nat Educ TV, 60. Media: Bronze, Marble. Dealer: Donald Morris Gallery 20082 Livernois Detroit MI 48221; Mekler Gallery Los Angeles CA. Mailing Add: Terry Dintenfass Inc 50 W 57th St New York NY 10021

SUTTON, GEORGE MIKSCH
PAINTER, ILLUSTRATOR
b Lincoln, Nebr, May 16, 98. Study: Bethany Col, BS, 23; ScD, 52; Univ Pittsburgh, 23-25; Cornell Univ, PhD, 32. Teaching: George Lynn Cross emer res prof zool, Univ Okla, presently. Pos: Emer cur birds, Stovall Mus, 68- Awards: Johns Burroughs Award, 62; Knight Cross Order of the Falcon, Iceland, 72. Mem: Wilson Ornithol Soc (past pres); Arctic Inst NAm; Cooper Ornithol Soc; Am Geog Soc; Am Ornithologists' Union (past councilman); plus others. Media: Watercolor. Publ: Auth & illusr, Iceland Summer, 61, Oklahoma Birds, 67 & Mexican Bird Portraits, 75, Univ Okla; auth & illusr, High Arctic, 71 & At a Bend in a Mexican River, 72, Eriksson; plus many others. Mailing Add: Stovall Mus Univ of Okla Norman OK 73069

SUTTON, PATRICIA
PAINTER
b New York, NY, Sept 9, 41. Study: Cornell Univ, 59-63, BFA; Brooklyn Mus Art Sch, summers 60-61; Art Students League, 63-64; Hunter Col, 64-68, MA. Work: Aldrich Mus of Contemp Art, Ridgefield, Conn; Joseph Hirshhorn Collection; Whitney Mus Am Art, New York; San Francisco Mus Fine Arts; Fogg Art Mus. Exhib: Lyrical Abstraction, Aldrich Mus of Contemp Art, 70 & Whitney Mus Am Art, 71; Highlights 1969-1970, 70 & Ten Years, 74, Aldrich Mus Contemp Art; Waves, Cranbrook Acad, Bloomfield Hills, Mich, 73; one-woman shows, Fairleigh Dickinson Univ, Rutherford, NJ, 68, four shows, Andre Emmerich Gallery, 70-75, Everson Mus, 70, Medici-Berenson Gallery, Fla, 72, 74 & 75 & Deutcher O'Reilly Gallery, 76. Teaching: Instr, Fairleigh Dickinson Univ, 68 & Hunter Col,

72; vis artist, San Francisco Art Inst, 74. Awards: First Prize, Scholastic Art Award, 59; NY State Coun on the Arts Grant & Am the Beautiful Fund Grant, Hoosick Falls Art Ctr, 71. Bibliog: Larry Aldrich (auth), Young Lyrical Painters, Art in Am, 11-12/69; Hilton Kramer (auth), Art: Two interesting talents make debut, New York times, 6/13/70 & Review, 10, 29/76; Grace Glueck (auth), Art People, New York Times, 9/17/76. Style & Technique: Oil on canvas; geometric abstraction. Media: Watercolor, Oil. Mailing Add: 11 Riverside Dr New York NY 10023

SUZUKI, JAMES HIROSHI
PAINTER
b Yokohama, Japan, Sept 19, 33. Study: Sch of Fine & Appl Art, Portland, Maine, 52; Corcoran Sch Art, 53-54; privately with Yoshio Markino. Work: Corcoran Gallery of Art, Washington, DC; Wadsworth Atheneum, Hartford, Conn; Rockefeller Inst, New York; Nat Mus Mod Art, Tokyo, Japan; Toledo Mus Art, Ohio. Exhib: Corcoran Gallery Art, 56, 58 & 60; Whitney Mus Am Art; Baltimore Mus Art, Md; Contemp Painters of Japanese Origin in Am, Inst Contemp Art, Boston; Cross-Currents, Am Fedn Arts, New York, 57-58; Everson Mus Art, Syracuse, NY, 58; Wadsworth Atheneum, 59; Waning Moon and Rising Sun, Mus Fine Arts of Houston, 59; San Francisco Mus Art, 63 & 64; Nat Mus Mod Art, Tokyo, 64; one-man show, Univ Calif, Berkeley, 63. Teaching: Instr, Univ Calif, Berkeley, 62-63 & Univ Ky, 66-68. Awards: Eugene Weiss Scholar, Corcoran Gallery Art, 54; John Hay Whitney Fel, 58; Larry Aldrich Prize, Silvermine Guild, 59. Mailing Add: 2003 MacArthur Blvd Oakland CA 94602

SUZUKI, KATSKO (KATSKO SUZUKI KANNEGIETER)
ART DEALER
b Nagoya, Japan. Study: Kinjyo Female Col, Nagoya; Bunka Fukuso Gakuin, Tokyo, Japan. Pos: Dir & pres, Suzuki Graphics, Inc, New York, 70-; juror Sumi-E Soc Am Exhib, 72. Bibliog: Article in Graphics: New York, 9/70; MaCnow (auth), article in High Fashion, 12/70; Kawabata (auth), article in Bungei Syunju Weekly, 1/71; R Lindsey (auth), article, New York Times, 11/13/72; E Stern (auth), article, New York Mag, 6/13/77. Specialty: Mainly specialized in graphics; many gallery artists are international; extended for small paintings, sculptures and other media at Suzuki Gallery (subsidiary). Publ: Auth, articles in Hanga Geijyutsu (Arts in Graphics), 74-75. Mailing Add: 38 E 57th St New York NY 10022

SUZUKI, SAKARI
PAINTER
b Iwateken, Japan; US citizen. Study: Calif Sch Fine Arts, San Francisco; Art Students League, Metrop scholar, 34. Work: High Mus Art, Atlanta, Ga; Dept Labor, Washington, DC. Comn: Mural, Willard Parker Hosp, New York, 37. Exhib: Corcoran Gallery Art, Washington, DC, 34; one-man shows, ACA Gallery, New York, 36, Artists Gallery, New York, 48 & 51 & Mandel Bros Art Gallery, Chicago, 55; Pa Acad Fine Arts, Philadelphia, 52. Teaching: Instr painting, Am Artists Sch, New York, 38-40. Pos: Scenic artist, Munic Opera, St Louis, Mo, 53-55; scenic artist, Starlight Theatre, Kansas City, Mo, 56-69; scenic artist, Gen Motors Futurama, 62-64; scenic artist, Lyric Opera, Chicago, 65-70. Awards: Am Artists Cong Prize, 36; Honorable Mention, Terry Nat Art Exhib, Miami, 52. Mem: United Scenic Artists Am. Style & Technique: Contemporary expressionism. Media: Oil. Mailing Add: 5040 Marine Dr Chicago IL 60640

SVENDSEN, LOUISE AVERILL
CURATOR
b Old Town, Maine, Nov 22, 15. Study: Wellesley Col, BA; Yale Univ, MA & PhD. Teaching: Instr hist of art, Duke Univ, Durham, NC, 43-45; asst prof hist of art, Goucher Col, Baltimore, Md, 45-50 & Am Univ, Washington, DC, 51-52; lectr, The Solomon R Guggenheim Mus, New York, 54-62. Pos: Assoc cur, The Solomon R Guggenheim Mus, 62-66, cur, 66- Publ: Auth, Rousseau, Redon and Fantasy, 68, auth, Ilya Bolotowsky, 74 & co-auth, The Solomon R Guggenheim Museum; Frank Lloyd Wright, Architect, 75, Guggenheim Mus. Mailing Add: 16 Park Ave New York NY 10016

SVENSON, JOHN EDWARD
SCULPTOR, COLLECTOR
b Los Angeles, Calif, May 10, 23. Study: Claremont Grad Sch, Calif; sculpture with Albert Stewart. Work: Alaska State Mus, Juneau; Ahmaoson Ctr, Los Angeles; City Mus & Nat Orange Show Permanent Collection, San Bernardino, Calif. Comn: Two hist panels, San Gabriel Mission Chapel, Calif, 58; bldg facade & sculpture, Purex Corp, Lakewood, Calif, 60; bronze Alaska Tlingit Medal, Soc Medalists Ann Issue, 72; medallion & sculpture, Alyeska Pipeline Serv, Anchorage; bas-relief, Alaska Mutual, Anchorage; plus others. Exhib: Otis Art Inst Galleries, Los Angeles, 60; Lang Galleries, Scripps Col, Claremont, 61; Los Angeles Co Mus Art, 62; Newman Galleries, Philadelphia, 71; Kennedy Galleries, New York, 72; Alaska State Mus; Green Galleries, Anchorage; plus others. Pos: Trustee, Alaska Indian Arts, Inc, Port Chilkoot, 67- Awards: First Prize, Greek Theater, Los Angeles, 51 & 54; two Awards for Excellence in Sculpture, Am Inst Archit, 57 & 61; First Prize, Laguna Art Festival, 61. Mem: Fel Nat Sculpture Soc; Soc Medalists, New York. Media: Wood, Fibreglass, by Antoine Barye & Paul Manship; paintings by Ramos Martinez & Henry Lee Stone. Mailing Add: PO Box 305 Green Valley Lake CA 92341

SWAIN, ROBERT
PAINTER
b Austin, Tex, Dec 7, 40. Study: Am Univ, Washington, DC, BA. Work: Corcoran Gallery of Art, Washington, DC; Walker Art Ctr, Minneapolis; Detroit Inst of Art, Mich; Albright-Knox Mus, Buffalo, NY; Everson Art Mus, Syracuse, NY. Comn: Painting (8 1/2ft x 20ft), Schering Labs, Bloomfield, NJ, comn by Skidmore, Owings & Merrill, New York, 70; painting (5ft x 10ft), Phillip Mallis of Kahn & Mallis Assocs, New York, 72. Exhib: The Art of the Real, Mus of Mod Art, New York, 68; one-man shows, Fischbach Gallery, New York, 68 & 69, Susan Caldwell Gallery, 74 & 76, Everson Art Mus, Syracuse, 74, Tex Gallery, 75 & Columbus Gallery of Fine Arts, Ohio, 76; 31st Biennial, Corcoran Gallery of Art, 69; The Structure of Color, Whitney Mus of Am Art, 71; Painting & Sculpture Today, Indianapolis Mus of Art, Ind, 74; Color as Language (traveling exhib, Latin Am), Mus of Mod Art, New York, 74-75. Awards: Guggenheim Fel, 69; Nat Endowment for Arts Grant, 76. Bibliog: Scott Burton (auth), Light, from Aten to Laser, MacMillan Co, 69; B Wasserman (auth), Modern Painting, Davis Publ, 70; Roberta Smith (auth), Rev, Artforum, 76. Style & Technique: Nonobjective painting. Media: Acrylic. Dealer: Susan Caldwell Inc 383 W Broadway New York NY 10013. Mailing Add: 57 Leonard St New York NY 10013

SWAIN, ROBERT FRANCIS
GALLERY DIRECTOR
b Halifax, NS, Oct 25, 42. Study: Carleton Univ, BA. Collections Arranged: Joan Frick, 74; Persian Rugs from Canadian Collections, 75; Robert Sinclair, 76. Pos: Dir, Gallery/Stratford. Mem: Can Mus Asn; Int Comt Mus; Ont Asn Art Galleries (dir). Mailing Add: 54 Romeo St Stratford ON N5A 4S9 Can

SWAN, BARBARA
PAINTER
b Newton, Mass, June 23, 22. Study: Wellesley Col, BA; Boston Mus Sch. Work: Philadelphia Mus Art; Boston Mus Art; Worcester Mus; Fogg Art Mus; Boston Pub Libr. Exhib: Carnegie Ann, 49; Contemporary American Painting, Univ Ill, 50; View 1960, Inst Contemp Arts, Boston, 60; Brooklyn Mus Biennial Print Exhib, 65; New Eng Women, De Cordova Mus, 75; Eight New Eng Artists, Works on Paper, Boston Mus of Fine Arts, 77. Teaching: Instr painting, Wellesley Col, 46-49; instr art, Milton Acad, 51-54; instr painting & drawing, Boston Univ, 60-65. Awards: Albert Whitin Traveling Fel, Boston Mus Art, 48; Assoc Scholar, Inst Independent Study, Radcliffe Col, 61-63; George Roth Prize, Philadelphia Print Club, 65. Style & Technique: Realist. Media: Oil. Dealer: Alpha Gallery 122 Newbury St Boston MA 02116. Mailing Add: 808 Washington St Brookline MA 02146

SWANSON, DEAN
ART CONSULTANT
b St Paul, Minn, Sept 7, 34. Study: Univ Minn, BA & MA. Collections Arranged: Robert Rauschenberg, 65; Richard Lindner, 69; Joan Miro Sculptures, 71; Morris Louis, 77. Teaching: Teaching asst, Univ Minn, 57-60. Pos: Asst cur, Walker Art Ctr, Minneapolis, 62, assoc cur, 64, chief cur, 67-77; exhibs coordr, Landmark Ctr, St Paul, Minn, 78- Mailing Add: 19 S First St Minneapolis MN 55401

SWANSON, J N
PAINTER, SCULPTOR
b Duluth, Minn, Feb 4, 27. Study: Col Arts & Crafts, Oakland, Calif; Carmel Art Inst; also with Donald Teague & Armin Hansen. Work: Cowboy Hall of Fame, Oklahoma City; BMA Collection, Kansas City; Read Mullin Collection, Phoenix; Sunset Mag Collection Art; Leaning Tree Mus, Boulder, Colo; Diamond M Mus, Tex. Comn: Pvt comn only. Exhib: Monterey Co Fair Prof Div, Calif, 67; Springville Regional Show, Utah; Cowboy Artists Ann Show, Hall of Fame, Okla, 70-75; Soc Western Artists, De Young Mus, San Francisco, 71; exhibs, Who's Who in Art Gallery, Carmel, Calif. Awards: San Francisco Best of Show Award, Monterey Co Fair, 67; Soc Western Artists Atelier Award, De Young Mus, 71. Bibliog: Ainsworth (auth), Cowboy in Art, World, 68; Paul Weaver (ed), Cowboy Artists Ann Exhib Bks, Northland, 69-75; Broder (auth), Bronzes of the American West, Abrams, 74 Mem: Cowboy Artists Am (vpres, 70). Style & Technique: Realistic and traditional; uses bristle brush. Media: Oil; Plastilene Clay. Res: Complete Western library for research into historical Western painting; first hand knowledge of the cowboy subject of present day. Collection: Several large paintings in oil of Western subject matter; collection of Mrs Swanson; sculpture. Mailing Add: Star Rte Box 120 Carmel Valley CA 93924

SWANSON, RAY V
PAINTER
b Alcester, SDak, Oct 4, 37. Study: Northrop Inst, BS, 60. Work: Indianapolis Mus Art; Riverside Art Collection Mus, Calif. Exhib: Wichita Nat Art Exhib, Kans, 70; Franklin Mint Gallery Am Art, 73-74; Capitol Bldg, Phoenix, Ariz, 75; Nat Acad Western Art, Cowboy Hall of Fame, 76. Pos: Judge, Traditional Art Show, San Bernardino, Calif, 69; art comt dir, George Phippen Mem Art Show, Prescott, Ariz, 76-78. Awards: Gold Medal, Nat Acad Western Art, Cowboy Hall of Fame, 75; Silver Medal, Royal Western Watercolor, Cowboy Hall of Fame, Fame, 75; Gold Medal, Franklin Mint Gallery, 75-76. Bibliog: J & J Ward (auth), Renaissance of Western Art, Franklin Mint Gallery, 74; Tom Cooper (auth), The Best of Arizona Highways, Ariz Hwys, 75; Royal B Hassrick (auth), Western Painting Today, Watson-Guptill Publ, 75. Mem: Prescott Fine Arts Asn. Style & Technique: Traditional realism. Media: Oil; Watercolor. Publ: Contribr, Artist of the Rockies, Colo Publ, 75; contribr, Arizona Highways, 75; contribr, Illuminator, Grand Cent Publ, 75. Dealer: Husberg Fine Arts Gallery Sedona AZ 86336. Mailing Add: 15 Perkins Dr Prescott AZ 86301

SWARD, ROBERT S
WRITER, ART EDITOR
b Chicago, Ill, June 23, 33. Study: Univ Ill, BA, 56; Univ Iowa, MA, 58. Work: Provincial Collection, Victoria, BC. Pos: Ed & publ, Soft Press, Victoria, 70-; ed & production coordr, Hancock House Publ, BC. Awards: MacDowell Colony & Yaddo Grants, 59-69; Guggenheim Fel, 64-65; D H Lawrence Fel, Univ NMex, 66. Mem: League of Can Poets; Signal Hill Poets Group. Style & Technique: Lithographs are free-form, pop, in collaboration with Peter Daglish; photography, graphic arts, fine printing and hand-type setting. Publ: Contribr, New American & Canadian Poetry, 73; auth, Letter to a Straw Hat (with graphics), 74; auth, Jurassic Shales, 75; ed, Cheers for Muktananda, 75; auth, Honey Bear on Lasqueti Island, BC, 78. Mailing Add: 1050 St David St Victoria BC Can

SWARTZ, BETH AMES
PAINTER
b New York, NY, Feb 5, 36. Study: Art Students League; Cornell Univ, BS, 57; NY Univ, MA, 60; and with Dorothy Fratt, 70-71. Work: Ariz State Univ Mem Union Collection & Mathews Ctr Collection; New Tucson Art Mus Permanent Collection; Valley Nat Bank Permanent Collection; Ariz Bank Permanent Collection. Exhib: Eight State Regional Watercolor Exhib (touring), 71-73; 8-West Biennial, Grand Junction, Colo, 74; Joslyn Art Mus, Omaha, Nebr, 74; Tex Fine Arts Asn 64th Ann, Laguna Gloria Mus, Austin, 75; Arizona/Women/75, Tucson Art Mus; Fine Arts Mus, Santa Fe, NMex, 76; Whitney Counterweight, New York, 77; Four-Corners Biennial, Phoenix Art Mus, 77; plus others. Teaching: Assoc, Exten Dept, Ariz State Univ, 63-74. Bibliog: B Cortright (auth), article in Artweek, 5/3/75 & Artspace, winter 78; William Peterson (auth), articles in Artspace, 77; Irene Clurman (auth), Ten works by ten artists reveal insights, Rocky Mountain News, 7/17/77; plus others. Mem: Nat & Ariz Art Educ Asns. Style & Technique: Abstract; ordering/disordering/reordering paper with mixed-media (fire, sunlight, earth); layered, textural works on paper, lyrical and luminiscent in feeling; nature-rooted. Media: Fire on Paper; Mixed-Media. Publ: Are we stifling our children's creativity?, Point West Mag, 63; Help your child create, Art Handbook for Parents, 65; auth, Inquiry into fire, Ariz Artist, fall 77. Dealer: c/o Suzanne Brown Art Wagon Gallery 7156 Main St Scottsdale AZ 85251. Mailing Add: 5346 E Sapphire Lane Scottsdale AZ 85253

SWARTZ, PHILLIP SCOTT
PAINTER, COLLECTOR
b Robinson, Ill, May 20, 36. Study: Eastern Ill Univ, BS(educ), 58, MS(educ), 63; Miami Univ, Ohio, grad studies. Work: J B Speed Mus, Louisville, Ky. Exhib: Viewpoint 75, Cincinnati Art Club, Ohio, 75; Miniature Painters, Sculptors & Gravers, Washington Arts Club, DC, 75, 76 & 77; Nat Small Painting Exhib Biennial, Gallery North, Mt Clemons, Mich, 76; Am Nat Miniature Exhib, Laramie Art Guild, Wyo, 76-77; Contemp Miniature (traveling exhib), Univ Mich, Ann Arbor, 77. Collections Arranged: Hamilton Campus, Miami Univ, Ohio. Pos: Coordr, Artist & Lectr Series, Miami Univ, 76- Awards: Award of Excellence, Northbrook Art League Invitational, 76; Honorable Mention, Ky State Fair, 77; Second Prize, Am Nat Miniature Exhib, Laramie Art Guild, 77. Mem: Alliance of Prof

Artists of Ohio, Ky & Ind; Fine Arts Coun, Hamilton, Ohio. Style & Technique: Reverse painting on glass in acrylic and enamel, verre eglomise. Media: Acrylic and Oil. Collection: Contemporary prints. Publ: Co-auth, The Scientific Interest of Robert W Gibbes, SC Mag of Hist, 65. Mailing Add: 3409 Amberway Ct Cincinnati OH 45239

SWARTZMAN, ROSLYN
PRINTMAKER, EDUCATOR
b Montreal, Que, Aug 17, 31. Study: Montreal Artists Sch; Montreal Mus Fine Arts; Ecole des Beaux Arts, with Albert Dumouchez. Work: Nat Gallery Can, Ottawa, Ont; Montreal Mus Fine Arts, Que; Bradford City Art Mus, Eng; Brooklyn Mus, NY; Winnipeg Art Gallery, Manitoba. Exhib: 2nd Brit Int Print Biennial, Bradford, 70; Int Traveling Exhib Graphics, Montreal, 71; La Bienal de Ibiza, Spain, 72-74; Que Artists, Milan, Italy, 74; 2nd Int Graphics Biennial, Miami, 75; Jewish Experience in the 20th Century, Mt St Vincent Univ, Halifax, NS; Can Landscape through Drawings & Prints, Mus Fine Arts, Montreal. Teaching: Teacher & dir graphics dept, Sayde Bronfman Ctr, Montreal, 71- Awards: First Prize Painting & Third Price Graphics, Que Prov Exhib Painting, Photog & Graphics, 57; Second Prize Painting, Concours Artistiques, Que, 58; G A Reid Award Etching, Soc Can Painter, Etchers & Engravers, 65. Mem: Royal Can Acad; Graphic Arts Coun Can; Print & Drawing Coun Can; Graphics Soc New Hampshire. Style & Technique: Deeply etched and embossed color etchings and collographs. Media: Intaglio; Bas-Relief Sculpture. Dealer: Gallery Pascal Graphics 334 Dundas St W Toronto ON Can. Mailing Add: 4174 Oxford St Montreal PQ H4A 2Y4 Can

SWARZ, SAHL
SCULPTOR
b New York, NY, May 4, 12. Study: Clay Club New York; Art Students League. Work: Whitney Mus Am Art, New York; Minneapolis Inst Fine Arts; NJ State Mus, Trenton; Richmond Mus Fine Arts, Va; Vatican Mus, Italy. Comn: Guardian (bronze), Brookgreen Gardens Mus, SC, 39; Equestrian Mem to Gen Bidwell, Buffalo, 49; symbolic wood figures, US Courthouse, Statesville, NC, 45; mall sculpture, Pittsfield, Mass, 71; fountain sculpture, State of NJ, Spruce Run Recreational Park, 72. Exhib: Whitney Mus Am Art Ann, 48-62; Pa Acad Fine Arts, 49-58; one-man shows, Sculpture Ctr, 54-74; Ill Biennial, 57 & 59; Bronzetto Int Padua, Italy, 59 & 61. Teaching: Instr sculpture, Brandeis Univ, 64-65; instr sculpture, Univ Wis-Madison, 66; asst prof sculpture, Columbia Univ, 66-78; instr sculpture, New Sch Social Res, 67-70. Awards: Am Acad Arts & Lett Grant, 55; J S Guggenheim Mem Found Grants, 55 & 58; Gov Purchase Prize, NJ State Mus, 65. Mem: Sculpture Ctr (assoc dir, 34-53). Style & Technique: Gradual development from figurative forms to non-figurative, with increasing emphasis on simple, basic structure. Media: Bronze, Steel. Publ: Auth & illusr, Blueprint for the Future of American Sculpture, 44; auth, Ilse Erythropel (monograph). Dealer: Sculpture Center 167 E 69th St New York NY 10021. Mailing Add: 351 Jay St Brooklyn NY 11201

SWARZENSKI, HANNS PETER THEOPHIL
ART HISTORIAN, WRITER
b Berlin, Ger, Aug 30, 03; US citizen. Study: Univ Bonn, PhD, 27; Fogg Art Mus, Harvard Univ, 27-28. Work: Berlin State Mus; Nat Gallery Art, Washington; Boston Mus Fine Arts. Collections Arranged: Rathbone Years, Boston Mus Fine Arts, 72; Zeit der Staufen, Stuttgart Landes Museum, 77. Teaching: Spec lectr medieval art, Warburg Inst, Univ London, 46-54. Pos: Res fel, Inst Advan Study, Princeton, NJ, 36-48; actg cur sculpture, Nat Gallery Art, Washington, DC, 44-46; asst cur painting, Boston Mus of Fine Arts, 48-58, cur decorative arts & sculpture, 53-72. Mem: Am Acad Arts & Sci. Res: Medieval art. Publ: Auth, Deutsche Buchmalerei des 13 Jahrhunderts, 36; auth, The Berthold Missal, 43; co-auth, English Sculptures of the 12th Century, 52; auth, Monuments of Romanesque Art, 53. Mailing Add: Haus Hollerberg 8121 Wilzhofen OBB Germany

SWAY, ALBERT
PAINTER, ETCHER
b Cincinnati, Ohio, Aug 6, 13. Study: Cincinnati Art Acad; Art Students League. Work: Metrop Mus Art, New York; New York Pub Libr; Carnegie Inst; Pa State Univ; Soc New York Hosp. Exhib: Libr Cong, 43-45; Albright-Knox Art Gallery, 51; Soc Am Graphic Artists, 51-; Royal Soc Painters, Etchers & Engravers, London, Eng, 54; Am-Japan Contemp Print Exhib, Tokyo, 67; plus many others. Teaching: Instr drawing & painting, New York Hosp League, 63-64. Awards: First Prize in Graphics, Cincinnati Mus Asn, 39. Mem: Soc Am Graphic Artists. Style & Technique: Realistic. Publ: Illusr filmstrips on New York State history, produced by Our York State, NY, 50-; med illusr, A Syllabus for Health Visitors, Navajo Tribal Coun, Ariz, 60; med illusr, Respiratory diseases, Nat Tuberculosis Asn, 61; med illusr, Hepatic Excretory Function (ser filmstrips); Am Gastroenterol Asn, 72; med illusr, Congenital Malforma tions of the Heart, Grune & Stratton, 75; plus med illus in sci jour. Mailing Add: PO Box 43 Kendall Park NJ 08824

SWEENEY, J GRAY
CURATOR, ART HISTORIAN
b Jacksonville, Fla, Nov 20, 43. Study: Univ NMex, BA, 66; Ind Univ, MA, 69, PhD, 75, study with Profs Louis Hawes, John Hacobus & Albert Elsen. Collections Arranged: Themes in American Painting, Grand Rapids Art Mus, 10-11/77; The Agrarian Landscape in American and French Painting, Tweed Mus of Art, Duluth, Minn, 12/77. Teaching: Asst prof 19th & 20th century Am painting, Grand Valley State Col, 71- Pos: Cur, Themes in Am painting, Grand Rapids Art Mus, 71-77. Mem: Col Art Asn. Res: Nineteenth century American landscape and genre painting. Publ: Auth, Themes in American Painting, Steketee-Van Huis, 77; auth, The Agrarian Landscape in American and French Painting, Univ Minn, 77; co-auth, The Permanent Collection of the Hackley Art Museum, Stekett-Van Huis, 78. Mailing Add: 335 Garfield NW Grand Rapids MI 49504

SWEENEY, JAMES JOHNSON
ART ADMINISTRATOR, LECTURER
b Brooklyn, NY, May 30, 00. Study: Georgetown Univ, AB, 22 & Hon LHD, 63; Jesus Col, Cambridge Univ, 22-24; Sorbonne, Paris, 25; Univ Siena, 26; Hon DFA, Grinnell Col, 57, Univ Mich, 60, Univ Notre Dame, 61 & Univ Buffalo, 62; Hon LHD, Rollins Col, 60, Col of the Holy Cross, 60 & Univ Miami, 68; Ripon Col, Hon ArtsD, 60. Collections Arranged: Many exhibs, Univ Chicago, Mus Mod Art, New York, Art Gallery Toronto, Va Mus Fine Arts, Mass Inst Technol, Mus Art Mod, Paris, Tate Gallery, London & Honolulu Acad Arts. Teaching: Lectr, many univs & mus, US, 35- Pos: Dir painting & sculpture, Mus Mod Art, New York, 45-46; dir, Guggenheim Mus, New York, 52-60; dir, Mus Fine Arts, Houston, 61-68, consult dir, 68-; gallery consult, Nat Capital Develop Comn, Canberra, Australia, 68-; mem vis comt visual & performing arts, Harvard Univ & fine arts, Fogg Art Mus, 69-; adv purchase, Arts Coun Northern Ireland, Belfast, 70-72; art adv, Israel Mus, 72-; also mem bd dirs, trustee, adv, fel or hon mem many art orgns, socs, comts, acad, workshops, asns, clubs, insts, coun & found, US & Europe. Awards: Chevalier, Legion d'Honneur, France, 55; Officier, Ordre des Arts et des Lett, Paris, 59; Art Am Award, 63. Mem: Asn Int Art les Moyens Audio-Visuels (vpres, 72-); hon mem Arts Club Chicago; hon mem Buffalo Fine Arts Acad; hon mem Int Coun Mus Mod Art; hon mem Am Inst Interior Designers; plus many others. Publ: Auth, Vision & Image, 68, African Sculpture, 70, Joan Miro, 70, Alexander Calder, 71 & Pierre Soulages, 72; plus many other bks, articles & films. Mailing Add: 120 East End Ave New York NY 10028

SWENEY, FRED
ILLUSTRATOR, PAINTER
b Holidaysburg, Pa, June 5, 12. Study: Cleveland Sch Art. Work: In pvt collections. Teaching: Instr, Ringling Sch Art, 49-78. Pos: Supvr, Leece-Neville Co; artist-illur, Brown & Bigelow, 49- Awards: Nat Offset Lithographic Award, Brown & Bigelow, 60, Lithographic Award, 61 & Graphic Arts Award, 62. Style & Technique: Extreme realism, patterned after the old masters in technique. Media: Oil. Publ: Auth & illusr, Techniques of Drawing and Painting Wildlife, 59; auth & illusr, Drawing and Painting Birds, 61; auth & illusr, Painting the American Scene in Watercolor, 64; illusr, Nat Geog; illusr & contribr, Sports Afield Mag. Mailing Add: 4576 Cooper Rd Sarasota FL 33582

SWENSEN, MARY JEANETTE HAMILTON (JEAN)
PAINTER, PRINTMAKER
b Laurens, SC, June 25, 10. Study: Columbia Univ, with Hans Mueller, BS, 56, with Arthur Young, MA(graphic arts), 60; Fine Arts Sch for Am, Fountainbleau, France, with Lucien Fontanerosa; Ariz State Univ, with Arthur Hahn, 5 summers. Work: Metrop Mus Art, New York; Nat Graphic Arts Collection, Smithsonian Inst, Washington, DC; Graphic Arts Collection, New York Pub Libr; Laurens Pub Libr, SC. Exhib: Soc Western Artists, M H de Young Mus, San Francisco, 64; Nat Art Roundup, Las Vegas, Nev, 65; Fine Arts Bldg, Colo State Fair, Pueblo, 65; Duncan Gallery, Paris, 74. Awards: Honorable Mention for Drawing, Soc Western Artists, 64; Duncan Gallery Prix de Paris, 74. Mem: Delta Phi Delta; Am Mensa Ltd; Int Platform Asn. Style & Technique: Lithography; Chinese style wash drawings in sumi and in acrylics on paper or canvas. Mailing Add: 684 W 99th Ave Denver CO 80221

SWENSON, ANNE
PAINTER, LECTURER
b Stafford Springs, Conn. Study: Art Students League; also with William Fisher, Vincent Drennan, Paul Giambertone & Tetsuya Kochi. Work: St Peter's Rectory, Staten Island, NY; pvt collection of Camillo Navarra, Italian architect. Exhib: Staten Island Mus, 55-61; Nat Arts Club, New York, 69 & Geometric Complexities, 77; Washington Mus Fine Arts, Hagerstown, Md, 71; Metrop Mus Art, 75 & 77; Avery Fisher Hall, Lincoln Ctr, 75 & 77; Snug Harbor Cult Ctr, Staten Island, NY, 76; Artists Equity Asn Exhib, Union Carbide Gallery, 77; Metrop Jr Mus Exhib (slide show of paintings with poetry), 77; Goldsboro Art Ctr, NC, 77. Teaching: Lectr & demonstr mosaics, Staten Island Mus, 59-; instr art & head dept, St Peter's Elem Sch, Staten Island, 60-62; lectr & demonstr painting, Susan Wagner High Sch, Staten Island, 74. Awards: Anna B Morse Gold Medal, Gotham Painters, 66; New York City Chap Second Place Award for Watercolor, Composers, Auth & Artists Am, 69, Nat Exhib Honorable Mention for Oil, 71. Bibliog: Bibliog with photos of work, Staten Island Advan, 59, 60 & 69; Anne Swenson, Composers, Authors & Artists of Am, Vol 26, No 1 & Vol 26, No 4. Mem: Burr Artists (dir, 67-); Artists Equity Asn of NY; Gotham Painters; Composers, Auth & Artists Am, Inc (treas, New York Chap, 70-72, historian, 72-); Fedn Staten Island Artists & Craftsmen. Media: Oil, Watercolor. Publ: Illusr, Indian Asn Am; auth, Rugs through the ages, New Bull Staten Island Mus, Vol 9, No 3. Mailing Add: 10 Phelps Pl Staten Island NY 10301

SWIFT, DICK
PRINTMAKER, EDUCATOR
b Long Beach, Calif, Nov 29, 18. Study: Los Angeles State Col, BA; Claremont Grad Sch, MFA; Chouinard Art Inst; Art Students League. Work: San Jose Col; Univ Ill; Cincinnati Mus Asn; Drake Univ; Zanesville Art Inst; plus many others. Exhib: One-man show, Santa Barbara Mus; Otis Art Inst, Calif Palace of Legion of Honor, Los Angeles Mus Art, Pasadena Mus Art & Pa Acad Fine Arts, 65-69; plus many other group & one-man shows. Teaching: Prof art, Calif State Univ, Long Beach, 58- Awards: Prizes, Am Color Print Soc, 65, Philadelphia Mus Art, 68 & Otis Art Inst, 69; plus many others. Mem: Am Color Print Soc; Los Angeles Print Soc (pres, 68-69). Media: Graphics. Mailing Add: Dept of Art Calif State Univ Long Beach CA 90840

SWIGART, LYNN S
PHOTOGRAPHER
b Kansas City, Mo, Aug 22, 30. Study: Bradley Univ, Peoria, Ill, BS(psychol, philos); also photog with Minor White & George Tice. Work: Carpenter Ctr for the Visual Arts, Harvard Univ, Cambridge, Mass. Exhib: One-man shows, Lakeview Ctr for Arts, Peoria, 71, Zone V Gallery, Watertown, Mass, 73, Enjay Gallery, Boston, 74, Knox Col, Galesburg, Ill, 75; Erie Art Ctr, Pa, 75; Williams Benton Mus, Univ of Conn, 77. Teaching: Instr photog, Multi-Media Arts Inst, Bradley Univ, summer 73 & 74. Mem: Lakeview Ctr for Arts; Ill Arts Coun Visual Arts Panel; Peoria Art Guild. Style & Technique: Primarily black and white prints in the naturalistic tradition. Publ: Contribr, Bradley Rev, 75 & Boundry, 2/76. Dealer: Peoria Art Guild 1831 N Knoxville Peoria IL 61603. Mailing Add: 1624 W Parkside Dr Peoria IL 61606

SWIGGETT, JEAN DONALD
EDUCATOR, PAINTER
b Franklin, Ind, Jan 6, 10. Study: Chouinard Inst Fine Art, Los Angeles, 30-31; San Diego State Univ, AB, 34; Univ Southern Calif, MFA, 39; Claremont Grad Sch, 50-52. Work: Long Beach Mus Art; Fine Arts Gallery, San Diego. Comn: Mural, Post Off, Franklin, Ind, 39; murals, SS President Jackson & SS President Adams, 40-41; illus, Psychol Today, 75. Exhib: Calif-Hawaii Regionals, San Diego Fine Arts Gallery, 71, 72 & 74; Reality-Illusion, Downey Mus Art, 72; Reality in Las Vegas, Univ Nev, 72; Southern Calif Regional Drawing & Print Show, 73, 74, 75, 76 & 77; Varieties of Visual Reality, Northern Ariz Univ, 75. Teaching: Teaching asst drawing, Univ Southern Calif, 40-41; instr painting, Wash State Col, 41-42; prof painting & drawing, San Diego State Univ, 46-77, emer prof, 77- Awards: San Diego Art Inst Ann, 71; Calif-Hawaii Regional Award, San Diego Fine Arts Gallery, 72; Jewish Community Ctr Award, San Diego, 73; plus others. Mem: Art Guild Fine Art Soc, San Diego (pres, 51-52, secy, 77-78). Style & Technique: Realist with classical and surrealist overtones. Media: Oil. Res: Romanesque architecture and sculpture. Mailing Add: 9275 Briarcrest Dr La Mesa CA 92041

SWINTON, GEORGE
PAINTER, WRITER
b Vienna, Austria, Apr 17, 17; Can citizen. Study: McGill Univ, BA, 46; Montreal Sch Art & Design, 47; Art Students League. Work: Nat Gallery Can; Vancouver Art Gallery; Winnipeg Art Gallery; Hamilton Art Gallery; Confederation Art Ctr, Charlottetown. Exhib: 2 retrospectives, Winnipeg Art Gallery; 4 Can Biennials; 3 Montreal Spring Exhibs; 11

Winnipeg Shows; many one-man shows. Teaching: Lectr art, Smith Col, 50-53; prof art, Univ Man, 54-, adj prof anthrop, 70- Awards: 3 Can Coun Grants. Res: Media: Oil, Watercolor. Res: Prehistoric and contemporary Eskimo art. Publ: Auth, Eskimo Sculpture/Sculpture Esquimaude, 65; illusr, Red River of the North, 67; co-auth, Sculpture/Inuit, 71; auth, Sculpture of the Eskimo, 72. Mailing Add: c/o Upstairs Gallery 266 Edmonton St Winnipeg MB R3C 1R9 Can

SWIRNOFF, LOIS
PAINTER, EDUCATOR
b Brooklyn, NY, May 9, 31. Study: Cooper Union, cert of grad, 51; Yale Univ, with Josef Albers, BFA, 53, MFA, 56. Work: Addison Gallery Am Art, Andover; Radcliffe Inst, Harvard Univ; Jewett Art Ctr, Wellesley Col. Exhib: Americans in Italy, Munson-Williams-Proctor Inst, Utica, NY; American Fulbright Painters, Duveen-Graham Gallery, New York, 57; Impressions Gallery & Swetzoff Gallery, Boston, 58-63; Boston Arts Festivals, 63-64; Affect/Effect, La Jolla Mus, Calif, 68; Radcliffe Inst for Independent Study, 74; Carpenter Ctr, Harvard Univ, 75; Wright Gallery, Univ Calif, Los Angeles, 77. Teaching: Instr art, Wellesley Col, 56-60; asst prof art, Univ Calif, Los Angeles, 63-68; lectr visual & environ studies, Harvard Univ, 68-75; assoc prof & chmn, Dept Art, Skidmore Col, 75- Awards: Fulbright Fel to Italy, 51-52; Radcliffe Inst Independent Study Fel, 61-63; Univ Calif Fel for Jr Fac, 67; auth, On color and form, Leonardo, Pergamon Press, 76. Style & Technique: Abstract. Media: Acrylic, Gouache, Oil. Mailing Add: Dept of Art Skidmore Col Saratoga Springs NY 12866

SYKES, (WILLIAM) MALTBY
PAINTER, PRINTMAKER
b Aberdeen, Miss, Dec 13, 11. Study: With Wayman Adams, John Sloan, Diego Rivera, Andre Lhote, Fernand Leger & Stanley William Hayter. Work: Mus Mod Art, New York; Stedlijk Mus, Amsterdam; Metrop Mus Art, New York; Boston Mus Fine Arts; Philadelphia Mus Art. Comn: Color engravings ed 210 prints, Trellis, Int Graphic Arts Soc, 55, Cathedral Interior, 58 & Floating Still Life, 62. Exhib: Salon d'Automne, Paris, 51; Int Biennial Contemp Color Lithography, Cincinnati Art Mus, 52; Am Watercolors, Drawings & Prints, Metrop Mus Art, New York, 52; Curator's Choice Exhib, Philadelphia Print Club, 56; Contemp Am Graphic Art, US Info Agency & Tour Abroad, 61. Teaching: Prof art, Auburn Univ, 42-77, artist in residence, 68-77, emer prof, 77- Awards: Albany Inst Hist & Art Purchase Award, Print Club, Albany, 63; Philip & Esther Klein Award, Am Color Print Soc, 65; Sabbatical Award, Nat Endowment Arts, 67-68. Mem: Soc Am Graphic Artists. Style & Technique: Black and white and color printmaking; semi-abstract. Media: Oil, Acrylic; Etching, Engraving, Lithograph. Publ: Auth, The Multimetal lithography process, Artists Proof, 68; contribr, Printmaking Today, Holt, Rinehart & Winston, rev ed, 72; contribr, The Print, Abrams, 75. Mailing Add: 712 Brenda Ave Auburn AL 36830

SYLVESTER, LUCILLE
PAINTER, WRITER
b Russia; US citizen. Study: Acad Julian, Paris, with Pierre Montezin; Art Students League, with Robert Brackman & Robert Phillips. Work: Tel Aviv Univ. Exhib: One-man show, Hammer Gallery, New York, 39; 1st Ann Contemp Drawings, Nat Acad Design, New York, 44-45; Allied Artists Am Ann, Nat Acad Design Galleries, 55; Nat Arts Club, New York, 57; Mus Art, Springville, Utah, 68. Teaching: Instr art, Jr High Schs, New York; lectr art, var schs, clubs & groups, 59- Pos: Juror, Queensboro Outdoor Art Ann, 52; chmn jury of awards, 3rd Ann Art Exhib Jewish Teachers Asn New York, 63. Awards: First Prize, Knickerbocker Artists Ann, 52; Lewis & Lewis Award, Catharine Lorillard Wolfe Art Club Ann, 57; Grumbacher Mat Award, 59. Bibliog: Article in New York Times, 3/27/38; Andrew Danzak (auth), article in Chelsea-Clinton News, 4/52; Gordon Sinclair (auth), Let's Be Personal (broadcast), CFRB, 2/9/65. Mem: Knickerbocker Artists (first vpres, 62-65, bd dirs, 69-71); fel Am Artists Prof League; Audubon Artists; Catharine Lorillard Wolfe Art Club; life mem Art Students League. Style & Technique: Traditional. Media: Oil. Publ: Auth, The meaning of art (play), Plays Mag, 11/47; auth, This Changing World: the Story of the Flag, 48; auth, Loyal Queen Esther, 56; auth & illusr, Portrait in Prose and Paint, 64; auth & illusr, six hist articles on New York, 68-69. Mailing Add: 200 W 20th St New York NY 10011

SYLVESTRE, GUY
ART CRITIC, WRITER
b Sorel, PQ, May 17, 18. Study: Col Ste Marie, Montreal; Univ Ottawa, MA. Pos: Ed, Gants du Ciel, 43-46; nat librn, Nat Libr, Ottawa, presently. Mem: Fedn Can Artists; Soc Ecrivains Can; Can Libr Asn; Royal Soc Can Acad Can Francaise. Publ: Auth, Anthologie de la Poesie Canadienne-Francaise, Beauchemin, 64 & 74; auth, Panorama des Lettres Canadiennes Francaises, 64 & Literature in French Canada, 67, EOQ; auth, Ecrivains Canadiens, HMH, 64 & McGraw, 67; auth, Structures Sociales du Canada Francais, Laval, 66; plus many others. Mailing Add: 1870 Rideau Garden Ottawa ON Can

SZABO, STEPHEN LEE
PHOTOGRAPHER
b Berwick, Pa, July 17, 40. Study: Art Ctr Col Design, Los Angeles, Calif; Pa State Univ. Work: Mus Mod Art, New York; Libr of Cong, Washington, DC; Int Mus Photog, George Eastman House, Rochester, NY; Corcoran Gallery Art, Washington, DC; Int Ctr Photog, New York. Exhib: Old Techniques by Young Photographers, Smithsonian Inst, Washington, DC, 73, Eastern Shore, Phillips Collection, Washington, DC, 73, Univ Kans, Lawrence, 76, Springfield Art Mus, Mo, 77, Hunter Mus Art, Chattanooga, Tenn, 77, Int Ctr Photog, NY, 77, Fine Arts Mus of the South, Mobile, Ala, 77 & Baltimore Mus Art, Md, 77. Bibliog: Paul Richard (auth), Of time and the photograph, Washington Post, 72; A dialogue with the present to document the past, Camera, 76; Mark Power (auth), Washington photographs and the contact print, Wash Rev of the Arts, 77. Style & Technique: Personal documentary, large format view camera; platinum printings. Publ: Illusr, Where We Live, Fed Home Loan Mortgage Corp, 73; auth-illusr, The Eastern Shore, Addison House, 76. Dealer: Kathleen Ewing 3615 Ordway St Washington DC 20016. Mailing Add: Quindacqua Ltd 3615 Ordway St Washington DC 20016

SZARAMA, JUDITH LAYNE
PRINTMAKER, INSTRUCTOR
b Stamford, Conn, Aug 12, 40. Study: Swain Sch Design, New Bedford, Mass, dipl. Work: Mint Mus, Charlotte, NC; Miami Art Ctr, Fla; Miami Pub Libr Lending Print Collection. Comn: Flight-tourist attractions on schedule of airline, Eastern Air Lines, Hartley Training Ctr, Miami, 69. Exhib: One-man show, Prints & Drawings, Baker Gallery, Coconut Grove, Fla, 67; Soc Am Graphic Artists 51st Print Ann, Kennedy Gallery, New York, 71; 33 Miami Artists, Miami Art Ctr, 71; 9th Nat Biennial Print Exhib, Silvermine Guild Artists, New Canaan, Conn, 72; Drawings, Ft Lauderdale Mus Arts, Fla, 72. Teaching: Instr anat & figure drawing, etching & painting, Miami Art Ctr; instr drawing, Div Archit Studies, RI Sch Design, 75, instr drawing & composition, Summer Workshop Prog, 75. Pos: Tech illusr, Eastern Air Lines, Miami, 67-70; asst to chmn grad studies, RI Sch Design, 73-75, dir exhib, 75- Awards: Mint Mus Purchase Award, 70; Outstanding Educator of Am, 75; Woman of the Yr, State of RI, 75. Bibliog: Frank Laurent (auth), Art, 68 & Bob Watters (auth), Where to let your art hang out, 71, Village Post, Coconut Grove. Mem: Mangrove (rec secy, 70). Media: Pencil, Graphic. Mailing Add: RI Sch of Design 2 College St Providence RI 02903

SZESKO, JUDITH CLARANN
See Jaidinger, Judith C

SZESKO, LENORE RUNDLE
PAINTER, PRINTMAKER
b Galesburg, Ill, Mar 13, 33. Study: Art Inst Chicago, BFA(drawing, painting, illus), 61, MFA(painting), 66; wood engraving with Adrian Troy. Work: Standard Oil Co, Chicago; NJ State Mus; Jayell Publ House, Miami, Fla; Springfield Col; Kemper Ins Co Collection, Long Grove, Ill. Exhib: Conn Acad Fine Arts 62nd Ann, Wadsworth Atheneum, Hartford, Conn, 72; Cedar City Ann Fine Art Exhib, Utah, 72-75; Contemp Am Graphics, Old Bergen Art Guild, Bayonne, NJ (traveling exhib), 72-76; Soc Am Graphic Artists 52nd Nat Print Exhib, New York & Chicago, 73; NH Print Club 1st & 2nd Int, Nashua, 73-74. Awards: Anonymous Prize Graphics, Nat Acad Design, New York, 70; James R Marsh Mem Purchase Prize, Hunterdon Art Ctr 16th Print, Clinton, NJ, 72; Muth Award, Miniature Painters, Sculptors & Gravers Soc of Washington, DC, 73; Award Highest Merit/Drawing, Miniature Art Soc of Fla Nat Exhib, 76. Mem: Audubon Artists, Inc, New York; Painters & Sculptors Soc NJ; Boston Printmakers, Mass; Miniature Art Soc NJ; La Watercolor Soc. Style & Technique: Composition-static and heiratic-subject matter, surrealist; technic careful and much attention to final detail. Media: Wood Engraving: Ink Drawing; Watercolor. Collection: American Indian and Pre-Columbian, some African art; antique furniture and dolls. Mailing Add: 835 S Ridgeland Ave Oak Park IL 60304

SZNAJDERMAN, MARIUS S
PAINTER, PRINTMAKER
b Paris, France, July 18, 26; US citizen. Study: Sch of Plastic Arts, Caracas, Venezuela, 47-48, with Rafael Monasterios, Ramon Martin Durban & Ventrillon-Horber; Columbia Univ, BS, 53, with printmaker Hans Mueller; T C Colombia, MFA, 58. Work: Galeria de Arte Nac, Caracas; Munic Mus of Graphic Arts, Maracaibo, Venezuela; Nat Inst of Cult & Fine Arts, Caracas; Yad Washem, Jerusalem; Morris Mus, Morristown, NJ. Exhib: One-man shows, Univ Ore Mus of Art, Portland, 62, Univ Merida Mus of Art, Venezuela, 66, Gallery of the Nat Inst of Cult & Fine Arts, Caracas, 72 & Mus of Contemp Art, Bogota, Colombia, 77; Contemp Hispanic Art Exhib, Latin Excellence, Xerox Ctr, Rochester, NY, 77; 1st Bienal of Am Printmaking, Munic Mus of Graphic Arts, Maracaibo, 77. Teaching: Instr art hist & painting, Sch of Visual Arts, New York, 65-71; lectr art appreciation, drawing & design, Fairleigh Dickinson Univ, Madison, NJ, 69-73; artist-in-residence, AIM Prog, NJ Pub Sch, 74- Pos: Dir, Galeria Venezuela, New York, 74- Mem: Mod Artists Guild of NJ (pres, 64-65). Style & Technique: Representational imagery with cubist and experssionistic influences; thematic subject matter. Media: Acrylic; Serigraph and Woodcut. Mailing Add: 242 Summit Ave Hackensack NJ 07601

SZOKE, JOHN
ART DEALER, PUBLISHER
US citizen. Study: NY Univ, BS, 72; Grad Sch Bus Admin, MBA, 73. Pos: Owner, John Szoke Graphics, New York. Mailing Add: c/o John Szoke Graphics 340 E 57th St New York NY 10022

T

TABACHNICK, ANNE
EDUCATOR, PAINTER
b Derby, Conn, July 28, 33. Study: Hans Hofmann Sch, 3 yrs scholar; Hunter Col, BA(anthrop); Univ Calif, Berkeley & NY Univ, grad study in art. Work: Hyde Collection, Glens Falls, NY; Mus of Univ Calif, Berkeley; Mus Of Univ Mass, Amherst; Radcliffe Col; Dayton Art Inst, Ohio. Exhib: Many one-woman shows in New York & other cities, 51-75; Mus Mod Art Traveling Show-Hofmann & His Students, 62; one-woman shows, Dayton Art Inst, 65, La State Univ Gallery, 75 & Hyde Collection, 76. Teaching: Instr art, Dayton Art Inst, 65-67; instr art, Harvard Univ, 68-69; prof painting, Md Inst Col Art, 70-; vis artist, La State Univ, Baton Rouge, 75. Pos: Reviewer, Art News, 66-67. Awards: Longview Found Award, 60; Radcliffe Inst Fels, Harvard Univ, 67-69; Creative Artists Pub Serv Fel, NY State Coun on Arts, 74. Bibliog: D Cochrane (auth), Hans Hofmann's students, 3/74 & Tabachnick-lyrical expressionist, 6/74, Am Artist. Style & Technique: Figurative, expressionist, calligraphic, colorist, unique special quality. Media: Acrylic on Canvas & Paper. Dealer: Aaron Berman Gallery 50 W 57th St New York NY. Mailing Add: 463 West St New York NY 10014

TABACK, SIMMS
ILLUSTRATOR, DESIGNER
b New York, NY, Feb 13, 32. Study: Cooper Union, BFA; Sch Visual Arts. Exhib: Soc Illusr Ann Exhib, 63-78; Art Dir Club Show; Am Inst Graphic Arts; Soc Publ Designers; Meade Libr; Type Dir Club. Teaching: Instr illus & design, Sch Visual Arts, New York, 67-78. Pos: Pres, Illustrators Guild, New York, 75-76; chairperson & illus discipline, Graphic Artists Guild, New York, 77- Awards: Cert of Merit, Soc Illusr Show & Ten Best Illus Children's Books, New York Times, 67. Mem: Soc of Illusr; Graphic Artists Guild. Style & Technique: Humerous and decorative, strongly influenced by American comic and cartoon tradition and European poster art. Media: Pen & Ink; Watercolor. Publ: Illusr, Please Share That Peanut, Harcourt-Brace, 67; illusr, Too Much Noise, Houghton-Mifflin, 68; illusr, Euphonia and the Flood, Parent's Mag Press, 76; illusr, Laughing Together, Four Winds Press, 77; auth-illusr, Joseph Had a Little Overcoat, Random House, 77. Dealer: Milton Newborn 135 E 54th St New York NY 10022. Mailing Add: 38 E 21st St New York NY 10010

TABUENA, ROMEO VILLALVA
PAINTER
b Iloilo City, Philippines, Aug 22, 21. Study: Univ Philippines, with Diosdado Lorenzo; Art Students League, Thekla M Barneys grant, 52-53, with Will Barnet; Acad Grande Chaumiere, Paris, with Goertz. Work: New York Pub Libr Print Div; Philippine Nat Mus, Manila; Palace Fine Arts, Mexico City; Mus Mod Arte, Mexico City; Mus Mod Art, Sao Paulo, Brazil. Comn: Filipiniana (mural), Govt Philippines, for Washington Embassy, 57. Exhib: One-man shows, Assoc Am Artists Galleries, New York, 53 & Palace Fine Arts, Mexico City, 62 & 69; Prize Winners Show, Whitney Mus Am Art, New York, 53; Tabuena Ten Yrs

Retrospective, Philippine Art Gallery, Manila, 59; Eighth Biennal Sao Paulo, Mus Mod Art, Brazil, 65. Teaching: Lectr art of today, Far Eastern Univ, 51; Galeria Bleue, Manila, Philippines, 74 & 78; Merrill Chase Galleries, Chicago, Ill, 77; Galeria Tere Haas, Mexico City, Mex, 74 & 78; I Bienal Ibero-Americana de Pintura, Mexico City, Mex, 78. Pos: Art dir, Eve News, Manila, 49-52. Awards: Gold Medal in Painting, Sch Fine Arts, Univ Philippines, 41; Second Prize, Art Asn Philippines Ann, 49. Bibliog: Emily Genauer (auth), Romeo V Tabuena, What's New, Abbot Labs, 55; Arias de la Canal (auth), Tabuena—Sensibilidad, Disciplinada & Poetica, El Norte, Mex, 69. Mem: Art Asn Philippines. Media: Acrylic, Oil, Watercolor. Publ: Auth, Tabuena (watercolor page), Am Artist Mag, 56; auth, Painting a still life, In: Painting in Acrylics, Watson-Guptill, 65. Dealer: Galeria Tere Haas Genova 2 Mexico City Mexico; Tasende Gallery Costera y Yanez Pinzon Acapulco Mexico. Mailing Add: Apdo Postal 114 Gto San Miguel de Allende Mexico

TAFF, BARBARA O'NEIL
ART DEALER
b Riverdale, Md, Oct 4, 51. Study: Am Univ, BA(art hist), 73. Pos: Assoc dir, Jane Haslem Gallery, Washington, DC, 71- Specialty: Contemporary American prints and paintings; political cartoons and comics. Mailing Add: 2121 P St NW Washington DC 20037

TAFT, FRANCES PRINDLE
ART HISTORIAN, LECTURER
b New Haven, Conn, Dec 12, 21. Study: Vassar Col; Yale Univ, grad sch, with George Heard Hamilton, George Kubler & Sumner McKnight Crosby. Teaching: Chmn liberal arts & instr art survey, 19th & 20th century art, pre-Columbian art, Cleveland Inst Art, 52-; instr, Cleveland Col, Case Western Reserve Univ. Pos: Actg dean, Cleveland Inst Art, 73-74. Mem: Cleveland Mus Art (trustee, 72-); Col Art Asn Am; Western Reserve Archit Historians (pres, 71-72); Art Asn Cleveland (purchasing comt); Jr Coun, Cleveland Mus Art (prog chmn, 72). Res: Pre-Columbian art in Mesoamerica & Peru. Interest: Active in Cleveland Art Asn, in Karamu House, in Cleveland Inst & in the Cleveland Mus Art. Collection: Small pre-Columbian collection and collection of painting, sculpture & prints with a focus on Cleveland artists. Mailing Add: 6 Pepper Ridge Rd Cleveland OH 44124

TAGGART, WILLIAM JOHN
PAINTER, INSTRUCTOR
b Buffalo, NY, Aug 8, 40. Study: Art Inst Chicago, BFA; Univ NMex, MA. Work: Int Arrivals Bldg, JFK Airport, New York; Installation, Pub Sch 3, New York; Univ NMex, Albuquerque; Art in the Embassies Prog, Bonn, Ger & New Delhi, India. Comn: Sculpture, Port Authority, New York, 73. Exhib: Paintings, Betty Parsons Gallery, New York, 74, Large Paintings Only, 75; Paintings, Sculpture & Drawings, Whitney Mus, New York, 74; Off the Wall, Pace Univ, New York, 74; New Directions in NY, Univ Maine, Portland, 75. Teaching: Instr printmaking, Cooper Union, New York, 68-71; instr visual fundamentals, York Community Col, 75. Style & Technique: Acrylic polymer color field paintings; bold color and shapes, abstract spatial paintings. Mailing Add: c/o Betty Parsons Gallery 24 W 57th St New York NY 10019

TAHEDL, ERNESTINE
STAINED GLASS ARTIST, PAINTER
b Vienna, Austria, Oct 10, 40; Can citizen. Study: Acad for Appl Arts, Vienna, Austria, with Franz Herbert, MA in Graphic Arts, 61; with Prof Heinrich Tahedl, collab in design & execution of stained glass works, 61-63. Work: Paintings represented in pub galleries in Vienna, San Salvador, Montpellier, France, London, Ont & Mus de Que, Can. Comn: Stained glass murals, Sisters of the Holy Cross, Edmonton, Alta, 64, The Sanctuary, Can Pavailion, Expo 67, Montreal, 67, Carefree Lodge, Toronto, Ont, 69 & 71, Mendel Art Gallery, Saskatoon, Sask, 70 & Fed Revenue Bldg, Quebec, Que, 71. Exhib: Cult Ctr of Lower Austria, 75; one-woman shows, Ecole des Beaux Arts, Montpellier, France, 75, Galerie les deux B, St Antoine sur Richelieu, Que, 76, Sisler Gallery, Toronto, Ont, 76, Gallery 93, Ottawa, Ont, 77, Lefebvre Gallery, Edmonton, Alta, 77 & Goethe Inst, Montreal, Que, 77. Awards: Bronze Medal, Vienna Int Exhib of Painting, 63; Allied Arts Medal, Royal Archit Inst of Can, 66; Can Coun Arts Award, 67. Mem: Royal Can Acad of Arts; Can Crafts Coun; Que Soc Prof Artists. Style & Technique: Abstract landscapes for printing and painting; abstract stained glass murals and sculpture. Dealer: Lefevbre Gallery 10238 123rd St Edmonton AB Can. Mailing Add: 1066 Beique Mont St Hilaire PQ J0L 1L0 Can

TAHIR, ABE M, JR
ART DEALER
b Greenwood, Miss, Feb 18, 31. Study: Univ Miss, BBA; George Washington Univ, MBA. Pos: Dir, Tahir Gallery. Specialty: Original prints. Publ: Auth, Hnizdovsky Woodcuts, 76. Mailing Add: 2220 Indiana St Houston TX 77019

TAIRA, FRANK
PAINTER, SCULPTOR
b San Francisco, Calif, Aug 21, 13. Study: Calif Sch Fine Arts; Art Students League; Columbia Univ. Work: In many pvt collections. Exhib: San Francisco Mus Arts, 40; one-man show, Hudson Guild Gallery, 67; Knickerbocker Artists, 68; Nat Arts Club, 68; Far Gallery, 69; Nat Acad of Design, New York, 76; Allied Artists of Am, 76. Teaching: Instr painting & drawing, Topaz Art Sch, Utah, 42-43. Awards: Award for one-man Show, Emily Lowe Found, 67; Nat Arts Club Award, 68; Hon Mention, Knickerbocker Artists, 68; plus others. Style & Technique: Realistic approach, with awareness of colors, lights and overall designs; direct welded bronze figures; handwrought creative jewelry. Media: Oil, Watercolor; Bronze. Mailing Add: 458 W 49th St New York NY 10019

TAIT, CORNELIA DAMIAN
PAINTER, SCULPTOR
b Philadelphia, Pa. Study: Graphic Sketch Club (Fleisher Art Memorial); Temple Univ, scholar, BS(educ); Tyler Sch Fine Arts, scholar, BFA(hon), MFA, with Antonio Cortizas, Raphael Sabatini & Boris Blai. Work: Temple Univ; Tyler Art Sch, Elkins Park, Pa; World Hq Christian Endeavor, Columbus, Ohio; Asociatia Romania, Bucharest; Nara Philos Study Ctr, Duncannon, Pa; plus others. Comn: Murals with musical themes, comn by Morris Rotenberg, Philadelphia, 46; portraits of church donors & 21 altar screen paintings (icons), Holy Trinity Romanian-Orthodox Cathedral, Detroit, 49-50; portrait of founder of Christian Endeavor, comn by Joseph Holton Jones; plus others. Exhib: One-man show, Woodmere Art Gallery, Philadelphia, 66, Romanian Libr, UN, New York, 74 & Biarritz & Paris, 75; Pa Acad Fine Arts, 66; Signs in Cloth, Nat Traveling Exhibs, US, 68-71; one-man retrospective, Bucharest, Timisoara & Cluj, Romania, 73; plus others. Teaching: Instr art, Settlement Music Sch, 42-44; instr sculpture, Philadelphia Mus Art, 44-45; instr art & supvr, Buckingham Friends Sch, 50-53; supvr art, Albington Twp Cult Ctr, 63; lectr, Violet Oakley Mem Found, Philadelphia, 73; lectr Romanian Libr, New York, 74; plus lectr to many art & church groups. Awards: Mania Blai Painting Award, Tyler Sch Fine Arts, 58; Painting Award, Phillips Mill Asn, New Hope, 65; Winner, Nat & Int Housing & Urban Develop Art Competition, 72-73; plus others. Bibliog: Interview, Romania Nat Radio & TV, 73; interview, Voice of Am, 73 & 74; interview, Radio Free Europe, 74; plus others. Mem: Artists Equity Asn; Philadelphia Art Alliance; Woodmere Art Gallery; US Platform Asn; Violet Oakley Mem Found. Style & Technique: From representational to abstract; from impasto knife and old master's technique interpretation of tempera on gesso to direct brush work. Media: Oil. Res: Byzantine architecture; folk and contemporary art of Romania; folk arts of the American Indians in the Southwest. Publ: Contribr, Process of Underpainting (film), 52; contribr, Friends J, 52; contribr, New Leaves, 65 & 66; contribr to var newspapers, 60's. Mailing Add: 10 Armour Rd Hatboro PA 19040

TAIT, KATHARINE LAMB
PAINTER, DESIGNER
b Alpine, NJ, June 3, 95. Study: Friends Sem, NY; Nat Acad Design; Art Students League; Cooper Union Art Sch. Comn: All nave & rose windows, Protestant & Roman Cath Chapels, US Marine Corps, Camp Lejeune, NC; all windows, Old Mariners Church, Detroit, Mich & Calvary Methodist Church, Dumont, NJ. Exhib: Guild Relig Archit, Detroit; Nat Arts Club, New York; Tenafly Pub Libr, NJ; Stained Glass Asn Am. Teaching: Instr design, Cooper Union Women's Art Sch, formerly. Pos: Artist & designer, J & R Lamb Studios. Mem: Nat Soc Mural Painters; Stained Glass Asn Am; Bergen Co Artists Guild. Publ: Auth & illusr, Children of Paris, New York Times Bk Rev; auth & illusr, A child's day in court, New York Times Mag. Mailing Add: Lambs Lane Box 102 Cresskill NJ 07626

TAJIRI, SHINKICHI
SCULPTOR, EDUCATOR
b Los Angeles, Calif, Dec 7, 23. Study: Art Inst Chicago, with Ossip Zadkine; with F Leger, Paris; Acad Grande Chaumiere, Paris. Work: Stedelijk Mus, Amsterdam; Mus Mod Art, New York; Louisiana, Copenhagen; Roysman Mus, Rotterdam; CNAC, Paris. Comn: AKU fountain, 60; Overhand Knot, Schiphol Airport, Amsterdam. Exhib: Stedelijk Mus, 60-67; Venice Biennial, 62; Andre Emmerich Gallery, New York, 65; Kunsthalle, Basel, Switz, 69; Kunsthalle Lund, Sweden, 71. Teaching: Guest prof sculpture, Minneapolis Col Art & Design, 64-65; prof sculpture, Stadtliche Höchschule für Bildende Kunste, West Berlin, Ger, 69- Awards: Golden Lion, 8th Int Festival Amateur Films, Cannes, France, 55; Mainichi Shibum Prize for Sculpture, Mainchi Newspapers, Tokyo, 63; Grand Prix, The Wet Dream Film Festival, Amsterdam, 70. Bibliog: L Freed (auth), Seltsame Spiele, Barmieyer & Nikel, 69. Publ: Auth, The Wall, 70; auth, Mayday, 70; auth, Land Mine, 70; ed, Portrait, Self-portrait & Measurements, 72; ed, The Vanishing Island, 74; plus others. Dealer: Cort Gallery Ostergade 24 Copenhagen Denmark. Mailing Add: Castle Scheres Limburg Baarlo Netherlands

TAKAI, TEIJI
PAINTER
b Osaka, Japan, Feb 5, 11. Study: Shinano Bashi Art Inst, Osaka. Work: Corcoran Gallery, Washington, DC; Mod Art Mus, Tokyo, Japan; Columbia Mus, SC; Uniontown Art Club, Pa; Wakayama Mod Art Mus, Japan. Exhib: Several one-man shows, Poindexter Gallery, 59-72; Whitney Mus Am Art Ann, New York, 59 & 61; Corcoran Biennial, 61-62; Carnegie Int, Pittsburgh, 61-62; Retrospective, Takashimaya Tokyo, 67. Teaching: Vis prof art, Winthrop Col, fall 70 & 72. Awards: Okada Prize, 40; Fukushima Prize, 64. Mem: Niki Art Asn; Int Artist Asn. Media: Oil. Mailing Add: c/o Poindexter Gallery 24 E 84th St New York NY 10028

TAKAL, PETER
PAINTER, PRINTMAKER
b Bucharest, Romania, Dec 8, 05; US citizen. Study: Paris, France. Work: Mus Mod Art, New York; Metrop Mus Art, New York; Whitney Mus Am Art, New York; Cleveland Mus Art; Los Angeles Co Mus Art; plus in over 100 mus collections in US & abroad. Comn: City Roofs (print), Print Club Cleveland, 56, Trees & Fields (print), 57; four prints, Int Graphic Arts Soc, New York, 56-65; Meditation (print), Assoc Am Artists, New York, 58; Of Man, Of Nature (suite of 20 lithographs), Tamarind Lithography Workshop, Los Angeles, 64; two prints, Hollander Workshop, New York, 69; plus others. Exhib: Pa Acad of the Fine Arts, 53-69; Whitney Mus Am Art Ann, 55-69; Recent Drawings USA, Mus Mod Art, New York, 56; one-man show, Cleveland Mus Art, 59 & Smithsonian Inst, 59-60; American Prints Today Traveling Exhib, Print Coun Am, 59, 62 & 63; White House, Washington, DC, 66 & 70; plus more than 50 one-man shows in US & abroad, 32-77. Teaching: Lectr art, Cleveland Mus Art, 58; artist in residence, Beloit Col Mus, 65; lectr art, Cent Col, 68. Awards: Fel, Yaddo Found, 61; Purchase Award, 3rd Nat Print Exhib, Pasadena Art Mus, 62; Ford Fel, Tamarind Lithography Workshop, 63-64; plus others. Bibliog: Pierre Mornand (auth), Takal portraitiste lineaire evocateur de l'insaisissable, Le Courrier Graphique, 37; Norman Kent (auth), What is good drawing, Am Artist Mag, 45; Leonia E Prasse & Louise Richards (auth), Recent Works of Peter Takal, Cleveland Mus Art, 58; plus others. Mem: Pa Acad of the Fine Arts (juror, 67); Print Club Philadelphia (juror, 58); Artists Equity Asn New York; Print Coun Am; Soc Am Graphic Artists; Am Color Print Soc (juror, 59). Media: Drill Point, Lithography. Publ: Auth, Selected Works of Peter Takal, Drawings & Poems, Int Univ, 45; auth & illusr, Drawings by Peter Takal, New Am Libr, 58; auth, Artist's Proof, Vol 1, No 2; illusr, Mother & Child in Modern Art, Duell, 64; auth, About the Invisible in Art, Wright Art Ctr, Beloit Col, 65; plus others. Dealer: Weyhe Gallery 794 Lexington Ave New York NY 10021; Van Straaten Gallery 646 N Michigan Ave Chicago IL 60611. Mailing Add: 40 Rue du Mole CH1201 Geneva Switzerland

TAKASHIMA, SHIZUYE VIOLET
INSTRUCTOR, PAINTER
b Vancouver, BC, Can, June 12, 28. Study: Ont Col Art, BA, 53; Fine Arts Inst, San Miguel, Mex (weaving), 65; Pratt Art Ctr Graphic Arts, New York, 66. Work: Nat Gallery, Ottawa, Can; Univ Sherbrooke, Que; Can Titanium Pigments Ltd, Montreal; Montreal Standard Publ Co, Montreal; Midland Computer Bldg, Syracuse, NY. Comn: Four Posters, Midwestern Regional Libr, Kitchener, Ont, 78. Exhib: Hamilton Art Gallery, Ont, 61; Hart House, Univ Toronto, 61; VI Biennial Exhib, Nat Gallery Ottawa, 65; Mystic Circle (traveling show), Burnaby Art Gallery, 74; five-man show, Montreal Mus Fine Arts, 65; four-man show, Art Gallery Ont, Toronto, 60; one-man shows, Burnaby Art Gallery, BC, 65 & 78 & Japanese Can Cult Ctr, Toronto, 74. Teaching: Instr drawing & painting, Forest Hill Learning Resources, 71 & Ont Col Art, Toronto, 76- Pos: Assoc ed, Rikka Mag (quarterly) & vol artist, Inner City Angels, Toronto, 76- Awards: Can Coun Grant, 71 & 73; Bronze Award, Can Asn Children's Libr Asn, 72. Bibliog: Robin Mathews (auth), Young Artists, Can Forum, 61; David P Silcox (auth), Young Artists, Can Art Mag, 62. Style & Technique: Figure painting with landscape; glaze technique in oils; watercolours: mixed media with coloured inks. Media: Oils with Lucite Medium: Watercolour, Etching. Interest: To bring meaningful art into the school to influence the young, for they are our future. Dealer: c/o Barbara Wells Gallery 13 Kaymar Dr Ottawa ON K1J 7C8 Can. Mailing Add: 21 Raglan Ave Toronto ON M6C 2K7 Can

TAKEMOTO, HENRY TADAAKI
CRAFTSMAN, SCULPTOR
b Honolulu, Hawaii, July 23, 30. Study: Univ Hawaii, BFA; Los Angeles Co Art Inst, MFA. Work: Smithsonian Inst. Exhib: 2nd Int Exhib Contemp Ceramics, Ostend, Belg, 59; 3rd Int Exhib Contemp Ceramics, Prague, Czech, 62; Studio Potter Exhib, Victoria & Albert Mus, London, Eng, 66-70; Objects: USA, Johnson Wax Collection Contemp Crafts, Smithsonian Inst, Washington, DC, 70-73; Contemp Ceramic Art, US, Can, Mex, Japan, 71-72. Teaching: Instr ceramics, Calif Sch Fine Arts, San Francisco; instr ceramics, Scripps Col, 65-69; former instr ceramics, Otis Art Inst. Pos: Designer & glaze chemist, Interpace Corp, 69- Awards: Double Purchase Prize, Wichita Art Asn, 59; Silver Medal for Sculpture, Ostend, Belg, 59; Bronze Medal, Mus Contemp Crafts, NY, 60; plus others. Media: Ceramics. Mailing Add: 3209 Landa Los Angeles CA 90039

TALABA, L (LINDA TALABA CUMMENS)
SCULPTOR, PRINTMAKER
b Detroit, Mich, July 15, 43. Study: Detroit Inst Technol, with Maxwell Wright; pvt instr With Lois Pety; Ill Wesleyan Univ, with Fred Brian, BFA; Southern Ill Univ, with David Folkman, master printmaker from Tamarind, Tom Walsh, sculptor & Lewis Brent Kington, Metalsmith, MFA. Work: Henry Ford Found Print Collection, Detroit; J B Speed Mus Traveling Print Collection, Tenn; Albion Univ Print Collection; Leopold Schepp Found Collection, New York; Detroit Art Inst Rental Gallery & Collection; plus others. Comn: Painting, Waterford Twp Bd Educ, 61; painting, Isaac E Crary, Jr High Sch, 63; painting, Burton Title & Abstract Co, Detroit, 67; bronze door ornaments, Little Grassy Mus, Southern Ill Univ, 70; bronze sculpture, Dir & Bur Budget, State of Ill, Springfield, 75; plus other comn by individuals. Exhib: Libr of Cong Print Show & Smithsonian Traveling Exhib, 65; one-man show, Renee Gallery, Detroit, 68 & Lewis Towers Gallery, Loyola Univ, 75; Drawings USA, St Paul, 75; Ball State Nat Drawing & Small Sculpture; plus others. Teaching: Guest artist sculpture, Springfield Art Asn, 74-; guest artist sculpture, Sangamon State Univ, 75- Pos: Treas, Delta Phi Delta, Bloomington, Ill, 63-64; lectr, Springfield Art Asn, 74- Awards: Nat Scholarships Inc, Grant in Metals, New York, 72; Ill State Mus Craftsmans Award, 75; Ball State Univ Nat Award for Sculpture, 75; plus others. Mem: Springboard Artists Asn, Springfield, Ill; Ill State Mus Hist Soc, Am Crafts Coun; Womens Caucus for Art. Style & Technique: Abstractive figurative to non-objective; cold forging copper, brass and bronze with leather and wood; cast bronze with lost-wax process and varied patinas. Media: Bronze, Plexiglas; Graphics, Intaglio & Serigraph. Publ: Illusr, Lakeland's Paradise (hist bk), Bd Educ Oakland County, Pontiac, Mich, 61; art ed, The Argus Newspaper, 62 & illusr, The Black Book (literary mag), 63-65, Ill Wesleyan Univ; illusr, Experimental Math Books, Cent Mid-Western Regional Educ Labs, 70; plus others. Dealer: Prairie House Gallery 213 S Sixth St Springfield IL 62701. Mailing Add: 825 S Glenwood Springfield IL 62704

TALBOT, JAROLD DEAN
MUSEUM DIRECTOR, EDUCATOR
b Solano, NMex, Aug 28, 07. Study: Cumming Sch of Art, Des Moines, Iowa; Grand Cent Sch of Art, New York; studied with Edmund Greacen, Ivan Olinsky, Keith Shaw Williams; Millikin Univ, AB, 51. Exhib: Nat Exhib of Am Art, New York, 36; Nat Acad of Design, New York, 37; Audubon Artists, New York, 48; Ohio Valley Oil & Water Color Show, Cincinnati, 54; Interior Valley Show, Cincinnati Art Mus, 58; Ann Exhib, Ill State Mus, Springfield, 59; 14th Ann Exhib, N Miss Valley Artists, 60. Collections Arranged: Ann Exhib Cent Ill Artists, 48-60; Tri-State Exhib of Painting & Sculpture, 60-63 & Nat WVa Centennial Exhib of Painting & Sculpture, 63, Huntington Galleries; Ann Exhib New Mexico Artists, Mus of Fine Arts, Santa Fe, 63; Photo Show, Orange Co, New York Hist Churches, 66-67. Teaching: Instr art, Bradley Univ, Peoria, Ill, 46; asst prof art, Millikin Univ, Decatur, Ill, 46-60. Pos: Dir, Decatur Art Ctr, Ill, 47-60, Huntington Galleries, WVa, 60-63, Fine Arts Gallery, Mus of Fine Art, Santa Fe, NMex, 63 & Smith Clove Mus of Folk-life, Monroe, NY, 64-71, cur, Hill-Stead Mus, Farmington, Conn, 72- Mem: Am Asn of Mus; Northeast Mus Conf, Am Asn of Mus; Nat Trust for Hist Preserv. Mailing Add: Hill-Stead Mus PO Box 353 Farmington CT 06032

TALBOT, JONATHAN
PRINTMAKER, PAINTER
b New York, NY, Nov 14, 39. Study: Brandeis Univ; New Sch Social Res; San Francisco Acad Art; wood engraving with Stefan Martin, painting with Gerald Lubeck & collage with Roderick Slater. Work: Free Libr Philadelphia; Drew Univ; Fairleigh Dickinson Univ; Toronto Cent Libr, Ont; Provincetown Hist Soc, Mass. Exhib: 25th Ann San Francisco Art Comn, 71; one-man shows, Fairleigh Dickinson Univ, 73, Drew Univ, 74; Arena 74, Binghamton, NY, 74; Assoc Am Artists, New York, 75; Mus Mod Art, New York, 76; plus others. Awards: Second Prize Graphics, Wash Sq Art Show, 73; Purchase Award, Cent New York Art Open, 75; Award, Arts Festival of Atlanta, Ga, 77; plus others. Bibliog: Creating an etching with aquatint, videotape, Media Dept, Fairleigh Dickinson Univ, 73. Mem: Salmagundi Club; Artists Equity; Silvermine Guild. Style & Technique: Traditional etchings and engravings, collage and aquatints and relief prints. Media: Etching, Engraving; Oil, Acrylic. Publ: Auth & illusr, Seals 2, NJ Music & Arts Mag, 10/73; illusr (frontpiece), A Portrait of the Artists as a Young Man, Easton Press, 77. Dealer: Assoc Am Artists 663 Fifth Ave New York NY 10003. Mailing Add: RD 2 Pine Island Turnpike Warwick NY 10990

TALBOT, WILLIAM (H M)
SCULPTOR
b Boston, Mass, Jan 10, 18. Study: Pa Acad Fine Arts, 36 & 41; with George Demetrios, Gloucester, Mass, 37-40; Acad Beaux Arts, Paris, France, 45-46. Work: Whitney Mus Am Art, New York; St Lawrence Univ; Earlham Col; Bryn Mawr Col; St John's Church, Washington, Conn. Comn: Fountain (with Carl Koch & G Kepes), Fitchburg Youth Libr, Mass, 50; fountain, Nat Coun State Garden Clubs Am Nat Hq, St Louis, Mo, 59; mem sculpture & stairwell, comn by Mrs Charles Belknap for Barnes Hosp Rehab Ctr, St Louis, 64. Exhib: Pa Acad Fine Arts Ann, 42, 49 & 66; Philadelphia Mus 3rd Int, 49; De Cordova & Dana Mus Sculpture Exhib, 49; Whitney Mus Am Art Sculpture Ann, 50, 51 & 63; one-man shows, Andrew Morris Gallery, New York, 63, Martin Schweig Gallery, St Louis, Mo, 65 & 69, Mattaleul Mus, Waterbury, Conn, 66, Frank Rehn Gallery, New York, 68 & 71, Arts Club, Chicago, 72 & Cherry Stone Gallery, Wellfleet, Mass, 76. Teaching: Vis prof sculpture, Univ Mich, spring 49. Awards: Prix de Rome, Am Acad Rome, 41; Cresson Traveling Fel, Pa Acad Fine Arts, 41, Steele Sculpture Prize, 49; Nat Inst Arts & Lett Award, 75. Bibliog: Peter Blake (auth), article in Archit Forum, 51; Edward Renouf (auth), The sculpture of William Talbot, Harvard Art Rev, spring-summer 67; D Meilach (auth), Contemporary Art with Stone, Crown, 69. Mem: Sculptors Guild (pres, 65-68, vpres publ, 68-72). Media: Concrete, Stained Glass. Dealer: Frank Rehn Gallery 655 Madison Ave New York NY 10021. Mailing Add: Bell Hill Washington CT 06793

TALLEUR, JOHN J
PRINTMAKER
b Chicago, Ill, May 29, 25. Study: Art Inst Chicago; Univ Chicago, BFA, 47; Iowa State Univ, MFA, 51. Work: Mus Mod Art, New York; Carnegie Inst, Pittsburgh; Metrop Mus, New York; Whitney Mus Am Art, New York; Art Inst Chicago. Comn: Print, Lakeside Studios, 72; print, Jewish Community Ctr, Kansas City, Mo, 72. Teaching: Instr printmaking, Carleton Col, 47-49; instr printmaking, St Paul Gallery & Sch Art, 49; prof printmaking, Univ Kans, 53- Pos: Hon cur prints, Univ Kans Mus Art, presently. Bibliog: Bret Waller (auth), John Talleur, Univ Kans Mus Art, 66. Media: Intaglio. Mailing Add: 242 Concord Lawrence KS 66073

TAM, REUBEN
PAINTER, EDUCATOR
b Kapaa, Hawaii, Jan 17, 16. Study: Univ Hawaii, BA, 37, fifth yr cert, 38; Calif Sch Fine Arts; Columbia Univ, with Meyer Schapiro; New Sch Social Res. Work: Mus Mod Art, New York; Metrop Mus Art, New York; Whitney Mus Am Art, New York; Brooklyn Mus; Nat Collection Fine Arts, Smithsonian Inst, Washington, DC. Exhib: Contemp Am Painting, Whitney Mus Am Art, New York, 41-65; Contemp Am Painting, Krannert Art Mus, Univ Ill, Urbana-Champaign, 49-69; Am Painting, Metrop Mus Art, New York, 53; Pittsburgh Int Exhib, Carnegie Inst Mus Art, 64 & 67; Landscape in Maine (1820-1970), Colby Col Art Mus, 70; one-man exhibs, Calif Palace of the Legion of Hon, 40, Honolulu Acad of Arts, 41 & 67, Portland Art Mus, Ore, 61, Ore State Univ, 66, Wichita Art Asn, Kans, 71, Sheldon Mem Art Gallery, Univ of Nebr, 76 & Telfair Acad of Arts & Sci, Savannah, Ga, 76. Teaching: Instr advan painting, Brooklyn Mus Art Sch, 46-75; prof painting, Ore State Univ, summer 66; vis artist, Ore State Syst Higher Educ, summer 71; vis prof art, Queens Col (NY), 73. Awards: First Nat Prize, Golden Gate Expos, San Francisco, 39; Guggenheim Fel, 48; First Prize, Brooklyn Mus Biennial, 52 & 56; First Prize, Nat Acad of Design Ann, 74 & 77. Bibliog: Burrey (auth), Reuben Tam; painter of the intimate landscape, Arts Mag, 2/58; Nordness & Weller (auth), Art USA Now, Viking, 62; Gussow (auth), A sense of place: the artist & the American land, Sat Rev, 72. Media: Oil, Acrylic, Ink. Dealer: Coe Kerr Gallery Inc 49 E 82nd St New York NY 10028. Mailing Add: 549 W 123rd St New York NY 10027

TAMAYO, RUFINO
PAINTER
b Oaxaca, Mex, 99. Work: Mus Mod Art, New York; Mus Art Mod, Paris, France; Mus Arte Mod, Rome, Italy; Mus Royale, Brussels, Belg; Phillips Mem Gallery, Washington, DC. Comn: Murals, Govt Mex, Palace Fine Arts, Mexico City, 52, Mus Nac Antropologia, Mexico City, 64 & UN, New York, 72; mural, Dallas Mus Fine Arts, 53; mural, UNESCO Bldg, Paris, 58. Exhib: One-man shows, San Francisco Mus Art, 53, Kunsternes Hus Oslo, Norway, 59, Phoenix Art Mus, Ariz, 68 & Biennal Venice. Awards: Oficiel Legion d'Honeur, France; Comendator Repub Italiana; Premio Nac Mex. Mem: Inst & Acad Arts & Lett; Acad Arte, Buenos Aires, Arg; Acad Diseno, Florence, Italy. Dealer: Perls Gallery 1016 Madison Ave New York NY 10021. Mailing Add: Callejon del Santisimo 12 San Angel Mexico DF Mexico

TAMBURINE, JEAN
PAINTER, ILLUSTRATOR
b Meriden, Conn, Feb 20, 30. Study: Traphagen, New York, 48-49; Art Students League, New York, with Jon Corbino & John Groth, 48-50; also with Elizabeth Gordon Chandler. Work: State Libr, Middletown, Conn; Nashville Pub Libr, Tenn; Strong Sch, Hartford, Conn; Middletown Pub Libr, Conn; plus others. Exhib: North Shore Arts Asn, Gloucester, Mass; Town & Country Club Exhib, West Hartford, Conn, 69; George Walter Vincent Smith Art Mus, Springfield, Mass; one-woman show, L'Heure Joyeux, Paris, France, 69; Pearl S Buck Found Exhib, Meriden Pub Libr, 72; Ellsworth Gallery, Simsbury, Conn, 76; plus others. Pos: Comnr, Conn Comn on Arts, State Conn, 63-65; chmn & organizer, Cult Comn for Art Appointments to Pub Bldg, 66-70. Mem: North Shore Arts Asn; Allied Artists Am; Arts & Crafts Asn; Int Platform; Women's Nat Book Asn. Style & Technique: Traditional oil, pen, ink and watercolor; sculpture, modelling, plasteleno to plaster to bronze. Publ: Auth & illusr, Almost Big Enough, 63 & I Think I Will, Go To The Hospital, 65, illusr, See Me Grow, 65 & auth & illusr, How Now, Brown Cow, 67, Abington Press; illusr, It's Nice To Be Little, Rand-McNally, 65; illusr, The Complete Peddlers Pack, Univ Tenn Press, 67; illusr, Something Was Missing, Follett, 69; illusr, Five Busy Bears, Rand-McNally, 69. Mailing Add: c/o The Bertolli Studio 73 Reynolds Dr Meriden CT 06450

TANGER, SUSANNA
PAINTER, WRITER
b Boston, Mass, June 9, 42. Study: Boston Mus Sch; Univ Colo; Univ Calif, Berkeley. Exhib: O K Harris Invitational, 72; Green Camp-Cooper Union Invitational, 73; Whitney Biennial, 75; Post Washington NY Cent Hall Gallery, 75; City of Paris Mus Mod Art, 75; PS 1, New York, 76; Hal Bromm Gallery, New York, 76; Galerie Rencontres, Paris, France, 76; Moore Col of Art Gallery, Philadelphia, 77; plus others. Style & Technique: Painting on canvas or wood; liquitex and graphite. Mailing Add: 141 Wooster St New York NY 10012

TANIA (SCHREIBER-MILICEVIC)
PAINTER, SCULPTOR
b Lodz, Poland, Jan 11, 24. Study: McGill Univ, MA, 42; Columbia Univ, PhD, ABD; Art Students League, with Yasuo Kuniyoshi, Morris Kantor & Vaclav Vytlacil, 48-51. Work: Rose Art Mus, Brandeis Univ; NY Univ; Morgan State Col; New York Civic Ctr Synagogue. Comn: Two walls, comn by New York City, Vest Pocket Parks, Brooklyn & Bronx, 67-68; outdoor sculpture (8ft x 18ft, aluminum), Albright Col, Reading, Pa, 72; sculpture (brushed aluminum, 8ft x 27ft), Dresdner Bank, New York, 72; plus others. Exhib: Two-man show, NY Univ Loeb Ctr, 64 & 67; Whitney Mus Am Art, New York, 64; Univ Va, 64 & 68; Milwaukee Art Inst, 65; Univ Del, 65; four-man show, Mus Mod Art, 69; Ringling Mus, Sarasota, Fla, 69; Jewish Mus, New York, 69; Finch Mus, New York, 71; Lincoln Ctr, New York, 72; Women Choose Women, New York Cult Ctr, 73; Artists of the Hamptons, Sotheby Parke Bernet, New York, 75; one-person show, Univ Ala, 76, plus others; Montclair Mus, NJ, 76; Andre Zarre Gallery, New York, 77; plus many others. Teaching: Instr fundamentals of design & drawing, NY Univ, 63-69; guest lectr, Pa Acad Fine Arts, 73, vis critic painting, 74-75; fac mem pub art in painting & sculpture, State Univ NY Col, Purchase, 75-76; vis assoc prof painting, Univ Ala, Tuscaloosa, 76. Pos: Dir bd & founding mem, City Walls Inc, New York. Mem: Art Students League; Guild Hall. Mailing Add: c/o Bertha Schaefer Galleries 41 E 57th St New York NY 10022

TANKSLEY, ANN
PAINTER
b Pittsburgh, Pa, Jan 25, 34. Study: Carnegie Inst Technol, with Samuel Rosenberg & Balcomb Green, BFA; Art Students League, with Norman Lewis. Work: Johnson Publ Co, Chicago. Exhib: Freedomways Exhib, Hudson River Mus, Yonkers, NY, 71; USA 1971, Carnegine Inst, Pittsburgh, 71; Rebuttal to Whitney Mus Exhib, Acts of Art Gallery, New

York, 71; Black Women Artists, Mt Holyoke Col, 72; Hon & Mrs Bruce Wright Collection Exhib, Fordham Univ, 74; plus numerous others. Style & Technique: Large monumental figures in oil and charcoal and muted earth tones which convey socially significant ideas. Media: Oil. Mailing Add: 18 Carlton Rd Great Neck NY 11021

TANNER, JAMES L
CRAFTSMAN
b Jacksonville, Fla, July 22, 41. Study: Fla A&M Univ, BA, 64; Aspen Sch Contemp Art, summer 64; Univ Wis-Madison, MS, 66, MFA, 67. Work: Johnson Wax Collection, Smithsonian Inst, Washington, DC; Del Mus of Art, Wilmington; Ill State Univ, Normal; Ray & Lee Grover Antiques, Inc, Cleveland, Ohio; North Hennepin State Jr Col, Minneapolis; Mankato State Univ. Exhib: Young America 1969, Mus Contemp Crafts, 69; Objects USA, circulated by Smithsonian Inst, 69-70; Glass 2000 BC-1971 AD, John Michael Kohler Art Ctr, Sheboygan, Wis, 71; Reflections on Glass, Long Beach Mus Art, 71-72; Toledo Glass Nat, 72. Bibliog: Daniel Wilson & David Wayne (auth), With These Hands, 70; Lee Nordness (auth), Objects USA, 70; Ray Grover & Lee Grover (co-auths), Contemporary Art Glass, Crown Publ Co, Inc, 75; Paul Donhauser (auth), The History of American Ceramics—Studio Potter, W C Brown, Kendall/Hunt Publ, 78. Mem: Nat Coun Educ Ceramic Arts; Am Craftsman Coun; Minn Craftsman Coun (bd dirs, 72-77). Media: Wood, Glass, Ceramics. Mailing Add: Rte 3 Box 189 Janesville MN 56048

TANNER, JOAN ELIZABETH
PAINTER
b Indianapolis, Ind, Nov 25, 35. Study: Univ Wis, BA, 57, teachers cert, 58. Work: Santa Barbara Mus Art. Exhib: 25 Calif Women of Art, Lytton Art Ctr, Los Angeles, 68; Wellinton-Ivest Collection, Inst Contemp Art, Boston, 68; 9 West, San Diego Mus Art, 69; Surrealism if Alive & Well in the West, Calif Inst Technol, 72; Abstraction: Alive-Well, State Univ NY Col Potsdam, 75. Mem: Los Angeles Inst Contemp Art. Style & Technique: Oil painting, mixed media oil painting, drawings on paper with collage and folded paper works. Dealer: Esther Bear Gallery 1125 High Rd Santa Barbara CA 93108. Mailing Add: 624 Olive Rd Santa Barbara CA 93108

TANNER, WARREN
ARTS ADVOCATE, PAINTER
b Brooklyn, NY, Sept 24, 42. Study: Hunter Col, BFA & MA(fine arts). Exhib: Hunter Col, New York, 64; 112 Greene St, New York, 74-75; Orgn of Independent Artists, Living Bldg, Commerce Dept, Washington, DC, Art in Pub Spaces, IRS Bldg, New York, Selena Gallery, Long Island Univ, Brooklyn, US Customs Court House, One Federal Plaza, 77 & Off of Educ Show, Off of Comnr Educ, Washington, DC, 78. Teaching: Vis lectr art & govt, Pratt Inst, Grad Div, 77; panelist art or polit, Artists Talk on Art, SoHo Ctr for Visual Arts, New York, 78. Pos: Founder, Orgn of Independent Artists, 76-, dir, 77-; panelist, First Nat Conf, Alternative Visual Arts Orgn, Santa Monica, Calif, 78. Awards: William Graff Scholar, Hunter Col, 64; Artist-in-Residence, Helen Wurlitzer Found, Taos, NMex, 76. Bibliog: Grace Glueck (auth), Art People/Weekend, New York Times, 6/10/77; Citiscope Morris Hirshfield, Channel 31 TV, New York, 12/77. Style & Technique: Geometric abstraction, color, sculpture. Mailing Add: 118 Prince St New York NY 10012

TARDO, (MANUEL) RODULFO
SCULPTOR
b Matanzas, Cuba, Feb 18, 19; US citizen. Study: Nat Fine Arts Sch, Havana, Cuba, prof(sculpture & drawing); Clay Club & Art Students League, scholar. Work: Nat Mus Cuba; Sch Archit, Havana; Sch Pedagogy, Havana Univ; Art Gallery Matanzas; Cathedral of St John the Divine, New York. Comn: Bust, Jackson Park, Elizabeth, NJ, 66; bust, Boulevard East, West New York, NJ, 68; eagles, Califano Mansion, Glen Cove, NY, 70; bust, Mother Cabrini Park, Newark, NJ, 75; image, Nat Shrine of Immaculate Conception, Washington, DC, 75-76. Exhib: Philadelphia Mus Art, 49; Mus Nat D'Art Mod, Paris, France, 51; Bienal Hispanoamericana de Arte, Madrid, Spain, 52; Brooklyn Mus, NY, 73; Metrop Mus of Art, New York, NY, 76; one-man shows, Galerie Int, New York, 71 & Cisnero Gallery, New York, 73. Teaching: Prof drawing, Sch Plastic Arts, Matanzas, 41-51, dir, 44-49, prof sculpture, 51-61. Pos: Dir, Art Mag, Matanzas, 50-52; mem, Seminar of Educ, Cuba, 56. Awards: Gold Medal, Tampa Univ, 52; Cuban Nat Art Competition, Bd Educ, Havana, 53; Honorable Mention, Audubon Artists, 74. Bibliog: Rodulfo Tardo, Art News, 2/70; Manuel Rodulfo Tardo, Arts Mag, 11/70; Jeanne Paris (auth), Rodulfo Tardo, Long Island Press, 71. Style & Technique: Volumes balanced against open spaces, allowing the sculpture breath; light and air combine to give a feeling of baroque; direct carving, welding. Dealer: Kromex Art Gallery One Rockefeller Plaza New York NY 10020. Mailing Add: 50-12 41st St Long Island City NY 11104

TARIN, GILBERTO A
PAINTER, PRINTMAKER
b San Antonio, Tex, Feb 19, 43. Study: Univ of Americas, Puebla, Mex, with Victor Cuevas & Fernando Belain; Our Lady of Lake Univ, San Antonio, Tex. Work: San Antonio Art League; SW Craft Ctr, San Antonio. Comn: Acrylic on canvas (6 ft x 18 ft), Julius P Foretich, Conroe, Tex, 77. Exhib: Inst Mexicano-Norteamericano de Rel Cult, Mexico City, 70; one-man shows, Galeria Rewi, Mexico City, 71 & Galeria Agustin Arrieta, Puebla, 72; Okla Art Mus, Oklahoma City, 74; Walker & Guthrie Art Ctr, Minneapolis, Minn, 74; McNay Art Inst, San Antonio, 77. Awards: Purchase Prize, Tex Watercolor Soc, 74; Cash Award, 26th Ann Tex Watercolor Soc, James K Naylor Mem, 75; First Prize, 47th Ann San Antonio Artists Exhib, Julian Onderdonk Mem, 77. Mem: Tex Watercolor Soc. Style & Technique: Modern impressionistic. Media: Pen & Ink, Gouache; Lithography. Dealer: Maggie L Reed 2222 Nacogdoches St San Antonio TX 78209. Mailing Add: 241 E French San Antonio TX 78212

TARNOPOL, GREGOIRE
PAINTER, COLLECTOR
b Odessa, Russia, Feb 24, 91; US citizen. Study: Acad Art, Munich; Acad Art, St Petersburg; Acad Art, Copenhagen. Exhib: Barzansky Gallery, New York, 41. Media: Gouache Collection: French modern, from Delacroix to Picasso. Mailing Add: 47 E 88th St New York NY 10028

TARSHIS, JEROME
WRITER, CURATOR
b New York, NY, June 27, 36. Study: Columbia Col, AB, 57. Pos: Guest cur, San Francisco Mus Mod Art, 75- Res: History of modernism and postmodernism in art and literature. Publ: Contribr, Village Voice, 59-61; contribr, Artforum, 70-72; contribr, Art News, 73-; contribr, Smithsonian & Christian Sci Monitor. Mailing Add: 1315 Polk St San Francisco CA 94109

TASCONA, ANTONIO TONY
PAINTER, SCULPTOR
b St Boniface, Man, Mar 16, 26. Study: Winnipeg Sch Art, dipl; Univ Man Sch Fine Arts. Work: Winnipeg Art Gallery, Man; Confederation Art Gallery & Mus Charlottetown, PEI; Art Gallery Ont, Toronto; Nat Gallery Can, Ottawa; Can Coun Collection, Ottawa. Comn: Aluminum bas relief, Man Centennial Art Ctr, 67-68; lacquer painting on aluminum, Winnipeg YWCA, 68; sculpture, Fletcher Argue Bldg, Univ Man, 69; epoxy resin disks, in steel rings, Fed Dept Pub Works for Freshwater Inst, Univ Man, 72. Exhib: Walker Art Ctr Biennial, Minneapolis, 58; Expos Concours Artistiques, Montreal Beaux Arts, 63 & Quebec Mus, 64; Can Prints & Drawings, Cardiff Commonwealth Arts Festival, Wales, 65; Nat Gallery Can Traveling Exhib Australia, 67; Nat Gallery Can Biennial, Ottawa, 68; one-man shows, Damjkar Galleries, Ribe, Denmark, 75, Windsor Pub Art Gallery, Ont, 78; Winnipeg Print Show, Can Cult Ctr, Paris, France, 76-77; Winnipeg Centennial Pub Libr Sculpture Competition, Man. Awards: Arts Medal Award, Royal Archit Inst Can, Ottawa, 70; Can Coun Arts Award Fel, 72; Can Silver Jubilee Medal, by Her Majesty, the Queen. Bibliog: Rene Ostiguey (auth), Western Canadian art, Vie Arts Montreal, 66; P Fry (auth), Tony Tascona, Artscanada, 72; plus others. Mem: Winnipeg Art Gallery (bd gov); Can Conf Artists; Can Artist Representation; Royal Can Acad Arts. Mailing Add: 151 Tache Ave St Boniface MB Can

TASGAL-KLIEGMAN, GERDA
PAINTER, SCULPTOR
b New York, NY. Study: Hunter Col; study with Oronzo Maldarelli; Hans Hoffman Sch Fine Arts, Scholar, study with Hans Hoffman; Graphic Arts Ctr, with Shiko Munakato. Work: US Educ Found, India. Exhib: Whitney Mus, New York; Mus NMex, Santa Fe; Massilon Mus, Ohio; Joslyn Mem Art Mus, Omaha, Nebr; Riverside Mus, New York; plus numerous others. Teaching: Studio instruction. Awards: First Prize for Sculpture, Knickerbocker Artists, 74. Bibliog: Reviews of work in New York Times & New York World-Telegram; plus others. Mem: Nat Asn Women Artists (prog comt); Knickerbocker Artists (exec bd); Artists Equity Asn NY; Allied Artists Am; Exp in Art & Technol. Style & Technique: Abstraction, cubism, figurative. Media: Oil; Assemblage; Calligraphic; Bronze. Mailing Add: 430 W 116th St New York NY 10027

TATHAM, DAVID FREDERIC
ART HISTORIAN
b Wellesley, Mass, Nov 29, 32. Study: Univ Mass, AB; Syracuse Univ, MA & PhD. Teaching: Prof hist art, Syracuse Univ, 68- Mem: Col Art Asn. Res: American painting and graphic arts of the nineteenth century. Publ: Auth, The Lure of the Striped Pig, Imprint Soc, 74; auth, John Henry Bufford, American Lithographer, Univ Press Va, 76; auth, Winslow Homer's Library, Am Art J, 77. Mailing Add: Dept of Fine Arts Syracuse Univ Syracuse NY 13210

TATISTCHEFF, PETER ALEXIS
ART DEALER
b New York, NY, Dec 12, 38. Study: Yale Univ, New Haven, Conn. Exhibitions Arranged: New Images, Figuration in American Painting, Queens Mus, NY, 11-12/74; New Figurative Painting Tour, 5-6/77; First Charleston Ann Tour, 10-11/77. Pos: Pres & dir, Tatistcheff & Co Inc, New York. Specialty: Contemporary American painting. Mailing Add: Tatistcheff & Co Inc 35 E 35th St New York NY 10016

TATOSSIAN, ARMAND
PAINTER
b Alexandria, Egypt, Sept 26, 48; Can citizen. Study: Painting with Adam Sherrif Scott, 66-69; Cararra Acad, Bergamo, Italy, mural techniques with Langarett, 70; also painting & lithography with Carzou, Paris, 71. Work: Nat Gallery, Ottawa; McGill Univ; Mus Quebec, Quebec City; Mt Royal Libr, PQ. Comn: Fight for Liberation (painting), Ecole Polytechnique, Athens, Greece, 74; paintings, Bank Can Nat, Montreal, 74. Exhib: One-man shows, Double Take Art Gallery, New York, 68, Molesworth Gallery, New York, 69, Galerie Gauvreau, Montreal, 71, Galerie Bernard Deroches, Montreal, 73 & Mus Nat, Armenia, USSR, 76. Teaching: Instr painting & drawing, Concordia Univ, 72- Bibliog: M Spicer (auth), Tatossian, Belarmin, 75. Mem: Royal Can Acad Art. Style & Technique: Figures and portraits in oil, acrylic and gouache; landscapes in strong vibrant colors and thick impastos. Media: Oil. Dealer: Galerie Bernard Desroches 1194 Sherbrooke St W Montreal PQ Can. Mailing Add: 2121 Tupper No 1411 Montreal PQ H3H 1P1 Can

TATRO, RONALD EDWARD
SCULPTOR, INSTRUCTOR
b Kankakee, Ill, Jan 12, 43. Study: Southern Ill Univ, BA & MFA. Work: Southern Ill Univ, Carbondale; Southwestern Col (Calif). Exhib: Two-man shows, Orr Gallery, San Diego, 73, Jewish Community Ctr, San Diego, 75 & Montalvo Ctr for the Arts, Saratoga, Calif, 77; The City is For People, San Diego Fine Arts Gallery, 73; 21st Ann All-Calif Show, Laguna Beach Mus Art, 75; one-man shows, San Diego Art Inst, 75 & Mira Costa Col, Oceanside, Calif, 76; San Diego Art Inst Ann, 75 & 76; 14th Ann Purchase Prize Competition, Riverside Art Ctr & Mus, Calif, 76; 22nd Ann All-Calif Show, Laguna Beach Mus Art, Calif, 76; Nat Small Sculpture Exhib, Cypress Col, Calif, 76; 15th Ann La Mirada Fiesta de Artes, Calif, 76; Crafts-Sculpture-Painting-Graphics, Orange Co Art Asn, Fullerton, Calif, 76; plus others. Teaching: Instr basic art, Southern Ill Univ, Carbondale, 66-67; asst prof art, Va State Col, 67-68; instr sculpture, Grossmont Col, 68- Mem: San Diego Art Inst (bd mem, 74-). Awards: Third Prize in Sculpture, San Diego Art Inst, 75; Juror's Award, Crafts-Sculpture-Painting-Graphics, Orange Co Art Asn, 76. Style & Technique: Contemporary, abstract, nonobjective; welding. Media: Steel. Mailing Add: 210 Highline Trail El Cajon CA 92021

TATSCHL, JOHN
CRAFTSMAN, SCULPTOR
b Vienna, Austria, June 30, 06. Study: Teachers Col, Vienna; Acad Appl Art & Acad Fine Arts, Master Sch Sculpture, Vienna. Work: Mus NMex, Santa Fe. Comn: Mural, US Post Off, Vivian, La; ten stained glass windows, St Michael Church, Albuquerque; stained glass windows, Am Bank Commerce, Albuquerque; stained glass for churches, Las Cruces, Los Alamos & Albuquerque, NMex; fountain, Roswell Mus; plus others. Exhib: Southwest Exhib, 46-56. Teaching: Asst prof, Park Col, 43-46; prof art, Univ NMex, 46-71. Awards: Purchase Awards, Roswell Mus & Mus NMex; Univ NMex Res Grants, 50 & 53; Am Inst Architects Award for Art in Archictecture, 63. Media: Wood, Glass, Bronze. Mailing Add: 1800 Las Lomas Rd NE Albuquerque NM 87106

TATTI, BENEDICT MICHAEL
SCULPTOR, PAINTER
b New York, NY, May 1, 17. Study: Masters Inst Roerich Mus, with L Slobodkin; Da Vinci Art Sch, with A Piccirilli; State Univ NY; Art Students League, with William Zorach & O Zadkine; Hans Hofmann Sch Art. Work: Harper's Row, Mr & Mrs Cass Canfield, New York;

Mr & Mrs Zero Mostel, New York; Dr Maurice Hexter, Fedn Jewish Philanthropies, New York; Boccour Paints, Mr & Mrs Sam Golden, NJ; Lasdon Found, Mr & Mrs Lloyd Lasdon, New York. Comn: Sundial, R W Bliss for Dumbarton Oaks, Washington, DC, 52; Bison, E Taylor for Tokyo Park, Japan, 60; D'Aragon Mem, A D'Aragon, Hartsdale, NY, 69; medallions of D Sarnoff, D Eisenhower & Mark Twain, Newell & Lennon, New York. Exhib: Artists for Victory, Metrop Mus Art, New York, 42; Pa Acad Fine Arts, Philadelphia, 50-54; Mus Mod Art, New York, 60; Claude Bernard Gallery, Paris, France, 60; Roko Gallery, New York, 67. Teaching: Instr sculpture & head dept, H S Art & Design; instr sculpture, Craft Students League, 66-67. Pos: Consult restoration, Alexanders Sculpture Studio, 46-72; sculptor-designer, Loewry-Smith Assocs, 52-65; artist in residence, Nat Ctr Experiments TV, San Francisco, 69. Awards: Creative Arts Prog Grant, NY State Coun Arts, 72; Medal of Honor for Sculpture, Painters & Sculptors Soc NJ, 72. Mem: Am Soc Contemp Artists; Sculptors League, New York; Painters & Sculptors Soc NJ (vpres). Dealer: Alexander Gallery 117 E 39th St New York NY 10016. Mailing Add: 214 E 39th St New York NY 10016

TAUBES, FREDERIC
PAINTER, WRITER
b Lvov, Poland, Apr 15, 00; US citizen. Study: Vienna Acad Fine Arts; Munich Art Acad, with F von Stuck & M Doerner; Bauhaus, Weimar, with J Itten. Work: Metrop Mus Art, New York; San Francisco Mus Art; De Young Mem Mus, San Francisco; Mills Col Collection, Oakland; William Rockhill Nelson Gallery, Kansas City; plus many others. Exhib: Over 100 one-man exhibs in mus & galleries in US. Teaching: Carnegie vis prof art, Univ Ill; vis prof art, Univ Wis, Univ Okla, Univ Hawaii, Colo State Col, State Teachers Col, Lansing, Mich, NY Univ, Cooper Union, Art Students League, plus many others; lectr art, Royal Col Art, Royal Soc Art, Slade Sch, London Univ, John Ruskin Sch Art, Art, Oxford Univ, Edinborough Col Art, Camberwell Sch Art & Crafts, plus many others. Pos: Contrib ed, Taubes Page, Am Artist Mag, 43-59; Am ed, The Artist Mag, with the Taubes Pages as ed feature, presently; columnist, Ask Taubes, Illusr Mag, presently. Awards: Hon Citations, New Iberia, San Antonio, Tex, Amarillo, Tex & Wheeling, WVa; Hon Colonel, State of NMex; Hon Admiral of Tecke, State of La. Mem: Fel Royal Soc Arts; fel Int Soc Arts & Lett. Res: Formulator of Taubes Varnishes & Copal Painting Media. Publ: Auth 40 bks on paint techniques & esthetics; contribr, Encycl Britannica: Yearbooks, Grolier Encycl & others. Mailing Add: Haverstraw NY 10927

TAUCH, WALDINE AMANDA
SCULPTOR, COLLECTOR
b Schulenburg, Tex. Study: With Pompeo Coppini. Work: Witte Mem Mus, San Antonio, Tex; Pan Handle Plains Hist Mus, Campos, Tex; Wesleyan Mus, Ga. Comn: Heroic monument to Bedford, Ind, State Ind, 22; The Doughboy Statue, Am Legion, Austin, Tex, 31; Moses Austin Monument, State Tex, 41; Higher Education, comn by Mr & Mrs Andrew Casoles for Trinity Univ (Tex), 68; Gen Douglas MacArthur, Howard Payne Col, Brownwood, Tex, 69. Exhib: Nat Sculpture Soc Traveling Show, 31; Women Painters & Sculptors, New York, 32; Coppini Acad Fine Arts, 54-; Witte Mem Mus; Nat Acad Design, New York; plus others. Bibliog: Shaffer (auth), Making the Texas Ranger of to-day, San Antonio Express, 61; John Field (auth), Unveiling of Gen Douglas MacArthur. Mem: Coppini Acad Fine Arts (sponsor, 57-, emer pres, 60-); fel Nat Sculpture Soc; Am Acad Arts & Lett; Panhandle Plains Hist Soc & Mus (dir arts, 72-73); fel Am Artists Prof League. Collection: Paintings by Van iest, Rolla Taylor, Harold Roney & Frank Garvari. Mailing Add: 115 Melrose Pl San Antonio TX 78212

TAULBEE, DAN J
PAINTER, ART DEALER
b Charlo, Mont, Apr 7, 24. Study: With pvt instructors. Work: Farnsworth Mus, Maine; Peabody Mus, Cambridge, Mass; Plains Indian Mus, Browning, Mont; C M Russell Mus, Helena, Mont; Southern Plains Mus, Anadarko, Okla. Exhib: Farnsworth Mus Show; Peabody Mus Show; Nat Acad Design, New York; Burr's Int Show; Heritage Am Art Gallery, Butte, Mont, 77. Pos: Owner, Heritage Am Art Gallery, Butte, Mont. Awards: Gold Medal, Burr Gallery. Mem: Grand Cent Watercolorists Soc. Media: Oil, Watercolor. Specialty: Historical plains Indian art and Western Americana. Dealer: Grand Central Galleries 40 Vanderbilt Ave New York NY 10017; La Galleria 2161 Ave de La Playa La Jolla CA 92037. Mailing Add: 2706 Nettie St Butte MT 59701

TAVENNER, PATRICIA (PAT)
COLLAGE ARTIST, PHOTOGRAPHER
b Doster, Mich, Mar 22, 41. Study: Mich State Univ, BA; Calif Col Arts & Crafts, Oakland, MFA. Work: San Francisco Mus Art; Oakland Mus Art, Calif; Mills Col; Kansas City Art Inst, Mo. Comn: Facade, Mus Contemp Crafts, New York, 71; sect of wall, Can Nat Res Libr, Ottawa, 73. Exhib: Small Formatt, Los Angeles Co Mus Art, Los Angeles, 69; Photo Media, Mus Contemp Crafts, New York, 71; Books by Artists, Moore Col, Philadelphia; Tampons, Inst Environ, Paris, France, 74; one-woman show, Mills Col, Oakland, 74; plus others. Teaching: Exploring creative energy on a psychic level & silk screen, Univ Calif, Berkeley Exten, 67-; asst prof art painting, Calif State Univ, San Jose, 72-73 women in the arts, Calif State Univ, San Francisco, 72-73. Bibliog: Donna Meilach (auth), Collage and Assemblage, Crown, 73. Mem: Womens Caucus for Art. Style & Technique: Collage, correspondence art, conceptual pieces, dominated by a photo image. Media: Montage. Publ: Contribr, International Image Directory, 73; contribr, Art et Communication Marginale, 74; contribr, Women See Women, 75; contribr, Art: A Womans Sensibility, 75; plus others. Mailing Add: Univ of Calif Exten 55 Laguna St San Francisco CA 94102

TAWNEY, LENORE
WEAVER, ASSEMBLAGE ARTIST
b Lorain, Ohio. Study: Univ Ill, 43-45; Inst Design, Ill, with Archipenko, 46-47; also with Martta Taipale, Finland, 54. Work: Mus Contemp Crafts, New York; Mus Mod Art, New York; Kunstegewerbe Mus, Zurich; Cleveland Inst of Art; Brooklyn Mus; Cooper-Hewitt Mus. Exhib: Brussels World's Fair, 59; Kunstegewerbe Mus, Zurich, 64; one-man shows, Art Inst Chicago, Contemp Crafts Mus, Seattle World's Fair & Staten Island Mus, New York, 61, Calif State Univ, Fullerton, 75 & Kansas City Art Inst, 77. Media: Linen, Collages. Dealer: Willard Gallery 29 E 72nd St New York NY 10021. Mailing Add: 64 Wooster St New York NY 10012

TAYLOR, BOB BYRON
CARTOONIST
b Stockton, Calif, July 21, 32. Study: Sacramento State Col, BA, 54. Exhib: Sports cartoonist, Sacramento Union, 49-54; ed & sports cartoonist, Dallas Times Herald, 58- Awards: Brotherhood Award, Nat Conf Christians & Jews, 64; Dept Defense Awards, 57 & 58; Dallas Press Club Award Best Cartoon of Yr, 68, 72 & 74. Mem: Am Asn Ed Cartoonists. Mailing Add: 13843 Waterfall Pl Dallas TX 75230

TAYLOR, FRAN (FRANCES JANE)
ART ADMINISTRATOR, PAINTER
b Philadelphia, Pa, Mar 2, 25. Study: Four yrs pvt study with Emilie DeS Atlee. Exhib: ADVAC Traveling Exhib for Award Winners, William Penn Mus, Harrisburg, Pa, 66; Philadelphia Art Festival, 67; Artist Equity Triennial Exhib, Philadelphia, 74; Am Artist Grand Nat Art Exhib, New York, 75; Nat Miniature Art Exhib, Nutley, NJ, 75. Pos: Freelance exhib dir for six firms, 60-68; exec dir, Cult Arts Ctr, Ocean City, NJ, 71 & Ocean City Sch Art, 74- Awards: Newtown Square Silver Medal, Women's Club Newtown Square, Pa, 64 & 66; Tavistock Gold Medal Best in Show, Perkiomen Valley Art League, Schwenksville, Pa, 66. Mem: Nat & Philadelphia Chap Artists Equity; Nat & NJ Chap Am Artists Prof League. Style & Technique: Landscapes, seascapes with palette knife; still life with brush. Media: Oil. Mailing Add: 500 Bay Ave Ocean City NJ 08226

TAYLOR, FREDERICK BOURCHIER
PAINTER, SCULPTOR
b Ottawa, Ont, July 27, 06. Study: McGill Univ, BArch, 30; Univ London Goldsmiths Col Art, with Stanley Anderson; London Co Coun Sch Arts & Crafts; Byam Shaw Sch Painting, with Ernest Jackson. Work: Nat Gallery Can, Ottawa; Pub Archives Can, Ottawa; Ont Heritage Collection; Montreal Mus Fine Arts; Can War Art Collection; plus many others. Comn: Etching, Govt Can, Ottawa, 32; etchings & painting for corps in Can & USA, 32-72; portraits, McGill Univ, 41-66; series of paintings, Algoma Steel Corp, Saulte Ste Marie, Ont, 46-47; plus many other pvt comn. Exhib: Ont Soc Artists, Toronto, 31-; Royal Can Acad Arts, Toronto, 31-72; many group & int traveling exhibs, Can, US & Mex, 31-78; Royal Inst Painters, London, 36. Teaching: Instr & lectr drawing & modeling, McGill Univ Sch Archit, 40-43. Pos: Chmn Que region, Fed Can Artists, 44-45, nat vpres, 45-46. Mem: Royal Can Acad Arts (coun & comts, 48-); Print & Drawing Coun Can. Style & Technique: Interpretative; representational. Media: Oil. Dealer: Walter Klinkhoff Gallery 1200 Sherbrooke St W Montreal PQ Can; Roberts Gallery 641 Yonge St Toronto ON Can. Mailing Add: Apartado Postal 101 San Miguel de Allende Gto Mexico

TAYLOR, GAGE
PAINTER
b Ft Worth, Tex, Jan 20, 42. Study: Univ of Tex, BFA, 65; Mich State Univ, MFA, 67. Work: Pioneer Mus, Stockton, Calif. Exhib: Other Landscapes & Shadowland, Univ of Southern Calif, 71; Imaginary Painting, San Jose State Univ, Calif, 72; Divergent Representation, Smithsonian Inst, Washington, DC, 73; Extraordinary Realities, Whitney Mus of Am Art, New York, 73; Our Land, Our Sky, Our Water, Expo 74, Spokane, Wash, 74; Baja, San Francisco Mus of Art, Calif, 75; Paris Biennale, Mus of Mod Art, Paris, 75; Alternative Realities, Mus of Contemp Art, Chicago, Ill, 76; Calif Painting & Sculpture, Mus of Mod Art, San Francisco, 76 & Nat Collection of Fine Arts, Washington, DC, 77; plus others. Teaching: Instr landscape painting, San Francisco Art Inst, 71; instr painting & drawing, pvt Studio, 72- Bibliog: Thomas Albright (auth), Visuals, Rolling Stone, 9/71; Mary Rourke (auth), Fantastic voyages, Newsweek, 7/77; Walter Hopps (auth Introd), Visions I, Pomegranate, 77. Style & Technique: Extremely detailed landscape & fantasy landscape paintings. Media: Oil, Gouache. Dealer: Gallery Rebecca Cooper 2130 P St NW Washington DC 20037; Zara Gallery 553 Pacific Ave San Francisco CA 94133. Mailing Add: Box 383 Woodacre CA 94973

TAYLOR, GRACE MARTIN
PAINTER, EDUCATOR
b Morgantown, WVa. Study: Pa Acad Fine Arts; WVa Univ, AB & MA; Ohio Univ; Art Inst Chicago; Art Students League; Bisttram Sch Art; Hans Hofmann Sch Fine Arts. Work: Am Color Print Soc; Hallmark Co; Charleston Art Gallery, WVa; plus many pvt collections. Exhib: Nat Acad Design, New York, 44 & 48; Am Watercolor Soc, New York, 58 & 59; Am Drawing Biennial, Norfolk Mus, 65; Contemp Gallery, Palm Beach, 67; one-man shows, Artist of the Yr, WVa Univ, 58 & 67 & WVa Univ Creative Arts Ctr, 74. Teaching: Assoc prof art & head dept, Mason Col Music & Fine Arts, 34-56; assoc prof art, Morris Harvey Col, 56-68; lectr, WVa Univ Div Exten Credit, 67-71. Pos: Dean, Mason Col Music & Fine Arts, 50-55, pres, 55-56. Awards: First Prize for Prints, Seven State Exhib, Va Intermont Col, 48; Three State Ann First Prize & Jurors Award, Huntington Galleries, 54 & 64; Citizen of the Yr in Art in WVa, WVa Rhododendron Arts Festival, 71 & First Prize Drawing, 74; Purchase Award Drawing, Allied Artists of WVa, WVa Arts Coun, 73. Bibliog: Haas & Packer (auth), Instruction in Audio-Visual Aids, 50 & Morris Davidson (auth), Painting with Purpose, 64, Prentice-Hall. Mem: Provincetown Art Asn; Allied Artists WVa (pres, 35-36); Am Asn Univ Prof; Int Platform Asn. Style & Technique: Abstract-architectonic with intuitive structuring of design; free yet controlled brushing to give paint visual plasticity and the mysterious quality of breathing in and out. Media: Oil, Casein, Acrylic. Collection: Portfolios of drawings and watercolors; paintings in all media. Mailing Add: 1604 Virginia St E Charleston WV 25311

TAYLOR, HARRY GEORGE
PRINTMAKER, PHOTOGRAPHER
b Detroit, Mich, Aug 17, 18. Study: Sch, Art Inst, Chicago, MFA, 49, studied with Boris Anisfeld, S W Hayter & Moise Smith. Work: Utah State Fine Arts, Capitol, Salt Lake City, Utah; Ogden Bd Educ Sch Mus, Utah; Co Sch Mus, Pleasant View, Utah. Comn: Eight ft wooden cross, 67 & 12ft wooden sculpture, 68, St James Church, Ogden, Utah; Mini-Show of Graphics, Ogden City Rd Educ, 70. Exhib: M H De Young Mus Nat Exhib, San Francisco, Calif, 60; one-man show, Salt Lake Art Ctr, Salt Lake City, Utah, 65-73; Soc Am Graphic Artists Ann Nat Print & Drawing Exhib, Chicago, Ill, 62; Calif Soc Printmakers Traveling Show, Vt, NY, Maine, Ohio, Mass, Pa, Iowa, Wis & others, 75-77; Utah Statewide Competition, 77. Teaching: Instr painting & drawing, St Bonaventure-Olean, NY, summer, 47; instr oil & watercolor, Weber State Col, Ogden, Utah, 59. Pos: Art dir, Meridian Publ Co, Ogden, Utah, 60-77. Awards: Purchase Awards, Chicago Veterans, US Army, 49 & Capiral Show, State of Utah, 52; First Place Graphics, 18th Ann Exhib, Ogden Palette Club, 77. Bibliog: James L Haseltine (auth), Catalog, Meridian Pub Co, 65; Bob Halliday (auth), 70 & Charlotte, 72, Salt Lake Tribune. Mem: Calif Soc Printmakers; Sch of the Art Inst Alumni Asn; Ogden Palette Club (vpres, 67); Venice Int. Style & Technique: Bold design; simplicity; clarity; conbined woodcut, etching & photo process. Media: Etching; Woodcut. Publ: Illusr, Improvement Era, Norman Press, 60; illusr, How to make a woodcut, Your Home, Meridian, 70; illusr, Hill Air Force Guide, US Air Force, 74; illusr, Exhibit for the Blind, Weber Col, 76; illusr, A Book of Korean Recipes, Twink Lee-Miller, 77. Mailing Add: 905 Rancho Blvd Ogden UT 84404

TAYLOR, HUGH HOLLOWAY
ART HISTORIAN, LECTURER
b Charlottesville, Va, July 18, 41. Study: Col of William & Mary, Williamsburg, Va, AB(art hist), 63; George Washington Univ, MA(art hist & theory), 65, with Lawrence Leite. Collections Arranged: Dir cataloging of collection of Washington Co Hist Soc, Pa, 76-77. Teaching: Teaching asst art hist, George Washington Univ, Washington, DC, 64-65; prof art

hist, Washington & Jefferson Col, Washington, Pa, 65- Pos: Assoc prof on the E M Kelso Chair of Art Hist, Washington & Jefferson Col, Washington, Pa, 65- Mem: Soc of Archit Historians; Nat Trust for Hist Preserv; Washington Co (Pa) Hist & Landmarks. Res: Nineteenth Century architecture of Western Pennsylvania. Mailing Add: 55 Main St West Middletown PA 15379

TAYLOR, JOHN C E
PAINTER, EDUCATOR
b New Haven, Conn, Oct 22, 02. Study: Acad Julian, Paris, France, 26-28; also with Walter Griffin, France, 26-28; Yale Univ, MA, 40. Work: Mus Am Art, New Britain, Conn; numerous pvt collections. Comn: Designs for wood carvings, Chapel, Trinity Col (Conn), 57-68, crypt chapel doors, 72; Westover award tablet, Westover Sch, Middlebury, Conn, 58; design for wood carvings, St James Church, Glastonbury, Conn, 62 & St Mary's by the Sea, Fenwick, Conn. Exhib: Spring Salon, Paris, 28; Corcoran Gallery Art Biennial, Washington, DC 35 & 39; Artists for Victory Traveling Exhib, 45-46; one-man retrospective, Trinity Col (Conn), 70. Teaching: Mem fac art, Lawrenceville Sch, NJ, 36-41; mem fac art, Trinity Col (Conn), 41-56, prof art hist, 56-70, head dept fine arts, 45-64; instr art hist, Loomis Sch, 55-72; retired. Pos: Scholar in residence, Loomis Sch, 70-72. Awards: Cooper Prize, Conn Acad Fine Arts, 35; Second Prize, New Orleans Art Asn, 46; Black & White Prize, Rockport Art Asn, 55. Bibliog: E A Jewell (auth), Exploring realism & abstraction, New York Times, 31; F Berkman (auth), Much avant-garde art profanation of nature, Hartford Times, 70; J Goldenthal (auth), Taylor work in retrospect, Hartford Courant, 70. Mem: Conn Acad Fine Arts; Rockport Art Asn; North Shore Arts Asn; Washington Arts Asn, Conn. Style & Technique: Realism. Media: Oil, Pencil. Mailing Add: 30 Four Mile Rd West Hartford CT 06107

TAYLOR, JOHN FRANK ADAMS
WRITER
b Dallas, Tex, Oct 8, 15. Study: Princeton Univ, AB(philos), 36, PhD, 40; Lewis & Clark Col, Hon LHD, 68. Comn: The Masks of Society (bk), written as Guggenheim fel, 63-64. Teaching: Fel art & archaeol, Princeton Univ, 41-42; prof & head dept lit & fine arts, Mich State Univ, 46-52, prof philos, 52- Pos: Dir, Humanities Res Ctr, Col Arts & Lett, Mich State Univ, 65-67. Awards: Distinguished Fac Award, Mich State Univ, 61. Res: Aesthetics, philosophy of art, theory of form and expression in the visual arts. Publ: Auth, The American artist: an essay on the uses of freedom, Centennial Rev Arts & Sci, 63; auth, The humanities in land grant universities, Sat Rev, 64; auth, Design & Expression in the Visual Arts, Dover, 64; auth, The art of encounter, Arts in Soc, 65; auth, The Masks of Society, Appleton, 66; plus many others. Mailing Add: 4539 Nakoma Dr Okemos MI 48864

TAYLOR, JOHN LLOYD
ART CRITIC, ART ADMINISTRATOR
b Muskegon, Mich, May 24, 35. Study: Muskegon Community Col, Mich, AA; Southern Ill Univ, BA & MA; Courtauld Inst Art, London Univ; Univ Denver. Collections Arranged: Options, 68; A Plastic Presence, 69; Giacometti: Complete Graphics, 70; Picasso in Milwaukee, 71; Eight Artists, 71; The Private World of George Segal, 73; Mr & Mrs Sidney Kohl Collection (assembled & cataloged), 73-75. Teaching: Asst prof art hist, Univ Wis-Milwaukee, 72-74. Pos: Dir, Madison Art Ctr, Wis, 65-67; dir exhib & collections, Milwaukee Art Ctr, 67-72; dir, Art Hist Galleries, Univ Wis-Milwaukee, 72-74; dir fine arts galleries, Univ Wis, Milwaukee, 76- Awards: Nat Endowment for Arts Fels for Mus Prof, 72 & 74. Mem: Col Art Asn Am; Int Coun Mus; Am Asn Mus (chmn accreditation vis comts); Arch Am Art; Int Inst Conserv. Res: Abstract expressionism. Publ: Auth, DeWain Valentine, 73 & Bob Stanley, 74, Art Int; auth, George Sugarman, Art in Am, 74; auth, Wisconsin printmaking workshops, Art News, 75; plus others. Mailing Add: 1559 N Prospect Ave Apt 309 Milwaukee WI 53202

TAYLOR, JOHN (WILLIAMS)
PAINTER
b Baltimore, Md, Oct 12, 97. Study: J Francis Smith Art Sch, 20-22; Art Students League, Los Angeles, with S McDonald Wright, 23; Art Students League, New York, with Boardman Robinson, 26-27; study in Paris, France, 29. Work: Va Mus, Richmond; Mus New Britain Inst, Conn; John Herron Mus, Indianapolis, Ind; Nat Acad Design Ranger Fund Collection, New York; Morse Gallery Art, Rollins Col, Fla. Comn: Mural painting for Richfield Springs Post Off, NY, Dept Interior Sect Fine Arts, 42. Exhib: Va Mus Art Biennial, 48; Carnegie Inst Int, Pittsburgh, 50; Pa Acad Fine Arts Ann, Philadelphia, 54; Whitney Mus Am Art Ann, New York, 59; Nat Acad Design Ann, New York, 61. Teaching: Instr painting, Art Students League Woodstock Summer Sch, 48-54; assoc prof painting & vis artist, Tulane Univ, 56, 58 & 59; prof painting & vis artist, Univ Fla, 60-62. Awards: John Barton Payne Medal & Purchase Award, Va Mus, 46; Citation & Grant, Am Acad Arts & Lett, 48; Guggenheim Fel, 54. Bibliog: Lawrence Campbell (auth), Poet of the Levee & the Level Sands, Art Students League New York News, 9/1/50 & John Taylor, Art News, 3/63; Ray Bethers (auth), How Paintings Happen, Norton, 51. Mem: Academician Nat Acad Design; life mem Woodstock Artists Asn (trustee, 65-70). Media: Oil, Gouache. Publ: Contribr, The Art of the Artist, Crown, 51. Mailing Add: Ulster Co Shady NY 12479

TAYLOR, JOSEPH RICHARD
SCULPTOR
b Wilbur, Wash, Feb 1, 07. Study: Univ Wash, BFA, 31, MFA(cum laude), 32; Univ Okla; Columbia Univ, 40. Work: Western Hemisphere Collection, IBM; De Golyer Collection, Univ Okla Libr; Philbrook Mus, Tulsa. Comn: W B Bizzell Mem Statue, Univ Okla, 50; three mem bronze busts, State Capitol Bldg, Oklahoma City, bronze plaque, comn by State Rep Carl Albert; bronze busts of John Zink, Tulsa, Bud Wilkenson, Univ Okla Football Coach & Joe Brandt, George L Cross & Paul Sharp, Presidents of Univ Okla; plus 200 portraits of children. Exhib: Kansas City Art Inst Ann Midwest Exhib, 33-40; New York World's Fair, 38-39; San Francisco World's Fair, 40; Mus Mod Art, New York, 40; Univ Okla Art Mus; plus others. Teaching: Prof art & head dept sculpture, Fine Arts Col, Univ Okla, 32-63, David Ross Boyd prof, 63-71, emer prof, 71- Pos: Lectr & art judge, art clubs & festivals, 69-; actg dir, Art Sch, Univ Okla. Awards: McDowell Art Colony Fel, Petersboro, NH, 40; Okla Hall of Fame, 60; Distinquished Serv Citation, Okla Univ, 77. Bibliog: Article in Fortune Mag, 4/61 & fall 69; article in Nat Sculpture Rev Mag, fall 70 & summer 71. Mem: Phi Beta Kappa; Okla Artists Asn (pres). Style & Technique: Realist. Media: Bronze, Wood, Stone. Mailing Add: 701 W Brooks St Norman OK 73069

TAYLOR, JOSHUA CHARLES
MUSEUM DIRECTOR, ART HISTORIAN
b Hillsboro, Ore, Aug 22, 17. Study: Mus Art Sch, Portland, Ore, 35-39; Reed Col, BA, 39, MA, 46; Princeton Univ, MFA, 49, PhD, 56. Teaching: Instr theatre, Reed Col, 39-41; instr hist art, Princeton Univ, 48-49; prof humanities & hist art, Univ Chicago, 49-63, William Rainey Harper prof humanities & prof art, 63-74. Pos: Dir, Nat Collection Fine Arts, 70- Awards: Quantrell Award, Univ Chicago, 56. Mem: Am Fedn of Arts (vpres); Nat Humanities Fac (mem bd); Asn Art Mus Dir; Col Art Asn Am (bd mem & vpres); Int Inst Conserv of Hist & Artistic Works; Benjamin Franklin fel Royal Soc Arts. Res: 19th and 20th century painting and artistic theory in Italy and United States. Publ: Auth, William Page, the American Titian, 57; auth, Learning to Look, 57; auth, Futurism, 61; auth, Graphic Works of Umberto Boccioni, 61; auth, Vedere Prima di Credere, 70; auth, To See is to Think, 75; auth, America as Art, 76. Mailing Add: 1250 31st St NW Washington DC 20007

TAYLOR, LISA
MUSEUM DIRECTOR
b New York, NY, Jan 8, 33. Study: Johns Hopkins Univ, 56-58; Georgetown Univ, 58-62; Corcoran Sch Art, 58-65; Parsons Sch Design, Hon DFA, 77. Comn: A Living Mus (film), Smithsonian Inst, 68. Pos: Admin asst, President's Fine Arts Comt, 58-62; membership dir, Corcoran Gallery Art, Washington DC, 62-66; prog dir, Smithsonian Inst, Washington, DC, 66-69; dir, Cooper-Hewitt Mus, New York, 69-; mem vis comt, Bank St Col & Fashion Inst Technol, presently. Awards: Exceptional Serv Award, Smithsonian Inst, 69; Bronze Apple Award, Indust Design Soc Am, 76; Thomas Jefferson Award, Am Soc Interior Designers, 76. Bibliog: Barbara Dubivsky (auth), Focus on: the Bazaar Woman, Harper's Bazaar, 5/73; Robert Mehlman (auth), Design comes to life, Indust Design, 9-10/76; Barbaralee Diamonstein (auth), The Cooper-Hewitt goes public, Art News, 9/76. Mem: Am Crafts Coun; Archit League; Mus Coun New York City; Mus Coun NY State. Publ: Contribr forwards to catalogs in: Winslow Homer, Smithsonian Inst, 72, An American Museum of Decorative Arts, McCorquodale Printers, Ltd, London, 73, Immovable Objects: Lower Manhattan, 75, Man Transforms, 76 & The Royal Pavilion at Brighton, 77, The Smithsonian Inst. Mailing Add: 1115 Fifth Ave New York NY 10028

TAYLOR, MARIE
SCULPTOR
b St Louis, Mo, Feb 22, 04. Study: Art Students League; Wash Univ Sch Art, 23-24. Work: St Louis Art Mus; also in many pvt collections. Comn: Main altar, St Paul's Church, Peoria, Ill, 60; Jefferson Mem Nat Expansion, St Louis Riverfront, for Mansion House, St Louis, 67. Exhib: Joslyn Mus Art; Kansas City Art Inst; Southern Ill Univ, Carbondale, 52; Brooks Mem Art Gallery, Memphis, Tenn, 55; Sculpture 1969, Span Int Pavillion, 69; plus others. Awards: Prizes, Cleveland Art Mus, St Louis Art Guild & Nat Asn Women Artists; plus others. Bibliog: M King (auth), Christmas exhibits at St Louis galleries, St Louis Post Dispatch, 12/12/69; Dona Z Meilach (auth), Creative carving, Turtle, 69 & Contemporary stone sculpture, Oracle, 70; plus many others. Mem: Sculptors Guild, NY. Style & Technique: Direct carver of stone; prefers to work with fieldstones or beachstone, granite. Mailing Add: 4607 Maryland Avc St Louis MO 63108

TAYLOR, MARY CAZORT
CURATOR, ART HISTORIAN
b Little Rock, Ark. Study: Washington Univ, St Louis, Mo, BFA, 53; Univ Mich, Ann Arbor, MA, 61, PhD, 70. Collections Arranged: Master Drawings from the National Gallery of Canada (travelling exhib), 69-70, Bronfman Gift Drawings (auth, catalogue), 74 & European Drawings from Canadian Collections (auth, catalogue, travelling exhib), 77, Nat Gallery Can, Ottawa. Teaching: Adj prof art hist, Carleton Univ, Ottawa, 77- Pos: Cur drawings, Nat Gallery Can, Ottawa, 70- Mem: Keepers of Pub Graphic Collections. Res: European drawings, concentration in North Italian, particularly Bolognese, late 18th century. Publ: Co-auth & ed, European Drawings from the National Gallery of Canada, Toronto, 69; auth, The pen and wash drawings of the Brothers Gandolfi, Master Drawings, Vol 14 (1976): 159-65. Mailing Add: Dept of Prints & Drawings Nat Gallery of Can Ottawa ON K1A 0M8 Can

TAYLOR, MICHAEL (LEACH)
SCULPTOR, GLASSWORKER
b Lewisburg, Tenn, May 10, 44. Study: Middle Tenn State Univ, BS; ETenn State Univ, MA & MFA; Penland Sch Arts & Crafts; Univ Wis; Univ Utah. Work: Corning Mus of Glass, NY; Lannon Found, Palm Beach, Fla; Tenn State Mus, Nashville; Mus fur Kunsthandiwerk, Frankfurt, WGer; Royal Leerdam Mus, Holland. Comn: Sculptural glass panel Vanderbilt Univ, Nashville, 73; two clear glass sculptures, Standard Oil Corp, Chicago, 75. Exhib: Nat Glass Exhib, Birmingham, Mich, 72; Am Crafts Coun Gallery, New York, 73; one-man shows, Del Mus of Art, Wilmington, 73 & Univ SC, Columbia, 73; Glass: Am, Europe & Japan, Mus fur Kunsthandiwerk, Frankfurt, WGer, 74; Contemp World Glass, Kunsthaus am Mus, Koln, WGer, 75; Contemp Art Glass Group Exhib, Lever House, New York, 76; Am Contemp Glass, Huntington Galleries, WVa, 76. Teaching: Instr glass sculpture, George Peabody Col, Nashville, 72-; vis artist, glass, Konfax Skolen, Stockholm, Sweden, 74 & Gerrit Rietuield Akad, Amsterdam, Holland, 74. Pos: Chmn arts fac, George Peabody Col, 76- Awards: Lewis Comfort Tiffany grant, Tiffany Found, 69; Thord Gray Fel, Am-Scand Found, 74; Fulbright-Hayes Scholar, 74. Bibliog: Richard Skull (auth), Michael Taylor: Glass (film), producer, Micki Colman, 68. Mem: Tenn Artists-Craftsmen Asn (pres, 70-71). Style & Technique: Blown, slumped, polished, cut, faceted and constructed glass. Media: Glass. Mailing Add: 2717 Elm Hill Pike Nashville TN 37214

TAYLOR, PRENTISS (HOTTEL)
LITHOGRAPHER, INSTRUCTOR
b Washington, DC, Dec 13, 07. Study: Art Students League, with Charles Locke, Eugene Fitsch, Anne Goldthwaite & others; also with Charles W Hawthorne. Work: Mus Mod Art, New York; Libr of Cong, Washington, DC; Phillips Collection, Washington, DC; Art Inst Chicago; Nat Collection Fine Arts; plus others. Comn: Mural in tempera for bath, comn by Mr & Mrs R F Flint, New Haven, Conn, 40; mural in oil, Christian Sci Hq, Washington, DC, 49. Exhib: Chicago Int Watercolors & Prints, Art Inst Chicago, 30's; Nat Print Exhib, Libr of Cong, Washington, DC, 43-; Painting Watercolor Graphics Ann, Whitney Mus Am Art, New York, 45; Painting in the US, 1946-1949, Carnegie Inst, Pittsburgh; Am Drawing Biennials, Norfolk Mus, Va, 60's; plus many others. Teaching: Lectr painting, Am Univ, 55-75. Pos: Pres, Artists Guild Washington; pres, Washington Watercolor Club; art therapist, St Elizabeth Hosp, Washington, DC, 43-54; art therapist, Chestnut Lodge, Rockville, Md, 58- Awards: Nat Print Exhib Purchase Awards, Libr of Cong, Washington, DC, 43-; Va Artists Purchase Awards in Watercolors, Va Mus Fine Arts, 43; Cannon Prize in Graphic Arts, Nat Acad Design, 54, Cert of Merit, 77. Bibliog: H Salpeter (auth), Prentiss Taylor, Coronet, 4/39; A Cohen (auth), Prentiss Taylor, DC Gazette, 70; Carl Zigrosser (auth), Prints & Their Creators, 74; plus others. Mem: Assoc Nat Acad Design (graphics class); Soc Am Graphic Artists; Philadelphia Water Color Club; Artists Equity Asn (bd mem, 71); Soc Washington Printmakers (pres, 42-76). Media: Watercolor, Graphic. Res: Art as psychotherapy; how art may reintegrate the disordered mind; talent/status vs expectancy achievement. Publ: Illusr, Negro Mother, 31; illusr, Scottsboro Limited, 32; illusr, Why Birds Sing, 33; illusr, American Herb Calendar, 37. Dealer: Kennedy Galleries 40 W 57th St New York NY 10019; Franz Bader 2124 Pennsylvania Ave NW Washington DC 20037. Mailing Add: 4520 Yuma St NW Washington DC 20016

TAYLOR, RENE CLAUDE
MUSEUM DIRECTOR
b London, Eng, Dec 9, 16. Pos: Dir, Museo de Arte de Ponce, PR, 62- Mailing Add: Museo de Arte de Ponce Ave Las Americas PO Box 1492 Ponce PR 00731

TAYLOR, ROBERT
ART CRITIC, WRITER
b Newton, Mass, Jan 19, 25. Study: Colgate Univ, AB, 47; Brown Univ Grad Sch, 48. Teaching: Vis lectr, Wheaton Col, 60-; lectr art hist, Boston Univ, 72-74. Pos: Art critic, Boston Herald, 52-67; Boston corresp, Pictures on Exhibit, 54-59; mem staff, Boston Globe Mag, 68-72, art critic, 72-, arts ed, 73-; Boston corresp, Art Gallery, 70- Publ: Auth, In Red Weather, 61; ed, publs, Inst Contemp Art, Boston, 67. Mailing Add: 1 Thomas Circle Marblehead MA 01945

TAYLOR, ROD ALLEN
ART ADMINISTRATOR, SCULPTOR
b Feb 29, 32; US citizen. Study: Va State Col, BS, 58; Ala State Univ, MEd, 72; Pa State Univ, PhD (art educ), 74. Work: Ghent Gallery, Norfolk, Va; Gallery One, Portsmouth, Va; Smith-Mason Art Int, Washington, DC; Bonbonniere Gallery, Managua, Nicaragua; The Little Art Gallery, Raleigh, NC. Exhib: 26th Ann Metrop Exhib, 63 & Creative Crafts Exhib, 64, Smithsonian Inst, Washington, DC; NY State Expo, Syracuse, 64; President's Park Art Fair, White House Park, Washington, DC, 65; 17th Area Exhib, Corcoran Gallery of Art, Washington, DC, 65; Tidewater Ann Outdoor Exhib, Norfolk, Va, 75. Teaching: Instr art educ, Ala State Univ, Montgomery, 68-70 & Pa State Univ, 72 & 74. Pos: Educ consult, Univ S Ala, Mobile, 70-72; chmn fine arts dept, Norfolk State col, Va, 74- Bibliog: Samella Lewis (ed), Black Artists on Art, Ward Ritchie Press, 71. Mem: Nat Art Educ Asn; Nat Conf of Artists; Southern Sculptors Soc. Style & Technique: Work in generally recognizable forms of humans and animals somewhat stylized. Media: Stone, Bronze. Publ: Auth, The Relationship of Art and Personality, 74. Mailing Add: 432 Longdale Crescent Chesapeake VA 23325

TAYLOR, ROSEMARY
CRAFTSMAN
b Joseph, Ore. Study: Cleveland Inst Art; NY Univ; Greenwich House. Exhib: One-man shows, Only Originals, NJ, 70, West Chester Col, 71; Artisan Gallery, Princeton, NJ, 72, Warren Libr, 72 & Georg Jensen, 72; Phillips Mill Gallery, Pa, 76; Craft Connection, Philadelphia, Pa, 77. Mem: NJ Designer-Craftsman; Artist-Craftsmen NY; Am Craft Coun. Style & Technique: Wheel-thrown sculpture. Media: Stoneware. Publ: Contribr, McCall's Needlework & Craft Mag. Mailing Add: Box 46 River Rd Lumberville PA 18933

TAYLOR, SANDRA ORTIZ
PAINTER, PRINTMAKER
b Los Angeles, Calif, Apr 27, 36. Study: Univ Calif, with William Brice & Sam Amato, BA; Iowa State Univ, with Byron Burford, MA. Work: Univ Iowa; Macy's Corp, New York; Univ Calif Res Libr, Los Angeles; Oakland Mus. Exhib: 3rd Ann Bay Area Regional Print Exhib, De Anza Col, 74; Palo Alto Print Invitational, Palo Alto Cult Ctr, 74; Photomorphosis, Berkeley Art Co-op, 75; Prints California, Oakland Mus & Contemp Graphics Ctr, Santa Barbara Mus, 75; 15th Nat Print Show, Bradley Univ, 75; Bicentennial Landscape Exhib, San Francisco Art Comn Gallery, 76; plus others. Teaching: Instr, San Francisco Community Col, 66- & Indian Valley Col, Marin, Calif, 74. Pos: Gallery asst, John Bolles Gallery, 70-71. Bibliog: Dwight Johnson (auth), rev in Palo Alto Times, 74; Lois Fishman (auth), article in Artweek, 74; Alfred Frankenstein (auth), article in San Francisco Chronicle, 74; plus others. Mem: Col Art Asn Am. Style & Technique: 3M color in color prints made from collages; paintings from slide projections of collages. Media: Acrylic, Oil; Graphic. Mailing Add: 31 Coleridge San Francisco CA 94110

TAYSOM, WAYNE PENDELTON
SCULPTOR, EDUCATOR
b Afton, Wyo, Oct 10, 25. Study: Univ Wyo; Columbia Univ; Univ Utah, BFA; Ecole Beaux-Arts, Paris; Teachers Col, Columbia Univ, MA; Cranbrook Acad Art. Work: Portland Art Mus; Ore State Univ Mem Union; Corvallis Clin, Ore; Univ Ore Erb Mem Union; US Nat Bank Ore, Portland. Comn: Archit sculpture, Lane Co Courthouse, Eugene; Corvallis Br, US Nat Bank Ore; fountain & doors, Ore State Univ Libr; coun chamber doors, Salem Civic Ctr, Ore; St Mary's Cath Church, Corvallis; plus many portrait & pvt comns. Exhib: One-man show, Portland Art Mus, 54, Paper Works, 72; Seattle World's Fair, 62; Am Crafts Coun, Western Craftsmen, 64; Hunnicutt Art Gallery, Hawaii, 67; plus many others. Teaching: Instr sculpture, Univ Ore, 51-52; prof sculpture, Ore State Univ, 53- Awards: Purchase Prize, Portland Art Mus, 56. Mem: Portland Art Asn; Corvallis Art Asn. Style & Technique: Modeller concerned with the human figure as a base; forms influenced strongly by gas welding; cast works more conservative. Mailing Add: Dept of Art Ore State Univ Corvallis OR 97331

TCHENG, JOHN T L
PAINTER
b Shanghai, China, Sept 21, 18; US citizen. Study: With S C Chao, Shanghai; with C C Wang, New York. Exhib: One-man shows from coast to coast, 56- Mem: Cincinnati Art Club. Media: Ink, Oil. Res: Chinese calligraphy; modern paintings. Mailing Add: Pine Studios PO Box 252 Ft Thomas KY 41075

TEAGUE, DONALD
PAINTER
b Brooklyn, NY, Nov 27, 97. Study: Art Students League; also with Norman Wilkinson, London. Work: Va Mus Fine Arts, Richmond; Frye Mus, Seattle; Air Force Acad, Colorado Springs; Mills Col Art Gallery; State of Calif Collection, Sacramento. Exhib: Am Watercolor Soc, New York; Mus Watercolor, Mexico City, Mex; Art Inst Chicago; Royal Watercolor Soc, London, Eng; Kyoto Mus, Japan. Awards: Gold Medal of Honor, Am Watercolor Soc, 53 & 64; Morse Gold Medal, Nat Acad Design, 62. Bibliog: Ernest Watson (auth), Donald Teague, illustrator, Am Artist, 44. Mem: Hon mem Am Watercolor Soc; Nat Acad Design; Salmagundi Club. Media: Watercolor. Mailing Add: PO Box 745 Carmel CA 93921

TEICHMAN, SABINA
PAINTER, SCULPTOR
b New York, NY. Study: Columbia Univ, BA & MA; also with Charles J Martin & Arthur J Young. Work: Whitney Mus Am Art; Butler Inst Am Art; Smithsonian Inst; Fogg Mus Art, Harvard Univ; San Francisco Mus Art. Exhib: Whitney Mus Am Art Ann; Art USA, 58; Provincetown Art Asn; Butler Inst Am Art Ann; Audubon Artists Ann; New York Cult Ctr; St Mary's Col, Md. Awards: Prize for Painting, Womens Westchester Ctr, 50. Bibliog: Baur & Goodrich (auth), Art of the 20th Century; Baron (auth), 31 Contemporary Artists; Frank Crotty (auth), Provincetown Profiles; Provincetown Painters, Everson Mus of Art, Syracuse, NY. Mem: Audubon Artists; Provincetown Art Asn. Media: Oil, Watercolor; Clay. Dealer: ACA Galleries 25 E 73rd St New York NY 10021. Mailing Add: 27 E 22nd St New York NY 10010

TEILHET, JEHANNE HILDEGARDE
ART HISTORIAN, LECTURER
b Palo Alto, Calif, May 16, 39. Study: Univ of Calif, Los Angeles, BA, 62, MA, 67 & PhD(art hist), 75; spec studies with Dr Guiart & Dr William Fagg, Europe, 64. Collections Arranged: Arts of East Africa, Los Angeles Mus of Sci & Indust, 67; Dimensions of Black (auth, catalog), La Jolla Mus of Art, 70; Dimensions of Polynesia (auth, catalog), San Diego Fine Arts Gallery, 73. Teaching: Tenured lect non-Western art hist, Dept of Visual Arts, Univ of Calif, San Diego, 68- Pos: Asst cur, Jos Mus, Nigeria, 67-68; consult ed, Tofua Press, San Diego, Calif, 75-77; filmmaker, Tapa Production in Tonga, 76- Awards: Rockefeller Found Award, Dimensions of Black, 69-70; Kress Found & Nat Endowment for the Arts Awards, Dimensions of Polynesia, 73. Res: Focus on non-Western arts of Africa Oceania and Nepal with especial interests in masking complexes & woman's art forms. Publ: Co-auth, Ancient Nigerian bronzes: lead isotope studies on metal sources, Nature, 76; auth, The Equivocal Nature of the Masking Tradition in Polynesia, Univ of Hawaii, 77-78; auth, The tradition of the Nava Durga in Bhaktapur, Nepal, Kailash, 77; auth, The Equivocal Role of Women Artists in Non-Literate Cultures, Heresies, 78. Mailing Add: 12744 Via Donada Del Mar CA 92014

TEILMAN, HERDIS BULL
CURATOR
b Paris, France; US citizen. Study: Barnard Col, BA; NY Univ Inst Fine Arts, 61 & 63-64; Univ Paris Inst Art & Archeol, 61-62. Pos: Secy-registr, Nat Serigraph Soc, 61; asst, Kunst pa Arbeidsplassen, Oslo, Norway, 62-63; cur painting & sculpture, Newark Mus, NJ, 68-70; asst dir, Mus Art, Carnegie Inst, 70-73, cur painting & sculpture, 73- Mem: Am Asn Mus; NE Mus Conf. Publ: Auth, Frank W Stokes, Meltzer Gallery, New York, 60; contribr, The Museum, Newark, 69; contribr, Carnegie Mag, 71-; auth, Forerunners of American Abstraction, 71; contrib ed, Catalogue of Painting Collection, 73; co-auth, Inaugural Exhibition of the Sarah Scaife Gallery, 74; co-auth, An Introduction to the Collections of the Museum of Art, Carnegie Inst, 77, plus others. Mailing Add: 4400 Forbes Ave Pittsburgh PA 15213

TEITZ, RICHARD STUART
MUSEUM DIRECTOR, ART HISTORIAN
b Fall River, Mass, July 18, 42. Study: Yale Univ, AB; Harvard Univ, MA. Collections Arranged: Etruscan Art, 67; Victoran Art, 69; Am Contemp Art, 69; Toulouse-Lautrec, 71; Marisol, 71; Escher, 71. Teaching: Instr archit hist, Boston Archit Ctr, 63-66; instr art hist, Clark Univ, 66-67. Pos: Dir, Wichita Art Mus, Kans, 67-69; assoc dir, Worcester Art Mus, Mass, 69-70, dir, 70- Mem: Col Art Asn Am; Asn Art Mus Dirs; Int Coun Mus; Am Asn Mus. Mus. Res: Classical and Renaissance art. Collection: Old master drawings. Publ: Auth, Masterpieces of Etruscan Art, 67; auth, Masterpieces of Religious Art, 67; auth, American Victoriana, 69. Mailing Add: 55 Salisbury St Worcester MA 01608

TEJEDA, CARLOS
PAINTER
b Mexico City, Mex, July 29, 04. Study: Self-taught. Work: Mus Mod Art, Vatican; Nat Palace, Mexico City; plus many others. Exhib: Tryon Gallery, London, 69; Palais an der Strudlhofstiege, Wien, Austria, 69; Walcheturm Gallery, Zurich, 69; Mus de Arte Mod, Chapultepec, Mex, 71; Club de Industriales, Mex, 72; Club de Banqueros, 78. Style & Technique: Oil painting, palette knife, watercolor; impressionism; etching. Mailing Add: AIDA 81 San Angel Inn Mexico DF Mexico

TELLER, JANE (SIMON)
SCULPTOR
b Rochester, NY. Study: Rochester Inst Technol; Barnard Col, BA; also with Ibram Lassaw. Work: Olsen Found, Stamford, Conn; Geigy Collection, Ardsley, NY; NJ State Mus, Trenton. Comn: Menorah (iron & Plexiglas) & Eternal Light (iron & Plexiglas), Temple Judea, Doylestown, Pa, 69; Newark Mus, NJ; Princeton Univ. Exhib: NJ State Mus, Trenton, 65-72; Newark Mus, NJ, 68; Sculptors Guild Ann, Lever House, New York, 61-; Hudson River Mus, Yonkers, NY, 71; Mus Mod Art, New York. Awards: Purchase Award, NJ State Mus, 71; Nat Asn Women Artists; 50th Anniversary Exhib Prize, Philadelphia Art Alliance. Bibliog: David R Campbell (auth), Art & architecture, Craft Horizons, 6/62; Donald Willcox (auth), Wood Design, Watson-Guptill, 68; Woodcraft, Golden Press, 76. Mem: Sculptors Guild; Artists Equity Asn. Style & Technique: Construction based on topographic form; involvement in the precariousness of balance and in variety of expression possible in tangent abstract forms; wood, shaped and roughly textured largely by hand; components positioned by dowels or lag screws. Media: Wood, Graphic. Mailing Add: 200 Prospect Ave Princeton NJ 08540

TEMES, MORTIMER (ROBERT)
CARTOONIST, DESIGNER
b Jersey City, NJ, Apr 15, 28. Study: Art Students League, with William McNulty, Jon Corbino, Frank Reilly & Robert B Hale, 47-49; NY Univ, BA, 53. Pos: Prof free lance cartoonist, 50-; dir spec serv, NJ Inst Technol, 58- Mem: Nat Cartoonists Soc; Cartoonists Guild. Style & Technique: Line and wash drawings. Media: Pen & Ink, Pencil, Watercolor. Publ: Illusr, Engineers & Engineering—Some Definitions, 68; illusr, Making Tomorrow Happen, 70; cartoons have appeared in many nat mags & cartoon anthologies. Mailing Add: 10 Sycamore Dr Hazlet NJ 07730

TEMPLE, MR & MRS ALAN H
COLLECTORS
Collection: Contemporary art. Mailing Add: 11 Paddington Rd Scarsdale NY 10583

TEN EYCK, CATRYNA (CATRYNA TEN EYCK SEYMOUR)
PAINTER
b New York, NY, June 30, 31. Study: Smith Col; Art Students League. Work: Nat Collection Fine Arts, Smithsonian Inst, Washington, DC; Calif Palace Legion Hon, San Francisco; Denver Art Mus; Honolulu Acad Arts; Munson-Williams-Proctor Inst, Utica, NY. Exhib: 60th Am Ann Exhib, Art Asn Newport, RI, 71; one-man show, New Sch Social Res, New York, 73; Ann Juried Exhib, Sahron Creative Arts Found, Conn, 74. Awards: First Prize for Graphics, Springfield Art League, 71; First Prize, Tanglewood Poster Design Competition, Berkshire Art Asn, 75. Mem: Southern Vt Artists, Inc; Cooperstown Art Asn. Style & Technique: Contemporary, clean-line, semi-representational. Media: Graphic, Acrylic. Publ: Auth, Enjoying the Southwest, Lippincott, 73. Dealer: Tunnel Gallery 232 E 59th St New York NY 10022. Mailing Add: Box 363 Salisbury CT 06068

TEN (JAN TEN BROEKE)
PAINTER, ART DEALER
b Marienberg, Netherlands, June 8, 30. Exhib: Crespi Gallery, 60; Newark Mus, 61; solo show, Flemington Studio Arts, NJ, 71, Upstairs Gallery, Somerville, NJ, 72 & Papermill Playhouse, Milburn, NJ, 72. Awards: Wally's Award, Plainfield Art Asn, 66, First Prize in Oils, 69; Tracy Long Mem Award, Summit Art Ctr, 66. Bibliog: Doris Brown (auth), Surrealist's exhibit opens, 5/3/70, Franklin artist, 8/8/71 & Dutch-born artist, 6/25/72, Sunday Home News. Mem: Hunterdon Co Art Ctr. Style & Technique: Sensualistic surrealism. Media: Oil. Specialty: Ethnic arts. Dealer: Geist Mill Studio Mill St Califon NJ 07830. Mailing Add: Box 158 RD 1 Somerset NJ 08873

TENNYSON, MERLE BERRY
PAINTER, PRINTMAKER
b Brandon, Miss, Mar 17, 20. Study: Miss State Col Women, BS; Univ Miss, MA; also with Ida Kohlmeyer, New Orleans, Andrew Bucci, Washington, DC, Alvin Sella, Univ Ala, Alex Russo, Frederick, Md, Tom Chimes, Philadelphia & Marie Hull, Jackson, Miss. Work: R W Norton Art Gallery, Shreveport, La; Miss Mus of Art, Miss Arts Comn; First Nat Bank, Unifirst; Deposit Guaranty Nat Bank, Jackson, Miss. Comn: Painting, comn by Mr & Mrs Francis Stevens, Washington, DC, 70; painting comn by Mr & Mrs Robert G Nichols, Jr, Jackson, Miss; Mr & Mrs Morris Lewis, Indianaola, Miss. Exhib: Nat Arts & Crafts, Miss Arts Festival, Jackson, 65, 69-71; Frontal Images, Miss Art Asn, Jackson, 67-69; Mid-South Exhib, Brooks Mem Art Gallery, Memphis, Tenn, 68 & 69; 47th Regional, Shreveport, 69; Delta Ann, Ark Art Ctr, Little Rock, 69 & 71; Edgewater Tri-State Ann, Biloxi, Miss. Teaching: Instr drawing & painting, Univ Miss Continuation Study Prog, 58-66. Awards: Regional Purchase Award, S Cent Bell Tel, 69, Lafont Art Colony Purchase Award, 70; Best in Show Award, Edgewater Ann, 73. Mem: Miss Art Asn (pres, 66-67, exec comt & bd dirs, 67-); Miss Arts Ctr (bd gov, 67-); Millsaps Col Arts & Lect Serv (bd dirs). Style & Technique: Acrylic, Oil; Etching, Serigraphy. Publ: Auth, Painting and Ceramics Used as Occupational Therapy in Working with the Mentally Ill, 58. Mailing Add: 1437 Rebel Dr Jackson MS 39211

TERENZIO, ANTHONY
PAINTER, EDUCATOR
b Settefrati, Italy, Feb 10, 23; US citizen. Study: Pratt Inst, BFA; Columbia Univ, MA; Am Art Sch, with Raphael Soyer & Jack Levine. Work: Lowe Ctr, Syracuse Univ. Exhib: Brooklyn Artists Biennial, Brooklyn Mus, 49; Butler Inst Am Art Biennial, Ohio, 57; Boston Arts Festival, 58; Eight From Connecticut, Wadsworth Atheneum, Hartford, 60; New Eng Drawing Exhib, Smith Col, 64. Teaching: Prof painting & drawing, Univ Conn, 55- Awards: Emily Lowe Award, 50; Ann Conn Artists First Award, Norwich Art Asn, 57, 60 & 75. Media: Oil, Watercolor. Mailing Add: 6 Forest Rd Storrs CT 06268

TERKEN, JOHN
SCULPTOR
b Rochester, NY, Jan 11, 12. Study: Beaux Arts Inst Design, with Chester Beach, Lee Lawrie & Paul Manship; NY Sch Fine & Indust Arts; Columbia Sch Fine Arts; also Europ art ctrs. Work: Roswell Mus, NMex; Gregory Mus, Hicksville, NY. Comn: Monument, Am Soc Prev Cruelty Animals Hq, New York, 55; Benjamin Franklin Mem, Franklin Nat Bank, Garden City, NY, 61; Eagle Fountain, Salisbury Park, East Meadow, NY, 61; New Horizons, Hempstead Town Plaza, 69; Richard Henry Dana Monument, San Juan Capistrano Hist Soc, Calif, 72; Colonial Lad Monument, East Meadow, NY, 77. Exhib: Nat Acad Design, New York, 68; Nat Arts Club, New York, 70; Hudson Valley Art Asn, Westchester, NY, 71; Acad Artists Asn, Springfield, Mass, 71; Nat Sculpture Soc, New York, 72. Teaching: Lectr sculpture, East Meadow High Sch. Pos: Advert mgr, Nat Sculpture Rev, 49-65, mem ed bd, 70-, mem, Bd Coop Educ Serv, Long Island Dist, 69-, deleg to Fine Arts Fedn New York, 70- Awards: Louis Comfort Tiffany Found Award, 49; Lindsey Morris Mem Prize, Nat Sculpture Soc, 65; Coun Am Artists Award, Am Artists Prof League, 72. Mem: Fel Nat Sculpture Soc (mem coun, 62-, secy, 68-70, first vpres, 77-78 & 78-79); fel Hudson Valley Art Asn; assoc Int Inst Conservators; Acad Artists Asn; Art League Nassau Co. Media: Bronze. Mailing Add: 386 Chambers Ave East Meadow NY 11554

TERMINI, CHRISTINE
ARTIST, ART DEALER
b Brooklyn, NY, Sept 30, 47. Study: Pratt Inst, BFA, study with Phillip Pearlstein; Hunter Col, MFA, study with Tony Smith & Robert Walker. Comn: Five paintings, 78th St Women's Ctr, 77; one painting, comn by John Reynolds Inc, Arch Diocese, New York, 78. Exhib: Audubon Artists, 74 & Nat Asn of Women Artists, 75, Nat Acad Galleries, New York; Artists Equity Asn of New York Exhibition (Union Carbide), 77; Ellenville Pub Libr & Mus, NY, 78; Heckscher Mus, Huntington, NY, 78. Teaching: Instr art, Bd of Educ, New York City High Schs, 70-75; lectr galleries, New Sch, Sch of Visual Arts, New York, 77-78. Pos: Art dir, Circle Galleries, New York, 76-77, Jack Gallerie, New York, 76-77, Gallerie La Grande Illusion, New York, 77, Neill Gallery, New York, 78- Bibliog: Chris Jones (auth), The 24 Hour Room, Am Home Mag, 5/77; Ann Kronenberg (auth), Current Exhibitions, Women in the Arts Newsletter, 8/77. Mem: Women in the Arts; Artists Equity Asn of New York; Found for the Community of Artists; Artists Referral & Telecommunications Soc. Style & Technique: Impressionistic color and style with rich impasto technique of applying paint. Media: Acrylic; Oil. Specialty: Discovering new and unusual talent in the contemporary style. Mailing Add: 243 E 78th St New York NY 10021

TERRELL, ALLEN TOWNSEND
SCULPTOR
b Riverhead, NY, Nov 2, 97. Study: Columbia Univ Sch Archit, cert proficiency, 21; Art Students League, with Edward McCartan; Pa Acad Fine Arts, with Albert Laessle; Ecoles Am Fontainebleau, France; Acad Julien, Paris, France; also with Charles Despiau. Work: Suffolk Co Hist Soc, Riverhead; Metrop Mus Art, New York & Mus City New York; Archives of Am Art, Smithsonian Inst, Washington, DC; Brooklyn Mus, NY. Comn: Vermil ye Medal, Franklin Inst, Philadelphia, Pa, 35; childrens playrm, 39 & cabin in class lounge (with John Marsman), 46, SS America, US Lines. Exhib: Nat Arts Club, 59; Allied Artists Am, 65; Nat Acad Design, 72; one-man show sculpture, Nat Arts Club, 75. Teaching: Instr watercolor & still life, Parsons Sch Design, 34-35. Awards: Bronze Medal of Hon for Sculpture, Nat Arts Club, 59; Awards Comt Prize for Sculpture, Allied Artists Am, 65; Dessie Greer Prize for Sculpture, Nat Acad Design, 72; Bronze Medal, Hort Soc NY. Mem: Fel Nat Sculpture Soc; Allied Artists Am; Am Watercolor Soc; Nat Arts Club; Pastel Soc Am. Media: High Fire Stoneware; Sculpture in Iron. Interest: Antique architectural drawings; drawings collections. Publ: Auth, Drawing for sculpture, Nat Sculpture rev, summer 74. Mailing Add: 42 Stuyvesant St New York NY 10003

TERRILL, EVELYN BEARD
ART ADMINISTRATOR, COLLECTOR
b Honolulu, Hawaii, Mar 13, 17. Study: Shipley Sch, Bryn Mawr, Pa, dipl. Pos: Exhib chmn, 70-75, mem bldg comt, 70-77 & pres bd of dir, 77, West Baton Rouge Mus, Port Allen. Mem: Found for Hist La, Baton Rouge. Collection: Eighteenth and twentieth century sporting prints, paintings, sculpture; modern Louisiana art. Mailing Add: Cinclare Plantation Brusley LA 70719

TERRIS, ALBERT
SCULPTOR, CALLIGRAPHER
b New York, NY, Nov 10, 16. Study: With Aaron J Goodelman, 33; Work Progress Admin Art Sch, New York; Beaux Arts Inst of Design, New York 33-34; City Col of New York, 36-39, BSS, 39, with George W Eggers; Inst of Fine Arts, New York Univ, 39-42, with Walter Friedlander, Richard Krautheimer & A Phillip McMahon. Comn: Signature piece (with Jimmy Ernst), for Pontiac Hour, Television, Playwrights 56, comn by Nat Broadcasting Co, 56; Sun (for Wide, Wide World), comn by Abe Liss of Electra Films, 58; Words: Strong, Weak, Argonne Nat Lab, Downers Grove, Ill, comn by Dr Ted Novy, 62. Exhib: One-man shows, Duveen/Graham Gallery, 58, Allan Stone Gallery, New York, 62, Artist Space 1975 & Gloria Cortella Gallery, New York, 77; Mus of Art, Carnegie Int, Pittsburgh, 58, 61; Brooklyn Mus Biennale, NY, 60; Sculpture Show, Mus of Mod Art, New York, 62; Bundy Int Sculpture Exhib, Waitsfield, Vt, 63; Treasures of 20th Century Art, Maremont Collection, Washington Gallery of Mod Art, Washington, DC, 64; Critics Choice, Sculpture Ctr of New York, 72; plus many others. Teaching: Guide-lectr, Metrop Mus of Art, New York, 41-42; teacher fine arts, Thomas Jefferson High Sch, Brooklyn, NY 48-54; assoc prof sculpture & theory of art, Dept of Art, Brooklyn Col, NY, 54- Pos: Deputy chmn in charge of Dept of Art, Sch of Gen Studies, Brooklyn Col, NY, 58-70. Awards: First Prize, Brooklyn Mus Biennial, John McKeen, 60. Bibliog: Sidney Geist (auth), Month in review, Arts Mag, 1/58; Michel Seuphor (auth), The Sculpture of this Century, George Brazillier, 60; James Schinneller (auth), Art, Experience & Self Discovery, Int Text Bk Co, Scranton, Pa, 2nd ed, 68. Style & Technique: Consolation of beauty—retinal. Media: Steel, Plaster, Terra Cotta, Acrylic. Publ: Contrib, Artists on the current scene, Arts Ann (4), 60; contrib, Sidney Geist, ed, The Private Myth, Tanager Gallery, 60; auth Retrospective 1950, 1975, metal sculpture, Freeport Mem Libr, 77. Dealer: Gloria Cortella Inc 41 E 57th St New York NY 10022. Mailing Add: 280 S Ocean Ave Freeport NY 11520

TERRY, DUNCAN NILES
DESIGNER, CRAFTSMAN
b Bath Maine, Nov 6, 09. Study: Sch Mus Fine Arts, Boston; Cent Sch Arts & Crafts, London; also with Ferdnand Leger, Paris. Comn: Carved glass windows, Riverside Church, New York, 50 & St James Episcopal Church, Long Branch, NJ, 62-67; windows & wood & stone mem, Trinity Cathedral, Trenton, NJ, 60-72; windows, doors & mem, All Saints Church, Torresdale, Pa, 60-72; stained glass, Bnai Emunah Synagogue, Tulsa, Okla, 62; windows, doors, facade & mosiac mural, St Marys Church, Kittanning, Pa, 67. Style & Technique: Developing new techniques in glass decoration and using them alone and in combination with established techniques. Media: Glass. Mailing Add: 1213 Lancaster Ave Rosemont PA 19010

TERRY, HILDA (HILDA TERRY D'ALESSIO)
CARTOONIST, ART DEALER
b Newburyport, Mass, June 25, 14. Study: Art Students League; Nat Acad Design; NY Univ. Comn: Fulton Fish Market (acrylics), comn by Sam Marg, New York, 71. Teaching: Instr cartooning, New Sch Social Res, 68; instr cartooning, New York Phoenix Sch Art & Design, 69-71. Pos: Dir, Hilda Terry Gallery, New York; computer animator, Kansas City Royals Stadium, Toronto Bluejays, Cleveland Indians, NJ Sports Complex, Denver Mile High Stadium, Atlanta Braves, Aloha Stadium, Hawaii & others. Awards: Wohelo Award, Camp Fire Girls; Best Waste-Not Cartoon, New York Times, 42; NCS Outstanding Animations Cartoonist, 76. Mem: Nat Cartoonists Soc. Specialty: Fine art humor. Interest: Computer animation. Publ: Auth, Teena (comic strip), 41-64; auth, Teena (comic bks), 46-49; auth, Originality in Art, 54; assoc ed, Art Collectors Almanac, 65. Mailing Add: 8 Henderson Pl New York NY 10028

TERRY, MARION (E)
PAINTER, ART CRITIC
b Evansville, Ind, June 4, 11. Study: Albright Art Sch; Univ Buffalo; also with Xavier Gonzalez. Work: New York Hosp Soc; Univ Bank, Coral Gables; Abbott Labs, Chicago; Ford Motor Co, Dearborn; Honeywell Mfg Co, Philadelphia. Comn: Living War Memorial (476 portraits of every Dade Co serviceman who lost his life in World War II); seven paintings, Com Bank, Winter Park, Fla; four paintings, First Nat Bank, Winter Park; City Nat Bank, Clearwater, Fla. Exhib: Southeastern Ann; Ford Motor Co Traveling Exhibs, 55, 57-58; Ft Worth, Tex, 58; Fla Gulf Coast Art, Clearwater, 71 & 73; St Petersburg Art Club; plus many others. Teaching: Instr painting, Craft Village, St Petersburg, 44-69; instr painting, C of C, Madeira Beach, Fla, 69-72; instr pvt classes. Pos: Art critic, Gulf Beach J. Awards: Award for Horses in the Surf, Gulf Coast, 71; Award for Pennsylvania Town, Art Guild, Treasure Island, Fla, 71, Award for Reflections, 72 & First Prize for Landscape in B Minor, 74; plus others, incl five prizes in Fla shows, 76-77. Mem: Fla Art Group; Fla Fedn Arts; Art Guild, Treasure Island. Style & Technique: Impressionist with some post-impressionist techniques. Media: Oil, Acrylic, Collages. Publ: Illusr, cover for 50th anniversary & auth, articles in St Petersburg Times. Dealer: By George St Petersburg Beach FL. Mailing Add: 14080 N Bayshore Dr Madeira Beach FL 33708

TESKE, EDUMND RUDOLPH
PHOTOGRAPHER
b Chicago, Ill, Mar 7, 11. Study: Huettle Art Sch, Chicago; Art Inst Chicago; Univ Chicago. Work: Mus Mod Art, New York; Chicago Art Inst; San Francisco Mus Mod Art; George Eastman House, Rochester, NY; Frederick Wight Gallery, Univ Calif Los Angeles. Comn: Photog to Frank Lloyd Wright, 36-52. Exhib: Contemp Photographs, Art Gallery, Univ Calif Los Angeles, 62; Sic Photographers, Krannert Art Mus, Univ Ill, 63; Three Photographers, Fine Arts Gallery, San Francisco State Col, 68; Light & Substance, Univ NMex, Albuquerque, 73; Through Ones Eyes, Muckenthaler Cult Ctr, Fullerton, Calif, 74; Photog 1974, Los Angeles Co Mus Art, 74; one-man shows, Pasadena Art Mus, Calif, 61, Santa Barbara Mus Art, Calif, 61, San Francisco Mus Art, 63, Art Inst Chicago, 70, Eastman House, Rochester, NY, 71, Lincoln Mus Art, Nebr, 71 & Univ Southern Calif, 73. Teaching: Asst prof art, Chouinard Art Inst, Los Angeles, 62-64; asst prof photog, Col Fine Arts, Univ Calif Los Angeles, 65- Pos: Fel, Taliesin Fel, Frank Lloyd Wright, Spring Green, Wis, 36-37. Awards: Grants, Frank Lloyd Wright, 36 & Nat Endowment for Arts, 75. Bibliog: Wright & Brownell (auth), Architecture & Modern Life, Harper & Bros, 37; Hitchcock (auth), In the Nature of Materials, Duell, Sloan & Pearce, 42; Eds of Time (auth), Life-the Art of Photography, Time-Life Books, 71. Style & Technique: Expressive by way of all the inherent technical possibilities of photography, including double image, solarization and duo-tone

solarization. Publ: Auth, Edmund Teske, pvt pub, 74. Dealer: Lee Witkin Witkin Gallery 41 E 57th St New York NY 10022. Mailing Add: 1652 N Harvard Blvd Los Angeles CA 90027

TETTLETON, ROBERT LYNN
PAINTER, EDUCATOR
b Ruston, La, Dec 23, 29. Study: La Polytech Inst, BA, 50; La State Univ, Baton Rouge, MA, 53. Exhib: La Art Comn, Baton Rouge, 52; Delgado Mus, New Orleans, La, 53; Gainesville Fine Arts Asn, Fla, 61; Mid-South Art Show, Brooks Mem Art Gallery, Memphis, Tenn, 69; one-man shows, Little Theater, Monroe, La, 54 & Mary Buie Mus, Oxford, Miss, 70. Teaching: Instr art, Northeast La State Col, 55-56; asst prof art, Univ Fla, 61-65; prof art, Univ Miss, 65-, chmn art dept, 65-76. Mem: Nat Art Educ Asn; Southeastern Col Art Asn (pres, 69-70); Gainesville Fine Arts Asn (pres, 65); Col Art Asn; Am Asn Univ Prof. Media: Oil. Mailing Add: 137 Leighton Rd Oxford MS 38677

TEVIS, GARY LEE
PRINTMAKER, PAINTER
b Council Bluffs, Iowa, July 9, 47. Study: Univ Nebr, Omaha, BS(art educ); Pratt Inst. Exhib: Midwest Biennial, Joslyn Art Mus, Omaha; Dickinson State Col Biennial, 69; Biggest Show of Little Painting, Louisville, Ky; Int Directory Arts; 40th Ann Springfield Art Exhib, Mo. Style & Technique: Realistic figures, mainly nude showing mans beliefs and the beauty of himself. Media: Pencil, Ink; Pastel, Acrylic. Mailing Add: 3639 S 51st St Omaha NE 68106

TEWI, THEA
SCULPTOR
US citizen. Study: Art Students League; Greenwich House; New Sch Social Res. Work: Nat Collection Fine Arts, Smithsonian Inst, Washington, DC; Cincinnati Art Mus; Norfolk Mus Arts & Scis, Va; Univ Notre Dame; Am Ins Co Corp Collection, Galveston, Tex; plus many others. Exhib: One-person shows, Village Art Ctr, New York, 61, La Boetie Gallery, New York, 66, 68 & 70, Notre Dame Gallery, 70, Main Place Gallery, Dallas, 71, Hallway Gallery, Washington, DC, 76 & Randall Gallery, New York, 77; 18th-20th Ann New Eng Exhib, Silvermine Guild Artists, 65 & 67-69; Nat Arts Club Exhib Relig Art, 66; Erie Summer Festival Arts, Pa State Univ, 68; 6th Biennial of Sculpture, Carrara, Italy, 69; plus many others. Awards: Medal of Honor & First Prize for Sculpture, Nat Asn Women Artists, 69, Sculpture Prize, 75 & 76; First Prize for Sculpture, Am Soc Contemp Artists, 71, 75 & 76; Nat Arts Club Medal of Merit, 74 & 75; plus others. Bibliog: D Meilach (auth), Contemporary Stone Sculpture, Crown, 70; Int Encycl Art, Ancona, Italy. Mem: Am Soc Contemp Artists; Sculptors League (pres, 71-); League Present Day Artists (hon pres); Nat Asn Women Artists (chmn sculpture jury, 69-72); Am Soc Contemp Artists. Media: Stone. Mailing Add: 100-30 67th Dr Forest Hills NY 11375

TEXIDOR, FERNANDO
PAINTER, GRAPHIC DESIGNER
b Barcelona, Spain, Oct 16, 07. Study: Univ Barcelona, MA; painting in Madrid, Paris, Barcelona, Mexico & New York. Work: Poster collection, Mus Mod Art, New York; Libr of Cong, Washington, DC; plus many others. Comn: Men's Apparels (mural), World's Fair, 39; designed Monument to Alice in Wonderland in Cent Park of New York with sculptor Jose DeCreft, 59 & The Animated & Musical Clock in New York Zoo, 65, both comn by George Delacorte. Exhib: Int Fair of Barcelona, 30; New York World's Fair, 39; Cancer Crusade in New York, 41; Army Air Corps Competition, 44 & Treas Dept-Defense Bond Competition, 44, Mus Mod Art, New York; plus many others. Pos: Art dir, Men's Apparel Reporter Mag, NY, 41-44; art consult, Am Fabrics Mag & Gentry, 46-47; art dir, Dell Publ Co, NY, 47-69. Awards: Prize Winner, Mural Contest at New York World's Fair, 39; Treas Dept Prizes, Army Air Corps & Defense Bond Poster Competition, 44. Bibliog: Articles & reproductions in Arts et Metiers Graphiques, Paris, 38, Art Dirs Club Ann, 39, 40, 45, 47, Life Mag, 6/59 & New York Times, 6/65; Raymond Ballinguer (auth), Layout, Reinhold, 56. Mem: Fundacio Joan Miro, Barcelona; Cult Hisp, Madrid; Mus Mod Art, Inst Graphic Arts & Hisp Inst, New York. Style & Technique: Stylized and abstract symbolism; graphic art in acrylic colors, painting and collage, oil and acrylic. Media: Mixed Media, Gouache, Oil. Mailing Add: 6248 Calle Rosa Scottsdale AZ 85251

TEXOON, JASMINE
PAINTER, INSTRUCTOR
b New York, NY, Sept 19, 24. Study: Nat Acad Design, with Gilford Beal, H Hildebrandt & Charles Hinton, 4 yrs with honors; Brooklyn Mus Art Sch, with Bocour; Art Students League, with Byron Browne. Work: Christ the King (mural), St Lawrence Sem, Mt Calvery, Wis; relig mural, Monastery St Lazarro Mus, Venice, Italy; painting, Col Armeno Permanent Collection, Venice; relig paintings, St Mary's Convent, Yonkers & Church Holy Cross Sch, New York; Sacrifice (painting), Juan Mus of Portub, Ala. Comn: Painting of home, comn by Mr & Mrs Zambetti, Sr, New York, 50; painting of boy & his dog, comn by Mr & Mrs Russell, New York, 54; three landscapes, comn by Mr & Mrs Alexander Walker, Yonkers, 67; portrait of a little girl, comn by Donata Pellegrini, Yonkers, 68. Exhib: Raymond Duncan Gallery, Paris, France, 62, 65, 68 & 69; Lynn Kotler Gallery, New York, 63; Int Exhib Drawings, Florence, Italy, 71; one-man shows, Manhattan Col, New York, 55 & Burr Gallery, New York, 59. Teaching: Instr pvt classes, 49-61 & 71-; instr art, New York City Bd Educ, 57- Pos: Occup therapist for prof patients, Bronx, NY, 55-62; occup therapist, Rockland State Hosp, 64- Awards: Honor for Art Work, Nat Acad Design Sch, 47; Prix de Paris, Ligoa Duncan Gallery, 62, 65, 68 & 69. Bibliog: Article in J Am, 59- Leonardo da Vinci, Cahiers d'Art, 70; Enciclopedia Internazionale Degli Artisti, Bugatti, 70. Mem: Life mem Art Students League; Burr Artists; Centro Studi E Scambi Internazionale Rome, Italy. Media: Oil. Mailing Add: 3523 Riverdale Ave New York NY 10463

TEYRAL, JOHN
PAINTER, INSTRUCTOR
b Yaroslav, Russia, June 10, 12. Study: Cleveland Inst Art; Boston Mus Fine Arts Sch; Grande Chaumiere, Paris; Accad Belli Arti, Florence, Italy. Work: Cleveland Mus Art; City of Cleveland, Ohio; Butler Inst Am Art; Pepsi Cola Collection; Montclair Mus Art, NJ. Comn: Mural, President Garfield Mem, Cleveland; Many portraits of prominent persons. Exhib: Carnegie Inst Int; Metrop Mus Art; Va Mus Fine Arts; Corcoran Gallery Art; Univ Nebr; plus many others. Collections Arranged: 32 Realists, Cleveland Inst Art, 72. Teaching: Instr drawing, Boston Mus Sch Fine Arts, 36-37; instr painting & drawing, Cleveland Inst Art, 39-77; retired. Awards: Prizes, Cleveland Mus Art, 41-61 & Butler Inst Am Art, 44; Fulbright Grant to Italy, 49 50; plus others. Publ: Encaustic—the hot wax medium, In: Portraits in the Making, Phoebe Flory Walker, G P Putnam's Sons, 48. Dealer: Harmon Gallery Naples FL 33940. Mailing Add: 2470 Kenilworth Rd Cleveland Heights OH 44106

THACHER, JOHN SEYMOUR
ART ADMINISTRATOR
b New York, NY, Sept 5, 04. Study: Yale Univ, BA, 27; Univ London, PhD, 36. Pos: Asst to dir, Fogg Mus Art, Cambridge, Mass, 36-40, asst dir, 40-46, exec off, Dumbarton Oaks Res Libr & Collection, 40-45, actg dir, 45-46, dir & treas, 46-69; trustee, Harvard Univ; trustee & assoc in fine arts, Yale Univ, 53-; former treas, Byzantine Inst, Inc, Washington, DC. Mem: Century Asn; Cosmos Club; assoc Int Inst Conserv Mus Objects; fel Pierpont Morgan Libr; Grolier Club; plus others. Publ: Auth, Paintings of Francisco de Herrara, the elder, Art Bull, 37. Mailing Add: 1692 31st St NW Washington DC 20007

THALACKER, DONALD WILLIAM
ART ADMINISTRATOR, ARCHITECT
b Detroit, Mich, July 29, 39. Study: Washington & Lee Univ, Lexington, Va, BA, 61; Univ of Calif, Berkeley, BA Archit, 67. Permanent installations arranged: Louise Nevelson, George Segal, Mark di Suvero, Isamu Noguchi, Jack Beal, Richard Hunt, Tony Smith, Al Held, Claes Oldenburg, Beverly Pepper, George Rickey, Leonard Baskin, Frank Stella, David von Schlegell, Peter Voulkos & Jack Youngerman, Nationwide pub art-in-archit exhib of permanently installed works in new Fed Bldg, US Gen Serv Admin, 73-77. Teaching: Lectr, New School Art in the Community Inst, New York, NY, 78, 9th and 10th Int Sculpture Conf, New Orleans, 76 & Toronto, 78, Fine Arts Fed of New York, 77. Pos: Dir, Art-in-Archit Prog, Gen Serv Admin, Washington, DC, 73- Bibliog: John Blair Mitchell (auth), Artists Equity National President, Art Workers News, 6/76; Jo Ann Lewis (auth), Art Critic, ARTnews Mag, 4/77; Barbara Rose (auth), Art Critic, Vogue Mag, 7/77; articles in London Economist, 5/21/77 & New York Times (ed) 9/17/77. Publ: Auth, The Art-in-Architecture Program of the US General Services Administration, Oakland Univ Press, Rochester, Mich. Mailing Add: 18th & F Sts Washington DC 20405

THALER, MILDRED G
ART DEALER, GALLERY DIRECTOR
b New York, NY, Oct 30, 21. Study: Hunter Col, New York, BA; Pratt Inst, Brooklyn, NY, BLS. Pos: Libr, Mus of French Art, French Inst, New York, 43-45; dir, The Marbella Gallery, Inc, New York, 71- Specialty: Nineteenth and early twentieth century American paintings. Mailing Add: 903 Madison Ave New York NY 10021

THEK, PAUL
SCULPTOR
b Brooklyn, NY, Nov 2, 33. Study: Cooper Union, New York, Art Students League, New York; Pratt Inst, New York, 51-54. Work: Stedelijk Mus, Amsterdam; Moderna Museet, Stockholm. Comn: Sets & costumes for the ballet Arena, comn by Glen Tetley, Nederlands Dans Theater, 69. Exhib: Carnegie Int, Pittsburgh, Pa, 67; The Obsessive Image, Inst of Contemp Arts, London, 68; Documenta 4, Kassel, W Ger, 68; Kunst der Sechziger Jahr, Wallraf-Richartz Mus, Cologne, 69; Galerie 20, Amsterdam, 69; Documenta 5, Kassel, W Ger, 72; one-man shows, Inst of Contemp Arts, London, 68, Stedelijk Mus, Amsterdam, 69, Moderna Museet, Stockholm 69 & 72 & Kunstmuseum, Lucerne Switz, 73. Awards: Fulbright Fel, 67. Bibliog: Mary Stewart (auth), In the Galleries: Paul Thek, Artsmagazine, New York, 11/67; B Caroir (auth), Individuelle Mythologien, Kunstwerk, Baden-Baden, 3/74; Paul Thek: entretien avec Harald Szeeman, article in Chroniques de l'Art Vivant, Paris 4/74. Publ: Auth, A Document Made by Paul Thek and Edwin Klein, Amsterdam/Stockholm, 69. Dealer: Galerie M E Thelen Lindenstrasse 20 5 Cologne Germany. Mailing Add: 58 E Third St New York NY 10003

THELIN, VALFRED P
PAINTER, LECTURER
b Waterbury, Conn, Jan 8, 34. Study: Layton Sch Art; Art Inst Chicagp; Int Design Conf Ctr, Insel Mainau, WGer; plus art seminars in six European countries & Mex. Work: Reading Mus, Pa; Ft Wayne Mus, Ind; Butler Inst Am Art, Youngstown, Ohio; Corcoran Gallery Art; Inst Cult Rels, Mexico City. Exhib: Watercolor USA, Springfield Mus, Mo, 63-72; Am Watercolor Soc, Nat Acad Galleries, New York, 63-72; Art in the Embassies, sponsored by Smithsonian Inst, Washington, DC, 68-73; Landscape 1 & Art Expo '72, De Cordova Mus, Lincoln, Mass, 70 & 72; Six by Eight, Philbrook Art Mus, Tulsa, Okla, 71. Awards: John Singer Sargeant Award, Watercolor USA, Springfield Mus, 68; Henry Ward Ranger Award, Audubon Artists, Nat Acad Design, 69; Barse Miller Mem Award, Am Watercolor Soc, 74. Bibliog: Joshua Kind (auth), Chicago, Art News, 2/66; Safer (auth), New York reviews, Arts Mag, 4/68; B Sheaks (auth), Painting with acrylics, Davis, 6/72. Mem: Ogunquit Art Asn (pres, 71-72); life mem Rockport Art Asn (juror); Pa Acad Fine Arts; Sarasota Art Asn (juror demonstrations, 72-73); Philadelphia Watercolor Soc. Media: Watercolor, Acrylic. Publ: Contribr, Art in Am, 3/67, 68 & 72 & The Art Gallery, 71 & 72; Watercolor page, Am Artist, 12/74; Master Class in Watercolor, Watson-Guptill, 75. Mailing Add: Box 473 Shore Rd Ogunquit ME 03907

THEPOT, ROGER FRANCOIS
PAINTER
b Landeleau, France, 25. Work: Mus Mod Art, New York; Mus d'Art Mod, Paris; Nat Gallery, Ottawa, Can; Art Gallery Ont, Toronto; Mendel Art Gallery, Saskatoon. Exhib: Construction and Geometry in Painting, Galerie Chalette, New York, 60; Ecole de Paris, Galerie Charpentier, Paris, 61; Prix Europe de Peinture, Ostende, Belg, 62; Thirteen French Artists, Nippon Gallery, Tokyo, 67; Canada 67, Mus Mod Art, New York, 67. Teaching: Instr colour, Ont Col Art, 67- Awards: Baxter Award, 67. Bibliog: M Seuphor (auth), La peinture abstraite, Flammarion, 62; G Rickey (auth), Constructivism—origins and evolution, Braziller, 67; Roger Francois Thepot, Ed Prisme, 72. Mem: Realites Nouvelles; Royal Can Acad Arts. Media: Acrylic, Gouache. Dealer: Gallery Moos Ltd 138 Yorkville Toronto ON Can. Mailing Add: 80 Alcina Ave Toronto ON M6G 2E8 Can

THIBAULT, CLAUDE
CURATOR, ART HISTORIAN
b Riviere Ouelle, Que, May 5, 48. Study: Laval Univ, Licence es Lettres, 72. Collections Arranged: Tresors des Communautes Religieuses de La Ville de Quebec (with catalog), 73; Le Diocese de Quebec, 1674-1974 (with catalog), 74; Francois Baillairge et son Oeuvre, 1759-1830 (with catalog), 75; L'Art du Quebec au lendemain de la Conquête 1760-1790 (with catalog), 77. Pos: Conserv ancient art Quebec, Mus Quebec, 72- Mem: Int Asn Art Critics; Asn Can Mus; Int Coun of Mus. Res: Ancient art of Quebec. Publ: Ed, La fin d'une epoque, Joseph-Pierre Ouellet, Architecte, 73. Mailing Add: Mus Quebec Parc des Champs de Bataille Quebec PQ Can

THIEBAUD, (MORTON) WAYNE
PAINTER, EDUCATOR
b Mesa, Ariz, Nov 15, 20. Study: Sacramento State Col, BA, 51 & MA, 52. Work: Mus Mod Art; Whitney Mus Am Art; Libr Cong; Albright-Knox Art Gallery; Washington Gallery Mod Art; plus many others. Comn: Fountain mobile structure, Calif State Fair, 52; mosaic mural, Munic Utility Dist Bldg, Sacramento, 59; producer 11 educ motion pictures, Bailey Films, Hollywood, Calif. Exhib: One-man shows, De Young Mem Mus, 62, Albright Mus, Kansas City, Mo, 66, Pasadena Art Mus, Calif, 67 & Whitney Mus Am Art, 71; Dayton Art Inst; Int Contemp Art, Houston, Tex; San Francisco Mus Art; Sao Paulo Biennale, Brazil, 68;

Documenta, Kassel, WGer, 72; Los Angeles Munic Mus, Calif, 73; Delphian Gallery, Sheridan, Ore, 77; plus many other group & one-man shows. Teaching: Chmn art dept, Sacramento City Col, 51; guest instr, San Francisco Art Inst, 58; prof art, Univ Calif, Davis, 60-; prof art & artist in residence, Cornell Univ, 66; artist in residence, Yale Univ, 74 & Rice Univ, 75. Awards: Scholastic Art Awards for films Space and Design, 61; Creative Res Found Grant, 61; DFA(hon), Calif Col Arts & Crafts, 74. Bibliog: Sam Hunter (ed), New Art Around the World: Painting and Sculpture, Abrams, 66; Lucy R Lippard (auth), Pop Art, Praeger, 66; Allen S Weller (auth), The Joys and Sorrows of Recent American Art, Univ Ill Press, 68. Publ: Auth, American rediscovered, 63 & Delights, 65. Mailing Add: Dept Art Univ Calif Davis CA 95616

THIELE, ROBERT RANSOM
PAINTER, SCULPTOR
b Milwaukee, Wis, July 12, 41. Study: Northland Col; Kent State Univ, BFA & MFA. Work: Ft Lauderdale Mus Arts. Comn: Mural-sized painting, Fla Bd Mus Dir for House of Rep Bldg, Tallahassee, 73-74. Exhib: Am Painting Ann, Soc Four Arts, 72; Hortt Memorial Competition, Ft Lauderdale Mus, 72-75 & 77; O K Harris Gallery, New York, 73 & one-man show, 78; Fla Creates Traveling Exhib, 73-74; Biennial Am Painting, Whitney Mus, New York, 75; Nat Drawing Invitational, Emporia Kans State Univ, 77 & 78. Teaching: Assoc prof art, Miami Dade Community Col, 69- Awards: Best in Show, Hortt Mem Competition, 72 & 77; Best in Show, Fla Creates Exhib, 73 & 74. Bibliog: Griffin Smith (auth), articles in Miami Herald & Art News, 70-; William Von Maurer (auth), Robert Thiele: defies convention, Miami News, 72; Jeanne Wolf (auth), Robert Thiele: In Portrait, Nat Educ TV, WPBT, Miami, 74; Griffin Smith (auth), article in Art News, 1/76; Ellen Edwards (auth), article in Art News, summer 77. Style & Technique: Concrete with constructions in laminated canvas, paint and glass. Mailing Add: Art Dept Miami Dade Community Col 11380 NW 27th Ave Miami FL 33167

THIERY, THOMAS ALLEN
PAINTER
b St John, Ind, Oct 16, 39. Study: Art Inst Chicago; Ind Univ; Taylor Univ; Moody Bible Inst; Western Mich Univ, BA; Eastern Mich Univ, MA. Work: Ferris State Col Collection Contemp Am Artists; Clark Equipment Co, Buchanan, Mich; Warning House, Elkhart, Ind. Exhib: Nat Arts Club Painting Exhib, 70; Mainstreams, 71-74; NMex Art League Nat Painting Exhib, 72-74; Toledo Mus Art Fedn Exhib, 72-75; Watercolor USA, 74. Awards: Best in Show, NMex Art League; Best in Show, Toledo Art Mus Fedn; Mainstreams '73 Award. Bibliog: Watercolor page, Am Artist, 75. Style & Technique: Representational; impressionistic. Media: Watercolor, Oil. Mailing Add: Box 54 Onsted MI 49265

THIES, CHARLES HERMAN
PAINTER, ART ADMINISTRATOR
b Poplar Bluff, Mo, Aug 22, 40. Study: Kans State Univ, MA(drawing & painting), study painting with Elmer Tomasch, 70; Kans Univ, printmaking with John Talleur, 66-67; Washington Univ, 64-65; Southeast Mo State Univ, BS(fine arts educ), 63. Work: Minn Mus of Art, St Paul. Comn: Exterior mural (36ft x 74ft), Ford Found Sponsored Prog at Kans State Univ, 69. Exhib: 14th Kans Artist Ann, Wichita Art Mus, 68; 18th Ann Exhib, 72 & Mid-South Biennial, 75, Brooks Mem Art Gallery, Memphis, Tenn; 43rd Ann Exhib, Springfield Art Mus, Mo, 75; Thirty Miles of Art, Nelson Gallery, Atkins Mus, Kansas City, Mo, 76; Western Ann Nat Drawing Exhib, Western Ill Univ, 76; Drawings/USA, Minn Art Mus, St Paul, 77; Joslyn Biennial, Joslyn Art Mus, Omaha, Nebr, 78. Teaching: Secondary instr drawing, design, painting & printmaking, McCluer N High Sch, Seaman High Sch & McCluer High Sch, 67-76; instr drawing, design & figure drawing, Florissant Valley Community Col, St Louis, Mo, 69-76 & 3-D design, Johnson Co Comunity Col, Overland Parks, Kans, 76. Pos: Asst dir of admis, Kansas City Art Inst, Mo, 76-77; admis rep (Colo), Kansas City Art Inst, 77- Awards: Painting Award, Exhib 70, St Louis, N Co Art Asn, 70; Drawing Award, Quincy Ill Fine Arts Asn, 71; Purchase, Drawings/USA 1977, Minn Mus of Art. Style & Technique: Realism, drawings in pencil. Media: Pencil; Oil. Mailing Add: 437 Elmira St Aurora CO 80010

THIRY, PAUL (ALBERT)
ARCHITECT, COLLECTOR
b Nome, Alaska, Sept 11, 04. Study: Ecole des Beaux Arts, Fontainebleau, dipl, 27; Univ Wash, BArchit, 28; St Martins Col, DFA, 70. Comn: State Libr, Capitol Comt, State of Wash, Olympia, 58; Embassy, US Dept State, Santiago, Chile, 60; Seattle Ctr Coliseum, City of Seattle, 64; Contemp Arts Pavilion, Seattle Art Mus, 64; World War II Monument, US 4th Inf Div, permanently located at Utah Beach, France, 68. Exhib: Salon d'Art Sacre, Mus Mod Art, Paris, 54; Nat Gold Medal Exhib, Archit League, New York, 56; Architectura Actual de Am, Madrid, 65; Ann Exhib, Nat Acad Design, New York, 68; New Am Archit, US Info Agency, New Delhi, India, 73. Pos: Mem & vchmn, Hist Am Bldg Surv, 56-61; prin architect, Century 21 Expos, Seattle, 57-62; mem, President's Coun for Pennsylvania Ave, 62-65; prof adv, Int Sculpture Competition Treaty Tower, Libby Dam, Mont, 74-75. Awards: Officier d'Acad, Repub of France, 50; Distinguished Citizen in the Arts, City of Seattle, 62; Herbert Adams Mem Medal, Nat Sculpture Soc, 74 & Henry Hering Medal, 76. Bibliog: Monogr, Nuestra Arquitectura, Arg, 7/49; Robert Koehler (auth), monogr, Pac Architect & Builder, Seattle, 2/61; Esther McCoy (auth), monogr, Arts & Archit, Los Angeles, 1/65. Mem: Hon mem Am Inst Interior Design; fel Am Inst Architects (chancellor, 62-64); hon mem Nat Sculpture Soc; academician Nat Acad Design; life mem Soc Archit Historians (dir, 67-70). Collection: Primitive arts of the Alaskan Eskimo and the Indians of the Northwest Coastal Areas. Publ: Auth, Architecture today, a symp, Liturgical Arts, 11/50; co-auth, Churches & Temples, Reinhold, 53; ed, Washington in transition, 1/63 & auth, Planning of Washington as a Capital, 4/74, Am Inst Architects J; auth, Architectural treatment of dams, Arts & Archit, 8/67; co-auth (with Mary Thiry), Eskimo Artifacts, Designed for Use, Super Publ Co, Seattle, Wash, 78. Mailing Add: 800 Columbia St Seattle WA 98104

THOLLANDER, EARL
ILLUSTRATOR, GRAPHIC ARTIST
b Kingsburg, Calif, Apr 13, 22. Study: Univ Calif, BA. Bibliog: Earl Thollander Discusses Painting, 4/54 & Artist reporter on tour, 3/60, Am Artist Mag; Adrian Wilson (auth), The Design of Books, Reinhold Studio Vista, 67; Diana Klemin (auth), The Illustrated Book, Clarkson N Potter, 70. Media: Pen Drawing, Acrylic, Watercolor. Publ: Auth & illusr, Back Roads of California, Sunset, 71; auth & illusr, Back Roads of New England, Potter, 74; auth & illusr, Barns of California, Calif Hist Soc, 74; auth & illusr, Back Roads of Arizona, Northland Press, 78; auth & illusr, Back Roads of Oregon, Potter, in press. Dealer: Depot Gallery Vintage 1870 Yountville CA 94599. Mailing Add: House in the Woods Murray Hill Calistoga CA 94515

THOM, ROBERT ALAN
ILLUSTRATOR, PAINTER
b Grand Rapids, Mich, Mar 4, 15. Study: Columbus Inst Fine Arts, Ohio; also with Robert Brackman. Work: Parke, Davis Co; Bohn Aluminum & Brass Co; Univ Md; Cranbrook Acad Arts; Kimberly-Clark Corp; plus others. Exhib: Vancouver Art Gallery, BC; Smithsonian Inst; Sheldon Swope Gallery Art; Ore Mus Nat Hist; Pioneer Mus, Stockton, Calif; plus many others. Mem: Soc Illusr; Bloomfield Art Asn. Publ: Auth & illusr, article on Wine Festival, Burgundy, France, In: Gourmet Mag, 61; North American Big Game Animals (ltd ed), Wilderness World. Mailing Add: 175 W Merrill St Birmingham MI 48011

THOMAS, ALMA WOODSEY
PAINTER
b Columbus, Ga, Sept 22, 91. Study: Howard Univ, BS, 24; Columbia Univ, MFA, 34; Am Univ, 50-60; also in Europe, 58, under auspices Temple Univ. Work: Corcoran Gallery Art & Smithsonian Inst Collection Fine Arts, Washington, DC; Fisk Univ Gallery Art, Nashville, Tenn; Whitney Mus Am Art, New York. Exhib: Howard Univ Gallery Art, 66 & 75; Franz Bader Gallery, Washington, DC, 68 & 70-74; Whitney Mus Am Art, 72; retrospective, Corcoran Gallery Art, 72; Martha Jackson Gallery, New York, 73 & 76. Teaching: Instr art, jr high sch, 24-60. Awards: Purchase Prize, Howard Univ, 63; Soc Washington Artists, 63, 68 & 71. Bibliog: Cedric Dover (auth), American Negro Art, Studio, 60; auto-biog sound filmstrip, Harcourt Brace Jovanovich, 73. Mem: Am Fedn Arts; Corcoran Gallery Art; Am Fedn Art; Washington Watercolor Asn; Smithsonian Inst. Style & Technique: Based on color and light inspired by nature and space; through simple, vari-colored bars have achieved interesting optical effects of movement and light presently concentrating on compositions utilizing only one color. Media: Oil, Acrylic. Dealer: Franz Bader Gallery 2124 Pennsylvania Ave NW Washington DC; Martha Jackson Gallery 521 W 57th St New York NY 10019. Mailing Add: 1530 15th St NW Washington DC 20005

THOMAS, BYRON
PAINTER
b Baltimore, Md, 1902. Study: Md Inst Art; Martinet Sch Art; Art Students League, Tiffany Found fel. Work: Pastime Bowling Alley, Mus Mod Art; Pine Trees, Pa Acad Fine Arts; Maples, Springfield Art Mus; US Dept Army; plus numerous pvt collections. Exhib: Numerous one-man and group shows in US & abroad. Teaching: Teacher painting, Cooper Union, 31-50. Pos: War artist, Life Mag, Europe, 43-44. Awards: Many prizes & awards. Mailing Add: 48 Elm St Woodstock VT 05091

THOMAS, ED B
EDUCATOR, LECTURER
b Cosmopolis, Wash, Nov 30, 20. Study: Columbia Univ; NY Univ; Univ Wash, BA & MFA. Comn: Recorded TV series for sch use, Man's Story, Treasure trips, Our neighbors, The Japanese, Electronic tour of Masterpieces of Korean Art, 58, Van Gogh, 59 & Treasures of Japan, 60, Seattle Art Mus. Exhib: Nat Serigraphy Soc; San Francisco Mus Art; Seattle Art Mus; regional exhibs, 50- Teaching: Lectr, weekly TV art prog, Seattle, 51-; instr art hist, Cornish Sch, Seattle, 52-58; from vis prof & lectr to assoc prof art, Western Wash State Col, 67- Pos: Cur educ, Seattle Art Mus & Seattle Ctr Art Pavilion, 51-54, educ dir, 54-61, asst dir, 61-63, assoc dir, 63-67; arts adv bd, Seattle World's Fair, 58-62; bd trustees, Allied Artists Seattle, 59-62; secy, Fine Arts, Inc, 62; vpres, Western Asn Art Mus, 63-64; bd trustees, Seattle Art Mus, 72-; art consult, People's Nat Bank of Wash. Awards: Prize for sch telecasts, Am Exhib of Educ Radio-TV Prog, Ohio Univ, 56; plus other TV awards. Mem: Pacific Art Asn (1st vpres, 60-62); Wash Art Asn; Nat Comt on Art Educ; Am Asn Mus; Northwest Printmakers (pres); plus others. Publ: Auth, Guide to Life's illuminations exhibit, Time, Inc, 58; auth, Mark Tobey, 59; ed & narrator, Chinese ink and watercolor (film), 61. Mailing Add: 1500 42nd St Seattle WA 98112

THOMAS, ELAINE FREEMAN
EDUCATOR, ART ADMINISTRATOR
b Cleveland, Ohio, July 21, 23. Study: Northwestern Univ, Evanston, 44; Tuskegee Inst, BS(magna cum laude), 45; Black Mountain Col, 45, with Josef Albers & Robert Motherwell; NY Univ, Bodden fel, MA, 49, with Hale Woodruff; Mexico City Col, 56; Berea Col, 61; Univ Paris, 66; Southern Univ Workshop, 68; Columbia Univ, 70. Collections Arranged: One-man exhib, Winston-Salem State Univ, 70; Discovery 70, Univ Cincinnati; George Washington Carver Exhib, White House, 71; Ala Black Artists Exhib, Birmingham Festival Art, 72; plus others. Teaching: Asst prof art & chmn dept, Tuskegee Inst, 45-, mus dir & cur, George W Carver Mus, 61-77. Pos: Mem expansion arts adv panel, Nat Endowment for the Arts; dir, Nat Hist Site Adv Coun, Tuskegee Inst. Awards: Distinguished Participation, Am Artists Prof League, 68; Beaux Arts Festival Award. Mem: Am Asn Mus; Col Art Asn Am; Nat Art Educ Asn; Nat Conf Artists; Ala Art League. Mailing Add: Chmn Dept of Arts Col of Arts & Sci Tuskegee Inst Tuskegee AL 36088

THOMAS, GEORGE R
EDUCATOR, ARCHITECT
b Portsmouth, Va, Dec 8, 06. Study: Univ NC, 24-25; Carnegie Inst Technol, BArch, 30; Columbia Univ, 38; study in Europe. Teaching: Instr art, Mary Washington Col, 35; from instr to prof archit & arts, Univ NH, 31-76, emer prof, 76-, dir art gallery, 37-76, chmn dept arts, 40-76. Mem: Am Inst Architects; Am Asn Univ Prof; NH Art Asn; Coun League NH Arts & Crafts; NH Soc Architects. Publ: Contribr, articles on archit design and educ to various publ. Mailing Add: Dept Arts Univ NH Durham NH 03824

THOMAS, HELEN (DOANE)
PAINTER, ART CRITIC
b Portland, Ore. Study: Philadelphia Col of Art, Pa & Art Students League, New York. Work: Chase Manhattan Bank, New York; Mus Univ of Wichita, Kans; Finch Mus, New York, Univ of Ala, Birmingham; New Eng Ctr Contemp Art, Brooklyn, Conn. Exhib: East Hampton Gallery, New York, 70; Albright-Knox Art Gallery, Buffalo, NY, 70-72; Philadelphia Mus Gallery, Pa, 72-75; Phoenix Gallery, New York, 73, 75, 77; Maison de la Cult, Cluses, France, 76; Maison de la Cult, Annemasse, France, 76; Ga Inst Technol, Atlanta, 76; Univ of Ala, Birmingham, 76. Pos: Treas, Phoenix Gallery, New York, 72-74, pres, 74- Mem: Nat Asn of Women Artists. Bibliog: Article on 1977 show, Arts Mag, 10/77. Style & Technique: Colorist, relationship of colors and flat surfaces of related opaque color resulting in the illusion of transparency. Media: Oil on Canvas. Dealer: Phoenix Gallery 30 W 57th St New York NY 10019. Mailing Add: 530 E 23rd St New York NY 10010

THOMAS, JOHN
PAINTER
b Bessemer, Ala, Feb 4, 27. Study: Univ Ga, 46-48; New Sch Social Res, New York, BA, 51; NY Univ, with William Baziotes, MA, 54; Univ Stranieri, Perugia, Italy, 54. Work: Hawaii State Found Cult & Arts Collection, Capitol Bldg, Honolulu, Hawaii Community Col, Hilo & Honoka'a State Off Bldg; Contemp Art Ctr of Hawaii, Honolulu. Exhib: 2nd Pac Coast

Biennial, Seattle Art Mus, Portland Art Mus, Santa Barbara Mus & San Francisco Legion of Honor, 57-58; Whitney Ann Am Art, New York, 59; Contemp Am Painting & Sculpture Biennial, Univ Ill, Champaign-Urbana, 61-65; Artists of Hawaii Ann Exhib, Honolulu Acad Arts, 65-; American Painting, 1966, Va Mus Fine Arts, Richmond, 66; Univ of Wis, Eau Claire, 76; Contemp Art Ctr of Hawaii, Honolulu, 76; Biblioteca Americana, Bucharest, Romania, 77. Teaching: Vis prof life drawing, State Univ Iowa, 62-63; prof art, Univ Hawaii, Manoa & Hilo, 65-67 & 70-74; vis artist painting, Univ Wash, 68-69. Awards: Huntington Hartford Found Fel Awards, 57 & 62; Tucson Arts Festival First Prize, Tucson Arts Ctr, 64; Ann Easter Art Festival First Prize, Hilo Arts & Crafts Asn, 74; Nat Endowment Arts grant (sets & costumes, opera Ka Lei No Kane), 77; Hawaii State Senate Congratulations (for Boy with Goldfish), 77. Bibliog: Betje Howell (auth), article in Am Artist, 2/78; Tanner Thomas & Siu Elliott (co-auths), Boy with Goldfish, multi-arts concept, Prem Honolulu Symphony Orchestra, 76. Mem: Komohana Artists Asn, Kailua-Kona (founding pres, 73-74). Style & Technique: Figures and foliage in prismatic colors and stereometric composition; semi-transparent oil technique. Media: Oil, Watercolor. Dealer: Laila Roster Contemp Arts Ctr 605 Kapiolani Blvd Honolulu HI 96813. Mailing Add: PO Box 1478 Kailua-Kona HI 96740

THOMAS, KATHERINE CASTELLANOS
ART ADMINISTRATOR, PAINTER
b Houston, Tex, Mar 7, 46. Study: Houston Mus Fine Arts; Laguna Gloria Art Mus Sch, Austin; Univ Tex, Austin, 65-70. Work: Lincoln First Federal, Spokane, Wash; Cheney CofC, Wash. Exhib: 24th & 25th Spokane Ann, 72 & 73; one-man shows, Gallery Three, Spokane, 73 & 74 & Kingsport Fine Arts Ctr, Tenn, 75. Collections Arranged: George Grosz, Eastern Wash State Col, 71 & Seattle Pac Col, 73; 19th Century Prints & Tsutomu Toguchi, Eastern Wash State Col, 73. Teaching: Instr drawing, Laguna Gloria Art Mus Sch, Austin, 69-70 & Eastern Wash State Col, 71-74. Pos: Art consult, USA Corps Engrs, Wash, 71-72; res dir, Art Exhib, Spokane World's Fair, 73-74; exec dir, Kingsport Fine Arts Ctr, Tenn, 74-76. Awards: Lincoln First Fed Purchase Award, 72; Cheney CofC Award for Downtown Refurbishment Design, 72. Bibliog: Opal Fleckenstein (auth), Visual arts (videotape), KSPS-TV, Spokane, 71; Gladys Guilbert (auth), New Breed of Northwest Artists, Sunday Mag, Spokesman-Rev, 73; Rebecca Hilton (auth), Art Center director, Johnson City Press-Chronicle, 75. Mem: Col Art Asn Am; Tenn State Arts Comn (mem community arts panel, 74-76); Am Asn Mus; Sullivan Co Am Revolutionary Bicentennial Comt (exec bd, 75-76); Tri-City Arts Coun (asst secy, 75-76). Style & Technique: Minimal designs; figure drawing. Media: Fabric, Acrylic, Conte, Charcoal. Publ: Contribr, Conceptual Design Statement..., 72; illusr, Frank Gallo, Northwestern Premier Exhib Brochure, 72; contribr, Our Land, Our Sky, Our Water, 72 & auth, Docent Training Program, Expo 74 Art Exhib; illusr, Historians' Bicentennial Newslett, 73-74. Mailing Add: 415 W Maple Johnson City TN 37601

THOMAS, LEW
PHOTOGRAPHER, ART WRITER
b San Francisco, Calif, Dec 19, 32. Study: Univ of San Francisco, BA, 60. Work: de Saisset Art Gallery, Univ of Santa Clara, Calif; La Mamelle's Art Ctr, San Francisco. Exhib: Photographic Corners, San Francisco Art Inst, 74; New Photog: San Francisco & Bay Area, Fine Arts Mus of San Francisco, 74; Rhinoceros, A Demonstration of Visual & Audial Poetic Experimentation, M H de Young Mem Mus, 75; 8 x 10, Mills Col, Oakland, Calif, 75; Vitruvian Context, 1472-1976, San Jose State Univ Art Gallery, 76; Exchange, SFO/DFW, San Francisco Mus of Mod Art, 76; West Coast Conceptual Photog, 76 & Photog & Lang, 76, La Mamelle's Arts Ctr. Collections Arranged: 8 x 10 (auth, catalog), Mills Col Art Gallery, Oakland, Calif, 75; Photog & Lang (ed, catalog), 76 & West Coast Conceptual Photog (ed, catalog), 76, La Mamelle's Arts Ctr. Awards: Photographer Fel, Nat Endowment for the Arts, 75 & Ilo Liston Mem Publ Award, Mills Col, 75. Style & Technique: Photography and language. Media: Images & text. Res: Theoretical. Publ: Auth, The Thinker, Fine Arts Mus San Francisco, 74; ed, Photography & ideology, Dumb Ox, 5/77. Mailing Add: 243 Grand View Ave San Francisco CA 94114

THOMAS, LIONEL ARTHUR JOHN
PAINTER, SCULPTOR
b Toronto, Ont, Can, Apr 3, 15. Study: John Russell Acad, Toronto; Ont Col Art, Toronto; Calif Sch Fine Art, San Francisco; also with Hans Hofmann, Provincetown, Mass. Work: Fla State Col, Lakeland; Nat Gallery, Ottawa; Art Gallery Toronto; Vancouver Art Gallery; Univ Victoria, BC. Comn: Bronze fountain, Edmonton City Hall, Alta, 58; Vancouver Pub Libr, 61; enamel doors, St Thomas More Col, Saskatoon, Sask, 62; BC Prov Govt Mus, Victoria, 68; oil on panels (with L & P Thomas), Student Union Bldg, Univ BC, 69. Exhib: Fine Arts Fac Exhib, Univ BC, 76, Myths, Legends, & Sci in Astrology & Astronomy, 77; one-man show, Vancouver Planetarium & Mus, 77. Teaching: Assoc prof design, Sch Archit, 50-64; assoc prof design, Univ BC, 64- Pos: Chmn, Comt Appl Design, BC Govt, Victoria, 65-68. Awards: Allied Arts Medal, Royal Archit Inst Can, 56. Bibliog: Stephen Franklin (auth), Artist and a briefcase, Weekend Mag, 58; article in BC Beautiful, spring 70; Mate Laoonsen (auth), Centauran, Vancouver Mag, 10/76; plus others. Mem: Royal Can Acad; Am Craftsmen Coun; Am Soc Archeologists; Can Fedn Artists; Ont Crafts Found; plus others. Mailing Add: Lassarre Bldg 403 Univ BC West Vancouver BC V6T 1W5 Can

THOMAS, ROBERT CHESTER
SCULPTOR
b Wichita, Kans, Apr 19, 24. Study: With David Green, Pasadena, Calif, 46-47 & Ossip Zadkine, Paris, 48-49; Univ Calif, Santa Barbara, BA, 51; Calif Col Arts & Crafts, MFA, 52. Work: Santa Barbara Mus Art, Calif; Univ Calif, Santa Barbara; Joseph H Hirshhorn Collection, Washington, DC. Comn: Painted wood sculpture, J Magnin, Century City, Calif, 66; bronze figure, Class of 1967, Univ Calif, Santa Barbara, 67; ceramic fountain, comn by Phyllis Plous, Santa Barbara, 68. Exhib: Int Salon de Mai, Paris, 49; San Francisco Mus Art, 52, 53, 56 & 57; one-man shows, Santa Barbara Mus Art, 55, La Jolla Art Ctr, Calif, 60 & Adele Bednarz Galleries, Los Angeles, 70-72 & 74; Retrospective, Univ Calif, Santa Barbara, 66; Adele Bednarz Galleries, Los Angeles, 76; Peppers Art Ctr, Univ Redlands, Calif, 76; Whatcom Mus Hist & Art, Bellingham, Wash, 78. Teaching: Prof sculpture, Univ Calif, Santa Barbara, 54- Awards: Bronze Medal for sculpture, City of Los Angeles, 49; Silver Medal for sculpture, Calif State Fair, 54; Purchase Prize for sculpture, Santa Barbara Mus Art, 59. Media: Stone, Wood, Bronze. Mailing Add: 38 San Mateo Ave Goleta CA 93017

THOMAS, STEFFEN WOLFGANG
SCULPTOR, PAINTER
b Fürth, Ger, Jan 7, 06; US citizen. Study: Sch Appl Arts, Nürnberg, Ger; Acad Fine Arts, Munich, Ger, with Herman Hahn, Bernhart Bleeker & Josef Wakerle. Work: High Mus, Atlanta, Ga; Agnes Scott Col, Decatur, Ga; State Capitol, Atlanta; Am Col Surg, Chicago; Univ Edinborough, Scotland. Comn: Bronze portrait bust of George Washington Carver, Tuskegee Inst, Ala, 45; bronze monument of Gov Eugene Talmadge, Talmadge Mem Comt, State Capitol Grounds, Atlanta, 49; bronze Ala Confederate monument, State of Ala, Vicksburg Nat Mil Park, Miss, 51; aluminum bas relief murals, Fulton Nat Bank, Atlanta, 54. Exhib: Glas Palast, Munich, 27; one-man show, High Mus, 36; Nat Sculpture Soc, New York, 48; Southeastern Art Show, Atlanta Art Asn, 49-51; Nat Soc Miniature Arts, Smithsonian Inst, Washington, DC, 52. Pos: Art dir Ga, Nat Youth Admin, 39-42. Awards: First & Purchase Prize for Head of Youth, City of Fürth, 25; hon mention, Fine Arts Acad, Munich, 28. Bibliog: Katerine Barnwell (auth), Artist's studio or lion's den, Atlanta J-Constitution Mag, 3/4/62; Ann Carter (auth), Reaching higher, Sun Atlanta J-Constitution, 2/2/69, Ethel Kerlin & staff (auth), Mr Steffen Thomas, WETV, 69. Style & Technique: Creative works in both representational and abstract fields. Media: Bronze. Mailing Add: 848 Mentelle Dr NE Atlanta GA 30308

THOMAS, TAMARA B
ART CONSULTANT
b Calif. Study: Univ Calif, Berkeley, BA(art hist). Collections Arranged: Security Pacific Nat Bank, 70; Blue Cross Southern Calif; The Taubman Co Inc; Hyatt Regency Hotels, Atlanta, New Orleans; plus many others. Pos: Pres, Fine Arts Services Inc, Los Angeles, 70- Mem: Mod & Contemp Art Coun, Los Angeles Mus of Art; Friends of Otis Art Inst, Los Angeles. Res: Cataloging of collections assembled; explanatory material on works acquired, bridging gap between public and contemporary art. Specialty: Consultation to corporations and real estate development architects and interior design firms on art acquisitions, display and integration. Mailing Add: Fine Arts Services Inc 107 S Irving Blvd Los Angeles CA 90004

THOMAS, WILLIAM RADFORD
EDUCATOR, PAINTER
b Waco, Tex, Nov 4, 30. Study: Univ Tex, Austin, BFA & PhD; NMex Highlands Univ, MA. Work: Israel Mus, Jerusalem; Dallas Mus Fine Arts, Tex; Oakland Mus, Calif; Laguna Gloria Art Mus, Austin, Tex; Simon Fraser Univ, Burnaby, BC; Comn: Altar, Holy Trinity Episcopal Church, Austin, 56; sculpture (welded steel), Bank of the Southwest, Houston, 63; sculpture (welded steel), Mercantile Bank of Houston, 64. Exhib: Palacio de Bellas Artes, Mex, 62; 19th Nat Print Exhib, Libr of Cong, Washington, DC, 62; Palacio de Bellas Artes, Mexico City, 62; The Guiding Hand, Ft Worth Art Ctr, Tex, 68; Nat Drawing Exhib, Southern Ill Univ, Carbondale, 75; Artists Stamp & Stamp Images, Simon Fraser Univ, Can, 75; Florence Mus, SC, 76; Image S Gallery, Atlanta, Ga, 76; Cabinet des Estampes, Mus d'Art et d'Hist, Geneva, Switz, 76; Berry Col, Mt Berry, Ga, 77; Langley Mus & Nat Exhib Centre, Ft Langley, BC, 77; Walter Phillips Gallery, Banff Centre, Alta, 77; Simcoe Co Mus, Minesing, Ont, 77; Nat Exhib Centre, Leaf Rapids, Man, 77; Grace Campbell Gallery, Prince Albert, Sask, 77; Prince George Art Gallery, BC, 77. Collections Arranged: Sculpture of Frank Gallo, 72, 19th Century Book Illustrations, 73, American Drawing, 73, Documents & Images, 73 & Environmental Communication—Graphic Arts of Signage & Display in Our Enviroment, 73, Eastern Wash State Col. Teaching: Instr drawing-painting, San Antonio Art Inst, Tex, 58-61; chmn dept art-photog, Amarillo Col, 64-67; asst prof design-prints, NTex State Univ, 67-68; admin asst dean fine arts, Univ Tex, Austin, 68-70; chmn dept art, Eastern Wash State Col, 70-74; chmn dept art, ETenn State Univ, 74- Awards: Purchase Awards, Tex Ann Painting & Sculpture, Dallas Mus Fine Arts, 59 & 29th Ann, Witte Mem Mus, San Antonio, 59; Award, Tex Watercolor Soc, 58. Bibliog: Richard Byrne (auth), In the guise of paintings, Phoenix, Austin, 68; Alfred Frankenstein (auth), Our land, our sky, our water, Expo 74, Spokane, 74; Ken Friedman (auth), Radford Thomas, Ecart Publ, Geneva, 75; plus others. Mem: Col Art Asn Am; Tenn Arts Comn (chmn visual arts adv panel); Nat Asn Schs Art; life mem Tex Fine Arts Asn. Style & Technique: Calligraphy, objective and nonobjective. Media: Ink; Water Soluble Media. Publ: Contribr, The Visual Arts, Telecourse, KSPA-TV, Spokane, Wash, 71; co-auth, A Conceptual Design Statement..., 72; ed, Ken Friedman: Sightings, E Wash State Univ, 74; auth, Development of a museum for Southwestern Univ, Georgetown, Texas, 74. Dealer: Image South Gallery 1931 Peachtree Rd NE Atlanta GA 30309. Mailing Add: Box 23740A E Tenn State Univ Johnson City TN 37601

THOMASON, TOM WILLIAM
JEWELER, ART DEALER
b Shawnee, Okla, Oct 28, 34. Study: Univ NMex, BFA, 60. Work: Am Inst Architects, Albuquerque, NMex. Comn: Bronze Sculpture, Arlene Vanderbilt Webb, New York, 67; Cross & Collection Plates, St Mark's Episcopal Church, Albuquerque, 68; Archit Awards, Am Inst Architects, Albuquerque, 69; Archit Medals, Univ NMex, 70; Desk Award Plaques, NMex Coun for Exceptional Children, 77. Exhib: Young Americans, Mus Contemp Crafts, New York, 62; Denver Own Your Own, Denver Art Mus, Colo, 62; Jewelry Int, Sch Am Craftsmen, Rochester Inst Technol, NY, 63; 1st Survey Contemp Am Crafts, Univ Tex Art Mus, Austin, 67; one-man show, Art Ministry, Tananarive, Magagascar, 67; Southwestrn Craftsmen, Dallas Mus of Fine Arts, Tex, 68; Silver & Gold, Corcoran Gallery of Art, Washington, DC, 72; Contemp Crafts Biennial, 1st Folk Art Mus, Santa Fe, NMex, 76. Collections Arranged: Contemporary Crafts Exhibition, New Mexico Pavilion, World's Fair, New York, 64; Santeros of New Mexico, Studio Gallery, Albuquerque, 68. Teaching: Guest artist, design, Univ Madagascar, Tananarive, 67. Pos: Owner & mgr, Studio Gallery, Albuquerque, 63-; design & sales adv, Zuni Arts & Crafts Coop, NMex, 68. Awards: Purchase Award, NMex Contemp Crafts, Am Inst Architects, Albuquerque, 70; First Prize, Metal, NMex Contemp Crafts, NMex State Fair, 73; First, Third & Fourth Prizes, Metal, Tulsa Gallery of Fine Arts, Okla, 73. Bibliog: Lois E Franke (auth), Handwrought Jewelry, McKnight & McKnight, 67. Mem: NMex Designer Craftsmen (vpres 62-65, pres, 65-66); Albuquerque Designer Craftsmen (pres, 62-65); Corrales Art Asn (vpres, 64 & 66); Albuquerque Gallery Asn (pres, 78); World Crafts Coun. Style & Technique: Sculpture and jewelry in metal using the lost wax and forging techniques; painting in oil, acrylic and water media; abstract. Media: Bronze for Sculpture; Silver and Gold for Jewelry; Oil for painting. Specialty: Contemporary art in painting, sculpture and art crafts. Publ: Contribr, Marcilla Chamberlain, auth, Making Metal Jewelry, Watson-Guptill, US & Pitman Ltd, Eng, 77. Mailing Add: 615 16th St NW Albuquerque NM 87104

THOMPSON, DAVID ELBRIDGE
See Hompson, Davi Det

THOMPSON, DONALD ROY
PAINTER, INSTRUCTOR
b Fowler, Calif, Mar 2, 36. Study: Calif State Univ, Sacramento, BA, 60, MA, 62. Work: Oakland Mus, Calif; Seattle First Nat Bank. Exhib: One-man shows, Galeria Carl Van Der Voort, San Francisco, 67 & Calif State Univ, Sacramento, 75; 40 Now California Painters, Tampa Bay Art Ctr, Fla, Ringling Mus Art, Sarasota, Fla, Fla State Univ & High Mus, Atlanta, Ga, 68; 2nd Brit Int Print Biennale, Bradford City Art Gallery & Mus, Eng, 70; Bay Area Artists Exhib, Oakland Mus, 75. Teaching: Instr art, Cabrillo Col, 71- Bibliog: Thomas Albright (auth), Gallery for elegant simplicity, San Francisco Chronicle, 9/28/67; Henry T Hopkins (auth), Visiting critic lauds exhibition, Tampa Tribune, 4/16/68; Charles Johnson (auth), Color is form and subject, Sacramento Bee, 1/26/75. Style & Technique: Color texturalist. Media: Acrylic on Canvas and various other surfaces. Mailing Add: 225 Union St Santa Cruz CA 95060

THOMPSON, DOROTHY BURR
ART HISTORIAN, LECTURER
b Delhi, NY, Aug 19, 00. Study: Bryn Mawr Col, AB, 23, European fel, 23, AM, PhD, 31; Wooster Col, hon DFA, 72. Collections Arranged: Comment in Clay, Royal Ont Mus, 47. Teaching: Lectr archaeol for circuit, Archaeol Inst Am, 40-; lectr class archaeol, Univ Toronto, 43-47; prof class archaeol, Univ Pa, 52 & 68; vis lectr archaeol, Oberlin Col, 68; prof class archaeol, Princeton Univ, 69-70; vis lectr, Univ Sydney, 72. Pos: Actg dir, Royal Ont Mus, 46-47. Mem: Archaeol Inst Am (exec comt, 48-52); mem Deutsches Archäologisches Inst. Res: Classical Greek subjects such as figurines, garden art and private life. Publ: Auth, Terracottas from Myrina in Museum of Fine Arts, Boston, privately publ, 34; auth, Swans and Amber (transl of Greek lyrics), Univ Toronto Press, 49; auth, Troy, the Terracotta Figurines of the Hellenistic Period, Princeton Univ Press, 63; auth, Ptolemaic Oinochoai and Portraits in Faience, Oxford Press, 73; contribr var jour. Mailing Add: Inst for Advan Study Princeton NJ 08540

THOMPSON, ERNEST THORNE
EDUCATOR, PAINTER
b St John, NB; US citizen. Study: Mass Sch Art, Boston; Mus Fine Art, Boston; independent European study. Work: Bibliot Nat, Paris; Nat Mus, Washington, DC; Univ Notre Dame; Col of New Rochelle; Farnsworth Mus, Rockland, Maine. Comn: Stations of the Cross, Univ Notre Dame, 24 & Football Championship Mem, 24; The Sacred Heart (mural), St Patrick's Church, McHenry, Ill, 25; Adventures of Don Quixote (murals), Oliver Hotel, South Bend, Ind, 26; Landmarks of New York (watercolor ser), Simpson, Thatcher & Bartlett, New York, 56. Exhib: Exhibs of Am Prints, Tate Gallery London, 27 & Bibliot Nat, Paris, 28; Fifty Prints of the Year, New York, 28; Ann exhibs, Am Watercolor Soc & Allied Artists of Am, New York, 49-74; Exchange Exhib, Royal Watercolor Soc, London, Am Watercolor Soc, 60. Teaching: Prof art & dir sch fine art, Univ Notre Dame, 22-29; prof art & chmn dept fine art, Col of New Rochelle, 29-67; dir, Huguenot Sch Art, New Rochelle, NY, 47-51. Pos: Vpres, Pemaquid Group of Artists, Bristol, Maine, 60-75; mem bd dirs, Maine Gallery, Wiscasset, 60-, dir, 62-75. Awards: Rudolf Lesch Award & Medal, Am Watercolor Soc, 56 & Lily Saportas Award, 64; Charles L Fox Award, Farnsworth Mus, Rockland, Maine, 74. Mem: Allied Artists of Am (pres, 65-67); Am Watercolor Soc (bd dirs, 62-64, 66-68); Chicago Soc Etchers; New Rochelle Art Asn (bd dirs, 40-45). Style & Technique: Watercolor and oil paintings are traditional in their approach to nature; emphasis upon sound drawing, composition and color. Media: Transparent Watercolor & Oil; Dry-Point. Publ: Auth, New England—Twelve Woodcuts, Univ Wash, 28; auth, Technique of the Modern Woodcut, Pencil Points Press, New York, 28. Dealer: Grand Cent Art Galleries New York NY 10017. Mailing Add: Muscongus Point Medomak ME 04551

THOMPSON, ERNEST THORNE, JR
SILVERSMITH, PAINTER
b South Bend, Ind, Nov 9, 28. Study: Huguenot Sch Art, with Courtney Allen, Charles R Kingnan, Ernest T Thompson, Sr, dipl; Sch of Mus Fine Arts, Boston, dipl, with Joseph L Sharrock, Sr & Hazel Olsen Brown. Work: Mus Sci, Boston, Mass; US Air Force Chapel, Bien Hoe, Vietnam; Corp Plate, Boston, Gt Brit. Comn: Industrial comns & pvt collections. Teaching: Dept head jewelry & silversmith, Boston Mus Sch, 61-70 & Portland Sch Art, 69- Pos: Trustee, Soc Arts & Crafts, 61-64; juror, Sterling Silver Design Competition, 75. Bibliog: Bill Cauldwell (auth), Stop, silversmith at work, Ford Times Mag, 10/69; Richard Stilwell (auth), Ernest Thompson unselfish in silver, Maine Guide Dir, 74. Style & Technique: Design spans from antique to modern, use of natural organic interpretations in all metals. Media: Gold, Silver, Bronze, Pewter. Mailing Add: Back Meadow Rd Damariscotta ME 04543

THOMPSON, F RAYMOND (RAY)
ILLUSTRATOR, WRITER
b Philadelphia, Pa, July 9, 05. Study: Temple Univ, 26-27 & 50-52; Mus Sch Art, Spring Garden Inst & Charles Morris Price Sch Journalism & Advert, Philadelphia. Media: Watercolor. Publ: Auth & illusr, Washington at Germantown, 71; auth & illusr, Betsy Ross, last of Philadelphia's free Quakers, 72; The walking purchase hoax, 73; Washington at Whitemarsh, 74; Benedict Arnold in Philadelphia, 75. Mailing Add: 1107 Montgomery Ave Ft Washington PA 19034

THOMPSON, GEORGE LOUIS
DESIGNER
b Winnetoon, Nebr, Oct 14, 13. Study: Univ Minn, BSA; Mass Inst Technol, MS. Work: Metrop Mus Art, New York; Palais Louvre, Paris; The Hermitage, Leningrad, USSR; William Rockhill Nelson Gallery Art, Kansas City, Mo; Nat Gallery Mod Art, New Delhi, India. Comn: Eisenhower Cup, comn by his cabinet, Washington, DC, 53; Papal Cup, Cardinal Spellman, New York, 56; Lafayette Medallion, Collection Pres Rene Coty, France, 57; Angel Stele, Kennedy Found, 62; Eleanor Roosevelt Mem, Libr, 71. Exhib: Five Steuben Traveling Exhibs, 36-53; New York World's Fair, 39-40; Designs in Glass by 27 Contemporary Artists, New York, 40; Brit Artists in Crystal, New York, 54; Poetry in Crystal, New York, 66. Pos: Sr designer, Steuben Glass, New York, 36- Awards: Boston Soc Archit Prize & Class Medal, Mass Inst Technol, 36. Bibliog: Poetry in crystal, 63 & Five masterworks, 72, Steuben Glass. Media: Glass. Mailing Add: Silver Springs Shores 611-A Midway Dr Ocala FL 32670

THOMPSON, (JAMES) BRADBURY
DESIGNER, ART DIRECTOR
b Topeka, Kans, Mar 25, 11. Study: Washburn Univ, AB, 34 & DFA, 65. Comn: Book design for ann of advert art, 43 & 54, graphic arts prod yearbk, 48 & 50, Westvaco Inspirations & Am Classics, 39-75, Homage to the book, 68 & The quality of life, 68; plus many others. Exhib: Int Exhib Graphic Art, Paris, 55, London, 56, Milan, Italy, 61, Amsterdam, 62 & Hamburg, Ger, 64; traveling one-man exhib, Am Inst Graphic Art, 58 & 75. Teaching: Vis critic, Sch Art & Archit, Yale Univ, 56-; bd gov, Philadelphia Col Art, 56-59. Pos: Art dir, Capper Publ, 34-38; art dir, Rogers, Kellogg, Stillson, Inc, 38-41; art dir, Off War Info, 42-45; art dir, Mademoiselle, 45-59; publ art dir, Street & Smith Publ, 45-59; consult, Westvaco Corp, 45-; res dir, Art News & Art News Ann, 45-72; art dir, Living for Young Homemakers, 47-49; consult, Famous Artists Sch, 59-, McGraw Hill Publ, 60-, Time-Life Bks, 64-70, Harvard Bus Rev, 64-67, Field Enterprises Educ Corp, 64- & Cornell Univ, 65-; bd trustees, Washburn Univ, 70; mem citizens stamp adv comt, Fed Design Prog Panel. Awards: Washburn Univ Distinguished Serv Award; Gold T-Square Award, Nat Soc Art Dirs, 50; Am Inst Graphic Arts Medal, 75; multiple awards, Art Dirs Club. Mem: Art Dirs Club (first vpres, exec comt); Soc Illusr; Am Inst Graphic Arts (bd dirs); Alliance Graphique Int; Nat Soc Art Dirs; plus others. Publ: Auth, The Monalphabet, 45 & Alphabet 26, 50. Mailing Add: Jones Park Riverside CT 06878

THOMPSON, JOANNE
PAINTER, SCULPTOR
b Chicago, Ill. Study: Univ Colo. Exhib: Nat Arts Club Gallery, New York, 65-69; Mus Fine Arts, Springfield, Mass, 65-70; Am Artists Prof League Grand Nat, New York, 66-70; Hammond Mus, Westchester, NY, 68. Teaching: Instr oil painting, Americana Galleries, 67-68. Mem: Am Artists Prof League; Artists Guild Chicago; Acad Artists; Catharine Lorillard Wolfe Prof Women's Club. Style & Technique: Paintings: representational; bronze sculptures, whimsical. Media: Oil, Bronze, Conte, Watercolor. Publ: Contribr, illusr & auth, Fun to Sketch with Pencil and Crayon, 73; illusr, Love Circles, reproductions of paintings, 78. Mailing Add: PO Box 5204 Huntington Beach CA 92646

THOMPSON, JUDITH KAY
PAINTER, LECTURER
b Kansas City, Kans, May 28, 40. Study: William Jewell Col, Liberty, Mo, 58-60; Kansas City Art Inst, Mo, 62-65, BFA(painting), study with Wilbur Niewald & Harold Bruder; Univ Cincinnati & Art Acad, Ohio, 65-67, MFA(painting); Aspen Sch Contemp Art, Colo, 68. Exhib: Solo shows, St Cloud State Univ, Kiehl Visual Arts Ctr Gallery, Minn, 74 & Country Gallery, Parkville, Mo, 78; Cincinnati 20th Ann Vicinity Show, Cincinnati Art Mus, 66; Tenth Midwest Bienniel, Joslyn Art Mus, Omaha, Neb, 68; Nat Drawing Invitational, Benedicta Arts Ctr, St Joseph, Minn, 70; 16th Nat Art Round-up, Lorenzi Park Gallery, Las Vegas, Nev, 72; Works on Paper-Women Artists, Brooklyn Mus, NY, 75; Nat Asn Women Artists Spring Ann, Nat Acad Galleries, New York, 76; Artists Choice, Women in the Arts, traveling to New York, Penn, & Va, 76-77; Women Artists 77, Univ Mo Kansas City, 77; Marietta Nat, Ohio, 78. Teaching: Instr painting & drawing, Benedicta Arts Ctr, 69; instr drawing, 2-D design & 3-D design, St Cloud State Univ, 69. Pos: Lectr Women Painters in History, 74-77. Awards: Goldie Paley Award Oil Painting, Nat Asn Women Artists Spring Ann, 76. Mem: Women in the Arts, New York; Nat Asn Women Artists. Style & Technique: Realist or representational; objects in life size or over life size; still-life and figures. Media: Oil. Dealer: Nelson Gallery of Art-Sales and Rental 45th and Oak Kansas City MO 64111. Mailing Add: 2003 NE Vivion Rd Kansas City MO 64118

THOMPSON, KENNETH WEBSTER
ILLUSTRATOR, PAINTER
b New York, NY, Apr 26, 07. Study: Grand Cent Sch Art; also with George Pierce Ennis. Work: Wartime illus, Libr of Cong, Washington, DC. Exhib: Am Watercolor Soc Ann; Soc Illusr; Nantucket Artists Asn; Nat Arts Club; Cerberus Gallery. Awards: Thirteen awards, Chicago Art Dir Club; three awards, NJ Art Dir Club; three awards, Am Inst Graphic Arts; seven awards, incl three medals, NY Art Dir Club; one award, Nat Arts Club. Mem: Life mem Soc Illusr (past dir); life mem Am Watercolor Soc; Nantucket Artists Asn (past dir); Artists Guild (past dir). Media: Gouache, Watercolor. Publ: Illusr, The continent we live on (series), 62-68; illusr, The sea, 66. Mailing Add: 20 W 11th St New York NY 10011

THOMPSON, LOCKWOOD
COLLECTOR
b Cleveland, Ohio, 01. Study: Williams Col, AB, 23; Harvard Law Sch, LLB, 26. Pos: Mem adv coun, Cleveland Mus Art, 49, mem adv bd; co-organizer & 1st pres, Cleveland Soc for Contemp Art, 61; mem int coun, Mus Mod Art, New York, 62; legal coun & mem comn accreditation, Nat Asn Schs Art. Collection: Contemporary art. Mailing Add: 11901 Carlton Rd Cleveland OH 44106

THOMPSON, MALCOLM BARTON
PAINTER, SCULPTOR
b Coraopolis, Pa, Dec 25, 16. Study: Pratt Inst, grad; Art Students League; also illus with Nicholas Riley. Comn: US Army in Action Ser, Pentagon, 49. Exhib: Soc Casein Artists, New York, 70; Slater Mem Mus, Norwich, Conn, 71; Conn Watercolor Soc, Hartford, Conn, 71; Mainstreams '71, Marietta, Ohio, 71; Am Watercolor Soc Traveling Exhibs, 72 & 73. Teaching: Instr watercolor & anat, McLane Art Inst, New York, 38-40. Awards: Marjorie Salembier Award, Conn Classic Arts, 68; First Prize, New Canaan Art Show, 70; Grumbacher Acrylic Award, Am Artists Prof League, 71 & 75. Mem: Am & Conn Watercolor Soc; Silvermine Guild Artists. Style & Technique: Painting my impressions of the beautiful in nature, interpreting the values of sunlight and air. Media: Acrylic, Watercolor. Dealer: Newman Galleries 1625 Walnut St Philadelphia PA 19103; Trend House Gallery 1113 Swan Ave Tampa FL 33606. Mailing Add: RFD 3 Georgetown CT 06829

THOMPSON, NANCY KUNKLE
GOLDSMITH, EDUCATOR
b Marion, Ind, Dec 31, 41. Study: Ball State Teachers Col, BS(art), 63; Ind Univ, MFA(jewelry design & metalsmithing), 68. Work: Ind Univ Mus Art, Bloomington; Greenville Co Mus Art, SC. Exhib: American Jewelry Today, Everhart Mus, Scranton, Pa, 67; For Men Only, Lee Nordness Gallery, New York, 71; Extraordinary Vehicles, J M Kohler Arts Ctr, Sheboygan, Wis, 74; Southeastern Crafts, Greenville Co Mus Art, SC, 74. Teaching: Asst prof jewelry & metalwork, Va Commonwealth Univ, 73- Pos: Richmond rep, WEB, 72-75. Awards: Exp Metalwork, Carnegie Found, 68; Slide Doc of Hist Jewelry-Ornamental Devices, Va Commonwealth Univ, 71. Bibliog: Foreward by Albert Elsen, Experimental Metalsmithing, Portfolio produced by Ind Univ, 68; Geff Reed (auth), Thompson/Kerrigan, Craft Horizons, 72. Mem: Am Crafts Coun; Washington DC Women's Art Registry; Soc NAm Goldsmiths. Style & Technique: Metal fabrication and/or casting techniques; miniature work which utilizes found images or objects. Media: Precious Metals; Nonmetallic Materials. Mailing Add: PO Box 7035 Richmond VA 23221

THOMPSON, PHYLLIS
EDUCATOR, PRINTMAKER
b Washington, DC, Oct 19, 46. Study: Philadelphia Col of Art, BFA, 68; Tyler Sch of Art, Temple Univ, Philadelphia, MFA, 72. Work: Philadelphia Mus of Art, Pa; First Pa Bank Collection, Philadelphia; Carlton Col Collection, Northfield, Minn. Exhib: Group show, Millennium, Mus of the Philadelphia Civic Ctr, 73; Directions in Afro-Am Art, Herbert F Johnson Mus, Ithaca, NY, 74; Benefit exhib, Political Prisoners in SAfrica, Stedelijk Mus, Amsterdam, 75; Carleton Col Art Exhib, Northfield, Minn, 75; The Beautiful Object, Bicentennial Exhib, Philadelphia Col of Art, 75; one-man show, Keystone Jr Col, La Plume, Pa, 76. Collections Arranged: Womens Work: American Art, Mus of the Philadelphia Civic Ctr, 74; Carleton College Art Exhibition, Northfield, Minn, 75; Contemporary Philadelphia Artists from the permanent collection of the Philadelphia Mus of Art, Moore Col of Art, Philadelphia, 75; The Beautiful Object, Bicentennial Exhibition, Philadelphia Col of Art, 76. Teaching: Asst prof printmaking, Cornell Univ, Ithaca, NY, 72-; artist-in-residence printmaking, Art Park, Lewiston, NY, summer 75. Pos: Workshop assoc, The Printmaking Workshop, New York, 76- Awards: Purchase Award, Carleton Col Art Exhib, Northfield, Minn, 75; Humanities Fac Res Grant, Cornell Univ, Ithaca, NY, 75. Mem: Nat Conf of Artists; African Am Inst, Educators to Africa, New York; Brandywine Graphics Workshop, Philadelphia. Style & Technique: Intaglio etchings & silkscreen prints; abstract images influenced by African & Indian design concepts. Media: Viscosity Printing with Color; Crayon Drawing. Mailing Add: Dept of Art Cornell Univ Ithaca NY 14850

THOMPSON, RICHARD CRAIG
PAINTER, SCULPTOR
b McMinnville, Ore, June 27, 45. Study: Ore State Univ, 63-65; Univ NMex, BFA, 67, MA, 72; painting with John Kacere; also lithography with Garo Antresian. Comn: Twenty Sculpture Pieces, Univ Md, 69; Impermanent Sculpture, Mich Arts Coun, Detroit, 74. Exhib: All Kinds of People, Washington Gallery Mod Art, DC, 68; Premise, Premises, Seattle Ctr, Wash, 73; Oregon Artists Under Thirty-Five, Portland Art Mus, Ore, 74; Biennial of Contemp Am Art, Whitney Mus, New York, 75; one-man shows, Univ Mont, Visual Arts Gallery, Missoula, 75 & Tyler Mus of Art, Tex, 78; Hill's Gallery, Santa Fe, NMex, 75-78; Mus NMex, 76-77; Harlan Gallery, Tucson, Ariz, 77; Phoenix Art Mus, Ariz, 77. Teaching: Lectr painting & drawing, Univ Albuquerque, 72-75; vis lectr color, Wayne State Univ, spring 74; instr design-color, Univ NMex, 75. Awards: Second Prize, Southwest Print & Drawing Exhib, 75; Alfred Morang Mem Award, Mus of NMex, 75; Juror's Prize, Phoenix Art Mus, Ariz. Bibliog: Charlotte Moser, New Mexico, open land and psychic elbow room, Artnews, 12/77. Style & Technique: Contemporary landscape and figure situations explored in an expressionistic manner in both two and three dimensions. Media: Mixed Media Constructions & Paintings. Dealer: Hill's Gallery 110 W San Francisco Santa Fe NM 87501. Mailing Add: 525 Wellesley SE Albuquerque NM 87106

THOMPSON, RICHARD E, JR
ART DEALER, COLLECTOR
b Oak Park, Ill, Dec 30, 39. Study: Univ Wis. Collections Arranged: Richard Thompson, Sr, 77. Pos: Dir, Richard Thompson Gallery, San Francisco, 77- Mem: Mus Soc of San Francisco. Specialty: Nineteenth-twentieth century American impressionists. Collection: Richard Thompson, Sr and Edward Potthast. Publ: Auth, Richard Thompson American Impressionist, privately publ, 77. Mailing Add: 80 Maiden Lane San Francisco CA 94108

THOMPSON, RICHARD EARL, SR
COLLECTOR, PAINTER
b Oak Park, Ill, Sept 26, 14. Study: Chicago Acad of Fine Arts, 30-31; Am Acad of Art, Chicago, 32-33; Art Inst of Chicago, 44. Work: Brigham Young Univ Collection, Salt Lake City, Utah; Johns Hopkins Hosp Collection, Baltimore, Md; Marquette Univ Collection, Milwaukee, Wis; Naval Art Collection, Pentagon, Washington, DC; Sears Roebuck Collection, Chicago. Comn: Portrait, comn by Casey Lambert, Lambert Pharmaceuticals, 73; landscape, comn by Joseph Uehline, Schlitz Brewing, Co, Milwaukee, Wis, 75; portraits, comn by Peter Marquardt, Mexico City, 75, Arthur MacArthur, Janesville, Wis, 75 & John Forester, Wausau, Wis for Yawkey-Woodson Mus, 76. Exhib: Bergstrom Art Ctr, Neenah, Wis, 65; Vincent Price Collection of Fine Art, USA, 65; Knickerbocker Artists, New York, 77. Teaching: Instr oil painting, Am Acad of Art, Chicago, 35-37. Pos: Painting mem, Pallette & Chisel Club, Chicago, 39-41. Awards: Nat High Sch Poster Contest, 32; George Washington Poster Contest, 32. Style & Technique: Landscape, figurative impressionist. Media: Oil on Canvas, Pastel and Charcoal. Collection: Homer, Loiseau, Murphy, J Francis, Jean Simon, Andrew Zorn; American impressionist painters. Publ: Contribr, Milwaukee J, 68-74; contribr (cover), Yankee Mag, spring 76 & fall 76. Mailing Add: 80 Maiden Lane San Francisco CA 94108

THOMPSON, ROBERT CHARLES
PAINTER, EDUCATOR
b Conroe, Tex, Nov 5, 36. Study: Univ Tex, BFA; Stephen F Austin State Univ, MA & MFA. Work: Southeast Ark Arts & Sci Ctr, Pine Bluff; First Nat Bank, Conway; Witte Mus, San Antonio, Tex; Pulaski Fed Savings & Loan Asn, Little Rock. Exhib: Young Artists Am, Xavier Univ, 60; Miniature Painter, Sculptors & Gravers Nat, Washington, DC, 68; Small Painting Nat Exhib, Univ Pac, 70; 4th Ann Nat Print & Drawing, Northern Ill Univ, 71; Ann Mid-South Exhib, Brooks Gallery, Memphis, Tenn, 71. Teaching: Asst prof art & art hist, Univ Cent Ark, 68- Awards: Tex Watercolor Soc Purchase Award, 65; Invitational Exhib Award, 13th Ann Ark Festival Arts, 70 & First Place Oils & Acrylics, 16th Ann, 73. Style & Technique: Representational style within an abstract emotional framework. Media: Oil, Acrylic, Watercolor. Mailing Add: Rte 3 Box 438 Conway AR 72032

THOMPSON, TAMARA (TAMARA THOMPSON BRYANT)
PAINTER, INSTRUCTOR
b Anderson, Ind, Apr 8, 35. Study: Univ Ky, BA(with hon in art); Ind Univ, MFA & study with Leon Golub, Creighton Gilbert & Rudy Pozzatti. Work: Ind Univ, Bloomington; Colgate Univ; Univ Ky; Headley Mus, Lexington, Ky. Exhib: One-man shows, Univ Ky & Ind Univ, Bloomington, 59 & NY Univ, Heights Campus, 64; 17 Connecticut Artists, Wadsworth Atheneum, Hartford, 60; Colgate Univ, 73 & 76; Arts of Cent New York 36th & 38th Ann, Munson-Williams-Proctor Inst, Utica, 73 & 75. Teaching: Instr art, Univ Ky, 65-66; instr fine arts, Colgate Univ, 72- Pos: Dir art classes, Wadsworth Atheneum, 59-61; vis artist in residence, Univ Ky, 65. Awards: First Prize, Hartford Soc Women Painters, 60 & 61. Bibliog: Exhib rev in Time Mag, New York Ed, 5/22/64. Style & Technique: Nonobjective painting; assemblage and collages. Media: Oil, Acrylic; Fabric & Mixed Media. Publ: Contribr, Drawings of the Italian Renaissance, Ind Univ, 58. Mailing Add: Box 54 Poolville NY 13432

THOMPSON, WADE
PAINTER, EDUCATOR
b Moorhead, Minn, July 30, 46. Study: Macalester Col, with Jerry Rudquist, BA, 68; Bowling Green State Univ, with Robert Mazur, MA, 71, MFA, 72. Work: Macalester Col; Bowling Green State Univ; Provincetown Art Asn, Mass; Sch Law, Temple Univ. Exhib: 17th Nat Exhib, Fall River Art Asn, Mass, 74; 63rd Nat Exhib, Laguna Gloria Art Mus, Austin, Tex, 74; Arena '74 Nat Exhib, Binghamton, NY, 74; one-man shows, Arnot Mus Art, Elmira, NY, 75 & Second Story Spring St Soc Gallery, New York, 76; 76 Nat Am Drawing Biennial (traveling exhib), Smithsonian Inst, Washington, DC, 76; Hansen Galleries, New York, 77; Alnico Gallery, New York, 77. Teaching: Asst prof art, Tyler Sch Art, Temple Univ, 72- Pos: Designer, Assoc Design, St Paul, Minn, 70-71. Awards: First Prize Merit in Painting, Arena '74 Nat Exhib, 74; Best of Show, Nat Cape Coral Art Exhib, Fla, 76; Purchase Award, Nat Graphics Competition, ProvinceProvincetown Art Asn, Mass, 76. Bibliog: Arena '74, WBNG-TV, Binghamton, NY, 74; Judith Hemphill (auth), People, Elmira Today, NY, 75; Madeleine Burnside (auth), rev in E Side Express, New York, 77. Mem: Col Art Asn Am; Am Asn Univ Prof. Style & Technique: Abstract expressionist, large canvases, gesture, movement, power and drama. Media: Acrylic, Mixed, Charcoal. Publ: Illusr, Prospectus, Minn Educ Asn, 70; illusr, Governor's Conference on Environmental Education, St Cloud, Minn, 70. Dealer: Alnico Gallery 123 Prince St New York NY 10012. Mailing Add: 313 Edgewood Dr Ambler PA 19002

THOMPSON, WILLIAM JOSEPH
EDUCATOR, SCULPTOR
b Denver, Colo, Apr 19, 26. Study: RI Sch Design, BFA, with Vladimir Raemaesch; Cranbrook Acad Art, MFA, with William McVey; Art Students League, Woodstock, NY, summer, with Kuniyoshi. Work: Bronze sculptures, Columbus Mus Fine Arts, Ohio, Ga Art Comn, Atlanta, Ga Mus, Athens, Pembroke State Col & Ga Power Co, Atlanta. Comn: Limestone relief, comn by architect for St Christopher's Church, Columbus, Ohio, 62; four portal high relief, First Congregational Church, Columbus, 64; portrait figure of J F Kennedy, Univ Dayton, 64; bronze portrait figure (14 ft) of R B Russell, State of Ga, 73-75; bronze group, Gov Comt for Ga Prisoner of War Mem, Americus, Ga, 73-76. Exhib: 20th, 21st & 22nd Southeastern Ann Exhibs, High Mus, Atlanta, 65, 66 & 67; one-man exhib, Grand Cent Mod, New York, 66; Southern Sculpture 67; Smithsonian Inst Traveling Exhib, 69-70; Ga Artists Exhib, High Mus, Atlanta, 72 & 74. Teaching: From instr to asst prof sculpture, Ohio State Univ, 54-64; from assoc prof to prof sculpture & drawing, Univ Ga, 64-, mem grad fac, 66- Pos: Chmn art comt, Archdiocese of Atlanta Liturgy Comt, 66-69. Awards: First Prize in Sculpture, Columbus Mus Fine Arts, 56; Columbus Chap, Am Inst Architects Award for Comn: St Andrew, 60; First Prize, Southern Sculpture 67. Bibliog: Articles in La Rev Mod, Paris, 68 & Atlanta Mag, Inc, 74. Mem: Nat Acad Design. Style & Technique: Strong organic form; carving in stone and wood, modeling for bronze. Media: Bronze; Carving. Mailing Add: 120 Cedar Circle Athens GA 30601

THOMSON, CARL L
PAINTER, DESIGNER
b Brooklyn, NY, Mar 6, 13. Study: Pratt Inst, with Arthur Schweider. Work: Salmagundi Club; Burr Artists Group. Exhib: Salmagundi Club Ann Watercolor & Oil Shows, 59-72. Teaching: Instr drawing, Salmagundi Club, 61-63. Pos: Advert designer, C Thomson Assoc, 47-59; art dir, Am Home Prod Corp, 59-70; owner, Thomson Studio & Gallery, New York, 70- Awards: Graphic Arts Award, Printing Industs Am, 69; Cert Spec Merit, Printing Industs Metrop New York, 70. Mem: Salmagundi Club (vpres & mem bd dirs). Media: Watercolor. Specialty: Contemporary and representational fine art. Mailing Add: 19 E 75th St New York NY 10021

THOMSON, WILLIAM DAVID
PAINTER
b Bristol, Conn, Mar 16, 31. Study: With Ernst Lohrmann, Meriden, Conn; Paier Art Sch, New Haven. Work: Butler Inst, Youngstown, Ohio; New Britain Mus Am Art, Conn; Williams Col, Mass; Berkshire Mus, Pittsfield, Mass; De Cordova Mus, Lincoln, Mass. Exhib: New York World's Fair, 65; Silvermine Guild New Eng; Am Watercolor Soc; Nat Acad; De Cordova Exhib-Humanism in New Eng. Awards: Ranger Fund Purchase Award, Nat Acad; Gold Medals, Allied Artists & Audubon Artists. Mem: Am Watercolor Soc; Conn Acad Fine Arts. Style & Technique: Expressive humanism. Media: Water Medium; Serigraphy. Mailing Add: 115 Arlington St Bristol CT 06010

THON, WILLIAM
PAINTER
b New York, NY, Aug 8, 06. Study: Art Students League, 24-25; Bates Col, hon DFA, 57. Work: Metrop Mus Art; Butler Inst Am Art; Munson-Williams-Proctor Inst, Utica, NY; Calif Palace of Legion of Honor, San Francisco; plus over 45 major US mus. Exhib: Corcoran Gallery Art, Washington, DC; Pa Acad Fine Arts, Philadelphia; Va Mus Fine Arts, Richmond; Art Inst Chicago; Whitney Mus Am Art, New York; plus many others. Pos: Trustee, Am Acad in Rome. Awards: Dawson Medal, Philadelphia Watercolor Club, 68; Altman Prize, Nat Acad Design, 69; Gold Medal of Honor, Am Watercolor Soc, 70; plus many others. Mem: Assoc Nat Acad Design; Salmagundi Club; Brooklyn Soc Art; Nat Inst Arts & Lett; Am Acad Arts & Lett. Dealer: Midtown Galleries 11 E 57th St New York NY 10022. Mailing Add: Port Clyde ME 04855

THORNDIKE, CHARLES JESSE (CHUCK)
CARTOONIST, WRITER
b Seattle, Wash, Jan 20, 97. Study: Univ Wash; Seattle Art Sch; Calif Sch Fine Arts; also with Lee F Randolph, Rudolph Schaefer, Harold Von Schmidt & Johonnot. Work: Smithsonian Inst, Washington, DC; Mus Natural Hist, New York; Mus Arts & Sci, Miami; Cartoonists Exchange, Pleasant Hill, Ohio; Washington Sch Art, DC. Exhib: Cartoon Mus, Orlando, Fla Travelling Exhib US Army, Europe; Celebrity Caricatures, Jockey Club, Miami, 73-76. Teaching: Instr cartooning & com art, Com Art Sch, 34-35, New York Sch Design, 35-36, Terry Art Sch, Miami, Fla, 49-51 & Univ Miami, 51- Pos: Art dir, Gen Motors Acceptance Corp, New York, 28-31; art dir, US Navy, 41-46. Mem: Jockey Club, Miami. Interest: Contributed 1,000 originals to colleges and collectors around the country, 77. Publ: Auth & illusr, The secrets of cartooning, House Little Bks, 35, The art of cartooning, 36, The art and use of the poster, 37, Arts and crafts for children, 38 & Oddities of nature (syndicated newspaper feature), 48. Mailing Add: 11660 Canal Dr North Miami FL 33161

THORNE, GORDON (KIT)
PAINTER, DESIGNER
b Stanway, Eng, Aug 21, 96; Can citizen. Study: Vancouver Sch Art, with Scott, Varley & McDonald; Goldsmiths Col, with Speed, Gardner & Stanley Anderson. Work: Centennial Mus, Vancouver, BC; Leningrad Arts, Russia; Vancouver Pub Libr; Lipsett Mus, Vancouver; Vancouver Art Gallery; Libr of Cong, Washington, DC. Comn: Blackstone Hotel, Vancouver, 68; Railway Mens Club, Vancouver, 72. Exhib: Western Art Circle, Vancouver, 52-71; Can Visual Arts, Toronto, 60-70; Fedn of Can Artists; one-man & quarterly group shows, Vancouver Art Gallery. Teaching: Instr art, Fedn Can Artists, 52-56. Mem: Charter mem & life mem Vancouver Mus Asn; Fedn of Can Artists; co-founder & life mem Western Art Circle; Can Painters & Etchers. Style & Technique: Realism into fantasy; abstract impressions, free technique. Media: Acrylic, Watercolor. Publ: Auth, Occasional notes of Vancouver and Victoria, 68; auth, Strolling and sketching, McNeil. Dealer: Art Emporium 2956 Granville St Vancouver BC Can; Artists of BC Gallery Vancouver BC Can. Mailing Add: 1460 Nelson St Vancouver BC V6G 1L8 Can

THORNHILL, ANNA
SCULPTOR, PAINTER
b Berlin, Ger, Aug 2, 40; Brit citizen. Study: St Martins Sch Art, London, dipl design; Royal Col Art, London, ARCA. Work: World Bank, Washington, DC; Hong Kong Mus Art; Hofstra Univ. Comn: Mosaic mural, P&O Shipping Lines, Ocean Terminal, Hong Kong, 66; two murals, August Films, Hq, New York, 69; mural, Johnson, Stokes & Master, Hong Kong, 69; painted sculpture, Wells TV, Hq, New York, 72; wall mural, Larry Spegel Productions, Tarzana, Calif, 73; tapestry, Ashland Oil. Exhib: Royal Acad Art, London, 62-64; County Hall, London, 63; Young Contemporaries, London; Brighton Mus Art, Eng, 64; one-woman show, Meisel Gallery, New York, 73; A Multi-Media Evening, Guggenheim Mus, New York, 77. Bibliog: Monogr on WOR-TV Prog, 72, 73 & NBC-TV Prog, 74; J R Klevin (auth), The Incredible Turned-On World of Anna Thornhill, Dialogue Systs, Inc, 74. Style & Technique: Multimedia, multi-material constructions and painted assemblages. Media: Wood; Plastic. Dealer: Louis K Meisel 141 Prince St New York NY 10012. Mailing Add: 205 Prince St New York NY 10012

THORNS, JOHN CYRIL, JR
DESIGNER, PAINTER
b Denver, Colo, Apr 14, 26. Study: Ft Hays State Univ, BA; Ind Univ, with Henry Hope & George Rickey, MA(art hist); Univ Iowa, with John Schulze & Lester Longman, MFA(archit design). Work: Hastings Col, Nebr; Friends of Art Collection, Kans State Univ; Marian Col, Wis; Hansen Mus, Logan, Kans. Comn: Bldg design, First Presby Church, Hays, Kans, 74; campanile design, Campus, Ft Hays Kans State Col, 75. Exhib: Kans Designers Show, Univ Kans, 55-63; Nat Decoration Arts Show, Wichita Art Asn Gallery, 58 & Kans Watercolor Soc, 72, 73, 74 & 75; Am Craftsman Coun Exhib, Mus Contemp Crafts, New York, 62 & 63; Watercolor USA, Springfield Art Mus, Mo, 63 & 64. Teaching: Mem fac, Ft Hays State Univ, 54-72, prof art hist & design & chmn dept art, 72- Pos: Pres, Hays Arts Coun, Kans, 72-74. Awards: Award Winner, Exhib Brochure Ser, Mid-Am Dist, Am Col Pub Rels Asn, 63; Cent State Bank Purchase Award for Collage Undergrowth, Kans Watercolor Soc Show, 74. Mem: Col Art Asn Am; Delta Phi Delta (ed, 66-70, pres, 70-73); Kans Watercolor Soc; Kans Art Educ Asn. Style & Technique: Landscape: Europe, Southwest, Plains. Media: Collage; Acrylic; Watercolor. Publ: Illusr, Frontier Mag, 57-62; contribr, Ft Hays Studies, Ser 1 & 2, 60 & 66, Ft Hays State Univ; ed, The Palette, spring 66-70 & 73. Mailing Add: 1103 Country Club Dr Hays KS 67601

THRALL, ARTHUR
PRINTMAKER, EDUCATOR
b Milwaukee, Wis, Mar 18, 26. Study: Wis State Col, Milwaukee, BS & MS; Univ Wis-Madison; Univ Ill, Urbana; Ohio State Univ. Work: Brit Mus, London, Eng; Libr Cong, Washington, DC; Art Inst Chicago; Brooklyn Mus, NY; Tate Gallery, London, Eng. Comn: 100 print ed, New York Hilton Hotel, 62. Exhib: Carnegie Inst Int Print Exhib, Pittsburgh, 51; Young American Printmakers, Mus Mod Art, New York, 53; one-man show, Smithsonian Inst, 60; 160th Ann, Pa Acad Art, Philadelphia, 64; 143rd Ann, Nat Acad Design, New York, 67. Teaching: Assoc prof art, Milwaukee-Downer Col, 56-64; prof art, Lawrence Univ, 64-; vis prof art, Univ Wis-Madison, 66-67. Awards: Louis Comfort Tiffany Found Fel Graphics, 63; Purchase Award, Brooklyn Mus 14th Ann, 63; Cannon Prize, Nat Acad Design 143rd Ann, 67. Bibliog: M Fish (auth), Arthur Thrall, Wis Architect, 65; D Anderson (auth), The Art of Written Forms, Holt Rinehart & Winston, 69. Mem: Soc Am Graphic Artists; Boston Printmakers; Audubon Artists. Media: Intaglio; Oil and Watercolor. Dealer: Associated American Artists 663 Fifth Ave New York NY 10022; Graphics Gallery 3 Embarcadero Ctr San Francisco CA 94111. Mailing Add: 59 Bellaire Ct Appleton WI 54911

THRELKELD, DALE
PAINTER, INSTRUCTOR
b Mo, Apr 11, 44. Study: Northeast Mo State Col, BS, 66; Ball State Univ, MA, 70; Southern Ill Univ, Edwardsville, MFA, 75. Work: Dulin Gallery Art, Knoxville, Tenn; Ark Arts Ctr, Little Rock; Brooklyn Mus of Art, NY; Ill State Mus, Springfield; St Lawrence Univ; Univ of the South. Exhib: Three Artists, Mitchell Mus of Art; Works on Paper, Krannert Gallery, Ind, 73; New Talent Exhib, Gimpel & Weitzenhoffer Gallery, New York, 74; Los Angeles Print Soc Nat Print Exhib, 74; 28th Ann Ill Invitational, Ill State Mus, 75; Unique Works on Paper, van Straaten Gallery, Chicago, 75. Teaching: Art instr drawing, Belleville Area Col, Ill, 71- Awards: Purchase Awards, Dulin Gallery Art, 70, Ark Arts Ctr, 71 & Ill State Mus, 75. Style & Technique: Varied. Media: Mixed Media. Dealer: Roy Boyd Gallery 233 E Ontario Chicago IL; van Straaten Gallery 646 N Michigan Ave Chicago IL 60611. Mailing Add: 24 Hilldale Dr Belleville IL 62223

THURLOW, FEARN CUTLER
CURATOR
b West Chester, Pa, Dec 5, 24. Study: Vassar Col, 42-44; Drew Univ, BA, 67; Newark Mus Trainee, 67; Rutgers Univ, 70-72. Teaching: Instr art hist, Drew Univ, Madison, NJ, 70-72. Pos: Coordr art sem, Drew Univ, 68-70, cur univ collection, 70-72; asst cur painting & sculpture, Newark Mus, NJ, 73, cur painting & sculpture, 73- Mem: Am Asn Mus; NE Mus Conf; Am Fedn Arts; Victorian Soc Am. Res: American painting and sculpture. Publ: Auth (catalogue), J Alden Weir, Montclair Art Mus, 72; auth, Newark's sculpture, Newark Mus Quart, winter 75; co-auth, As The Seasons Turn: Southwest Indian Easel Painting and Related Arts, Newark Mus Quart, spring, 77. Mailing Add: RD 2 Mendham NJ 07945

THURSTON, JACQUELINE BEVERLY
PHOTOGRAPHER, EDUCATOR
b Cincinnati, Ohio, Jan 27, 39. Study: Carnegie-Mellon Univ, BFA(painting), 61; Stanford Univ, MA(painting), 62. Work: Int Mus of Photog, George Eastman House, Rochester, NY; Oakland Mus, Calif; Univ NMex Mus, Albuquerque; plus many pvt collections. Comn: Photographs & paintings with Ralph Morocco & Wayne Hoy, comn by Western Electric for City of San Jose, San Jose Munic Airport, 74. Exhib: Contemp Photogr VII (travelling exhib), Int Mus of Photography, George Eastman House, Rochester, NY 72; Observations/Translations—Four Photogr, Oakland Mus, Calif, 72; Two Photogr, Oakland Mus, 75; Photography 2, Jack Glenn Gallery, Newport Beach, Calif, 75; Am Photogr: Past into Present, Seattle Mus of Art, Wash, 76; one-person show, Susan Spiritus Gallery, Newport Beach, 77. Teaching: Prof design & printmaking, San Jose State Univ, Calif, 75- Awards: Nat Endowment for the Arts Photogr Fel, 76 & 78. Mem: Soc Photographic Educators. Style & Technique: Small scale black and white photographic prints. Publ: Co-auth with Ronald Carraher, Optical Illusions and the Visual Arts, Van Nostrand Reinhold, 66. Mailing Add: 1321 Crane St Menlo Park CA 94025

THWAITES, CHARLES WINSTANLEY
PAINTER
b Milwaukee, Wis, Mar 12, 04. Study: Univ Wis; Layton Sch Art. Work: Univ Wis; Gimbel Collection; Edgar Kaufman Collection; Milwaukee Art Ctr. Comn: Murals, US Post Off, Greenville, Mich, Plymouth & Chilton, Wis & Windom, Minn; portraits, pres of St John's Col, Annapolis, Md & Santa Fe, NMex; mural designs for fed bldgs, Pub Bldgs Admin. Exhib: Eight shows, Mus NMex, Santa Fe, 55-68; one-man show, St John's Col, 65; Southwest Biennials, 66-68; Fedn Rocky Mountain States Eight States Exhib, 68; Carnegie Inst Int; Nat Gallery Art; Chicago Art Inst; Corcoran Biennials, Washington, DC; Pa Acad Fine Arts; Metrop Mus Art, New York; Whitney Mus Am Art, New York; Nat Acad Design, New York; Walker Art Ctr, Minneapolis; Palace of the Legion of Honor, San Francisco; Nelson-Atkins Gallery, Kansas City; Colorado Springs Fine Arts Ctr, Colo; Mus NMex, Santa Fe; Univ Minn Traveling Exhib of Govt Art 1930-1940, 77-78; plus many other nat & regional exhibs. Pos: Artist in residence, St John's Col, Santa Fe, NMex, 73-74. Awards: Forty-eight State Mural Competition Prize, 39; Prizes & Medal, Calif Palace of Legion of Honor, 46. Bibliog: Article in The Studio, London, Eng, Vol 131, No 634; Dr Francis V O'Connor (auth), Federal art patronage, Univ Md, 66; Forbes Watson (auth), American painting today, Am Fedn Arts. Style & Technique: Non-objective in a flexible range of techniques. Mailing Add: Box 4454 Santa Fe NM 87502

TIBBS, THOMAS S
LECTURER
b Indianapolis, Ind, Aug 30, 17. Study: Univ Rochester, AB & MFA; Columbia Univ. Exhib: Craftsmanship in a Changing World, 56; Louis Comfort Tiffany Retrospective, 58; Six Decades of American Painting, 61; Affect & Effect, 68; Jose de Rivera Forty Year Retrospective, 72. Teaching: Lectr art hist, Calif State Univ, San Diego, 69- Pos: Assoc dir educ, Rochester Mem Art Gallery, 47-52; dir, Huntington Galleries, WVa, 52-56; dir, Mus Contemp Crafts, New York, 56-60; dir, Des Moines Art Ctr, Iowa, 60-68; dir, La Jolla Mus Contemp Art, 68-73. Mem: Am Asn Mus; Asn Art Mus Dir; fel Royal Soc Art, London. Mailing Add: Dept of Art San Diego State Univ San Diego CA 92115

TICE, GEORGE ANDREW
PHOTOGRAPHER, AUTHOR
b Newark, NJ, Oct 13, 38. Study: Newark Vocational & Tech High Sch, NJ, 55. Work: Metrop Mus of Art, New York; Mus of Mod Art, New York; Art Inst of Chicago; Bibliot Nat, Paris, France; Victoria & Albert Mus, London, Eng. Comn: Two 55ft photog murals, Field Mus of Natural Hist, Chicago, 75; three wall photographs, Miami Int Airport, Fla, 77. Exhib: Five one-man shows, Witkin Gallery, New York, 69-77; one-man shows, Art Inst of Chicago, 71, Metrop Mus of Art, New York, 72, NJ State Mus, Trenton, 76, Susan Spiritus Gallery, Newport Beach, Calif, 76 & Werkstatt fur Fotografie, Berlin, WGer, 77; group shows, Smithsonian Inst, Washington, DC, 73 & Whitney Mus of Am Art, New York, 74. Teaching: Instr master class photog, The New Sch, New York, 70- Awards: Grand Prix, Festival d'Arles, France, 73; Nat Endowment for Arts Fel, 73; Guggenheim Fel, 73-74. Media: Photographs; Photography Books. Publ: Co-auth, Fields of Peace, Doubleday, 70; auth, Paterson, Rutgers Univ, 72; co-auth, Seacoast Maine, Doubleday, 73; auth, Urban Landscapes, Rutgers Univ, 75; auth, Artie Van Blarcum, Addison House, 77. Dealer: The Witkin Gallery 41 E 57th St New York NY 10022. Mailing Add: 323 Gill Lane 9B Iselin NJ 08830

TIERNEY, PATRICK LENNOX
ART HISTORIAN, EDUCATOR
b Weston, WVa, Jan 28, 14. Study: Univ of Calif, Los Angeles, EdB(cum laude), 36; Columbia Univ, New York, MA, 44; Sogetsu-Ryu, Tokyo, Japan, Seizan I, 52. Teaching: Chmn arts fac, Pasadena City Col, Calif, 46-71; lectr, Univ of Calif, Los Angeles & San Diego, 52-71; assoc dean col of fine arts & prof hist of Oriental art, Univ of Utah, 71- Awards: Emmy, Acad Television Arts & Sci, 67; Honors Citation, Resolution of Bd of Trustees, Pasadena City Col, Calif, 71. Mem: Pacificulture Found, Pasadena, Calif (dir, mus div, 61-70, mem bd dir, Asian Mus, 61-); Acad of Television Arts & Sci; Salt Lake Art Ctr (mem bd dir, 71-); Japan-Am Soc, Southern Calif (dir, 72-). Res: Folk art of Japan. Publ: Co-auth, Japan, Int Publ, 58; co-auth, Chanoyu, as a form of non literary art criticism, Chanoyu J, Kyoto, 76. Mailing Add: 3758 Adonis Dr Salt Lake City UT 84117

TIETZ, EVELYNE
PAINTER
b Grants, NMex. Study: Finch Col, with Leon Kroll & Louise Stinnet; Univ Ariz, BFA(art educ); Cappello Sch Art, Florence, Italy, with Gastone Canessa; also with Ramon Froman & Nathan Robinson. Work: El Paso Mus Art; Oshkosh Mus, Wis; plus many in pvt collections. Comn: Oil painting, El Paso Symphony Debutante Ball, 75. Exhib: El Paso Art Asn, 69; El Paso Mus Art, 60-73; Benedictine Brandy Co Exhib, New York, 70-74; Midwest Biennial, Omaha, 73. Teaching: Teacher art, Tucson, Phoenix & El Paso Pub Schs, 5 yrs. Awards: Best in Oil, El Paso Art Asn, 69; Sun Carnival Show Purchase Prize, El Paso Mus Art, 69; Benedictine Brandy Co Art Awards, 70, 73 & 74. Mem: El Paso Art Asn; Tex Art Asn; Am Fedn Arts; Nat Soc Arts & Lett. Style & Technique: Contemporary realism; portraits. Media: Oil. Dealer: Two Twenty Two Gallery Fortune Coronado Towers Mesa St El Paso TX 79912. Mailing Add: 711 Rim Rd El Paso TX 79902

TIFFANY, MARGUERITE BRISTOL
PAINTER, WEAVER
b Syracuse, NY. Study: Syracuse Univ, BS; Columbia Univ, MA; Newark Sch Fine & Appl Arts, cert; Parsons Sch, New York, cert; NY Univ; also with Emile Walters, Iceland & William Zoroch, New York. Exhib: NJ State Ann, Montclair Mus, 33, 34, 35 & 37; Ogunquit Art Ctr Ann, Maine, 41-70; Am Artistic Prof League Ann, Spring Lake, NJ, 41-71; Newark Mus, 72 & 76; Gotham Painters, New York, 74-78; plus 5 one-woman shows, NJ. Teaching: Prof art, Rutgers Univ, 25-40; William Paterson Col, 29-56; Fairleigh Dickinson Univ, 56-65. Pos: Art Comt, NJ chmn, Metrop Opera Guild, 52-58; state pres, Nat League Am Penwomen, 66-68; NJ state pres, Assoc Handweavers, 68-70. Awards: Cert, contrib art educ, Eastern Arts Asn, 60; hon mention ribbon, State Fedn Womens Clubs NJ, 72. Mem: Am Artists Prof League, NJ Chap; Paterson Art League; Eastern Arts Asn; Gotham Painters; Int Miniature Soc. Style & Technique: Representative. Media: Oil, Watercolor. Publ: Auth, Art and picture study (monogr), NJ Dept Educ, 30; Educ Mag (art issue), 2/46; contribr, Art education in principle and practice, 33; Art room planning guide, Dept Educ, Trenton, NJ, 60-63; illusr, two articles, Newark Sunday News, 4/12 & 4/14/70. Mailing Add: 330 E 33rd St Paterson NJ 07504

TIFT, MARY LOUISE
PRINTMAKER
b Seattle, Wash, Jan 2, 13. Study: Univ Wash, BFA; Art Ctr Col Design; San Francisco State Col. Work: Philadelphia Mus Art, Pa; Brooklyn Mus, NY; Seattle Art Mus, Wash; Achenbach Print Collection, San Francisco Palace Legion of Honor; Bell Tel Co Ill Print & Drawing Collection, Chicago; Libr of Cong, Washington, DC. Exhib: 2nd Brit Biennale Prints, Yorkshire, Eng, 70; 5th Int Triennal Colored Graphics, Grenchen, Switz, 70; Graphics 71, circulated by Smithsonian Inst; 5th Int Print Biennale, Cracow, Poland, 72; 1st Int Print Biennale, Segouia, Spain, 74; US Mission to UN, Geneva, Switz, 74; World Print Competition, San Francisco Mus of Mod Art & tour in US & Can, 77; one-man show, Gumps' Gallery, San Francisco, Calif, 77. Teaching: Asst prof design, Calif Col Arts & Crafts, Oakland, 49-57. Pos: Coordr design, San Francisco Art Inst, 57-60. Awards: Purchase Awards, Northwest Printmakers Int, 69, Print Club Philadelphia, 69 & 74 & Nat Exhib Prints, Nat Gallery, Washington, DC, 73. Mem: Calif Soc Printmakers (coun mem, 70-72); Los Angeles Printmakers Soc; Print Club Philadelphia. Style & Technique: Romantic realism and colorist. Media: Etching, Silkscreen. Mailing Add: 607 Chapman Dr Corte Madera CA 94925

TIGERMAN, STANLEY
PAINTER, ARCHITECT
b Chicago, Ill, Sept, 20, 30. Study: Mass Inst Technol, 48-49; Inst Design, 49-50; Yale Univ, BArch, 60 & MArch, 61. Comn: Modular structure, Metrop Structures, Chicago, 71. Exhib: Soc Contemp Artists Show, Art Inst Chicago, 65; Eight Chicago Artists, Walker Art Ctr, Minneapolis, Minn, 65; one-man shows, Evanston Art Ctr, Ill, 69, Art Res Ctr, Kansas City, Mo, 69 & Springfield Arts Asn, Ill, 70. Teaching: Prof archit & art, Univ Ill, Chicago Circle, 65-71. Pos: Prin, Stanley Tigerman & Assocs, Chicago, 62- Awards: Graham Found Fel

advan study fine arts, 65; Honor Awards, Nat Am Inst Architects & Housing & Urban Develop, 70 & Chicago Chap Am Inst Architects, 71. Bibliog: R A M Stern (auth), New Directions in American Architecture, Braziller, 69; Faulkner & Ziegfield (auth), Art Today, Holt, Rinehart & Winston, 69; Dahinden (auth), Urban Structures of the Future, Praeger, 72. Mem: Am Inst Architects; Yale Art Asn (past pres); Ill Arts Coun; Yale Club NY; Arts Club Chicago. Media: Acrylic. Publ: Contribr, Young architects in America, Zodiac Int, 64; contribr, Instant city, Archit J Hui, 66; contribr, City shape 21, Toshi Jutaku, Tokyo, 68; auth, Formal generators of structure, Leonardo Mag, 68. Mailing Add: 920 N Michigan Ave Chicago IL 60611

TILLENIUS, CLARENCE (INGWALL)
PAINTER, WRITER
b Sandridge, Man, Aug 31, 13. Study: Teulon Col, with A J Musgrove; Univ Winnipeg, hon LLD, 70. Comn: Collection of wildlife painting, Monarch Life Assurance Co, Winnipeg, 54-75; dioramas, habitat groups, Nat Mus Can, Ottawa, Ont, 60-72, BC Mus, Victoria, 65-70 & Mus Alta, Edmonton, 72-74; dioramas, paintings, Man Mus Man & Nature, Winnipeg, 69-75. Exhib: Two one-man shows, London Art Gallery, London Shute Inst, 54; one-man exhib, Monarch Life Bldg, 62, Whitney Gallery Western Art, Cody, Wyo, 64, Man Mus Man & Nature, 74 & Glenbow-Alta Inst, 75. Teaching: Lectr art appreciation, Man, 50-52; lectr wildlife painters, Glenbow Inst, 70; dir wildlife drawings, Okanagan Summer Sch Arts, Penticton, BC, 73- Pos: Diorama dir, Nat Mus Can, Ottawa, 62-72. Awards: Man Centennial Medal Honor, Gov Gen, Prov Man, 72. Bibliog: Walter Wilwerding (auth), Clarence Tillenius, Illustrator, 52; Peter Kelly & Paul Guyot (co-auth), Tillenius on the Prairies (film), Can Broadcasting Corp, 63; Eric Mitchell (auth), Clarence Tillenius, Nature Can Mag, 73. Mem: Soc Animal Artists; life mem Man Naturalist Soc (pres & past pres). Style & Technique: Impressionistic; watercolor freely handled; pen and ink, charcoal, drybrush, detailed but loosely rendered realistic. Media: Oil, Watercolor. Res: Lifetime study of wild animals, wilderness travels across North America into Yukon and the arctic. Publ: Illusr, Little Giant, 51; illusr & auth, Fur Bearers of Canada, 51; illusr & auth, Monarchs of the Canadian Wilds, 54-75; auth, Sketchpad Out of Doors, 2 eds, 56-62; illusr, Orphan of the North, 58. Dealer: Loch Art Gallery 306 St Marys Rd Winnipeg MB Can. Mailing Add: 441 Dominion St Winnipeg MB R3G 3M8 Can

TILLEY, LEWIS LEE
PAINTER, FILM MAKER
b Parrott, Ga, May 17, 21. Study: High Mus Sch Art, 37-39; Emory Univ, 37-39; Univ Ga, BFA, 42; Colorado Springs Fine Arts Ctr, with Boardman Robinson, Adolph Dehn & John Held, 42-45; Inst Allende, Mex, MFA, 68. Work: Post Card No 2, Colorado Springs Fine Arts Ctr, Colo; Canon City Art Ctr, Colo; State Fair Colo Collection; Ga Art Asn; Southern States Art League. Comn: Mural, Broadmoor Cheyenne Mountain Zoo, Colorado Springs, 58; dragon wall mural, Victor Hornbein House, Denver, 59; mural, First Nat Bank, Colorado Springs, 59; four polyester resin sculptures, Colorado Springs Eye Clin, 60; exterior wall mural, Horace Mann Jr High Sch, Colorado Springs, 62. Exhib: Am Fedn Arts; Graphic Arts Chicago; Denver Ann & Biennial; Artists West of Mississippi; Washington Cathedral Relig Exhib. Teaching: Instr painting, life drawing & design, Colorado Springs Fine Arts Ctr, 45-51; prof art, painting, graphic design & drawing, Southern Colo State Col, 65- Pos: Producer & dir, Alexander Film Co, 58-62; communications media adv, US Agency Int Develop, Ind Univ, 62-64. Awards: First Purchase Award for oil, Canon City Blossom Festival, 69; First Purchase Award for oil, Colo State Fair, 70. Bibliog: Discovery No 49, Mod Photog, 58. Style & Technique: Image maker. Media: Oil, Acrylic. Publ: Auth, History of writing and painting, 63; illusr, English with the twins, 63; illusr, History of medicine, 63; ed, The story of Nok culture, 63. Mailing Add: 30 Mesa Rd Colorado Springs CO 80903

TILLIM, SIDNEY
PAINTER, INSTRUCTOR
b Brooklyn, NY, June 16, 25. Study: Syracuse Univ, BFA, 50. Work: Michener Collection, Univ Tex, Austin; Ludwig Collection, Neue Galerie, Aachen, Ger; Weatherspoon Art Gallery, Univ NC, Greensboro; Joseph H Hirshhorn Mus & Sculpture Garden; NJ State Mus, Trenton. Exhib: Contemp Realism in Figure & Landscape, Wadsworth Atheneum, Hartford, Conn, 64; J B Speed Art Mus, Louisville, Ky, 65; Realism Now, Vassar Col Art Gallery, Poughkeepsie, NY, 68; Aspects of New Realism, Milwaukee Art Ctr, 69; 22 Realists, 70 & Ann, 72, Whitney Mus Am Art; 30th Ann, Chicago Art Inst, 70; one-man shows, Robert Schoelkopf Gallery, New York, 65 & 67, Noah Goldowsky Gallery, New York, 69 & 74, Edmonton Art Gallery, Alta, 73 & 76 & Tibor de Nagy Gallery, New York, 77. Teaching: Instr art hist & drawing, Pratt Inst, 64-68; instr art hist & painting, Bennington Col, 66- Pos: Contrib ed, Arts, 59-65; contrib ed, Artforum, 65-69. Awards: Painting grants, Nat Endowment for the Arts, 74 & Ingram-Merrill Found, 76. Style & Technique: History and narrative painter, oil on canvas. Publ: Auth, The Ideal and the literal sublime, Artforum, 5/76; auth, Notes on narrative and history painting, Artforum, 5/77. Dealer: Tibor de Nagy Gallery 29 W 57th St New York NY 10019. Mailing Add: 166 E 96th St New York NY 10028

TILLOTISON, ROBBIE
PAINTER, INSTRUCTOR
b Denton, NC, Nov 8, 50. Study: Appalachian State Univ, BA; Univ of NC, Greensboro, MFA. Work: R J Reynolds Tobacco Co Nat Hq, Winston-Salem, NC; Appalachian State Univ, Boone, NC; Brevard Col, NC; Manhattan Theatre Club, New York; Burlington Industs, Greensboro. Exhib: 34th Ann Painting Competition Exhib, NC Mus of Art, Raleigh, 76; Weatherspoon Art Gallery, Univ of NC, Greensboro, 74; 1st Southeastern Artists Invitational, Southeastern Ctr for Contemp Art, 77; one-man show, Southeastern Ctr for Contemp Art, Winston-Salem, 74, Wiener Gallery, New York, 75 & Aames Gallery, New Soho Talent, 75, New York, 75. Pos: Dir, Appalachian State Univ Art Prog, New York, 74- Awards: Chancellor's Award, Annual Grad Exhib, Univ of NC, Greensboro, 74; Best in Show, Greenhill Art Gallery, Burlington Industs, 75. Bibliog: Bob Colacello (auth), Andy Warhol's Interview, 2/75; Brantley Mewbonne, After Dark, 12/76; William Zimmer, Arts Mag, 2/77. Style & Technique: Figurative (expressionistic paper painting). Media: Acrylic Painting on Paper with Cray-pas; Frottage method. Publ: Co-auth, Zelda (Fitzgerald) Still Lives, Feminist Art J, spring 75. Dealer: Nonson Gallery 133 Wooster St New York NY 10012. Mailing Add: 67 Vestry St New York NY 10013

TIMMAS, OSVALD
PAINTER
b Estonia, Sept 17, 19; Can citizen. Study: Tartu State Univ; Atelier Sch Tartu & Tallinn, Estonia, with Nicholas Kummits & Gunther Reindorff. Work: London Art Mus, Ont; Art Gallery Hamilton; Art Gallery Windsor; Rodman Hall Art Ctr, St Catharines, Ont; Erie Art Ctr, Pa. Exhib: Can Watercolors, Drawings & Prints, Nat Gallery Can, Ottawa, 66; Audubon Artists, 66-69, Am Watercolor Soc, 66, 67 & 69 & Nat Acad Design, 67, 68 & 71, New York; Royal Can Acad Arts, Nat Gallery Can, 70; plus one-man shows. Awards: Medal & Award for creative aquarelle, Audubon Artists, 67 & 68; Major Award for watercolor painting, Coutts-Hallmark Co Can, 69 & 70; John Labatt Ltd Award, 71. Bibliog: Anthony Ferry (auth), A floating world, 2/20/65 & It's now time for Timmas, 11/11/65, Toronto Star; Stevens (auth), Osvald Timmas, La Rev Mod, 11/66. Mem: Royal Can Acad Arts; Am Watercolor Soc; Can Soc Painters Watercolor; Ont Soc Artists (vpres, 71-75). Style & Technique: Creative abstraction; often impregnating the painting with natural ferric oxides. Media: Watercolor, Acrylic. Dealer: Merton Gallery 68 Merton St Toronto 7 ON Can; Gallerie Fore 405 Selkirk Ave Winnipeg 4 Can. Mailing Add: 776 Marlee Ave Toronto ON M6B 1L1 Can

TIMMINS, WILLIAM FREDERICK
PAINTER, ILLUSTRATOR
b Chicago, Ill. Study: Am Acad Art, Chicago; Art Students League, with George Bridgman; Grand Cent Art Sch, New York, with Harvey Dunn & Mario Cooper. Work: Longyear Found Mus, Boston; House of Four Winds, Calif Hist Bldg, Monterey. Comn: Mural, Independent Savings & Loan Asn, Salinas, Calif, 72; also many comns for pvt portraits and paintings. Exhib: One-man show, Perry House Gallery, 67 & 73; Village Artistry, Carmel, Calif, 76; Pepper Tree Ranch Western Art Ctr, Santa Cruz, Calif, 77; Sioux Falls Civic Fine Arts Ctr, SDak, 77. Mem: Soc Western Artists. Style & Technique: Representational, emphasizing light and shade, textures and atmospheric moods. Media: Oil, Watercolor. Publ: Illusr, Boy Scout Handbook, 68 & Winnie the Pooh, Western Publ, 68. Dealer: Village Artistry Dolores Ave & Ocean Ave Carmel CA 93921; A Huney Gallery 3746 Sixth Ave San Diego CA 92103. Mailing Add: PO Box 5685 Carmel CA 93921

TIMMS, PETER ROWLAND
MUSEUM DIRECTOR
b Philadelphia, Pa, Aug 26, 42. Study: Brown Univ, Providence, RI, BA, 64; Harvard Univ, MA, 69 & PhD(anthrop), 76. Pos: Dir, Fitchburg Art Mus, Mass. Publ: Auth, Flint Implements of the Old Stone Age, Shire, United Kingdom, 74. Mailing Add: 70 Prichard St Fitchburg MA 01420

TIMS, MICHAEL WAYNE
See Bronson, AA

TING, WALASSE
PAINTER
b Shanghai, China, Oct 13, 29. Work: Mus Mod Art, New York; Guggenheim Mus, New York; Carnegie Inst, Pittsburgh; Stedelijk Mus, Amsterdam, Holland; Israel Nat Mus, Jerusalem. Exhib: Paul Facchetti, Paris, France, 54; Martha Jackson Gallery, 60; Carnegie Inst Int, 61, 64, 67 & 70; Galerie Birch, 63; Galerie ed France, 68; Lefebre Gallery, 71. Awards: Guggenheim Fel, 70. Publ: Auth, My Shit & My Love, 61; auth, One Cent Life, 64; auth, Chinese Moonlight, 67; auth, Hot & Sour Soup, 69; auth, Green Banana, 71. Dealer: Lefebre Gallery 47 E 77th St New York NY 10028. Mailing Add: 100 W 25th St New York NY 10001

TINNING, GEORGE CAMPBELL
PAINTER
b Saskatoon, Sask, Feb 25, 10. Study: Elliot O'Hara Sch, Maine; Art Students League. Work: Nat Gallery Art, Ottawa, Ont; Nat War Mus, Ottawa, Ont; Montreal Mus Fine Arts, PQ; Ford Motor Co, Dearborn, Mich; Charlottetown Art Mus, P E I; Montreal Star, PQ. Comn: Mural, Jenkins Valve Co, Lachine, Que, 60; mural, Bank Montreal, 61; murals, Ritz Carlton Hotel, Montreal, 67. Teaching: Pvt classes. Pos: War artist, hist sect, Can Army, 43-46. Awards: Dow Awards for watercolor, 42 & 48, Montreal Mus Fine Arts. Mem: Academician Royal Can Acad Art; Can Soc Painters Watercolour. Media: Watercolor, Acrylic. Publ: Auth, Can Art, spring, 49; auth & illusr, Lincoln Mercury Times, 50-59. Dealer: Continental Galleries Inc Drummond St Montreal PQ Can. Mailing Add: Apt 52 1509 Sherbrooke St W Montreal PQ H3G 1M1 Can

TIRANA, ROSAMOND (MRS EDWARD CORBETT)
PAINTER
b New York, NY, Jan 29, 10. Study: Swarthmore Col, BA, 31; London Sch Econ, 31-32; Univ Geneva, 31 & 32; painting with Bernice Cross, E R Rankine & Hans Hofmann. Exhib: Corcoran Gallery Art, Washington, DC, 56-59 & 66; Provincetown Art Asn, Mass, 57-65; Art for Embassies, Nat Collection Fine Arts, 68, US Embassy, Turkey, 69; Franz Bader Gallery, Washington, DC, 69; plus others. Pos: Foreign corresp, Chicago Daily News, London Clarion & Milwaukee Leader, 32-34. Awards: Prizes, Lycee Mooiere, Paris, 24; Va Regional Exhib, 59; Washington Post Area Competition, 59. Mem: Am Fedn Arts. Mailing Add: 3500 35th St NW Washington DC 20016

TOBEY, ALTON S
PAINTER, LECTURER
b Middletown, Conn, Nov 5, 14. Study: Yale Univ Sch Fine Arts, BFA, 37, MFA, 47. Work: Jewish Mus, New York; Nat Acad Design Edwin Abbey Collection, NY; Mus of City New York; Wadsworth Atheneum, Hartford, Conn; Smithsonian Inst, Washington, DC. Comn: Mural for Campfield Ave Libr, comn by Charles Goodwin, 37; mural, East Hartford Post Off, 38; Life of Gen MacArthur (six murals), Edwin Abbey Mural Fund for MacArthur Mem, 65; two murals on anthrop, Smithsonian Mus Natural Hist, 67; 14 murals on Am hist, comn by dir of Proj 14, Chadds Ford, Pa, 70. Exhib: Conn Acad Fine Arts, 34-37; City Ctr Galleries, 50-53; Riverside Mus, 52-54; one-man shows, Burliuk Gallery, New York, 53, Trinity Col, Hartford, Conn, 70, Katonah Gallery, NY, 73, Galerie Alliance, Copenhagen, Denmark, 74, Am Ctr, Stockholm, Sweden, 75 & Portrait Gallery, Westport, Conn, 76; Norfolk Mus Arts & Sci, 66; Loeb Ctr, NY Univ, 69-71; Sarah Lawrence Col, Bronxville, NY; Silvermine Guild, New Canaan, Conn; Univ Pa Art Mus, Philadelphia; Hudson River Mus, Yonkers, NY; Albany Mus, NY. Teaching: Instr & lectr styles, techniques & hist art, Yale Sch Fine Arts, 45-49; lectr hist art, City Col New York, 50-51. Pos: Pres, Mamaroneck Art Guild. Mem: Abraxas; Silvermine Artists Guild (dir); Artists Equity New York (dir, 70-); Nat Soc Mural Painters (vpres, 72-). Media: Oil, Acrylic. Mailing Add: 296 Murray Ave Larchmont NY 10538

TOBIAS, ABRAHAM JOEL
PAINTER, SCULPTOR
b Rochester, NY, Nov 21, 13. Study: Cooper Union Art Sch, 30-31; Art Students League, 31-33; Fed Art Proj, New York, 38-40. Work: Brooklyn Mus, NY; Los Angeles Co Mus Art; New York Pub Libr; Rochester Pub Libr, NY. Comn: The Student (fresco mural), Howard Univ, Washington, DC, 45; two war mem fresco panels, James Madison High Sch, Brooklyn, acrylic mural, Domestic Rels Ctr, Dept Pub Works, New York, 56; two Plexiglas panels for entrance, Polytech Inst Brooklyn, 58; mosaic & terrazzo mural, Henrietta Szold Sch, New York Bd Educ, 60. Exhib: Mus Mod Art, New York; San Francisco Mus; Brooklyn Mus; Adelphia Col; Archit League New York; plus many others. Teaching: Lectr mural painting, Howard Univ, 45; artist in residence, Adelphi Univ, 47-57; lectr mural painting, Asn Am Cols Prog, 52 & 55; inst artist, Polytech Inst Brooklyn, 70- Pos: Art dir, Intelligence Div, US Air

Forces, Washington, DC, 43-44; graphic designer, Off Strategic Serv, Washington, DC, 44-45. Awards: Award for Mural Painting, Archit League New York, 52. Bibliog: Joseph L Young (auth), Mosaics: Principles & Practice, Reinhold, 64; Lawrence N Jensen (auth), Synthetic Painting Media, Prentice Hall, 64; Louis Botto (auth), In the know, Look Mag, 69. Media: Plastic, Metal, Stone. Publ: Auth, Mural painting, 2/57 & auth, A mural painting for science & technology, 3/69, Am Artist Mag. Mailing Add: 98-51 65th Ave Rego Park NY 11374

TOBIAS, JULIUS
SCULPTOR, INSTRUCTOR
b New York, NY, Aug 27, 15. Study: Atelier Fernand Leger, Paris, 49-52. Work: Pasadena Mus Art, Calif. Exhib: Pa Acad Fine Arts, Philadelphia, 58; Mus Mod Art Traveling Exhib, Tokyo, 59; New Eng Exhib, Silvermine, Conn, 60; Whitney Mus Am Art Sculpture Ann, 68; Indianapolis Mus Art, Ind, 70. Teaching: Instr painting, New York Inst Technol, 66-71; instr sculpture, Queens Col (NY), 71-74; vis artist, Ind Univ, Bloomington, 74-75; vis artist, Univ Minn, Minneapolis, 77; vis artist, Univ NC, Greensboro, 78. Awards: NY Cult Coun Found Creative Artists Pub Serv Prog Grant, 71; grant, NY Cult Coun Found, 71 & 78; fel, Guggenheim Mem Found, 72-73; grant, Mark Rothko Found, 73; grant, Nat Endowment for the Arts, 75-76. Bibliog: Barbara Rose (auth), A gallery without walls, Art Am, 3-4/68; James R Mellow (auth), Two sculptors worlds apart, 1/31/71 & Peter Schjeldahl (auth), A journey well worth making, 1/20/74, New York Times; Corinne Robins (auth), Julius Tobias: a decade of spatial dialogue, Arts Mag, 3/77; Judith Lopes Cardozo (auth), reviews, Artforum Mag, 12/77. Media: Concrete. Dealer: Tony Allesandro Gallery 489 Broome St New York NY 10013. Mailing Add: 9 Great Jones St New York NY 10012

TOBIAS, ROBERT PAUL
PAINTER, SCULPTOR
b Reading, Pa, Dec 14, 33. Study: Ariz State Univ, BS(appl arts, ceramics), 64, MFA(sculpture), 69. Work: Matthews Ctr, Ariz State Univ, Tempe; Univ Ariz Mus Art, Tucson; Wis State Univ, Platteville; Ariz Western Col, Yuma; Phoenix Col, Ariz. Comn: Painting, comn by Mr & Mrs Michael Pulitzer, Tucson, 74; monumental sculpture, La Placita, City of Tucson, 74. Exhib: Painting, 1973 Four Corners Exhib, Phoenix & 1974 Mainstreams, Marietta Col, Ohio; sculpture, Nelson Art Mus, Kansas City, Mo, 70, Yuma Invitational, 73 & Arizona's Outlook '74, Tucson Art Ctr. Teaching: Instr design, Univ Kans, Lawrence, 69-71; assoc prof sculpture & design, Univ Ariz, Tucson, 71- Awards: Sculpture Purchase Award, Wis State Univ, Platteville, 67; Painting Award, 1972 Yuma Invitational, Ariz Western Col; Sculpture Exhib Award, Tucson Art Mus, 74. Bibliog: Tobias show in Lawrence, Kansas City Star, 3/22/70; Darrell Dobraus (auth), Artists review, Desert Silhouette, Tucson, 10/75. Style & Technique: Constructivist. Dealer: Ankrum Gallery 657 N La Cienega Blvd Los Angeles CA 90069. Mailing Add: Dept of Art Univ Arizona Tucson AZ 85721

TOBIN, ROBERT L B
COLLECTOR, PATRON
b San Antonio, Tex, Mar 12, 34. Study: Univ Tex. Collections Arranged: Explosion: Color: Paris: 1909, Spoleto, 70; Eugene Berman, A Retrospective, Spoleto, 73 & Univ Tex, 75. Collection: Theatre art; modern American painting and drawing; fine prints. Mailing Add: 173 Ira Lee Rd San Antonio TX 78218

TODD, LOUISE (LOUISE TODD COPE)
WEAVER, INSTRUCTOR
b Ventnor, NJ, June 17, 30. Study: Syracuse Univ, BA(fine arts); Grinnell Col; Haystack Mountain Sch Crafts. Work: NC Mus Art, Raleigh; Del Art Mus, Wilmington; Kutz State Col Collection, Pa; Riggs, Councilman, Michaels & Downs Ins Co, Baltimore. Comn: Weaving (6'x8' tapestry), comn by Irving Grief, Stevenson, Md, 69; Weaving (8' icelandic wool), Kutztown State Col, 71; weaving (6' window panels), comn by Dr Samuel Kron, Philadelphia, 71. Exhib: Fur & Feather, Mus Contemp Craft, New York, 71; Weaving Unlimited, DeCordova Mus, Mass, 71; Art in Fiber, Knoll Int, Washington, DC, 73; Invisible Artist, Philadelphia Mus Art, 73-74; Women's Work, American Art, Civic Ctr Mus, Philadelphia Nat Exhib, 74. Teaching: Teacher fibers, Haystack Sch Crafts, 69; chmn dept textiles, Moore Col Art, 70-74; teacher textiles, Penland Sch Crafts, NC, summers 70-72; tutor textiles, Wincester Sch Art, Eng, summer 73; teacher fibers, var workshops in US, Eng & Can. Awards: Am Crafts Coun Nat Merit Award, 69; NC Mus Art Purchase Award, 71; Del Art Mus Purchase Award, 70. Bibliog: Donald J Willcox (auth), Body Covering: International Perspectives, Regnery, 73; Virginia Harvey (auth), article in Threads in Action, 72. Mem: World Crafts Coun; Am Crafts Coun; Philadelphia Coun Prof Craftsmen. Style & Technique: Fibers and fiber techniques to express ideas and concepts, including tapestry, knotting and netting. Media: Fiber. Publ: Auth, Clothing (auth), Shuttle, Spindle & Dyepot Mag, 72. Mailing Add: c/o Helen Drutt Gallery 1625 Spruce St Philadelphia PA 19103

TODD, MICHAEL CULLEN
SCULPTOR, PAINTER
b Omaha, Nebr, June 20, 35. Study: Univ Notre Dame, BFA, 57; Univ Calif, Los Angeles, MA, 59. Work: Whitney Mus Am Art, New York; Los Angeles Co Mus Art; Southwestern Col, Chula Vista, Calif. Exhib: Whitney Mus Am Art Sculpture Ann, 64-70; Sculpture of 60's, Los Angeles Co Mus Art, 65 & Philadelphia Mus, 66; Living Am Art, Maeght Found, France, 71; Exhibs Large Scale Sculpture, Lippincott Corp; Zabriski Gallery, New York, 74; plus others. Teaching: Instr sculpture, Bennington Col, 66-68; asst prof sculpture, Univ Calif, San Diego, 68- Awards: Woodrow Wilson Fel, 59; Fulbright Fel, France, 61. Bibliog: T Garver (auth), Recent Sculpture 1968-70, Univ Calif, Los Angeles & Salk Inst, 69; L Goldberg (auth), Sculpture, Circle Series, 1970-72, Art Gallery, Calif State Univ, Fullerton, 72. Mem: Mus Mod Art; Whitney Mus Am Art; Fine Art Gallery, San Diego. Media: Steel, Aluminum. Mailing Add: 2422 Silver Ridge Ave Los Angeles CA 90039

TOIGO, DANIEL JOSEPH
PAINTER
b Albia, Iowa, May 20, 12. Study: Apprenticeship with Herb Olsen, Dale Nichols & Ben Stahl; Chouinard Art Inst, with William Moore. Work: Paintings, State Capitol Bldg, Sacramento, San Diego Art Inst, Santa Paula CofC & Ahmanson Collection, Los Angeles, Calif. Exhib: Los Angeles All City Art Festival, 67-71; Frye Mus, Seattle, Wash, 68; Santa Paula Ann Art Exhib, 68-71; Am Artists Prof League Grand Nat, 68-72; Calif State Fair, Sacramento, 70-71; Ft Hayes State Univ, Kans. Teaching: Pvt instr landscape, 45- Awards: Los Angeles All City Purchase Award, Howard Ahmanson, 68 & 69; San Diego Art Inst Award, Walter Scott, 68; Am Artists Prof League Award, 71 & 75. Bibliog: Artist—Dan Toigo (film), Chico State Col, 70; article in Am Artist Mag, 7/76. Mem: Fel Am Artists Prof League; Am Inst Fine Arts; Calif Art Club; San Gabriel Fine Arts Asn (dir, 67- Style & Technique: Traditional realism to impressionistic. Media: Oil, Watercolor. Mailing Add: 5278 Ellenwood Dr Los Angeles CA 90041

TOLEDO, FRANCISCO
PAINTER, SCULPTOR
b Juchitan, Mexico, July 17, 40. Study: Taller Libre del Grabado, Mexico City; with Stanley William Hayter, Paris, 60-65. Work: Mus Mod Art, New York, Philadelphia, Paris & Mexico City; New York Pub Libr; Tate Gallery, London; Kunstnaneshus Mus, Oslo. Exhib: Ft Worth Art Ctr, 59; Galerie Karl Flinker, Paris, 63; Arvil Gallery, Mexico City, 70, 74 & 75; Martha Jackson Gallery, New York, 74. Bibliog: A Pieyre d Mandiargues (auth), article in 20th Century, 12/64; J Canaday (auth), Small packages, New York Times, 12/8/64; Elaine L Johnson (auth), article in Art in Am, 1-28/71. Style & Technique: Work is deeply rooted in the native artistic traditions and mythology of Mexico; paintings, gouaches and graphics; also sculpture and ceramics and most recently tapestry. Media: Oil, Watercolor, Graphic. Mailing Add: c/o Arvil Gallery Humburgo 241 Mexico DF Mexico

TOLGESY, VICTOR
SCULPTOR
b Miskolc, Hungary, Aug 22, 28; Can citizen. Work: Nat Gallery Can, Ottawa; Etherington Art Ctr, Queen's Univ, Ont; Charlottetown Confedn Art Gallery, P E I, Can; Waterloo Univ, Ont; Willistead Art Gallery, Windsor, Ont. Comn: Hungarian freedom monument, Can-Hungarian Fedn, Toronto, 66; sculpture for Expo '67; sculpture, Jeffery Hall, Queen's Univ, 71; sculptures, Ottawa Pub Libr, 72. Exhib: Sculpture 67, Toronto, 67; Royal Can Acad Show, 67 & Montreal & Charlottetown, 71; 11th Winnipeg Show, 68; Ont Soc Artists 100th Ann Exhib, Toronto, 72. Awards: Can Coun Sr Fel, 65; Sculpture Prize, Royal Can Acad, Waterloo Univ, 67; Sculpture Prize, Soc Can Artists, 71. Mem: Royal Can Acad Arts. Media: Laminated plywood, Metals. Mailing Add: 90 Kirby Rd Ottawa ON K2B 6A3 Can

TOLL, BARBARA ELIZABETH
ART DEALER, CURATOR
b Philadelphia, Pa, June 8, 45. Study: Goucher Col, Towson, Md, AB, 67; Radcliffe Col, 67; Pratt Inst, New York, MFA, 69. Pos: Dir, Hundred Acres Gallery, New York, 70-77; freelance cur & pvt dealer, 77- Specialty: Young artists; photo-realism, conceptual, funk and abstract art. Mailing Add: 138 Prince St New York NY 10012

TOLLES, BRYANT FRANKLIN, JR
MUSEUM DIRECTOR, ART LIBRARIAN
b Hartford, Conn, Mar 14, 39. Study: Yale Univ, BA, 61 & MAT, 62; Boston Univ, PhD(hist), 70. Teaching: Asst dean & instr hist, Tufts Univ, Medford, Mass 65-71. Pos: Asst dir & libr, NH Hist Soc, Concord, 72-74; dir & libr, Essex Inst, Salem, Mass, 74- Mem: Am Hist Asn; Orgn of Am Historians; Soc of Archit Historians; Nat Trust for Hist Preserv; Soc for the Preserv of New England Antiq. Res: New England architectural history, late 18th and 19th century. Interest: American architectural history. Publ: Auth, Textile Mill Architecture in East Central New England, Essex Inst Hist Collection, 71; auth, The College edifice (1801-1807) at the University of Vermont, Vermont Hist, 72; auth, College architecture in New England in printed & sketched views, Antiques, 73; auth, Gridley J F Bryant and the first building for Tufts College, Old-Time New England, 73; auth, New Hampshire Architecture: A Guide, Univ Press of New Eng, 78. Mailing Add: Box 122 Center Sandwich NH 03227

TOLMIE, KENNETH DONALD
PAINTER, ILLUSTRATOR
b Halifax, NS, Sept 18, 41. Study: Mt Allison Univ, Sackville, NB, BFA(honors), with Alex Colville. Work: Nat Gallery of Can, Ottawa, Ont; Montreal Mus of Fine Arts, Que; Hirshhorn Collection, Washington, DC; Calif Col of Arts & Crafts, Oakland; Burnaby Art Gallery, BC. Exhib: One-man shows, Dorothy Cameron Gallery, Toronto, Ont, 63, Lofthouse Gallery, Ottawa, 69, Wells Gallery, Ottawa, 74 & 75; New Images from Canada, Banfer Gallery, New York, 63; Royal Acad of Art Summer Show, London, Eng, 63; Nat Gallery of Can Watercolors, Prints & Drawings, Ottawa, 64 & 66; Magic Realism in Can, London Art Mus, Ont, 66; Atlantic Award Exhib, Dalhousie Univ Gallery, Halifax, 67; Can Printmakers Showcase, Ottawa, 73; 7th Biennial Exhib, Burnaby Art Gallery, BC, 73; 40th Ann Exhib, Can Soc of Graphic Art, Univ Western Ont, 73. Pos: Chmn, Visual Arts, Ottawa, 75-76. Awards: Purchase Prizes, Burnaby Art Gallery, 73, McIntosh Gallery, Univ Western Ont, 73 & Contemp Can Graphics, Carleton Univ, 74. Bibliog: B L Smiley (auth), Profile: Ken Tolmie, In Review, Autumn 1976. Style & Technique: Realistic images. Media: Acrylic or Egg Tempera; Pencil & Pen & Ink Drawings. Publ: Auth & illusr, Tale of an Egg, Oberon Press, 75. Dealer: Wallack Galleries 202 Bank St Ottawa On Canada. Mailing Add: RR 3 Bridgetown NS B0S 1C0 Can

TOMASINI, WALLACE J
ART ADMINISTRATOR, ART HISTORIAN
b Brooklyn, NY, Oct 19, 26. Study: Univ Mich, AB, 49, AM, 50, PhD, 53; Univ Florence, Fulbright grant, 51-52; NY Univ Inst Fine Arts, 54-57. Teaching: Instr hist of art, Finch Col, 54-57; asst prof hist of art, Univ Iowa, 57-61, assoc prof, 61-64, prof, 64-, dir, Sch Art & Art Hist, 72- Awards: Am Numismatic Soc Grant, 57; Am Philos Soc Grant, 58. Mem: Am Numismatic Soc; Mid-Am Col Art Conf (mem bd dirs); Int Exchange of Scholars (mem adv screening comt); Sixteenth Century Studies (mem ed bd); Midwest Art Hist Soc; Renaissance Soc; Am Hist Asn; Col Art Asn Am. Res: Social and economic determinants of Italian Renaissance art; Late Imperial and Barbaric numismatics. Publ: Auth, Report on Visigothic Numismatic Research, 62; auth, Exhibition Catalogue: Drawing & the Human Figure 1400-1964, 64; auth, The Barbaric Tremissis in Spain & Southern France, Anastasius to Leovigild (numismatic notes & monogr 152), 64; contribr, 17th Century Art Essay (CIC Exhib Catalogue), 73. Mailing Add: 729 N Linn St Iowa City IA 52240

TOMCHUK, MARJORIE
PRINTMAKER
b Manitoba, Can, Oct 16, 33; US citizen. Study: Univ Mich, BA, 57, MA, 61; Long Beach State Col, 62; Sophia Univ, Japan; Pratt Graphics Ctr, NY. Work: Nat Air & Space Mus, Smithsonian Inst, Washington, DC; Denver Art Mus; Decordova Mus; Davison Art Ctr, Conn; Libr of Cong, Washington, DC; Butler Inst of Am Art, Youngstown, Ohio; Mus of Native Am Cult, Spokane, Wash; Univ Club of Chicago, Ill; Nelson Gallery, Kansas City, Mo; Tacoma Art Mus, Wash. Exhib: Nat Print Exhib, Ueno Mus, Tokyo, 63; Nat Print Exhib, Brooklyn Mus, 70; Boston Printmakers Nat Print Exhib, Lincoln, Mass, 71 & 73; Am Prints, F15 Gallery, Moss, Norway, 73; 23rd Ann Print Exhib, Libr Cong, 73. Awards: Boston Nat Print Show, Purchase Prizes, Decordova Mus, 71 & 73; Nat Arts Club Award, New York, 72; Stamford Art Club First Prize, 73. Mem: Silvermine Guild Artists (bd mem, 73-); Philadelphia Print Club; Stamford Art Asn; Pratt Graphics Ctr; Audubon Artists. Style & Technique: Original prints usually etchings with the use of three to five colors; realistic themes drawn with considerable detail. Media: Etching. Mailing Add: 44 Horton Lane New Canaan CT 06840

TOMES, MARGOT LADD
ILLUSTRATOR
b Yonkers, NY. Study: Pratt Inst, Brooklyn, NY. Work: Kerlan Col, Univ of Minn, Minneapolis; Hunter Col, New York; Univ of Ala. Comn: Illusr, Coward, McCann & Geoghegan, Seabury Press, Holiday House, G P Putnam's Sons, J P Lippincott, Thomas Y Crowell, New York & Bowmar Inc, Calif, 67- Pos: Illusr of Children's Books, Coward, McCann & Geoghegan, Seabury Press, Holiday House, B P Putnam's Sons, J P Lippincott, Thomas Y Crowell, New York & Bowmar Inc, Calif, 67- Awards: One of Ten Best Books of the Year, New York Times, 77. Style & Technique: Gouche, pen and ink with overlays. Geoghegan, Publ: Illusr, King George's Head was Made of Lead, Coward, McCann & Geoghegan, 74, Little Sister and the Month Brothers, Seabury Press, 76, Phoebe and the General, Coward, McCann & Geoghegan, 77, Jack and the Wonder Beans, G P Putnam's Sons, 77 & Giant Poems, Holiday House, 78. Mailing Add: 172 E 80 New York NY 10021

TOMIDY, PAUL J
ART ADMINISTRATOR, PAINTER
b Utica, NY, Mar 5, 44. Study: Pratt Inst, Brooklyn, NY, BFA, 66; Mills Col, Oakland, Calif, MFA, 73. Exhib: Everson Art Mus, Syracuse, NY, 69; Oakland Mus, Calif, 77. Collections Arranged: Thirty Year Retrospective of Ralph DuCasse (auth, catalog), 76, Ansel Adams-Roi Partridge Exhib, 77 & Calif Soc of Printmakers (auth, catalog), 78, Mills Col Art Gallery, Oakland, Calif. Pos: Acting dir, Mills Col Art Gallery, Oakland, Calif, 7/76. Style & Technique: Large abstract minimal paintings. Media: Acrylic. Mailing Add: c/o Mills Col Art Gallery Oakland CA 94613

TOMKINS, CALVIN
ART WRITER
b Orange, NJ, Dec 17, 25. Study: Princeton Univ, BA. Pos: Staff writer, The New Yorker, Mag, 61- Publ: Auth, The Bride and the Bachelors, Viking Press, 65; auth, Merchants and Masterpieces: The Story of the Metropolitan Museum of Art, E P Dutton, 70; auth, Living Well Is the Best Revenge, 71 & auth, The Scene: Reports on Post-Modern Art, 76, Viking Press; auth, Paul Strand: Sixty Years of Photographs, Aperture, 76. Mailing Add: c/o The New Yorker 25 W 43rd St New York NY 10036

TOMKO, GEORGE PETER
ART HISTORIAN, CURATOR
b Cleveland, Ohio, Mar 17, 36. Study: Case Western Reserve Univ, Cleveland, Ohio, BA, 57, 57-63 & 65. Collections Arranged: Roland P Murdock Collection (auth, catalog), Wichita Art Mus, 72; Paintings from Midwestern University Collections, 73; Arts Symposium: Exhibit of work by guest speakers Philip Pearlstein, Robert Smithson, Peter Blake & Otto Muehl, 74; John Silk Deckard Retrospective, 74. Teaching: Instr art hist, Dickinson Col, Carlisle, Pa, 63-64; asst prof art hist, Ohio Univ, Athens, 65-67; asst prof art hist, Transylvania Col, Lexington, Ky, 67-68. Pos: Cur of collections, Wichita Art Mus, 70-72; gallery dir, Ohio State Univ, 72-74; dir, Parrish Art Mus, 75; cur of Western collections, Joslyn Art Mus, Omaha, Nebr, 77- Mem: Col Art Asn; Am Asn of Mus. Res: Nineteenth and twentieth century American painting and sculpture. Publ: Contrib, The Frederick W Schumacher Collection, The Columbus Gallery of Fine Arts, Columbus Gallery of Fine Arts, 76. Mailing Add: 2200 Dodge St Omaha NE 68102

TOMLINSON, FLORENCE KIDDER
PAINTER
b Austin, Ill. Study: Colt Sch Art, dipl; Stillwater Art Colony; Univ Minn Summer Sch; Univ Wis, teachers cert; also with Ralph Pearson, Frederick Taubes & Myra Werten. Work: Milwaukee Art Inst, Wis; lithograph, Nat League Am Pen Women, Washington, DC; oil paintings, Oshkosh Paper Co & Madison Pub Libr, Wis; plus pvt collections. Comn: History of Cooperation (mural in oil), Midland Coop, Inc, Minneapolis, Minn, 48; Trade and Industry (mural in oil), Madison Tech Col, 55; plus many pvt commissions. Exhib: Nat Exhib Prints, Libr of Cong, Washington, DC, 45-54; Northwest Printmakers 18th Int, Seattle, Wash, 46; Walker Art Gallery Regional Exhib, Minneapolis, 46; Soc Am Graphic Artists, Kennedy Galleries, New York, 53; Wisconsin Painters & Sculptors, Milwaukee Art Inst, 61. Teaching: Instr figure & portrait painting & design, Madison Adult Voc Sch, 30-62; instr art, Shorewood Sch, 40-41; instr drawing, Univ Wis Summer Art Tour Europe, 61. Awards: Purchase Award for Eve (wood engraving), Milwaukee Art Inst, 44; award for Sharkies (oil painting), Wis Salon Art, 56; First Award for Dreams (lithograph), Nat League Am Pen Women, 64. Bibliog: Al Sessler (auth), The Tomlinson exhibition, 52 & Elizabeth Gould (auth), A thing about clowns, 68, Wis State J; Frank Custer (auth), Mrs Tomlinson's record, Capitol Times, 11/18/61; Dorish Goodhue (auth), About our cover, Pen Woman, 1/69. Mem: Artists of Mid-West; Artists Equity Asn; Madison Art Asn; hon mem Madison Art Guild; Nat League Am Pen Women. Media: Oil, Watercolor. Publ: Illusr & contribr, Design in nature's silhouettes, Country Life in Am, 39; illusr & contribr, Wood engravings, Wis Hort, 44; illusr, Am Bee J, 48 & 49; illusr & contribr, Block prints are fun, Nature Mag, 56; contribr, House & Garden. Mailing Add: 703 Glenway St Madison WI 53711

TOMPKINS, ALAN
PAINTER, EDUCATOR
b New Rochelle, NY, Oct 29, 07. Study: Columbia Univ, BA; Yale Univ, BFA. Comn: Mural paintings comn by US Treas Dept for post off at Indianapolis, Ind, 36, Martinsville,Ind, 37 & Boone, NC, 40; mural painting, Gen Elec Co, Bridgeport, Conn, 44; mural painting, Cent Baptist Church, Hartford, Conn, 58. Exhib: Ind Artists Ann, 37-38; Art Inst Chicago Ann, 38; Conn Acad Ann, 52-71. Teaching: Instr painting, Cooper Union Art Sch, 38-43; lectr painting, Columbia Univ, 46-51; prof painting & art hist, Univ Hartford, 51-74, retired. Pos: Dir, Hartford Art Sch, Univ Hartford, 57-69; comnr, Fine Arts Comn, Hartford, 59-69; vchancellor, Univ Hartford, 60-74. Awards: First Prize for painting, 68-70, Conn Acad. Mem: Conn Acad (vpres, 70-72); Conn Watercolor Soc. Style & Technique: Semi-abstract landscape and figure; oils on canvas. Res: 20th century art. Mailing Add: 11 Milburn Dr Bloomfield CT 06002

TONEY, ANTHONY
PAINTER, INSTRUCTOR
b Gloversville, NY, June 28, 13. Study: Syracuse Univ, BFA; Teachers Col, Columbia Univ, MA & EdD. Work: Whitney Mus Am Art, Nat Acad Design & Syracuse Univ, NY; Univ Ill, Urbana; Teachers Col, Columbia Univ; plus others. Comn: Murals, Bowne Hall, 68 & six panels, Brockway Cafeteria, St Mary's Dorm, Syracuse, NY, 71; plus many others. Exhib: Carnegie Inst Int, 49; Whitney Mus Am Art Ann, 50-60; Pa Acad Fine Arts Ann, 50-68; Audubon Artists Ann, 55-78; Nat Acad Design Ann, 60-78; plus others. Teaching: Instr creative art, Hofstra Univ, 52-55; instr creative painting, New Sch Social Res, 52-; instr creative painting, Five Towns Music & Art Found, 52-; instr, Rockland Ctr for Arts, 74-76. Awards: Childe Hassam Purchase Award, Nat Inst Arts & Lett, 68 & 76; Medals of Honor, Audubon Artists, 68 & 75; Benjamin Altman Prize, Nat Acad, 75. Mem: Nat Acad Design; Audubon Artists (mem bd, 75-); Nat Soc Mural Painters (treas, 73-76); Artists Equity Asn (mem bd dirs, 71-72); Int Inst Arts & Lett. Media: Oil. Publ: Contribr, article in Reality, 55; contribr, Tune of the calliope, 57; ed, 150 masterpieces of drawing, 65; auth, Creative painting and drawing, 66; auth, article on painting, Family Creative Workshop, 75; auth, article in Leonardo, 10/77; auth, Painting and Drawing—Discovering Your Own Visual Language, Prentice-Hall, NJ, 78. Dealer: ACA Gallery 25 E 73rd St New York NY 10021. Mailing Add: 16 Hampton Pl Katonah NY 10536

TONG, MARVIN ENOCH
MUSEUM DIRECTOR
b Springfield, Mo, June 26, 22. Study: Southwest Mo State Univ, BS; Univ of Ark, MA. Collections Arranged: Santos of the Southwest, 63, Contemporary American Indian Art, 63 & Oklahoma College Student Art, 67, Mus of the Great Plains, Lawton, Okla; Black Art of Texas, Centre on the Strand, Galveston, Tex, 72; Selected works of Rose O'Neill, Ralph Foster Mus, Point Lookout, Mo, 75. Teaching: Lectr art hist, Mus of the Great Plains, Lawton, Okla, 62-68. Pos: Dir & founder, Mus of the Great Plains, Lawton, Okla, 60-69; dir, Mus of the Great Lakes, Bay City, Mich, 69-70; exec dir, Centre on the Strand, Galveston, Tex, 71-73; dir, Ralph Foster Mus, Sch of the Ozarks, Point Lookout, 75- Mem: Mountain-Plains Mus Conf (chmn, 63-64); Okla Arts & Humanities Coun (bd mem, 63-69); Mich Arts Coun (bd mem, 70); Am Asn of Mus (mem coun, 63-64); Okla Mus Asn (pres, 63-68). Res: Art of the West. Publ: Auth, The Cox Site, Am Antiq, 59; auth, The great plains awaits, 63 & auth, A university of the great plains, 67, Great Plains J. Mailing Add: Ralph Foster Mus The Sch of the Ozarks Point Lookout MO 65726

TOOKER, GEORGE
PAINTER, PRINTMAKER
b Brooklyn, NY, Aug 5, 20. Study: Phillips Acad, grad, 38; Harvard Univ, AB, 42; Art Students League, 43-44, with Reginald Marsh, Kenneth Hayes Miller & Harry Sternberg. Work: Whitney Mus Am Art, New York; Metrop Mus Art, New York; Mus Mod Art, New York; Walker Art Ctr, Minneapolis; Nat Collection of Fine Arts, Smithsonian Inst, Washington, DC. Exhib: Art Inst Chicago; 28th Venice Biennial; Mus Mod Art; Metrop Mus Art; Corcoran Gallery Art; Retrospective, Jaffee-Friede Gallery, Hopkins Ctr, Dartmouth Col, Hanover, NH, 67, Fine Arts Mus of San Francisco, Calif Palace of the Legion of Honor, Mus of Contemp Art, Chicago, Whitney Mus of Am Art, New York & Indianapolis Mus of Art, Ind, 74-75. Teaching: Instr, Art Students League, 65-68. Awards: Nat Inst Arts & Lett Grant, 60. Mem: Nat Acad Design, New York. Mailing Add: c/o Frank Rehn Gallery 655 Madison Ave New York NY 10021

TOPERZER, THOMAS RAYMOND
PAINTER, GALLERY DIRECTOR
b Homestead, Pa, Aug 12, 39. Study: Sterling Col, 59-61; Southwestern Col (Kans), BA, 63; Univ Nebr-Lincoln, Woods fel, 69-70, MFA, 70. Work: Des Moines Art Ctr, Iowa; Springfield Art Mus, Mo; Rochester Art Ctr, Minn; Blanden Art Mus, Iowa. Exhib: Iowa Artists, Des Moines Art Ctr; New Horizons, Chicago; Nat Drawing, San Francisco Mus Art; Nat Prints & Drawings, Okla Art Ctr, Mid-America, Kansas City-St Louis, 74. Teaching: Asst prof arts mgt, Ill State Univ, 72- Pos: Dir, Blanden Art Mus, 70-71; dir, Rochester Art Ctr, 71-72; asst dir, Mus & Galleries, Ill State Univ, 72, dir, Univ Galleries, Ctr Visual Arts Gallery, 73-, ed, Univ Mus Newslett, 75- Mem: Am Asn Mus. Dealer: One Hundred Eighteen: An Art Gallery Harmon Pl Minneapolis MN 55403. Mailing Add: 1202 Belt Ave Normal IL 61761

TOPOL, ROBERT MARTIN
COLLECTOR
b New York, NY, Mar 9, 25. Collection: Frescos, oils and sculptures. Mailing Add: 825 Orienta Ave Mamaroneck NY 10543

TORAL, MARIA TERESA
ENGRAVER, DESIGNER
b Madrid, Spain. Study: Escuela Artes y Oficios, Madrid; Taller Ciudadela, Inst Nac Bellas Artes, Mex; also with Guillermo Silva Santamaria & Yukio Fukasawa. Work: Mus Arte Mod, Mex; Mus Arte Contemp, Chile; Univ Mus, Tex; Living Arts Found, New York; Joods Historisch Mus, Amsterdam. Exhib: Bienal de Chile, 63; Salon del OPIC, Mex, 66; Exposicion Solar, Inst Bellas Artes, Mex, 68; Salon de Grabado, Salon Plastica Mexicana, 69, 70 & 72; Int Miniature Prints Exhib, Pratt Graphics Ctr, New York, 69 & 71. Bibliog: Margarita Nelken (auth), Siete anos de grabado de Maria Teresa Toral, Acta Politecnica, 68. Mem: Salon Plastica Mexicana; Pratt Ctr Contemp Printmaking. Media: Ink, Oil, Collage. Mailing Add: c/o Galeria Misrachi Genova 20 Mexico DF Mexico

TORBERT, DONALD ROBERT
EDUCATOR, ART HISTORIAN
b Bluerock, Ohio, Dec 21, 10. Study: Ohio State Univ, BA, MA; Univ Minn, PhD; also with Boardman Robinson & Sol Wilson. Collections Arranged: State Centennial Exhib of Architecture, Minneapolis Inst Arts, 58. Teaching: Instr design & watercolor, Ohio State Univ, 34-36; instr design, Univ La, summer 39 & Univ Syracuse, NY, summer 40; prof art hist, Univ Minn, 36- Pos: Mem, Comt on Urban Environment, 68- & Heritage Preserv Comn, 72-, City Minneapolis; mem state rev comt, Nat Roster Hist Places, State Minn, 70- Awards: Post-doctoral Fulbright, Paris, 59-60. Mem: Col Art Asn; Soc Archit Historians. Res: Scandinavian sources of wood-framed architecture in United States. Publ: Auth, A Century of Art & Architecture, Univ Minn, 58; auth, A Century of Minnesota Architecture, Minneapolis Inst Arts, 58; auth, Significant Architecture in the History of Minneapolis, City Planning Comn & Minneapolis Chap of Am Inst Architects, 69-73. Mailing Add: 2116 Irving Ave S Minneapolis MN 55405

TORBERT, MARGUERITE BIRCH
DESIGNER, WRITER
b Faribault, Minn, Sept 30, 12. Study: Univ Minn, BA; Univ Iowa, MA. Pos: Cur of design & ed, Design Quart, Walker Art Ctr, 50-63; film dir, Minnimath, Nat Sci Found, 65-70; interior designer, Int Design Ctr, 72- Mailing Add: 2116 Irving Ave S Minneapolis MN 55405

TORBERT, STEPHANIE BIRCH
PHOTOGRAPHER, EDUCATOR
b Wichita Falls, Tex, May 31, 45. Study: Univ NMex, BFA, 68; Sch for Am Craftsman, Rochester Inst Technol, NY, 68; Visual Studies Workshop, State Univ NY, Buffalo, MFA, 71. Work: Minneapolis Inst Arts, Minn; Int Mus Photography, George Eastman House, Rochester; Mus NMex, Santa Fe; Univ Minn Art Gallery, Minneapolis. Exhib: Light Gallery, New York, 73; 20th Century Am Photog, Photographic Gallery, Kansas City, Mo, 74; Peter M David Gallery Color Invitational, Minneapolis, 75; Minneapolis Col Art & Design, 77; Minn Survey: Six Photogrs, Minneapolis Inst Arts & Nat Endowment for the Arts, 78; one-person shows, Minneapolis Inst Arts, 70, Walker Art Ctr, Minneapolis, 73 & Int Mus

Photog, George Eastman House, Rochester, NY, 78. Teaching: Instr photog, N Hennepin Community Col, Minneapolis, 74-75 & Minneapolis Col Art & Design, 77- Pos: Visual arts panel, Minn State Arts Bd, 76- Awards: Minn State Arts Bd Artists Fel, 74; Bush Found Artists Fel, Minneapolis, 76-77; Nat Endowment for the Arts Grant, Minn Survey: Six Photogr, 77. Mem: Soc Photog Educ. Media: Cibachrome, Non-Silver Process. Mailing Add: 3824 Harriet Ave S Minneapolis MN 55409

TORFFIELD, MARVIN
SCULPTOR
b New York, NY, July 25, 43. Study: Pratt Inst, BFA, 65; Skowhegan Sch Painting & Sculpture, 66; Yale Univ Sch Art & Architecture, MFA, 70. Exhib: Jewish Mus, New York, 69; Carpenter Ctr for Visual Arts, Harvard Univ, 72; Seagram Bldg, Seagram Plaza, New York, 73; Whitney Mus, New York, 74; Artists Space, New York, 75; Projects in Nature, Merriewold West, Far Hills, NJ, 75; New Sculpture: Plans & Proj, Fine Arts Bldg, New York, 76; Paula Cooper Gallery, New York, 77. Teaching: Asst in sculpture, Yale Univ Sch Art & Archit, 68-70; resident artist, Branford Col, 69-70; vis fellow, Mass Inst Technol, 70; res fellow, Harvard Univ, 71-72. Awards: Nat Endowment Arts Grant, 70-71; CAPS Fel, 75-76; Guggenheim Fel, 75-76. Style & Technique: Structures that reflect sound. Mailing Add: 50 Greene St New York NY 10013

TORMEY, JAMES
PAINTER, DESIGNER
b New York, NY. Study: Pratt Inst; Art Students League, with William Zorach, five yrs. Exhib: Nat Acad Design, 69-74, Allied Artists Am, 71, Audubon Artists, 71-74 & Gallery Madison 90, New York. Media: Oil. Mailing Add: c/o Gallery Madison 90 1248 Madison Ave New York NY 10028

TORNHEIM, NORMAN
SCULPTOR
b Chicago, Ill, Sept 16, 42. Study: Art Ctr Col Design, BS, 66; Calif State Univ, San Diego, MA, 75. Work: Las Vegas Art Mus, Nev; Marietta Col, Ohio; Arkansas Arts Ctr, Little Rock; Smith Col, Northampton, Mass; Ind Univ. Comn: Sculpture, comn by Mr & Mrs Stern, Calif, 76; Sculpture, comn by Mr & Mrs Lewis, Calif, 77; sculpture comn by Dr I Mori, Calif, 77. Exhib: Mainstreams 76, Marietta Col, Ohio, 76; Calif Craftsmen, Monterey Mus Art, Calif, 76; Designer-Craftsmen 76, Richmond Art Ctr, Calif, 76; Nat Competition 77, Dahl Fine Arts Ctr, 77; Calif Craftsmen, E B Crocker Art Mus, Sacramento, 77; Goldsmiths USA, Univ Wash, Seattle, 77; Musical Instruments, The Smithsonian Inst, Washington, DC, 78-80. Collections Arranged: Golden West Col Invitational, 78. Teaching: Instr wood, metal & leather, San Diego State Univ, Calif, 72-75; instr wood, metal, leather & clay, Golden West Col, Huntington Beach, Calif, 75- Awards: Jurors Award, Las Vegas Art Mus, 75; Purchase Award, Ark Art Ctr, 76; Merit Award, Nat Competition 77, Dahl Fine Arts Ctr, 77. Bibliog: Dona Z Meilach (auth), Wood Objects as Functional Sculpture, Crown, 76. Style & Technique: Mixed media, wood, clay, leather and metal. Media: Clay, Porcelain, low fire, underglaze, luster. Publ: Contribr, Artweek, 76-77. Mailing Add: 238 Colton Newport Beach CA 92663

TORREANO, JOHN FRANCIS
PAINTER, LECTURER
b Flint, Mich, Aug 17, 41. Study: Cranbrook Acad Art, BFA, 63; Ohio State Univ, MFA, 67; also with Robert King & Hoyt L Sherman. Work: Whitney Mus Am Art, New York; Larry Aldrich Mus Contemp Art, Ridgefield, Conn; Michener Collection, Univ Tex; Chase Manhattan Bank; Mus Art, RI Sch Design, Providence. Exhib: One-man shows, John Doyle Gallery, Chicago, Susan Caldwell Gallery & Artists Space, New York; Paula Cooper Gallery, New York; Neuberger Mus, Purchase, NY. Teaching: Asst prof painting, Univ SDak, 67-68; instr painting, Sch Visual Arts, 69-70; vis artist, Art Inst Chicago, 72; instr painting, State Univ NY at Purchase & grad prog, Goddard Col, 73-75; vis artist, NS Col Art & Design, Halifax, 75; vis lectr, Ohio State Univ, Columbus, 75. Bibliog: Jeremy Gilbert-Rolfe (auth), rev, 74, Carter Ratcliff (auth), The paint thickens, summer 76 & Jeff Perone (auth), Approaching the decorative, 12/76, Artforum. Style & Technique: Somewhat of a medieval style, employing the use of wooden column shapes or canvases with huge wooden frames with glass jewels as star-marks swimming in oil paint. Media: Acrylic. Mailing Add: 103 Franklin St New York NY 10013

TOSCHIK, LARRY
PAINTER, WRITER
b Milwaukee, Wis, July 17, 22. Study: Wis Art Acad, scholar; Layton Art Sch, Milwaukee. Work: Ariz State Univ Col Bus Admin; Riveredge Found, Calgary; Am Diplomatic Mission, Peking, China. Comn: Battlefield monument, 361st Inf 91st Div Mil Cemetery, Florence, Italy, 44; 30 paintings (wildlife), Hallmark Permanent Collection, 69-71; 20 silver medallions, Ducks Unlimited Inc, Chicago, 74; four wildlife lithographs, Franklin Mint; ltd ed porcelain plates, Artists of the World. Exhib: Mem Union, Ariz State Univ, 62; Nat Cowboy Hall of Fame, Oklahoma City, Okla, 73; Waterfowl Festival, Easton, Md, 73; Pac Flyway Show, Santa Rosa, Calif, 75. Pos: Art dir, Larry Toschik Art Studio, Phoenix, Ariz, 50-60 & Bur Publ, Ariz State Univ, 60-65. Awards: 3M Co Design Award, 62; Ducks Unlimited Inc Artist of the Year, 75-76; two awards, Printing Indust of Am, 77. Style & Technique: Impressionistic realism by brush; wildlife subjects. Media: Oil, Watercolor. Publ: Illusr, 15 juv novels, David McKay, 54-60; auth & illusr, Arizona the quail garden, 10/71, Whispering skies of Arizona (complete issue), 3/73 & Shadowed trails (complete issue), 2/76, Ariz Highways Mag; auth & illusr, SC Wildlife (supplement), 9-10/73; illusr, Wildlife Techniques Manual. Dealer: Austin Gallery 7103 Main St Scottsdale AZ 85251; Petersen Gallery 9433 Wilshire Blvd Beverly Hills CA 90212. Mailing Add: Box 305 Pine AZ 85544

TOTH, CARL WAYNE
PHOTOGRAPHER
b Cleveland, Ohio, Dec 7, 47. Study: Rochester Inst of Technol, AAS, 68; State Univ of New York, Buffalo, BA, 70, MFA, 72, with Donald Blumberg. Work: Int Mus of Photog at George Eastman House, Rochester, NY; Visual Studies Workshop, Rochester; Mus of Mod Art, New York; Australian Nat Gallery, Canberra; Detroit Inst of Art, Mich. Exhib: One-man show, Int Mus of Photog at George Eastman House, 72; three-man show, Visual Studies Workshop, 72; Dog Show, 73, Recent Acquisitions, 73 & Locations in Time, 77, Int Mus of Photog at George Eastman House; Photography Unlimited, William Hayes Fogg Art Mus, Cambridge, Mass, 74; Young American Photographers, Kalamazoo Inst of Arts, 75; Recent Acquisitions, Detroit Inst of Art, 77. Teaching: Head dept photog, Cranbrook Acad of Art, Bloomfield Hills, Mich, 72- Awards: Photogr Fel, Nat Endowment fot the Arts, 75. Bibliog: Photography Year, Time Life Books, 73; Exhibition Review, Artforum, 1/75. Mem: Soc for Photog Educ. Style & Technique: Multi-frame hand colored photographs; black & white photographs. Dealer: Light Gallery 724 Fifth Ave New York NY 10019. Mailing Add: 29 Academy Way Bloomfield Hills MI 48013

TOULIS, VASILIOS (APOSTOLOS)
PRINTMAKER, PAINTER
b Clewiston, Fla, Mar 24, 31. Study: Univ Fla, BDes, with Fletcher Martin & Carl Holty; Pratt Inst, BFA, with Richard Lindner, Fritz Eichenberg, Jacob Landau & Walter Rogalski. Work: US State Dept, Washington, DC; Mus Arte Mod, Mexico City, Mex; Caravan House, New York. Comn: Portfolio of prints, Ctr for Contemp Printmaking, 68. Exhib: Brooklyn Mus, NY, 66; Fleishcer Mem, Philadelphia, 66; Mus Arte Mod, Mexico City, 67; Int Miniature Print Exhib, 68; New Paltz Nat Print Exhib, 68; plus others. Teaching: Lectr serigraphic printmaking, Univ RI, 67 & Pratt Inst Seminar, 69; head graphic workshops, Pratt Inst, 66-, instr printmaking, 69-71, assoc prof & head undergrad printmaking, 71-; dir silk screen workshops, The Artists Collective, Hartford, Conn, 73- Pos: Printmaking adv to dir, Hudson River Mus, New York. Awards: Tiffany Found Grant in Printmaking, 67. Mem: Am Asn Univ Prof. Mailing Add: RFD 3 Putnam Valley NY 10579

TOUSIGNANT, CLAUDE
PAINTER, INSTRUCTOR
b Montreal, PQ, Dec 23, 32. Study: Sch Art & Design, Montreal; Acad Ranson, Paris. Work: Nat Gallery Can; Phoenix Art Mus, Ariz; Larry Aldrich Mus, Ridgefield, Conn; York Univ; Mus Contemp Art, Montreal & Quebec; plus others. Exhib: Solomon R Guggenheim Mus, New York, 65; Can Art, Paris, Rome & Brussels; Lausanne, Switz, 68; Mass Inst Technol, Cambridge; Washington Gallery Mod Art; Retrospective, Nat Gallery Can, 73-75; plus many other group exhibs & 13 one-man shows. Teaching: Instr design, Sch Art & Design, Montreal. Pos: Pres, Claude Tousignant, Inc. Awards: Prize, Salon de la Jeune Peinture, 62 & Centennial Exhib, 67; Rome Prize, 73. Mem: Artistes Prof de Montreal; Royal Can Acad Arts. Style & Technique: Hard-edge. Mailing Add: 3684 St Laurent Montreal PQ Can

TOVISH, HAROLD
SCULPTOR, EDUCATOR
b New York, NY, July 31, 21. Study: Columbia Univ, 40-43; Ossip Zadkine Sch Sculpture, Paris, 49-50; Acad Grande Chaumiere, Paris, 50-51. Work: Whitney Mus Am Art & Mus Mod Art, New York; Minneapolis Inst of Art; Walker Art Ctr; Smithsonian Inst, Washington, DC; Hirshhorn Mus, Washington, DC; Solomon R Guggenheim Mus, NY; Boston Mus Fine Art, Mass; Philadelphia Mus Art, Pa; Art Inst Chicago. Comn: Epitaph (sculpture), State of Hawaii, 70. Exhib: 28th Venice Biennial, Italy, 56; Carnegie Inst Int, 58; Recent Sculpture: USA, Mus Mod Art, New York, 59; Whitney Mus Am Art Ann, 66; Int Award Exhib, Solomon R Guggenheim Mus, 68; Boston Mus of Fine Art, 77; Inst of Contemp Art, Boston, 77; plus others including one-man shows. Teaching: Asst prof sculpture & drawing, Univ Minn, 51-54; vis prof sculpture, Univ Hawaii, 64-70; prof art, Boston Univ, 71- Awards: Am Inst Arts & Lett Grant, 60 & 71; sculptor in residence, Am Acad, Rome, 66; Guggenheim Fel, 67. Bibliog: H Harvard Arneson (auth), New talent, Art in Am, 54. Mem: Boston Visual Artists Union. Media: Bronze. Dealer: Terry Dintenfass Inc 50 W 57th St New York NY 10019. Mailing Add: 164 Rawson Rd Brookline MA 02146

TOWN, HAROLD BARLING
PAINTER, WRITER
b Toronto, Ont, June 13, 24. Study: Ont Col Art, grad, 44; hon LHD, York Univ, 66. Work: Tate Gallery, London; Mus Mod Art, New York; Stedelijk Mus, Amsterdam, Holland; Solomon R Guggenheim Mus, New York; Nat Gallery Can. Comn: Mural on canvas, Ont Hydro Comn, St Lawrence Seaway Power Proj, 57; decorative exterior enamel frieze, North York Pub Libr, Toronto, 59; two-part mural & sculptural screen, Toronto Int Airport, Malton, Can Govt, 62; mural on canvas, Queens Park Proj, Ont Govt, 69. Exhib: Cezanne & Structure in Modern Painting, Guggenheim Mus, 63; Documenta, Kassel, Ger, 64; Can Govt Pavilion, Expo '67 & Expo '70, Osaka, Japan; one-man shows, Venice Biennial, Italy, 56, 64 & 72; retrospective, Art Gallery Windsor, 75. Pos: Mem bd gov, Ont Art Col, 71. Awards: Fel, Inst Cult Hispanica, Arte de Am y Espana, Madrid, 63; Officer, Order Can, 68 & 10th Anniversary Medal; hon fel, Founders Col, York Univ. Bibliog: R Fulford (auth), The multiplicity of Harold Town, Arts Can, 4/71; David Silcox (auth), The First Exhibition of New Work, 1969/73, 73 & Albert Franck (auth), Keeper of the Lanes, 74, McClelland & Stewart. Mem: Royal Can Acad. Publ: Illusr, Love where the nights are long, 62; auth, Enigmas, 64; co-auth, Drawings of Harold Town, 69; auth, Silent stars, sound stars, film stars, 71; co-auth (with Tom Thomson), The Silence and the Storm, MacMillan & Stewart, 77. Dealer: Waddington Galleries 33 Hazelton Ave Toronto ON Can. Mailing Add: 9 Castle Frank Crescent Toronto ON M4W 3A2 Can

TOWNLEY, HUGH
SCULPTOR, PRINTMAKER
b Lafayette, Ind, Feb 6, 23. Study: Univ Wis, 46-48; also with Ossip Zadkine, Paris, 48-49; London Co Coun Arts & Crafts, 49-50. Work: Mus Mod Art; Whitney Mus Am Art; Boston Mus Fine Arts; Fogg Mus Art, Harvard Univ; Los Angeles Co Mus Art. Comn: Cast concrete reliefs & archit walls, Old Stone Bank, Bristol, RI, 65; wood relief, Bristol Hosp, Conn, 69; three concrete pieces, Class of 65, Brown Univ, Providence, RI, 70; three hanging wood sculptures, Retail Palnning Corp, Nashville, Tenn, 71; three concrete pieces, State of Ky Comprehensive Training Ctr, Somerset, Ky, 72. Exhib: New Talent Show, Mus Mod Art, 55; Carnegie Inst Biennial, 58; Am Painting & Sculpture, Univ Ill, 61 & 63; Ann Drawings & Sculpture, Whitney Mus Am Art, 62 & 63; 65th Am Painting & Sculpture Exhib, Art Inst Chicago, 64; one-man shows, Bell Gallery, Brown Univ, 72, Univ Ore, Eugene, 76, Schochet Gallery, Newport, 77 & Western Carolina Univ, Cullowhee, NC, 78; two-man show, Univ Ore Mus Art, 75; Dartmouth Col, 75; Keene State Univ, NH, 76; Wingspread Gallery, Northeast Harbour, Maine, 77; Inst Contemp Art, Boston, 77. Teaching: Instr sculpture & drawing, Layton Sch Art, Milwaukee, 51-56; asst prof sculpture, Beloit Col, 56-57; asst prof sculpture & drawing, Boston Univ, 57-61; prof art, Brown Univ, 61-; vis prof, Univ Calif, Berkeley, 61; vis lectr, Harvard Univ, 67; vis prof, Univ Calif, Santa Barbara, 68; vis lectr, Ft Wright Col, 71. Awards: Grant for Creative Work in Art, Nat Inst Arts & Lett, 67; Gov Award, State of RI Coun Arts, 72; Ore Sculpture Symposium, Eugene, 74. Media: Wood, Concrete, Lithography. Mailing Add: 1 Resolute Ln Bristol RI 02809

TOWNSEND, J BENJAMIN
ART CRITIC, ART HISTORIAN
b Stillwater, NY, Feb 17, 18. Study: Princeton Univ, BA, 40; Harvard Univ, MA, 42; Yale Univ, PhD, 51. Collections Arranged: This New Man: a Discourse in Portraits (with catalog), 68 & Presidential Portraits (with catalog), 68, Nat Portrait Gallery, Smithsonian Inst; Martha Visser 't Hooft: Paintings & Drawings, 1950-1973 (with catalog), 73 & Six Corporate Collectors (with catalog), 75, Charles Burchfield Ctr. Teaching: Prof art & lit, State Univ NY Buffalo, 57-, chmn master of arts in humanities, 60-66 & chmn dept art & art hist, 69-71. Pos: Asst dir, Nat Portrait Gallery, Smithsonian Inst, 67-68. Res: Selective, annotated bibliography of 19th century American painting for Archives of American Art; an edition of the journals of Charles Burchfield. Publ: Auth, 100: The Buffalo Fine Arts Academy, 1862-1962, Albright-Knox Art Gallery, 62. Mailing Add: 879 W Ferry St Buffalo NY 14209

TOWNSEND, JOHN F
SCULPTOR, PAINTER
b La Crosse, Wis. Study: Carroll Col, Waukesha, Wis, BS, 51; Minneapolis Sch of Art, 53-55; Univ of Minn Grad Sch, MFA, 59. Work: Mus of Fine Art, Boston, Mass; Rose Mus, Brandeis Univ, Waltham, Mass; Allentown Art Mus, Pa; Chase Manhattan Bank, New York; World Bank, Washington, DC. Exhib: White on White, De Cordova Mus, Lincoln, Mass, 65; Art for US Embassies, Inst of Contemp Art, Boston, 66; Optical Art (traveling exhib), Mus of Mod Art, New York, 66-68; Small Paintings for Mus Collections, Am Fedn of Art Traveling Exhib, 67-68; one-man shows, John Townsend-15 Black and White Paintings, Mus of NMex Art Gallery, Santa Fe, 60, Releif Sculpture, Byron Gallery, New York, 66 & Eleanor Rigelhaupt Gallery, Boston, 67 & Work in Progress, Ward-Nasse Gallery, Boston, 70. Teaching: Instr sculpture & painting, Eastern NMex Univ, Portales, 59-60; from instr to full prof sculpture, drawing & design, Univ of Mass, Amherst, 60-; part-time instr painting, Mt Holyoke Col, South Hadley, Mass, 61-62. Pos: Dir of art exhibs, 60-64 & dir grad art prog, 71-74, Univ of Mass, Amherst. Awards: First Award Sculpture, Second Ann Univ Arts Faculty Exhib, Argus Gallery, Madison, NJ, 63; Crane Co Award, 17th Ann Exhib of Painting & Drawing, 68 & 15th Spring Exhib, Berkshire Mus, Pittsfield, Mass. Bibliog: Dona Z Meilach (auth), Contemporary Art with Wood, Crown Publ Inc, New York, 68. Style & Technique: Abstract, assemblage/constructivist approach in both paint and sculpture. Media: Acrylic on Canvas; Wood. Mailing Add: 118 Aubinwood Rd Amherst MA 01002

TOWNSEND, MARVIN J
CARTOONIST, ILLUSTRATOR
b Kansas City, Mo, July 2, 15. Study: Kansas City Art Inst; Col Com Art Sch. Work: Syracuse Univ Permanent Collection, NY. Media: Ink brush. Publ: Strips, gag cartoons & illus for trade, bus & prof mags, 41-; auth, Oshco (cartoon strip), Nat Safety News, 58-; auth, Moontoons jokes and riddles, 70 & Ghostly ghastly cartoons, 71; Laugh it up, 74; auth, Sillyettes (weekly cartoon strip), The Star, World News Corp. Mailing Add: 631 W 88th St Kansas City MO 64114

TOWNSEND, STORM D
SCULPTOR, LECTURER
b London, Eng, Aug 31, 37. Study: London Univ, NDD, ATC, Goldsmiths' Col Art, 6 yrs, with Harold Parker & Ivor Roberts Jones. Work: Fine Arts Mus NMex, Santa Fe. Comn: Life-size portrait in bronze, comn by David Cargo, Gov NMex, 67. Exhib: Fine Arts Biennial, Mus of NMex, 65 & Sculpture Invitational, 67; Mainstreams '71, Marietta Col, Ohio, 71; Nat Directions Exhib, Albuquerque, NMex, 72; one-person shows, Discovery Gallery, Santa Fe, 75, Gallery Marquis, Denver, Colo, 75, Studio-Gallery, Albuquerque, NMex, 77 & Gallery Eleven, Lubbock, Tex, 77; Shidoni Summer Outdoor Exhib, 75; Survey of Contemp NMex Sculpture, NMex Mus Fine Art, Santa Fe, 76. Teaching: Instr sculpture, Pojoaque Art Ctr, Santa Fe, 65-66, Col of Santa Fe, 73-75 & Univ Albuquerque, NMex, 76; lect & workshops in studios & mus, currently. Awards: Jajasan Siswa Lokantara Resident Fel to study the arts in Indonesia, 60-61; Resident Fels, Huntington Hartford Found, Calif, 63 & Helene Wurlitzer Found, Taos, NMex, 64. Style & Technique: Stylized figurative realism; modeled clay and tooled gypsums for bronze. Media: Cast Metal. Mailing Add: PO Box 1165 Corrales NM 87048

TRACHTMAN, ARNOLD S
PAINTER
b Lynn, Mass, Oct 5, 30. Study: Mass Sch of Art, BFA; Sch of the Art Inst of Chicago, MFA. Work: Fogg Art Mus, Harvard Univ, Cambridge, Mass; Addison Gallery of Am Art, Andover Mass; Wiggin Collection, Boston Pub Libr, Mass; Boston Mus of Fine Arts. Exhib: Art with a Message, 73, Painting Invitational, 75 & Boston 78, an Invitational of Painting and Sculpture, 78, Brockton Art Ctr, Mass; Watergate Galerie Borjeson, Malmo, Sweden, 74; one-man shows, Inst of Contemp Art, Boston, 70 & Addison Gallery of Am Art, Andover Mass, 76. Teaching: Instr art, Lynnfield High Sch, Mass, 70- Mem: Boston Visual Artist Union (chmn, 71; prog comt, 74, 76 & 78; gallery exhib comt, 75). Style & Technique: Critical realism, attempt to make visible through visual metaphor, the state of contemporary society. Media: Acrylic, Watercolor; Drawing. Mailing Add: 27 Dana St Cambridge MA 02138

TRACY, BERRY BRYSON
CURATOR, HISTORIC PRESERVATIONIST
b Hampton, Iowa, Sept 4, 33. Study: Parson's Sch Design, with Robert J Castle, 52; Univ Iowa, BA(Am studies), 55; Attingham Park Adult Col, Shropshire, Eng, with George Trevelyan, 55; Newark Mus, mus philos & techniques with Katherine Coffey, 60. Comn: Criteria & Proposals for an 18th Century French Illinois Room, Chicago Hist Soc, 60; Critique on the Historic Furnishings of Boscobel, Boscobel Restoration, Inc, 75; re-restoration of Boscobel, 76-77. Exhib: Classical America, 1815-1845 (with catalog), Newark Mus, 63; 19th Century America, Furniture & Other Decorative Arts (with catalog), Metrop Mus, 70. Pos: Historical technician, Dept Conservation, State Ill, 57-60; adv for restoration and furnishing of Pierre Menard Home, Vandalia State Capitol & Shawneetown Bank, State Ill, 57-60, Bartow-Pell Mansion, Pelham, NY, 67-, Old Merchant's House, New York, 70-, Abigail Adams-Smith House, New York, 70-, Morris-Jumel Mansion, New York, 74-, Bull-Jackson House, Orange Co, NY, 74- & Exec Mansion, Albany, 75-; cur decorative arts, Newark Mus, 60-64; asst cur, Metrop Mus Art, New York, 64-65, assoc cur, 65-68, cur, 68-72, cur in chg Am Wing, 73-; mem, Spec Fine Arts Comt, US Dept of State, Washington, DC, 71-77 & 77- Bibliog: John Canaday (auth), Good show in Newark, New York Times, 6/2/63; Marvin D Schwartz (auth), Classical America 1815-1845, Art Quart, summer 63; Jay Cantor (auth), Critic's view of 19th century America, Winterthur Portfolio, 72. Mem: Friends of Attingham (bd dir, 70-74); Mus of City of New York; Nat Soc Arts & Lit; Nat Trust Hist Preservation; Newark Mus. Res: 18th and 19th century American decorative arts and architecture, furniture and cabinetmakers of Federal New York, 1786-1826. Publ: Auth, 19th Century American Furniture in the Collection of the Newark Museum, 61 & auth, English Pottery in the Collection of the Newark Museum, 62, Newark Mus; auth, Late classical styles in American silver, 1810-1830, Antiques Mag, 12/64. Mailing Add: PO Box 633 Goshen NY 10924

TRACY, (LOIS) BARTLETT
PAINTER, WRITER
b Jackson, Mich. Study: Rollins Col, 29; with Hans Hofmann, 45-46; Mich State Univ, MA, 58; New Col Workshop, 65, with Balcomb Greene, Afro, James Brooks, Marca-Relli & Sid Solomon. Work: Air & Space Mus, Smithsonian Inst, Washington, DC; Norton Gallery Art, Palm Beach, Fla; Univ Va, Charlottesville; Univ NC, Chapel Hill; Southeastern Col, Univ Ky. Exhib: Nat Asn Women Artists, New York, 40-60; Fla Artists Group Traveling Shows, 40-72; Assoc Artists NC Traveling Shows, 60-63; Audubon Artists, New York; Southeastern Shows, Atlanta, Ga; Four Arts Soc, Palm Beach, Fla, 77; Harmon Gallery, Naples, Fla, 78; plus others. Teaching: Instr, Univ Va Exten, 52-59 & 64-65; head dept art, Clinch Valley Col, 53-58; head dept art, Southeastern Col, Univ Ky, 64-66; head dept art, Edison Jr Col, Ft Myers, Fla, 68- Pos: Pres, NH Art Asn; mem bd, Nat Asn Women Artists, Pen & Brush & Assoc Artists NC & Am Pen Women; adjudacator, Manatee Co Art Ctr, 75-77. Awards: First Award, Fla Artists Group, 68; Watercolor Award, Southeastern Ann, High Mus Art; Gold Medal, New York World's Fair, State of Fla; plus others. Bibliog: Cosmic artist, Yankee, 7/49; Bartlett Tracy, NH Profiles, 4/52. Mem: Am Asn Univ Prof; Fla Artists Group; Sarasota Art Asn; Galerie Int New York. Style & Technique: Collages on raw canvas, using gesso and printing the backgrounds; raw vinyl as medium. Media: Acrylic, Oil. Publ: Auth, Painting principles and practices, 65, 67, 69 & 71; auth, The art of art. Dealer: Center St Gallery Winter Park FL 32789; Buyways Gallery 5255 Ocean Blvd Sarasota FL 33581. Mailing Add: 580 Artist Ave Englewood FL 33533

TRAHER, WILLIAM HENRY
PAINTER, LECTURER
b Rock Springs, Wyo, Apr 6, 08. Study: Nat Acad Design, 30-33; Yale Univ Sch Fine Art, 38-39. Work: Diorama backgrounds, Denver Mus Natural Hist. Comn: De Witt Ark Post Off, 41, US Treas Dept; cloud recognition mural, Williams Air Force Field, Ariz, 43; wilderness murals, Columbia Savings & Loan, Pueblo, Colo, 68; four landscape murals, St Louis Arch, Nat Park Serv, 70. Exhib: 5th Int Exhib Lithography & Wood Engraving, Art Inst Chicago, 36; New Horizons in American Art, Mus Mod Art, New York, 36; 2nd Nat Exhib Am Art, Munic Art Comt, New York, 37; Fine Art in Advertising, Art Dir Club, New York, 50; Surrealism, Mus Mod Art, Denver Art Mus, 62. Pos: Art dir, Philip H Gray Advert Agency, 45-47; artist & researcher, Jeppesen Map Co, Denver, 52-53; tech illusr, Lowry AFB, Denver, 53-54; chief artist, Denver Mus Natural Hist, 54- Awards: Purchase Prize, Penny Art Fund, Colo Fedn Woman's Clubs, 36; Beaux Arts Inst Design Award, 38; medal for originality, 6th Southwest Int Exhib, 55. Bibliog: J Devran (auth), Studio in a cigarette case, Rocky Mountain Life, 1/48; D Evans (auth), A maker of visions, Denver Mag, 6/65; J Jellico (auth), Giant in the museum, Am Artist, 4/74. Media: Acrylic. Publ: Illusr, Stars and Men, Bobbs, New York & Arnolds, London, 39; illusr, Wyoming design, state series, Container Corp, 49; illusr, Index of American design, Christensen, 54; illusr, US Golf Asn Ann, 60; auth, The artist cornered, Photog Soc Am J, 65. Mailing Add: 2331 Niagara St Denver CO 80207

TRAKAS, GEORGE
SCULPTOR
b Quebec, Que, May 11, 44. Study: Sir George Williams Univ, Montreal, 62-63; New Sch Social Res; Brooklyn Mus Art Sch; Hunter Col; NY Univ, BS. Work: Solomon R Guggenheim Mus. Exhib: Projects: Pier 18, Mus Mod Art, New York, 71; Ten Young Artists: Theodoron Awards, Guggenheim Mus, New York, 71; 12 Statements: Beyond the 60's, Detroit Inst Art, 72; one-man show, City Univ Grad Ctr, New York, 75; Projects in Nature, Far Hills, NJ, 75; Artpark, Lewiston, NJ, 76; Nassau Co Mus, Roslyn, NY, 76; Documenta 6, Kassel, WGer, 77; Scale & Environment, Walker Art Ctr, Minneapolis, 77. Style & Technique: Construction & demolition. Media: Building Materials. Bibliog: Paul Stimson (auth), rev in Art in Am, Vol 63 (Sept-Oct, 75); Kate Linker (auth), George Trakas & the syntax of space, Arts Mag, Vol 50 (Jan, 76); Barbara Baracks (auth), Artpark: the new aesthetic playground, Artforum, Vol 15 (Nov, 76). Publ: Contribr, Outcrops, Avalanche, fall 71; contribr (catalogue essays), Projects in Nature, 75 & Artpark, 76. Mailing Add: PO Box 395 New York NY 10013

TRAKIS, LOUIS
SCULPTOR
b New York, NY, June 22, 1927. Study: Cooper Union, BFA; Columbia Univ; Art Students League; Politechneion, Athens, Greece; Fulbright grants, Acad Fine Arts, Rome, Italy, 1959-60 & 1960-1961. Exhib: Laurel Gallery, New York, 49; Gallery Creuze, Paris, France; Metrop Mus of Art, Tokyo; Appunto Gallery, Rome; Galleria re Magi, Milan, Italy; Corcoran Gallery, Washington, DC; Brooklyn Mus, NY; Feingarten Gallery, NY; Benson Gallery, Bridgehampton, LI, NY. Teaching: Instr sculpture, Philadelphia Col of Art, Columbia Univ, New Sch for Social Res & Southhampton Col; assoc prof art, Manhattanville Col, 76- Awards: Comfort Tiffany Found Award/Sculpture, 61 & 63. Mailing Add: 532 16th St Brooklyn NY 11215

TRANK, LYNN EDGAR
EDUCATOR, PAINTER
b Cook, Nebr, Feb 24, 18. Study: Univ of Nebr, BFA; Washington Univ, BFA; Univ of Iowa, MFA; Ohio State Univ, PhD; study with Alfredo Zalce, Mexico. Work: Joslyn Art Mus, Omaha; Des Moines Art Ctr, Iowa; Evansville Mus of Art, Ind; Philadelphia Library Print Collection, Pa; Sheldon Swope Art Gallery, Terre Haute, Ind. Exhib: 57th Ann Am Exhib (watercolor & drawings), Art Inst of Chicago, 46, 1st Biennial Painting and Prints, Walker Art Ctr, 47; 6th Bradley Nat Ann, Peoria, Ill, 55; Drawing & Small Sculptures Nat, Muncie, Ind, 55, 56, 58, 59; Nat Print Show, Wichita, Kans, 56; Craft Exhib Invitational 59, Art Gallery, Muncie, 58; Watercolor USA, Springfield, Mo, 63-64; Wabash Valley Exhib, Sheldon Swope Gallery, Terre Haute, 70-72. Teaching: Prof drawing, painting & printmaking, Eastern Ill Univ, Charleston, 53- Awards: Tri Kappa Soc Graphic Arts Award, Tri-State Exhib, 55, 56; Wabash Valley Labor Coun Prize, Wabash Valley Exhib, Terre Haute, 70. Mem: Col Art Asn. Style & Technique: Transparent watercolor on canvas-landscape. Media: Intaglio-collagraph in printmaking-semi-abstract. Publ: Illusr, Febold Feboldson, Univ Nebr Press, 48; contribr, The Print, Creative Graphics, New York, 59. Mailing Add: 10 W Johnson Charleston IL 61920

TRAPP, FRANK ANDERSON
ART ADMINISTRATOR, ART HISTORIAN
b Pittsburgh, Pa, June 13, 22. Study: Carnegie Inst Technol, BA, 43; Harvard Univ, MA, 47, PhD, 52. Teaching: From instr to asst prof art hist, Williams Col, 51-56; from asst prof to prof art hist, Amherst Col, Mass, 56-, chmn dept fine arts, 63- Pos: Dir, Mead Art Gallery, Amherst Col, 65- Awards: Fulbright Scholar, 49-50; Nat Endowment for Humanities Sr Fel, 71-72. Mem: Col Art Asn. Publ: Auth, Art nouveau aspects of early Matisse, Art J, fall 67; auth, Expo 1867 revisited, Apollo, 2/69; auth, Attainment of Delacroix, Johns Hopkins Press, 70; auth, Aged lion returns: Jean-Leon Gerome, Burlington Mag, 5/73; auth, South Kensington Exhibition of 1874, Connoisseur, 12/74. Mailing Add: 71 Spring St Amherst MA 01002

TRAUB, CHARLES H
EDUCATOR, PHOTOGRAPHER
b Louisville, Ky, Apr 6, 45. Study: Univ of Ill, Champaign, BA, 67; Inst of Design, Ill Inst of Technol, MS(photog), 71, with Aaron Siskind & Eugene Meatyard. Work: Visual Studies Workshop, Rochester, NY; Mus of Mod Art, New York; Art Inst of Chicago, Ill; Fogg Mus, Harvard Univ, Cambridge, Mass; Int Mus of Photog, Rochester, NY. Exhib: Photographs of Charles Traub, Art Inst of Chicago, 75; The City, Mus of Contemp Art, Chicago, 77; one-man show, Light Gallery, New York, 77; Contemp Photog, Fogg Mus, 77; Five Photogr, Halstead 831 Gallery, Birmingham, Mich, 77. Teaching: Vis artist, Franconia Col, NH, 73-74; chmn dept & prof photog, Columbia Col, Chicago, Ill, 71- Pos: Free lance photogr, 69-; pres, Photog Adv Group, Chicago, Ill, 75-77. Mem: Soc of Photog Educ; Col Art Asn. Style & Technique:

Black and white and color still photographs, silver process, all formats. Dealer: Light Gallery 724 Fifth Ave New York NY 10019. Mailing Add: 907 Aislie St Chicago IL 60640

TRAUERMAN, MARGY ANN
PAINTER, INSTRUCTOR
b Sioux Falls, SDak. Study: Iowa State Univ, BFA; Am Acad Art; Art Students League. Exhib: Am Watercolor Soc Ann, 53-68; NY Figurative Painting & Traveling Exhib, 71; one-man shows, Chatham Col, Pittsburgh, 61, First Street Gallery, New York, 72, 74 & 77 & Landmark Gallery, McAllen, Tex, 75. Teaching: Instr art, Art & Design High Sch, New York, 52-78; instr art, Queens Col, New York, spring 75. Awards: Hon mention, Knickerbocker Artists Ann, 57; award, 67 & medal, 68, Painters & Sculptors Soc NJ. Bibliog: David Loeffler Smith (auth), Celebrated women artists, 1/62 & Heritage of the thirties, 10/62, Am Artist; Watercolor page, Am Artist, 7/74. Mem: Soc Painters & Sculptors NJ; Am Watercolor Soc. Media: Watercolor. Dealer: First Street Gallery 118 Prince St New York NY 10012. Mailing Add: 2 W 67th St New York NY 10023

TRAVANTI, LEON EMIDIO
PAINTER, DESIGNER
b Kenosha, Wis, Aug 5, 36. Study: Cranbrook Acad of Arts, MFA, 60; Layton Sch of Art, BFA, 59. Work: Milwaukee Art Ctr; Bergstrom Mus, Neenah, Wis; Rahr Art Ctr, La Crosse, Wis; Univ of Mo; Univ of Wis. Comn: Paintings & drawings, Ansul Int, Brussels, Belgium, 74, Lane Ltd, Sydney, Australia, 74-75 & Malaysia Ancom, Quala Lumpour, Malaysia, 75; mural for Union Bldg, Univ Wis Student Union, 69; painting, First Wis Nat Bank for pres off, 76. Exhib: Carnegie Inst, 53 & 54; Walker Art Ctr Biennial, Minneapolis, Minn, 56; Butler Inst of Am Art, Youngstown, Ohio, 56; Chicago Art Inst, 56 & 58; Philadelphia Acad of Art, 57; Nat Acad of Design, New York, 58; St Paul Art Ctr, Nat Drawing Exhib, traveling, 59; Detroit Inst of Art, 60; Milwaukee Renaissance Competition, Marine Bank collection, 60; Wis Marine Bank Invitational, 65; Milwaukee Art Ctr Biennials; Columbia Col, Mo, 78; Fitzsimmons, New York, 78. Teaching: Prof art & design, Univ Wis, Milwaukee, 64-; vis prof art, Univ Mo, Columbia, 77-78; vis lectr graphic design, Parsons Sch of Design, summer 77. Pos: Art dir, Wis Archit & Milwaukee mag, Schmidt Publ, 60-64; dir graphic design, Sch Fine Arts, Univ Wis, 64-74. Awards: Purchase Prizes, Milwaukee Renaissance, 60 & Wis Invitational, 65, Milwaukee Marine Bank; Metal Award, Brotherhood of Man, Strelsin Found, 64. Bibliog: Walter Herdig (ed), Ann Report Paintings, Graphis Ann, 66-67 & 75-76; auth (unsigned), Paintings in reports, Print Mag, 76 & Current Am Paintings, La Revue Moderne, Paris, 60. Mem: Milwaukee Advert Club; Soc of Typographic Arts; Milwaukee Soc of Communicating Arts. Style & Technique: Abstractions drawn from urban life. Media: Acrylic in Glazing, Layered Applications with Foil. Dealer: Betty Levin c/o Art Options Inc 49 E 53rd St New York NY 10022. Mailing Add: 2847 N Farwell Ave Milwaukee WI 53211

TRAVERS, GWYNETH MABEL
PRINTMAKER
b Kingston, Ont, Apr 6, 11. Study: Queen's Univ, BA, 33; Queen's Summer Sch; also with Andre Bieler, Ralph Allen & George Swinton. Work: Acadia Univ, Wolfsville, NS; Nat Gallery Can, Ottawa; Queen's Univ, Kingston; Montreal Mus Fine Arts, PQ; Winnipeg Art Gallery, Man. Exhib: Can Painter-Etchers & Engravers, Toronto, Ont, 57-70; Winnipeg Show, Man, 58-60; Nat Gallery Can Biennial, Ottawa, 58 & 71; Agnes Etherington Art Ctr, Queen's Univ, Kingston, 60-69; Brockville I O D E Exhib, 69 & 71; one-woman show, Gallery Schonberger, Kingston, 75. Awards: Reid Award, Can Painter-Etchers & Engravers, 58; Dept Educ, PQ, 63 & First Prize in graphics, 65, Expos Provincial. Mailing Add: 234 Albert St Kingston ON Can

TRAVIS, DAVID B
CURATOR, ART HISTORIAN
b Omaha, Nebr, Jan 31, 48. Study: Univ of Chicago, BA(art hist), Smithsonian Inst, Res fel, 72. Collections Arranged: Exhibitions of photography, Art Inst of Chicago, 73-; Photographs from the Julien Levy Collection: Starting with Atget (auth, catalog), 77; Photographs from the Andre Jammes Collection: Niepce to Atget (ed, catalog), 77. Teaching: Lectr hist of photog, Sch of the Art Inst of Chicago, 74. Pos: Asst cur photog, Art Inst of Chicago, 74-77, assoc cur photog, 77- Publ: Ed, Micro fiche Survey of the Collection of Photographs, Art Inst of Chicago/Univ of Chicago Press, 77. Mailing Add: The Art Inst of Chicago Mich Ave at Adams St Chicago IL 60603

TRAVIS, DAVID HAIL
ART DEALER, COLLECTOR
b Dallas, Tex, Dec 25, 31. Study: Extensive study in art and art appreciation with parents, Kathryne Hail Travis and Olin Herman Travis. Pos: Owner, Artisan's Gallery, 63- Mem: Lincoln Co Art Asn (pres, 69-). Specialty: Modern Western art, mostly young artists of exceptional quality. Collection: Wide range of Southwestern art, with watercolors, etchings, lithos and drawings. Mailing Add: PO Drawer T Ruidoso NM 88345

TRAVIS, OLIN (HERMAN)
PAINTER
b Dallas, Tex, Nov 15, 88. Study: Art Inst Chicago, 5 yrs. Work: Tex Fine Arts Mus, Austin; Highland Park Art Mus; Dallas Mus Fine Arts; also many portraits & landscapes in pvt collections. Comn: Eutra, East Tex Rm, Hall of State, Dallas; Love Field Airport, Tex; habitat backgrounds for Dallas Mus Natural Hist & Corpus Christi Mus, Tex. Exhib: San Francisco Nat; plus many others. Teaching: Instr art, San Antonio Art Inst; instr art, Austin Col, Sherman, Tex. Pos: Founder & dir, Dallas Art Inst, 24-44; dir, Dallas Art Asn, 8 yrs. Awards: Gold Medal for Portraiture, Art Inst Chicago; First Landscape Award, Southern States Art League, Memphis; plus many others. Media: Oil. Mailing Add: 8343 Santa Clara Dr Dallas TX 75218

TREADWELL, HELEN
PAINTER, DESIGNER
b Chihuahua, Mex. Study: Vassar Col; Sorbonne, Paris, France. Comn: Many murals in hotels & clubs in US, also Hotel Bermudiana, Hamilton, Bermuda, Hotel O'Higgins, Chile, Chase Manhattan Bank, San Juan, PR, Marine Midland, NY & others; five mosaic murals, New York Pub Sch Syst; many others in ships, trains & pvt homes; mosaic panels, Church of the Word Lutheran, Rochester, NY. Exhib: One-man shows, Arthur Newton Gallery, Rockefeller Ctr, Archit League, Crespi Gallery & Contemp Gallery, 34-65. Awards: Spec Award for Mural Paintings in Munic Bldgs, Chile; Presidential Medal for Extraordinary Serv in Promotion of Relationship Between Archit & Fine Arts of Mural Painting & Sculpture, Archit League, 69. Mem: Nat Soc Mural Painters (pres, 63-68); Archit League (first vpres, 52-54 & 64-66, mem exec comt); US Comn Int Asn Art (treas); Fine Arts Fedn New York (vpres); Artists Equity Asn; plus others. Mailing Add: 33 W 67th St New York NY 10023

TREASTER, RICHARD A
PAINTER, INSTRUCTOR
b Lorain, Ohio, July 14, 32. Study: Cleveland Inst Art, BFA. Work: Butler Inst Am Art, Canton Art Inst & Miami Univ, Ohio; Lehigh Univ, Bethlehem, Pa; Nat Acad Design, New York; Cleveland Mus of Art, Ohio; Southern Alleghenies Mus of Art, Loretto, Pa; Clara M Eagle Gallery, Murray State Univ, Ky; Wittenberg Univ, Springfield, Ohio. Exhib: 200 Years Am Watercolor, Metrop Mus Art, 66; View of Contemp Am Watercolor, Cleveland Inst Art, 68; Mainstream Int, 68-72; Watercolor USA, 72; Cleveland May Show, 75; one-man shows, Charleston Art Gallery, WVa & Southern Alleghenies Mus of Art, Loretto, Pa, 77. Teaching: Instr painting, Cooper Sch Art, Cleveland, 66-67; instr painting, Cleveland Inst Art, 66- Awards: Mainstreams Award of Excellence, Marietta Col, 69; Emily Goldsmith Award, Am Watercolor Soc, 69; Ohio Fine Arts Coun Honorarium, 71. Bibliog: Ralph Fabri (auth), Medal of merit, Today's art, 8/66; Norman Kent (auth), Richard Treaster—American artist, Am Artist, 1/72; Susan E Meyer (auth), Forty Watercolorists and How They Work. Mem: Am Watercolor Soc. Style & Technique: Realist, American painter. Media: Watercolor, Egg Tempera. Dealer: A B Closson Jr Co 400 Race St Cincinnati OH 45202. Mailing Add: 1228 Virginia Ave Lakewood OH 44107

TREBILCOCK, PAUL
PAINTER
b Chicago, Ill, Feb 13, 02. Study: Univ Ill; Art Inst Chicago; also study in Europe. Work: Art Inst Chicago; Cranbrook Mus; Cincinnati Mus; US Embassy, London, Eng; plus many univs & cols. Comn: Many portraits of prominent persons. Awards: William Randolph Hearst Prize, 26, Frank G Logan Medal & First Prize, 28, Art Inst Chicago; First Hallgarten Prize, Nat Acad Design, 31. Bibliog: Ernest Watson (auth), Paul Trebilcock, Am Artist Mag, 12/44 & Paul Trebilcock, portrait painter, In: Twenty Painters and How They Work, Watson-Guptill, 50. Mem: Nat Acad Design; Century Asn; Chelsea Arts Club, London, Eng. Media: Oil. Dealer: Portraits Inc 41 E 57th St New York NY 10022. Mailing Add: 44 W 77th St New York NY 10024

TREDENNICK, DOROTHY W
ART HISTORIAN, LECTURER
b Bristol, Conn, Oct 5, 14. Study: Norwich Art Sch, 32-34; Berea Col, AB(hist), 43, AB(polit sci), 43; Univ Mich, Gen Educ Bd fel, 50-51, MA(art hist), 51. Teaching: Instr art, Norwich Art Sch, 33-34; prof art hist & humanities, Berea Col, 46-70, Morris Belknap prof art, 70-, co-chmn dept art, 54-70; lectr, US & Asia. Pos: Assoc dir, Slater Mem Mus, 39-43. Awards: Seabury Award for Excellence in Teaching, Berea Col, 62; Fulbright Award Chinese Civilization, 63; summer sem grant, Nat Endowment Humanities, Univ Calif, 77. Mem: Col Art Asn; Southern Humanities Conf; Phi Kappa Phi; Am Asn Univ Prof; Am Asn Univ Women. Publ: Co-auth, This is Our Best, 55; co-auth, Kress Study Collection, 61; auth, Living by Design, 63; auth, Art & Protestant Church Today, 66; auth, Design for Living, 68. Mailing Add: Box 1834 Berea Col Berea KY 40404

TREESE, WILLIAM R
ART LIBRARIAN, PAINTER
b Burlington, Wash, Dec 7, 32. Study: Art Inst of Chicago, BFA, 60; Stanford Univ, MA, 61; Drexel Univ, Philadelphia, MLS, 64. Pos: Art librn, Free Libr, Philadelphia, 61-64; art librn, Univ Calif, 66- Mem: Art Libr Soc of NAm. Style & Technique: Paintings in acrylics. Publ: Co-auth, Computerized approach to art exhibition catalogues, Libr Trends, 1/75; ed, Catalogs of the Art Exhibition Catalog Collection of the Arts Library, University of California, Santa Barbara, Somerset House, 77. Mailing Add: Arts Library Univ Calif Santa Barbara CA 93106

TREIMAN, JOYCE WAHL
PAINTER
b Evanston, Ill, May 29, 22. Study: Univ Iowa, BFA. Work: Whitney Mus Am Art, New York; Art Inst Chicago; Denver Art Mus, Colo; Oberlin Allen Art Mus; Grunwald Found, Univ Calif, Los Angeles. Exhib: American Painting, Art Inst Chicago, 46-60; American Painting & Sculpture, Univ Ill, 50-63; Whitney Mus Am Art, New York, 51-53, 57 & 58; Carnegie Inst Int, Pittsburgh, 55 & 57; Recent Painting: The Figure, Mus Mod Art, New York, 62; Am Acad of Arts & Lett, 74-76; San Francisco Art Inst Ann, Calif, 77; Retrospective 1947-1977, Munic Art Gallery, Los Angeles; Contemp Am Monotypes (travelling exhib), Smithsonian Inst, Washington, DC, 78-80. Teaching: Vis prof painting, Art Ctr Col Design, summer 68; vis prof painting, San Fernando Valley State Col, 68-69; vis lectr painting, Univ Calif, Los Angeles, 69-70. Awards: Tiffany Fel, 47; Logan Prize, Art Inst Chicago, 51; Tamarind Lithography Fel, Ford Found, 62. Style & Technique: Figurative paintings, generally multi-figure compositions. Media: Oil. Dealer: Forum Gallery 1018 Madison Ave New York NY 10021; Tortue Gallery 2917 Santa Monica Blvd Santa Monica CA 90404. Mailing Add: 712 Amalfi Dr Pacific Palisades CA 90272

TRENTHAM, GARY LYNN
EDUCATOR, FIBER ARTIST
b Gleason, Tenn, Dec 7, 39. Study: Murray State Univ, BA, 61, MA, 65; Ind Univ, Bloomington, MFA, 72, with Budd Stalnaker & Joan Sterrenberg. Work: Steuben Glass, New York; Ind Univ, Bloomington Collection of Vpres of Corning Glass, NY; Auburn Univ, Ala. Exhib: Piedmont Crafts Exhib, Mint Mus of Art, Charlotte, NC, 73-74 & 76; Southern Tier Artist & Crafts Exhib, Corning Mus, NY, 74; Objects: Basketry Techniques, Am Craftsman, New York, 75; 7th Int Biennial of Tapestry, Centre Int de la Tapisserie Ancienne et Mod, Lausanne, Switz, 75; Fiber Structures, Carnegie Inst, Pittsburgh, 76; 2nd Int Exhib of Miniature Textiles, Brit Craft Centre, London, 76; Source Detroit, Cranbrook Acad of Art, Bloomfield Hills, Mich, 76; Exhib of Contemp & Hist Baskets, Peabody Mus of Harvard, Worcester, Mass, 76; Textiles: Past & Prologue, Greenville Co Mus of Arts, SC, 76; Basket Invitational, Florence Duhl Gallery, New York, 77. Teaching: Assoc instr textiles, Ind Univ, Bloomington, 69-72; assoc prof textile design, Auburn Univ, 72- Pos: Art instr, Lilburn High Sch, Mo, 61-64; art instr, Lone Oak High Sch, Paducah, Ky, 64-68; instr Proj 8, Jetton Jr High, Paducah, 68-69; asst in art series for elementary schs, Ind Univ, 68-69. Awards: Fiber Prize, Marietta Col Crafts Regional, Ohio, 73; Res & Exhib Expense Awards, Auburn Univ, 74-77; First Prize Fiber, El Paso Designer Craftsmen, Tex, 77. Mem: Am Crafts Coun; World Crafts Coun; Ala Crafts Coun. Style & Technique: Coiled and erratic half-hitch knotted basket forms, basically of linen, neutral colors. Publ: Contribr, D Meilach, auth, Modern Approach to Basketry, Crown, 74; contribr, articles in Craft Horizons, 74 & 76; contribr, articles in quart Rev of Design, Japan, 75; contribr, Ed Rossbach, auth, The New Basketry, Van Nostrand, 76; contribr, Decorative Art & Modern Interiors, Studio Vista, London, 77. Dealer: Florence Duhl Gallery 33 W 54th New York NY 10019. Mailing Add: Spidle Hall Auburn Univ Auburn AL 36830

TRENTON, PATRICA JEAN
ART HISTORIAN
b Los Angeles, Calif, May 14, 27. Study: Univ Calif, Berkeley & Los Angeles, BA, MA(art hist), PhD candidate, 78. Collections Arranged: Colorado Collects Historic Western Art: The Nostalgia of the Vanishing West (auth, catalogue), 73, Paintings from the Philip Anschutz Collection, 73, Picturesque Images from Taos and Santa Fe (auth, catalogue), 74 & Robert Rockwell Foundation, Mini-Exhibition of the West, Denver Art Mus, 74. Pos: Cur Am art, Denver Art Mus, Colo, 69-74. Awards: Nat Award by Graphics Art Industry for Am Art, Denver Art Mus Collection, 69; Bicentennial-Centennial Comnr's Seal for Scholarship for book, Harvey Otis Young, 75; Rockefeller Fel, Univ Calif Los Angeles, 77. Mem: Col Art Assoc. Res: Landscapists in the West during the 19th century. Publ: Co-auth, American Art from the Denver Art Museum Collection, 69 & auth, Harvey Otis Young, 1840-1901: The Lost Genius, Denver Art Mus, 75; co-auth, The Rocky Mountains: A Vision for the Artists of the Nineteenth Century, Clarkson Potter, New York, (in prep). Mailing Add: Anchorage West 1401 S Knoll Ave Pasadena CA 91109

TRIANO, ANTHONY THOMAS
PAINTER, EDUCATOR
b Newark, NJ, Aug 25, 28. Study: Newark Sch Fine & Indust Art, 46-50; with Reuben Nakian, 47-52; also with Samuel Brecher. Work: Newark Mus, NJ; Lowe Mus, Coral Gables, Fla; Paterson State Col, Wayne, NJ; Hartford Art Found, Conn; Seton Hall Univ, South Orange, NJ; plus othes. Exhib: Five Newark Artists, Newark Mus, 58; Albert Landry Galleries, New York, NY, 59 & 62; East Hampton Collectors, Guild Hall, Long Island, NY, 62; Gallery Selections, J L Hudson Gallery, Detroit, 64; New Jersey & the Artist, NJ State Mus, Trenton, 65; Boochever Art Collection, Paterson State Col, 68; Images of James Joyce, Montclair Mus, NJ, 75; Time, Life & Hope, Univ of Ala, Huntsville, Ala, 78; plus others. Teaching: Artist in residence & prof art, Seton Hall Univ, 70- Pos: US Govt art surveyor & consult, 72. Awards: 25th Ann NJ State Art Award, Montclair Mus, 57; Purchase Award, Newark Mus, 59. Bibliog: Mike Berg (auth), The Life & World of Triano, Seton Hall Univ, 68; William Sheppard (auth), Inside the Arts, produced on WNYC TV by Brooklyn Col, 70; D Simon (auth), Profiles, TV prog produced by Seton Hall Univ, 71. Media: Oil. Publ: Illusr, Exploring nature's rythms, 60 & illusr, Duck fever, 61, Abbott Labs; contribr, H & G colors for your personal bed & bath, 56 & contribr, House of color, 67, House & Garden. Mailing Add: Art Dept Seton Hall Univ South Orange NJ 07079

TRIEFF, SELINA
PAINTER, INSTRUCTOR
b Brooklyn, NY, Jan 7, 34. Study: Art Students League, study with Morris Kantor; Hans Hofmann Sch, study with Hofmann; Brooklyn Col, BA, study with Rothko & Reinhardt, 55. Work: Brooklyn Mus; New York Pub Libr; Inst for Human Develop. Exhib: Contemp Am Figure Painting, Wadsworth Atheneum, 64; Women Choose Women, New York Cultural Ctr, 72; Women's Art, Stanford Mus, 72; Work on Paper, Brooklyn Mus, 75; Butler Inst Ann, 77. Teaching: Instr drawing, New York Inst of Technol, 75-; vis artist painting, Notre Dame Univ, Ind, 76. Awards: CAPS Grant, New York Coun on the Arts, 76; Second Prize, Goddard Col Ann, 76; Purchase Prize, View from the Ctr, Bayonne Community Ctr, 78. Mem: Women in the Arts; Womens Caucus, Col Art Asn. Style & Technique: Expressive figurative painting. Media: Oil; Charcoal. Dealer: Prince St Gallery 106 Prince St New York NY 10012. Mailing Add: 803 Greenwich St New York NY 10014

TRIESTER, KENNETH
PAINTER, SCULPTOR
b New York, NY, Mar 5, 30. Study: Univ Miami; Univ Fla, BArch, 53. Work: Norton Gallery, Palm Beach, Fla; Miami Mus Mod Art, Fla; Fla Supreme Ct, Tallahassee. Comn: Family of God (limited ed of bronze menoras), 69 & series of six bronze plaques depicting hist of Jews, United Jewish Appeal; series of ten paintings depicting 4,000 yr hist of Jews, Temple Israel, Miami. Exhib: Greenwich Gallery, New York; Mus Fine Arts, Columbus, Ga; Lowe Art Gallery, Coral Gables, Fla; Contemp Art Mus, Houston, Tex; High Mus, Atlanta, Ga; plus several one-man shows. Awards: First Prize for Four Conversations (sculpture), Nat Ceramic Exhib, Lowe Art Gallery, 53. Mem: Blue Dome Soc, Miami; Fla Sculptural Soc; Southern Asn Sculptors. Style & Technique: Photopainting, a new technique of combining photographs and paintings. Mailing Add: 2699 S Bayshore Dr Coconut Grove FL 33133

TRIMM, H WAYNE
ILLUSTRATOR
b Albany, NY, Aug 16, 22. Study: Cornell Univ, 40; Augustana Col, BS, 48; Kans State Univ, 49; Cor Forestry, Syracuse Univ, MS, 53. Comn: Dioramas, Springfield Mus Art; three ecol dioramas, Augustana Col, 67; movie for Audubon Screen Tour, 68-69; diorama, Good Samaritan Ctr, Clear Lake, SDak, 74; mural, Gilboa-Blenheim Mus, 74. Exhib: Am Bird Artists Traveling Exhib, sponsored by Audubon Artists; Joslyn Mus Art; Buffalo Mus Sci; San Jose State Univ; New York Coliseum Sportsman's Show; plus others. Teaching: Lectr conserv, wildlife painting & Alaskan bowhunting; instr nature & sci illus, State Univ NY, Albany. Pos: Art dir, Conservationist Mag, Div Educ Serv, NY State Dept Environ Conserv, 53-73, art dir, 73- Mem: Columbia Co Arts & Crafts; Soc Animal Artists; hon mem Tuscarora Indian Tribe; Am Ornithologists Union. Style & Technique: Field sketches; finished paintings in watercolor, oil and acrylic. Publ: Illusr, Manual of museum techniques, 48 & The mammals of California and its coastal waters, 54; illusr, Collier's Encycl, 60-61; field paintings for The birds of Tikal, 63-64 & The birds of Colorado, 66; contribr, illus to Audubon Mag, NY State Conservationist, Time-Life Nature Bks, Nat Wildlife Mag & Mammals of New York (bk); plus others. Mailing Add: Sketch Book Farm Chatham NY 12037

TRINIDAD, FRANCISCO FLORES CORKY, JR
CARTOONIST
b Manila, Philippines, May 26, 39. Study: Univ Ateneo de Manila, AB(jour), 60. Pos: Cartoonist, Philippines Herald, 60-69; ed cartoonist syndicated comic strip Nguyen Charlie, 66-; syndicated ed cartoonist, Honolulu Star-Bull, Los Angeles Times, 69- Awards: Foreign Journalism Award, Univ Calif, Los Angeles, 67; Montreal Salon Cartoons Award, 67. Publ: Auth, Nguyen Charlie, 68; Not in this War; Aloha Eden. Mailing Add: 263 Kawaihae St Honolulu HI 96825

TRIPLETT, MARGARET L
PAINTER
b Vermillion, SDak, Dec 30, 05. Study: Univ Iowa, BA; Boston Mus Fine Arts Sch; Yale Univ, MA; also with Grant Wood. Work: Munson-Williams-Proctor Inst, Utica, NY; Slater Mem Mus, Norwich, Conn. Exhib: Am Watercolor Soc; Conn Watercolor Soc; De Cordova & Dana Mus; Slater Mus Art; Lyman Allyn Mus; Art in Transition: A Century of the Mus Sch, Mus of Fine Arts, Boston, 77; plus others. Teaching: Instr art, Norwich Art Sch, 29-43, dir, 43-70; retired. Pos: Trustee, Hartford Art Sch, Univ Hartford, 62-70; dir, Innovation I, Eastern Conn State Col, Willimantic, 75. Awards: Jesse Smith Noyes Found Grant, 69; Second Prize, Mystic Art Asn Juried Show, 77. Mem: Conn Art Asn; Conn Watercolor Soc; Mystic Art Asn (bd dirs, 72); life mem Nat Educ Asn; plus others. Publ: Co-auth, The Norwich Art School, a study of the directors, in combination with an on-going study of former students, 71. Mailing Add: 1 Prunier Ct Norwich CT 06360

TRIPP, WALLACE WHITNEY
ILLUSTRATOR
b Boston, Mass, June 26, 40. Study: Boston Mus Sch, dipl (graphic arts); Keene State Col, BEd(Eng); Univ of NH. Awards: Boston Globe/Horn Bk Illus Award (for Granfa' Grig had a Pig), 77. Mem: Author's Guild. Style & Technique: Pen and ink with watercolor used in traditional and realistic manner; mainly humorous; anthropomorphic animal subject. Publ: Illusr & ed, A Great Big Ugly Man Came Up and Tied His Horse to Me, Little, Brown, 73; auth & illusr, Sir Toby Jingle's Beastly Journey, Coward, McCann, 76; illusr & ed, Granfa' Grig Had a Pig, Little, Brown, 76; Illusr, Pawprints Greeting Cards. Mailing Add: Hancock NH 03449

TRISSEL, JAMES NEVIN
PAINTER, EDUCATOR
b Davenport, Iowa, Nov 7, 30. Study: State Univ Iowa, BA; Colo State Col, MA; State Univ Iowa, MFA. Work: Univ Wis; Beloit Col; Colo Col; Colorado Springs Fine Arts Ctr. Exhib: One-man show, Beloit Col, 57, & Colorado Springs Fine Arts Ctr, 66 & 72, Ankrum Gallery, Los Angeles, 76; Wis Salon, 58; El Paso Biennial, 64 & 66. Teaching: Instr art, Beloit Col, 58-60; asst prof art & art theory, Univ Calif, Los Angeles, 60-64; assoc prof art & art hist, Colo Col, 64-70, prof art, 70-, chmn dept art, 71-77. Pos: Pos: Actg dir, Wright Art Ctr, Beloit Col, 58-59; dir, Univ Exten Prog in Art, Univ Calif, Los Angeles, 62-64. Dealer: Carlin Galleries 710 Montgomery Ft Worth TX 76107; Ankrum Gallery 657 N La Cienega Blvd Los Angeles CA 90069. Media: Oil. Mailing Add: 1724 N Tejon St Colorado Springs CO 80907

TRIVIGNO, PAT
PAINTER, EDUCATOR
b New York, NY, Mar 13, 22. Study: Tyler Sch Art; NY Univ; Columbia Univ, BA & MA. Work: Solomon R Guggenheim Mus, New York; Brooklyn Mus, NY; Everson Mus, Syracuse, NY; New York Times; Gen Elec Corp. Comn: Murals, Lykes Steamship Lines & Cook Conv Ctr, Memphis. Exhib: Whitney Mus Am Art Ann; Art Inst Chicago; Pa Acad Fine Arts; Am Acad Arts & Lett; Univ Ill Biennial; plus 12 one-man shows. Teaching: Prof art, Tulane Univ La, 50-; chmn art dept. Bibliog: Articles in New York Times, 10/8/50 & 1/10/60; R Pearson (auth), Modern Renaissance in American Art, Harper. Style & Technique: Abstract painter. Media: Acrylic, Oil. Dealer: Galleria Bonino 5 W 57th St New York NY 10019. Mailing Add: 1831 Marengo St New Orleans LA 70115

TRLAK, ROGER
PAINTER, DESIGNER
b Chicago, Ill, June 27, 34. Study: Art Inst Chicago, 52-56 & 71; also with Gustan Likan, Joseph Schmidt, Briggs Dyer & Leroy Nieman. Work: Art Inst Chicago; Union League Club. Comn: Design logotype, Scottsdale Ctr Arts, 74. Exhib: One-man shows, Vincent Price Gallery, 68 & Art Harris Gallery, 72 & 73; Chicago & Vicinity, 70-71; Scottsdale Fine Arts, 72-75; Scottsdale One Hundred, 75. Pos: Dir, RST Galerie, Scottsdale, currently. Awards: Silver Medal Graphics, 74; Soc Illusr Award, 74; Hermes Award, 74. Bibliog: Jo Miller (auth), Starting a print collection, Am Artists, 10/75. Mem: Life mem Art Inst Alumni Asn; Chicago Artists Guild; Soc Typographical Arts; Chicago Soc Etchers; DuPage Art League. Style & Technique: Abstractionist painter and etcher. Media: Oil. Res: Ivan Albrights graphics. Specialty: American masters, including Albright, Avery, Bellows, Benton, Davies, Hirsch, Kuhn, Marsh, Sloan, Soyer, Weber & Wood. Mailing Add: 4660 E Mockingbird Ln Phoenix AZ 85028

TROP-BLUMBERG, SANDRA (SANDRA TROP BLUMBERG)
ART ADMINISTRATOR
b Brooklyn, NY. Study: NY Univ, BS(cum laude); Everson Mus Art. Collections Arranged: Frank Gillette (video; with catalog), 74; Sachakolin (drawings & sculpture), 74; John Willenbecher (paintings; with catalog), 75; David Hayes (sculpture; with catalog), 75; Leila Katzen (sculpture; with catalog), 75; Charles James (costume design; with catalog); Ant Farm 20-20 Vision (multimedia), 75; plus others. Pos: Cur traveling exhibs, Everson Mus Art, Syracuse, NY, 72, asst to dir, 73, actg dir, 74, asst dir, 74- Mem: Int Coun Mus (int comt mus & collections mod art); Lowe Art Ctr Bd, Syracuse Univ; Am Asn Mus. Mailing Add: Everson Mus Art 401 Harrison St Syracuse NY 13202

TROSKY, HELENE ROTH
PRINTMAKER, WRITER
b Monticello, NY. Study: New Sch Social Res, with Kuniyoshi Egas; Manhattanville Col, BA, with Al Blaustein & John Ross. Work: Wichita Mus of Art; Sheldon Swope Mus of Art, Terre Haute, Ind; Staten Island Mus. Exhib: Nat Asn Women Artists, Nat Acad Design Galleries, 67-69; Conn Acad Fine Arts, 67 & 68; Charles Z Mann Gallery, 67 & 69; Silvermine Guild, 68-70; one-person shows, Hudson River Mus, Yonkers, NY, 69, Wichita Mus of Art, Kans, 77 & Silvermine Guild of Artists, 78. Teaching: Art dir, Westchester Co Music & Art Camp, 65, 66, 71 & 72; lectr art hist, Brandeis Univ Women, 66-; instr printmaking, Manhattanville Col, 71- Pos: Columnist, Muse roundup, Harrison Independent Greenburgh Rec & Yonkers Rec, 60-; art consult, Westchester Libr Syst, 65-70; dir, 2nd Regional Plan, New York, 65- Awards: Westchester Art Soc Award, 67; Northern Westchester Award, 68; Nat Asn Women Artists Award, 69. Mem: Silvermine Guild; Conn Acad Fine Arts; Westchester Art Soc (exec dir & chmn bd, 60-); Artists Equity New York; Nat Asn Women Artists; plus others. Style & Technique: Expressionist style, collograph technique; cast paper; heavy textured prints using found objects incorporated into expressionist images. Dealer: Raydon Gallery 1091 Madison Ave New York NY 10028. Mailing Add: Yarmouth Rd Purchase NY 10577

TROVA, ERNEST TINO
SCULPTOR, PAINTER
b St Louis, Mo, Feb 19, 27. Work: Hirshhorn Mus, Washington, DC; Whitney Mus Am Art, New York; Guggenheim Mus, New York; Mus Mod Art, New York; Aldrich Contemp Art Mus, Ridgefield, Conn. Exhib: Documenta IV, Kassel, Ger; Los Angeles Co Mus Art; Solomon R Guggenheim Mus; Nat Mus Mod Art, Tokyo, Japan; Tapestry Show, Pace Editions, Inc, New York, 72; 5th Int Poster Biennial, Warsaw, Poland, 74; Hirshhorn Mus, 74; plus others. Bibliog: Donald Miller (auth), Ernest Trova as neo-surrealist, Art Inst, 9/70; David Zack (auth), Trova, Esquire, 10/73; Jean Lipman & Helen M Franc (auth), Bright Stars: American Painting & Sculpture Since 1776, New York, 76. Dealer: Pace Gallery 32 E 57th St New York NY 10022. Mailing Add: 6 Layton Terr St Louis MO 63124

TROVATO, JOSEPH S
PAINTER
b Guardavalle, Italy, Feb 6, 12. Study: Art Students League; Nat Acad Design; Sch Related Arts & Sci, Utica, NY; Munson-Williams-Proctor Inst Sch Art; Hamilton Col, hon DFA, 63. Work: Munson-Williams-Proctor Inst; Utica Col; Libr Cong, Washington, DC. Exhib: Munson-Williams-Proctor Inst; Utica Col; Albany Inst Hist & Art; E W Root Art Ctr, Hamilton Col; Everson Mus Art. Collections Arranged: Charles Burchfield, 62; 50th Anniversary Exhib of the Armory Show, 63; Edward Hopper, 64; Learning About Pictures from Mr Root, 65; 125 Years of New York Painting and Sculpture for NY State Coun on the Arts; The Nature of Charles Burchfield (mem exhib with catalog), Munson-Williams-Proctor Inst, 70. Teaching: Vis asst prof art, Hamilton Col, 65-66. Pos: Asst to dir, Munson-Williams-Proctor Inst, 39-; in charge exhib prog, Edward W Root Art Ctr, Hamilton Col, 58-; field researcher for NY State, Arch Am Art for the New Deal and the Arts, 64-65; consult, NY State Coun on the Arts. Publ: Contribr, Art in Am. Mailing Add: 12 Hamilton Pl Clinton NY 13323

TRUAX, KAREN
PHOTOGRAPHER
b Vermillion, SDak, May 17, 46. Study: Ariz State Univ, with Jack Stuler & Eric Kronengold, BFA(summa cum laude), 74; Univ NMex, with Van Deren Coke & Beaumont Newhall, working on MFA, presently. Work: Yale Univ; Intermont Col, Bristol, Va; Mus of NMex, Santa Fe; Phoenix Col, Ariz; Albuquerque Art Coun, NMex. Exhib: Heavy-Light, Pasadena City Col, Calif, 74; Women in Photog, Friends of the Crafts Mus, Seattle, 75; Is There a Female Camera?, Neikrug Gallery, New York, 75; one-person show, Focus Gallery, San Francisco, 75; Women of Photography: an Historial Survey, San Francisco Mus Art, 75; New Portfolios, Montgomery Art Gallery, Pomona, Calif, 76; Friends of Photog, Carmel, Calif, 77. Style & Technique: Photography, surreal hand colored black and white photographs. Publ: Contribr, Camera Mag, Lucerne, Switz, 73; contribr, Women See Woman, New York, 75; contribr, Camera 35, contribr, New Mexico Portfolio, Ctr of the Eye Photog Collaborative, Santa Fe, NMex, 76. Dealer: Hill's Gallery 110 W San Francisco Santa Fe NM 87501; Limner Gallery 7145 Main St Scottsdale AZ 85251. Mailing Add: 1038 Vassar Dr NE Albuquerque NM 87106

TRUBNER, HENRY
ART HISTORIAN
b Munich, Ger, June 10, 20; US citizen. Study: Fogg Art Mus, Harvard Univ, BA & MA. Collections Arranged: Chinese Ceramics; Arts of T'ang Dynasty, Los Angeles Co Mus Art, 52 & 57 (with catalog); Arts of Han Dynasty, Chinese Art Soc, Asia House, 61 (with catalog); Ceramic Art Japan: 100 Masterpieces from Japanese Collections (with catalog), Seattle Art Mus, Nelson Art Gallery, Asia House & Los Angeles Co Mus Art, 72-73; Int Symp on Japanese Ceramics, Seattle Art Mus, 72. Teaching: Assoc prof Asian art, Univ Toronto, 58-68. Pos: Cur Oriental art, Los Angeles Co Mus Art, 47-58; cur Far Eastern dept, Royal Ont Mus, Toronto, 58-68; cur dept Asian art, Seattle Art Mus, Wash, 68-, assoc dir, 75- Mem: Asia Soc (mem adv comt); Japan Soc; CULCON (mus interchange subcomt); Oriental Ceramic Soc, London; Col Art Asn Am. Res: Japanese and Chinese ceramics. Publ: Co-auth, Art treasures from Japan, 65-66; co-auth, Asiatic art in the Seattle Art Mus, Kodansha Int, Tokyo, 73. Mailing Add: Seattle Art Mus Volunteer Park Seattle WA 98102

TRUBY, BETSY KIRBY
PAINTER, ILLUSTRATOR
b Winchester, Va, Nov 8, 26. Study: Hiram Col; Cleveland Sch Art; NMex Inst Mining & Technol; Univ NMex; also with David Moneypenny, Oden Hillenkramer & Joe Morello. Work: Int Moral Re-Armament Ctr, Mackinaw Island, Mich; Cancer Res & Treatment Ctr, Albuquerque; Geronimo Springs Art Mus, Truth or Consequences, NMex; Gallery Southwestern Art, Old Town, Albuquerque; La Quinta Mus, Albuquerque. Comn: Portraits of three grandchildren of Gov John Simms, NMex, comn by Lillian Hutchinson, 65-68; Indian child portrait, NMex Easter Seal Soc, 69; three Indian paintings, First Presby Church, Albuquerque, 72-73; historical portrait, Synod Southwest, Presby Church, 75; two paintings reproduced as Christmas cards, Cyctic Fibrosis Found, NMex, 76 & 77. Cystic Fibrosis Found, NMex, 76 & 77. Exhib: Fine Arts Gallery, Carnegie Inst, Pittsburgh, 46; NMex Fiesta Biennial, State Mus, Santa Fe, 64 & 68; Nat Alpine Holiday Exhib, Ouray, Colo, 68; Nat Art Show, Lawton, Okla, 74; Nat League Am Pen Women Mid-Ad Cong, Phoenix, Ariz, 75. Teaching: Instr ceramics, US Pub Health Hosp, 48-49; instr ceramics, Ohio Pub Sch Syst, 49-50. Pos: Exhib chmn, NMex Art League, Albuquerque, 63-64; secy, Yucca Art Gallery, Albuquerque, 69-70, asst dir, 70-71, cur, 74-75; mem nat scholar comt, Nat League Am Pen Women, 76-, mem state bd, 76-77. Awards: Second Prize Oil Portrait, Southern Regional, Nat League Am Pen Women, Boulder, Colo, 65 & First Premium Pastel Portrait, Nat Mid-Ad, Salt Lake City, 73; Second Premium Pastel Portrait, NMex State Fair, 73, First Premium, 76. Bibliog: Flo Wilkes (auth), B Truby-retrospect, Albuquerque J, 67; Vivian Woods (auth), Arts & artists, Nevadan, 72; J Bonnette (auth), The Creative Process, KNME TV, Univ NMex, 73. Mem: Nat League Am Pen Women (secy, Yucca Br, 68-69, vpres, 70-71); Artists Equity; NMex Art League (exhib chmn, 63-64). Style & Technique: Portraits; southwestern landscapes; objective or realistic. Media: Oil, Pastel. Publ: Cover illusr, Flags, 73 & Let Our Light Shine, 74. Mailing Add: 6609 Loftus Ave NE Albuquerque NM 87109

TRUDEAU, YVES
SCULPTOR
b Montreal, PQ, Dec 3, 30. Study: Ecole Beaux Arts Montreal, sr matriculant with Marie Mediatrice. Work: Mus Quebec; Galerie Nat Can; Mus Art Contemp Montreal; Mus Art Prague, Czech; Mus Plein Air D'Ostrava, Czech. Comn: Vivace, J M C Camp Musical, Mont-Orford, PQ, 60; Vie Interieur, comn by N D De L'Enfant, Sherbrooke, PQ, 66; Phare Du Cosmos, Expo 67, Universe Plaza, 67; concrete relief, Univ Sherbrooke; bronze relief, Ecole Arts & Metiers De Riviere-Du-Loup, PQ, 68. Exhib: 3rd Int Contemp Sculpture Biennial, Mus Rodin, France, 66, Panorama Sculpture Quebec, 70; Int Symp Sculpture, Ostrava, 69; one-man show, Mus Quebec, 70; Biennale Middleheim, Anvers, Belg, 71; Premiere Biennale Petite Sculpture, Budapest, Hungary, 71. Teaching: Prof sculpture, Ecole Beaux-Arts Montreal, 67-69; prof sculpture concept & metal, Univ Que, Montreal. Awards: Can Coun Awards, 63 & 69; Ministere Educ Quebec Award, 70-71. Bibliog: Robert Guy (auth), Yves Trudeau, sculptor, Asn Sculpteurs Quebec, 71. Mem: Royal Can Acad Arts; Can Conf Arts (councellor, 67-68); Asn Sculpterus Quebec (pres, 60-66); Int Conf Mus; Int Asn Plastic Art. Media: Bronze, Plexiglas, Steel. Publ: Auth, article in Metiers D'Arts Quebec, 63; co-auth, Catalogue, Galerie Nat Can, 66; auth, Confrontation 67 (catalog), 67. Mailing Add: 5429 Ave Durocher Outremont Montreal PQ H2V 3X9 Can

TRUETTNER, WILLIAM
ART ADMINISTRATOR
Pos: Cur 18th & 19th century painting & sculpture, Nat Collection Fine Arts. Mailing Add: Nat Collection Fine Art 8th & G St NW Washington DC 20560

TRUEX, VAN DAY
PAINTER, DESIGNER
b Delphos, Kans, Mar 5, 04. Study: Parsons Sch Design, New York; Kans Wesleyan, DFA. Work: Calif Palace Legion of Honor, San Francisco; Mus Kans State Univ, Manhattan; Nelson Rockhill Mus, Kansas City, Mo; Philadelphia Mus Art, Pa; Metrop Mus Art, New York. Teaching: Pres, Parsons Sch Design, 41-51. Pos: Designer, Yale & Towne Mfg Co, 51-53; designer, Tiffany & Co, 51- Awards: Chevalier, Legion d'honneur, France, 51. Dealer: Graham Gallery 1014 Madison Ave New York NY 10021. Mailing Add: 84560 Menerbes France

TRUITT, ANNE (DEAN)
SCULPTOR
b Baltimore, Md, Mar 16, 21. Study: Bryn Mawr Col, BA, 43; Inst Contemp Art, Washington, DC, 48-49; Dallas Mus Fine Arts, 50. Work: Univ Ariz Mus Art, Tucson; Nat Collection Fine Arts, Washington, DC; Mus Mod Art; Whitney Mus Am Art; Walker Art Ctr. Exhib: One-woman shows, Andre Emmerich Gallery, 63, 65, 69 & 75, Baltimore Mus Art, 69 & 74, Pyramid Gallery, 71, 73, 75 & 77, Whitney Mus Am Art, 74 & Corcoran Gallery Art, 74. Awards: Guggenheim Fel, 71; Nat Endowment Arts, 72 & 77. Bibliog: Gregory Battcock (auth), Minimal Art, a Critical Anthology, Dutton, 68; Clement Greenberg (auth), Anne Truitt: American artist, Vogue, 68 & article in Art Int, Vol 11, No 4. Media: Wood, Acrylic. Dealer: Andre Emmerich 41 E 57th St New York NY 10021; Pyramid Gallery 2121 P St NW Washington DC 20037. Mailing Add: 3506 35th St NW Washington DC 20016

TRUMAN, JOCK CURTIS
ART DEALER, COLLECTOR
b Minneapolis, Minn, Sept 4, 20. Study: Univ Cincinnati, 38-41; Harvard Grad Sch Design, with Gabo, Albers, Kepes, Hyman Bloom, 46-50. Pos: Owner-operator, Thirty-Five River St, Inc, Boston, 50-58; asst to dir, Robert Isaacson Gallery, New York, 58-61; with Betty Parsons Gallery, New York, 61-75, dir, 70-75; dir, Parsons-Truman Gallery, New York, 75-76; dir, Truman Gallery, 76- Specialty: Modern art. Collection: Modern art. Publ: Ed & publ, 57th St Rev, 66-67. Mailing Add: 38 E 57th St New York NY 10022

TSAI, HSIAO HSIA
PAINTER, SCULPTOR
b China; US citizen. Study: Nat Col Art China, BFA; Univ Okla scholar & MFA; Cleveland State Univ, Ohio, hon PhD, 78; scholar study sculpture & portrait. Exhib: Laguna Gloria Art Mus, 61-64, 66 & 75; Nat Acad Galleries, 68, 72-75; El Paso Mus, Tex, 72; Jess Besser Mus, 75; Charles & Emma Frye Mus Pensacola Art Ctr, 75; Mus Fine Arts, Dallas, 76; plus many others. Awards: Silver Medal Int Competition, NY, 70; Watercolor Abstract Art Ctr, Tex, 74, 76 & 77; First Award in Watercolor, Mus Fine Arts, Dallas, 76. Mem: Hon mem Int Asn Art. Publ: Auth, Principles of Chinese painting adapted to modern needs; Translation from the Mustard seed garden treatise; plus others. Mailing Add: Hsiao-Hsia Tsai Gallery Fine Art 1437 Casa Verde Dr Corpus Christi TX 78411

TSAI, WEN-YING
SCULPTOR, PAINTER
b Amoy, China, Oct 13, 28; US citizen. Study: Univ Mich, ME, 53; Art Students League, 53-57; grad fac polit & social sci, New Sch Social Res, 56-58. Work: Tate Gallery, London; Centre Nat d'Art Contemporain, Paris; Kaiser Wilhem Mus, Krefeld, Ger; Albright-Knox Art Gallery, Buffalo, NY; Whitney Mus Am Art, New York. Exhib: One-man shows, Hayden Gallery, Mass Inst of Technol, Cambridge, Ont Sci Ctr, Toronto, Galerie Francoise Meyer, Brussels, Belg, 71, Corcoran Gallery of Art, Washington, DC, Denise René Gallery, New York & Paris, 72, Musée d'Art Contemporain, Montreal, Que, Galerie Denise René Hans Mayer, Dusseldorf, Ger, 73, Museo de Arte Contemporaneo de Caracas, 75 & Wildenstein Art Ctr, Houston, Tex, 78; The Responsive Eye, 65 & The Machine Show, 68, Mus Mod Art, New York; Cybernetic Serendipity, Inst Contemp Arts, London, 68; 3rd Salon Int Galeries Pilotes, Mus Cantonal Beaux Arts, Lausanne, Switz, 70; Pittsburgh Int, Carnegie Inst Mus Art, 70. Pos: Proj engr, Guy B Panero, Engineers, New York, 56-60; proj mgr, Cosentini Assocs, Engineers, New York, 62-63. Awards: Whitney Fel, 63; Ctr Advan Visual Studies Fel, Mass Inst Technol, 69-71; design in steel award, Am Iron & Steel Inst, 71. Bibliog: Art for tomorrow-the 21st century, produced on CBS-TV, 69; Jonathan Benthall (auth), Cybernetic sculpture of Tsai, Studio Int, 3/69; Fred Barzyk (auth), Video variations (with Boston Symphony Orchestra), produced on WGBH-TV, 71. Style & Technique: Abstract in style, technique varies; utilizing harmonic vibration, electronic feed back control with high frequency flash light, etc. Media: Stainless Steel. Dealer: Wildenstein Art Ctr Houston TX. Mailing Add: 154 Hester St New York NY 10013

TSCHACBASOV, NAHUM
PAINTER, PRINTMAKER
b Baku, Russia, Aug 30, 99; US citizen. Study: Lewis Inst, Chicago; Armour Inst Technol; Columbia Univ; also in Paris, France. Work: Metrop Mus Art & Whitney Mus Am Art, New York; State Dept, Washington, DC; Dallas Mus Fine Arts, Tex; Tel-Aviv Mus, Israel; Philadelphia Mus Art; plus many others. Exhib: Carnegie Inst Int, Pittsburgh; Art Inst Chicago; Corcoran Gallery Art, Washington, DC; Va Mus Fine Arts, Richmond; Univ Tex, Austin; plus many other group & one-man shows in the US & Europe. Teaching: Former instr, Am Artists Sch & Art Students League. Pos: Owner, Tschacbasov Sch Fine Arts; pres, Am Arch World Art, Inc. Awards: Pepsi-Cola Award, 47. Mem: An Am Group. Style & Technique: Versatile, creative, etc. Publ: Publ, two portfolios of etchings, 47; auth & publ, The American library compendium and index of world art, 61 & An illustrated survey of western art; contribr, articles to Art Students League Quart & Numero. Mailing Add: 222 W 23rd St New York NY 10011

TSE, STEPHEN
INSTRUCTOR, PAINTER
b Hong Kong, Oct 20, 38; US citizen. Study: Washburn Univ, Topeka, Kans, BFA; Univ Idaho, MFA; also with Jack Tworkov. Work: Univ Ore Mus of Art, Eugene; Univ Idaho Mus, Moscow; Battelle NW Permanent Collection, Richland, Wash; Big Bend Community Col, Wash; Jaid Gallery, Wash. Comn: Sculpture panels with painting, Student Union, Univ Idaho, 65. Exhib: One-man shows, Univ Idaho Mus, 66, Kiku Gallery of Fine Art, Seattle, Wash, 75, Jaid Gallery, Wash, 76, Wash State Arts Comn Purchase Grant Exhib, 76, Garnegie Ctr Gallery, Wash, 76; Univ Ore Mus of Art, 77, Kirsten Gallery, Seattle, 77 & Art Gallery, Spokane Falls Community Col, 78; Cheney Cowles Mem Mus, Spokane, Wash, 75-76; 2nd Nat Exhib of Works on Paper, Dana Fine Arts Ctr, Springfield Col, Mass, 76; Nat Cape Coral Ann Art Exhib, Fla, 77-78. Teaching: Chmn art dept, Big Bend Community Col, 66- Awards: Battelle Purchase Award, Columbia Basin Col, 75; Wash State Arts Comn Purchase Award, Big Bend Community Col, 76; First Place Award, Bicentennial Art Exhib Gallery, 76, Wenatchee Valley Col, 76. Mem: Wash Art Asn; Oriental Ceramic Soc, London. Style & Technique: Oil painting, pottery. Media: Oil and Watercolor; Clay. Dealer: Kirsten Gallery

5320 Roosevelt Way NE Seattle WA 98105. Mailing Add: 957 S Garden Dr Moses Lake WA 98837

TSELOS, DIMITRI THEODORE
ART HISTORIAN, WRITER
b Kerasea, Greece, Oct 21, 01; US citizen. Study: Univ Chicago, PhB, 26 & MA, 28; Princeton Univ, Carnegie Found scholarships, 28-32, MA, 29, MFA, 31 & PhD, 33; Inst Fine Arts, NY Univ, 29-30, with Richard Offner & Walter Cook; also with Charles R Morey. Teaching: From instr medieval & mod art to assoc prof, Inst Fine Arts, NY Univ, 31-49; lectr mod art, Swarthmore Col, 37-41, Univ Southern Calif, summers 37-41 & Vassar Col, 42-43; vis prof, Bryn Mawr Col, 44-46; prof art, Univ Minn, 49-71, prof emer & consult, 71-; distinguished vis prof, Northwestern Univ, 77. Awards: Fulbright Res Grants, Greece, 55-56 & 63-64. Mem: Col Art Asn Am; Archaeol Inst Am; Soc Archit Historians; Am Asn Univ Prof; Minn Hist Soc. Res: Medieval painting; modern architecture; modern Greek art. Publ: Auth, Exotic influences in the architecture of F L Wright, Mag Art, 53; auth, The sources of the Utrecht psalter miniatures, 55; auth, Modern illustrated books, 59; auth, Defensive addenda on the origins of the Utrecht psalter, Art Bull, 67; auth, F L Wright and world architecture, J Archit Historians, 69. Mailing Add: 1494 Branston St St Paul MN 55108

TSEU, ROSITA HSU
ART ADMINISTRATOR, INSTRUCTOR
b Peking, People's Republic of China, Jan 6, 16; US citizen. Study: Col Municipal Francaise, Shanghai, 30-36; Ecole des Beaux Arts, Paris; Sochow Art Acad, Shanghai; Otis Art Inst, Los Angeles; Brit Com Inst, 47. Comn: Portraits, Adm Jarret, USA Navy, retired, 52; protraits, Mme Chang Hsueh Liang, 62, Rabbi Willner, (deceased), 63, Anna Chennault, 70. Exhib: One-man show, San Gabriel Fine Arts Gallery, 77. Teaching: Portrait classes in own studio, 70- Pos: Managing dir, Sergie Bongart Sch of Art, 75- Style & Technique: Impressionist. Media: Mixed Media, Oil, Pastel, Acrylic. Dealer: Katona Gallery 11971 San Vincenti Blvd Brentwood CA 90049; Oriental Interior Gallery 24582 Hawthorne Blvd Torrance CA 90505. Mailing Add: 6869 Pacific View Dr Hollywood CA 90068

TSUCHIDANA, HARRY SUYEMI
PAINTER
b Waipahu, Hawaii, May 28, 32. Study: Honolulu Acad Arts, Hawaii; Corcoran Sch Art, Washington, DC. Work: Honolulu Acad Arts; State Found Cult & Arts, Honolulu; Free Libr Philadelphia. Exhib: Young Talent, Corcoran Gallery Art, 56; Ankrum Gallery, Los Angeles, 67; one-man shows, Libr Hawaii, Honolulu, 61, Gima's Gallery, Honolulu, 63 & Contemp Arts Ctr Hawaii, Honolulu, 66. Awards: John Hay Whitney Fel, 59. Media: Oil. Mailing Add: 1271 S King St Honolulu HI 96814

TSUTAKAWA, GEORGE
SCULPTOR, PAINTER
b Seattle, Wash, Feb 22, 10. Study: With Alexander Archipenko, 36; Univ Wash Sch Art, BFA, 37, MFA, 50. Work: Seattle Art Mus, Wash; Denver Art Mus, Colo; Santa Barbara Mus Art; Henry Art Gallery, Univ Wash, Seattle. Comn: Fountain sculpture, in bronze, Jefferson Plaza, Indianapolis, Ind, 71; Rain Fountain (stainless steel), Design Ctr NW, Seattle, 73; Somerset Fountain (bronze), Troy, Mich, 74; aluminum fountain sculpture, Expo 74, Spokane, Wash; bronze fountain sculpture, NW Med Ctr, Bellingham, Wash, 76. Exhib: 3rd Biennial, Sao Paulo, Brazil, 55; San Francisco Painting & Sculpture Ann, San Francisco Mus Art, 55, 58 & 60; 3rd Pac Coast Biennial, Santa Barbara Mus Art, 59; 66th Ann Exhib Western Art, Denver Art Mus, 60; Int Art Festival, Amerika Haus, Berlin, EGer, 66. Teaching: Prof art, Univ Wash, 46- Awards: Award for Obos No 5 (wood), Santa Barbara Mus Art, 59; Awards for Obos No 9 (wood), San Francisco Mus Art & Denver Art Mus, 60. Bibliog: Martha Kingsbury (auth), Art of the Thirties, Univ Wash Press, 72; Rachael Griffin & Kingsbury (auth), Art of the Pacific Northwest, Smithsonian Inst, 74; Benjamin Forgey (auth), article in Smithsonian Mag, 75. Media: Bronze, Watercolor. Mailing Add: 3116 S Irving St Seattle WA 98144

TUBIS, SEYMOUR
PAINTER, PRINTMAKER
b Philadelphia, Pa, Sept 20, 19. Study: Temple Univ; Philadelphia Mus Sch; Art Students League; with Georges Braque; Acad Grande Chaumiere, Paris; Inst d'Arte, Florence, Italy; also with Hans Hofmann. Work: Metrop Mus Art, New York; Libr of Cong, Washington, DC; Soc Am Graphic Artists, New York; Univ Calgary, Alta; US Dept of State, Washington, DC & Embassies in Asia, Europe & Africa. Exhib: Carnegie Inst Int, Pittsburgh, 48; Nat Exhib Prints, Drawings & Watercolors, Metrop Mus Art, 52; Traveling Exhib Am Prints, Royal Soc London, 54; Int Exhib Graphics, Seattle Art Mus, 68; retrospective, Mus NMex, Santa Fe, 64; Dallas Mus of Art, 70; Seattle Art Mus, 71; Washington-Baltimore Experimental Prints, Antioch Col, 73; Univ Maine, Augusta, 74; Mediterranea Paintings, Prints & Sculpture, Discovery Gallery, Santa Fe, 75. Teaching: Instr painting, design & graphic arts, Inst Am Indian Arts, 62-, chmn dept fine arts, 65- Pos: Artist-designer, New York Times, 59-62. Awards: Noyes Mem Prize for intaglio, Soc Am Graphic Artists, 48; Fourth Purchase Award in painting, Joe & Emily Lowe Found, 50; First Prize in watercolor, Mus NMex, 75. Bibliog: Michelle Seuiere (auth), Les exposition Seymour Tubis, Opera, 7/26/50; John MacGregor (auth), Seymour Tubis experiments with printmkaing, Pasatiempo, 8/27/67; Martha Buddeke (auth), Seymour Tubis takes two directions, J Arts, Albuquerque J, 11/21/71. Mem: Life mem Art Students League; Soc Am Graphic Artists; Col Art Asn Am; Santa Fe Designer/Craftsmen. Media: Oil, Intaglio, Bronze, Wood, Bone. Publ: Contribr, 72nd ann, Royal Soc Painters, Etchers & Engravers, 54; contribr, Western review, Western NMex Univ, 66; illusr, Pembroke Mag; illusr, Yerma, Santa Fe NMex, 71; contribr, Indian painters and white patrons, El Palacio, 71. Dealer: Los Llanos Gallery 72 E San Francisco Santa Fe NM 87501; The New West Gallery 2935C Louisiana NE Albuquerque NM 87110. Mailing Add: 947 Acequia Madre Santa Fe NM 87501

TUCHMAN, MAURICE
MUSEUM CURATOR
b Jacksonville, Fla, Nov 30, 36. Study: Nat Univ Mex; City Col New York, BA, 57; Columbia Univ, MA, 59. Collections Arranged: Five Younger Calif Artists, 65; Edward Kienholz, 66; Irwin-Price, 66; John Mason, 66; Am Sculpture of 60's, 67 (with catalog); Soutine, 68 (with catalog); Art & Technol, 71 (with catalog); 11 Los Angeles Artists, Arts Coun Gt Brit, 71 (with catalog). Pos: Art ed mod art sect, Columbia Encycl, 62; mem curatorial & lect staff, Guggenheim Mus, 62-64, organizer, summer 64; sr cur of mod art, Los Angeles Co Mus Art, 64- Awards: Fulbright Scholar, 60-61. Mailing Add: Los Angeles Co Mus Art 5905 Wilshire Blvd Los Angeles CA 90036

TUCHMAN, PHYLLIS
ART HISTORIAN, ART CRITIC
b Passaic, NJ, Jan 4, 47. Study: Sarah Lawrence Col Summer Session in Florence, 67; Boston Univ, BA(distinction in fine arts), 68; Inst of Fine Arts, NY Univ, MA, 73, with Robert Goldwater, Robert Rosenblum & William S Rubin. Teaching: Instr art hist, Sch of Visual Arts, New York, 72-75; adj lectr art hist, Hunter Col, 76- Pos: Mem ed bd, Marsyas, New York, 71-74. Res: Twentieth century sculpture; art of the 1960s; nineteenth century American sculpture. Publ: Auth, An interview with Anthony Caro, Artforum, 72; auth, Alexander Calder's Almaden Mercury Fountain, Marsyas, 73; auth, POP & I, Art News, 74; auth, Minimalism and critical response, Artforum, 77; auth, Carl Andre, Artforum, 78. Mailing Add: 333 E 79th St New York NY 10021

TUCKER, ANNE
CURATOR, PHOTO HISTORIAN AND CRITIC
b Baton Rouge, La, Oct 18, 45. Study: Randolph-Macon Women's Col, Lynchburg Va, BA(art hist), 67; Rochester Inst of Technol, AAS(photog), 68; Visual Studies Workshop, MFA, photo hist and mus procedure with Nathan Lyons and Beaumont Newhall, 70. Collections Arranged: Photographs of Women, Mus of Mod Art, New York, 71; The Target Collection of American Photography (traveling to five cities; ed, catalog), Mus of Fine Arts, Houtong, 77; Photographic Crossroads: The PhotoLeague (touring five mus; auth, catalog), Ottawa, 78; George Krause: Photographs, Mus of Fine Arts, 78. Teaching: Vis lectr photographic hist, Cooper Union, New York, 72-75; affiliate artist in photographic hist, Univ of Houston, 76- Pos: Res asst, George Eastman House, Rochester, NY, 68-70; curatorial intern, Photog dept, Mus of Mod Art, 70-71; adjunct cur, Mus of Fine Arts, 76- Mem: Soc for Photog Educ (bd mem, 76-; secy, 77-); Col Art Asn. Res: Concentrated on 20th century American photographs; interest in the absences and gaps in current photographic history. Publ: Auth & ed, The Woman's Eye, Alfred A Knopf, New York, 73; auth, Photography in America: Problems of a Show and Catalogue, Afterimage, 75; co-auth with Lee Witkin, Rare Books and Photographs (catalog one), Witkin Gallery, 71. Mailing Add: 1403 Banks St Houston TX 77006

TUCKER, CHARLES CLEMENT
PAINTER
b SC, Sept 13, 13. Study: Art Students League, scholar & with Frank Vincent DuMond, Ivan G Olinsky & George B Bridgman. Work: Rayburn Bldg, Washington, DC; Mass Inst Technol, Cambridge; Mint Mus, Charlotte, NC; 4th Circuit Ct Appeals, Richmond Fed Bldg, Va; Univ NC, Charlotte; plus numerous other univs & mus throughout the US. Comn: James Francis Byrnes, former Secy State, James P Richards, Ambassador to Mid East, Mrs O Max Gardner, Dr Mary Martin Sloop & J Spencer Bell. Exhib: Metrop Mus Art, 42, Nat Acad Design, 50, Coun Am Artist Socs, 66, Hudson Valley Art Asn, 68-72 & Allied Artist Am, 71-72, New York. Awards: First Award, NC Nat Exhib, 58 & 59; Dirs Award, Coun Am Artist Soc, 66; Artist of Year, Charlotte-Mecklenburg Bi-Centennial, 68. Bibliog: Legette Blythe (auth), Miracle in the Hills, McGraw, 53 & Call Down the Storm, Holt, 58; Works of Art, US Capitol. Mem: Allied Artist Am; Hudson Valley Art Asn; life mem Art Students League; Am Artist Prof League; Int Platform Asn. Mailing Add: 3621 Arborway Dr Charlotte NC 28211

TUCKER, GLENN F
ART CRITIC, COLLECTOR
b Tullahoma, Tenn, May 28, 36. Study: Univ Tenn, BFA, 58, MA, 59; All Souls Col, with A L Ronse; also in Eng. Pos: Art critic, San Antonio Light, 63- Awards: Journalist of the Year, Incarnate Word Col, 65. Collection: Elizabethan sketches, stage designs, original prints and graphics. Publ: Auth, Behind the flower portrait, Harvard Quart, 67; auth, Shakespeare and painting, 69 & auth, The man in the Grafton portrait, 71, Sewanee Rev; auth, What is an original print, Southwestern Art, 73. Mailing Add: 10014 Broadway San Antonio TX 78217

TUCKER, JAMES EWING
MUSEUM CURATOR, PAINTER
b Rule, Tex, Aug 13, 30. Study: Midwestern Univ; Univ Tex, Austin, BFA; Univ Iowa, MFA. Work: Miss Art Asn, Jackson; NC State Univ, Raleigh; Pine Bluff Art Ctr, Ark; Witte Mus, San Antonio. Collections Arranged: Art on Paper, 65-77, Cone Collection & Dillard Collection, Weatherspoon Art Gallery. Pos: Cur, Weatherspoon Art Gallery, 59-, ed, Bull, 65- Media: Oil, Watercolor, Graphics. Mailing Add: 632 Scott Ave Greensboro NC 27403

TUCKER, MARCIA
ART HISTORIAN, CURATOR
b New York, NY, Apr 11, 40. Study: Ecole du Louvre & Acad Grande Chaumiere, Paris, France, 59-60; Conn Col, BA(fine arts), 61; NY Univ Inst Fine Arts, MA, 69. Collections Arranged: Anti-Illusion: Procedures/Materials, 69, Robert Morris, 70 (with catalog), The Structure of Color, 71, James Rosenquist & Bruce Nauman (with catalog), Retrospective Exhibs, 72 & 73, Lee Krasner, Joan Mitchell & Al Held Exhibs, 1975 Biennial: Contemporary Art, 73-75, Whitney Mus Am Art, New York. Teaching: Instr art, Univ RI, 66-68; instr art, City Univ New York, 67-68; instr art, Sch Visual Arts, 69-73; guest lectr, cols, univs & inst. Pos: Cur, William N Copley Collection, 63-66; ed assoc, ArtNews, 65-69; assoc cur, Whitney Mus Am Art, 69-76; dir, The New Mus, New York, 76- Publ: Auth, Ferdinand Howald Collection of American paintings (catalogue), 69; auth, PreNaumanology, 12/70 & The anatomy of a brush stroke: recent paintings by Joan Snyder, 5/71, Artforum; auth, Early Work by Five Contemporary Artists & Bad Painting (exhib catalogues), The New Mus; plus others. Mailing Add: The New Mus 65 Fifth Ave New York NY 10021

TUCKER, PERI
WRITER, ILLUSTRATOR
b Kashau, Austria-Hungary, July 25, 11; US citizen. Study: Columbus Sch Fine Arts; also with E C Van Swearingen. Exhib: Regional Ann, 40-46, Akron Art Inst, Ohio; Touring Show, Ohio Watercolor Soc, 43; one-man show, Fla Gulf Coast Art Ctr, Belleair, Fla, 67; Whiskey Painters of Am Nat Shows (travelling exhib), Akron Art Inst, Ohio, 73, 26 E Art Ctr, Tulsa, Okla, 75, De Colores Gallery, Denver, Colo, 76 & Strongs Gallery, Cleveland, Ohio, 77. Pos: Free-lance writer & artist, 67- Style & Technique: Finished art adheres to free style of my quick sketches done from life. Media: Watercolor, Ink. Publ: Children's bk illusr, Saalfield Publ Co, 38-51; art writer & news artist, Akron Beacon J, 42-51 & St Petersburg Times, 52-66. Mailing Add: 201 Driftwood Lane Harbor Bluffs Largo FL 33540

TUCKER, RICHARD DERBY
PAINTER
b New York, NY, Dec 7, 03. Study: Art Students League, 19 & 49-53. Exhib: Univ Maine, Orono, 61-74; Frank Rehn Gallery, New York, 61-74. Mem: Founding mem Maine Coast Artists, Rockport. Media: Oil, Acrylic Ink. Dealer: Frank Rehn Gallery 655 Madison Ave New York NY 10021. Mailing Add: Box 127 Camden ME 04843

TUCKER, WILLIAM G
ART WRITER, SCULPTOR
b Cairo, Egypt, Feb 28, 35; Brit citizen. Study: Oxford Univ, BA(mod hist), 58; Cent Sch of Art & St Martin's Sch of Art, London, 59-61. Work: Tate Gallery, London; Mus of Mod Art, New York; Brit Mus, London; Walker Art Ctr, Minneapolis; Kroller-Muller Mus, Otterlo,

Holland. Comn: Angel (sculpture), Livingston Develop Corp, Lanark, Scotland, 76. Exhib: 2nd Biennale des Jennes, Paris, 61; New Generation, Whitechapel Art Gallery, Eng, 65; London, The New Scene, Walker Art Ctr, Minneapolis, 66; Eight Young Brit Sculptors, Stedelijk, Amsterdam, 66; Primary Structures, Jewish Mus, New York, 66; Guggenheim Int Sculpture, Solomon R Guggenheim Mus, New York, 67; Dokumenta 6, Kassel, Ger, 68; Int Exhib of Contemp Art, Atheneum Helsinki, 69; retrospective, Leeds City Art Gallery, Eng, 70; Brit Painting & Sculpture 1960-70, Nat Gallery of Art, Washington, DC, 70; 36th Venice Biennale, 72; Brit Sculptors, 72, Royal Acad, London, 72; The Condition of Sculpture, Hayward Gallery, London, 75. Bibliog: Norbert Lynton (auth), Latest Developments in British Sculpture, Art & Lit II, 64. Style & Technique: Abstract sculptor. Media: Wood/Steel. Res: History of sculpture. Publ: Auth, Early Modern Sculpture, Oxford Univ Press, 74; articles in Studio Int, Art in Am, Tracks, plus others. Dealer: Robert Elkon Gallery 1063 Madison Ave New York NY 10028. Mailing Add: Nova Scotia Col of Art & Design 5163 Duke St Halifax NS B3J 3J6 Can

TUDOR, TASHA
ILLUSTRATOR, WRITER
b Boston, Mass, Aug 28, 15. Study: Boston Mus Fine Arts Sch. Comn: Creator of the Tasha Tudor Christmas Cards. Exhib: Currier Gallery Art. Publ: Auth & illusr, A is for Annabelle, Walck, 54, Rand, 71; auth & illusr, One is One, Hale, 56, Rand, 71; auth & illusr, Corgiville Fair, Crowell, 71; auth & illusr, The Dolls Christmas, 72 & auth & illusr, A Tale for Easter, 73, Walck; plus many others. Mailing Add: c/o David McKay Co 750 Third Ave New York NY 10017

TUFTS, ELEANOR M
ART HISTORIAN
b Exeter, NH. Study: Simmons Col, Span with Edith F Helman, BS; Radcliffe Col, Renaissance with Millard Meiss, also Rembrandt with Jakob Rosenberg, MA; NY Univ Inst Fine Arts, Span painting with Jose Lopez-Rey, PhD. Teaching: Asst prof art hist, Univ Bridgeport, 66-68; assoc prof Baroque art, Southern Conn State Col, 68-74; prof women artists & chairperson div fine arts, Southern Methodist Univ, 74- Awards: Nat Endowment for Humanities Summer Res Grant, 74. Mem: Col Art Asn Am. Res: Monograph on Luis Melendez; women artists of the past. Publ: Auth, Albertinellis rediscovered at Yale, 68 & auth, Bellows & Goya, 71, Art J; auth, Luis Melendez: documents on his life & work, 72 & auth, A second self-portrait by Luis Melendez, 74, Art Bull; auth, Our Hidden Heritage: Five Centuries of Women Artists, 74. Mailing Add: Div of Fine Arts Southern Methodist Univ Dallas TX 75275

TULK, ALFRED JAMES
PAINTER
b London, Eng, Oct 3, 99; US citizen. Study: Oberlin Col; Nat Acad Design, cert; Art Students League, cert; Yale Univ Sch Art, BFA, 23; Inst Bellas Artes, Guanajuato, Mex, MFA, 63. Work: Birmingham Mus Art, Ala; Orlando Pub Libr, Fla. Comn: Stained glass window, Col WAfrica, Monrovia, Liberia, 40; murals, Salvation Army Hosp, Flushing, NY, 48; Iconastasis, Franciscan Monastery, New Canaan, Conn, 52; mural, D A Long Co Bldg, Hamden, Conn, 59; three murals, Picuris Indian Pueblo, Penasco, NMex, 63. Exhib: One-man shows, Recent Paintings, Art Mus, Stamford, Conn, 60 & 62, Recent Paintings, Stiles Col, Yale Univ, New Haven, 65, Exhib of Paintings, Mus Art, Birmingham, 68, Instructors Show, Art League, Bradenton, Fla, 68, Expressionistic Paintings, United Gt Hall, New Haven, Conn, 71; Mus Art, Bridgeport, Conn, 72; Quinnipiac Col, New Haven, Conn, 73; Westfield Atheneum, Mass, 74; Burnett Gallery, Amherst, Mass, 74; Post Col, Waterbury, Conn, 75; Albertus Magnus Col, New Haven, 77. Teaching: Instr drawing & painting, Dept Adult Educ, City of Stamford, 54-58; instr drawing & painting, Art Guild North Haven, 65-70. Pos: Dir dept mural painting, Rambusch Decorating Co, New York, 26-46; gen designer, Karl Hackert Studios, Chicago, 46-72; assoc designer, Studios of George Payne, Paterson, NJ, 48-52. Awards: Drawing Prize, Yale Art Sch, 21; Bronze Medal, Beaux Arts Inst Design, 22; First Prize for oil painting, Greenwich Art Sch, 58. Mem: Nat Soc Mural Painters; New Haven Arts Coun; North Haven Art Guild (adv). Media: Oil, Watercolor. Mailing Add: 210 Upper State St North Haven CT 06473

TUNICK, DAVID
ART DEALER
b Greenwich, Conn, Nov 17, 43. Study: Williams Col, BA(art hist), 66. Pos: Pres, David Tunick, Inc, New York, 66- Mem: Art Dealers Asn Am; Antiqn Booksellers' Asn Am; Int League Antiqn Booksellers; Chambre Syndicale de l'Estampe, Paris. Specialty: Original prints and drawings from the 15th century to circa 1950; particular emphasis on prints by Dürer, Rembrandt, Tiepolo, Degas, Whistler, and other Old Masters, impressionists, cubists, and German expressionists. Publ: Auth, Old Master & Modern Prints (ser of ann catalogs), 71-78; auth, Twenty-One Prints by Tissot (catalog), 72; auth, Viscount Downe collection of Rembrandt etchings, an auction review, 73 & auth, Anatomy of an auction: the Kornfeld sale of Old Masters, 74, articles in Print Collector's Newsletter; co-auth, Sixty-Five Prints by James McNeill Whistler (catalog), 75. Mailing Add: 12 E 80th St New York NY 10021

TURANO, DON
SCULPTOR, MEDALIST
b New York, NY, Mar 9, 30. Study: Sch Indust Art, with Albino Cavalido; Corcoran Sch Art, with Heinz Warneke; Skowhegan Sch Painting & Sculpture, with H Tovish; Rinehart Sch Sculpture, with R Puccinelli. Comn: Silver & wood mace, Am Col Physicians, Philadelphia, 64; carved oak panels, First Presby Church, Royal Oak, Mich, 65; limestone figures, Cathedral of St Peter & St Paul, Washington, DC, 69; four arks (locust wood), Temple Micah, Washington, DC, 71; Silver Medallion, Univ Notre Dame, Ind, 72. Exhib: Pa Acad Fine Arts, Philadelphia, 63; St Louis Mus, Mo, 64; Univ Colo, Boulder, 65; Audubon Ann, Nat Acad Design Galleries, 66; Xerox Corp, Rochester, NY, 71. Teaching: Instr sculpture, George Washington Univ, 61-65; instr sculpture, Corcoran Sch Art, 61-65. Awards: First Prize, Corcoran Gallery Art, 66; First Prize, Festival Relig Art, 67; First Prize, George Washington Univ, 68. Mem: Nat Sculpture Soc; assoc Washington Relig Art Comn. Media: Bronze, Wood. Mailing Add: 2625 Connecticut Ave NW Washington DC 20008

TURANO, JANE VAN NORMAN
ART EDITOR, ART WRITER
b Glen Ridge, NJ, Feb 20, 51. Study: Smith Col, BA, 73. Pos: Asst ed, The American Art Jour, New York, 73-75, auth bk rev, 74-, ed, 75- Mem: Decorative Arts Chap, Soc Archit Historians; New-York Hist Soc; Victorian Soc Am; Nat Trust for Hist Preservation; Am Art Hist Caucus of the Col Art Asn (secy, 78). Res: The American mind as reflected in American decorative arts of the 18th and 19th century and the relationship of American art to American literature, music and cultural history. Publ: Contribr to Am Art J & Antique Mo. Mailing Add: The Am Art Journal 40 W 57th St Fifth Floor New York NY 10019

TURK, RUDY H
MUSEUM DIRECTOR, ART HISTORIAN
b Sheboygan, Wis, June 24, 27. Study: Univ Wis; Univ Tenn; Ind Univ; Univ Paris, Fulbright scholar, 56-57. Collections Arranged: The Works of John Roeder, Richmond Art Ctr, Calif, 61-62; Contemporary Glass, Fine Arts Gallery San Diego, 67; Paintings by Tom Holland, 68, The World of David Gilhooly, 69 & Enamels by June Schwarcz, 70, Ariz State Univ. Teaching: Prof art, Ariz State Univ, 67-77. Pos: Art historian & dir art gallery, Univ Mont, 57-60; dir, Richmond Art Ctr, 60-65; asst dir, Fine Arts Gallery San Diego, 65-67; dir, Univ Art Collections, Ariz State Univ, 67- Awards: Award of Merit, Calif Col Fine Arts, 65; Golden Crate Award, Western Asn Art Mus, 74. Mem: Western Asn Art Mus; Asn Am Mus; Col Art Asn Am. Res: Contemporary art; 18th century French art; humanities; American ceramics. Collection: 18th century French prints; contemporary American art. Publ: Auth, I L Udell, Univ Art Collections, 71; co-auth, Scholder/Indians, Northland, 72; co-auth, The Search for Personal Freedom, William C Brown, Vols I & II, 4th ed, 72, 5th ed, 77; plus critical studies, art catalogues & art reviews. Mailing Add: Univ Art Collections Ariz State Univ Tempe AZ 85281

TURNBULL, BETTY
CURATOR
b Hollywood, Calif, Aug 4, 24. Study: Los Angeles Valley Col (art hist, design, drawing & painting), 56-59. Exhibitions Organized: Art of the Northwest Indian & Alaska Eskimo, Fine Arts Patrons of Newport Harbor, 68; Directly Seen: New Realism, 70, Art of the Indian Southwest Newport Harbor Art Mus & Pasadena Mus of Art, 71, Mary Cassatt (catalog text), 74, The Flute and the Brush: Indian Miniatye Paintings, 76, The Last Time I Saw Ferus (catalog text), 76 & David Park Retrospective (catalog text), 77, Newport Harbor Mus. Pos: Cur of Art, 69-72, actg dir, 72-73, cur of art, 73-77 & cur of exhibs & collections, 77-, Newport Harbor Art Mus, Calif. Mailing Add: Newport Harbor Art Mus 850 San Clemente Drive Newport Beach CA 92660

TURNER, ALAN
PAINTER
b New York, NY, July 6, 43. Study: City Col New York, BA, 65; Univ Calif, Berkeley, MA(painting), 67. Comn: Lithograph, Kunstvereine, Hamburg, Ger, 71. Exhib: One-man shows, Galerie Neuendorf, Cologne, Ger, 71 & Carl Solway Gallery, Cincinnati, 74 & 77 & New York, 75 & 77; Stadtische Kunsthalle, Recklinghausen, Ger, 73; Whitney Mus Am Art Biennial Exhib, 75. Awards: Univ Calif Alumni Asn Traveling Fel, 67; Award for Painting, Univ Calif, 67; Nat Endowment for the Arts Individual Fel Grant, 77. Style & Technique: Realist. Media: Oil. Mailing Add: 196 Bowery New York NY 10012

TURNER, ARTHUR CHARLES
PAINTER, INSTRUCTOR
b Houston, Tex, 40. Study: North Tex State Univ, Denton, BA, 62; The Sch of the Dallas Mus of Fine Arts, Tex, 63; Cranbrook Acad of Art, Bloomfield Hills, Mich, MFA, 66. Work: The Mus of Fine Arts, Houston, Tex; Cranbrook Acad of Art, Bloomfield Hills; Sam Houston State Univ, Huntsville, Tex; ALCOA Corp, Detroit, Mich; Am Tel & Telegraph Co, New York. Exhib: Drawings From Seventeen States, Mus of Fine Arts, Houston, 65; Third Ann Piedmont Graphics, The Mint Mus of Art, Charlotte, NC, 67; Nineteenth & Twentieth Ann Exhib of the Tex Watercolor Soc, The Witte Mus, San Antonio, Tex, 68 & 69; Drawings From Nine States, The Drawing Biennial XXIV, Norfolk Mus of Art, Va, 71; Tex Painting & Sculpture 71, Dallas Mus of Fine Arts, 71; Artists Biennial 73, New Orleans Mus of Art, La, 73; 24th & 29th Ann Exhib, Tex Watercolor Soc, McNay Mus, San Antonio, 73 & 78; Houston Area Exhib, Blaffer Gallery, Univ of Houston, 74; one-man shows, Art Gallery, Madison Col, Harrisonburg, Va, 67 & 74, Columbia Mus of Art, SC, 68, Art Studio Gallery, Sam Houston State Univ, Huntsville, 71, Beaumont Art Mus, Tex, 72 & Art Mus of South Tex, Corpus Christi, 73. Dealer: Moody Gallery 2015-J W Gray Houston TX 77019. Mailing Add: 2419 Julian Houston TX 77009

TURNER, BRUCE BACKMAN
PAINTER
b Worcester, Mass, Oct 28, 41. Work: Mem Sloan-Kettering Cancer Ctr, New York; Cheshire Pub Libr, Conn; also pvt collections throughout the US. Exhib: Ogunquit Art Ctr Ann Exhibs, Maine, 71 & 72; Am Artists Prof League Grand Nat, New York, 71 & 72; Hudson Valley Art Asn Ann, White Plains, NY, 72; Chautauqua Art Asn Nat Exhib, 72; North Shore Arts Asn Ann, East Gloucester, Mass, 72; 2nd Greater New Orleans Nat Exhib, La, 72; Acad Artists Asn Ann, Springfield Mus Art, Mo; Attleboro Mus Ann, Mass, 75; Am Fortnight Exhib, Hong Kong, China, 75; Mainstreams, Marietta Col, Ohio, 76; plus others. Teaching: Pvt classes oil painting, Rockport, Mass, 71-72. Awards: Mrs Helen Logan Award for Ogunquit Spume, Chautauqua Nat, 72; Seley Purchase Prize, Salmagundi Club, 76; Shumaker Award, Rockport Art Asn, Mass, 76; plus many others. Mem: Am Artists Prof League; Rockport Art Asn; North Shore Arts Asn; Acad Artists Asn; Salmagundi Club. Style & Technique: Oil paintings, done in traditional style, landscapes and seascapes. Media: Oil. Mailing Add: 4 Story St Rockport MA 01966

TURNER, (CHARLES) ARTHUR
PAINTER, INSTRUCTOR
b Houston, Tex, Nov 17, 40. Study: NTex State Univ, BA, 62; Cranbrook Acad Art, Bloomfield Hills, Mich, MFA, 66, with Zoltan Shepeshy. Work: Mus Fine Arts, Houston; Alcoa Aluminum Co, Detroit, Mich; The Galleries, Cranbrook Acad Art; Del Mar Col, Corpus Christi, Tex; Am Tel & Tel Co, New York. Exhib: Prints 1966, State Univ NY Potsdam, 66; Drawing Soc Nat, Am Fedn Art, New York, 70; 24th Am Drawing Biennial, Norfolk Mus Art, Va, 71; The Other Coast, Calif State Col, Long Beach, 71; Art Mus South Tex, Corpus Christi, 73; Artists Biennial, New Orleans Mus of Art, 73; The Prism Series, Moody Gallery, Houston, Tex, 76; Ten From Houston, The Art Ctr, Waco, Tex, 77. Teaching: Asst prof painting, Madison Col (Va), 66-68; instr painting, Sch Art, Mus Fine Arts, Houston, 69- Awards: Second Award, Southwestern Watercolor Soc 7th Ann, 71; First Purchase Award, Beaumont Art Mus 20th Ann, 71; First Award, Art Found Ann, Art Mus South Tex, 73. Bibliog: Richard Hutchens (auth), Arthur Turner—painter, Forum, summer 68; Arthur Turner, Facets, 6/69; Edwy B Lee (auth), Arthur Turner, drawings, Art Voices/South, 3/78. Mem: Tex Fine Arts Asn; Tex Watercolor Soc; Col Art Asn Am. Style & Technique: Abstract impressionism. Media: Oil, Charcoal, Watercolor. Dealer: Moody Gallery 2015 W Gray Houston TX 77019. Mailing Add: 2419 Julian Houston TX 77009

TURNER, DICK
CARTOONIST
b Indianapolis, Ind, Aug 11, 09. Study: John Heron Art Inst; De Pauw Univ, AB; Chicago Acad Fine Arts; Cleveland Art Sch. Mem: Nat Cartoonist Soc. Media: Ink. Publ: Auth & illusr, Carnival (cartoon panel), 40- Mailing Add: c/o Nat Cartoonists Soc 9 Ebony Ct Brooklyn NY 11229

TURNER, EVAN HOPKINS
MUSEUM DIRECTOR
b Orono, Maine, Nov 8, 27. Study: Harvard Univ, AB, MA & PhD; Sir George Williams Univ, hon LHD, 65; Swarthmore Col, hon LHD, 67; Temple Univ, hon DL, 74. Teaching: Adj prof art hist, Univ Pa, 70- Pos: Lectr & res asst, Frick Collection, New York, 53-56; gen cur & asst dir, Wadsworth Atheneum, Hartford, Conn, 55-59; dir, Mont Mus Fine Arts, 49-65; dir, Philadelphia Mus Art, 64-77. Mem: Am Asn Mus; Asn Art Mus Dirs ((pres, 75-76); Benjamin Franklin fel Royal Soc Arts; Am Fedn Arts (bd mem). Res: Thomas Eakins; 18th century American sculpture. Mailing Add: PO Box 7646 Philadelphia PA 19101

TURNER, JAMES THOMAS, SR
SCULPTOR, PAINTER
b Denver, Colo, Mar 15, 33. Study: Famous Artist Course; Western Brass & Foundry; also sculpture with Edgar Britton. Work: White House; Crawford State Bank, Nebr; Can Bank Seattle; in pvt collection of John Wayne & Sen Fred Harris, Okla. Comn: Joseph (wood carving), St Joseph High Sch, Denver, 69; Seven Days of Creation (wood carved door), Cath Church, Fairplay, Colo, 71; Four Horsemen of the Apocalypse (door), Four Horsemen Art Gallery, Fairplay, 72. Exhib: Pacific Northwest Indian Ctr, Spokane, Wash, 73; Death Valley Days, Calif, 74; C M Russell Art Auction & Sale, Great Falls, Mont, 74; Miniature Painters, Engravers & Sculptors Soc, 74; Calif Int Artist of the Year, 74; also one-man shows, in Zurich, Switz, 73 & Hong Kong, 74. Bibliog: Steve Cady (auth), A Casting for the President, Channel 7 TV, Denver, 71-72; 100 Years of Western Art, Channel 6, Denver; Patricia Janis Broder (auth), Bronzes of the American West, Abrams, 74. Mem: Denver Art Mus; Am Fedn Arts; Artists Equity. Style & Technique: Realism; architectual art. Dealer: Gallery A Taos NM 87571; Four Horsemen Gallery Stapleton Plaza Denver CO 80201. Mailing Add: 5930 Coal Mine Rd Littleton CO 80123

TURNER, JANET E
PRINTMAKER, EDUCATOR
b Kansas City, Mo, Apr 7, 14. Study: Stanford Univ, AB, 36; Kansas City Art Inst, with Thomas H Burton, dipl, 41; Claremont Col, with Millard Sheets & Henry McFee, MFA, 47; Columbia Univ, EdD, 60. Work: Metrop Mus Art, New York; Philadelphia Mus Art, Pa; Victoria & Albert Mus, London; Bibliotheque Nat, Paris; Libr of Cong & Smithsonian Inst, Washington, DC. Exhib: American Painting Today, 50 & Watercolors & Prints, 52, Metrop Mus Art, New York; 9th Nat Exhib, Libr of Cong, Washington, DC, 51; Nat Acad Design, New York, 61; 4th Int Bordighera Biennale, Italy. Teaching: Instr art, Girl's Collegiate Sch, 42-47; asst prof art, Stephen F Austin State Col, 47- 56; from asst prof to prof art, Chico State Col, 59- Pos: Pres, Nat Serigraph Soc, 57-59, vpres, 59-62. Awards: Guggenheim Fel, 53; Cannon Prize, Nat Acad Design, 61; Outstanding Prof Award, Calif State Univ & Col System, 75. Mem: Academician Nat Acad Design; Soc Am Graphic Artists; Nat Asn Women Artists; Am Color Print Soc; Calif Soc of Printmakers. Style & Technique: Designed realism style; printmaking: relief serigraph or intaglio serigraph mixtures; paintings: colored inks on scratchboard. Dealer: Kabutoya Gallery 900 North Point San Francisco CA 94109; Arts & Crafts Chico CA 95926. Mailing Add: 567 E Lassen Sp 701 Chico CA 95926

TURNER, JANICE KAY
ART DEALER
b Muskegon, Mich, May 8, 38. Study: Ray-Vogue Sch Design; Otis Art Inst; also painting with Mitsumi Kanemitsu & drawing with Charles White. Pos: Dir, Janus Gallery, currently. Bibliog: Laurie Gottlieb (auth), article in Home Mag, Los Angeles Times, 1/75. Mem: Artists Equity. Specialty: Contemporary paintings, graphics. Mailing Add: Janus Gallery 21 Market St Venice CA 90291

TURNER, JOSEPH
PATRON
b New York, NY, Feb 6, 92. Study: Jefferson Med Col, BS & MD. Interest: Kodachrome photography (non-profit) of works of art and donating the transparencies to museums and universities. Mailing Add: 1150 Park Ave New York NY 10028

TURNER, NORMAN HUNTINGTON
PAINTER
b Storm Lake, Iowa, July 11, 39. Study: Univ Colo, 57-58; Univ Iowa, 58-60; New York Studio Sch, 64-66. Exhib: Painterly Realism, Am Fedn Arts Traveling Show, US & Can, 69-71; The Representational Spirit, State Univ NY Albany, 70; New England Landscapes, Fleming Mus, Vt, 71; Drawing Each Other, Brooklyn Mus, 71; New Paintings from the Del Water Gap, Hopper House, Nyak, NY, 77; Ingber Gallery, 77; one-man shows, Green Mountain Gallery, New York, 72-75. Pos: Critic, Arts Mag, 77- Bibliog: Lawrence Campbell (auth), rev in Art News, 11/72; Laura Schwartz (auth), rev, 2/73, Ellen Lubell (auth), rev, 4/75 & Allen Ellenzweig (auth), rev, 4/77, Arts Mag; Ved Perl (auth), rev, Art in Am, 5-6/77. Media: Oil on Canvas, Drawing. Dealer: Barbara Ingber c/o Ingber Gallery 3 E 78th St New York NY 10021. Mailing Add: 602 Carlton Ave Brooklyn NY 11238

TURNER, RALPH JAMES
SCULPTOR, PAINTER
b Ashland, Ore, Oct 24, 35. Study: Reed Col, BA(painting), 58, with calligrapher, Lloyd Reynolds; Portland Art Mus Sch, dipl, 58, with painter, Louis Bunce; Portland State Col, 59; Univ Ore, MFA(sculpture), 62, with Jan Zach, Gerald di Guisto; science courses at Univ Ariz, 65, 72 & 73. Work: Syracuse Univ; Catalina Observator, Univ Ariz, Tucson; Flandrau Planetarium, Tucson; Hayden Planetarium, New York; Nat Aeronautical & Space Admin-Ames, San Francisco. Comn: Portrait sculpture of Tom Stant (bronze), comn by Donald Stant, Tucson, 63; triptych wood relief (black walnut), Cent Presby Church, Syracuse, 68; two polychromed scale models of Jupiter (fiberglass), Nat Aeronautical & Space Admin-Ames, Moffett Field, San Francisco, 74 & 76; portrait sculpture of Dr Gerard Kuiper (bronze), Univ Ariz, Tucson, 75; model of Phobos (Martian moon, fiberglass), comn by Jurgen Blunch, Hamburg, Ger, 76 with copies to Cornell Univ, Nat Aeronautical & Space Admin-Ames & Air & Space Mus, Smithsonian Inst. Exhib: A Series of Sculpture, Univ Ore Mus of Art, Eugene, 62; Ralph J Turner, Sculpture, Tucson Art Ctr, 63 & Univ Ariz, Tucson, 64; three-man exhib, Space & Art, Rainbow Gallery, Cannon Beach, Ore, 76; Planets & Progs: A Retrospective, Delphian Found, Sheridan, Ore, 77 & Williamette Sci & Technol Ctr, Eugene, 77. Teaching: Instr sculpture, Univ Ariz, Tucson, 62-65; asst prof design & drawing, Syracuse Univ, NY, 66-69; art coordr graphics, humanities & sculpture, Pima Col, Tucson, 70-72. Pos: Res assoc planetary models, Lunar & Planetary Lab, Univ Ariz, Tucson, 64-73; co-dir/designer, Rock Creek Experimental Sta, 73- Awards: Third Prize/Sculpture, Ariz State Fair, 64; Nat Endowment for the Humanities fel, 72-73. Bibliog: Sculpture by Ralph J Turner, NW Rev, Univ Ore, 63; Alexandra Schmeckebier (auth), Murals & sculpture on the campus of Syracuse Univ, Syracuse Univ Art Mus, 68; Fred Crafts (auth), Is it art or science, Eugene Register Guard, 77. Mem: Portland Art Mus. Style & Technique: Scale relief models made of planets or planetary surfaces (these are art and science artifacts); acrylic paintings on Plexiglas, in hexagonal matrices, based on computer-aided designs; wood carvings influenced by planetary forms. Media: Stone, Wood; Acrylic on Plexiglas, Ink. Publ: Auth, The Northeast Rim of Tycho, Lunar & Planetary Commun, Vol 8 (1970); auth, Extraterrestrial landscapes through the eyes of a sculptor, Leonardo, Vol 5 (1972); auth, A model of the eastern portion of Schroter's Valley, Lunar & Planetary Commun, Vol 10 (1973); auth, A model of Phobos, Icarus, Cornell Univ, 77; auth, Modeling and mapping Phobos, Sky & telescope, 77-78. Dealer: Lawrence Gallery Hwy 18 Bellvue OR 97378. Mailing Add: Rte 2 Box 167 Sheridan OR 97378

TURNER, RAYMOND
SCULPTOR
b Milwaukee, Wis, May 25, 03. Study: Milwaukee Art Inst; Layton Sch Art; Wis State Univ; Beaux Arts Inst, New York. Work: Ft Wadsworth, Staten Island, NY; Smithsonian Inst, Washington, DC; Baseball Hall of Fame, Cooperstown, NY. Comn: Commemorative coins of Robert E Lee, Nat Commemorative Soc, 68, Fats Waller, Am Negro Commemorative Soc, 70, Theodore Roosevelt, Int Fraternal Commemorative Soc, 70, Emily Dickinson, Soc Commemorative Femmes Celebres, 70, Eddie Rickenbacker, Nat Commemorative Soc, 73 & Evacuation of Boston by British, American Bicentennial Commemorative Soc, 76. Exhib: Detroit Art Inst, 27; Salon Aulomne, Paris, 28; Pa Acad Fine Arts, Philadelphia, 40; Nat Acad Design, New York, 67; Nat Sculpture Soc, New York, 72; Sports of the Olympics, Nat Art Mus of Sport, New York, 72; New York City WPA Art Exhib, Parsons Sch of Design, 77. Awards: August Helbig Prize for Man, Detroit Art Inst, 27; Guggenheim Found Fel, 28; Pauline Law Prize for Girl, Allied Artists Am, 66. Mem: Fel Nat Sculpture Soc. Media: Wood, Bronze. Mailing Add: 51 Seventh Ave S New York NY 10014

TURNER, ROBERT CHAPMAN
EDUCATOR, CERAMIST
b Port Washington, NY, July 22, 13. Study: Swarthmore Col, BA; Pa Acad Fine Arts; State Univ NY Col Ceramics, Alfred Univ, MFA. Work: Walker Art Ctr, Minneapolis; Univ Ill, Urbana; Smithsonian Inst, Washington, DC; Los Angeles Co Fair Asn; Lannan Found, Palm Beach, Fla. Exhib: Int Ceramic Exhib, Palais Miramar, Brussels, Belg, 58, Nat Mus Art, Buenos Aires, Arg, 63 & Victoria & Albert Mus, London, Eng, 72; one-man exhibs, Alta Col Art, Calgery, 74, Yaw Gallery, Birmingham, Miss, 77, Brooks Mem Art Gallery, Memphis, Tenn, 78 & Florence Duhl Gallery, New York, NY, 78. Teaching: Instr ceramics, Black Mountain Col, 49-51; prof ceramic art, State Univ NY Col Ceramics, Alfred Univ, 58 , actg head div art & design, 74-76; instr ceramic art, Penland Sch Crafts, summers 69-71 & 74. Awards: Int Exhib Ceramics Silver Medal, Cannes, France, 54; Silver Medal, Third Int Cong Contemp Ceramics, Prague, Czech, 62; Ceramic Art USA Award, 66; State Univ NY Chancellor's Award for excellence in teaching, 74. Bibliog: Daniel Rhodes (auth), Robert Turner, 57 & Howard Yana Shapiro (auth), Bob Turner, 72, Craft Horizons. Mem: Nat Coun Educ Ceramic Arts; NY State Craftsmen; fel Am Crafts Coun; Int Acad Ceramics, Geneva, Switz. Style & Technique: Stoneware vessels; thrown, altered, geometric. Media: Clay. Mailing Add: Cook Rd Alfred Station NY 14803

TURNER, THEODORE ROY
PAINTER, EDUCATOR
b Frederick Hall, Va, Jan 10, 22. Study: Richmond Prof Inst, Col William & Mary, BFA, 43; New Sch Social Res, New York, 46-50, painting with Abraham Rattner & printmaking with Louis Shanker; NY Univ Inst Fine Arts, MA, 50. Work: New York Pub Libr Print Collection; Va Mus Fine Arts, Richmond; Miss Art Asn, Jackson; Dartmouth Col, Hanover, NH; Univ Va, Charlottesville. Exhib: Brooklyn Mus Print Ann, 51 & 55; Am Fedn Arts Traveling Exhib Prints, 55; Va Mus Biennials, 59, 67 & 71; Watercolor USA, Springfield, Mo, 64; one-man shows, Babcock Galleries, New York, 68 & 69. Teaching: Instr medieval archit, Dartmouth Col, 50-52; assoc prof painting, Univ Va, 52-, actg chmn, McIntire Dept Fine Arts, 62-67; vis artists, Roanoke Fine Arts Ctr, Va, 71. Awards: Cert Distinction & Purchase Award, Va Mus Fine Arts, 59; Purchase Award, 20th Watercolor Nat, Miss Art Asn, 61; Painting Award, 18th Irene Leache Mem, Norfolk Mus, 66. Bibliog: Sue Dickinson (auth), Theodore Turner, Richmond Times-Dispatch, 6/23/68; Theodore Turner, New York Mag, 6/24/68; Larry Campbell (auth), Theodore Turner's watercolors, Art News, 12/69. Mem: Va Ctr Creative Arts (adv bd, 71-72). Media: Watercolor, Oil. Dealer: Babcock Galleries 805 Madison Ave New York NY 10021. Mailing Add: 916 Old Farm Rd Charlottesville VA 22903

TURNURE, JAMES HARVEY
EDUCATOR, ART HISTORIAN
b Yonkers, NY, July 8, 24. Study: Princeton Univ, AB, MFA(art hist), PhD. Teaching: Instr, Cornell Univ, Ithaca, NY, 53-58, asst prof, 58-64, assoc prof, 64-68; prof, Bucknell Univ, Lewisburg, Pa, 69-, Samuel H Kress Prof art hist, 74- Mem: Col Art Asn Am; Ist per la Storia Dell'arte Lombarda. Res: Interpretation of evidence in archaeology and art history. Publ: Auth, Statuette of Imhotep, Rec of Art Mus, Princeton Univ, 52, auth, Princeton's enigmatic relief, 63; auth, Late style of Ambrogio Figino, Art Bulletin, 65; auth, Etruscan ritual armor..., Am J Archaeol, 65; contribr, Il Duomo di Milano, Edizioni La Rete, 69. Mailing Add: RD 1 Box 398A Lewisburg PA 17837

TUROFF, MURIEL PARGH
SCULPTOR, PAINTER
b Odessa, Russia, Mar 1, 04; US citizen. Study: Art Students League; Pratt Inst; Univ Colo. Work: Smithsonian Inst Portrait Gallery, Washington, DC; Jewish Mus, New York. Comn: Enamel on copper artifacts, comn by St James Lutheran Church, Coral Gables, Fla, 74. Exhib: Syracuse Mus Art, NY, 45; Mus Natural Hist, New York, 58; Cooper Union Mus, New York, 60; Lowe Mus Beaux Arts, Miami, Fla, 68; YM-YWHA, Miami, Fla, 71; Bicardi Gallery, Miami, 76. Teaching: Instr art & ceramics, Riverdale Neighborhood House, New York, 43-47; instr ceramics in occup ther, Vet Hosp, Bronx, 45-46; instr basic design, Westchester Co Ctr, 59-61; instr enamelling, Miami Art Ctr, 70-75. Awards: Blue Ribbon for best in show, Blue Dome Art Fel, 66 & 73; Second Prize, YM-YWHA, 71. Mem: Artists Equity Asn; Fla Sculptors; Blue Dome Art Fel (treas, 64-68); Fla Craftsmen. Style & Technique: Realism with abstraction. Media: Metal, Enamel. Publ: Auth, How to Make Pottery, Crown, 49. Mailing Add: 517 Gerona Ave Coral Gables FL 33146

TURRELL, JAMES ARCHIE
ARTIST
b Los Angeles, Calif, May 6, 43. Study: Pomona Col, BA, 65; Univ Calif, Irvine, 65-66; Claremont Grad Sch, MA, 73. Work: Stedelijk Mus, Amsterdam; Holland; Cascina Tavernia, Museo Ambientale, Milano, Italy; Villa Schiebler, Quarto Oggiaro, Milano, Italy; Villa Panza, Varese, Italy. Comn: Roden Crater, Ariz, Dia Art Found, New York, 77. Exhib: Light Projections, Pasadena Art Mus, Calif, 67; Light Spaces, Main & Hill Studio, Los Angeles, 69 & 70; Art & Technol, Los Angeles Co Mus of Art, Los Angeles, 70; 3D into 2D: Drawing for Sculpture, The New York Cultural Ctr, New York, 73; Lichtprojecties En Lichtruimten, Stedelijk Mus, Amsterdam, 76; Light Space, Arco Ctr for Visual Art, Los Angeles, 76; one-man shows, Pasadena Art Mus, 67 & Stedelijk Mus, 76. Teaching: Lectr, Univ Calif, Los Angeles, summer 68; lectr, Univ Calif, Riverside, 71; vis artist, Pomona Col, Claremont, Calif,

71-73; vis artist, Claremont Grad Sch, 72-73; lectr, Univ Calif, Irvine, winter 74. Awards: Nat Endowment for the Arts, 68; Guggenheim, 74; Nat Endowments Matching Grant/Nat Endowment for the Arts, 75. Bibliog: John Coplans (auth), James Turrell: Projected Light Images, Artforum, New York, 10/67; Barbara Rose (auth), A Gallery Without Walls, Art in Am, New York, 3-4/68; New directions in Calif sculpture, article in Arts Mag, New York, summer 70; Melinda Wortz (auth), Exposure to Process, Art News, New York, 1/77; Germano Celanj (auth), Ambiente/Arte Dal Futurismo, Edizioni La Biennale Di Venezia, 76; Barbara Radice (auth), Un Pezzo Fatto Nel Cielo, Data, Milano, Italy, 2-3/77. Style & Technique: Light & space. Dealer: Heiner Friedrich Inc 393 Broadway New York NY 10012; Nick Wilder 8225 1/2 Santa Monica Blvd Los Angeles CA 90046. Mailing Add: Back-O-Beyond Sedona AZ 86336

TUTTLE, RICHARD
PAINTER
b Rahway, NJ. Study: Trinity Col (Conn); Cooper Union. Work: James A Michener Found; Nat Gallery, Can; Corcoran Gallery Art, Washington, DC; Kaiser-Wilhelm Mus, Ger; plus other pub & pvt collections. Exhib: One-man shows, Betty Parsons Gallery, 65-74, Galeria Schmela, Dusseldorf, 68, NY, 70, Mus Fine Art, Dallas, 71 & Mus Mod Art, New York, Nicholas Wilder Gallery, Los Angeles, 69, Albright-Knox Art Gallery, Buffalo, NY, 70, Mus Fine Art, Dallas, 71 & Mus Mod Art, New York, 72; Anti Illusion: Procedures/Materials, Whitney Mus Am Art, 69, Retrospective, 75; Corcoran Gallery Art 31st Biennial, 69; Soft Art, NJ State Mus, 69; Am Paintings of 60's, Am Fedn Arts, 69; Documenta, Kassel, WGer, 72; plus others. Bibliog: The avant garde: subtle, cerebral, elusive, Time, 11/2/68; This is the loose paint generation, Nat Observer, 8/4/69; Robert Pincus-Witten (auth), The art of Richard Tuttle, Artforum, 2/70; plus many others. Publ: Contribr, Art Int. Mailing Add: c/o Betty Parsons Gallery 24 W 57th St New York NY 10019

TWARDOWICZ, STANLEY JAN
PAINTER, PHOTOGRAPHER
b Detroit, Mich, July 8, 17. Study: Meinzinger Art Sch, Detroit, 40-44; Skowhegan Sch Painting & Sculpture, Maine, summers 46 & 47. Work: Mus Mod Art, New York; Los Angeles Co Mus Art; NY Univ; Fogg Art Mus; Vassar Col Art Gallery. Exhib: Art Inst Chicago, 54, 55 & 61; five exhibs, Mus Mod Art, 57-69; Mus Fine Arts, Boston, 66; one-man shows, Peridot Gallery, New York, 56-70; retrospective, Heckscher Mus, Huntington, NY, 74. Teaching: Instr art, Ohio State Univ, 46-51; asst prof art, Hofstra Univ, 65- Awards: Guggenheim Found Fel, 56-57. Mailing Add: 57 Main St Northport NY 11768

TWAROGOWSKI, LEROY ANDREW
DRAFTSMAN, EDUCATOR
b Chicago, Ill, Sept 12, 37. Study: Art Inst of Chicago, 55-59; Univ Kans, Lawrence, BFA, 61, MFA, 65. Work: Southern Colo State Univ, Pueblo; Ft Hays State Univ, Hays, Kans; Hastings Col, Nebr; US Nat Bank, Omaha, Nebr; Mountain Bell Corp, Denver, Colo. Exhib: 2nd All-Colo Competitive Exhib, Denver Art Mus, 74; 2nd Brit Int Drawing Biennale, Middlesbrough, Eng, 75; Drawings USA/75 Biennale, Minn Mus of Art, St Paul, 75; Spree/Colo Celebration of the Arts, Denver, 76; Rocky Mountain Drawing & Painting Exhib, Aspen Found for the Arts, Colo, 77. Teaching: Prof drawing, Colo State Univ, 67- Style & Technique: Figurative, representational. Media: Graphite. Mailing Add: 1501 Welch St Ft Collins CO 80521

TWIGGS, LEO FRANKLIN
PAINTER, EDUCATOR
b St Stephen, SC, Feb 13, 34. Study: Claflin Col, Orangeburg, SC; Art Inst Chicago; NY Univ, with Jason Seley & Hale Woodruff; Univ Ga, with Sam Adler. Work: Johnson Publ Co, Chicago; Spring Mills, New York; Wachovia Bank & Trust Co, NC; City of Atlanta, Ga; Herbert F Johnson Mus, Cornell Univ. Exhib: Sch Art & Arch, Univ Cincinnati, 70; Nat Exhib Black Artists, Washington, DC, 71; Artists USA, Carnegie Inst Int, Pittsburgh, 71; Salute to Black Artists, NJ State Mus, Trenton, 72; Directions in Afro-American Art, Cornell Univ, 74; Studio Mus, New York, NY. Teaching: Prof art, SC State Col, Orangeburg, currently. Pos: Dir art prog & Whittaker Gallery, 71- Awards: Best in show, Nat Conf Artists, 69; Award of Distinction, Smith Mason Gallery, 71; Merit Prize, Guild SC Artists, 75. Bibliog: J Edward Atkinson (auth), Black dimensions in contemporary American art, 70; Mary Mebane (auth), article in Instr Mag, 72; Thomas W Leavitt (auth), Directions in Afro-American art, Cornell Univ, 75. Mem: Col Art Asn Am; Nat Art Educ Asn; Nat Conf Artists (chmn, educ div, 72); Guild SC Artists (vpres, 74); SC Mus Comn. Style & Technique: Batik as a painting medium; after several waxings and dippings, adhering the fabric to a hard surface and paint it with dyes. Publ: Auth, articles in Explor Educ, 70, Design Mag, 72, Negro Educ Rev, 72, Sch Arts, 72 & Mus News, 72. Mailing Add: PO Box 1691 SC State Col Orangeburg SC 29117

TWIGGS, RUSSELL GOULD
PAINTER
b Sandusky, Ohio, Apr 29, 98. Study: Carnegie-Mellon Univ. Work: Whitney Mus Am Art, New York; Wadsworth Atheneum, Hartford, Conn; Mus Art, Carnegie Inst Int, Pittsburgh; Brooklyn Mus, NY; Westmoreland Co Mus Art, Greensburg, Pa. Exhib: Abstr & Surrealist Painting, Art Inst Chicago, 47; Whitney Mus Am Art Ann, 55; five Carnegie Inst Int, 55-67; Mus Mod Art Drawing Show, 56; Corcoran Gallery Art, Washington, DC, 57. Pos: Massier, Carnegie-Mellon Univ, 24- Awards: Carnegie Inst Group Prize, Assoc Artists Pittsburgh, 49; Second Prize for painting, Cincinnati Art Mus, 55; Mrs Henry J Heinz, II Award, 62. Bibliog: Paul Lancaster (auth), The artist, Wall St J, 57; Connie Kienzle (auth), Russell Twiggs, Roto-Pittsburgh Press, 71. Mem: Pittsburgh Plan Art. Style & Technique: Abstract-flow. Media: Acrylic. Dealer: Pittsburgh Plan for Art 1251 N Negley Ave Pittsburgh PA 15206. Mailing Add: 652 Maryland Ave Pittsburgh PA 15232

TWITTY, JAMES (WATSON)
PAINTER, PRINTMAKER
b Mt Vernon, NY, Apr 13, 16. Study: Art Students League, with Edwin Dickenson, Stephen Greene & Morris Kantor; Univ Miami, with Xavier Gonzalez & Eliot O'Hara. Work: Nat Gallery Art & Corcoran Gallery Art, Washington, DC; Brooklyn Mus, NY; Baltimore Mus Art, Md; Mus Fine Art, Dallas; plus others. Exhib: One-man shows, Corcoran Gallery Art, 66, Lehigh Univ, Bethlehem, Pa, 67, David Findlay Galleries, New York, 71, 73-74, 76 & 78, McNay Art Inst, San Antonio, Tex, 72, George Washington Univ, 75, Hokin Gallery, Chicago, 76 & Bettina Gallery, Zurich, Switz, 77; plus others. Teaching: Assoc prof painting, Corcoran Sch Art, 64-74; lectr fine arts, George Washington Univ, 64-74; exchange prof painting, Leeds Col Art, Eng, 67-68; vis prof painting, Miami Art Ctr, Fla, 70; vis prof painting, San Antonio Art Inst, Tex, 72. Awards: Allied Artists Am Award, 61; Soc Wash Art Award, 65; First Ann Exhib Award, Miami, 66. Bibliog: Frank Getlein (auth), A Washington artist in a New York setting, Washington DC Star-News, 73. Mem: Life mem Art Students League. Media: Acrylic, Silkscreen. Dealer: David Findlay Galleries 984 Madison Ave New York NY 10021. Mailing Add: 1600 South Eads St Apt 1234-S Arlington VA 22202

TWOMBLY, CY
PAINTER
b Lexington, Va, Apr 25, 28. Study: Boston Mus Sch Fine Arts, 48-49; Washington & Lee Univ, 50; Art Students League, 51; Black Mountain Col, 52, with Frank Kline & Robert Motherwell. Work: RI Sch Design; Whitney Mus Am Art, New York; Mus Mod Art, New York; also pvt collections in New York, Chicago, Washington, DC & Europe. Exhib: NY Univ, 67; Whitney Mus Am Art Ann, New York, 67; one-man shows, Milwaukee, 68 & Nicholas Wilder Gallery, 69; Herron Inst Art, Indianapolis, 69; Guggenheim Mus, New York, 76; Mus Mod Art, 76; plus others. Teaching: Head dept art, Southern Sem & Jr Col, Buena Vista, Va, 55-56. Awards: Va Mus Fine Arts Fel for Travel in Europe & Africa, 52-53. Bibliog: Pierre Restany (auth), Lyrisme et Abstraction, Edizioni Apollinairi, Milan, 60. Mailing Add: c/o Leo Castelli Gallery 420 W Broadway New York NY 10013

TWORKOV, JACK
PAINTER
b Biala, Poland, Aug 15, 00; US citizen. Study: Columbia Univ, 20-23, hon LHD, 72; Nat Acad Design, 23-25; Art Students League, 25-26. Work: Albright-Knox Art Gallery, Buffalo; Cleveland Mus Fine Art; Mus Mod Art, New York; Nat Collection Fine Art, Smithsonian Inst, Washington, DC; Whitney Mus Am Art, New York; plus others. Exhib: New American Painting, Int Traveling Show, Nionia, 58; Osaka Festival, Gutai 9, 58; Documenta II, Kassel, Ger, 59; American Abstract Expressionists, Guggenheim Mus, 61; Whitney Mus Am Art Ann, 69-71. Teaching: Leffingwell prof art & chmn dept, Yale Univ, 63-69; vis prof painting, Cooper Union, 70-72; vis prof painting, Columbia Univ, spring 73. Awards: William A Clark Prize & Corcoran Gold Medal, Corcoran Gallery Art, 63; Guggenheim Fel, 71. Bibliog: D Ashton (auth), The Unknown Shore, Little, 62; L Slate (auth), Jack Tworkov (film), Nat Educ TV, 63; Ed Bryant (auth), Jack Tworkov, Whitney Mus, 64; plus others. Publ: Auth, The wandering soutine, 11/50 & auth, Flowers & realism, 5/54, Art News; auth, articles in It Is, spring 58, autumn 58 & 59. Mailing Add: 161 W 22nd St New York NY 10011

TYLER, KENNETH EUGENE
PRINT PUBLISHER, PRINTMAKER
b East Chicago, Ind, Dec 13, 31. Study: Art Inst of Chicago, 49-52, 54-57, BAE, 57; Ind Univ, 51-52; Chicago Univ, 55-57; John Herron Sch of Art, MAE, 63. Work: Mus of Mod Art, New York; Los Angeles Co Mus of Art, Los Angeles; San Diego Mus; Sheldon Swope Art Gallery, Terra Haute, Ind; Nat Mus of Australia, Camberra. Teaching: Teacher art & theatre & scene shop dir, Evanston Township High Sch, 57-58. Pos: Tech dir, Tamarind Lithography Workshop, 64-65; dir, Gemini GEL, 66-73; dir, Tyler Graphics Ltd, 74- Awards: Ford Grant, 63; grant, Nat Coun on Visual Arts for Res & Develop Work in Lithography, 67. Bibliog: Riva Castleman (auth), Technics & Creativity; Gemini GEL, Mus of Mod Art, New York, 70; Reaching Out: Master Printer Kenneth Tyler (16mm color film, 35 minutes), Avery/Tirce Productions, 74; Judith Goldman (auth), Art Off the Picture Press—Tyler Graphics Ltd, Hofstra Univ, 77. Mailing Add: PO Box 294 Bedford Village NY 10506

TYLER, VALTON
PRINTMAKER, PAINTER
b Texas City, Tex, Mar 30, 44. Study: Dallas Art Inst, Tex, 67. Work: Tyler Mus Art, Tex. Exhib: First Fifty Prints, Pollock Galleries, Southern Methodist Univ, Dallas & Tyler Mus Art, 72; 8th Ann New Talent in Printmaking, Assoc Am Artists, New York, 72; one-man show, Galerie Claude Jongen, Brussels, Belg, 77. Bibliog: Reynolds (auth), The fifty prints—Valton Tyler, Southern Methodist Univ Press, 72. Style & Technique: Oil painting—surrealist. Media: Aquatint. Mailing Add: c/o Valley House Gallery 6616 Spring Valley Rd Dallas TX 75240

TYSON, MARY (MRS KENNETH THOMPSON)
PAINTER
b Sewanee, Tenn, Nov 2, 09. Study: Grand Cent Art Sch, with George P Ennis, Howard Hildebrandt & Wayman Adams; New Sch Social Res, with Julian Levi. Work: Artists Asn Nantucket Permanent Collection; Guild Hall Collection. Exhib: Int Exhib, Brooklyn Mus, 35 & 37; Am Watercolor Soc Ann; Nat Arts Club Watercolor Exhib, 68-75; Addison Gallery, Andover; one-man shows, Bruce Mus, Greenwich, Conn & Present Day Club, Princeton, NJ, 71. Awards: Solo Award, 69, Elizabeth Morse Genius Mem Award, 70 & Award, 71, 73, 75 & 77, Pen & Brush Club; Award, Guild Hall, East Hampton, 77. Mem: Life mem Am Watercolor Soc; Pen & Brush Club; Easthampton Guild Hall; Nat Arts Club. Media: Watercolor. Mailing Add: 20 W 11th St New York NY 10011

TYSON, RAE JULIAN
ART ADMINISTRATOR, SCULPTOR
b Lockport, NY, Jan 3, 44. Study: Ball State Univ; Niagara Univ; Univ of Buffalo, Parsons Col, BA, 67. Work: H F Johnson Mus, Ithaca, NY. Exhib: 03-23-03, Nat Gallery of Can, Ottawa, 77; NY State Artist Series, Johnson Mus, Ithaca, 77; Artwords and Bookworks, Los Angeles Inst of Contemp Art, Calif, 78; Artist Books, Chicago Art Inst, 78; one-man shows, Vehicule Gallery, Montreal, 76, Hallwalls Gallery, Buffalo, 77 & Marion Locks Gallery, Philadelphia, 78. Collections Arranged: Artpark: The Program in Visual Arts (contribr, catalog), 75-78. Teaching: Guest lectr contemp art, Cranbrook, RI Sch of Design, Chicago Art Inst, Walker Art Ctr, NS Col of Art & Design, plus many others, 74- Pos: Consult, Various States, Art Agencies, 74; visual arts dir, Artpark, Lewiston, NY, 74-; fel, Inst for Art & Urban Res, New York, 75. Bibliog: Lucy R Lippard (auth), A is for Artpark, Art in Am, 74; Barbara Baracks (auth), Artpark: the New Aesthetic Playground, Artform, 76; Michael Blackwood (auth), Artpark People (film), Blackwood Productions, 77. Mem: Am Crafts Coun; Can Crafts Coun; Northeast Mus Asn; Col Art Asn. Style & Technique: Minimal floor pieces, drawings. Media: Steel; Wood; Charcoal; Paint Stick on Paper. Publ: Auth, Rae Tyson: Drawings, 76 & Drawings II, 78, Journeyman Press. Mailing Add: 511 Lake St Wilson NY 14172

TYTELL, LOUIS
PAINTER
b New York, NY, Jan 8, 13. Study: City Col New York, BS, 34; Columbia Univ, MA, 35; Skowhegan Sch Painting & Sculpture; New Sch Social Res. Work: Newark Mus; Corcoran Gallery of Art; Wickersham Gallery, Univ NC, Raleigh; Libr of Cong Print Collection, Washington, DC. Exhib: 110 American Painters, Walker Art Ctr, 44; Pa Acad Fine Arts Ann, 49 & 66; Nat Acad Design Ann, 62, 66 & 68; Nat Inst Arts & Lett, 67; Mus Mod Art Lending Serv Gallery, 73-78; Edward Hopper House, Nyack, NY, 78. Teaching: Chmn art dept, High Sch Music & Art, 61-67 & 69-75; assoc prof art, City Col New York, 67-69. Awards: Tiffany Fel, 62; Am Inst Arts & Lett Grant, 67. Media: Oil, Pastel. Dealer: Roko Gallery 90 E Tenth St New York NY 10003. Mailing Add: 107 Green Rd West Nyack NY 10994

U

UBANS, JURIS K
PAINTER, EDUCATOR
b Riga, Latvia, July 12, 38; US citizen. Study: Yale Univ, with William Bailey, 65; Syracuse Univ, BFA, 66, with Ainslee Burke & Frederick Hauck; Pa State Univ, MFA, 68, with Enrique Montenegro & Eugenio Battisti. Work: Yale Univ; Syracuse Univ; Pa State Univ; Univ Maine, Portland-Gorham; plus pvt collections. Comn: A Season in Hell (ballet visuals), Syracuse Univ, NY, 66; Good Woman of Setzvan (teater visuals), Univ Maine, Portland-Gorham, 72, Renascence (planetarium visuals), 75 & From Morn Till Midnight (theater visuals), 76; Photography Maine 1973 (poster, catalogue & cert design), Maine State Comn on Arts & Humanities, 73. Exhib: Everson Mus Art, Syracuse, 66; Munson-Williams-Proctor Inst, Utica, NY, 66; Mem Art Gallery, Rochester, NY, 66; Nat Print Exhib, State Univ NY Col, Potsdam, 67; Bradley-Print Show, Peoria Art Ctr, Ill, 68; Imprint-Nat Print Exhib, Kutztown State Col, Pa, 68-69; Nat Exhib Prints & Drawings, Okla Art Ctr, Okla, 69-70; Statements in Media, Haystack Traveling Exhib, east coast, 72-73; solo shows, Univ Maine, August, 74 & Univ of the South, Sewanee, Tenn, 78; First Light, Humboldt State Univ, Col of Redwoods & Humboldt Arts Coun, Calif, 75-76. Collections Arranged: As It Was (auth, ed, catalogue), 74, Ben Shahn-Photographs (auth & ed, catalogue), 76 & Walker-Evans-Photographs, 78, Univ Maine, Portland-Gorham. Teaching: From asst prof to assoc prof painting, film, photog & drawing, Univ Maine, Portland-Gorham, 68-; coordr Soleri sem, Haystack Mountain Sch, Deer Isle, Maine, summer 71. Pos: Dir art gallery, Univ Maine, Portland-Gorham, 68-, chmn art dept, 74-; pres bd dir, Film Study Ctr, Portland, 72- Awards: Helen B Stoeckel Fel, Yale Univ, 66; Hiram Gee Fel, Lowe Art Ctr, Syracuse, NY, 65; Gregory Batcock Prize, Independent Filmmakers, 68. Mem: Col Art Asn; Nat Asn Sch of Art; Mus Mod art; Am Film Inst; Int Mus Photog, George Eastman House, Rochester, NY. Style & Technique: Formal and additive; photomechanical process. Media: Oil, Mixed Media. Publ: Auth & ed (catalogue), John Ford Film Retrospective, Univ Maine, Portland-Gorham, 70; contribr, Eugenio Battisti, auth, Piero Della Francesca, 73; contrbr, Note Sulla Prospettiva Riniscrimentale, Arte Lombarda, 70. Mailing Add: Dept of Art Univ Maine Portland Gorham Gorham ME 04038

UBERTALLI, HECTOR
PAINTER, SCULPTOR
b Arg, Mar 28, 28; US citizen. Study: Acad Fine Arts, Buenos Aires; also with Juan Hohmann, Ana Weiss Rossi & Felix Aranguren, Buenos Aires. Exhib: Pan Am Union, Washington, DC, 61; Am Embassy, Buenos Aires, 62; Collection Sculpture Old Testament, New York Worlds Fair, 64; Columbia Mus Art, SC, 65; also in Palm Beach Galleries, 65- Teaching: Pvt instr. Bibliog: M Mulhare (auth), Hector Ubertalli, Am Artist, 10/61; H Adams (auth), Hector Ubertalli, Palm Beach Life, 1/72; article in Palm Beach Daily News, 4/28/74. Mem: Smithsonian Inst, Washington, DC, Soc Four Arts; Norton Mus; Fla Artists Group. Style & Technique: Landscapes; uses palette knife. Media: Acrylic. Mailing Add: 2919 N Dixie Hwy West Palm Beach FL 33407

UCHIMA, ANSEI
PRINTMAKER, PAINTER
b Stockton, Calif, May 1, 21. Work: Art Inst Chicago; Rijks Mus, Amsterdam; Libr of Cong, Washington, DC; Philadelphia Mus, Pa; Metrop Mus Art, New York. Exhib: Tokyo Int Print Biennials, 57 & 60; Grenchen Int Print Triennials, 58, 61 & 70; 5th Sao Paulo Int Biennial, 59; Vancouver Int Print Exhib, 67; 35th Venice Int Biennial, 70. Teaching: Mem fac printmaking, Sarah Lawrence Col, 62-; lectr printmaking, Columbia Univ, 68- Awards: Guggenheim Fel, 62-63 & 70-71. Mem: Soc Am Graphic Artists; Japan Print Asn. Style & Technique: Woodcuts in watercolors; watercolor. Mailing Add: 652 W 163rd St New York NY 10032

UCHIMA, TOSHIKO
PAINTER
b Manchuria, China; Japanese citizen. Study: Kobe Col, Japan, BA; and with Ryohei Koiso. Work: Art Inst Chicago; Hampton Inst, Va; Brooklyn Mus. Exhib: One-woman shows, Osaka, Japan, 57, Drawings, Mich State Univ, 63 & Collages, Box Assemblages, New York, 75; Grenchen Int Print Triennial, Switz, 58; Art Inst Chicago, 60; Southern France, 75; Tokyo, Japan, 76; New York, NY, 77. Style & Technique: Collage, box assemblages, drawing and prints. Publ: Contribr, Sphynx (portfolio prints & poems), 54. Mailing Add: 652 W 163rd St New York NY 10032

UDEL, JOAN ERBE
See Erbe, Joan

UDINOTTI, AGNESE
SCULPTOR, PAINTER
b Athens, Greece, Jan 9, 40; US citizen. Study: Ariz State Univ, BA & MA. Work: Phoenix Art Mus, Ariz; Chicago Med Sch; Ariz State Univ, Tempe; Stanford Mus of Art; Univ Utah; Ministry of Educ, Athens. Comn: Steel doors, Wilson Jones & Assocs, Scottsdale, Ariz, 70 & Imagineering, Tucson, Ariz, 72; relief, comn by Mrs M Ehrlich, Phoenix, 70; steel diptych, comn by Har Oude Jans, Amsterdam, Holland, 72; outdoor sculpture, comn by Glendale Community Col, 74. Exhib: One-man shows, Vorpal Galleries, San Francisco, 68, 71 & 75, Art Forms Gallery, Athens, 69, 71, 75 & 77 & Ariz Chap Arts & Humanities Traveling Exhib, 71-72; Southwestern Biennial, Phoenix Art Mus, 71; Galerie Balans, Amsterdam, Holland, 73-75 & 77. Teaching: Workshop leader welded sculpture, Orme Sch Fine Arts Prog, Mayer, Ariz, 71 & 72; Univ Southern Calif, summer 72. Awards: Hellenic Am Union Sculpture Award, 68; Sculpture Prize, Phoenix Art Mus 1st Biennial, 71; Solomos Prize for sculpture, Panos Nikoli Tselepi, Athens, 71. Bibliog: Seiden Mellach (auth), Direct Metal Sculpture, Crown, 66 & Creating Art from Anything, Reilly & Lee, 68. Media: Steel, Oil. Publ: Udinotti, Northland Press & Macabre love songs and aphorisms, Greek Publ, Kedros; My Udinotti J, Vol 1, Amaranth Press, 77. Mailing Add: c/o 4215 N Marshall Way Scottsdale AZ 85251

UDVARDY, JOHN WARREN
SCULPTOR, PAINTER
b Elyria, Ohio. Study: Skowhegan Sch Painting & Sculpture, scholar, summer 57; Cleveland Inst Art, scholar, 55-58, BFA, 63; Yale Univ, scholar, 64-65, MFA, 65. Work: Cleveland Inst Art; Betty Parsons Gallery, New York; Columbia Broadcasting Syst, New York; Fogg Mus, Cambridge, Mass; Princeton Univ, NJ. Comn: Design of symbol & emblem for Ecol Action RI, 70. Exhib: One-man shows, Michael Walls Gallery, San Francisco, 67, Bristol Art Mus, RI, 69, Cleveland Inst Art, 70, Annmary Brown Mem, Providence, RI, 71, Woods-Gerry Gallery, Providence, 73 & 76, Wheaton Col, Norton, Mass, 74, Any Art Gallery, Warren, RI, 75 & Schochet Gallery, Newport, RI, 77; Young New Eng Painters, Sarasota, Fla, Portland, Maine & Manchester, NH, 69; Smith Col, Northampton, Mass, 77. Teaching: Instr drawing, Cleveland Inst Art, 62-63; asst printmaking, Yale Univ, 64-65; asst prof painting & design, Brown Univ, 65-73; chmn, Freshman Found Div, RI Sch Design, 73-77, prof design, 78- Pos: Critic & guest lectr, Atlanta Sch Art, Ga, 70; vis critic, RI Sch Design, 70, 71 & 73; guest lectr, Dartmouth Col, 73 & Univ NH, Durham, 73; rep & adv, Inst Am Indian Art, Santa Fe, NMex, 74; mem visual arts adv panel, RI State Coun on the Arts, 76-78. Awards: Mary C Page Europe Traveling Scholar, Cleveland Inst Art, 60-61. Mem: Mass Archaeol Soc; Nat Audubon Soc; RI Zoo Soc. Media: Wood, Branch, Stick. Publ: Illusr, Los, fall 68 & spring 70, Art J, winter 73 & Art in Am, 3-4/75. Dealer: Suzanne Schochet Gallery Brick Market Pl Newport RI 02840. Mailing Add: 900 Hope St Bristol RI 02809

UELSMANN, JERRY
PHOTOGRAPHER
b Detroit, Mich, June 11, 34. Study: Rochester Inst Technol, BFA, 57; Ind Univ, MS, 58, MFA, 60. Work: Mus Mod Art, New York; Philadelphia Mus Art; Art Inst Chicago; Nat Gallery Can, Ottawa; Int Mus Photog, George Eastman House, Rochester, NY. Exhib: Photography in America 1850-1965, Yale Univ Art Gallery, 65; Photography in the Twentieth Century, George Eastman House in collab with Nat Gallery Can, 67; one-man shows, Mus Mod Art, New York, 67, Philadelphia Mus Art, 70 & Art Inst Chicago, 72; Witkin Gallery, New York, 75 & 78; San Francisco Mus of Mod Art, 77. Teaching: Prof photog, Univ Fla, 60-, Grad res prof art, 74- Awards: Guggenheim Fel, 67; Grant, Univ Fla, 70; Photog Fel, Nat Endowment Arts, 73. Bibliog: W E Parker (auth), Eight Photographs: Jerry Uelsmann, Doubleday, 70; John Ward (auth), The Criticism of Photography as Art: the Photographs of Jerry Uelsmann, Univ Fla, 70; Silver Meditations (monogr), Morgan & Morgan, 75. Mem: Founding mem Soc Photog Educ; fel Royal Photog Soc Gt Brit. Publ: Contribr, Contemp Photog, 64, Camera, 67, Aperture, 67, 68 & 70, Life, 69 & Infinity. Dealer: Witkin Gallery 41 E 57th St New York NY 10022. Mailing Add: 5701 SW 17th Dr Gainesville FL 32608

UHRMAN, CELIA
PAINTER, WRITER
b New London, Conn, May 14, 27. Study: Brooklyn Col, BA & MA, 53; Brooklyn Mus Art Sch, 56-57; Teachers Col, Columbia Univ, 61; City Univ New York, 66. Work: Brooklyn Col; Ovar Mus; govt bldgs in Spain & Portugal. Exhib: 2nd All New England Drawing, Lyman Allyn Mus, New London, Conn, 60; 26th Ann Contemp Am Paintings, Soc Four Arts, Palm Beach, Fla, 64; Premi Int Dibeaux, Joan Miro, Barcelona, Spain, 70; 26th Expos Int d'Art Contemporain, Luxembourg, 74; Des Beaux-Arts Exhib, Monaco, Monte-Carlo, 69, 70 & 72. Teaching: Teacher art & spec talent classes, Lefferts Jr High Sch, Brooklyn, NY, 58-59. Awards: George Washington Medal of Honor, USA, Freedoms Found, Valley Forge, Pa, 64; Silver Medal, Centro Studi E Scambi, 69 & Gold Medal, 72; Academic Laurel, 27th Int Exhib Contemp Art, Moka Club, Paris, 74 & others. Bibliog: Jim Burns Talk Show (interview), WECT-TV, Wilmington, NC, 7/10/73; Rev in Int News, Int Arts Bull, 75; Div Gen Educ, NY Univ, Part IV (film), 58. Mem: Centro Studi E Scambi Int, Rome (hon US rep, 70- & mem int exec comt); Int Arts Guild, Monte-Carlo (commandeur mem arts & lett, 66); Int Platform Asn (art group, 70). Style & Technique: Impressionistic oils, free style and realistic watercolors. Media: Oil, Watercolor. Publ: Auth, A Pause for Poetry for Children, 73; auth, The Chimps are Coming (novel), 75; and others. Mailing Add: 1655 Flatbush Ave Brooklyn NY 11210

UHRMAN, ESTHER
PAINTER, WRITER
b New London, Conn, July 7, 21. Study: Traphagan Sch Fashion, (design & illus), 55; New York City Community Col, AA, 74; Cornell Univ & Col New Rochelle. Work: Ovar Mus, Portugal; Mohican Hotel, New London, Conn; var pub bldgs in Spain. Exhib: 65th Ann Nat Exhib of Washington Watercolor Soc, Smithsonian Inst, 62; Tribute to Southeastern Connecticut, Mohican Hotel, Conn CofC, New London, 62; Uhrman Show of Water Colors, Brooklyn & Staten Island Flatbush CofC, Rivoli, Brooklyn, 63; Premi Int Dibuix Joan Miro, Barcelona, Spain, 70; 26th Expos Int Art Contemp, Luxembourg, 74. Awards: Silver Medal Olympic Design, Ital Govt, 68; Golden Windmill Radio Drama Award, Holland, 71; Dipl of Honor Palme, Int Arts Guild, Monaco, 72. Bibliog: Charles Richman (auth), articles in Brooklyn Rec, 57-; article in Flatbusha, 60; articles in Int Arts Bull, 72- Mem: Centro Studi e Scambi Int, Rome (hon US rep, 74-); Int Arts Guild, Monte Carlo (commandeur mem arts & lett, 66-); Int Platform Asn (art group, 71-). Style & Technique: Realistic-seascapes, landscapes, circus, gypsy. Media: Oil, Watercolor. Publ: Auth, Cover Your Walls, Diet Indust, 57; auth, Gypsy Logic, 70; auth, Mocking ghost, Life is Tremendous, 72; auth, Brotherhood, Pub Employee Press, 74. Mailing Add: 1655 Flatbush Ave Apt C602 Brooklyn NY 11210

ULBRICHT, JOHN,
PAINTER
b Havana, Cuba, Nov 6, 26; US citizen. Study: Art Inst Chicago, dipl, 50. Work: Denver Art Mus; Nat Portrait Gallery, London; State Univ NY, Buffalo; Pasadena Art Mus; Columbus Gallery Fine Arts, Ohio & others. Comn: Portrait, Mrs Betty Ford, comn by Pres Gerald Ford, 75; portrait, Chief Judge David Bazelon, Collection US Fed Court House, Washington, DC, 76. Exhib: Spanish Contemp Art, Brussels, Helsinki & Berlin, 61 & 63; Homage to Miro, Col Archit, Palma de Mallorca, 73; one-man shows, 12 Spanish Portraits, Pavilion of Spain, New York World's Fair, 65, Richard DeMarco Gallery, Edinburgh, 69 & Iolas-Velasco Gallery, Madrid, 72; plus others in the US & Europe. Pos: Asst dir, Denver Art Mus, 52-53. Awards: John Quincy Adams Foreign Travel Fel, Art Inst Chicago, 50. Bibliog: Camilo Cela (auth), John Ulbricht: 12 Spanish Portraits, Papeles de Son Armadans, 65; Ruthven Todd (auth), Portraits cubed, Art News Mag, 69; Josep Melia (auth), John Ulbricht, Ed Rayuela, Madrid, 74. Style & Technique: Figurative; portraits and floral/vegetable subjects and landscapes on large scale; oil glazes and scumbles on canvas. Media: Oil on Canvas. Dealer: Sala Pelaires Gallery Pelaires 23 Palma de Mallorca Spain. Mailing Add: Es Clapes 85 Galilea Mallorca Spain

ULLBERG, J KENT
SCULPTOR
b Göteborg, Sweden, July 15, 45. Study: Swedish State Sch Art, cert(drawing & sculpture); Swedish Mus Natural Hist, anat, 4 yrs; Mus Des Sci Naturelles, Orleans, France. Work: Swedish Mus Natural Hist, Stockholm; Münster Mus, Münster, Vestfalen, WGer; Botswana Nat Art Gallery, Gaborone, Botswana, Africa; Mus des Sci Naturelles, Orleans; Denver Mus Natural Hist. Exhib: Nat Art Gallery, Gaborone, 72; 61st Ann Exhib, Allied Artists Am, New York, 74; 150th Ann Exhib, Nat Acad Design, New York, 75; Arvada Fine Arts Ctr, Colo, 76; Helsingborg Artmuseum, Sweden, 76; 44th Ann Nat Sculpture Soc, New York, 77; Nat Cowboy Hall of Fame, Oklahoma City, Okla, 77; Birger Sandzen Mem Gallery, Lindsborg, Kans, 77; Los Angeles Co Mus, 77. Pos: Cur, Nat Mus & Art Gallery, Botswana, Africa, 71-74; cur/consult, Denver Mus Natural Hist, 74-76. Awards: Helen Foster Barnett Price, Nat Acad Design, 75; Merit Award, Colo Celebration Arts, 75. Mem: Assoc mem Allied Artists Am; Soc of Animal Artists, New York. Style & Technique: Impressionistic, animal

and figure. Media: Bronze. Dealer: De Colores Gallery 2817 E Third Ave Denver CO 80206; Sportsman's Edge Ltd 136 E 74th St New York NY 10021. Mailing Add: 1758 Clermont St Denver CO 80220

ULLMAN, MRS GEORGE W
COLLECTOR
Collection: French furniture and paintings, Louis XV and Louis XVI periods; Haitian paintings; contemporary paintings of Philip Curtis; Spanish paintings, 17th and 18th century on painted furniture & glass. Mailing Add: 4642 N 56th St Phoenix AZ 85018

ULLMAN, HAROLD P
COLLECTOR
b Chicago, Ill, Jan 30, 99. Study: Univ Mich Sch Engr. Pos: Bd mem, Los Angeles Co Mus Art, 59-64; bd mem, Pasadena Art Mus, 65-; bd mem, Grunwald Ctr Graphic Arts, Univ Calif, Los Angeles. Collection: Rouault graphics; sculpture from India and Nepal; primitive art; part of collection shown at Denver Art Museum, 75. Mailing Add: 800 Woodacre Rd Santa Monica CA 90402

ULLRICH-ZUCKERMAN, B
PAINTER, PHOTOGRAPHER
b Evanston, Ill. Study: Northwestern Univ, BA(with hons in Eng), 30; Art Inst Chicago, BFA, 34; with Boris Anisfeld & Francis Chapin; also with Edward Weston, 42; Univ Chicago, MA, 48. Work: Remembrance of Things Past, Univ Ariz Collection Am Painting, Tucson; photog in Hall of Justice, San Francisco, Calif; Midwest Color Slide Art Collection, Chicago Main Pub Libr, Ill; plus in many pvt collections throughout USA. Exhib: Art Inst Chicago, 37, 39 & 50; Pa Acad Fine Arts, 38-39; Corcoran Gallery Art, Washington, DC, 39; Portland Art Asn, Ore, 39; San Francisco Mus Mod Art, 39, 41 & 70; Seattle Art Mus, Wash, 40; Riverside Mus, NY, 40; Detroit Inst Art, Mich, 40; one-person shows, San Francisco Mus Art, 40, Humanist House, San Francisco, 72, Univ Pac, Stockton, Calif, 76 & Photog Ctr, San Francisco, 77; Cent Am Traveling Exhib, 41; Painting in the United States, Carnegie Inst, Pittsburgh, Pa, 41, 43 & 44; de Young Mus, San Francisco, 43 & 70; Renaissance Soc, Univ Chicago, 53-64; Photography at Mid Century, Eastman House, Rochester, NY, 59; Western Asn Art Mus Traveling Drawing Show, 66-68; Zellerbach Gallery, San Francisco, 67-68 & 74; Focus Gallery, San Francisco, 75; Calif Expo, Sacramento, 77; One Market Plaza Gallery, San Francisco, 78. Teaching: Instr pvt classes, 46- Mem: Artists Equity Asn (secy Chicago chap, 55-56); San Francisco Women Artists (secy artists coun, 74-75); Int Ctr Photography, New York. Publ: Contribr, Am Heritage, 2/65; reproduced painting, Mardi Gras; contribr (photog), Imogen's Sign, In: Imogen Cunningham, an Interview (film), shown 75 & Visual Dialog Mag, fall 77; contribr, Imogen After Ninety, 78. Mailing Add: 2254 42nd Ave San Francisco CA 94116

ULRICH, EDWIN ABEL
COLLECTOR, PATRON
b Brooklyn, NY, Dec 23, 97. Collections Arranged: Three Generations of the American Family of Painters....Waugh, 1814-1973, 77. Pos: Dir, Edwin A Ulrich Mus, Hyde Park, 56- Collection: American art, specializing in Frederick J Waugh, 1861-1940; has given Frederick J Waugh Collection to Wichita State Univ and donated a trust to support the collection; in recognition, Bd of Regents named the new univ mus, Edwin A Ulrich Mus of Art; also loaned paintings to Smithsonian Inst for traveling exhib, 69-71; paintings have been exhibited in various cities and mus. Mailing Add: Edwin A Ulrich Mus Albany Post Rd Hyde Park NY 12538

UMANA, ALFONSO
PAINTER, SCULPTOR
b Bogota, Colombia, Feb 17, 08; US citizen. Work: Metrop Mus Art, New York; Cornell Univ Mus; New York Pub Libr; Harvard Univ Libr. Pos: Designer of sets for ballet; designer, illusr & publ of rare books. Style & Technique: Contemporary. Media: Iron, Marble; painter in all media. Mailing Add: 35 E 19th St New York NY 10003

UMLAUF, CHARLES
SCULPTOR
b Mich, July 17, 11. Study: Art Inst Chicago, with Albin Polasek; Chicago Sch Sculpture, with Viola Norman. Work: Krannert Art Mus, Univ Ill, Urbana; Des Moines Art Ctr, Iowa; Metrop Mus Art, New York; Okla Art Ctr; Mus Fine Arts, Houston, Tex; plus nine other Tex mus. Comn: Marble reredos relief, St Michael & All Angels Church, Dallas, Tex, 61; Spirit of Flight (bronze fountain sculpture), Lovefield Airport, Dallas, 61; Torch Bearers (bronze), Univ Tex, Austin, 63; Icarus (bronze), Phillips Petrol Bldg, Bartlesville, Okla, 64; Family Group (three figural bronze), Houston Mus Natural Sci, Tex, 72. Exhib: American Sculpture, Metrop Mus Art, New York, 51; Int Relig Biennial, Salzburg, Austria, Ger, Spain & Eng, 58-59; 20th Ceramic Int, Everson Mus, Syracuse, NY & tour, 59-60; 161st Ann, Pa Acad Fine Arts, Philadelphia, 66; two retrospectives, Gallery House, Dallas, 59 & Univ Tex Art Mus, Austin, 67; plus 30 solo exhibs in New York & Italy. Teaching: Prof sculpture, Univ Tex, Austin, 52- Awards: Guggenheim Grant, 49-50; Purchase Award, Ford Found, 60; Univ Tex Grant, 66. Bibliog: Gibson A Danes (auth), The sculpture of Charles Umlauf, Valley House Publ, 59; Donald B Goodall (auth), Charles Umlauf, Sculptor, Univ Tex Press, 67; Earl Miller (film dir), Bronze Sculpture (in the making), produced by Univ Tex, 69. Style & Technique: Modelled work excels in liveliness and great sensitivity; in his carved pieces the severe technique forces him to temper his exuberance and he arrives at formulations close to those of the classical sculptors from the Greek to Brancusi. Media: Bronze, Marble. Dealer: Valley House Gallery 6616 Spring Valley Rd Dallas TX 75240; John Klep Gallery 1711 S Post Oak Rd Houston TX 77027. Mailing Add: 506 Barton Blvd Austin TX 78704

UMLAUF, KARL A
PAINTER
b Chicago, Ill, May 16, 39. Study: Univ Tex, Austin, BFA, 57-61; Yale Univ, fel, summer 60; Cornell Univ, MFA. Work: New Orleans Mus Art, La; Everson Mus, Syracuse, NY; Joslyn Art Mus, Omaha; Silvermine Guild Artists; Dallas Mus Art. Exhib: 14th Ann Delta Exhib, Ark Art Ctr, 72; Project South, Southwest Ft Worth Art Ctr, 72; Potsdam Nat Print & Drawing Exhib, State Univ NY Potsdam, 72; Artist Biennial, New Orleans Mus, 73; Midwest Biennial, Joslyn Art Mus, 74. Teaching: Asst instr painting & drawing, Cornell Univ, 61-63; instr painting & drawing, Univ Pa, 63-65; asst prof painting & drawing, Univ Northern Iowa, 65-66; chmn grad prog, ETex State Univ, 67-74; vis prof art, Ind Univ, Bloomington, 74-75. Awards: First Prize & Purchase Award, Everson Mus, 62; First Prize, Okla Art Ctr, 70; First Prize, Evansville Mus Art, 75. Style & Technique: Acrylic lacquer on vacuum formed uvex-Plexiglas. Dealer: Valley House Gallery Spring Valley Rd Dallas TX; DuBose Gallery Houston TX. Mailing Add: 109 Royal Ln Commerce TX 75428

UNDERWOOD, EVELYN NOTMAN
PAINTER
b St Catharines, Ont; US citizen. Study: Pratt Inst, grad; Berkshire Summer Sch Art, grad; State Univ NY Buffalo; Millard Fillmore Col; also with Charles Burchfield, Millard Sheets, Ernest Watson & Rex Brandt. Work: Roswell Park Inst, Buffalo, NY; Vet Hosp, Buffalo. Exhib: Butler Inst Am Art 19th Ann, Youngstown, Ohio, 54; Indust Niagara Art Exhib, 65; Int Platform Asn Art Shows, Sheraton Hotel, Washington, DC, 70 & 71; Burchfield Ctr, State Univ NY Col Buffalo, 70 & 72; Nat League Am Pen Women Regionals, New York; plus others. Teaching: Instr art, Buffalo Pub Schs; instr, Buffalo Mus Sci, 50-51; instr art, Arcade Cent Sch, NY, 63-64. Awards: First Prize, Nat Leagure Am Pen Women; Paul Lindsay Sample Mem Award, Chautauqua Nat Art Show, 73; Outstanding Merit Award, 1st Ann Erie Co Art Festival, 74; Gold Medal & Gold Patron Award, Buffalo Soc of Artists, 77. Mem: Int Platform Asn; Buffalo Soc Artists; Nat League Am Pen Women (deleg, Assoc Art Orgn Western NY, 68-72). Style & Technique: Watercolor: use both wet and dry method, dry method often used with casein white. Publ: Illusr, Bulletin Millard Fillmore Hosp, 56; illusr, cover, Pen Woman, Vol 47, No 4. Mailing Add: 362 Linden Ave East Aurora NY 14052

UNGER, MARY ANN
SCULPTOR
b New York, NY, May 10, 45. Study: Mt Holyoke Col, BA, 67; Berkeley Univ of Calif, grad study with Voulkas, B Hudson & R Melchert; Columbia Univ, MFA, study with Balden, Sugarman & T Harrison, 75. Exhib: Ten Downtown, Ten Years, project studio one, New York, 77; Organization of Independent Artist, Battery Park, NY, 77; Nat Parks Comn, New York, 78; 7th Ann Contemp Reflections, Aldrich Mus of Art, Ridgefield, Conn, 78. Teaching: Instr printmaking and drawing, Montclair State Col, Upper Mt NJ & ceramics, sculpture & painting, Mt St Vincent, Riverdale, NY, 77- Style & Technique: Modular, organic/geometric dichotomy cast in various materials, wax, bonded iron & ceramic. Mailing Add: 5 E 3rd St New York NY 10003

UNTERSEHER, CHRIS CHRISTIAN
SCULPTOR
b Portland, Ore, May 14, 43. Study: San Francisco State Col, BA, 65; Univ Calif, Davis, MA, 67. Work: Objects USA, Johnson Wax Collection, Racine, Wis; Allan Stone Galleries Collection, New York; Jim Newman Found, San Francisco, Calif; Oakland Mus, Calif. Exhib: Objects USA, Johnson Wax Collection, int traveling show, 69-73; 20 Americans, Mus Contemp Crafts, New York, 71; one-man shows, Hansen-Fuller Gallery, San Francisco, 67-70 & De Young Mus, San Francisco, Calif, 68 & 77; Clay, Whitney Mus, New York, 74; Quay Ceramics Gallery, San Francisco, 75 & 77. Teaching: Instr ceramics, Univ Calif, Davis, 68-69; instr ceramics, Univ Cincinnati, 69-70; chmn ceramics dept, Univ Nev, Reno, 70- Awards: Purchase Award, Mem Union Art Gallery, Univ Calif, Davis, 68. Bibliog: David Zack (auth), Art news: nut art in quake time, 70; Nordness (auth), Objects: USA, Viking, 70; Lowell Darling (auth), Clay without tears, Art Ctr World, 71. Mem: Am Crafts Coun. Style & Technique: Sculptural orientation using white clay, both porcelain and earthenware. Dealer: Quay Ceramics Gallery 560 Sutter St San Francisco CA 94102. Mailing Add: Dept of Art Univ of Nev Reno NV 89507

UNWIN, NORA SPICER
PAINTER, PRINTMAKER
b Surbiton, Eng. Study: Leon Underwood Studio; Kingston Sch Art; ARCA; also with George Demetrios, Boston & Donald Stoltenberg, De Cordova Mus, Lincoln. Work: Brit Mus & Victoria & Albert Mus, London, Eng; Metrop Mus Art, New York; Libr Cong, Washington, DC; Wiggin Collection, Boston Pub Libr. Exhib: Royal Acad, London, Eng; Bibliot Nat, Paris, France; Worcester Art Mus, Mass; Springfield Mus Art, Mass; Metrop Mus Art, New York. Awards: Prize for Graphics, Nat Acad Design, 58; Prize for Watercolor, Boston Watercolor Soc, 65; Prize for Graphics, Cambridge Art Asn, 68. Mem: Nat Acad Design; Soc Am Graphic Artists; Boston Printmakers (exec bd); Boston Watercolor Soc; NH Art Asn. Media: Watercolor, Collage, Graphics. Publ: Auth & illusr, Proud Pumpkin, Joyful the Morning, 63, Two Too Many, 63 & The Midsummer Witch, 66, McKay; auth & illusr, Sinbad the Cygnet, John Day Co, 70. Mailing Add: Pine-Apple Cottage Old Street Rd Peterborough NH 03458

UPELNIEKS, ARTHUR
PAINTER
b Latvia-Valle, July 10, 11; US citizen. Study: Latvian Nat Art Inst, Riga. Work: Bavarian State Art Mus, Ger; also in many pvt collections. Exhib: Numerous one-man shows in Ger, 46-54; Am Artists Prof League, 73-75. Awards: For Fisherman, Am Artists Prof League, 73, for Monhegan Island, Maine, 74 & for Monhegan Coast, 75. Mem: Am Artists Prof League. Style & Technique: Seascapes; palette knife and brush. Media: Oil. Dealer: Leopold Laudsberger Inc 48 W 27th St New York NY 10001. Mailing Add: 132-06 Rockaway B Blvd Belle Harbor New York NY 11694

UPJOHN, EVERARD MILLER
ART HISTORIAN
b Scranton, Pa, Nov 7, 03. Study: Harvard Univ, AB, 25, MArch, 29. Teaching: Asst prof hist art, Univ Minn, Minneapolis, 29-35; from asst prof to prof hist art, Columbia Univ, 35-70, prof emer art hist, 70- Res: History of American architecture. Publ: Auth, Richard Upjohn, architect and churchman, 39; co-auth, History of world art, 49, rev ed, 58; contribr, Encycl American, 50; co-auth, Highlights, an illustrated history of art, 63. Mailing Add: 47-06 U Meadow Lakes Hightstown NJ 08520

UPTON, JOHN DAVID
EDUCATOR, ART HISTORIAN
b Des Moines, Iowa, May 4, 32. Study: Calif Sch of Fine Arts, Univ Rochester, with Minor White & Beaumont Newhall; Univ Calif, Berkeley; Calif State Univ Long Beach, BA & Grad Study (art hist). Work: Mass Inst Technol Creative Photog Collection, Cambridge; Photog in the Fine Arts Collection, Metrop Mus of Art, New York. Exhib: Photography in the Fine Arts, Metrop Mus of Art, New York, 63; 15 American Photographers, Houston Mus of Contemp Art, 64; one-man shows, Mass Inst Technol Creative Photography Gallery, Cambridge, 65 & Camerawork Gallery, Costa Mesa, Calif, 68; Light 7, Mass Inst Technol Art Gallery, Cambridge, 68. Collections Arranged: The Equivalent, 66, Zen Art, 67, Orange Coast Col; The Photograph as: Metaphor, Object & Document of Concept (auth, catalog), 74 & The Photograph as Artifice (auth, catalog), 78, Calif State Univ Long Beach; Emerging Southern Calif Photographers (contribr, catalog essay), 76. Teaching: Prof hist of photog & creative photog, Orange Coast Col, Costa Mesa, Calif, 63-; vis lectr hist of photog, Univ Calif Los Angeles, 75; vis lectr hist of photog, Calif State Univ Fullerton, 75- Pos: Chmn dept of photog & asst chmn div of fine arts, Orange Coast Col, Costa Mesa, Calif, 63- Bibliog: Minor White (auth), Photographers Northwest, Aperture, Vol 11 No 3, 64; Robert Routh (auth), An Educator's Educator, Petersen's Photog, 12/75. Mem: Soc for Photog Educ (mem bd trustees, 75-); Friends of Photog (mem bd trustees, 74-); Adv Comt Ctr of Creative Photog,

Univ Ariz; Los Angeles Ctr of Photog Studies. Res: Photographic historian, extensive research in the history of photography since 1900, especially Alfred Steiglitz, Minor White & Edward Weston. Publ: Contribr, New Vision of the 70's, Photographers Choice, Addison House, 75; co-auth, Photography, Little, Brown & Co, 76. Mailing Add: 1725 Ashland Ave Santa Monica CA 90405

UPTON, RICHARD THOMAS
PAINTER, PRINTMAKER
b Hartford, Conn. Study: Univ Conn, BFA; Ind Univ, MFA. Work: Nat Collection of Fine Arts, Smithsonian Inst, Washington, DC; Mus Mod Art, New York; Victoria & Albert, Mus, London, Eng; Bibliot Nat, Paris, France; Montreal Mus Fine Art, Can. Comn: Eros Thanatos Suite (German poem & woodcuts), Interlaken Corp, Providence, RI, 67; Salamovka Poster (limited ed silkscreen), Okla Art Ctr, Oklahoma City, 74; River Road Suite, 76 & Robert Lowell at 66 (suite of drawings), 77, Salmagundi Mag for the Humanities. Exhib: L'Estampe Contemporaine, Galerie Mansart, Bibliot Nat, France, 69; Sala Int, Palacio de Bellas Artes, Mexico City, Mex, 69; Sept Graveures un Sculpteur de Medailles, Musee Denon, Chalon-Sur Saome, France, 73; Brit Int Print Biennale, US Sect touring Eng, 73; Recent Acquisitions 1969-1973, Bibliot Nat, Paris, France, 74; The Delaware Water Gap, Corcoran Gallery Art, Washington, DC, 75; Everson Mus Art, Syracuse, NY, 75; Nat Collection Prints & Poetry, Libr of Cong, Washington, DC, 76-77; Retrospective of prints from Elvehejm Art Ctr, Atelier 17, France, 77; Okla Art Ctr, 77; Tweed Mus Art, Duluth, Minn, 77; Weatherspoon Art Gallery, Greensboro, NC, 77. Collections Arranged: Salamovka Series and Other New Paintings (auth, catalog), Oklahoma Art Ctr, Oklahoma City, 74. Awards: Fulbright Fel; Nat Educ Asn grant, Artists for Environ; Interlaken Corp Designer Award, Providence, RI, 67. Bibliog: James Kiehl (auth), Richard Upton's Credo, Salmagundi Mag for the Humanities; Laurence Schmeckebier (auth), Richard Upton: 1960-1970, Syracuse Univ, 70; Harry Gaugh (auth), Richard Upton New Paintings-Prints, Hartwick Col. Style & Technique: Figurative. Media: Oil and Water Based Media; Lithography; Intaglio. Publ: Auth, Impressions-A Paris Suite, 64, co-auth, Credo, 68 & co-auth, Eros Thanatos, 68, Interlaken Corp; co-auth, Models, 75 & River Road, 75, Erebus Press. Dealer: Weyne Gallery Lexington Ave New York NY; Townhouse Galleries 2400 E Las Olas Blvd Ft Lauderdale FL 33301. Mailing Add: 113 Regent St Saratoga Springs NY 12866

URBAN, MYCHAJLO RAPHAEL
SCULPTOR, PAINTER
b Luka, Ukraine, Sept 27, 28; US citizen. Study: Univ Chicago, 56-59; Sch Art Inst Chicago, BFA, 59; Ill Inst Technol, with Misch Kohn, 64-65. Work: Concordia Teachers Col, River Forest, Ill. Exhib: Ravinia Festival Art Exhib, Highland Park, Ill, 59; 64th Ann Artists Chicago & Vicinity, 61; 161st Ann, Pa Acad fine Art, Philadelphia, 66; 13th Ball State Univ Ann, Muncie, Ind, 67; 150 Years Ill Traveling Show, 69-71. Teaching: Instr sculpture, Evanston Art Ctr, 70- Awards: Edward L Ryerson Foreign Traveling Fel, 59; Prizes, Art Inst Chicago & Univ Wis-La Crosse, 65. Bibliog: D Z Meilach (auth), Contemporary Art with Wood, Crown, 68 & Creative Carving, Reilly & Lee, 69. Media: Plywood, Welded Steel, Acrylic. Dealer: Michael Wyman Gallery 233 E Ontario St Chicago IL 60611. Mailing Add: 6432 N Clark Chicago IL 60626

URBAN, REVA
PAINTER, SCULPTOR
b Brooklyn, NY, Oct 15, 25. Study: Art Students League, Carnegie scholar, 43-45. Work: Mus Mod Art, New York; Art Inst Chicago; Univ Mus, Berkeley; Finch Col Mus, New York; Averthorp Gallery, Jenkintown, Pa. Exhib: Pittsburgh Int, 58-; 1st Biennale Chrislicher Kunst der Gegenwart, Salzburg, Austria, 58; Continuity & Change, Wadsworth Atheneum, Hartford, Conn, 62; Documenta III, Kassel, Ger, 64; Seven Decades-Crosscurrents in Modern Art 1895-1965, exhib at ten New York galleries, 65; seven one-person shows, New York, Washington, DC, Chicago & Ger. Awards: Tamarind Fel. Bibliog: Sam Wagstaff, Jr (auth), Reva, Am Abstract Painters & Sculptors, 62; Peter Selz (auth), Reva Urban, Univ Art Collections, 66. Style & Technique: Paintings, shaped canvas and sculpture involve organic shapes. Media: Oil, Aluminum. Mailing Add: 845 Eighth Ave New York NY 10019

URQUHART, TONY
SCULPTOR, PAINTER
b Niagara Falls, Ont, Apr 9, 34. Study: Albright Art Sch, dipl, 56; Univ Buffalo, BFA, 58; Yale Univ Summer Sch, fel, 55. Work: Nat Gallery Can, Ottawa; Art Gallery Ont, Toronto; Winnipeg Art Gallery; Walker Art Ctr, Minneapolis, Minn; Mus Mod Art. Comn: Twelve murals, Niagara Falls, Skylon Tower, CPR Restaurants, 65; mural, Prov Ont Govt Bldg, 67; Christmas card, comn by Can Coun, 73-74. Exhib: Carnegie Inst Int, Pittsburgh, 58; Guggenheim Int, New York, 58; Paris Biennial, France, 63; Art Am & Spain, Madrid, Barcelona, Rome & Paris, 64; Sculpture '67, Toronto, 67; Art Gallery of Ont, Toronto, 68; Nat Gallery of Can, Ottawa, 74; Changing Visions: The Can Landscape, Art Gallery of Ont & Art Gallery of Edmonton, Alta, 76; plus others. Teaching: Lectr lettering, Univ Buffalo, 57-58; lectr basic design, McMaster Univ, 66-67; asst & assoc prof basic design & fine art, Univ Western Ont, 67-72; prof fine art, Univ Waterloo, 72- Pos: Artist in residence, Univ Western Ont, 60-63 & 64-65. Awards: Baxter Award, Ont Soc Artists Exhib, 61; Can Coun Fel, 63 & 67. Bibliog: J Russell Harper (auth), Painting in Canada, Univ Toronto Press, 66; Dorothy Cameron (auth), A reunion with Tony Urquhart, 4/5/71, Arts Can; J Vastokas (auth), The interdimensional landscape, architypal imagery in the work of Tony Urquhart, Arts Can, 5/73. Mem: Can Artists Representation (nat secy, 68-72); Can Conf Arts (bd gov, 70-73, 2nd vpres, 71); Art Gallery Ontario (trustee, 74-75). Style & Technique: Painted plywood boxes which have hinged doors and can be manipulated into many different positions, changing both the plastic appearance and the philosophical meaning. Publ: Illusr, A sketchbook of Canadian and European drawings, 63 & The Broken Ark—A Book of Beasts, 71. Dealer: Nancy Poole Studio Waterloo St London & Toronto. Mailing Add: c/o BauXi Gallery 3003 Granville St Vancouver BC V6H 3J8 Can

URRY, STEVEN
SCULPTOR
b Chicago, Ill, Sept 5, 39. Study: Chicago Art Inst, 57-59; Univ Chicago, BA, 59. Work: Chicago Art Inst. Comn: Monumental sculpture, Libr Bldg, Loyola Univ, Ill, 69. Exhib: Hemisphere, Am Pavillion, Tex, 68; Univ Nebr Ann, 70; Whitney Mus Am Art, New York, 70; Art Inst Chicago, 70; Chicago Eight Sculptors, Pioneer Plaza Ctr. Media: Aluminum. Mailing Add: c/o Zabriskie Gallery 29 W 57th St New York NY 10019

URSO, RICHARD CARL
SCULPTOR
Study: Silvermine Col Art; Art Students League; Calif Col Arts & Crafts. Work: Univ Maine, Augusta; Maine State Comn Arts & Humanities; St Josephs Manor, Portland, Maine; Mid-Maine Med Ctr; also in pvt collections. Comn: Both pvt & pub comns. Exhib: Ann New Eng Exhib, Silvermine Guild Artists, 66 & 68; Ann Kaiser Ctr Mezzanine Gallery Exhib, East Bay Artist Asn, Oakland, 71; Maine Coast Artists Asn, 73; Hadassah Ann Art Exhib, Bangor, Maine, 74; Italian-Am Artists in USA Invitational, Stone Park, Ill, 77. Awards: Gold Medal/Sculpture, Stone Park, Ill, 77. Mem: Artists Equity Asn. Style & Technique: Direct carving, modeling and casting, ranging from representational to abstract and free form. Media: Wood, Terracotta, Cast Work. Mailing Add: PO Box 252 Danville CA 94526

URUETA, CORDELIA
PAINTER
b Mexico City, Mex, Sept 16, 08. Study: High sch & col, Mexico City, Buenos Aires, Agr & New York; Free Sch Painting, Churubusco, Mex. Work: Mus Mod Art, Mexico City, Tel Aviv, Israel & Houston, Tex; Galeria de Arte Mexicano, Mexico City; Inst Nac Bellas Artes, Mexico City. Exhib: I & II Interamericana Biennial, Mexico City, 58 & 60; VI & X Int Biennial, Sao Paulo, Brazil, 61 & 69; Contemp Mexican Art, Mus Mod Art, Tokyo & Kyoto, Japan, 74-75. Awards: Hon Mention, II Interamericana Biennial, 60 & VI Int Biennial, Sao Paulo, 61; First Prize, Salon Plastica Mexicana, 66 & 68. Style & Technique: Abstract; portrayal of the new social changes. Media: Oil on Canvas. Dealer: Galeria de Arte Mexicano Calle Milan 18 Mexico DF Mexico. Mailing Add: Calle Texas 38 Mexico DF Mexico

USHENKO, AUDREY ANDREYEVNA
PAINTER, ART HISTORIAN
b Princeton, NJ, July 28, 45. Study: Ind Univ, BA, 65; Art Inst Chicago; Northwestern Univ, MFA, 67, PhD, 78, with George M Cohen. Exhib: Ind Artists Salon, Indianapolis Mus, 66-68; Phalanx Four & Phalanx Five, Chicago, 67 & 68; one-woman shows, Sloan Galleries, Valparaiso, Ind, 68 & 70, Gary Art Ctr & Louisville, Ky, 74, Second Story Spring St Soc, New York, 76, Gov's State Univ, 77 & Viridian Gallery, New York, 78; American Landscape, Ind State Univ, 74; Critic's Choice, Chicago, 76. Teaching: Instr art, Valparaiso Univ, 68-73; instr art, Allen R Hite Inst, Univ Louisville, 73-74; asst prof, Northwestern Univ, 74-75. Style & Technique: New painterly realism. Media: Oil. Res: Late 18th century English topographical watercolors. Dealer: Viridian Gallery 24 W 57th St New York NY 10019; Gallery 1134 1134 W Washington St Chicago IL 60651. Mailing Add: 1424 N Kedvale Ave Chicago IL 60651

USHER, ELIZABETH REUTER
ART LIBRARIAN, LECTURER
b Seward, Nebr. Study: Concordia Teachers Col, Seward, dipl; Univ Nebr, BScEd; Univ Ill, LSc; Cranbrook Acad of Art, Bloomfield Hills, Mich; NY Univ. Pos: Librn, Cranbrook Acad of Art, Bloomfield Hills, 45-48; catalog/reference librn, Metrop Mus of Art, New York, 48-53, head cataloguer, 53-54, actg head of libr, 54-57, chief, Art Reference Libr, 57-68, chief librn, 68- Mem: Art Libr Soc/NAm. Res: Art librarianship; bibliography. Interest: Modern art history. Publ: Auth, Rare Books and the Art Museum Library, Spec Libr, 1/61; auth, Continuing Bibliography for the Fine Arts in the United States, Colloques Int, Paris, 3/69; auth, The Metropolitan Museum of Art Library (Research and Reference) (Memorial Name: The Thomas J Watson Library), In: Allen Kent & Harold Lancour, ed, Encyclopedia of Library & Information Science Vol XVII, Dekker, 76. Mailing Add: 5 Peter Cooper Rd New York NY 10010

USUI, FRANCES ELIZABETH
See Pratt, Frances

USUI, KIICHI
CURATOR
b Tokyo, Japan, Dec 2, 31. Study: Tokyo Univ Arts, BFA; Art Students League with Morris Kantor; Univ Mich, MA(oriental art hist). Collections Arranged: Art of the Decade, 1960-1970, 71; Japanese Ink Painting of the Edo Period, 72; American Realism Post Pop, 73; Found Industrial Objects-Unintended Art, 73; Minoru Yamasaki, A Retrospective, 74; Art of the T'ang Dynasty, 75. Teaching: Asst prof studio art, Oakland Univ, Rochester, Mich, 66-71. Pos: Cur, Meadow Brook Art Gallery, Oakland Univ, 71- Bibliog: Franz Schulze (auth), How good-looking can a dashboard be, Art News, 1/74; Joan M Hartman (auth), Report from America, Oriental Art, autumn, 73 & Yamasaki taped interview, Progressive Architecture, 3/75. Mem: Asia Soc; Japan Soc; Am Asn Mus; Detroit Inst Art; Meadow Brook Gallery Assoc. Mailing Add: Meadow Brook Art Gallery Oakland Univ Rochester MI 48063

UTESCHER, GERD
DESIGNER, SCULPTOR
b Germany; US citizen. Study: Studied drawing, graphics & sculpture with Prof Wadim Falileef; Acad of Fine Arts, Berlin, MA. Work: Fleisher Art Memorial, Philadelphia; Lafayette Col, Easton, Pa. Comn: Stage design, Bavarian State Opera & pvt theaters, 46-48; Freedom Fountain (bronze), Philadelphia Fel Comn & City of Philadelphia, 64; Compassion (bronze), Philadelphia Gen Hosp, 66; St Joseph (bronze), Sisters of St Joseph, Whitemarsh, Pa, 68; Tree of Life (bronze), Pa Col of Podiatric Med, Philadelphia, 75. Exhib: Philadelphia Art Alliance, 57-59; Philadelphia Mus of Art, 60; Pa Acad Fine Arts, 60-61; Detroit Art Inst, 60. Collections Arranged: Numerous sculpture exhibitions & student & faculty shows, Philadelphia Art Alliance, 60-69. Teaching: Instr sculpture, Pa Acad Fine Arts, 60-64 & Philadelphia Mus of Art, 62-69; instr sculpture & three-dimensional design, Philadelphia Col of Art, 62-68. Pos: Chmn sculpture comt, Philadelphia Art Alliance, 60-69. Awards: Special Arts Award for teaching sculpture to the blind, Philadelphia Asn for the Blind; Philadelphia Art Alliance Prize, Regional Exhib, 57. Bibliog: A Sailer (auth), Applied plastic art, Gebrauchs Graphik, Munich, 3/50; Sculpture of the Blind, WCAU-TV, Philadelphia, 61-62; Fairmount Park Asn, Sculpture of the City, Walker Publ, 74. Mem: Artists Equity; Philadelphia Art Alliance; Int Asn of Art-UNESCO (US mem exec bd, 76-). Media: Direct Plaster and Wax for Bronze, Terra Cotta. Dealer: E W Colwin Assoc 343 S Fifth St Philadelphia PA 19106. Mailing Add: Villa Angela 17021 Allasio Italy

UTHCO, T R (JOHN EMIL HILLDING)
SCULPTOR
b Seattle, Wash, July 29, 44. Study: Kansas City Art Inst, BFA; Md Inst Col Art, MFA. Work: Palace of Fine Arts, San Francisco; Portland Ctr Visual Art, Ore; Whitney Mus Arch, New York; Wilkeson Mus Mod Art, Wash. Comn: Colossal Faucet, Bullitt Found, Seattle, 72; Oly, Olympia Brewing Co, 72; World's Largest Sculpture Show, Seattle Arts Comn, 73; Inflated Dollar, Better Bus Bur, Washington, DC, 74. Exhib: NW Ann, Seattle Art Mus, 65; Futures, Instant City, Mills Col, 71; Truthco, Vancouver Art Mus, BC, 74; Great Moments, Palace of Fine Arts, San Francisco, 75; Bill Ding, Media Burn, Ant Farm, San Francisco, 75. Awards: First Prize 8mm Film, Exp Col, Univ Wash, 71; Noble Prize, Ant Farm, San Francisco, 75. Bibliog: Shultz (auth), Their art belongs to Dada, Esquire, 8/74; Agostini (auth), T R Uthco, Domus, Italy, summer 75. Style & Technique: Inflated plastic sculpture of monumental sizes (600'). Media: Conceptual, avant-garde. Mailing Add: Box H Wilkeson WA 98396

UTTECH, THOMAS MARTIN
PAINTER, EDUCATOR
b Merrill, Wis, Oct 27, 42. Study: Layton Sch Art, BFA; Univ Cincinnati, MFA. Work: Milwaukee Art Ctr; Univ Wis-Madison. Exhib: Wis Painters & Sculptors Exhib, 72-74; Not in NY Gallery, Cincinnati, Ohio, 74; Directions, Milwaukee Art Ctr, 75; Artists of Chicago & Vicinity, 75; Whitney Mus Am Art Ann, New York, 75; Beauty of the Beast, Images of Animals in Am Art & The Human Image in Am Art of the 70s, John Michael Kohler Art Ctr, 77; Regenbögen für eine bessere Wüttembergishe Kunstverein, Stuttgart, Ger, 77; two-man exhib (with Jerome Krause), Visions from the Northwoods, Milwaukee Art Ctr, 77. Teaching: Assoc prof painting, drawing & photog, Univ Wis-Milwaukee, 68- Awards: Top Exhib Award, Wis Painters & Sculptors, Milwaukee Art Ctr, 73; Peninsula Sch Art Grant, Fish Creek, Wis, 73; Univ Wis Res Grant, 75. Bibliog: C Kohlman (auth), article in Midwest Art; Claudia Strohm (auth), Door County Creations (30 min interview), Channel 10, Milwaukee, 7/75; Amy Goldin (auth), New Whitney Biennial: pattern emerging, Art Am, 5-6/75. Mem: Wis Painters & Sculptors (pres, 73-76). Style & Technique: Rather controlled landscapes, spooky woods, large paintings, personal images. Media: Oil, Photographs. Publ: Illusr, A roadless area revisited, Audubon Mag, 75; illusr, Earth Care, Sierra Club & Audubon Soc, 75. Dealer: Not in NY Gallery 314 W Fourth St Cincinnati OH 45202. Mailing Add: 2582 N Cramer St Milwaukee WI 53211

UZIELLI, GIORGIO
COLLECTOR
b Florence, Italy, June 5, 03. Study: Univ Florence, LLD. Mem: Am-Italy Soc (pres). Collection: Aldine editions; first editions of Dante; paintings and bronzes. Mailing Add: 1107 Fifth Ave New York NY 10028

V

VACCARINO, ROBIN
SCULPTOR, PAINTER, PRINTMAKER
b Seattle, Wash, Aug 14, 28. Study: Los Angeles City Col; Los Angeles Valley Col; Univ of Calif, Los Angeles; Otis Art Inst, MFA(magna cum laude), 66. Work: De Cordova Mus, Mass; Otis Mus Collection, Los Angeles; Library of Congress, Washington, DC; Minot State Col, NDak. Comn: Murals, oil canvas, Latham & Watkins, Atlantic Richfield Plaza, 72; polychrome aluminum sculptures, Credit Lyonnais Int, Los Angeles, 75, Bank of Boston Int, Los Angeles, 75, Fluor Corp, Irvine, Calif, 77 & Hyatt Regency, Dallas, Tex, 78. Exhib: Los Angeles Printmaking Soc Ann, 68, 77; La Jolla Mus Nat Invitational, Calif, 69; Long Beach Mus of Art, Ann New Artist, Calif 69; Otis Mus 50th Anniv Exhib, Los Angeles, 69; Library of Congress Nat Print Exhib, Washington, DC, 69; Calif State Col Faculty Exhib, Northridge, 73; Exhib of Graphics, San Jose Mus of Art, Calif, 74; Univ of Calif, Santa Cruz, 77. Teaching: Instr printmaking & drawing, Calif State Univ, Northridge, 72-73; instr adv drawing, Otis Art Inst, 74- Pos: Co-founder & co-dir, Triad Graphic Workshop, N Hollywood, Calif, 66-; pres & co-owner, Art Source Inc, Los Angeles, 76- Awards: First Award, Otis Mus 50th Anniv, Otis Asn, 69; Purchase Awards, De Cordova Mus, Mass, 72 & Minot State Col Mus, 77. Bibliog: Joseph Mugaini (auth), Drawing, A Search for Form, Reinholt, New York, 66; Innovative Printmakers in Southern Calif, Southwest Art Mag, 73; article in Artweek, 74. Mem: Los Angeles Printmaking Soc. Style & Technique: Equivocal form, spatial ambiguity, color vibrations. Media: Polychromed Aluminum or Brass for Sculpture; Oil on Canvas for Painting; Etching and Silkscreen for Printmaking. Dealer: Art Source Inc 8687 Melrosa Ave Los Angeles CA 90069. Mailing Add: 3593 Berry Dr Studio City CA 91604

VACCARO, LUELLA GRACE
CERAMIST, PAINTER
b Miles City, Mont, June 2, 34. Study: Univ Wash, Seattle; Univ Calif, Berkeley; workshops with Peter Voulkas. Work: Antonio Prieto Collection, Mills Col, Oakland, Calif; Ceramics Monthly Collection, Columbus, Ohio. Exhib: Ceramic & Sculpture Ann, Butler Inst Am Art, Youngstown, Ohio, 58 & 66; Nat Print Exhib, Honolulu Acad Art, Hawaii, 59; 32nd & 33rd Int Print Exhib, Seattle Art Mus, Wash, 61-62; 13th Southwest Print Exhib, Dallas Mus Fine Arts, 63; Kans Designer Craftsman, Lawrence, 64, 65, 66, 68, 71 & 77; Kans Artist-Craftsman, Mulvane Art Ctr, Topeka, Kans, 71-73; two-person show, Seventh St Gallery, Lawrence, Kans, 77; Italian Cult Ctr, Stone Park, Ill, 77; one-artist shows, Univ of Kans, 66 (125 pieces) & Lawrence City Libr, 67 (40 pieces). Awards: Laguna Gloria Award, Tex Fine Arts Asn, Austin, 61; Kans Designer Craftsman Award, Kans Univ Art Mus, Lawrence, 68; Ceramic Monthly Award, Ceramics Monthly, Columbus, Ohio, 71. Style & Technique: Abstract expressionist. Media: Oil Paint; Stoneware Clay. Dealer: Crafts Incredible Gallery 7217 Mission Rd Prairie Village KS 66208. Mailing Add: 535 Kansas St Lawrence KS 66044

VACCARO, NICK DANTE
PAINTER, EDUCATOR
b Youngstown, Ohio, Apr 09, 31. Study: Univ Wash, BA, 58; Univ Calif, Berkeley, MA, 60; also with David Park. Work: San Francisco Art Asn; Dallas Mus Fine Art; Montgomery Mus Fine Art, Ala; Univ Calif, Berkeley; Youngstown Univ, Ohio. Comn: Mosaic, Pac Coast Paper Mills, Seattle, 57. Exhib: Butler Inst Ann, Youngstown, 56 & 59; Seattle Art Mus, Wash, 57, 58 & 62; Oakland Art Mus, Calif, 58; San Francisco Art Mus Ann, 58; Riverside Mus Print Int, New York, 59; Libr of Cong, Washington, DC, 60; Okla Art Ctr, Oklahoma City, 60, 61, 64, 65, 66 & 76; Dallas Mus of Fine Arts, Tex, 61, 62 & 63; Munic Art Mus, Los Angeles, Calif, 61; Isaac Delgado Mus, New Orleans, La, 61 & 63; Calif Palace of Legion of Honor, San Francisco, 61; DeYoung Mus, San Francisco, 62; Denver Art Mus, Colo, 62; Houston Mus of Fine Arts, Tex, 63; Mid-Am, Nelson Gallery, Kansas City, 64-66 & 70; two-person show, Seventh St Gallery, Lawrence, Kans, 77; one-man shows, Univ of Tex, Austin, 61, Wichita Univ, Kans, 67, Univ of Okla, Norman, 72 & Univ of Kans, Lawrence, 73. Teaching: Instr drawing & painting, Dept Art, Univ Tex, 60-61, asst prof drawing color, Sch Archit, 61-63; prof drawing & painting, Univ Kans, 63-, chmn dept art, 63-67; vis artist, Pa State Univ, 70. Awards: Purchase Awards, San Francisco Mus Art, 58, Dallas Mus Fine Arts, 61 & Montgomery Mus Fine Art, 62. Style & Technique: Poetic formalism, painterly and linear techniques. Media: Mixed Media. Publ: Illusr, Tex Quart, Vol 5, No 1; illusr, Image, Univ Tex, Austin, 63; auth, Gorky's debt, Art J, 63. Mailing Add: 535 Kansas St Lawrence KS 66044

VACCARO, PATRICK FRANK (PATT VACCARO)
PRINTMAKER, PAINTER
b New Rochelle, NY. Study: Ohio State Univ; Youngstown State Univ, BS(art educ). Work: US Govt for Foreign Embassies; Butler Inst Am Art, Youngstown, Ohio; St Peter's Col, Jersey City, NJ; Hoyt Inst, Pa; Aurora Art Ctr, Ill; Bethany Theological Sem, Oakwood, Ill; Farnsworth Mus, Wellesley Col, Mass; Canton Art Inst, Ohio. Comn: Preservation Print, Friends Am Art, Youngstown, 69. Exhib: Boston Libr Tour Italy, 55-59; Boston Printmakers Ann, Boston Mus Fine Arts, 55-; Am Colorprint Soc Ann, Philadelphia, 59-; Butler Inst Am Art Midyears, Youngstown, 62-67; Cleveland Mus Art Nat US Tour, 67. Teaching: Instr art, Youngstown Pub Schs, 52-; instr art, Youngstown State Univ, 59-70. Pos: Trustee, Soc NAm Artists, 71-72. Awards: First Graphics Awards, Butler Inst Am Art, 58-72; First Watercolor Awards, Anniston, Ala, 62; Medal of Honor in Graphics, Painters & Sculptors Soc NJ, 63; First Watercolor Awards, Aurora Art Ctr, Ill, 64; Quaker Storage Award, Am Colorprint Soc, 69. Mem: Boston Printmakers; Am Colorprint Soc; Painters & Sculptors Soc NJ. Style & Technique: Printmaking, serigraphy; painting, stylized realism to total abstraction. Media: Serigraphy. Publ: Illusr, Christian Herald; illusr, Together, Methodist Monthly, 69; illusr, Presby-Westminster Press, 71-72. Dealer: Dorothy Yepez Gallery 301 E 64th St 12-D New York NY 10021. Mailing Add: 7078 Oak Dr Poland OH 44514

VACHON, CASSANDRASU DHOOGE-QUINN
See Quinn, Sandi

VALENSTEIN, ALICE
PAINTER, COLLECTOR
b New York, NY, Feb 12, 04. Study: Teachers Col, Columbia Univ, study with Winold Reiss, Morris Davidson, Victor Candell & Leo Manso. Work: Staten Island Mus, NY; Emily Lowe Mus, Coral Gables, Fla; Hofstra Univ, NY; Miami Mus Mod Art, Fla; Mills Col, Oakland, Calif. Exhib: One-woman shows, Krasner Gallery, NY, Carus Gallery, NY, Katonah Gallery, NY, Miami Mus Mod Art & Alonzo Gallery, NY. Pos: Interior decorator, Alice Starr Interior Decorator, 27- Awards: Scarsdale Art Asn; Westchester Arts; Brandeis Univ. Mem: Nat Asn Women Artists; Hudson River Mus; Mus Mod Art; Whitney Mus. Style & Technique: Abstract collage and watercolors; figurative and abstract acrylic and oil. Collection: Contemporary fellow artists. Dealer: Jack Alonzo 30 W 57th St New York NY 10021. Mailing Add: 20 Heathcote Rd Scarsdale NY 10583 New York NY 20 Heathcote Rd Scarsdale NY 10583

VALENTINE, DEWAIN
SCULPTOR
b Ft Collins, Colo, Aug 27, 36. Study: Univ Colo, BFA, 58, MFA, 60; Yale-Norfolk Art Sch, Yale Univ fel, 58. Work: Whitney Mus Am Art, New York; Los Angeles Co Mus Art; Pasadena Art Mus; Milwaukee Art Ctr; Stanford Univ Art Mus. Exhib: Whitney Mus Am Art Ann, 66, 68 & 70; Sculpture of the Sixties, Los Angeles Co Mus Art, 66; Plastic Presence, Jewish Mus, New York, Milwaukee Art Ctr & San Francisco Art Mus, 69; 14 Sculptors: The Industrial Edge, Walker Art Ctr, 69; Art Inst Chicago Am Ann, 70; plus others. Teaching: Instr design & drawing, Univ Colo, 58-61; instr plastics, Univ Calif, Los Angeles, 65-67. Bibliog: Kurt Von Mier (auth), An interview with DeWain Valentine, 5/68 & Plagens (auth), Five artists—Ace Gallery, 10/71, Artforum; E A Danielli (auth), DeWain Valentine, Art Int, 11/69. Media: Polyester Resin. Mailing Add: 69 Market St Venice CA 90291

VALERIO, JAMES ROBERT
PAINTER, EDUCATOR
b Chicago, Ill, Dec 2, 38. Study: Art Inst of Chicago, BFA, 66, Anne Louis Raymond fel & MFA, 68; spec study with Seymour Rosofsky. Work: Long Beach Mus of Art, Calif; Ill Bell Telephone Co. Exhib: Twelve Painters & the Human Figure, Santa Barbara Mus of Art, Calif, 73; Seperate Realities, Los Angeles Munic Gallery, Calif, 73; Super Realist Vision, De Cordova Mus, Lincoln, Mass, 73; one-man shows, Michael Walls Gallery, New York, 74 & John Berggruen Gallery, San Francisco, 77; Selections in Contemp Realism, Akron Art Inst, Ohio, 74; Current Concerns, Part 2, Los Angeles Inst of Contemp Art, Calif, 75; Painting & Sculpture in Calif: The Mod Era, Nat Col of Fine Arts of the Smithsonian Inst, Washington, DC & San Francisco Mus of Art, 76-77. Teaching: Asst prof art, Rock Valley Col, Rockford, Ill, 68-70; assoc prof art, Univ Calif, Los Angeles, 70- Awards: Purchase Award, Long Beach Mus of Art, 70; Creative Arts Award fel, Univ Calif, Los Angeles, 76. Style & Technique: Realist painting. Media: Paint. Mailing Add: 16807 Magnolia Blvd Encino CA 91436

VALIER, BIRON (FRANK)
PAINTER, PRINTMAKER
b West Palm Beach, Fla, Mar 13, 43. Study: Cranbrook Acad Art, BFA; Yale Univ, MFA; Univ Ark; Woodstock Artist's Asn Graphic Workshop; Art Students League; Norton Gallery & Sch Art; Palm Beach Jr Col; Fla State Univ; Mexico City Col. Work: Butler Inst Am Art, Youngstown, Ohio; DeCordova Mus, Lincoln, Mass; Mus Fine Arts, Boston; Norton Gallery Contemp Collection, West Palm Beach; Print Collection, Boston Pub Libr. Exhib: Nat Acad Design Ann, New York, 65; Young Printmakers 1967 Traveling Exhib, 67; New Talent Show, Alpha Gallery, Boston, 69; Landscape II, DeCordova Mus, Lincoln, 71; Food Show, Inst Contemp Art, Boston, 72. Teaching: Instr art, Wheelock Col, 69-72; part-time instr, RI Col, fall 72. Awards: Purchase Prize, Butler Inst Am Art, 66; Award of Merit, Fla State Fair Fine Arts Exhib, 66 & 68; Boston Printmakers Exhib Purchase Prize, DeCordova Mus, 71. Bibliog: Peter Fierz (auth), New talent: James Piskoti, Biron Valier, Kunstnachrichten, 11/69; Robert Taylor (auth), Biron Valier's work tough, bold, Boston Globe, 11/10/72; Katherine Nahum (auth), Biron Valier; trains of thought, Newton Times, 11/8/72. Mem: Boston Visual Artist's Union; Am Fedn Arts. Style & Technique: Acrylic and aluminum collages.Publ: Contribr, Paula's Dream World of Trains, 72. Dealer: Athena Gallery 135 W Elm St New Haven CT 06515. Mailing Add: 2 Park Rd Belmont MA 02178

VALINSKI, DENNIS JOHN
SCULPTOR, LECTURER
b Carbondale, Pa, Nov 30, 46. Study: Univ Dayton Art Inst, BFA; Sch of Chicago Art Inst, MFA; studied with Richard Stankiewitz. Work: Storm King Art Ctr, Cornwall, NY; Johnson Mus, Ithaca, NY; Contemp Art Ctr, Cincinnati, Ohio. Comn: Two environ sculptures, Storm King Art Ctr, Cornwall, NY, 73-74; aerial sculpture, Cincinatti, Contemp Arts Ctr, Ohio, 73; aerial sculpture, Arts & Humanities Coun, Tulsa, Okla, 75; monumental fabric sculpture, Mus Contemp Crafts, New York, 76; monumental fabric sculpture, Mus Contemp Art, Teehran, Iran, 77. Exhib: All Ohio Paintings & Sculpture, Dayton Art Inst, Ohio, 67-68; Sculpture in the Park, Van Saun Park, Paramus, NJ, 71 & 74; one-man shows, Gallery at 210, New York, 73, 74 & 76 & Waterside Plaza, Pub Arts Coun, New York, 76; Sculpture in the Fields, Storm King Art Ctr, Cornwall, NY, 73 & 74; Art Park, Forest Gales & Moulting, Lewiston, NY, 74; Chicago & Vicinity Exhib, 74 & James Nelson Raymond Traveling Fel Exhib, Art Inst Chicago, Ill, 75; 20th Anniversary Exhib, Mus Contemp Crafts, New York, 76. Teaching: Lectr sculpture, Sarah Lawrence Col, Bronxville, NY & Univ Tulsa, Okla, fall 75; panelist, Art & the Community Inst, New Sch for Social Res, New York, 77. Bibliog: Grace Glueck (auth), Art people New York Times, 6/76; Sally DeVaney (auth), Art in space, Art Gallery Mag, 8-9/76; Skip Landen (auth), Celebration Artists (film), Nat Endowment for the Arts, 77-78. Style & Technique: Environmental, monumental and small scale sculpture in various materials, primarily fabric, rattan, steel mesh and cable and natural woods. Media: All.

Dealer: Doris Gaines Gallery at 210 Fifth Ave New York NY 10010. Mailing Add: 266 River Rd Edgewater NJ 07020

VALIUS, TELESFORAS
GRAPHIC ARTIST
b Riga, Latvia, July 10, 14; Can citizen. Study: Kaunas Sch Fine Arts, 37; Ont Col Educ, 66. Work: Vytautas Mus, Kaunas, Lithuania; Art Mus Fine Arts, Vilnius, Luthuania; Art Mus, London, Ont; Mus Fine Arts, Montreal, PQ; Art Inst Ont, Toronto. Exhib: Canadian Religious Art Today, Regis Col, Jesuit Seminary, Scarboro, Ont, 63; 30th Ann Exhib Am Color Print Soc, Asn Am Artists, New York, 69; Color Prints of the Americas, NJ State Mus, Cult Ctr, Trenton, 70; Exhib Prints sponsored by Can Soc Graphic Arts & Can Embassy, Washington, DC, 71; Canadian Prints & Drawings, sponsored by Can Soc Graphic Arts, Inst Studies Educ Tour, 71. Teaching: Prof graphic arts, Vilnius Acad Art, 42-44; head graphic arts, Ecole des Arts et Metiers, Freiburg, 46-49; instr art, Winston Churchill Col. Pos: Pres, Lithuanian Art Inst, 49-57; pres, Soc Can Painters, Etchers & Engravers, 62-65; pres, Can Soc Graphic Art, 65-66. Awards: C W Jeffery's Award, Can Soc Graphic Art, 58; Sterling Trust Award, Soc Can Painters, Etchers & Engravers, 61; Centennial Siver Medal, Can Govt, 67. Bibliog: Albert Bechtold (auth), Telesforas Valius, Ourer's L'Imprimerie de Lustenau, 45; Algimantas Mackus (auth), Telesforas Valius, Luthuanian Mag, 64; Alginmantas Banelis (auth), Su Telesforu Valiumi, Luthuanian Cult Mag, 70. Mem: Am Colo Print Soc; life fel Int Inst Arts & Lett; Int Platform Asn; hon mem Int Acad Lit, Arts & Sci. Dealer: Picture Loan Gallery 3 Charles St W Toronto ON Can. Mailing Add: 84 Pine Crest Rd Toronto ON M6P 3G5 Can

VALLEE, JACK (LAND)
PAINTER
b Wichita Falls, Tex, Aug 23, 21. Study: Midwestern Univ; Art Students League, with Reginald Marsh, Howard Trafton & Frank DuMond. Work: Springfield Mus Art; Univ Okla; Okla Art Ctr; Berkshire Mus, Pittsfield, Mass; Holyoke Mus Art. Exhib: Am Watercolor Soc, 58-65; Conn Acad Fine Arts, 59-65; Holyoke Mus, 64 & 68; Fisher Gallery, Washington, DC, 65 & 68; plus others. Awards: Okla Art Festival, 62-64; McDowell Colony Fel, 63; Watercolor USA, 64. Mem: Allied Artists Am; Washington Watercolor Club; Am Watercolor Soc; Nat Arts Club; Asn Okla Artists. Media: Watercolor. Mailing Add: 1216 NE 50th St Oklahoma City OK 73111

VALLEE, WILLIAM OSCAR
PAINTER
b South Paris, Maine, June 18, 34. Study: Univ Alaska. Work: Many in pvt collections. Exhib: Anchorage Fur Rendezvous, 63; Easter Arts Festival, 63; Alaska Festival Music & Art, 63 & 64; one-man shows, Anchorage Petrol Club, 63 & Anchor Galleries, 63. Pos: Instituted (in coop with Am Artists Prof League), Am Art Wk, 63; treas, Soc Alaskan Arts, 63; co-founder, Alaska-Int Cult Arts Ctr; bd dirs & co-founder, Anchorage Community Art Ctr; pres & chmn bd, Alaska Map Serv, Inc. Awards: Anchorage Fur Rendezvous, 63; Easter Art Festival, 63; Artist of the Month, Alaska Art Guild, 63. Mem: Alaska Art Guild (pres & chmn, 64); Alaska Watercolor Soc (pres, 63-); Am Soc Photogrammetry; Am Artist Prof League. Media: Watercolor. Mailing Add: 4118 Irene Dr Anchorage AK 99504

VALTMAN, EDMUND
CARTOONIST
b Tallinn, Estonia, May 31, 14; US citizen. Study: Pvt studios, 36-39; Tallinn Art & Appl Art Sch, 42-44. Work: Lyndon Johnson Libr, Austin, Tex; Univ Southern Miss Libr; Univ Cincinnati Libr; State Hist Soc Mo, Columbia; Wichita State Univ Libr, Kans. Exhib: The Great Challenge, Ed Cartoon Exhib, Washington, Tokyo & London, 58-59; Politics 1960, Columbia Univ, New York, 60; Int Salon Cartoons, Montreal, PQ, 68-71; World Cartoon Festival, Knokke-Heist, Belg, 71; one-man cartoon exhib, Trinity Col, Hartford, Conn, 65. Awards: Pub Interest Award, Nat Safety Coun, 58; Pulitzer Prize for Cartooning, Columbia Univ, 62; Frank Tripp Award, Gannett Newspapers, 63. Mem: Asn Am Ed Cartoonists; Nat Cartoonists Soc; Conn Acad Fine Arts. Media: India Ink. Collection: Editorial cartoons. Mailing Add: 41 Foothills Way Bloomfield CT 06002

VAN AALTEN, JACQUES
PAINTER
b Antwerp, Belg, Apr 12, 07. Study: Nat Acad Design, 26-30, grad; Art Students League, 32-34; Acad Grande Chaumiere, Paris, 55; Tulane Univ La, 70-71. Work: Portrait of Pope Pius XII, Vatican Mus Permanent Collection, Rome; Relig Ministry Bldg, Jerusalem; Truman Libr, Independence, Mo; La State Art Collection, New Capitol Bldg, Baton Rouge; Rockport Art Asn, Mass; plus many others in pvt collections in USA & abroad. Exhib: Nat Acad of Design, New York, NY, 30; fresco mural, Straubenmuller Textile High Sch, New York, 38-39; Whitney Mus, 40; Beaux Arts, New York, 40; Archit League, New York, 40; Soc of Independent Artists, New York, 40; Munic Artists, New York, 41; Detroit Inst Art Mus, Mich, 46; Isaac Delgado Mus Art, New Orleans, 58-59; Rockport Art Asn, Mass, 62-71; Mus-Norton Gallery, Palm Beach, Fla, 63; La Artists Group, La Art Comn Gallery, Old Capitol Bldg, Baton Rouge; plus many other group & one-man shows. Teaching: Instr art, Nassau Conserv Art, Long Island, NY, 40; instr art, van Aalten Studio Sch, Detroit, 44-47. Awards: Suydam Medal, 30; Tiffany Scholar, 30; Silver Pontifical Medal, received from Pope Pius XII, Vatican City, Rome, Italy, 56. Mem: Life mem Rockport Art Asn; life mem Art Students League; Nat Soc Mural Painters; Isaac Delgado Mus Art Asn. Style & Technique: Realism, impressionism and abstraction in miscellaneous and varied techniques. Mailing Add: Lyndhurst K-1043 Deerfield Beach FL 33441

VAN ARSDALE, DOROTHY THAYER
ART ADMINISTRATOR
b Malden, Mass, Jan 14, 17. Study: Simmons Col, BS(bus admin). Collections Arranged: Art Treasure of Turkey, 66, Tunisian Mosaics, 67, Colonial Art from Ecuador, 68 & Swiss Drawing, 69, Washington, DC & nat tour; Selection of New Belgian Painting, Fla & nat tour, 71; Discovering American Artists Series. Pos: Chief traveling exhib serv, Smithsonian Inst, Washington, DC, 64-70; dir, Dorothy T Van Arsdale Assocs, Traveling Exhib Serv, Alexandria, Va. Awards: Knight, Order Dannebrog, King of Denmark, 71. Mem: Am Asn Mus; Int Coun Mus. Publ: Contribr, Paintings & Drawings, 66, Sculptures & Drawings, 66, Islamic Art from the Collection of Edwin Binney, III, 66 & Carl-Henning Pedersen, 69; contribr & ed, 140 Years of Danish Glass (catalogue), 68. Mailing Add: 407 N Washington St Alexandria VA 22314

VANASSE, LOUIS RAYMOND
COLLECTOR, INSTRUCTOR
b Northampton, Mass, Jan 22, 31. Study: St Michael's Col, AB(Eng); Univ of Mass, MA(Eng). Teaching: Instr humanities, Northampton Sch System, Mass, 60- Awards: John Hay Fel, Studies in the Humanities, Williams Col, 62; Fulbright-Hays Grant, study in Ghana, W Africa, African Art, Univ Mass, 74. Collection: Twentieth century American Artists. Mailing Add: 17 Aubinwood Rd Amherst MA 01002

VAN ATTA, HELEN ULMER
COLLECTOR
b Midland, Tex, Mar 3, 14. Mem: Art Collectors Club. Collection: Contemporary American art. Mailing Add: 4850 Preston Rd Dallas TX 75205

VAN BRUNT, PHILIP G
ART DIRECTOR, ASSEMBLAGE ARTIST
b Kobe, Japan, Mar 31, 35; US citizen. Study: Chaffey Col, Ontario, Calif, AA; Otis Art Inst, Los Angeles, MFA, 60; also with Arthur Ames. Work: Santa Barbara Mus Art, Calif; Salk Inst, La Jolla; Lyman Allyn Mus, New London, Conn; Presidente Mus, Guadalajara, Mex; Carnegie Inst, Pittsburgh, Pa. Comn: Processional Cross, St Mark's Episcopal Church, Upland, Calif, 64; oil painting, Gen Foods Corp, Calif, 65; Enamel Mural, pvt residence, Los Angeles, 69; mural, collage, Clinton Nat Bank, Conn, 74. Exhib: Enamels' Mus Contemp Crafts, New York, 59; Los Angeles Co Mus Art, Calif, 59-61; 17 Conn Artists, Slater Mem Mus, Norwich, Conn, 72; one-man show, La Jolla Art Mus, 68 & Lyman Allyn Mus, New London, Conn, 74. Teaching: Instr painting, Lyman Allyn Mus, summers; instr, Westridge Sch, Pasadena, Calif, 63-64; dir art, Williams Sch, New London, Conn, 72- Pos: Asst dir, Downey Mus Art, Downey, Calif, 60-65. Awards: Gold Medal, Nat Orange Show, San Bernardino, Calif, 58. Bibliog: Jean Yoder (auth), Titanic epilogue, Commutator J. Mem: Otis Art Assoc, Los Angeles. Style & Technique: Collage, painting & box construction; restoration of antique objects, specializing in trompe l'oeil finishes. Media: Found Objects. Publ: Contribr, Joseph Mugnaini (auth), Oil Painting, 72; illusr, Choristers guild letters, 74-75. Dealer: Henri Gallery 1500 21st St NW Washington DC 20036. Mailing Add: 110 Hempstead St New London CT 06320

VAN BUREN, HELEN RAE
PAINTER, ART DEALER
b Marshalltown, Iowa, July 17, 19. Study: San Antonio Art Inst; San Francisco Art Inst; Inst Allende, San Miguel de Allende, Mex; also with Peter Lanyon, James Twitty & James Pinto. Work: Laguna Gloria Mus, Austin, Tex; Witte Mus, San Antonio; Farm & Home Savings & Loan Asn, Austin; Embassy, Sierra Leone, Africa; among others. Exhib: Tex Watercolor Soc, San Antonio, 62-75; Tex Fine Arts Asn, Austin, 63; Okla Fine Arts Seven State Regional, Oklahoma City, 67; Watercolor USA, Springfield, Mo, 68; Crossroads of America, Chicago, 75. Awards: First Purchase Prize, San Antonio Art League, 63 & Tex Fine Arts Asn, 63; Purchase Prize, Howard Wolf, Inc, New York, 74. Bibliog: Artist of the month, River Art Group Bull, San Antonio, 75. Mem: Tex Watercolor Soc (exhib chmn, 72-74, treas, 75-); San Antonio Art League; Contemp Artists Group (pres, 72-74); River Art Group; Laredo Art League. Style & Technique: Impressionistic and nonobjective; collage. Media: Acrylic, Watercolor. Mailing Add: 338 Albany San Antonio TX 78209

VAN BUREN, RAEBURN
ILLUSTRATOR, CARTOONIST
b Pueblo, Colo, Jan 12, 91. Study: Art Students League, 13. Work: Boston Univ Libr; Syracuse Univ. Teaching: Lect, Comic Strip Art. Pos: Creator of United Feature Syndicated Comic Strip Abbie & Slats, over 350 daily newspapers. Awards: Cartoonist of the Year, B'nai B'rith, Philadelphia, 58; Reuben Award/Story Strips Category, Nat Cartoonist Soc, 76. Mem: Charter mem Nat Cartoonists Soc; life mem Soc Illusr; Artists & Writers Soc. Publ: Contribr illus, Sat Eve Post, Collier's, Redbook, New Yorker, McClure Syndicate & King Features Syndicate, plus others. Mailing Add: 21 Clover Dr Great Neck NY 11021

VAN BUREN, RICHARD
SCULPTOR
b Syracuse, NY, 1937. Study: Mexico City Col; Univ Mex; San Francisco State Col. Work: Mus Mod Art, New York; Walker Art Ctr, Minneapolis; Nat Gallery Australia, Canberra; Art Mus STex, Corpus Christi. Comn: Three-unit wall sculpture, Walker Art Ctr, 71. Exhib: Primary Structures, Jewish Mus, New York, 66; Whitney Sculpture Ann, Whitney Mus Am Art, New York, 68 & 70; Milwaukee Art Mus, 69 & 71; Finch Col, New York, 69; Art Inst Chicago, 69 & 72; Akron Art Inst, Ohio, 70; Walker Art Ctr, Minneapolis, 71; Albright-Knox Art Gallery, Buffalo, NY, 71; Contemp Art Mus, Houston, 72; Harvard Univ, 73; Contemp Arts Ctr, Cincinnati, 73; Indianapolis Mus Art, Ind, 74; Va Mus Fine Arts, Richmond, 74; New York Cult Ctr, 74; plus others. Bibliog: Phyllis Tuchman (auth), An interview with Richard Van Buren, 12/69 & Susan Heineman (auth), Richard Van Buren, 4/75, Artforum; Carter Ratcliff (auth), Solid color, Art News, 5/72. Mailing Add: c/o Paula Cooper Gallery 155 Wooster St New York NY 10012

VANCE, GEORGE WAYNE
CERAMIST, SCULPTOR
b Macomb, Ill, Oct 29, 40. Study: Knox Col, BA, 62; Univ Iowa, MA, 68; Univ Colo, MFA, 72. Work: Wis State Univ-Platteville. Comn: Casserole, Sheldon Mem Gallery, Lincoln, Nebr, 69. Exhib: 10th Ann Rochester Festival Relig Art, NY, 68; Iscals, Tex Technol Col Mus, 69; Kitchen Keramik Exhib, Sheldon Mem Gallery, 69; Midwest Biennial, Joslyn Mus, Omaha, Nebr, 70-72; Objects 73, Colo Ctr for Arts. Teaching: Instr ceramics, Dak State Col, 68-70. Awards: First Prize Sculpture, Rochester Festival Relig Art, 68; First Prize Sculpture, 70 & Jurors Award, 71, Own Your Own, Southern Colo State Col. Bibliog: Paul Arnold (auth), article in Craft Horizons, 68; Ray Schemore (auth), article in Craft Horizons, 70. Mem: Am Crafts Coun. Media: Clay. Mailing Add: Jamestown Star Rte Boulder CO 80302

VANCO, JOHN LEROY
ART ADMINISTRATOR, PHOTOGRAPHER
b Erie, Pa, Aug 21, 45. Study: Allegheny Col, BA(art hist & hist); Whitney Mus Am Art. Pos: Exec dir, Erie Art Ctr, 68- Awards: Best Prof, ESFA Photog Exhib, 72. Publ: Auth, What Ever Happened to Louis Eilshemius?, 67; contribr, American Art & Western Wildlife, 72; illusr, Roger Misiewicz: Wolfman of the Blues, 72; auth, Graphic Work of The Vienna Secession (catalog); auth, Multiplemedia (catalog). Mailing Add: 1317 Parade St Erie PA 16503

VAN DE BOVENKAMP, HANS
SCULPTOR
b Barneveld, Holland, June 1, 38. Study: Archit Sch Amsterdam, 57; Univ Mich, Ann Arbor, BScDes, 61. Comn: Sculpture Del Trust Co, Wilmington, 70; Kennilworth Mgt, NY, 71, Jewish Inst Geriatrics Care, Lake Success, NY, 72, Home Fed Savings & Loan Bank, Minneapolis, 73 & 74 & Southpark Shopping Ctr Mall, Moline, Ill, 74; plus others. Exhib: Benson Gallery, Bridgehampton, NY, 69, 75 & 78; Lever House, New York, 69 & 73-78; Dayton's, Minn, 71; Storm King Art Ctr, Cornwall, NY, 73-74; Aquarius Int, Caracas, Venezuela, 74-75; Am Inst of Arts & Lett, New York, 76; Arnot Art Mus, Elmira, NY, 76; Nat Acad of Design, New York, 77; plus others. Awards: Emily Lowe Award, 64; I-80 Nebr

Award, 75. Style & Technique: Large outdoor forms dealing with negative imagery; welded aluminum and stainless steel. Mailing Add: Box 837 Tillson NY 12486

VANDENBERGE, PETER WILLEM
SCULPTOR
b Voorberg, Zuid-Holland, Neth, Oct 16, 35; US citizen. Study: Art Acad, The Hague, Neth; Calif State Univ, Sacramento, BA; Univ Calif, Davis, MA. Work: Henry Gallery, Univ Wash, Seattle; Mus Contemp Crafts, New York; Johnson Collection Am Crafts, Racine, Wis; Crocker Art Gallery, Sacramento; Burpee Art Mus, Rockford, Ill. Comn: Three glazed relief tile murals, San Francisco City Col, 71; Hall of Flowers, Golden Gate Park, San Francisco, 72; public murals, San Francisco Arts Comn, City of San Francisco; glazed tile relief, Contra Costa Jr Col Dist Off, John F Gordon Educ Ctr, Martinez, Calif, 75. Exhib: Objects USA, Johnson Collection Am Crafts Traveling Exhib, 69-70; Clay Works, Mus Contemp Crafts, 71; Int Ceramic Exhib, Victoria & Albert Mus, London, 72; Four Ceramic Sculptors from California, Alan Frumkin Gallery, New York, 73, Calif Ceramic Sculptors I & II, 74, Five Ceramic Sculptors from Calif, Chicago, 75; Clay, Whitney Mus Am Art, New York, 74; Fendrick's Gallery, Washington, DC, 76; Campbell Mus Contemp Crafts, Cranbrook Acad Art, Bloomfield Hills, Mich, 76; plus others. Teaching: Asst prof ceramics & sculpture, San Francisco State Univ, 66-73; asst prof ceramics & sculpture, Calif State Univ, Sacramento, 73- Awards: Madeleine Cortese Williams Found Award, 63 & 66; Purchase Award for Sculpture, Home Savings & Loan Assoc, Los Angeles, 73. Bibliog: D Zack (auth), Mythology, California ceramics, Art & Artist Mag, London, 9/69, Nut art in quake time, Art News, 70 & Laugh in clay, Craft Horizon Mag, 71. Style & Technique: Figurative expressionist attitudes using sculptural techniques of carving and handbuilding. Media: Stoneware, Porcelain; Clay, Terra Cotta. Dealer: Allan Frumkin 41 57th St New York NY 10022. Mailing Add: 713 37th St Sacramento CA 95819

VANDERLIP, DIANNE PERRY
GALLERY DIRECTOR, EDUCATOR
b Toledo, Ohio, Apr 20, 41. Study: Ohio Univ, BFA; NY Univ; Pratt Inst. Collections Arranged: Recorded Activities (with catalog), 70; Artists Books (with catalog), 73; N, E, W, S & Middle (with catalog), 75; Alphons Schilling Stereoptics, 75; John Sloan/Robert Henri: Their Philadelphia Yrs, 76; Alan Shields' Environments, 77; Robert Hudson, 77. Teaching: Prof aesthetics, Moore Col Art, 68- Pos: Dir, Vanderlip Gallery, Philadelphia, 66-68; dir, Moore Col Art Gallery, 68-78; cur & consult, Dechert, Price & Rhoads, Philadelphia, 74-; panelist & consult, Nat Endowments Arts, Washington, DC, 74-; cur of contemp art, Denver Art Mus, 78- Awards: Award of Excellence, Philadelphia Art Dir Club, 71. Bibliog: Dore Ashton (auth), Beyond literalism, Art Mag, 69; Lucy Lippard (auth), Dematerialization of Art, Praeger, 73; Dianne Kelder (auth), Artists books, Art in Am, 74. Mem: Am Asn Mus; Am Fedn Arts; Soc Arts & Lett. Collection: Contemporary paintings and drawings by American artists. Publ: Ed, More Ray Gun Poems by Claes Oldenburg, 74; ed, Hopi Kachina Dolls, 75. Mailing Add: Denver Art Mus 100 W 14 Ave Pkwy Denver CO 80204

VAN DER MARCK, JAN
MUSEUM DIRECTOR
b Roermond, Netherlands, Aug 19, 29. Study: Univ Nijmegen, BA, MA & PhD(hist art), 56; Univ Utrecht; Columbia Univ. Exhibitions Organized: Charles Biederman, 65 & Lucio Fontana, 66, Walker Art Ctr, Minneapolis; Pictures to be Read/Poetry to be Seen, 67, Christo: Wrap in Wrap Out, 69, Moholy-Nagy, 69 & Art by Telephone, 69, Mus Contemp Art, Chicago; American Art: Third Quarter Century, 73, Seattle Art Mus; Arman, Mus Contemp Art, La Jolla, Calif, 74, Herbert Bayer, 77, Lucio Pozzi, 77 & Alain Kirili, 78. Teaching: Assoc prof art hist, Univ Wash, Seattle, 72-74. Pos: Cur, Gemeentemuseum, Arnhem, Netherlands, 59-61; dep dir fine arts, Seattle World's Fair, 61-62; cur, Walker Art Ctr, Minneapolis, 63-67; dir, Mus Contemp Art, Chicago, 67-70; dir, Valley Curtain Corp, 71-72; dir, Dartmouth Col mus & galleries, 74- Awards: Fel, Netherlands Orgn Pure Res, 54-55; fel, Rockefeller Found, 57-59. Mem: Am Fed Arts (nat exhib comt, 68-); Am Asn Mus Dir. Publ: Auth, Romantische Boekillustratie in Belgie, Romen, 56; auth, Lucio Fontana, Connaissance, 74; auth, George Segal, Abrams, 75; also articles in Artforum, Art in Am & other jour. Mailing Add: Wildwood Dr West Lebanon NH 03784

VAN DERPOOL, JAMES GROTE
ART HISTORIAN
b New York, NY, July 21, 03. Study: Mass Inst Technol, BArch; Harvard Univ, MFA; Am Acad Rome, Italy; Atelier Gromort; Ecole Beaux Arts, Paris, France. Teaching: Prof hist archit, Univ Ill, 32-39, head dept art, 39-46; prof archit & head Avery Libr, Columbia Univ, 46-60, actg archit dean & assoc dean, 59-61. Pos: Consult var hist preserv projs, 50-; archit ed, Columbia Encycl, 52-54; chmn design construct, Hist St Luke's Church, Smithfield, Va, 52-56; co-ed, Complete Libr World Art, 57-62; exec dir, Landmarks Preserv Comn New York, 62-65; chmn design ballroom wing, Grace Mansion, New York, 64. Awards: George McAneny Medal, Am Scenic & Hist Preserv Soc, 64. Mem: Benjamin Franklin fel Royal Soc Arts, London; fel Am Inst Archit; Soc Archit Historians (nat pres, 55-57); Int Fund for Monuments (trustee); Col Art Asn Am; Am Scenic & Hist Preserv Soc (trustee, 36-). Interest: Historic preservation; Renaissance painting and eighteenth century American arts. Collection: Italian, Dutch and American paintings. Publ: Contribr, Art Bull, Soc Archit Hist J, Encycl Britannica & others. Mailing Add: 95 Ocean Way Santa Monica CA 90402

VANDER SLUIS, GEORGE J
PAINTER, EDUCATOR
b Cleveland, Ohio, Dec 18, 15. Study: Cleveland Inst Art; Colorado Springs Fine Arts Ctr; Fulbright scholar, Italy, 51-52. Work: Rochester Mem Art Gallery, NY; Everson Mus Art, Syracuse, NY; Munson-Williams-Proctor Inst, Utica, NY; State Univ NY Albany; Hamline Univ, St Paul, Minn; plus many others. Comn: Mural, Post Off, Rifle, Colo, 40 & Riverton, Wyo, 41, US Govt Sect Fine Arts; Barn Door decorations in NY State, NY State Coun Arts grant, 66; wall painting, Hotel Syracuse, City Walls New York & NY State Coun Arts, 71; designed two US airmail stamps, 71. Exhib: American Paintings 1945-1957, Minneapolis Inst Arts, 57; Contemporary Painting & Sculpture, Univ Ill, 61; 125 Years of New York Painting & Sculpture, NY State Expos, Syracuse, 66; American Art, White House, Washington, DC, 66; The Door, Mus Contemp Crafts, New York, 68; one-man shows, J Seligmann Gallery, New York, 59, Royal Marks Gallery, New York, 62, 63 & 64; Krasner Gallery, New York, 68, 69 & 71, Everson Mus of Art, Syracuse, NY, 77 & Syracuse Univ Lubin House, New York, 78; plus many other group & one-man shows. Teaching: Instr painting & drawing, Colo Fine Arts Ctr, 40-42 & 45-47; prof painting & drawing, Syracuse Univ, 47- Awards: Jurors' Award, Rochester Mem Art Gallery, 58 & 69. Bibliog: J Albino (auth), Barn door painting, Dodge News, 11/67; articles in New York Times, 4/7/67 & Syracuse New Times, 6/5/71. Style & Technique: Circular images referring to astronomical phenomena, moons, planets and galaxies. Media: Acrylic. Mailing Add: Sch of Art Syracuse Univ Syracuse NY 13210

VAN DER STRAETEN, VINCENT ROGER
ART DEALER
b New York, NY, June 9, 29. Pos: Dir, Van Der Straeten Gallery, New York. Mem: Art & Antique Dealers League Am (vpres). Specialty: Contemporary American, English and French paintings, master graphics and sculpture. Mailing Add: 136 E 79th St New York NY 10021

VAN DER VOORT, AMANDA VENELIA
PAINTER
b Alliance, Ohio. Study: Pratt Inst, grad; Grand Cent Sch Art; Metrop Sch Art; Nat Acad Sch Fine Arts; Columbia Univ; NY Univ; also with Helen Lorenz, Ogden Pleisner, Romanovsky, Robert Philipp, Dong Kingman & Howard Hildebrandt. Comn: Painting of El Jardin, comn by W Alton Jones, La Gorce Island, Fla, 61; portrait of Mrs Rosen, comn by Dr Theodore Rosen, New York, 63; flower painting, comn by E H Blanchard, Warwick, NY, 67; High St, Rockport, Mass, comn by Dr J Wolfe, Houston, Tex, 68; Gloxinias, comn by George E Martin, Greenwich, Conn, 71. Exhib: Allied Artists Am, New York, 56-57; Am Artists Prof League, New York, 56-78; Nat Acad Design, New York, 57; Hudson Valley Art Asn, White Plains, NY, 59-78; Acad Artists Asn, Springfield, Mass, 65-75. Pos: Dir & rec secy, Hudson Valley Art Asn, 66-; dir & first vpres, Pen & Brush, 67-; dir nat bd, Am Artists Prof League, 70- Awards: For Figure Painting, Catharine Lorillard Wolfe Art Club, 70 & Art Soc Old Greenwich, 71; Best in Show for Oil Portrait, Conn State Fedn Women's Clubs, 72. Mem: Catharine Lorillard Wolfe Art Club (dir & chmn nat exhib, 60-75); Kent Art Asn, Conn; Nat League Am Pen Women (art chmn, 72-77); fel Nat Acad Design; fel Royal Soc Arts, London. Style & Technique: Traditional and representational. Media: Oil, Watercolor, Graphics. Mailing Add: 17 Stonehedge Dr S Greenwich CT 06830

VAN DE WIELE, GERALD
PAINTER
b Detroit, Mich, 1932. Study: Art Inst Chicago; Black Mountain Col. Work: Baltimore Mus Art; Borg Warner Corp, Chicago; Singer Mfg Co; Owens Corning Fiberglas Corp; Coca-Cola Co; also in pvt collections. Exhib: Albright-Knox Art Gallery, Buffalo, 63; Riverside Mus, New York, 64 & 66; Smithsonian Inst Traveling Exhib, 68; Ill Wesleyan Univ, Bloomington, 68; Peridot Gallery, New York, 69; plus others. Awards: Nat Coun Arts Grant, 68. Mailing Add: c/o Art Options 49 E 53rd St New York NY 10022

VAN DOMMELEN, DAVID B
ART WRITER, FIBER ARTIST
b Grand Rapids, Mich, Aug 21, 29. Study: Harrington Interior Design Inst, cert; Mich State Univ, BA & MA; also with Abraham Rattner & Mariska Karasz. Work: Mich State Univ Mus of Art, East Lansing; Arrowmont Sch of Crafts, Gatlinburg, Tenn; Am Home Econ Asn Collection, Washington, DC; Marshall Field Permanent Collection, Chicago; Portland Mus of Fine Arts, Maine. Exhib: Group Traveling Show, Smithsonian Inst, Washington, DC, 57-78; Invention with Thread, Montclair Art Mus, NJ, 61; one-man shows, Nashville Art Ctr, Tenn, 61, Univ Maine Mus of Art, Orono, 62, Portland Mus of Art, Maine, 63, Kalamazoo Art Ctr Mus, Mich, 66, Univ Iowa, Iowa City, 67 & WVa State Univ Mus, Institute, 75; plus many others. Collections Arranged: Retrospective 1956-1968, Pa State Univ, 68. Teaching: Prof art educ, Pa State Univ, 59-; summer instr, Haystack Sch of Crafts, 62, 63 & 74; guest prof, Univ Iowa, 66-69; summer instr, Arrowmont Schs of Crafts, 70-76. Awards: Fishburn Award, Int Understanding, Educ Press Am, 73. Bibliog: John Peter (auth), Sewing machine art, Look Mag, 8/61, Ruth Bunker (auth), David Van Dommelen, Cross-Country Craftsman, 10/62. Mem: Nat Art Educ Asn; Nat Craftsman's Asn (mem bd dirs, 75-77). Style & Technique: Tapestries in contemporary idiom utilizing weaving, machine stitchery and applique. Media: Fiber. Publ: Co-auth, Design at Work: Its Forms and Functions, Pa State Univ, 61; auth, Decorative Wall Hangings, 62 & auth, Walls: Enrichment and Ornamentation, 65, Funk & Wagnalls; auth, Designing and Decorating Interiors, John Wiley, 65; auth, New Uses for Old Cannonballs, Funk & Wagnalls, 66. Mailing Add: 1981 Highland Dr State College PA 16801

VAN DUINWYK, GEORGE PAUL
METALSMITH, INSTRUCTOR
b New York, NY, Sept 30, 41. Study: Calif State Univ, Northridge, BA, 64, with Frederick Lauritzen; Calif State Univ, Long Beach, MA, 71, with Alvin A Pine; RI Sch of Design, MFA, 72, with John A Prip. Work: Oakland Mus, Calif. Exhib: Mod Am Metalsmithing & Jewelry, Corcoran Gallery of Art, Washington, DC, 72; Int Jewelry Exhib, Munich, WGer, 73-74; Jewelry Invitational, Albright-Knox Mus, Buffalo, NY, 74; World Silver Fair, Mexico City, Mex, 74; Contemp Crafts of N, Cent & S Am, Univ of Colo, 74; 275 Yrs of Am Metalsmithing, Mus of Contemp Crafts, New York, 75; Goldsmiths 77, Phoenix Art Mus, Ariz, 77; Profiles of US Jewelry, Tex Tech Univ, Lubbock, 77. Teaching: Assoc prof metalsmithing, Calif State Univ, Long Beach, 72-73; adj prof metalsmithing, RI Sch of Design, 73-74. Pos: Craftsman-in-residence, RI State Coun on the Arts, 76-77; dir tech resources, Jewelry Inst, Providence, RI, 77- Awards: Purchase Award, The Metal Experience, Oakland Mus, 71; Design Award, Designer/Craftsman 77, Richmond Art Ctr, Calif, 76; Nat Endowment for the Arts Grant, Slide Jury Proj, 77. Bibliog: Ralph Turner (auth), Modern Jewelry, Eng publ, 76; Thelma Newman (auth), The Container Book, Chilton, 77; Oppi Untracht (auth), Jewelry Techniques, Doubleday 77. Mem: Sco NAm Goldsmiths; Am Crafts Coun. Style & Technique: Constructions in precious and nonprecious metals of whimsical container and mask-like jewelry forms. Dealer: Art Wear 28 W 74th St New York NY 10021 Mailing Add: 28 Ayrault St Newport RI 02840

VANESS, MARGARET HELEN
PAINTER, PRINTMAKER
b Seattle, Wash, Nov 6, 19. Study: Univ Wash, BFA(printmaking), BFA(painting) & MFA; Drexel Univ; spec study with Francis Cellentano & Glen Alps. Work: US Embassies in Athens, Bogata, Bierut, Caracas, Copenhagen, Seoul, Managua, Lima, Lagos, Dar es Salaam & Tanzania; Cheney-Cowles Mus, Spokane, Wash; Pratt-Manhatten Ctr Gallery, New York; World Print Orgn, San Francisco, Calif; Evergreen State Col Libr Collection, Olympia, Wash; plus others. Comn: Two ed of ten prints each, USIA, 73; Mural, Med Ctr, Boeing Co, Philadelphia, Pa, 74. Exhib: Wash State Capitol Mus, Olympia, 64; Northwest Ann, Seattle Art Mus, Wash, 65 & 67; Pacific-Northwest Arts & Crafts Print Invitational, 70; Judkin Mem Am Mus, Bath, Eng, Pratt Manhatten, New York, 72-74; 60th Ann, Del Art Mus, Wilmington, 74; Philadelphia Art Alliance, Pa, 75; one-person show, Greenhill-Lower Merion, Philadelphia, Pa, 76; Nat Print Exhib, Cheney-Cowles Mus, Spokane Wash, 77; plus others. Collections Arranged: Group Exhibs, Burien Arts Asn Festival of Arts, 66-69; King Co Arts Comn, Seattle Arts Comn Touring Exhib, 71, Exhib of Prints, 72. Teaching: Instr painting & drawing, Burien Arts Gallery Sch, Seattle, Wash, 68-69; asst printmaking Univ Wash, Seattle, 71-73. Pos: Trustee & charter mem, Burien Arts Asn, Seattle, Wash, 65-69; illusr, Boeing Co, Seattle, Wash, 72-73 & 78 & Philadelphia, Pa, 74-75; illusr, Du Pont Co, Wilmington, Del, 73-74. Awards: First Award Painting, Boeing Co, 68; First Awards Print, Pac Northwest Arts & Crafts Asn, 70 & 71 & others. Bibliog: Carolyn Wright (auth), Thesis

exhibit at Henry Gallery, Univ Washington Daily, 6/73; Andrew Seraphin (auth), Four printmakers in Gallery F, Art Alliance Bull, 4/75. Mem: Col Art Asn, New York; Philadelphia Print Club. Style & Technique: Interaction of color and universal space; hard-edge painting; color and texture abstract prints; systemic. Media: (Painting) Acrylic and Mixed; (Printmaking) Collagraph and Serigraphy. Publ: Auth, Color/Light and Time, (in prep). Mailing Add: 17128 Second Southwest Seattle WA 98166

VAN GINKEL, BLANCHE LEMCO
ARCHITECT, EDUCATOR
b Can. Study: McGill Univ, BArch; Harvard Univ, MCP. Exhib: Wo de Co Exhib, Tokyo, Japan, 60; Plan for Old Montreal, Place Ville Marie, Montreal, Que, 63; Midtown Manhattan Plan Exhib, Art Dir Club & New York Cult Ctr, New York, 72; Work of van Ginkel Assoc, Columbia Univ, New York, 73; Spectrum Can, Royal Can Acad of Arts, Montreal, 76. Teaching: Asst prof archit, Univ Pa, Philadelphia, 51-57; dir archit, Univ Toronto, Ont, 77- Pos: Rep to Can Conf of Arts, Ottawa, Royal Archit Inst of Can, 71-74; mem adv comt on design, Nat Capital Planning Comn, 77-; chmn, Massey Awards, Ottawa, Ont, 77- Awards: Massey Medal, 64; Grand Prix for Film, Int Fedn Housing & Planning, 56. Bibliog: New patterns for a metropolis, Archit Forum, 10/71; Les effets reel . . . , Archit Concept, 5/73. Mem: Royal Can Acad of Arts; Few Royal Archit Inst of Can. Publ: Auth, The form of the core, J Am Inst Planner, 2/61; ed & contribr, Automobile Issue of Can Art, 62; contribr, Phenomenon of Pollution, Harvest House, 66; ed & contribr, Expo 67 Architectural Design, 67; contribr, Aesthetic considerations, In: Urban Problems, Holt Rinehart & Winston, 71. Mailing Add: Sch of Archit Univ Toronto 230 College St Toronto ON M5S 1A1 Can

VAN HOESEN, BETH (MRS MARK ADAMS)
PRINTMAKER
b Boise, Idaho, June 27, 26. Study: Stanford Univ, BA; San Francisco Art Inst; San Francisco State Col; Escuela Esmeralda, Mex; Acad Fontainbleau; Acad Grande Chaumiere; Acad Julian. Work: San Francisco Mus; Brooklyn Mus; Mus Mod Art, New York; Smithsonian Inst, Washington, DC; Victoria-Albert Mus, London. Exhib: Two Decades of American Prints, 16th Nat Print Exhib, Brooklyn Mus, 47-68; 116th Ann Exhib, Pa Acad Fine Arts, 65; Amerikanische Radierugen, touring exhib ten printmakers, US Info Bur; Contemporary Prints from Northern California, Art in Embassies Prog, US State Dept, 66; Graphics '71, West Coast USA, Univ Ky, 71. Awards: San Francisco Mus Art 25th Ann, 61; Pasadena Mus Purchase Award, 4th Biennial Print Exhib, 64; Hawaii Nat Biennial, 71. Bibliog: One woman renaissance in prints, Esquire, 55; A portfolio by Beth Van Hoesen, Ramparts, summer 64; Mendelowitz (auth), A History of American Art, Holt, 70. Mem: San Francisco Women Artists; Calif Soc Printmakers. Style & Technique: Realism; dry point, aquatint. Media: Intaglio. Publ: Illusr, A Collection of Wonderful Things, Scrimshaw, 72. Dealer: Gumps Gallery 250 Post San Francisco CA 98216; Hansen-Fuller Gallery 228 Grant Ave San Francisco CA 94108. Mailing Add: 3816 22nd St San Francisco CA 94114

VAN HOOK, DAVID H
PAINTER, ART ADMINISTRATOR
b Danville, Va, Dec 25, 23. Study: Univ SC, with Edmund Yaghijian. Work: Jacksonville Mus Art, Fla; Greenville Co Mus, SC; C & S Nat Bank, Columbia, SC; murals, Caughman Rd Sch, Columbia; Columbia Mus Art. Exhib: Mint Mus, Charlotte, NC, 66; Columbia Mus Art, 67; C & S Nat Bank Exhib, 68; Pfeiffer Col, Misenheimer, NC, 69; Contemp Artist of SC Tricentennial Exhib, Columbia, Greenville & Charleston, SC, 70; plus many other group & one-man shows. Collections Arranged: Jasper Johns Print Traveling Exhibit, 71; Eight Washington Artists, 71. Pos: Registr, Columbia Mus Art, 51-58, asst to dir, 58-60, cur exhibs, 61- Awards: Rose Talbert Award, 54; Hon Award, Columbia Mus Art, 59; Purchase Prize, Guild SC Artists, 61. Mem: Guild SC Artists; Am Asn Mus; Southeastern Mus Conf. Mailing Add: Columbia Mus Art Bull & Senate Sts Columbia SC 29201

VAN LEER, MRS W LEICESTER
COLLECTOR
b Warwick, NY, Jan 29, 05. Study: Smith Col; also with Mary Turlay Robinson. Collection: Includes works by Delacroix, Matisse, Boudin, Dufy, Burchfield, Wyeth, Prendergast, Davies, Bishop, Homer, Segonzac, Marin, Cropsey, Utrillo, Beal, Andrew Wyeth & others. Mailing Add: 12 E 73rd St New York NY 10017

VAN LEUNEN, ALICE LOUISE
TEXTILE ARTIST, INSTRUCTOR
b Evansville, Ind, Feb 7, 43. Study: Smith Col, BA, 65; Ind Univ, 66-67. Comn: Three-dimensional textile hanging, Deluxe 2 Restaurant, Seattle, Wash, 76; textile panels, Playboy Club, Chicago, 78. Exhib: Bodycraft Exhib, Portland Art Mus, Ore, 73; Valley Art Asn Ann, Pac Univ, Forest Grove, Ore, 75; 76 Nat Traveling Exhib Competition, Univ Ore Mus of Art, Eugene, 76; Useful Objects, Contemp Crafts Gallery, Portland, 76; NW Designer-Craftsmen Group Exhib, Bellevue Art Mus, Wash, 76 & Boise Gallery Art, Idaho, 78; three-woman exhib, Contemp Crafts Gallery, Portland, 77 & Maude Kerns Gallery, Eugene, 78; Duo Exhib, Univ Ore Mus of Art, 78. Teaching: Seminar instr, Dept Fine Arts, Univ Ore, 78- Pos: Asst dir, Delphian Gallery-Delphian Found, 77-; artist-in-residence, Delphian Univ, 78. Awards: Cash Award, & Traveling Exhib, 76 Traveling Exhib Competition, Univ Ore Mus of Art, 6/76; Honorable Mention, 6th Ann Exhib, Corvallis Art Ctr, 11/76; US Deleg to World Crafts Coun Conf, Kyoto, Japan, 78. Bibliog: Elyse & Mike Sommer (auths), Wearable Crafts, Crown, 76; Northwest Designer-Craftsmen, NW Designer-Craftsmen Mag, Frank Potter & Assocs, Seattle, 76. Mem: Artists Equity; NW Designer Craftsmen, Inc, Seattle; Ore Designer-Craftsmen Guild; Am Crafts Coun, NW Region. Style & Technique: All textile techniques, with emphasis on woven and constructed two and three-dimensional forms; designs frequently relate to natural environment. Media: Fiber and Paper. Dealer: LaForge-Cohan 407 SW 11th Portland OR 97204. Mailing Add: Delphian Found Rte 2 Box 195 Sheridan OR 97378

VAN LOEN, ALFRED
SCULPTOR, EDUCATOR
b Oberhausen-Osterfeld, Ger, Sept 11, 24; US citizen. Study: Royal Acad Art, Amsterdam, Holland, 41-46. Work: Metrop Mus Art & Mus Mod Art, New York; Brooklyn Mus, NY; Nat Mus, Jerusalem, Israel. Comn: Brass fountain, James White Community Ctr, Salt Lake City, Utah, 58; Peace Window, Community Church, New York, 63; Crescendo State Univ NY Agr & Tech Col Farmingdale, 69; Jacob's Dream (brass), Little Neck Jewish Ctr, NY, 70; bronze & acrylic symbolic portrait of Guy Lombardo, Hall of Fame, Stony Brook, NY, 72. Exhib: Whitney Mus Am Art Ann, New York, 67; Emil Walters Gallery, New York, 68; Stony Brook Mus, 68; Heckshen Mus, Huntington, NY, 71 & 74; Nassau Community Col, NY, 72. Teaching: Instr, Hunter Col, 53-54; instr, NShore Community Art Ctr, NY, 55-61; assoc prof sculpture, C W Post Col, Long Island Univ, 62- Pos: Art dir, South Huntington Pub Libr. Awards: First Prize, Village Art Ctr, 49; Louissa Robbins Award, Silvermine Guild Artists, 56; First Prize Sculpture, Am Soc Contemp Artists, 64. Bibliog: Paul Mocsanyi (auth), Alfred Van Loen, Channel Press, 60; Mark Smith (auth), Alfred Van Loen, portrait, Long Island Mag, 64; Sculptured emotion of A V L, Mod Castings, 65. Mem: Artists Equity Asn; Am Soc Contemp Artists; Am Crafts Coun; Long Island Univ Pioneer Club; Huntington Artists Group, Hecksher Mus. Style & Technique: Direct approach to stone and all other carving materials. Media: Stone, Acrylic. Publ: Auth, Simple Methods of Sculpture, Channel Press, 58; auth, Instructions to Sculpture, C W Post Col, 66; auth, Origin of Structure & Design, Hamilton Press, 67; auth, Drawings by Alfred Van Loen, Harbor Gallery Press, 69. Dealer: Harbor Gallery 43 Main St Cold Spring Harbor NY 11724. Mailing Add: 221 Beverly Rd Huntington Station NY 11746

VANN, LOLI (MRS LILIAN VAN YOUNG)
PAINTER
b Chicago, Ill, Jan 7, 13. Study: Art Inst Chicago; also with Sam Ostrowsky. Work: Chaffey Col, Ontario, Calif; Hollenbeck High Sch, Los Angeles. Exhib: Exhib Am Paintings, Carnegie Inst, Pittsburgh; Am Painting, Metrop Mus Art, New York; Corcoran Gallery Art Biennial, Washington, DC; Am Paintings & Int Watercolor Exhibs, Art Inst Chicago. Awards: Purchase Prize, Chaffey Community Art Asn; Hon Mention, Calif Watercolor Soc; Second Prize, Los Angeles Co Mus Art. Style & Technique: Human, emotional and romantic approach; rhythmical seouences line, form, color; fluid, calligraphic application of paint. Media: Oil, Watercolor, Pastel. Mailing Add: 2293 Panorama Terr Los Angeles CA 90039

VAN OORDT, PETER
PAINTER, DESIGNER
b Rotterdam, Neth, Apr 4, 03; US citizen. Study: Acad Rotterdam, Neth; Sch Appl Arts, Utrecht; Royal Acad, Amsterdam; Grosvenor Sch Arts, London. Work: Art Mus Honolulu, Hawaii; Santa Barbara Mus Fine Arts, Calif. Exhib: Inst of Fine Arts, Peking, China, 36 & 40; Honolulu Acad Arts, Hawaii, 40; Los Angeles Co Mus Art, 48; Santa Barbara Mus Fine Art, Calif, 51; Duncan Galleries, Paris, 74. Pos: Travel poster artist, Brit Railways, Ralph & Brown Studios, 32-39; background artist for cartoon films, Warner Bros, London & Hollywood, 47-49; designer, Lamb Studios (ecclesiastical arts), Northvale, NJ, 55-73. Style & Technique: Watercolor, acrylic & casein; stylized landscape & graphic design for bookcovers & letterheads. Mailing Add: 217 Hungry Hollow Rd Spring Valley NY 10977

VAN RIPER, PETER
PRINTMAKER, PERFORMANCE ARTIST
b Detroit, Mich, July 8, 42. Study: Univ NC, BA(art hist, Far Eastern hist); Univ Tokyo, MA(Far Eastern art hist); Univ Mich, grad study. Work: Everson Mus Art, Syracuse, NY; Oakland Mus, Calif. Exhib: One-man shows, US Info Serv Japan performance tour, 74, video & graphics exhib, Everson Mus, 75; Kunst Bleibt Kunst, Kunstverein Art Mus, Cologne, Ger, 74; Southland Video Anthology, Long Beach Mus Art, Calif, 75; Holography 75 First Decade, Int Ctr Photog, New York. Teaching: Teacher multi-media art, Calif Inst of Arts, Valencia, 70-73. Awards: Traveling Exhib Award, Western Asn of Art Mus, 74. Mem: Editions/Sch of Holography, Ann Arbor, Mich & San Francisco (pres); Fluxus, New York. Style & Technique: Multi-media performance, laser holography, photographic silk screen. Publ: Auth, It, 75; contribr, Southland Video Anthology, 75. Dealer: Upstairs Gallery 1457 Grant Ave San Francisco CA 94133. Mailing Add: 537 Broadway New York NY 10012

VAN ROEKENS, PAULETTE (MRS ARTHUR MELTZER)
PAINTER
b France, Jan 1, 96; US citizen. Study: Philadelphia Sch Design for Women; Pa Acad Fine Arts, Philadelphia; Graphic Sketch Club; also with Henry Snell, Joseph Pierson & Leopold Seyfeert; Moore Col Art, LHD, 61. Work: Pa Acad Fine Arts, Philadelphia; Reading Mus, Pa; Woodmere Art Gallery, Philadelphia; Sch Design for Women Alumnae, Philadelphia; Allentown Mus, Pa. Exhib: Corcoran Gallery Art, Washington, DC; Pa Acad Fine Arts, Philadelphia; Art Inst Chicago; Carnegie Inst, Pittsburgh; Nat Acad Design, New York; 14 solo shows. Teaching: Instr, Graphic Sketch Club, 20-27; asst prof painting & drawing, Moore Col Art, 23-61. Awards: Bronze Medal First Prize, Philadelphia Sketch Club; Gold Medal First Prize, Plastic Club; Mary T Mason Prize, Woodmere Art Gallery, 65. Style & Technique: Colorful, impressionistic. Media: Oil, Pastel. Mailing Add: 1521 Welsh Rd Huntingdon Valley PA 19006

VAN ROIJEN, HILDEGARDE GRAHAM
GRAPHIC ARTIST, SCULPTOR
b Washington, DC, Nov 1, 15. Study: Rollins Col; Am Univ; Corcoran Gallery Sch Art, Washington, DC. Work: Drawings of Egypt, Brooklyn Mus, NY. Comn: Watercolor, Jr League Hq, Washington, DC. Exhib: Am House, Vienna, Austria; Va Mus, Richmond; Corcoran Gallery Art, Washington, DC; Galerie im Ram Hof, Frankfurt, Ger, 74; Kunstler Haus-Galerie, Vienna, Austria, 74; West Point Mil Acad, 77. Pos: Art therapist, St Elizabeth's Hosp, Washington, DC. Awards: First for Pride's Sin, Univ Va, Charlottesville, 71. Mem: Artists Equity Asn; WAS; Northern Va Artists; Washington Printmakers. Media: Metal, Graphics. Mailing Add: 2911 M St-Rear Washington DC 20007

VAN SCHLEY (EVANDER DUER VAN SCHLEY)
VIDEO ARTIST, FILMMAKER
b Montreal, Can, Apr 21, 41; US citizen. Work: Everson Mus, Syracuse, NY; N M Rothschild and Sons, London; Eastman House, Rochester, NY. Exhib: Place & Process, Edmonton Art Gallery, Can, 69; Information, Mus of Mod Art, New York, 70; Software, Jewish Mus, New York, 70; Encentros de Pamplona, Spain, 71; Kuntsmarkt, Cologne, 73; Books of Artists, Moore Col of Art, Philadelphia, Pa, 74; Circuit, A Travelling Video Int, Everson Mus & US Tour, 74; Artists Della West Coast, Francoise Lambert Galleria, Milan, 74; Video CAYC, Paris, France, 75; one-man show, Everson Mus, Syracuse, NY, 73. Bibliog: W Sharp (auth), Different Strokes for Different Folks, Avalanche Mag, New York, 7/73; Art En Cours, article in Art Press, Paris, summer 74; Schley & Alder (auth), World Run, A Global Art Piece, Flash Art, Milan, 10/74. Publ: Auth, Signs, Santa Monica, Calif, 72; co-auth (with Billy Alder), World Run, Long Beach, Calif, 76. Dealer: Francoise Lambert, Milan, Italy; Ursula Wevers, Projection Gallery, Cologne, WGer. Mailing Add: c/o Great Balls of Fire Inc 3666 Barry Ave Los Angeles CA 90066

VAN SUCHTELEN, ADRIAN
PRINTMAKER, EDUCATOR
b Semarang, Indonesia, June 18, 41; US citizen. Study: El Camino Col, Calif; Otis Art Inst, Los Angeles, BFA, MFA, 66; also with Joseph Hirsch, Moishe Smith & Joseph Mugnaini. Work: Inst Fine Arts, Salt Lake City, Utah; NMex State Univ; Riverside Mus, Calif; Salt Lake Art Ctr; Utah State Univ. Comn: Art work on film Young Lovers, Samuel Goldwyn Studios, Los Angeles, 64. Exhib: Drawing Soc Nat Exhib, Am Fedn Arts, NY, 70-72; Colorprint USA, Tex, 74; Davidson Nat Print & Drawing Exhib, NC, 75; Pratt Graphics Ctr Int Print Exhib, NY, 75; one-man show, Salt Lake Art Ctr, 75; plus others. Teaching: Asst prof drawing, Utah State Univ, 67- Awards: First Place Purchase Award, Utah Inst Fine Arts, 68; Purchase Award, NMex State Univ, 71; Ben & Abbey Grey Found Purchase Award, Salt Lake Art Ctr,

72. Bibliog: Color Print USA, Tex Tech Univ, 74. Mem: Graphics Soc. Style & Technique: Combination figurative; geometric drawing; color intaglio printmaking. Media: Conte, India Ink; Relief & Etching Intaglio. Publ: Contribr, Drawing A Search for Form, 65; auth & illusr, Lifetime Career Schools, Correspondence Art Course, 67; contribr, Oil Painting, Techniques and Materials, 69; The Hidden Elements of Drawing, 73. Dealer: Heritage Gallery 718 N La Cienega Blvd Los Angeles CA 90069. Mailing Add: 655 East 1800 N Logan UT 84321

VAN TONGEREN, HAROLD (HERK)
SCULPTOR
b Holland, Mich, Aug 19, 43. Study: Studied in Europe, 62-64; Univ Colo, BA, 69, MFA, 70. Work: Burnaby Art Gallery, Vancouver, BC, Can; Weatherspoon Art Gallery, Greensboro, NC; Univ Colo Art Collection. Exhib: 39th Ann Southeast, Mint Mus, Charlotte, NC, 73; one-man shows, Weatherspoon Art Gallery, Greensboro, NC, 73, San Diego State Univ, Calif, 75 & Burnaby Art Gallery, Vancouver, BC, 77; 13th Ann, Riverside Art Mus, Calif, 76. Teaching: Instr sculpture design, Univ NC, Greensboro, 71-74; asst prof sculpture design, San Diego State Univ, Calif, 75-77. Pos: Exec dir, Johnson Atelier, Princeton, NJ, 77-; ed, Sculptor's News Exchange, Arlington, Va, 77- Awards: Honorable Mention, Calif Small Images, Calif State Univ, Los Angeles, 76. Media: Mixed. Publ: Auth, Proceeding of the 9th Nat/Int Sculpture Conference (Ceramic Shell Techniques and the Casting of Saul Baizermans Symphony Pastorale Number II), Int Sculpture Ctr, 77. Mailing Add: c/o Ettl Farm Rosedale Rd Princeton NJ 08540

VAN VEEN, STUYVESANT
PAINTER
b New York, NY, Sept 12, 10. Study: City Col New York; Pa Acad Fine Arts; Nat Acad Design; Art Students League; New York Sch Indust Art; also with Daniel Garber, Thomas Benton & David Karfunkel. Work: Norfolk Mus Arts & Sci, Va; Newark Mus, NJ; Fairleigh Dickinson Univ, NJ; Smithsonian Inst, Washington, DC; New York Hist Soc. Comn: Pittsburgh Panorama (mural), Pittsburgh Post Off, Courthouse, comn by US Treas Dept, 37; The Story of Pharmacy (mural), New York World's Fair, World's Fair Corp, 38; Synthesis (mural) & Security (mural), for courtrooms in Philadelphia Munic Ct Bldg, Philadelphia Art Comn; Bridge of Wings (mural), Wright-Patterson AFB, Ohio Hq Bldg, USAF, 45; Dodgers Victories (murals), for seven lobbies at Ebbets Field Apts, Brooklyn, NY, HFH Corp, 63. Exhib: Carnegie Int, Pittsburgh, 29 & 43; Am Ann, Art Inst Chicago Century Progress, six from 33-46; Cincinnati Mus Ann, five from 36-49; Whitney Mus Am Art Ann, 39-40; Nat Acad Design Ann, 65-69. Teaching: Pvt art classes, 30-41; instr & supvr painting & drawing, Cincinnati Art Acad, 46-49; assoc prof art, City Col New York, 49-75. Pos: Res assoc, Dept Anthrop, Columbia Univ, 35-38; art dir, Cincinnati Ord Dist, War Dept, 42-43; co-founder & set designer, Stage Inc, Cincinnati Civic Theater, 48-49; art & mural consult, Int Fair Consult, 62-63. Awards: Childe Hassam Purchase Award, Am Acad Arts & Lett, 61; Nelson Whitehead Prize, Am Soc Contemp Artists, 66; Prize, New Eng Ann, Silvermine Guild Artists, 68. Mem: Am Watercolor Soc; Nat Soc Painters Casein (bd dirs, 53); Nat Soc Mural Painters (treas, 60); Artists Equity Asn (pres, 58-59); Am Acad & Inst of Arts & Lett; Audubon Soc of Artists; WPA Artists of New York, Inc; corp mem, MacDowell Colonists; life mem Art Students League. Media: Oil, Watercolor, Gouache. Publ: Illusr, Fortune Mag, 35; illusr, Gesture & Environment, Kings Crown, 41; illusr, The Rebel Mail Runner, Holiday, 54; illusr, Garibaldi, Random, 57; illusr, The Art of Making the Dance, Rinehart, 60; illusr & comment, Gesture, Race & Culture, Mouton, 72. Dealer: ACA Gallery 25 E 73rd St New York NY 10021. Mailing Add: 320 Central Park W New York NY 10025

VAN VLIET, CLAIRE
PRINTMAKER
b Ottawa, Ont, Can, Aug 9, 33. Study: San Diego State Univ, AB, 52; Claremont Grad Sch, MFA, 54. Work: Nat Gallery, Washington, DC; Philadelphia Mus Art; Montreal Mus Fine Arts; Cleveland Mus Art; Victoria & Albert Mus, London. Exhib: Philadelphia Arts Festival, Philadelphia Mus Art, 62; Claire Van Vliet Prints, The Print Club, Philadelphia, 63, 66 & 71; Kunst zu Kafka, traveling exhib in Ger, 75; The Janus Press 1955-76, The Print Club, 76; Claire Van Vliet & The Janus Press, Wiggin Gallery, Boston Pub Libr, 77; 500 Years of Print Making, Metrop Mus Philippines, 77. Teaching: Asst prof printmaking, Philadelphia Col Art, 59-65. Bibliog: Scott David (auth), Claire Van Vliet Prints, Fleming Mus, Univ Vt, 70; Ruth Fine Lehrer (auth), The Janus Press 1955-75, Fleming Mus, Univ Vt, 75 & Claire Van Vliet Paperworks, The Janus Press, 78. Mem: Soc Printers Boston; The Print Club, Philadelphia. Style & Technique: Romantic landscapes in color work; expressionist in black and white. Media: Relief and Lithography Paper. Publ: Illusr & ed, Sky and Earth-Variable Landscape, Janus Press, 70; auth & illusr, Satellite, Mus Mod Art, 71; illusr & ed, The Tower of Babel-an Anthology, Janus Press, 75. Dealer: AAA 1614 Latimer St Philadelphia Pa 19103. Mailing Add: RD2 West Burke VT 05871

VAN VRANKEN, ROSE (ROSE VAN VRANKEN HICKEY)
SCULPTOR, PRINTMAKER
b Passaic, NJ, May 15, 19. Study: Pomona Col, BA(art, with hon); Art Students League, 3 yrs with William Zorach & Robert Laurent; New York Univ Grad Inst Fine Arts, art hist 1 yr; Univ Iowa, MA(sculpture), 43, sculpture with Humbert Albrizio & printmaking with Mauricio Lasansky; hon DFA, Ricker Col, Maine, 76. Work: Tex Fine Arts Asn, Laguna Gloria Mus, Austin; Des Moines Art Ctr, Iowa; Houston Pub Libr, Tex; Coventry Cathedral, Eng; Mitchell Energy Corp Col, Houston. Exhib: One-person shows, Pasadena Art Mus, Calif, 46, Madison Art Ctr, Wis, 68, Barnwell Art Ctr, Shreveport, La, 73 & Rosenberg Libr, Galveston Tex, 75; Nat Asn of Women Artists Ann, Nat Acad, New York, 51-77; Nat Asn of Women Artists Travelling Show, Stedelijk Mus, Amsterdam, 56-57; Houston Mus of Fine Arts, 63; two-man show, Sculpture, Univ Wis-Madison, 64; Beloit Col, 64-68; Lever House, New York, 65; Audubon Artists Nat Ann, Nat Acad, New York, 65; Print Show, 67 & Sculpture Show, 77, Union Carbide Corp, New York; Acad Artists Asn Ann, Mus Fine Arts, Springfield, Mass, 68-77; Tyler Mus Ann, 69; Milwaukee Art Ctr Sales & Rental Gallery, Wis; Southern Sculptors Asn Nat Ann, 73-75; Tex Fine Arts Asn Nat Ann, Laguna Gloria Mus, 75; Beaumont Mus, Tex, 75; Art in Embassies Prog, US State Dept, 77-78. Teaching: Research asst art hist, Univ Iowa, 42-43; instr sculpture & mem bd dir, Madison Art Ctr Mus, Wis, 65-68; instr sculpture, Jewish Community Ctr, Houston, 69-70, Art League of Houston, 70-74 & Continuing Educ Prog, Rice Univ, 75- Awards: Medal of Honor for Graphics, Nat Asn Women Artists, 52; 1st Prize Sculpture, Des Moines Art Ctr, 53; Portrait Award Sculpture, Catharine Lorillard Wolfe Nat Art Exhib, New York, 69. Bibliog: Archives Am Art, Smithsonian Inst, Washington, DC. Mem: Tex Soc Sculptors (vpres, 74-75; pres Gulf Coast Chap, 75-76); Nat Asn Women Artists; Acad Artists Asn; Southern Asn Sculptors. Style & Technique: Simplified realism to abstract and semi-abstract, based on nature. Media: Direct Carving in Stone & Wood, Casting in Polished Bronze. Dealer: John Klep Gallery 1711 S Post Oak Rd Houston TX 77056; Gilman Galleries 103 E Oak Chicago IL 60611. Mailing Add: 435 Tallowood Houston TX 77024

VAN WERT, GORDON FRANKLIN
SCULPTOR, INSTRUCTOR
b Redlake, Minn, Mar 21, 52. Study: Inst of Am Indian Arts; also with Allan Houser & Douglas Hyde. Work: Whitney Mus of Am Art, New York; Buffalo Bill Mus, Cody, Wyo; Inst of Am Indian Arts Mus. Exhib: Arts & Crafts Show, 73-77, Sculpture I, 74 & Sculpture II, 75, Heard Mus, Phoenix, Ariz; plus others. Teaching: Instr sculpture, Inst of Am Indian Arts, 73-74; instr sculpture, Native Americans of Community Action, 77- Awards: Honorable Mention, Scottsdale Nat, Ariz, 75; Honorable Mention, 75 & First in Stone, 76, Heard Mus, Phoenix, Ariz. Style & Technique: Free-style and work from shape of the stone and not models. Media: Stone; Welded Steel. Mailing Add: 15 N San Francisco St PO Box 572 Flagstaff AZ 86002

VAN WINKLE, LESTER G
SCULPTOR, EDUCATOR
b Greenville, Tex, Jan 11, 44. Study: ETex State Univ, BS; Univ Ky, MA; aslo sculpture with Michael D Hall. Work: Arrowmont Sch Arts & Crafts, Gatlinburg, Tenn; Dade Co Jr Col, Miami. Exhib: Sculpt 70, Corcoran Gallery Art, Washington, DC, 70; Whitney Biennial of Painting & Sculpture, Whitney Mus, New York, 73; one-man shows, Henry Gallery, Washington, 73-75 & Webb Parsons Gallery, Bedford, NY, 74-75; Waves Exhib, Cranbrook Acad Art Galleries, 74. Teaching: Asst prof sculpture, Va Commonwealth Univ, 69- Style & Technique: Representational. Dealer: Henri Gallery 1500 21st St NW Washington DC 20036. Mailing Add: 1823 W Grace Ave Richmond VA 23220

VAN WOLF, HENRY
SCULPTOR, PAINTER
b Regensburg, Bavaria, Apr 14, 98; US citizen. Study: Munich Art Sch, 12-16; sculpture & bronze technique with Ferdinand von Miller, 19-22 & 23-26. Comn: Fernando (bronze statue of Indian), Van Nuys Mall, Calif; Mem Bust of Einstein (bronze), Albert Einstein Med Ctr, Philadelphia, Pa; sculpture group, Garden Grove, Calif; sculptured bronze doors, St Nicholas Episcopal Church, Encino, Calif; Monument of Martin Luther King, Jr (bronze), Martin Luther King Elem Sch, Compton, Calif; plus many others. Exhib: Brooklyn Mus, NY; Springfield Mus Art; Int Contemp Relig Sculptured Medals, Rome, Italy, 63; Int Exhib Contemp Sculptured Medals, Athens, Greece, 66 & Paris, France, 67; plus many others. Awards: Los Angeles City Art Exhib, 49, 66 & 70; Nat Award, Nat Sculpture Soc, 62; seven awards, Valley Art Build, 48-72; plus over 40 top awards. Mem: Nat Sculpture Soc; fel Am Inst Fine Arts; Valley Artist's Guild (founder & past pres); Traditional Artists Soc (dir coun). Style & Technique: Traditional and classic style. Media: Antique Patinated Bronze, Wood. Mailing Add: 5417 Hazeltine Ave Van Nuys CA 91401

VAN WYK, HELEN
PAINTER, LECTURER
b Fair Lawn, NJ. Study: Art Students League; New Sch Social Res; also with Maximilian Aureal Rasko. Work: Norfolk Mus Arts & Sci, Va; Bergen Co Mus, NJ; St Vincent's Col, Latrobe, Pa; Minneapolis Club; Livonia Sch Syst, Mich. Comn: Mural, comn by Joseph Grumbacher, Exec Off, M Grumbacker, Inc, New York, 63; portraits, comn by Pamela Charles, Cindy Adams, Paolo Pansa & others. Exhib: Acad Artists, Springfield, Mass, 53 & 57; Audubon Artists, New York, 54, 55 & 63; Nat Acad Design, New York, 54, 55 & 64; Silvermine Guild Artists, Conn, 59. Pos: Ed, Palette Talk, Grumbacher, Inc, 67- Awards: John C Pierson Prize, Ogunquit Art Ctr, Maine, 49; First Prize for Still Life, Catharine Lorillard Wolfe Art Club, 55; Curtis Mem Award, Rockport Art Asn, 72 & 73. Bibliog: Walter Brooks (auth), Art of Acrylic Painting, Grumbacher, 69; Herb Rogoff (auth), Each demonstration a challenge, Am Artist Mag, 69. Mem: Rockport Art Asn; NShore Arts Asn, Mass; Grand Cent Art Galleries, New York. Style & Technique: Portraits and still lifes in traditional manner. Media: Oil, Acrylic. Publ: Co-auth, Casselwyk Book on Oil Painting, privately publ, 61; auth, Acrylic Portrait Painting, Watson-Guptil, 70; auth, Helen Van Wyk's Successful Color Mixtures, Art Instr Assocs, 73. Mailing Add: 2 Briarstone Rd Rockport MA 01966

VAN YOUNG, OSCAR
PAINTER
b Vienna, Austria; US citizen. Study: Art Acad, Odessa, Russia; with Sam Ostrowsky, Paris & Chicago; Calif State Univ, Los Angeles, BA & MA. Work: Los Angeles Co Mus Art, Calif; Chaffey Col, Ontario, Calif; Frye Mus, Seattle; Int Lithography & Engraving, Chicago; Mother & Child (drawing), Santa Barbara Mus, Calif. Exhib: Am Paintings & Int Watercolor Shows, Art Inst Chicago; Nat Acad, New York; Calif Palace of Legion of Honor; Pa Acad; Encycl Britannica Collection; Golden Gate World's Fair Expos, San Francisco; Va Mus Biennial; Corcoran Gallery Art Biennial, Washington, DC; one-man shows, Art Inst of Chicago, Los Angeles Co Mus of Art, Los Angeles, Copenhagen Galleri, Solvang, Calif, San Francisco Mus of Art, Pasadena Art Mus, Santa Barbara Mus, Calif, James Vigeveno Galleries, Westwood, Calif & Cowie Galleries, Los Angeles; Retrospective, San Bernardino Valley Col Gallery of Art. Teaching: Instr advan painting, Otis Art Inst, 54-56; instr design, painting & drawing, Pasadena City Col, 59-73; asst prof advan painting, Los Angeles State Univ, 61-63. Awards: Bartels Prize, Art Inst Chicago; Purchase Prize, Chaffey Col; Purchase Award, Frye Mus. Bibliog: Ronald D Scofield (auth), California painter turns against early realism, Santa Barbara; Joseph Mugnaini (auth), Oil Painting Techniques & Materials, Van Nostrand Reinhold Co, 69; Janice Lovoos (auth), Painting for the joy of it, SW Art, 7/77. Style & Technique: Post-impressionist to expressionist; color applied amorphously, superimposed by calligraphic lines. Media: Oil. Dealer: Copenhagen Galleri Solvang CA 93463. Mailing Add: 2293 Panorama Terr Los Angeles CA 90039

VARGA, FERENC
SCULPTOR
b Szekesfehervar, Hungary; US citizen. Study: Acad Fine Arts, Budapest, Hungary, with Prof Eugene Broy & Prof Prof Francis Sidlo; govt scholar, Italy, 38 & France, 42. Work: Nat Art Gallery, Budapest; Mus Fine Arts, Budapest; Vatican Mus, Rome, Italy; Mus Zurich, Switz. Comn: Portrait, VRegent of Hungary, Budapest, 42; monument, City of Windsor, Ont, Can, 50; group of statues, Ft Lincoln Mem, Washington, DC, 55 & 8ft bronze statue of Patrick Henry, 78; monument, City of Detroit, Mich, 66; bust, Ford Auditorium, Detroit, 72; 9ft bronze statue of Cardinal J Mindszenty, New Brunswick, NJ, 76. Exhib: Nat Art Gallery, Budapest, 42; Exhib Ecclesiastical Arts Guild, Detroit, 52; Nat Sculpture Soc, New York, 59; one-man show, Masters' Gallery, Toronto, Ont, 64; Eszterhazy Gallery, Palm Beach, Fla, 71. Teaching: Assoc prof sculpturing, Acad Fine Arts, Budapest, 28-40. Awards: Lord Rotheremere Award, 28 & Ballo-Ede Scholar, Govt, Hungary, 42; Medal of Bethlehem Distinction, Fine Arts & Sci Soc of Church of Hungary, 47. Bibliog: Dr E Schwartz (auth), Ferenc Varga, Ons Volk (Brussels), 49 & Last uns nach Bethlehem eilen, Am-Ung Verlag (Cologne), 59; J P Danglade (auth), Magnificent statue of the Christ by sculptor, Varga, The Cemeterian (Columbus), 62. Mem: Fine Arts & Sci Soc of Church of Hungary, Budapest; Acad Cath Hungarica Sci Atrib Prov, Vatican City; Nat Sculpture Soc. Style & Technique:

Classical-modern sculpture. Media: Bronze, Marble, Wood. Mailing Add: 296 NE Sixth Ave Delray Beach FL 33444

VARGA, MARGIT
PAINTER, WRITER
b New York, NY, May 5, 08. Study: Art Students League, with Boardman Robinson & Robert Laurent. Work: Metrop Mus Art; Springfield Mus Fine Arts, Mass; Univ Ariz, Tucson; IBM Collection; Pa Acad Fine Arts. Comn: Mural for lobby, Kidder, Meade & Co, Paramus, NJ. Exhib: Whitney Mus Am Art, 51; Univ Ill, 51; Art Inst Chicago; Carnegie Inst; Corcoran Gallery Art. Pos: Art ed, Life Mag, 36-56, asst art dir, 56-60; art consult, Time, Inc, 60-70. Style & Technique: Poetic realist. Media: Oil. Dealer: Midtown Galleries 11 E 57th St New York NY 10022. Mailing Add: Box 784 Hildreth Lane Bridgehampton NY 11932

VARGAS, RUDOLPH
SCULPTOR
b Uruapan, Mex, Apr 20, 04; US citizen. Study: San Carlos Acad Fine Arts, Mexico City, Mex. Work: Hand woodcarved Madonna, Vatican Mus, Rome, Italy; 30 works of hand woodcarved statues & panels, Santa Teresita Hosp, Duarte, Calif; Life of Father Junipero Serra (five scenes), San Juan Capistrano Mission, Calif; scenes of life of Christ, San Frenando Mission, Calif. Comn: Large figures, Reno, Nev; Albert Pyke (bronze bust), Scottish Rite Cathedral, Pasadena, Calif. Exhib: One-man show, Santa Teresita Hosp, Duarte, 72. Pos: Sculptor, Warner Bros Studios, 67; sculptor, Walt Disney Studios, 68-70. Bibliog: Phil Gilkerson (auth), Southland Artist, 65; Garcia Mendez (auth), Ideas: Eventos Latinos, 69; article in Enciclopedia Internazionale Degli Artisti, Bugatti Editore, 70-71. Mailing Add: c/o Goez Art Gallery 3757 E First St Los Angeles CA 90063

VARGO, JOHN
EDUCATOR, PAINTER
b Cleveland, Ohio, Aug 9, 29. Study: Cleveland Inst Art, with Louis Bosa. Work: Cleveland Mus Art; Syracuse Univ; Munson-Williams-Proctor Inst, Utica, NY; LeMoyne Col, Syracuse. Comn: The Erie Canal (mural), First Fed Savings Syracuse, 60. Exhib: Cooperstown 35th Ann Exhib, NY, 70; Rochester Finger Lakes Exhib, NY, 71; one man shows, Pa State Univ, New Kensington, 69, May Mem, Syracuse, 70 & LeMoyne Col, 71. Teaching: Prof illus & serigraph, Syracuse Univ, 58- Pos: Illusr, Advance Art, Cleveland, 51-58. Awards: Eagan Pres Plaza Award, NY State Fair, 64, Popular Prize, 64; First Prize for Portrait Painting, Cooperstown Art Asn, 70; Award for Painting, Mem Art Gallery, Univ Rochester, 71. Bibliog: Anna W Olmsted (auth), rev, 4/19/70 & Ann Hartranft (auth), rev, 12/12/71, Syracuse Herald-Am; Gordon Muck (auth), article in Syracuse Post Standard, 12/6/71. Media: Tempera, Watercolor. Mailing Add: 6319 Danbury Dr Jamesville NY 13078

VARIAN, ELAYNE H
ART ADMINISTRATOR, ART HISTORIAN
b San Francisco, Calif. Study: Art Inst Chicago; Univ Chicago, MA. Collections Arranged: Art in Process, I, II, III & IV, 65-69; Art Nouveau, 69; Art Deco, 70; N Dimensional Space, 70; Artists' Videotape Performances, 71; Prints from Hollanders Workshop, 72; Women in the Arts Festival, 72; Mr & Mrs George Rickey's Private Collection: Constructivist Art, 72. Teaching: Instr museology, Finch Col, 65-75. Pos: Asst to pres, Duveen Bros, Inc, 53-62; dir & cur, Contemp Wing, Finch Col Mus Art, 64-; adv, NY State Coun Arts, 67-; dir & trustee, Heathcote Art Found, New York; past pres, Attingham Summer Sch, Eng; mem, Mayor's Citizens Comt & Gov Citizens Comt; mem, Artists' Cert Comt, New York Dept Cult Affairs; trustee, Loch Haven Art Ctr, Orlando, Fla; adv/juror, Nat Endowment for the Arts, 75-76; adv/critic, Contemp Art/Southeast, 76-; cur contemp art, John & Mable Ringling Mus of Art, 77- Awards: MacDowell Colony Fel. Mem: Am Asn Mus; Int Coun Mus; Col Art Asn Am; Gallery Asn NY State (co-dir exhib comt, 72). Publ: Contribr, Art in Am, Arts Mag & Art Int. Mailing Add: 1310 Lake Shore Dr Orlando FL 32803

VARNEDOE, JOHN KIRK TRAIN
ART HISTORIAN
b Savannah, Ga, Jan 18, 46. Study: Williams Col, BA; Stanford Univ, MA & PhD. Teaching: Asst prof, Stanford Univ, Calif, 73-74 & Columbia Univ, New York, 74- Awards: David E Finley Fel, Nat Gallery Art, Washington, DC, 70-72; fel for independent study, Nat Endowment for the Humanities, 77-78. Res: Articles and lectures on work of Rodin, especially drawings, and Gustave Caillebotte, plus other modern art topics. Publ: Co-auth, The Drawings of Rodin, 71; ed, Modern Portraits: The Self and Others, 76; ed & co-auth, Gustave Caillebotte: A Retrospective Exhibition, 76; co-auth (with Elizabeth Streicher), Graphic Works of Max Klinger, 77. Mailing Add: 146 W 75th St New York NY 10023

VARNUM, ZOË SHIPPEN
See Shippen, Zoë

VASA (VASA VELIZAR MIHICH)
SCULPTOR, EDUCATOR
b Yugoslavia, Apr 25, 33; US citizen. Study: Sch Appl Art, Beograd, Yugoslavia, 47-51, dipl; Acad Appl Art, Beograd, 52-54, dipl. Work: Mus Mod Art, Beograd; Denver Art Mus, Colo; Hirshhorn Collection & Phillips Collection, Washington, DC; Wilhelm Lehmbruck Mus, Ger; plus many others including pvt collections. Comn: Wood inlay mural, Hotel Metropol, Beograd, 57; plastic sculpture, Frederick Weisman, Toyota Auto Industs, Japan, 71; plastic sculpture, Max Palevsky, Palm Springs, Calif, 71; plastic sculpture, Winmar Co, Inc, Severence Ctr, Cleveland, 72; plastic sculpture, United Aircraft, Hartford, Conn, 75. Exhib: New Modes in California Painting & Sculpture, La Jolla Mus Art, Calif, 66; Univ Ill Biennial Exhib Contemp Painting & Sculpture, Champaign, 67; American Sculpture of the Sixties, Los Angeles Co Mus Art, Calif, 67; 73rd Western Ann, Inaugural Exhib, Denver Art Mus, Colo, 71; Vasa Sculptures, Mus Mod Art, Beograd, 72; plus many others including one-man shows. Teaching: Prof art, Univ Calif, Los Angeles, 67-; assoc prof visual fundamentals, Univ Southern Calif, 70-71. Awards: Grant, Univ Calif, Los Angeles, 70; Judith Thomas Found Grant, 71; Creative Arts Inst, Univ Calif, 72-73 & 75-76; plus others. Bibliog: William Wilson (auth), Sculpture by Vasa in USC Show, Los Angeles Times, 70; Larry Aldrich (auth), New Talents USA, Art in Am, 7-8/66; plus others. Media: Laminated Acrylic Plexiglas. Mailing Add: 360 Sunset Ave Venice CA 90291

VASILS, ALBERT
PAINTER, ILLUSTRATOR
b Siberia, Russia, May 3, 15; US citizen. Study: Col Arts & Crafts, Riga, Latvia, 35-38; Col Arts & Crafts, Birmingham, Eng, 52-53; Mich State Univ, BFA, 62, MA, 63. Work: US Archives & NASA Permanent Collection, Nat Gallery Art, Washington, DC; Kresge Art Gallery, Mich State Univ; East Lansing Pub Libr; also in pvt collections throughout the world. Comn: Portrait of President J F Kennedy, Owasso High Sch Class, Mich, 64 & Mrs Joanna North, Pinecrest Elem Sch, East Lansing, 70; among others. Exhib: Detroit Inst Arts, 65; Flint Inst Arts, 67; Creativity '72, Americana Hotel, NY & Hilton, Chicago, 72; D'Art Graphico-Plastique, Paris, 74; Les Sur Independants, Paris, 74-77; plus others. Pos: Illusr, Mich State Univ, 62- Awards: Cert for Creativity '72, Art Direction Mag, 72; Las Palmas de Oro, Asoc Belgo-Hispanica, Paris, 74; Les laureats du Prix de Paris, 77. Mem: Am Fedn Arts; Lansing Community Art Gallery; Lansing Art Guild. Style & Technique: Contemporary, personal. Media: Acrylic, Oil, Ink-Pen, Pencil. Res: Adventures into two dimension. Interest: Ink drawings, paintings; contemporary, personal (Vasilism) two dimensional compositions. Publ: Illusr, Friendship on the Wing, Raven Printing, 75. Dealer: Ligoa Duncan Galleries 1046 Madison Ave New York NY 10021. Mailing Add: 511 Charles St East Lansing MI 48823

VASQUEZ J, ALBERTO
WEAVER
b Teotitlan del Valle, Mex, Sept 26, 41. Study: Study with Manuel Vasquez (father). Work: Alliance Francais, Mexico City; Cortez' Palace, Cuernavaca, Mex; Palace Fine Arts, Oaxaca; Wells Fargo Bank, Santa Cruz, Calif; Ger Cult Ctr, Mexico City. Comn: Woven murals, Abraham Lincoln, US Embassy, Mexico City, 66, Puerto Rican Coat of Arms, PR Embassy, Mexico City, 66-67, Feathered Coyote (Moctezuma), Volkerunde Mus, Vienna, 68, Picasso Reproduction (Nature's Death), Jose Kleigerman Art Gallery, Guadalajara, Mex, 71 & Conjunccion del Universa, comn by Leonardo Nierma, Mexico City, 73. Bibliog: Sarapes y Tapices, article in La Prensa, Mexico City, 2/4/71; El Taento de un Artesano, article in El Sol de Mex, Mexico City, 4/2/73; Mgt Koch (auth), Indian handweaver, Sentinel, Santa Cruz, Calif, 72. Style & Technique: Weaving on hand loom. Mailing Add: Av Juarez 42 Teotitlan del Valle Oaxaca Mexico

VASS, GENE
PAINTER, SCULPTOR
b Buffalo, NY, July 28, 22. Work: Mus Mod Art, New York; Whitney Mus Am Art, New York; Guggenheim Mus, New York; Albright-Knox Art Gallery, Buffalo; Baltimore Mus, Md; plus others including many in pvt collections. Exhib: Carnegie Inst Int, 65; Whitney Ann, Whitney Mus Am Art, 65 & New Acquisitions, 69; New Acquisitions, Guggenheim Mus, 66; Select Artists, Des Moines Art Ctr, Iowa, 67; plus many others. Media: Oil, Ink; Wood. Mailing Add: 159 Mercer St New York NY 10012

VAUGHAN, CLIFFORD
CARTOONIST
b Manchester, Eng, Mar 20, 11; US citizen. Study: Manchester Sch Art, 25-30. Work: Oil & sculpture works in pvt collections in Eng. Pos: Free-lance cartoonist, 30-; staff cartoonist, Newark Star-Ledger, 54- Mailing Add: 211-09 73rd Ave New York NY 11364

VAUX, RICHARD
PAINTER
b Greensburg, Pa, Sept 15, 40. Study: Miami Univ, BFA, 63; Northern Ill Univ, MFA, 69. Work: Hofstra Univ, Hempstead, NY; Northern Ill Univ; Nassau Community Col, Garden City, NY; C W Post Col, Greenvale, NY; Univ Mass, Amherst. Exhib: NY State Pavilion, New York World's Fair; Dayton Art Inst, Ohio, 63; Butler Inst Am Art, Youngstown, Ohio, 68; Stamford Mus, Conn, 70; Minn Mus Art, St Paul, 71. Teaching: Asst prof art, Adelphi Univ, 72. Awards: Awards for Painting, Hofstra Univ Ann, 63 & Westchester Art Ann, 70; Award for Drawing, Northern Ill Univ Ann, 68. Style & Technique: Glazing acrylics utilizing incidental light and its illumination potential; abstraction impressionist, landscape. Media: Acrylic, Oil, Graphics. Mailing Add: c/o James Yu Gallery 393 W Broadway New York NY 10012

VAZAN, WILLIAM JOSEPH
CONCEPTUAL ARTIST, PHOTOGRAPHER
b Toronto, Ont, Nov 18, 33. Study: Ont Col Art, Toronto; L'Ecole des Beaux-Arts, Paris, France; Sir George Williams Univ. Work: Nat Gallery Can, Ottawa; Philadelphia Mus Art; Power Gallery Contemp Art, Sydney, Australia; Montreal Mus Fine Arts; plus others. Comn: Floor Sculpture, Air Can, Montreal, 70; Taped Sculpture Court, Art Gallery Ont, Toronto, 70; Seasons' Calendar, Govt Can, Dept Pub Works, Terrebonne, PQ, 75. Exhib: 45 degrees 30 minutes N - 73 degrees 36 minutes W, Montreal, 71; Worldline, 25 cities worldwide, 71; Topographies, Montreal, 72; Contacts, Montreal & worldwide, 73; Les Traces, Quebec, 74; Obras Recientes, Buenos Aires, Arg, 75; Scannings, Antwerp, Belg, 76; Planetary Works, Toronto, Ont & Paris, France, 77; York Palms, Toronto, 77; Winnipeg Globes, 78; plus others. Exhibitions Arranged: Forty-five degrees 30 minutes N - 73 degrees 36 minutes W, 71. Awards: Concours Artistique Laureat, Govt Quebec, 70; Can Coun Grants, Ottawa, 73-75. Bibliog: Gilles Toupin (auth), La geographie de Bill Vazan, Vie des Arts, 72; J P Boyer (auth), A l'esthetique de l'idee, Ateliers, 72. Mem: Vehicule Art Inc, Montreal (treas, 72-73, pres, 73-74); Soc Quebec Prof Artists. Style & Technique: Actions, rituals, documented in print, photos and video. Media: Natural Elements & Forces. Publ: Auth, Worldline, 71; auth, Contacts, 73; co-auth, Conceptual art: transformation of natural & of cultural environments, Leonardo, 74. Dealer: Galerie Gilles Gheerbrant 2130 Crescent St Montreal PQ Can. Mailing Add: 6245 Ave de Carignan Montreal PQ Can

VAZQUEZ, JUAN JULIAN
COLLECTOR
b Madrid, Spain. Study: Univ Madrid, MD. Teaching: Asst prof psychiat, Abraham Lincoln Sch Med, 65- Mem: AMA; Am Psychiat Asn; AAAS; Royal Soc Health. Collection: Spanish artists and American, mostly Vincent Arcilesi. Mailing Add: 3920 N Lake Shore Dr Chicago IL 60613

VAZQUEZ, PAUL
PAINTER
b Brooklyn, NY, Sept 19, 33. Study: Ohio Wesleyan Univ, BFA, 56; Univ Ill, Kate Neal Kinley fel & MFA, 57. Work: Butler Inst Am Art, Youngstown, Ohio; Univ Ill, Urbana; Ball State Teachers Col, Muncie, Ind. Exhib: Allen Stone Gallery, New York, 70; Galerie Biesj, Amsterdam, Holland, 70; American Painting, Chicago Inst Am Art, 72; Gallery Ariadne, New York; one-man shows, Paley & Lowe Gallery, 71, 72 & 73, shows in Köln, Ger & Vienna, Austria, 75, David Findlay Gallery, New York, NY, 76 & 78 & Gallery 99, Miami Beach, Fla, 77. Teaching: Instr art hist, Bennett Col, 63-66; asst prof humanities, Western Conn State Col, 66-69; assoc prof drawing & painting, Univ Bridgeport, 69- Awards: Purchase Award, Butler Inst Am Art, 58; Conn Comn Arts Grant for Painting, 74. Dealer: David Findlay Gallery 984 Madison Ave New York NY 10021. Mailing Add: 205 Savoy St Bridgeport CT 06606

VEGA, EDWARD
SCULPTOR, PRINTMAKER
b Deming, NMex, Oct 13, 38. Study: NMex State Univ, Las Cruces, BFA, 68; Univ NMex, Albuquerque, MA, 70; lithog with Garo Antreasian; drawing with Ilya Bolotowsky; sculpture with Charlie Mattox. Work: Sculpture Competition Model, Univ NMex Art Gallery,

Albuquerque. Exhib: Mainstreams '69, Marietta, Ohio; Southwest Fine Arts Biennial, Santa Fe, NMex, 72; Graphics '73, Western NMex Univ, Silver City; 50th Regional Art Exhib, Shreveport, La, 73. Teaching: Instr sculpture, NMex State Univ, 71- Pos: App by Gov Apodaca to NMex Arts Comn. Awards: Third Pl Purchase Award for Sculpture, Univ NMex, 75; Res Grant Sculpture, NMex State Univ, 75. Style & Technique: Constructions made of wood, canvas & vacuum formed Plexiglas; wall sculptures; drawings and lithographs with a combination of vacuum formed areas. Media: Sculpture; Graphics. Mailing Add: Dept of Art NMex State Univ Las Cruces NM 88003

VELARDE, PABLITA
PAINTER, ILLUSTRATOR
b Santa Clara Pueblo, NMex, Sept 19, 18. Study: US Indian Sch, Santa Fe, with Dorothy Dunn. Comn: Murals, Maisel Bldg, Albuquerque, 40; Bandelier Nat Monument Mus, NMex, 46; Foote Cafeteria, Houston, 57; Western Skies Hotel, Albuquerque, 58. Exhib: Denver Art Mus; M H de Young Mem Mus, San Francisco; Mus NMex; Calif Palace Legion of Honor, San Francisco; Philbrook Art Ctr; plus others. Teaching: Painting demonstrations, KOB TV, Albuquerque. Awards: Palmes Academique, Fr Govt, 55; Grand Prizes, Gallup Ceremonial, NMex, 55-59; NMex State Fair, 59; plus others. Mem: Art League NMex; Nat League Am Pen Women; Inter-Tribap Indian Ceremonial Asn. Publ: Illusr, cover of Indians of Arizona; auth & illusr, Old Father, the Story Teller, 60. Mailing Add: 805 Adams St NE Albuquerque NM 87100

VELJKOVIC, ANDREV
ART DEALER
b Belgrade, Yugoslavia, Dec 3, 46. Collections Arranged: 1st Biennial of Yugoslav Art, Alternative Ctr for Int Arts, New York, 1/18-2/28/78. Pos: Dir, United Art Group-1, 75-; pres, Assoc Group of Artists -1 Inc, 76-; pres, Yugoslav Asn of Visual Artists-1 Artists-1, Inc, 76- Bibliog: Diana Loercher (auth), Wit, realism in Yugoslav art, Christian Sci Monitor, 2/78; Stevan Stanic (auth), Oaza u Njujorku, NIN, 2/78. Specialty: Yugoslav art. Mailing Add: 701 W 179th St Suite 35 New York NY 10033

VENOR, ROBERT GEORGE
PAINTER, EDUCATOR
b Montreal, Que, Can, Jan 12, 31. Study: Sir George Williams Univ, 53; Ecole des Beaux-Arts, 54. Work: Montreal Mus of Fine Arts; Mus du Que, Quebec City; Art Gallery of Ont, Toronto; Confederation Art Gallery & Mus, PEI; Collection of Canadian Art, Sir George Williams Univ. Exhib: Survey 70, Montreal Mus Fine Arts, 70; 3D into the 70s (traveling exhib), Art Gallery of Ont, 70-71; Pluriel 71, Mus des Beaux-Arts, Que, 71; New Media, Can Nat Exhib, Toronto, 71; Canada Banners, Burnaby Art Gallery, BC, 72; Eight Canadian Printmakers, Confederation Art Gallery, PEI, 73; Canada Banners Co, Saidye Bronfman Ctr, Montreal, 73 & Mus du Que, 73; SAPQ, Can Cult Ctr, Paris, France, 75; Contemporary American Painting, Lehigh Univ, Pa, 76; one-man show, West Broadway Gallery, New York, 75. Teaching: Instr painting, Univ Que, 72-; instr drawing & painting, Concordia Univ, 75-77. Awards: Que Ministere des Affaired Culturelles Grant, 68 & 72; Can Coun Art Grant, 69. Bibliog: Virginia Nixon (auth), Color is the secret word, Montreal Gazette, 3/24/73; Guy Robert (auth), L'Art au Quebec, 76; John Gruen (auth), On Art, The Soho Weekly News, 3/27/75. Mem: Soc des Artists Professionels du Que (treas, 75-76); Can Artist Representation. Style & Technique: Printmaking, banners, paintings and sculpture. Media: Painting. Mailing Add: 3774 St Johns Rd Dollard Des Oreaux PQ H9G 2H5 Can

VENTIMIGLIA, JOHN THOMAS
SCULPTOR, INSTRUCTOR
b Augusta, Maine, Jan 12, 43. Study: Sch Art, Syracuse Univ, BFA, 65; Rinehart Sch, Md Inst Art, MFA(sculpture), 67; with N Carlberg, G Hartigan, D Hare, R Engman. Exhib: New Talent/Sculpture in the Park, DeCordova Mus Art, Lincoln, Mass, 73; Hildreth Gallery, Nasson Col, Springvale, Maine, 74; Maine Coast Artists Gallery, Rockport, 75 & 77; Ogunquit Mus Art, Maine, 75; 76 Maine Artists, Augusta Mus, 76; Maine Sculpture 76, Univ of Maine, 76; Barn Gallery, Ogunquit, Maine, 77; Cape Split Pl, Addison, Maine, 77. Teaching: Instr sculpture, design & drawing, Portland Sch Art, Maine, 72-78. Pos: Asst to Piotr Kowlaski, Int Sculpture Symp, Calif State Univ, Long Beach, 65; dir, Portland Sch Art, Outdoor Sculpture Exhib Series, 73-78. Awards: Scholar, Showhegan Sch Painting & Sculpture, 64; First Prize, 3rd Ann Bridgeton Arts Festival, Maine, 73. Bibliog: Lynn Franklin (auth), Making of a sculptor, 72; 76 Maine Artists (exhib catalog), Maine State Bicentennial Comn, 76. Style & Technique: Shapes and lines in steel suggestive of skeletal and tensional stress, reaching, moving with air currents, fragile. Media: Steel. Mailing Add: RFD 2 Box 100 Sebago Lake ME 04075

VENTURI, ROBERT
ARCHITECT
b Philadelphia, Pa, June 25, 25. Study: Princeton Univ, AB, 47, MFA, 50; Oberlin Col, DFA(hon), 77; Rome Prize Fel, Am Acad in Rome, 54-56. Comn: Guild House, with Rauch, Cope & Lippincott Assoc Architects, Friends Neighborhood Guild, Philadelphia, 63; addition & renovation of Allen Mem Art Mus, Oberlin Col, Ohio, 76; Franklin Court, with Rauch, Nat Park Serv, Philadelphia, 76. Exhib: Work of Venturi & Rauch, Whitney Mus of Am Art, New York, 71 & Pa Acad of the Fine Arts, Philadelphia, 75; Invisible Artist, Philadelphia Mus of Art, 74; Suburban Alternatives: 11 American Projs, Am Archit Exhib, Venice Biennale, 76; 200 Yrs of Am Archit Drawing, Cooper-Hewitt Mus, New York, 77; Drawings for a More Mod Archit, The Drawing Ctr, New York, 77; Archit 1: An Exhib, Leo Castelli Gallery, New York, 77; Roma Interrota, Incontri Int d'Arte, Rome, 77-78. Teaching: From asst to assoc prof archit, Univ Pa, 51-65; Davenport Prof archit, Yale Univ, 66-70; mem panel of visitors archit, Univ Calif, Los Angeles, 66-68. Pos: Partner, Venturi & Rauch Architects & Planning, Philadelphia, 64-; architect-in-residence, Am Acad in Rome, Italy, 66, trustee, 69-74; mem bd adv, Dept Art & Archaeol, Princeton Univ, 69-72 & Sch of Archit & Urban Design, 77- Awards: First Prize & Award of Comn, Math Bldg Competition, Yale Univ, 70; Arnold W Brunner Mem Prize in Archit recipient, 73; Hon Award, Franklin Court, Am Inst of Architects, 77. Bibliog: Vincent Scully (auth), American Architecture & Urbanism, Praeger, 69; Robert A M Stern (auth), New Directions in American Architecture, Braziller, 69; Yukio Futagowa, Global Architecture, EDITA, Tokyo, 76. Mem: Pa Soc of Architects; Am Inst of Architects. Publ: Co-auth, Learning from Las Vegas, Mass Inst Technol Press, 72; auth, Complexity and Contradiction in Architecture, Mus of Mod Art, 66. Mailing Add: 333 S 16th St Philadelphia PA 19102

VERMES, MADELAINE
CRAFTSMAN
b Hungary, Sept 15, 15. Study: Alfred Univ; Craft Students League; Greenwich House Potters. Work: Cooper Union Mus; Mus Int delle Ceramiche, Faenza, Italy. Exhib: Coliseum, New York, 57; Art League Long Island, NY, 58; Int Ceramic Arts, Smithsonian Inst, Washington, DC; Philadelphia Art Alliance, Pa; one-man show, Brentano's Gallery, New York, 57; plus many other group & one-man shows. Mem: Artist-Craftsmen New York; Nat League Am Pen Women; York State Craftsmen. Mailing Add: 315 E 65th St Apt 10F New York NY 10021

VERMETTE, LUCE
ART CRITIC, ART HISTORIAN
b Montreal, Que, Apr 14, 48. Study: Univ Montreal, BA(hist art). Teaching: Instr Can art, Univ Que, Montreal, 72-73. Pos: Historian, Nat Parks & Hist Sites, Dept Indian Affairs, Gov Can, 73- Mem: Musee des Beaux-Arts, Montreal; Conf Can Arts; Asn Advan Hist Archit; Art Preservation Technol; Heritage Can. Res: Canadian and popular art. Publ: Contribr, Viedes Arts, 71-; contribr, Decormag, 73-74; ed, Les Objets Familiers de nos Ancetres, L'Homme, 74. Mailing Add: 7 Richard Tauraine St Ottawa ON K1Y 2X1 Can

VERMEULE, CORNELIUS CLARKSON, III
ART HISTORIAN, WRITER
b Queenstown, Ireland, Aug 10, 25; US citizen. Study: Harvard Univ, AB, 47, MA, 51; Univ Col, Univ London, PhD, 53. Work: Mus Fine Arts, Boston; Nat Mus, Pylos, Hellas; Morphou-Omorfo Mus, Cyprus. Collections Arranged: Many exhibs, Fogg Mus Art, 50-72; Sir John Soane's Mus, London; Mus Fine Arts, Boston. Teaching: Asst prof fine arts, Univ Mich, Ann Arbor, 53-55; asst prof archaeol, Bryn Mawr Col, 55-57; prof classics, Yale Univ, 72-73. Pos: Asst, Sir John Soane's Mus, 51-53; cur classical art, Mus Fine Arts, Boston, 57-, actg dir, 72-73; cur coins, Mass Hist Soc, Boston, 69- Mem: Life mem Col Art Asn Am; Soc of Antiquaries; fel Royal Numismatic Soc; life fel Am Numismatic Soc (mem coun, 60-); life mem Archaeol Inst Am; life mem Hellenic & Roman Soc. Res: European painting, Greek and Roman art; numismatics. Interest: Classical and Neo-classical style, Greek sculptural technique. Collection: Green and Roman art; drawings; all on loan to Museum of Fine Arts, Boston. Publ: Auth, European Art & the Classical Past, 64; auth, Roman Imperial Art in Greece & Asia Minor, 68; auth, Polykleitos, 69; auth, Numismatic Art in America, 71; co-auth, Greek, Etruscan & Roman Art, 72; auth, Greek Sculpture & Roman Taste, 77. Mailing Add: Mus of Fine Arts Boston MA 02115

VERNER, ELIZABETH O'NEILL
ETCHER, WRITER
b Charleston, SC, Dec 21, 83. Study: Pa Acad Fine Arts; Slade Sch, London; Kyoto. Work: Libr Cong; Kyoto Int Mus; Metrop Mus, New York; Boston Mus; Denver Mus. Exhib: One-woman retrospectives, Gibbes Art Gallery, Charleston, 63; one-woman shows, Manila, Philippines, 64, Spartanburg, SC, 70, Columbia, SC, 71, Sumter, SC, 71, Beaufort, SC, 72 & Atlanta, Ga, 77. Bibliog: Tezza (auth), Woman I don't know, Preservation News, Charleston, 69; Bussman (auth), Born Charlestonian, State Publ Co, 69; Thomas (auth), Fifty Years in Art, Sandlapper Mag, 75. Style & Technique: Preservationist; etcher of architecture; portraits of Gullah Negro and his environment. Media: Pastel. Publ: Auth, Prints & Impressions of Charleston, Bostic & Thornley, 40; Mellowed by Time, 41; Other Places, 45; Stonewall Ladies, 63. Mailing Add: 38 Tradd St Charleston SC 29401

VEROSTKO, ROMAN JOSEPH
EDUCATOR, ART HISTORIAN
b Tarrs, Pa, Sept 12, 29. Study: Art Inst of Pittsburgh, dipl; St Vincent Col & Seminary, Latrobe, Pa, BA, 55; Pratt Inst, MFA, 61; New York Univ; Columbia Univ; Atelier 17, Paris. Teaching: Prof art hist, Minneapolis Col Art & Design, Minn, 68-75. Pos: Staff ed art & archit, New Catholic Encyclo, Catholic Univ, Washington, 64-68; acad dean, Minneapolis Col Art & Design, 75- Bibliog: C J McNaspy (auth), Art & the New Catholic Encyclo, Am, 3/67; F Debuyst (auth), Sculptures de Ciment, Roman Verostko, Art D'Eglise, 68. Mem: Col Art Asn; Am Asn Univ Prof; World Future Soc. Res: Changing roles of the artist in our society. Publ: Auth, Abstract Art and the Liturgy, Liturgical Arts, 62; auth, Abstract Art and the Church, New Catholic Encyclo, 68; auth-illusr, The Celebration of Man, Jubilee, 68; auth, Experience in Community: The New Art, Liturgical Arts, 72; auth, Le Sacre et la Profane, Art D'Eglise, 75. Mailing Add: 5535 Clinton Ave S Minneapolis MN 55419

VERSHBOW, MR & MRS ARTHUR
COLLECTORS
Mr Vershbow, b Boston, Mass, Mar 22, 22; Mrs Vershbow, b Boston, Mass, June 12, 24. Study: Mr Vershbow, Mass Inst Technol, BS & MS; Mrs Vershbow, Radcliffe Col, AB. Collection: Prints, particularly works by Redon, Piranesi and Callot; illustrated books, especially 15th to 17th centuries. Mailing Add: Box 52 Boston MA 02125

VERZYL, JUNE CAROL
ART DEALER, COLLECTOR
b Huntington, NY, Feb 5, 28. Study: Parsons Sch of Design. Pos: Dir, Verzyl Gallery, 66- Bibliog: Jane Margold (auth), Galleries struggle with an image, Newsday, 3/31/67. Specialty: Contemporary American painting, graphics and sculpture. Collection: Contemporary American work, including Filmus, Refregier, Benda, Twardowicz, Clawson and Christopher; also a large collection of New England gravestone rubbings. Mailing Add: 377 Rte 25A Northport NY 11768

VERZYL, KENNETH H
ART DEALER, DRAFTSMAN
b Long Island City, NY, Sept 18, 22. Study: NY State Agr & Tech Inst, grad, 42. Work: Nicholas Roerich Mus, New York; East Northport Pub Libr, New York. Exhib: One-man shows, Confederate General Officers, Mus of Confederacy, Richmond, Va (illusr catalog), 72, Recent Drawings, Performing Arts Found Gallery, Huntington Sta, NY, 72, Drawings of Poets & Authors, Syosset Pub Libr, NY, 72, Drawings by Kenneth H Verzyl, Nicolas Roerich Mus, New York, 73, Berkshire Mus, Pittsfield, Mass, 74 & Hilson Gallery, Deerfield Acad, Mass. Pos: Dir, Verzyl Gallery, Northport, NY, 66- Bibliog: Malcom Preston (auth), Power of the pen, Newsday, Garden City, NY, 72; Martin Curry (auth), New art display has psychological impact, Observer, Northport, NY, 72. Mem: Guild Hall, Easthampton, NY; Heckscher Mus, Huntington; Am Fedn Arts, New York. Style & Technique: Impressionist drawings & prints, linear webs carefully drawn, concentric and parallel lines in drawings; prints are hand rubbed impressionist. Media: Steel Pen and India Ink on Vellum Paper. Specialty: Contemporary American paintings, sculpture and graphics. Dealer: Studio II New York Ave Huntington NY 11743. Mailing Add: 25 Bevin Rd Asharoken NY 11768

VEVERS, ANTHONY MARR
PAINTER, EDUCATOR
b London, Eng, May 20, 26; US citizen. Study: Yale Univ, BA, 50; Accad Belle Arte, Florence, Italy, 50; Hans Hofmann Sch, New York, 52-53. Work: Isaac Delgado Mus, New Orleans; Univ Mass, Amherst; Purdue Univ, Lafayette, Ind; Fairleigh Dickinson Univ, NJ; J H Hirshhorn Collection. Exhib: Am Acad Arts & Lett, New York, 64; Younger Painters, Yale Univ, 65; Pa Acad Fine Arts Ann, 66; Evansville Mus Show, Ind, 67; 350th Anniversary Exhib New Eng Art, Mass, 71; Provincetown Painters, Everson Mus, Syracuse, NY, 77; one-man shows, Artist's Space Gallery, New York, NY, 76 & Long Point Gallery,

Provincetown, Mass, 78. Teaching: Lectr painting, Univ NC, Greensboro, 63-64; prof painting & art hist, Purdue Univ, Lafayette, 64-; vis staff, Fine Arts Work Ctr, Provincetown, Mass, 70-71, consult, 71- Pos: Consult, Ind State Arts Comn, 65-66; vpres, Art Asn Provincetown, 71-74. Awards: Grants, Nat Coun Arts, 67 & Purdue Univ, 70; New Eng Painting & Sculpture Prize, 71. Style & Technique: Collage and sand to make pictures with acrylic as a binding medium. Media: Oil, Mixed Media. Dealer: Babcock Galleries 805 Madison Ave New York NY 10021. Mailing Add: Dept of Creative Arts Purdue Univ Lafayette IN 47907

VIAN, ORFEO
EDUCATOR, PRINTMAKER
b Portogruaro, Prov, Venice, Italy, Dec 10, 24; US citizen. Study: John Herron Art Sch, BFA; Ind Univ, Bloomington, MFA. Work: The Print Club of Albany, NY; St John's Univ, Jamaica, NY; Butler Univ, Indianapolis, Ind; Calif Col of Arts & Crafts, Oakland. Comn: One edition of original prints for portfolios by six outstanding pritmakers alumni of Herron Art Sch Garo Antreasian, John Bernhardt, Edwin Fulwider, Misch Kohn, George Jo Mess & Orfeo Vian, comn by Alumni Asn of John Herron Art Sch, Indianapolis, 49. Exhib: 3rd Nat Print Ann Exhib, Brooklyn Mus, New York, 49; 46th Ann Watercolor and Print Exhib, Pa Acad of Fine Arts, 48; 3rd Biennial Open Nat Print Exhib, Print Club of Albany, NY, 49; 7 Artisti USA, Academia di Belle Arti, Perugia, Italy, 71; Three New York Artist, Northern Ill Univ, DeKalb, 72; two-man show, Ind Central Univ, Indianapolis, 65 & 71; one-man shows, St John's Univ, Jamaica, NY, 76 & Bellarmine Col, Louisville, Ky, 65. Teaching: Vis prof printmaking, Notre Dame, Ind, summer 60; prof printmaking & hist of art, St John's Univ, Jamaica, 65- Pos: Mem bd of dir, Ind Printmaker Soc, 51-52; treas, Ind Artists Club Inc, 54-56. Awards: Purchase Prize, 3rd Biennial Open Nat Print Exhib, Print Club of Albany, NY, 49; Work of Excellence in any medium, Ind Artists Exhib, Herron Alumni Asn, 54; Purchase Prize, Ind Artists Club, Mr & Mrs H C Krannert, 55. Mem: The Graphics Soc; Col Art Asn of Am. Style & Technique: Expressionist, using the media of woodcut and sometimes silkscreen black and white from brutally direct to soft and gentle, mostly representational. Media: Woodcut & Silkscreen. Mailing Add: 6 Horseshoe Lane Commack NY 11725

VICENTE, ESTEBAN
PAINTER
b Turegeno, Spain, Jan 20, 04; US citizen. Study: Acad Belles Artes, Madrid, Spain. Work: Whitney Mus Am Art, Mus Mod Art & Metrop Mus Art, New York; Nat Collection Fine Arts, Smithsonian Inst, Washington, DC; Tate Gallery, London. Exhib: Eighth St Art Show, 49; Mus Mod Art, New York; Guggenheim Mus, New York; Art Inst Chicago; Inst Contemp Art, Boston; Carnegie Int, Pittsburgh; Whitney Mus Am Art Ann; plus many others. Teaching: Instr art, Black Mountain Col, 48; instr art, Univ Calif, Berkeley, 54 & 58, NY Univ, 59-69, Yale Univ, 60-61 & Univ Calif, Los Angeles, 62; artist in residence, Des Moines Art Ctr, 65, Princeton Univ, 65-66 & 69-72 & Honolulu Acad Fine Arts, 69; teacher, New York Studio Sch, 65-75. Awards: Purchase Awards, 60 & 61 & Tamarind Fel, 62, Ford Found; Childe Hassam Purchase Award, Am Acad Arts & Lett, 71; Robert Motherwell Fel. Bibliog. Elaine De Kooning (auth), Vicente paints a collage, Art News, 52; John Ashberry (auth), article in Art News, 5/72; John Gruen (auth), article in New York Times, 3/75. Style & Technique: Abstraction concerned with time and space; color defining that ideal-a synthesis of Spanish tradition with American abstract work of the 1940's and 1950's. Media: Oil, Collage. Dealer: Fischbach Gallery 29 W 57th St New York NY 10019. Mailing Add: 1 W 67th St Apt 606 New York NY 10023

VICKERS, GEORGE STEPHEN
EDUCATOR
b St Catharines, Ont, Dec 19, 13. Study: McMaster Univ, BA; Harvard Univ, AM. Teaching: Prof & chmn dept fine arts, Univ Toronto. Awards: Harvard Univ Jr Fel, 39-42. Publ: Co-auth, Art and Man (3 vols), 64; contribr, Art Bull & Burlington Mag. Mailing Add: 31 Rosedale Rd Toronto ON M4W 2P5 Can

VICKERY, CHARLES BRIDGEMAN
PAINTER
b Hinsdale, Ill, July 16, 13. Study: Art Inst Chicago; Am Acad Fine Art, Chicago; also with Ben Stahl. Work: Univ Club, Chicago; Union League Club, Chicago; prints, Royal Acad, London. Exhib: Rockport Art Asn, Mass; Union League Club; Ackerman Gallery, London; Springfield Mus, Ill; Pallette & Chisel Acad, Chicago. Awards: Diamond Medal Award, Pallette & Chisel Acad, 68; Waters of the World Prize, NShore Art Asn, Gloucester, 70; Union League Club Prize, 72. Bibliog: Eleanor Jewett (auth), article in Chicago Tribune, 45; C J Bulliet (auth), article in Chicago Daily News, 8/51. Mem: Palette & Chisel Acad (dir, 67-69); Rockport Art Asn; NShore Art Asn. Style & Technique: Realistic style; direct brushwork, dark to light, warm to cool. Media: Oil, Acrylic. Dealer: W Russell Button Gallery 955 Center St Douglas MI 49406. Mailing Add: 4533 Wolf Rd Western Springs IL 60558

VICKREY, ROBERT REMSEN
PAINTER
b New York, NY, Aug 20, 26. Study: Yale Univ, BA; Art Students League; Yale Sch Fine Arts, BFA; also with Kenneth Hayes Miller & Reginald Marsh. Work: Syracuse Univ; Metrop Mus Art & Whitney Mus Am Art, New York; Butler Inst Am Art; Mus Arte Mod, Rio de Janeiro. Comn: Covers for Time Mag; also portraits & bk jackets. Exhib: Whitney Mus Am Art; Mus Mod Art, New York; Santa Barbara Mus, Calif; Mus Fine Arts, Houston; Univ Nebr. Awards: Edwin Austin Abbey Mural Fel, 49; Am Watercolor Soc, 56; Nat Acad Design, 58. Mem: Am Watercolor Soc; Audubon Artists; Nat Acad Design. Media: Tempera. Dealer: Midtown Galleries 11 E 57th St New York NY 10022. Mailing Add: RFD 1 Box 445 Orleans MA 02653

VICTOR, MARY O'NEILL
MUSEUM DIRECTOR
b Boston, Mass, Dec 27, 24. Study: Boston Univ, 43-47. Collections Arranged: American Watercolors 1850-1972, 72; Art of Ancient Orthodoxy, 72; Where the Action Is (sports in art), 73; Art of the Old West, 74; Chop Art: American Motorcycle Design, 75; Cleveland Woodward: Painter by God's Good Light, 76; Southern Antiques and Folk Art, 76; Jewish Art: A Continuing Heritage, 77; Wildlife Art: American Sculpture, 77. Pos: Registr, Mus Fine Arts, Boston, 64-69; dir, Fine Arts Mus of the South, Mobile, 69-; mem bd dirs, Mobile Opera Asn, 73- Mem: Am Asn Mus; Am Fedn Arts. Collection: 19th and 20th century American paintings and sculpture and graphics. Mailing Add: Fine Arts Mus of the South Mobile AL 36608

VIDAL, HAHN
PAINTER
b Hamburg, Ger, Mar 11, 19; US citizen. Study: With Eduardo Couce Vidal. Work: Eduardo Sivori, Mus Artes Plasticas, Buenos Aires, Arg; Juan B Castagnino, Mus Cuidad Rosario, Arg; Mus Seattle, Wash; Mus Mobile, Ala; Hist Mus Taiwan, China; plus many others. Comn: Hahn Vidal Rm, Boca Raton Hotel & Club, Fla, 69. Exhib: Okla Mus Art, Oklahoma City, 70 & 72; Grand Cent Art Gallery, 70 & 73; Dayton, Ohio, 70 & 73; Arvest, Boston, 74 & 77; Valencia, Spain, 75 & 77; Wichita Art Asn, Kans, 78; plus others. Mem: Grand Cent Art Galleries; Salmagundi Club; Soc Illusr. Style & Technique: Impressionistic; strong, free use of brush and palette knife; captures the lush radiance of flowers at full bloom. Media: Oil. Dealer: Grand Cent Art Gallery Inc 40 Vanderbilt Ave New York NY 10019. Mailing Add: 345 W 58th St New York NY 10019

VIELEHR, WILLIAM RALPH
SCULPTOR
b Chicago, Ill, Jan 6, 45. Study: Univ Colo, 63-66; Colo State Univ, BFA, 69; also with Frank Gallo. Work: Designer Craftsman Collection, Boulder, Colo; Chicago Mus Contemp Art; Embarcadero Ctr, San Francisco; Northern Ill Univ. Comn: Outdoor sculpture, Gerry Bean, Boulder, 68; Aluminum & Bronze Mask, Gilman Gallery, Chicago, 74. Exhib: One-man show, Gilman Gallery, 71 & 74; Joslyn Art Mus, Omaha, Nebr, 72 & 74; Denver Art Mus, 72; Allrich Gallery, San Francisco, 75; Attitudes Gallery, Denver, 75; Sebastian Moore Gallery, Denver, 77. Teaching: Vis artist sculpture workshop, Jefferson Co Schs, 71-72 & Colo State Univ, 73. Awards: Purchase Prize, Designer Craftsmen Asn, 72. Style & Technique: Male and female figurative sculpture modeled in clay, body forms fragmented. Media: Polished Cast Bronze & Aluminum. Dealer: Gilman Gallery 102 E Ohio Chicago IL 60611; Marilyn Marsh 1034 Logan St Denver CO 80203. Mailing Add: 2715 Elm Boulder CO 80303

VIERA, RICARDO
PAINTER, PRINTMAKER
b Ciego de Avila, Cuba, Dec 15, 45; US citizen. Study: Sch of the Mus of Fine Arts, Boston, dipl; Tufts Univ, BFA; RI Sch of Design, Providence, MFA. Work: Allentown Art Mus, Pa; Cleveland Art Mus, Ohio; Canton Art Inst, Ohio; Miami-Dade Pub Libr, Fla; Lehigh Univ, Bethlehem, Pa. Exhib: One-man show, Inst of Contemp Art, Boston, 73; Davidson Nat Print & Drawing Competition, Davidson Col, NC, 73; RI Mus of Art, Providence, 74; Colorprint USA, Tex Tech Univ, Lubbock, 74; Am Painters in Paris, France, 76; Transitions in Art, Mus of Fine Arts, Boston, 77, Allentown Art Mus, PA, 77; plus many others. Collections Arranged: Six Hispanic Artists, Boston City Hall Gallery, 74; 21st-23rd Annual Contemporary American Painting, 75-77, Pennsylvania Printmakers, 76, Arthur Bowen David (1862-1928) (traveling exhib), 76, Lehigh Univ; American Figure Drawing, Lehigh Univ & Victorian Col of Art, Melbourne, Australia, 76. Teaching: Instr printmaking/painting, Lehigh Univ, 74-75, asst prof printmaking/painting, 75- Pos: Dir exhibs & collection, Lehigh Univ, 74-, chmn pro-tempore univ, 77-78. Awards: Elizabeth H Bartol Scholarship, Boston Mus of Fine Arts Sch, 71-72; Cintas fel, Cintas Found, Inst of Int Educ, 74-75; Mellon Found Grant, 78-80; plus over 25 Purchase Awards, Prizes & Honorable Mentions. Bibliog: Ricardo Viera/Illustraciones Enlace, Nueva Revista Hispanoamericana, 76; Linda Weintraub (auth), Art Show reveals dual nature of man, Morning Call, Allentown, Pa, 76; Robert Godfrey (auth), Ricardo Viera at Westminister, Westminister Col, New Wilmington, Pa, 76. Mem: Col Art Asn; Am Asn of Univ Prof; Am Asn of Mus; Pratt Graphics. Style & Technique: Colorist/abstractionist interested in textures, lines and light; lithography. Media: Oil, Acrylic, Enamel Spray and Oil Crayon. Publ: Illusr, Dr Fernando Ortiz, auth, Los Negros Brujos, Ed Universal, Miami, Fla, 73; illusr, Libro Quinto de Lectura Gramatica y Ortografia, Leal & Sanchez Boudy, Miami, 75; illusr, Introduccion al Estudio de la Civilizacion Espanola, Barroso, Miami, 76; auth, Arte Visual en la Palabra de Lydia Cabrera, Festschriften/Ed Universal, 77; auth, From Limestones to aluminum plate lithography, RI Sch of Design Bull, 77. Mailing Add: Box 63 Rd 3 Northampton PA 18067

VIERTHALER, ARTHUR A
CRAFTSMAN, EDUCATOR
b Milwaukee, Wis, Sept 15, 16. Study: Milwaukee State Teachers Col, BS; Univ Wis, MS. Comn: Many comns for jewelry, relig articles & others. Exhib: Int Exhib, Paris, France; Midwestern Designers; Smithsonian Traveling Exhib; Designer-Craftsmen Traveling Exhibs; Wis State Fair; plus others. Teaching: Lectr on Pre-Historic Design, Contemporary Design, Natural Phenomena of Design Elements in Minerals, Gemstones, Mining for Gemstones & others; instr art, Madison Pub Schs; prof art, Art Dept, Univ Wis-Madison, currently. Awards: Award, St Paul Art Gallery, Minn; Award, Rochester Mus; Award, Miss River Exhib, 61; and others. Mailing Add: Rt 1 Box 110 Fort Pierce FL 33450

VIESULAS, ROMAS
PRINTMAKER, EDUCATOR
b Lithuania, Sept 11, 18; US citizen. Study: Ecole des Arts et Metiers, Ger, grad; Ecole des Beaux Arts, Paris. Work: Mus Mod Art, New York; Mus Mod Art, Kamakura, Japan; Bibliot Nat, Paris; Art Gallery, NSW, Sydney, Australia; Nat Gallery Art, Washington, DC. Comn: Spring (ed), Print Club, Philadelphia, 65; Up-on (100 prints), Int Graphic Arts Soc, New York, 68. Exhib: Whitney Mus Am Art Ann, 66; Biennial Graphic Arts, Krakow, Poland, 66, 68 & 70; Two Decades of American Prints 1947-1968, Brooklyn Mus, 69; 35th Biennial of Venice & one-man show, Italy, 70; Int Biennial of Graphic Arts & Multiples, Segovia, Spain, 74; Int Graphic, Kunsthalle Bremen, Bremen, WGer, 76; Int Graphic, Stockholm Nationalmuseum, Stockholm, Sweden, 76; 30 Yrs of Am Printmaking, Brooklyn Mus, NY, 76-77; Pintores de los Paises Balticos, Mus of Contemp Art of Caracas, Venezuela, 77; Am Prints of the 20th Century, Philadelphia Mus of Art, Pa, 77-78. Teaching: Prof printmaking, Tyler Sch Art, Temple Univ, 60- Awards: Guggenheim Fels, 58, 64 & 69; Tamarind Fel, 60; Medal, Biennial Graphic Arts, Krakow, 70. Bibliog: Jules Heller (auth), Printmaking Today, Holt, Rinehart & Winston, 72; Workshop problems of oversize relief prints, Leonardo, Vol 7, 74. Mem: Print Club Philadelphia; Soc Am Graphic Artists. Style & Technique: Relief media intaglio; inkless reliefs. Media: Graphics. Dealer: Weyhe Gallery 794 Lexington Ave New York NY 10021. Mailing Add: Dept of Printmaking Tyler Sch Arts Temple Univ Philadelphia PA 19126

VIGIL, VELOY JOSEPH
PAINTER, PRINTMAKER
b Denver, Colo, Mar 5, 31. Study: Colo Inst of Art, Denver. Work: Colorado Springs Fine Arts Ctr, Colo; Home Savings & Loan Asn of Los Angeles, Calif; Armour Dial Res Ctr, Scottsdale, Ariz; Am Greetings Corp, Cleveland, Ohio. Comn: Posters, Art Wagon Gallery, Scottsdale & Hall Gallery, Ft Worth, 77. Exhib: Nat Acad of Design & Nat Acad Galleries, New York, 62; Watercolor USA Ann, Springfield Art Mus, Mo, 65; Nat Watercolor Soc Ann, Laguna Beach Art Mus, Calif, 67; Am Watercolor Soc, Nat Acad Galleries, New York, 68; one-man shows, Carlson-Lowe Galleries, Taos, NMex, 75, Art Wagon Gallery, Scottsdale, Ariz, 76-77 & Hall Gallery, Ft Worth, Tex, 76-77; Indian Arts & Crafts Exhib, Heard Mus, Phoenix, Ariz, 76. Collections Arranged: Nat Watercolor Soc Travel Show, Embassy of Switz, 72 & Va Mus of Fine Arts, Richmond, 73-74. Awards: Winslow Homer Award, Springfield Art Mus, Mo, 70; Franklin Murphy Award, Ankrum Gallery, Los Angeles, Calif, 72; Avery Mem Award, Heard Mus Guild, Phoenix, 76. Bibliog: Article in Les Ed de la Revue Moderne, Paris, 70; Claudia Reinhardt (auth), Veloy J Vigil, Artists of the Rockies, Spring

1976; Lawrence Kaplan (auth), Nostalgia—the golden memory, SW Art, 1/77. Mem: Nat Watercolor Soc (1st vpres, 74-75). Style & Technique: Figurative abstract-expressionism. Media: Watercolor and Acrylic. Mailing Add: 836 S Hilda St Anaheim CA 92806

VIGTEL, GUDMUND
ART ADMINISTRATOR
b July 9, 25; US citizen. Study: Isaac Grunewald's Sch Art, Stockholm, 43-44; Univ Ga, BFA, 52, MFA, 53. Collections Arranged: The New Tradition, 63; An Anthology of Modern American Art, 64; The Beckoning Land, 71; The Modern Image, 72; The Düsseldorf Academy & the Americans, 73; plus numerous others. Pos: Admin asst, Corcoran Gallery Art, 54-57, asst to dir, 57-61, asst dir, 61-63; dir, High Mus Art, 63- Mem: Am Asn Mus; Asn Art Mus Dirs. Publ: Auth numerous exhib catalogues. Mailing Add: High Mus Art 1280 Peachtree St NE Atlanta GA 30309

VIHOS, GEORGE
PAINTER
b Detroit, Mich, Feb 18, 37. Study: Art Inst Chicago, 59-63. Work: Wayne State Univ Med Sch. Exhib: Regional Mich Artist, Detroit Inst Art, 60 & 65; Biennial Drawing, Art Inst Chicago, 62; Nat Religious Art, Cranbrook Acad Art, Bloomfield Hills, Mich, 65; Made in Detroit, Franklin Siden Gallery, Detroit, 68; Michigan Focus, Flint Inst Art, 74-75. Teaching: Instr drawing & painting, Soc Arts & Crafts, Detroit, 66-68 & Wayne State Univ, 68-71; instr drawing, painting & art hist, Roeper Sch, Bloomfield Hills, 70-75. Pos: Visual arts coordr, Mich State Coun Arts, 67-68; artist in residence, Pontiac Creative Art Ctr, Mich, summer 68 & Manistique, Mich, summer 71. Awards: Tiffany Grant for Painting & Drawing, 68; Fulbright-Hays Fel, Florence, Italy, 69. Bibliog: Morley Driver (auth), Detroits ten most promising artists, D A C News, 2/67; Joy Hakanson (auth), Made in Detroit, Midwest Art News, 68 & rev in Detroit News, 4/70. Style & Technique: Linear crayon surface. Media: Oil Crayon & Pencil; Canvas. Dealer: Mrs Lee Hoffman 2945 Woodward Bloomfield Hills MI 48013. Mailing Add: 344 Brown Birmingham MI 48009

VILDER, ROGER
KINETIC ARTIST
b Beyrouth, Lebanon, Nov 29, 38; Can citizen. Study: Sir George Williams Art Sch, dipl; Sir George Williams Univ, BFA; McGill Univ. Work: Mus Contemp Art, Montreal. Comn: Kinetic works, Montreal World's Fair, 70-71 & Can Govt, Osaka, Japan, 70; kinetic wall, Ministry External Affairs, Ottawa, 71-72. Exhib: Artists 68, Art Gallery Ont, Toronto, 68; Concours Quebec Prov, Mus Contemp Art, Montreal, 68, 69 & 71; Some More Beginning, Brooklyn Mus, 69; 11th & 12th Winnipeg Biennial, Man, 69-71; Kinetics, Hayward Gallery, London, Eng, 70. Teaching: Prof painting & sculpture, Mus Art Sch, Montreal, 67-69; prof advan design, Sir George Williams Univ, 69-70; prof painting & sculpture, Col Old Montreal. Awards: Concours Artistique PQ, Mus Contemp Art, 68; Can Arts Coun Grants, 69-70 & 71-72. Bibliog: Frank Popper (auth), Kinetics art, Studio Vista, Holland, 68; William Townsend (auth), Canadian art today, Studio Int, London, 70; Jasia Reichardt (auth), Kinetics, Archit Design, London, 71. Mem: Quebec Sculptor Asn (mem exec comt, 69-, counr, 69-71); Asn Artistes Prof Quebec (adv & mem exec comt, 70-71); Can Artist Rels. Publ: Auth, Sculpture and lights, Artscanada, 12/68; auth, Lumiere dans l'art, Forces, spring 69; ed, London exhibitions, Arts Mag, 11/70; auth, Technology and art, Studio Int, 11/70; auth, Le paradoxe magique de Roger Vilder, Vie Arts, fall 71. Dealer: The Electric Gallery 272 Avenue Rd Toronto ON Can. Mailing Add: 410 Champagneur Ave Montreal PQ H2V 3P5 Can

VILLA, CARLOS
PAINTER
b Dec 11, 36. Study: San Francisco Art Inst, BFA, 61; Mills Col, MFA, 63. Exhib: Park Pl Group, Daniel's Gallery, New York, 65; Park Pl Invitational, Park Pl Gallery, New York, 65; 2nd Ann Arp to Artschwager Exhib, Goldowsky Gallery, New York, 67; one-man shows, Poindexter Gallery, New York, 67, San Francisco Art Inst, Calif, 69, Sacramento State Col Gallery, Calif, 69, Hansen Fuller Gallery, San Francisco, 71, 74 & 78, San Jose State Col Gallery, Calif, 72, Nancy Hoffman Gallery, New York, 73 & 75, Emanuel Walter Gallery, San Francisco Art Inst, 73 & E B Crocker Art Gallery, Sacramento, 77; two-man exhibs, Wyndham Col, Vt, 68 & San Francisco Art Inst, 69; Indianapolis Mus Art, Ind, 72; de Young Mus, San Francisco, 72; Whitney Mus Am Art Ann, New York, 72; Contemp Art Ctr, Cincinnati, Ohio, 73; Contemp Am Painting & Sculpture, Krannert Art Mus, Univ Ill, Urbana-Champaign, 74; San Francisco Mus, 74; San Francisco Art Inst, 76; Calif Show: The Mod Era, San Francisco Mus, Calif & Nat Collection Fine Arts, Washington, DC, 76-77; Calif Bay Area Art—Update, Huntsville Mus Art, Ala, 77; New in the Seventies, Univ Tex, Austin, 77; plus others. Teaching: Asst, Mills Col, 61-63; asst, Studio 1, Oakland, Calif, 61-63; instr, Tel Hill Neighborhood Ctr, Urban Arts, San Francisco, 69-70; chmn interdept studies, San Francisco Art Inst, currently; asst prof art, Calif State Univ, Sacramento, currently. Awards: Hon Mention, Richmond Art Ctr Ann, 58; Nat Endowment for the Arts Grant, 73; Adeline Kent Award, San Francisco Art Inst, 73. Bibliog: Rev, 12/70 & Emily Wasserman (auth), article, 1/71, Artforum. Mailing Add: 1664 Grove St San Francisco CA 91317

VILLAFRANCA, LEONOR MORALES DE
ART HISTORIAN, ART CRITIC
b Mexico City, Mex, Dec 17, 35. Study: Univ Iberoamericana, Mex, MA(hist art). Teaching: Teacher mod art, Univ Iberoamericana, 66-73, teacher art criticism, 74- & head art dept, 72-; tech secy, Coord of Univ Exten, Nat Univ of Mex, 77- Awards: Hon Mention for Thesis, Univ Iberoamericana, 65. Mem: Int & Mex Asns Art Critics. Publ: Auth, Plastica, weekly article in Revista Manana, 66-74. Mailing Add: Av Desierto de los Leones 4184 Mexico 20 DF Mexico

VILLENEUVE, JOSEPH ARTHUR
PAINTER
b Chicoutimi, PR, Jan 4, 10. Work: Mus Beaux Arts Montreal; Mus Quebec; Nat Gallery Can, Ottawa. Exhib: Mus Quebec; Vancouver Art Gallery; Galerie Art Can, Chicoutimi; Galerie Morency, Montreal; Galerie Waddington, Montreal. Awards: Chevalier Membre de l'Orde du Canada. Bibliog: Arthur Villeneuve's Quebec Chronicles (exhib catalog), Montreal Mus Fine Arts. Dealer: Galerie Morency 1564 St Denis Montreal PQ Can. Mailing Add: 669 Rue Tache Chicoutimi PQ Can

VINCENT, TOM
PAINTER
b Kansas City, Mo, 1930. Study: Kansas City Art Inst, BFA & MFA. Work: Kansas City Art Inst; Springfield Mus Fine Arts, Mo; Atlanta Mus, Ga; Montclair Art Mus, NJ; Milwaukee Art Ctr, Wis. Comn: Painting, Charles S Gehrie Presto Int, 40; Jazz (painting), Venice Film Festival, 62; mural, Schering Corp, 68; mural, Montclair Travel Bollinger, 71. Exhib: Mus Mod Art, New York; Corcoran Gallery Art, Washington, DC; Pa Acad Fine Arts, Philadelphia; Galerie Cernushi, New York & Paris. Teaching: Instr drawing, Montclair Art Mus, 70- Awards: Speiser Mem Award for Procession, 62; Silvermine Guild Award for Composition, 69; Montclair Mus Award for Triptich, 70. Bibliog: Russel O Woody (auth), Polymer Painting, Van Nostrand, 71. Mem: Pa Acad Fine Arts; Am Watercolor Soc; United Scenic Artists. Style & Technique: From realism to non-objective. Media: Polymer, Liquitex, Oil. Dealer: Galerie Cernushi Paris 8 France; Pisces Gallery Wellfleet MA 02667. Mailing Add: c/o Caravan de France Cernuschi Galleries 121 E 57th St New York NY 10022

VINER, FRANK LINCOLN
SCULPTOR, DESIGNER
b Worcester, Mass, Aug 9, 37. Study: Sch Worcester Art Mus; Yale Univ, BFA, 61, MFA, 63. Work: Rose Art Mus, Brandeis Univ; Milwaukee Art Ctr; Riverside Mus, New York. Comn: Five wearable sculptures, Berkshire Int, 68; yellow environ room, Wadsworth Atheneum, Hartford, Conn, 69. Exhib: Eccentric Abstraction, Fischbach Gallery, New York, 66; Options, Directions, Milwaukee Art Ctr & Mus Contemp Art, Chicago, 68; Whitney Mus Am Art Sculpture Ann, New York, 68; Op Losse Schroeven/Square Tags in Round Holes, Stedelijk Mus, Amsterdam, 69; A Plastic Presence, Jewish Mus, New York, Milwaukee Art Ctr & San Francisco Mus Art, 70. Teaching: Instr fine art, Sch Visual Arts, New York, 63-; vis artist, Univ Colo Grad Sch Art, Boulder, 72; Rhinehart critic sculpture, Md Inst Art, 72. Bibliog: D Judd (auth), Hard edge painting, Arts Mag, 2/63; H Kramer (auth), And now eccentric abstraction, New York Times, 11/66; L R Lippard (auth), Collected Essays in Art Criticism, 71. Media: Vinyl, Cheesecloth, Dyes. Publ: Contribr, Art by Telephone (recording), Mus Contemp Art Chicago, 69; contribr, If I Had a Mind...Concept-Art Project-Art, 71. Dealer: 55 Mercer Gallery 55 Mercer St New York NY 10013. Mailing Add: 163 Bowery New York NY 10002

VIRET, MARGARET MARY (MRS FRANK IVO)
PAINTER, INSTRUCTOR
b New York, NY, Apr 18, 13. Study: Terry Art Sch; Miami Art Sch; Miami Art Ctr; Univ Miami; also with Dong Kingman, Eliot O'Hara, Xavier Gonzalez, Eugene Massin, Georges Sellier & Jack Amoroso; plus many other prominent instrs. Work: Norton Gallery; Lowe Art Gallery. Comn: Cuba Home Scene, Miami Woman's Club, 63; ballet scenes, Pauline Hill Co, Miami, 65; Spring Flowers (watercolors), Fla C of C, 69; Fla Everglades Scene for wall, Capt Gene, 70; Fla Flowers for wall, Laura, Pompano Beach, Fla. Exhib: Tampa Art Mus, 55; Fla Fedn Art, 55-56; Bass Art Mus, Miami Beach, 55-57, 62 & 63; Lowe Art Gallery, 60, 62 & 70; American Contemporary, Four Arts Soc, 65; plus others. Teaching: Instr art, Miami Art League, 55-56; instr art, Adult Classes, YWCA & YMCA, Miami, 63-68; instr art adult classes, Dade Co Schs, 68- Pos: Chmn, Dade Co Art Chmn, 56-58; art dir, Fla Fedn Women's Clubs, 56-63; pres, Laramore Rader Poetry Group, Miami, 70-72; art dir, Miami Women's Club, 67-, dir fine arts, 77-78. Awards: Best Watercolor for Florwers, Fla Fedn Women's Clubs, 61; Best Watercolor for Marine, Bass Art Mus, 62; Best Watercolor for Flowers, Burdines Coral Gables Art Club, 63. Bibliog: Violet Barker (auth), Dade County, Community Press, 63; Irene Gramling (auth), Sphinx, Franklin Press, 65 & 66; Edna Chauser (auth), Cultural Alliance, Chase, 71. Mem: Miami Art League (pres, 55-56); Fla Fedn Art (vpres, 56-58); hon mem Hibiscus Fine Arts Guild; hon mem Allied Arts NMiami; life mem Miami Palette Club. Style & Technique: Realistic impressionism. Media: Watercolor, Oil, Acrylic. Mailing Add: 294 NE 55th Terr Miami FL 33137

VISCO, ANTHONY SALVATORE
EDUCATOR, SCULPTOR
b Philadelphia, Pa, Sept 13, 48. Study: Fleischer Art Mem, Philadelphia; Philadelphia Col of Art; Accad delle Belle Art, Florence, Italy; Skowhegan Sch of Painting & Sculpture, Maine. Comn: Portrait, D Tredici, Florence, Italy, 71; Landscape drawing, M Pietrini, Sulmona, Italy, 73; terra cotta portrait, Mr Charles Ogg, Philadelphia, 75; bronze portrait, Mem to Gen Baker, comn by Mrs Baker, Valley Forge Mil Acad, Wayne, Pa, 76; bronze crucifix & bronze baptismal fount lid, Church of St Anastasia, Newtown Sq, Pa, 76. Exhib: One-man shows, Capital Bldg, Harrisburg, Pa, 66, Italian Trade Comn, Barclay Hotel, Philadelphia, 76; Ann Student Exhib, Philadelphia Col of Art, 66-70; Invitational, Acad of Mus, Philadelphia, 75; Kenmore Gallery, Philadelphia, 75; 41st Eucharistic Cong, Exhib of Liturgical Arts, Civic Ctr, Philadelphia, 76. Teaching: Instr sculpture, Philadelphia Col of Art, 76-, Creuzberg Ctr, Radnor, Pa, 76- Pos: Art instr, Recreation Ctr for Older People, Philadelphia, summer 1968; apprentice, Waler Erlbacher, Elkins Park, Pa, summer 1970; sculpture technician, Skowhegan Sch, Maine, summer 1975. Awards: State scholar, Philadelphia Col of Art, 66-70; Fulbright-Hayes Scholar, Florence, Italy, 70-71; Greenshields Award, Pvt Studio Work, Can, 75-76. Style & Technique: Figurative, naturalistic, humanistic; allegorical. Media: Clay; Wax; Bronze. Mailing Add: c/o Sandy Webter 2018 Locust St Philadelphia PA 19103

VISSER'T HOOFT, MARTHA
PAINTER
b Buffalo, NY, May 25, 06. Study: Acad Julien, Paris, 22. Work: Albright-Knox Art Gallery, Buffalo; Whitney Mus Am Art, New York; Columbia Mus Art, SC; Rollins Col Mus Art; Munson-Williams-Proctor Inst, Utica, NY. Exhib: American Painting Today, Metrop Mus Art, New York, 50; Carnegie Inst Int, Pittsburgh, 52; Art Inst Chicago, 56; Artistas Brasileros Americanos, Mus Mod Art, Sao Paulo, Brazil; one-man show, Charles Burchfield Ctr, State Univ NY Col Buffalo, 73. Awards: Purchase Award, Columbia Mus Art, 59; Second Prize in Oil, Chautauqua Inst Art, 64; NY State Univ Buffalo Community Coun Award, 75; plus others. Bibliog: J Benjamin Townsend (auth), Martha Visser't Hooft Paintings & Drawings, 1950-1973, State Univ NY Col Buffalo Alumni Found, 73. Mem: Hon mem Buffalo Fine Art Acad, Albright-Knox Gallery; Charles Burchfield Ctr, State Univ NY Col Buffalo; Patteran Artists Soc. Style & Technique: Semi-abstract in gouache; hard-edge nonobjective in acrylic. Dealer: More-Rubin Gallery Buffalo NY. Mailing Add: 64 Cleveland Ave Buffalo NY 14222

VITALE, LYDIA MODI
MUSEUM DIRECTOR, CURATOR
b New York, NY. Study: Scholar Award, Art Students League, New York; apprentice of Hans Hoffman, New York; internship, Museo Nac de Hist, 45-46 & Museo Nac de Antropologia, 58, Mexico City; studies in art conserv & restoration, Univ Calif, Davis, 70. Collections Arranged: Art Nouveau, 68, Fish-Fox-Kos: Concept Art, 71, Westward HO: Russell, Remington, Price & Hansen, 76 & New Deal Art: California (ed, catalogue; comprehensive survey of art during fed patronage 1932-42), 76, de Saisset Art Gallery & Mus, Univ Santa Clara. Pos: Display dir, Prince Matchabelli, Inc, New York; art dir & set/costume designer, Actor's Workshop, San Francisco, 56-57; dir, cur & art instr, Triton Mus of Art, San Jose, Calif, 65-67; dir, de Saisset Art Gallery & Mus, Univ Santa Clara, 67- Awards: Adolph's Found grant, 74, Calif Arts Comn Grant, 74 & Nat Endowment for the Humanities grant & exten, 74 & 75, New Deal Art, California. Mem: Western Asn of Am Mus (exec secy, 69-71); Am Asn Art Mus; Bay Area Lawyers for the Arts; Archeoclub d'Italia (bd dirs, currently). Publ: Ed catalogues, Twenty Color Photographs: Light Abstractions, Wynn Bullock, 72, Fletcher Benton: Selected Works 1964-74, 74 & Scholder Collects Scholder 1965-75 Retrospective, 75, de Saisset Art Gallery & Mus; co-ed, James W McManus: Survey of

Selected Works 1967-77, de Saisset Art Gallery & Mus, 77. Mailing Add: Univ Santa Clara Santa Clara CA 95053

VIVENZA, FRANCESCA
GRAPHIC ARTIST, PAINTER
b Rome, Italy, May 4, 41. Study: High Sch Fine Art, Milan, Italy; Acad Belle Arti Brera, Milan; frescos with Gianfilippo Usellini. Comn: Geology & Metamorphosis of Sci (drawings), Univ Toronto Mining Bldg, 74; mural, Toronto Peace Convention, 76. Exhib: One-man shows, Albert White Gallery, Toronto, 72, 74 & 76, Galleria Clovasso, Milan, 75, Galleria Agrifoglio, Milan, 76 & Pub Libr, Cambridge, Ont, 77; Scan, Vancouver Art Gallery, 74; graphics with open studio, Pollock Gallery, Toronto, 75 & Glenbow-Alta Inst, Calgary, 75; Prints from Open Studio, touring exhib, Art Gallery of Ont, 75; plus others, incl showings in Paris & London in 76-77. Teaching: Prof hist art, Secondary Schs, Milan & Como, Italy, 67-69; guest artist, Humber Col, fall 74; artist-in-residence, Scarborough Col, Ont. Bibliog: Jean-Loup Bourget (auth), Vivenza, Vie des Arts, Montreal, fall 71; K Kirtzweiser (auth), Vivenza, 3/20/71 & Globe & Mail, Toronto, 4/13/74; C Morgan (auth), Artist of outside-inside, Mosaico, 75; J Purdie (auth), article in Globe & Mail, 1/31/76; plus others. Style & Technique: Concentration of movement and color built around message. Media: Pen & Ink; Oil. Dealer: A White Gallery 25 Prince Arthur Ave Toronto ON Can. Mailing Add: 73 Ellerbeck St Toronto ON M4K 2V2 Can

VODICKA, RUTH KESSLER
SCULPTOR
b New York, NY Study: City Col New York; with O'Connor Barrett; Sculpture Ctr, New York; Art Students League, 56-57 & 59; New Sch Social Res, 65; NY Univ, 69; Empire State Col Prog, 75- Work: Norfolk Mus, Va; Montclair State Col, NJ; Grayson Co State Bank, Sherman, Tex. Comn: Eternal Light (bronze sculpture), Temple of Jewish Community Ctr, Harrison, NJ, 65. Exhib: Whitney Mus Ann, New York, 52-57; Am Fedn Arts Traveling Exhib, 57-58; Galerie Claude Bernard, Paris, 60; Walk-Through-Dance-Through-Sculpture, New York Cult Arts Festival, Bryant Park, 67; Sculpture for the Dance, Hudson River Mus, Yonkers, NY, 73; plus many solo shows, 56- Teaching: Instr sculpture, Queens Youth Ctr, Bayside, 53-56; instr sculpture, Emanuel Midtown YM & WHA, New York, 66-69; instr sculpture, Great Neck Arrandale Sch, 69-70; vis artist, Hillside Sch, Hastings-on-Hudson, 73-74. Awards: Joseph W Beatman Award for Best Work in Any Medium & First Prize, Silvermine Guild Artists, 57; Medal of Honor, Painters & Sculptors Soc NJ, 62; Julia Ford Pew Prize, Nat Asn Woman Artists, 66; plus others. Bibliog: Louis Calta (auth), Multi-purpose sculpture on view in Bryant Park, New York Times, 10/67; Environmental happening, Journal News, Mt Kisco, 9/73; They Choreograph to sculpture (cover), Patent Trader, 10/73. Mem: Am Soc Contemp Artists; Audubon Artists; Nat Asn Women Artists; Sculptors Guild (exec bd, 75); Women in Arts. Style & Technique: Participatory environmental sculpture with dance/music/poetry/theatre to become total theatre. Media: Bronze, Brass, Wood. Publ: Contribr, Feminist Art J, 72, Women & Art, 72, Artworkers Newslett, 73-75. Mailing Add: 97 Wooster St New York NY 10012

VO-DINH, MAI
PAINTER, PRINTMAKER
b Hue, Vietnam, Nov 14, 33; US citizen. Study: Sorbonne, Fac Lett, 56; Acad Grande Chaumiere, 57; Ecole Nat Superieure Beaux-Arts, 59. Work: Mus Mod Art, Paris; Mus Rouen; Schiedam Mus, Holland; Nashville Mus, Tenn; Wash Co Mus Fine Arts, Md. Exhib: Collection Harry L Bradley, Milwaukee Art Ctr, Wis, 62; Little Show, Mus Sect, The Guild Hall, East Hampton, NY, 67; Invitational Ann, Carroll Reece Mus, Johnson City, Tenn, 70; one-man shows, Synechia Arts Ctr, Middletown, NY, 74 & Wash Co Mus Fine Arts, Md, 76. Awards: Christopher Award, Christopher Found, New York, NY, 75. Bibliog: Sidney Fields (auth), A Voice for Vietnam, New York Daily News, 2/71; Rena Andrews (auth), The Fine Arts, Denver Post, 4/71; Libbie Powell (auth), International Recognized Artist, The Daily Mail, Hagerstown, Md, 11/74. Mem: Artists Equity Asn New York; Int Asn Artists. Style & Technique: Semi-abstract; use of chalk and woodcut collage. Media: Oil, Acrylic; Woodblock Printing. Publ: Illusr, The Cry of Vietnam, Unicorn, Santa Barbara, Calif, 68; auth & illusr, The Toad is the Emperor's Uncle, Doubleday, NY, 70; auth & illusr, The Jade Song, Chelsea House, NY, 70; illusr, First Snow, Knopf, NY, 74; illusr, The Raft is Not the Shore, Beacon Press, Boston, 75. Dealer: The Hendricks Art Collection 6502 Hillmead Rd Bethesda MD 20034; Suzuki Graphics 38 E 57th St New York NY 10022. Mailing Add: Stonevale RFD 1 Burkittsville MD 21718

VOELKER, JOHN
PAINTER, DESIGNER
b Givens, Ohio. Study: Columbus Col Art & Design, Ohio, 53-57; design workshop with Canzani; advan painting with Kuehn. Work: Columbus Gallery Fine Arts, Ohio; Abilene Mus Fine Arts, Tex. Comn: Posters, Cerebral Palsy Found, 56; Tex Fine Arts Asn, Dallas, 71 & Logo Design Bicentennial with Tex Fine Arts Asn, 75. Exhib: Ultimate Concerns, Prints & Drawings, Ohio Univ, 63 & 64; Artists of Gulf States & Tex, Delgado Mus, New Orleans, 64 & 66; Chautauqua Exhib Am Art, NY, 67; 11th Ann Prints & Drawings, Okla Art Ctr, Oklahoma City, 69; Southwest Painting Ann, Albuquerque, NMex, 70. Pos: Art coordr, Coronet Packaging, Dallas, 61-75. Awards: Permanent Collection Choice, Ultimate Concerns, Ohio Univ, 63; Haydon Calhoun Gallery Award, Painting & Sculpture Ann, Dallas Mus Fine Arts, 64; Best of Show, Tex Fine Arts Asn, 72. Bibliog: Article in Columbus Sunday Mag, Dispatch, 3/56; article in Dallas Times Herald, 10/76. Mem: Artists Equity, Dallas; Tex Fine Arts Asn (vpres, 70-71, pres, 71-72 & 75-76, dir publ, 73-75); Artists Coalition of Tex. Style & Technique: Acrylic, printmaking. Dealer: Adelle Taylor 3317 McKinney Dallas TX. Mailing Add: 4135 University Dallas TX 75205

VOGEL, DONALD
PRINTMAKER, INSTRUCTOR
b Poland, Dec 24, 02; US citizen. Study: Parson Sch Design; Columbia Univ, BS & MA. Work: Seattle Art Mus; Pa State Univ; Metrop Mus Art, New York; Munson-Williams-Proctor Inst; Soc Am Graphic Artists; plus others. Exhib: Brooklyn Mus, 50; Am Fedn Arts Traveling Exhib, 50; Royal Soc Painters, Etchers & Engravers, 54; Calif Western Univ, San Diego, 60; Pratt Graphic Art Ctr, 64; plus many others. Teaching: Instr art, High Sch Art & Design, New York. Awards: Munson-Williams-Proctor Inst, 43; Northwest Printmakers, 43 & 46; Libr of Cong, 50. Mem: Soc Am Graphic Artists. Publ: Contribr, Print Collector's Quart, La Rev Mod & others. Mailing Add: 415 E 52nd St New York NY 10022

VOGEL, DONALD S
PAINTER, ART DEALER
b Milwaukee, Wis, Oct 21, 17. Study: Corcoran Gallery Art, Washington, DC; Art Inst Chicago; Work Prog Admin Easel Proj, Chicago. Work: Ft Worth Art Ctr, Tex; Dallas Mus Fine Arts; Beaumont Mus Art, Tex; Mobile Art Ctr, Ala; Philbrook Art Ctr, Tulsa, Okla. Exhib: One-man shows, Mobile Art Gallery, Ala, 69, Philbrook Mus Art, Tulsa, 69, Beaumont Art Mus, Tex, 70, Schoener Gallery, San Antonio, 75 & Robert Rice Gallery, Houston, 75. Collections Arranged: Clara McDonald Williamson, 66 & Velox Ward (with catalog), 72, Amon Carter Mus Art, Ft Worth; Valton Tyler (with catalog), Southern Methodist Univ, 72. Pos: Dir, Valley House Gallery, Inc. Awards: Bronze Medal, Am Acad Rome, 42; Dallas Allied Arts Ann Awards, Dallas Mus Fine Arts, 44-46; 8th Tex Gen Exhib Award, Houston Mus Fine Arts, 46. Mem: Art Dealers Asn Am; Am Fedn Arts; Dallas Mus Fine Arts. Specialty: Paintings and sculpture of the nineteenth and twentieth centuries. Publ: Co-auth & ed, Passion: Georges Roualt (catalog), 62; co-auth, Aunt Clara, 66; ed, The Paintings of Hugh H Breckenridge (catalog), 67. Mailing Add: Valley House Gallery Inc 6616 Spring Valley Rd Dallas TX 75240

VOGEL, MR & MRS HERBERT
COLLECTORS
Mr Herbert Vogel b New York, NY, Aug 16, 22; Mrs Dorothy Vogel b Elmira, NY, May 14, 35. Study: Mr Vogel, NY Univ Inst Fine Arts, with Erwin Panofsky, Alfred Salmony, Richard Offner & Walter Friedlaender; Mrs Vogel, Syracuse Univ, BA, 57; Univ Denver, MA, 58. Exhib: Selections from the Collection of Dorothy & Herbert Vogel, Clocktower, New York, 75; Painting, Drawing & Sculpture of the 60's & 70's from the Dorothy & Herbert Vogel Collection, Inst Contemp Art, Univ Pa, 75 & Contemp Arts Ctr, Cincinnati, Ohio, 75-76; Works from the Collection of Dorothy & Herbert Vogel, Univ of Mich Mus of Art, 77. Bibliog: Lucio Pozzi (auth), Una straordinaria collezione delle avanguardie, Bolaffiarte, 6/73; Anthony Haden-Guest (auth), A new art-world legend, NY Mag, 4/28/75; Grace Glueck (auth), Art Notes: The 'in' couple, NY Times, 5/4/75. Collection: Contemporary drawing, sculpture and painting. Mailing Add: 305 E 86th St New York NY 10028

VOGL, DON GEORGE
PAINTER, PRINTMAKER
b Milwaukee, Wis, July 22, 29. Study: Art Inst Chicago & Univ Chicago, BAE, 57; Univ Wis-Milwaukee, MS(art educ), 58. Work: Art Gallery, Univ Notre Dame, Ind; Alverno Col, Milwaukee; Mt Mary Col, Milwaukee; Cardinal Stritch Col, Milwaukee. Comn: Wood constructions, Immaculate Conception Church, Hartford, Mich, 69; square reliefs & wood constructions, St Mark's Church, Niles, Mich, 70; wall hanging, Law Libr, Notre Dame Univ, 75; construction, Methodist Church, Stevenville, Mich; railroad bridge over Michigan Ave, S of Plaza, South Bend, Ind. Exhib: Chicago Vicinity Show, 65; Watercolor USA, Springfield, Mo, 68; Tri-State Graphics Show, Louisville, Ky, 74; Indianapolis Painters & Sculptors, 75. Teaching: Instr art, Marygrove Col, Detroit, 61-63; assoc prof painting & graphics, Univ Notre Dame, 63- Pos: Vpres, Visual Improvement Prog, South Bend, 74-75. Awards: 1st Award Painting, Wis State Fair, 58; La Vera Pohl Award, Wis Painters & Sculptors, 60; 2nd Award Graphics, Salamonie Art Show, Warren, Ind, 74. Bibliog: Rudy Pozatti (auth), Indiana Printmakers, Ind Art Educ Asn, 12/74. Mem: Am Col Art Asn. Style & Technique: Fanciful figurative style; dominant use of line; new emphasis on delicate or subtle colo; lyrical style in painting. Media: Lithography with Spray Paint and Watercolor Added; Paintings in Acrylic and Oil. Dealer: Deson-Zaks 226 E Ontario St Chicago IL 60611. Mailing Add: 851 Park Ave South Bend IN 46616

VOLKIN, HILDA APPEL
PRINTMAKER, PAINTER
b Boston, Mass, Sept 24, 33. Study: Mass Col Art, BS, 54; Radcliffe Col, MA, 56. Work: Cleveland Mus Art, Ohio; Univ NMex, Albuquerque; Massillon Mus, Ohio; Beth-Israel, West Temple, Cleveland. Exhib: Massillon Mus Ann, 64 & 73; Canton Art Inst Ann, Ohio, 67-73; Cleveland Mus Art Travel Exhib, 71 & May Shows, 73 & 74; SPAR Nat Art, Shreveport, La, 73; Gov's Gallery, State House, Santa Fe, NMex, 75; Mus Fine Arts, Santa Fe, 77; SW Print & Drawing Biennial Exhib, NMex State Univ, Las Cruces, 77. Teaching: Art instr, Cuyahoga Community Col, Metro Campus, Cleveland, 72; instr painting, Univ NMex, Los Alamos, 74- Pos: Dir, Fuller Lodge Art Ctr, 77- Awards: Purchase Award for Watercolor, Massillon Mus, 66; Third Prize for Serigraphs, Canton Art Inst, Ohio, 68; Graphics Award, Cleveland Mus Art, 74. Mem: Mus NMex; NMex Asn Art Mus. Style & Technique: Hand printed combining silk screen with acrylics, oil and pencil in paintings. Mailing Add: 405 Cheryl Ave White Rock NM 87544

VOLLMER, RUTH
SCULPTOR
b Munich, Ger; US citizen. Work: Nat Collection Fine Arts, Smithsonian Inst, Washington, DC; Mus Mod Art Whitney Mus Am Art, New York; NY Univ Art Collection; Rose Art Mus, Brandeis Univ; plus many others including pvt collections. Comn: Mus Mod Art Exhibs, Art in Progress, 15th Anniversary Exhib, 44, Elements of Stage Design, toured USA, 47-50 & several children's art dept, including Brussels World's Fair, 58; relief mural for lobby, New York; sculpture to each of 15 founders on 25th anniversary, CED, 67. Exhib: Mus Mod Art Lending Serv, New York, 63-; For Eyes & Ears, Cordier Ekstrom Gallery, New York, 64; Whitney Mus Am Art Ann, 64-70; 2nd Salon Int Galeries Pilotes, Lausanne, Switz, 66; one-person shows, Everson Mus Art, Syracuse, NY, 74, Neuberger Mus, State Univ NY, Purchase, NY, 76 & Columbus, Ohio, 76; plus numerous other group & one-person shows. Bibliog: B H Friedman (auth), The quiet world of Ruth Vollmer, Art Int, Vol 9, No 12; Robert Smithson (auth), Quasi-infinities & the waning of space, Arts Mag, Vol 41, No 1, Sol LeWitt(auth), Paragraphs on conceptual art, Artforum, summer 67; plus many others. Mem: Am Abstract Artist; Sculptors Guild. Style & Technique: Construction, conceptual. Media: Plastic and Metal. Dealer: Betty Parsons Gallery 24 W 57th St New York NY 10019. Mailing Add: 25 Central Park W New York NY 10023

VOLPE, ROBERT
PAINTER, LECTURER
b New York, NY, Dec 13, 42. Study: Sch Art & Design, New York; New Sch Social Res, New York; also printmaking with John Ross. Work: South Street Seaport Mus, New York; State Univ NY Downstate Med Ctr Collection. Exhib: Conf House Asn, 69-78; one-man shows, Kottler Galleries, New York, 70, South Street Seaport Mus, 74, Nahas Gallery, New York, 75-77 & Salmagundi Club, New York, 76-78; Nacal Official Naval Combat Artist Group, 76-78. Pos: Cur, Antietam Nat Mus, Sharpsburg, Md, 72-78; mem bd dirs, Found Community Artist, New York, 72-75; dir, Art Identification Unit, City of New York Police Dept, 72-78; bd dirs, Art Cent Ltd, New York, 74-78. Awards: President's Award for Graphics, Salmagundi Club, New York, 77; Metrop Mus Art Acrylic Award, 77; Graphic Awards, Guggenheim Mus, 77 & Sch Visual Art, New York, 77. Bibliog: George Krimsky (auth), Meet Volpe the Bibliog: Laurie Adams (auth), Art-Cop, Dodd Meade, 75; Barry Cunningham (auth), Newest breed, New York Post, 75; articles in Wall St J & New York Mag, 78. Style & Technique: Seascapes, New York harbor tug boats; dry brush. Media: Oil on Canvas; Watercolor; Printmaking. Mailing Add: c/o Salmagundi Club 47 Fifth Ave New York NY 10003

VOM SIEBENSTEIN
See Siebner, Herbert Johannes

VON GUNTEN, ROGER
PAINTER
b Zurich, Switz, Mar 29, 33. Study: Kunstgewerbeschule Zurich, 48-53; Iberoamerican Univ, Mex, 59-60. Work: Mus Arte Mod, Mexico City; Univ Oaxaca, Mex; Mus Univ Veracruzana, Xalapa, Mex; Centro Arte Mod, Guadalajara, Mex. Comn: Paintings, Mex Pavilions, Expo 67, Montreal & Hemisfair, 68, San Antonio, 68; murals, Mex Pavilion, Expo 67, Osaka, Japan, 69 & Centro Arte Mod, Guadalajara, Mex, 70. Exhib: 20th Biennial Watercolors, Brooklyn Mus, NY, 58; Confrontacion 66, Mus Bellas Artes, Mexico City, 66; 2nd Bienal Coltejer, Medellin, Colombia, 70; Fifteen of Mexico's Artists, Phoenix Art Mus, 73; Contemporary Mexican Art, Nat Mus Art, Tokyo, 74; Art Contemporani l'Latino-Americá, Museu de l'Empordá, Figueras, Catalonio, Spain, 76; Siete Pintores Contemporaneos, Palacio de Bellas Artes, Mexico City, Mex, 77; one-man show, Galerie Bettie Thommen, Basel, Switz, 77. plus others. Awards: Soc Amigos Acapulco First Prize, 2nd Festival Pictorico Acapulco, Mex, 64. Bibliog: J Garcia Ponce (auth), Nueve pintores, Mexicanos, Ed Era, Mex, 68 & Aparicion de lo invisible, Ed Siglo XXI, Mex, 68; Damian Bayon (auth), Aventura plastica Hispanoamericana, Ed Fondo de Cultura Economica, Mex, 74. Style & Technique: Structural expressionism-neofigurative. Media: Oil, Acrylic. Mailing Add: c/o Galeria Juan Martin Amberes 17 Mexico City Mexico

VON HUENE, STEPHAN R
SCULPTOR
b Los Angeles, Calif, Sept 15, 32. Study: Pasadena City Col, 50-52; Univ Calif, Los Angeles, 52-53 & 63-65, MA; Chouinard Art Inst, 55-59, BFA. Work: Los Angeles Co Mus; Pasadena Art Mus, Calif; Southwestern Col, Chula Vista, Calif; Whitney Mus Am Art, New York; Exploratorium, San Francisco. Exhib: American Sculpture of the 60's, Los Angeles Co Mus, 67; Electro-Magica, Int Elec Arts Exhib, Tokyo, Japan, 69; Sound Sculpture, Vancouver Art Gallery, BC, 73; Sehen um Zu Hören, Kunsthalle, Düsseldorf, WGer, 76; Bild Raum Klang, Bonn, WGer, 76; one-man shows, Whitney Mus Am Art, 70, San Francisco Mus, 71, Los Angeles Co Mus, 71, Chicago Mus Contemp Art, 74 & Inge Bhecker Gallery, Bochum, WGer, 77. Teaching: Teacher drawing, painting & sculpture, Chouinard Art Inst, Los Angeles, 64-70; teacher drawing & sculpture, Calif Inst Arts, Valencia, 71-, assoc dean, 72-76, actg dean, 76-77. Awards: Nat Endowment Grant, 74; Deutscher Akad Austauschdienst Berlin Grant, 76. Bibliog: Articles in Artforum, 1/68 & 10/69, Mizue, Japan, 7/73 & Ikebana Sogetsu, Number 114, 77. Style & Technique: Sound sculpture. Mailing Add: Calif Inst Arts 24700 McBean Pkwy Valencia CA 91355

VON MEYER, MICHAEL
SCULPTOR
b Russia, June 10, 94; US citizen. Study: Calif Sch Fine Arts, San Francisco. Work: Daily Californian Newspaper Bldg, Salinas; House Off Bldg, Washington, DC; US Post Off, Santa Clara, Calif; Church of Transfiguration, Denver, Colo; Marina Heights, Vallejo, Calif. Comn: St Innocent Eastern Orthodox Church, Encino, Calif; St Therese's Shrine, Fresno, Calif; Russian Orthodox Holy Trinity Cathedral, San Francisco; Russian Cath Ctr; Beach Chalet, San Francisco. Exhib: San Francisco Mus Art; Corcoran Gallery Art, Washington, DC; Oakland Art Gallery, 36; Pomeroy Galleries, San Francisco, 66; Monterey Peninsula Mus Art, 69. Awards: Winner, Woman's Art Asn San Francisco, 26; Bronze Medal, Oakland Art Gallery 4th Ann Sculpture, 34. Bibliog: E M Polley (auth), Art & artists, Sun Times Herald, Vallejo, Calif; Robert Hagan (auth), The walls they left behind, San Francisco Mag, 64; Ann Gold (auth), Shades of Imperial Russia, San Francisco Sunday Examiner & Chronicle, 11/20/77. Mailing Add: c/o Hoover Gallery 710 Sansome St San Francisco CA 94111

VON NEUMANN, ROBERT A
SCULPTOR, EDUCATOR
b Berlin, Ger, Nov 15, 23; US citizen. Study: Sch Art Inst Chicago, BFA; Univ Wis, MS. Work: Des Moines Art Ctr, Iowa; Detroit Mus Art; Newark Mus Art, NJ; Ill State Univ, Normal; Ind State Col, Indianapolis. Comn: Sculpture to illus article in Playboy Mag, 69 & 72. Exhib: Aspects of Christian Art, Newark Mus Art, 56; Craftsmen in a Changing World, Mus Contemp Crafts, New York, 57; American Crafts, Am Pavilion, World's Fair, Brussels, Belg, 58; American Decorative Arts, Europe, US & Near East, US State Dept, 59-61; Int Sterling Silver Flatware Design Competition, Europe & US, 60-61. Teaching: From instr to asst prof art, Iowa State Teachers Col, 50-55; prof art, Univ Ill, Urbana. Awards: Chosen by competition to study with Baron Frik Fleming, Court Silversmith to King of Sweden, 50; Award, 1st Int Design Competition for Sterling Silver Flatware, 60; Award to Study Japanese Handicraft Industries, Int Coop Comn, 60. Bibliog: Elizabeth Drews (auth), The Creative Personality (series of films), Dept Educ, Mich State Univ, 58. Mem: Am Craftsmens Coun. Media: Clay, Wood, Metal. Publ: Auth, The decorative arts: an aesthetic stepchild?, Col Arts J, 60; auth, The Design and Creation of Jewelry, Chilton, 60 & rev ed, 72. Mailing Add: c/o Gilman Gallery 103 E Oak St Chicago IL 60611

VON REBHAN, ELINOR ANNE
SLIDE LIBRARIAN
b Northampton, Mass, Oct 10, 45. Study: Sweet Briar Col, BA(art hist), 67. Pos: Slide librn, Nat Gallery of Art, 68- Mem: Art Libr Soc of NAm. Mailing Add: Nat Gallery of Art Washington DC 20565

VON SCHLEGELL, DAVID
SCULPTOR
b St Louis, Mo, May 25, 20. Study: Univ Mich, 40-42; Art Students League, 46-48. Work: Whitney Mus Am Art, New York; Hirshhorn Mus, Washington, DC; Carnegie Inst, Pittsburgh; Mass Inst Technol, Cambridge, Mass; H F Johnson Mus, Cornell Univ, Ithaca, NY. Comn: Sculpture, Lannon Found, Palm Beach, Fla, 69, Storm King Art Ctr, Mountainville, 70, Harbor Towers, Boston, 72, Duluth, Minn, 75 & Philadelphia, 76. Exhib: Whitney Ann, 60-68 & Lipman Found, 69, Whitney Mus Am Art, New York; Carnegie Int, Pittsburgh, 70; Sculpture for New Spaces, Walker Art Ctr, Minneapolis, 71; Middleheim Biennial, Belg, 71; Univ Wash, 71; plus many other group & one-man shows. Teaching: Vis lectr sculpture, Univ Calif, Santa Barbara, 68; instr painting, Sch Visual Arts, 68-69; vis instr sculpture, Cornell Univ, 69-70; dir studies sculpture, Yale Univ, 71- Awards: Purchase Prize, Carnegie Int, 67; St Buttolph Award, 69; Nat Found Arts, 69 & Guggenheim, 74. Bibliog: Jacobs (auth), The artist speaks: D V S, Art in Am, 5-6/68; 2 outdoor pieces, Dus Arts, 5-6/73. Mailing Add: c/o Pace Gallery 32 E 57th St New York NY 10022

VON SCHLIPPE, ALEXEY
PAINTER, EDUCATOR
b Moscow, Russia, Sept 12, 15; US citizen. Study: Acad Fine Arts, Berlin, Ger; pvt studies in Rome, Italy; Royal Art Mus, Brussels, Belg, with Prof Phillipot. Work: West Berlin Gallery, Ger; Munich Gallery; Slater Mus, Norwich, Conn. Exhib: Hartford Watercolor, 63, 65 & 66; New England Artists, Boston, 67; New Haven Art Festival, 68-73; Munich Int Europ Summer Show, Ger, 72-78. Teaching: Asst prof art appreciation & hist, Univ Conn, 63-68, assoc prof design, 68-, prof art appreciation & hist & design, 77- Awards: First Prize, Norwich Free Acad, 62; Second Prize, Hartford Atheneum, 64. Bibliog: Rev in Art Rev, 67 & Univ Conn Chronicle, 2/73. Mem: Am Soc Psychopathology of Expression, US chapter. Style & Technique: Semi-abstract expressive realism. Media: Oil over Egg Tempera; Watercolor. Mailing Add: 18 Caulkins Rd Norwich CT 06360

VON WIEGAND, CHARMION
PAINTER, WRITER
b Chicago, Ill. Study: Barnard Col, Columbia Univ; also Byzantine art hist with Wittemore, Florentine & Siena, painting with Richard Offner & Oriental art with Riefstahl. Work: Mus Mod Art, New York; Whitney Mus Am Art, New York; Cincinnati Art Mus, Ohio; Seattle Art Mus; Joseph Hirshhorn Mus, Washington, DC. Comn: Painting, Container Corp Am. Exhib: Women, Peggy Guggenheim's Art of This Century, 45; Classic Tradition in Contemporary Art, Walker Art Inst, 53; Konkrete Kunst: 50 Years Development, Zurich, Switz, 60; Art & Writing, Stedelijk Mus, Amsterdam & Baden-Baden, Ger, 63; Mondrian, DeStijl & Their Impact, Marlboro-Gerson Gallery, 64. Pos: Pres, Am Abstr Artists, 51-53. Awards: Award, Soc Typographic Arts, Chicago, 68; First Prize in Painting on Tibetan Theme, 6th Relig Biennale, Cranbrook Acad Art, Mich, 69. Media: Oil. Collection: Tibetan art; constructivists. Publ: Auth, The meaning of Mondrian, J Aesthet, 43; auth, The Rissian art, In: Encycl Arts, 46; auth, The Oriental tradition and abstract art, In: The World of Abstract Art; auth, Memoir on Mondrian, Arts Ann, 61. Mailing Add: 333 E 34th St New York NY 10016

VOORHEES, DONALD EDWARD
PAINTER, LITHOGRAPHER
b Neptune, NJ, May 6, 26. Study: Acad Arts, Newark, NJ, with Stanley Turnbull, Avery Johnson & Edmund Fitzgerald; Art Students League, with Mario Cooper, John Pike & Edgar Whitney. Exhib: NJ Watercolor Soc State Ann, Morris Mus & Monmouth Mus, 54-; Knickerbocker Artists Ann, Nat Arts Club, 71-75; Am Watercolor Soc Ann, 72 & 75, Nat Traveling Exhib, 72 & 75; Hudson Valley Artists Ann, 75. Teaching: Instr watercolor, Guild Creative Arts, Shrewsbury, NJ, 64-; instr watercolor, Shore Art Ctr, Long Branch, NJ, 74-; pvt art classes. Pos: Mem art adv comt, Monmouth Co Bd Freeholders, 69- Awards: Mary Lawrence Award, NJ Watercolor Soc State Ann, 71; First Prize, Guild of Creative Art State Ann, 75; Muriel Alvord Award, Hudson Valley Artists Ann, 75; plus others. Mem: NJ Watercolor Soc (pres, 75-76); Artist's Fel; Int Soc of Artists; Salmagundi Club; Guild Creative Art; Monmouth Art Found; Metrop Mus Art; plus others. Style & Technique: Realistic watercolorist. Dealer: Donald Voorhees Gallery 35 Center Ave Atlantic Highlands NJ 07716. Mailing Add: 35 Center Ave Atlantic Highlands NJ 07716

VOOS, WILLIAM JOHN
ART ADMINISTRATOR, PAINTER
b St Louis, Mo, July 2, 30. Study: Wash Univ Sch Fine Arts, BFA, 52; Univ Kans, MFA, 53; NY Univ, US Arts & Humanities Art Admin fel, 67. Work: Rend Lake Col Collection, Mt Vernon, Ill; Mus Contemp Art, Recife, Brazil. Comn: Mural, Army Educ Ctr, Ft Bragg, NC, 54; playground mural, Ferguson Park Comn, Mo, 60. Exhib: One-man show, Lafayette Art Ctr, Ind, 66 & Northern State Col, 74; Fac Shows, Steinberg Hall, Wash Univ, 68-72; Atlanta Col Art Fac Show, High Mus Art, 75; Mus Contemp Art, Recife, Brazil, 75. Teaching: Assoc prof art & chmn humanities div, Florissant Valley Community Col, 64-68; assoc prof art & assoc dean sch fine arts, Wash Univ, 68-73; dean, Atlanta Col Art, 73-75, pres, 75- Awards: Harmon Watercolor Prize, 62 & Crunden Prize, 70, St Louis Artists Guild; Semi-Finalist, Urban Walls Design Competition, Atlanta, Ga, 73. Mem: Col Art Asn Am; Southeastern Col Art Asn; Nat Coun Art Adminrs; Nat Asn Sch Art (exec bd mem, 70-73); Union of Independent Cols of Art (mem exec bd). Style & Technique: Abstract painting. Media: Acrylic, Watercolor. Mailing Add: 3229 Wendwood Dr Marietta GA 30062

VORHEES, D LAWREY
PAINTER, INSTRUCTOR
b Cleveland, Ohio, Sept 12, 15. Study: Ohio Univ, AB; Columbia Univ; also with Chas Martin & Chas Burchfield & study in workshops in London, Eng. Comn: Pen & wash paintings of homes, business houses & others on a regular basis in London. Exhib: Royal Soc Marine Artists, 6 yrs; Artists of Chelsea, 6 yrs; Royal Soc Brit Artists, 6 yrs; Royal Inst Watercolor Painters, 6 yrs; one-man show, London, 75. Teaching: Art supvr, Pub Sch, Eaton, Ohio, 37-41 & Normandy, Mo, 41-43; art dir, Kirkwood High Sch, Mo, 46-53. Mem: NMex Watercolor Soc. Style & Technique: Bold, dramatic designed interpretation; pen and washes. Media: Watercolor. Mailing Add: 1709 Pedregoso Pl Albuquerque NM 87123

VORIS, ANNA MAYBELLE
CURATOR
b Mt Rainier, Md, Aug 5, 20. Study: George Washington Univ, BA; Cath Univ Am, MA; Johns Hopkins Univ. Pos: Cur Spanish painting, Nat Gallery Art, Washington, DC. Mailing Add: 4801 Kenmore Ave Alexandria VA 22304

VORWERK, E CHARLSIE
PAINTER, ILLUSTRATOR
b Tennga, Ga, Jan 28, 34. Study: Ga State Col Women, AB; com art study, 2 yrs. Work: Mamie Padgett Collection, Ga Col. Comn: Bicentennial mural, Fine Arts Coun, Summerville, SC, 75; designs for altar kneelers, St Paul's Episcopal Church, 75; official city flag, City Coun & YWCO, Summerville, 75; plus other individuals & companies. Exhib: 23rd SC Artists Exhib, Charleston, 68; Ann Exhib Miniature Painters, Sculptors & Gravers Soc, Washington, DC, 70-75; Miniature Art Soc NJ, Paramus, 71-75; 23rd & 24th Gran Prix Int Peiture de Deauville, France, 72 & 73; 9th & 10th Gran Prix Peinture de la Cote D'Azur, Cannes, France, 73 & 74. Teaching: Pvt group art classes for children & adults. Pos: Billboard designer, Vanesco Poster, Chattanooga, Tenn; fashion illustrator, Lovemans; cartographic draftsman, Tenn Valley Authority; free lance com artist. Awards: Honorable Selection & Traveling Exhib, Gran Int Deauville, 72 & Finalist & Traveling Exhib, 73; ribbons in minor local and state exhibs. Bibliog: Rev in La Rev Mod, Paris, France, 71, 73 & 74, Il Giornale D'Italia & Iltempo, 73; John Biola (auth), SC art happenings, Sunshine Artists, 75. Mem: League Charleston Artists (secy, 75, 76 & 77); Summerville Artist Guild (exhib chmn); Charleston Artists Guild (exhib comt, 73); Guild SC Artists; Miniature Art Soc NJ; Am Art Soc (contribr artist). Style & Technique: Interpretive realism in all medias; direct pigment; no mixing except on canvas. Media: Acrylic, Watercolor; Pen & Ink, Pastel. Publ: Contribr, Methodist Cookbook SC Low Country, 73; contribr & coordr, YWCA Calendar, 75; illusr, low country tourists brochures, for various orgns & Episcopal church periodicals and brochures; illusr, Tales and Taradiddles, 76 & Epitaphs of St Paul's Cemetary 1858-1978, 77. Dealer: Chester Smith Seaside Art Gallery PO Box 1 Nags Head NC 27959. Mailing Add: 315 W Carolina Ave Summerville SC 29483

VOSE, ROBERT CHURCHILL, JR
ART DEALER
b Boston, Mass, Mar 30, 11. Study: Harvard. Pos: Treas, Vose Galleries of Boston, 53-76, pres, 76- Bibliog: J Post (auth), The Old Family Business, Yankee Mag, 73. Mem: Copley Soc, Boston (mem bd, 50-60). Res: Alvan Fisher, 1792-1863; Ralph Blakelock, 1847-1919. Specialty: Eighteenth, nineteenth and early twentieth century American paintings; to a lesser degree, eighteenth and nineteenth century English and nineteenth century French paintings. Publ: Auth, Alvan Fisher, American Pioneer in Landscape and Genre, Conn Hist Soc, 62. Mailing Add: Vose Galleries of Boston Inc 238 Newbury St Boston MA 02116

VOTH, ANDREW CHARLES
ART ADMINISTRATOR, PAINTER
b Akron, Ohio, Aug 4, 47. Study: Cuyahoga Valley Art Ctr; Akron Art Inst; Madison Sch of Art, Conn; Ambassador Col, BA; also with Jack Richard & Robert Brackman. Comn: Designed four specialty restaurants on Queen Mary, Long Beach, 74; four paintings for Pasadena Off, Bateman, Eichler, Hill, Richard Inc, Los Angeles, 74; portrait, Metcalf Galleries, South Pasadena, Calif, 76; custom paintings & bookplates, comn by Warren Mason, La Jolla, Calif, 76-77. Exhib: One-man shows, Ambassador Col, Pasadena, 70 & 74 & Longpre Gallery, La Canada, 75; Huntington-Sheraton Gallery, Pasadena 74; Holiday Inn, Pasadena, 76-77; Pasadena Festival of the Arts, 76 & 77. Teaching: Chmn art dept, Imperial High Sch, Pasadena, 70-73; lectr art, Ambassador Col, 73-76. Pos: Dir publ, Ambassador Col, 73-75, dir art, 75-76, art dept chmn & dir galleries, 77-; chmn art show, Pasadena Festival of the Arts, 76-77. Awards: Second Place, Oil, San Gabriel Art Asn, 75. Mem: San Gabriel Fine Arts Asn; Am Inst of Arts in Europe (bd mem, 77); Pasadena Arts Coun. Style & Technique: Traditional; landscape, still life, portraits. Media: Oil, Watercolor. Publ: Illusr, W Dankenbrig, auth, Creation, Triumph, 75; co-auth, A Guide to Oil Painting, Ambassador Int Cult Found, 77. Mailing Add: 625 Linda Vista Ave Pasadena CA 91105

VOULKOS, PETER
SCULPTOR, EDUCATOR
b Bozeman, Mont, Jan 29, 24. Study: Mont State Univ, BS, hon LHD, 68, Calif Col Arts & Crafts, MFA. Work: Baltimore Mus Art, Md; Denver Art Mus; Smithsonian Inst, Washington, DC; Japanese Craft Mus; San Francisco Mus Art; plus many others. Exhib: Brussels World's Fair, 58; Seattle World's Fair, 62; Int Sculpture Exhib, Battersea Park, London, 63; Los Angeles State Col, 64; Univ Calif, Irving, 66; Whitney Mus Am Art, 70; one-man shows, San Francisco Mus Art, 72, Kansas City Art Inst, 75 & Detroit Inst Art, 76; plus many others. Teaching: Instr, Archie Bray Found, Black Mountain Col, Los Angeles Co Art Inst, Mont State Univ, Greenwich House Potter & Teachers Col, Columbia Univ; prof art & design, Univ Calif, Berkeley, 59- Awards: Silver Medal, Int Ceramic Exhib, Ostend, Belg, 54; Gold Medal, Int Ceramic Exhib, Cannes, France; Rodin Mus Prize in Sculpture, I Paris Biennial, 59; plus many others. Bibliog: Lee Nordness (auth), Objects: USA, London, 70; M Leopold (auth), Los Angeles letter, Art Int, summer 73. Mailing Add: 1306 Third St Berkeley CA 94710

VOYER, SYLVAIN JACQUES
PAINTER
b Edmonton, Alta, Jan 22, 39. Study: Alta Col Art, Calgary, with Deli Sacilotto. Work: Nat Gallery Can, Ottawa; Edmonton Art Gallery; Willistead Art Gallery, Windsor, Ont; Univ Calgary. Exhib: 6th Biennial Can Painting, Nat Gallery Can, 65 & Can Watercolors, Prints & Drawings, 66; Edmonton Art Gallery, 71. Pos: Mem bd, Edmonton Art Gallery, 72- Mem: Can Artist Representation (rep, 71 & 72). Media: Acrylic. Mailing Add: 10024 102nd St Edmonton AB T5J 0V6 Can

VRANA, ALBERT S
SCULPTOR
b Cliffside Park, NJ, Jan 25, 21. Study: Univ Miami. Work: Captive (cast bronze), Atlanta Mem Art Ctr, Ga; War Flower (bronze), Lowe Art Gallery, Univ Miami, Fla; Fuego (wood), Univ Miami. Comn: Sand cast stone relief for Miami Beach Pub Libr Rotunda, City Miami Beach, Fla, 62; cast stone relief from styrofoam molds, US Govt for Fed Off Bldg, Jacksonville, Fla, 66; cast stone relief from styrofoam molds, Morris Burk, Prof Arts Ctr, Miami, 66; free-standing monument (ferro cement & bronze), Allen House, Miami Beach, 69; monumental mural (ferro cement & hammered bronze), State of Fla for Fla Int Univ, Miami, 72. Exhib: One-man shows, Lowe Art Gallery, Univ Miami, 60 & 63, Fairleigh Dickinson Univ Art Gallery, Madison, NJ, 64, ACA Galleries, New York, 66 & Berenson Gallery, Miami, 68, 69 & 72; Long Boat Key Art Ctr, Fla, 73. Teaching: Instr sculpture, Miami-Dade Jr Col, 66-67; instr sculpture, Penland Sch, summers 68- Awards: Tiffany Grant, 63. Bibliog: Art Mandler (auth), Artist in Concrete (film), produced by Portland Cement Asn, 66; Le beton sculpte par moulage, Batir Mag, Paris, 67; Harry Forgeron (auth), Sculptured structures molded in plastic foam, New York Times, 67. Mem: Sculptors of Fla (vpres, 65). Style & Technique: Hugh sheets of plastic foam laminated and carved to form molds in which are cast concrete walls and columns which are integral parts of the architecture. Media: Bronze, Architectural Concrete. Publ: Contribr, Sculpture from Plastics, 67; contribr, Spiel mit Form und Struktur, 68; contribr, Contemporary Art with Wood, 68; contribr, Plastics as an Art Form, 69; contribr, Contemporary Stone Sculpture, 70. Dealer: Harmon Gallery 1258 Third St S Naples FL 33940; IFA Galleries Inc 2623 Connecticut Ave Washington DC 20008. Mailing Add: Rte 3 Box 330 C F Bakersville NC 28705

VYTLACIL, VACLAV
PAINTER, EDUCATOR
b New York, NY, Nov 1, 92. Study: Art Inst Chicago; Art Students League; Bavarian Royal Acad Art, Munich, Ger; Hans Hofmann Sch Art, Munich. Work: Whitney Mus Am Art, New York; Metrop Mus Art, New York; Pa Acad Fine Arts, Philadelphia; Duncan Philips Mus Art, Washington, DC; Rochester Mus Art, NY. Exhib: Whitney Mus Am Art, New York, 40-62; Carnegie Inst Int, Pittsburgh, 42, 44 & 45; Artists for Victory, Metrop Mus Art, New York, 44; Pa Acad Fine Arts, Philadelphia, 52; Duncan Philips Mus Art, Washington, DC, 55; Southern Vt Art Ctr, Manchester & Univ Notre Dame, 75; Retrospective, Montclair Art Mus, NJ, 75; plus many others. Teaching: Instr art, Minneapolis Sch Art, 17-21; lectr mod art & artist in residence, Univ Calif, Berkeley, 28-29; instr art, Calif Col Arts & Crafts, summers 36 & 37; lectr hist art & chmn dept art, Queen's Col, 42-45; instr art, Colorado Springs Fine Art Ctr, 51-53; instr art, Univ Ga, 68; instr painting & lectr hist mod art, Art Students League. Pos: Jury mem, Pepsi-Cola Nat Art Competition, 48; regional jury mem, Nat Exhib Art, Metrop Mus Art, New York, 50. Awards: Hon Mention, Soc Am Artists, Art Inst Chicago, 14, William M R French Gold Medal, 36. Mem: Fedn Mod Painters & Sculptors; Am Abstract Artists; Art Students League. Media: Oil, Acrylic, Tempera. Mailing Add: Old Kings Hwy Sparkill NY 10976

W

WAANO-GANO, JOE
PAINTER, LECTURER
b Salt Lake City, Utah, Mar 3, 06. Study: T N Lukits Acad Art; Hanson Puthuff Art Sch; Univ Southern Calif; also with Dean Cornwell. Work: Southwest Mus, Los Angeles; Gardena High Sch, Calif; Hist & Art Mus, Los Angeles; Cedar City High Sch, Utah; Bur Indian Affairs, Washington, DC. Comn: Sioux Ghost Dance Chant (mural), Ticket Off, Rapid City, SDak, 30 & Sacred Deerskin Dance (mural), Ticket Off, San Francisco, 44, Western Air Lines; mural for children's ward, Los Angeles Gen Hosp, 30; Theme (mural) & Education (mural), Sherman Indian Inst, Arlington, Calif, 34. Exhib: Am Artists Prof League, New York, 40-; Nat Ann Indian Art Exhib, Indian Ctr, Los Angeles, 55-69; Am Indian Artists Nat Exhib, Philbrook Mus, Tulsa, Okla, 57-; Nat Am Indian Exhib, Scottsdale, Ariz, 60-; Ctr Arts Indian Am, Washington, DC, 64-68. Pos: Bd dirs, Painters & Sculptors, Los Angeles, 50-64, pres, 62-63. Awards: Award for Moonlight Madonna, Int Madonna Festival, 52; Award for Flight of the Great Head, Tulsa Indian Women's Club, 63; Award for Chief Strong Bear, Greek Theatre, 65. Bibliog: Ada Wallis (auth), Cherokee Indian, gifted artist, Widening Horizons, 60; Jeanne Snodgrass (auth), Joe Waano Gano, Am Indian Painters, 68; Marion Gridley (auth), Joe Waano Gano, Indians of Today, 71. Mem: Valley Artists Guild (pres, 51-52); Artists of the Southwest (bd dirs, 51-); fel Am Artists Prof League; fel Am Inst Fine Art; life mem Traditional Art Guild of Paramount. Style & Technique: From Amerindian picto-graphic line and flat treatment to 3-D broken color via palatte knife. Media: Oil, Watercolor, Acrylic. Publ: Auth & illusr, Art of the American Indian, Western Art Rev, 51. Mailing Add: 8926 Holly Pl Los Angeles CA 90046

WACHSTETER, GEORGE
ILLUSTRATOR
b Hartford, Conn, Mar 12, 11. Work: New York Pub Libr Theatre Collection; US Steel Collection; NBC Collection; plus works in pvt collections. Exhib: One-man traveling exhib for NBC Book of Stars, 58. Pos: Illusr for major advert agencies, theatrical & motion picture productions, 36-; illusr for CBS, ABC, NBC radio & TV networks, 37-; weekly contribr illus & caricature to drama pages, New York Herald Tribune, 41-50; contribr illus & caricature drama & political pages, New York Times, 38-50, TV artist, 50-51; caricaturist for Theatre Guild on the Air, produced by US Steel, 45-63; drama artist, New York J-Am, 56-63, TV mag cover artist, 58-63; drama artist, New York World Tel, 64-66; syndicated feature illusr for Hallmark TV Drama Series, 64-69. Style & Technique: In illustration-realism, rendered in free pen line; in caricature-stylized approach rendered in precise line. Media: Ink, Watercolor. Publ: Illusr, NBC Book of Stars, Simon & Schuster, 57. Mailing Add: 85-05 Elmhurst Ave Elmhurst NY 11373

WADDELL, EUGENE
PAINTER, COLLECTOR
b Charlottesville, Va, Oct 7, 25. Study: Duquesne Univ; Univ Pittsburgh, BS; Carnegie Inst Technol, murals with Claude Hurd; Cooper Union; NY Univ; also with A Raymond Katz, Buell Mullen, Ludwig Deschenek & others. Work: NY Tel Bldg, White Plains; IBM, Armonk, NY & Stamford; Dexter Corp, Windsor Locks, Conn; Lathrop Mem Gallery, Pawling, NY; Am Can Co, Greenwich, Conn; plus others. Comn: City scene murals, Ayer/Jorgenson/MacDonald, Los Angeles, 67; typography mural, Matrotype Co, Ltd, Eng, 68; still life mural, Bass & Ullman, New York, 69; Exuberance (mural), Wheelabrater-Frye, New York, 70; abstract murals, Humbert & Jones, New York, 71. Exhib: Berkshire Mus, Pittsfield, Mass, 66; Mayan II Gallery, Watch Hill, RI, 69; Nationwide Art Gallery, Fairfield, Conn, 70; Automation House Gallery, New York, 74; Mus Mod Art, New York; plus many others. Teaching: Instr art, Stormville Art Sch, 50-52; instr new methods of painting, River House, Pawling, NY & Dover Jr High Sch, 71; guest instr art, Holiday Hills, Pawling, 73 & 74; creator & instr application of chem & nitre-acryloid-polyester in painting. Pos: Pres, Pyap Int Ltd, 68- Awards: Award for Divine Comedy, Nat Gallery, 68; Award for Carnival, Mountain View Gallery Exhib, sponsored by President Nixon, Princess Grace & Dr Jonas Salk, Scranton, Pa, 72; First Prize for Seascape, Art League Hudson Valley, 73. Bibliog: Many articles in mags & newspapers in US & Europe. Mem: Life fel Royal Soc Art, London, Eng; Archit League New York; Nat Coun Arts & Govt; Inst Contemp Arts, London; Allied Artists Am; plus many others. Style & Technique: 42 different techniques, using chemicals and industrial custom-made paints. Media: Industrial Paints. Collection: Sculpture and paintings. Mailing Add: Pawling NY 12564

WADDELL, JOHN HENRY
SCULPTOR
b Des Moines, Iowa, Feb 14, 21. Study: Art Inst Chicago, BFA, MFA, BAE & MAE. Work: Phoenix Art Mus, Ariz; Univ Ariz, Tucson; Ariz State Univ, Tempe; Kenyon Col; Valley Nat Bank, Ariz. Comn: Dance Mother, Phoenix Art Mus, 59-62; That Which Might Have Been, Unitarian Church, Phoenix, 63-64; The Family, Maricopa Co Complex, 65-67; Dance, Phoenix Civic Ctr, 70-74. Exhib: One-man shows, La Jolla Mus, 62, Phoenix Art Mus, 60, 63 & 64 & Hellenic Am Union, Athens, Greece, 66; touring one-man show, Ariz, 69. Teaching: Asst prof art, Inst Design, Chicago, 55-57; prof art, Ariz State Univ, 57-61 & 64; Master Apprentice Prog, 72- Awards: Ariz Comn Art & Humanities Grant, 70-74; Nat Found Art & Humanities Grant, 71-72; Man of the Yr, Valley of the Sun Chap, Nat Soc Arts & Lett, 75. Bibliog: Harry Wood (auth), Soul, 67; Man of Bronze (film), 75. Media: Bronze. Mailing Add: Star Rte 252A Cottonwood AZ 86326

WADDINGHAM, JOHN ALFRED
ARTIST-ILLUSTRATOR
b London, Eng, July 9, 15; US citizen. Study: Coronado Sch Fine Arts, Calif, 53-54; Portland Art Mus, 40-45; Univ Portland, 46-47; also with Rex Brandt, Eliot O'Hara & George Post. Work: Portland Art Mus; Bush House, Salem, Ore; Univ Ore Mus; Vincent Price Collection; Ford Times Collection. Comn: Mural Genesis, St Barnabas Episcopal Church, Portland, 60. Teaching: Teacher watercolor, Ore Soc Artists, 54-56. Pos: Promotion art dir, Ore J, Portland, 46-59; mem staff, Oregonian, Portland, 59, ed art dir, 59-; proprietor, John Waddingham Hand Prints, 65- Awards: Gold Medal, Italy, 76; Award for Newspaper Illus, 76. Bibliog: Featured artist, Am Artist, 5/67. Mem: Portland Art Mus; Portland Art Dirs Club (past pres). Style & Technique: Drawings of old Portland landmarks and houses; watercolor landscape. Mailing Add: 955 SW Westwood Dr Portland OR 97201

WADE, JANE
ART DEALER
b Dallas, Tex, June 30, 25. Study: Univ Ariz; in Europe; Curt Valentin Gallery, New York; Otto Gerson Gallery, New York. Collections Arranged: Drawings by Sculptors, Smithsonian Inst & US Tour. Pos: Secy & asst, Curt Valentin Gallery, 48-56; secy & assoc, Otto Gerson Gallery, 56-63; vpres, Marlborough-Gerson Gallery, 63-64; juror, Mid-West Ann, William

Rockhill Nelson Gallery Art, Kansas City, Mo; owner & dir, Jane Wade Ltd. Bibliog: Jay Jacobs (auth), By appointment only, Art in Am, 7-8/67; By appointment only, Newsweek, 9/4/67; By appointment only, Time, 8/3/70. Mem: Art Dealers Asn Am. Specialty: Twentieth century painting and sculpture. Mailing Add: 45 E 66th St New York NY 10021

WADE, ROBERT SCHROPE
PHOTOGRAPHER, SCULPTOR
b Austin, Tex, Jan 6, 43. Study: Univ Tex, Austin, BFA, 65; Univ Calif, Berkeley, MA, 66. Work: Okla Art Ctr, Oklahoma City; Witte Mus, San Antonio, Tex; Mountainview Col, Dallas; Chicago Telephone Co; Chase Manhattan Bank, New York. Comn: Map of the United States (300 ft-outdoor), for Bicentennial '76, Northwood Contemp Coun & Nat Endowment, near Dallas. Exhib: Whitney Contemp Ann, Whitney Mus Am Art, New York, 69 & 73; one-man shows, Kornblee Gallery, New York, 71, 74 & 76 & Smither-Delahunty Gallery, Dallas, 72 & 75; Contemp Arts Mus, Houston, 75; 112 Greene St, New York, 75. Teaching: Instr, McLennan Col, 66-70; artist in residence, Northwood Inst, 70-72, dir, Northwood Exp Art Inst, Dallas, 72-77; asst prof, NTex State Univ, Denton, 73- Pos: Mem, Tex Comn Arts & Humanities, 75- Awards: Nat Endowment Grants, 73 & 74. Bibliog: Robert Pincus-Witten (auth), New York, Artforum, 12/71; Jozanne Rabyor (auth), Robert Wade at Delahunty, Art in Am, 5/75; Janet Kutner (auth), Dallas, Art News, 6/75. Style & Technique: Hand tinted photo sensitized canvas and photomurals, also environmental installations. Dealer: Kornblee Gallery 20 W 57th St New York NY 10019. Mailing Add: c/o Delahunty Gallery 2611 Cedar Springs Dallas TX 75201

WAGNER, CHARLES H
ART ADMINISTRATOR, INSTRUCTOR
b Baltimore, Md. Study: Md Inst Col Art, BFA; Johns Hopkins Univ; Yale Univ, MFA. Work: Md Inst Col Art; Western Md Col, Westminster. Exhib: Print Exhib, Yale Univ, 61; one-man show, Towson State Col, 73; Baltimore Watercolor Club, Md, 73-75; Western Md Col, 75. Teaching: Dept chmn sec art, Baltimore Co Pub Schs, Md, 55-70; instr drawing & painting, Md Inst Col Art, Baltimore, 50-; instr design, Towson State Col, Md, 72-73. Pos: Dir, Md Inst, Towson Sch, Md, 60-; supvr art instr, Howard Co Pub Sch, Columbia, Md, 70- Awards: Bronze Medal (figure painting), Md Inst, 55; First Prize (design), Nat Educ Asn, 65; John Hay Fel, Yale Univ, 60-61. Mem: Nat Art Educ Asn; Md Art Asn; Baltimore Watercolor Club. Publ: Illusr, Baltimore County Serves the Nation, 59; contribr, art curriculum guides, 60-75; auth, Classroom Discipline, 60; auth, Team Teaching in Art, 74. Mailing Add: Regwood Rd Hydes MD 21082

WAGNER, G NOBLE
PAINTER, SCULPTOR
b Pa, Nov 20, 07. Study: Temple Univ Tyler Sch Art, BFA, MFA, 59. Work: Philadelphia Art Mus; Albright-Knox Art Gallery, Buffalo, NY; Chemical Bank, NY; Monsanto Chem Corp, NY; First Pa Bank, Philadelphia. Exhib: Philadelphia Print Club, 69; Nat Print & Watercolor Exhib, Pa Acad Fine Arts, 69; New York State Fair, Syracuse, 69; Cheltenham Art Centre Ann Regional Sculpture Exhib, Philadelphia Civic Ctr, 71-78; Philadelphia Art Mus, 72; Fairmount Park, Azelea Garden, 75; Temple Music Festival, Ambler, Pa, 75; one-man exhibs, Philadelphia Art Alliance, 69, Franklin & Marshall Col, Lancaster, Pa, 69, Cheltenham Art Centre, Pa, 69, Lehigh Univ, Pa, 72, Hartley Gallery, New York, NY, 73 & Marian Locks Gallery, Philadelphia, Pa, 71-78. Teaching: Instr art & philos, 51-56; instr art, Oak Lane Co Day Sch, Temple Univ, 59-60, instr art educ, Univ, 60-65, instr art educ, Elem Educ Teachers for State Cert, 62-63; instr philos art educ, Cheltenham Twp Art Centre, 61-, instr painting & sculpture, 62- Pos: Co-founder & dir educ, Cheltenham Sch Fine Arts, Cheltenham Twp Art Centre, 40-, pres, 41-42, chmn bd gov, 42-43, established Aegean Sch Fine Arts, Greece; mem coun, Exp Art & Technol, 67; mem coun, Pa Art Educ Asn, 69; dir art tours abroad, 63 & 66. Awards: Tyler Alumni Award, Temple Univ, 68 & 70; First Addie Rubin Mem Award, 22nd Ann Award Exhib, 69 & Print Exhib Award, 71, Cheltenham Art Centre. Mem: Pa Acad Fine Arts; Philadelphia Print Club; Mus Mod Art, New York; Philadelphia Mus Art; Philadelphia Art Alliance. Style & Technique: Painting and sculpture of polished aluminum or stainless steel, some enameled; post-minimal, hard-edge, strong, direct, often archetypical. Res: The nature of a meaningful art education course for elementary education student teachers. Mailing Add: 7955 Waltham Rd Cheltenham PA 19012

WAGNER, GORDON PARSONS
ASSEMBLAGE ARTIST, SMALL ENVIRONMENTAL ARTIST
b Redondo Beach, Calif, Apr 13, 15. Study: Univ Calif, Los Angeles; Chouinard Art Inst, Los Angeles. Work: Denver Mus Art; Ahmanson Collection, Los Angeles; Metro Media, New York; Standard Oil Co Chicago; Sodertalje Konsthall, Stockholm, Sweden. Exhib: Corcoran Gallery Biennial, Washington, DC, 57-61; 66 Signs in Neon, Mus Mod Art, Washington, DC, 66; Los Angeles Sculpture, Munic Art Gallery, 65; Three American Artists, Am Embassy, London, Eng, 72; Small Environments, Univ Southern Ill, Carbondale, 72; Trio, Los Angeles Munic Art Mus, Calif, 72; Ironic Reality, San Jose Mus, Calif, 74; Assemblage, Los Angeles Inst of Contemp Art, Calif, 75; Sculptors of NMex, Mus of NMex, Sante Fe, 76; Beyond the Garden Wall, Downey Mus, Calif, 77; Architektenhuis, Gent, Belg, 78; plus many others. Awards: Purchase Award for Night Scene Amusement Pier, Ahmanson Collection, 56; Purchase Award for Sky Festival, Denver Mus Art, 59; Award, Nat Watercolor Soc, 67. Bibliog: Virginia Copeland (auth), Objects trouve, Southwest Art Mag, 3/73; Jan de Breucker (auth), Magic surrealism, Spectator Mag, Brussels, 74; Michael Leopold (auth), Art of the 70's, Art Int Mag, summer 74; plus others. Mem: Nat Watercolor Soc; Los Angeles Inst Contemp Art. Style & Technique: Combination of painting and sculpture in a surreal style, in boxes or small environments. Dealer: Vorpal Gallery Soho 465 W Broadway New York NY 10012; Gallery of Contemp Art One LeDoux St Taos NM 87571. Mailing Add: 2305 Effie St Los Angeles CA 90026

WAGNER, JOHN PHILIP
PAINTER
b Philadelphia, Pa, July 29, 43. Study: Philadelphia Col Art, BFA; Md Inst Col Art, MFA; spec study with David Hare & Dennis Leon. Comn: Poly-chrome sculpture, Baltimore Parks Comn, Md, 65. Exhib: Baltimore Mus Art Regional Show, 65; Soc Illusrs Show, New York, 69; Southwest Fine Arts Biennial, Santa Fe, NMex, 70; Artists of Santa Fe, 77. Teaching: Instr drawing, Md Inst Col Art, summer 68. Pos: Nat Endowment Arts NMex State artist in residence, 70-71. Awards: Rinehart Sch Sculpture Fel, 65. Publ: Illusr, Grove Press & Evergreen Rev, 68-69; illusr, Avante Garde Mag, 69; illusr, NMex Mag, 69; illusr, children bks for Macmillan & Crowell Collier, 69-70; contribr, Western Rev, 72. Mailing Add: c/o Jamisons Galleries 111 E San Francisco St Santa Fe NM 87501

WAGNER, MERRILL
PAINTER
b Seattle, Wash, June 12, 35. Study: Sarah Lawrence Col, BA, 57; Art Students League, New York, 59-63, study with Edwin Dickenson, George Grosz & Julian Levy. Comn: Permanent Installation, Project Studio One Inst for Art & Urban Resources, 78. Exhib: 26 Contemporary Women Artists, Aldrich Mus, Ridgefield, Conn, 71; Christmas Show, Art Lending Service, Penthouse, Mus of Mod Art, 71; Grids, Inst of Contemporary Art, Philadelphia, Pa, 72; 55 Mercer, traveling show, The Gallery Asn of New York, 74; Outside the City Limits: Landscape by New York, 77; Post Minimal Artists, 78 Nobe Gallery, New York, 78; many one-person shows, Mercer St Gallery, 70, 71, 74, 76 & 77, Truman Gallery, 77 & Julian Pretto, 78, New York. Bibliog: Robert Pincus-Witten, Artforum, 2/72, Ellen Lubell, Arts Mag, 6/76 & Tiffany Bell, Arts Mag, 2/78, all reviews of one-person shows. Mem: Am Abstract Artists. Style & Technique: Oil paintings and drawings made with tape. Media: Oil Paint; Pastel or Crayon with Tape. Dealer: Julian Pretto 176 Franklin St New York NY 10013; Truman Gallery 38 E 57th St New York NY 10022. Mailing Add: 17 W 16 New York NY 10011

WAGNER, RICHARD ELLIS
PAINTER
b Trotwood, Ohio, June 18, 23. Study: Antioch Col; Dayton Art Inst, Ohio; Univ Colo, BFA & MFA. Work: Denver Art Mus, Colo; Libr of Cong, Washington, DC; Dartmouth Col, Hanover, NH; De Cordova Mus, Lincoln, Mass; Rochester Mus, NY. Comn: Murals, Horizon House, Naples, Fla, 71. Exhib: Recent Drawings USA, Mus Mod Art, New York, 56; Art USA, Madison Sq Garden, 58; Boston Arts Festival, Mass, 58, 60 & 62; Jefferson Arts Festival, New Orleans, 69; Youngstown Art Festival, Butler Inst Am Art, 70; plus over 40 one-man shows, 53- Teaching: Assoc prof art, Dartmouth Col, 53-66. Awards: Purchase Prizes, Denver Art Mus, 50 & Libr of Cong, 52; City of Manchester Award, Currier Gallery, Manchester, NH, 56. Style & Technique: Realistic, strong light and atmosphere to create mood. Media: Acrylic, Oil. Publ: Illusr, Ford Times, 58-70. Dealer: Grand Cent Art Galleries 40 Vanderbilt Ave New York NY 10017. Mailing Add: 249 Commerce St Naples FL 33940

WAGONER, ROBERT B
PAINTER, SCULPTOR
b Marion, Ohio, July 13, 28. Study: With Burt Procter & Olaf Weighorst. Work: Leanin' Tree Publ Mus, Boulder, Colo; Winthrop Rockefeller Collection. Exhib: Death Valley 49ers, Calif, 61; two-man shows, Scottsdale, Ariz, 72 & 73 & three-man show, 74; Mont Hist Soc, Helena, 74; Preview 76, Texas Gallery, Dallas, 75. Pos: Dir, Death Valley 49ers, 69- Awards: First Award & Top Artists Award, Death Valley 49ers, 72 & 73 & First Award, 74, 75 & 76. Bibliog: Ed Ainsworth (auth), Cowboy in Art, World Publ Co, 68; James Serven (auth), Cattle, guns and cowboys, Ariz Hwys Mag, 70; Robert Wolenik (auth), Colorful west of Robert Wagoner, Westerner, 1-2/73. Style & Technique: Traditional, western-type subjects. Media: Oil, Watercolor; Canvas, Masonite. Dealer: Trailside Galleries Scottsdale AZ 85251; Tex Art Gallery 1400 Main St Dallas TX 75202. Mailing Add: 2710 Highland Dr Bishop CA 93514

WAHLING, B JON
SCULPTOR, WEAVER
b Council Bluffs, Iowa, Apr 14, 38. Study: Kansas City Art Inst & Sch Design, BFA, 62; Haystack Mountain Sch Crafts, Deer Isle, Maine, summers 63-65; Cranbrook Acad Art, MFA, 64; also with Maija Grotell & Glen Kauffman. Work: Columbus Gallery Fine Arts, Ohio; Massillon Mus, Ohio; Yager Gallery, Hartwick College; Univ Art Mus, Univ Tex, Austin. Comn: Fibre sculpture hangings, comn by James Beam, Architect for Scioto Country Club, Columbus, 65. Exhib: Sculpture in Fibre, Mus Contemp Craft, New York, 72; Fibre Structure, Denver Art Mus, 72; 7th Beaux Arts Designer/Cr aftsmen Regional, Columbus Gallery Fine Arts, 73; Con texture Nat Exhib, Ft Wayne Pub Libr Exhib, 74; Seven Weavers, Univ Art Mus, Univ Tex, Austin, 74; Fibre Structures, Heinz Gallery of the Mus of Art, Carnegie Inst Int, Pittsburgh, Pa, 76; two-man show, Packard Gallery, Columbus Gallery of Fine Arts, Ohio, 77. Teaching: Instr weaving, Arts & Crafts Ctr, Columbus Recreation & Parks Dept, Ohio, 64-; instr weaving, Penland Sch Crafts, NC, summers 66, 67 & 71. Awards: Craftsmen USA Nat Merit Award, Mus Contemp Crafts, New York, 66; Ten Outstanding Young Men Award, Columbus Jaycees, 72; Bordens Award for Outstanding Design in Fibre, 7th Beaux Arts Designer/Craftsmen Exhib, 73. Mem: Am Crafts Coun; Ohio Designer Craftsmen (trustee, 73-74); hon mem Cent Ohio Weavers Guild. Style & Technique: Fibre sculpture in woven and knotted technique. Media: Fibre, Metal. Dealer: Ed Miller Assoc 300 Scioto Urbana OH 43078. Mailing Add: 44 Stimmel St Columbus OH 43206

WAISLER, LEE
PAINTER, PRINTMAKER
b Los Angeles, Calif, Feb 25, 38. Study: Univ Southern Calif; Univ Calif, Los Angeles. Work: Bibliot Nat, Paris, France; Victoria & Albert Mus, London, Eng; Kunsthaus, Zurich, Switz; Jewish Mus, New York; Atkins Mus Fine Art, Kansas City, Mo. Style & Technique: Paintings are from expressive figurative to abstract figurative; graphics and color etchings employ varied combinations of intaglio and relief; multiple panel etchings. Media: Tempera, Acrylic & Aquatint. Dealer: Carl Schlosberg Fine Arts 4825 Havenhurst Ave Encino CA 91316. Mailing Add: 15456 Valley Vista Sherman Oaks CA 91403

WAITT, ALDEN HARRY
PAINTER, ART ADMINISTRATOR
b Orlando, Fla, Dec 22, 92. Study: Mass Inst Technol, BS, 14, MS, 27; Trinity Univ Tex, 55-57; Art Ctr San Antonio, with Cecil Casebier, 56-57; San Antonio Art Inst, 57-, with Stamos, Yunkers, Oliveria, Lanyon & Twitty. Work: Lang Collection, Marion Koogler McNay Art Mus, San Antonio; Univ Tex Health Sci Ctr, San Antonio; US Auto Asn Hq, San Antonio; Nat Bank of Ft Sam Houston, San Antonio; Palacio de Bellas Artes, Int Gallery, Mexico City. Exhib: SW Tex State Univ, San Marcos, 62; State Mus Monterey, Mex, 63; Int Salon Art by Chemists Chicago, 65 & 67; one-man shows, Laguna Gloria Art Mus, Austin, Tex, 60s, Beaumont Art Mus, Tex, 62, McNay Art Mus, 67 & Univ Tex Health Sci Ctr, 70 & 73; retrospective, San Antonio Art Inst, 77. Pos: Chmn & pres, San Antonio Art Inst, 59-77, exec dir, 64-76; trustee & bd mem, McNay Art Mus & Inst, 66- Awards: Best Landscape, River Art Group, 5 yrs in succession; Purchase Prizes, San Antonio Local Artists, Frost Bros & Tex Fine Arts Asn. Mem: River Art Group (pres, 57-58); Tex Fine Arts Asn (exec bd trustee, 59-62); Contemp Artists Group, San Antonio. Style & Technique: Contemporary realist; landscapes of Tex, New Eng & Portugal. Media: Oil, Lithography. Dealer: Schoener Galleries 10710 Mt Tipton San Antonio TX 78213. Mailing Add: 211 Brightwood Pl San Antonio TX 78209

WAITZKIN, STELLA
SCULPTOR, PAINTER
b New York, NY. Study: Alfred Univ; NY Univ; Columbia Univ; also with Meyer Shapiro & Hans Hofmann. Work: Richmond Mus Fine Arts, Va; Newark Mus, NJ; Butler Mus Am Art, Ohio; Calhoun Col, Yale Univ; Wis Univ Ctr for 20th Century Studies. Exhib: Destruction Show, Finch Col Mus, 68 & Recent Acquisitions, 74; one-woman show, Serious Literature, Calhoun Col, Yale Univ, 74; Potsdam Plastics, NY Univ, 75; Contemp Am Sculpture, Va Mus Downtown Gallery, 75; James Yu Exhib, 75; Renwick Gallery,

Smithsonian Inst, Washington, DC; Nat Collection Fine Arts, Washington, DC; plus others. Teaching: Guest lectr, Columbia Univ Grad Sch, 73. Awards: Yaddo Found Fels, 73 & 74; MacDowell Found Fels, 74 & 75; Louis Comfort Tiffany Grant, 77. Bibliog: Taylor Mead, Studio Art (film); D Holmes (auth), article in Arch Am Art, 71; articles in Arts Mag, 73 & 74. Style & Technique: Painting in three dimensional sculptured books; some transparent, others opaque. Media: Sandstone, Polyester Resin. Publ: Reproductions & articles in art publs; film work. Dealer: Fendrick Gallery 3059 M St NW Washington DC 20007; Peter David Gallery 430 Oak Grove Minneapolis MN 55403. Mailing Add: 222 W 23rd St New York NY 10011

WALBURG, GERALD
SCULPTOR, EDUCATOR
b Berkeley, Calif, May 5, 36. Study: Calif Col Arts & Crafts, 54-56; Calif State Univ, San Francisco, BA, 65; Univ Calif, Davis, MFA, 67. Work: Storm King Art Ctr, Mountainville, NY; San Francisco Mus Art, Calif; Oakland Mus; Stanford Mus, Stanford Univ; City of San Francisco. Exhib: One-person shows, San Francisco Mus Art, 67 & 69, Royal Marks Gallery, NY, 69, Crocker Art Gallery, Sacramento, 73, Artists Contemp Gallery, San Francisco, 73, Diablo Valley Col, Pleasant Hill, Calif, 75 & Charles Campbell Gallery, San Francisco, 76; Expo 70 Mus, Osaka, Japan, 70; Joslyn Art Mus, Omaha, Nebr, 70; Oakland Mus, Calif, 71 & 74; Storm King Art Ctr, Mountainville, NY, 73-74; Baltimore Mus Art, Md, 73; Soc of the Four Arts, Palm Beach, Fla, 74; New York Cult Ctr, 75; plus others. Teaching: Assoc prof art, Calif State Univ, Sacramento, 68- Bibliog: Kurt Von Meier (auth), Bay area, Arts Mag, 3/71; John Fitzgibbon (auth), Sacramento, Art in Am, 12/71. Mailing Add: 1734 34th St Sacramento CA 95816

WALCH, JOHN LEO
PAINTER, SCULPTOR
b Oklahoma City, Okla, Jan 14, 18. Study: Loyola Univ, Chicago, BA, 39; Sch of the Chicago Art Inst, 35-41; studied sculpture with Bernard Frazier, painting with Herny Hensche, Robert E Wood, Edgar Whitney, John Pike, Mel Crawford & Milford Zornes & graphic art with Emilio Amero. Work: Fogg Mus of Art, Cambridge, Mass; Philbrook Art Ctr, Tulsa, Okla; Okla Mus of Art, Oklahoma City; Mabee-Gerrer Mus, Shawnee, Okla; Kirkpatrick Found, Oklahoma City. Comn: Crucifix (large sculpture), Church of the Madeline, Tulsa, Okla, 49-50; four large sculptures, six paintings and liturgical design, Archdiocese of Oklahoma City, for Ctr for Christain Renewal, 58-59; paintings, Seminary of the Immaculate Conception, Huntington, NY, 64; Stations of the Cross, sculpture & liturgical design, Church of Christ The King, Oklahoma City, 64; two murals, Church of St James, Oklahoma City, 71 & 77. Exhib: Int Exposition of Mod Sacred Art, Vatican City, Rome, Italy (reproduction in catalog), 50; Eight-State Exhib, 58 & 72 & Nat Print & Drawing Exhib, 71, Okla Art Ctr, Oklahoma City; Contemp Christian Arts Gallery, New York, 61; Birger Sandzein Mus, Linsberg, Kans, 63; one-man shows, Okla Art Ctr, Oklahoma City, 50 & 63; Philbrook Art Ctr, Tulsa, Okla, 57 & Southern Plains Indian Mus, Anadarko, Okla, 62. Teaching: Vis instr figure drawing & painting, Briar Cliff Col, Sioux City, Iowa, 65-66; numerous workshops figure & portrait drawing, Okla Art Guild, Oklahoma City, 70- Pos: Nat pres, The Catholic Art Asn, 49-54; consult & design, St John Damascene, Studio of Liturgical Art, 58-; diocesan dir of art, Roman Catholic Diocese of Oklahoma City, 58-72; bd of dirs, Okla Art Guild, Oklahoma City, 65-; bd of trustees, Okla Mus of Art, 68- Awards: Third Prize, Nat Sacred Heart Contest, Xavier Univ & Apostleship of Prayer, 56; Second in Watercolor, Nat Art Ann, Gilcrease Mus, Tulsa, 58; Purchase Award, Okla Ann Exhib, Philbrook Art Ctr, Tulsa, 61. Bibliog: Ada King Wallace (auth), Widening Horizons, Okla ed Vol 15 No 4, Ada K Wallace, Los Angeles, Calif, 56; articles in Okla Today Mag, State of Oklahoma, 57- & Orbit Mag, Okla Publishing Co, Oklahoma City, 77; Margaret Harold (auth), Prize-Winning Graphics, Allied Publ Inc, Ft Lauderdale, Fla, 62. Mem: Okla Art Guild (bd of dir, 65-). Style & Technique: Realist. Media: Painting, Oil & Acrylic; Sculpture, Bronze & Hydracal. Collection: Religious Art and extensive and varied collection of oriental cloisonne. Publ: Contribr, Catholic Art Quarterly, Catholic Art Asn, 50-54; illusr, Roman Missal, Catholic Bk Publ Co, NY, 64; illusr, Catholic Art Calendar, Cathloic Church Extension Soc, Chicago, 67-71. Dealer: Karl Newman c/o St Thomas More Book Stall 1745 N W 16th St Oklahoma City OK 73106. Mailing Add: 317 N Blackwelder Oklahoma City OK 73106

WALD, SYLVIA
PAINTER, SCULPTOR
b Philadelphia, Pa. Study: Moore Inst Art, Philadelphia. Work: Mus Mod Art, Metrop Mus Art & Whitney Mus Am Art, New York; Guggenheim Mus; Nat Gallery Art, Washington, DC; Brooklyn Mus, NY; plus others. Exhib: One-woman show, Constructions & Collage, Benson Gallery, Bridgehampton, Long Island, NY, 77; Curator's Choice, Smithsonian Inst & Tour US, 54; 50 Yrs Am Art, Mus Mod Art & Tour Europe, 55; American Prints Today, 62; US Info Serv Show, Palacio Bellas Artes, Mex, 64; Women Choose Women, NY Cult Ctr, 73. Bibliog: Seiberling (auth), Looking into Art, Henry Holt, 59; The art of printmaking, In: Master Prints from Nineteenth & Twentieth Centuries, Libr of Cong & Univ Nebr Art Gallery, 66; Harvey Daniels (auth), Printmaking, 72; Zigrosser (auth), Prints and Their Creators—A World History, 74. Mem: Am Fedn Arts. Mailing Add: 37 E Fourth St New York NY 10003

WALDMAN, PAUL
PAINTER
b Erie, Pa, 1936. Study: Brooklyn Mus Art Sch; Pratt Inst. Work: Mus Mod Art, New York; Smithsonian Inst, Washington, DC; Brooklyn Mus, NY; Los Angeles Co Mus Mod Art, Los Angeles; Hirshhorn Mus, Washington, DC. plus many others. Exhib: Group Paintings & Prints, Sch Visual Arts, 68; 2nd Kent Invitational, Ohio, 68; Group Show From Collection, Newark Mus, 68; Dominant Female, Finch Col Mus Art, 68; Knoedler Gallery, 71; Hirshhorn Mus, 74; plus many others. Teaching: Instr, Greenwich Art Ctr, spring 63; instr, New York Community Col, 63-64; instr, Brooklyn Mus Art Sch, 63-67; vis artist, Ohio State Univ, 66; vis prof, Univ Calif, Davis, spring 66; instr, Sch Visual Arts, 66- Pos: Ford Found artist in residence, 65. Mailing Add: c/o Leo Castelli Gallery 420 W Broadway New York NY 10012

WALKER, GEORGE R P, JR
ART DEALER, FINE ARTS FRAMER
b Columbia, SC, Sept 9, 32. Pos: Pres, G Walker Gallery, Columbia, SC. Specialty: Original art; antique and fine art; fine art framing. Mailing Add: 1127 Gregg St Columbia SC 29201

WALKER, HERBERT BROOKS
SCULPTOR, MUSEUM DIRECTOR
b Brooklyn, NY, Nov 30, 27. Study: Art Students League, with Harry Sternberg & Robert B Hale, 43; Yale Sch Fine Arts, BFA, with R Eberhardt, R Zallinger, Graziani, R Albers & De Konning. Work: Photographs of Antonio Gaudis Work, Mus Mod Art, New York; Barbados Mus, BWI; Walker Mus. Comn: Paintings, movie, photographs, Gahagan Dredging, Orinoco River, Venezuela, 53-54; paintings & photographs, US Steel, Cerro Bolivar, Venezuela; earth sculpture, Walker Mus, 60. Exhib: One-man shows, Stony Brook Mus, Long Island, NY, 52, Barbados Mus, 54 & IORC, Abadan, Iran, 58; Walker Mus, 60-; Rodin Mus, 70. Collections Arranged: Oil Exhibs, IORC, Abadan, Iran, 58 & 59; spec exhibs for pub schs, 60-72 & Walker Mus, Fairlee, Vt, 60- Teaching: Instr art, Thetford Acad, 64-66. Pos: Materials prod head, IROC, Abadan, Iran, 58-59; dir, Walker Mus, 59- Bibliog: H Brooks Walker, 1951, Eye Mag, Yale Univ, 67. Mem: Life mem Art Students League; Yale Arts Alumni Asn. Media: Sheet Metal, Bronze. Publ: Illusr, Gaudi, Mus Mod Art, 57. Mailing Add: Walker Mus Fairlee VT 05045

WALKER, JAMES ADAMS
PAINTER, PRINTMAKER
b Connersville, Ind, Jan 24, 21. Study: Western Mich Univ, BS, 46; Univ Mich, 47-48; Teachers Col, Columbia Univ, MA, 49, prof dipl, 58; E Carolina Univ, 49-56; Claremont Grad Sch, 59; Mich State Univ, MFA, 61. Work: Dullin Gallery Art, Knoxville, Tenn; Flint Inst Arts, Mich; Mercyhurst Col, Erie, Pa; Western Mich Univ, Kalamazoo; Butler Inst Am Art, Youngstown, Ohio. Exhib: 19th Nat Competition Prints, Libr of Cong, Washington, DC, 63; 14th & 15th Nat Brooklyn Mus Print Exhib, 64 & 66; 32nd Nat Graphic Arts Drawing Exhib, Wichita Art Asn, Kans, 65; 11th Nat Biennial Print Exhib, Print Club Albany, NY, 66. Teaching: Art supvr & critic instr, E Carolina Univ, 49-56; art instr, Northern Community High Sch, Flint, 56-66; art instr, Nat Music Camp, Interlochen, Mich, summer 63; assoc prof art, Kent State Univ, Warren, Ohio, 66- Awards: Purchase Award, 25th Ann Mich Acad Sci, Arts & Lett, 66; Hugh J Baker Mem Prize for Prints, 43rd Ann Hoosier Salon, Indianapolis, 67; First Print Purchase Award, Butler Inst Am Art, 68 & 77. Bibliog: Arne W Randall (auth), Murals for schools, Davis, Mass, 56; Charles E Meyer (auth), Papers of the Michigan Academy of Science, Arts & Letters, Univ Mich, 62; Eleanor Nelson (auth), Faculty Focus, Kent State Univ, 71. Mem: Mich Acad Sci, Arts & Lett (chmn fine arts sect, 65-67); Trumbull Art Guild (bd dirs & bd trustees, 69-75); Kalamazoo Inst Arts; Canton Art Inst; Steel Valley Art Teachers Asn. Style & Technique: Mainly serigraphs and watercolors; abstract and geometric abstract; semi-realistic watercolors. Publ: Auth, Newsprint, paste & chicken wire, 50, Let's scribble a mural, 53 & Buttermilk & chalk drawing, 54, Sch Arts Mag; auth, Cypress knees, Indust Arts Mag, 59. Mailing Add: 8778 Gull Rd Richland MI 49083

WALKER, JOY
PAINTER, PRINTMAKER
b Tacoma, Wash, July 17, 42. Study: Univ Paris at the Sorbonne, 62-63; Univ Ore, BA(honors), 64; Columbia Univ, 65; New York Studio Sch, 65-67. Work: Art Gallery of Ont, Toronto; Can Coun Art Bank, Ottawa; Dept of External Affairs, Ottawa; Robert McLaughlin Gallery, Oshawa, Ont; Agnes Etherinton Art Ctr, Kingston, Ont. Comn: Olympic print (with lithographer, Deli Sacilotto), York Univ, Toronto, 76. Exhib: One-man shows, Morris Gallery, Toronto, 71-76 & André Zarre Gallery, New York, 77; Recent Can Painting & Sculpture, State Univ NY, Buffalo, 73; A Response to the Environment, Rutgers Univ, NJ, 75; Dartmouth Col Friends Regional Art Show, Hanover, NH, 75; Abstractions (traveling exhib), Montreal, Paris, London & Stratford, Ont, 76-77; Ontario Now II, Hamilton Art Gallery, Ont, 77; Painting Now, Agnes Etherington Art Ctr, Kingston, 77. Teaching: Instr painting, Banff Ctr, Alta, Can, summer 75; instr painting, York Univ, Ont, 76-78. Awards: Print Winner, Editions I, Ont Arts Coun, 74; Arts Grant, Prov of Ont, 74 & 76; Arts Grant, Can Coun, 75. Bibliog: Walter Klepac (auth), rev in Artscanada, 5/76; Peter White (auth), rev in Toronto Globe & Mail, 1/77. Style & Technique: Abstract color, impressment. Media: Acrylic/Oil; Silkscreen. Dealer: André Zarre Gallery 41 E 57th New York NY 10022. Mailing Add: 567 Queen St W Toronto ON M5V 2B6 Can

WALKER, LARRY
PAINTER, EDUCATOR
b Franklin, Ga, Oct 22, 35. Study: High Sch of Music & Art, New York; Highland Park Jr Col, Mich; Wayne State Univ, Detroit. Work: Pioneer Mus & Haggin Art Gallery, Stockton, Calif; Univ of the Pac, Stockton; Oakland Mus, Calif; Delta Mem Hosp, Antioch, Calif; San Joaquin Delta Col, Stockton. Comn: Oil on canvas mural (6ft x 15ft), Univ of the Pac, 65; oil painting, comn by San Joaquin Co Health Soc for Congressman J McFall's Washington Off, 66; drawing, comn by Hannaham & Johnson Eng Consult for A Lee Mus, New York, 70; photo-collage mural (8ft x 8ft), comn by Benjamin Holt Found for San Joaquin Delta Col, 74. Exhib: Am Watercolor Soc 101st Ann, New York, 68; Watercolor USA, Springfield, Mo, 68-69; Wichita Centennial Nat Art Exhib, Kans, 70; Black Untitled II/Dimensions of the Figure, Oakland Mus, Calif, 71; Cal Expo Ann, Exposition Gallery, Sacramento, Calif, 71-76; Crocker Kingsley Ann, E B Crocker Mus, Sacramento, 72 & 77; West Coast 74: The Black Image, E B Crocker Mus, Sacramento & Los Angeles Munic Art Gallery, 74; Northern Calif Arts Ann, Exposition Gallery, Calif Expos, Sacramento, 76; Festac (2nd World Black & African Festival of Arts & Cult, Lagos, Nigeria, 77. Teaching: Prof painting, drawing & art educ, Univ of the Pac, 64- Pos: Art instr, Detroit Pub Sch System, 58-64; chmn art dept, Univ of the Pac, 73- Awards: B H Armstrong Cash Award, Watercolor USA, B H Armstrong Fund, 69; First Award/Painting, Stockton Art League 26th Ann, Dr & Mrs Spracher, 76. Bibliog: Samella Lewis & Ruth Waddy (auths), The Black Artist on Art, Vol I, Contemp Crafts Publ, 69; Afro-American Slide Collection, Univ of S Ala, 69. Mem: Nat Conf of Artists; Nat Coun of Art Adminrs (mem bd dirs, 76-78, chmn, 77-78); Stockton Arts Comn (vchairperson, 76-). Style & Technique: Symbolic abstraction. Media: All Painting and Drawing Media. Publ: Co-auth, Fantasy, form & fun, Sch Art Mag, 70; Larry Walker, Artist/Teacher, article in Black Art—an int quart, summer 77. Dealer: Collectors Gallery Oakland Mus 1000 Oak St Oakland CA 94607. Mailing Add: 202 San Fernando Stockton CA 95210

WALKER, MARY CAROLYN
SILVERSMITH, DESIGNER
b Lancaster, Pa, Oct 24, 38. Study: Pa State Univ, BS(home art); Rochester Inst of Technol Sch for Am Craftsmen, with Don Drumm & Eleanor Moty. Exhib: Young Am 1962, Mus of Contemp Crafts, New York, 62; Am Jewelry Today, Everhart Mus, Scranton, Pa, 63; Marietta Col Crafts Regional, Ohio, 72; Southern Tier Arts & Crafts Show, Corning, NY, 73; First World Silver Fair, Mexico, 74; Spec Exhib for Nat Gov's Conf, 76. Pos: Partner, Tamcraft Products Co, Neffsville, Pa, 60- Awards: First Prize Metals, Harrisburg Arts Festival, 72; Best in Show, 73 & First Prize Jewlery, 76, Pa Guild of Craftsman. Bibliog: R Stevens (auth), Arts decoratifs, La Revue Mod des Arts et de la vie, France, 12/72. Mem: Am Crafts Coun (secy, NE Region, 71-74); Pa Guild of Craftsman (treas, 70-71, pres, 72, vpres, 73); Harrisburg Craftsmen (pres, 70, secy 72 & treas, 73); Nat Asn of Handcraftsmen. Style & Technique: One of a kind, limited edition jewelry working directly with silver to create original constructions in silver. Media: Sterling Silver. Mailing Add: 22 Conway Dr Mechanicsburg PA 17055

WALKER, MORT
CARTOONIST
b El Dorado, Kans, Sept 3, 23. Study: Univ Mo, BA. Work: Bird Libr, Syracuse Univ; Boston Univ Libr; Kans State Univ; Montreal Humor Pavilion; Smithsonian Inst. Exhib: Metrop Mus Art, New York, 52; Brussels World's Fair, 64; Mus Louvre, Paris, 65; New York World's Fair,

67; Expo, Montreal, 69. Pos: Creator of Beetle Bailey, King Features Syndicate, 50-, Hi & Lois, 54-, Sam's Strip, 61-63, Boner's Ark, 68- & Sam & Silo, 77; pres, Mus of Cartoon Art, Rye, NY. Awards: Reuben Award, Nat Cartoonists Soc, 54, Best Humor Strip Plaques, 66 & 69; Silver Lady, Banshees Soc, 55; Award, Il Secolo XIX, Italy, 72; Adamson Award, Sweden, 75; Power of Printing Award, 77; Segar Award, 77. Bibliog: Many articles, bks & TV specials. Mem: Nat Cartoonists Soc (pres, 60); Newspaper Comics Coun; Artists & Writers Asn. Media: Ink. Publ: Ed, Nat Cartoonists Soc Album, 61, 65 & 72; auth, Most, 71; auth, Land of Lost Things, 72; auth, Hi and Lois (7 vols); auth & illusr, Beetle Bailey (20 vols) & Backstage at the Strips, 76. Dealer: Graham Gallery 1014 Madison Ave New York NY 10021. Mailing Add: c/o King Features 235 E 45th St New York NY 10017

WALKER, PETER RICHARD
PAINTER
b New York, NY, Sept 18, 46. Study: Art Students League; Provincetown Workshop; Cooper Union, BFA, 68. Work: Minn Mus, St Paul; Butler Inst Am Art, Youngstown, Ohio. Exhib: One-man shows, Terry Dintenfass Gallery, New York, 68 & 74; Four Arts Soc, 73; Drawings USA, Minn Mus, 73; Butler Inst Mid-Year Show, 74. Awards: First Salao de Arte de Lagos, Portugal, 70; Ball State Univ Drawing Award, 74; Butler Inst Purchase Award, 74. Style & Technique: Realist; classical underpainting. Media: Acrylic, Pencil. Mailing Add: c/o Carson & Barnes Circus Box J Hugo OK 74743

WALKER, MR & MRS RALPH
COLLECTORS
Collection: Antiques and contemporary art. Mailing Add: 17 Fort George Hill New York NY 10040

WALKER, ROBERT MILLER
EDUCATOR
b Flushing, NY, Dec 10, 08. Study: Princeton Univ, BA, 32, MFA, 36; Harvard Univ, PhD, 41. Teaching: Instr, Williams Col, 36-38; asst prof art hist, Swarthmore Col, 41-47, chmn dept, 41-71, assoc prof, 47-52, prof, 52-73, emer prof, 73- Mem: Col Art Asn Am; Soc Archit Historians; Philadelphia Print Club; Am Archaeol Soc; Print Coun Am; plus others. Mailing Add: 212 Elm Ave Swarthmore PA 19081

WALKER, SANDRA RADCLIFFE
PAINTER
b Milton, Pa, Aug 25, 37. Exhib: Biennial, Corcoran Gallery Art, Washington, DC, 74; 19th Nat Juried Show, Chatauqua, NY, 76; Mainstreams, Marietta, Ohio, 76 & 77; Watermedia Exhib, Rocky Mt Nat, Golden, Colo, 76-77; Watercolor USA 1977, Springfield Art Mus, Mo, 77; Nat Watercolor Soc Traveling Exhib, Los Angeles, Calif, 77; solo show, Spectrum Gallery, Georgetown, Washington, DC, 77. Awards: H Lester Cooke Found Grant, Washington, DC, 77. Bibliog: Anon (auth), The Watercolor Page—Sandra Walker, Am Artist Mag, 2/77. Mem: Nat Watercolor Soc; Washington Watercolor Soc. Style & Technique: Realistic, architectural; mostly inner-city scenes. Media: Watercolor. Dealer: Spectrum Gallery 3033 M St Washington DC 20007 Mailing Add: 1904 York Dr Woodbridge VA 22191

WALKER, WILLIAM BOND
ART LIBRARIAN
b Brownsville, Tenn, Apr 15, 30. Study: Bisttram Sch of Fine Art, Taos, NMex & Los Angeles Calif, 48-49, with Emil Bisttram; State Univ Iowa, Iowa City, BA, 53, with Mauricio Lasansky, Howard Warshaw, James Lechay & Stuart Edie; Rutgers Univ Grad Sch of Libr Serv, MSLS, 58. Pos: Cataloger/reference librn, Libr of Metrop Mus of Art, New York, 57-59; chief librn, Art Reference Libr, Brooklyn Mus, NY, 59-64; chief librn, Libr of the Nat Collection of Fine Arts & the Nat Portrait Gallery, Smithsonian Inst, Washington, DC, 64- Bibliog: Marge Byers (auth), Personality: Bill Walker, Nat Collection of Fine Arts Calendar, 8/76. Mem: Am Libr Asn; Col Art Asn; Art Libr Soc of NAm (nat chmn, 75); Spec Libr Asn Mus Div (nat chmn, 61-62); Spec Libr Asn Picture Div. Res: American sculpture of 18th-20th century; art library classification at Library of Congress. Interest: American art; American portraiture. Publ: Auth, Notes on the scope and collections of the NCFA/NPG library, Spec Libr Asn Mus Div Bull, spring 68; auth, Art books & periodicals: Dewey and LC (classification), Libr Trends, Vol 23 (Jan, 75). Mailing Add: 3325 N 23rd Rd Arlington VA 22201

WALKER, WILLIAM WALTER
MURALIST
b Birmingham, Ala, May 9, 27. Study: Colubmus Col Art & Design, Ohio, cert. Work: Family Love (mural), Southside Community Art Ctr, Chicago; Emancipation Proclamation (bicentennial painting), Chicago Tribune & Jack O'Grady Galleries. Comn: Wall of Respect, OBAC, Chicago, 67; St Bernard Wall (mural), Archdiocese of Detroit, 68; Peace & Salvation Wall, Nat Endowment Humanities & TPO, Chicago, 70; St Marcellus (murals), Nat Endowment for Humanities & Rev D Kendricks, 71-73; History Packing House Worker (mural), Amalgamated Meat Cutters Union & Chicago Arts Coun, 75. Exhib: 47th Ann, Columbus Gallery Fine Arts, Ohio, 52. Teaching: Teacher mural painting, Highland Park High Sch, Ill, spring, 71. Awards: Earl C Derby Award, Columbus Gallery Fine Arts, 52; City Beautification Award, Richard J Daley, Mayor Chicago, 71. Bibliog: Roger E Hoyt (auth), Explosion of a dormant art form: Chicago's murals, Chicago Hist, 74; AM America, Chicago Public Art, ABC/TV, 75; Mural Art, NBC/TV, 75. Mem: Internation Walls, Inc (founder & pres, 75). Style & Technique: Exterior and interior walls. Media: Oil. Mailing Add: 6155 S Vernon Chicago IL 60637

WALKEY, FREDERICK P
MUSEUM DIRECTOR
b Belmont, Mass, May 29, 22. Study: Duke Univ; Boston Mus Fine Arts Sch; Tufts Col, BSEd. Pos: Exec dir, De Cordova Mus, Lincoln, Mass, currently. Mem: New Eng Conf (pres); Am Asn Mus; Am Fedn Arts. Mailing Add: De Cordova Mus Sandy Pond Rd Lincoln MA 01773

WALL, BRIAN
SCULPTOR
b London, Eng, Sept 5, 31. Study: Luton Col Art, Eng; with Barbara Hepworth, 54-58. Work: Tate Gallery, London; Nat Gallery, Dublin; Art Gallery NSW, Sidney; Oakland Mus; Univ Art Mus, Berkeley. Comn: Thornaby (sculpture), New Town Ctr, Thornaby, Eng, 68. Exhib: One-man shows, Sch Archit, London, Eng, 57, Quay Gallery, San Francisco, 74, Braunstein/Quay Gallery, San Francisco, 76, Univ Nev, Las Vegas, 76 & Sculpture Now Gallery, New York, 77; 2nd Paris Biennale, Mus Mod Art, 61; Sculpture of the Sixties, Tate Gallery, 65; Sculpture 1960-66, Battersea Park, London, 66; Inst Contemp Art, London, 70; British Sculptors '72, Royal Acad Art, London, 72; Public Sculpture/Urban Environment, Oakland Mus, 74; Retrospective, James Willis Gallery, 76; City of Palo Alto Outdoor Sculpture Exhib, Calif, 77; Queen's Silver Jubilee Exhib, London, 77; Max Hutchinson Gallery Group, Houston, Tex, 77. Teaching: Chmn sculpture dept, Cent Sch Art & Design, London, 64-72; prof sculpture, Univ Calif, Berkeley, 69- Bibliog: Charles Spencer (auth), Brian Wall, sculptor of simplicity, Studio Int, 3/66; G S Whittet (auth), Question and artist: Brian Wall, Sculpture Int, 10/69; Hilton Kramer (auth), article in New York Times, 5/13/77. Style & Technique: Abstract. Media: Steel. Dealer: Braunstein Quay Gallery 560 Sutter St San Francisco CA 94162. Mailing Add: 1824 Grant Ave San Francisco CA 94133

WALL, RALPH ALAN
PAINTER, ILLUSTRATOR
b Hobart, Ind, Aug 1, 32. Study: Univ Okla; Oklahoma City Univ, BS; also with Tom Lovell. Work: Bimson Collection, Valley Nat Bank, Phoenix, Ariz; Fidelity Bank Collection, Oklahoma City; Oklahoma City Univ; Mountain Oyster Club, Tucson, Ariz; Big Chief Collection, Ardmore, Okla. Comn: Prints of Indian Headdresses (series), Big Chief Roofing, Ardmore, Okla, 75. Exhib: Two-man show, Oklahoma City Univ, 70; one-man shows, Lodge on the Desert, Tucson, Ariz, 71, Goddard Ctr, Ardmore, Okla & Ponca City Art Ctr, Okla, 72; Oklahoma Mus Art, Red Ridge, Oklahoma City, 73; Mus of the SW, Midland, Tex, 76; two-man show, Glasser's, San Antonio, 78. Pos: Pres, Art Dir Club, Houston, 66-67. Awards: Am Inst Graphic Art Award (packaging), 67; Gold Medal, 1974 Portfolio Western Art, Franklin Mint, 74. Bibliog: Fredie Steve Harris (auth), Horse painter, Cattleman, 9/74 & Franklin Mint Paint, Paint Horse J, 11/74; Gary K Hill (auth), Indian artist, Houston Chronicle, 3/74. Mem: Artists Equity; hon mem Mountain Oyster Club, Tucson. Style & Technique: Historical and contemporary American West, primarily dealing with Plains Indian. Media: Acrylic, Oil, Pencil & Ink, Photography. Publ: Illusr, American Horseman, 9/73, Paint Horse J (cover), 1/75 & 11/75; illusr, Leanin Tree Greeting Card Series, 77 & Okla Today, Summer 1976; illusr, Dean Krakel, auth, Adventures in Western Art, 77. Mailing Add: 3706 Nottingham Houston TX 77005

WALL, SUE
PAINTER, PRINTMAKER
b Cleveland, Ohio, Feb 18, 50. Study: Ohio Univ, BFA, 71, MFA, 73. Work: Cleveland Mus Art; Canton Art Inst Mus, Ohio; Butler Inst Am Art, Youngstown, Ohio; Univ Iowa Mus Art; Kenneth Beck Ctr for Cult Arts, Cleveland. Exhib: Nat Acad Ann Exhib, Nat Acad Galleries, New York, 75; Philbrook Gallery, Tulsa, Okla, 75; Catharine Lorillard Wolfe Exhib, New York, 75; Butler Ann Mid-Year Show, Youngstown, 75-77; Cleveland May Show, Cleveland Mus of Art, 75-77; Audubon Artists Ann Exhib, 75-78, Allied Artists Ann Exhib, 76 & Nat Soc Painter in Casein & Acrylic Ann, 77, Nat Acad Galleries, New York; one-person shows, Gallery Madison 90, New York, 74, 76 & 78, Zainesville Art Ctr, Ohio, 75, Hamilton Gallery, Des Moines, Iowa, 75, Strong's Gallery, Cleveland, 75 & 77, Canton Art Inst, Ohio, 76, Gallery 200, Columbus, 76 & Piccolo Mondo, Palm Beach, Fla, 76 & 78. Awards: Grumbacher Cash Award, 79th Ann Catahrine Lorillard Wolfe, 75; Truman Award, 150th Ann Nat Acad Exhib, 75; First Prize, Am Nat Miniature Show, Laramie Art Guild, 76. Bibliog: Rhoda Levinsohn, Sue Wall, Sunday Plain Dealer, 75 & Art Look 102, Apple Publ, S Africa, 9/76; Millie Wolff, Sue Wall, Palm Beach Daily News, 2/78. Mem: New Organization of Visual Arts; Audubon Artists; Nat Soc Painters in Casein & Acrylic. Style & Technique: Representational, dealing with architecture. Media: Acrylic on Canvas. Mailing Add: 144 W 72nd St New York NY 10023

WALLACE, DAVID HAROLD
ART HISTORIAN, MUSEUM CURATOR
b Baltimore, Md, Dec 24, 26. Study: Lebanon Valley Col, BA; Columbia Univ, MA & PhD. Pos: Asst ed, NY Hist Soc, New York, 52-56; mus cur, Independence Nat Hist Park, Philadelphia, 58-68; asst chief, Br Mus Opers, Nat Park Serv, 68-71, chief, 71-73, chief Br Reference Serv, 74- Res: American artist biographies. Publ: Co-auth, Dictionary of artists in America, 1564-1860, NY Hist Soc, 57; auth, John Rogers, the People's Sculptor, 67. Mailing Add: 9 W Third St Frederick MD 21701

WALLACE, ELIZABETH S
ART ADMINISTRATOR, SCULPTOR
b Mankato, Kans. Study: Washburn Univ, AB; Univ Nebr, BFA, MFA; also with Thomas Sheffield. Work: Elder Gallery, Lincoln, Nebr. Exhib: One-person shows, Nebr Wesleyan Univ, Lincoln, 66, Haymarket Art Gallery, 70 & Elder Gallery, 74, Lincoln, Nebr. Teaching: Instr ceramics, Nebr Wesleyan Univ, Lincoln, 72-, asst prof sculpture & art hist, 76- Pos: Head art dept, Nebr Wesleyan Univ, Lincoln, 76-; dir, Elder Gallery, Lincoln, 76-; dir, Univ Place Art Ctr & Wesleyan Lab Gallery, 77- Mem: Nebr Art Asn (bd trustees, 76-); Lincoln Arts Coun (bd trustee, 77-); Wesleyan Arts Coun (pres, 75-76); Nebr Crafts Coun; Am Crafts Coun. Style & Technique: Basically ceramic, but composites of media and techniques. Mailing Add: 420 Lakewood Lincoln NE 68510

WALLACE, JOHN EDWARD
PAINTER, EDUCATOR
b St Louis, Mo, Dec 29, 29. Study: Washington Univ, with Paul Burlin & Carl Holty, BFA; Ind Univ, Bloomington, with Alton Pickens, MFA; Skowhegan Sch Painting & Sculpture, with Jack Levine. Work: St Louis Art Mus, Mo; Detroit Inst Arts, Mich. Comn: Mural in true fresco, South Solon Meeting House, Maine, 54; sculpture panel in bronze, Aquatic House, St Louis Zool Gardens, Mo, 59. Exhib: Denver Art Mus, Colo, 52; 147th Ann Painting & Sculpture, Pa Acad Fine Arts, 52; 7th Ann Nat Print Exhib, Brooklyn Mus, NY, 53; Momentum Midcontinental, Inst Design, Ill Inst Technol, Chicago, 54; Cincinnati Art Mus, Ohio, 55; Mus Fine Arts, Dallas, Tex, 55; US Info Agency Traveling Exhib, Japan, Australia, India & Near East, 57-59; Artist in Residence Exhib, Roswell Mus & Art Ctr, NMex, 68; Skowhegan Ann, New York, 66-69; Bertrand Russell Centenary, Nottingham, Eng, 73. Collections Arranged: New Art Asn Exhib, Col Art Asn Am, 59th Ann Meeting, 71. Teaching: Prof painting & sculpture, Prairie State Col, Chicago Heights, Ill, 68- & chmn art dept, 71-74; vis artist, painting & sculpture, Governors State Univ, Park Forest South, Ill, Nat Endowment Arts Grant, summers 73 & 74; instr true-fresco mural, Truro Ctr for the Arts, Castle Hill, Mass, summers 76, 77 & 78. Pos: Interregional coordr (Chicago area), New Art Asn, NY, 70-71 & co-ed, Nat Newslett, winter 71; organizer & co-chmn, New Directions for Studio Teaching, 59th Ann Col Art Asn Am, 71. Awards: Purchase Awards, St Louis Art Mus, 50, 52 & 54; Margaret Day Blake Fel in Fresco, Skowhegan Sch Painting & Sculpture, 54; Resident Fel in Painting, Huntington Hartford Found, Calif, 60. Mem: Col Art Asn Am; Mid-West Col Art Conf. Style & Technique: Painterly approach to the figure in interiors and landscapes; Media: Acrylic, Oil, True-Fresco. Mailing Add: PO Box 362 Truro MA 02666

WALLACE, LYSBETH (MAI)
WEAVER, DESIGNER
b Hopkinsville, Ky. Study: Univ Ky; Kansas City Art Inst; Cranbrook Acad of Art, Bloomfield Hills, Mich with Maija Grotell & Marianne Strengell. Work: Evansville Mus of Arts & Sci, Ind; Berea Col, Ky. Comn: Woven tapestries, comn by Sarah Myers for dress shop, 74 & Illusive Sun for pvt home, 77, Hopkinsville, Ky; woven geometric design wall hanging (2

panels), comn by Gray Construction Co, Production Credit Asn Bldg, Glasgow, Ky, 76; Mss for learning (abstract Books; woven inlay tapestry), comn by Town & Country Garden Club for Pub Libr, Hopkinsville, 77; Woven Art Nouveau Tree, comn by Howard Gray for lake house, Barren River Lake, Glasgow, Ky, 77. Exhib: Wichita Decorative Arts, Wichita Art Mus, Kans, 49; Designer/Craftsmen, Detroit Mus of Art, 51; Alumni Show, Cranbrook Acad of Art, 54; Contemp Handweaving II (traveling show), Joslyn Art Mus, Omaha, Nebr, 59-60; Eight State Craft Show, J B Speed Mus, Louisville, Ky, 60-66 & 76; Designer/Craftsmen Show, Univ Kans, 63; Int Craft Show, Calif State Univ, Northridge, 63; Mid-State Craft Show, Evansville Mus of Arts & Sci, Ind, 63-65 & 77. Teaching: Instr design, Washburn Univ, Topeka, Kans, 46-48; from instr to asst prof weaving, Southern Ill Univ, Carbondale, 55-60; asst prof weaving, Ill State Univ, Normal, 61-65; from asst prof to prof weaving & design, Western Ky Univ, 65- Pos: Handweaving expert, UN Tech Assistance Admin, Manila, Philippines, 51-53. Awards: Anonymous Award, Designer/Craftsman, Univ Kans, 63; Purchase Award, Mid-State Craft Show, Malcom Koch, 67; Purchase Award, Berea Biennial, Berea Col, 70. Bibliog: Betty Pepies (auth), New fibers for old forms, Living for Young Homemakers, 52; Patricia K Brooks (auth), Experiment in the Philippines, Carft Horizons, 54. Mem: Col Art Asn; Am Craftsmen Coun; KY Guild of Artist & Craftsmen. Style & Technique: Abstract as well as somewhat naturalistic geometric forms; white on white and color; woven tapestry wall hangings. Media: Weaving and Ceramic. Publ: Auth, Handweaving in the Philippines, UN, 53; auth, Tapestry weaver in the mid-west, 60 & Lysbeth Wallace teaches weaving, 61, Handweaver & Craftsman; illusr, Lucile Van Cleve Wallace, auth, Recollections & Recipes, Circulation Serv, Kansas City, Nov 77. Dealer: Swearingen-Haynie Gallery Brownsboro Ctr Brownsboro Rd Louisville KY 40207. Mailing Add: 563 E Main Bowling Green KY 42101

WALLACE, SONI
PAINTER
b London, Eng, Apr 18, 31; US citizen. Study: Silvermine Art Guild, New Canaan, Conn; Mus Mod Art, with Zolten Hecht; Pratt Graphics, New York. Work: Gibbes Art Mus, Charleston, SC; Univ Ala Mus. Comn: Three covers for mag, Distinguished Resorts, 68, 70 & 71. Exhib: Conn Watercolor Soc 31st Ann, Fairfield Univ, 69; Love/Peace, Am Greetings Gallery, NY, 69; Northwest Printmakers 41st Int Exhib, Seattle Art Mus, 70; solo shows, Pacem-in-Terris Gallery, New York, 70, Danbury Libr Gallery, Conn, 71 & Phoenix Gallery, New York, 75. Awards: Max Granick Award, Am Soc Contemp Artists, NY, 71; Award, Washington Art Asn, Conn, 72; Am Soc Contemp Artists Ann, 74. Mem: Nat Asn Women Artists (prog chmn, 72-73); Am Soc Contemp Artists; Silvermine Guild Artists; Washington Art Asn; Women in the Arts. Style & Technique: Vivid abstract acrylics in which suggestions of glazing terrains shape a resonant geometry; areas conjoint along a horizontal axis, rising to a vertical axis against a field of united color. Media: Acrylic, Watercolor. Mailing Add: 150 E 77th St New York NY 10021

WALLER, AARON BRET
MUSEUM DIRECTOR, ART HISTORIAN
b Liberal, Kans, Dec 7, 35. Study: Univ Kans, Lawrence; Kansas City Art Inst & Sch of Design, BFA, 57; Univ Kans, Lawrence, MFA, 58; Univ Oslo, Norway. Collections Arranged: School for Scandal: Thomas Rowlandson's London (co-auth, catalogue), 67 & The Waning Middle Ages (ed, catalogue), 69, Univ Kans; Images of Love & Death in Late Medieval and Renaissance Art (ed, catalogue), 75 & Works from the Collection of Dorothy & Herbert Vogel (auth, catalogue), 77, Univ Mich. Teaching: Asst prof art hist, Univ Kans, Lawrence, 64-70; assoc prof art hist, Univ Mich, Ann Arbor, 73- Pos: Dir, Mus of Art, Univ Kans, Lawrence, 68-70; head, Dept Pub Educ, Metrop Mus of Art, New York, 70-73; dir, Mus of Art, Univ Mich, 73- Mem: Asn Art Mus Dirs; Intermuseum Conserv Asn (pres, 77-78); Am Asn of Mus; Col Art Asn. Res: Graphic arts, 20th century art. Mailing Add: Univ Mich Mus of Art Ann Arbor MI 48109

WALMSLEY, WILLIAM AUBREY
LITHOGRAPHER
b Tuscumbia, Ala, Oct 9, 23. Study: Univ Ala, BFA, 51 & MA, 53; Art Students League; Acad Julian, Paris; Tamarind Lithography Workshop, Los Angeles. Work: Mus Mod Art, New York; Libr Cong, Washington, DC; Tate Gallery, London, Eng; Hawaii Acad Art, Honolulu; Ohio State Univ, Columbus. Exhib: Nat Print Exhib, Honolulu Acad Art, Hawaii, 74; Davidson Print Exhib, NC, 74; Philadelphia Print Club Int, Pa, 75; Libr Cong, Print Exhib, Washington, DC, 75; Soc Am Graphic Artist Print Exhib, New York, 75. Teaching: Prof lithography, Fla State Univ, Tallahassee, 62; vis artist lithography, Northern Ill Univ, Dekalb, summer 73; vis artist lithography, Penland Sch Crafts, Spruce Pine, NC, summer 75 & 77. Awards: Purchase Awards, Colorprint USA, Tex Tech, Lubbock, 72 & Potsdam Prints, NY, 72; Second Purchase Award, 12th Ann Calgary Graphic, Alta, 72. Bibliog: Emil Weddige (auth), Lithography, Int Textbk Co, 66; Clare Romano & John Ross (co-auth), Complete Screenprint & Lithography, Freepress, Macmillan, 74; Mem: Southeastern Graphic Coun (pres, 76-78); Southeastern Col Art Conf (bd dir, 77-80); Soc Am Graphic Arts; Calif Soc Printmakers; Boston Printmakers; Southern Graphics Coun. Style & Technique: Lithography, including color and fluorescent color lithographs. Collection: Prints by Goya, Picasso, Callot, Ernst, Beckman, Matisse & Piranesi. Mailing Add: 1536 Cristobal Dr Tallahassee FL 32303

WALSH, JOHN, JR
CURATOR, EDUCATOR
b Mason City, Wash, Dec 9, 37. Study: Yale Univ, BA; Univ Leiden, Netherlands; Columbia Univ, MA, PhD. Teaching: From adj prof to prof art hist, Barnard Col & Columbia Univ, 70-77. Pos: Lectr & curatorial asst, Frick Collection, New York, 66-68; from assoc for higher educ to assoc cur of Europ paintings to cur of Europ paintings, Metrop Mus of Art, New York, 68-75; Mrs R W Baker cur of paintings, Mus of Fine Arts, 77- Mem: Yale Univ Art Gallery Governing Bd; Mus of Mod Art, New York (mem trustee comt on educ); Col Art Asn; Am Asn of Mus. Mailing Add: Mus of Fine Arts Boston MA 02115

WALSH, JOHN STANLEY
PAINTER, WRITER
b Brighton, Eng, Aug 16, 07. Study: London Cent Sch Art, Eng. Work: Montreal Mus Fine Arts; Toronto Art Mus. Exhib: Am Watercolor Soc, 61; Can Soc Painter in Water Colour; Can Soc Graphic Art; Royal Can Acad Art; numerous one-man shows, Montreal, New York & Toronto. Teaching: Lectr watercolor painting. Mem: Can Watercolor Soc; Can Soc Graphic Art. Media: Watercolor. Publ: Contribr, Am Artists, New York Times, Esquire, Harper's Bazaar & Field & Stream; plus others. Mailing Add: 142 52nd Ave Lachine PQ H8T 2W9 Can

WALSH, PATRICIA RUTH
PAINTER
b Cleveland, Ohio. Study: Col Mt St Joseph, Cincinnati, BA; Art Students League; Syracuse Univ, NY, MFA. Exhib: Northwest Printmakers Int, Seattle Art Mus, 65; Paintings, Calif Col Arts & Crafts Gallery, Oakland, 69; Pollution Show, Oakland Mus, 70; Three Watercolorists, San Jose Civic Art Ctr, 73; Spaces & Places, Palo Alto Cult Ctr, 75. Teaching: Staff, Dayton Art Inst, 56-57; asst prof fine arts, Nazareth Col, Rochester, NY, 57-65; prof fine arts, Calif Col Arts & Crafts, 65- Style & Technique: Realistic material is organized to make a statement basically formal and sculptural. Media: Oil, Watercolor. Publ: Illusr, Boy & the Stars, Golden Quill Press, 65. Mailing Add: c/o Graphics Gallery Three Embarcadero Ctr San Francisco CA 94111

WALTER, MAY E
COLLECTOR, PATRON
Pos: Mem art adv coun, Univ Notre Dame; secy, trustee & mem exec comt, Am Craftsman's Coun, 62-77, hon trustee, 77- Interest: Patron, New York University Art Collection, Notre Dame University. Collection: Twentieth Century Masters, includes Cubism and Futurism. Mailing Add: 923 Fifth Ave New York NY 10021

WALTER, PAUL F
COLLECTOR, PATRON
b Mt Vernon, NY, July 29, 35. Study: Oberlin Col, Ohio; Columbia Univ, New York. Donations for Pub Collections: Los Angeles Co Mus Art, Calif; Allen Art Mus, Oberlin Col, Ohio; Princeton Univ Mus, NJ. Collection Exhib: Indian Art from Paul Walter Collection, Oberlin, Ohio, 69; Indian Drawings from Paul Walter Collection, Los Angeles Co Mus & 12 other US mus; Agnes Martin Retrospective, Pasadena, Calif, 74; Indian Painting, Asia House Gallery, New York, 74; Brice Marden Retrospective, Guggenheim Mus, New York, 75. Pos: Trustee, Walter Found, Princeton, NJ, Byrd Hoffman Found, New York & The Kitchen Ctr, New York, 67- mem adv comt, Princeton Art Mus, 75- Mem: Mus Mod Art, NY; Metrop Mus Art; Asia Soc; Guggenheim Mus; Los Angeles Co Mus Art. Interest: Art education, avant garde music and video. Collection: Extensive collection of Indian paintings; avant garde paintings, drawings and sculpture; photographs; Whistler prints and old master prints. Mailing Add: 52 Arreton Rd Princeton NJ 08540 Princeton NJ Princeton NJ

WALTER, VALÉRIE HARRISSE
SCULPTOR
b Baltimore, Md. Study: Md Inst, Baltimore; Art Students League; apprentice to Augustus Lukeman; Hunter Col; Col Notre Dame, Md; McCoy Col, Johns Hopkins Univ. Work: Gen Umberto Nobile, Aeronaut Ministry, Rome, Italy; Gorilla, John Daniel II & Bamboo (life-size bronze gorillas), Baltimore Zoo; three sculptures of gorillas, Dept Anthrop, Johns Hopkins Univ. Comn: Geheimrat Carl van Noorden (marble bust), Frankfurt, Ger & Vienna, 34; Charlotte (bronze head), comn by Dr Mason Faulkner Lord, Baltimore, 57; bronze bas-relief, Dr & Mrs W Waldemar W Argow, Unitarian Church, Baltimore, 62; Toni (bronze), comn by Mrs Richard O'Brien; Nathalie (bronze bust), comn by Mr J Sawyer Wilson. Exhib: Corcoran Gallery Art, Washington, DC; Pa Acad Fine Arts, Philadelphia; Paris Salon; San Francisco Mus Art; Hispanic Mus, New York. Awards: First Prize for Sculpture, Soc Washington Artists Ann. Media: Marble, Teak, Mahogany. Mailing Add: 202 E 31st Baltimore MD 21218

WALTERS, BILLIE
CERAMIST
b Colman, Tex, Mar 12, 27. Study: Univ Colo; Univ NMex; also with Hal Reigger, Ariz, Paul Soldner, NMex, Don Reitz, NMex & William Daley and Carl Paak. Work: Alta Col Art, Edmonton; Univ NMex; Everson Mus Slide Collection, Syracuse, NY. Exhib: Everson Mus, Syracuse, NY, 72; Ceramics Int, 73, Calgary, Alta, 73; Ceramic Conjunction, Brand Mus Art, Glendale, Calif, 73-74; Crafts Biennial, Int Folk Art Mus, Santa Fe, NMex, 74; Crafts V, Mus Albuquerque, NMex, 74; Raku Invitational Exhib, Elements Gallery, Greenwich, Conn, 77; Clay, Fiber & Metal Exhib Invitational, Bronx Mus, NY, 78. Pos: Crafts Rep, Bd NMex Arts & Crafts Fair, 74-75; Southwest cur, Women's Caucus for Art Exhib, Bronx Mus, NY, 78. Awards: Purchase Award, Ceramics Int, 73; Third Pl Award, Lake Superior Craft Biennial, 73; Purchase Award, Crafts V, Mus Albuquerque, 74. Bibliog: W R Mitchell (auth), Ceramic Art of the World 1973, Govt Can, Alta, 73; Susan Keith (auth), Raku & Zen, Albuquerque J, 11/3/74. Mem: Am Crafts Coun; World Crafts Coun; NMex Potters Asn; Albuquerque Designer-Craftsman. Mailing Add: 3835 Rio Grande Blvd NW Albuquerque NM 87107

WALTERS, ERNEST
PAINTER
b Elizabethtown, Ky, Nov 11, 27. Study: Univ Louisville; Univ Miami; French Studio Schs. Work: Mus Mod Art, New York; Israel Mus, Jerusalem; Stedelijk Mus, Amsterdam, Neth; Albertina, Vienna, Austria; Mus d'Art Mod, Brussels, Belg. Exhib: IFA Galleries, Washington, DC; Galerie d'Egmont, Brussels, Belg; Galerie Richter, Wiesbaden, Ger; Siemens, Overbeck Gallery, Lubeck; Galerie Kumar, Vienna, Austria. Style & Technique: Linear abstract. Media: Oil. Publ: Auth, Wiener Schwarzweiss (a portfolio of drawings), 68; auth, An astonished survivor (poems & typographical drawings), 73. Dealer: IFA Galleries 2623 Connecticut Ave NW Washington DC 20008. Mailing Add: 257 Foster Knoll Dr Joppa MD 21085

WALTERS, SYLVIA SOLOCHEK
PRINTMAKER, INSTRUCTOR
b Milwaukee, Wis, Aug 24, 38. Study: Univ Wis, Madison, BS, MS, MFA. Work: Elvejhem Collection, Madison; US Info Agency; Francis McCray Gallery, Western NMex Univ; Ky Arts Comn, Louisville; First Nat Bank of Boston. Exhib: 14th, 15th, 23rd & 26th Boston Printmakers, DeCordova Mus, 61, 62, 71 & 74; Eight State Prints, J B Speed Mus, 73; Mid-Am V, Nelson Atkins & St Louis Mus, 74; 3rd Hawaii Nat Prints, Honolulu Acad, 75; 3rd Graphics Biennial Metrop Mus & Art Ctr, Miami, 77; Contemp Am Prints, Fendrick Gallery, 62; Black & White Prints, Philadelphia Print Club, 69; 11th & 12th Nat Silvermine Guild Prints, New Cannan, Conn, 76 & 78; Contemp Issues, Works by Women on Paper, Los Angeles, 77; Univ Utah Mus, 77; Blaffer Gallery, Univ Houston, 77. Teaching: Instr printmaking, Layton Sch of Art, 63-64; instr drawing, Doane Col, 67-68 & St Louis Univ, 68-69; assoc prof drawing, Univ Mo, St Louis, 69- Pos: Graphic & book designer, Univ Wis Press, 64-67; dir Gallery 210, Univ Mo, 74-; chmn dept art, Univ Mo, 77-; bd dir, Art Coord Coun for the area, 76- Awards: Purchase Awards, Eight State Print Exhib, Ky Arts Comn, 73, Graphics 71, Western NMex Univ & Los Angeles Printmaking Soc, Graphic Group, 74. Bibliog: Donald Anderson (auth), The Art of Written Forms, Holt, Rinehart, Winston, 69; Nancy Rice (auth), Sylvia Solochek Walters, The St Louis Seen, fall 77; Marlene Schiller (auth), article Am Artist (in prep), 78. Mem: Col Art Asn; Women's Caucus for Art; Boston Printmakers; Los Angeles Printmakers Soc; Art Coord Coun for the area (bd dir). Media: Woodcut and Relief Prints, Lithography. Publ: Auth, American Women Printmakers, Gallery 210, Univ Mo, St Louis, 75; auth, Art on the Mississippi, 4/76 & Place, Race & Rights in St Louis, summer 76, Women Artist News. Dealer: Assoc Am Artists 663 Fifth Ave New York NY 10022. Mailing Add: 7414 Melrose Ave St Louis MO 63130

WALTON, DONALD WILLIAM
GALLERY DIRECTOR, WRITER
b Cleveland, Ohio, Aug 13, 17. Study: Western Reserve Univ, BA; John Huntington Art Sch. Pos: Dir fine arts, Franklin Mint, 69-74, managing dir, Franklin Mint Gallery Am Art, 74-77, cur, Hallmark Collection, 77- Awards: Doc on Norman Rockwell, Int Film Festival & NY Film Festival, 74. Mem: Nat Sculpture Soc; Am Fedn Arts; Am Asn Mus; Philadelphia Print Club; Philadelphia Mus Art. Specialty: Publishes and markets art collectibles and graphics. Publ: Auth, Art is to Enjoy, 63; auth, Norman Rockwell Biography, 78. Mailing Add: 330 E Bridlespur Dr Kansas City KS 64114

WALTON, FLORENCE GOODSTEIN (GOODSTEIN-SHAPIRO)
PAINTER, ART HISTORIAN
b New York, NY, July 22, 31. Study: Cooper Union, 50-51; City Col New York, BS(art educ), 52; Hans Hofmann Sch Fine Arts, 56-57; Univ Minn, MA(art hist), 73. Work: Bonython Gallery, Sydney, Australia; Martin Luther King Collection, Atlanta, Ga; Augsburg Col Collection, Minneapolis; Juana Mordo Gallery, Madrid, Spain. Exhib: Am Watercolor Soc, Smithsonian Inst, Washington, DC, 63; Cooper Union Gallery, New York, 67; Los Angeles Co Mus Art, 69; Boynthon Art Gallery, Sydney, 69; Tweed Gallery, Univ Minn, Duluth, 71; Hamline Univ, St Paul, Minn, 76. Teaching: Instr art hist, Lakewood State Jr Col, 71- Pos: Art prog dir, Emanuel-Midtown Y Community Ctr, 63-65; secy & pub rels dir, Aspects Gallery, New York, 64-66; dir, Artists Against War Exhib, New York, 67-68. Awards: STA Award for Excellence, Art Inst Chicago, 54. Bibliog: New voices, Village Voice, 3/64; Artist paints death, Australian, 9/30/69; Shades of Whispering Glades, Sydney Morning-Herald, 9/30/69. Mem: Col Art Asn Am; Am Inst Archaeol; Exp Art & Technol. Media: Oil, Charcoal, Pastel. Res: Pre-Hellenic Greek ware; Goya's black paintings; Indian Gupta architecture. Publ: Auth, Lumen room, Technol & Environ, 70. Mailing Add: 8066 Ruth St NE Minneapolis MN 55432

WALTON, HARRY A, JR
COLLECTOR
b Covington, Va, Sept 24, 18. Study: Univ Va, 37; Columbia Univ, 39; Lynchburg Col, AB, 39. Exhib: Works have been exhibited in libraries at: Trinity Col, Washington, DC, Col William & Mary, Norfolk Mus Art & Sci, Univ Va & Lynchburg Col. Mem: Fel Pierpont-Morgan Libr, NY; Univ Va Bibliog Soc. Collection: Early books and manuscripts, Bibles, fine binding, Aldinae and first editions. Mailing Add: White Oak Dairy Box 790 Covington VA 24426

WALTON, MARION (MARION WALTON PUTNAM)
SCULPTOR
b New Rochelle, NY, Nov 19, 99. Study: Bryn Mawr Col; Art Students League; Acad Grande Chaumiere, Paris, with Antoine Bourdelle. Work: Lincoln Mus, Nebr; plus many pvt collections in US, France & Sweden. Comn: World's Fair, US Govt, 39; Post Off mural, US Govt; plus many pvt comn for portraits, gardens & interiors. Exhib: Mus Mod Art, New York; Whitney Mus Am Art, New York; Metrop Mus Art, New York; Art Inst Chicago; La Jeune Sculpture, Rodin Mus, Paris, France; Pa Acad Fine Arts; Philadelphia Mus Art; Triennale Europ de Sculpture, Palais Royal, Paris; plus many others. Teaching: Prof sculpture, Sarah Lawrence Col, 50-51. Mem: Sculptors Guild; Artists Equity Asn. Media: Marble, Bronze, Wood. Mailing Add: 49 Irving Pl New York NY 10003

WALTON, WILLIAM
PAINTER,
b Jacksonville, Ill, Aug 20, 09. Study: Univ Wis, AB, 31; Ill Col, LHD, 46. Work: Corcoran Gallery; Phillips Mem Gallery. Exhib: Six one-man shows in Washington & New York. Pos: Chmn, US Comn Fine Arts, 63-71; trustee, Kennedy Mem Libr. Mailing Add: 236 W 26th St New York NY 10001

WALTZER, STEWART PAUL
ART DEALER, PAINTER
b New York, NY, Mar 17, 48. Study: NY Univ, BA, 69, MA, 70; Columbia Univ; New York Studio Sch; also with Irving Sandler, Audrey Flack, Chuck Close & Kenneth Noland. Exhib: City Univ New York. Pos: Dir, Andre Emmerich Gallery Downtown, 72-74, Tibor de Nagy Gallery, 74-77 & Meredith Long Contemp, 77- Style & Technique: Abstract art oriented toward color. Specialty: American 20th century contemporary and modern painting and sculpture. Dealer: Gloria Cortella Gallery 41 E 57th St New York NY 10021. Mailing Add: c/o Meredith Long Contemp 7 W 57th St New York NY 10019

WANDS, ALFRED JAMES
PAINTER
b Cleveland, Ohio, Feb 19, 04. Study: Cleveland Art Inst, BFA; Western Reserve Univ, BS; Univ Colo; Acad Julien, Paris; John Huntington Inst. Work: Cleveland Art Mus; Brooklyn Mus Arts & Sci; Calif Palace of Legion of Honor, San Francisco; Denver Art Mus; Kansas City Art Inst, Mo. Comn: Five Colorado landscapes, Denver Pub Schs, 46; Christ in the Temple (mural), Grant Ave Methodist Church, Denver, 47; mural of Rocky Mountains, YMCA of the Rockies, Denver, 67; mural elk, Rocky Mountain Nat Park, Estes Park, Colo, 75. Exhib: Carnegie Inst Int, Pittsburgh; Corcoran Art Gallery Biennial, Washington, DC; Art Inst Chicago Am Ann; Kansas City Art Inst Midwestern Ann, Mo; Denver Art Mus Ann. Teaching: Instr painting, Cleveland Art Inst, 26-30; prof painting & drawing, Colo Women's Col, Denver, 30-47; instr painting, Univ Colo, Denver, 47-50. Pos: Chmn, Denver Art Comn, 45-61. Awards: Silver Medal, Kansas City Art Inst, 42; Purchase Award, Brooklyn Mus Arts & Sci, 45; Purchase Award for Watercolor, Calif Palace of Legion of Honor, 50. Mem: Denver Artists Guild (pres, 32, 41 & 63); Ohio Watercolor Soc; Carmel Art Asn; Col Art Asn Am (secy, Colo Chap, 36-42). Style & Technique: Realist-some semi-modern. Media: Oil, Watercolor. Publ: Auth, How to Paint Mountains, 75. Dealer: Studio Art Gallery San Carlos & Ocean Carmel CA 93921. Mailing Add: 2065 Ivanhoe St Denver CO 80207

WANG, CHI-CHIEN
PAINTER
b Soochow, China, Feb 14, 07. Study: Soochow Univ, grad. Work: Brooklyn Mus Art, NY; Art Mus, Princeton Univ, NJ; Bank of Am, San Francisco; Fogg Mus, Boston. Exhib: The New Chinese Landscape, Six Contemporary Chinese Artists, 66; De Young Mem Mus, San Francisco, 68; Indianapolis Mus Art, 72; Fogg Mus, Harvard Univ, 73; Watercolor Soc, Nat Acad Art & Design, New York, 74. Teaching: Prof art, Shanghai Acad Art, 33-34; vis lectr, Columbia Univ, New York, 51-52 & Univ Calif, Berkeley, 68-69; chmn art dept, Chinese Univ, Hong Kong, 62-64. Mem: China Inst. Style & Technique: Landscape, watercolor on oriental paper. Mailing Add: 190 E 72nd St New York NY 10021

WANG, SAMUEL
PHOTOGRAPHER, PRINTMAKER
b Peking, China, Apr 4, 39; US citizen. Study: Augustana Col, Sioux Falls, BA, 64; Univ Iowa, MFA, 66. Work: Greenville Co Mus of Art, SC; Ga State Univ, Atlanta; Mint Mus of Art, Charlotte, NC; Cent Washington Univ, Ellensburg; Asheville Art Mus, NC. Comn: E R photo-serigraph, Piedmont Mortgage and Loan, Greenville, 74. Exhib: Photo/Graphics, Int Mus of Photog & Univ NMex Art Mus, 71; Contemp Directions, Addison Gallery of Am Art, 75; Piedmont Graphics, Greenville Co Mus, SC 75 & 77; Silver & Silk, Mus of Hist & Technol, Smithsonian Inst, 75-77; one-man shows, Photoserigraphs, Mint Mus of Art, 70, Greenville Co Mus of Art, 72 & 77, Univ Ore Mus, 73, Univ of Iowa Mus Art, 75 & Univ Notre Dame, 78. Teaching: Assoc prof photog & printmaking, Clemson Univ, SC, 66-; vis artist photog & graphics, Penland Sch of Crafts, NC, summer 70 & 74. Pos: Mem bd dir, The Soc for Photog Educ, New York, 73-77; chmn, State Art Collections Comm, SC, 77-78. Bibliog: David Featherstone (auth), Art Week, 73; Joe Earle (auth), Artist Collects Photography as His Raw Material, Greenville, Piedmont, 77. Mem: Soc for Photog Educ (bd dir, 73-77; chmn of grants, 73-77); Guild of SC Artists; Southeastern Col Art Conf. Style & Technique: Serigraphy with photographic images. Media: Photoserigraphy; Photography. Publ: Illusr, South Carolina Architecture 1670-1970, SC Tricentennial Comn, 70. Mailing Add: 108 Poole Lane Clemson SC 29631

WANG, YINPAO
PAINTER, WRITER
b Suchow, China, Mar 11, 15; US citizen. Study: Chao Tung Univ, BA; Univ Pa, MBA. Work: Henry Ford Mus, Detroit; Detroit Art Mus; China Inst in Am, New York; Gracie Mansion, New York; James Cash Penney Collections, New York. Exhib: One-man shows, Art Students League, 38, Frank & Meier Galleries, Portland, 49, Detroit Art Mus, 58, Woodmere Galleries, Philadelphia, 60, Shaffer Galleries, Philadelphia, 62, Columbia Univ, New York, 68, Sino-Am Cult Asn, Taipei, Taiwan, 69, Nat Mus, Taipei, Taiwan, 70, Jefferson Univ, Philadelphia, 71 & annually at Ward Eggleston Galleries, New York, Crespi Galleries, New York & Lynn Kottler Galleries, New York. Teaching: Instr painting, Art Students League, 37-38; prof art, Kwang Si Univ, 46-47. Pos: Founder, Peking Art Asn, China, 34; vpres, Chinese Art League in New York, 37-41. Awards: Merit Award, Grumbacher, 54; Int Awards, Am Inst Interior Designers, 61 & 63; Spec Award, Int Platform Asn, 65; plus others. Mem: Fel Royal Soc Arts, London; hon mem Kappa Pi; life mem Harrisburg Art Asn; art mem Philadelphia Art Alliance; Nat Soc Arts & Lett. Style & Technique: Neo-classic Chinese traditional painting fused with impressionistic reality; modern materials and colors are selectively introduced. Media: Watercolor. Publ: Contribr, The Mysterious Fifth Dimension, 58; auth, Techniques of Chinese Painting, 70, We Live in Art, 70, Thoughts in Chinese Art, 72, First Generation, 75 & Our Social Life, 76. Mailing Add: 87 Kent Dr East Greenwich RI 02818

WAPP, JOSEPHINE MYERS
DESIGNER, INSTRUCTOR
b Apache, Okla, Feb 10, 12. Study: Univ Okla; Univ NMex, Albuquerque; Southwestern Col (Kans); Okla State Univ, BS; Western Mont Col, NDEA scholar, 66; Santa Fe Indian Sch; and with Dr Kenneth Chapman & Dorothy Leibes; study abroad. Work: Arts & Crafts Bd, Washington, DC; Mus Southern Plains, Anadarko, Okla. Exhib: Ctr Arts of Indian America, Washington, DC; Needle & Thread Exhib, Mus Contemp Crafts, New York; Contemp Mus, Wichita, Kans; Contemp Crafts, Univ Kans; Comparative Show Old & New Indian Crafts, Scotland, Ger, Turkey, Mex & Chile. Teaching: Teacher arts & crafts, Chillocco Indian Sch, Okla, 34-63, Intermountain Sch, Brigham City, Utah & Bur Indian Affairs Arts & Crafts Workshop, summer 58; instr, Inst Am Indian Arts, Santa Fe, NMex, 63- Pos: Consult, Indn Studies Workshop, 73- Awards: Bur Indian Affairs Incentive Award for Indian Cult Workshop & Dance, Inst Am Indian Arts, 67. Mem: Nat Indian Educ Asn; Nat Indian Women's Asn. Publ: Contribr, Dance with Indian Children, Educ Res Develop Am Indian Cult, 72; contribr, El Palacio, 74. Mailing Add: Inst of Am Indian Arts Santa Fe NM 87501

WARASHINA, M PATRICIA
CERAMIC SCULPTOR, EDUCATOR
b Spokane, Wash. Study: Univ Wash, Seattle, BFA, MFA. Work: Everson Art Mus, Syracuse, NY; Nelson Gallery of Art, Kansas City, Mo; Detroit Art Inst, Mich; Henry Art Gallery, Seattle, Wash; John Michael Kohler Arts Ctr, Sheboygan, Wis. Exhib: 10th Int Exhib of Ceramic Art, Smithsonian Inst, Washington, DC, 65; Contemp Ceramic Art, US, Can, Mex, Japan, Nat Mus of Mod Art, Tokyo, 71; Int Exhib of Ceramics, Victoria & Albert Mus, London, Eng, 72; Sensible Cup Int Exhib, Sea of Japan Expos, Kanazawa, Japan, 73; Clay, Whitney Mus of Am Art, New York, 74; 1st World Crafts Exhib, Ont Sci Ctr, Toronto, 74; The Collector, Mus of Contemp Crafts, New York, 74; NW 77 Exhib, Mod Art Pavilion, Seattle Ctr, Wash, 77. Teaching: Instr art, Wis State Univ, Platteville, 64-65; instr art, Eastern Mich Univ, Ypsilanti, 66-68; prof art, Univ Wash, Seattle, 70- Style & Technique: Low-fire ceramic sculpture. Media: Clay; Drawing. Dealer: Polly Freidlander Art Gallery 89 Yesler Way Seattle WA 98104. Mailing Add: 1404 E Lynn Seattle WA 98112

WARBURG, EDWARD M M
COLLECTOR
b White Plains, NY, June 5, 08. Study: Harvard Col, BS, 30; Brandeis Univ, hon DHL; Jewish Inst Relig, Hebrew Union Col. Teaching: Art instr, Bryn Mawr Col, 31-33. Pos: Mem archaeol exped to photograph Islamic archit, Iran, 33; staff mem, Mus Mod Art, 34-35; trustee, Am-Israel Cult Found; chmn, Am Patrons of Israel Mus; founder & hon trustee, Mus Mod Art, New York; hon trustee, Inst Int Educ. Collection: Contemporary art. Mailing Add: 900 Park Ave New York NY 10021

WARD, EVELYN SVEC
FIBRE ARTIST
b Solon, Ohio. Study: Otterbein Col, BA; Sorbonne, Paris. Work: Cleveland Mus of Art & Cleveland Trust Collection, Ohio. Exhib: May Shows, Cleveland Mus of Art, 53-; Fibre Art by Am Artists, Ball State Univ, Muncie, Ind, 72; Weaving-Off Loom, Fairtree Gallery, New York & Galeria del Sol, Santa Barbara, Calif, 73; Ohio Craft Invitational, Mansfield Art Ctr, Ohio, 75; Fibre Structures, Mus of Art, Carnegie Inst, Pittsburgh, Pa, 76; one-person show, Recent Works in Fibre, Ross Widen Gallery, Cleveland, 77. Collections Arranged: Fiberworks, Cleveland Mus of Art (auth, catalog), 77. Pos: Textile asst, Cleveland Mus of Art, 50-55. Awards: Juror mention, May Show, Cleveland Mus of Art, 57 & 67. Bibliog: D Z Meliach (auth), Art from Fibres and Fabrics, 72 & Virginai C Bath (auth), Lace, 74, Henry Regnery Co; Elyse Sommer (auth), Inventive Fibre Crafts, Prentice-Hall Inc, 76. Mem: Textile Arts Club (pres, 64-66); Women's Comt, Cleveland Inst of Art; Am Crafts Coun; Ohio Designer Craftsmen; Cleveland Soc for Contemp Art. Style & Technique: Cloth and thread manipulation for three-dimensional and relief sculptures and webs. Dealer: Ross Widen Gallery 5120 Mayfield Rd Cleveland OH 44124. Mailing Add: 27045 Solon Rd Solon OH 44139

WARD, JOHN LAWRENCE
ART HISTORIAN, PAINTER
b East Orange, NJ, Feb 6, 38. Study: Hamilton Col, BA; Yale Univ, MA(art hist); Univ NMex, MFA(painting). Work: Univ NMex. Exhib: One-man shows, Rollins Col, Winter Park, Fla, 70, Fla Tech Univ, Orlando, 76 & Univ of Fla, Gainesville, 76; Artist-Teacher in Fla Univ, Ringling Mus, Sarasota, Fla, 70; Southeastern Biennale, Isaac Delgado Mus, New Orleans, 71 & New Orleans Mus Art, 75; The Human Presence, Jacksonville Art Mus, Fla, 74; Southeastern Ctr for Contemp Art, Winston-Salem, NC, 75. Teaching: Assoc prof art hist, Univ Fla, 62-64 & 66- Mem: Col Art Asn. Style & Technique: Realist. Media: Oil on Canvas. Res: Flemish painting, pictorial space construction and perception; criticism of photography. Publ: Auth, A new look at the Friedsam Annunciation, Vol L, 68, A proposed reconstruction of an altarpiece by Rogier Van der Weyden, Vol LIII, 71 & Hidden symbolism in Jan Van Eyck's Annunciations, Vol LVII, 75, Art Bulletin; auth, The criticism of photography as art: The photographs of Jerry Uelsmann, 70; auth, Van der Weyden, Encycl Universalis. Mailing Add: Art Dept AFA Univ of Fla Gainesville FL 32611

WARD, LYLE EDWARD
PAINTER, EDUCATOR
b Topeka, Kans, Feb 4, 22. Study: Stevens Point State Teachers Col, Wis, 43; Kansas City Univ, 50; Kansas City Art Inst, BFA, 51, MFA, 52; also with Miron Sokole, New York. Work: Brooklyn Mus, NY; Corcoran Gallery, Washington, DC; Butler Inst Am Art, Youngstown, Ohio; Mus Art, Univ Okla, Norman; Mulvane Art Mus, Topeka. Exhib: One-man shows, Kansas City Art Inst, 60, Superior St Gallery, Chicago, 60 & Univ Miss, Oxford, 72; Contemporary Americans, Ark Arts Ctr, Little Rock, 66; Ark State Pavilion, Hemisfair, San Antonio, Tex, 68; Inaugural Exhib Artists USA, State Univ NY Col Oswego, 68; Kansas State Col, Pittsburgh, 69; Ellis Gallery, Springfield, Mo, 69; Univ Miss, Oxford, 72; Avanti Galleries, New York, 75; Breedlove Fine Arts Ctr, Ft Smith, Ark, 76; Treishman Gallery, Hendrix Col, Conway, Ark, 76. Teaching: Assoc prof art & chmn dept, Col of the Ozarks, Clarksville, Ark, 56- Awards: Arts Festival Award, Worthen Bank, Little Rock, 60 & 62; First Prize, Delta Exhib, Ark Arts Ctr, 63, 65 & 67; 18th Arts Festival Award, Ft Smith Festival Bd, Ark, 68. Bibliog: Peggy Robertson (auth), article in Ark Gazette, Little Rock, 74; Gordon Brown (auth), rev in Arts Mag, 75. Mem: Col Art Asn Am; Mid-Am Art Asn; Southeast Art Conf. Style & Technique: Large works executed in oil on canvas using a palette knife; all are abstract-figurative paintings stated in dark sombre field of color. Media: Oil. Dealer: Avanti Galleries 145 E 72nd St New York NY 10021. Mailing Add: 610 Johnson St Clarksville AR 72830

WARD, LYND (KENDALL)
ILLUSTRATOR, WRITER
b Chicago, Ill, June 26, 05. Study: Teachers Col, Columbia Univ, BS, 26; Staatliche Akad Graphische Kunst, Leipzig, Ger, 26-27. Work: Libr Cong; New York World's Fair, 39; Nat Acad Design; Newark Mus; Metrop Mus Art; Montclair Art Mus, NJ. Exhib: Am Art Cong; New York World's Fair, 39; Nat Acad Design; John Herron Art Inst. Awards: Prize, Nat Acad Design, 49, John Taylor Arms Mem Prize, 62; Samuel F B Morse Gold Medal, 66; Rutgers Medal, 69; plus others. Mem: Academician Nat Acad Design; Soc Am Graphic Artists (pres, 53-59); Soc Illusr. Publ: Auth & illusr (novels in woodcuts), God's Man, 29, Madman's Drum, 30, Song Without Words, 36 & Vertigo, 37; auth & illusr, Nic of the Woods, 65; plus others. Mailing Add: Lambs Ln Cresskill NJ 07626

WARD, VELOX BENJAMIN
PAINTER
b Mount Vernon, Tex, Dec 21, 01. Work: Smithsonian Inst, Washington, DC; Am Nat Collection; Am Nat Ins Co, Galveston, Tex; Amon Carter Mus, Ft Worth, Tex; Longview Mus & Art Ctr, Tex. Comn: Paintings of old homesteads for Mrs Jean Roberts, Longview, 62, Mrs Henry Foster, Longview, 67, Mrs Nila Boatner, Longview, 69, Mrs Joan Cotton, Longview, 69 & Mobil Oil Co, 75. Exhib: Heirloom House, Inc, Dallas, 65; Tex Painting & Sculpture Exhib, Dallas Mus Fine Arts, 66; The Sphere of Art, Hemisfair 68, San Antonio: Amon Carter Mus, 72. Style & Technique: Primitive. Media: Oil. Publ: Auth, Texans, their Land & History. Mailing Add: 2303 Stardust Longview TX 75601

WARD, WILLIAM EDWARD
DESIGNER, PAINTER
b Cleveland, Ohio, Apr 4, 22. Study: Western Reserve Univ, BS, 47, MA, 48; Cleveland Inst Art, dipl, 47; Columbia Univ, 50. Work: Cleveland Mus Art; Akron Art Inst, Ohio; Cleveland Art Asn; Cleveland Trust Bank. Comn: Firemen's Memorial (sculpture), Cleveland Fire Dept, 68; official seal for Sch of Med & Case Western Reserve Univ, 69; traveling exhib for George Gund Collection Western Art, New York, 72; mural, Harris Corp, Cleveland, 75. Exhib: One-man shows, Painting & Photography, Cleveland Inst Art, 48 & Acrylics & Watercolors, Ross Widen Gallery, Cleveland, 73; Cleveland Inst Art Fac Exhib, 60-; Wheaton Col, Ill, 69; Ohio Fine Arts Exhib, Massilon Mus Art, Ohio, 75. Collections Arranged: All special exhibition and permanent collection installations, Cleveland Mus Art, 58- Teaching: Instr calligraphy, Cleveland Inst Art, 60-, instr watercolor, 67-69. Pos: Educ & Oriental Depts asst, Cleveland Mus Art, 47-57, designer, 57- Awards: First Prize in Textile Design, Cleveland Mus Art May Show, 57; City Canvas Competition Comn Award, Cleveland Area Arts Coun, 75. Mem: Int Design Conf; City of Cleveland Fine Arts Adv Comt; Cleveland Soc Contemp Art; Print Club Cleveland; The Rowfant Club. Style & Technique: Abstract landscapes; wet-transition technique. Media: Watercolor, Acrylic. Collection: Folk art of Oaxaca, Mexico area and Kalighat paintings from the Calcutta region, India. Dealer: Ross Widen Gallery 5120 Mayfield Rd Cleveland OH 44124. Mailing Add: 27045 Solon Rd Solon OH 44139

WARDER, WILLIAM
PAINTER, EDUCATOR
b Guadalupita, NMex, July 23, 20. Study: Univ NMex, with Raymond Jonson, Kenneth Adams & Randall Davey, BFA; Art Students League, with Louis Bouche & Morris Kantor; Univ Calif, Los Angeles. Work: Art Mus NMex, Santa Fe; NMex State Fair Collection, Albuquerque; Mus Albuquerque; Raton Mus, NMex. Comn: Tom Sawyer & Huck, Works Progress Admin Arts Proj, 36; mural Army life, Ft Warren, Wyo, 43; New Mexico Scene, Radio Sta KABQ, Albuquerque, 55; NMex hist murals, Int State Bank, Raton, 70. Exhib: Am Watercolor Soc, Nat Acad, New York, 48; Audubon Artists Exhib, 48; New York World's Fair Ford Pavillion Nat Exhib, 64; Watercolor USA, Springfield, Mo, 64 & 73; Southwest Fine Arts Biennial, Mus NMex, 74. Teaching. Artist-in-sch, Las Vegas, NMex, 71-73 & Espanola, 74-75, Albuquerque, 74-78. Pos: Art consult, West Las Vegas Pub Schs, 73-74; art consult, NMex Dept Educ, 73-78. Awards: Purchase Award, Mus NMex, 64; Purchase & Grand Prize Awards, NMex State Fair, 64 & 65; Nat Endowment Arts Grants, 71-75. Bibliog: Senator Peter Domenici (auth), speech entered into US Cong Rec, 6/25/73; Artist-in-schools, NMex Sch Rev, Spring 74 & Fall 77. Mem: Inst Platform Assoc. Style & Technique: Varying degrees of abstraction, predominantly landscape and design. Media: Watercolor, Oil. Res: Distinguishing the self and person as two entities in the individual that relate to intrinsic creativity and the extrinsic social productivity as bases for educational orientations. Publ: Auth, Alternative Approach in Education Using Art as the Medium, 74. Dealer: Jamison Gallery 111 E San Francisco St Santa Fe NM 87501. Mailing Add: PO Box 8123 Albuquerque NM 87198

WARDLAW, GEORGE MELVIN
PAINTER
b Baldwyn, Miss, Apr 9, 27. Study: Memphis Acad Arts, BFA, 51; Univ Miss, with David Smith & Jack Tworkov, MFA, 65. Exhib: American Crafts, Smithsonian Inst, Washington, DC, 52; Recent Still Life, RI Sch Design, Providence, 66; Inside-Outside, Smith Col Mus Art, Northampton, Mass, 66; Contemporary Art at Yale, Yale Univ Art Gallery, New Haven, Conn, 66; Abstract Paintings, DeCordova Mus, Lincoln, Mass, 71. Teaching: Asst prof design, State Univ NY Col New Paltz, 56-63; assoc prof painting & exec off, Yale Univ, 64-68; prof painting & chmn dept, Univ Mass, Amherst, 68- Media: Acrylic. Mailing Add: 47 Morgan Circle Amherst MA 01002

WARDLE, ALFRED HILL
SILVERSMITH, JEWELER
b Englewood, NJ, May 29, 33. Study: Art Inst Pittsburgh; Sch Am Craftsmen, Rochester Inst Technol, AAS & BS; Syracuse Univ Sch Art. Comn: Mem punch bowl, Rochester Inst Technol, 56; silver chalice with gold cross, Grace Episcopal Church, Utica, NY, 60; silver chalice, Westminster Presby Church, Utica, 62; large tree of life, Temple Addas Israel, Rome, NY, 66; presidential maces, Mohawk Valley Community Col, Utica, 69 & State Univ of NY, Col of Technol, Utica, 75. Exhib: Smithsonian Inst Traveling Exhib, 58; Crafts Exhib, Mus Mod Art, Caracas, Venezuela, 61; RI Arts Festival Show, Providence, 63; one-man show, Three Rivers Arts Festival, Pittsburgh, 66; two-man show, Munson-Williams-Proctor Inst, Utica, 68. Teaching: Instr metal arts, Norwich Free Acad, Conn, 59-60; instr silversmithing, Munson-Williams-Proctor Inst. Pos: Color coordr rstoration comt, Unitarian Church Barneveld, NY, 70-72. Awards: Young Americans Second Prize, Mus Contemp Crafts, 54; Hollow Ware First Prize, RI Arts Festival, 63; Crafts First Prize, Syracuse Regional Art Show, 63-65. Bibliog: Nicolas Haney, Trilling & Lee (auth), Art for Young America, Bennett Co, 60. Mem: Soc of NAm Goldsmiths; Cooperstown Art Asn; Ziyara Temple AAONMS of Utica; NY State Craftsmen. Media: Sterling Silver, Gold. Mailing Add: RD 1 Hinman Rd Barneveld NY 13304

WARDWELL, ALLEN
GALLERY DIRECTOR
b New York, NY, Jan 18, 35. Study: Yale Univ, BA, 57; NY Univ, MA, 60. Collections Arranged: Yakutat South Indian Art of the Northwest Coast (auth, catalogue), 64, The Sculpture of Polynesia (auth, catalogue), 67 & The Art of the Sepik River (auth, catalogue), 71, Art Inst of Chicago; Gold of Ancient America (auth, catalogue), Mus of Fine Arts, Boston, 68. Pos: Asst cur of primitive art, Art Inst of Chicago, 60-63, cur primitive art, 63-73, actg cur of decorative arts, 64-70 & asst dir mus serv, 70-72; dir, Asia House Gallery, 74- Mem: Yale Univ Art Gallery trustees; Asn of Am Mus Dirs; Indo-US Subcomn on Educ & Cult. Publ: Contribr, Bibliography Northwest Coast Indian Art, Mus of Primitive Art, Art Inst of Chicago, 70. Mailing Add: 112 E 64th St New York NY 10021

WARDY, FREDERICK
SCULPTOR, PAINTER
b Los Angeles, Calif, Nov 18, 37. Study: Univ Calif, Los Angeles, BA, 60; Chouinard Art Inst, 65. Work: Arnot Mus, Elmira, NY; Minn Mus Art; First Nat Bank Chicago. Comn: Large outdoor wood sculpture, NY State Coun Arts, 74. Exhib: Whitney Ann, 72. Pos: Cur traveling exhib, US Info Agency, Japan, 73. Media: Acrylic on Canvas. Dealer: Willard Gallery 29 E 72nd St New York NY 10021. Mailing Add: 70 Thomas St New York NY 10013

WARHOL, ANDY
PAINTER, CRAFTSMAN
b Cleveland, Ohio, Aug 8, 31. Study: Carnegie Inst Technol. Work: Albright-Knox Art Gallery, Buffalo; Los Angeles Co Mus Art; Mus Mod Art; Whitney Mus Am Art; Walker Art Ctr, Minneapolis; plus others. Exhib: The 1960's, Mus Mod Art, 67; Documenta IV, Kassel, Ger, 68; Directions I: Options, Milwaukee Art Ctr, 68; The Development of the Imagery, Magnin Gallery, 75; Baltimore Mus Art, 75; Art Inst Chicago; Whitney Mus Am Art; Metrop Mus Art; Contemp Art Ctr, Cincinnati; plus others. Awards: Sixth Film Cult Award, 64; Los Angeles Film Festival Award, 64. Bibliog: Gregory Battcock (ed), Minimal Art: A Critical Anthology, Dutton, 68; plus many others. Mem: Film Co-op. Dealer: Leo Castelli Gallery 4 E 77th St New York NY 10021. Mailing Add: Andy Warhol Enterprises 860 Broadway New York NY 10003

WARK, ROBERT RODGER
ART ADMINISTRATOR, ART HISTORIAN
b Edmonton, Alta, Oct 7, 24; US citizen. Study: Univ Alta, BA & MA; Harvard Univ, MA & PhD. Teaching: Instr art, Harvard Univ, 52-54; instr art, Yale Univ, 54-56; lectr art, Calif Inst Technol, 60-; lectr art, Univ Calif, Los Angeles, 65- Pos: Cur art, Huntington Libr & Art Gallery, 56- Mem: Col Art Asn Am; Asn Art Mus Dirs. Res: English art of the Georgian period. Publ: Ed, Sir Joshua Reynolds, Discourses on Art, 59; auth, Early British Drawings in the Huntington Collection 1700-1750, 69; auth, Drawings by John Flaxman in the Huntington Collection, 70; auth, Ten British Pictures 1740-1840; auth, Drawings by Thomas Rowlandson in the Huntington Collection, 75; plus others. Mailing Add: Henry E Huntington Libr & Art Gallery San Marino CA 91108

WARKOV, ESTHER
PAINTER
b Winnipeg, Man, Oct 12, 41. Study: Winnipeg Sch Art, 58-61. Work: Nat Gallery, Ottawa; Mus Fine Arts, Montreal; Vancouver Art Gallery; Winnipeg Art Gallery; Beaver Brook Art Gallery, Fredricton, NB. Exhib: Expo '67, Montreal, 67; Marlborough Godard Exhib, 73; Mus Mod Art, Paris, 73; Albright Knox Art Gallery, Buffalo, 74. Awards: Can Coun Bursaries, 67-72; Can Coun Grant, 73-74. Bibliog: Esther Warkov, Can Broadcasting Corp, 73. Mem: Royal Can Acad Arts. Style & Technique: Figurative multi-panelled canvases. Media: Oil. Dealer: Marlborough Godard Ltd 1490 Sherbrooke W Montreal PQ Can. Mailing Add: 341 Matheson Ave Winnipeg MB R2W 0C9 Can

WARNEKE, HEINZ
SCULPTOR
b Bremen, Ger, June 30, 95; US citizen. Study: Kunstschule, Bremen; Staatliche Kunstgewerbe Schule & Acad, masters degree; with Blossfeld, Haberkamp, Wakele & others. Work: Art Inst Chicago; Corcoran Gallery Art, Washington, DC; Brookgreen Gardens, Georgetown, SC; Santa Fe Mus, NMex; The Immigrant, P Samuel Mem, Fairmount Park, Philadelphia; Nat Collection Am Art, Smithsonian Inst. Comn: Prodigal Son (granite),

Washington Cathedral, DC, 38, Last Supper, tympanium at s portal, 55 & entire decoration of clerestory at s transcept, 56-60; granite elephant group, comn by pvt group for Philadelphia Zool Gardens, 63; portrait plaque of Allen C Dulles, pvt comn for CIA Bldg, Langley, Va, 69. Exhib: Salon des Tuileries, Paris, France, 29; Art Inst Chicago Ann, 30; Pa Acad Fine Arts Ann, Philadelphia, 34-42; Mus Mod Art Ann, New York, 36-46; Whitney Mus Am Art Ann, New York, 36-46. Teaching: Head sculpture, Warneke Sch Art, 40-42; head sculpture, Corcoran Sch Art, 43-68; prof sculpture, George Washington Univ, 43-68. Pos: Mem, Ger Monuments Comn, World War I, Bucharest, Romania, 14-18. Awards: Logan Prize for Best in Show, 30; Widener Gold Medal, Pa Acad Fine Arts, 35; Washington DC Artists Ann First Prize, Corcoran Gallery Art, 43-44; plus others. Bibliog: Olin Dows (auth), Art for housing tenants, Mag Art, 11/38; Walter Nathan (auth), Living forms: the sculptor Heinz Warneke, Parnassus Mag, 2/41; New Last Supper, Life Mag, 9/19/55. Mem: Nat Acad Design; fel Nat Sculpture Soc; assoc Salon des Tuileries; New Eng Sculptors Soc; life fel Int Inst Arts & Lett. Media: Granite. Publ: Auth, First & last & sculptor, Mag Art, 2/39. Mailing Add: The Mowings East Haddam CT 06423

WARNER, BOYD, JR
PAINTER
b Kaibeto, Ariz, May 26, 37. Work: In the pvt collections of James T Bialec, Phoenix, Ariz, Dick Van Dyke, Cave Creek, Ariz, Alan Alda, Senator & Mrs Barry Goldwater, Ariz, James Buchanan, Okla, Dr Gentile, Mesa, Ariz, Glenn Ford and others. Exhib: Scottsdale Nat Indian Art & Crafts Show, 68-71; Inter Tribal Ceremonial, Gallup, NMex, 68-72; Heard Mus Indian Art Show, Phoenix, 69-71; Ariz State Fair, Phoenix, 69-71; 27th Indian Art Show, Philbrook Art Ctr, Tulsa, Okla, 72; one-man shows, Garelick's Gallery, Scottsdale, Ariz, 77 & Birmingham Gallery Inc, Mich, 77. Awards: Elkus Mem Award, Inter Tribal Ceremonial, 71; First and Second Place Award in Mixed Media 72; Grand Award for portrait of A Smiling Indian, Scottsdale Nat Indian Art Show, 75; First Award for painting Shalako, NMex State Fair, 74; First & Second Award, NMex State Fair, 76. Mailing Add: 606 N Fourth St Apt 1 Phoenix AZ 85004

WARNER, HARRY BACKER, JR
WRITER
b Chambersburg, Pa, Dec 19, 22. Pos: Art critic & writer on art, Hagerstown Herald-Mail, Md, 43- Mailing Add: 423 Summit Ave Hagerstown MD 21740

WARNER, JO
PAINTER
b Clayton, NMex, Apr 30, 31. Study: Univ Colo, Boulder, BFA; Skowhegan Sch Painting & Sculpture, Maine, with Jack Levine & Henry V Poor; Art Students League, with Morris Kantor & Byron Brown. Exhib: Tenth Street, Mus Contemp Art, Houston, Tex, 59; Recent American Painting & Sculpture, Mus Mod Art Circulating Exhib, 61-63; West Side Artists-New York City, Riverside Mus, 64; Kutztown State Col Mus, Pa, 75; Tenth St Days—The Co-ops of the 50s, New York, NY, 77; solo exhibs, Univ Wis-Eau Claire Mus, 64 & Phoenix Gallery, New York, 72 & 76. Awards: Award & Ganeles Prize/Sculpture, Nat Asn of Women Artists, 74. Media: Oil; Collage; Wood. Dealer: Phoenix Gallery 30 W 57th St New York NY 10019. Mailing Add: 142 West End Ave New York NY 10023

WARNER, LUCY ANN
WEAVER, DESIGNER
b Northampton, Mass, Apr 16, 37. Study: Univ Colo, BA, 58; Univ NMex, BA(art educ), 61; Cranbrook Acad Art MFA(weaving & textile design), 64. Work: Detroit Inst Arts, Mich. Comn: Upholstery fabric for off exec dir, Harvey McWilliam, St Mary's Hosp, Richmond, Va, 65; wall hanging, comn by Robert W Stewart, Richmond, Va, 66; wall hanging, comn by Robert Klein, 67; interior fabrics for apt in Hancock Bldg, comn by Beverly Niemiec, Touchstone Gallery, Chicago, 75. Exhib: Am Craftsmen, Mus Contemp Crafts, New York, 66; Nat Crafts Exhib, Univ NMex Art Mus, 68; Crafts Southwest 70; Los Angeles Co Fair, Pomona, 70; Int Designer Craftsmen, El Paso Exhib, 71; Southwest Crafts Exhib, Am Crafts Coun Gallery, New York, 72. Teaching: Instr weaving, Univ NMex Community Col, 69-71. Pos: Res craftsman, Va Mus Fine Arts, Richmond, 64-66. Awards: Purchase Award, Mich Artist Craftsmen Exhib, Am Inst Interior Designers, 64; Nat Merit Award, Southeastern Craftsmen, Am Crafts Coun, 66; Excellence in Weaving, Textiles NMex, 74, Mus Albuquerque, 74. Bibliog: Art in Arts in Va, 65; Jeanne Bonnette (producer), guest artist Creative Process series, KNME-TV, 71; Arthur Sussman (producer), artist film interview, TV 7 Art News, KOAT-TV, 75. Mem: Am Crafts Coun; World Crafts Coun; NMex Designer-Craftsmen (pres, 69-70); Albuquerque Designer-Craftsmen. Style & Technique: Weaving for interiors varies from very colorful and bold pieces, sometimes three dimensional, to very subtle open woven tapestries; other textile techniques also used, usually in combination with weaving. Media: Fibers. Dealer: Hills Gallery 110 San Francisco St Santa Fe NM 87501; Mariposa Gallery 113 Romero NW Albuquerque NM 87104. Mailing Add: 1908 Griegos Rd NW Albuquerque NM 87107

WARREN, BETTY
PAINTER
b New York, NY. Study: Nat Acad Design; Cape Sch Art, with Henry Hensche. Work: Albany Inst Hist & Art, NY; State Univ NY, Albany; Fourth Regiment Armory, New York, NY; Albany Law Sch, NY; Hartwick Col, Oneonta, NY; NY State Supreme Court, Albany; Grand Lodge Masons NY State, New York. Exhib: Artists of the Mohawk, Hudson Region, Schenectady, NY, 60-71; Allied Artists Am, New York, 65 & 67; Am Watercolor Soc, New York, 66; Nat Arts Club Nat, New York, 69-71; Knickerbocker Artists, New York; over 25 one-man shows in mus & galleries. Teaching: Instr painting & drawing, Albany Inst Hist & Art, 59-; owner & dir, Malden Bridge Sch Art, NY, 65- Awards: Purchase Prizes, Albany Inst Hist & Art, 50 & 64; Gold Medal, Catharine Lorillard Wolfe Art Club; Grand Prize, Cooperstown 29th Ann Exhib. Bibliog: Norman Kent (auth), The paintings of Betty Warren, Am Artist, 67; rev in Grand Cent Galleries Yearbk, 67, 69 & 70. Mem: Grand Cent Art Galleries; Nat Arts Club; Am Artists Prof League; Nat League Am Pen Women; Pen & Brush. Media: Oil, Pastel. Dealer: Grand Cent Art Galleries Hotel Biltmore New York NY 10017; Portraits Inc 41 E 57th St New York NY 10022. Mailing Add: 76 Western Ave Albany NY 12203

WARREN, FERDINAND EARL
PAINTER, ART ADMINISTRATOR
b Independence, Mo, Aug 1, 99. Study: Kansas City Art Inst. Work: Metrop Mus Art, New York; Brooklyn Mus Art, NY; Rochester Mem Gallery, Youngstown, Ohio; Currier Gallery Art, Springfield, NH; NASA Permanent Collection, Nat Gallery Art, Washington, DC. Comn: Two war bond posters, US Treas Dept, 43; History of the Printed Word (mural), Foote & Davies, Atlanta, 57; Robert Frost (portrait from life), Agnes Scott Col, Decatur, Ga, 58; copper enamel cross, St Agnes Episcopal Church, Atlanta, 63; Apollo 14 (painting), NASA, Washington, DC, 71. Exhib: Richmond Va Ann, 48-49; Corcoran Gallery Art, Washington, DC, 49; Art in the Embassies, US Dept State, 66-70; Nat Acad Design Ann, New York; Carnegie Int, Pittsburgh. Pos: Artist in residence, Univ Ga, 50-51; chmn dept art, Agnes Scott Col, 52-69. Awards: Silver Medal, Am Watercolor Soc, 50; Purchase Prize, Butler Inst Am Art, 54; Edwin Palmer Prize, Nat Acad Design, 61. Bibliog: Forbes Watson (auth), Painting Today; Ernest Watson (auth), Composition in Landscape. Mem: Nat Acad Design. Media: Oil. Mailing Add: 227 E Hancock St Decatur GA 30030

WARREN, JULIANNE BUSSET BAKER
PHOTOGRAPHER
b Lima, Ohio, May 8, 16. Work: Pub Libr Cincinnati & Hamilton Co; Truman Libr, Austin, Tex; Smithsonian Inst. Comn: Photographs of seven US Presidents; Prime Minister Wilson, London; Princess Margaret. Exhib: Cincinatti Art Mus, 59; Shillito's Dept Store, Cincinnati, 61; Jewish Community Ctr, Cincinnati, 70; Cincinnati Woman's Club, 74; one-man shows, Pub Libr Cincinnati & Hamilton Co, 67 & Exhib of Collection, 78. Pos: Mgr, Photo-finishing Co, Cincinnati, 41-48; Photogr radio station, 50-52; news photogr, Cincinnati Post, 52-68. Awards: First Prize, Nat Heirloom Contest, 59; First Prize, Newspaper Guild's Page-One Ball, 61; two prizes. Best Women's Page Photography, Univ Mo, 65. Mem: Asn Am Edit Cartoonists (historian, 71-). Publ: Contribr & illusr, Press Photography, MacMillan, , 61; co-auth, Cincinnati in Color, Hastings House, 78. Mailing Add: 1815 William Howard Taft Rd Cincinnati OH 45206

WARREN, L D
EDITORIAL CARTOONIST
b Wilmington, Del, Dec 27, 06. Work: Cincinnati Art Mus, Eden Park, Ohio; Pub Libr of Cincinnati & Hamilton Co; Univ Cincinnati; Lyndon B Johnson Libr, Austin, Tex; Mus Cartoon Art, Greenwich, Conn. Comn: Numerous cartoon illus for bks, mag & brochures over a period of many yrs. Exhib: Cartoon Exhib, Metrop Mus Art, New York, 54; Int Salon of Cartoons, Int Pavillon of Humor, Montreal, 68-74; Asn Am Ed Cartoonist Exhib, World Cartoon Gallery, Skopje, Yugoslavia, 69 & 71 & Nat Portrait Gallery, London, 70; Editorial Cartoons by L D Warren, Cincinnati Art Mus, 74. Teaching: Guest instr cartooning, Art Acad Cincinnati, 57. Pos: Staff artist, Camden Courier-Post, NJ, 25-27; cartoonist, Philadelphia Rec, 27-47; ed cartoonist, Cincinnati Equirer, 47- Awards: Freedoms Found Awards, 49-73; Nat Headliners Club Award, 61; Best Cartoon of the Sixties, Nat Found Hwy Safety, 71; Martha Kinney Cooper Ohioana Bk Award (Social Hist & Journalism Graphics), Columbus, Ohio, 77. Bibliog: Joseph Eble (auth), As L D sees the world, Pictorial Mag, Cincinnati Enquirer, 66; Judge John W Peck (auth), Federal judge talks about comics, The Cartoonist, 67; Jud Hurd (auth), Want to be a cartoonist?, Cartoonist Profiles, 69. Mem: Asn Am Ed Cartoonists (vpres, 60 & 75); Nat Cartoonists Soc; Cincinnati Art Mus. Media: Ink, Crayon. Publ: Illusr, Penny Penguin (informative comic bk for children), Stern & Co, 35; illusr, Terry & Bunky Play Football, Terry & (in Japanese, 49) & Terry & Bunky Play Basketball (series of children's sports bks), Putnam, 45-51; co-auth (with Walter C Langsam), The World and Warren's Cartoons, Exposition Press, NY, 77. Mailing Add: 1815 William Howard Taft Rd Cincinnati OH 45206

WARREN, MELVIN CHARLES
PAINTER, SCULPTOR
b Los Angeles, Calif, Mar 19, 20. Study: Fed Art Corresp, 36; Tex Christian Univ, 49-53. Work: Cowboy Hall of Fame & Western Heritage Ctr, Oklahoma City; Lyndon B Johnson Libr, Austin, Tex. Comn: Bronze to celebrate 150th anniversary, Tex Rangers Commemorative Found, 72; Tex Longhorn Steer (bronze ed of 60), Gov Dolph Briscoe, Tex, for 40th Southern Governors' Conf, 74; commemorative bronze (ed of 100), Tex & Southwestern Cattle Raisers Asn, 76. Exhib: Nat Cowboy Hall of Fame & Western Heritage Ctr, Oklahoma City, 68-72; Phoenix Art Mus, Ariz, 73, 74, 76 & 77. Awards: Gold Medal in Oil, Franklin Mint, 73 & 74; Colt Medal, Colt Indust, 73 & 74; Gold Medal in Oil, Cowboy Artist of Am, 74, Colt Award & Gold Medal/Drawing, 75 & Silver Medal/Drawing, Cowboy Artist of Am Exhib, Phoenix Art Mus, Ariz, 77. Bibliog: Dean Kraker (auth), Director National Cowboy Hall of Fame, Persimmon Hill, 12/70; Dr John Diffily (auth), Director of education-Amon Carter Mus, Am Artist, 7/75 & article in Southwest Art, 10/76; article in Mzuri Drumbeat, Mzuri Safair Found. Mem: Cowboy Artists of Am (vpres, 72-73); Coppini Acad Fine Arts. Style & Technique: Western art, sharp focus realism to accent near objects. Publ: Illusr, Frontier Forts of Texas, Tex Press, 66; Trails of the Southwest, Premberton Press, 68. Mailing Add: PO Box 369 Clifton TX 76634

WARREN, PETER WHITSON
See Whitson

WARRINER, LAURA B
PAINTER
b Tulsa, Okla, Jan 18, 43. Study: Okla Baptist Univ; Oklahoma City Univ. Exhib: Nat Watercolor Soc 54th Ann, Laguna Beach Mus, Calif, 74; Watercolor USA, Springfield Art Ctr, Mo, 74; Nat Acad Design, 149th Ann Exhib, 107th Ann Exhib Am Watercolor Soc & Allied Artists Am 60th Ann Exhib, Nat Acad Design Galleries, New York 74 & 75. Awards: Award for Watercolor, Allied Artists Am 60th Ann Exhib, 74; Barbara Vassilieff Award for Flowers-Still Life, Allied Artists Am 61st Ann Exhib, 75; Century Award of Merit, Rocky Mountain Nat Watermedia Exhib, 75. Bibliog: Ralph Fabri (auth), Flower painting in all media, 2/74 & Can you succeed in art without really trying, 9/74, Today's Art. Mem: Nat Watercolor Soc; Okla Watercolor Asn; Southwestern Watercolor Soc (pres, 73-74). Style & Technique: Loose impressionistic watercolors. Media: Watercolor, Drawing. Mailing Add: 1700 NW 39th St Oklahoma City OK 73118

WARSHAW, HOWARD
PAINTER
b New York, NY, Aug 14, 20. Study: Pratt Inst; Nat Acad Design Sch; Art Students League. Work: Carnegie Inst, Pittsburgh; Pa Acad Fine Arts, Philadelphia; Santa Barbara Mus Art, Calif; Los Angeles Co Mus Art, Calif; Univ Southern Calif Collection. Comn: Murals, Wyle Res, El Segundo, Calif, 53, Ortega Commons, Univ Calif, Santa Barbara, 60, Revelle Commons, Univ Calif, San Diego, 67, Bowdoin Col Libr, Brunswick, Maine, 69 & Univ Calif, Los Angeles, Reed Neurol Res Ctr, 71. Exhib: Corcoran Gallery Art, Washington, DC; Guggenheim Mus & Whitney Mus Am Art, New York; Carnegie Int, Pittsburgh; Mus Art Mod, Paris. Teaching: Prof art, Univ Calif, Santa Barbara, 55- Awards: First Prize for Oil Painting & First Prize for Watercolor, Los Angeles Co Mus Art Centennial, 50. Media: Acrylic, Offset Lithography. Interest: Originated a graduate program in which offset lithography and video tape are used as media for drawing. Publ: Auth, The return of naturalism as the avant-garde, Nation, 60; auth, The wild goose chase for reality, Ctr Mag, 69. Dealer: Larcada Gallery 23 E 67th St New York NY 10021; Adelle Bednarz 902 N La Cienega Blvd Los Angeles CA 90069. Mailing Add: 250 Toro Canyon Rd Carpinteria CA 93013

WARSINSKE, NORMAN GEORGE, JR
SCULPTOR, PAINTER
b Wichita, Kans, Mar 4, 29. Study: Univ Mont, BA; Kunstwerkschule, Darmstadt, Ger; Univ Wash, BA. Comn: Bronze fountains, King Co Med Bldg, Seattle, 65 & Theodora Retirement Home, Seattle, 66; brass & steel screen, Yellowstone Boy's Ranch, Billings, Mont, 69; gold leaf steel stabile, IBM Bldg Lobby, Seattle, 71; stainless stabile, Seattle First Nat Bank, Bellevue, 75. Exhib: Northwest Ann, Seattle Art Mus, 59-65; Santa Barbara Invitational, Calif, 63; Sculpture, Los Angeles Co Mus Art, 64; one-man show, Northwest Craft Ctr, Seattle, 69-70; Woodside Gallery, Seattle, 73. Teaching: Asst instr drawing, Univ Wash, 58-59. Awards: First Prize for Sculpture, Bellevue Art Festival, 60; Best of All Categories, Henry Art Gallery, 66. Bibliog: Louis Redstone (auth), Art in Architecture, McGraw, 68; M R Heinley (auth), Norman Warsinske—metal artistry, Designers W, 6/70. Mem: Seattle Munic Art Comn (vpres, 65-69); Northwest Craft Ctr (pres, 65-70). Style & Technique: Contemporary bold forms based on nature. Media: Metal, Bronze, Steel, Acrylic. Publ: Illusr cover, Am Inst Architects J, 8/71. Dealer: Miller-Pollard Inc 4538 University Way NE Seattle WA 98105 Mailing Add: 3823 94th NE Bellevue WA 98004

WASEY, JANE
SCULPTOR
b Chicago, Ill, June 28, 12. Study: With Paul Landowski, Paris; Simon Moselsio, New York; also with John Flanagan & Heinz Warneke. Work: Ariz State Univ, Tempe; Univ Colo; Dartmouth Col; Univ Nebr; Pa Acad Fine Arts; Whitney Mus Am Art, New York; plus others. Exhib: Art Inst Chicago; Brooklyn Mus; Univ Chicago; Detroit Inst Arts; one-man shows, Montross Gallery, 34, Delphic Studio, 35, Philbrook Art Ctr, 49, Weathervanes Contemp, New York, 54 & Kraushaar Galleries, 56 & 71; plus others. Teaching: Instr sculpture, Bennington Col, 48-49; pvt art classes, 50-60. Awards: First Prizes for Sculpture, Parrish Art Mus & Guild Hall, NY; Mrs John Henry Hammond Award, Nat Asn Women Artists, 51; Phillips Mem Prize, Archit League, 55; plus others. Bibliog: Brumme (auth), Contemporary American Sculpture; Anton Henze (auth), Contemporary Church Art; Design for learning, Town & Country, 10/49; plus others. Mem: Sculptor's Guild; Nat Asn Women Artists; Nat Sculpture Soc; Audubon Artists. Media: Stone, Wood. Dealer: Kraushaar Galleries 1055 Madison Ave New York NY 10028. Mailing Add: Box 61 Lincolnville ME 04849

WASHBURN, GORDON BAILEY
MUSEUM DIRECTOR
b Wellesley Hills, Mass, Nov 7, 04. Study: Deerfield Acad; Williams Col, AB, 28; Fogg Mus Art, Harvard Univ; Williams Col, Hon MFA, 38; Allegheny Col, Hon DFA, 59; Univ Buffalo, Hon DFA, 62; Washington & Jefferson Col, Hon DFA, 68 & LHD, 74. Collections Arranged: Pittsburgh International (triennially); French Painting 1100-1900 & Pictures of Everyday Life-Genre Painting in Europe, 1500-1900, Carnegie Inst; American Painting in the 1950's, Am Fedn Arts, 68; three exhibs per yr, Asia House Gallery, 61-74. Teaching: Lectr art hist. Pos: Dir, Albright Art Gallery, Buffalo, NY, 31-42; dir, Mus Art, RI Sch Design, 42-49; dir dept fine arts, Carnegie Inst, Pittsburgh, 50-62; dir, Asia House Gallery, New York, 61-74, emer dir, 74- Awards: Guggenheim Fel, 49-50; Chevalier, Legion of Honor, 52; Comdr, Royal Order N Star, Sweden, 73. Mem: Col Art Asn Am; Asn Art Mus Dirs; Am Asn Mus. Mailing Add: Asia House Gallery 112 E 64th St New York NY 10021

WASHBURN, JOAN T
ART DEALER
b New York, NY, Dec 26, 29. Study: Middlebury Col, BA. Collections Arranged: Jean Xceron (1890-1967)—Paintings from 1930-1940, 71; Joshua Johnston (1796-1824), 71; Martin Johnson Heade (1819-1904)—Paintings after 1880, 72; William Trost Richards (1833-1905); Am Abstract Artists of the 1930s & 40s, 77; Morgan Russell (1886-1953), 78. Pos: Dir, Washburn Gallery, New York. Specialty: 19th and 20th century American painting and sculpture. Mailing Add: Washburn Gallery 42 E 57th St New York NY 10022

WASHBURN, STAN
PRINTMAKER, PAINTER
b New York, NY, Jan 2, 43. Study: Calif Col Arts & Crafts, Oakland, BFA, 67 & MFA, 68. Work: Chicago Art Inst; Achenbach Found for Graphic Arts, San Francisco; Calif Palace of Legion of Honor, San Francisco Libr Cong, Washington, DC; Mus of Fine Arts, Boston, Mass. Exhib: Davidson Nat Print & Drawing Competition, NC, 73-75; Prints Calif, Oakland Mus Art, 75; Int Miniature Print Competition, Pratt Graphics Ctr, New York, 75 & 77; 24th Nat Exhib Prints, Libr Cong, Washington, DC, 75, Hassam Fund Purchase Prize Exhib, Am Acad of Arts & Lett, New York, 75 & 76; one-man show, Achenbach Found for Graphic Arts, Calif Palace of Legion of Honor, 77. Awards: Pennell Fund Purchase, Libr 75; Purchase Award, Int Miniature Print Collection, Pratt Graphics Ctr, New York, 77. Bibliog: One-half hour spec, KQED-TV, San Francisco, 75. Mem: Calif Soc Printmakers. Style & Technique: Representational, traditional technique. Media: Etching; Oil. Publ: Auth & illusr, True History of the Death by Violence of George's Dragon, 74, illusr, Schinocephalic Waif, 75; illusr, Great Wheadle Tragedy, Godine, 75. Dealer: Pucker/Safrai 171 Newbury St Boston MA 02116. Mailing Add: 2010 Virginia St Berkeley CA 94709

WASHINGTON, JAMES W, JR
PAINTER, SCULPTOR
b Gloster, Miss. Study: Nat Landscape Inst; also with Mark Tobey; Grad Theol Union's Ctr Urban Black Studies, Berkeley, Calif, Hon DFA, 75. Work: Seattle Art Mus, Wash; San Francisco Art Mus. Comn: The Creation (series 4), YWCA, Seattle, 66; The Creation (series 6), Seattle Pub Libr, 67; The Creation (series 7-10), Seattle First Nat Bank Main Br, 68; busts of hist men, Progress Plaza, Philadelphia, 69; The Creation (series 5), Meany Jr High Sch, Seattle, 70; Woodchuck Sunning (sculpture), Frankfurt, WGer, 74. Exhib: 3rd Pac Coast Biennial, Santa Barbara Mus Art, Calif, 59; Willard Gallery, New York, 60-64; Northwest Today, Seattle World's Fair, 62; Grosvenor Gallery Int Exhib, London, 64; Expo '70, Osaka, Japan, 70; Art of the Pac Northwest, Nat Collection of Fine Arts, Washington, DC, 74; one-man exhibs, Foster/White Gallery, Seattle, Wash, 68, 70, 72, 74 & 76 & An Am Baptist Sculptor's Exhib for the Third Biennial, San Diego, Calif, 77. Pos: Secy, Seattle Chap, Artists Equity Asn, 49-53, pres, 60-62; mem gov coun art, State of Wash, 59-60, state art comnr, 61-66. Awards: Award for Bird Hatching, Oakland Munic Art Mus, 57; Award for Wounded Bird, Seattle World's Fair, 62; Gov Sculpture Award, 70. Bibliog: Ann Faber (auth), James Washington's stone sculpture excellence, Seattle Post Intelligence, 56; Pauline Johnson (auth), James Washington speaks, Art Educ J, 68. Mem: Int Platform Asn. Style & Technique: Conventional. Media: Oil, Tempera, Pastel; Granite, Marble. Mailing Add: 1816 26th Ave Seattle WA 98122

WASSER, PAULA KLOSTER
EDUCATOR, PAINTER
b Hatton, NDak. Study: Univ Minn; Minneapolis Sch Art; Univ NDak, BS, 26; Stanford Univ, MA, 31, grad study, 48; Univ Mex, grad study, 33; Univ Southern Calif, 39; also study var art schs. Exhib: Phoenix Fine Arts Asn; Tucson Fine Arts Festival; Ariz Art Guild; Ariz State Fair; Univ Nev, Reno; one-man shows, Phoenix, Ariz; plus others. Teaching: Instr art, Grand Forks Jr High Sch, NDak, 23-25; supvr student art, State Teachers Col, Valley City, NDak, 26-27; actg head dept art, Ariz State Univ, 27-33, head dept, 33-54, prof art, 49-64, cur Am collection, 50-64, emer prof art, 65- Mem: Hon life mem & fel Int Inst Arts & Lett; Delta Phi Delta; Col Art Asn Am; Am Asn Mus; Nat Art Educ Asn. Style & Technique: Expressionist, abstractionist and realist; employ loose, bold and free movement as well as precise and measured. Media: Oil, Acrylic, Watercolor. Publ: Compiled brochures of College Collection, 50-52, 55-56 & 59-63; auth, The Arizona State College Collection of American Art, 54; co-auth, A Guide for the Improvement of the Teaching of Art in the Schools of Arizona; contribr, Am Homes Mag & Design; plus others. Mailing Add: 181 Lassen Circle Vacaville CA 95688

WASSERMAN, ALBERT
PAINTER, DESIGNER
b New York, NY, Aug 22, 20. Study: Art Students League, 37-39, with Charles Chapman; Nat Acad Design, 38-40; with Sidney Dickinson; US Army Univ, France. Work: Traphagen Collection, Ariz. Comn: Many pvt portrait comns. Exhib: Nat Acad Design, New York, 41; Allied Artists Am, New York, 41-72; NJ Painters & Sculptors Soc, 41-72; Am Watercolor Soc, New York, 53-69; Audubon Artists, New York, 60. Teaching: Instr & lectr, Jackson Heights Art Asn, 55-; instr & lectr, Nat Art League, 67-69. Pos: Graphic design consult, var agencies, 48- Awards: Pulitzer Prize Scholar, 40 & Obrig Prize, 41, Nat Acad Design; Friedrichs Prize, Allied Artists Am, 41. Bibliog: Ethel Traphagen (auth), article in Fashion Digest, 54. Mem: Salmagundi Club; Allied Artists Am; NJ Painters & Sculptors Soc; assoc Am Watercolor Soc; Nat Art League; Artists Equity Asn. Style & Technique: Realist, impressionist; direct oil (alla prima). Mailing Add: 34-24 82nd St New York NY 11372

WASSERMAN, BURTON
PAINTER, PRINTMAKER
b Brooklyn, NY, Mar 10, 29. Study: Brooklyn Col, BA, with Burgoyne Diller & Ad Reinhardt; Columbia Univ, MA & EdD. Work: Philadelphia Mus Art, Pa; Munson-Williams-Proctor Inst, Utica, NY; Del Art Ctr, Wilmington; Montreal Mus Fine Arts; NJ State Mus, Trenton; plus others. Comn: Relief triptych, Mr & Mrs Herbert Kurtz, Melrose Park, Pa, 71. Exhib: 21st Am Drawing Biennial, Norfolk Mus Arts & Sci, 65; Art Alliance, Philadelphia, 66-77; USA Pavilion, Int Expos, Osaka, Japan, 70; Color Prints of the Americas, NJ State Mus, 70; Int Graphics Exhib, Montreal Mus Art, 71; Silkscreen: History of a Medium, Philadelphia Mus Art, 71-72; Benjamin Mangel Gallery, Bala-Cynwyd, Pa, 72-77; plus others. Teaching: Prof art, Glassboro State Col, 60- Awards: Brickhouse Drawing Prize, 21st Am Drawing Biennial, Norfolk Mus Arts & Sci, 65; Ryan Purchase Prize, Art from NJ Ann Exhib, NJ State Mus, 67; Esther-Philip Klein Award, Am Color Print Soc Ann, 70; plus others. Mem: Artists Equity Asn (nat pres, 71-73); Am Color Print Soc (mem exec coun, 65-78); Philadelphia Watercolor Club (vpres, 70-76). Style & Technique: Pure plastic concrete, constructivist forms; non-representational, hard-edge abstraction; geometric art. Media: Oil, Silkscreen, Spray Enamels. Publ: Auth articles in Am Artist, Art Educ, Sch Arts, Arts & Activities & many more, 59-72; auth, Modern Painting: the Movements, the Artists, Their Work, 70 & co-auth, Basic Silkscreen Printmaking, 71, Davis, Mass; auth, Bridges of Vision: the Art of Prints & the Craft of Printmaking, NJ State Mus, 70; auth, Exploring the Visual Arts, Davis, Mass, 76. Dealer: Benjamin Mangel Gallery 202 Bala Ave Bala Cynwyd PA 19004. Mailing Add: 204 Dubois Rd Glassboro NJ 08028

WASSERMAN, JACK
ART HISTORIAN, ART ADMINISTRATOR
b New York, NY, Apr 27, 21. Study: Washington Sq Col, NY Univ, BA; NY Univ Inst Fine Arts, with Karl Lehmann & Richard Krautheimer, MA & PhD. Teaching: Instr art, Univ Conn, 53-60; asst prof art, Ind Univ, Bloomington, 60-62; prof Renaissance art, Univ Wis-Milwaukee, 62-75; prof art hist & dean, Tyler Sch Art, Temple Univ, Philadelphia, 75- Awards: Am Coun Learned Soc Grant, 70; Am Philos Soc Grant, 71; Kress Found Grant, 75. Mem: Col Art Asn Am; Soc Archit Historians (bd dirs, 70-); Royal Soc Arts; Amici de Brera. Publ: Auth, Quirinal Palace in Rome, 63 & The dating & patronage of Leonardo's Burlington House cartoon, 71, Art Bull; auth, Ottaviano Mascarino, Accad di San Luca, Rome, 66; auth, Michelangelo's Virgin & Child with St Anne at Oxford, Burlington Mag, 69; auth, Leonardo da Vinci, Abrams, 75. Mailing Add: Tyler Sch of Art Beech & Penrose Sts Philadelphia PA 19126

WASSERMAN, JEANNE L
CURATOR, ART HISTORIAN
b New York, NY, Mar 19, 15. Study: Fieldston, Ethical Cult Schs, New York; Radcliffe Col, AB, 36; Boston Univ, 46-48. Collections Arranged: Daumier Sculpture: A Critical & Comparative Study (with catalog), 5-6/69; Six Sculptors & Their Drawings (with catalog), 71; Recent Figure Sculpture (with catalog), 72; Metamorphoses in 19th Century Sculpture (with catalog), 75-76. Pos: Trustee, Inst Contemp Art, Boston, 62-; res asst to dir, Fogg Art Mus, Harvard Univ, 62-69, hon cur 19th & 20th century sculpture, 69-, vis to art mus, 66-; cur, 180 Beacon Collection Contemp Art, Boston, 67-74; vis, Sch Mus Fine Arts, Boston, 69- Res: 19th and 20th century sculpture with special interest and research in the authentication and dating of cast editions. Mailing Add: 52 Malia Terr Chestnut Hill MA 02167 Boston MA 52 Malia Terr Chestnut Hill MA 02167

WATERHOUSE, CHARLES HOWARD
ILLUSTRATOR, PAINTER
b Columbus, Ga, Sept 22, 24. Study: Newark Sch Fine & Indust Art; also with Steven R Kidd. Work: USMC Mus, US Navy Combat Art Collection & USAAF Collections, Washington, DC; Rutgers Univ, New Brunswick, NJ; NJ Bell Tel Co, Newark. Comn: Marines in the Revolution, 74, Vietnam Refugees, 75 & Marines in Mexican War, USMC, 75-76; Hamilton's Battery, Class of 24, Rutgers Univ, 74; Tarawa Beach Head, L P H Tarawa, US Navy, 75. Exhib: One-man shows, NJ State Mus, Trenton, US Naval Acad, Annapolis, Md, Los Angeles Mus Nat Hist, San Francisco City Hall & Soc Illusrs, New York, 75. Teaching: Instr, lectr & demonstr illus, Newark Sch Fine & Indust Art, 55-73. Pos: Staff artist, Prudential Ins Co, 50-55; free-lance illusr, Nat Publ & Books, 55-73; artist in residence, USMC, 73. Bibliog: Norman Kent (auth), Vietnam drawings, Am Artist, 68, Ed Fleming (auth), Vietnam Sketchbook, AP News Features, 68; F B Nihart (auth), Paintings by Charles Waterhouse, Marine Corps Publ, 75. Mem: Soc Illusr; Salmagundi Club; Nat Soc Mural Painters; USMC Combat Corresp; NACAL Artists. Style & Technique: Decorative line thru realistic paint. Media: Acrylic, Ink. Publ: Illusr, Outdoor Life, Argosy, Saga, Reader's Digest & others, 55-; illusr, Grosset, Dunlap, Viking, Am, & Rutgers Press, 55-; auth & illusr, Vietnam Sketchbook from Delta to DMZ, 68; auth & illusr, Vietnam War Drawings, Air, Land & Sea, 70; illusr, Marines in the Revolution, 75. Mailing Add: 67 Dartmouth St Edison NJ 08817

WATERHOUSE, RUSSELL RUTLEDGE
PAINTER
b El Paso, Tex, Aug 11, 28. Study: Tex A&M Univ, BS, 50; Art Ctr Col Design, Pasadena, Calif, 54-56. Work: Tex Tech Univ Mus Art, Lubbock; El Paso Mus Art; Tex A&M Univ, College Station; Univ Tex, El Paso. Exhib: Baker Collectors Gallery, Lubbock, 65; one-man show, El Paso Mus Art, 72, Wichita Falls Tex Cult Ctr & Mus Art, 72 & Tex A&M Univ, 77. Pos: Mem, Tex Comn Arts & Humanities, 70-75. Media: Watercolor. Publ: Illusr, Goodbye to a River, Knopf, 60; illusr, The Legal Heritage of El Paso, 63 & Pass of the North, 68, Tex Western Press. Mailing Add: 5500 Westside Dr El Paso TX 79932

WATERMAN, DONALD CALVIN
DESIGNER, EDUCATOR
b Erie, Pa, Aug 17, 28. Study: Cleveland Inst Art, dipl; Syracuse Univ, BFA & MFA. Comn: Rayas Collection Textiles, Maharam Fabric Corp, New York, 66, Opel I & II Collection Textiles, 69 & Solar-Loc Malimo Collection, 72; Taxco (wallcovering mural), Imperial Wallpaper Mill, Inc, Cleveland, Ohio, 69; Square-rigger (wall covering mural), F Schumacher, Inc, New York, 69. Exhib: 9th & 11th Regional, Everson Mus Art, Syracuse, NY, 61 & 63; Rochester Finger Lakes, NY, 63 & 64. Teaching: Instr silk screen printing, Mex City Col, Mex, 53; instr indust design & design, Syracuse Univ, 55-60, prof fabric design, 60-, chmn dept textile arts, 70- Pos: Chief designer, Indust Ruiz-Galindo, SA, Mexico City, 53-55; resident designer, Am Pavilion-Int Trade Fair, Zagreb, Yugoslavia, summer 56, Bari, Italy, 57 & Lima, Peru, 59. Style & Technique: Decorative textile & wall covering. Media: Mixed Media, Silk Screen; Landscapes, Watercolor. Publ: Auth, Lugar a Vivir, Construccion Moderna, Mex, 5-6/55; auth, Triennale Report, Indust Design, 11/57. Mailing Add: 7398 Silverwood Dr Manlius NY 13104

WATERS, HERBERT (OGDEN)
PRINTMAKER, EDUCATOR
b Swatow, China, Nov 15, 03; US citizen. Study: Denison Univ, PhB; Pa Sch Indust Art; Art Inst Chicago; Harvard Univ Grad Sch Fine Art. Work: Metrop Mus Art, New York; Libr Cong, Washington, DC; Boston Mus Fine Art; Boston Pub Libr; Springfield Art Mus, Mass. Comn: Book illus, Stephen Day Press, Brattleboro, Vt, 40 & 41; membership print, Rochester Print Club, NY, 52; baptistry mural, Campton Baptist Church, NH, 54; mem bookplates, Denison Univ Libr, 59 & 72. Exhib: New York World's Fair Art Exhib, 39; Am Watercolors Prints & Drawings, Metrop Mus, New York, 52; Boston Print Makers Exhib, 52-; Soc Am Graphic Artists, 60-; Appalachian Corridors I & II, Charleston, WVa, 68 & 70. Teaching: Vis prof graphic art, art hist & painting, Univ NH, summers 46-59; teacher studio & art hist, Holderness Sch, Plymouth, NH, 46-60; from asst prof to emer prof, Alderson-Broaddus Col, 61. Awards: John Taylor Arms Purchase Award Graphic Art, Soc Am Graphic Artists, 54; Prize in Watercolor, WVa Centennial, 63; Award Graphic Art, Appalachian Corridors I & II, 68 & 70. Mem: Nat Acad Design; Soc Am Graphic Artists; Boston Print Makers Soc; NH Art Asn (pres, 60). Style & Technique: Wood engraving on end-grain boxwood, usually in black and white; fine detail; creating a rich pattern; landscapes; self-proofed on hand press. Media: Wood Engraving Prints, Watercolor Painting. Publ: Illusr, New England year, 40; illusr, New England days, 41; contribr, New Hampshire art calendar, 74. Mailing Add: Upper Mad River Rd Campton NH 03223

WATERSTON, HARRY CLEMENT
PAINTER
b New York, NY, Mar 15, 09. Study: NY Sch Fine & Appl Art; Art Students League; NY Univ Sch Educ, BS(sci); also studied watercolor with Eliot O'Hara, Edgar Whitney & Mario Cooper. Work: Hudson River Mus, Yonkers, NY; lithograph, Smithsonian Inst, Washington, DC; lithograph, Mus Graphic Arts, New York. Exhib: Grand Nat, Am Artists Prof League, 62, 74, 75 & 76; Watercolor Show, Nat Arts Club, 63; Hudson Valley Art Asn; Cross-section Show, Artists Equity Asn, 75 & 77; Bronx Mus, 76 & 77; Audubon Artists, 77. Teaching: Teacher art, New York High Schs, 30-37. Awards: Anne G Morse Medal, Gotham Painters Show, 62. Mem: Fel Am Artists Prof League; Artists Equity Asn, NY (bd mem, 75); Art Students League; Nat Coun Art in Jewish Live (vchmn, 70-). Style & Technique: Wet-in-wet technique; landscapes and abstract. Media: Watercolor. Publ: Contribr, Sketches of Riverdale, Riverdale Press, 66- Dealer: Continental Art Gallery 72-21 Austin St Forest Hills NY 11375; Lexington Art Gallery 968 Lexington Ave New York NY. Mailing Add: 4555 Henry Hudson Pkwy New York NY 10471

WATERSTREET, KEN (JAMES KENT WATERSTREET)
PAINTER
b Ogden, Utah, July 18, 40. Study: Calif State Univ, Sacramento, BA, 63, MA, 69. Work: E B Crocker Art Gallery, Sacramento; Univ Southern Ill; Stuart M Speiser Collection; Calif State Univ, Sacramento; Oakland Mus, Calif. Exhib: Human Concern/Personal Torment, Whitney Mus of Am Art, New York, 69 & Mus of Univ Calif, 70; Sacramento Sampler, Long Beach Mus, Calif & E B Crocker Art Gallery, Sacramento, 73; Photo Realism 1973 (traveling exhib), Louis M Speiser Collection, 73-75; Some Realists, Hathorn Gallery, Skidmore Col, Saratoga Springs, NY, 74; Aspects of Realism, Gallery Moos Ltd, Toronto, 74; one-man shows, Louis K Meisel Gallery, New York, 74 & 77; Watercolors & Drawings/American Realists, Louis K Meisel Gallery, 75; Abstraction-Alive & Well, State Univ Col at Potsdam Art Gallery, NY, 75; Hue & Far Cry of Color, Ft Wayne Mus, Ind, 76. Pos: Comnr, Sacramento Metrop Arts Comn, 77, 78. Media: Oil on canvas. Dealer: Louis K Meisel Gallery 141 Prince St New York NY 10012. Mailing Add: 3218 Tobari Ct Sacramento CA 95821

WATFORD, FRANCES MIZELLE
PAINTER, GALLERY DIRECTOR
b Thomasville, Ga, Sept 6, 15. Study: Hilton Leech Art Sch, summers 52-59; Sarasota Sch Art, Portas Studio & Ringling Sch Art, Fla, summers 59-64; spec workshop with Dong Kingman, Columbua, Ga, 66; Famous Artists Sch, grad, 69. Work: Montgomery Mus Fine Arts, Ala; Birmingham Mus Art, Ala; Houston Mem Libr, Dothan, Ala; Dothan High Sch Gallery; Ala Arts & Humanities Coun, Montgomery. Comn: Portraits for pvt collections, Dothan, 58 & 62, Elba, Ala, 60 & 64 & Graceville, Fla, 60; murals for pvt collections, Dothan, 64-66. Exhib: Exhibs, Ala Art League, 51-77; Dothan-Wiregrass Art League, 61-75; Bienniale Int Vichy, France, 64; Honored Exhibitor, Birmingham, Ala, 66; Arts & Crafts Festival Dothan, 71-77; Nat Exhib, Watercolor Soc of Ala; Faces & Voices of Ala Women, Int Women's Yr traveling exhib, 77; one-man shows, Montgomery Mus Fine Arts, 61, Dothan, 61, 64 & 70 & Columbus Mus Arts & Crafts, Ga, 66; plus others. Teaching: Pvt art classes, 49-; instr printmaking, George Wallace Community Col, 77. Pos: Dir, Attic Gallery, Dothan, 58-; free-lance artist. Awards: Purchase Awards, 58-61 & 59 & Cline Award, 66, Ala Art League; Dipl d'Honneur, Bienniale Vichy, 64; Best of Show Purchase Award, Houston Arts & Crafts Festival, Dothan, Ala, 73, 75 & 77. Bibliog: L'art a l'etranger, 10/63 & En province, 1/65, La Rev Mod; Grace Burgess (auth), Student showcase, Famous Artists Mag, 11/71. Mem: Ala Art League (regional vpres, 63-67); Watercolor Soc Ala (regional vpres, 56); Arts & Crafts Festival Dothan (receiving comt, 71-77); Dothan Wiregrass Art League; Houston Arts & Humanities Coun. Style & Technique: Creative interpretation as opposed to realistic; abstract base; emphasis on composition; contemporary, but not non-objective. Media: Watercolor, Acrylic, Oil. Specialty: Paintings and collage in all media. Mailing Add: 106 Montezuma Ave Dothan AL 36301

WATHALL, BETTIE GERALDINE
See Becker, Betty

WATIA, TARMO
PAINTER, EDUCATOR
b Detroit, Mich, May 11, 38. Study: Univ Mich, BS(design), 60 & MFA, 62. Work: Boise Art Gallery, Idaho; Boise Cascade Bldg, Idaho; Kiser Medical, Portland, Ore. Exhib: 52nd Ann, Detroit Art Inst, Mich, 61; Graphics 71, Nat Print & Drawing Exhib, Silver City, NMex, 71; 38th Ann Idaho, Boise Art Gallery, 74; 16th Ann Prints & Drawings, Okla Art Ctr, Oklahoma City, 74; Watercolor USA, Springfield, Mo, 75; 53rd Ann Nat Art Exhib, Springville Mus of Art, Utah, 77; Ninth Ann Arts & Crafts Festival, Coeur D'Alene, Idaho. Teaching: Instr art, Southern Ore Col, Ashland, 66-69; asst prof art, Boise State Univ, Idaho, 69- Awards: Hon Mention, Wenatchee, Wash, 71; Second Place Award, Rock Spring, Wyo, 72; Purchase Award, Boise Art Gallery, Idaho, 74; Cash Award/Painting, Ninth Ann Arts & Crafts Festival, Coeur D'Alene, Idaho. Style & Technique: Colorist, figure, landscape, still life & abstract. Media: Oil, Gouache. Mailing Add: 1015 N Tenth St Boise ID 83702

WATKINS, EILEEN FRANCES
ART CRITIC
b Long Island, NY, Nov 22, 50. Study: Marywood Col, BA(Eng). Pos: Art ed, Newark Star-Ledger, currently; judge, TWA Newark High Schs Art Contest, 74-75; judge, West Hudson Arts Show, 75. Mailing Add: Star-Ledger Star-Ledger Plaza Newark NJ 07101

WATROUS, JAMES SCALES
PAINTER, ART HISTORIAN
b Winfield, Kans, Aug 3, 08. Study: Univ Wis, BS, MA & PhD. Work: Lawrence Univ; Kans State Univ. Comn: Symbols of Printing (mural), Webcrafters Press, Madison, Wis, 52; Justice (aluminum), Wis Bar Ctr, Madison, 58; The Conjurer (mosaic mural), Wash Univ, St Louis, Mo, 59; Man: Creator of Order & Disorder, 64, Symbols of Communication, 72 & Mem Libr, 77 (mosaics), Univ Wis. Teaching: Prof art hist, Univ Wis-Madison, 41-76, Hagen Frof art hist, 64-76, chmn dept art hist, 52-61. Awards: Inst Advan Educ Fac Fel, Italy, 54; Award of Merit, Wis Chap Am Inst Architects, 62; Wis Gov Award in Arts, 69. Mem: Wis Arts Found (bd dir, 75-); Midwest Art Hist Soc (bd dir, 74-75); Mid-Am Col Art Asn (pres, 59); Col Art Asn Am (pres, 62-64); Nat Soc Mural Painters. Res: Technical studies in the fine arts. Publ: Auth, The Craft of Old-Master Drawings, Univ Wis, 57. Mailing Add: 2809 Sylvan Ave Madison WI 53705

WATROUS, JOHN
MUSEUM DIRECTOR
b Riverside, Calif, Aug 24, 42. Study: Pvt study with Lucienne Bloch, 69; Humboldt State Univ, AB, 73; NMex Highlands Univ, MA, 74; Mus Training Prog, Univ Calif, Berkeley, 76-77. Collections Arranged: Charles Schulz, 74, Jim Rosen, 74, Innocent Vision: Living Folk Artists, Films by Gentner/Birdsall & Musical Instruments of Richard Waters, 74-77, Carroll Barnes (ed, catalogue), 75, Marguerite Wildenhain, 75, Southern California Photographers, The Photograph Transformed, The Photographic Landscape, Geometrics in Quilts, Baskets, The Shape of Things, A B Heinsbergen, Architectural Rendering & Contemporary Fiber and Fabric in California, 75-77, Invitational Drawing (auth, catalogue), 76, Three Bay Area Painters (auth & illusr, catalogue), Nat Invitational Drawing Show & Contemporary National Print Show, 76-77, Figurative Sculpture, 77, Santa Rosa Jr Col. Teaching: Instr design & sculpture, Santa Rose Jr Col, Calif, 74- Pos: Dir, Santa Rosa Jr Col Art Gallery, 74-; juror, Sonoma Co Arts Coun, 74-75, mem bd trustees, 75; adv bd, Evolution Art Inst, Petaluma, Calif, 75- Bibliog: Gerrye Payne (auth), African mask show review, 76 & John Kessel (auth), Figurative Sculpture show, 77, Artweek; Sophie Jensen (auth), Richard Waters show opening, The Press, Santa Rosa, 78. Mem: Sonoma Co Arts Coun; Western Asn of Art Mus; Dada Processing Inst, Sebastopol, Calif. Publ: Auth, Hein, Lapp, Quandt, Rosen, Yates, Santa Rosa Jr Col, 75. Mailing Add: 7190 Witter Rd Sebastopol CA 95472

WATSON, ALDREN AULD
DESIGNER, ILLUSTRATOR
b Brooklyn, NY, May 10, 17. Study: Yale Univ, 35; Art Students League, with George Bridgman, Charles Chapman, Robert Brackman, William Auerbach-Levy & others. Work: Illus bks in libr, US, Can, Europe & pvt collections. Comn: Mural, SS Pres Hayes, Thomas Crowell Co Off, 64. Exhib: Fifty Bks Shows, Soc Illusr Ann; New Eng Textbk Shows. Pos: Textbk designer, D C Heath & Co, Boston, 65-66; chief ed curric oriented mat, Silver Burdett Co, Morristown NJ, 66-; official NASA artist, Apollo 8, 68; consult art dir, Houghton Mifflin, Boston, 68-72. Awards: Prize, Domesday Bk Illus Competition, 45. Bibliog: Chap in Forty Illustrators & How They Work. Mem: Author's Guild. Style & Technique: Brush and ink with colored inks; pen and ink; black and color washes; watercolor and gouache. Publ: Auth & illusr, My Garden Grows, 62 & Maple Tree Begins, 70, Viking; auth & illusr, Hand Bookbinding, 63, 68 & 75; auth & illusr, Village Blacksmith, 58 & Country Furniture, 74, Crowell; illusr, Vt Life Mag & Country J; plus many others. Mailing Add: PO Box 482 Brattleboro VT 05301

WATSON, CLARISSA H
ART DEALER
b Ashland, Wis. Study: Layton Art Sch, Milwaukee; Univ Wis-Milwaukee; Milwaukee-Downer Col, BA; Country Art Sch, with Harry Sternberg. Collections Arranged: Long Island Artists Washington, DC, 67; The Collectors' Collections, Adelphi Univ, Garden City, Long Island, 68; Gabriel Spat (1890-1967) Retrospective, Fine Arts Asn Willoughby, Cleveland, Ohio, 70; Nobility of the Horse in Art—to Save America's Wild Horses, Washington, DC, 71. Pos: Dir-founder, Country Art Sch, Westbury, Long Island, 53-68; dir & co-founder, Country Art Gallery, Locust Valley, Long Island, 53-; art consult, Adelphi Univ, 67-69; dir film festivals, 7 Village Arts Coun, Locust Valley, 69-71; dir-producer, Mediaeval Christmas Festival, Locust Valley, 70-73. Specialty: Nineteenth and twentieth century American realism and American and European naifs. Publ: Auth, The art virus, This Wk Mag, 64; auth, Ateliers of Paris, 65 & The art balloon, 67, Locust Valley Leader; auth, Art as an investment, Oyster Bay Guardian, Long Island, 66; ed, The Artists' Cookbook, Stevenson, 71; auth, Fourth Stage of Gainsborough Brown, McKay, 77. Mailing Add: Country Art Gallery 113 Forest Ave Locust Valley NY 11560

WATSON, DARLIENE KEENEY
PAINTER
b Amarillo, Tex, Mar 16, 29. Study: Univ Colo, BFA; Art Inst Chicago; Malden Bridge Sch Art, NY; also with Dick Goetz, Oklahoma City & New York; Lui-Sang Wong, San Francisco

& Ho Nien Au, Taiwan. Exhib: Tenth through Fourteenth Exhibs, Sumie Soc Am, 73-77; Art Barn, Artists Equity & Nat Parks, 74; Art League Northern Va; Fairfax County Coun Arts; Potomac Valley Watercolor Soc; Southern Watercolor Soc; var local & regional shows in East & Southwest US. Awards: First Prize, Sumie Soc Am, 73 & 75; Third Prize, St Peter's 5th Ann Exhib, 75; Equal Merit Award, Potomac Valley Watercolor Soc, 77. Bibliog: Widening Horizons in Creative Arts, Ada King Wallis, 61. Mem: Sumie Soc Am (chap pres, 75-77); Fairfax County Coun Arts; Potomac Valley Watercolor Soc; Washington Women's Arts Ctr. Style & Technique: Nature painting in Oriental brush painting technique with a style which is a blending of the East and West. Media: Watercolor, Acrylic. Mailing Add: 9617 Jomar Dr Fairfax VA 22032

WATSON, HALEN RICHTER
CERAMIST, SCULPTOR
b Laredo, Tex, May 10, 26. Study: Scripps Col, Calif, BA, 47; Clarement Grad Sch & Univ Ctr, MFA, 59; spec work with Bernard Leach, 50; Swed Govt grant, Stockholm, Sweden, 52053; spec work with Marguerite Wildenhain, 60; Alfred Univ, NY, 66. Work: Witte Mem Mus, San Antonio, Tex; Wichita Art Asn, Kans; Pitzer Col, Claremont, Calif; Pasadena Mus of Art, Calif. Comn: Ceramic tilc murals (50ft x 10ft), Lobby, Laredo Nat Bank, Tex, 58; stairwell, grill units & off dividers Tyler Bank & Trust Co, Tex, 59; ceramic units & lettering, Exterior of Scottish Rite Masonic Temple, Los Angeles, comn by Millard Sheets, 62; 24ft ceramic sculpture, Nueces Co Courthouse, comn by Bicentennial Comt, Corpus Christi, Tex, 76; 16ft ceramic sculpture, Mall del Norte, Laredo, Tex, comn by Enterprise Develop Assocs, 77. Exhib: Ceramic Art, Univ Chicago, 54; one-woman shows, Long Beach State Col, 64, Ceramic Sculpture, Marion Koogler McNay Mus of Art, San Antonio, Tex, 72, Okla Art Ctr, Oklahoma City, 72 & Wichita Art Asn, Kans, 72; 2nd Nat Ceramic Exhib, San Jose State Col, Calif, 65; Media Explored, Laguna Beach Mus, Calif, 67; Artist as Craftsman—Craftsman as Artist, Long Beach Mus of Art, 67; 25 Yrs of Ceramic Art, Scripps Col, 69; 1st Ann Exhib of Ceramic Art Women's Bldg, Los Angeles, 74; plus others. Teaching: Instr ceramics, Chaffey Col, Ontario, Calif, 50-52 & Mt San Antonio Col, Walnut, Calif, 55-57; full prof ceramics, Otis Art Inst, Los Angeles, 58- Pos: Chmn ceramics dept, Otis Art Inst 59-; artist-in-residence, Claremont Men's Col, Calif, 77-78. Awards: Frost Bros Award & Estill Gray Purchase Award, Witte Mem Mus, 51. Bibliog: Beverly Johnson (auth), From established artists come exciting new forms, Home Mag, Los Angeles Times, 2/72; Kim Blair (auth), Potter's career is shaping up, Los Angeles Times, 3/72; John P Simoni (auth), Excellent shows around the state, Wichita Eagle, 3/72. Mem: Southern Calif designer Craftsmen; Design Div, Am Ceramic Soc; Artists Equity; Calif Design; Laredo Art Asn. Style & Technique: Many areas of ceramics from porcelain pots to unusually large, stylized and/or abstract stoneware sculptures, as well as murals; work includes low and high temperature, wheel and hand-built work. Publ: Contribr, Richard B Petterson, auth, Twenty-five years of ceramic art, Ceramic Monthly, 70; contribr, Glenn C Nelson, auth, Ceramics: A Potter's Handbook, Holt, Rinehart, Winston, 3rd ed, 71; contribr, Leon I Nigrosh, auth, Claywork: Form and Idea in Ceramic Design, Davis Publ, 75. Dealer: Barbara Beretich Gallery 8 Bonita & Harvard Rd Claremont CA 91711. Mailing Add: 520 E Sixth St Claremont CA 91711

WATSON, LYNDA
JEWELER, METALSMITH
b Orange, Calif. Study: Orange Coast Col, AA; Rochester Inst of Technol; Chapman Col; Calif State Univ, Long Beach, BA, MA, MFA. Work: Objects USA, Johnson's Wax Co; Mus of Contemp Crafts, New York. Exhib: Calif Design IX, X, XI, 76 Pasadena Mus & Calif Design Ctr, 67 & 70, 72-74; Crafts of the Americas (traveling), under Auspices of Smithsonian, 75-77; Forms in Metal, 275 Yrs of Am Metalsmithing, Mus of Contemp Crafts, Renwick Gallery, Cranbrook Acad, 75 (traveled under Smithsonian) 75-77; Jewelers USA, Calif State Univ, Gullerton, 76; Creative Jewelry, Design Ctr, Manila, Phillipines, 76; The Metalsmith, Soc NAm Jewelers, Univ of Washington, Phoenix Art Mus, 77; Art in Crafts, Bronx Mus, 77; Landscape, New Views, Cornell Univ, 78. Teaching: Instr Jewelry metal, Calif State Univ, Los Angeles, 69, Cabrillo Col, 70- & Colo Mountain Col, summers 74-77. Pos: Designer/Production artist, Buzza Cardoza Greeting Card Co, 61-65; designer, Hencury Head Workshop. 65-69 & Signature V Collection, Reed and Barton Silversmiths, 76-78. Awards: Nat Endowment for the Arts Craftsman's Grant, 77-78. Bibliog: Ralph Turner (auth), Contemporary Jewelry, Van Nostrand, Reinhold, 75; Olivia Emery (auth), Craftsman Lifestyle, Calif Design, 77; Analee Gold (auth), Crafts in Industry, Craft Horizons, 8/77. Mem: Am Crafts Coun; World Crafts Coun; Soc NAm Goldsmiths. Style & Technique: Metal worker, mostly fabrication. Media: Fine and Sterling Silver, Copper, Brass & Plastic. Publ: Contribr, Jewelry Techniques, Craft Horizons, Calif Design, Objects USA, Crafts of the Modern World, Body Jewelry, Contemporary Crafts of the Americas & Contemporary Jewelry, 78. Mailing Add: 2691 E Cliff Dr Santa Cruz CA 95062

WATSON, ROBERT
PAINTER
b Martinez, Calif, Feb 28, 23. Study: Univ Calif; Univ Ill; Univ Wis. Work: Calif Palace of Legion of Honor, San Francisco; Rochester Univ, NY; Fry Mus, Seattle, Wash; Univ of Utah, Salt Lake City; St Mary's Col, Moraga, Calif; Boise Art Mus, Idaho; Milwaukee Art Mus, Wis. Exhib: Fifth Ann Exhib Contemp Am Art, Calif Palace of Legion of Honor, 52; Calif State Fair, Sacramento, 53; Exhib Contemp Am Art, Univ Ill, 54; Nat Acad Design, New York, 54. Awards: First Prize, Calif State Fair, 54. Bibliog: Arthur Watson (auth), article in Am Artist, 9/53; Jan Jennings (auth), article in Southwest Art, 6/77. Mem: Soc Western Artists. Style & Technique: Neo-Romantic technique; 17th century oil painting technique. Mailing Add: c/o Serendipity Gallery 11628 1/2 Barrington Ct Los Angeles CA 90049

WATSON, ROSS
ART HISTORIAN
b Bangor, NIreland, July 29, 34. Study: Pembroke Col, Cambridge, BA(hist with hon), 56, MA, 59; Courtauld Inst Art, London, dipl (hist art, with distinction), 63. Collections Arranged: Arranged and cataloged, Brit Coun Exhib 18th Century English Watercolors, Rijks Mus, Amsterdam, Albertina, Vienna, 66; J M W Turner from Mellon Collection, Nat Gallery Art, Washington, DC, 69, John Constable from Mellon Collection, 69, Joseph Wright Derby, from Mellon Collection, 69-70, William Hogarth from Mellon Collection, 70-71, Eye of Thomas Jefferson, Bicentennial Exhib, 76. Pos: Asst keeper, City Mus & Art Gallery, Birmingham, Eng, 63-66; asst cur, Paul Mellon Collection, Washington, DC, 66; cur, Nat Gallery Art, Washington, DC, 66-77. Mem: Col Art Asn Am; Walpole Soc; Asn Irish Art Hist. Res: 18th century European, particularly British painting. Publ: Auth, Queen Christina's pictures, Hist Today, 64; auth, Francis Wheatley in Ireland, Apollo, 65; co-auth, Renaissance furniture, Antiques Int, 66; auth, Guardi and the visit of Pius VI to Venice in 1782, Nat Gallery Art Report & Studies Hist Art, 67; auth, Irish portraits in American Collections, Irish Georgian Soc Bull, 69. Mailing Add: 5414 Cathedral Ave NW Washington DC 20016

WATSON, SYDNEY HOLLINGER
DESIGNER
b Toronto, Ont, Apr 6, 11. Work: Nat Gallery Can, Ottawa; Queen's Univ, Kingston, Ont; McLaughlin Gallery, Oshawa, Ont; Hart House, Univ Toronto; McMichael Conserv Collection Art, Toronto. Comn: Mural (oil on canvas), Bd Rm, Imp Oil Head Off, Toronto, 55; acrylic wall paintings, Chapel, Trinity Col Sch, Port Hope, Ont, 65; mosaic mural, Head Off, Can Imperial Bank Com, Montreal, PQ, 66; sand blasted slate mural, Excelsior Life Ins Head Off, Toronto, 67; exterior wall panels (porcelain on steel), Chem Bldg, Univ Toronto, 68. Exhib: Ont Soc Artists; Royal Can Acad Arts; Can Soc Painters Watercolor; Can Group Painters. Teaching: Instr design, Ont Col Art, 46-49, vprin, 49-54, prin, 54-70. Awards: Art Dirs Club Medal, Toronto, 64; Can Centennial Medal, Govt Can, 67; Royal Can Acad Arts Medal, 68. Mem: Royal Can Acad Arts (mem coun); Ont Soc Artists (pres, 54-57); Can Group Painters (dir, 68-). Publ: Auth & illusr, lettering text, W W Gage, Toronto, 55; auth & illusr, A History of Printing, Gaylord Printing Co, Toronto, 58. Dealer: Roberts Gallery 641 Yonge St Toronto ON Can. Mailing Add: 2 Nesbitt Dr Toronto ON Can

WATSON, WENDY
ILLUSTRATOR, WRITER
b Patterson, NJ, July 7, 42. Study: Bryn Mawr Col, BA; studied painting & drawing with Jerry Farnsworth & Daniel Greene; illustrating with Aldren Watson (father). Exhib: Am Inst Graphic Arts Children's Book Show, New York, 68 & 72; Children's Book Coun Showcase, 72; The Mental Picture, Am Inst Graphic Arts, 72; Brooklyn Art Books for Children, 73 & 74; Biennial Illustrations, Bratislava, Yugoslavia, 73. Awards: Nomination for Father Fox's Pennyrhymes, Nat Book Award (children's div), 72. Bibliog: Horn Book, 10/71 & 10/72. Mem: Author's Guild. Style & Technique: Pen & Ink, Pen & ink with watercolor. Publ: Ed & illusr, Fisherman Lullabies, 68; co-auth & illusr, Hedgehog & the Hare, 69; illusr, Father Fox's Pennyrhymes, 71, Birthday Goat, 71, Quips & Quirks, 75 & Lollipop, 76. Mailing Add: c/o Thomas Y Crowell Co 10 E 53rd St New York NY 10022

WATTENMAKER, RICHARD J
ART HISTORIAN, MUSEUM DIRECTOR
b Philadelphia, Pa, Feb 22, 41. Study: Univ Pa, BA; NY Univ, Inst Fine Arts, MA, PhD. Collections Arranged: The Art of William Glackens (with catalogue), 67; The Art of Charles Pendergast (with catalogue), 68; The Art of Jean Hugo (with catalogue), 73; The Fauves (with catalogue), 75; Puvis de Chavannes and The Modern Tradition (with catalogue), 75; The Dutch Cityscape in the 17th century and its Sources (with catalogue), 77. Pos: Dir, Rutgers Univ Art Gallery, 66-69; chief cur, Art Gallery of Ont, Toronto, 72- Mem: Col Art Asn. Res: Nineteenth and twentieth century European painting; Renaissance and Post-Renaissance European painting; American painting and decorative art. Publ: Auth, Art Gallery of Ontario (illus handbk/cat), Art Gallery of Ont, 74. Mailing Add: c/o Art Gallery of Ont Grange Park Toronto ON M5T 1G4 Can

WATTS, ROBERT M
CONCEPTUAL ARTIST, DESIGNER
b US, June 14, 23. Study: Univ Louisville, BME, 44; Art Students League, 46-48; Columbia Univ, AM, 51. Work: Mod Museet, Stockholm; Houston Art Mus; Albright-Knox Art Mus, Buffalo; Art Inst Chicago. Exhib: New Media, New Forms II, Martha Jackson Gallery, New York, 60; Assemblage, 61 & The Machine, 68, Mus Mod Art; Whitney Mus Am Art Ann Contemp Am Sculpture, 65; Happening & Flexus, Koelnischer Kunstverein, Köln, Ger, 71. Teaching: Prof film & mixed media, Rutgers Univ, New Brunswick, 52-, univ res coun grant for film & mixed media, 64-71; Carnegie Corp vis artist & consult, Univ Calif, Santa Cruz, 68. Awards: Exp Workshop Award, Carnegie Corp, 64. Bibliog: Max Kosloff (auth), Pop culture & the new vulgarians, Art Int, 62; Brian O'Dougherty (auth), Art: machines in revolt, 62 & Grace Glueck (auth), If its art you want..., 67, New York Times. Mem: Life mem Art Students League. Media: Mixed Media. Publ: Co-auth, Newspaper, 63; auth, Flexus, assorted events & objects, 64-72; auth, Postage stamps, fluxpost, 65; contribr, The Arts on Campus: the Necessity for Change, 70; co-auth, Proposals for Art Education, 70. Mailing Add: RD 3 Bangor PA 18013

WAUFLE, ALAN DUANE
MUSEUM DIRECTOR, ART HISTORIAN
b Hornell, NY, Feb 11, 51. Study: Col of William & Mary, BA; Duke Univ, MA. Collections Arranged: McConnell Art Collection, 77 & Antique Quilts & Coverlets of Gaston County, 77, Gaston Co Art & Hist Mus. Pos: Dir, Gaston Co Art & Hist Mus, Dallas, NC, 76- Mem: Am Asn of Mus; SE Mus Conf. Res: Iconography of works celebrating the 1571 Battle of Lepanto. Mailing Add: 1411 Quail Woods Rd Gastonia NC 28052

WAUTERS, ANDRE
ART DEALER, COLLECTOR
b Liege, Belg, July 11, 21. Study: Col Melle-lez-Gand; Col St Jean Berchmans, Brussels; Ecole Nat Superieure d'Archit et des Arts Visuels; art hist with Paul Fierens & Luc Haesaerts. Collections Arranged: First Mid-Western Exhibition of Belgian Painters, 5 cities, 61-62; Belgian Engravings, 13 cities, 64-65. Pos: Cult secy, Consulate Gen Belgium, Chicago, 58-65; in charge art res & promotion, Mosan-Lambert, New York, 65- Awards: Brit Coun Grant, 47. Specialty: Old and modern master drawings, Flemish and Belgian paintings. Mailing Add: 1014 Madison Ave New York NY 10021

WAXMAN, BASHKA PAEFF
See Paeff, Bashka

WAYNE, JUNE
PAINTER
b Chicago, Ill. Work: Bibliot Nat, France; Bibliot Royale Bruxelles; Mus Mod Art, New York; Nat Collection Fine Art, Smithsonian Inst, Washington, DC; Rosenwald Collection, Alverthorpe Gallery, Jenkintown, Pa. Exhib: Tidal Waves & Visas: Tapestries & Lithography, June Wayne La Demeure, Paris, 75; From Lurcat to Today: Masterpieces of Tapestry, La Royale Belge, Bruxelles, Belg. Pos: Dir, Tamarind Lithography Workshop & adv, Tamarind Inst, Univ NMex, 60-; mem bd dirs, Grunwald Graphic Arts Found, Univ Calif, Los Angeles, 65-75, mem exec comt & adv to chancellor, Arts Mgt Prog, Grad Sch Admin, 69-; mem overseers comt, Sch Visual & Environ Arts, Harvard Univ, 71-76. Awards: Prix du Biennale, Int Estampes Epinal, 71 & 73; For film, Golden Eagle, Cine, Documentary Category Nomination for an Academy Award, 74. Bibliog: Baskett (auth), The Art of June Wayne, Abrams, 68; Dominique De Santi (auth), Les Tempetes de June Wayne, Le Monde, Paris; Bernard Kester (auth), The tapestries of June Wayne, Craft Horizons, 74; plus others. Dealer: Gallery La Demeure Pl St Sulpice Paris 6 France; Peter Plone Assocs 1108 N Tamarind Ave Los Angeles CA 90038. Mailing Add: 1108 N Tamarind Ave Los Angeles CA 90038

WEARE, SHANE
PRINTMAKER
b England, Aug 29, 36. Study: Royal Col Art, London, Eng, ARCA(printmaking), 63; Univ Iowa, asst etching, 63-64. Work: Brit Mus, London; Lib Libr Cong, Washington, DC; Brooklyn Mus, NY; Art Inst Chicago; San Francisco Mus Art. Exhib: Int Exhib Graphic Art, Ljubljana, Yugoslavia, 66; Brit Int Print Biennale, 68; 22nd Ann Print Exhib, Boston Mus, 70; World Print Competition, San Francisco Mus Art, 73; one-man show, Calif Palace of Legion of Honor, City of San Francisco, 73; 20th Nat Print Exhib, Brooklyn Mus, New York, 77. Awards: Purchase Awards, Los Angeles Soc Printmakers, 68-74, City of San Francisco, 72, City of Palo Alto, 74 & Univ Colo, 74; Spaces Between Prog Award, KQED-TV, San Francisco, 75. Bibliog: John Brunsden (auth), Technique of Etching & Engraving, Batsford, 66. Mem: Calif Soc Printmakers (vchmn, 72-73). Style & Technique: Printmaking, etching. Dealer: William Sawyer Gallery 3045 Clay St San Francisco CA 94118. Mailing Add: 6449 Harwood Ave Oakland CA 94618

WEAVER, JOHN BARNEY
SCULPTOR
b Anaconda, Mont, Mar 28, 20. Study: Art Inst Chicago, Albert Kuppenhiemer scholar, 41, dipl; monumental sculpture with Albin Polasek. Work: Bronzes, Charles Russell, Statuary Hall, Washington, DC, Double Equestrian, Fort Walsh, Sask & Archaic Indian, NY State Mus, Albany; The Bullwhacker, Helena, Mont; heads & figures, Anthrop Hall, Smithsonian Inst. Comn: Three Indians, Nat Geog Soc, Washington, DC, 63; The Stake (bronze), Prov Mus & Arch, Alta, 67; The Trader, Edmonton Libr Plaza, Alta, 73; Service to the North (bronze frieze), RCMP Hq, Edmonton, 74; bronze relief, Observ Lounge, Libby Dam, Mont, 75. Exhib: Chicago & Vicinity, Art Inst Chicago, 47; 1st Exhib Old Northwest Territory, Springfield, Ill, 47; Denver Art Mus 54th Ann, 48; Wis Painters & Sculptors, Milwaukee Art Inst, 51; 68th Exhib Soc Washington Artists, Natural Hist Bldg, Washington, DC, 61. Teaching: Instr life drawing, Layton Sch Art, Milwaukee, 46-51. Pos: Sculptor, Mont Hist Soc, 55-60; sculptor, Smithsonian Inst, 61-66. Awards: Alta Achievement Award for Excellence in Sculpture, 77. Bibliog: R T Taylor (auth), Jack Weaver—sculptor, Mont Inst Arts, 55; Ruth Bowen (auth), Alberta art in bronze, My Golden West, 70; B Schwartz (auth), Talented Hands, CBC-TV, Edmonton, 70. Mem: Nat Sculpture Soc. Style & Technique: Traditional realism. Media: Bronze. Dealer: Mont Gallery & Book Shop Box 181 11th & California Helena MT 59601. Mailing Add: 10904-126th St Edmonton AB Can

WEBB, FRANK (FRANCIS H WEBB)
PAINTER, DESIGNER
b North Versailles, Pa, Sept 14, 27. Study: Art Inst of Pittsburgh, with Edgar A Whitney, Syd Solomon & John Jellico. Work: Butler Inst of Am Art, Youngstown, Ohio; PPG Found, Pittsburgh; United Steelworkers Int Hq, Pittsburgh; Am Bank, Austin, Tex; Aluminum Co of Am Hq. Comn: Historical illus of Hanover Fair, WGer, United States Steel, Pittsburgh, 76. Exhib: Midyear Ann, Butler Inst of Am Art, Youngstown, Ohio, 68-73; Washington & Jefferson Col, Washington, Pa, 71; Chautauqua Exhib of Am Art Ann, NY, 71; Am Watercolor Soc Ann, Nat Acad, New York, 71-72 & 74-76; Nat Arts Club Open Ann, Nat Arts Club Galleries, New York, 71, 73 & 77; Marietta Col Mainstreams Ann, Ohio, 71, 74, 76 & 77; Watercolor USA, Springfield Mus of Art, Mo, 72; Audubon Artists, Nat Acad, New York, 73, 74, 77 & 78; Allied Artists, Nat Acad, New York, 73, 76 & 77; W Tex Watercolor Ann, Mus of Tex Tech Univ, Lubbock, 76; Cape Coral Nat Ann, Edison Community College, Fort Myers, Fla, 76; plus many others. Teaching: Guest lectr painting, Carnegie-Mellon Univ, Pittsburgh, 73-76 & Louisville Art Ctr, Ky, 76; guest instr painting, Southwestern Watercolor Soc, Dallas, Tex, 77. Pos: Pres, Phillips Studio, Pittsburgh, 57- Awards: Sizek Award, Butler Midyear Ann, Butler Inst of Am Art, Youngstown, Ohio, 73; Bronze Medal of Honor, Am Watercolor Soc, 76; Winsor & Newton Medal, Audubon Artists Ann, 77. Mem: Am Watercolor Soc; Philadelphia Water Color Club; Knickerbocker Artists; Hudson Valley Art Asn; Pittsburgh Watercolor Soc (pres, 74-77). Style & Technique: Landscapes. Media: Watercolor. Publ: Illusr, Bicentennial Calendar, 75 & History of Steelmaking Calendar, 77, US Steel; illusr, Ford Times, 77. Mailing Add: 108 Washington St Pittsburgh PA 15218

WEBB, SPIDER
TATTOOIST, PHOTOGRAPHER, SCULPTOR
b Mar 3, 44. Study: Art Students League; Am Art Sch, BFA; Sch Visual Arts, New York, MFA; Inst Allende, Mex. Work: Mus of Mod Art, New York; Metrop Mus, New York; Louvre, France; Whitney Mus of Am Art, New York; San Francisco Mus of Fine Art, Calif. Comn: Portraits, photographs, Muhammad Ali, NYCA Gallery, New York, Willem de Kooning, East Hampton, NY, Stella, Foto Gallery, New York, Larry Rivers, Neikrug Gallery, New York & Toni Brown, High Times Mag, Neikrug Gallery, 78. Exhib: One-man shows, Brata Gallery, New York, 68-72 & 74, Royal Acad of Arts, London, 75, Galerie Muwro, Hamburg, Ger, 76, Levitan Gallery, New York, 76-77, NYCA Gallery, 76-78, Neikrug Galleries, 78 & Foto Gallery, 78. Teaching: Lectr on work at cols & univs around country. Pos: Prof art, Inst Allendo, Mex, 71-72. Bibliog: Larry Rivers (auth), Spider Webb-Tattoo (film), Pvt Publ, 76; G Schioartwan (auth), 501—Global Village (film), New York Coun on the Arts, 76; History as we lived it 1976, articles publ by Assoc Press, 76. Mem: Tattoo Club of Am (pres, 60-). Style & Technique: Tattooist; Photographer. Publ: Auth, Heavily Tattooed Men & Women, McGraw-Hill, 76; auth, X-1000, R Mutt Fine Art Publ, New York, 77; auth, Bi-Sexual Draggons, Bochner Press, New York, 78; auth, The Tattoo Revolution & My Autobiography, Simon & Schuster, New York, in prep. Dealer: Graphic Represenatives 91 Eighth Ave Parkslope Brooklyn NY 11215; Neikrug Galleries Inc 224 E 68th St New York NY. Mailing Add: 112 W First St Mt Vernon NY 10550

WEBB, VIRGINIA LOUISE
PAINTER
b Brooklyn, NY, June 2, 20. Study: Art Students League; Julian Acad, Paris, France; landscape painting with Jay Connaway, Pawlet, Vt; portrait painting with Wallace Bassford, North Truro, Mass. Work: Berkshire Mus, Pittsfield, Mass; Mus Fine Arts, Springfield, Mass; Benedictine Abbey Collection, Fecamp, France; Laurance Rockefeller's Woodstock Inn Collection; Southern Vt Art Ctr, Exhib: Berkshire Art Asn, Pittsfield, Mass, 56, 62, 63 & 74; Benedictine Art Award Show, New York, 69; Southern Vt Art Ctr, Manchester, Vt, 70; Acad Artists Asn, Springfield, Mass, 72-74; Allied Artists Am, New York, 74. Awards: Berkshire Art Asn Award for Summer Still Life, 62; Purchase Award for Abandoned, Mus Fine Arts, 71; Muriel Alvord Mem Award for Apples & Pears, 72. Bibliog: Charles Bonenti (auth), Self portrait of an elusive Gemini, Bennington Banner Newspaper, 71. Mem: Southern Vt Artists, Inc (chmn art comt & trustee, 71); Southern Vt Br Nat League Am Pen Women, Washington, DC(treas, 72 & mem chmn, 75); Acad Artists Asn; Berkshire Art Asn; Chaffee Art Ctr. Style & Technique: Oil landscapes, still life and portraits in impressionist style. Media: Oil Painting; Pentel Drawing. Dealer: Gallery 2 Woodstock VT; Doll & Richards 172 Newbury Boston MA. Mailing Add: Canterbury Rd Manchester Center VT 05255

WEBER, ALBERT JACOB
PAINTER, EDUCATOR
b Chicago, Ill, July 10, 19. Study: Art Inst Chicago, BFA; Mexico City Col, MAA. Exhib: Pa Acad Fine Arts, 50, 52, 59 & 60; five shows, Univ Mich, 56-69; Soc Washington Printmakers, 57 & 60; Detroit Inst Art, 57, 60 & 66; Am Fedn Arts Traveling Exhibs, 58-60; plus many other group & one-man shows. Teaching: Instr, Mexico City Col; prof art, Univ Mich, Ann Arbor, 55- Awards: Prize, Grand Rapids Art Gallery, 58; Purchase Prizes, Butler Inst Am Art, 59-61; Purchase Prize, Graphic Art & Drawing Exhib, Olivet Col, Mich, 62; plus others. Mem: Ann Arbor Art Asn. Mailing Add: 554 Elizabeth Apt 4 Ann Arbor MI 48104

WEBER, HULDA
See Katz, Hilda

WEBER, IDELLE
PAINTER
b Chicago, Ill. Study: Scripps Col; Univ Calif, Los Angeles, BA & MA. Work: Nat Collection Fine Arts, Washington, DC; Va Mus, Richmond; Worcester Art Mus, Mass; Albright-Knox Art Gallery, Buffalo, NY; Yale Univ Art Gallery, New Haven, Conn. Exhib: Mus Mod Art, 56, 61-62, traveling exhib, Rothman Art Prog, 76-78; Bertha Schaefer Gallery, New York, 62-64 & Hundred Acres Gallery, 73 & 75; Guggenheim Mus, New York, 64; Worcester Art Mus, 65; Wadsworth Atheneum, Hartford, Conn, 66 & 74; Art Ctr, C W Post Col, 74; Wichita State Univ, Kans, 75; Art Gallery, Yale Univ, 75; Whitney Downtown, New York, 75; Realismus und Realitat, Darmstadt, WGer, 75; Nat Collection Fine Arts, 76; McNay Art Inst, San Antonio, 76; O K Harris Gallery, 77; City Univ New York, 78; plus others. Awards: Nat Scholastic Art Awards, Scripps Col. Bibliog: Ellen Lubell (auth), Idelle Weber, Arts Mag, spring 77; Michael Greenwood (auth), Realism, naturalism and symbolism, ArtsCanada, 77; Joshua Taylor (auth), America as Art, 77. Style & Technique: Photo-realism. Media: Etching, Oil, Watercolor. Mailing Add: c/o O K Harris 383 W Broadway New York NY 10013

WEBER, JAN
PAINTER
b Lafayette, Ind. Study: Univ NMex; pvt instructors. Work: Gov Mansion, Santa Fe, NMex; Bataan Mem Hosp, Albuquerque, NMex. Exhib: NMex Biennial, Santa Fe; El Paso Sun Carnival, Tex; Hoosier Art Salon, Indianapolis, Ind, travel exhib; Southern Colo State Col, Pueblo; NMex Arts & Crafts, Albuquerque. Teaching: Instr painting & drawing, Art Ctr Sch, Albuquerque, 66-69; instr painting & drawing, Kirtland AFB, 67-72; instr painting & drawing, Sandia Base, Albuquerque, 67-74. Pos: Bd mem, NMex Arts & Crafts, 74-75; judge, NMex Arts & Crafts, Buick Com Show, Rio Grande Arts & Crafts & Albuquerque City High Schs. Mem: Artists Equity; Nat League Am Pen Women. Style & Technique: Experimental; impressionist. Media: Oil, Acrylic. Dealer: Kachina Gallery 114 Old Santa Fe Trail Santa Fe NM 87501. Mailing Add: 7133 Kiowa Ave NE Albuquerque NM 87110

WEBER, JEAN M
ART ADMINISTRATOR, EDUCATOR
b Boston, Mass, Apr 2, 33. Study: Brown Univ; RI Sch Design, BA; Edinburgh Univ; State Univ Iowa. Collections Arranged: The Summer Place, 70; American Impressions, 70; Commedia dell'Arte, 71; Objects & Images, 71; Tantric Art of Tibet, 72; Ceramic Arts of China, 74; Doughty Porcelains, 75; Viewpoints: The American Land, 76; Fairfield Porter's Maine, 77. Teaching: Adj assoc prof, Southampton Col, 70- Pos: Dir, Jr Art Gallery, Louisville, Ky, 66-69; asst & actg dir, Parrish Art Mus, Southampton, NY, 69-70, dir, 70- Awards: Danforth Found Fel, 54-55; Int Mus Sem Award, NY State Coun Art, Metrop Mus, 72. Mem: Am Asn Mus (mem accreditation comn, 76-); Am Fedn Arts; Nat Art Educ Asn; Int Coun Mus; NY State Asn Mus (mem coun, 77-). Publ: Auth, articles in Am Art Rev, Museologist & Mus News. Mailing Add: Henry St Sag Harbor NY 19963

WEBER, JOHN
ART DEALER
Pos: Pres, John Weber Gallery. Specialty: Contemporary art. Mailing Add: 420 W Broadway New York NY 10012

WEBER, JOHN PITMAN
MURALIST, EDUCATOR
b Washington, DC, Dec 6, 42. Study: Harvard Col, VA(cum laude), 64; Fulbright-Hayes Scholar, Atelier 17, Paris, 64-66, with S Hayter & Jean Helion; Ecole des Beaux Arts; Art Inst of Chicago, MFA(painting), 68, with Yoshida & Halsted. Comn: Wall of Choices (30ft x 60ft), comn by Nat Endowment for the Arts, Christopher House Settlement, Chicago, 70; Fuertes Somos Ya (350 sq ft), Ruiz Belvis Ctr, Mus of Contemp Art, Chicago, 71; Solidarity (stair cycle with Jose Guerrero, United Elec Workers, Chicago, 74; The Builders (500 sq ft, with Celia Radek, Nat Endowment for the Arts Grant, Ato Z Equip, Chicago, 75; Tilt (16ft x 90ft), comn by Nat Endowment for the Arts, Maas Park, Chicago, 76. Exhib: Artists' Response, Univ Northern Ill, DeKalb, 68; Murals for the People, Mus of Contemp Art, Chicago, 71; one-man show, Valparaiso Univ, Ind, 72 & Guerbois Two Gallery, Chicago, 78; Housing & Urban Develop Nat Community Art Competition, Nat Collection of Fine Art, Washington, DC, 73; On Chicago Walls, Chicago Pub Libr Cult Ctr, 73; Radical Attitudes Toward the Gallery, Art Net, London, Eng, 77. Teaching: Assoc prof studio art & art hist, Elmhurst Col, Ill, 68-; adj asst prof mural art, Sch of Art Inst of Chicago, 73-75; vis artist mural workshop, Univ NDak, Grand Forks, 75. Pos: Dir & founding mem, Chicago Mural Group, Chicago, 70-; pres, Community Mural Proj, Chicago, 74-; dir, Corridor Arts Prog, Chicago, 75-76; vis lectr, Escuela Nat de Pintura, Mexico, 76. Awards: Chicago Beautiful Comt Award, Sheffield & Barry Mural, 72 & Wilton/Diversey Mural, 73; Award for study in Mexico, Elmhurst Col Alumni Asn, 72. Bibliog: Julio Solorzano (auth), Pintando la calle, Revista de Revistas, 72; Janet Bloom (auth), Changing walls, Archit Forum, 5/73; Robert Sommer (auth), Street Art, Links Books, 75. Mem: Art Inst of Chicago Alumni Asn; Nat Murals Network; Chicago Artists Coalition. Style & Technique: Simplified human figure and objects used evocatively and narratively, post-cubist, pre-pop style affinities. Media: Oil, acrylic, enamels on brick, cement, canvas and paper. Publ: Auth, Murals as people's art, In: Les Etats Unis en Movement, DeNoel, Paris, 72; auth, Letters on art, TRA, 72; co-auth, Children's murals, Urban Rev, 76; co-auth, A critical context for community murals, El Gallo Illus, 77; co-auth, Toward a People's Art, The Contemporary Mural Movement, Dutton, 77. Dealer: Guerbois 2 Gallery 1133 W Webster Chicago IL 60614. Mailing Add: 4830 N Springfield Chicago IL 60625

WEBSTER, LARRY
DESIGNER, PAINTER
b Arlington, Mass, Mar 18, 30. Study: Mass Col Art, BFA; Boston Univ, MS. Work: De Cordova Mus, Lincoln, Mass; Grand Rapids Art Mus, Mich; Munic Gallery, Davenport, Iowa; Springfield Art Mus, Mo; Art Mus, Colby Col, Waterville, Maine. Exhib: Nat Acad Design, New York, 70; Allied Artists Am, 71; Am Watercolor Soc, New York, 72;

Watercolor USA. Teaching: Asst prof typographic design, hist type & watercolor painting, Mass Col Art, 64-65. Pos: Package designer, Union Bag & Paper Corp, 53-54; illusr, USA, 54-56; graphic designer, vpres & dir, Thomas Todd Co, Boston, 56- Awards: Obrig Prize for Watercolor, Nat Acad Design, 68 & 70; Silver Medal of Honor, Am Watercolor Soc, 68 & 72; Gold Medal of Honor, Allied Artists Am, 71. Mem: Nat Acad Design; Am Watercolor Soc; Allied Artists Am; Soc Printers, Boston; Boston Watercolor Soc. Style & Technique: From Traditional realism to abstract expressionism; from transparent watercolor to opaque acrylic. Media: Watercolor, Acrylic. Mailing Add: 116 Perkins Row Topsfield MA 01983

WEBSTER, STOKELY
PAINTER
b Evanston, Ill, Aug 23, 12. Study: With Lawton Parker, Paris, 22; Art Students League; Nat Acad Design; Yale Univ Sch Fine Arts, with Wayman Adams. Work: Mus of City New York; Elliot Mus, Fla. Comn: Many portrait comn. Exhib: Nat Acad Design, New York, 45-; Salon des Artiste Francais, Paris, 70-73; Salon d'Automne, Paris, 73-74; Chicago Art Inst; one-man shows, Eric Gallery, New York, 75. Awards: First Halgarten Prize, Nat Acad Design. Style & Technique: American post-impressionist and personal style. Media: Oil, Graphic, Etching. Dealer: Eric Galleries 61 E 57th St New York NY 10022. Mailing Add: 309 Deer Park Ave Dix Hills NY 11746

WECHTER, VIVIENNE THAUL
EDUCATOR, PAINTER
b New York, NY. Study: Jamaica Teachers Col, with Hunter, BP; Columbia Univ; NY Univ; Pratt Inst; Sculpture Ctr, New York; Art Students League; with Robert Beverly Hale & de Creeft; Morris Davidson Sch Mod Art; Union Grad Sch, NY, PhD. Work: Corcoran Gallery Art, Washington, DC; Berkeley, Calif; Rose Mus, Brandeis, Mass; Everson Mus, Syracuse, NY; Johnson Mus, Cornell Univ, Ithaca, NY; Neuberger Mus, Purchase, NY; Ft Lauderdale Mus, Fla; Notre Dame Mus, South Bend, Ind; Jewish Mus, New York; Mus Fine Art, Houston & Ft Worth, Tex. Exhib: Art: USA; Provincetown Art Asn; Mus Mod Art, New York; Riverside Mus, New York; Fedn Mod Painters & Sculptors; plus many one-man shows. Teaching: Artist in residence, Fordham Univ, 64-, chmn acquisitions & exhibs, 64-, prof inter-arts, 67-; vis artist, Kans City Art Inst, Marist Col, Md Inst Col of Art & others. Pos: Dir, Urban Arts Corps, 68-; chmn univ coalition, Bronx Coun Arts, 70-77; dir, Bronx Mus Art, 71-77, first vpres, currently; moderator weekly broadcast arts & humanities, Today's World. Awards: Riverside Mus; Am Soc Artists; Jersey City Mus. Bibliog: G Brown (auth), article, 68 & R Gurin (auth), article, 68, In: Arts Mag. Mem: Soc Esthetics; Col Art Asn Am; Fedn Mod Painters & Sculptors (exec comt, 71-, vpres, currently); Am Soc Artists; Kappa Pi. Style & Technique: Abstract symbolism; poetry and painting together. Publ: Illusr, The Park of Jonas, 67; ed, Five Museums Come to Fordham, 68; ed, Visual Fordham, 69 & 70; auth, A View From the Ark, Barlenmir House, 72; contribr, Reconsidering the Nonfigurative in Painting. Mailing Add: Fac Mem Hall Fordham Univ Bronx NY 10458

WECKER, CHRISTOPH ULRICH
ART ADMINISTRATOR
b Heilbronn, WGer, Dec 9, 21. Study: Tubingen, Ger, PhD(polit sci & econ). Pos: Dir, Goethe House New York, 75- Mailing Add: 1014 Fifth Ave New York NY 10028

WEDDIGE, EMIL
LITHOGRAPHER, EDUCATOR
b Sandwich, Ont, Dec 23, 07; US citizen. Study: Eastern Mich Univ, BS; Univ Mich, MDes; also with Emil Ganse, Morris Kantor & E Desjobert, France. Work: Metrop Mus Art, New York; Cape Kennedy, Fla; Libr Cong, Washington, DC; Philadelphia Mus Art; Detroit Art Inst. Comn: Lithography in color, Chrysler Motor Car Co, 55; suite of lithographs in color, Parke, Davis & Co, 56; History of Paper (suite), Dow Chem Co, 57; portrait of a city, Detroit Edison Co, 58; Sesquicentennial Suite, Univ Mich, 66. Exhib: Joseph Pennel Exhib, 34-68; Am Color Print Soc, 48-71; Print Club, 48-71; Biennial Color Print Exhib, 52 & 54; Van Gogh Mem Exhib, Pontoise, France, 60. Teaching: Instr art, Eastern Mich Univ, 36-37; prof art, Univ Mich, Ann Arbor, 38-73, emer prof, 73- Awards: Founders Prize, Detroit Inst Arts, 42; Best Print Award, Am Color Print Soc, 56; James Cleating Print Prize, Michigan Exhib, 64. Bibliog: Article in Statesman, India, 60; Joy Hakanson (auth), Art, Detroit News, 69; William Tall (auth), Art, Detroit Freepress, 69. Mem: Am Fedn Arts; Am Color Print Soc; Print Club; Print Coun Am; Int Platform Asn (spec adv to art chmn, 68-). Style & Technique: Stone lithography. Publ: Auth, Lithography, 66. Dealer: Birmingham Gallery 1028 Haynes St Birmingham MI 48011. Mailing Add: 870 Stein Rd Ann Arbor MI 48103

WEDIN, WINSLOW ELLIOTT
ARCHITECT
b Minneapolis, Minn, Sept 30, 33. Study: Univ Minn, BA(art) & BArch; St Paul Sch Art; Auburn Univ; Fla State Univ, MA, also with Ralph Rapson, Edward Young, Christian Schmidt & Elof Wedin. Work: In pvt collections only. Comn: Ensculptic III (environ sculpture in plastic), comn by Mr & Mrs James Littlejohn, 66; mural around hall, Knights of Columbus, Crystal City, Minn; testing lab on I-75, State of Fla, 74. Exhib: Minn State Fair, St Paul, 56-64; Lutheran Brotherhood Exhib, 58; Collector's Gallery, Minneapolis, 62; Univ Women's Club, St Paul, 63 & 64; one-man show, Ransey Jr Col, St Paul, 68. Teaching: Asst prof archit, Auburn Univ, 68-70; asst prof educ facilities, Fla State Univ, 71-73, asst prof housing design, 73- Pos: Free lance architect, 60-; design consult, Int Design Ctr, Minneapolis, 66-69. Awards: Second Prize for Jewelry, Minn State Fair, 59; First Prize for Sculpture, Soc Minn Sculptors, 62. Bibliog: Sometimes there are those more determined, Northwest Architect, 68; House made from spray foam, Life Mag, 3/70; Cindy Miller (auth), Condo living, Tallahassee Democrat, 75. Mem: Soc Minn Sculptors (vpres, 66-68); Lemoyne Art Found, Tallahassee; Walker Art Found, Minneapolis; World Futures Soc, Tallahassee (pres, 74-); Ctr Aesthet Exploration, Washington, DC (co-founder). Style & Technique: Bold cubistic and often free form sculptural massing, utilizing natural patinas; environmental sculpture. Media: Wood, Concrete, Plastic. Publ: Contribr, Educational Environments for Latin America, Fla State Univ, 71; co-auth, The Open Media Center, Drexel Univ, 72; co-auth, The Responsive House, Mass Inst Technol, 74; auth, The Copper Bannana, Elixir Inst Tallahassee, 75. Mailing Add: 220-5 N Belmont Rd Tallahassee FL 32301

WEEBER, GRETCHEN
PAINTER
b Albany, NY. Study: Albany Inst Hist & Art; Inst Allende, San Miguel de Allende, Mex; also with Betty Warren. Work: Rensselaer Co Hist Soc, Troy, NY; Home Savings Bank, Albany; NY State Conf Mayors, Albany; First Lutheran Church, Albany; Robert Appleton Collection, Albany; plus others in pvt collections. Exhib: Eastern States Expos, Springfield, Mass, 59, 61, 64 & 65; Cooperstown Ann, NY, 60-68; Rensselaer Co Hist Soc, Troy, NY, 60-68; Greater Schenectady Exhib, NY, 60-66; NY State Expos, Syracuse, 62 & 64; Berkshire Ann, Pittsfield, Mass, 64, 67 & 68; Artists Asn Nantucket, Kenneth Taylor Galleries, Mass, 69-; Artists of the Upper Hudson, Albany Inst Hist & Art, 70; plus many other group & one-man shows. Awards: Raymond Scofield Prize for Best Watercolor, Albany Artists Group, 64; First Prize, Rennselaer Co Hist Soc, 68; Georgie Walling Award for Nantucket Subjects, Artists Asn Nantucket, 76. Mem: Artists Asn Nantucket (bd mem, 72-73). Style & Technique: Watercolors are loosely executed and often influenced by natural forms, such as shells and wildflowers. Dealer: The Granary Old South Wharf Nantucket MA 02554. Mailing Add: 11 N Liberty St Nantucket Island MA 02554

WEEDMAN, KENNETH RUSSELL
SCULPTOR, PAINTER
b Little Rock, Ark, Sept 26, 39. Study: Memphis Acad Art; Univ Tulsa, with Alexandre Hogue & Duayne Hatchet, BA & MA. Work: Ark Arts Ctr, Little Rock; Cincinnati Mus Art, Ohio; Masur Mus Art, Monroe, La; Univ Tulsa; Baldwin-Wallace Art & Drama Ctr, Berea, Ohio. Exhib: Conn Acad, Wadsworth Atheneum Mus, 66; Artist of Southeast & Tex Biennials, New Orleans City Art Mus, 66, 71 & 75; Past Jurors, Okla Art Ctr, Oklahoma City, 69; one-man shows, Bienville Gallery, New Orleans, 71 & Art & Drama Ctr Galleries, Baldwin-Wallace Col, 73. Teaching: Instr sculpture, Sul Ross State Col, Alpine, Tex, 65-66; vis artist, Nicholls State Univ, Thibodaux, La, 70-71; asst prof sculpture, Cumberland Col, Williamsburg, Ky, 68- Pos: Ed, Sculpture Quart, Southern Asn Sculptures, 74-75. Awards: Purchase Award, 6th Delta Exhib, Ark Arts Ctr, 63; Award of Merit for Sculpture, Univ Tulsa, 64 & Nebr Wesleyan Univ, 66. Bibliog: Harold D Cole (auth), Kenneth Weedman, Baldwin-Wallace Col, 73; Dona Z Meilach (auth), Soft Sculpture, Crown Publ, 74. Mem: Am Craft Coun; Col Art Asn of Am. Media: Plastic, Steel; Acrylic, Watercolor. Publ: Illusr, Nimrod, 64; illusr, Tragos, 70; contribr, Sculpture Quart, 74 & 75. Mailing Add: PO Box 790 CC Sta Williamsburg KY 40769

WEEGE, WILLIAM
PRINTMAKER, EDUCATOR
b Milwaukee, Wis. Study: Univ Wis-Milwaukee; Univ Wis-Madison, MA, 67, MFA, 68. Work: Akron Art Inst; Brooklyn Mus; Art Inst Chicago; Frankfurt Libr, Ger; Mus Mod Art, New York; plus many others. Exhib: US Pavilion, World's Fair, Japan, 70; 7th Int Biennial Exhib Prints, Tokyo, 70; Beyond Realism, Assoc Am Artists, New York, 70; Mechanics in Printmaking, 70 & Artist as Adversary, 70, Mus Mod Art, New York; Large Print Show, Whitney Mus Am Art, 71; plus many other group & one-man shows. Teaching: From instr lettering to assoc prof art, Univ Wis-Madison, 67- Pos: Dir photo-offset area proj, Univ Wis-Madison, 67-68, graphics area specialist, 68; dir exp workshop for Smithsonian Inst, 35th Venice Biennale, summer 70; dir, Shenanigan Press, Ltd, Venice, Italy. Style & Technique: Printings, mixed graphic media, unique prints usually flouted and realistic images. Mailing Add: Box 259 Rte 1 Barneveld WI 53507

WEEKES, SHIRLEY MARIE
PAINTER
b Buffalo, NY, May 9, 17. Study: Detroit Art Acad; Detroit Soc Arts & Crafts; Burnley Sch Prof Art, Seattle, Wash; Univ Wash with Fred Anderson; also with Sergei Bongart (award of scholar); Master Painter Prog with Carl Morris, Port Townsend, Wash. Work: Charles & Emma Frye Mus, Seattle; Washington Mutual Bank Collection; Craftsman Press Collection. Exhib: One-woman shows, Frye Mus, Seattle, 67 & 72, Challis Galleries, Laguna Beach, Calif, 70, 72 & 74 & Haines Gallery, Seattle, 73 & 75; West Coast Oil Show, Frye Mus, 67-69; Puget Sound Show, Frye Mus, Seattle, 65, 66, 68, 71-75; Okla Mus of Art, 77. Awards: Craftsman Press Award, Craftsman Press, 65; 7th Ann Puget Sound Show, Frye Mus, Seattle, 65 & West Coast Oil Show, 68; Northwest Watercolor Show, Northwest Watercolor Soc, 72. Mem: Soc Western Artists; Northwest Watercolor Soc; Okla Watercolor Asn. Style & Technique: Abstracted impressionist, landscape, still life, figurative. Media: Acrylic, Watercolor & Oil. Dealer: Challis Galleries 1390 S Coast Hwy Laguna Beach CA 92653. Mailing Add: 203 Pine Tree Lane Norman OK 73069

WEEKS, EDWARD F
ART HISTORIAN, MUSEOLOGIST
b Boston, Mass. Study: Goethe Inst, Graffing, Ger, cert, 61; Columbia Univ, BS(art hist), 62; Inst Fine Arts, NY Univ, MA, 70, with Robert Goldwater & Colin Eisler; Inst Arts Admin, Harvard Univ, cert, 73. Exhib Arranged: Contemporary Selections, 71; Art of Spain Since 1300, 71; Veronese and His Studio: In American Collections (with catalog), 72; American Watercolors: 1850-1972 (with catalog); Enchantress: Berthe Morisot (with catalog), 73; German Masters of 20th Century Art (with catalog), 74; Downtown Club Collection, 19th Century American Paintings from Thomas Birch to Charles Russell (catalog with color reproductions), 74; Art of the Old West, 74. Teaching: Instr mod sculpture, Univ Ala, Birmingham, spring 75. Pos: Asst dir, Cummer Gallery Art, Jacksonville, Fla, 62-65; exec asst to dir, Albright-Knox Art Gallery, Buffalo, NY, 67-69; selector, Am Fedn Arts Mus Purchase Fund Collection, 68; cur, High Mus Art, Atlanta, Ga, 69-70; cur, Birmingham Mus Art, Ala, 70-; guest art critic, Birmingham News, 70-; art consult, Downtown Club Collection, 73-, Eye Found Hosp, 73- & Birmingham Civic Ctr, 74- Mem: Nat Inst Arts & Lett; Am Asn Mus; Southeastern Mus Asn; Col Art Asn Am; Birmingham Festival Arts (visual arts comt, 70-, co-chmn, 71-73 & 75). Res: Western paintings and sculpture since 1400; 20th century sculpture and painting; Flemish and Dutch painting, 1500-1630. Interest: Organizing major Old Master exhibits from American collections (currently preparing Tiepolos in American collections). Collection: American paintings, watercolors, prints and photography, 19th and 20th centuries; Pre-Columbian art. Mailing Add: 201 Mountain Ave Birmingham AL 35213

WEEKS, H J
ART ADMINISTRATOR, ART CRITIC
b Hollywood, Calif, Dec 27, 27. Study: Chouinard Art Sch, Los Angeles; Univ Calif, Los Angeles, BA; Art Ctr Sch, Los Angeles; Univ Southern Calif, MA. Collections Arranged: Statements, Oakland Mus (with catalog); Reflections on Glass, Long Beach Mus Art, Portland Art Mus, Phoenix Art Mus (with catalog); Southern California Early Hard Edge Painters, Long Beach Mus Art. Teaching: Asst prof mus admin, Grad Exp Courses, 70- Pos: Educ cur, Long Beach Mus Art, 59-64; dir, Richmond Calif Art Ctr, 65-67; art coordr, Ollendorff Fine Arts, 72-75. Mem: Bay Area Lawyers for the Arts; Am Asn Mus; Western Asn Art Mus. Res: Emphasis on contemporary art, especially California art of this century. Publ: Contribr, Artforum, 60-65, Artweek, 70-, San Jose Mercury-News, 75- & Art Voices/South, 77- Mailing Add: 455 Vallejo St Apt 112 San Francisco CA 94133

WEEKS, JAMES (DARRELL NORTHRUP)
PAINTER, EDUCATOR
b Oakland, Calif, Dec 1, 22. Study: Calif Sch Fine Arts, 40-42 & 46-48; Hartwell Sch Design, 47; Escuela Pintura, Mexico City. Work: Corcoran Gallery Art, Washington, DC; San Francisco Mus Art; Am Fedn Art, New York; Howard Univ, Washington, DC; Oakland Mus. Comn: Am 76 (painting), US Dept of the Interior traveling exhib, 76; painting, Boston 200 Bicentennial Exhib, 76. Exhib: Corcoran Gallery, 63; Carnegie Int, Pittsburgh, 64; one-man shows, San Francisco Mus Art, 65 & Boston Univ Art Gallery, 71; Expo '70, Osaka, Japan; Calif Painting & Sculpture—The Mod Era, San Francisco Mus of Art & Corcoran Gallery, Washington, DC, 76; James Weeks 30 Yr Retrospective—Paintings & Drawings, Brandeis

Univ & Oakland Mus, 78. Teaching: At San Francisco Art Inst, 58-67 & Univ Calif, Los Angeles, 67-70; assoc prof grad painting, Boston Univ, 70- Awards: Nat Endowment Arts grant/painting, 77-78. Bibliog: A Ventura (auth), James Weeks: the plain path, Arts Mag, 2/64; James Weeks, paintings, Felix Landau Gallery, 64. Dealer: Charles Campbell Gallery 647 Chestnut St San Francisco CA 94133. Mailing Add: 11 Notre Dame Rd Bedford MA 01730

WEEMS, KATHARINE LANE
SCULPTOR
b Boston, Mass, Feb 22, 99. Study: May Sch, Boston; Sch Mus Fine Arts, Boston; also with Anna Hyatt Huntington, Brenda Putnam, Charles Grafly & George Demetrios. Work: Mus Fine Arts, Boston; Mus Sci, Boston; Colby Col Art Mus, Maine; Glenbow Found Mus, Alta; Brookgreen Gardens, SC. Comn: Brick carvings of geog distribution of animals of World, two life-size bronze chinos & entrance doors, Biol Labs, Harvard Univ; Lotta Fountain, Esplanade, Boston; US Legion of Merit & Medal for Merit, US Govt; Goodwin Medal, Mass Inst Technol, Cambridge, Mass. Exhib: Paris Salon, France; Nat Acad Design, New York. Awards: Widener Gold Medal, Philadelphia Acad Fine Arts, 27; Speyer Prize, 31, 63, 73 & 75 & Saltus Gold Medal for Merit, 60, Nat Acad Design. Bibliog: From Clay to Bronze (film), Harvard Univ & Mus Fine Arts, Boston; Patricia Barnard (auth), The Contemporary Mouse, Coward, 54. Mem: Nat Acad Design; Nat Sculpture Soc (mem coun, 49); Nat Inst Arts & Lett; Guild Boston Artists; Archit League New York. Dealer: Guild of Boston Artists 162 Newbury St Boston MA 02116. Mailing Add: PO Box 126 Manchester MA 01944

WEESE, MYRTLE A
PAINTER
b Roslyn, Wash, Oct 30, 03. Study: Los Angeles Co Art Inst; also with George Flower & Ejnar Hansen. Work: Paintings & portraits in pvt collections. Exhib: One-man shows, Bowers Mem Mus, Santa Anna, Sierra Madre City Hall, Los Angeles City Hall, Descanso Gardens, 61 & Sierra Madre, 67; plus others. Awards: Prizes, Brea Women's Club, 61 & Las Artistas, 61, Gold Medal, Greek Theatre, Los Angeles, 61. Mem: Scand-Am Soc; Am Inst Fine Arts; Las Artistas Art Club; Prof Artists Los Angeles. Style & Technique: Classic in portrait and figure; oil, no varnish; underpainting; color harmony. Mailing Add: 12821 Fourth St 18 Yucaipa CA 92309

WEGMAN, WILLIAM
PHOTOGRAPHER, VIDEO ARTIST
b Holyoke, Mass. Dec 2, 43. Study: Mass Col Art, Boston, BFA, 65; Univ Ill, Urbana-Champaign, MFA, 67. Work: Whitney Mus Am Art, New York; Mus Mod Art, New York & Paris; Los Angeles Co Mus Art; Int Mus Photog, Rochester, NY. Comn: Semi-buffet color video tape, WGBH, Boston, 74-75; video tape rev, Channel 13, WNET, New York, 75. Exhib: Open Circuits, Everson Mus, Syracuse, 72; Some Recent American Art from Museum of Modern Art, New York, in Sydney, Australia, 73; Whitney Biennial, New York, 73 & 76; Paris Biennial, 73; Video the New Wave, WNET Broadcast, 74; plus others. Awards: Guggenheim Fel, 75; Nat Endowment Arts Grant, 75-76. Bibliog: Jane Livingston (auth), William Wegman, Los Angeles Co Mus Art, 73; Liza Bear (auth), interview, Avalanche, winter/spring 73; Maud Lauin (auth), Notes on William Wegman, Artforum, 3/75. Style & Technique: Short, humorous video tapes, often with dog. Publ: Auth, Pathetic readings, Avalanche Mag, 74; contribr, Paris Rev, fall 74. Dealer: Sonnabend 420 W Broadway New York NY 10013. Mailing Add: 27 Thames St New York NY 10007

WEGNER, NADENE R
METALSMITH, INSTRUCTOR
b Sheboygan, Wis, Feb 18, 50. Study: Univ Wis-Milwaukee, BFA, 72; Tyler Sch Art, Temple Univ, MFA, 75. Work: Tyler Sch Art, Temple Univ, Philadelphia, Pa. Exhib: Wis Directions, Milwaukee Art Ctr, Wis, 75; Forms in Metal, Mus Contemp Crafts, New York, 75; Statements in Sterling, Lever House, New York, 75; Craftwork 76, Metrop Mus & Art Ctr, Miami, Fla, 76; Intent: Jewelry/Metal, Edinboro, Pa, 76; Women's Art Symp, Terre Haute, Ind, 77; Copper, Brass & Bronze Competition, Tucson, Ariz, 77; Profiles of US Jewelry, Lubbock, Tex, 77. Teaching: Instr metalsmithing & Jewelry, Louisville Sch Art, Anchorage, Ky, 75- Awards: 53rd Wisconsin Designer/Craftsman Award, 74; Honorable Mention, Statements in Sterling, Sterling Guild Am, 75; Merit Award, Ky Art Exhib, 76. Bibliog: Metalsmithing USA, 75 & New York Metal, 76, Craft Horizons; Marcia Chamberlain (auth), Metal Jewelry Techniques, Watson-Guptill, 76. Mem: Am crafts Coun; Soc NAm Goldsmiths. Style & Technique: Fabrication of hollow forms utilizing fabrication and casting techniques. Media: Silver and Delrin. Mailing Add: PO Box 3 Sulphur KY 40070

WEHR, WESLEY CONRAD
PAINTER
b Everett, Wash, Apr 17, 29. Study: Univ Wash, BA & MA; also with Mark Tobey. Work: Munic Gallery Mod Art, Dublin, Ireland; Boymans-Van Beuningen Mus, Rotterdam; Nat Collection Fine Arts, Smithsonian Inst; Baltimore Mus; Brooklyn Mus. Exhib: Osaka World's Fair, 70; retrospective, Whatcom Mus Hist & Art, Bellingham, Wash, 70; Shepherd Gallery, New York, 73; Humboldt Gallery, San Francisco, 74; Gallerie Rosenau, Bern, Switz, 76; one-man show, Basel, Switz, 77; Gallerie Mod Art, Munich, Ger, 77; Gallerie Radechi, Bonn, Ger, 78. Media: Mixed Media. Mailing Add: Henry Art Gallery Univ of Wash Seattle WA 98195

WEIDENAAR, REYNOLD HENRY
ETCHER, PAINTER
b Grand Rapids, Mich, Nov 17, 15. Study: Kendall Sch Design, 35-36; Kansas City Art Inst, scholar, 38-40. Work: Libr Cong, Washington, DC; Detroit Inst Arts, Mich; Nat Gallery SWales, Liverpool, Eng; Honolulu Acad Fine Arts, Hawaii; Hackley Art Gallery, Muskegon, Mich. Comn: Murals, church hist, La Grave Ave Christian Reformed Church, 65 & Urban Renewal, Mich Consol Gas Co, Grand Rapids. Exhib: Regular exhibitor, Nat Acad Design, Detroit Inst Arts & Libr Cong. Teaching: Instr life drawing & painting, Kendall Sch Design, 56-74. Awards: Guggenheim Found Award, 44; Tiffany Found Scholar, 48. Mem: Nat Acad Design; Soc Am Graphic Artists; Am Watercolor Soc. Style & Technique: Realistic and conservative; satirical; romanticism. Media: Watercolor, Resin-Oil. Publ: Auth, Our Changing Landscape, Wake-Brook House, 70. Dealer: June 1 Gallery Fine Art Bellamy Lane Bethlehem CT 06751. Mailing Add: 4041 Pointe o' Woods Ct SE Apt 108 Grand Rapids MI 49508

WEIDNER, MARILYN KEMP
CONSERVATOR, LECTURER
b Floral Park, NY, Jan 10, 28. Study: Pratt Inst; Hofstra Univ, BA; Univ Pa; Minna Horowitz Nagel-Metrop Mus Art; Takashi Sugiura-Freer Gallery Art. Teaching: Adj prof conserv art on paper, NY State Univ, Cooperstown Grad Progs, 71-74. Pos: Asst registrar, Mus Mod Art, New York, 51-56; registrar, Brooklyn Mus, 56-58; conservator, pvt practice, Philadelphia, 58-78; dir, Conserv Ctr for Art & Hist Artifacts, Philadelphia, 78- Mem: Fel Int Inst Conserv Art & Hist Artifacts; Am Inst Conserv Art & Hist Artifacts (chmn paper comt, 65-72); Peale Club; Pa Acad Fine Arts; Inst Paper Conserv, London. Publ: Contribr, Damage and Deterioration of Art on Paper, Studies in Conservation, Int Inst Conserv Art & Hist Artifacts, 67; contribr, A vacuum table of use in paper conservation, Am Inst Conserv Art & Hist Artifacts Bull, 74; contribr, Repair of Wall Charts from Cloister Edhrata, Pa Conserv & Restoration of Pictorial Art, Butterworth's, 76. Mailing Add: 612 Spruce St Philadelphia PA 19106

WEIDNER, ROSWELL THEODORE
PAINTER, INSTRUCTOR
b Reading, Pa, Sept 18, 11. Study: Pa Acad Fine Arts, Philadelphia, Cresson Foreign traveling scholar, 35; Barnes Found, Merion, Pa. Work: Pa Acad Fine Arts; Philadelphia Mus Art; Pa State Univ; Metrop Mus Art, New York; Libr Cong, Washington, DC. Comn: Portraits, of Herman Beerman, Univ, Pa, 68, Robert C Sale, Conn State Libr, Hartford, 69 & Clair R McCollough, Nat Asn Broadcasters, Washington, DC, 70. Exhib: Pa Acad Fine Arts Ann, Philadelphia, 36-70; World's Fair, New York, 39; Directions Am Painting, Carnegie Inst, Pittsburgh, Pa, 43; Drawing Soc 2nd Eastern Cent Exhib, Philadelphia Mus Art, 70; 24th Am Drawing Biennial, Norfolk Mus Arts & Sci, Va & Smithsonian Traveling Exhib, 71; one-man exhib, Newman Galleries, Philadelphia, Pa, 78. Teaching: Sr instr painting, Pa Acad Fine Arts, 38-; instr painting, Philadelphia Col Art, 49-51. Pos: Mem exhib comt, Philadelphia Art Alliance, 65-70. Awards: Fel prize, Pa Acad Fine Arts Ann, 43; Dawson Mem Medal, Philadelphia Watercolor Club, 64-72 & 76; Percy Owens Award, 75. Mem: Fel Pa Acad Fine Arts (pres, 54-67, vpres, 67-72); Philadelphia Watercolor Club (bd dirs, 65-72); Artists Equity Asn; Print Club Philadelphia; Int Inst Conserv Hist & Artistic Works. Style & Technique: Romantic realism. Media: Oil, Charcoal, Pastels. Mailing Add: 612 Spruce St Philadelphia PA 19106

WEIL, LISL
ILLUSTRATOR, WRITER
b Vienna, Austria; US citizen. Pos: Auth & illusr of over 100 children's books; concert illusr with major symphony orchestras, US; concert illustrations on nationwide TV specials. Mailing Add: 25 Central Park W New York NY 10023

WEIL, STEPHEN EDWARD
MUSEUM EXECUTIVE, LECTURER
b New York, NY, June 24, 28. Study: Brown Univ, AB, 49; Columbia Univ, LLB, 56. Pos: Vpres & gen mgr, Marlborough-Gerson Gallery, New York, 63-67; adminr, Whitney Mus of Am Art, New York, 67-74; deputy dir, Hirshhorn Mus & Sculpture Garden, Smithsonian Inst, 74- Mem: Am Asn Mus (coun mem, mem exec comt, treas, 75-); Volunteer Lawyers for the Arts, NY (mem adv bd, 75-); Opportunity Resources for the Arts (mem adv bd, 74-); H Lester Cooke Found (mem adv bd, 75-). Publ: Auth var articles in Art in Am, Law Libr J, Mus News & Print Collectors Newsletter, 70-77; co-ed, Legal & Business Problems of Artists, Art Galleries & Museums, 73 & co-auth, Art Works: Law, Policy, Practice, 74, Practising Law Inst. Mailing Add: Hirshhorn Mus & Sculpture Garden Smithsonian Inst Washington DC 20560

WEILER, MELODY M
PRINTMAKER, EDUCATOR
b Santa Monica, Calif, Mar 4, 47. Study: State Univ NY, Buffalo, BFA; Ohio Univ, MFA; also with Harvey Breverman, Seymour Drumlevitch, Donald Roberts & Harvey Daniels. Work: Ohio Univ, Athens; Kemper Gallery, Kansas City, Mo. Comn: Ceramic & screened mural, Ohio Univ, Athens, 70-71; cover design, Glass Eye Productions, Los Angeles, 76; posters, Hollins Col, Va & Murray State Univ, Ky, 76-77; airbrushed shirts & masks, Mr Jerry Ziegman, Los Angeles, 77. Exhib: Western NY Art Exhib, Albright-Knox Art Gallery, Buffalo, 69; Young Printmakers, Herron Sch of Art, Ind, 70; High Mus of Art, Atlanta, Ga, 72; Nelson-Atkins Art Mus, Kansas City, Mo, 74; Four Artists, Morgan Art Gallery, Shawnee Mission, Kans, 75; A Pictorial Hist of the World, Kemper Gallery, Kansas City, Mo, 75; Fiber Art, Broadway Gallery, Kansas City, Mo, 76; one-person show, Hollins Col, Va, 77; Fell's Point Gallery, Baltimore, Md, 78. Teaching: Instr printmaking/design, Atlanta Sch of Art, Ga, 71-72; instr found design, Kansas City Art Inst, Mo, 72-73; asst prof printmaking, Murray State Univ, 75- Awards: Res grant, Hand Papermaking, Murray State Univ, 76-77 & 77-78; Workshop grant, Printing & Papermaking, Ky Arts Comn & Nat Endowment for the Arts, 77, Hand Bookbinding, 78. Bibliog: Carolyn Robertson (auth), Designing shirts, Kansas City Star, 74; Richard A Matthews (auth), Shirtworks (16mm film), 76; Jerry Speight (auth), Airbrush painting, Ky Artist & Craftsman, 77. Mem: Col Art Asn; Ctr for the Bk Arts; Pvt Libr Asn; Printing Hist Soc; Int Paper Historians. Style & Technique: Fantasy juxtapositions; airbrush and stencil printing on fabric. Media: Acrylic; Serigraphy. Publ: Contribr, Simple Printmaking with Children, 72 & Exploring Printmaking for Young People, 72, Van Nostrand Reinhold; illusr, A Pictorial History of the World, Kemper Gallery, 75; contribr (photog coverage), The Painted Vega, 75 & illusr (cover design), Southern Exposure, 76, Glass Eye Productions; contribr, Creating Handmade Paper, Crown, 78. Mailing Add: Dept of Art Murray State Univ Murray KY 42071

WEIL-GARRIS, KATHLEEN
See Garris, Kathleen

WEILL, ERNA
SCULPTOR, INSTRUCTOR
b Frankfurt am Main, Ger; US citizen. Study: Univ Frankfurt, with Helene von Beckerath; also with John Hovannes, New York. Work: Ga Mus Art, Athens; Birmingham Mus, Ala; Jewish Mus, New York; Hyde Park Libr, New York; Israel Mus, Hebrew Univ, Jerusalem; plus many others. Comn: Bronze archit sculptures, Teaneck Jewish Ctr, NJ, 55, White Plains Jewish Ctr, NY, 58 & Temple Har El, Jerusalem, Israel, 63; bronze portrait sculptures, Linus Pauling, Portula Valley, Calif, Martin Buber, Hebrew Univ, Leonard Bernstein, Dr Martin Luther King & Elie Wiesel; plus many more. Exhib: New York World's Fair; NJ State Mus, Trenton; Brooklyn Mus; Montclair Mus; Newark Mus; plus one-man shows, NY & NJ, 51-72. Teaching: Instr sculpture, Brooklyn Mus, Forest Hills Pub Schs, Forest Hills Jewish Ctr & Teaneck Jewish Ctr; instr sculpture, Adult Educ Prog, Ft Lee, NJ; pvt instr, sculpture; lectr, Fairleigh Dickinson Univ; lectr, var clubs & temples, NJ. Awards: Mem Found Jewish Cult grant for relig sculpture; Best in Sculpture, Artist-Craftsman, New York, 75. Bibliog: Bernard Buranelli (auth), World of Erna Weill, Rec Mag, 64; Avram Kampf (auth), Contemporary synagogue art, Union Am Hebrew Congregations, 65. Mem: Artists Equity Asn New York; New York Soc Artists Craftsmen; Mod Artists Guild, NJ; Sculptors Affil Art Ctr. Style & Technique: Simplified forms and basic shapes to transmit intensity. Media: Stone, Metal, Concrete. Publ: Auth, Any child can model in clay, Design; co-auth, article in, Crisis, 10/65; contribr, Libr J & NJ Educ Rev. Mailing Add: 886 Alpine Dr Teaneck NJ 07666

WEIN, ALBERT W
SCULPTOR, PAINTER
b New York, NY, July 27, 15. Study: Md Inst, 27-29; Nat Acad Design; Grand Cent Sch Art; Beaux Arts Inst, with Hans Hofmann. Work: Vatican Mus Numismatic Collection, Vatican City; NY Univ Hall of Fame; Jewish Mus, New York; Brookgreen Gardens, SC; Palm Springs Desert Mus, Calif. Comn: Exterior sculptures, Hillside Mem Park, Los Angeles, 60-68; exterior, St Michael's Episcopal Church, Anaheim, Calif, 67; bas-relief panels, Univ Wyo Phys Sci Ctr, 68; 25th Anniversary Medal, UN, 70; granite bas-relief, Libby Dam Treaty Tower & designer medal for Libby Dam Dedication, Libby, Mont, 75. Exhib: Whitney Mus Am Art Ann, New York, 50; Am Sculpture, Metrop Mus Art, New York, 51; San Francisco Mus Art Ann, 57; one-man show, Jewish Mus, 58; 30 yr retrospective, Palm Springs Desert Mus, 69. Teaching: Vis prof sculpture, Univ Wyo, 65-67; mem fac, Nat Acad of Design, 77-78. Awards: Prix de Rome, Am Acad Rome, 47 & 48; Tiffany Found fel, 49; Huntington Hartford Found fel, 55. Bibliog: J Lovoos (auth), Art of Albert Wein, Am Artist, 1/63 & Art rev, Christian Sci Monitor, 4/67. Mem: Fel Am Acad Rome; assoc fel Nat Acad of Design; fel Int Inst Arts & Lett; fel Huntington Hartford Found; fel Nat Sculpture Soc. Media: Bronze, Marble; Paint. Mailing Add: PO Box 311 Scarborough NY 10510

WEINBAUM, JEAN
PAINTER, SCULPTOR
b Zurich, Switz, 26. Study: Zurich Sch Fine Arts, 42-46; Acad Grande Chaumiere; Ecole Paul Colin; Acad Andre L'Hote, 47-48. Work: Mus Mod Art, Paris, France; Nat Collection Fine Arts, Washington, DC; Univ Art Mus, Berkeley, Calif; Stanford Univ Mus, Calif; Calif Palace of Legion of Honor, San Francisco. Comn: Eleven stained glass windows, Chapelle de Mosloy, 51; rosette stained glass, Berne sur Oise, 55; 22 stained glass windows, St Pierre du Regard, 57; Wall of Light (monumental stained glass window), Escherange, 62; eight windows, Lycee de Jeunes Filles, Bayonne, France, 66. Exhib: Mus Mod Art, Paris, 62, 63 & 65; one-man shows, Galerie Smith-Andersen, Palo Alto, Calif, 70, 71, 73 & 75, Calif Palace of Legion of Honor, 71, Musee Arts Decoratifs, Lausanne, Switz, 72 & Bildungszentrum, Gelsenkirchen, Ger, 72; plus many other group & one-man shows. Bibliog: Francois Mathey & others (auth), Vitrail Francais, In: Tendances Modernes, Ed Deux Mondes, Paris, 58; Robert Sowers (auth), Stained Glass: an Architectural Art, Universe Bks, New York, 65; Shuji Takashina (auth), Stained glass works by Jean Weinbaum, Space Design, Tokyo, 9/67. Style & Technique: Abstract colorpainting with symbolic meanings inspired from Zen Buddhism and philosophies of ancient Tibet, India and china. Media: Watercolor, Oil, Stained Glass. Dealer: Galerie Smith-Andersen 200 Homer St Palo Alto CA 94301. Mailing Add: PO Box 40291 San Francisco CA 94140

WEINBERG, DANIEL
ART DEALER
b Chicago, Ill, Dec 25, 33. Study: San Diego State Univ, BA, 56. Specialty: Contemporary art. Mailing Add: 2140 Bush St San Francisco CA 94115

WEINBERG, ELBERT
SCULPTOR, EDUCATOR
b Hartford, Conn, May 27, 28. Study: Hartford Art Sch, with Henry Kreis; RI Sch Design, with Waldemar Raemisch; Yale Univ Sch Fine Arts. Work: Mus Mod Art, New York; Whitney Mus Am Art & Jewish Mus, New York; Boston Mus Fine Arts, Mass; Wadsworth Athenaeum, Hartford. Comn: Bronze procession (sculpture), Mr & Mrs Albert List, Jewish Mus, 59; Jacob Wrestling with Angel (sculpture), Brandeis Univ, Waltham, Mass, 64; Shofar (bronze), Rockdale Temple, Cincinnati, Ohio, 69; Justice (bronze), Boston Univ Law Sch Lobby, 74; Bronze Procession 2, Beth El Temple, West Hartford, Conn, 75. Exhib: Whitney Mus Am Art, New York, 57, 58, 60 & 64; Carnegie Int, Pittsburgh, Pa, 58 & 61; Sculpture USA, Mus Mod Art, New York, 59; 64 Americans Exhib, Art Inst Chicago, Ill, 61; Hirschhorn Collection, Guggenheim Mus, New York, 62. Teaching: Instr sculpture, Cooper Union, 56-59; vis prof sculpture, Boston Univ, 70- & Tyler Sch Art, Temple Abroad. Awards: Prix de Rome, Am Acad Rome, 51-53; Guggenheim fel, 59; Sculpture Award, Am Inst Arts & Lett, 69. Bibliog: Articles & photographs in several bks. Mem: Sculptors Guild, New York. Style & Technique: Direct wax for bronze; plastics in recent expressionist group of work. Dealer: Grace Borgenicht Gallery 1018 Madison Ave New York NY 10021; Alpha Gallery 121 Newbury St Boston MA 02116. Mailing Add: Via Appia Antica 20 Rome Italy

WEINBERG, EPHRAIM
ART ADMINISTRATOR, EDUCATOR
b Philadelphia, Pa, Apr 28, 38. Study: Philadelphia Col of Art; Univ Pa. Teaching: Lectr, Bournmouth Col of Art, Eng, 64-65; prof, Bucks Co Community Col, Newton, Pa, 67-68; prof, Philadelphia Col of Art, 69-71; prof, Sch of the Art Inst of Chicago, 71-77. Pos: Dean, Pa Acad of Fine Arts, 77- Mem: Nat Asn of Arts Adminr; Nat Art Educ Asn; Nat Asn of Sch of Art. Mailing Add: Pa Acad of Fine Arts Broad & Cherry Sts Philadelphia PA 19102

WEINBERG, H BARBARA
ART HISTORIAN
b New York, NY. Study: Barnard Col, BA; Columbia Univ, MA, PhD(art hist, archaeol). Teaching: Assoc prof art hist, Queens Col, City Univ of NY & Grad Sch, 72- Mem: Col Art Asn of Am; Victorian Soc in Am. Res: Nineteenth century American painting. Publ: Auth, The Decorative Work of John La Farge, Garland, 77. Mailing Add: Dept Art Queens Col City Univ NY Flushing NY 11367

WEINER, ABE
PAINTER, INSTRUCTOR
b Pittsburgh, Pa, Nov 5, 17. Study: Carnegie Inst Technol, cert painting & design, 41, with Robert Gwathmey & Samuel Rosenberg. Work: Hillman Libr, Univ Pittsburgh. Comn: Painting & mosaic on aluminum, Alcoa Co Pittsburgh; painting, PPG Industs. Exhib: Assoc Artists Pittsburgh, 40-72 & Shows, 46-49, Carnegie Inst; Carnegie Inst Int, Pittsburgh, 50; Contemp Soc Exhib, Art Inst Chicago, 52; 50 Most Promising Artists US, Metrop Mus Art, 53. Teaching: Instr painting, Arts & Crafts Ctr, 57-60; instr painting & drawing & asst dir, Ivy Sch Prof Art, 61-; instr painting, Irene Kaufman Ctr, 65- Awards: First Prize & Second Prize, 41 & 45, Judge's Prize, 59 & Purchase Award, 74 & 75, Assoc Artists Pittsburgh; Three Rivers Festival Purchase Award, 68. Mem: Assoc Artists Pittsburgh. Style & Technique: Surrealism with emphasis on texture. Media: Acrylic, Dry Pigment. Mailing Add: 1636 Denniston Ave Pittsburgh PA 15217

WEINER, EGON
SCULPTOR
b Vienna, Austria, July 24, 06; US citizen. Study: Sch Arts Crafts, Acad Fine Arts, Vienna. Work: Syracuse Mus Fine Arts; Augsburg Col, Minneapolis; Augustana Col, Rock Island, Ill; plus others. Comn: Portrait bust of Dr Eric Oldberg (bronze), for Med Ctr, Chicago, 72; bronze busts of Nobel Prize Winner Willy Brandt, Harvard Univ, 72 & Ernest Hemingway, Oak Park Libr, Ill, 74; heads of Secy of State Henry Kissinger, 77 & Diana, daughter of Apollo 8 Astronaut Anders, 77; plus others. Exhib: Art Inst Chicago, 60-71; Art Inst Oslo Ann Exhib, 71, 73 & 75-76; US Info Serv Libr, Am Embassy, Oslo, 72-73; plus many others. Teaching: Lectr, US & abroad; prof sculpture & life drawing, Art Inst Chicago, 45-71, emer prof, 71-; vis prof art, Augustana Col, 56. Pos: Educ consult, Film of Del Prado Mus, Madrid, Spain, 69; educ consult, Int Film Bur, Chicago. Awards: Gold Medal, Munic Art League, Chicago, 69; Gold Medal, Soc Arts & Lett, 70; Austrian Cross of Honor First Class for Sci & Art, 77; plus others. Mem: Life fel Int Inst Arts & Lett; Munic Art League, Chicago (dir, 61-64); Cliff Dwellers of Chicago; hon life mem Alumni Asn Sch of Art Inst Chicago; Nat Inst Arts & Lett (adv coun, 68-70); plus others. Media: Stone, Wood, Steel and Bronze. Mailing Add: 835 Michigan Ave Evanston IL 60202

WEINER, LAWRENCE CHARLES
ARTIST
b Bronx, NY, Feb 10, 40. Work: Mus Mod Art, New York; Vanabbe Mus, Eindhoven, Netherlands; Stäticshes Mus Mönchengladbach, W Ger; Gentofte Kummunes Kunstbibliotek, Hellerup, Denmark; Nat Gallery of Australia, Canberra. Exhib: Concept Art, Stadisches Mus, Leverkusen, Ger, 69; Information, Mus of Mod Art, New York, 70; Koncept Kunst, Westfalischer Kunstverein, Munster, Ger, 71; Venice Bienniale, Videogalerie Schum, Venice; Idea & Image in Recent Art, Art Inst Chicago, Ill, 74; Art/On Art, Kolnischer Kunstverein, Cologne; one-man shows, Westfalischer Kunstverein, Munster, Ger, 72, Staditisches Mus Monchengladbach, Ger, 73; Van Abbemuseum Eindhoven, Netherlands, 76; Inst Contemp Art, London, 76; Kunstalle Basel, Switz, 76 & Laguna Gloria Mus, Austin, Tex. Awards: Deutscher Akadomischer Austamschdient Fel, 75; Nat Endowment for the Arts Fel, 76-77. Publ: Auth, Statements, Siegelaub, New York, 68; auth, A Primer, Documenta Five, 72; auth, Within Forward Motion, Kabinet Fur Aktuelle Kunst, 73; auth, Various Manners with Various Things, Inst Contemp Art, London, 76; auth, Works, Printed Matter, 77. Mailing Add: c/o Leo Castelli 420 W Broadway New York NY 10012

WEINER, TED
COLLECTOR, PATRON
b Ft Worth, Tex, Mar 9, 11. Pos: Dir, Palm Springs Desert Mus, Calif, 67- Awards: Culture Award, WTex CofC, 67. Interest: Experimental art class for gifted children, Ft Worth. Collection: Contemporary paintings and sculpture, including works by Henry Moore, Maillol, Marino Marini, Modigliani, Lipchitz, Picasso, Callery, Voulkos, Chadwick, Noguchi, Calder, Laurens, Marchs, de la Fresneye, de Stael, Tamayo, Parker & Kline; selection exhibited at University of Texas at Austin, 66 & Palm Springs Desert Museum, 69. Mailing Add: Ted Weiner Oil Properties 2601 Ridgmar Plaza Ft Worth TX 76116

WEINER, TESS MANILLA
See Manilla, Tess

WEINGARTEN, HILDE (KEVESS)
PAINTER, PRINTMAKER
b Berlin, Ger; US citizen. Study: Art Students League, with Morris Kantor; Cooper Union Art Sch, with Morris Kantor, Robert Gwathmey & Will Barnet, cert, 47, BFA, 76; Pratt Graphics Ctr. Work: Brooklyn Mus; Herbert F Johnson Mus, Cornell Univ; Israel Mus, Jerusalem; New York Pub Libr Print Collection; Fogg Art Mus, Harvard Univ. Exhib: Philadelphia Art Alliance, 54; Denver Art Mus, 54; Rochester Mem Art Gallery, 54; Albright Art Gallery, Buffalo, 55; Cleveland Mus of Art, 55; Dallas Mus of Fine Art, 56; Brooklyn Mus, NY, 58, 63, 71, 74, 76 & 77; New York World's Fair, 65; Graphics 71 Print Exhib, Western NMex Univ, Silver City, 71; Audubon Artists, Nat Acad Design, New York, 71, 73, 75, 77 & 78; Palazzo Vecchio, Florence & Pompeiian Pavilion, Naples, Italy, 72; Pratt Graphics Ctr Annuals, 72-77; plus many other group & six one-artist shows. Awards: Patrons of Art Prize for Oil Painting, Painters & Sculptors Soc NJ, 70; Winsor & Newton Award for Oil Painting, Am Soc Contemp Artists, 71; Donna Miller Mem Prize for Etching, Nat Asn Women Artists, 75. Mem: Artists Equity Asn, New York (bd dirs, 64-72); Nat Asn Women Artists (mem graphics jury, 73-75 & oil jury, 75-77); League Present Day Artists; Am Soc Contemp Artists; Painters & Sculptors Soc NJ. Style & Technique: Semi-abstract; Media: Intaglio, Collagraph, Oil, Acrylic. Publ: Illusr, Tune of the calliope, 58 & German folksongs, 68. Mailing Add: 140 Cadman Plaza W Brooklyn NY 11201

WEINHARDT, CARL JOSEPH, JR
MUSEUM DIRECTOR, WRITER
b Indianapolis, Ind, Sept 22, 27. Study: Harvard Univ, AB(magna cum laude), 48, MA, 49, MFA, 55; Christian Theol Sem, Indianapolis, HHD, 67. Collections Arranged: Five Centuries German Prints, Metrop Mus Art, 56, 18th Century Design, 60; Four Centuries American Art, Minneapolis Inst Arts, 63; Pavel Tchelitchew, Gallery Mod Art, 64, Lovis Corinth, 65; Treasures From Metrop, Indianapolis Mus Art, 70. Teaching: Lectr archit, Boston Archit Ctr, 54-55; lectr fine art, Columbia Univ, 58-60. Pos: Staff mem, Metrop Mus Art, 55-58, assoc cur prints & drawings, 58-60; dir, Minneapolis Inst Arts, 60-62, dir, Gallery Mod Art, New York, 62-65; dir, Indianapolis Mus Art, 65-75; dir, Villa Vizcaya & Gardens, Miami, Fla, 76; secy, Cult Execs Coun Greater Miami; mem steering comt, Miami Downtown Develop Auth; coordr, Metrop Dade Co Art Inst. Bibliog: Caroline Geib (auth), A Challenge Accepted, Time-Life Broadcasts, 71. Mem: Asn Art Mus Dirs; Nat Soc Arts & Lett (nat adv); Drawing Soc (nat comt); Olana Preserv (trustee); Miami Design Preserv League (vpres). Publ: Auth, The Etchings of Canaletto, Metrop Mus Art, 56; auth, Beacon Hill, Bostonian Soc, 58; auth, The James Ford Bell American Wing, Minneapolis Inst Art, 63; auth, Newport preserved, Art Am, 65; auth, A Catalogue of European Paintings in the Indianapolis Museum of Art, 71. Mailing Add: 3251 S Miami Ave Miami FL 33129

WEINMAN, ROBERT ALEXANDER
SCULPTOR
b New York, NY, Mar 19, 15. Study: Nat Acad Design; Art Students League; Hobart Sculptor's Welding Course; also sculpture with A A Weinman, Lee Lawrie, Paul Manship, E McCartan, C Jennewein & J E Fraser. Work: Brookgreen Gardens, SC. Comn: Limestone tympana, Our Lady Queen of Martyrs Church, Forest Hills, NY, 39; bronze elk, Elks, Walla Walla, Wash, 48; bronze doors, Armstrong Libr, Baylor Univ, Waco, Tex, 51; athletic medals, Nat Collegiate Athletic Asn, 52; Morning Mission (bronze), Tulsa, Okla, 62. Exhib: Nat Acad Design Ann, 37, 38, 49 & 53; Pa Acad Fine Art Ann, 38 & 39; Allied Artists Am, 46, Sculpture Int, Philadelphia, 49; Nat Sculpture Soc, 52, 60, 65, 69 & 70. Awards: Hon Mention for Sculpture, Allied Artists Am, 46; Mrs Louis Bennett Prize, Nat Sculpture Soc, 52; J S Saltus Medal, Am Numismatic Soc, 64 & Sculptor of the Yr Gold Medal Award, 75. Mem: Academician Nat Acad Design; fel Nat Sculpture Soc (secy, 62-65, first vpres, 65-68 & 70-73, pres, 73-76); Soc Animal Artists; Collectors Art Medals (charter dir, 71). Style & Technique: Representational; modeling in clay, cast in plaster for reproduction by others in metal, stone or wood. Publ: Contribr, articles in, Nat Sculpture Rev, 62-75. Mailing Add: Cross River Rd RD 3 Bedford NY 10506

WEINRIB, DAVID
SCULPTOR
b Brooklyn, NY, 1924. Study: Brooklyn Col; State Univ NY, Alfred. Work: Los Angeles Co Mus of Art, Calif; Whitney Mus of Art; Walker Art Ctr. Minneapolis, Minn. Exhib: Ann, Whitney Mus of Am Art, 64-65 & 66-67; VIII Sao Paulo Biennial, 65; New York Univ, 65; American Sculpture of the Sixties, Los Angeles Co Mus, 67; Southern Ill Univ, 67; Univ Ill, 69; one-man shows, Howard Wise Gallery, 63 & Royal Marks Gallery, 66 & 71. Teaching: Instr, Sch of Visual Arts, New York. Awards: J S Guggenheim Fel, 68. Mailing Add: c/o Royal Marks Gallery 29 E 64th St New York NY 10021

WEINSTEIN, FLORENCE
PAINTER, SCULPTOR
b New York, NY, June 5, 95. Study: Adelphi Col, BA, 16; Subjects of the Artist Sch, New York, 48-49; Black Mountain Col, NC, 49-50; study with Motherwell, 49-50; Hofmann Sch, Provincetown, Mass, 52. Work: Edwin A Ulrich Mus of Art, Wichita, Kans; New Paltz Univ Mus, New York; Marist Col, Poughkeepsie, NY; Norfolk Mus of Arts & Sci, VA; Russel Sage Col, Troy, NY. Exhib: Eleven Painters—One Sculptor, Riverside Mus, New York, 55; Art US, New York, 58; Int Carnegie Inst, Pittsbirgh, Pa, 58-59; 40 Yrs Am Collage, Buecker & Harpsichords, New York, 74; 10th St Days, Soho, New York, 77. Mem: Woodstock Art Asn (mem bd dir, 52-); Artists Club, New York. Style & Technique: Nonrepresentational lyric abstraction; ceramic sculpture, collage montage. Mailing Add: 246 E 46th St New York NY 10017

WEINSTEIN, MR & MRS JOSEPH
COLLECTORS, PATRONS
Mr Weinstein, b New York, NY, Nov 13, 99. Study: Mr Weinstein, Harvard Univ; Mrs Weinstein, Simmons Col. Collection: Picasso, Cezanne, Renoir, Rouault, Soutine, Max Weber, Balcomb Greene, Rodin, Zogbaum, Zorach and others; also African sculpture. Mailing Add: 211 Central Park W New York NY 10024

WEISBERG, RUTH ELLEN
PRINTMAKER, EDUCATOR
b Chicago, Ill, July 31, 42. Study: Accad di Belli Arte, Perugia, Italy, Laurea; Univ Mich, BS & MA; Atelier 17, Paris, with S W Hayter. Work: Bibliot Nat of France; Chicago Art Inst; Detroit Inst of Art; New York Pub Libr; Norwegian Nat Collection. Comn: Together Again (ed of 150 lithographs), Midwest Regional Orgn for Rehabilitation & Training, 75; The Gift (ed of 60 lithographs), Univ Synagogue, Los Angeles, 75. Exhib: Innovations in Intaglio, Detroit Inst of Art, 69; one-person show, Munic Gallery, Oslo, Norway, 72, Univ Tex, Dallas, 77, Oglethorpe Univ, Atlanta, 77, El Camino Col, Los Angeles, 77, Alice Simsar Gallery, Ann Arbor, 77; Eight Artist-Teachers, Contemp Graphics, Santa Barbara Mus, Calif, 75; Works on Twin Rocker Paper, Indianapolis Mus, 75; Artist's Proof: The Multiple Image, Fine Arts Mus of San Francisco, 76; two-person shows, Union Gallery, Ariz State Univ, 76 & Palos Verdes Art Gallery, Los Angeles, 76; Works by Women on Paper, Nat Invitational, Women's Bldg, Los Angeles, 77. Teaching: Asst prof fine arts, Eastern Mich Univ, Ypsilanti, 66-67; assoc prof fine arts, Univ Southern Calif, Los Angeles, 70-; assoc dean, Univ Southern Calif, 74-75 & 76-77. Awards: Purchase Award, Los Angeles Printmaking Soc, Griffin Press, 76. Bibliog: V Thorson (auth), Sensory visions of Ruth Weisberg, Womanspace J, 8/73. Mem: Los Angeles Printmaking Soc (pres, 74-76); Graphic Arts Coun, Los Angeles Co Mus (mem exec bd, 76-77); Women's Caucus for Art (mem nat adv bd, 77-80); Artist for Econ Action; Malaspina Printmakers Soc. Style & Technique: Expressive and subjective depictions of reality. Media: Lithography; Drawing. Publ: Illusr, Tom O'Bedlam's Song, 69 & auth & illusr, The Shtsthl, A Journey & A Memorial, 72, Kelyn, Press. Mailing Add: 2421 Third St Santa Monica CA 90405

WEISGARD, LEONARD JOSEPH
ILLUSTRATOR, WRITER
b New Haven, Conn, Dec 13, 16. Study: Pratt Inst; New Sch Social Res; also with Alexei Brodovich. Exhib: Metrop Mus Art; Mus Mod Art, New York; Worcester Mus; Waterbury Mus; plus throughout the Soviet Union. Teaching: Instr art, Booth Free Sch. Pos: Dir exhibs, Mattatuck Hist Soc; mem greeting card art selection, UNICEF; scenic & costume designer. Awards: Caldecott Award, Am Libr Asn; Awards, Am Inst Graphic Arts. Bibliog: Articles in, Horn Bk Mag. Publ: Auth over 13 bks; illusr over 250 bks for children. Mailing Add: Jelshøjgard Traelløse 4160 Herlufmagle Denmark

WEISMANN, DONALD LEROY
EDUCATOR, PAINTER
b Milwaukee, Wis, Oct 12, 14. Study: Univ Wis-Milwaukee, BS; Univ Minn; Univ Wis-Madison, PhM; St Louis Univ; Harvard Univ, Carnegie Corp scholar, 41; Ohio State Univ, PhD. Work: Butler Inst Am Art, Youngstown, Ohio; Chrysler Mus, Provincetown, Mass; Columbia Mus Art, SC; D D Feldman Collection, Humanities Res Ctr, Univ Tex, Austin; Witte Mus, San Antonio, Tex. Comn: Mural, Ill Centennial Bldg, Springfield, 41; TV videotape ser, Mirror of Western Art, Nat Educ TV, 60 & Visual Arts, Ford Found & US Off Educ, 61; films, Terlingua, 71 & Station X, 75, Pub Broadcast Corp; Azimuth, 76. Exhib: Ann Exhib Am Art, 40-41 & Int Watercolor Exhib, 42, Art Inst Chicago, Ill; Ann Exhib Art US & Territories, Butler Inst Am Art, 57-58; Gulf-Caribbean Exhib, Houston Mus Fine Arts, Tex, 58; World's Fair, New York, 64-65; Colorado Springs Fine Arts Ctr, Colo; Cincinnati Mus of Art, Ohio; Corcoran Gallery of Art, Washington, DC; Dallas Mus of Fine Arts, Tex; Inst of Contemp Arts, Boston, Mass; Toledo Mus of Art, Ohio. Collections Arranged: Ulfert Wilke Retrospective, 53 & Victor Hammer Retrospective, 54, Univ Ky, Lexington. Teaching: Assoc prof, NTex State Univ, summer 40; asst prof art & art hist, Ill State Univ, 40-42 & 46-48; asst prof art hist, Wayne State Univ, 49-51; prof art & head dept, Univ Ky, 51-54; prof art, Univ Tex, Austin, 54-, chmn dept, 54-58, grad prof art hist, 58-, univ prof in arts, 64-, chmn comp studies, 67-72. Awards: Purchase Award for Painting, Butler Inst Am Art, 57; Bromberg Award for Excellence in Teaching, Univ Tex, Austin, 65; Lett of Commendation for Enhancement of Arts in Am, President of US, 72. Mem: Nat Coun Arts; Nat Humanities Fac; Am Asn Univ Prof; Tex Fine Arts Asn. Style & Technique: Romantic, abstract, allegorical surrealism; sui generis technique. Media: Collage, Film. Res: Creative process in art and science; language and visual form. Publ: Auth, Jelly was the Word, 65; auth & illusr, Language & Visual Form, 68; auth, Visual Arts as Human Experience, 70; auth & illusr, Why Draw?, 74; auth, The 12 Cadavers of Joe Mariner, 77. Dealer: Carlin Galleries 710 Montgomery St Ft Worth TX 76107. Mailing Add: Academic Ctr 18 Univ of Tex Austin TX 78712

WEISS, ANTON
PAINTER, ART DIRECTOR
b Belgrade, Yugoslavia, Mar 29, 36. Study: Villach Art Inst, Austria; Art Students League; Watkins Inst, Nashville; Univ Tenn. Work: Parthenon, Nashville; Watkins Inst; First Am Nat Bank, Nashville; ETex Art Asn, Longview. Comn: Cityscape of Franklin, Tenn, Harpeth Nat Bank, 73. Exhib: Trans-Mississippi Painting, The Lewis James & Nelle Stratton Davis Art Gallery, 64; Cent South Exhib, Nashville, 66-74; Jr Serv League, Longview, 68-69; Tenn All-State Exhib, Nashville, 69; Winston-Salem Competitive Exhib, NC. Pos: Art dir, Watkins Inst, 74- Awards: Cent South Exhib Parthenon Purchase Award, Tenn Art League, 68 & 70; Tenn All-State Exhib Award, First Am Nat Bank, 69 & 70. Bibliog: The Voice, Paul Hamilton Galleries, 71. Mem: Tenn & Southern Watercolor Socs; Tenn Art League (pres, 75). Style & Technique: Abstract expressionism. Media: Acrylic; Bronze. Dealer: Thanhardt-Burger Corp LaPorte IN 46350. Mailing Add: 6224 Bresslyn Rd Nashville TN 37205

WEISS, HARVEY
SCULPTOR
b New York, NY, Apr 10, 22. Study: Nat Acad Design; Art Students League; and with Ossipe Zadkine, Paris. Work: Albright-Knox Art Gallery; Krannert Mus; Silvermine Guild Collection; Nelson Rockefeller Collection; Joseph H Hirshhorn Collection; plus others. Comn: Menorah, Temple B'nai Zion, Shreveport, La, 67; relief, Mt Vernon Synagogue, NY, 69; relief, Conn Off Bldg, Westport, 71. Exhib: Five one-man shows, Paul Rosenberg & Co, 59-70; one-man show, Silvermine Guild, 68; retrospective, Fairfield Univ, 70; Am Inst Arts & Lett, 70; Sculptor's Guild Ann Shows. Teaching: Asst prof sculpture, Adelphi Univ, Garden City, NY, currently. Awards: Three Ford Found Purchase Awards; Olivetti Award, New Eng Ann Exhib, 69; Nat Inst Arts & Lett Grant, 70. Mem: Sculptors Guild (pres, 70-71); Silvermine Guild Artists (bd trustees, 68-70); Auth Guild. Media: Bronze, Welded Brass. Publ: Auth & illusr, Ceramics, 64, Paint Brush & Palette, 66, Collage & Construction, 70, Gadget Book, 71 & Lens & Shutter, 71; plus others. Dealer: Paul Rosenberg & Co 20 E 79th St New York NY 10021. Mailing Add: 42 Maple Lane Greens Farms CT 06436

WEISS, JOHN JOSEPH
PHOTOGRAPHER
b Philadelphia, Pa, Jan 31, 41. Study: Temple Univ, BS, 63; Mass Inst Technol, with Minor White, 69-73; RI Sch of Design, MFA, 73. Work: Mus Mod Art, New York; Addison Gallery of Am Art, Andover, Mass; Del Art Mus, Wilmington; The Photog Place, Philadelphia. Exhib: Addison Gallery of Am Art, Andover, Mass, 73; Washington Gallery of Photog, DC, 75; Del Art Mus, Wilmington, 75; Mass Inst Technol Creative Photog Gallery, Cambridge, 76; Galerie de l'Instant, Paris, France, 77. Teaching: Instr photog, Mass Inst Technol, 69-73; asst prof photog, Univ Del, Newark, 75- Style & Technique: Black and white photography addressed to inner essences. Media: Photography. Publ: Contribr, articles in Aperture, 72 & 74; contribr to Camera, 73 & Philadelphia Photo Rev, 77; contribr, Portraits, Mod Photog, 77; auth, A darkroom philosophy, Camera 35, 77. Mailing Add: Dept of Art Univ Del Newark DE 19711

WEISS, LEE (ELYSE C WEISS)
PAINTER
b Inglewood, Calif, May 22, 28. Study: Calif Col Arts & Crafts, 46-47; also with N Eric Oback, 57 & Alexander Nepote, 58. Work: Nat Collection Fine Arts, Smithsonian Inst, Washington, DC; Nat Acad Design, New York; Phillips Collection, Washington, DC; Exec Residence, State Wis; Springfield Mus Art, Mo; plus many others. Comn: Am Artist & Water Resources, one of 40 Am artists chosen for Bur Reclamation Art Proj, US Dept Interior, 71. Exhib: Calif Palace of the Legion of Honor, San Francisco, 62; Am Watercolor Soc, New York, 65-; Pa Acad Fine Arts, Philadelphia, 65 & 68; Landscape as Interpreted by Twenty-two Artists, Minneapolis Inst Fine Arts, Minn, 66; American Artist & Water Reclamation, Nat Gallery Art, Washington, DC, 72; San Jose Mus Art, Calif, 74; Nat Air & Space Mus, Smithsonian Inst, Washington, DC, 78; plus many other group & one-man shows. Awards: Medal of Hon for Watercolor, Knickerbocker Artists, 64; seven awards, 65-75 & Purchase Award, 67, Watercolor USA, Springfield Mus; Emily Lowe Award, 66, Henry Ward Ranger Fund Purchase Award, 67 & Martha T McKinnon Award, 73, Am Watercolor Soc; plus many others. Bibliog: Gerald F Brommer (auth), Transparent Watercolor: Ideas & Techniques, 73 & Landscapes, 77, Davis; Susan E Meyer, Forty Watercolorists & How They Work, Watson-Guptill, 76; article in Today's Art, 3/77. Mem: Am Watercolor Soc; Calif Nat Watercolor Soc; Wis Painters & Sculptors; Wis Watercolor Soc. Style & Technique: Landscape, with emphasis on close-up views of nature; very large format, often using monoprint process; strictly transparent. Media: Watercolor. Publ: Co-auth, Lee Weiss watercolors, Col Printing & Publ, 71; auth, article in, Watercolor Page, Am Artist Mag, 9/72. Dealer: Franz Bader Gallery 2124 Pennsylvania Ave NW Washington DC 20037; Oehlschaeger Galleries 107 E Oak Chicago IL 60611. Mailing Add: 106 Vaughn Ct Madison WI 53705

WEISS, PEG
ART HISTORIAN, CURATOR
Study: Syracuse Univ, BA, 54, PhD, 73; Univ Munich & Syracuse Univ, MA, 60. Exhibitions Arranged: Medieval Art in Upstate NY, 74, Art Deco Environment, 76 & Animal Kingdom in American Art, 77, Everson Mus. Teaching: Vis asst prof art hist, Columbia Univ, 74-75; adj asst prof art hist, Syracuse Univ, 74- Pos: Publ cur, Everson Mus, Syracuse NY, 74, cur collections, 75- Awards: German Govt Scholar, 56-57; Fulbright Scholar, 67-68; Millard Meiss Publ Fund Award, 77. Mem: Col Art Asn Am; Int Comt Mus; Am Asn Mus; Am Soc Aesthetics. Res: Major research area concerns turn-of-the-century and origins of abstraction, especially Kandinsky studies. Publ: Auth, Graphic art of Kandinsky, Art News, 3/74; auth, Kandinsky & the Jugendstil Arts & Crafts Movement, Burlington Mag, 5/75; auth, Kandinsky the Utopian focus, Arts Mag, 4/77; auth, Kandinsky: Symbolist Poetics & Theater in Munich, Pantheon, summer 77; Kandinsky in Munich—The Formative Jugendstil Years, Princeton Univ (in prep). Mailing Add: 238 Scottholm Terr Syracuse NY 13224

WEISSMAN, JULIAN PAUL
ART WRITER, ART DEALER
b New York, NY, June 28, 43. Study: Hobart Col, Geneva, NY, BA. Pos: Art Critic, The Press, 73-77; ed assoc, writer & reviwer, Art New Mag, New York, 74-; mgr, Susan Caldwell Gallery Inc, New York, 74-75,; mgr, Gloria Cortella Inc (gallery), New York, 76-77; dir, Alexander F Milliken Inc, (gallery), New York, 78- Res: Impressionism; German expressionism; the Bauhaus; 20th century sculpture; contemporary art and artists who live and work in New York. Specialty: Contemporary art gallery, primarily devoted to showing recent works by younger artists who live and work in New York. Publ: Auth, Standoff in Soho, Art News Mag, 74; auth, What's wrong at the Whitney?, The Press, -Vol 3 No 3, 75; auth, Master Atget... (photog) & Portraits of the Artists, Art News Mag, 76; auth, Here comes the taxman, Soho Weekly News, 76; auth, Dazzling Drawings are Redefining the Art, The Press, Vol 4 No 1, 76. Mailing Add: 60 Thomas St New York NY 10013

WEITZENHOFFER, A MAX
ART DEALER
b Oklahoma City, Okla, Oct 30, 39. Study: Univ Okla, BFA. Pos: Dir, Gimpel & Weitzenhoffer Ltd. Mem: Art Dealers Asn Am. Specialty: 20th century American and European paintings and sculpture. Mailing Add: 1040 Madison Ave New York NY 10021

WEITZMANN, KURT
EDUCATOR, ART HISTORIAN
b Almerode, Ger, Mar 7, 04; US citizen. Study: Univ Munster; Univ Wurzburg; Univ Vienna; Univ Berlin, PhD, 29; Univ Heidelberg, hon Dr, 67; Univ Chicago, hon Dr, 68. Teaching: Assoc prof art & archaeol, Princeton Univ, 45-50, prof art & archaeol, 50-72, emer prof, 72-; vis lectr art & archaeol, Yale Univ, 54-55; vis prof art & archaeol, Univ Alexandria, 60; guest prof art & archaeol, Univ Bonn, 62; vis scholar, Dumbarton Oaks, Washington, DC. Pos: Stipend, Ger Archaeol Inst, Greece, 32 & Berlin, 32-34; permanent mem, Inst Advan Study, 35-72; consult cur, Metrop Mus Art. Awards: Prix Gustave Schlumberger, Acad Inscriptions & Belles Lett, Paris, France, 69. Mem: Fel Medieval Acad Am; Ger Archaeol Inst; Am Philos Soc; Col Art Asn Am; Archaeol Inst Am. Res: Late classical, Byzantine and medieval art; expeditions to Mt Athos & Mt Sinai. Publ: Co-auth, Die Byzantinische Elfenbeinskulpturen des XXIII Jahrhunderts, Vols I & II, 30 & 34; auth, Illustrations in Roll & Codex, 47, rev ed, 70; auth, Greek Mythology in Byzantine Art, 51; co-auth, A Treasury of Icons, 67; auth, Studies in Late Classical & Byzantine Manuscript Illumination, 71. Mailing Add: 30 Nassau St Princeton NJ 08540

WELCH, JAMES HENRY
COLLECTOR
b Cleveland, Ohio, June 21, 31. Study: Western Pa Horological Inst, Pittsburgh, certified watchmaker; Col Wooster, BA. Mem: Nat Asn Watch & Clock Collectors (pres, Ohio Valley Chap, 64-65). Collection: 17th, 18th and early 19th century decorative watches including enamel automaton repousse and complicated watches; 18th century English musical clocks; American paintings, Hudson River, 19th century portraits and still lifes; British 19th century landscapes and portraits; French Barbizon School landscapes; Oriental rugs. Mailing Add: James K Welsh & Sons Trading Co 325 McKinley NW Canton OH 44702

WELCH, JAMES WYMORE
PAINTER
b Omaha, Nebr, June 7, 28. Study: George Washington Univ, BA; Univ Omaha, study with Anna C Myers; Acad Fine Arts, Tokyo, Japan, with Shiguru Yamamoto; Keio Univ, Hiyoshi, Japan, study with Daisuke Sakai; Sch of Fine Arts, Seoul, Korea, study with Kim Il Han; study with Mark Rothko. Work: Nat Mus, Seoul; Joslyn Mem Mus, Omaha; Nat Mus Mod Art, Tokyo; Xerox Corp, Richmond, VA; Fed Reserve Bank Collection, Richmond. Comn: Poster panel designs, US State Dept Arts Abroad Prog, Washington, DC, 63; acrylic mural, Univ Panama, Repub Panama, 59. Exhib: Mid-West Artists Exhib, Joslyn Mem Mus, Omaha, 45-46; Japan Fine Arts Festival, Nat Mus Mod Art, Tokyo & Kyoto, Japan, 48-50; Oriental Art Trends for Today, Fine Arts Pavillion, Osaka, Japan, 50; Ann Invitational, Palacio de Fine Arts, Panama City, Republic Panama, 59-60; Presidential Fine Arts Show, Duk-Soo Palace, Seoul, 63; 13th Biennial Show, Valentine Mus, Richmond, 74; Ann Federated Arts Show, June Jubilee, Richmond, 77. Teaching: Guest instr abstract painting, Univ Panama, 58-60; guest lectr Western US art, US State Dept/Korean Govt, Seoul, 63-64. Pos: Artist-in-residence, Southern Bankshares Inc, Richmond, 76- Awards: First Prize, Armed Forces Far East Command Art Show, Tokyo, 49; Presidential Award, Presidential Fine Arts Show, Seoul, 63; Purchase Award, Shockoe Slip Art Fair, Xerox Corp, 76. Mem: West End Artists Asn, Richmond; Federated Arts Coun, Richmond; Va Mus of Fine Arts, Richmond; Int Soc Artists, Marion, Ohio. Style & Technique: Traditional style in palette knife technique and non-specific abstracts using hard edge technique. Media: Oil; Acrylic. Dealer: Eric Schlinder Gallery 2305 E Broad St Richmond VA 23223. Mailing Add: 1500 Park Ave Richmond VA 23220

WELCH, MR & MRS ROBERT G
COLLECTORS
Mr Welch b Kewanee, Ill, July 9, 15. Study: Stanford Univ, AB, 37. Mem: Cleveland Mus Art; Mus Mod Art, New York (Cleveland growth bd); Cleveland Soc Contemp Art. Mailing Add: 16800 S Woodland Rd Cleveland OH 44120

WELCH, ROGER
SCULPTOR, CONCEPTUAL ARTIST
b Westfield, NJ, Feb 10, 46. Study: Miami Univ, Ohio, BFA, 69; Whitney Mus Independent Study Prog, 70-71; Sch of the Chicago Art Inst, MFA, 71. Work: Georgia Mus of Art, Athens; Wallraf-Richartz Mus, Cologne, Ger; Milwaukee Art Ctr, Wis; Lund Kunsthalle, Lund, Sweden; Haus Lange Mus, Krefeld, Ger. Comn: The O J Simpson Project (multi-media work), Albright-Knox Art Gallery, Buffalo, NY, 77. Exhib: Documenta 5, Kassel, Ger, 72; Project 74, Wallraf-Richartz Mus, Cologne, 74; Narrative Art, Palais Des-Beaux-Arts, Brussels, Belg, 74; Interventions in Landscapes, Mass Inst of Technol, Cambridge, 74; Art Now 74, Kennedy Ctr, Washington, DC, Camera Art, Lund Kunsthalle, Sweden, 75; Video Art, Museo Carillo Gil, Mexico City, 77; one-man shows, Roger Welch, Milwaukee Art Ctr, 75, Albright-Knox Art Gallery, Buffalo, 77, Univ Southern Calif, Los Angeles, 77, Galerie Hans Mayer, Denise Rene, Dusseldorf, Ger, 77 & Alberta College of Art, Calgary, Can, 78. Collections Arranged: The Solomon Collection, Sarah Lawrence Col, 76; Collection for Jimmy Carter, Georgia Mus of Art, 77. Teaching: Vis instr studio art, Univ Calif, Irvine, 1/5/78-4/1/78. Awards: Creative Artists Pub Serv Grant, NY State Coun of the Arts, 73 & 76; Nat Endowment for the Arts Grant, 74. Bibliog: Philip Smith (auth), Roger Welch, Arts Mag, 75; Frank Popper (auth), Art Action & Participation, NY Univ Press, 75; Sam Hunter (auth), Mod Art, Abrams & Co, 77. Style & Technique: Works involving use of photography, drawing and hand written or typed text, also multi-media installation pieces. Publ: Contrib, Tracks—A Journal of Artist's Writings, Herbert George Publ, spring Vol 1 No 2, 75; auth, Roger Welch (catalogue), Milwaukee Art Ctr, 75; contrib, Unbuilt America, McGraw-Hill, 76; contribr, The Individual in a Social World, Addison-Wesley, 77; contribr, The Big Jewish Book, Doubleday, 78. Dealer: John Gibson Gallery 392 W Broadway New York NY 10012. Mailing Add: 87 E Houston St New York NY 10012

WELLER, ALLEN STUART
EDUCATOR, ART HISTORIAN
b Chicago, Ill, Feb 1, 07. Study: Univ Chicago, PhB, 27, PhD, 42; Princeton Univ, MA, 29; Ind Cent Col, hon LLD, 65; Univ Fla, hon DFA, 77. Collections Arranged: Contemporary American Painting & Sculpture, Krannert Art Mus, 48-53, biennially, 55-74. Teaching: Prof hist art, Univ Mo-Columbia, 29-47; prof hist art, head dept, dean col fine & appl arts & dir mus, Univ Ill, 47-75; vis prof, Univ Minn, Univ Colo, Univ Calif, Univ RI & Ore State Univ. Awards: Legion of Merit, USAF, 46. Mem: Fel Royal Soc Arts London; fel Nat Asn Schs Art; Col Art Asn Am (bd dirs); Soc Archit Historians; Nat Asn Schs Art (bd dirs). Res: Italian Renaissance; contemporary American painting and sculpture. Publ: Auth, Francesco de Giorgio, 1439-1501, 42; auth, Abraham Rattner, 56; Art USA Now, 62; auth, Joys and Sorrows of Recent American Art, 68. Mailing Add: 412 W Iowa St Urbana IL 61801

WELLER, JOHN SIDNEY
PAINTER, PRINTMAKER
b Rockford, Ill, July 7, 28. Study: Chicago Acad Fine Arts, 47-49; Univ Ill, Urbana, BFA, 55, MFA, 57. Work: Metrop Mus Art, New York; Burpee Gallery, Rockford, Ill; MacArthur Arts Ctr, Little Rock, Ark. Exhib: Soc Am Graphic Artists, 59; Pa Acad Fine Arts, 62; 19th Mo Show, St Louis, 63; 16th Mid-Am Exhib, Kansas City, 65; Ten Missouri Painters, Mo Coun Arts, 66. Teaching: Prof art, Univ Mo-Columbia, 58- Awards: Robert H Ochard Award, 19th Mo Show, 63; Hon Mention, 16th Mid-Am Ann, 65; Lida & Jay Herndon Smith Fund Prize for Prints, St Louis Artist Guild, 72. Mailing Add: 1008 Pheasant Run Dr Columbia MO 65201

WELLINGTON, DUKE
PAINTER
b Kans, Aug 9, 96. Study: Kans State Col; Los Angeles Art Ctr; Art Students League; and with Eliot O'Hara, Edgar A Whitney, Hayward Veal, Doel Reed, Alice Harold Murphy, Reed Schmickle & Joseph Fleck. Work: Graphica, NY; Hoover Mus, Joplin; in many pvt collections, incl Maurice Chevalier, Paris, Irving Berlin, NY & Gustav S Eyssell, NY. Exhib: Kansas City Mo Art Asn, Kansas City Mus, 57; Kans Painters Show, Kans State Col Pittsburg, 58; Ozark Artist Guild, Joplin, Mo, 58; Spiva Art Ctr, Joplin, 59; Wichita Art Mus, 68. Pos: Art dir, Tex Theatre, San Antonio, 24-26, Paramount Theatres, New York, 27-36 & Nat Screen Serv, Los Angeles, Calif, 46-56; demonstr art, NBC/KOAM Educ TV, Pittsburg, 66-67; art therapy prog at rehabilitation hospitals. Awards: Ozark Artist Guild Award for Clown Lou Jacobs, 58; Spiva Art Ctr Award for Hens, 59; Kans Painters Show Award for Finitude, 59. Bibliog: Robert Kelly (auth) San Antonio boy promoted, San Antonio Eve News, 5/25/28; George Britt (auth), Lure movie fans, NY World Telegram, 10/7/32; R E Brenner (auth), Duke, artist deluxe, Signs of the Times, Cincinnati, Ohio, 2/32. Mem: Spiva Art Ctr (mem bd dirs); life mem Scene & Pictorial Painters Int; Wichita Art Mus. Style & Technique: Perceptual impressionism. Media: Oil. Publ: Auth, Theory and practice of poster art, Signs of Times Publ Co, 34. Dealer: Reynolds Gallery Taos NM 87571. Mailing Add: Ranchos de Taos NM 87557

WELLIVER, NEIL G
PAINTER
b Millville, Pa, July 22, 29. Study: Philadelphia Mus Col Art; Yale Univ, with Albers, Diller, Brooks & Marcarelli. Work: Whitney Mus Am Art; Vassar Col Mus Art; Brandeis Univ, Waltham, Mass; Hirshhorn Mus, Washington, DC; Mus Fine Arts, Boston. Comn: Portrait, Bishop of Portland, Maine, 76; 41st Int Eucharist Cong, Philadelphia, 76. Exhib: Nat Arts Club, 59; Am Fedn Arts Traveling Exhib, 60 & 68; RI Sch Design, 64; Pa Acad Fine Arts, 65 & 77; Jewish Mus, New York, 68; Realism Now, Vassar Col, 68; Four Views, NJ State Mus, 70; The New Landscape, Boston Univ, 72; Whitney Mus Am Art, New York, 72 & 73; Okla Art Ctr, Contemp Landscape Painting, Okla Art Ctr, Tulsa, 75; 1st Int Biennial of Figurative Painting, Tokyo & Osaka, Japan, 75; Art Inst Chicago, 75; Candid Painting: Am Genre 1950-1975, De Cordova Mus, Lincoln, Mass, 75; Am 76 (traveling exhib), US Dept Interior, 76-78; Univ Mo, Kansas City, 77; NC Mus Art, Raleigh, 77; Am Realism, William & Mary Col, Va, 78; plus many others. Teaching: With dept fine art, Grad Sch Fine Arts, Univ Pa, currently. Pos: Critic painting, Cooper Union Art Sch, 54-57; critic painting, Yale Univ, Univ Pa & Md Inst Col Art. Awards: Morse Fel, 60-61; Skowhegan Award, 75. Bibliog: Welliver's travels, Art News, 68; Rudolph Burckhardt (prod), Green Wind (film), 70. Publ: Contribr, Bicentennial Exhib catalogue, US Dept Interior, 75; contribr, Art News, Craft Horizons & Perspecta. Dealer: Fischbach Gallery 29 W 57th St New York NY 10019; Brooke Alexander 20 W 57th St New York NY 10019. Mailing Add: RD 2 Lincolnville ME 04849

WELLS, BETTY CHILDS
ILLUSTRATOR, PAINTER
b Baltimore, Md, Dec 7, 26. Study: Johns Hopkins Univ, 46; Md Inst Art, grad, 48, scholar, 49. Work: New Zealand Nat Gallery Art, Wellington; Peale Mus, Baltimore; Am Univ; Univ Md Sch Law; Toronto Pub Libr. Comn: Interior murals (plaster & mosaic), Taylor Manor Psychiat Ctr, Ellicott City, Md, 69; interior murals (mosaic), Lake Clifton Sch, Baltimore, 71; exterior mural (bas relief in stone), Violetville Recreation Ctr, Baltimore, 72; exterior mural (mosaic), Templeton Sch, Baltimore, 73. Exhib: New York Soc Illusr, 48; Audubon Artists Ann, Nat Acad Art, New York, 65; one-woman shows, Int Gallery, Baltimore, 66 & Baltimore Mus Art, 74; Syracuse Univ, NY, 76; US Supreme Court, Washington, DC, 76-78. Teaching: Instr basic drawing, Md Inst Art, 46-48. Pos: Freelance courtroom illusr, Washington Post, 72-77; freelance courtroom illusr, WTOP, Washington, DC, 73-74; courtroom illusr, NBC, 74- Awards: Henry Walters First Prize in Fine Arts, Md Inst Art, 48; Second Prize, New York Soc-Illusr Show, 48; Best in Show, Easton Acad Arts, Md, 66. Bibliog: Larry Lewis (auth), Quick on the draw, Md Living, News Am Mag, 70; Mildred Weiler Tyson(auth), Courtroom illustrator, Christian Sci Monitor, 73; Robert Leslie (auth), Walls designed by Betty Wells, Idea, Japan, Vol 23, No 130. Mem: Artists Equity Asn (pres, Md Chap, 66-68); Md Inst Art Alumni; Baltimore Mus Art. Style & Technique: Drawings are swift, fluid, modulated pen and ink with dry brush; paintings art in acrylic, thin and thick, combining realism and abstract; abstract murals in mosaic and mixed media. Publ: Contribr, Designing and Making Mosaics, Davis, 71; contribr, Arts for Architecture, Dept Housing & Urban Develop, 73; illusr, Supreme Court on Nixon Tapes, New York Times, US News & World Report, 74 & Newsweek, 10/77 & 12/77; illusr (covers), Am Bar Asn J, 3/77 & Litigation, Winter 1976. Mailing Add: 727 Nottingham Rd Baltimore MD 21229

WELLS, CHARLES ARTHUR, JR
SCULPTOR
b New York, NY, Dec 24, 35. Study: With Leonard Baskin. Work: Whitney Mus Am Art, New York; Nat Portrait Gallery, Washington, DC; Pa State Univ Mus; Smith Col Mus Art, Northampton, Mass; Princeton Univ Art Mus, NJ; plus others. Awards: John Taylor Arms Award, 63; Nat Inst Arts & Lett, 64; Am Acad Rome, 64-66. Bibliog: C Chetham (auth), article in Mass Rev, 64. Style & Technique: Stone carving; etching. Mailing Add: Vallecchia-Castello Lucca 55040 Italy

WELLS, JAMES LESESNE
PAINTER, LITHOGRAPHER
b Atlanta, Ga, Nov 2, 02. Study: Lincoln Univ; Teachers Col, Columbia Univ, BS, MA; Nat Acad Design, with Frank Nankivell. Work: IBM Collection; Hampton Inst; Univ Kans; Thayer Mus Art; Valentine Mus Art; plus others. Exhib: Nat & Int Group Show, Soc Washington Printmakers, Prints of Two Worlds, Stampe di Due Mondi, Philadelphia Mus Art & Temple Univ, Rome, Italy & Exhib & Symposium on Black Arts, Cleveland Mus Art, 67; two-man show, Carl Van Vechtan Gallery Art, Fisk Univ, 67; one-man show, Smith-Mason Gallery, Washington, DC, 69 & 73, Paintings & Prints, Van Vechtan Gallery Art, 72 & 75 & Howard Univ Gallery of Art, 77; group show, Afro-American Images, State Armory, Wilmington, Del, 69; Megraciones—An Exhib of Afro-Am Graphic Artists (travelling exhib to SAm & Cent Am), Mus de Arte Mod, La Tetulia, Calis, Colombia, 76; plus many other group & one-man shows. Teaching: Prof art, Howard Univ, retired, 68.

Awards: Purchase Award for Talladega Col, Am Fedn Arts, 64; James Van der Zee Award, Afro-Am Hist & Cult Mus & Brandywine Graphic Workshop, Philadelphia, 77; Hon Mention, Nat Collection of Art & High Sch Graphic Arts V, 77. Bibliog: Anacostia Neighborhood Mus, Barnett-Aden Collection,, Smithsonian Inst Press, 74; David Driskell (auth), Two Centuries of Black American Art, Alfred A Knopf, 76. Mem: Am Fedn Arts; Washington Watercolor Club. Mailing Add: 1333 R St NW Washington DC 20009

WELLS, JULIAN CARLYLE
See Carlyle, Julian

WELLS, LYNTON
PAINTER
b Baltimore, Md, Oct 21, 40. Study: RI Sch Design, BFA, 62; Cranbrook Acad Art, MFA, 65. Work: Mus Mod Art, New York; Dallas Mus Fine Art, Tex. Exhib: One-man shows, Everson Mus Art, Syracuse, NY, 71, Cuningham Ward, New York, 73 & 74, Sable-Castelli, Toronto, 74-78, Andre Emmerich, New York, 75 & 77 & Zurich, 76, Clair Copley, Los Angeles, 76 & Graphic Stake, San Francisco, 77. Awards: Nat Endowment for Arts Grant, 75. Bibliog: Carol Chelz (auth), Lynton Wells, Everson Mus Art, 71; Bruce Boice (auth), rev in Artforum, 5/73. Mailing Add: c/o Droll/Kolbert Gallery 724 Fifth Ave New York NY 10019

WELLS, MAC
PAINTER
b Cleveland, Ohio, Feb 3, 25. Study: Oberlin Col, BA, 48; Cooper Union, 48-49; also with Nahum Tschacbasov & Yasuo Kuniyoshi. Work: Michener Collection, Univ Tex, Austin; Aldrich Mus, Ridgefield, Conn; Herron Mus Art, Indianapolis, Ind; Purdue Univ, West Lafyaette; Univ Mass, Amherst. Comn: Three-dimensional card, Mus Mod Art, New York, NY, 65. Exhib: One-man shows, Aegis Gallery, New York, 63, A M Sachs Gallery, New York, 65 & 67, Max Hitchinson Gallery, New York, 70 & 72 & Susan Caldwell Gallery, New York, 75. Teaching: Asst prof, gen studio, Hunter Col, 66-; instr painting & design, Moore Col Art, Philadelphia, 66-72; instr painting, Skowhegan Sch Painting & Sculpture, Maine, 69. Bibliog: Article in, New Talent, Art in Am, 7&8/65; Lucy Lippard (auth), New York letter, Art Int, 11/20/65. Mem: Am Abstr Artists. Media: Acrylic, Watercolor. Mailing Add: 64 Grand St New York NY 10013

WENGER, MURIEL JUNE
ART DEALER, COLLECTOR
b Brooklyn, NY, June 11, 15. Study: Brooklyn Col, BA; La Jolla Mus Contemp Art. Exhibs Arranged: Mex Govt exhib of Colonial Art of 18th Century, Fine Arts Gallery San Diego, 69 & Phoenix Art Mus, 69; first one-man exhib in US of works of Ung-No Lee, Wenger Gallery, La Jolla, 74. Pos: Assoc dir, Galerias Carlota, Tijuana & Mexico City, Mex, 64-71; co-dir, Wenger Gallery, La Jolla & San Francisco, 69- Specialty: Contemporary art including tapestry; consultants for corporate collections. Mailing Add: PO Box 312 La Jolla CA 92038

WENGER, SIGMUND
ART DEALER, ART CONSULTANT
b Brooklyn, NY, Nov 20, 10. Study: NY Univ, BA. Exhibs Arranged: Francisco Icaza, La Jolla Mus Contemp Art, 66, Phoenix Art Mus, 67, Long Beach Mus, 68 & Ariz State Univ, 68; Antonio Rodriguez Luna, Fine Arts Gallery San Diego, 67; Marta Palau, Fine Arts Gallery San Diego, 69, Univ Tex, 70, Long Beach Mus, 70 & Ariz State Univ, 70; also organized first solo exhib US of sculpture of Marta Pan, Wenger Gallery, San Francisco, 70 & Univ Southern Calif, 72. Pos: Dir, Galerias Carlota, Tijuana & Mexico City, Mex, 63-72; co-dir, Wenger Gallery, La Jolla & San Francisco, 69- Specialty: Contemporary art; tapestry; consultants corporate collections. Mailing Add: PO Box 312 La Jolla CA 92038

WENTWORTH, MURRAY JACKSON
PAINTER, INSTRUCTOR
b Boston, Mass, Jan 18, 27. Study: Art Inst Boston. Work: Farnsworth Mus Art, Rockland, Maine; Springfield Mus Art, Mo; First Nat Bank, Boston; DeCordova Mus, Lincoln, Mass; Utah State Univ, Logan. Exhib: Metrop Mus Art, New York, 66; Mex Art Inst & Watercolor Mus, Mexico City, 68; Butler Inst Am Art, Youngstown, Ohio, 69; Brockton Fuller Mem Mus, Mass, 70; DeCordova Mus, Mass, 77; one-man shows, Farnsworth Mus, 72 & Guild of Boston Artists, 77. Teaching: Instr watercolor, Art Inst Boston, 57-77; instr watercolor, pvt & watercolor workshops, 77- Awards: Ranger Fund Purchase Prize, Nat Acad Design, 65; Nat Arts Club Bronze Medal Hon, 68; Am Watercolor Soc Bronze Medal Hon, 69. Mem: Am Watercolor Soc; Allied Artists Am; Boston Watercolor Soc (vpres, 71-); Guild Boston Artists; assoc Nat Acad Design. Media: Watercolor. Publ: Contribr, watercolor page, Am Artist Mag, 70. Mailing Add: 132 Central St Norwell MA 02061

WERNER, ALFRED
CRITIC, WRITER
Study: Univ Vienna; NY Univ Inst Fine Arts. Teaching: Lectr hist mod art, Guggenheim Mus, Mus Mod Art, Nat Gallery Art & Jewish Mus; instr art hist, Wagner Col, City Col New York & Rutgers State Univ. Pos: US corresp, Pantheon, Munich, Ger; bk rev ed, Am Artist, New York. Awards: Prof Honoris Causa, Austrian Govt, 67; Officer's Cross, Ger Order Merit. Mem: Int Asn Art Critics. Publ: Twenty bks published including works on Modigliani, Pascin, Chagall & Barlach; contribr to Soutine, Art J, Am Artist, Art & Artists, Progressive. Mailing Add: 230 W 54th St New York NY 10019

WERNER, DONALD (LEWIS)
PAINTER, PHOTOGRAPHER
b Fresno, Calif, Feb 2, 29. Study: Fresno State Col, BA, with Adolf & Ella Odorfer & Jane Gale; Chouinard Art Inst, Los Angeles; also costuming with Majorie Best. Work: Murals, Dan River Mills, Wellington Sears & Martex, New York; Fresno Art Ctr, Calif; Hudson River Mus, Yonkers, NY. Comn: Collage murals, New York World's Fair. Exhib: Many one-man shows, Gallery 84, New York, 59-75, Painting & Photog, Fresno Art Gallery, 67, Photog, Focus Gallery, San Francisco, 68, Painting & Photog, Hudson River Mus, 69 & 72 & Photog, St Paul Civic Ctr, Minn, 70. Collections Arranged: Art in Westchester, 69, African Art, 71, Light, Motion, Sound, 71, Sky, Sand & Spirits, 72, 20th Century Sculpture, 72 & Light & Lens-Methods of Photography (with catalog), 73, Hudson River Mus; Mus of the Am Indian, New York, NY, 78; The Echo of Their Drums, Customs House, New York, NY, 78. Pos: Display designer, Seventeen Mag, 11 yrs; store designer & displayer, Gimbels, 68-69; mus artist & designer, Hudson River Mus, 68-75. Awards: First Prize for Watercolor, Fresno Art Ctr, 60. Bibliog: Beeching (auth), Theatrical displays and display techniques (film), Scope Prod, 69. Media: Watercolor, Collage Photography. Publ: Auth, photogr & designer, Reflections of Winter: Summer Comes Too Fast, Holt, Rhinehart & Winston, 78. Dealer: Gallery 84 1046 Madison Ave New York NY 10016. Mailing Add: 65 W 92nd St New York NY 10025

WERNER, FRITZ
PAINTER
b Vienna, Austria, US citizen. Study: Acad Fine Arts, Vienna, Munich & Paris. Work: Phoenix Art Mus; Oklahoma City Art Mus; Syracuse Art Mus; Cincinnati Art Mus; Circuit Court of Appeal, Chicago; Princeton Univ. Comn: Okla Hall of Fame, Oklahoma City; Princeton Univ; Am Univ, Washington, DC; State House, Montpelier, Vt; also portrait comns of William Howard Taft, Pres of US, Sen Robert Taft, Warren Austin, US Ambassador to UN, William S Knudsen, former pres Gen Motors Corp & Achmed Ziwar Pascha, former pres Egypt. Exhib: Le Salon, Paris; Terzia Biennale Romana, Rome; two one-man shows, Wildenstein Art Gallery, New York; Nat Acad Design, New York; Galleria Whitcomb, Buenos Aires, Arg. Awards: Gundel Portrait Prize, State of Austria; Scholarship, Acad Fine Arts, Vienna, Austria. Style & Technique: Impressionist. Media: Oil, Pastel, Watercolor. Mailing Add: Apt 9-D 1001 Genter St La Jolla CA 92037

WERNER, NAT
SCULPTOR
b New York, NY, Dec 8, 08. Study: City Col New York, BA; Columbia Univ, MA; Art Students League, with Robert Laurent. Work: Whitney Mus Am Art, New York; Lyman Allen Mus, New London, Conn; Mt Sinai Hosp, Detroit; Tel Aviv Mus, Israel; Howard Univ Gallery, Washington, DC. Comn: Bas-relief, Fowler Post Off, Ind; sculptures, New York World's Fair, 39, Argus Res, New York, bronze, New York Eng Soc & wood, James Madison High Sch, New York. Exhib: Whitney Mus Am Art Ann, 36-63; Pa Acad Fine Arts, 39-56; Brussels Int, 46; Fairmount Int, Philadelphia, 50; Art USA, New York, 58-59; one-man show, Benson Gallery, Bridgehampton, NY, 73, 75 & 78. Teaching: Instr sculpture, Stuyvesant Adult Ctr, 60- Awards: First Hon Mentions, New York World's Fair, 39 & New Orleans Sculpture, 42; First Prize, Guildhall Easthampton, 53-54; Purchase Award, Southampton Col, Long Island, 76. Mem: Sculptors Guild (pres, 63-65). Style & Technique: Cubism. Dealer: Benson Gallery, Bridgehampton NY 11932; ACA Galleries 25 E 73rd St New York NY 10021. Mailing Add: 225 E 21st St New York NY 10010

WERNER (CHARLES GEORGE WERNER)
EDITORIAL CARTOONIST
b Marshfield, Wis, Mar 23, 09. Study: Oklahoma City Univ; Northwestern Univ. Work: Mo State Hist Soc; Syracuse Univ, NY; Wis State Hist Soc, Madison; Addison Gallery Am Art, Andover, Mass. Exhib: Asn Am Ed Cartoonists travel tour. Pos: Ed cartoonist, Daily Oklahoman, 35-41; chief ed cartoonist, Chicago Sun, 41-47; ed cartoonist, Indianapolis Star, 47- Awards: Pulitzer Prize, 38; First Place Award, Nat Found Highway Safety, 71; Award for Caricature, Int Salon Art, Montreal, 73. Mem: New York Cartoonists Soc; Asn Am Ed Cartoonists (pres, 69). Style & Technique: Ink; Brush & Crayon. Mailing Add: 4445 Brown Rd Indianapolis IN 46226

WERNER-VAUGHN, SALLE
PAINTER
b Tex. Work: San Francisco Mus of Mod Art, Calif; Akron Art Inst, Ohio; Lomas-Nettleton Co, Dallas, Tex; Am Tel & Tel, New York. Exhib: Biennial Exhib Painting & Sculpture Show, Whitney Mus, New York, 73; Contemporary Watercolors, Akron Art Inst, Ohio, Indianapolis, Ind & Rochester, NY, 76; Helen Serger, La Boetie Inc, New York, 77; one-man show, Tyler Mus of Art, Tex, 73. Teaching: Founder experimental art, Art Involvement & Motivation, 70- Bibliog: Patsy Swank (auth), Salle Werner (film), Dallas Educ TV, 72. Media: Watercolor, Oil. Mailing Add: 2235 Brentwood Houston TX 77019

WERNESS, HOPE B
ART HISTORIAN
b Del Rio, Tex, Feb 10, 43. Study: Univ Calif, Santa Barbara, BA, 65 & PhD, 72; Tulane Univ, MA. 68. Teaching: Vis lectr art hist, San Jose State Univ, Calif, 76-77; asst prof art hist, Calif State Col, Stanislaus, Turlack, Calif, 77- Mem: Col Art Asn. Res: Nineteenth century art history, specializing in Van Gogh, twentieth century art history, pre-columbian and primitive art. Mailing Add: 3201 N Olive Ave Turlock CA 95380

WERTH, KURT
ILLUSTRATOR
b Leipzig, Ger; US citizen. Study: State Acad Graphic Arts, Leipzig, with Walter Tiemann, grad. Work: Mus Fine Arts, Leipzig. Comn: Murals for canteens in many factories in Ger, 30-34. Media: Wood, Inks. Publ: Illusr, Shakespeare: Troilus & Cressida, 25, Merry Miller, 52 & One Mitten Lewis, 55; auth & illusr, Monkey, the Lion & the Snake, 67 & Lazy Jack, 70; plus many others. Mailing Add: 645 W 239th St Bronx NY 10463

WESCHLER, ANITA
SCULPTOR, PAINTER
b New York, NY. Study: Parsons Sch Design, grad; Nat Acad Design; Pa Acad Fine Arts, with Albert Laessle; Art Students League, with William Zorach; Columbia Univ; Barnes Found. Work: Whitney Mus Am Art, Amherst Univ; Brandeis Univ; Wichita State Mus; Yale Univ; plus other pub & pvt collections. Comn: Sculpture, US Treas Dept, var portraits, US Post Off, Ekin, NC; ten life-size portrait heads (bronze), Inst for Achievement of Human Potential, Philadelphia. Exhib: Group shows, Whitney Mus Am Art, Nat Inst Arts & Lett, Metrop Mus Art, Philadelphia Mus Art, Mus Mod Art, plus others; also 40 one-man shows nationwide, 64- Pos: Deleg to US Comt Int Asn Art; deleg, Fine Arts Fedn New York. Awards: Prizes, Corcoran Gallery Art & San Francisco Mus Art; Audubon Artists Medal of Honor; MacDowell Colony & Yaddo Fels. Mem: Archit League; Fedn Mod Painters & Sculptors; Nat Asn Women Artists; Sculptor's Guild (mem exec bd). Style & Technique: Abstract; painting with synthetic glazes; representational. Media: Cast Stone, Bronze, Plastic, Aluminum. Publ: Auth, Nightshade, Colony Press; auth, Sculptor's Summary. Mailing Add: 136 Waverly Pl New York NY 10014

WESLEY, JOHN
PAINTER
b Los Angeles, Calif, Nov 25, 28. Work: Albright-Knox Art Gallery, Buffalo, NY; Hirschhorn Mus and Sculpture Garden, Smithsonian Inst, Washington, DC; Mus Mod Art; Univ Rochester; Univ Tex. Exhib: Gallery of Mod Art, Washington, DC, 65; Noveau Realisme, Palais des Beaux-Arts, Brussels, Belg, 67; The Figure Int, Am Fedn of Arts, New York, 67-68; 1968, Whitney Mus of Art, 69; Indianapolis Mus of Art, Ind, 69; Documenta V, Kassel, Ger, 72; one-man show, Univ Rochester, 74. Teaching: Instr, Sch Visual Arts, New York, 70-73. Dealer: Robert Elkon Gallery 1063 Madison Ave New York NY 10028. Mailing Add: 52 Barrow St New York NY 10014

WESSEL, CHARLENE FREIMUTH
ART ADMINISTRATOR
b Duluth, Minn, Sept 21, 20. Study: Univ Minn, BA; NY Univ, with Adler. Pos: Stylist, Nicholas Murray Photographer, New York, 45-48; asst dir, Westchester Art Workshop,

White Plains, NY, 73- Mem: Co Westchester Parks Recreation Conservation; NY State Parks Recreation Conservation; Coun Arts. Mailing Add: Westchester Art Workshop County Center White Plains NY 10606

WESSEL, HENRY, JR
PHOTOGRAPHER
b Teaneck, NJ, July 28, 42. Study: Pa State Univ, BA, 66; State Univ NY, Buffalo, Visual Studies Workshop, MFA, 72. Work: Mus Mod Art, New York; Nat Gallery Can, Ottawa; Int Mus of Photog, George Eastman House, Rochester, NY; Sheldon Art Gallery, Univ Nebr, Lincoln; Philadelphia Mus of Art. Exhib: Mus Mod Art, New York; Nat Gallery of Can, Ottawa; Int Mus of Photog, Goerge Eastman House; Pasadena Art Mus, Calif; Visual Studies Workshop, New York; Light Gallery, New York; Vision & Expresssion, 69, Contemp Photog V, 70 & New Topographics, 75x(traveling 75, George Eastman House (traveling Exhibs); one-man shows, Mus Mod Art, New York, 73 & Pa State Univ, 74. Teaching: Instr, Pa State Univ, 67-69; instr, Ctr of the Eye, Aspen, Colo, 73, Univ Calif, Berkeley, 73 & San Francisco Art Inst, 73-; asst prof, San Francisco State Univ, Calif, 74; vis artist, Univ Calif, Davis, 77; vis lectr, Calif Col of Arts & Crafts, 77. Awards: Guggenheim Fel, 71 & 78; Nat Endowment for the Arts Grant, 74 & 76. Bibliog: Articles in Modern Photography, 7/73, Art News, 9/73, Camera, Lucerne, Switz, 5/74, Afterimage, Vol 3 No 1 & Vol 2 No 8 & Art in Am, 1/76. Mailing Add: Box 475 Point Richmond CA 94807

WESSELMANN, TOM
PAINTER
b Cincinnati, Ohio, Feb 23, 31. Study: Hiram Col; Univ Cincinnati, BA; Art Acad Cincinnati; Cooper Union Art Sch, cert. Work: Albright-Knox Art Gallery, Buffalo, NY; Mus Mod Art & Whitney Mus Am Art, New York; Suermondt Mus, Aachen, Ger; Atkins Mus Fine Arts, Kansas City, Mo; plus others. Exhib: One-man shows, Tanager Gallery, 61, Green Gallery, 62, 64 & 65 & Sidney Janis Gallery, New York, 66, 68, 70, 72, 74 & 76; Mus Contemp Art, Chicago, Ill, 69; De Cordova Mus, Lincoln, Mass, 69; plus many other group & one-man shows. Media: Oil. Dealer: Sidney Janis Gallery 6 W 57th St New York NY 10019. Mailing Add: RD 1 Box 36 Long Eddy NY 12760

WESSELS, GLENN ANTHONY
PAINTER
b Capetown, SAfrica, Dec 15, 95. Study: Univ Calif, AB(psychol), 31; Calif Col Arts & Crafts, BFA, 26; Hoffman Schule Bildende Kunst, Munich, 28-30; Univ Calif, Berkeley, MA(art), 32; and with Andre Lhote & Karl Hofer. Work: San Francisco Mus Art, Calif; Oakland Art Mus, Calif; Univ Calif Art Mus; Seattle Mus Art, Wash; Vancouver Mus Art, BC. Exhib: Santa Barbara Mus, Calif, 46; San Francisco Art Asn Exhibs, 50-68; Oakland Art Mus Exhibs, 50-68; Chrysler Mus, Provincetown; Univ Ill. Teaching: Prof compos materials art, Calif Col Arts & Crafts, 31 42; prof drawing, painting & art philos, Univ Calif, Berkeley, 46-63, emer prof, 63-67. Pos: Art critic, San Francisco Fortnightly, 31-33; art ed, San Francisco Argonaut, 34-40; supvr, Works Proj Admin, 35-39; regional gen chmn, Nat Art Week, 41. Awards: Grant, 65 & Citation, 71, Univ Calif, Berkeley; First Award for Painting, San Francisco Mus Ann, San Francisco Art Asn, 55. Mem: San Francisco Art Inst (bd trustees, 63-72); Friends of Photography, Carmel (bd trustees, 68-75); Oakland Mus (bd trustees, 68-73). Style & Technique: Expressionist; abstractions based chiefly on landscape. Media: Oil, Acrylic. Mailing Add: 2873 Hilltop Dr Placerville CA 95667

WEST, AMY M
PAINTER
b New York, NY, May 31, 36. Study: Fr Inst Art, 46; with Michael Lensen, Nutley, NJ, 52; Cornell Univ Univ, AB, 57; Art Students League, with Rudolph Baranik. Work: Cornell Univ Student Collection. Exhib: Painters & Sculptors Soc NJ Exhib, Jersey City Mus, 74 & Nat Arts Club, New York, 74; Art Ctr of Oranges Nat Exhib, East Orange, NJ, 74 & 75; Springville Mus Art 51st Nat Exhib, Utah, 75; Soc Painters in Casein & Acrylic, Nat Acad Arts, New York, 75. Awards: DeWitt Savings & Loan Award for Oil, Painters & Sculptors Soc, 74, Robert Simmons Award, 75; Directors Award, Art Ctr Oranges, 74. Mem: Painters & Sculptors Soc NJ; Silvermine Guild Artists; affil mem Art Ctr of Northern NJ. Style & Technique: Abstract expressionism; combination of paper collage and acrylic paints on canvas; colored ink washes with linear overlays. Media: Oil, Acrylic. Dealer: Gallery 84 1046 Madison Ave New York NY 10021. Mailing Add: 1 McCain Ct Closter NJ 07624

WEST, CLARA FAYE
PAINTER, CONSERVATOR
b Coffeeville, Miss, May 8, 23. Study: Corcoran Sch Art, Washington, DC, with Eugen Weisz, Nicolai Cikovsky & Heinz Warneke; also with Jaska Shaffran. Work: Mitchell Mem Libr, Miss State Univ; S D Lee Mus, Columbus, Miss; plus others. Comn: Ten portrait of univ pres, 74 & US Sen John C Stennis, Class of 23, Miss State Univ; portrait plaques of three univ pres & 13 trustees, State Bd of Inst of Higher Learning, comn by Res & Develop Ctr, Jackson, Miss, 75-78; six portraits of univ pres & six portrait drawings, Jackson State Univ, Miss, 77; Harvey Cromwell portrait, Cromwell Commun Ctr, comn by Miss Univ Women, 77; plus over 400 portraits and over 300 restorations in pub & pvt collections. Exhib: Mary Buie Mus, Oxford, Miss, 49; Mid-South Exhib, Brooks Mem Gallery, Memphis, 59; one-man shows, West Memphis Libr, Ark, 59; Miss State Univ, 65-67 & 72 & Hogarth Student Ctr, Miss Univ Women, 70-77. Teaching: Guest instr portrait painting, Miss Univ Women, 69-73. Awards: First Prize for Seeds for Britain (poster), Brit War Relief Soc, 43. Mem: Am Inst Conservators Hist & Artistic Works; Art Asn Columbus (pres, 72-73); Miss Art Asn; Style & Technique: Realistic, impressionist. Media: Oil, Acrylic. Mailing Add: 410 Tenth St S Columbus MS 39701

WEST, CLIFFORD BATEMAN
PAINTER, FILM MAKER
b Cleveland, Ohio, July 4, 16. Study: Cleveland Sch Art; Adams State Teachers Col, BA; Colorado Springs Fine Arts Ctr; Cranbrook Acad Art, MA; and with Boardman Robinson, Arnold Blanch & others. Work: Massillon Mus Art; Iowa State Teacher's Col; Cranbrook Mus Art. Comn: Murals, Rackham Mem Bldg, Detroit, Mich, Casa Contenta Hotel, Guatemala, Vet Mem Bldg, Detroit, Colorado State Hist Soc, Denver, Alamosa Nat Bank, Colo & City Bank, Detroit. Exhib: Int Watercolor Exhib, Chicago, Ill, 40; Pa Acad Fine Arts, Philadelphia, 47; Nat Acad Design, New York, 48; Premier of Eduard Munch Films, Guggenheim Mus, New York, 68; Premier of Nesch Films, Detroit Mus Art, 72. Teaching: Head dept art, Kingswood Sch, 40-54; instr drawing anat, Cranbrook Acad Art, 40-54. Pos: Co-founder & pres, Ossabow Island Proj, 61- Awards: Prix de Rome, Alumni Prize, 39; Cine Golden Eagle Award for film Harry Bertoia's Sculpture, 69; Gold Medal, Mich Acad Arts, Sci & Lit, 69. Style & Technique: Figurative, expressionistic. Media: Oil, Film. Mailing Add: 225 Lone Pine Rd Bloomfield Hills MI 48013

WEST, E GORDON
ADMINISTRATOR, PAINTER
b Salt Lake City, Utah, June 1, 33. Study: Art Inst Chicago; Univ Louisville, BS. Comn: San Antonio (painting reproduced on cover telephone bk), Southwestern Bell Tel Co, 72; wildlife series of drawings, Arts Limited Ltd, San Antonio, 74; painting, San Antonio Chap, Geol Soc Am, 75; among others. Exhib: Southern Ind-Ky, Louisville, 53-54; Tex Watercolor Ann, San Antonio, 63-77; Tex Fine Arts Ann, Austin, 65, 67 & 68; Watercolor USA, Springfield, Mo, 66; Southwestern Watercolor, Dallas, 69. Pos: Post arts & crafts dir, Ft Leonard Wood, Mo, 57-60; dir arts & crafts prog, Hq, Fifth US Army, 61-73; chief arts & crafts prog, Hq, US Air Force, 73-77, chief, Recreation Sect, 77- Awards: Allen Hite Art Scholar, Univ Louisville, 51-54; Tex Watercolor Ann Awards, var times, 66-76; Southwestern Watercolor Regional Award, 69. Mem: Tex Watercolor Soc (pres, 66-67); San Antonio Art League (vpres, 65); Men of Art Guild of San Antonio. Style & Technique: Realism. Media: Watercolor. Dealer: Charles Spano c/o Glassers Art Gallery 1522 N Main St San Antonio TX 78212; Hope Kaplan c/o Odyssey Art Gallery 2222 Breezewood San Antonio TX 78209. Mailing Add: 8610 Norwich Dr San Antonio TX 78217

WEST, RICHARD VINCENT
MUSEUM DIRECTOR, ART HISTORIAN
b Prague, Czech, Nov 26, 34; US citizen. Study: Univ Calif, Santa Barbara, BA(with highest honors), 61; Akad Bildenden Kunste, Vienna, 61-62, with Wotruba; Univ Calif, Berkeley, MA(art hist), 65. Collections Arranged: Section d'Or (with catalog), 67-68; Language of the Print (with catalog), 68-69; Rockwell Kent: The Early Years (with catalog), 69; Pre-Rembrandtists (with catalog), 74; Munich & Am Realism, 78. Pos: Cur & dir, Bowdoin Col Mus Art, 67-72; dir, E B Crocker Art Gallery, 73- Awards: Ford Fel, 65-67; Smithsonian Fel, 71. Mem: Asn Art Mus Dir; Am Asn Mus; Western Asn Art Mus (pres, 75-77); Sacramento Regional Arts Coun (trustee); Col Art Asn. Publ: Auth, Painters of the Section d'Or, 67 & Walker Art Building Murals, 72. Mailing Add: E B Crocker Art Gallery 216 O St Sacramento CA 95814

WEST, VIRGINIA M
FIBER SCULPTOR, WRITER
b Boston, Mass. Study: Goucher Col; Philadelphia Col Textiles; Md Inst Col Art. Work: Baltimore Mus Art; Del Art Mus; Com Credit Exec Off Suite, Baltimore, Md; Goucher Col Kraushaar Gallery, Baltimore; Peterson Howell & Heather, Hunt Valley, Md. Comn: Ark curtain, Shaarei Zion Synagogue, Baltimore, Md, 68; wall hanging, Greif Gallery, Stevenson, Md, 69, Galleries III, Charlottesville, Va, 70; Mr & Mrs Richard Steigelman, Monkton, Md, 72 & 75 & Designed Interiors, Baltimore, Md, 74. Exhib: Crafts 1970, Boston, Mass, 70; Contemp Crafts Exhib, Del Art Mus, Wilmington, 70-75; Md Artists Exhib, Baltimore, 70 & 75; Fibre Art American Artists, Ball State Univ, 72; Mus Contemporary Crafts, New York, 72. Teaching: Teacher weaving, fiber sculpture & basketry as a textile art, Md Inst Col Art, 69- Awards: Baltimore Outdoor Art Festival, 68; First Award, Creative Crafts Biennial, 68; Purchase Award, Baltimore Mus Art, 70. Mem: Am Crafts Coun (secy, rep, 69-72); Md Crafts Coun (pres, 62-64); Baltimore Weavers Guild (pres, 59-61). Style & Technique: Contemporary woven and constructed fiber sculpture & wall hangings. Media: Fiber. Res: Basketry styles and techniques. Publ: Auth, Finishing Touches for the Handweaver, 68; auth, feature articles, Handweaver & Craftsmen Mag, 69, 70 & 72; auth, feature articles, Shuttle, Spindle & Dyepot, 72 & 73; auth, feature articles, Craft Horizons, 10/75, 12/75 & 8/76; auth, The Art of Fiber, Studio Vista Publ, summer 76; auth, feature articles, Vie des Art, 6/78; auth, feature articles, Baltimore Sunday Sun. Mailing Add: Grasty Rd RFD 7 Baltimore MD 21208

WEST, W RICHARD (DICK)
EDUCATOR, PAINTER
b Darlington, Okla, Sept 8, 12. Study: Haskell Inst; Bacone Col; Univ Okla, BFA & MFA; Univ Redlands; hon DFA, Baker Univ, Baldwin City, Kans, 76; also with Olaf Nordmark. Work: Smithsonian Inst, Washington, DC; Joslyn Mem Art Mus, Omaha, Nebr; Philbrook Art Ctr, Tulsa, Okla; Gilcrease Mus, Tulsa; Bacone Col, Okla. Comn: Post off mural, Okemah, Okla, 41; bas-relief panels, Univ Redlands, Calif, 60's; Crucifixion (sculpture), NAm Indian Ctr, Chicago, 60's. Exhib: Esquire Theater Art Gallery, Chicago, 56; Philbrook Art Ctr, 58; Bacone Col, 67; Civic Ctr, Muskogee, Okla, 69; Kansas City Mus Hist & Sci, Mo, 71. Teaching: Dir oil painting & perspective, Bacone Col, 47-70; dir Indian art & sculpture, Haskell Indian Jr Col. Awards: Citation of Indian Arts & Crafts, 60; First Place for Sculpture, Philbrook Art Ctr Nat Show, 60; Waite Phillips Award, 64. Bibliog: Ed Shaw (auth), Another Face of Jesus (filmstrip of life & works), Am Baptist Films, 69; Charles Waugaman (auth), Cheyenne Artist, Friendship Press, 70; Dorothy Elliot (auth), Dick West Artist, Kansas, 71. Style & Technique: Religious paintings and woodcarvings. Res: Indian art. Mailing Add: RR 1 Box 447 Ft Gibson OK 74434

WESTCOAST, WANDA
SCULPTOR, EDUCATOR
b Seattle, Wash, Oct 31, 35. Study: Univ Wash, BA & MFA(painting); and with Alden Mason, Wendell Brazeau & Walter Isaacs. Exhib: Centennial Exhib, San Francisco Art Inst, 71; Henry Gallery, Seattle, Wash, 60, 61 & 72; Invisible-Visible, Long Beach Art Mus, Calif, 72; Los Angeles Co Art Mus, 72, 73 & 75; Whitney Mus Am Art Biennial, 75; Los Angeles Inst Contemp Art, Calif. Teaching: Asst prof, Univ Wash, 59-60; assoc prof, Calif State Univ, Los Angeles, 61-, chairperson art dept, 67-68; instr, Santa Monica City Col, 66; chairperson dept humanities, Otis Art Inst, Los Angeles, 74- Pos: Guest cur, Calif State Univ, Los Angeles, 64; secy exec bd, Pac Arts Asn, 62-63; chairperson & founder, Womanspace, Los Angeles, 70-72. Awards: Northwest Craft Awards, Univ Wash, 59 & 60; artist in residence, Summer Sch Arts, Port Townsend, Wash & Alaska State Art Comn, 6/75; Leadership Award, YWCA Ann, 77. Bibliog: Joseph Young (auth), Rev in Art Int, 4/20/70; Lucy Lippard (auth), rev in Artforum, 12/30/70 & Women's imagery, Ms Mag, 3/73; J Dematrakas (auth), Womanspace (film), 74. Media: Plastic. Publ: Auth, Art Series, Educ TV, Channel 9, Seattle, 60, Channel 9, Los Angeles, 63 & Channel 28, 64. Mailing Add: 26 Brooks Ave Venice CA 90291

WESTERMANN, HORACE CLIFFORD
SCULPTOR
b Los Angeles, Calif, Dec 11, 22. Study: Art Inst Chicago; and with Paul Weighardt. Work: Whitney Mus Am Art, New York; Art Inst Chicago, Ill; Los Angeles Co Mus Art. Exhib: Surrealist Art, Mus Mod Art, New York, 60; retrospective, Los Angeles Co Mus Art, 68 & Mus Contemp Art, Chicago, 69; Documenta, Ger, 70 & 72. Awards: Nat Arts Coun, 67. Media: Woods, Metals. Mailing Add: Box 28 Brookfield Center CT 06805

WESTERMEIER, CLIFFORD PETER
PAINTER, EDUCATOR
b Buffalo, NY, Mar 4, 10. Study: Buffalo Sch Fine Arts; Pratt Inst Art Sch; New York Sch Fine & Appl Arts; Univ Buffalo, BS; Univ Colo, PhD. Work: Albright-Knox Art Gallery; Nat Cowboy Hall of Fame & Western Heritage, Oklahoma City, Okla. Comn: Many pvt portrait

commissions. Exhib: Albright-Knox Art Gallery; Am Watercolor Soc; Syracuse Mus Fine Art; Boulder, Colo; one-man show, Tucson, Ariz; plus other group & one-man shows. Teaching: Instr art, Buffalo Sch Fine Art, 35-44; instr art, Univ Buffalo, 35-44; instr hist, Univ Colo, 44-46; asst prof hist, St Louis Univ & Maryville Col, 46-52; prof hist, Univ Ark, Fayetteville, 52-64; guest lectr, Univ Tex, 54; guest lectr, Univ Colo, Boulder, 57 & 59, prof hist, 64- Awards: Patteran, 39 & 40. Style & Technique: Contemporary; realistic. Publ: Auth, Man, Beast, Dust: The Story of Rodeo, 47; auth & illusr, Trailing the Cowboy, 55 & Who Rush to Glory, 58; auth, Colorado's First Portrait, Univ NMex, 70; contribr, Britannica Jr & Encycl Britannica. Mailing Add: 1703 Columbine Ave Boulder CO 80302

WESTERVELT, ROBERT F
ART HISTORIAN, CERAMIST
b New York, NY, Apr 6, 28. Study: Williams Col, AB; Claremont Grad Sch, MFA; Emory Univ, PhD. Work: Delgado Mus, New Orleans; High Mus of Atlanta, Ga; Frank Wingate Collection of Contemp Am Ceramics, Syracuse Univ; Scripps Col Collection, Claremont, Calif. Comn: Ceramic decoration (with Joseph Amisano, archit), Visual Arts Bldg, Univ Ga, 59. Exhib: Georgia Artists, Smithsonian, Washington, DC, 64; Scripps Col Invitational, Claremont, 69. Teaching: Assoc prof of hist of Am painting, pottery, design & sculpture, Agnes Scott Col, Decatur, Ga, 57- Awards: Cash grant, Atlanta Arts Festival, 64; Purchase Awards, Delgado Mus & Arts Festival of Atlanta. Mem: Ga Designer Craftsman. Style & Technique: Stoneware pottery design. Media: Clay and Bronze. Publ: Auth, The whig painter of Missouri, Am Art J, Kennedy Gallery, 70. Mailing Add: 332 S McDonough St Decatur GA 30030

WESTFALL, CAROL D
SCULPTOR, EDUCATOR
b Everett, Pa, Sept 7, 38. Study: RI Sch of Design, BFA; Maryland Inst , Col of Art, MFA. Work: Goucher Col Collection, Towson, Md; Del Mus of Art, Wilmington; NJ State Mus, Trenton; Polylok Corp Collection, New York; PD 100, Architects, Mexico City. Comn: Nine Batiks, R F Kennedy Family Collection, 70 & three batiks, L B Johnson Family Collection, 70, Washington Gallery of Art, DC. Exhib: Corning Mus, NY, 71; one-woman shows, Turner Gallery, Johns Hopkins Univ, Baltimore, Md, 72, Conde Gallery, Inst Allende, San Miguel de Allende, Mex, 75, Florence Duhl Gallery, New York, 76 & Galeria Kin, Mexico City, 76; Washington Co Mus, Hagerstown, Md, 72; Del Mus of Art, Wilmington, 73; Baltimore Mus of Art, Md, 74; 7th Biennial of Tapestry, Mus Contonal des Beaux Arts, Lausanne, Switz, 75; Auditorium Gallery, NJ State Mus, Trenton, 75; Mus of Art, Carnegie Inst Int, Pittsburgh, Pa, 76; Mus of Contemp Crafts, New York, 76. Teaching: Instr fibers & fabrics, Md Inst, Baltimore, 68-73; asst prof fibres & fabrics, Montclair State Col, NJ, 73-; guest instr, Teachers Col, Columbia Univ, New York, 77 & Sch for Am Craftsmen, Rochester Inst of Technol, 77. Awards: Morton & Sophie Macht Found Award, Baltimore Mus of Art, 72; Levi Sculpture Award, Baltimore Mus of Art, 74; Governor's Purchase Award, NJ Biennial , State of NJ, 75. Bibliog: Articles in Crafts Horizons, 69-77. Mem: Handweavers Guild of Am; Am Crafts Coun; NJ State Coun on the Arts, Artists in Schs Prog; World Crafts Coun. Style & Technique: Off-and-on loom woven forms with surface design. Media: Mixed Media. Publ: Co-auth, Plaiting Step by Step, Watson-Guptill, 76. Dealer: Florence Duhl Galley 31 W 54th St New York NY 10019. Mailing Add: Dept Fine Arts Montclair State Col Upper Montclair NJ 07043

WESTIN, ROBERT H
ART HISTORIAN
b St Paul, Minn, Jan 11, 46. Study: Univ Minn, BA, 68; Pa State Univ, MA, 70 & PhD, 78; Birbeck Col, Univ London, with Sir Nikolas Pevsner & Sir John Summerson. Collections Arranged: Figurative Drawings from Windsor Castle of the Roman Baroque; Collection of Her Majesty the Queen; Carlo Maratti and His Contemporaries (co-auth, catalogue), Mus of Art, Pa State Univ, 75. Teaching: Asst prof renaissance-baroque art hist, Ariz State Univ, Tempe, 73- Pos: Admin asst, chmn dept art, 74-75 & asst dean & acad dean Col Fine Arts, Ariz State Univ, 76-77. Awards: Nat defense Educ Art Title IV, US Govt, 71-72; Ariz State Univ Fac Fel, 74. Mem: Col Art Asn; Mid-Am Col Art; Rocky Mountain Conf of Brit Studies; Art Historians of Southern Calif; Am Asn Univ Prof. Res: Research on collections of Metropolitan Museum of New York, Philadelphia Museum of Art and the collection of Janos Scholz, Cooper-Hewitt Union; Roman Baroque sculpture and Michelangelo. Publ: Auth, Antonio Raggi's death of St Cecilia, The Art Bull, 74; co-auth, Contributions to the late chronology of Giuseppe Mazzuoli, Burlington Mag, 74. Mailing Add: 2318 W Portobello Ave Mesa AZ 85202

WESTLUND, HARRY E
MASTER PRINTER, ART DEALER, COLLECTOR
b Chicago, Ill, Nov 20, 41. Study: Calif State Col, Long Beach, BA, 67; Tamarind Inst, Albuquerque, Master Printer, 70. Work: Pasadena Mus, Calif; Gruenwald Found, Univ Calif, Los Angeles; Mus of Mod Art, New York, Los Angeles Co Mus of Art, Los Angeles; Tamarind Inst Collection, Univ NMex. Exhib: Eight Tamarind Printers, Motel Gallery, Albuquerque, Nmex; New Multiples, San Diego; Art of the Master Printer, Robinson Galleries, Houston, Tex; Collectors Exhib, Starline Gallery, Albuquerque, 78. Pos: Shop mgr, Lakeside Studios, Mich, 71; mgr, Tamarind Publ, Tamarind Inst, 72-75; litho/silkscreen staff printer, Cirrue Ed, Hollywood, Calif, 75-76; dir Serigraphs Custom Silkscreen Workshop, Albuquerque, 76- Specialty: Publishing, custom printing, silkscreen process. Collection: Contemporary; Old Master. Publ: Auth, Polymer Reversal Technique as Applied to Zinc Plates, Tamarind, 71. Mailing Add: 502 Mullen Rd NW Albuquerque NM 87107

WESTWATER, ANGELA KING
ART DEALER, ART EDITOR
b Columbus, Ohio, July 6, 42. Study: Smith Col, BA; NY Univ, MA. Pos: Asst dir, Ctr Int Studies, NY Univ, 67-69; res assoc, Inst Govt & ed, Ga Govt Rev, Univ Ga, 69-71; managing ed, Artforum, 72-75; trustee, Louis Comfort Tiffany Found; partner, Sperone, Westwater, Fischer Inc, New York, 75- Specialty: Contemporary painting and sculpture. Mailing Add: Sperone Westwater Fischer Inc 142 Greene St New York NY 10012

WETHEY, HAROLD EDWIN
ART HISTORIAN
b Port Byron, NY, Apr 10, 02. Study: Cornell Univ, AB; Harvard Univ, MA, PhD. Teaching: From instr to asst prof art hist, Bryn Mawr Col, 34-38; asst prof art hist, Washington Univ, 38-40; assoc prof art hist, Univ Mich, Ann Arbor, 40-46, prof art hist, 46-; vis prof art, Univ Tucuman, Arg, 43; US State Dept vis prof art, Univ Mex, summer 60. Pos: Contribr ed, Handbk of Latin-Am Studies, 46-59; mem ed staff, Art Bull, 65-71. Awards: Fel, Am Coun Learned Soc, 36 & 63-64; Russel lectureship, 64-65 & Guggenheim Fel, 71-72, Univ Mich, Ann Arbor; plus others. Mem: Col Art Asn Am; Hispanic Soc Am; Acad de S Fernando; Soc Peruana Historia; plus others. Interest: Spanish and Latin American art; Italian Renaissance and Baroque art. Publ: Auth, Alonso Cano, Painter, Sculptor & Architect, 55; auth, El Greco & His School, 62; auth, Titian, the Religious Paintings, 69; auth, Titian, Vol II, The Portraits, 71; auth, Titian, Vol III, Mythological & Historical Paintings, 75; plus many others including contribr to leading encyclopedias & mags. Mailing Add: 1510 Cambridge Rd Ann Arbor MI 48104

WETHINGTON, WILMA ZELLA
PAINTER
b Clinton, Iowa, Apr 15, 18. Study: Clinton High Sch; Marshall Univ, Huntington, WVa; Wichita State Univ; also with Mario Cooper, John Pike, Charles R Kinghan, Tom Hill, Clayton Henri Staples, Robert Wood & others. Work: Univ Wyo, Laramie; Wichita State Univ, Kans; Episcopal Diocese Kans, Topeka; Briarcroft Savings & Loan Asn, Lubbock, Tex; Parsons Art Mus, Kans. Comn: Life-sized portrait of Miss America, comn by Gov Wm Avery, 66; portrait of Pres Emory Lindquist, comn by Wichita State Univ, 70; portrait of Bishop Edward Turner, comn by Episcopal Diocese, Kans, 74. Exhib: Am Watercolor Soc, New York, 72; Hudson Valley Art Asn, New York, 72-74; Southwestern Watercolor Soc, Dallas, Tex, 73, 74; New Orleans Int Art Mart, 74; Nat Soc Painters in Casein & Acrylic, New York, 75. Teaching: Pvt art instr, Wichita, Kans, 50-; instr painting, McConnell Air Base, Wichita, spring, 73. Pos: Secy, Artist Guild, Wichita, Kans, 74-75. Awards: First Prize, 8th West Biennial, Grand Junction Art Mus, Colo, 70; Best of Show, North Platte Artists Guild, Nebr, 73; First Award in Watercolor, Okla Mus Art, 75. Mem: Am Watercolor Soc; Hudson Valley Art Asn; Salmagundi Club, New York; Kans Watercolor Soc. Style & Technique: Realistic landscapes in watercolor. Media: Oil, Pastel. Dealer: Accent Frames & Gallery 2819 E Central Wichita KS 67214. Mailing Add: 2 Linden Dr Wichita KS 67206

WETHLI, MARK CHRISTIAN
PAINTER, DRAFTSMAN
b Westfield, NY, Nov 9, 49. Study: Univ Miami, BFA & MFA. Exhib: One-man shows, Corcoran & Corcoran Gallery, Miami, 73 & Univ of Northern Iowa Art Gallery, Cedar Falls, 76; Drawings, Nancy Hoffman Gallery, New York, 74 & Summer Invitational, 77; Works on Paper, Va Mus, Richmond, 74; Whitney Mus Biennial Exhib, New York, 75; Ten Am Realists, DM Gallery, London, 75. Teaching: Instr painting, Barry Col, Miami, 74; asst prof of art, painting & drawing, Univ of Northern Iowa, Cedar Falls, 76- Awards: Grad painting grant, Univ Miami, 73; Artist's Workshop Grant, Fine Arts Coun, Fla, 74; Nat Endowment Arts Artist's Grant, 74. Style & Technique: Realist interiors. Media: Oil on Canvas, Acrylic on Paper, Graphite on Paper. Dealer: Nancy Hoffman Gallery 429 W Broadway New York NY 10012. Mailing Add: 2909 Rainbow Dr Cedar Falls IA 50613

WEXLER, GEORGE
PAINTER, EDUCATOR
b Brooklyn, NY, Jan 18, 25. Study: Cooper Union Sch Art; NY Univ, BA; Mich State Univ, MA. Work: Norfolk Mus Art, Va; Walter P Chrysler Collection, New York; State Univ NY Albany; NY Univ Collection; NY State Legis Collection, Albany. Comn: Murals, Detroit, Mich, 55 & Milwaukee, Wis, 56, Victor Gruen Assocs. Exhib: Landscape in America, New Sch Social Res, 63; one-man shows, Angeleski Gallery, New York, 61, Albany Inst Art, NY, 66, First St Gallery, New York, 72 & 75 & Schenectady Mus Art, NY, 72. Teaching: Asst prof design, Mich State Univ, 50-57; prof painting, State Univ NY Col New Paltz, 57- Awards: Hon mention, Michiana, South Bend, Ind, 54; hon mention, Ball State Ann Drawing Exhib, Ind, 62; Painting Prize, Mid-Hudson Ann, Albany Inst Art, 63-65. Bibliog: Gussow (auth), Sense of Place, Sat Rev, 72. Style & Technique: Realistic, traditional. Media: Oil. Dealer: First Street Gallery 118 Prince St New York NY 10012. Mailing Add: 359 Springtown Rd New Paltz NY 12561

WEXLER, JEROME LEROY
PHOTOGRAPHER, CHILDREN'S BOOK ILLUSTRATOR
b New York, NY, Feb 6, 23. Study: Self-taught. Style & Technique: Straight forward scientific photogtaphy, mostly close-up photography where the image on the film runs from one-tenth lifesize to twenty times lifesize. Publ: Illusr, My Puppy is Born, 73; Bulbs, Corms and Such, 74; The Harlequin Moth, 75; A Chick Hatches, 76 & The Amazing Dandelion, 77, William Morrow. Mailing Add: 4 Middle Lane Wallingford CT 06492

WEYHE, ARTHUR
SCULPTOR
b New York, NY. Work: Everson Mus Art, Syracuse, NY; Herbert F Johnson Mus Art, Cornell Univ; Neuberger Mus, Purchase, NY; William Benton Mus of Art, Storrs, Conn; Storm King Art Ctr, Mountainville, NY; Hudson River Mus, Yonkers, NY. Exhib: Spectrum Gallery, New York, 71; Benson Gallery, Bridgehampton, NY, 73; Sculpture in the Park, Paramus, NJ, 74; NY Sculpture Selected by Ivan Karp, William Patterson Col, Wayne, NJ, 74; 55 Mercer Gallery, New York, 75; O K Harris Gallery, New York, 76. Mailing Add: 140 Sullivan St New York NY 10012

WEYHE, MRS ERHARD
ART DEALER
Specialty: Art books and art. Mailing Add: 794 Lexington Ave New York NY 10021

WHEELER, CLEORA CLARK
DESIGNER, ILLUMINATOR
b Austin, Minn. Study: Univ Minn, BA & cert eng drafting & advan eng drafting, 43; Barson's Sch of Design (formerly New York Sch Fine & Appl Art). Work: Brass wall plaque, libr Kappa Kappa Gamma House, Univ Minn, Minneapolis; complete collection of bookplates in libr at Brown Univ, Columbia Univ, Harvard Univ & New York Pub Libr; bookplate collection, Spec Collections Dept, Univ of Minn Libr; plus other univ & pub libr. Exhib: Am Bookplate Soc Ann, 16-25; Bookplate Asn Int, 26-36; New York Times Bk Fair, 37; Nat Collection Fine Arts, Smithsonian Inst, Washington, DC, 46-66; Exhib of Bookplate Mat, Univ of Minn Libr, 56; Bookplates, 14th Ann Int Cong of Int Ex Libris Soc, Elsinore, Denmark, 72. Awards: First Award in Design, Minn State Art Soc, 13 & Nat League Am Pen Women, 50; Silver Chalice Achievement Award, Kappa Kappa Gamma, 52. Mem: Nat League Am Pen Women (pres, Minn Br, 40-42, state pres, 42-44, nat chmn design, 44-46, nat chmn heraldic art, 54-56 & nat chmn illum & inscriptions, 64-66). Collection: Bookplates. Publ: Auth, On Behalf of Accuracy, Am Soc Bookplate Collectors & Designers Yrbk, 33; auth, ser of six articles on bookplates, In: Minn Med, 7-12/57, reprinted in Univ Minn Bull, 7/72. Mailing Add: 1376 Summit Ave St Paul MN 55105

WHEELER, DOUG
PAINTER
b Globe, Ariz, Dec 29, 39. Study: Santa Monica City Col, Calif, 58-59; Univ Calif, Los Angeles, 59-60; Chouinard Art Inst, Los Angeles, 60-64, BFA, 64. Work: Stedelijk Mus, Amsterdam; Chicago Art Inst, Ill. Exhib: Stanford Univ, Palo Alto, Calif, 68; Robert Irwin, Doug Wheeler, Fort Worth Art Ctr, Tex, 69; Prospectus 69, Kunsthalle, Dusseldorf, 69; Kompas IV, Stedelijk Mus, Eindhoven, 69; Larry Bell, Robert Irwin, Doug Wheeler, Tate Gallery, London, 70; 3D into 2D (traveling), New York Cult Ctr, New York, 73; Biennale

de Paris, France, 73; 71st Am Exhib, Chicago Art Inst, 74; Four from Five, Cailf, New York Sch of Visual Arts, Corocran Mus, Washington, DC, 75; PS 1, New York, 76; Ambient Art, Venice Biennale, 76; one-man show, Pasadena Mus of Art, Calif, 68. Teaching: Instr, Col Creative Studies, Univ Calif, Santa Barbara, 78- Awards: New Talent Award, Los Angeles Co Mus of Art, Calif, 66; Nat Endowment for the Arts Grant, Washington, DC, 68 & 77; Guggenheim Fel, New York, 71. Bibliog: William Wilson (auth), Electric Art, Los Angeles Times, 68; John Coplans (auth), Doug Wheeler-Light Paintings, 3/70 & Peter Plagens (auth), Doug Wheeler-Riko Mizuno Gallery, 9/74, Artforum, New York. Style & Technique: Spatial tension in an environmental context through manipulation of known structure or experience by establishing focus through sensate means; light/shadow/sound, silence or physical alterations. Dealer: Riko Mizuno Gallery 669 La Cienega W Hollywood Calif; Galleria Salvatore Ala 3 Mameli Milan Italy. Mailing Add: 2623 Main St Santa Monica CA 90405

WHEELER, MARK
ILLUSTRATOR, DESIGNER
b Bellingham, Wash, Sept 26, 43. Study: Burnley Sch of Professional Art, dipl, Seattle, Wash; Western Washington State Univ (graphic arts); seminar in Marketing Arts, Calvin Goodman, Los Angeles, 77. Work: Japan Mus of Art, Tatayama. Comn: Serigraph series, Northern Commercial Co, Anchorage, Alaska, 74; Indust illus, Ketchikan Pulp Co, 75; Watercolors, Division of Marine Transportation, State of Alaska, 75; Watercolors, Princess Cruises, 75; Five murals (4ft x 12ft), Nat Bank of Alaska, Ketchikan Br, 76. Exhib: All Alaska Shows, Anchorage, 74-76; Advert Fedn of Alaska Ann Invitational Auction, 75 & 76; one-man shows, Art Ctr Mus, Anchorage, Alaska, 72-77 & The Gallery (Alaska Watercolor Soc), Anchorage, 76. Teaching: Instr watercolor, Northern Commercial Co, Anchorage, 73-74 & Wrangell Arts Coun, Alaska, 78- Pos: Owner, Mark Wheeler Publishing, Ketchikan, 58-; staff artist, The Seattle Times, Wash, 65-66; art dir, Pacific Standard Life Insurance Co, Burlingame, Calif, 67 & Sterling Theatres, Seattle, 68. Bibliog: Stanton H Patty (auth), A Spoof on All Things Alaskan, The Seattle Times, 9/17/72; Rod Cardwell (auth), Faces and Places, Tacoma New Tribune, 2/4/73; Richard Foley (auth), Mark Wheeler—Alaskan Artist, The Southeastern Log, 10/77. Mem: Alaska Watercolor Soc (charter mem); AnchorageArts Coun; The Alaska Press Club; The Advert Found of Alaska. Style & Technique: Realistic and traditional transparent watercolorist; primary subjects are historic building that require extensive research for historic accuracy. Media: Transparent Watercolor, Pen & Ink, Acrylic. Publ: Auth & illusr, Half Baked Alaska, Mark Wheeler Publ, 72; illusr, Country Station and Country Scene, Haddad's Fine Arts Inc, 73, Cannery Notes, Alaskan Traditions, 73, A Portfolio of Twelve Alaskan Watercolors, Northern Commercial Co, 74 & A Sunny Day in Ketchikan, Alaska Fed Saving & Loan, 78. Mailing Add: 320 Bawden St No 701 Ketchikan AK 99901

WHEELER, ORSON SHOREY
SCULPTOR, LECTURER
b Barnston, PQ, Sept 17, 02. Study: Bishop's Univ, BA & hon DCL, 76; Royal Can Acad, Montreal; Cooper Union; Nat Inst Archit Educ; Nat Acad Design; also study in Europe. Comn: Bust, Can Pac Railways; bust, Court House, Montreal, PQ; Supreme Court, Ottawa; Robinson Residence for Retired Teachers, Cowansville, PQ; sculpture, Dow Chem Can, Ltd; plus many others including many in pvt Collections in US & Can. Exhib: Nat Acad Design, New York, 40; Smith Col, 45; Ottawa, 50; Quebec City, PQ, 51 & 60; Montreal Mus Fine Arts, 52-57; plus many others. Teaching: Lectr fine arts, Sir George William Univ; seasonal lectr archit, McGill Univ. Pos: Chmn permanent collection, Can Handicrafts Guild, 44-64, co-chmn, 64- Awards: Dominican Govt Centennial Medal, 67. Bibliog: Quebec Arts '58, film produced by CBC, Madones et Abstractions (Fr version), shown at Brussels World's Fair, 58. Mem: Sculpture Soc Can (treas, 52-67); Royal Can Acad Art. Interest: Made over 200 scale models of world famous buildings to illustrate the history of architecture, models exhibited at Montreal Museum Fine Arts, 55. Mailing Add: 1435 Drummond St Montreal PQ H3G 1W4 Can

WHEELER, ROBERT G
ART ADMINISTRATOR
b Kinderhook, NY, Sept 20, 17. Study: Syracuse Univ; Columbia Univ; NY State Col Teachers. Teaching: Instr Am art hist & art appreciation, Russell Sage Col, Albany Div, 50-56. Pos: Asst dir, Albany Inst Hist & Art, 47-49, dir, 49-56; dir res & publ, Sleepy Hollow Restorations, 56-68; dir crafts, Henry Ford Mus, 68-69, vpres res & interpretation, 69- Mem: Am Asn Mus (pres northeastern conf, 53-54 & 67-68); Am Fedn Arts. Interest: Lectr on 17th, 18th & 19th century arts and crafts of the Hudson Valley. Publ: Contribr, Antiques Mag, Am Collector, New York Hist Soc Bull, New York Hist, New York Sun & New York World-Tel & Sun. Mailing Add: 24516 Bashian Dr Novi MI 48050

WHEELOCK, ARTHUR KINGSLAND, JR
CURATOR, EDUCATOR
b Worcester, Mass, May 13, 43. Study: Williams Col, BA, 65; Harvard Univ, PhD, 73. Teaching: Asst prof Northern Baroque art, Univ of Md, College Park, 74- Pos: Cur Dutch & Flemish painting, Nat Gallery of Art, Washington, DC, 76- Awards: David E Finley Fel, Nat Gallery of Art, 71-74. Mem: Col Art Asn. Res: Dutch and Flemish art of the 17th century, primarily Vermeer and Rembrandt; artists' techniques; problems of optics and perspective. Publ: Co-auth, Underdrawings in some paintings by Cornelis Engebrechtsz, Oud-Holland, 73; auth, Carel Fabritius: perspective & optics in Delft, Nederlands Kunsthistorisch Jaarboek, 73; auth, Perspective, Optice & Delft Artists Around 1650, Garland Press, 77; auth, Constantijn Huygens & early attitudes towards the camera obscura, Hist of Photog, 77; auth, De geschiedenis en bekoring van 'De Molen, De Kroniek van het Rembrandthuis, 77. Mailing Add: 3418 Rodman St Washington DC 20008

WHIDDEN, CONNI (CONSTANCE)
PAINTER, INSTRUCTOR
b Cambridge, Mass. Study: Boston Mus Sch Fine Arts, 32-38, Sturdivant traveling fel Europe, 38-39; also with Hans Hofmann & Ferdinand Leger. Work: US Embassy, Brussels; St George's Gallery, London; Boston Mus Fine Arts; Smithsonian Inst; Honolulu Acad Art. Exhib: New Selection of Works by Contemporary Artists, St George's Gallery, London, 46; Salon de Mai, Paris, 50; NJ State Mus Ann, 67-68; one-woman show, Reflections of Hawaii, Honolulu Acad Art Mus, 70; Contemporary American Drawings, Cranbrook Acad Art Mus Flint Inst Art, 75; Selection Paintings, Detroit Inst of Arts, 76; 50s Show, NoHo Gallery, New York, NY, 77-78; Now Show, Landmark Gallery, New York, 77-78, 50s, Gallery Asn of NY State traveling show, two yrs. Teaching: Instr painting, Chelsea Studios, London, 45-47; instr drawing & painting, Cranbrook Acad Art Mus, 72- Pos: Artist mem, Bank St Col Art Educ Eval Comt, Ford Found, 68; artist lectr, Princeton Univ Art Mus, 69; vis artist, Ind Univ, 71; artist lectr, Cranbrook Acad Art, 72-75. Awards: Nat Scholar Art Educ, Harvard Univ, 39; Purchase Award, Anglo-French Ctr, London, 47. Mem: Mich Watercolor Soc; Birmingham Soc Painters; Arch Am Art, Detroit Inst Art. Style & Technique: Lyrical expressionism. Media: Acrylic and Oil on Canvas; Wash & Pastel. Dealer: Birmingham Gallery Inc Haynes Birmingham MI 48011. Mailing Add: Castine ME 04421

WHIPPLE, BARBARA (MRS GRANT HEILMAN)
PRINTMAKER, WRITER
b San Francisco, Calif. Study: Swarthmore Col, BA, 43; Rochester Inst Technol, BS, 56; Tyler Sch, Temple Univ, MFA, 61. Work: Newark Pub Libr, NJ; Elizabethtown Col, Pa; Lancaster Country Day Sch, Pa. Comn: Woodcut prints, Jr League & Lancaster Pub Libr, Pa. Exhib: One-man shows, Swarthmore Col, Pa, 64 & 74, Elizabethtown Col, Pa, 71 & Lebanon Valley Col, Annville, Pa, 73; Centenary Col, 74; Marion Court, Lancaster, Pa, 73. Teaching: Instr art, Mem Art Gallery, Univ Rochester, 55-58; instr art, Rochester Sch Deaf, 56-58; asst prof art, Geneseo State Teachers Col, 58-59; instr printmaking, Elizabethtown Col, 74-76; instr drawing, Franklin & Marshall Col, 74. Awards: Best of Show & Purchase Prize, Lib Relig Art Exhib, Denver, Colo, 67; First Prize, Lancaster Open Award, Pa, 68; Juror's Award, Reading Regional, Pa, 69. Bibliog: Barbara Whipple, printmaker, La Rev Mod, 1/66. Mem: Philadelphia Watercolor Club; Philadelphia Art Alliance; Artists Equity Asn; Swarthmore Col (trustee, 70-75); Old Bergen Art Guild. Publ: Auth, Luigi Rist: printmaker, 71, William E Sharer, painter, 73, Ford Ruthling, master of the ball point pen, 73, Cecilia Beaux, 74, Fremont Ellis, 75, Charles Berninghaus, 76 & Marilyn Markowitz, 78, Am Artist. Mailing Add: Box 609 Buena Vista CO 81211

WHIPPLE, ENEZ MARY
ART ADMINISTRATOR
b Syracuse, NY. Study: Syracuse Univ, BS(jour); Syracuse Univ, NY. Teaching: Adj prof humanities, Southampton Col, Long Island Univ, 71. Pos: Exec dir, Guild Hall E Hampton, 48- Mem: Am Fedn Arts; Long Island Mus Asn; Am Asn Mus; NY State Asn Mus. Mailing Add: Guild Hall of East Hampton 158 Main St East Hampton NY 11937

WHITAKER, FREDERIC
PAINTER, WRITER
b Providence, RI, Jan 9, 91. Study: RI Sch Design, 07-11. Work: Metrop Mus Art, New York; Boston Mus Fine Arts, Mass; Hispanic Mus, New York; Frye Mus, Seattle, Wash; Salt Lake City Art Mus, Utah. Exhib: Am Watercolor Soc, New York, 38-77; Nat Acad Design, New York, 45-72; Royal Watercolor Soc, London, 62; Watercolor USA Ann, Springfield, Mo, 62-72; Metrop Mus Art Centennial Am Watercolor Soc, 66. Teaching: Pvt instr watercolor, 58-64. Pos: Designer, Gorham Co, Providence, 16-21; designer, Tiffany Co, New York, 22. Awards: Silver Medal, Am Watercolor Soc, 49; Best in Show, Am Artists Prof League Grand Nat, 69; Best in Show for All Media, Springville Art Asn, Utah, 70. Bibliog: Norman Kent (auth), Watercolor Methods, 55 & Susan Meyer (auth), Twenty-four Watercolorists, 72, Watson-Guptill; Janice Lovoos (auth), Frederic Whitaker, Northland, 72. Mem: Am Watercolor Soc (pres, 49-56); Nat Acad Design (vpres, 56-57); fel Royal Soc Arts; Audubon Artists (pres, 43-46); Int Asn Plastic Arts (vpres, 54-61). Style & Technique: Representational. Media: Transparent Watercolor. Publ: Auth, 85 monographs in, Am Artist, 56-72; auth, Whitaker on Watercolor, 63 & Guide to Painting Better Pictures, 65, Van Nostrand Reinhold. Dealer: A Huney Gallery 3746 Sixth Ave San Diego CA 92103. Mailing Add: 1579 Alta La Jolla Dr La Jolla CA 92037

WHITAKER, IRWIN A
EDUCATOR, CRAFTSMAN
b Wirt, Okla, Oct 19, 19. Study: San Jose State Col, BA; Claremont Col, MFA, with Richard Pettersen. Work: Detroit Art Inst. Exhib: Many nat & regional exhibs. Teaching: Instr ceramics, Southern Ore Col, 49-50; prof ceramics, Mich State Univ, 50- Awards: First Award for Ceramics, Calif State Fair, 49; Purchase Award for Ceramics, Univ Nebr, 59; Purchase Award for Enamel, Detroit Inst Art, 62. Media: Ceramics, Enamels, Plastics. Publ: Auth, Crafts and craftsmen, 67; co-auth, with Emily Whitaker, A Potter's Mexico, 78. Mailing Add: 4721 Ottawa Dr Okemos MI 48864

WHITAKER, WILLIAM
PAINTER, EDUCATOR
b Chicago, Ill, Mar 5, 43. Study: Univ Utah, BA; Otis Art Inst. Work: Brigham Young Univ. Comn: Design illus, Capital Records, Inc, 69, Church of Jesus Christ Latter-day Saints, 69-73 & Brigham Young Univ, 69-75; plus many other illus & portraits. Exhib: Utah Inst Arts, 72-73 & 76; Nat Acad Western Art, Oklahoma City, 75, 76 & 77; Nat Cowboy Hall of Fame traveling show, 76. Teaching: Assoc prof art & design, Brigham Young Univ, 69-77, dir, Art Inst, 78- Pos: Advert mgr, Capital Records Inc, Hollywood, Calif, 68-69. Awards: Gold Medal, Nat Acad of Western Art, Oklahoma City, 76 & Silver Medal, 77. Bibliog: Articles in Ariz Hwy, 4/74 & 7/75. Style & Technique: Figure. Media: Oil, Pastel. Mailing Add: 2846 Marrcrest Circle W Provo UT 84601

WHITCOMB, JON
PAINTER, ILLUSTRATOR
b Weatherford, Okla, June 9, 06. Study: Ohio Wesleyan Univ, 23-27; Ohio State Univ, AB, 28. Teaching: Mem fac portrait painting, Famous Artists Sch. Pos: Poster artist, RKO Theatres, Chicago, 28-29; art advert, Cleveland, 30-34; vpres, Charles E Cooper, Inc, Advert Art, New York, 35-64. Style & Technique: Portrait painting. Publ: Illusr & auth, articles in Cosmopolitan; illusr, Ladies Home J, McCall's & Redbook. Mailing Add: 211 E 70th St Apt 34-B New York NY 10021

WHITE, ALBERT
ART DEALER, COLLECTOR
b Toronto, Ont. Pos: Pres, Albert White Gallery. Mem: Prof Art Dealers Asn of Can. Specialty: Modern art, Moore, Picasso, Miro, Chagall; primitive art, Africa, New Guinea, Pre-Columbian. Collection: Primitive art. Publ: Auth, Albert White on art investment, Toronto Life, 4/74. Mailing Add: 25 Prince Arthur Ave Toronto ON Can

WHITE, AMOS, IV
CERAMIST, PHOTOGRAPHER
b Montgomery, Ala. Study: Ala State Univ, BS, 58; Sculpture Studio, with Isaac S Hathaway, 58; Univ Southern Calif, MFA, 61; Long Island Univ, grad study, 66. Work: Quinn Gallery, Univ Southern Calif; Lemoyne Art Found, Tallahassee, Fla. Exhib: Designer-Craftsmen USA, 60 & Young Americans, 62, Mus Contemp Crafts, New York; Am Fedn Arts Traveling Exhib, 63; 18th Nat Decorative Arts & Ceramics Exhib, Wichita, 64; Outstanding Atlantic Seaboard Artists, Jacksonville, Fla, 73; plus many others. Teaching: Assoc prof ceramics, Fla A&M Univ, Tallahassee, 61-69; assoc prof ceramics, Bowie State Col, Md, 69-, assoc prof photog, 70-, chmn art dept, 69- Awards: Design West, Los Angeles Mus Sci & Indust, 60; Merit Award, Am Craftsmen's Coun, 61; Ceramic Award, Fla State Fair Fine Arts Comn, 65. Bibliog: Lewis & Waddy (auth), Black artists/art, Contemp Crafts, 69; J W Chase (auth), Afro-American Art & Crafts, Von Nostrand-Reinhold, 71. Mem: Fla Craftsmen (pres, 69); Am Craftsmen's Coun, New York (Fla state councilman, 68-69); Md Fedn Art; Nat Coun Art Adminr; Col Art Asn Am. Style & Technique: High fire reduction glazed stoneware; ceramic designs are contemporary. Media: Clay. Mailing Add: 12307 Rockledge Dr Bowie MD 20715

WHITE, BRUCE HILDING
SCULPTOR
b Bay Shore, NY, July 11, 33. Study: Univ Md, BA; Columbia Univ, MA & PhD. Work: Ind Mus Arts & Sci, Evansville; Western Ill Univ; Columbia Univ; Northern Ill Univ; Omaha Nat Bank, Nebr. Comn: Stainless steel sculpture, Rogers Libr & Mus Art, Laurel, Miss; Aluminum Sculpture, Maraine Valley Community Col & Law Firm Seyfarth, Shaw, Fairweather & Geraldson, Chicago; Corten Steel Sculpture, Crystal Lake High Sch, Ill & Bicentennial, Hinsdale, Ill. Exhib: Three Large Sculpture Ann, Blossom Kent Festival, Ohio, 69-71; Chicago & Vicinity Artists 72nd & 73rd Ann, Art Inst Chicago, 69 & 71; Sculpture Nat, Purdue Univ, Ind, 70; 12th Midwest Biennial, Joslyn Art Mus, Omaha, Nebr, 72. Teaching: Prof sculpture & area chmn sculpture & crafts, Dept Art, Northern Ill Univ, 68- Style & Technique: Constructivist-abstract. Media: Welded & Fabricated in Sheet & Cast Metal. Mailing Add: c/o Fairweather Hardin Gallery 101 E Ontario St Chicago IL 60611

WHITE, CHARLES WILBERT
PAINTER, EDUCATOR
b Chicago, Ill, Apr 2, 18. Study: Art Inst Chicago; Art Students League; Taller Grafica Mex; Columbia Col (Ill), hon DFA. Work: Metrop Mus Art & Whitney Mus Am Art, New York; Los Angeles Co Mus Art, Calif; Dresden Mus Art, Ger; Govt of Ghana. Comn: Murals, Assoc Negro Press, 40, Chicago Pub Libr, Ill, 43, Hampton Inst, Va, 43 & Mary McLeod Bethune Libr, Los Angeles, 78. Exhib: Howard Univ, Washington, DC, 67; Am Drawings of the Sixties, New Sch Art Ctr, New York, 69; Five Famous Black Artists, Mus Fine Arts, Boston, Mass, 70; Krannert Art Mus, Champaign, Ill, 71; Three Graphic Artists, Los Angeles Co Mus Art, 71; Teaching: Instr art, Southside Art Ctr, Chicago, 39-40; resident artist, Howard Univ, 45; instr art, Workshop Sch Art, 50-53; prof drawing, Otis Art Inst, 65- Awards: Julius Rosenwald Fel, 42 & 43; Childe Hassam Award, Am Acad Art, 65. Bibliog: A Locke (auth), Negro in Art, 40; B Horowitz (auth), Images of Dignity, Drawings of Charles White, Ward Ritchie, 67; Louis Robinson (auth), Charles White, Ebony Mag, 7/67. Mem: Black Acad Arts & Lett (exec bd mem, 69-); assoc Nat Acad Design; Nat Conf Artists; Otis Art Assocs. Style & Technique: Figurative. Media: Oil Washes, Charcoal, Ink. Publ: Illusr, Four took freedom, 67 & illusr, Black History, 68, Doubleday. Mailing Add: c/o Heritage Gallery 718 N La Cienega Blvd Los Angeles CA 90069

WHITE, DEBORAH
ART DEALER
b Toronto, Can. Study: Univ Toronto, BA; Univ Florence, spec cert. Exhibitions Arranged: Fernand Leger, 71; Picasso, 74; Henry Moore, 74; Chagall, 76; Dubuffet, 77. Pos: Dir, Albert White Gallery. Mem: Can Prof Art Dealers Asn. Specialty: Modern art, international artists, Moore, Chagall, Picasso, Leger, Miro, Lichtenstein, and others; primitive and pre-Columbian art. Mailing Add: 25 Prince Arthur Toronto ON Can

WHITE, DORIS A
PAINTER
b Eau Claire, Wis. Study: Art Inst Chicago. Exhib: Butler Inst Am Art, Youngstown, Ohio; Am Watercolor Soc, New York; Art Alliance, Philadelphia; Inst Arte Mex; Ill Mus, Springfield; plus many others. Awards: Grand Award, Am Watercolor Soc; Ranger Fund Purchase Award, Nat Acad Design & RCA Victor Purchase Award, Lowe Gallery; Assoc Mem Award, Allied Artists Am; plus others. Mem: Nat Acad Design; Calif Watercolor Soc; Am Watercolor Soc; Philadelphia Watercolor Club; Wis Watercolor Soc. Mailing Add: Rte 1 Jackson WI 53037

WHITE, FRANKLIN
PAINTER, DRAFTSMAN
b Richmond, Va, 1943. Study: Skowhegan Sch Painting & Sculpture, Maine, 66; Brooklyn Mus Art Sch, 67-68; Nat Collection Fine Arts Internship, 69-70; Howard Univ, BFA, 69, MFA, 71. Work: Woodward Found, Washington, DC; Am Fedn Arts; Stern Found, Washington, DC; Washington Post; Corcoran Gallery of Art, Washington, DC. Comn: Three multi-color serigraphs, The Workshop, Washington, DC, 72 & 78. Exhib: Still Life Today, Am Fedn of Arts, New York, 70; Contemp Black Artists in Am, Whitney Mus Am Art, New York, 71; 2nd Ann Exhib Washington Artists, Phillips Collection, DC, 72; Corcoran Mus Art, 72 & 75; Directions in Afro-Am Art, Johnson Mus, Cornell Univ, Ithaca, NY, 74; Black Am Contemp Art, US Info Agency Art in Embassie Prog, 74; AFL-CIO Labor Studies Ctr, Silver Spring, Md, 75 & Wash Project for the Arts, 75; 77 Artists, Wash Project for the Arts, 77; Decorator's Show House, 77; Kennedy Gallery Salutes Skowhegan, 78; one-man shows, Corcoran Gallery, Washington, DC, 72, Jefferson Pl Gallery, 72 & 74, AFL-CIO Labor Studies Ctr, 75 & Gallery Rebecca Cooper, Washington, DC, 75 & 77. Teaching: Instr painting & drawing, Georgetown Univ & Md Sch of Arts & Design; artist-in-residence painting & drawing, DC Pub Sch & DC Comn on the Arts, 70-71; instr drawing & painting, Corcoran Gallery Art Sch, 75- Pos: Info guide intern, Nat Collection Fine Arts, 69-70. Awards: Painting Award, Skowhegan Sch Arts & Design; Nat Endowment for the Arts Grant, 70-71. Bibliog: Roberta Smith (auth), Directions in Afro-American Art, Artforum, 75; Henri Ghent (auth), article in Art in Am, 1-2/75; Benjamin Forgery (auth), Washington DC Round-up, Artnews, 2/75. Mailing Add: c/o Gallery Rebecca Cooper 2130 P St NW Washington DC 20037

WHITE, IAN MCKIBBIN
ART ADMINISTRATOR, DESIGNER
b Honolulu, Hawaii, May 10, 29. Study: Cate Sch; Harvard Col, BA(archit), 51, Harvard Univ Grad Sch Design, 51-52; Univ Calif, Los Angeles, 57-58; Bowdoin Col, Maine, hon degree. Comn: Designed, Frieda Shiff Warburg Sculpture Garden, Brooklyn Mus, New York, 66; designed, Peary-McMillan Arctic Mus, Bowdoin Col, Brunswick, Maine, 67. Pos: Asst dir, Brooklyn Mus, New York, 64-67; dir, Calif Palace Legion of Honor, San Francisco, 68; dir mus, Calif Palace Legion of Honor & M H deYoung Mem Mus, San Francisco, 70-; mem adv mus panel, Nat Endowment for Arts, 73; trustee, The Corning Mus of Glass, Corning, NY. Awards: Silver Medal for Oil Painting, Cate Sch, 47. Mem: US Nat Comt Int Coun Mus; Am Asn Mus (adv coun, 64-); Am Asn Mus Dir (vpres, 75); Am Fedn Arts (trustee, 71-). Publ: Auth, articles in, Curator, Vol 10, No 1 & San Francisco Examiner, 67. Mailing Add: M H de Young Mem Mus Calif Palace of Legion of Honor San Francisco CA 94121

WHITE, JACK
PAINTER
b Raleigh, NC, July 23, 31. Study: Morgan State Col, Baltimore, BS(art educ), 58. Work: Crouse-Irving Mem Hosp, Syracuse, NY; Munson-Williams-Proctor Inst, Utica, NY; Everson Mus of Art, Syracuse; Univ Art Gallery, State Univ NY, Albany; Gallery of Art, Morgan State Univ. Comn: Grand Opening (poster design), Cult Resources Coun, Civic Ctr, Syracuse, 76; logo design, Educ Opportunity Ctr, State Univ NY, Syracuse, 77. Exhib: Munson-Williams-Proctor Inst, Utica, 71; Directions in Afro-Am Art, Herbert F Johnson Mus, Cornell Univ, Ithaca, NY, 74; Everson Mus of Art, 74; Gallery of Art, Morgan State Univ, 75; Schenectady Mus Fine Art, NY, 75; Exposure Four, Mem Art Gallery, Rochester, NY, 75; Artist & Texture, Allentown Art Mus, Pa, 76; Ashville Art Mus, NC, 77. Teaching: Adj prof painting, Le Moyne Col, Syracuse, 73-; prof painting & drawing, Col Visual & Performing Arts, Syracuse Univ, 74- Bibliog: Group Portrait, Cable Arts TV, Pub Broadcasting Serv, 74; Nancy Tobin Willig (auth), Anger & heritage, Art News, 74; Ruth Ann Appelhof (auth), Jack White, Syracuse Guide, 76. Style & Technique: Hard-edge with painterly approach. Media: Acrylic. Publ: Illusr, Reflections from a Morning Sunbeam, 67, Soul, La La, 67 & Squash Flowers, 68, Dodge Graphic Press, Utica. Mailing Add: 141 W Pleasant Ave Syracuse NY 13205

WHITE, JOHN M
PAINTER, CONCEPTUAL ARTIST
b San Francisco, Calif, May 10, 37. Study: Patri Sch of Art Fundamentals, San Francisco, 62-65; Otis Art Inst, Los Angeles, MFA, 69. Work: Los Angeles Co Art Mus, Los Angeles; Oakland Mus Art, Calif; Whitney Mus Am Art, New York; St Louis Art Mus, Mo. Exhib: Four Los Angeles Sculptors, Contemp Mus Art, Chicago, 72; New Work, New Talent, Los Angeles Co Art Mus, 74; Drawing Show, Newport Harbor Art Mus, 75; Am Drawings, Gallerie Farideh Cadot, Paris, France, 76; Autobiographical Fantasies, Los Angeles Inst Contemp Art, 76; one-man shows, Betty Gold Gallery, Los Angeles, 74, Gallerie Doyle, Paris, 74, Freidus Gallery, New York, 76, Barbara Okun Gallery, St Louis, 77 & Baum-Silverman Gallery, Los Angeles, 78; performances, Vancouver Art Gallery, BC, 74, Miami-Dade Community Col, Fla, 75, St Louis Mus Contemp Art, 77 & Chicago Art Inst, 78. Teaching: Vis artist performance workshop, Claremont Grad Sch, 77- & Otis Art Inst, 77- Awards: New Talent Award, Los Angeles Co Art Mus, 72; Nat Endowment for the Arts Grant, 76-77. Mem: Los Angeles Inst of Contemp Art. Style & Technique: Conceptual art; performance. Media: Multi-Media. Mailing Add: 1320 Pacific Ave Venice CA 90291

WHITE, LEO
CARTOONIST
b Holliston, Mass, Apr 8, 18. Study: Sch Practical Art, Boston; Evans Sch Cartooning, Cleveland. Pos: Sports & ed cartoonist, Patriot-Ledger, Quincy, Mass. Publ: Auth & illusr, Hockey stars, Toronto Tel News Serv, TV starscramble, Columbia Features, New York, Little people's puzzle, United Features & Crosswords for kids, Fawcett. Mailing Add: Patriot-Ledger 13 Temple Pl Quincy MA 02169

WHITE, NORMAN TRIPLETT
SCULPTOR
b San Antonio, Tex, Jan 7, 38. Study: Harvard Col, with T Lux Feininger, 55-59, BA(biol), 59. Work: Nat Gallery Can, Ottawa, Art Bank, Ottawa. Exhib: Some More Beginnings, Exp in Art & Technol Show, Brooklyn Mus, New York, 68; Norm White at the Electric Gallery, Toronto, 71; Int Art Fairs, Basel, Switz, 73 & 74; Le Musee Electrique, Mus Contemp Art, Montreal, 74; retrospective, Vancouver Art Gallery, BC. Awards: Can Coun Bursaries, 69-71. Style & Technique: Unarbitrary mimicing of the efficiency, flexibility and diversity of biological systems. Media: Electronics, Plastic. Dealer: Electric Gallery 272 Avenue Rd Toronto ON Can. Mailing Add: 30 St Andrew's St Toronto ON M5T 1K6 Can

WHITE, PHILIP BUTLER
PAINTER, COLLECTOR
b Chicago, Ill, Jan 23, 35. Study: Univ Southern Calif, BFA(painting). Exhib: Butler Inst Am Art, Youngstown, Ohio, 64; Ill State Mus, Springfield, 70; Am Watercolor Soc, New York, 71; Union League Club, Chicago, 74; Nat Acad Design, New York, 75. Awards: First Prize, Ill State Fair, 65; First Prize, Union League, Chicago, 67; Thomas B Clark Award, Nat Acad Design, 70. Style & Technique: Traditional realism. Media: Oil, Egg Tempera. Collection: Contemporary realistic art. Dealer: Oehlschlaeger Gallery 107 E Oak Chicago IL 60611. Mailing Add: 710 Clinton Pl River Forest IL 60305

WHITE, RALPH
PAINTER, EDUCATOR
b Minneapolis, Minn, Jan 3, 21. Study: Minneapolis Col Art & Design, cert, 42; Pratt Inst, cert, 46. Work: Minneapolis Inst Art; Everson Mus, Syracuse, NY; Mem Mus, Corpus Christi, Tex; Wright State Univ, Dayton, Ohio; St Mary's Col of Md. Exhib: Denver Art Mus 59th Western Art Ann, 53; Butler Inst Am Art 22nd Ann Midyear Show, 57; Tex Contemp Artists Knoedler Gallery, New York (circulated nationally); Watercolor USA, Springfield Art Mus, Mo, 71 & 77; Ralph White Acrylics, Palacio de Bellas Artes, Mexico City, 72-73. Teaching: Prof studio art, Univ Tex, Austin, 46-, actg chmn dept art, 67-73. Awards: Vanderlip Fel, Minn Sch Art, 42; Purchase Award, Minneapolis Inst Art, 42; Onderdonk Purchase Award, Tex Paint & Sculpture Ann, Witte Mus, 49. Bibliog: Richard Teller Hirsch (auth), Tale Painting Tells, Alcalde, Univ Tex, 12/70; Eleanor Freed (auth), 2 views of space, Houston Post, 2/6/72; Margaret T Dry (auth), Laguna Gloria Spotlights Ralph White, Austin Am Statesman, 1/5/75. Mem: Tex Watercolor Soc; Tex Asn Fine Arts (adv bd, 73-76); Dallas Ft Worth Soc Visual Commun; Austin Prof Artists (pres, 59). Style & Technique: Nonobjective space, form color, kinetic. Media: Acrylic, Watercolor. Mailing Add: 407 Buckeye Trail Austin TX 78746

WHITE, ROBERT (WINTHROP)
SCULPTOR, EDUCATOR
b New York, NY, Sept 19, 21. Study: With Joseph Weisz, Minich, 32-34; also with John Howard Benson, RI Sch Design, 38-42 & 46; and with Waldemar Raemisch. Work: Brooklyn Mus, NY; RI Sch Design Mus, Providence; Springfield Mus, Mass. Comn: Life size bronze fountain, Mr & Mrs Amyas Ames, Martha's Vineyard, Mass, 57; bronze, St Anthony of Padua Sch, Northport, NY, 59; A E Verrill Silver Medal, Peabody Mus Natural Hist, Yale Univ, 60; three wooden & metal figures, Mrs Hester Pickman, St Michael's Roman Cath Church, Bedford, Mass, 60-66; bronze relief portrait of Joseph Wilson, Xerox Corp, Stamford, Conn, 72. Exhib: Pa Acad Ann, Philadelphia, 50; Int Exhib Relig Art, Stazione Marittima, Trieste, Italy, 58; Continuing Tradition of Realism in American Art, Hirschl & Adler Galleries, New York, 62; Eight Americans, Amsterdam, Breda, Nymegen, Holland, 69; Representational Spirit, Univ Art Gallery, Albany, NY, 70. Teaching: Instr life drawing, Parsons Sch Design, New York, 49-52; assoc prof life drawing, State Univ NY, Stony Brook, 62- Pos: Resident sculptor, Am Acad Rome, Italy, 69-70 & Skowhegan Sch of Painting & Sculpture, 74. Awards: Am Acad Rome Fel, 52-55; Nat Acad Design Proctor Mem Prize, 62; Farfield Found Grant, 69. Style & Technique: Anti-style and anti-mannerist; anti-experimental technique, dominating material. Media: Bronze, Terra-Cotta, Stone, Wood. Publ: Illusr, Enchanted, Pantheon, 51 & Confessions of Nat Turner, Harper's Mag, 67. Dealer: James Graham & Sons 1014 Madison Ave New York NY 10021. Mailing Add: Moriches Rd St James NY 11780

WHITE, ROGER LEE
PAINTER, SCULPTOR
b Shelby, Ohio, Nov 27, 25. Study: Miami Univ, BFA; Univ Denver, MA; Univ Colo; Univ Okla; also study with Mark Rothko, Jimmie Ernst, Wendell H Black & Carl Morris. Work:

Okla Art Ctr, Oklahoma City; Oklahoma City Univ; Miami Univ Sch Art, Oxford, Ohio; Univ Okla Mus Art, Norman; Okla Printmakers Soc. Exhib: Philbrook Art Ctr, Tulsa, Okla, 56-72; Okla Art Ctr, 56-72; Southwest Painters & Sculptors, Houston, Tex, 63; Nelson Gallery Art, Kansas City, Mo, 64; Okla Univ Mus Art, Norman, 70. Teaching: Asst prof & chmn art dept, Col of the Ozarks, 57-58; spec instr studio courses, Okla Sci & Arts Found, 58-69; assoc prof studio courses & chmn art dept, Oklahoma City Univ, 58-69. Pos: Dir, Silver Mountain Summer Art Sch, Empire, 59-72; dir, C & W Art Gallery, 65-68; dir, Silver Mountain Art Gallery, Georgetown, Colo, 69-72; producer, cinematographer & artist, Focal Point Assocs, Oklahoma City, 71- Awards: Philbrook Mus Art, 59-60; 20th Ann Exhib Okla Artists, 60; Okla Printmakers 5th Nat Exhib Contemp Art, 63. Bibliog: Betty Neukom (auth), Silver mountain, Silver Mountain Art Studios. Mem: Asn Okla Artists; Okla Printmakers Soc (exec bd). Media: Oil, Watercolor, Welded Sculpture. Dealer: Silver Mountain Art Studio Empire CO 80438. Mailing Add: 1424 Northwest 105 Oklahoma City OK 73114

WHITE, RON
ART CRITIC, ART EDITOR
b San Antonio, Tex, Nov 4, 44. Study: St Mary's Univ, BA, 69, MA, 76. Pos: Fine arts ed, San Antonio Express & News, 72- Mailing Add: PO Box 2171 San Antonio TX 78297

WHITE, RUTH
ART DEALER, COLLECTOR
b New York, NY. Study: With Kurt Seligmann. Pos: Owner, Ruth White Gallery. Specialty: Contemporary paintings, sculpture and graphics. Collection: Kurt Seligmann; Ozenfant; paintings and sculpture by various young American artists. Mailing Add: Shadybrook Village 8405 Byron Lane Sarasota FL 33580

WHITEHILL, FLORENCE (FITCH)
PAINTER
b Hillsdale, NY. Study: Mass Col Art, Boston; Grand Cent Sch Art, New York. Work: New York Hist Soc; East Hampton Soc, NY; Tamassee Daughters Am Revolution Sch, SC. Exhib: Allied Artists Am, Nat Acad Design Galleries, New York, 44 & 52; Am Artists Prof League Grand Nat, New York, 47-78; Catharine Lorillard Wolfe Art Club Ann, 49-78; Acad Artists Asn, Fine Arts Mus, Springfield, Mass, 56-58, 64 & 67; Nat League Am Pen Women Biennial, Smithsonian Inst, Washington, DC, 58. Awards: Best in Show, 53 & Best Watercolor, 68, Catharine Lorillard Wolfe Art Club; Award of Honor for Watercolor, Nat League Am Pen Women, 58. Bibliog: Mary Barbara Reinmuth (auth), Pen woman, New York Br, Nat League Am Pen Women, winter 57-58. Mem: Catharine Lorillard Wolfe Art Club (pres, 53-56, corresp secy, 59-71); Am Artists Prof League; Acad Artists Asn; Nat League Am Pen Women (state art chmn, 64-66, NY br treas, 72-78); life fel Royal Soc Arts, London. Style & Technique: Traditional. Media: Watercolor. Mailing Add: 7 Peter Cooper Rd New York NY 10010

WHITEHILL, WALTER MUIR
WRITER, ART HISTORIAN
b Cambridge, Mass, Sept 28, 05. Study: Harvard Univ, AB, 26, AM, 29, with A Kingsley Porter; Courtauld Inst, Univ London, PhD, 34, with W G Constable & Alfred Clapham. Teaching: Tutor fine arts, Harvard Univ, 26-28, Allston Burr Sr Tutor, Lowell House, 52-56, lectr hist, 56-57. Pos: Asst dir, Peabody Mus Salem, 36-46; dir & librn, Boston Atheneum, 46-73, emer, 73-; trustee, Mus Fine Arts, Boston, 53- Bibliog: L H Butterfield (ed), Walter Muir Whitehill, a record, Antheonsen Press, 58; complete bibliog in, Bull Bibliog, F W Faxon Co, 73; Walter Muir Whitehill...A Bibliography, Boston Athenaeum, 74. Mem: Col Art Asn Am; hon mem Art Workers Guild (London); hon mem Boston Soc Architects; hon mem Am Inst Architects. Res: Spanish Romanesque architecture and manuscripts; architecture and topography of Boston; histories of various museums, libraries and institutions. Publ: Auth, Spanish Romanesque Architecture of the Eleventh Century, 41 & 68; auth, Boston Public Library, A Centennial History, 56; auth, Boston, A Topographical History, 59 & 68; auth, Museum of Fine Arts, Boston, A Centennial History, 70; auth, Boston Statues, 70. Mailing Add: 44 Andover St North Andover MA 01845

WHITEMAN, EDWARD RUSSELL
PAINTER
b Buffalo, NY, Dec 16, 38. Study: Univ Buffalo Albright Art Sch, AA. Exhib: Whitney Biennial Contemp Am Art, New York, 75; North, East, South West & Middle, Moore Col traveling show, 75-76; Artist Biennial, New Orleans Mus Art, 75; USIA Works Selected from Artist Biennial, New Orleans (traveling), 75-77; Eight State Exhib Paintings & Sculpture, Okla Art Ctr, 75. Awards: Adam, Meldrum & Anderson Award, 26th Western NY, Albright-Knox Art Gallery, 59; Ester A Bensley & C E Meyer Award, Sequicentennial, Concord, NY, 62; Purchase Award, New Orleans Mus Art, 75. Bibliog: Jean Nathan (auth), Newswatch Art, Channel 6 News, 75. Style & Technique: Abstract. Media: Liquitex, Pastel. Dealer: Galerie Simonne Stern 516 Royal St New Orleans LA 70230; David Findlay Galleries 984 Madison Ave New York NY 10021. Mailing Add: 601-603 Constantinople New Orleans LA 70115

WHITEN, COLETTE
SCULPTOR, INSTRUCTOR
b Birmingham, Eng, Feb 7, 45; Can citizen. Study: Ont Col of Art, AOCA. Work: Nat Gallery of Can, Ottawa; Art Gallery of Ont, Toronto; Art Bank, Ottawa. Comn: Sculpture, Dept Pub Works, 77. Exhib: 8th Biennale de Paris, Mus d'Art Mod de la Ville de Paris, France, 73; Some Can Women Artists, Nat Gallery, Ottawa, 75; Eight from Toronto, Winnipeg Art Gallery, Man, 75; Sculpture, Vancouver Art Gallery, BC, 76; Forum 76, Montreal Mus of Fine Arts, Que, 76; Ont Now, A Survey of Contemp Art, Kitchener-Waterloo Gallery, Art Gallery of Hamilton, 76; Celebration of the Body, Agnes Etherinton, Art Centre, Queen's Univ, Kingston, Ont, 76; one-person show, London Art Gallery, Ont, 78. Teaching: Instr concept develop, Ont Col of Art, Toronto, 74- Awards: Eaton Traveling Scholar, 72; Can Arts Coun Bursary, 73 & 76. Bibliog: John Noel Chandler (auth), Colette Whiten: her working and her work, Artscanada, Vol 24 (1972); Joyce Zemans (auth), The sculpture of Colette Whiten, Art Mag, Vol 6 (1974); Gary Michael Dault (auth), reviews in Artscanada, 75-76. Style & Technique: Plaster casting. Media: Plaster, Wood. Mailing Add: c/o Carmen Lamanna Gallery 840 Yonge St Toronto ON M4W 2H1 Can

WHITESELL, JOHN D
PRINTMAKER
b Hamilton, Ohio, Dec 1, 42. Study: Earlham Col, Richmond, Ind, BA; Miami Univ, Ohio, with Robert Wolfe, Jr; Ind Univ with Rudy Pozzatti & Marvin Lowe, MFA. Work: Bradford City Art Gallery, Yorkshire, Eng; Libr Cong, Washington, DC; Miami Art Ctr, Fla; US Info Agency, Prints in Embassies Prog. Comn: Vermillion Seven (suite of prints), comn & publ by Univ SDak, 75. Exhib: Nat Print, Libr Cong, 71 & 73; 5th Ann Nat Exhib Prints, San Diego, Calif, 72; 1st Int Graphics Biennial, Miami, Fla, 73; Nat Print Los Angeles, 73; Bradley Nat Print Show, Peoria, Ill, 75. Teaching: Assoc prof printmaking, Univ Louisville, Ky, 73- Awards: Third Award, Miami Print Int, 73; Purchase Awards, Libr Cong, 73 & Bradley Univ, 75. Media: Silkscreen; Lithographs. Mailing Add: Dept of Art Univ of Louisville Louisville KY 40208

WHITESIDE, WILLIAM ALBERT, II
PAINTER, EDUCATOR
b Bradenton, Fla, Aug 1, 25. Study: Ringling Sch Art, Sarasota; Fla State Univ, BS(art educ), MFA, 66; also with Karl Zerbe & Arthur Deshaies. Work: Fla State Univ; Rosenberg Mem Libr, Galveston, Tex; First Hutchings-Sealy Nat Bank, Galveston; First Nat Bank, Sweetwater; High Hampton Inn & Country Club, Cashiers, NC. Exhib: Am Watercolor Soc, New York, 65; Fla Pavilion, New York World's Fair, 65; Butler Inst Am Art Midyear Show, Youngstown, Ohio, 66 & 67; 3rd Monroe Ann, Masur Mus Art, La, 66; 7th Ann Nat Western Art Show, San Antonio, Tex, 69; Baker Gallery Fine Arts, Lubbock, Tex, 77. plus var one-man shows. Teaching: Instr art, Fla State Univ, 64-65; instr art, NTex State Univ, 66-68; artist in residence, High Hampton Inn & Country Club, 69-75; instr painting, Western Carolina Univ, summer 73-75. Awards: Purchase Award, Tex Watercolor Soc, I Miller Shoes, 74 & Sharon's World, 74; Transparent Watercolor Award, Tex Watercolor Soc, 73. Mem: Southwestern, Southern & Tex Watercolor Socs. Style & Technique: Traditional; figurative landscapes. Media: Watercolor, Acrylic, Egg Tempera. Mailing Add: PO Box 522 Cashiers NC 28717

WHITLEY, PHILIP WAFF
SCULPTOR
b Rocky Mount, NC, Nov 24, 43. Study: Univ NC, Chapel Hill, BA & MFA. Work: Mint Mus Art, Charlotte, NC; Greenville Co Mus Art, SC; Vardell Gallery, St Andrews Presby Col, Laurinburg, NC; Springs Mills, Lancaster, SC. Exhib: Southern Sculpture: 68, Southern Asn Sculptors, Columbia, SC, 68; Ann Springs Mills Art Show, 69; Ann Piedmont Painting & Sculpture Exhib, Charlotte, NC, 70; two-man show, Greenville Co Mus Art, 71. Teaching: Instr art, St Andrews Presby Col, 69-70; artist in residence, Greenville Co Mus Art Sch, 71- Mem: Guild SC Artists; Greenville Art Guild. Media: Steel, Bronze. Mailing Add: 116 Cammer Ave Greenville SC 29607

WHITLOCK, JOHN JOSEPH
ART ADMINISTRATOR, EDUCATOR
b South Bend, Ind, Jan 7, 35. Study: Ball State Univ, BS, 57, MA, 63; Ind Univ, EdD. Work: Ball State Univ, Muncie, Ind; Hanover Col, Ind. Exhib: Drawings & Small Sculpture Show, Ball State Univ, 57; one-man shows, Hanover Col, 63 & 67-69, Guild Gallery, Louisville, Ky, 64, Ind Univ Matrix Gallery, Bloomington, Ind, 69 & Franklin Col, Ind, 69. Collections Arranged: Senufo Door/A Study of its Iconography, 70; Ghana Door/A Study of its Origin, 70; Return to Humanism, 71; Carroll Cloar, 76; Japanese Woodblock Prints, 77; Bill Eggleston Photographs, 77; Richard Hunt Sculpture, 77; Recent Media, 77. Teaching: Art teacher & supvr, Union City, Iowa, 57-59; art dir & teacher, Madison, Ind, 59-64; instr educ, Hanover Col, 64-66, asst prof art, 66-69; teaching assoc art educ, Ind Univ, Bloomington, 69-70; prof arts & humanities, Elgin Community Col, 70-72; prof, Mus Studies Prog, Southwestern at Memphis, 73-; prof museology, Memphis State Univ, 76. Pos: Dir & cur, Burpee Art Mus, Rockford, Ill, 70-72; dir, Brooks Mem Art Gallery, Memphis, Tenn, 72- Awards: Ball State Univ Fine Arts Purchase Award, 57. Mem: Am Asn Mus; Southwestern Asn of Mus; Tenn Asn of Mus; Int Coul of Mus; Asn Art Mus Dirs. Publ: Auth, Art in the small college, Midwest Art Educ Conf, Houston, Tex, 65; auth, Reproduction was better than the painting, Art Educ, 71; auth, Return to Alexandria, Viewpoints, Ind Univ, 76; auth, articles in Mus Studies & Mus Scope, 76. Mailing Add: c/o Brooks Art Gallery Overton Park Memphis TN 38112

WHITLOW, TYREL EUGENE
PAINTER, INSTRUCTOR
b Lynn, Ark, Aug 31, 40. Study: Ark State Univ, with Dan F Howard, BA; Inst Allende, San Miguel Allende, Mex, with James Pinto, MFA. Work: Pulaski Savings & Loan Asn Relig Collection, Little Rock, Ark. Exhib: 5th Monroe Ann, Masur Mus Art, Monroe, La, 68; Contemp Southern Art Exhib, Memphis, 68; 10th Ann Delta Art Exhib, Ark Arts Ctr, Little Rock, 68; Print & Drawing Nat, Northern Ill Univ, 70; Ill State Fair, Springfield, Ill, 72; Butler Inst Am Art Mid-Year Exhib, Youngstown, Ohio. Teaching: Instr art, Ill Valley Community Col, 68- Awards: Top Award, Contemp Southern Art Exhib, 68; Purchase Award, Ark Arts Festival, Pulaski Fed Loan & Savings, Little Rock, 68; Watercolor Award, Ark State Watercolor Exhib, 68. Mem: Am Fedn Arts; Rockford Art Asn; Lakeview Art Ctr; Nat Art Asn; Soc Art Historians. Style & Technique: Expressionist-realist. Media: Oil. Dealer: Burpee Mus of Art 737 N Main St Rockford IL 61103; Collection Gallery Princeton IL 61356. Mailing Add: Ill Valley Community Col RR 1 Oglesby IL 61348

WHITMAN, ROBERT
FILMMAKER, ENVIRONMENTAL ARTIST
b New York, NY, 1935. Study: Rutgers Univ, New Brunswick, NJ, 53-57, BA, 57; Columbia Univ, NY. Work: Mus of Contemp Art, Chicago; Jewish Mus, New York. Exhib: New Forms—New Media, Martha Jackson Gallery, New York, 60 & 61; Eleven From the Reuben Gallery, Guggenheim Mus, New York, 65; Projected Art, Finch Col, New York, 67; Six Artists, Six Exhibs, Walker Art Ctr, Minneapolis, Minn, 68; Expo 70, Osaka, Japan, 70; Art & Technol, Los Angeles Co Mus Art, Los Angeles, Calif, 71; Projected Images, Walker Art Ctr, 74; one-man shows, Rutgers Univ, New Brunswick, NJ, 59, Jewish Mus, New York, 68, Mus of Contemp Art, Chicago, 68 & Mus Mod Art, New York, 73. Bibliog: Jan Livingston (auth), Some Thoughts on Art and Technology, Studio Int, London, 6/71; Jack Burnham (auth), Corporate Art, Artforum, New York 10/71; George Segal (auth), Bob Whitman and Things..., Art & Artists, London, 11/72. Style & Technique: Environments and films. Dealer: Pace Gallery 32 E 57th St New York Ny; Bykert Gallery 24 E 81 St New York NY 10028. Mailing Add: 85 White St New York NY 10013

WHITMORE, COBY
PAINTER, ILLUSTRATOR
b Dayton, Ohio, June 11, 13. Study: Art Inst Chicago. Work: The Pentagon, Washington, DC, US Air Force Acad; New Britain Mus Am Art, Conn; Syracuse Univ, NY. Exhib: One-man show, Am Soc Illustrators, New York, 48. Pos: Apprentice, Haddon Sundblom, Chicago, 32-35; artist with Carl Jensen, Cincinnati, 38-39; artist, Grauman Studios, Chicago, 39-43; artist, Charles E Cooper, Inc, New York, 42- Awards: Cert of Distinctive Merit, Art Dirs Club, Philadelphia, 54; Award for Merit, 33rd Ann Nat Exhib Advert & Ed Art & Design, 54; Ann Award for Outdoor Advert, Art Dirs Club, Chicago. Mem: Am Soc Illustrators. Publ: Illusr cover page, Sat Eve Post, Good Housekeeping, Ladies Home J, McCalls & Cosmopolitan. Mailing Add: 6 N Calibogue Cay Sea Pines Hilton Head Island SC 29928

WHITMORE, LENORE K
PAINTER
b Lemont, Pa, Aug 9, 20. Study: Pa State Univ, BS; Herron Sch Art; Provincetown Workshop; and with Garo Antresian, Will Barnet, Edward Manetta, Victor Candell & Leo Manso. Work: John Calvert Collection; G D Sickert Collection; Indianapolis Found; DePauw Univ, Jerone Picker Collection. Exhib: Eastern Mich Nat Polymer Exhib, 68; Audubon Artists Exhibs; Int de Femme, 69; Painters & Sculpturs Soc NJ; traveling exhib, US, 75. Teaching: Instr lit & painting, Ridgewood Sch Art, 69 & 70. Pos: Pres, Indianapolis Art League Found, 59-64. Awards: Motorola Nat Art Exhib Awards, 61 & 62; Mark A Brown Award in Composition, Hoosier Salon, 63; Permanent Pigments Award, Painters & Sculptors Soc NJ, 68. Mem: Nat Asn Women Artists; Pen & Brush Club; Mod Artists Guild; Indianapolis Art League; Ind Artists Club. Media: Mixed Media. Mailing Add: Box 802 203 Oak St Ridgewood NJ 07450

WHITNEY, EDGAR ALBERT
PAINTER, INSTRUCTOR
b New York, NY, Apr 16, 91. Study: Cooper Union; Art Students League; Nat Acad Design; Columbia Univ; Grand Cent Sch Art; also with Jay Comaway, Eliot O'Hara & Charles W Hawthorne. Work: Farnsworth Mus, Rockland, Maine; Nat Acad Design, NY; Art Club St Petersburg; Lake Worth Art Asn, Fla; pvt collection of Lawrence Rockefeller. Exhib: Am Watercolor Soc; Nat Art League; Nat Acad Design, 71 & 72. Teaching: Instr watercolor & compos, Pratt Inst, 38-52; instr, NY Bot Gardens; creator-instr, Whitney Watercolor Tours. Pos: Art dir, McCann Erickson, New York; contrib ed, Am Artist Mag. Awards: Audubon Artists Award, 58; Nat Art League Award, 52-58; Nat Acad Ranger Fund Purchase Prize, 69. Bibliog: David Clark (auth), Watercolor Holiday, Universal Films, Hollywood, Calif. Mem: Am Watercolor Soc (treas, 54-60); Philadelphia Watercolor Club; life mem Art Students League; hon life mem Southwestern Watercolor Socs; hon life mem La Watercolor Socs. Media: Watercolor. Publ: Auth, Watercolor: the Hows and Whys, 58 & Complete Guide to Watercolor, 65, Watson-Guptill; auth, Watercolor & casein articles, In: Grolier Encycl; plus others. Dealer: Downtown Gallery 532 Chartres New Orleans LA 70130; Schramm Galleries 1507 E Las Olas Blvd Ft Lauderdale FL 33301. Mailing Add: 19-70 81st St Jackson Heights NY 11370

WHITNEY, JOHN HAY
ART ADMINISTRATOR, COLLECTOR
b Ellsworth, Maine, Aug 17, 04. Study: Yale Univ, 22-26, hon MA; Oxford Univ, 26-27; Kenyon Col, hon LHD; Colgate Univ, hon LLD, 58; Brown Univ, hon LLD, 58; Exeter Univ, hon LLD, 59; Colby Col, hon LLD, 59; Columbia Univ, hon LLD, 59. Pos: Bd dirs & vpres, Saratoga Performing Arts Ctr; trustee, Mus Mod Art, New York; trustee & vpres, Nat Gallery Art. Awards: Benjamin Franklin Medal, Royal Col Art, Eng; Legion Merit; Chevalier, Fr Legion Honneur; plus others. Collection: Carpets and tapestries. Mailing Add: 110 W 51st St New York NY 10020

WHITNEY, MAYNARD MERLE
SCULPTOR, EDUCATOR
b Cedar Rapids, Iowa, Dec 18, 31. Study: Iowa Wesleyan Col, BA, 58; Univ Calif, Los Angeles, 60; Univ Iowa, 61; Univ Ore, MFA(sculptor), 65. Work: Joslyn Art Mus, Omaha, Nebr; Sheldon Art Gallery, Lincoln, Nebr; Denver Art Mus, Colo; Elder Art Gallery, Nebr Wesleyan Univ, Lincoln; Omaha Nat Bank, Nebr. Comn: Hanging Plexiglas sculpture, Ford-Warren Libr, Denver Pub Libr, 75. Exhib: Mid-Am III, Kansas City & St Louis Art Mus, 70; 40th Ann Exhib, Springfield Art Mus, Mo, 70; 21st Denver Metrop Exhib, Denver Art Mus, 72; Artrain (toured nine western states), 73; 13th Midwest Biennial, Joslyn Art Mus, Omaha, 74; 14th Ann Own Your Own Show, Pueblo Art Ctr, Colo, 74; one-man shows, Sheldon Art Gallery, Lincoln, 70 & Kansas State Univ, Manhattan, 71. Teaching: Chmn of dept of art, sculpture and other art, Nebr Wesleyan Univ, Lincoln, 65-72 & Colo Women's Col, Denver, 72- Awards: Creative Teaching Award, Nebr Wesleyan Univ, 67; Mus Purchase, 11th Midwest Biennial, Joslyn Art Mus, Omaha, 70; Purchase Award, 6th Ann Midland Exhib, Omaha Nat Bank, 70. Style & Technique: Abstract, geometric sculptures exploiting the inherent beauty of colored plexiglas with natural and artifical light sources. Media: Plexiglas; Wood. Mailing Add: 3128 S Ouray St Aurora CO 80013

WHITNEY, WILLIAM KUEBLER
PAINTER, ART HISTORIAN
b New Orleans, La, July 6, 21. Study: Corcoran Sch of Art, Washington, DC, 40-42, with still life painter, N Cikovsky, Sr; Wayne State Univ, Detroit, 56-57; Cranbrook Acad of Art, Bloomfield Hills, Mich, BFA & MFA, 58, with Zoltan Sepeshy. Work: Mus of Cranbrook Acad of Art. Comn: Exterior mural painting, Olivet Col Libr, Mich, 61, interior mural painting with Charlotte Whitney, Theatre, 73. Exhib: Soc of Washington Artists Ann, 42 & Corcoran Biennial of Am Art, 45, Corcoran Gallery of Art, Washington, DC; Honolulu Artists Ann, Honolulu Acad of Art, 44; Mich Artists Ann, Detroit Inst of Art, Mich, 47; Works in Progress in Mich, Detroit Inst of Art, 48-49; one-man show, Drawings of 19th Century Mid-Mich Bldgs, Octagon House, Am Inst of Archit, Washington, DC, 72, Drawings of Florence, Univ Calif, Davis, Ball State Univ, Muncie, Ind & Battle Creek Art Ctr, Mich, 74-75; Battle Creek 100, Battle Creek Art Ctr, 77; plus others. Collections Arranged: Paintings by Norman LaLiberte, 52 & Sculpture by Joseph Bulone, 55, Whitney Gallery, Birmingham, Mich; 22 Michigan Artists at Olivet, 73, Paintings by Irving Althage, 74 & Paintings by Michael Cassino, 76, Armstrong Mus, Olivet Col, Mich. Teaching: From instr to prof art hist & painting-drawing, Olivet Col, 59- Pos: Co-dir, Whitney Galleries, Birmingham, Mich, 50-59; head art dept, Olivet Col, 60-75, dir, Armstrong Mus, 72- Awards: Bronze Medal/Still Life, Soc Washington Artists, DC, 42; Award of Merit, Mich Acad of Sci, Arts & Lett, 50. Bibliog: Joy Hakanson (auth), House is home and gallery, Detroit News, 3/54; Nancy Crawley (auth), Paving the way to innovative art, Battle Creek Enquirer & News, 4/77. Mem: Soc of Archit Historians; Battle Creek Artists' Guild; Am Asn of Univ Prof; Nat Trust for Hist Preserv. Style & Technique: Designed realism, with buildings as subject matter. Media: Acrylic; Metalcraft; Technical Pen Drawing. Res: Melanesian art and culture; bronze doors of St Zeno, Vernoa, Italy; 19th century American houses in the midwest. Collection: Nineteenth and twentieth century paintings, prints and drawings. Publ: Illusr, Drawings of Florence, Olivet Col, 71. Mailing Add: 614 Summer St Olivet MI 49076

WHITSON (PETER WHITSON WARREN)
DRAFTSMAN, COLLAGE ARTIST
b Concord, Mass, Sept 7, 41. Study: Univ NH, with Christopher Cook, John Hatch & John Laurent, BA, 63; Univ Iowa, with Byron Burford, James Lechay & Hans Breder, MA & MFA, 67. Work: Univ NH; Univ Iowa; Kansas City Art Inst; Mod Museet, Stockholm, Sweden; Galeria Teatru Studio, Warsaw, Poland. Exhib: One-man shows, Western Dakota Junk Co Show, Eastern Mont Col, 69, SLUJ Int, 73, Univ Buffalo, NY, 70, SLUJ Int, Colby Col, NH, 74, SLUJ Int, State Univ NY, Fredonia, 75; Pictorial History of the World, Kansas City Art Inst, 75; NY Univ; Mod Museet, Stockholm; Rotterdam Acad, Netherlands; Galeria Teatru Studio, Warsaw; Nat Art Gallery, Wellington, NZ; plus many other corresp art shows in US & Can, 69- Teaching: Asst drawing, Univ Iowa, 65-67; from instr to asst prof drawing, Eastern Mont Col, 67-77, prof, 77- Pos: Pres, Western Dakota Junk Co, Billings, Mont, 69-; pres, Lost Lady Mining Co, Billings, 70-; pres, Al's Ham-'N'-Egger & Body Shop, Billings, 71-; ed & publr, SLUJ Press, 75- Mem: United SLUJ Workers; Am Asn Univ Prof; Am Fedn Teachers; Nat Acad Conceptualists. Style & Technique: Primarily neo-dada collage with plays on 19th century romanticism and eroticism in direct reaction to the neo-dada cult of ugliness. Publ: Auth, Western Dakota Junk Co Junker Flyer, 70-72; auth, Lost Lady Newslett, 70-72; Al's Ham-'N'-Egger & Body Shop Again (poems & drawings), Basilisk Press, 74; Change (process collage), 75; The SLUJ Book, SLUJ Press, 76; plus auth & contribr to many other corresp art publs, 69-75. Mailing Add: Western Dakota Junk Co 315 S 34th St Billings MT 59101

WHITTY-JOHNSON, PATRICIA
PAINTER
b New Orleans, La, Mar 28, 43. Study: Newcomb Art Sch, Tulane Univ, BFA, with Ida Kohlmeyer; Washington Univ, St Louis, Mo, MFA, with Arthur Osver; Rome, Italy, 68-69. Work: Okla Art Ctr, Oklahoma City. Exhib: Drawing & Small Sculpture Show, Ball State Univ, Muncie, Ind, 65, 70 & 71; 20th Mo Show, St Louis Art Mus, 66; Artists of the SE & Tex, New Orleans Mus of Art, 67, 71 & 73; Mostra, Am Acad, Rome, Italy, 68; Tex Painting & Sculpture Exhib, Dallas Mus Fine Arts, 71; one-person shows, E Tex State Univ, 71, Emden Gallery, St Louis, Mo, 72, 74 & 76 & Loft-on-Strand Gallery, Galveston, Tex, 77; 13th & 14th Ann Okla Exhib of Painting, Okla Art Ctr, 71-72; 12th Midwest Biennial, Joslyn Mus of Art, Omaha, Nebr, 72; SW Graphics, San Antonio, Tex, 72; two-person show, Vincent Mann Gallery, New Orleans, 74. Teaching: Vis artist, St Louis Community Col, 78. Pos: Co-dir, Johnson-Whitty Gallery, New Orleans, 75-; co-chmn & founder, Vis Artists Prog, Newcomb Art Sch, Tulane Univ, 76- Awards: Molly Palfrey Mem, Newcomb Art Sch, 65; First Prize, Young St Louis Artists, St Louis Artists' Guild, 66; Second Prize, SW Graphics, San Antonio, Tex, 72. Bibliog: Alberta Collier (auth), The world of art, Times Picayune, 1/74; Suzanne Fosberg (auth), Johnson-Whitty's artists for the 70s, Courier, 5/76; George E Jordan (auth), Local artists reveal images of themselves, Times Picayune, 10/77. Mem: Artists Equity. Style & Technique: New realism painting. Media: Oil; Pencil. Mailing Add: 6820 Rugby Ct New Orleans LA 70126

WHYTE, RAYMOND A
PAINTER
b Canmore, Alta, Aug 3, 23. Study: Art Students League, with Edwin Dickinson; Venice, Paris & Madrid; Univ Toronto. Work: Crocker Art Mus, Sacramento, Calif; De Beers Mus SAfrica. Comn: Mural, Austral Oil Co, Houston, Tex, 65; triptych, Gerald B Kara, New York, 68; memorabilia (oil), Bernard G Cantor, Beverly Hills, Calif, 70; Dr Hector Giancarlo, Englewood, NJ; large triptych, B Gerald Cantor, New York, 77; plus many other portrait & painting comns. Exhib: Nat Acad, 49-; one-man shows, Galerie DeTours, San Francisco, 62-78, De Saisset Art Mus, Santa Clara, Calif, 67, Crocker Art Mus, Sacramento, Calif, 67 & E Kuhlik Gallery, New York, 72; Family Portraits 1730-1976, Philadelphia Mus of Art. Bibliog: Doug Scott (auth), Profiles in progress, San Francisco Examr, 8/2/64; Kevin Sanders (auth), Contemporary surrealists, ABC TV Art Rev, 2/3/72; John Angelini (auth), Profile in Whyte, NJ Music & Arts, 6/77. Media: Oil. Dealer: Galerie DeTours 559 Sutter St San Francisco CA 94102. Mailing Add: 30 Fayson Lakes Rd Kinnelon NJ 07405

WICK, PETER ARMS
CURATOR
b Cleveland, Ohio, May 17, 20. Study: Yale Univ, BA, BArch; NY Univ Inst Fine Arts; Fogg Art Mus, Harvard Univ, MA. Pos: Asst cur, Dept Prints & Drawings, Boston Mus Fine Arts, 62-64; dir, Print Coun Am, 65; governor, Gore Place, Waltham-Watertown, Mass, 65; asst dir, Fogg Art Mus, Harvard Univ, 66-67, asst cur, Houghton Libr, 67-70, cur printing & graphic arts, 70-75. Interest: Prints and drawings. Publ: Auth, Jacques Villion: Master of Graphic Art (exhib catalog) & Honore Daumier Anniversary Exhibition Catalogue, 58, Boston Mus Fine Arts; ed, Maurice Prendergast, Watercolor Sketchbook, 1899, New York Graphic Soc, 60; auth, A Summer Sketchbook by David Levine, 63; co-auth, Arts of the French Book, 1900-1965: Illustrated Books of the School of Paris, Southern Methodist Univ, 67; plus others. Mailing Add: 41 W Cedar St Boston MA 02114

WICKISER, RALPH LEWANDA
ART ADMINISTRATOR, PAINTER
b Greenup, Ill, Mar 20, 10. Study: Art Inst Chicago, 28-31; Eastern Ill Univ, BA, 34, hon PhD, 56; Vanderbilt & Peabody, Tiffany fel, 34-35, MA, 35, PhD, 38. Work: Delgado Mus, New Orleans, La; Lehigh Univ, Bethlehem, Pa; La Art Comn, Baton Rouge; Mint Mus, Charlotte, NC; High Mus, Atlanta, Ga. Exhib: Libr Cong Ann Print Exhib, 48; George Vinet Traveling Exhib Relig Prints, 52-58; Whitney Mus Am Art Ann, 53-; State Dept Exhib Color Lithographs travel through Europe, 54-56; New Realism, Suffolk Mus, Stony Brook, NY, 71; United Nations, New York, 75; Lotus Gallery, New York, 76 & 77; Savage Gallery, Boston, 77; Mikelson Gallery, Washington, DC, 77; Newman Gallery, Philadelphia, 77. Teaching: From instr to prof painting & chmn dept, La State Univ, 37-56; prof painting & dir div art educ, State Univ NY Col New Paltz, 56-59; prof painting, Pratt Inst, 59-, chmn art educ dept, 59-65. Awards: Grant for One Yr Painting & Study, 52. Bibliog: Artist as a teacher, Col Art J, winter 51-52. Mem: Col Art Asn Am. Media: Oil. Res: Art theory and art education. Interest: Figure and landscape painting. Publ: Auth, Introduction to Art Activities, 47; contribr, Education of the Artist, 51; contribr, Contemporary Painter's Attitude Toward Tradition, 55; auth, Introduction to Art Education, 57; co-auth, Higher Education & the Arts. Mailing Add: Pratt Inst Brooklyn NY 11205

WICKS, EUGENE CLAUDE
PAINTER, EDUCATOR
b Coleharbor, NDak, Oct 7, 31. Study: Univ Colo, BFA, MFA, 59. Work: Art Inst Chicago, Ill; Philadelphia Print Club, Pa; Lakeview Art Ctr, Peoria, Ill; Decatur Art Ctr, Ill; Am Fedn Arts Overseas Collection. Exhib: Libr Cong, Washington, DC, 59; Brooklyn Mus Print Exhib, 60, 62 & 64; Northwest Printmakers Ann Exhib, 60-68; 1st Biennial Exhibs of Prints, Art Inst Chicago, 62; Philadelphia Acad 185th Ann, 63; one-man show, Edinburgh Col of Art, Scotland, 64 & Western Mich Univ, Kalamazoo, 75, plus others. Teaching: Prof painting, Univ Ill, Urbana, 59-, asst head dept art, 61-67, assoc head, 68-77, head, 77- Pos: Vis artist, Dept Art, Univ Colo, summer 63; dir, Nat Asn of Schs of Art, 75- Awards: Purchase Awards, 1st Biennial, Art Inst Chicago, 62, Print Exhib, 62 & 24th Ann, Decatur Art Ctr, 68. Mem: Nat Asn Schs Art; Nat Coun Art Adminr; Col Art Asn. Style & Technique: Naturalistic; glaze technique in oil. Mailing Add: 2121 Gunn Dr Champaign IL 61820

WIDMER, GWEN ELLEN
PHOTOGRAPHER, EDUCATOR
b Chicago, Ill, Mar 10, 45. Study: Goshen Col, Ind, BA, 67; Sch the Art Inst of Chicago, MFA, 73. Work: J B Speed Art Mus, Louisville, Ky; Madison Art Ctr, Wis; Kalamazoo Inst of Arts, Mich; Humboldt State Univ Arcata, Calif. Exhib: Photogr Midwest, Walker Art Ctr, Minneapolis, 73; one-person shows, Lightfall Gallery, Evanston Art Ctr, Ill, 74, Madison Art Ctr, Wis, 75 & Midway Studios, Univ Chicago, 76; Artemisia Gallery, Chicago, 75; Young

Am Photogr, Kalamazoo Inst of Arts, Mich, 75; Photographic Exhib, Speed Art Mus, Louisville, 76; Four Midwestern Photogr, Camerawork Gallery, San Francisco, 77. Teaching: Instr photog, Univ Ill, Urbana/Champaign, 72-74; instr photog, Univ Northern Iowa, Cedar Falls, 76- Awards: Photog Fel, Nat Endowment for the Arts, 75; Third Prize, Bicentennial Exhib of Photog, Andromeda Gallery, Buffalo, NY, 77; Purchase Award, Light II, Humboldt State Univ, 77. Mem: Soc for Photog Educ. Style & Technique: Hand colored silver prints. Media: Photography; Painting. Publ: Contribr (catalogue), Photographers Midwest Invitational, Walker Art Ctr, 73; contribr, Popular Photography, Vol 75 (2), Ziff-Davis, 74; contribr, Young American Photographers, Kalamazoo Inst of Art, 75; contribr (catalogue), J B Speed Art Museum's 1976 Photographic Exhibit, Speed Art Mus, 76; contribr, Color, Life Libr of Photography, Time-Life Bks, 78. Mailing Add: 703 Iowa St Cedar Falls IA 50613

WIDSTROM, EDWARD FREDERICK
SCULPTOR
b Wallingford, Conn, Nov 1, 03. Study: Detroit Sch Art; Art Students League. Work: New Haven Paint & Clay, Inc, Conn; Brookgreen Gardens, SC; Benton Col, Conn; Meriden Art & Crafts Asn, Conn; also in pvt collections. Comn: 36 Presidents of US, Int Silver Co, Meriden, 39-70; portrait reliefs, St Stevens Sch, Bridgeport, Conn, 50, Munic Bldg, Meriden, 66 & Marionist Sch, Thompson, Conn, 68. Exhib: Nat Acad Design, New York, 40-75; Nat Sculpture Soc, New York, 60-77; Hudson Valley Art Asn, White Plains, NY, 60-72; Am Artists Prof League, New York, 69-71; Coun Am Artists, New York. Awards: Dir Award, Coun Am Artists Soc, 64; Pres Award, Am Artists Prof League, 70; Silver Medal, Nat Sculpture Soc, 72, John Spring Award, 73, C P Dietsch Award, 75. Mem: Nat Sculpture Soc; Am Artists Prof League; Hudson Valley Art Asn; Conn Acad Fine Arts; Meriden Arts & Crafts Asn. Media: Bronze, Metal. Mailing Add: 21 Lydale Pl Meriden CT 06450

WIEDENHOEFT, RENATE
PHOTOGRAPHER, ART HISTORIAN
b Berlin, Ger, Nov 23, 42. Study: Univ Wis, Madison; Autodidact; also with Dr Ron Weidenhoeft. Collections Documented: Cleveland Mus of Art, Ohio; Metrop Mus of Art, NY; Louvre, Paris, France; Wallraf-Richartz Mus, Cologne, Ger; Permanenten, Bergen; Nat Gallery in Oslo, Sweden; Thorvaldsen Mus, Copenhagen, Denmark; Kunsthistorisches Mus, Vienna, Acad Fine Art, Vienna, Austria; Nat Gallery in Palazzo Barberini, Rome, Italy; Galleria Borghese, Rome; Palazzo Corsini, Rome; Gallerie Nazionale di Capodimonte, Naples; Gallerie dell' Accademia, Venice. Pos: Co-founder, partner & pres, Saskia Cult Doc (principle activity is the photography of art & archit, the cataloging of images & the distribution of color transparencies to mus & universities throughout the world), 66- Style & Technique: Super-realism, with uncanny sharpness of line, verisimilitude and durability; unique speciality, exquisite details. Res: Western European art and architecture from the Renaissance to early 20th century. Publ: Auth, Saskia Cultural Documentation, pvt publ, 77. Mailing Add: Saskia 3156 Plateau Dr Salt Lake City UT 84109

WIEDENHOEFT-WESLER, ANITA KAE
METALSMITH
b Unity, Wis, Mar 18, 47. Study: Univ Wis, BA, 71, BS, 73, MFA, 77. Work: Nat Collection Fine Arts, Smithsonian Inst, Washington, DC. Exhib: Craft Multiples, Smithsonian Inst, 75 & 76; 1976 Intent: Jewelry/Metal, Bruce Gallery, Edinboro, Pa, 76; The Object as Poet, Mus of Contemp Crafts, New York & Renwick Gallery, Smithsonian Inst, 76-77; Lake Superior 77, Tweed Mus of Art, Duluth, Minn, 77; Beaux Arts, Columbus Gallery of Fine Arts, Ohio, 77. Awards: Wis Arts Bd Fel, 77. Mem: Wis Designer Craftsmen; Soc of NAm Goldsmiths; Am Crafts Coun. Media: Metal. Mailing Add: 721 E Gorham Madison WI 53703

WIEDERSPAN, STAN
ART ADMINISTRATOR, PAINTER
b Holdredge, Nebr, Dec 24, 38. Study: Hastings Col, Nebr, BA; Univ Iowa, Iowa City, MA & MFA. Teaching: Head dept art, Iowa Wesleyan Col, Mt Pleasant, 65-73. Pos: Mem, Iowa Arts Coun, 71-73; dir, Cedar Rapids Art Ctr, 73- Style & Technique: Painting in a color field style reminiscent of Turner on 4'x6' format. Media: Oil on Canvas. Mailing Add: 1051 20th St SE Cedar Rapids IA 52403

WIEGAND, ROBERT
PAINTER, VIDEO ARTIST
b Mineola, NY, May 15, 34. Study: Albright Art Sch, Buffalo, NY; State Univ NY Buffalo, BS(art educ); NY Univ. Work: New York Dept Parks; Lever Bros Co, New York; Noble Found & Reliance Savings Bank, New York. Exhib: Mus Mod Art, 69; Jewish Mus, 70; Newark Mus, 72; Kitchen Ctr, 74; Anthology Film Arch, 75; Bicentennial Banners, Hirshhorn Mus & Sculpture Garden, Washington, DC, 76; The Hue & Far Cry of Color, Ft Wayne Mus of Art, Ind, 76; Am Artists Celebrate the Bicentennial, US Info Agency Travelling Exhib, 76; plus other group & one-man shows. Teaching: Instr, St Ann's Episcopal Sch. Awards: New York Bd Trade Award, 70; Rockefeller Found Travelling Artist's fel, 77. Bibliog: Graphics in the Environment, Graphic Design of the World, Kodansha Pub, Japan, 74; Ira Schneider & Beryl Korot (ed), Video Art, Harcourt Brace, 74; New American Art, Compton's Yrbk, Encycl Britannica, 75. Mailing Add: 16 Greene St New York NY 10013

WIELAND, JOYCE
PAINTER, FILM MAKER
b Toronto, Ont, 1931. Study: Cent Tech Sch, grad. Work: Nat Gallery Can; Montreal Mus Fine Arts, Can; Philadelphia Mus Art; Mus Mod Art Film Archives, New York; Royal Belg Film Archives; plus many other painting & film works in collections of univs, galleries & film archives. Comn: Bill's Hat (mixed media), Art Gallery Ont, 67. Exhib: The Wall-Art for Architecture Traveling Exhib, Art Gallery Ont, 69 & Rothmans Art Gallery, Stratford, Ont, 70; Oberhausen Film Festival, Austria, 69; Survey '70-Realism(e)s, Montreal Mus Fine Arts & Art Gallery Ont, 70; Eight Artists from Canada, Tel Aviv Mus, Israel, 70; Directors' Fortnight, Cannes Film Festival, France, 70; plus many others. Awards: Can Coun Grant, 66 & 68; Prizes for Rat Life & Diet in North America, 3rd Independent Filmmakers' Festival, New York, 68. Mem: Royal Can Acad Arts. Dealer: Isaacs Gallery 832 Yonge St Toronto ON Can. Mailing Add: 137 Summerhill Ave Toronto ON M4T 1B1 Can

WIENER, LOUISE WEINGARTEN
ART ADMINISTRATOR, ART WRITER
b Bridgeport, Conn, Oct 31, 40. Study: Bryn Mawr Col, BA(art hist); Spec study under Elizabeth Mongan at Alverthorpe Rosenwald Collection; Inst Fine Art, NY Univ. Collections Arranged: Homage to Siqueiros, High Mus of Art, Atlanta, Ga, for Orgn Am States Gen Assembly, 74 & Palacio de Belles Artes, Mexico City, 75; Festival of Women in the Arts, Atlanta, 75. Pos: Publ dir, Assoc Am Artists, New York, 62-67; pres, Louise Wiener Art Promotions, New York, 67-71; art critic, Atlanta Mag, 72-73; co-dir, Urban Walls/Atlanta, 73-74; exec dir, Festival of Women in the Arts, Atlanta, 75; spec asst cult affairs, Off of the Secy, US Dept of Com, 77- Bibliog: Articles in Atalnta Mag, 72-73 & Creative Loafing, 73-75. Res: Economics of cultural affairs. Mailing Add: 6 Pinehurst Circle Chevy Chase MD 20015

WIENER, PHYLLIS AMES
PAINTER
b Iowa City, Iowa, Sept 17, 21. Study: Univ Iowa, 40-41; Univ Mo, 43-44; Univ Minn, 52, 54 & 56, with Cameron Booth; Inst Allende, San Miguel, Mex, with Pinto, 61. Work: Minneapolis Art Inst; Walker Art Ctr, Minneapolis; Patrick Lannon Collection, Chicago; Am Asn Univ Women; Grand Rapids Art Mus. Exhib: Walker Biennial, 52-64; US State Dept Traveling Show, 62; Pa Acad Fine Arts, Philadelphia, 64; Butler Inst Art, Youngstown, Ohio, 65; one-man show, Minneapolis Art Inst, 67; plus others. Teaching: Instr oil painting, Walker Art Ctr, 60-66; instr composition, Univ Minn Exten Div, 62-72; instr watercolor painting, St Catherines Col, summers 73 & 74. Awards: Walker Art Ctr Biennial Awards, 54, 58 & 62; Minneapolis Inst Art Awards, 55, 58 & 62. Mem: Artists Equity Asn (pres, Minn Chap, 55-56, secy, 74-75); Womens Art Registry Minn. Style & Technique: Figure Compositions and aerial landscapes. Media: Watercolor, Acrylic. Dealer: Art Lending Gallery 430 Oak Grove Minneapolis MN 55403. Mailing Add: Box 37B E Star Rte Two Harbors MN 55616

WIER, GORDON D (DON)
DESIGNER, PAINTER
b Orchard Lake, Mich, June 14, 03. Study: Univ Mich, AB; Chicago Acad Fine Arts; Grand Cent Sch Art; and with J Scott Williams. Work: Detroit Inst Art; Mus Royaux Art et Hist, Brussels, Belg; also in pvt collections of King H M Baudouin I, Belg, King Frederick IX & Queen Ingrid, Denmark, Crown Prince Akihito, Japan & others. Exhib: Baltimore Watercolor Club; Del River Art Asn; Soc Decorators; two one-man shows, Bridgeport, Conn. Teaching: Instr, Grand Cent Sch Art, 28-35. Pos: Designer, Steuben Glass, 45-51, art designer, 52-69; designer, Corning Glass Works, 49-50. Awards: Cert of Excellence, Inst Graphic Arts, 50 & 51. Style & Technique: Realism obtained through mixed media. Mailing Add: 3601 Husted Dr Chevy Chase MD 20015

WIEST, KAY VAN ELMENDORF
PAINTER, PHOTOGRAPHER
b Little Rock, Ark, May 24, 15. Study: Art Inst Chicago, with Louis Rittman; Am Acad Art, Chicago, with St John; London City & Guilds Sch, Eng, with Middleton Todd; L'Ecole des Beaux Artes, Paris, with Msr Souverbie; Univ NMex, Albuquerque, with Raymond Jonson. Work: Univ NMex Sch Jour, Albuquerque; Nat Hq Pen Women, Washington, DC; NMex Fine Arts Mus, Santa Fe. Comn: Battle Scenes of WW II, Vet Foreign Wars Post 401, 47-48; mural of Albuquerque, 49; plus many others. Exhib: Int Exhib, Stevens Hotel, Chicago, 42; Newton Art Gallery, New York, 46; Univ NMex, Albuquerque, 50; Univ Ind, Indianapolis, 58; NMex Fine Arts Mus, Santa Fe, 67. Teaching: Teacher portrait painting, Europe, Africa & US, 36-56; teacher portrait painting & photog, Inst Am Indian Arts, Santa Fe, 63-75; pvt classes com arts, photog & portraiture, 48- Awards: First Prize Portraiture, Int Art Show, Chicago, 42; Portraiture, La Gallerie de Boetie, Paris, 45; First Prize Portraiture, Botts Gallery, Albuquerque, NMex, 53. Mem: Prof Photog Am. Style & Technique: Portraiture, old world methods and modern techniques, oil and pastel; photography, artifacts, art work, studio techniques, black and white, color. Publ: Contribr-photogr, Art of the Americas, Ancient and Hispanic, Crowell Press, 70-71; contribr-photog, Ariz Hwy Mag, 1/72, John F Kennedy Ctr Perfoming Arts Catalog, 73, A History of the American Indian, Univ NMex, 74 & Encycl of Indians of the Americas, Scholarly Press, 75. Mailing Add: 2596 Calle Delfino Santa Fe NM 87501

WIGGINS, BILL
PAINTER
b Roswell, NMex, Sept 24, 17. Study: NMex Mil Inst, Roswell; Abilene Christian Col; Am Shrivenham Univ, Eng, with Francis Speight; Fed Art Proj, Work Proj Admin, Roswell. Work: Roswell Mus & Art Ctr. Exhib: Newport 43rd Ann, RI, 54; Low Ruins Nat, Tubac, Ariz, 65; 5th Arts Nat, Tyler, Tex, 68; Mainstreams 68, Marietta Col, Ohio; Ark State Univ Nat, Jonesboro, 70. Teaching: Instr art, Roswell Mus & Art Ctr, 55-63. Bibliog: Elena Montes (auth), Bill Wiggins of Roswell, NMex Mag, 10/65; United States art, La Rev Mod, Paris, 12/65. Mem: Artists Equity Asn. Style & Technique: Realistic and expressionistic, specializing in large faces and heads. Media: Oil. Mailing Add: 711 W Eighth St Roswell NM 88201

WIGHT, FREDERICK S
PAINTER, ART ADMINISTRATOR
b New York, NY, June 1, 02. Study: Univ Va, BA; Harvard Univ, MA. Work: Los Angeles Co Mus Art, Los Angeles; Roswell Art Mus, NMex; Palm Springs Desert Mus, Calif. Exhib: One-man shows, M H de Young Mem Mus, San Francisco, Calif, 56, Pasadena Art Mus, Calif, 56, Fine Arts Gallery San Diego, Calif, 60, Esther Robles Gallery, Los Angeles, Calif, 60, Long Beach Mus Art, Calif, 61 & Palm Springs Desert Mus, Calif, 69. Collections Arranged: Jacques Lipchitz Retrospective, 63, Kurt Schwitters, 65, Henri Matisse Retrospective, 66, Negro in American Art, 66, Jean Arp Memorial, 68 & Gerhard Marcks Retrospective, 69; plus many others. Teaching: Instr art hist, Univ Mich, 50; instr art hist, Harvard Univ, 51; prof 20th century art, Univ Calif, Los Angeles, 53-73, chmn dept art, 63-66. Pos: Assoc dir, Inst Contemp Art, Boston, Mass; dir, Frederick S Wight Galleries, Univ Calif, Los Angeles, 53-73. Awards: Nat Endowment Arts Grant, 73; 25th Anniversary Award & Medal, Nat Gallery. Mem: Int Asn Art Critics; Univ Calif Los Angeles Art Coun. Style & Technique: Representational, abstract. Media: Oil on Canvas, Wood. Publ: Auth, Morris Graves, 56, Hans Hofmann, 57, Arthur G Dove, 58, Richard Neutra, 58 & Modigliani, 61; auth, Potent Images, Macmillan, 76; plus many others. Mailing Add: 405 Hilgard Ave Los Angeles CA 90024

WIITASALO, SHIRLEY
PAINTER
b Toronto, Ont, Can, 1949. Work: Can Coun Art Bank, Ottawa; Nat Gallery of Can, Ottawa; Owens Art Gallery, Mt Allison Univ, Sackville, NB; Mem Univ Art Gallery, St John's Nfld. Exhib: Can Cult Ctr, Paris, 73; Contemp Ont Art, Art Gallery of Ont, Toronto, 74; Carmen Lamanna at Owens Art Gallery, Mt Allison Univ, Sackville, NB, 75; Some Canadian Women Artists, Nat Gallery of Can, Ottawa, 75; Ont Now-A Survey of Contemp Art, Kitchener-Waterloo Gallery, Art Gallery of Hamilton, Ont, 76; 17 Canadian Artists-A Protean View, Vancouver Art Gallery, BC, 76; Kunsthalle, Basel, Switz, 78. Bibliog: Angelo Sgabellone (auth), Reviews, Queen St Mag, Vol 2, No 2 (1974); Gary Dault (auth), Two unusually fine paintings, Toronto Star, 9/27/74 & Shirley Wiitasalo..., Art Mag, Vol 6, No 20 (1975). Style & Technique: Stencil painting on canvas; representational. Media: Oil on Canvas. Mailing Add: 840 Yonge St Toronto ON M4W 2H1 Can

WILBERT, ROBERT JOHN
PAINTER, EDUCATOR
b Chicago, Ill, Oct 9, 29. Study: Univ Ill, BFA, 51, MFA, 54. Work: Saginaw Mus, Mich; South Bend Art Ctr, Ind; Kalamazoo Art Ctr, Mich; Macomb Co Community Col, Warren, Mich; Wayne State Univ, Detroit. Exhib: American Watercolors, Drawings & Prints, Metrop Mus Art, 52; Butler Inst Am Art 25th Midyear Ann, 60; Pa Acad Fine Arts 156th Ann, 61;

one-man shows, Donald Morris Gallery, Detroit, 62-72 & Wayne State Univ, 74; A Survey of Contemporary Art, J B Speed Art Mus, Louisville, Ky, 65; Flint Inst Arts & DeWaters Art Ctr, Mich, 71; Kresge Art Ctr, Mich State Univ, Lansing, 71; Eastern Mich Univ, Ypsilanti, 72; Cranbrook Acad Art Gallery, Bloomfield Hills, Mich, 72; Kalamazoo Art Ctr, Mich, 73; Slusser Art Ctr, Univ Mich, Ann Arbor, 74 & 76; Detroit Inst Arts, 76; Henry Ford Community Col, Dearborn, Mich, 76; Teaching: Instr painting, Flint Inst Arts, Mich, 54-56; prof painting, Wayne State Univ, 56- Awards: 4th Biennial Michiana Regional Award, South Bend Art Ctr, 66; Gallery Award, Mich State Fair, 67; 57th Exhib Mich Artists Werbe Award, Detroit Inst Arts, 69. Media: Oil, Watercolor. Dealer: Donald Morris Gallery 20082 Livernois Detroit MI 48221. Mailing Add: Dept of Art & Art Hist Wayne State Univ Detroit MI 48202

WILCOX, GORDON CUMNOCK
PAINTER
b Boston, Mass, Aug 12, 34. Study: Sch Practical Art, Boston; Art Students League, with Olinsky & Dickinson; Nat Acad Design. Comn: Portrait of Sen Kenneth Keating, 64. Exhib: Panhandle-Plains Hist Mus, Canyon, Tex, 65; Expos Intercontinentale, France, 67 & Monaco, 68; Wichita Centennial Nat Art Exhib, Kans, 70; one-man shows, Wickersham Gallery, New York, 68 & Southampton Gallery, Southampton, NY, 76. Awards: Hon Mention, Smithsonian Inst, Washington, DC, 63 & Guild Hall, Easthampton, NY, 75; John Duck Award, Parrish Art Mus, Southampton, NY, 71. Mem: Guild Hall; Parrish Art Mus. Style & Technique: Wet on wet technique resulting in soft, misty landscapes and seascapes. Media: Watercolor. Mailing Add: 400 E 88th St New York NY 10028

WILDE, JOHN
PAINTER, EDUCATOR
b Milwaukee, Wis, Dec 12, 19. Study: Univ Wis, BS & MS. Work: Whitney Mus Am Art, New York; Pa Acad Fine Arts, Philadelphia; Art Inst Chicago; Detroit Inst Art; Wadsworth Atheneum, Hartford, Conn. Exhib: Contemp Am Art, Univ Ill Biennial, 48-65; Whitney Mus Am Art, 52-68; 52 Americans Under 36, 54 & Contemp Drawing USA, 58, Mus Mod Art; Pittsburgh Int Contemp Painting & Sculpture, Carnegie Inst Int, 58; Art USA Now, US, Europe & Eastern mus, 62-66; Magic Realism in Am, Am Fedn of Arts Travelling Exhib, 64-65; Drawing: USA, St Paul Art Ctr, Minn, 64-67 & 71; Contemp Fantastic Drawings Int, Univ Chicago, 65; Art Across Am (travelling exhib), Wildenstein Galleries, New York, 65-66; retrospective, Milwaukee Art Ctr, 67; Three Centuries of the Nude in American Art 1675-1975, New York Cult Ctr, 75 & Minneapolis Inst of Arts, 76; Am Master Drawings & Watercolors (From Colonial Times to the Present), Minneapolis Inst of Arts, 76, Whitney Mus of Am Art, New York, 76 & San Francisco Fine Arts Mus, 77; Contemp Am Drawing, Fine Arts Gallery, San Diego, 77. Teaching: Alfred Sessler Distinguished Prof Art, Univ Wis-Madison, 69- Awards: Lambert Purchase Award, Pa Acad Fine Art, 63; Childe Hassam Purchase Award, Nat Acad Design, 65; Purchase Award, Butler Inst Am Art, 68. Bibliog: Lee Nordness (ed), Art USA Now, Viking Press, 63; Una E Johnson (auth), 20th Century Modern Drawings, Shorewood, 67; Theodore Stebbins, Jr (auth), American Master Drawings & Watercolors, Harper & Row, 76. Style & Technique: Work is meticulous, tight, pointed, scrutinizing, intense and introspective. Media: Oil, Pencil, Silverpoint. Dealer: Everett Oehlschlaeger Galleries 107 E Oak St Chicago IL 60611; Veldman Galleries 330 E Mason St Milwaukee WI 53202. Mailing Add: RFD 1 Evansville WI 53536

WILDENHAIN, FRANS
POTTER
b Leipzig, Ger, June 5, 05; US citizen. Study: Weimar Bauhaus; Acad Amsterdam, Holland. Work: Smithsonian Inst, Washington, DC; Rochester Mem Art Gallery, NY; Everson Mus, Syracuse, NY; Stedelijk Mus, Amsterdam; Boymans Mus, Rotterdam; plus many others. Comn: Mural, Strasenburgh Lab, Rochester, NY; Nat Libr Med, Bethesda, Md; Summit Hosp, Overlook, NY; Rochester Inst Technol, Rochester Student League. Exhib: Mus Contemp Crafts, 56 & 62-64; Miami Nat, 57 & 58; Brussels World's Fair, 58; Syracuse Invitational, 71; Am Crafts Coun Gallery, New York; plus many others. Teaching: From prof ceramics to emer prof, Sch Am Craftsman, Rochester Inst Technol. Awards: Fairchild Award, Rochester; Award, Brussels World's Fair; plus many others. Bibliog: Article in Crafts Horizons. Mem: Am Crafts Coun; World Crafts Coun. Publ: Contribr, Am Artist Mag & Crafts Horizons. Mailing Add: 6 Laird Ln Pittsford NY 14534

WILDER, MITCHELL ARMITAGE
ART ADMINISTRATOR
b Colorado Springs, Colo, Aug 19, 13. Study: McGill Univ, AB, 35; Univ Calif, Berkeley. Pos: Dir, Colorado Springs Fine Arts Ctr, 45-53; dir, Abby Aldrich Rockefeller Collection, Williamsburg, Va, 54-58; dir, Chouinard Art Inst, Los Angeles, 58-61; dir, Amon Carter Mus, Ft Worth, 61-; mem adv bd environ planning, Bur Reclamation, US Dept Interior, 66-, comnr, Indian Arts & Crafts Bd, 67-70; mem adv comt, Vatican Mus, 73-77; mem adv coun, Nat Mus Act, 74-77. Mem: Asn Art Mus Dirs. Publ: Santos, The Religious Folk Art of New Mexico, Taylor Mus, 43. Mailing Add: Box 2365 Ft Worth TX 76101

WILEY, WILLIAM T
PAINTER
b Bedford, Ind, Oct 21, 37. Study: San Francisco Art Inst, BFA, 60, MFA, 62. Work: San Francisco Mus Art; Whitney Mus Am Art, New York; Mus Mod Art, New York; Los Angeles Co Mus Art; Oakland Mus, Calif. Exhib: Univ Nev Ann Art Festival, Reno, 69; Looking West, Joslyn Art Mus, Omaha, Nebr, 70; Kompas IV Exhib, Stedelijk van Abbemuseum, Eindhoven & Dortmund, Netherlands, 70 & Kunsthalle, Berne, Switz, 70; Retrospective, Univ Calif, Berkeley, 71; one-man shows, Studio Marconi, Milan, Italy, 71, Art Inst Chicago, 72, Corcoran Gallery Art, Washington, DC, 72 & Mus Mod Art, New York, 75; E B Crocker Art Gallery, Sacramento, 72; Documenta, Kassel, WGer, 72; Ringling Mus, Sarasota, Fla, 72; Albright-Knox Art Gallery, Buffalo, NY, 72; Whitney Mus Am Art, New York, 73; Corcoran Gallery Art, Washington, DC, 75; JPL Fine Arts, London, 75; plus others. Teaching: Assoc prof art, Univ Calif, Davis, 62- Awards: Sculpture Purchase Award, Los Angeles Co Mus Art, 67; Purchase Prize, Whitney Mus Am Art, 68; Nealie Sullivan Award, San Francisco Art Inst, 68; plus others. Bibliog: James R Mellow (auth), Realist William Wiley, New York Times, 10/11/70; John Perrault (auth), Toward a new metaphysics, Village Voice, 10/15/70; Cecile McCann (auth), Probing the western ethic, Artweek, 5/15/71; plus others. Publ: Co-auth, The Great Blondino (film), shown Belg Film Festival, 67; contribr, Over Evident Falls (theater event), Sacramento State Col, 68; auth, Man's Nature (film), shown Hansen Fuller Gallery, 71. Dealer: Hansen Fuller Gallery 228 Grant Ave San Francisco CA 94108. Mailing Add: Box 654 Woodacre CA 94973

WILF, ANDREW JEFFREY
PAINTER
b Los Angeles, Calif, Aug 25, 49. Study: Compton City Col, Calif; Long Beach City Col, Calif; Otis Art Inst, Los Angeles. Comn: Billboard, with D J Hall & Nat Endowment for the Arts, Eyes & Ears, 76. Exhib: Portrait Painting 70-75, Allan Frumkin Gallery, New York, 75; Biennial Exhib, Whitney Mus Am Art, New York, 75; 4x8, Newport Harbor Mus, Newport Beach, Calif, 75; one-man shows, Comsky Gallery, Beverly Hills, Calif, 75, Albert Contreras Gallery, Los Angeles, 76 & 77 & Los Angeles Inst of Contemp Art, 77; Five Realist, Mt St Mary's Col, Los Angeles, 76; Figure in Contemp Realism, Long Beach City Col, Calif, 76; Realist Painting Los Angeles, ARCO Ctr for Visual Art, Los Angeles, 78. Bibliog: Amy Goldin (auth), Pattern emerging, Art in Am, 5-6/75; Melinda Wortz (auth), Emerging California talent, Art Week, 6/75; Martha Alf (auth), Andrew Wilf's portraits, Art Week, 10/75. Style & Technique: Realism. Media: Acrylic on Canvas. Dealer: Albert Contreras Gallery 2120 N Cahuenga Blvd Los Angeles CA 90068. Mailing Add: 7880 Seville Ave Walnut Park CA 90255

WILKE, HANNAH
SCULPTOR, INSTRUCTOR
b New York, NY, Mar 7, 40. Study: Temple Univ, BFA, 61, BS, 62. Work: Albright-Knox Art Gallery, Buffalo, NY; Allen Art Mus, Oberlin, Ohio; Brooklyn Mus, NY; Power Inst, Sydney, Australia; Metro-Media, Channel 5, New York. Comn: Mural (latex), comn by Carl Solway Gallery for Ponderosa Systs, Dayton, Ohio, 74; greeting card, Mus Mod Art, New York, 77. Exhib: One-woman shows, Sculpture & Drawing, Ronald Feldman Fine Arts, NY, 72, 74 & 75, Drawing & Sculpture Show, Margo Leavin Gallery, Los Angeles, 74 & 76, London Mus, Ont, 77 & Albright-Knox Art Gallery, 77; Newark Akron Inst, 72; Am Women Artists, Kunsthau Hamburg, WGer, 72; Contemp Arts Ctr, Cincinnati, Ohio, 73; Whitney Mus Biennial, New York, 73; Woman Choose Woman & Soft Sculpture, NY Cult Ctr, 73; ICA Gallery, Boston, 74; Indianapolis Mus, Ind, 74; Brooklyn Mus, NY, 74; Graz Austria, 74; 5 Americans in Paris, Galerie Gerald Piltzer, France, 75; Marrianne Deson Gallery, Chicago, 75; Albright-Knox Art Gallery, 75; Bronx Mus, NY, 75; 26th Berlin Festival, 76; Whitney Mus Am Art, New York, 76. Teaching: Instr sculpture, Sch Visual Arts, NY, 74- Pos: Cur, Store Days, 70-77. Awards: Sculpture Award, Creative Arts Prog Serv, NY State Coun Arts, 74; Nat Endowment for the Arts, 76. Bibliog: Cindy Nemser, 4 Artists of sensuality, Arts, 74; Mark Savitt (auth), Hannah Wilke, the pleasure principle, Arts Mag, 9/75; Ruth Iskin (auth), Conversation with Hannah Wilke, Visual Dialogue, Vol 2 (1977). Style & Technique: Spontaneous gestural compositions; sensual and erotic; early feminist art since 1959; folding, pouring, involving movement in sculpture and drawing. Media: Gum, Latex Rubber, Terra-cotta; Video. Publ: Contribr, Woman's sensibility, Art, 75; contribr, Flash Art, 5/75; auth, My Father's Brother's Wife's Mother, Heresies, 78. Mailing Add: 62 Greene St New York NY 10012

WILKE, ULFERT S
PAINTER, ART ADMINISTRATOR
b Bad Tölz, Ger, July 14, 07; US citizen. Study: With Willy Jaeckel, 23; Arts & Crafts Sch, Brunswick, 24-25; Acad Grande Chaumiere, 27-28; Acad Ranson, Paris, 27-28; Harvard Univ, 40-41; State Univ Iowa, MA, 47. Work: Philadelphia Mus, Pa; Solomon R Guggenheim Mus, New York; Cleveland Mus Art, Ohio; Whitney Mus Am Art, New York; Mus Tel Aviv, Israel. Exhib: Younger Am Artists; Solomon R Guggenheim Mus, 54; Italy Rediscovered, Smithsonian Traveling Exhib, 55-56; Lettering by Mod Artists, Mus Mod Art, New York, 64; Tokyo Biennial, tour Japan, 67; Ulfert Wilke, Recent Works, Des Moines Art Ctr, Columbus Gallery Fine Arts, Joslyn Art Mus & San Francisco Mus Art, 70-71; Jodi Scully Gallery, Los Angeles, 76; Recent Calligraphic Paintings, Arts Club of Chicago, 77; Gurewitsch Gallery, New York, 78. Collections Arranged: Oscar Kokoschka, Kalamazoo Inst Arts, 40; As Found, Inst Contemp Art, Boston, 66; Very Small Paintings, Objects & Works on Paper, Univ Iowa Mus Art, 72. Teaching: Asst prof art, Univ Louisville, 48-55; vis grad prof painting, Univ Ga, 55-56; assoc prof art, Rutgers Univ, New Brunswick, 62-67. Pos: Head dept art & dir, Kalamazoo Col & Inst Arts, Mich, 40-42; art & educ dir, Springfield Art Asn, Ill, 46-47; dir, Univ Iowa Mus Art, 68-75. Awards: Albrecht Durer Prize, Ger, 27; Guggenheim Found Fels Study in Europe, 59-60 & 60-61. Bibliog: J Langsner (auth), Art, 11/61 & G Nordland (auth), Calligraphy & the art of Ulfert Wilke, 4/71, Art Int. Mem: Asn Am Mus Dirs. Media: Oil, Acrylic. Publ: Illusr, portfolios, Music to Be Seen, 56, Fragments From Nowhere, 58 & One, Two & More, 60; An Artist Collects-Ulfert Wilke Selections from Five Continents, 75. Mailing Add: Box 211 Rte 3 Solon IA 52333

WILKINS, DAVID GEORGE
ART HISTORIAN, MUSEUM DIRECTOR
b Battle Creek, Mich, Sept 12, 39. Study: Oberlin Col, BA, 61; Univ Mich, MA, 63 & PhD, 69. Teaching: Assoc prof art hist, Dept Fine Arts, Univ Pittsburgh, 67- Pos: Dir, Univ Art Gallery, Univ Pittsburgh, 76- Mem: Col Art Asn; Soc of Archit Historians; Renaissance Soc of Am. Res: History of western painting, including American 19th century and American architecture. Publ: Auth, American painting collection at Pittsburgh, Am Art Rev, 75; contribr, Art in nineteenth century Pittsburgh, Univ Art Gallery, 77. Mailing Add: Univ Art Gallery Univ Pittsburgh Pittsburgh PA 15260

WILKINSON, CHARLES K
MUSEUM CURATOR
b London, Eng, Oct 13, 97. Study: Slade Sch & Univ Col, Univ London, 15-17 & 19-20. Teaching: Adj prof, Columbia Univ, 64-69; adj prof, NY Univ, 66-67. Pos: Mem Egyptian exped, Metrop Mus Art, 20-32, Iranian exped, 32-40, sr res fel, 42-47, assoc cur Near Eastern archaeol, 47-53, cur, 53-63, emer cur, 63-; Hagop Kevorkian cur Mid East art & archaeol, Brooklyn Mus, 69-74, emer cur, 74- Mem: Am Oriental Soc; Am Schs Oriental Res; Am Inst Iranian Studies; Archaeol Inst Am; Century Asn. Mailing Add: Sharon CT 06069

WILKINSON, KIRK COOK
ART DEALER, PAINTER
b New York, NY, Nov 23, 09. Study: Parson's Sch Design; watercolor painting with Felice Waldo Howell. Work: Scarborough Art Gallery, NY; Pocker Art Gallery, New York; Kendall Art Gallery, Wellfleet, Mass. Exhib: Art Dir Club New York, 34-; Art Dir Club Philadelphia, 54 & 56; Jr League Westchester Ann, 66-69; Westchester Art Asn Ann, 69; Cape Cod Art Asn Ann, 70-72; plus others. Teaching: Instr graphics & ann lectr, Parson's Sch Design, 31-52. Pos: Art dir, Country Life, Am Home Mag, NY, 35-36; art dir, House Beautiful Mag, New York, 36-37; art dir, Conde Nast, New York, 37-39; art dir, Women's Day Mag, New York, 38-70; pres & organizer, Parson's Sch Design Alumni Coun, 44; owner, Kendall Art Gallery. Awards: Gold Medal, New York Art Dir Club, 54; Gold Medal, Philadelphia Art Dir Club; Second Prize Watercolor, Jr League Westchester Show, 69; plus others. Bibliog: Charles Coiner (auth), Commentary on the art & layout of Women's Day, Art Direction Mag, 4/54. Mem: Am Fedn Arts; Soc Illusr; Century Asn; Dutch Treat Club; Provincetown Art Asn; plus others. Style & Technique: Contemporary realism, sea and shore related subjects. Media: Watercolor, Casein, Acrylic. Specialty: Contemporary art, sculpture and ceramics. Publ: Auth, Let's talk about your pictures, Popular Photog, 4/54; auth, Lighting is the news, 10/59 & New thinking man, 2/62, Art Direction. Dealer: Kendall Art Gallery Inc Wellfleet MA 02667; Hambleton Gallery Old South Wharf Nantucket MA 02554. Mailing Add: c/o Kendall Art Gallery Box 742 Wellfleet MA 02667

WILKINSON, RUTH MURPHY
COLLECTOR, PATRON
b Fairfield Plantation, Ark, Jan 28, 21. Study: La State Univ, BA. Mem: Friends of Anglo Am Art Mus, La State Univ (pres, 74; bd mem, 70-); West Baton Rouge Art Mus, Port Allen (bd mem, 70-; pres & chmn bd, 75-76). Interest: Development of small parish museum and building activities of museums; collecting. Collection: Louisiana paintings. Mailing Add: Rt 2 Box 83 Port Allen LA 70767

WILL, JOHN A
PRINTMAKER, PAINTER
b Waterloo, Iowa, June 30, 39. Study: Univ Iowa, MFA, 64; Rijsacadamie von Beeldende Kunston, Amsterdam, 64-65; Tamarind, Albuquerque, NMex, Ford Found grant, 70-71. Work: New York Pub Libr; Art Inst Chicago; Libr of Cong; Mus NMex, Santa Fe; Glenbow Art Gallery, Calgary. Exhib: Libr Cong Nat Print Exhib, 73; Int Triennial Original Color Graphics, Grenchen, Switz, 73; Brit Int Print Biennial, Bradford, Yorkshire, 74; 2nd Miami Graphics Int Biennial, Fla, 75; 11th Int Biennial Graphic Art, Ljubljana, Yugoslavia, 75; plus others. Teaching: Asst prof drawing, Univ Wis-Stout, 65-70; resident artist, Yale Univ, summer 66 & Peninsula Sch Art, Fish Creek, Wis, summer 68; assoc prof lithography, Univ Calgary, 71-; instr, Nova Scotia Col Art & Design, summers 73-75 & 77. Awards: Fulbright Fel, Holland, 64-65. Media: Graphics, Painting. Mailing Add: Dept of Art Univ of Calgary Calgary AB Can

WILL, MARY SHANNON
CERAMIST, INSTRUCTOR
b Ithaca, NY, Sept 9, 44. Study: Univ Iowa, 64-68; Univ NMex, 70-71; Archie Bray Found, 74. Work: Glenbow Art Gallery, Calgary, Alta; Alta Art Found, Edmonton: Univ Calgary, Alta. Exhib: West 71, Edmonton Art Gallery, Alta, 71; Ceramics Int, Calgary, Alta, 73; Design Can Crafts Awards, Ottawa, Ont, 74; Contemp Ceramic Sculpture, Univ BC, Vancouver, 74; Five Calgary Ceramists, Glenbow Art Gallery, 74; Hist of Ceramics in Alta, Edmonton Art Gallery, 75; Alta Art Found Overseas Exhib, London, Brussels, Paris, New York, 75-76; Eight from Calgary, House of Ceramics, Vancouver, BS, 77. Teaching: Guest instr ceramics, Tuscarora Pottery Sch, Nev, 69 & 75. Bibliog: Five Calgary ceramists, Ceramics Mo, 75. Style & Technique: Abstract sculpture; lowfire white earthenware and multi-fire glaze techniques; raku and highfire processes. Media: Ceramic. Mailing Add: 1720 9A St SW Calgary AB T2T 3E6 Can

WILLARD, CHARLOTTE
ART CRITIC, WRITER
Study: NY Univ; Columbia Univ, BA; New Sch Social Res, with Jose de Creeft. Pos: Art ed, Look, 50-55; contrib ed, Art Am, 58-68; art critic, New York Post, 64-68. Awards: MacDowell Colony Fel, 71-72. Res: Renaissance painting. Publ: Contribr, Story Behind Painting, 60, Moses Soyer, 61, What is a Masterpiece, 64, Cezanne to Op Art, 71 & Frank Lloyd Wright, 72. Mailing Add: 340 E 63rd St New York NY 10021

WILLE, O LOUIS
SCULPTOR
b Apr 27, 17; US citizen. Study: Univ Minn, MA. Work: Univ Minn Gallery; Sculpture Ctr, New York. Exhib: Minneapolis Art Inst; Walker Art Ctr; Denver Art Mus; San Francisco Mus Art; Everson Mus, Syracuse. Style & Technique: Direct carving or welding without use of model. Media: Wood, Stone, Bronze. Mailing Add: 200 W Main Aspen CO 81611

WILLENBECHER, JOHN
SCULPTOR, PAINTER
b Macungie, Pa, May 5, 36. Study: Brown Univ, BA, 58; NY Univ Inst Fine Arts, 58-61. Work: Whitney Mus Am Art, New York; Albright-Knox Art Gallery, Buffalo, NY; James A Michener Found Collection, Univ Tex, Austin; Hirshhorn Mus & Sculpture Garden, Washington, DC; Solomon R Guggenheim Mus, New York. Exhib: Mixed Media & Pop Art, Albright-Knox Art Gallery, Buffalo, 63; Paintings & Constructions of the 1960's, RI Sch Design, Providence, 64; Young Americans, Whitney Mus Am Art, New York, 65; Kunst-Lucht-Kunst, Stedelijk Mus, Eindhoven, Holland, 66; John Willenbecher, Everson Mus Art, Syracuse, NY, 75. Teaching: Lectr painting, Philadelphia Col Art, 72-73. Bibliog: David Bourdon (auth), Out there with Willenbecher, 9/68 & Joseph McElroy (auth), Through the labyrinth: The art of John Willenbecher, 3/75, Art Int; William Wilson (auth), John Willenbecher: Pyramids, spheres & labyrinths, Arts Mag, 3/75. Mailing Add: 145 W Broadway New York NY 10013

WILLER, JIM
SCULPTOR, PAINTER
b Fulham, Eng, Feb 25, 21; Can citizen. Study: Hornsey Sch Art, London, Eng; Royal Acad, Amsterdam; Winnipeg Sch Art & Univ Man, BA, 52. Work: Nat Gallery Can, Ottawa; Winnipeg Art Gallery, Man; Univ Winnipeg; Univ Man; Vancouver Art Gallery. Comn: Post-tensioned concrete sundial & two hanging screens, Polo Park Shopping Ctr, Winnipeg, 59; mural (concrete), Charleswood Hotel, Winnipeg, 61; aluminum & steel sculpture, Greenwin Award for Arts, Toronto, 69; five murals for Image I, Vancouver, 70-71; light-sensitive sculpture, BC Inst Technol, 75. Exhib: Can Scholar Winner's Abroad Exhib, Nat Gallery Ottawa, 56; Can Biennial, 56-57; Univ Man Exhib Winnipeg Artists, 61; Sculpture '67, Toronto City Hall, 67; 3D into the 70's, East Can on Tour, 70; plus others. Teaching: Instr design, Vancouver Sch Art, 64-65. Awards: Can Govt Overseas Grant, 54; Can Award to Netherlands, Imp Tobacco Prize, 67-68; Greenwin Award Arts, Toronto, 69. Mem: Can Artists (rep). Style & Technique: Kinetic sculpture. Publ: Auth, Paramind (novel), McClelland & Stewart, 73. Dealer: Bau-xi Gallery 3003 Granville St Vancouver BC Can. Mailing Add: Sunset Beach West Vancouver BC Can

WILLET, HENRY LEE
CRAFTSMAN
b Pittsburgh, Pa, Dec 7, 99. Study: Princeton Univ; Univ Pa; with father, William Willet; Europ study & travel; Lafayette Col, hon DArt, 51; Geneva Col, hon LHD, 66; Ursinus Col, hon LHD, 67; St Lawrence Univ, hon DFA, 72. Work: Children's Gallery, Metrop Mus Art, New York. Comn: Stained glass, Cadet Chapel, West Point Mil Acad, 10-75, Am Lutheran Church, Oslo, Norway, 66, Hall of Sci, New York World's Fair, 67, Nat Presby Church Ctr, Washington, DC, 68, St Mary's Cath Church, 70 & Coral Ridge Presby Church, Ft Lauderdlae, Fla, 75; stained glass & tower window, San Francisco Grace Cathedral, 66. Exhib: One-man shows, Columbia Mus Art, SC, 61, Atlanta Art Asn, Ga, 61, Taft Mus, Cincinnati, Ohio, 69 & Mus Am Art, New Britain, Conn, 71; Archit Glass, Mus Contemp Crafts, New York, 68. Teaching: Instr hist stained glass, Philadelphia Sch Apprentices Stained Glass, 63-; instr sem symbolism & color, Nantucket Sch Ecclesiastical Needlery, summer 71. Pos: Pres, Willet Stained Glass Studios, 30-65, chmn bd, 65- Awards: Medal of achievement, Philadelphia Art Alliance, 52; Conover Award, Guild Relig Archit, 63; Frank P Brown Medal, Franklin Inst, 71; Relig Heritage of Am Award, 71. Bibliog: Article in, Time, 10/11/37; A new luster in churches, Life, 4/11/55; Anne Hoene (auth), Stained glass—what future?, Art Gallery, 12/68. Mem: Hon mem Am Inst Architects; fel Stained Glass Asn Am (pres, 42-44); Benjamin Franklin Soc; fel Royal Soc Arts, London; Guild Relig Archit; fel Am Soc Church Archit. Publ: Co-auth, Stained glass, In: Encycl Americana, 48. Mailing Add: 10 E Moreland Ave Philadelphia PA 19118

WILLIAMS, BENJAMIN FORREST
MUSEUM CURATOR, ART HISTORIAN
b Lumberton, NC, Dec 24, 25. Study: Corcoran Sch Art, with Eugene Weisz; George Washington Univ, AA; Univ NC, AB; Columbia Univ, Paris Exten, Ecole du Louvre; Netherlands Inst Art Hist; Art Students League New York. Work: Atlanta Art Asn; NC Mus Art; Duke Univ; Greenville Civic Art Gallery, NC; Knoll Assoc, New York. Exhib: Va Intermont, Bristol; Weatherspoon Gallery, Greensboro; Person Hall Gallery, Chapel Hill, NC; Asheville Art Mus; Am Fedn Arts traveling exhibs; plus many others. Collections Arranged: Francis Speight-Retrospective; Sculptures of Tilmann Riemenschneider; Carolina Charter Tercentenary Exhibition; Young British Art; North Carolina Collects; Retropsectives for Josef Albers, Hobson Pittman, Jacob Marling, Victor Hammer, Fedor Zakharov, Henry Pearson & the collections of the NC Mus Art; assisted with, Rembrandt & His Pupils & E L Kirchner. Pos: In chg of Ann NC Artists' Exhib; prin investr, Black Mountain Col Res Proj; gen cur, NC Mus Art, currently. Awards: Ronsheim Mem Award, Corcoran Sch Art, 46; Washington Soc Arts, 47; Prizes, Southeastern Ann, 47. Mem: Am Asn Mus; Southeastern Mus Conf; Col Art Asn Am. Publ: Contribr articles on 19th century American painting & sculpture to NC Mus Art Bull & NC Hist Rev. Mailing Add: NC Mus of Art Raleigh NC 27611

WILLIAMS, CHESTER LEE
SCULPTOR, EDUCATOR
b Durham, NC, July 24, 44. Study: NC Cent Univ, BA, 68; Univ Mich, MFA, 71. Work: Student Union Gallery, NC Cent Univ, Durham, Voorhees Col Libr, Denmark, SC; Art Dept Gallery, Univ Mich, Ann Arbor; Univ Gallery, Appalachian State Univ, Boone, NC; Black Arch Mus & Res Ctr, Fla A&M Univ, Tallahassee. Comn: Sculpture, bronze casting, comn by Dr Oscar Cole, New York, 71 & Dr & Mrs Robert Zakarin, Tallahassee, 77; painting & sculpture, Fla A&M Univ, 77-78; bronze bust of Johnathan Gibbs, Fine Arts Coun of Fla, Div Cult Affairs, State of Fla, Tallahassee, 77-78. Exhib: Univ Mich Mus of Art, Ann Arbor, 71; Garden's Gallery, Raliigh, NC, 71; LeMoyne Art Found, Tallahassee, 75; Appalachian State Univ, 75; Univ W Fla, Pensacola, 75; Howard Univ Galleries, Washington, DC, 76; Ala State Univ, Montgomery, 77. Collections Arranged: Richard Hunt Print's Show, Fla A&M Univ Gallery, 75; plus others. Teaching: Instr creative woodwork, Sch Design, Durham, NC, 68-69; asst prof sculpture & art appreciation, Voorhess Col, Denmark, SC, 71-74; asst prof sculpture & painting, Fla A&M Univ, 74- Pos: Illusr, Nat Air Pollution Control Ctr, Durham, NC, 69-70. Bibliog: Belle Cool (auth), Sculpture Exhibited, The Appalachian, 75; Melissa Klinzing (auth), Chester Williams: It's Ironic, New Look, 76; Jerome A Grey (auth), Conjugal Unity, Black Art: An Int Quarterly, 77. Mem: Col Art Asn of Am; Nat Conf Aritsts; Southern Asn Sculptors Inc; LeMoyne Art Found. Style & Technique: Highly polished bronze sculpture. Media: Bronze Casting. Mailing Add: 950 Richardson Trail Tallahassee FL 32301

WILLIAMS, GARTH MONTGOMERY
ILLUSTRATOR, DESIGNER
b New York, NY, Apr 16, 12. Study: Westminster Sch Art, London, Eng; ARCA, spec talent scholar painting & exten scholar. Exhib: Royal Acad Arts Ann, London, 33-35 & 41; Exhib Original Textile Designs, Cotton Bd, Cent Gallery, Manchester, Eng, 41. Awards: Prix de Rome for Sculpture, Soc Rome Scholars, London, 36. Publ: Illusr, Stuart Little, 45, illusr, Charlotte's Web, 52, illusr, The Little House Books, 53, auth & illusr, The Adventures of Benjamin Pink, 51 & auth & illusr, The Rabbit's Wedding, 58, Harper & Row; plus others. Mailing Add: Apartado Postal 123 Guanajuato GTO Mexico

WILLIAMS, GERALD
SCULPTOR, POTTER
b Asansol, India, Jan 5, 26; US citizen. Study: Cornell Col; Notre Dame Col, NH, hon DFA, 71. Work: Fitchburg Art Mus, Mass; Syracuse Univ, NY; Objects USA, Johnson Collection. Comn: Ceramic mural, Sunapee & resin mural, Laconia, State of NH; resin mural, Int Paper Box Machine Co, Nashua, NH; ceramic mural, Sheen, Finney, Bass & Green Law Off, Manchester. Exhib: Am Studio Pottery, Victoria & Albert Mus, London, Eng, 67, Ceramic Int, 72; Syracuse Ceramic Nat, 70; one-man shows, Contemp Crafts Mus, New York, 69 & Currier Gallery Art, Manchester, 70. Teaching: Instr sculpture, Currier Gallery Sch Art, 52-72; instr ceramics, Dartmouth Col, 64-65; instr ceramics, Haystack Sch Crafts. Pos: Trustee, Soc Arts & Crafts, Boston, 67-72; mem adv bd, NH Comn Arts. Bibliog: Nordness (auth), Objects: USA, 70. Mem: NH Art Asn; League NH Craftsmen. Media: Clay. Res: Wet-firing process; photo-resist process. Publ: Auth, Textiles of Oaxaca, 64; contribr, Craft Horizons, 69; ed, The Studio Potter, 72. Mailing Add: RFD 1 Goffstown NH 03045

WILLIAMS, HIRAM DRAPER
PAINTER, EDUCATOR
b Indianapolis, Ind, Feb 11, 17. Study: Williamsport Sketch Club, with George Eddinger; Pa State Univ, BS, with Victor Lowenfeld & MEd, with Hobson Pittman & Lowenfeld. Work: Mus Mod Art & Whitney Mus Am Art, New York; Milwaukee Art Ctr; Nat Art Collection & Corcoran Gallery Art, Washington, DC. Exhib: Art USA: Painting, Mus Mod Art, 61; Art USA II; Carnegie Inst Int, Pittsburgh, 64; Art Across Am, 65; Art: USA: Now, 66. Teaching: Asst prof art educ, Univ Southern Calif, 53-54; asst prof art educ, Univ Tex, Austin, 54-60, res grant, 58; prof painting, Univ Fla, 60- Awards: D D Feldman Award, 58; Guggenheim Found Fel, 63. Bibliog: Donald Weisman (auth), Recent paintings of Hiram Williams, Univ Tex Quart, 59; William B Stephens (auth), On creating & teaching, Col Art J, summer 71. Media: Oil. Publ: Auth, Notes for a Young Painter, Prentice-Hall, 63; co-auth, Forms, Univ Tex, 69. Dealer: Nordness Galleries 140 E 81st St New York NY 10028. Mailing Add: 2804 NW 30th Terr Gainesville FL 32601

WILLIAMS, JOHN ALDEN
ART HISTORIAN
b Ft Smith, Ark, Sept 6, 28. Study: Am Univ Beirut, 50-51; Univ Munich, 51-52, with Hans Sedlmayer; Univ Ark, BA(hist & philos), 53; Princeton Univ, MA & PhD(oriental studies), 53-57; further work under Sir K A C Creswell in Cairo on hist of Islamic art & archit, 57-59. Teaching: Asst & assoc prof Islamic studies, McGill Univ, Montreal, Que, Can, 59-66; dir & prof, Ctr for Arabic Studies, Am Univ Cairo, 66-73; prof art hist & Middle East studies, Univ Tex, Austin, 76- Pos: Asst field dir, Am Ctr for Res in Egypt, 57-59. Res: History of Islamic art and architecture. Publ: Ed, Islam In: Great Religions of Modern Man, George Braziller Inc, 61; contribr, The Ottoman Monuments of Cairo Colloque International sur l'Historie du Caire, Ministry of Cult, 70; ed, Themes of Islamic Civilization, Univ Calif Press, 71; co-auth, Art and Architecture of Cairo (405 slides with commentary) & auth, Islamic

Architecture of the Yemen (80 slides with commentary), Visual Educ Inc, 77. Mailing Add: c/o Ctr for middle East Studies Univ Tex Austin TX 78703

WILLIAMS, JOHN WESLEY
ART HISTORIAN
b Memphis, Tenn, Feb 25, 28. Study: Duke Univ; Yale Univ, BA; Univ Mich, PhD. Teaching: From instr to assoc prof Medieval art, Swarthmore Col, Pa, 60-72; prof Medieval art, Univ Pittsburgh, 72- Pos: Chmn fine arts dept, Swarthmore Col, 71-72. Awards: Fulbright-Hays Res Grant, Spain, 64 & 69. Mem: Col Art Asn Am. Res: Spanish medieval art. Publ: Auth, Romanesque Bible of San Millan, JWCI, 65; auth, Valeranica and the Scribe Florentine, Madrider Mitteilungen, 70; auth, San Isidoro: evidence for a new history, Art Bull, 73; auth, Early Spanish Manuscript Illumination, George Braziller, Inc, 77; plus others. Mailing Add: 749 S Linden Ave Pittsburgh PA 15208

WILLIAMS, LEWIS W, II
ART HISTORIAN
b Champaign, Ill, Apr 24, 18. Study: Univ Ill, BFA, 46, MFA, 48; Univ Chicago, PhD, 58. Teaching: Instr art hist, Univ Mo-Columbia, 48-50; asst art hist, Northwestern Univ, Evanston, 53-55; prof art hist, Beloit Col, 55- Pos: Dir, Assoc Cols Midwest Arts London & Florence, Florence, Italy, 71-72. Awards: Teacher of Yr, Beloit Col, 66. Mem: Col Art Asn Am; Am Asn Univ Prof (pres local chap, 67). Res: American sculpture. Mailing Add: Dept of Art Beloit Col Beloit WI 53511

WILLIAMS, MARY FRANCES
ART HISTORIAN, LECTURER
b Providence, RI, Apr 26, 05. Study: Radcliffe Col, BA, MA & PhD. Collections Arranged: 41st-61st Ann Loan Exhibitions of American Art, Randolph-Macon Woman's Col. Teaching: Asst prof art, Hollins Col, 36-39; asst prof art, Mt Holyoke Col, 39-42; prof art hist & cur, Randolph-Macon Woman's Col, 52-73; retired. Pos: Mem, Va State Art Comn, 56-70. Awards: Jonathan Fay Prize, 27 & Caroline Wilby Prize, 31, Radcliffe Col; Gillie A Larew Distinguished Teaching Award, Randolph-Macon Woman's Col, 72. Mem: Nat League Am Penwomen; Lynchburg Fine Arts Ctr; Phi Beta Kappa; Archaeol Inst Am; Alliance Francaise. Publ: Auth, Catalogue of the collection of American art at Randolph-Macon Woman's College, 65 & 2nd ed, 77; auth, Paintings as Teachers, Am Art Rev, 2/78. Mailing Add: 239 Westmoreland St Lynchburg VA 24503

WILLIAMS, MARYLOU LORD STUDY
MUSEUM DIRECTOR, PAINTER
b Neodesha, Kans. Study: Beloit Col, BA, 62; Univ Wis, Madison, MA(art), 65; study with Victor D'Amico, New York Univ & Inst of Mod Art. Work: New York Univ Art Collection; Beloit Col Permanent Collection, Wright Art Ctr, Wis; Janesville Art League Gallery, Wis; Hawaii State Found on Cult & the Arts, Honolulu; Contemp Arts Ctr-Hawaii Gallery, Honolulu. Comn: Series of five charcoal drawings, General Motors Assembly Div Plant, Janesville, 54; oil painting, Wis Scene, Merchants & Savings Bank, Janesville, 65; assemblage for lanai, Ossipoff, Snyder, Roland & Getz Architects, Honolulu, 72. Exhib: Artists of Hawaii, Honolulu Acad of Arts, 72; Wis Painters & Sculptors, Milwaukee Art Ctr, 66 & 67; Conn Ann, Wadsworth Athenaeum, Hartford, Conn, 66; Three Artists, Sneed-Hillman Gallery, Rockford, Ill, 67; two-person show, Paintings-Collages-Assemblages, Bradley Galleries, Milwaukee, 76; Burpee Art Mus, Rockford, 77; Art for the Out-of-Doors, Paul Waggoner Gallery, Chicago, Ill, 77; one-man show, Collages—Marylou Williams, The Foundry Gallery, Honolulu, 71 & 73. Collections Arranged: Georgia O'Keefe (with catalogue), Daland Fine Arts Ctr, Kohler Gallery, Milton Col, Wis, 4/20-5/10/65. Teaching: Chmn & asst prof of art hist, design & gallery dir, Milton Col, Wis, 64-67; art coordr, elementary through community col, Dept Educ, Pago Pago, Am Samoa, 76-71; instr mus sch, Honolulu Acad Arts, summer 70, 71 & 73; instr mus sch, Bernice P Bishop Mus, Honolulu, 71-72. Pos: Dir & owner, Devlin Gallery, Janesville, 60-65; dir & cur, Theodore Lyman Wright Art Ctr, Beloit Col, Wis, 75- Awards: First Award, Beloit & Vicinity Exhib, Art League of Beloit, 61; First Award, Rockford & Vicinity Exhib, Rockford Art Asn, 65; First of Top Ten Award, Wis Painters, Sculptures, Milwaukee Art Ctr, Wis, 66. Bibliog: Webb Anderson (auth), Rev/Critique, Honolulu Star Bull & Advert, 4/2 & 6/4/72. Mem: Am Asn of Mus; Midwest Mus Asn; Wis Fed of Mus; Wis Painters & Sculptors League; Hawaii Artists League. Style & Technique: Collage and assemblage compositions which empahsize harmonious combinations of shape, color and surfaces derived from found objects and materials. Media: Assemblage. Res: Study in depth of Polynesian bark cloth. Dealer: Patricia Sneed c/o Sneed-Hillman Gallery 2024 Harlem Blvd Rockford IL 61103. Mailing Add: 2528 Riverview Dr Janesville WI 53545

WILLIAMS, NEIL
PAINTER, FILM MAKER
b Bluff, Utah, Aug 19, 34. Study: Calif Sch Fine Arts, BFA, 59. Work: Whitney Mus Am Art, New York; Richmond Mus, Calif; Mass Inst Technol, Cambridge. Exhib: One-man exhibs, Green Gallery, 64, Dwan Gallery, 66, Andre Emmerich Gallery, New York, 66 & 68 & Logiudice Gallery, 72; Walter Kelly Gallery, 73. Bibliog: Richard Hirsch (auth), Private affinities & public users, Arts Mag, Vol 40, No 7; John Perraeult (auth), Systematic painting, Artforum, 11/66; Lucy Lippard (auth), Peverse perspectives, Art Int, 3/67. Mailing Add: PO Box 114 Sagaponack NY 11962

WILLIAMS, RANDALPH ANDREW
EDUCATOR, PAINTER
b New York, NY, Apr 30, 47. Study: New York Univ, BS(art educ), 70; Concordia Col, Sir George Williams Univ, Montreal, Que, Can, MA(art educ), 72. Work: New York State Off Bldg, Harlem; The City of New York Art Collection. Comn: Dance sculpture, comn by Rika Burnham for Helen Adams, Shelia Kaminisky & Danie Co, 77. Exhib: Sir George Williams Univ, Montreal, 71; Henry St Settlement, New York, 75; Whitney Counterweight, James Yu Gallery, Soho, NY, 77; Goddard Riverside, Col Show, 78; one-man shows, Just Above Midtown Gallery, 75, 76 & 77 & Studio Mus, Harlem, NY, 77. Teaching: Instr fel sculpture, Sir George Williams Univ, Montreal, 70-71; art educ, art hist & educ, Metrop Mus of Art, New York, 72- Awards: Workspace for Artists, Painting/Installation, New York Art & Urban Resource Ctr, 77-78. Bibliog: Barbara Cavaliere (auth), Rev, Arts Mag, 2/77; Hilton Kramer (auth), Rev, New York Times, 4/8/77; Linda Bryant & Mary Phillips (auths), Contextures, Just Above Midtown Inc, 3/78. Style & Technique: Painting abstract minimal structures with use of blacks and blues with linean color lines; collages, brown paper bag geometric string collages. Media: Acrylic Paints; Collages. Publ: Ed, Black Creations (inst for Afro-Am Affairs), New York Univ, 72-75. Mailing Add: 219 Bowery New York NY 10002

WILLIAMS, RAYMOND LESTER
PAINTER, INSTRUCTOR
b Lenoir City, Tenn, Nov 10, 26. Study: Chicago Acad of Fine Arts, cert, study with Edgar Whitney, John Pellew, Edmound Fitzgerald & Zolton Zabo. Work: United Tel Co, Bristol, Tenn; Dobyns-Bennett High Sch & Tenn Eastman Co, Kingsport; Carrol Reese Mus & Tipton-Haynes Mus, Johnson City, Tenn. Comn: Hist Landmark paintings, Kingsport Merchants Asn, Tenn, 76. Exhib: Tenn State Mus, Nashville, 73; Atlanta Arts Festival, Ga, 73-74; Va Beach Boardwalk Show, Va, 73-75; Southeastern Art Festival, Winston-Salem, NC, 76-78; Pensacola Art Show, Fla, 75; and many one-man shows. Pos: Graphic artist, Kingsport, 50-74 & painter fine arts, 75-78, Tenn Eastman Co. Awards: First Place Watercolors, Johnson City Sears Show, 72; Best of Show, Jonesboro Days, City of Jonesboro, Tenn, 75; Best of Show, Kingsport Bank Show, Kingsport Art Guild, 75. Mem: Tenn Watercolor Soc (dist dir, 74-75); Atlanta Artist; Tenn Artist; Kingsport Art Gulid (pres, 75-76); Int Soc Artists. Style & Technique: Watercolor all techniques, realistic, impressionistic and semi-abstract landscapes flora and fauna. Mailing Add: 122 E Market St Kingsport TN 37660

WILLIAMS, ROGER
SCULPTOR
b Dayton, Ohio, 1943. Study: Cornell Univ, BArchit, 66; Hunter Col, 66-67. Exhib: Drawing Show, Bennington Col, Vt, 72; David Gallery, Rochester, NY, 72; Allen Ctr Competition, Houston, 73; Sculpture by Roger Williams, Usdan Gallery, Bennington, 73; Janie C Lee Gallery, Houston, 74. Pos: Dir, Art Acad of Cincinnati, 77- Bibliog: Ellen Lubell (auth), rev in Arts Mag, 1/75. Dealer: Andre Emmerich Gallery Inc 41 E 57th St New York NY 10022. Mailing Add: 6300 Park Rd Cincinnati OH 45243

WILLIAMS, TODD
SCULPTOR, PAINTER
b Savannah, Ga, Jan 6, 39. Study: City Col New York; Sch Visual Arts, New York, cert & scholar, 64. Work: Smithsonian Inst, Washington, DC. Comn: Sculpture, Mex Govt, Olympic Village, Mexico City, 68; sculpture, Mary Bethune Towers, New York, 70; wall painting, New York Parks Dept, Livingston & Bond Sts, Brooklyn, 70; sculptures, New York Bd Educ, I S 167, Bronx, 73 & Boys & Girls High Sch, Brooklyn, 75. Exhib: Colored Sculpture, Oakland Art Mus, 65; Witte Mem Mus, Madison, Wis, 66; Cranbrook Acad of Art, Bloomfield Hills, Mich, 66; Books, Boxes & Things, Jewish Mus, New York, 69; Contemp Black Artists, Whitney Mus Am Art, New York, 71; Banners, Nat Mus, Singapore, 76 & Hirshhorn Mus, Washington, DC, 76. Collections Arranged: Colored Sculpture, Am Fedn of Art, 65; Ten Negro Artists from the United States Dakar, Senegal, US State Dept, 65; Small Sculpture from the United States, 71 & Bicentennial Banners, 76, Smithsonian Inst. Teaching: Adj instr sculpture, Brooklyn Col, NY, 73-76; asst prof sculpture, Columbia Univ, New York, 76- Pos: Bd mem, City Walls Inc, New York. Awards: John Hay Whitney Found Fel, 65; J Clawson Mills Fel, Archit League of New York, 66. Style & Technique: Geometric and organic forms in laminated wood and fabricated metals. Media: Mixed-Media. Dealer: Richard Larcada 23 E 67th St New York NY 10021. Mailing Add: 310 Atlantic Ave Brooklyn NY 11201

WILLIAMS, WALTER (HENRY)
PAINTER, PRINTMAKER
b Brooklyn, NY, Aug 11, 20. Study: Brooklyn Mus Art Sch, 51-55; Skowhegan Sch Painting & Sculpture, summer 53; also with Ben Shahn, spring 52. Work: Whitney Mus Am Art, New York; Brooklyn Mus; Nat Gallery Arts, Washington, DC; Riverside Mus, New York; Metrop Mus Art, New York. Exhib: Whitney Mus Ann, 53-63; Int Watercolor Biennial, Brooklyn Mus, 63; Corner, Charlottenborg, Copenhagen, Denmark, 63; Pa Acad Ann, 66; Nat Acad Design 147th Ann, 72. Teaching: Artist in residence, Fisk Univ, 68-69. Awards: John Hay Whitney Found Fel, 55; Nat Inst Arts & Lett Grant, 60; Adolph & Clara Obrig Prize, Nat Acad Design, 72. Bibliog: Cedric Dover (auth), American Negro art, Studio, London, 58; Janet Erickson & Adelaide Sproul (auth), Printmaking Without a Press, Reinhold, 67. Mem: Billed Kunstnernes Forbund, Denmark. Mailing Add: c/o Terry Dintenfass Inc 50 W 57th St New York NY 10019

WILLIAMS, WARNER
SCULPTOR, DESIGNER
b Henderson, Ky, Apr 23, 03. Study: Berea Col; Herron Art Inst; Art Inst Chicago, BFA. Work: Martin Luther King bas-relief portrait, King Mem, Atlanta, Ga; Albert Schweitzer medallion, Schweitzer Mem Mus, Switz; Queen Marie medal, Vienna Diplomatic Acad & Theresianische Acad; Thomas Edison Commemorative Medal, Smithsonian Inst & Edison Mus, East Orange, NJ; Helen Keller medallion, 35 schs for blind, US; plus many other mem, medals, medallions, bas-reliefs & busts. Pos: Resident artist, Culver Mil Acad, Ind, 40-68. Awards: Six awards, Hoosier Salon, 28-42; Award, City of Chicago, 38; Prize, Art Inst Chicago, 41; plus others. Mem: Chicago Art Club; Chicago Art Asn; Hoosier Salon; Nat Sculpture Soc. Mailing Add: Geodesic Dome Studio Culver IN 46511

WILLIAMS, WAYNE FRANCIS
SCULPTOR
b Newark, NY, July 22, 37. Study: Syracuse Univ, BFA, 58, MFA, 62, Chaloner Found fel, 58 & 59; Skowhegan Sch Painting & Sculpture, summer 56-57, with Harold Touish. Work: Ministry Pub Educ Collections, Brussels, Belg; Murdock Collection, Wichita Mus, Kans; Whitney Found Collection, Cornell Univ; Nebr Art Asn, Univ Nebr-Lincoln; NY State Univ Col Albany. Comn: Life size welded sculpture, North Rose Wolcott Sch, NY, 72. Exhib: Belg Salon des Beaux Arts, Mus voor Schone Kunsten, Ghent, Belg, 60; one-man shows, Maynard Walker Gallery, 61 & 64 & Frank Rehn Gallery, New York, 74; New York Art Dealers Exhib, Park Bernet Gallery, New York, 64. Teaching: Instr drawing, Syracuse Univ, 60-63; assoc prof drawing & sculpture, Community Col Finger Lakes, 68- Awards: Louis Comfort Tiffany Found Award for Sculpture, 64. Bibliog: John Canaday (auth), Wayne Williams-Maynard-Walker, New York Times, 10/64; Dorothy Hall (auth), Williams at Rehn, Park East, New York, 4/74; Roberta Olson (auth), Wayne Williams-Rehn, Arts Mag, 6/74. Style & Technique: Figurative, genre and animal subjects; direct metal techniques, welded and formed ferrous and non-ferrous metals. Media: Steel, Copper, Brass. Publ: Auth, The art program at Community College of Finger Lakes, NY State Art Teachers Mag, 5/74. Dealer: John Clancy c/o Frank Rehn Gallery 655 Madison Ave New York NY 10021. Mailing Add: RD 3 Gardner Rd Newark NY 14513

WILLIAMS, WILLIAM TERENCE
PAINTER, EDUCATOR
b Wilkes-Barre, Pa, Nov 13, 41. Study: Wilkes Col, with J Philip Richards, BS(art); Univ RI; Pratt Inst, with Calvin Albert & Arthur Young, MS(art). Work: Pratt Inst, Brooklyn; Slater Mem Mus, Norwich, Conn; Owensboro Area Mus, Ky; Hancock Co Collection, Hawesville, Ky; City Hall of Owensboro. Comn: Riverboat on the Ohio (8 ft x 24 ft mural), Lincoln Fed Savings & Loan, Owensboro, 73, 6 ft x 15 ft mural, exterior of home, 74; Pictures at an Exhibition (multi-media presentation of 850 slides, 20 drawings & 12 paintings), Owensboro Symphony Orchestra, Moussorgsky-Ravel's (videotaped for TV), 74; 8 ft x 9 ft abstract mural, Off foyer, Drs Meister & Blakeman, Owensboro, 75; 9 ft x 10 ft abstract mural, off foyer, Dr Jon Fisher, Dent Arts Bldg, Owensboro, 75. Exhib: 101st Am Watercolor Soc Show & Traveling Exhib, 68-69; Connecticut Realists, Slater Mem Mus, Norwich, Conn, 69; New York Life Ins Co Calendar Show, Grand Cent Art Galleries, New York, 73; Realism 74, Owensboro Arts Ctr, 74; Ky Hist Events Traveling Celebration Art Show, 74-75. Teaching:

Chmn art dept, Fitch Jr High Sch, Groton, Conn, 64-66; instr watercolor, Adult Educ Prog, Groton Sch Syst, 65-66; chmn art, Mitchell Col, New London, 67-70; instr painting, Lyman Allan Mus, New London Art League, Conn, 68-70; asst prof art, Ky Wesleyan Col, 70- Pos: Artist in residence, Hillcrest Inn, Ogunquit, Maine, summer 71. Awards: Patriotic Purchase Award & First Place in Watercolor, Second Ann Ky Arts Exhib, Hancock Co, 74; First Place Purchase Award in Graphics, Bardstown Exhib, Ky, 74; First Place Owensboro Supergraphics Contest, Thompson Homes & Citizens Security Bank, 75. Bibliog: Emery (auth), Contemporary art in America, La Rev Mod, 68. Mem: Owensboro Art Guild (bd mem, 70-72 & 75, pres, 73-74); Soc NAm Artists; Hancock Co Cult Enrichment Comt, Inc (consult, 73-75); Mayor's Art Comn, Owensboro (chmn var subcomts, 73-). Style & Technique: Realistic still life, landscape and figure paintings, drawings and graphics. Media: Watercolor, Oil; Relief, Intaglio. Dealer: Owensboro Arts Ctr 18th St Owensboro KY 42301. Mailing Add: 218 Wilder Dr Owensboro KY 42301

WILLIAMSON, JASON H
PAINTER, ART DEALER
b Bristol, Va, Mar 20, 26. Study: Emory & Henry Col, Va; Vesper George Sch of Art, Boston, Mass, cert. Exhib: Va Intermont Seven State Regional, 51-54; Va State Artists, Richmond, 54, 55 & 74; Am Watercolor Soc, 65, 74-77; Watercolor USA, Springfield, Mo, 63, 72 & 74; Nat Watercolor Soc, 77; South Cent, 71, 72; Tenn Watercolor Soc, Traveling show, 72-75; one-man shows, East Tenn State Univ, Johnson City, 54, Memphis Acad of Arts, Tenn, 60, 67, Emory and Henry Col, Va, 67, Tenn Tech Univ, 73 & Ark Arts Ctr, Pine Bluff, 74 and many others. Comn: Signed and numbered reproduction color prints, comn by Grey Stone Press, Nashville, Tenn. Teaching: Dept head advert art, The Memphis Acad of Art, Tenn, 60-69; pvt classes and workshops, artist watercolor & oil. Pos: Art dir, S E Massengill Co, Bristol, Tenn, 49-56 & Plough Inc, Memphis, 56-58; free lance advert art, Memphis, 58-62; advert art studio head, Williamson—Parker, 62-75; gallery owner, Golden Fleece Art Gallery, Memphis, 70-75 & Carefree, Ariz, 76- Awards: John Young Hunter, Am Watercolor Soc, 74; General Award, Nat Watercolor Soc, 76; Colo Watermedia Award, Rocky Mountain Nat, 77. Bibliog: Watercolor Page, Am Artist Mag, 6/78. Mem: Am Watercolor Soc; Nat Watercolor Soc; Southern Watercolor Soc; Tenn Watercolor Soc (hon lifetime); Memphis Watercolor Group (hon lifetime). Style & Technique: Transparent watercolor plus experimental watercolor both transparent and opaque. Media: Watercolor, Oil. Specialty: Watercolor and oil. Interest: Support many worthwhile art organizations. Dealer: Golden Fleece Art Gallery 42 Easy St Carefree AZ 85331. Mailing Add: PO Box 1943 Cave Creek AZ 85331

WILLIAMSON, MARGARET THOMPSON
See Patch, Peggie

WILLIG, NANCY TOBIN
ART CRITIC
b New York, NY, Aug 31, 43. Study: Syracuse Univ Sch Art, BFA, 65. Pos: Art dir, Buffalo Mag, 65-75, asst ed, 65-69; art critic, Courier Express, Buffalo, 71-77, ed, Sunday Mag, 78-; free lance writer, ArtNews, New York Times & Progressive Archit, currently. Awards: Awards for Ed Content & Visual Content for Buffalo Mag, Am Asn Com Publ, 66-71; Merit Award for Criticism, Am Newspaper Guild, 75. Mem: Hon mem Patteran Soc. Mailing Add: Courier Express 787 Main St Buffalo NY 14240

WILLIS, ELIZABETH BAYLEY
ART HISTORIAN, COLLECTOR
b Somerville, Mass, May 9, 02. Study: Univ Wash, AB, with Lyonel Feininger, Mark Tobey & Morris Graves. Pos: Assoc, Willard Gallery, New York, 43-46; cur, Henry Gallery, Univ Wash, 46-48; cur, San Francisco Mus Art, 48-50; actg asst dir, Calif Palace Legion of Honor, 50-51; consult decorative arts, prod & mkt, Mingei Kan, Tokyo, 51-52; mem UN Tech Asst Bd for Taiwan, Vietnam, India & Morocco, 52-59; consult textile export, India, 55-57. Res: Tribes of India's northeast frontier (1959-1964), especially their arts and textiles; textile arts of India; folk arts of Japan. Collection: Artifacts, pottery and textiles from Tibet, Bhutan, Japan & Morocco, now in the Permanent Collection of the Smithsonian Institution; costumes and textiles from the same countries now in Permanent Collections of the University of Washington and the Washington State Museum; Ming and Ch'ing paintings in a private collection. Mailing Add: 7740 NE North St Bainbridge Island WA 98110

WILLIS, JAY STEWARD
SCULPTOR, INSTRUCTOR
b Fort Wayne, Ind, Oct 22, 40. Study: Univ Ill, Urbana, BFA(sculpture), 61, study with Frank Gallo & Roger Majorweiz; Univ Calif, Berkeley, MA(sculpture), 66, study with Donald Haskin, Harold Paris, Jacques Schnier & Peter Voulkos. Work: Moore Col of Art, Pa; Del Mar Col, Corpus Christie, Tex; Am Tel & Tel, Chicago; Am Inst of Archit, Washington, DC; Home Savings & Loan, Los Angeles. Comn: Multiple Structures, Cirus Ed, 73; sculpture comn by Terry Inch, Los Angeles, 74; sculpture (with Bob Smith), ABC Century City, Los Angeles, 75; sculpture (with Don Brewer), ALCOA, Univ Southern Calif sculpture garden, Los Angeles, 78. Exhib: 17th Exhib of Prints & Drawings, Dallas Mus of Fine Arts, Tex, 67; Nat Drawing Exhib, San Francisco Mus of Art, 70; Metal Experience, Oakland Mus, Calif, 71; Basel Art Festival, Switz, 73-75; Wall Objects, La Jolla Contemp Mus of Art, Calif, 73; Four by Eight, New Port Beach Harbor Art Mus, Calif, 75; Current Concerns...100 plus Current Directions in Southern Calif Art, Los Angeles Inst of Contemp Art, 75 & 77; one-man shows, Fisher Gallery, Univ Southern Calif, Los Angeles (catalogued), 78, Del Mar Col, Corpus Christie, Tex, Cirrus Gallery Ltd, Los Angeles, 72-75 & 78, plus others. Teaching: Instr sculpture, Univ Ariz, Tucson, 66-69; assoc prof sculpture, Univ Southern Calif, Los Angeles, 69- Awards: Hon mention, Nat Sculpture Exhib, Southern Asn Sculptors (traveling show), 67; Purchase Award, Am Drawing 1968, Moore Col of Art, Philadelphia, Pa, 68; Purchase & Hon mention, Am Art Festival, Home Saving & Loan, 70, 73 & 75. Bibliog: Articles in Artweek, 71-73 & 75-78; articles in Artforum, 71, 72 & 78; Art Mag, 4/73. Style & Technique: Conceptual sculptor dealing with illusions utilizing glass, light metal, video and photography. Mailing Add: 3802 S Grand Los Angeles CA 90037

WILLIS, SIDNEY F
PAINTER
b Newark, NJ, Dec 14, 30. Study: Vesper George Sch Art, grad, continued study with Robert D Hunter. Exhib: Southern Vt Artists, 72; Jordan Show, Boston, Mass, 73; Ogunquit Art Ctr, Maine, 74; Am Artists Prof League, New York, 74; Coun Am Artists Show, New York. Teaching: Instr painting & drawing, Vesper George Art Sch, Boston, Mass, 67-69 & Sharon Art Ctr, Peterborough, NH, 65- Awards: Grand Prize, Jordan Show, Boston, 58 & 62; First Prize, Ogunquit Art Ctr, Maine, 61; and many others. Mem: Guild Boston Artists; NH Art Asn; Southern Vt Artists; Am Artists Prof League; Paste Soc of Am. Style & Technique: Contemporary impressionism. Media: Acrylic and Oil. Mailing Add: Box 151 Bennington NH 03442

WILLIS, THORNTON
PAINTER
b Pensacola, Fla, May 25, 36. Study: Auburn Univ, Ala; Univ Southern Miss, Hattiesburg, BS; Univ Ala, MA. Work: Whitney Mus Am Art, New York; Rochester Mem Gallery, NY; Aldrich Mus Contemp Art, Ridgefield, Conn; New Orleans Mus Art, La; CBS Bldg, New York; Exhib: Lyrical Abstraction, Aldrich Mus, 69 & Whitney Mus, 71; New Work, New York, Am Fedn Art, 70-71; Paley & Lowe Inc, New York, 70-72; one-man show, New Orleans Mus Art, 72. Teaching: Instr drawing, Wagner Col, Staten Island, NY, 67-68; artist in residence, La State Univ, New Orleans, 70-71. Awards: Merit Award, Munic Gallery, Jackson, Miss, 65; Hon Mention, Munic Gallery, Birmingham, Ala, 66; Fac Res Grant for Painting, Wagner Col, Staten Island, NY, 68. Bibliog: Richard Lanier (auth), New Work; New York, catalog, Am Fedn Arts, 70; Carter Ratcliff (auth), Reviews-Previews, Art News, 5/71; Ted Calas (auth), Pluralist Tendencies, Art Gallery Mag, 3/72. Style & Technique: Color field expressionist. Media: Plastic, Oil, Acrylic. Dealer: O K Harris Gallery 383 W Broadway New York NY 10012. Mailing Add: 85-87 Mercer St New York NY 10012

WILLIS, WILLIAM HENRY, JR
EDUCATOR
b Boston, Mass, Oct 29, 40. Study: Marlboro Col, VT, BA; Yale Univ, New Haven, Conn, MFA. Pos: Dir admis, The Art Inst of Boston, 67-74, dir, 74-76 & pres, 76- Mailing Add: 88 Marginal St Chelsea MA 02150

WILLSON, ROBERT
SCULPTOR, EDUCATOR
b Mertzon, Tex, May 28, 12. Study: Univ Tex, BA; Univ Bellas Artes, Guanajuato, Mex, MFA; and with Jose Clemente Orozco. Work: Mus Correr, Venice, Italy; Nat Glass Mus, Murano, Italy; Nat Mus, Auckland, NZ; Witte Art Mus, San Antonio, Tex; Lowe Art Mus, Coral Gables, Fla; Univ Tex Art Mus, Austin; McNay Art Inst, San Antonio, Tex; Corning Glass Mus, NY. Comn: Glass sculptures, Harmon Gallery, Naples, Fla, 69; ceramic sculptures, comn by Mrs Robert Hoffman, Naples, 70; glass sculpture doorway, comn by Herbert Martin, Miami, Fla, 72; enamel sculpture, Exec Plaza, Miami, 72. Exhib: Painting & Sculpture Nat, San Francisco Mus Art, 57; Int Glass Sculpture, Venice, Italy, 64, 66, 68, 73 & 76; one man shows, Robert Willson Glass Sculpture, Mus Correr, Venice, 68, Ringling Art Mus, Sarasota, Fla, 70 & Corning Mus Glass, NY, 71; Biennale Exhib, Venice, 72; Int Glass Sculpture, Lowe Art Mus, Coral Gables, Fla, 73; Tex Mus Tour, 78. Collections Arranged: 3500 Years Colombian Art, Lowe Art Mus, 60; Fragments of Egypt, Peoria Art Mus, 69. Teaching: Chmn dept art, Tex Wesleyan Col, 40-48; prof art, Univ Miami, 52-57. Pos: Dir, Coun Ozark Artists, 50-52; pres & dir, Fla Craftsmen, 52-58. Awards: Nat Hon Mention for Sculpture, San Francisco Mus Art, 57; Shell Co Fund Grants for Glass Sculpture, 71 & 73; Fla State Grand Medal Award Winner for Sculpture, Garden Mod Art, Miami, 72. Bibliog: Roland Fleischer (auth), Some recent experiments in glass, 65 & Paul Perrot (auth), Robert Willson—sculptor in glass, 69, Col Art J; Frank Wills (auth), Robert Willson glass sculpture, Mnemosyne, 68. Mem: Col Art Asn Am; Am Asn Mus. Style & Technique: Abstracted symbolism and American Indian visual forms. Media: Glass, Ceramic, Porcelain, Watercolor. Res: History of glass as sculpture; history of ceramic sculpture. Publ: Ed, Kress Collection, 61 & auth, Art concept in Clay, 67, Univ Miami; auth, College-level Art Curriculum in Glass, Dept Health, Educ & Welfare, 68. Dealer: Galerie 99 1135 Kane Concourse Bay Harbor Island Miami FL 33154; Harmon Art Gallery 1258 Third St S Naples FL 33940. Mailing Add: 1127 Cedar Elm Dr San Antonio TX 78230

WILMARTH, CHRISTOPHER MALLORY
SCULPTOR, DRAFTSMAN
b Sonoma, Calif, June 11, 43. Study: Cooper Union, BFA, 65. Work: Mus Mod Art, New York; Philadelphia Mus; Art Inst Chicago; Woodward Found, Washington, DC; Metrop Mus, New York. Exhib: Whitney Ann, Whitney Mus Am Art, New York, 66, 68 & 70; one-man shows, Graham Gallery, New York, 68, Paula Cooper Gallery, New York, 71 & 72, Wadsworth Atheneum, Conn, 74 & St Louis Mus, 75; Am Ann, Art Inst Chicago, 72; Grey Art Gallery, New York; plus others. Teaching: Adj prof sculpture, Cooper Union, 69-; vis critic sculpture, Yale Univ, 71-72. Awards: Nat Coun Arts Grant, 69; Guggenheim Mem Fel, 70-71; Howard Found Fel, 72. Bibliog: Joseph Masheck (auth), rev in, Artforum, 6/72; Hilton Kramer (auth), rev in New York Sunday Times, 12/8/74 & 1/20/78; Kate Linker (auth), rev in, Arts Mag, 4/75. Media: Glass, Steel, Paper. Mailing Add: PO Box 203 Canal St Sta New York NY 10013

WILMERDING, JOHN
ART HISTORIAN, CURATOR
b Boston, Mass, Apr 28, 38. Study: Harvard Col, AB, 60; Harvard Univ, AM, 61 & PhD, 65; also Am art with Benjamin Rowland. Collections Arranged: Nineteenth Century America: Painting & Sculpture, Metrop Mus Art, New York, 70; The Art of Fitz Hugh Lane, Farnsworth Art Mus, Rockland, Maine, 74; The Natural Paradise, Painting in America 1800-1950, Mus Mod Art, New York, 76; American Marine Painting, Va Mus Fine Arts, Richmond, 76; 100 American Drawings from the J D Hatch Collection, Nat Gallery of Ireland, 76. Teaching: Leon E Williams Prof of Am art, Dartmouth Col, Hanover, NH, 65-77; vis lectr Am art, Yale Univ, New Haven, Conn, 72; vis prof Am art, Harvard Univ, Cambridge Mass, 76. Pos: Vpres, Shelburne Mus, Vt, 66-; trustee, Wyeth Endowment for Am Art, Boston, 66- & Found for Art Educ, New York, 75-; cur of Am art & sr cur, Nat Gallery of Art, Washington, DC, 77- Awards: Humanities Fac Develop Grant, Dartmouth Col, 70-71; Guggenheim Found Fel, 73-74. Mem: Am Studies Asn; Col Art Asn (mem ed bd, art bull, 76-80). Res: Luminist painting, drawing and photography; John F Peto; the late work of Eakins. Publ: Auth, A History of American Marine Painting, Little, Brown & Co, 68; auth, Robert Salmon, Painter of Ship & Shore, Boston Pub Libr, 71; auth, Fritz Hugh Lane, 71 & Winslow Homer, 72, Praeger; auth, American Art, Pelican/Penguin, 76. Mailing Add: Cur of Am Art Nat Gallery of Art Washington DC 20565

WILMETH, HAL TURNER
ART HISTORIAN, PAINTER
b Lincoln, Nebr, July 9, 17. Study: Kansas City Art Inst, with Thomas Hart Benton, BFA; Univ Chicago, with W Middeldorf & O Von Simson, MA; Univ Degli Studii, Florence, Italy, with Longhi & Salmi. Work: Univ Okla. Teaching: Instr art hist, Univ Nebr, 48-54; dean students, art hist & humanities, Calif Col Arts & Crafts, 55-60; chmn dept art hist, Dominican Col, 61- Pos: Dir, Gumps Art Gallery, San Francisco, 54-60. Awards: Fulbright Grant, Italy, 49-51. Mem: Am Asn Univ Prof; Col Art Asn. Mailing Add: 96 Half Moon Rd Novato CA 94947

WILSON, ALDEN CHANDLER
ARTS ADMINISTRATOR
b Morgantown, WVa, Feb 23, 47. Study: Colby Col, BA. Pos: Exec dir, Maine Comn Arts & Humanities, 74- Mem: Assoc Coun Arts; Nat Assembly State Art Agencies; New Eng Found for the Arts (pres). Mailing Add: Clifford Round North Edgecomb ME 04556

WILSON, BEN
PAINTER, LECTURER
b Philadelphia, Pa, June 23, 13. Study: Nat Acad Design, 31-33; City Col New York, with Eggers, BSS, 35; Acad Julien, Paris, France, 53-54. Work: Everhart Mus, Scranton, Pa; Fairleigh Dickinson Collection Self Portraits; Norfolk Mus, Va; Faberge Collection, Ridgefield, NJ; Almeras Collection, Paris. Exhib: Riverside Mus, 55; Newark Mus, 56, triennial, 61; nine exhibs, Montclair Mus, 56-72; Everhart Mus, 65 & 66; NJ Pavilion, New York World's Fair, 65-66; one-man show, Bergen Community Mus, 74. Teaching: Instr painting & drawing, City Col New York, 46-48; instr life drawing, Jamesine Franklin Sch Art, 50; lectr mod art, NY Univ, 62-68; instr, Art Ctr of Northern NJ, 65-68. Pos: Art critic, TAO, 76-77. Awards: Agnes B Noyes Award for Watercolor, 59 & Skinner Award for Abstract Oils, 63, Montclair Mus; Ford Found Resident Artist, Everhart Mus, 65. Bibliog: Bugatti (auth), International Encyclopedia of Artists, Univ Europa, 70-71. Mem: Mod Artists Guild (vpres, 63); Assoc Artists NJ. Style & Technique: Abstract constructivist. Media: Oil. Publ: Auth, Cobra, Artists Proof, 66. Dealer: Galerie A G rue de l'universite, Paris, France. Mailing Add: 596 Broad Ave Ridgefield NJ 07657

WILSON, CARRIE LOIS
GALLERY DIRECTOR, LECTURER
b Philadelphia, Pa, Sept 15, 44. Study: Barnard Col, Columbia Univ, BA(art hist), 66; philosophy of Aesthetic Realism with its founder, Eli Siegel, 69- Teaching: Consult, The Kindest Art, Aesthetic Realism Found, 72- Pos: Co-dir, Terrain Gallery, 72- Specialty: Contemporary American prints, drawings and paintings; exhibitions showing that the Aesthetic Realism of Eli Siegel is true. Mailing Add: c/o Terrain Gallery 141 Greene St New York NY 10012

WILSON, CHARLES BANKS
PAINTER, LITHOGRAPHER
b Springdale, Ark, Aug 6, 18. Study: Art Inst Chicago, lithography with Francis Chapin, painting with Louis Ritman & Boris Anisfeld & watercolor with Hubert Ropp. Work: Metrop Mus Art, New York; Corcoran Gallery Art, Washington, DC; Gilcrease Inst Am Hist & Art, Tulsa, Okla; US Capitol Speaker's Gallery; Smithsonian Inst, Washington, DC. Comn: 50 Watercolors, Ford Motor Co, 51-69; oil mural, comn by J D Rockefeller, Jr, Jackson Lake Lodge, Wyo, 55; portraits of Thomas Gilcrease, Gilcrease Inst Am Hist & Art, 57, Will Rogers, Okla Press Asn, Oklahoma City, 61, Sen Robert Kerr & Jim Thorpe; rotunda murals, Okla State Legis, 63; rotunda murals, Okla Capitol, 76. plus others. Exhib: Int Watercolor Exhib, Art Inst Chicago, 39; Am Watercolor Exhib, Springfield, Mo, 70; some 200 nat & regional exhibs. Teaching: Head art, Northeastern Okla Agr & Mech Col, 47-60. Awards: Gov's Art Award, 76; Distinguished Serv Citation, Univ Okla, 76; Okla Hall of Fame, 77. Bibliog: An Indian party, Collier's Mag, 7/42; Hold before the young, Okla Today, 69; Painting mural portraits, Am Artist, 11/69; Names We Never Knew (TV film documentary), 74. Style & Technique: Representational. Media: Egg Tempera, Oil. Publ: Illusr, Treasure Island, 48, Company of Adventures, 49, Mustangs, 52 & Geronimo, 58; auth, Indians of Eastern Oklahoma; plus others. Mailing Add: 100 N Main St Miami OK 74354

WILSON, DAVID PHILIP
PORTRAIT PAINTER
b Monongahela, Pa, Aug 12, 09. Study: Carnegie Inst Technol Col Painting & Design, BFA; Child-Walker Sch Art, scholar in portrait painting with Charles Hopkinson. Work: Ohio Hist Mus, Wapakoneta; State Capitol Collection, Austin, Tex; Ohio State Capitol Bldg, Columbus; also in pvt collections of business & pvt individuals. Comn: Portraits of Potter Stewart & Harold Burton (Supreme Court Justices), twelve col presidents, dozens of deans of Ohio State Univ, Trinity Univ & others, numerous surgeons & med men incl Dr Zollinger, Dr Meiling, Dr Klassen & Dr Von Haam, Neil Armstrong & John Glenn, President L B Johnson, seven Ohio governors, Anchor Hocking Glass execs Gushman & Hetzel, Miles Labs pres George Orr, Arch Moore (WVa gov), six chmn of Youngstown Sheet & Tube, Paul G Benedum of Pittsburgh, John McConnell of Worthington, Ind, three dirs of Battell Mem Inst, Columbus, Ohio, Douglas Mansfield (publ), A G Loos, chmn of Loos Co, Conn, & numerous others. Exhib: New Directions, Carnegie Mus, Pittsburgh; Art Inst Chicago All Am Show & Nat Traveling Exhib; Cleveland Mus Art May Shows, 46 & 47; also numerous private shows. Teaching: Instr compos, Cleveland Inst Art, 46-48; artist in residence portrait painting, Trinity Univ, 63-68. Mem: Coppini Acad Fine Arts, Tex; Chagrin Falls Art Asn, Ohio (pres-founder, 47-49). Style & Technique: Realistic with particular attention to individuals' color, characteristics, and spirit. Media: Oil, Pastel. Dealer: Harmon Gallery 1258 Third St S Naples FL 33940; Sigoloff Gallery San Antonio TX. Mailing Add: 340 West Ave Naples FL 33940

WILSON, EDWARD N
SCULPTOR, EDUCATOR
b Baltimore, Md, Mar 28, 25. Study: Univ Iowa, BA & MA; Univ NC. Work: Howard Univ; State Univ NY Binghamton; plus numerous pvt collections. Comn: JFK (park design & sculpture), City of Binghamton & Sun Bull Fund, NY, 66-69; Second Genesis (aluminum sculpture), City of Baltimore for Lake Clifton Sch, Md, 70-71; Mem in bronze, Harlem Commonwealth Coun, 72; Middle Passage (concrete & bronze), City of New York, Brooklyn, 73-75; stainless steel & bronze sculpture, Ralph Ellison Libr, Oklahoma City, 75. Exhib: NC Mus Art, Raleigh, NC, 55, 61 & 62; 155th Ann Exhib Am Painting & Sculpture, Pa Acad Fine Arts & Detroit Inst Arts, 60; Am Negro Art, Univ Calif, Los Angeles, 66, Univ Calif, Davis, 66, San Diego & Oakland, Calif, 67; Artists of Cent New York, Munson-Williams-Proctor Mus, 66-68; 30 Contemporary Black Artists, nat circulated, 68-70; 200 Yrs Black Am Art, nat circulated, 76-77; JFK Mem Maquettes Collection, San Francisco Mus, 77. Teaching: Prof sculpture, State Univ NY Binghamton, 64-, chmn dept art & art hist, 68-72. Pos: Resident artist, Humanities Div, Western Mich Univ, 69. Awards: Award for Sculpture, Md Artists 24th Ann, Baltimore Mus Art, 56; Purchase Prize for Sculpture, New Vistas in Am Art, Howard Univ, 61; Fel, State Univ NY, 66-68. Bibliog: Cedric Dover (auth), American Negro art, NY Graphic Soc, 60; Art & rebuttal, Christian Sci Monitor, 4/21/71; H Hope (auth), article in, Art J, spring Vol 31, No 3. Mem: Col Art Asn Am (bd dirs, 70, secy & chmn artists comt, 71-); State Univ NY- Wide Comt Arts. Publ: Auth, Contemporary sculpture: some trends & problems, 63; auth, Statement, Arts in Soc, fall-winter, 68-69; auth, CAA & Negro colleges, Art J, winter 68-69. Mailing Add: Dept of Art & Art Hist State Univ of New York Binghamton NY 13901

WILSON, GEORGE LEWIS
PAINTER
b Windsor, NC, Sept 30, 30. Study: Art Inst, Pittsburgh, Pa; Sch Visual Arts, New York; Nat Acad Sch Fine Art, New York. Work: Johnson Publ, Inc, Chicago; Howard Univ, Washington, DC; Bowie State Col, Md; Clinica Limonar, Malaga, Spain. Comn: Portrait of Msgr Hart, comn by Our Lady of Lord Church, New York, 62; portrait of J R Jones, comn by Carver Dem Club, NY; 2 oil paintings, comn by Pub Sch 186, NY, 64; 2 oil paintings, comn by NY-Long Island Libr, West Middle Island, 66; portrait of Bishop Nichols, comn by Salem Methodist Church, New York, 69. Exhib: One-man shows, Depicting our Youth, Fisk Univ, Nashville, Tenn, 64, Recent Exhib, Hudson Guild, New York, 68 & Schenectady Mus, NY, 76; Allied Artists Am Ann, Nat Acad, New York, many times; Mainstream, Marietta Col Int, 70-71; Contemporary, Springville Mus Ann, Utah, 74 & 76; Bronx Mus Ann, New York, 75, 76 & 77; Lever House, 78. Collections Arranged: Contemporary Black Artists, Oakland Mus, 66; Afro-American Exhib, Brooklyn Mus, 68; Harlem Contemporaries, Studio Mus, Harlem, 68. Awards: Emily Lowe Competition Award, Joe & Emily Lowe Found, 63; travel grant, Washington Sq Outdoor Art Exhib, Inc, 71; First Prize for Figure Painting, Atlantic City Boardwalk, 74 & 76. Bibliog: Lindsay Patterson (auth), Negro in Mus & Art, Publ Co Inc, 67; Herbert Temple (auth), Perspectives, Johnson Publ, 73. Mem: Bronx Coun Arts. Style & Technique: Post impressionist; spontaneous; youthful subjects. Media: Oil, Pastel. Dealer: Smith-Mason Gallery 1207 Rhode Ave NW Washington DC 20005. Mailing Add: 4197 Park Ave Bronx NY 10457

WILSON, HELEN J
TAPESTRY ARTIST, SCULPTOR
b Salina, Kans. Study: Univ Ore, BA; Col Arts & Crafts, Oakland, Calif; Univ Calif, Berkeley. Work: Utah State Univ, Logan; Sheldon Mus, Univ Nebr-Lincoln. Exhib: Mus NMex, Santa Fe, 65; Fiber, Clay & Metal, St Paul, Minn, 66; Nat, Regional Merit Award Winners, Mus Contemp Crafts, New York, 67; one-woman show, Hopkins Ctr, Dartmouth Col, 68 & Stanford Univ, 77. Delgado Mus, New Orleans, La, 72. Teaching: Hon lectr weaving tapestry, Univ Calif, Davis, 66 & New Orleans Weaver's Guild, 72; hon lectr textile construct, Univ Colo Fine Arts Dept, 69-70; lect & workshop, Stanford Univ, 77. Awards: Best of Show, Colo Artist Craftsmen, 65 & Mus NMex, 65; Nat Merit Award, Am Craftsmen Coun, 66. Bibliog: Duncan Pollack (art critic), article in Rocky Mountain News, 70; Paul Soldner (auth), rev, 71 & George Woodman (auth), rev, 6/75, Craft Horizons. Mem: Rogue Valley Weaver's Guild; Colo Artist Craftsmen. Style & Technique: Fabric collage tapestry; handwoven loom tapestry; off-loom constructions; fiber sculpture. Dealer: Hill's Gallery 110 W San Francisco Santa Fe NM 87501. Mailing Add: 1495 Woodland Dr Ashland OR 97520

WILSON, JANE
PAINTER
b Seymour, Iowa, Apr 29, 24. Study: Univ Iowa, BA & MA. Work: Mus Mod Art, New York; Whitney Mus Am Art, New York; Wadsworth Atheneum, Hartford, Conn; NY Univ; Rockefeller Inst, New York; plus many others. Exhib: Whitney Mus Am Art, New York, 63 & 68; Smithsonian Traveling Exhib, 68; Newport Festival Art, 68; Univ Iowa, 69; Finch Col, NY, 69; plus many others. Teaching: Instr art hist, Pratt Inst, 67-69. Awards: Tiffany Grant, 67. Mailing Add: c/o Graham Galleries 1014 Madison Ave New York NY 10021

WILSON, JOHN
PAINTER, PRINTMAKER
b Boston, Mass, Apr 14, 22. Study: Sch Mus Fine Arts, Boston, dipl; Tufts Univ, BS(educ); Fernand Leger's Sch, Paris; Inst Politecnico, Esmeralda Sch Art & Escuela Artes del Libro, Mexico City. Work: Mus Fine Arts, Boston; Smith Col Mus Art, Northampton, Mass; Mus Mod Art, New York; Atlanta Univ, Ga; Dept Fine Arts, Govt France. Exhib: Master Prints from the Mus Collections, Mus Mod Art, New York, 49; Young Am Painters, Metrop Mus Art, New York, 50; Mus Int Biennial Color Lithography, Cincinnati, Ohio, 53; Afro-American Artists, Mus Fine Arts, New York & Boston, 70; Highlights from Univ Collection, High Mus Art, Atlanta, Ga, 73. Teaching: Teacher art, New York Bd Educ, 59-64; assoc prof art, Boston Univ, 64- Awards: Boston Mus Sch Travel Fel, James William Paige, 46; John Hay Whitney Fel for study in Mex, 50; Best Cover Design, Int Fedn Periodicals Press, Paris, 71. Mem: Elmo Lewis Sch Fine Arts, Inc, Boston (bd dirs). Style & Technique: Figurative, realist. Media: Oil, Pastel, Lithography, Etching. Publ: Co-illusr, New Worlds of Reading, Harcourt, 59, American Negro Art, Graphic Soc, NY, 60, Who Look at Me, Crowell, NY, 69, 17 Black Artists, Dodd Mead Co, New York, 71 & Land of Progress, Ginn, 75. Mailing Add: 44 Harris St Brookline MA 02146

WILSON, MARTHA STOREY
MIXED-MEDIA ARTIST, MUSEUM DIRECTOR
b Philadelphia, Pa, Dec 18, 47. Study: Wilmington Col, Ohio, BA; Dalhousie Univ, Halifax, NS, Can, MA & studies for PhD. Exhib: Circa 7500 (traveling exhib of women conceptual artists), 73-74; Autogeography, Downtown Whitney Mus Am Art, New York, 75; Four Evenings, Four Days, Whitney Mus of Am Art, New York, 76. Teaching: Lectr lit, NS Col of Art & Design, 72-74; lectr 20th century art, Brooklyn Col, NY, 75. Pos: Exec dir, Franklin Furnace Archives Inc, 76- Bibliog: Lucy R Lippard (auth), Six Years: The Dematerialization of the Art Object, Praeger, 73; Lucy R Lippard (auth), From the Center: Feminist Essays on Women's Art, Dutton, 76. Mem: Col Art Asn; Gallery Asn NY State. Style & Technique: Performance, videotape, written texts, photographs and slides. Media: Mixed-Media. Publ: Auth, TruckFuckMuck, 75 & The Arnotated Alice, 76, privately publ. Mailing Add: 112 Franklin St New York NY 10013

WILSON, MAY
SCULPTOR
b Baltimore, Md, Sept 28, 05. Work: Whitney Mus Am Art, New York; Baltimore Mus; Goucher Col, Baltimore; Corcoran Gallery Art, Washington, DC; Dela Banque de Pariset, Brussels, Belg. Exhib: New Idea, New Media Show, Martha Jackson Gallery, New York, 60; Mus Mod Art Traveling Assemblage, New York, 62; Am Fedn Arts Patriotic Traveling Show, New York, 68; Human Concern Show, 69 & Whitney Sculpture Ann, 70, Whitney Mus Am Art. Awards: Baltimore Mus Art Show Awards, 52 & 59. Bibliog: Bill Wilson (auth), Grandma Moses of the underground, Art & Artists, 5/68; Woo who? May Wilson (film), Amalie Rothschild, 70; May Wilson (videotape), Lee Ferguson, 7/14/71. Style & Technique: Assemblages of junk material painted over with one color. Mailing Add: 208 W 23rd St New York NY 10011

WILSON, MORTIMER, JR
PAINTER, ILLUSTRATOR
b Jan 10, 06. Study: Art Students League, with George Bridgeman & Frank V DuMond, 24-29. Work: Paintings are in many pvt collections. Comn: Portrait of Mrs Michael Pulitzer & son. Exhib: Pa Acad Fine Arts; Obrien's Art Emporium, Scottsdale, Ariz, 75 & 77. Bibliog: Barbara Cortright (auth), article in Am Artist, 75. Mem: Soc Illusr. Style & Technique: Portrait and genre paintings. Publ: Illustrations appeared with writings of Frans Werfel, Louis Bromfield, Ursula Parrot, Ben Hecht, Paul Gallico, G R Wylier & others. Mailing Add: Box 353 Tubac AZ 85640

WILSON, NICHOLAS JON
PAINTER
b Seattle, Wash, June 7, 47. Work: Walter Bimson Collection Western Art, Phoenix, Ariz; Okla Cowboy Hall of Fame, Oklahoma City. Exhib: C M Russell Exhib & Auction, Great Falls, Mont, 72-74; Safari Club Exhib, Las Vegas, Nev, 73; Royal Western Watercolor

Competition, Cowboy Hall of Fame, 74 & 75; Nat Acad Western Art, 74 & 75; Kansas City Soc Western Art, Mo, 75; Soc Animal Artists Exhib, Westport, Conn, New York & Oklahoma City, 78; Audubon Soc-Eastman Kodak Co Wildlife Exhib, New York, 78. Pos: Cur exhib, Ariz-Sonora Desert Mus, Tucson, 70-72. Bibliog: Adina Wingate (auth), Nick Wilson: Wildlife Artist, SW Art Mag, 4/74; Wildlife Artist Nick Wilson, article in Outdoor Am, 6/77. Mem: Soc Animal Artists. Style & Technique: Defined realism done in opaque watercolor on board with close detail scratched out of surface with an engraver's tool. Media: Gouche; Stone Lithography. Publ: Illusr, The Chukar Partridge, Nev Fish & Game, 69. Dealer: Mill Pond Press Inc 204 S Nassau St Venice FL 33959. Mailing Add: 1708 S Magnolia Ave Tucson AZ 85711

WILSON, RICHARD BRIAN
PAINTER, INSTRUCTOR
b Wichita, Kans, June 12, 44. Study: Calif State Univ, San Jose, BA & MA. Work: Downey Art Mus, Calif; San Jose Univ Art Mus, Calif; Cabrillos Col, Aptos, Calif. Exhib: Contemp Calif Artists, travel show, Calif Arts Comn, 69-70; Looking West, Joslin Art Mus, Omaha, Nebr, 70; Northwest Printmakers 41st Int, Seattle, Wash, 70; Drawings, 1st Ann Nat, St Johns Univ, New York, 70; one-man show (paintings), Reed Col Art Mus, Portland, Ore, 73. Teaching: Instr art, Shasta Col, Redding, Calif, 68- Awards: Third Prize (painting), 1st Ann Grand Galleria Nat Art Show, 72; Purchase Prize, 15th Printing Ann, Downey Mus, 72; Second Prize (painting), 5th Ann North Valley Art Show, Redding, 73. Bibliog: Thomas Albright (auth), Impressive look West, 11/29/70 & Old tradition revitalized, 6/8/74, San Francisco Chronicle; Henry J Seldis (auth), Wilshire district/art walk, Los Angeles Times, 10/1/71. Style & Technique: Chromatic abstraction; acrylic emulsion sprayed onto sized canvas. Media: Painting; Drawing. Mailing Add: c/o Hank Baum Gallery Three Embarcadero Ctr San Francisco CA 94111

WILSON, ROWLAND BRAGG
CARTOONIST
b Dallas, Tex, Aug 3, 30. Study: Univ Tex, BFA, 52; Columbia Univ, 52-54. Pos: Freelance cartoonist, New York, 52-54 & 57-; animation cartoonist, Keitz & Herndon, Dallas, 54; art dir, Young & Rubicam, New York, 57-64; daily comic strip, Noon, 67-; resident designer, Richard Williams Animation Ltd, 73-75. Awards: First Prize Com, 3rd Int Animation Festival, 75; Bronze Lion Award, Venice Animation Festival, 75; Grand Prix, Irish Animation Festival, 75; plus others. Publ: Auth, The White of Their Eyes, 63; illusr, Bigger Than a Breadbox, 67, Tubby & the Lantern, 72 & Tubby & the Poobah, 72. Mailing Add: c/o Phil Kimmelman & Assoc 65 E 55th St New York NY 10022

WILSON, SYBIL
PAINTER, DESIGNER
b Tulsa, Okla, Mar 20, 23. Study: Art Students League, with Ernest Fiene; Yale Univ Sch Art & Archit, with Josef Albers, BFA & MFA; also with Anni Albers. Work: NY Univ Collection; Univ Ky Collection; Univ Mass Collection; Univ Bridgeport Collection; Chase Manhattan Bank Collection; plus others. Exhib: One-man shows, Grand Cent Mod Gallery, New York, 62 & 65, East Hampton Gallery, New York, 70 & Woods, Gerry Gallery, RI Sch Design, 72; Retinal Art in US Traveling Exhib, 66. Teaching: Prof art, Univ Bridgeport, 54-; adj prof art, RI Sch Design, 70-72. Awards: Am Inst Graphic Arts 50 Best Bks Award, 60. Media: Acrylic. Publ: Ed, Anni Albers: On Designing, Pellango Press, 60. Dealer: East Hampton Gallery 450 W 27th St New York NY 10025. Mailing Add: 66 Rennell St Bridgeport CT 06602

WILSON, TOM MUIR
DESIGNER
b Bellaire, Ohio, Dec 6, 30. Study: WVa Inst Technol; Cranbrook Acad Art, BFA; Rochester Inst Technol, MFA. Exhib: One-man shows, Rochester, NY & Wheeling, WVa, 57, 59 & 61; Boston Art Festival, 61; Photog Exhib, George Eastman House, Rochester, 63; Western NY Ann, Buffalo, 63 & 64; Art of Two Cities, Minneapolis, 65; plus others. Teaching: Prof art & instr photog & graphic design, Minneapolis Sch Art; instr photog, Rochester Inst Technol, assoc prof photog arts, 77-; instr sculpture & design, Nazareth Col, Rochester. Pos: Designer exhib galleries, George Eastman House Mus Photog, 61-62; free lance photogr & graphic designer, New York, Rochester & Minneapolis, 61- Awards: Award for Sculpture, Art Inst Am Inst Architects, 56; Prize, Philadelphia Print Club, 61. Media: Graphic. Mailing Add: Col of Graphic Arts & Photog Rochester Inst of Technol Rochester NY 14623

WILSON, WARREN BINGHAM
EDUCATOR, SCULPTOR
b North Farmington, Utah, Nov 4, 20. Study: Utah State Univ, BS(educ); State Univ Iowa, MFA(sculpture). Work: Utah State Univ, Logan; Utah Capitol Bldg Collection, Salt Lake City; Utah State Fair Asn, Salt Lake City; Brigham Young Univ, Provo, Utah; State Univ Iowa, Iowa City, plus others. Comn: Exterior steel sculpture, Holladay Law Offices, Pocatello, Idaho, 60 & Utah State Training Sch, 62. Exhib: Ann Painting & Sculpture Exhib, Denver Art Mus, 51; Regional Graphics Show, Colorado Springs Fine Arts Ctr, 51; Traveling Show of Utah Artists, Santa Fe Art Mus, 53; Ceramic & Sculpture Exhib, Wichita Art Ctr, 60; Ceramic Conjunction, Brand Art Ctr, Glendale, Calif, 73; one-man show, Traveling Exhib of Wood Sculpture, Western Asn of Art Mus through Western States, 62-64; 20-Year Restrospective, Brigham Young Univ, 70; plus many others. Teaching: Asst prof sculpture & printmaking, Utah State Univ, 49-54; prof sculpture & ceramics, Brigham Young Univ, 54-; vis lectr ceramics, Univ Calif, Davis, 68. Mem: Southwest Regional Assembly of Craftsmen (Utah rep, 61-65); Utah Designer Craftsmen (pres, 63-65); Art Teachers in Higher Educ, Nat Art Educ Asn (Utah chmn, 69-73); Nat Coun on Educ for the Ceramic Arts. Awards: Purchase Award, Ann Fine Arts Exhib, Utah State Inst of Fine Arts & Fine Arts Exhib, Utah State Fair Bd, 52; Fel Resident, Huntington Hartford Found, 61. Bibliog: Articles in Craftsmen of the Southwest, 65; Margaret Ellis (auth), Vessels of the Lord, The New Era, LDS Church, 73; Articles in Primitive Pottery in Provo, Ceramic Monthly, 74. Style & Technique: Rough hewn wood sculpture of figures; abstract compositions of combined thrown sections for ceramic sculpture. Media: Native Fruit Woods, Cherry, Peach; Red Stoneware Clay within Mat Glaze. Mailing Add: 1000 Briar Ave Provo UT 84601

WILSON, WILLIAM HARRY
ART HISTORIAN, CURATOR
b Philadelphia, Pa, Nov 26, 39. Study: Baylor Univ, BA, 64; Pa State Univ, MA, 66; Harvard Univ, PhD, 74. Teaching: Asst prof art hist, Trinity Univ, San Antonio, Tex, 68-69; instr art hist, Univ Mass, Boston, 69-70; assoc prof art hist, Univ Conn, Storrs, 70- Pos: Cur collections, Ringling Mus Art, 77- Mem: Col Art Asn. Res: Seventeenth century Dutch art; history of the graphic arts; history of photography. Publ: Co-auth, Poesia e simboli nel caravaggio, Palatino, 66; auth, An Unpublished Giordano Bozzetto, Harvard Univ, 67; auth, Transformations: a seventeenth century Dutch portrait by Jan de Bray, Benton Mus Bull, 72; auth, The Circumcision, a drawing by Romeyn de Hooghe, Master Drawings, 75; auth, Revolutionary street poster workshop: Boston, spring, 1970, Print Collector's Newsletter, 76. Mailing Add: Ringling Mus Art PO Box 1838 Sarasota FL 33578

WILSON, WILLIAM S, III
ART WRITER
b Baltimore, Md, Apr 7, 32. Study: Univ Va, BA, 53; Yale Univ, MA, 65, PhD, 61. Publ: Auth, Robert Morris: hard questions and soft answers, 69 & Dan Flavin: fiat lux, 70, Art News; auth, John Willenbecher: pyramids and labyrinths, 75 & Ralph Humphrey, 75, Arts; auth, Ralph Humphrey: an apology for painting, Artforum, 77. Mailing Add: 458 W 25th St New York NY 10001

WILSON, YORK
PAINTER
b Toronto, Ont, Dec 6, 07. Study: Cent Tech Sch, Toronto; Ont Col Art. Work: Nat Gallery Can; Nat Mus Art Mod, Paris; Mus Mod Art, Mex; Birla Acad Mus, Calcutta, India; Art Gallery Ont. Comn: Murals, McGill Univ, Montreal, 54, Imp Oil, Toronto, 57, O'Keefe Ctr, Toronto, 59 & Gen Hosp, Port Arthur, 65; mosaic, Carleton Univ, Ottawa, 70. Exhib: New York World's Fair, 39; Carnegie Int, Pittsburgh, Pa, 52; Bienial Sao Paulo, Brazil, 63; Main Gallery, Mus Galliera, 63; one-man show, Bellas Artes, Mex, 69. Awards: Winnipeg Show Award, 56, Baxter Award, Toronto, 60; Can Centennial Medal, 67. Bibliog: Mural (film), Crawley Films, 57; Michael Foytenay (auth), York Wilson (film), Nat Film Bd, 62; Michel Seuphor (auth), York Wilson (catalog), 64. Mem: Royal Can Acad; Ont Soc Artists (pres, 46-49); Can Group Painters (pres, 68). Publ: Illusr, Face at the bottom of the world, Hagiwara Sukitaro Publ, Tokyo. Dealer: Roberts Gallery 641 Yonge St Toronto ON Can; Wallack Galleries 202 Bank St Ottawa ON Can. Mailing Add: 41 Alcina Ave Toronto ON M6G 2E7 Can

WILWERS, EDWARD MATHIAS
EDUCATOR, ILLUSTRATOR
b Chicago, Ill, Feb 4, 18. Study: Drake Univ, BFA; Ohio Univ, MFA; also with Karl Mattern, Yasuo Kuniyoshi & Milford Zornes. Comn: Oil painting, comn by Dr & Mrs Robert Eilers, Merion, Pa, 71; watercolor, comn by Dr & Mrs Sascha Schnittmann, San Jose, Calif, 72; acrylic, comn by Dr & Mrs Harvey Ashmead, Ogden, Utah, 73; watercolor, comn by Dr & Mrs George Pratt, Washington, DC, 74; oil painting, comn by Mr & Mrs Avery Shinn, Russellville, Ark, 75; oil painting, Dr & Mrs Jim Ed McGee, Dardanelle, Ark, 77. Exhib: Kappa Pi Nat Hon Art Fraternity, Nacogdoches, Tex, 63 & Mt Pleasant, Iowa, 65; one-man shows, Saga Gallery, Taos, NMex, 66, Ark Found Fine Arts, Russellville, 67 & Triton Mus Art, San Jose, Calif, 68. Teaching: Prof art & head dept, Ark Tech Univ, Russellville, 60- Pos: Designer, Hutcheson Displays, Inc, Omaha, Nebr, 51-58; illusr, D & H Assoc, Ogden, Utah, 59-60. Mem: Kappa Pi; Nat Coun Art Adminr; Southeastern Col Art Conf; Mid-Am Art Conf. Publ: Illusr, Nuclear Energy Conf (portfolio), 61; illusr, Arkansas Polytechnic College (promotion booklet), 63; illusr, Blanchard Springs Caverns (booklet), US Forest Serv, 66; Dardanelle Reservoir (booklet), US Corp Engrs, 68; illusr, Pleasure Boating on the Arkansas River, Ark Parks & Tour Dept, 70. Mailing Add: Rte 4 Bayou Lane Russellville AR 72801

WIMAN, BILL
PAINTER, EDUCATOR
b Roscoe, Tex, Nov 12, 40. Study: E Tex State Univ, BS; Univ Fla, MFA. Work: Butler Inst of Am Art, Youngstown, Ohio; Okla Art Ctr, Oklahoma City; Witte Mem Mus, San Antonio, Tex; Am Tel & Tel, New York; Mus of Arts & Sci, Evansville, Ind. Exhib: Project S/SW-Younger Am Artists, Ft Worth Art Ctr, Tex, 70; Tex Painting & Sculpture: The 20th Century, Owens Art Ctr, Dallas, Tex, 71; Stuart M Speiser Collection of Photorealism, Witte Mem Mus, San Antonio, 74; Talent: USA, Jacksonville Art Mus, Fla, 76; one-man show, Art Mus of S Tex, Corpus Christie, 76. Teaching: Asst prof painting, E Tex State Univ, 66-71; assoc prof painting, Univ Tex, Austin, 72- Awards: Purchase Awards, Mid-States Art Exhib, Mus of Arts & Sci, Evansville, 71, 10th Monroe Nat Ann, Masur Mus of Art, La, 74 & 38th Ann Midyear Show, Butler Inst of Am Art, 74. Bibliog: Utterback (auth), Tex rev, Artforum, 1/71. Style & Technique: Photo-realist. Media: Oil. Dealer: Hansen Gallery 70-72 Wooster St New York NY 10012. Mailing Add: 3405 Perry Lane Austin TX 78731

WIMBERLEY, FRANK WALDEN
PAINTER, SCULPTOR
b Pleasantville, NJ, Aug 31, 26. Study: Howard Univ, with Lois M Jones, James Wells & James Porter. Work: Mus Mod Art, New York; Storefront Mus, New York. Exhib: C W Post Col, NY, 69; Whitney Rebuttal, Acts of Art Gallery, New York, 71; Hudson River Mus, Yonkers, NY, 71; Seton Hall Univ, NJ, 71; Dutchess Co Col, NY, 72. Mem: Guild Hall, East Hampton, NY. Media: Collage. Mailing Add: 99-11 35th Ave Corona NY 11368

WINCHESTER, ALICE
ART EDITOR
b Chicago, Ill, July 26, 07. Study: Smith Col, BA, 29. Pos: Ed, Mag Antiques, 38-72; temporary cur, Whitney Mus Am Art, 72-74. Mem: Furniture Hist Soc; Am Ceramic Circle; Nat Trust for Hist Preserv; Conn Hist Soc. Res: American decorative arts; American folk art. Publ: Co-ed, Primitive Painters in America 1750-1950, 50; auth, How to Know American Antiques, 51; ed, Antiques Treasury of Furniture & Other Decorative Arts, 59, Collectors & Collections, 61 & Living with Antiques, 63; auth, Versatile Yankee, The Art of Jonathan Fisher 1768-1847, 73; co-auth, Flowering of American Folk Art 1776-1876, 74. Mailing Add: 4 Currituck Rd Newtown CT 06470

WINDEKNECHT, MARGARET BRAKE
FIBER ARTIST
b Alma, Mich, June 27, 36. Study: Univ Mich, BSDes; Memphis State Univ, MEd; study with Ted Hallman, Virginia I Harvey & Else Regensteiner. Work: Carroll B Reese Mus, Johnson City, Tenn; Ark Art Ctr, Little Rock; Tenn State Mus, Nashville; Com Union Bank Collection, Nashville; Cook Industs Collection, Memphis. Comn: Cardweaving, Unitarian Church Elliot Mem, Memphis, 77; loom-controlled, St John's United Methodist Church, Memphis, 78. Exhib: Miss River Craft Show, Brooks Mem Art Gallery, Memphis, 73, 75 & 77; Marietta Col Crafts Nat, Hermann Fine Arts Ctr, Marietta, Ohio, 74; Fiber Structures, Heinz Gallery Mus Art, Carnegie Inst, Pittsburgh, Pa, 76; Superior 77, Tweed Mus of Art, Duluth, Minn, 77; Intent 78—Fabrics, Bruce Gallery, Edinboro, Pa, 78. Awards: Purchase Award, 6th Biennial, Tenn Artist-Craftsmen, 76; Purchase Awards, 9th & 10th Prints, Drawings & Craft Shows, Ark Art Ctr, 76 & 77. Bibliog: C Thilenius (auth), Creative Monk's Belt, Shuttle, Spindle & Dyepot, 77; Burry & Calonius (auths), Weaving, City of Memphis Mag, 78. Mem: Handweavers Guild Am; Am Crafts Coun; Tenn Artist-Craftsman's Asn. Style & Technique: Loom-controlled weaving, cardweaving, off-the-loom fiber techniques, batik, use of all natural fibres. Media: Fiber. Publ: Contribr, Designing for Crafts, Scribners, 75; contribr, Fiber Structures, Van Nostrand Rein, 76; co-auth, Computer Aided Study of Weaving Design, Inst Soc Am, 76; auth, Creative Monk's Belt, HTH Publ, 77; auth, Creative Overshot, HTH Publ, 78. Mailing Add: 5143 Chiswood Cove Memphis TN 38134

WINDROW, PATRICIA (PATRICIA WINDROW KLEIN)
PAINTER, ILLUSTRATOR
b London, Eng, Sept 12, 23; US citizen. Work: Parrish Mus, Southampton, NY. Comn: Mural, Tinker Nat Bank, Setauket, NY, 56 & Port Jefferson, NY, 68; mural, Geide's Inn, Centerport, NY, 64; mural, Franklin Savings Bank, Garden City, NY. 65. Exhib: Allied Artists Am, New York, 69 & 73. Teaching: Pvt instr, 60-; instr, Lincoln Sq Acad, New York, 67-72; instr, Prof Children's Sch, New York, 74- Awards: Frist Prize in Oils for the Kite, Guild Hall Ann Mem Exhib, Easthampton, 57; First Prize for Shrouded Muchacha, Catharine Lorillard Wolfe Club, New York, 68; First Prize for Still Life, Miniature Art Soc New York Ann, 70. Mem: Allied Artists Am. Style & Technique: Representational and super-realism still life; trompe l'oeil; still water seascapes; smooth, meticulous style. Media: Oil. Publ: Illusr, The Long White Road, 57; illusr, My Best Friends are Dinosaurs, 61; auth & illusr, The Beautiful Blacks Coloring Book, Phantom, 70. Dealer: Harbor Gallery Main St Cold Spring Harbor NY 11724. Mailing Add: 71 Thompson Haypath Setauket NY 11733

WINER, DONALD ARTHUR
MUSEUM CURATOR, INSTRUCTOR
b St Louis, Mo, Oct 26, 27. Study: Univ Mo, BS & MA. Collections Arranged: William Singer, Jr Retrospective, 67; Edwin W Zoller Retrospective, 68; Pennsylvania '71; George Hetzel Retrospective, 72; Pennsylvania Heritage, 72; Edward Redfield Retrospective, 73; Jack Bookbinder Retropsective, 74. Teaching: Instr painting, drawing & art hist, Elizabethtown Col, 69- Pos: Cur, Springfield Art Mus, Mo, 54-57; asst dir, Brooks Art Gallery, Memphis, Tenn, 57-59; dir, Montgomery Mus Fine Arts, Ala, 59-62; dir, Everhart Mus Art & Sci, 62-66; cur, Pa Collection Fine Arts, Pa Hist & Mus Comn, 66- Mem: Am Asn Mus; Northeastern Mus Conf; Pa Guild Craftsmen; Mid-State Artists; Gallery Doshi. Style & Technique: Abstract. Media: Ceramics. Res: Pennsylvania painters; pottery of Pennsylvania. Collection: American earthenware, especially slip decorated red ware. Mailing Add: 3112 Schoolhouse Lane Harrisburg PA 17109

WINES, JAMES N
SCULPTOR
b Oak Park, Ill, June 27, 32. Study: Syracuse Univ Sch Art, BA, 55. Work: Albright-Knox Art Gallery, Buffalo; Stedelijk Mus, Amsterdam, Holland; Whitney Mus Am Art, New York; Tate Gallery, London, Eng; Walker Art Ctr, Minneapolis. Comn: Lobby sculpture, Dana Arts Ctr, Colgate Univ, Hamilton, NY, 67; sculpture for mall, State Capitol Bldg, Albany, NY, 68; sculpture for lobby, Treadwell Corp, New York, 68; showrooms, Best Products Co Inc, Houston, 75 & Sacramento, 77; Ghost Parking Lot, Nat Shopping Ctrs, Hamden, Conn, 78. Exhib: Whitney Mus Am Art Sculpture Biennial, New York, 61-67; American Sculpture, Sao Paulo Biennial, Brazil, 63; Pittsburgh Int, 64; American Sculpture, Walker Art Ctr, Minneapolis, 64; International Sculpture, Tate Gallery, London, 65; Columbia Univ, New York, 73; Whitney Mus Am Art, New York, 73; Mus Mod Art, New York, 75; Venice Biennale, Italy, 75; Archit Marginales, Pompidou Ctr, Paris, France, 75; Experimental Archit, CAYC Mus, Buenos Aires, Arg, 77; Illusions of Reality (traveling exhib of eight mus, Australia), 77-78. Teaching: Instr environ art, Sch Visual Art, 65-; instr environ workshop, NY Univ, 65-; instr, NJ Sch Archit, 75-; Mellon prof, Cooper Union, New York, 77- Pos: Dir, Site, Inc, New York, 69-; mem, Arts & Bus Coop Coun, New York, 71-; mem, Fed Design Assembly, Washington, DC, 72; mem arts adv coun, Bicentennial Celebration, Washington, DC, 72; pres, SITE, Inc. Awards: Design in Steel, Iron & Steel Inst, 71; Nat Endowment for Archit, 73; Nat Endowment for Arts Grant, 74. Bibliog: David Sellin (auth), James Wines—Sculpture, Colgate Univ, 66; Judith Goldman (auth), SITE-ations, Art News, 10/75; Gerald Allen (auth), Bringing in the business, Archit Record, 3/77. Publ: Auth, The case for site-oriented art, Landscape Archit, 7/71; auth, Site, Art & Artists, London, 10/71; co-auth, Street art, TA/BK, Holland, 1/72; co-auth, Peekskill melt, Art Gallery, 3/72; auth, The case for the big duck, Archit Forum, 4/72. Dealer: Marlborough Gallery 41 E 57th St New York NY 10022. Mailing Add: 60 Greene St New York NY 10022

WINFIELD, RODNEY M
ARTIST
b New York, NY, Feb 6, 25. Study: Univ Miami, 43; Cooper Union, 44-45. Work: Steinberg Gallery; Wash Univ, St Louis & pvt collections. Exhib: One-man shows, Galerie Creuze, Paris, 50, Martin Schweig Gallery, St Louis; Pope Pius Libr, St Louis Univ; Pallette Bleau, Paris. Exhib: City Art Mus, St Louis. Comn: Three dimensional windows, Shaare Zedec, St Louis, 58; bronze & steel Ark Wall, Temple Israel, St Louis, 62; doors, interior artifacts, Good Samaritan Hosp, Chapel, Mt Vernon, Ill, 68; space window, Washington Cathedral, 73; designer, Apostle Spoons, Franklin Mint. Teaching: Prof art, Maryville Col, 64- Pos: Designer, Emil Frei Assocs, St Louis, 53-; designer, Winfield Jewelry, St Louis, 70- Mailing Add: 4444 Laclede Pl St Louis MO 63108

WING, ROBIN STEWART
ART DEALER, ART ADMINISTRATOR
b Los Angeles, Calif, Feb 17, 47. Study: Calif State Univ, Northridge, 64-71, BA(anthrop), 69, BA(art) BA(art), 71, study with Lance Richbourg, Marvin Hardin, Robert von Sternberg & Walter Gabrielson. Teaching: Instr wildlife art, Wing Gallery, Pierce Col, Woodland Hills, Calif, 77. Pos: Gallery dir-owner, Wing Gallery, Encino, Calif, 75- Bibliog: William G Cotner (auth), Developing an Affirmative Action Program for Wildlife Art, Decor Mag, Com Publ Co, 3/77. Specialty: Wildlife art; introduction of children, through various programs, especially educational programs, to art; emphasis on art in the world around us. Mailing Add: c/o The Wing Gallery 17310 Ventura Blvd Encino CA 91316

WINGATE, ADINA (R)
ART WRITER, LECTURER
b Berkeley, Calif, June 17, 49. Study: Case Western Reserve Univ, Ohio, BA(art hist, cum laude); Cleveland Inst of Art, Ohio. Teaching: Lectr, Univ of Ariz, Tucson, 76- & Corcoran Gallery of Art, Washington, DC, 2/77. Pos: Art writer, Arizona Daily Star, Tucson, Ariz, 73-76; publicist & media coord, Tucson Mus of Art, 76-; freelance art critic, cur & lectr contemp southwestern painting, sculpture, printmaking & photog, 73- Res: Documentation and art criticism pertaining to contemporary American art in the Southwest; interview documentation of living Southwestern painters, sculptors, printmaker and photographers; lecturer on contemporary American Southwestern art. Publ: Auth, articles in Craft Horizon, 74-, Currant, 74-76, Artweek, 74-76 & Artspace, 75-; contribr, Contemporary Artists, St Martins Press, 77. Mailing Add: PO Box 302 Tucson AZ 85701

WINGATE, ARLINE (HOLLANDER)
SCULPTOR
b New York, NY. Work: Syracuse Univ Mus, NY; Nat Mus Stockholm, Sweden; Ghent Mus Belg; Farnsworth Mus, Rockland, Maine; Wichita Univ Mus; Newark Mus; Parrish Mus of Southampton, NY; Guild Hall Mus, East Hampton, NY; Norfolk Mus, Va; Birmingham Mus, Ala; Lawrence Univ Mus, NY; J Walter Thompson Collection; Joseph H Hirshhorn Collection; plus many others incl pvt collections. Exhib: Metrop Mus Art & Whitney Mus Am Art, New York; Wadsworth Atheneum Mus; San Francisco Mus, Calif; Baltimore Mus, Md; plus many others in Paris, France, Belg, Buenos Aires, Arg, London, Eng & US incl five one-man shows. Dealer: Frank Rehn Gallery 655 Madison Ave New York NY 10021. Mailing Add: PO Box 335 East Hampton NY 11937

WINGATE, ROBERT BRAY
ILLUSTRATOR, CURATOR
b Harrisburg, Pa, Sept 21, 25. Study: Lebanon Valley Col, AB, 48; Pa Acad Fine Arts, summer 48; Johns Hopkins Med Sch, MA(art as appl to med), 51; Drexel Univ, MS(libr sci), 60; Sussex Univ, ScD, 71. Pos: Med illusr, Walter Reed Army Med Ctr, Washington, DC, 54-56 & Ophthalmological Found, Inc, New York, 56-60; free lance illusr, 60-; chief rare bks & spec collections, Pa State Libr, Harrisburg, 65- Mem: Life fel Royal Soc Arts, London; affil Royal Soc Med, London; Bibliog Soc Am. Style & Technique: Carbon-dust on stipple board; ink-line; mixed media. Res: History of medicine and medical illustration; history of printing and bookbinding. Publ: Illusr, Berens & King, co-auth, An Atlas of Ophthalmic Surgery, Lippincott, 61; illusr, Fasanella, auth, Modern Advances in Cataract Surgery, Lippincott, 63; illusr, Fasanella, auth, Management of Complication in Eye Surgery, Saunders, 65; illusr, von Noorden & Maumenee, co-auth, Atlas of Strabismus, Mosby, 67, 2nd ed, 73; illusr, King & Wadsworth, co-auth, An Atlas of Ophthalmic Surgery, Lippincott, 70. Mailing Add: 136 Shell St Harrisburg PA 17109

WINKEL, NINA
SCULPTOR, LECTURER
b Westfalen, Ger, May 21, 05; US citizen. Study: Staedel Mus Sch, Frankfurt, Ger. Work: Wall panel, Keene Valley Libr, NY. Comn: Lassiter Mem, Lassiter Family, Charlotte, NC; Early Moravians (wall panels), Hanes Corp, Winston-Salem, NC; War Mem, Seward Park High Sch, New York; Group of Children, City of Wiesbaden, Albert Schweitzer Sch. Exhib: Int Fairmount Park Exhib; Am Acad Arts & Lett; one-man show, Univ Notre Dame, 54; many shows, Nat Acad Design; retrospective, Sculpture Ctr, 72. Teaching: Instr sculpture, Clay Club Servicemen Canteen, 42-46. Awards: E Watrous Gold Medal, 45 & Samuel F B Morse Gold Medal, 64, Nat Acad Design; Bronze Medal, Nat Sculpture Soc, 67-71. Bibliog: Nancy Dryfoos (auth), Nina Winkel, Nat Sculpture Rev, 71. Mem: Fel Nat Sculpture Soc (secy, 65-68); Nat Acad Design; Sculptors Guild; Sculpture Ctr (pres, 70-73, emer pres). Style & Technique: Realistic to semi-abstract, according to subject and intention; welding, modeling and carving techniques. Media: Copper, Terra-cotta. Res: Antiques; Byzantine mosaics. Publ: Auth, var articles on sculpture & mosaics in periodicals. Mailing Add: Keene Valley NY 12943

WINKLER, DIETMAR R
DESIGNER, EDUCATOR
b Loewenberg, Ger. Study: Kunstschule Alsterdamm, Hamburg, Ger; RI Sch Design, Providence; also with Max Mahlmann, Hamburg. Work: Nat Arch, Washington, DC. Comn: Photog & design, Champion Paper, New York, 70; Centennial Symbol, Wellesley Col, 73. Exhib: New England Book Show, 64 & 70; Am Inst Graphic Arts, New York, 67-72; New York Type Dirs Club, 67-75; Typomundus, 70; New York Art Dirs Club, 72. Teaching: Design curric, Simmons Col, 65-73; assoc prof visual design & dir grad prog visual design, Southeastern Mass Univ, 73-76, dean col fine & appl arts, 75-76; prof design & chmn art dept, Inst Design, Ill Inst Technol, 76- Pos: Design dir, Off Publ, Mass Inst Technol, 66-70, design & art dir, WGBH-TV Educ Found, Boston, 70-73; design dir, Harvard Bus Sch, 72-; design consult, Fed Graphics Improvement Prog, Nat Endowment Arts, 73-; design workshop & direction, Univ NH, 75. Awards: Award of Merit & Excellence, Type Dirs Club, 67-72 & 75; Award of Excellence, CA Mag, 68 & 69; Award of Merit, Art Dirs Club, 74. Bibliog: Article in CA Mag, Vol 13, No 4; Objective visual design, recent American developments, Graphis, 73; J J de Lucio-Meyer (auth), Publicity for higher education in the USA, Novum, 7/73. Mem: Am Inst Graphic Arts (bd dirs, 70-72). Style & Technique: Controlled, highly organized hard edged non-objective structures and constructions; animation. Media: Plastic, Video, Film. Publ: Auth, Influencing the design future, Design Quart, 74. Mailing Add: Inst Design Ill Inst Technol 3360 S State St Chicago IL 60616

WINKLER, MARIA PAULA
PAINTER, EDUCATOR
b Krakow, Poland, Oct 24, 45; US citizen. Study: Univ Pa, Philadelphia, BA(art & art hist), study with Karl Umlauf; Pa State Univ, State Col, MFA(painting & drawing), study with Enrigue Montenegro & PhD(art educ), study with Kenneth Beittel. Work: Pa State Univ, State Col; Boise Gallery of Art, Idaho. Exhib: Nat Drawing & Small Sculpture Exhib, Ball State Univ, Muncie, Ind, 70; New York Exhib of Paintings, Sculpture & Graphics, Avanti Galleries, New York, 71; New Generation Drawing, Cheney Cowles Mem State Mus, Spokane, Wash, 73; NMex Int Art Exhib, Clovis, NMex, 76; Int Women's Slide Exhib, sponsored by the Ford Found, New York, 76; Invitational Group Show, Fine Arts Gallery, Univ BC, Vancouver, Can, 77. Collections Arranged: Images of Women, Linda Farris Gallery, Seattle, Wash, 75; West Coast Women's Show, Bau-Xi Gallery, Vancouver, 76; For The Birds, Fine Arts Gallery, Univ BC, Vancouver, 77; Works From Crown Printers & David Shapiro, Artist's Gallery, Vancouver, 77. Teaching: Asst prof art & art educ, Boise State Univ, Idaho, 73-75; asst prof art educ, Univ PC, Vancouver, 75-77 & Calif State Univ, Sacramento, 77- Pos: Tech illusr, Aerojet Gen Corp, Sacramento, 63; vis lectr, Art Dept, Pa State Univ, State Col, 72-73. Awards: Margaret A Fleishman Creativity Award, Univ Pa, 66; Hon mentions, 16th Reg Art Exhib, Art League, Hazeltown, Pa, 69 & NMex Int Art Exhib, Clovis-Portales Art Coun, 76. Bibliog: Patti McCoy (auth), Interview: Maria Winkler-Green, Women Aritst Group of the of the NW News & Media Report to Women, 77. Mem: Nat Art Educ Asn; Nat Art Educ Asn Women's Caucus (treas, 77-); Calif Art Educ Asn (N area higher educ rep, 78-); Sacramento Regional Arts Coun. Style & Technique: Realism and magic realism, figurative works on paper. Media: Mixed-media; Drawing, Acrylic. Res: Research and writings on techniques of teaching art appreciation to teachers and museum volunteers. Publ: Illusr, Art Magic, Impulse and Control, A Guide to Viewing, Prentice-Hall, 73; illusr, Handbook for Student Teaching in Secondary Schools, Boise State Univ, 75; auth, The Curriculum Board Game, Calif State Univ, Sacramento, 77. Dealer: Zara Gallery 553 Pacific Ave San Francisco CA 94133; Linda Farris Gallery 322 2nd Ave Seattle WA 98104. Mailing Add: c/o Art Dept Calif State Univ Sacramento CA 95819

WINNINGHAM, GEOFF
PHOTOGRAPHER
b Jackson, Tenn, Mar 4, 43. Study: Rice Univ, BA(Eng), 65; Ill Inst Technol, MS(photog), 68 with Aaron Siskind. Work: Mus Mod Art, New York; Boston Mus Fine Arts; Mus Fine Arts, Houston; Int Mus Photog, Rochester, NY; Princeton Univ,; Carpenter Ctr, Harvard Univ. Comn: Courthouses of Tex (photographs), Seagrams Co, New York, 75. Exhib: Mus Fine Arts, Houston, 74; Witkin Gallery, New York, 75; Cronin Gallery, Houston, 77. Teaching: Asst prof photog, Univ St Thomas, Houston, 68-69; assoc prof photog, Rice Univ, Houston, 69- Awards: Corp for Pub Broadcasting Award, 72; Guggenheim Found fel, 72; Nat Endowment Arts photog fel, 75 & 77. Bibliog: E A Carmean (ed), Geoff Winningham

Photographs, Mus Fine Arts, Houston, 74. Publ: Auth, Friday Night in the Coliseum, 71; auth, Going Texan, 72. Dealer: Cronin Gallery 2008 Peven St Houston TX 77019. Mailing Add: 2020 Wroxton Houston TX 77005

WINOGRAND, GARRY
PHOTOGRAPHER, LECTURER
b New York, NY, Jan 14, 28. Study: City Col of New York; Columbia Col; New Sch for Social Res, with Alexi Brodovich. Work: George Eastman House, Rochester, NY; Mus Mod Art, New York; Smithsonian Inst, Washington, DC; Libr Congress; Ft Worth Mus of Art, Tex. Comn: The Great Am Rodeo Show (80 photogs), Ft Worth Mus of Art, 76. Exhib: Five Unrelated Photogrs, Mus Mod Art, New York, 63; Towards a New Social Landscape, George Eastman House, 66; New Documents, Mus of Mod Art, New York, 69; Ten Photogrs, Am Pavillion, Osaka World's Fair, Japan, 69; The Animals, Mus Mod Art, New York, 70; one-man shows, Light Gallery, 72 & 75, The Great Am Rodeo Show, Ft Worth Art Mus, 76. Teaching: Instr photog, Inst Design, Ill Inst Technol, Chicago, 71-72; lectr photog, Univ Tex, Austin, 73- Media: 35 mm Black and White Photography. Publ: Auth, The Animals, Mus Mod Art, New York, 70; contribr, Documentary Photography, Time-Life Bks, 72; contribr, 1974 Photography Annual, Time-Life Bks, 74; auth, Women are Beautiful, Light Gallery, 75; auth, Grossmont College Show (catalogue), Grosmont Col Gallery, 76. Dealer: Light Gallery 724 Fifth Ave New York NY 10019. Mailing Add: 1817 E Oltorf No 2053 Austin TX 78741

WINOKUR, JAMES L
COLLECTOR, PATRON
b Philadelphia, Pa, Sept 12, 22. Study: Univ Pa, BS(econ), 43. Pos: Trustee & mem mus art comt, Carnegie Inst, 67-; vpres & gov, Pittsburgh Plan for Art, 67-; fel Mus Art, Carnegie Inst, 68-; trustee & vchmn, Sarah Scaife Found, 72-; art critic, Greensburg Tribune-Rev, 74- Interest: Joseph Goto, Ameriean sculptor in welded steel. Collection: Cobra paintings, drawings and sculpture including Carl-Henning Pedersen, Jorn, Corneille, Alechinsky, Ubac, Reinhoud and others; 20th century American paintings, drawings and sculpture including John Kane, Wines, Sam Francis, Joseph Goto and others; prints from Old Masters to the 20th century. Mailing Add: 5625 Darlington Rd Pittsburgh PA 15217

WINOKUR, PAULA COLTON
CERAMIST
b Philadelphia, Pa, May 13, 35. Study: Temple Univ, BFA, BSEd, 58, with Rudolf Staffel; Alfred Univ, New York, 58. Work: Witte Mus of Art, San Antonio, Tex; Philadelphia Mus of Art; Del Mus of Art, Wilmington; Alberta Potters Asn/Int Ceramic Soc, Switz; Utah Mus of Art, Salt Lake City. Comn: Series of large planters, comn by Ford & Earl Archit Designers, Detroit, First Nat Bank, Chicago, 69; ltd ed patrons plate, Friends Select Sch, Philadelphia, 75. Exhib: Young Americans, Mus Contemp Crafts, New York, 58 & 62; 22nd & 23rd Ceramic Nat, Everson Mus, Syracuse, NY, 62 & 64; Craftsmen USA, Mus of Contemp Crafts, 66; 19th Ann Scripps Col Ceramics Invitational, 66; Ceramics Int, 73, Calgary, Alta, Can, 73; Pa Crafts 74, William Penn Mus, Harrisburg, Pa, 74; Am Crafts Coun & US Info Agency 20 Potters (traveling exhib), 73-77; Contemp Ceramics, William Penn Mus, 74; Baroque 74, Mus of Contemp Crafts, 74; Soup Tureens, 76, Campbell Mus, Camden, NJ, 76; Philadelphia: 300 Yrs of Am Art, Philadelphia Mus of Art, 76; 100 Artists Celebrate 100 Yrs, Fairtree Gallery & Xerox Gallery, 76. Teaching: Lectr ceramics, Philadelphia Col of Art & Beaver Col, Glenside, Pa, 73- Pos: Treas, Philadelphia Coun of Prof Craftsmen, 68-74; state rep, NE Regional Assembly of Am Crafts Coun, 73-77. Awards: Merit Award, Craftsmen USA, Am Crafts Coun, 66; Prize, Ceramics Int 73, Calgary, Alta, 73; Nat Endowment for the Arts Craftsmen's Fel, 76. Mem: Am Crafts Coun; Nat Coun on Educ in Ceramic Arts. Style & Technique: Art nouveau and romantic influences in hand-built porcelain containers; using celadon glazes in reduction atmosphere. Publ: Co-auth, The light of Rudolph Staffel, Craft Horizions, 77. Dealer: Helen Druitt Gallery 1625 Spruce St Philadelphia PA 19103. Mailing Add: 435 Norristown Rd Horsham PA 19044

WINOKUR, ROBERT MARK
CERAMIST, EDUCATOR
b Brooklyn, NY, Dec 24, 33. Study: Temple Univ, BFA, 56 with Rudolph Staffel; NY State Col of Ceramics, Alfred, MFA, 58. Work: Lannan Found, Palm Beach, Fla; Int Acad of Ceramics, Lucerne, Switz; Alberta Potters Asn, Calgary, Alta, Can; Philadelphia Mus of Art, Pa. Comn: Twenty large planters, comn by Ford & Earl Archit Designers, Detroit, Mich; First Nat Bank, Chicago, Ill, 69; coffee pots, Arts/Objects USA, Lee Nordness Galleries, New York, 73, Holy Water Font, comn by Bishop McDevitt, Temple Univ Newman Ctr, 76. Exhib: Young Americans, Mus of Contemp Crafts, New York, 62; 22nd-25th Ceramic Nat, Everson Mus, Syracuse, NY, 62-68; 19th Ann Scripps Col Invitational, Claremont, Calif, 66; Craftsmen 67 & 73, Philadelphia Civic Ctr Mus, 67 & 73; Am Crafts 76, Mus of Contemp Art, Chicago, 76; Philadelphia: 300 Years of Am Art, Philadelphia Mus of Art, 76; Soup Toureens, Campbell Mus, Camden, NJ, 76; Super Mud Masters Show, Hub Gallery, Pa State Univ, 77. Collections Arranged: Container Show, Nat Ceramics & Glass Show, Pa Coun on the Arts Grant, Tyler Sch of Art, Temple Univ, 75. Teaching: Coordr two-deminisional visual design dept, N Tex State Univ, Denton, 58-63; area chmn ceramics, Tyler Sch of Art, Temple Univ, 66- Pos: Proj dir, Philadelphia Ceramic Speakers Consortium, Pa Coun on the Arts in assoc with Tyler Sch of Art, Moore Col & Philadelphia Col of Art. Awards: Fourth Prize, Ceramic Art of the World, Int Acad of Ceramics & Alta Potters Asn, 73; participant, 2nd Int Ceramic Symposium, Nat Endowment for the Arts & Tenn Arts Comn, Gatlingburg, 75. Bibliog: Hahn & Elisari (auths), Clay Artists, doc film, 75; Charlotte Sewalt (auth), An Interview with Robert Winokur, Ceramics Mo, 9/77. Mem: Am Crafts Coun; Nat Coun on Educ in the Ceramic Arts (br dir, 69-70; ed, Speakers Guide, 70; vpres, 72-73; prog chmn, 75); Philadelphia Coun of Professional Craftsmen. Style & Technique: Thrown and assembled off-wheel; selected surfaces drawn upon and painted with slips, engobles and wood ash glazes. Media: Salt-glazed Stoneware. Publ: Auth, The Tyler School of Art of Temple University, Ceramics Mo, 75; co-auth, The light of Rudolph Staffel, Craft Horizions, 77. Dealer: Helen Druitt Gallery 1625 Spruce St Philadelphia PA 19103. Mailing Add: 435 Norristown Rd Horsham PA 19044

WINSHIP, FLORENCE SARAH
ILLUSTRATOR
b Elkhart, Ind. Study: Chicago Acad Fine Arts; Art Inst Chicago. Publ: Illusr, Woofus & Miss Sniff, Santa's Surprise, The Night Before Christmas & The Bird Book; plus many other bks for children. Mailing Add: 1111 Oxford Rd Deerfield IL 60015

WINSLOW, JOHN RANDOLPH
PAINTER, EDUCATOR
b Washington, DC, July 5, 38. Study: Princeton Univ, BA, 60; Yale Univ, BFA, 62 & MFA, 63. Work: New Orleans Mus Art, La; Kemper Ins Group, Chicago. Exhib: New Talent, Conn Acad Fine Arts, New Britain, 68; Eastern Cent Regional Drawing, Philadelphia Mus Art, 70; Am Fedn Arts Drawing Soc, Nat Travel Exhib, 70-71; Figurative Painters, Corcoran Gallery Art, 73-74; Living American Artists & the Figure, Pa State Univ Mus Art, 74. Teaching: Grad instr drawing, Yale Univ Sch Art, 62-63; asst prof painting & drawing, Cath Univ, Washington, DC, 69-74, assoc prof, 74- Pos: Staff artist, New Haven Redevelop Agency, 63-69. Awards: Scholar Award, Yale Univ Sch Art, 61-63; Louis Comfort Tiffany Award for Painting, Louis Comfort Tiffany Found, 64-65; Silvermine Award, New England Ann, Silvermine Guild, 68. Bibliog: John Canaday (auth), Upset by vision & expression in Philadelphia, NY Times, 7/19/70; Benjamin Forgey (auth), Winslow, top of the galleries, Wash Star-News, 1/27/73; Paul Richard (auth), Looking through windows, Wash Post, 1/23/73. Mem: Artists Equity Asn, Washington, DC (1st vpres, 74-). Style & Technique: Figurative, representational. Media: Oil, Canvas. Mailing Add: c/o Studio Gallery 1735 Connecticut Ave NW Washington DC 20009

WINSOR, V JACQUELINE
SCULPTOR
b Nfld, Can, Oct 20, 41; US citizen. Study: Yale Summer Sch Art & Music, 64; Mass Col Art, BFA, 65; Rutgers Univ, MFA, 67. Work: Mus Mod Art, New York; Whitney Mus Am Art, New York; Australia Nat Gallery, Canberra; Detroit Inst Arts, Mich; Mus d'Arte Mod, Paris, France. Exhib: American Women Artists, Hamburg Kunsthaus, Ger, 72; one-woman Shows, Nova Scotia Col Art & Design, Halifax, 72, Contemp Arts Ctr, Cincinnati & San Francisco Mus Art, 76; Va Commonwealth Univ, Richmond, 72; Paula Cooper Gallery, New York, 72; Whitney Mus Am Art Ann of Painting & Sculpture, 73, Recent Acquisitions, 74; plus others. Teaching: Instr art introd & ceramics, Douglass Col, 67; instr art introd, Middlesex Co Col & Newark State Teachers' Col, 68 & 69; instr ceramics, Mills Col Educ, 68 & 71; instr graphics, Loyola Univ, New Orleans, summer 69; instr ceramics, Greenwich House Pottery Sch, New York, 69-72; instr sculpture, Sch Visual Arts, New York, 71 & 75; instr art introd, Hunter Col, 72-75. Awards: NY State Coun on the Arts Grant, 73-74; Nat Endowment for the Arts Grant, 74-75; Matter Award, 74. Bibliog: Grace Glueck (auth), Art notes, New York Times, 5/30/71; Elizabeth Bear (auth), Rumbles, 9/71 & Interview with Jackie Winsor, spring 72, Avalanche; Lucy Lippard (auth), article in Artforum, 2/74; plus others. Dealer: Paula Cooper Gallery 155 Wooster New York NY 10012. Mailing Add: 112 Mercer St New York NY 10012

WINTER, CLARK
SCULPTOR
b Cambridge, Mass, Apr 4, 07. Study: Harvard Univ, AB; Ind Univ, MFA; Fontainebleau Acad Art; Art Students League. Work: Mus Art, Carnegie Inst; Aldrich Mus Contemp Art. Comn: Pittsburgh Hilton Hotel; Hall of Sci, Carnegie-Mellon Univ; Pittsburgh Arts & Crafts Ctr; also pvt comn by Katherine Cornell. Exhib: Am Sculpture Exhib, Metrop Mus Art, 51; Sculpture Ann, Whitney Mus Am Art, 54; San Francisco Mus Art, 54; 3rd Int, Philadelphia Mus Art; Soc Sculptors. Teaching: Instr, Ind Univ, 47-49; head dept sculpture, Kansas City Art Inst, 49-53; vis assoc prof, Univ Calif, Berkeley, 53 & 55; assoc prof sculpture, Carnegie-Mellon Univ, 55-72, emer prof, 72- Mailing Add: 595 Fairhills Dr San Rafael CA 94901

WINTER, GERALD GLEN
PAINTER, EDUCATOR
b Milwaukee, Wis, Sept 1, 36. Study: Univ Wis-Milwaukee, BFA, Madison, MS & MFA. Work: Milwaukee Art Ctr; Lowe Mus, Univ Miami, Coral Gables, Fla. Exhib: Corcoran Biennial of Am Painting, 63; one-man shows, Gordon Craig Gallery, Miami, Fla, 68, Allis Art Libr, Milwaukee, 68, Span Int Pavillion, St Louis, 70, Miami-Dade Community Col, Fla, 75 & Lowe Mus, Univ Miami, 75; 34th & 35th Exhib of Contemp Am Painting, Palm Beach, Fla, 72 & 73; Phases of New Realism, Lowe Mus, Univ Miami, 72; 14th-19th Ann Hortt Mem Exhib, Ft Lauderdale Mus, Fla, 72-77; 33 Miami Artists, Miami Art Ctr. Teaching: Prof & chmn art dept, Univ Miami, 65- Awards: Second Prize, Wis Painters & Sculptors Exhib, Milwaukee Art Ctr, 60; Ford Found Purchase Award, 62; Third Prize, Corcoran Gallery of Art Biennial, 62. Mem: Col Art Asn. Style & Technique: Fantasies, surrealistic subject matter treated in a half realistic, half primitive technique. Media: Oil, Acrylic. Dealer: Joy Horwich Gallery 333 E Ontario St Chicago IL 60611. Mailing Add: 6629 SW 62nd Terr Miami FL 33143

WINTER, H EDWARD
ENAMELIST, WRITER
b Pasadena, Calif, Oct 14, 08. Study: Cleveland Inst Art; Kunstgewerbeschule, Vienna, Austria, with Josef Hoffman & Michael Powolny. Work: Cleveland Mus Art, Ohio; Everson Mus Art, Syracuse, NY; Butler Mus Am Art, Youngstown, Ohio; NY State Col Ceramics Gallery, Alfred; Mus Sci & Indust, Chicago. Comn: Murals (enamel processing), Ferro Corp lobby, Cleveland, 34-35; Flora & Fauna (mural), US Govt Post Off, Cassville, Mo, 41; mural, Alpine Village Restaurant, Cleveland, 51; mural, Crown Filtration Plant, Rocky River, 53; mural, Mott Bldg, Internal Revenue, Cleveland, 64. Exhib: Nat Ceramic, Everson Mus Art, Syracuse, 51; Massillon Mus Art, Ohio, 68; Mansfield Art Mus, Ohio, 69. Teaching: Teacher enameling, Cleveland Inst Art, 35-37 & Old White Art Colony, White Sulphur Springs, WVa, 36. Pos: Adv ed, Design Mag, 75- Awards: First Prize, Cleveland Art Mus, 33; First Prize, Ceramics of Western Hemisphere, Everson Mus, Syracuse, 41; Spec Award, Horace Potter, Cleveland Mus Art, 53. Mem: Western Reserve Hist Soc, Cleveland; Fel Royal Soc Art, London; Am Ceramic Soc. Style & Technique: Decorative, flora and fauna; abstract expressionist; painting, sgraffito, foil inlay, transparent and opaque surfaces on copper, steel, silver and aluminum. Media: Enameling Metals. Publ: Auth, Enamel Art on Metals, 58 & auth, Enameling for Beginners, 61, Watson-Guptill; auth, Enamel Painting Techniques, Praeger, London, 70; contribr, Ceramic Soc Bull, Am Artist Mag, Mag Am Art, London Studio Mag & Popular Ceramics. Mailing Add: 11020 Magnolia Dr Cleveland OH 44106

WINTER, LUMEN MARTIN
SCULPTOR, PAINTER
b Ellery, Ill, Dec 12, 08. Study: Grand Rapids Jr Col; Cleveland Sch Art; Nat Acad Design; also study in France & Italy. Work: Washington Co Mus, Hagerstown, Md; Libr Cong, Washington, DC; Mus of Art in Sport, Madison Sq Garden, New York; Grand Rapids Art Mus, Mich; Kans State Hist Soc; Mus Contemp Art, Dallas; Columbus Mus Arts & Crafts, Ga; Vatican, Rome, Italy; plus many others. Comn: Lady of the Thruways (bronze figure), Knights of Columbus Don Bosco Shrine, Haverstraw on the Hudson, NY, 59; mosaic & bas-relief sculpture for chapels, US Air Force Acad, Colorado Springs, Colo, 60-61; Apollo 13 official medallion for Capt James A Lovell, Jr, Houston, 70; Titans mural (oil on linen), UN, New York, 72; space age mosaic, AFL-CIO Hq Bldg, Washington, DC, 72; 5ft x 40ft bas relief frieze, Gerald R Ford Ctr, Grand Rapids, Mich, 76. Exhib: Nat Acad Design, New York; Int Color Lithography, Cincinnati Art Mus, 44; Am Fedn of Art; Nat Soc of Mural Painters; Am Watercolor Soc Ann & Traveling Shows, 50-; Int Watercolor, Pa Acad Fine Arts, Philadelphia, 51; Geneva, Switz, 55; plus others. Pos: Vpres, Archit League New York, 55-57; art juror, various art shows. Awards: Purchase Award, Nat Acad Design, 65; Peterson Award, Salmagundi Club, 69; Medallion, New York Bicentennial, Am Numismatic Soc, 72. Bibliog: Norman Kent & Ernest Watson (auth), Lumen Martin Winter, Am Artist Mag, 50, 52, 59 & 66; Ralph Fabri (auth), Lumen Martin Winter, Today's Art, 66. Mem: Salmagundi

Club (comts & juries, 50-); Am Watercolor Soc; Nat Soc Mural Painters (vpres, 53-55); New Rochelle Art Asn (pres, 52-54). Style & Technique: Reconstruction of full size Last Supper. Media: Marble and Bronze; Watercolor, Oil. Res: Art works of Leonardo da Vinci. Publ: Co-auth, The Last Supper of Leonardo da Vinci, Coward McCann, 53; auth, A People's Art, Kans Quart, Kans State Univ, Manhattan, 77. Mailing Add: 1600 Old Pecos Trail Santa Fe NM 87501

WINTER, ROGER
PAINTER, EDUCATOR
b Denison, Tex, Aug 17, 34. Study: Univ Tex, BFA, 56; Univ Iowa, MFA, 60; Brooklyn Mus Sch, Beckmann scholar, 60. Work: Mus Art, Univ Okla, Norman; Dallas Mus Fine Arts, Tex; Southern Methodist Univ, Dallas; Oak Cliff Savings & Loan, Dallas; Longview Mus & Art Ctr, Tex. Exhib: Tex Painting & Sculpture, 20th Century Dallas, 71-62; two-man show, Whitte Mus, San Antonio, Tex, 67; one-man shows, Pollock Gallery, 68 & One i at a Time, 71, Southern Methodist Univ, Dallas & Delgado Mus, New Orleans, La, 68. Teaching: Instr painting, Ft Worth Art Ctr, 61; instr painting, Dallas Mus Fine Arts, 62-68; prof painting, Southern Methodist Univ, 65- Pos: Installation asst, Dallas Mus Contemp Arts, 62-63; gallery tours & lectr, Dallas Mus Fine Arts, 63- Awards: Purchase Award, Univ Okla Art Mus, 62; Top Award, Dallas Ann, Dallas Mus Fine Arts, 64. Bibliog: Film on work produced on KERA-TV, Dallas, 71. Style & Technique: Figurative. Media: Oil, Serigraphy, Collage. Dealer: Delahunty Inc 2611 Cedar Springs Dallas TX 75201. Mailing Add: 3228 Rankin Dallas TX 75205

WINTER, RUTH
PAINTER
b New York, NY, Jan 17, 13. Study: NY Univ, BS, 31, MA, 32; Art Students League, with Corbino, Bosa & Morris Kantor, 57-61. Work: In collections of Reginald Cabral, Provincetown, Mass, Marlo Lewis, Scarsdale, NY, Mr Frantz, Great Neck, NY, Lawrence Koenisberg, South Lawrence, NY & Semour S Alter, West Hempstead, NY. Exhib: Am Art at Mid-Century, Orange, NJ, 57; Nat Asn Women Art- ists, 57-68 & 74; Art USA, Provincetown, Mass, 58; Brooklyn Mus, 60; Nat Acad Design, 60. Awards: Marcia Brady Tucker Prize, Nat Asn Women Artists, 57; Max Low Award, 59; Mr & Mrs Gomes Award, Mahopac Art League, 59. Bibliog: Robert M Coates (auth), Art galleries, New Yorker, 5/57; Stuart Preston (auth), Art: a game of styles, New York Times, 5/57; Painting televised, Boston, 7/58. Mem: Nat Asn Women Artists; life mem Art Students League New York; Mahopac Art League. Media: Abstraction from nature, with emphasis on perceiving the larger vision. Media: Oil. Mailing Add: 98-50 67th Ave Rego Park NY 11374

WINTER, THELMA FRAZIER
SCULPTOR, ENAMELIST
b Gnadenhutten, Ohio, Dec 17, 03. Study: Cleveland Inst Art, dipl(painting, design & ceramics), sculpture, 29-30; Ohio State Univ, ceramics with Arthur E Baggs; Ohio State Univ Med Sch, Anat, 33; Case Western Res Univ, BC(educ), 35. Work: Cleveland Mus Art; City of Cleveland Munic Collection; Everson Mus Art, Syracuse, NY; Butler Mus Am Art, Youngstown, Ohio; Western Res Hist Soc Collection. Comn: Arisen Christ (ecclesiastical enamel), St Mary's Romanian Orthodox Church of Cleveland, 60; enamel decoration, Colby Col, Waterville, Maine, 65; Annunciation (ecclesiastical enamel) Cath Diocese of Cleveland, 68 & Last Supper, 71. Exhib: May Shows, Ann, Cleveland Mus Art, 33-60; Golden Gate Int, San Francisco, 39; Contemp Ceramics Western Hemisphere, Syracuse, NY, 41; Ceramic Nat, Everson Mus Art, Syracuse, NY, 39-59; Butler Mus Am Art, Youngstown, Ohio, 64. Teaching: Chmn art dept, Laurel Sch, Shaker Heights, Ohio, 39-45; instr 3-D design ceramics, Cleveland Inst Art, 45-51; instr compos & painting, Cleveland Mus Art, 50-54; instr, Col Club Cleveland, 60- Awards: First Prize for Night & Young Moon (ceramic sculpture), Nat Ceramic, Everson Mus, 39, Jugglers, Int Bus Mach, 49 & US Potter's Award for King Bird, 59. Mem: Fel Royal Soc Art, London; Alumni Asn Cleveland Inst Art; Nat Asn Am Pen Women. Style & Technique: Painting, decorative, semi-abstract; sculpture, stylized, decorative. Media: Sculpture, Ceramic; Painting, Enamels & Sgraffito. Publ: Contribr, Art of ceramic sculpture, Am Artist, 39; contribr, Ceramic art in America, Am Ceramic Soc J, 55; auth, Art & Craft of Ceramic Sculpture, Appl Sci Publ, London, 73. Mailing Add: 11020 Magnolia Dr Cleveland OH 44106

WINTERS, DENNY
PAINTER
b Grand Rapids, Mich, Mar 17, 07. Study: Art Inst Chicago; Chicago Acad Fine Arts; Acad Julien, Paris, France. Work: Philadelphia Mus Art, Pa; San Francisco Mus Art, Calif; Colby Col Mus; Butler Inst Am Art; Univ Maine, Orono. Exhib: Mus Mod Art, New York; Art Inst Chicago; Pa Acad Fine Arts, Philadelphia; San Francisco Mus Art; Carnegie Inst, Pittsburgh; one-man shows, Univ Maine, Orono, 78, Barridoff Gallery, Portland, Maine, 78 & Payson Mus, Portland, Maine, 78; plus numerous other group & one-man shows. Awards: Guggenheim Fel, 48; Butler Inst Am Art Purchase Prize; Denver Mus First Prize Ann Art Show; First Ann Skowhegan Award for Outstanding Achievement, Maine, 73. Style & Technique: Semi-abstract, calligraphic brush strokes, severely edited material. Publ: Illusr, Full Fathom Five & Savage Summer; jacket design, Wilderness River. Mailing Add: Rockport ME 04856

WINTERS, JOHN L
PAINTER, PRINTMAKER
b Zalite, Latvia, Dec 10, 35; US citizen. Study: RI Sch Design, BFA; Tulane Univ, MFA; Inst Allende, San Miguel Allende, Mex. Work: Miss State Col Women Art Gallery, Columbus. Comn: Print on William Faulkner, Univ Miss. Exhib: Artists of the Southeast & Texas, Delgado Mus, New Orleans, La, 69; 57th Nat, Jackson, Miss, 67; Southeastern Graphics Coun traveling exhib, 73-75; Nat Drawing Exhib, Southern Ill Univ, Carbondale, 75; 19th Mid-South Biennial, Brooks Art Gallery, Memphis, Tenn, 75. Teaching: Instr drawing, painting & printmaking, Miss State Col Women, 65-70; assoc prof drawing, painting & printmaking, Univ Miss, 70- Mem: Southeastern Col Art Conf; Am Asn Univ Prof; Southern Graphics Coun. Style & Technique: Surrealistic and expressionistic. Media: Oil, Intaglio. Mailing Add: PO Box 144 University MS 38677

WINTERSTEEN, BERNICE MCILHENNY
ART ADMINISTRATOR, COLLECTOR
b Philadelphia, Pa, June 16, 03. Study: Smith Col, BA; Ursinius Col, hon LHD, 65; Villanova Univ, hon DFA, 67; Wilson Col, DFA, 68; Moore Col Art, DFA, 68; LaSalle Col, LHD. Pos: Bd gov & trustee, Womens Comt, Philadelphia Mus Art, 47-64, pres, 64-68; organizer & first chmn vis comt, Smith Col Art Mus, 51; bd gov, Philadelphia Mus Col Art, 55-64; adv coun mem, Princeton Univ Mus Art, 58-; mem vis comt, design & visual arts dept, Harvard Univ, 64-; hon chmn, Nat Trust Preserv Conf, Philadelphia, 66; chmn, Philadelphia Art Festival, 67; hon chmn, Philadelphia Friends Am Mus Britain; mem mayor's comt for 1976 Bicentennial Observ & 1976 World's Fair Comt; dir, Atheneum Libr, mem Am civilization adv coun & mem comt develop of res in sci, Univ Pa; plus many civic, art & state positions. Awards: Distinguished Daughter of Pennsylvania, 64; Gimbel Award, 66. Mem: Philadelphia Art Comn; charter mem Philadelphia Ctr Performing Arts. Collection: 19th and 20th century French painting and sculpture; French Impressionist and Post-Impressionist paintings, including nineteen paintings by Ficasso and Matisse's Lady in Blue. Mailing Add: 402 Grays Lane House 100 Grays Lane Haverford PA 19041

WIPER, THOMAS WILLIAM
INSTRUCTOR, PAINTER
b San Francisco, Calif, June 1, 38. Study: Univ Ariz, with Charles Littler, BFA & MFA; Univ Calif, Berkeley, with Carl Kasten. Exhib: Regional exhibs, 64- Teaching: Instr, Foothill Col, 65-66; instr, Univ Ariz, 66-68. Pos: Dir educ, Tucson Mus Art, Ariz, 68-75; assoc fac, Pima Community Col, Tucson, 75- Mem: Am Fedn Arts; Tucson Coun Arts. Style & Technique: Abstract. Media: Mixed Media, Watercolor. Mailing Add: 305 S Mission Tucson AZ 85705

WIRTSCHAFTER, BUD
FILM MAKER, INSTRUCTOR
b Atlantic City, NJ, Jan 11, 24. Study: Art Students League, 46-47; New Sch Social Res, 47-49; Hans Hoffman Sch Fine Arts, New York, 47-49; Acad de Belli Arti, Italy, BA, 53. Exhib: Festival Di Popoli, Florence, Italy, 67; Spoletto Film Festival, 67; San Francisco Film Festival, 68; Cannes Film Festival, 70; 2 Media Environments, Neighborhood, 68 & Sale of a Memory, 75; plus many others. Teaching: Instr film, New Sch Social Res, 70-73, dir, Workshop Extended Cinema, 70-; instr film, City Col New York, 70- Pos: Dir, Soho Media Coop, 74- Bibliog: R Schekner (auth), interview in Tulane Drama Rev, spring 68 & Living it out on E 7th St, Urban Rev, 4/68; J Wilcock (auth), interview in autobiography 23& Sex Life a Warhol. Mem: Experiments in Art & Technol; Filmmakers Cinemateque; New Am Cinema Group; life mem Art Students League; Filmmakers Coop. Style & Technique: Experimental documentary. Publ: Dialogue, NBC-TV, New York, 65; Point of View, WOR-TV, New York, 66; I'm Here Now, Brandon Films, New York, 66; Ten Down Town, NYC-TV, New York, 69; plus others. Mailing Add: Soho Media Coop 154 Spring St New York NY 10012

WISE, GENEVA H (HOLCOMB)
PAINTER, COLLECTOR
b Pittsburg, Kans. Study: Okla State Univ, BA; with Doel Reed, Edward N Walker, David DeAllende, Elinor Evans, Dale McKinney, Milford Zornes, George Post & Father John Walch. Work: Okla State Univ; plus many pvt collections. Exhib: Eight State Exhib, Southwest Am Art, Okla Art Ctr, Oklahoma City, 61 & 64; NMex Biennial, Santa Fe Fine Arts Ctr, 62; Nat Small Painting Exhib, NMex Art Guild, 71 & 72; Southwestern Watercolor Soc, Dallas, 67 & 73; Okla State Univ, 75; Okla Mus Art, Oklahoma City, Ann Artists Salon, Okla Mus Art, Oklahoma City, 76 & 77; 15th Ann, Temple Emanu-El, Dallas, Tex. Pos: Arts chmn, Am Asn Univ Women, 77. Awards: Asel Materials Co Award, Dallas, 67; Award for Watercolor, Stillwater Okla Art Guild, 73; Award, Fidelity Bank Ann, Oklahoma City, 73. Bibliog: Rev in La Rev Mod, 2/72; Caralee Strock Stanard (auth), biog & photo, Adelphian Mag, 74. Mem: Okla Watercolor Asn; Okla Art Guild; Southwestern Watercolor Soc (Dallas chap); Stillwater Art Guild; Watercolor Okla (historian, 73-74). Style & Technique: Fluid style; frequently work wet in wet on watercolors; collage on watercolors; contemporary feeling. Media: Watercolor (transparent), Acrylic. Collection: Doel Reed aquatint; Dale McKinney silk screen; J J McVicker intaglio; Richard Morton lithograph; Kaethe Kollwitz etching and others. Mailing Add: 305 S Monroe St Stillwater OK 74074

WISE, HOWARD
ART ADMINISTRATOR
b Cleveland, Ohio, Nov 6, 03. Study: Clare Col, Cambridge Univ, BA(hons); Western Reserve Univ; Cleveland Inst Art. Pos: Estab Howard Wise Gallery of Present Day Painting & Sculpture, Cleveland, 57; dir, Howard Wise Gallery, New York, 60-71; founder, Electronic Arts Intermix, Inc, 71- Interest: Fostering the use of video (half inch portable TV) as a means of individual expression and communication. Mailing Add: 84 Fifth Ave New York NY 10011

WISNOSKY, JOHN G
PAINTER, EDUCATOR
b Springfield, Ill, Mar 21, 40. Study: Yale Univ Summer Sch Art, 61; Univ Ill, Urbana, BFA, 62, MFA, 64. Work: Honolulu Acad Arts, Hawaii; Southern Ill Univ, Carbondale; Contemp Arts Ctr, Hawaii, Honolulu; State Hawaii Found Cult & Arts; Mint Mus, Charlotte, NC. Comn: Pan Pac hall design, Hawaii Pavilion, Osaka World's Fair, 70; sculpture, Ewa Beach Publ Libr, Oahu, Hawaii, 71; flora pacifica design, Ethnobotanical Expos, 71. Exhib: Northwest Printmakers Int, Seattle, Wash, 65; Soc Am Graphic Artists, New York, 65; Presentation Artist Show in conjunction with Boston Printmakers, Boston Mus Fine Art, 66; Drawings-USA, St Paul Art Ctr, Minn, 67; Am Printmakers Exhib, Otis Art Inst, 68. Teaching: Instr painting & design, Va Polytech Inst & State Univ, 64-66; assoc prof & chmn, Univ Hawaii, 66- Pos: Owner, J Wisnosky Design Serv, 70- Awards: Henry B Shope Prize, Soc Am Graphic Artists, 65; Purchase Award, Honolulu Acad Arts, 70. Bibliog: Jean Charlot (auth), rev in, Honolulu Star-Bull, 9/13/67, 1/12/71 & 7/1/71; Webster Anderson (auth), rev in, Honolulu Advertiser, 3/9/69 & 6/30/71. Mem: Honolulu Printmakers (pres, 69-70); Hawaii Painters & Sculptors League (pres, 69-70). Dealer: Downtown Gallery 125 Merchant St Honolulu HI 96813. Mailing Add: Univ of Hawaii 2535 The Mall Honolulu HI 96822

WISSEMANN-WIDRIG, NANCY
PAINTER
b Jamestown, NY. Study: Syracuse Univ, NY; Ohio Univ, Athens. Work: Canton Art Inst, Ohio; Univ Kans Mus Fine Arts; Port Authority of New York; Nat Shawmut Bank, Boston, Mass; Minn Mining & Mfg Co. Exhib: Western New York Artists, Albright-Knox Art Gallery, Buffalo, NY, 64; Am Acad of Arts & Lett, 69; Landscape, Baltimore Mus Fine Arts, 73; A Sense of Place, Univ Nebr, 73-74; one-person show, Tibor de Nagy Gallery, New York, 74 & 77; Contemp Landscape, Okla Art Ctr, Oklahoma City, 75; Expressions from Maine, Hobe Sound Gallery, Fla, 76; Pepperdine Univ, Malibu, Calif, 76; Hamline Univ, St Paul, Minn, 76; Headley Mus, Lexington, Ky, 76. Awards: Outstanding Realist, Western New York Artists, Albright-Knox Art Gallery, 64; Purchase Award, Am Acad of Arts & Lett, Childe Hassam Fund, 69. Bibliog: Ellen Stevens (auth), What's happening way out here?, New Directions, 77; Norman Turner (auth), Nancy Wissemann-Widrig, Arts Mag, 12/77. Mem: E End Arts & Humanities (Long Island, NY adv bd). Style & Technique: Painterly realist; attentive and sympathetic examination of one's everyday surroundings. Media: Acrylic, Oil. Dealer: Tibor de Nagy 29 W 57th St New York NY 10019. Mailing Add: Box 524 Southold NY 11971

WITHAM, VERNON CLINT
PAINTER, COLLECTOR
b Eugene, Ore, Dec 6, 25. Study: Univ Ore; Calif Sch Fine Arts, San Francisco. Work: Univ Ore Mus Art, Eugene; Univ Wyo Mus Art, Laramie. Exhib: Under 25, Seligmann Gallery,

New York, 49; Artists of Oregon, Portland Art Mus, 53; one-man show, Calif Palace of Legion of Honor, San Francisco, 60; Maxwell Gallery, San Francisco, 61; American Landscape, Peridot Gallery, New York, 68. Teaching: Resident artist, Univ Wyo, 71- Awards: Purchase Award, Northwest Painting Ann, 72. Style & Technique: Emperical experience and conceptual idea; painting and charting properties, structures and processes of physical and mental world. Media: Mixed Media. Collection: Antique primitive art from around the world. Publ: Co-auth, 12 new painters (serigraph folio), 53; contribr, insert 4, Written Palette, 62. Dealer: Grandtour Gallery 622 SW 12th Portland OR 97205. Mailing Add: 2100 Greiner Eugene OR 97405

WITHERS, JOSEPHINE
ART HISTORIAN, ART WRITER
b Cambridge, Mass, July 3, 38. Study: Oberlin Col, BA, 60; Columbia Univ, PhD, 71. Collections Arranged: Julio Gonzalez, Sculpture and Drawings, Mus Mod Art, New York, 68; Mixed Bag, Univ Md Art Gallery, 73. Teaching: Asst prof art hist, Temple Univ, Philadelphia, Pa, 68-69; asst prof 20th century art, 70- & Women in Art, 78-, Univ Md, College Park. Awards: Aelioian Fel, Oberlin Col, 64; Gen Res Bd, Univ Md, 72 & 77. Mem: Col Art Asn; Women's Caucus for Art; Washington Women's Art Ctr (bd dir, 76-77); Conf of Women in the Visual Arts (steering comt, 72). Res: Twentieth century art, concentrating on European art of the 1930s; American women artists of the nineteenth and twentieth century. Publ: Auth, Phillips Simpkin, Made in Philadelphia, Philadelphia Inst of Contemp Art, 73; auth, The Artistic Collaboration of Picasso and Gonzalez, Art J, winter 76; auth, The Famous Fur-Lined Teacup and The Anomyous Meret Oppenheim, Arts Mag, 11/77; auth, Julio Gonzalez, Sculpture in Iron, New York Univ Press, 77. Mailing Add: 2122 Decatur Pl NW Washington DC 20008

WITHROW, WILLIAM J
ART ADMINISTRATOR
b Toronto, Ont, Sept 30, 26. Study: Univ Toronto, BA, 50, BEd, 55 & MEd, 58, MA, 60. Teaching: Head art dept, Earl Haig Col, 51-59. Pos: Dir, Art Gallery Ont, Toronto, 60- Awards: Can Centennial Medal, 67. Mem: Can Mus Asn; Am Asn Mus; Am Asn Art Mus Dirs; Can Art Mus Dirs Orgn; Can Nat Comt for Int Coun Mus. Publ: Auth, Sorel Etrog sculpture, 67 & Contemporary Canadian painting, 72. Mailing Add: c/o Art Gallery of Ont Grange Park Toronto ON Can

WITKIN, ISAAC
SCULPTOR, INSTRUCTOR
b Johannesburg, SAfrica, May 10, 36; US citizen. Study: St Martins Sch Art, London, with Anthony Caro; also with Henry Moore, Eng. Work: Joseph Hirshhorn Mus, Washington, DC; Tate Gallery, London, Eng; Worcester Art Mus, Mass; Ill State Univ. Comn: Sculpture, Storm King Art Ctr, Mountainville, NY, 70; sculpture, Springfield, Mass, 75. Exhib: One-man shows, Elkon Gallery, Waddington Gallery & Marlborough Gallery, 63-; Paris Bienale, Mus Mod Art, 65; Primary Structures, Jewish Mus, New York, 65; New Generation, White Chapel Gallery, London, 65; Condition of Sculpture, Hayward Gallery, London, 75. Teaching: Instr sculpture, St Martins Sch Art, 63-65; instr sculpture, Bennington Col, 65-; instr sculpture, Parsons Sch Design, 75- Awards: Co-Winner First Prize, Paris Bienale, 65. Bibliog: James Mellows (auth), article in New York Times, 71; Bill Lipke (auth), film for Vt Coun Arts, 72; Neil Marshad (auth), film for Nat Educ TV, 75. Mem: Mass Arts & Humanities Found. Style & Technique: Abstract, using welded steel construction. Media: Steel. Publ: Auth, Thames and Hudson, Modern Eng Sculpture, 67; contribr, Minimal Art, Dutton, 68; auth, Alistair Healpine Gift, Tate Gallery, 71; contribr, New York Mag, 4/9/73. Dealer: Marlborough Gallery Inc 40 W 57th St New York NY 10019. Mailing Add: 136 W 24th St New York NY 10011

WITKIN, JEROME PAUL
PAINTER, EDUCATOR
b Brooklyn, NY, Sept 13, 39. Study: Cooper Union Art Sch, 57-60; Skowhegan Sch Painting & Sculpture; Berlin Acad, WGer, Pulitzer traveling fel, 60; Univ Pa, MFA, 70. Work: Minn Mus Art, St Paul; Univ NH, Durham; B K Smith Gallery, Lake Erie Col; Univ Maine, Portland-Gorham; Canton Art Inst, Ohio. Exhib: One-man shows, Morris Gallery, New York, 62-64 & Kraushaar Galleries, New York, 73 & 76; Transatlantics, US Artists in Eng, US Embassy, London, 66; Drawings USA, Minn Mus Art, 71; Drawings, Kraushaar Gallery, New York, 71. Teaching: Instr drawing, Md Inst Art, Baltimore, 63-65; lectr painting, Manchester Col Art, Eng, 65-67; vis prof design, drawing & painting, Moore Col, 68-71; assoc prof art, Syracuse Univ, 71- Awards: Guggenheim Found Fel Painting, 63-64; First Julius Hallgarten Prize, Nat Acad Design, 73. Style & Technique: Romantic and painterly style; technique is a rough and alive alla-prima in oils on large canvases. Dealer: Kraushaar Galleries 80th St & Madison Ave New York NY 10021. Mailing Add: Lowe Art Ctr Syracuse Univ Syracuse NY 13210

WITMEYER, STANLEY HERBERT
ART ADMINISTRATOR, DESIGNER
b Palmyra, Pa, Feb 14, 13. Study: Sch Art & Design, Rochester Inst Technol, dipl; State Univ NY Col Buffalo, BS; Syracuse Univ, MFA; Univ Hawaii, with Ben Norris. Work: Pvt collections. Exhib: Rochester Mem Art Gallery; Albright-Knox Gallery, Buffalo; Honolulu Acad Fine Arts; Everson Mus, Syracuse. Teaching: Instr art, Cuba Pub Schs, NY, 39-44; prof painting & design, Sch Art Design, Rochester Inst Technol, 46-52. Pos: Dir sch art & design, Rochester Inst Technol, 52-68, assoc dean col fine & appl arts, 68- Awards: Distinguished Alumni Awards, State Univ NY Col Buffalo, 68 & Rochester Inst Technol, 71; Athletic Hall of Fame Award, Rochester Inst Technol, 71. Mem: Rochester Torch Club (pres, 52); Nat Art Educ Asn; Rochester Art Club (pres, 56); Rochester Inst Technol Alumni Asn (pres, 52); NY State Art Teachers Asn. Media: Watercolor, Mixed Media. Collection: American printmakers and painters. Publ: Auth, articles in, Everyday Art, Design Mag, Sch Arts, Nat Art Educ J & NY Art Teachers Bull. Mailing Add: 300 Sunnyside Dr Rochester NY 14623

WITOLD-K (KACZANOWSKI)
PAINTER, SCULPTOR
b Warsaw, Poland, May 15, 32; US citizen. Study: eng & archit, Acad Fine Arts, Warsaw, with Prof W Fangor & Prof H Tomaszewski. Work: Mus Fine Arts, Houston, Tex; Mus NMex, Santa Fe; Phoenix Art Mus, Ariz; Nat Libr, Paris, France; Whitney Mus, New York. Comn: Murals, Int Fairs, Poznan & Leipzich, 57-59; 57-59; mural, Polish exhib, Moscow, USSR, 60; Auschwitz (mural), Govt Poland, 61; painting, United Bank Calif, Beverly Hills, 71; painting, Conoco Oil Co, Houston, Tex, 74; mural, Mainstreet Art Festival, Houston, 75. Exhib: ZPAP Gallery, Warsaw, Poland, 60; Galerie 3 plus 2, Paris, France, 66; Aux Bateliers, Brussels, Belg, 67; La Pochade Gallerie, Paris, France, 68; Seton Hall Univ Gallery, South Orange, NJ, 71; Simpliciano Galeria, Milan, Italy, 72; Otis Art Inst, Los Angeles, 73; St John's Col, Santa Fe, NMex, 74. Teaching: Lectr art philos, Seton Hall Univ, 71. Bibliog: Michel Casse (ed), Le Crevasses du Ciel, Paris, 67; Ifal & French TV, joint interviews with Nurejev & Jiji Jamaire, 72; Am Film Inst, Who is Mr K?, documentary, 74; Am Printmakers, 74. Dealer: Max Hutchinson Gallery 127 Green St New York NY 10012. Mailing Add: 1119 Welch Houston TX 77006

WITT, JOHN
PAINTER, PRINTMAKER
b Wilmington, Del, Jan 30, 40. Study: Philadelphia Col Art, BFA, 62; Univ Md Grad Sch; Brooklyn Mus Sch Art. Work: Smithsonian Inst, USMC Combat Art Collections, US Navy Combat Art Collection, Pentagon & US Army, Off Chief Mil Hist, Washington, DC. Exhib: Smithsonian Inst Vietnam Exhib, Washington, DC, 69; Nat Arts Club, New York, 72; Hudson Valley Art Asn Ann, White Plains, NY, 72; Audubon Artists Ann, New York, 73; Am Artists Prof League Ann, New York, 73. Pos: Combat artist, USMC Civilian Comn, 68 & 69; combat artist, US Navy, 73 & 76; courtroom trial artist, ABC News, 74. Awards: Gold Medal, Hudson Valley Art Asn, 72; Best in Show, Nat Arts Club, New York, 72; Gold Medal, Louis E Seley NACAL Award, 78. Bibliog: US Army, Executive Corridor Section of the Army, USGPO, 66; Mark Goodman (auth), Trial of art, New Times Mag, 5/17/74; Col Raymond Henri (auth), Combat art since 1775, Marine Corps Gazette, 74. Mem: Soc Illusr (mem exec comt, 74-78); Hudson Valley Art Asn; Audubon Artists; Am Artists Prof League. Style & Technique: Representational/Documentary; oil, acrylic, watercolor, pastel, woodcuts & serigraphs. Publ: Auth & illusr, Vietnam, Sterling, 72; illusr, Mitchell/Stans Trial, Newsweek Mag, 74; illusr, Mitchell/Stans Trial Courtroom Drawings, ABC News, 74; illusr, Marine Corps Gazette, 74; illusr, Portraits of Valor, USMC, 74. Mailing Add: RD 1 Baptist Church Rd Yorktown Heights NY 10598

WITT, NANCY CAMDEN
SCULPTOR, PAINTER
b Richmond, Va, Oct 24, 30. Study: Randolph-Macon Woman's Col; Old Dominion Univ, BA; Va Commonwealth Univ, MFA. Work: Valentine Mus, Richmond; Chrysler Mus, Norfolk, Va; Mint Mus, Charlotte, NC; RMC, Ashland; RMWC, Lynchburg; Univ Va, Charlottesville; Va Mil Inst, Lexington. Comn: Portrait, Ferrum Col, VA, 69; mobile construct, Philip Morris Tobacco Co, Richmond, 69-70; mural, Security Fed Savings & Loan Co, Richmond, 71. Exhib: Va Mus Biennial, Richmond, 61-73; Miami Nat Painting Exhib, Coral Gables, Fla, 64; Southeastern Exhib, Atlanta, Ga, 64; Southeastern Exhib Prints & Drawings, Jacksonville, Fla, 65; Mainstreams, 75, 76 & 77, Marietta, Ohio; Int Woman Artists Exhib, 76. Teaching: Actg chmn dept art, Richard Bland Col, Col William & Mary, 61-63 & 64-65. Awards: Purchase Prize, Exec Towers Sculpture, Va Comn on Arts & Humanities, 75; Award, Int Woman Artists Exhib, 76. Media: Oil; Constructions. Dealer: Scott-McKennis Fine Art 3465 W Cary St Richmond VA 23221. Mailing Add: Rte 3 Box 643 Ashland VA 23005

WITTEMAN, ALISA WELLS
PHOTOGRAPHER
b Erie, Pa. Study: Ansel Adam Workshop, 61; Nathan Lyons Workshop, Rochester, NY, 61-62 & 65-66. Work: Inst Mus Photog, George Eastman House, Rochester; Krannert Art Mus, Univ Ill, Champaign; Pasadena Art Mus, Calif; NMex Fine Arts Mus; Visual Studies Workshop. Exhib: Int Mus Photog, George Eastman House, 63-70; Photog USA, De Cordova Mus, Lincoln, Mass, 67; Contemp Photographs, Univ Calif, Los Angeles, 67; The Photograph as Object: 1843-1969 (traveling show), Art Gallery of Ont & Nat Gallery of Can, 69-70; Photographs of Women by Women, Baldwin Gallery, Toronto, 72; one-person shows, State Univ NY, Buffalo, 72, Mus NMex, Santa Fe, 73 & Moncton Art Gallery, 75; Gli Americani, Fotografi Oggi, Italy, 73; Light & Lens, Hudson River Mus, 73; An Inquiry into the Aesthetics of Photog, Nat Gallery of Can, 74; Women of Photog, San Francisco Mus Art & Seattle Art Mus, 75; Mus NMex, 75; Exhib Women Artists, Berlin, WGer, 77; plus many others. Pos: Assoc cur, Int Mus Photog, George Eastman House, 62-69; asst to dir, Visual Studies Workshop, Rochester, 69-72; free lance photogr, Taos, NMex, 72- Awards: Creative Artists Pub Serv Grant, NY, 72; Nat Endowment for the Arts Fel, 72; Western State Art Found Grant, 75. Bibliog: Mike Weaver (auth), New American Photography, Form, 68; Anne Tucker (auth), The Women's Eye, Knopf, 73; Women of Photography, San Francisco Mus of Photog, 75. Style & Technique: Camera work as a means toward self awareness and understanding of the inner/outer world I touch upon. Publ: Contribr, Photography in the 20th century, Horizon Press, 67; contribr, The Photograph as Object, 1843-1969, Nat Gallery of Can, 69; contribr, The Figure in the Landscape, Int Mus Photog, George Eastman House, 70; contribr, The Art of Photography, Life Series, 71; contribr, New Mexico Portfolio, Ctr of the Eye, 76. Dealer: Stables Art Gallery Taos NM 87571. Mailing Add: Box DDD Taos NM 87571

WITTMANN, OTTO
ART ADMINISTRATOR
b Kansas City, Mo, Sept 1, 11. Study: Harvard Univ. Collections Arranged: Splendid Century, Masterpieces from France; Painting in Italy in 18th Century; Age of Rembrandt; Art of Van Gogh. Teaching: Instr art hist, Skidmore Col, 38-41. Pos: Cur, Hyde Collection, Glens Falls, NY, 38-41; asst dir, Portland Mus Art, Ore, 41; assoc dir, Toledo Mus Art, 53-59, dir, 59-77, emer dir, 77-, vpres, consult & art adv, 77-, ed, Mus News, 14 yrs; trustee & consult, Los Angeles Co Mus of Art, Los Angeles, 77-; mem, Nat Endowment Arts Mus Adv Panel. Awards: Officer, Legion Honor, France; Commander, Order of Merit, Italy; Officer, Order of Orange-Nassau, Netherlands & Order Arts & Lett, France. Mem: Asn Art Mus Dir (pres, 71-72); Am Asn Mus (vchmn); Mus Asn Eng. Nat Collection Fine Arts Comn; Col Art Asn Am (former dir). Publ: Co-auth, Travellers in Arcadia; auth numerous articles in art mags. Mailing Add: Toledo Mus of Art Box 1013 Toledo OH 43697

WOEHRMAN, RALPH
PRINTMAKER, DRAFTSMAN
b Cleveland, Ohio, 1940. Study: Kent State Univ; Cleveland Inst Art, BFA(printmaking), 66; Cranbrook Acad Art, MFA(printmaking), 72. Work: Ohio Fine Arts Coun, Columbus; Minneapolis Mus Art, St Paul, Minn; Corcoran Gallery, Washington, DC; Osaka Univ, Niniwa Col Arts, Japan; Ringling Mus, Sarasota, Fla. Comn: 40 prints, Univ Print Club, Cleveland. Exhib: Nat Ann Print, Brand Libr Art Ctr, Los Angeles; Ann Soc Am Graphic Artists, New York; Drawings, USA, Minneapolis Mus Art, St Paul, Minn; Seattle Print Int Ann, Wash; Libr of Cong Print Exhib, Washington, DC, 75; 20th Nat Print Exhib, Brooklyn Mus, NY, 77. Teaching: Instr, Memphis Acad Art, 66-67; instr, Cleveland Inst Art, 75- Awards: Agnes Gund Award, Cleveland Inst Art, 66; Ohio Arts Coun, Columbus; Tiffany Grant, Louis Comfort Tiffany Found, 73. Bibliog: Articles in Art Int, 6/74 & Art Mag, 6/74. Style & Technique: Realism, drawings and prints. Media: Colored Pencil, Ink, Acrylic; Mezzotint, Lithographs. Dealer: Kingpitcher Gallery 303 S Craig Pittsburgh PA 15213. Mailing Add: 4350 S Hilltop Chagrin Falls OH 44022

WOELFFER, EMERSON
PAINTER
b Chicago, Ill, July 27, 14. Study: Art Inst Chicago; Inst Design, Chicago, BA & hon DFA. Work: Art Inst Chicago; Whitney Mus Am Art & Mus Mod Art, New York; Univ Ill; plus

others. Exhib: Gallery 16, Graz, Austria, 65; one-man shows, Santa Barbara Mus, Calif, 64, David Stuart Gallery, Los Angeles, Calif, 65- 65 & 69, Quay Gallery, San Francisco, Calif, 68, Jodi Scully Gallery, Los Angeles, 72, Poindexter Gallery, New York, Newport Harbor Mus of Art, Newport Beach, Calif, Phillips Collection, Washington, DC & Gruenebaum Gallery, New York; Calif Inst Arts, 72; plus many other group & one-man shows. Teaching: Instr, Sch Design, Chicago, 42; vis prof, Black Mountain Col, 49; instr, Colo Springs Fine Arts Ctr, 50; instr, Chouinard Art Inst, 59; vis prof painting, Univ Southern Calif, summer 62. Pos: Topog draftsman, USAAF, 39-40; resident artist, Honolulu Acad Arts, Hawaii, 70. Awards: Guggenheim Found Fel, France, Italy, Spain & Eng, 67-68; Purchase Award, All City Art Festival, 68; Raymond A Speiser Mem Prize, Pa Acad Fine Arts, 68; plus others. Bibliog: Archives Am Art, Smithsonian Inst, Washington, DC. Media: Oil, Acrylic. Collection: African, New Guinea & pre-Columbian works; surrealist paintings. Mailing Add: 475 Dustin Dr Los Angeles CA 90065

WOELL, J FRED
CRAFTSMAN, SCULPTOR
b Evergreen Park, Ill, Feb 4, 34. Study: Park Col; Univ Ill, Urbana, BA(econ), 56 & BFA(art educ), 60; Univ Wis, Madison, MS & MFA(art metal), 62; Cranbrook Acad Art, Bloomfield Hills, Mich, MFA(sculpture), 69. Work: Objects, USA, Smithsonian Mus, Washington, DC; US Info Agency, Washington, DC; Sheldon Mem Art Gallery, Univ Nebr-Lincoln. Exhib: Young Americans, Mus Contemp Crafts, New York, 62 & one-man show, 67; Objects USA, travel exhib, S C Johnson Wax Corp, 69-; Goldsmith 70, St Paul Art Ctr, Minn; Goldsmiths, Renwick Gallery, Washington, DC, 74. Collections Arranged: Crafts of the Americas, Colo State Univ, Ft Collins, 75. Teaching: Asst prof art metal, Univ Wis-Madison, 69-70 & Univ Wis, Whitewater, 71-73. Pos: Asst to sculptor Frank Gallo, Urbana, Ill, 65-67; asst dir, Haystack Mountain Sch Crafts, Deer Isle, Maine, 73-74. Bibliog: J Fred Woell, Craft Horizons, 3/68; Lee Nordness (auth), Objects USA, Viking Press, 70; Mondale (auth), Politics in Art, Lerner Publ, 72. Mem: Am Craftsman Coun. Style & Technique: Assembly found objects and images into small sculpture and jewelry. Media: Casting Brass; Bronze, Silver. Publ: Illusr, Photography in the crafts, 75. Mailing Add: Deer Isle ME 04627

WOFFORD, PHILIP
PAINTER, WRITER
b Van Buren, Ark, Aug 14, 35. Study: Univ Ark, BA, 57; Univ Calif, Berkeley, 57-58. Work: Whitney Mus Am Art, New York; Michener Found Collection, Austin, Tex; RI Sch Design, Providence. Exhib: San Francisco Mus Ann, 58; Whitney Mus Ann Exhib Am Painting, 69 & 72; Corcoran Gallery Art, Washington, DC. Teaching: Instr art, NY Univ Exten, 64-68; instr art, Bennington Col, 69- Awards: Woodrow Wilson Fel; Nat Endowment Arts Fel. Bibliog: Carter Ratcliff (auth), New informalists, Art News, 2/70; Peter Scheldajl (auth), Return to the sublime, New York Times, 4/18/71. Publ: Auth, article in, Art Now: New York, 70; auth, Grand Canyon Search Ceremony, Barlenmir House, 72; In the Belly of the Shark, Random House, 72; work in, Poetry Rev, 4/75. Dealer: Andre Emmerich Gallery 41 E 57th St New York NY 10022. Mailing Add: RD 2 Hoosick Falls NY 12090

WOGSTAD, JAMES EVERET
EDUCATOR, ILLUSTRATOR
b Lordsburg, NMex, Sept 24, 39. Study: San Antonio Col, cert, 59; Univ Tex, Austin, BFA, 61, MFA, 68. Comn: Original graphics prog, Univ Tex Med Sch, San Antonio, 68-69; dioramic backgrounds & natural hist graphic displays, Witte Mus, San Antonio, 70-74. Teaching: Assoc prof art & chmn dept, San Antonio Col, 68- Pos: Lead illusr, Creative Commun, Houston, 62-63; chief illusr, Finger Contract Supply, Houston, 63-65; preparator-cur, Witte Mus, 70-74; ed-illusr, Replica in Scale, 72- Mem: Col Art Asn Am. Tex Asn Schs Art (parliamentarian, 69-70, secy-treas, 70-74); Tex Jr Col Teachers Asn (vchmn art sect, 69-70, chmn, 70-71). Style & Technique: Technical illustrations in transparent watercolor and gouache; heavy impasto; acrylics. Media: Acrylic on Canvas; Black Ink on Paper. Publ: Illusr, Any Time is Party Time, 67, Auschuitz, 67 & Belsen, 67, Naylor. Mailing Add: 4014 Belle Grove San Antonio TX 78230

WOITENA, BEN S
SCULPTOR, EDUCATOR
b San Antonio, Tex, Mar 24, 42. Study: Univ Tex, Austin, BFA, 61-64; Univ Southern Calif, MFA, 68-70. Work: Houston Mus of Fine Arts, Tex. Exhib: Main St 72, Contemp Art Mus, Houston, Tex, 72; Monumental Sculpture, Houston, 75; Collector's Exhib, Houston Mus of Fine Arts, 75; Gulf Coast Sculpture Exhib, Galveston, Tex, 76. Teaching: Instr sculpture, Houston Mus of Fine Arts Mus Sch, 71- Bibliog: Ann Holmes (auth), Houston: The Second City for Art?, Art News, 75; Roberta Smith (auth), Twelve Days of Texas, Art in Am, 76; Actual Yardage Gained (30 minute doc), Channel 8, Nat Educ Television, KUHT, Houston, 76. Style & Technique: Welded metal. Dealer: McGaughy Art Consulting Firm 120 Portland Houston TX 77006. Mailing Add: 1410 Cook Houston TX 77006

WOJCIK, GARY THOMAS
SCULPTOR
b Chicago, Ill, Feb 26, 45. Study: Art Inst Chicago, BFA; Univ Ky, MA. Work: High Mus Art, Atlanta, Ga; New York Port Authority, NY; Chicago Park Dist, Hyde Park, Chicago. Exhib: Whitney Sculpture Ann, Whitney Mus Am Art, 68; Univ Ill Biennial Painting & Sculpture Exhib, 69; Soc Contemp Art 29th Ann, Art Inst Chicago, 69; Viewpoints Painting & Sculpture Invitational, Colgate Univ, 70; Painting & Sculpture 1972, Storm King Art Ctr, Mountainville, NY, 72. Teaching: Part-time asst prof sculpture, Ithaca Col. Awards: Art Inst Chicago Traveling Fel. Bibliog: Rev in New York Times, 11/29/70, Art News Mag, 1/29/71 & Art Int, 2/20/71. Media: Welded Metal. Dealer: Kornblee Art Gallery 20 W 57th St New York NY 10019. Mailing Add: 273 Bundy Rd Ithaca NY 14850

WOJTYLA, HASSE (WALTER JOSEPH WOJTYLA)
PAINTER, DRAFTSMAN
b Chicago, Ill, Feb 10, 33. Study: Art Inst of Chicago; Univ of Ill, BFA(painting); Univ Cincinnati, MFA; Brooklyn Mus Art Sch. Exhib: Nat Drawing Competition, San Francisco Mus of Art, 55; Int Drawing Competition, State Univ of Educ, Potsdam, NY, 60; Tenth Ann Nat Exhib of Painting & Sculpture, Ringling Mus of Art, Sarasota, Fla, 60; Brooklyn & Long Island Artists Biennial Exhib, Brooklyn Mus of Art, 60; Art in Am Exhib, New York, 62; All Ohio Painting & Sculpture Exhib, Dayton Art Inst, 66; Calif-Hawaii Biennial, Fine Arts Gallery of San Diego, 76 & 78; one-man show, Recent Paintings, Fine Arts Gallery of San Diego, 75. Teaching: Instr painting & drawing, San Diego State Univ, Calif, 76. Awards: Singer & Sons Prize, Artists of Chicago & Vicinity, Art Inst of Chicago, 56; Painting Award, All Calif Juried Exhib, Laguna Beach Mus of Art, 76; Painting Award, Calif Ann Award Show, Jewish Community Ctr, San Diego, 77. Mem: Artists Equity Asn Inc. Style & Technique: Interperative figure painting with brush and pallete knife. Media: Oil Painting, Mixed-media; Ink Drawing, Charcoal Drawing. Mailing Add: 621 4th Ave San Diego CA 92101

WOLBER, PAUL J
PAINTER, EDUCATOR
b Deer Creek, Ill, June 23, 35. Study: Ill State Univ; Southern Ill Univ, Edwardsville; Bob Jones Univ, BS & MA. Work: Evansville Mus Art, Ind; Franklin Life Ins Co, Springfield, Ill; Mitchell Mus Art, Mt Vernon, Ill; Bob Jones Univ, Greenville, SC; Ill State Mus, Springfield, Ill. Exhib: Ill State Mus, Springfield, 74; Grand Galleria Nat Ann, Seattle, 74; Springville Mus Nat Ann, Utah, 74; Gov Exhib, 30 Ill Artists, Springfield, 75; two-man show, Opapi Gallery, Southern Ill Univ, Edwardsville, 75. Teaching: Assoc prof art, Spring Arbor Col, Mich, 76- Pos: Art educ consult, State Off Pub Instr, Springfield, Ill, 74-75. Awards: Robert Cooke Enlow Mem Purchase Award, Evansville Mus Arts & Sci, 73; Nat Small Painting Award, NMex Art League, Albuquerque, 74 & 75; Outstanding Educ Am Award, 72 & 75. Bibliog: Abner Hershberger (ed), Monnonite Artists Contemporary, 1975, Goshen Col Art Gallery; Glen P Ives (auth), Museum object of the week, Sunday Courier, Evansville, Ind, 10/6/74; Howard Derrickson (auth), rev in The Advocate, Greenville, 1/28/75. Mem: Mid Am Col Art Asn; Ill Art Educ Asn; Nat Art Educ Asn; Bond Co Art & Cult Asn (vpres, 73-74). Style & Technique: Formal/realist style based on mid-west subjects. Media: Oil, Acrylic; Opaque, Semi-Opaque. Mailing Add: 1660 Chapel Rd Parma MI 49269

WOLF, JACK CLIFFORD
WRITER, PAINTER
b Omaha, Nebr, May 25, 22. Study: Creighton Univ, BS, 47; State Univ NY Col Brockport, MA, 69; State Univ NY, Buffalo, PhD, 72. Exhib: Fedn Brit Artists Gallery, London, 62; Hove Mus, Eng, 62; 3rd Gran Prix Int, Salon Bosio, Monte Carlo, Monaco, 62; Univision Gallery, Newcastle-on-Tyne, Eng, 63; one-man show, Woodstock Gallery, London, 63. Teaching: Assoc prof English, State Univ NY Col Brockport, 70- Awards: Fel Award for Writing, State Univ NY, 73. Mem: Mod Lang Asn. Style & Technique: Abstract. Media: Oil. Publ: Auth, Payoff of Fever Street, 62; ed, Past, Present & Future Perfect, ed, Ghosts, Castles & Victims, 74 & ed, Tales of the Occult, 75, Fawcett; co-auth, Professional Framing for the Amateur, 74. Mailing Add: 218 Dartmouth St Rochester NY 14607

WOLFE, ANN (ANN WOLFE GRAUBARD)
SCULPTOR, INSTRUCTOR
b Mlawa, Poland; US citizen. Study: Hunter Col, BA; studies sculpture in Manchester, Eng & Paris, France; Acad Grande Chaumiere, with Despiau & Vlerick. Work: Morris Raphael Cohen Libr, City Univ New York; Jerusalem Mus Art, Israel; Nat Mus Korea, Seoul; Mus Western Art, Moscow, Russia; Wangensteen-Phillips Med Ctr, Univ Minn. Comn: Dr Morris R Cohen (bronze head), alumni of City Univ New York, 43; Pres Syngman Rhea (bronze head), Dr R Oliver, Washington, DC, 47; Dr W R Ramsey (bronze head), Children's Hosp, St Paul, Minn, 57; welded relief in steel & bronze, Mt Zion Temple, St Paul, 65; Dr O H Wangensteen (bronze head), alumni of dept surg, Univ Minn, 65. Exhib: One-man shows, Grace Horne Gallery, Boston, 41, Walker Art Ctr, Minneapolis, 55, Minneapolis Inst Arts, 64, Adele Bednarz Galleries, Los Angeles, 66, 3rd Sculpture Int, Philadelphia Mus Art, Pa, 49. Teaching: Instr pvt sutdio, 62-70; instr sculpture, Minnetonka Ctr Arts & Educ, 71- Awards: Allied Artists Am, 36; Soc Washington Artists, 44 & 45; Minneapolis Inst Arts, 51. Style & Technique: Abstract, occasionally figurative. Publ: Contribr, Worcester Tel-Gazette, 40-60. Dealer: Grand Cent Gallery 961 Grand Ave St Paul MN 55105; Fairweather-Hardin Galleries 101 E Ontario Chicago IL 60611. Mailing Add: 2928 Dean Pkwy Minneapolis MN 55416

WOLFE, JAMES
SCULPTOR
b New York, NY, Apr 28, 44. Study: Solebury Sch, grad. Exhib: Contemporary Sculpture, Phillips Collection, Washington, DC, 72; New England Sculpture, Dartmouth Col, Hanover, NH, 73; Contemporary American Artists, Cleveland Mus Art, 74; Monumenta, Newport, RI, 74; one-man shows, Andre Emmerich Gallery, 73, 74 & 75. Pos: Tech dir, Theater Dept & tech asst, Sculpture Dept, Bennington Col. Bibliog: J Mascjeck (auth), Notes on Caro influence; five sculptors from Bennington, Artforum, 4/72; Jeanne Siegel (auth), rev in Art News, 2/73; Ellen Lubell (auth), James Wolfe, Arts Mag, 6/75. Dealer: Andre Emmerich Gallery Inc 41 E 57th St New York NY 10022. Mailing Add: Valentine Lane Bennington VT 05201

WOLFE, LYNN ROBERT
STAINED GLASS ARTIST, PAINTER
b Red Cloud, Nebr, Sept 11, 17. Study: Univ Nebr, BA; Univ Colo, with Max Beckman, MA; Paris Atelier with Ossip Zadkine. Work: Univ Nebr State Mus, Lincoln; Univ Colo, Boulder. Comn: Copper doors, Danforth Chapel, Colo State Univ, Ft Collins, 54; mosaic (stained glass), McPherson Chapel, Durango, Colo, 60; stained glass window, Norgren Chapel, Denver, 65; stained glass windows, St Aidans Episcopal Church, Boulder, 70; polyester hanging sculpture, Midland Fed Savings, Westminster, Colo, 73. Exhib: Hallmark Int, Wilderstein Gallery, New York, 52; Nat Drawing & Small Sculpture, Muncie, Ind, 58; Mus Contemp Crafts, New York, 59; one-man show, Variation on a landscape theme, Colorado Springs Fine Arts Ctr, 74; Western Artists, Denver Art Mus, 72. Teaching: Instr sculpture, Univ Nebr, Lincoln, 45-46; vis artist watercolor, Univ Alaska, summer 46; prof painting, Univ Colo, Boulder, 47- & chmn dept fine arts, 72-74. Pos: Cur collections, Univ Colo, Boulder, 64-74. Awards: Hallmark Art Award, Hall Bros Inc, 52; Sculpture Award, Ball State Teachers Col, 58; Univ Colo Fac Fel, 67. Bibliog: M E Bevlin (auth), Design through Discovery, Holt, 70. Mem: Boulder Fine Arts Ctr; Boulder Arts & Humanities Coun. Style & Technique: Lyrical abstractions derived from landscapes. Media: Acrylic, Canvas; Stained Glass, Faceted Dalles. Mailing Add: 701 Euclid Boulder CO 80302

WOLFE, MAURICE RAYMOND
MUSEUM DIRECTOR, EDUCATOR
b Paris, France, Oct 13, 24; US citizen. Study: Univ Calif, Berkeley, BA, MA, grad study; Fr Govt fel to Univ Paris at Sorbonne. Collections Arranged: Art Mobilier of the Djukas of Surinam, Pacific Northwest & Eskimo Material Culture, Meso-American Prehistory, Mohave Desert Culture, African Musical Instruments & Domestic Objects & The Art of New Guinea, 74-75, The Cuna of Panama—Arts & Crafts, West Africa, Aboriginal Australian Art from Expo 74 & California Gatherers & Hunters, Circa 1776 (Bicentennial celebration), 75-76, Oceanic Cultures: Emphasis on American Trust Territories, Folk Art of Mexico & Archaeology, 77-78, Merritt Col Anthrop Mus. Teaching: Instr, Merritt Col, Oakland, 62-, prof prehist art, 72- Pos: Dir, Merritt Col Anthrop Mus, 73- Mem: Am Asn Mus; Western Art Asn; Calif Archaeol Soc. Mailing Add: 225 Canon Dr Orinda CA 94563

WOLFE, MILDRED NUNGESTER
PAINTER, DESIGNER
b Celina, Ohio, Aug 23, 12. Study: Athens Col; Univ Montevallo, AB, 32; Dixie Art Colony, with J Kelly Fitzpatrick; Art Students League, with Will Barnet; Chicago Art Inst; Colorado Springs Fine Arts Ctr, with Boardman Robinson, MA, 44. Work: Miss Art Asn, Jackson; Lauren Rogers Mus, Laurel, Miss; Print Collection, Libr Cong, Washington, DC;

Montgomery Mus Fine Arts, Ala; Middle South Utilities, Changing South Mag Collection, New Orleans. Comn: Orpheus (mosaic), McDowell Br Libr, Jackson, 58; Stations of the Cross, comn by Monsignor Joseia Chatham for St Richards, Jackson, 60; David (mosaic), comn by Elizabeth Kingford for St Dominic's Hosp, Jackson, 61; chapel window (stained glass), Frist Baptist Church, Hazelhurst, Miss, 65; symbolic windows, Independent Methodist Episcopal Church, Jackson, 71-74. Exhib: Southern Painters, McDowell Galleries, New York, 38; Nat Exhib Prints, Libr Cong, 44; Grumbacher Int Exhib, Lakeland, Fla, 52; Painters of Southeastern US, Univ SFla, 62; Bertrand Russell Peace Found Exhib, Nottingham, Eng, 73; Lauren Rogers Mus of Art, Laurel, Miss, 77; Old Capitol Mus, Jackson, Miss, 77 & 77-78. Teaching: Prof hist art & printmaking, Millsaps Col, 58-68. Awards: First Prize for Cotton Pickers, Southern Painter, McDowell Gallery, 38; First Prize for Watercolor, Miss Art Asn, 46; Award of Merit for Still Life, Grumbacher Int Exhib, 52. Mem: Miss Art Asn. Style & Technique: Painting arises out of feeling evoked by nature. Mailing Add: c/o Wolfe Gallery 4308 Old Canton Rd Jackson MS 39211

WOLFE, ROBERT, JR
PRINTMAKER, PAINTER
b Oxford, Ohio, May 15, 30. Study: Miami Univ, BFA, 52; Cincinnati Art Acad, 55; Univ Iowa, scholar, 59, with M Lasansky, MFA(printmaking), 60. Work: Cincinnati Art Mus, Ohio; New York Pub Libr; Dayton Art Inst, Ohio; Ohio State Univ; Univ Wis-Madison. Comn: Five color intaglios, Miami Univ, 71. Exhib: One-man shows, Prints, Paintings, Drawings, Dayton Art Inst, Ohio, 68 & Prints & Drawings, Grinnell Col, Iowa, 77; Five Contemp Printmakers, Northern Ariz Univ, 74; Engravings Am, Albrecht Gallery, Mus Art, St Joseph, Mo, 74; New American Graphics, Univ Wis-Madison, 75; Nine Midwest Printmakers, Mt St Joseph Col, Cincinnati, Ohio, 77. Teaching: Instr design, Clarion Col, Pa, 61-62; prof printmaking, Miami Univ, 62- Pos: Artist-illusr, US Army, 52-54. Awards: Res Grant, Miami Univ, 71; Purchase Award, New American Graphics, Univ Wis-Madison, 75; Res Grant for zinc relief printing, Miami Univ, Ohio, 78. Media: Oil; Intaglio, Lithography. Dealer: Malton Gallery Hyde Park Cincinnati OH. Mailing Add: 418 Bowden Lane Oxford OH 45056

WOLFE, TOWNSEND DURANT
PAINTER, ART ADMINISTRATOR
b Hartsville, SC, Aug 15, 35. Study: Ga Inst Technol; Atlanta Art Inst, BFA; Cranbrook Acad Art, MFA; Inst Art Admin, Harvard Univ, cert. Work: Ark Arts Ctr, Little Rock; Mint Mus Art, Charlotte, NC; Okla Arts Ctr, Oklahoma City; Miss Art Asn, Jackson; Carroll Reece Mem Mus, ETenn State Univ. Exhib: Ball State Teacher's Col Drawing Nat, Muncie, Ind, four shows, 59-67; Mead Painting of Yr Exhib, Atlanta, 62; Watercolors USA, Springfield, Mo, 63-64; Audubon Artist Nat, New York, 64-65; Bucknell Ann Drawing Nat, Lewisberg, Pa, 65. Teaching: Instr painting & drawing, Memphis Acad Arts, Tenn, 59-64; instr painting & drawing, Scarsdale Studio Workshop, NY, 64-65. Pos: Dir, Wooster Community Art Ctr, Danbury, Conn, 65-68; art dir, Upward Bound Proj, Danbury, summers 66-68; exec dir, Ark Arts Ctr, 68- Awards: M J Kaplan Painting Award, Nat Soc Casein Painters, 65; Silvermine Guild Award Painting, 18th Ann New Eng Exhib, 67; Award Merit & Purchase Prize, 57th Nat Painting Exhib, Miss Art Asn, 67. Mem: Am Asn Mus; Am Fedn Arts; Southeastern Asn Mus. Media: Oil, Bronze. Mailing Add: Ark Arts Ctr MacArthur Park Little Rock AR 72203

WOLFF, RICHARD EVANS
STAINED GLASS ARTIST, DESIGNER
b New York, NY, May 12, 42. Study: Boston Univ, BFA, 64; Syracuse Univ, MFA, 66. Work: (Stained glass windows in pub bldgs), Cathedral of the Immaculate Conception, Syracuse, NY; Christ Episcopal Church, NY; St Mary's Episcopal Church, Staten Island, NY; Holy Trinity Church, Bermuda. Comn: Centennial windows, Crouse Col, Syracuse Univ, 70; 2 nave windows, St John's Church, Pembroke, Bermuda, 73; 4 song windows, United Church of Fayetteville, NY, 74; Trumansburg windows, comn by Dr Donald Bidwell, 74-75; sacristy windows, St Mary's Church, NY, 75. Teaching: Assoc prof glass & drawing, Syracuse Univ, 67- Mem: Fel Royal Col Arts. Style & Technique: Glass design executed in all techniques; leaded glass, glass applique, dalle de verre. Mailing Add: 115 Buffington Rd Syracuse NY 13224

WOLFF, WILLIAM H
ART DEALER
b Brussels, Belg, Apr 15. 06; US citizen. Pos: Owner, William H Wolff Inc, 59- Mem: Asia Soc, NY; Nat Antique & Art Dealers Asn Am; Am Asn Dealers in Ancient, Oriental & Primitive Art. Specialty: Far Eastern anitquities; stone and bronze sculptures; Indian miniature paintings. Mailing Add: William H Wolff Inc 22 E 76th St New York NY 10021

WOLINS, JOSEPH
PAINTER
b Atlantic City, NJ, Mar 26, 15. Study: Nat Acad Design, 31-35; WPA Fed Art Proj, New York, 35-42. Work: Metrop Mus Art, New York; Norfolk Mus Arts & Sci, Va; Albrecht Mus, St Joseph, Mo; Fiske Univ Art Gallery, Ala; Ein Harod Mus, Israel. Exhib: Corcoran Gallery Art Biennial, Washington, DC, 47; Pa Acad Fine Arts Ann, Philadelphia, 48; Whitney Mus Am Art Ann, 49-53; Mus Mod Art Ann, Sao Paulo, Brazil, 62; Butler Inst Am Art Ann, Youngstown, Ohio, 65. Awards: Mark Rothko Found Award for Painting, 71; Award, Nat Inst of Arts & Lett, 76. Mem: Artists Equity Asn; Audubon Artists; Am Soc Contemp Artists. Media: Oil, Watercolor. Mailing Add: 463 West St New York NY 10014

WOLPERT, ELIZABETH DAVIS
PAINTER, INSTRUCTOR
b Ft Washington, Pa, Sept 12, 15. Study: Moore Col Art, BFA; Pa State Univ, MAEd; and with Hobson Pittman. Work: Woodmere Art Gallery, Philadelphia, Pa; Pa State Univ, University Park; Temple Univ, Philadelphia; Bob Jones Univ, Greenville, SC; Univ Miami, Coral Gables. Exhib: Pa Acad Fine Arts, Philadelphia, 48; Philadelphia Mus Art, 62; Butler Inst Art, Youngstown, Ohio, 65; many shows, Woodmere Art Gallery; Cheltenham Art Ctr, 66; plus many one-man shows. Teaching: Instr art, pub & pvt schs, 38- Awards: Charles K Smith First Prize & First Mem Prize, Woodmere Art Gallery, 53; First Purchase Prizes, Junto, Philadelphia, 58-59. Mem: Artists Equity Asn; Philadelphia Art Alliance; Philadelphia Mus Art; Woodmere Art Gallery; Nat Art Educ Asn. Style & Technique: Representational. Media: Oil. Mailing Add: Meadows Apt 140 Ambler PA 19002

WOLSKY, JACK
PAINTER, EDUCATOR
b Rochester, NY, Aug 5, 30. Study: Rochester Inst Technol, AS, 51; State Univ NY Col Buffalo, BS, 55, MS, 57. Work: Rochester Mem Art Gallery, NY; New Britain Mus Am Art, Conn; Munson-Williams Proctor Inst, Utica, NY; Rochester Inst Technol; State Univ NY Brockport. Exhib: Am Fedn Arts Exhib, Turkey, Iran & Pakistan; 154th Exhib, Pa Acad Fine Arts; State Univ NY Arts Convocation Exhib, Albright-Knox Gallery; Chautauqua Exhib Am Art; Univ Omaha Nat Exhib. Teaching: Prof studio art, State Univ NY Col Brockport, 59- Awards: Lillian Fairchild Award, Univ Rochester, 70; Distinguished Alumnus Award, State Univ NY Buffalo, 71; Fac Exchange Scholar, State Univ NY, 74. Bibliog: Talis Bergmanis (auth), Exuberant art of Jack Wolsky, Dem & Chronicle Publ, 12/13/70; Karen Ibrahim (auth), Abstract art of Jack Wolsky, News & Rev, Rochester Inst Technol, 71; Evolution of a moment, Channel 21 TV, Rochester, NY, 74. Style & Technique: Abstract organic forms utilizing glazing techniques. Media: Acrylic, Lacquer. Dealer: Oxford Gallery 267 Oxford St Rochester NY 14607. Mailing Add: 295 Washington St Spencerport NY 14559

WOLSKY, MILTON LABAN
PAINTER
b Omaha, Nebr, Jan 23, 16. Study: Univ Nebr, Omaha; Art Inst Chicago; and with Julian Levi & Hans Hofmann, New York. Work: Gov Mansion, State of Nebr; US Embassy, Lebanon; Air Force Hist Soc; US Nat Bank, Omaha. Exhib: Am Watercolor Soc, New York, 53; one-man exhib, Joslyn Art Mus, Omaha, 60; Nebr Centennial, Sheldon Art Gallery, Lincoln, 67. Teaching: Instr painting, Joslyn Art Mus, 58-62. Awards: First Award & Purchase Prize, Gov Art Show, 64. Style & Technique: Inventive, painterly organizations of the real world. Media: Oil. Collection: Wolsky Collection of contemporary paintings; donation to Joslyn Art Mus, 67. Publ: Auth, Basic Elements of Painting, 59; auth & illusr, Rock People, 70. Mailing Add: 5804 Leavenworth St Omaha NE 68106

WONG, CHING
PAINTER, WRITER
b Canton, China, Oct 24, 36. Study: Nat Cent Univ China, MFA; Art Students League; Pratt Graphics Ctr, New York. Work: Philbrook Art Mus, Okla; Honolulu Acad Art, Hawaii; Hong Kong City Hall Mus; Honolulu City Hall; Hawaii State Found Cult & Art. Comn: Mural, US Jaycees, Tulsa, 72; painting, United Airlines, Hawaii, 72. Exhib: Honolulu Acad Art, 70-75; Japan Print Asn Exhib, Tokyo Munic Mus, 72; US Am Nat Print Exhib, Hawaii, 73 & 78; Le Salon Exposision Tricentenaire, 73; Int Exhib Print, Norway, 74; Nat Watercolor Soc Exhib, Calif, 75; Hong Kong Art Ctr, 76. Pos: Traveling art critic, Lion Art Mag, 75- Awards: Gold Medal, Nat Woodcutters Exhib, China, 70; Acquisition Award, Hawaii State Found Cult & Art, 71-75; Acquisition Award, Honolulu Acad Art, 75. Mem: Honolulu Printmakers Asn; Pratt Graphics Ctr, New York; Hong Kong Chinese Contemp Artists Guild; Nat Watercolor Soc; Los Angeles Printmakers Soc. Style & Technique: Changing styles in modern European and Oriental techniques. Media: Oil, Watercolor, Etching. Publ: History of Chinese Ancient Arts, 67. Dealer: Downtown Art Gallery 125 Merchant St Honolulu HI 96802. Mailing Add: 3669 Hilo Pl Honolulu HI 96816

WONG, FREDERICK
PAINTER, INSTRUCTOR
b Buffalo, NY, May 31, 29. Study: Univ NMex, BFA & MA. Work: Butler Inst Am Art, Youngstown, Ohio; Atlanta Art Asn, Ga; Reading Mus Art, Pa; Philbrook Art Ctr, Tulsa, Okla; Neuberger Collection, Purchase, NY. Exhib: Los Angeles Co Mus Art, 59; Butler Inst Am Art, Youngstown, 60; Am Watercolor Soc, New York, 60-69; Watercolor USA, Springfield, Mo, 63; Mainstreams '69, Marietta, Ohio, 69. Teaching: Instr form & structure, Pratt Inst, 66-69; instr painting, drawing, calligraphy & design, Hofstra Univ. Awards: Butler Midyear Ann Bronze Medal, Butler Inst Am Art, 60; Gold Medal, Nat Arts Club, 61; Mainstreams '69 Award of Excellence, Marietta Col, 69. Mem: Am Watercolor Soc; Allied Artists Am. Media: Watercolor. Publ: Auth, Oriental Watercolor Techniques, Watson-Guptill, 77. Dealer: Self 77 Chambers St New York NY 10007. Mailing Add: 315 Riverside Dr New York NY 10025

WONG, JASON
MUSEUM DIRECTOR
b Long Beach, Calif, May 12, 34. Study: Long Beach City Col, AA, 54; Univ Calif, Los Angeles, BA, 63. Collections Arranged: Seven Decades of Design, organized through Calif Arts Comn grant for state tour, 67-68; Art of Alexander Calder—Gouaches, western states tour, 70; Max Beckmann Graphics, Nat Tour, 73; Photo/Synthesis Nat Invitational Exhib, NY State Coun on the Arts, 76-77. Pos: Asst cur, Long Beach Mus Art, 59-64; art dir, Audiorama Corp, Am-Quest Int, 64-65; cur, Long Beach Mus Art, 65, dir, 65-72; dir, Tucson Art Ctr, 72-73; dir visual arts div, Spokane World's Fair, 74; asst dir, Herbert F Johnson Mus Art, Cornell Univ, 74-77; prof museology, Syracuse Univ, 78- Pos: Cur, Joe & Emily Lowe Art Gallery, Syracuse Univ, 78- Awards: Nat Educ Asn Grant for Res in Museological Studies, 72. Mem: Am Asn Mus. Publ: Auth, exhib catalog introd, Art Int, 10-11/76. Mailing Add: Joe & Emily Lowe Art Gallery Sims Hall Syracuse Univ Syracuse NY 13210

WONNER, PAUL (JOHN)
PAINTER
b Tucson, Ariz, Apr 24, 20. Study: Calif Col Arts & Crafts; Univ Calif, Berkeley, MA, MLS. Work: Guggenheim Mus, New York; San Francisco Mus Art; Nat Collection Fine Arts, Smithsonian Inst, Washington, DC; Oakland Mus, Calif; Joseph H Hirshhorn Found; plus others. Exhib: Carnegie Inst, Pittsburgh, 58 & 64; Whitney Mus Am Art, New York, 59; Art Inst Chicago, 61 & 64; Univ Ill, 61, 63 & 65; Mus Mod Art, New York, 62; plus many others. Teaching: Instr painting, Univ Calif, Los Angeles, 63-64; instr painting, Otis Art Inst, 66-68. Mailing Add: 1151 Keeler Berkeley CA 94708

WOOD, BEATRICE
CERAMIST, EDUCATOR
b San Francisco, Calif. Study: Pottery with Glen Luckens, Otto & Gertrud Natzler & Viveka & Otto Heino. Work: Metrop Mus Art, New York; Newark Mus, NJ; Mus Int dell Ceramiche Faeaza, Italy. Exhib: Calif Palace of the Legion of Honor, San Francisco; Honolulu Acad of Art; M H de Young Mem Mus, San Francisco; Mus Contemp Crafts, New York; Phoenix Art Mus, Ariz; Santa Barbara Mus Art, Calif; Takishamaya Gallery, Tokyo, Japan; Tucson Art Ctr, Ariz. Teaching: Instr pottery, Happy Valley Sch, Ojai, Calif, 55-60. Awards: Richard Gump Award, Syracuse; Hon Mention, Mus Mod Art, New York. Bibliog: Frances Nauman (auth), I shock myself, Arts Mag, 5/77. Mem: Am Crafts Asn. Style & Technique: Lustre and decorative ware. Dealer: Zachary Waller 7930 Vulcan Dr Los Angeles CA 90046. Mailing Add: 8560 Hwy 150 Ojai CA 93023

WOOD, HARRY EMSLEY, JR
EDUCATOR, PAINTER
b Indianapolis, Ind, Dec 10, 10. Study: Univ Wis, BA & MA; Ohio State Univ, MA & PhD; Acad Belli Arti, Florence, Italy, with Ottono Rosai; and with John Frazier, Provincetown, Mass & Emil Bisttram, Taos, NMex. Work: Mem Union, Ariz State Univ; Phoenix Art Mus, Ariz; Nat Portrait Gallery, Smithsonian Inst, Washington, DC. Comn: Murals, Gt Cent Ins Co, Peoria, Ill; plus many portraits of prominent people. Exhib: Florence, Italy, 50; Phoenix Art Mus, 61; Phoenix & Tucson Ann, 62; Ariz State Univ; Northern Ariz Univ; plus other group & one-man shows. Teaching: Prof art, Ill Wesleyan Univ, 42-44; dean col fine arts,

Bradley Univ, 44-50; prof art, Ariz State Univ, 54-76, chmn dept, 54-66, emer prof art, 76- Pos: Art critic, Scottsdale Progress, Ariz, 74-77. Awards: Purchase Prize, Artist Guild, 59. Mem: Col Art Asn Am; Nat Art Educ Asn (nat coun, 58-62); Pac Art Asn (pres, 58-60); Ariz Art Educ Asn (pres, 54-55); Ariz Hist Soc. Publ: Auth, Lew Davis, 25 years of painting in Arizona, 61, Soul, an interpretation of That which might have been, Birmingham, 63, A sculpture by John Waddell & Faces of Abraham Lincoln, 70; auth, articles in, Lincoln Herald, 75; auth & illusr, The Sphinkus Has No Noise—An Egyptian Adventure, 77. Mailing Add: 104 Vista del Cerro Tempe AZ 85281

WOOD, JAMES ARTHUR (ART)
CARTOONIST, LECTURER
b Miami, Fla, June 6, 27. Study: Washington & Lee Univ, BA; Mich State Univ. Work: Libr Cong, Washington, DC; Permanent Libr Collection, Univ Va, Charlottesville; Univ Akron Collection, Ohio; William Allen White Collection, Univ Kans; Truman Libr Collection. Exhib: Brussels World's Fair, 58; one-man show, Pittsburgh Press, 59; Great Challenge, Int Cartoon Exhib, 59-60; Cartoon Show, Nat Portrait Gallery, 72. Pos: Ed cartoonist, Richmond Newsleader, 50-56; chief political cartoonist, Pittsburgh Press, 56-63; cartoonist & dir info, US Independent Tel Asn, 63- Awards: Freedoms Found Awards, 53, 54 & 58-60; Golden Quill Awards, 60 & 62; Huevos de Onix, Mexico City, 77. Mem: Asn Am Ed Cartoonist (bd mem, 59-63, pres, 75-); Nat Cartoonists Soc; Nat Press Club. Media: Pen & Ink, Crayon. Mailing Add: 7008 Tilden Lane Rockville MD 20852

WOOD, JAMES NOWELL
ART HISTORIAN, ART ADMINISTRATOR
b Boston, Mass, Mar 20, 41. Study: Williams Col, BA; Inst Fine Arts, NY Univ, MA. Pos: Asst to dir, Metrop Mus Art, New York, 67-68; asst cur, dept 20th century art, 68-70; cur, Albright-Knox Art Gallery, Buffalo, NY, 70-73, assoc dir, 73- Res: 19th and 20th century American and European painting, sculpture and decorative arts. Publ: Auth, Rockne Krebs, 71; auth, Six Painters, 71; auth, Max Bill: Painting, Sculpture, Graphics, 74; auth, Era of Exploration, 75. Mailing Add: Albright-Knox Art Gallery Buffalo NY 14222

WOOD, JIM (JAMES REID WOOD)
PAINTER, DESIGNER
b Suffern, NY, Feb 14, 42. Study: Lehigh Univ, BFA(art hist), 63; Pratt Inst, 63-65, with Gabriel Laderman & Lennart Anderson. Work: Phoenix Art Mus, Ariz; Mus of Fine Arts, Santa Fe, NMex; Long Beach Mus Art, Calif; Lehigh Univ, Bethlehem, Pa; Springfield Art Mus, Mo. Comn: Concert series poster, Col Santa Fe, NMex, 77. Exhib: Five shows, NMex & SW Fine Arts Biennials, Mus NMex, Santa Fe, 69-76; Midwest Biennial, Joslyn Art Mus, Omaha, Nebr, 72; Four-Corners Biennial, Phoenix Art Mus, Ariz, 73; Am Watercolor Soc Biennial, Springfield, Mo, 75; Fine Arts Ctr, Colorado Springs, 75; Five from NMex, Long Beach Mus Art, 76. Awards: Purchase Awards, Four-Corners Biennial, 73 & Watercolor USA, Southern Mo Mus Asn, 75; Visual Arts Fel Grant, Western States Art Found & Nat Endowment for the Arts, 76-77. Bibliog: William Peterson (auth), Camera obscura/camera lucida: Abdalla & Wood, Artspace Mag, 77. Style & Technique: Photo-derived still lifes and portraits. Media: Acrylic, Watercolor. Dealer: Janus Gallery 110 Galisteo St Santa Fe NM 87501; The Gallery Rose 9025 Santa Monica Blvd Los Angeles CA 90069. Mailing Add: 706 Sosaya St Santa Fe NM 87501

WOOD, ROBERT E
PAINTER, INSTRUCTOR
b Gardena, Calif, Feb 4, 26. Study: Pomona Col, BA; Claremont Grad Sch, with Millard Sheets, Phil Dike & Jean Ames, MFA. Work: Butler Inst Am Art, Youngstown, Ohio; West Tex Mus, Lubbock; Lytton Financial Corp, Los Angeles; Riverside Art Ctr & Mus, Calif; Wichita Art Asn & Mus, Kans. Exhib: Am Watercolor Soc, New York, 54 & 58-75; Watercolor USA, Springfield, Mo, 63-73; Watercolor West, Riverside, Calif, 69-75; Nat Watercolor Soc, 60-75; Nat Acad Design, New York. Teaching: Instr art, Univ Minn, Duluth, 52-55; instr art, Claremont Grad Sch, Calif, 58; dir watercolor, Robert E Wood Summer Sch Painting, Green Valley Lake, 61- Awards: Nat Watercolor Soc, Calif, 58-73; Am Watercolor Soc, New York, 69 & 71; Watercolor West, Riverside, 70-75. Bibliog: San Bernardino Valley Col, Visit to the artist's studio, Educ/TV, 66. Mem: Am Watercolor Soc (vpres, 68-74); Nat Watercolor Soc; Nat Acad Design; Watercolor West; West Coast Watercolor Soc. Style & Technique: Landscapes and figure painting, personally stylized, direct and free translations of nature. Media: Watercolor; Drawing. Publ: Auth, Robert E Wood, advocate thorough preparation, Am Artist Mag, 68; auth & producer, The search for a creative watercolor, cassette & slides, 72; co-auth, Watercolor Workshop, 74. Dealer: Challis Galleries 1390 South Coast Hwy PO Box 1356 Laguna Beach CA 92652. Mailing Add: 33135 Maple Lane PO Box 216 Green Valley Lake CA 92341

WOODARD, TOM L
ART DEALER, CRITIC
b Gallup, NMex, Aug 15, 36. Study: Univ Ariz, Tucson. Collections Arranged: Numerous shows in Gallup for Indian artists, as well as exhibitions throughout the US & Europe. Pos: Owner, Woodard's Indian Arts, Gallup; judge, Scottsdale Nat Indian Art Coun, Navajo Tribal Fair, Santa Fe Indian Market & Heard Mus, Phoenix. Res: Study of Indian art. Specialty: American Indian art. Collection: Extensive collection of all Indian artists since 1900. Mailing Add: Woodard's Indian Arts 224 W Coal Ave Gallup NM 87301

WOODEN, HOWARD EDMUND
MUSEUM DIRECTOR, ART CRITIC
b Baltimore, Md, Oct 10, 19. Study: Johns Hopkins Univ, BS & MA. Collections Arranged: Rose Hulman Institute Collection of British Watercolors (with catalog), 67-72; Sculptures by Ernst Eisenmayer, 67-68; John Silk Deckard: 1960-1970, 70-71; B M Jackson Retrospective, 75; Thomas Nast—19th Century Am Artist & Political Satirist, 75; 5000 Yrs of Art from the Metrop Mus (inaugural exhib of the new Wichita Art Mus), 77. Teaching: Fulbright instr, Athens Col, 51-52; lectr art hist, Univ Evansville, 55-63; assoc prof, Univ Fla, 63-66; assoc prof art hist, Ind State Univ, Terre Haute, 67-75. Pos: Dir, Sheldon Swope Art Gallery, Terre Haute, 66-75; dir, Wichita Art Mus, 75- Awards: Fulbright Grant, US Dept State, 51-52. Mem: Col Art Asn Am; Am Asn Mus; Soc Archit Historians; Archaeol Inst Am. Res: British watercolor painting of the 18th and 19th centuries; American architecture of the 19th century; meaning in contemporary art. Publ: Auth, Architectural heritage of Evansville, 62; auth, Fifty paintings and sculptures from the collection of Sheldon Swope Art Gallery, 72; plus numerous articles & brochures. Mailing Add: Wichita Art Mus 619 Stackman Dr Wichita KS 67203

WOODHAM, DERRICK JAMES
SCULPTOR
b Blackburn, Eng, Nov 5, 40. Study: SE Essex Tech Col Sch Art, intermediate dipl design; Hornsey Col Arts & Crafts, nat dipl design; Royal Col Art, dipl. Work: Tate Gallery, London, Eng; Mus Contemp Art, Nagaoka, Japan. Comn: Sculpture, comn by J Meeker, Ft Worth, Tex, 69; sculpture, comn by S P Steinberg, Newlett, NY, 71; sculpture, comn by North Jersey Cult Coun, Paramus, NJ. Coun, Paramus, NJ. Exhib: New Generation, 1965, Whitechapel Gallery, London, 65; Paris Biennale, Mus Art Mod, 65; Primary Structures, Jewish Mus, New York, 66; British Sculpture of the 60's, Nash House Gallery, London, 70; Der Geist Surrealismus, Baukunst Galerie, Köln, WGer, 71; Sculpture in the Park, Paramus, NJ, 71 & 74; Wright State Univ Gallery, 76; Nat Sculpture Exhib traveling exhib, 76-77; Artists Choose Artists, Tweed Mus, Duluth, 77; one-man show, Jewish Mus, 69. Teaching: Instr sculpture, Philadelphia Col Art, 68-70; asst prof art forms found, Univ Iowa Sch Art, 70-73; mem dept art, Univ Ky, currently. Awards: Stuyvesant Found Bursary, 65; Prix de la Ville, Sculpture, Paris Biennale, 65. Bibliog: Grace Gluek (auth), British sculptures, Art in Am, 66; Robert Kudielka, Abscheid vom Object, Kunstwerke, 10/68; Otto Kulturman (auth), The New Sculpture, Praeger, 69; Teruo Fujieda (auth), Form & Structure, Kodansha Ltd, 72. Mailing Add: Dept of Art Univ of Ky Lexington KY 40506

WOODHAM, JEAN
SCULPTOR, EDUCATOR
b Midland City, Ala, Aug 16, 25. Study: Auburn Univ, BA; Sculpture Ctr, New York; Univ Ill, Kate Neal Kinley Mem fel. Work: Massillon Mus Permanent Collection, Ohio; Nuclear Ship Savannah; Telfair Acad Arts & Sci, Savannah, Ga; Alfred Khouri Mem Collection, Norfolk Mus Arts & Sci, Va; Westport Permanent Collection, Conn. Comn: Fountain sculptures, Flintkote Corp Hq, White Plains, NY, 68-69, Gen Tel & Electronics Hq, Stamford, Conn, 73 & Tex Eastern Transmission, Houston Ctr, Tex, 74-75; fountain pieces, Gen Elec Credit Corp, Stamford, Conn, 71-72; Scholar's Sphere (four and one-half ton sculpture), Harry S Truman High Sch, New York, 77. Exhib: Pa Acad Fine Arts Ann, Philadelphia, 50-54; Womens Int Art Club, New Burlington Gallery, London, Eng, 55; New Eng Ann, Silvermine Guild, Conn, 55-60; US Info Agency Exhibs, Arg, Brazil, Chile & Mex, 63; Selected Sculptors Guild, Albright-Knox Art Gallery, Buffalo, NY, 71; plus others. Teaching: Head dept sculpture, Silvermine Guild Artists, 55-56; instr sculpture, Stamford Mus, Conn, 67-69; vis asst prof sculpture, Auburn Univ, 70, assoc prof, Auburn Univ, 74-75. Pos: Chmn sculpture, New York Fedn Women's Clubs, 50-51; mem bd mgrs, Silvermine Guild Artists. 58-60; mem exec bd, Sculptors Guild Inc, New York, 77-78. Awards: Jacobs Award for Best Sculpture & Beatman Award for Best of Show, New Eng Ann, 60; Audubon Artists Medal for Creative Sculpture, 62; Medals of Honor for Sculpture, Nat Asn Women Artists, 66 & 74. Bibliog: Jean Woodham-Sculptress, Veritas Corp, 66; Dr L Funderburk (auth), Art in Public Places in the United States, Bowling Green Univ, 75; Suzanne Benton (auth), Art of Welded Sculpture, 76. Mem: Sculptors Guild (treas, 60-65, exec bd, 66-68, secy, 72-); Archit League New York; Audubon Artists (juror, 64); Artists Equity Asn; Nat Asn Women Artists (juror, 60, 61 & 63-66, chmn sculpture, 65-66). Style & Technique: Large scale sculptures for outdoor environments, using industrial methods such as gas, arc & tungsten tig stands for inert gas welding of metals. Mailing Add: 26 Pin Oak Lane Westport CT 06880

WOODLOCK, ETHELYN HURD
PAINTER
b Hallowell, Maine, June 9, 07. Study: Copley Sch Commercial Art, Boston, Mass. Work: Valley Hosp, Ridgewood, NJ; Carlson Collection, Ramsey, NJ; Hickory Art Mus, SC; Bergen Community Mus, NJ; UN Bldg, New York. Exhib: 64th Am Show, Art Inst Chicago, 61; Contemporary Portraits, Fitchburg Art Mus, Mass, 62; Awards Artists Exhib, Montclair Art Mus, 66; Contemporary American Realism, Hammond Mus, Salem, NY, 68; two-man show, Bergen Community Mus, 71. Awards: Best Traditional Oil, Nat Asn Women Artists, 73; Gold Medal, Catharine Lorillard Wolfe, 73; Award of Highest Merit, Tri-State Bergen Co Artists Guild, 75, among others. Bibliog: Rodger (auth), Nonverbal communication, Am Soc Clin Hypnosis, 72. Mem: Nat Asn Women Artists; Catharine Lorillard Wolfe Art Club; Am Artists Prof League; Allied Artists Am. Style & Technique: Surrealistic. Media: Oil. Mailing Add: 15 Franklin Ave Midland Park NJ 07432

WOODNER, IAN
COLLECTOR
Mem: Art Collectors Club. Collection: Ancient art, Ethnographica and Near East. Mailing Add: 39 W 67th St New York NY 10023

WOODRUFF, HALE A
PAINTER, EDUCATOR
b Cairo, Ill, Aug 26, 00. Study: John Herron Art Inst, Indianapolis, Ind, Fogg Art Mus, Harvard Univ; Acad Scandinave & Acad Mod, Paris; Morgan State Col, hon DFA; also fresco painting with Diego Rivera, Mex; Atlanta Univ, hon PhD, 72. Work: Newark Mus, NJ; Metrop Mus of Art, New York; High Mus of Art, Atlanta, Ga; Indianapolis Mus of Art, Ind; Johnson Publ Co, Chicago; Libr Cong, Washington, DC; IBM Collection; Howard Univ, Washington, DC; Lincoln Univ, Jefferson City, Mo; plus other pub & pvt collections. Exhib: Galerie Jeune Peinture, Paris; First Nat Exhib Am Art, New York; Whitney Mus Am Art; one-man shows, Int Print Soc, State Mus NC, Chapel Hill & Greensboro; plus other group & one-man shows at mus, cols, schs & galleries throughout US. Teaching: Lectr, Drew Univ, Denver Mus, Univ Mass, Amherst, Queensboro Jewish Ctr, Vassar Col, Univ Colo, Boulder & many other clubs, schs & art groups throughout US; prof art educ, NY Univ, emer prof, 68- Pos: Art dir, Atlanta Univ; US deleg, First World Conf of Negro Arts, Dakar, Senegal, 66; lectr US art & artists, US State Dept tour of five WAfrican countries, 66. Awards: Julius Rosenwald Fel Continued Creativity Art, 43-45; Bronze Award & Hon Mention, Harmon Found; First Award, High Mus Art, Atlanta; Citation for Serv to Community & Art, Mayor Abraham Beame, New York, NY; plus others. Bibliog: Alain Locke (auth), Negro art past & present & article, In: Am Mag Art; Ralph M Pearson (auth), Experiencing pictures, Simon & Schuster, New art education, Harpers & article, In: Forum Mag; Ralph McGill (auth), article, In: Atlanta Constitution; plus others. Mem: NJ Soc Artists. Style & Technique: Semi-abstract. Media: Oil, Watercolor. Dealer: Arch of Am Art 41 E 65th St New York NY 10021. Mailing Add: 22 E Eighth St New York NY 10003

WOODS, GURDON GRANT
SCULPTOR, EDUCATOR
b Savannah, Ga, Apr 15, 15. Study: Art Students League; Brooklyn Mus Sch; San Francisco Art Inst, Hon DArts, 66. Work: City of San Francisco. Comn: Steel fountain & concrete relief panels, IBM Corp, San Jose, Calif; aluminum fountain, Paul Masson Winery, Saratoga, Calif; concrete panels, McGraw-Hill, Novato, Calif; plus others. Exhib: San Francisco Art Inst Ann; San Francisco Art Festivals; Denver Mus Ann; Sao Paulo Biennial; Southern Sculpture Ann; Janus Gallery, Los Angeles, 76; Los Angeles Munic Art Gallery, 77; Los Angeles Co Mus of Art, 78; plus others. Teaching: Instr sculpture, San Francisco Art Inst, 55-65; prof art, Univ Calif, Santa Cruz, 66-74, chmn dept, 66-70. Pos: Dir, Col San Francisco Art Inst, 55-65; sculptor mem, San Francisco Art Comn, 54-56; sculptor mem, Santa Cruz Art Comn, 70-74; dir, Otis Art Inst, Los Angeles, 74-77; asst dir, Los Angeles Co Mus of Natural Hist, 77- Awards: Four Purchase Awards, San Francisco Art Festivals; plus other grants & citations.

Mem: San Francisco Art Inst (exec dir, 55-64). Media: Concrete; Paper. Mailing Add: 3109 Coolidge Ave Los Angeles CA 90066

WOODS, RIP
PAINTER, EDUCATOR
b Idabel, Okla, Aug 15, 33. Study: Ariz State Univ, MAE, 58. Work: Phoenix Art Mus, Ariz; Ariz State Univ, Tempe; Ark State Univ, Jonesboro; Yuma Fine Arts Ctr, Ariz; Ariz Western Col, Yuma. Comn: Relief-assemblage mural (with Ray Fink), Nat Housing Industs, Phoenix, 70; mosaic & bas relief painting (with Ray Fink), Greyhound-Armour, Phoenix, 71. Exhib: Drawing USA, Calif Palace of Legion of Honor, San Francisco, 60; one-man show, Phoenix Art Mus, 68; Art on Paper, Weatherspoon Gallery, NC, 69; Ill Bell Traveling Exhib, Chicago, 70-71; 73rd Western Ann, Denver, Colo, 71; Ariz Print Competition traveling exhib, 76; Ariz Outlook traveling exhib, 76; Invitational Exhib, Univ of Minn, Duluth, 77; FESTAC Visual Art Exhib, Lagos, Nigeria, 77. Teaching: Prof painting & drawing, Ariz State Univ, 65-; assoc prof painting, Colorado Springs Fine Art Ctr, Colo, summer 67. Media: Mixed Media. Mailing Add: Col of Fine Arts Ariz State Univ Tempe AZ 85281

WOODS, SARAH LADD
COLLECTOR, PATRON
b Lincoln, Nebr, May 8, 95. Study: Wellesley Col, BA; Univ Nebr, LHD. Pos: Patron, past pres & life trustee, Nebr Art Asn. Interest: Thomas C Woods Collection, Sheldon Gallery, University of Nebraska. Collection: Contemporary American. Mailing Add: 2475 Lake St Lincoln NE 68502

WOODS, TED
SCULPTOR, CRAFTSMAN
b Akron, Ohio, Jan 1, 48. Study: Ariz State Univ, with Ben Goo, BFA & MFA. Work: Ariz State Univ; also numerous pvt collections. Exhib: 7th Nat Sculpture & Drawing Exhib, Corpus Christi, Tex, 73; 12th Ann Drawing & Small Sculpture Show, Muncie, Ind, 74; 9th Southwestern, Yuma, Ariz, 74; 64th Ann Nat Exhib, Laguna Gloria Art Mus, Tex, 75; Four Corners Biennial '75, Phoenix Art Mus, Ariz; Small Sculptures: Nat, Cypress Col, Calif, 76; 1st Ann Wood-in-Art Exhib, Ariz State Univ, Tempe, 77; 10th Biennial Craft Exhib, El Paso Mus of Art, Tex, 77. Teaching: Nat Endowment Arts artist in residence, Mesa, Ariz, 72-73; vis staff instr sculpture, Glendale Community Col, 73- Awards: Spec Award Sculpture, Dimensions '73; Purchase Award, 9th Southwestern, Yuma; First Place Wood, 10th Biennial Craft Exhib, 77. Mem: Artist-Blacksmith's Asn NAm; Am Crafts Coun; Southern Asn Sculptors, Inc. Style & Technique: Juxtaposition of shapes and line in space, balance, counterbalance, color and texture (applied-inherent) utilizing wood and metal in all fabrication phases. Media: Metal, Plastics, Wood. Dealer: Cactus Flower 7137 Stetson Dr Scottsdale AZ 85251. Mailing Add: 964 E Ninth Dr Mesa AZ 85204

WOODS, WILLIS FRANKLIN
MUSEUM DIRECTOR
b Washington, DC, July 25, 20. Study: Brown Univ, AB; Am Univ; Univ Ore. Teaching: Instr art, Palm Beach Jr Col, 58-62. Pos: Asst dir, Corcoran Gallery Art, Washington, DC, 47-49; dir, Norton Gallery & Sch Art, West Palm Beach, Fla, 49-62; dir, Detroit Inst Arts, 62-73, hon trustee, Founders Soc; dir, Seattle Art Mus, 74- Mem: Am Asn Mus; Am Asn Mus Dirs. Mailing Add: Seattle Art Mus Volunteer Park Seattle WA 98112

WOODSIDE, GORDON WILLIAM
ART DEALER, COLLECTOR
b Seattle, Wash. Study: Univ Wash. Pos: Dir, Gordon Woodside Galleries, Seattle. Specialty: Artists of the Pacific Northwest. Collection: Representative works by prominent artists of the Northwest. Mailing Add: 803 E Union St Seattle WA 98122

WOODSON, DORIS
EDUCATOR, PAINTER
b Richmond, Va, Jan 13, 29. Study: Xavier Univ, New Orleans, BA; Commonwealth Univ, Richmond, Va, MFA. Work: Bank of Va, Richmond; Univ Pa. Exhib: 11th Ann Piedmont Painting Show, Mint Mus, Charlotte, NC, 71; Mainstreams 71, Int Painting, Marietta, Ohio, 71; Virginia Artists, Va Mus, Richmond, 71 & 75; Artists Showcase Gallery, Virginia Beach, Va, 73. Teaching: Instr painting, Richard Bland Col, Petersburg, Va, 69; asst prof painting & drawing, Va State Col, Petersburg, 69- Pos: Dir gallery, Va State Col, Petersburg, 69- Awards: Petersburg Art Festival, Petersburg Area Art Leagues, 68-74; Norfolk Art Festival, Tidewater Artists Asn, 73; Lynchburg Art Festival, Lynchburg Art Asn, 74. Mem: Richmond Artists Asn (secy, 68-69); Petersburg Art League. Style & Technique: Hard edged/realism, figure painting, non objective 3-dimensional constructions, light and shadow interest. Media: Acrylic, Plexiglas. Mailing Add: 20007 Roosevelt Ave Colonial Heights VA 23834

WOODSON, SHIRLEY ANN
PAINTER, EDUCATOR
b Pulaski, Tenn, Mar 3, 36. Study: Wayne State Univ, BFA, MA; Art Inst Chicago. Work: Dulin Gallery Art, Knoxville, Tenn; Detroit Pub Schs, Mich. Exhib: Childe Hassam Found Purchase Exhib, Acad Arts & Lett, New York, 68; Mich Artists Exhib, Detroit Inst Arts, 60; Collaboration: Painter & Poet, Shirley Woodson, Dudley Randall Arts Extended Gallery, Detroit, 69; Chico State Col Watercolor Invitational, 72; one-man show, Howard Univ, 75. Teaching: Instr painting, design, drawing & art hist, Highland Park Community Col, 66-; instr painting, Wayne State Univ, 74. Pos: Dir exhib, Arts Extended Gallery, 63-71. Awards: Purchase Prize, Print & Drawing Exhib, Dulin Gallery Art, Knoxville, Tenn, 65; Fel, MacDowell Colony, 66-67. Bibliog: Louise Bruner (auth), Black artists in America, Toledo Blade, 69; Joy Hakanson (auth), Art, Woodson-Randall, Detroit News, 4/69; Leonead Pack Bailey (auth), Broadside Poets and Artists, Broadside Press, 74. Dealer: Celia A Woodson & Edsel Reid 17215 San Juan Detroit MI 48221. Mailing Add: 5656 Oakman Blvd Detroit MI 48204

WOODWARD, CLEVELAND LANDON
PAINTER, ILLUSTRATOR
b Glendale, Ohio, June 25, 00. Study: Cincinnati Art Acad, scholar, 23-26; Charles Hawthorne's Cape Cod Sch Art, summer 24; Brit Art Acad, Rome, Italy, 28-29. Work: Mus Fine Arts, Mobile, Ala; Arctic Mus, Brunswick, Maine; Boardman Press, Nashville, Tenn; United Lutheran Publ House, Philadelphia; Christian Bd Publ, St Louis, Mo. Comn: Samuel & Eli (mural), Seventh Presby Church, Cincinnati, Ohio, 49; painting for Donald B MacMillan of Arctic Mus, Brunswick, Maine, 52; 16 watercolor illus for World Bible, World Publ Co, 62; Peter & John (mural), West Eng Baptist Church, Mobile, 72; plus others. Exhib: Cincinnati Art Mus Spring Exhib, 25; one-man shows, Traxel Art Gallery, Cincinnati, 29, Mus Fine Art, Mobile, 68, 71 & 77 & Percy Whiting Mus, Fairhope, Ala, 69 & 71. Teaching: Lectr Biblical art, schs, cols & mus, many yrs; instr oil painting, Eastern Shore Acad Fine Arts, 72- Pos: Co-founder & mem first bd dirs, Cape Cod Art Asn. Bibliog: Article in Am Artist Mag, 5/73. Mem: Eastern Shore Art Asn (bd dirs, 71-74); Eastern Shore Acad Fine Arts (adv comt). Style & Technique: Direct in oil with very little preparatory drawing; watercolor technique is wet on wet. Media: Oil, Watercolor. Publ: Illusr, By an Unknown Disciple, Harper Bros, The Other Wise Man, Harper Bros, Painting Christ Head, Abingdon & The Shepherds and the Angel, Standard Publ. Dealer: Orleans Art Gallery Main St Orleans Cape Cod MA 02653; Koch Galleries 162 S Lawrence St Mobile AL 36602. Mailing Add: 354 Boone Lane Fairhope AL 36532

WOODWARD, HELEN M
PAINTER, COLLECTOR
b Orange Co, Ind, July 28, 10. Study: John Herron Art Inst; Cape Cod Sch of Art, study with Jerry Farnsworth; Art Students League, study with Robert Brackman; Wayman Adams; Elliot O'Hara & Frank Schoonover. Work: Ind Univ, Music Hall, Bloomington, Ind; J W Armbruster Collections, Bronxville, New York; Cincinnati Bible Seminary, Ohio; plus others. Comn: Portraits, Head of Engineering Sch, Agriculture, Dean & head of Pub Relations, Purdue Univ, Woman Benefactor, Finch Col & Industrialist, Little Sisters of the Poor Hospital. Exhib: Hoosier Salon, Chicago, Ill, 28 & 30; Ind State Fair, 30; Objectivity in Contemp Painting, Herron Mus of Art, 63; Jefferson Life Insurance Bldg, 75; Portraits & Flowers, Ind Nat Bank, 77; Midwestern Art Mus, Evansville, Ind; Ind Artists Exhib; Ind Artists Club Prizes; Portrait Files of the Smithsonian Inst, Nat Gallery of Fine Arts. Awards: Popular Vote, Herron Art Mus, Booth Tarkington, 39; Excellence in Painting, Exhib of Objectivity, John Herron Art Mus, 63; Merit Award, Ind Artists Exhib, L S Ayres, 74. Bibliog: Mrs L F Smith (auth), Executive Chair, Hoosier Salon, 60 & Corbin Potrkk (auth), Art Critic, Indianapolis Star; Marion Garmel (auth), Art Critic, Indianapolis News. Mem: Ind Artists Club; Ind Mus of Art; Contemp Club of Ind; Ind Art League. Style & Technique: Begins painting with lights, darks and medium tones, bringing up detail last; brilliant colors. Collection: Small collection of Charles W Hawthorne, Farnsworth, Eliot O'Hare, watercolor; autograph signed letters; George Stubbs, Bonheuer, Danton, King of Bavaria, Lord Byran, Marie Teresse, Whistler, Chalon; Fine old Japanese Prints. Publ: Contribr, Rotogravure Section, Chicago Tribune, 30; contribr, La Review Moderine, Paris, France, 35; contribr, Booklets of Herron Mus of Art, 63; contribr, Indianapolis Star; contribr, Indianapolis News. Mailing Add: 5849 Winthrop Ave Indianapolis IN 46220

WOODWARD, WILLIAM
PAINTER, EDUCATOR
b Washington, DC, Mar 11, 35. Study: Abbott Sch Art, Corcoran Sch Art, Am Univ, BA & MA, Washington, DC; Acad de Belli Arti, Florence, Italy. Work: Art in Embassies Prog. Comn: Welded steel sculpture, Wilco Bldg, 63, drawing, The White House, 68, mural, United Brotherhood Teamsters, 69, Washington, DC; mural, Eutaw Sch, Baltimore, 68; mural, George Washington Masonic Temple, Alexandria, Va, 74. Exhib: One-man shows, Mickelson Gallery, Washington, DC, 66-74, Hirschl & Adler Gallery, New York, 71, John State Col, Vt, 74 & Washington Co Mus Fine Art, Hagerstown, Md, 75; Adams-Davidson Gallery, Washington, DC, 74. Teaching: Instr painting, Corcoran Sch Art, Washington, DC, 65-69; asst prof painting, George Washington Univ, Washington, DC, 69- Awards: Painting Fel in Italy, Leopold Schepp Found, 57-59; Mary Graydon Scholar, Am Univ, 53-57 & Teaching Fel, 58-61. Bibliog: Leroy Aarons (auth), Artist refuses to nonconform, Washington Post, 10/23/66; Rafael Sqirru (auth), The Washington mannerists: the foresight to look backwards, Americas, Vol 19, No 1; Legrace N Benson (auth), The Washington scene, Art Int, Vol 13, No 10; Jill Weschsler (auth), William Woodward: Traditional themes, modern methods, Am Artist, 12/76. Style & Technique: Figures in landscapes, acrylic underpainting, overpainting in oils, glazing and alla prima technique. Publ: Auth bk rev, Art in America, 1760-1860, 69, contribr, Leonardo da Vinci, 70 & Dreamers of Decadence, 72, Washington Post. Mailing Add: 1314 28th St NW Washington DC 20007

WOODY, (THOMAS) HOWARD
SCULPTOR, EDUCATOR
b Salisbury, Md, Sept 26, 35. Study: Richmond Prof Inst, BFA; E Carolina Univ, MA; Univ Iowa; Art Inst Chicago; Kalamazoo Art Ctr; Univ Ky. Work: Miami Mus Mod Art, Fla; Mint Mus Art, Charlotte, NC; Birmingham Mus Art, Ala; Columbus Mus Arts & Crafts, Ga; Royal Ont Mus, Toronto. Exhib: Smithsonian Touring Sculpture Exhib, 69; Agora 2, Mus D'Art Mod, Strasbourg, France, 74; atmospheric one-man presentations, Int Cult Centrum, Antwerp, Belg, 74, Arnolfini Gallery, Bristol, Gt Brit, 75 & Mint Mus Art, Charlotte, NC, 75. Teaching: Instr sculpture, Roanoke Fine Art Ctr, Va, 59-61; assoc prof sculpture, Pembroke State Univ, 62-67; prof sculpture, Univ SC, 67-, Russell Creative Res Award, 72. Awards: Spec Citation Award, Atlanta Festival Sculpture, 68; SC State Art Collection Award, SC Arts Comn, 71 & 74. Bibliog: J A Morris (auth), Contemporary artists of South Carolina, Greenville Co Mus Art, 70; C Rossignol (auth), Agora 2, Mus D'Art Mod, Strasbourg, 74; D Z Meilach (auth), Soft sculpture, Crown Publ, 74. Mem: Southern Asn Sculptors (pres, 65-70); Nat Sculpture Ctr (adv, 66-); Guild SC Artists (mem bd, 69); SC Craftsmen (mem bd, 68); Southeastern Col Art Conf. Style & Technique: Lighter than air launched, free floating atmospheric sky sculpture. Media: Sky Sculpture, Assemblage. Publ: Auth, Atmospheric sky sculpture, Studio Int, 6/74; auth, Kinetic environmental art: sky sculpture, Leonardo, summer 74; auth, Atmospheric sculpture: concepts, procedures & events, Sculpture Quart, winter 74; auth, Atmospheric sculpture: an event, not an object, Vol 7, No 1 & Atmospheric concepts, Vol 6, No 2, Southeastern Col Art Conf Rev. Mailing Add: 433 Arrowwood Rd Columbia SC 29210

WOOF, MAIJA (MAIJA GEGERIS ZACK PEEPLES)
PAINTER
b Riga, Latvia, Nov 21, 42. Study: Univ Calif, Davis, BA, 64, MA, 65; also with William T Wiley, Robert Arneson & Wayne Thiebaud. Work: Crocker Art Gallery, Sacramento, Calif; La Jolla Mus Art, Calif; Matthews Art Ctr, Tempe, Ariz; San Francisco Mus Art; Norman MacKenzie Art Gallery, Regina, Sask. Comn: Beast rainbow painting, City of San Francisco, Civic Ctr, 67; rainbow house, pvt party, San Francisco, 67-68; ceiling murals, Rainbow House, San Francisco, 67-68; crocheted, woven & sewn beast curtains, Univ Calif Art Bldg, Davis, 71. Exhib: One-man shows, Candy Store Gallery, Folsom, Calif, 65-77 & Mem Union Art Gallery, Davis, Calif, 75; Grotesque Show, San Francisco, Boston, & Philadelphia, 69; Sacramento Sampler 1, Crocker Art Gallery, Oakland Mus & Brazil, 71-72; The World of Woof, Ariz, 71-72; Beast Retrospective, Univ Calif Gallery, Davis, 72; San Francisco Bay Area Printmakers, Cincinnati Mus of Art, Ohio, 73; San Francisco Art Mus, 73-75; Cup & Goblet, Univ Nev, Reno, 74; Calif Ceramics Exhib, Calif State Fair Expo, Sacramento, 74; Rainbow Show, De Young Mus, San Francisco, 74-75; Beastie Sheikcup, Sea of Japan Exhib, Tokyo, 74; Calif Women Artists, Sacramento State Capitol, 75; Three Calif Artists, Univ Calif, Davis Gallery, 76; Crossroads Gallery, 76; Bounty of Beasties, Am River Col, Sacramento, 77. Collections Arranged: The Nut Show, for Kaiser-Aetna, Tahoe Verdes, Calif, 72. Teaching: Instr art, Laney Col, Oakland, 68-69; instr art, Univ Calif, Davis, 71-72; instr art, Sierra Col, Rocklin, Calif, 71-73. Awards: Award, Ceramics Excellence, Calif State Fair, 74. Bibliog: Andrew Gale (auth), An art original, Sacramento Bee, 71; Corinne Geeting (auth), California's Joan of Art, Lifestyle, 75. Media: Oil, Acrylic, Clay, Thread, Dye. Dealer:

Candy Store Gallery 605 Sutter St Folsom CA 95630. Mailing Add: 2586 King Richard Dr El Dorado Hills CA 95630

WOOLFENDEN, WILLIAM EDWARD
ART ADMINISTRATOR, ART HISTORIAN
b Detroit, Mich, June 27, 18. Study: Wayne State Univ, BA & MA. Pos: Asst cur Am art, Detroit Inst Arts, 45-49, dir educ, 49-60; asst dir, Arch Am Art, Detroit, 60-62, exec dir, 62-64, dir, 64-70, dir, Arch Am Art, Smithsonian Inst, New York, 70-; mem vis comt, Dept Am Paintings & Sculpture, Metrop Mus Art, New York; adv drawings, Minn Mus Art, St Paul. Mem: Am Asn Mus; Col Art Asn Am; Soc Archit Historians; Nat Trust Hist Preservation. Res: American art; American drawings. Mailing Add: 219 E 69th St New York NY 10021

WORTH, CARL
ART ADMINISTRATOR
b New York, NY, June 30, 35. Study: Univ Calif, Berkeley, BA, 60, MA(painting), 61. Exhib: Development of 70 exhibs of diverse work by Bay Area Artists. Pos: Asst cur decorative arts, Cooper Union Mus, New York, 62-64; set designer, Actors' Workshop, San Francisco, 66; dir community arts, City of Berkeley, Calif, 67-, developer, Romare Bearden Mural Proj for Berkeley City Coun Chambers, 73. Mem: Western Asn Art Mus (co-chmn conf, 72); Berkeley Civic Art Comn (secy, 70-); Civic Art Found, Berkeley (bd dirs, 70-); Alameda Co Neighborhood Arts Prog (bd dirs, 74-). Mailing Add: Berkeley Art Ctr 1275 Walnut St Berkeley CA 94709

WORTH, KAREN
SCULPTOR
b Philadelphia, Pa, Mar 9, 24. Study: Tyler Art Sch, Temple Univ; Pa Acad Fine Arts; Acad Grande Chaumiere, Paris. Work: Smithsonian Inst; West Point Acad, NY; Am Jewish Hist Asn, Boston; Jewish Mus, New York; Israel Govt Coins & Medals Div, Jerusalem. Comn: Portraits, Mimi Murray, New York & Braj Kumar Nehru, India, 59 & many others; Space Age (medal), Soc Medalists, 63; Hist Jews of Am, Judaic Heritage Soc, 69; Presidents USA, Whittnauer Precious Metals Guild, 74; Bicentennial Presidents (medal), Galaxies Unlimited Inc, 75. Exhib: Nat Acad, New York, 65; Lever House, New York, 66-; Ceramic Sculpture of Western Hemisphere. Teaching: Pvt sculpture classes, 72-73. Pos: Co-chmn, Sculptors Pen & Brush, New York, 64-66. Awards: Second Place for Sculpture, Ceramic Sculpture Western Hemisphere, 41; Pa Acad Fine Arts Award for Sculpture, 42; Allied Artists Am Award for Sculpture, 65. Bibliog: Dr Clain-Stephanelli (auth), History of Medal Making; Ed Trautman (auth), Almanac, Franklin Mint, 68. Mem: Fel Nat Sculpture Soc (coun, 69-); Fine Arts Fedn New York (deleg, 67-). Style & Technique: Contemporary representational. Media: Clay, Bronze. Mailing Add: 19 Henry St Orangeburg NY 10962

WORTH, PETER JOHN
SCULPTOR, ART HISTORIAN
b Ipswich, Eng, Mar 16, 17; US citizen. Study: Ipswich Sch Art, 34-37; Royal Col Art, London, 37-39, ARCA, 46, with E W Tristram, Paul Nash, Edward Bawden, Douglas Cockerell, Roger Powell & others. Work: Denver Art Mus; Joslyn Art Mus; Permanent Collection, Sheldon Gallery Art, Univ Nebr. Exhib: San Francisco Mus Art, 50; Nelson Gallery Art, 50, 53, 54 & 57; Art Inst Chicago, 51; Walker Art Ctr, 51, 52 & 56; Denver Art Mus, 52, 53, 55-57 & 60-63. Teaching: Prof art hist, Univ Nebr, Lincoln. Mem: Egypt Explor Soc, London; Col Art Asn Am. Res: Stylistic transformations in late antique and early medieval art, especially in iconography. Publ: Photogr, Life Library of Photography, 70; photogr, Bilder, Stuttgart, 70. Mailing Add: Dept of Art Woods Hall Univ of Nebr Lincoln NE 68508

WORTHEN, WILLIAM MARSHALL
SCULPTOR
b Wellsberg, WVa, Mar 1, 43. Study: Univ NMex, BS. Exhib: NMex Prof Invitational, Albuquerque, 68 & 72; Mainstreams, Marietta , Ohio, 71 & 72; The West Artists & Illustrators, Tucson Art Ctr, Ariz, 72. Awards: Award for Falcon, NMex State Fair, 67, Award for Falcon on Gauntlet & Buffalo, 71. Dealer: Gallery A E Kit Carson Rd Taos NM 87571. Mailing Add: 920 Nashville Ave SW Albuquerque NM 87105

WORTZ, MELINDA FARRIS
GALLERY DIRECTOR, ART CRITIC
b Ann Arbor, Mich, Apr 30, 40. Study: Radcliffe Col, BA(cum laude), 62; Otis Art Inst, 62-63; Univ Calif, Los Angeles, MA, 70; also with John Altoon. Exhibitions Arranged: Art & Marriage, Husband & Wife Artists of the 20th Century, Univ Calif, Riverside, 73, Earth, Sea, Sky, 74; Robert Motherwell in California Collections (with catalog), Otis Art Inst, Los Angeles, 74; German Expressionist Painting & Sculpture, Pasadena Art Mus, 74; Irvine Milieu, La Jolla Mus Contemp Art, 75. Teaching: Asst prof issues in art, Calif State Univ, Long Beach, 72-75 & Calif State Univ, Los Angeles, 74-75; lectr, Univ Calif, Irvine, currently. Pos: Gallery dir, Univ Calif, Riverside, 72-74 & Univ Calif, Irvine, currently; Southern Calif ed, Artweek, currently; contribr ed, Arts Mag, Art Gallery, Art News & Archit Dig, currently. Res: Contemporary American art. Publ: Auth, Seven Southern California Artists (catalog), Cirrus Gallery, Los Angeles, 74; auth, Dewain Valentine (exhib catalog), Long Beach Mus Art, 75; auth, Ludwig Redl (catalog essay), 75. Mailing Add: 580 Prospect Blvd Pasadena CA 91103

WOSTREL, NANCY J
PAINTER
b San Diego, Calif. Study: Study with John C Pellew, 70 & 71; Famous Artists Sch, cert, 72. Exhib: Am Watercolor Soc, Nat Acad Galleries, New York, 72 & 76; San Diego Watercolor Soc Golden State Ann, 73-76; Watercolor W, Riverside, Calif, 75 & 77; Rocky Mt Nat Watermedia Exhib, Golden, Colo, 76 & 77; one-man show, Knowles Art Ctr, La Jolla, Calif, 77. Awards: Purchase Awards, San Diego Watercolor Soc Ann, 73 & 76; First Prize Watercolor, Inst Award, San Diego Art Inst Exhib, 75. Bibliog: Richard Reilly (auth), Frost Poems Inspire Art, San Diego Union, Copley Publ, 77; Jan Jennings (auth), Sensitive Watercolors on View, Evening Tribune, Copley Publ, 77. Mem: San Diego Watercolor Soc (catalogue Chmn, 76); Watercolor W; Am Watercolor Soc. Style & Technique: Representational landscapes and lyrical interpretations of figures and surrounding flora in watercolor. Media: Watercolor. Publ: Auth, North Light Mag, Fletcher Art Serv Inc, 76. Dealer: Knowles Art Ctr 7420 Girard Ave LaJolla CA 92037; Milcir Gallery 118 Main St Tiburon CA 94920. Mailing Add: 2505 Montclair St San Diego CA 92104

WRAY, DICK
PAINTER
b Houston, Tex, Dec 5, 33. Study: Univ Houston. Work: Albright-Knox Art Gallery, Buffalo; Mus Fine Arts, Houston. Exhib: Mus Contemp Art, Houston, 61; Southwest Painting & Sculpture, Houston, 62; Hemisfair, Houston, 68; Homage to Lithography, Mus Mod Art, New York, 69. Awards: Purchase Prize, Ford Found, 62; Purchase Prize, Mus Fine Arts, Houston, 63. Mailing Add: 1206 Peveto Houston TX 77008

WRAY, MARGARET
PAINTER, CERAMIST
b Galveston, Tex. Study: San Antonio Art Inst, Tex; Inst Allende, San Miguel de Allende, Mex; also with Theodores Stamos, Adja Yonkers, Nathan Olivera, Fletcher Martin, Millard Sheets, Dong Kingman & Rex Brandt. Work: Collection of Susan Thomas, Inc, New York; Lady of the Lake Col, San Antonio, Tex; Hutching-Sealy Bank, Galveston, Tex; The Charles Urchel Collection, San Antonio; Mr & Mrs Ronald Morrison, Corona Del Mar, Calif. Comn: The Waterfall (watercolor), C W Miller, Medina Ranch, Tex; The Nellie B (watercolor), Alton E Robertson, San Antonio; Ranch Map, Hugh Fitzsimmons, San Pedro Ranch, Corrizo Springs, Tex. Exhib: Tex Fine Arts, Austin, 58-67 & 73; 16th Southwestern Print & Drawing, Mus Fine Arts, Dallas, 66; Art Mus of Southwest, Corpus Christi, Tex, 70; Tex Watercolor Soc & circuits, 70, 71 & 74; 17th Delta Ann Art, Ark Art Ctr, Little Rock, 74. Awards: Purchase Prize, Susan Thomas, Inc, San Antonio, 63; Purchase Prize (landscape), Mr & Mrs John K Mitchell, Houston; Tex Woman's Club Award (Color Etude), Houston, 72. Bibliog: Glen Tucker (auth), Today, art scene, San Antonio Light; Joseph Cain (auth), Art new & reviews, Caller Times, Corpus Christi, 7/73. Mem: Tex Watercolor Soc (pres, 60-61); Contemp Artist Group (treas, 65-67); Am Fedn Arts; Tex Arts Asn; San Antonio Art League. Style & Technique: Abstract color; collages; abstracted landscapes. Media: Acrylic on Canvas; Watercolor. Mailing Add: c/o Odyssey Gallery 2222 Breezewood San Antonio TX 78209

WRIGHT, BARTON ALLEN
PAINTER, ILLUSTRATOR
b Bisbee, Ariz, Dec 21, 20. Comn: Wupatki Nat Monument, Ft Union Nat Monument, Babbitt Stores. Exhib: La Jolla Art Asn, Calif, 69; Festival of Arts, Lake Oswego, 71; Winged Arts Gallery, Sedona, 70; Parlor Gallery, Ore, 71-75; Thorne Gallery, Scottsdale, 74 & 75. Collections Arranged: M R F Colton, 58; G E Burr, 59; Indian Artists, 60; Western Artists, 62; Paul Dyck, 64; American Art, 65; Flagstaff Art, 66; Southwest Art, 68; Widforss, 69; Santa Fe Indian Art, 70; Nat Park Illustrated, 71; N Fechin, 72. Pos: Cur arts & exhib, Mus Northern Ariz, 55-58, cur, Mus, 58-77; sci dir, Mus of Man, 77- Publ: Illusr, San Caetano, 55, Throw Stone, 61, Little Cloud, 62 & Dinosaurs of Northern Arizona, 68; auth, This is a Hopi Kachina, 64, Kachina's, a Hopi Artist's Documentary, 73, Unchanging Hopi, 75, Pueblo Shields, 76, Hopi Kachinas, the Complete Guide, 77 & others. Mailing Add: Mus of Man 1350 El Prado Balboa Park San Diego CA 92101

WRIGHT, BERNARD
PAINTER, GRAPHIC ARTIST
b Pittsburgh, Pa, Feb 23, 38. Study: Otis Art Inst, Los Angeles, 69-70; Los Angeles Trade Tech Col, 71-74. Work: New York Pub Libr; Howard Univ, Washington, DC; Libr Cong; Morehouse Col, Atlanta, Ga; Los Angeles Pub Libr. Comn: Numerous furniture and garment exclusive designs. Exhib: Los Angeles City Hall Rotunda Gallery, 67; Alley Gallery, Beverly Hills, 68; Florenz's Art Gallery, Los Angeles, 69; Fine Arts Gallery, San Diego, Calif, 69; Phillip E Freed Gallery Fine Arts, Chicago, 69; Emerald Gallery, Diplomat Hotel, Hollywood Beach, Fla, 70; NJ State Mus, Trenton, 72; Detroit Inst Arts, 74; Univ Southern Calif, Fisher Art Galleries, Los Angeles, 74; Calif Mus Sci & Indust, Los Angeles, 75; plus others. Pos: Pres & co-founder, Westly & Wright Products, Los Angeles, 72- Mem: Art W Asn Inc, (mem bd dir, 67-73); Int Platform Asn; Artist Equity Asn. Style & Technique: A blend of fantasy, abstraction and structured organization sparkling with vibrant, breathing color, employing the continual play of light against broad areas; through softness of line, deep psychological impacts of figures are revealed. Media: Oil, Ink. Mailing Add: c/o Edward Smith & Co PO Box 8990 Los Angeles CA 90008

WRIGHT, CATHARINE MORRIS
PAINTER, WRITER
b Philadelphia, Pa, Jan 26, 99. Study: Philadelphia Sch Design Women, 17-18; also with Henry B Snell & Leopold Seyffert. Work: Pa Acad Fine Arts, Philadelphia; Philadelphia Mus Art; Woodmere Art Gallery; Univ Pa; Nat Acad Design. Comn: Many pvt portrait comns. Exhib: Pa Acad Fine Arts, 18-52; Corcoran Gallery Art, 21-41; Nat Acad Design, 30-52; Am Watercolor Soc; Carnegie Inst. Teaching: Founder, Fox Hill Sch Art, 50-69. Awards: Second Hallgarten Prize, Nat Acad Design, 33; Prize, Allied Artists Am, 41; Prize, Silvermine Guild Artists, 55. Mem: NAm Watercolor Soc; Audubon Artists; Allied Artists Am; Philadelphia Watercolor Club (vpres, 49-57); Newport Art Asn; Nat Acad Design. Media: Oil, Watercolor. Publ: Auth, The Simple Nun, 29, Seaweed Their Pasture, 46 & The Color of Life, 57; plus prose & verse in nat mags including Atlantic Monthly, Sat Eve Post & many others. Dealer: Vos Galleries of Boston Inc 238 Newbury St Boston MA 02116. Mailing Add: Fox Hill Jamestown RI 02835

WRIGHT, FRANK
PAINTER, PRINTMAKER
b Washington, DC, Oct 10, 32. Study: Am Univ, BA, 54; Univ Ill, Urbana, MA, 57; Fogg Mus, Harvard Univ, fel, 60-61. Work: Bibliot Nat, Paris; Nat Collections Fine Arts, Washington, DC; Univ Seattle Law Sch, Wash. Comn: Deepbite etching demonstration plate & ed, Lessing J Rosenwald, Jenkintown, Pa, 68. Exhib: One-man shows, Watkins Gallery, 59, Mickelson Gallery, 65, Gallery Marc, 71 & Adams, Davidson Galleries, Inc, 75, Washington, DC; two-man show, Galeria Nice, Buenos Aires, Arg, 65; plus others. Teaching: Instr master drawing, Corcoran Sch Art, Washington, DC, 66-70; asst prof design & graphics, George Washington Univ, 70- Awards: Nat Soc Arts & Lett Scholar, 50-54; Leopold Schepp Found Fel Europ Studies, 56-58; Paul J Sachs Fel Graphic Arts, Print Coun Am, 59-62; plus others. Bibliog: Rafael Squirru (auth), Washington mannerists or the foresight to look backward, Americas, 1/57. Style & Technique: Figurative; oil glazes as used in 17th century as technique in painting; engraving in the manner of Albrecht Dürer and Lucas Vin Leyden as technique in printmaking. Media: Oil; Graphics. Publ: Auth, Why I love to engrave, G W Forum, Vol 7, No 1 (winter 77). Dealer: The Ledroit Bldg 810 F St NW Rm 102 Washington DC 20004. Mailing Add: 3520 Bradley Lane Chevy Chase MD 20015

WRIGHT, FRANK COOKMAN
PAINTER, INSTRUCTOR
b Cincinnati, Ohio, June 6, 04. Study: Yale Univ, AB, with Sydney Dickenson & Eugene Sarage; Grand Cent Sch Art, with Edmund Graecen; Nat Acad Design Sch, with Dean Cornwell; also with Dimitri Romanovsky. Work: Elliott Mus, Stuart, Fla; Tarrytown Publ Libr, NY; also in pvt collections, 47 states & 18 countries. Comn: Gateway Arch—St Louis, Nat Marine Serv, 66; plus many portraits. Exhib: Macbeth Galleries, 35; one-man shows, Benszic Galleries, Washington, DC & Copley Soc, Boston; Newport Art Asn, RI; Am Artists Prof League Grand Nat; Hudson Valley Art Asn; plus others. Teaching: Pvt art classes; lectr & demonstr radio & TV progs. Pos: Ed, News Bull, 59- Awards: First Prize for Portraits, Hudson Valley Art Asn, 35; Hon Mention for Oil Landscapes, Am Artists Prof League, 62.

Mem: Am Artists Prof League (pres, 67-); Coun Am Artist Socs (pres, 68-); Hudson Valley Art Asn (pres, 31-37, dir); fel Am Inst Fine Arts; Copley Soc, Boston. Style & Technique: Clarity, precision, and architectural balance of design. Media: Oil, Acrylic. Publ: Contribr many editorials, articles & rev. Mailing Add: 222 E 71st St New York NY 10021

WRIGHT, G ALAN
SCULPTOR
b Seattle, Wash, Mar 31, 27. Study: Honolulu Sch Art; also with Willson Stamper & Ralston Crawford. Work: Johnson Wax Collection; Seattle Art Mus; Denver Art Mus. Comn: The Great Gull (bronze), D E Skinner, Seattle Sci Pavillion, World's Fair, 62; bronze lion cub, First Nat Bank, Spokane, Wash, 63; bronze owl, City Hall, Renton, Wash, 68; bronze crane, Seattle First Nat Bank, 69; crane, First Nat Bank, Tacoma, Wash, 69. Exhib: Northwest Ann Show, Seattle Art Mus, 62-65; Gov Invitational Exhib, Wash, 67; Sara Roby Gallery, Racine, Wis, 68; Whitney Mus Am Art, New York, 68; Lee Nordness Gallery, New York, 68 & 69. Pos: Serigraph artist, Honolulu Acad Arts, Hawaii; bd dirs & founding mem, Allied Art, Renton, 62-64; pres, Renton Art Festival, 62-64; comnr, Mayor's Art Comn, Renton, 62-65. Awards: First Prizes, Renton Art Festival, 62 & 64; First Prize, New Arts & Crafts Fair, Bellevue, Wash, 63; Ford Found Purchase Award, 64. Bibliog: Article in Christian Sci Monitor, 62 & 64; J Canaday (auth), article in New York Times, 68; M Randlett (auth), Living Artists of the Pacific Northwest, 72. Media: Bronze, Stone. Dealer: Gordon Woodside Gallery 803 E Union St Seattle WA 98122; Lee Nordness Galleries 236-238 E 75th St New York NY 10021. Mailing Add: Preston WA 98050

WRIGHT, HAROLD DAVID
ILLUSTRATOR, PAINTER
b Rosine, Ky, June 13, 42. Study: Harris Sch Advert Art, Nashville, Tenn; watercolor in Italy, and with Beth Harris. Work: Tenn State Mus, Nashville. Comn: Portraits of Civil War Generals, General's Retreat, Franklin, Tenn, 74. Exhib: Cent South Show, Parthenon, Nashville, 74; Sardella Art Show, Atlanta, Ga, 74. Pos: Artist, Newspaper Printing Corp, Nashville, 62-66; art dir, Buntin & Assocs Advert, 66-69; partner, Nova Group, Nashville, 69-; vpres, Graystone Press, Nashville, 73- Awards: Best of Show, Art Dirs Club Nashville, 68; First Award Fine Art Competition, 73. Mem: Art Dirs Club Nashville (vpres, 70). Style & Technique: Realism. Media: Watercolor, Tempera. Publ: Illusr, Civil War in Middle Tennessee, 65; illusr, Nashville Tennessean Mag, 66; illusr, Tenn Conservationist Mag, 74-75; painter limited ed prints, Graystone Press, 73-75. Dealer: Graystone Press & Gallery 207 Louise Ave Nashville TN 37203. Mailing Add: Rte 1 Cedar Grove Rd Cross Plains TN 37049

WRIGHT, NINA KAIDEN
ART CONSULTANT
b New York, NY, May 18, 31. Study: Emerson Col, BA. Pos: Mem nat adv coun, Mus Graphic Art, New York; mem art adv coun, New York Bd Trade; consult to Philip Morris for Two Hundred Years of North American Indian Art & When Attitudes Become Form; consult to Mead Corp for European Painters Today; consult to Am Motors Co, Gulf & Western Industries, Bristol-Myers, Coca-Cola, J C Penney, Capital Res & others; pres, Ruder & Finn Fine Arts, currently. Mailing Add: Ruder & Finn Fine Arts 110 E 59th St New York NY 10022

WRIGHT, STANLEY MARC
PAINTER, INSTRUCTOR
b Irvington, NJ, May 24, 11. Study: Sch Fine Art, Pratt Inst, grad with highest honors, 33; Jerry Farnsworth Sch Art, Tiffany Found fel, 35. Work: Portraits, of Gov Deane C Davis & Sen George D Aiken, State House, Montpelier, Vt, Joe Kirkwood, Golf Hall of Fame, Foxberg, Pa, George A Wolf, Med Ctr, Univ Kans & A G Mackay, Med Ctr, Burlington, Vt. Comn: Portrait & landscape paintings, US & Europe. Exhib: Metrop Mus Art; Brooklyn Mus; Newark Mus; Montclair Mus; Cong Galleries, Washington, DC; one-man show, House of Representatives, US Capitol, Washington, DC, 76. Teaching: Head portrait & landscape, Newark Sch Fine Arts, 44-50; instr portrait & landscape & dir, Wright Sch Art, Stowe, Vt, 50-; lectr, demonstr & instr painting, many orgn. Awards: Many prizes for nat exhibs & one-man shows. Bibliog: Articles in Cue Mag, Vt Life Mag, Times, Newark News, Free Press & others. Mem: Salmagundi Club; Audubon Artists; Fel Int Inst Arts & Lett; hon mem Vt Artists; Vt Coun Arts. Style & Technique: Portraits-realistic; landscapes-realistic, impressionistic, abstract; prints-polymergraphs. Media: Oil, Watercolor, Acrylic. Mailing Add: RFD 2 Stowe VT 05672

WRIGHT, MR & MRS WILLIAM H
COLLECTORS
Collection: Modern paintings and watercolors; pre-Columbian sculpture, mostly from Colima, Mexico. Mailing Add: 12921 Evanston St Los Angeles CA 90049

WRIGHTSMAN, CHARLES BIERER
COLLECTOR
b Pawnee, Okla, June 13, 95. Study: Stanford Univ, 14-15; Columbia Univ, 15-17. Pos: Trustee, Metrop Mus Art, New York, chmn bd trustees, Inst Fine Arts. Collection: Ethnographica, ancient art. Mailing Add: First City Nat Bank Bldg 1021 Main St Houston TX 77002

WRISTON, BARBARA
ART HISTORIAN, LECTURER
b Middletown, Conn, June 29, 17. Study: Oberlin Col, AB; Brown Univ, AM. Pos: Dir mus ed, Art Inst Chicago, 61- Mem: Am Asn Mus; Benjamin Franklin fel Royal Soc Arts; Soc Archit Historians (pres, 60-61); Furniture Hist Soc; Victorian Soc. Res: 17th and 18th century English and American architecture and furniture. Publ: Auth, When does architecture become history, Inland Architect, 62; auth, Who was the architect of the Indiana Cotton Mill, 1848-1850?, J Soc Archit Historians, 5/65; auth, Joiner's tools in The Art Institute of Chicago, 67 & The Howard Van Doren Shaw Memorial Collection in the Art Institute of Chicago, 69, Mus Studies; auth, Visual Arts in Illinois, 68. Mailing Add: Art Inst of Chicago Michigan Ave at Adams St Chicago IL 60603

WU, I-CHEN
CALLIGRAPHER, PAINTER
b Ochen, Hupeh, China, Nov 25, 27. Study: 10 yrs classical Chinese studies; Nat ChungHsina Univ Taiwan, BA, 58; Univ Mo-Columbia, 68; Calif State Univ, San Jose, MA, 74; Univ of Ariz, Tucson, doctoral work, 78- Work: Calligraphers Asn Prov Taiwan, Chung Hsing Village; Nat Hist Mus Taiwan, China; Prov Mus Victoria, BC; Chinese Art Gallery San Francisco; San Jose Mus Art. Exhib: Art Gallery, Prov Govt Taiwan, 64; Chinese Pavilion, Montreal World's Fair, 67; Chinese Pavilion, HemisFair, San Antonio, Tex, 68; Prov Mus Victoria, 70; Calif Inst Technol, 71; Chinese Info Serv, New York, NY, 76. Teaching: Instr Chinese painting, Univ Calif, San Francisco, 72-73; lectr Chinese painting, Mills Col, Oakland, 74, San Francisco Community Col, 74-75, Univ Nev, Reno, 76-77 & Univ of Ariz, Tucson, 78- Pos: Art inspector, Taiwan Prov Dept Educ, 53-66. Awards: First Place, Essay San Min Chu I, Prov Govt Taiwan, 64; Second Place, Columbia Art League & Bank Am Show, 67; Second Pl, Chinese Renaissance Asn, 73 & 74 & Third Place, 77. Mem: Chinese Calligraphers' Asn; Art Soc China; Soc Confucius-Mencius, Taiwan; Asian Art Soc San Francisco. Style & Technique: Chinese ink-wash painting, Chinese calligraphy. Media: Chinese Color. Res: Late Ming painters and Yang Chow School. Collection: Chinese calligraphy and painting from Yuan to the present. Publ: Ed, Chinese Political Set Up, 57; ed, Introduction to Chinese Painting, Univ Mo, 67; ed, Patterns of Chinese Landscape Painting, KWED-TV, San Francisco, 74; auth, articles of Chinese art exhibs in US, Taiwan Cent Daily News, 68-72. Mailing Add: 1683 Christopher St San Jose CA 95122

WU, LINDA YEE CHAU
SCULPTOR, EDUCATOR
b Canton, China, July 4, 19; US citizen. Study: Calif Sch Fine Arts, 39-42; Nat Acad Design, 42-44; Sch Painting & Sculpture, Columbia Univ, 44-50. Comn: Bas-relief, Chinese Community, New York, 52; portrait of Sam Y Ong, Republican Club Chinatown, New York, 75. Exhib: Allied Artists Am Ann Exhibs, 47-; Audubon Artists Ann Exhibs; Nat Acad Design Ann Exhibs; Nat Sculpture Soc Ann Exhibs; Int Sculpture Third, Philadelphia Art Mus, 49. Teaching: Dean students, New York Chinese Sch, 60-74, prin, 74- Pos: Mem ed bd, Nat Sculpture Rev, 72. Awards: Dessie Greer Prize for Sculpture, Nat Acad Design, 65; Anna Hyatt Huntington Gold Medal, Catharine Lorillard Wolfe Art Club, 68; Gold Medal of Honor for Sculpture, Allied Artists Am, 73. Mem: Nat Acad Design; fel Nat Sculpture Soc (counr, 72-74); Allied Artists Am; Pen & Brush Art Club; Knickerbocker Artists (chmn jury sculpture awards, 74). Style & Technique: Between traditional and contemporary with Chinese influence. Mailing Add: Studio 209-10 185 Canal St New York NY 10013

WUERMER, CARL
PAINTER, FINE ART APPRAISER
b Munich, Ger, Aug 3, 00; US citizen. Study: Art Inst Chicago, 20-24; Art Students League. Work: High Mus Art, Atlanta, Ga; IBM Corp Art Collection, Endicott, NY; Encycl Britannica Collection Am Art; Royal Globe Ins Co, London; Syracuse Univ Art Collection, NY. Exhib: Var ann, Am Painting & Sculpture, Art Inst Chicago & Nat Acad Design; Corcoran Gallery Art Bi-Ann, 32, Painting in US, Carnegie Inst, 46-49; 5th Ann Painting & Sculpture, Grover M Hermann Fine Arts Ctr, Marietta, Ohio, 72. Awards: J Francis Murphy Mem Prize, Nat Acad Design, 28; Popular Vote Prize, Carnegie Inst, 49; Hon Mention, Allied Artists Am 58th Ann, 71. Bibliog: G Pagano (auth), The Encyclopedia Britannica Collection of American Painting, 46. Mem: Grand Cent Art Galleries; Allied Artists Am; Artists Fel (pres, 57-59); Hudson Valley Art Asn. Media: Oil. Res: For the appraisal of the Frick Collection, New York, High Museum of Art Collection, Eleutherian Mills-Hagley Foundation Collection, Wilmington, Delaware and others. Mailing Add: RFD 253 B Woodstock NY 12498

WUJCIK, THEO
PRINTMAKER, EDUCATOR
b Detroit, Mich, Jan 29, 36. Study: Soc Arts & Crafts Art Sch, Detroit, dipl; Creative Graphic Workshop, New York; Tamarind Lithography Workshop, Calif, Ford Found Grant, 67-68. Work: Mus Mod Art, New York; Los Angeles Co Mus Art; Amon Carter Mus Western Art, Ft Worth; Pasadena Art Mus, Calif; Libr Cong, Washington, DC. Exhib: Int Original Prints, Calif Palace of Legion of Honor, San Francisco, 64; Boston Printmakers 19th Ann, Mus Fine Arts, Boston, 67; 17th Print Nat, Brooklyn Mus, NY, 70; Prints by Seven, Whitney Mus Am Art, New York, 70; Int Miniature Print Exhib, Pratt Graphic Art Ctr, New York, 71; 20th Nat Print Exhib, Brooklyn Mus, NY, 77. Teaching: Instr graphics, Soc Arts & Crafts Art Sch, 64-70; assoc prof lithography, Univ SFla, 72- Pos: Co-founder, Detroit Lithography Workshop, 68-70; shop dir, Graphicstudio, Univ SFla, 70- Awards: Louis Comfort Tiffany Found Award Graphics, 64. Media: Graphic. Dealer: Brooke Alexander Inc 20 W 57th St New York NY 10019. Mailing Add: 411 Berwick Ave Tampa FL 33617

WUNDER, RICHARD PAUL
ART HISTORIAN, ART ADMINISTRATOR
b Ardmore, Pa, May 31, 23. Study: Harvard Univ, AB, 49, MA, 50, PhD, 55. Collections Arranged: The Architect's Eye, Cooper Union Mus, 62; Theater Drawings from the Donald Oenslager Collection, Minneapolis Inst Arts & Yale Univ Art Gallery, 63-64; Frederic Edwin Church, Nat Collection Fine Arts, Smithsonian Inst, 66. Teaching: John Hamilton Fulton Prof, Middlebury Col, 75- Pos: Asst to dir, Fogg Art Mus, Harvard Univ, 53-54; cur drawings & prints, Cooper Union Mus, 55-64; cur & asst dir, Nat Collection Fine Arts, Smithsonian Inst, 64-69; dir, Cooper-Hewitt Mus Design, 69-70. Awards: John Thornton Kirkland Fel, Harvard Univ, 54. Mem: Col Art Asn Am; Drawing Soc (dir, 64-72); Soc l'Histoire l'Art Francais; Arch Am Art (adv bd, 68-); Art Quart (adv bd, 67-). Res: Italian and French drawings of the 17th and 18th centuries; American painting, sculpture and drawings of the 19th century. Publ: Auth, Extravagent Drawings of the 18th Century, Lambert-Spector, 62; auth, Architectural & Ornament Drawings, Univ Mich Mus, 65; auth, Hiram Powers, Vermont sculptor, Woodstock Hist Soc, Vt, 74; auth, Architectural, Ornament, Landscape & Figure Drawings, Middlebury Col, 75. Mailing Add: Brookside Orwell VT 05760

WUNDERLICH, RUDOLF G
ART DEALER
b Tarrytown, NY, Nov 13, 20. Study: NY Univ. Pos: Pres, Kennedy Galleries, Inc. Specialty: American art, paintings of the 18th, 19th and 20th centuries; Western Americana, paintings and sculpture; Old Master engravings, modern fine prints; work of modern American Masters in paintings, sculpture and graphics. Mailing Add: Kennedy Galleries Inc 40 W 57th St-Fifth Floor New York NY 10019

WUNDERMAN, JAN (LILJAN DARCOURT WUNDERMAN)
PAINTER, PRINTMAKER
b Winnipeg, Man, Jan 22, 21; US citizen. Study: Otis Art Inst, Los Angeles, Calif, 42; Brooklyn Mus of Art Sch, 54-56, with Reuben Tam. Work: Loeb Collection, NY Univ; Alfred Khouri Collection, Norfolk Mus, Va; Ball State Univ Art Gallery, Muncie, Ind; Univ SC Art Gallery, Columbia; Post Col, Long Island, NY. Comn: Eight paintings, New York City off, White, Weld & Co, 68; paintings, New York, Tulsa & Ft Worth off, Arthur Young & Co, 73; painting, Commercial Union Bank, Nashville, Tenn, 75; painting, New York off, Bank of Am, 76; painting, New York off, The Boston Co, 77. Exhib: Pasadena Mus, Calif, 44; Los Angeles Co Mus Art, Los Angeles, 45; one-person shows, Gastine Gallery, Los Angeles, 45, Angeleski Gallery, New York, 61, Roko Gallery, New York, 63-77 & Easthampton Guild Gallery, Long Island, NY, 66; Brooklyn Mus, NY, 56; Philadelphia Mus Art, 56-62; Riverside Mus, New York, 59; Pa Acad of Fine Arts, Philadelphia, 59-65; Butler Inst Am Art, Youngstown, Ohio, 59-66; Mus de Bellas Artes, Buenos Aires, Arg, 60; Pan Pac Exhib of Young Painters, Osaka & Tokyo, Japan, 60; Bergen Co Mus, NJ, 63; Va Mus Fine Arts, Richmond, 67; Eggleston Gallery, New York. Pos: Chairperson exhib comt, N Shore Community Arts Ctr, Long Island, 65-66. Awards: Ohashi Award, Pan Pac Exhib, Japanese Comt of Cult Affairs, Japan,

61; Emily Lowe Found Award, Univ Miami, Fla, 65; Medal of Honor, Nat Asn of Women Artists, 68. Mem: Nat Asn of Women Artists (chairperson, Nat Jury Comt, 77-78); Artists Equity; Am Soc Contemp Artists. Style & Technique: Abstract; large paintings based on natural forms. Media: Oil, Acrylic; Black & White Intaglio Prints. Publ: Contribr, with Charlotte Rubenstein, American Women Artists, Hart Press, Calif, 78. Dealer: Roko Gallery 90 E Tenth St New York NY 10003. Mailing Add: 131 E 19th St New York NY 10003

WURDEMANN, HELEN (BARONESS ELENA GUZZARDI)
ART ADMINISTRATOR, COLLECTOR
b Milwaukee, Wis. Study: Univ Wis, BA. Collections Arranged: Monthly exhibitions of paintings and sculptures by Southern California artists. Pos: Dir, Los Angeles Art Asn Galleries, 50-; Western art reporter & writer, Art in Am, 54-65; art critic, Los Angeles Mirror News, 60-61. Awards: Citations from City & Co of Los Angeles, 52 & 54; Arts & Humanities Award, Nat Watercolor Soc, 74. Mem: Los Angeles Art Asn & Galleries (dir); Univ Calif, Los Angeles Art Coun (treas); Los Angeles Mus Art & Print Coun; hon mem Nat Watercolor Soc & Women Painters of the West. Collection: Lithographs by Daumier & Goya; drawings by Macdonald-Wright, Stephen Longstreet, Helen Lundeberg & Lorser Feitelson; paintings. Mailing Add: Los Angeles Art Asn Galleries 825 N La Cienega Blvd Los Angeles CA 90069

WYATT, STANLEY
PAINTER, EDUCATOR
b Denver, Colo, Sept 20, 21. Study: Columbia Col, with Frank Mechau, BA, 43; Art Inst Chicago, 46; Columbia Univ, with Meyer Shapiro, MA, 47; Brooklyn Mus, with Rufino Tamayo, 48. Work: NAm-Mexican Cult Inst, Mexico City; Packaging Inst, Toronto, Can; Nyack Pub Libr, NY. Comn: Illus, Nat Educ Asn J, 52-65, Columbia Univ Alumni News, 53-57, New York Times Mag, 57-61, Col Entrance Bd Rev, 59-72 & Rockefeller Univ Rev, 68. Exhib: Barnard Col, New York, 59; Regis Col, Denver, 61; La Galeria Collectionistas, Mexico City, 62; NAm-Mexican Cult Inst, Mexico City, 63; Casa Italiana, Columbia Univ, New York, 71. Teaching: Assoc prof art & chmn dept, Waynesburg Col, 49-51; instr art, Columbia Univ, 52-60; assoc prof art, City Col New York, 60-; assoc prof art & chmn dept, Rockland Community Col, 61-63. Pos: Dir dept art, Del Piombo Art Ctr, 59-61; art dept rep, Baruch Sch, 61-69; supvr art dept, Eve Div, City Col New York, 69-72. Awards: Brainard Sr Prize, Columbia Col, 43; Distinction in Illustration, Am Asn Alumni Mags, 57; Gold Ribbon for Prints, 5th Ann Bergen Mall Exhibs, 66. Bibliog: Graphic art of Stanley Wyatt, Anon, Univ Mich, 70. Mem: Fel Royal Soc Arts, London; Salmagundi Club; Newcomen Soc NAm; United Fedn Col Teachers. Media: Oil, Tempera, Graphite. Publ: Ed, Jester, Columbia Univ, 43; auth, Thanks to Shanks, 58; illusr, Poetry of the Damned, Peter Pauper, 60; illusr, 20th Century Views & 20th Century Interpretations, 60-72 & The Great American Forest, 65, Prentice-Hall. Mailing Add: 75 River Rd Grand View-on-Hudson NY 10960

WYBRANTS-LYNCH, SHARON
PAINTER, INSTRUCTOR
b Miami Beach, Fla, Sept 29, 43. Study: Art Students League, 53-54 & 68; with Antiono Gattorno, 58-60; Sullins Col, AA, 61-63; RI Sch Design, 63; Ohio Wesleyan Univ, BFA, 65; Ind Univ, grad work, 66-68; Hunter Col, MA(painting), 73. Work: Ohio Wesleyan Univ; Western Ill Univ. Exhib: One-person show, Soho 20 Gallery, New York, 73 & 74; Eye of Woman, Hobart & William Smith Cols, 74; Am Acad Arts & Lett, 74; Year of the Woman, Bronx Mus Arts, NY, 75. Teaching: Teacher art & curric consult, Elem & High Schs, Spencer & Gosport, Ind, 66-68. Awards: Childe Hassam Fund Purchase Award, Am Acad Arts & Lett, 74. Bibliog: Judith Van Baron & Ellen Lubell (auth), rev in Arts Mag, 3/74 & 12/74; John Gruen (auth), Eight Soho shows, Soho Weekly News, 10/74. Mem: Soho 20 Gallery Inc (mem bd dirs & head legal comt, 73-); Women in the Arts. Style & Technique: Expressionist realism, primarily portraiture. Media: Acrylic, Pastel. Mailing Add: 670 West End Ave New York NY 10025

WYCKOFF, SYLVIA SPENCER
PAINTER, EDUCATOR
b Pittsburgh, Pa, Nov 14, 15. Study: Col Fine Arts, Syracuse Univ, BFA, 37, MFA, 44. Work: Radio Sta WSYR, Syracuse, NY; R E Dietz Co, Syracuse; also in pvt collections. Exhib: Munson-Williams-Proctor Inst, Utica, NY; Mem Art Gallery, Rochester, NY; Everson Mus Art, Syracuse; Cooperstown Art Asn, NY; Nat Asn Women Artists, New York. Teaching: Prof watercolor & drawing & chmn, Freshman Core Progs Dept, Syracuse Univ, 42- Awards: First Prize for Watercolor, Syracuse Regional, 45; League Prize for Watercolor, Nat League Am Pen Women Nat Show, 48; Gordon Steele Award, Assoc Artists Syracuse, 68. Mem: Nat Asn Women Artists; Nat League Am Pen Women; Assoc Artists Syracuse; Daubers Club Syracuse. Media: Watercolor. Mailing Add: 2 Seminary St Cazenovia NY 13035

WYETH, ANDREW NEWELL
PAINTER
b Chadds Ford, Pa, July 12, 17. Study: With N C Wyeth; Harvard Univ, hon DFA, 55; Colby Col, hon DFA, 55; Dickinson Col, hon DFA, 58; Swarthmore Col, hon DFA, 58. Work: Metrop Mus Art, New York; Mus Fine Arts, Boston; Los Angeles Co Mus Art; Art Inst Chicago; Farnsworth Mus, Rockland, Maine; plus many others. Exhib: Currier Gallery Art, Manchester, NH; Pa Acad Fine Arts, Philadelphia; Fogg Art Mus, Mass; Univ Ariz, Tucson; Mus Fine Arts, Boston; Nat Mus of Mod Art, Tokyo, Japan; Nat Mus of Mod Art, Kyoto, Japan; Metrop Mus of Art, New York; plus many others. Awards: Pa Acad Fine Arts; Carnegie Inst; Am Watercolor Soc; Associé Etranger de l'Institut de France; plus many others. Bibliog: Richard Merryman (auth), Andrew Wyeth, Houghton. Mem: Nat Acad Design, Audubon Artists; Am Watercolor Soc; Nat Acad Arts & Lett; Am Acad Arts & Lett. Media: Tempera, Watercolor. Mailing Add: c/o Coe Kerr Gallery 49 E 82nd St New York NY 10028

WYETH, HENRIETTE (MRS PETER HURD)
PAINTER
b Wilmington, Del, Oct 22, 07. Study: Normal Art Sch, Boston; Pa Acad Fine Arts; also with N C Wyeth. Work: Wilmington Soc Fine Arts; Roswell Mus Art; New Britain Mus Art, Conn; Lubbock Mus Art, Tex; Tex Tech Univ; portraits in pvt collections. Exhib: Carnegie Inst, Pittsburgh; Art Inst Chicago; Metrop Mus Art, New York; Roswell Mus Art, NMex; New York City & others. Awards: Four First Prizes, Wilmington Soc Fine Arts; Pa Acad Fine Arts. Mailing Add: Sentinel Ranch San Patricio NM 88348

WYETH, JAMES BROWNING
PAINTER
b Wilmington, Del, July 6, 46. Work: William Farnsworth Mus, Rockland, Maine; Brandywine River Mus, Chadds Ford, Pa; Del Art Mus, Wilmington. Bibliog: Joseph Roody (auth), Another Wyeth, Look Mag, 4/2/68; Wyeth Phenomenon (film), CBS TV, 69; Richard Meryman (auth), Wyeth Christmas, Life Mag, 12/17/71. Mem: Nat Acad Design; Am Watercolor Soc; Nat Endowment Arts. Media: Oil, Watercolor. Mailing Add: Chadds Ford PA 19317

WYMAN, WILLIAM
CRAFTSMAN
b Boston, Mass, June 13, 22. Study: Mass Col Art, BS; Columbia Univ, MA; Alfred Univ. Work: Des Moines Art Ctr; St Paul Gallery Art; Mus Contemp Crafts; Everson Mus Art; Smithsonian Inst; plus others. Comn: Ceramic monument, Weymouth High Sch, 65. Exhib: Work exhibited in every major ceramic exhib nat & int incl Metrop Mus Art, Inst Contemp Arts, Boston, Victoria & Albert Mus, London, World Ceramic Exhib, New York, Brussels World's Fair; plus many others. Teaching: Workshops & lect, many univs, cols & art orgn, US & Can; instr ceramics & sculpture, Boston Mus Fine Arts Sch, currently. Pos: Operator, Herring Run Pottery, East Weymouth. Awards: RI Festival Arts; Smithsonian Inst; Am Crafts Coun; plus others. Mem: Am Crafts Coun; Am Asn Univ Prof. Mailing Add: Boston Mus Fine Arts Sch 230 The Fenway Ave Boston MA 02115

WYNGAARD, SUSAN ELIZABETH
ART LIBRARIAN
b Madison, Wis, Oct 16, 47. Study: Univ Wis, Madison, BA & MLS; Univ Per Stranieri, Siena, Italy, cert; Taos Valley Weaving Sch, with Kristina Wilson. Pos: Asst librn, Univ Calif, Santa Barbara, 74- Mem: Women's Caucus for Art; Art Libr Soc/NAm (vchmn, 77-, chmn elect, 78 & contribr, newsletter, 75-). Res: Bibliography of American women in the arts 1900 to the present. Interest: Collecting and indexing of art exhibition catalogues. Publ: Co-auth, Printed catalogues of the Art Exhibition Catalogue Collection of the Arts Library, Univ Calif, Santa Barbara, Somerset House, Cambridge, Eng & Teaneck, NJ, 77. Mailing Add: Arts Libr Univ Calif Santa Barbara CA 93106

WYNN, DONALD JAMES
PAINTER, LECTURER
b Brooklyn, NY, Sept 26, 42. Study: Pratt Inst, BFA, 67; Ind Univ, MFA, 69. Exhib: 22 Realists, Whitney Mus Am Art, 70; The Realist Revival, Am Fedn Arts Traveling Exhib, NY Cult Ctr, 72; New American Realism, Galleria Il Fante Di Spade, Rome, Italy, 72; The Figure in Recent Am Painting, St John's Univ, New York, 75; Parsons Sch of Design; Del Mus, Wilmington; Michael C Rockefeller Arts Ctr, State Univ NY Cortland; Gallery Hartmann, Munich, WGer; one-man shows, Allentown Art Mus, Pa, 72, Albany Inst Hist & Art, NY, 74, Gallery 38 E, New York, 74, Artist's Space Gallery, New York, 74, Alpha Gallery, Boston, 75, Hudson Walker Gallery, Provincetown, Robert Schoelkopf Gallery, New York, Ctr for Music, Drama & Art, Lake Placid, NY, NY State Legislature Off Bldg, Albany, Kemerer Mus, Adirondack Mus, 77-78. Pos: Guest artist, Yale Univ, 70; guest artist, Skidmore Col, 71; vis artist, Ohio Univ, 72; vis artist, Art Inst Chicago, 72-73; guest artist, Moore Col Art, 74; fine arts coordr, Adirondack Lakes Ctr for the Arts, currently. Awards: Elizabeth T Greenshields Mem Found Grant, 70; Residence Grant, Fine Arts Work Ctr, Provincetown, 71; CAPS Grant, NY State Coun Arts, 75. Bibliog: James Monte (auth), 22 Realists, Whitney Mus Am Art, 70; Carter Ratcliff (auth), New York, Art Int Mag, 4/70; Gerritt Henry (auth), A realist twin bill, Art News Mag, 1/73; Judith Tannenbaum (auth), Don Wynn, Arts Mag, 1/77. Style & Technique: Representational, realist. Mailing Add: Durant Rd Blue Mountain Lake NY 12812

WYNNE, ALBERT GIVENS
PAINTER
b Colorado Springs, Colo, Jan 3, 22. Study: Univ Denver; Iowa Wesleyan Col, BA; Univ Iowa, MA; also with S Carl Fracassini, Boardman Robinson, James Lechay & others. Exhib: Joslyn Art Mus; Butler Inst Am Art; Anchorage, Alaska; Am Fedn Arts Traveling Exhib; Roswell, NMex; plus many others. Teaching: Hon instr, Univ Colo, Colorado Springs Fine Arts Ctr. Awards: Prizes, Anchorage Art Exhib & Des Moines Art Ctr. Mailing Add: 7420 Swan Rd Colorado Springs CO 80908

WYNSHAW, FRANCES
ART DEALER, ART COLLECTOR
b New York, NY. Pos: Former dir, Avanti Galleries, New York. Specialty: Contemporary American and European art. Mailing Add: 157 E 72nd St New York NY 10021

WYRICK, CHARLES LLOYD, JR (PETE)
MUSEUM DIRECTOR, WRITER
b Greensboro, NC, May 5, 39. Study: Davidson Col, BA; Univ NC, MFA; Univ Mo. Exhib: Corcoran Biennial Exhib Am Painting, 67; Assoc Artists NC Ann, 68; Univ Va Print Exhib, 68. Collections Arranged: Art from the Ancient World, The Human Figure in Art, A Wyeth Portrait & Light as a Creative Medium, Va Mus Fine Arts, 66-68; Contemporary American Paintings from the Lewis Collection, Del Art Mus, 74; Va Mus, Philadelphia Art Alliance, Carspecken-Scott Gallery & Wilmington Friends Sch, 77-78. Teaching: Instr, Stephens Col, 64-66. Pos: Artmobile coordr & asst head prog div, Va Mus Fine Arts, Richmond, 66-68; exec dir, Asn Preservation Va Antiq, 68-70; pres, Fine Arts Consults, Richmond, 71-73; art critic, Richmond News Leader, 71-73; dir, Del Art Mus, 73- Mem: Am Asn Mus; Col Art Asn Am; Soc Archit Historians; Asn Art Mus Dirs; Victorian Soc Am. Res: Contemporary American painting; eighteenth to twentieth century American architecture. Publ: Auth, Art & urban aesthetics (weekly column), Richmond News Leader; auth, A Wyeth Portrait, 67 & Contemporary Art at the Virginia Museum, 72, Arts in Va; auth, Richmond's 17th Street Market, 73. Dealer: Carspecken-Scott Gallery Wilmington DE. Mailing Add: 2301 Kentmere Pkwy Wilmington DE 19806

WYSE, ALEXANDER JOHN
PAINTER, SCULPTOR
b Gloucestershire, Eng, Sept 8, 38; Can citizen. Study: Cheltenham Col Art, Gloucestershire; Royal Col Art, London. Work: Mem Univ, Nfld; Can Coun Collection. Exhib: Brit Young Contemporaries; first Can one-man show, Pa Acad Fine Arts Peale Gallery; Arwin Galleries, Detroit; Pollock Gallery, Toronto, Ont; Opening of Henry Moore Wing, 74 & Through Looking Glass, 74, Ont Art Gallery; Landscape-Canada-Roots & Promise, Image & Symbol (traveling exhib), Art Gallery Ont, 75-76; Oh Canada (traveling exhib), London Art Gallery, Ont, 76-77; Changing Visions—Appletree (traveling exhib of Can & eastern US), 76-77; Hamilton Art Gallery, Ont, 77; 17 Can Artists: A Protean View, Vancouver Art Gallery, BC, 77. Teaching: Instr engraving, Northwest Territories, Can, 62-63. lectr, Ont Elem Schs, 71 & 73. Awards: Am Inst Graphic Arts Award, Alphabet Book, 68 & One to Fifty Book, 73; Can Coun Grants, 68, 70 & 73; Can Design Coun Award, The Look of Books, 74. Media: Tin, Oil, Wood, Glass, Ink. Publ: Co-auth (with Anne Wyse), Alphabet Book, 68-69 & One to Fifty Book, 73, Univ Toronto; co-auth (with Anne Wyse), The Ottawa Book, 78. Dealer: Arwin Galleries 222 Grand River W Detroit MI 48226. Mailing Add: 125 Noel St Ottawa ON Can

Y

YAGHJIAN, EDMUND
PAINTER, INSTRUCTOR
b Harpoot, Armenia; US citizen. Study: RI Sch Design, BFA; Art Students League, with Stuart Davis. Work: New York Pub Libr; NY Univ; High Mus Art, Atlanta, Ga; Gibbes Art Mus, Charleston, SC; West Point Mus, NY; plus many other including over 500 in pvt collections. Exhib: New York World's Fair; San Francisco World's Fair; Carnegie Int, Pittsburgh, 36; Whitney Mus Am Art, New York, 40; Metrop Mus Art, New York, 41; 40 Year Retrospective, Univ SC, 72; plus many other group & one-man shows. Teaching: Instr art, Art Students League, 38-42; guest instr painting, Univ Mo, 44-45; head dept art, Univ SC, 45-66, artist in residence, 66-72; instr painting, Columbia Mus Art, 72- Awards: Numerous prizes & awards in local & regional shows. Mem: Am Fedn Arts; Col Art Asn Am; Southeastern Col Art Asn (pres); life mem Art Students League; SC Artists Guild (pres & founder). Media: Acrylic. Mailing Add: 1510 Adger Rd Columbia SC 29205

YANISH, ELIZABETH
SCULPTOR, LECTURER
b St Louis, Mo. Study: Wash Univ; Denver Univ; also with Frank Varra, Wilbur Verhelst, Edgar Brittor, Marian Buchan & Angelo DiBenedetto. Work: Tyler Mus, Tex; Colo State Bank, Denver, Martin-Marietta Co, Denver; Colo Womens Col; Ball State Col. Comn: Carved doors, eternal light, Menorah, BMH Synagogue, Denver, 72-74; complete interior, Har Ha Shem Congregation, Boulder, 74; Relief Tree (bronze), Beth Israel Hosp, Denver, 74; mem relief, Denver Gen Hosp, 75. Exhib: Denver Art Mus Exhib, 61-75 & Western Ann, 65; Midwest Biennial, Joslyn Mus, Omaha, Nebr, 68; Int Exhib, Lucca, Italy, 71; one-man show, Woodstock Gallery, London, Eng, 73; Artrain, Mich Fine Arts Coun, 74. Teaching: Lectr contemp sculpture, var cols & univs. Pos: Trustee, Denver Ctr Performing Arts, 73-75; chmn, Visual Arts Festival, Bicentennial, 74-75; bd educ, Arts in Elem Educ, 77-78. Awards: Purchase Award Golden Web, Colo Women's Col, 63; McCormick Award, Ball State Univ, 61; Purchase Award, Tyler Mus, Tex, 65. Bibliog: Article in Artforum, 63, Jim Mills (auth), var feature stories, Denver Post Art Ed, 64-75; John Manson (auth), Artists of the Rockies, 74. Mem: Artists Equity Asn (pres, 63); Rocky Mountain Liturgical Arts; Allied Sculptors Colo; Denver Coun Arts (pres, 73-75). Style & Technique: Contemporary sculpture; welded fabricated bronze highly polished; various woods in one work. Media: Welded Steel, Bronze, Copper. Mailing Add: 131 Fairfax Denver CO 80220

YANOSKY, TOM
PAINTER, DESIGNER
b Colver, Pa, Sept 12, 18. Study: Corcoran Sch Art, Washington, DC, with Eugen Weisz; Am Univ, with Jack Tworkov; Phillips Mem Gallery, with Karl Knaths. Work: Phillips Collection, Washington, DC; George Washington Univ; Libr Cong. Comn: History of Cartography, US Army Topographic Ctr, Washington, DC, 65. Exhib: Pennell Show, Libr Cong, 47 & 52; Corcoran Area Show, 56; Soc Washington Artists Area Shows; Southwestern Invitational, Ariz, 73 & 74; Four Corners Biennial, Phoenix, 75; one-man shows, Arts Club, Washington, DC, 62, Artist Mar, Washington, DC, 63, Harlan Gallery, Tucson, Ariz, 73 & Thompson Gallery, Phoenix, Ariz, 76. Pos: Pres, Soc Washington Artists, 67-68. Awards: First Award for Prints & Drawings, Times-Herald, Washington, DC, 46; Libr Cong Purchase Award, Joseph & E Pennell Fund, 47; First Award for Painting, Soc Washington Artists, 68. Style & Technique: Geometric abstract, emphasis on formal relationships and design; color field painting; constructions. Media: Acrylic on Canvas; Painted Reliefs (Constructions); Bas Reliefs and Small Sculptures; Masks (Wood); Drawing; Jewelry Design. Dealer: Thompson Gallery 2020 N Central Ave Phoenix AZ 85004. Mailing Add: 3502 E Cochise Rd Phoenix AZ 85024

YANOW, RHODA MAE
PAINTER, ILLUSTRATOR
b Newark, NJ. Study: Newark Arts Club; Parsons Sch Design; Newark Sch Fine & Indust Arts; Heritage Art Sch; Nat Acad Design, with Henry Gasser, Daniel Greene, Harvey Dinnerstein & John Grabach. Work: West Orange Home for Senior Citizens, NJ; Newark Pub Libr. Exhib: 78th Ann Open Exhib, Catharine Lorillard Wolfe Art Club, Inc, 74; Nat Arts Club Pastel Show, 74; Muhlenberg Col Festival of Arts, 75; Am Artists Prof League Grand Nat Exhib, 75; Salmagundi Club Watercolor Show, 75. Awards: Andrews/Nelson/Whitehead Award, Nat Arts Club, 74; Coun Am Artist Socs Award, Am Artists Prof League Grand Nat, 75; Louis La Beaum Mem Award, Nat Acad Design, 75; Hudson Artists' Award, Bergen Community Mus, 76; Dr Ralph Weiler Prize, 77; Fairlawn Art Asn Award, 77; Ray A Jones Mem Award for Traditional Painting, 77; Silvermine Guild of Artists Award, 77; Award, Greenwich Village Spring Show, 77; James A Suydam Bronze Medal, 77; Anna Hyatt Huntington Silver Medal, 77; Catharine Lorillard Wold Art Club Gold Medal, 77; Hon Mention, Audubon Artists, 78. Bibliog: Ruthann Williams (auth), Graven images, NJ Music & Arts, 6/74. Mem: Am Artists Prof League; Philadelphia Water Color Club; Catharine Lorillard Wolfe Art Club; Salmagundi Club; Pastel Soc of Am (corresp secy, 75). Style & Technique: Representational pastel portraits of contemporary people. Media: Pastels, Pen & Ink, Oil. Publ: Contribr & illusr, NJ Music & Arts, 74 & 75; contribr, Star Ledger & other local newspapers. Dealer: Hait Gallery 2A Inwood Pl Maplewood NJ 07040. Mailing Add: 12 Korwel Circle West Orange NJ 07052

YARBROUGH, LEILA KEPERT
PRINTMAKER, PAINTER
b Katoomba, NSW, Australia, Mar 23, 32; US citizen. Study: Univ Fla; Atlanta Sch of Art, Ga. Work: Chrysler Mus, Norfolk, Va; Augusta Mus Art, Ga; Piedmont Col, Demorest, Ga; Loch Haven Art Ctr, Orlando, Fla; Great Smoky Mts Nat Park Art Collection, Gatlinburg, Tenn. Exhib: Drawing Soc Nat Travel Exhib, Am Fedn Arts, 65-66; Eastern US Drawing Competition, Cummer Gallery of Art, Jacksonville, Fla, 70; Contemporary American Drawing V: Norfolk, Smithsonian Inst Travel Exhib, 71-73; 34th Ann Contemp Am Painting, Soc of Four Arts, Palm Beach, Fla, 72; Ga Artists II, High Mus of Art, Atlanta, 72; 1st Nat Monoprint/Monotype, Oglethorpe Univ, Atlanta, Ga, 73; 64th Ann, Conn Acad Fine Arts, Hartford, 74; Am Drawings, Portsmouth Community Art Ctr, Va, 76. Awards: Am Drawing Purchase Award, Norfolk Mus, 71; First Prize, The Single Impression, Oglethorpe Univ, Atlanta, 73; Great Smoky Mts Nat Park Purchase Award, US Govt Art Purchase Prog, 74. Bibliog: Martin Sharter (auth), Art, Atlanta Mag, 12/73. Mem: Atlanta Art Workers Coalition. Style & Technique: Large innovative color etchings based on nature. Media: Intaglio, Monoprints; Casein; Mixed. Dealer: Artists Assoc Inc 3261 Roswell Rd NE Atlanta GA 30305. Mailing Add: 5147-1 Roswell Rd NE Atlanta GA 30342

YARDLEY, RICHARD QUINCY
CARTOONIST
b Baltimore, Md, Mar 11, 03. Study: Md Inst Art. Pos: Polit cartoonist, Morning Sun, 34-39, ed cartoonist, 49-66, ed cartoonist, Baltimore Sun, 66-72; auth & illusr syndicated comic panel, Our Ancestors by Quincy. Mem: Nat Cartoonists Soc; Nat Ed Cartoonists Soc; Nat Press Club. Publ: Contribr cartoons, New Yorker, Reporter Mag. Mailing Add: 4413 Sedgwick Rd Baltimore MD 21210

YASKO, CARYL ANNE
MURALIST
b Racine, Wis, Mar 11, 41. Study: Dominican Col, Wis, sculpture with Monica Gabriel & painting with Branislov Bak, grad, 63. Comn: Nat Endowment for Arts murals, Under City Stone, Hyde Park, Chicago, 72, Health of the People, Razem, Chicago, 73, I Am the People, Logan Square, Chicago, 74 & Polish-American Mural, Chicago; Lemont Bicentennial Mural, Lemont Hist Soc Bicentennial Comn, 75. Exhib: On Chicago Walls, Chicago Pub Libr, 73 & Chicago State Univ, 74; Civic Sculpture, Appleton, Neenah & Menasha, Wis, 77. Teaching: Dir & instr, Cove Sch, Racine, Wis, 57-63; lectr murals, Loop Jr Col, Valparaiso Univ, Art Inst Chicago & Cherokee Lane Elem Sch, Adelphi, Md, 72-; instr, Art Inst Chicago, 75 & 76 & Oakton Community Col, Morton Grove, Ill, 77. Pos: Artist in residence, City of Racine, 65; co-founder & co-dir, Art Tillers, Chicago, 71-73; dir, Chicago Group Mural Workshop, 73-76. Awards: Chicago Beautiful Award, Mayor Daley, 75 & 76. Bibliog: Harold Haydon (auth), article in Compton's Encycl Yearbk, 75; Whitney Gould (auth), The Cosmos is on the Wall, Madison Press Connection, 77; Murals over America, In These Times, 77. Mem: Chicago Mural Group (bd mem); Chicago Artist Coalition. Media: Oil, Watercolor. Publ: Contribr, Art Workers News, 73, New Art Examr, 74 & Nat Murals Newsletter, 78; auth, Big art, Environmental Commun, 77. Mailing Add: 136 Whiton St Whitewater WI 53190

YASSIN, ROBERT ALAN
MUSEUM DIRECTOR, ART HISTORIAN
b Malden, Mass, May 22, 41. Study: Dartmouth Col, BA, 62; Univ Mich, Ann Arbor, MA(hist art), 65, Samuel H Kress Found fel, 68-70; Yale Univ, Ford fel, 66-68. Collections Arranged: Contemporary Art at Yale Yale, Univ Mich, 66, Art & the Excited Spirit (with catalog), 72; Helen W & Robert M Benjamin Collection, Yale Univ, 67, American Art from Alumni Collections, 68; Victor Higgins Retrospective (with catalog), Indianapolis Mus Art, 75, Harrison Eiteljorg Collection of Western American Art, 76; Leonard Baskin, 76; Painting & Sculpture Today, 76; Art in Bus Collections, 77. Teaching: Instr graphic arts & mus practice & co-dir joint mus training prog, Univ Mich, Ann Arbor, 70-73; adj prof, Herron Sch of Art, Ind Univ-Purdue Univ, Indianapolis, 76- Pos: Ed, Yale Univ Art Gallery Bull, 66-68; asst dir, Mus Art, Univ Mich, Ann Arbor, 70-72, ed, Art Bull, 70-73, assoc dir & actg dir, Mus, 73; chief cur, Indianapolis Mus Art, 73-75, actg dir, 75, dir, 75- Mem: Col Art Asn Am; Am Asn Mus; Asn Art Mus Dir; Nat Trust Hist Preservation; Mus Conserv Asn (chmn exec comt, 77-); Midwest Mus Asn. Res: Late 19th and 20th century American art; 19th century British painting. Mailing Add: 1200 W 38th St Indianapolis IN 46208

YASUDA, ROBERT
PAINTER
b Lihue, Kauai, Hawaii, Nov 14, 40. Study: Pratt Inst, BFA, 62, MFA, 64. Work: Brooklyn Mus, NY; Libr Cong, Washington, DC; State of Hawaii Found of the Arts. Exhib: Prospect 68, Dusseldorf, Ger, 68; Albright-Knox Art Gallery, Buffalo, NY, 75; one-man shows, The Clocktower, Inst for Art & Urban Resources, 76 & Betty Parsons Gallery, New York, 77; Proj Space I, Inst for Art & Urban Resources Rooms, New York, 76; Arte Fiera 77, Bologna, Italy, 77; 35th Biennial Corcoran Gallery Art, Washington, DC, 77; plus others. Style & Technique: Large quiet installations with large scale painted walls, leaning paintings and corner paintings. Media: Acrylic Emulsion, Multi-Layering Technique. Dealer: Betty Parsons Gallery 24 W 57th St New York NY 10019. Mailing Add: 429 W Broadway New York NY 10012

YATER, GEORGE DAVID
PAINTER
b Madison, Ind, Nov 30, 10. Study: John Herron Art Sch, 28-32, dipl; Cape Sch Art, Provincetown, with Henry Hensche, summers 31-34; also with Edwin Dickinson & Richard Miller. Work: Chrysler Collection, Norfolk Art Gallery, Va; Ford Motor Co, Dearborn, Mich; Paper Mill Playhouse, Millburn, NJ; Ind Univ, Bloomington; Arch Am Art, Smithsonian Inst, Washington, DC. Comn: Mural, Provincetown-Boston Airline, Provincetown Airport, 76. Exhib: World's Fair, New York, NY, 39; Nat Acad Design, New York; Pa Acad Fine Arts, Philadelphia; Am Watercolor Soc, New York; Indianapolis Mus Art; Chrysler Art Mus, Provincetown, Mass; Provincetown Painters 1890s-1970s, Everson Mus of Art, Syracuse, NY & Provincetown Art Asn & Mus, Provincetown, Mass, 77. Pos: Dir, Provincetown Art Asn, 47-61; dir, Sarasota Art Asn, 55-56; dir & instr, Middletown Fine Arts Ctr, 70-71. Awards: Alumni Prize, Ind Artists Ann, John Herron Art Mus, 53; Outstanding Oil, Hoosier Salon, Indianapolis, 54; First Prize for Oil, Falmouth Artists Guild, 61, 69 & 75. Bibliog: Ernie Pyle (auth), article in Scripps-Howard Feature, 36; Jack Stinnet (auth), In New York, AP Feature, 36; Robert Hatch (auth), At the tip of Cape Cod, Horizon Mag, 61. Style & Technique: Realist work with traditional materials and methods. Media: Oil, Watercolor. Publ: More than 75 watercolors have been used as illus in Ford Times, Lincoln-Mercury Times & New Eng Journeys, 52-66. Mailing Add: Castle Rd Truro MA 02666

YATES, SHARON DEBORAH
PAINTER
b Rochester, NY, Apr 3, 42. Study: Syracuse Univ, scholar to Florence, Italy, 63, BFA, 64; Tulane Univ La, MFA, 66. Work: Okla Art Ctr, Oklahoma City. Exhib: Am Fedn Arts Traveling Exhib, New York, 67-; Okla Art Ctr 10th Ann, 68; Mainstreams '70, Marietta Col Fine Arts Ctr, Ohio, 70; Exhib Contemp Realists, Cleveland Inst, 72; one-man show, Univ Louisville, Ky, 67; plus many others. Teaching: Instr printmaking, painting & drawing, Univ Louisville, 66-68; instr painting & drawing, Md Inst Col Art, 68- Pos: Am Beautiful Fund of Natural Area Coun artist in residence, 70. Awards: Grand Prize, Mainstreams, 70; Prix de Rome, 72. Bibliog: Barbara Gold (auth), Art!? (film), Channel 2, Baltimore, Md, 3/72. Media: Oil. Publ: Contribr, A Sense of Place, The Artist & The American Land, 72. Mailing Add: 701 Druid Park Lake Dr Baltimore MD 21217

YEATTS, JAMES MCKINNEY
ART DEALER, PAINTER
b Roanoke, Va, Mar 31, 22. Study: Univ Va, BS, 47; Prince Univ, MFA, 49, with Jean Labatu, also with John Canaday. Work: Va Mus Fine Arts, Richmond; Roanoke Fine Arts Ctr, Va; Va Military Inst, Lexington; Hollins Col, Va; Va Polytech Inst & State Univ, Blacksburg. Comn: Painting, Gov Linwood Holton, Gov's mansion, Richmond, 73. Exhib: One-man shows, Univ Va, Charlottesville, 62, Eric Schindler Gallery, Richmond, 69, Walter Rawls Mus, Norfolk, 70, Mary Baldwin Col, Lynchburg, 71, Va Polytech Inst, 74, Cassell Gallery II, New Orleans, La, 77 & Emory & Henry Col, Va, 78. Pos: Owner, Yeatts Gallery, Roanoke.

Awards: Best in Abstract, Roanoke Sidewalk Art Show, 69; Purchase Award, Va Area Art Show, Shenandoah Life Insurance Co, 70; Best in Show, Gallery 28, Am Asn Univ Women, 78. Media: Oil on Canvas, Pastel on Board. Dealer: William Dale Gallery 828 Chartres St New Orleans LA 70116. Mailing Add: 364 Walnut Ave SW Roanoke VA 24016

YEH, CAROL
PRINTMAKER
b Lackawanna, NY, Dec 25, 38. Study: Yale Univ Summer Sch, Norfolk, Conn; Smith Col, Northampton, Mass, BA, 61, with Leonard Baskin; Acad de la Grande Chaumière, Paris, France; Univ Iowa, Iowa City, MA, 66, with Mauricio Lasansky; Acad de Bellas Artes, San Fernando, Madrid, Spain. Work: Ohio Univ Art Mus, Athens; New York Pub Libr; Everson Mus of Art, Syracuse, NY; Harvard Univ Libr, Cambridge; Yale Univ Libr, New Haven. Exhib: Am Drawing Biennial XXI, Norfolk Mus Arts & Sci, Va, 65; Smithsonian Inst Travel Am Drawings, 65-66; Northwest Printmakers, 37th Int, Seattle, Wash, & Portland, Ore, 66; two-man show, Drawings, Fleischer Anhalt Gallery, Los Angeles, 69; one-woman shows, Prints & Drawings, Houghton House, Geneva, NY, 75 & Prints, Everson Mus Luncheon Gallery, Syracuse, NY, 77. Awards: Fulbright Grant to Spain, 66-67, Yaddo Fel, 72 & Macdowell Colony Fel, 72. Style & Technique: Abstract narrative in autographic line. Media: Drawing; Intaglio. Publ: Auth & illusr, Etched Portraits of Ernest Hemingway, 61; illusr, Red Flower, 61; auth & illusr, Houdini, 71; illusr, Ragtime, 76; illusr, Hawthorne, 77. Dealer: Zeitlin & Ver Brugge 815 N La Cienega Los Angeles CA 90025. Mailing Add: Box 11 Fayette NY 13065

YEKTAI, MANOUCHER
PAINTER
b Tehran, Iran, Dec 22, 22; US citizen. Study: Univ Tehran; Ecole Superior Beaux Arts, Paris, with Auzenfant, 45-47; Art Students League, 47-48. Work: Baltimore Mus Art, Md; Mus Mod Art, New York; Everson Mus, Syracuse, NY; Hirshhorn Mus, Washington, DC; also many pub & pvt collections. Exhib: Gumps Gallery, San Francisco, 59, 64 & 65; Piccadilly Gallery, London, 61 & 70; Anderson-Meyer Gallery, Paris, 62; Mus Mod Art, 62; Art Inst Chicago, 63; Gertrude Kasle Gallery, Detroit, 65-70; Benson Gallery, Bridgehampton, NY, 67, 72, 73 & 75; plus many others. Media: Oil. Mailing Add: 225 W 86th St New York NY 10024

YENAWINE, BRUCE HARLEY
ART ADMINISTRATOR, EDUCATOR
b Urbana, Ill, Dec 30, 49. Study: Univ Louisville, Ky, BA. Teaching: Lectr sr sem aesthetics, Louisville Sch of Art, Ky, 77- Pos: Assoc dir, Louisville Sch of Art, 73-74, dir, 74- Awards: Cardinal Award, Univ Louisville, 72; Outstanding contribr to arts, Art Ctr Asn, 74. Mem: Nat Asn of Sch of Art (mem bd dir & chmn comt on res & develop, 76-); Nat Soc of Arts & Lit; Ky Art Educ Asn; Ky Asn of Mus. Publ: Contribr, Anchorage Revisited, Libr Nat, 76. Mailing Add: 11300 Ridge Rd Anchorage KY 40223

YEREX, ELTON
PAINTER, EDUCATOR
b Neepawa, Man, Feb 10, 35. Study: Univ Man, BFA; Univ Mich, Ann Arbor, MFA; Wayne State Univ, MA(art hist). Work: Art Gallery Windsor. Exhib: Mich Artists Exhib, Detroit Inst Arts, 67 & 68; Soc Can Artists, Toronto, 68 & 70; Agnes Etherington Ann Exhib, Kingston, 71; Ann Southwestern Ont Artists Exhib, Windsor, 72; one-man shows, Mushroom Gallery, Windsor, 74 & Nancy Poole Studio, Toronto, 74 & 75. Teaching: Lectr studio art, Univ Windsor, 65-68; prof studio art, Univ Guelph, 68- Media: Acrylic on Canvas. Dealer: Nancy Poole Studio 16 Hazelton Toronto ON Can. Mailing Add: 15 Oxford Guelph ON N1H 2M4 Can

YIANNES, (IORDANIDIS)
SCULPTOR, CERAMIST
b Athens, Greece, Dec 16, 43. Study: Umanitaria Art Inst, Milan, Italy, scholar, 62; Brooklyn Mus Art Sch, scholar, 67-70; Max Beckmann scholar, 71-72. Exhib: NY Univ, 70; Brooklyn Mus, 71; Brockton Art Ctr, 72; International Contemporary Artistic Ceramics, Italy, 72; Whitney Mus Am Art Clay Exhib, 74. Teaching: Instr ceramics, Queens Col, summer 70; instr ceramics, Brooklyn Mus Art Sch, 70-; instr ceramics, Brooklyn Col, 72- Awards: First Prize in Ceramics, Alfred Parker, 69. Bibliog: Serry Suris (auth), Brooklyn Museum, 12/72, Craft Horizons; cover of Ramparts Mag, 5/71; Lisa Hammel (auth), article, New York Times, 3/77. Mem: Am & World Craft Couns. Style & Technique: Clay sculpture, wheel thrown forms; mixed media using ceramic materials. Media: Clay. Dealer: Allan Stone Gallery 48 E 86th St New York NY 10028. Mailing Add: 19 Commerce St New York NY 10014

YOAKUM, DELMER J
PAINTER, DESIGNER
b St Joseph, Mo, Dec 6, 15. Study: Chouinard Art Inst & Jepson Art Inst, Los Angeles; Kansas City Art Inst; Univ Southern Calif. Work: Butler Inst Am Art, Youngstown, Ohio; San Diego Art Mus, Calif; Nat Watercolor Soc; Las Vegas Art League; Glendale Savings & Loan, Calif; Pa Acad of Fine Arts, Philadelphia; DeYoung Mus, San Francisco, Calif; John Ringling Mus, Sarasota, Fla; Pasadena Mus, Calif; Calif Palace of the Legion of Hon, San Francisco; Tucson Art Mus, Calif; Calif State Fair, Sacramento; Assoc Am Artist Galleries; Va Mus; Mainstreams, Marietta, Ohio; Ariz State Fair, Phoenix. Exhib: Los Angeles Mus, Calif, 47-58; Butler Inst Am Art, 53-75; Nat Watercolor Soc, Los Angeles, 54-74; Watercolor USA, Springfield, Mo, 66-74; Nat Acad Design, New York, 70. Teaching: Instr art, Sedona, Ariz. Pos: Scenic artist, Motion Picture Studios, Hollywood, Calif, 52-72. Awards: Edouvard Manet Award, Frye Art Mus, 58 & 63; Best of Show, City of Avalon, Calif, 67; John Marin Mem Award, Watercolor USA, 71. Mem: Nat Watercolor Soc (past pres); hon life mem Inglewood Art League; Sedona Arts Ctr; Nat Soc Lit & Arts. Style & Technique: Contemporary realism. Media: Oil, Watercolor. Dealer: Garelick's Gallery Inc 7145 Main St Scottsdale AZ 85251. Mailing Add: 57 Chapel Hills Rd Sedona AZ 86336

YOCHIM, LOUISE DUNN
PAINTER
b Jitomir, Ukraine, July 18, 09; US citizen. Study: Art Inst Chicago, cert, 32, BAE, 42, MAE, 52; Univ Chicago, 56. Work: Bir-Bejan, Russia; Eilat Mus, Israel; Bernard Horwich Ctr, Chicago; Northeastern Ill Univ, Chicago; A Werbe Gallery, Detroit. Exhib: Chicago & Vicinity Exhib, Art Inst Chicago, 35-44; Chicago Soc Artists Exhib, Riverside Mus, New York, 51; Nat Exhib, Terry Mus Art, Fla, 52; Assoc Artists Gallery, Washington, DC, 62; one-woman show, Northeastern Ill Univ, 72; plus many others. Teaching: Instr art, Chicago Pub High Sch, Ill, 34-50; instr art, Chicago Acad Fine Arts, 51-52; instr art, Chicago Teachers Col, 60-61. Pos: Art supvr, Chicago Pub Schs, 50-71; consult art, elem & high schs, 71-; consult art, Rand McNally Publ, 67-; consult art, Encycl Britannica, 68- Awards: Todros Geller Award for Painting, Am Jewish Arts Club, 48-61; Award, Chicago Soc Artists, 53. Bibliog: Frank Holland (auth), Renaissance unit's show to cap season, Chicago Sun Times, 57; Doris Lane Butler (auth), Winnetka to open art fair season, Chicago Daily News, 57; Frank Getlein (auth), Associated Artists, Sunday Star, Washington, DC, 62. Mem: Chicago Soc Artists (pres, 72-78); Renaissance Soc Art; Nat Art Educ Asn; Nat Comt Art Educ. Media: Oil, Watercolor. Publ: Auth, Building Human Relationships Through Art, 54, Perceptual Growth in Creativity, 67, Art in Action, 69 & Role & Impact: The Chicago Society of Artists, 78. Dealer: Four Arts Gallery 1629 Oak Ave Evanston IL 60203. Mailing Add: 9545 Drake Ave Evanston IL 60203

YOKOI, RITA
SCULPTOR, PAINTER
b New York, NY, Aug 26, 38. Study: Alfred NY State Col of Ceramics, Alfred Univ, 56-59; San Francisco Art Inst, Agnes Brandenstein Mem Scholar, 59-61, BFA(with hon), 61; Tokyo Univ of Art, Japan, Fulbright Fel Ceramics, 62-63; Univ Calif Berkeley, 66-70, MA(art & sculpture), 70. Exhib: Eighth Int Exhib of Ceramic Art, Smithsonian Inst, Washington, DC, 61; Young Americans, Mus of Contemp Crafts, New York, 62; M H DeYoung Mem Mus, San Francisco, 68; Calif Crafts VI, Pacific Dimensions, E B Crocker Art Gallery, Sacramento, Calif, 69; three woman exhib, Exploration/Perception/Growing, Oakland Art Mus, Calif, 70; The Last Plastics Show, Calif Inst of the Arts, Valencia, 72; Twenty-one Artists, Invisible/Visible, Long Beach Mus of Art, on tour to Mills Col, Oakland, Alta, Can & Southern Methodist Univ, 72; Collage & Assemblage in Southern Calif, Los Angeles Inst Contemp Art, 75; Imagination, Los Angeles Inst Contemp Art, 76; The Artist & The Mask, Craft & Folk Art Mus, Los Angeles, 77; Downtown Dog Show, DeYoung Mus Downtown Ctr, San Francisco, 77; Artwords-Bookworks, Los Angeles Inst of Contemp Art, 78; 100 plus Current Directions in Southern Calif Art, Los Angeles Inst Contemp Art, 78; one-woman shows, Cactus Images, Gallery 707, Los Angeles, 73, Mt St Mary's Col, Los Angeles, 76, New Paintings and Sculpture by Rita Yokoi, Jacqueline Anhalt Gallery, Los Angeles, 77 & One Hundred Flamingos, Otis Art Inst Gallery, Los Angeles, 77. Exhibitions Arranged: Attitudes Towards Space: Environmental Art (cur, auth, intro to catalogue), Mt St Mary's Col, Los Angeles, 77. Teaching: Instr ceramics, YWCA, San Francisco, 61, Zion Lutheran Church Sch, San Francisco, 66, Mendocino Art Ctr, Calif, 69, Oakland Evening Sch, summers, 69-71; instr ceramics & sculpture, San Francisco Community Col, 66-72; instr intro to art, Fresno City Col, Calif, fall 72; lectr sculpture, Calif State Univ, Fresno, 71-73; instr design & advert to grad students, Otis Art Inst, 73-75; lectr sculpture, Univ Calif, Los Angeles, 73-75; asst prof art, Mt St Mary's Col, 75-76; adj fac, Antioch Col-W. Los Angeles, fall 76; vis artist, Claremont Grad Sch, spring 78. Awards: Purchase award, San Francisco Art Festival, City of San Francisco, 61; Purchase Award, Ceramics 70, Col San Mateo, Calif, 70; Acad Yr Res grant, Univ Calif, Los Angeles, 74-75. Bibliog: Melinda Wortz (auth), Female Fantasies, Fine Arts Gallery, Univ Calif, Irvine, 2/77; Ruth Askey (auth), Relationships Interpreted, Artweek, Oakland, 11/77; Henry J Seldis (auth), Quirks of world we live in, Los Angeles Times, 12/26/77. Mem: Los Angeles Inst Contemp Art; Calif Confederation of the Arts; Otis Asn; Artists for Economic Action; Women's Caucus for Art; Col Art Asn. Style & Technique: Environmental sculpture, sculpture, painting, drawing and photography. Media: Mixed. Publ: Contribr, Women's Month Group Show (intro to catalogue), Calif State Univ, Fresno, 3/73; contribr, Women's Studies in Art and Art History, Col Art Asn of Am, 1/74; auth, An afternoon of events, Artweek, 4/20/74; contribr, By Our Own Hands, Double X, Santa Monica, Calif, 77. Mailing Add: 4577 S Centinela Ave Los Angeles CA 90066

YOKOMI, RICHARD KOJI
PAINTER
b Denver, Colo, Mar 12, 44. Study: Chouinard Art Inst, BS, 65. Work: Pasadena Art Mus, Calif. Exhib: USA West Coast, Kunstverein, Hamburg, WGer, 72; State of Calif Painting (traveling exhib), 72-73; 15 Abstract Artists—Los Angeles, Santa Barbara Mus, 74; Painting & Sculpture in Calif, The Mod Era, San Francisco Mus Mod Art, 76 & Smithsonian Inst, Washington, DC, 77. Style & Technique: Abstract painting, acrylic on canvas. Dealer: Nickolas Wilder Gallery 8225 1/2 Santa Monica Blvd Los Angeles CA 90046. Mailing Add: 3666 Division St Los Angeles CA 90065

YOSHIDA, RAY KAKUO
PAINTER, EDUCATOR
b Kapaa, Kauai, Hawaii, Oct 3, 30. Study: Art Inst Chicago, BA; Syracuse Univ, MFA; Univ Chicago; Univ Hawaii; also with A D Reinhardt. Work: Everson Mus, Syracuse, NY; Art Inst Chicago; Mus des 20, Jahrhunderts, Vienna; Am Tel & Tel, New York; Ball State Univ, Muncie, Ind. Exhib: Spirit of the Comics, Inst Contemp Art, Univ Pa, 69; Chicago & Vicinity Exhibs, Art Inst Chicago, 69, 71 & 77; Am Painting, Indianapolis Mus Art, 72 & 77; 12th Bienal de Sao Paulo, Brazil, 73; Mus Contemp Art, Chicago; Brooklyn Mus; plus others. Teaching: Frank Harrold Sellers Prof, Art Inst Chicago, 60- Awards: Thomas C Thompson Purchase Prize, Everson Mus, 53; Walter M Campana Prize, 60, Frank G Logan Medal & Prize, 71, Virgine K Headberg Prize, 77, Art Inst Chicago. Bibliog: Franz Schulze (auth), Chicago Art, Follett, 72; articles in Art Int & Art News. Mem: Art Inst Chicago. Media: Oil, Acrylic. Dealer: Phyllis Kind Gallery 226 E Ontario Chicago IL 60611. Mailing Add: 1944 N Wood Chicago IL 60622

YOSHIMURA, FUMIO
SCULPTOR
b Kamakura, Japan, Feb 22, 26. Study: Tokyo Univ Arts, MFA, 49. Work: Philadelphia Art Mus; Pa Acad Fine Arts, Philadelphia; Albright-Knox Gallery, New York; Gobett-Brewster Gallery, New Plymouth, NZ; Power Gallery of Contemp Art, Sydney, Australia; Univ of Mass, Amherst; Univ Pa, Int House, Philadelphia. Comn: Mobile, Haskell & Sells, Philadelphia. Exhib: Pa Acad Fine Arts, 71; Photo Realism, Wadsworth Atheneum, Conn, 73; Nancy Hoffman Gallery, New York, 73 & 76; Tokyo Bienale, 74; Galleri Arnesen, Copenhagen, Denmark, 74; Realism/Realisme, Rothman's Pall Mall traveling exhib, Can, 76; Object as Poet, Renwick Gallery, Smithsonian Inst, Washington, DC, 76; Norton Gallery of Art, Fla, 77. Style & Technique: Detailed or simplified forms of common subjects in piece or in group. Media: Natural White Wood. Dealer: Marian Locks Gallery 1524 Walnut St Philadelphia PA 19102; Nancy Hoffman Gallery New York NY. Mailing Add: 5 E Third St New York NY 10003

YOUKELES, ANNE
PAINTER, PRINTMAKER
b Bad Ischl, Austria; US citizen. Study: Kunstgewerbeschule Vienna, Austria; Acad de la Grande Chaumière, Paris; Ohio State Univ; painting with Alexander Dobkin & Rudolf Baranik; printmaking with Sidney Chafetz & Carol Summers. Work: Philadelphia Mus Art; Rosenwald Collection, Smithsonian Inst; Bibliothèque Nat, Paris; Minneapolis Mus Art, Minn; De Cordova Mus, Mass. Comn: Editions of prints, Int Graphic Arts Soc, 72, Jewish Mus, 73 & Print Club, Philadelphia, 75. Exhib: Second British Int Biennial, Bradford, Eng, 70; Pratt Miniature Shows, 71 & 74; L'Estampe Contemp a la Bibliothèque Nat, 73; New Am Prints-40 Artists Traveling Exhib, 73; New Brunswick Mus, St John, 73; Queens Talent, Queens Mus, NY, 75; Art Today USA II, Mod Art Mus, Tehran, Iran, 77; one-person shows, Marion Locks Gallery, Philadelphia, 73 & 77 & Dubins Gallery, Los Angeles, 78. Awards: Purchase Prizes, Pratt Miniature Show, Boston Printmakers Ann & Philadelphia Print Club.

Bibliog: Gabor Peterdi (auth), Printmaking, MacMillan Publ Co, New York, 72 & Ross & Romano (auths), Techniques in Printmaking, 74. Mem: Soc Am Graphic Artists (coun mem, 73-); Boston Printmakers; Silvermine Guild Artists; Am Colorprint Soc; Print Club, Philadelphia. Style & Technique: All work three-dimensional; prints are silkscreened, cut, folded and applied to a background; paintings are painted on canvas and stretched on wood. Media: Silkscreen; Acrylic. Dealer: Marian Locks Gallery 1524 Walnut St Philadelphia PA 19102. Mailing Add: 81-42 193rd St Jamaica NY 11423

YOUNG, CHARLES ALEXANDER
EDUCATOR, PAINTER
b New York, NY, Nov 17, 30. Study: Hampton Inst, BS; NY Univ, with Hale Woodruff, MA; Cath Univ Am. Work: Fisk Univ Art Gallery, Nashville; Kennedy Inst; Fayetteville State Univ, NC; Scottish Bank, Fayetteville, NC. Exhib: Cent South Art Exhib, Nashville, 67; one-man show, Smith-Mason Gallery, 69 & Agra Gallery, Washington, DC, 72; Afro-American Images, Wilmington, Del, 71; Nat Exhib Black Artists, Washington, DC, 71. Teaching: Instr art, Fayetteville State Univ, 60-63; asst prof art, Tenn A&I Univ, 63-68; prof art & chmn dept, Fed City Col, 68- Awards: First & Second Prizes, First Open Exhib, Fayetteville, 62. Bibliog: Samella Lewis & Ruth G Waddy (auth), Black Artists on Art, Vol 2, Contemp Crafts, 71; J Edward Atkinson (auth), Black Dimensions in Contemporary American Art, New Am Libr, 71; Theresa, Dickeson, Cederholm (auth), Afro-American Artists, Trustees Boston Libr, 73. Mem: Col Art Asn; Nat Art Educ Asn; DC Comn Arts. Style & Technique: Abstract; expressionism. Media: Oil, Acrylic. Mailing Add: 8104 W Beach Dr NW Washington DC 20012

YOUNG, CLIFF
PAINTER, INSTRUCTOR
b New Waterford, Ohio, Dec 27, 05. Study: Art Inst Pittsburgh; Art Inst Chicago; Nat Acad Design; also with George Oberteuffer, Charles Schroeder, John Norton, J Wellington Reynolds & Harvey Dunn. Work: USN Art Gallery & USMC Collection, Washington, DC; Fed Hall, New York. Comn: Murals, St Francis Monastery, Utuado, PR, 58, Berkshire Life Ins Co, Pittsfield, Mass, 61, Church of Our Lady of Victory, New York, 62, Norweg Children's Home, Brooklyn, NY, 63, Pub Sch 232, Queens, NY, 65 & US Capitol, Washington, DC, 70- Teaching: Vis asst prof, Pratt-NY Phoenix Sch Design, 67-77; instr painting, Salmagundi Club, New York, 70- Mem: Archit League New York; Salmagundi Club (chmn art comt, 70-71); Nat Soc Mural Painters (treas, 71-72); Soc Illusr; Artists Guild (pres, 72). Style & Technique: Representational. Media: Oil, Acrylic. Publ: Auth, Figure Drawing Without a Model, 46; auth, Drawing Drapery, 47; auth, Figure Construction, 66. Mailing Add: 56 W 45th St New York NY 10036

YOUNG, DOUG Y H
PAINTER
b Honolulu, Hawaii. Study: Coe Col, Iowa, BA(art); Univ Hawaii; NY Univ; also with Duane Hanson, Ivan Karp & O K Harris. Work: State Found on Cult & the Arts, Hawaii; City & Co of Honolulu; Honolulu Acad of Arts. Comn: 75th Anniversary airbrush painting, Alexander & Baldwin, Inc, 75; two watercolors, Castle & Cooke, Inc, 75. Exhib: One-man shows, Coe Col Art Gallery, Iowa, 73, Young-Hawaii Works of Art, Honolulu, 74, Advertiser Contemp Arts Ctr, Honolulu, 75; Space, Los Angeles, 77 & Gima's, Honolulu, 78; 25th Iowa Artists Exhib, Des Moines Art Ctr, 73; Art Hawaii One, 75 & Art Hawaii Showcase 1976, Honolulu Acad of Arts; Calif-Hawaii Biennial 1976, Fine Arts Gallery, San Diego, 76. Collections Arranged: Artists of Hawaii, City & Co of Honolulu, Toronto, Can, 74; Arta Contemporana in Hawaii, Bucharest, Romania, 77. Teaching: Instr polyester resin casting, Coe Col, Iowa, 73. Awards: Hawaii Watercolor & Serigraph Soc Award, 75-76; Juror's Award, Easter Art Show, Honolulu, 74-75; Calif-Hawaii Biennial Award, Fine Arts Gallery, San Diego, 76. Style & Technique: Airbrush and acrylic enamel on Plexiglass; realistic local Hawaiian imagery. Media: Watercolor. Mailing Add: 927 Prospect St 1602 Honolulu HI 96822

YOUNG, JOHN CHIN
PAINTER, COLLECTOR
b Honolulu, Hawaii, Mar 26, 09. Work: Hawaii State Found Cult & Arts, Honolulu; Honolulu Acad Arts; Smithsonian Inst Art in Embassy Prog, Washington, DC; Dept Educ Hawaii State Artmobile Prog, Honolulu. Comn: Oil mural painting, Hana Ranch, Maui, Hawaii. Exhib: American Art Today, Metrop Mus Art & Va Art Mus, 50 & 58; one-man shows, Los Angeles Co Mus Art, Calif Palace of Legion of Honor, Honolulu Acad Art, Portland Art Mus, 74 & Honolulu Acad of Arts, 77; Pac Heritage Traveling Exhib to Berlin. Teaching: Instr painting, Honolulu Acad Art, 60-61. Pos: Art critic, Honolulu Star Bull, 65-66; chmn cult activities comt, East West Ctr, Honolulu, 71-72; dir, John Young Gallery. Awards: First Prize in Watercolors, 50, First Prize in Oil Painting, 54 & Best in Show, 55, Honolulu Acad Art. Mem: Hawaii Painters & Sculptors League (pres); Tennent Art Found (trustee, 72). Media: Oil. Collection: Oriental, pre-Columbian, African and Oceanic art works. Mailing Add: Kahala Hilton Honolulu HI 96816

YOUNG, JOSEPH E
ART HISTORIAN, CURATOR
b Los Angeles, Calif, Sept 8, 39. Study: Univ Calif, Los Angeles, MA, 78. Pos: West Coast Ed, USA, Art Int, 70-71; asst cur, prints & drawings, Los Angeles Co Mus of Art, 65- Mem: Print Coun of Am; Art Hist of Southern Calif; Col Art Asn of Am; Art Coun, KCET Pub Serv Television Sta, Channel 28, Los Angeles. Res: The History of European and American drawings and prints; the theory and criticism of art; history of American art. Publ: Auth, Jasper Johns: An Appraisal, Art Int, 69; auth, Pages and Fuses: An Extended View of Robert Rauchenberg, The Print Collectors Newsletter, 74; ed, Old Master Drawings from American Collections, 76 & auth, French Drawings and Prints from the Permanent Collection (1480-1961), 77, Los Angeles Co Mus of Art. Mailing Add: 5905 Wilshire Blvd Los Angeles CA 90036

YOUNG, JOSEPH LOUIS
SCULPTOR, ART ADMINISTRATOR
b Pittsburgh, Pa, Nov 27, 19. Study: Westminster Col, AB, 41, Hon LLD, 60; Boston Mus Sch Fine Art, hon grad, 51; Carnegie Inst Technol; Mass Inst Technol; Cranbrook Acad Art; Art Students League; also with Karl Zerbe, David Aronson, Mitchell Siporin, Oskar Kockoshka & Gyorgy Kepes. Comn: Sixteen stained glass windows, Congregation Beth Sholom, San Francisco, 65; west apse, Nat Shrine Immaculate Conception, Washington, DC, 67; History of Math (mosaic murals), Math Sci Bldg, Univ Calif, Los Angeles, 70; The Triforium (multi-media tower), Los Angeles Mall, 70-75; 30ft theme sculpture, City of La Mirada Civic Theatre, 78; plus over 40 major archit comns throughout the USA. Exhib: Ten Year Retrospective, Art in Architecture, Palm Springs Desert Mus, 63; Int Exhib Muralists, Brussels, Belg, 65; VII Triennale, UNESCO, Varna, Bulgaria, 73; one-man shows, Archit League New York, 51 & Falk Raboff Gallery, Los Angeles, 53. Teaching: Instr art hist, Tufts Col, Medford, Mass, 50; instr painting, Boston Mus Sch Fine Arts, 50; dir, Mosaic Workshop, 55-; artist in residence, Brandeis Inst, 62-; chmn dept archit arts, Santa Barbara Art Inst, 70-75; lectr, Art in Architecture at var insts of higher learning. Pos: Owner, Art in Architecture, 53-; designer 400th Anniversary of Michelangelo, Italian Trade Comn; nat vpres, Artists Equity Asn, 61-62; nat vpres, Nat Soc Mural Painters, 71-72; art consult, City of Huntington Beach, 73-74; head exhib design, Bowers Mus, Santa Ana, 77; field adminr, CETA Arts Prog, Los Angeles, 78. Awards: Am Acad Rome, Italy, 51; Huntington Hartford Found Fel, 52; Cavaliere, Repub Italy, 75; plus var awards, Am Inst Archit. Mem: Fel Int Inst Arts & Lett; Nat Sculpture Ctr, Lawrence, Kans; Nat Soc Mural Painters; Artists for Econ Action (bd mem); Artists Equity Asn (bd mem). Style & Technique: Correlation of light-sound in architectural environments. Media: Multi-Media. Publ: Auth, Bibliography of Mural Painting in USA, 46; auth, A Plan for Mural Painting in Israel, 52; auth, The World of Mosaic (film), Univ Calif, Los Angeles, 57; auth, Arts & crafts in architecture, Creative Crafts, Vol 2, No 1; auth, Mosaics: Principles & Practice, Reinhold, 63; auth, Dialogues in Art, KNBC-TV Series, 67; auth, The Triforium (film), 75. Mailing Add: 1434 S Spaulding Ave Los Angeles CA 90019

YOUNG, KENNETH VICTOR
PAINTER, DESIGNER
b Louisville, Ky, Dec 12, 33. Study: Ind Univ; Univ Louisville, BS. Work: Corcoran Gallery Art, Washington, DC; Va Nat Bank, Alexandria; Johnson Publ Co, Chicago; Am Tel & Tel, New York; Fisk Univ, Nashville. Exhib: Inst Contemp Arts, Washington, DC, 67; Baltimore Mus, 69; Ill Bell Co, Chicago, 71; Indianapolis Mus, 72; Corcoran Gallery Art, 74. Collections Arranged: Music Machines, Hall of Graphic Arts, Women & Politics, Gandhi Centennial Exhib, Explorers NZ. Teaching: Instr painting, Louisville Pub Sch, 62-63; instr design & painting, Corcoran Sch Art, 70- Pos: Designer, Smithsonian Inst, 64- Bibliog: B Rose (auth), Black artist in America, Art in Am, 70. Style & Technique: Color-field painting acrylic stain on unprimed canvas. Media: Watercolor on Paper and Pellon. Dealer: Franz Bader 2124 Pennsylvania Ave Washington DC 20037. Mailing Add: 1930 Columbia Rd No 303 Washington DC 20009

YOUNG, LILIAN VAN
See Vann, Loli

YOUNG, MAHONRI S
WRITER
b New York, NY, July 23, 11. Study: Dartmouth Col, AB; NY Univ, MA. Exhibitions Arranged: Howald, Brit Art & Boudin, Irish Art. Teaching: Instr hist art, Sarah Lawrence Col, 41-50. Pos: Actg dir, Munson-Williams-Proctor Inst, 51-53; dir, Columbus Gallery Fine Arts, 53-76. Publ: Am corresp, Apollo Mag; auth, Old George, 40; auth, The Paintings of George Bellows, 73; auth, The Eight: The Realist Revolt in American Painting, 73; auth, Early American Moderns: Painters of the Stieglitz Group, 74; auth, American Realists: Homer to Hopper, 77. Mailing Add: Box 754 Bridgehampton NY 11932

YOUNG, MARJORIE WARD
PAINTER
b Chicago, Ill, June 25, 10. Study: Art Inst Chicago Sat Sch, 25-27, Day Sch, 28-32; with William B Schimmel, 55-56, Jossey Bilan, 58-62, Edgar A Whitney, 69, 71 & 75, Richmond Yip, 70, & J Douglas Greenbowe & Milford Zornes, 72 & Robert Wood, 77. Work: Ariz Bank, Phoenix; First Nat Bank Ariz, Phoenix; Walter Bimson Collection, Phoenix; Phoenix Country Club; Western Serum Co, Tempe, Ariz. Exhib: 16th Ann Tucson Festival Art, Ariz, 66; Fine Arts Festival SDak State Univ, 69; 2nd Ariz Watercolor Biennial, Phoenix Art Mus, 70; Nat Diamond Biennial, Nat League Am Pen Women, Washington, DC, 72; Catherine Lorillard Wolf 77th Ann, 73; Ariz Watercolor Asn Show in Taiwan, 74; Watercolor Southwestone, Albuquerque, 76; Watercolor SW Two, Tucson, 76; 110th Ann Am Watercolor Soc, New York, 77. Teaching: Instr drawing & watercolor, Phoenix Art Mus, 70-72 & 77. Pos: Background artist, Fleischer, Famous & Paramount Studios, Miami, Fla, 38-42; gallery dir, Phoenix YWCA, 70-78. Awards: Second in Watercolor for Filibusters, Low Ruins Spring Nat, Tubac, Ariz, 65; Hon Mention for A Study in Brief, Nat Diamond Biennial, 72 & First in Watercolor & Best of Show for Pencil Sketch, League Show, 75, Nat League Am Pen Women. Mem: Ariz Artists Guild (pres, 61-62); Ariz Watercolor Asn (pres, 68); Nat League Am Pen Women (br art chmn, 72); Phoenix Art Mus Fine Arts Asn; hon mem Contemp Watercolorists Ariz. Style & Technique: Transparent watercolor and drawings with felt tip pen and pencil. Publ: Illusr, Many Lives of the Lynx, 64; illusr, Functional Spanish, 68. Dealer: O'Brien's Art Emporium 7122 Stetson Dr Scottsdale AZ 85251. Mailing Add: 320 W Montecito Phoenix AZ 85013

YOUNG, MILTON
PAINTER, SCULPTOR
b Houston, Tex, Oct 6, 35. Study: Los Angeles City Col, AA; Calif State Univ, Los Angeles, BA. Work: Malcolm X Col, Chicago. Comn: Black & white mural, Compton Communicative Arts Acad, Calif, 71. Exhib: One-man show, Brockman Gallery, Los Angeles, 70; Black American Artist, Lobby Gallery, Ill Bell, Chicago, 71; UCLA Four in One, Dickson Art Ctr, Los Angeles, 72; West Coast 74 Black Image, Crocker Art Gallery, Sacramento, 74; Tex Fine Arts Asn, Austin, 75. Collections Arranged: Jean Arp, Univ Calif, Los Angeles, 68, Japanese Prints, 69, Picasso, 70, George Rickey, 71, Decade in Retrospect, 74, African Art in Motion, 74, Medieval Ceramics, 75. Bibliog: Article in, Good Housekeeping, 2/67; Joe Young (auth), article in Art Int, 3/70; Lewis & Waddy (auth), article in, Black Artist on Art, 71. Mem: Art West Asn; Los Angeles Art Asn. Style & Technique: Hard-edge abstraction; strong emphasis on color juxtaposition. Media: Acrylic; Wood, Stone. Publ: Contribr, Coast Mag, 71 & Tuesday Mag, 73. Mailing Add: 1307 Park Ave Inglewood CA 90302

YOUNG, PETER FORD
PAINTER
b Pittsburgh, Pa, Jan 2, 40. Study: Chouinard Art Inst, Los Angeles, 57-58; Pomona Col, 58-60; Art Students League, New York, 60-61; New York Univ, BA(art hist), 63. Work: Albright-Knox Mus, Buffalo, NY; Guggenheim Mus & Mus Mod Art, New York; Aldrich Mus, Conn & NY. Comn: Graphic, Lincoln Ctr, Newport Jazz Festival, 72. Exhib: Ann Exhib of Contemp Am Painting, Whitney Mus, New York, 67-68; 31st Biennial—Contemp Painting, Corcoran Gallery, Washington, DC, 69; Nine Young Artists, Theodoran Awards, Guggenheim Mus, 69 & Ann Exhib of Contemp Painting, Whitney Mus, New York, 70; Six Painters, Albright-Knox Mus, Buffalo, 71; Eight Artists, Art Mus of South Tex, Corpus Christie, 74; Eight Artists, Miami Mus of Art, Fla, 74; El Color Como Lenguaje, Exhib of Mus of Mod Art, New York Int Prog, 75-76. Teaching: Vis artist, Oberlin Col, Ohio, 70 & Pima Col, Tucson, Ariz, 76. Bibliog: Barbara Rose (auth), Gallery Without Walls, Art in Am, 3/68; Ellen Johnson (auth), A Chronology of the Work, Artforum, 4/71; Elizabeth Baker(auth), Peter Young and David Dias, Art News, 9/71. Style & Technique: Acrylic on canvas. Dealer: Richard Bellamy 333 Park Ave S New York NY 10010. Mailing Add: c/o Todas Casas de Boruca Bisbee AZ 85063

YOUNG, ROBERT JOHN
PAINTER
b Vancouver, BC, Aug 8, 38. Study: Univ BC, BA(art hist); City & Guilds of London Sch of Art, Eng; Vancouver Sch of Art, dipl graphics. Work: Can Coun Art Bank, Ottawa; Govt of BC Prov Collection; London Borough of Camden, Eng; Vancouver Art Gallery; Montreal Mus Fine Arts. Comn: Christmas card Clothworkers Guild, London, 63; portrait, comn by Paul William White, London, 73; portrait, comn by Donna MacDonald, London, 76. Exhib: One-man shows, Redfern Gallery, London, 71, 73 & 75 & Vancouver Art Gallery, 74; Bradford Print Biennale, City Art Gallery & Mus, Eng, 73; Realismus und Realitat, Darmstadt, WGer, 75; Time Mag, Can Canvas, Across Can, 75-76; Can Cult Ctr, Embassy, Paris, 76; Vancouver Art Gallery, BC, 76-77; Marlborough-Godard, Toronto & Montreal, 76-77. Teaching: Instr painting, Banff Sch of Fine Arts, Alta, 75; vis artist, Royal Col Art, London, 76, Vancouver Sch Art, 77 & Alta Col Art, 78. Bibliog: Doris Shadbolt (auth), Robert Young, The Implacable Image, Vanguard, Vancouver Art Gallery, 77. Style & Technique: Photo-based painting, oil on linen. Media: Oil; Intaglio Printmaking. Dealer: Mira Godard 22 Hazelton Ave Toronto ON Can; Redfern Gallery 20 Cork St London ON Can. Mailing Add: 3940 Quebec Vancouver BC V5V 3K8 Can

YOUNG, TOM (WILLIAM THOMAS YOUNG)
PAINTER, EDUCATOR
b Huntington, WVa, Oct 7, 24. Study: John Herron Art Inst; Cincinnati Art Acad; Univ Ala, BFA & MA(fine arts); Ohio State Univ; Chouinard Art Inst; Univ Southern Calif; Columbia Univ, EdD; also with Hans Hofmann, New York. Work: Cincinnati Art Mus; Univ Southern Ill; Univ Ala, Tuscaloosa; Wagner Col; Univ New Orleans. Comn: Mural, US Air Base, Altus, Okla, 43. Exhib: Metrop Young Artist Show, Nat Arts Club, 59; Selection of Contemporary American Art, Kansas City Art Inst, 60; Retrospective Exhib Painting & Drawings, Ark Art Ctr, 61; Exhib Recent Paintings, Columbia Univ, 69; After Twenty Years, Birmingham Mus Art, 71; Tenth St Days, Pleiades Gallery, New York, 77; Now Show, Landmark Gallery, New York, 77. Teaching: Prof fine arts & chmn dept, Wagner Col, 53-69; head prof art, Auburn Univ, 69-70; prof fine arts, Univ New Orleans, 70-, chmn dept, 70-78. Pos: Illusr exp aircraft, Douglas Aircraft Corp, Los Angeles, 52-53; art dir, Good Health Mag, New York, 53-57; cover designer, Electronic Design Mag, New York, 55-56; design & color consult, Royal Metal Mfg Co, 56-57; color consult, New Orleans Dock Bd, 71-72. Awards: Most Distinguished Painting, Nat Watercolor Exhib, Birmingham Mus Art, 54; Weissglass Award, State Island Mus, 55; Hon Mention, New York City Ctr Gallery, 56. Mem: New Orleans Mus Art (bd trustees, 73-); Col Art Asn Am. Style & Technique: Abstraction. Media: Oil, Watercolor. Mailing Add: Dept of Fine Arts Univ of New Orleans New Orleans LA 70122

YOUNGERMAN, JACK
PAINTER
b Louisville, Ky, 1926. Study: Univ NC, Chapel Hill; Univ Mo-Columbia; Ecole des Beaux Arts, Paris, France. Work: Albright-Knox Art Gallery, Buffalo; Art Inst Chicago; Corcoran Gallery Art, Washington, DC; Whitney Mus Am Art, New York; Nat Collection Fine Arts; Phillips Collection, Washington, DC; plus many others. Exhib: Corcoran Biennial Traveling Exhib, 67; American Prints Today, Mus Art, Munson-Williams-Proctor Inst, Utica, NY, 68; Whitney Ann, 69; L'Art Vivant aux Etats-Unis, Fondation Maeght, Paris, 70; Carnegie Inst Int, 71; one-man shows, Portland Ctr for Visual Arts, Ore, 72, Seattle Art Mus, Wash, 72 & Arts Club of Chicago Chicago, 73; plus many others. Pos: Designer state sets & costumes, Histoire de Vasco, Paris, 56 & Death Watch, New York, 58. Awards: Nat Coun Arts & Sci Award, 66. Bibliog: Portrait—Jack Youngerman, Art in Am, 9-10/68; Drawings by Jack Youngerman, Harpers, 10/68; Barbara Rose (auth), Getting it physical, Vogue, 2/71; plus many others. Dealer: Pace Gallery 32 E 57th St New York NY 10022. Mailing Add: 130 W Third New York NY 10012

YOUNGLOVE, RUTH ANN (MRS BENJAMIN RHEES LOXLEY)
PAINTER
b Chicago, Ill, Feb 14, 09. Study: Univ Calif, Los Angeles, BE; also with Orrin A White & Marion K Wachtel. Work: Bank of Am, Pasadena, Calif; El Tovar Hotel, Grand Canyon, Ariz. Exhib: Nat Watercolor Soc, Los Angeles, 67; Laguna Beach Art Asn Gallery, 71; one-woman shows, Flintridge Prep Sch, La Can, 72, Community Serv Ctr, Pasadena, 72-75, Altadena Pub Libr, Calif, 75 & Pasadena Soc of Artists Sales Gallery, 76-77. Teaching: Docent, Pacificulture Mus, Pasadena, currently. Awards: Second Prize for Landscape, Artists League Seal Beach, 68; Fourth Prize in Painting, Pasadena Presby Church Exhib. Mem: Pasadena Soc Artists (patron chmn, 58-68); life mem Laguna Beach Art Asn; Nat Watercolor Soc; assoc Am Watercolor Soc. Style & Technique: Simplified designing with landscape forms people can recognize, with emphasis on composition; landscape painting, linoleum block printing, weaving. Media: Watercolor, Linoleum Block Print. Mailing Add: 1180 Yocum St Pasadena CA 91103

YOUNGQUIST, JACK
DRAFTSMAN
b Crookston, Minn, Sept 19, 18. Study: Univ Minn, BA; Minn Sch Art; Univ Iowa, MFA; Art Students League; Slade Sch, Univ London; Inst Allende, San Miguel Allende, Mex; NY Univ. Work: Minn Inst Art, Minneapolis; Minn Mus Art, St Paul; NDak State Univ, Fargo; Moorhead State Col, Minn; Univ Iowa, Iowa City. Exhib: Drawing USA, St Paul, 71; Manisphere Int, Winnipeg, 71; Red River Ann, Moorhead, 72 & 77; Ball State Drawing Exhib, Muncie, Ind; Minneapolis Art Inst Biennial. Teaching: Instr calligraphy, Minn Sch Art, 54-59; instr, Univ Minn Exten, 57-58; prof drawing, Moorhead State Univ, 61- Pos: Bd dirs, Red River Art Ctr, Moorhead, 66-68. Awards: Purchase Award, Drawings USA, St Paul, 71; Merit Award, Minn State Art Exhib, 74; Bronze Medal, 16th Midwest Artists, Moorhead, Minn, 75. Mem: Col Art Asn Am. Style & Technique: Representational figure drawings with contemporary amibiguities. Dealer: Rourke Art Gallery 523 S Fourth St Moorhead MN 56560; Kilbride Art Gallery 3208 Hennepin Ave Minneapolis MN. Mailing Add: Art Dept Moorhead State Univ Moorhead MN 56560

YOUNGSBLOOD, NAT
PAINTER, ILLUSTRATOR
b Evansville, Ind, Dec 28, 16. Study: Univ NMex, Albuquerque, with Millard Sheets; Am Acad Art, Chicago; also with Barse Miller, Raymond Joahnson, Ralph Douglass & Howard Mosby. Work: Nat Marine Mus; Buhl Planetarium & Inst Popular Sci, Pittsburgh; Indiana Univ Pa; Calif State Col, Pa. Comn: Oil portraits (indust leaders), for Pittsburgh Press, Pa, 56; mural, US Steel Corp, Pittsburgh; portrait President Kennedy, Metro News Serv, 61; Five hist paintings, Ft Pitt Mus, Pittsburgh; oil paintings (pioneer life), Pittsburgh Pa Bicentennial, 75. Exhib: Carnegie Inst Art for Indust, 54; Bantam Books Nat Competition, 57; Pittsburgh Art Dirs Soc, 59; Golden Quill Competition, 61; Pennational Exhib, 65. Teaching: Instr painting & design, LaRoche Col & Art Inst Pittsburgh, 74. Pos: Art dir, Carter, Johne & Taylor Advert, 39-42; cartoonist, illusr & painter, Pittsburgh Press, 46- Awards: First Place, Carnegie Inst Art for Indust, 54; First Place, Golden Quill Competition, 63; First Place, Pennational Exhib, 66. Bibliog: Margaret Harold (auth), Prize winning art, Allied Publ, Ind, 67; Norman Kent(auth), 100 Watercolor Techniques, Watson-Guptill, 68; Art Inst Pittsburgh, Careers in Art (film), 75. Mem: Pittsburgh Watercolor Soc; Pittsburgh Art Dirs Soc. Style & Technique: Impressionist. Media: Watercolor, Oil. Res: American Plains Indian; American colonial history and pioneer life in Pennsylvania. Interest: Impressionist landscapes, watercolor and oil; historical scenes of pioneer life in Pennsylvania. Publ: Ed, 101st Airborne Division Picture History, 45; auth, Watercolor page, Am Artist Mag, 59. Dealer: Margaret M Youngblood 6300 Katson NE Albuquerque NM 87109. Mailing Add: Gateway Towers 25G Pittsburgh PA 15222

YOURITZIN, GLENDA GREEN
PAINTER, ART HISTORIAN
b Weatherford, Tex, Feb 4, 45. Study: Tex Christian Univ, BFA(magna cum laude), 67; Kress Fel, 67-70; Tulane Univ, MA(art hist), 70. Work: Mus of the City of New York; Nat Mus Hist & Technol, Smithsonian Inst, Washington, DC; Williams Col Mus of Art, Williamstown, Mass; State of Okla Art Collection, Okla Art Ctr, Oklahoma City; Univ Okla, Norman. Comn: Portrait of Hon Allen J Ellender, Ellender Mem, Houma, La, 72; portrait of A Hyatt Mayor, comn by sitter, Mus of City of New York, 74; portrait of S Lane Faison, Jr, comn by sitter & Williams Col, Williams Col Mus, 76. Exhib: One-person shows, Art Gallery, NTex State Univ, Denton, 74, Mus of the SW, Midland, Tex, 75, Mus of Art, Univ Okla, Norman, 75, Okla Mus of Art, Oklahoma City, 76 & Philbrook Art Ctr, Tulsa, Okla, 78; 1975 Bicentennial Nat Art Exhib, Art Gallery, Univ Tex, Arlington, 75; 18th Ann Eight State Exhib of Painting & Sculpture, Okla Art Ctr, Oklahoma City, 76; SW Tarrant Co Ann, Ft Worth Mus of Art, Tex, 76; 1976 SW Fine Arts Biennial, Mus of Fine Arts, Santa Fe, NMex, 76; 19th Ann Eight State Exhib of Painting & Sculpture, Okla Art Ctr, 77. Teaching: Instr art hist, Tulane Univ, New Orleans, La, 69-72; guest artist painting, Univ Okla, Norman, 72-75, vis instr art hist, 73-76. Pos: Cur collections, Newcomb Col Sch of Art, New Orleans, 69-72; res asst, Kimbell Art Mus, Ft Worth, Tex, 68-69; artist-in-residence, Okla Arts & Humanities Coun, 77-78. Bibliog: V Kimbell (auth), A new search for humanism in art: an interview with Glenda Youritzin, 1/74 & Jim Ramses (auth), A feminine humanist: Glenda Youritzin, 9/76, SW Art; Boo Browning (auth), More than meets the eye (the art of Glenda Youritzin), Okla Mo, 1/78. Mem: Col Art Asn. Style & Technique: Realist, figurative. Media: Oil. Mailing Add: 1721 Oakwood Dr Norman OK 73069

YOURITZIN, VICTOR KOSHKIN
ART HISTORIAN, EDUCATOR
b New York, NY, Dec 20, 42. Study: Williams Col, BA(cum laude), 64; Sch of Archit, Columbia Univ, 64-65; Inst Fine Arts, NY Univ, MA, 67; Cert Mus Training, Inst of Fine Arts & Metrop Mus Art, New York, 69. Collections Arranged: The Poetry of the Body: Paintings by Paul Peck (ed, catalogue), Vanderbilt Univ, 69, (ed, catalogue), Tulane Univ, 70 & Dallas Health & Sci Mus, 74-78. Teaching: Instr art hist, Vanderbilt Univ, Nashville, Tenn, 68-69 & Newcomb Col, Tulane Univ, New Orleans, 69-72; asst prof art hist, Univ Okla, Norman, 72- Pos: Mem accessions comt, Okla Mus of Art, Oklahoma City, 76-, bd trustees, 78- Awards: Ford Found Fel, Dept of Am Painting & Sculpture, Metrop Mus of Art, New York, 67-68. Mem: Col Art Asn; Midwest Art Hist Soc. Res: Nineteenth and twentieth century art; museology. Publ: Auth, Tchelitchew's Hide & Seek, winter 64-65 & A museum course at Newcomb College, spring 71, Art J; auth, The irony of Degas, Gazette des Beaux-Arts, 1/76; auth, The architect as statesman, Archit Minn, 1/78. Mailing Add: 1721 Oakwood Dr Norman OK 73069

YRISARRY, MARIO
PAINTER
b Manila, Philippines, Mar 29, 33; US citizen. Study: Queens Col, NY, BA; Cooper Union. Work: Whitney Mus Am Art, New York; Baltimore Mus Art; Indianapolis Mus Art; Rose Art Mus, Brandeis Univ, Mass; Mus of Art, Carnegie Inst, Pittsburgh, Pa. Comn: Poster, Albert A List Found, Lincoln Ctr, New York, 72; Tamarind Inst, NMex, Ford Found grant, 73. Exhib: American Painting & Sculpture, Indianapolis Mus Art, 70; Structure of Color, 71 & Recent Acquisitions, 73, Whitney Mus Am Art, New York, 71; Grids, Int Contemp Art, Univ Pa, 72; The International Style in America, Lowe Art Mus, Univ Miami, Coral Gables, Fla, 74; Pattern Painting, Project Studio One, Long Island City, NY, 77. Bibliog: Donald Judd (auth), rev in Arts Mag, 10/64; Carter Ratcliff (auth), rev in News, 12/69; Robert Pincus-Witten (auth), New York, Artforum, 2/70; John Perreault (auth), Issues in pattern painting, Artforum, 11/77; Harcourt Brace Javonovich Films (auth), Contemporary Artists at Work: Volume II, San Francisco, Calif, 78. Style & Technique: Abstract, color investigations of processes and patterns; brushed and sprayed acrylic on sized canvas. Publ: Auth, The new work, first person singular-2, Art Gallery, Conn, 5/71; Patterns, Tracks, NY, Vol 1, No 1, 74. Mailing Add: 297 Third Ave New York NY 10010

YRIZARRY, MARCOS
PAINTER, GRAPHIC ARTIST
b Mayaguez, PR, Oct 7, 36. Study: Acad Cent San Fernandeo, Madrid, Spain. Work: Mus Mod Art, New York; Bibliot Nat, Paris, France; Ponce Mus, PR; Univ PR, Rio Piedras. Exhib: Int Graphic Biennial, Yugoslavia, 67 & Poland, 68; Galeria Colibri, San Juan, PR; Casa de las Americas, Havana, Cuba. Awards: Medalla de Oro del XV Salon, Madrid, Spain; Premio Javier Baez, Casa de las Americas. Mailing Add: Box 1734 San Juan PR 00903

YUDIN, CAROL
PRINTMAKER, PAINTER
b Brooklyn, NY. Study: Pratt Graphic Ctr, with Sid Hammer, Michael Ponce de Leon, Roberto di Lamonica, Andrew Stasik & painting with Michael Lenson. Work: NJ State Mus, Trenton; Jersey City Mus, NJ; St Peter's Col, Jersey City; Miniature Art Soc NJ, Paramus; Belleville Pub Libr, NJ. Comn: Tree of Life, Congregation Ahavath Achim, Belleville, 65. Exhib: Art from NJ, NJ State Mus, 69; 4th Int Miniature Print Exhib, 71; 7th Triennial NJ Artists, Newark Mus, NJ, 71; 31st Ann Painters & Sculptors Soc NJ, 71; Nat Asn Women Artists, Jersey City & New York, 71; Audubon Artists, Nat Acad, New York. Teaching: Instr oil painting, Nutley Adult Sch, 66-76; instr oil painting, Temple Emanuel, Paterson, NJ, 66-69. Awards: Purchase Awards, NJ State Mus, 69, Painters & Sculptors Soc NJ, 69 & Nat Miniature Art Soc Exhib, 70; Edna P Stauffer Mem Award, Audubon Artists, New York, 77. Mem: Nat Asn Women Artists (graphic juror, 72-75 & 77-78); Painters & Sculptors Soc NJ (secy, 62-70, pres, 71-73); Hunterdon Art Ctr; Printmaking Coun NJ (art dir, 77-); Audubon Artists, New York (corresp secy, 76-77). Style & Technique: Abstract and fanciful interpretation of the range and variety of things found in nature; photo-negative etchings. Dealer: Pratt Graphic Ctr Gallery 160 Lexington Ave New York NY 10016. Mailing Add: 490 Joralemon St Belleville NJ 07109

YUNKERS, ADJA
PAINTER, EDUCATOR
b Riga, Latvia, July 15, 00; US citizen. Study: Leningrad, Paris, Berlin & Rome. Work: Represented in over 82 insts including Mus Mod Art, Guggenheim Mus, Whitney Mus Am Art & Metrop Mus Art, New York & Albright-Knox Art Gallery, Buffalo, NY. Comn: A

Human Condition (mural), Syracuse Univ, 66; tapestry for student union, State Univ NY Stony Brook, 67. Exhib: Numerous group shows including, Abstract Expressionists & Imagists, Guggenheim Mus, New York, 61, The New American Painting & Sculpture: The First Generation, Mus Mod Art, New York, 69, Etats Unis, Fondation Maeght, St Paul de Venice, France & Mus Arte Mod, Mexico City, 75; plus many others including over 40 one-man shows. Teaching: Instr art, New Sch Social Res, 47-56; instr art, Cooper Union, 56-67; instr art, Barnard Col, 69-; instr summer sessions at several Western univs. Pos: Ed, Creation, Ars & Ars-Portfolio, Stockholm, 42-45; vis critic, Columbia Univ, 67-69. Awards: Guggenheim Fel, 49-50 & 54-55; Ford Found Grant, 60; plus numerous other awards. Media: Graphics, Pastel, Oil. Publ: Ed, Prints in the Desert, 50; illusr, Octavio Paz (auth), bk on poetry & Richard Wilbur (auth), To Ona (poem). Mailing Add: 217 E 11th St New York NY 10003

YURISTY, RUSSELL MICHAEL
DESIGNER, SCULPTOR
b Goodeve, Sask, Mar 23, 36. Study: Univ Sask, Saskatoon, BA; Univ Wis-Madison, MS. Work: Norman Mackenzie Art Gallery, Regina, Sask; Sask Arts Bd; Regina Pub Libr, Sask; Can Coun Collection; Can Arts Bank. Comn: Wooden elephant, Village of Silton, Sask, 71; wooden animals playground, Expo Can, Can Island, Spokane, Wash, 74; wooden polar bear, Dept Pub Works, Ottawa, Churchill, Man, 75. Exhib: Sensible Int Cup Show, Osaka, Japan, 73; Canada Trajectories 73, Mus Mod Art, Paris, 73; Canadian Craft, 74, York Univ & Guild Show, Toronto, 74; Ceramica Americana, Coe Col, 74; Cicansky, Fafard, James, Yuristy, L'Atitude 53 Gallery, Edmonton, 74. Teaching: Instr drawing & graphics, Univ Sask, Regina, 67-71. Pos: Dir, Creative Playgrounds, Silton, Sask, 70-71; pres, Yuristy Enterprise Ltd, Silton, Sask, 74- Awards: Scholar Award, Sask Arts Bd, 66; Can Coun Bursary, Ottawa, 72-73 & 73-74. Style & Technique: Huge wooden animal sculptures incorporating playhouses inside with slide coming out; also small ceramic sculptures and drawings. Publ: Contribr, Russ Yuristy, his notes, stoneboats, elephants & friends, Arts Can, fall 72. Dealer: Galerie Royale 2107 Fourth St SW Calgary AB Can. Mailing Add: PO Box 65 Silton SK Can

YUST, DAVID E
PAINTER, EDUCATOR
b Wichita, Kans, Apr 3, 39. Study: Birger Sandzen; Wichita State Univ; Kans State Univ; Univ Kans, BFA, 63; Univ Ore, MFA, 69. Work: Denver Art Mus; Mulvane Art Ctr, Topeka, Kans; Okla Art Ctr, Oklahoma City; Univ Ore, Eugene; Wichita Art Mus, Kans. Comn: Pizza Hut Corp Off, Wichita, Kans. Exhib: 73rd Western Ann, Denver Art Mus, 71; Colo/Nebr Exchange Exhib, Friends of Contemporary Art, Denver/Joslyn Art Mus, Omaha, Nebr, 73; 15th Ann 8-State Exhib Painting & Sculpture, Okla Art Ctr, 73; one-man shows, Wichita Art Mus, 73, Habatat Galleries, Dearborn, Mich, 74, Sol Del Rio Gallery, San Antonio, Tex, 75, Denver Art Mus, 76, Rourke Gallery, Moorhead, Minn, 77 & Joseph Magnin Gallery, Denver, 77; 20 Colo Artists, Denver Art Mus, 77. Teaching: Assoc prof painting & drawing, Colo State Univ, 65- Awards: US State Dept Award, Am Embassy Arts Prog, 66-68; Purchase Awards, 11th Biennial, Kans State Univ, 70, Colo State Univ, 70 & Okla Art Ctr, 73. Style & Technique: Exploration of symmetry and how it can function in painting; two and three-dimensional works on canvas stretched over laminated wood and plywood structures. Media: Lithography, Acrylic, Silkscreen. Dealer: ADI Gallery 530 McAllister St San Francisco CA 94102; Sol Del Rio 1020 Townsend Ave San Antonio TX 78209. Mailing Add: 1301 Patton Ft Collins CO 80521

YVON, JOSEPH
See Fafard, Joe

Z

ZABARSKY, MELVIN JOEL
PAINTER, EDUCATOR
b Worcester, Mass, Aug 21, 32. Study: Sch Worcester Art Mus; Ruskin Sch Drawing & Fine Arts, Univ Oxford; Sch Fine & Appl Arts, Boston Univ, BFA; Univ Cincinnati, MFA. Work: Mus Mod Art, New York; De Cordova Mus, Lincoln, Mass; Addison Gallery Am Art, Andover, Mass; Wiggins Collection, Boston Pub Libr; Currier Gallery Art, Manchester, NH. Exhib: One-man exhibs, Boris Mirski Gallery, Boston, 62, Tragos Gallery, Boston, 66 & De Cordova Mus, 70; Surreal Images, De Cordova Mus, 68; New Eng Painters Traveling Exhib, Ringling Mus, Sarasota, Fla, 69. Teaching: Instr painting, Swain Sch Design, New Bedford, Mass, 60-64; asst prof painting, Wheaton Col, 64-69; prof painting, Univ NH, 69- Awards: Painting Prize, Boston Arts Festival, 62; Ford Found Grant in humanities, 68. Bibliog: B Schwartz (auth), Humanism in 20th Century Art, Praeger, 73. Style & Technique: Symbolic narrative realist in style, rich, volumetric and tonal in painting technique. Media: Oil. Mailing Add: Dept of Art Univ NH Durham NH 03824

ZABOROWSKI, DENNIS J
PAINTER, EDUCATOR
b Cleveland, Ohio, Jan 31, 43. Study: Cleveland Inst of Art, cert, 61-65; Yale Univ, BFA, 65 & MFA, 68 with Jack Tworkov & Bernard Chaet. Work: Mint Mus of Art, Charlotte, NC; NC Nat Bank, NC Collection; Rauch Indust Inc, Gastonia, NC; Ackland Art Mus, Chapel Hill, NC. Comn: Youth Ctr mural, New Haven Redevlop Agency, 68. Exhib: Ann Cleveland May Show, Cleveland Mus of Art, 65; Arts Festival of Atlanta, Ga, 69; 4th Ann James River Art Exhib, Mariners Mus, Newport News, Va, 70; 3rd Am Exhib, Washington & Lee Univ Mus, Lexington, Va, 71; Realism in NC, Mint Mus of Art, Charlotte, 74; 18th Ann Spring Art show, Lancaster, SC, 76; 39th Ann NC Artists Exhib, NC Mus of Art, Raleigh, 76. Collections Arranged: Fac Choice Exhib, Va Polytech Inst, Blackburg, Va, 71; New Talent Show, Allan Stone Gallery, New York, 75; 200 Yrs of the Visual Arts in NC, NC Mus of Art, Raleigh, 76; one-person show, Gallery of Contemp Art, Winston-Salem, NC, 72. Teaching: Assoc prof painting, drawing & design, Univ of NC, Chapel Hill, 68-; asst prof design, Duke Univ, Durham, NC, 72. Pos: Mem adv bd, Ackland Mus of Art, Chapel Hill, NC, 71- & Art Sch, Carrboro, NC, 76- Awards: Purchase Awards, NC Artists Exhib, Rauch Indust, 73 & Realism in NC, Mint Mus of Art, Charlotte, 74; Best Oil Painting, Spring Mills Exhib, Spring Mills Corp, 75. Mem: Nat Asn of Schs of Art. Style & Technique: Large scale realist oil painting with meticulously rendered surfaces. Media: Oil on Canvas. Mailing Add: 1001 Dawes St Chapel Hill NC 27514

ZABRISKIE, VIRGINIA M
ART DEALER
b New York, NY. Study: Washington Sq Col, NY Univ, BA; NY Univ Inst Fine Arts, MA. Pos: Dir, Zabriskie Gallery, 54- Mem: Art Dealers Asn (bd dirs). Specialty: 20th century American art. Mailing Add: 29 W 57th St New York NY 10019

ZACH, JAN
PAINTER, SCULPTOR
b Slany, Czech, July 27, 14; US citizen. Study: Superior Sch Indust Arts, Prague; Acad Fine Arts, Prague; also with Angelo Zeyer. Comn: Czech Pavilion, New York World's Fair, 38-39; monument to Dr M Amaro, founder of Colegio de Calaguazes (archit Oscar Niemeyer), Cataguazes, MG, Brazil, 50-51; Prometheus, Univ Ore, Eugene, 59; sculptures & relief, New Eugene City Hall, Ore, 64; Can-Can (kinetic sculpture), Meier & Frank, Valley River Ctr, Eugene, 68. Exhib: Retrospective, Mus Belas Artes, Rio de Janeiro, Brazil, 45, Victoria Art Gallery, BC, Can, 52 & Mus Art, Univ Ore, Eugene, 59; one-man show, Portland Art Mus, Ore, 68; 73rd Western Ann, Denver, 71. Teaching: Teacher painting, Banff Sch Fine Arts, Univ Alta, 51-52; pvt instr painting & sculpture, own art sch, Victoria, BC, 51-57; prof sculpture, Sch Archit, Univ Ore, Eugene, 58- Awards: Hon Mention, Northwest Ann, Seattle Art Mus, Wash, 56; Award, Off Sci & Scholar Res, Univ Ore, 66; Cash Award Res, Chapelbrook Found, Boston, 68. Bibliog: Marques Rebelo (auth), Works by Jan Zach, Ed Vecchi, Rio de Janeiro, 49; Don Horter (auth), Work of Jan Zach (film), New York & Eugene, 68; Frank J Malina (auth), Kinetic Art: Theory & Practice, Dover Publ, 74. Mem: Nat Sculpture Ctr, Univ Kans (bd mem); Artists Equity Asn; Czech Soc Arts & Sci in Am Inc. Style & Technique: Interested in light, motion and organic nature of Pacific Northwest; in wood stone, steel, welding, neon and casting in aluminum, bronze and cement. Publ: Auth, The Contribution of the Czechoslovak Sculpture to the World of Art (abstr), 62; auth, The influence of experiment, accident & design on sculpture casting, 4th Nat Sculpture Conf, 66; auth, Imagery, light & motion in my sculpture, Leonardo, Gt Brit, 70. Mailing Add: 25113 Lamb Rd Elmira OR 97437

ZACHA, GEORGE WILLIAM
PAINTER, SCULPTOR
b Garland, Tex, Jan 19, 20. Study: Univ Calif, 40-41 & 47-48; George Washington Univ, BA, 51; Corcoran, Washington, DC, study with Heinz Warneke; Studio Hinna, Rome, Italy, 51-52; study with Ruth Cravath, 70-75. Exhib: First Show of Am Painters in Europe, Bordighera, Italy, 52; Int Cult Ctr, Guatemala, 68; Sutro Libr, San Francisco, Calif, 75; Serigraphs, Calif State Libr, Sacramento, 76; Sculpture, Palazzo Durini, Milano, Italy, 77; Watercolor/Sculpture, Bay Window Gallery, Mendicino, Calif, 77; Art Ctr, Eureka, Calif, 78. Pos: Founder, dir, Mendocino Art Ctr, 59- Bibliog: Chandler Brossard (auth), A Young Man Saves An Old Town, Look Mag, 8/62 & Where Artists Live, Horizions No 15, US Info Serv. Style & Technique: Classically inspired bronzes, representational prints and transparent watercolor to capture mood rather than emotion. Collection: Primarily small sculptures, bronze, stone, wood with international approach. Dealer: Bay Window Gallery 560 Main St Mendicino CA 95460. Mailing Add: PO Box 484 Main Mendocino CA 95460

ZACHARIAS, ATHOS
PAINTER
b Marlborough, Mass, June 17, 27. Study: Art Students League, summer 52; RI Sch Design, BFA, 52; Cranbrook Acad Art, MFA, 53. Work: Mus Art, Providence, RI; Inst Contemp Art, Boston; Kalamazoo Inst Art, Mich; Phoenix Art Mus, Ariz; Westinghouse Corp, Pittsburgh. Comn: Decor for Manhattan Festival Dancers, comn by Robert Ossorio, New York, 63. Exhib: NC Mus Art, Raleigh, 59; Pan-Pacific Show, Kyoto, Japan, 61; one-man shows, Gallery Mayer, 61, Louis Alexander Gallery, 63, Landmark Gallery, 73 & James Yu Gallery, 77, New York. Teaching: Instr painting, Brown Univ, 53-55; instr painting, Parsons Sch Design, 63-65; asst prof painting, Wagner Col, 69- Awards: Best in Show Award, Guild Hall, 61; Longview Found Grant, 62; Festival Arts Purchase Award, Southampton Col, 68. Style & Technique: Geometric fantasy rendered with spray gun and printing technique. Media: Acrylic. Publ: Illusr, cover in Sci & Technol, 63. Mailing Add: 463 West St Apt B-946 New York NY 10014

ZACK, DAVID
DESIGNER, WRITER
b New Orleans, La, June 12, 38. Study: Univ Chicago, MA, 59; Jesus Col, Cambridge Univ, 61-62; also with Roy De Forest, Bob Arneson, Raymond Williams & Alexander Kok. Work: Can Art Writers Arch, Regina, Sask; Nut Art Arch, Aurora, Ont. Comn: Rainbow House (with Maija Gegeris), Woof Univ, San Francisco, 67-69; Dodge Place (with Ruth Walsh), Can Art Writers, Silton, Sask, 72-74; Ordure Mural (with Ann Wilson, Robert Buechler & Ray Johnson), Byrd Hoffman Ctr, New York, 74; Greer Court (with Vi Snell), Local Housing Authority, Regina, 75; Pluto Ctr (with Jane Ashdown), Regina, 75. Exhib: Nut Art Show, Univ Calif, Berkeley Exten Gallery, 68, Calif State Col, Hayward, 71 & MacKenzie & Mendel Galleries, Sask, 71; one-man show, Ecart Gallery, Geneva, Switz, 74 & Coe Col, 75. Teaching: Lectr humanities, San Francisco Art Inst, 65-68; lectr art hist, Univ Sask, 70-72. Pos: Critic, KQED-TV, San Francisco, 65-67; pres, Woof Univ, 65-70; dir, Can Art Writers, 70-74; dir, Art Cause Commun Co, 74- Awards: Travel Award, Univ PR, 61; Video Doc, Sask Dept Cult-Youth, 72; Art in Am, Nat Endowment Arts, 73. Bibliog: Ron Gabe (auth), Dream city, File, 72; Beke Laszlo (auth), Nut art, Budapest Hungary Art Paper, 73; Jon Armleder (auth), De l'arte marginale Ecart, Elements, 74. Mem: Int Artists Cooperation (corresp); Participation Proj Found (corresp). Style & Technique: Free personal fantasy, precise line detail, humorous tendency. Media: Designer of Displays & Publ; Collages. Publ: Auth, California myth making, Art & Artists, 69; auth, Nut art in quake time, Art News, 70; article in Basic Art, 71; auth, Art McKay's roots with Regina five, Artscanada, 72; Mail on mail art, Art in Am, 73. Mailing Add: PO Box 794 Regina SK S4P 3A8 Can

ZAFRAN, ERIC MYLES
CURATOR, ART HISTORIAN
b Malden, Mass, Apr 19, 46. Study: Tilton Sch, NH, 63; Brandeis Univ, BA, 67; Inst Fine Arts, NY Univ, MA, 70, PhD, 73. Collections Arranged: The Mask and the Eye (graphics by Redon & Ensor), Rose Art Mus, spring 67; Master Paintings from the Hermitage (co-auth & ed, catalogue), Nat Gallery, 75; Homage to the Louvre, French Paintings in the Chrysler Collection, Chrysler Mus at Norfolk, 76; Treasures from the Chrysler Museum (co-auth, catalogue), Tenn Fine Arts Ctr, Cheekwood, Nashville, 77. Teaching: Assoc prof Rembrandt, City Col New York, 75-76; assoc adj northern paintings, Old Dominion Univ, 77- Pos: Curatorial asst, Rose Art Mus, Waltham, Mass, 65-67; print cataloguer, Parke-Bernet Galleries, New York, 68-71; res asst, Metrop Mus of Art, New York, 72-75; chief cur, Chrysler Mus at Norfolk, 76- Mem: Col Art Asn. Publ: Auth, The Virgin of Cambron: an alledged case of image desecration, J Jewish Art, 77; auth, Jan Victors and the Bible, Bull of Israel Mus, 77. Mailing Add: 800 Graydon Ave Norfolk VA 23507

ZAHN, CARL FREDERICK
DESIGNER, ART ADMINISTRATOR
b Louisville, Ky, Mar 9, 28. Study: Harvard Univ, AB, 48. Exhib: Fifty Books Exhibition, Am Inst Graphic Arts, 60-76; one-man show, Dreitzer Gallery, Brandeis Univ, 69. Pos: Graphics

designer, Mus Fine Arts, Boston, 56-, ed-in-chief, 71- Mem: Am Inst Graphic Arts (bd dirs, 68-71); Soc Printers. Mailing Add: 479 Huntington Ave Boston MA 02115

ZAIDENBERG, ARTHUR
SCULPTOR, WRITER
b New York, NY. Study: Art Students League; Nat Acad Design, New York; Beaux Arts, Paris; also in Rome & Munich. Work: Metrop Mus; Brooklyn Mus; New York Pub Libr; Albany Mus. Comn: SS Rotterdam (mural), Holland Am Line, 70; also many murals in hotels & pub bldgs in US. Exhib: One-man shows, Albany Mus, 65 & Bellas Artes, Mex, 72. Teaching: Instr drawing, NY Univ, 43-44; instr drawing, Inst San Miguel, Mex, 72-73. Awards: Sally Jacobs Award, Woodstock Artists Asn, 69. Mem: Woodstock Artists Asn. Media: Welded Steel, Oil. Publ: Auth, Studies in Figure Drawing, Doubleday, 60; auth, Out of Line, 61 & auth, Anyone Can Paint, 65, Crown; auth, Prints, 64 & auth, Anyone Can Sculpt, 74, Harper. Dealer: Galerie San Miguel San Miguel Allende Guanajuato Mexico. Mailing Add: Apdo 318 Calle de Las Moras Guanajuato San Miguel Allende Mexico

ZAJAC, JACK
SCULPTOR, PAINTER
b Youngstown, Ohio, Dec 13, 29. Study: Scripps Col, 49-53; also with Millard Sheets, Henry McFee & Sueo Serisawa; Am Acad in Rome. Work: Mus Mod Art, New York; Los Angeles Mus Art; Pa Acad Fine Arts, Philadelphia; Milwaukee Art Inst; Matthews Collection, Ariz State Univ, Tempe; plus others. Comn: Reynolds Metals Co, 68. Exhib: Drawings by Sculptors, Smithsonian Inst, circulated in the US, 61-63; American Painting, Va Mus Fine Arts, Richmond, 62; Fifty California Artists, Whitney Mus Mod Art, New York, 62-63; retrospectives, Newport Harbor Art Mus, Balboa, Calif, 65, Temple Univ, Rome, 69, Santa Barbara Mus, 75 & Fine Arts Gallery San Diego, 75; plus many others. Teaching: Instr, Pomona Col, 59. Awards: Prix de Rome, 54, 56 & 57; Am Acad Arts & Lett Grant, 58; Guggenheim Fel, 59. Bibliog: Henry J Seldis & Ulfert Wilke (auth), The Sculpture of Jack Zajac, Gallard Press, 60; Allen S Weller (auth), The Joys and Sorrows of Recent American Art, Univ Ill, 68. Dealer: Fairweather Hardin Gallery 101 E Ontario Ave Chicago IL 60611. Mailing Add: c/o Forum Gallery 1018 Madison Ave New York NY 10021

ZAKANYCH, ROBERT
PAINTER
b Elizabeth, NJ, May 24, 35. Work: Whitney Mus Am Art, New York; Munich Mus Mod Art, WGer; Philadelphia Mus, Pa; Wadsworth Atheneum, Hartford, Conn; Phoenix Mus, Ariz. Exhib: Int Drawing Show, Iarmstadt, Ger, 71; Structure of Color, 71 & Recent Acquisitions, 71, Whitney Mus Am Art; one-man shows, Reese Palley, New York, 70 & 71, Cuningham Ward, New York, 73 & 74; Contemp Arts Soc, Chicago Art Inst, 72. Bibliog: David Shirey (auth), Lyrical abstraction show at Whitney, New York Times, 5/29/71; Marcia Tucker (auth), The structure of color, Whitney Mus Am Art, 71; Robert Hughes (auth), Three bold newcomers, Time, 3/13/72. Mailing Add: 18 Warren St New York NY 10007

ZAKIN, MIKHAIL
SCULPTOR, EDUCATOR
b US citizen. Study: Sch of Mus Fine Arts, Boston, Mass; Art Students League, sculpture with William Zorach & Albino Manca; also ceramics, with Karen Karnes & David Weirib. Work: Mus Arts & Sci, Salt Lake City, Utah. Exhib: Morris Mus Arts & Sci, Morristown, NJ, 71-72; US Salt Potters, Mus Contemp Crafts, New York, 74; Brooklyn Mus, NY, 74-76; Am Potters, Mus Arts & Sci, Salt Lake City, 75; Four US Potters, Fair Tree Gallery, 75; Pratt Grad Sch, New York, 75-77; Brooklyn Col, 75-77; Baruch Col, New York, 75-77. Collections Arranged: Rochester Shop & Gallery, NY, 70; Hunterdon Art Ctr, Clinton, NJ, 72; Nat Conf Ceramic Educators, 75; Sarah Lawrence Col, 76; Women's Interart Ctr, 76. Teaching: Advan ceramics instr, Greenwich House Pottery, 71-75; head ceramics dept, Brooklyn Mus Art Sch, 72-75; head ceramics dept, Sarah Lawrence Col, 76- Pos: Founder & dir, Old Church Cult Ctr & Sch of Art, Demarest, NJ, 74-; staff reviewer by-line column, Craft Horizons, 74-; traveling sem leader, Potters Sem in Eng, 76, Craft in Relation to Cult, Japan, 77 & Mexico—The Folk Potter, 78; co-founder, Scotland-North Coast Continuum, 78- Awards: Lebensburger Found Grant, 74; Craftsmen's Fel, NJ Coun on Arts, 75 & Nat Endowment for the Arts, 76. Mem: Am Crafts Coun; World Crafts Coun; Nat Conf Ceramic Educators; TenaKill Potters Guild (founder & vpres, 74); NY Artist Craftsman. Style & Technique: Sculpture with salt-glaze. Media: Clay. Mailing Add: 37 County Rd Closter NJ 07624

ZALESKI, JEAN M
PAINTER, ART ADMINISTRATOR
b Malta, Europe; US citizen. Study: Art Students League; New Sch for Social Res, New York; Pratt Inst, New York; Parsons Sch of Design, New York; Moore Col of Art, Philadelphia; also with Harry Sternberg, Ernest Fiene and Sumi-e painting with Motoi Oi. Work: Hofstra Univ, Garden City, NY; Brooklyn Polytechnic Inst. Comn: Paintings, Inst of Life Insurance, New York, Easter Seal Human Resources Ctr, New York, Great Neck Sch Dist, NY & Sewhanaka High Sch Dist, Franklin Square, NY. Exhib: Art: USA 1969, New York; Four Artists, Frick Mus, Pittsburgh, Pa, 70; Nat Acad Design, New York, 70-71; one-person shows, Neikrug Gallery, New York, 71 & Adelphia Univ, 76; Faces, Philadelphia Mus Art, 71; Equity Artists, Philadelphia Civic Ctr, 71; Am Women Artists, Palazzo Vecchio, Florence, Italy, 72; Int Women's Arts Festival, Milan, Italy, 73; Works on Paper—Women Artists, 75, Brooklyn Mus, NY, 75; Eleven Contemp Women Artists, Sweetbriar Col, Va, 77. Teaching: Instr drawing & painting & art dir, Studio 733 Art Sch, Great Neck, NY, 63-67; instr life drawing, Hussian Col of Art, Philadelphia, 70-71; instr drawing & painting, Am Studies Ctr, Naples, Italy, 72-73 & Northern Atlantic Treaty Orgn Hq, Naples, 72-73; adj lectr painting, Brooklyn Col, 74-76; adj lectr painting, Hofstra Univ, Hempstead, NY, 77. Pos: Exec coordr, Women in the Arts Found, 75-; bd dir, Visual Dialog Mag, 77-; spec appt 5-mem adv comt, White House, Washington, DC, 3/77. Awards: MacDowell Fel, 71; Gold Medal, Int Arts Festival, Milan, 73; Va Ctr for Creative Arts Fel, 75-78. Bibliog: C A White (auth), rev in Art News, 70; Dorothy Grafly (auth), rev in Philadelphia Art in Focus, 71; Malcolm Preston (auth), On art, Newsday, 75. Mem: Int Asn of Art; Nat Women Studies Asn (task force adv bd, 76-); Artists Equity; Found for Community of Artists, New York. Style & Technique: Expressionistic, using abstracted nature forms; pasture-forms. Media: Acrylic; Paper Work of Gouache; Ink & Pencil; Oil. Publ: Illusr, Woman to Woman: European Feminists, Staragoubski, 74; auth, Report from an art colony, Woman in the Arts Newsletter, 76; auth, Women in the arts, Women's Caucus for Art Newsletter, 77; auth, The College Art Association: in-depth report, Women in the Arts Newsletter, 77. Mailing Add: 463 West St 503D New York NY 10014

ZALLINGER, JEAN DAY
ILLUSTRATOR, INSTRUCTOR
b Boston, Mass, Feb 15, 18. Study: Mass Col of Art, cert(drawing & painting), 35-39; Yale Sch Fine Arts, BFA, 42. Work: Paint & Clay Club, Permanent Collection, Univ Southern Miss. Teaching: Instr drawing, 67- & fourth yr illus, Paier Sch of Art, Hamden, Conn, 74- Pos: Tech illus draftsman, Applied Physics Lab, Univ of Washington, Seattle, 51-53. Awards: Jr Lit Guild Award for Turned to Stone, 65 & I Watch Flies, 77; Outstanding Sci Children's Book, Nat Sci & Children's Book Coun, 76; Nat Sci Teachers Awards for Biography of a Fish Hawk & I Watch Flies, 77. Mem: Paint & Clay Club, New Haven, Conn. Style & Technique: Full color, egg tempera or colored pencil; mylar; prismacolor; black and white illustration. Publ: Illusr, I Like Beetles, Holiday House, 75; illusr, Herbs and Spices—Weeds—Botnany, Golden Press, 76; illusr, Sounds in the Sea, Morrow Bk, 77; illusr, Biography of a Fish Hawk, Putnam Bk, 77; illusr, I Watch Flies, Holiday House, 77. Mailing Add: 5060 Ridge Rd North Haven CT 06473

ZALLINGER, RUDOLPH FRANZ
PAINTER, EDUCATOR
b Irkutsk, Siberia, Nov 12, 19; US citizen. Study: Yale Sch Fine Arts, Yale Univ, BFA, 42, MFA, 71. Work: Seattle Art Mus; Yale Peabody Mus Natural Hist; Berkeley Col, Yale Sch Med, Yale Univ; New Brit Mus Am Art, Conn. Comn: Age of Reptiles, fresco, Peabody Mus, Yale Univ, 42-47 & Age of Mammals, fresco, 61-67. Exhib: Northwest Ann Exhib, Seattle Art Mus, 40, 41, 50 & 51; New Directions, Yale Gallery of Fine Arts, 49; Fac Exhib, Joseloff Gallery, Hartford Art Sch, Univ Hartford, 62-64, 68, 70, 72, 74 & 76-78; 32 Realists, Cleveland Inst Art, 72-; Sanford Low Mem Exhib, New Brit Mus Am Art, 76; 200 Yrs of Am Illus, NY Hist Soc Mus, 76-77. Teaching: Instr & asst prof drawing & painting compos, Yale Sch Fine Arts, 42-50; asst & assoc prof & prof drawing & painting compos, Hartford Art Sch, Univ Hartford, 61- Pos: Artist-in-residence, Peabody Mus Natural Hist, Yale Univ, 52- Awards: Hon Mention, Prix-de-Rome, Am Acad Rome, 41; Pulitzer Prize for Painting, Columbia Univ, 49; Postage Stamp Commemoration for Age of Reptiles mural, 70. Bibliog: Lawrence Rasie (auth), Rudolph Zallinger, Dinosaur Man, Hartford Courant, Sunday, 74; Carl O Dunbar (auth), Recollections of the Renaissance of Peabody Mus Exhibs, Discovery Mag, Peabody Mus, 76; John Ostrum (auth), The Age of Reptiles, Discovery Mag Supplement 1, Peabody Mus, 77. Mem: New Haven Paint & Clay Club (vpres, 48-49; pres, 76- 78); Puget Sound Group Northwest Painters. Style & Technique: Realism with oil and egg tempera; interpretive realism in frescos. Media: Egg-tempera, Oil. Publ: Illusr, World We Live In, Life, 55; illusr, Giant Golden Book of Dinosaurs, Golden Press, 18th printing, 60; illusr, Wonders of Life on Earth, 60 & Epic of Man, 61, Life; illusr, Worlds of the Past, Golden Press, 72. Mailing Add: 5060 Ridge Rd North Haven CT 06473

ZALSTEM-ZALESSKY, MRS ALEXIS
COLLECTOR
Collection: Contemporary art. Mailing Add: Cloud Wald Farm New Milford CT 06776

ZAMMITT, NORMAN
SCULPTOR
b Toronto, Ont, Feb 3, 31; US citizen. Study: Pasadena City Col, scholar, AA, 57; Otis Art Inst, scholar, MFA, 61. Work: Mus Mod Art, New York; Hirshhorn Mus, New York; Libr Cong, Washington, DC; Otis Art Gallery, Los Angeles; Larry Aldrich Mus, Conn. Exhib: Mus Mod Art, New York, 65 & Show of New Acquisitions, 67; American Sculpture of the Sixties, Los Angeles Co Mus Art & Philadelphia Mus Art, 67; Felix Landau at Studio Marconi, Milan, Italy, 70; Metromedia, Los Angeles; Corcoran Gallery, Washington, DC; one-man shows, Beverly Hills & Los Angeles, Calif & New York, 62-72, Los Angeles Co Mus of Art, 77 & Corcoran Gallery, Washington, DC, 78. Awards: Tamarind fel, 67; Guggenheim Mem Found fel, 68. Bibliog: Various articles in Art Int, Artforum, Art in Am & Los Angeles Times. Style & Technique: Painting three dimensional art. Mailing Add: 233 N Wilson Ave Pasadena CA 91106

ZAMPARELLI, MARIO ARMOND
DESIGNER, COLLECTOR
b New York, NY. Study: Pratt Inst; Univ Paris. Comn: Murals in acrylic, Trans World Airlines; graphic works & environ designs for Kimberly-Clark, Union Bank, Hughes Airwest & Summa Corp. Pos: Owner, Mario Armond Zamparelli & Co; pres, Art Index, Inc. Awards: J W Alexander Medal, City of New York; Haskel Traveling Fel, Pratt Inst; Paul Hoffman Gold Medal. Bibliog: Articles in Esquire Mag, Sundancer Mag & Los Angeles Times. Specialty: International art curatorial and exhibition service. Collection: Renaissance art, contemporary and ethnic art. Mailing Add: Art Index Inc Suite 208 17000 Ventura Blvd PO Box 2500 Encino CA 91316

ZANTMAN, J B
ART DEALER
b Sumbawa, Dutch East Indies, Dec 27, 19; US citizen. Study: Pvt instr, Netherlands. Pos: Pres, Zantman Art Galleries, Ltd, Dallas, Tex, Carmel & Palm Desert, Calif. Specialty: Living artists from US and France. Mailing Add: PO Box 5818 Carmel CA 93921

ZAPKUS, KESTUTIS EDWARD
PAINTER
b Dabikine, Lithuania, Apr 22, 38; US citizen. Study: Art Inst Chicago, BFA, 60; Syracuse Univ, Ryerson fel, 60, MFA, 62. Work: Stedelijk Mus, Amsterdam, Holland; Hirshhorn Mus, Washington, DC; Va Mus Fine Arts, Richmond; Hunter Mus Art, Chattanooga, Tenn; Art Inst Chicago; plus pvt collections, US & Paris, France. Exhib: Six Americans Signal, Paris, 64; Whitney Mus Am Art Ann, 69; one-man shows, Gres Gallery, Chicago, 62, Stable Gallery, 68 & Paula Cooper Gallery, New York, 71; Indianapolis Mus Art, Ind, 70 & 74; Madison Art Ctr, Wis, 72; Contemp Arts Ctr, Cincinnati, 73; Inst Contemp Art, Boston, 75; Middlebury Col, Vt, 75; Butler Inst Am Art, Youngstown, Ohio, 76; plus others. Awards: Invitational First Prize, Chicago Arts Festival, 63. Media: Acrylic, Oil. Dealer: Paula Cooper Gallery 155 Wooster New York NY 10012. Mailing Add: 35 Bond St New York NY 10012

ZARAND, JULIUS JOHN
PAINTER, RESTORER
b Nagyvarad, Hungary, June 27, 13; Can citizen. Study: Royal Acad, dipl & dipl educ; also with Oskar Kokoschka, Salzburg, Austria. Work: City Hall, Halifax, NS; Yokahama Univ Gallery, Japan. Comn: Portrait of Pope Pius XII, comn by Prime Cardinal of Hungary, 38; portrait, comn by Lord Thompson, Toronto, 54; murals, St Bridgid Church, Toronto, 55; portrait of Sir John Thompson, City of Halifax, NS, 68; portraits of all presidents of the co, Maritime Telegraph & Telephone Co, Halifax, NS; portrait of Roy Charles, comn by Am Nat Red Cross for Tidewater Chapter, Norfolk, Va. Exhib: One-man shows, Halifax Libr, 64, Norfolk, Va, 67, Lafayette Art Ctr, Ind, 69, Purdue Univ Gallery, 69 & Zwicker's Gallery, Halifax, 70. Teaching: Asst prof fine arts, St Mary's Univ, Halifax, 56-65. Style & Technique: Direct painting with brush; portrait and marine scenes. Media: Oil, Egg Tempera. Dealer: Zwicker's Gallery Ltd 5415 Doyle St Halifax NS Can. Mailing Add: RR 2 Tatamagouche NS Can

ZAVEL (ZAVEL SILBER)
SCULPTOR, PRINTMAKER
b Latvia, Mar 29, 10; US citizen. Study: Vicar Art Sch, Detroit, Mich; Art Inst Chicago; Univ Southern Calif; also with Charles Despiau, Paris, Vira Mockina & William Sherwood, France. Comn: Abstr sculpture, comn by Mr & Mrs Albert Miller, Detroit, 54; metal sculpture & fireplace, comn by Mr & Mrs George Hall, Pittsburgh, 65; bronze centerpieces, comn by Mr & Mrs Phil Brant, Detroit, 69 & Dr & Mrs Leonard Brant, Port Richmond, Calif, 70. Exhib: Salon Carnot, Paris, 36; Detroit Inst Fine Arts, 55; Am Ceramic Soc, Los Angeles, 58; Am Art, Orange, NJ, 62; Old Print Ctr, New York, 70. Mailing Add: 463 West St Apt 648 New York NY 10014

ZEIDENBERGS, OLAFS
SCULPTOR
b Latvia, Mar 17, 36; US citizen. Study: Univ Hartford, BFA, 61; Yale Univ, MFA, 63. Work: Morse Col, Yale Univ; Valley Bank & Trust Co, Springfield, Mass; Avon Corp, Rye, NY; McGraw-Hill Corp, New York; Unitarian Soc New Haven, Hamden, Conn. Comn: Fountain sculpture, New Brit Redevelop Corp, 69; lobby sculpture, Blue Cross Conn, North Haven, 73; lobby sculpture, Paine, Webber, Jackson & Curtis, Inc, Stamford, Conn, 74. Exhib: Outdoor Sculpture, DeCordova Mus, Lincoln, Mass, 69; Four Sculptors, Univ Conn, 69 & Small Packages, 71; Mainstreams 74, Marietta Col, 74; Tex Fine Arts Asn Ann, Austin, 75. Teaching: Assoc prof sculpture, Southern Conn State Col, 66- Awards: Silvermine Guild Artists Award, 65 & 70, New Haven Festival Arts Award, 69 & Conn Acad Fine Arts Award, 70 & 74. Mem: Conn Acad Fine Arts (coun mem, 70-); Conn Artists 33. Style & Technique: Geometric abstract constructions and structures. Media: Metal, Plastics. Mailing Add: Dept of Art Southern Conn State Col New Haven CT 06515

ZEIDLER, EBERHARD HEINRICH
DESIGNER, ARCHITECT
b Braunsdorf, Ger, Jan 11, 26; Can citizen. Study: Bauhaus Weimar, cand arch, 45-48; Karlsruhe Univ, Dipl Ing, 49. Comn: Designer, Korah Collegiate & Voc Sch, Sault Ste Marie, Ont, 67-68, Ruddy Gen Hosp, Whitby, Ont, 68-70, McMaster Univ Health Sci Ctr, 68-72, Ont Place, Lake Ont, 69-71 & Eaton Ctr, Toronto, 73-77. Teaching: Lectr archit design, Univ Toronto, 53-55. Pos: Guest speaker, var world confs; mem var archit juries, incl, Can Archit Yearbk Award, 67, M R Design Awards, 73 & 22nd Progressive Archit Awards Prog, 74; sr partner, Zeidler Partnership-Architects. Awards: Over 30 nat & int design awards. Mem: Academician Royal Can Acad Arts; fel Royal Archit Inst Can; Ont Asn Architects; corp mem Royal Inst Brit Architects; Order Architects of Que. Publ: Auth, Healing the Hospital-McMaster Health Science Centre: Its Conception & Evolution, 74; plus many articles in leading prof mags. Mailing Add: 98 Queen St E Toronto ON Can

ZEISLER, RICHARD SPIRO
COLLECTOR, PATRON
b Chicago, Ill, Nov 28, 16. Study: Amherst Col, BA; Harvard Univ. Mem: Int Coun Mus Mod Art (bd dirs, chmn prog comt); gov life mem Art Inst of Chicago; life mem Metrop Mus, New York; Brandeis Univ (fine arts awards adv comt); Mt Holyoke Col (art adv comt); fel Pierpont Morgan Libr. Collection: European painting of the 20th century. Mailing Add: 767 Fifth Ave New York NY 10022

ZEITLIN, HARRIET BROOKS
PRINTMAKER, PAINTER
b Philadelphia, Pa, Feb 12, 29. Study: Pa Acad of Fine Arts, Univ Pa, BFA, 46-50; Barnes Found, 49 & 50; Univ Calif, Los Angeles, 63-69. Work: Libr Congress; US Info Serv, Am Embassy, New Delhi, India. Exhib: A Bicentennial Suite, Santa Barbara Mus of Art, Monterey Penensula Mus of Art, Calif State Univ, Long Beach & US Info Serv (traveling exhib), US Libr, Madras, Calcutta, Bombay & New Delhi, India, 76; 11 Women Artists, Santa Monica Col, 77; Original Masks by Outstanding Contemp Artists, Craft & Folk Art Mus, Los Angeles, 77; Calif Artists, San Antonio & Austin, Tex; Los Angeles Printmaking Soc Korean Exhib, 77. Teaching: Artist in Communities Grant in Painting & Printmaking, Calif Arts Coun, Vista Del Mar, Los Angeles, 77. Pos: Exec bd mem, Los Angeles Printmaking Soc, 64-69; artist/community relations & exec bd mem, Graphic Arts Coun of Los Angeles Co Mus of Art, 73-75; corresp secy, Artists for Economic Action, 73-74, vpres, 75-76, pres, 77- & exec dir CETA Title VI, Art in Public Places Grant, 77-78. Mem: Los Angeles Inst Contemp Art; Graphic Arts Coun, Los Angeles Co Mus of Art (exec bd, 73-75). Style & Technique: Collage paintings including acrylics, photoetching, fabric, photogtaphs, pencil, pastel and found materials, depicting dances of India. Media: Printmaking & Painting. Publ: Auth, A Community of Artists, Graphic Arts Coun Newsletter, Vol IX No 4, Los Angeles Co Mus, 74; auth, Presidents Report, Artist for Economic Action Newsletters, 77-78. Dealer: Carol Shep 3629 Grandview Blvd Los Angeles CA 90066; Suzanne Gross 1726 Sansom St Philadelphia PA. Mailing Add: 202 S Saltair Ave Los Angeles CA 90049

ZEITLIN, JACOB ILRAEL
ART DEALER, COLLECTOR
b Racine, Wis, Nov 4, 02. Pos: Owner & dir, Zeitlin & Ver Brugge Gallery, 28- Mem: Print Coun, Los Angeles Co Mus; Gruenwald Collection, Univ Calif, Los Angeles (founder, mem, trustee). Specialty: Graphic arts, old and modern, especially old masters; also Breughel and Kollwitz. Collection: Peter Breughel and the Elder Prints. Mailing Add: 815 N La Cienega Blvd Los Angeles CA 90060

ZELANSKI, PAUL JOHN
PAINTER
b Hartford, Conn, Apr 13, 31. Study: Cooper Union, cert, 55; Yale Univ, BFA, 57; Bowling Green State Univ, MA, 58. Work: Univ Mass, Amherst; Slater Mus, Norwich, Conn; Manchester Community Col, Conn; Hampshire Col, Northampton, Mass. Exhib: New England in Five Parts, De Cordova Mus, Lincoln, Mass; CREIA, Hartford Univ Carpenter Ctr, Boston; New Directions in Painting, Univ Mass, Amherst; Hard Eye, Amel Gallery, New York; Conn Painters & Sculptors Show, Hartford Arts Festival, Wadsworth Atheneum, 73. Teaching: Instr painting, drawing & design, NTex State Univ, 58-61; instr painting, Ft Worth, Tex, 61-62; assoc prof art, Univ Conn, 62-76, prof, 76- Awards: Purchase Award, Hartford Arts Festival, 72; Painting Prize, Norwich Ann, 73; Painting Prize, New Haven Paint & Clay Club, 74; Smith & Westen Award, Springfield Ann, 75-76. Bibliog: Alan Graham Collier (auth), Form, Space and Vision, Prentice-Hall; Barnard Chaet (auth), Artists at work, Webb. Mem: Mystic Art Asn (bd dirs, 62-); Conn Acad Fine Arts; Berkshire Art League; Springfield Art League; New Haven Paint & Clay Club. Media: Acrylic, Plexiglas. Mailing Add: Dept of Art U-99 Univ Conn Storrs CT 06268

ZELENAK, EDWARD JOHN
SCULPTOR
b St Thomas, Ont, Nov 9, 40. Study: Meinszinger Sch Art, Detroit, Mich; Ft Worth Art Ctr, Tex; Ont Col Art, Toronto. Work: Cantonnal Mus, Lausanne, Switz; Nat Gallery Can, Ottawa; Ont Art Gallery, Toronto; Rothman's Ltd, Stratford, Ont; Dept Pub Works, Toronto. Comn: Major outdoor sculpture, Nat Gallery Can, 72, Dept Pub Works, Toronto, 73 & North York, 76, Rothman's Art Gallery, 73 & Northfield Minn, Carleton Col, 73; major sculpture, Prov Dept Pub Works, Kitchener, Ont, 77. Exhib: One-man exhib, Major Outdoor Sculpture, Nat Art Ctr, Ottawa, 69; Tendence Actuelles, Galerie de France, Paris, 69; 3rd Int Pioneer Galleries Exhib: Cantonnal Mus, Lausanne & Mus Mod Art, Paris, 70; 49th Parallels, Ringling Mus, Sarasota, Fla & Mus Contemp Art, Chicago, 71; Washington, Northfield, Milwaukee major touring sculpture, Minn State Art Coun & Henry Gallery, 73-74. Awards: Can Coun Jr Arts Grant, 68-71, Sr Arts Grant, 73-75; Prov Ont Coun Arts Grant in Aid, 74. Bibliog: Jean Noel Chandler (auth), article in Artscanada, 4/69; Barry Lord (auth), articles in Art in Am, 1-2/69; R Naasgard (auth), article in Artscanada, 6/73. Mem: Royal Can Acad Acad Arts. Style & Technique: Large, monumental outdoor works; strong personal style; all fabrication done in studio. Media: Metal, Fiberglas. Dealer: Carmen Lamanna Gallery 840 Yonge St Toronto ON Can. Mailing Add: RR 3 West Lorne ON N0L 2P0 Can

ZELT, MARTHA
PRINTMAKER, INSTRUCTOR
b Washington, Pa, Nov 16, 30. Study: Conn Col; Pa Acad Fine Arts; New Sch Social Res, with Antonio Frasconi; Mus Arte Mod, Brazil, with John Friedlaender; Univ NMex, with Garo Antreasian; Temple Univ, BA. Work: Philadelphia Free Libr, Pa; Pa Acad Fine Arts; Philadelphia Mus of Art; George Allen Smith Collection of Yale Univ Art Gallery. Exhib: Salao Arte Mod, Rio de Janeiro, Brazil, 61; Int Bienale, Sao Paulo, Brazil, 61; Pa Acad Fine Arts Nat Ann, 61-70; one-man shows, Pa Acad Peale Galleries, 72 & Print Club, 75; 30 Yrs Am Printmaking, Brooklyn Mus, 76; New Ways With Paper, Nat Collection of Fine Arts, Washington, DC. Teaching: Instr silkscreen, Pa Acad Fine Arts, 68-; instr printmaking, Philadelphia Col Art, 69-; resident printmaker, Va Mus Fine Arts, 75- Pos: Dir graphic workshop prof artists, Pa Acad Fine Arts, 63-65; demonstrating artist & printmaker, Prints in Progress, Philadelphia, 63-71; secy, Exp in Art & Technol, Inc, Philadelphia, 68. Awards: Cresson Traveling Award, 54 & Scheidt Mem Traveling Award, Pa Acad Fine Arts; Print Club Fel, 65. Mem: Print Club; fel Pa Acad Fine Arts; Am Color Print Soc (bd). Style & Technique: Drawings and prints combining print techniques with sewing on paper and fabric; nonobjective, using flat planes and color lines. Mailing Add: 1811 Chestnut St Philadelphia PA 19103

ZETLIN, FAY (FLORENCE ANSHEN ZETLIN)
PAINTER
b Boston, Mass, Oct 9, 06. Study: Pembroke Col, AB(cum laude), 28. Work: Houston Mus Fine Arts, Tex; Phillip Morris Res Tower, Richmond, Va; Parthenon Mus, Memphis, Tenn; Mint Mus Fine Arts, Charlotte, NC; First & Merchants Bank, Richmond & br, Va. Comn: Earthworks design, Diggs Park Playground, Norfolk Redevelopment & Housing Authority, Va, 72; libr mural (8ft x 36ft), Old Dominion Univ, Norfolk, 76-77. Exhib: Va Mus Fine Arts Biennial, Richmond, 60; McClung Mus Gallery, Tex, 61; Nat Print & Drawing Exhib, Dulin Gallery, Knoxville, Tenn, 64 & 70; High Mus Art, Atlanta, Ga, 64; Ann Piedmont Exhib, Mint Mus, Charlotte, NC, 64; Parthenon Mus, Memphis, Tenn, 64; Art on Paper, Weatherspoon Art Gallery, Greensboro, NC, 65; Irene Leache Mem Exhib, Chrysler Mus at Norfolk, Va, 74; Southeastern Ann, Ball State Univ Art Gallery, 77; one-person shows, Col Mus, Hampton Inst, Va, 72, Va Commonwealth Univ, 73, Franz Bader Gallery, Washington, DC, 73 & Chrysler Mus at Norfolk, 77; plus others. Teaching: Artist-in-residence, Old Dominion Univ, 69- Pos: Vis artist, Va Wesleyan Col, 65-66 & Huntingdon Col, Montgomery, Ala, 76. Awards: Piedmont Purchase Award, Ann Exhib, Mint Mus, 64; Parthenon Mus Purchase Award, Ann Exhib, 64; Nat Found for the Arts grant, Va Comn for the Arts & Humanities, 77. Bibliog: Stefan Grunewald (auth), In Fay Zetlin's Studio (doc), Pub Television WHRO, Norfolk, 70; Creating a natural environment for urban children, Brown Univ Mag, 73. Mem: Women in Art. Style & Technique: Abstract symbolic shape in color field paintings; an iconic image made with spray gun and poured paint. Media: Acrylic on Canvas. Publ: Co-auth, with Ernest Mauer, Plastics Fables, Saturday Press, 69. Mailing Add: 7300 Heron Lane Norfolk VA 23505

ZEVON, IRENE
PAINTER
b New York, NY, Nov 24, 18. Study: With Nahum Tschacbasov. Work: Butler Inst Am Art, Youngstown, Ohio; La Jolla Art Ctr, Calif; Kenosha Pub Mus, Wis; Mary Buie Mus, Oxford, Miss; Univ Ga Mus, Athens; plus many others including pvt collections. Exhib: Kenosha Pub Mus, Wis; St Louis Pub Libr, Mo; Long Island Univ, NY; Nat Acad Design, New York; Nat Asn Women Artists Ann, New York, 72; plus many other group & one-woman shows in univs, mus & galleries. Awards: Marion K Haldenstein Mem Prize, Nat Asn Women Artists, 72. Mem: Nat Asn Women Artists. Style & Technique: Hard-edge abstract. Media: Oil. Mailing Add: 222 W 23rd St New York NY 10011

ZIB, TOM (THOMAS A ZIBELLI)
CARTOONIST
b Mt Vernon, NY. Study: Grand Cent Sch Art; Com Illus Studios. Publ: Contribr, Sat Rev & Weight Watchers, 72, Sat Eve Post, Nat Enquirer & Reader's Digest, 73. Mailing Add: 167 E Devonia Ave Mt Vernon NY 10552

ZIEGLER, JACQUELINE (JACQUELINE CHALAT-ZIEGLER)
SCULPTOR, EDUCATOR
b Mt Vernon, NY, Feb 23, 30. Study: With Frederick V Guinzburg, 43, Ruth Nickerson, 44, Columbia Univ, sculpture with Oronzio Maldarelli & casting with Ettore Salvatore, 47; Art Students League, life drawing with Klonis, 48; Univ Chicago, AB, 48; Fashion Inst Technol, 48-50; Royal Acad Fine Arts, Copenhagen, Denmark, 60-62. Work: Many Hands (3-ton wood carving), Govt of Nigeria, Enugu, Nigeria; Judge Charles Fahy (bronze portrait), Georgetown Law Libr, Washington, DC; Portrait Plaques, Onondaga Community Col, Syracuse, NY; Bushwoman of the Kalahari, Smithsonian Inst, Washington, DC; Ecce Homo, Jesuit Curia, Rome; Edith Stein Mem, Our Lady of Victory Church, New York, 78. Exhib: Charlottenborg, Copenhagen, Denmark, 62; Nat Collection of Fine Arts, Washington, DC, 63; Washington Gallery Art, 66; Everson Mus, Syracuse, NY, 72; one-man shows, St Peter's Gallery, Soc Art, Relig & Cult, New York, 75 & Everson Mus, Syracuse, NY, 79. Teaching: Prof & dir fine arts, Lemoyne Col, Syracuse, NY, 69- Bibliog: P Scala (auth), Begotten not made (film), ABC-TV, Syracuse, NY, 74. Mem: Nat Soc Am Pen Women: Am Aesthetic Soc; Soc for Art, Relig & Cult; Col Art Asn Am. Style & Technique: Figurative; expressionist; direct technique. Media: Clay, Wood & Stone; Acrylic, Painting. Mailing Add: 321 Hurlburt Rd Syracuse NY 13224

ZIEGLER, LAURA
SCULPTOR
b Columbus, Ohio. Study: Columbus Art Sch; Ohio State Univ; Cranbrook Acad; and with Peride Fazzini, Rome. Work: Hirshhorn Mus & Sculpture Garden, Washington, DC; Columbus Gallery Fine Art, Ohio; Hopkins Art Ctr, Dartmouth Col. Comn: 21 ft steel &

colored Plexiglas cross, St Stephen's Episcopal Church, Columbus, Ohio, 51; Burning Bush (44 ft welded copper), Temple Israel, Columbus, 59; plus many portraits. Exhib: Int Venice Biennial, 56-58; Inst Contemp Arts, Boston, 67; one-artist shows, Dartmouth Col, 74, Columbus Gallery Fine Art, 75 & Judah L Magnes Mem Mus, Berkeley, Calif, 76-77. Pos: Resident artist, Dartmouth Col, spring 74. Awards: Fulbright scholar, 49. Bibliog: Diane Cochran (auth), Laura Ziegler's portraits in Terra-cotta, Am Artist, 75. Style & Technique: Polychromed terra-cotta portraits; bronze sculptures. Mailing Add: c/o Forum Gallery 1018 Madison Ave New York NY 10021

ZIEMANN, RICHARD CLAUDE
PRINTMAKER, EDUCATOR
b Buffalo, NY, July 3, 32. Study: Albright Art Sch; Yale Univ, BFA & MFA; painting with Albers & Brooks; printmaking with Peterdi; drawings with Chaet. Work: Brooklyn Mus, NY; Silvermine Guild Art; Seattle Art Mus, Wash; De Cordova & Dana Mus; Libr Cong & Nat Gallery Art, Washington, DC; plus many others. Comn: Print Editions for Int Graphic Arts Soc, 58 & 60, Yale Univ Alumni Asn, 60 & Pan-Am Airlines, 62. Exhib: American Prints Today Touring Exhib, most maj print exhibs, 58-65, 24 mus, 62-63 & Paris Biennale, 63; one-man shows, Springfield Col, 66, Allen R Hite Art Inst, Univ Louisville, 67, Alpha Gallery, Boston, 67 & Univ Conn Art Gallery, 68; Oversize Prints, Whitney Mus Am Art. Teaching: Asst prof art, Hunter Col, 66; instr printmaking, Yale Univ Summer Sch, 66-67; assoc prof art, Lehman Col, currently. Pos: Supvr, Graphic Workshop in Graphic Arts USA Touring Exhib, Soviet Union, 63-64; artist in residence, Dartmouth Col, summer 71. Awards: Fulbright Grant to Netherlands, 58-59; Nat Inst Arts & Lett Grant, 66; Tiffany Found Grant, 60-61; plus many others. Mem: Soc Am Graphic Artists. Dealer: Jane Haslem Gallery 1669 Wisconsin Ave NW Washington DC 20007; Alpha Galleries 121 Newbury St Boston MA 02116. Mailing Add: Dept of Art Lehman Col Bronx NY 10465

ZIERLER, WILLIAM
ART DEALER
b New York, NY, Oct 5, 28. Study: Washington & Jefferson Col. Pos: Pres & dir, William Zierler Gallery, 68- Specialty: 20th century American and European paintings and sculpture. Publ: Contribr, Arts Mag, 4/71. Mailing Add: 360 E 72nd St New York NY 10021

ZIETZ, STEPHEN JOSEPH
ART LIBRARIAN, ART HISTORIAN
b Mobile, Ala, July 24, 49. Study: Spring Hill Col, Mobile, BA(Eng lit), 71; Villa Schifanoia Grad Sch of Fine Arts, Florence, Italy, MA(art hist), 73; Emory Univ, Atlanta, Ga, MLn, 75. Pos: Art librn, Joint Univ Libr, Vanderbilt Univ, 75-77; head libr, Fine Arts Libr, Lake Placid Sch of Art, 77-78; art librn, State Univ NY, Col at Purchase, 78- Mem: Art Libr Soc NAm. Res: 17th century Italian painting as related to the Counter-Reformation. Interest: Graphic artists and art. Mailing Add: 5 High St Bedford Hills NY 10507

ZIFF, JERROLD
ART HISTORIAN, COLLECTOR
b Los Angeles, Calif, Dec 20, 28. Study: Occidental Col, BA, 51; Univ Southern Calif, MA, 54; Harvard Univ, PhD, 59. Collections Arranged: French Masters: Rocco to Romanticism (co-auth, catalog), Univ Calif, Los Angeles, 60-61; George F Mc Murray Collection of 19th century American Paintings, Trinity Col, Hartford, Conn, 68; Drawings from Four Collections (co-auth, catalog), 73 & II (auth, catalog), Univ Ill. Pos: Asst prof 19th century art, Univ Calif, Los Angeles, 58-66; prof 18th & 19th century art, Trinity Col, Hartford, 66-69; prof 18th & 19th century art & drawings, Univ Ill, Champaign, 69- Mem: Col Art Asn; Midwest Art Hist Soc; Turner Soc. Res: Art of J M W Turner; old master drawings. Collection: Old master and 19th century drawings. Mailing Add: 140 Fine Arts Bldg Univ Ill Champaign IL 61820

ZILCZER, JUDITH KATY
ART HISTORIAN, CURATOR
b Waterbury, Conn, Nov 6, 48. Study: George Washington Univ, Washington, DC, BA, 69 & MA, 71; Univ Del, PhD, 75. Collections Arranged: The Noble Buyer: John Quinn, Patron of the Avant-Garde (auth, catalogue), Hirshhorn Mus & Sculpture Garden, Washington, DC, 78. Teaching: Instr art hist, Univ Del, Newark, 74; asst prof art hist & prof lectr Am studies, George Washington Univ, 75-76. Pos: Historian, Hirshhorn Mus & Sculpture Garden, 74- Awards: Unidel Found Fel, Univ Del, 71-73; Smithsonian Fel, Nat Collection of Fine Arts, 73-74; Penrose Fund res grant, Am Philos Soc, 76-77. Mem: Col Art Asn; Women's Caucus for Art. Res: Nineteenth and twentieth century art; history of patronage. Publ: Auth, The world's new art center: modern art exhibitions in New York City, 1913-1918, Arch of Am Art J, 74; auth, Robert J Coady, forgotten spokesman for avant-garde culture in America, Am Art Rev, 75; contribr, Avant-garde painting and sculpture in America, 1910-1925, Del Art Mus, 75; auth, Primitivism and New York Dada, Arts Mag, 77. Mailing Add: c/o Hirshhorn Mus & Sculpture Garden Independence Ave & Eighth St SW Washington DC 20560

ZILKA, MICHAEL JOHN
EDUCATOR, STUDIO DIRECTOR
b Oak Park, Ill, Oct 19, 47. Study: Ill State Univ, BS; Univ Wis, with Donald Reitz & Bruce Breckenridge, MFA. Exhib: Scripps Col; Art Ctr, Evanston, Ill; Rochester Art Ctr, Minn. Teaching: Instr ceramics, Milton Col, Wis, 70-71; instr, Oxbow Summer Sch Painting, Saugatuck, Mich, 70-75; instr ceramics & design, Stephens Col, 72- Pos: Dir (ceramics grant), Mich Arts Coun, 75. Awards: Lakefront Festival Art First Prize, Milwaukee, Wis, 72. Mem: Nat Coun Educr in Ceramic Arts. Media: Ceramic; Watercolor. Mailing Add: Dept of Art Stephens Col Columbia MO 65201

ZIMILES, MURRAY
PAINTER, EDUCATOR
b New York, NY, Nov 30, 41. Study: Univ Ill, BFA; Cornell Univ, MFA; Ecole Nat Superieure Beaux-Arts, Paris. Work: Brooklyn Mus, NY; New York Pub Libr; Rosenwald Collection; Nat Collection Fine Arts; US Embassy, Bogata, Colombia. Exhib: Prints from Portfolios, Brooklyn Mus, 70; 4th Bienal Am Grabado, Santiago, Chile, 70; one-man shows, Zingale Gallery, New York, 71, Kunstnerforbundet Gallery, Oslo, Norway, 72, New Talent Forum Gallery, 74, Vassar Col Gallery, 77 & Sindin Galleries, New York, 78. Teaching: Instr printmaking, Pratt Graphics Ctr, New York, 68-71; asst prof drawing & printmaking, Silvermine Col Art, New Canaan, Conn, 68-71; asst prof drawing & printmaking, State Univ NY, New Paltz, 72-77; assoc prof drawing & printmaking, State Univ NY, Purchase, 77- Awards: Found Etats-Unis Fel, Paris, 65-66; Royal Norweg Govt Fel, 71; State Univ NY res grant, 76. Bibliog: New talent, Artist Proof Ann, 71; article, Arts Mag, 1/78. Publ: Co-auth, The technique of fine art lithography, 70, Early American mills, 73; The contemporary lithographic workshop around the world, 74. Dealer: Sindin Galleries 1035 Madison Ave New York NY. Mailing Add: RFD 1 Millerton NY 12546

ZIMMERMAN, ELYN
SCULPTOR
b Philadelphia, Pa, Dec 16, 45. Study: Univ Calif, Los Angeles, BA(psychol), 68, MFA, 72; and with Robert Irwin & Richard Diebenkorn. Work: Los Angeles Co Mus Art, Los Angeles; Whitney Mus Am Art. Exhib: Factor Collection, Pasadena Mus Art, Calif, 73; one-women exhib, Univ Art Mus, Berkeley, 74, Baxter Gallery, Calif Inst Technol, Pasadena, 75, Broxton Gallery, Los Angeles, 76 & 77 & Inst Art & Urban Resources, PS 1, New York, 77; 5 Women Artists, Univ Nev, Las Vegas, 75; Sense of Reference, Mandeville Art Gallery, La Jolla, Calif, 75; Whitney Mus Am Art Biennial, New York, 75; Three Women Artists, Fisher Gallery, Univ Southern Calif, Los Angeles; Biennale, Sydney, Australia; Palomar Col, Calif, 77. Teaching: Instr painting, Calif State Univ, Humboldt, 72-73, Mills Col, Oakland, 73-75, Calif State Univ, San Francisco, 74-75, Calif Inst for the Arts, 77-78. Awards: Nat Endowment for the Arts Artist's fel, 76; New Talent Award, Los Angeles Co Mus of Art, 76. Bibliog: Sharon Smith (auth), Women who make movies, Hopkinson & Blake, 74; Kirk Varnedoe (auth), Artifact or fact art, Arts Mag, 6/75; Nancy Marmer (auth), Los Angeles, Artforum, 5/77. Mem: Los Angeles Inst Contemp Art (bd dir, 76-). Media: Use of various media, dependent on given situation for exhibition and intent of work. Mailing Add: PO Box 1112 Venice CA 90291

ZIMMERMAN, KATHLEEN MARIE
PAINTER, COLLAGE ARTIST
b Floral Park, NY, Apr 24, 23. Study: Art Students League; Nat Acad Sch Fine Arts. Work: Butler Inst Am Art, Youngstown, Ohio; Sheldon Swope Art Gallery, Terre Haute, Ind; Univ Wyo Art Mus, Laramie; Lowe Art Mus, Univ Miami, Coral Gables, Fla; NC Mus Art, Raleigh; and others. Exhib: Art USA, 58; Silvermine Guild, Conn, 62; Nat Acad Design, 69, 75, 76 & 77; one-man show, Westbeth Gallery, 73 & 74, Am Watercolor Soc, 75, 76 & 77, New York & others. Teaching: Instr drawing & painting, Midtown Sch Art, New York, 47-52. Awards: Scholar, John F & Anna Lee Stacey Found, 54; six Prizes, Nat Asn Women Artists, 57-76; Henry Ward Ranger Fund Purchase, Nat Acad of Design, 76; plus others. Bibliog: James Mellow (auth), art rev in New York Times, 2/17/73; Beverly Chesler (auth), Pictures on exhibit, Art Rev, 5-6/77; Hilton Kramer (auth), New York Times, Art Rev, 6/10/77. Mem: Nat Asn Women Artists; Audubon Artists. Style & Technique: Semi-abstract painting; abstract and semi-abstract collage. Media: Oil, Acrylic, Paper. Publ: Co-illusr, Diet for a Small Planet, 71. Mailing Add: 463 West St A1110 New York NY 10014

ZIMMERMAN, PAUL WARREN
PAINTER, EDUCATOR
b Toledo, Ohio, Apr 29, 21. Study: John Herron Art Sch, BFA. Work: Pa Acad Fine Arts, Philadelphia; Houston Mus Fine Art; Butler Inst Am Art, Youngstown, Ohio; Springfield Mus Fine Art, Mass; Wadsworth Atheneum, Hartford, Conn. Comn: Mural, First New Haven Nat Bank, Conn, 65. Exhib: Indiana Artists Exhibition, John Herron Art Mus, Indianapolis, 57; American Painting & Sculpture, Univ Ill, 61; Pa Acad Fine Arts, Philadelphia, 62; 144th Ann Exhib, Nat Acad Design, New York, 69; Midyear Show, Butler Inst Am Art, Youngstown, 70. Teaching: Prof painting & design, Univ Hartford Art Sch, 47- Awards: First Prize, Conn Watercolor Soc, 64; Altman Landscape Prize for Second Place, Nat Acad Design, 67, First Place, 69. Bibliog: Henry Pitz (auth), Paintings of Paul Zimmerman, Am Artist Mag, 1/60. Mem: Nat Acad Design; Conn Acad Fine Arts; Conn Watercolor Soc (pres, 52-53). Media: Oil. Dealer: Munson Gallery New Haven CT; Korn Bluth Gallery Fair Lawn NJ. Mailing Add: 257 Victoria Rd Hartford CT 06114

ZIMMERMAN, WILLIAM HAROLD
PAINTER, ILLUSTRATOR
b Dillsboro, Ind, Oct 1, 37. Study: Cincinnati Art Acad. Work: Cincinnati Mus Natural Hist, Ohio; Ind State Mus, Indianapolis; Pomona Col, Calif. Exhib: Cincinnati Animal Art Show, 66; Soc Animal Artists Ann, New York, 67; one-man shows in New York, San Francisco, Chicago, Cincinnati & Columbus, Ohio. Awards: Award for Magpie, Cincinnati Animal Art Show, 66. Bibliog: Oscar Godbout (auth), Wood, field and stream, New York Times, 10/18/64; Bill Thomas (auth), Dillsboro's Audubon, Nat Observer, 11/12/65; Jay Shuler (auth), A real artist has to work for himself, Carolina Outdoors, 9/71. Mem: Soc Animal Artists; Nat Soc Lit & Arts. Style & Technique: Gouache, glazing technique on illustration board. Publ: Co-auth & illusr, Topflight, speed index to waterfowl, 66; auth, Waterfowl of North America, 74. Mailing Add: RR 3 Box 36 Nashville TN 47448

ZIMON, KATHY ELIZABETH
ART LIBRARIAN
b Szeged, Hungary, Feb 20, 41; Can citizen. Study: Univ BC, BA(art hist), 66, BLS, 69, MA(art hist), 70. Pos: Fine arts librn, Univ Calgary Libr, Alta, 69- Mem: Can Libr Asn; Can Asn of Spec Libr & Info Serv (newsletter ed, 75-; vchmn art sect, 77-78); Univ Art Asn of Can; Art Libr Soc NAm. Mailing Add: Libr Div Fine Arts Univ Calgary Calgary AB T2N 1N4 Can

ZINGALE, LAWRENCE
PAINTER
b Florida, NY, Aug 12, 38. Work: Int Mus of Folk Art, Santa Fe, NMex. Exhib: Magic Spaces, Contemp Folk and Primitive Painting, Stamford Mus, Conn, 74; Int Mus of Folk Art, Santa Fe, 76; The All-Am Dog, Mus of Folk Art, New York, 77-78; The Am Game, Wilson Art Ctr, Rochester, NY, 78. Bibliog: Carol Odevseff (auth), One in Thirty Million, Times Herald Record, 73; Stelio Tomei (auth), I Naifs, Passera & Agosta, Rome, 74; Dr Robert Bishop (auth), The All-American Dog, Avon Publ, New York, 77. Style & Technique: Primitive or naive; oil or acrylic on canvas. Mailing Add: c/o American Hurrah Antiques 316 E 70 New York NY 10021

ZIOLKOWSKI, KORCZAK
SCULPTOR
b Boston, Mass, Sept 6, 08. Work: San Francisco Art Mus; Judge Baker Guidance Ctr, Boston; Symphony Hall, Boston; Vassar Col; marble portraits of Paderewski, Georges Enesco, Artur Schnable, Wilbur L Cross, John F Kennedy & Crazy Horse at Crazy Horse Mem. Comn: Noah Webster Statue (marble), Town Hall Lawn, West Hartford, Conn; granite portrait of Wild Bill Hickok, Deadwood, SDak; Chief Sitting Bull (granite portrait), Mobridge, SDak; Robert Driscoll, Sr (marble), First Nat Bank Black Hills, Rapid City, SDak; carving mountain into equestrian figure of Sioux Chief Crazy Horse at request of Indians as mem to Indians of NAm, Custer, SDak, 48- Pos: Chmn bd, Crazy Horse Found; asst to Cutzon Borglum, Mount Rushmore Nat Mem, SDak. Awards: First Sculptural Prize for Marble Portrait of Paderewski, New York World's Fair, 39. Mem: Nat Sculpture Soc. Mailing Add: Crazy Horse Custer SD 57730

ZIPKIN, JEROME R
COLLECTOR
b New York, NY. Study: Princeton Univ. Mem: Art Collectors Club. Collection: Contemporary paintings and sculpture. Mailing Add: 1175 Park Ave New York NY 10028

ZIRKER, JOSEPH
PRINTMAKER, LECTURER
b Los Angeles, Calif, Aug 13, 24. Study: Univ Calif, Los Angeles, 43-44, 46-47; Univ Denver, BFA, 49; with Jules Heller & Francis de Erdely, Univ Southern Calif, MFA, 51; Tamarind Lithography Workshop, printer fel, 62-63 & res fel, 64. Work: Brooklyn Art Mus, NY; Tamarind Archives, Tamarind Lithography Workshop; Stanley Freenean Collection, Los Angeles Co Mus; Martin Gluck Collection, San Diego Mus, La Jolla Art Ctr; Achenbach Found, Palace of Legion of Honor, San Francisco. Exhib: New Dimensions of Lithography, Tamarind Lithographs, Univ Southern Calif, 64; Calif Printmakers, Achenbach Found, Palace of Legion of Honor, 71; Int Inst Exp Printmaking, Santa Cruz, Calif, 75; New Ways With Paper, Nat Collection of Fine Arts, Smithsonian Inst, Washington, DC, 77-78; one-man shows, Calif Palace of Legion of Honor, San Francisco, 74 & De Saisset Art Gallery & Mus, Univ Santa Clara, Calif, 75. Teaching: Lectr printmaking, Univ Southern Calif, 63; instr, Chouinard Art Inst, Los Angeles, 63; instr drawing, San Jose City Col, 66- Pos: Dir, Joseph Press, Venice, Calif, 63-64. Awards: 3rd Nat Print Exhib Award, Bradley Univ, Ill, 52; 2nd Nat Exhib of Prints, Univ Southern Calif, 52; 7th Ann Print Exhib, Brooklyn Mus, 53. Mem: Col Art Asn Am. Style & Technique: Both abstract and representational formal relationships in the making of drawings and monotypes; techniques: the combining of drawing, painting, collage and printmaking methods and materials. Publ: Cover designs for Baja California 1533-1950, 51; Embryo, a literary quarterly, 54-55; Art is One Exhibition (catalog), 61. Dealer: Gallerie Smith-Andersen Homer Ave & Emerson St Palo Alto CA 94301 Mailing Add: 451 O'Connor St Palo Alto CA 94303

ZISLA, HAROLD
PAINTER, EDUCATOR
b Cleveland, Ohio, June 28, 25. Study: Cleveland Inst Art; Western Reserve Univ, BS(educ) & AM. Exhib: Cleveland Mus Art; South Bend Michiana; John Herron Art Mus; Ft Wayne Art Mus; Kalamazoo Art Inst; plus others. Teaching: Instr, South Bend Art Ctr, 53-; instr, Ind Univ Exten, South Bend, 55; assoc prof, Ind Univ, South Bend. Pos: Dir & bd mem, South Bend Art Ctr, 57- Mailing Add: Ind Univ Northside at Greenlawn South Bend IN 46615

ZIVIC, WILLIAM THOMAS
PAINTER, SCULPTOR
b Ironwood, Mich, Aug 31, 30. Work: City of Tucson; Univ Ariz; Pima Col; Lockheed Aircraft, Los Angeles; Grissmer Corp, Indianapolis, Ind; plus over 1,000 pvt collections, US, Europe, Africa & Asia. Comn: Paintings, Great Western Bank, Phoenix, 73; painting, Ariz Bank, Tucson, 75; painting, US Postal Serv, 75. Exhib: Tucson Art Ctr Ann, 74; Alamo Kiwanis Art Show, San Antonio, 74; Casa Grande Art Fiesta, Ariz, 75; Tubac Art Festival, Ariz, 75. Mem: Tucson Art Ctr; Casa Grande Art Asn; Santa Cruz Valley Art Asn. Style & Technique: Realistic Western art work. Media: Pen, Watercolor, Oil & Acrylic; Bronze. Publ: Illusr, Tucson Bi-Centennial Mag, 75; illusr, Southwest Memories, 75. Dealer: Trailside Galleries PO Box 858 Jackson WY 83001. Mailing Add: 1516 Turquoise Vista Tucson AZ 85710

ZLOTNICK, DIANA SHIRLEY
COLLECTOR, PATRON
b Los Angeles, Calif, Sept 3, 27. Study: Calif State Univ, Los Angeles, BS, 48. Work: Donated to Los Angeles Co Mus Art, La Jolla Mus Contemp Art, Fisk Univ & Calif State Univ, Northridge. Exhib: Andy Warhol Factory Additions, from collection, Calif State Univ, Hayward, 68-69; The Diana Zlotnick Collection, Calif State Univ. Los Angeles, 69; Contemporary Collector, Diana Zlotnick, Montgomery Gallery, Claremont Cols. Teaching: Lectr understanding & collecting art through direct experience, Univ Southern Calif, 72-75. Pos: Exec secy, Aesthet Res Coun, 68; pvt asst, Pasadena Art Mus, 70-71; publ, Newslett on the Arts, Los Angeles, 71- Bibliog: Art Seidenbaum (auth), Home is where the art is, 11/19/65, Dianne Thomas (auth), How to collect art worth $80,000 on pin money, 11/16/69 & Donna Scheibe (auth), Young artists aided in struggle, 2/23/73, Los Angeles Times. Mem: Los Angeles Inst Contemp Art (pub info officer, 74-75); Los Angeles Co Art Mus Art Rental Gallery; hon mem Newport Harbor Art Mus, Otis Art Assoc & Mus Sci & Indust. Interest: Supportive role for the art community via Newsletter on the Arts providing continuous exposure for emerging and established artists of varied aesthetic attitudes on the basis of quality; consulting service for artists in community, dealers and curators; refer artists to sources for exhibiting works and selectively arranging for dealers and curators to view work of interest to them. Collection: Reveals the wedding of assemblage and pop art images in the fusion of painting and sculpture in California since the sixties. Mailing Add: 2968 Dona Susana Dr Studio City CA 91604

ZOELLNER, RICHARD C
PRINTMAKER, PAINTER
b Portsmouth, Ohio, June 30, 08. Study: Cincinnati Art Acad. Work: Mus Mod Art, New York; Philadelphia Mus Art; Brooklyn Mus Art, NY; Pa Acad Fine Arts, Philadelphia; Andover Mus Am Art, Mass. Exhib: Ann Painting Exhib, Pa Acad Fine Arts, 55; Festival Arts, Birmingham Mus Art, Ala, 63; Am Color Print Soc, Philadelphia, 63; 18th Ann Piedmont Graphic Exhib, Mint Mus, Charlotte, NC, 71; 23rd Nat Exhib Prints, Libr of Cong, Washington, DC, 73. Teaching: Instr art, Cincinnati Art Mus, 45-48; prof art, Univ Ala, 48- Pos: Vis artist, Mary Washington Col, 51, Univ Miss, 52-53 & Univ Fla, 53-54. Awards: Award for Images on Paper, Miss Art Asn, 71; Award, 13th Dixie Ann, Montgomery Mus Fine Art, 72; Purchase Award, 23rd Nat Exhib Prints, Libr of Cong, 73. Mem: Soc Am Graphic Artists; Am Color Print Soc; Graphics Soc. Media: Intaglio. Mailing Add: 14 Guilds Wood Tuscaloosa AL 35401

ZOLOTOW, MILTON
DESIGNER, EDUCATOR
b New York, NY, May 29, 20. Study: Art Students League, 37-39 & 46; Cavanaugh Sch of Lettering & Design, New York, 39; Escuela de Pintura y Escultura, Mex, 48-49. Teaching: Instr commun design, Art Ctr Col of Design, 76-; instr design, Calif Inst of the Arts, 77- Pos: Art dir, Atherton Mogge Privett, Los Angeles, 55-59; partner, Gollin, Bright & Zolotow, 59-61; graphic designer, own studio, Los Angeles, 66- Awards: Gold Medal, New York Art Dirs Club, 60 & Los Angeles Art Dirs Club, 71; Zellerbach Award, Los Angeles Art Dirs Club, 71. Mem: Los Angeles Art Dirs Club; Craft & Folk Art Mus, Los Angeles (bd trustees, 77-). Publ: Contribr, Peter Palazzo & the Sunday papers, Communication Arts Mag, 64, /going to camp in LA, Media Agency Clients Mag, 65, The design conference at Aspen, Art Direction Mag, 70, Art, useful or useless, Communication Arts Mag, 76 & Next stop Pasadena, Art Direction Mag, 76. Mailing Add: 10227 Chrysanthemum Lane Los Angeles CA 90024

ZONIA, DHIMITRI
PAINTER, MURALIST
b St Louis, Mo, June 12, 21. Study: Independent study in Italy & Eng. Work: Butler Inst Am Art, Youngstown, Ohio; Ark Art Ctr, Little Rock; Okla Art Ctr, Oklahoma City; Art Gallery, Del Mar Col, Corpus Christie, Tex; Mus Relig Art, Green Lake, Wis. Exhib: Four-man show, Brooks Mem Mus, Memphis, Tenn, 64; Benedictine Art Awards, Hannover Galleries, New York, 65; Mo State Coun Arts, travel exhib, 67; one-man show, Albrecht Mus, St Joseph, Mo, 73; Midyear Show, Butler Inst Am Art, Youngstown, Ohio, 74, Harlin Mus, West Plains, Mo, 77, St Louis Artists Guild, 77; Palais des Congress, Paris, France, 76; Tattershall Castle Gallery, Victoria Embankment, London, Eng, 78. Awards: Harlin Mus Trustee's Award, West Plains, Award, Del Mar Col, 74, Ark Art Ctr, Little Rock, 74 & Butler Inst Am Mo, 77; Chattanooga Nat Award, Tenn, 77; William K Bixby Award, St Louis Artist's Guild, 77. Bibliog: Viola R Greason (auth), Dhimitri Zonia, 11/27/68 & Shirley Althoff (auth), Byzantine artist, 8/29/71, St Louis Dem; Floyd Bowser (auth), Aspiring artist, St Louis Post Dispatch, 4/26/70. Style & Technique: New realism; super realistic. Media: Oil; Etching. Publ: Auth, Some thoughts on book illustrating, CPH Commentator, 74; co-auth, Arise My Love, Concordia Publ Co, 75. Mailing Add: 4680 Karamar Dr St Louis MO 63128

ZORETICH, GEORGE STEPHEN
PAINTER, EDUCATOR
b Monessen, Pa, June 19, 18. Study: Pa State Univ, BS(art educ) & MA(studio art); Columbia Univ & Syracuse Univ, grad study; also with Hobson Pittman & Ivan Mestrovic. Work: Butler Art Inst, Youngstown, Ohio; Pa State Univ Mus, University Park; St Albans Sch, Washington, DC; Indiana State Univ, Pa; Kutztown State Col, Pa. Comn: Open Hearth (mural), Mineral Industs, Pa State Univ, 58. Exhib: Six Pa Acad Fine Arts Ann, 49-67; nine Butler Art Inst Ann, 50-67; four Corcoran Biennials, Washington, DC, 53-61; San Francisco Art Mus 84th Ann, 65; Nat Acad Design 150th Ann, 75. Teaching: From instr to prof art, Pa State Univ, University Park, 46- Awards: Hon Mention for Painting, Butler Art Inst, 54 & Moravian Col Invitational, 70; Barse Miller Mem Award for Watercolor, Nat Acad Design, 75. Bibliog: James Schineller (auth), Art-search-self discovery, Int Textbk, 60; Yar Chomicky (auth), Watercolor Paintings, Prentice-Hall, 68. Style & Technique: Lyrical abstraction, dealing with landscape and space; field relationships, including structural elements and calligraphy. Media: Oil, Acrylic. Publ: Auth, Woodcut, Everyday Art, spring 60; co-auth, Prints & Printmaking, Pa State Univ, 60; co-auth, Drawing, Lock Haven Rev, 73. Mailing Add: 144 Spring Hill Lane State College PA 16801

ZORNES, JAMES MILFORD
PAINTER, DESIGNER
b Camargo, Okla, Jan 25, 08. Study: With F Toles Chamberlin & Millard Sheets, 35-38; Otis Art Inst, 38; Pomona Col, 46-50. Work: Metrop Mus Art, New York; Los Angeles Co Mus Art; Butler Inst Am Art, Youngstown, Ohio; Nat Acad Design, New York; White House Collection, Washington, DC; plus many others including pvt collections. Comn: Murals for post off at Campo, Tex, 37 & Claremont, Calif, 38, US Govt. Exhib: Chicago Int Watercolor Exhib, Art Inst Chicago, 38; San Francisco World's Fair, 38-40; Metrop Mus Art, New York, 41; 96th Ann Am Watercolor Soc, 63; Watercolor USA, 72; plus many others. Teaching: Instr painting, Otis Art Inst, 38-46; instr painting, Pomona Col, 46-50; instr painting, Univ Calif, Santa Barbara, 48-49. Pos: Off army artist, US Govt, 43-45. Awards: Award for In the Cove, Nat Acad Design; William Tuthill Prize for Well at Guadalupe, 38; Am Artist Medal for Beach Party, 63; plus many others. Bibliog: Article in Am Artist Mag, 11/63; Edgar A Whitney (auth), Complete guide to watercolor painting, 65; One Hundred Watercolor Techniques, Watson-Guptill, 68; plus others. Mem: Assoc Nat Acad Design; Am Watercolor Soc; Nat Watercolor Soc (past pres); West Coast Watercolor Soc (former vpres); Riverside Art Asn (bd dirs, 66-67). Style & Technique: Abstract realism, transparent watercolor and other media. Publ: Auth, A Journey to Nicaragua, Univ of Okla Press, Norman, 77. Mailing Add: PO Box 24 Mt Carmel UT 84755

ZOROMSKIS, KAZIMIERAS
PAINTER, INSTRUCTOR
b Lithuania; US citizen. Study: Vilna Art Acad, BA, 42; Vienna Art Acad, Masters dipl, 45; Rome Royal Art Acad, Italy, spec fresco studies, 46. Work: Miguel deFaguaga y Solana, Madrid, Spain; Sun Times Bldg, Chicago; State Mus, Vilna, Lithuania. Exhib: 23rd Salon de Otono, Nat Mus Mod Art, Madrid, Spain, 49; Art Inst Chicago Ann, 53 & 56; 159th All Am, Pa Acad Fine Arts, Philadelphia, 64; Dealers Choice Exhib, Huntington Hartford Mus, New York, 67-68; Corcoran Gallery, Washington, DC, 73. Teaching: Prof fine arts, Univ Javeriana, Bogota, Colombia, 50-51; instr perspective & oil painting, Newark Sch Fine & Indust Art, 68- Bibliog: Many articles & rev in Am, Span & Lithuanian Mags & papers; also in Lithuanian Encycl, 66. Style & Technique: Changing from early abstract to abstract new reality; three dimensional; optical illusion. Media: Oil on Canvas. Mailing Add: 163 W 23rd St New York NY 10011

ZOX, LARRY
PAINTER
b Des Moines, Iowa, May 31, 36. Study: Univ Okla; Drake Univ; Des Moines Art Ctr, with George Grosz. Work: Whitney Mus Am Art, New York; Mus Fine Arts, Houston, Tex; Joseph H Hirshhorn Collection; Des Moines Art Ctr; Mus Mod Art, New York; plus many others. Exhib: First Indian Triennale, 68; The Direct Image, Worcester Art Mus, Mass, 69; Whitney Mus Am Art Ann, New York, 69-70 & 72; Indianapolis Mus Art, Ind, 72; one-man retrospective, Whitney Mus Art, 73; Palm Springs Desert Mus, Calif, 73; plus others. Teaching: Artist in residence, Juniata Col, 64; guest critic, Cornell Univ, 67; artist in resident, Univ NC, Greensboro, 67; instr art, Sch Visual Arts, 67-; instr art, Dartmouth Col, winter 69. Awards: Guggenheim Fel, 67; Nat Coun Arts Award, 69. Mailing Add: c/o Andre Emmerich Gallery 41 E 57th St New York NY 10022

ZUCCARELLI, FRANK EDWARD
PAINTER
b Pa, Oct 23, 21. Study: Newark Sch Fine & Indust Art, with William J Aylward & John Grabach; Art Students League, with Robert Philip; Kean Col NJ, BA. Work: US Navy & Marine Mus, Washington, DC; Marine Corps Base, Barstow, Calif; Abraham Sharpe Found & Malcolm Forbes Collection, New York. Comn: Paintings for US Navy, Newport RI, 71 & Washington, DC, 75; Dahlgren Weapons Lab, Va, 71 & Mediter Sixth Fleet, 72; Apollo-Soyuz Test Proj (recovery of astronauts in Pac), 75. Exhib: Newark Sch Indust & Fine Arts Alumni Show, Newark Mus, NJ; USN Combat Art Collection, Salmagundi Club, New York; Am Artists Prof League Grand Nat, 70 & 77; Hudson Valley Art Asn Ann Open Show, 77. Teaching: Pvt instr oils, 58-; instr oils & pictorial illus, Spectrum Inst, Somerville, NJ, 72- Awards: Salmagundi Club Prize, 69 & 77; H H Heydenryk Award, Pastel Soc of Am, 77; Pastel Soc of Am Award, Am Artist Prof League Grand Nat, 77. Bibliog: Doris Brown (auth), New England—artist's forte, New Brunswick Home News, 68 & Artist's assignment pays off, Sun Home News, New Brunswick, 71; Colleen Zirnite (auth), Artist speaks of many things, Spectator, 72. Mem: Naval Art Coop & Liaison Comt (combat artist); Salmagundi Club

(resident artist & juror); fel Am Artists Prof League; Pastel Soc of Am. Style & Technique: Traditional. Media: Oil and Pastel. Mailing Add: 61 Appleman Rd Somerset NJ 08873

ZUCKER, BARBARA M
SCULPTOR, INSTRUCTOR
b Philadelphia, Pa, Aug 2, 40. Study: Univ Mich, BS(design), 62; Cranbrook Acad Art, Bloomfield Hills, Mich; Kokoschka Sch Vision, Salzburg, Austria, 61; Hunter Col, MA, 77. Work: Whitney Mus Am Art; pvt collections of Lowell Nesbitt, Milton Brutten, Helen Herrick & Claes Oldenburg. Exhib: 26 Contemporary Women Artists, Aldrich Mus Art, Ridgefield, Conn, 71; one-woman shows, Douglass Col, Rutgers Univ, New Brunswick, NJ, 73, Focus, Philadelphia Civic Ctr Mus, 74, 112 Greene St Gallery, 76 & Robert Miller Gallery, New York, 78; Seven Sculptors, Inst Contemp Art, Boston, 74. Teaching: Docent lectr, Whitney Mus Am Art, 73-; instr art, La Guardia Community Col, Queens, NY, 74-77; instr, Fordham Univ, Lincoln Ctr, New York, 74-; artist in residence, Princeton Univ, fall 75 & Fine Arts Work Ctr, Provincetown, winter 75; artist-in-residence, Fla State Univ, 76; instr, Philadelphia Col of Art, 77-78. Pos: Co-founder, AIR Gallery, New York, NY, 72; Ed assoc, Art News Mag, 74- Awards: Hon Soc, Univ Mich, 52; Col Art Asn Am, MFA, 75; Nat Endowment Arts Fel Grant, 75; Purchase Prize, Ulster Co Coun, NY, 77. Bibliog: Hermine Freed (auth), Barbara Zucker, video, 72; Rosemary Mayer (auth), rev in Arts Mag, 73; Dough Krimp (auth), rev in Art Int, 73; Jeff Perrone (auth), Ten approaches to the decorative, Artforum, 76; Jay Gorney (auth), Barbara Zucker, Arts Mag, 77; Five years of fresh AIR, MS Mag, 1/78. Style & Technique: Unusual materials; celastic, hydrocal, rubber latex, flocking, paste jewels, anodized aluminum. Media: Sculpture; Organic Abstraction. Publ: Contribr, Art News, 74-75; contribr, Village Voice (centerfold), 7/2/75 & 7/9/75 & article on Red Grooms, 76; auth, article on Florine Stettheimer (American painter), Art News, 2/76. Mailing Add: 21 E Tenth St New York NY 10003

ZUCKER, BOB
PHOTOGRAPHER, DESIGNER
b New York, NY, Dec 10, 46. Study: Hunter Col, BA; and with Philippe Halsman, New York. Work: Libr of Cong. Comn: Photos, 19th Century Pub Sculpture, Metrop Mus, 73; Sculpture of Isodor Konti, Hudson River Mus, 74; Historic Architectural Documentation of Old Westchester Co Courthouse Complex, Co of Westchester, 74; Bicentennial Exhib, Venturi & Rauch AIA & Whitney Mus, 75; Am Bicentennial: Signs of Life in the City, Renwick Gallery, Smithsonian Inst, 75. Exhib: 19th Century Public Sculpture in New York Parks, 73; Collection of Norbert Schimmel-Ancient Art, 72; Sakakke-Textile Art from West Africa-African Am Inst, 75. Teaching: Instr photog, City Univ New York. Style & Technique: Large format, black and white and color, still photography applied to exhibitions and publications. Publ: Auth, American Architecture: Westchester County, 77. Mailing Add: 3 Burbank Ct Greenlawn Ct NY 11740

ZUCKER, JACQUES
PAINTER
b Radom, Poland, June 15, 00; US citizen. Study: Bezalel Art Sch, Jerusalem; Acad Grande Chaumiere; Colarossi Acad, Paris; Nat Acad, New York. Work: Bezalel Art Mus, Jerusalem; Mus Mod Art, Tel-Aviv, Israel; Helena Rubenstein Mus, Tel-Aviv; Mus Mod Art, Paris; plus many others including pvt collections in France, Israel, Eng, Sweden, Japan, US & world over. Exhib: Mus Mod Art, New York; Carnegie Inst Int, Pittsburgh; Pa Acad Fine Arts, Philadelphia; Art Inst Chicago; Whitney Mus Am Art, New York; plus many other group shows including twenty-eight one-man shows. Bibliog: Harry Salpeter (auth), article in Esquire Mag, 38; Claude Roger (auth), Marx: Jacques Zucker, Paul Petrides Ed, 12/69; articles in Menorah & Coronet Mag. Mem: Artists Equity Asn; Fedn Artists & Sculptors. Style & Technique: Romantic expressionism, painting apres la nature. Media: Oil, Pastel, Watercolor. Interest: High art qualities and expression. Dealer: Schoeneman Galleries 823 Madison Ave New York NY 10021. Mailing Add: 44 W 77th St New York NY 10024

ZUCKER, JOSEPH I
PAINTER
b Chicago, Ill, May 21, 41. Study: Miami Univ, 59-60; Art Inst Chicago, BFA & MFA. Work: Walker Art Ctr, Minneapolis. Exhib: Chicago & Vicinity Show, Art Inst Chicago, 64; Walker Art Ctr, 68; New American Abstract Painting, Madison Art Ctr, 72; Prospect, Dusseldorf, Ger, 73; Bykert Gallery, New York, 74. Teaching: Instr painting, Minneapolis Sch Art, 66-68, Sch Visual Arts, New York, 68-71 & NY Univ, 71-74. Mailing Add: c/o Leonard B Stern & Co 274 Madison Ave New York NY 10016

ZUCKER, MURRAY HARVEY
PAINTER, SCULPTOR
b New York, NY, Dec 14, 20. Work: AFL-CIO Hq, Washington, DC; Community Blood Coun, New York; Omaha Nat Bank, Nebr; Butler Inst of Am Art, Ohio. Comn: Paintings, Atlantic Richfield Co, New York, 68, Technicon Corp, Ardsley, NY, 69 & Police Benevolent Asn, New York, 70. Exhib: 32nd Ann, Audubon Artists, New York, 74; 20th Ann, Ball State Teachers Col, Muncie, Ind, 74; 21st Ann, Nat Soc Painters in Casein & Acrylic, New York, 74; Annuals, Am Soc Contemp Artists, New York, 75 & 77; Artists Equity of New York, 75 & 77. Awards: Hon mention, Pa Acad Fine Arts, 66; B F Morrow Award, Am Vet Soc Artists, 72; Heydenryk Award, Am Soc Contemp Artists, 75 & First Prize for Graphics, 76. Bibliog: C Crane (auth), Contemporary collages, Interiors, 5/70; Gerald F Brommer (auth), Collaging with Paper, Davis Publ, Inc, 78. Mem: Int Platform Asn; Artists Equity Asn; Am Soc Contemp Artists; Am Soc Interior Designers. Style & Technique: Abstract hard edged organic forms applied in flat bold color. Media: Unique Bronze, Acrylic, Collage. Mailing Add: 253 E 62nd St New York NY 10021

ZUCKERBERG, STANLEY M
PAINTER
b New York, NY, Sept 13, 19. Study: Pratt Inst; Art Students League; also with George Bridgman, Harold Von Schmidt, Norman Rockwell, Nick Riley, Khosrov Ajootian & Alexander Kostello. Work: Grand Cent Art Galleries, New York. Exhib: Grand Cent Art Galleries; Allied Am Artists Ann, Nat Acad, New York; Blair Gallery, Santa Fe, NMex; La Galeria, Sedona, Ariz. Awards: Todays' Art Award, Todays' Art Mag, 66; David Wu Ject Key Mem Award, Allied Artists Am; First Prize, Southern Shore Artists Asn. Bibliog: Ralph Fabri (auth), Marine breakwater, Todays' Art Mag, 67; Henry Gasser (auth), Stanley Zuckerberg On The Waterfront, Am Artist Mag, 6/74; John Legakes (auth), Days of my love, Publ Weekly. Mem: Allied Artists Am; Artists Fel; Am Artists Prof League; Salmagundi Club; Soc Illusr New York. Style & Technique: Realism in oil, specializing in waterfront subjects. Media: Oil with Brush, Oil with Knife. Mailing Add: 21 Old Farm Rd Levittown NY 11756

ZUGOR, SANDOR
PAINTER
b Brod, Yugoslavia, Feb 7, 23; US citizen. Study: Acad Fine Art, Budapest, 41-45, with Istvan Szonyi; Hungarian Acad Rome, fel, 46-48, graphics with Varga Nandor Lajos. Work: Mus Fine Art Budapest; Gallery of Mod Art, Taipei, Taiwan; Butler Inst of Am Art, Youngstown, Ohio; Munic Mus Budapest; Ministry Cult Affairs, Vienna. Exhib: Nat Mus Hist, Taipei, Taiwan; Budapest Nat Exhibs, Nat Gallery Art, 54 & 55; Young Americans, Mus Contemp Crafts, New York, 62; Brooklyn Mus, 69; Palacio Bellas Artes, Mexico City, 72; Nat Mus Hist Gallery, Repub China, 74; plus others. Teaching: Lectr drawing, Brooklyn Col Adult Educ, 66-71. Awards: First Prize for Peace & War, Fedn Hungarian Artists, 54. Media: Etching; Acrylics, Oil. Mailing Add: 463 West St New York NY 10014

ZULPO-DANE, BILL
PHOTOGRAPHER
b Pasadena, Calif, Nov 12, 38. Study: Univ Calif, Berkeley, BA(art & polit sci), 64 & MA(painting), 68. Work: Mus Mod Art, New York; Nat Gallery Can, Ottawa. Exhib: One-man shows, Painting, Sculpture, Snapshots, Reese Palley Gallery, San Francisco, 70, Unfamiliar Places, A Message from Bill Dane, Mus Mod Art, New York, 73, Ctr Creative Photog, Univ Ariz, Tucson, 76 & De Young Mus, San Francisco, 77; Landscape Discovery, Hofstra Univ, Long Island, NY, 73; Recent Am Still Photog, Edinburg Art Ctr, Scotland, 76; Concerning Photog, Photogr Gallery, London, 77. Awards: Fel in Photog, Guggenheim Mem Found, 73-74; Nat Endowment for the Arts photog fel, 76 & 78. Style & Technique: Still photography. Publ: Contribr, The Snapshot, Aperture Publ, 74; contribr, On Time, Mus Mod Art Calendar, 75. Mailing Add: 410 Washington Ave Point Richmond CA 94801

ZUNIGA, FRANCISCO
SCULPTOR
b San Jose, Costa Rica, Dec 31, 11. Work: Middelheim Mus, Antwerpen, Belg; Fogg Art Mus, Cambridge, Mass; Fine Arts Galleries San Diego; Mus Arte Mod, Mexico City, Mex; Phoenix Art Mus, Ariz. Comn: Monument, Nuevo Laredo, Mex, 58; Monumento a Cuauhtemoc, Quito, Ecuador, 61; Fuentes Monumentales, Chapultepec, Mexico City, 62; reliefs, Edigicio Secretaria de Communicaciones; Estatua a Benito Juarez, Gobierno de Michoacan, Morelia, Mich. Exhib: 3rd Sculpture Int, Philadelphia Mus Art, 49; Expos F Zuniga, Mus Nac, San Jose, Costa Rica, 54; Kunst Mexikaner, Köln, Ger, 59; Expos Zuniga, Fine Arts Gallery San Diego & Phoenix Art Ms, 71. Awards: Primer Piemio Escultura, Costa Rica, Expos Art Centro Americano, 35; Premio for Diego Rivera, 2nd Biennial Inter-Am Art, 60; Premio Adquisicion, Inst Nac Bellas Artes. Bibliog: Rosa Gonzalez (auth), Dictionnaire de la Sculpture Moderne, Paris, 60; Ali Chumxcero (auth), Zuniga, Misrachi, Mexico, 69. Dealer: Galeria Tasende Ave M Aleman Acapulco Guerrero Mexico. Mailing Add: Privada de Xontepec 9 Tlalpan Mexico DF México

ZVER, JAMES M
PAINTER, PRINTMAKER
b Chicago, Ill, May 30, 35. Study: Art Inst of Chicago, 53-57; Univ Chicago, BFA, 53-57; Cornell Univ, MFA(grad teachingassistantship), 67-69. Work: Speed Mus of Art, Louisville, Ky; Brown Univ, Providence, RI; Univ Tex, Houston; Mills Col, Oakland, Calif; Herron Mus of Art, Indianapolis, Ind. Exhib: Chicago Artists Exhib, Art Inst of Chicago, 57-58; Los Angeles to New York, Drawings of the sixties (numerous mus and univs throughout the US), 67; Painting & Sculpture Today, Herron Mus of Art, 67-68; Contemp Painting Exhib, Silvermine Guild of Artists, 68; Contemp Reflections, Larry Aldrich Mus, Ridgefield, Conn, 75; one-man shows, Durlacher Brother Gallery, New York, 66, Larcada Gallery, New York, 68, Emily Lowe Gallery, Hofstra Univ, Hempstead, New York, 72 & The Soho Ctr for Visual Artists, 76. Teaching: Instr graphics, Pratt Graphics Art Ctr, New York, 65-67, Sch of Visual Arts, New York, 69-70 & painting & graphics, Hofstra Univ, Hempstead, 70-76. Bibliog: Article in Art News, 66; Grace Gluck (auth), Soho Artists, New York Times, 74; Emily Geneaur (auth), 10 Downtown Artists, New York Post, 74. Mem: Alumni Asn, Sch of the Art Inst of Chicago. Style & Technique: Primarily large wall collages made of a fiber-glass material involving use of photographic Silk screen process. Media: Painting and Related Collage Pieces; Lithography; Silkscreen. Dealer: Andreas Brown c/o Gotham Book Mart Gallery 41 W 47th St New York NY 10017; Fredrick Merida c/o Merida Gallery 415 Westport Rd Louisville KY 40207. Mailing Add: 16 Greene St New York NY 10013

ZWEERTS, ARNOLD
PAINTER, EDUCATOR
b Bussum, Neth, 18; US citizen. Study: Sch for Arts & Crafts & Sch for Art Teacher Training, Royal Acad Art, Amsterdam; Royal Acad Art, Copenhagen, Denmark; Acad Belli Arti, Ravenna, Italy; Inst Allende, Univ Guanajunto, Mex, MFA; also study with Jos Rovers, Riseby, Orselli, Signoriny & Kortlang. Work: Stedelijk Mus, Amsterdam; Collection of the State, The Hague, Neth; also pvt collections in Denmark, Eng, Norway, Holland, US & Mex. Comn: Mosaics, Hengelo, Neth, 54, Lockhorst, Koldewyn, Van Eyck, Rotterdam Architects, 55-56, Chicago Process Gear Co, 61, Boulder Med Arts Bldg, Colo, 63-64 & Lombard Dental Med Bldg, 72, 73 & 74; mosaic (8ft x 8ft), Postville Sch House, Wis, 76-77. Exhib: One-man shows, Amsterdam, Neth, 48 & Chicago Merchandise Mart, 60; St Paul Gallery Art, Minn, 62; Art Inst Chicago, 66; The Barn—A Vanishing Landmark, SDak & Mo, 77; plus many others. Teaching: Instr mosaic & color, Kingston Upon Thames, Surrey, Eng, 51-53; instr appreciation of art, Stedelijk Mus, Rijkmus, Amsterdam, 54-57; asst prof drawing & painting, Art Inst Chicago, 57-73; lectr, dept fine arts, Loyola Univ Chicago, 68- Awards: First Prize/Printmaking, Civic Fine Arts Asn, Sioux Falls, 76; Award of Hon, 63 Salon, Madison Art Mus, 77; Art Award Nomination, Best Single Art Work in Chicago & Vicinity, Chicago Art Awards, 77. Bibliog: Pieter Scheen (auth), Lexicon Nederlandse Beeldende Kunstenaars 1750-1950, Part II, Kunsthandel P Scheen N V, The Hague, 70. Style & Technique: Expressionist oil paintings, mosaic woodcuts. Publ: Auth, articles in Bussumsche Courant, 50; auth, A renaissance in architectural art?, Delphian Quart, Vol 43, No 4. Mailing Add: Postville School House Rte 1 Box 53 Blanchardville WI 53516

ZWICK, ROSEMARY G
SCULPTOR, PRINTMAKER
b Chicago, Ill, July 13, 25. Study: Univ Iowa, with Phillip Guston & Abrizio, BFA, 45; Art Inst Chicago, with Max Kahn, 45-47; De Paul Univ, 46. Work: Oak Park Libr Collection, Ill; Albion Col Print Collection, Mich; Reavis Sch Collection, Chicago; Phoenix Pub Schs Collection, Ariz; Crow Island Sch, Winnetka, Ill; plus others. Comn: Two sculpture animal forms, Wonderland Shopping Ctr, Livonia, Mich, 60; wall relief, Motorola Co, Chicago, 62; sculpture, Temple B'nai Jenoshua, Morton Grove, Ill, 68; large seated figure, Blue Island Libr, Ill, 71. Exhib: Art Inst Chicago, 54-78; Ceramic Nat, Everson Mus Art, Syracuse, NY, 60, 62 & 64; Soc Washington Printmakers, Nat Mus, Washington, DC, 64; Mundelein Col, Chicago, 64-71; Indianapolis Mus Art, 70-78; Bicentennial Sculpture, E Leyden Sch Libr, 77. Pos: Staff artist, Jr Arts & Activities Mag, 45-47; assoc, Four Arts Gallery, Evanston, Ill, 62- Bibliog: John B Kenny (auth), Ceramic design, Chilton, 63; Wesley Buchwald (auth), Craftsmen in Illinois, Ill Art Educ Asn, 65. Mem: Renaissance Soc, Univ Chicago; Am Craftsmen Soc; Chicago Soc Artists. Style & Technique: Semi-abstract to abstract, slab built,

welded sculpture. Media: Ceramics. Specialty: Japanese prints midwestern artists and craftsmen. Dealer: Collector's Showroom 325 N Wells Chicago IL 60654; Four Arts Gallery 1629 Oak Ave Evanston IL 60201. Mailing Add: 1720 Washington St Evanston IL 60202

ZWICKER, LEROY JUDSON
PAINTER
b Halifax, NS, Can, July 21, 06. Study: NS Col of Art, DFA; Skowhegan Sch of Art, Maine, with Jack Levine & Henry Varnum Porr; also with Alfred Pellan, St Rose, Que. Work: Nat Gallery of Can, Ottawa, Ont; Art Gallery of NS, Halifax. Exhib: Paris Salon, France; Brit Empire Exhib, London, Eng; Nat Gallery of Can, Ottawa; Royal Can Acad of Art, Toronto; Montreal Art Asn, Que; NS Soc of Artists, Halifax; Maritime Art Asn, St John, NB; Can Soc of Watercolors, Toronto; one-man show, Leroy Zwicker in Retrospect, Art Gallery of NS, Halifax, 75. Mem: NS Soc of Artists; Maritime Art Asn. Style & Technique: Traditional to abstract. Media: Oil. Dealer: Manuge Art Dealer Hollis St Halifax NS Can. Mailing Add: 588 Younge Ave Halifax NS B3H 2V5 Can

Geographic Index

ALABAMA

Auburn

Hatfield, Donald Gene Painter, Educator
Olson, Douglas John Painter, Educator
Ross, Conrad Harold Printmaker, Educator
Ross, Janice Koenig Painter
Sykes, (William) Maltby Painter, Printmaker
Trentham, Gary Lynn Educator, Fiber Artist

Bessemer

Leader, Garnet Rosamonde Art Administrator

Birmingham

Barnett, Ed Willis Photographer, Writer
Creecy, Herbert Lee, Jr Painter, Sculptor
Farmer, John David Art Historian, Art Administrator
Hames, Carl Martin Art Dealer, Collector
Howard, Richard Foster Art Administrator
Hulsey, William Hansell Collector
Lewis, Ronald Walter Painter, Instructor
Price, Rosalie Pettus Painter
Rankin, Don Painter
Shelton, Robert Lee Designer, Educator
Stewart, Arthur Painter
Weeks, Edward F Art Historian, Museologist

Dothan

Watford, Frances Mizelle Painter, Gallery Director

Fairhope

Gatling, Eva Ingersoll Museum Consultant, Art Historian.
Woodward, Cleveland Landon Painter, Illustrator

Hartselle

Howell, Elizabeth Ann (Mitch) Painter, Illustrator

Huntsville

Bayer, Jeffrey Joshua Educator, Sculptor
Bowles, Thomas Andrew, III Art Administrator, Art Historian
Boyd, Lakin Educator, Printmaker
Hudson, Ralph Magee Art Historian, Educator
Parrish, David Buchanan Painter
Pearson, Clifton Sculptor, Educator
Pope, Mary Ann Irwin Painter
Pope, Richard Coraine Painter, Designer
Reeves, James Franklin Art Historian, Collector
Rubin, Donald Vincent Sculptor
Savas, Jo-Ann (Mrs George T Savas) Painter, Instructor

Jacksonville

Page, Bill Painter, Educator

Mentone

Graham, John Meredith, II Art Administrator

Mobile

Altmayer, Jay P Collector
Blackburn, Lenora Whitmire Collector
Conlon, James Edward Sculptor, Art Historian
Figures, Alfred Painter, Educator
Kennedy, James Edward Painter, Sculptor
Koch, William Emery Art Dealer, Collector
Lassiter, Vernice (Vernice Lassiter Brown) Painter
Victor, Mary O'Neill Museum Director

Montgomery

Britt, Al Painter, Educator
Brooks, Louise Cherry Collector, Ceramist
Robert, Henry Flood, Jr Museum Director

Opelika

Furr, Jim Painter, Printmaker

Ozark

Deloney, Jack Clouse Painter, Illustrator

South Birmingham

Schnorrenberg, John Martin Art Historian, Art Administrator

Tuscaloosa

Zoellner, Richard C Printmaker, Painter

Tuskegee

Thomas, Elaine Freeman Educator, Art Administrator

Tuskegee Institute

Jarkowski, Stefania Agnes Painter, Educator

University

Brough, Richard Burrell Educator, Designer
Sella, Alvin Conrad Painter, Educator

ALASKA

Anchorage

Appel, Keith Kenneth Painter, Printmaker
Ard, Saradell (Saradell Ard Frederick) Educator, Painter
Austin, Pat Printmaker, Educator
Birdsall, Byron Painter
Conaway, Gerald Sculptor, Painter
Cooke, Jody Helen Painter, Educator
Gordon, Josephine Painter
Hedman, Teri Jo Printmaker, Painter
Kimura, William Yusaburo Painter
Owens, Tennys Bowers Art Dealer
Pitcher, John Charles Painter
Regat, Jean Jacques Sculptor, Muralist
Regat, Mary E Sculptor, Muralist
Shadrach, Jean H Painter, Art Dealer
Shalkop, Robert Leroy Museum Director, Art Historian
Sommer, Wassily Painter, Educator
Vallee, William Oscar Painter

Cordova

Bugbee, Joan Scott Sculptor, Educator

Fairbanks

Berry, William David Illustrator, Sculptor
Brody, Arthur William Printmaker, Painter
Choy, Terence Tin-Ho Painter, Educator

Juneau

De Armond, Dale B Printmaker
Munoz, Rie (Marie Angelina Munoz) Painter, Printmaker

Ketchikan

Wheeler, Mark Illustrator, Designer

Palmer

Machetanz, Fred Painter, Lithographer

ARIZONA

Bisbee

Gilbert, Herb Painter, Graphic Artist
Young, Peter Ford Painter

Carefree

Harris, Robert George Painter, Illustrator

Cave Creek

Cox, Marion Averal Painter, Instructor
Patch, Peggie (Margaret Thompson Williamson) Painter, Art Dealer
Sproul, Ann Stephenson Painter
Williamson, Jason H Painter, Art Dealer

Cottonwood

Waddell, John Henry Sculptor

ARIZONA (cont)

Flagstaff

Anderson, James P Sculptor, Educator
Brookins, Jacob Boden Craftsman, Sculptor
Horn, Bruce Printmaker, Educator
Monthan, Guy Photographer, Educator
Owen, Bill Painter, Sculptor
Van Wert, Gordon Franklin Sculptor, Instructor

Glendale

Dewey, Kenneth Francis Painter, Illustrator

Green Valley

Porter, J Erwin Painter

Hotevilla

Loloma, Charles Jeweler, Designer

Kingman

Schliefer, Stafford Lerrig Painter, Lecturer

Mayer

Polk, Frank Fredrick Sculptor

Mesa

Halbach, David Allen Painter, Instructor
O'Dell, Erin (Anne) Painter, Designer
Slater, Gary Lee Sculptor
Westin, Robert H Art Historian
Woods, Ted Sculptor, Craftsman

Oracle

McGrew, Bruce Elwin Painter, Instructor
Rush, Andrew Printmaker, Painter

Paradise Valley

Keane, Bil Cartoonist
McCall, Robert Theodore Painter, Illustrator
Micale, Albert Painter, Illustrator
Ruskin, Lewis J Collector, Patron

Phoenix

Airola, Paavo Painter, Writer
Bales, Jewel Painter
Bermudez, Jose Ygnacio Sculptor, Painter
Blair, Helen (Helen Blair Crosbie) Sculptor, Illustrator
Broadley, Hugh T Art Historian, Art Administrator
Brown, Suzanne Goldman Gallery Owner, Art Historian
Burns, Sid Sculptor, Collector
Cole, Frances Painter
Dignac, Geny (Eugenia M Bermudez) Sculptor, Painter
Fink, Ray (Raymond Russell) Sculptor, Educator
Frerichs, Ruth Colcord Painter
Golubic, Theodore Sculptor, Designer
Grigsby, Jefferson Eugene, Jr Educator, Painter
Hack, Phillip S & Patricia Y Collectors
Heit, Steven Robert Art Dealer
Hickman, Ronald Dean Museum Director
Hill, John Conner Designer, Publisher
Houlihan, Patrick Thomas Museum Director
Jacobson, Arthur Robert Painter, Printmaker
Jacobson, Ursula Mercedes Painter, Sculptor
Kniffin, Ralph Gus Pen and Ink Artist
Knudson, Robert LeRoy Painter
Mahaffey, Merrill Dean Painter, Instructor
McCarthy, Frank C Painter
Monongye, Preston Lee Silversmith, Goldsmith
Moore, Ina May Instructor, Painter
Morez, Mary Painter, Illustrator
Norton, Mary Joyce Painter
Phillips, Irving W Cartoonist, Illustrator
Pritzlaff, Mr & Mrs John, Jr Collectors
Quinn, Brian Grant Sculptor
Richter, Hank Painter, Sculptor
Riley, Roy John Painter, Designer
Sutherland, Marylou Art Librarian
Trlak, Roger Painter, Designer
Ullman, Mrs George W Collector
Warner, Boyd, Jr Painter
Yanosky, Tom Painter, Designer
Young, Marjorie Ward Painter

Pine

Toschik, Larry Painter, Writer

Pinewood

Carpenter, Earl L Painter

Prescott

Chethlahe (David Chethlahe Paladin) Painter, Designer
Moreton, Russell Painter
Polland, Donald Jack Sculptor
Sommer, Frederick Painter, Photographer, Landscape Architect
Swanson, Ray V Painter

Rimrock

Dyck, Paul Painter, Art Director

Scottsdale

Abeita, Jim Painter
Armstrong, John Albert Art Administrator, Printmaker
Austin, Jo-Anne Jordan Art Dealer
Curtis, Philip Campbell Painter
Davis, Lew E Painter
Dorr, Goldthwaite Higginson, III Art Dealer
Gentry, Warren Miller Instructor, Painter
Goo, Benjamin Sculptor, Painter
Greenbowe, F Douglas Painter
Hampton, John W Painter, Sculptor
Heller, Jules Printmaker, Writer
Huldermann, Paul F Art Dealer, Lecturer
Lang, Margo Terzian Painter
Lehrer, Leonard Painter, Educator
Love, Paul Van Derveer Gallery Director, Art Historian
Manning, Reg (West) Cartoonist, Writer
Metz, Gerry Michael Painter, Instructor
O'Brien, William Vincent Art Dealer
Sanderson, Raymond Phillips Sculptor
Schimmel, William Berry Painter, Lecturer
Scholder, Fritz Painter, Printmaker
Soleri, Paolo Architect-Environmental Planner, Sculptor
Swartz, Beth Ames Painter
Texidor, Fernando Painter, Graphic Designer
Udinotti, Agnese Sculptor, Painter

Second Mesa

Coochsiwukioma, DH (Del Honanie) Painter, Sculptor
Kabotie, Fred Painter, Designer

Sedona

Beeler, Joe (Neil) Painter
Lunge, Jeffrey (Roy) Painter
Pendleton, Mary Caroline Handweaver, Writer
Reynolds, James Elwood Painter
Turrell, James Archie Artist
Yoakum, Delmer J Painter, Designer

Sun City

Bittner, Hans Oskar Painter, Illustrator
Bolster, Ella S Designer, Weaver
Luitjens, Helen Anita Instructor, Painter
Salter, John Randall Sculptor, Painter

Tempe

Bush, Donald John Art Historian, Educator
Dawson, John Allan Painter
DeMatties, Nick Frank Printmaker
Gillingwater, Denis Claude Painter, Sculptor
Gully, Anthony Lacy Art Historian
Jay, Bill Photographic Historian, Art Critic
Kampen, Michael Edwin Art Historian, Illustrator
Lewis, William R Instructor, Painter
Schmidt, Randall Bernard Sculptor, Educator
Stuler, Jack Photographer, Educator
Turk, Rudy H Museum Director, Art Historian
Wood, Harry Emsley, Jr Educator, Painter
Woods, Rip Painter, Educator

Tubac

Jenkinson, Geoffrey Painter
Wilson, Mortimer, Jr Painter, Illustrator

Tucson

Billmyer, John Edward Craftsman, Educator
Bredlow, Tom Designer, Blacksmith
Conant, Howard Somers Painter, Art Editor
Cone, Gerrit Craig Art Administrator
Croft, Michael Flynt Goldsmith, Educator
De Grazia, Ettore Ted Painter
Denniston, Douglas Painter, Educator
Gottschalk, Max Jules Designer, Instructor
Grygutis, Barbara Ceramist
Hanna, Boyd Everett Painter, Printmaker
Haskin, Donald Marcus Educator, Sculptor
Heric, John F Sculptor
Hupp, Frederick Duis Painter, Educator
Jones, Harold Henry Art Administrator, Photographer
Loney, Doris Howard Painter
Martin, Lucille Caiar (Mrs Hampton Martin) Painter
McMillan, Robert W Painter, Educator
Miller, Nancy Tokar Painter, Instructor
Pleasants, Frederick R Collector, Patron
Reich, Sheldon Art Historian
Sles, Steven Lawrence Painter, Poet
Stefan, Ross Painter
Tobias, Robert Paul Painter, Sculptor
Wilson, Nicholas Jon Painter
Wingate, Adina (R) Art Writer, Lecturer
Wiper, Thomas William Instructor, Painter
Zivic, William Thomas Painter, Sculptor

Williams

Cartledge, Roseanne Catherine Graphic Artist
Seaman, Drake F Painter

Window Rock

Gorman, Carl Nelson (Kin-ya-onny Beyeh) Painter, Lecturer

Yuma

Anderson, Brad J Cartoonist
Meinig, Laurel Art Administrator

ARKANSAS

Arkadelphia

Linn, John William Art Administrator, Art Writer
Raybon, Phares Henderson Painter, Educator

Clarksville

Ward, Lyle Edward Painter, Educator

Conway

Larsen, Patrick Heffner Painter, Sculptor
Thompson, Robert Charles Painter, Educator

Eureka Springs

Freund, Harry Louis Painter, Illustrator

Fayetteville

Cockrill, Sherna Painter, Instructor
Jensen, Cecil Leon Cartoonist
Reif, Rubin Painter, Educator

Jonesboro

Lindquist, Evan Printmaker, Educator
Mitchell, Robert Ellis Goldsmith, Educator

Little Rock

Graham, Bill (William Karr) Cartoonist
Kellogg, Maurice Dale Painter, Lecturer
Mapes, Doris Williamson Painter
Rembert, Virginia Pitts Art Historian
Schmidt, Frederick Lee Painter, Educator
Wolfe, Townsend Durant Painter, Art Administrator

Russellville

Wilwers, Edward Mathias Educator, Illustrator

Scott

Altvater, Catherine Tharp Painter

State University

Richards, Karl Frederick Educator, Painter

CALIFORNIA

Agoura

Hayden, Michael Sculptor

Alameda

Berlin, Beatrice Winn Printmaker, Painter
Perez, Vincent Painter, Instructor

Altadena

Green, David Oliver Sculptor, Educator
Outterbridge, John Wilfred Art Administrator, Painter, Sculptor

Anaheim

Macaray, Lawrence Richard Painter, Educator

Apple Valley

Hay-Messick, Velma Painter
Messick, Ben (Newton) Painter, Instructor

Arcadia

Hawkins, Thomas Wilson, Jr Painter, Instructor
Navratil, Amy R Art Librarian
Roysher, Hudson (Brisbine) Designer, Art Administrator

Arcata

Anderson, William Thomas Printmaker, Painter
Berry, Glenn Painter, Educator
Bullen, Reese Ceramist, Calligrapher
Knight, Thomas Lincoln, Jr Educator, Photographer
Land-Weber, Ellen E Photographer, Educator
LaPlantz, David Craftsman, Educator
Price, Leslie Kenneth Painter, Educator
Schuler, Melvin Albert Sculptor, Painter

Bakersfield

Rippey, Clayton Painter, Educator

Balboa Island

Schlup, Elaine Smitha Designer, Jeweler

Bayside

Bettiga, Floyd Henry Educator, Painter

Beaumont

Meltzer, Robert Hiram Instructor, Painter

Belvedere

Ludekens, Fred Painter, Illustrator

Benicia

Shannonhouse, Sandra Lynne Sculpture, Ceramist

Berkeley

Akawie, Thomas Frank Educator, Painter
Anderson, David Paul Sculptor, Instructor
Aylon, Helene Painter
Bechtle, Robert Alan Painter
Bischoff, Elmer Nelson Painter, Educator
Blos, May (Elizabeth) Illustrator, Painter
Blos, Peter W Painter, Instructor
Bony, Jean Victor Educator, Art Historian
Browne, Tom Martin Sculptor, Painter
Cahill, James Francis Art Historian, Educator
Candau, Eugenie Art Librarian
Cheney, Sheldon Writer, Art Historian
Chipp, Herschel Browning Educator, Curator
Davis, Jerrold Painter
Ettlinger, Leopold David Art Historian
Feldman, Bella Tabak Sculptor
Gantz, Jeanne A Printmaker, Art Administrator
Goetzl, Thomas Maxwell Art Writer, Lawyer, Educator
Gordin, Sidney Sculpture, Educator
Hoare, Tyler James Sculptor, Printmaker
Holland, Tom Painter
Kasten, Karl Albert Painter, Printmaker
Leon, Dennis Sculptor
Lipofsky, Marvin B Sculptor, Glass Blower
Loberg, Robert Warren Painter, Instructor
Loran, Erle Painter, Writer
Prestini, James Libero Sculptor, Designer
Ross, David Anthony Curator, Lecturer
Ruvolo, Felix Emmanuele Painter, Educator
St John, Terry N Painter, Curator
Sargent, Richard Painter, Curator
Sekimachi, Kay Weaver, Instructor
Selz, Peter H Art Historian
Shere, Charles Everett Art Critic
Shimizu, Yoshiaki Art Historian, Educator
Shoemaker, Peter Painter, Educator
Simpson, David Painter, Educator
Slusky, Joseph Sculptor, Instructor
Snelgrove, Walter H Painter
Voulkos, Peter Sculptor, Educator
Washburn, Stan Printmaker, Painter
Wonner, Paul (John) Painter
Worth, Carl Art Administrator

Beverly Hills

Brown, Harry Joe, Jr Collector
Cantor, B Gerald Collector
Chesney, Lee R, Jr Printmaker, Painter
Elmo, James Painter, Sculptor
Glover, Robert Leon Sculptor, Painter
Halff, Robert H Collector
Lewin, Bernard Art Dealer, Collector
Longstreet, Stephen Painter, Writer, Art Historian
Price, Vincent Collector, Art Dealer
Rifkind, Robert Gore Collector
Rustvold, Katherine Jo Art Dealer, Gallery Director
Secunda, (Holland) Arthur Painter, Collage Artist
Shane, Frederick E Painter, Educator

Big Sur

Owings, Margaret Wentworth Painter, Collage in Stitchery

Bishop

Wagoner, Robert B Painter, Sculptor

Blue Lake

Benson, Robert Franklin Painter, Instructor

Bodega

Morehouse, William Paul Painter, Sculptor

Bolinas

Carpenter, Arthur Espenet Craftsman, Lecturer
Harris, Paul Sculptor
Okamura, Arthur Painter

Brea

Foley, Kyoko Y Instructor, Painter

Burbank

Asmar, Alice Painter, Printmaker
Riley, Art (Arthur Irwin) Painter, Photographer

Burlingame

Lilienthal, Mr & Mrs Philip N, Jr Collectors

Calistoga

Thollander, Earl Illustrator, Graphic Artist

Cambria

Clark, Robert Charles Painter, Lecturer
Hamilton, Frank Moss Painter, Architect

Canoga Park

Hampton, Roy (George LeRoy Hampton) Painter

Cardiff

Sekula, Allan Video Artist, Art Critic

Carmel

Adams, Ansel Easton Photographer
Alinder, James Gilbert Photographer, Museum Director
Bates, Bill Cartoonist
Chang, Dai-Chien Painter
Cost, James Peter Painter
Crispo, Dick Painter, Printmaker
Dooley, Helen Bertha Painter, Art Dealer
Dowling, Daniel Blair Editorial Cartoonist
Enyeart, James Lyle Art Historian, Museum Director
Garcia, Danny Painter
Huth, Hans Art Historian
Huth, Marta Painter, Photographer
Jacobs, Ralph, Jr Painter
Lagorio, Irene R Painter, Printmaker
Laycox, (William) Jack Painter, Designer

CALIFORNIA (cont)

Mason, Harold Dean Printmaker, Painter
Miner, Ralph Hamlin Art Dealer, Designer
Mitchell, Donald Art Administrator, Art Dealer
Norman, Emile Painter, Sculptor
Oehler, Helen Gapen Painter, Lecturer
Shoemaker, Vaughn Editorial Cartoonist, Painter
Skalagard, Hans Marine Painter, Lecturer
Teague, Donald Painter
Timmins, William Frederick Painter, Illustrator
Zantman, J B Art Dealer

Carmel Valley

Baker, Eugene Ames Painter, Serigrapher
Cunningham, J Painter, Educator
Ketcham, Henry King (Hank) Cartoonist
Parker, Alfred Illustrator
Swanson, J N Painter, Sculptor

Carpinteria

Fine, Jud Sculptor
Plous, Phyllis Curator
Warshaw, Howard Painter

Castro Valley

Hunkler, Dennis Francis Painter, Printmaker
Kohn, Misch Painter, Printmaker

Chatsworth

Elder, David Morton Sculptor, Art Administrator
Harden, Marvin Painter, Educator

Chico

Epting, Marion Austin Printmaker, Educator
Feldhaus, Paul A Educator, Printmaker
Hornaday, Richard Hoyt Painter, Educator
McManus, James William Sculptor, Instructor
Turner, Janet E Printmaker, Educator

Chula Vista

Lewis, Marcia Jeweler-Metalsmith, Instructor

Claremont

Ackerman, Gerald Martin Art Historian, Educator
Ames, Arthur Forbes Painter, Educator
Ames, Jean Goodwin Designer, Painter
Benjamin, Karl Stanley Painter, Instructor
Blizzard, Alan Painter, Educator
Casanova, Aldo John Sculptor, Educator
Dike, Philip Latimer Painter, Designer
Furman, David Stephen Sculptor, Educator
Hueter, James Warren Sculptor, Painter
Humble, Douglas Gallery Director, Sculptor
Klotz-Reilly, Suzanne Ruth Painter, Sculptor
McIntosh, Harrison Edward Ceramist, Designer
Mix, Walter Joseph Painter, Educator
Pahl, James Robert, II Museum Director
Simon, Leonard Ronald Art Administrator, Art Writer
Steadman, David Wilton Art Historian, Gallery Director
Stewart, Albert T Sculptor
Watson, Halen Richter Ceramist, Sculptor

Clovis

Laury, Jean Ray (Jean Ray Bitters) Designer, Writer

Compton

Slater, Van E Printmaker, Educator

Corona Del Mar

Brandt, Rexford Elson Painter, Printmaker
DeLap, Tony Sculptor
Partch, Virgil Franklin, II Cartoonist, Illustrator
Procter, Burt Painter

Corte Madera

Potter, (George) Kenneth Painter, Designer
Tift, Mary Louise Printmaker

Costa Mesa

Green, Martin Leonard Painter, Printmaker
Kushner, Dorothy Browdy Painter, Instructor
Muller, Jerome Kenneth Collector, Art Dealer
Romans, Van Anthony Sculptor/Designer, Gallery Director
Serisawa, Sueo Painter

Cotati

Hudson, Robert H Sculptor

Culver City

De Larios, Dora Sculptor, Potter

Cupertino

Robinson, Wahneta Theresa Curator, Art Historian

Dana Point

McLaughlin, John D Painter

Danville

Urso, Richard Carl Sculptor

Davis

Arneson, Robert Carston Sculptor, Educator
McElroy, Nancy Lynn Sculptor, Designer
Petersen, Roland Conrad Painter, Printmaker
Thiebaud, (Morton) Wayne Painter, Educator

Del Mar

Antin, Eleanor Conceptual Artist, Video Artist
Braley, Jean Duffield Printmaker, Painter
Fredman, Faiya R Sculptor, Painter
Harrison, Helen Mayer Conceptual Artist, Photographer
Harrison, Newton A Ecological Artist, Educator
Herman, Vic Painter, Illustrator—Children's Books
Hewitt, Jean Clifford Art Dealer, Collector
Patterson, Patricia Film Critic, Painter
Snow, Cynthia Reeves Painter, Educator
Teilhet, Jehanne Hildegarde Art Historian, Lecturer

Downey

Steen, Ronald Earl Museum Director, Instructor

El Cajon

Lawrence, Jaye A Sculptor
Lawrence, Les Ceramist, Sculptor
Tatro, Ronald Edward Sculptor, Instructor

El Cerrito

Law, Carol L Printmaker, Performance Artist

El Dorado Hills

Woof, Maija (Maija Gegeris Zack Peeples) Painter

Encinitas

Perine, Robert Heath Painter
Provder, Carl Painter, Instructor
Rosler, Martha Rose Video Artist, Art Critic

Encino

Hoowij, Jan Painter
Hubenthal, Karl Samuel Cartoonist
Valerio, James Robert Painter, Educator
Wing, Robin Stewart Art Dealer, Art Administrator
Zamparelli, Mario Armond Designer, Collector

Escondido

Sternberg, Harry Painter, Graphic Artist

Eureka

Marak, Louis Bernard Ceramic Sculptor, Educator

Fairfax

Schulz, Cornelia Painter
Shaw, Richard Blake Sculptor
Stinski, Gerald Paul Painter, Collector

Felton

Cochran, Dewees (Dewees Cochran Helbeck) Designer, Painter

Folsom

McHugh, Adeliza Sorenson Art Dealer, Collector

Fresno

Bolomey, Roger Henry Sculptor, Art Historian
Herman, Susan L Painter, Printmaker
Maass, Richard Andrew Art Administrator
Maughelli, Mary L Painter, Lithographer
McCoon, Betty Jean Painter, Sculptor
McNitt, Miriam D Craftsman, Instructor
Musselman, Darwin B Painter, Educator
Pickford, Rollin, Jr Painter

Fullerton

Arnold, Florence M Painter
Cannon, Margaret Erickson Painter, Lecturer
Frankel, Dextra Educator Gallery Director
Partin, Robert (E) Painter, Educator

Garden Grove

Ortlieb, Robert Eugene Sculptor, Graphic Artist

Glendale

Ackerman, Frank Edward Painter, Designer
Gill, Gene Painter, Printmaker
Herman, Alan David Designer, Writer
Hoffberg, Judith Ann Art Librarian, Art Consultant
Moure, Nancy Dustin Wall Curator, Writer

Goleta

Thomas, Robert Chester Sculptor

Green Valley Lake

Svenson, John Edward Sculptor, Collector
Wood, Robert E Painter, Instructor

Gualala

Sheets, Millard Owen Designer, Painter

Guerneville

Barrio, Raymond Writer, Painter

Hemet

Hutchison, Elizabeth S Painter

Hillsborough

Siberell, Anne Hicks Printmaker, Illustrator

Hollywood

Band, Max Painter, Sculptor
Huntington, Daphne Painter, Muralist
Ruscha, Edward Joseph Painter, Filmmaker
Sauls, Frederick Inabinette Sculptor, Painter
Souza, Paul Marciel Painter, Instructor
Tseu, Rosita Hsu Art Administrator, Instructor

Huntington Beach

Thompson, Joanne Painter, Sculptor

Imperial Beach

Garman, Ed Painter, Writer

Indian Wells

Love, Rosalie Bowen Painter, Instructor

Indio

Edens, Lettye P Art Dealer, Painter

Inglewood

Young, Milton Painter, Sculptor

Inverness

Foote, Howard Reed Artist, Printmaker
Onslow Ford, Gordon M Painter
Storer, Inez Mary Painter, Art Dealer

Kentfield

Galli, Stanley Walter Illustrator, Painter
Moquin, Richard Attilio Sculptor, Educator

Kenwood

Hein, Max Printmaker, Instructor

La Jolla

Adler, Sebastian J Museum Director
Baxter, Patricia Huy Curator
Byrne, Charles Joseph Designer
Forester, Russell Painter
Geisel, Theodor Seuss (Dr Seuss) Illustrator, Writer
Ingraham, Esther Price Painter
Inverarity, Robert Bruce Designer, Museum Director
Jones, Douglas McKee (Doug) Painter, Art Dealer
Key-Oberg, Ellen Burke Sculptor
Lonidier, Fred Spencer Conceptual Artist, Photographer
Luna (Antonio Rodriguez Luna) Painter
Mark, Bendor Painter
McGilvery, Laurence Antiquarian Book Dealer, Publisher
McReynolds, (Joe) Cliff Painter, Instructor
Monaghan, Eileen (Mrs Frederic Whitaker) Painter
O'Hara, (James) Frederick Printmaker
Reilly, Richard Art Critic
Stewart, John Lincoln Educator, Writer
Stratton, Dorothy (Mrs William A King) Painter, Printmaker
Wenger, Muriel June Art Dealer, Collector
Wenger, Sigmund Art Dealer, Art Consultant
Werner, Fritz Painter
Whitaker, Frederic Painter, Writer

La Mesa

Blackmun, Barbara Winston Educator, Art Historian
Coffelt, Beth Art Administrator, Writer
Kimball, Wilford Wayne, Jr Draftsman, Lithographer
Lebeck, Carol E Ceramist
Swiggett, Jean Donald Educator, Painter

La Verne

Brown, Reynold Painter, Illustrator

Lafayette

Beaumont, Mona M Painter, Printmaker
Schnier, Jacques Sculptor

Laguna Beach

Anderson, Ivan Delos Painter, Printmaker
Blacketer, James Richard Painter, Art Dealer
Burchfield, Jerry Lee Photographer, Educator
Challis, Richard Bracebridge Art Dealer
Darrow, Paul Gardner Painter, Educator
De Mille, Leslie Benjamin Painter
Enman, Tom Kenneth Painter, Museum Director
Gasparian, Armen Tigran Instructor, Painter
Jones, Barbara Nester Painter
Kaplan, Leonard Art Dealer, Painter
Kauffman, Robert Craig Painter, Sculptor
Kinghan, Charles Ross Painter
Peche, Dale C Painter
Sassone, Marco Painter
Scheu, Leonard Painter, Lecturer
Solomon, David Painter, Designer

Laguna Hills

Armstrong, Roger Joseph Painter, Cartoonist
Beson, Roberta (Roberta Beson Hill) Painter, Art Administrator
Hill, Dale Logan Painter, Instructor

Lagunitas

Holman, Arthur (Stearns) Painter

Lake Arrowhead

Vigil, Veloy Joseph Painter, Printmaker

Larkspur

Defeo, Jay Painter, Photographer
Frances, Harriette Anton Painter, Printmaker

Loleta

Graves, Morris Painter

Long Beach

Bledsoe, Jane Kathryn Art Historian, Art Administrator
Ferreira, (Armando) Thomas Educator, Sculptor
Glenn, Constance White Art Administrator, Art Historian
Swift, Dick Printmaker, Educator

Los Altos

Bunn, Cecine Cole Painter, Lecturer
Hobbs, (Carl) Fredric Sculptor, Film Maker

Los Altos Hills

Silver, Pat Draftsman, Art Dealer

Los Angeles

Adler, Billy (Telethon) Sculptor, Photographer
Alhilali, Neda Multimedia Artist, Sculptor
Anhalt, Jacqueline Richards Art Dealer
Ankrum, Joan Art Dealer
Aron, Kalman Painter
Asher, Betty M Collector
Bailey, Walter Alexander Painter, Writer
Baker, George Sculptor
Bass, Joel Painter
Baum, Hank Art Dealer, Lecturer
Bednarz, Adele Art Dealer
Berg, Phil Collector, Patron
Berman, Nancy Mallin Museum Director, Art Historian
Beydler, Gary Earl Sculptor, Photographer
Biberman, Edward Painter, Lecturer
Blankfort, Dorothy Collector
Blankfort, Michael Collector
Bloch, E Maurice Art Historian, Educator
Blumberg, Ron Painter, Instructor
Bowater, Marian Art Dealer, Collector
Bowman, Ruth Educator, Art Historian
Brendel, Bettina Painter, Lecturer
Brewer, Donald J Museum Director, Art Historian
Brice, William Painter, Educator
Broderson, Morris Painter
Brody, Mr & Mrs Sidney F Collectors
Brooks, Lois Ziff Textile Artist, Educator
Bueno, Jose (Joe Goode) Sculptor, Painter
Burkhardt, Hans Gustav Painter, Collector
Burton, Gloria Sculptor, Painter
Byrnes, James Bernard Museum Director, Art Historian
Card, Greg S Sculptor, Painter
Cho, David Sculptor
Chuey, Robert Arnold Painter, Lecturer
Clayberger, Samuel Robert Painter, Educator
Clemens, Paul Painter, Writer
Clothier, Peter Dean Art Administrator, Art Critic
Colverson, Ian Printmaker, Lecturer
Conrad, Paul Francis Cartoonist
Copley, Claire Strohn Art Dealer, Lecturer
Cremean, Robert Sculptor
Crown, Keith Allen Painter, Educator
Curran, Darryl Joseph Photographer, Printmaker
D'Andrea, Jeanne Art Administrator, Designer
Darricarrere, Roger Dominique Sculptor, Stained Glass Artist
Davidson, J LeRoy Art Historian
Davis, Alonzo Joseph Visual Artist, Art Administrator
Davis, L Clarice Art Book Dealer, Art Historian
De Bretteville, Sheila Levrant Designer, Instructor
Dentzel, Carl Schaefer Museum Director, Writer
Dillon, Paul Sanford Painter
Dimondstein, Morton Sculptor, Painter
Donahue, Kenneth Museum Director, Art Historian
Doolin, James Lawrence Painter, Instructor
Douke, Daniel W Painter, Educator
Dreiband, Laurence Painter
Edge, Douglas Benjamin Sculptor, Photographer
Edwards, Joy M Art Dealer
Ellis, George Richard Museum Director
Elsky, Herb Sculptor
Epler, Venetia Painter, Muralist
Ewing, Edgar Louis Painter
Feinblatt, Ebria Art Historian
Feitelson, Lorser Painter
Fels, C P Painter, Writer
Fenci, Renzo Sculptor
Fender, Tom Mac Sculptor
Fichter, Herbert Francis Printmaker, Painter
Fichter, Robert Photographer
Finch, Keith Bruce Painter
Finkelstein, Max Sculptor, Instructor
Flick, Robert Photographer, Educator
Francis, Sam Painter
Gibson, George Painter, Art Administrator
Gilbert, Arthur Collector, Patron
Glasgow, Lukman Gallery Director, Sculptor
Glicksman, Hal Gallery Director, Educator
Goedike, Shirl Painter

CALIFORNIA (cont)
Gold, Betty Art Dealer
Gonzalez, Jose Luis Art Administrator, Restorer
Goodman, Calvin Jerome Art Consultant, Lecturer
Gordon, Joni Art Dealer, Collector
Goulds, Peter J Art Dealer, Designer
Greaves, James L Conservator
Greenwald, Alice (Alice Marian Greenwald-Ward) Curator, Lecturer
Grieger, (Walter) Scott Sculptor
Guerriero, Henry Edward Sculptor
Hamilton, John Printmaker
Hammer, Armand Collector, Art Dealer
Hamrol, Lloyd Sculptor
Hansen, Robert Painter
Heinecken, Robert Friedli Photographer, Educator
Heinz, Susan Art Administrator
Henderson, Victor (Lance) Painter, Photographer
Hernandez, Anthony Louis Photographer
Herschler, David Sculptor
Hoopes, Donelson Farquhar Museum Curator, Art Historian
Horowitz, Benjamin Art Administrator, Art Dealer
Hough, Richard Photographer, Designer
Huebler, Douglas Sculptor
Hugo, Joan (Dowey) Art Librarian, Art Writer
Irwin, Robert Painter
Isaacs, Claire Naomi Gallery Director
Iskin, Ruth Evelyn Art Historian, Educator
Jackson, Suzanne Fitzallen Painter, Writer
Johnston, Ynez Painter, Printmaker
Jones, William Ezelle Curator, Lecturer
Kahlenberg, Mary Hunt Art Historian, Curator
Kalavrezou-Maxeiner, Ioli Art Historian
Kanemitsu, Matsumi Painter, Lecturer
Kaplan, Julius David Art Historian
Kataoka, Mits Designer, Video Artist
Kazor, Virginia Ernst Curator
Kester, Lenard Painter
Kim, Bongtae Painter, Printmaker
Kisner, Bernard Collector
Klein, Cecelia F Art Historian, Educator
Kovinick, Philip Peter Researcher, Writer
Kreitzer, David Martin Painter
Kuwayama, George Curator, Art Historian
Lacy, Suzanne Performance Artist, Educator
Landau, Felix Art Dealer
Landau, Mitzi Art Dealer, Curator
Landers, Bertha Painter, Printmaker
Lark, Raymond Painter, Draftsman
Larsen, Susan C Art Historian, Art Critic
Lecoque Painter, Writer
Leeper, John P Painter
Lem, Richard Douglas Painter
Leonard, Leon Lank, Sr Painter, Sculptor
Leopold, Michael Christopher Art Critic
Lewis, Samella Sanders Painter, Art Historian
Lloyd, Gary Marchal Sculptor, Educator
Logan, Gene Adams Sculptor, Painter
Lubner, Martin Paul Painter
Ludmer, Joyce Pellerano Art Librarian, Art Historian
Lundeberg, Helen (Helen Lundeberg Feitelson) Painter
Mason, John Sculptor
McCracken, John Harvey Sculptor, Painter
McMillan, Jerry Edward Photographer, Sculptor
Mekler, Adam Art Dealer, Curator
Mesaros, Ron Photographer
Milant, Jean Robert Art Dealer
Miller, George Conceptual Artist, Writer
Mirano, Virgil Marcus Photographer, Educator
Moore, Russell James Museum Director, Art Administrator
Natzler, Otto Ceramist, Sculptor
Newman, Louis Art Dealer, Gallery Director
Orr-Cahall, Anona Christina Curator, Art Historian
Owens, Mary (Mary Louis Schnore) Painter
Pajaud, William Etienne Painter
Pal, Pratapaditya Curator, Art Historian
Phillips, Gifford Collector, Writer
Pillin, Polia Painter, Ceramist
Platus, Libby Fibre Sculptor, Lecturer
Poole, Richard Elliott Painter, Instructor
Porter, Albert Wright Educator, Painter
Preble, Michael Andrew Art Administrator, Educator
Quinn, Noel Joseph Painter, Instructor
Rachel, Vaughan Photographer, Writer
Raul Esparza S (Raul Esparza Sanchez) Muralist, Sculptor
Raven, Arlene Writer, Art Critic
Rebert, Jo Liefeld Painter, Lecturer
Redding, Steve Art Dealer, Collector
Robles, Esther Waggoner Art Dealer, Collector
Ross, Kenneth Art Administrator
Rossman, Ruth Scharff Painter, Instructor
Royce, Richard Benjamin Master Printer, Printmaker
Rubin, Arnold Gary Art Historian
Saar, Betye Assemblage & Collage Artist
Sargent, Margaret Holland Painter, Designer
Schaffner, Ruth S Art Dealer
Schrut, Sherry Painter, Printmaker
Schwandner, Kathleen M Art Dealer, Collector
Schwarz, Kurt L Art Dealer, Art Historian
Seletz, Emil Sculptor
Serisawa, Ikuo Art Dealer
Sherwood, Richard E Patron, Collector
Silverman, Ronald H Educator, Writer
Simon, Norton Collector
Sklar, Dorothy Painter
Smith, Alexis (Patricia Anne) Conceptual Artist
Smith, Robert Lewis Museum Director, Educator
Smith, Victor Joachim Painter, Educator
Snow, Lee Erlin Designer, Instructor
Squires, Norma-Jean Sculptor, Painter
Stead, Rexford Arthur Art Administrator, Art Historian
Steele, Emily Sculptor, Glass Artist
Stuart, David Art Dealer
Stussy, Jan Painter, Educator
Stussy, Maxine Kim Sculptor
Takemoto, Henry Tadaaki Craftsman, Sculptor
Teske, Edumnd Rudolph Photographer
Thomas, Tamara B Art Consultant
Todd, Michael Cullen Sculptor, Painter
Toigo, Daniel Joseph Painter
Tuchman, Maurice Museum Curator
Vaccarino, Robin Sculptor, Painter, Printmaker
Vann, Loli (Mrs Lilian Van Young) Painter
Van Schley (Evander Duer Van Schley) Video Artist, Filmmaker
Van Young, Oscar Painter
Vargas, Rudolph Sculptor
Waano-Gano, Joe Painter, Lecturer
Wagner, Gordon Parsons Assemblage Artist, Small Environmental Artist
Watson, Robert Painter
Wayne, June Painter
White, Charles Wilbert Painter, Educator
Wight, Frederick S Painter, Art Administrator
Willis, Jay Steward Sculptor, Instructor
Woelffer, Emerson Painter
Woods, Gurdon Grant Sculptor, Educator
Wright, Bernard Painter, Graphic Artist
Wright, Mr & Mrs William H Collectors
Wurdemann, Helen (Baroness Elena Guzzardi) Art Administrator, Collector
Yokoi, Rita Sculptor, Painter
Yokomi, Richard Koji Painter
Young, Joseph E Art Historian, Curator
Young, Joseph Louis Sculptor, Art Administrator
Zeitlin, Harriet Brooks Printmaker, Painter
Zeitlin, Jacob Ilrael Art Dealer, Collector
Zolotow, Milton Designer, Educator

Los Gatos

Kruskamp, Janet Painter, Instructor
Maltby, Hazel Farrow Weaver, Designer

Los Olivos

Cody, John (Alexis) Sculptor

Malibu

Albuquerque, Lita Painter, Lecturer
Bowman, Bruce Painter, Art Writer
Davis, Ronald Wendel Painter, Printmaker
Eino (Eino Antti Romppanen) Sculptor
Ellison, Nancy Painter, Photographer
Fredericksen, Burton Baum Curator, Art Historian
Frel, Jiri Art Historian, Curator
Garrett, Stephen Museum Director

Mendocino

Bothwell, Dorr Painter, Printmaker
Zacha, George William Painter, Sculptor

Menlo Park

Fanning, Robbie Art Writer, Lecturer
Friend, David Painter, Educator
Mozley, Anita Ventura Curator, Art Historian
Smith, Albert E Painter
Stout, George Leslie Art Consult
Thurston, Jacqueline Beverly Photographer, Educator

Mill Valley

Allan, William George Painter, Educator
Anderson, Jeremy Radcliffe Sculptor, Educator
Ihle, John Livingston Printmaker, Educator
O'Hanlon, Richard E Sculptor
Padula, Fred David Film Maker, Photographer
Saul, Peter Painter
Sherry, William Grant Painter, Sculptor

Millbrae

Nepote, Alexander Painter, Educator

Modesto

Remsing, (Joseph) Gary Painter, Sculptor

Montebello

Shubin, Morris Jack Painter, Lecturer

Montecito

Bayer, Herbert Painter, Designer
Ludington, Wright S Collector, Patron
Lutz, Dan S Painter
Pattee, Rowena Serigrapher, Painter

Monterey

Bradford, Howard Printmaker, Painter
Dedini, Eldon Lawrence Cartoonist
Henderson, Lester Kierstead Photographer, Art Dealer
Limber, Trudy C Art Dealer

Monterey Park

Arcuri, Frank J Sculptor, Photographer

Morgan Hill

Freimark, Robert (Matthew) Printmaker, Painter

Mount Baldy

Ramstead, Edward Oliver, Jr Painter, Illustrator

Mountain Center

Olsen, Frederick L Potter, Sculptor

Mountain View

Dzigurski, Alex Painter

Napa

Garnett, William Ashford Photographer, Educator

Newport Beach

Alf, Martha Joanne Painter, Writer
Feuerstein, Roberta Art Dealer
Garver, Thomas H Curator, Writer
Moonier, Syliva Art Restorer, Painter
Tornheim, Norman Sculptor
Turnbull, Betty Curàtor

North Hollywood

Brommer, Gerald F Painter, Writer
D'Agostino, Vincent Painter
Danieli, Fidel Angelo Painter, Art Critic
Kovner, Saul Painter
La Vigne, Robert Clair Painter, Designer
Smith, Lyn Wall Art Writer, Painter

Northridge

Fricano, Tom S Painter, Printmaker

Novato

Wilmeth, Hal Turner Art Historian, Painter

Oakland

Battenberg, John Sculptor, Educator
Beasley, Bruce Sculptor
Boiger, Peter Sculptor
Clark, Claude Lecturer, Painter
Colescott, Robert H Painter, Instructor
Cornin, Jon Painter, Instructor
Dhaemers, Robert August Printmaker, Educator
Diamond, Paul Photographer
Foosaner, Judith Ann Painter
Ford, Harry Xavier Educator, Art Administrator
Garwood, Audrey Painter, Printmaker
Hardy, David Whittaker, III Painter, Instructor
Hartman, Robert Leroy Painter, Educator
Jensen, Gary Painter, Film Maker
Kirk, Jerome Sculptor
Lederer, Wolfgang Designer, Educator
Levine, Marilyn Anne Sculptor, Educator
Levine, Martin Printmaker
Lewis, John Conard Sculptor, Glassblower
Lopez, Michael John Ceramist
Marshall, Kerry Art Administrator, Instructor
Martin, Fred Thomas Painter
McCann, Cecile Nelken Art Editor, Art Critic
McLean, Richard Thorpe Painter, Educator
Melchert, James Frederick Sculptor, Educator
Mendenhall, Jack Painter, Instructor
Neubert, George Walter Sculptor, Curator
Paris, Harold Persico Sculptor
Ramos, Melvin John Painter, Educator
Rees, Joseph F Sculptor
Richardson, Sam Painter, Educator
Rishell, Robert Clifford Painter, Sculptor
Rogers, Barbara Joan Painter
Saunders, Raymond Jennings Painter, Educator
Schoener, Jason Painter, Educator
Siegriest, Lundy Painter
Suzuki, James Hiroshi Painter
Tomidy, Paul J Art Administrator, Painter
Weare, Shane Printmaker

Ojai

Armitage, Frank Medical Illustrator, Painter
Dominique, John August Painter
Mayers, John J Collector
Wood, Beatrice Ceramist, Educator

Orange

Cumming, Robert H Conceptual Artist
Holste, Thomas James Painter, Instructor
Smith, Thelma deGoede Painter, Teacher

Orinda

Clymer, Albert Anderson Painter
Wolfe, Maurice Raymond Museum Director, Educator

Oro Grande

Bender, Bill Painter

Pacheco

Fon, Jade Painter, Instructor

Pacific Grove

Jolley, Geraldine H (Jerry) Painter, Sculptor

Pacific Palisades

Brokaw, Lucile Painter
Campbell, Richard Horton Painter, Printmaker
Hannah, John Junior Printmaker, Educator
Janelsins, Veronica Illustrator, Painter
Longman, Lester Duncan Art Historian
Sherman, Z Charlotte Painter
Treiman, Joyce Wahl Painter

Pacifica

Baird, Roger Lee Sculptor, Silversmith

Palm Desert

Rich, Frances L Sculptor, Draftsman

Palm Springs

Caniff, Milton Arthur Cartoonist
Morgan, Warren Dean Art Dealer, Designer

Palo Alto

Boyle, Keith Painter, Educator
Glanz, Andrea Elise Museum Director, Educator
Lobdell, Frank Painter
Ranes, Chris Painter, Printmaker
Zirker, Joseph Printmaker, Lecturer

Pasadena

Carmichael, Jae Painter, Art Administrator
Cole, Max Painter, Instructor
Dutton, Pauline Mae Art Librarian
Dyer, Carolyn Price Art Critic, Tapestry Artist
Edmondson, Leonard Etcher
Holo, Selma Reuben Art Historian, Curator
Hundley, David Holladay Art Dealer, Educator
Jackson, Richard Norris Painter
Kubly, Donald R Designer, Art Administrator
Levy, Hilda Painter
Perkins, Constance M Educator, Art Writer
Smith, Barbara Turner Instructor, Video Artist
Trenton, Patrica Jean Art Historian
Voth, Andrew Charles Art Administrator, Painter
Wortz, Melinda Farris Gallery Director, Art Critic
Younglove, Ruth Ann (Mrs Benjamin Rhees Loxley) Painter
Zammitt, Norman Sculptor

Paso Robles

Miller, Vel Painter, Sculptor

Pebble Beach

Kaller, Robert Jameson Art Dealer
Mortensen, Gordon Louis Printmaker, Painter

Petaluma

Beery, Eugene Brian Painter
Fuller, Mary (Mary Fuller McChesney) Sculptor, Writer
McChesney, Robert Pearson Painter
Reichek, Jesse Printmaker, Painter

Piedmont

Johnson, Doris Miller (Mrs Gardiner Johnson) Painter
Murray, Joan Art Critic, Photographer

Placerville

Wessels, Glenn Anthony Painter

Point Richmond

Wessel, Henry, Jr Photographer
Zulpo-Dane, Bill Photographer

Port Costa

De Forest, Roy Dean Painter, Sculptor

Rancho Mirage

Portanova, Joseph Domenico Portrait Sculptor, Designer

Rancho Santa Fe

Jones, Claire (Deann Burtchaell) Painter, Instructor

Redding

Oldham, Berton Jepsen Printmaker, Instructor

Redwood City

Bowman, Richard Painter
Strong, Charles Ralph Painter, Educator

Reseda

Anaya, Stephen Raul Printmaker
Sider, Deno Painter, Sculptor

Richmond

Evjen, Rudolph Berndt Sculptor, Painter
Haley, John Charles Painter, Sculptor
Kim, Ernie Ceramist, Art Administrator
Pinkerton, Clayton (David) Painter
Soult, James Thomas Curator, Graphic Artist

Riverside

Brinkerhoff, Dericksen Morgan Art Historian, Educator
Deal, Joe Photographer
deGooyer, Kirk Alan Gallery Director, Art Administrator
Garrett, Alan Thomas Museum Director, Sculptor
Seyle, Robert Harley Sculptor, Designer

Running Springs

Solberg, Morten Edward Painter

Sacramento

Adan, Suzanne Rae Painter, Instructor
Clisby, Roger David Curator, Art Historian
Else, Robert John Educator, Painter
Kaltenbach, Stephen James Painter, Sculptor
LaPena, Frank Raymond Painter, Art Historian
Marcus, Irving E Painter, Graphic Artist
Moment, Joan Painter, Educator
Riegel, Michael Byron Metalsmith

CALIFORNIA (cont)
Rippon, Ruth Margaret Ceramist, Educator
Vandenberge, Peter Willem Sculptor
Walburg, Gerald Sculptor, Educator
Waterstreet, Ken (James Kent Waterstreet) Painter
West, Richard Vincent Museum Director, Art Historian
Winkler, Maria Paula Painter, Educator

Salinas

Butterbaugh, Robert Clyde Sculptor, Educator
De Groat, George Hugh Painter, Printmaker

San Bernardino

Lintault, Roger Paul Educator, Sculptor

San Clemente

Berg, Barry Painter, Mail Artist

San Diego

Alden, Gary Wade Art Conservator
Antin, David A Art Critic, Writer
Beach, Warren Painter
Cohen, Harold Artist-Theorist, Educator
Conrad, John W Educator, Ceramist
Cordy-Collins, Alana (Alana Kathleen Cordy-Collins Riesland) Art Historian, Instructor
Davisson, Darrell Art Historian, Lecturer
Fisch, Arline Marie Goldsmith, Educator
Fisher, Sarah Lisbeth Art Conservator
Friedman, Kenneth Scott Sculptor, Educator
Gardiner, Henry Gilbert Art Administrator, Art Historian.
Hughes, Donald N Printmaker, Draftsman
Imana, Jorge Garron Painter
Jackson, Everett Gee Painter, Illustrator
Jennings, Jan Art Critic, Writer
Jung, Kwan Yee Painter
Jung, Yee Wah Painter
Kilian, Austin Farland Painter, Educator
Kornmayer, J Gary (John) Painter, Photographer
Lopez, Rhoda Le Blanc Sculptor, Educator
Meilach, Dona Z Art Writer, Photographer
Morgan, Frank James Sculptor
Rigby, Ida Katherine Art Historian
Salla, Salvatore Painter, Instructor
Schultz, Caroline Reel Painter, Lecturer
Sherman, Lenore (Walton) Painter, Lecturer
Strasen, Barbara Elaine Painter, Environmental Artist
Tibbs, Thomas S Lecturer
Wojtyla, Hasse (Walter Joseph Wojtyla) Painter, Draftsman
Wostrel, Nancy J Painter
Wright, Barton Allen Painter, Illustrator

San Francisco

Acton, Arlo C Sculptor
Adams, Mark Designer, Painter
Albright, Thomas Art Critic, Writer
Alexander, Kenneth Lewis Cartoonist
Allrich, M Louise Barco Art Dealer
Anargyros, Spero Sculptor
Asawa, Ruth (Ruth Asawa Lanier) Sculptor, Graphic Artist
Ascott, Roy Assemblage Artist, Educator
Bartlett, Scott Film Maker
Benton, Fletcher Sculptor
Berggruen, John Henry Art Dealer
Bolles, John S Art Dealer, Collector
Bolton, James Painter, Lecturer
Bottini, David M Sculptor
Bowers, Cheryl Olsen Painter, Lecturer
Brawley, Robert Julius Educator, Painter
Breschi, Karen Lee Sculptor
Brooks, (John) Alan Painter, Instructor
Camarata, Martin L Educator, Printmaker
Cameron, Elsa S Curator, Art Administrator
Castellon, Rolando Curator, Painter
Clark, G Fletcher Sculptor
Close, Marjorie (Perry) Painter, Lecturer
Conner, Bruce Painter, Film Maker
Connor, Linda Stevens Photographer, Instructor
Cortright, Steven M Printmaker, Painter
Cox, E Morris Collector
Davis, Stephen A Painter
Dern, F Carl Sculptor
Dickinson, Eleanor Creekmore Painter, Graphic & Video Artist
Elder, Muldoon Painter, Sculptor
Elliott, Lillian Weaver, Designer
Evans, Henry Printmaker
Fitch, George Hopper Collector, Patron
Folsom, Karl Leroy Printmaker, Photographer
Foster, Barbara Lynn Printmaker, Instructor
Fox, Terry Alan Sculptor
Frankenstein, Alfred Victor Art Critic, Art Historian
Freeman, Phyllis (Therese) Mixed Media, Lecturer
Frey, Viola Sculptor, Painter
Fried, Alexander Art Critic
Fried, Howard Lee Sculptor
Fuller, Diana Art Dealer
Gagliani, Oliver Photographer
Gecse, Helene Painter, Etcher
Glassman, Joel A Video Artist, Photographer
Goddard, Vivian Painter
Goldeen, Dorothy A Art Dealer
Goldstein, Daniel Joshua Printmaker, Sculptor
Gooch, Gerald Painter
Graham, F Lanier Art Administrator, Educator
Grant, James Sculptor
Graysmith, Robert Editorial Cartoonist
Gutkin, Peter Sculptor
Gutmann, John Painter, Educator
Hack, Howard Edwin Painter
Hansen, Wanda Art Dealer
Henderson, Mike (William Howard Henderson) Painter
Henry, Jean Painter, Instructor
Hershman, Lynn Lester Sculptor
Herstand, Arnold Painter, Art Administrator
Hinkhouse, Forest Melick Art Consultant
Hoover, F Herbert Art Dealer, Writer
Hoover, Margaret Pomeroy Collector, Researcher
Hopkins, Henry Tyler Museum Director, Educator
Howard, David Photographer, Instructor
Howard, Robert Boardman Sculptor
Howe, Thomas Carr Museum Director
Howell, Raymond Painter, Photographer
Hyson, Jean Painter
Iannetti, Pasquale Francesco Paolo Art Dealer, Collector
Ida, Shoichi Printmaker, Sculptor
Jess (Jess Collins) Painter, Collage Artist
Johnson, Robert Flynn Curator, Art Historian
Johnston, Helen Head Art Dealer
Jones, David Lee Painter, Sculptor
Karlstrom, Paul Johnson Art Historian, Art Administrator
King, Hayward Ellis Gallery Director
Koblick, Freda Sculptor
Kohn, William Roth Painter, Educator
Kolawole, Lawrence Compton Painter, Sculptor
Kos, Paul Joseph Sculptor, Educator
Kussoy, Bernice (Helen) Sculptor
Lefebvre d'Argence, Rene-Yvon Museum Director
Leighton, Thomas Charles Painter, Instructor
Levin, Morton D Printmaker, Painter
Lew, Weyman Michael Painter, Printmaker
Linhares, Philip E Painter, Curator
Lipzin, Janis Crystal Film Maker
Loeffler, Carl Eugene Art Publisher, Art Administrator
Lomahaftewa, Linda (Linda Joyce Slock) Painter, Educator
Lowinsky, Simon L Art Dealer
Lupper, Edward Painter
Mackenzie, David Painter
Majdrakoff, Ivan Painter, Educator
Maradiaga, Ralph Gallery Director, Designer
Marioni, Tom Sculptor, Curator
McGill, Robert Lee Painter, Instructor
Meyer, Thomas Vincent Art Dealer
Miller, Mrs Robert Watt Patron
Mohr, Pauline Catherine Art Conservator, Restorer
Moore, Michael Shannon Painter
Mundt, Ernest Karl Sculptor, Educator
Nelson, Jane Gray Art Librarian
Neri, Manuel Sculptor
Neto, G Reis (Gilda Reis Netopuletti) Painter
Nong Painter, Sculptor
Pearson, Louis O Sculptor
Pennuto, James William Mixed-Media Artist
Phillips, Donna-Lee Photographer, Writer
Pomeroy, James Calwell, Jr Performance Artist, Sculptor
Posey, Ernest Noel Painter, Instructor
Posner, Richard Perry Glass Artist, Lecturer
Post, George (Booth) Painter, Educator
Potts, Don Sculptor, Educator
Quandt, Elizabeth (Elizabeth Quandt Barr) Printmaker
Rabow, Rose Art Dealer, Collector
Raciti, Cherie Painter, Sculptor
Redd Ekks (Robert Norman Rasmussen) Sculptor, Ceramist
Reichman, Fred (Thomas) Painter
Reilley, Patrick Richard Art Dealer, Appraiser
Renk, Merry Designer, Sculptor
Robinson, C David Architect, Collector
Rose, Mary Anne Painter, Art Administrator
Rumsey, David MacIver Environmental Artist, Collector
St Amand, Joseph Painter
Sanchez, Carol Lee Painter
Sapien, Darryl Rudolph Performance Artist
Satty, Wilfried Graphic Artist, Film Maker
Sawyer, William Art Dealer, Collector
Seligman, Thomas Knowles Curator, Art Administrator
Serra, Rudy Sculptor
Shangraw, Clarence Frank Art Historian, Curator
Shangraw, Sylvia Chen Art Historian, Curator
Shelton, Gilbert Key Cartoonist, Illustrator
Sheppard, Joseph Sherly Painter, Sculptor
Sinton, Nell (Walter) Painter
Smith, Howard Ross Museum Curator
Sovary, Lilly Painter, Designer
Staprans, Raimonds Painter, Sculptor
Stephens, Richard Alan Art Administrator, Painter
Stevens, Marjorie Painter
Stofflet, Mary Art Critic, Art Historian
Summers, Carol Printmaker
Tarshis, Jerome Writer, Curator
Tavenner, Patricia (Pat) Collage Artist, Photographer
Taylor, Sandra Ortiz Painter, Printmaker
Thomas, Lew Photographer, Art Writer
Thompson, Richard E, Jr Art Dealer, Collector
Thompson, Richard Earl, Sr Collector, Painter
Ullrich-Zuckerman, B Painter, Photographer
Van Hoesen, Beth (Mrs Mark Adams) Printmaker
Villa, Carlos Painter
von Meyer, Michael Sculptor
Wall, Brian Sculptor
Walsh, Patricia Ruth Painter
Weeks, H J Art Administrator, Art Critic
Weinbaum, Jean Painter, Sculptor
Weinberg, Daniel Art Dealer
White, Ian McKibbin Art Administrator, Designer
Wilson, Richard Brian Painter, Instructor

San Geronimo

Hedrick, Wally Bill Sculptor, Painter
Raffael, Joseph Painter
Raffael, Judith K Painter, Stained Glass Artist

San Jose

Abbatecola (Oronzo) Painter, Sculptor
Chapman, Robert Gordon Jeweler, Painter
Dixon, Albert George, III Museum Director, Educator
Hunter, John H Painter, Educator
Schnittmann, Sascha S Sculptor
Wu, I-Chen Calligrapher, Painter

San Juan Capistrano

Honeyman, Robert B, Jr Collector

San Luis Obispo

Gray, Gladys Painter, Muralist
Paradise, Phil (Herschel) Painter, Sculptor
Reynolds, Robert Painter, Educator
Ruggles, Joanne Beaule Printmaker, Educator

San Marcos

Baldwin, Russell W Information Artist, Gallery Director
Freeman, Robert Lee Painter, Sculptor

San Marino

Medearis, Roger Painter, Lithographer
Wark, Robert Rodger Art Administrator, Art Historian

San Mateo

Gilbert, Alma Magdalena Art Dealer, Museum Director
Mancini, John Painter, Illustrator

San Pedro

Bassler, James W Fiber Artist
Crutchfield, William Richard Painter, Printmaker
McCafferty, Jay David Video Artist

San Rafael

Evans, Paul Fredric Art Historian, Writer/Consultant
Greaves, Fielding Lewis Writer, Photographer
Larsen, D Dane Ceramist, Sculptor
Sister Adele Photographer, Educator
Winter, Clark Sculptor

Santa Ana

De Coursey, John Edward Collector, Art Dealer
Karwelis, Donald Charles Painter, Lecturer
Rhodes, Reilly Patrick Art Museum Director

Santa Barbara

Backus, Standish, Jr Painter, Muralist
Badash, Sandi Borr Painter, Fabric Designer
Braiden, Rose Margaret J Art Historian, Illustrator
Brown, Gary Hugh Painter, Educator
Catalan, Edgardo Omar Painter, Educator
Cavat, Irma Painter, Educator
Craner, Robert Rogers Painter, Educator
Dole, William Painter, Educator
Dorra, Henri Art Historian, Educator
Eguchi, Yasu Painter
Farwell, Beatrice Art Historian
Fenton, Howard Carter Painter, Educator
Firfires, Nicholas Samuel Painter
Frame, Robert (Aaron) Painter
Gebhard, David Gallery Director, Art Historian
Hammond, Ruth MacKrille Painter
Irvin, Fred Maddox Illustrator, Painter
Jarvaise, James J Painter
Mallory, Margaret Collector, Producer
Mills, Paul Chadbourne Museum Director
Moir, Alfred Art Historian
Morrison, Doris Painter, Art Administrator
Parshall, Douglass Ewell Painter
Setterberg, Carl Georg Painter, Illustrator
Tanner, Joan Elizabeth Painter
Treese, William R Art Librarian, Painter
Wyngaard, Susan Elizabeth Art Librarian

Santa Clara

Hawkins, Myrtle H Painter, Writer
Vitale, Lydia Modi Museum Director, Curator

Santa Cruz

Alford, Gloria K Sculptor, Printmaker
Auvil, Kenneth William Educator, Printmaker
Marx, Nicki D Assemblage Artist, Sculptor
McClellan, Douglas Eugene Painter
Nutzle, Futzie (Bruce John Kleinsmith) Graphic Artist, Cartoonist
Thompson, Donald Roy Painter, Instructor
Watson, Lynda Jeweler, Metalsmith

Santa Monica

Baldessari, John Anthony Conceptual Artist
Berlant, Tony Artist
Bongart, Sergei R Painter, Instructor
Bordeaux, Jean Luc Art Historian, Curator
Chicago, Judy Painter
Davis, Phil Douglas Painter, Instructor
Diebenkorn, Richard Painter
Haines, Richard Painter
Hill, William Mansfield Art Historian, Museum Director
Karpel, Eli Sculptor, Instructor
Kayser, Stephen S Educator, Writer
McMillen, Michael Chalmers Environmental Artist, Sculptor
Mesches, Arnold Painter, Educator
Mullican, Lee Painter, Educator
Okulick, John A Sculptor
Owyang, Judith Francine Art Critic
Ruppersberg, Allen Rawson Conceptual Artist
Segalove, Ilene Judy Video Artist, Photographer
Stern, Irene Monat Painter
Stern, Jan Peter Sculptor
Ullman, Harold P Collector
Upton, John David Educator, Art Historian
Van Derpool, James Grote Art Historian
Weisberg, Ruth Ellen Printmaker, Educator
Wheeler, Doug Painter

Santa Monica Canyon

Andrews, Oliver Sculptor

Santa Rosa

Barr, Roger Terry Sculptor, Painter
Lienau, Daniel Clifford Art Dealer, Collector
Rosen, James Mahlon Painter, Art Historian

Santa Ynez

Peake, Channing Painter

Saratoga

Caswell, Helen Rayburn Painter, Writer

Sausalito

Baltz, Lewis Photographer
Beall, Dennis Ray Printmaker, Educator
Kuhlman, Walter Egel Painter, Educator
Schwarcz, June Therese Craftsman

Sebastopol

Barnes, Carroll Sculptor
Barnhart, C Raymond Assemblage Artist, Instructor
Lichty, George M Cartoonist
Moulton, Susan Gene Art Administrator, Art Historian
Palmer, Mabel (Evelyn) Painter
Watrous, John Museum Director

Sherman Oaks

Carl, Joan Sculptor, Graphic Artist, Designer
de la Vega, Enrique Miguel Sculptor, Designer
Engle, Chet Painter, Sculptor
Schlosberg, Carl Martin Art Dealer
Stern, Jean Art Historian, Consultant
Stérn, Louis Art Dealer, Appraiser
Waisler, Lee Painter, Printmaker

Sierra Madre

Randall, (Lillian) Paula Sculptor, Designer

Simi Valley

Harris, Murray A Collector, Commercial Artist

Solvang

Aronson, Cliff Art Dealer
St John, John Milton Painter, Muralist

Sonoma

Anderson, Gunnar Donald Painter, Illustrator
Christensen, Ted Painter, Printmaker
Mercer, John Douglas Photographer, Publisher

South Laguna

Dreaper, Richard Edward Art Dealer, Art Historian
Hardy, Robert Gallery Director, Ceramist
Jones, John Paul Painter, Printmaker
Strombotne, James Painter

South Pasadena

Askin, Walter Miller Painter, Educator
Ballatore, Sandra Lee Art Critic, Instructor
Schary, Susan Painter

Spring Valley

Clark, John Dewitt Sculptor
Greene, Ethel Maud Painter

Stanford

Eisner, Elliot Wayne Educator
Eitner, Lorenz E A Art Historian, Museum Director
Elsen, Albert Edward Art Historian
Mendelowitz, Daniel Marcus Painter, Writer
Oliveira, Nathan Painter
Proctor, Gifford MacGregor Sculptor, Designer

Stanton

Barton, Phyllis Grace Art Writer, Art Agent

Stockton

Dennison, Keith Elkins Museum Director, Art Historian
Gyermek, Stephen A Educator
Reynolds, Richard (Henry) Sculptor, Painter
Walker, Larry Painter, Educator

Studio City

Block, Irving Alexander Painter, Educator
Harwood, June Beatrice Painter, Instructor
Zlotnick, Diana Shirley Collector, Patron

Suisun

Stone, Gwen Painter, Printmaker

Sunnyvale

Lock, Charles L Painter, Illustrator

CALIFORNIA (cont)

Sylmar

Gebhardt, Harold Sculptor, Educator
Gebhardt, Peter Martin Sculptor

Tarzana

Bromberg, Faith Painter
Burroughs, John Coleman Painter, Illustrator
Rosenthal, Rachel Sculptor

Thousand Oaks

Janss, Edwin, Jr Collector
Martino, Antonio P Painter

Tiburon

Baird, Joseph Armstrong, Jr Writer, Art Dealer

Topanga

Alexander, Peter Sculptor
Jennings, Thomas Painter, Printmaker
Schley, Evander Duer (Van) Conceptual Artist, Photographer

Torrance

Everts, Connor Painter, Printmaker

Trinidad

Groth, Bruno Sculptor

Tujunga

Kerr, Kenneth A Painter, Designer

Turlock

McGee, Winston Eugene Painter
Parton, Ralf Sculptor, Instructor
Werness, Hope B Art Historian

Twentynine Palms

Hilton, John William Painter, Illustrator

Vacaville

Wasser, Paula Kloster Educator, Painter

Valencia

Fitzpatrick, Robert John Art Administrator
Mandel, John Painter
Von Huene, Stephan R Sculptor

Vallejo

Salmon, Donna Elaine Illustrator
Salmon, Raymond Merle Cartoonist, Educator

Van Nuys

Penny, Aubrey John Robert Painter
Van Wolf, Henry Sculptor, Painter

Venice

Asher, Michael Artist
Askevold, David Video Artist
Bengston, Billy Al Painter
Bieser, Natalie Painter
Boyce, Richard Sculptor
Brewster, Michael Sculptor, Educator
Burden, Chris Conceptual Artist, Sculptor
Cheng, Fu-Ding Filmmaker, Painter
Colorado, Charlotte Painter
Cooper, Ron Painter, Sculptor
Dill, Guy Girard Sculptor
Dill, Laddie John Painter, Sculptor
Divola, John Manford, Jr Photographer
Eversley, Frederick John Sculptor
Falkenstein, Claire Sculptor
Fay, Joe Painter, Printmaker
Forst, Miles Painter
Gordon, John S Sculptor, Educator
Graham, Robert Sculptor
Hirsch, Gilah Yelin Painter, Educator
Kisch, Gloria Sculptor
Omar, Margit Painter, Educator
O'Shea, Terrence Patrick Painter, Sculptor
Sturgeon, John Floyd Video Artist
Sturman, Eugene Painter, Sculptor
Suarez, Magdalena Frimkess Painter, Sculptor
Turner, Janice Kay Art Dealer
Valentine, DeWain Sculptor
Vasa (Vasa Velizar Mihich) Sculptor, Educator
Westcoast, Wanda Sculptor, Educator
White, John M Painter, Conceptual Artist
Zimmerman, Elyn Sculptor

Ventura

Koch, Gerd (Herman) Painter, Educator
Lochrie, Elizabeth Davey Painter, Sculptor
Moser, Julon Painter
Smith, Robert Alan Painter, Instructor

Walnut Creek

Bernard, Felix S Art Dealer
Dennis, Charles Houston Cartoonist
Hunter, Leonard LeGrande, III Sculptor, Educator
Partridge, Roi Landscape Etcher
Pneuman, Mildred Y Painter
Stiegelmeyer, Norman Earl Painter, Sculptor

Walnut Park

Wilf, Andrew Jeffrey Painter

West Covina

Cross, Watson, Jr Painter, Instructor

Westwood

Dey, Kris Sculptor, Designer

Whitethorn

Gill, James (Francis) Painter, Sculptor

Woodacre

Martin, William Henry (Bill) Painter, Sculptor
Snyder, William B Painter, Instructor
Taylor, Gage Painter
Wiley, William T Painter

Woodland Hills

Reed, Hal Painter, Sculptor

Yucaipa

Weese, Myrtle A Painter

COLORADO

Arvada

Lyon, Hayes Paxton Painter

Aspen

Chesley, Paul Alexander Photographer
Soldner, Paul Edmund Sculptor, Ceramist
Wille, O Louis Sculptor

Aurora

Thies, Charles Herman Painter, Art Administrator
Whitney, Maynard Merle Sculptor, Educator

Boulder

Anker, Suzanne C Sculptor
Drewelowe, Eve Painter, Sculptor
Eades, Luis Eric Painter, Educator
Forsman, Chuck (Charles Stanley Forsman) Painter, Educator
Geck, Francis Joseph Painter, Designer
Goodacre, Glenna Painter, Sculptor
Iwamasa, Ken Educator, Artist
Johnson, James Alan Painter, Educator
Kuczun, Ann-Marie Painter
Matthews, Gene Painter, Educator
Matthews, Wanda Miller Printmaker
Neher, Fred Cartoonist
Praeger, Frederick A Collector, Publisher
Shark, Herman R Master Printer, Printmaker
Vance, George Wayne Ceramist, Sculptor
Vielehr, William Ralph Sculptor
Westermeier, Clifford Peter Painter, Educator
Wolfe, Lynn Robert Stained Glass Artist, Painter

Buena Vista

Whipple, Barbara (Mrs Grant Heilman) Printmaker, Writer

Cherry Hills

Howell, Frank Painter

Cherry Hills Village

Strawn, Melvin Nicholas Painter, Sculptor

Colorado Springs

Arnest, Bernard Painter, Educator
Hansen, Arne Rae Museum Director, Art Administrator
Jones, Tom Douglas Kinetic Artist, Lecturer
Tilley, Lewis Lee Painter, Film Maker
Trissel, James Nevin Painter, Educator
Wynne, Albert Givens Painter

Crested Butte

O'Connor, Harold Thomas Goldsmith, Instructor

Denver

Bach, Otto Karl Museum Director, Writer
Brauer, Connie Ann Designer, Metalsmith
Clurman, Irene Art Critic
DeMaree, Elizabeth Ann (Betty) Painter, Collector
Dragul, Sandra Kaplan Painter, Printmaker
Fulton, W Joseph Consultant, Lecturer
Graese, Judy (Judith Ann) Pyrography, Illustrator
Hansen, Frances Frakes Educator, Painter
Jacob, Ned Painter, Sculptor
Katz, Eunice Painter, Sculptor
Kelley, Ramon Painter
Kirkland, Vance Hall Painter, Collector
Maytham, Thomas Northrup Museum Director, Lecturer
Michael, Gary Art Writer, Painter
Mills, James Art Critic, Collector
Musick, Archie L Painter, Writer
Oliphant, Patrick Bruce Editorial Cartoonist
Ragland, Bob Painter, Lecturer
Rainey, John Watts Painter, Collector
Rivoli, Mario Illustrator, Painter
Rosen, Beverly Doris Painter, Educator
Schiff, Jean Draftsman, Video Artist
Sprout, Francis Allen Painter, Educator
Swensen, Mary Jeanette Hamilton (Jean) Painter, Printmaker
Traher, William Henry Painter, Lecturer
Ullberg, J Kent Sculptor
Vanderlip, Dianne Perry Gallery Director, Educator

Wands, Alfred James Painter
Yanish, Elizabeth Sculptor, Lecturer

Elizabeth

Bunn, Kenneth Rodney Painter, Sculptor
Kaplinski, Buffalo Painter

Englewood

Jellico, John Anthony Art Director, Painter

Estes Park

Simoni, John Peter Painter, Educator

Fort Collins

De Waal, Ronald Burt Collector
Forsyth, Robert Joseph Art Historian, Collector
Getty, Nilda Fernandez Educator, Metalsmith
Jacobs, Peter Alan Art Administrator, Printmaker
Kittelson, John Henry Painter, Sculptor
Twarogowski, Leroy Andrew Draftsman, Educator
Yust, David E Painter, Educator

Georgetown

Baehler, Wallace R Art Dealer, Collector

Glen Haven

Sorby, J Richard Painter, Educator

Golden

Clark, R Dane Painter, Designer
Deaton, Charles Sculptor, Architect
Poduska, T F Lecturer, Painter

Greeley

Schumacher, Herbert Charles Ceramist, Educator

Gunnison

Johnson, Lee Painter, Educator
Julio, Pat T Educator, Craftsman

Lakewood

DeAndrea, John Louis Sculptor
Denton, Pat Painter, Instructor
Knaub, Raymond L Painter, Instructor
Lang, Rodger Alan Ceramist, Educator

Littleton

Bartlett, Fred Stewart Art Administrator
Britton, Edgar Sculptor
Jagman, Ed Painter
Retzer, Howard Earl Collector, Painter
Turner, James Thomas, Sr Sculptor, Painter

Longmont

Adams, Robert Hickman Photographer

Loveland

Simmons, Cleda Marie Painter

Nederland

Fernie, John Chipman Sculptor, Instructor

Pueblo

Helgoe, Orlin Milton Painter, Educator

Rollinsville

Brakhage, James Stanley Film Maker, Lecturer

CONNECTICUT

Ashford

Spencer, Harold Edwin Art Historian, Painter

Bethany

Herbert, Robert L Art Historian

Bethel

Ajay, Abe Painter, Sculptor
Farris, Joseph Cartoonist, Painter

Bloomfield

Tompkins, Alan Painter, Educator
Valtman, Edmund Cartoonist

Branford

Hilles, Susan Morse Collector, Patron

Bridgeport

Vazquez, Paul Painter
Wilson, Sybil Painter, Designer

Bridgewater

Abbett, Robert Kennedy Painter
Levy, Julien Educator, Writer

Bristol

Thomson, William David Painter

Brookfield Center

Beall, Joanna Painter, Sculptor
Westermann, Horace Clifford Sculptor

Brooklyn

Sufi (Ahmad Antung) Sculptor, Craftsman

Byram

List, Vera G Patron, Collector

Canaan

Ritchie, Andrew C Art Administrator, Art Historian

Chester

Killam, Walt Painter, Art Dealer
Schueler, Jon R Painter, Lecturer

Clinton

Mays, Victor Illustrator

Cornwall Bridge

Gray, Cleve Painter, Sculptor
Sloane, Eric Illustrator, Writer

Cos Cob

Chapin, Louis (Le Bourgeois) Writer, Art Critic
Kane, Margaret Brassler Sculptor

Coventry

Hayes, David Vincent Sculptor

Danbury

Hooton, Arthur Painter

Darien

Black, Lisa Painter
Newman, Ralph Albert Cartoonist, Writer

Deep River

Field, Richard Sampson Curator, Art Historian
Jensen, Pat Painter

East Haddam

Warneke, Heinz Sculptor

East Haven

Gardner, Joan A Painter, Film Maker
Mancusi-Ungaro, Carol Caruso Conservator

East Killingly

Lent, Blair Illustrator, Writer

Fairfield

Dal Fabbro, Mario Sculptor, Writer
Glaser, Bruce Art Historian, Educator
Riley, Bernard Joseph Painter

Falls Village

Lathrop, Dorothy P Illustrator, Writer
Lathrop, Gertrude K Sculptor

Farmington

Lavoy, Walter Joseph Jeweler, Educator
Talbot, Jarold Dean Museum Director, Educator

Georgetown

D'Aulaire, Edgar Parin Illustrator, Lithographer
D'Aulaire, Ingri (Mortenson) Parin Writer, Illustrator
Thompson, Malcolm Barton Painter, Sculptor

Greens Farms

Batuz Painter, Sculptor
Reid, Charles Art Writer, Painter
Weiss, Harvey Sculptor

Greenwich

Balazs-Pottasch, Gyongyi Painter
Barrie, Erwin S Painter
Birnbaum, Mildred Gallery Director, Painter
Brown, William Ferdinand, II Illustrator, Writer
Cherepov, George Painter, Instructor
Fields, Fredrica H Stained Glass Artist, Glass Engraver
Gimbel, Mrs Bernard F Collector, Patron
Kaep, Louis Joseph Painter
Lust, Herbert Art Historian, Collector
Lust, Virginia Art Dealer
Momiyama, Nanae Painter, Educator
Motherwell, Robert Painter, Printmaker
Simpson, Tommy Hall Painter, Sculptor
Van Der Voort, Amanda Venelia Painter

Groton

MacGillis, Robert Donald Painter, Illustrator
Nelson, Harry William Painter, Printmaker

Groton Long Point

Fix, John Robert Sculptor, Silversmith

Guilford

Gonzales, Shirley Art Critic, Writer

Hamden

Keller, Deane Educator, Painter
Lichtenberg, Manes Painter
MacClintock, Dorcas Sculptor

CONNECTICUT (cont)

Hartford

Atkinson, Tracy Museum Director
Coppola, Andrew Sculptor, Draftsman
Elliott, James Heyer Museum Director
Huntington, John W Collector, Patron
Keller, Andrea Miller Curator
Mahoney, Michael R T Art Historian, Educator
Mitchell, Clifford Painter, Architect
Zimmerman, Paul Warren Painter, Educator

Ivoryton

Bendig, William Charles Painter, Publisher
Jensen, Leo (Vernon) Sculptor, Painter
Ramanauskas, Dalia Irena Painter, Draftsman

Kent

Steig, William Cartoonist, Sculptor

Killingworth

Harris, William Wadsworth, II Painter

Lakeville

Blagden, Thomas P Painter
Dzubas, Friedel Painter

Litchfield

Beineke, Dr & Mrs J Frederick Collectors
Landeck, Armin Painter, Engraver

Lyme

Hardin, Adlai S Sculptor

Madison

Bauermeister, Mary Hilde Ruth Sculptor
Connery, Ruth M Painter
Davies, Kenneth Southworth Painter, Instructor
Maestro, Giulio Marcello Illustrator, Painter
Morris, Robert Clarke Painter, Educator

Manchester

Geoffrey, Syed Iqbal (Jafree) Art Administrator

Mansfield Center

Forman, Kenneth Warner Painter, Educator

Meriden

Scalise, Nicholas Peter Painter
Tamburine, Jean Painter, Illustrator
Widstrom, Edward Frederick Sculptor

Middletown

Frazer, John Thatcher Film Maker, Painter
Gourevitch, Jacqueline Painter
Green, Samuel Magee Art Historian, Painter
Risley, John Hollister Sculptor, Educator

Monroe

Bogart, Richard Jerome Painter
Shrady, Frederick C Sculptor

Moodus

Guy, James M Painter, Educator

Mystic

Aalund, Suzy Painter, Miniaturist
Bates, Gladys Edgerly Sculptor
Olson, Joseph Olaf Designer, Painter

New Britain

Ferguson, Charles Painter, Art Historian
Guzman-Forbes, Robert Painter, Illustrator
Mill, Eleanor Illustrator, Painter

New Canaan

Barton, Jean L Painter, Designer
Cavalli, Dick Cartoonist
Eberman, Edwin Art Administrator, Educator
Finch, Ruth Woodward Patron, Photographer
Geerlings, Gerald Kenneth Graphic Artist, Architect
MacLean, Arthur Painter
Margolies, Ethel Polacheck Painter, Art Administrator
Richards, Walter DuBois Painter, Printmaker
Roesch, Kurt (Ferdinand) Painter
Saxon, Charles David Cartoonist, Illustrator
Soby, James Thrall Writer, Critic
Tomchuk, Marjorie Printmaker

New Fairfield

Austin, Darrel Painter
Domanska, Janina Illustrator
Nevelson, Mike Sculptor
Smith, Joseph Anthony Painter, Illustrator

New Haven

Bailey, William H Painter
Bloomgarden, Judith Mary Art Librarian
Burke, James Donald Art Historian, Curator
Carter, David Giles Art Consultant, Museum Director
Chaet, Bernard Painter, Educator
Forge, Andrew Murray Art Writer, Painter
Friedman, Joan Marcy Curator, Art Librarian
Fussiner, Howard Painter
Garston, Gerald Drexler Painter
Gruppe, Charles Painter
Halaby, Samia Asaad Painter, Educator
Johnson, Lester F Painter, Educator
Koch, Robert Art Historian, Writer
Kubler, George Alexander Art Historian, Writer
Lambert, Nancy S Art Librarian
Mermin, Mildred (Shire) Painter
Norris, Andrea Spaulding Art Historian
Pelli, Cesar Architect
Prown, Jules David Art Historian
Rannit, Aleksis Art Historian
Scully, Vincent Art Historian, Educator
Shestack, Alan Museum Director, Art Historian
Zeidenbergs, Olafs Sculptor

New London

Bonamarte, Lou Painter, Designer
Hendricks, Barkley Leonnard Painter
Lukosius, Richard Benedict Painter, Educator
Mayhew, Edgar De Noailles Educator, Museum Director
Straight, Robert Larry Painter, Educator
Van Brunt, Philip G Art Director, Assemblage Artist

New Milford

Crawford, Mel Painter, Illustrator
Stewart, Dorothy S Painter
Zalstem-Zalessky, Mrs Alexis Collector

Newington

Martin, G W Painter, Educator

Newtown

Caparn, Rhys (Rhys Caparn Steel) Sculptor
Fradon, Dana Cartoonist
Getz, Ilse Painter, Collage & Assemblage Artist
Inman, Pauline Winchester Printmaker, Illustrator
Kijanka, Stanley Joseph Painter
Winchester, Alice Art Editor

Niantic

Dennis, Roger Wilson Painter

Noank

Brackman, Robert Painter, Educator
Stein, Fritz Henry Art Dealer
Stein, Harve Painter, Restorer

Norfolk

Kelemen, Pal Art Historian

North Haven

Tulk, Alfred James Painter
Zallinger, Jean Day Illustrator, Instructor
Zallinger, Rudolph Franz Painter, Educator

Norwalk

Chappell, Warren Draftsman, Graphic Artist
Egleson, Jim (James Downey) Printmaker-Etcher, Painter
Frasconi, Antonio Illustrator, Painter
Lasker, Joseph (L) Painter, Illustrator
Pellew, John Clifford Painter
Perry, Charles O Sculptor

Norwich

Gualtieri, Joseph P Museum Director, Painter
Radin, Dan Painter
Triplett, Margaret L Painter
von Schlippe, Alexey Painter, Educator

Old Greenwich

Giles, Newell Walton, Jr Painter

Old Lyme

Chandler, Elisabeth Gordon Sculptor
Peterson, Roger Tory Illustrator, Writer

Orange

Albers, Anni Designer, Graphic Artist

Oxford

Chaplin, George Edwin Painter, Educator
Fuge, Paul H Sculptor

Plainville

Brzozowski, Richard Joseph Painter

Portland

Glasson, Lloyd Sculptor, Educator

Putnam

Davis, Wayne Lambert Painter, Illustrator

Quaker Hill

McCabe, Maureen M Collage Artist

Ridgefield

Benton, Suzanne E Sculptor, Art Writer
Busino, Orlando Francis Cartoonist
Drummond, Sally Hazelet Painter
Perlin, Bernard Painter, Illustrator
Ross, Alexander Painter
Sendak, Maurice Bernard Writer, Illustrator

Riverside

Thompson, (James) Bradbury Designer, Art Director

Rowayton

Flora, James Royer Illustrator, Painter
Peterdi, Gabor F Painter, Printmaker
Squadra, John Painter, Instructor

Roxbury

Arnason, H Harvard Art Historian, Writer
Bart, Elizabeth (Elizabeth Bart Gerald) Painter, Designer
Ericson, Dick Cartoonist, Illustrator
Kappel, Philip Writer, Etcher
Kuhn, Bob Illustrator, Painter
Morath, Inge (Inge Morath Miller) Photographer

Salisbury

Blagden, Allen Painter
Osborn, Elodie C (Mrs Robert C Osborn) Art Administrator
Osborn, Robert Illustrator, Satiric Artist
Ten Eyck, Catryna (Catryna Ten Eyck Seymour) Painter

Sandy Hook

Sidenius, W Christian Designer, Light Artist

Sharon

Magee, Alderson Graphic Artist, Painter, Collector
McIntosh, Harold Painter
Wilkinson, Charles K Museum Curator

Sherman

Blume, Peter Painter
Schmid, Richard Alan Painter
Soltesz, Frank Joseph Painter

South Kent

Aymar, Gordon Christian Painter, Art Historian

Southbury

Folds, Thomas McKey Art Consultant, Educator
Frishmuth, Harriet Whitney Sculptor
Johnson, Edvard Arthur Painter, Educator
Lariar, Lawrence Cartoonist, Writer
Merrill, David Kenneth Painter

Southport

Hutchins, Maude Phelps McVeigh Sculptor

Stamford

Bechtle, C Ronald Painter
Burt, David Sill Sculptor, Writer
Bushmiller, Ernie Paul Cartoonist
Calrow, Robert F Instructor, Painter
Couturier, Marion B Art Dealer, Collector
Gonzalez-Tornero, Sergio Painter, Printmaker
Hausman, Fred S Sculptor, Designer
Metzger, Robert Paul Curator, Educator
Nakian, Reuben Sculptor
Schanker, Louis Printmaker, Painter

Sterling

Holden, Raymond James Painter, Illustrator

Stonington

Burchard, Peter Duncan Illustrator, Photographer
Cale, Robert Allan Printmaker

Stony Creek

London, Jeff Designer, Lecturer

Storrs

Crossgrove, Roger Lynn Painter, Educator
Gregoropoulos, John Painter
Rovetti, Paul F Museum Director
Terenzio, Anthony Painter, Educator
Zelanski, Paul John Painter

Tolland

Doudera, Gerard Educator, Painter

Uncasville

McCloy, William Ashby Painter, Printmaker

Voluntown

Caddell, Foster Painter, Instructor

Wallingford

Neff, John A Painter, Designer
Wexler, Jerome LeRoy Photographer, Children's Book Illustrator

Warren

Abrams, Herbert E Painter, Lecturer

Washington

Gilbert, Albert Earl Painter, Illustrator
Parker, Robert Andrew Painter
Porter, Priscilla Manning Craftsman, Instructor
Renouf, Edward Pechmann Painter, Sculptor
Talbot, William (H M) Sculptor

Washington Depot

Frazier, Paul D Sculptor

Watertown

Cajori, Charles F Painter

West Cornwall

Mangravite, Peppino Gino Painter, Lecturer
Simont, Marc Illustrator

West Hartford

Barton, Eleanor Dodge Educator
Hanson, Bernard A Art Administrator
Miller, Jean Johnston Art Librarian, Art Historian
Taylor, John C E Painter, Educator

West Redding

Dieringer, Ernest A Painter
Giusti, George Designer, Sculptor

Weston

Bleifeld, Stanley Sculptor, Instructor
Cadmus, Paul Painter, Printmaker
Fogel, Seymour Painter, Sculptor
Nonay, Paul Painter
Rand, Paul Painter, Designer

Westport

Boulton, Joseph L Sculptor, Designer
Chernow, Ann Painter, Instructor
Chernow, Burt Instructor, Museum Director
Dobrin, Arnold Jack Illustrator
Dohanos, Stevan Illustrator, Painter
Fisher, Leonard Everett Painter, Illustrator
Gramatky, Hardie Painter, Writer
Hurd, Justin G (Jud) Cartoonist
Kovatch, Jak Gene Printmaker, Educator
Rabut, Paul Illustrator, Painter
Reed, Walt Arnold Art Historian, Writer
Skemp, Robert Oliver Painter
Woodham, Jean Sculptor, Educator

Willimantic

Mazzocca, Gus (Augustus Nicholas Mazzocca) Printmaker, Educator

Wilton

Darrow, Whitney, Jr Cartoonist
Franco, Robert John Sculptor, Educator
King, Warren Thomas Cartoonist
Lipman, Jean Art Editor, Writer
Prdy, Donald R Painter
Roberts, Priscilla Warren Painter
Stuart, Kenneth James Art Director

Windsor

Meyer, Frank Hildbridge Printmaker, Instructor

Woodbridge

Crosby, Sumner McKnight Art Historian
Ingalls, Eve Painter, Instructor
Lytle, Richard Painter, Educator

Woodbury

Leighton, Clare Engraver, Writer

DELAWARE

Felton

Kohut, Lorene Painter

Greenville

Reynolds, Nancy Du Pont Sculptor

Hockessin

Parks, Charles Cropper Sculptor
Parks, Christopher Cropper Sculptor, Painter

Newark

Allen, Margaret Prosser Painter, Educator
Breslin, Wynn Painter, Sculptor
Craven, Wayne Art Historian, Writer
Da Cunha, Julio Educator, Painter
Homer, William Innes Art Historian, Educator
Moss, Joe (Francis) Sculptor, Painter
Rowe, Charles Alfred Painter, Designer
Weiss, John Joseph Photographer

Rockland

Harvey, (William) Andre Sculptor

Smyrna

Bailey, Richard H Sculptor

Wilmington

Colombo, Charles Painter
Elzea, Rowland Procter Museum Curator, Painter
Hayes, Tua Painter
Layton, Richard Painter
Martone, William Robert Painter, Instructor
McFarren, Grace Painter
Nichols, Eleanor Cary Designer, Silversmith
Raley, Mr & Mrs Robert L Collectors
Rhoads, Eugenia Eckford Painter
Wyrick, Charles Lloyd, Jr (Pete) Museum Director, Writer

Winterthur

Hummel, Charles Frederick Curator

DELAWARE (cont)

Schwartzbaum, Paul Martin Conservator
Smith, James Morton Museum Director, Historian
Sommer, Frank H Art Librarian, Art Writer
Stoner, Joyce Hill Conservator, Art Editor

DISTRICT OF COLUMBIA

Washington

Adams, William Howard Art Administrator, Collector
Atlas, Martin & Liane W Collectors
Bader, Franz Art Dealer, Collector
Baker, Sarah Marimda Painter
Beall, Karen F Curator
Berkowitz, Leon Painter
Biddle, James Art Administrator, Collector
Biddle, Livingston Ludlow, Jr Art Administrator
Bingham, Lois A Art Administrator, Lecturer
Block, Huntington Turner Art Insuror
Bookatz, Samuel Painter, Sculptor
Boulton, Jack Art Administrator
Bowman, Jean (Jean Bowman Magruder) Painter, Illustrator
Braunstein, H Terry Mixed-Media Artist
Breeskin, Adelyn Dohme Art Administrator
Broude, Norma Freedman Art Historian, Educator
Brown, David Alan Art Historian, Curator
Brown, John Carter Museum Director
Carmean, E A, Jr Art Historian, Curator
Carter, Albert Joseph Museum Curator
Cavanaugh, John W Sculptor
Chapman, Howard Eugene Art Director, Cartoonist
Chase, William Thomas (W Thomas Chase) Art Conservator
Cogswell, Margaret Price Art Administrator
Comes, Marcella Painter, Photographer
Cooper, Rebecca (Rebecca Cooper Eisenberg) Art Dealer, Collector
Cooper, Theodore A Art Dealer
Costigan, Constance Christian Designer, Painter
D'Arista, Robert Painter, Educator
Davis, Gene Painter
Dean, James Art Administrator, Painter
de Looper, Willem Painter, Art Administrator
De Weldon, Felix George Weihs Sculptor, Architect
DiPerna, Frank Paul Photographer, Instructor
Donaldson, Jeff R Painter, Art Administrator
Downing, Thomas Painter
Eisenstein, Mr & Mrs Julian Collectors
Faul, Roberta Heller Consultant, Writer
Fendrick, Barbara Cooper Art Dealer
Ferber, Elise Van Hook Art Administrator, Curator
Fern, Alan Maxwell Art Historian, Art Administrator
Ferriter, Clare Painter, Collage Artist
Flint, Janet Altic Curator, Art Historian
Fontanini, Clare Educator, Sculptor
Foshag, Merle Painter
Garrard, Mary DuBose Art Historian, Lecturer
Garson, Inez Curator
Gerdts, Abigail Booth Art Administrator, Art Historian
Gilliam, Sam Painter
Gomez-Sicre, Jose Art Administrator, Art Critic
Gramberg, Liliana Painter, Printmaker
Green, Eleanor Broome Gallery Director, Art Historian
Grossman, Maurizia M Art Dealer, Gallery Director
Grossman, Sheldon Museum Curator, Art Historian
Grubar, Francis Stanley Art Historian, Lecturer
Gumpert, Gunther Painter
Haden, Eunice (Barnard) Painter, Illustrator
Hand, John Oliver Art Historian, Curator
Hanks, David Allen Curator
Hanks, Nancy Art Administrator
Hart, Robert Gordon Art Administrator
Haslem, Jane N Art Dealer
Hay, George Austin Painter, Filmmaker
Herblock (Herbert Lawrence Block) Cartoonist
Herman, Lloyd Eldred Museum Director
Herzbrun, Helene McKinsey Painter, Instructor
Hopps, Walter Art Administrator
Howland, Richard Hubbard Art Historian, Writer
Isham, Sheila Eaton Painter
Jackson, Virgil V Cartoonist, Illustrator
Jones, Lois Mailou (Mrs V Pierre-Noel) Painter, Designer
Kagy, Sheffield Harold Painter, Sculptor
Kamen, Gloria Illustrator, Painter
Kerr, John Hoare Art Administrator, Art Historian
Kinney, Gilbert Hart Collector, Art Administrator
Klavans, Minnie Painter, Sculptor
Knox, Katharine McCook Art Historian, Collector
Krebs, Rockne Sculptor
Kreeger, David Lloyd Patron, Collector
Lane, H Palmer Art Dealer
Lastra, Luis Art Dealer
Laub-Novak, Karen Painter, Printmaker
Lazzari, Pietro Sculptor, Painter
Leisher, William Rodger Conservator
Lewis, Douglas Art Historian, Art Curator
Lewton, Jean Louise Art Editor, Art Administrator
Lewton, Val Edwin Designer, Painter
Libhart, Myles Laroy Art Administrator, Art Writer
Livingston, Jane S Art Critic, Curator
Loar, Peggy A Curator, Arts Administrator
Lowe, Harry Art Administrator, Designer
Lunn, Harry, Jr Art Dealer
MacDonald, William Allan Art Historian, Educator
Marshall, Mara Painter
McBryde, Sarah Elva Painter, Printmaker
McCabe, Cynthia Jaffee Curator, Art Historian
McCabe, Lawrence Sculptor
McGowin, Ed Sculptor, Painter
McGrath, Kyran Murray Art Administrator
Meader, Jonathan Grant (Ascian) Printmaker, Painter
Mellon, Paul Collector, Art Administrator
Miles, Ellen Gross Art Historian, Curator
Millard, Charles Warren, III Curator, Writer
Mitchell, Eleanor Fine Arts Specialist, Librarian
Mondale, Joan Adams Craftsperson
Moore, E Bruce Sculptor
Neslage, Oliver John, Jr Art Dealer
Nuki (Daniel Millsaps) Painter, Writer
Pablo (Paul Burgess Edwards) Painter, Educator
Parkhurst, Charles Gallery Director, Curator
Perlmutter, Jack Painter, Printmaker
Perrot, Paul N Art Administrator, Lecturer
Phillips, Laughlin Museum Director
Phillips, Marjorie Museum Director, Painter
Pierce, Delilah W Painter, Educator
Pierre-Noel, Vergniaud Designer
Pope, Annemarie Henle Art Administrator
Pope, John Alexander Historian, Museum Director
Powell, Earl Alexander, III Curator, Art Historian
Power, Mark Photographer, Critic
Puryear, Martin Sculptor
Rankine, V V Sculptor, Painter
Ratzenberger, Katharine M Art Librarian
Rennie, Helen (Sewell) Painter, Designer
Richard, Paul Art Critic
Richman, Robert M Art Administrator, Writer
Rigsby, John David Painter, Art Administrator
Robbins, Warren M Museum Director, Educator
Robertson, Charles J Art Administrator
Robison, Andrew Museum Curator, Writer
Rosenzweig, Phyllis D Curatorial Assistant
Ross, Marvin Chauncey Museum Curator, Art Historian
Russell, Helen Diane Art Historian
Rust, David E Art Historian, Collector
Sadik, Marvin Sherwood Gallery Director, Art Historian
Sandground, Mark Bernard, Sr Collector, Patron
Schlaikjer, Jes (Wilhelm) Painter, Illustrator
Schmutzhart, Berthold Josef Sculptor, Educator
Schmutzhart, Slaithong Chengtrakul Instructor, Sculptor
Scott, David Winfield Art Administrator
Sellin, David Art Historian, Curator
Shapley, Fern Rusk Curator, Writer
Shapley, John Art Historian
Shaw, Renata Vitzthum Art Librarian
Sherman, Claire Richter Art Historian, Educator
Shute, Roberta E Sculptor, Painter
Sickman, Jessalee Bane Painter, Instructor
Silberfeld, Kay Conservator
Sivard, Robert Paul Painter
Smith, Alfred James, Jr Painter, Sculptor
Smith, Arthur Hall Painter, Art Educator
Solmssen, Peter Art Administrator
Spandorf, Lily Gabriella Painter
Spencer, John R Art Historian, Art Administrator
Stamm, Geoffrey Eaton Art Administrator, Art Historian
Stapp, William F Curator
Stevenson, A Brockie Painter
Stewart, Robert Gordon Curator, Art Historian
Stovall, Luther McKinley (Lou) Printmaker
Straight, Michael Collector
Szabo, Stephen Lee Photographer
Taff, Barbara O'Neil Art Dealer
Taylor, Joshua Charles Museum Director, Art Historian
Taylor, Prentiss (Hottel) Lithographer, Instructor
Thacher, John Seymour Art Administrator
Thalacker, Donald William Art Administrator, Architect
Thomas, Alma Woodsey Painter
Tirana, Rosamond (Mrs Edward Corbett) Painter
Truettner, William Art Administrator
Truitt, Anne (Dean) Sculptor
Turano, Don Sculptor, Medalist
Van Roijen, Hildegarde Graham Graphic Artist, Sculptor
von Rebhan, Elinor Anne Slide Librarian
Walker, Sandra Radcliffe Painter
Walker, William Bond Art Librarian
Watson, Ross Art Historian
Weil, Stephen Edward Museum Executive, Lecturer
Wells, James Lesesne Painter, Lithographer
Wheelock, Arthur Kingsland, Jr Curator, Educator
White, Franklin Painter, Draftsman
Wilmerding, John Art Historian, Curator
Winslow, John Randolph Painter, Educator
Withers, Josephine Art Historian, Art Writer
Woodward, William Painter, Educator
Young, Charles Alexander Educator, Painter
Young, Kenneth Victor Painter, Designer
Zilczer, Judith Katy Art Historian, Curator

FLORIDA

Bay Harbor Islands

Kessler, Edna Leventhal Painter, Printmaker
Silverman, Sherley C Painter, Sculptor

Boca Raton

Dorst, Claire V Painter, Educator
Dorst, Mary Crowe Instructor, Artist

Russo, Kathleen L Art Historian
Shanks, Bruce McKinley Editorial Cartoonist

Bonita Springs

Lam, Jennett (Brinsmade) Painter, Educator

Bradenton

Cogswell, Dorothy McIntosh Educator, Painter

Cantonment

Carey, John Thomas Educator, Art Historian

Cape Coral

Korjus, Veronica Maria Elisabeth Painter, Lecturer

Clearwater

Kennedy, J William Painter

Clermont

Amateis, Edmond Romulus Sculptor

Cocoa Beach

Roever, Joan Marilyn Illustrator Children's Books, Dioramist

Coconut Grove

Busch, Julia M Writer, Sculptor
Massin, Eugene Max Painter, Educator
Triester, Kenneth Painter, Sculptor

Coral Gables

Ahlander, Leslie Judd Curator, Art Critic
Baratte, John J Museum Director
Freeman, Gertrude Consultant, Collector
Lehman, Arnold L Museum Director, Art Historian
Neijna, Barbara Sculptor
Schmitt, Marilyn Low Art Historian
Smith, Griffin (Mary-Griffin Smith Hoeveler) Art Critic
Turoff, Muriel Pargh Sculptor, Painter

Crystal River

Doolittle, Warren Ford, Jr Painter, Educator

Davie

Hanson, Duane Sculptor, Instructor

Daytona Beach

Broemel, Carl William Painter, Illustrator

De Land

Libby, Gary Russel Museum Director, Art Historian
Messersmith, Fred Lawrence Painter, Educator
Shaw, Elsie Babbit Sculptor, Painter

Deerfield Beach

Sitton, John M Painter, Lecturer
Van Aalten, Jacques Painter

Delray Beach

Schang, Frederick, Jr Collector
Stell, H Kenyon Educator, Painter
Varga, Ferenc Sculptor

Edgewater

Stowman, Annette Burr Painter

Englewood

Pinto, Biagio Painter
Tracy, (Lois) Bartlett Painter, Writer

Fort Lauderdale

Batt, Miles Girard Painter, Instructor
Bessemer, Auriel Muralist, Illustrator

Fort Pierce

Kenny, Patrick Gerald Painter, Illustrator
Vierthaler, Arthur A Craftsman, Educator

Fort Walton Beach

Simpson, Marilyn Jean Painter, Instructor

Gainesville

Craven, Roy Curtis, Jr Gallery Director, Educator
Grissom, Eugene Edward Educator, Printmaker
Hodges, Stephen Lofton Painter
Holbrook, Hollis Howard Muralist, Painter
Holbrook, Vivian Nicholas Painter, Art Administrator
Isaacson, Marcia Jean Draftsman, Educator
Kerslake, Kenneth Alvin Printmaker, Educator
Naylor, John Geoffrey Sculptor, Educator
O'Connor, John Arthur Painter, Educator
Purser, Stuart Robert Painter, Educator
Sabatella, Joseph John Art Administrator, Painter
Shiner, Nate Painter, Educator
Skelley, Robert Charles Educator, Printmaker
Uelsmann, Jerry Photographer
Ward, John Lawrence Art Historian, Painter
Williams, Hiram Draper Painter, Educator

Hallandale

Gallo, Enzo D Sculptor
Jewell, Kester Donald Curator

Hawthorne

Burnham, Lee Sculptor, Painter

Hialeah

Sherwood, A (Frances Ann Crane) Sculptor, Designer

Hollywood

Hicken, Russell Bradford Art Consultant, Lecturer
Schreck, Michael Henry Painter, Sculptor
Somers, H Painter

Jacksonville

Bear, Marcelle L Collector, Painter
Brownett, Thelma Denyer Painter
Dodge, Joseph Jeffers Painter
Edelson, Elihu Art Critic, Instructor
Eden, F Brown Painter, Printmaker
Gefter, Judith Michelman Photographer
Koscielny, Margaret Sculptor, Painter
Pringle, Burt Evins Graphic Artist, Aquarellist

Lake Worth

Kirkwood, Larry Thomas Designer, Printmaker

Lakeland

Stoddard, Donna Melissa Educator, Gallery Director

Largo

Levitan, Israel (Jack) Sculptor, Lecturer
Tucker, Peri Writer, Illustrator

Leesburg

Humes, Ralph H Sculptor

Longboat Key

Allen, Margo (Mrs Harry Shaw) Sculptor, Painter
Bendell, Marilyn Painter, Instructor
Cord, Orlando Painter
Rogers, Leo M Collector
Rowan, Frances Physioc Painter, Printmaker

Lutz

Bailey, Oscar Photographer, Educator

Lynn Haven

Ferguson, Edward Robert Painter, Printmaker

Madeira Beach

Terry, Marion (E) Painter, Art Critic

Maitland

Maas, Arnold (Marcolino) Instructor, Painter

Mandarin

Dempsey, Bruce Harvey Museum Director

Miami

Bergling, Virginia Catherine (Mrs Stephen J Kozazcki) Art Book Dealer, Publisher
Bogaev, Ronni (Ronni Bogaev Greenstein) Lecturer, Painter
Cano, Margarita Art Librarian, Painter
Carulla, Ramon Painter
Chow Chian-Chiu Painter, Art Historian
Chow Leung Chen-Ying Painter
Cianfoni, Emilio Conservator, Painter
Couper, James M Painter, Educator
Fleming, Betty Corcoran Art Dealer
Harrison, Joseph Robert, Jr Collector, Patron
Jennings, Frank Harding Lecturer, Painter
Kahn, A Michael Painter, Designer
Kent, H Latham Gallery Director, Painter
Lis, Janet Chapman Painter
Martinez-Maresma, Sara (Sara Martinez) Painter
McAllister-Kelly Painter
Musgrave, Shirley H Educator, Photographer
Reiling, Susan Wallace Curator, Art Historian
Riveron, Enrique Painter, Sculptor
Romoser, Ruth Amelia Painter, Sculptor
Salinas, Baruj Painter, Graphic Artist
Storm, Larue Painter, Sculptor
Strickland, Thomas J Painter
Thiele, Robert Ransom Painter, Sculptor
Viret, Margaret Mary (Mrs Frank Ivo) Painter, Instructor
Weinhardt, Carl Joseph, Jr Museum Director, Writer
Winter, Gerald Glen Painter, Educator

Miami Beach

Bass, John Collector, Patron
Bernay, Betti Painter
Gains, Jacob Painter
Hoff, (Syd) Cartoonist, Writer
Luria, Gloria Art Dealer
Rosenblum, Sadie Skoletsky Painter, Sculptor
Schein, Eugenie Painter, Printmaker

Miami Shores

Hollinger, (Helen Wetherbee) Painter, Lecturer

Naples

Geiger, Edith Rogers Painter
Kelsey, Muriel Chamberlin Sculptor

FLORIDA (cont)
Meek, J William, III Art Dealer, Collector
Oppenheim, Samuel Edmund Painter
Orr, Elliot Painter
Roach, Ruth S Jeweler, Designer
Summy, Anne Tunis Painter
Wagner, Richard Ellis Painter
Wilson, David Philip Portrait Painter

New Smyrna Beach

Leeper, Doris Marie Painter, Sculptor

North Miami

Curtiss, George Curt Painter, Illustrator
Thorndike, Charles Jesse (Chuck) Cartoonist, Writer

Ocala

Thompson, George Louis Designer

Odessa

Gelinas, Robert William Painter, Educator

Orange Park

Hunt, Courtenay Painter, Instructor

Orlando

Crane, Roy (Campbell) Cartoonist, Writer
Ivey, James Burnett Cartoonist, Collector
Miyamoto, Wayne Akira Painter, Printmaker
Perry, William M Cartoonist
Varian, Elayne H Art Administrator, Art Historian

Ormond Beach

Strickland, Allen Painter

Osprey

Buzzelli, Joseph Anthony Painter, Sculptor

Ozona

Smith, Oliver Painter

Palm Beach

Akston, Joseph James Collector, Patron
Artinian, Artine Collector
Brams, Joan Painter, Sculptor
Brown, James Monroe, III Museum Director
Dame, Lawrence Art Critic, Writer
Gordon, John Art Administrator, Art Historian
Hare, Channing Painter
Hare, Stephen Hopkins Painter
Hokin, Grace E Art Dealer, Collector
Huldah (Huldah Cherry Jeffe) Painter
Koni, Nicolaus Sculptor, Lecturer
Levin, Jeanne Painter, Collector
Lukin, Philip Collector
Ness, Evaline (Mrs Arnold A Bayard) Illustrator, Writer
Phillips, John Goldsmith Museum Curator
Rautbord, Dorothy H Collector, Patron
Sanchez, Thorvald Painter
Shippen, Zoe (Zoe Shippen Varnum) Painter

Ponte Vedra Beach

Draper, Josiah Everett Painter

Port Charlotte

Randall, Ruth Hunie Designer

Riviera Beach

Hibel, Edna Painter, Lithographer

Saint Augustine

Calkin, Carleton Ivers Painter, Restorer
Roberds, Gene Allen Printmaker, Sculptor

Saint Petersburg

Crane, James Painter, Cartoonist
Defenbacher, Daniel S Designer, Lecturer
Dickey, Helen Pauline Painter
Gellman, Beah (Mrs William C McNulty) Painter, Sculptor
Goldberg, Norman Lewis Writer, Lecturer
Hill, Polly Knipp Etcher, Painter
Klarin, Winifred Erlick Painter
Malone, Lee H B Museum Director
McVeigh, Miriam Temperance Painter
Rigg, Margaret Ruth Painter, Calligrapher
Schwarz, Felix Conrad Painter, Educator
Schwarz, Myrtle Cooper Designer, Mosaic Artist
Sutherland, Sandy Painter

Sanibel

Snyder, James Wilbert (Wilb) Painter

Sarasota

Behl, Marjorie Painter
Campbell, Dorothy Bostwick Painter, Sculptor
De Diego, Julio Painter, Illustrator
Eliscu, Frank Sculptor
Farnsworth, Jerry Painter, Writer
Floethe, Richard Illustrator, Designer
Gregory, Bruce Painter, Instructor
Harmon, Foster Art Dealer
Held, Philip Painter, Instructor
Hodgell, Robert Overman Printmaker, Sculptor
Hopper, Frank J Painter, Illustrator
Hoppes, Lowell E Cartoonist
Laufman, Sidney Painter
Morse, John D Art Editor
Oehlschlaeger, Frank J Art Dealer
Olds, Elizabeth Painter, Printmaker
Osborne, Robert Lee Painter, Educator
Parton, Nike Painter, Sculptor
Perkins, Robert Eugene Art Administrator
Pollack, Peter Photographer, Writer
Posey, Leslie Thomas Sculptor, Instructor
Rowland, Elden Hart Painter
Sawyer, Helen (Helen Sawyer Farnsworth) Painter, Writer
Shaw, Harry Hutchison Painter
Solomon, Syd Painter, Instructor
Sweney, Fred Illustrator, Painter
White, Ruth Art Dealer, Collector
Wilson, William Harry Art Historian, Curator

South Miami

Bailey, James Arlington, Jr Painter, Restorer

Spring Hill

Foster, Hal Cartoonist, Painter

Stillwater Island

Camins, Jacques Joseph Painter, Printmaker

Stuart

Hutchinson, Janet L Museum Director, Collector
Mosley, Zack T Illustrator, Cartoonist

Sunrise

Berkowitz, Henry Painter, Designer

Tallahassee

Burggraf, Ray Lowell Painter, Educator
Deshaies, Arthur Printmaker
Harper, William Enamelist, Educator
Holschuh, (George) Fred Sculptor
Hurst, Ralph N Sculptor, Educator
Johnson, Ivan Earl Educator, Designer
Kuhn, Marylou Educator, Painter
Walmsley, William Aubrey Lithographer
Wedin, Winslow Elliott Architect
Williams, Chester Lee Sculptor, Educator

Tamarac

Gould, Stephen Sculptor, Collector

Tampa

Aguayo, Oscar Art Administrator, Gallery Director
Bell, James M Art Administrator
Cardoso, Anthony Painter, Instructor
Covington, Harrison Wall Painter, Educator
Cox, Ernest Lee Sculptor, Educator
Fager, Charles J Educator, Ceramist
Kronsnoble, Jeffrey Michael Painter, Educator
Nazarenko, Bonnie Coe Painter
Pappas, George Educator, Painter
Rosenquist, James Painter
Wujcik, Theo Printmaker, Educator

Temple Terrace

Kashdin, Gladys S Painter, Educator
Saff, Donald Jay Printmaker, Art Administrator

Venice

Lewin, Mr & Mrs Robert L Art Publishers

Vero Beach

Brightwell, Walter Painter

West Palm Beach

Becker, Martin Earle Publisher, Patron
Grove, Edward Ryneal Medalist/Sculptor, Painter
Grove, Jean Donner Sculptor
Houser, Jim Painter, Educator
Knapp, Sadie Magnet Painter, Sculptor
Leff, Rita Printmaker, Painter
Madigan, Richard Allen Art Administrator
Mueller, Trude Sculptor
Norton, Ann Sculptor
Ubertalli, Hector Painter, Sculptor

Winter Haven

Ives, Elaine Caroline Painter

Winter Park

Genius, Jeannette (Jeannette M McKean) Painter, Designer
McKean, Hugh Ferguson Painter, Educator

GEORGIA

Athens

Arnholm, Ronald Fisher Designer, Educator
Clements, Robert Donald Educator, Sculptor
Collier, Graham (Alan Graham-Collier) Writer, Painter
Dodd, Lamar Painter, Educator
Edmonston, Paul Educator, Art Editor
Feldman, Edmund Burke Educator, Art Critic
Hammond, Gale Thomas Printmaker, Educator
Herbert, James Arthur Painter, Film Maker
Lukasiewicz, Ronald Joseph Printmaker, Art Administrator
Marriott, William Allen Painter, Educator
Moore, Ethel Curator, Art Historian
Paul, William D, Jr Museum Director, Painter
Thompson, William Joseph Educator, Sculptor

Atlanta

Beattie, George Art Administrator, Painter
Bhalla, Hans Painter, Art Historian
Borochoff, (Ida) Sloan Painter
Bruno, Santo Michael Painter, Lecturer
Chase, Allan (Seamans) Sculptor, Designer
Colarusso, Corrine Camille Painter, Instructor
Cone-Skelton, Annette Painter, Art Editor
Crouse, John L (Jay) Art Dealer, Photographer
Davis, Ben H Painter, Video Artist
De Noronha, Maria M (Mrs David Gallman) Painter, Lecturer
Dodd, Ed (Edward Benton) Cartoonist
Edvi Illes, Emma Designer, Tapestry Artist
Edvi Illes, George Painter, Sculptor
Fenton, Julia Ann Multi-media Artist, Art Administrator
Frazer, James Nisbet, Jr Photographer
Gillette, W Dean Painter, Art Dealer
Greco, Anthony Joseph Painter, Sculptor
Harris, Julian Hoke Sculptor, Architect
Heath, David C Art Dealer
Kiah, Virginia Jackson Painter, Museum Director
McAdoo, Donald Eldridge Painter, Printmaker
Menaboni, Athos Rudolfo Painter
Meserole, Vera Stromsted Painter, Art Administrator
Mills, Lev Timothy Printmaker, Sculptor
Patterson, Curtis Ray Sculptor, Instructor
Rasmussen, Keith Eric Printmaker, Instructor
Shute, Ben E Painter
Simon, Jewel Woodard Painter, Sculptor
Sipe, Gary Robert Art Librarian
Smith, Ben Printmaker
Smith, Ross Ransom Williams Art Dealer, Collector
Thomas, Steffen Wolfgang Sculptor, Painter
Vigtel, Gudmund Art Administrator
Yarbrough, Leila Kepert Printmaker, Painter

Augusta

Klopfenstein, Philip Arthur Painter, Art Administrator

Carrollton

Bobick, Bruce Painter, Educator

Chamblee

McLean, James Albert Educator, Printmaker

Clayton

Singleton, Robert Ellison Painter, Printmaker

Columbus

Shorter, Edward Swift Painter, Collector

Decatur

Burnett, W C, Jr Art Critic
Canaday, Ouida Gornto Painter, Educator
Howett, John Art Historian
Shead, S Ray Painter, Printmaker
Staven, Leland Carroll Educator, Painter
Warren, Ferdinand Earl Painter, Art Administrator
Westervelt, Robert F Art Historian, Ceramist

Farmington

Chappelle, Jerry Leon Educator, Sculptor

Good Hope

Ransom, Henry Cleveland, Jr Painter

Jekyll Island

Fiore, Rosario Russell Sculptor

Macon

Daugherty, Marshall Harrison Sculptor, Art Administrator
Rice, Anthony Hopkins Sculptor, Painter

Marietta

Voos, William John Art Administrator, Painter

Rome

Mew, Tommy Painter, Educator, Conceptual Artist

Savannah

Anderson, William Sculptor, Photographer
Gaudieri, Alexander V J Museum Director
Seraphin, Joseph Anthony Art Dealer, Publisher

Statesboro

Solomon, Bernard Alan Printmaker, Educator

HAWAII

Hauula

Hayward, Peter Painter, Sculptor

Honolulu

Belshe, Mirella Monti Sculptor, Art Historian
Browne, Robert M Collector, Patron
Charlot, Jean Painter, Art Historian
Cooper, Lucille Baldwin Painter, Sculptor
Ecke, Betty Tseng Yu-Ho Painter, Art Historian
Engle, Barbara Jean Painter, Printmaker
Feher, Joseph Designer, Painter
Foster, James W, Jr Art Administrator
Haar, Francis Photographer, Film Maker
Harvey, Donald Gilbert Sculptor, Instructor
Higa, Charles Eisho Painter, Instructor
Hudson, Winnifred Painter
Jameikis, Brone Aleksandra Designer, Instructor
Karawina, Erica (Mrs Sideny C Hsiao) Painter, Stained Glass Artist
Kenda, Juanita Echeverria Painter, Writer
Kimura, Sueko M Painter, Educator
Kingrey, Kenneth Designer, Educator
Kjargaard, John Ingvard Painter, Printmaker
Kobayashi, Katsumi Peter Painter, Lecturer
Kowalke, Ronald Leroy Painter, Printmaker
Link, Howard Anthony Curator
Loring, Clarice Painter, Muralist
Lux, Gwen (Gwen Lux Creighton) Sculptor
Maehara, Hiromu Painter, Designer
Marozzi, Eli Raphael Sculptor, Instructor
Norris, (Robert) Ben Painter, Educator
Pohl, Louis G Painter, Printmaker
Preis, Alfred Art Administrator, Architect
Roster, Fred Howard Sculptor, Educator
Roster, Laila Bergs Gallery Director, Art Critic
Russell, Shirley Ximena (Hopper) Painter
Salmoiraghi, Frank Photographer, Instructor
Shutt, Ken Sculptor, Painter
Stasack, Edward Armen Painter, Printmaker
Trinidad, Francisco Flores Corky, Jr Cartoonist
Tsuchidana, Harry Suyemi Painter
Wisnosky, John G Painter, Educator
Wong, Ching Painter, Writer
Young, Doug Y H Painter
Young, John Chin Painter, Collector

Kahului

Miller, Barbara Darlene Painter, Instructor

Kailua

Hartwell, Patricia Lochridge Art Administrator
Stamper, Willson Young Painter

Kailua-Kona

Thomas, John Painter

Kaneohe

Hee, Hon-Chew Painter, Gallery Director

Keaau

Rhodes, James Melvin Glass Blower, Sculptor

Lahaina

Sato, Tadashi Painter, Sculptor
Schuman, Robert Conrad Painter, Weaver

Lihue

Lai, Waihang Painter, Instructor

Pahoa

Charlot, Martin Day Painter, Illustrator

Volcano

Morrison, Bee (Berenice G) Weaver
Morrison, Boone M Photographer, Art Administrator

IDAHO

Boise

Auth, Robert R Painter, Printmaker
Huff, Howard Lee Educator, Photographer
Killmaster, John H Painter, Muralist
Kober, Alfred John Educator, Sculptor
Snyder, Kim Lawrence Curator, Painter
Watia, Tarmo Painter, Educator

Moscow

Kirkwood, Mary Burnette Painter

Sun Valley

Bennett, Don Bemco Painter, Printmaker
deLory, Peter Photographer, Instructor

Tetonia

Connolly, Jerome Patrick Painter, Muralist

ILLINOIS

Alton

Freund, Will Frederick Painter, Educator

Arlington Heights

Rebbeck, Lester James, Jr Painter, Sculptor

Aurora

Ford, Ruth Vansickle Painter, Educator
Narus, Marta Maria Margareta Art Dealer

Barrington

Hofer, Ingrid (Ingeborg) Painter, Instructor
Schnackenberg, Roy Painter, Sculptor

ILLINOIS (cont)

Belleville

Hesse, Don Cartoonist
Threlkeld, Dale Painter, Instructor

Bloomington

Butler, James D Printmaker, Painter
George, Raymond Ellis Printmaker, Educator
Gregor, Harold Laurence Painter, Educator
Holder, Kenneth Allen Painter, Educator
Myers, Joel Philip Artist in Glass, Educator

Carbondale

Fink, Herbert Lewis Painter, Educator
Johnson, Evert Alfred Art Administrator, Painter
Kington, Louis Brent Sculptor, Educator
Plochmann, Carolyn Gassan Painter

Champaign

Betts, Edward Howard Painter, Educator
Britsky, Nicholas Painter, Educator
Bushman, David Franklin Painter, Educator
Christison, Muriel B Museum Director, Educator
Edwards, Gwendolyn Tyner Art Dealer, Gallery Director
Elkin, Beverly Dawn Art Dealer
Fehl, Philipp P Painter, Art Historian
Gammon, Juanita-La Verne Painter, Educator
Grucza, Leo (Victor) Painter, Educator
Gunter, Frank Elliott Painter, Educator
Hilson, Douglas Painter, Educator
Perkins, Ann Art Historian
Rae, Edwin C Art Historian
Rowan, Dennis Michael Printmaker, Educator
Shipley, James R Educator, Designer
Sinsabaugh, Art Photographer, Educator
Sprague, Mark Anderson Painter, Educator
Stephens, Curtis Designer, Photographer
Wicks, Eugene Claude Painter, Educator
Ziff, Jerrold Art Historian, Collector

Charleston

Moldroski, Al R Painter, Educator
Shull, Carl Edwin Painter, Educator
Sorge, Walter Painter, Printmaker
Stapp, Ray Veryl Educator, Painter
Trank, Lynn Edgar Educator, Painter

Chicago

Albright, Malvin Marr Painter, Sculptor
Allen, (Harvey) Harold Photographer, Art Historian
Allen, Jane Addams Art Editor, Art Critic
Ames, (Polly) Scribner Painter
Amft, Robert Painter, Photographer
Anderson, Howard Benjamin Collage Artist, Photographer
Arnold, Ralph Moffett Painter, Educator
Aubin, Barbara Painter, Instructor
Ball, Walter Neil Painter, Educator
Barazani, Morris Educator, Painter
Bennett, Rainey Painter
Bensinger, B Edward, III Collector
Berdich, Vera Printmaker, Painter
Block, Mr & Mrs Leigh B Collectors
Booth, Laurence Ogden Sculptor, Architect
Brown, Buck Cartoonist
Burck, Jacob Cartoonist, Painter
Burroughs, Margaret T G Lecturer, Painter
Campoli, Cosmo Sculptor, Educator
Chalmers, E Laurence, Jr Art Administrator, Educator
Chapman, Dave Designer
Colker, Edward Painter, Graphic Artist
Cooper, Anthony J Painter, Instructor
Crane, Barbara Bachmann Photographer, Educator
Cruz, Emilio Painter, Instructor
Danhausen, Eldon Sculptor
Darling, Sharon Sandling Curator, Art Historian
Davidson, Herbert Laurence Painter
Davidson, Suzette Morton Designer, Collector
de Lama, Alberto Painter
Donson, Jerome Allan Gallery Director, Art Dealer
Doyle, John Lawrence Printmaker, Painter
Duckworth, Ruth Sculptor, Ceramist
Dunn, Cal Painter, Film Maker
Edwards, Stanley Dean Painter, Illustrator
Fabion, John Sculptor, Educator
Fairweather, Sally H Art Dealer
Feiffer, Jules Cartoonist, Writer
Feldman, Arthur Mitchell Museum Director
Ferrari, Virginio Luig Sculptor, Educator
Findlay, Helen T Art Dealer
Fischetti, John Cartoonist
Florsheim, Richard A Painter, Printmaker
Friedland, Ruth Volid Art Dealer
Galen, Elaine Painter, Sculptor
Garrison, Eve Painter
Gehr, Mary (Mary Ray) Printmaker, Painter
Gerard, Paula (Mrs Herbert Renison) Printmaker, Painter
Ginzel, Roland Painter, Printmaker
Glauber, Robert H Writer, Curator
Gonzalez, Jose Gamaliel Art Administrator, Designer
Gray, Richard Art Dealer
Greene-Mercier, Marie Zoe Sculptor, Draftsman
Grossman, Grace Cohen Curator, Art Historian
Guthman, Leo S Collector
Guthrie, Derek Art Critic, Painter
Halkin, Theodore Sculptor, Painter
Hanson, Philip Holton Painter
Hardin, Shirley G Art Dealer
Hatch, W A S Printmaker, Educator
Haydon, Harold (Emerson) Painter, Educator
Henry, John Raymond Sculptor
Himmelfarb, John David Painter
Horn, Milton Sculptor, Writer
Hubbard, Robert Sculptor
Hunt, Richard Howard Sculptor
Indeck, Karen Joy Art Dealer, Collector
Irving, Donald J Art Administrator, Writer
Jaidinger, Judith C (Judith Clarann Szesko) Printmaker, Painter
Jakstas, Alfred John Museum Conservator
Joachim, Harold Museum Curator
John, Nancy Regina Art Librarian
Kapsalis, Thomas Harry Painter, Sculptor
Kearney, John (W) Sculptor, Art Administrator
Keefe, Katharine Lee Curator
Kelly, Walter W Art Dealer
Kenney, Estelle Koval Art Therapist, Painter
Kestnbaum, Gertrude Dana Collector
Kind, Joshua B Educator, Art Critic
Kind, Phyllis Art Dealer
King, Elaine A Curator, Photography Critic
Klement, Vera Painter, Educator
Klindt, Steven Art Administrator, Photographer
Koga, Mary Photographer
Kowalski, Dennis Allen Artist
Lanyon, Ellen Painter, Printmaker
Lauffer, Alice A Painter, Printmaker
Lerner, Nathan Bernard Photographer, Painter
Lewis, Phillip Harold Curator
Lipschultz, Maurice A Collector
Love, Richard Henry Art Dealer, Art Writer
Marandel, J Patrice Curator
Maremont, Arnold H Collector
Markus, Mrs Henry A Collector
Maser, Edward Andrew Art Historian, Educator
Mauldin, Bill Cartoonist, Writer
Maurer, Evan Maclyn Art Historian, Curator
Maurice, Alfred Paul Printmaker, Educator
McNear, Everett C Painter, Designer
Messick, Dale Cartoonist
Michod, Susan A Painter
Middaugh, Robert Burton Painter
Mintz, Harry Painter
Morishita, Joyce Chizuko Art Historian, Painter
Morrison, Keith Anthony Painter, Educator
Myers, C Stowe Designer
Naeve, Milo M Art Administrator, Art Historian
Nickle, Robert W Painter, Educator
Parfenoff, Michael S Educator, Printmaker
Paschke, Edward F (Ed) Painter, Illustrator
Peart, Jerry Linn Sculptor
Pen, Rudolph Painter
Phillips, Bertrand D Painter, Photographer
Piatek, Francis John Painter
Polimenakos, Carmon Art Administrator
Postiglione, Corey M Art Dealer, Educator
Prekop, Martin Dennis Sculptor, Educator
Ramberg, Christina (Christina Ramberg Hanson) Painter
Ray, Robert Arthur Sculptor, Architect
Regensteiner, Else (Friedsam) Designer
Rogovin, Mark Muralist, Educator
Rosenthal, John W Slide Maker, Photographer of Art
Rosofsky, Seymour Painter, Printmaker
Rossi, Barbara Painter, Printmaker
Salomon, Lawrence Sculptor, Educator
Schiller, Beatrice Painter, Graphic Artist
Schooler, Lee Collector
Schwartz, Carl E Painter, Instructor
Schwartz, William S Painter, Lithographer
Sewell, Jack Vincent Museum Curator
Shaddle, Alice Sculptor, Painter
Siegel, Irene Painter
Sonnenschein, Hugo Patron, Art Historian
Speyer, A James Curator
Spongberg, Grace Painter, Photographer
Stipe, William S Painter
Suzuki, Sakari Painter
Tigerman, Stanley Painter, Architect
Traub, Charles H Educator, Photographer
Travis, David B Curator, Art Historian
Urban, Mychajlo Raphael Sculptor, Painter
Ushenko, Audrey Andreyevna Painter, Art Historian
Vazquez, Juan Julian Collector
Von Neumann, Robert A Sculptor, Educator
Walker, William Walter Muralist
Weber, John Pitman Muralist, Educator
White, Bruce Hilding Sculptor
Winkler, Dietmar R Designer, Educator
Wriston, Barbara Art Historian, Lecturer
Yoshida, Ray Kakuo Painter, Educator

Chicago Ridge

Sorell, Victor Alexander Art Historian, Art Administrator

De Kalb

Beard, Richard Elliot Painter, Educator
Caldwell, Eleanor Educator, Jeweler
Even, Robert Lawrence Educator
Mahmoud, Ben Painter

Decatur

Klaven, Marvin L Painter, Educator

Deerfield

Houskeeper, Barbara Sculptor, Painter
Winship, Florence Sarah Illustrator

Dekalb

Des Plaines

Grubert, Carl Alfred Cartoonist

East Peoria

Benz, Lee R Printmaker, Watercolorist

Edwardsville

Hampton, Phillip Jewel Painter, Educator
Huntley, David C Painter, Educator

Malone, Robert R Painter, Printmaker
Ryden, Kenneth Glenn Sculptor

Elizabeth

Locker, Thomas Painter

Elmhurst

Jorgensen, Sandra Painter, Educator
Kauffman, (Camille) Andrene Painter, Muralist

Evanston

Avison, David Photographer
Bouras, Harry D Sculptor, Painter
Breckenridge, James D Art Historian
Burnham, Jack Wesley Art Critic, Art Administrator
Gillies, Jean Art Critic, Art Historian
Hurtig, Martin Russell Painter, Sculptor
Pomerantz, Louis Art Conservator, Lecturer
Weiner, Egon Sculptor
Yochim, Louise Dunn Painter
Zwick, Rosemary G Sculptor, Printmaker

Evergreen Park

Miller, Jan Painter, Designer

Flossmoor

Gilbert, Arnold Martin Collector

Geneva

Ehresmann, Donald Louis Art Historian, Educator
Ehresmann, Julia Moore Art Writer, Instructor

Glencoe

Calapai, Letterio Printmaker

Glenview

Barnett, Earl D Designer, Painter
Bramson, Phyllis Halperin Painter, Instructor
Shapiro, Irving Painter, Instructor

Greenville

Hallmark, Donald Parker Art Historian, Curator

Groveland

Mitchell, Dow Penrose Printmaker, Educator

Highland Park

Arenberg, Mr & Mrs Albert L Collectors
Bentley, Claude Painter, Muralist
Esserman, Ruth Painter
Fischer, Jo Cartoonist
Flax, Serene Painter
Spitz, Barbara S Printmaker

Hillside

Chase, Robert M Art Dealer, Collector

Hinsdale

Larsen, Ole Painter, Illustrator

Hubbard Woods

Ludgin, Earle Collector

Joliet

Brulc, Lillian G Painter, Sculptor

Kingston

Driesbach, David Fraiser Printmaker, Educator

Lake Bluff

MacAlister, Paul Ritter Designer, Collector

Lake Forest

Judson, Sylvia Shaw Sculptor
Lockhart, James Leland Illustrator, Painter
Pounian, Albert Kachouni Painter, Educator
Schulze, Franz Educator, Art Critic

Lake Villa

Robertson, Joan Elizabeth (Joan Elizabeth Mitchell) Curator, Draftsman

Lane

Calhoun, Larry Darryl Ceramist

Lombard

Ahlstrom, Ronald Gustin Collage Artist

Macomb

Czach, Marie Museum Director, Curator
Davis, James Wesley Painter, Writer
Jones, Frederick George Printmaker, Educator
Loomer, Gifford C Educator, Painter
Parker, Samuel Murray Printmaker, Painter

Mahomet

Perlman, Raymond Educator, Illustrator

Merrionette Park

Maldre, Mati Photographer, Educator

Metamora

Hedden-Sellman, Zelda Painter, Instructor

Moline

Ramsauer, Joseph Francis Painter, Art Administrator
Stone, Alex Benjamin Art Dealer, Collector

Morton Grove

Berman, Steven M Painter, Printmaker

Naperville

Parke, Walter Simpson Painter, Illustrator

New Lenox

Merfeld, Gerald Lydon Painter

Normal

Carswell, Rodney Painter, Educator
Hoover, Francis Louis Collector, Appraiser
Mawdsley, Richard W Goldsmith, Educator
Toperzer, Thomas Raymond Painter, Gallery Director

Normal-Bloomington

Mills, Frederick Van Fleet Art Administrator, Educator

Northbrook

Eitel, Cliffe Dean Painter, Designer
Endsley, Fred Starr Photographer, Video Artist

Northfield

Boz, Alex (Alex Bozickovic) Painter, Lecturer
Glass, Henry P Designer
Iervolino, Joseph Anthony Art Dealer, Collector
Iervolino, Paula Art Dealer, Collector

Oak Brook

Perry, Richard C Art Dealer, Collector

Oak Lawn

Jachna, Joseph David Photographer, Educator

Oak Park

Jones, Dan Burne Art Historian, Painter
Lennon, Timothy Painting Conservator
Sokol, David Martin Art Historian, Art Administrator
Szesko, Lenore Rundle Painter, Printmaker

Oglesby

Whitlow, Tyrel Eugene Painter, Instructor

Park Forest

Payne, John D Sculptor, Educator

Park Ridge

Fedelle, Estelle Painter, Lecturer
Steinfels, Melville P Painter, Designer

Payson

St Maur, Kirk (Kirk Seymour McReynolds) Sculptor, Educator

Peoria

Cooley, Adelaide Nation Painter, Ceramist
Cooley, William, Jr Collector, Patron
Fromberg, LaVerne Ray Art Administrator, Painter
Kottemann, George & Norma Collectors
Peterson, John Douglas Art Administrator, Designer
Swigart, Lynn S Photographer

Peoria Heights

Buster, Jacqueline Mary Art Dealer, Lecturer

Quincy

Irwin, George M Patron, Collector
Mejer, Robert Lee Painter, Educator
Morrison, Fritzi Mohrenstecher Painter, Lecturer

Ringwood

Pearson, James Eugene Instructor, Sculptor

River Forest

Holt, Charlotte Sinclair Medical Illustrator, Sculptor
Sloan, Jeanette Pasin Painter, Printmaker
White, Philip Butler Painter, Collector

Riverside

Howlett, Carolyn Svrluga Educator, Designer

Riverwoods

Pinkowski, Emily Joan Painter

Rockford

Heflin, Tom Pat Painter, Designer

ILLINOIS (cont)

McGonagle, William Albert Art Administrator
Pinzarrone, Paul Painter
Sneed, Patricia M Art Dealer, Collector

Roscoe

Bond, Oriel Edmund Illustrator, Painter

Saint Charles

Hessing, Valjean McCarty Painter, Illustrator
Morrison C L Art Writer, Art Critic

Schaumburg

Martyl (Martyl Schweig Langsdorf) Painter

Springfield

Bealmer, William Gallery Director, Educator
Evans, Robert James Painter, Museum Curator
Formigoni, Maurie Monihon Painter, Sculptor
Hodge, Roy Garey Painter, Instructor
Madden, Betty I Art Historian, Painter
Madura, Jack Joseph Painter, Instructor
Talaba, L (Linda Talaba Cummens) Sculptor, Printmaker

Sycamore

Peck, Lee Barnes Jeweler, Educator

Urbana

Bradshaw, Glenn Raymond Painter, Educator
Creese, Walter Littlefield Educator
Gallo, Frank Sculptor, Educator
Jackson, Billy Morrow Painter
Lecky, Susan Painter
Replinger, Dot (Dorothy Thiele) Weaver, Designer
Schultz, Harold A Painter, Educator
Smith, Ralph Alexander Writer, Educator
Weller, Allen Stuart Educator, Art Historian

Villa Park

Parker, John William Painter, Educator

Washington

Sunderland, Nita Kathleen Educator, Sculptor

Western Springs

Gilmore, Roger Art Administrator, Educator
Vickery, Charles Bridgeman Painter

Wheaton

Hunter, Miriam Eileen Educator, Art Administrator
Steffler, Alva W Educator, Curator

Wilmette

Drower, Sara Ruth Painter, Illustrator

Winnetka

Alsdorf, James W Patron, Collector
Pattison, Abbott Sculptor, Painter

Woodstock

Gould, Chester Cartoonist

INDIANA

Albany

Patrick, Alan K Potter

Bloomington

Barnes, Robert M Painter, Educator
Cole, Bruce Art Historian, Educator
Eikerman, Alma Jeweler, Designer
Jacquard (Jerald Wayne Jackard) Sculptor, Educator
Kleinbauer, W Eugene Art Historian
Lowe, Marvin Printmaker, Painter
Markman, Ronald Painter
Martz, Karl Ceramist, Educator
McGarrell, James Painter, Educator
Pozzatti, Rudy O Printmaker, Painter
Sieber, Roy Educator, Curator
Solley, Thomas Treat Museum Director

Borden

Marsh, (Edwin) Thomas Potter, Educator

Culver

Williams, Warner Sculptor, Designer

Elkhart

Gilbert, Clyde Lingle Painter

Evansville

Blevins, James Richard Art Administrator, Educator
Eilers, Fred (Anton Frederick), Painter, Designer
Gumberts, William A Collector, Patron
Miley, Les Ceramist, Educator
Streetman, John William, III Art Administrator

Fort Wayne

Brown, Peggy Ann Painter
Krushenick, John Painter, Educator
McBride, James Joseph Painter, Watercolorist
Sandeson, William Seymour Cartoonist

Gosport

Irvine, Betty Jo Art Librarian, Instructor

Granger

Langland, Harold Reed Sculptor, Educator

Greencastle

French, Ray H Printmaker, Sculptor
Meehan, William Dale Painter, Designer

Indianapolis

Block, Amanda Roth Painter, Printmaker
Brucker, Edmund Painter, Educator
Clowes, Allen Whitehill Collector, Patron
Daily, Evelynne B Painter, Printmaker
Davis, Harry Allen Painter, Educator
Eagerton, Robert Pierce Printmaker, Painter
Eiteljorg, Harrison Collector, Patron
Hale, Jean Graham Illustrator, Art Administrator
Mari (Mari M Eagerton) Craftsman, Painter
Mino, Yukata Art Historian, Curator
Rauch, John G Collector, Patron
Roberson, Samuel Arndt Architectural Historian, Educator
Rubins, David Kresz Sculptor
Werner (Charles George Werner) Editorial Cartoonist
Woodward, Helen M Painter, Collector
Yassin, Robert Alan Museum Director, Art Historian

Kouts

Cooper, Wayne Painter, Graphic Artist

Lafayette

Pijanowski, Eugene M Metalworker, Instructor
Pijanowski, Hiroko Sato Metalworker, Instructor
Vevers, Anthony Marr Painter, Educator

Michigan City

Harbart, Gertrude Felton Painter, Instructor

Morgantown

Boyce, Gerald G Educator, Painter

Muncie

Griner, Ned H Educator, Craftsman
Nichols, Alice W Painter, Educator
Nitz, Thomas L Designer, Educator
Rollman-Shay, Ed & Charlotte Painters, Printmakers
Story, William Easton Painter, Gallery Director

Munster

Meeker, Barbara Miller Educator, Painter

New Albany

Engle, George Richard Printmaker

New Carlisle

Droege, Anthony Joseph, II Educator, Painter

Notre Dame

Lauck, Anthony Joseph Sculptor, Educator

Reelsville

Peeler, Richard Potter, Sculptor

Saint Mary Of The Woods

Newport, Esther Painter

South Bend

Holmes, Paul James & Mary E Collectors
Schorgl, Thomas Barry Curator, Printmaker
Vogl, Don George Painter, Printmaker
Zisla, Harold Painter, Educator

Terre Haute

Bowne, James Dehart Museum Director, Art Historian
Engeran, Whitney John, Jr Art Administrator, Painter
Evans, Robert Graves Sculptor, Educator
Friedman, Alan Sculptor, Designer
Hay, Dick Sculptor, Educator
Lamis, Leroy Sculptor, Educator
Porter, Elmer Johnson Painter, Educator
Reddington, Charles Leonard Painter, Gallery Director
Rensch, Roslyn (Roslyn Maria Erbes) Art Historian, Writer

Vincennes

Beard, Marion L Patterson Educator, Painter

West Lafayette

Beelke, Ralph G Educator
Revington, George D, III Collector

IOWA

Ames

Benson, Martha J Gallery Director, Sculptor
Meixner, Mary Louise Painter, Educator

Burlington

Schramm, James Siegmund Collector, Patron

Cedar Falls

Campbell, Marjorie Dunn Painter, Educator
Eliason, Shirley (Shirley Eliason Haupt) Mixed-Media Artist, Instructor
Estabrook, Reed Photographer, Educator
Herrold, Clifford H Educator, Craftsman
Lash, Kenneth Educator, Writer
Page, John Henry, Jr Printmaker, Painter
Ruffo, Joseph Martin Printmaker, Designer
Shaman, Sanford Sivitz Gallery Director, Curator
Wethli, Mark Christian Painter, Draftsman
Widmer, Gwen Ellen Photographer, Educator

Cedar Rapids

Barth, Charles John Educator, Printmaker
Kocher, Robert Lee Painter, Educator
Stamats, Peter Owen Collector, Patron
Wiederspan, Stan Art Administrator, Painter

Cherokee

Hoge, Robert Wilson Museum Director, Educator
Laposky, Ben Francis Designer, Photographer

Coralville

Foster, Stephen C Art Historian, Art Writer

Davenport

Hoffman, Larry Gene Museum Director

Des Moines

Demetrion, James Thomas Art Administrator
Kawa, Florence Kathryn Painter
Kirschenbaum, Jules Painter, Educator
Reece, Maynard Painter, Illustrator

Dubuque

Gibbs, Tom Sculptor

Indianola

Ragland, Jack Whitney Painter, Printmaker

Iowa City

Achepohl, Keith Anden Educator, Printmaker
Alexander, Margaret Ames Art Historian
Breder, Hans Dieter Sculptor, Video Artist
Bundy, Stephen Allen Sculptor, Instructor
Burford, Byron Leslie Painter, Educator
Choo, Chunghi Metalsmith, Fabric Designer
Cuttler, Charles David Art Historian
Gorder, Clayton J Painter, Educator
Lasansky, Mauricio L Printmaker
Moser, Joann Curator, Art Historian
Muhlert, Jan Keene Museum Director
Parry, Ellwood Comly III Art Historian
Patrick, Genie H Painter, Instructor
Patrick, Joseph Alexander Painter, Educator
Schmidt, Julius Sculptor
Schulze, John H Photographer, Educator
Sprague, Nancy Kunzman Sculptor
Tomasini, Wallace J Art Administrator, Art Historian

Jefferson

Finson, Hildred A Children's Book Illustrator

Marion

Morrison, Art Jens Ceramist, Instructor

Marshalltown

Sigrin, Michael E Art Administrator, Museum Director

Mason City

Leet, Richard Eugene Museum Director, Painter

Mitchellville

Olson, Gary Spangler Sculptor, Instructor

Orange City

Kaericher, John Conrad Printmaker, Educator

Solon

Myers, Virginia Anne Printmaker, Educator
Wilke, Ulfert S Painter, Art Administrator

Waterloo

Alling, Clarence (Edgar) Museum Director, Ceramist
Held, Alma M Painter

KANSAS

Ellsworth

Rogers, Charles B Painter, Museum Director

Emporia

Eppink, Helen Brenan Painter
Eppink, Norman R Printmaker, Painter
Hall, Rex Earl Painter, Educator
Johnson, Donald Ray Art Historian, Printmaker

Fredonia

LaDow, Jesse Collector, Patron

Hays

Kuchar, Kathleen Ann Painter, Instructor
Moss, Joel C Painter, Educator
Nichols, Francis N, II Printmaker, Educator
Stevanov, Zoran Painter, Sculptor
Thorns, John Cyril, Jr Designer, Painter

Kansas City

Walton, Donald William Gallery Director, Writer

Lawrence

Brejcha, Vernon Lee Glassblower, Instructor
Carey, James Sheldon Educator, Ceramist
Eldredge, Charles Child, III Museum Director, Art Historian
Enggass, Robert Art Historian
Kehde, Martha Elizabeth Art Librarian
Larsen, Erik Art Historian, Educator
Li, Chu-Tsing Art Administrator, Art Historian
McKay, John Sangster Educator, Art Administrator
Schira, Cynthia Jones Weaver
Shimomura, Roger Yutaka Painter, Educator
Stokstad, Marilyn Art Historian, Educator
Sudlow, Robert N Painter, Educator
Talleur, John J Printmaker
Vaccaro, Luella Grace Ceramist, Painter
Vaccaro, Nick Dante Painter, Educator

Leawood

Selonke, Irene A Painter

Manhattan

Larmer, Oscar Vance Painter, Educator
Maddox, Jerrold Warren Educator, Painter
Ohno, Mitsugi Glassblower

McPherson

Robinson, Mary Ann Art Administrator, Educator

Mission

Bandel, Lennon Raymond Painter
Morgan, James Sherrod Collector

Overland Park

Sickbert, Jo Painter

Pittsburg

Krug, Harry Elno Printmaker, Educator
Russell, Robert Price Educator, Painter

Shawnee Mission

Morgan, Myra Jean Art Dealer

Topeka

Hunt, Robert James Art Administrator, Educator
Peters, Larry Dean Curator, Gallery Director

Wichita

Amsden, Floyd T Collector, Patron
Beren, Stanley O Patron
Bernard, David Edwin Printmaker, Educator
Blameuser, Mary Fleurette Painter, Instructor
Bosin, Blackbear Painter, Designer
Boyd, John David Educator, Printmaker
Bush, Martin Harry Museum Director, Art Historian
Connett, Dee M Educator, Painter
Dickerson, Betty Painter, Lecturer
Goldman, Louis & Sondra Art Dealers
Graves, Mr & Mrs John W Collectors
Hood, Gary Allen Printmaker, Curator
Kincade, Arthur Warren Collector, Patron
Kiskadden, Robert Morgan Painter, Educator
Kurdian, Haroutiun Harry Writer, Collector
Rouse, John R Curator, Collector
Sanderson, Charles Howard Painter, Instructor
Wethington, Wilma Zella Painter
Wooden, Howard Edmund Museum Director, Art Critic

KENTUCKY

Alexandria

Storm, Howard Painter

Anchorage

Koebbeman, Skip Educator, Sculptor
Yenawine, Bruce Harley Art Administrator, Educator

Augusta

Greene, Lois D Art Dealer

KENTUCKY (cont)

Bardstown

Albro, Jeannette (Jeannette Louise Cantrell) Art Dealer, Collector
Cantrell, Jim Painter, Ceramist

Berea

Pross, Lester Fred Educator, Painter
Tredennick, Dorothy W Art Historian, Lecturer

Bowling Green

Forrester, Charles Howard Sculptor, Educator
Kakas, Christopher Printmaker, Painter
Oakes, John Warren Painter, Art Administrator
Schieferdecker, Ivan E Printmaker
Stomps, Walter E, Jr Painter, Educator
Wallace, Lysbeth (Mai) Weaver, Designer

Fort Thomas

Tcheng, John T L Painter

Lexington

Colt, Priscilla C Museum Director
Foose, Robert James Painter, Designer
Freeman, Richard Borden Art Historian, Educator
Petro, Joseph (Victor), Jr Painter, Illustrator
Pierce, James Smith Art Historian, Sculptor
Roloff, John Scott Ceramist, Sculptor
Woodham, Derrick James Sculptor

Louisville

Bratcher, Dale Painter
Bright, Barney Sculptor
Chodkowski, Henry, Jr Painter, Educator
Coates, Ann S Slide Curator, Art Historian
Covi, Dario A Art Historian
Haynie, Hugh Cartoonist
Kloner, Jay Martin Art Historian, Art Administrator
Kohlhepp, Norman Painter, Printmaker
Laugesen, Madelyn A Art Dealer, Patron
Morgan, William Art Historian, Preservationist
Nay, Mary Spencer Painter, Educator
Page, Addison Franklin Museum Director
Stoll, Mrs Berry Vincent Collector
Whitesell, John D Printmaker

Morehead

Altschuler, Franz Illustrator, Educator
Booth, Bill Educator

Murray

Boyd, Karen White Weaver, Tapestry Artist
Head, Robert William Painter, Educator
Rice, Philip Somerset Painter, Educator
Weiler, Melody M Printmaker, Educator

Owensboro

Williams, William Terence Painter, Educator

Princeton

Granstaff, William Boyd Painter, Illustrator

Richmond

Halbrooks, Darryl Wayne Painter, Educator
Isaacs, Ron Painter, Instructor

Shepherdsville

Lesch, Alma Wallace Textile Craftsman, Educator

Sulphur

Kaulitz, Garry Charles Painter, Printmaker
Wegner, Nadene R Metalsmith, Instructor

Williamsburg

Weedman, Kenneth Russell Sculptor, Painter

LOUISIANA

Baton Rouge

Bacot, Henry Parrott Art Historian
Bova, Joe Sculptor, Ceramist
Broussard, Jay Remy Museum Director, Painter
Cox, Richard William Art Historian, Writer
Crespo, Michael Lowe Painter, Educator
Daugherty, Michael F Educator, Sculptor
Dufour, Paul Arthur Painter, Designer
Durieux, Caroline Wogan Printmaker
Harris, Harvey Sherman Painter, Educator
Hayden, Frank Educator, Sculptor
May, William L Collector
O'Neill, John Patton Painter, Illustrator
Pramuk, Edward Richard Painter, Educator
Price, Anne Kirkendall Art Critic
Sachse, Janice R Painter, Printmaker

Brusly

Terrill, Evelyn Beard Art Administrator, Collector

Cecilia

Landry, Richard Miles Photographer, Video Artist

Lafayette

Love, Frances Taylor Museum Director, Writer
Rodrigue, George G Painter

Lake Charles

Holcombe, R Gordon, Jr Collector, Patron

Mamou

Savoy, Chyrl Lenore Sculptor, Educator

Metairie

Kohlmeyer, Ida (R) Painter

New Orleans

Amoss, Berthe Illustrator, Educator
Bernstein, Joseph Collector, Patron
Bullard, Edgar John, III Museum Director, Art Historian
Collier, Alberta Art Critic
Davis, Mr & Mrs Walter Collectors, Patrons
Eckert, Lou Art Dealer, Painter
Emery, Lin (Lin Emery Braselman) Sculptor
Frank, Charles William Wood Carver, Art Writer
Glasgow, Vaughn Leslie Curator, Art Historian
Golden, Rolland Harve Painter
Gordy, Robert P Painter
Gregory, Angela Sculptor, Educator
Harter, John Burton Curator, Painter
Horton, Jan E Painter, Writer
Jordan, George Edwin Art Critic, Art Historian
Jordan, Jack Art Administrator, Sculptor
Kern, Arthur (Edward) Educator, Sculptor
Koss, Gene H Sculptor, Educator
Labiche, Walter Anthony Art Administrator, Instructor
Lamantia, James Painter, Collector
Mason, Bette Painter
Muniot, Barbara King Art Dealer, Collector
Reddix, Roscoe Chester Painter, Educator
Rockmore, Noel Painter
Scott, John Tarrell Educator, Sculptor, Printmaker
Steg, J L Printmaker
Struppeck, Jules Sculptor, Educator
Trivigno, Pat Painter, Educator
Whiteman, Edward Russell Painter
Whitty-Johnson, Patricia Painter
Young, Tom (William Thomas Young) Painter, Educator

Port Allen

Wilkinson, Ruth Murphy Collector, Patron

Ruston

Berguson, Robert Jenkins Painter, Educator
Strother, Joseph Willis Art Administrator, Painter

Shreveport

Cadle, Ray Kenneth Painter, Craftsman
Morgan, Arthur C Sculptor
Morgan, Gladys B Painter, Instructor
Sloan, Richard Painter, Illustrator

Thibodaux

Garzon-Blanco, Armando Designer, Painter

MAINE

Alfred

Benson, S Patricia (McMahon) Printmaker

Bangor

D'Amico, Augustine A Collector, Patron

Bath

Ipcar, Dahlov Illustrator, Painter

Boothbay Harbor

Cavanaugh, Tom Richard Painter, Educator
Eames, John Heagan Etcher, Painter

Bristol

Klebe, Gene (Charles Eugene) Painter, Writer

Brunswick

Beam, Philip Conway Art Administrator, Educator
Cornell, Thomas Browne Painter, Printmaker
Fiori, Dennis Andrew Art Administrator, Museum Director
Rakovan, Lawrence Francis Printmaker, Painter

Camden

Iselin, Lewis Sculptor
Tucker, Richard Derby Painter

Cape Neddick

Kuhn, Brenda Art Historian

Cape Porpoise

Bacon, Peggy Painter, Writer

Casco Village

Dibner, Martin Museum Director

Castine

Ortman, George Earl Painter, Sculptor
Whidden, Conni (Constance) Painter, Instructor

Clinton

Matthews, Harriett Sculptor

Cushing

Collins, John Ireland Painter

Damariscotta

Melville, Grevis Whitaker Painter, Printmaker
Thompson, Ernest Thorne, Jr, Silversmith, Painter

Deer Isle

Merritt, Francis Sumner Painter, Designer
Woell, J Fred Craftsman, Sculptor

East Boothbay

Hook, Frances A Illustrator

Edgecomb

Dean, Nicholas Brice Printmaker, Photographer

Farmington

Scheibe, Fred Karl Painter, Curator
Stucki, Margaret Elizabeth Painter, Writer

Georgetown

Montgomery, Claude Painter, Etcher

Gray

Niss, Robert Sharples Art Critic, Illustrator

Hancock

Holmbom, James William Painter
Moise, William Sidney Painter

Harborside

McCloskey, Robert Painter, Illustrator

Kennebunkport

Penney, Bruce Barton Painter

Kittery

Fein, B R Painter, Lecturer

Lewiston

Isaacson, Philip Marshal Art Critic, Writer

Lincolnville

Wasey, Jane Sculptor
Welliver, Neil G Painter

Medomak

Thompson, Ernest Thorne Educator, Painter

Monhegan Island

Hudson, Jacqueline Painter, Graphic Artist

Newcastle

Coggeshall, Calvert Painter

North Berwick

Hardy, (Clarion) Dewitt Painter, Art Administrator

North Edgecomb

Wilson, Alden Chandler Arts Administrator

Ogunquit

Ehrig, William Columbus Painter
Strater, Henry Painter
Thelin, Valfred P Painter, Lecturer

Orono

Hartgen, Vincent Andrew Painter, Educator
Lewis, Michael H Painter, Educator

Port Clyde

Thon, William Painter

Portland

Barry, William David Curator
Collins, William Charles Painter, Art Administrator
Eide, John Photographer, Instructor
Elowitch, Annette Art Dealer, Antique Dealer
Elowitch, Robert Jason Art Dealer, Patron
Holverson, John Museum Director, Curator
Muench, John Painter, Graphic Artist
Ubans, Juris K Painter, Educator

Richmond

Knox, Elizabeth Ann Painter

Rockland

Hadlock, Wendell Stanwood Museum Director
Peladeau, Marius Beaudoin Art Writer, Museum Director

Rockport

Winters, Denny Painter

Sebago Lake

Ventimiglia, John Thomas Sculptor, Instructor

South Harpswell

Burchess, Arnold Painter, Sculptor
Etnier, Stephen Morgan Painter

South Portland

Douglas, Edwin Perry Painter, Instructor

South Thomaston

Spaulding, Warren Dan Painter, Lecturer

Stonington

Muir, Emily Lansingh Painter, Designer

Sunset

Barrett, Thomas R Painter, Instructor
Mancuso, Leni (Leni Mancuso Barrett) Painter, Instructor

Waldoboro

Parnall, Peter Designer, Illustrator

Waterville

Carpenter, James Morton Art Historian

West Boothbay Harbor

Hemenway, Nancy (Mrs Robert D Barton) Tapestry Artist, Designer

Winter Harbor

Browne, Syd J Painter

York

Hallam, Beverly (Linney) Painter, Lecturer
Laurent, John Louis Painter, Educator
Moore, Robert Eric Painter
Smart, Mary-Leigh Collector, Patron

York Village

Simoneau, Everett Hubert Illustrator, Painter

MARYLAND

Baltimore

Allwell, Stephen S Sculptor
Baney, Ralph Ramoutar Sculptor
Baney, Vera Ceramist, Printmaker
Berge, Henry Sculptor
Bowron, Edgar Peters Curator, Art Historian
Bransky, Miriam (Miriam Ann Gilden) Art Dealer, Painter
Brown, Hilton Edward Educator, Painter
Buitron, Diana M Curator, Art Historian
Carlberg, Norman Kenneth Sculptor, Instructor
Covey, Victor Charles B Conservator
Crosby, Ranice W Medical Illustrator, Educator
Czestochowski, Joseph Stephen Gallery Director
Daniel, Suzanne Garrigues Art Historian
Embry, Norris Painter
Erbe, Joan (Mrs Joan Erbe Udel) Painter
Fendell, Jonas J Educator, Painter
Flannery, Thomas Cartoonist
Ford, John Gilmore Collector
Freudenheim, Tom Lippmann Museum Director
Gilchriest, Lorenzo Constructionist, Educator
Goldstein, Gladys Hack Painter
Green, Morris Baldwin Painter, Instructor
Halpern, Lea Ceramist, Painter Study: Acad in Amsterdam, drawing, painting, sculpture & ceramics with Bert Nienhuis; Reiman Art Sch, Berlin, dr terdam, d
Hammond, Leslie King Art Historian, Writer
Harris, Dr & Mrs S Elliott Collectors
Hartigan, Grace Painter
Hershberg, Israel Painter, Instructor
Hill, Dorothy Kent Museum Curator
Holgate, Jeanne Painter, Illustrator
Ireland, Richard Wilson (Dick) Painter, Instructor
Johnston, William Ralph Art Historian, Art Administrator
Jones, James Edward Printmaker, Painter
Katzen, Hal Zachery Art Dealer
Katzenberg, Dena S Curator
King, Edward S Art Historian
Klitzke, Theodore Elmer Art Historian
Kornblatt, Barbara Rodbell Art Dealer
Kramer, Reuben Sculptor
Long, Glenn Alan Art Historian, Writer
Maril, Herman Painter
Martin, Keith Morrow Painter
Mitchell, John Blair Painter, Educator
Moscatt, Paul N Painter, Instructor
Oppenheimer, Selma L Painter
Quisgard, Liz Whitney Painter, Sculptor
Randall, Richard Harding, Jr Gallery Director, Art Historian
Rembski, Stanislav Painter, Writer
Richardson, Brenda Museum Curator, Writer
Richardson, Frank, Jr Muralist
Rosen, Israel Collector
Rosenthal, Gertrude Art Historian, Art Administrator
Rothschild, Amalie (Rosenfeld) Sculptor, Painter
Sangiamo, Albert Educator, Painter
Satorsky, Cyril Printmaker, Illustrator

MARYLAND (cont)
Scarpitta, Salvatore Sculptor
Scuris, Stephanie Sculptor, Educator
Shackelford, Shelby Painter
Shecter, Mark Painter
Slorp, John Stephen Calligrapher, Instructor
Somerville, Romaine Stec Curator, Art Administrator
Sparks, John Edwin Printmaker, Instructor
Stoneham, John Art Librarian
Streett, Tylden Westcott Sculptor, Educator
Walter, Valerie Harrisse Sculptor
Wells, Betty Childs Illustrator, Painter
West, Virginia M Fiber Sculptor, Writer
Yardley, Richard Quincy Cartoonist
Yates, Sharon Deborah Painter

Bel Air

Montenegro, Enrique E Painter

Bethesda

Ayoroa, Rodolfo (Rudy) E Painter
Cable, Maxine Roth Sculptor
Dawdy, Doris Ostrander Writer, Art Historian
Duffy, Betty Minor Art Dealer
Holvey, Samuel Boyer Sculptor, Designer
Larson, Jane (Warren) Ceramist, Art Writer
Lee, Dora Fugh Painter, Sculptor
Maddox, Jerald Curtis Curator, Art Historian
Mion, Pierre Riccardo Illustrator, Painter
Sarnoff, Lolo Sculptor, Collector

Bowie

White, Amos, IV Ceramist, Photographer

Bozman

Ernst, James Arnold Painter, Instructor

Brookeville

Canby, Jeanny Vorys Art Historian, Curator

Burkittsville

Vo-Dinh, Mai Painter, Printmaker

Cabin John

Green, Tom Instructor, Sculptor

Cambridge

Garbisch, Edgar William & Bernice Chrysler Collectors

Chevy Chase

Asher, Lila Oliver Printmaker, Painter
Breitenbach, Edgar Art Historian
Calfee, William Howard Sculptor
Fruhauf, Aline Painter, Printmaker
Kainen, Jacob Painter, Printmaker
Kranking, Margaret Graham Painter, Instructor
Wiener, Louise Weingarten Art Administrator, Art Writer
Wier, Gordon D (Don) Designer, Painter
Wright, Frank Painter, Printmaker

Clarksville

Kressley, Margaret Hyatt Painter, Printmaker

Clear Spring

Etchison, Bruce Art Conservator, Painter

College Park

Levitine, George Art Historian
Lynch, James Burr, Jr Art Historian
Shaw, Courtney Ann Art Librarian, Art Historian

Crofton

Cusick, Nancy Taylor Painter
Phillips, Gordon Dale Painter, Sculptor

Drayden

Egeli, Peter Even Painter, Illustrator

Easton

Lederer, Kurt Collector

Elkton

Phillips, Melita Ahl Sculptor, Painter

Fort Washington

Grady, Ruby McLain Painter, Sculptor

Frederick

Gates, Harry Irving Sculptor, Painter
Russo, Alexander Peter Painter, Educator
Wallace, David Harold Art Historian, Museum Curator

Gaithersburg

Balance, Jerrald Clark Painter, Sculptor

Glenelg

Niese, Henry Ernst Painter, Film Maker

Hagerstown

Kotun, Henry Paul Museum Director
Roberts, Clyde Harry Painter, Instructor
Warner, Harry Backer, Jr Writer

Hyattsville

Driskell, David Clyde Painter, Educator

Hydes

Wagner, Charles H Art Administrator, Instructor

Joppa

Walters, Ernest Painter

Kensington

Cave, Leonard Edward Sculptor, Educator
McWhinnie, Harold James Printmaker, Educator

Linthicum Heights

Paul, Bernard H Craftsman

Monkton

Leake, Eugene W Painter

New Windsor

Still, Clyfford Painter

Owings Mills

Kissel, William Thorn, Jr Sculptor
Robison, Joan Settle Art Librarian

Point Of Rocks

Larson, Blaine (Gledhill) Painter, Instructor

Potomac

Chieffo, Clifford Toby Painter, Printmaker
Nossal, Audrey Jean Painter, Writer

Queenstown

Houghton, Arthur A, Jr Art Administrator

Riverdale

Clapsaddle, Jerry Painter

Rockville

Edwards, Ellender Morgan Printmaker, Photographer
Pierce, J Michael Printmaker, Instructor
Pruitt, Lynn Sculptor, Gallery Director
Safer, John Sculptor
Wood, James Arthur (Art) Cartoonist, Lecturer

Sandy Spring

Crockett, Gibson M Cartoonist, Painter

Severna Park

Stephany, Jaromir Photographer, Educator

Silver Spring

Bynum, E Anderson (Esther Pearl) Lithographer, Art Administrator
Glick, Paula Florence Art Dealer, Collector
Lapinski, Tadeusz (A) Printmaker, Educator
MacDonald, Kevin John Graphic Artist
Peiperl, Adam Kinetic Artist
Roberts, Lucille D (Malkia) Painter, Educator

Takoma Park

Rode, Meredith Eagon Printmaker, Educator

Towson

Johnson, Lincoln Fernando Educator, Art Writer

MASSACHUSETTS

Amesbury

Dailey, Daniel Owen Sculptor, Designer

Amherst

Ablow, Joseph Painter, Educator
Cohen, Michael S Potter
Davies, Hugh Marlais Art Historian, Gallery Director
Grillo, John Painter
Hendricks, James (Powell) Painter, Educator
Matheson, Donald Roy Printmaker, Educator
Morgan, Charles H Writer
Norton, Paul Foote Art Historian, Educator
Patterson, William Joseph Educator, Printmaker
Roskill, Mark Wentworth Art Historian, Art Critic
Schmalz, Carl (Nelson, Jr) Painter, Educator
Stevens, Nelson L Painter, Educator
Townsend, John F Sculptor, Painter
Trapp, Frank Anderson Art Administrator, Art Historian
Vanasse, Louis Raymond Collector, Instructor
Wardlaw, George Melvin Painter

Andover

Cook Christopher Capen Art Administrator
Hayes, Bartlett Harding, Jr Art Administrator, Writer

Arlington

Dahill, Thomas Henry, Jr Painter, Educator
Rosenberg, Jakob Writer
Slavit, Ann L Sculptor, Painter

Ashfield

Lund, Jane Painter, Ceramist

Bedford

Weeks, James (Darrell Northrup) Painter, Educator

Belmont

Barbarossa, Theodore C Sculptor
Hodgson, James Stanley Art Librarian
Reynolds, Joseph Gardiner Designer
Valier, Biron (Frank) Painter, Printmaker

Beverly

Broudo, Joseph David Educator, Ceramist

Boston

Apel, Barbara Jean Printmaker, Educator
Arthur, John C Curator, Gallery Director
Barreres, Domingo Painter, Educator
Benedikt, Michael Writer, Art Critic
Binning, Robin Printmaker, Sculptor
Blake, Peter Jost Architect, Critic
Cataldo, John William Educator, Calligrapher
Chandler, Dana C, Jr (Akin Duro) Painter, Educator
Channing, Susan Rose Art Administrator, Photographer
Cormier, Robert John Painter, Instructor
Cox, Gardner Painter
Cox, J W S Painter, Instructor
Crite, Allan Rohan Painter, Illustrator
Cunningham, Charles C, Jr Art Administrator
Danikian, Caron Le Brun Writer, Art Critic
Darr, William Humiston Art Historian, Painter
Dolloff, Frank Wesley Conservator
Douaihy, Saliba Painter
Driscoll, Edgar Joseph, Jr Art Critic
Dunn, Roger Terry Art Dealer, Lecturer
Enos, Chris Photographer, Art Administrator
Fairbanks, Jonathan Leo Curator
Fillman, Jesse R Collector
Fink, Alan Art Dealer
Ghikas, Panos George Painter, Educator
Gibran, Kahlil George Sculptor
Gilmartin, Garry M Illustrator
Hadley, Rollin van Nostrand Museum Director
Haley, Patience E (Patience E Haley Ghikas) Painter, Art Conservator
Highberg, Stephanie Wenner Instructor, Painter
Hopkins, Benjamin Art Librarian
Hunter, Robert Douglas Painter, Instructor
Hyde, Andrew Cornwall Art Administrator, Art Consultant
Kanegis, Sidney S Art Dealer
Katayama, Toshihiro Designer, Educator
Kelley, Donald Castell Gallery Director, Art Librarian
Krakow, Barbara L Art Dealer
Kramer, Jack N Painter, Educator
Le Pelley, Guernsey Cartoonist
Livingston, Virginia (Mrs Hudson Warren Budd) Painter, Illustrator
McKie, Todd Stoddard Painter, Printmaker
Moeller, Robert Charles, III Art Historian, Art Administrator
Peabody, Amelia Sculptor
Pezzati, Pietro Painter
Pinckney, Stanley Painter, Tapestry Artist
Prokopoff, Stephen Stephen Museum Director, Art Historian
Pucker, Bernard H Art Dealer
Ranalli, Daniel Photographer, Art Administrator
Robb, Mr & Mrs Sidney R Collectors
Rolly, Ronald Joseph Art Dealer
Safford, Ruth Perkins Painter
Salmon, Larry Curator
Sayre, Eleanor Axson Curator
Schwartz, Henry Painter, Instructor
Searles, Stephen Sculptor
Shatter, Susan Louise Painter
Shooter, Tom Painter
Sisson, Laurence P Painter
Sproat, Christopher Townsend Sculptor
Stebbins, Theodore Ellis, Jr Art Historian, Art Administrator
Vermeule, Cornelius Clarkson, III Art Historian, Writer
Vershbow, Mr & Mrs Arthur Collectors
Vose, Robert Churchill, Jr Art Dealer
Walsh, John, Jr Curator, Educator
Wick, Peter Arms Curator
Wyman, William Craftsman
Zahn, Carl Frederick Designer, Art Administrator

Bradford

Burgy, (Donald Thomas) Conceptual Artist

Brewster

Stoltenberg, Donald Hugo Painter, Printmaker

Brockton

Minutillo, Richard G Curator, Art Historian

Brookfield

Knight, Jacob Jaskoviak Painter, Illustrator

Brookline

Alcalay, Albert S Painter
Barron, Ros Painter, Video Artist
Berger, Jason Painter, Printmaker
Kay, Reed Educator, Painter
Little, Nina Fletcher Collector, Art Historian
Maynard, William Painter, Educator
Nagano, Paul Tatsumi Painter, Designer
Papo, Iso Painter
Pineda, Marianna (Marianna Pineda Tovish) Sculptor
Rogers, Miriam Assemblage Artist
Slone, Sandi Painter, Instructor
Swan, Barbara Painter
Tovish, Harold Sculptor, Educator
Wilson, John Painter, Printmaker

Cambridge

Abramowicz, Janet Printmaker, Sculptor
Ackerman, James S Art Historian, Educator
Agoos, Herbert M Collector
Andersen, Wayne Vesti Art Historian, Educator
Bloom, Hyman Painter
Burgess, David Lowry Environmental Artist
Campbell, David Paul Painter
Capp, Al Cartoonist
Casey, Jacqueline Shepard Designer, Design Director
Chadwick, Whitney Art Historian, Educator
Cohen, Joan Lebold Art Historian, Photographer
Cohn, Marjorie B Conservator, Art Historian
des Rioux, Deena (Victoria Coty) Painter, Designer
Feininger, T Lux Painter, Writer
Fisher, Elaine Photographer, Educator
Freedberg, Sydney Joseph Art Historian, Educator
Freitag, Wolfgang Martin Art Librarian, Art Historian
Fried, Michael Art Critic
Gabin, George Joseph Painter, Instructor
Garvey, Eleanor Art Administrator
Hadzi, Dimitri Sculptor, Printmaker
Hanfmann, George M A Curator, Educator
Ihara, Michio Sculptor
Jewell, William M Educator, Painter
Kepes, Gyorgy Painter, Educator
Kitzinger, Ernst Art Historian
Loehr, Max Museum Curator, Educator
Mazur, Michael Painter, Educator
Mongan, Agnes Art Administrator, Art Historian
Norfleet, Barbara Pugh Curator, Educator
Oberhuber, Konrad J Art Historian, Curator
Paeff, Bashka (Bashka Paeff Waxman) Sculptor
Parry, Marian (Marian Parry Feld) Illustrator, Printmaker
Piene, Otto Sculptor, Painter
Preusser, Robert Ormerod Painter, Educator
Rabb, Mr & Mrs Irving W Collectors
Rathbone, Perry Townsend Museum Director
Reimann, William P Sculptor, Educator
Rey, H A Illustrator, Writer
Roberts, Helene Emylou Art Librarian
Saarinen, Lilian Sculptor
Sussman, Elisabeth Sacks Curator
Trachtman, Arnold S Painter

Charlemont

Behl, Wolfgang Sculptor, Educator

Charlestown

Delgado-Guitart, Jose Painter, Serigrapher
MacLean-Smith, Elizabeth Sculptor, Lecturer

Chatham

Hovey, Walter Read Art Historian, Lecturer

Chelsea

Willis, William Henry, Jr Educator

Chester

Hollingworth, Keith William Sculptor

Chestnut Hill

Abdell, Douglas Sculptor
Plaut, James S Art Administrator, Writer
Saltonstall, Elizabeth Painter
Sharf, Frederic Alan Art Historian, Collector
Wasserman, Jeanne L Curator, Art Historian

Chilmark

Scott, Henry (Edwards), Jr Painter, Educator

Cohasset

Kowal, Dennis J Sculptor, Writer

Conway

Mallary, Robert Sculptor, Educator

Cummaquid

Barber, Samir Painter

Dennis

Geissbuhler, Arnold Sculptor

Dorchester

Lewis, Elma Ina Art Administrator
MacNutt, Glenn Gordon Painter, Illustrator

Dover

Celli, Paul Painter, Educator

Duxbury

Bengtz, Ture Museum Director, Painter

Easthampton

Moser, Barry Illustrator, Printmaker

Fitchburg

Timms, Peter Rowland Museum Director

MASSACHUSETTS (cont)

Framingham

Gordon, Joy L Museum Director, Educator

Framingham Center

Schiff, Lonny Painter, Art Restorer

Georgetown

Nick, George Painter, Educator

Gloucester

Aarons, George Sculptor
Benham, Robert Charles Painter
Coburn, Ralph Painter, Designer
Curtis, Roger William Painter, Art Dealer
Duca, Alfred Milton Sculptor, Painter
Gage, Harry (Lawrence) Painter, Designer
Grasso, Doris (Ten-Eyck) Painter, Sculptor
Gruppe, Emile Albert Painter
Hancock, Walker (Kirtland) Sculptor
Jeswald, Joseph Painter
Margulies, Joseph Painter, Etcher
Movalli, Charles Joseph Art Writer, Painter
Safford, Arthur R Lecturer, Painter
Shore, Mary Painter
Solman, Joseph Painter, Educator

Great Barrington

Agar, Eunice Jane Educator, Painter

Harwich Port

Gilbertson, Charlotte Painter

Hingham

Pierce, Patricia Jobe Art Dealer, Writer
Reardon, Mary A Painter
Rose, Samuel Painter

Holyoke

Hamel, Bernard Franklin Painter

Housatonic

Hillman, Arthur Stanley Printmaker, Instructor

Huntington

Stankiewicz, Richard Peter Sculptor, Educator

Hyannis

Brooks, Robert Art Dealer, Painter

Hyde Park

Pinardi, Enrico Vittorio Sculptor, Painter

Kingston

Brenner, Mabel Painter
Joyce, Marshall Woodside Painter, Instructor

Lenox

Hatch, John Davis Art Consultant, Art Historian

Leverett

Fornas, Leander Printmaker, Instructor

Lexington

Bakanowsky, Louis J Environmental Artist, Designer
Berman, Vivian Printmaker
Cascieri, Arcangelo Sculptor, Educator
Filipowski, Richard E Sculptor, Educator
Franco, Barbara Curator
Kumler, Kipton (Cornelius) Photographer, Lecturer

Lincoln

Steczynski, John Myron Educator, Painter
Walkey, Frederick P Museum Director

Longmeadow

Catok, Lottie Meyer Painter

Manchester

Lothrop, Kristin Curtis Sculptor
Oleksiw, Michael Nicholas, II Art Dealer, Sculptor
Weems, Katharine Lane Sculptor

Marblehead

Taylor, Robert Art Critic, Writer

Marshfield

Greenamyer, George Mossman Sculptor, Educator

Mattapan

Gaither, Edmund B Museum Director, Art Historian

Medford

Stern, Gerd Jacob Sculptor, Kinetic Artist

Medway

Burnett, Calvin Graphic Artist, Illustrator

Melrose

Camlin, James A Painter

Milton

Martin, Marianne Winter Art Historian
Martin, William Barriss, II Sculptor, Designer

Montague

Coughlin, Jack Printmaker, Sculptor

Nantucket

Hicken, Philip Burnham Painter, Instructor
Koch, Virginia Greenleaf Painter
Shunney, Andrew Painter

Nantucket Island

Perrin, C Robert Painter, Illustrator
Weeber, Gretchen Painter

Natick

Abany, Albert Charles Painter, Printmaker
Geller, Esther (Esther Geller Shapero) Painter, Printmaker
Leax, Ronald Allen Sculptor

Needham Heights

Castano, Elvira Art Dealer, Collector
Castano, Giovanni Art Dealer, Painter

New Bedford

Angelo, Domenick Michael Sculptor
Frauwirth, Sidney Collector
Neugebauer, Margot Designer, Craftsman
Smith, David Loeffler Painter, Educator

Newton

Bahm, Henry Painter
Bohlen, Nina (Celestine Eustis Bohlen) Painter
Garber, Susan R Art Administrator, Lecturer
Grippe, Florence (Berg) Painter, Potter
Grippe, Peter J Sculptor, Printmaker
Hurwitz, Sidney J Painter, Printmaker
Jencks, Penelope Instructor, Sculptor

Newton Center

Cobb, Ruth Painter
Glaser, Samuel Collector
Kupferman, Lawrence Painter

Newtonville

Polonsky, Arthur Painter, Educator
Skinner, Orin Ensign Designer

North Amherst

Brown, Jeffrey Rogers Art Dealer, Art Historian

North Andover

Whitehill, Walter Muir Writer, Art Historian

North Brookfield

Neal, (Minor) Avon Writer, Printmaker
Parker, Ann (Ann Parker Neal) Photographer, Printmaker

North Hatfield

Minisci, Brenda (Eileen) Sculptor, Ceramist

North Scituate

Pappas, Marilyn Collage Artist, Educator

North Tewksbury

Kaufman, Mico Sculptor

Northampton

Chetham, Charles Museum Director
Cohen, H George Painter, Educator
MacDonald, William L Architectural Historian
Offner, Elliot Sculptor, Printmaker

Norwell

Wentworth, Murray Jackson Painter, Instructor

Onset

Halberstadt, Ernst Painter, Sculptor
Mellor, George Edward Educator, Sculptor

Orleans

Vickrey, Robert Remsen Painter

Pittsfield

Henry, Stuart (Compton) Museum Director, Painter

Provincetown

Couper, Charles Alexander Painter, Instructor
De Nagy, Eva Painter
Forsberg, Jim Painter, Printmaker
Hensche, Henry Painter, Instructor
Jensen, Claud Craftsman
Jensen, Marit Painter, Serigrapher
Kaplan, Joseph Painter
Malicoat, Philip Cecil Painter

Rayner, Ada (Ada Rayner Hensche) Painter
Rizk, Romanos Painter, Instructor
Stout, Myron Stedman Painter

Quincy

White, Leo Cartoonist

Reading

Nordstrand, Nathalie Johnson Painter

Revere

Cretara, Domenic Anthony Painter, Educator

Rockport

Beaman, Richard Bancroft Painter
Bissell, Phil Cartoonist, Illustrator
Davidson, Allan Albert Painter, Sculptor
Harper, Eleanor O'Neil Painter
Hill, J Tweed Painter
LaFreniere, Isabel Marcotte Painter
Martin, Mary Finch Art Director
Martin, Roger Painter, Graphic Artist
Morrell, Wayne (Beam) Painter
Murphy, Gladys Wilkins Painter, Craftsman
Murphy, Herbert A Architect, Painter
Nicholas, Thomas Andrew Painter
Pearson, Marguerite Stuber Painter
Pettibone, John Wolcott Art Administrator, Graphic Artist.
Recchia, Richard (Henry) Sculptor
Ricci, Jerri Painter
Schlemm, Betty Lou Painter
Strisik, Paul Painter
Turner, Bruce Backman Painter
Van Wyk, Helen Painter, Lecturer

Rowley

Ahl, Henry C Painter, Writer
Jacques, Michael Louis Printmaker, Educator

Roxbury

Avedisian, Edward Painter
Crump, Walter Moore Printmaker, Painter

Salem

Tolles, Bryant Franklin, Jr Museum Director, Art Librarian

Segreganset

Macomber, Allison Painter, Sculptor

Sharon

Avakian, John Painter, Instructor

Sheffield

Friedman, Benno Photographer
Philbrick, Margaret Elder Printmaker, Painter

Sherborn

Pickhardt, Carl Painter, Printmaker

Somerville

Corish, Joseph Ryan Painter
Leja, Michael Joseph Curator, Art Critic

South Boston

Quinn, Sandi (Cassandrasu Dhooge-quinn Vachon) Instructor, Calligrapher

South Dennis

Pride, Joy Painter, Writer

South Hadley

DeLonga, Leonard Anthony Sculptor, Educator
Holcomb, Grant Art Historian, Educator
Seace, Barry William Printmaker, Educator

South Harwich

Sahrbeck, Everett William Painter

Spencer

Elliott, Bruce Roger Printmaker, Educator

Springfield

Muhlberger, Richard Charles Museum Director

Stockbridge

Boris, Bessie Painter
Garel, Leo Painter
Jones, Franklin Reed Painter, Art Writer
Kalischer, Clemens Photographer, Gallery Director
Rockwell, Norman Illustrator

Stoughton

Hoffman, Marilyn Friedman Gallery Director

Sudbury

Aronson, David Painter, Sculptor
McSheehy, Cornelia Marie Printmaker

Sunderland

Kamys, Walter Painter, Educator

Topsfield

Webster, Larry Designer, Painter

Truro

Craig, Nancy Ellen Painter
Johnson, Joyce Instructor, Sculptor
Preston, Malcolm H Critic, Painter
Wallace, John Edward Painter, Educator
Yater, George David Painter

Tyringham

Brown, Jeanette H Collector, Art Administrator
Davis, Donald Robert Painter, Art Dealer
Picken, George Painter, Printmaker

Vineyard Haven

Berresford, Virginia Painter, Muralist

Waban

Goldstein, Nathan Art Writer, Painter

Waltham

Belz, Carl Irvin Museum Director
Neuman, Robert S Painter, Educator

Ware

Chase, Alice Elizabeth Educator, Writer

Wayland

Bentov, Mirtala Sculptor
Dergalis, George Painter, Sculptor
Rodman, Ruth M Printmaker

Wellesley

Borgo, Ludovico Art Historian
O'Gorman, James Francis Art Historian
Rayen, James Wilson Painter, Educator

Wellfleet

Dickinson, Edwin Painter
Lechay, James Painter
Wilkinson, Kirk Cook Art Dealer, Painter

Wenham

Fransioli, Thomas Adrian Painter, Printmaker

West Cambridge

Coolidge, John Art Historian

West Harwich

Bush, Lucile Elizabeth Painter, Educator

West Newton

Schon, Nancy Quint Sculptor, Instructor

West Roxbury

Altmann, Henry S Painter, Educator
Sorokin, Maxine Ann Painter, Educator

West Springfield

Reichert, Donald O Painter, Museum Director

Weston

Mariano, Kristine Painter

Wilbraham

Gale, William Henry Painter, Designer
Stevens, Richard Clive Painter, Illustrator

Williamstown

Brooke, David Stopford Museum Director
Brooks, John H Art Administrator, Educator
Cunningham, Charles Crehore Curator, Lecturer
Faison, Samson Lane, Jr Museum Director, Educator
Hamilton, George Heard Museum Director, Art Historian
Johnson, Eugene Joseph Art Historian
Rinehart, Michael Art Librarian, Editor
Robinson, Franklin W Art Administrator, Art Historian
Schneider, Julie (Saecker) Painter
Stoddard, Whitney Snow Art Historian

Wilmington

Ballou, Anne MacDougall Printmaker

Winchester

Dobbins, James Joseph Cartoonist

Wollaston

Smongeski, Joseph Leon Painter, Designer

Worcester

Bumgardner, Georgia Brady Curator, Art Historian
Cronin, Robert (Lawrence) Painter
Dresser, Louisa Art Administrator, Art Historian
Farber, Mrs George W Collector
Graziani, Sante Painter, Muralist
Haswell, Hollee Art Librarian, Painter
Hovsepian, Leon Painter, Designer
Italiano, Joan Nylen Sculptor, Educator
Krueger, Donald W Painter, Educator
Mattern, Penny Greig Art Librarian
McCorison, Marcus Allen Librarian
Nigrosh, Leon Isaac Designer, Instructor
Orze, Joseph John Art Administrator, Sculptor
Priest, T Painter, Printmaker

MASSACHUSETTS (cont)
Riley, Chapin Collector
Shepard, Lewis Albert Art Dealer, Art Historian
Teitz, Richard Stuart Museum Director, Art Historian

Yarmouth Port

Hitch, Jean Leason Painter
Hitch, Robert A Painter

MICHIGAN

Adrian

Cervenka, Barbara Educator, Painter

Albion

Brunkus, Richard Allen Printmaker, Curator

Alma

Kirby, Kent Bruce Printmaker, Photographer

Alpena

Bodem, Dennis Richard Museum Director

Ann Arbor

Arnheim, Rudolf Educator, Writer
Bayliss, George Painter, Art Administrator
Cassara, Frank Painter, Printmaker
Eisenberg, Marvin Art Historian, Educator
Gooch, Donald Burnette Painter
Iglehart, Robert L Educator
Kamrowski, Gerome Painter, Educator
La More, Chet Harmon Painter, Sculptor
Lewis, William Arthur Painter, Art Administrator
McClure, Thomas F Sculptor, Educator
McMillan, Constance Painter
Palazzola, Guy Art Administrator, Educator
Poinier, Arthur Best Cartoonist
Reider, David H Designer, Photographer
Sawyer, Charles Henry Museum Director
Smith, Sherry Weaver, Educator
Stephenson, John H Sculptor, Educator
Waller, Aaron Bret Museum Director, Art Historian
Weber, Albert Jacob Painter, Educator
Weddige, Emil Lithographer, Educator
Wethey, Harold Edwin Art Historian

Berrien Springs

Constantine, Greg John Painter, Educator

Birmingham

Fredericks, Marshall Maynard Sculptor
Kasle, Gertrude Art Consultant, Collector
Michaels, Glen Sculptor, Painter
Morris, Donald Fischer Art Dealer
Morris, Florence Marie Art Dealer
Robinson, Sally W Painter, Printmaker
Stewart, Norman (William) Printmaker, Instructor
Thom, Robert Alan Illustrator, Painter
Vihos, George Painter

Bloomfield Hills

Hall, Julie Ann Art Writer, Collector
Hall, Michael David Sculptor, Educator
Mitchell, Wallace (MacMahon) Museum Director, Painter
Siden, Harriet Field Art Librarian, Collector
Slade, Roy Painter, Gallery Director
Toth, Carl Wayne Photographer
West, Clifford Bateman Painter, Film Maker

Brighton

Nestor, Lulu B Painter, Art Administrator

Canton

Mandziuk, Michael Dennis Painter, Serigrapher

Cass City

Ritter, Richard Quintin Glass Blower

Coloma

Martmer, William P Painter, Photographer

Detroit

Arwin, Kathleen G Art Dealer
Arwin, Lester B Art Dealer
Asante, Kwasi Seitu (Robin Okeeffer Harper) Art Historian, Painter
Basset, Brian Willard Editorial Cartoonist
Bostick, William Allison Painter, Calligrapher
Broner, Robert Printmaker, Painter
Burnett, Patricia Hill Painter, Sculptor
Colby, Joy Hakanson Art Critic, Art Consultant
Cummings, Frederick James Art Administrator, Art Historian
Downs, Linda Anne Curator, Art Administrator
Driver, Morley-Brooke Lister Art Critic, Collector
Elam, Charles Henry Art Administrator, Art Historian
Goodman, Brenda Joyce Painter, Instructor
Hill, Draper Editorial Cartoonist, Art Historian
Jacobsson, Sten Wilhelm John Designer, Sculptor
Johnson, Lester L Painter, Instructor
Kachadoorian, Zubel Painter, Educator
Kan, Michael Art Historian, Art Administrator
King, Henri Umbaji Painter, Illustrator
Kozlow, Richard Painter, Lecturer
Midener, Walter Sculptor, Instructor
Miles, Cyril Painter, Instructor
Mosby, Dewey Franklin Curator, Art Historian
Peck, William Henry Curator, Art Historian
Redstone, Louis Gordon Architect, Art Writer
Rivard, Nancy J Curator, Art Historian
Roland, Arthur Painter, Educator
Rossen, Susan F Art Historian, Art Editor
Scheyer, Ernst Art Historian, Lecturer
Schuster, Eugene Ivan Art Dealer, Art Historian
Slusser, James Bernard Art Dealer, Kinetic Artist
Stark, Shirley Sculptor
Stephenson, Susanne G Ceramist
Wilbert, Robert John Painter, Educator
Woodson, Shirley Ann Painter, Educator

Dexter

Mason, Alice Frances Lithographer, Painter
Rush, Jon N Sculptor, Educator

East Lansing

Alexander, Robert Seymour Educator, Designer
Brainard, Owen Painter, Educator
Church, C Howard Painter
De Blasi, Anthony Armando Painter
Hu, Mary Lee Metalsmith, Educator
Ishikawa, Joseph Museum Director, Lecturer
Logan, David George Educator, Metalsmith
McChesney, Clifton Painter, Educator
Vasils, Albert Painter, Illustrator

Flint

Davidek, Stefan Painter
Hodge, G Stuart Museum Director

Grand Rapids

Collins, Paul Painter
Danielson, Phyllis I Art Administrator, Fiber Artist
Inslee, Marguerite T Painter, Collector
Koster, Marjory Jean Printmaker
Myers, Fred A Museum Director
Sweeney, J Gray Curator, Art Historian
Weidenaar, Reynold Henry Etcher, Painter

Grandville

McIver, John Kolb Painter

Grosse Pointe

Nobili, Louise Educator, Painter

Grosse Pointe Farms

Krentzin, Earl Sculptor, Silversmith
Muccioli, Anna Maria Painter, Sculptor

Hartland

Stemelos, Electra Georgia Mousmoules Painter, Instructor

Highland Park

Brose, Morris Sculptor

Kalamazoo

Asbel, Joseph Art Dealer
Gammon, Reginald Adolphus Educator, Painter
Greaver, Hanne Printmaker
Greaver, Harry Art Administrator, Painter
Harrison, Carole Educator, Sculptor
Hefner, Harry Simon Painter, Educator
Johnston, Robert Porter Sculptor, Art Historian
Kemper, John Garner Painter, Designer
Meyer, Charles Edward Art Historian, Ceramist
Sheridan, Helen Adler Art Librarian

Lakeside

King, Clinton Blair Painter, Printmaker

Lansing

Jungwirth, Irene Gayas (I Gayas Jungwirth) Painter, Stained Glass Artist

Lawton

Laslo, Patricia Louise Sculptor, Instructor

Marquette

Gorski, Richard Kenny Educator, Graphic Artist

Mason

Leepa, Allen Painter, Educator

Midland

Breed, Charles Ayars Sculptor, Educator

Mount Pleasant

Bambas, Thomas Reese Metalsmith
Born, James E Sculptor

Muskegon

Howarth, Shirley Reiff Museum Director, Art Historian

Niles

Milonadis, Konstantin Sculptor

Northville

Chaffee, John W Sculptor, Lecturer

Novi

Wheeler, Robert G Art Administrator

Oak Park

Barr, David John Sculptor, Painter
Rosen-Queralt, Jann Sculptor, Designer

Okemos

de Martelly, John Stockton Painter, Printmaker
Taylor, John Frank Adams Writer
Whitaker, Irwin A Educator, Craftsman

Olivet

Whitney, William Kuebler Painter, Art Historian

Onsted

Thiery, Thomas Allen Painter

Owosso

Harsh, Richard Painter, Educator

Parma

Wolber, Paul J Painter, Educator

Plymouth

DeLauro, Joseph Nicola Sculptor, Educator

Pontiac

Lyons, Ian Raymond Art Administrator, Collector

Richland

Walker, James Adams Painter, Printmaker

Rochester

Brun, Thomas Sculptor, Instructor
Usui, Kiichi Curator

Royal Oak

McCarty, Lorraine Chambers Painter, Instructor

Saginaw

Chester, Janie Kathleen Museum Director, Educator

Saint Clair Shores

Burns, Sheila Painter, Lecturer
Burns, Stan Painter, Sculptor
Cartmell, Helen Painter, Art Administrator

Troy

Cloud, Jack L Gallery Owner, Publisher

West Bloomfield

Siden, Franklin Art Dealer, Lecturer
Simper, Frederick Painter

West Olive

Boeve, Edgar Gene Educator, Painter

Whitmore Lake

Davis, Philip Charles Photographer, Educator

Williamston

Lawton, James L Sculptor, Educator

Ypsilanti

Calkins, Kingsley Mark Painter, Educator
Iden, Sheldon Painter, Educator

MINNESOTA

Albert Lea

Herfindahl, Lloyd Manford Painter

Bemidji

Smith, Kent Alvin Sculptor

Collegeville

Hendershot, J L Printmaker, Educator
Petheo, Bela Francis Painter, Printmaker

Duluth

Boyce, William G Museum Director, Educator
Brush, Leif Sound Sculptor, Instructor

Excelsior

Nash, Katherine E Sculptor, Educator

Golden Valley

Jardine, Donald Leroy Art Editor, Educator

Hastings

Koestner, Don Painter

Janesville

Tanner, James L Craftsman

Mankato

Finkler, Robert Allan Educator, Painter
Hapke, Paul Frederick Painter, Educator
Spurgin, John Edwin Art Administrator, Painter

Minneapolis

Beal, Graham William John Curator, Lecturer, Historian
Bjorklund, Lee Painter, Educator
Booth, Cameron Painter
Bradbury, Ellen A Curator, Art Historian
Burpee, James Stanley Painter, Instructor
Busa, Peter Painter, Sculptor
Byrne, James Richard Video Artist
Caglioti, Victor Painter, Sculptor
Conaway, James D Painter, Educator
Cooper, Frederick Alexander Art Historian
Fisher, Carole Gorney Painter, Sculptor
Flick, Paul John Painter, Collector
Friedman, Martin Museum Director
Gawboy, Carl Painter, Art Historian
Graham, Richard Marston Sculptor, Educator
Hallman, Gary Lee Photographer
Hausman, Jerome Joseph Educator
Hedberg, Gregory Scott Curator, Art Historian
Hendler, Raymond Painter, Sculptor
Holen, Norman Dean Sculptor, Educator
Humleker, Ruth S Art Administrator
Johnson, James Edwin & Sandra Kay Graphic Designers
Justus, Roy Braxton Cartoonist
Kouba, Leslie Carl Art Dealer, Painter
Larkin, Eugene Designer, Educator
Larson, Philip Seely Artist, Art Historian
Long, Scott Cartoonist
Lyons, Lisa Curator, Art Historian
Marcheschi, (Louis) Cork Sculptor, Educator
McCannel, Mrs Malcolm A Collector
McNally, Sheila John Educator, Art Historian
Morris, Edward A Painter, Illustrator
Munzer, Aribert Painter, Educator
Myers, Malcolm Haynie Printmaker, Painter
Nielsen, Stuart Painter
Parsons, Merribell Maddux Curator, Art Administrator
Peterson, Harold Patrick Art Librarian, Art Editor
Poor, Robert John Art Historian
Preuss, Roger Painter, Writer
Quick, Birney MacNabb Painter, Instructor
Richardson, Phyllis A Art Administrator, Painter
Rollins, Jo Lutz Art Dealer, Painter
Rose, Thomas Albert Sculptor
Rowan, Herman Painter, Educator
Rudquist, Jerry Jacob Painter, Instructor
Sachs, Samuel, II Art Historian, Museum Director
Saltzman, William Painter, Designer
Scherer, Herbert Grover Art Librarian, Art Historian
Sheppard, Carl Dunkle Art Historian
Slettehaugh, Thomas Chester Painter, Educator
Smith, Justin V Collector
Stoller, John Chapman Art Dealer
Stones, Margaret Alison Art Historian
Sussman, Bonnie K Art Dealer, Collector
Torbert, Donald Robert Educator, Art Historian
Torbert, Marguerite Birch Designer, Writer
Torbert Stephanie Birch Photographer, Educator
Verostko, Roman Joseph Educator, Art Historian
Walton, Florence Goodstein (Goodstein-Shapiro) Painter, Art Historian
Wolfe, Ann (Ann Wolfe Graubard) Sculptor, Instructor

Minnetonka

Lack, Richard Frederick Painter, Instructor

Moorhead

Boe, Roy Asbjorn Art Historian, Educator
Youngquist, Jack Draftsman

Nisswa

Smith, Paul Roland Painter, Educator

Red Wing

Biederman, Charles (Karel Joseph) Sculptor

Rochester

Gagnon, Charles Eugene Sculptor

Saint Cloud

Ellingson, William John Educator, Printmaker

Saint Paul

Boese, Alvin William Researcher, Collector
Caponi, Anthony Sculptor, Educator
Celender, Donald Dennis Art Historian, Conceptual Artist
Follett, Jean Frances Sculptor, Painter
Grey, Mrs Benjamin Edwards Collector, Patron
Headley, Sherman Knight Museum Director, Patron
Kielkopf, James Robert Painter
Lasansky, Leonardo da Iowa Educator, Printmaker
Leach, Frederick Darwin Painter, Art Historian
Lein, Malcolm Emil Art Administrator, Designer
Lupori, Peter John Educator, Sculptor
Montequin, Francois-Auguste de Art Historian, Writer
Morrison, George Painter
Niemeyer, Arnold Matthew Collector, Patron
Nowytski, Sviatoslav (Slavko) Film Maker, Photographer

MINNESOTA (cont)

Ott, Jerry Duane Painter
Price, Michael Benjamin Sculptor
Rahja, Virginia Helga Painter, Art Administrator
Randell, Richard K Sculptor
Swanson, Dean Art Consultant
Tselos, Dimitri Theodore Art Historian, Writer
Wheeler, Cleora Clark Designer, Illuminator

Saint Peter

Buranabunpot, Pornpilai Designer, Weaver
Granlund, Paul Theodore Sculptor, Instructor
Palmgren, Donald Gene Painter, Photographer

Thief River Falls

Hagglund, Irvin (Arvid) Cartoonist

Two Harbors

Wiener, Phyllis Ames Painter

White Bear Lake

Larkin, John E, Jr Collector, Patron

Winona

Murray, Floretta May Painter, Educator

Zumbrota

Lee, Margaret F Painter

MISSISSIPPI

Bay Saint Louis

Kimbrough, (Sara) Dodge Painter

Cleveland

Britt, Sam Glenn Educator, Painter
Norwood, Malcolm Mark Painter, Educator

Clinton

Gore, Samuel Marshall Painter, Sculptor

Columbus

Ambrose, Charles Edward Painter, Educator
Dice, Elizabeth Jane Craftsman, Educator
Frank, David Potter, Educator
Nawrocki, Thomas Dennis Printmaker, Educator
Stringer, Mary Evelyn Educator, Art Historian
Summer, (Emily) Eugenia Painter, Sculptor
West, Clara Faye Painter, Conservator

Hattiesburg

Bowman, Jeff Ray Art Administrator, Educator

Itta Bena

Johnston, William Edward Painter, Educator

Jackson

Hull, Marie (Atkinson) Painter
Tennyson, Merle Berry Painter, Printmaker
Wolfe, Mildred Nungester Painter, Designer

McComb

Holmes, Ruth Atkinson Painter, Sculptor

Oxford

Allen, Jere Hardy Painter, Educator
Gross, Charles Merrill Educator, Sculptor
Hamblett, Theora Painter, Illustrator
Tettleton, Robert Lynn Painter, Educator

Silver City

Slaughter, Lurline Eddy Painter

Summit

Dawson, Bess Phipps Painter, Art Dealer

Tupelo

Francis, Jean Thickens Painter, Sculptor
Francis, Madison Ke, Jr Sculptor, Printmaker

University

Winters, John L Painter, Printmaker

MISSOURI

Cape Girardeau

Parker, James Varner Art Administrator, Designer

Columbia

Bartlett, Donald Loring Sculptor, Educator
Berneche, Jerry Douglas Educator, Painter
Bussabarger, Robert Franklin Sculptor, Painter
Cameron, Brooke Bulovsky Educator, Printmaker
Christ-Janer, Arland F Painter, Printmaker
Collins, Marcia Reed Art Librarian
Kabak, Robert Painter, Educator
Larson, Sidney Painter, Conservator
McCauley, Gardiner Rae Educator, Painter
McKinin, Lawrence Educator, Painter
Moulton, Rosalind Kimball Photographer
Peckham, Nicholas Architect, Designer
Rugolo, Lawrence Screenprinter, Educator
Stack, Frank Huntington Painter, Printmaker
Weller, John Sidney Painter, Printmaker
Zilka, Michael John Educator, Studio Director

Crestwood

Geis, Milton Arthur Painter, Designer

Florissant

Fousek, Frank Daniel Printmaker, Painter

Jefferson City

Parks, James Dallas Art Historian, Painter

Kansas City

Bassin, Joan Art Historian, Educator
Bransby, Eric James Muralist, Educator
Brody, Myron Roy Sculptor
Cadieux, Michael Eugene Educator, Painter
Carstenson, Cecil C Sculptor, Lecturer
Clare, Stewart Research Artist
Crist, William Gary Sculptor, Educator
Eaton, Thomas Newton Cartoonist, Illustrator
Ehrlich, George Art Historian
Field, Lyman Art Administrator, Collector
Goheen Ellen Rozanne Curator, Art Historian
Goldman, Lester Painter
James, Frederic Painter
Kitta, George Edward Printmaker, Graphic Artist
Lottes, John William Art Administrator
Marshall, James Duard Conservator, Painter
McKim, William Wind Printmaker, Painter
Miller, Lee Anne Painter, Printmaker
Reinhart, Margaret Emily Painter
Sickman, Laurence Chalfant Stevens Art Administrator, Art Historian
Thompson, Judith Kay Painter, Lecturer
Townsend, Marvin J Cartoonist, Illustrator

Kirksville

Jorgenson, Dale Alfred Art Administrator, Aesthetician

Kirkwood

Reinhardt, Siegfried Gerhard Painter, Designer

Maryville

Hageman, Charles Lee Educator, Designer
Sunkel, Robert Cleveland Art Historian, Art Administrator

Nevada

Chew, Harry Painter, Educator

Osage Beach

Roth, James Buford Art Consultant

Ozark

Armstrong, Bill Howard Painter, Educator

Point Lookout

Tong, Marvin Enoch Museum Director

Rogersville

Elkins, (E) Lane Educator, Potter

Saint Charles

Eckert, William Dean Painter, Art Historian
Moerschel, Chiara Painter

Saint James

Lacy, Robert Eugene Painter

Saint Joseph

Ray, Jim Museum Director

Saint Louis

Crane, Michael Patrick Photographer, Performance Artist
Duhme, H Richard, Jr Sculptor, Educator
Engelhardt, Thomas Alexander Editorial Cartoonist
Fett, William F Instructor, Painter
Fifield, Mary Administrator, Writer
Hicks, Leon Nathaniel Printmaker
Hilligoss, Martha M Art Librarian
Jones, Howard William Painter, Sculptor
Krukowski, Lucian Painter, Educator
Kultermann, Udo Art Historian, Educator
Leven, Arline Claire Museum Curator
May, Morton David Collector, Patron
Newman, (John) Christopher Sculptor, Educator
Nickel, Jim H Painter, Sculptor
Osver, Arthur Painter
Palmer, Lucie Mackay Painter, Lecturer
Pulitzer, Mr & Mrs Joseph, Jr Collectors
Quinn, William Painter
Schactman, Barry Robert Painter, Educator
Schweiss, Ruth Keller Sculptor, Designer
Seppa, Heikki Markus Goldsmith, Silversmith, Educator
Smith, Helen M Illustrator, Painter
Springer, Lynn Elise Curator
Taylor, Marie Sculptor
Trova, Ernest Tino Sculptor, Painter
Walters, Sylvia Solochek Printmaker, Instructor
Winfield, Rodney M Artist
Zonia, Dhimitri Painter, Muralist

Sainte Genevieve

Bowman, Dorothy (Louise) Painter, Printmaker

Springfield

Albin, Edgar A Educator, Art Critic
Bonacker, Joyce Sybil Painter, Art Dealer
Ettinger, Susi Steinitz Painter, Lecturer
Ivy, Gregory Dowler Painter
Kieferndorf, Frederick George Painter, Educator
Landwehr, William Charles Museum Director
Latham, Catherine Doris Gallery Director, Painter
Richardson, James Lewis Educator, Printmaker
Shuck, Kenneth Menaugh Museum Director, Painter

Warrensburg

Ellis, Edwin Charles Educator

Webster Groves

Boccia, Edward Eugene Painter

MONTANA

Anaconda

Brimhall, Mary Jane Museum Director

Babb

Racine, Albert Batiste Woodcarver

Bigfork

Fellows, Fred Painter, Sculptor
Morgan, Darlene Painter

Billings

Forbes, Donna Marie Museum Director
Morrison, Robert Clifton Printmaker, Painter
Ralston, James Kenneth Painter, Illustrator
Steele, Benjamin Charles Painter, Educator
Whitson (Peter Whitson Warren) Draftsman, Collage Artist

Bozeman

Alexander, William C Art Administrator, Ceramist
Bashor, John W Educator, Painter
Bronson, Clark Everice Sculptor, Painter
Ferguson, Frank Wayne Intermedia Artist
Helzer, Richard Brian Metalsmith, Educator

Browning

Scriver, Robert Macfie (Bob) Sculptor

Butte

Taulbee, Dan J Painter, Art Dealer

Choteau

Boussard, Dana Sculptor

Dillon

Corr, James Donat Painter, Gallery Director

Great Falls

Cordingley, Mary Bowles Painter
Halko, Joe Sculptor, Painter
Stevenson, Branson Graves Painter, Printmaker

Lakeside

Lynde, Stan Cartoonist, Painter

Lodge Grass

Red Star, Kevin Francis Painter, Illustrator

Missoula

Barton, Bruce Walter Painter, Educator
Collier, Ric Sculptor, Museum Director
Dew, James Edward Educator, Painter
Eder, Earl Painter
Hook, Walter Painter, Printmaker
Hunt, David Curtis Museum Director, Writer

Rollins

Lebkicher, Anne Ross Painter, Art Administrator

Somers

Smith, Cecil Alden Painter, Illustrator

NEBRASKA

Grand Island

Christensen, Val Alan Printmaker, Instructor

Kearney

Peterson, Larry D Painter, Instructor

Lexington

Sheldon, Olga N (Mrs A B Sheldon) Patron, Collector

Lincoln

Eisentrager, James A Painter
Geske, Norman Albert Museum Director, Educator
Howard, Dan F Painter, Educator
Jacobshagen, N Keith, II Painter, Photographer
Lux, Gladys Marie Painter
Nelson, Jon Allen Curator, Art Historian
Ross, Douglas Allan Sculptor, Instructor
Rowan, C Patrick Sculptor, Educator
Seyler, David W Sculptor, Educator
Spence, Robert Art Historian
Wallace, Elizabeth S Art Administrator, Sculptor
Woods, Sarah Ladd Collector, Patron
Worth, Peter John Sculptor, Art Historian

Omaha

Birdman, Jerome M Art Administrator, Educator
Blackwell, John Victor Art Historian, Educator
Bradshaw, Lawrence James Instructor, Painter
Buchanan, Sidney Arnold Instructor, Sculptor
Doll, Donald Arthur Educator, Photographer
Hill, Peter Painter, Educator
Hiller, Betty R Gallery Director, Curator
Lubbers, Leland Eugene Sculptor, Educator
Majeski, Thomas H Printmaker, Instructor
Tevis, Gary Lee Printmaker, Painter
Tomko, George Peter Art Historian, Curator
Wolsky, Milton Laban Painter

Wayne

Lesh, Richard D Painter, Instructor

NEVADA

Boulder City

Burk, Anna Darlene Art Dealer

Gardnerville

Lawrence, James A Painter, Photographer

Incline Village

Smith, Henry Holmes Photographer, Educator

Las Vegas

Beckmann, Robert Owen Painter, Muralist
Holder, Tom Painter
Lesnick, Stephen William Painter, Instructor
Marchese, Lamar Vincent Art Administrator, Photographer
Marchese, Patricia Davis Art Administrator, Printmaker
Misch, Allene K Collector, Painter
Poppelman, Raymond James Art Dealer, Collector
Reber, Mick Sculptor, Painter
Rozzi, (James A) Painter, Sculptor

Reno

Ball, Lyle V Painter, Illustrator
Cooper, Phillis Sculptor
Jacobson, Yolande (Mrs J Craig Sheppard) Sculptor
Sheppard, John Craig Painter, Educator
Unterseher, Chris Christian Sculptor

Virginia City

Bromund, Cal E Painter

NEW HAMPSHIRE

Bennington

Willis, Sidney F Painter

Campton

Waters, Herbert (Ogden) Printmaker, Educator

Canaan

Walker, Joy Painter, Printmaker

Center Conway

Jordan, Robert Painter, Educator

Concord

Chandler, John William Painter, Instructor
Hoffmann, Lilly Elisabeth Weaver, Instructor

Durham

Hatch, John W Painter, Educator
Thomas, George R Educator, Architect
Zabarsky, Melvin Joel Painter, Educator

Exeter

Lyford, Cabot Sculptor, Painter

Francestown

Milton, Peter Winslow Printmaker

Goffstown

Williams, Gerald Sculptor, Potter

NEW HAMPSHIRE (cont)

Hancock

Dombek, Blanche M Sculptor
Tripp, Wallace Whitney Illustrator

Hanover

Boghosian, Varujan Sculptor, Educator
Lathrop, Churchill Pierce Art Historian
Ruzicka, Rudolph Illustrator, Designer

Harrisville

Meitzler, (Herbert) Neil Painter, Designer

Jackson

Beal, Mack Sculptor

Jaffrey

Hillsmith, Fannie Painter

Keene

Lourie, Herbert S Painter, Educator

Littleton

Bradley, Peter Alexander Painter, Art Dealer

Lyme

Schmeckebier, Laurence E Art Historian, Sculptor

Manchester

Doty, Robert McIntyre Art Administrator
Eshoo, Robert Painter

Marlborough

Harris, Paul Stewart Art Historian

Mason

Jones, Elizabeth Orton Illustrator, Writer

Meredith

Olitski, Jules Painter, Sculptor

Northwood

Abeles, Sigmund Printmaker, Sculptor

Peterborough

Unwin, Nora Spicer Painter, Printmaker

Plymouth

Quinn, Raymond John Illustrator, Painter

Portsmouth

Labrie, Rose Painter, Writer

Raymond

Beardsley, Barbara H Conservator

Warner

Nemec, Nancy Printmaker

West Lebanon

van der Marck, Jan Museum Director

Westmoreland

Isaak, Nicholas, Jr Painter, Printmaker

Wilmot Flat

de Paola, Tomie Illustrator, Designer

NEW JERSEY

Asbury

Anderson, John S Sculptor
Konrad, Adolf Ferdinand Painter

Asbury Park

Cleary, Fritz Sculptor, Art Critic

Atlantic City

Palley, Reese Art Dealer

Atlantic Highlands

Voorhees, Donald Edward Painter, Lithographer

Barnegat Light

Rothman, Sidney Gallery Director, Art Critic

Bayonne

Gary, Jan (Mrs William D Gorman) Painter, Printmaker
Gorman, William D Painter, Graphic Artist

Beach Haven

Martell, Barbara Bentley Painter

Belleville

Yudin, Carol Printmaker, Painter

Berkeley Heights

Lorentz, Pauline Painter, Instructor

Blairstown

Lenney, Annie Painter

Bloomfield

Anderson, Robert Raymond Painter, Instructor
Schwacha, George Painter

Brick Town

Smart, Wini Painter, Art Dealer

Bridgeton

Peterson, Chester G Graphic Designer

Bridgewater

Mockers, Michel M True Fresco Painter

Brigantine

Pierotti, John Cartoonist

Butler

Angelini, John Michael Painter, Art Director

Caldwell

Lewis, Nat Brush Painter, Instructor
Mueller, M Gerardine Sculptor, Educator

Califon

Burger, W Carl Educator, Painter
Sandol, Maynard Painter

Carlstadt

Howell, Marie W Designer, Instructor

Chatham

DeCaprio, Alice Painter, Instructor
Manhold, John Henry Sculptor

Cherry Hill

Conrad, George Educator, Printmaker
Horn, Stuart Alan Graphic Artist, Writer

Clarksburg

Arias-Misson, Alain Visual Poet, Graphic Artist

Cliffside Park

LaMarca, Howard J Designer, Educator

Clifton

Hamer, Marilou Heilman Art Dealer, Lecturer

Closter

West, Amy M Painter
Zakin, Mikhail Sculptor, Educator

Colonia

Isaacs, Carole Schaffer Collector, Patron

Colts Neck

Schweitzer, Gertrude Painter, Sculptor

Cranford

Dawley, Joseph William Painter, Art Dealer
Lieber, France Printmaker, Painter

Cresskill

Baker, Dina Gustin Painter
Mayen, Paul Designer
Radoczy, Albert Painter
Tait, Katharine Lamb Painter, Designer
Ward, Lynd (Kendall) Illustrator, Writer

Demarest

Racz, Andre Painter, Printmaker

Denville

Agopoff, Agop Minass Sculptor
Johnson, Avery Fischer Painter, Instructor

Dover

Kearns, James Joseph Sculptor, Painter

East Brunswick

Bloom, Donald Stanley Painter
Bradshaw, Robert George Painter, Educator
Cantor, Robert Lloyd Educator, Designer

East Windsor

Lee-Smith, Hughie Painter, Lecturer

Edgewater

Case, Elizabeth Painter, Writer
Valinski, Dennis John Sculptor, Lecturer

Edison

Waterhouse, Charles Howard   Illustrator, Painter

Elberon

Stamaty, Stanley   Cartoonist, Illustrator

Emerson

Stark, Bruce Gunsten   Cartoonist

Englewood

Anuszkiewicz, Richard Joseph   Painter
Casarella, Edmond   Sculptor, Printmaker
Grushkin, Philip   Designer, Instructor
Ross, John T   Printmaker, Educator
Shore, Richard Paul   Sculptor

Fair Lawn

Birkin, Morton   Painter
Schwab, Eloisa (Mrs A H Rodriguez)   Painter

Finesville

Kozlow, Sigmund   Painter, Instructor

Flanders

Margoulies, Berta (Berta Margoulies O'Hare) Sculptor, Educator

Fords

G'Miglio (Gloria Miglionico)   Photographer

Fort Lee

Cohen, Stephen Donald   Illustrator, Courtroom Artist
Creatore, Mary-Alice   Sumie Artist, Painter
Grosz, Franz Joseph   Painter, Designer
Ortlip, Paul Daniel   Painter

Freehold

Lyle, Charles Thomas   Art Administrator

Frenchtown

Saalburg, Allen Russel   Painter, Printmaker

Gladstone

Duvoisin, Roger   Writer, Illustrator

Glassboro

Wasserman, Burton   Painter, Printmaker

Glen Gardner

Hunt, Kari   Sculptor, Writer
Kuehn, Gary   Sculptor, Graphic Artist

Glen Ridge

Jensen, Alfred   Painter
Kato, Kay   Cartoonist, Illustrator
Konopka, Joseph   Painter

Hackensack

Sznajderman, Marius S   Painter, Printmaker

Haddon Heights

Chalmers, Mary Eilleen   Illustrator

Haddonfield

Byrd, Robert John   Illustrator, Instructor
Sandecki, Albert Edward   Painter, Instructor

Hampton

Bubb, Nancy (Jane)   Sculptor, Curator

Hasbrouck Heights

Perham, Roy Gates   Painter

Hawthorne

Falconieri, Virginia   Painter, Instructor

Hazlet

Temes, Mortimer (Robert)   Cartoonist, Designer

Highland Park

Buros, Luella   Painter, Designer

Hightstown

Upjohn, Everard Miller   Art Historian

Hillside

Homitzky, Peter   Painter
Reale, Nicholas Albert   Painter, Instructor

Hoboken

Santlofer, Jonathan   Painter

Hopewell

Friedman, Marvin   Illustrator, Collector
Ispanky, Laszlo   Sculptor, Designer

Irvington

Grabach, John R   Painter, Instructor

Iselin

Tice, George Andrew   Photographer, Author

Island Heights

English, John Arbogast   Painter

Jamesburg

Hui, Ka-Kwong   Craftsman, Educator
Minnick, Esther Tress   Painter
Schaffer, Rose   Painter, Lecturer

Jersey City

Craft, Douglas D   Painter, Educator
Grundy, John Owen   Patron, Writer
Harms, Elizabeth   Painter
Magnan, Oscar Gustav   Painter, Sculptor
Mazzone, Domenico   Sculptor, Painter
Mount, Pauline Ward   Painter, Sculptor
Murphy, Catherine E   Painter
Robinson, Charles K   Art Administrator, Writer
Serra-Badue, Daniel   Painter, Educator
Stevens, Edward John, Jr   Painter, Educator

Keasbey

Sosnowitz, Henry Abram   Collector, Patron

Kendall Park

Sway, Albert   Painter, Etcher

Kenilworth

Shor, Bernice Abramowitz   Art Editor

Kingston

Cook, Peter (Geoffrey)   Painter

Kinnelon

Whyte, Raymond A   Painter

Lakewood

Burgues, Irving Carl   Sculptor, Painter
Clinedinst, Katherine Parsons   Painter, Lecturer

Lebanon

Neal, Reginald H   Painter, Educator

Leonardo

De Lue, Donald   Sculptor

Leonia

Birmelin, August Robert   Painter, Printmaker
Dickerson, Daniel Jay   Painter, Educator
Friedensohn, Elias   Painter, Sculptor
Johnson, Selina (Tetzlaff)   Museologist, Museum Historian
Resek, Kate Frances   Painter

Little Silver

Hart, Betty Miller   Painter, Graphic Artist

Livingston

Bearman, Jane Ruth   Painter, Illustrator

Loveladies

Kelly, Leon   Painter

Madison

Galles, Arie Alexander   Educator, Art Administrator
Henry, Sara Lynn   Art Historian, Art Critic
Smith, R Harmer   Painter, Etcher

Mahwah

Peck, Judith   Sculptor, Educator

Manasquan

Markow, Jack   Cartoonist, Painter

Mantua

Stankard, Paul Joseph   Craftsman, Glass Artist

Maplewood

Dee, Leo Joseph   Painter
Feldman, Hilda (Mrs Neville S Dickinson) Painter, Educator
Joffe, Bertha   Designer
Nardone, Vincent Joseph   Painter
Rose, Roslyn   Printmaker, Instructor

Margate

Myers, Legh   Sculptor

Mendham

Hobbie, Lucille   Painter, Illustrator
Notaro, Anthony   Sculptor
Thurlow, Fearn Cutler   Curator

Midland Park

Woodlock, Ethelyn Hurd   Painter

Milford

Carter, Clarence Holbrook   Painter, Designer

NEW JERSEY (cont)

Monmouth Beach

Domareki, Joseph Theodore Painter, Sculptor

Monmouth Junction

Hardaway, Pearl (Pearl Hardaway Reese) Painter

Montclair

Day, Worden Sculptor, Printmaker
De Leeuw, Leon Painter, Sculptor
Gamble, Kathryn Elizabeth Museum Director

Moorestown

Eisenstat, Benjamin Painter, Illustrator

Morris Plains

Ferris, (Carlisle) Keith Illustrator, Painter

Morristown

Frelinghuysen, Mr & Mrs Peter H B, Jr Collectors
Krugman, Irene Sculptor

Mount Holly

Giannotti, John J Sculptor, Educator

Mountainside

Devlin, Harry Illustrator, Painter

New Brunswick

Cate, Phillip Dennis Art Historian, Curator
Goodyear, John L Painter, Art Administrator

New Vernon

Bross, Albert L, Jr Painter

Newark

Auth, Susan Handler Curator, Archaeologist
Ayaso, Manuel Painter, Sculptor
Baretski, Charles Allan Art Librarian, Art Historian
Bartle, Dorothy Budd Curator, Lecturer
Burns, G Joan Art Librarian
Curtis, Phillip Houston Curator, Lecturer
Dane, William Jerald Art Librarian
Jones, Ben Painter, Sculptor
Maldjian, Vartavar B Painter, Weaver
Miller, Samuel Clifford Museum Director
Rabin, Bernard Art Restorer
Reynolds, Valrae Curator
Watkins, Eileen Frances Art Critic

North Bergen

Makarenko, Zachary Philipp Painter, Sculptor

North Haledon

Heusser, Eleanore Elizabeth Painter

Nutley

Carlin, James Painter
Schwinger, Sylvia Art Dealer, Painter

Oakland

Rodman, Selden Writer, Collector

Ocean City

Taylor, Fran (Frances Jane) Art Administrator, Painter

Orange

Damron, John Clarence Painter, Illustrator

Paramus

Jacobs, Helen Nichols Painter

Park Ridge

De Pol, John Engraver, Designer

Parsippany

Schonwalter, Jean Frances Painter, Instructor

Paterson

Civitello, John Patrick Painter
Tiffany, Marguerite Bristol Painter, Weaver

Perth Amboy

Hari, Kenneth Painter, Printmaker

Piscataway

Silkotch, Mary Ellen Painter

Pitman

Ottiano, John William Educator, Sculptor

Pittstown

Marsh, Anne Steele Painter, Printmaker

Plainfield

Graziano, Florence V Mercolino Painter, Sculptor
Helfond, Riva Painter, Printmaker
Seidel, Alexander Carl-Victor Painter, Designer

Pluckemin

Hart, Morgan Drake Painter, Instructor

Pompton Plains

Hopper, Marianne Seward Painter, Art Dealer

Princeton

Bannard, Walter Darby Painter, Art Critic
Boretz, Naomi Painter, Educator
Brodsky, Judith Kapstein Printmaker, Painter
Brown, Gwyneth King (Mrs Joseph Brown) Painter
Brown, Joseph Sculptor, Educator
Bunnell, Peter Curtis Educator, Curator
George, Thomas Painter, Printmaker
Goreleigh, Rex Painter, Printmaker
Greenbaum, Dorothea Schwarcz Sculptor, Graphic Artist
Heckscher, William Sebastian Art Historian
Jones, Frances Follin Curator
Kelleher, Patrick Joseph Art Historian, Art Consultant
Kuehn, Frances Painter
Lavin, Irving Art Historian
Lee, Rensselaer Wright Art Historian
Martin, Charles E Designer, Painter
Morales, Armando Painter
Savage, Naomi Photographer
Schmidt, Mary Morris Art Librarian
Schnessel, S Michael Art Writer, Art Dealer
Snyder, Barry Art Dealer, Collector
Stevens, Elisabeth Goss Writer, Art Critic
Teller, Jane (Simon) Sculptor
Thompson, Dorothy Burr Art Historian, Lecturer
Van Tongeren, Harold (Herk) Sculptor
Walter, Paul F Collector, Patron
Weitzmann, Kurt Educator, Art Historian

Ramsey

Hertzberg, Rose Painter, Printmaker

Randolph

Sarsony, Robert Painter, Printmaker

Red Bank

Graupe-Pillard, Grace Painter
McIlvain, Douglas Lee Instructor

Ridgefield

Wilson, Ben Painter, Lecturer

Ridgefield Park

Botto, Richard Alfred Painter, Instructor

Ridgewood

Burns, Paul Callan Painter, Instructor
Lane, Marion Jean Arrons Painter, Instructor
Whitmore, Lenore K Painter

Ringwood

Barbour, Arthur J Painter, Writer

River Edge

Fish, George A Painter
Friedberg, Ray E Painter, Instructor

Roosevelt

Landau, Jacob Painter, Printmaker
Prestopino, Gregorio Painter

Roselle

Silins, Janis Painter

Rutherford

Barnwell, John L Painter
Laurer, Robert A Educator
Petrie, Ferdinand Ralph Painter, Illustrator

Somers Point

Morningstern, Harry V Painter, Illustrator

Somerset

Albrecht, Robert A Collector, Illustrator
Allen, Tom, Jr Sculptor, Designer
Menthe, Melissa Art Librarian, Photographer
Ten (Jan Ten Broeke) Painter, Art Dealer
Zuccarelli, Frank Edward Painter

South Brunswick

Segal, George Sculptor

South Orange

De Foix-Crenascol, Louis Art Historian, Educator
Gasser, Henry Martin Painter, Writer
Gelman, Milton Collector
Lipton, Barbara B Art Writer, Curator
Singer, Esther Forman Painter, Art Critic
Triano, Anthony Thomas Painter, Educator

Stockholm

Jauss, Anne Marie Painter, Illustrator

Stockton

Farnham, Alexander Painter, Writer
Schoenherr, John Carl Illustrator, Painter

Summit

Davis, Gerald Vivian Painter
Palmer, Fred Loren Collector, Patron

Teaneck

Barry, Robert Thomas Conceptual Artist
Feigl, Doris Louise Painter
Girona, Julio Painter
Weill, Erna Sculptor, Instructor

Tenafly

Krauser, Joel Instructor, Printmaker
Price, George Cartoonist

Tinton Falls

St Tamara Painter, Printmaker

Titusville

Ring, Edward Alfred Art Publisher, Collector

Trenton

Anderson, Winslow Designer, Painter
Brooks, Wendell T Printmaker, Educator
Buki, Zoltan Curator, Art Administrator
Cummins, Karen Gasco Art Administrator
Diodato, Baldo Painter, Sculptor
Goldstein, Howard Painter, Educator
Greco, Frank Painter
Lehman, Mark Ammon Educator, Sculptor
Roebling, Mary G Collector, Patron
Selig, J Daniel Museum Director, Curator
Sloshberg, Leah Phyfer Museum Director

Union

Bailin, Hella Painter
Josimovich, George Painter, Designer

Union City

Korn, Elizabeth P Painter, Illustrator

Upper Montclair

Beerman, Miriam H Painter
Coes, Kent Day Painter, Designer
Kawecki, Jean Mary Sculptor, Gallery Director
McQuillan, Frances C Painter, Instructor
Westfall, Carol D Sculptor, Educator

Ventnor City

Harris, Marian D Painter
Robbins, Hulda D Painter, Printmaker

Watchung

Bolley, Irma S Painter, Designer

Wayne

Battcock, Gregory Art Critic, Art Historian
De Nike, Michael Nicholas Sculptor
Paris, Lucille M Painter

Weehawken

Churchill, Diane Painter
Groshans, Werner (Emil) Painter

West Orange

Hunter, Graham Cartoonist
Schreiber, Eileen Sher Painter, Lecturer
Yanow, Rhoda Mae Painter, Illustrator

Westfield

Becker, Natalie Rose Painter
Devine, William Charles Art Dealer, Collector

Wood-Ridge

Lynds, Clyde William Sculptor

Woodstown

DeShazo, Edith Kind Art Critic, Art Historian

Wyckoff

Carpenter, E Painter

NEW MEXICO

Abiquiu

Johnson, Douglas Walter Painter
O'Keeffe, Georgia Painter

Alamogordo

Stevens, William Ansel, Sr Painter, Illustrator

Albuquerque

Abdalla, Nick Painter, Educator
Abrams, Jane Eldora Printmaker, Educator
Adams, Clinton Painter, Lithographer
Antreasian, Garo Zareh Painter, Lithographer
Barrow, Thomas Francis Photographer, Instructor
Black, Frederick (Edward) Painter
Booth, Judith Gayle Curator
Brody, Jacob Jerome Museum Director, Educator
Bunting, Bainbridge Art Historian
Chapian, Grieg Hovsep Painter, Conservator
Chavez, Joseph Arnold Sculptor, Craftsman
Cikovsky, Nicolai, Jr Art Historian, Educator
Coke, F Van Deren Educator, Photographer
de Borhegyi, Suzanne Sims Art Administrator
Etter, Howard Lee Painter, Lecturer
Garver, Jack Painter, Draftsman
Hahn, Betty Photographer, Educator
Hammersley, Frederick Painter
Hardin, Helen Painter
Harrison, Pat (Broeder) Painter
Haut, Claire (Joan) Designer, Painter
Hurley, Wilson Painter
Jaffe, Ira Sheldon Educator, Art Administrator
Johnson, Arthur Harold Curator
Jonson, Raymond Painter, Gallery Director
Kerr, James Wilfrid Painter, Lecturer
La Fon, Julia Anna Painter, Craftsman
Landis, Ellen Jamie Curator, Art Historian
Long, Frank Weathers Sculptor, Jeweler
Mabry, Jane Painter, Art Dealer
Marks, George B Painter
Martin, Agnes Bernice Painter
Mattox, Charles Painter, Educator
McIlroy, Carol Jean Painter, Art Dealer
Moyers, Wm Painter, Sculptor
Nadler, Harry Painter, Educator
Nelson, Mary Carroll Art Writer, Painter
Newhall, Beaumont Art Historian, Writer
Noggle, Anne Curator, Photographer
Owens, Al Curtis Painter, Draftsman
Ramirez, Joel Tito Painter, Illustrator
Reed, Michael Arthur Art Writer, Art Editor
Rivard, J Bernard Painter
Robb, Peggy Hight Painter
Sabo, Betty Jean Painter, Art Dealer
Salamone, Gladys L Painter
Skinner, Elsa Kells Illustrator, Painter
Skolle, John Painter, Writer
Smith, Sam Painter, Educator
Sommers, John Sherman Lithographer, Educator
Sowers, Miriam R Painter, Writer
Sussman, Arthur Painter
Tatschl, John Craftsman, Sculptor
Thomason, Tom William Jeweler, Art Dealer
Thompson, Richard Craig Painter, Sculptor
Truax, Karen Photographer
Truby, Betsy Kirby Painter, Illustrator
Velarde, Pablita Painter, Illustrator
Vorhees, D Lawrey Painter, Instructor
Walters, Billie Ceramist
Warder, William Painter, Educator
Warner, Lucy Ann Weaver, Designer
Weber, Jan Painter
Westlund, Harry E Master Printer, Art Dealer, Collector
Worthen, William Marshall Sculptor

Angel Fire

Niblett, Gary Lawrence Painter

Cerrillos

Sarkisian, Paul Painter

Continental Divide

Long, C Chee Sculptor, Painter

Corrales

Ingram, Jerry Cleman Painter, Designer
Orr, Veronica Marie (Veronica Marie Ingram) Jeweler, Collector
Townsend, Storm D Sculptor, Lecturer

El Prado

Boughton, William Harrison Painter, Educator

El Rito

Haas, Lez Painter, Educator

Espanola

Lonewolf, Joseph Potter
Medicine Flower, Grace Potter
Naranjo, Michael Alfred Sculptor, Lecturer
Romero, Mike Painter, Collector

Farmington

Farm, Gerald E Painter

Gallup

Aitson, Marland Konad Painter, Craftsman
Guadagnoli, Nello T Art Dealer
Ha-So-De (Narcisco Abeyta) Illustrator Children's Books, Painter
Woodard, Tom L Art Dealer, Critic

Glenwood

Howard, Cecil Ray Painter, Sculptor

Glorieta

Greeley, Charles Matthew Painter, Instructor

Grants

Lowney, Bruce Stark Painter, Printmaker

Hobbs

Easley, Loyce Rogers Painter, Ceramist
Garey, Pat Draftsman, Painter

Jemez Pueblo

Momaday, Al Painter

Las Cruces

Guzevich, Kreszenz (Cynthia) Painter, Instructor
Joost-Gaugier, Christiane L Art Administrator, Art Historian
Moffitt, John Francis Painter, Art Historian

NEW MEXICO (cont)
Richards, Lee Educator, Jeweler
Smith, Jo-an Designer, Jeweler
Vega, Edward Sculptor, Printmaker

Las Vegas

Mirabal, Miguel Enrique Ceramist, Educator

Mesilla Park

Hauser, Alonzo Painter, Sculptor

Montezuma

Schooley, Elmer Wayne Painter, Educator

Ojo Caliente

Renner, Eric Painter, Photographer

Penablanca

Lovato, Charles Fredric Painter

Placitas

Sewards, Michele Bourque Lithographer, Craftsman

Portales

Gikas, Christopher Educator, Sculptor
Hamlett, Dale Edward Educator, Painter

Quemado

McGrew, Ralph Brownell Painter

Ranchos De Taos

Wellington, Duke Painter

Roswell

Du Jardin, Gussie Painter, Printmaker
Ebie, William Dennis Art Administrator, Painter
Jimenez, Luis Alfonso, Jr Sculptor
Ott, Wendell Lorenz Museum Director, Painter
Wiggins, Bill Painter

Ruidoso

Snidow, Gordon E Painter, Sculptor
Travis, David Hail Art Dealer, Collector

Ruidoso Downs

Knapp, Tom Sculptor, Painter

San Juan

Namingha, Dan Printer, Sculptor, Printmaker

San Patricio

Hurd, Peter Painter, Writer
Meigs, John Liggett Painter, Art Historian
Wyeth, Henriette (Mrs Peter Hurd) Painter

Sandia Park

Eagleboy, Wayne Painter, Craftsman

Santa Fe

Ahvakana, Ulaaq (Lawrence Reynold Ahvakana) Sculptor, Glass Blower
Bacigalupa, Andrea Designer, Painter
Benge, David Philip Ceramist, Designer
Blaz, Georgia Lee Craftsman, Painter
Boni, Delmar Painter, Instructor
Boylan, John Lewis Painter, Printmaker
Burgess, Joseph James, Jr Art Dealer, Art Writer, Painter
Cannon, T C (Tom Wayne) Painter, Printmaker
Caponigro, Paul Photographer
Conley, Zeb Bristol, Jr Collector, Art Dealer
Constable, Rosalind Collector, Writer
Cook, Richard Lee Sculptor, Educator
Dailey, Charles Andrew (Chuck) Museum Director, Painter
Dickerson, Tom Painter, Ceramist
Dillingham, Rick (James Richard II) Ceramist, Art Dealer
Ellis, Fremont F Painter
Ettenberg, Franklin Joseph Painter, Draftsman
Fincher, John H Painter, Educator
Gallenkamp, Patricia Art Dealer
Gilpin, Laura Photographer, Writer
Gobin, Henry (Delano) Painter
Gross, Earl Painter, Lecturer
Hanbury, Una Sculptor
Haozous, Robert L Sculptor
Harrill, James Painter
Henrickson, Paul Robert Painter, Writer
Hill, Jim Sculptor
Hill, Megan Lloyd Painter, Art Dealer
Hotvedt, Kris J Printmaker, Instructor
Houser, Allan C Sculptor, Painter
Humphrey, Donald Gray Gallery Director, Lecturer
Jamison, Margaret Conry Art Dealer
Johnson, Harvey William Painter
Johnson, James Ralph Painter, Writer
Johnson, (Leonard) Lucas Painter, Illustrator
Keener, Anna Elizabeth Painter, Printmaker
King, William Alfred Educator, Painter
Kramer, James Painter
Latham, Barbara Painter, Illustrator
Lefranc, Margaret (Margaret Lefranc Schoonover) Painter, Illustrator
Leon, Ralph Bernard Painter, Illustrator
Lippincott, Janet Painter
Longley, Bernique Painter, Sculptor
Lougheed, Robert Elmer Illustrator, Painter
Lovato, Manuelita Instructor, Museologist
Lovell, Tom Painter, Illustrator
Montoya, Geronima Cruz (Po-Tsu-Nu) Painter, Instructor
Moses, Forrest (Lee), (Jr) Painter
Nalder, Nan Painter, Designer
Naumer, Helmuth Painter
New, Lloyd H (Lloyd Kiva) Art Administrator, Designer
Pardington, Joyce Elizabeth Weaver, Designer
Pardington, Ralph Arthur Ceramist, Sculptor
Porter, Eliot Furness Photographer, Writer
Rogers, Peter Wilfrid Painter
Ruthling, Ford Painter
Schultz, Roger d Painter, Sculptor
Scott, Sam Painter, Instructor
Sims, Agnes Painter, Sculptor
Smith, Bradford Leaman Sculptor, Jeweler
Sprang, Elizabeth Lewis Painter, Lithographer
Steinke, Bettina Painter
Strel, Donald O Museum Director
Thwaites, Charles Winstanley Painter
Tubis, Seymour Painter, Printmaker
Wagner, John Philip Painter
Wapp, Josephine Myers Designer, Instructor
Wiest, Kay Van Elmendorf Painter, Photographer
Winter, Lumen Martin Sculptor, Painter
Wood, Jim (James Reid Wood) Painter, Designer

Shiprock

Cohoe, Grey Printmaker, Writer

Silver City

Humphrey, S L Painter, Illustrator
McCray, Dorothy M Printmaker, Educator

Taos

Bell, Larry Stuart Sculptor
Boyer, Jack K Museum Director, Curator
Catusco, Louis Painter, Sculptor
Cook, Howard Norton Painter, Lecturer
Crumbo, Minisa Painter, Graphic Artist
Dasburg, Andrew Michael Painter
Egri, Ted Sculptor
Ellis, Robert Carroll Painter, Printmaker
Ganthiers, Louise Marie Painter
Gorman, R C Painter, Art Dealer
Harmon, Barbara Sayre Painter, Children's Book Illustrator
Harmon, Cliff Franklin Painter
Kloss, Gene (Alice Geneva Glasier) Etcher, Painter
Mandelman, Beatrice M Painter
Manzo, Anthony Joseph Painter, Instructor
Mitchell, Jeffrey Malcolm Museum Director, Painter
Price, Kenneth Printmaker, Sculptor
Ray, Robert (Donald) Painter, Sculptor
Reed, Doel Painter
Ribak, Louis Painter
Richards, Tally Art Dealer, Art Writer
Robles, Julian Painter, Sculptor
Scott, Jonathan Painter
Simpson, Lee Painter
Solomon, Hyde Painter
Stewart, Charles Carl Painter, Sculptor
Witteman, Alisa Wells Photographer

White Rock

Volkin, Hilda Appel Printmaker, Painter

NEW YORK

Albany

Frinta, Mojmir Svatopluk Art Historian, Writer
Liddle, Nancy Hyatt Art Administrator, Gallery Director
Rosen, Hy(man) (Joseph) Cartoonist
Schafer, Alice Pauline Printmaker
Warren, Betty Painter

Albertson

Madsen, Viggo Holm Printmaker, Craftsman

Alfred

Randall, Theodore A Sculptor, Educator

Alfred Station

Turner, Robert Chapman Educator, Ceramist

Almond

Phelan, Linn Lovejoy Designer

Altamont

Cowlèy, Edward P Painter, Educator

Amagansett

Durham, William Painter, Printmaker
Gwathmey, Robert Painter
Opper, John Painter
Perret, George Albert Writer, Lecturer

Amenia

Hale, Nathan Cabot Sculptor, Writer
Simon, Howard Illustrator, Painter

Angola

Haug, Donald Raymond Painter, Instructor

Annandale-On-Hudson

Phillips, Matt Painter

Ardsley

Lysun, Gregory Painter, Restorer

Ardsley-On-Hudson

Griggs, Maitland Lee Collector

Armonk

Gressel, Michael L Sculptor

Asharoken

Verzyl, Kenneth H Art Dealer, Draftsman

Astoria

Azaceta, Luis Cruz Painter
Drummond, (I G) Painter, Sculptor

Auburn

Long, Walter Kinscella Museum Director, Painter

Aurora

Roberts, William Edward Painter, Educator

Babylon

Eckelberry, Don Richard Painter
Jolley, George B Sculptor, Designer

Baldwin

Carter, Granville W Sculptor, Instructor

Barneveld

Wardle, Alfred Hill Silversmith, Jeweler

Bay Shore

Ciuca, Eugen Sculptor, Painter

Bayridge

Chung, Roger K Art Dealer, Painter

Bayshore

Hendricks, Donald Teves Painter, Sculptor

Bayside

Goldstein, Milton Printmaker, Educator
Kotzky, Alex Sylvester Cartoonist
Niemann, Edmund E Painter

Bayville

Montana, Pietro Sculptor, Painter

Bearsville

Klitgaard, Georgina Painter, Muralist

Bedford

McDonnell, Joseph Anthony Sculptor
Roth, David Painter
Weinman, Robert Alexander Sculptor

Bedford Hills

Brussel-Smith, Bernard Printmaker
Carter, Bernard Shirley Painter, Instructor
Zietz, Stephen Joseph Art Librarian, Art Historian

Bedford Village

Canfield, Jane (White) Sculptor
Tyler, Kenneth Eugene Print Publisher, Printmaker

Beechhurst

Karpel, Bernard Art Librarian, Art Editor

Binghamton

Ippolito, Angelo Painter, Educator
Lindsay, Kenneth C Art Historian, Writer
Martin, Keith Art Administrator, Painter
Schwartz, Aubrey E Printmaker
Stein, Roger Breed Art Historian, Educator
Wilson, Edward N Sculptor, Educator

Blauvelt

Leber, Roberta (Roberta Leber McVeigh) Ceramist, Instructor
Plummer, John H Art Administrator, Educator

Bloomington

Ruffing, Anne Elizabeth Painter

Blue Mountain Lake

Wynn, Donald James Painter, Lecturer

Brainard

Johnsen, May Anne Painter, Etcher

Briarcliff Manor

Adler, Myril Printmaker, Painter

Briarwood

Consuegra, Hugo Painter, Architect

Bridgehampton

Benson, Elaine K G Art Dealer, Writer
Newbill, Al Painter
Norquist, Ryl Art Dealer
Prohaska, Ray Painter, Illustrator
Varga, Margit Painter, Writer
Young, Mahonri S Writer

Brockport

Marx, Robert Ernst Painter, Printmaker
Mirko (Wolodymyr Walter Pylyshenko) Collector, Painter
Rosenberg, Charles Michael Writer, Art Historian

Bronx

Allen, Patricia (Patricia Allen Bott) Painter, Art Critic
Baron, Hannelore Collage Artist
Berg, Siri Painter, Instructor
Byars, Donna Sculptor, Collage Artist
Davis, Walter Lewis Painter
Fastove, Aaron (Aaron Fastovsky) Painter
Florio, Sal Erseny Sculptor
Goodelman, Aaron J Sculptor
Jaffe, Irma B Art Historian
Kallem, Henry Painter
Kassoy, Bernard Painter, Printmaker
Kassoy, Hortense Sculptor, Painter
Katz, Leo Painter, Writer
Kaye, George Painter
Rosenberg, Bernard Art Publisher, Book Dealer
Wechter, Vivienne Thaul Educator, Painter
Werth, Kurt Illustrator
Wilson, George Lewis Painter
Ziemann, Richard Claude Printmaker, Educator

Bronxville

Carlson, Jane C Painter
D'Amato, Janet Potter Illustrator, Craftsman
Poucher, Elizabeth Morris Sculptor
Seckler, Dorothy Gees Art Critic, Painter

Brookhaven

Delihas, Neva C Sculptor

Brooklyn

Accurso, Anthony Salvatore Illustrator, Painter
Adler, Lee Painter, Printmaker
Anderson, Lennart Printmaker, Instructor
Bard, Joellen Painter
Baumbach, Harold Painter, Printmaker
Beerman, Herbert Painter, Educator
Benedict, Nan M Painter, Educator
Bertoni, Dante H Painter, Illustrator
Bidner, Robert D H Painter, Art Director
Bothmer, Bernard V Curator, Art Historian
Botwinick, Michael Museum Director
Bove, Richard Painter, Educator
Brooks, Bruce W Painter
Burns, Jerome Painter
Burns, Josephine Painter
Clipsham, Jacqueline Ann Ceramist, Educator
Colon-Morales, Rafael Painter
Comito, Nicholas U Painter, Illustrator
Cramer, Abraham Painter, Cartoonist
Cuffari, Richard J Illustrator, Instructor
d'Andrea, Albert Philip Educator, Sculptor
Delson, Elizabeth Painter, Printmaker
Demartis, James J Painter
Dorn, Ruth (Ruth Dornbush) Painter
Estern, Neil Sculptor
Faunce, Sarah Cushing Museum Curator
Federe, Marion Painter, Graphic Artist
Fein, Stanley Painter, Illustrator
Fife, Mary (Mrs Edward Laning) Painter
Fuerst, Shirley Miller Sculptor, Painter
Gardner, Andrew Bradford Printmaker, Painter
Gardner, Susan Ross Painter, Printmaker
Gironda, R Painter, Sculptor
Grado, Angelo John Painter, Illustrator
Guiffreda, Mauro Francis Painter, Printmaker
Gurr, Lena Painter, Printmaker
Hamwi, Richard Alexander Painter
Hanan, Harry Cartoonist
Henderson, Jack W Painter, Instructor
Kaminisky, Jack Allan Educator, Photographer
Katzive, David H Art Administrator
Kish, Maurice Painter
Kolin, Sacha Sculptor, Painter
Kramer, Paul Designer
Kupferman, Murray Painter, Sculptor
La Noue, Terence David Painter, Sculptor
Lerner Levine, Marion Painter, Instructor
Le Roy, Harold M Painter, Lecturer
Lewin, Keith Kerton Painter, Instructor
Magazzini, Gene Painter
Malta, Vincent Educator, Painter
Manilla, Tess (Tess Manilla Weiner) Painter
Mark, Marilyn Painter
Marlor, Clark Strang Art Historian, Collector
McNeil, George J Painter, Educator
Midgette, Willard Franklin Painter, Printmaker
Nagano, Shozo Painter
Neals, Otto Painter, Sculptor
Nemser, Cindy Art Critic, Writer
O'Lenick, David Charles Art Administrator, Educator
Ostrowitz, Judith Maura Sculptor, Art Administrator
Pate, Lee Printmaker
Perry, Kathryn Powers Painter
Punia, Constance Edith Painter
Ranson, Nancy Sussman Painter, Serigrapher
Reich, Nathaniel E Painter
Rennick, Dan Painted Constructions, Painter
Rhoden, John W Sculptor
Richmond, Frederick W Collector, Patron
Robbins, Frank Cartoonist, Illustrator
Robinson, Margot (Margot Steigman) Painter, Sculptor
Rogalski, Walter Printmaker, Lecturer
Rubin, Irwin Painter, Designer
Saito, Seiji Sculptor
Scharff, Constance Kramer Printmaker, Painter
Schneider, Noel Sculptor
Shaw, (George) Kendall Painter, Instructor

NEW YORK (cont)
Sherker, Michael Z Painter, Educator
Shimoda, Osamu Sculptor, Painter
Stegman, Patricia (Patricia Stegman Snyder) Painter
Stelzer, Michael Norman Sculptor
Swarz, Sahl Sculptor
Trakis, Louis Sculptor
Turner, Dick Cartoonist
Turner, Norman Huntington Painter
Uhrman, Celia Painter, Writer
Uhrman, Esther Painter, Writer
Weingarten, Hilde (Kevess) Painter, Printmaker
Wickiser, Ralph Lewanda Art Administrator, Painter
Williams, Todd Sculptor, Painter

Brooklyn Heights

Schucker, Charles Painter

Buffalo

Berlyn, Sheldon Painter, Printmaker
Breverman, Harvey Painter, Printmaker
Brock, Robert W Sculptor, Educator
Buck, Robert Treat, Jr Art Historian, Museum Director
Cathcart, Linda Louise Curator, Art Historian
Cohen, Harold Larry Designer, Educator
Cuthbert, Virginia Painter
Elliott, Philip Clarkson Painter, Educator
Gordon, Violet Illustrator, Writer
Hamouda, Amy Sculptor, Video Artist
Hatchett, Duayne Sculptor, Educator
Johnson, Charlotte Buel Art Historian, Educator
Knox, Seymour H Patron
Krims, Leslie Robert Conceptual Artist, Photographer
Levick, Mr & Mrs Irving Collectors
Martin, Margaret M Painter, Designer
McIvor, John Wilfred Printmaker, Painter
Nash, Steven Alan Art Historian, Art Administrator
Nichols, Donald Edward Designer, Educator
Paterson, Anthony R Sculptor, Educator
Piccillo, Joseph Painter, Educator
Prochownik, Walter A Lecturer, Painter
Puchalski, Gregory John Correspondence Artist, Photographer
Schultz, Douglas George Curator
Sharits, Paul Jeffrey Film Artist, Educator
Sisti, Anthony J (Tony) Collector, Painter
Smith, Gordon Mackintosh Museum Director
Townsend, J Benjamin Art Critic, Art Historian
Visser't Hooft, Martha Painter
Willig, Nancy Tobin Art Critic
Wood, James Nowell Art Historian, Art Administrator

Buskirk

Goossen, Eugene Coons Writer, Educator
Johanson, Patricia (Maureen) Sculptor, Architect

Campbell

Billeci, Andre George Sculptor, Educator
Greenly, Colin Intangible Art, Sculptor

Canaan

Knight, Frederic Charles Painter

Canton

Holladay, Harlan H Art Historian, Painter
Lowe, J Michael Sculptor, Educator
Schweizer, Paul Douglas Art Historian, Curator

Carmel

Lee, Robert J Painter, Educator
Mitchell, James E Illustrator, Painter
Sorel, Edward Illustrator, Writer

Cazenovia

Pirkl, James Joseph Designer, Educator
Wyckoff, Sylvia Spencer Painter, Educator

Centerport

Lewicki, James Illustrator, Educator

Chappaqua

Bode, Robert William Designer, Painter
Fagg, Kenneth (Stanley) Illustrator, Sculptor
Reibel, Bertram Sculptor, Graphic Artist

Charlotteville

Artschwager, Richard Ernst Painter, Sculptor
Bower, Gary David Painter
Pettibone, Richard H Painter

Chatham

Johansen, Anders Daniel Painter
Trimm, H Wayne Illustrator

Chautauqua

Morgan, Maritza Leskovar Painter, Illustrator

Cheektowaga

Bisone, Edward George Painter, Illustrator

Clarence

Crume, Gregg Sculptor, Mosaic Artist

Clinton

Palmer, William C Painter, Educator
Penney, James Painter, Educator
Trovato, Joseph S Painter

Cochecton Center

Loewer, Henry Peter Illustrator, Printmaker

Cold Spring

Margules, Gabriele Ella Illustrator, Painter
Marzollo, Claudio Sculptor

Cold Spring Harbor

Ginsburg, Max Painter, Illustrator
Maione, Robert Painter
Moss, Milton Painter
Pfahl, Charles Anton, III Painter
Schneiderman, Dorothy Art Dealer

Commack

Vian, Orfeo Educator, Printmaker

Congers

Gussow, Alan Painter, Writer

Cooperstown

Jones, Louis C Museum Director
Keck, Sheldon Waugh Educator, Art Conservator

Coram

Manetta, Edward J Art Administrator, Painter

Corning

Buechner, Thomas Scharman Museum Director, Painter
Hurd, Zorah Illustrator, Painter
Schulze, Paul Designer

Corona

Wimberley, Frank Walden Painter, Sculptor

Cortland

DiGiusto, Gerald N Sculptor

Cross River

Smith, Lawrence Beall Painter, Illustrator

Croton-On-Hudson

Harari, Hananiah Painter

Cutchogue

Abbott, Dorothy I Sculptor

Delmar

Jones, W Louis Painter, Sculptor

Dix Hills

Ames, Lee Judah Illustrator, Writer
Moy, May (Wong) Painter, Lecturer
Schlam, Murray J Sculptor
Webster, Stokely Painter

Dobbs Ferry

Cadge, William Fleming Designer, Photographer
Lissim, Simon Painter, Designer
Rothschild, Lincoln Sculptor, Writer

Douglaston

Starrs, Mildred Painter

Eagle Bridge

Moses, Betty (Betty Moses McCart) Painter

East Amherst

Garver, Walter Raymond Painter, Instructor

East Aurora

Underwood, Evelyn Notman Painter

East Chatham

Hogrogian, Nonny Illustrator
Lehman, Irving Painter, Sculptor
Rickey, George W Sculptor

East Elmhurst

Oi, Motoi Painter, Instructor

East Hampton

Bontecou, Lee Assemblage Artist, Sculptor
Brooks, James Painter
Carey, Ted Collector, Designer
Craig, Martin Sculptor, Restorer
De Kooning, Willem Painter
Ernst, Jimmy Painter, Educator
Hoffmann, Arnold, Jr Painter, Art Director
Ikeda, Masuo Printmaker
Jacobs, Jay Art Writer, Critic
Krasner, Lee Painter
Lassaw, Ibram Sculptor
Little, John Painter, Sculptor
Long, Hubert Sculptor
Morris, Kyle Randolph Painter
Nivola, Constantino Sculptor
Ossorio, Alfonso A Painter, Sculptor
Whipple, Enez Mary Art Administrator
Wingate, Arline (Hollander) Sculptor

East Hills

Newmark, Marilyn (Marilyn Newmark Meiselman) Sculptor

East Meadow

Finke, Leonda Froelich Sculptor, Draftsman
Terken, John Sculptor

East Norwich

Solomon, Ruth B Art Administrator

East Patchogue

Desoto, Rafael M Painter, Illustrator

East Setauket

Farrell, Stephanie Krauss Curator

East Williston

Simel, Elaine Printmaker, Painter

Eaton

Faller, Marion Photographer, Educator

Elmhurst

Berkon, Martin Painter
Wachsteter, George Illustrator

Elmira

Macdonnell, Cameron Painter, Sculptor

Elmont

Rogers, John Painter, Lecturer
Schary, Emanuel Painter

Endicott

Hart, John Lewis Cartoonist

Erieville

Malinowski, Jerome Joseph Sculptor, Designer

Essex

Lowry, Bates Art Historian, Art Critic

Fair Haven

Fuller, John Charles Art Historian, Photographer

Fairport

Peters, Carl W Painter

Fayette

Yeh, Carol Printmaker

Fayetteville

Goodnow, Frank A Painter, Educator
Pollock, Merlin F Painter
Smith, Lawson Wentworth Sculptor, Educator

Floral Park

Moss, Irene Painter

Florida

Gray, Don Painter, Art Critic

Flushing

Bergere, Richard Illustrator, Painter
Kochta, Ruth (Martha) Painter
Koras, George Sculptor
Ludwig, Eva Sculptor
Pincus-Witten, Robert A Art Historian, Writer
Rosenthal, Seymour Joseph Painter, Lithographer
Slatkes, Leonard Joseph Art Historian
Weinberg, H Barbara Art Historian

Forest Hills

De Bellis, Hannibal Sculptor, Medalist
Leeds, Annette Painter
Lombardo, Josef Vincent Art Historian, Educator
Pearlstein, Seymour Painter, Educator
Tewi, Thea Sculptor

Franklin Square

Indiviglia, Salvatore Joseph Painter, Instructor
Newer, Thesis Painter
Soloway, Reta Painter, Lecturer

Freehold

Maltzman, Stanley Printmaker, Painter

Freeport

Brown, Marion B Painter
de Kooning, Elaine Marie Catherine Painter, Writer
Terris, Albert Sculptor, Calligrapher

Fresh Meadows

Silber, Maurice Painter, Illustrator

Garden City

Jennerjahn, W P Educator, Painter
Linder, Stasia Painter, Educator

Garnerville

Harvey, Dermot Kinetic Artist

Garrison

Asoma, Tadashi Painter
Clifton, Michelle Gamm Sculptor, Printmaker
Flavin, Dan Artist, Writer
Locke, Charles Wheeler Painter, Printmaker

Geneva

Bate, Norman Arthur Educator, Printmaker

Gilbertsville

Eckmair, Frank C Printmaker

Glen Cove

Knipscher, Gerard Allen Painter
Paris, Jeanne C Art Critic, Writer

Glen Head

Mason, Lauris Lapidos Art Dealer, Writer

Gloversville

Schulman, Jacob Collector

Goshen

Tracy, Berry Bryson Curator, Historic Preservationist

Grand Island

Hill, Richard Wayne Painter, Photographer

Grand View-On-Hudson

Wyatt, Stanley Painter, Educator

Great Neck

Beck, Margit Painter, Educator
Berne, Gustave Morton Collector
Eckstein, Ruth Printmaker, Painter
Filmus, Tully Painter, Lecturer
Goldsmith, Elsa M Painter
Gorelick, Shirley Painter, Printmaker
Housman, Russell F Painter, Instructor
Lieberman, Harry Painter
Meyer, Seymour W Sculptor
Mills, Agnes Sculptor, Printmaker
Moglia, Luigi (John) Painter, Instructor
Quat, Helen S Printmaker, Painter
Richmond, Lawrence Collector
Schuller, Grete Sculptor
Schutz, Estelle Painter, Printmaker
Seidler, Doris Painter, Printmaker
Shapiro, David Painter, Art Historian
Tanksley, Ann Painter
Van Buren, Raeburn Illustrator, Cartoonist

Greenport

Daisy (Daisy Black Langhauser) Painter, Art Dealer

Greenvale

Miller, Joan Vita Museum Director

Groton

Colby, Victor E Sculptor, Educator

Halesite

Steward, Donn Horatio Printmaker, Master Printer

Hamilton

Clancy, Patrick Painter, Video Artist
Loveless, Jim Educator, Painter
Paulson, Alan Sculptor

Hannibal

Eckersley, Thomas Cyril Photographer, Educator

Harrison

Neustadter, Edward L Collector, Patron

Hastings-On-Hudson

Catti (Catherine James) Painter, Enamelist
Freedman, Maurice Painter
Halley, Donald M, Jr Museum Director
Madigan, Mary Jean Smith Curator, Writer
Nardin, Mario Sculptor
Sklar-Weinstein, Arlene (Joyce) Painter, Printmaker

Haverstraw

Taubes, Frederic Painter, Writer

Hawthorne

Oechsli, Kelly Illustrator

Hempstead

Feriola, James Philip Painter, Art Administrator
Jacobs, David (Theodore) Sculptor, Educator

Hicksville

Landy, Jacob Art Historian

NEW YORK (cont)

High Falls

Bishop, Benjamin Painter, Educator

Highland Falls

Heberling, Glen Austin Painter, Illustrator

Holland

Blair, Jeanette Anne Painter
Blair, Robert Noel Painter, Sculptor

Holland Patent

Christiana, Edward Painter, Instructor

Hollis

Davies, Theodore Peter Printmaker, Painter
Mau, Hui-Chi Painter

Honeoye Falls

Coffey, Douglas Robert Painter, Educator

Hoosick Falls

Haerer, Carol Painter
Wofford, Philip Painter, Writer

Huntington

Brodsky, Stan Painter, Educator
Buckley, Mary L (Mrs Joseph M Parriott) Painter, Educator
Engel, Michael Martin, II Painter, Illustrator
Fludd, Reginald Joseph Painter, Instructor

Huntington Station

Mann, Katinka Painter, Printmaker
Van Loen, Alfred Sculptor, Educator

Hyde Park

Ulrich, Edwin Abel Collector, Patron

Irvington

Chinni, Peter Anthony Sculptor, Painter
Holden, Donald Art Editor, Art Administrator

Ithaca

Atwell, Allen Educator, Painter
Calkins, Robert G Art Historian
Daly, Norman Painter, Sculptor
Evett, Kenneth Warnock Painter
Gilbert, Creighton Eddy Art Historian
Grippi, Salvatore William Painter, Educator
Hartell, John (Anthony) Painter
Holliday, Judith Art Librarian
Kahn, Peter Painter, Designer
Leavitt, Thomas Whittlesey Museum Director, Art Historian
Mahoney, James Owen Painter, Educator
O'Connor, Stanley James Art Historian, Educator
Poleskie, Stephen Francis Painter, Printmaker
Press, Nancy Neumann Curator, Educator
Richenburg, Robert Bartlett Painter, Sculptor
Seley, Jason Sculptor
Squier, Jack Leslie Sculptor, Educator
Thompson, Phyllis Educator, Printmaker
Wojcik, Gary Thomas Sculptor

Jackson Heights

Cardman, Cecilia Painter
de Gerenday, Laci Anthony Sculptor
Farian, Babette S Painter, Designer
Freund, Tibor Painter, Muralist
Judkins, Sylvia Painter
Kappel, R Rose (Mrs Irving Gould) Printmaker
Whitney, Edgar Albert Painter, Instructor

Jamaica

Cade, Walter, III Painter
Haber, William Art Dealer, Collector
Krigstein, Bernard Painter, Illustrator
Lloyd, Tom Sculptor
Lowe, Joe Hing Painter, Instructor
Pascual, Manolo Sculptor, Instructor
Youkeles, Anne Painter, Printmaker

Jamesville

Andrews, Michael Frank Synaesthetic Educator
Vargo, John Educator, Painter

Jefferson

Hacklin, Allan Dave Painter

Jericho

Gross, Sandra Lerner Painter, Lecturer
Kaplan, Marilyn Painter
Ross, Beatrice Brook Painter
Singer, Arthur B Illustrator, Painter

Katonah

Askin, Arnold Samuel Collector
Baur, John I H Museum Director, Writer
Giobbi, Edward Gioachino Painter
Lipinsky de Orlov, Lino S Painter, Illustrator
Samerjan, George E Designer, Painter
Simpson, William Kelly Art Historian, Educator
Toney, Anthony Painter, Instructor

Keene Valley

Winkel, Nina Sculptor, Lecturer

Kendall

Markusen, Thomas Roy Designer, Metalsmith

Kenoza Lake

D'Arcangelo, Allan M Painter

Kew Gardens

Brennan, Francis Edwin Art Director, Editorial Cartoonist
Seeman, Helene Zucker Art Librarian, Art Dealer

Kings Point

Schulhof, Mr & Mrs Rudolph B Collectors

La Fayette

Gernhardt, Henry Kendall Sculptor, Ceramist

Lake Placid

Bartnick, Harry William Painter, Educator

Lake Success

Jerviss, Joy Printmaker
Leaf, Ruth Printmaker, Instructor
Roman, Shirley Printmaker

Lansing

Hoyt, Dorothy (Dorothy Hoyt Dillingham) Painter

Larchmont

Adamy, George E Educator, Sculptor
Fitzgerald, Edmond James Painter, Lecturer
Lefcourt, Irwin Art Dealer
Medrich, Libby E Sculptor
Tobey, Alton S Painter, Lecturer

Latham

Callner, Richard Painter, Educator

Levittown

Chestney, Lillian Illustrator, Painter
Kaplan, Stanley Printmaker, Educator
Schachter, Justine Ranson Graphic Artist, Illustrator
Zuckerberg, Stanley M Painter

Lily Dale

Davis, Robert Tyler Art Administrator, Art Historian

Lockport

Penney, Charles Rand Collector, Patron

Locust Valley

Bush-Brown, Albert Writer, Educator
Howell, Douglass (Morse) Painter, Art Historian
Johnson, Ray Painter
Samuels, Harold & Peggy Art Historians, Art Dealers
Watson, Clarissa H Art Dealer

Long Beach

Altabe, Joan Berg Painter, Muralist

Long Eddy

Wesselmann, Tom Painter

Long Island

Catan-Rose, Richard Painter, Educator
Gruppe, Karl Heinrich Sculptor
Mina-Mora, Dorise Olson Painter
Mina-Mora, Raul Jose Painter, Illustrator

Long Island City

Davison, Robert Painter, Designer
Garchik, Morton Lloyd Painter, Printmaker
Glorig, Ostor Painter
Gussow, Roy Sculptor
Noguchi, Isamu Sculptor
Tardo, (Manuel) Rodulfo Sculptor

Mamaroneck

Goldberger, Mr & Mrs Edward Collectors, Patrons
Gumpel, Hugh Painter
Lekberg, Barbara Hult Sculptor
Sloan, Robert Smullyan Painter, Art Dealer
Topol, Robert Martin Collector

Manhasset

Catchi (Catherine O Childs) Painter, Sculptor
Harvey, Jacqueline Painter
Payson, Mr & Mrs Charles S Collectors

Manlius

Burke, E Ainslie Painter, Educator
Cortese, Don F Printmaker, Instructor
Groat, Hall Pierce Painter
Waterman, Donald Calvin Designer, Educator

Merrick

Cariola, Robert J Painter, Sculptor
Pearlman, Etta S Painter

Middletown

Blumenthal, Fritz Painter, Printmaker
Ericson, Beatrice Painter

Mill Neck

Burrows, Selig S Collector, Patron

Millbrook

Bluhm, Norman Painter
Della-Volpe, Ralph Eugene Painter, Educator
Klosty, James Michael Photographer, Writer
Streeter, Tal Sculptor

Millerton

Helck, (Clarence) Peter Illustrator, Writer
Zimiles, Murray Painter, Educator

Millwood

Galanin, Igor Ivanovich Painter, Illustrator

Monsey

Mesibov, Hugh Painter, Instructor

Monticello

De Hoyos, Luis Collector

Mount Kisco

Jones, Amy (Amy Jones Frisbie) Sculptor, Printmaker
Laskey, Dr & Mrs Norman F Collectors

Mount Morris

Dickinson, David Charles Printmaker, Lecturer

Mount Vernon

Olsen, Ernest Moran Designer, Painter
Seliger, Charles Painter, Designer
Webb, Spider Tattootist, Photographer, Sculptor
Zib, Tom (Thomas A Zibelli) Cartoonist

Mountainville

Stern, H Peter Collector

Neponsit

Mount, Charles Merrill Painter

New Berlin

Huot, Robert Painter, Filmmaker

New City

Kessler, Leonard H Illustrator
Mayhew, Richard Painter, Illustrator
Rosse, Maryvonne Sculptor

New Hampton

Sinnard, Elaine (Janice) Painter, Sculptor

New Paltz

Bohan, Peter John Art Historian, Painter
Kammerer, Herbert Lewis Sculptor
Lewen, Si Painter
Martin, Alexander Toedt Educator, Painter
Minewski, Alex Painter, Educator
Munsterberg, Hugo Art Historian, Educator
Raleigh, Henry Patrick Painter, Writer
Shaw, Ernest Carl Sculptor
Wexler, George Painter, Educator

New Rochelle

Beling, Helen Sculptor, Instructor
FeBland, Harriet Painter, Sculptor
Greene, Theodore R Art Dealer
Gross, Irene (Irene Gross Berzon) Painter, Sculptor
Lantz, Michael F Sculptor
Liljegren, Frank Painter, Instructor
Meizner, Paula Sculptor
Montlack, Edith Painter
Nechis, Barbara (Friedman) Painter
Perlmutter, Merle Printmaker, Instructor
Schlanger, Jeff Sculptor
Seckel, Paul Bernhard Painter, Printmaker
Slotnick, Mortimer H Painter

New York

Aach, Herb Painter, Writer
Abish, Cecile Sculptor, Instructor
Abramovitz, Mr & Mrs Max Collectors
Abrams, Harry N Publisher, Collector
Abrams, Ruth Painter
Acconci, Vito Sculptor
Adams, Alice Sculptor
Addams, Charles Samuel Cartoonist
Adel, Judith Art Director, Designer
Adler, Robert Painter
Adler, Samuel (Marcus) Painter, Educator
Adlmann, Jan Ernst Curator
Adrian, Barbara (Mrs Franklin Tramutola) Painter, Collector
Agostinelli, Mario Painter, Sculptor
Agostini, Peter Sculptor
Ahlskog, Sirkka Craftsman, Sculptor
Ahn, Don C Painter, Art Dealer
Alajalov, Constantin Painter, Illustrator
Albert, Calvin Sculptor, Educator
Albertazzi, Mario Painter, Art Critic
Alcopley, L Painter, Graphic Artist
Aldrich, Larry Art Collector
Allen, Roberta Conceptual Artist
Allner, Walter H Painter, Designer
Alloway, Lawrence Educator, Art Critic
Alonzo, Jack J Art Dealer, Collector
Alper, M Victor Educator, Writer
Alpert, George Photographer, Gallery Director
Altschul, Arthur G Collector, Patron
Amino, Leo Sculptor, Instructor
Amster, Sally Painter
Anbinder, Paul Art Publisher, Collector
Anderson, David K Art Dealer, Collector
Anderson, Dennis Ray Art Dealer, Art Historian
Anderson, Doug Illustrator
Andre, Carl Sculptor
Andrejevic, Milet Painter
Andrews, Benny Painter, Lecturer
Angel, Rifka Painter
Anspach, Ernst Collector
Anthony, William Graham Painter, Draftsman
Antonakos, Stephen Sculptor
Antonovici, Constantin Sculptor, Lecturer
Aparicio, Gerardo Painter
Appel, Eric A Painter, Sculptor
Appel, Karel Painter, Sculptor
Apple, Jacki (Jacqueline B) Post-Conceptual Artist, Curator
Applebroog, Ida H Conceptual Artist, Sculptor
Apt, Charles Painter
Arakawa (Shusaku) Painter
Arcilesi, Vincent J Painter, Instructor
Arman Sculptor
Armstrong, Thomas Newton, III Art Administrator, Art Historian
Aronson, Sanda Sculptor
Asch, Stan (Stanley William Aschemeier) Cartoonist
Ascher, Mary Painter, Printmaker
Ashbaugh, Dennis John Painter
Ashbery, John Lawrence Art Critic
Ashby, Carl Painter, Instructor
Asher, Elise Painter, Sculptor
Ashton, Dore Art Critic, Art Historian
Askild, Anita (Anita Askild Feinstein) Designer, Weaver
Athena Painter, Sculptor
Atirnomis (Rita Simon) Painter, Printmaker
Attie, Dotty Drawer
Ault, Lee Addison Collector, Art Dealer
Avedon, Richard Photographer
Aycock, Alice Sculptor
Azara, Nancy J Sculptor, Educator
Azuma, Norio Serigrapher, Painter
Baber, Alice Painter, Printmaker
Bach, Mickey (Milton Francis) Cartoonist
Baeder, John Painter
Baer, Alan Art Administrator
Baer, Norbert Sebastian Educator
Bailey, Malcolm C W Painter, Illustrator
Bakaty, Mike Painter, Sculptor
Baker, Elizabeth C Art Editor, Critic
Baker, Jill Withrow Illustrator, Painter
Baker, Richard Brown Collector
Baker, Walter C Collector
Balog, Michael Painter, Sculptor
Banerjee (bimal) Graphic Artist, Painter
Banning, Jack (John Peck Banning, Jr) Art Dealer, Lecturer
Baranik, Rudolf Painter, Instructor
Barbera, Joe Cartoonist
Bardazzi, Peter Painter
Bareiss, Walter Collector
Barnes, Curt (Curtis Edward) Painter, Instructor
Barnet, Will Painter, Printmaker
Baro, Gene Art Critic, Lecturer
Barowitz, Elliott Painter, Instructor
Barr, Alfred Hamilton, Jr Art Historian, Art Administrator
Barr, Norman Painter
Barrett, Bill Sculptor, Educator
Barr-Sharrar, Beryl Painter, Writer
Barth, Frances Painter
Bartholet, Elizabeth Ives Art Dealer, Art Consultant
Bartlett, Jennifer Losch Painter, Writer
Barton, August Charles Designer, Painter
Barton, John Murray Painter, Art Dealer
Barzun, Jacques Writer, Art Critic
Baskerville, Charles Painter, Muralist
Bass, Ruth Gilbert Educator, Painter
Baxter, Douglas W Art Dealer
Baynard, Ed Painter
Beal, Jack Painter
Bean, Jacob Curator
Bearden, Romare Howard Painter
Beatty, Frances Fielding Lewis Art Historian, Art Critic
Beauchamp, John R Instructor, Painter
Beck, Doreen Editor, Writer
Beck, Rosemarie (Rosemarie Beck Phelps) Painter, Educator
Beck, Stephen R Painter, Educator
Beckley, Bill Post-Conceptual Artist
Beery, Arthur O Painter
Beker, Gisela Painter
Belkin, Arnold Painter, Muralist
Bell, Charles S Painter
Bellamy, Richard Art Dealer
Benglis, Lynda Sculptor, Painter
Benn, Ben Painter
Bennett, Harriet Painter
Benney, Robert Painter, Illustrator
Benno, Benjamin G Painter, Sculptor
Benton, William Collector
Ben-Zion Painter, Sculptor
Berge, Carol Lecturer, Writer
Bergen, Sidney L Art Dealer
Berger, Oscar Graphic Artist
Berkman, Aaron Painter, Gallery Director
Berman, Aaron Art Dealer, Collector
Berman, Ariane R Painter, Printmaker
Bernstein, Judith Painter, Lecturer
Bernstein, Theresa Painter, Art Historian
Berthot, Jake Painter
Besser, Arne Charles Painter
Betensky, Rose Hart Painter, Art Administrator
Bettmann, Otto Ludwig Art Historian
Bhavsar, Natvar Prahladji Painter
Bianco, Pamela Ruby Painter
Bigelow, Chandler, II Painter

NEW YORK (cont)
Bingham, Mrs Harry Payne Collector
Bishop, Isabel (Mrs Harold G Wolff) Painter, Etcher
Bishop, James Painter
Bishop, Robert Charles Museum Director, Art Writer
Black, Mary Childs Art Historian, Curator
Black, Shirley Painter
Blackwell, Thomas Leo Painter
Bladen, Ronald Sculptor
Blaine, Nell Painter
Blanc, Peter (William Peters Blanc) Sculptor, Painter
Blanchard, Carol Painter, Graphic Artist
Blatas, Arbit Painter
Blaustein, Alfred H Painter, Printmaker
Block, Adolph Sculptor, Instructor
Blodgett, Anne Washington Painter
Bloom, Jason Art Dealer, Curator
Blumenthal, Margaret M Designer
Boardman, Seymour Painter
Bochner, Mel Conceptual Artist, Art Writer
Bogarin, Rafael Printmaker
Bogorad, Alan Dale Illustrator
Bohnen, Blythe Painter
Bollinger, William Conceptual Artist
Bonevardi, Marcelo Painter, Sculptor
Bonino, Alfredo Art Dealer
Boone, Mary Art Dealer
Booth, George Warren Painter, Illustrator
Boothe, Power Robert Painter
Borgatta, Isabel Case Sculptor, Educator
Borgatta, Robert Edward Painter, Educator
Borgenicht, Grace (Grace Borgenicht Brandt) Art Dealer, Collector
Borofsky, Jon Painter
Boros, Billi (Mrs Philip Bisaccio) Painter, Writer
Borstein, Elena Painter, Lecturer
Bostwick, Mr & Mrs Dunbar W Collectors
Boterf, Chester Arthur (Check) Painter, Lecturer
Botero, Fernando Sculptor
Botkin, Henry Painter, Writer
Bourdon, David Art Critic
Bourgeois, Louise Sculptor
Boutis, Tom Painter
Bowen, Helen Eakins Painter
Bowie, William Sculptor
Bowling, Frank Painter
Bowman, Ken Painter
Boxer, Stanley (Robert) Sculptor, Painter
Brach, Paul Henry Painter
Brainard, Joe Graphic Artist, Painter
Brandfield, Kitty Painter
Brandt, Warren Painter
Bransom, (John) Paul Painter, Illustrator
Braunstein, Ruth Art Dealer
Brecher, Samuel Painter, Printmaker
Breiger, Elaine Painter, Printmaker
Brenner, Leonard J Painter
Brigadier, Anne Painter, Lecturer
Briggs, Ernest Painter
Brody, Jacqueline Art Editor
Bromm, Hal Art Dealer, Lecturer
Brown, Jonathan Art Administrator, Art Historian
Brown, Judith Gwyn Illustrator, Painter
Brown, Milton Wolf Art Historian
Brown, Peter C Painter, Educator
Brown, Rhett Delford (Harriett Gurney Brown) Fiber Artist, Illustrator
Brown, Robert Delford Conceptual Artist
Brown, Robert K Art Dealer, Bibliographer
Browne, Vivian E Art Administrator, Painter
Browning, Colleen Painter
Bruder, Harold Jacob Painter, Educator
Brumer, Miriam Instructor, Painter
Brumer, Shulamith Sculptor, Instructor
Bruno, Phillip A Art Dealer, Collector
Brusca, Jack Painter
Bry, Edith Glass Artist
Bryant, Linda Goode Art Dealer, Art Historian
Buczak, Brian Elliot Painter, Sculptor
Buecker, Robert Gallery Director, Painter
Bultman, Fritz Sculptor, Painter
Bunch, Clarence Educator, Sculptor
Bunshaft, Mr & Mrs Gordon Collectors
Bunts, Frank Painter
Burch, Claire R Painter, Writer
Burckhardt, Rudy Photographer, Film Maker
Burden, Carter Collector
Burnham, Elizabeth Louese Museum Registrar, Art Administrator
Burton, Scott Sculptor, Conceptual Artist
Byard, Carole Marie Painter, Illustrator
Byron, Charles Anthony Art Dealer
Cady, Dennis Vern Art Conservator, Painter
Calas, Nicolas Writer
Calcagno, Lawrence Painter
Califano, Edward Christopher Art Dealer, Publisher
Callahan, Harry Photographer
Campbell, Gretna Painter, Educator
Campbell, (James) Lawrence Painter, Writer
Campbell, Kenneth Sculptor, Painter
Campbell, Vivian (Vivian Campbell Stoll) Collector, Writer
Campus, Peter Video Artist
Canaday, John Edwin Art Critic
Canepa, Anna L Video Expert
Canin, Martin Painter
Canright, Sarah Anne Painter
Capa, Cornell Photographer, Museum Director
Carewe, Sylvia Painter, Tapestry Artist
Carlson, Alexander Art Dealer, Lecturer
Carlson, Cynthia J Painter, Instructor
Caro, Francis Art Dealer
Carr, Sally Swan Sculptor
Carroll, Robert Joseph Painter, Illustrator
Cartwright, Constance B & Carroll L Collectors
Cassanelli, Victor Vi Painter
Castelli, Leo Art Dealer
Castile, Rand Gallery Director
Castleman, Riva Curator, Art Historian
Castoro, Rosemarie Painter, Sculptor
Cavallon, Giorgio Painter
Cecere, Ada Rasario Painter
Cecere, Gaetano Sculptor, Lecturer
Cernuschi, Alberto C Art Dealer, Art Critic
Chalk, Mr & Mrs O Roy Collectors
Chamberlain, Betty Art Administrator, Writer
Chamberlain, John Angus Sculptor
Chambers, Karen Sue Art Historian, Art Dealer
Chapman, Mrs Gilbert W Collector, Patron
Chase, Doris (Totten) Sculptor, Film Maker
Chase, Saul Alan Painter
Chen, Hilo Painter
Chen, Tony (Anthony Young Chen) Illustrator, Collector
Chen Chi Painter
Chermayeff, Ivan Designer, Painter
Chinn, Yuen Yuey Painter
Christensen, Dan Painter
Christensen, Ronald Julius Printmaker, Painter
Christo (Javacheff) Sculptor
Chryssa, (Vardea) Sculptor
Chwast, Seymour Designer, Illustrator
Ciarrochi, Ray Painter
Cicero, Carmen L Painter
Cikovsky, Nicolai Painter, Muralist
Citron, Minna Wright Painter, Printmaker
Clancy, John Art Dealer
Clark, Michael Vinson Painter
Clark, William W Art Historian
Clarke, John Clem Painter
Clerk, Pierre Painter, Sculptor
Close, Chuck Painter
Clutz, William Painter
Cohen, Arthur A Collectors
Cohen, Elaine Lustig Painter, Designer
Cohen, Hy Painter
Cohen, Jean Painter, Lecturer
Cohen, Wilfred P Collector, Patron
Cohn, Richard A Art Dealer
Cole, Donald Painter
Cole, Joyce Painter
Cole, Sylvan, Jr Art Dealer, Writer
Colin, Georgia T Collector, Designer
Colin, Ralph Frederick Collector
Collins, Christiane C Art Historian, Art Librarian
Collins, George R Art Historian
Condeso, Orlando Printmaker
Condit, Louise Art Administrator
Conforte, Renee Art Dealer
Conover, Robert Fremont Printmaker, Painter
Constant, George Painter
Constantine, Mildred Art Historian
Cook, Gladys Emerson Illustrator, Painter
Cooney, Barbara (Mrs Charles Talbot Porter) Illustrator, Writer
Cooper, Mario Painter, Sculptor
Cooper, Paula Art Dealer
Cooper, Wendy Ann Curator
Copeland, Lawrence Gill Educator, Designer
Copeland, Lila Painter, Printmaker
Copley, William Nelson Painter
Corbin, George Allen Art Historian, Writer
Corse, Mary Ann Painter, Sculptor
Corso, Patrick Painter, Sculptor
Cortella, Gloria Charlene Art Dealer
Cortlandt, Lyn Painter
Cote, Alan Painter
Cotsworth, Staats Painter
Cowles, Mr & Mrs Gardner Collectors
Cowles, Russell Painter
Cox, Allyn Painter
Crawford, John McAllister, Jr Collector, Patron
Crawford, Ralston Painter, Lithographer
Crawford, William II Cartoonist, Sculptor
Creamer, Paul Lyle Art Dealer
Crile, Susan Painter
Crimi, Alfred D Painter, Instructor
Crimp, Douglas Art Critic, Art Historian
Crispo, Andrew John Art Dealer, Collector
Cronbach, Robert M Sculptor
Crovello, William George Painter, Sculptor
Crum, Jason Roger Painter, Muralist
Crystal, Boris Painter
Culbertson, Janet Lynn (Mrs Douglas Kaften) Painter, Instructor
Culkin, John Michael Art Administrator, Educator
Cummings, David William Painter
Cummings, Nathan Collector
Cuningham, Elizabeth Bayard (Mrs E W R Templeton) Art Dealer
Cunningham, (Charles) Bruce Painter
Cunningham, Francis Painter
Cutler, Ethel Rose Painter, Designer
Cyril, R Painter, Designer
d'Alessio, Gregory Cartoonist, Illustrator
Dali, Salvador Designer, Painter
Damaz, Paul F Writer, Collector
Danenberg, Bernard Art Dealer
Daniels, David M Collector, Patron
Dank, Leonard Dewey Medical Illustrator, Audio-Visual Consultant
Daphnis, Nassos Painter, Sculptor
Daphnis-Avlon, Helen Painter, Sculptor
Darboven, Hanne Conceptual Artist, Graphic Artist
Darton, Christopher Painter
Daskaloff, Gyorgy Painter
Dauterman, Carl Christian Art Historian, Lecturer
David, Don Raymond Painter, Instructor
Davidovitch, Jaime Painter
Davidson, Marshall Bowman Art Critic, Writer
Davidson, Maxwell, III Art Dealer
Davila, Carlos Painter, Printmaker
Davis, Bradley Darius Painter
Davis, Douglas Matthew Artist, Critic
Davis, Ellen N Art Historian
Davis, George Cartoonist, Illustrator
Davis, Leroy Art Dealer
Dawson, Eve Painter
Day, John Painter, Educator
Day, Lucien B Painter, Art Dealer
Day, Robert James Cartoonist
deAK, Edit Art Critic, Curator
Dean, Abner Illustrator, Writer
Dean, Peter Painter
De Botton, Jean Philippe Painter, Sculptor
de Champlain, Vera Chopak Painter
Dechar, Peter Painter
Decker, Lindsey Sculptor

De Creeft, Jose Sculptor, Educator
Dee, Elaine Evans Art Historian
Deem, George Painter
Degen, Paul Illustrator
De Graaff, Mr & Mrs Jan Collectors, Patrons
Dehn, Virginia Painter
Dehner, Dorothy Sculptor, Printmaker
DeKay, John Painter
De Knight, Avel Painter
de Kolb, Eric Collector, Writer
DeLamonica, Roberto Printmaker, Educator
Delaney, Joseph Painter, Writer
De La Verriere, Jean-Jacques Jeweler, Enamelist
de Lesseps, Tauni Sculptor, Painter
Delford Brown, Robert Sculptor, Environmental Artist
de Lisio, Michael Sculptor
Dellis, Arlene B Art Administrator
Del Valle, Joseph Bourke Design Consultant
De Marco, Jean Antoine Sculptor
De Maria, Walter Sculptor
De Martini, Joseph Painter
de Miskey, Julian Sculptor, Printmaker
De Monte, Claudia Educator, Conceptual Video Artist
De Montebello, Guy-Philippe Lannes Art Administrator
de Nagy, Tibor (J) Art Dealer, Collector
Denby, Jillian Painter
Denes, Agnes C Multimedia Artist, Conceptual Artist
De Niro, Robert Sculptor, Painter
De Rivera, Jose Sculptor
De Ruth, Jan Painter, Writer
Diao, David Painter
Dibbets, Jan Artist
di Gioia, Frank Painter
Dillon, C Douglas Art Administrator, Collector
Di Meo, Dominick Painter, Sculptor
Dine, James Painter, Sculptor
Dinnerstein, Simon A Painter
Dintenfass, Terry Art Dealer
Di Suvero, Mark Painter, Sculptor
Dobbs, John Barnes Painter
Dobkin, John Howard Art Administrator
Dockstader, Frederick J Art Consultant,
Dodd, Lois Painter, Educator
Dogancay, Burhan Cahit Painter
Donati, Enrico Painter, Sculptor
Donneson, Seena Printmaker, Sculptor
Dorfman, Bruce Painter, Instructor
Dorsky, Morris Art Historian, Educator
Doumato, Lamia Art Librarian, Researcher
Dowden, Anne Ophelia Todd Painter, Illustrator
Downey, Juan Sculptor, Educator
Doyle, Thomas J Sculptor, Instructor
Draper, William Franklin Painter
Dreitzer, Albert J Collector, Patron
Drexler, Lynne Painter
Drexler, Paul Eugene Art Dealer
Driggs, Elsie Painter
Droll, Donald E Art Dealer
Dryfoos, Nancy Sculptor
Duane, Tanya Painter, Collage Artist
Duback, Charles S Painter, Printmaker
Dubin, Ralph Painter, Sculptor
Duff, John Ewing Sculptor
Dugmore, Edward Painter
Duis, Rita (Rita Duis Astley-Bell) Painter
Dulac, Margarita Walker Painter, Art Critic
Dunbar, Jill H Art Writer, Art Critic
Duncan, (Eleanore) Klari Painter, Instructor
Dunkelman, Loretta Painter
Dunnington, Mrs Walter Grey Collector, Patron
Dunwiddie, Charlotte Sculptor
Dupuy, Jean Multimedia Artist
Duran, Robert Painter
Dworzan, George R Painter, Sculptor
Eastman, John, Jr Art Administrator
Eddy, Don Painter
Edelheit, Martha Painter, Filmmaker
Edelson, Mary Beth Lecturer, Conceptual Artist
Edwards, Ethel (Mrs Xavier Gonzalez) Painter
Efrat, Benni Sculptor
Einstein, Gilbert W Art Dealer
Eisenberg, Sonja Miriam Painter, Photographer
Eisinger, Harry Painter
Eitingon, Brigitte Art Dealer
Ekstrom, Arne H Art Dealer
Elderfield, John Art Historian, Curator
Eliot, Lucy Carter Painter
Elkon, Robert Art Dealer, Collector
Elliott, Ronnie Painter
Elliott, Scott Cameron Art Dealer, Collector
Ellis, Richard Painter, Illustrator
Elman, Emily Painter, Educator
Eloul, Kosso Sculptor
Elwell, Chip Master Printer, Printmaker
Emil, Arthur D Collector
Emmerich, Andre Art Dealer, Writer
Endo, Robert Akira Art Dealer
Engelhard, Mr & Mrs Charles Collectors
Engelson, Carol Painter
Englander, Gertrud Ceramist
Ente, Lily Sculptor, Printmaker
Ericson, Ernest Illustrator, Instructor
Eriquezzo, Lee M Painter
Esman, Rosa M Art Dealer, Collector
Esterow, Milton Art Editor, Publisher
Estes, Richard Painter
Ets, Marie Hall Illustrator, Writer
Ettinghausen, Richard Art Administrator, Educator
Evans, John Painter, Collage Artist
Everett, Len G Painter
Ewald, Elin Lake Art Dealer, Art Writer
Eyen, Richard J Art Dealer, Designer
Facci, Domenico (Aurelio) Sculptor, Instructor
Faden, Lawrence Steven Painter, Sculptor
Fahlen, Charles Sculptor
Fangor, Voy Painter
Faragasso, Jack Illustrator, Painter
Farber, Maya M Painter
Fares, William O Painter
Farrell, Patric Museum Director, Writer
Farruggio, Remo Michael Painter
Fasano, Clara Sculptor
Faulconer, Mary (Fullerton) Painter, Designer
Faulkner, Frank Painter
Faurer, Louis Photographer
Fausett, (William) Dean Painter, Etcher
Fedele, Frank D Art Dealer, Publisher
Feder, Ben Designer, Painter
Feigen, Richard L Art Dealer, Collector
Feigenbaum, Harriet (Mrs Neil Chamberlain) Sculptor
Feigin, Marsha Printmaker, Painter
Feinman, Stephen E Art Dealer
Feld, Stuart Paul Curator
Feldman, Ronald Art Dealer
Feldstein, Mary Collector, Art Librarian
Felt, Mr & Mrs Irving Mitchell Collectors
Fenton, Alan Painter, Instructor
Ferber, Herbert Sculptor, Painter
Ferguson, Kathleen Elizabeth Sculptor
Figert, Sam A Art Dealer, Writer
Finck, Furman J Painter, Instructor
Findlay, David B Art Dealer
Fingesten, Peter Graphic Artist, Educator
Finkelstein, Louis Educator, Painter
Finn, David Illustrator, Photographer
Finnegan, Sharyn Marie Gallery Director, Painter
Fiore, Joseph A Painter, Educator
Fischbach, Marilyn Cole Art Dealer, Collector
Fischer, John J Painter, Sculptor
Fish, Janet I Painter
Fisher Joel A Painter, Writer
Fishko, Bella Art Dealer
Fisk, Evi Ester Painter
Flack, Audrey L Painter, Instructor
Fleck, Irma L Art Administrator
Fleischman, Lawrence Art Dealer, Collector
Flexner, James Thomas Writer, Art Historian
Flinn, Elizabeth Haight Educator
Floeter, Kent Sculptor
Fohr, Jenny Sculptor, Instructor
Fondren, Harold M Art Dealer
Foote, Nancy Art Editor, Art Critic
Ford, John Charles Painter
Fosburgh, James Whitney Painter, Writer
Fosdick, Sina G Art Administrator, Collector
Foulkes, Llyn Painter
Fourcade, Xavier Art Dealer
Fowler, Mel Painter, Printmaker
Frampton, Hollis Filmmaker
Francis, Sherron Painter
Frank, Mary Sculptor
Frank, Peter Solomon Art Critic, Curator
Frankenberg, Robert Clinton Illustrator, Instructor
Frankenthaler, Helen Painter
Franzen, Joan C Art Administrator
Fraser, Douglas (Ferrar) Art Historian, Educator
Frater, Hal Painter
Frazier, Le Roy Dyyon Painter, Sculptor
Freed, Hermine Video Artists, Writer
Freed, William Painter
Freedman, Doris C Art Administrator
Freeman, Margaret B Museum Curator, Writer
Freeman, Mark Painter, Printmaker
Freilich, Ann Painter
Freilicher, Jane Painter
Frick, Helen Clay Art Library Director
Fried, Theodore Painter, Etcher
Friedman, B H Writer
Fromboluti, Sideo Painter
Fromer, Mrs Leon Collector
Frumkin, Allan Art Dealer
Fry, Edward Fort Art Historian, Art Critic
Fugate-Wilcox, Terry Sculptor
Fukui, Nobu Painter, Printmaker
Fuller, Emily (Emily Fuller Kingston) Painter, Sculptor
Furman, Aaron & Joyce Art Dealers, Collectors
Gahman, Floyd Painter
Garbaty, Marie Louise Collector, Patron
Gardiner, Robert David Lion Collector
Garris, Kathleen (Kathleen Weil-Garris) Educator, Art Historian
Gary, Dorothy Hales Collector, Writer
Gear, Josephine Art Historian, Art Writer
Geber, Hana Sculptor, Instructor
Gebhardt, Roland Sculptor, Designer
Gechtoff, Sonia Painter
Gee, Helen Art Consultant
Geissman, Robert Glenn Illustrator, Designer
Geist, Sidney Sculptor, Art Critic
Gekiere, Madeleine Painter, Film Maker
Gelb, Jan Painter, Printmaker
Gelber, Samuel Painter, Educator
Geldzahler, Henry Curator
Gellis, Sandy L Sculptor
Genauer, Emily Art Critic, Writer
Genn, Nancy Painter
Gentile, Gloria Irene Designer, Sculptor
Gerardia, Helen Painter, Printmaker
Gerdts, William H Art Historian, Educator
Gerst, Hilde W Art Dealer
Ghent, Henri Critic, Writer
Giambertone, Paul Sculptor
Gianakos, Cristos Sculptor
Gianakos, Steve Sculptor, Painter
Gibson, Ralph H Photographer
Gifford, J Nebraska Painter
Gikow, Ruth (Ruth Gikow Levine) Painter
Gilbert, Lionel Painter, Instructor
Gilchrist, Elizabeth Brenda Art Editor
Gillespie, Dorothy Merle Painter, Art Administrator
Gillespie, Gregory Joseph Painter
Gilvarry, James Collector
Giorgi, Vita Printmaker, Painter
Giraudier, Antonio Painter, Writer
Gladstone, M J Art Administrator, Writer
Glaeser, Ludwig Curator
Glaser, Milton Designer, Illustrator
Glass, Wendy D Art Dealer, Collector
Glezer, Nechemia Art Dealer, Art Historian
Glickman, Maurice Sculptor, Writer
Gliko, Carl Albert Painter
Glimcher, Arnold B Art Dealer, Writer
Globus, Dorothy Twining Gallery Director, Curator

NEW YORK (cont)
Gluckman, Morris Painter
Glueck, Grace (Helen) Writer
Goddard, Donald Art Editor, Art Writer
Goell, Abby Jane Painter, Printmaker
Goertz, Augustus Frederick Painter
Goff, Lloyd Lozes Painter, Illustrator
Goings, Ralph Painter
Golbin, Andree Painter, Illustrator
Gold, Leah Painter, Printmaker
Gold, Sharon Cecile Painter
Goldberg, Michael Painter
Golden, Eunice Painter, Film Maker
Goldfarb, Roz Art Administrator, Sculptor
Goldin, Leon Painter, Educator
Goldowsky, Noah Art Dealer
Goldring, Nancy Deborah Graphic Artist, Educator
Goldschmidt, Lucien Art Dealer
Goldsmith, Barbara Writer, Art Critic
Goldsmith, C Gerald Collector, Patron
Goldstein, Jack Mixed-Media Artist
Goldstein, Julius Painter, Instructor
Goldstone, Mr & Mrs Herbert Collectors
Golinkin, Joseph Webster Painter, Printmaker
Gollin, Mr & Mrs Joshua A Collectors, Patrons
Golub, Leon Albert Painter
Gomez, Sita Painter
Gomez-Quiroz, Juan Manuel Painter, Printmaker
Gongora, Leonel Painter, Educator
Gonzalez, Xavier Painter, Sculptor
Goodbred, Ray Edw Painter, Instructor
Goodman, Bertram Painter
Goodman, James Neil Art Dealer, Collector
Goodman, Marian Art Dealer, Art Publisher
Goodnough, Robert Painter
Goodrich, Lloyd Museum Officer, Writer
Gorchov, Ron Painter
Gordon, Albert F Art Dealer
Gordon, John Art Dealer, Collector
Gordon, Leah Shanks Writer
Gordon, Martin Art Dealer, Collector
Gorney, Jay Philip Art Dealer
Gorsline, Douglas Warner Painter, Illustrator
Gottlieb, Abe Collector, Patron
Goulet, Lorrie (Lorrie J De Creeft) Sculptor, Instructor
Graham, Daniel H Conceptual Artist
Graham, James Art Dealer
Graham, Margaret Bloy Children's Book Illustrator
Graham, Robert Claverhouse Art Dealer, Collector
Grausman, Philip Sculptor
Graves, Bradford Sculptor, Educator
Graves, Nancy Stevenson Painter, Sculptor
Green, Denise G Painter
Green, George D Painter
Green, Wilder Art Administrator, Architect
Greenbaum, Marty Painter, Sculptor
Greenberg, Clement Writer, Art Critic
Greenberg, Gloria Painter, Designer
Greenberg, Irwin Painter, Instructor
Greene, Balcomb Painter
Greene, Daniel E Painter
Greenleaf, Kenneth Lee Sculptor
Greenspan, Mr & Mrs George Collectors
Greenwald, Charles D Collector, Patron
Greenwald, Dorothy Kirstein Collector
Greenwald, Sheila Ellen Illustrator
Grey, Estelle (Estelle Ashby) Painter, Sculptor
Grigoriadis, Mary Painter
Groell, Theophil Painter, Instructor
Grooms, Red Painter
Gross, Alice (Alice Gross Fish) Sculptor
Gross, Chaim Sculptor, Instructor
Grossen, Francoise Instructor, Sculptor
Grosser, Maurice Art Writer, Painter
Grossman, Nancy Sculptor, Painter
Grosvenor, Robert Sculptor
Groth, John August Illustrator, Painter
Grotz, Dorothy Rogers Painter
Gruen, John Art Critic
Gruskin, Mary Josephine Art Dealer
Guerrero, Jose Painter
Gundelfinger, John Andre Painter, Instructor
Gurewitsch, Edna P Art Dealer, Art Historian
Gusella, Ernest Video Artist
Haacke, Hans Christoph Sculptor
Haas, Helen (Helen Haas de Langley) Sculptor
Haas, Richard John Printmaker, Painter
Haber, Ira Joel Sculptor, Writer
Haber, Leonard Collector, Designer
Habergritz, George Joseph Painter, Sculptor
Hackenbroch, Yvonne Alix Curator, Writer
Hadler, Warren Arnold Art Dealer
Haessle, Jean-Marie Georges Painter, Printmaker
Hafif, Marcia Painter, Instructor
Hahn, Stephen Art Dealer
Hale, Robert Beverly Art Administrator, Instructor
Hall, Susan Painter
Halpern, Nathan L Collector
Hamilton, Patricia Rose Art Dealer, Curator
Hammer, Victor J Art Dealer
Hammond, Harmony Painter, Sculptor
Hampton, Lucille Charlotte Sculptor
Hare, David Sculptor
Harkavy, Minna Sculptor
Harlow, Frederica Todd Art Historian, Art Dealer
Harmon, Lily Painter, Sculptor
Harnett, Mr & Mrs Joel William Collectors
Harris, Ann Sutherland Art Historian, Art Administrator
Harris, Margo Liebes Sculptor
Harrison, Tony Painter, Educator
Harriton, Abraham Painter
Harsley, Alex Gallery Director, Instructor
Hart, Agnes Painter, Instructor
Hart, Bill Art Dealer
Hart, Harold Rudolf Art Dealer
Hartford, Huntington Collector, Patron
Hartwig, Cleo Sculptor
Hasen, Burt Stanly Painter
Haskell, Barbara Curator
Hatfield, David Underhill Painter
Hauptman, Susan Ann Draftsman
Hayward, Jane Art Historian, Curator
Hazen, Joseph H Collector
Hazlitt, Don Robert Painter
Healy, Anne Laura Sculptor, Educator
Healy, Julia Schmitt Painter, Art Critic
Heckscher, Morrison Harris Curator, Art Historian
Heiloms, May Painter
Heineman, Bernard, Jr Collector
Heinemann, Peter Painter, Instructor
Heise, Myron Robert Painter
Held, Al Painter
Heliker, John Edward Painter, Educator
Helioff, Anne Graile (Mrs Benjamin Hirschberg) Painter
Heller, Ben Art Dealer, Collector
Heller, Dorothy Painter
Heller, Goldie (Mrs Edward W Greenberg) Collector
Helman, Phoebe Sculptor
Hemphill, Herbert Waide Curator, Lecturer
Hendricks, David Charles Painter, Visual Artist
Hendricks, Geoffrey Painter, Environmental Artist
Henry, Robert Painter, Educator
Henselmann, Caspar Sculptor
Herbert, David Art Dealer, Collector
Herfield, Phyllis Anne Illustrator, Printmaker
Herman, Joyce Elaine Art Dealer, Collector
Herrera, Carmen Painter
Hess, Emil John Painter, Sculptor
Hess, Thomas B Art Critic, Writer
Heyman, Mr & Mrs David M Collectors
Hickins, Walter H Sculptor, Graphic Artist
Higa, (Yoshiharu) Painter, Photographer
Higgins, Dick Designer, Printmaker
Hightower, John B Art Administrator
Highwater, Jamake Art Critic, Lecturer
Hildebrand, June Mary Ann Printmaker
Hill, Clinton J Painter, Educator
Himler, Ronald Norbert Illustrator, Painter
Hines, John M Painter
Hinman, Charles B Painter, Sculptor
Hios, Theo Painter, Graphic Artist
Hirsch, David W (Dave) Cartoonist
Hirsch, Joseph Painter
Hirschfeld, Albert Graphic Artist
Hitchcock, Henry Russell Art Historian, Art Critic
Hobson, Katherine Thayer Sculptor
Hodgkins, Rosalind Selma Painter
Hofer, Evelyn Photographer
Hoff, Margo Painter, Collage Artist
Hoffeld, Jeffrey Art Historian, Gallery Director
Hoffman, Martin (Joseph) Painter, Illustrator
Hoffman, Nancy Art Dealer
Hoie, Claus Painter, Etcher
Hollerbach, Serge Painter, Instructor
Hollingsworth, Alvin Carl Painter, Instructor
Hollister, Paul Painter, Writer
Holt, Nancy Louise Sculptor, Film Maker
Holton, Leonard T Cartoonist
Holtz, Itshak Jack Painter, Printmaker
Hood, Ethel Painter Sculptor
Hooker, Mrs R Wolcott Collector, Patron
Hooton, Bruce Duff Art Dealer, Critic
Hopkins, Budd Painter
Hopkins, Peter Painter, Educator
Hornak, Ian John Painter
Horowitz, Nadia Painter, Designer
Horowitz, Mr & Mrs Raymond J Collector
Horowitz, Saul Collector
Horton, Carolyn Art & Book Conservator
Horwitt, Will Sculptor
Hovell, Joseph Sculptor
Hoving, Thomas Art Consultant
Howard, Linda Sculptor
Howat, John Keith Curator, Art Historian
Howe, Nelson S Designer, Assemblage Artist
Howell, Hannah Johnson Art Librarian
Hoy, Anne Tawes Art Historian, Art Editor
Hoyt, Whitney F Painter, Collector
Hsiao, Chin Painter, Sculptor
Huchthausen, David Richard Glass Artist, Sculptor, Lecturer
Hughes, Robert S F Art Critic, Lecturer
Hui, Helene Painter, Film Maker
Hultberg, John Phillip Painter
Humphrey, Ralph Painter
Hunter, Sam Art Historian
Hunter-Stiebel, Penelope (Penelope Hunter Stiebel) Curator
Huntington, Jim Sculptor
Hurt, Susanne M Painter
Hutchinson, Max Art Dealer
Hutchinson, Peter Arthur Conceptual Artist
Hutsaliuk, Lubo Painter
Hutton, Leonard Art Dealer
Huxtable, Ada Louise Critic
Iimura, Taka Filmmaker, Video Artist
Indiana, Robert Painter, Sculptor
Ingber, Barbara Art Dealer, Collector
Inokuma, Guenichiro Painter
Inoue, Kazuko Painter, Lecturer
Insel, Paula Art Dealer, Art Administrator
Insley, Will Painter
Inukai, Kyohei Painter, Sculptor
Inzerillo, Gian Del Valentino Art Dealer, Collector
Iolas, Alexander Art Dealer
Ireland, Patrick (Brian O'Doherty) Artist
Isenburger, Eric Painter
Israel, Marvin Designer, Painter
Isserstedt, Dorothea Carus Art Dealer, Art Historian
Itchkawich, David Michael Printmaker
Iwamoto, Ralph Shigeto Painter
Izacyro (Isaac Jiro Matsuoka) Painter
Izuka, Kunio Sculptor
Jachmann, Kurt M Collector
Jackson, Ward Painter, Editor
Jacobs, Jim Painter
Jacobs, Ted Seth Painter
Jacobs, William Ketchum, Jr Collector
Jacquemon, Pierre Painter
Jacquette, Yvonne Helene (Yvonne Helen Burckhardt) Painter, Educator
Jaffe, Nora Sculptor, Painter

Jaffe, Mrs William B Collector
Jagger, Gillian Painter, Sculptor
James, Christopher P Photographer
Janis, Conrad Art Dealer, Collector
Janis, Sidney Art Dealer, Writer
Janowsky, Bela Sculptor, Instructor
Jansen, Angela Bing Printmaker, Photographer
Janson, Horst Woldemar Art Historian
Jaramillo, Virginia Painter
Jarvis, Lucy Collector, Filmmaker
Jaudon, Valerie Painter
Ject-Key, Elsie Painter
Jeffers, Wendy Jane Painter, Curator
Jelinek, Hans Graphic Artist, Educator
Jenkins, Paul Painter
Jennings, Francis Sculptor, Painter
Jenrette, Pamela Anne Painter, Costume Designer
Johns, Jasper Painter
Johnson, Buffie Painter, Lecturer
Johnson, Cecile Ryden Painter, Publisher
Johnson, Daniel LaRue Sculptor, Painter
Johnson, J Stewart Curator
Johnson, Marian Willard Art Dealer
Johnson, Miani Guthrie Art Dealer
Johnson, Philip Cortelyou Collector, Architect
Johnson, Una E Curator, Writer
Jonas, Joan Video Artist, Conceptual Artist
Jones, Edward Powis Painter, Sculptor
Jones, Jerry Sculptor, Painter
Jordan, Christine Painter
Joseph, Cliff (Clifford Ricardo) Painter, Art Therapist
Josten, Mrs Werner E Collector
Joukhadar, Moumtaz A N Art Dealer, Painter
Judd, Donald Clarence Sculptor
Judson, Jeannette Alexander Painter
Jules, Mervin Painter, Educator
Julian, Lazaro Painter, Designer
Juszczyk, James Joseph Painter
Kacere, John C Painter
Kahan, Alexander Art Dealer
Kahane, Melanie (Melanie Kahane Grauer) Designer
Kahn, Susan B Painter
Kahn, Wolf Painter
Kaiser, Diane Sculptor, Educator
Kaish, Luise Sculptor
Kaish, Morton Painter, Educator
Kalina, Richard Seth Painter
Kallem, Herbert Sculptor
Kallir, Otto Art Dealer, Art Historian
Kamihira, Ben Painter
Kan, Diana Painter, Lecturer
Kane, Bob Paul Painter
Kaplan, Alice Manheim Patron, Collector
Kaplan, Jacques Collector
Kaplan, Muriel Sheerr Sculptor, Designer
Kaprow, Allan Painter, Educator
Karp, Ivan C Art Dealer, Lecturer
Karp, Richard Gordon Painter
Kasak, Nikolai (Kazak) Sculptor-Painter, Theoretition
Kasuba, Aleksandra Environmental Artist
Katz, Alex Painter
Katz, Hilda (Hilda Weber) Painter, Printmaker
Katz, Morris Painter
Katzen, Lila (Pell) Sculptor, Educator
Katzen, Philip Art Dealer, Curator
Katzman, Herbert Painter, Instructor
Kaufman, Edgar, Jr Designer, Writer
Kaufman, Jane A Painter, Instructor
Kaufman, Joe Illustrator
Kaufman, Nancy Art Administrator
Kaufmann, Robert Carl Art Librarian
Kawabata, Minoru Painter, Instructor
Kawara, On Conceptual Artist
Kaz, Nathaniel Sculptor, Instructor
Kaz (Lawrence Katzman) Designer, Cartoonist
Keats, Ezra Jack Illustrator, Writer
Keen, Helen Boyd Painter, Collector
Keith, Eros Illustrator, Painter
Kelder, Diane M Art Historian, Art Critic
Kelly, Ellsworth Painter, Sculptor
Kelly, James Painter
Kempton, Greta Painter
Kepalas (Elena Kepalaite) Sculptor, Painter
Kepets, Hugh Michael Painter
Kerns, Ed (Johnson, Jr) Painter
Kerr, Berta Borgenicht Art Dealer, Collector
Kertess, Klaus D Art Dealer, Art Historian
Kessler, Alan Painter, Sculptor
Kessler, Shirley Painter, Instructor
Khendry, Janak Kumar Art Administrator, Sculptor
Kidd, Steven R Illustrator, Instructor
Kienbusch, William Austin Painter
Kimball, Yeffe Painter
Kimmel-Cohn, Roberta Art Dealer, Designer
Kimura, Riisaburo Painter, Printmaker
King, Ethel May Collector, Patron
King, William Dickey Sculptor
Kingman, Dong M Painter, Illustrator
Kingsley, April Art Critic, Lecturer
Kinigstein, Jonah Painter, Designer
Kinstler, Everett Raymond Painter, Instructor
Kipp, Lyman Sculptor
Kirk, Michael Printmaker
Kirschenbaum, Bernard Edwin Sculptor
Kirstein, Mr & Mrs Lincoln Collectors
Kiselewski, Joseph Sculptor
Kitaj, R B Painter, Printmaker
Klabunde, Charles Spencer Printmaker, Painter
Kleemann, Ron Painter
Kleiman, Alan Painter, Sculptor
Klein, Doris Painter
Klein, Sandor C Painter, Sculptor
Kline, Alma Sculptor
Klonis, Stewart Painter, Art Director
Kluver, Billy (Johan Wilhem Kluver) Art Administrator, Technical Consultant
Knight, Hilary Illustrator, Designer
Knigin, Michael Jay Painter, Printmaker
Knowles, Alison Performance Artist, Printmaker
Knowlton, Monique Art Dealer, Collector
Koch, Edwin E Sculptor, Painter
Koch, John Painter, Collector
Kocherthaler, Mina Painter
Kocsis, Ann Painter
Koehler, Henry Painter
Koerner, Daniel Painter, Cartoonist
Kolbert, Frank L Art Dealer
Kolodner, Nathan K Art Dealer
Koltun, Frances Lang Collector, Lecturer
Komor, Mathias Art Dealer
Konigsberg, Harvey Painter
Konzal, Joseph Sculptor
Koppelman, Chaim Printmaker, Educator
Koppelman, Dorothy Painter, Gallery Director
Koren, Edward B Cartoonist, Illustrator
Korman, Barbara Sculptor, Instructor
Korman, Harriet R Painter
Korot, Beryl Video Artist
Koshalek, Richard Museum Director
Kosuth, Joseph Conceptual Artist
Kotin, Albert Painter, Educator
Kottler, Lynn Art Dealer
Kovachevich, Thomas Painter
Kowing, Frank Eugene Painter
Kozloff, Joyce Painter
Kozloff, Max Art Critic
Kramarsky, Mrs Siegried Collector
Kramer, Hilton Art Critic
Kraner, Florian G Painter, Educator
Krashes, Barbara Painter, Instructor
Krasner, Oscar Art Dealer
Kraushaar, Antoinette M Art Dealer
Kreznar, Richard J Sculptor, Painter
Kriensky, (Morris E) Painter, Sculptor
Kruger, Barbara Conceptual Artist
Kruger, Louise Sculptor
Krushenick, Nicholas Painter
Kubota, Shigeko Video Curator, Video Artist
Kuchel, Konrad Art Administrator
Kuh, Howard Painter
Kuh, Katharine Art Critic, Art Consultant
Kulicke, Robert M Painter, Craftsman
Kup, Karl Art Historian
Kurahara, Ted Painter, Educator
Kurhajec, Joseph A Sculptor
Kurz, Diana Painter, Educator
Kushner, Robert Ellis Painter, Designer
Kuwayama, Tadaaki Painter
Laderman, Gabriel Painter, Educator
La Hotan, Robert L Painter
Laine, Lenore Painter
Laliberte, Norman Painter
Lamb, Adrian Painter
Lampert, Dorrie Painter, Designer
Lancaster, Mark Painter
Landfield, Ronnie (Ronald T) Painter, Instructor
Landis, Lily Sculptor
Landry, Albert Art Dealer
Landsman, Stanley Sculptor
Lane, Alvin Seymour Collector
Lang, Daniel S Painter
Langner, Nola Illustrator Children's Books
Laning, Edward Painter
Lansner, Fay Painter
Lapiner, Alan C Art Dealer
Larcada, Richard Kenneth Art Dealer
Larsen, Jack Lenor Designer, Weaver
Lasch, Pat Painter
Lasker, Mrs Albert D Collector
Law, Pauline Elizabeth Painter
Lawrence, Marion Art Historian
Lay, Patricia Anne Sculptor
Lebedev, Vladimir Painter
Lebish, Harriet Shiller Art Dealer
Lee, Eleanor Gay Painter
Leech, Merle Eugene Sculptor, Printmaker
Lefebre, John Art Dealer
Leff, Juliette Painter, Educator
Lehr, Janet Art Dealer
Leiber, Gerson August Printmaker, Painter
Leitman, Norman Art Dealer
Lekakis, Michael Nicholas Sculptor
Lembeck, John Edgar Painter
Leonardi, Hector Painter, Instructor
Lerman, Doris (Harriet) Painter, Sculptor
Lerman, Leo Writer, Art Historian
Lerman, Ora Painter, Sculptor
Lerner, Abe Book Designer, Photographer
Lerner, Abram Museum Director
Lerner, Alexander Collector
Lerner, Marilyn Ann Painter
Lerner, Richard J Art Dealer
Lerner, Sandy R Painter, Lithographer
Leslie, Alfred Painter
Leven, Ruth Ann Art Administrator
Leventhal, Ruth Lee Painter, Sculptor
Levering, Robert K Painter, Illustrator
Levi, Josef Painter
Levi, Julian (E) Painter, Educator
Levin, Gail Curator, Art Historian
Levin, Kim (Kim Pateman) Art Critic, Painter
Levine, David Illustrator, Painter
Levine, Jack Painter
Levine, Les Sculptor, Curator
Levinson, Fred (Floyd) Designer, Cartoonist
Levinson, Mon Sculptor
Levit, Herschel Painter, Illustrator
Levitt, Alfred Painter, Prehistorian
Lev-Landau (Samuel David Landau) Painter
Levy, David Corcos Photographer, Educator
Levy, Mayra Phyllis Art Administrator
Levy, Stuart D Gallery Director, Art Dealer
Levy, Tibbie Painter
Lewis, Elizabeth Matthew Art Librarian, Painter
Lewis, Golda Assemblage Artist, Papermaker
Lewis, Norman Wilfred Painter, Instructor
Lewison, Florence (Mrs Maurice Glickman) Writer, Art Dealer
Le Witt, Sol Sculptor
Liberman, Alexander Photographer, Writer
Lieb, Vered (Vered Shapiro-Lieb) Art Writer, Painter
Lieberman, William S Art Administrator
Ligare, David H Painter
Liles, Raeford Bailey Painter, Sculptor
Li Marzi, Joseph Painter, Instructor
Lindner, Richard Painter
Linn, Steven Allen Sculptor
Linsky, Mr & Mrs Jack Collectors
Lipman, Howard W Collector

NEW YORK (cont)

Lippard, Lucy Rowland Writer
Lippold, Richard Sculptor
Lipsky, Pat Painter
Lipton, Seymour Sculptor
Lipton, Sondra (Sahlman) Painter, Sculptor
Liszt, Maria Veronica Painter, Designer
Littman, Robert R Art Administrator, Art Historian
Livingston, Charlotte (Mrs Francis Vendeveer Kughler) Painter, Art Administrator
Livingston, Sidnee Painter
Llorente, Luis Painter, Designer
Lock, Charles K Art Dealer
Loeb, Mr & Mrs John L Collectors
Loew, Michael Painter
London, Alexander Collector, Illustrator
London, Barbara Curator
Longo, Vincent Painter, Educator
Lorber, Richard Art Writer, Educator
Lorber, Stephen Neil Painter, Printmaker
Loring, John Painter, Printmaker
Love, Iris Cornelia Art Historian
Love, Joseph Painter
Lucas, Charles C, Jr Collector
Lucchesi, Bruno Sculptor
Lucioni, Luigi Painter, Etcher
Luck, Robert Educator, Curator
Luisi, Jerry Sculptor, Instructor
Lukin, Sven Painter
Lund, David Painter
Lunde, Karl Roy Art Historian, Writer
Lusker, Ron Painter
Lutze Sculptor, Consultant, Art Dealer
Lye, Len Sculptor, Kinetic Artist
Lynes, Russell Writer, Critic
MacGarvey, Bernard B Painter
MacIver, Loren Painter
MacKay, Hugh Art Dealer
MacKendrick, Lilian Painter
Madsen, Loren Wakefield Sculptor
Magriel, Paul Collector
Malbin, Lydia Winston Collector
Mallory, Nina A Educator, Art Historian
Mallory, Ronald Sculptor
Manca, Albino Sculptor
Mandel, Howard Painter, Sculptor
Mankowski, Bruno Sculptor
Mann, Andy Video Artist
Mann, David Art Dealer
Manship, John Paul Painter, Sculptor
Manso, Leo Painter, Educator
Manton, Jock (Archimedes Aristides Giacomantonio) Sculptor, Art Administrator
Manville, Elsie Painter
Marais (Mary Rachel Brown) Painter
Marazzi, William C P Painter
Marberger, A Aladar Art Dealer
Marca-Relli, Conrad Painter
Marchisotto, Linda A Art Dealer
Marcus, Marcia Painter
Marden, Brice Painter, Educator
Marder, Dorie Painter, Serigrapher
Margo, Boris Painter, Printmaker
Margolies, John Video Artist, Photographer
Marisol, Escobar Sculptor
Mark, Phyllis Sculptor
Markel, Kathryn E Art Dealer
Markell, Isabella Banks Painter, Graphic Artist
Marks, Mr & Mrs Cedric H Collector, Patron
Marks, Claude Painter, Writer
Marks, Royal S Art Dealer, Collector
Marks, Stanley Albert Collector
Marron, Donald B Collector
Marshall, Richard Donald Curator, Art Historian
Marsicano, Nicholas Painter, Educator
Marsteller, William A Collector
Marter, Joan M Art Historian, Art Critic
Martin, Knox Painter, Sculptor
Martin, Richard (Harrison) Art Historian, Art Administrator
Martin, Thomas Painter, Instructor
Masheck, Joseph Daniel Editor, Art Historian
Mason, Frank Herbert Painter, Instructor
Matisse, Pierre Art Dealer
Matta-Clark, Gordon Sculptor
Mattiello, Roberto Painter, Sculptor
Mavian, Salpi Miriam Painter
Max, Peter Designer, Illustrator
Maxwell, William C Painter, Printmaker
Mayer, Bena Frank Painter
Mayer, Grace M Curator, Collector
Mayer, Ralph Painter, Writer
Mayer, Rosemary Sculptor
Maynard, Valerie Sculptor, Lecturer
Mayor, Alpheus Hyatt Art Historian, Writer
Mayorga, Gabriel Humberto Painter, Sculptor
McCall, Anthony Film Maker, Conceptual Artist
McCarthy, Denis Painter
McCartin, William Francis Painter
McColley, Sutherland Curator
McCormick, Harry Painter
McCormick, Jo Mary (Jo Mary McCormick-Sakurai) Painter, Illustrator
McCoy, Ann Painter, Draftsman
McCoy, Jason Art Dealer
McCray, Porter A Art Administrator
McDarrah, Fred William Photographer, Writer
McFadden, Mary Collector, Designer
McKesson, Malcolm Forbes Painter, Sculptor
McKinney, Donald Art Dealer
McKnight, Eline Printmaker
McKnight, Thomas Frederick Painter
McLanathan, Richard B K Art Consultant, Writer
McMahon, James Edward Art Dealer
McShine, Kynaston Leigh Curator
Meadmore, Clement L Sculptor
Mehring, Howard William Painter
Meier, Richard Alan Architect
Meisel, Louis Koenig Art Dealer, Art Historian
Melikian, Mary Painter
Mellon, James Printmaker, Painter
Meltzer, Anna E Painter, Instructor
Meltzer, Doris Art Dealer, Printmaker
Mendelson, Haim Painter, Printmaker
Meneeley, Edward Sculptor
Meng, Wendy Painter
Merkin, Richard Marshall Painter, Printmaker
Messer, Thomas M Museum Director, Art Historian
Metz, Frank Robert Painter, Art Director
Metzger, Evelyn Borchard Painter, Sculptor
Meyer, Mr & Mrs Andre Collectors
Meyer, Felicia Painter
Meyer, Susan E Art Editor & Writer
Meyer, Ursula Sculptor, Photographer
Meyerowitz, William Painter
Meyers, Dale (Mrs Mario Cooper) Painter, Instructor
Michals, Duane Photographer
Michaux, Ronald Robert Art Dealer
Michelson-Bagley, Henrietta Sculptor, Painter
Middleman, Raoul F Painter, Instructor
Mieczkowski, Edwin Painter
Mikus, Eleanore Painter, Lecturer
Milch, Harold Carlton Art Dealer
Milder, Jay Painter, Sculptor
Miles, Jeanne Patterson Painter, Sculptor
Milette, Clemence M Painter
Milholland, Richard Alexander Painter
Miller, David Stuart Art Dealer
Miller, Donald Richard Sculptor
Miller, Dorothy Canning Art Consultant
Miller, Mrs G Macculloch Collector
Miller, Richard Kidwell Painter
Miller, Richard McDermott Sculptor
Miller, Robert Peter Art Dealer
Milliken, Alexander Fabbri Art Dealer, Collector
Millonzi, Victor Sculptor
Mills, Margaret Art Administrator
Miralda, Antoni Sculptor
Miss, Mary Sculptor
Mitchell, Fred Painter
Mitchell, Joan Painter
Mitchell, Peter Todd Painter
Mittleman, Ann Painter
Miyasaki, George Joji Printmaker, Painter
Miyashita, Tad Painter
Mock, Richard Basil Painter, Environmental Artist
Model, Elisabeth D Sculptor
Mogensen, Paul Painter
Monaghan, William Scott Painter, Sculptor
Monroe, Gerald Painter, Educator
Monroe, Robert Photographer
Mont, Betty Art Dealer
Mont, Frederick Art Dealer
Moore, Barbara Archivist
Moore, Peter Photographer, Archivist
Moore, Robert James Painter, Instructor
Morgan, Norma Gloria Painter, Engraver
Morgan, Theodora Art Writer
Morley, Malcom Painter
Morris, Robert Sculptor
Morse, Mitchell Ian Art Dealer, Restorer
Morton, Robert Alan Publisher, Art Writer
Moseley, Ralph Sessions Painter
Moses, Ed Painter
Moskowitz, Robert S Painter
Moy, Seong Painter, Graphic Artist
Moyer, Roy Painter, Art Administrator
Muehsam, Gerd Art Librarian, Art Writer
Mullen, Buell Painter
Muntadas, Antonio Media Artist
Murata, Hiroshi Painter, Printmaker
Murphy, Hass Sculptor, Draftsman
Murray, Albert (Ketcham) Painter
Murray, Elizabeth Painter
Murray, John Michael Painter
Murray, Robert (Gray) Sculptor
Myers, Forrest Warden Sculptor
Myers, John B Art Dealer
Naiman, Lee E Art Dealer
Nakazato, Hitoshi Painter, Printmaker
Nama, George Allen Printmaker, Painter
Namuth, Hans Photographer, Film Maker
Nathan, Helmuth Max Educator, Painter
Nathans, Rhoda R Photographer
Natkin, Robert Painter
Nauman, Bruce Sculptor
Navas, Elizabeth S Collector, Patron
Neel, Alice Painter
Neikrug, Marjorie Art Dealer
Neiman, LeRoy Painter, Printmaker
Nesbitt, Lowell (Blair) Painter, Lecturer
Neuberger, Roy R Collector, Patron
Neustein, Joshua Painter, Art Critic
Nevelson, Louise Sculptor
Newhouse, Bertram Maurice Art Dealer
Newhouse, Clyde Mortimer Art Dealer, Art Historian
Newman, Arnold Photographer
Newman, Elias Painter, Writer
Newsom, Barbara Ylvisaker Writer
Newton, Douglas Art Administrator, Museum Director
Niblock, Phill Film Maker, Composer
Nichols, James William Painter
Nicholson, Ben Painter
Niizuma, Minoru Sculptor
Nirvanno, Comet (Vincent Romano) Painter, Photographer
Noble, Joseph Veach Museum Director
Nochlin, Linda (Linda Pommer) Art Historian, Educator
Noel, Georges Painter
Nordhausen, A Henry Painter
Nordness, Lee Art Dealer
Norman, Dorothy (S) Writer, Photographer
Norton, Rob Roy, Jr Painter
Norvell, Patsy Sculptor, Environmental Artist
Nosoff, Frank Painter
Notarbartolo, Albert Painter
Novak, Barbara (Mrs Brian O'Doherty) Art Historian, Educator
Novros, David Painter
Nuala (Elsa De Brun) Painter
Ocampo, Miguel Painter
O'Connell, Edward E Photographer, Printmaker
O'Connor, Francis Valentine Art Historian, Lecturer
Odate, Toshio Conceptual Artist, Instructor
Oenslager, Donald Mitchell Stage Designer
Offin, Charles Z Collector, Art Critic

Ohashi, Yutaka Painter
Ohlson, Douglas Dean Painter
Ohrbach, Jerome K Collector
Okada, Kenzo Painter
O'Kelley, Mattie Lou Painter
Okoshi, Eugenia Sumiye Painter, Printmaker
Oldenburg, Claes Thure Sculptor
Oldenburg, Richard Erik Museum Director
Oliver, Richard Bruce Curator
Oloffson, Werner Olaf Painter, Photographer
Olugebefola, Ademola Painter, Designer
Ono, Yoko Filmmaker
Oppenheim, Dennis A Sculptor
Order, Trudy Painter
Orenstein, Gloria Feman Writer, Art Historian
Orkin, Ruth (Mrs Morris Engel) Photographer, Film Maker
Orling, Anne Art Consultant, Painter
Ortiz, Ralph Sculptor
Oscarsson, Victoria Constance Gunhild Art Dealer, Administrator
Oster, Gerald Painter, Graphic Artist
Ostuni, Peter W Painter
Osze, Andrew E Sculptor, Painter
O'Toole, James St Laurence Art Dealer, Art Historian
Owen, Frank (Franklin Charles Owen) Painter
Pace, Stephen S Painter, Printmaker
Pacileo, Dolores Margaret Environmental Artist, Art Administrator
Paik, Nam June Video Artist
Paley, Mr & Mrs William S Collectors
Papageorge, Tod Photographer
Parish, Betty Waldo Painter, Writer
Parker, James Painter
Parker, Nancy Winslow Illustrator, Painter
Parker, Raymond Painter
Parkinson, Elizabeth Bliss Patron, Collector
Parsons, Betty Bierne Painter, Art Dealer
Pascal, David Painter, Cartoonist
Passuntino, Peter Zaccaria Painter, Sculptor
Paternosto, Cesar Pedro Painter
Patten, David John Editor, Art Librarian
Payne, Lan Painter, Filmmaker
Payor, Eugene Painter, Illustrator
Payson, Dale Constance Illustrator, Painter
Pearl, Marilyn Art Dealer
Pearlstein, Philip Painter, Educator
Pease, Roland Folsom, Jr Art Critic, Collector
Pei, I M (Ieoh Ming Pei) Architect
Pekarsky, Mel (Melvin Hirsch) Painter, Educator
Pellicone, Marie Gallery Director
Pellicone, William Painter
Pels, Albert Painter, Art Administrator
Penn, Irving Photographer
Perless, Robert Sculptor
Perlman, Joel Leonard Sculptor, Instructor
Perls, Klaus G Art Dealer
Perreault, John Art Critic, Multi-Media Artist
Perret, Nell Foster Painter
Perry, Edward (Ted) Samuel Art Administrator
Persky, Robert S Gallery Director, Art Dealer
Pesner, Carole Manishin Art Dealer
Petlin, Irving Painter
Pettet, William Painter
Pfeifer, Marcuse Art Dealer, Gallery Owner
Pharr, Mr & Mrs Walter Nelson Collectors
Philipp, Robert Painter
Picard, Lil Painter, Sculptor
Pilgrim, James F Curator, Art Historian
Pindell, Howardena Doreen Painter, Curator
Pines, Ned L Collector
Pinto, Angelo Raphael Painter, Etcher
Pisano, Ronald George Art Historian, Curator
Pizitz, Silvia Collector, Patron
Placzek, Adolf Kurt Art Librarian, Art Historian
Plagens, Peter Painter, Educator
Plunkett, Edward Milton Painter, Lecturer
Poindexter, Elinor Fuller Art Dealer
Pollard, Donald Pence Designer, Painter
Pollaro, Paul Painter
Polsky, Cynthia Artist, Art Administrator
Ponce de Leon, Michael Printmaker; Painter
Pond, Clayton Painter, Printmaker
Poons, Larry Painter
Poor, Anne Painter
Porter, Liliana Instructor, Printmaker
Posen, Stephen Painter
Poses, Mr & Mrs Jack I Collectors
Posner, Donald Art Historian
Post, Anne B Sculptor, Graphic Artist
Powell, Leslie (Joseph) Painter, Designer
Pozzi, Lucio Painter
Prager, David A Collector
Prakapas, Eugene Joseph Art Dealer
Pratt, Dallas Patron, Collector
Pratt, Frances (Frances Elizabeth Usui) Painter, Illustrator
Prentice, David Ramage Painter, Designer
Prins, (J) Warner Painter, Illustrator
Pusey, Mavis Painter, Printmaker
Quaytman, Harvey Painter
Rabinovich, Raquel Painter, Sculptor
Rabinovitch, William Avrum Painter
Rabinowitch, Royden Leslie Sculptor
Rabkin, Leo Painter, Sculptor
Rachelski, Florian W Painter, Sculptor
Radulovic, Savo Painter, Craftsman
Rafsky, Jessica C Collector
Raggio, Olga Art Administrator, Curator
Rain, Charles (Whedon) Painter
Rappin, Adrian Painter
Raskins, Ellen Illustrator, Designer
Ratcliff, Carter Art Critic, Writer
Ratkai, George Painter, Sculptor
Rauschenberg, Robert Painter
Rave, Georgia Painter, Educator
Raydon, Alexander R Art Dealer, Collector
Recanati, Dina Sculptor
Reddy, Krishna N Printmaker, Sculptor
Reed, David Fredrick Painter
Reed, Harold Art Dealer
Reginato, Peter Sculptor
Rehberger, Gustav Painter, Draftsman
Reiback, Earl M Sculptor, Painter
Reid, Robert Dennis Painter, Instructor
Reiner, Mr & Mrs Jules Collectors, Patrons
Reisman, Philip Painter, Illustrator
Relis, Sandy Painter, Sculptor
Remington, Deborah Williams Painter
Renouf, Edda Painter, Printmaker
Reopel, Joyce Draftsman
Resika, Paul Painter
Resnick, Marcia Aylene Photographer, Conceptual Artist
Resnick, Milton Painter
Rewald, John Art Historian, Educator
Reynal, Jeanne Mosaic Artist
Rice, Dan Painter
Rice, Shelley Enid Art Critic, Art Historian
Rich, Garry Lorence Painter
Richard, Betti Sculptor
Richards, Bill Painter, Educator
Richardson, Gretchen (Mrs Ronald Freelander) Sculptor
Riess, Lore Painter, Printmaker
Rifkin, Dr & Mrs Harold Collectors
Ringgold, Faith Painter, Sculptor
Rinhart, George R Art Dealer, Collector
Ripps, Rodney Painter
Rivera, Frank Painter
Robbin, Anthony Stuart Painter
Roberts, Colette (Jacqueline) Art Critic, Art Administrator
Robins, Corinne Art Critic, Writer
Roby, Sara (Mary Barnes) Collector, Patron
Rockburne, Dorothea Sculptor
Rockefeller, Mr & Mrs David Collectors
Rockefeller, John Davison, III Collector, Patron
Rockefeller, Mrs Laurance S Collector
Rockefeller, Nelson Aldrich Collector, Patron
Roesler, Norbert Leonhard Hugo Collector
Rogovin, Howard Sand Painter
Rohlfing, Christian Art Administrator, Curator
Rojtman, Mrs Marc B Collector
Roller, Marion Bender Sculptor, Painter
Romano, Clare Camille Printmaker, Painter
Romano, Emanuel Glicen Painter, Illustrator
Romano, Salvatore Michael Sculptor, Painter
Romano, Umberto Roberto Painter, Sculptor
Rome, Harold Collector, Painter
Romeu, Joost A Conceptual Artist
Rosati, James Sculptor, Educator
Rose, Barbara E Art Historian, Art Writer
Rose, Bernice Berend Curator
Rose, Herman Painter, Printmaker
Rose, Leatrice Painter, Instructor
Rose, Peter Henry Art Dealer
Rosenberg, Alex Jacob Publisher, Editor
Rosenberg, Carole Halsband Art Editor, Art Dealer
Rosenberg, Harold Writer, Educator
Rosenblum, Jay Painter
Rosenblum, Robert Art Historian
Rosenborg, Ralph M Painter
Rosenhouse, Irwin Jacob Printmaker, Illustrator
Rosenquit, Bernard Painter, Printmaker
Rosenthal, Mrs Alan H Collector
Rosenthal, Stephen Painter
Rosenthal, Tony (Bernard) Sculptor
Ross, Charles Sculptor
Roston, Arnold Artist, Educator
Roszak, Theodore Painter, Sculptor
Rotan, Walter Sculptor
Rotenberg, Harold Painter
Roth, Frank Painter
Rothschild, Judith Painter
Rotterdam, Paul Z Painter
Rowell, Margit Art Historian
Ruben, Richards Painter, Educator
Rubin, Lawrence Art Dealer, Collector
Rubin, William Art Curator, Art Historian
Rubinstein, Susan R Photographer
Ruda, Edwin Painter
Ruddley, John Art Administrator, Painter
Russell, Philip C Painter, Instructor
Ruta, Peter Paul Painter, Editor
Ryerson, Margery Austen Painter, Etcher
Ryman, Robert Painter
Saari, Peter H Painter, Sculptor
Sachs, A M Art Dealer, Collector
Sadek, George Educator, Designer
Saidenberg, Daniel Art Dealer
Saidenberg, Eleanore B Art Dealer, Collector
St Clair, Michael Art Dealer
Salemme, Lucia (Autorino) Painter, Writer
Salt, John Painter
Salzman, Rick Video Artist, Sculptor
Samaras, Lucas Sculptor
Samburg, Grace (Blanche) Painter, Lithographer
Sampliner, Mr & Mrs Paul H Collectors
Samuels, Gerald Painter, Sculptor
Samuels, John Stockwell, 3d Collector, Patron
Sanchez, Emilio Painter
Sandback, Frederick Lane Sculptor
Sande, Rhoda Art Dealer
Sandler, Barbara Painter
Sandler, Irving Harry Art Historian, Educator
Saphire, Lawrence M Art Writer
Saret, Alan Daniel Sculptor
Sarnoff, Arthur Saron Painter
Sarnoff, Robert W Collector
Sasaki, Tomiyo Painter, Video Artist
Sato, Masaaki Painter, Printmaker
Savelli, Angelo Painter, Sculptor
Savitz, Frieda (Frieda Savitz Laden) Painter, Educator
Schab, Margo Pollins Art Dealer
Schapiro, Meyer Educator, Art Historian
Schapiro, Miriam Painter
Scharf, William Painter
Schary, Saul Illustrator, Painter
Scherr, Mary Ann Goldsmith, Designer
Schimansky, Donya Dobrila Art Librarian, Art Historian
Schimmel, Norbert Collector
Schlemowitz, Abram Sculptor
Schloss, Arleen P (Arleen P Kelly) Multi Media Artist, Painter
Schmidt, Arnold Alfred Painter, Sculptor
Schmidt, Harvey Lester Illustrator, Writer
Schneebaum, Tobias Painter
Schneemann, Carolee Filmmaker, Performance Artist, Writer
Schneider, Ira Video Artist, Lecturer
Schneider, Jo Anne Painter

NEW YORK (cont)

Schneider, Lisa Dawn Art Dealer, Art Critic
Schneier, Donna Frances Art Dealer
Schnurr-Colflesh, E Painter
Schoelkopf, Robert J, Jr Art Dealer
Schoen, Mr & Mrs Arthur Boyer Collectors
Scholz, Janos Collector, Art Historian
Schorr, Justin Painter, Educator
Schrag, Karl Painter
Schreyer, Greta L Painter, Lecturer
Schulte, Mr & Mrs Arthur D Collectors
Schulz, Charles Monroe Cartoonist
Schumsky, Felicie Roberta Art Publisher
Schuselka, Elfi Printmaker, Sculptor
Schutz, Prescott Dietrich Art Dealer
Schwabacher, Ethel K Painter, Art Critic
Schwalb, Susan Graphic Artist, Painter
Schwalbach, Mary Jo Painter, Sculptor
Schwartz, Barbara Ann Painter, Writer
Schwartz, Eugene M Collector, Patron
Schwartz, Marvin D Art Historian
Schwartz, Sing-Si Photographer
Schwartz, Therese Painter, Writer
Schwarz, Gladys Painter
Schwedler, Wm A Painter
Schweitzer, M R Art Dealer, Collector
Scott, Arden Sculptor
Scott-Gibson, Herbert Nathaniel Art Administrator, Educator
Seery, John Painter
Segy, Ladislas Art Dealer, Collector
Seide, Charles Painter, Educator
Seligmann, Herbert J Art Writer
Semmel, Joan Painter
Seplowin, Charles Joseph Sculptor
Serger, Helen Art Dealer
Serniak, Regina Painter, Writer
Serra, Richard Sculptor
Seyffert, Richard Leopold Painter, Instructor
Shahly, Jehan Painter
Shapiro, Babe Painter
Shapiro, Daisy Viertel Collector, Patron
Shapiro, David Painter
Shapiro, Frank D Educator, Painter
Shapiro, Joel (Elias) Sculptor
Shapshak, Rene Sculptor
Sharp, Anne Painter, Printmaker
Sharp, Harold Illustrator
Sharp, Willoughby Art Administrator, Video Artist
Sharpe, David Flemming Painter, Printmaker
Shechtman, George Henoch Art Dealer
Shecter, Pearl S Painter
Sherman, Sarai Painter, Designer
Sherrod, Philip Lawrence Painter
Shibley, Gertrude Painter
Shikler, Aaron Painter
Shostak, Edwin Bennett Sculptor
Shoulberg, Harry Painter
Showell, Kenneth L Painter
Shuff, Lily (Lillian Shir) Painter, Engraver
Sideris, Alexander Painter
Siegel, (Leo) Dink Illustrator
Sievan, Maurice Painter
Sigel, Barry Chaim Painter
Sihvonen, Oli Painter
Silberstein-Storfer, Muriel Rosoff Instructor, Painter
Sills, Thomas Albert Painter
Silverberg, Ellen Ruth Art Dealer
Silverman, Burton Philip Painter, Illustrator
Simkin, Phillips M Sculptor
Simon, Bernard Sculptor, Instructor
Simon, Helene Sculptor
Simon, Sidney Sculptor, Painter
Simonds, Charles Frederick Sculptor, Architect
Simpson, Merton D Painter, Art Dealer
Sims, Patterson Curator
Sinaiko, Arlie Sculptor, Collector
Sirena (Contessa Antonia Mastrocristino Fanara) Painter, Collector
Sirugo, Salvatore Painter
Skolnick, Arnold Painter, Graphic Artist
Slack, Dee Painter
Slavin, Arlene Painter
Slavin, Neal Photographer
Sleigh, Sylvia Painter, Instructor
Slivka, David Sculptor
Slivka, Rose Art Editor
Sloane, Patricia Hermine Painter
Smith, Albert Comic Artist, Art Editor
Smith, Alvin Painter, Educator
Smith, Mrs Bertram Collector, Patron
Smith, George W Sculptor, Educator
Smith, Paul J Museum Director
Smith, Shirlann Painter
Smith, Tony Sculptor
Smith, Vincent D Painter
Smith-Gordon, Nannette Art Dealer
Smyth, David Richard Sculptor
Snelson, Kenneth D Sculptor
Snyder, Seymour Illustrator, Instructor
Soffer, Sasson Sculptor
Sokole, Miron Painter, Educator
Solinger, David M Collector, Patron
Solodkin, Judith Printmaker, Educator
Solomon, Gerald Art Dealer
Solomon, Holly Art Dealer, Collector
Solomon, Richard H Art Publisher, Print Dealer, Collector
Solomon, Mr & Mrs Sidney L Collectors
Sommerburg, Miriam Painter, Sculptor
Sonday, Milton Franklin, Jr Curator
Sonenberg, Jack Painter
Sonfist, Alan Painter
Sonneman, Eve Photographer, Film Maker
Sonnenberg, Mr & Mrs Benjamin Collectors
Sonnier, Keith Environmental Artist, Video Artist
Soreff, Helen Painter
Soroka, Margery Painter
Soyer, Isaac Painter, Instructor
Soyer, Raphael Painter
Spaeth, Eloise O'Mara Collector, Writer
Spark, Victor David Art Dealer
Spaventa, George Sculptor
Spector, Naomi Art Dealer, Writer
Speiser, Stuart M Collector, Patron
Spelman, Jill Sullivan Painter
Spence, Andy Painter
Sperakis, Nicholas George Painter, Printmaker
Spero, Nancy Painter
Speyer, Nora Painter
Spiegel, Sam Collector
Spitzer, Frances R Collector
Spohn, Clay (Edgar) Painter, Instructor
Spruyt, E Lee Painter, Printmaker
Stachelberg, Mrs Charles G Collector, Patron
Stacy, Donald L Painter, Educator
Stadler, Albert Painter
Staempfli, George W Art Dealer, Painter
Staley, Allen Art Historian
Stamm, John Davies Collector
Stamm, Ted Painter, Artist
Stamos, Theodoros (S) Painter
Stampfle, Felice Art Curator, Writer
Standen, Edith Appleton Art Historian
Stanley, Bob Painter
Stapleton, Joseph F Instructor, Painter
Stasik, Andrew J Printmaker, Gallery Director
Steckel, Anita Painter, Collage Artist
Stefanelli, Joseph J Painter
Stefanotty, Robert Alan Art Administrator
Stein, Claire A Art Administrator
Stein, Ronald Jay Sculptor
Stein, Walter Painter, Sculptor
Steinberg, Saul Cartoonist
Steiner, Julia Bourne Collector, Patron
Steiner, Michael Sculptor
Steiner, Paul Writer
Steir, Pat Painter
Stella, Frank Painter
Stellings, Alexa Art Dealer
Stenbery, Algot Painter
Stern, Leonard B Art Dealer, Collector
Sterne, Dahli Painter, Sculptor
Sterne, Hedda Painter
Stevens, May Painter
Stewart, Jack Painter, Educator
Stiebel, Eric Art Dealer
Stiebel, Gerald Gustave Art Dealer
Stillman, E Clark Collector
Stoessel, Henry Kurt Painter, Designer
Stokes, Thomas Phelps Painter
Stoloff, Carolyn Painter
Stoloff, Irma Sculptor
Stone, Sylvia Sculptor
Stralem, Donald S Collector, Patron
Strautmanis, Edvins Painter, Sculptor
Strider, Marjorie Virginia Sculptor
Stronghilos, Carol Painter
Stroud, Peter Anthony Painter, Educator
Stuart, Michelle Painter, Sculptor
Sturtevant, Elaine F Painter, Filmmaker
Suba, Susanne Painter, Illustrator
Sugarman, George Sculptor, Painter
Sugimoto, Henry Y Painter
Sullivan, Jim Painter
Sultan, Altoon Painter
Suttman, Paul Sculptor
Sutton, Patricia Painter
Suzuki, Katsko (Katsko Suzuki Kannegieter) Art Dealer
Svendsen, Louise Averill Curator
Swain, Robert Painter
Sweeney, James Johnson Art Administrator, Lecturer
Sylvester, Lucille Painter, Writer
Szoke, John Art Dealer, Publisher
Tabachnick, Anne Educator, Painter
Taback, Simms Illustrator, Designer
Taggart, William John Painter, Instructor
Taira, Frank Painter, Sculptor
Takai, Teiji Painter
Tam, Reuben Painter, Educator
Tanger, Susanna Painter, Writer
Tania (Schreiber-Milicevic) Painter, Sculptor
Tanner, Warren Arts Advocate, Painter
Tarnopol, Gregoire Painter, Collector
Tasgal-Kliegman, Gerda Painter, Sculptor
Tatistcheff, Peter Alexis Art Dealer
Tatti, Benedict Michael Sculptor, Painter
Tawney, Lenore Weaver, Assemblage Artist
Taylor, Lisa Museum Director
Teichman, Sabina Painter, Sculptor
Termini, Christine Artist, Art Dealer
Terrell, Allen Townsend Sculptor
Terry, Hilda (Hilda Terry D'Alessio) Cartoonist, Art Dealer
Texoon, Jasmine Painter, Instructor
Thaler, Mildred G Art Dealer, Gallery Director
Thek, Paul Sculptor
Thomas, Helen (Doane) Painter, Art Critic
Thompson, Kenneth Webster Illustrator, Painter
Thomson, Carl L Painter, Designer
Thornhill, Anna Sculptor, Painter
Tillim, Sidney Painter, Instructor
Tillotison, Robbie Painter, Instructor
Ting, Walasse Painter
Tobias, Julius Sculptor, Instructor
Toll, Barbara Elizabeth Art Dealer, Curator
Tomes, Margot Ladd Illustrator
Tomkins, Calvin Art Writer
Tooker, George Painter, Printmaker
Torffield, Marvin Sculptor
Tormey, James Painter, Designer
Torreano, John Francis Painter, Lecturer
Trakas, George Sculptor
Trauerman, Margy Ann Painter, Instructor
Treadwell, Helen Painter, Designer
Trebilcock, Paul Painter
Trieff, Selina Painter, Instructor
Truman, Jock Curtis Art Dealer, Collector
Tsai, Wen-Ying Sculptor, Painter
Tschacbasov, Nahum Painter, Printmaker
Tuchman, Phyllis Art Historian, Art Critic
Tucker, Marcia Art Historian, Curator
Tudor, Tasha Illustrator, Writer
Tunick, David Art Dealer
Turano, Jane Van Norman Art Editor, Art Writer
Turner, Alan Painter
Turner, Joseph Patron
Turner, Raymond Sculptor
Tuttle, Richard Painter
Twombly, Cy Painter
Tworkov, Jack Painter
Tyson, Mary (Mrs Kenneth Thompson) Painter

Uchima, Ansei Printmaker, Painter
Uchima, Toshiko Painter
Umana, Alfonso Painter, Sculptor
Unger, Mary Ann Sculptor
Upelnieks, Arthur Painter
Urban, Reva Painter, Sculptor
Urry, Steven Sculptor
Usher, Elizabeth Reuter Art Librarian, Lecturer
Uzielli, Giorgio Collector
Van Buren, Richard Sculptor
Van Der Straeten, Vincent Roger Art Dealer
Van De Wiele, Gerald Painter
Van Leer, Mrs W Leicester Collector
Van Riper, Peter Printmaker, Performance Artist
Van Veen, Stuyvesant Painter
Varnedoe, John Kirk Train Art Historian
Vass, Gene Painter, Sculptor
Vaughan, Clifford Cartoonist
Vaux, Richard Painter
Veljkovic, Andrev Art Dealer
Vermes, Madelaine Craftsman
Vicente, Esteban Painter
Vidal, Hahn Painter
Vincent, Tom Painter
Viner, Frank Lincoln Sculptor, Designer
Vodicka, Ruth Kessler Sculptor
Vogel, Donald Printmaker, Instructor
Vogel, Mr & Mrs Herbert Collectors
Vollmer, Ruth Sculptor
Volpe, Robert Painter, Lecturer
Von Schlegell, David Sculptor
Von Wiegand, Charmion Painter, Writer
Wade, Jane Art Dealer
Wagner, Merrill Painter
Waitzkin, Stella Sculptor, Painter
Wald, Sylvia Painter, Sculptor
Waldman, Paul Painter
Walker, Mort Cartoonist
Walker, Mr & Mrs Ralph Collectors
Wall, Sue Painter, Printmaker
Wallace, Soni Painter
Walter, May E Collector, Patron
Walton, Marion (Marion Walton Putnam) Sculptor
Walton, William Painter
Waltzer, Stewart Paul Art Dealer, Painter
Wang, Chi-Chien Painter
Warburg, Edward M M Collector
Wardwell, Allen Gallery Director
Wardy, Frederick Sculptor, Painter
Warhol, Andy Painter, Craftsman
Warner, Jo Painter
Washburn, Gordon Bailey Museum Director
Washburn, Joan T Art Dealer
Wasserman, Albert Painter, Designer
Waterston, Harry Clement Painter
Watson, Wendy Illustrator, Writer
Wauters, Andre Art Dealer, Collector
Weber, Idelle Painter
Weber, John Art Dealer
Wecker, Christoph Ulrich Art Administrator
Wegman, William Photographer, Video Artist
Weil, Lisl Illustrator, Writer
Weiner, Lawrence Charles Artist
Weinrib, David Sculptor
Weinstein, Florence Painter, Sculptor
Weinstein, Mr & Mrs Joseph Collectors, Patrons
Weissman, Julian Paul Art Writer, Art Dealer
Weitzenhoffer, A Max Art Dealer
Welch, Roger Sculptor, Conceptual Artist
Wells, Lynton Painter
Wells, Mac Painter
Werner, Alfred Critic, Writer
Werner, Donald (Lewis) Painter, Photographer
Werner, Nat Sculptor
Weschler, Anita Sculptor, Painter
Wesley, John Painter
Westwater, Angela King Art Dealer, Art Editor
Weyhe, Arthur Sculptor
Weyhe, Mrs Erhard Art Dealer
Whitcomb, Jon Painter, Illustrator
Whitehill, Florence (Fitch) Painter
Whitman, Robert Filmmaker, Environmental Artist
Whitney, John Hay Art Administrator, Collector
Wiegand, Robert Painter, Video Artist
Wilcox, Gordon Cumnock Painter
Wilke, Hannah Sculptor, Instructor
Willard, Charlotte Art Critic, Writer
Willenbecher, John Sculptor, Painter
Williams, Randalph Andrew Educator, Painter
Williams, Walter (Henry) Painter, Printmaker
Willis, Thornton Painter
Wilmarth, Christopher Mallory Sculptor, Draftsman
Wilson, Carrie Lois Gallery Director, Lecturer
Wilson, Jane Painter
Wilson, Martha Storey Mixed-Media Artist, Museum Director
Wilson, May Sculptor
Wilson, Rowland Bragg Cartoonist
Wilson, William S, III Art Writer
Wines, James N Sculptor
Winsor, V Jacqueline Sculptor
Wirtschafter, Bud Film Maker, Instructor
Wise, Howard Art Administrator
Witkin, Isaac Sculptor, Instructor
Wolff, William H Art Dealer
Wolins, Joseph Painter
Wong, Frederick Painter, Instructor
Woodner, Ian Collector
Woodruff, Hale A Painter, Educator
Woolfenden, William Edward Art Administrator, Art Historian
Wright, Frank Cookman Painter, Instructor
Wright, Nina Kaiden Art Consultant
Wu, Linda Yee Chau Sculptor, Educator
Wunderlich, Rudolf G Art Dealer
Wunderman, Jan (Liljan Darcourt Wunderman) Painter, Printmaker
Wybrants-Lynch, Sharon Painter, Instructor
Wyeth, Andrew Newell Painter
Wynshaw, Frances Art Dealer, Art Collector
Yasuda, Robert Painter
Yektai, Manoucher Painter
Yiannes, (Iordanidis) Sculptor, Ceramist
Yoshimura, Fumio Sculptor
Young, Cliff Painter, Instructor
Youngerman, Jack Painter
Yrisarry, Mario Painter
Yunkers, Adja Painter, Educator
Zabriskie, Virginia M Art Dealer
Zacharias, Athos Painter
Zajac, Jack Sculptor, Painter
Zakanych, Robert Painter
Zaleski, Jean M Painter, Art Administrator
Zapkus, Kestutis Edward Painter
Zavel (Zavel Silber) Sculptor, Printmaker
Zeisler, Richard Spiro Collector, Patron
Zevon, Irene Painter
Ziegler, Laura Sculptor
Zierler, William Art Dealer
Zimmerman, Kathleen Marie Painter, Collage Artist
Zingale, Lawrence Painter
Zipkin, Jerome R Collector
Zoromskis, Kazimieras Painter, Instructor
Zox, Larry Painter
Zucker, Barbara M Sculptor, Instructor
Zucker, Bob Photographer, Designer
Zucker, Jacques Painter
Zucker, Joseph I Painter
Zucker, Murray Harvey Painter, Sculptor
Zugor, Sandor Painter
Zver, James M Painter, Printmaker

Newark

Williams, Wayne Francis Sculptor

Newburgh

Jackson, Hazel Brill Sculptor
Mayhall, Dorothy A Art Administrator

Niagara Falls

Slawinski, Joseph Muralist, Conservator

North Babylon

Evans, Nancy Painter

North Bellmore

Schreiber, Martin Sculptor, Painter

North Haven

Brook, Alexander Painter

North Salem

Hammond, Natalie Hays Painter, Museum Director
Savitt, Sam Painter, Illustrator

North Tarrytown

Gursoy, Ahmet Painter

Northport

Benda, Richard R Painter
Geyer, Luise Margot Collector
Twardowicz, Stanley Jan Painter, Photographer
Verzyl, June Carol Art Dealer, Collector

Nyack

Aronson, Boris Designer, Painter
Borne, Mortimer Sculptor, Painter
Dahlberg, Edwin Lennart Painter

Oceanside

Laguna, Muriel Painter

Odessa

Hilton, Eric G Designer, Lecturer

Old Chatham

Kratina, K George Sculptor

Oneida

Colway, James R Painter

Oneonta

Johnson, Donald Marvin Metalsmith
Mahlke, Ernest D Sculptor, Educator
Parish, Jean E Painter, Educator

Orangeburg

Harootian, Khoren Der Painter, Sculptor
Worth, Karen Sculptor

Ossining

Krust, Walter Painter, Sculptor

Oswego

Baitsell, Wilma Williamson Art Administrator, Craftsman
DiPasquale, Dominic Theodore Silversmith, Educator
O'Connell, George D Printmaker, Educator
Saunders, Aulus Ward Painter, Educator
Seawell, Thomas Robert Printmaker, Painter
Stark, George King Educator, Sculptor
Sullins, Robert M Painter, Educator

Oyster Bay

Bothmer, Dietrich Felix Von Art Historian, Art Administrator

Quogue

Kuehnl, Claudia Ann Jeweler, Educator

NEW YORK (cont)

Palisades

Breer, Robert C Sculptor, Film Maker
Knowlton, Grace Farrar Sculptor

Pawling

Waddell, Eugene Painter, Collector

Peekskill

Levine, Seymour R Collector
Osyczka, Bohdan Danny Painter, Illustrator
Rocklin, Raymond Sculptor, Lecturer

Pelham

Boal, Sara Metzner Painter, Instructor
Rutsch, Alexander Painter, Sculptor

Piermont

Davidson, Morris Painter

Pine Plains

Becker, Charlotte (Mrs Walter Cox) Illustrator, Painter

Pittsford

Johnston, Robert Harold Art Administration, Art Historian
Perry, Mary-Ellen Earl Curator
Wildenhain, Frans Potter

Plainview

Coheleach, Guy Joseph Painter, Illustrator
Liberi, Dante Painter, Sculptor
Margulies, Isidore Sculptor

Plattsburgh

Lochridge, Sudie Katherine Art Administrator, Art Historian

Pleasant Valley

Beck, Curt Werner Art Conservator, Art Editor

Pleasantville

Bettinson, Brenda Educator, Painter
Cawein, Kathrin Printmaker, Illuminator
Handville, Robert T Painter, Illustrator
Harmon, Eloise (Norstad) Sculptor
Peck, Stephen Rogers Instructor, Painter
Robinson, Jay Thurston Painter

Poolville

Bryant, Edward Albert Museum Director, Art Historian
Thompson, Tamara (Tamara Thompson Bryant) Painter, Instructor

Port Chester

Blattner, Robert Henry Painter, Illustrator

Port Jefferson

Flecker, Maurice Nathan Painter, Educator

Port Washington

Aaron, Evalyn (Wilhelmina) Painter
Barooshian, Martin Painter, Printmaker
Kleinholz, Frank Painter, Writer

Potsdam

Gibson, Roland Collector, Curator
Goldsmith, Benedict Isaac Gallery Director, Educator
Hildreth, Joseph Alan Printmaker, Painter

Poughkeepsie

Askew, Pamela Art Historian, Writer
Forman, Alice Painter, Designer
Havelock, Christine Mitchell Art Historian
Lindmark, Arne Painter, Lecturer
McNamara, Mary Jo Art Historian, Curator
Morrin, Peter Patrick Art Historian, Art Administrator
Pickens, Alton Painter, Instructor
Reynard, Carolyn Cole Painter, Instructor
Rubenstein, Lewis W Painter, Printmaker

Poughquag

Lidov, Arthur Herschel Painter, Sculptor

Pound Ridge

Bender, Beverly Sterl Sculptor, Designer
Ferro, Walter Printmaker

Purchase

Blum, Shirley Neilsen Art Historian
Danes, Gibson Andrew Educator
Gray, Robert Hugh Educator
Trosky, Helene Roth Printmaker, Writer

Purdy Station

McGee, William Douglas Painter, Educator

Putnam Valley

Padovano, Anthony John Sculptor, Lecturer
Toulis, Vasilios (Apostolos) Printmaker, Painter

Queens

Archie, James Lee Artist

Queens Village

Jonynas, Vytautas K Sculptor, Painter
Kilgore, Al Cartoonist

Red Hook

Lax, David Painter

Rego Park

Aronson, Irene Hilde Designer, Painter
Kanidinc, Salahattin Designer, Calligrapher
Pacheco, Maria Luisa Painter
Tobias, Abraham Joel Painter, Sculptor
Winter, Ruth Painter

Rhinebeck

Krevolin, Lewis Designer, Craftsman

Richmond Hill

Eres, Eugenia Painter

Ridgewood

Negri, Rocco Antonio Illustrator, Painter

Riverdale

Carmel, Hilda Anne Painter
De La Vega, Antonio Painter, Designer
Hnizdovsky, Jacques Painter, Printmaker
Menkes, Sigmund Painter
Morris, George North Painter, Writer

Rochester

Barschel, Hans J Designer, Photographer
Brown, Bruce Robert Painter, Sculptor
Christensen, Hans-Jorgen Thorvald Designer, Craftsman
Doherty, Robert J Museum Director, Educator
Feuerherm, Kurt K Painter
Holm, Milton W Painter
Mahey, John A Gallery Director
Menihan, John Conway Painter, Designer
Paley, Albert Raymond Goldsmith, Designer
Sheppard, Luvon Art Administrator, Educator
Smith, Keith A Photographer, Printmaker
Stern, Mr & Mrs Arthur Lewis Collectors
Wilson, Tom Muir Designer
Witmeyer, Stanley Herbert Art Administrator, Designer
Wolf, Jack Clifford Writer, Painter

Rock City Falls

Davidson, Robert William Sculptor, Educator

Rockville Centre

Knief, Janet (Helen Jeanette) Painter

Rocky Point

England, Paul Grady Painter, Educator

Roslyn

Kenny, Lisa A Painter, Sculptor
Kenny, Thomas Henry Painter

Roslyn Estates

Pall, Dr & Mrs David B Collectors

Roslyn Heights

Gach, George Painter, Sculptor
Rotholz, Rina Printmaker
Sonnenberg, Frances Sculptor, Instructor

Rush

Keyser, William Alphonse, Jr Craftsman, Educator

Rye

Bisgyer, Barbara G (Barbara G Cohn) Sculptor
Drew, Joan Printmaker, Sculptor
Guion, Molly Painter
Morgan, Frances Mallory Sculptor

Sag Harbor

Billings, Henry Painter, Illustrator
Bolotowsky, Ilya Painter, Educator
Fink, Louis R Painter, Photographer
Knee, Gina (Mrs Alexander Brook) Painter, Etcher
Lipman-Wulf, Peter Sculptor, Printmaker
Weber, Jean M Art Administrator, Educator

Sagaponack

Butchkes, Sydney Painter, Sculptor
Dash, Robert (Warren) Painter
Dunlap, Loren Edward Painter, Instructor
Georges, Paul Painter
Williams, Neil Painter, Film Maker

Saint James

White, Robert (Winthrop) Sculptor, Educator

Salem

Garrett, Stuart Grayson, Jr Painter, Educator

Salt Point

Sellers, William Freeman Sculptor, Educator

Sands Point

Holliday, Betty Painter, Photographer

Saranac Lake

Kindermann, Helmmo Photographer, Educator
Patchett, Daniel Claude Art Administrator, Painter

Saratoga Springs

Brodie, Regis Conrad Artist, Potter
Cunningham, J Sculptor
Pardon, Earl B Craftsman, Educator
Swirnoff, Lois Painter, Educator
Upton, Richard Thomas Painter, Printmaker

Saugerties

Martinelli, Ezio Sculptor

Scarborough

Wein, Albert W Sculptor, Painter

Scarsdale

Abel, Ray Illustrator, Designer
Bernstein, Sylvia Painter, Sculptor
Breinin, Raymond Painter, Sculptor
Callisen, Sterling Art Historian, Lecturer
Frackman, Noel Art Critic, Lecturer
Hibbard, Howard Art Historian, Writer
Kaufman, Irving Painter, Educator
Kearl, Stanley Brandon Sculptor
Kline, Harriet Painter, Printmaker
Morgan, Barbara Brooks Painter, Photographer
Peter, George Painter, Instructor
Ries, Martin Painter, Art Historian
Roda (Rhoda Lillian Sablow) Designer, Painter
Temple, Mr & Mrs Alan H Collectors
Valenstein, Alice Painter, Collector

Scottsville

Castle, Wendell Keith Designer, Sculptor
Meyer, Fred (Robert) Sculptor, Painter

Sea Cliff

Spampinato, Clemente Sculptor

Setauket

Badalamenti, Fred Painter, Gallery Director
Bishop, Marjorie Cutler Painter
Guilmain, Jacques Art Historian, Educator
O'Sullivan, Daniel Joseph Painter
Remsen, John Everett, II Art Consultant, Painter
Windrow, Patricia (Patricia Windrow Klein) Painter, Illustrator

Shady

Hofsted, Jolyon Gene Sculptor, Educator
Ruellan, Andree Painter
Taylor, John (Williams) Painter

Shelter Island

Coelho, Luiz Carlos Painter, Printmaker
Mosca, August Painter, Instructor
Shields, Alan J Designer, Painter

Shoreham

Smith, Leon Polk Painter, Sculptor
Spier, Peter Edward Illustrator, Writer

Sidney

McClelland, Jeanne C Printmaker

Skaneateles

Hing, Allan Mark Educator, Interior Designer

Snyder

Cohen, Adele Sculptor, Painter

Somers

Adelman, Dorothy (Lee) McClintock Printmaker, Painter

South Butler

Caster, Bernard Harry Painter, Enamelist

Southampton

Eshraw, Ra Painter, Illustrator
Fuller, Sue Sculptor
Lichtenstein, Roy Painter, Sculptor
Rivers, Larry Painter

Southold

Wissemann-Widrig, Nancy Painter

Sparkill

Vytlacil, Vaclav Painter, Educator

Spencer

Nowack, Wayne Kenyon Painter, Assemblage Artist

Spencerport

Wolsky, Jack Painter, Educator

Spring Valley

Van Oordt, Peter Painter, Designer

Staten Island

Bernstein, Gerald Painter, Restorer
Czimbalmos, Magdolna Paal Painter
Czimbalmos, Szabo Kalman Painter, Educator
Lorenzani, Arthur Emanuele Sculptor
Mailman, Cynthia Painter
Moroz, Mychajlo Painter
Mulcahy, Freda Painter, Art Administrator
Nelson, Carey Boone Sculptor
Noble, John A Painter, Lithographer
O'Brien, Marjorie (Marjorie O'Brien Rapaport) Painter, Printmaker
Salerno, Charles Sculptor, Educator
Sticker, Robert Edward Painter
Swenson, Anne Painter, Lecturer

Stephentown

Jackson, William Davis Sculptor, Designer

Stone Ridge

Sanders, Joop A Painter

Stony Brook

Ellinger, Ilona E Painter, Educator
Reboli, Joseph John Painter, Illustrator
Stitt, Susan (Margaret) Museum Director

Stony Point

Dienes, Sari Sculptor, Printmaker
Johnson, Cletus Merlin Sculptor, Painter

Stormville

St John, Bruce Art Administrator, Art Historian

Suffern

Pousette-Dart, Richard Painter

Swan Lake

Sokolowski, Linda Robinson Printmaker, Painter

Syosset

Rosenthal, Gloria M Painter

Syracuse

Appelhof, Ruth A Art Historian, Painter
Bakke, Karen Lee Fiber Artist, Educator
Bakke, Larry Hubert Educator, Painter
Catlin, Stanton L Museum Director, Art Historian
Dibble, Charles Ryder Educator, Painter
Dwyer, James Eugene Painter, Educator
Freundlich, August L Educator
Gibbs, Craig Stevens Sculptor, Educator
Jerry, Michael John Educator, Craftsman
Jones, George Bobby Painter, Synaesthetic Artist
Kuchta, Ronald A Museum Director, Lecturer
Mack, Rodger Allen Sculptor, Educator
Nelson, Jack D Sculptor
Pulos, Arthur Jon Industrial Designer, Design Educator
Ridlon, James A Sculptor, Educator
Scala, Joseph (A) Sculptor, Educator
Seames, Clarann Painter, Illustrator
Sellers, John Lewis Educator, Designer
Tatham, David Frederic Art Historian
Trop-Blumberg, Sandra (Sandra Trop Blumberg) Art Administrator
Vander Sluis, George J Painter, Educator
Weiss, Peg Art Historian, Curator
White, Jack Painter
Witkin, Jerome Paul Painter, Educator
Wolff, Richard Evans Stained Glass Artist, Designer
Wong, Jason Museum Director
Ziegler, Jacqueline (Jacqueline Chalat-Ziegler) Sculptor, Educator

Tappan

Lo Medico, Thomas Gaetano Sculptor, Designer
Nickford, Juan Sculptor, Educator

Tarrytown

Butler, Joseph Thomas Art Historian, Writer
Kipniss, Robert Painter, Lithographer

The Springs

Fine, Perle Painter, Educator

Tillson

Van de Bovenkamp, Hans Sculptor

Tonawanda

Bolinsky, Joseph Abraham Sculptor, Educator

Tuxedo Park

Domjan, Joseph (also Spiri) Painter, Graphic Artist

Upper Grandview

Dash, Harvey Dwight Art Administrator, Painter

Upper Nyack

Larraz, Julio Fernandez Painter

NEW YORK (cont)

Utica

Cimbalo, Robert W Sculptor, Graphic Artist
Dwight, Edward Harold Museum Director
Loy, John Sheridan Painter
Murray, William Colman Collector, Patron
Pribble, Easton Painter, Instructor
Sabine, Julia Art Librarian

Valley Cottage

Greene, Stephen Painter
Heaton, Maurice Designer, Craftsman

Valley Stream

Hart, Allen M Painter, Educator

Van Hornesville

Romeling, W B Painter

Voorheesville

O'Connor, Thom Printmaker

Wainscott

Porter, (Edwin) David Painter, Sculptor

Wantagh

Chin, Ric Lecturer, Painter
Glaser, David Painter

Warwick

Bogdanovic, Bogomir Painter, Lecturer
Franck, Frederick S Painter, Writer
Talbot, Jonathan Printmaker, Painter

Washingtonville

Mangold, Robert Peter Painter
Mangold, Sylvia Plimack Painter

Water Mill

Jackson, Lee Painter
Jordan, Barbara Schwinn Painter, Illustrator

West Falls

Lindemann, Edna M Museum Director, Educator

West Hempstead

Hornung, Clarence Pearson Designer, Writer

West Nyack

Tytell, Louis Painter

Westbury

Honig, Mervin Painter, Painting Conservator
Ludman, Joan Hurwitz Art Dealer, Art Writer
Sherbell, Rhoda Sculptor, Collector
Surrey, Milt Painter

White Plains

Lazarus, Marvin P Photographer
Nickerson, Ruth (Ruth Nickerson Greacen) Sculptor
Wessel, Charlene Freimuth Art Administrator

Williamsville

Banta, Melissa Wiekser Art Dealer, Collector

Wilson

Tyson, Rae Julian Art Administrator, Sculptor

Woodhaven

Csoka, Stephen Painter, Etcher
Manuella, Frank R Designer, Painter

Woodmere

Ginsburg, Estelle Painter, Sculptor

Woodside

Fax, Elton Clay Painter, Writer
Fluek, Toby Painter, Graphic Artist
Goldszer, Bath-Sheba Painter, Graphic Artist
Leitman, Samuel Painter

Woodstock

Angeloch, Robert (Henry) Painter
Chavez, Edward Arcenio Painter, Sculptor
Currie, Bruce Painter
Fortess, Karl E Painter, Printmaker
Foster, Holland Painter, Sculptor
Guston, Philip Painter
Hague, Raoul Sculptor
Handell, Albert George Painter
Johnson, Fridolf Lester Designer, Writer
Lee, Doris Painter, Illustrator
Lenssen, Heidi (Mrs Fridolf Johnson) Painter, Lecturer
Lieberman, Meyer Frank Painter, Printmaker
Magafan, Ethel Painter
Neustadt, Barbara (Barbara Meyer) Printmaker, Lecturer
Pachner, William Painter
Pike, John Illustrator, Painter
Plath, Iona Designer, Writer
Refregier, Anton Painter
Small, Amy Gans Sculptor, Instructor
Wuermer, Carl Painter, Fine Art Appraiser

Yonkers

Clive, Richard R Painter
Corwin, Sophia M Sculptor, Painter
DeGroat, Diane L Illustrator, Designer
Gallo, William Victor Cartoonist
Sarff, Walter Painter, Designer
Scott, Walter Painter, Architect

Yorktown Heights

Kaupelis, Robert John Painter, Writer
Laventhol, Hank Painter, Printmaker
Putnam, Wallace (Bradstreet) Painter, Writer
Witt, John Painter, Printmaker

NORTH CAROLINA

Albemarle

Moose, Talmadge Bowers Painter, Instructor

Asheville

Cooke, Samuel Tucker Painter, Draftsman
Gray, Robert Ward Art Administrator
Martin, Doris-Marie Constable Designer, Sculptor
Ruble, Ronald L Printmaker, Painter

Bakersville

Vrana, Albert S Sculptor

Belmont

Logan, Juan Leon Sculptor
Mintich, Mary Ringelberg Sculptor, Craftsman

Blowing Rock

Moose, Philip Anthony Painter, Illustrator

Burnsville

Bernstein, William Joseph Designer, Glassblower

Cashiers

Whiteside, William Albert, II Painter, Educator

Chapel Hill

Cindric, Michael Anthony Sculptor, Educator
Folda, Jaroslav (Thayer, III) Art Historian
Howard, Robert A Sculptor, Educator
Immerwahr, Sara Anderson Art Historian, Writer
Kinnaird, Richard William Painter, Educator
Kuspit, Donald Burton Art Historian, Art Critic
Nelson, Robert Allen Printmaker, Painter
Ness, (Albert) Kenneth Painter, Designer
Noe, Jerry Lee Sculptor, Educator
Prange, Sally Bowen Ceramic Artist
Saltzman, Marvin Painter, Printmaker
Schlageter, Robert William Art Administrator
Sloane, Joseph Curtis Art Historian
Sturgeon, Mary C Art Historian, Archaeologist
Zaborowski, Dennis J Painter, Educator

Charlotte

Bloch, Milton Joseph Art Administrator, Museum Director
Dalton, Harry L Collector, Patron
Delhom, Mary Mellanay Curator, Art Historian
Ferguson, Garth Michele Art Historian, Educator
Franklin, Ernest Washington, Jr Collector
Gebhardt, Ann Stellhorn Painter, Educator
Kortheuer, Dayrell Painter, Conservator
Melberg, Jerald Leigh Curator, Collector
Musgrove, Stephen Ward Art Administrator, Curator
Tucker, Charles Clement Painter

Concord

Holt, Margaret McConnell Patron, Collector

Cullowhee

Kelly, Isaac Perry Craftsman, Educator
Lewis, Jackson Pittman Sculptor

Davidson

Grosch, Laura Painter, Printmaker
Jackson, Herb Painter, Educator

Durham

Hall, Louise Educator, Art Historian
Markman, Sidney David Art Administrator, Art Historian
Mueller, Earl George Art Historian, Educator
Pendergraft, Norman Elveis Museum Director, Art Historian
Pratt, Vernon Gaither Painter, Educator
Semans, James Hustead Patron
Smith, Susan Carlton Illustrator, Painter
Stars, William Kenneth Educator, Museum Director
Sunderland, Elizabeth Read Art Historian

Gastonia

Waufle, Alan Duane Museum Director, Art Historian

Goldsboro

Cowan, Thomas Bruce Painter

Greensboro

Barker, Walter William Painter, Writer
Bass, David Loren Painter
Blahove, Marcos Painter
Carpenter, Gilbert Frederick (Bert) Painter, Museum Director
Gregory, Joan Educator, Painter
Krebs, Patricia (Patricia Krebs Barker) Art Critic
Miller, Eva-Hamlin Painter, Educator
Tucker, James Ewing Museum Curator, Painter

Greenville

Blakeslee, Sarah (Sarah Blakeslee Speight) Painter
Chamberlain, Charles Ceramist, Educator
Crawley, Wesley V Sculptor, Educator
Edmiston, Sara Joanne Educator, Designer
Farnham, Emily Painter, Writer
Gordley, Marilyn F M Painter, Educator
Gordley, Metz Tranbarger Painter
Hartley, Paul Jerome Painter, Educator
Reep, Edward Arnold Painter, Educator
Satterfield, John Edward Jeweler, Educator
Sexauer, Donald Richard Printmaker, Educator
Speight, Francis Painter, Educator
Stanforth, Melvin Sidney Educator, Printmaker

Kinston

Pearson, Henry C Painter

Milton

Gatewood, Maud Florance Painter

Morganton

Stacks, William Leon Painter, Art Restorer

North Wilkesboro

Nichols, Ward H Painter
Printmaker

Raleigh

Bier, Justus Museum Director, Writer
Bireline, George Lee Painter, Educator
Broderson, Robert Painter
Domit, Moussa M Museum Director, Art Historian
Hertzman, Gay Mahaffy Art Administrator, Art Historian
Jenkins, Mary Anne K Painter, Instructor
Williams, Benjamin Forrest Museum Curator, Art Historian

Salisbury

Hood, Walter Kelly Art Historian, Painter

Smithfield

Creech, Franklin Underwood Painter, Printmaker

Spruce Pine

Littleton, Harvey K Sculptor, Educator

Tryon

Quest, Charles Francis Painter, Educator
Quest, Dorothy (Johnson) Portrait Painter

Walnut Cove

Nygren, John Fergus Glassblower

Weaverville

Gilmartin, F Thomas Art Director, Instructor

Wilmington

Evans, Minnie Painter
Howell, Claude Flynn Painter, Educator

Winston-Salem

Browning, Dixie Burrus Painter
Dance, Robert Bartlett Painter, Printmaker
Gray, Thomas Alexander Museum Director
King, Joseph Wallace (Vinciata) Painter
Mangum, William (Goodson) Sculptor
Oubre, Hayward Louis Sculptor, Educator
Potter, Ted Painter, Art Administrator
Saunders, Edith Dariel Chase Painter, Instructor

Zirconia

Blakely, Joyce (Carol) Painter, Instructor

NORTH DAKOTA

Dickinson

Navrat, Den (Dennis Edward Navrat) Printmaker, Educator

Grand Forks

McElroy, Jacquelyn Ann Printmaker, Educator
Paulsen, Brian Oliver Painter
Reuter, Laurel J Gallery Director, Lecturer
Rogers, John H Sculptor, Educator
Schaefer, Ronald H Printmaker, Educator

Minot

Schwieger, C Robert Printmaker, Educator

OHIO

Akron

Coplans, John (Rivers) Art Administrator, Art Editor
Drumm, Don Sculptor, Craftsman
Ertman, Earl Leslie Art Historian, Educator
Rogers, P J Printmaker, Graphics

Alliance

Cleveland, Helen Barth Art Administrator, Instructor

Athens

Ahrendt, Christine Painter
Baldwin, John Educator, Sculptor
Hostetler, David Sculptor, Educator
Kortlander, William (Clark) Painter
Roberts, Donald Educator, Printmaker
Silverman, David Frederick Sculptor, Educator

Bay Village

Blazey, Lawrence Edwin Designer, Painter

Beachwood

Davis, David Ensos Sculptor

Berea

Cole, Harold David Art Historian, Educator
Myers, Jack Fredrick Painter, Instructor

Bowling Green

Lee, Briant Hamor Scenographer, Art Historian
Ocvirk, Otto G Sculptor, Printmaker

Brecksville

Miller, John Paul Jeweler, Instructor

Canal Winchester

Craig, Eugene Editorial Cartoonist

Canton

Welch, James Henry Collector

Chagrin Falls

Woehrman, Ralph Printmaker, Draftsman

Chillicothe

Gough, Robert Alan Painter
Ohman, Richard Michael Painter, Instructor

Cincinnati

Batchelor, Anthony John Printmaker, Instructor
Brod, Stanford Painter, Educator
Cornelius, Francis DuPont Conservator, Painter
Driesbach, Walter Clark, Jr Sculptor, Instructor
Fabe, Robert Painter, Educator
Findsen, Owen Kenneth Art Critic
Fischer, Mildred (Gertrude) Designer, Tapestry Artist
Foster, April Printmaker, Instructor
Goodridge, Lawrence Wayne Painter, Sculptor
Hanna, Katherine Art Administrator
Hayes, Robert T Painter, Printmaker
Knipschild, Robert Painter, Educator
Krody, Barron J Designer, Instructor
Maciel, Mary Oliveira Illustrator, Educator
McClure, Constance M Instructor, Painter
Merkel, Jayne (Silverstein) Art Historian, Writer
Miotke, Anne E Painter, Instructor
Rice, Harold Randolph Educator, Writer
Rogers, Millard Foster, Jr Museum Director, Art Historian
Solway, Carl E Art Dealer
Stewart, John P Printmaker, Painter
Swartz, Phillip Scott Painter, Collector
Warren, Julianne Busset Baker Photographer
Warren, L D Editorial Cartoonist
Williams, Roger Sculptor

Cleveland

Aidlin, Jerome Sculptor, Instructor
Bickford, George Percival Collector
Cassill, Herbert Carroll Printmaker, Educator
Chiara, Alan Robert Painter
Combes, Willard Wetmore Cartoonist
Conover, Claude Sculptor, Ceramist
Czuma, Stanislaw J Art Historian, Curator
Denis, Paul Andre S Painter, Instructor
Drewal, Henry John Art Historian, Educator
Erdelac, Joseph Mark Collector, Patron
Gibson, Walter Samuel Art Historian, Art Writer
Goldberg, Kenneth Paul Art Historian, Art Librarian
Hornung, Gertrude Seymour Art Historian, Lecturer
Jankowski, Joseph P Painter, Educator
Kropf, Joan R Museum Director
Lee, Sherman Emery Museum Director
McVey, Leza Sculptor, Weaver
McVey, William M Sculptor, Educator
Miller, Leon Gordon Designer, Printmaker
Morse, A Reynolds Collector
Osrin, Raymond Harold Cartoonist
Putnam, Mrs John B Collector
Rebeck, Steven Augustus Sculptor
Seltzer, Phyllis Printmaker, Painter
Shepherd, Dorothy G (Mrs Ernst Payer) Museum Curator
Sloane, Phyllis Lester Painter, Printmaker
Taft, Frances Prindle Art Historian, Lecturer
Thompson, Lockwood Collector

OHIO (cont)
Welch, Mr & Mrs Robert G Collectors
Winter, H Edward Enamelist, Writer
Winter, Thelma Frazier Sculptor, Enamelist

Cleveland Heights

Dubaniewicz, Peter Paul Painter
Henning, Edward Burk Curator, Art Historian
Jones, Marvin Harold Printmaker, Painter
Kowalski, Raymond Alois Painter
Krausz, Laszlo Painter
McCullough, Joseph Art Administrator, Painter
Schreckengost, Viktor Designer, Sculptor
Silver, Thomas C Sculptor, Educator
Teyral, John Painter, Instructor

Clinton

Neumann, William A Educator, Goldsmith

Columbus

Bishop, Budd Harris Museum Director
Black, David Evans Sculptor
Chafetz, Sidney Printmaker, Educator
Close, Dean Purdy Art Dealer, Collector
Clover, James B Sculptor, Educator
Gatrell, Marion Thompson Educator, Painter
Gatrell, Robert Morris Educator, Painter
Goodwin, Louis Payne Cartoonist
Jocda (Joseph Charles Dailey) Painter
Kuehn, Edmund Karl Painter, Lecturer
Mason, Phillip Lindsay Painter, Printmaker
Massey, Charles Wesley, Jr Printmaker, Educator
Nicodemus, Chester Roland Sculptor, Designer
Simson, Bevlyn A Painter, Printmaker
Sisson, Jacqueline D Librarian, Writer
Stull, Robert J Sculptor, Art Administrator
Wahling, B Jon Sculptor, Weaver

Cuyahoga Falls

Boedeker, Arnold E (Boedie) Illustrator, Painter
Moon, Marc Instructor, Painter
Richard, Jack Painter, Gallery Director

Dayton

Colt, Thomas C, Jr Museum Director
Cooper, Rhonda Curator, Instructor
David, Honore Salmi Educator
Evans, Bruce Haselton Museum Director, Art Historian
Foley, Kathy Kelsey Curator, Art Historian
Koepnick, Robert Charles Sculptor, Educator
Mathis, Kenneth Lawrence Art Historian, Educator
Ostendorf, (Arthur) Lloyd, Jr Painter, Instructor
Pinkney, Helen Louise Art Administrator, Art Historian
Raffel, Alvin Robert Painter, Instructor
Spurlock, William Henry, II Gallery Director, Art Historian

Delaware

Getz, Dorothy Sculptor
Kalb, Marty Joel Painter
Stewart, Jarvis Anthony Educator, Painter

Dublin

Chadeayne, Robert Osborne Painter
Sander, Dennis Jay Architect, Designer

Euclid

Bates, Kenneth Francis Enamelist, Craftsman

Gambier

Dwyer, Eugene Joseph Art Historian
Garhart, Martin J Printmaker
Gunderson, Barry L Sculptor
Slate, Joseph Frank Painter, Writer

Gates Mills

Clague, John Rogers Sculptor

Georgetown

Ruthven, John Aldrich Painter, Lecturer

Grand Rapids

Labino, Dominick Glass Blower, Sculptor

Hamilton

George, Richard Allan Painter
Phelps, Nan Dee Painter, Photographer

Hiram

Jagow, Ellen T Painter

Hudson

Matteson, Ira Sculptor, Draftsman

Kent

Flint, Leroy W Painter, Educator
Grossman, Morton Painter, Educator
Kitner, Harold Educator
Morrow, Robert Earl Educator, Muralist
Myers, Richard Lewis Educator, Film Maker
Novotny, Elmer Ladislaw Painter, Educator
O'Sickey, Joseph Benjamin Painter, Educator
Petrochuk, Konstantin Photographer, Film Maker
Saucy, Claude Gerald Painter, Educator

Lakeview

Earl, Jack Eugene Sculptor

Lakewood

Treaster, Richard A Painter, Instructor

Mansfield

Butts, H Daniel, III Museum Director

Medina

Kleidon, Dennis Arthur Educator, Designer

Melrose

Burt, Clyde Edwin Ceramist, Educator

Mentor

Pierce, Diane (Diane Pierce Huxtable) Painter, Illustrator

New Richmond

Kelley, Donald William Printmaker, Sculptor

North Lima

Mohn, Cheri (Ann) Painter

North Madison

Gabriel, Hannelore Goldsmith

North Olmsted

Curry, Noble Wilbur Painter, Printmaker

Oberlin

Arnold, Paul Beaver Educator, Printmaker
Artz, Frederick B Art Historian, Writer
Bongiorno, Laurine Mack Art Historian
Butler, Marigene H Conservator
Epstein, Annabel Wharton Art Historian
Huemer, Christina Gertrude Art Librarian
Johnson, Ellen Hulda Art Historian, Art Critic
Pearson, John Painter, Instructor
Rosenzweig, Daphne Lange Art Historian, Collector
Spear, Richard Edmund Educator, Museum Director

Oxford

Davis, Willis Bing Painter, Ceramist
Wolfe, Robert, Jr Printmaker, Painter

Painesville

Kangas, Gene Sculptor, Collector

Parma

Jergens, Robert Joseph Painter, Educator
Pearman, Sara Jane Art Historian, Art Librarian

Perrysburg

Brunner, Louis Katherine (Mrs Paul Orr) Art Critic, Writer

Poland

Dennison, Dorothy (Dorothy Dennison Butler) Painter, Lithographer
Parella, Albert Lucian Painter, Designer
Vaccaro, Patrick Frank (Patt Vaccaro) Printmaker, Painter

Ravenna

Schar, Stuart Art Administrator

Rocky River

Kuekes, Edward D Cartoonist

Sandusky

Brown, Daniel Quilter (Dan Q) Illustrator, Cartoonist

Seven Hills

Stanczak, Julian Painter, Instructor

Shaker Heights

Hess, Stanley William Art Librarian
Korow, Elinore Maria Painter

Solon

Schepis, Anthony Joseph Educator, Painter
Ward, Evelyn Svec Fibre Artist
Ward, William Edward Designer, Painter

South Euclid

Cintron, Joseph Painter, Instructor
Merrill, Ross M Painting Conservator, Painter

Springfield

Catron, Patricia D'Arcy Art Administrator
Morgan, Helen Bosart Sculptor
Schlump, John Otto Educator, Printmaker

Sylvania

Chapman, Walter Howard Painter, Illustrator
Golden, Libby Printmaker, Painter

Toledo

Autry, Carolyn (Carolyn Autry Elloian) Printmaker, Instructor

Elloian, Peter Printmaker, Instructor
Hutton, William Museum Curator
Luckner, Kurt T Curator
Mandle, Earl Roger Art Administrator, Art Historian
McGlauchlin, Tom Glassblower, Potter
Wittmann, Otto Art Administrator

Urbana

Miller, Nancy Sculptor, Graphic Artist

West Richfield

Laessig, Robert Painter, Illustrator

Wooster

Gouma-Peterson, Thalia Art Historian

Worthington

Severino, Dominick Alexander Educator, Art Administrator

Wyoming

Gross, Mr & Mrs Merrill Jay Collectors, Patrons

Yellow Springs

Bell, Evelyn Behnan Printmaker, Photographer
Jordan, James William Art Historian, Painter
McCaslin, Walter Wright Art Critic, Writer

Youngstown

Butler, Joseph (Green) Art Administrator, Painter
McDonough, John Joseph Collector, Patron
Murray, Richard Deibel Painter, Sculptor
Singer, Clyde J Painter

OKLAHOMA

Ada

Lafon, Dee J Painter, Sculptor
Sieg, Robert Lawrence Sculptor, Enamelist

Broken Arrow

Broadd, Harry Andrew Painter, Art Historian

Chandler

Packer, Clair Lange Painter, Writer

Checotah

Beaver, Fred Painter, Lecturer

Chickasha

Allen, Constance Olleen Webb Painter, Jewelry Designer
Bailey, Clark T Sculptor, Educator
Good, Leonard Painter, Educator

Edmond

Muno, Richard Carl Sculptor, Art Director
Rayburn, Bryan B Art Administrator

Fort Gibson

West, W Richard (Dick) Educator, Painter

Goodwell

Kachel, Harold Stanley Museum Director, Educator

Hugo

Walker, Peter Richard Painter

Idabel

Stevenson, Harold Painter

Lawton

Morton, Richard H Painter, Illustrator

Locust Grove

Stone, Willard Designer, Sculptor

Miami

Wilson, Charles Banks Painter, Lithographer

Midwest City

Jones, Reita Painter

Muskogee

Hill, Joan (Chea-se-quah) Painter, Illustrator

Norman

Bavinger, Eugene Allen Painter, Educator
Bogart, George A Painter
Corsaw, Roger D Educator, Craftsman
Gunning, Eleonore Victoria Painter
Henkle, James Lee Sculptor, Educator
Hobbs, Joe Ferrell Art Administrator, Sculptor
Oliveira, V'Lou Ceramist, Instructor
Olkinetzky, Sam Painter, Museum Director
Sutton, George Miksch Painter, Illustrator
Taylor, Joseph Richard Sculptor
Weekes, Shirley Marie Painter
Youritzin, Glenda Green Painter, Art Historian
Youritzin, Victor Koshkin Art Historian, Educator

Oklahoma City

Alaupovic, Alexandra V Sculptor, Educator
Bell, Coca (Mary Catlett Bell) Painter
Belle, Anna (Anna Belle Birckett) Painter
Davis, J Ray Painter, Printmaker
Faris, Brunel De Bost Painter, Instructor
Goetz, Edith Jean Painter, Instructor
Goetz, Richard Vernon Painter, Instructor
Grass, Patty Patterson Painter
Krakel, Dean Museum Administrator, Art Historian
Kuebler, George F Art Administrator, Educator
Lopina, Louise Carol Illustrator, Painter
McAninch, Beth Painter
McChristy, Quentin L Painter, Designer
Menchaca, Juan Curator, Painter
Merchant, Pat (Jean) Instructor, Painter
Riley, Gerald Patrick Craftsman, Sculptor
Seabourn, Bert Dail Painter, Illustrator
Silberman, Arthur Art Library Director, Lecturer
Vallee, Jack (Land) Painter
Walch, John Leo Painter, Sculptor
Warriner, Laura B Painter
White, Roger Lee Painter, Sculptor

Okmulgee

Jones, Ruthe Blalock Painter

Pawhuska

Free, John D Painter, Sculptor

Prague

Hrdy, Olinka Muralist, Designer

Stillwater

McVicker, J Jay Painter, Educator
Smith, B J Museum Director, Instructor
Wise, Geneva H (Holcomb) Painter, Collector

Tahlequah

Cochran, George McKee Painter, Writer
Hagerstrand, Martin Allan Museum Director, Art Adminstrator

Tulsa

Allen, Clarence Canning Painter
Allen, Loretta B Painter, Designer
Coker, Carl David Painter, Educator
Crumbo, Woody Painter, Printmaker
Godsey, Glenn Educator, Painter
Gussman, Herbert Collector, Patron
Hogue, Alexandre Painter, Lithographer
Manhart, Thomas Arthur Educator, Ceramist
Place, Bradley Eugene Educator
Schellstede, Richard Lee Art Dealer
Snodgrass, Jeanne Owens (Mrs M Eugene King) Museologist, Art Historian

Wagoner

Dennis, Cherre Nixon Painter, Etcher

Woodward

Kemoha (George W Patrick Patterson) Painter, Art Historian

OREGON

Ashland

Wilson, Helen J Tapestry Artist, Sculptor

Astoria

Klep, Rolf Museum Director, Illustrator

Beaverton

Cheshire, Craig Gifford Painter, Educator

Corvallis

Chappell, Berkley Warner Painter, Printmaker
Crozier, William K, Jr Craftsman, Designer
Gunn, Paul James Painter, Educator
Jameson, Demetrios George Painter, Printmaker
Levine, Shepard Painter, Educator
Sandgren, Ernest Nelson Painter, Educator
Sponenburgh, Mark Art Historian, Sculptor
Taysom, Wayne Pendelton Sculptor, Educator

Dallas

Casey, John Joseph Educator, Painter

Elmira

Zach, Jan Painter, Sculptor

Eugene

Baker, Ralph Bernard Painter, Educator
Buckner, Kay Lamoreux Painter
Buckner, Paul Eugene Sculptor
Donnelly, Marian Card Art Historian
Gronbeck, Jean Painter
Jacobsen, Michael A Art Historian
Krause, LaVerne Erickson Painter, Printmaker
Kutka, Anne (Mrs David McCosh) Painter
McCosh, David J Painter
McFee, June King Educator, Writer
Paul, Ken (Hugh) Printmaker, Painter

OREGON (cont)

Paulin, Richard Calkins Museum Director, Craftsman
Witham, Vernon Clint Painter, Collector

Lake Oswego

Hoffman, Elaine Janet Painter

Lincoln City

Banister, Robert Barr Art Dealer, Painter

Oregon City

Kelly, Lee Sculptor

Port Orford

Rippon, Tom Michael Sculptor

Portland

Beebe, Mary Livingstone Art Administrator
Bimrose, Arthur Sylvanus, Jr Cartoonist
Bunce, Louis DeMott Painter
Feldenheimer, Edith Collector
Gilkey, Gordon Waverly Curator, Educator
Griffin, Rachael S Art Administrator, Writer
Halvorsen, Ruth Elise Painter, Writer
Hardy, Thomas (Austin) Sculptor
Heidel, Frederick (H) Painter, Educator
Jenkins, Donald John Museum Director, Art Historian
Johanson, George E Painter, Printmaker
Kennedy, Leta Marietta Craftsman
McLarty, William James (Jack) Painter, Instructor
Morris, Carl Painter
Morris, Hilda Sculptor, Painter
Newton, Francis John Museum Director
Rhyne, Charles Sylvanus Art Historian, Gallery Director
Schnitzer, Arlene Director Art Dealer, Collector
Schulz, William Gallagher Sculptor, Painter
Sheehan, Evelyn Painter
Waddingham, John Alfred Artist-Illustrator

Rainier

Lewis, Mary Sculptor, Illustrator

Salem

Hall, Carl Alvin Painter, Instructor
Hero, Peter deCourcy Art Administrator, Art Historian

Sheridan

Turner, Ralph James Sculptor, Painter
Van Leunen, Alice Louise Textile Artist, Instructor

Talent

Cornell, David E Ceramist, Sculptor

West Linn

Murphy, Chester Glenn Painter

PENNSYLVANIA

Abington

Pease, David G Painter, Instructor

Alburtis

Kyriakos, Aleko Sculptor

Allentown

Berman, Bernard Collector
Berman, Muriel Mallin Collector, Patron
Berman, Philip I Collector, Patron
Gregg, Richard Nelson Museum Director, Writer
Hoffman, Richard Peter Painter
MacDonald, Gayle Coleman Art Restorer, Lecturer
Miley, Mimi Conneen Educator, Curator
Moller, Hans Painter

Allison Park

Osby, Larissa Geiss Painter

Altoona

Russell, (George) Gordon Painter

Ambler

Thompson, Wade Painter, Educator
Wolpert, Elizabeth Davis Painter, Instructor

Apollo

Kalinowski, Eugene M Painter, Sculptor
Kerstetter, Barbara Ann Painter, Instructor

Arcola

Mitchell, Henry (Weber) Sculptor

Ardmore

Atlee, Emilie DeS Painter, Instructor

Audubon

Snyder, Toni Goessler Goldsmith, Printmaker

Bala-Cynwyd

Mangel, Benjamin Art Dealer
Shalit, Mitzi (Mildred M Shalit) Art Consultant, Art Dealer

Bangor

McInerney, Gene Joseph Painter
Watts, Robert M Conceptual Artist, Designer

Barto

Bertoia, Harry Sculptor, Graphic Artist

Berwyn

Fry, Guy Painter

Bethel Park

Bolmgren, Donna Hollen Educator, Painter

Bethlehem

Redd, Richard James Painter

Bloomsburg

Roberts, Percival R Art Administrator, Painter

Blue Bell

Martino, Eva E Painter, Sculptor
Martino, Giovanni Painter

Broomall

Ingram, Judith Printmaker, Collage Artist

Bryn Mawr

Aichele, Kathryn Porter Art Historian
Janschka, Fritz Painter, Graphic Artist

Bucks County

Rosenwald, Barbara K Collector

Camp Hill

Bartlett, Robert Webster Painter, Designer

Carlisle

Sellers, Charles Coleman Art Historian

Carversville

Barger, Raymond Granville Sculptor
Clark, Fred, Jr Museum Director, Collector

Chadds Ford

Duff, James H Museum Director, Art Administrator
Haskell, Harry Garner, Jr Collector
McCoy, John W, (II) Painter, Educator
Wyeth, James Browning Painter

Chambersburg

Harris, Josephine Marie Educator, Art Historian

Cheltenham

Day, Larry (Lawrence James Day) Painter, Instructor
Wagner, G Noble Painter, Sculptor

Cheyney

Hemphill, Pamela Art Historian

Christiana

Miller, Daniel Dawson Painter, Sculptor
Rohrer, Warren Painter, Instructor

Clarion

Hobbs, Robert Dean Art Administrator, Printmaker

Cochranville

Sazegar, Morteza Painter

Cornwall

Quinn, Henrietta Reist Collector

Cornwells Heights

Feld, Augusta Painter, Printmaker

Downingtown

Bostelle, Thomas (Theodore) Painter, Sculptor

Doylestown

Bye, Ranulph (DeBayeux) Painter, Educator

Duncansville

Atkyns, (Willie) Lee, Jr Painter, Art Administrator

East Stroudsburg

Strauser, Sterling Boyd Painter

Easton

Higgins, (George) Edward Sculptor
Salemme, Antonio Painter, Sculptor
Salemme, Martha Painter

Edinboro

Ko, Anthony Printmaker, Educator
Laing, Richard Harlow Art Administrator, Designer
Mitra, Gopal C Painter, Printmaker
Nicholas, Donna Lee Ceramist, Educator

Elkins Park

Clark, Jon Frederic Educator, Glass Blower
Davidson, Abraham A Educator, Writer
Fine, Ruth Eileen Curator, Printmaker
Goodman, Sidney Painter
Lechtzin, Stanley Craftsman, Educator

Erdenheim

Strawbridge, Edward R Painter

Erie

Ahlgren, Roy B Instructor, Printmaker
Burke, Daniel V Painter, Educator
Higgins, Edward Koelling Craftsman, Educator
Higgins, Mary Lou Craftsman
Kaiser, Vitus J Painter
Kelleher, Daniel Joseph Painter, Instructor
Plavcan, Joseph Michael Painter, Sculptor
Sanders, Andrew Dominick Painter, Instructor
Schabacker, Betty Barchet Painter, Lecturer
Sundberg, Carl Gustave Enamelist, Art Director
Sundberg, Wilda (Regelman) Painter
Vanco, John Leroy Art Administrator, Photographer

Farmington

Kujundzic, Zeljko D Ceramist, Sculptor

Fort Washington

Thompson, F Raymond (Ray) Illustrator, Writer

Freeburg

Bucher, George Robert Educator, Sculptor

Gibsonia

De Coux, Janet Sculptor

Gladwyne

Stegeman, Charles Painter, Educator

Glen Campbell

Mallory, Larry Richard Painter, Instructor

Greensburg

Chew, Paul Albert Art Administrator, Lecturer
Filkosky, Josefa Sculptor, Educator

Harmony

Hulmer, Eric Claus Curator-Conservator

Harrisburg

Leff, Jay C Collector
Winer, Donald Arthur Museum Curator, Instructor
Wingate, Robert Bray Illustrator, Curator

Hatboro

Tait, Cornelia Damian Painter, Sculptor

Haverford

Lloyd, Mrs H Gates Collector, Patron
Schutte, Thomas Frederick Art Administrator
Wintersteen, Bernice McIlhenny Art Administrator, Collector

Havertown

Fish, Richard G Painter, Designer
Gasparro, Frank Sculptor, Instructor

Horsham

Winokur, Paula Colton Ceramist
Winokur, Robert Mark Ceramist, Educator

Huntingdon Valley

Meltzer, Arthur Painter
Van Roekens, Paulette (Mrs Arthur Meltzer) Painter

Indiana

Kipp, Orval Painter, Educator
Reynolds, Ralph William Educator, Painter

Jenkintown

Brown, Bo Cartoonist
Dioda, Adolph T Sculptor, Instructor
Fuhrman, Esther Sculptor
Katz, Theodore (Harry) Educator, Painter
Langman, Richard Theodore Art Dealer
Rosenwald, Lessing Julius Collector, Patron

Johnstown

Bradley, Ida Florence Painter, Instructor
Sheehe, Lillian Carolyn Painter

Kempton

Hesketh Sculptor

Kennett Square

Greenleaf, Esther (Hargrave) Painter, Potter

King Of Prussia

Diehl, Sevilla S Painter

Kutztown

Quirk, Thomas Charles, Jr Painter, Educator

Lancaster

Kermes, Constantine John Painter, Printmaker
Lipman, Stan Sculptor, Instructor

Lederach

Hallman, H Theodore, Jr Craftsman

Lemont

Altman, Harold Printmaker, Educator

Lewisburg

Turnure, James Harvey Educator, Art Historian

Ligonier

Cornelius, Marty Painter, Illustrator

Lumberville

Katsiff, Bruce Photographer, Educator
Taylor, Rosemary Craftsman

Manheim

Steinmetz, Grace Ernst Titus Painter, Lecturer

Mansfield

Sakaoka, Yasue Sculptor, Instructor

Martins Creek

Fink, Laurence B Educator, Photographer
Snyder, Joan Painter

McKean

Kemenyffy, Steven Ceramist, Educator
Kemenyffy, Susan B Hale Ceramist, Printmaker

Mechanicsburg

Walker, Mary Carolyn Silversmith, Designer

Mechanicsville

Coiner, Charles Toucey Painter

Media

Berd, Morris Painter, Educator
Hildebrandt, William Albert Painter, Art Administrator
House, James Charles, Jr Sculptor, Educator

Melrose Park

Blai, Bert Instructor, Ceramic Artist
Sabatini, Raphael Painter, Educator

Mendenhall

Boucher, Tania Kunsky Art Dealer, Painter

Merion

Sankowsky, Itzhak Painter, Sculptor

Merion Station

Newman, Libby Painter, Printmaker
Robb, David M Educator, Art Historian

Millersville

Hay, Ike Sculptor, Educator

Narberth

Donohoe, Victoria Art Critic, Writer
McGovern, Robert F Painter, Sculptor

New Hope

Haenigsen, Harry William Cartoonist
Moore, Beveridge Painter

Newtown Square

Martino, Edmund Painter, Designer
Roberts, Gilroy Sculptor
Serwazi, Albert B Painter

Norristown

Grimley, Oliver Fetterolf Painter, Sculptor
Rapp, Lois Painter

Northampton

Viera, Ricardo Painter, Printmaker

Ottsville

Rudy, Charles Sculptor

Philadelphia

Andrade, Edna Wright Educator, Painter
Angelo, Emidio Cartoonist, Painter
Anliker, Roger (William) Painter, Educator
Auth, Tony (William Anthony Auth, Jr) Editorial Cartoonist
Ballinger, Louise Bowen Instructor, Writer
Barber, Ronald Art Administrator
Bateman, Ronald C Painter

PENNSYLVANIA (cont)

Bayard, Mary Ivy Art Librarian
Belfiore, Gerardo Painter, Instructor
Benson, Gertrude Ackerman Writer, Art Critic
Bernstein, Benjamin D Collector
Blackburn, Morris (Atkinson) Painter, Printmaker
Blai, Boris Sculptor, Lecturer
Bobrowicz, Yvonne P Instructor, Fiber Artist
Bookbinder, Jack Painter, Printmaker
Bowling, Jack Silversmith, Printmaker
Boyle, Richard J Museum Director, Writer
Burgart, Herbert Joseph Educator, Art Administrator
Burko, Diane Painter, Educator
Bushnell, Marietta P Art Librarian
Campbell, Malcolm Art Historian, Educator
Cederstrom, John Andrew Painter, Instructor
Cramer, Richard Charles Painter, Educator
Daley, William P Ceramist, Sculptor
Delehanty, Suzanne E Art Administrator
Dessner, Murray Painter
D'Harnoncourt, Anne (J) Art Historian, Curator
Dillon, Mildred (Murphy) Painter, Printmaker
Dolan, Margo Art Dealer, Collector
Drutt, Helen Williams Gallery Director, Art Historian
East, N S, Jr Designer, Sculptor
Edmunds, Allan Logan Printmaker, Art Administrator
Emerson, Edith Painter, Curator
Etting, Emlen Painter, Illustrator
Ewing, Thomas R Painter, Instructor
Falter, John Illustrator
Fenton, Beatrice Sculptor
Ferrer, Rafael Painter, Sculptor
Ferris, Edythe Painter, Graphic Artist
Forman, Nessa Ruth Art Editor
Franklin, Charlotte White Painter, Sculptor
Freeland, William Lee Painter, Sculptor
Frudakis, Evangelos William Sculptor
Fuller, R Buckminster Design Scientist
Garcia, Ofelia Art Administrator, Printmaker
Gaul, Arrah Lee Painter
Gold, Albert Painter, Educator
Goodyear, Frank H, Jr Art Historian, Curator
Greenwood, Paul Anthony Sculptor, Instructor
Gross, Estelle Shane Art Dealer
Gundersheimer, Herman (Samuel) Art Historian
Hahn, Maurice & Roslyn Art Dealers
Hanes, James (Albert) Painter
Hanlen, John (Garrett) Painter, Instructor
Havard, James Pinkney Painter
Hood, (Thomas) Richard Printmaker, Designer
Hoptner, Richard Sculptor
Howard, Humbert L Painter
Hutton, Dorothy Wackerman Designer, Printmaker
Jacobs, Harold Painter, Sculptor
Johnson, Homer Painter
Johnson, Lois Marlene Printmaker, Educator
Jolles, Arnold H Art Administrator, Conservator
Jones, (Charles) Dexter (Weatherbee), III Sculptor
Kaplan, Jerome Eugene Printmaker
Kardon, Janet Curator, Art Historian
Kettner, David Allen Artist, Educator
Keyser, Robert Gifford Painter, Educator
Kimmelman, Harold Sculptor
Klein, Esther M Patron, Collector
Knobler, Lois Jean Painter
Knobler, Nathan Sculptor, Educator
Kotala, Stanislaw Waclaw Painter, Art Librarian
Kramrisch, Stella Curator, Educator
Kushner-Weiner, Anita May Painter
Lang, J T Printmaker, Lecturer
Lasuchin, Michael Printmaker, Painter
Le Clair, Charles Painter, Educator
Lee, Manning de Villeneuve Illustrator, Painter
Lee, Richard Allen Painter, Collector
Limont, Naomi Charles Printmaker, Instructor
Locks, Marian Art Dealer, Collector
Lueders, Jimmy C Painter, Instructor
Maitin, Samuel (Calman) Designer, Painter
Makler, Hope Welsh Art Dealer
Mangione, Patricia Anthony Painter
Martinet, Marjorie D Painter
Marzano, Albert Painter, Designer
McGarvey, Elsie Siratz Curator, Lecturer
McGinnis, Christine Painter
McIlhenny, Henry Plumer Collector
McNulty, Kneeland Curator
Medoff, Eve Artist, Writer
Merrick, James Kirk Painter
Metzker, Ray K Photographer, Educator
Moskowitz, Shirley (Mrs Jacob W Gruber) Painter, Sculptor
Neff, Edith Painter, Instructor
Nelson, Leonard Painter, Instructor
Omwake, Leon, Jr Painter, Sculptor
Paone, Peter Printmaker, Painter
Perkins, G Holmes Architect, Educator
Pitz, Molly Wood Painter
Pretsch, John Edward Cartoonist, Illustrator
Quigley, Michael Allen Art Administrator
Rainey, Froelich Gladstone Art Administrator, Writer
Ray, Deborah Painter, Illustrator
Reinsel, Walter N Painter
Remenick, Seymour Painter
Richardson, Constance (Coleman) Painter
Richardson, Edgar Preston Art Historian
Rishel, Joseph John, Jr Curator
Rosenfeld, Richard Joel Art Dealer
Sacklarian, Stephen Painter, Sculptor
Scanga, Italo Sculptor, Educator
Searles, Charles Robert Painter
Sevy, Barbara Snetsinger Art Librarian
Seymour, Rachel Collector, Patron
Shatalow, Vladimir Mihailovich Painter
Shores, (James) Franklin Painter
Siegel, Adrian Photographer, Painter
Sloan, Louis Baynard Painter, Conservator
Soviak, Harry Painter, Instructor
Staffel, Rudolf Harry Ceramist, Instructor
Stewart, Lizbeth McNett Sculptor, Ceramist
Stewart, Patricia Kaye Art Critic, Art Administrator
Stubbs, Robert Art Administrator
Todd, Louise (Louise Todd Cope) Weaver, Instructor
Turner, Evan Hopkins Museum Director
Utescher, Gerd Designer, Sculptor
Venturi, Robert Architect
Viesulas, Romas Printmaker, Educator
Visco, Anthony Salvatore Educator, Sculptor
Wasserman, Jack Art Historian, Art Administrator
Weidner, Marilyn Kemp Conservator, Lecturer
Weidner, Roswell Theodore Painter, Instructor
Weinberg, Ephraim Art Administrator, Educator
Willet, Henry Lee Craftsman
Zelt, Martha Printmaker, Instructor

Phoenixville

Crowell, Lucius Painter, Sculptor
Hopkins, Kendal Coles Painter

Pine Grove Mills

Chomicky, Yar Gregory Educator, Painter

Pineville

Smith, William Arthur Painter, Printmaker

Pittsburgh

Arkus, Leon Anthony Museum Director
Berman, Rebecca Robbins Gallery Director, Painter
Binai, Paul Freye Painter, Art Curator
Brown, Larry K Painter, Sculptor
Cantini, Virgil D Painter, Sculptor
Caplan, Jerry L Sculptor, Educator
Dixon, Sally Foy Film Curator, Lecturer
Feller, Robert L Conservation Scientist
Gabriel, Robert A Sculptor
Gardner, Robert Earl Printmaker, Educator
Gentry, Herbert Painter
Gordon, Anne W Art Librarian
Gruber, Aaronel De Roy Sculptor, Kinetic Artist
Haskins, John Franklin Art Historian, Educator
Hearn, M F (Millard Fillmore Hearn, Jr) Art Administrator, Art Historian
Heller, Reinhold August Art Historian
Hungerford, Cyrus Cotton Cartoonist
Karn, Gloria Stoll Painter, Instructor
Katz, Joseph M Collector, Patron
Koerner, Henry Painter, Designer
Landreau, Anthony Norman Art Administrator, Weaver
Lepper, Robert Lewis Educator, Sculptor
Lewis, Virginia Elnora Museum Director, Art Historian
Libby, William C Painter, Writer
Meister, Maureen I Art Writer
Miller, Donald Art Critic, Writer
Owsley, David Thomas Museum Curator
Pershing, Louise Painter, Sculptor
Rice, Norman Lewis Painter, Educator
Selwitz, Ruth F Painter, Printmaker
Sheon, Aaron Art Historian
Teilman, Herdis Bull Curator
Twiggs, Russell Gould Painter
Webb, Frank (Francis H Webb) Painter, Designer
Weiner, Abe Painter, Instructor
Wilkins, David George Art Historian, Museum Director
Williams, John Wesley Art Historian
Winokur, James L Collector, Patron
Youngsblood, Nat Painter, Illustrator

Pleasant Valley

Opie, John Mart Painter, Printmaker

Plumsteadville

Amarotico, Joseph Anthony Painter, Conservator

Pottstown

Kratz, Mildred Sands Painter
Slider, Dorla Dean Painter

Reading

Dietrich, Bruce Leinbach Museum Director, Art Administrator

Ridgway

McCloskey, Eunice LonCoske Painter, Writer

Rochester

Marino, Albert Joseph Collector

Rosemont

Terry, Duncan Niles Designer, Craftsman

Selinsgrove

Putterman, Florence Grace Painter

Seven Valleys

Gorski, Daniel Alexander Sculptor, Painter

Sewickley

Heinz, Mr & Mrs Henry J, II Collectors, Patrons

Sharon

Dunn, Nate Painter, Instructor

Shavertown

Simon, Herbert Bernheimer Sculptor, Educator

Shippensburg

Bentz, Harry Donald Art Administrator, Painter

Solebury

Anthonisen, George Rioch Sculptor

Souderton

Bock, William Sauts-Netamux'we Illustrator, Painter

Springfield

Bates, Betsey Illustrator, Designer

Spring House

Garvan, Beatrice Bronson Curator, Art Historian

State College

Frost, Stuart Homer Educator, Painter
McCoy, Wirth Vaughan Painter, Educator
Van Dommelen, David B Art Writer, Fiber Artist
Zoretich, George Stephen Painter, Educator

Sunbury

Karniol, Hilda Painter, Instructor

Swarthmore

Hollister, Valerie (Dutton) Painter
Walker, Robert Miller Educator

Titusville

Herpst, Martha Jane Painter

Trucksville

Colson, Chester E Painter, Educator

Unionville

Parks, Eric Vernon Sculptor

University Park

Hull, William Floyd Museum Director
Hyslop, Francis Edwin Art Historian
Lawrence, Howard Ray Designer, Educator
Smith, Elizabeth Jean Art Librarian

Upper Black Eddy

Bosa, Louis Painter

Wallingford

Mark, Enid (Epstein) Printmaker, Painter

Warrington

Keene, Paul Painter

Washington Crossing

Ceglia, Vincent Painter, Instructor
Kemble, Richard Printmaker, Sculptor

Waterford

Stull, Jean Himrod Painter, Instructor

Wayne

Cooke, Donald Ewin Writer, Designer
Dobie, Jeanne Painter, Instructor
Hoffman, Edward Fenno, III Sculptor
Key, Ted Cartoonist
Megargee, Lawrence Anthony (Laurie) Painter, Illustrator

West Chester

Baldwin, Richard Wood Illustrator, Sculptor
Hawthorne, Jack Gardner Educator, Painter
Jamison, Philip (Duane, Jr) Painter

West Grove

Allman, Margo Sculptor, Printmaker

West Middletown

Taylor, Hugh Holloway Art Historian, Lecturer

Williamsport

Shipley, Roger Douglas Sculptor, Educator

Wyncote

Jansen, Catherine Sandra Photographer, Instructor
Larson, William G Photographer
Moore, John J Painter, Educator

Wynnewood

Gill, Sue May Painter, Sculptor
Greenwood, William James Painter, Conservator
Maxwell, John Painter
Merriam, Ruth Conservator, Collector

Wyomissing

Elliott, B Charles, Jr Art Consultant, Art Historian

Zionsville

Stark, Melville F Painter, Educator

RHODE ISLAND

Bristol

Goff, Thomas Jefferson Sculptor, Medalist
Knowlton, Daniel Gibson Bookbinder
Townley, Hugh Sculptor, Printmaker
Udvardy, John Warren Sculptor, Painter

Coventry

Beaudoin, Andre Eugene Press Manufacturer, Photographer

Cranston

Casey, Elizabeth Temple Curator
Crooks, W Spencer Painter, Lecturer

East Greenwich

Wang, Yinpao Painter, Writer

East Providence

Peterson, A E S Painter

Jamestown

Wright, Catharine Morris Painter, Writer

Johnston

Smith, Donald C Educator, Painter

Kingston

Brown, Marvin Prentiss Painter, Sculptor
Leete, William White Painter

Lincoln

Loughlin, John Leo Painter, Lecturer
Senior, Dorothy Elizabeth Painter

Little Compton

Schmidt, Katherine (Katherine Schmidt Shubert) Painter

Newport

Bach, Dirk Painter, Educator
Barry, Robert E Illustrator, Art Administrator
Cathers, James O Sculptor, Educator
Cooper, Marve H Painter, Art Dealer
Gaines, Alan Jay Painter, Printmaker
Nesbitt, Alexander John Educator, Calligrapher
Silvia, Judith Heidler Richardson Art Dealer, Museum Director
van Duinwyk, George Paul Metalsmith, Instructor

Peace Dale

Eichenberg, Fritz Illustrator, Printmaker
Petrie, Sylvia Spencer Printmaker, Painter

Providence

Blodgett, Peter Sculptor, Educator
Chihuly, Dale Patrick Glass Artist, Designer
Day, Martha B Willson Painter, Collector
Ewing, Bayard Art Administrator, Collector
Feldman, Walter (Sidney) Painter, Educator
Geran, Joseph, Jr Sculptor, Painter
Goto, Joseph Sculptor
Grear, James Malcolm Designer, Educator
Hall, Lee Art Administrator, Painter
Helander, Bruce Paul Painter, Art Administrator
Macaualy, David Alexander Designer, Illustrator
Morin, Thomas Edward Sculptor, Educator
Ockerse, Thomas Designer, Educator
Ostrow, Stephen Edward Art Historian, Museum Director
Peers, Gordon Franklin Painter, Educator
Pilavin, Selma F Patron
Prince, Arnold Sculptor, Educator
Ryder, Mahler Bessinger Painter, Illustrator
St Florian, Friedrich Gartler Educator, Designer
Szarama, Judith Layne Printmaker, Instructor

Wakefield

Rohm, Robert Sculptor

Westerly

Day, Chon (Chauncey Addison) Cartoonist

SOUTH CAROLINA

Charleston

Clark, Chevis Delwin Painter, Instructor
Halsey, William Melton Painter, Educator
Herold, Donald G Museum Director
Hirsch, Willard Newman Sculptor
Janson, Anthony Fredrick Art Historian
Johnson, Diane Chalmers Art Historian
Karesh, Ann Bamberger Painter, Sculptor

SOUTH CAROLINA (cont)

McCallum, Corrie (Mrs William Halsey) Painter, Printmaker
Verner, Elizabeth O'Neill Etcher, Writer

Chesnee

Cook, August Charles Painter, Engraver

Clemson

McGee, Olivia Jackson Painter, Illustrator
Wang, Samuel Photographer, Printmaker

Cleveland

Lewis, Don Potter, Sculptor

Columbia

Bardin, Jesse Redwin Painter, Instructor
Barnwell, F Edward Curator, Registrar
Condon, Lawrence James Painter, Instructor
Craft, John Richard Museum Director
Davis, John Sherwood Potter, Art Administrator
Edwards, James F Video Artist, Photographer
Hampton, Ambrose Gonzales, Jr Collector
Hansen, Harold John Educator, Painter
Hathaway, Walter Murphy Museum Director
Lafaye, Nell Murray Painter, Educator
Ledyard, Walter William Sculptor
Mack, Charles Randall Educator, Art Writer
Marin, Kathryn Garrison Painter, Printmaker
McWhorter, Elsie Jean Painter, Sculptor
Mitchell, Dana Covington, Jr Collector
Mullen, Philip Edward Artist
Ochs, Robert David Collector, Patron
O'Neil, John Joseph Art Administrator, Designer
Quinsac, Annie-Paule Art Historian, Writer
Saunders, J Boyd Printmaker, Educator
Sennema, David C Art Administrator, Educator
Van Hook, David H Painter, Art Administrator
Walker, George R P, Jr Art Dealer, Fine Arts Framer
Woody, (Thomas) Howard Sculptor, Educator
Yaghjian, Edmund Painter, Instructor

Gaffney

Boggs, Mayo Mac Sculptor, Educator

Greenville

Alberga, Alta W Art Historian, Painter
Appleman, David Earl Designer, Painter
Blair, Carl Raymond Painter, Educator
Bopp, Emery Painter, Educator
Coburn, Bette Lee Dobry Painter
Dreskin, Jeanet Steckler Painter, Instructor
Flowers, Thomas Earl Painter, Educator
Hodge, Scottie Art Dealer, Art Administrator
Hunter, Robert Howard Painter, Printmaker
Koons, Darell J Painter, Instructor
Morris, Jack Austin, Jr Museum Director, Writer
Petty, John L, Jr Museum Director, Conservator
Whitley, Philip Waff Sculptor

Hilton Head Island

Bowler, Joseph, Jr Portrait Artist, Illustrator
Greer, Walter Marion Painter
Whitmore, Coby Painter, Illustrator

Isle Of Palms

Knerr, Sallie Frost Painter, Printmaker

Johns Island

Mawicke, Tran Painter, Illustrator

Orangeburg

Twiggs, Leo Franklin Painter, Educator

Rock Hill

Freeman, David L Painter, Educator
Lewandowski, Edmund D Painter, Art Administrator

Spartanburg

Bramlett, Betty Jane Art Administrator, Painter
Du Pre, Grace Annette Painter

Summerville

Vorwerk, E Charlsie Painter, Illustrator

Wadmalaw Island

McKoy, Victor Grainger Sculptor

SOUTH DAKOTA

Brookings

Bunce, Fredrick William Draftsman, Art Historian
Nelson, Signe (Signe Nelson Stuart) Painter
Stuart, Joseph Martin Painter, Museum Director

Custer

Ziolkowski, Korczak Sculptor

Sioux Falls

Eide, Palmer Sculptor, Designer
Grupp, Carl Alf Painter, Printmaker

Springfield

Gettinger, Edmond Walter Educator, Painter

Vermillion

Howe, Oscar Painter, Educator

Westport

Gibson, James D Art Administrator, Painter

TENNESSEE

Brentwood

Frace, Charles Lewis Illustrator, Painter

Chattanooga

Cress, George Ayers Painter, Educator
Hazard, Jim (Ovington) Art Critic, Art Editor
Michalove, Carla Maria Educator, Curator
Scarbrough, Cleve Knox, Jr Museum Director, Art Historian
Shumacker, Elizabeth Wight Painter, Instructor

Clarksville

Bryant, Olen L Sculptor, Educator
Crouch, Ned Philbrick Sculptor, Curator

Collegedale

Childers, Malcolm Graeme Printmaker Photographer

Cross Plains

Wright, Harold David Illustrator, Painter

Gatlinburg

Gray, Jim Painter, Sculptor
Schulz, Ken Painter, Lecturer

Jackson

Carmichael, Donald Ray Painter, Educator
Grissom, Kenneth Ryland, II Painter
Robinson, Grove Educator, Painter

Jefferson City

Cleveland, Robert Earl Art Administrator, Educator

Johnson City

Gold, Debra Lynn Metalsmith, Instructor
Thomas, Katherine Castellanos Art Administrator, Painter
Thomas, William Radford Educator, Painter

Kingsport

Williams, Raymond Lester Painter, Instructor

Knoxville

Le Fevre, Richard John Painter, Designer
Leland, Whitney Edward Painter, Educator
McKeeby, Byron Gordon Printmaker, Educator
McNabb, William Ross Gallery Director
Stevens, Walter Hollis Painter, Educator

Lookout Mountain

Lynch, Mary Britten Painter, Instructor

Maryville

Langston, Loyd H Art Dealer, Collector

Memphis

Allgood, Charles Henry Art Historian, Painter
Anthony, Lawrence Kenneth Sculptor, Educator
Bennett, Jamie Jeweler, Instructor
Califf, Marilyn Iskiwitz Painter, Designer
Callicott, Burton Harry Painter, Calligrapher
Cloar, Carroll Painter
Easterwood, Henry Lewis Educator, Tapestry Artist
Faiers, Edward Spencer (Ted) Painter, Printmaker
Goodman, Benjamin Patron
Govan, Francis Hawks Educator, Painter
Johnson, Dana Doane Educator, Painter
Knowles, Richard H Painter, Writer
Lehman, Louise Brasell Painter
Lincoln, Fred Clinton Designer, Ceramist
Moss, Morrie Alfred Collector
Pekar, Ronald Walter Painter, Educator
Penczner, Paul Joseph Painter
Rawlinson, Jonlane Frederick Painter, Instructor
Riseling, Robert Lowell Educator, Painter
Riss, Murray Photographer, Educator
Roberson, William Weaver
Rust, Edwin C Sculptor, Art Administrator
Sanderson, Robert Wright Art Dealer
Seyfried, John Louis Sculptor
Shook, Georg Painter
Smith, Dolph Painter, Educator
Whitlock, John Joseph Art Administrator, Educator
Windeknecht, Margaret Brake Fiber Artist

Morristown

Ortmayer, Constance Sculptor, Educator

Nashville

Bissell, Charles Overman Cartoonist

Bodo, Sandor Painter, Sculptor
Brumbaugh, Thomas Brendle Art Historian, Writer
Caldwell, Benjamin Hubbard, Jr Collector, Art Historian
Hazlehurst, Franklin Hamilton Art Historian, Educator
Hill, John Alexander Collector
Hooks, Earl J Educator, Sculptor
Jarman, Walton Maxey Collector
Jones, Theodore Joseph Sculptor, Printmaker
King, Myron Lyzon Art Dealer
Martin, Rose Breyer Collector
Pilsk, Adele Inez Art Administrator
Pletcher, Gerry Painter, Printmaker
Pogue, Stephanie Elaine Printmaker, Educator
Ridley, Gregory D, Jr Painter, Sculptor
Sublett, Carl C Painter, Educator
Taylor, Michael (Leach) Sculptor, Glassworker
Weiss, Anton Painter, Art Director
Zimmerman, William Harold Painter, Illustrator

Sewanee

Carlos, (James) Edward Painter, Art Administrator
Duncan, Richard Hurley Printmaker, Educator

Signal Mountain

Collins, Jim Educator, Sculptor

TEXAS

Abilene

Kwiecinski, Chester Martin Museum Director, Painter
Suter, Sherwood Eugene Educator, Painter

Amarillo

Caballero, Emilio Educator, Painter
Childers, Betty Bivins Collector, Patron
Daviee, Jerry Michael Curator, Writer
Fraze, Denny T Artist, Art Administrator
Livesay, Thomas Andrew Museum Director
McCracken, Patrick Ed Painter, Educator

Arlington

Brouillette, Al Painter, Instructor
Bruno, Vincent J Art Historian, Art Administrator
Grandee, Joe Ruiz Painter, Gallery Director
Rascoe, Stephen Thomas Painter, Educator
Sullivan, Max William Art Administrator

Austin

Baranoff, Mort Printmaker, Painter
Beitz, Lester U Painter, Illustrator
Bowlt, John Art Historian, Educator
Brettell, Richard Robson Art Historian
Brezik, Hilarion Painter, Educator
Bucknall, Malcolm Roderick Painter
Chesney, Lee Roy, III Printmaker, Educator
Davis, Marian B Art Historian, Curator
Deming, David Lawson Sculptor, Educator
Fearing, Kelly Painter, Educator
Fisher, James Donald Sculptor, Museum Director
Forsyth, Constance Painter, Printmaker
Francis, Bill Dean Designer, Educator
George, Walter Eugene, Jr Architect, Designer
Goodall, Donald Bannard Art Administrator
Grieder, Terence Art Historian
Guerin, John William Painter, Educator
Hale, Kenneth John Lithographer, Painter
Hatgil, Paul Sculptor
Hess, Joyce Art Librarian
High, Timothy Griffin Printmaker, Instructor
Houser, Caroline Mae Art Historian
Kelpe, Paul Painter
Lee, Russell Photographer, Educator
Likan, Gustav Painter, Instructor
Lindlof, Edward Axel, Jr Illustrator, Lecturer
Marshall, Bruce Illustrator, Painter
Mayer, Susan Martin Educator, Painter
Milliken, Gibbs Painter, Educator
Pena, Amado Maurilio, Jr Painter, Illustrator
Phillips, James Art Historian, Painter
Popinsky, Arnold Dave Sculptor, Ceramist
Prescott, Kenneth Wade Educator, Writer
Ravel, Dana B Art Dealer
Reese, Thomas Ford Art Historian, Educator
Ruben, Leonard Designer, Educator
Schmandt-Besserat, Denise Art Historian, Archaeologist
Spruce, Everett Franklin Painter, Printmaker
Umlauf, Charles Sculptor
Weismann, Donald Leroy Educator, Painter
White, Ralph Painter, Educator
Williams, John Alden Art Historian
Wiman, Bill Painter, Educator
Winogrand, Garry Photographer, Lecturer

Beaumont

Coe, Matchett Herring Sculptor

Bellaire

Parsons, David Goode Sculptor, Educator

Brenham

Malina, Frank Joseph Art Editor, Painter

Canyon

Cornette, Mary Elizabeth Art Dealer, Painter
Mayes, Steven Lee Art Administrator, Printmaker

Clifton

Boren, James Erwin Painter, Lecturer
Warren, Melvin Charles Painter, Sculptor

Clint

Herring, Jan(et Mantel) Painter, Writer

Commerce

McGough, Charles E Printmaker, Educator
Umlauf, Karl A Painter

Corpus Christi

Cain, Joseph Alexander Painter, Educator
Gallander, Cathleen S Museum Director
Lambert, Eddie Printmaker, Painter
Locke, Michelle Wilson Curator, Art Historian
Tsai, Hsiao Hsia Painter, Sculptor

Dallas

Albrecht, Mary Dickson Sculptor, Painter
Allumbaugh, James Sculptor, Educator
Altermann, Tony Art Dealer
Bodnar, Peter Painter, Educator
Bond, Roland S Collector
Briggs, Judson Reynolds Painter
Brotherton, Naomi Painter, Instructor
Burford, William E Art Dealer, Art Administrator
Bywaters, Jerry Painter, Art Historian
Calle, Paul Painter, Writer
Childers, Richard Robin Painter
Clark, Nancy Kissel Sculptor
Clifford, Jutta Art Dealer
Comini, Alessandra Art Historian, Lecturer
Dozier, Otis Painter, Printmaker
Emerson, Walter Caruth Educator, Writer
Ficklen, Jack Howells Cartoonist
Froman, Ramon Mitchell Painter
Gantz, Ann Cushing Art Dealer, Painter
Green, George Thurman Sculptor, Painter
Harris, Leon A, Jr Collector, Patron
Hunter, Debora Photographer, Educator
Jones, Lois Swan Art Historian, Lecturer
Jordan, William B Museum Director, Art Historian
Judd, De Forrest Hale Painter, Educator
Kahn, Annelies Ruth Ceramist, Instructor
Kahn, Ralph H Art Dealer, Lecturer
Kelley, Chapman Painter, Art Dealer
Koch, Arthur Robert Painter, Educator
Komodore, Bill Painter, Sculptor
Kutner, Janet Art Critic, Lecturer
Leeber, Sharon Corgan Sculptor
Lunsford, John (Crawford) Art Historian, Curator
Marcus, Betty Collector, Patron
Marcus, Stanley Collector
McClanahan, William J Cartoonist
McCullough, David William Painter, Sculptor
Meadows, Algur H Patron
Mudge, Edmund Webster, Jr Collector
Murchison, John D Collector
Murdock, Robert Mead Museum Curator, Art Historian
Nagler, Edith Kroger Painter
Nagler, Fred Painter
Parker, Harry S, III Museum Director
Piccolo, Thomas Frank Sculptor, Jeweler
Scholder, Laurence Printmaker, Educator
Smither, Edward Murray Art Dealer
Taylor, Bob Byron Cartoonist
Travis, Olin (Herman) Painter
Tufts, Eleanor M Art Historian
Tyler, Valton Printmaker, Painter
Van Atta, Helen Ulmer Collector
Voelker, John Painter, Designer
Vogel, Donald S Painter, Art Dealer
Wade, Robert Schrope Photographer, Sculptor
Winter, Roger Painter, Educator

Denton

Corpron, Carlotta Mae Educator, Photographer
Davis, D Jack Educator, Art Administrator
Davis, Donald Jack Educator
Erdle, Rob Painter, Educator
Havis, C Kenneth Gallery Director, Designer
Mattil, Edward L Educator, Writer
Smith, Donald Eugene Art Administrator, Educator

Driftwood

Scott, Curtis S Ceramist, Educator

Dumas

Stallwitz, Carolyn Painter, Photographer

Edinburg

Field, Philip Sidney Painter, Printmaker

El Paso

Acosta, Manuel Gregorio Painter, Sculptor
Archer, Dorothy Bryant Painter, Instructor
Canaris, Patti Ann Painter
Carter, Frederick Timmins Painter, Illustrator
de Turczynowicz, Wanda (Mrs Eliot Hermann) Designer, Painter
Drake, James Printmaker, Sculptor
Enriquez, Gaspar Designer, Instructor
Fulton, Fred Franklin Painter
Garnsey, Clarke Henderson Art Historian, Educator
Grissom, Freda Gill Painter, Silversmith
Hill, Ed Art Dealer, Collector
Janzen, Loren Gene Printmaker, Educator
Kolliker, William Augustin Painter, Graphic Artist
Lea, Tom Painter, Illustrator
Martin, Loretta Marsh Painter, Cartoonist
Martinez, Ernesto Pedregon Instructor, Muralist
Massey, Robert Joseph Painter, Educator

TEXAS (cont)
Rakocy, William (Joseph) Painter
Schuster, Cita Fletcher (Sarah E) Art Dealer, Appraiser
Sipiora, Leonard Paul Museum Director, Writer
Tietz, Evelyne Painter
Waterhouse, Russell Rutledge Painter

Fort Worth

Brown, Richard F Museum Director
Cantey, Sam Benton, III Collector
Carlin, Electra Marshall Art Dealer
Clark, Carol Canda Curator
Conn, David Edward Printmaker
Cross, Maria Concetta Painter, Collector
Fuller, Adelaide P & William Marshall Collectors
Henslee, Jack Painter, Illustrator
Johnson, Ruth Carter Collector, Patron
Jones, Anthony Educator, Painter/Sculptor
Lincoln, Richard Mather Ceramist, Educator
Malone, James William Artist
Pruitt, A Kelly Painter, Sculptor
Smith, Emily Guthrie Painter
Stegall, James Park Painter, Instructor
Stone, John Lewis, Jr Painter
Strother, Virginia Vaughn Painter
Sullivan, Ruth Wilkins Art Historian, Curator
Weiner, Ted Collector, Patron
Wilder, Mitchell Armitage Art Administrator

Galveston

Atkins, Billy W Art Administrator, Painter
Bott, H J Sculptor, Assemblagist
Deats, Margaret (Margaret Deats Bott) Art Dealer, Art Writer
Glasco, Joseph M Painter, Sculptor

Glen Rose

Summers, Robert Painter, Sculptor

Hamilton

Rice, James William, Jr Illustrator, Sculptor

Houston

Alexander, John E Painter
Andrews, Victoria L Art Dealer
Biggers, John Thomas Educator, Painter
Boynton, James W Painter, Printmaker
Bunker, George Painter, Printmaker
Camblin, Bob Bilyeu Painter
Camfield, William Arnett Art Historian
Carlin, Robert Eugene Painter, Art Historian
Casas, Fernando Rodriguez Painter, Draftsman
Cobb, Virginia Horton Painter, Lecturer
Collins, Lowell Daunt Painter, Art Dealer
Conrad, Nancy R Painter
David, Dianne Art Dealer, Collector
Dreyer, Margaret Webb Painter, Art Dealer
Erdman, R H Donnelley Art Dealer
Evans, Burford Elonzo Painter, Lecturer
Goldberg, Arnold Herbert Painter
Goldberg, Chaim Painter, Printmaker
Guenther, Peter W Art Historian
Hammett, Polly Horton Instructor, Painter
Hickman, David Coleman Painter, Educator
Hood, Dorothy Painter
Hooks, Charles Vernon Art Dealer, Collector
Jewesson, Kenneth R Art Administrator
Laird, E Ruth Sculptor
Lansdon, Gay Brandt Instructor, Printmaker
Lesher, Marie Palmisano Sculptor
Link, Val James Jeweler, Educator
Long, Meredith J Art Dealer
Love, Jim Sculptor
Ludtke, Lawrence Monroe Sculptor
Metyko, Michael Joseph Curator, Artist
Moody, Elizabeth Chambers Art Dealer
Moser, Charlotte Art Critic
O'Neil, John Painter, Educator
Pelham-Keller, Richard Monroe Art Dealer, Designer
Poulos, Basilios Nicholas Painter, Educator
Pulido, Guillermo Aguilar Sculptor, Video Artist
Robinson, Thomas Art Dealer, Collector
Rodriguez, Joe Bastida Art Director, Painter
Rodriguez, Ralph Noel Curator, Painter
Shaw, Donald Edward Painter, Sculptor
Smith, Ray Winfield Collector, Art Historian
Speers, Teryl Townsend Painter, Educator
Stack, Gael Z Educator, Painter
Storm, Mark (Kennedy) Painter, Illustrator
Stout, Richard Gordon Painter
Tahir, Abe M, Jr Art Dealer
Tucker, Anne Curator, Photo Historian and Critic
Turner, Arthur Charles Painter, Instructor
Turner, (Charles) Arthur Painter, Instructor
Van Vranken, Rose (Rose Van Vranken Hickey) Sculptor, Printmaker
Wall, Ralph Alan Painter, Illustrator
Werner-Vaughn, Salle Painter
Winningham, Geoff Photographer
Witold-k (Kaczanowski) Painter, Sculptor
Woitena, Ben S Sculptor, Educator
Wray, Dick Painter
Wrightsman, Charles Bierer Collector

Huntsville

Ahysen, Harry Joseph Painter, Educator
Breitenbach, William John Sculptor, Draftsman
Eastman, Gene M Painter, Art Administrator
Geeslin, Lee Gaddis Painter, Educator
Lea, Stanley E Printmaker, Painter

Irving

Novinski, Lyle Frank Painter, Educator

Kerrville

Burt, Dan Painter

Kingsville

Rutland, Emily Edith Painter
Scherpereel, Richard Charles Educator, Painter

La Feria

Borglum, James Lincoln de la Mothe Sculptor, Photographer

Longview

Elias, Harold John Painter, Lecturer
Jeter, Randy Joe Drawer, Educator
Statman, Jan B Painter, Instructor
Ward, Velox Benjamin Painter

Lubbock

Cheatham, Frank Reagan Painter, Designer
Dixon, Kenneth Ray Painter, Gallery Director
Funk, Charlotte M Weaver
Funk, Verne J Ceramist, Educator
Gibbons, Hugh (James) Painter, Educator
Hanna, Paul Dean, Jr Printmaker, Painter
Hastie, Reid Educator, Writer
Hillis, Richard K Designer, Painter
Howze, James Dean Educator, Painter
Kreneck, Lynwood Printmaker
Morrow, Terry Draftsman, Printmaker
Stephen, Francis B Jeweler, Instructor

Marfa

Gervasi, Frank Painter

Medina

Carrington, Joy Harrell Painter, Illuminator

Mission

McClendon, Maxine (Maxine McClendon Nichols) Painter, Craftsman

Nacogdoches

Schlicher, Karl Theodore Painter, Educator

Odessa

Pool, Nelda Lee Art Appraiser, Art Dealer

Port Arthur

Broussard, Normaj Collector, Painter
Carron, Maudee Lilyan Painter, Sculptor

Richardson

Brown, John Hall Painter, Architect
Curtis, Mary Cranfill Printmaker, Painter
Dreskin-Haig, Jeanet Elizabeth Painter, Printmaker
McNary, Oscar L Painter
Pederson, Molly Fay Painter, Sculptor

San Angelo

Schmidt, Stephen Museum Director

San Antonio

Bristow, William Arthur Painter, Educator
Casas, Melesio Painter, Educator
Duncan, Ruth Painter
Fainter, Robert A Educator, Painter
Fuchs, Mary Tharsilla Educator
Kent, Jack Illustrator
Lee, Amy Freeman Painter, Lecturer
Leeper, John Palmer Museum Director
McGregor, Jack R Museum Director
Naylor, Alice Stephenson Painter
Pace, Margaret Bosshardt Designer, Painter
Quirarte, Jacinto Art Historian, Educator
Rodgers, Jack A Art Administrator
Roney, Harold Arthur Painter, Lecturer
Rowe, Reginald M Painter, Sculptor
Sigoloff, Violet Bruce Art Dealer, Painter
Tarin, Gilberto A Painter, Printmaker
Tauch, Waldine Amanda Sculptor, Collector
Tobin, Robert L B Collector, Patron
Tucker, Glenn F Art Critic, Collector
Van Buren, Helen Rae Painter, Art Dealer
Waitt, Alden Harry Painter, Art Administrator
West, E Gordon Administrator, Painter
White, Ron Art Critic, Art Editor
Willson, Robert Sculptor, Educator
Wogstad, James Everet Educator, Illustrator
Wray, Margaret Painter, Ceramist

San Marcos

Boyd, Donald Edgar Photographer, Art Dealer
Looney, Norman Painter, Instructor

Sherman

Fisher, Vernon Painter, Educator
Neidhardt, Carl Richard Art Administrator, Painter

Texarkana

Caver, William Ralph Sculptor, Painter

Tyler

Gentry (Augustus Calahan, Jr) Painter
Stephens, William Blakely Educator, Painter

Waco

Harris, Paul Rogers Museum Director, Educator
Kemp, Paul Zane Printmaker
McClanahan, John Dean Painter, Educator
Smith, John Bertie Educator, Painter
Stewart, William Painter

Waxahachie

Nichols, Jeannettie Doornhein Painter

UTAH

Brigham City

Huchel, Frederick M Museum Director, Curator

Lehi

Jarvis, John Brent Painter

Lindon

Speed, (Ulysses) Grant Sculptor

Logan

Elsner, Larry Edward Sculptor, Educator
Kusama, Tetsuo Fiber Artist
Lindstrom, Gaell Painter, Educator
Smith, Moishe Printmaker
Van Suchtelen, Adrian Printmaker, Educator

Mount Carmel

Zornes, James Milford Painter, Designer

Ogden

Collett, Farrell Reuben Painter, Educator
Taylor, Harry George Printmaker, Photographer

Provo

Andrus, James Roman Printmaker, Painter
Barsch, Wulf Erich Painter, Printmaker
Burnside, Wesley M Art Historian, Painter
Coleman, Michael Painter, Etcher
De Jong, Gerrit, Jr Lecturer, Writer
Magleby, Francis R (Frank) Painter, Educator
Myer, Peter Livingston Kinetic Artist, Museum Director
Whitaker, William Painter, Educator
Wilson, Warren Bingham Educator, Sculptor

Salt Lake City

Christensen, Larry R Art Director, Painter
Christensen, Sharlene Painter, Instructor
Cutler, Grayce E Painter, Writer
Dibble, George Painter, Art Writer
Dodworth, Allen Stevens Museum Director, Printmaker
Dunn, O Coleman Collector
Fairbanks, Avard Sculptor
Friberg, Arnold Illustrator, Painter
Hicks, Harold Jon (Jack) Sculptor
Johnston, Richard M Sculptor, Educator
Koga, Dean Art Librarian, Craftsman
Olpin, Robert Spencer Art Historian, Curator
Phillips, Bonnie Art Dealer
Rasmussen, Anton Jesse Painter, Art Administrator
Sanguinetti, Eugene F Art Administrator, Lecturer
Smith, Frank Anthony Painter
Snow, Vivian Douglas Painter, Educator
Tierney, Patrick Lennox Art Historian, Educator
Wiedenhoeft, Renate Photographer, Art Historian

South Jordan

Fraughton, Edward James Sculptor

Springville

Marshall, Robert Leroy Educator, Painter
Rose, Timothy G Art Administrator, Museum Director

VERMONT

Barre

Gaylord, Frank Chalfant Sculptor, Designer

Barton

Baker, Anna P Painter, Graphic Artist
Miller, Dolly (Ethel B) Painter

Bennington

Adams, Pat Painter, Instructor
Held, Julius S Educator, Writer
Wolfe, James Sculptor

Braintree

Robbins, Daniel J Art Historian, Museum Director

Brattleboro

Watson, Aldren Auld Designer, Illustrator

Brookfield

Newton, Earle Williams Art Administrator, Collector

Burlington

Colburn, Francis Peabody Artist

Castleton

Robinson, Robert Doke Painter, Educator

Charlotte

Aschenbach, (Walter) Paul Sculptor

Craftsbury

Mainardi, Patricia M Painter, Writer

Dorset

Kouwenhoven, John A Writer, Educator

East Corinth

Hewitt, Francis Ray Painter, Educator

Fairlee

Walker, Herbert Brooks Sculptor, Museum Director

Grafton

Hunter, Mel Painter, Printmaker
Schoener, Allon Art Consultant

Jericho

Haversat, Lillian Kerr Art Dealer

Londonderry

Shokler, Harry Painter, Serigrapher

Lowell

Kramer, Marjorie Anne Painter

Ludlow

Schietinger, James Frederick Sculptor, Photographer

Manchester

Pleissner, Ogden Minton Painter

Manchester Center

Abbe, Elfriede Martha Sculptor, Engraver
Armstrong, Jane Botsford Sculptor
Montague, James L Painter
Rath, Hildegard Painter, Lecturer
Webb, Virginia Louise Painter

Marlboro

Heiskell, Diana Painter, Designer

Middlebury

Bumbeck, David A Printmaker, Educator
Healy, Arthur K D Painter, Lecturer
Hunisak, John Michael Art Historian, Educator
Mitcham, Georgia Whitman Sculptor
Reiff, Robert Frank Art Historian, Painter

Morrisville

Barrett, Robert Dumas Painter, Educator

Orwell

Jensen, John Edward Painter, Designer
Wunder, Richard Paul Art Historian, Art Administrator

Pittsford

Frick, Robert Oliver Painter, Instructor

Putney

Forakis, Peter Sculptor
Ginnever, Charles Sculptor

Randolph

Robbins, Eugenia S Art Writer, Art Editor

Rutland

Johnson, Katherine King Art Administrator, Painter

Saint Johnsbury

Carlyle, Julian (Julian Carlyle Wells) Collage Artist, Sculptor

South Shaftsbury

Noland, Kenneth Painter

Springfield

Baldwin, Harold Fletcher Sculptor, Painter
Eldredge, Mary Agnes Sculptor
Eldredge, Stuart Edson Painter

Stowe

Wright, Stanley Marc Painter, Instructor

Waitsfield

Carpenter, Harlow Museum Director

West Burke

Boylen, Michael Edward Craftsman, Art Administrator
Van Vliet, Claire Printmaker

West Townshend

Court, Lee Winslow Painter

VERMONT (cont)

Weston

Landon, Edward August   Printmaker, Painter

Winooski

Buchman, James Wallace   Sculptor

Woodstock

Albright, Ivan Le Lorraine   Artist
Gyra, Francis Joseph, Jr   Instructor, Painter
Thomas, Byron   Painter

Worcester

Jensen, Hank   Sculptor

VIRGINIA

Alexandria

Adams, Katherine Langhorne   Painter, Sculptor
Bailey, Worth   Art Historian
Banks, Anne Johnson   Sculptor, Printmaker
Caples, Barbara Barrett   Printmaker, Painter
Conger, Clement E   Curator
Day, Horace Talmage   Painter, Art Director
Doolin, Mary N   Art Dealer, Collector
Evans, Grose   Art Historian
Godwin, Robert Kimball   Painter
Jamieson, Mitchell   Painter
Keeler, David Boughton   Art Administrator, Painter
Keena, Janet Laybourn   Painter
Lacy, Bettie   Museum Director
Lanou, Tobie E   Art Critic, Art Administrator
Luray, J (J Luray Schaffner)   Printmaker, Designer
Marker, Mariska Pugsley   Painter, Collector
Marker, Ralph E   Painter, Collector
Myers, Denys Peter   Art Historian, Lecturer
Nash, Veronica F   Art Dealer, Collector
Richards, Jeanne Herron   Etcher, Painter
Sanborn, Herbert J   Lithographer, Painter
Singletary, Robert Eugene   Graphic Artist, Muralist
Spagnolo, Kathleen Mary   Printmaker, Illustrator
Van Arsdale, Dorothy Thayer   Art Administrator
Voris, Anna Maybelle   Curator

Annandale

McLean, Roddy (Verneda Rodriguez)   Painter, Instructor
Spink, Frank Henry, Jr   Writer, Painter

Arlington

Castro, Alex   Painter, Bookmaker
Fenical, Marlin E   Painter, Photographer
Gast, Carolyn Bartlett (Carolyn B Lutz)   Illustrator, Illuminator
Gast, Michael Carl   Painter
Harlan, Roma Christine   Painter
Reed, Paul Allen   Painter, Instructor
Twitty, James (Watson)   Painter, Printmaker

Ashburn

Pickens, Vinton Liddell   Painter

Ashland

Longaker, Jon Dasu   Educator, Writer
Witt, Nancy Camden   Sculptor, Painter

Bent Mountain

Harrington, William Charles   Sculptor, Educator

Blacksburg

Carter, Dean   Sculptor, Educator
Harman, Maryann Whittemore   Painter
Huggins, Victor, (Jr)   Painter, Educator
Long, Sandra Tardo   Designer, Graphic Artist
Sarvis, Alva Taylor   Printmaker

Bridgewater

Beer, Kenneth John   Educator, Sculptor

Bumpass

Renick, Charles Cooley   Sculptor, Educator

Charlottesville

Barbee, Robert Thomas   Painter, Graphic Artist
Burr, Horace   Curator, Collector
Clark, Eliot Candee   Painter
Dunnigan, Mary Catherine   Art Librarian
Hagan, James Garrison   Sculptor, Instructor
Hartt, Frederick   Art Historian
Markowski, Eugene David   Painter
Moxey, Keith Patricio Fleming   Art Historian
Priest, Hartwell Wyse   Painter, Printmaker
Smith, Charles (William)   Painter
Turner, Theodore Roy   Painter, Educator

Chesapeake

Taylor, Rod Allen   Art Administrator, Sculptor

Christiansburg

Kass, Ray   Painter

Clifton

Hennesy, Gerald Craft   Painter

Colonial Heights

Woodson, Doris   Educator, Painter

Covington

Walton, Harry A, Jr   Collector

Ettrick

Macklin, Anderson D   Art Administrator, Potter

Fairfax

Watson, Darliene Keeney   Painter

Fairfax Station

Jackson, Vaughn L   Painter, Illustrator

Falls Church

Fredrick, Eugene Wallace   Printmaker, Educator
Grosse (Carolyn Ann Gawarecki)   Painter, Instructor
Kumm, Marguerite Elizabeth   Painter, Printmaker
Land, Ernest Albert   Painter
Liu, Ho   Collector, Painter
Robinson, Charlotte   Painter, Printmaker

Farmville

Bishop, Barbara Lee   Educator, Printmaker

Fredericksburg

Robertson, D Hall   Painter

Great Falls

Pollack, Reginald Murray   Painter, Writer

Hampton

Clifton, Jack Whitney   Instructor, Painter
Jones, Allan Dudley   Painter, Educator

Harrisonburg

Caldwell, Martha Belle   Educator, Art Historian
Crable, James Harbour   Multi-Media Artist, Instructor

Herndon

Pisani, Joseph   Designer, Painter

Lexington

Doyon, Gerard Maurice   Gallery Director, Art Historian
Ju, I-Hsiung   Painter, Educator

Lynchburg

Williams, Mary Frances   Art Historian, Lecturer

McLean

Anderson, Gwendolyn Orsinger (Orsini)   Enamelist, Instructor
Basset, Gene   Political Cartoonist
Beggs, Thomas Montague   Fine Arts Consultant, Painter
Lawson, Edward Pitt   Art Administrator
O'Connell, Ann Brown   Painter, Collector
Stark, Ron   Photographer

Middletown

Chumley, John Wesley   Painter

Midlothian

Baldridge, Mark S   Editor, Goldsmith

Newport News

Anglin, Betty Lockhart   Educator, Painter
Sheaks, Barclay   Painter

Norfolk

Amaya, Mario Anthony   Museum Director, Writer
Chrysler, Walter P, Jr   Collector
Clark, Mark A   Curator
Jackson, A B   Educator, Painter
Jones, Herb (Leon Herbert Jones, Jr)   Painter, Printmaker
Knorr, Jeanne Boardman   Craftsman, Educator
Lesley, Parker   Art Historian, Museum Curator
Lewis, Don S, Sr   Art Dealer, Painter
Lewis, Donald Sykes, Jr   Art Historian, Art Dealer
Matson, Elina   Weaver
Matson, Greta (Greta Matson Khouri)   Painter
Zafran, Eric Myles   Curator, Art Historian
Zetlin, Fay (Florence Anshen Zetlin)   Painter

Portsmouth

Sibley, Charles Kenneth   Painter, Educator

Powhatan

Binford, Julien   Painter, Sculptor

Reston

Drewes, Werner   Painter, Printmaker
Mahlmann, John James   Art Administrator

Richmond

Apgar, Nicolas Adam   Painter, Educator
Archer, Edmund   Painter
Bedno, Edward   Designer, Educator

Brandt, Frederick Robert Printmaker, Museum Exhibition Director
Brown, Catharine Homan Potter
Bumgardner, James Arliss Painter, Educator
Campbell, Jewett Educator, Painter
Cossitt, Franklin D Sculptor, Art Editor
DePillars, Murry N Art Administrator, Illustrator
Desmidt, Thomas H Painter, Educator
Freed, David Printmaker, Painter
Gaines, William Robert Art Historian, Painter
Haynes, George Edward Painter, Illustrator
Hompson, Davi Det (David Elbridge Thompson) Conceptual Artist
Ipsen, Kent Forrest Glassworker, Educator
Johnson, Charles W, Jr Art Historian, Educator
Kevorkian, Richard Painter
Klein, Beatrice T Painter, Printmaker
MacNelly, Jeffrey Kenneth Cartoonist
Martin, Bernard Murray Painter
Mavroudis, Demetrios Sculptor, Educator
McKennis, Gail Printmaker, Painter
Mooz, R Peter Museum Director
Perry, Regenia Alfreda Art Historian
Pollak, Theresa Educator, Painter
Thompson, Nancy Kunkle Goldsmith, Educator
Van Winkle, Lester G Sculptor, Educator
Welch, James Wymore Painter

Roanoke

Yeatts, James McKinney Art Dealer, Painter

Springfield

Hoffman, Helen Bacon Painter

Staunton

Desportes, Ulysse Gandvier Painter, Art Historian

Sterling

Criquette (Ruth DuBarry Montague) Painter, Writer

Suffolk

Godwin, Judith Whitney Painter, Designer

Urbanna

Genders, Richard Atherstone Painter, Designer

Vienna

Gonzales, Carlotta (Mrs Richard Lahey) Painter, Sculptor
Lahey, Richard (Francis) Painter, Lecturer
Summerford, Ben Long Painter, Educator

Warrenton

Hara, Teruo Potter, Sculptor

Williamsburg

Baker, Grace Painter
Roseberg, Carl Andersson Sculptor, Art Historian
Rumford, Beatrix Tyson Art Administrator

WASHINGTON

Anacortes

McCracken, Philip Sculptor

Bainbridge Island

Willis, Elizabeth Bayley Art Historian, Collector

Bellevue

Carter, Dudley Christopher Sculptor
Levine, Reeva (Anna) Miller Painter, Instructor
Reese, William Foster Painter
Warsinske, Norman George, Jr Sculptor, Painter

Bellingham

Hanson, Lawrence Sculptor, Educator
Johnston, Thomas Alix Printmaker, Painter
Marsh, David Foster Educator, Painter

Bothell

Peck, James Edward Painter, Designer

Chelan

Cox, John Rogers Painter

Cheney

Sage, Bill B Ceramist, Educator

Eastsound

Bevlin, Marjorie Elliott Painter, Writer

Edmonds

Marshall, John Carl Craftsman

Ellensburg

Sahlstrand, James Michael Photographer, Educator
Sahlstrand, Margaret Ahrens Printmaker, Craftsman
Spurgeon, Sarah (Edna M) Painter, Educator

Fpo Seattle

Block, Joyce Calligrapher, Instructor

Grapeview

Hoover, John Jay Sculptor, Painter

Issaquah

Skelly, Barbara Jean Designer, Enamelist, Metalsmith

La Conner

Anderson, Guy Irving Painter

Long Beach

Callahan, Kenneth Painter

Mercer Island

Correa, Flora Horst Painter

Moses Lake

Tse, Stephen Instructor, Painter

Olympia

Haseltine, James Lewis Art Administrator, Painter
Haseltine, Maury (Margaret Wilson Haseltine) Painter
Hopkins, Kenneth R Museum Director, Art Administrator

Poulsbo

Ewald, Louis Painter, Designer

Preston

Wright, G Alan Sculptor

Pullman

Coates, Ross Alexander Art Historian, Painter
Monaghan, Keith Painter, Educator

Reardan

Chester, Charlotte Wanetta Painter, Printmaker

Renton

Arnautoff, Jacob Victor Sculptor, Painter

Seattle

Acker, Perry Miles Painter, Educator
Alps, Glen Earl Educator, Printmaker
Anderson, Gordon Sculptor, Designer
Arnold, Richard R Designer, Painter
Banks, Virginia Painter
Bravmann, Rene A Art Historian, Educator
Bush, Beverly Painter, Sculptor
Celentano, Francis Michael Painter
Clark, Sarah Ann Curator, Lecturer
Cowles, Charles Curator, Collector
Dailey, Michael Dennis Painter, Educator
Du Pen, Everett George Sculptor, Educator
Eckstein, Joanna Collector, Patron
Foster, Donald Isle Art Dealer
Goldberg, Joseph Wallace Painter
Gonzales, Boyer Painter, Educator
Gray, Marie Elise Painter
Grove, Richard Museum Director, Writer
Harrington, La Mar Art Administrator, Art Historian
Herard, Marvin T Sculptor, Educator
Holm, Bill Art Historian, Curator
Horiuchi, Paul Painter
Johnson, Pauline B Educator, Writer
Jones, Robert Cushman Painter
Kenny, Bettie Ilene Cruts (BIK) Painter, Writer
Kirsten-Daiensai, Richard Charles Painter, Printmaker
Kohler, Mel (Otto) Art Dealer
Kottler, Howard William Sculptor, Educator
Kuvshinoff, Bertha Horne Painter
Kuvshinoff, Nicolai Painter, Sculptor
Lawrence, Jacob Painter, Educator
Lynch, Jo (Marilyn Blanche) Painter, Illustrator
Maki, Robert Richard Sculptor
Mason, Alden C Painter, Educator
Mendoza, David C Art Dealer, Art Writer
Moseley, Spencer Altemont Painter, Educator
Nadalini, (Louis Ernest) Painter
Pacific, Gertrude Painter, Designer
Portmann, Frieda Bertha Anne Painter, Sculptor
Praczukowski, Edward Leon Painter, Educator
Rapp, Ebba (Ebba Rapp McLauchlan) Sculptor, Painter
Rising, Dorothy Milne Painter, Illustrator
Ritchie, William Printmaker, Video Artist
Sawada, Ikune Painter
Seders, Francine Lavinal Art Dealer
Selig, Mr & Mrs Manfred Collectors, Patrons
Spafford, Michael Charles Educator, Painter
Sperry, Robert Ceramist, Film Maker
Thiry, Paul (Albert) Architect, Collector
Thomas, Ed B Educator, Lecturer
Trubner, Henry Art Historian
Tsutakawa, George Sculptor, Painter
Vaness, Margaret Helen Painter, Printmaker
Warashina, M Patricia Ceramic Sculptor, Educator
Washington, James W, Jr Painter, Sculptor
Wehr, Wesley Conrad Painter
Woods, Willis Franklin Museum Director
Woodside, Gordon William Art Dealer, Collector

WASHINGTON (cont)

Spokane

Adkison, Kathleen (Gemberling) Painter
Askman, Tom K Painter, Educator
Fleckenstein, Opal R Painter, Educator
Patnode, J Scott Printmaker, Lecturer

Steilacoom

Grigor, Margaret Christian Sculptor
Schwidder, Ernst Carl Sculptor, Designer

Tacoma

Johnson, Kenn Elmer Painter, Curator
Kowalek, Jon W Museum Director, Lecturer
McGrath, James Arthur Art Administrator, Painter
Moe, Richard D Art Administrator
Rennels, Frederic M Sculptor

Vancouver

Hansen, James Lee Sculptor

Wenatchee

Graham, Walter Painter, Sculptor

Wilkeson

Uthco, T R (John Emil Hillding) Sculptor

WEST VIRGINIA

Charleston

Atkins, Rosalie Marks Painter
Black, Mary McCune Curator, Painter
Blumberg, Barbara Griffiths Painter, Instructor
Cain, James Frederick, Jr Printmaker, Museum Curator
Keane, Lucina Mabel Painter, Printmaker
McNamara, Raymond Edmund Printmaker, Painter
Taylor, Grace Martin Painter, Educator

Elkins

Reed, Jesse Floyd Painter, Printmaker

Fairmont

Smigocki, Stephen Vincent Printmaker, Graphic Artist

Harpers Ferry

Preissler, Audrey Painter

Huntington

Emerson, Roberta Shinn Museum Director
Ettling, Ruth (Droitcour) Printmaker, Painter
Hage, Raymond Joseph Art Dealer, Collector
Polan, Lincoln M Collector
Polan, Nancy Moore Painter

Morgantown

Couch, Urban Painter, Educator
Petersen, Will Printmaker, Art Writer

Parkersburg

Burnside, Katherine Talbott Painter

Saint Albans

Keeling, Henry Cornelious Painter, Educator

Wheeling

Peace, Bernie (Kinzel) Painter

Williamstown

Gerhold, William Henry Painter, Educator
Sheng, Shao Fang Painter, Craftsman

WISCONSIN

Appleton

Livingstone, Biganess Painter, Educator
Thrall, Arthur Printmaker, Educator

Barneveld

Weege, William Printmaker, Educator

Beloit

Boggs, Franklin Painter, Educator
Malsch, Ellen L Painter, Instructor
Olson, Richard W Educator, Painter
Williams, Lewis W, II Art Historian

Blanchardville

Zweerts, Arnold Painter, Educator

Colgate

Jensen, Dean N Art Writer, Art Critic

Dane

Anderson, Donald Myers Art Writer, Calligrapher

Ellison Bay

Austin, Phil Painter, Lecturer

Evansville

Wilde, John Painter, Educator

Fish Creek

Becker, Bettie (Bettie Geraldine Wathall) Painter

Glendale

Gruen, Shirley Schanen Painter

Hollandale

Colescott, Warrington W Printmaker, Educator
Myers, Frances Printmaker

Jackson

White, Doris A Painter

Janesville

Williams, Marylou Lord Study Museum Director, Painter

Kenosha

Goray, John C Painter, Instructor

Lake Geneva

Herr, Richard Joseph Sculptor, Instructor
Salter, Richard Mackintire Painter, Photographer

Madison

Bohrod, Aaron Painter, Educator
Breckenridge, Bruce M Ceramic Artist, Educator
Butts, Porter Art Historian, Art Administrator
Byrd, D Gibson Educator, Painter
Handler, Audrey Glass Artist, Educator
High, Freida Printmaker, Educator
Kreilick, Marjorie E Mosaic Artist, Educator
Logan, Frederick Manning Educator, Writer
Lotterman, Hal Painter, Educator
McCready, Eric Scott Museum Director, Art Historian
Meeker, Dean Jackson Printmaker, Painter
Overland, Carlton Edward Curator, Art Historian
Starks, Elliott Roland Art Administrator, Educator
Tomlinson, Florence Kidder Painter
Watrous, James Scales Painter, Art Historian
Weiss, Lee (Elyse C Weiss) Painter
Wiedenhoeft-Wesler, Anita Kae Metalsmith

Marinette

La Malfa, James Thomas Sculptor, Educator

Mazomanie

Massaro, Karen Thuesen Ceramist, Sculptor

Menomonie

Fumagalli, Barbara Merrill Printmaker, Illustrator
Fumagalli, Orazio Educator
Hannibal, Joseph Harry Educator, Printmaker

Milwaukee

Auer, James Matthew Art Critic, Writer
Balsley, John Gerald Painter, Sculptor
Berman, Fred J Painter, Photographer
Bradley, Dorothy Art Dealer, Painter
Bradley, Mrs Harry Lynde Collector
Brink, Guido Peter Painter, Sculptor
Brulc, Dennis Printmaker, Painter
Burkert, Robert Randall Painter, Printmaker
Colt, John Nicholson Painter, Educator
Danoff, I Michael Curator, Art Historian
Flagg, Mr & Mrs Richard B Collectors
Goodrich, Susan Painter
Green, Edward Anthony Art Director, Designer
Grotenrath, Ruth Painter
Henning, Paul Harvey Photographer, Art Dealer
Kaiser, Charles James Painter
Kao, Ruth (Yu-Hsin) Lee Fiber Artist, Educator
Key, Donald D Art Critic, Writer
Kohl, Barbara Collector, Painter
Lacktman, Michael Educator, Designer
Luntz, Irving Art Dealer
Melamed, Abraham Collector, Patron
Meredith, Dorothy Laverne Weaver, Educator
Nordland, Gerald John Gallery Director, Art Critic
Ozonoff, Ida Painter
Pierce, Danny P Sculptor, Printmaker
Posner, Judith L Art Dealer, Collector
Priebe, Karl Painter
Rahill, Margaret Fish Curator, Art Critic
Revor, Remy Designer, Educator
Rosenblatt, Adolph Painter, Sculptor
Rosenblatt, Suzanne Maris Painter, Draftsman
Schellin, Robert William Painter, Educator
Sister Thomasita (Mary Thomasita Fessler) Sculptor, Educator
Stonebarger, Virginia Painter, Instructor
Summ, Helmut Painter, Educator
Taylor, John Lloyd Art Critic, Art Administrator
Travanti, Leon Emidio Painter, Designer
Uttech, Thomas Martin Painter, Educator

Mount Horeb

Hamady, Walter Samuel Graphic Artist, Papermaker
Laird, Mary (Mary Laird Hamady) Graphic Artist, Illustrator

Oshkosh

Donhauser, Paul Stefan Sculptor

Platteville

Ross, James Matthew Educator, Painter

Racine

Bogucki (Edwin Arnold Bogucki) Sculptor, Painter
Johansen, Robert Painter
Mathis, Emile Henry, II Art Dealer, Collector
Richard, George Mairet Museum Director
Rozman, Joseph John Painter, Printmaker

Ripon

Breithaupt, Erwin M Educator, Art Historian

Sheboygan

Kohler, Ruth DeYoung Museum Director, Curator

Waukesha

Penkoff, Ronald Peter Educator, Printmaker

Whitewater

Yasko, Caryl Anne Muralist

WYOMING

Byron

Hopkinson, Harold I Painter, Collector

Casper

Goedicke, Jean Painter, Instructor
Naegle, Stephen Howard Painter, Sculptor

Cheyenne

Hayes, Laura M Curator, Art Historian
Paulley, David Gordon Painter

Cody

Fillerup, Mel Painter
Hassrick, Peter H Museum Director, Art Historian
Hopkinson, Glen Spencer Painter, Sculptor
Jackson, Harry Andrew Painter, Sculptor
McCracken, Harold Art Administrator, Art Historian

Jackson Hole

Kerswill, J W Roy Painter
Schwiering, Conrad Painter

Laramie

Berg, Thomas Painter
Berger, Jerry Allen Curator
Deaderick, Joseph Painter, Educator
Evans, Richard Painter, Educator
Flach, Victor H Designer, Writer
Forrest, James Taylor Museum Director, Art Historian
Mueller, Henrietta Waters Painter, Sculptor
Russin, Robert I Sculptor, Educator

Rock Springs

Halseth, Elmer Johann Patron, Collector
Kenney, Allen Lloyd Educator, Museum Director

Sheridan

Bolinger, Truman Sculptor
Martinsen, Ivar Richard Painter, Educator

Story

Smyth, Ed Illustrator, Painter

Teton Village

Clymer, John F Painter, Illustrator

Wapiti

Bama, James E Painter

PUERTO RICO

Aguadilla

Loro, Anthony Pivotto Art Dealer, Painter

Catano

Dirube, Rolando Lopez Painter, Sculptor

Miramar

Homar, Lorenzo Printmaker, Painter

Ponce

Balmaceda, Margarita S Educator, Art Writer
Micheli, Julio Painter, Printmaker
Taylor, Rene Claude Museum Director

Rio Piedras

Balossi, John Sculptor, Painter
Batista, Tomas Sculptor, Instructor
Buscaglia, Jose Sculptor
Delano, Jack Illustrator, Photographer
Fontanez, Carmelo Painter, Educator
Hernandez-Cruz, Luis Painter, Educator

San German

Carrero, Jaime Painter, Instructor

San Juan

Alicea, Jose Printmaker
Irizarry, Carlos Painter, Printmaker
Marin, Augusto Painter, Educator
Marrozzini, Luigi Art Dealer
Molina, Antonio J Painter, Art Critic
Rodriguez-Morales, Luis Manuel Art Administrator, Educator
Romano, Jaime (Luis) Painter
Yrizarry, Marcos Painter, Graphic Artist

VIRGIN ISLANDS

Christiansted

Baringer, Richard E Painter, Designer

Saint Croix

Caimite (Lynne Ruskin) Painter, Illustrator
Hawes, Charles Painter, Illustrator

Saint John

Low, Joseph Painter, Printmaker

CANADA

ALBERTA

Banff

Leighton, David S R Art Administrator

Calgary

Atkins, Gordon Lee Designer, Architect
Chalke, John Ceramist, Sculptor
Dodd, Eric M Gallery Director, Educator
Esler, John Kenneth Printmaker
Gilhooly, David James, III Sculptor
Hall, John (Scott) Educator, Painter
Hushlak, Gerald Marshall Painter
Kostyniuk, Ronald P Sculptor, Educator
Mabie, Don Edward Mixed-Media Artist, Painter
Mignosa, Santo Ceramist, Sculptor
Ohe, Katie (Minna) Sculptor, Instructor
O'Neil, Bruce William Painter, Instructor
Pfeifer, Bodo Painter, Sculptor
Roukes, Nicholas M Kinetic Artist, Writer
Sawai, Noboru Printmaker, Educator
Snow, John Printmaker, Painter
Spickett, Ronald John, (Sr) Painter, Instructor
Will, John A Printmaker, Painter
Will, Mary Shannon Ceramist, Instructor
Zimon, Kathy Elizabeth Art Librarian

Edmonton

Cantine, David Painter
Cardinal, Douglas Joseph Henry Architect
Darrah, Ann Clarke Lecturer, Painter
Davey, Ronald A Art Historian, Educator
Dmytruk, Ihor Painter
Haynes, Douglas H Painter, Educator
Knowlton, Jonathan Painter
Manarey, Thelma Alberta Printmaker, Painter
Voyer, Sylvain Jacques Painter
Weaver, John Barney Sculptor

Lethbridge

Beny, Roloff Photographer, Writer

BRITISH COLUMBIA

Burnaby

Shadbolt, Jack Leonard Painter

Campbell River

Andrews, Sybil (Sybil Andrews Morgan) Graphic Artist

Chase

Crittenden, John William Neil Painter, Printmaker

Duncan

Hughes, Edward John Painter

Nelson

Emery, Charles Anthony Gallery Director

North Vancouver

Baxter, Iain Environmental Artist, Designer
Baxter, Ingrid Gallery Director
Harman, Jack Kenneth Sculptor, Educator
Perry, Frank Sculptor
Peter, Friedrich Gunther Calligrapher, Educator

BRITISH COLUMBIA (cont)

Port Washington

Glyde, Henry George   Painter, Educator

Richmond

Reid, (William) Richard   Painter

Valemount

Dyson, John Holroyd   Painter

Vancouver

Balkind, Alvin Louis   Fine Arts Curator
Dwyer, Melva Jean   Art Librarian, Art Historian
Falk, Gathie   Sculptor, Painter
Fish, Robert (Robert James Field)   Sculptor, Educator
Flakey Rose Hip (Glenn Alun Lewis)   Designer, Sculptor
Guderna, Ladislav   Painter, Illustrator
Jarvis, Donald   Painter, Instructor
Kanee, Ben   Collector
Knox, George   Art Historian
Korner, John (John Michael Anthony Koerner)   Painter
Longstaffe, John Ronald   Collector
Morris, Michael   Painter
Murraygreen, Ryan   Painter, Paper Artist
Onley, Toni   Painter
Prince, Richard Edmund   Sculptor, Educator
Rimmer, David McLellan   Film Artist
Sawyer, Alan R   Art Consultant
Sjolseth, Minn Solveig   Painter, Printmaker
Thorne, Gordon (Kit)   Painter, Designer
Urquhart, Tony   Sculptor, Painter
Young, Robert John   Painter

Victoria

Bates, Maxwell Bennett   Painter, Lithographer
Gore, Tom   Curator, Photographer
Harvey, Donald   Painter, Lecturer
Jorgensen, Flemming   Painter
Lansdowne, James Fenwick   Painter
Mayhew, Elza   Sculptor
Page, Robin   Painter
Segger, Martin Joseph   Art Historian, Museum Director
Siebner, Herbert (Vom Siebenstein)   Painter, Muralist
Skelton, Robin   Art Writer, Collage Artist
Sward, Robert S   Writer, Art Editor

West Vancouver

Bell, Alistair Macready   Printmaker, Painter
Davidson, Ian J   Collector, Patron
Edwards, Allan W   Collector, Illustrator
Felter, James Warren   Painter, Curator
Jones, Bill   Painter, Assemblage Artist
Koochin, William   Sculptor, Instructor
Lennie, Beatrice E C   Sculptor, Designer
Norris, Leonard Matheson   Cartoonist, Illustrator
Smith, Gordon   Painter
Thomas, Lionel Arthur John   Painter, Sculptor
Willer, Jim   Sculptor, Painter

Westbank

Lyon, Harold Lloyd   Painter

Winlaw

Foulger, Richard F   Serigrapher, Painter

MANITOBA

Fort Garry

Hammer, Alfred Emil   Painter, Art Administrator

Saint Boniface

Tascona, Antonio Tony   Painter, Sculptor

Winnipeg

Bigger, Michael Dinsmore   Sculptor, Instructor
Davis, Ann   Curator, Art Historian
ECKHARDT, Ferdinand   Art 'istorian, Museum Director
Eyre, Ivan   Painter, Sculptor
Head, George Bruce   Painter, Designer
Leathers, Winston Lyle   Painter, Printmaker
Mol, Leo   Sculptor
Reichert, Donald Karl   Painter, Educator
Smith, Ernest John   Architect, Designer
Swinton, George   Painter, Writer
Tillenius, Clarence (Ingwall)   Painter, Writer
Warkov, Esther   Painter

NEW BRUNSWICK

Fredericton

Donaldson, Marjory (Rogers)   Curator, Painter
Lumsden, Ian Gordon   Curator

Moncton

Clermont, Ghislain   Art Historian, Art Critic
Roussel, Claude Patrice   Sculptor, Instructor

Sackville

Adams, Glenn Nelson   Painter
Hammock, Virgil Gene   Educator, Painter

Saint John

Ross, Fred (Joseph)   Painter, Instructor

NEWFOUNDLAND

Ferryland

Squires, Gerald Leopold   Painter, Educator

Saint Catherine's

Pratt, Mary Frances   Painter

Saint John's

Bell, Peter Alan   Painter, Art Critic
Perlin, Rae   Painter

Tors Cove

Lapointe, Frank   Painter, Printmaker

NORTHWEST TERRITORIES

Cape Dorset

Kenojuak (Kenojuak Ashevak)   Printmaker, Sculptor

NOVA SCOTIA

Bridgetown

Tolmie, Kenneth Donald   Painter, Illustrator

Canning

Metson, Graham   Painter, Art Historian

Cherry Hill

Greer, John Sydney   Sculptor

Chester Basin

Croft, Lewis Scott   Painter

Dartmouth

Forrestall, Thomas De Vany   Sculptor, Painter

Halifax

Berlind, Robert   Painter
Brownhill, Harold   Painter, Illustrator
Cameron, Eric   Art Administrator, Painter
Fernandes, Michael Adrian   Painter, Instructor
Fraser, Carol Hoorn   Painter
Hofman, Kate   Art Dealer, Collector
Jackson, Sarah   Sculptor, Graphic Artist
Law, C Anthony   Painter
Lindgren, Charlotte   Weaver
Mackay, Donald Cameron   Painter, Art Historian
Murchie, Donald John   Art Librarian
Tucker, William G   Art Writer, Sculptor
Zwicker, Leroy Judson   Painter

Kentville

Fox, Charles Harold   Craftsman
Fox, Winifred Grace   Craftsman, Painter

Liverpool

Savage, Roger   Painter, Printmaker

Mabou

Leaf, June   Painter, Sculptor

Mahone Bay

Larson, Orland   Goldsmith, Designer

Peggy's Cove

de Garthe, William Edward   Painter, Sculptor

Sydney

Mould, Lola Frowde   Painter

Tatamagouche

Zarand, Julius John   Painter, Restorer

Wolfville

Colville, Alexander   Painter, Printmaker

Yarmouth

Pierce, Elizabeth R   Painter

ONTARIO

Alexandria

Harper, John Russell   Art Historian

Alton

Nevitt, Richard Barrington Educator, Illustrator

Ancaster

Panabaker, Frank S Painter

Ayton

Roberts, William Griffith Painter

Barrie

Stuart, Donald Alexander Designer/Craftsman, Instructor

Burlington

Mansaram, Panchal Collage Artist, Photographer

Caledon East

Hogbin, Stephen James Sculptor

Campbellville

Hanson, Jean (Mrs Jean Elphick) Painter, Designer

Carlisle

Brender a Brandis, Gerard William Printmaker, Illustrator

Don Mills

Bayefsky, Aba Painter, Printmaker

Dundas

Holbrook, Elizabeth Bradford Sculptor

Gananoque

Russell, John Laurel Art Dealer, Collector

Grimsby

Lukas, Dennis Brian Painter, Educator

Guelph

Bachinski, Walter Joseph Sculptor, Printmaker
Chu, Gene Printmaker, Lecturer
Yerex, Elton Painter, Educator

Hamilton

Courtney, Keith Townsend Curator
Cumming, Glen Edward Museum Director
MacDonald, Thomas Reid Painter
Rabinowitch, David Sculptor

Ingersoll

Crawford, Catherine Betty Painter

Kingston

Aird, Neil Carrick Goldsmith, Designer
Allen, Ralph Painter, Educator
Andrew, David Neville Painter, Educator
Bieler, Andre Charles Painter, Printmaker
Dorn, Peter Klaus Designer
Finley, Gerald Eric Art Historian
Heywood, J Carl Painter, Printmaker
Hodgson, Trevor Painter, Photographer
Macdonald, Grant Painter, Illustrator
Polzer, Joseph Art Historian
Schonberger, Fred Painter, Sculptor
Travers, Gwyneth Mabel Printmaker

Kitchener

Goetz, Peter Henry Painter, Lecturer

Locust Hill

Bieler, Ted Andre Educator, Sculptor

London

Ariss, Herbert Joshua Painter, Illustrator
Barrio-Garay, Jose Luis Art Administrator, Art Historian
Becker, Helmut Julius Printmaker
Bice, Clare Art Administrator, Painter
Chambers, John Painter, Film Maker
Dale, William Scott Abell Art Historian
De Kergommeaux, Duncan Painter, Educator
Lorcini, Gino Sculptor
Messer, Brenda Ruth Slide Curator

MacDonald's Corners

Reitzenstein, Reinhard Environmental Artist

Milton

Bateman, Robert McLellan Painter

Mississauga

Bakken, Haakon Art Administrator, Jeweler
Broomfield, Adolphus George Painter, Designer
La Pierre, Thomas Painter, Printmaker
McKinley, Donald Lloyd Educator, Designer
McKinley, Ruth Gowdy Ceramist, Designer
Sabelis, Huibert Collector, Painter

Newmarket

Hall, John A Painter, Educator

Niagara On The Lake

Jones, Jacobine Sculptor
Scott, Campbell Printmaker, Sculptor

Oakville

Chesterton, David Educator, Graphic Artist

Odessa

Holmes, David Bryan Painter

Oshawa

Hilts, Alvin Sculptor

Ottawa

Betteridge, Lois Etherington Silver & Goldsmith, Lecturer
Boggs, Jean Sutherland Museum Director, Art Historian
Borcoman, James Curator
Boyd, James Henderson Printmaker, Sculptor
Burnett, David Grant Art Historian, Art Critic
Cohen, Lynne G Photographer, Lecturer
Coughtry, John Graham Painter, Sculptor
Dickson, Jennifer Joan Photographer, Printmaker
Emori, Eiko Graphic Designer
Groves, Naomi Jackson Writer, Painter
Harris, Lawren Phillips Painter, Educator
Hubbard, Robert Hamilton Art Historian
Hyde, Laurence Painter, Designer
James, Geoffrey Art Administrator
Karsh, Yousuf Photographer
Laskin, Myron, Jr Curator, Art Historian
MacDonald, Colin Somerled Writer, Publisher
Masson, Henri Painter
Ostiguy, Jean-Rene Painter, Curator
Schoeler, Paul Jean Rene Architect
Smith, Gord Sculptor, Painter
Stolow, Nathan Art Conservator, Lecturer
Sylvestre, Guy Art Critic, Writer
Taylor, Mary Cazort Curator, Art Historian
Tolgesy, Victor Sculptor
Vermette, Luce Art Critic, Art Historian
Wyse, Alexander John Painter, Sculptor

Peterborough

Bierk, David Charles Painter, Gallery Director
Nind, Jean Painter, Printmaker

Pickering

Semak, Michael Photographer, Educator

Pointe-Au-Baril

Lumbers, James Richard Painter, Designer

Port Credit

Roberts, Thomas (Kieth) Painter

Port Hope

Blackwood, David (Lloyd) Painter, Printmaker.

Rexdale

Kramolc, Theodore Maria Painter, Designer

Rockwood

Mitchell, Beresford Strickland Designer, Illustrator

St Catharines

Harris, Alfred Peter Painter, Art Administrator

Scarborough

McCarthy, Doris Jean Painter, Instructor

Stratford

Green, Art Painter
Swain, Robert Francis Gallery Director

Tamworth

Saxe, Henry Sculptor

Thornhill

MacDonald, Thoreau Illustrator, Designer

Toronto

Aarons, Anita Craftsman, Art Critic
Aldwinckle, Eric Designer, Painter
Altwerger, Libby Painter, Graphic Artist
Arbuckle, Franklin Painter, Illustrator
Astman, Barbara Anne Photographer, Multi-Media Artist
Banz, George Writer, Architect
Barrett, Barbara Art Administrator, Painter
Barry, Anne Meredith Printmaker, Instructor
Bell, Philip Michael Art Administrator, Art Historian
Bell, R Murray Collector
Birnberg, Gerald H Art Dealer
Birnberg, Ruth Carrel Art Dealer
Blazeje, Zbigniew Sculptor, Painter
Bodolai, Joseph Stephen Film Maker, Sculptor
Bronson, A A (Michael Wayne Tims) Post-Conceptual Artist, Writer
Campbell, Colin Keith Video Artist
Carr-Harris, Ian Redford Sculptor, Photographer
Cattell, Ray Painter, Art Director
Clark, Paraskeva Painter
Collier, Alan Caswell Painter
Dagys, Jacob Sculptor
Daly, Kathleen (Kathleen Daly Pepper) Painter
Danby, Ken Painter, Printmaker

ONTARIO (cont)

De Pedery-Hunt, Dora Sculptor, Designer
Deutsch, Peter Andrew Painter
Diamond, Abel Joseph Designer, Architect
Dimson, Theo Aeneas Designer
Drutz, June Painter, Educator
DuBois, Macy Architect, Art Critic
Duff, Ann MacIntosh Painter, Printmaker
Engel, Walter F Art Critic, Art Dealer
Etrog, Sorel Sculptor, Painter
Ewen, Paterson Painter, Educator
Favro, Murray Mixed-Media Artist, Painter
Filipovic, Augustin Sculptor, Painter
Fleisher, Pat Art Critic, Artist
Fleming, Allan Robb Designer, Calligrapher
Fournier, Alexander Paul Painter, Printmaker
Freifeld, Eric Painter, Educator
Gage, Frances M Sculptor
Gale, Peggy Art Writer
Gauthier, Joachim George Painter
Goldhamer, Charles Painter
Graham, K M Painter
Gregor, Helen Frances Designer, Educator
Hagan, (Robert) Frederick Printmaker, Painter
Harding, Noel Robert Video Artist, Environmental Artist
Haworth, B Cogill (Mrs Peter Haworth) Painter
Heath, David Martin Educator, Photographer
Holmes, Reginald Painter, Photographer
Horne, (Arthur Edward) Cleeve Painter, Sculptor
Housser, Yvonne McKague Painter, Designer
Isaacs, Avrom Art Dealer
Iskowitz, Gershon Painter
Joy, Nancy Grahame Illustrator, Educator
Kaye, David Haigh Textile Artist, Designer
Kinoshita, Gene Architect
Kopmanis, Augusts A Sculptor
Kravis, Janis Designer, Architect
Kramer, Burton Designer
Kurelek, William Painter
Lamanna, Carmen Art Dealer, Art Restorer
Lee, Raymond Man Designer, Lecturer
Letendre, Rita Painter
Luz, Virginia Painter
MacGregor, John Boyko Painter, Art Administrator
MacKenzie, Hugh Seaforth Painter
Mah, Peter Painter, Instructor
Manning, Jo Printmaker
Markle, Jack M Art Dealer, Sculptor
Markle, Sam Art Dealer, Sculptor
Martin, Bernice Fenwick Painter, Printmaker
Martin, Langton Painter, Printmaker
Martin, Ron Painter
McElcheran, William Hodd Designer, Sculptor
McGeoch, Lillian Jean Painter, Sculptor
Meredith, John Painter
Miezajs, Dainis Painter, Instructor
Milrad, Aaron M Collector, Art Lawyer
Mirvish, David Art Dealer
Mochizuki, Betty Ayako Painter
Moos, Walter A Art Dealer
Motter, Dean Roger Illustrator, Designer
Nakamura, Kazuo Painter
Neddeau, Donald Frederick Price Painter, Designer
Newman, John Beatty Painter, Instructor
Oesterle, Leonhard Freidrich Sculptor, Educator
Ogilvie, Will (William Abernethy) Painter
Partridge, David Gerry Painter, Sculptor
Pehap, Erich K Painter, Graphic Artist
Perkins, A Alan Printmaker, Enamelist
Pigott, Marjorie Painter
Popescu, Cara Sculptor, Painter
Reeves, John Alexander Photographer
Ronald, William Painter
Rutherford, Erica Painter
Sandberg, Hannah Painter, Educator
Schaefer, Carl Fellman Painter
Sime, John Art Administrator
Simon, Ellen R Designer, Stained Glass Artist
Sing Hoo (Sing Hoo Yuen) Sculptor, Painter
Sisler, Rebecca Sculptor, Art Administrator
Snow, Michael Painter, Film Maker
Solomon, Daniel Painter
Steele, Lisa Video Artist
Steiger, Frederic Painter
Takashima, Shizuye Violet Instructor, Painter
Thepot, Roger Francois Painter
Timmas, Osvald Painter
Town, Harold Barling Painter, Writer
Valius, Telesforas Graphic Artist
Van Ginkel, Blanche Lemco Architect, Educator
Vickers, George Stephen Educator
Vivenza, Francesca Graphic Artist, Painter
Watson, Sydney Hollinger Designer
Wattenmaker, Richard J Art Historian, Museum Director
White, Albert Art Dealer, Collector
White, Deborah Art Dealer
White, Norman Triplett Sculptor
Whiten, Colette Sculptor, Instructor
Wieland, Joyce Painter, Film Maker
Wiitasalo, Shirley Painter
Wilson, York Painter
Withrow, William J Art Administrator
Zeidler, Eberhard Heinrich Designer, Architect

Waterloo

Izumi, Kiyoshi Architect, Educator

Waubaushene

Gould, John Howard Painter, Film Maker

West Bay

Debassige, Blake R Illustrator, Painter

West Lorne

Redinger, Walter Fred Sculptor
Zelenak, Edward John Sculptor

Willowdale

Ebsen, Alf K Designer
Gilling, Lucille Printmaker
Jaworska, Tamara Painter, Designer
Robb, Charles (Charles Robert Bush) Painter

Windsor

Pufahl, John K Educator, Printmaker
Saltmarche, Kenneth Charles Painter, Art Administrator

PRINCE EDWARD ISLAND

Summerside East

Barton, Georgie Read Painter, Sculptor

QUEBEC

Baie-D'Urfe

Bouchard, Lorne Holland Painter, Illustrator

Chicoutimi

Villeneuve, Joseph Arthur Painter

Dollard Des Oreaux

Venor, Robert George Painter, Educator

Dorval

Daoust, Sylvia Sculptor
Simpkins, Henry John Painter, Illustrator

Hudson

Cosgrove, Stanley Painter
McLaren, Norman Film Maker

Hudson Heights

Braitstein, Marcel Sculptor, Educator

Lachine

Walsh, John Stanley Painter, Writer

Laval City

Pellan (Alfred) Painter

Longueuil

Goulet, Claude Educator, Painter

Matane

Picher, Claude Art Administrator, Painter

Mont St Hilaire

Bonet, Jordi Sculptor, Muralist
Tahedl, Ernestine Stained Glass Artist, Painter

Montreal

Almond, Paul Film Maker
Barry, Frank (Barry Francis Leopold) Painter, Educator
Beament, Harold Painter
Beament, Tib (Thomas Harold) Painter, Instructor
Besner, J Jacques Sculptor, Educator
Briansky, Rita Prezament Painter, Printmaker
Bruneau, Kittie Painter
Cardinal, Marcelin Painter
Chicoine, Rene Draftsman, Educator
Cleaver, Elizabeth Illustrator, Printmaker
Cooke, Edwy Francis Painter, Educator
Dansereau, Mireille Film Maker
Feist, Warner David Graphic Artist, Painter
Fox, John Painter
Gaucher, Yves Printmaker, Painter
Gerin-Lajoie, Guy Architect
Gersovitz, Sarah Valerie Printmaker, Painter
Gottschalk, Fritz Designer, Lecturer
Harder, Rolf Peter Designer, Painter
Hebert, Julien Sculptor, Designer
Jackson, Ruth Amelia Curator
Kahane, Anne Sculptor
Kwartler, Alexander Painter, Sculptor
Lacroix, Richard Painter, Printmaker
Lambert, Phyllis Architect, Collector
Lewis, Stanley Sculptor, Printmaker
London, Elca Art Dealer
McEwen, Jean Painter
Menses, Jan Painter, Printmaker
Molinari, Guido Painter, Sculptor
Morris, Kathleen Moir Painter
Muhlstock, Louis Painter
Pinsky, Alfred Painter, Educator
Prent, Mark Environmental Artist, Sculptor
Prezament, Joseph Painter
Roberts, (William) Goodridge Painter
Roch, Ernst Designer, Graphic Artist
Rostand, Michel Painter
Scott, Marian (Dale) Painter
Selchow, Roger Hoffman Painter, Sculptor
Steinhouse, Tobie (Thelma) Painter, Printmaker
Street, John Michael Painter
Surrey, Philip Henry Painter
Swartzman, Roslyn Printmaker, Educator
Tatossian, Armand Painter
Tinning, George Campbell Painter
Tousignant, Claude Painter, Instructor
Trudeau, Yves Sculptor
Vazan, William Joseph Conceptual Artist, Photographer
Vilder, Roger Kinetic Artist
Wheeler, Orson Shorey Sculptor, Lecturer

Nicolet

Mercier, Monique Painter, Tapestry Artist

Old Chelsea

Mason, William Clifford Film Maker, Painter

Outremont

Ferron, Marcelle Glass Artist
Jaque, Louis Painter

Perce

Guite, Suzanne Painter, Sculptor

Piedmont

Smith, John Ivor Sculptor, Educator

Portneuf

Beauchemin, Micheline Painter, Weaver

Quebec

Crouton, Francois (Francois LaFortune) Art Administrator, Photographer
Iacurto, Francesco Painter, Instructor
Lemieux, Irenee Painter
Plamondon, Marius Gerald Sculptor, Craftsman
Thibault, Claude Curator, Art Historian

Saint Agathe Des Monts

Miller, H McRae Sculptor, Painter

Saint Lambert

Archambault, Louis Sculptor, Educator

Sainte-Adele

Rousseau-Vermette, Marietta Tapestry Artist

Sherbrooke

Cantieni, Graham Alfred Painter, Art Administrator
Holcomb, Adele Mansfield Art Historian

Sillery

Lemieux, Jean Paul Painter

Terrebonne

Hurtubise, Jacques Painter

Val-Saint-Michel

Potvin, Daniel Painter, Glass Blower

Westmount

Caiserman-Roth, Ghitta Painter, Printmaker

SASKATCHEWAN

Craven

Cicansky, Victor Sculptor

Dundurn

Bentham, Douglas Wayne Sculptor

Lumsden

Nugent, John Cullen Sculptor, Educator

Moose Jaw

Mann, Vaughan (Vaughan Grayson) Painter, Printmaker

Pense

Fafard, Joe (Joseph Yvon) Sculptor

Regina

Dillow, Nancy E (Nancy Elizabeth Robertson) Art Administrator, Art Historian
Lee, Roger Educator, Curator
McKay, Arthur Fortescue Painter, Educator
Nulf, Frank Allen Painter, Educator
Zack, David Designer, Writer

Saskatoon

Bornstein, Eli Educator, Sculptor
Knowles, Dorothy Elsie (Dorothy Elsie Perehudoff) Painter
Lindner, Ernest Painter
Perehudoff, William W Painter
Rogers, Otto Donald Painter, Educator

Silton

Yuristy, Russell Michael Designer, Sculptor

OTHER COUNTRIES

AUSTRALIA

Kelly, William Joseph Educator, Painter
Samstag, Gordon Painter, Sculptor

BRITISH WEST INDES

Miller, Mariann (Mariann Helm) Painter

COLOMBIA

Betancourt, R Arenas Sculptor

DENMARK

Weisgard, Leonard Joseph Illustrator, Writer

ENGLAND

Aliki (Aliki Brandenberg) Illustrator, Writer
Baskin, Leonard Sculptor, Graphic Artist
Blake, John Clemens Filmmaker
Cottingham, Robert Painter
Cowles, Fleur Painter, Writer
Fassett, Kaffe Havrah Painter, Textile Constructor
Gablik, Suzi Writer, Painter
Hubbard, John Painter
Lijn, Liliane Sculptor, Art Writer
Muensterberger, Werner Collector, Writer
Smith, Hassel W, Jr Painter

FRANCE

Benoit, Jean Sculptor, Conceptual Artist
Biala, Janice Painter
Brustlein, Daniel Painter
Chase-Riboud, Barbara Dewayne Sculptor, Draftsman
Crotto, Paul Painter, Sculptor
Diska Sculptor
Gysin, Brion Painter
Hicks, Sheila Tapestry Artist
Kerkovius, Ruth Painter
Koenig, John Franklin Painter
Levee, John H Painter, Sculptor
Masurovsky, Gregory Draftsman, Printmaker
Parker, Bill Painter
Pfriem, Bernard Painter
Spencer, Eleanor Patterson Writer, Art Historian
Stoianovich, Marcelle Painter
Truex, Van Day Painter, Designer

GERMANY, FEDERAL REPUBLIC OF

Bowers, Lynn Chuck Painter
Brecht, George Conceptual Artist, Assemblage Artist
Iannone, Dorothy Painter
Kanovitz, Howard Painter
Swarzenski, Hanns Peter Theophil Art Historian, Writer

GREECE

Ford, Charles Henri Painter, Photographer

GUATEMALA

Nichols, Dale William Writer, Designer

INDIA

Morley, Grace L McCann Museologist, Writer

IRELAND

Baer, Jo Painter, Writer
Brady, Charles Michael Painter

ISRAEL

Alexenberg, Melvin (Menahem) Educator, Painter

ITALY

Baxter, Robert James Painter
Buba, Joy Flinsch Sculptor, Illustrator
Congdon, William (Grosvenor) Painter
Cook, Robert Howard Sculptor
d'Almeida, George Painter

ITALY (cont)
DeLuigi, Janice Cecilia Sculptor, Painter
De Tolnay, Charles Art Historian, Writer
French, Jared Painter, Sculptor
Friscia, Albert Joseph Painter, Sculptor
Guggenheim, Peggy Collector, Patron
Hebald, Milton Elting Sculptor, Printmaker
Jones, Elizabeth Sculptor, Medalist
Lavatelli, Carla Sculptor, Weaver
Leong, James Chan Painter
Lionni, Leo Sculptor, Painter
Marinsky, Harry Sculptor, Painter
Noordhoek, Harry Cecil Sculptor, Painter
Pepper, Beverly Sculptor, Painter
Puccinelli, Raimondo Sculptor, Graphic Artist
Rockwell, Peter Barstow Sculptor, Lecturer
Schloss, Edith Painter, Art Critic
Schulthess, Amalia Sculptor, Painter
Selvig, Forrest Hall Art Historian, Writer
Smyth, Craig Hugh Art Administrator, Art Historian
Weinberg, Elbert Sculptor, Educator
Wells, Charles Arthur, Jr Sculptor

JAPAN

Kusama, Yayoi Sculptor, Painter

MALTA

Pick, John Art Administrator

MEXICO

Acuna, Victor Miguel Art Dealer
Amor, Ines Art Dealer
Anguiano, Raul Muralist, Painter
Angulo, Chappie Painter, Illustrator
Anzures, Rafael Educator, Art Critic
Aquino, Edmundo Painter, Printmaker
Baigts, Juan Art Writer, Lecturer
Baz, Marysole Worner Painter, Sculptor
Bejar, Feliciano Sculptor, Painter
Beraha, Enrique Misrachi Art Dealer
Bragar, Philip Frank Painter, Printmaker
Brooks, Frank Leonard Painter, Writer
Byron, Gene Painter, Designer
Cabrera, Geles Sculptor
Calderon, Juan Architect, Painter
Castro (Pacheco Fernando) Painter
Catlett, Elizabeth Sculptor, Printmaker
Cervantes, Pedro Sculptor
Cesar, Gaston Gonzalez Sculptor
Chavez-Morado, Jose Painter, Educator
Coen, Arnaldo Painter
Colina, Armando G Art Dealer
Coronel, Pedro Painter, Sculptor
Corzas, Francisco Painter, Printmaker
Costa, Olga Painter, Collector
Cruz, Hector Painter
Cuevas, Jose Luis Painter, Illustrator
de Kuper, Merle Portnoy Gallery Director
Dickinson, William Stirling Lecturer, Art Administrator
Donde, Olga Painter
Edie, Stuart Painter
Escobedo, Augusto Ortega Sculptor, Painter
Escobedo, Helen Environmental Sculptor
Felguerez, Manuel Painter, Sculptor
Friedeberg, Pedro Painter, Sculptor
Garcia Ponce, Fernando Painter
Gerzso, Gunther Painter
Giampaoli, James Francis Painter, Printmaker
Gironella, Alberto Painter, Illustrator
Goeritz, Mathias Sculptor, Designer
Gordon, Maxwell Painter
Gurria, Angela Sculptor
Herrera, Raul Othon Painter
Icaza (Francisco de Icaza) Painter, Sculptor
Joskowicz, Alfredo Film Maker, Art Critic
Kaspe, Vladimir Architect, Educator
Kestenbaum, Lothar J Sculptor, Educator
Lagunes, Maria (Maria Lagunes Hernandez) Sculptor, Painter
Manrique, Jorge Alberto Art Critic, Art Historian
Martin, Fletcher Painter
Maxwell, Robert Edwin Painter, Graphic Artists
Merida, Carlos Painter
Messeguer, Villoro Benito Painter, Sculptor
Mora, Francisco Painter, Printmaker
Moyssen, Xavier Art Critic, Art Historian
Nakatani, Carlos Painter, Printmaker
Nierman, Leonardo M Painter, Sculptor
Ocejo (Jose Garcia) Painter
O'Gorman, Juan Painter, Muralist
Ordonez, Efren Painter, Sculptor
Ortiz Macedo, Luis Architect, Art Historian
Palau, Marta Tapestry Artist, Painter
Paredes, Limon Mariano Engraver, Painter
Parra, Thomas (Garcia) Painter, Instructor
Pinto, James Painter, Sculptor
Ramirez, Gabriel Painter
Ramirex-Vazquez, Pedro Designer, Architect
Ramos-Prida, Fernando Painter
Reindorf, Samuel Painter
Rodriguez, Oscar Painter, Sculptor
Rojo, Vicente Painter
Sakai, Kazuya Painter, Art Editor
Salazar, Juan Painter, Designer
Saldivar, Jaime Painter
Samuelson, Fred Binder Painter, Instructor
Soriano, Juan Painter, Sculptor
Stahl, Ben (Albert) Painter, Illustrator
Tabuena, Romeo Villalva Painter
Tamayo, Rufino Painter
Taylor, Frederick Bourchier Painter, Sculptor
Tejeda, Carlos Painter
Toledo, Francisco Painter, Sculptor
Toral, Maria Teresa Engraver, Designer
Urueta, Cordelia Painter
Vasquez J, Alberto Weaver
Villafranca, Leonor Morales De Art Historian, Art Critic
Von Gunten, Roger Painter
Williams, Garth Montgomery Illustrator, Designer
Zaidenberg, Arthur Sculptor, Writer
Zuniga, Francisco Sculptor

NETHERLANDS

DeWit, Floyd Tennison Sculptor, Painter
Tajiri, Shinkichi Sculptor, Educator

NEW ZEALAND

Hirsch, Richard Teller Museum Director, Critic

NIGERIA

Mount, Marshall Ward Art Historian, Art Administrator

PERU

Davis, John Harold Gallery Director, Illustrator

SPAIN

Harlow, Robert E Painter
Harvey, Robert Martin Painter
Hollander, Gino F Painter, Art Dealer
Meigs, Walter Painter
Narotzky, Norman David Painter, Printmaker
Ulbricht, John, Painter

SWITZERLAND

Takal, Peter Painter, Printmaker

VENEZUELA

Neumann, Hans Collector
De Tonnancour, Jacques G Painter, Instructor

Professional Classifications Index

ADMINISTRATOR

Adams, William Howard
Adlmann, Jan Ernst
Aguayo, Oscar
Aldrich, Larry
Alexander, William C
Amaya, Mario Anthony
Apel, Barbara Jean
Ard, Saradell (Saradell Ard Frederick)
Armstrong, John Albert
Armstrong, Thomas Newton, III
Arnold, Richard R
Atkins, Billy W
Atkyns, (Willie) Lee, Jr
Ault, Lee Addison
Baer, Alan
Baitsell, Wilma Williamson
Bakken, Haakon
Barber, Ronald
Barooshian, Martin
Barr, Alfred Hamilton, Jr
Barrett, Barbara
Barrio-Garay, Jose Luis
Barry, Robert E
Bartle, Dorothy Budd
Bartlett, Fred Stewart
Bayer, Jeffrey Joshua
Bayliss, George
Beal, Graham William John
Bealmer, William
Beam, Philip Conway
Beattie, George
Beebe, Mary Livingstone
Bell, James M
Bell, Philip Michael
Benson, Martha J
Bentz, Harry Donald
Berger, Jerry Allen
Beson, Roberta (Roberta Beson Hill)
Betensky, Rose Hart
Bice, Clare
Biddle, James
Biddle, Livingston Ludlow, Jr
Bingham, Lois A
Birdman, Jerome M
Bjorklund, Lee
Blackmun, Barbara Winston
Bledsoe, Jane Kathryn
Blevins, James Richard
Bloch, Milton Joseph
Bookbinder, Jack
Booth, Bill
Booth, Judith Gayle
Bostick, William Allison
Bothmer, Dietrich Felix Von
Boulton, Jack
Bowman, Jeff Ray
Boylen, Michael Edward
Bradley, Dorothy
Braiden, Rose Margaret J
Bramlett, Betty Jane
Breeskin, Adelyn Dohme
Broadley, Hugh T
Brookins, Jacob Boden
Brooks, Bruce W
Brooks, John H
Brown, Jeanette H
Brown, John Carter
Brown, Jonathan
Browne, Vivian E
Bruno, Vincent J
Buki, Zoltan
Burford, William E
Burgart, Herbert Joseph
Burke, James Donald
Burnham, Elizabeth Louese
Butler, Joseph (Green)
Butts, Porter
Bynum, E Anderson (Esther Pearl)
Cameron, Elsa S
Cameron, Eric
Cantieni, Graham Alfred
Cartledge, Roseanne Catherine
Casey, Jacqueline Shepard
Catan-Rose, Richard
Cathers, James O
Catron, Patricia D'Arcy
Chalmers, E Laurence, Jr
Chamberlain, Betty
Channing, Susan Rose
Chiara, Alan Robert
Cleveland, Helen Barth
Cleveland, Robert Earl
Clothier, Peter Dean
Coffelt, Beth
Cogswell, Margaret Price
Colin, Ralph Frederick
Collins, Christiane C
Collins, William Charles
Condit, Louise
Cone, Gerrit Craig
Cone-Skelton, Annette
Cook Christopher Capen
Coolidge, John
Cooper, Marve H
Cox, J W S
Craven, Roy Curtis, Jr
Culkin, John Michael
Cummings, Frederick James
Cummins, Karen Gasco
Cunningham, Charles C, Jr
D'Andrea, Jeanne
Danielson, Phyllis I
Dash, Harvey Dwight
Daugherty, Marshall Harrison
Davis, D Jack
Davis, Donald Jack
Davis, John Sherwood
Davis, Robert Tyler
Dean, James
De Foix-Crenascol, Louis
deGooyer, Kirk Alan
Delehanty, Suzanne E
Dellis, Arlene B
de Looper, Willem
Demetrion, James Thomas
De Montebello, Guy-Philippe Lannes
DePillars, Murry N
Desmidt, Thomas H
Dibble, Charles Ryder
Dickinson, William Stirling
Dietrich, Bruce Leinbach
Dillon, C Douglas
Dillow, Nancy E (Nancy Elizabeth Robertson)
Dobkin, John Howard
Dolan, Margo
Donaldson, Jeff R
Donson, Jerome Allan
Doty, Robert McIntyre
Downs, Linda Anne
Dresser, Louisa
Driskell, David Clyde
Duff, James H
Eastman, Gene M
Eastman, John, Jr
Eberman, Edwin
Ebie, William Dennis
Eckert, William Dean
Edmunds, Allan Logan
Elam, Charles Henry
Elder, David Morton
Elias, Harold John
Elliott, B Charles, Jr
Engeran, Whitney John, Jr
Ettinghausen, Richard
Even, Robert Lawrence
Ewing, Bayard
Farrell, Patric
Farrell, Stephanie Krauss
Faul, Roberta Heller
Feldman, Arthur Mitchell
Feldstein, Mary
Fenton, Julia Ann
Ferber, Elise Van Hook
Fern, Alan Maxwell
Field, Lyman
Fifield, Mary
Fincher, John H
Fiori, Dennis Andrew
Fisher, James Donald
Fitzpatrick, Robert John
Fleck, Irma L
Ford, Harry Xavier
Forst, Miles
Fosdick, Sina G
Foster, James W, Jr
Franzen, Joan C
Fraze, Denny T
Freedman, Doris C
Freitag, Wolfgang Martin
Freundlich, August L
Fromberg, LaVerne Ray
Fulton, W Joseph
Fumagalli, Orazio
Gabriel, Robert A
Galles, Arie Alexander
Gantz, Jeanne A
Garber, Susan R
Garcia, Ofelia
Garvey, Eleanor
Geoffrey, Syed Iqbal (Jafree)
Geran, Joseph, Jr
Gerdts, Abigail Booth
Gibson, George
Gibson, James D
Gikas, Christopher
Gillespie, Dorothy Merle
Gilmore, Roger
Gladstone, M J
Glaser, Bruce
Glenn, Constance White
Glick, Paula Florence
Goldfarb, Roz
Gomez-Sicre, Jose
Gonzalez, Jose Gamaliel
Gonzalez, Jose Luis
Goodall, Donald Bannard
Goodyear, John L
Gordley, Metz Tranbarger
Gordon, John
Gordon, Joy L
Graham, F Lanier
Graham, John Meredith, II
Gray, Robert Hugh
Gray, Robert Ward
Gray, Thomas Alexander
Graziani, Sante
Green, Wilder
Gregory, Joan
Griffin, Rachael S
Griner, Ned H
Grissom, Eugene Edward
Hagerstrand, Martin Allan
Hale, Jean Graham
Hale, Robert Beverly
Hall, Lee
Hammer, Alfred Emil
Hanks, Nancy
Hansen, Arne Rae
Hanson, Bernard A
Hardy, (Clarion) Dewitt
Harrington, La Mar
Harris, Alfred Peter
Harris, Ann Sutherland
Hart, Allen M
Hart, Robert Gordon
Hartwell, Patricia Lochridge
Haseltine, James Lewis
Hausman, Jerome Joseph
Hayes, Bartlett Harding, Jr
Hayes, Laura M
Head, Robert William
Hearn, M F (Millard Fillmore Hearn, Jr)
Heinz, Susan
Helander, Bruce Paul
Heller, Jules
Henry, John Raymond
Hero, Peter deCourcy
Herstand, Arnold
Hertzman, Gay Mahaffy
Hess, Stanley William
Hicks, Harold Jon (Jack)
Hightower, John B
Hildebrandt, William Albert
Hobbs, Joe Ferrell
Hobbs, Robert Dean
Hodge, Scottie
Holbrook, Vivian Nicholas

ADMINISTRATOR (cont)
Holden, Donald
Holliday, Betty
Hooton, Bruce Duff
Hopkins, Kenneth R
Hopps, Walter
Horowitz, Benjamin
Houghton, Arthur A, Jr
Howarth, Shirley Reiff
Humleker, Ruth S
Hunt, Robert James
Hunter, Miriam Eileen
Hyde, Andrew Cornwall
Insel, Paula
Irvine, Betty Jo
Irving, Donald J
Isaacson, Philip Marshal
Jacobs, Peter Alan
Jaffe, Ira Sheldon
James, Geoffrey
Jardine, Donald Leroy
Jeswald, Joseph
Jewesson, Kenneth R
Johnson, Joyce
Johnson, Katherine King
Johnson, Robert Flynn
Johnston, Robert Harold
Johnston, William Ralph
Jolles, Arnold H
Jones, Anthony
Jones, Harold Henry
Joost-Gaugier, Christiane L
Jordan, Jack
Jorgenson, Dale Alfred
Kaiser, Diane
Kan, Michael
Karlstrom, Paul Johnson
Kataoka, Mits
Katzive, David H
Kaufman, Nancy
Kaye, George
Kearney, John (W)
Kelly, Isaac Perry
Kenney, Estelle Koval
Kerr, John Hoare
Khendry, Janak Kumar
Kim, Ernie
Kinney, Gilbert Hart
Kirby, Kent Bruce
Klaven, Marvin L
Kloner, Jay Martin
Klopfenstein, Philip Arthur
Kluver, Billy (Johan Wilhem Kluver)
Kocher, Robert Lee
Krakel, Dean
Krashes, Barbara
Kubly, Donald R
Kuchel, Konrad
Kuebler, George F
Labiche, Walter Anthony
Laing, Richard Harlow
Landreau, Anthony Norman
Lanou, Tobie E
Lawson, Edward Pitt
Leach, Frederick Darwin
Leader, Garnet Rosamonde
Lebkicher, Anne Ross
Leighton, David S R
Lein, Malcolm Emil
Leven, Ruth Ann
Levitine, George
Levy, Mayra Phyllis
Lewandowski, Edmund D
Lewis, Elma Ina
Lewis, Michael H
Lewis, Virginia Elnora
Lewton, Jean Louise
Li, Chu-Tsing
Libby, Gary Russell
Libhart, Myles Laroy
Liddle, Nancy Hyatt
Lieberman, William S
Linn, John William
Littman, Robert R
Livingston, Charlotte (Mrs Francis Vendeveer Kughler)
Loar, Peggy A
Lochridge, Sudie Katherine
Loeffler, Carl Eugene
Logan, Frederick Manning
Lottes, John William
Lowe, Harry
Ludmer, Joyce Pellerano
Lukasiewicz, Ronald Joseph
Lyle, Charles Thomas
Lyons, Ian Raymond
Maass, Richard Andrew
MacGregor, John Boyko
Macklin, Anderson D
Madigan, Mary Jean Smith
Madigan, Richard Allen
Mahlmann, John James
Mandle, Earl Roger
Manetta, Edward J
Manton, Jock (Archimedes Aristides Giacomantonio)
Marchese, Lamar Vincent
Marchese, Patricia Davis
Margolics, Ethel Polacheck
Markman, Sidney David
Marshall, Kerry
Martin, Keith
Martin, Loretta Marsh
Martin, Richard (Harrison)
Mason, Phillip Lindsay
Mattil, Edward L
Mayer, Susan Martin
Mayes, Steven Lee
Mayhall, Dorothy A
McCauley, Gardiner Rae
McColley, Sutherland
McCracken, Harold
McCray, Porter A
McGonagle, William Albert
McGough, Charles E
McGrath, James Arthur
McGrath, Kyran Murray
McGregor, Jack R
McKay, John Sangster
McMillan, Robert W
Meinig, Laurel
Mellon, Paul
Merchant, Pat (Jean)
Meserole, Vera Stromsted
Miller, Joan Vita
Miller, Lee Anne
Mills, Frederick Van Fleet
Mills, Margaret
Milrad, Aaron M
Mitchell, Donald
Moe, Richard D
Moeller, Robert Charles, III
Mongan, Agnes
Moore, Russell James
Morrison, Boone M
Morrison, Doris
Moseley, Spencer Altemont
Mount, Marshall Ward
Moxey, Keith Patricio Fleming
Moyer, Roy
Mulcahy, Freda
Murray, William Colman
Musgrove, Stephen Ward
Nash, Steven Alan
Neddeau, Donald Frederick Price
Neidhardt, Carl Richard
Nelson, Jon Allen
Nelson, Robert Allen
New, Lloyd H (Lloyd Kiva)
Newton, Douglas
Oakes, John Warren
O'Lenick, David Charles
Olpin, Robert Spencer
Olson, Richard W
O'Neil, John Joseph
Orze, Joseph John
Osborn, Elodie C (Mrs Robert C Osborn)
Osborne, Robert Lee
Oscarsson, Victoria Constance Gunhild
Ostrowitz, Judith Maura
Outterbridge, John Wilfred
Pacileo, Dolores Margaret
Palazzola, Guy
Palmer, William C
Parker, James Varner
Parsons, Merribell Maddux
Patchett, Daniel Claude
Peace, Bernie (Kinzel)
Pearson, Clifton
Perkins, Robert Eugene
Perrot, Paul N
Perry, Edward (Ted) Samuel
Peterson, John Douglas
Pettibone, John Wolcott
Picher, Claude
Pick, John
Pilsk, Adele Inez
Pinkney, Helen Louise
Plaut, James S
Plummer, John H
Polimenakos, Carmon
Polsky, Cynthia
Pope, Annemarie Henle
Potter, Ted
Preble, Michael Andrew
Preis, Alfred
Press, Nancy Neumann
Putterman, Florence Grace
Quigley, Michael Allen
Quinn, Sandi (Cassandrasu Dhooge-quinn Vachon)
Quirarte, Jacinto
Raggio, Olga
Rahja, Virginia Helga
Rainey, Froelich Gladstone
Ramsauer, Joseph Francis
Ranalli, Daniel
Rasmussen, Anton Jesse
Rathbone, Perry Townsend
Raybon, Phares Henderson
Rayburn, Bryan B
Richard, George Mairet
Richards, Karl Frederick
Richardson, Phyllis A
Richman, Robert M
Rigsby, John David
Ritchie, Andrew C
Roberts, Colette (Jacqueline)
Roberts, Percival R
Robertson, Charles J
Robinson, Charles K
Robinson, Franklin W
Robinson, Mary Ann
Rodgers, Jack A
Rodriguez, Ralph Noel
Rodriguez-Morales, Luis Manuel
Rohlfing, Christian
Rose, Mary Anne
Rose, Timothy G
Ross, Kenneth
Rovetti, Paul F
Roysher, Hudson (Brisbine)
Ruddley, John
Ruffo, Joseph Martin
Rumford, Beatrix Tyson
Rumsey, David MacIver
Russell, Philip C
Rust, Edwin C
Sabatella, Joseph John
Sachs, Samuel, II
Saff, Donald Jay
Saltmarche, Kenneth Charles
Sanders, Andrew Dominick
Sanguinetti, Eugene F
Sawyer, Charles Henry
Schar, Stuart
Schlageter, Robert William
Schlump, John Otto
Schmeckebier, Laurence E
Schmidt, Stephen
Schnorrenberg, John Martin
Schorgl, Thomas Barry
Schutte, Thomas Frederick
Scott, David Winfield
Scott-Gibson, Herbert Nathaniel
Selig, J Daniel
Seligman, Thomas Knowles
Sellers, John Lewis
Sennema, David C
Severino, Dominick Alexander
Shaman, Sanford Sivitz
Shapiro, Babe
Sharp, Willoughby
Sheppard, Luvon
Sherbell, Rhoda
Sherwood, Richard E
Sickman, Laurence Chalfant Stevens
Sigrin, Michael E
Sime, John
Simon, Leonard Ronald
Sisler, Rebecca
Sister Thomasita (Mary Thomasita Fessler)
Sloane, Joseph Curtis
Smith, Donald Eugene
Smyth, Craig Hugh
Sokol, David Martin
Solmssen, Peter
Solomon, Ruth B
Somerville, Romaine Stec
Sorell, Victor Alexander
Spear, Richard Edmund
Spence, Robert
Spencer, John R
Spurgin, John Edwin
Stamm, Geoffrey Eaton
Stars, William Kenneth
Stead, Rexford Arthur
Stebbins, Theodore Ellis, Jr
Stefanotty, Robert Alan
Stein, Claire A
Stephens, Richard Alan
Stevens, Edward John, Jr
Stewart, Jack
Stewart, Patricia Kaye
Stomps, Walter E, Jr
Strawn, Melvin Nicholas
Streetman, John William, III
Strother, Joseph Willis
Stubbs, Robert
Stull, Robert J
Sullivan, Ruth Wilkins
Sunkel, Robert Cleveland
Sweeney, James Johnson
Tanner, Warren
Taylor, Fran (Frances Jane)
Taylor, John Lloyd
Taylor, Joshua Charles
Taylor, Michael (Leach)
Taylor, Rod Allen
Terrill, Evelyn Beard
Thacher, John Seymour
Thalacker, Donald William
Thies, Charles Herman
Thomas, Katherine Castellanos
Thomas, William Radford
Tomasini, Wallace J
Tomidy, Paul J
Tracy, Berry Bryson
Trakis, Louis
Trapp, Frank Anderson
Traub, Charles H
Trop-Blumberg, Sandra (Sandra Trop Blumberg)
Trovato, Joseph S
Truettner, William
Tseu, Rosita Hsu
Tyson, Rae Julian
Ubans, Juris K
Van Arsdale, Dorothy Thayer
Vanderlip, Dianne Perry
Van Derpool, James Grote
Van Hook, David H
Van Tongeren, Harold (Herk)
Vigtel, Gudmund
Villafranca, Leonor Morales De
Voos, William John
Voth, Andrew Charles
Wagner, Charles H
Wahling, B Jon
Waitt, Alden Harry

Walker, William Bond
Wallace, Elizabeth S
Wardwell, Allen
Wark, Robert Rodger
Warren, Ferdinand Earl
Wasserman, Jack
Waterman, Donald Calvin
Wattenmaker, Richard J
Waufle, Alan Duane
Weber, Jean M
Wecker, Christoph Ulrich
Weeks, H J
Weidner, Marilyn Kemp
Weinberg, Ephraim
Wessel, Charlene Freimuth
West, E Gordon
Westin, Robert H
Wheeler, Robert G
Whipple, Enez Mary
White, Ian McKibbin
Whitehill, Walter Muir
Whitlock, John Joseph
Whitney, John Hay
Wickiser, Ralph Lewanda
Wicks, Eugene Claude
Wiener, Louise Weingarten
Wilder, Mitchell Armitage
Wilke, Ulfert S
Willis, William Henry, Jr
Wilson, Alden Chandler
Wing, Robin Stewart
Winter, Gerald Glen
Wintersteen, Bernice McIlhenny
Wise, Howard
Witmeyer, Stanley Herbert
Wittmann, Otto
Wogstad, James Everet
Wolfe, Townsend Durant
Wood, James Nowell
Woods, Gurdon Grant
Woolfenden, William Edward
Worth, Carl
Wunder, Richard Paul
Wurdemann, Helen (Baroness Elena Guzzardi)
Yenawine, Bruce Harley
Young, Joseph Louis
Zacha, George William
Zahn, Carl Frederick
Zaleski, Jean M

ARCHITECT

Atkins, Gordon Lee
Bakanowsky, Louis J
Banz, George
Baringer, Richard E
Blake, Peter Jost
Bolles, John S
Booth, Laurence Ogden
Brown, John Hall
Calderon, Juan
Cardinal, Douglas Joseph Henry
Chapman, Dave
Consuegra, Hugo
Damaz, Paul F
Deaton, Charles
De Larios, Dora
De Weldon, Felix George Weihs
Diamond, Abel Joseph
Downey, Juan
DuBois, Macy
Fuller, R Buckminster
Geerlings, Gerald Kenneth
George, Walter Eugene, Jr
Gerin-Lajoie, Guy
Glaser, Samuel
Goeritz, Mathias
Goldeen, Dorothy A
Green, Wilder
Hamilton, Frank Moss
Harris, Julian Hoke
Holschuh, (George) Fred
Izumi, Kiyoshi
Johnson, Philip Cortelyou
Kaspe, Vladimir
Kinoshita, Gene
Kravis, Janis
Lambert, Phyllis
Lawrence, Howard Ray
MacDonald, William L
Mallory, Nina A
Meier, Richard Alan
Mitchell, Clifford
Montequin, Francois-Auguste de
Murphy, Herbert A
Oliver, Richard Bruce
Ortiz Macedo, Luis
Peckham, Nicholas
Pei, I M (Ieoh Ming Pei)
Pelli, Cesar
Perkins, G Holmes
Preis, Alfred
Ramirez-Vazquez, Pedro
Ray, Robert Arthur
Redstone, Louis Gordon
Robinson, C David
Sander, Dennis Jay
Saret, Alan Daniel
Schoeler, Paul Jean Rene
Scott, Walter
Simonds, Charles Frederick
Smith, Ernest John
Soleri, Paolo
Sommer, Frederick
Thalacker, Donald William
Thiry, Paul (Albert)
Thomas, George R
Tigerman, Stanley
Van Ginkel, Blanche Lemco
Venturi, Robert
Wedin, Winslow Elliott
Wines, James N
Yeatts, James McKinney
Zeidler, Eberhard Heinrich

ART DEALER

Acuna, Victor Miguel
Ahn, Don C
Albro, Jeannette (Jeannette Louise Cantrell)
Allrich, M Louise Barco
Alonzo, Jack J
Altermann, Tony
Amor, Ines
Anderson, David K
Anderson, Dennis Ray
Anderson, Gwendolyn Orsinger (Orsini)
Andrews, Victoria L
Anhalt, Jacqueline Richards
Ankrum, Joan
Aronson, Cliff
Arwin, Kathleen G
Arwin, Lester B
Ault, Lee Addison
Austin, Jo-Anne Jordan
Bader, Franz
Baehler, Wallace R
Baird, Joseph Armstrong, Jr
Banister, Robert Barr
Banning, Jack (John Peck Banning, Jr)
Banta, Melissa Wiekser
Bartholet, Elizabeth Ives
Barton, John Murray
Barton, Phyllis Grace
Baum, Hank
Baxter, Douglas W
Bednarz, Adele
Bellamy, Richard
Benson, Elaine K G
Beraha, Enrique Misrachi
Bergen, Sidney L
Berggruen, John Henry
Berman, Aaron
Bernard, Felix S
Birnberg, Gerald H
Birnberg, Ruth Carrel
Blacketer, James Richard
Bloom, Jason
Bolles, John S
Bonacker, Joyce Sybil
Bonino, Alfredo
Boone, Mary
Borgenicht, Grace (Grace Borgenicht Brandt)
Boucher, Tania Kunsky
Bowater, Marian
Boyd, Donald Edgar
Bradford, Howard
Bradley, Dorothy
Bradley, Peter Alexander
Bransky, Miriam (Miriam Ann Gilden)
Braunstein, Ruth
Bromm, Hal
Brooks, Robert
Brown, Jeffrey Rogers
Brown, Robert K
Brownett, Thelma Denyer
Bruno, Phillip A
Bryant, Linda Goode
Burford, William E
Burgess, Joseph James, Jr
Burton, Gloria
Buster, Jacqueline Mary
Byron, Charles Anthony
Califano, Edward Christopher
Carlin, Electra Marshall
Carlson, Alexander
Caro, Francis
Castano, Elvira
Castano, Giovanni
Castelli, Leo
Cernuschi, Alberto C
Challis, Richard Bracebridge
Chambers, Karen Sue
Chase, Robert M
Chung, Roger K
Clancy, John
Clifford, Jutta
Cohn, Richard A
Cole, Sylvan, Jr
Colina, Armando G
Collins, Lowell Daunt
Conforte, Renee
Conley, Zeb Bristol, Jr
Cooper, Paula
Cooper, Rebecca (Rebecca Cooper Eisenberg)
Cooper, Theodore A
Copley, Claire Strohn
Cornette, Mary Elizabeth
Cortella, Gloria Charlene
Couturier, Marion B
Creamer, Paul Lyle
Crispo, Andrew John
Cross, Maria Concetta
Crouse, John L (Jay)
Cuningham, Elizabeth Bayard (Mrs E W R Templeton)
Curtis, Roger William
Daisy (Daisy Black Langhauser)
Danenberg, Bernard
David, Dianne
Davidson, Maxwell, III
Davis, Donald Robert
Davis, Leroy
Dawley, Joseph William
Dawson, Bess Phipps
Day, Lucien B
Deats, Margaret (Margaret Deats Bott)
De Coursey, John Edward
De Nagy, Eva
de Nagy, Tibor (J)
Devine, William Charles
Dillingham, Rick (James Richard II)
Dintenfass, Terry
Donson, Jerome Allan
Doolin, Mary N
Dorr, Goldthwaite Higginson, III
Dreaper, Richard Edward
Drexler, Paul Eugene
Droll, Donald E
Drutt, Helen Williams
Duffy, Betty Minor
Dunn, Roger Terry
Eckert, Lou
Edens, Lettye P
Edwards, Gwendolyn Tyner
Edwards, Joy M
Einstein, Gilbert W
Eitingon, Brigitte
Ekstrom, Arne H
Elkin, Beverly Dawn
Elkon, Robert
Elliott, Scott Cameron
Elowitch, Annette
Elowitch, Robert Jason
Emmerich, Andre
Endo, Robert Akira
Engel, Walter F
Erdman, R H Donnelley
Esman, Rosa M
Ewald, Elin Lake
Eyen, Richard J
Fairweather, Sally H
Fedele, Frank D
Feigen, Richard L
Feinman, Stephen E
Feldman, Ronald
Fendrick, Barbara Cooper
Feuerstein, Roberta
Figert, Sam A
Findlay, David B
Findlay, Helen T
Fink, Alan
Fischbach, Marilyn Cole
Fishko, Bella
Fleischman, Lawrence
Fleming, Betty Corcoran
Fondren, Harold M
Foster, Donald Isle
Fourcade, Xavier
Friedland, Ruth Volid
Frumkin, Allan
Fuller, Diana
Furman, Aaron & Joyce
Gallenkamp, Patricia
Gantz, Ann Cushing
Gerst, Hilde W
Gilbert, Alma Magdalena
Gilbertson, Charlotte
Gillette, W Dean
Glass, Wendy D
Glezer, Nechemia
Glick, Paula Florence
Glimcher, Arnold B
Gold, Betty
Goldeen, Dorothy A
Goldman, Louis & Sondra
Goldowsky, Noah
Goldschmidt, Lucien
Goodman, James Neil
Goodman, Marian
Gordon, Albert F
Gordon, John
Gordon, Joni
Gordon, Martin
Gorman, R C
Gorney, Jay Philip
Goulds, Peter J
Graham, James
Graham, Robert Claverhouse
Gray, Richard
Greene, Lois D
Greene, Theodore R
Gross, Estelle Shane
Grossman, Maurizia M
Gruskin, Mary Josephine
Guadagnoli, Nello T
Gurewitsch, Edna P
Haber, William

ART DEALER (cont)
Hadler, Warren Arnold
Hage, Raymond Joseph
Hahn, Maurice & Roslyn
Hahn, Stephen
Hamer, Marilou Heilman
Hames, Carl Martin
Hammer, Armand
Hammer, Victor J
Hansen, Wanda
Hardin, Shirley G
Harlow, Frederica Todd
Harmon, Foster
Hart, Bill
Hart, Harold Rudolf
Haslem, Jane N
Haversat, Lillian Kerr
Heath, David C
Heit, Steven Robert
Heller, Ben
Henderson, Lester Kierstead
Henning, Paul Harvey
Herbert, David
Herman, Joyce Elaine
Hewitt, Jean Clifford
Hill, Ed
Hill, Megan Lloyd
Hodge, Scottie
Hoffeld, Jeffrey
Hoffman, Nancy
Hoffmann, Arnold, Jr
Hofman, Kate
Hokin, Grace E
Hooks, Charles Vernon
Hooton, Bruce Duff
Hoover, F Herbert
Hopper, Marianne Seward
Horowitz, Benjamin
Howlett, Carolyn Svrluga
Huldermann, Paul F
Hundley, David Holladay
Hunter, Mel
Hutchinson, Max
Hutton, Leonard
Iannetti, Pasquale Francesco Paolo
Iervolino, Joseph Anthony
Iervolino, Paula
Indeck, Karen Joy
Ingber, Barbara
Insel, Paula
Inzerillo, Gian Del Valentino
Iolas, Alexander
Jamison, Margaret Conry
Janis, Conrad
Janis, Sidney
Johnson, Marian Willard
Johnson, Miani Guthrie
Johnston, Helen Head
Jones, Douglas McKee (Doug)
Joukhadar, Moumtaz A N
Kahan, Alexander
Kahn, Ralph H
Kaller, Robert Jameson
Kallir, Otto
Kanegis, Sidney S
Kaplan, Leonard
Kaplan, Muriel Sheerr
Karp, Ivan C
Katzen, Hal Zachery
Katzen, Philip
Kelley, Chapman
Kent, H Latham
Kerr, Berta Borgenicht
Kertess, Klaus D
Killam, Walt
Kimmel-Cohn, Roberta
Kind, Phyllis
King, Myron Lyzon
Knowlton, Monique
Koch, William Emery
Kohler, Mel (Otto)
Kolbert, Frank L
Kolodner, Nathan K
Komor, Mathias
Kornblatt, Barbara Rodbell
Kottler, Lynn
Kouba, Leslie Carl
Krakow, Barbara L
Krasner, Oscar
Kraushaar, Antoinette M
Lamanna, Carmen
Landau, Felix
Landau, Mitzi
Landry, Albert
Lane, H Palmer
Langman, Richard Theodore
Langston, Loyd H
Lapiner, Alan C
Larcada, Richard Kenneth
Lastra, Luis
Laugesen, Madelyn A
Lebish, Harriet Shiller
Lefcourt, Irwin
Lefebre, John
Lehr, Janet
Leitman, Norman
Lerner, Richard J
Le Roy, Harold M
Levy, Stuart D
Lewin, Bernard
Lewis, Don S, Sr
Lewis, Donald Sykes, Jr
Lewison, Florence (Mrs Maurice Glickman)
Lieber, France
Lienau, Daniel Clifford
Limber, Trudy C
Lock, Charles K
Locks, Marian
London, Elca
Long, Meredith J
Loro, Anthony Pivotto
Love, Richard Henry
Lowinsky, Simon L
Ludman, Joan Hurwitz
Lunn, Harry, Jr
Luntz, Irving
Luria, Gloria
Lust, Virginia
Lutze
Mabry, Jane
MacKay, Hugh
Makler, Hope Welsh
Mangel, Benjamin
Mann, David
Manrique, Jorge Alberto
Marberger, A Aladar
Marchisotto, Linda A
Markel, Kathryn E
Markle, Jack M
Markle, Sam
Marks, Royal S
Marrozzini, Luigi
Mason, Lauris Lapidos
Mathis, Emile Henry, II
Matisse, Pierre
McCoy, Jason
McFarren, Grace
McHugh, Adeliza Sorenson
McIlroy, Carol Jean
McKennis, Gail
McKinney, Donald
McMahon, James Edward
Meek, J William, III
Meisel, Louis Koenig
Mekler, Adam
Meltzer, Doris
Mendoza, David C
Meyer, Thomas Vincent
Michaux, Ronald Robert
Milant, Jean Robert
Milch, Harold Carlton
Miller, David Stuart
Miller, Robert Peter
Milliken, Alexander Fabbri
Miner, Ralph Hamlin
Mirvish, David
Mitchell, Donald
Mont, Betty
Mont, Frederick
Moody, Elizabeth Chambers
Moos, Walter A
Morgan, Myra Jean
Morgan, Warren Dean
Morris, Donald Fischer
Morris, Florence Marie
Morse, Mitchell Ian
Muller, Jerome Kenneth
Muniot, Barbara King
Myers, John B
Naiman, Lee E
Narus, Marta Maria Margareta
Nash, Veronica F
Neikrug, Marjorie
Neslage, Oliver John, Jr
Newhouse, Bertram Maurice
Newhouse, Clyde Mortimer
Newman, Louis
Nordness, Lee
Norman, Emile
Norquist, Ryl
O'Brien, William Vincent
Oehlschlaeger, Frank J
Orling, Anne
Oscarsson, Victoria Constance Gunhild
O'Toole, James St Laurence
Owens, Tennys Bowers
Palley, Reese
Patch, Peggie (Margaret Thompson Williamson)
Pearl, Marilyn
Pelham-Keller, Richard Monroe
Perls, Klaus G
Perry, Richard C
Persky, Robert S
Pesner, Carole Manishin
Pfeifer, Marcuse
Phillips, Bonnie
Pierce, Patricia Jobe
Poindexter, Elinor Fuller
Pool, Nelda Lee
Poppelman, Raymond James
Posner, Judith L
Prakapas, Eugene Joseph
Pratt, Frances (Frances Elizabeth Usui)
Price, Vincent
Pucker, Bernard H
Rabow, Rose
Ravel, Dana B
Raydon, Alexander R
Redding, Steve
Reed, Harold
Reilley, Patrick Richard
Richards, Tally
Rinhart, George R
Robinson, Thomas
Robles, Esther Waggoner
Rollins, Jo Lutz
Rolly, Ronald Joseph
Rose, Peter Henry
Rosenberg, Carole Halsband
Rothman, Sidney
Royce, Richard Benjamin
Rubin, Lawrence
Russell, John Laurel
Rustvold, Katherine Jo
Sabo, Betty Jean
Sachs, A M
Saidenberg, Daniel
Saidenberg, Eleanore B
St Clair, Michael
Samuels, Harold & Peggy
Sanchez, Emilio
Sande, Rhoda
Sanderson, Robert Wright
Sawyer, William
Schab, Margo Pollins
Schaffner, Ruth S
Schellstede, Richard Lee
Schlosberg, Carl Martin
Schneider, Lisa Dawn
Schneiderman, Dorothy
Schneier, Donna Frances
Schnessel, S Michael
Schnitzer, Arlene Director
Schoelkopf, Robert J, Jr
Schumsky, Felicie Roberta
Schuster, Cita Fletcher (Sarah E)
Schuster, Eugene Ivan
Schutz, Prescott Dietrich
Schwandner, Kathleen M
Schwarz, Kurt L
Schweitzer, M R
Seders, Francine Lavinal
Seeman, Helene Zucker
Segy, Ladislas
Seraphin, Joseph Anthony
Serger, Helen
Serisawa, Ikuo
Shadrach, Jean H
Shalit, Mitzi (Mildred M Shalit)
Shechtman, George Henoch
Shepard, Lewis Albert
Siden, Franklin
Sigoloff, Violet Bruce
Silverberg, Ellen Ruth
Silvia, Judith Heidler Richardson
Simpson, Merton D
Sirena (Contessa Antonia Mastrocristino Fanara)
Sloan, Robert Smullyan
Slusser, James Bernard
Smart, Wini
Smith, Albert E
Smith, Ross Ransom Williams
Smither, Edward Murray
Sneed, Patricia M
Snyder, Barry
Solomon, Gerald
Solomon, Holly
Solomon, Richard H
Solway, Carl E
Spark, Victor David
Spector, Naomi
Staempfli, George W
Stein, Fritz Henry
Stein Harve
Stellings, Alexa
Stern, Jean
Stern, Leonard B
Stern, Louis
Stewart, Charles Carl
Stiebel, Eric
Stiebel, Gerald Gustave
Stoller, John Chapman
Stone, Alex Benjamin
Stuart, David
Sussman, Bonnie K
Suzuki, Katsko (Katsko Suzuki Kannegieter)
Szoke, John
Taff, Barbara O'Neil
Tahir, Abe M, Jr
Tatistcheff, Peter Alexis
Ten (Jan Ten Broeke)
Termini, Christine
Thaler, Mildred G
Thomason, Tom William
Thompson, Richard E, Jr
Thompson, Richard Earl, Sr
Thomson, Carl L
Toll, Barbara Elizabeth
Travis, David Hail
Trlak, Roger
Truman, Jock Curtis
Tunick, David
Turner, Janice Kay
Tyler, Kenneth Eugene
Van Der Straeten, Vincent Roger
Veljkovic, Andrev
Verzyl, June Carol
Verzyl, Kenneth H
Vogel, Donald S
Vose, Robert Churchill, Jr
Wade, Jane
Walker, George R P, Jr
Waltzer, Stewart Paul
Washburn, Joan T
Watson, Clarissa H
Wauters, Andre
Weber, John
Weinberg, Daniel

Weitzenhoffer, A Max
Welch, James Henry
Wenger, Muriel June
Wenger, Sigmund
Westlund, Harry E
Westwater, Angela King
Weyhe, Mrs Erhard
White, Albert
White, Deborah
White, Ruth
Wilkinson, Kirk Cook
Williamson, Jason H
Wilson, Carrie Lois
Wing, Robin Stewart
Wolff, William H
Woodard, Tom L
Woodside, Gordon William
Wunderlich, Rudolf G
Wynshaw, Frances
Zabriskie, Virginia M
Zantman, J B
Zeitlin, Jacob Ilrael
Zierler, William

ARTIST-THEORIST

Cohen, Harold

ASSEMBLAGE ARTIST

Ahrendt, Christine
Ajay, Abe
Arman
Ascott, Roy
Aubin, Barbara
Bakke, Karen Lee
Barnhart, C Raymond
Benge, David Philip
Benson, Martha J
Berg, Barry
Berman, Fred J
Boghosian, Varujan
Bontecou, Lee
Botkin, Henry
Bott, H J
Bramson, Phyllis Halperin
Brecht, George
Bruno, Santo Michael
Buczak, Brian Elliot
Burton, Scott
Byars, Donna
Cable, Maxine Roth
Cho, David
DeCaprio, Alice
Dienes, Sari
Dillon, Paul Sanford
Di Meo, Dominick
Elliott, Ronnie
Fincher, John H
Fisher, Carole Gorney
Flick, Paul John
Foulkes, Llyn
Freeman, Phyllis (Therese)
Freilich, Ann
Friedberg, Ray E
Getz, Ilse
Gilchriest, Lorenzo
Goell, Abby Jane
Gordon, John S
Grossman, Nancy
Habergritz, George Joseph
Halberstadt, Ernst
Hamady, Walter Samuel
Hamouda, Amy
Houskeeper, Barbara
Howe, Nelson S
Humble, Douglas
Jones, Bill
Jones, James Edward
Koch, Arthur Robert
Kowing, Frank Eugene
Kushner, Robert Ellis
Leax, Ronald Allen
Lewis, Golda
Lynch, Mary Britten
Markle, Sam
Marx, Nicki D
McCabe, Maureen M
McChesney, Robert Pearson
McNitt, Miriam D
Micheli, Julio
Miller, George
Nelson, Jack D
Nowack, Wayne Kenyon
Olson, Gary Spangler
Olson, Richard W
Outterbridge, John Wilfred
Parker, Nancy Winslow
Paulin, Richard Calkins
Reich, Nathaniel E
Relis, Sandy
Rennick, Dan
Renouf, Edward Pechmann
Richardson, Frank, Jr
Rivoli, Mario
Roberts, Donald
Rogers, Miriam
Rosenquit, Bernard
Saar, Betye
Schachter, Justine Ranson
Selchow, Roger Hoffman
Shelton, Robert Lee
Shore, Mary
Silberstein-Storfer, Muriel Rosoff
Smith, Lawson Wentworth
Sovary, Lilly
Spaulding, Warren Dan
Sprang, Elizabeth Lewis
Storer, Inez Mary
Storm, Howard
Tawney, Lenore
Thompson, Tamara (Tamara Thompson Bryant)
Thorne, Gordon (Kit)
Thornhill, Anna
Van Brunt, Philip G
Wagner, Gordon Parsons
Warner, Jo
Winters, Denny
Wiper, Thomas William
Zirker, Joseph

BOOK DEALER

Banta, Melissa Wiekser
Bergling, Virginia Catherine (Mrs Stephen J Kozazcki)
Brown, Robert K
Burk, Anna Darlene
Caddell, Foster
Canepa, Anna L
Colescott, Robert H
Crouse, John L (Jay)
Davis, L Clarice
Gordon, Martin
Haber, William
Isserstedt, Dorothea Carus
Mason, Lauris Lapidos
McGilvery, Laurence
Moore, Barbara
Rosenberg, Bernard
Rosenfeld, Richard Joel
Smith-Gordon, Nannette
Weissman, Julian Paul
Winter, H Edward

CALLIGRAPHER

Anderson, Donald Myers
Berguson, Robert Jenkins
Block, Joyce
Bostick, William Allison
Bullen, Reese
Callicott, Burton Harry
Cataldo, John William
Chin, Ric
Chung, Roger K
Ebsen, Alf K
Ecke, Betty Tseng Yu-Ho
Fleming, Allan Robb
Foley, Kyoko Y
Giannotti, John J
Grushkin, Philip
Haar, Francis
Hammer, Alfred Emil
Held, Philip
Johnson, Fridolf Lester
Kanidinc, Salahattin
Krauser, Joel
LaMarca, Howard J
Leitman, Samuel
Marin, Augusto
Martin, Loretta Marsh
McLean, Roddy (Verneda Rodriguez)
Mueller, M Gerardine
Nesbitt, Alexander John
Offner, Elliot
Oi, Motoi
Peter, Friedrich Gunther
Petheo, Bela Francis
Pope, Mary Ann Irwin
Pope, Richard Coraine
Quinn, Sandi (Cassandrasu Dhooge-quinn Vachon)
Ramirez, Joel Tito
Rigg, Margaret Ruth
Riley, Roy John
Sandberg, Hannah
Sarvis, Alva Taylor
Schachter, Justine Ranson
Scharff, Constance Kramer
Terris, Albert
Turner, Ralph James
Wong, Frederick
Wu, I-Chen

CARTOONIST

Addams, Charles Samuel
Alexander, Kenneth Lewis
Anderson, Brad J
Angelo, Emidio
Armstrong, Roger Joseph
Arnosky, James Edward
Asch, Stan (Stanley William Aschemeier)
Auth, Tony (William Anthony Auth, Jr)
Bach, Mickey (Milton Francis)
Barbera, Joe
Basset, Brian Willard
Basset, Gene
Bates, Bill
Bimrose, Arthur Sylvanus, Jr
Bissell, Charles Overman
Bissell, Phil
Brennan, Francis Edwin
Brown, Bo
Brown, Buck
Brown, Daniel Quilter (Dan Q)
Brown, William Ferdinand, II
Brownhill, Harold
Burck, Jacob
Bushmiller, Ernie Paul
Busino, Orlando Francis
Caniff, Milton Arthur
Capp, Al
Cavalli, Dick
Chapman, Howard Eugene
Cochran, George McKee
Combes, Willard Wetmore
Conrad, Paul Francis
Craig, Eugene
Cramer, Abraham
Crane, James
Crane, Roy (Campbell)
Crawford, William H
Crockett, Gibson M
Cronin, Robert (Lawrence)
d'Alessio, Gregory
Darrow, Whitney, Jr
Davis, George
Day, Chon (Chauncey Addison)
Day, Robert James
Dean, Abner
Dedini, Eldon Lawrence
Delano, Jack
Dennis, Charles Houston
Devlin, Harry
Dobbins, James Joseph
Dodd, Ed (Edward Benton)
Dowling, Daniel Blair
Eaton, Thomas Newton
Engelhardt, Thomas Alexander
Ericson, Dick
Farris, Joseph
Feiffer, Jules
Ficklen, Jack Howells
Fischer, Jo
Fischetti, John
Flannery, Thomas
Foster, Hal
Fradon, Dana
Gallo, William Victor
Goodwin, Louis Payne
Gould, Chester
Graham, Bill (William Karr)
Graysmith, Robert
Grubert, Carl Alfred
Haenigsen, Harry William
Hagglund, Irvin (Arvid)
Hanan, Harry
Harris, Murray A
Hart, John Lewis
Haynie, Hugh
Herblock (Herbert Lawrence Block)
Hesse, Don
Hessing, Valjean McCarty
Hill, Draper
Hirsch, David W (Dave)
Hoff, (Syd)
Holton, Leonard T
Hoppes, Lowell E
Hubenthal, Karl Samuel
Hungerford, Cyrus Cotton
Hunter, Graham
Hurd, Justin G (Jud)
Ivey, James Burnett
Jackson, Virgil V
Jensen, Cecil Leon
Justus, Roy Braxton
Kassoy, Bernard
Kato, Kay
Kaz (Lawrence Katzman)
Keane, Bil
Kent, Jack
Ketcham, Henry King (Hank)
Key, Ted
Kilgore, Al
King, Warren Thomas
Koerner, Daniel
Koren, Edward B
Kotzky, Alex Sylvester
Kuekes, Edward D
Lariar, Lawrence
Leet, Richard Eugene
Le Pelley, Guernsey
Levinson, Fred (Floyd)
Lichty, George M
Long, Scott
Lynde, Stan

CARTOONIST (cont)
MacNelly, Jeffrey Kenneth
Manning, Reg (West)
Markow, Jack
Martin, Charles E
Martin, Loretta Marsh
Mauldin, Bill
McClanahan, William J
Messick, Dale
Mosley, Zack T
Motter, Dean Roger
Neher, Fred
Newman, Ralph Albert
Niss, Robert Sharples
Norris, Leonard Matheson
Nutzle, Futzie (Bruce John Kleinsmith)
Oliphant, Patrick Bruce
Osrin, Raymond Harold
Partch, Virgil Franklin, II
Pascal, David
Perry, William M
Phillips, Irving W
Pierotti, John
Poinier, Arthur Best
Pretsch, John Edward
Price, George
Riveron, Enrique
Robbins, Frank
Rosen, Hy(man) (Joseph)
Salmon, Raymond Merle
Sandeson, William Seymour
Saxon, Charles David
Schulz, Charles Monroe
Shanks, Bruce McKinley
Sharp, Harold
Shelton, Gilbert Key
Shoemaker, Vaughn
Siegel, (Leo) Dink
Smith, Albert
Stamaty, Stanley
Stark, Bruce Gunsten
Steig, William
Steinberg, Saul
Stevens, William Ansel, Sr
Taylor, Bob Byron
Temes, Mortimer (Robert)
Terry, Hilda (Hilda Terry D'Alessio)
Thorndike, Charles Jesse (Chuck)
Townsend, Marvin J
Trinidad, Francisco Flores Corky, Jr
Turner, Dick
Valtman, Edmund
Van Buren, Raeburn
Vasils, Albert
Vaughan, Clifford
Walker, Mort
Warren, L D
Werner (Charles George Werner)
Wheeler, Mark
White, Leo
Wilson, Rowland Bragg
Wood, James Arthur (Art)
Yardley, Richard Quincy
Yokoi, Rita
Youngsblood, Nat
Zib, Tom (Thomas A Zibelli)

CERAMIST

Alexander, William C
Alling, Clarence (Edgar)
Anderson, Winslow
Aronson, Sanda
Bacigalupa, Andrea
Baney, Vera
Benge, David Philip
Blai, Bert
Blazey, Lawrence Edwin
Bova, Joe
Breckenridge, Bruce M
Brodie, Regis Conrad
Brooks, Louise Cherry
Broudo, Joseph David
Brown, Catharine Homan
Bugbee, Joan Scott
Bullen, Reese
Burt, Clyde Edwin
Calhoun, Larry Darryl
Caplan, Jerry L
Carey, James Sheldon
Chalke, John
Chamberlain, Charles
Chappelle, Jerry Leon
Christensen, Ted
Clipsham, Jacqueline Ann
Cohen, Michael S
Conover, Claude
Conrad, John W
Cooley, Adelaide Nation
Cornell, David E
Corsaw, Roger D
Crowell, Lucius
Daley, William P
Davis, John Sherwood
Davis, Willis Bing
De Larios, Dora
Dice, Elizabeth Jane
Dickerson, Tom
Dillingham, Rick (James Richard II)
Donhauser, Paul Stefan
Duckworth, Ruth
Earl, Jack Eugene
Easley, Loyce Rogers
Elkins, (E) Lane
Englander, Gertrud
Fager, Charles J
Ferreira, (Armando) Thomas
Frank, David
Funk, Verne J
Furman, David Stephen
Gernhardt, Henry Kendall
Gilhooly, David James, III
Greeley, Charles Matthew
Greenleaf, Esther (Hargrave)
Grippe, Florence (Berg)
Grygutis, Barbara
Halpern, Lea
Hara, Teruo
Hardy, Robert
Hay, Dick
Higgins, Edward Koelling
Higgins, Mary Lou
Hofsted, Jolyon Gene
Hooks, Earl J
Hudson, Robert H
Jencks, Penelope
Kahn, Annelies Ruth
Kelly, Isaac Perry
Kemenyffy, Steven
Kemenyffy, Susan B Hale
Kennedy, Leta Marietta
Kerstetter, Barbara Ann
Kim, Ernie
Klitgaard, Georgina
Knowlton, Grace Farrar
Koss, Gene H
Krevolin, Lewis
Kujundzic, Zeljko D
Lang, Rodger Alan
Larsen, D Dane
Larson, Jane (Warren)
Lawrence, Les
Lebeck, Carol E
Leber, Roberta (Roberta Leber McVeigh)
Lehman, Mark Ammon
Levine, Marilyn Anne
Lewis, Don
Lincoln, Fred Clinton
Lincoln, Richard Mather
Loloma, Charles
Lonewolf, Joseph
Lopez, Michael John
Lund, Jane
Macklin, Anderson D
Manhart, Thomas Arthur
Marak, Louis Bernard
Marsh, (Edwin) Thomas
Martz, Karl
Mason, John
Massaro, Karen Thuesen
McCann, Cecile Nelken
McIntosh, Harrison Edward
McKinley, Ruth Gowdy
McVey, Leza
McWhinnie, Harold James
Medicine Flower, Grace
Meyer, Charles Edward
Mignosa, Santo
Miley, Les
Mirabal, Miguel Enrique
Moquin, Richard Attilio
Morrison, Art Jens
Moss, Joel C
Natzler, Otto
Nicholas, Donna Lee
Nicodemus, Chester Roland
Nigrosh, Leon Isaac
Noble, Joseph Veach
Norwood, Malcolm Mark
Oliveira, V'Lou
Olsen, Frederick L
Pardington, Ralph Arthur
Paterson, Anthony R
Patrick, Alan K
Patterson, Curtis Ray
Pearson, Clifton
Peeler, Richard
Phelan, Linn Lovejoy
Pillin, Polia
Pilsk, Adele Inez
Popinsky, Arnold Dave
Prange, Sally Bowen
Randall, Ruth Hunie
Randall, Theodore A
Redd Ekks (Robert Norman Rasmussen)
Rippon, Ruth Margaret
Roloff, John Scott
Sage, Bill B
Schellin, Robert William
Schietinger, James Frederick
Schlanger, Jeff
Schmutzhart, Slaithong Chengtrakul
Schulz, William Gallagher
Schumacher, Herbert Charles
Scott, Curtis S
Sewards, Michele Bourque
Shannonhouse, Sandra Lynne
Silverman, David Frederick
Skinner, Elsa Kells
Soffer, Sasson
Sperry, Robert
Spongberg, Grace
Staffel, Rudolf Harry
Stephenson, John H
Stephenson, Susanne G
Stevenson, Branson Graves
Stewart, Lizbeth McNett
Takemoto, Henry Tadaaki
Taylor, Rosemary
Thomas, Steffen Wolfgang
Tornheim, Norman
Tse, Stephen
Turner, Robert Chapman
Unterseher, Chris Christian
Vaccaro, Luella Grace
Vance, George Wayne
Vandenberge, Peter Willem
Vermes, Madelaine
Wallace, Elizabeth S
Walters, Billie
Warashina, M Patricia
Watia, Tarmo
Watson, Halen Richter
Westervelt, Robert F
Whitaker, Irwin A
White, Amos, IV
Wildenhain, Frans
Will, Mary Shannon
Williams, Gerald
Wilson, Warren Bingham
Winokur, Paula Colton
Winokur, Robert Mark
Winter, Thelma Frazier
Wood, Beatrice
Wray, Margaret
Wyman, William
Yiannes, (Iordanidis)

COLLAGE ARTIST

Aach, Herb
Adler, Myril
Ahlstrom, Ronald Gustin
Ahrendt, Christine
Ajay, Abe
Albertazzi, Mario
Alcopley, L
Anderson, Howard Benjamin
Appel, Eric A
Archer, Dorothy Bryant
Ashby, Carl
Atkins, Rosalie Marks
Baker, Jill Withrow
Banerjee (bimal)
Bardazzi, Peter
Baron, Hannelore
Bart, Elizabeth (Elizabeth Bart Gerald)
Batchelor, Anthony John
Bearman, Jane Ruth
Beaumont, Mona M
Becker, Bettie (Bettie Geraldine Wathall)
Beerman, Miriam H
Benda, Richard R
Berman, Fred J
Bhalla, Hans
Birnbaum, Mildred
Boris, Bessie
Bothwell, Dorr
Boutis, Tom
Bove, Richard
Bradshaw, Glenn Raymond
Breiger, Elaine
Brigadier, Anne
Brommer, Gerald F
Brown, Peggy Ann
Brown, Rhett Delford (Harriett Gurney Brown)
Bry, Edith
Buczak, Brian Elliot
Bunker, George
Byars, Donna
Cade, Walter, III
Cadieux, Michael Eugene
Cardinal, Marcelin
Carlyle, Julian (Julian Carlyle Wells)
Churchill, Diane
Cleaver, Elizabeth
Coburn, Ralph
Colorado, Charlotte
Crable, James Harbour
Curran, Darryl Joseph
Davis, Walter Lewis
Day, John
Debassige, Blake R
Degen, Paul
Deming, David Lawson
Dillon, Paul Sanford
Dole, William
Driggs, Elsie
Duane, Tanya
Dugmore, Edward
Duvoisin, Roger
Eckstein, Ruth
Elliott, Ronnie
Endsley, Fred Starr
Evans, John

Everts, Connor
Farber, Maya M
Faris, Brunel De Bost
Ferriter, Clare
Feuerherm, Kurt K
Fraze, Denny T
Frazier, Le Roy Dyyon
Freeman, Phyllis (Therese)
Gablik, Suzi
Gardner, Joan A
Geiger, Edith Rogers
Getz, Ilse
Gilchriest, Lorenzo
Glasco, Joseph M
Goell, Abby Jane
Goertz, Augustus Frederick
Goldstein, Gladys Hack
Goldstein, Milton
Gregory, Joan
Grossman, Nancy
Halsey, William Melton
Hamwi, Richard Alexander
Handville, Robert T
Hanlen, John (Garrett)
Harlow, Robert E
Haseltine, Maury (Margaret Wilson Haseltine)
Hay-Messick, Velma
Herman, Susan L
Hertzberg, Rose
Hill, Joan (Chea-se-quah)
Hoare, Tyler James
Hobbs, Robert Dean
Hoff, Margo
Holste, Thomas James
Horn, Stuart Alan
Howe, Nelson S
Hudson, Winnifred
Humble, Douglas
Hunter, John H
Hutton, Dorothy Wackerman
Ingram, Judith
Jeffers, Wendy Jane
Jenkins, Mary Anne K
Jess (Jess Collins)
Kaish, Luise
Keeling, Henry Cornelious
Kelleher, Daniel Joseph
Kilian, Austin Farland
Kitta, George Edward
Kjargaard, John Ingvard
Knerr, Sallie Frost
Knorr, Jeanne Boardman
Koch, Arthur Robert
Kohl, Barbara
Korman, Barbara
Korn, Elizabeth P
Kornmayer, J Gary (John)
Koster, Marjory Jean
Krasner, Lee
Kuchar, Kathleen Ann
Kuczun, Ann-Marie
Kusama, Yayoi
Latham, Catherine Doris
Lea, Stanley E
Leax, Ronald Allen
Lesch, Alma Wallace
Levering, Robert K
Lewen, Si
Little, John
Longstreet, Stephen
Ludwig, Eva
Lynds, Clyde William
Mabie, Don Edward
Mancuso, Leni (Leni Mancuso Barrett)
Mansaram, Panchal
Margolies, Ethel Polacheck
Martin, Keith Morrow
Martin, Roger
McCabe, Maureen M
McClanahan, John Dean
McKay, John Sangster
Miller, Dolly (Ethel B)
Miller, George
Miller, Nancy Tokar
Miyashita, Tad
Monaghan, William Scott
Morrison, George
Moskowitz, Shirley (Mrs Jacob W Gruber)
Narotzky, Norman David
Nay, Mary Spencer
Nonay, Paul
Nowack, Wayne Kenyon
Olson, Gary Spangler
Orling, Anne
Owings, Margaret Wentworth
Ozonoff, Ida
Pappas, Marilyn
Parker, James Varner
Payne, John D
Pearlman, Etta S
Peiperl, Adam
Perry, Kathryn Powers
Plunkett, Edward Milton
Prentice, David Ramage
Provder, Carl
Ramos-Prida, Fernando
Ramsauer, Joseph Francis
Reich, Nathaniel E
Reichert, Donald O
Romoser, Ruth Amelia
Rosenthal, Gloria M
Rothschild, Judith
Ryder, Mahler Bessinger
Saar, Betye
Schabacker, Betty Barchet
Scharff, Constance Kramer
Schneemann, Carolee
Scholder, Laurence
Schulze, John H
Secunda, (Holland) Arthur
Seidler, Doris
Selchow, Roger Hoffman
Shaddle, Alice
Sharp, Anne
Sheehan, Evelyn
Simmons, Cleda Marie
Skelton, Robin
Smith, Alexis (Patricia Anne)
Smith, Bradford Leaman
Smith, Vincent D
Speers, Teryl Townsend
Spero, Nancy
Sprague, Mark Anderson
Steckel, Anita
Stevens, Marjorie
Stoianovich, Marcelle
Stone, Gwen
Storer, Inez Mary
Storm, Larue
Szesko, Lenore Rundle
Tanner, Joan Elizabeth
Tavenner, Patricia (Pat)
Taylor, Michael (Leach)
Taylor, Sandra Ortiz
Thornhill, Anna
Tracy, (Lois) Bartlett
Uchima, Toshiko
Van Brunt, Philip G
Van Buren, Helen Rae
Vevers, Anthony Marr
Wagner, Gordon Parsons
Warner, Jo
Watford, Frances Mizelle
Weinstein, Florence
West, Amy M
Whitson (Peter Whitson Warren)
Williams, Marylou Lord Study
Wilson, Helen J
Winter, Roger
Winters, Denny
Woodson, Shirley Ann
Young, Charles Alexander
Zack, David
Zimmerman, Kathleen Marie
Zucker, Murray Harvey
Zver, James M

COLLECTOR

Abramovitz, Mr & Mrs Max
Abrams, Harry N
Adams, William Howard
Adrian, Barbara (Mrs Franklin Tramutola)
Agoos, Herbert M
Akston, Joseph James
Albrecht, Robert A
Albro, Jeannette (Jeannette Louise Cantrell)
Aldrich, Larry
Alonzo, Jack J
Alsdorf, James W
Altmayer, Jay P
Altschul, Arthur G
Amsden, Floyd T
Anbinder, Paul
Anderson, David K
Anspach, Ernst
Arenberg, Mr & Mrs Albert L
Artinian, Artine
Arwin, Lester B
Asher, Betty M
Askin, Arnold Samuel
Atkyns, (Willie) Lee, Jr
Atlas, Martin & Liane W
Ault, Lee Addison
Bader, Franz
Baehler, Wallace R
Baird, Joseph Armstrong, Jr
Baker, Richard Brown
Baker, Walter C
Banta, Melissa Wiekser
Bareiss, Walter
Barton, Phyllis Grace
Bass, John
Baum, Hank
Bear, Marcelle L
Bednarz, Adele
Beineke, Dr & Mrs J Frederick
Bell, R Murray
Bensinger, B Edward, III
Bentley, Claude
Benton, William
Berg, Phil
Berman, Aaron
Berman, Bernard
Berman, Muriel Mallin
Berman, Philip I
Berne, Gustave Morton
Bernstein, Benjamin D
Bernstein, Joseph
Bickford, George Percival
Biddle, James
Bingham, Mrs Harry Payne
Birdman, Jerome M
Blackburn, Lenora Whitmire
Blankfort, Dorothy
Blankfort, Michael
Block, Mr & Mrs Leigh B
Boese, Alvin William
Bolles, John S
Bond, Roland S
Borgenicht, Grace (Grace Borgenicht Brandt)
Bostwick, Mr & Mrs Dunbar W
Bowater, Marian
Bradley, Mrs Harry Lynde
Brody, Mr & Mrs Sidney F
Brooks, Louise Cherry
Broussard, Normaj
Brown, Harry Joe, Jr
Brown, Jeanette H
Browne, Robert M
Brunkus, Richard Allen
Bruno, Phillip A
Bunshaft, Mr & Mrs Gordon
Burden, Carter
Burford, William E
Burk, Anna Darlene
Burkhardt, Hans Gustav
Burns, Sid
Burnside, Wesley M
Burr, Horace
Burrows, Selig S
Byron, Charles Anthony
Caldwell, Benjamin Hubbard, Jr
Campbell, Vivian (Vivian Campbell Stoll)
Cantey, Sam Benton, III
Cantor, B Gerald
Carey, Ted
Cartwright, Constance B & Carroll L
Castano, Elvira
Chalk, Mr & Mrs O Roy
Chapman, Mrs Gilbert W
Chase, Robert M
Childers, Betty Bivins
Chrysler, Walter P, Jr
Clare, Stewart
Clark, Fred, Jr
Clowes, Allen Whitehill
Cohen, Arthur A
Cohen, Wilfred P
Colin, Georgia T
Colin, Ralph Frederick
Conley, Zeb Bristol, Jr
Constable, Rosalind
Cooley, William, Jr
Cooper, Rebecca (Rebecca Cooper Eisenberg)
Costa, Olga
Couturier, Marion B
Cowles, Charles
Cowles, Mr & Mrs Gardner
Cox, E Morris
Crawford, John McAllister, Jr
Crispo, Andrew John
Cummings, Nathan
Cunningham, Charles Crehore
Dalton, Harry L
Damaz, Paul F
D'Amico, Augustine A
Daniels, David M
Davidson, Ian J
Davidson, Suzette Morton
Davis, John Harold
Davis, Mr & Mrs Walter
Day, Martha B Willson
De Coursey, John Edward
De Graaff, Mr & Mrs Jan
De Hoyos, Luis
de Kolb, Eric
Delhom, Mary Mellanay
DeMaree, Elizabeth Ann (Betty)
de Nagy, Tibor (J)
Devine, William Charles
De Waal, Ronald Burt
Dillon, C Douglas
Dolan, Margo
Dreitzer, Albert J
Driver, Morley-Brooke Lister
Dunn, O Coleman
Dunnington, Mrs Walter Grey
Dyck, Paul
Eckstein, Joanna
Edwards, Allan W
Eisenstein, Mr & Mrs Julian
Eiteljorg, Harrison
Elkon, Robert
Elliott, Scott Cameron
Emil, Arthur D
Engelhard, Mr & Mrs Charles
Erdelac, Joseph Mark
Esman, Rosa M
Evans, Nancy
Ewing, Bayard
Farber, Mrs George W
Feigen, Richard L
Feldenheimer, Edith
Feldstein, Mary
Felt, Mr & Mrs Irving Mitchell
Field, Lyman
Fillman, Jesse R
Finn, David
Fischbach, Marilyn Cole
Fitch, George Hopper

COLLECTOR (cont)
Flagg, Mr & Mrs Richard B
Fleischman, Lawrence
Flick, Paul John
Ford, John Gilmore
Forsyth, Robert Joseph
Fosdick, Sina G
Frank, Charles William
Franklin, Ernest Washington, Jr
Frauwirth, Sidney
Freeman, Gertrude
Frelinghuysen, Mr & Mrs Peter H B, Jr
Friedman, Marvin
Fromer, Mrs Leon
Fuller, Adelaide P & William Marshall
Furman, Aaron & Joyce
Garbaty, Marie Louise
Garbisch, Edgar William & Bernice Chrysler
Gardiner, Robert David Lion
Gary, Dorothy Hales
Gebhardt, Harold
Gelman, Milton
Geyer, Luise Margot
Gibson, Roland
Gilbert, Alma Magdalena
Gilbert, Arnold Martin
Gilbert, Arthur
Gilkey, Gordon Waverly
Gilvarry, James
Gimbel, Mrs Bernard F
Glaser, Samuel
Glass, Wendy D
Glezer, Nechemia
Glick, Paula Florence
Goetzl, Thomas Maxwell
Goldberger, Mr & Mrs Edward
Goldsmith, C Gerald
Goldstone, Mr & Mrs Herbert
Gollin, Mr & Mrs Joshua A
Goodman, Calvin Jerome
Goodman, James Neil
Gordon, John
Gordon, Joni
Gottlieb, Abe
Graham, Robert Claverhouse
Grass, Patty Patterson
Graves, Mr & Mrs John W
Gray, Thomas Alexander
Greenspan, Mr & Mrs George
Greenwald, Charles D
Greenwald, Dorothy Kirstein
Grey, Mrs Benjamin Edwards
Griggs, Maitland Lee
Gross, Mr & Mrs Merrill Jay
Gruber, Aaronel De Roy
Guggenheim, Peggy
Gumberts, William A
Gussman, Herbert
Guthman, Leo S
Haber, Leonard
Haber, William
Hack, Phillip S & Patricia Y
Hadzi, Dimitri
Hage, Raymond Joseph
Halff, Robert H
Hall, Julie Ann
Hall, Michael David
Halpern, Nathan L
Halseth, Elmer Johann
Hames, Carl Martin
Hammer, Armand
Hampton, Ambrose Gonzales, Jr
Harnett, Mr & Mrs Joel William
Harris, Leon A, Jr
Harris, Murray A
Harris, Dr & Mrs S Elliott
Harrison, Joseph Robert, Jr
Hartford, Huntington
Haskell, Harry Garner, Jr
Hazen, Joseph H
Heath, David C
Heineman, Bernard, Jr
Heinz, Mr & Mrs Henry J, II
Heller, Ben
Heller, Goldie (Mrs Edward W Greenberg)
Hemphill, Herbert Waide
Henrickson, Paul Robert
Herbert, David
Herman, Joyce Elaine
Hewitt, Jean Clifford
Heyman, Mr & Mrs David M
Hill, Ed
Hill, John Alexander
Hilles, Susan Morse
Hirshhorn, Joseph H
Hofman, Kate
Hokin, Grace E
Holcombe, R Gordon, Jr
Holmes, Paul James & Mary E
Holt, Margaret McConnell
Honeyman, Robert B, Jr
Hooker, Mrs R Wolcott
Hooks, Charles Vernon
Hoover, Francis Louis
Hoover, Margaret Pomeroy
Hopkinson, Harold I
Horowitz, Mr & Mrs Raymond J
Horowitz, Saul
Hovey, Walter Read
Hoyt, Whitney F
Hulsey, William Hansell
Hunt, Kari
Huntington, John W
Iannetti, Pasquale Francesco Paolo
Iervolino, Joseph Anthony
Iervolino, Paula
Indeck, Karen Joy
Ingber, Barbara
Inslee, Marguerite T
Inzerillo, Gian Del Valentino
Iolas, Alexander
Irwin, George M
Isaacs, Carole Schaffer
Ivey, James Burnett
Jachmann, Kurt M
Jacobs, William Ketchum, Jr
Jaffe, Mrs William B
Janis, Conrad
Janss, Edwin, Jr
Jarman, Walton Maxey
Jarvis, Lucy
Johnson, Philip Cortelyou
Johnson, Robert Flynn
Johnson, Ruth Carter
Josten, Mrs Werner E
Kanee, Ben
Kangas, Gene
Kaplan, Alice Manheim
Kaplan, Jacques
Kaplan, Muriel Sheerr
Kasle, Gertrude
Katz, Joseph M
Keane, Lucina Mabel
Keen, Helen Boyd
Kelleher, Patrick Joseph
Kerr, Berta Borgenicht
Kestnbaum, Gertrude Dana
Killam, Walt
Kincade, Arthur Warren
King, Ethel May
Kinney, Gilbert Hart
Kirkland, Vance Hall
Kirstein, Mr & Mrs Lincoln
Kisner, Bernard
Klein, Esther M
Knowlton, Monique
Knox, Katharine McCook
Koch, John
Koch, William Emery
Kohl, Barbara
Koltun, Frances Lang
Kottemann, George & Norma
Kramarsky, Mrs Siegried
Kreeger, David Lloyd
Kurdian, Haroutiun Harry
LaDow, Jesse
Lamantia, James
Lambert, Phyllis
Lane, Alvin Seymour
Langston, Loyd H
Larkin, John E, Jr
Lasker, Mrs Albert D
Laskey, Dr & Mrs Norman F
Lederer, Kurt
Lee, Richard Allen
Leff, Jay C
Lerner, Alexander
Levick, Mr & Mrs Irving
Levin, Jeanne
Levine, Seymour R
Lewin, Bernard
Lienau, Daniel Clifford
Lilienthal, Mr & Mrs Philip N, Jr
Linsky, Mr & Mrs Jack
Lipman, Howard W
Lipschultz, Maurice A
List, Vera G
Little, Nina Fletcher
Liu, Ho
Lloyd, Mrs H Gates
Locks, Marian
Loeb, Mr & Mrs John L
London, Alexander
Longstaffe, John Ronald
Loran, Erle
Lucas, Charles C, Jr
Ludgin, Earle
Ludington, Wright S
Lukin, Philip
Lust, Herbert
Lyons, Ian Raymond
MacAlister, Paul Ritter
Magee, Alderson
Magriel, Paul
Malbin, Lydia Winston
Mallory, Margaret
Marcus, Betty
Marcus, Stanley
Maremont, Arnold H
Marino, Albert Joseph
Marker, Mariska Pugsley
Marker, Ralph E
Marks, Mr & Mrs Cedric H
Marks, Royal S
Marks, Stanley Albert
Markus, Mrs Henry A
Marlor, Clark Strang
Marron, Donald B
Marsteller, William A
Martin, Rose Breyer
Mathis, Emile Henry, II
Maurice, Alfred Paul
May, Morton David
May, William L
Mayer, Grace M
Mayers, John J
McCannel, Mrs Malcolm A
McDonough, John Joseph
McFadden, Mary
McHugh, Adeliza Sorenson
McIlhenny, Henry Plumer
McKean, Hugh Ferguson
McNear, Everett C
Meek, J William, III
Meisel, Louis Koenig
Mekler, Adam
Melamed, Abraham
Melberg, Jerald Leigh
Mellon, Paul
Meltzer, Doris
Mendoza, David C
Merriam, Ruth
Meyer, Mr & Mrs Andre
Miller, Mrs G Macculloch
Milliken, Alexander Fabbri
Mills, James
Milrad, Aaron M
Mirko (Wolodymyr Walter Pylyshenko)
Mirvish, David
Misch, Allene K
Mitchell, Dana Covington, Jr
Moir, Alfred
Molina, Antonio J
Morgan, James Sherrod
Morse, A Reynolds
Moss, Morrie Alfred
Mudge, Edmund Webster, Jr
Muensterberger, Werner
Muller, Jerome Kenneth
Muniot, Barbara King
Munsterberg, Hugo
Murchison, John D
Murray, Joan
Murray, William Colman
Namuth, Hans
Nash, Veronica F
Navas, Elizabeth S
Neuberger, Roy R
Neumann, Hans
Neustadter, Edward L
Newman, Arnold
Newman, Louis
Niemeyer, Arnold Matthew
Nutzle, Futzie (Bruce John Kleinsmith)
Ochs, Robert David
Offin, Charles Z
Ohrbach, Jerome K
Orr, Veronica Marie (Veronica Marie Ingram)
Osborn, Elodie C (Mrs Robert C Osborn)
Paley, Mr & Mrs William S
Pall, Dr & Mrs David B
Palmer, Fred Loren
Parker, Ann (Ann Parker Neal)
Parkinson, Elizabeth Bliss
Parsons, Betty Bierne
Patten, David John
Payson, Mr & Mrs Charles S
Pease, Roland Folsom, Jr
Penney, Charles Rand
Perry, Richard C
Pettibone, John Wolcott
Pharr, Mr & Mrs Walter Nelson
Phillips, Gifford
Pilavin, Selma F
Pines, Ned L
Pizitz, Silvia
Pleasants, Frederick R
Polan, Lincoln M
Polsky, Cynthia
Pool, Nelda Lee
Pope, Annemarie Henle
Poppelman, Raymond James
Poses, Mr & Mrs Jack I
Posner, Judith L
Praeger, Frederick A
Prager, David A
Pratt, Dallas
Price, Vincent
Pritzlaff, Mr & Mrs John, Jr
Pulitzer, Mr & Mrs Joseph, Jr
Putnam, Mrs John B
Quinn, Henrietta Reist
Rabb, Mr & Mrs Irving W
Rabkin, Leo
Rabow, Rose
Rafsky, Jessica C
Rainey, John Watts
Raley, Mr & Mrs Robert L
Rauch, John G
Rautbord, Dorothy H
Ray, Jim
Raydon, Alexander R
Redding, Steve
Reeves, James Franklin
Retzer, Howard Earl
Revington, George D, III
Richmond, Frederick W
Richmond, Lawrence
Rifkin, Dr & Mrs Harold
Rifkind, Robert Gore
Riley, Chapin
Ring, Edward Alfred
Rinhart, George R
Robb, Mr & Mrs Sidney R
Robinson, C David
Robinson, Thomas

Robison, Andrew
Robles, Esther Waggoner
Roby, Sara (Mary Barnes)
Rockefeller, Mr & Mrs David
Rockefeller, John Davison, III
Rockefeller, Mrs Laurance S
Rockefeller, Nelson Aldrich
Rodman, Selden
Roebling, Mary G
Roesler, Norbert Leonhard Hugo
Rogers, Leo M
Rojtman, Mrs Marc B
Rome, Harold
Romero, Mike
Rosen, Israel
Rosenberg, Carole Halsband
Rosenthal, Mrs Alan H
Rosenwald, Barbara K
Rosenwald, Lessing Julius
Rosenzweig, Daphne Lange
Rouse, John R
Rubin, Lawrence
Rumsey, David MacIver
Ruskin, Lewis J
Russell, John Laurel
Rust, David E
Sabelis, Huibert
Sachs, A M
Sachse, Janice R
Saidenberg, Eleanore B
Sampliner, Mr & Mrs Paul H
Samuels, John Stockwell, 3d
Sandground, Mark Bernard, Sr
Sarnoff, Lolo
Sarnoff, Robert W
Sawyer, William
Schang, Frederick, Jr
Schimmel, Norbert
Schoen, Mr & Mrs Arthur Boyer
Schooler, Lee
Schramm, James Siegmund
Schulhof, Mr & Mrs Rudolph B
Schulman, Jacob
Schulte, Mr & Mrs Arthur D
Schwandner, Kathleen M
Schwartz, Eugene M
Schweitzer, M R
Seders, Francine Lavinal
Segy, Ladislas
Selig, Mr & Mrs Manfred
Seymour, Rachel
Shapiro, Daisy Viertel
Sharf, Frederic Alan
Sheldon, Olga N (Mrs A B Sheldon)
Sherbell, Rhoda
Sherwood, A (Frances Ann Crane)
Sherwood, Richard E
Shorter, Edward Swift
Simon, Norton
Sinaiko, Arlie
Sirena (Contessa Antonia Mastrocristino Fanara)
Skelton, Robin
Smart, Mary-Leigh
Smith, Mrs Bertram
Smith, Justin V
Smith, Ray Winfield
Smith, Ross Ransom Williams
Sneed, Patricia M
Snyder, Barry
Solinger, David M
Solman, Joseph
Solomon, Holly
Solomon, Richard H
Solomon, Mr & Mrs Sidney L
Sonnenberg, Mr & Mrs Benjamin
Sosnowitz, Henry Abram
Spaeth, Eloise O'Mara
Speiser, Stuart M
Spiegel, Sam
Spitzer, Frances R
Spurgeon, Sarah (Edna M)
Stachelberg, Mrs Charles G
Stamats, Peter Owen
Stamm, John Davies
Stein, Fritz Henry
Steiner, Paul
Stephens, Richard Alan
Stern, Mr & Mrs Arthur Lewis
Stern, H Peter
Stern, Leonard B
Stevens, Edward John, Jr
Stillman, E Clark
Stinski, Gerald Paul
Stoll, Mrs Berry Vincent
Stone, Alex Benjamin
Straight, Michael
Stralem, Donald S
Stubbs, Robert
Stull, Robert J
Sussman, Bonnie K
Swartz, Phillip Scott
Tarnopol, Gregoire
Tauch, Waldine Amanda
Temple, Mr & Mrs Alan H
Terrill, Evelyn Beard
Thiry, Paul (Albert)
Thompson, Lockwood
Thompson, Richard E, Jr
Thompson, Richard Earl, Sr
Tobin, Robert L B
Topol, Robert Martin
Travis, David Hail
Truman, Jock Curtis
Tucker, Glenn F
Ullman, Mrs George W
Ullman, Harold P
Ulrich, Edwin Abel
Uzielli, Giorgio
Valenstein, Alice
Vanasse, Louis Raymond
Van Atta, Helen Ulmer
Van Derpool, James Grote
Van Leer, Mrs W Leicester
Vazquez, Juan Julian
Vershbow, Mr & Mrs Arthur
Verzyl, June Carol
Vogel, Mr & Mrs Herbert
Von Wiegand, Charmion
Waddell, Eugene
Walker, Mr & Mrs Ralph
Wall, Sue
Walmsley, William Aubrey
Walter, May E
Walter, Paul F
Walton, Harry A, Jr
Warburg, Edward M M
Wauters, Andre
Weiner, Ted
Weinstein, Mr & Mrs Joseph
Welch, Mr & Mrs Robert G
Wenger, Muriel June
Westermeier, Clifford Peter
Westlund, Harry E
White, Albert
White, Philip Butler
Whitney, John Hay
Wilkinson, Ruth Murphy
Willis, Elizabeth Bayley
Winokur, James L
Wintersteen, Bernice McIlhenny
Wise, Geneva H (Holcomb)
Witham, Vernon Clint
Wood, James Arthur (Art)
Woodner, Ian
Woods, Sarah Ladd
Woodside, Gordon William
Woodward, Helen M
Wright, Mr & Mrs William H
Wrightsman, Charles Bierer
Wurdemann, Helen (Baroness Elena Guzzardi)
Wynshaw, Frances
Young, John Chin
Zalstem-Zalessky, Mrs Alexis
Zamparelli, Mario Armond
Zeisler, Richard Spiro
Zeitlin, Jacob Ilrael
Ziff, Jerrold
Zipkin, Jerome R
Zlotnick, Diana Shirley

CONCEPTUAL ARTIST

Abish, Cecile
Alexenberg, Melvin (Menahem)
Allen, Roberta
Antin, Eleanor
Apple, Jacki (Jacqueline B)
Applebroog, Ida H
Baldessari, John Anthony
Baldwin, Russell W
Barry, Robert Thomas
Beckley, Bill
Berg, Barry
Blake, John Clemens
Boal, Sara Metzner
Bochner, Mel
Bollinger, William
Bott, H J
Bowman, Dorothy (Louise)
Brecht, George
Bronson, A A (Michael Wayne Tims)
Brown, Robert Delford
Burden, Chris
Burgess, David Lowry
Burgy, (Donald Thomas)
Burton, Scott
Card, Greg S
Celender, Donald Dennis
Conaway, Gerald
Crane, Michael Patrick
Cumming, Robert H
Darboven, Hanne
Davis, Ben H
Davis, Douglas Matthew
Davis, Phil Douglas
Dean, Peter
deGooyer, Kirk Alan
Delford Brown, Robert
De Monte, Claudia
Denes, Agnes C
Dignac, Geny (Eugenia M Bermudez)
Dupuy, Jean
East, N S, Jr
Edelson, Mary Beth
Edwards, James F
Endsley, Fred Starr
Feigenbaum, Harriet (Mrs Neil Chamberlain)
Fenton, Julia Ann
Ferguson, Frank Wayne
Fernie, John Chipman
Fine, Jud
Fisher Joel A
Foulkes, Llyn
Fried, Howard Lee
Fugate-Wilcox, Terry
Fulton, Fred Franklin
Gillingwater, Denis Claude
Goldstein, Jack
Graham, Daniel H
Greenly, Colin
Hamouda, Amy
Hari, Kenneth
Harrison, Helen Mayer
Harrison, Newton A
Hoffman, Martin (Joseph)
Hompson, Davi Det (David Elbridge Thompson)
Horn, Stuart Alan
Hurley, Wilson
Hutchinson, Peter Arthur
Ida, Shoichi
Ispanky, Laszlo
Jansen, Angela Bing
Jennings, Frank Harding
Jonas, Joan
Jones, Bill
Kawara, On
Kosuth, Joseph
Krims, Leslie Robert
Kruger, Barbara
Lacy, Suzanne
Lax, David
Levine, Les
Levine, Reeva (Anna) Miller
Levinson, Mon
Le Witt, Sol
Loeffler, Carl Eugene
Lonidier, Fred Spencer
MacGillis, Robert Donald
Mackenzie, David
Max, Peter
McCall, Anthony
Metyko, Michael Joseph
Mew, Tommy
Mignosa, Santo
Miller, George
Milonadis, Konstantin
Misch, Allene K
Mullen, Buell
Muntadas, Antonio
Nauman, Bruce
Nelson, Harry William
Notarbartolo, Albert
Ockerse, Thomas
Odate, Toshio
Okulick, John A
Oppenheim, Dennis A
Pennuto, James William
Petrochuk, Konstantin
Pettibone, Richard H
Phillips, Donna-Lee
Pomeroy, James Calwell, Jr
Puchalski, Gregory John
Pulido, Guillermo Aguilar
Ramos, Melvin John
Resnick, Marcia Aylene
Romeu, Joost A
Rosenthal, Rachel
Ruppersberg, Allen Rawson
Salzman, Rick
Sapien, Darryl Rudolph
Schley, Evander Duer (Van)
Schneider, Ira
Segalove, Ilene Judy
Sekula, Allan
Sharits, Paul Jeffrey
Sigel, Barry Chaim
Simkin, Phillips M
Smith, Alexis (Patricia Anne)
Smith, Barbara Turner
Solomon, David
Sorby, J Richard
Sturgeon, John Floyd
Tanner, Warren
Torffield, Marvin
Trakas, George
Turner, Ralph James
Van Riper, Peter
Vazan, William Joseph
Walker, William Walter
Watts, Robert M
Welch, Roger
Wheeler, Doug
White, John M
Whitson (Peter Whitson Warren)
Willer, Jim
Willis, Jay Steward
Wilson, Martha Storey

CONSERVATOR

see also **Restorer**

Alden, Gary Wade
Amarotico, Joseph Anthony
Beardsley, Barbara H
Beck, Curt Werner
Butler, Marigene H
Cady, Dennis Vern
Chapian, Grieg Hovsep
Chase, William Thomas (W Thomas Chase)
Cianfoni, Emilio
Cohn, Marjorie B

CONSERVATOR (cont)
Cornelius, Francis DuPont
Covey, Victor Charles B
Craig, Martin
Demartis, James J
Dennis, Roger Wilson
Dolloff, Frank Wesley
Etchison, Bruce
Feller, Robert L
Feuerherm, Kurt K
Fisher, Sarah Lisbeth
Greaves, James L
Greenwood, William James
Haley, Patience E (Patience E Haley Ghikas)
Homitzky, Peter
Honig, Mervin
Horton, Carolyn
Howell, Douglass (Morse)
Hulmer, Eric Claus
Jakstas, Alfred John
Jarkowski, Stefania Agnes
Jolles, Arnold H
Jones, Allan Dudley
Keck, Sheldon Waugh
Knowlton, Daniel Gibson
Kortheuer, Dayrell
Larson, Sidney
Leisher, William Rodger
Lennon, Timothy
Lewis, Don S, Sr
MacDonald, Gayle Coleman
Mancusi-Ungaro, Carol Caruso
Marshall, James Duard
Merriam, Ruth
Merrill, Ross M
Minewski, Alex
Mohr, Pauline Catherine
Pennuto, James William
Petty, John L, Jr
Pomerantz, Louis
Robinson, Charles K
Sandecki, Albert Edward
Schlicher, Karl Theodore
Schmutzhart, Berthold Josef
Schwartzbaum, Paul Martin
Sidenius, W Christian
Silberfeld, Kay
Slawinski, Joseph
Sloan, Robert Smullyan
Stars, William Kenneth
Stein, Fritz Henry
Stolow, Nathan
Stoner, Joyce Hill
Weidner, Marilyn Kemp
West, Clara Faye
Young, Cliff

CONSULTANT

Adamy, George E
Alper, M Victor
Andrew, David Neville
Archie, James Lee
Asbel, Joseph
Auth, Susan Handler
Baehler, Wallace R
Barnes, Carroll
Baro, Gene
Bartholet, Elizabeth Ives
Barzun, Jacques
Bass, David Loren
Baum, Hank
Bealmer, William
Beardsley, Barbara H
Bednarz, Adele
Beebe, Mary Livingstone
Beggs, Thomas Montague
Belfiore, Gerardo
Belle, Anna (Anna Belle Birckett)
Benedikt, Michael
Benjamin, Karl Stanley
Berger, Jerry Allen
Bessemer, Auriel
Bier, Justus
Bloom, Jason
Bloomgarden, Judith Mary
Blos, May (Elizabeth)
Booth, Bill
Botkin, Henry
Bowman, Jeff Ray
Breeskin, Adelyn Dohme
Breitenbach, Edgar
Brookins, Jacob Boden
Burgart, Herbert Joseph
Burns, Jerome
Byrne, Charles Joseph
Byrnes, James Bernard
Canepa, Anna L
Cannon, Margaret Erickson
Casey, Elizabeth Temple
Casey, Jacqueline Shepard
Cathers, James O
Chaffee, John W
Chapin, Louis (Le Bourgeois)
Colby, Joy Hakanson
Colorado, Charlotte
Colt, Priscilla C
Cooley, Adelaide Nation
Cordy-Collins, Alana (Alana Kathleen Cordy-Collins Riesland)
Crouch, Ned Philbrick
Curtis, Phillip Houston
Danikian, Caron Le Brun
Dank, Leonard Dewey
De Coursey, John Edward
Dennison, Keith Elkins
DeShazo, Edith Kind
Diamond, Abel Joseph
Dickerson, Tom
Dockstader, Frederick J
Dunn, Roger Terry
Elliott, B Charles, Jr
Eriquezzo, Lee M
Evans, Paul Fredric
Faul, Roberta Heller
Fedele, Frank D
Feinman, Stephen E
Fiori, Dennis Andrew
Fleming, Betty Corcoran
Flick, Robert
Folds, Thomas McKey
Fraughton, Edward James
Freeman, Gertrude
Freundlich, August L
Friedland, Ruth Volid
Fulton, W Joseph
Gagnon, Charles Eugene
Gaines, Alan Jay
Gee, Helen
Gilchrist, Elizabeth Brenda
Glass, Wendy D
Gold, Betty
Goldberg, Kenneth Paul
Goldeen, Dorothy A
Goldhamer, Charles
Gomez-Sicre, Jose
Goodman, Calvin Jerome
Goreleigh, Rex
Gorman, Carl Nelson (Kin-ya-onny Beyeh)
Gottschalk, Fritz
Gottschalk, Max Jules
Graham, F Lanier
Gray, Robert Ward
Greene, Theodore R
Gregory, Angela
Gross, Mr & Mrs Merrill Jay
Gursoy, Ahmet
Hage, Raymond Joseph
Hammond, Leslie King
Hanks, David Allen
Harris, William Wadsworth, II
Harriton, Abraham
Hatch, John Davis
Hayes, Bartlett Harding, Jr
Hayes, Laura M
Heath, David C
Heinz, Susan
Held, Julius S
Heller, Goldie (Mrs Edward W Greenberg)
Herbert, David
Herman, Alan David
Hess, Stanley William
Hicken, Russell Bradford
Hinkhouse, Forest Melick
Hodgson, James Stanley
Hoffberg, Judith Ann
Hoffman, Martin (Joseph)
Hoover, Francis Louis
Horne, (Arthur Edward) Cleeve
Hornung, Gertrude Seymour
Hoving, Thomas
Howard, Richard Foster
Howe, Thomas Carr
Hubbard, Robert Hamilton
Hyde, Andrew Cornwall
Iannetti, Pasquale Francesco Paolo
Irwin, George M
Isaacs, Avrom
Jakstas, Alfred John
Jardine, Donald Leroy
Jordan, Barbara Schwinn
Kaep, Louis Joseph
Karpel, Bernard
Kasle, Gertrude
Katzive, David H
Kaufman, Nancy
Keener, Anna Elizabeth
Kelleher, Patrick Joseph
Kerr, James Wilfrid
Kirkwood, Larry Thomas
Klein, Cecelia F
Kravis, Janis
Kuehn, Edmund Karl
Kuh, Katharine
Landau, Mitzi
Lanou, Tobie E
Lebedev, Vladimir
Leff, Juliette
Lewin, Keith Kerton
Lewis, Don S, Sr
Lewis, Golda
Luck, Robert
Luntz, Irving
Luria, Gloria
Lutze
Maas, Arnold (Marcolino)
MacDonald, Gayle Coleman
Mack, Charles Randall
Malinowski, Jerome Joseph
Marks, Royal S
Marlor, Clark Strang
Martinez, Ernesto Pedregon
McColley, Sutherland
McLanathan, Richard B K
Mekler, Adam
Mendoza, David C
Merritt, Francis Sumner
Milch, Harold Carlton
Miller, Dorothy Canning
Miller, Eva-Hamlin
Mitchell, Eleanor
Moore, Barbara
Morley, Grace L McCann
Newman, Libby
Newton, Earle Williams
Nitz, Thomas L
Nordness, Lee
Norfleet, Barbara Pugh
O'Connor, Francis Valentine
Orling, Anne
Pacileo, Dolores Margaret
Pena, Amado Maurilio, Jr
Peterson, John Douglas
Pfeifer, Marcuse
Pirkl, James Joseph
Poduska, T F
Polimenakos, Carmon
Pope, Annemarie Henle
Pounian, Albert Kachouni
Pratt, Vernon Gaither
Priest, T
Quick, Birney MacNabb
Rathbone, Perry Townsend
Regensteiner, Else (Friedsam)
Remsen, John Everett, II
Robbins, Daniel J
Robinson, Grove
Rogovin, Mark
Rosenthal, Gertrude
Roston, Arnold
Roth, James Buford
Rowe, Charles Alfred
Ruddley, John
St John, Bruce
St John, Terry N
Sawyer, Alan R
Sawyer, William
Schmidt, Stephen
Schmutzhart, Berthold Josef
Schnitzer, Arlene Director
Schoener, Allon
Scholz, Janos
Schuster, Cita Fletcher (Sarah E)
Sellin, David
Seyler, David W
Shalit, Mitzi (Mildred M Shalit)
Siden, Franklin
Silberman, Arthur
Slater, Van E
Smart, Mary-Leigh
Smither, Edward Murray
Solway, Carl E
Souza, Paul Marciel
Starks, Elliott Roland
Stern, Jean
Stomps, Walter E, Jr
Stout, George Leslie
Stronghilos, Carol
Swanson, Dean
Swarzenski, Hanns Peter Theophil
Thomas, Tamara B
Thomas, William Radford
Tracy, Berry Bryson
Tredennick, Dorothy W
Truman, Jock Curtis
Upelnieks, Arthur
Van Der Straeten, Vincent Roger
Van Ginkel, Blanche Lemco
Varian, Elayne H
Wade, Jane
Walker, William Walter
Watson, Aldren Auld
Weeks, H J
Wehr, Wesley Conrad
Wenger, Sigmund
Werner, Alfred
White, Ruth
Wilson, Carrie Lois
Winchester, Alice
Wright, Nina Kaiden
Yochim, Louise Dunn
Zamparelli, Mario Armond
Zeisler, Richard Spiro
Zucker, Bob

CRAFTSMAN

Aarons, Anita
Ahlskog, Sirkka
Aitson, Marland Konad
Allman, Margo
Arnautoff, Jacob Victor
Atkins, Rosalie Marks
Baitsell, Wilma Williamson
Bakken, Haakon
Baldridge, Mark S
Bambas, Thomas Reese
Bassler, James W
Bates, Kenneth Francis
Beaudoin, Andre Eugene
Bernstein, William Joseph
Betteridge, Lois Etherington

Bittner, Hans Oskar
Blaz, Georgia Lee
Blazey, Lawrence Edwin
Blumberg, Barbara Griffiths
Boylen, Michael Edward
Brejcha, Vernon Lee
Brooks, Lois Ziff
Brown, Catharine Homan
Buranabunpot, Pornpilai
Byrne, Charles Joseph
Cadle, Ray Kenneth
Cantor, Robert Lloyd
Cantrell, Jim
Carpenter, Arthur Espenet
Carter, Dudley Christopher
Castle, Wendell Keith
Chamberlain, Charles
Chapman, Robert Gordon
Chappelle, Jerry Leon
Chavez, Joseph Arnold
Christensen, Hans-Jorgen Thorvald
Clark, Jon Frederic
Cohen, Michael S
Conover, Claude
Cornell, David E
Corsaw, Roger D
Crozier, William K, Jr
Daily, Evelynne B
Danielson, Phyllis I
Davis, John Sherwood
Dice, Elizabeth Jane
Dillingham, Rick (James Richard II)
Drumm, Don
Eagleboy, Wayne
Ellingei, Ilona E
Fields, Fredrica H
Fisch, Arline Marie
Foote, Howard Reed
Fox, Charles Harold
Fox, Winifred Grace
Frank, David
Funk, Charlotte M
Funk, Verne J
Gabriel, Hannelore
Glasson, Lloyd
Glorig, Ostor
Griner, Ned H
Grygutis, Barbara
Hallman, H Theodore, Jr
Handler, Audrey
Haut, Claire (Joan)
Heaton, Maurice
Henkle, James Lee
Herrold, Clifford H
Hicks, Sheila
Higgins, Edward Koelling
Higgins, Mary Lou
Hill, John Conner
Hill, Richard Wayne
Hoffmann, Lilly Elisabeth
Hofsted, Jolyon Gene
Hogbin, Stephen James
Holm, Bill
Hostetler, David
Howard, Cecil Ray
Hu, Mary Lee
Hui, Ka-Kwong
Ipsen, Kent Forrest
Jensen, Claud
Jerry, Michael John
Johnson, Donald Marvin
Johnson, Ivan Earl
Johnston, Robert Harold
Julio, Pat T
Kemenyffy, Steven
Kennedy, Leta Marietta
Keyser, William Alphonse, Jr
Kington, Louis Brent
Knorr, Jeanne Boardman
Knowlton, Daniel Gibson
Koga, Dean
Kolawole, Lawrence Compton
Krevolin, Lewis
Kulicke, Robert M
Kupferman, Murray
Lacktman, Michael
La Fon, Julia Anna
Lang, Rodger Alan
LaPlantz, David
Laury, Jean Ray (Jean Ray Bitters)
Lawrence, Jaye A
Leber, Roberta (Roberta Leber McVeigh)
Lechtzin, Stanley
Lesch, Alma Wallace
Levine, Marilyn Anne
Lewis, Golda
Lewis, John Conard
Lonewolf, Joseph
Lux, Gladys Marie
Madsen, Viggo Holm
Marak, Louis Bernard
Mari (Mari M Eagerton)
Marsh, Anne Steele
Marsh, (Edwin) Thomas
Marshall, John Carl
McClendon, Maxine (Maxine McClendon Nichols)
McGlauchlin, Tom
McIntosh, Harrison Edward
McKinley, Donald Lloyd
McNitt, Miriam D
McWhinnie, Harold James
Medicine Flower, Grace
Menihan, John Conway
Mintich, Mary Ringelberg
Mirabal, Miguel Enrique
Mitchell, Robert Ellis
Mondale, Joan Adams
Murphy, Gladys Wilkins
Myers, Joel Philip
Naegle, Stephen Howard
Neugebauer, Margot
Nicholas, Donna Lee
Nigrosh, Leon Isaac
Oliveira, V'Lou
Olsen, Frederick L
Oster, Gerald
Ottiano, John William
Pardon, Earl B
Paul, Bernard H
Pearson, James Eugene
Peck, Lee Barnes
Pijanowski, Eugene M
Pijanowski, Hiroko Sato
Plamondon, Marius Gerald
Plath, Iona
Porter, Priscilla Manning
Portmann, Frieda Bertha Anne
Prestini, James Libero
Radulovic, Savo
Replinger, Dot (Dorothy Thiele)
Riley, Gerald Patrick
Ritter, Richard Quintin
Robertson, Joan Elizabeth (Joan Elizabeth Mitchell)
Rogers, John H
Royce, Richard Benjamin
Roysher, Hudson (Brisbine)
Sage, Bill B
Sahlstrand, Margaret Ahrens
Schellin, Robert William
Scherr, Mary Ann
Schlup, Elaine Smitha
Schwarcz, June Therese
Scott, Curtis S
Sellers, John Lewis
Sewards, Michele Bourque
Sheng, Shao Fang
Sieg, Robert Lawrence
Simon, Ellen R
Skelly, Barbara Jean
Smith, Alfred James, Jr
Soleri, Paolo
Staffel, Rudolf Harry
Stankard, Paul Joseph
Stapp, Ray Veryl
Starks, Elliott Roland
Stephens, Curtis
Stuart, Donald Alexander
Sufi (Ahmad Antung)
Takemoto, Henry Tadaaki
Tanner, James L
Tatschl, John
Taylor, Rosemary
Terry, Duncan Niles
Thomason, Tom William
Todd, Louise (Louise Todd Cope)
Torbert Stephanie Birch
Tornheim, Norman
Trentham, Gary Lynn
Van Dommelen, David B
van Duinwyk, George Paul
Van Leunen, Alice Louise
Vermes, Madelaine
Wahling, B Jon
Walker, Mary Carolyn
Warashina, M Patricia
Ward, Evelyn Svec
Wardle, Alfred Hill
Warhol, Andy
Warner, Lucy Ann
Warsinske, Norman George, Jr
West, Virginia M
Willet, Henry Lee
Winokur, Paula Colton
Winokur, Robert Mark
Woell, J Fred
Wood, Beatrice
Woods, Ted
Wyman, William

CRITIC

Aarons, Anita
Ahlander, Leslie Judd
Albin, Edgar A
Albright, Thomas
Allen, Jane Addams
Alloway, Lawrence
Alper, M Victor
Andrews, Benny
Antin, David A
Anzures, Rafael
Appelhof, Ruth A
Ashbery, John Lawrence
Ashton, Dore
Aubin, Barbara
Auer, James Matthew
Baker, Elizabeth C
Ballatore, Sandra Lee
Bannard, Walter Darby
Baro, Gene
Barrio-Garay, Jose Luis
Barzun, Jacques
Bass, Ruth Gilbert
Bassin, Joan
Battcock, Gregory
Beatty, Frances Fielding Lewis
Benedikt, Michael
Benson, Elaine K G
Benson, Gertrude Ackerman
Blake, Peter Jost
Bourdon, David
Bowlt, John
Boyd, Donald Edgar
Bromm, Hal
Bruner, Louise Katherine (Mrs Paul Orr)
Burnett, David Grant
Burnett, W C, Jr
Burnham, Jack Wesley
Canaday, John Edwin
Cernuschi, Alberto C
Chadwick, Whitney
Chapin, Louis (Le Bourgeois)
Chipp, Herschel Browning
Ciuca, Eugen
Cleary, Fritz
Clermont, Ghislain
Clothier, Peter Dean
Clurman, Irene
Colby, Joy Hakanson
Cole, Harold David
Collier, Alberta
Constable, Rosalind
Coplans, John (Rivers)
Cossitt, Franklin D
Crimp, Douglas
Dame, Lawrence
Danieli, Fidel Angelo
Danikian, Caron Le Brun
Davis, Douglas Matthew
deAK, Edit
De Bretteville, Sheila Levrant
DeShazo, Edith Kind
Donaldson, Jeff R
Donohoe, Victoria
Driscoll, Edgar Joseph, Jr
Driver, Morley-Brooke Lister
DuBois, Macy
Dulac, Margarita Walker
Dunbar, Jill H
Dyer, Carolyn Price
Dzubas, Friedel
Eckelberry, Don Richard
Edelson, Elihu
Engel, Walter F
Feldman, Edmund Burke
Findsen, Owen Kenneth
Fleisher, Pat
Foote, Nancy
Foster, Stephen C
Frackman, Noel
Frank, Peter Solomon
Frankenstein, Alfred Victor
Freeman, David L
Fried, Alexander
Fried, Michael
Friedman, Kenneth Scott
Fry, Edward Fort
Fuller, John Charles
Geist, Sidney
Genauer, Emily
Ghent, Henri
Gillies, Jean
Goddard, Donald
Goldsmith, Barbara
Gomez-Sicre, Jose
Gonzales, Shirley
Goodrich, Lloyd
Gottschalk, Max Jules
Gray, Don
Greenberg, Clement
Greene, Theodore R
Gruen, John
Guthrie, Derek
Hall, Julie Ann
Hammock, Virgil Gene
Haydon, Harold (Emerson)
Hayes, Bartlett Harding, Jr
Hazard, Jim (Ovington)
Healy, Julia Schmitt
Heinz, Susan
Henrickson, Paul Robert
Henry, Sara Lynn
Hess, Thomas B
Highwater, Jamake
Hirsch, Richard Teller
Hitchcock, Henry Russell
Hoffeld, Jeffrey
Hooton, Bruce Duff
Howett, John
Hughes, Robert S F
Huxtable, Ada Louise
Isaacson, Philip Marshal
Jacobs, Jay
Jaffe, Ira Sheldon
Jay, Bill
Jennings, Jan
Jensen, Dean N
Johnson, Ellen Hulda
Johnson, Lincoln Fernando
Jordan, George Edwin
Joskowicz, Alfredo
Kaspe, Vladimir
Kelder, Diane M
Key, Donald D
Kind, Joshua B

CRITIC (cont)
King, Elaine A
Kingsley, April
Kozloff, Max
Kramer, Hilton
Kratz, Mildred Sands
Krebs, Patricia (Patricia Krebs Barker)
Kuh, Katharine
Kultermann, Udo
Kuspit, Donald Burton
Kutner, Janet
Lagorio, Irene R
Lanou, Tobie E
Larsen, Susan C
Lecky, Susan
Lee, Rensselaer Wright
Leja, Michael Joseph
Leopold, Michael Christopher
Levin, Kim (Kim Pateman)
Lewton, Val Edwin
Libby, Gary Russell
Linn, John William
Livingston, Jane S
Longaker, Jon Dasu
Lorber, Richard
Loring, John
Lowry, Bates
Lunde, Karl Roy
Lynes, Russell
Maddox, Jerald Curtis
Marter, Joan M
McCann, Cecile Nelken
McCaslin, Walter Wright
McCormick, Jo Mary (Jo Mary McCormick-Sakurai)
Meister, Maureen I
Merkel, Jayne (Silverstein)
Miller, Donald
Mills, James
Molina, Antonio J
Morgan, William
Morrison C L
Moser, Charlotte
Moyssen, Xavier
Mozley, Anita Ventura
Murray, Joan
Nemser, Cindy
Neustein, Joshua
Newsom, Barbara Ylvisaker
Niss, Robert Sharples
Nordland, Gerald John
Offin, Charles Z
Orenstein, Gloria Feman
Osze, Andrew E
Owens, Al Curtis
Owyang, Judith Francine
Paredes, Limon Mariano
Paris, Jeanne C
Patterson, Patricia
Pease, Roland Folsom, Jr
Perkins, Constance M
Perreault, John
Pincus-Witten, Robert A
Plagens, Peter
Pool, Nelda Lee
Power, Mark
Preston, Malcolm H
Price, Anne Kirkendall
Rahill, Margaret Fish
Raven, Arlene
Reilly, Richard
Rice, Shelley Enid
Richard, Paul
Rigby, Ida Katherine
Roberts, Colette (Jacqueline)
Robins, Corinne
Rosenberg, Harold
Roskill, Mark Wentworth
Rosler, Martha Rose
Roster, Laila Bergs
Rothman, Sidney
Sakaoka, Yasue
Saltmarche, Kenneth Charles
Sandground, Mark Bernard, Sr
Schloss, Edith
Schneider, Lisa Dawn
Schulze, Franz
Schwabacher, Ethel K
Seckler, Dorothy Gees
Sekula, Allan
Shere, Charles Everett
Singer, Esther Forman
Skelton, Robin
Smith, Griffin (Mary-Griffin Smith Hoeveler)
Smith, Henry Holmes
Soby, James Thrall
Spurlock, William Henry, II
Steen, Ronald Earl
Steiner, Paul
Stevens, Elisabeth Goss
Stewart, Patricia Kaye
Stofflet, Mary
Sylvestre, Guy
Tarshis, Jerome
Taylor, John Frank Adams
Taylor, John Lloyd
Taylor, Robert
Thomas, Helen (Doane)
Town, Harold Barling
Townsend, J Benjamin
Tuchman, Phyllis
Tucker, Anne
Tucker, Glenn F
Turano, Jane Van Norman
Turner, Norman Huntington
Upelnieks, Arthur
Vermette, Luce
Villafranca, Leonor Morales De
Warner, Harry Backer, Jr
Watkins, Eileen Frances
Wattenmaker, Richard J
Weeks, H J
Weissman, Julian Paul
White, Ron
Willard, Charlotte
Willig, Nancy Tobin
Wilson, William Harry
Wilson, William S, III
Wingate, Adina (R)
Winokur, James L
Wong, Ching
Woodard, Tom L
Wooden, Howard Edmund
Wortz, Melinda Farris
Young, Joseph E
Zoromskis, Kazimieras

CURATOR

Ahlander, Leslie Judd
Apple, Jacki (Jacqueline B)
Arthur, John C
Atirnomis (Rita Simon)
Auth, Susan Handler
Bacot, Henry Parrott
Bailey, Worth
Balkind, Alvin Louis
Barnwell, F Edward
Barry, William David
Bass, David Loren
Baxter, Patricia Huy
Beal, Graham William John
Beall, Karen F
Bean, Jacob
Berger, Jerry Allen
Bice, Clare
Binai, Paul Freye
Black, Mary Childs
Black, Mary McCune
Bloom, Jason
Booth, Judith Gayle
Borcoman, James
Bordeaux, Jean Luc
Bothmer, Bernard V
Bowron, Edgar Peters
Boyer, Jack K
Bradbury, Ellen A
Brandt, Frederick Robert
Brown, David Alan
Brunkus, Richard Allen
Bubb, Nancy (Jane)
Buitron, Diana M
Buki, Zoltan
Bundy, Stephen Allen
Bunnell, Peter Curtis
Burke, James Donald
Butler, Joseph Thomas
Cain, James Frederick, Jr
Cameron, Elsa S
Canby, Jeanny Vorys
Canepa, Anna L
Carmean, E A, Jr
Carter, Albert Joseph
Carter, David Giles
Casey, Elizabeth Temple
Castellon, Rolando
Cate, Phillip Dennis
Cathcart, Linda Louise
Catlin, Stanton L
Chester, Janie Kathleen
Chieffo, Clifford Toby
Clark, Carol Canda
Clark, Mark A
Clark, Sarah Ann
Clisby, Roger David
Coates, Ann S
Conger, Clement E
Cooper, Rhonda
Cooper, Wendy Ann
Courtney, Keith Townsend
Cowles, Charles
Cunningham, Charles Crehore
Curtis, Phillip Houston
Czach, Marie
Czuma, Stanislaw J
Dailey, Charles Andrew (Chuck)
Danoff, I Michael
Darling, Sharon Sandling
Daviee, Jerry Michael
Davis, Ann
Davis, Marian B
Dean, James
Delhom, Mary Mellanay
D'Harnoncourt, Anne (J)
Dixon, Sally Foy
Donaldson, Marjory (Rogers)
Downs, Linda Anne
Dresser, Louisa
Elderfield, John
Elzea, Rowland Procter
Emerson, Edith
Evans, Robert James
Fairbanks, Jonathan Leo
Farrell, Stephanie Krauss
Faunce, Sarah Cushing
Feinblatt, Ebria
Feld, Stuart Paul
Felter, James Warren
Ferber, Elise Van Hook
Field, Richard Sampson
Fine, Ruth Eileen
Flick, Robert
Flint, Janet Altic
Foley, Kathy Kelsey
Franco, Barbara
Frank, Peter Solomon
Frankel, Dextra
Fredericksen, Burton Baum
Freeman, Margaret B
Frel, Jiri
Friedman, Joan Marcy
Gaither, Edmund B
Garson, Inez
Garvan, Beatrice Bronson
Garver, Thomas H
Geck, Francis Joseph
Geldzahler, Henry
Gibson, Roland
Glaeser, Ludwig
Glasgow, Vaughn Leslie
Glauber, Robert H
Glicksman, Hal
Globus, Dorothy Twining
Goheen Ellen Rozanne
Goodyear, Frank H, Jr
Gore, Tom
Govan, Francis Hawks
Green, Eleanor Broome
Greenwald, Alice (Alice Marian Greenwald-Ward)
Griffin, Rachael S
Grossman, Grace Cohen
Grossman, Sheldon
Hackenbroch, Yvonne Alix
Hallmark, Donald Parker
Hamilton, Patricia Rose
Hand, John Oliver
Hanfmann, George M A
Hanks, David Allen
Hanna, Katherine
Harrington, La Mar
Harter, John Burton
Haskell, Barbara
Havelock, Christine Mitchell
Hayes, Laura M
Hayward, Jane
Heckscher, Morrison Harris
Hedberg, Gregory Scott
Hemphill, Herbert Waide
Henning, Edward Burk
Hershman, Lynn Lester
Hill, Dorothy Kent
Hiller, Betty R
Holm, Bill
Holo, Selma Reuben
Holverson, John
Hood, Gary Allen
Hoopes, Donelson Farquhar
Howat, John Keith
Howett, John
Hubbard, Robert Hamilton
Huchel, Frederick M
Hulmer, Eric Claus
Hummel, Charles Frederick
Hunter-Stiebel, Penelope (Penelope Hunter Stiebel)
Hutton, William
Jackson, Ruth Amelia
Jeffers, Wendy Jane
Jewell, Kester Donald
Joachim, Harold
Johnson, Arthur Harold
Johnson, Evert Alfred
Johnson, J Stewart
Johnson, Kenn Elmer
Johnson, Robert Flynn
Johnson, Una E
Jones, Frances Follin
Jones, William Ezelle
Kahlenberg, Mary Hunt
Kardon, Janet
Katzen, Philip
Katzenberg, Dena S
Kazor, Virginia Ernst
Keefe, Katharine Lee
Kelleher, Patrick Joseph
Keller, Andrea Miller
King, Elaine A
Kingsley, April
Kluver, Billy (Johan Wilhem Kluver)
Kohler, Ruth DeYoung
Kramrisch, Stella
Krushenick, John
Kubota, Shigeko
Kuwayama, George
Landau, Mitzi
Landis, Ellen Jamie
Larson, Sidney
Laskin, Myron, Jr
Lee, Roger
Leja, Michael Joseph
Leven, Arline Claire
Levin, Gail
Levine, Les
Lewis, Douglas
Lewis, Phillip Harold
Lewis, Virginia Elnora

Li, Chu-Tsing
Lienau, Daniel Clifford
Linhares, Philip E
Link, Howard Anthony
Lipton, Barbara B
Livesay, Thomas Andrew
Livingston, Jane S
Loar, Peggy A
Locke, Michelle Wilson
Loehr, Max
London, Barbara
Loran, Erle
Luck, Robert
Luckner, Kurt T
Lumsden, Ian Gordon
Lunsford, John (Crawford)
Lyons, Lisa
Maddox, Jerald Curtis
Madigan, Mary Jean Smith
Magnan, Oscar Gustav
Mandle, Earl Roger
Manrique, Jorge Alberto
Marandel, J Patrice
Marioni, Tom
Marshall, Richard Donald
Marter, Joan M
Mathis, Kenneth Lawrence
Maurer, Evan Maclyn
Mayer, Grace M
Mayor, Alpheus Hyatt
McCabe, Cynthia Jaffee
McGarvey, Elsie Siratz
McGonagle, William Albert
McNamara, Mary Jo
McNulty, Kneeland
McShine, Kynaston Leigh
Mekler, Adam
Melberg, Jerald Leigh
Menchaca, Juan
Messer, Brenda Ruth
Metyko, Michael Joseph
Metzger, Robert Paul
Michalove, Carla Maria
Miles, Ellen Gross
Miley, Mimi Conneen
Millard, Charles Warren, III
Miller, Joan Vita
Mino, Yukata
Minutillo, Richard G
Moeller, Robert Charles, III
Moore, Ethel
Morrison C L
Mosby, Dewey Franklin
Moser, Joann
Moure, Nancy Dustin Wall
Mozley, Anita Ventura
Murdock, Robert Mead
Musgrove, Stephen Ward
Naeve, Milo M
Nelson, Jane Gray
Nelson, Jon Allen
Neubert, George Walter
Noggle, Anne
Norfleet, Barbara Pugh
Norris, Andrea Spaulding
Oberhuber, Konrad J
Oliver, Richard Bruce
Olpin, Robert Spencer
Orr-Cahall, Anona Christina
Ostiguy, Jean-Rene
Overland, Carlton Edward
Owsley, David Thomas
Pajaud, William Etienne
Pal, Pratapaditya
Parkhurst, Charles
Parsons, Merribell Maddux
Peck, William Henry
Perry, Mary-Ellen Earl
Peters, Larry Dean
Phillips, John Goldsmith
Pilgrim, James F
Pindell, Howardena Doreen
Pisano, Ronald George
Plous, Phyllis
Pomeroy, James Calwell, Jr
Powell, Earl Alexander, III
Press, Nancy Neumann
Raggio, Olga
Rahill, Margaret Fish
Reeves, James Franklin
Reiling, Susan Wallace
Reynolds, Valrae
Richardson, Brenda
Rishel, Joseph John, Jr
Rivard, Nancy J
Robertson, Joan Elizabeth (Joan Elizabeth Mitchell)
Robinson, Wahneta Theresa
Robison, Andrew
Rodriguez, Ralph Noel
Rohlfing, Christian
Rose, Bernice Berend
Rosenthal, Gertrude
Rosenzweig, Phyllis D
Ross, David Anthony
Ross, Marvin Chauncey
Rouse, John R
Rubin, William
Russell, Helen Diane
Rust, David E
St John, Terry N
Salmon, Larry
Sargent, Richard
Sayre, Eleanor Axson
Scheibe, Fred Karl
Schorgl, Thomas Barry
Schultz, Douglas George
Schweizer, Paul Douglas
Selig, J Daniel
Seligman, Thomas Knowles
Sellin, David
Sewell, Jack Vincent
Shaman, Sanford Sivitz
Shangraw, Clarence Frank
Shangraw, Sylvia Chen
Shapley, Fern Rusk
Shepherd, Dorothy G (Mrs Ernst Payer)
Sieber, Roy
Sims, Patterson
Smith, Howard Ross
Snyder, Kim Lawrence
Solomon, Ruth B
Somerville, Romaine Stec
Sonday, Milton Franklin, Jr
Soult, James Thomas
Speyer, A James
Springer, Lynn Elise
Spurlock, William Henry, II
Stampfle, Felice
Stapp, William F
Steffler, Alva W
Stein, Harve
Stern, Jean
Stewart, Robert Gordon
Stokstad, Marilyn
Sullivan, Ruth Wilkins
Sunkel, Robert Cleveland
Sussman, Elisabeth Sacks
Svendsen, Louise Averill
Swarzenski, Hanns Peter Theophil
Sweeney, J Gray
Tatistcheff, Peter Alexis
Taylor, Mary Cazort
Teilman, Herdis Bull
Thibault, Claude
Thomas, Elaine Freeman
Thurlow, Fearn Cutler
Toll, Barbara Elizabeth
Tomko, George Peter
Tracy, Berry Bryson
Travis, David B
Trubner, Henry
Tuchman, Maurice
Tucker, Anne
Tucker, James Ewing
Tucker, Marcia
Turnbull, Betty
Usui, Kiichi
Vanderlip, Dianne Perry
Van Hook, David H
Veljkovic, Andrev
Vitale, Lydia Modi
Volpe, Robert
Voris, Anna Maybelle
Wallace, David Harold
Walsh, John, Jr
Walton, Donald William
Wasserman, Jeanne L
Weiss, Peg
Weitzmann, Kurt
Wheelock, Arthur Kingsland, Jr
Wick, Peter Arms
Wilkinson, Charles K
Wilmerding, John
Winer, Donald Arthur
Wingate, Robert Bray
Wong, Jason
Young, Joseph E
Zafran, Eric Myles
Zilczer, Judith Katy

DESIGNER

Aarons, Anita
Abel, Ray
Ackerman, Frank Edward
Adel, Judith
Albers, Anni
Aldwinckle, Eric
Alexander, Robert Seymour
Alicea, Jose
Aliki (Aliki Brandenberg)
Allen, Loretta B
Allen, Tom, Jr
Allner, Walter H
Altschuler, Franz
Ames, Arthur Forbes
Ames, Jean Goodwin
Anderson, Donald Myers
Anderson, Gordon
Anderson, Winslow
Angelini, John Michael
Appleman, David Earl
Archie, James Lee
Arnautoff, Jacob Victor
Arnholm, Ronald Fisher
Arnold, Richard R
Aronson, Boris
Askild, Anita (Anita Askild Feinstein)
Atkins, Gordon Lee
Bacigalupa, Andrea
Badash, Sandi Borr
Bakanowsky, Louis J
Bakke, Karen Lee
Bakken, Haakon
Ballou, Anne MacDougall
Baringer, Richard E
Barnett, Earl D
Barschel, Hans J
Bart, Elizabeth (Elizabeth Bart Gerald)
Bartlett, Robert Webster
Barton, August Charles
Barton, Jean L
Barton, Phyllis Grace
Bassler, James W
Bates, Betsey
Batt, Miles Girard
Baxter, Iain
Beaudoin, Andre Eugene
Bedno, Edward
Bender, Beverly Sterl
Benge, David Philip
Berkowitz, Henry
Bernstein, William Joseph
Blaz, Georgia Lee
Blazey, Lawrence Edwin
Blumenthal, Margaret M
Bode, Robert William
Boeve, Edgar Gene
Bolley, Irma S
Bolster, Ella S
Bosin, Blackbear
Boulton, Joseph L
Boussard, Dana
Bradshaw, Lawrence James
Brauer, Connie Ann
Bredlow, Tom
Bristow, William Arthur
Brod, Stanford
Broemel, Carl William
Brommer, Gerald F
Brookins, Jacob Boden
Brooks, Lois Ziff
Broomfield, Adolphus George
Brough, Richard Burrell
Brown, Gary Hugh
Buranabunpot, Pornpilai
Burgess, Joseph James, Jr
Burt, Clyde Edwin
Butterbaugh, Robert Clyde
Byrne, Charles Joseph
Byron, Gene
Cadge, William Fleming
Califf, Marilyn Iskiwitz
Cantor, Robert Lloyd
Cardman, Cecilia
Carewe, Sylvia
Carey, James Sheldon
Carey, Ted
Carl, Joan
Carpenter, Arthur Espenet
Carter, Clarence Holbrook
Casey, Jacqueline Shepard
Castle, Wendell Keith
Catti (Catherine James)
Chapman, Dave
Chappelle, Jerry Leon
Chase, Allan (Seamans)
Cheatham, Frank Reagan
Chermayeff, Ivan
Chestney, Lillian
Chethlahe (David Chethlahe Paladin)
Chihuly, Dale Patrick
Childers, Malcolm Graeme
Choo, Chunghi
Chwast, Seymour
Clark, R Dane
Clayberger, Samuel Robert
Clymer, Albert Anderson
Coburn, Ralph
Cochran, Dewees (Dewees Cochran Helbeck)
Coes, Kent Day
Cohen, Elaine Lustig
Cohen, Harold Larry
Colin, Georgia T
Colker, Edward
Cooke, Donald Ewin
Copeland, Lawrence Gill
Corpron, Carlotta Mae
Costigan, Constance Christian
Crittenden, John William Neil
Crozier, William K, Jr
Cutler, Ethel Rose
Cyril, R
Dailey, Daniel Owen
Daily, Evelynne B
Dali, Salvador
D'Andrea, Jeanne
Dank, Leonard Dewey
Davidson, Suzette Morton
Davison, Robert
De Bretteville, Sheila Levrant
Defenbacher, Daniel S
DeGroat, Diane L
De La Vega, Antonio
de la Vega, Enrique Miguel
Del Valle, Joseph Bourke
de Paola, Tomie
De Pedery-Hunt, Dora
De Pol, John
des Rioux, Deena (Victoria Coty)
Dey, Kris
Diamond, Abel Joseph
Dice, Elizabeth Jane
Dimson, Theo Aeneas

DESIGNER (cont)
Dorn, Peter Klaus
Drummond, (I G)
Dufour, Paul Arthur
Ebsen, Alf K
Edmiston, Sara Joanne
Edvi Illes, Emma
Edwards, Allan W
Eide, Palmer
Eikerman, Alma
Eilers, Fred (Anton Frederick)
Eitel, Cliffe Dean
Elliott, Lillian
Emori, Eiko
Enriquez, Gaspar
Ewald, Louis
Farian, Babette S
Fassett, Kaffe Havrah
Faulconer, Mary (Fullerton)
Feder, Ben
Feher, Joseph
Feist, Warner David
Feriola, James Philip
Ferron, Marcelle
Fifield, Mary
Fisch, Arline Marie
Fischer, Mildred (Gertrude)
Fish, Richard G
Fisher, Leonard Everett
Flach, Victor H
Flakey Rose Hip (Glenn Alun Lewis)
Fleming, Allan Robb
Floethe, Richard
Foose, Robert James
Forman, Alice
Francis, Bill Dean
Frankel, Dextra
Friedman, Alan
Fuhrman, Esther
Fuller, R Buckminster
Gage, Harry (Lawrence)
Gale, William Henry
Gardner, Andrew Bradford
Garzon-Blanco, Armando
Gebhardt, Roland
Geck, Francis Joseph
Geis, Milton Arthur
Geissman, Robert Glenn
Genius, Jeannette (Jeannette M McKean)
George, Walter Eugene, Jr
Geran, Joseph, Jr
Getty, Nilda Fernandez
Giannotti, John J
Gilbert, Herb
Giusti, George
Glaser, David
Glaser, Milton
Glaser, Samuel
Glass, Henry P
Glover, Robert Leon
Godwin, Judith Whitney
Golubic, Theodore
Gonzalez, Jose Gamaliel
Gorman, Carl Nelson (Kin-ya-onny Beyeh)
Gottschalk, Fritz
Gottschalk, Max Jules
Goulds, Peter J
Govan, Francis Hawks
Grear, James Malcolm
Greenberg, Gloria
Grissom, Kenneth Ryland, II
Grosz, Franz Joseph
Grushkin, Philip
Gursoy, Ahmet
Haber, Leonard
Haley, Patience E (Patience E Haley Ghikas)
Hall, John A
Hallman, H Theodore, Jr
Hansen, Frances Frakes
Hanson, Jean (Mrs Jean Elphick)
Hausman, Fred S
Hayes, Robert T
Head, George Bruce
Healy, Julia Schmitt
Heaton, Maurice
Hebert, Julien
Heflin, Tom Pat
Heiskell, Diana
Heller, Goldie (Mrs Edward W Greenberg)
Hemenway, Nancy (Mrs Robert D Barton)
Henkle, James Lee
Herman, Alan David
Hicks, Sheila
Higgins, Dick
Hill, John Conner
Hillis, Richard K
Hillman, Arthur Stanley
Hilton, Eric G
Hing, Allan Mark
Hoare, Tyler James
Hoffman, Martin (Joseph)
Holvey, Samuel Boyer
Hood, (Thomas) Richard
Hornung, Clarence Pearson
Horowitz, Nadia
Hough, Richard
Howe, Nelson S
Howell, Marie W
Howlett, Carolyn Svrluga
Howze, James Dean
Hrdy, Olinka
Hundley, David Holladay
Hurd, Zorah
Hutton, Dorothy Wackerman
Ingram, Jerry Cleman
Inverarity, Robert Bruce
Israel, Marvin
Jackson, William Davis
Jacobson, Ursula Mercedes
Jacobsson, Sten Wilhelm John
Jameikis, Brone Aleksandra
Jaworska, Tamara
Jenrette, Pamela Anne
Jensen, John Edward
Joffe, Bertha
Johanson, Patricia (Maureen)
Johnson, Edvard Arthur
Johnson, Fridolf Lester
Johnson, James Edwin & Sandra Kay
Jolley, George B
Josimovich, George
Julian, Lazaro
Kabotie, Fred
Kahane, Melanie (Melanie Kahane Grauer)
Kahn, A Michael
Kahn, Peter
Kanidinc, Salahattin
Kaplan, Muriel Sheerr
Karawina, Erica (Mrs Sideny C Hsiao)
Kataoka, Mits
Katzive, David H
Kaufman, Edgar, Jr
Kaye, David Haigh
Kaz (Lawrence Katzman)
Kemper, John Garner
Kenny, Thomas Henry
Kerr, Kenneth A
Kessler, Edna Leventhal
Kessler, Leonard H
Keyser, William Alphonse, Jr
Kimmel-Cohn, Roberta
Kingrey, Kenneth
Kinoshita, Gene
Kirkwood, Larry Thomas
Kleidon, Dennis Arthur
Knight, Hilary
Knowlton, Daniel Gibson
Koerner, Henry
Korman, Barbara
Korow, Elinore Maria
Kowalski, Raymond Alois
Kramer, Burton
Kramer, Paul
Kramolc, Theodore Maria
Kravis, Janis
Krody, Barron J
Kubly, Donald R
Kushner, Robert Ellis
Lacktman, Michael
Laing, Richard Harlow
LaMarca, Howard J
Lampert, Dorrie
Laposky, Ben Francis
Larkin, Eugene
Larsen, Jack Lenor
Larson, Orland
Lasuchin, Michael
Laury, Jean Ray (Jean Ray Bitters)
La Vigne, Robert Clair
Lawrence, Howard Ray
Laycox, (William) Jack
Lederer, Wolfgang
Lee, Raymond Man
Le Fevre, Richard John
Lein, Malcolm Emil
Lennie, Beatrice E C
Lerner, Abe
Lerner, Nathan Bernard
Levinson, Fred (Floyd)
Lewis, John Conard
Lewton, Val Edwin
Lincoln, Fred Clinton
Lissim, Simon
Liszt, Maria Veronica
Llorente, Luis
Loloma, Charles
Lo Medico, Thomas Gaetano
London, Jeff
Long, Frank Weathers
Long, Sandra Tardo
Lowe, Harry
Ludekens, Fred
Lumbers, James Richard
Luray, J (J Luray Schaffner)
Lynch, Jo (Marilyn Blanche)
MacAlister, Paul Ritter
Macaualy, David Alexander
Maehara, Hiromu
Maitin, Samuel (Calman)
Malinowski, Jerome Joseph
Maltby, Hazel Farrow
Maltzman, Stanley
Maradiaga, Ralph
Markle, Jack M
Markle, Sam
Markusen, Thomas Roy
Martin, Charles E
Martin, Doris-Marie Constable
Martin, G W
Martin, Margaret M
Martin, William Barriss, II
Martino, Edmund
Marzano, Albert
Massey, Charles Wesley, Jr
Mayen, Paul
McChristy, Quentin L
McElcheran, William Hodd
McElroy, Nancy Lynn
McFadden, Mary
McIntosh, Harrison Edward
McKinley, Donald Lloyd
McKinley, Ruth Gowdy
McNear, Everett C
McNitt, Miriam D
Meehan, William Dale
Meitzler, (Herbert) Neil
Menihan, John Conway
Merritt, Francis Sumner
Meserole, Vera Stromsted
Miller, Leon Gordon
Miner, Ralph Hamlin
Mintich, Mary Ringelberg
Mitchell, Beresford Strickland
Morgan, Warren Dean
Muir, Emily Lansingh
Myers, C Stowe
Nagano, Paul Tatsumi
Nalder, Nan
Nama, George Allen
Neff, John A
Nelson, Jack D
Nesbitt, Alexander John
Ness, (Albert) Kenneth
Neugebauer, Margot
New, Lloyd H (Lloyd Kiva)
Nichols, Alice W
Nichols, Donald Edward
Nichols, Eleanor Cary
Nicodemus, Chester Roland
Nigrosh, Leon Isaac
Nitz, Thomas L
Ockerse, Thomas
O'Connor, Harold Thomas
O'Dell, Erin (Anne)
Oenslager, Donald Mitchell
Olsen, Ernest Moran
Olson, Douglas John
Olugebefola, Ademola
O'Neil, John Joseph
Pace, Margaret Bosshardt
Pacific, Gertrude
Paley, Albert Raymond
Pardington, Joyce Elizabeth
Parella, Albert Lucian
Parker, James Varner
Parnall, Peter
Peck, James Edward
Peckham, Nicholas
Pelham-Keller, Richard Monroe
Perlman, Raymond
Peter, Friedrich Gunther
Peterson, Chester G
Peterson, John Douglas
Peterson, Larry D
Pierre-Noel, Vergniaud
Pirkl, James Joseph
Pisani, Joseph
Plath, Iona
Pollard, Donald Pence
Pope, Richard Coraine
Portanova, Joseph Domenico
Posner, Richard Perry
Potter, (George) Kenneth
Powell, Leslie (Joseph)
Prentice, David Ramage
Prestini, James Libero
Pride, Joy
Priest, T
Pringle, Burt Evins
Proctor, Gifford MacGregor
Pulos, Arthur Jon
Quinn, Noel Joseph
Ramirez-Vazquez, Pedro
Ramstead, Edward Oliver, Jr
Rand, Paul
Randall, (Lillian) Paula
Randall, Ruth Hunie
Raskins, Ellen
Reale, Nicholas Albert
Reardon, Mary A
Reider, David H
Reinhardt, Siegfried Gerhard
Renk, Merry
Rennie, Helen (Sewell)
Replinger, Dot (Dorothy Thiele)
Revor, Remy
Reynolds, Joseph Gardiner
Rice, Philip Somerset
Richards, Lee
Rigg, Margaret Ruth
Riley, Gerald Patrick
Roach, Ruth S
Robb, Peggy Hight
Roberson, William
Roberts, Gilroy
Roch, Ernst
Roda (Rhoda Lillian Sablow)
Romans, Van Anthony
Rosen-Queralt, Jann
Rothschild, Amalie (Rosenfeld)
Rousseau-Vermette, Mariette
Rowe, Charles Alfred
Roysher, Hudson (Brisbine)
Ruben, Leonard
Rubin, Irwin

Ruffo, Joseph Martin
Rugolo, Lawrence
Ruzicka, Rudolph
Saar, Betye
Sadek, George
St Florian, Friedrich Gartler
Sander, Dennis Jay
Sarff, Walter
Sargent, Margaret Holland
Scherr, Mary Ann
Schlup, Elaine Smitha
Schoener, Allon
Schreckengost, Viktor
Schrut, Sherry
Schulze, Paul
Schwarz, Myrtle Cooper
Schweiss, Ruth Keller
Seidel, Alexander Carl-Victor
Sekimachi, Kay
Seliger, Charles
Sellers, John Lewis
Seltzer, Phyllis
Senior, Dorothy Elizabeth
Serniak, Regina
Seyle, Robert Harley
Sheets, Millard Owen
Sherman, Sarai
Shipley, James R
Sidenius, W Christian
Silver, Pat
Simmons, Cleda Marie
Simon, Ellen R
Singleton, Robert Ellison
Skelley, Robert Charles
Skinner, Orin Ensign
Skolnick, Arnold
Sloan, Jeanette Pasin
Smith, Ernest John
Smith, Jo-an
Smongeski, Joseph Leon
Snow, Lee Erlin
Snyder, Kim Lawrence
Solomon, David
Sorby, J Richard
Stanforth, Melvin Sidney
Steinfels, Melville P
Stephens, Curtis
Stevanov, Zoran
Stoessel, Henry Kurt
Strawn, Melvin Nicholas
Street, John Michael
Stuart, Donald Alexander
Sufi (Ahmad Antung)
Taback, Simms
Temes, Mortimer (Robert)
Texidor, Fernando
Thompson, George Louis
Thompson, (James) Bradbury
Thompson, Wade
Thomson, Carl L
Thorns, John Cyril, Jr
Toral, Maria Teresa
Torbert, Marguerite Birch
Tormey, James
Town, Harold Barling
Travanti, Leon Emidio
Treadwell, Helen
Trlak, Roger
Truex, Van Day
Uhrman, Esther
Utescher, Gerd
Vanco, John Leroy
Van Ginkel, Blanche Lemco
Van Oordt, Peter
Van Wolf, Henry
Vierthaler, Arthur A
Viner, Frank Lincoln
Vitale, Lydia Modi
Voelker, John
Walker, Mary Carolyn
Wallace, Lysbeth (Mai)
Wallace, Soni
Wapp, Josephine Myers
Ward, William Edward
Warner, Lucy Ann
Warriner, Laura B
Wasserman, Albert
Waterman, Donald Calvin
Watson, Aldren Auld
Watson, Sydney Hollinger
Watson, Wendy
Watts, Robert M
Webb, Frank (Francis H Webb)
Webb, Spider
Webster, Larry
Werner, Donald (Lewis)
Wethli, Mark Christian
Wheeler, Cleora Clark
Wheeler, Mark
White, Ian McKibbin
White, Robert (Winthrop)
Wier, Gordon D (Don)
Wilkinson, Kirk Cook
Williams, Garth Montgomery
Williams, Warner
Wilson, Sybil
Wilson, Tom Muir
Wilwers, Edward Mathias
Winfield, Rodney M
Winkler, Dietmar R
Witmeyer, Stanley Herbert
Wolfe, Mildred Nungester
Wolff, Richard Evans
Wood, James Arthur (Art)
Wood, Jim (James Reid Wood)
Wright, Bernard
Yanosky, Tom
Young, Kenneth Victor
Yudin, Carol
Yuristy, Russell Michael
Zahn, Carl Frederick
Zamparelli, Mario Armond
Zeidler, Eberhard Heinrich
Zolotow, Milton
Zucker, Bob
Zuckerberg, Stanley M

DIRECTOR

Ackerman, Frank Edward
Adel, Judith
Anderson, Winslow
Angelini, John Michael
Bedno, Edward
Bidner, Robert D H
Blattner, Robert Henry
Boros, Billi (Mrs Philip Bisaccio)
Brennan, Francis Edwin
Bumgardner, Georgia Brady
Cadle, Ray Kenneth
Carlos, (James) Edward
Cartmell, Helen
Casey, Jacqueline Shepard
Cattell, Ray
Channing, Susan Rose
Chapman, Howard Eugene
Christensen, Larry R
Cochran, Dewees (Dewees Cochran Helbeck)
Coes, Kent Day
Day, Horace Talmage
de Borhegyi, Suzanne Sims
De La Vega, Antonio
Del Valle, Joseph Bourke
De Pol, John
Dickey, Helen Pauline
Enos, Chris
Feher, Joseph
Fenical, Marlin E
Fleming, Allan Robb
Franco, Robert John
Frick, Helen Clay
Garcia, Ofelia
Gentile, Gloria Irene
Gilmartin, F Thomas
Goldstein, Jack
Gonzalez, Jose Gamaliel
Gordon, Joy L
Gray, Thomas Alexander
Green, Edward Anthony
Groth, John August
Hee, Hon-Chew
Hoffmann, Arnold, Jr
Jellico, John Anthony
Kelly, Walter W
Klindt, Steven
Klonis, Stewart
Knipscher, Gerard Allen
Kowalski, Raymond Alois
Lerner, Abe
Loughlin, John Leo
Love, Frances Taylor
Malinowski, Jerome Joseph
Marks, Royal S
Martin, Mary Finch
Mayen, Paul
Miller, Jan
Muniot, Barbara King
Muno, Richard Carl
Neddeau, Donald Frederick Price
Osborn, Elodie C (Mrs Robert C Osborn)
Paris, Jeanne C
Petersen, Will
Postiglione, Corey M
Pringle, Burt Evins
Quirarte, Jacinto
Rabinovitch, William Avrum
Rankin, Don
Reibel, Bertram
Robinson, Charles K
Rodriguez, Joe Bastida
Rosenthal, John W
Rubin, Irwin
Ruta, Peter Paul
Sawyer, Charles Henry
Schulze, Paul
Seabourn, Bert Dail
Simpson, Marilyn Jean
Smongeski, Joseph Leon
Steffler, Alva W
Stewart, John Lincoln
Stuart, Kenneth James
Sundberg, Carl Gustave
Taulbee, Dan J
Thompson, (James) Bradbury
Tyler, Kenneth Eugene
Veljkovic, Andrev
Viret, Margaret Mary (Mrs Frank Ivo)
Walker, William Walter
Waufle, Alan Duane
Weissman, Julian Paul
White, Deborah
White, Ruth
Youngsblood, Nat
Zilka, Michael John

DRAFTSMAN

Anthony, William Graham
Asmar, Alice
Attie, Dotty
Ball, Walter Neil
Batchelor, Anthony John
Benno, Benjamin G
Boccia, Edward Eugene
Borofsky, Jon
Breitenbach, William John
Brender a Brandis, Gerard William
Brown, Larry K
Buckner, Kay Lamoreux
Buckner, Paul Eugene
Bunce, Fredrick William
Caparn, Rhys (Rhys Caparn Steel)
Casas, Fernando Rodriguez
Chappell, Warren
Chase-Riboud, Barbara Dewayne
Chicoine, Rene
Clayberger, Samuel Robert
Clipsham, Jacqueline Ann
Clutz, William
Cooke, Samuel Tucker
Coppola, Andrew
Corr, James Donat
Crawford, Catherine Betty
Daly, Kathleen (Kathleen Daly Pepper)
Davison, Robert
Dee, Leo Joseph
Dole, William
Elliott, Bruce Roger
Ellis, Edwin Charles
Ettenberg, Franklin Joseph
Favro, Murray
Follett, Jean Frances
Freeman, David L
Fromboluti, Sideo
Fulton, Fred Franklin
Garey, Pat
Garhart, Martin J
Garver, Jack
George, Richard Allan
George, Thomas
Gibbons, Hugh (James)
Greene-Mercier, Marie Zoe
Gregor, Helen Frances
Guerin, John William
Gwathmey, Robert
Hamwi, Richard Alexander
Hart, Betty Miller
Hauptman, Susan Ann
Haut, Claire (Joan)
Head, Robert William
Hobbs, (Carl) Fredric
Holbrook, Elizabeth Bradford
Hood, Dorothy
Horn, Milton
Howze, James Dean
Hughes, Donald N
Isaacson, Marcia Jean
Iwamasa, Ken
Iwamoto, Ralph Shigeto
Jeter, Randy Joe
Johnson, Doris Miller (Mrs Gardiner Johnson)
Kaericher, John Conrad
Kaupelis, Robert John
Kelly, William Joseph
Kettner, David Allen
Kimball, Wilford Wayne, Jr
Klavans, Minnie
Knobler, Nathan
La Pierre, Thomas
Lark, Raymond
Lasansky, Leonardo da Iowa
Lincoln, Fred Clinton
Looney, Norman
Maki, Robert Richard
Mancuso, Leni (Leni Mancuso Barrett)
Marriott, William Allen
Martin, Thomas
Marx, Robert Ernst
Masurovsky, Gregory
Matteson, Ira
Mayes, Steven Lee
McCoy, Ann
McGrew, Ralph Brownell
Medearis, Roger
Menses, Jan
Miotke, Anne E
Moldroski, Al R
Morrison, Boone M
Morrow, Terry
Mullen, Philip Edward
Murphy, Hass
Nagler, Edith Kroger
Newman, John Beatty
Olkinetzky, Sam
Olson, Douglas John
Osborn, Robert
Owens, Al Curtis
Palmgren, Donald Gene
Pineda, Marianna (Marianna Pineda Tovish)
Postiglione, Corey M

DRAFTSMAN (cont)

Ramanauskas, Dalia Irena
Rehberger, Gustav
Reimann, William P
Reopel, Joyce
Rich, Frances L
Rode, Meredith Eagon
Rosenblatt, Suzanne Maris
Roszak, Theodore
Rowan, C Patrick
Sangiamo, Albert
Sapien, Darryl Rudolph
Schactman, Barry Robert
Schiff, Jean
Schwalb, Susan
Schwieger, C Robert
Scott, Jonathan
Snyder, William B
Speyer, Nora
Spurgeon, Sarah (Edna M)
Stuart, Michelle
Thompson, Donald Roy
Twarogowski, Leroy Andrew
Urquhart, Tony
Verzyl, Kenneth H
Von Gunten, Roger
Warshaw, Howard
Wethli, Mark Christian
Wheeler, Doug
White, Franklin
Whitney, William Kuebler
Whitson (Peter Whitson Warren)
Wilde, John
Wilmarth, Christopher Mallory
Wojtyla, Hasse (Walter Joseph Wojtyla)
Youngquist, Jack

EDITOR

Allen, Jane Addams
Amaya, Mario Anthony
Anbinder, Paul
Baker, Elizabeth C
Baldridge, Mark S
Bartle, Dorothy Budd
Beck, Curt Werner
Bornstein, Eli
Brody, Jacqueline
Bronson, A A (Michael Wayne Tims)
Califano, Edward Christopher
Chase, Robert M
Cogswell, Margaret Price
Comes, Marcella
Conant, Howard Somers
Cone-Skelton, Annette
Coplans, John (Rivers)
Crane, Michael Patrick
Crimp, Douglas
Davidson, Marshall Bowman
deAK, Edit
Edmonston, Paul
Esterow, Milton
Fanning, Robbie
Fenton, Julia Ann
Fleisher, Pat
Foote, Nancy
Forman, Nessa Ruth
Frank, Peter Solomon
Gettinger, Edmond Walter
Gilchrist, Elizabeth Brenda
Goddard, Donald
Goldsmith, Barbara
Haden, Eunice (Barnard)
Hanes, James (Albert)
Hazard, Jim (Ovington)
Helck, (Clarence) Peter
Hibbard, Howard
Holden, Donald
Hoy, Anne Tawes
Ireland, Patrick (Brian O'Doherty)
Jackson, Ward
Jardine, Donald Leroy
Jennings, Jan
Karpel, Bernard
Kelder, Diane M
Kozloff, Max
Kramer, Hilton
Kuh, Katharine
Lerman, Leo
Lerner, Abe
Lewton, Jean Louise
Lieb, Vered (Vered Shapiro-Lieb)
Lipman, Jean
Lorber, Richard
Mabie, Don Edward
MacDonald, Colin Somerled
Malina, Frank Joseph
Manrique, Jorge Alberto
Martin, Richard (Harrison)
Masheck, Joseph Daniel
McCann, Cecile Nelken
Meeker, Barbara Miller
Meister, Maureen I
Messer, Brenda Ruth
Meyer, Susan E
Mills, Frederick Van Fleet
Morse, John D
Newsom, Barbara Ylvisaker
Niss, Robert Sharples
Nuki (Daniel Millsaps)
Patten, David John
Peterson, Harold Patrick
Pincus-Witten, Robert A
Posner, Judith L
Puchalski, Gregory John
Reed, Michael Arthur
Rice, Shelley Enid
Rinehart, Michael
Robbins, Eugenia S
Rosenberg, Alex Jacob
Rosenberg, Carole Halsband
Rosenthal, Gertrude
Rossen, Susan F
Ruta, Peter Paul
Sakai, Kazuya
Schlicher, Karl Theodore
Schmidt, Mary Morris
Schneider, Ira
Schoener, Allon
Shor, Bernice Abramowitz
Slivka, Rose
Smith, Albert
Stampfle, Felice
Stoner, Joyce Hill
Sward, Robert S
Tolles, Bryant Franklin, Jr
Townsend, J Benjamin
Turano, Jane Van Norman
Van Tongeren, Harold (Herk)
Watkins, Eileen Frances
Werner, Alfred
Westwater, Angela King
White, Ron
Winchester, Alice
Wright, Frank Cookman
Young, Joseph E
Zlotnick, Diana Shirley

EDUCATOR
(College/University)

Aach, Herb
Abdalla, Nick
Abeles, Sigmund
Ablow, Joseph
Abrams, Jane Eldora
Achepohl, Keith Anden
Acker, Perry Miles
Ackerman, Gerald Martin
Ackerman, James S
Adamy, George E
Adler, Samuel (Marcus)
Agar, Eunice Jane
Agostini, Peter
Ahysen, Harry Joseph
Akawie, Thomas Frank
Alaupovic, Alexandra V
Albert, Calvin
Alexander, Margaret Ames
Alexander, Robert Seymour
Alexenberg, Melvin (Menahem)
Alf, Martha Joanne
Allan, William George
Allen, Jere Hardy
Allen, Margaret Prosser
Allen, Ralph
Allgood, Charles Henry
Alloway, Lawrence
Allumbaugh, James
Alper, M Victor
Alpert, George
Alps, Glen Earl
Altman, Harold
Altmann, Henry S
Altschuler, Franz
Ambrose, Charles Edward
Amoss, Berthe
Andersen, Wayne Vesti
Anderson, Donald Myers
Anderson, James P
Anderson, Jeremy Radcliffe
Anderson, William Thomas
Andrew, David Neville
Andrews, Michael Frank
Andrews, Oliver
Andrus, James Roman
Anglin, Betty Lockhart
Anliker, Roger (William)
Anthony, Lawrence Kenneth
Antin, David A
Antin, Eleanor
Antreasian, Garo Zareh
Anzures, Rafael
Apel, Barbara Jean
Apgar, Nicolas Adam
Appel, Keith Kenneth
Appelhof, Ruth A
Appleman, David Earl
Archambault, Louis
Arcuri, Frank J
Ard, Saradell (Saradell Ard Frederick)
Armstrong, Bill Howard
Arneson, Robert Carston
Arnest, Bernard
Arnheim, Rudolf
Arnold, Paul Beaver
Arnold, Ralph Moffett
Aronson, David
Aschenbach, (Walter) Paul
Ascott, Roy
Asher, Lila Oliver
Askin, Walter Miller
Askman, Tom K
Atwell, Allen
Aubin, Barbara
Austin, Pat
Auvil, Kenneth William
Azara, Nancy J
Bach, Dirk
Bacot, Henry Parrott
Baer, Norbert Sebastian
Bailey, Clark T
Bailey, Oscar
Baird, Joseph Armstrong, Jr
Baker, Ralph Bernard
Bakke, Karen Lee
Bakke, Larry Hubert
Baldridge, Mark S
Baldwin, John
Baldwin, Russell W
Ball, Walter Neil
Balmaceda, Margarita S
Balossi, John
Bambas, Thomas Reese
Banks, Anne Johnson
Baranoff, Mort
Barazani, Morris
Barbee, Robert Thomas
Barker, Walter William
Barnes, Curt (Curtis Edward)
Barnes, Robert M
Barreres, Domingo
Barrett, Bill
Barrett, Robert Dumas
Barron, Ros
Barry, Anne Meredith
Barry, Frank (Barry Francis Leopold)
Barschel, Hans J
Barth, Charles John
Bartlett, Donald Loring
Bartnick, Harry William
Barton, Bruce Walter
Barton, Eleanor Dodge
Bashor, John W
Bass, Ruth Gilbert
Bassin, Joan
Bate, Norman Arthur
Battcock, Gregory
Battenberg, John
Bavinger, Eugene Allen
Bayer, Jeffrey Joshua
Bayliss, George
Bealmer, William
Beam, Philip Conway
Beard, Marion L Patterson
Beard, Richard Elliott
Beck, Margit
Beck, Rosemarie (Rosemarie Beck Phelps)
Beck, Stephen R
Bedno, Edward
Beelke, Ralph G
Beer, Kenneth John
Beerman, Herbert
Belshe, Mirella Monti
Benedict, Nan M
Benedikt, Michael
Benglis, Lynda
Bentz, Harry Donald
Benz, Lee R
Berd, Morris
Berguson, Robert Jenkins
Berlyn, Sheldon
Berman, Steven M
Bernard, David Edwin
Berneche, Jerry Douglas
Bernstein, Judith
Berry, Glenn
Bettiga, Floyd Henry
Bettinson, Brenda
Betts, Edward Howard
Bieler, Andre Charles
Bieler, Ted Andre
Bier, Justus
Biggers, John Thomas
Billeci, Andre George
Billmyer, John Edward
Birdman, Jerome M
Bireline, George Lee
Birkin, Morton
Birmelin, August Robert
Bischoff, Elmer Nelson
Bishop, Barbara Lee
Bishop, Benjamin
Bjorklund, Lee
Black, David Evans
Blackmun, Barbara Winston
Blackwell, John Victor
Blair, Carl Raymond
Blaustein, Alfred H
Blevins, James Richard
Blizzard, Alan
Bloch, E Maurice
Block, Irving Alexander
Blodgett, Peter
Bobick, Bruce
Boccia, Edward Eugene
Bodnar, Peter
Boe, Roy Asbjorn
Boeve, Edgar Gene
Bogart, George A

Boggs, Franklin
Boggs, Mayo Mac
Boghosian, Varujan
Bohan, Peter John
Bohrod, Aaron
Bolinsky, Joseph Abraham
Bolomey, Roger Henry
Bolotowsky, Ilya
Bony, Jean Victor
Booth, Bill
Bopp, Emery
Boretz, Naomi
Borgatta, Isabel Case
Borgatta, Robert Edward
Born, James E
Bornstein, Eli
Borstein, Elena
Boughton, William Harrison
Bove, Richard
Bowlt, John
Bowman, Bruce
Bowman, Jeff Ray
Bowman, Ruth
Boyce, Gerald G
Boyce, William G
Boyd, James Henderson
Boyd, John David
Boyd, Lakin
Boyle, Keith
Brackman, Robert
Bradbury, Ellen A
Bradshaw, Glenn Raymond
Bradshaw, Robert George
Brainard, Owen
Braitstein, Marcel
Bransby, Eric James
Bravmann, Rene A
Brawley, Robert Julius
Breckenridge, Bruce M
Breed, Charles Ayars
Breitenbach, William John
Breithaupt, Erwin M
Brejcha, Vernon Lee
Brewster, Michael
Brezik, Hilarion
Brice, William
Brinkerhoff, Dericksen Morgan
Bristow, William Arthur
Britsky, Nicholas
Britt, Al
Britt, Sam Glenn
Brock, Robert W
Brod, Stanford
Brodsky, Stan
Brody, Jacob Jerome
Brody, Myron Roy
Brooks, Bruce W
Brooks, John H
Brooks, Lois Ziff
Brooks, Wendell T
Broude, Norma Freedman
Broudo, Joseph David
Brough, Richard Burrell
Brown, Gary Hugh
Brown, Hilton Edward
Brown, Jonathan
Brown, Joseph
Brown, Larry K
Brown, Peter C
Brownett, Thelma Denyer
Brucker, Edmund
Bruder, Harold Jacob
Brumbaugh, Thomas Brendle
Bruno, Vincent J
Bryant, Edward Albert
Bryant, Olen L
Bucher, George Robert
Buckley, Mary L (Mrs Joseph M Parriott)
Buckner, Kay Lamoreux
Buckner, Paul Eugene
Bullen, Reese
Bumbeck, David A
Bumgardner, James Arliss
Bunch, Clarence
Bunker, George
Bunnell, Peter Curtis
Buranabunpot, Pornpilai
Burchess, Arnold
Burchfield, Jerry Lee
Burford, Byron Leslie
Burgart, Herbert Joseph
Burger, W Carl
Burggraf, Ray Lowell
Burke, Daniel V
Burke, E Ainslie
Burke, James Donald
Burkhardt, Hans Gustav
Burko, Diane
Burnham, Jack Wesley
Burr, Horace
Bush, Donald John
Bush, Lucile Elizabeth
Bush-Brown, Albert
Bushman, David Franklin
Bussabarger, Robert Franklin
Butler, Marigene H
Butterbaugh, Robert Clyde
Bye, Ranulph (DeBayeux)
Byrd, D Gibson
Caballero, Emilio
Cadieux, Michael Eugene
Cahill, James Francis
Cain, Joseph Alexander
Cajori, Charles F
Calas, Nicolas
Caldwell, Eleanor
Caldwell, Martha Belle
Calkins, Kingsley Mark
Calkins, Robert G
Callner, Richard
Camarata, Martin L
Cameron, Brooke Bulovsky
Campbell, Gretna
Campbell, Jewett
Campbell, Malcolm
Campbell, Marjorie Dunn
Campoli, Cosmo
Cannon, Margaret Erickson
Cantini, Virgil D
Cantor, Robert Lloyd
Caplan, Jerry L
Caponi, Anthony
Carey, James Sheldon
Carey, John Thomas
Carlos, (James) Edward
Carmichael, Donald Ray
Carpenter, Gilbert Frederick (Bert)
Carpenter, James Morton
Carrero, Jaime
Carswell, Rodney
Carter, Dean
Casanova, Aldo John
Casas, Melesio
Casey, John Joseph
Cassara, Frank
Castro (Pacheco Fernando)
Cataldo, John William
Catan-Rose, Richard
Cathers, James O
Cavanaugh, Tom Richard
Cavat, Irma
Cave, Leonard Edward
Ceglia, Vincent
Celentano, Francis Michael
Celli, Paul
Cervenka, Barbara
Chadwick, Whitney
Chaet, Bernard
Chafetz, Sidney
Chalmers, E Laurence, Jr
Chamberlain, Charles
Chandler, Dana C, Jr (Akin Duro)
Chapian, Grieg Hovsep
Chapin, Louis (Le Bourgeois)
Chaplin, George Edwin
Chapman, Robert Gordon
Chappell, Berkley Warner
Chase, Alice Elizabeth
Chavez-Morado, Jose
Cheatham, Frank Reagan
Cheshire, Craig Gifford
Chesney, Lee R, Jr
Chesney, Lee Roy, III
Chester, Janie Kathleen
Chesterton, David
Chetham, Charles
Chew, Harry
Chew, Paul Albert
Chicoine, Rene
Chipp, Herschel Browning
Chodkowski, Henry, Jr
Chomicky, Yar Gregory
Choy, Terence Tin-Ho
Christensen, Hans-Jorgen Thorvald
Christison, Muriel B
Chu, Gene
Cikovsky, Nicolai, Jr
Cindric, Michael Anthony
Clark, Jon Frederic
Clayberger, Samuel Robert
Clements, Robert Donald
Cleveland, Robert Earl
Clipsham, Jacqueline Ann
Clover, James B
Coffey, Douglas Robert
Cogswell, Dorothy McIntosh
Cohen, H George
Cohen, Harold
Cohen, Harold Larry
Cohn, Marjorie B
Cohoe, Grey
Coke, F Van Deren
Coker, Carl David
Colby, Victor E
Cole, Bruce
Cole, Harold David
Colescott, Warrington W
Colker, Edward
Collett, Farrell Reuben
Collier, Graham (Alan Graham-Collier)
Collins, George R
Collins, Jim
Collins, William Charles
Colson, Chester E
Colt, John Nicholson
Comini, Alessandra
Conant, Howard Somers
Conaway, James D
Conlon, James Edward
Conn, David Edward
Connett, Dee M
Connor, Linda Stevens
Conrad, George
Conrad, John W
Constantine, Greg John
Cook, Richard Lee
Cooke, Edwy Francis
Cooke, Jody Helen
Coolidge, John
Cooper, Rhonda
Copeland, Lawrence Gill
Cordy-Collins, Alana (Alana Kathleen Cordy-Collins Riesland)
Corpron, Carlotta Mae
Corsaw, Roger D
Couch, Urban
Coughlin, Jack
Couper, James M
Covi, Dario A
Covington, Harrison Wall
Cox, Ernest Lee
Crable, James Harbour
Craft, Douglas D
Cramer, Richard Charles
Crane, Barbara Bachmann
Crane, James
Craven, Roy Curtis, Jr
Craven, Wayne
Crawley, Wesley V
Creese, Walter Littlefield
Crespo, Michael Lowe
Cress, George Ayers
Cretara, Domenic Anthony
Crile, Susan
Crist, William Gary
Cronbach, Robert M
Crosby, Ranice W
Crossgrove, Roger Lynn
Crown, Keith Allen
Culkin, John Michael
Czimbalmos, Szabo Kalman
Da Cunha, Julio
Dahill, Thomas Henry, Jr
Dailey, Michael Dennis
Dale, William Scott Abell
d'Alessio, Gregory
Daly, Norman
d'Andrea, Albert Philip
Danes, Gibson Andrew
Danhausen, Eldon
Danieli, Fidel Angelo
Danoff, I Michael
D'Arcangelo, Allan M
D'Arista, Robert
Darrow, Paul Gardner
Daugherty, Michael F
Davey, Ronald A
David, Honore Salmi
Davidson, Abraham A
Davis, D Jack
Davis, Donald Jack
Davis, Harry Allen
Davis, J Ray
Davis, James Wesley
Davis, Marian B
Davis, Phil Douglas
Davis, Philip Charles
Davisson, Darrell
Day, John
Deaderick, Joseph
Deal, Joe
De Blasi, Anthony Armando
De Creeft, Jose
De Foix-Crenascol, Louis
De Kergommeaux, Duncan
DeLamonica, Roberto
DeLap, Tony
DeLauro, Joseph Nicola
De Leeuw, Leon
Della-Volpe, Ralph Eugene
DeLonga, Leonard Anthony
DeLuigi, Janice Cecilia
DeMatties, Nick Frank
De Monte, Claudia
Denniston, Douglas
de Paola, Tomie
Desmidt, Thomas H
Desoto, Rafael M
Devlin, Harry
Dew, James Edward
Dhaemers, Robert August
Dibble, Charles Ryder
Dice, Elizabeth Jane
Dickerson, Daniel Jay
Dickinson, David Charles
DiGiusto, Gerald N
Dillow, Nancy E (Nancy Elizabeth Robertson)
DiPasquale, Dominic Theodore
Dixon, Albert George, III
Dodd, Eric M
Dodd, Lamar
Doherty, Robert J
Dole, William
Doll, Donald Arthur
Donson, Jerome Allan
Doolittle, Warren Ford, Jr
Dorra, Henri
Dorsky, Morris
Dorst, Claire V
Doudera, Gerard
Douke, Daniel W
Downey, Juan
Doyon, Gerard Maurice
Drewal, Henry John
Driskell, David Clyde
Droege, Anthony Joseph, II
Duckworth, Ruth
Duhme, H Richard, Jr
Duncan, Richard Hurley
Du Pen, Everett George

EDUCATOR(cont)

Dwyer, Eugene Joseph
Dwyer, James Eugene
Eades, Luis Eric
Earl, Jack Eugene
East, N S, Jr
Easterwood, Henry Lewis
Eberman, Edwin
Eckersley, Thomas Cyril
Eckert, William Dean
Edmiston, Sara Joanne
Edmonston, Paul
Edwards, James F
Ehresmann, Donald Louis
Ehrlich, George
Eide, Palmer
Eikerman, Alma
Eilers, Fred (Anton Frederick)
Eisenberg, Marvin
Eisenstat, Benjamin
Eisner, Elliot Wayne
Eitner, Lorenz E A
Elder, David Morton
Elkins, (E) Lane
Ellinger, Ilona E
Ellingson, William John
Elliott, Bruce Roger
Elliott, Philip Clarkson
Ellis, Edwin Charles
Elman, Emily
Else, Robert John
Elsen, Albert Edward
Elsner, Larry Edward
Emerson, Walter Caruth
Engeran, Whitney John, Jr
Enggass, Robert
Enos, Chris
Eppink, Norman R
Epting, Marion Austin
Erdle, Rob
Ertman, Earl Leslie
Esler, John Kenneth
Estabrook, Reed
Ettinghausen, Richard
Evans, Grose
Evans, Richard
Evans, Robert Graves
Ewen, Paterson
Fabe, Robert
Fabion, John
Fager, Charles J
Fainter, Robert A
Faison, Samson Lane, Jr
Faller, Marion
Farnham, Emily
Farnsworth, Jerry
Farwell, Beatrice
Fearing, Kelly
Fehl, Philipp P
Feldhaus, Paul A
Feldman, Arthur Mitchell
Feldman, Edmund Burke
Feldman, Walter (Sidney)
Feldstein, Mary
Feller, Robert L
Fels, C P
Fenci, Renzo
Fendell, Jonas J
Fenton, Howard Carter
Ferguson, Garth Michele
Ferrari, Virginio Luig
Ferreira, (Armando) Thomas
Field, Richard Sampson
Fifield, Mary
Filipowski, Richard E
Filkosky, Josefa
Fincher, John H
Fingesten, Peter
Fink, Herbert Lewis
Fink, Laurence B
Fink, Ray (Raymond Russell)
Finkelstein, Louis
Finkelstein, Max
Finkler, Robert Allan
Finley, Gerald Eric
Fisch, Arline Marie
Fisher, Elaine
Fisher, Vernon
Flach, Victor H
Fleckenstein, Opal R
Flecker, Maurice Nathan
Flick, Robert
Flinn, Elizabeth Haight
Flint, Leroy W
Flowers, Thomas Earl
Folsom, Karl Leroy
Fontanez, Carmelo
Fontanini, Clare
Foosaner, Judith Ann
Ford, Harry Xavier
Ford, Ruth Vansickle
Forman, Kenneth Warner
Formigoni, Maurie Monihon
Fornas, Leander
Forrest, James Taylor
Forrester, Charles Howard
Forsman, Chuck (Charles Stanley Forsman)
Francis, Bill Dean
Frank, David
Frankel, Dextra
Fraser, Douglas (Ferrar)
Frazer, John Thatcher
Frazier, Paul D
Fredrick, Eugene Wallace
Freedberg, Sydney Joseph
Freeman, Richard Borden
Freifeld, Eric
Freimark, Robert (Matthew)
Freund, Will Frederick
Freundlich, August L
Fricano, Tom S
Frick, Robert Oliver
Friedman, Kenneth Scott
Friend, David
Frinta, Mojmir Svatopluk
Frost, Stuart Homer
Fuchs, Mary Tharsilla
Fulton, W Joseph
Fumagalli, Orazio
Funk, Verne J
Furman, David Stephen
Galles, Arie Alexander
Gallo, Frank
Gammon, Juanita-La Verne
Gammon, Reginald Adolphus
Garcia, Ofelia
Gardner, Robert Earl
Garey, Pat
Garnett, William Ashford
Garnsey, Clarke Henderson
Garrard, Mary DuBose
Garrett, Stuart Grayson, Jr
Garris, Kathleen (Kathleen Weil-Garris)
Gatrell, Marion Thompson
Gatrell, Robert Morris
Gebhard, David
Gebhardt, Ann Stellhorn
Gebhardt, Harold
Geck, Francis Joseph
Geeslin, Lee Gaddis
Gekiere, Madeleine
Gelber, Samuel
Gelinas, Robert William
Genders, Richard Atherstone
George, Raymond Ellis
Gerdts, William H
Gerhold, William Henry
Gernhardt, Henry Kendall
Geske, Norman Albert
Gettinger, Edmond Walter
Getty, Nilda Fernandez
Ghikas, Panos George
Giannotti, John J
Gibbons, Hugh (James)
Gibson, Walter Samuel
Gikas, Christopher
Gilbert, Creighton Eddy
Gilbert, Herb
Gilchriest, Lorenzo
Gilkey, Gordon Waverly
Gilmore, Roger
Ginnever, Charles
Glanz, Andrea Elise
Glaser, Bruce
Glasson, Lloyd
Glicksman, Hal
Glover, Robert Leon
Glyde, Henry George
Godsey, Glenn
Goeritz, Mathias
Goetzl, Thomas Maxwell
Gold, Albert
Golden, Eunice
Goldin, Leon
Goldring, Nancy Deborah
Goldsmith, Benedict Isaac
Goldstein, Howard
Goldstein, Milton
Golub, Leon Albert
Gongora, Leonel
Gonzales, Boyer
Gooch, Donald Burnette
Gooch, Gerald
Good, Leonard
Goodall, Donald Bannard
Goodnow, Frank A
Goossen, Eugene Coons
Gorder, Clayton J
Gordin, Sidney
Gordley, Marilyn F M
Gordley, Metz Tranbarger
Gordon, John S
Gordon, Joy L
Gorski, Daniel Alexander
Gorski, Richard Kenny
Goulet, Claude
Gourevitch, Jacqueline
Graham, F Lanier
Graham, Richard Marston
Graves, Bradford
Gray, Don
Gray, Robert Hugh
Grear, James Malcolm
Green, Art
Green, Edward Anthony
Green, Samuel Magee
Greenamyer, George Mossman
Greene, Stephen
Gregor, Harold Laurence
Gregor, Helen Frances
Gregoropoulos, John
Gregory, Joan
Grigsby, Jefferson Eugene, Jr
Griner, Ned H
Grippe, Peter J
Grippi, Salvatore William
Grissom, Eugene Edward
Gross, Charles Merrill
Grossman, Morton
Grucza, Leo (Victor)
Grupp, Carl Alf
Guenther, Peter W
Guerin, John William
Guilmain, Jacques
Gundersheimer, Herman (Samuel)
Gunn, Paul James
Gunter, Frank Elliott
Guston, Philip
Guthrie, Derek
Gutmann, John
Guy, James M
Gyermek, Stephen A
Haas, Lez
Hadzi, Dimitri
Hagan, (Robert) Frederick
Hageman, Charles Lee
Hahn, Betty
Halaby, Samia Asaad
Halbrooks, Darryl Wayne
Hall, Carl Alvin
Hall, John (Scott)
Hall, Louise
Hall, Michael David
Hall, Rex Earl
Hallmark, Donald Parker
Halsey, William Melton
Hamady, Walter Samuel
Hamlett, Dale Edward
Hammock, Virgil Gene
Hammond, Gale Thomas
Hampton, Phillip Jewel
Handler, Audrey
Hanfmann, George M A
Hanna, Paul Dean, Jr
Hannah, John Junior
Hannibal, Joseph Harry
Hansen, Frances Frakes
Hansen, Harold John
Hansen, James Lee
Hansen, Robert
Hanson, Lawrence
Hapke, Paul Frederick
Hara, Teruo
Harden, Marvin
Harding, Noel Robert
Hardy, Robert
Harper, William
Harrington, William Charles
Harris, Harvey Sherman
Harris, Josephine Marie
Harris, Lawren Phillips
Harris, Paul Rogers
Harsh, Richard
Hartgen, Vincent Andrew
Hartley, Paul Jerome
Hartman, Robert Leroy
Hartt, Frederick
Haskin, Donald Marcus
Haskins, John Franklin
Hastie, Reid
Hatch, John W
Hatch, W A S
Hatchett, Duayne
Hatfield, Donald Gene
Hauptman, Susan Ann
Hausman, Jerome Joseph
Havelock, Christine Mitchell
Hawthorne, Jack Gardner
Hay, Dick
Hay, Ike
Hayden, Frank
Haydon, Harold (Emerson)
Haynes, Douglas H
Hazlehurst, Franklin Hamilton
Head, Robert William
Healy, Anne Laura
Heath, David Martin
Hefner, Harry Simon
Heidel, Frederick (H)
Hein, Max
Heinecken, Robert Friedli
Held, Julius S
Helgoe, Orlin Milton
Heliker, John Edward
Heller, Jules
Helzer, Richard Brian
Hemphill, Pamela
Hendershot, J L
Henderson, Mike (William Howard Henderson)
Hendler, Raymond
Hendricks, Geoffrey
Hendricks, James (Powell)
Henkle, James Lee
Henry, Robert
Herard, Marvin T
Herbert, James Arthur
Herbert, Robert L
Hernandez-Cruz, Luis
Herrold, Clifford H
Hess, Stanley William
Hewitt, Francis Ray
Hibbard, Howard
Hickman, David Coleman
Higgins, Edward Koelling
High, Freida
High, Timothy Griffin
Hill, Clinton J
Hill, Peter
Hilson, Douglas
Hilton, Eric G
Hing, Allan Mark

Hirsch, Gilah Yelin
Hitchcock, Henry Russell
Hobbs, Robert Dean
Hofsted, Jolyon Gene
Hogbin, Stephen James
Hoge, Robert Wilson
Holcomb, Grant
Holder, Kenneth Allen
Holen, Norman Dean
Holladay, Harlan H
Holm, Bill
Holste, Thomas James
Homer, William Innes
Hood, (Thomas) Richard
Hooks, Earl J
Hopkins, Peter
Horn, Bruce
Hornaday, Richard Hoyt
Hornung, Gertrude Seymour
Hostetler, David
House, James Charles, Jr
Houser, Jim
Howard, Dan F
Howard, Robert A
Howe, Oscar
Howell, Claude Flynn
Howett, John
Howze, James Dean
Hu, Mary Lee
Hudson, Ralph Magee
Huff, Howard Lee
Huggins, Victor, (Jr)
Hui, Ka-Kwong
Hundley, David Holladay
Hunisak, John Michael
Hunt, Robert James
Hunter, Debora
Hunter, John H
Hunter, Leonard LeGrande, III
Hunter, Miriam Eileen
Hunter, Robert Howard
Hunter, Sam
Huntley, David C
Hupp, Frederick Duis
Hurst, Ralph N
Hurtig, Martin Russell
Hurwitz, Sidney J
Hyslop, Francis Edwin
Iden, Sheldon
Iglehart, Robert L
Ihle, John Livingston
Ippolito, Angelo
Irving, Donald J
Isaacson, Marcia Jean
Iskin, Ruth Evelyn
Italiano, Joan Nylen
Iwamasa, Ken
Izumi, Kiyoshi
Jachna, Joseph David
Jackson, A B
Jackson, Billy Morrow
Jackson, Herb
Jacobs, David (Theodore)
Jacobs, Harold
Jacobsen, Michael A
Jacobshagen, N Keith, II
Jacobson, Arthur Robert
Jacquard (Jerald Wayne Jackard)
Jacques, Michael Louis
Jacquette, Yvonne Helene (Yvonne Helen Burckhardt)
Jaffe, Ira Sheldon
Jankowski, Joseph P
Janson, Horst Woldemar
Janzen, Loren Gene
Jaque, Louis
Jardine, Donald Leroy
Jelinek, Hans
Jennerjahn, W P
Jergens, Robert Joseph
Jerry, Michael John
Jeter, Randy Joe
Jewell, William M
Johnson, Charles W, Jr
Johnson, Charlotte Buel
Johnson, Dana Doane
Johnson, Donald Ray
Johnson, Edvard Arthur
Johnson, Ellen Hulda
Johnson, Ivan Earl
Johnson, James Alan
Johnson, Lester F
Johnson, Lincoln Fernando
Johnson, Lois Marlene
Johnson, Pauline B
Johnston, Richard M
Johnston, Robert Harold
Johnston, Robert Porter
Johnston, William Medford
Jones, Frederick George
Jones, John Paul
Jones, Lois Swan
Jones, Louis C
Jones, Marvin Harold
Jones, Robert Cushman
Jones, Theodore Joseph
Jordan, James William
Jordan, Robert
Jordan, William B
Jorgensen, Sandra
Jorgenson, Dale Alfred
Joseph, Cliff (Clifford Ricardo)
Joy, Nancy Grahame
Ju, I-Hsiung
Judd, De Forrest Hale
Jules, Mervin
Julio, Pat T
Kabak, Robert
Kachel, Harold Stanley
Kaericher, John Conrad
Kahn, Peter
Kaiser, Charles James
Kaiser, Diane
Kaish, Morton
Kalavrezou-Maxeiner, Ioli
Kalb, Marty Joel
Kaminisky, Jack Allan
Kammerer, Herbert Lewis
Kamrowski, Gerome
Kamys, Walter
Kao, Ruth (Yu-Hsin) Lee
Kaplan, Stanley
Kaprow, Allan
Kashdin, Gladys S
Kaspe, Vladimir
Kataoka, Mits
Katayama, Toshihiro
Katsiff, Bruce
Kaufman, Irving
Kaupelis, Robert John
Kay, Reed
Kayser, Stephen S
Keck, Sheldon Waugh
Keeling, Henry Cornelious
Keene, Paul
Keener, Anna Elizabeth
Keller, Deane
Kelly, Isaac Perry
Kelly, William Joseph
Kemble, Richard
Kemenyffy, Steven
Kemenyffy, Susan B Hale
Kemp, Paul Zane
Kennedy, James Edward
Kenney, Allen Lloyd
Kepes, Gyorgy
Kern, Arthur (Edward)
Kerslake, Kenneth Alvin
Kestenbaum, Lothar J
Kettner, David Allen
Keyser, Robert Gifford
Keyser, William Alphonse, Jr
Kieferndorf, Frederick George
Kilian, Austin Farland
Killmaster, John H
Kim, Bongtae
Kind, Joshua B
Kindermann, Helmmo
King, William Alfred
Kingrey, Kenneth
Kipp, Lyman
Kipp, Orval
Kirschenbaum, Jules
Kiskadden, Robert Morgan
Kitner, Harold
Kitzinger, Ernst
Klaven, Marvin L
Kleidon, Dennis Arthur
Klein, Cecelia F
Klement, Vera
Knight, Thomas Lincoln, Jr
Knipschild, Robert
Knobler, Nathan
Knowles, Richard H
Knowlton, Jonathan
Knox, George
Ko, Anthony
Kobayashi, Katsumi Peter
Kober, Alfred John
Koch, Arthur Robert
Koch, Gerd (Herman)
Koch, Robert
Kocher, Robert Lee
Koebbeman, Skip
Koepnick, Robert Charles
Kohlmeyer, Ida (R)
Kohn, William Roth
Kolliker, William Augustin
Koons, Darell J
Koppelman, Chaim
Koras, George
Korn, Elizabeth P
Kos, Paul Joseph
Koss, Gene H
Kostyniuk, Ronald P
Kotin, Albert
Kottler, Howard William
Kouwenhoven, John A
Kovatch, Jak Gene
Kowalski, Dennis Allen
Kramer, Jack N
Kramrisch, Stella
Kraner, Florian G
Krause, LaVerne Erickson
Kreilick, Marjorie E
Kreneck, Lynwood
Krevolin, Lewis
Kreznar, Richard J
Kronsnoble, Jeffrey Michael
Krueger, Donald W
Krug, Harry Elno
Krukowski, Lucian
Krushenick, John
Kubler, George Alexander
Kuchar, Kathleen Ann
Kuebler, George F
Kuehnl, Claudia Ann
Kuhlman, Walter Egel
Kuhn, Marylou
Kultermann, Udo
Kurahara, Ted
Kurz, Diana
Kuspit, Donald Burton
Lacktman, Michael
Laderman, Gabriel
Lafaye, Nell Murray
Lagunes, Maria (Maria Lagunes Hernandez)
Lam, Jennett (Brinsmade)
LaMarca, Howard J
Lamis, Leroy
La More, Chet Harmon
Landis, Ellen Jamie
Land-Weber, Ellen E
Landy, Jacob
Lang, Rodger Alan
Langland, Harold Reed
Lapinski, Tadeusz (A)
LaPlantz, David
Larkin, Eugene
Larmer, Oscar Vance
Larsen, Erik
Larson, William G
Lasansky, Leonardo da Iowa
Lasansky, Mauricio L
Lash, Kenneth
Lasuchin, Michael
Lauck, Anthony Joseph
Laurent, John Louis
Laurer, Robert A
Lavoy, Walter Joseph
Lawrence, Howard Ray
Lawrence, Jacob
Lawrence, Les
Lawton, James L
Lax, David
Lay, Patricia Anne
Lea, Stanley E
Leathers, Winston Lyle
Leavitt, Thomas Whittlesey
Lechtzin, Stanley
Le Clair, Charles
Lederer, Wolfgang
Lee, Rensselaer Wright
Lee, Robert J
Lee, Roger
Lee, Russell
Lee, Sherman Emery
Leeber, Sharon Corgan
Leepa, Allen
Le Fevre, Richard John
Leff, Juliette
Lehrer, Leonard
Leland, Whitney Edward
Lembeck, John Edgar
Leon, Dennis
Lepper, Robert Lewis
Lerman, Ora
Lerner, Nathan Bernard
Lesh, Richard D
Lesley, Parker
Levi, Julian (E)
Levine, Marilyn Anne
Levine, Shepard
Levitine, George
Levy, David Corcos
Levy, Julien
Lewicki, James
Lewis, Michael H
Lewis, William Arthur
Libby, Gary Russell
Libby, William C
Lincoln, Richard Mather
Lindemann, Edna M
Linder, Stasia
Lindquist, Evan
Lindstrom, Gaell
Link, Val James
Linn, John William
Lintault, Roger Paul
Lipman-Wulf, Peter
Lipofsky, Marvin B
Lissim, Simon
Littleton, Harvey K
Livingstone, Biganess
Lloyd, Gary Marchal
Lobdell, Frank
Loehr, Max
Logan, David George
Logan, Frederick Manning
Lomahaftewa, Linda (Linda Joyce Slock)
Lombardo, Josef Vincent
Long, Glenn Alan
Longaker, Jon Dasu
Longman, Lester Duncan
Longo, Vincent
Loomer, Gifford C
Looney, Norman
Lopez, Rhoda Le Blanc
Lorber, Richard
Lotterman, Hal
Lourie, Herbert S
Love, Iris Cornelia
Love, Paul Van Derveer
Loveless, Jim
Lowe, J Michael
Lowe, Marvin
Lowry, Bates
Lubbers, Leland Eugene
Lukas, Dennis Brian
Lukosius, Richard Benedict
Lund, David
Lunde, Karl Roy

EDUCATOR(cont)
Lunsford, John (Crawford)
Lupori, Peter John
Lye, Len
Lynch, James Burr, Jr
Lytle, Richard
Macaray, Lawrence Richard
MacDonald, William Allan
Maciel, Mary Oliveira
Mack, Charles Randall
Mack, Rodger Allen
Macklin, Anderson D
Maddox, Jerrold Warren
Madsen, Viggo Holm
Madura, Jack Joseph
Magleby, Francis R (Frank)
Mahlke, Ernest D
Mahoney, James Owen
Mahoney, Michael R T
Maldre, Mati
Mallary, Robert
Mallory, Nina A
Malone, Robert R
Malta, Vincent
Manetta, Edward J
Manhart, Thomas Arthur
Manrique, Jorge Alberto
Manso, Leo
Marak, Louis Bernard
Marcheschi, (Louis) Cork
Marcus, Irving E
Marcus, Marcia
Margo, Boris
Marlor, Clark Strang
Marsh, David Foster
Marsh, (Edwin) Thomas
Marshall, John Carl
Marshall, Robert Leroy
Marsicano, Nicholas
Marter, Joan M
Martin, Alexander Toedt
Martin, Bernard Murray
Martin, G W
Martinsen, Ivar Richard
Martz, Karl
Maser, Edward Andrew
Mason, Phillip Lindsay
Massey, Charles Wesley, Jr
Massey, Robert Joseph
Massin, Eugene Max
Matheson, Donald Roy
Mathis, Kenneth Lawrence
Matteson, Ira
Matthews, Gene
Matthews, Harriett
Mattox, Charles
Maughelli, Mary L
Maurice, Alfred Paul
Mavroudis, Demetrios
Mawdsley, Richard W
Maxwell, William C
Mayhew, Edgar De Noailles
Maynard, William
Mayor, Alpheus Hyatt
Mazur, Michael
McCarthy, Denis
McCauley, Gardiner Rae
McChesney, Clifton
McClanahan, John Dean
McCloy, William Ashby
McClure, Thomas F
McCoy, Wirth Vaughan
McCracken, Patrick Ed
McCray, Dorothy M
McElroy, Jacquelyn Ann
McFee, June King
McGarrell, James
McGill, Robert Lee
McGough, Charles E
McGovern, Robert F
McGowin, Ed
McIlvain, Douglas Lee
McIvor, John Wilfred
McKay, Arthur Fortescue
McKay, John Sangster
McKean, Hugh Ferguson
McKeeby, Byron Gordon
McKinin, Lawrence
McKinley, Donald Lloyd
McLean, James Albert
McLean, Richard Thorpe
McMillan, Jerry Edward
McMillan, Robert W
McNally, Sheila John
McNamara, Raymond Edmund
McNeil, George J
McVey, William M
McWhinnie, Harold James
Meehan, William Dale
Meeker, Barbara Miller
Meeker, Dean Jackson
Meixner, Mary Louise
Mejer, Robert Lee
Melchert, James Frederick
Mellor, George Edward
Meredith, Dorothy Laverne
Mesches, Arnold
Mesibov, Hugh
Messersmith, Fred Lawrence
Metzger, Robert Paul
Metzker, Ray K
Mew, Tommy
Meyer, Charles Edward
Meyer, Ursula
Michalove, Carla Maria
Micheli, Julio
Mignosa, Santo
Miley, Les
Miller, Richard McDermott
Milliken, Gibbs
Mills, Frederick Van Fleet
Mills, Lev Timothy
Milrad, Aaron M
Minewski, Alex
Minisci, Brenda (Eileen)
Mintich, Mary Ringelberg
Minutillo, Richard G
Miotke, Anne E
Mirabal, Miguel Enrique
Mirano, Virgil Marcus
Mirko (Wolodymyr Walter Pylyshenko)
Mitchell, Dow Penrose
Mitchell, John Blair
Mitchell, Robert Ellis
Mittleman, Ann
Mix, Walter Joseph
Miyasaki, George Joji
Moffitt, John Francis
Moir, Alfred
Moment, Joan
Momiyama, Nanae
Monaghan, Keith
Monroe, Gerald
Montequin, Francois-Auguste de
Monthan, Guy
Moore, John J
Morin, Thomas Edward
Morrin, Peter Patrick
Morris, Robert Clarke
Morrison, Keith Anthony
Morrison, Robert Clifton
Morrow, Robert Earl
Morrow, Terry
Moseley, Spencer Altemont
Moss, Joel C
Moulton, Rosalind Kimball
Moy, Seong
Muehsam, Gerd
Mueller, Earl George
Mueller, Henrietta Waters
Mueller, M Gerardine
Mullican, Lee
Mundt, Ernest Karl
Munsterberg, Hugo
Munzer, Aribert
Murray, Elizabeth
Murray, Floretta May
Murraygreen, Ryan
Musgrave, Shirley H
Musselman, Darwin B
Myers, Joel Philip
Myers, Richard Lewis
Myers, Virginia Anne
Nadler, Harry
Nash, Katherine E
Nash, Steven Alan
Navrat, Den (Dennis Edward Navrat)
Nawrocki, Thomas Dennis
Nay, Mary Spencer
Naylor, John Geoffrey
Neal, Reginald H
Nelson, Jack D
Nepote, Alexander
Nesbitt, Alexander John
Neugebauer, Margot
Nevitt, Richard Barrington
Newhall, Beaumont
Newman, (John) Christopher
Newport, Esther
Newton, Earle Williams
Nicholas, Donna Lee
Nichols, Donald Edward
Nichols, Francis N, II
Nick, George
Nickford, Juan
Nickle, Robert W
Nitz, Thomas L
Nobili, Louise
Nochlin, Linda (Linda Pommer)
Noe, Jerry Lee
Norris, (Robert) Ben
Norton, Paul Foote
Norvell, Patsy
Norwood, Malcolm Mark
Novak, Barbara (Mrs Brian O'Doherty)
Novinski, Lyle Frank
Novotny, Elmer Ladislaw
Nulf, Frank Allen
Oberhuber, Konrad J
Ockerse, Thomas
O'Connell, George D
O'Connor, John Arthur
O'Connor, Stanley James
O'Connor, Thom
Ocvirk, Otto G
Offner, Elliot
O'Gorman, James Francis
O'Gorman, Juan
O'Hanlon, Richard E
Ohlson, Douglas Dean
Ohman, Richard Michael
O'Lenick, David Charles
Olkinetzky, Sam
Olson, Douglas John
Olson, Richard W
Omar, Margit
O'Neil, John
O'Neil, John Joseph
Onley, Toni
Opper, John
Orenstein, Gloria Feman
Orze, Joseph John
O'Sickey, Joseph Benjamin
Ottiano, John William
Oubre, Hayward Louis
Pablo (Paul Burgess Edwards)
Page, Bill
Page, John Henry, Jr
Palazzola, Guy
Palmgren, Donald Gene
Pappas, George
Pappas, Marilyn
Pardon, Earl B
Parfenoff, Michael S
Paris, Harold Persico
Parker, John William
Parker, Samuel Murray
Parsons, David Goode
Partin, Robert (E)
Paterson, Anthony R
Patnode, J Scott
Patrick, Joseph Alexander
Paul, Ken (Hugh)
Paulin, Richard Calkins
Payne, John D
Pearlstein, Philip
Pearlstein, Seymour
Peck, Judith
Peck, Lee Barnes
Peckham, Nicholas
Peers, Gordon Franklin
Pekarsky, Mel (Melvin Hirsch)
Pendergraft, Norman Elveis
Penney, James
Perkins, Ann
Perkins, Constance M
Perkins, G Holmes
Perlman, Joel Leonard
Perlman, Raymond
Perry, Edward (Ted) Samuel
Perry, Regenia Alfreda
Peter, Friedrich Gunther
Peterdi, Gabor F
Petersen, Roland Conrad
Peterson, Larry D
Petheo, Bela Francis
Petro, Joseph (Victor), Jr
Petrochuk, Konstantin
Phillips, Donna-Lee
Piccillo, Joseph
Piccolo, Thomas Frank
Pierce, Delilah W
Pinardi, Enrico Vittorio
Pincus-Witten, Robert A
Pineda, Marianna (Marianna Pineda Tovish)
Pinsky, Alfred
Pinto, Angelo Raphael
Pirkl, James Joseph
Place, Bradley Eugene
Plagens, Peter
Plummer, John H
Pogue, Stephanie Elaine
Poleskie, Stephen Francis
Pollak, Theresa
Polonsky, Arthur
Ponce de Leon, Michael
Popinsky, Arnold Dave
Porter, Albert Wright
Porter, Elmer Johnson
Posey, Ernest Noel
Postiglione, Corey M
Potts, Don
Poulos, Basilios Nicholas
Pounian, Albert Kachouni
Power, Mark
Praczukowski, Edward Leon
Pramuk, Edward Richard
Pratt, Vernon Gaither
Preble, Michael Andrew
Prekop, Martin Dennis
Prescott, Kenneth Wade
Press, Nancy Neumann
Prestini, James Libero
Preusser, Robert Ormerod
Pribble, Easton
Price, Leslie Kenneth
Price, Michael Benjamin
Prince, Arnold
Prohaska, Ray
Pross, Lester Fred
Pufahl, John K
Pulos, Arthur Jon
Purser, Stuart Robert
Puryear, Martin
Putterman, Florence Grace
Quest, Charles Francis
Quest, Dorothy (Johnson)
Quirarte, Jacinto
Quirk, Thomas Charles, Jr
Racz, Andre
Rae, Edwin C
Raggio, Olga
Raleigh, Henry Patrick
Ramos, Melvin John
Ramsauer, Joseph Francis
Ranes, Chris
Rannit, Aleksis
Rascoe, Stephen Thomas
Rasmussen, Anton Jesse

Rave, Georgia
Ray, Robert Arthur
Raybon, Phares Henderson
Rayen, James Wilson
Redd, Richard James
Redd Ekks (Robert Norman Rasmussen)
Reddix, Roscoe Chester
Reed, Jesse Floyd
Reed, Paul Allen
Reep, Edward Arnold
Reese, Thomas Ford
Reichert, Donald Karl
Reichman, Fred (Thomas)
Reid, (William) Richard
Reider, David H
Reif, Rubin
Reiff, Robert Frank
Reimann, William P
Rembert, Virginia Pitts
Renick, Charles Cooley
Resnick, Marcia Aylene
Revor, Remy
Rewald, John
Reynolds, Richard (Henry)
Reynolds, Robert
Rhyne, Charles Sylvanus
Rice, Harold Randolph
Rice, James William, Jr
Rice, Norman Lewis
Rice, Shelley Enid
Richards, Bill
Richards, Karl Frederick
Richards, Lee
Richardson, James Lewis
Richardson, Sam
Richenburg, Robert Bartlett
Ridlon, James A
Rigby, Ida Katherine
Rigg, Margaret Ruth
Rippey, Clayton
Rippon, Ruth Margaret
Riseling, Robert Lowell
Risley, John Hollister
Riss, Murray
Robb, David M
Robbins, Daniel J
Roberson, Samuel Arndt
Roberts, Lucille D (Malkia)
Robinson, Franklin W
Robinson, Grove
Robinson, Mary Ann
Robinson, Robert Doke
Rode, Meredith Eagon
Rodriguez-Morales, Luis Manuel
Rogers, John H
Rogers, Otto Donald
Rogovin, Mark
Rohm, Robert
Roland, Arthur
Romano, Clare Camille
Rosati, James
Rose, Mary Anne
Roseberg, Carl Andersson
Rosen, Beverly Doris
Rosenberg, Charles Michael
Rosenberg, Harold
Roskill, Mark Wentworth
Ross, Conrad Harold
Ross, James Matthew
Roster, Fred Howard
Roston, Arnold
Roukes, Nicholas M
Rowan, C Patrick
Rowan, Dennis Michael
Rowan, Herman
Rozman, Joseph John
Ruben, Leonard
Ruben, Richards
Rubin, William
Ruddley, John
Ruggles, Joanne Beaule
Rugolo, Lawrence
Rush, Jon N
Russell, Robert Price
Russin, Robert I
Russo, Alexander Peter
Russo, Kathleen L
Rutherford, Erica
Ruvolo, Felix Emmanuele
Sabatella, Joseph John
Sadek, George
Sage, Bill B
Sahlstrand, James Michael
Sahlstrand, Margaret Ahrens
St Florian, Friedrich Gartler
St Maur, Kirk (Kirk Seymour McReynolds)
Salmon, Raymond Merle
Saltzman, Marvin
Salzman, Rick
Samuels, Gerald
Sandberg, Hannah
Sander, Dennis Jay
Sandgren, Ernest Nelson
Sangiamo, Albert
Sanguinetti, Eugene F
Sarvis, Alva Taylor
Satorsky, Cyril
Satterfield, John Edward
Saucy, Claude Gerald
Saunders, J Boyd
Saunders, Raymond Jennings
Savitz, Frieda (Frieda Savitz Laden)
Savoy, Chyrl Lenore
Sawai, Noboru
Sawyer, Charles Henry
Scala, Joseph (A)
Scanga, Italo
Schactman, Barry Robert
Schaefer, Ronald H
Schapiro, Meyer
Schellin, Robert William
Schepis, Anthony Joseph
Scherpereel, Richard Charles
Schieferdecker, Ivan E
Schiff, Jean
Schlemowitz, Abram
Schlicher, Karl Theodore
Schlump, John Otto
Schmalz, Carl (Nelson, Jr)
Schmandt-Besserat, Denise
Schmidt, Frederick Lee
Schmidt, Julius
Schmidt, Randall Bernard
Schmutzhart, Berthold Josef
Schneider, Ira
Schoener, Jason
Scholz, Janos
Schooley, Elmer Wayne
Schorr, Justin
Schucker, Charles
Schultz, Harold A
Schulze, Franz
Schulze, John H
Schumacher, Herbert Charles
Schwarz, Felix Conrad
Schwarz, Myrtle Cooper
Schweizer, Paul Douglas
Schwidder, Ernst Carl
Schwieger, C Robert
Scott, Curtis S
Scott, Henry (Edwards), Jr
Scott, John Tarrell
Scott-Gibson, Herbert Nathaniel
Scully, Vincent
Scuris, Stephanie
Seace, Barry William
Seames, Clarann
Seide, Charles
Seley, Jason
Sella, Alvin Conrad
Sellers, John Lewis
Sellers, William Freeman
Selz, Peter H
Semak, Michael
Sennema, David C
Seppa, Heikki Markus
Serniak, Regina
Serra-Badue, Daniel
Severino, Dominick Alexander
Sexauer, Donald Richard
Seyler, David W
Shapiro, Frank D
Shapley, John
Sharits, Paul Jeffrey
Shepherd, Dorothy G (Mrs Ernst Payer)
Sheppard, Luvon
Sherker, Michael Z
Sherman, Claire Richter
Shestack, Alan
Shimizu, Yoshiaki
Shimomura, Roger Yutaka
Shiner, Nate
Shipley, James R
Shipley, Roger Douglas
Shoemaker, Peter
Shull, Carl Edwin
Siden, Franklin
Sieber, Roy
Sieg, Robert Lawrence
Sigrin, Michael E
Silverman, David Frederick
Silverman, Ronald H
Simkin, Phillips M
Simon, Herbert Bernheimer
Simoni, John Peter
Simpson, David
Simpson, William Kelly
Sinsabaugh, Art
Sisson, Jacqueline D
Sister Adele
Sister Thomasita (Mary Thomasita Fessler)
Sitton, John M
Skelley, Robert Charles
Slate, Joseph Frank
Slater, Van E
Slatkes, Leonard Joseph
Slavin, Arlene
Slavit, Ann L
Slawinski, Joseph
Slettehaugh, Thomas Chester
Sloane, Joseph Curtis
Slotnick, Mortimer H
Slusky, Joseph
Smith, Arthur Hall
Smith, Barbara Turner
Smith, David Loeffler
Smith, Donald Eugene
Smith, Frank Anthony
Smith, John Bertie
Smith, John Ivor
Smith, Lawson Wentworth
Smith, Ralph Alexander
Smith, Robert Lewis
Smith, Sam
Smith, Sherry
Smith, Thelma deGoede
Smith, Victor Joachim
Sokol, David Martin
Sokole, Miron
Solman, Joseph
Solodkin, Judith
Solomon, Bernard Alan
Solomon, David
Sommer, Wassily
Sommers, John Sherman
Sorell, Victor Alexander
Sorokin, Maxine Ann
Spafford, Michael Charles
Spaulding, Warren Dan
Spear, Richard Edmund
Speight, Francis
Spence, Robert
Spencer, Eleanor Patterson
Spencer, Harold Edwin
Sprague, Mark Anderson
Sprout, Francis Allen
Spruce, Everett Franklin
Spurgin, John Edwin
Squier, Jack Leslie
Stack, Frank Huntington
Stack, Gael Z
Stacy, Donald L
Stanforth, Melvin Sidney
Stankiewicz, Richard Peter
Stapp, Ray Veryl
Stark, George King
Stark, Melville F
Starks, Elliott Roland
Stars, William Kenneth
Staven, Leland Carroll
Steele, Benjamin Charles
Steen, Ronald Earl
Steffler, Alva W
Steg, J L
Stegeman, Charles
Stein, Roger Breed
Stell, H Kenyon
Stephany, Jaromir
Stephens, Curtis
Stephens, Richard Alan
Stephens, William Blakely
Stephenson, John H
Stephenson, Susanne G
Stevanov, Zoran
Stevens, Walter Hollis
Stewart, Jarvis Anthony
Stoddard, Donna Melissa
Stokstad, Marilyn
Stoneham, John
Stoner, Joyce Hill
Storm, Howard
Stout, Richard Gordon
Straight, Robert Larry
Strasen, Barbara Elaine
Stringer, Mary Evelyn
Strong, Charles Ralph
Strother, Joseph Willis
Stroud, Peter Anthony
Struppeck, Jules
Stuart, Joseph Martin
Stuler, Jack
Sturgeon, Mary C
Sublett, Carl C
Sudlow, Robert N
Sullins, Robert M
Sullivan, Jim
Sullivan, Max William
Sullivan, Ruth Wilkins
Summ, Helmut
Summerford, Ben Long
Sunderland, Elizabeth Read
Sunderland, Nita Kathleen
Sunkel, Robert Cleveland
Sussman, Elisabeth Sacks
Suter, Sherwood Eugene
Swift, Dick
Swinton, George
Swirnoff, Lois
Sykes, (William) Maltby
Tabachnick, Anne
Tajiri, Shinkichi
Talbot, Jarold Dean
Talleur, John J
Tam, Reuben
Tatham, David Frederic
Taylor, John C E
Taylor, Joshua Charles
Taysom, Wayne Pendelton
Teilhet, Jehanne Hildegarde
Terenzio, Anthony
Termini, Christine
Tettleton, Robert Lynn
Thiebaud, (Morton) Wayne
Thiele, Robert Ransom
Thomas, Elaine Freeman
Thomas, George R
Thomas, Robert Chester
Thomas, William Radford
Thompson, Nancy Kunkle
Thompson, Phyllis
Thompson, Robert Charles
Thompson, Tamara (Tamara Thompson Bryant)
Thompson, Wade
Thompson, William Joseph
Thorns, John Cyril, Jr
Thrall, Arthur
Thurston, Jacqueline Beverly
Tierney, Patrick Lennox

EDUCATOR(cont)
Tillotison, Robbie
Tobias, Robert Paul
Tomasini, Wallace J
Toney, Anthony
Torbert, Donald Robert
Toth, Carl Wayne
Toulis, Vasilios (Apostolos)
Tovish, Harold
Townley, Hugh
Townsend, J Benjamin
Trakis, Louis
Trank, Lynn Edgar
Traub, Charles H
Travanti, Leon Emidio
Tredennick, Dorothy W
Trentham, Gary Lynn
Triano, Anthony Thomas
Trissel, James Nevin
Trivigno, Pat
Trudeau, Yves
Tsutakawa, George
Tuchman, Phyllis
Tufts, Eleanor M
Turk, Rudy H
Turner, Evan Hopkins
Turner, Janet E
Turner, Robert Chapman
Turner, Theodore Roy
Turnure, James Harvey
Twarogowski, Leroy Andrew
Twiggs, Leo Franklin
Ubans, Juris K
Umlauf, Charles
Upton, John David
Urquhart, Tony
Ushenko, Audrey Andreyevna
Vaccarino, Robin
Vaccaro, Nick Dante
Valerio, James Robert
Vanderlip, Dianne Perry
Van Derpool, James Grote
Vander Sluis, George J
Van Dommelen, David B
Van Ginkel, Blanche Lemco
Van Leunen, Alice Louise
Van Suchtelen, Adrian
Van Winkle, Lester G
Varnedoe, John Kirk Train
Vasa (Vasa Velizar Mihich)
Vazquez, Paul
Venor, Robert George
Ventimiglia, John Thomas
Verostko, Roman Joseph
Vevers, Anthony Marr
Vian, Orfeo
Vickers, George Stephen
Viera, Ricardo
Viesulas, Romas
Villa, Carlos
Villafranca, Leonor Morales De
Vogl, Don George
von Schlippe, Alexey
Voos, William John
Voth, Andrew Charles
Voulkos, Peter
Wade, Robert Schrope
Walburg, Gerald
Walker, James Adams
Walker, Larry
Walker, Robert Miller
Wall, Brian
Wallace, John Edward
Wallace, Lysbeth (Mai)
Walters, Sylvia Solochek
Wang, Samuel
Ward, John Lawrence
Ward, Lyle Edward
Wark, Robert Rodger
Warshaw, Howard
Wasser, Paula Kloster
Wasserman, Burton
Wasserman, Jack
Waterman, Donald Calvin
Waters, Herbert (Ogden)
Watia, Tarmo
Watrous, James Scales
Watson, Halen Richter
Weber, Albert Jacob
Weber, Idelle
Weber, Jean M
Weber, John Pitman
Wechter, Vivienne Thaul
Weddige, Emil
Wedin, Winslow Elliott
Weege, William
Weeks, James (Darrell Northrup)
Weiler, Melody M
Weinberg, Elbert
Weinberg, Ephraim
Weisberg, Ruth Ellen
Weismann, Donald Leroy
Weiss, Peg
Weitzmann, Kurt
Weller, Allen Stuart
Weller, John Sidney
Wells, Mac
Werness, Hope B
Wessel, Henry, Jr
West, W Richard (Dick)
Westcoast, Wanda
Westermeier, Clifford Peter
Westervelt, Robert F
Westfall, Carol D
Wexler, George
Wheelock, Arthur Kingsland, Jr
White, Amos, IV
White, Charles Wilbert
White, Jack
Whitehill, Walter Muir
Whitesell, John D
Whiteside, William Albert, II
Whitlock, John Joseph
Whitney, Maynard Merle
Whitson (Peter Whitson Warren)
Wickiser, Ralph Lewanda
Wicks, Eugene Claude
Widmer, Gwen Ellen
Wiederspan, Stan
Wilbert, Robert John
Wilde, John
Wiley, William T
Williams, Chester Lee
Williams, Hiram Draper
Williams, John Alden
Williams, John Wesley
Williams, Lewis W, II
Williams, Todd
Williams, William Terence
Willis, William Henry, Jr
Willson, Robert
Wilson, Edward N
Wilson, John
Wilson, Sybil
Wilson, Warren Bingham
Wilson, William Harry
Wiman, Bill
Winkler, Dietmar R
Winkler, Maria Paula
Winokur, Paula Colton
Winokur, Robert Mark
Winslow, John Randolph
Winter, Gerald Glen
Winter, Roger
Wisnosky, John G
Withers, Josephine
Witkin, Jerome Paul
Wogstad, James Everet
Woitena, Ben S
Wolber, Paul J
Wolf, Jack Clifford
Wolfe, Lynn Robert
Wolfe, Maurice Raymond
Wolff, Richard Evans
Wolsky, Jack
Wong, Frederick
Wood, Beatrice
Wood, Harry Emsley, Jr
Woodham, Jean
Woodruff, Hale A
Woods, Gurdon Grant
Woods, Rip
Woodson, Doris
Woody, (Thomas) Howard
Worth, Peter John
Wright, Frank
Wriston, Barbara
Wujcik, Theo
Wunder, Richard Paul
Wyatt, Stanley
Wyckoff, Sylvia Spencer
Wynn, Donald James
Yeatts, James McKinney
Yenawine, Bruce Harley
Yerex, Elton
Yiannes, (Iordanidis)
Yoshida, Ray Kakuo
Young, Charles Alexander
Young, Joseph Louis
Young, Kenneth Victor
Young, Tom (William Thomas Young)
Youngquist, Jack
Youritzin, Victor Koshkin
Yunkers, Adja
Yust, David E
Zabarsky, Melvin Joel
Zaborowski, Dennis J
Zach, Jan
Zafran, Eric Myles
Zakin, Mikhail
Zallinger, Jean Day
Zallinger, Rudolph Franz
Zelanski, Paul John
Ziegler, Jacqueline (Jacqueline Chalat-Ziegler)
Ziemann, Richard Claude
Zietz, Stephen Joseph
Zilka, Michael John
Zimiles, Murray
Zimmerman, Paul Warren
Zisla, Harold
Zolotow, Milton
Zoretich, George Stephen
Zoromskis, Kazimieras
Zweerts, Arnold

ENAMELIST

Anderson, Gwendolyn Orsinger (Orsini)
Bates, Kenneth Francis
Bennett, Jamie
Buzzelli, Joseph Anthony
Caballero, Emilio
Cantini, Virgil D
Caster, Bernard Harry
Catti (Catherine James)
Croft, Michael Flynt
De La Verriere, Jean-Jacques
Dodd, Lois
Greenleaf, Esther (Hargrave)
Harper, William
Jensen, Claud
Johnson, Donald Marvin
Killmaster, John H
Lai, Waihang
Marshall, John Carl
Neumann, William A
Ostuni, Peter W
Perkins, A Alan
Robinson, Jay Thurston
Scheibe, Fred Karl
Schrut, Sherry
Schwarcz, June Therese
Sheehe, Lillian Carolyn
Sheng, Shao Fang
Sieg, Robert Lawrence
Skelly, Barbara Jean
Smith, Jo-an
Spongberg, Grace
Sundberg, Carl Gustave
Thomas, Lionel Arthur John
Turoff, Muriel Pargh
Whitaker, Irwin A
Winter, H Edward

ENVIRONMENTAL ARTIST

Abish, Cecile
Alhilali, Neda
Appel, Eric A
Archambault, Louis
Bakanowsky, Louis J
Baxter, Iain
Bayer, Herbert
Benton, Suzanne E
Berg, Barry
Besner, J Jacques
Bolomey, Roger Henry
Brandfield, Kitty
Brewster, Michael
Brulc, Dennis
Burgess, David Lowry
Burton, Scott
Butterbaugh, Robert Clyde
Buzzelli, Joseph Anthony
Cable, Maxine Roth
Campus, Peter
Canaris, Patti Ann
Card, Greg S
Castoro, Rosemarie
Christo (Javacheff)
Clancy, Patrick
Crane, Michael Patrick
Crist, William Gary
Dean, Peter
Delford Brown, Robert
Denes, Agnes C
Dignac, Geny (Eugenia M Bermudez)
Escobedo, Helen
Feigenbaum, Harriet (Mrs Neil Chamberlain)
Forst, Miles
Foulkes, Llyn
Fuerst, Shirley Miller
Fugate-Wilcox, Terry
Fuge, Paul H
Gellis, Sandy L
Glass, Henry P
Goldstein, Daniel Joshua
Gordon, John S
Goulet, Claude
Graves, Bradford
Green, Tom
Greenbaum, Marty
Greenly, Colin
Gregor, Harold Laurence
Haessle, Jean-Marie Georges
Halkin, Theodore
Harding, Noel Robert
Harrison, Helen Mayer
Harrison, Newton A
Harvey, Dermot
Hayden, Michael
Healy, Anne Laura
Hemenway, Nancy (Mrs Robert D Barton)
Henderson, Victor (Lance)
Hendricks, Geoffrey
High, Timothy Griffin
Hildebrand, June Mary Ann
Hollinger, (Helen Wetherbee)
Irwin, Robert
Jocda (Joseph Charles Dailey)
Johanson, Patricia (Maureen)
Kasuba, Aleksandra
Katzen, Lila (Pell)
Kerr, James Wilfrid
Kirschenbaum, Bernard Edwin
Knowles, Alison
Kowalski, Dennis Allen
Krebs, Rockne
Lacy, Suzanne

London, Jeff
Mahaffey, Merrill Dean
Martin, William Barriss, II
Mattiello, Roberto
McMillen, Michael Chalmers
Metyko, Michael Joseph
Mock, Richard Basil
Moon, Marc
Nauman, Bruce
Neijna, Barbara
Norvell, Patsy
Okamura, Arthur
Oppenheim, Dennis A
Pacilco, Dolores Margaret
Palau, Marta
Pekar, Ronald Walter
Pekarsky, Mel (Melvin Hirsch)
Perreault, John
Pierce, James Smith
Prent, Mark
Pulido, Guillermo Aguilar
Rapp, Lois
Reitzenstein, Reinhard
Ringgold, Faith
Roston, Arnold
Rumsey, David MacIver
Salomon, Lawrence
Sandback, Frederick Lane
Saret, Alan Daniel
Schiff, Jean
Schneemann, Carolee
Schultz, Caroline Reel
Seyfried, John Louis
Shadrach, Jean H
Sharits, Paul Jeffrey
Simkin, Phillips M
Simonds, Charles Frederick
Slavit, Ann L
Smyth, David Richard
Sonnier, Keith
Sproat, Christopher Townsend
Stankard, Paul Joseph
Strasen, Barbara Elaine
Stuart, Michelle
Sturgeon, John Floyd
Swirnoff, Lois
Talbot, William (H M)
Ten Eyck, Catryna (Catryna Ten Eyck Seymour)
Thek, Paul
Torffield, Marvin
Toschik, Larry
Trakas, George
Tsai, Wen-Ying
Turrell, James Archie
Valinski, Dennis John
Van Riper, Peter
Vazan, William Joseph
Vodicka, Ruth Kessler
Vrana, Albert S
Waitt, Alden Harry
Watts, Robert M
Wedin, Winslow Elliott
Wheeler, Doug
Whitman, Robert
Williams, Randalph Andrew
Wines, James N
Wirtschafter, Bud
Woody, (Thomas) Howard
Yokoi, Rita
Zimmerman, William Harold

FILMMAKER

Almond, Paul
Baldessari, John Anthony
Balog, Michael
Bartlett, Scott
Blake, John Clemens
Block, Irving Alexander
Bodolai, Joseph Stephen
Boulton, Jack
Bowman, Dorothy (Louise)
Brakhage, James Stanley
Breer, Robert C
Burckhardt, Rudy
Chambers, John
Chase, Doris (Totten)
Cheng, Fu-Ding
Conner, Bruce
Conrad, George
Crawford, Ralston
Dansereau, Mireille
deAK, Edit
Delano, Jack
Dixon, Sally Foy
Dunn, Cal
Edelheit, Martha
Elder, Muldoon
Ford, Charles Henri
Frampton, Hollis
Frazer, John Thatcher
Fried, Howard Lee
Gardner, Joan A
Gekiere, Madeleine
Golden, Eunice
Goldstein, Jack
Gould, John Howard
Graham, Daniel H
Graves, Nancy Stevenson
Haar, Francis
Harding, Noel Robert
Hay, George Austin
Herbert, James Arthur
Holt, Nancy Louise
Horton, Jan E
Huggins, Victor, (Jr)
Hui, Helene
Hunter, Leonard LeGrande, III
Huot, Robert
Hutchinson, Peter Arthur
Hyde, Laurence
Icaza (Francisco de Icaza)
Iimura, Taka
Jarvis, Lucy
Jensen, Gary
Joskowicz, Alfredo
Karwelis, Donald Charles
Klosty, James Michael
Komodore, Bill
Lecoque
Lent, Blair
Levy, Julien
Lewis, Elizabeth Matthew
Lewis, Michael H
Lipman, Stan
Lipzin, Janis Crystal
Mallory, Margaret
Maradiaga, Ralph
Marrozzini, Luigi
Mason, William Clifford
McCall, Anthony
McLaren, Norman
Miles, Cyril
Murray, John Michael
Myers, Richard Lewis
Namuth, Hans
Nauman, Bruce
Ness, (Albert) Kenneth
Niblock, Phill
Niese, Henry Ernst
Noble, Joseph Veach
Nowytski, Sviatoslav (Slavko)
Ono, Yoko
Orkin, Ruth (Mrs Morris Engel)
Padula, Fred David
Pattee, Rowena
Payne, Lan
Petrochuk, Konstantin
Pollack, Reginald Murray
Pulido, Guillermo Aguilar
Richardson, Frank, Jr
Richter, Hank
Rimmer, David McLellan
Rosenblatt, Adolph
Rosenblatt, Suzanne Maris
Rosenthal, John W
Rozman, Joseph John
Ruscha, Edward Joseph
Rutherford, Erica
Sasaki, Tomiyo
Satty, Wilfried
Sauls, Frederick Inabinette
Schneemann, Carolee
Sharits, Paul Jeffrey
Sherman, Sarai
Simonds, Charles Frederick
Snow, Michael
Sonneman, Eve
Sperry, Robert
Stewart, William
Strider, Marjorie Virginia
Sturtevant, Elaine F
Tajiri, Shinkichi
Tilley, Lewis Lee
Torbert, Marguerite Birch
Van Schley (Evander Duer Van Schley)
Waitzkin, Stella
Wayne, June
Weismann, Donald Leroy
West, Clifford Bateman
Whitman, Robert
Whitney, Edgar Albert
Wieland, Joyce
Williams, Neil
Winningham, Geoff
Wirtschafter, Bud

GALLERY DIRECTOR

see also **Museum Director**

Aguayo, Oscar
Albro, Jeannette (Jeannette Louise Cantrell)
Alpert, George
Anderson, Gwendolyn Orsinger (Orsini)
Anthony, Lawrence Kenneth
Arthur, John C
Badalamenti, Fred
Baldwin, Russell W
Baxter, Ingrid
Bealmer, William
Bednarz, Adele
Benson, Martha J
Bergen, Sidney L
Berggruen, John Henry
Berkman, Aaron
Berman, Aaron
Berman, Rebecca Robbins
Bernard, Felix S
Bettmann, Otto Ludwig
Bierk, David Charles
Birnbaum, Mildred
Booth, Bill
Bowater, Marian
Bradshaw, Lawrence James
Bromm, Hal
Brooks, Robert
Brown, Robert K
Brown, Suzanne Goldman
Buecker, Robert
Bumbeck, David A
Burchfield, Jerry Lee
Burford, William E
Califano, Edward Christopher
Canepa, Anna L
Castile, Rand
Cate, Phillip Dennis
Catlin, Stanton L
Close, Dean Purdy
Cloud, Jack L
Cooper, Marve H
Corr, James Donat
Craven, Roy Curtis, Jr
Crouse, John L (Jay)
Czestochowski, Joseph Stephen
Dane, William Jerald
Davies, Hugh Marlais
Davis, Donald Robert
Davis, John Harold
De Coursey, John Edward
deGooyer, Kirk Alan
de Kuper, Merle Portnoy
Dixon, Kenneth Ray
Dodd, Eric M
Donson, Jerome Allan
Douke, Daniel W
Doyon, Gerard Maurice
Dunn, Roger Terry
Eckert, Lou
Edwards, Gwendolyn Tyner
Elkin, Beverly Dawn
Elliott, B Charles, Jr
Emery, Charles Anthony
Erdle, Rob
Feinman, Stephen E
Felter, James Warren
Feuerstein, Roberta
Finnegan, Sharyn Marie
Flint, Leroy W
Frankel, Dextra
Friedland, Ruth Volid
Frumkin, Allan
Fumagalli, Orazio
Furman, Aaron & Joyce
Gage, Harry (Lawrence)
Gebhard, David
Gilbert, Alma Magdalena
Gilbertson, Charlotte
Glasgow, Lukman
Glass, Wendy D
Glick, Paula Florence
Glicksman, Hal
Globus, Dorothy Twining
Goldman, Louis & Sondra
Goldsmith, Benedict Isaac
Gottschalk, Fritz
Grado, Angelo John
Grady, Ruby McLain
Grandee, Joe Ruiz
Green, Eleanor Broome
Greene, Theodore R
Grossman, Maurizia M
Hamel, Bernard Franklin
Hames, Carl Martin
Hardy, Robert
Harlow, Frederica Todd
Harsley, Alex
Hartgen, Vincent Andrew
Haversat, Lillian Kerr
Havis, C Kenneth
Hay-Messick, Velma
Hendershot, J L
Hiller, Betty R
Hoffeld, Jeffrey
Hoffman, Marilyn Friedman
Howard, Cecil Ray
Huchel, Frederick M
Humphrey, Donald Gray
Iolas, Alexander
Isaacs, Claire Naomi
Jarkowski, Stefania Agnes
Johnson, Evert Alfred
Jonson, Raymond
Joseph, Cliff (Clifford Ricardo)
Kaericher, John Conrad
Kalischer, Clemens
Kawecki, Jean Mary
Kelley, Donald Castell
Kent, H Latham
Killam, Walt
King, Hayward Ellis
Klaven, Marvin L
Klebe, Gene (Charles Eugene)
Klement, Vera
Kobayashi, Katsumi Peter
Koppelman, Dorothy
Kornblatt, Barbara Rodbell
Kramer, Jack N
Krausz, Laszlo
Krevolin, Lewis
Kuvshinoff, Bertha Horne
Kuvshinoff, Nicolai
Landau, Mitzi
Langman, Richard Theodore
Latham, Catherine Doris
Lathrop, Churchill Pierce

GALLERY DIRECTOR (cont)
Levy, Stuart D
Lewis, Don S, Sr
Lewis, Donald Sykes, Jr
Liddle, Nancy Hyatt
Lienau, Daniel Clifford
Linhares, Philip E
Littman, Robert R
Lochridge, Sudie Katherine
Loro, Anthony Pivotto
Lumsden, Ian Gordon
Madigan, Richard Allen
Mahey, John A
Mangel, Benjamin
Maradiaga, Ralph
Marberger, A Aladar
Maser, Edward Andrew
McColley, Sutherland
McKean, Hugh Ferguson
McNabb, William Ross
Meeker, Barbara Miller
Mejer, Robert Lee
Micale, Albert
Michaux, Ronald Robert
Miller, Eva-Hamlin
Miller, Jan
Miller, Joan Vita
Moos, Walter A
Muniot, Barbara King
Narus, Marta Maria Margareta
Nitz, Thomas L
Nordland, Gerald John
Oakes, John Warren
Oscarsson, Victoria Constance Gunhild
Pablo (Paul Burgess Edwards)
Paradise, Phil (Herschel)
Parkhurst, Charles
Parsons, Betty Bierne
Patch, Peggie (Margaret Thompson Williamson)
Patnode, J Scott
Pellicone, Marie
Pels, Albert
Perkins, Constance M
Perreault, John
Persky, Robert S
Peters, Larry Dean
Pfeifer, Marcuse
Prakapas, Eugene Joseph
Pruitt, Lynn
Randall, Richard Harding, Jr
Rasmussen, Anton Jesse
Ravel, Dana B
Reilley, Patrick Richard
Reuter, Laurel J
Rhyne, Charles Sylvanus
Rice, Philip Somerset
Richard, Jack
Richards, Tally
Romans, Van Anthony
Rosenberg, Carole Halsband
Roster, Laila Bergs
Rustvold, Katherine Jo
Sadik, Marvin Sherwood
Scala, Joseph (A)
Schnitzer, Arlene Director
Schnorrenberg, John Martin
Schonberger, Fred
Schwinger, Sylvia
Seders, Francine Lavinal
Shaman, Sanford Sivitz
Silins, Janis
Simoneau, Everett Hubert
Sisti, Anthony J (Tony)
Slade, Roy
Smith, Albert E
Smith, B J
Snyder, Barry
Spurlock, William Henry, II
Starrs, Mildred
Stasik, Andrew J
Staven, Leland Carroll
Stein, Fritz Henry
Stoddard, Donna Melissa
Strong, Charles Ralph
Suzuki, Katsko (Katsko Suzuki Kannegieter)
Swain, Robert Francis
Sznajderman, Marius S
Tatistcheff, Peter Alexis
Termini, Christine
Thaler, Mildred G
Thiele, Robert Ransom
Thomas, George R
Thomason, Tom William
Toperzer, Thomas Raymond
Turner, Janice Kay
Ubans, Juris K
Vanderlip, Dianne Perry
Van Der Straeten, Vincent Roger
Van Leunen, Alice Louise
Viera, Ricardo
Vose, Robert Churchill, Jr
Voth, Andrew Charles
Walton, Donald William
Wardwell, Allen
Washburn, Gordon Bailey
Watford, Frances Mizelle
Wethington, Wilma Zella
White, Ruth
Wilson, Carrie Lois
Wing, Robin Stewart
Withrow, William J
Wortz, Melinda Farris
Yeatts, James McKinney

GLASS BLOWER

Ahvakana, Ulaaq (Lawrence Reynold Ahvakana)
Balog, Michael
Bernstein, William Joseph
Brejcha, Vernon Lee
Carey, James Sheldon
Chihuly, Dale Patrick
Clark, Jon Frederic
Dailey, Daniel Owen
Furman, David Stephen
Handler, Audrey
Ipsen, Kent Forrest
Kangas, Gene
Labino, Dominick
Lewis, John Conard
Lipofsky, Marvin B
Myers, Joel Philip
Nygren, John Fergus
Ohno, Mitsugi
Pearson, Clifton
Pijanowski, Eugene M
Posner, Richard Perry
Potvin, Daniel
Rhodes, James Melvin
Ritter, Richard Quintin
Sandground, Mark Bernard, Sr
Stankard, Paul Joseph
Taylor, Michael (Leach)

GOLDSMITH

Aird, Neil Carrick
Allen, Constance Olleen Webb
Baldridge, Mark S
Bennett, Jamie
Betteridge, Lois Etherington
Brauer, Connie Ann
Caldwell, Eleanor
Croft, Michael Flynt
Getty, Nilda Fernandez
Gold, Debra Lynn
Grissom, Freda Gill
Hageman, Charles Lee
Harper, William
Helzer, Richard Brian
Kington, Louis Brent
Larson, Orland
Long, Frank Weathers
Mitchell, Robert Ellis
Monongye, Preston Lee
Neumann, William A
O'Connor, Harold Thomas
Orr, Veronica Marie (Veronica Marie Ingram)
Paley, Albert Raymond
Peck, Lee Barnes
Pijanowski, Hiroko Sato
Renk, Merry
Seppa, Heikki Markus
Snyder, Toni Goessler
Thomason, Tom William
Thompson, Nancy Kunkle
van Duinwyk, George Paul
Wardle, Alfred Hill

GRAPHIC ARTIST

Ackerman, Frank Edward
Albers, Anni
Alcopley, L
Alf, Martha Joanne
Allen, Roberta
Altwerger, Libby
Anderson, Howard Benjamin
Arias-Misson, Alain
Arnholm, Ronald Fisher
Asawa, Ruth (Ruth Asawa Lanier)
Atkins, Gordon Lee
Bailey, Worth
Baker, Anna P
Ball, Lyle V
Banerjee (bimal)
Barbee, Robert Thomas
Barr, Roger Terry
Barrett, Barbara
Baskin, Leonard
Beaumont, Mona M
Becker, Bettie (Bettie Geraldine Wathall)
Bedno, Edward
Beitz, Lester U
Berger, Oscar
Bertoia, Harry
Black, Lisa
Blanchard, Carol
Blos, May (Elizabeth)
Blos, Peter W
Boal, Sara Metzner
Bolton, James
Brainard, Joe
Brumer, Miriam
Bucknall, Malcolm Roderick
Burger, W Carl
Burnett, Calvin
Byrd, Robert John
Byrne, Charles Joseph
Cardinal, Marcelin
Carl, Joan
Cartledge, Roseanne Catherine
Castellon, Rolando
Cavat, Irma
Ceglia, Vincent
Chappell, Warren
Chesterton, David
Cikovsky, Nicolai
Cimbalo, Robert W
Coburn, Ralph
Colker, Edward
Colson, Chester E
Coppola, Andrew
Creech, Franklin Underwood
Crittenden, John William Neil
Cronin, Robert (Lawrence)
Cross, Watson, Jr
Crumbo, Minisa
Dank, Leonard Dewey
Darboven, Hanne
De Bretteville, Sheila Levrant
DeCaprio, Alice
De La Vega, Antonio
Del Valle, Joseph Bourke
DeMaree, Elizabeth Ann (Betty)
Denton, Pat
Dickinson, Eleanor Creekmore
Di Meo, Dominick
Dinnerstein, Simon A
Dooley, Helen Bertha
Dorn, Peter Klaus
Drower, Sara Ruth
Ebsen, Alf K
Eckmair, Frank C
Evans, Minnie
Faris, Brunel De Bost
Federe, Marion
Feigl, Doris Louise
Fein, Stanley
Feist, Warner David
Ferguson, Frank Wayne
Ferris, Edythe
Fingesten, Peter
Fink, Herbert Lewis
Fish, Richard G
Fleming, Allan Robb
Fluek, Toby
Foley, Kyoko Y
Foster, Holland
Franck, Frederick S
Frasconi, Antonio
Freeman, Robert Lee
Gardner, Andrew Bradford
Gast, Carolyn Bartlett (Carolyn B Lutz)
Gefter, Judith Michelman
Geis, Milton Arthur
Gentile, Gloria Irene
Gilbert, Herb
Golbin, Andree
Goldring, Nancy Deborah
Goldszer, Bath-Sheba
Gorman, Carl Nelson (Kin-ya-onny Beyeh)
Gorman, William D
Gorski, Richard Kenny
Gough, Robert Alan
Greenbaum, Dorothea Schwarcz
Grippe, Florence (Berg)
Haden, Eunice (Barnard)
Hamady, Walter Samuel
Hamlett, Dale Edward
Harder, Rolf Peter
Harris, Marian D
Hart, Betty Miller
Hausman, Fred S
Haut, Claire (Joan)
Herfield, Phyllis Anne
Herman, Alan David
Hios, Theo
Hirschfeld, Albert
Hobbs, (Carl) Fredric
Hoffman, Martin (Joseph)
Hollander, Gino F
Horn, Stuart Alan
Howe, Nelson S
Hudson, Jacqueline
Hueter, James Warren
Ingalls, Eve
Ispanky, Laszlo
Iwamoto, Ralph Shigeto
Jackson, Lee
Jackson, Sarah
Janschka, Fritz
Jelinek, Hans
Jennings, Thomas
Jeter, Randy Joe
Johnson, James Edwin & Sandra Kay
Jones, Ruthe Blalock
Kamen, Gloria
Katz, Theodore (Harry)
Kemper, John Garner
Kirsten-Daiensai, Richard Charles
Kitta, George Edward
Kleidon, Dennis Arthur
Kniffin, Ralph Gus

Kramer, Burton
Kreznar, Richard J
Kuehn, Gary
Labiche, Walter Anthony
Lagorio, Irene R
Laird, Mary (Mary Laird Hamady)
LaMarca, Howard J
Landry, Richard Miles
Lederer, Wolfgang
Lew, Weyman Michael
Lewen, Si
Llorente, Luis
Loewer, Henry Peter
Long, Sandra Tardo
Lorentz, Pauline
Loughlin, John Leo
Low, Joseph
Lynch, Jo (Marilyn Blanche)
Lynch, Mary Britten
MacDonald, Kevin John
MacDonald, Thoreau
Magee, Alderson
Maldre, Mati
Malsch, Ellen L
Manuella, Frank R
Markell, Isabella Banks
Marsicano, Nicholas
Martin, Margaret M
Mason, William Clifford
Maxwell, Robert Edwin
Mayer, Rosemary
McClure, Constance M
McCoon, Betty Jean
McElroy, Nancy Lynn
Miller, Vel
Mills, Lev Timothy
Monthan, Guy
Moore, Robert James
Moose, Talmadge Bowers
Morgan, Warren Dean
Morningstern, Harry V
Morrison, Robert Clifton
Mosca, August
Motter, Dean Roger
Nagano, Paul Tatsumi
Nash, Katherine E
Neff, John A
Newman, Louis
Norton, Mary Joyce
Nutzle, Futzie (Bruce John Kleinsmith)
Ohman, Richard Michael
Order, Trudy
Peterson, Chester G
Pettibone, John Wolcott
Piatek, Francis John
Pickens, Vinton Liddell
Pirkl, James Joseph
Plochmann, Carolyn Gassan
Post, Anne B
Pratt, Vernon Gaither
Pringle, Burt Evins
Rapp, Lois
Renouf, Edward Pechmann
Reynolds, Ralph William
Robbins, Hulda D
Roberds, Gene Allen
Roch, Ernst
Rodriguez, Oscar
Romero, Mike
Romoser, Ruth Amelia
Ross, Fred (Joseph)
Ross, Janice Koenig
Salinas, Baruj
Samerjan, George E
Sanchez, Carol Lee
Sarnoff, Arthur Saron
Satty, Wilfried
Schachter, Justine Ranson
Schiller, Beatrice
Schwalb, Susan
Seames, Clarann
Shapiro, David
Siebner, Herbert (Vom Siebenstein)
Slusky, Joseph
Smigocki, Stephen Vincent
Soult, James Thomas
Stack, Gael Z
Steckel, Anita
Sternberg, Harry
Stevens, Richard Clive
Stoessel, Henry Kurt
Sudlow, Robert N
Swiggett, Jean Donald
Sylvester, Lucille
Szesko, Lenore Rundle
Tasgal-Kliegman, Gerda
Taylor, Grace Martin
Texidor, Fernando
Thollander, Earl
Thorne, Gordon (Kit)
Tolmie, Kenneth Donald
Tucker, James Ewing
Valius, Telesforas
Van Der Voort, Amanda Venelia
Vaness, Margaret Helen
Van Roijen, Hildegarde Graham
Vasils, Albert
Vivenza, Francesca
Webb, Frank (Francis H Webb)
Weidner, Roswell Theodore
Whiteman, Edward Russell
Winkler, Maria Paula
Witt, John
Wright, Barton Allen
Wright, Bernard
Wright, Harold David
Young, Marjorie Ward
Yrizarry, Marcos
Zolotow, Milton

HISTORIAN

Ackerman, Gerald Martin
Ackerman, James S
Aichele, Kathryn Porter
Albin, Edgar A
Alexander, Margaret Ames
Allen, (Harvey) Harold
Allgood, Charles Henry
Andersen, Wayne Vesti
Anderson, Dennis Ray
Appelhof, Ruth A
Armstrong, Thomas Newton, III
Arnason, H Harvard
Artz, Frederick B
Asante, Kwasi Seitu (Robin Okeeffer Harper)
Ashton, Dore
Askew, Pamela
Aymar, Gordon Christian
Bach, Otto Karl
Bacot, Henry Parrott
Bailey, Worth
Baretski, Charles Allan
Baro, Gene
Barr, Alfred Hamilton, Jr
Barrio-Garay, Jose Luis
Barry, William David
Barton, Eleanor Dodge
Bassin, Joan
Battcock, Gregory
Beal, Graham William John
Beardsley, Barbara H
Beatty, Frances Fielding Lewis
Becker, Martin Earle
Bell, Philip Michael
Belshe, Mirella Monti
Benson, Gertrude Ackerman
Berman, Nancy Mallin
Bernstein, Theresa
Bettinson, Brenda
Bettmann, Otto Ludwig
Bhalla, Hans
Billmyer, John Edward
Black, Mary Childs
Blackmun, Barbara Winston
Blackwell, John Victor
Bledsoe, Jane Kathryn
Bloch, E Maurice
Bloom, Jason
Blum, Shirley Neilsen
Boe, Roy Asbjorn
Boggs, Jean Sutherland
Bohan, Peter John
Bongiorno, Laurine Mack
Bony, Jean Victor
Borcoman, James
Bordeaux, Jean Luc
Borgo, Ludovico
Bothmer, Bernard V
Bothmer, Dietrich Felix Von
Botwinick, Michael
Bowles, Thomas Andrew, III
Bowlt, John
Bowman, Ruth
Bowne, James Dehart
Bowron, Edgar Peters
Bradbury, Ellen A
Braiden, Rose Margaret J
Brandt, Frederick Robert
Bravmann, Rene A
Breckenridge, James D
Breitenbach, Edgar
Breithaupt, Erwin M
Brettell, Richard Robson
Brewer, Donald J
Brinkerhoff, Dericksen Morgan
Broadd, Harry Andrew
Broadley, Hugh T
Broude, Norma Freedman
Brown, David Alan
Brown, Jeffrey Rogers
Brown, John Carter
Brown, Jonathan
Brown, Milton Wolf
Brown, Suzanne Goldman
Brumbaugh, Thomas Brendle
Bryant, Edward Albert
Bryant, Linda Goode
Buck, Robert Treat, Jr
Bullard, Edgar John, III
Bumgardner, Georgia Brady
Bunce, Fredrick William
Bunting, Bainbridge
Burnett, David Grant
Burnside, Wesley M
Burr, Horace
Bush, Donald John
Bush, Martin Harry
Butler, Joseph Thomas
Butts, Porter
Byrnes, James Bernard
Bywaters, Jerry
Cadieux, Michael Eugene
Cahill, James Francis
Caldwell, Benjamin Hubbard, Jr
Caldwell, Martha Belle
Calkin, Carleton Ivers
Calkins, Robert G
Callisen, Sterling
Camfield, William Arnett
Campbell, Malcolm
Canby, Jeanny Vorys
Carey, John Thomas
Carlin, Robert Eugene
Carmean, E A, Jr
Carpenter, James Morton
Carter, David Giles
Castano, Elvira
Cate, Phillip Dennis
Cathcart, Linda Louise
Catlin, Stanton L
Celender, Donald Dennis
Chadwick, Whitney
Chambers, Karen Sue
Chandler, Dana C, Jr (Akin Duro)
Charlot, Jean
Chase, Alice Elizabeth
Cheney, Sheldon
Chew, Paul Albert
Chow Chian-Chiu
Cikovsky, Nicolai, Jr
Clark, William W
Clermont, Ghislain
Clisby, Roger David
Coates, Ann S
Coates, Ross Alexander
Cohen, Joan Lebold
Cohn, Marjorie B
Coke, F Van Deren
Cole, Bruce
Cole, Harold David
Collier, Graham (Alan Graham-Collier)
Collins, Christiane C
Collins, George R
Comini, Alessandra
Conlon, James Edward
Conrad, George
Constantine, Mildred
Coolidge, John
Cooper, Frederick Alexander
Corbin, George Allen
Cordy-Collins, Alana (Alana Kathleen Cordy-Collins Riesland)
Covi, Dario A
Cox, Richard William
Craven, Wayne
Crimp, Douglas
Crite, Allan Rohan
Crosby, Sumner McKnight
Cummings, Frederick James
Curtis, Phillip Houston
Cutler, Ethel Rose
Cuttler, Charles David
Czuma, Stanislaw J
Dale, William Scott Abell
Daniel, Suzanne Garrigues
Danieli, Fidel Angelo
Danoff, I Michael
Darling, Sharon Sandling
Darr, William Humiston
Dauterman, Carl Christian
Davey, Ronald A
Davidson, Abraham A
Davidson, J LeRoy
Davidson, Marshall Bowman
Davies, Hugh Marlais
Davis, Ann
Davis, Ellen N
Davis, L Clarice
Davis, Marian B
Davis, Robert Tyler
Davisson, Darrell
Dawdy, Doris Ostrander
de Borhegyi, Suzanne Sims
Dee, Elaine Evans
De Foix-Crenascol, Louis
Delhom, Mary Mellanay
Dennison, Keith Elkins
DeShazo, Edith Kind
Desportes, Ulysse Gandvier
De Tolnay, Charles
D'Harnoncourt, Anne (J)
Dibble, Charles Ryder
Dillow, Nancy E (Nancy Elizabeth Robertson)
Donaldson, Jeff R
Donnelly, Marian Card
Donohoe, Victoria
Dorra, Henri
Dorsky, Morris
Doyon, Gerard Maurice
Dreaper, Richard Edward
Dresser, Louisa
Drewal, Henry John
Driskell, David Clyde
Drutt, Helen Williams
Dwyer, Eugene Joseph
Dwyer, Melva Jean
Dyck, Paul
Ecke, Betty Tseng Yu-Ho
Eckert, William Dean
Eckhardt, Ferdinand
Ehresmann, Donald Louis
Ehrlich, George
Eisenberg, Marvin

HISTORIAN (cont)

Eitner, Lorenz E A
Elam, Charles Henry
Elderfield, John
Eldredge, Charles Child, III
Ellinger, Ilona E
Ellis, Edwin Charles
Elsen, Albert Edward
Elzea, Rowland Procter
Enggass, Robert
Enyeart, James Lyle
Epstein, Annabel Wharton
Ertman, Earl Leslie
Ettlinger, Leopold David
Evans, Bruce Haselton
Evans, Grose
Evans, Paul Fredric
Farmer, John David
Farnham, Emily
Farrell, Patric
Farwell, Beatrice
Fehl, Philipp P
Feigen, Richard L
Feinblatt, Ebria
Feldman, Edmund Burke
Ferguson, Charles
Ferguson, Garth Michele
Fern, Alan Maxwell
Ferris, (Carlisle) Keith
Field, Richard Sampson
Fingesten, Peter
Finley, Gerald Eric
Flexner, James Thomas
Flint, Janet Altic
Folda, Jaroslav (Thayer, III)
Foley, Kathy Kelsey
Forrest, James Taylor
Forsyth, Robert Joseph
Foster, Stephen C
Frankenstein, Alfred Victor
Fraser, Douglas (Ferrar)
Fredericksen, Burton Baum
Freedberg, Sydney Joseph
Freeman, Richard Borden
Freitag, Wolfgang Martin
Frel, Jiri
Freundlich, August L
Frinta, Mojmir Svatopluk
Fry, Edward Fort
Fuller, John Charles
Gaines, William Robert
Gaither, Edmund B
Gardiner, Henry Gilbert
Garnsey, Clarke Henderson
Garrard, Mary DuBose
Garris, Kathleen (Kathleen Weil-Garris)
Garvan, Beatrice Bronson
Garver, Thomas H
Gatling, Eva Ingersoll
Gawboy, Carl
Gear, Josephine
Gebhard, David
Gerdts, Abigail Booth
Gerdts, William H
Geske, Norman Albert
Gibson, Walter Samuel
Gilbert, Creighton Eddy
Gillies, Jean
Glaser, Bruce
Glasgow, Vaughn Leslie
Glenn, Constance White
Glezer, Nechemia
Goheen Ellen Rozanne
Goldberg, Kenneth Paul
Goldberg, Norman Lewis
Goodyear, Frank H, Jr
Gordon, John
Gouma-Peterson, Thalia
Graham, F Lanier
Green, Eleanor Broome
Green, Samuel Magee
Grieder, Terence
Grossman, Grace Cohen
Grossman, Sheldon
Grubar, Francis Stanley
Guenther, Peter W
Guilmain, Jacques
Gully, Anthony Lacy
Gundersheimer, Herman (Samuel)
Gurewitsch, Edna P
Hall, Louise
Hallmark, Donald Parker
Hamilton, George Heard
Hamilton, Patricia Rose
Hammond, Leslie King
Hand, John Oliver
Harlow, Frederica Todd
Harper, John Russell
Harrington, La Mar
Harris, Ann Sutherland
Harris, Josephine Marie
Harris, Paul Stewart
Hartt, Frederick
Haskell, Barbara
Haskins, John Franklin
Hassrick, Peter H
Hatch, John Davis
Havelock, Christine Mitchell
Hayes, Laura M
Hayward, Jane
Hazlehurst, Franklin Hamilton
Hearn, M F (Millard Fillmore Hearn, Jr)
Heckscher, Morrison Harris
Heckscher, William Sebastian
Hedberg, Gregory Scott
Held, Julius S
Heller, Reinhold August
Hemphill, Herbert Waide
Hemphill, Pamela
Henning, Edward Burk
Henry, Sara Lynn
Herbert, Robert L
Hero, Peter deCourcy
Hertzman, Gay Mahaffy
Hess, Thomas B
Hibbard, Howard
Hill, Draper
Hill, William Mansfield
Hinkhouse, Forest Melick
Hirsch, Richard Teller
Hitchcock, Henry Russell
Hoffeld, Jeffrey
Hoge, Robert Wilson
Holcomb, Adele Mansfield
Holcomb, Grant
Holladay, Harlan H
Hollister, Paul
Holm, Bill
Holo, Selma Reuben
Holverson, John
Homer, William Innes
Hood, Walter Kelly
Hoopes, Donelson Farquhar
Hornung, Clarence Pearson
Hornung, Gertrude Seymour
Houser, Caroline M
Hovey, Walter Read
Howarth, Shirley Reiff
Howat, John Keith
Howell, Douglass (Morse)
Howett, John
Howland, Richard Hubbard
Hoy, Anne Tawes
Hubbard, Robert Hamilton
Huchel, Frederick M
Hudson, Ralph Magee
Hunisak, John Michael
Hunter, Sam
Huth, Hans
Hutton, William
Hyslop, Francis Edwin
Immerwahr, Sara Anderson
Iskin, Ruth Evelyn
Isserstedt, Dorothea Carus
Jacobsen, Michael A
Jaffe, Ira Sheldon
Jaffe, Irma B
Janson, Anthony Fredrick
Janson, Horst Woldemar
Jay, Bill
Jenkins, Donald John
Johnson, Charles W, Jr
Johnson, Charlotte Buel
Johnson, Dana Doane
Johnson, Diane Chalmers
Johnson, Donald Ray
Johnson, Ellen Hulda
Johnson, Eugene Joseph
Johnson, Lincoln Fernando
Johnston, Robert Porter
Johnston, William Ralph
Jones, Anthony
Jones, Dan Burne
Jones, Lois Swan
Jones, Louis C
Joost-Gaugier, Christiane L
Jordan, George Edwin
Jordan, James William
Jordan, William B
Kahlenberg, Mary Hunt
Kalavrezou-Maxeiner, Ioli
Kallir, Otto
Kampen, Michael Edwin
Kan, Michael
Kaplan, Julius David
Kardon, Janet
Karlstrom, Paul Johnson
Kelder, Diane M
Kelemen, Pal
Kelleher, Patrick Joseph
Kemoha (George W Patrick Patterson)
Kerr, John Hoare
Kertess, Klaus D
King, Edward S
Kingsley, April
Kirstein, Mr & Mrs Lincoln
Kitzinger, Ernst
Klein, Cecelia F
Kleinbauer, W Eugene
Klitzke, Theodore Elmer
Kloner, Jay Martin
Knox, George
Knox, Katharine McCook
Koch, Robert
Kortlander, William (Clark)
Kouwenhoven, John A
Krakel, Dean
Kubler, George Alexander
Kuhn, Brenda
Kultermann, Udo
Kup, Karl
Kuspit, Donald Burton
Kuwayama, George
Landis, Ellen Jamie
Landy, Jacob
LaPena, Frank Raymond
Larsen, Erik
Larsen, Susan C
Larson, Philip Seely
Laskin, Myron, Jr
Lathrop, Churchill Pierce
Laurer, Robert A
Lavin, Irving
Lawrence, Marion
Leach, Frederick Darwin
Leavitt, Thomas Whittlesey
Lee, Briant Hamor
Lee, Rensselaer Wright
Lee, Sherman Emery
Lehman, Arnold L
Lehman, Mark Ammon
Lerman, Leo
Lesley, Parker
Levin, Gail
Levit, Herschel
Levitine, George
Levitt, Alfred
Lewis, Donald Sykes, Jr
Lewis, Douglas
Lewis, Samella Sanders
Lewis, Virginia Elnora
Li, Chu-Tsing
Lindsay, Kenneth C
Lipton, Barbara B
Little, Nina Fletcher
Littman, Robert R
Lochridge, Sudie Katherine
Lombardo, Josef Vincent
Long, Glenn Alan
Longaker, Jon Dasu
Longman, Lester Duncan
Longstreet, Stephen
Love, Iris Cornelia
Love, Richard Henry
Lowry, Bates
Ludmer, Joyce Pellerano
Lumsden, Ian Gordon
Lunde, Karl Roy
Lust, Herbert
Lynch, James Burr, Jr
Lyons, Lisa
MacDonald, William Allan
MacDonald, William L
Mack, Charles Randall
Mackay, Donald Cameron
Madden, Betty I
Maddox, Jerald Curtis
Mahoney, Michael R T
Mallory, Nina A
Mandle, Earl Roger
Markman, Sidney David
Marlor, Clark Strang
Marshall, Richard Donald
Marter, Joan M
Martin, Marianne Winter
Martin, Richard (Harrison)
Maser, Edward Andrew
Masheck, Joseph Daniel
Mathis, Kenneth Lawrence
Maurer, Evan Maclyn
Mayhew, Edgar De Noailles
Mayor, Alpheus Hyatt
McCabe, Cynthia Jaffee
McCracken, Harold
McCready, Eric Scott
McMillan, Robert W
McNally, Sheila John
McNamara, Mary Jo
Meigs, John Liggett
Meisel, Louis Koenig
Merkel, Jayne (Silverstein)
Messer, Thomas M
Metson, Graham
Meyer, Charles Edward
Miles, Ellen Gross
Miley, Mimi Conneen
Miller, Jean Johnston
Mino, Yukata
Minutillo, Richard G
Moeller, Robert Charles, III
Moffitt, John Francis
Moir, Alfred
Molina, Antonio J
Mongan, Agnes
Montequin, Francois-Auguste de
Moore, Barbara
Moore, Ethel
Moore, Peter
Morgan, Charles H
Morgan, William
Morishita, Joyce Chizuko
Mosby, Dewey Franklin
Moser, Charlotte
Moser, Joann
Moulton, Susan Gene
Mount, Marshall Ward
Moure, Nancy Dustin Wall
Moxey, Keith Patricio Fleming
Moyssen, Xavier
Mozley, Anita Ventura
Mueller, Earl George
Muhlert, Jan Keene
Munsterberg, Hugo
Murdock, Robert Mead
Myers, Denys Peter
Naeve, Milo M
Nash, Steven Alan
Nelson, Jon Allen
Newhall, Beaumont
Newhouse, Clyde Mortimer
Newton, Earle Williams

Nochlin, Linda (Linda Pommer)
Norris, Andrea Spaulding
Norton, Paul Foote
Novak, Barbara (Mrs Brian O'Doherty)
Novinski, Lyle Frank
Oberhuber, Konrad J
Ochs, Robert David
O'Connor, Francis Valentine
O'Connor, Stanley James
O'Gorman, James Francis
Olpin, Robert Spencer
Orenstein, Gloria Feman
Orr-Cahall, Anona Christina
Ortiz Macedo, Luis
Osborne, Robert Lee
Ostrow, Stephen Edward
O'Toole, James St Laurence
Overland, Carlton Edward
Pal, Pratapaditya
Parker, John William
Parks, James Dallas
Parry, Ellwood Comly III
Paulin, Richard Calkins
Pearman, Sara Jane
Peck, William Henry
Pendergraft, Norman Elveis
Perkins, Ann
Perry, Regenia Alfreda
Phillips, James
Pierce, James Smith
Pilgrim, James F
Pincus-Witten, Robert A
Pinkney, Helen Louise
Pisano, Ronald George
Placzek, Adolf Kurt
Plunkett, Edward Milton
Polzer, Joseph
Poor, Robert John
Pope, John Alexander
Posner, Donald
Powell, Earl Alexander, III
Prokopoff, Stephen Stephen
Prown, Jules David
Pulos, Arthur Jon
Quinsac, Annie-Paule
Quirarte, Jacinto
Rae, Edwin C
Ralston, James Kenneth
Randall, Richard Harding, Jr
Rannit, Aleksis
Rathbone, Perry Townsend
Reed, Walt Arnold
Reese, Thomas Ford
Reeves, James Franklin
Reich, Sheldon
Reiff, Robert Frank
Rembert, Virginia Pitts
Rensch, Roslyn (Roslyn Maria Erbes)
Rewald, John
Rhyne, Charles Sylvanus
Rice, Shelley Enid
Richardson, Edgar Preston
Ries, Martin
Rigby, Ida Katherine
Rinhart, George R
Ritchie, Andrew C
Rivard, Nancy J
Robb, David M
Robbins, Daniel J
Roberson, Samuel Arndt
Robinson, Franklin W
Robinson, Wahneta Theresa
Robison, Andrew
Rogers, Millard Foster, Jr
Rose, Barbara E
Roseberg, Carl Andersson
Rosen, James Mahlon
Rosenberg, Charles Michael
Rosenberg, Jakob
Rosenblum, Robert
Rosenthal, Gertrude
Rosenzweig, Daphne Lange
Rosenzweig, Phyllis D
Ross, Marvin Chauncey
Rossen, Susan F
Rowell, Margit
Rubin, Arnold Gary
Rubin, William
Russell, Helen Diane
Russo, Kathleen L
Rust, David E
Sachs, Samuel, II
Sadik, Marvin Sherwood
Saff, Donald Jay
Samuels, Harold & Peggy
Sawyer, Alan R
Scarbrough, Cleve Knox, Jr
Schapiro, Meyer
Scherer, Herbert Grover
Scheyer, Ernst
Schimansky, Donya Dobrila
Schmandt-Besserat, Denise
Schmeckebier, Laurence E
Schmidt, Mary Morris
Schmitt, Marilyn Low
Schnorrenberg, John Martin
Scholz, Janos
Schuster, Eugene Ivan
Schwartz, Marvin D
Schwarz, Kurt L
Schweizer, Paul Douglas
Scott, David Winfield
Scott, Henry (Edwards), Jr
Scully, Vincent
Segger, Martin Joseph
Sellers, Charles Coleman
Sellin, David
Selvig, Forrest Hall
Selz, Peter H
Shalkop, Robert Leroy
Shangraw, Clarence Frank
Shangraw, Sylvia Chen
Shapiro, David
Shapley, Fern Rusk
Shapley, John
Sharf, Frederic Alan
Shaw, Courtney Ann
Sheon, Aaron
Shepard, Lewis Albert
Sheppard, Carl Dunkle
Sherman, Claire Richter
Shestack, Alan
Shimizu, Yoshiaki
Sickman, Laurence Chalfant Stevens
Sieber, Roy
Silberman, Arthur
Silins, Janis
Simpson, William Kelly
Slatkes, Leonard Joseph
Slawinski, Joseph
Smith, James Morton
Smith, Lyn Wall
Smith, Ray Winfield
Smyth, Craig Hugh
Snodgrass, Jeanne Owens (Mrs M Eugene King)
Sokol, David Martin
Sonnenschein, Hugo
Sorell, Victor Alexander
Spear, Richard Edmund
Spence, Robert
Spencer, Eleanor Patterson
Spencer, Harold Edwin
Spencer, John R
Sponenburgh, Mark
Sprout, Francis Allen
Staley, Allen
Stamm, Geoffrey Eaton
Standen, Edith Appleton
Stead, Rexford Arthur
Steadman, David Wilton
Stebbins, Theodore Ellis, Jr
Steen, Ronald Earl
Stein, Roger Breed
Stell, H Kenyon
Stephany, Jaromir
Stern, Jean
Stewart, Robert Gordon
Stitt, Susan (Margaret)
Stoddard, Whitney Snow
Stofflet, Mary
Stokstad, Marilyn
Stones, Margaret Alison
Stringer, Mary Evelyn
Stucki, Margaret Elizabeth
Sturgeon, Mary C
Sullivan, Ruth Wilkins
Sunderland, Elizabeth Read
Sunkel, Robert Cleveland
Sussman, Elisabeth Sacks
Sweeney, J Gray
Taft, Frances Prindle
Tatham, David Frederic
Taylor, Hugh Holloway
Taylor, John Frank Adams
Taylor, Joshua Charles
Taylor, Mary Cazort
Teilhet, Jehanne Hildegarde
Teitz, Richard Stuart
Thibault, Claude
Thomas, Lionel Arthur John
Thompson, Dorothy Burr
Tierney, Patrick Lennox
Tolles, Bryant Franklin, Jr
Tomasini, Wallace J
Tomko, George Peter
Torbert, Donald Robert
Tracy, Berry Bryson
Trapp, Frank Anderson
Travis, David B
Tredennick, Dorothy W
Trenton, Patrica Jean
Trubner, Henry
Tselos, Dimitri Theodore
Tuchman, Phyllis
Tucker, Anne
Tucker, Marcia
Tufts, Eleanor M
Turano, Jane Van Norman
Turk, Rudy H
Turnure, James Harvey
Upjohn, Everard Miller
Upton, John David
Ushenko, Audrey Andreyevna
Van Derpool, James Grote
Varnedoe, John Kirk Train
Vermette, Luce
Vermeule, Cornelius Clarkson, III
Verostko, Roman Joseph
Wallace, David Harold
Ward, John Lawrence
Wark, Robert Rodger
Wasserman, Jack
Wasserman, Jeanne L
Watrous, James Scales
Watson, Ross
Wattenmaker, Richard J
Waufle, Alan Duane
Weeks, Edward F
Weinberg, H Barbara
Weinhardt, Carl Joseph, Jr
Weisberg, Ruth Ellen
Weiss, Peg
Weller, Allen Stuart
Werner, Alfred
Werness, Hope B
West, Richard Vincent
Westin, Robert H
Wethey, Harold Edwin
Wheelock, Arthur Kingsland, Jr
Whitehill, Walter Muir
Whitney, William Kuebler
Wiedenhoeft, Renate
Wilkins, David George
Willard, Charlotte
Williams, Benjamin Forrest
Williams, John Alden
Williams, John Wesley
Williams, Lewis W, II
Williams, Mary Frances
Willis, Elizabeth Bayley
Wilmerding, John
Wilmeth, Hal Turner
Wilson, William Harry
Wingate, Adina (R)
Withers, Josephine
Wood, James Nowell
Wooden, Howard Edmund
Woolfenden, William Edward
Worth, Peter John
Wortz, Melinda Farris
Wriston, Barbara
Wunder, Richard Paul
Yassin, Robert Alan
Young, Joseph E
Youritzin, Glenda Green
Youritzin, Victor Koshkin
Zietz, Stephen Joseph
Ziff, Jerrold
Zilczer, Judith Katy

ILLUMINATOR

Andre, Carl
Balog, Michael
Carrington, Joy Harrell
Carstenson, Cecil C
Cawein, Kathrin
Ceglia, Vincent
Ebsen, Alf K
Gast, Carolyn Bartlett (Carolyn B Lutz)
Hart, Allen M
Haworth, B Cogill (Mrs Peter Haworth)
Mack, Charles Randall
Nuala (Elsa De Brun)
Quinn, Sandi (Cassandrasu Dhooge-quinn Vachon)
Slotnick, Mortimer H
Wheeler, Cleora Clark
Wheeler, Doug

ILLUSTRATOR

Abel, Ray
Accurso, Anthony Salvatore
Ahl, Henry C
Alajalov, Constantin
Albrecht, Robert A
Alicea, Jose
Aliki (Aliki Brandenberg)
Allen, Loretta B
Altabe, Joan Berg
Altschuler, Franz
Ames, Lee Judah
Amoss, Berthe
Anderson, Doug
Angelo, Emidio
Angulo, Chappie
Arbuckle, Franklin
Ariss, Herbert Joshua
Armitage, Frank
Bailey, Malcolm C W
Baker, Jill Withrow
Baldwin, Richard Wood
Ball, Lyle V
Barbour, Arthur J
Bartlett, Robert Webster
Bates, Betsey
Bearman, Jane Ruth
Beaver, Fred
Beitz, Lester U
Benney, Robert
Bergere, Richard
Berry, William David
Bertoni, Dante H
Bessemer, Auriel
Besser, Arne Charles
Billings, Henry
Bissell, Phil
Bittner, Hans Oskar
Blattner, Robert Henry
Blos, May (Elizabeth)

ILLUSTRATOR (cont)
Bode, Robert William
Boedeker, Arnold E (Boedie)
Bogorad, Alan Dale
Bonamarte, Lou
Bond, Oriel Edmund
Booth, George Warren
Boren, James Erwin
Bouchard, Lorne Holland
Bowler, Joseph, Jr
Bowman, Jean (Jean Bowman Magruder)
Braiden, Rose Margaret J
Bransom, (John) Paul
Brender a Brandis, Gerard William
Broemel, Carl William
Brown, Daniel Quilter (Dan Q)
Brown, Gary Hugh
Brown, Judith Gwyn
Brown, Rhett Delford (Harriett Gurney Brown)
Brown, William Ferdinand, II
Brownhill, Harold
Buba, Joy Flinsch
Burchard, Peter Duncan
Burroughs, John Coleman
Byard, Carole Marie
Bye, Ranulph (DeBayeux)
Byrd, Robert John
Caimite (Lynne Ruskin)
Campbell, Dorothy Bostwick
Carroll, Robert Joseph
Carter, Frederick Timmins
Chalmers, Mary Eilleen
Chapman, Walter Howard
Charlot, Martin Day
Chestney, Lillian
Chwast, Seymour
Cimbalo, Robert W
Clymer, John F
Cohen, Stephen Donald
Cohoe, Grey
Comito, Nicholas U
Condon, Lawrence James
Cook, Gladys Emerson
Cooke, Donald Ewin
Cooney, Barbara (Mrs Charles Talbot Porter)
Crawford, Mel
Crite, Allan Rohan
Crosby, Ranice W
Cuevas, Jose Luis
Cuffari, Richard J
Curtiss, George Curt
d'Alessio, Gregory
D'Amato, Janet Potter
Damron, John Clarence
Dank, Leonard Dewey
D'Aulaire, Ingri (Mortenson) Parin
Davis, George
Davis, John Harold
Davis, Wayne Lambert
Dean, Abner
Dean, Nicholas Brice
Debassige, Blake R
De Diego, Julio
Degen, Paul
DeGroat, Diane L
Delano, Jack
Deloney, Jack Clouse
Deming, David Lawson
de Paola, Tomie
DePillars, Murry N
Desoto, Rafael M
Devlin, Harry
Dewey, Kenneth Francis
Dickinson, William Stirling
Dine, James
Dobrin, Arnold Jack
Dohanos, Stevan
Domanska, Janina
Domjan, Joseph (also Spiri)
Dowden, Anne Ophelia Todd
Driesbach, Walter Clark, Jr
Drower, Sara Ruth
Duvoisin, Roger
Eaton, Thomas Newton
Eckelberry, Don Richard
Edwards, Allan W
Edwards, Stanley Dean
Egeli, Peter Even
Egleson, Jim (James Downey)
Eichenberg, Fritz
Eisenstat, Benjamin
Ellis, Richard
Emerson, Edith
Engel, Michael Martin, II
Ericson, Dick
Ericson, Ernest
Eshraw, Ra
Etting, Emlen
Evans, Burford Elonzo
Fagg, Kenneth (Stanley)
Falter, John
Faragasso, Jack
Fassett, Kaffe Havrah
Fein, Stanley
Feininger, T Lux
Ferris, (Carlisle) Keith
Ferro, Walter
Firfires, Nicholas Samuel
Fish, Richard G
Floethe, Richard
Flora, James Royer
Foose, Robert James
Foster, Hal
Fowler, Mel
Frace, Charles Lewis
Freund, Harry Louis
Friberg, Arnold
Friedman, Marvin
Fumagalli, Barbara Merrill
Gaines, Alan Jay
Galanin, Igor Ivanovich
Galli, Stanley Walter
Gast, Carolyn Bartlett (Carolyn B Lutz)
Geber, Hana
Gefter, Judith Michelman
Geisel, Theodor Seuss (Dr Seuss)
Geissman, Robert Glenn
Gersovitz, Sarah Valerie
Gilbert, Albert Earl
Gilmartin, Garry M
Ginsburg, Max
Gironella, Alberto
Glaser, Milton
Godsey, Glenn
Goff, Lloyd Lozes
Gooch, Donald Burnette
Gordon, Violet
Gorski, Richard Kenny
Grado, Angelo John
Granstaff, William Boyd
Graysmith, Robert
Greenberg, Irwin
Greenwald, Sheila Ellen
Groth, John August
Guderna, Ladislav
Guzman-Forbes, Robert
Hamblett, Theora
Hampton, John W
Handville, Robert T
Harmon, Lily
Harris, Robert George
Hawes, Charles
Hawkins, Myrtle H
Haworth, B Cogill (Mrs Peter Haworth)
Hay, George Austin
Haynes, George Edward
Heberling, Glen Austin
Helck, (Clarence) Peter
Henslee, Jack
Herfield, Phyllis Anne
Herring, Jan(et Mantel)
Hessing, Valjean McCarty
Hildebrand, June Mary Ann
Hildebrandt, William Albert
Hill, Draper
Hill, Joan (Chea-se-quah)
Hilton, John William
Himler, Ronald Norbert
Hodge, Roy Garey
Hodgell, Robert Overman
Holden, Raymond James
Holgate, Jeanne
Holt, Charlotte Sinclair
Holton, Leonard T
Hook, Frances A
Hopper, Frank J
Hornung, Clarence Pearson
Horton, Jan E
Howell, Elizabeth Ann (Mitch)
Hunter, Graham
Huntington, Daphne
Hurd, Zorah
Icaza (Francisco de Icaza)
Inman, Pauline Winchester
Irvin, Fred Maddox
Jackson, Everett Gee
Jackson, Vaughn L
Jackson, Virgil V
Janelsins, Veronica
Jenkins, Mary Anne K
Jess (Jess Collins)
Johnson, Fridolf Lester
Johnson, James Ralph
Johnson, Kenn Elmer
Johnson, (Leonard) Lucas
Johnson, Selina (Tetzlaff)
Jones, Elizabeth Orton
Jones, James Edward
Jones, Ruthe Blalock
Joy, Nancy Grahame
Kamen, Gloria
Kampen, Michael Edwin
Kato, Kay
Kaufman, Joe
Keith, Eros
Kenda, Juanita Echeverria
Kenny, Patrick Gerald
Kerr, Kenneth A
Kessler, Leonard H
Kidd, Steven R
King, Henri Umbaji
Kinigstein, Jonah
Klep, Rolf
Knight, Jacob Jaskoviak
Koren, Edward B
Kornmayer, J Gary (John)
Kraner, Florian G
Krigstein, Bernard
Kuhn, Bob
Kurelek, William
Labrie, Rose
Laessig, Robert
Laird, Mary (Mary Laird Hamady)
Larsen, Ole
Latham, Barbara
Lathrop, Dorothy P
Lea, Tom
Lederer, Wolfgang
Lee, Doris
Lee, Manning de Villeneuve
Lee, Robert J
Lefranc, Margaret (Margaret Lefranc Schoonover)
Leighton, Clare
Leon, Ralph Bernard
Levering, Robert K
Levine, David
Levit, Herschel
Lewen, Si
Lewicki, James
Lewin, Keith Kerton
Lewis, Mary
Lidov, Arthur Herschel
Lieberman, Harry
Lindlof, Edward Axel, Jr
Lipinsky de Orlov, Lino S
Lis, Janet Chapman
Livingston, Virginia (Mrs Hudson Warren Budd)
Llorente, Luis
Lock, Charles L
Lockhart, James Leland
Loewer, Henry Peter
London, Alexander
Lopina, Louise Carol
Lovell, Tom
Lyon, Harold Lloyd
Macaualy, David Alexander
Macdonald, Grant
MacDonald, Thoreau
MacGillis, Robert Donald
Maciel, Mary Oliveira
Mackay, Donald Cameron
MacNutt, Glenn Gordon
Maestro, Giulio Marcello
Malta, Vincent
Mancini, John
Margules, Gabriele Ella
Marshall, Bruce
Martin, Margaret M
Mawicke, Tran
Mayhew, Richard
Mays, Victor
McBride, James Joseph
McCall, Robert Theodore
McCloskey, Robert
McCormick, Jo Mary (Jo Mary McCormick-Sakurai)
Mill, Eleanor
Mion, Pierre Riccardo
Mitchell, Beresford Strickland
Mitchell, James E
Moore, Michael Shannon
Moose, Philip Anthony
Moose, Talmadge Bowers
Mora, Francisco
Morez, Mary
Morgan, Maritza Leskovar
Morningstern, Harry V
Morris, Edward A
Morton, Richard H
Moser, Barry
Mosley, Zack T
Moy, May (Wong)
Moyers, Wm
Musselman, Darwin B
Neff, John A
Negri, Rocco Antonio
Ness, Evaline (Mrs Arnold A Bayard)
Neustadt, Barbara (Barbara Meyer)
Nevitt, Richard Barrington
Niss, Robert Sharples
Norris, Leonard Matheson
Oechsli, Kelly
Olugebefola, Ademola
O'Neill, John Patton
Osborn, Robert
Ostendorf, (Arthur) Lloyd, Jr
Osyczka, Bohdan Danny
Pajaud, William Etienne
Paredes, Limon Mariano
Parker, Alfred
Parker, Nancy Winslow
Parnall, Peter
Parry, Marian (Marian Parry Feld)
Partch, Virgil Franklin, II
Paschke, Edward F (Ed)
Paulley, David Gordon
Payor, Eugene
Payson, Dale Constance
Pena, Amado Maurilio, Jr
Perez, Vincent
Perlin, Bernard
Perlman, Raymond
Perrin, C Robert
Peterson, Roger Tory
Petrie, Ferdinand Ralph
Petro, Joseph (Victor), Jr
Phillips, Irving W
Pierce, Diane (Diane Pierce Huxtable)
Pisani, Joseph
Plunkett, Edward Milton
Polonsky, Arthur
Pratt, Frances (Frances Elizabeth Usui)
Pretsch, John Edward
Prins, (J) Warner

Rabut, Paul
Ramirez, Joel Tito
Ramstead, Edward Oliver, Jr
Rand, Paul
Raskins, Ellen
Ray, Deborah
Red Star, Kevin Francis
Reece, Maynard
Richards, Walter DuBois
Rising, Dorothy Milne
Rivoli, Mario
Robbins, Frank
Robertson, D Hall
Rockwell, Norman
Roever, Joan Marilyn
Roland, Arthur
Romano, Emanuel Glicen
Rose, Samuel
Rosenblatt, Suzanne Maris
Rosen-Queralt, Jann
Ruzicka, Rudolph
Ryder, Mahler Bessinger
Salmoiraghi, Frank
Salmon, Donna Elaine
Sarnoff, Arthur Saron
Saunders, J Boyd
Savitt, Sam
Saxon, Charles David
Schachter, Justine Ranson
Schlaikjer, Jes (Wilhelm)
Schmidt, Harvey Lester
Schneebaum, Tobias
Schultz, Caroline Reel
Seabourn, Bert Dail
Seames, Clarann
Searles, Charles Robert
Seltzer, Phyllis
Sendak, Maurice Bernard
Setterberg, Carl Georg
Sharp, Harold
Shelton, Gilbert Key
Sheppard, John Craig
Shook, Georg
Siegel, (Leo) Dink
Sigel, Barry Chaim
Silber, Maurice
Silver, Pat
Silverman, Burton Philip
Simmons, Cleda Marie
Simon, Howard
Simoneau, Everett Hubert
Simont, Marc
Singer, Arthur B
Sivard, Robert Paul
Skinner, Elsa Kells
Sloan, Richard
Sloane, Eric
Smith, Cecil Alden
Smith, Helen M
Smith, Joseph Anthony
Smith, Lawrence Beall
Smith, Susan Carlton
Smyth, Ed
Snyder, Seymour
Soltesz, Frank Joseph
Sorel, Edward
Spagnolo, Kathleen Mary
Spink, Frank Henry, Jr
Stahl, Ben (Albert)
Stamaty, Stanley
Stark, Bruce Gunsten
Statman, Jan B
Stevens, Richard Clive
Stevens, William Ansel, Sr
Storm, Mark (Kennedy)
Stuart, Kenneth James
Suba, Susanne
Sutton, George Miksch
Sway, Albert
Sweney, Fred
Tamburine, Jean
Taylor, Harry George
Thollander, Earl
Thom, Robert Alan
Thompson, F Raymond (Ray)
Thompson, Kenneth Webster
Tolmie, Kenneth Donald
Tomes, Margot Ladd
Tompkins, Alan
Treaster, Richard A
Trimm, H Wayne
Tripp, Wallace Whitney
Truby, Betsy Kirby
Tucker, Peri
Tudor, Tasha
Van Buren, Raeburn
Van Vliet, Claire
Vasils, Albert
Velarde, Pablita
Vo-Dinh, Mai
Voelker, John
Vorwerk, E Charlsie
Wachsteter, George
Waddingham, John Alfred
Wagner, John Philip
Walch, John Leo
Wall, Ralph Alan
Ward, Lynd (Kendall)
Warren, L D
Warriner, Laura B
Washburn, Stan
Wasserman, Albert
Waterhouse, Charles Howard
Waterhouse, Russell Rutledge
Watson, Aldren Auld
Weisgard, Leonard Joseph
Wells, Betty Childs
Werth, Kurt
Wexler, Jerome LeRoy
Whitcomb, Jon
White, Robert (Winthrop)
Whitmore, Coby
Williamson, Jason H
Wilson, John
Wilson, Mortimer, Jr
Wilwers, Edward Mathias
Windrow, Patricia (Patricia Windrow Klein)
Wingate, Robert Bray
Winters, Denny
Witt, John
Wogstad, James Everet
Wolsky, Milton Laban
Woodward, Cleveland Landon
Wright, Harold David
Yanow, Rhoda Mae
Youngsblood, Nat
Zallinger, Jean Day
Zallinger, Rudolph Franz
Zimmerman, William Harold
Zuckerberg, Stanley M

ILLUSTRATOR—CHILDREN'S BOOKS

Abel, Ray
Aliki (Aliki Brandenberg)
Allen, Loretta B
Ames, Lee Judah
Amoss, Berthe
Anderson, Gunnar Donald
Arnosky, James Edward
Bacon, Peggy
Barowitz, Elliott
Barry, Robert E
Bate, Norman Arthur
Becker, Charlotte (Mrs Walter Cox)
Blair, Helen (Helen Blair Crosbie)
Bock, William Sauts-Netamux'we
Bowman, Bruce
Brown, Judith Gwyn
Burnett, Calvin
Byrd, Robert John
Chalmers, Mary Eilleen
Chen, Tony (Anthony Young Chen)
Chestney, Lillian
Cleaver, Elizabeth
Coheleach, Guy Joseph
Connolly, Jerome Patrick
Cooke, Donald Ewin
Crawford, Mel
D'Aulaire, Edgar Parin
De Botton, Jean Philippe
DeGroat, Diane L
Duncan, (Eleanore) Klari
Duvoisin, Roger
Ets, Marie Hall
Ferguson, Kathleen Elizabeth
Finson, Hildred A
Fisher, Leonard Everett
Frankenberg, Robert Clinton
Frasconi, Antonio
Friedman, Marvin
Garchik, Morton Lloyd
Golbin, Andree
Gold, Albert
Gorsline, Douglas Warner
Graese, Judy (Judith Ann)
Graham, Margaret Bloy
Gramatky, Hardie
Graysmith, Robert
Graziano, Florence V Mercolino
Hale, Jean Graham
Harmon, Barbara Sayre
Ha-So-De (Narcisco Abeyta)
Herman, Vic
Hessing, Valjean McCarty
Himler, Ronald Norbert
Hogrogian, Nonny
Ingram, Jerry Cleman
Ipcar, Dahlov
Jauss, Anne Marie
Keats, Ezra Jack
Keith, Eros
Kent, Jack
Kessler, Leonard H
Knight, Hilary
Korn, Elizabeth P
Kurelek, William
Langner, Nola
Lasker, Joseph (L)
Latham, Barbara
Lent, Blair
Macaualy, David Alexander
Maestro, Giulio Marcello
Masurovsky, Gregory
McMillan, Constance
Micale, Albert
Motter, Dean Roger
Negri, Rocco Antonio
Olds, Elizabeth
Parry, Marian (Marian Parry Feld)
Payson, Dale Constance
Pohl, Louis G
Prohaska, Ray
Ramirez, Joel Tito
Rappin, Adrian
Raskins, Ellen
Ray, Deborah
Rey, H A
Rice, James William, Jr
Richter, Hank
Roever, Joan Marilyn
Romeu, Joost A
Rosenhouse, Irwin Jacob
Sarnoff, Arthur Saron
Savitt, Sam
Schary, Saul
Schoenherr, John Carl
Siberell, Anne Hicks
Simon, Ellen R
Smith, Susan Carlton
Spier, Peter Edward
Squires, Norma-Jean
Taback, Simms
Tamburine, Jean
Thompson, Joanne
Thorndike, Charles Jesse (Chuck)
Timmins, William Frederick
Tripp, Wallace Whitney
Wagner, John Philip
Warren, L D
Watson, Wendy
Weil, Lisl
Wexler, Jerome LeRoy
Williams, Garth Montgomery
Winship, Florence Sarah

INSTRUCTOR
(Studio/Art School)

Abbatecola (Oronzo)
Abish, Cecile
Adams, Pat
Adan, Suzanne Rae
Adelman, Dorothy (Lee) McClintock
Adler, Myril
Ahlgren, Roy B
Ahn, Don C
Amarotico, Joseph Anthony
Amino, Leo
Anderson, David Paul
Anderson, John S
Anderson, Lennart
Anderson, Robert Raymond
Archer, Dorothy Bryant
Armstrong, Roger Joseph
Aronson, Irene Hilde
Aronson, Sanda
Atlee, Emilie DeS
Autry, Carolyn (Carolyn Autry Elloian)
Avakian, John
Bailin, Hella
Baird, Roger Lee
Ballatore, Sandra Lee
Ballinger, Louise Bowen
Baranik, Rudolf
Barber, Samir
Bardin, Jesse Redwin
Barnet, Will
Barnhart, C Raymond
Barr, Norman
Barr, Roger Terry
Barrett, Thomas R
Barrio, Raymond
Barrow, Thomas Francis
Bartlett, Jennifer Losch
Batchelor, Anthony John
Batista, Tomas
Batt, Miles Girard
Beauchamp, John R
Beerman, Miriam H
Belfiore, Gerardo
Bendell, Marilyn
Benjamin, Karl Stanley
Benson, Robert Franklin
Berg, Siri
Betteridge, Lois Etherington
Bigger, Michael Dinsmore
Blackburn, Morris (Atkinson)
Blai, Bert
Blakely, Joyce (Carol)
Bleifeld, Stanley
Block, Adolph
Block, Amanda Roth
Blos, Peter W
Blumberg, Barbara Griffiths
Blumberg, Ron
Bobrowicz, Yvonne P
Bohnen, Blythe
Bolmgren, Donna Hollen
Bonacker, Joyce Sybil
Bongart, Sergei R
Boni, Delmar
Botto, Richard Alfred
Bradley, Ida Florence
Bradley, Peter Alexander
Bradshaw, Lawrence James
Brady, Charles Michael
Bramson, Phyllis Halperin
Braunstein, H Terry
Brecher, Samuel

INSTRUCTOR(cont)
Breiger, Elaine
Brender a Brandis, Gerard William
Breschi, Karen Lee
Brodsky, Judith Kapstein
Brooks, (John) Alan
Brotherton, Naomi
Brown, Peggy Ann
Brown, Reynold
Brumer, Shulamith
Brun, Thomas
Bruner, Louise Katherine (Mrs Paul Orr)
Bruno, Santo Michael
Brush, Leif
Buchanan, Sidney Arnold
Bunce, Louis DeMott
Bundy, Stephen Allen
Bunts, Frank
Burns, Paul Callan
Burpee, James Stanley
Byrd, Robert John
Cale, Robert Allan
Calrow, Robert F
Canaday, Ouida Gornto
Carlson, Cynthia J
Carter, Bernard Shirley
Cascieri, Arcangelo
Cassill, Herbert Carroll
Catalan, Edgardo Omar
Cavanaugh, Tom Richard
Cecere, Ada Rasario
Chandler, John William
Chavez, Joseph Arnold
Chen, Tony (Anthony Young Chen)
Cherepov, George
Chernow, Ann
Chernow, Burt
Chester, Charlotte Wanetta
Chin, Ric
Christensen, Larry R
Christensen, Sharlene
Christensen, Val Alan
Christiana, Edward
Ciarrochi, Ray
Cintron, Joseph
Clancy, Patrick
Clark, Chevis Delwin
Cleveland, Helen Barth
Clifton, Jack Whitney
Cockrill, Sherna
Colarusso, Corrine Camille
Cole, Max
Condon, Lawrence James
Cone-Skelton, Annette
Conover, Robert Fremont
Cooper, Anthony J
Cooper, Mario
Cormier, Robert John
Cornin, Jon
Cortese, Don F
Couper, Charles Alexander
Cox, J W S
Craner, Robert Rogers
Cretara, Domenic Anthony
Crimi, Alfred D
Crooks, W Spencer
Cross, Watson, Jr
Crum, Jason Roger
Crump, Walter Moore
Cruz, Emilio
Csoka, Stephen
Cuffari, Richard J
Cunningham, Francis
Dailey, Daniel Owen
Daley, William P
Damron, John Clarence
David, Don Raymond
Davidson, Herbert Laurence
Davies, Kenneth Southworth
Davis, Gene
Day, Larry (Lawrence James Day)
De Botton, Jean Philippe
De Bretteville, Sheila Levrant
DeCaprio, Alice
de Champlain, Vera Chopak
deLory, Peter
Del Valle, Joseph Bourke
DeMaree, Elizabeth Ann (Betty)
Denis, Paul Andre S
Denton, Pat
De Tonnancour, Jacques G
Dickinson, Eleanor Creekmore
di Gioia, Frank
Dioda, Adolph T
DiPerna, Frank Paul
Dobie, Jeanne
Doolin, James Lawrence
Dorfman, Bruce
Dorst, Mary Crowe
Douglas, Edwin Perry
Draper, William Franklin
Dreiband, Laurence
Dreskin, Jeanet Steckler
Dubaniewicz, Peter Paul
Duncan, (Eleanore) Klari
Dunlap, Loren Edward
Dunn, Nate
Dworzan, George R
Dwyer, James Eugene
Ebie, William Dennis
Eckmair, Frank C
Edelson, Elihu
Edge, Douglas Benjamin
Edwards, Allan W
Ehresmann, Julia Moore
Eide, John
Eliason, Shirley (Shirley Eliason Haupt)
Elloian, Peter
Engle, Barbara Jean
Enriquez, Gaspar
Ericson, Ernest
Ernst, James Arnold
Eshoo, Robert
Esserman, Ruth
Ettenberg, Franklin Joseph
Ewing, Thomas R
Falconieri, Virginia
Faragasso, Jack
Faris, Brunel De Bost
Feher, Joseph
Feldman, Hilda (Mrs Neville S Dickinson)
Fenton, Alan
Fernandes, Michael Adrian
Ferriter, Clare
Fett, William F
Finck, Furman J
Fiore, Joseph A
Fitzgerald, Edmond James
Fix, John Robert
Flack, Audrey L
Flick, Paul John
Fludd, Reginald Joseph
Fohr, Jenny
Foley, Kyoko Y
Fon, Jade
Foster, April
Foster, Barbara Lynn
Frances, Harriette Anton
Frankenberg, Robert Clinton
Frazer, James Nisbet, Jr
Frey, Viola
Fried, Howard Lee
Friedberg, Ray E
Froman, Ramon Mitchell
Frudakis, Evangelos William
Gains, Jacob
Gardner, Joan A
Garel, Leo
Garhart, Martin J
Garrett, Alan Thomas
Garver, Walter Raymond
Gasparian, Armen Tigran
Gasparro, Frank
Gentile, Gloria Irene
Gentry, Warren Miller
George, Richard Allan
Gibbs, Craig Stevens
Gilbert, Lionel
Gilhooly, David James, III
Goetz, Edith Jean
Goetz, Richard Vernon
Gold, Debra Lynn
Goldstein, Gladys Hack
Goldstein, Julius
Goodbred, Ray Edw
Goodman, Brenda Joyce
Goodridge, Lawrence Wayne
Goray, John C
Gottschalk, Max Jules
Goulet, Lorrie (Lorrie J De Creeft)
Grabach, John R
Grado, Angelo John
Granlund, Paul Theodore
Graupe-Pillard, Grace
Gray, Jim
Greco, Anthony Joseph
Greeley, Charles Matthew
Green, Morris Baldwin
Greenberg, Irwin
Greenwood, Paul Anthony
Gregory, Bruce
Gross, Chaim
Grosse (Carolyn Ann Gawarecki)
Grossen, Francoise
Groth, John August
Grushkin, Philip
Gumpel, Hugh
Gundelfinger, John Andre
Guzevich, Kreszenz (Cynthia)
Gyra, Francis Joseph, Jr
Hacklin, Allan Dave
Hafif, Marcia
Hagan, James Garrison
Hale, Kenneth John
Hale, Robert Beverly
Hall, John A
Hammett, Polly Horton
Hammond, Harmony
Hanlen, John (Garrett)
Harbart, Gertrude Felton
Hardy, David Whittaker, III
Hart, Agnes
Harvey, Dermot
Harvey, Donald Gilbert
Harwood, June Beatrice
Hasen, Burt Stanly
Haug, Donald Raymond
Hawkins, Thomas Wilson, Jr
Healy, Julia Schmitt
Hedden-Sellman, Zelda
Hedrick, Wally Bill
Heinemann, Peter
Helander, Bruce Paul
Helck, (Clarence) Peter
Held, Philip
Helfond, Riva
Helgoe, Orlin Milton
Helman, Phoebe
Henderson, Jack W
Henry, Jean
Hensche, Henry
Herpst, Martha Jane
Herr, Richard Joseph
Hershberg, Israel
Herzbrun, Helene McKinsey
Hicken, Philip Burnham
Hickins, Walter H
Highberg, Stephanie Wenner
Hillman, Arthur Stanley
Hofer, Ingrid (Ingeborg)
Hoffmann, Lilly Elisabeth
Hollerbach, Serge
Hollingsworth, Alvin Carl
Holste, Thomas James
Homar, Lorenzo
Horowitz, Nadia
Hotvedt, Kris J
Housman, Russell F
Hovsepian, Leon
Howard, David
Howell, Marie W
Hunt, Courtenay
Hunter, Robert Douglas
Hupp, Frederick Duis
Hurt, Susanne M
Iacurto, Francesco
Indiviglia, Salvatore Joseph
Ingalls, Eve
Ireland, Richard Wilson (Dick)
Isaacs, Ron
Jackson, Virgil V
Jacobs, Helen Nichols
Jameikis, Brone Aleksandra
Janowsky, Bela
Jansen, Catherine Sandra
Jarvis, Donald
Jencks, Penelope
Jennings, Frank Harding
Jensen, John Edward
Johanson, George E
Johnson, Joyce
Johnson, Lester L
Jones, Claire (Deann Burtchaell)
Jones, Franklin Reed
Jones, Herb (Leon Herbert Jones, Jr)
Jordan, Barbara Schwinn
Joyce, Marshall Woodside
Kapsalis, Thomas Harry
Karn, Gloria Stoll
Karniol, Hilda
Karpel, Eli
Katzen, Lila (Pell)
Kaufman, Jane A
Kaulitz, Garry Charles
Kaz, Nathaniel
Keene, Paul
Kelleher, Daniel Joseph
Kellogg, Maurice Dale
Kemble, Richard
Kennedy, Leta Marietta
Kessler, Shirley
Kidd, Steven R
Kinstler, Everett Raymond
Kirby, Kent Bruce
Kirk, Michael
Knaub, Raymond L
Knigin, Michael Jay
Knorr, Jeanne Boardman
Koestner, Don
Koga, Mary
Kolliker, William Augustin
Koochin, William
Korjus, Veronica Maria Elisabeth
Korman, Barbara
Kowalski, Raymond Alois
Kozlow, Sigmund
Kranking, Margaret Graham
Krashes, Barbara
Krauser, Joel
Krigstein, Bernard
Krody, Barron J
Kruskamp, Janet
Kushner, Dorothy Browdy
Kutka, Anne (Mrs David McCosh)
Labiche, Walter Anthony
Lack, Richard Frederick
Laguna, Muriel
Lai, Waihang
Lambert, Eddie
Landfield, Ronnie (Ronald T)
Lane, Marion Jean Arrons
Lang, J T
Lansdon, Gay Brandt
Larson, Blaine (Gledhill)
Laslo, Patricia Louise
Leber, Roberta (Roberta Leber McVeigh)
Leeds, Annette
Leighton, Thomas Charles
Leitman, Samuel
Leonard, Leon Lank, Sr
Leonardi, Hector
Lerner Levine, Marion
Lesnick, Stephen William
Levin, Morton D
Levine, Reeva (Anna) Miller
Levitan, Israel (Jack)
Lewis, Marcia
Lewis, Nat Brush

Lewis, Norman Wilfred
Lewis, Ronald Walter
Lewis, William R
Lieber, France
Lieberman, Meyer Frank
Likan, Gustav
Liljegren, Frank
Limont, Naomi Charles
Lincoln, Fred Clinton
Lindmark, Arne
Linhares, Philip E
Long, Sandra Tardo
Lorentz, Pauline
Lovato, Manuelita
Love, Rosalie Bowen
Lowe, Joe Hing
Lucchesi, Bruno
Lueders, Jimmy C
Luisi, Jerry
Luitjens, Helen Anita
Lutze
Maas, Arnold (Marcolino)
MacKenzie, Hugh Seaforth
Mahaffey, Merrill Dean
Majdrakoff, Ivan
Maldre, Mati
Mallory, Larry Richard
Malsch, Ellen L
Malta, Vincent
Maltby, Hazel Farrow
Mancuso, Leni (Leni Mancuso Barrett)
Manuella, Frank R
Manzo, Anthony Joseph
Marden, Brice
Markowski, Eugene David
Marshall, Kerry
Martin, Doris-Marie Constable
Martin, Fred Thomas
Martin, Roger
Martin, Thomas
Martinez, Ernesto Pedregon
Martone, William Robert
Mason, Alden C
Mason, Frank Herbert
McCallum, Corrie (Mrs William Halsey)
McCarty, Lorraine Chambers
McClure, Constance M
McCoy, John W, (II)
McGee, Olivia Jackson
McGeoch, Lillian Jean
McGlauchlin, Tom
McKennis, Gail
McNitt, Miriam D
McQuillan, Frances C
McReynolds, (Joe) Cliff
McVey, Leza
McWhorter, Elsie Jean
Mellon, James
Meltzer, Anna E
Meltzer, Robert Hiram
Mendenhall, Jack
Meng, Wendy
Merkel, Jayne (Silverstein)
Messick, Ben (Newton)
Metz, Gerry Michael
Meyer, Frank Hildbridge
Meyers, Dale (Mrs Mario Cooper)
Middleman, Raoul F
Midener, Walter
Miezajs, Dainis
Miles, Cyril
Milholland, Richard Alexander
Miller, Barbara Darlene
Miller, John Paul
Miller, Nancy Tokar
Milonadis, Konstantin
Minewski, Alex
Misch, Allene K
Mohn, Cheri (Ann)
Montoya, Geronima Cruz (Po-Tsu-Nu)
Moore, Ina May
Moose, Talmadge Bowers
Moquin, Richard Attilio
Morgan, Gladys B
Morgan, Maritza Leskovar
Moscatt, Paul N
Motter, Dean Roger
Myers, Jack Fredrick
Myers, Malcolm Haynie
Nelson, Leonard
Nestor, Lulu B
Newman, John Beatty
Nichols, Eleanor Cary
Nichols, Jeannettie Doornhein
Nossal, Audrey Jean
O'Connor, Harold Thomas
Odate, Toshio
Oesterle, Leonhard Freidrich
Ohe, Katie (Minna)
Oi, Motoi
Oldham, Berton Jepsen
Oliveira, V'Lou
Olson, Gary Spangler
O'Neil, Bruce William
Ortlieb, Robert Eugene
Ortman, George Earl
Ostendorf, (Arthur) Lloyd, Jr
O'Sullivan, Daniel Joseph
Osyczka, Bohdan Danny
Paley, Albert Raymond
Parker, Alfred
Parker, James
Parra, Thomas (Garcia)
Parshall, Douglass Ewell
Parton, Ralf
Pascual, Manolo
Patrick, Genie H
Patterson, William Joseph
Pearson, James Eugene
Pearson, John
Pearson, Marguerite Stuber
Pease, David G
Peck, James Edward
Peck, Stephen Rogers
Pels, Albert
Pen, Rudolph
Perez, Vincent
Perlmutter, Jack
Perlmutter, Merle
Perreault, John
Peter, George
Pettibone, John Wolcott
Pfriem, Bernard
Pierce, J Michael
Pijanowski, Eugene M
Pijanowski, Hiroko Sato
Pike, John
Pinzarrone, Paul
Pomeroy, James Calwell, Jr
Poole, Richard Elliott
Porter, Liliana
Porter, Priscilla Manning
Posey, Leslie Thomas
Provder, Carl
Quick, Birney MacNabb
Quinn, Noel Joseph
Raffel, Alvin Robert
Rawlinson, Jonlane Frederick
Reale, Nicholas Albert
Reddington, Charles Leonard
Red Star, Kevin Francis
Rehberger, Gustav
Reid, Robert Dennis
Reisman, Philip
Remsing, (Joseph) Gary
Reynard, Carolyn Cole
Richards, Walter DuBois
Rishell, Robert Clifford
Ritchie, William
Rizk, Romanos
Roberson, William
Roberts, Clyde Harry
Roberts, Donald
Rodriguez, Ralph Noel
Rogalski, Walter
Rohrer, Warren
Roney, Harold Arthur
Rose, Leatrice
Rose, Roslyn
Rose, Samuel
Rosenblum, Jay
Ross, Douglas Allan
Ross, John T
Rossi, Barbara
Rossman, Ruth Scharff
Roster, Laila Bergs
Rousseau-Vermette, Mariette
Roussel, Claude Patrice
Rowan, Frances Physioc
Rubenstein, Lewis W
Rubins, David Kresz
Rudquist, Jerry Jacob
Ruffo, Joseph Martin
Saar, Betye
Salemme, Lucia (Autorino)
Samuelson, Fred Binder
Sanchez, Carol Lee
Sandler, Irving Harry
Saunders, Edith Dariel Chase
Savas, Jo-Ann (Mrs George T Savas)
Schon, Nancy Quint
Schulz, Ken
Schuman, Robert Conrad
Schwartz, Carl E
Schwartz, Henry
Scott, Sam
Searles, Stephen
Sekimachi, Kay
Seyffert, Richard Leopold
Shapiro, Irving
Shaw, (George) Kendall
Sheehe, Lillian Carolyn
Shelton, Robert Lee
Sheppard, Joseph Sherly
Sherman, Lenore (Walton)
Shumacker, Elizabeth Wight
Sickman, Jessalee Bane
Sider, Deno
Silberstein-Storfer, Muriel Rosoff
Silverman, Sherley C
Simon, Sidney
Simpson, Marilyn Jean
Singleton, Robert Ellison
Sklar-Weinstein, Arlene (Joyce)
Skolnick, Arnold
Sleigh, Sylvia
Slone, Sandi
Slorp, John Stephen
Smith, Emily Guthrie
Smith, Joseph Anthony
Smith, Robert Alan
Smith, Thelma deGoede
Snyder, Seymour
Snyder, William B
Sokole, Miron
Solomon, Syd
Soloway, Reta
Souza, Paul Marciel
Soviak, Harry
Soyer, Isaac
Speers, Teryl Townsend
Spickett, Ronald John, (Sr)
Sprague, Mark Anderson
Squadra, John
Staffel, Rudolf Harry
Stanczak, Julian
Stapleton, Joseph F
Steadman, David Wilton
Steckel, Anita
Steczynski, John Myron
Stefanelli, Joseph J
Stegall, James Park
Steinmetz, Grace Ernst Titus
Stelzer, Michael Norman
Stemelos, Electra Georgia Mousmoules
Stevenson, A Brockie
Stewart, Jack
Stewart, Norman (William)
Stoessel, Henry Kurt
Stoltenberg, Donald Hugo
Stonebarger, Virginia
Storm, Larue
Stowman, Annette Burr
Streett, Tylden Westcott
Stronghilos, Carol
Stuart, Donald Alexander
Stull, Jean Himrod
Szarama, Judith Layne
Taggart, William John
Takashima, Shizuye Violet
Takemoto, Henry Tadaaki
Tatro, Ronald Edward
Taylor, Prentiss (Hottel)
Teyral, John
Thepot, Roger Francois
Thomas, Ed B
Thompson, Donald Roy
Threlkeld, Dale
Tiffany, Marguerite Bristol
Tillim, Sidney
Todd, Louise (Louise Todd Cope)
Tracy, (Lois) Bartlett
Trauerman, Margy Ann
Trieff, Selina
Trosky, Helene Roth
Tseu, Rosita Hsu
Tubis, Seymour
Turner, Arthur Charles
Turner, (Charles) Arthur
Van Wyk, Helen
Vega, Edward
Viner, Frank Lincoln
Viret, Margaret Mary (Mrs Frank Ivo)
Vogel, Donald
Wagner, Charles H
Waldman, Paul
Walsh, Patricia Ruth
Wapp, Josephine Myers
Warner, Lucy Ann
Waterstreet, Ken (James Kent Waterstreet)
Watson, Lynda
Webb, Frank (Francis H Webb)
Wegner, Nadene R
Weidner, Roswell Theodore
Weill, Erna
Weiner, Abe
Wellington, Duke
Werner-Vaughn, Salle
West, E Gordon
Wethington, Wilma Zella
Whidden, Conni (Constance)
Whipple, Barbara (Mrs Grant Heilman)
White, Bruce Hilding
White, Franklin
White, Robert (Winthrop)
Whiten, Colette
Whitlow, Tyrel Eugene
Whitney, Edgar Albert
Wilke, Hannah
Willis, Jay Steward
Wilson, Carrie Lois
Wilson, Richard Brian
Windrow, Patricia (Patricia Windrow Klein)
Winer, Donald Arthur
Wiper, Thomas William
Witkin, Isaac
Woehrman, Ralph
Wolfe, Ann (Ann Wolfe Graubard)
Wolpert, Elizabeth Davis
Wolsky, Jack
Wood, Robert E
Woodson, Shirley Ann
Woof, Maija (Maija Gegeris Zack Peeples)
Wright, Frank Cookman
Wright, Stanley Marc
Wyman, William
Yaghjian, Edmund
Yates, Sharon Deborah
Young, Cliff
Zelt, Martha
Zirker, Joseph

JEWELER

Aird, Neil Carrick
Allen, Constance Olleen Webb
Bakken, Haakon
Baldwin, Harold Fletcher
Bambas, Thomas Reese
Bell, Evelyn Behnan
Bennett, Jamie
Busch, Julia M
Caldwell, Eleanor
Chapman, Robert Gordon
Chase-Riboud, Barbara Dewayne
Conaway, Gerald
Croft, Michael Flynt
Crozier, William K, Jr
De La Verriere, Jean-Jacques
Dhaemers, Robert August
Eikerman, Alma
Elkins, (E) Lane
Enriquez, Gaspar
Fisch, Arline Marie
Fix, John Robert
Fox, Charles Harold
Fox, Winifred Grace
Gabriel, Hannelore
Grissom, Freda Gill
Hageman, Charles Lee
Harper, William
Helzer, Richard Brian
Herrold, Clifford H
Higgins, Edward Koelling
Higgins, Mary Lou
Hu, Mary Lee
Jackson, William Davis
Jensen, Claud
Johnson, Donald Marvin
Jungwirth, Irene Gayas (I Gayas Jungwirth)
Kearl, Stanley Brandon
Kuehnl, Claudia Ann
LaPlantz, David
Lavoy, Walter Joseph
Lechtzin, Stanley
Leeber, Sharon Corgan
Lewis, Marcia
Link, Val James
Loloma, Charles
Long, Frank Weathers
Mattil, Edward L
Mawdsley, Richard W
Miller, John Paul
Mitchell, Robert Ellis
Monongye, Preston Lee
Neugebauer, Margot
Neumann, William A
Nichols, Eleanor Cary
Orr, Veronica Marie (Veronica Marie Ingram)
Ottiano, John William
Peck, Lee Barnes
Piccolo, Thomas Frank
Pijanowski, Eugene M
Pijanowski, Hiroko Sato
Renk, Merry
Richards, Lee
Roach, Ruth S
Satterfield, John Edward
Scherr, Mary Ann
Schlup, Elaine Smitha
Sheng, Shao Fang
Skelly, Barbara Jean
Smith, Bradford Leaman
Smith, Jo-an
Stephen, Francis B
Taira, Frank
Thompson, Nancy Kunkle
van Duinwyk, George Paul
Vierthaler, Arthur A
Wagner, Merrill
Walker, Mary Carolyn
Wardle, Alfred Hill
Wegner, Nadene R
Wiedenhoeft-Wesler, Anita Kae

KINETIC ARTIST

Barnes, Carroll
Besner, J Jacques
Billeci, Andre George
Bowles, Thomas Andrew, III
Brewster, Michael
Bundy, Stephen Allen
Cho, David
Cooper, Ron
Crist, William Gary
Delihas, Neva C
Emery, Lin (Lin Emery Braselman)
Eversley, Frederick John
Favro, Murray
Flavin, Dan
Freund, Tibor
Freund, Will Frederick
Friscia, Albert Joseph
Fugate-Wilcox, Terry
Gebhardt, Peter Martin
Goldstein, Daniel Joshua
Goulet, Claude
Gruber, Aaronel De Roy
Harvey, Dermot
Hayden, Michael
Hill, Jim
Holvey, Samuel Boyer
Izuka, Kunio
Jackson, William Davis
Jacobs, Harold
Jones, Tom Douglas
Laposky, Ben Francis
Lijn, Liliane
Lye, Len
Lynds, Clyde William
Malina, Frank Joseph
Margulies, Isidore
Mark, Phyllis
Milonadis, Konstantin
Myer, Peter Livingston
Natzler, Otto
Oster, Gerald
Peiperl, Adam
Pershing, Louise
Poleskie, Stephen Francis
Prent, Mark
Prince, Richard Edmund
Reiback, Earl M
Roukes, Nicholas M
Schneemann, Carolee
Seyfried, John Louis
Sidenius, W Christian
Slusser, James Bernard
Squires, Norma-Jean
Stephen, Francis B
Stern, Gerd Jacob
Talbot, William (H M)
Tsai, Wen-Ying
Valinski, Dennis John
Vilder, Roger
Warsinske, Norman George, Jr
Winkler, Dietmar R

LECTURER

Ablow, Joseph
Abrams, Herbert E
Adamy, George E
Airola, Paavo
Albin, Edgar A
Albrecht, Mary Dickson
Albuquerque, Lita
Alcalay, Albert S
Alpert, George
Anderson, Gwendolyn Orsinger (Orsini)
Andrews, Benny
Andrews, Oliver
Antin, David A
Austin, Phil
Aymar, Gordon Christian
Baber, Alice
Baigts, Juan
Balance, Jerrald Clark
Banning, Jack (John Peck Banning, Jr)
Barker, Walter William
Barnett, Ed Willis
Baro, Gene
Bartle, Dorothy Budd
Bartlett, Scott
Barton, August Charles
Bates, Kenneth Francis
Baum, Hank
Beal, Graham William John
Beal, Jack
Beard, Marion L Patterson
Beaver, Fred
Bechtle, C Ronald
Bendell, Marilyn
Benglis, Lynda
Benson, Gertrude Ackerman
Benton, Suzanne E
Berge, Carol
Berman, Aaron
Berman, Muriel Mallin
Bernstein, Judith
Biberman, Edward
Bingham, Lois A
Blai, Boris
Boeve, Edgar Gene
Bogaev, Ronni (Ronni Bogaev Greenstein)
Bogdanovic, Bogomir
Bolster, Ella S
Bolton, James
Bookbinder, Jack
Boren, James Erwin
Boterf, Chester Arthur (Check)
Bothwell, Dorr
Bowers, Cheryl Olsen
Bowman, Jeff Ray
Boz, Alex (Alex Bozickovic)
Bradshaw, Robert George
Brakhage, James Stanley
Brendel, Bettina
Brigadier, Anne
Bromm, Hal
Broudo, Joseph David
Brouillette, Al
Brown, Joseph
Brown, Marvin Prentiss
Brown, Reynold
Browning, Dixie Burrus
Bruno, Santo Michael
Bunn, Cecine Cole
Burko, Diane
Burnett, Patricia Hill
Burnham, Jack Wesley
Burns, Sheila
Burroughs, Margaret T G
Bush, Martin Harry
Buster, Jacqueline Mary
Butler, Joseph Thomas
Bywaters, Jerry
Caldwell, Eleanor
Calkin, Carleton Ivers
Callisen, Sterling
Cannon, Margaret Erickson
Cano, Margarita
Capp, Al
Carlson, Alexander
Carmichael, Jae
Carpenter, Arthur Espenet
Carter, Clarence Holbrook
Casey, Elizabeth Temple
Castoro, Rosemarie
Catti (Catherine James)
Cecere, Gaetano
Challis, Richard Bracebridge
Chandler, Dana C, Jr (Akin Duro)
Chase, Alice Elizabeth
Chen, Tony (Anthony Young Chen)
Chester, Janie Kathleen
Chin, Ric
Chu, Gene
Chuey, Robert Arnold
Clare, Stewart
Clark, Claude
Clark, Nancy Kissel
Clark, Robert Charles
Clark, Sarah Ann
Cleary, Fritz
Cleveland, Robert Earl
Close, Marjorie (Perry)
Cobb, Virginia Horton
Cochran, George McKee
Cohen, Jean
Cohen, Joan Lebold
Cohen, Lynne G
Cole, Bruce
Collins, George R
Collins, Lowell Daunt
Collins, William Charles
Colverson, Ian
Comini, Alessandra
Cook, Howard Norton
Cooper, Rhonda
Copley, Claire Strohn
Corish, Joseph Ryan
Corwin, Sophia M
Crane, Barbara Bachmann
Criquette (Ruth DuBarry Montague)
Cunningham, Charles Crehore
Curtis, Phillip Houston
Daniel, Suzanne Garrigues
Danikian, Caron Le Brun
Darrah, Ann Clarke
Dauterman, Carl Christian
Davidson, Marshall Bowman
Davis, Phil Douglas
Davisson, Darrell
Day, Larry (Lawrence James Day)
Debassige, Blake R
Defenbacher, Daniel S
De Groat, George Hugh
De Jong, Gerrit, Jr
Delgado-Guitart, Jose
Delhom, Mary Mellanay
Denes, Agnes C
De Nike, Michael Nicholas
De Noronha, Maria M (Mrs David Gallman)
Dergalis, George
Dickinson, David Charles
Dickinson, William Stirling
Dienes, Sari
Dixon, Sally Foy
Donneson, Seena
Dooley, Helen Bertha
Doty, Robert McIntyre
Dreaper, Richard Edward
Dubaniewicz, Peter Paul
Dunn, Roger Terry
Eckelberry, Don Richard
Eckstein, Joanna
Edelson, Elihu
Eisenstat, Benjamin
Elias, Harold John
Emerson, Edith
Enos, Chris
Ernst, Jimmy
Etter, Howard Lee
Ettinger, Susi Steinitz
Evans, Burford Elonzo
Evans, Grose
Evans, Paul Fredric
Fanning, Robbie
Farian, Babette S
Fedelle, Estelle
Fein, B R
Feist, Warner David
Ferguson, Kathleen Elizabeth
Fichter, Herbert Francis
Finn, David
Fisher, Elaine
Fisher Joel A
Fleischman, Lawrence
Foster, Barbara Lynn

Foster, Stephen C
Frace, Charles Lewis
Frackman, Noel
Franck, Frederick S
Franco, Robert John
Frank, Charles William
Frank, Peter Solomon
Fraughton, Edward James
Freeman, David L
Freitag, Wolfgang Martin
Fricano, Tom S
Frick, Robert Oliver
Friend, David
Fry, Edward Fort
Fuller, R Buckminster
Fulton, W Joseph
Gablik, Suzi
Gaines, Alan Jay
Gaines, William Robert
Garber, Susan R
Garrard, Mary DuBose
Garvan, Beatrice Bronson
Garver, Thomas H
Gawboy, Carl
Gellman, Beah (Mrs William C McNulty)
Gillette, W Dean
Glasgow, Vaughn Leslie
Gliko, Carl Albert
Goedicke, Jean
Goetz, Peter Henry
Goldberg, Kenneth Paul
Goldberg, Norman Lewis
Goldeen, Dorothy A
Gomez-Sicre, Jose
Goodman, Calvin Jerome
Goodrich, Lloyd
Gorski, Daniel Alexander
Gottschalk, Fritz
Gould, John Howard
Gould, Stephen
Grass, Patty Patterson
Green, Martin Leonard
Greenwald, Alice (Alice Marian Greenwald-Ward)
Gregg, Richard Nelson
Gregory, Angela
Grigsby, Jefferson Eugene, Jr
Gross, Earl
Gross, Sandra Lerner
Grubar, Francis Stanley
Guerriero, Henry Edward
Guion, Molly
Gundersheimer, Herman (Samuel)
Gussow, Alan
Haar, Francis
Haden, Eunice (Barnard)
Hahn, Betty
Hale, Nathan Cabot
Hale, Robert Beverly
Hall, Carl Alvin
Hall, Julie Ann
Hall, Michael David
Hallam, Beverly (Linney)
Hamer, Marilou Heilman
Hammond, Harmony
Hammond, Leslie King
Hanks, David Allen
Hare, David
Harlow, Frederica Todd
Harris, Ann Sutherland
Harris, Murray A
Harsley, Alex
Harvey, Donald
Haskins, John Franklin
Havelock, Christine Mitchell
Haversat, Lillian Kerr
Havis, C Kenneth
Hawkins, Myrtle H
Hay, Dick
Hayes, Bartlett Harding, Jr
Healy, Arthur K D
Hemenway, Nancy (Mrs Robert D Barton)
Hemphill, Herbert Waide
Hensche, Henry
Herold, Donald G
Herring, Jan(et Mantel)
Hicken, Russell Bradford
Highwater, Jamake
Hill, Draper
Hill, Richard Wayne
Hoff, (Syd)
Hoffman, Richard Peter
Hollister, Paul
Holschuh, (George) Fred
Homitzky, Peter
Honig, Mervin
Hood, Gary Allen
Hoover, F Herbert
Hornung, Gertrude Seymour
Hovey, Walter Read
Howell, Douglass (Morse)
Huchthausen, David Richard
Hudson, Ralph Magee
Hughes, Robert S F
Huldermann, Paul F
Humphrey, Donald Gray
Hunter-Stiebel, Penelope (Penelope Hunter Stiebel)
Imana, Jorge Garron
Inoue, Kazuko
Irvine, Betty Jo
Irwin, Robert
Ishikawa, Joseph
Jacob, Ned
Jacobsen, Michael A
Jagger, Gillian
Jay, Bill
Jennings, Frank Harding
Johnson, Buffie
Johnson, James Edwin & Sandra Kay
Johnson, Robert Flynn
Jones, Lois Mailou (Mrs V Pierre-Noel)
Jones, Lois Swan
Jones, Tom Douglas
Jones, William Ezelle
Jordan, George Edwin
Ju, I-Hsiung
Jungwirth, Irene Gayas (I Gayas Jungwirth)
Kahn, Ralph H
Kaish, Luise
Kan, Diana
Karp, Ivan C
Karwelis, Donald Charles
Kaspe, Vladimir
Kato, Kay
Kellogg, Maurice Dale
Kennedy, James Edward
Kenny, Bettie Ilene Cruts (BIK)
Kerr, James Wilfrid
Kerswill, J W Roy
Kind, Joshua B
King, Hayward Ellis
Kingsley, April
Klein, Cecelia F
Klein, Esther M
Knowles, Richard H
Koblick, Freda
Koch, Robert
Koltun, Frances Lang
Konrad, Adolf Ferdinand
Korjus, Veronica Maria Elisabeth
Kornblatt, Barbara Rodbell
Kouwenhoven, John A
Kovinick, Philip Peter
Kowal, Dennis J
Kowalek, Jon W
Kowalski, Dennis Allen
Kozlow, Richard
Kramer, Burton
Kratina, K George
Kriensky, (Morris E)
Kropf, Joan R
Kuchta, Ronald A
Kuehn, Edmund Karl
Kumler, Kipton (Cornelius)
Kurz, Diana
Kutner, Janet
Kuvshinoff, Bertha Horne
Kuvshinoff, Nicolai
LaFreniere, Isabel Marcotte
Lahey, Richard (Francis)
Lang, J T
Langland, Harold Reed
Langman, Richard Theodore
Laning, Edward
Larsen, Jack Lenor
Laub-Novak, Karen
Lee, Raymond Man
Lee-Smith, Hughie
Leighton, Thomas Charles
Leitman, Samuel
Lerner, Marilyn Ann
Lerner, Sandy R
Lesher, Marie Palmisano
Levine, Jack
Levitan, Israel (Jack)
Levitt, Alfred
Lewis, Stanley
Lindlof, Edward Axel, Jr
Lis, Janet Chapman
Littleton, Harvey K
Lochrie, Elizabeth Davey
Logan, Frederick Manning
London, Jeff
Loughlin, John Leo
Love, Frances Taylor
Luck, Robert
Lukas, Dennis Brian
Lunsford, John (Crawford)
Lysun, Gregory
MacDonald, Gayle Coleman
MacLean-Smith, Elizabeth
Madden, Betty I
Mandziuk, Michael Dennis
Mangravite, Peppino Gino
Marcus, Marcia
Marker, Mariska Pugsley
Marks, Claude
Martin, Fred Thomas
Mason, Alice Frances
Mason, Phillip Lindsay
Massaro, Karen Thuesen
Mayer, Susan Martin
Maynard, Valerie
Maytham, Thomas Northrup
McCall, Robert Theodore
McCloskey, Eunice LonCoske
McCullough, Joseph
McGarrell, James
McGarvey, Elsie Siratz
McGowin, Ed
McLanathan, Richard B K
McVey, William M
Meisel, Louis Koenig
Mercer, John Douglas
Merritt, Francis Sumner
Messersmith, Fred Lawrence
Metzger, Robert Paul
Mikus, Eleanore
Miller, Donald
Mockers, Michel M
Moise, William Sidney
Moldroski, Al R
Momiyama, Nanae
Morrison C L
Morrison, Fritzi Mohrenstecher
Moser, Charlotte
Moy, May (Wong)
Moy, Seong
Mozley, Anita Ventura
Murray, Joan
Murray, John Michael
Myers, Denys Peter
Myers, Joel Philip
Naeve, Milo M
Naranjo, Michael Alfred
Nechis, Barbara (Friedman)
Nestor, Lulu B
Neustadt, Barbara (Barbara Meyer)
Newman, Arnold
Newman, Libby
Nonay, Paul
Norfleet, Barbara Pugh
Norvell, Patsy
O'Brien, Marjorie (Marjorie O'Brien Rapaport)
O'Connor, Francis Valentine
Oehler, Helen Gapen
O'Gorman, James Francis
Osborne, Robert Lee
Padovano, Anthony John
Palmer, Lucie Mackay
Palmer, William C
Paone, Peter
Paris, Jeanne C
Parker, Alfred
Parker, Ann (Ann Parker Neal)
Patch, Peggie (Margaret Thompson Williamson)
Patnode, J Scott
Perret, George Albert
Perrin, C Robert
Perry, Regenia Alfreda
Peterson, Larry D
Platus, Libby
Poduska, T F
Pomerantz, Louis
Pool, Nelda Lee
Posner, Judith L
Posner, Richard Perry
Pribble, Easton
Prochownik, Walter A
Quinn, Sandi (Cassandrasu Dhooge-quinn Vachon)
Ragland, Bob
Rainey, Froelich Gladstone
Ranson, Nancy Sussman
Rath, Hildegard
Raven, Arlene
Rebert, Jo Liefeld
Reep, Edward Arnold
Refregier, Anton
Regensteiner, Else (Friedsam)
Rehberger, Gustav
Reichert, Donald O
Reilley, Patrick Richard
Rensch, Roslyn (Roslyn Maria Erbes)
Resnick, Marcia Aylene
Richardson, Frank, Jr
Rigby, Ida Katherine
Robbins, Warren M
Roberds, Gene Allen
Robison, Andrew
Rockwell, Peter Barstow
Rodriguez-Morales, Luis Manuel
Rogalski, Walter
Rogers, John
Rogovin, Mark
Roland, Arthur
Rose, Mary Anne
Rosenthal, Rachel
Ross, David Anthony
Rotholz, Rina
Ruben, Leonard
Russell, Helen Diane
Ruthven, John Aldrich
Sabatini, Raphael
St John, Bruce
Sanchez, Carol Lee
Sandberg, Hannah
Sandground, Mark Bernard, Sr
Sanguinetti, Eugene F
Sarff, Walter
Sassone, Marco
Sawyer, Alan R
Schabacker, Betty Barchet
Schaffer, Rose
Scheibe, Fred Karl
Scheyer, Ernst
Schimmel, William Berry
Schlemowitz, Abram
Schliefer, Stafford Lerrig
Schreiber, Eileen Sher
Schreyer, Greta L
Schucker, Charles
Schueler, Jon R
Schultz, Caroline Reel
Schultz, Harold A

LECTURER (cont)

Schulz, Ken
Schwartz, Marvin D
Schwarz, Felix Conrad
Scott, Henry (Edwards), Jr
Segy, Ladislas
Sellin, David
Semak, Michael
Semmel, Joan
Serra, Rudy
Sheon, Aaron
Sherman, Lenore (Walton)
Shubin, Morris Jack
Siden, Franklin
Sieber, Roy
Silberman, Arthur
Silins, Janis
Sitton, John M
Skalagard, Hans
Skolnick, Arnold
Sleigh, Sylvia
Slettehaugh, Thomas Chester
Smith, Alfred James, Jr
Smith, Ray Winfield
Smith, Ross Ransom Williams
Snow, Lee Erlin
Solinger, David M
Soreff, Helen
Sovary, Lilly
Spaulding, Warren Dan
Speers, Teryl Townsend
Sprout, Francis Allen
Spurlock, William Henry, II
Stegeman, Charles
Steiner, Julia Bourne
Steinmetz, Grace Ernst Titus
Stephens, Richard Alan
Stevens, May
Stofflet, Mary
Stolow, Nathan
Stoneham, John
Strisik, Paul
Summ, Helmut
Sweeney, James Johnson
Swenson, Anne
Sylvester, Lucille
Taft, Frances Prindle
Tait, Cornelia Damian
Takal, Peter
Tam, Reuben
Taylor, Hugh Holloway
Taylor, John Frank Adams
Taylor, Robert
Terris, Albert
Thelin, Valfred P
Thomas, Ed B
Thomas, Helen (Doane)
Thomas, John
Thompson, Dorothy Burr
Thompson, Judith Kay
Threlkeld, Dale
Tibbs, Thomas S
Torreano, John Francis
Townsend, Storm D
Traher, William Henry
Trakas, George
Trakis, Louis
Treaster, Richard A
Tredennick, Dorothy W
Trentham, Gary Lynn
Trosky, Helene Roth
Tuchman, Phyllis
Tucker, Marcia
Turner, Theodore Roy
Uchima, Ansei
Uhrman, Esther
Upton, John David
Usher, Elizabeth Reuter
Valinski, Dennis John
Van Der Straeten, Vincent Roger
Van Tongeren, Harold (Herk)
Van Wyk, Helen
Volpe, Robert
Wang, Yinpao
Washington, James W, Jr
Webb, Spider
Wechter, Vivienne Thaul
Weidner, Marilyn Kemp
Weil, Stephen Edward
Weiner, Abe
Weinhardt, Carl Joseph, Jr
Welch, James Wymore
Wethington, Wilma Zella
Wheeler, Orson Shorey
Whidden, Conni (Constance)
Whitaker, William
Whitehill, Walter Muir
Whitney, Edgar Albert
Willard, Charlotte
Williams, Mary Frances
Williams, William Terence
Wilson, Ben
Wilson, Martha Storey
Wilson, William S, III
Winchester, Alice
Wines, James N
Wingate, Adina (R)
Winkel, Nina
Winkler, Dietmar R
Winogrand, Garry
Winokur, Paula Colton
Winokur, Robert Mark
Wong, Jason
Wood, James Arthur (Art)
Wortz, Melinda Farris
Wright, Frank
Wriston, Barbara
Wynn, Donald James
Yasko, Caryl Anne
Ziegler, Jacqueline (Jacqueline Chalat-Ziegler)
Zornes, James Milford
Zucker, Barbara M

LIBRARIAN

Baretski, Charles Allan
Bayard, Mary Ivy
Bettmann, Otto Ludwig
Bloomgarden, Judith Mary
Burns, G Joan
Busch, Julia M
Bushnell, Marietta P
Candau, Eugenie
Cano, Margarita
Collins, Christiane C
Collins, Marcia Reed
Crouton, Francois (Francois LaFortune)
Dane, William Jerald
Doumato, Lamia
Dunnigan, Mary Catherine
Dutton, Pauline Mae
Dwyer, Melva Jean
Ehresmann, Julia Moore
Feldstein, Mary
Freitag, Wolfgang Martin
Frick, Helen Clay
Friedman, Joan Marcy
Goldberg, Kenneth Paul
Gordon, Anne W
Haswell, Hollee
Hess, Joyce
Hess, Stanley William
Hilligoss, Martha M
Hodgson, James Stanley
Hoffberg, Judith Ann
Holliday, Judith
Hopkins, Benjamin
Howell, Hannah Johnson
Huemer, Christina Gertrude
Hugo, Joan (Dowey)
Irvine, Betty Jo
John, Nancy Regina
Karpel, Bernard
Kaufmann, Robert Carl
Kehde, Martha Elizabeth
Kelley, Donald Castell
Koga, Dean
Kotala, Stanislaw Waclaw
Lambert, Nancy S
Lipton, Barbara B
Lipzin, Janis Crystal
Ludmer, Joyce Pellerano
Mattern, Penny Greig
McCorison, Marcus Allen
Menthe, Melissa
Messer, Brenda Ruth
Miller, Jean Johnston
Mitchell, Eleanor
Moore, Barbara
Muehsam, Gerd
Murchie, Donald John
Navratil, Amy R
Nelson, Jane Gray
Patten, David John
Pearman, Sara Jane
Peterson, Harold Patrick
Placzek, Adolf Kurt
Ratzenberger, Katharine M
Rinehart, Michael
Roberts, Helene Emylou
Robison, Joan Settle
Sabine, Julia
Scherer, Herbert Grover
Schimansky, Donya Dobrila
Schmidt, Mary Morris
Seeman, Helene Zucker
Sevy, Barbara Snetsinger
Shaw, Courtney Ann
Shaw, Renata Vitzthum
Sheridan, Helen Adler
Siden, Harriet Field
Silberman, Arthur
Sipe, Gary Robert
Sisson, Jacqueline D
Smith, Elizabeth Jean
Sommer, Frank H
Stoneham, John
Sutherland, Marylou
Tolles, Bryant Franklin, Jr
Treese, William R
Usher, Elizabeth Reuter
von Rebhan, Elinor Anne
Walker, William Bond
Wyngaard, Susan Elizabeth
Zietz, Stephen Joseph
Zimon, Kathy Elizabeth

LITHOGRAPHER

see also **Printmaker**

Abdalla, Nick
Anderson, Howard Benjamin
Andrade, Edna Wright
Antreasian, Garo Zareh
Bates, Maxwell Bennett
Beny, Roloff
Berg, Thomas
Blameuser, Mary Fleurette
Bynum, E Anderson (Esther Pearl)
Dash, Robert (Warren)
D'Aulaire, Edgar Parin
Degen, Paul
Dennison, Dorothy (Dorothy Dennison Butler)
Elliott, Bruce Roger
Eriquezzo, Lee M
Evans, Burford Elonzo
Ferguson, Edward Robert
Graham, K M
Guiffreda, Mauro Francis
Hale, Kenneth John
Hewitt, Francis Ray
Hirsch, Joseph
Hogue, Alexandre
Ida, Shoichi
Kimball, Wilford Wayne, Jr
Lang, J T
Lapinski, Tadeusz (A)
Lerner, Sandy R
Mark, Enid (Epstein)
Mason, Alice Frances
Massey, Charles Wesley, Jr
Maughelli, Mary L
Medearis, Roger
Narotzky, Norman David
Sanborn, Herbert J
Shark, Herman R
Sloan, Jeanette Pasin
Solodkin, Judith
Sommers, John Sherman
Sprang, Elizabeth Lewis
Stoianovich, Marcelle
Taylor, Prentiss (Hottel)
Voorhees, Donald Edward
Walmsley, William Aubrey
Weddige, Emil
Whitaker, William
Wilson, Charles Banks

MEDALIST

Aldwinckle, Eric
Allen, Tom, Jr
Anargyros, Spero
Anthonisen, George Rioch
Bugbee, Joan Scott
Cook, Robert Howard
Coppola, Andrew
d'Andrea, Albert Philip
De Bellis, Hannibal
De Nike, Michael Nicholas
Dryfoos, Nancy
Edvi Illes, George
Eliscu, Frank
Frudakis, Evangelos William
Goff, Thomas Jefferson
Gregory, Angela
Grigor, Margaret Christian
Grove, Edward Ryneal
Hancock, Walker (Kirtland)
Holbrook, Elizabeth Bradford
Jacobs, Peter Alan
Jacobsson, Sten Wilhelm John
Jones, (Charles) Dexter (Weatherbee), III
Jones, Elizabeth
Kaufman, Mico
Kujundzic, Zeljko D
Macomber, Allison
Mankowski, Bruno
Miller, Donald Richard
Miller, Richard McDermott
Newmark, Marilyn (Marilyn Newmark Meiselman)
Nicodemus, Chester Roland
Parella, Albert Lucian
Pineda, Marianna (Marianna Pineda Tovish)
Posey, Leslie Thomas
Reed, Hal
Roberts, Gilroy
Roseberg, Carl Andersson
Rosse, Maryvonne
Rotholz, Rina
Rush, Jon N
Svenson, John Edward
Turano, Don
Van Wolf, Henry
Weinberg, Elbert

MOSAIC ARTIST

Ames, Arthur Forbes
Blameuser, Mary Fleurette
Califf, Marilyn Iskiwitz
Cariola, Robert J
Cox, Allyn
Crume, Gregg

de Turczynowicz, Wanda (Mrs Eliot Hermann)
Eide, Palmer
Fogel, Seymour
Gach, George
Golden, Libby
Jung, Yee Wah
Kjargaard, John Ingvard
Kreilick, Marjorie E
Lewis, Elizabeth Matthew
Mueller, M Gerardine
Newport, Esther
Partridge, David Gerry
Pattee, Rowena
Reardon, Mary A
Reynal, Jeanne
Ruta, Peter Paul
Schwarz, Myrtle Cooper
Seyle, Robert Harley
Smith, Emily Guthrie
Sommerburg, Miriam
Steinfels, Melville P
Tait, Katharine Lamb
Tobias, Abraham Joel
Watrous, James Scales
Zweerts, Arnold

MURALIST

Ahysen, Harry Joseph
Alcopley, L
Aldwinckle, Eric
Allen, Tom, Jr
Altabe, Joan Berg
Amen, Irving
Anderson, Guy Irving
Andrade, Edna Wright
Anguiano, Raul
Arcilesi, Vincent J
Arnold, Richard R
Asante, Kwasi Seitu (Robin Okeeffer Harper)
Backus, Standish, Jr
Barnes, Carroll
Barr, Norman
Barton, John Murray
Baskerville, Charles
Beal, Jack
Beaver, Fred
Beckmann, Robert Owen
Beitz, Lester U
Belkin, Arnold
Benedict, Nan M
Benge, David Philip
Bentley, Claude
Berkowitz, Leon
Berresford, Virginia
Besner, J Jacques
Bessemer, Auriel
Biberman, Edward
Billings, Henry
Bireline, George Lee
Bittner, Hans Oskar
Boccia, Edward Eugene
Bock, William Sauts-Netamux'we
Bonamarte, Lou
Bonet, Jordi
Bookatz, Samuel
Bransby, Eric James
Brown, Hilton Edward
Brulc, Lillian G
Burt, Clyde Edwin
Buzzelli, Joseph Anthony
Byard, Carole Marie
Callahan, Kenneth
Cardinal, Marcelin
Cariola, Robert J
Case, Elizabeth
Cecere, Ada Rasario
Celender, Donald Dennis
Chesley, Paul Alexander
Cikovsky, Nicolai
Cleveland, Helen Barth
Colt, John Nicholson
Comes, Marcella
Condon, Lawrence James
Connolly, Jerome Patrick
Cook, Howard Norton
Cox, Allyn
Crane, Barbara Bachmann
Crimi, Alfred D
Crowell, Lucius
Crum, Jason Roger
Czimbalmos, Szabo Kalman
Davis, Alonzo Joseph
Day, Horace Talmage
De Botton, Jean Philippe
De Larios, Dora
DePillars, Murry N
De Weldon, Felix George Weihs
Dirube, Rolando Lopez
Drummond, (I G)
Dubaniewicz, Peter Paul
Dunkelman, Loretta
Edelson, Mary Beth
Eitel, Cliffe Dean
Epler, Venetia
Ewald, Louis
Ferris, (Carlisle) Keith
Fitzgerald, Edmond James
Fransioli, Thomas Adrian
Frazer, James Nisbet, Jr
Freund, Harry Louis
Freund, Tibor
Goff, Lloyd Lozes
Gold, Albert
Goldstein, Gladys Hack
Gonzalez, Jose Gamaliel
Goreleigh, Rex
Gray, Cleve
Gray, Gladys
Graziani, Sante
Green, Martin Leonard
Halberstadt, Ernst
Hall, John A
Hanlen, John (Garrett)
Harrison, Newton A
Haydon, Harold (Emerson)
Heberling, Glen Austin
Hee, Hon-Chew
Henderson, Victor (Lance)
Herfindahl, Lloyd Manford
Holbrook, Hollis Howard
Hollander, Gino F
Hoover, John Jay
Hopper, Frank J
Hovsepian, Leon
Hrdy, Olinka
Huntington, Daphne
Hurley, Wilson
Imana, Jorge Garron
Jackson, Suzanne Fitzallen
Jacobs, Ted Seth
Jaque, Louis
Jaudon, Valerie
Jenkins, Mary Anne K
Jensen, Pat
Johnson, Buffie
Johnson, Selina (Tetzlaff)
Jung, Kwan Yee
Jung, Yee Wah
Kauffman, (Camille) Andrene
Keene, Paul
Kemoha (George W Patrick Patterson)
Kester, Lenard
Killmaster, John H
Kinigstein, Jonah
Klitgaard, Georgina
Koch, Virginia Greenleaf
Kotin, Albert
Kreilick, Marjorie E
Kupferman, Murray
Laning, Edward
Larson, Sidney
Lassiter, Vernice (Vernice Lassiter Brown)
Laury, Jean Ray (Jean Ray Bitters)
Lax, David
Lazzari, Pietro
Lea, Tom
Leathers, Winston Lyle
Levee, John H
Lewis, Don
Lewis, Elizabeth Matthew
Lewis, Norman Wilfred
Lis, Janet Chapman
Lloyd, Tom
Lochrie, Elizabeth Davey
Loew, Michael
Lorcini, Gino
Loring, Clarice
Loring, John
Lunge, Jeffrey (Roy)
Macdonnell, Cameron
Magafan, Ethel
Magazzini, Gene
Magleby, Francis R (Frank)
Mangione, Patricia Anthony
Manship, John Paul
Marin, Augusto
Martin, Fletcher
Martin, G W
Martin, Lucille Caiar (Mrs Hampton Martin)
Martinez, Ernesto Pedregon
Martone, William Robert
Martyl (Martyl Schweig Langsdorf)
Marx, Nicki D
Massin, Eugene Max
Mattiello, Roberto
Maynard, Valerie
McCall, Robert Theodore
McCarty, Lorraine Chambers
McChesney, Clifton
McChesney, Robert Pearson
McClure, Constance M
McCoy, Ann
McCullough, David William
McDonnell, Joseph Anthony
McKie, Todd Stoddard
Merrick, James Kirk
Merrill, David Kenneth
Mesches, Arnold
Mesibov, Hugh
Messeguer, Villoro Benito
Messick, Ben (Newton)
Michaels, Glen
Midgette, Willard Franklin
Miller, Nancy
Moon, Marc
Mora, Francisco
Morehouse, William Paul
Morrow, Robert Earl
Mullen, Buell
Murray, Richard Deibel
Neff, Edith
Nesbitt, Lowell (Blair)
Neto, G Reis (Gilda Reis Netopuletti)
Noel, Georges
O'Gorman, Juan
Olson, Joseph Olaf
Ortlip, Paul Daniel
Ostuni, Peter W
Pace, Margaret Bosshardt
Palmer, William C
Parton, Ralf
Pekarsky, Mel (Melvin Hirsch)
Penney, James
Peters, Carl W
Pinto, Biagio
Quisgard, Liz Whitney
Rakocy, William (Joseph)
Ralston, James Kenneth
Raul Esparza S (Raul Esparza Sanchez)
Reardon, Mary A
Refregier, Anton
Regat, Jean Jacques
Regat, Mary E
Richard, Jack
Richardson, Frank, Jr
Riley, Bernard Joseph
Ringgold, Faith
Rippey, Clayton
Rivoli, Mario
Robertson, D Hall
Rogers, Peter Wilfrid
Rogovin, Mark
Romero, Mike
Ronald, William
Rose, Samuel
Ross, Fred (Joseph)
Rousseau-Vermette, Mariette
Rubenstein, Lewis W
St John, John Milton
Salemme, Lucia (Autorino)
Samerjan, George E
Schanker, Louis
Scheibe, Fred Karl
Schliefer, Stafford Lerrig
Seidel, Alexander Carl-Victor
Shadbolt, Jack Leonard
Shaw, Harry Hutchison
Sheets, Millard Owen
Sherker, Michael Z
Sibley, Charles Kenneth
Siebner, Herbert (Vom Siebenstein)
Sigel, Barry Chaim
Simon, Sidney
Singletary, Robert Eugene
Sitton, John M
Skemp, Robert Oliver
Slawinski, Joseph
Smart, Wini
Smith, Cecil Alden
Smith, Vincent D
Smith, William Arthur
Snow, Vivian Douglas
Spandorf, Lily Gabriella
Spurgeon, Sarah (Edna M)
Steinfels, Melville P
Stevens, Nelson L
Stevenson, Branson Graves
Stewart, Arthur
Stewart, Jack
Storm, Mark (Kennedy)
Strickland, Thomas J
Stroud, Peter Anthony
Stucki, Margaret Elizabeth
Sussman, Arthur
Tait, Cornelia Damian
Texoon, Jasmine
Thomas, John
Thorne, Gordon (Kit)
Thwaites, Charles Winstanley
Tobey, Alton S
Tobias, Abraham Joel
Tompkins, Alan
Treadwell, Helen
Van Aalten, Jacques
Van Brunt, Philip G
Vandenberge, Peter Willem
Vickery, Charles Bridgeman
Vrana, Albert S
Waddell, Eugene
Wagner, G Noble
Walker, William Walter
Wallace, John Edward
Warner, Boyd, Jr
Warshaw, Howard
Watrous, James Scales
Watson, Halen Richter
Weber, John Pitman
Welch, James Wymore
West, Clifford Bateman
Whitney, William Kuebler
Williams, William Terence
Willson, Robert
Wilson, Charles Banks
Wilson, York
Winter, H Edward
Woodruff, Hale A
Woodward, William
Wybrants-Lynch, Sharon
Yasko, Caryl Anne
Yoakum, Delmer J
Young, Cliff
Young, Joseph Louis
Zaidenberg, Arthur

MURALIST (cont)
Zallinger, Rudolph Franz
Zonia, Dhimitri

MUSEOLOGIST

Berg, Phil
Brown, John Carter
Carter, David Giles
Catlin, Stanton L
Condit, Louise
Craft, John Richard
Crouton, Francois (Francois LaFortune)
Cummins, Karen Gasco
Dailey, Charles Andrew (Chuck)
Dockstader, Frederick J
Dyck, Paul
Feldman, Arthur Mitchell
Fiori, Dennis Andrew
Gaines, William Robert
Harrington, La Mar
Herold, Donald G
Hoge, Robert Wilson
Holverson, John
Howard, Richard Foster
Hunter-Stiebel, Penelope (Penelope Hunter Stiebel)
Inverarity, Robert Bruce
Jakstas, Alfred John
Johnson, Evert Alfred
Jones, Frances Follin
Keeler, David Boughton
Lewis, Phillip Harold
Lochridge, Sudie Katherine
Lovato, Manuelita
Madigan, Mary Jean Smith
Marsh, Anne Steele
Mayer, Susan Martin
McGrath, Kyran Murray
McLanathan, Richard B K
Morley, Grace L McCann
Parsons, Merribell Maddux
Pendergraft, Norman Elveis
Perrot, Paul N
Perry, Mary-Ellen Earl
Pope, Annemarie Henle
Reiling, Susan Wallace
Richardson, Brenda
Rovetti, Paul F
Russell, Helen Diane
Scala, Joseph (A)
Schmidt, Stephen
Schwartz, Marvin D
Segger, Martin Joseph
Selig, J Daniel
Sheon, Aaron
Snodgrass, Jeanne Owens (Mrs M Eugene King)
Sponenburgh, Mark
Stead, Rexford Arthur
Streetman, John William, III
Ullman, Mrs George W
Wallace, David Harold
Weeks, Edward F
Weil, Stephen Edward
Werner, Donald (Lewis)
Whitlock, John Joseph
Williams, Benjamin Forrest
Williams, Randalph Andrew
Wong, Jason

MUSEUM DIRECTOR

Adler, Sebastian J
Adlmann, Jan Ernst
Alinder, James Gilbert
Alling, Clarence (Edgar)
Amaya, Mario Anthony
Arkus, Leon Anthony
Armstrong, Thomas Newton, III
Atkinson, Tracy
Bach, Otto Karl
Baratte, John J
Barrow, Thomas Francis
Bass, John
Baur, John I H
Belz, Carl Irvin
Bengtz, Ture
Berman, Nancy Mallin
Bier, Justus
Bishop, Budd Harris
Bishop, Robert Charles
Bloch, Milton Joseph
Bodem, Dennis Richard
Boggs, Jean Sutherland
Botwinick, Michael
Boulton, Jack
Bowles, Thomas Andrew, III
Bowne, James Dehart
Boyce, William G
Boyer, Jack K
Boyle, Richard J
Brewer, Donald J
Brimhall, Mary Jane
Brody, Jacob Jerome
Brooke, David Stopford
Broussard, Jay Remy
Brown, James Monroe, III
Brown, John Carter
Brown, Richard F
Bryant, Edward Albert
Buck, Robert Treat, Jr
Buechner, Thomas Scharman
Bullard, Edgar John, III
Bush, Martin Harry
Butts, H Daniel, III
Byrnes, James Bernard
Cabrera, Geles
Capa, Cornell
Carmichael, Jae
Carpenter, Gilbert Frederick (Bert)
Carpenter, Harlow
Carter, David Giles
Chernow, Burt
Chester, Janie Kathleen
Chetham, Charles
Chew, Paul Albert
Chipp, Herschel Browning
Christison, Muriel B
Clark, Fred, Jr
Coke, F Van Deren
Collier, Ric
Colt, Priscilla C
Colt, Thomas C, Jr
Craft, John Richard
Cumming, Glen Edward
Cunningham, Charles Crehore
Czach, Marie
Dailey, Charles Andrew (Chuck)
de Borhegyi, Suzanne Sims
Dempsey, Bruce Harvey
Dennison, Keith Elkins
Dentzel, Carl Schaefer
Dibner, Martin
Dietrich, Bruce Leinbach
Dixon, Albert George, III
Dockstader, Frederick J
Dodworth, Allen Stevens
Doherty, Robert J
Domit, Moussa M
Donahue, Kenneth
Duff, James H
Dwight, Edward Harold
Eckhardt, Ferdinand
Eitner, Lorenz E A
Eldredge, Charles Child, III
Elliott, B Charles, Jr
Elliott, James Heyer
Ellis, George Richard
Emerson, Roberta Shinn
Enman, Tom Kenneth
Enyeart, James Lyle
Evans, Bruce Haselton
Faison, Samson Lane, Jr
Farmer, John David
Farrell, Patric
Feldman, Arthur Mitchell
Ferguson, Charles
Fiori, Dennis Andrew
Fisher, James Donald
Forbes, Donna Marie
Forrest, James Taylor
Freudenheim, Tom Lippmann
Friedman, Martin
Gaither, Edmund B
Gallander, Cathleen S
Gamble, Kathryn Elizabeth
Garrett, Alan Thomas
Garrett, Stephen
Gatling, Eva Ingersoll
Gaudieri, Alexander V J
Geske, Norman Albert
Gilbert, Alma Magdalena
Glanz, Andrea Elise
Goodrich, Lloyd
Gordon, Joy L
Gray, Thomas Alexander
Greaver, Harry
Green, Eleanor Broome
Gregg, Richard Nelson
Grove, Richard
Gualtieri, Joseph P
Hadley, Rollin van Nostrand
Hadlock, Wendell Stanwood
Hagerstrand, Martin Allan
Halley, Donald M, Jr
Hallmark, Donald Parker
Hamilton, George Heard
Hammond, Natalie Hays
Hanna, Katherine
Hansen, Arne Rae
Harris, Paul Rogers
Hartt, Frederick
Hassrick, Peter H
Hathaway, Walter Murphy
Headley, Sherman Knight
Heinz, Susan
Henry, Stuart (Compton)
Herman, Lloyd Eldred
Herold, Donald G
Hickman, Ronald Dean
Hill, William Mansfield
Hinkhouse, Forest Melick
Hirsch, Richard Teller
Hodge, G Stuart
Hoffman, Larry Gene
Hoge, Robert Wilson
Holverson, John
Hopkins, Henry Tyler
Hopkins, Kenneth R
Houlihan, Patrick Thomas
Howard, Richard Foster
Howarth, Shirley Reiff
Howe, Thomas Carr
Huchel, Frederick M
Hull, William Floyd
Hunt, David Curtis
Hutchinson, Janet L
Inverarity, Robert Bruce
Ishikawa, Joseph
Ivey, James Burnett
Jenkins, Donald John
Jones, Louis C
Jordan, William B
Kachel, Harold Stanley
Katzive, David H
Kenney, Allen Lloyd
Kiah, Virginia Jackson
Klep, Rolf
Kohler, Ruth DeYoung
Koshalek, Richard
Kotun, Henry Paul
Kowalek, Jon W
Kropf, Joan R
Krushenick, John
Kuchta, Ronald A
Kwiecinski, Chester Martin
Lacy, Bettie
Landwehr, William Charles
Lauck, Anthony Joseph
Laurer, Robert A
Leavitt, Thomas Whittlesey
Lee, Sherman Emery
Leeper, John Palmer
Leet, Richard Eugene
Lefebvre d'Argence, Rene-Yvon
Lehman, Arnold L
Lein, Malcolm Emil
Lerner, Abram
Lewis, Virginia Elnora
Libby, Gary Russell
Lindemann, Edna M
Long, Walter Kinscella
Malone, Lee H B
Mandle, Earl Roger
Mayhew, Edgar De Noailles
Maytham, Thomas Northrup
McCready, Eric Scott
McFadden, Mary
McGregor, Jack R
Meinig, Laurel
Messer, Thomas M
Miller, Joan Vita
Miller, Samuel Clifford
Mills, Paul Chadbourne
Mitchell, Jeffrey Malcolm
Mitchell, Wallace (MacMahon)
Moore, Russell James
Mooz, R Peter
Morley, Grace L McCann
Morrin, Peter Patrick
Morris, Jack Austin, Jr
Muhlberger, Richard Charles
Muhlert, Jan Keene
Myer, Peter Livingston
Myers, Fred A
Newton, Douglas
Newton, Earle Williams
Newton, Francis John
Noble, Joseph Veach
Oldenburg, Richard Erik
Olkinetzky, Sam
Ostrow, Stephen Edward
Ott, Wendell Lorenz
Page, Addison Franklin
Pahl, James Robert, II
Parker, Harry S, III
Paul, William D, Jr
Paulin, Richard Calkins
Peladeau, Marius Beaudoin
Perrot, Paul N
Peterson, John Douglas
Petty, John L, Jr
Phillips, Laughlin
Pope, John Alexander
Powell, Earl Alexander, III
Prokopoff, Stephen Stephen
Rainey, Froelich Gladstone
Rathbone, Perry Townsend
Ray, Jim
Rhodes, Reilly Patrick
Richard, George Mairet
Robbins, Daniel J
Robbins, Warren M
Robert, Henry Flood, Jr
Robinson, Franklin W
Rogers, Charles B
Rogers, Millard Foster, Jr
Rose, Timothy G
Rovetti, Paul F
Sachs, Samuel, II
Sanguinetti, Eugene F
Scarbrough, Cleve Knox, Jr
Schmidt, Stephen
Schorgl, Thomas Barry
Segger, Martin Joseph
Selig, J Daniel
Shalkop, Robert Leroy
Shapshak, Rene
Shestack, Alan
Shuck, Kenneth Menaugh
Silvia, Judith Heidler Richardson
Sipiora, Leonard Paul
Sloane, Joseph Curtis
Sloshberg, Leah Phyfer
Smith, Gordon Mackintosh

Smith, James Morton
Smith, Paul J
Smith, Robert Lewis
Solley, Thomas Treat
Spear, Richard Edmund
Stars, William Kenneth
Stead, Rexford Arthur
Steadman, David Wilton
Steen, Ronald Earl
Stitt, Susan (Margaret)
Story, William Easton
Strel, Donald O
Stuart, Joseph Martin
Sullivan, Max William
Talbot, Jarold Dean
Taylor, Joshua Charles
Taylor, Lisa
Taylor, Rene Claude
Teitz, Richard Stuart
Thomas, Elaine Freeman
Timms, Peter Rowland
Tolles, Bryant Franklin, Jr
Tong, Marvin Enoch
Townsend, J Benjamin
Turk, Rudy H
Turner, Evan Hopkins
Ulrich, Edwin Abel
Vanco, John Leroy
van der Marck, Jan
Varian, Elayne H
Victor, Mary O'Neill
Vigtel, Gudmund
Vitale, Lydia Modi
Walker, Herbert Brooks
Walkey, Frederick P
Wallace, David Harold
Waller, Aaron Bret
Wardwell, Allen
Watrous, John
Wattenmaker, Richard J
Waufle, Alan Duane
Wecker, Christoph Ulrich
Weil, Stephen Edward
Weinhardt, Carl Joseph, Jr
Weller, Allen Stuart
West, Richard Vincent
Whitlock, John Joseph
Wiederspan, Stan
Wilder, Mitchell Armitage
Wilkins, David George
Wilkinson, Ruth Murphy
Williams, Marylou Lord Study
Wilson, Martha Storey
Wittmann, Otto
Wolfe, Maurice Raymond
Wong, Jason
Wooden, Howard Edmund
Woods, Willis Franklin
Wright, Barton Allen
Wyrick, Charles Lloyd, Jr (Pete)
Yassin, Robert Alan

PAINTER

Acrylic, Oil

Aalund, Suzy
Aaron, Evalyn (Wilhelmina)
Abany, Albert Charles
Abbatecola (Oronzo)
Abbett, Robert Kennedy
Abdalla, Nick
Abeita, Jim
Abrams, Herbert E
Achepohl, Keith Anden
Acker, Perry Miles
Acosta, Manuel Gregorio
Adams, Glenn Nelson
Adams, Katherine Langhorne
Adams, Mark
Adan, Suzanne Rae
Adkison, Kathleen (Gemberling)
Adler, Lee
Adler, Robert
Adler, Samuel (Marcus)
Adrian, Barbara (Mrs Franklin Tramutola)
Agostinelli, Mario
Ahl, Henry C
Ahrendt, Christine
Ahysen, Harry Joseph
Airola, Paavo
Ajay, Abe
Akawie, Thomas Frank
Albertazzi, Mario
Albin, Edgar A
Alexander, John E
Alf, Martha Joanne
Allen, Clarence Canning
Allen, Margo (Mrs Harry Shaw)
Allen, Patricia (Patricia Allen Bott)
Allgood, Charles Henry
Allman, Margo
Altabe, Joan Berg
Altman, Harold
Altmann, Henry S
Altschuler, Franz
Altvater, Catherine Tharp
Amarotico, Joseph Anthony
Amen, Irving
Ames, Jean Goodwin
Amster, Sally
Anderson, Gunnar Donald
Anderson, Ivan Delos
Anderson, Robert Raymond
Andrade, Edna Wright
Andrejevic, Milet
Andrus, James Roman
Angel, Rifka
Angelo, Emidio
Angeloch, Robert (Henry)
Anguiano, Raul
Angulo, Chappie
Anthony, William Graham
Anzures, Rafael
Appel, Karel
Appleman, David Earl
Aquino, Edmundo
Archer, Dorothy Bryant
Archer, Edmund
Arcilesi, Vincent J
Ard, Saradell (Saradell Ard Frederick)
Armitage, Frank
Armstrong, Roger Joseph
Arnest, Bernard
Arnholm, Ronald Fisher
Arnold, Florence M
Arnold, Richard R
Aronson, Boris
Asante, Kwasi Seitu (Robin Okeeffer Harper)
Ashbaugh, Dennis John
Asher, Elise
Asher, Lila Oliver
Askild, Anita (Anita Askild Feinstein)
Asoma, Tadashi
Athena
Atirnomis (Rita Simon)
Atkins, Rosalie Marks
Atkyns, (Willie) Lee, Jr
Atlee, Emilie DeS
Austin, Darrel
Auth, Robert R
Avakian, John
Aylon, Helene
Aymar, Gordon Christian
Azaceta, Luis Cruz
Azuma, Norio
Baber, Alice
Bach, Dirk
Bach, Otto Karl
Bacigalupa, Andrea
Badash, Sandi Borr
Baeder, John
Baer, Jo
Bailey, James Arlington, Jr
Bailey, Malcolm C W
Bailey, Walter Alexander
Bailey, William H
Baker, Dina Gustin
Baker, Grace
Baker, Ralph Bernard
Bakke, Larry Hubert
Balance, Jerrald Clark
Balazs-Pottasch, Gyongyi
Bales, Jewel
Ball, Lyle V
Ball, Walter Neil
Balossi, John
Bama, James E
Bandel, Lennon Raymond
Banister, Robert Barr
Bannard, Walter Darby
Baranik, Rudolf
Baranoff, Mort
Barber, Samir
Bard, Joellen
Bardazzi, Peter
Bardin, Jesse Redwin
Baringer, Richard E
Barnes, Curt (Curtis Edward)
Barnet, Will
Barnett, Earl D
Barnwell, John L
Barooshian, Martin
Barowitz, Elliott
Barr, David John
Barr, Norman
Barreres, Domingo
Barrett, Robert Dumas
Barrio, Raymond
Barron, Ros
Barr-Sharrar, Beryl
Bart, Elizabeth (Elizabeth Bart Gerald)
Bartlett, Robert Webster
Bartnick, Harry William
Barton, August Charles
Barton, Georgie Read
Bashor, John W
Baskerville, Charles
Bass, David Loren
Bass, Ruth Gilbert
Bateman, Robert McLellan
Bateman, Ronald C
Bates, Betsey
Bates, Maxwell Bennett
Batt, Miles Girard
Batuz
Bayer, Herbert
Baynard, Ed
Baz, Marysole Worner
Beach, Warren
Beall, Joanna
Beaman, Richard Bancroft
Beament, Harold
Bear, Marcelle L
Beard, Marion L Patterson
Beard, Richard Elliott
Beattie, George
Beauchamp, John R
Beaumont, Mona M
Bechtle, Robert Alan
Beck, Margit
Beck, Rosemarie (Rosemarie Beck Phelps)
Beck, Stephen R
Becker, Bettie (Bettie Geraldine Wathall)
Becker, Charlotte (Mrs Walter Cox)
Becker, Natalie Rose
Beckmann, Robert Owen
Beeler, Joe (Neil)
Beerman, Miriam H
Beery, Arthur O
Beery, Eugene Brian
Behl, Marjorie
Bejar, Feliciano
Beker, Gisela
Belkin, Arnold
Bell, Charles S
Bell, Coca (Mary Catlett Bell)
Bell, Evelyn Behnan
Bell, Peter Alan
Belle, Anna (Anna Belle Birckett)
Benda, Richard R
Bendell, Marilyn
Bender, Bill
Benedict, Nan M
Benham, Robert Charles
Benjamin, Karl Stanley
Bennett, Don Bemco
Bennett, Rainey
Benney, Robert
Benno, Benjamin G
Bentley, Claude
Beny, Roloff
Berd, Morris
Berg, Thomas
Berger, Jason
Berguson, Robert Jenkins
Berkman, Aaron
Berkowitz, Leon
Berlind, Robert
Berlyn, Sheldon
Berman, Ariane R
Berman, Fred J
Berman, Rebecca Robbins
Berman, Steven M
Bernay, Betti
Berneche, Jerry Douglas
Bernstein, Gerald
Bernstein, Sylvia
Bernstein, Theresa
Berresford, Virginia
Berry, Glenn
Berthot, Jake
Betensky, Rose Hart
Bettinson, Brenda
Betts, Edward Howard
Bevlin, Marjorie Elliott
Bhavsar, Natvar Prahladji
Bianco, Pamela Ruby
Biberman, Edward
Bice, Clare
Bidner, Robert D H
Bieler, Andre Charles
Bierk, David Charles
Bieser, Natalie
Bigelow, Chandler, II
Binai, Paul Freye
Binford, Julien
Bireline, George Lee
Birkin, Morton
Birnbaum, Mildred
Bischoff, Elmer Nelson
Bishop, Benjamin
Bishop, Isabel (Mrs Harold G Wolff)
Bishop, James
Bishop, Marjorie Cutler
Black, Frederick (Edward)
Black, Lisa
Blacketer, James Richard
Blackwell, Thomas Leo
Blagden, Thomas P
Blahove, Marcos
Blaine, Nell
Blair, Carl Raymond
Blair, Jeanette Anne
Blair, Robert Noel
Blakely, Joyce (Carol)
Blakeslee, Sarah (Sarah Blakeslee Speight)
Blameuser, Mary Fleurette
Blatas, Arbit
Block, Amanda Roth
Blodgett, Anne Washington
Bloom, Donald Stanley
Bloom, Hyman
Blos, Peter W
Bluhm, Norman
Blumberg, Barbara Griffiths
Blumberg, Ron
Blumenthal, Fritz
Boal, Sara Metzner
Boardman, Seymour
Boccia, Edward Eugene
Bock, William Sauts-Netamux'we

PAINTER (cont)
Boedeker, Arnold E (Boedie)
Boeve, Edgar Gene
Bogaev, Ronni (Ronni Bogaev Greenstein)
Bogart, George A
Bogart, Richard Jerome
Bogdanovic, Bogomir
Bogorad, Alan Dale
Bogucki (Edwin Arnold Bogucki)
Bolmgren, Donna Hollen
Bolotowsky, Ilya
Bolton, James
Bond, Oriel Edmund
Bonevardi, Marcelo
Bongart, Sergei R
Boni, Delmar
Bookbinder, Jack
Booth, Cameron
Booth, George Warren
Boothe, Power Robert
Bopp, Emery
Boren, James Erwin
Boretz, Naomi
Borgatta, Robert Edward
Boris, Bessie
Borofsky, Jon
Borstein, Elena
Bosa, Louis
Bosin, Blackbear
Bostelle, Thomas (Theodore)
Bostick, William Allison
Boterf, Chester Arthur (Check)
Bothwell, Dorr
Botto, Richard Alfred
Bouchard, Lorne Holland
Boucher, Tania Kunsky
Boughton, William Harrison
Bouras, Harry D
Boutis, Tom
Bove, Richard
Bowen, Helen Eakins
Bower, Gary David
Bowers, Cheryl Olsen
Bowers, Lynn Chuck
Bowler, Joseph, Jr
Bowling, Frank
Bowman, Bruce
Bowman, Jean (Jean Bowman Magruder)
Bowman, Ken
Bowman, Richard
Boxer, Stanley (Robert)
Boylan, John Lewis
Boz, Alex (Alex Bozickovic)
Bradford, Howard
Bradley, Dorothy
Bradley, Peter Alexander
Bradshaw, Robert George
Brady, Charles Michael
Bragar, Philip Frank
Brainard, Owen
Braley, Jean Duffield
Brams, Joan
Brandfield, Kitty
Brandt, Warren
Bransky, Miriam (Miriam Ann Gilden)
Brawley, Robert Julius
Breiger, Elaine
Brendel, Bettina
Brenner, Mabel
Breslin, Wynn
Brice, William
Brigadier, Anne
Brightwell, Walter
Bristow, William Arthur
Britt, Sam Glenn
Broadd, Harry Andrew
Brodsky, Judith Kapstein
Brodsky, Stan
Brody, Arthur William
Bromberg, Faith
Bromund, Cal E
Broner, Robert
Brook, Alexander
Brooks, Bruce W
Brooks, Frank Leonard
Brooks, James
Brooks, (John) Alan
Brooks, Robert
Broomfield, Adolphus George
Bross, Albert L, Jr
Brough, Richard Burrell
Brouillette, Al
Broussard, Normaj
Brown, Bruce Robert
Brown, Judith Gwyn
Brown, Peggy Ann
Brown, Peter C
Browne, Syd J
Browne, Tom Martin
Browne, Vivian E
Brownett, Thelma Denyer
Browning, Colleen
Brucker, Edmund
Bruder, Harold Jacob
Brulc, Lillian G
Bruneau, Kittie
Bruno, Vincent J
Brusca, Jack
Brustlein, Daniel
Brzozowski, Richard Joseph
Buckley, Mary L (Mrs Joseph M Parriott)
Bucknall, Malcolm Roderick
Buckner, Kay Lamoreux
Buecker, Robert
Bueno, Jose (Joe Goode)
Bumgardner, James Arliss
Bunce, Louis DeMott
Bunker, George
Bunn, Cecine Cole
Bunts, Frank
Burford, Byron Leslie
Burger, W Carl
Burgess, Joseph James, Jr
Burggraf, Ray Lowell
Burke, Daniel V
Burke, E Ainslie
Burkert, Robert Randall
Burko, Diane
Burnett, Calvin
Burnett, Patricia Hill
Burns, Jerome
Burns, Josephine
Burns, Paul Callan
Burns, Sheila
Burns, Stan
Burnside, Katherine Talbott
Buros, Luella
Burpee, James Stanley
Burroughs, Margaret T G
Burt, Dan
Busch, Julia M
Butchkes, Sydney
Butler, James D
Butler, Joseph (Green)
Byard, Carole Marie
Byrd, D Gibson
Byron, Gene
Caddell, Foster
Cade, Walter, III
Cadmus, Paul
Cady, Dennis Vern
Caglioti, Victor
Caimite (Lynne Ruskin)
Cain, Joseph Alexander
Caiserman-Roth, Ghitta
Cajori, Charles F
Calderon, Juan
Calkin, Carleton Ivers
Calkins, Kingsley Mark
Calle, Paul
Callicott, Burton Harry
Camblin, Bob Bilyeu
Cameron, Eric
Camins, Jacques Joseph
Campbell, David Paul
Campbell, Gretna
Campbell, (James) Lawrence
Campbell, Jewett
Campbell, Richard Horton
Canin, Martin
Cannon, T C (Tom Wayne)
Canright, Sarah Anne
Cantine, David
Cantrell, Jim
Cardman, Cecilia
Cardoso, Anthony
Carlin, James
Carlin, Robert Eugene
Carlos, (James) Edward
Carlson, Cynthia J
Carlson, Jane C
Carmichael, Donald Ray
Carmichael, Jae
Carpenter, Earl L
Carrero, Jaime
Carrington, Joy Harrell
Carron, Maudee Lilyan
Carswell, Rodney
Carter, Clarence Holbrook
Carter, Frederick Timmins
Cartmell, Helen
Carulla, Ramon
Casarella, Edmond
Casas, Fernando Rodriguez
Casas, Melesio
Cassanelli, Victor Vi
Cassara, Frank
Castano, Giovanni
Castellon, Rolando
Caswell, Helen Rayburn
Catchi (Catherine O Childs)
Catok, Lottie Meyer
Cattell, Ray
Catusco, Louis
Cavallon, Giorgio
Cavanaugh, Tom Richard
Cavat, Irma
Caver, William Ralph
Celentano, Francis Michael
Cervenka, Barbara
Chadeayne, Robert Osborne
Chambers, John
Chapian, Grieg Hovsep
Chaplin, George Edwin
Chapman, Howard Eugene
Chapman, Walter Howard
Chappell, Berkley Warner
Charlot, Martin Day
Chase, Saul Alan
Chavez-Morado, Jose
Cheatham, Frank Reagan
Chen Chi
Cherepov, George
Chernow, Ann
Cheshire, Craig Gifford
Chesney, Lee R, Jr
Chethlahe (David Chethlahe Paladin)
Chieffo, Clifford Toby
Childers, Richard Robin
Chinn, Yuen Yuey
Chinni, Peter Anthony
Chodkowski, Henry, Jr
Christensen, Ronald Julius
Christensen, Ted
Christiana, Edward
Chuey, Robert Arnold
Churchill, Diane
Ciarrochi, Ray
Cicero, Carmen L
Cikovsky, Nicolai
Cintron, Joseph
Civitello, John Patrick
Clapsaddle, Jerry
Clark, Claude
Clark, Eliot Candee
Clark, Michael Vinson
Clark, R Dane
Clark, Robert Charles
Clarke, John Clem
Cleveland, Robert Earl
Clifton, Jack Whitney
Clifton, Michelle Gamm
Clinedinst, Katherine Parsons
Clive, Richard R
Cloar, Carroll
Close, Chuck
Close, Dean Purdy
Close, Marjorie (Perry)
Clutz, William
Clymer, Albert Anderson
Coburn, Bette Lee Dobry
Cochran, George McKee
Coelho, Luiz Carlos
Coen, Arnaldo
Coffey, Douglas Robert
Coggeshall, Calvert
Cogswell, Dorothy McIntosh
Coheleach, Guy Joseph
Coiner, Charles Toucey
Coker, Carl David
Colarusso, Corrine Camille
Cole, Donald
Cole, Joyce
Cole, Max
Coleman, Michael
Collier, Alan Caswell
Collins, John Ireland
Collins, Lowell Daunt
Collins, Paul
Collins, William Charles
Colon-Morales, Rafael
Colson, Chester E
Colt, John Nicholson
Colville, Alexander
Colway, James R
Conant, Howard Somers
Congdon, William (Grosvenor)
Connery, Ruth M
Connett, Dee M
Connolly, Jerome Patrick
Conrad, Nancy R
Constantine, Greg John
Consuegra, Hugo
Coochsiwukioma, DH (Del Honanie)
Cook, August Charles
Cook, Gladys Emerson
Cook, Peter (Geoffrey)
Cooley, Adelaide Nation
Cooper, Anthony J
Cooper, Lucille Baldwin
Cooper, Mario
Cooper, Marve H
Cooper, Ron
Cooper, Wayne
Copeland, Lila
Copley, William Nelson
Cord, Orlando
Corish, Joseph Ryan
Cormier, Robert John
Cornelius, Marty
Cornell, Thomas Browne
Cornin, Jon
Coronel, Pedro
Corr, James Donat
Correa, Flora Horst
Cortlandt, Lyn
Cortright, Steven M
Corzas, Francisco
Costa, Olga
Couper, Charles Alexander
Court, Lee Winslow
Covington, Harrison Wall
Cowan, Thomas Bruce
Cowles, Fleur
Cox, Gardner
Cox, Marion Averal
Craft, Douglas D
Craig, Nancy Ellen
Cramer, Richard Charles
Craner, Robert Rogers
Crawford, Mel
Crawford, Ralston
Creatore, Mary-Alice
Creech, Franklin Underwood
Creecy, Herbert Lee, Jr
Cretara, Domenic Anthony
Crile, Susan
Criquette (Ruth DuBarry Montague)

Crittenden, John William Neil
Croft, Lewis Scott
Cronin, Robert (Lawrence)
Crooks, W Spencer
Cross, Maria Concetta Catherine
Cross, Watson, Jr
Crotto, Paul
Crovello, William George
Crowell, Lucius
Crown, Keith Allen
Crum, Jason Roger
Crumbo, Minisa
Crump, Walter Moore
Cruz, Emilio
Cruz, Hector
Crystal, Boris
Culbertson, Janet Lynn (Mrs Douglas Kaften)
Cummings, David William
Cunningham, (Charles) Bruce
Cunningham, Francis
Cunningham, J
Currie, Bruce
Curry, Noble Wilbur
Curtis, Mary Cranfill
Curtis, Philip Campbell
Curtis, Roger William
Cusick, Nancy Taylor
Cuthbert, Virginia
Cutler, Grayce E
Czimbalmos, Magdolna Paal
Da Cunha, Julio
D'Agostino, Vincent
Dagys, Jacob
Dailey, Charles Andrew (Chuck)
Dailey, Michael Dennis
Daisy (Daisy Black Langhauser)
d'Alessio, Gregory
d'Almeida, George
Daly, Kathleen (Kathleen Daly Pepper)
Damron, John Clarence
Dance, Robert Bartlett
Danieli, Fidel Angelo
Daphnis-Avlon, Helen
D'Arista, Robert
Darr, William Humiston
Darrah, Ann Clarke
Darton, Christopher
Dasburg, Andrew Michael
Dash, Harvey Dwight
Daskaloff, Gyorgy
David, Don Raymond
Davidek, Stefan
Davidson, Allan Albert
Davidson, Herbert Laurence
Davidson, Morris
Davies, Kenneth Southworth
Davis, Alonzo Joseph
Davis, Bradley Darius
Davis, Donald Robert
Davis, Gene
Davis, Harry Allen
Davis, Lew E
Davis, Phil Douglas
Davis, Ronald Wendel
Davis, Walter Lewis
Dawley, Joseph William
Dawson, Bess Phipps
Dawson, Eve
Dawson, John Allan
Day, Horace Talmage
Day, John
Deaderick, Joseph
Dean, Peter
Debassige, Blake R
De Blasi, Anthony Armando
Dechar, Peter
De Diego, Julio
Dee, Leo Joseph
Deem, George
Defeo, Jay
De Forest, Roy Dean
de Garthe, William Edward
deGooyer, Kirk Alan
De Groat, George Hugh
Dehn, Virginia
De Kergommeaux, Duncan
De Knight, Avel
de Kooning, Elaine Marie Catherine
de Lama, Alberto
Delaney, Joseph
De La Vega, Antonio
De Leeuw, Leon
de Lesseps, Tauni
Della-Volpe, Ralph Eugene
Deloney, Jack Clouse
DeLonga, Leonard Anthony
Delson, Elizabeth
DeLuigi, Janice Cecilia
de Martelly, John Stockton
De Mille, Leslie Benjamin
de Miskey, Julian
Denby, Jillian
Denis, Paul Andre S
Dennis, Cherre Nixon
Dennis, Roger Wilson
Dennison, Dorothy (Dorothy Dennison Butler)
Denniston, Douglas
De Ruth, Jan
Desmidt, Thomas H
des Rioux, Deena (Victoria Coty)
Deutsch, Peter Andrew
Devlin, Harry
Dew, James Edward
De Weldon, Felix George Weihs
Dewey, Kenneth Francis
Dibble, Charles Ryder
Dibble, George
Dickerson, Betty
Dickerson, Daniel Jay
Dickey, Helen Pauline
Diebenkorn, Richard
Diehl, Sevilla S
Dieringer, Ernest A
di Gioia, Frank
Dike, Philip Latimer
Dillon, Paul Sanford
Dinnerstein, Simon A
Dobbs, John Barnes
Dodd, Lois
Dodge, Joseph Jeffers
Dominique, John August
Donaldson, Marjory (Rogers)
Donde, Olga
Dooley, Helen Bertha
Doolin, James Lawrence
Dorn, Ruth (Ruth Dornbush)
Dorst, Claire V
Douaihy, Saliba
Doudera, Gerard
Douglas, Edwin Perry
Douke, Daniel W
Dragul, Sandra Kaplan
Draper, William Franklin
Dreiband, Laurence
Dreskin, Jeanet Steckler
Drewelowe, Eve
Drewes, Werner
Drexler, Lynne
Dreyer, Margaret Webb
Driggs, Elsie
Droege, Anthony Joseph, II
Drummond, Sally Hazelet
Drutz, June
Duback, Charles S
Dubin, Ralph
Duca, Alfred Milton
Duis, Rita (Rita Duis Astley-Bell)
Du Jardin, Gussie
Dulac, Margarita Walker
Duncan, (Eleanore) Klari
Duncan, Ruth
Dunkelman, Loretta
Dunlap, Loren Edward
Dunn, Cal
Du Pre, Grace Annette
Durham, William
Dworzan, George R
Dwyer, James Eugene
Dyson, John Holroyd
Dzigurski, Alex
Dzubas, Friedel
Eagleboy, Wayne
Eames, John Heagan
Easley, Loyce Rogers
Eastman, Gene M
Ebie, William Dennis
Ecke, Betty Tseng Yu-Ho
Eckert, Lou
Eckert, William Dean
Eckstein, Ruth
Eddy, Don
Edelheit, Martha
Eden, F Brown
Edge, Douglas Benjamin
Edie, Stuart
Edvi Illes, George
Edwards, Stanley Dean
Egeli, Peter Even
Ehrig, William Columbus
Eilers, Fred (Anton Frederick)
Eisenberg, Sonja Miriam
Eisentrager, James A
Eisinger, Harry
Elder, Muldoon
Eldredge, Stuart Edson
Eliason, Shirley (Shirley Eliason Haupt)
Eliot, Lucy Carter
Elliott, Ronnie
Ellis, Richard
Ellis, Robert Carroll
Ellison, Nancy
Else, Robert John
Elzea, Rowland Procter
Engelson, Carol
Engeran, Whitney John, Jr
Engle, Barbara Jean
Engle, Chet
Engle, George Richard
English, John Arbogast
Enman, Tom Kenneth
Eppink, Helen Brenan
Eppink, Norman R
Eres, Eugenia
Ericson, Beatrice
Ericson, Ernest
Ernst, James Arnold
Eshoo, Robert
Eshraw, Ra
Estes, Richard
Etnier, Stephen Morgan
Ettenberg, Franklin Joseph
Etter, Howard Lee
Etting, Emlen
Ettinger, Susi Steinitz
Evans, Burford Elonzo
Evans, John
Evans, Richard
Everett, Len G
Evett, Kenneth Warnock
Evjen, Rudolph Berndt
Ewald, Louis
Ewing, Edgar Louis
Eyre, Ivan
Fabe, Robert
Faden, Lawrence Steven
Fagg, Kenneth (Stanley)
Faiers, Edward Spencer (Ted)
Fainter, Robert A
Falconieri, Virginia
Farber, Maya M
Fares, William O
Farm, Gerald E
Farnham, Alexander
Farruggio, Remo Michael
Faulkner, Frank
Fax, Elton Clay
Fay, Joe
FeBland, Harriet
Feder, Ben
Feigin, Marsha
Feigl, Doris Louise
Fein, Stanley
Feininger, T Lux
Feist, Warner David
Felter, James Warren
Fenton, Alan
Fenton, Howard Carter
Ferber, Herbert
Ferguson, Edward Robert
Feriola, James Philip
Ferris, (Carlisle) Keith
Ferris, Edythe
Fett, William F
Feuerherm, Kurt K
Fichter, Herbert Francis
Field, Philip Sidney
Fife, Mary (Mrs Edward Laning)
Figures, Alfred
Fillerup, Mel
Fincher, John H
Fine, Perle
Fink, Louis R
Finkelstein, Louis
Finn, David
Finson, Hildred A
Fiore, Joseph A
Firfires, Nicholas Samuel
Fish, Richard G
Fisher Joel A
Fisher, Vernon
Fisk, Evi Ester
Flack, Audrey L
Fleckenstein, Opal R
Flecker, Maurice Nathan
Fleisher, Pat
Flint, Leroy W
Flowers, Thomas Earl
Fludd, Reginald Joseph
Fluek, Toby
Foley, Kyoko Y
Foosaner, Judith Ann
Ford, Ruth Vansickle
Forester, Russell
Forge, Andrew Murray
Forman, Alice
Forman, Kenneth Warner
Formigoni, Maurie Monihon
Forsberg, Jim
Forsman, Chuck (Charles Stanley Forsman)
Fortess, Karl E
Fosburgh, James Whitney
Foster, Holland
Fournier, Alexander Paul
Fousek, Frank Daniel
Fowler, Mel
Fox, John
Frace, Charles Lewis
Frame, Robert (Aaron)
Frances, Harriette Anton
Francis, Sherron
Franklin, Charlotte White
Fransioli, Thomas Adrian
Fraser, Carol Hoorn
Frater, Hal
Fraze, Denny T
Frazer, John Thatcher
Frazier, Le Roy Dyyon
Fredericksen, Burton Baum
Freedman, Maurice
Freeman, David L
Freeman, Mark
Freeman, Robert Lee
Freilich, Ann
Freilicher, Jane
Freund, Harry Louis
Freund, Tibor
Frick, Robert Oliver
Friedensohn, Elias
Froman, Ramon Mitchell
Fromberg, LaVerne Ray
Fromboluti, Sideo
Fruhauf, Aline
Fuerst, Shirley Miller
Fukui, Nobu
Fuller, Emily (Emily Fuller Kingston)
Furr, Jim
Fussiner, Howard

PAINTER (cont)
Gabin, George Joseph
Gach, George
Gahman, Floyd
Gaines, William Robert
Galanin, Igor Ivanovich
Gale, William Henry
Galen, Elaine
Gammon, Juanita-La Verne
Gammon, Reginald Adolphus
Gantz, Ann Cushing
Garcia, Danny
Garcia Ponce, Fernando
Gardner, Joan A
Gardner, Susan Ross
Garey, Pat
Garman, Ed
Garnsey, Clarke Henderson
Garrison, Eve
Garston, Gerald Drexler
Garver, Jack
Garver, Walter Raymond
Garwood, Audrey
Gary, Jan (Mrs William D Gorman)
Gasparian, Armen Tigran
Gast, Michael Carl
Gatewood, Maud Florance
Gatrell, Robert Morris
Gaul, Arrah Lee
Gauthier, Joachim George
Gawboy, Carl
Gebhardt, Harold
Gebhardt, Peter Martin
Gechtoff, Sonia
Gehr, Mary (Mary Ray)
Geis, Milton Arthur
Geissman, Robert Glenn
Gekiere, Madeleine
Gelber, Samuel
Gelinas, Robert William
Gellman, Beah (Mrs William C McNulty)
Genius, Jeannette (Jeannette M McKean)
Gentry, Warren Miller
George, Richard Allan
Georges, Paul
Geran, Joseph, Jr
Gerardia, Helen
Gerhold, William Henry
Gersovitz, Sarah Valerie
Gerzso, Gunther
Gettinger, Edmond Walter
Giampaoli, James Francis
Gibbons, Hugh (James)
Gibson, James D
Gikow, Ruth (Ruth Gikow Levine)
Gilbert, Albert Earl
Gilbert, Clyde Lingle
Gilbert, Herb
Gilbert, Lionel
Gilbertson, Charlotte
Giles, Newell Walton, Jr
Gillespie, Dorothy Merle
Gillespie, Gregory Joseph
Gillette, W Dean
Gilmartin, F Thomas
Ginsburg, Estelle
Giobbi, Edward Gioachino
Giraudier, Antonio
Girona, Julio
Gliko, Carl Albert
Glorig, Ostor
Godwin, Judith Whitney
Godwin, Robert Kimball
Goedicke, Jean
Goedike, Shirl
Goell, Abby Jane
Goertz, Augustus Frederick
Goetz, Edith Jean
Goetz, Richard Vernon
Goff, Lloyd Lozes
Goings, Ralph
Golbin, Andree
Gold, Sharon Cecile
Goldberg, Arnold Herbert
Goldberg, Chaim
Goldberg, Joseph Wallace
Golden, Rolland Harve
Goldin, Leon
Goldman, Lester
Goldsmith, Elsa M
Goldstein, Howard
Goldstein, Nathan
Goldszer, Bath-Sheba
Golub, Leon Albert
Gomez, Sita
Gomez-Quiroz, Juan Manuel
Gonzales, Boyer
Gonzales, Carlotta (Mrs Richard Lahey)
Gonzalez, Jose Luis
Gonzalez-Tornero, Sergio
Good, Leonard
Goodacre, Glenna
Goodbred, Ray Edw
Goodman, Brenda Joyce
Goodman, Sidney
Goodrich, Susan
Goodridge, Lawrence Wayne
Goray, John C
Gorchov, Ron
Gordley, Marilyn F M
Gordley, Metz Tranbarger
Gordon, Josephine
Gordy, Robert P
Gore, Samuel Marshall
Gorelick, Shirley
Gorman, R C
Gorski, Daniel Alexander
Gorsline, Douglas Warner
Gough, Robert Alan
Gould, John Howard
Gourevitch, Jacqueline
Graham, Walter
Grandee, Joe Ruiz
Granstaff, William Boyd
Grass, Patty Patterson
Graupe-Pillard, Grace
Graves, Morris
Gray, Gladys
Gray, Jim
Greco, Anthony Joseph
Greco, Frank
Greeley, Charles Matthew
Green, Art
Green, Denise G
Green, George D
Green, Martin Leonard
Green, Samuel Magee
Greenberg, Gloria
Greenberg, Irwin
Greene, Ethel Maud
Greene, Stephen
Greenleaf, Esther (Hargrave)
Greenwood, William James
Greer, Walter Marion
Gregor, Harold Laurence
Gregory, Bruce
Grey, Estelle (Estelle Ashby)
Grigoriadis, Mary
Grigsby, Jefferson Eugene, Jr
Grissom, Freda Gill
Grissom, Kenneth Ryland, II
Groat, Hall Pierce
Groell, Theophil
Gronbeck, Jean
Grosch, Laura
Groshans, Werner (Emil)
Gross, Earl
Gross, Irene (Irene Gross Berzon)
Gross, Sandra Lerner
Grosser, Maurice
Grossman, Morton
Grosz, Franz Joseph
Grotz, Dorothy Rogers
Grove, Edward Ryneal
Groves, Naomi Jackson
Gruber, Aaronel De Roy
Grucza, Leo (Victor)
Grupp, Carl Alf
Gruppe, Charles
Gruppe, Emile Albert
Gualtieri, Joseph P
Guderna, Ladislav
Guerin, John William
Guerrero, Jose
Guerriero, Henry Edward
Guiffreda, Mauro Francis
Guion, Molly
Gumpel, Hugh
Gundelfinger, John Andre
Gunter, Frank Elliott
Gursoy, Ahmet
Gussow, Alan
Guston, Philip
Guy, James M
Gwathmey, Robert
Hack, Howard Edwin
Haerer, Carol
Haessle, Jean-Marie Georges
Haines, Richard
Halaby, Samia Asaad
Halbrooks, Darryl Wayne
Halko, Joe
Hall, John (Scott)
Hall, Susan
Hallam, Beverly (Linney)
Halpern, Lea
Halvorsen, Ruth Elise
Hamblett, Theora
Hamel, Bernard Franklin
Hamlett, Dale Edward
Hammersley, Frederick
Hammond, Harmony
Hammond, Ruth MacKrille
Hampton, John W
Hampton, Phillip Jewel
Hampton, Roy (George LeRoy Hampton)
Handell, Albert George
Handville, Robert T
Hanes, James (Albert)
Hanna, Boyd Everett
Hanna, Paul Dean, Jr
Hansen, Frances Frakes
Hanson, Jean (Mrs Jean Elphick)
Hapke, Paul Frederick
Harari, Hananiah
Hardaway, Pearl (Pearl Hardaway Reese)
Harden, Marvin
Harder, Rolf Peter
Hardin, Helen
Hardy, David Whittaker, III
Hari, Kenneth
Harlan, Roma Christine
Harlow, Robert E
Harman, Maryann Whittemore
Harmon, Cliff Franklin
Harmon, Lily
Harms, Elizabeth
Harper, Eleanor O'Neil
Harrill, James
Harris, Alfred Peter
Harris, Marian D
Harris, Robert George
Harrison, Pat (Broeder)
Harrison, Tony
Harsh, Richard
Hart, Agnes
Hart, Betty Miller
Hart, Morgan Drake
Hartell, John (Anthony)
Harter, John Burton
Hartigan, Grace
Hartman, Robert Leroy
Harvey, Donald
Harvey, Jacqueline
Harwood, June Beatrice
Haseltine, James Lewis
Haseltine, Maury (Margaret Wilson Haseltine)
Hasen, Burt Stanly
Hastie, Reid
Haswell, Hollee
Hatchett, Duayne
Hatfield, Donald Gene
Haug, Donald Raymond
Hausman, Fred S
Haworth, B Cogill (Mrs Peter Haworth)
Hay, George Austin
Hayes, Tua
Haynes, Douglas H
Haynes, George Edward
Hayward, Peter
Hazlitt, Don Robert
Head, George Bruce
Hedden-Sellman, Zelda
Hedman, Teri Jo
Hedrick, Wally Bill
Heflin, Tom Pat
Heinemann, Peter
Heise, Myron Robert
Held, Alma M
Held, Philip
Helfond, Riva
Helgoe, Orlin Milton
Heliker, John Edward
Helioff, Anne Graile (Mrs Benjamin Hirschberg)
Henderson, Jack W
Henderson, Mike (William Howard Henderson)
Hendler, Raymond
Hendricks, Barkley Leonnard
Hendricks, David Charles
Hendricks, Donald Teves
Hendricks, Geoffrey
Hendricks, James (Powell)
Hennesy, Gerald Craft
Henry, Jean
Henry, Robert
Henslee, Jack
Herbert, James Arthur
Herfindahl, Lloyd Manford
Hernandez-Cruz, Luis
Herpst, Martha Jane
Herrera, Raul Othon
Herring, Jan(et Mantel)
Hershberg, Israel
Hertzberg, Rose
Herzbrun, Helene McKinsey
Hess, Emil John
Heusser, Eleanore Elizabeth
Hewitt, Francis Ray
Hibel, Edna
Hicken, Philip Burnham
Hickman, David Coleman
Highberg, Stephanie Wenner
Hildreth, Joseph Alan
Hill, Clinton J
Hill, J Tweed
Hill, Joan (Chea-se-quah)
Hill, Peter
Hill, Polly Knipp
Hillis, Richard K
Hilson, Douglas
Hilton, John William
Himler, Ronald Norbert
Himmelfarb, John David
Hines, John M
Hinman, Charles B
Hios, Theo
Hirsch, Gilah Yelin
Hirsch, Joseph
Hitch, Jean Leason
Hitch, Robert A
Hnizdovsky, Jacques
Hobbie, Lucille
Hodge, Roy Garey
Hodgell, Robert Overman
Hodges, Stephen Lofton
Hodgkins, Rosalind Selma
Hoff, Margo
Hoffman, Helen Bacon
Hoffmann, Arnold, Jr
Hogue, Alexandre
Holbrook, Vivian Nicholas
Holder, Kenneth Allen
Holgate, Jeanne
Hollander, Gino F

Hollerbach, Serge
Holliday, Betty
Hollinger, (Helen Wetherbee)
Hollingsworth, Alvin Carl
Hollister, Paul
Hollister, Valerie (Dutton)
Holm, Milton W
Holman, Arthur (Stearns)
Holmbom, James William
Holmes, David Bryan
Holmes, Reginald
Holtz, Itshak Jack
Honig, Mervin
Hood, Dorothy
Hooton, Arthur
Hoover, John Jay
Hopkins, Budd
Hopkins, Kendal Coles
Hopkins, Peter
Hopkinson, Glen Spencer
Hopper, Frank J
Hornak, Ian John
Horne, (Arthur Edward) Cleeve
Horton, Jan E
Houser, Allan C
Houser, Jim
Houskeeper, Barbara
Housser, Yvonne McKague
Howard, Dan F
Howell, Claude Flynn
Howell, Frank
Hoyt, Dorothy (Dorothy Hoyt Dillingham)
Hoyt, Whitney F
Hsiao, Chin
Hubbard, John
Hudson, Jacqueline
Hudson, Winnifred
Huggins, Victor, (Jr)
Hughes, Edward John
Hui, Helene
Hull, Marie (Atkinson)
Hultberg, John Phillip
Humble, Douglas
Humphrey, S L
Hunkler, Dennis Francis
Hunt, Courtenay
Hunter, Robert Douglas
Hunter, Robert Howard
Hupp, Frederick Duis
Hurd, Zorah
Hurley, Wilson
Hurt, Susanne M
Hurtubise, Jacques
Hurwitz, Sidney J
Hushlak, Gerald Marshall
Hutchison, Elizabeth S
Hyson, Jean
Iacurto, Francesco
Iden, Sheldon
Indiana, Robert
Ingraham, Esther Price
Ingram, Judith
Inokuma, Guenichiro
Inoue, Kazuko
Inslee, Marguerite T
Ipcar, Dahlov
Ippolito, Angelo
Irvin, Fred Maddox
Isaacs, Ron
Isaak, Nicholas, Jr
Isenburger, Eric
Isham, Sheila Eaton
Iskowitz, Gershon
Israel, Marvin
Ives, Elaine Caroline
Iwamoto, Ralph Shigeto
Jackson, Billy Morrow
Jackson, Everett Gee
Jackson, Harry Andrew
Jackson, Herb
Jackson, Lee
Jackson, Richard Norris
Jackson, Suzanne Fitzallen
Jackson, Vaughn L
Jacob, Ned
Jacobs, Harold
Jacobs, Helen Nichols
Jacobs, Ralph, Jr
Jacobshagen, N Keith, II
Jacobson, Arthur Robert
Jacquemon, Pierre
Jacquette, Yvonne Helene (Yvonne Helen Burckhardt)
Jaffe, Nora
Jagow, Ellen T
Jameson, Demetrios George
Janelsins, Veronica
Janschka, Fritz
Jaque, Louis
Jaramillo, Virginia
Jarkowski, Stefania Agnes
Jarvis, Donald
Jarvis, John Brent
Jaudon, Valerie
Jauss, Anne Marie
Ject-Key, Elsie
Jeffers, Wendy Jane
Jenkinson, Geoffrey
Jennerjahn, W P
Jennings, Francis
Jennings, Thomas
Jensen, Gary
Jensen, Leo (Vernon)
Jensen, Marit
Jensen, Pat
Jess (Jess Collins)
Jewell, William M
Jocda (Joseph Charles Dailey)
Johansen, Anders Daniel
Johanson, George E
Johanson, Patricia (Maureen)
Johnsen, May Anne
Johnson, Buffie
Johnson, Doris Miller (Mrs Gardiner Johnson)
Johnson, Harvey William
Johnson, Homer
Johnson, James Alan
Johnson, James Ralph
Johnson, Katherine King
Johnson, Lee
Johnson, (Leonard) Lucas
Johnson, Lester L
Johnston, Thomas Alix
Johnston, William Edward
Johnston, William Medford
Jolley, Geraldine H (Jerry)
Jones, Allan Dudley
Jones, Amy (Amy Jones Frisbie)
Jones, Barbara Nester
Jones, Douglas McKee (Doug)
Jones, Franklin Reed
Jones, Howard William
Jones, James Edward
Jones, John Paul
Jones, Marvin Harold
Jones, Robert Cushman
Jones, W Louis
Jordan, Barbara Schwinn
Jordan, Christine
Jordan, James William
Jordan, Robert
Jorgensen, Flemming
Jorgensen, Sandra
Joseph, Cliff (Clifford Ricardo)
Josimovich, George
Joukhadar, Moumtaz A N
Joyce, Marshall Woodside
Judd, De Forrest Hale
Judkins, Sylvia
Judson, Jeannette Alexander
Julian, Lazaro
Jung, Kwan Yee
Jung, Yee Wah
Juszczyk, James Joseph
Kabak, Robert
Kabotie, Fred
Kagy, Sheffield Harold
Kahn, Susan B
Kahn, Wolf
Kainen, Jacob
Kaiser, Charles James
Kaiser, Diane
Kaiser, Vitus J
Kaish, Morton
Kakas, Christopher
Kalb, Marty Joel
Kalina, Richard Seth
Kallem, Henry
Kamihira, Ben
Kamys, Walter
Kane, Bob Paul
Kanemitsu, Matsumi
Kanovitz, Howard
Kaplan, Joseph
Kaplan, Marilyn
Kapsalis, Thomas Harry
Karesh, Ann Bamberger
Karn, Gloria Stoll
Karp, Richard Gordon
Karwelis, Donald Charles
Kasak, Nikolai (Kazak)
Kasten, Karl Albert
Katayama, Toshihiro
Katz, Alex
Katz, Eunice
Katz, Morris
Katzman, Herbert
Kauffman, Robert Craig
Kaufman, Irving
Kaufman, Jane A
Kaupelis, Robert John
Kawa, Florence Kathryn
Kawabata, Minoru
Kay, Reed
Keeling, Henry Cornelious
Keen, Helen Boyd
Keena, Janet Laybourn
Keener, Anna Elizabeth
Kelleher, Daniel Joseph
Keller, Deane
Kelley, Chapman
Kelley, Ramon
Kellogg, Maurice Dale
Kelly, James
Kelly, Leon
Kelly, William Joseph
Kelpe, Paul
Kemper, John Garner
Kenda, Juanita Echeverria
Kennedy, James Edward
Kenney, Estelle Koval
Kenny, Lisa A
Kenny, Patrick Gerald
Kenny, Thomas Henry
Kent, H Latham
Kepalas (Elena Kepalaite)
Kermes, Constantine John
Kerns, Ed (Johnson, Jr)
Kerstetter, Barbara Ann
Kerswill, J W Roy
Kessler, Alan
Kessler, Edna Leventhal
Kessler, Shirley
Kester, Lenard
Kevorkian, Richard
Keyser, Robert Gifford
Kiah, Virginia Jackson
Kieferndorf, Frederick George
Kielkopf, James Robert
Kijanka, Stanley Joseph
Kilian, Austin Farland
Kimbrough, (Sara) Dodge
Kimura, Sueko M
King, Clinton Blair
King, Henri Umbaji
King, William Alfred
Kinghan, Charles Ross
Kinnaird, Richard William
Kipniss, Robert
Kirkland, Vance Hall
Kirkwood, Larry Thomas
Kirkwood, Mary Burnette
Kirschenbaum, Jules
Kirsten-Daiensai, Richard Charles
Kish, Maurice
Kiskadden, Robert Morgan
Kitner, Harold
Kjargaard, John Ingvard
Klabunde, Charles Spencer
Klarin, Winifred Erlick
Klavans, Minnie
Klaven, Marvin L
Kleidon, Dennis Arthur
Kleiman, Alan
Klein, Beatrice T
Klein, Doris
Klein, Medard
Klein, Sandor C
Klement, Vera
Kline, Harriet
Kloss, Gene (Alice Geneva Glasier)
Knapp, Tom
Knaub, Raymond L
Knee, Gina (Mrs Alexander Brook)
Knief, Janet (Helen Jeanette)
Knight, Frederic Charles
Knight, Jacob Jaskoviak
Knipscher, Gerard Allen
Knipschild, Robert
Knobler, Lois Jean
Knowles, Dorothy Elsie (Dorothy Elsie Perehudoff)
Knowles, Richard H
Knowlton, Jonathan
Knox, Elizabeth Ann
Knudson, Robert LeRoy
Kobayashi, Katsumi Peter
Koch, Edwin E
Koch, Gerd (Herman)
Koch, John
Koch, Virginia Greenleaf
Kocherthaler, Mina
Kochta, Ruth (Martha)
Koehler, Henry
Koenig, John Franklin
Koestner, Don
Koga, Dean
Kohl, Barbara
Kohlmeyer, Ida (R)
Kohn, William Roth
Kohut, Lorene
Kolin, Sacha
Konigsberg, Harvey
Konopka, Joseph
Koons, Darell J
Koppelman, Dorothy
Korjus, Veronica Maria Elisabeth
Korner, John (John Michael Anthony Koerner)
Korow, Elinore Maria
Kortheuer, Dayrell
Kotala, Stanislaw Waclaw
Kotin, Albert
Kouba, Leslie Carl
Kovachevich, Thomas
Kovner, Saul
Kowalski, Raymond Alois
Kozloff, Joyce
Kozlow, Richard
Kozlow, Sigmund
Kramer, Jack N
Kramer, Marjorie Anne
Kramolc, Theodore Maria
Krashes, Barbara
Krasner, Lee
Krause, LaVerne Erickson
Krauser, Joel
Krausz, Laszlo
Kreitzer, David Martin
Kressley, Margaret Hyatt
Kriensky, (Morris E)
Krigstein, Bernard
Kronsnoble, Jeffrey Michael
Krushenick, John
Kruskamp, Janet
Krust, Walter
Kuehn, Frances
Kuh, Howard
Kuhlman, Walter Egel
Kuhn, Bob
Kumm, Marguerite Elizabeth

PAINTER (cont)
Kupferman, Lawrence
Kupferman, Murray
Kurz, Diana
Kusama, Yayoi
Kushner, Dorothy Browdy
Kushner, Robert Ellis
Kuwayama, Tadaaki
Kwiecinski, Chester Martin
Labiche, Walter Anthony
Labrie, Rose
Lack, Richard Frederick
Lacroix, Richard
Lacy, Robert Eugene
Lafaye, Nell Murray
Lafon, Dee J
La Fon, Julia Anna
LaFreniere, Isabel Marcotte
Laguna, Muriel
Lahey, Richard (Francis)
La Hotan, Robert L
Laine, Lenore
Lam, Jennett (Brinsmade)
Lamantia, James
Lamb, Adrian
Lambert, Eddie
Lampert, Dorrie
Lancaster, Mark
Land, Ernest Albert
Landers, Bertha
Landfield, Ronnie (Ronald T)
Landreau, Anthony Norman
Lane, Marion Jean Arrons
Lang, Daniel S
Lang, Margo Terzian
Laning, Edward
La Noue, Terence David
Lansdon, Gay Brandt
Lanyon, Ellen
LaPena, Frank Raymond
La Pierre, Thomas
Lapointe, Frank
Lark, Raymond
Larmer, Oscar Vance
Larsen, Ole
Larson, Blaine (Gledhill)
Lasker, Joseph (L)
Laub-Novak, Karen
Lauffer, Alice A
Laufman, Sidney
Laurent, John Louis
La Vigne, Robert Clair
Law, C Anthony
Law, Pauline Elizabeth
Lawrence, Jacob
Lax, David
Laycox, (William) Jack
Lea, Stanley E
Leach, Frederick Darwin
Lebedev, Vladimir
Lebkicher, Anne Ross
Lecky, Susan
Le Clair, Charles
Lee, Doris
Lee, Eleanor Gay
Lee, Margaret F
Lee, Richard Allen
Leeds, Annette
Leepa, Allen
Leeper, Doris Marie
Leeper, John P
Lee-Smith, Hughie
Leete, William White
Leff, Juliette
Leff, Rita
Lefranc, Margaret (Margaret Lefranc Schoonover)
Lehrer, Leonard
Leighton, Thomas Charles
Leland, Whitney Edward
Lem, Richard Douglas
Lembeck, John Edgar
Lemieux, Irenee
Lenney, Annie
Lenssen, Heidi (Mrs Fridolf Johnson)
Leon, Ralph Bernard
Lerman, Ora
Lerner, Marilyn Ann
Lerner, Sandy R
Lerner Levine, Marion
Le Roy, Harold M
Lesnick, Stephen William
Letendre, Rita
Levee, John H
Leventhal, Ruth Lee
Levering, Robert K
Levi, Julian (E)
Levin, Kim (Kim Pateman)
Levine, Reeva (Anna) Miller
Levit, Herschel
Lev-Landau (Samuel David Landau)
Levy, Tibbie
Lew, Weyman Michael
Lewin, Keith Kerton
Lewis, Michael H
Lewis, Nat Brush
Lewis, Norman Wilfred
Lewis, Ronald Walter
Lewton, Val Edwin
Libby, William C
Libhart, Myles Laroy
Lichtenberg, Manes
Lichty, George M
Lieb, Vered (Vered Shapiro-Lieb)
Lieber, France
Lieberman, Harry
Ligare, David H
Likan, Gustav
Liljegren, Frank
Li Marzi, Joseph
Limont, Naomi Charles
Linder, Stasia
Lindmark, Arne
Lindner, Ernest
Lindner, Richard
Linhares, Philip E
Linn, John William
Lipinsky de Orlov, Lino S
Lippincott, Janet
Lipsky, Pat
Lipton, Sondra (Sahlman)
Lis, Janet Chapman
Liszt, Maria Veronica
Livingston, Sidnee
Livingstone, Biganess
Locke, Charles Wheeler
Locker, Thomas
Loew, Michael
Logan, Gene Adams
Long, C Chee
Long, Sandra Tardo
Long, Walter Kinscella
Loomer, Gifford C
Looney, Norman
Lopina, Louise Carol
Loran, Erle
Lorentz, Pauline
Lotterman, Hal
Lougheed, Robert Elmer
Lovato, Charles Fredric
Love, Rosalie Bowen
Loveless, Jim
Lovell, Tom
Lowe, Joe Hing
Lowney, Bruce Stark
Loy, John Sheridan
Lueders, Jimmy C
Lukas, Dennis Brian
Lumbers, James Richard
Luna (Antonio Rodriguez Luna)
Lund, David
Lundeberg, Helen (Helen Lundeberg Feitelson)
Lusker, Ron
Lutz, Dan S
Lux, Gladys Marie
Luz, Virginia
Lynch, Jo (Marilyn Blanche)
Lynch, Mary Britten
Lynde, Stan
Lynds, Clyde William
Lyon, Harold Lloyd
Lyon, Hayes Paxton
Lysun, Gregory
Lytle, Richard
Maas, Arnold (Marcolino)
Mabry, Jane
Macaray, Lawrence Richard
MacDonald, Colin Somerled
Macdonald, Grant
MacDonald, Thomas Reid
MacGillis, Robert Donald
MacGregor, John Boyko
Machetanz, Fred
MacKendrick, Lilian
Macklin, Anderson D
MacLean, Arthur
MacNutt, Glenn Gordon
Maddox, Jerrold Warren
Madura, Jack Joseph
Maestro, Giulio Marcello
Magazzini, Gene
Magleby, Francis R (Frank)
Mahaffey, Merrill Dean
Mahmoud, Ben
Mailman, Cynthia
Mainardi, Patricia M
Maione, Robert
Maitin, Samuel (Calman)
Majdrakoff, Ivan
Makarenko, Zachary Philipp
Maldjian, Vartavar B
Malone, James William
Malone, Robert R
Malta, Vincent
Manarey, Thelma Alberta
Mancini, John
Mandel, Howard
Mandel, John
Mandelman, Beatrice M
Mandziuk, Michael Dennis
Manetta, Edward J
Mangione, Patricia Anthony
Mangold, Sylvia Plimack
Mangravite, Peppino Gino
Mann, Katinka
Mann, Vaughan (Vaughan Grayson)
Manso, Leo
Manuella, Frank R
Manville, Elsie
Manzo, Anthony Joseph
Mapes, Doris Williamson
Marais (Mary Rachel Brown)
Marazzi, William C P
Marcus, Irving E
Marcus, Marcia
Marden, Brice
Marder, Dorie
Margolies, Ethel Polacheck
Mariano, Kristine
Mari (Mari M Eagerton)
Marin, Augusto
Marin, Kathryn Garrison
Mark, Marilyn
Marker, Mariska Pugsley
Marker, Ralph E
Markman, Ronald
Markow, Jack
Marks, George B
Marozzi, Eli Raphael
Marriott, William Allen
Martell, Barbara Bentley
Martin, Agnes Bernice
Martin, Alexander Toedt
Martin, Bernard Murray
Martin, Bernice Fenwick
Martin, Keith Morrow
Martin, Lucille Caiar (Mrs Hampton Martin)
Martin, Roger
Martin, Ron
Martinez-Maresma, Sara (Sara Martinez)
Martino, Antonio P
Martino, Edmund
Martino, Eva E
Martino, Giovanni
Martone, William Robert
Martyl (Martyl Schweig Langsdorf)
Marx, Robert Ernst
Marzano, Albert
Mason, Alden C
Mason, Bette
Mason, Frank Herbert
Mason, Harold Dean
Mason, Phillip Lindsay
Mason, William Clifford
Massin, Eugene Max
Masson, Henri
Matson, Greta (Greta Matson Khouri)
Matthews, Gene
Maughelli, Mary L
Mavian, Salpi Miriam
Mawicke, Tran
Maxwell, John
Mayer, Bena Frank
Mayer, Ralph
Mayer, Susan Martin
Maynard, William
Mazzone, Domenico
McAdoo, Donald Eldridge
McAllister-Kelly
McBryde, Sarah Elva
McCarthy, Doris Jean
McCartin, William Francis
McCarty, Lorraine Chambers
McCauley, Gardiner Rae
McChesney, Clifton
McChesney, Robert Pearson
McChristy, Quentin L
McClanahan, William J
McClellan, Douglas Eugene
McClendon, Maxine (Maxine McClendon Nichols)
McCloskey, Eunice LonCoske
McClure, Constance M
McCormick, Harry
McCosh, David J
McCoy, Wirth Vaughan
McCracken, Patrick Ed
McCullough, David William
McCullough, Joseph
McGee, William Douglas
McGee, Winston Eugene
McGeoch, Lillian Jean
McGill, Robert Lee
McGinnis, Christine
McGovern, Robert F
McGrath, James Arthur
McGrew, Bruce Elwin
McGrew, Ralph Brownell
McIlroy, Carol Jean
McInerney, Gene Joseph
McIntosh, Harold
McIver, John Kolb
McKeeby, Byron Gordon
McKesson, Malcolm Forbes
McKie, Todd Stoddard
McKim, William Wind
McKinin, Lawrence
McKnight, Thomas Frederick
McLarty, William James (Jack)
McLaughlin, John D
McLean, Richard Thorpe
McMillan, Constance
McNamara, Raymond Edmund
McNary, Oscar L
McNear, Everett C
McQuillan, Frances C
McReynolds, (Joe) Cliff
McVeigh, Miriam Temperance
McVicker, J Jay
Meader, Jonathan Grant (Ascian)
Medearis, Roger
Meehan, William Dale
Mehring, Howard William
Meitzler, (Herbert) Neil
Meixner, Mary Louise
Melikian, Mary
Meltzer, Anna E
Meltzer, Arthur

Melville, Grevis Whitaker
Menaboni, Athos Rudolfo
Mendelson, Haim
Mendenhall, Jack
Meng, Wendy
Merchant, Pat (Jean)
Mercier, Monique
Mermin, Mildred (Shire)
Merrick, James Kirk
Merrill, David Kenneth
Merrill, Ross M
Mesches, Arnold
Meserole, Vera Stromsted
Messersmith, Fred Lawrence
Messick, Ben (Newton)
Metson, Graham
Metz, Frank Robert
Metzger, Evelyn Borchard
Mew, Tommy
Meyer, Frank Hildbridge
Meyerowitz, William
Michael, Gary
Micheli, Julio
Michod, Susan A
Middleman, Raoul F
Midgette, Willard Franklin
Mieczkowski, Edwin
Milder, Jay
Miles, Cyril
Miles, Jeanne Patterson
Milette, Clemence M
Miller, Dolly (Ethel B)
Miller, Jan
Miller, Lee Anne
Miller, Mariann (Mariann Helm)
Miller, Nancy Tokar
Miller, Vel
Mina-Mora, Dorise Olson
Mina-Mora, Raul Jose
Mintz, Harry
Mion, Pierre Riccardo
Miotke, Anne E
Mirko (Wolodymyr Walter Pylyshenko)
Misch, Allene K
Mitchell, Fred
Mitchell, John Blair
Mitchell, Peter Todd
Mitra, Gopal C
Mittleman, Ann
Mix, Walter Joseph
Miyamoto, Wayne Akira
Miyasaki, George Joji
Mochizuki, Betty Ayako
Mockers, Michel M
Moffitt, John Francis
Mohn, Cheri (Ann)
Moise, William Sidney
Molina, Antonio J
Moller, Hans
Momaday, Al
Moment, Joan
Momiyama, Nanae
Monaghan, Eileen (Mrs Frederic Whitaker)
Monaghan, Keith
Monongye, Preston Lee
Monroe, Gerald
Montenegro, Enrique E
Montgomery, Claude
Montlack, Edith
Moon, Marc
Moonier, Syliva
Moore, Beveridge
Moore, John J
Moore, Michael Shannon
Moore, Robert Eric
Moore, Robert James
Moose, Philip Anthony
Moose, Talmadge Bowers
Morales, Armando
Moreton, Russell
Morgan, Darlene
Morgan, Gladys B
Morgan, Norma Gloria
Morishita, Joyce Chizuko
Morley, Malcom
Morningstern, Harry V
Moroz, Mychajlo
Morrell, Wayne (Beam)
Morris, Carl
Morris, Kyle Randolph
Morris, Michael
Morrison, Doris
Morrison, George
Morrison, Keith Anthony
Morrison, Robert Clifton
Mortensen, Gordon Louis
Mosca, August
Moscatt, Paul N
Moseley, Ralph Sessions
Moseley, Spencer Altemont
Moses, Betty (Betty Moses McCart)
Moses, Forrest (Lee), (Jr)
Moss, Irene
Moss, Milton
Mould, Lola Frowde
Movalli, Charles Joseph
Moy, Seong
Moyers, Wm
Muench, John
Muir, Emily Lansingh
Mulcahy, Freda
Mullen, Buell
Mullen, Philip Edward
Muller, Jerome Kenneth
Mullican, Lee
Munoz, Rie (Marie Angelina Muroz)
Murata, Hiroshi
Murphy, Catherine E
Murphy, Chester Glenn
Murray, Albert (Ketcham)
Murray, Elizabeth
Murray, Floretta May
Murray, Richard Deibel
Musselman, Darwin B
Myers, Jack Fredrick
Myers, Malcolm Haynie
Myers, Virginia Anne
Nadalini, (Louis Ernest)
Nadler, Harry
Naegle, Stephen Howard
Nagano, Shozo
Nagler, Edith Kroger
Nagler, Fred
Nakamura, Kazuo
Nakatani, Carlos
Nakazato, Hitoshi
Nalder, Nan
Namingha, Dan
Nardone, Vincent Joseph
Nathan, Helmuth Max
Natkin, Robert
Navrat, Den (Dennis Edward Navrat)
Nay, Mary Spencer
Naylor, Alice Stephenson
Nazarenko, Bonnie Coe
Neals, Otto
Neddeau, Donald Frederick Price
Neel, Alice
Neff, Edith
Negri, Rocco Antonio
Neidhardt, Carl Richard
Neiman, LeRoy
Nelson, Harry William
Nelson, Leonard
Nelson, Mary Carroll
Nelson, Robert Allen
Nelson, Signe (Signe Nelson Stuart)
Nesbitt, Lowell (Blair)
Neto, G Reis (Gilda Reis Netopuletti)
Neustein, Joshua
Newbill, Al
Newer, Thesis
Newman, John Beatty
Newman, Libby
Newport, Esther
Niblett, Gary Lawrence
Nicholas, Thomas Andrew
Nichols, Alice W
Nichols, Dale William
Nichols, Jeannettie Doornhein
Nichols, Ward H
Nick, George
Nickel, Jim H
Nielsen, Stuart
Niemann, Edmund E
Nierman, Leonardo M
Niese, Henry Ernst
Nind, Jean
Nirvanno, Comet (Vincent Romano)
Nobili, Louise
Noble, John A
Noordhoek, Harry Cecil
Nordhausen, A Henry
Nordstrand, Nathalie Johnson
Norman, Emile
Norton, Mary Joyce
Norton, Rob Roy, Jr
Norwood, Malcolm Mark
Nosoff, Frank
Novotny, Elmer Ladislaw
Novros, David
Nuki (Daniel Millsaps)
Nutzle, Futzie (Bruce John Kleinsmith)
Oakes, John Warren
O'Brien, Marjorie (Marjorie O'Brien Rapaport)
Ocampo, Miguel
Ocejo (Jose Garcia)
O'Connor, John Arthur
Oehler, Helen Gapen
O'Hanlon, Richard E
Ohashi, Yutaka
Ohlson, Douglas Dean
Ohman, Richard Michael
Okada, Kenzo
Okoshi, Eugenia Sumiye
Oleksiw, Michael Nicholas, II
Olitski, Jules
Oliveira, Nathan
Olsen, Ernest Moran
Olson, Douglas John
Olson, Joseph Olaf
Omar, Margit
Omwake, Leon, Jr
O'Neil, Bruce William
Onley, Toni
Opie, John Mart
Oppenheim, Samuel Edmund
Oppenheimer, Selma L
Order, Trudy
Ordonez, Efren
Orling, Anne
Ortlip, Paul Daniel
Osby, Larissa Geiss
O'Sickey, Joseph Benjamin
Ostendorf, (Arthur) Lloyd, Jr
Oster, Gerald
Ostuni, Peter W
O'Sullivan, Daniel Joseph
Ott, Jerry Duane
Ott, Wendell Lorenz
Oubre, Hayward Louis
Outterbridge, John Wilfred
Owen, Bill
Owens, Mary (Mary Louis Schnore)
Ozonoff, Ida
Pace, Stephen S
Pacheco, Maria Luisa
Pachner, William
Pacific, Gertrude
Packer, Clair Lange
Page, Bill
Palazzola, Guy
Palmer, Mabel (Evelyn)
Palmer, William C
Palmgren, Donald Gene
Papo, Iso
Pappas, George
Paredes, Limon Mariano
Parella, Albert Lucian
Paris, Lucille M
Parish, Jean E
Parke, Walter Simpson
Parker, Bill
Parker, James
Parker, Nancy Winslow
Parker, Raymond
Parker, Samuel Murray
Parks, James Dallas
Parra, Thomas (Garcia)
Parrish, David Buchanan
Parsons, Betty Bierne
Partin, Robert (E)
Pascal, David
Paschke, Edward F (Ed)
Passuntino, Peter Zaccaria
Patchett, Daniel Claude
Paternosto, Cesar Pedro
Patrick, Genie H
Patrick, Joseph Alexander
Paul, Ken (Hugh)
Paulley, David Gordon
Payne, Lan
Peace, Bernie (Kinzel)
Pearson, Henry C
Pearson, Marguerite Stuber
Pease, David G
Peck, James Edward
Peck, Stephen Rogers
Pederson, Molly Fay
Pellan (Alfred)
Pellew, John Clifford
Pellicone, William
Pels, Albert
Pen, Rudolph
Penczner, Paul Joseph
Penkoff, Ronald Peter
Penny, Aubrey John Robert
Perehudoff, William W
Perez, Vincent
Perham, Roy Gates
Perlin, Rae
Perlmutter, Jack
Perry, Kathryn Powers
Pershing, Louise
Peter, George
Peterdi, Gabor F
Peters, Carl W
Petersen, Roland Conrad
Peterson, Larry D
Peterson, Roger Tory
Petlin, Irving
Petrie, Ferdinand Ralph
Petrie, Sylvia Spencer
Petro, Joseph (Victor), Jr
Pettet, William
Pettibone, Richard H
Pezzati, Pietro
Pfahl, Charles Anton, III
Pfriem, Bernard
Phelps, Nan Dee
Philbrick, Margaret Elder
Phillips, Bertrand D
Phillips, Gordon Dale
Phillips, Marjorie
Phillips, Matt
Phillips, Melita Ahl
Piatek, Francis John
Picher, Claude
Pickens, Alton
Pickens, Vinton Liddell
Pickford, Rollin, Jr
Pierce, Delilah W
Pierce, Diane (Diane Pierce Huxtable)
Pierce, Elizabeth R
Pillin, Polia
Pindell, Howardena Doreen
Pinkerton, Clayton (David)
Pinkowski, Emily Joan
Pinto, Biagio
Pinto, James
Pinzarrone, Paul
Plagens, Peter

PAINTER (cont)
Plavcan, Joseph Michael
Pleissner, Ogden Minton
Pletcher, Gerry
Plochmann, Carolyn Gassan
Pneuman, Mildred Y
Pohl, Louis G
Pollak, Theresa
Pollard, Donald Pence
Pollaro, Paul
Pollock, Merlin F
Polsky, Cynthia
Ponce de Leon, Michael
Poole, Richard Elliott
Poor, Anne
Posen, Stephen
Potvin, Daniel
Poulos, Basilios Nicholas
Pounian, Albert Kachouni
Powell, Leslie (Joseph)
Pozzatti, Rudy O
Praczukowski, Edward Leon
Pramuk, Edward Richard
Pratt, Frances (Frances Elizabeth Usui)
Pratt, Mary Frances
Pratt, Vernon Gaither
Prdy, Donald R
Preissler, Audrey
Preston, Malcolm H
Prestopino, Gregorio
Preuss, Roger
Prezament, Joseph
Pribble, Easton
Price, Leslie Kenneth
Price, Rosalie Pettus
Priest, Hartwell Wyse
Priest, T
Procter, Burt
Pross, Lester Fred
Provder, Carl
Pruitt, A Kelly
Punia, Constance Edith
Quat, Helen S
Quest, Dorothy (Johnson)
Quinn, Raymond John
Quinn, William
Quirk, Thomas Charles, Jr
Rabinovich, Raquel
Rabinovitch, William Avrum
Raciti, Cherie
Radin, Dan
Radoczy, Albert
Raffael, Joseph
Raffael, Judith K
Raffel, Alvin Robert
Ragland, Bob
Ragland, Jack Whitney
Rahja, Virginia Helga
Rainey, John Watts
Rakocy, William (Joseph)
Raleigh, Henry Patrick
Ralston, James Kenneth
Ramberg, Christina (Christina Ramberg Hanson)
Ramirez, Gabriel
Ramos, Melvin John
Ramos-Prida, Fernando
Ramsauer, Joseph Francis
Ramstead, Edward Oliver, Jr
Ranes, Chris
Rankine, V V
Ransom, Henry Cleveland, Jr
Ranson, Nancy Sussman
Rapp, Ebba (Ebba Rapp McLauchlan)
Rapp, Lois
Rappin, Adrian
Rascoe, Stephen Thomas
Rasmussen, Anton Jesse
Rasmussen, Keith Eric
Rath, Hildegard
Rave, Georgia
Ray, Deborah
Raybon, Phares Henderson
Rayen, James Wilson
Rayner, Ada (Ada Rayner Hensche)
Reale, Nicholas Albert
Rebbeck, Lester James, Jr
Reber, Mick
Reboli, Joseph John
Reddington, Charles Leonard
Reddix, Roscoe Chester
Red Star, Kevin Francis
Reece, Maynard
Reed, David Fredrick
Reed, Doel
Reed, Hal
Reed, Paul Allen
Reese, William Foster
Refregier, Anton
Regat, Mary E
Reich, Nathaniel E
Reichert, Donald Karl
Reichert, Donald O
Reichman, Fred (Thomas)
Reid, Charles
Reid, Robert Dennis
Reid, (William) Richard
Reiff, Robert Frank
Reindorf, Samuel
Reinhart, Margaret Emily
Reinsel, Walter N
Reisman, Philip
Rembski, Stanislav
Remenick, Seymour
Remington, Deborah Williams
Remsen, John Everett, II
Renner, Eric
Rennick, Dan
Rennie, Helen (Sewell)
Renouf, Edward Pechmann
Resek, Kate Frances
Resika, Paul
Reynard, Carolyn Cole
Reynolds, James Elwood
Reynolds, Richard (Henry)
Reynolds, Robert
Rhoads, Eugenia Eckford
Ribak, Louis
Rice, Dan
Rice, Philip Somerset
Rich, Garry Lorence
Richards, Bill
Richards, Karl Frederick
Richardson, Constance (Coleman)
Riess, Lore
Rigsby, John David
Riley, Art (Arthur Irwin)
Riley, Bernard Joseph
Riley, Roy John
Ripps, Rodney
Riseling, Robert Lowell
Rishell, Robert Clifford
Rising, Dorothy Milne
Rivard, J Bernard
Rivera, Frank
Riveron, Enrique
Rizk, Romanos
Robb, Charles (Charles Robert Bush)
Robb, Peggy Hight
Robbin, Anthony Stuart
Roberts, Lucille D (Malkia)
Roberts, Percival R
Roberts, Priscilla Warren
Roberts, Thomas (Kieth)
Roberts, William Edward
Roberts, William Griffith
Robertson, D Hall
Robinson, Charlotte
Robinson, Margot (Margot Steigman)
Robinson, Mary Ann
Robinson, Robert Doke
Robison, Joan Settle
Roda (Rhoda Lillian Sablow)
Rodrigue, George G
Roever, Joan Marilyn
Rogers, Barbara Joan
Rogers, Otto Donald
Rogers, P J
Rohrer, Warren
Rojo, Vicente
Rollman-Shay, Ed & Charlotte
Romano, Jaime (Luis)
Romano, Salvatore Michael
Romero, Mike
Romoser, Ruth Amelia
Ronald, William
Roney, Harold Arthur
Rose, Leatrice
Rose, Mary Anne
Rose, Samuel
Rosen, Beverly Doris
Rosen, James Mahlon
Rosenblatt, Adolph
Rosenblatt, Susan Maris
Rosenblum, Jay
Rosenhouse, Irwin Jacob
Rosenquist, James
Rosenthal, Gloria M
Rosenthal, Seymour Joseph
Rosofsky, Seymour
Ross, Alexander
Ross, Beatrice Brook
Ross, Fred (Joseph)
Ross, Janice Koenig
Rossman, Ruth Scharff
Roster, Laila Bergs
Rotenberg, Harold
Roth, David
Rothschild, Amalie (Rosenfeld)
Rothschild, Judith
Roussel, Claude Patrice
Rowan, Frances Physioc
Rowan, Herman
Rowe, Charles Alfred
Rowe, Reginald M
Rowland, Elden Hart
Rozzi, (James A)
Ruben, Richards
Ruble, Ronald L
Ruda, Edwin
Rudquist, Jerry Jacob
Ruellan, Andree
Ruscha, Edward Joseph
Russell, (George) Gordon
Russell, Philip C
Russell, Robert Price
Russell, Shirley Ximena (Hopper)
Ruta, Peter Paul
Rutherford, Erica
Ruthling, Ford
Rutland, Emily Edith
Ryerson, Margery Austen
Saalburg, Allen Russel
Saari, Peter H
Sabatella, Joseph John
Sabelis, Huibert
Sabo, Betty Jean
Sachse, Janice R
Sacklarian, Stephen
Sahrbeck, Everett William
St Amand, Joseph
St John, John Milton
St John, Terry N
St Tamara
Sakai, Kazuya
Salamone, Gladys L
Salazar, Juan
Salemme, Antonio
Salemme, Martha
Salinas, Baruj
Salt, John
Salter, John Randall
Salter, Richard Mackintire
Saltonstall, Elizabeth
Saltzman, Marvin
Saltzman, William
Samburg, Grace (Blanche)
Samuels, Gerald
Samuelson, Fred Binder
Sanchez, Thorvald
Sandberg, Hannah
Sanders, Andrew Dominick
Sanders, Joop A
Sanderson, Charles Howard
Sandler, Barbara
Sandol, Maynard
Santlofer, Jonathan
Sargent, Margaret Holland
Sargent, Richard
Sarkisian, Paul
Sarsony, Robert
Sassone, Marco
Sato, Masaaki
Sato, Tadashi
Satorsky, Cyril
Saucy, Claude Gerald
Saunders, Aulus Ward
Saunders, Edith Dariel Chase
Savas, Jo-Ann (Mrs George T Savas)
Savelli, Angelo
Savitz, Frieda (Frieda Savitz Laden)
Savoy, Chyrl Lenore
Sawada, Ikune
Sazegar, Morteza
Scalise, Nicholas Peter
Schabacker, Betty Barchet
Schactman, Barry Robert
Schapiro, Miriam
Scharf, William
Schary, Emanuel
Schary, Saul
Schary, Susan
Schellin, Robert William
Schepis, Anthony Joseph
Scheu, Leonard
Schiff, Lonny
Schiller, Beatrice
Schimmel, William Berry
Schlemm, Betty Lou
Schlicher, Karl Theodore
Schloss, Edith
Schmidt, Arnold Alfred
Schnackenberg, Roy
Schneebaum, Tobias
Schneider, Jo Anne
Schnurr-Colflesh, E
Schoener, Jason
Schoenherr, John Carl
Schonberger, Fred
Schonwalter, Jean Frances
Schooley, Elmer Wayne
Schorr, Justin
Schreck, Michael Henry
Schreiber, Eileen Sher
Schreiber, Martin
Schreyer, Greta L
Schucker, Charles
Schueler, Jon R
Schultz, Caroline Reel
Schultz, Harold A
Schultz, Roger d
Schuman, Robert Conrad
Schuster, Cita Fletcher (Sarah E)
Schwab, Eloisa (Mrs A H Rodriguez)
Schwabacher, Ethel K
Schwacha, George
Schwartz, Carl E
Schwartz, Henry
Schwarz, Felix Conrad
Schwarz, Gladys
Schwedler, Wm A
Schwiering, Conrad
Schwinger, Sylvia
Scott, Jonathan
Scott, Marian (Dale)
Scott, Sam
Scott, Walter
Seabourn, Bert Dail
Seace, Barry William
Seaman, Drake F
Seames, Clarann
Searles, Charles Robert
Secunda, (Holland) Arthur
Seide, Charles
Seidler, Doris
Seliger, Charles

Seltzer, Phyllis
Selwitz, Ruth F
Semmel, Joan
Serisawa, Sueo
Serniak, Regina
Serra-Badue, Daniel
Serwazi, Albert B
Setterberg, Carl Georg
Seyffert, Richard Leopold
Shaddle, Alice
Shadrach, Jean H
Shahly, Jehan
Shane, Frederick E
Shapiro, Babe
Shapiro, David
Shapiro, David
Sharp, Anne
Sharpe, David Flemming
Shatalow, Vladimir Mihailovich
Shatter, Susan Louise
Shaw, Elsie Babbitt
Shaw, (George) Kendall
Shecter, Mark
Shecter, Pearl S
Sheehan, Evelyn
Sheehe, Lillian Carolyn
Sheets, Millard Owen
Sheppard, Joseph Sherly
Sherker, Michael Z
Sherman, Lenore (Walton)
Sherrod, Philip Lawrence
Sherry, William Grant
Shibley, Gertrude
Shields, Alan J
Shimomura, Roger Yutaka
Shiner, Nate
Shipley, Roger Douglas
Shippen, Zoe (Zoe Shippen Varnum)
Shoemaker, Peter
Shoemaker, Vaughn
Shokler, Harry
Shook, Georg
Shooter, Tom
Shore, Mary
Shores, (James) Franklin
Shorter, Edward Swift
Shoulberg, Harry
Showell, Kenneth L
Shuck, Kenneth Menaugh
Shuff, Lily (Lillian Shir)
Shull, Carl Edwin
Shunney, Andrew
Sickbert, Jo
Sickman, Jessalee Bane
Sideris, Alexander
Siegel, Adrian
Sievan, Maurice
Sigoloff, Violet Bruce
Sihvonen, Oli
Silins, Janis
Silverberg, Ellen Ruth
Silverman, Sherley C
Simel, Elaine
Simon, Howard
Simpkins, Henry John
Simpson, David
Simpson, Lee
Simpson, Marilyn Jean
Simpson, Merton D
Simson, Bevlyn A
Singer, Arthur B
Singer, Clyde J
Singer, Esther Forman
Singletary, Robert Eugene
Singleton, Robert Ellison
Sinnard, Elaine (Janice)
Sinton, Nell (Walter)
Sisson, Laurence P
Sisti, Anthony J (Tony)
Sitton, John M
Sivard, Robert Paul
Sjolseth, Minn Solveig
Skalagard, Hans
Skemp, Robert Oliver
Skinner, Elsa Kells
Sklar, Dorothy
Sklar-Weinstein, Arlene (Joyce)
Skolle, John
Skolnick, Arnold
Slack, Dee
Slater, Van E
Slaughter, Lurline Eddy
Slavit, Ann L
Sleigh, Sylvia
Sles, Steven Lawrence
Slider, Dorla Dean
Sloan, Jeanette Pasin
Sloan, Louis Baynard
Sloan, Richard
Sloan, Robert Smullyan
Sloane, Phyllis Lester
Slone, Sandi
Slorp, John Stephen
Slotnick, Mortimer H
Smart, Wini
Smith, Albert E
Smith, Alfred James, Jr
Smith, Arthur Hall
Smith, B J
Smith, Cecil Alden
Smith, Charles (William)
Smith, David Loeffler
Smith, Donald C
Smith, Frank Anthony
Smith, Gordon
Smith, Hassel W, Jr
Smith, Lawrence Beall
Smith, Paul Roland
Smith, Robert Alan
Smith, Thelma deGoede
Smith, Vincent D
Smongeski, Joseph Leon
Smyth, David Richard
Snow, Cynthia Reeves
Snow, Lee Erlin
Snyder, Seymour
Snyder, William B
Solberg, Morten Edward
Solinger, David M
Solman, Joseph
Solomon, Daniel
Solomon, David
Solomon, Hyde
Solomon, Syd
Soloway, Reta
Soltesz, Frank Joseph
Somers, H
Sommer, Frederick
Sommer, Wassily
Sommerburg, Miriam
Sorby, J Richard
Soriano, Juan
Souza, Paul Marciel
Soviak, Harry
Sowers, Miriam R
Soyer, Isaac
Soyer, Raphael
Spafford, Michael Charles
Spaulding, Warren Dan
Spaventa, George
Spelman, Jill Sullivan
Spence, Andy
Speyer, Nora
Spickett, Ronald John, (Sr)
Spohn, Clay (Edgar)
Sprague, Mark Anderson
Sprang, Elizabeth Lewis
Spruce, Everett Franklin
Squadra, John
Squires, Gerald Leopold
Stack, Frank Huntington
Stacks, William Leon
Stacy, Donald L
Stadler, Albert
Stamm, Ted
Stamper, Willson Young
Stanley, Bob
Stapleton, Joseph F
Staprans, Raimonds
Starrs, Mildred
Stasack, Edward Armen
Statman, Jan B
Staven, Leland Carroll
Steele, Benjamin Charles
Stefan, Ross
Stegall, James Park
Stegeman, Charles
Stegman, Patricia (Patricia Stegman Snyder)
Steiger, Frederic
Stein, Walter
Steinfels, Melville P
Steinhouse, Tobie (Thelma)
Stell, H Kenyon
Stemelos, Electra Georgia Mousmoules
Stenbery, Algot
Stephens, William Blakely
Stern, Irene Monat
Sternberg, Harry
Sterne, Dahli
Stevanov, Zoran
Stevens, May
Stevens, Nelson L
Stevens, Richard Clive
Stevens, Walter Hollis
Stevens, William Ansel, Sr
Stevenson, A Brockie
Stewart, Arthur
Stewart, Jack
Stewart, Jarvis Anthony
Stewart, John P
Stewart, William
Sticker, Robert Edward
Stiegelmeyer, Norman Earl
Stinski, Gerald Paul
Stokes, Thomas Phelps
Stoloff, Carolyn
Stoltenberg, Donald Hugo
Stomps, Walter E, Jr
Stone, John Lewis, Jr
Storm, Howard
Stout, Myron Stedman
Stout, Richard Gordon
Stowman, Annette Burr
Strater, Henry
Stratton, Dorothy (Mrs William A King)
Strauser, Sterling Boyd
Strautmanis, Edvins
Strawbridge, Edward R
Strawn, Melvin Nicholas
Strickland, Allen
Strickland, Thomas J
Strisik, Paul
Strong, Charles Ralph
Strother, Joseph Willis
Strother, Virginia Vaughn
Stroud, Peter Anthony
Stuart, Joseph Martin
Stucki, Margaret Elizabeth
Stull, Robert J
Sturtevant, Elaine F
Stussy, Jan
Sublett, Carl C
Sudlow, Robert N
Sugarman, George
Sugimoto, Henry Y
Sullins, Robert M
Sullivan, Jim
Sultan, Altoon
Summer, (Emily) Eugenia
Summerford, Ben Long
Summers, Robert
Summy, Anne Tunis
Surrey, Milt
Surrey, Philip Henry
Suter, Sherwood Eugene
Sutherland, Sandy
Sutton, Patricia
Suzuki, Sakari
Swain, Robert
Swanson, J N
Swanson, Ray V
Swartz, Beth Ames
Swartz, Phillip Scott
Sway, Albert
Sweney, Fred
Swenson, Anne
Swiggett, Jean Donald
Swinton, George
Sykes, (William) Maltby
Sylvester, Lucille
Tabachnick, Anne
Tabuena, Romeo Villalva
Taggart, William John
Tahedl, Ernestine
Taira, Frank
Takai, Teiji
Takashima, Shizuye Violet
Talbot, Jonathan
Talleur, John J
Tam, Reuben
Tanger, Susanna
Tanksley, Ann
Tanner, Joan Elizabeth
Tatossian, Armand
Taulbee, Dan J
Taylor, Fran (Frances Jane)
Taylor, Gage
Taylor, Grace Martin
Taylor, John C E
Taylor, John (Williams)
Taylor, Marie
Taylor, Sandra Ortiz
Tcheng, John T L
Teichman, Sabina
Tejeda, Carlos
Ten Eyck, Catryna (Catryna Ten Eyck Seymour)
Ten (Jan Ten Broeke)
Tennyson, Merle Berry
Terenzio, Anthony
Termini, Christine
Terry, Marion (E)
Tettleton, Robert Lynn
Tevis, Gary Lee
Texoon, Jasmine
Thelin, Valfred P
Thepot, Roger Francois
Thiery, Thomas Allen
Thies, Charles Herman
Thollander, Earl
Thom, Robert Alan
Thomas, Alma Woodsey
Thomas, Helen (Doane)
Thomas, John
Thomas, Katherine Castellanos
Thompson, Donald Roy
Thompson, Ernest Thorne
Thompson, Joanne
Thompson, Judith Kay
Thompson, Malcolm Barton
Thompson, Richard Earl, Sr
Thompson, Robert Charles
Thompson, Tamara (Tamara Thompson Bryant)
Thompson, Wade
Thomson, William David
Thorns, John Cyril, Jr
Thrall, Arthur
Thwaites, Charles Winstanley
Tiffany, Marguerite Bristol
Tigerman, Stanley
Tillim, Sidney
Timmas, Osvald
Timmins, William Frederick
Tinning, George Campbell
Tobey, Alton S
Todd, Michael Cullen
Toigo, Daniel Joseph
Toledo, Francisco
Tolmie, Kenneth Donald
Tomidy, Paul J
Tomlinson, Florence Kidder
Tompkins, Alan
Toney, Anthony
Toperzer, Thomas Raymond
Toral, Maria Teresa
Tormey, James
Torreano, John Francis
Toschik, Larry
Tousignant, Claude

PAINTER (cont)
Townsend, John F
Trachtman, Arnold S
Traher, William Henry
Travanti, Leon Emidio
Travis, Olin (Herman)
Trebilcock, Paul
Treese, William R
Triano, Anthony Thomas
Trieff, Selina
Triester, Kenneth
Trissel, James Nevin
Trivigno, Pat
Trlak, Roger
Truby, Betsy Kirby
Tse, Stephen
Tsuchidana, Harry Suyemi
Tucker, James Ewing
Tucker, Richard Derby
Turner, Alan
Turner, Arthur Charles
Turner, Bruce Backman
Turner, (Charles) Arthur
Turner, Norman Huntington
Turner, Ralph James
Turner, Theodore Roy
Twardowicz, Stanley Jan
Twiggs, Russell Gould
Tyler, Valton
Tyson, Mary (Mrs Kenneth Thompson)
Tytell, Louis
Ubans, Juris K
Ubertalli, Hector
Udinotti, Agnese
Uhrman, Celia
Uhrman, Esther
Ulbricht, John
Ullrich-Zuckerman, B
Urban, Mychajlo Raphael
Urban, Reva
Urueta, Cordelia
Ushenko, Audrey Andreyevna
Uttech, Thomas Martin
Vaccarino, Robin
Vaccaro, Luella Grace
Vaccaro, Nick Dante
Valenstein, Alice
Valerio, James Robert
Valier, Biron (Frank)
Van Buren, Helen Rae
Vander Sluis, George J
Van Der Voort, Amanda Venelia
Vaness, Margaret Helen
Van Hook, David H
Van Oordt, Peter
Van Roekens, Paulette (Mrs Arthur Meltzer)
Van Suchtelen, Adrian
Van Veen, Stuyvesant
Van Wyk, Helen
Vasils, Albert
Vass, Gene
Vaux, Richard
Vazquez, Paul
Venor, Robert George
Vicente, Esteban
Vickery, Charles Bridgeman
Vidal, Hahn
Vierthaler, Arthur A
Vigil, Veloy Joseph
Villeneuve, Joseph Arthur
Vincent, Tom
Visser't Hooft, Martha
Vitale, Lydia Modi
Vivenza, Francesca
Vo-Dinh, Mai
Voelker, John
Vogel, Donald S
Vogl, Don George
Von Gunten, Roger
von Schlippe, Alexey
Von Wiegand, Charmion
Voos, William John
Vorwerk, E Charlsie
Voyer, Sylvain Jacques
Vytlacil, Vaclav
Wagner, Gordon Parsons
Wagner, Merrill
Wagner, Richard Ellis
Wagoner, Robert B
Waitt, Alden Harry
Walch, John Leo
Walker, Joy
Walker, Larry
Walker, Peter Richard
Walker, Sandra Radcliffe
Wall, Ralph Alan
Wall, Sue
Wallace, John Edward
Wallace, Soni
Walsh, Patricia Ruth
Walters, Ernest
Walton, Florence Goodstein (Goodstein-Shapiro)
Waltzer, Stewart Paul
Wands, Alfred James
Ward, John Lawrence
Ward, Lyle Edward
Ward, Velox Benjamin
Ward, William Edward
Warder, William
Wardlaw, George Melvin
Wardy, Frederick
Warkov, Esther
Warner, Boyd, Jr
Warren, Betty
Warren, Ferdinand Earl
Warshaw, Howard
Warsinske, Norman George, Jr
Washburn, Stan
Wasser, Paula Kloster
Wasserman, Albert
Waterhouse, Charles Howard
Waterstreet, Ken (James Kent Waterstreet)
Watford, Frances Mizelle
Watia, Tarmo
Watson, Robert
Wayne, June
Weber, Idelle
Webster, Stokely
Weedman, Kenneth Russell
Weekes, Shirley Marie
Weeks, James (Darrell Northrup)
Weese, Myrtle A
Weidenaar, Reynold Henry
Weidner, Roswell Theodore
Weiler, Melody M
Weinbaum, Jean
Weingarten, Hilde (Kevess)
Weiss, Anton
Welch, James Wymore
Wellington, Duke
Wells, Mac
Werner-Vaughn, Salle
Wesselmann, Tom
Wessels, Glenn Anthony
West, Amy M
West, Clara Faye
Westcoast, Wanda
Wethli, Mark Christian
Wexler, George
Whidden, Conni (Constance)
Whitaker, Frederic
White, Charles Wilbert
White, Doris A
White, Franklin
White, Jack
White, Philip Butler
White, Ralph
White, Roger Lee
Whiteside, William Albert, II
Whitlow, Tyrel Eugene
Whitmore, Lenore K
Whitney, William Kuebler
Whitty-Johnson, Patricia
Wickiser, Ralph Lewanda
Wicks, Eugene Claude
Wiederspan, Stan
Wiegand, Robert
Wiener, Phyllis Ames
Wiggins, Bill
Wiitasalo, Shirley
Wilbert, Robert John
Wilde, John
Wilf, Andrew Jeffrey
Wilke, Ulfert S
Wilkinson, Kirk Cook
Willenbecher, John
Williams, Hiram Draper
Williams, Randalph Andrew
Williams, Raymond Lester
Williams, Todd
Williamson, Jason H
Willis, Sidney F
Willis, Thornton
Wilson, Ben
Wilson, Charles Banks
Wilson, David Philip
Wilson, George Lewis
Wilson, John
Wilson, Richard Brian
Wilson, Sybil
Wiman, Bill
Windrow, Patricia (Patricia Windrow Klein)
Winkler, Maria Paula
Winslow, John Randolph
Winter, Gerald Glen
Winter, Lumen Martin
Winter, Roger
Winter, Ruth
Winter, Thelma Frazier
Winters, Denny
Winters, John L
Wise, Geneva H (Holcomb)
Wissemann-Widrig, Nancy
Witkin, Jerome Paul
Witt, Nancy Camden
Woelffer, Emerson
Wogstad, James Everet
Wojtyla, Hasse (Walter Joseph Wojtyla)
Wolber, Paul J
Wolfe, Lynn Robert
Wolfe, Robert, Jr
Wolfe, Townsend Durant
Wolins, Joseph
Wolpert, Elizabeth Davis
Wolsky, Jack
Wolsky, Milton Laban
Wong, Ching
Wood, Jim (James Reid Wood)
Woodlock, Ethelyn Hurd
Woodruff, Hale A
Woodson, Doris
Woodson, Shirley Ann
Woodward, Cleveland Landon
Woodward, Helen M
Woof, Maija (Maija Gegeris Zack Peeples)
Wray, Margaret
Wright, Barton Allen
Wright, Bernard
Wright, Catharine Morris
Wright, Frank
Wright, Frank Cookman
Wuermer, Carl
Wunderman, Jan (Liljan Darcourt Wunderman)
Wyatt, Stanley
Wybrants-Lynch, Sharon
Wyeth, Henriette (Mrs Peter Hurd)
Wyeth, James Browning
Wynn, Donald James
Yaghjian, Edmund
Yanosky, Tom
Yarbrough, Leila Kepert
Yasko, Caryl Anne
Yasuda, Robert
Yater, George David
Yates, Sharon Deborah
Yektai, Manoucher
Yerex, Elton
Yoakum, Delmer J
Yokoi, Rita
Yokomi, Richard Koji
Yoshida, Ray Kakuo
Youkeles, Anne
Young, Cliff
Young, John Chin
Young, Milton
Young, Peter Ford
Young, Robert John
Young, Tom (William Thomas Young)
Youritzin, Glenda Green
Yrisarry, Mario
Yust, David E
Zabarsky, Melvin Joel
Zaborowski, Dennis J
Zaidenberg, Arthur
Zakanych, Robert
Zaleski, Jean M
Zallinger, Rudolph Franz
Zapkus, Kestutis Edward
Zarand, Julius John
Zeitlin, Harriet Brooks
Zelanski, Paul John
Zetlin, Fay (Florence Anshen Zetlin)
Ziegler, Jacqueline (Jacqueline Chalat-Ziegler)
Zimiles, Murray
Zimmerman, Kathleen Marie
Zimmerman, Paul Warren
Zingale, Lawrence
Zisla, Harold
Zivic, William Thomas
Zoellner, Richard C
Zonia, Dhimitri
Zoretich, George Stephen
Zoromskis, Kazimieras
Zuccarelli, Frank Edward
Zucker, Jacques
Zucker, Murray Harvey
Zuckerberg, Stanley M
Zugor, Sandor
Zweerts, Arnold
Zwick, Rosemary G
Zwicker, Leroy Judson

All Media

Aach, Herb
Abrams, Ruth
Accurso, Anthony Salvatore
Adams, Clinton
Adams, Pat
Adelman, Dorothy (Lee) McClintock
Adler, Myril
Agar, Eunice Jane
Ahn, Don C
Alajalov, Constantin
Alberga, Alta W
Albright, Ivan Le Lorraine
Albright, Malvin Marr
Alcalay, Albert S
Alcopley, L
Alexander, Robert Seymour
Allan, William George
Allen, Constance Olleen Webb
Allen, Jere Hardy
Allen, Loretta B
Allen, Margaret Prosser
Allen, Ralph
Allner, Walter H
Ambrose, Charles Edward
Ames, Arthur Forbes
Ames, (Polly) Scribner
Amft, Robert
Anderson, Guy Irving
Anderson, Winslow
Andrews, Benny
Andrews, Sybil (Sybil Andrews Morgan)
Antreasian, Garo Zareh
Anuszkiewicz, Richard Joseph
Aparicio, Gerardo

Apgar, Nicolas Adam
Appel, Eric A
Appel, Keith Kenneth
Appelhof, Ruth A
Apt, Charles
Arakawa (Shusaku)
Arbuckle, Franklin
Archie, James Lee
Ariss, Herbert Joshua
Armstrong, Bill Howard
Arnautoff, Jacob Victor
Arnold, Ralph Moffett
Aron, Kalman
Aronson, Irene Hilde
Artschwager, Richard Ernst
Ascher, Mary
Ashby, Carl
Asher, Elise
Askin, Walter Miller
Askman, Tom K
Asmar, Alice
Atkins, Billy W
Atkins, Rosalie Marks
Atwell, Allen
Aubin, Barbara
Avedisian, Edward
Ayaso, Manuel
Ayoroa, Rodolfo (Rudy) E
Backus, Standish, Jr
Badalamenti, Fred
Bahm, Henry
Bailin, Hella
Baker, Anna P
Baker, Eugene Ames
Baker, Jill Withrow
Baldwin, Harold Fletcher
Baldwin, John
Baldwin, Richard Wood
Balsley, John Gerald
Band, Max
Barazani, Morris
Barbee, Robert Thomas
Bardin, Jesse Redwin
Barnes, Robert M
Barr, Roger Terry
Barrett, Barbara
Barrett, Thomas R
Barrie, Erwin S
Barth, Frances
Barton, Bruce Walter
Barton, John Murray
Baumbach, Harold
Bavinger, Eugene Allen
Bayefsky, Aba
Bayliss, George
Beal, Jack
Beard, Marion L Patterson
Bearden, Romare Howard
Beerman, Herbert
Beitz, Lester U
Bendig, William Charles
Benglis, Lynda
Bengston, Billy Al
Bengtz, Ture
Bennett, Harriet
Benson, Robert Franklin
Ben-Zion
Berg, Siri
Bergere, Richard
Berguson, Robert Jenkins
Berkowitz, Henry
Bermudez, Jose Ygnacio
Bernstein, Judith
Berthot, Jake
Besser, Arne Charles
Bhalla, Hans
Biala, Janice
Bieler, Andre Charles
Billings, Henry
Birmelin, August Robert
Bisone, Edward George
Blackburn, Morris (Atkinson)
Blai, Bert
Blanc, Peter (William Peters Blanc)
Blanchard, Carol
Blaustein, Alfred H
Blazeje, Zbigniew
Blazey, Lawrence Edwin
Blizzard, Alan
Block, Irving Alexander
Blume, Peter
Bode, Robert William
Bodnar, Peter
Bodo, Sandor
Boggs, Franklin
Bohlen, Nina (Celestine Eustis Bohlen)
Bohnen, Blythe
Bohrod, Aaron
Bonacker, Joyce Sybil
Bonamarte, Lou
Bonet, Jordi
Bookatz, Samuel
Bornstein, Eli
Borochoff, (Ida) Sloan
Boros, Billi (Mrs Philip Bisaccio)
Bosa, Louis
Botkin, Henry
Bott, H J
Botto, Richard Alfred
Boutis, Tom
Bowers, Cheryl Olsen
Bowman, Dorothy (Louise)
Bowman, Richard
Boyce, Gerald G
Boyle, Keith
Boynton, James W
Brackman, Robert
Bradshaw, Lawrence James
Bramlett, Betty Jane
Brandfield, Kitty
Brandt, Rexford Elson
Bransby, Eric James
Bransom, (John) Paul
Brecher, Samuel
Brenner, Leonard J
Breverman, Harvey
Briansky, Rita Prezament
Briggs, Ernest
Briggs, Judson Reynolds
Brink, Guido Peter
Britsky, Nicholas
Brod, Stanford
Broderson, Morris
Broderson, Robert
Broemel, Carl William
Brooks, Bruce W
Brooks, Frank Leonard
Broudo, Joseph David
Broussard, Jay Remy
Brown, Gary Hugh
Brown, Gwyneth King (Mrs Joseph Brown)
Brown, Hilton Edward
Brown, John Hall
Brown, Peter C
Brumer, Miriam
Bruno, Santo Michael
Buczak, Brian Elliot
Buechner, Thomas Scharman
Burchess, Arnold
Burckhardt, Rudy
Burnham, Lee
Burroughs, John Coleman
Busa, Peter
Bush, Beverly
Bush, Lucile Elizabeth
Bushman, David Franklin
Bussabarger, Robert Franklin
Bywaters, Jerry
Caballero, Emilio
Cadle, Ray Kenneth
Calcagno, Lawrence
Calfee, William Howard
Califf, Marilyn Iskiwitz
Callahan, Kenneth
Callner, Richard
Camarata, Martin L
Canaday, Ouida Gornto
Cannon, Margaret Erickson
Cano, Margarita
Cantini, Virgil D
Cardinal, Marcelin
Cardman, Cecilia
Carewe, Sylvia
Carpenter, Gilbert Frederick (Bert)
Caster, Bernard Harry
Castoro, Rosemarie
Castro (Pacheco Fernando)
Catalan, Edgardo Omar
Catan-Rose, Richard
Cecere, Ada Rasario
Cederstrom, John Andrew
Ceglia, Vincent
Celli, Paul
Chaet, Bernard
Chapian, Grieg Hovsep
Charlot, Jean
Chavez, Edward Arcenio
Chermayeff, Ivan
Chester, Charlotte Wanetta
Chew, Harry
Childers, Malcolm Graeme
Chinn, Yuen Yuey
Christensen, Dan
Cianfoni, Emilio
Citron, Minna Wright
Ciuca, Eugen
Clancy, Patrick
Clayberger, Samuel Robert
Clemens, Paul
Clerk, Pierre
Cleveland, Helen Barth
Clymer, John F
Coates, Ross Alexander
Cochran, Dewees (Dewees Cochran Helbeck)
Cockrill, Sherna
Cohen, Adele
Cohen, Elaine Lustig
Cohen, Jean
Colarusso, Corrine Camille
Colker, Edward
Collett, Farrell Reuben
Colombo, Charles
Comes, Marcella
Comito, Nicholas U
Conaway, Gerald
Conaway, James D
Condon, Lawrence James
Conner, Bruce
Constantine, Greg John
Coochsiwukioma, DH (Del Honanie)
Cook, Howard Norton
Cooke, Jody Helen
Cooke, Samuel Tucker
Cooper, Wayne
Cordingley, Mary Bowles
Cornette, Mary Elizabeth
Corso, Patrick
Corwin, Sophia M
Costa, Olga
Costigan, Constance Christian
Cote, Alan
Couch, Urban
Coughtry, John Graham
Cowles, Russell
Cox, Allyn
Crable, James Harbour
Cramer, Abraham
Crane, James
Crespo, Michael Lowe
Cress, George Ayers
Crimi, Alfred D
Crispo, Dick
Crite, Allan Rohan
Crumbo, Woody
Crystal, Boris
Csoka, Stephen
Culbertson, Janet Lynn (Mrs Douglas Kaften)
Curtiss, George Curt
Cutler, Ethel Rose
Cyril, R
Czimbalmos, Szabo Kalman
Da Cunha, Julio
Daily, Evelynne B
Daly, Norman
Daphnis, Nassos
D'Arcangelo, Allan M
Darrow, Paul Gardner
Dash, Robert (Warren)
D'Aulaire, Edgar Parin
D'Aulaire, Ingri (Mortenson) Parin
Davidovitch, Jaime
Davies, Theodore Peter
Davis, Ben H
Davis, Gerald Vivian
Davis, James Wesley
Davis, Stephen A
Davis, Willis Bing
Davison, Robert
Day, Lucien B
Day, Martha B Willson
De Botton, Jean Philippe
de Champlain, Vera Chopak
De Diego, Julio
Deem, George
De Grazia, Ettore Ted
DeGroat, Diane L
Delford Brown, Robert
Delgado-Guitart, Jose
de Looper, Willem
Demartis, James J
De Nagy, Eva
De Niro, Robert
De Noronha, Maria M (Mrs David Gallman)
DePillars, Murry N
Dergalis, George
Desportes, Ulysse Gandvier
DeWit, Floyd Tennison
Diao, David
Dickerson, Tom
Dickinson, Edwin
Dill, Laddie John
Dillon, Mildred (Murphy)
Dimondstein, Morton
Dine, James
Diodato, Baldo
Dirube, Rolando Lopez
Di Suvero, Mark
Dodd, Lamar
Dogancay, Burhan Cahit
Dohanos, Stevan
Domareki, Joseph Theodore
Domjan, Joseph (also Spiri)
Donati, Enrico
Donneson, Seena
Doolittle, Warren Ford, Jr
Dorfman, Bruce
Dozier, Otis
Drake, James
Dreskin-Haig, Jeanet Elizabeth
Driskell, David Clyde
Duane, Tanya
Dubaniewicz, Peter Paul
Dugmore, Edward
Dunkelman, Loretta
Dunn, Nate
Dyck, Paul
Eades, Luis Eric
Eagerton, Robert Pierce
Eckelberry, Don Richard
Edens, Lettye P
Eder, Earl
Egleson, Jim (James Downey)
Eguchi, Yasu
Eide, Palmer
Eisenstat, Benjamin
Eitel, Cliffe Dean
Elias, Harold John
Eliot, Lucy Carter
Ellinger, Ilona E
Elliott, Philip Clarkson
Ellis, Fremont F
Elmo, James
Embry, Norris
England, Paul Grady
English, John Arbogast
Epler, Venetia
Erbe, Joan (Mrs Joan Erbe Udel)
Eriquezzo, Lee M

PAINTER (cont)
Ernst, Jimmy
Escobedo, Augusto Ortega
Esserman, Ruth
Etchison, Bruce
Etrog, Sorel
Evans, Minnie
Evans, Robert James
Everts, Connor
Ewing, Thomas R
Fabe, Robert
Faiers, Edward Spencer (Ted)
Falk, Gathie
Fangor, Voy
Faragasso, Jack
Faris, Brunel De Bost
Farnsworth, Jerry
Farris, Joseph
Fassett, Kaffe Havrah
Faulconer, Mary (Fullerton)
Fausett, (William) Dean
Fearing, Kelly
Fedelle, Estelle
Federe, Marion
Feher, Joseph
Fehl, Philipp P
Feitelson, Lorser
Feld, Augusta
Feldman, Walter (Sidney)
Felguerez, Manuel
Fellows, Fred
Fels, C P
Fenical, Marlin E
Ferguson, Charles
Ferriter, Clare
Feuerherm, Kurt K
Filipovic, Augustin
Filmus, Tully
Finch, Keith Bruce
Finck, Furman J
Fine, Ruth Eileen
Fink, Herbert Lewis
Finkler, Robert Allan
Fischer, John J
Fisher, Carole Gorney
Fisher, Leonard Everett
Fisk, Evi Ester
Fitzgerald, Edmond James
Floethe, Richard
Florsheim, Richard A
Fogel, Seymour
Foose, Robert James
Foote, Howard Reed
Ford, Charles Henri
Ford, John Charles
Foulkes, Llyn
Fox, Winifred Grace
Francis, Sam
Frankenberg, Robert Clinton
Frankenthaler, Helen
Frasconi, Antonio
Free, John D
Freed, William
Freeland, William Lee
Freimark, Robert (Matthew)
Freund, Will Frederick
Friberg, Arnold
Fricano, Tom S
Fried, Theodore
Friend, David
Fulton, Fred Franklin
Gains, Jacob
Galli, Stanley Walter
Garcia, Danny
Garrett, Stuart Grayson, Jr
Gates, Harry Irving
Gebhardt, Ann Stellhorn
Gebhardt, Peter Martin
Gecse, Helene
Geeslin, Lee Gaddis
Geiger, Edith Rogers
Genn, Nancy
Gentry (Augustus Calahan, Jr)
George, Thomas
Gervasi, Frank
Getz, Ilse
Gifford, J Nebraska
Gilbertson, Charlotte
Gill, James (Francis)
Gill, Sue May
Gillespie, Dorothy Merle
Gilliam, Sam
Ginzel, Roland
Giorgi, Vita
Gironella, Alberto
Glasco, Joseph M
Gluckman, Morris
Glyde, Henry George
Goddard, Vivian
Godsey, Glenn
Godwin, Judith Whitney
Goeritz, Mathias
Goetz, Richard Vernon
Gold, Albert
Goldberg, Michael
Golden, Eunice
Golden, Libby
Goldhamer, Charles
Goldstein, Gladys Hack
Goldstein, Julius
Gongora, Leonel
Gonzalez, Xavier
Gooch, Donald Burnette
Gooch, Gerald
Goodman, Bertram
Goodnough, Robert
Goodnow, Frank A
Goodyear, John L
Gorder, Clayton J
Gordon, Maxwell
Gordon, Violet
Goreleigh, Rex
Gorman, Carl Nelson (Kin-ya-onny Beyeh)
Gorman, William D
Gould, Stephen
Goulet, Claude
Govan, Francis Hawks
Grabach, John R
Grado, Angelo John
Grady, Ruby McLain
Graham, K M
Gramberg, Liliana
Grasso, Doris (Ten-Eyck)
Graves, Nancy Stevenson
Gray, Cleve
Gray, Don
Graziani, Sante
Graziano, Florence V Mercolino
Green, George Thurman
Green, Tom
Greenbaum, Marty
Greene, Balcomb
Greene, Daniel E
Greenwood, William James
Gregoropoulos, John
Grillo, John
Grippe, Florence (Berg)
Grippi, Salvatore William
Gronbeck, Jean
Grooms, Red
Grossman, Nancy
Grosz, Franz Joseph
Grotenrath, Ruth
Gruen, Shirley Schanen
Guite, Suzanne
Gumpert, Gunther
Gunn, Paul James
Gurr, Lena
Gutmann, John
Guzevich, Kreszenz (Cynthia)
Guzman-Forbes, Robert
Gyra, Francis Joseph, Jr
Gysin, Brion
Haas, Lez
Haas, Richard John
Hacklin, Allan Dave
Hafif, Marcia
Hagan, (Robert) Frederick
Halberstadt, Ernst
Hale, Kenneth John
Haley, John Charles
Halkin, Theodore
Hall, Carl Alvin
Hall, Rex Earl
Halsey, William Melton
Hammer, Alfred Emil
Hammock, Virgil Gene
Hammond, Ruth MacKrille
Hanlen, John (Garrett)
Hannibal, Joseph Harry
Hanson, Philip Holton
Harbart, Gertrude Felton
Harden, Marvin
Hare, Channing
Harris, Harvey Sherman
Harris, William Wadsworth, II
Harriton, Abraham
Hart, Allen M
Hartley, Paul Jerome
Harvey, Robert Martin
Hatfield, David Underhill
Hauser, Alonzo
Hawes, Charles
Hawkins, Myrtle H
Hawkins, Thomas Wilson, Jr
Haydon, Harold (Emerson)
Hay-Messick, Velma
Hazlitt, Don Robert
Head, Robert William
Healy, Julia Schmitt
Heberling, Glen Austin
Hee, Hon-Chew
Heidel, Frederick (H)
Heiloms, May
Heiskell, Diana
Helander, Bruce Paul
Held, Al
Helfond, Riva
Helgoe, Orlin Milton
Heller, Dorothy
Hendricks, Geoffrey
Henrickson, Paul Robert
Henry, Stuart (Compton)
Hensche, Henry
Herfield, Phyllis Anne
Herfindahl, Lloyd Manford
Herman, Vic
Herrera, Carmen
Herrera, Raul Othon
Herstand, Arnold
Hertzberg, Rose
Higa, (Yoshiharu)
Hill, Dale Logan
Hill, Joan (Chea-se-quah)
Hillsmith, Fannie
Hios, Theo
Holbrook, Hollis Howard
Holden, Raymond James
Holder, Tom
Holladay, Harlan H
Holland, Tom
Holmes, Ruth Atkinson
Holtz, Itshak Jack
Homar, Lorenzo
Homitzky, Peter
Hood, Walter Kelly
Hook, Walter
Hoowij, Jan
Hopkinson, Harold I
Hopper, Marianne Seward
Horiuchi, Paul
Housman, Russell F
Hovespain, Leon
Howard, Cecil Ray
Howard, Humbert L
Howell, Raymond
Hubenthal, Karl Samuel
Hudson, Robert H
Huldah (Huldah Cherry Jeffe)
Hunter, Mel
Huntington, Daphne
Huntley, David C
Hutsaliuk, Lubo
Hyde, Laurence
Icaza (Francisco de Icaza)
Imana, Jorge Garron
Indiviglia, Salvatore Joseph
Inoue, Kazuko
Insley, Will
Inukai, Kyohei
Inverarity, Robert Bruce
Ireland, Richard Wilson (Dick)
Ispanky, Laszlo
Ivy, Gregory Dowler
Izacyro (Isaac Jiro Matsuoka)
Jackson, A B
Jackson, Virgil V
Jacobs, Ted Seth
Jacobson, Ursula Mercedes
Jacquard (Jerald Wayne Jackard)
Jagger, Gillian
Jaidinger, Judith C (Judith Clarann Szesko)
James, Frederic
Jamieson, Mitchell
Jankowski, Joseph P
Jarvaise, James J
Jarvis, John Brent
Jaworska, Tamara
Jellico, John Anthony
Jenkins, Mary Anne K
Jenkins, Paul
Jennings, Francis
Jenrette, Pamela Anne
Jensen, Alfred
Jergens, Robert Joseph
Jeswald, Joseph
Johns, Jasper
Johnson, Cletus Merlin
Johnson, Daniel LaRue
Johnson, Doris Miller (Mrs Gardiner Johnson)
Johnson, Edvard Arthur
Johnson, Kenn Elmer
Johnson, Lee
Johnson, Lester F
Johnston, Ynez
Jolley, Geraldine H (Jerry)
Jones, Ben
Jones, Edward Powis
Jones, George Bobby
Jones, Herb (Leon Herbert Jones, Jr)
Jones, Jerry
Jones, Lois Mailou (Mrs V Pierre-Noel)
Jones, Ruthe Blalock
Jonson, Raymond
Ju, I-Hsiung
Jules, Mervin
Jungwirth, Irene Gayas (I Gayas Jungwirth)
Kahn, A Michael
Kahn, Peter
Kalinowski, Eugene M
Kaltenbach, Stephen James
Kamrowski, Gerome
Kaplan, Leonard
Kaplinski, Buffalo
Kaprow, Allan
Karniol, Hilda
Karp, Richard Gordon
Kashdin, Gladys S
Kass, Ray
Kassoy, Bernard
Katz, Hilda (Hilda Weber)
Katz, Leo
Katz, Morris
Kauffman, (Camille) Andrene
Kaulitz, Garry Charles
Keane, Lucina Mabel
Kearns, James Joseph
Keene, Paul
Keith, Eros
Kelley, Ramon
Kelly, Ellsworth
Kemoha (George W Patrick Patterson)
Kempton, Greta
Kenny, Bettie Ilene Cruts (BIK)
Kepes, Gyorgy
Kepets, Hugh Michael
Kerkovius, Ruth

Kerr, James Wilfrid
Kienbusch, William Austin
Killmaster, John H
Kim, Bongtae
Kimball, Yeffe
Kimura, William Yusaburo
King, Joseph Wallace (Vinciata)
Kinigstein, Jonah
Kinstler, Everett Raymond
Kipp, Orval
Kittelson, John Henry
Klein, Doris
Klein, Medard
Kleinholz, Frank
Klitgaard, Georgina
Klotz-Reilly, Suzanne Ruth
Knigin, Michael Jay
Knowles, Richard H
Koch, Arthur Robert
Koch, Edwin E
Kocsis, Ann
Koerner, Daniel
Koerner, Henry
Kohlhepp, Norman
Kolawole, Lawrence Compton
Komodore, Bill
Koni, Nicolaus
Konrad, Adolf Ferdinand
Korman, Harriet R
Korn, Elizabeth P
Kortlander, William (Clark)
Kowalke, Ronald Leroy
Kowing, Frank Eugene
Kozlow, Sigmund
Kramer, Marjorie Anne
Kraner, Florian G
Kressley, Margaret Hyatt
Kreznar, Richard J
Krukowski, Lucian
Krushenick, Nicholas
Kuchar, Kathleen Ann
Kuhn, Marylou
Kurahara, Ted
Kurz, Diana
Kuvshinoff, Bertha Horne
Kuvshinoff, Nicolai
LaFreniere, Isabel Marcotte
Lagorio, Irene R
Laguna, Muriel
Landfield, Ronnie (Ronald T)
Landon, Edward August
Larsen, Patrick Heffner
Larson, Sidney
Lassiter, Vernice (Vernice Lassiter Brown)
Latham, Barbara
Laventhol, Hank
Lazzari, Pietro
Lea, Tom
Leake, Eugene W
Leathers, Winston Lyle
Lechay, James
Lecoque
Lee, Robert J
Le Fevre, Richard John
Leff, Rita
Lekakis, Michael Nicholas
Lerner, Nathan Bernard
Lesh, Richard D
Leslie, Alfred
Levi, Josef
Levin, Jeanne
Levin, Morton D
Levine, Jack
Levine, Shepard
Levinson, Mon
Levitt, Alfred
Levy, Hilda
Lewandowski, Edmund D
Lewicki, James
Lewis, Elizabeth Matthew
Lewis, Ronald Walter
Liberi, Dante
Liberman, Alexander
Lichtenstein, Roy
Lidov, Arthur Herschel
Likan, Gustav
Liles, Raeford Bailey
Lindstrom, Gaell
Lionni, Leo
Little, John
Liu, Ho
Llorente, Luis
Lobdell, Frank
Loberg, Robert Warren
Lochrie, Elizabeth Davey
Lockhart, James Leland
Lomahaftewa, Linda (Linda Joyce Slock)
Loney, Doris Howard
Longley, Bernique
Longstreet, Stephen
Lorber, Stephen Neil
Loring, Clarice
Loring, John
Loro, Anthony Pivotto
Lourie, Herbert S
Love, Joseph
Lowe, Marvin
Lubner, Martin Paul
Lucioni, Luigi
Ludekens, Fred
Lukin, Sven
Lupper, Edward
Lyle, Charles Thomas
Mabry, Jane
Macdonald, Grant
Macdonnell, Cameron
MacGregor, John Boyko
MacIver, Loren
Mackay, Donald Cameron
MacNutt, Glenn Gordon
Macomber, Allison
Maehara, Hiromu
Magee, Alderson
Magnan, Oscar Gustav
Mahoney, James Owen
Malina, Frank Joseph
Mallory, Larry Richard
Malsch, Ellen L
Maltzman, Stanley
Mangold, Robert Peter
Manilla, Tess (Tess Manilla Weiner)
Manship, John Paul
Marca-Relli, Conrad
Margulies, Joseph
Mariano, Kristine
Maril, Herman
Mark, Bendor
Markell, Isabella Banks
Marks, Claude
Marks, George B
Marshall, James Duard
Marshall, Mara
Marsicano, Nicholas
Martin, Charles E
Martin, Fletcher
Martin, Fred Thomas
Martin, G W
Martin, Keith
Martin, Knox
Martin, Langton
Martin, Loretta Marsh
Martin, Thomas
Martin, William Henry (Bill)
Martinsen, Ivar Richard
Mason, Alice Frances
Mattiello, Roberto
Mattox, Charles
Maurice, Alfred Paul
Max, Peter
Maxwell, Robert Edwin
Maxwell, William C
Mayer, Bena Frank
Mayhew, Richard
Mayorga, Gabriel Humberto
McAllister-Kelly
McCall, Robert Theodore
McCallum, Corrie (Mrs William Halsey)
McCarthy, Denis
McClanahan, John Dean
McCloskey, Robert
McCloy, William Ashby
McCoon, Betty Jean
McCoy, John W, (II)
McCracken, John Harvey
McCray, Dorothy M
McEwen, Jean
McFarren, Grace
McGarrell, James
McIvor, John Wilfred
McMillan, Robert W
McNeil, George J
McWhorter, Elsie Jean
Meeker, Barbara Miller
Meeker, Dean Jackson
Mejer, Robert Lee
Mellon, James
Menchaca, Juan
Menihan, John Conway
Menkes, Sigmund
Menses, Jan
Meredith, John
Merfeld, Gerald Lydon
Merkin, Richard Marshall
Mesibov, Hugh
Messeguer, Villoro Benito
Metzger, Evelyn Borchard
Meyer, Felicia
Meyer, Fred (Robert)
Micale, Albert
Middaugh, Robert Burton
Mikus, Eleanore
Miller, Barbara Darlene
Miller, Eva-Hamlin
Miller, Richard Kidwell
Milliken, Gibbs
Mills, Agnes
Mina-Mora, Raul Jose
Minewski, Alex
Mitchell, Clifford
Mitchell, James E
Mitchell, Joan
Mitchell, Wallace (MacMahon)
Miyashita, Tad
Mock, Richard Basil
Moerschel, Chiara
Moldroski, Al R
Molinari, Guido
Monaghan, William Scott
Montana, Pietro
Montoya, Geronima Cruz (Po-Tsu-Nu)
Mora, Francisco
Morez, Mary
Morgan, Barbara Brooks
Morris, Edward A
Morris, George North
Morris, Kathleen Moir
Morris, Robert Clarke
Mosca, August
Moser, Julon
Moses, Ed
Moskowitz, Robert S
Moskowitz, Shirley (Mrs Jacob W Gruber)
Motherwell, Robert
Moulton, Susan Gene
Mount, Charles Merrill
Mount, Pauline Ward
Moyer, Roy
Mueller, Henrietta Waters
Muhlstock, Louis
Mullen, Philip Edward
Munzer, Aribert
Murphy, Gladys Wilkins
Murphy, Herbert A
Nalder, Nan
Nama, George Allen
Narotzky, Norman David
Naumer, Helmuth
Neff, Edith
Neiman, LeRoy
Ness, (Albert) Kenneth
Neuman, Robert S
Newman, Elias
Nichols, Donald Edward
Nonay, Paul
Nong
Norris, (Robert) Ben
Norton, Rob Roy, Jr
Nossal, Audrey Jean
Notarbartolo, Albert
Novinski, Lyle Frank
Nowack, Wayne Kenyon
Nulf, Frank Allen
Ocejo (Jose Garcia)
Oi, Motoi
Okamura, Arthur
O'Keeffe, Georgia
O'Kelley, Mattie Lou
Olds, Elizabeth
Olkinetzky, Sam
Onslow Ford, Gordon M
Opper, John
Orr, Elliot
Ortman, George Earl
Osborne, Robert Lee
Ossorio, Alfonso A
Owen, Frank (Franklin Charles Owen)
Pablo (Paul Burgess Edwards)
Pacheco, Maria Luisa
Page, John Henry, Jr
Page, Robin
Palau, Marta
Paone, Peter
Papo, Iso
Paradise, Phil (Herschel)
Paris, Lucille M
Parker, John William
Parks, Christopher Cropper
Parshall, Douglass Ewell
Parton, Nike
Pattee, Rowena
Payor, Eugene
Pearlman, Etta S
Pearlstein, Philip
Pearlstein, Seymour
Pehap, Erich K
Pekar, Ronald Walter
Pekarsky, Mel (Melvin Hirsch)
Pellicone, William
Perlin, Bernard
Petheo, Bela Francis
Phillips, James
Piatek, Francis John
Piccillo, Joseph
Picken, George
Pierce, J Michael
Pike, John
Pinardi, Enrico Vittorio
Pinsky, Alfred
Pinto, Angelo Raphael
Pisani, Joseph
Plochmann, Carolyn Gassan
Poduska, T F
Polan, Nancy Moore
Pollack, Reginald Murray
Polonsky, Arthur
Poons, Larry
Pope, Mary Ann Irwin
Porter, (Edwin) David
Porter, J Erwin
Portmann, Frieda Bertha Anne
Posey, Ernest Noel
Postiglione, Corey M
Potter, Ted
Pozzi, Lucio
Prentice, David Ramage
Pride, Joy
Prochownik, Walter A
Prohaska, Ray
Purser, Stuart Robert
Pusey, Mavis
Putnam, Wallace (Bradstreet)
Putterman, Florence Grace
Quaytman, Harvey
Quest, Charles Francis
Racz, Andre
Radulovic, Savo
Ragland, Bob

PAINTER (cont)
Ragland, Jack Whitney
Rakovan, Lawrence Francis
Ramirez, Joel Tito
Rand, Paul
Ratkai, George
Rauschenberg, Robert
Reardon, Mary A
Rebert, Jo Liefeld
Reed, Jesse Floyd
Reep, Edward Arnold
Rehberger, Gustav
Reiback, Earl M
Reif, Rubin
Reindorf, Samuel
Reinhardt, Siegfried Gerhard
Relis, Sandy
Remsing, (Joseph) Gary
Resnick, Milton
Retzer, Howard Earl
Reynolds, Ralph William
Ricci, Jerri
Rice, Anthony Hopkins
Rice, Norman Lewis
Richard, Jack
Richards, Walter DuBois
Richardson, Sam
Richenburg, Robert Bartlett
Richter, Hank
Ridley, Gregory D, Jr
Ridlon, James A
Ries, Martin
Riley, Bernard Joseph
Ringgold, Faith
Rivers, Larry
Roberts, Donald
Roberts, (William) Goodridge
Robinson, Grove
Robinson, Jay Thurston
Robinson, Sally W
Rockmore, Noel
Rodriguez, Oscar
Rodriguez, Ralph Noel
Roesch, Kurt (Ferdinand)
Rogers, Charles B
Rogers, Peter Wilfrid
Rogovin, Howard Sand
Roland, Arthur
Romano, Clare Camille
Romano, Emanuel Glicen
Romano, Umberto Roberto
Rome, Harold
Rose, Herman
Rosenblum, Sadie Skoletsky
Rosenborg, Ralph M
Rosenquit, Bernard
Ross, James Matthew
Rossi, Barbara
Rostand, Michel
Roston, Arnold
Roszak, Theodore
Rotenberg, Harold
Roth, Frank
Rotterdam, Paul Z
Rozman, Joseph John
Ruben, Leonard
Rubenstein, Lewis W
Rubin, Irwin
Ruddley, John
Russo, Alexander Peter
Rutsch, Alexander
Ruvolo, Felix Emmanuele
Ryman, Robert
Sabatini, Raphael
Safford, Arthur R
Saldivar, Jaime
Salemme, Lucia (Autorino)
Salla, Salvatore
Saltmarche, Kenneth Charles
Samerjan, George E
Samstag, Gordon
Samuels, Gerald
Samuelson, Fred Binder
Sanchez, Carol Lee
Sanchez, Emilio
Sanderson, Charles Howard
Sandgren, Ernest Nelson
Sandler, Barbara
Sankowsky, Itzhak
Saret, Alan Daniel
Sarff, Walter
Sarnoff, Arthur Saron
Saul, Peter
Sauls, Frederick Inabinette
Saunders, J Boyd
Savage, Roger
Savas, Jo-Ann (Mrs George T Savas)
Savitt, Sam
Sawyer, Helen (Helen Sawyer Farnsworth)
Scanga, Italo
Schaffer, Rose
Schanker, Louis
Scharff, Constance Kramer
Schein, Eugenie
Scherpereel, Richard Charles
Schlaikjer, Jes (Wilhelm)
Schliefer, Stafford Lerrig
Schmid, Richard Alan
Schmidt, Frederick Lee
Schmidt, Katherine (Katherine Schmidt Shubert)
Scholder, Fritz
Schrag, Karl
Schrut, Sherry
Schulthess, Amalia
Schulz, William Gallagher
Schutz, Estelle
Schwalbach, Mary Jo
Schwartz, Therese
Schwartz, William S
Schwarz, Felix Conrad
Schwarz, Gladys
Schweitzer, Gertrude
Scott, Henry (Edwards), Jr
Seckel, Paul Bernhard
Seckler, Dorothy Gees
Seery, John
Selonke, Irene A
Senior, Dorothy Elizabeth
Shadbolt, Jack Leonard
Shaw, Elsie Babbitt
Shaw, Harry Hutchison
Shead, S Ray
Sheaks, Barclay
Shecter, Mark
Sheehan, Evelyn
Shelton, Robert Lee
Sheppard, John Craig
Sheppard, Luvon
Sherman, Sarai
Sherman, Z Charlotte
Sherwood, A (Frances Ann Crane)
Shikler, Aaron
Shimoda, Osamu
Shuff, Lily (Lillian Shir)
Shumacker, Elizabeth Wight
Shute, Ben E
Shute, Roberta E
Sibley, Charles Kenneth
Sider, Deno
Siebner, Herbert (Vom Siebenstein)
Siegel, Irene
Siegriest, Lundy
Sigel, Barry Chaim
Silber, Maurice
Silkotch, Mary Ellen
Sills, Thomas Albert
Silverman, Burton Philip
Simon, Jewel Woodard
Simon, Sidney
Simoneau, Everett Hubert
Simoni, John Peter
Simpson, Merton D
Simpson, Tommy Hall
Sims, Agnes
Sing Hoo (Sing Hoo Yuen)
Sirena (Contessa Antonia Mastrocristino Fanara)
Sirugo, Salvatore
Sister Thomasita (Mary Thomasita Fessler)
Skalagard, Hans
Slade, Roy
Slate, Joseph Frank
Slavin, Arlene
Sloane, Patricia Hermine
Smith, Alvin
Smith, Gord
Smith, Gordon
Smith, Helen M
Smith, Joseph Anthony
Smith, Leon Polk
Smith, Lyn Wall
Smith, Paul Roland
Smith, Sam
Smith, Shirlann
Smith, Victor Joachim
Smith, William Arthur
Snelgrove, Walter H
Snidow, Gordon E
Snow, John
Snow, Michael
Snow, Vivian Douglas
Snyder, Joan
Snyder, Kim Lawrence
Sokole, Miron
Sonfist, Alan
Soreff, Helen
Sorge, Walter
Sorokin, Maxine Ann
Sovary, Lilly
Spandorf, Lily Gabriella
Speight, Francis
Spencer, Harold Edwin
Sperakis, Nicholas George
Sprout, Francis Allen
Spruyt, E Lee
Staempfli, George W
Stahl, Ben (Albert)
Stamos, Theodoros (S)
Stanczak, Julian
Stark, Melville F
Starrs, Mildred
Stefanelli, Joseph J
Steinke, Bettina
Sterne, Hedda
Stevens, Walter Hollis
Stewart, Charles Carl
Stewart, Dorothy S
Stewart, Norman (William)
Still, Clyfford
Stipe, William S
Stoessel, Henry Kurt
Stone, Gwen
Stonebarger, Virginia
Storer, Inez Mary
Storm, Larue
Storm, Mark (Kennedy)
Story, William Easton
Straight, Robert Larry
Stratton, Dorothy (Mrs William A King)
Strombotne, James
Stronghilos, Carol
Sturman, Eugene
Stussy, Jan
Suarez, Magdalena Frimkess
Suba, Susanne
Sullins, Robert M
Summ, Helmut
Sussman, Arthur
Sutton, George Miksch
Swan, Barbara
Swensen, Mary Jeanette Hamilton (Jean)
Swirnoff, Lois
Sznajderman, Marius S
Tait, Cornelia Damian
Takal, Peter
Tamayo, Rufino
Tania (Schreiber-Milicevic)
Tanner, Warren
Tascona, Antonio Tony
Tasgal-Kliegman, Gerda
Tatossian, Armand
Tatti, Benedict Michael
Taubes, Frederic
Taylor, Frederick Bourchier
Taylor, John C E
Terris, Albert
Texidor, Fernando
Texoon, Jasmine
Teyral, John
Thiebaud, (Morton) Wayne
Thomas, Byron
Thomas, Lionel Arthur John
Thomas, Steffen Wolfgang
Thomas, William Radford
Thompson, Richard Craig
Thon, William
Thorns, John Cyril, Jr
Thwaites, Charles Winstanley
Tietz, Evelyne
Tillenius, Clarence (Ingwall)
Tilley, Lewis Lee
Ting, Walasse
Tirana, Rosamond (Mrs Edward Corbett)
Tobias, Abraham Joel
Tobias, Robert Paul
Toulis, Vasilios (Apostolos)
Town, Harold Barling
Tracy, (Lois) Bartlett
Treadwell, Helen
Treiman, Joyce Wahl
Triester, Kenneth
Trova, Ernest Tino
Trovato, Joseph S
Tsai, Hsiao Hsia
Tschacbasov, Nahum
Tse, Stephen
Tubis, Seymour
Tucker, Charles Clement
Tulk, Alfred James
Turner, James Thomas, Sr
Tuttle, Richard
Twitty, James (Watson)
Twombly, Cy
Tworkov, Jack
Udvardy, John Warren
Umana, Alfonso
Umlauf, Karl A
Underwood, Evelyn Notman
Upton, Richard Thomas
Vaccaro, Patrick Frank (Patt Vaccaro)
Van De Wiele, Gerald
Vann, Loli (Mrs Lilian Van Young)
Van Roijen, Hildegarde Graham
Van Veen, Stuyvesant
Van Young, Oscar
Varga, Margit
Vaux, Richard
Velarde, Pablita
Viera, Ricardo
Vihos, George
Viret, Margaret Mary (Mrs Frank Ivo)
Volkin, Hilda Appel
Volpe, Robert
Vorwerk, E Charlsie
Voth, Andrew Charles
Waano-Gano, Joe
Waddell, Eugene
Wagner, Charles H
Wagner, G Noble
Wagner, John Philip
Waisler, Lee
Walch, John Leo
Waldman, Paul
Wallace, Soni
Walton, William
Warhol, Andy
Warner, Boyd, Jr
Warren, Melvin Charles
Warriner, Laura B
Washington, James W, Jr
Watson, Darliene Keeney
Webb, Virginia Louise
Weber, Albert Jacob
Weber, Jan
Wechter, Vivienne Thaul
Wein, Albert W

Weiner, Abe
Weinstein, Florence
Weismann, Donald Leroy
Weller, John Sidney
Welliver, Neil G
Wells, Betty Childs
Werner, Donald (Lewis)
Werner, Fritz
West, W Richard (Dick)
Wethington, Wilma Zella
Whitaker, William
Whitcomb, Jon
White, John M
Whiteman, Edward Russell
Whitmore, Coby
Whyte, Raymond A
Wieland, Joyce
Wight, Frederick S
Wiley, William T
Will, John A
Williams, Benjamin Forrest
Williams, Marylou Lord Study
Williams, Neil
Williams, Walter (Henry)
Williams, William Terence
Wilmeth, Hal Turner
Wilson, Jane
Wilson, Mortimer, Jr
Wilson, York
Wilwers, Edward Mathias
Wimberley, Frank Walden
Winer, Donald Arthur
Wisnosky, John G
Witham, Vernon Clint
Witold-k (Kaczanowski)
Witt, John
Wofford, Philip
Wolf, Jack Clifford
Wolfe, Mildred Nungester
Wonner, Paul (John)
Wood, Harry Emsley, Jr
Wood, Robert E
Woods, Rip
Woodward, William
Wray, Dick
Wright, Stanley Marc
Wu, I-Chen
Wynne, Albert Givens
Wyse, Alexander John
Yanow, Rhoda Mae
Yeatts, James McKinney
Yochim, Louise Dunn
Young, Charles Alexander
Young, Kenneth Victor
Young, Tom (William Thomas Young)
Youngerman, Jack
Youngsblood, Nat
Yrizarry, Marcos
Yunkers, Adja
Zach, Jan
Zacharias, Athos
Zajac, Jack
Zamparelli, Mario Armond
Zeitlin, Harriet Brooks
Zevon, Irene
Zietz, Stephen Joseph
Ziric, William Thomas
Zox, Larry
Zucker, Jacques
Zucker, Joseph I

Egg Tempera

Allen, Patricia (Patricia Allen Bott)
Amarotico, Joseph Anthony
Andrejevic, Milet
Azaceta, Luis Cruz
Baxter, Robert James
Binford, Julien
Bishop, Isabel (Mrs Harold G Wolff)
Braiden, Rose Margaret J
Bratcher, Dale
Brenner, Mabel
Cadmus, Paul
Campbell, David Paul
Chavez-Morado, Jose
Chestney, Lillian
Chumley, John Wesley
Clark, Robert Charles
Coheleach, Guy Joseph
Cotsworth, Staats
Cox, Gardner
Danby, Ken
Dance, Robert Bartlett
Davis, Wayne Lambert
De Diego, Julio
de Lesseps, Tauni
de Martelly, John Stockton
de Turczynowicz, Wanda (Mrs Eliot Hermann)
Diehl, Sevilla S
di Gioia, Frank
Drutz, June
Eldredge, Stuart Edson
Engle, Chet
Etter, Howard Lee
Fastove, Aaron (Aaron Fastovsky)
Flint, Leroy W
Forrestall, Thomas De Vany
French, Jared
Gerhold, William Henry
Ghikas, Panos George
Graves, Morris
Guderna, Ladislav
Hack, Howard Edwin
Harrison, Pat (Broeder)
Holmes, David Bryan
Hood, Walter Kelly
Howell, Frank
Hurd, Peter
Jones, Anthony
Kruskamp, Janet
Kurelek, William
Lawrence, Jacob
Lewis, Nat Brush
Lieberman, Meyer Frank
Lindner, Ernest
Lumbers, James Richard
Macdonald, Grant
MacKenzie, Hugh Seaforth
Magafan, Ethel
Makarenko, Zachary Philipp
Manarey, Thelma Alberta
Massey, Robert Joseph
McAdoo, Donald Eldridge
McIntosh, Harold
McKim, William Wind
Medearis, Roger
Megargee, Lawrence Anthony (Laurie)
Meigs, John Liggett
Montgomery, Claude
Musick, Archie L
Musselman, Darwin B
Ocejo (Jose Garcia)
Osze, Andrew E
Patterson, William Joseph
Pellicone, William
Perret, Nell Foster
Peter, George
Petro, Joseph (Victor), Jr
Rankin, Don
Rosenthal, Seymour Joseph
Rosenthal, Stephen
Sargent, Richard
Schaefer, Carl Fellman
Schoenherr, John Carl
Schulz, Ken
Shatalow, Vladimir Mihailovich
Shook, Georg
Sievan, Maurice
Steele, Benjamin Charles
Stone, John Lewis, Jr
Summers, Robert
Tarnopol, Gregoire
Thomson, William David
Tolmie, Kenneth Donald
Tooker, George
Treaster, Richard A
Underwood, Evelyn Notman
Vargo, John
Vickrey, Robert Remsen
von Schlippe, Alexey
Vytlacil, Vaclav
West, Clara Faye
White, Philip Butler
Whiteside, William Albert, II
Wilson, Charles Banks
Winter, Thelma Frazier
Wright, Harold David
Wyatt, Stanley
Wyeth, Andrew Newell
Zarand, Julius John

Miscellaneous Media

Ablow, Joseph
Achepohl, Keith Anden
Adler, Robert
Ahrendt, Christine
Aitson, Marland Konad
Albrecht, Mary Dickson
Albuquerque, Lita
Aldwinckle, Eric
Alexenberg, Melvin (Menahem)
Alhilali, Neda
Anderson, William Thomas
Andrew, David Neville
Angel, Rifka
Angelini, John Michael
Anglin, Betty Lockhart
Angulo, Chappie
Anliker, Roger (William)
Ariss, Herbert Joshua
Armitage, Frank
Aronson, David
Asante, Kwasi Seitu (Robin Okeeffer Harper)
Atlee, Emilie DeS
Auth, Robert R
Avakian, John
Bacon, Peggy
Bailey, Malcolm C W
Bakaty, Mike
Baker, Sarah Marimda
Balazs-Pottasch, Gyongyi
Bandel, Lennon Raymond
Banerjee (bimal)
Barker, Walter William
Barsch, Wulf Erich
Bartlett, Jennifer Losch
Barton, Bruce Walter
Barton, Jean L
Bass, Joel
Beaman, Richard Bancroft
Beament, Tib (Thomas Harold)
Beauchemin, Micheline
Beker, Gisela
Belfiore, Gerardo
Benn, Ben
Berdich, Vera
Berg, Barry
Berkon, Martin
Bernstein, Theresa
Bhavsar, Natvar Prahladji
Biggers, John Thomas
Bjorklund, Lee
Blagden, Allen
Blaine, Nell
Blake, John Clemens
Blaz, Georgia Lee
Block, Joyce
Bloom, Donald Stanley
Bogaev, Ronni (Ronni Bogaev Greenstein)
Bohan, Peter John
Bohnen, Blythe
Boni, Delmar
Bosin, Blackbear
Botero, Fernando
Bowers, Cheryl Olsen
Boz, Alex (Alex Bozickovic)
Brach, Paul Henry
Brainard, Joe
Bramson, Phyllis Halperin
Braunstein, H Terry
Breinin, Raymond
Breslin, Wynn
Brice, William
Britt, Al
Brodie, Regis Conrad
Brokaw, Lucile
Bromberg, Faith
Bronson, Clark Everice
Brown, Larry K
Brown, Marvin Prentiss
Brown, Reynold
Browning, Dixie Burrus
Brulc, Dennis
Bruneau, Kittie
Bunn, Kenneth Rodney
Bunts, Frank
Burck, Jacob
Burgess, David Lowry
Burgues, Irving Carl
Burke, Daniel V
Burke, E Ainslie
Burns, Stan
Burnside, Wesley M
Cadieux, Michael Eugene
Cain, James Frederick, Jr
Cajori, Charles F
Calle, Paul
Calrow, Robert F
Campbell, Kenneth
Campbell, Marjorie Dunn
Cantieni, Graham Alfred
Card, Greg S
Carmel, Hilda Anne
Carroll, Robert Joseph
Carulla, Ramon
Case, Elizabeth
Casey, John Joseph
Cassanelli, Victor Vi
Castro, Alex
Catti (Catherine James)
Cavat, Irma
Chambers, John
Chandler, Dana C, Jr (Akin Duro)
Chandler, John William
Chang, Dai-Chien
Chapman, Dave
Chapman, Robert Gordon
Chen, Hilo
Chesney, Lee Roy, III
Chicago, Judy
Choy, Terence Tin-Ho
Christensen, Ronald Julius
Christ-Janer, Arland F
Church, C Howard
Clark, Eliot Candee
Clark, Michael Vinson
Close, Chuck
Coburn, Bette Lee Dobry
Coburn, Ralph
Coen, Arnaldo
Cohen, H George
Colescott, Robert H
Collier, Graham (Alan Graham-Collier)
Collins, Paul
Colorado, Charlotte
Conant, Howard Somers
Cone-Skelton, Annette
Conn, David Edward
Constant, George
Copeland, Lila
Copley, William Nelson
Cornin, Jon
Correa, Flora Horst
Corse, Mary Ann
Cosgrove, Stanley
Cost, James Peter
Cottingham, Robert
Couper, Charles Alexander
Couper, James M
Cowley, Edward P
Cox, Gardner

PAINTER (cont)
Cox, John Rogers
Cox, Marion Averal
Creatore, Mary-Alice
Crile, Susan
Crockett, Gibson M
Crossgrove, Roger Lynn
Cuevas, Jose Luis
Cunningham, (Charles) Bruce
Cusick, Nancy Taylor
Dahill, Thomas Henry, Jr
Dali, Salvador
D'Amato, Janet Potter
Davila, Carlos
Davis, Bradley Darius
Davis, Donald Robert
Davis, J Ray
Davis, Jerrold
Day, Larry (Lawrence James Day)
DeKay, John
De Knight, Avel
De Kooning, Willem
de Lesseps, Tauni
De Martini, Joseph
Denton, Pat
Desoto, Rafael M
Dessner, Murray
De Tonnancour, Jacques G
de Turczynowicz, Wanda (Mrs Eliot Hermann)
Dickinson, Eleanor Creekmore
Diehl, Sevilla S
Dillon, Paul Sanford
Di Meo, Dominick
Dmytruk, Ihor
Dodge, Joseph Jeffers
Donaldson, Jeff R
Downing, Thomas
Draper, Josiah Everett
Drewelowe, Eve
Drummond, (I G)
Dufour, Paul Arthur
Duis, Rita (Rita Duis Astley-Bell)
Dunkelman, Loretta
Duran, Robert
East, N S, Jr
Edvi Illes, George
Elliott, Ronnie
Elman, Emily
Emerson, Edith
Ettling, Ruth (Droitcour)
Evans, Nancy
Ewen, Paterson
Fainter, Robert A
Farian, Babette S
Farruggio, Remo Michael
Faulkner, Frank
Feigl, Doris Louise
Fein, B R
Fendell, Jonas J
Fernandes, Michael Adrian
Ferrer, Rafael
Fett, William F
Figures, Alfred
Fine, Perle
Fink, Louis R
Finnegan, Sharyn Marie
Fish, Janet I
Fleckenstein, Opal R
Flick, Paul John
Flora, James Royer
Flowers, Thomas Earl
Follett, Jean Frances
Forester, Russell
Foster, Barbara Lynn
Foster, Hal
Francis, Jean Thickens
Franck, Frederick S
Fraser, Carol Hoorn
Fredman, Faiya R
Freed, David
Freed, William
Freedman, Maurice
French, Jared
Frey, Viola
Friedberg, Ray E
Friedeberg, Pedro
Friscia, Albert Joseph
Frost, Stuart Homer
Fuller, Emily (Emily Fuller Kingston)
Gablik, Suzi
Galen, Elaine
Ganthiers, Louise Marie
Gardner, Andrew Bradford
Garel, Leo
Garrison, Eve
Gary, Jan (Mrs William D Gorman)
Garzon-Blanco, Armando
Gaucher, Yves
Gechtoff, Sonia
Gehr, Mary (Mary Ray)
Geissman, Robert Glenn
Gelb, Jan
Geller, Esther (Esther Geller Shapero)
Gentry, Herbert
Gianakos, Steve
Gill, Gene
Gillingwater, Denis Claude
Ginsburg, Max
Giobbi, Edward Gioachino
Giraudier, Antonio
Glaser, David
Glover, Robert Leon
Goetz, Edith Jean
Gold, Leah
Goldin, Leon
Goldstein, Milton
Golinkin, Joseph Webster
Goo, Benjamin
Goodman, Brenda Joyce
Goodyear, John L
Gordy, Robert P
Gorman, R C
Graves, Nancy Stevenson
Gray, Marie Elise
Green, Denise G
Greenbaum, Dorothea Schwarcz
Greenberg, Gloria
Greer, Walter Marion
Grimley, Oliver Fetterolf
Gross, Sandra Lerner
Gualtieri, Joseph P
Guthrie, Derek
Habergritz, George Joseph
Hall, John A
Hall, Lee
Hamel, Bernard Franklin
Hampton, John W
Handell, Albert George
Hansen, Harold John
Hansen, Robert
Hare, Stephen Hopkins
Harris, Lawren Phillips
Hartigan, Grace
Hatch, John W
Haut, Claire (Joan)
Havard, James Pinkney
Havis, C Kenneth
Haynes, Douglas H
Hedden-Sellman, Zelda
Helck, (Clarence) Peter
Heliker, John Edward
Henderson, Victor (Lance)
Herman, Susan L
Hernandez-Cruz, Luis
Hildebrandt, William Albert
Hill, Megan Lloyd
Hilton, John William
Hodge, Roy Garey
Hodgson, Trevor
Hoffman, Helen Bacon
Hoie, Claus
Holbrook, Vivian Nicholas
Hollinger, (Helen Wetherbee)
Hollingsworth, Alvin Carl
Holmbom, James William
Holste, Thomas James
Horowitz, Nadia
Housser, Yvonne McKague
Howe, Oscar
Howze, James Dean
Hubbard, John
Hull, Marie (Atkinson)
Humphrey, Ralph
Hunkler, Dennis Francis
Hunt, Courtenay
Hunter, John H
Huot, Robert
Hupp, Frederick Duis
Hutchison, Elizabeth S
Huth, Marta
Hutton, Dorothy Wackerman
Iannone, Dorothy
Iden, Sheldon
Ingalls, Eve
Irizarry, Carlos
Irvin, Fred Maddox
Israel, Marvin
Jackson, Suzanne Fitzallen
Jackson, Vaughn L
Jacobs, Jim
Jaque, Louis
Jenkinson, Geoffrey
Jensen, Pat
Johnson, Avery Fischer
Johnson, Dana Doane
Johnson, Douglas Walter
Johnson, Homer
Johnson, Ray
Johnston, William Edward
Jones, Allan Dudley
Jones, Bill
Jones, David Lee
Jones, Douglas McKee (Doug)
Jones, Howard William
Kacere, John C
Kachadoorian, Zubel
Kanemitsu, Matsumi
Kaplan, Joseph
Karawina, Erica (Mrs Sideny C Hsiao)
Kaye, George
Keeler, David Boughton
Keen, Helen Boyd
Keena, Janet Laybourn
Kelley, Chapman
Kennedy, J William
Kerns, Ed (Johnson, Jr)
Kettner, David Allen
Kielkopf, James Robert
Kimura, Riisaburo
King, Clinton Blair
Kinnaird, Richard William
Kitaj, R B
Klavans, Minnie
Kleemann, Ron
Knapp, Sadie Magnet
Knight, Jacob Jaskoviak
Knobler, Lois Jean
Knowles, Dorothy Elsie (Dorothy Elsie Perehudoff)
Kocher, Robert Lee
Kohl, Barbara
Kohn, Misch
Kohut, Lorene
Kornmayer, J Gary (John)
Kovner, Saul
Kramolc, Theodore Maria
Krasner, Lee
Kreitzer, David Martin
Krueger, Donald W
Kuehn, Edmund Karl
Kujundzic, Zeljko D
Kulicke, Robert M
Kupferman, Murray
Kutka, Anne (Mrs David McCosh)
Kwartler, Alexander
Laderman, Gabriel
Lagunes, Maria (Maria Lagunes Hernandez)
Lai, Waihang
Laliberte, Norman
La More, Chet Harmon
Lampert, Dorrie
Landeck, Armin
Lansdowne, James Fenwick
Lansner, Fay
Larraz, Julio Fernandez
Lasch, Pat
Latham, Catherine Doris
Layton, Richard
Leaf, June
Lebedev, Vladimir
Lebkicher, Anne Ross
Lee, Amy Freeman
Lee, Briant Hamor
Lee, Eleanor Gay
Lee, Manning de Villeneuve
Lee, Margaret F
Lee-Smith, Hughie
Lehman, Louise Brasell
Leighton, Thomas Charles
Lemieux, Jean Paul
Leonardi, Hector
Leong, James Chan
Lerman, Doris (Harriet)
Lerner, Sandy R
Lev-Landau (Samuel David Landau)
Lewen, Si
Lewis, Samella Sanders
Li Marzi, Joseph
Livingston, Sidnee
Livingstone, Biganess
Long, C Chee
Longo, Vincent
Love, Paul Van Derveer
Loveless, Jim
Lowe, Joe Hing
Lukosius, Richard Benedict
Lund, David
Lupper, Edward
Lynch, Jo (Marilyn Blanche)
Mabie, Don Edward
MacGarvey, Bernard B
MacKendrick, Lilian
Mackenzie, David
Malina, Frank Joseph
Mancuso, Leni (Leni Mancuso Barrett)
Mandelman, Beatrice M
Manville, Elsie
Margo, Boris
Margules, Gabriele Ella
Mark, Marilyn
Marker, Mariska Pugsley
Markowski, Eugene David
Marsh, Anne Steele
Marshall, Robert Leroy
Martinet, Marjorie D
Martmer, William P
Massey, Robert Joseph
Mau, Hui-Chi
Mayer, Ralph
Mazur, Michael
McAninch, Beth
McCarthy, Frank C
McCormick, Jo Mary (Jo Mary McCormick-Sakurai)
McGowin, Ed
McGrath, James Arthur
McKay, Arthur Fortescue
McKesson, Malcolm Forbes
McKinin, Lawrence
McMillen, Michael Chalmers
McReynolds, (Joe) Cliff
Meigs, Walter
Merida, Carlos
Mermin, Mildred (Shire)
Metz, Gerry Michael
Metzger, Evelyn Borchard
Michelson-Bagley, Henrietta
Milholland, Richard Alexander
Miller, Daniel Dawson
Miller, Nancy Tokar
Mitchell, Jeffrey Malcolm
Mochizuki, Betty Ayako
Mohn, Cheri (Ann)
Momaday, Al
Monaghan, Keith
Montague, James L

Morehouse, William Paul
Morgan, Darlene
Morgan, Maritza Leskovar
Moroz, Mychajlo
Morris, Hilda
Murray, John Michael
Neal, Reginald H
Neto, G Reis (Gilda Reis Netopuletti)
Nichols, Alice W
Nichols, James William
Nichols, Jeannettie Doornhein
Nicholson, Ben
Nickle, Robert W
Noel, Georges
Noland, Kenneth
Norton, Rob Roy, Jr
Nosoff, Frank
Novotny, Elmer Ladislaw
Nuala (Elsa De Brun)
Ogilvie, Will (William Abernethy)
O'Gorman, Juan
Olson, Richard W
Olugebefola, Ademola
O'Neil, John
O'Neill, John Patton
Onley, Toni
Ortlip, Paul Daniel
O'Shea, Terrence Patrick
Ostiguy, Jean-Rene
Osver, Arthur
Owens, Al Curtis
Owings, Margaret Wentworth
Packer, Clair Lange
Palmer, Lucie Mackay
Panabaker, Frank S
Parish, Betty Waldo
Parish, Jean E
Parker, James
Partridge, David Gerry
Pattison, Abbott
Paul, William D, Jr
Peake, Channing
Pearson, John
Pearson, Marguerite Stuber
Peche, Dale C
Peck, Stephen Rogers
Peers, Gordon Franklin
Penney, Bruce Barton
Penney, James
Pennuto, James William
Perlin, Rae
Peterson, A E S
Petrie, Sylvia Spencer
Pezzati, Pietro
Pfeifer, Bodo
Philbrick, Margaret Elder
Philipp, Robert
Picard, Lil
Pickhardt, Carl
Piene, Otto
Pindell, Howardena Doreen
Plunkett, Edward Milton
Poleskie, Stephen Francis
Pollak, Theresa
Pond, Clayton
Popescu, Cara
Potter, (George) Kenneth
Pousette-Dart, Richard
Powell, Leslie (Joseph)
Preissler, Audrey
Preusser, Robert Ormerod
Priebe, Karl
Prins, (J) Warner
Quisgard, Liz Whitney
Rabut, Paul
Rachelski, Florian W
Rain, Charles (Whedon)
Rainey, John Watts
Rath, Hildegard
Ray, Robert (Donald)
Redd, Richard James
Red Star, Kevin Francis
Reed, Paul Allen
Reichert, Donald Karl
Rembski, Stanislav
Renouf, Edda
Richardson, Phyllis A
Rigg, Margaret Ruth
Rigsby, John David
Riley, Bernard Joseph
Rippey, Clayton
Riseling, Robert Lowell
Rizk, Romanos
Robbins, Hulda D
Robles, Julian
Romoser, Ruth Amelia
Rosenthal, Rachel
Ross, Beatrice Brook
Rossman, Ruth Scharff
Roussel, Claude Patrice
Rowan, C Patrick
Russell, (George) Gordon
Ryden, Kenneth Glenn
Saari, Peter H
Sabelis, Huibert
Salinas, Baruj
Sandberg, Hannah
Sangiamo, Albert
Saski, Tomiyo
Saunders, Edith Dariel Chase
Saunders, Raymond Jennings
Schaefer, Carl Fellman
Schiff, Lonny
Schloss, Arleen P (Arleen P Kelly)
Schneider, Julie (Saecker)
Schoenherr, John Carl
Schreiber, Eileen Sher
Schucker, Charles
Schulz, Cornelia
Schwabacher, Ethel K
Schwartz, Barbara Ann
Seidel, Alexander Carl-Victor
Sella, Alvin Conrad
Selwitz, Ruth F
Shackelford, Shelby
Shane, Frederick E
Shaw, Donald Edward
Shecter, Pearl S
Shooter, Tom
Shore, Mary
Silberstein-Storfer, Muriel Rosoff
Silver, Pat
Simmons, Cleda Marie
Simon, Howard
Skolle, John
Sles, Steven Lawrence
Slider, Dorla Dean
Smith, Dolph
Smith, Emily Guthrie
Sokolowski, Linda Robinson
Sonenberg, Jack
Soriano, Juan
Spafford, Michael Charles
Spero, Nancy
Spohn, Clay (Edgar)
Spurgeon, Sarah (Edna M)
Spurgin, John Edwin
Stack, Gael Z
Stapp, Ray Veryl
Steckel, Anita
Steczynski, John Myron
Steinmetz, Grace Ernst Titus
Steir, Pat
Stella, Frank
Stenbery, Algot
Stevens, Edward John, Jr
Stevenson, Branson Graves
Stevenson, Harold
Stiegelmeyer, Norman Earl
Stoianovich, Marcelle
Strasen, Barbara Elaine
Street, John Michael
Stuart, Michelle
Sundberg, Carl Gustave
Suzuki, James Hiroshi
Takashima, Shizuye Violet
Tamburine, Jean
Tanger, Susanna
Tarin, Gilberto A
Thepot, Roger Francois
Thiele, Robert Ransom
Thomas, Katherine Castellanos
Thompson, Ernest Thorne, Jr
Thompson, Joanne
Thompson, Wade
Threlkeld, Dale
Tillotison, Robbie
Turner, Janet E
Turoff, Muriel Pargh
Twiggs, Leo Franklin
Tytell, Louis
Uchima, Toshiko
Ullrich-Zuckerman, B
Underwood, Evelyn Notman
Unwin, Nora Spicer
Urban, Reva
Van Aalten, Jacques
Van Der Voort, Amanda Venelia
Van Hook, David H
Van Roekens, Paulette (Mrs Arthur Meltzer)
Venor, Robert George
Vevers, Anthony Marr
Vicente, Esteban
Villa, Carlos
Viret, Margaret Mary (Mrs Frank Ivo)
Vivenza, Francesca
Waddell, John Henry
Wagner, Merrill
Waitzkin, Stella
Walker, Herbert Brooks
Walton, Florence Goodstein (Goodstein-Shapiro)
Warner, Boyd, Jr
Warren, Betty
Wasserman, Burton
Wehr, Wesley Conrad
Weingarten, Hilde (Kevess)
Wells, Lynton
Weschler, Anita
Wesley, John
Westermeier, Clifford Peter
Wethli, Mark Christian
White, Charles Wilbert
White, Doris A
White, John M
Wier, Gordon D (Don)
Wiest, Kay Van Elmendorf
Willis, Thornton
Wilson, George Lewis
Wiper, Thomas William
Woodson, Doris
Woof, Maija (Maija Gegeris Zack Peeples)
Wyatt, Stanley
Wybrants-Lynch, Sharon
Yanow, Rhoda Mae
Zver, James M

Sand

Bishop, Marjorie Cutler
Chethlahe (David Chethlahe Paladin)
Crystal, Boris
Fredman, Faiya R
Hampton, Lucille Charlotte
Hart, Agnes
Noel, Georges
Owens, Al Curtis
Ramos-Prida, Fernando
Stewart, Arthur

Watercolor

Aalund, Suzy
Aaron, Evalyn (Wilhelmina)
Accurso, Anthony Salvatore
Acker, Perry Miles
Ackerman, Frank Edward
Adams, Glenn Nelson
Ahysen, Harry Joseph
Airola, Paavo
Aitson, Marland Konad
Allen, Margo (Mrs Harry Shaw)
Allen, Patricia (Patricia Allen Bott)
Allgood, Charles Henry
Altvater, Catherine Tharp
Altwerger, Libby
Amster, Sally
Angelini, John Michael
Anglin, Betty Lockhart
Anzures, Rafael
Arcilesi, Vincent J
Armstrong, Roger Joseph
Arnholm, Ronald Fisher
Ashby, Carl
Austin, Phil
Auth, Robert R
Aymar, Gordon Christian
Baber, Alice
Baeder, John
Bales, Jewel
Ball, Lyle V
Balossi, John
Bama, James E
Banister, Robert Barr
Banks, Virginia
Barbour, Arthur J
Barnett, Earl D
Barnwell, John L
Barr, Norman
Barrett, Robert Dumas
Barron, Ros
Barr-Sharrar, Beryl
Bart, Elizabeth (Elizabeth Bart Gerald)
Bartlett, Robert Webster
Barton, August Charles
Barton, Georgie Read
Barton, Jean L
Baskerville, Charles
Bates, Maxwell Bennett
Batt, Miles Girard
Baynard, Ed
Beach, Warren
Beall, Joanna
Beaver, Fred
Bechtle, C Ronald
Bechtle, Robert Alan
Becker, Natalie Rose
Beery, Arthur O
Behl, Marjorie
Beker, Gisela
Bell, Alistair Macready
Bell, Coca (Mary Catlett Bell)
Bell, Peter Alan
Belle, Anna (Anna Belle Birckett)
Benda, Richard R
Bender, Bill
Bennett, Don Bemco
Benney, Robert
Bentz, Harry Donald
Benz, Lee R
Berd, Morris
Berger, Jason
Berkman, Aaron
Berneche, Jerry Douglas
Bernstein, Gerald
Bernstein, Sylvia
Berresford, Virginia
Berry, William David
Berthot, Jake
Bertoni, Dante H
Bettiga, Floyd Henry
Betts, Edward Howard
Bevlin, Marjorie Elliott
Bieser, Natalie
Birdsall, Byron
Bireline, George Lee
Birkin, Morton
Black, Mary McCune
Black, Shirley
Blackwood, David (Lloyd)
Blagden, Thomas P
Blahove, Marcos
Blaine, Nell
Blair, Jeanette Anne

PAINTER (cont)
Blair, Robert Noel
Blameuser, Mary Fleurette
Blattner, Robert Henry
Bloom, Donald Stanley
Blumberg, Barbara Griffiths
Blumberg, Ron
Boal, Sara Metzner
Bobick, Bruce
Bock, William Sauts-Netamux'we
Boedeker, Arnold E (Boedie)
Bogdanovic, Bogomir
Bolley, Irma S
Booth, George Warren
Boren, James Erwin
Boretz, Naomi
Borgatta, Robert Edward
Boris, Bessie
Borne, Mortimer
Bosa, Louis
Bosin, Blackbear
Bostick, William Allison
Boutis, Tom
Bove, Richard
Bower, Gary David
Bowers, Lynn Chuck
Bradley, Dorothy
Bradley, Ida Florence
Bradshaw, Glenn Raymond
Bradshaw, Robert George
Bragar, Philip Frank
Brandfield, Kitty
Bratcher, Dale
Brawley, Robert Julius
Breslin, Wynn
Brezik, Hilarion
Brightwell, Walter
Brodsky, Stan
Broemel, Carl William
Brommer, Gerald F
Brooks, Frank Leonard
Brooks, (John) Alan
Brooks, Robert
Broomfield, Adolphus George
Brotherton, Naomi
Brough, Richard Burrell
Brouillette, Al
Brown, Judith Gwyn
Brown, Marion B
Browne, Syd J
Brownhill, Harold
Browning, Dixie Burrus
Brucker, Edmund
Bruno, Vincent J
Brzozowski, Richard Joseph
Burch, Claire R
Burger, W Carl
Burns, Paul Callan
Burns, Sheila
Buros, Luella
Burroughs, Margaret T G
Burt, Dan
Burton, Gloria
Butler, Joseph (Green)
Bye, Ranulph (DeBayeux)
Bynum, E Anderson (Esther Pearl)
Caballero, Emilio
Caimite (Lynne Ruskin)
Cain, Joseph Alexander
Calkins, Kingsley Mark
Calrow, Robert F
Camlin, James A
Campbell, David Paul
Campbell, Dorothy Bostwick
Campbell, (James) Lawrence
Canaris, Patti Ann
Cantrell, Jim
Caplan, Jerry L
Caples, Barbara Barrett
Cardman, Cecilia
Carlin, James
Carlin, Robert Eugene
Carlos, (James) Edward
Carlson, Jane C
Carmichael, Donald Ray
Carmichael, Jae
Carpenter, E
Carrero, Jaime
Carrington, Joy Harrell
Carron, Maudee Lilyan
Carter, Bernard Shirley
Cartmell, Helen
Casarella, Edmond
Castano, Giovanni
Catchi (Catherine O Childs)
Catok, Lottie Meyer
Cattell, Ray
Cervenka, Barbara
Chadeayne, Robert Osborne
Chapman, Dave
Chapman, Howard Eugene
Chapman, Walter Howard
Chen, Tony (Anthony Young Chen)
Chen Chi
Cheng, Fu-Ding
Cheshire, Craig Gifford
Chiara, Alan Robert
Chin, Ric
Chomicky, Yar Gregory
Chow Chian-Chiu
Chow Leung Chen-Ying
Christensen, Larry R
Christensen, Sharlene
Christiana, Edward
Chumley, John Wesley
Ciarrochi, Ray
Cikovsky, Nicolai
Clark, Chevis Delwin
Clark, Eliot Candee
Clark, Paraskeva
Clark, Robert Charles
Clifton, Michelle Gamm
Clinedinst, Katherine Parsons
Clive, Richard R
Close, Chuck
Cobb, Ruth
Cobb, Virginia Horton
Coes, Kent Day
Cogswell, Dorothy McIntosh
Cohen, Hy
Cole, Frances
Collins, John Ireland
Colson, Chester E
Colt, John Nicholson
Colway, James R
Conrad, Nancy R
Cook, Gladys Emerson
Cooke, Donald Ewin
Cooke, Edwy Francis
Cooley, Adelaide Nation
Cooper, Lucille Baldwin
Cooper, Mario
Cornin, Jon
Corr, James Donat
Correa, Flora Horst
Cotsworth, Staats
Cowan, Thomas Bruce
Cox, Gardner
Cox, J W S
Cox, Marion Averal
Craft, Douglas D
Craner, Robert Rogers
Crawford, Catherine Betty
Crawford, Mel
Creatore, Mary-Alice
Croft, Lewis Scott
Crooks, W Spencer
Cross, Maria Concetta
Cross, Watson, Jr
Crossgrove, Roger Lynn
Crown, Keith Allen
Crumbo, Minisa
Crutchfield, William Richard
Crystal, Boris
Currie, Bruce
Curry, Noble Wilbur
Cutler, Grayce E
D'Agostino, Vincent
Dahlberg, Edwin Lennart
Dailey, Michael Dennis
Daisy (Daisy Black Langhauser)
d'Almeida, George
Damron, John Clarence
Danby, Ken
Dance, Robert Bartlett
d'Andrea, Albert Philip
Darr, William Humiston
Dash, Harvey Dwight
David, Don Raymond
Davidek, Stefan
Davidson, Allan Albert
Davidson, Morris
Davis, Harry Allen
Davis, Wayne Lambert
Day, Horace Talmage
Deaderick, Joseph
Dean, James
DeCaprio, Alice
De Leeuw, Leon
Deloney, Jack Clouse
DeLuigi, Janice Cecilia
DeMaree, Elizabeth Ann (Betty)
de Martelly, John Stockton
De Mille, Leslie Benjamin
Denis, Paul Andre S
Dennis, Cherre Nixon
Dennis, Roger Wilson
Denniston, Douglas
de Turczynowicz, Wanda (Mrs Eliot Hermann)
Dew, James Edward
Dewey, Kenneth Francis
Dibble, George
Dickerson, Betty
Diehl, Sevilla S
di Gioia, Frank
Dike, Philip Latimer
Dixon, Kenneth Ray
Dobie, Jeanne
Dodd, Lois
Dole, William
Dominique, John August
Dooley, Helen Bertha
Dorst, Claire V
Doudera, Gerard
Dowden, Anne Ophelia Todd
Doyle, John Lawrence
Dragul, Sandra Kaplan
Draper, Josiah Everett
Drewes, Werner
Dreyer, Margaret Webb
Drower, Sara Ruth
Drutz, June
Duback, Charles S
Dubin, Ralph
Duff, Ann MacIntosh
Duis, Rita (Rita Duis Astley-Bell)
Duncan, Ruth
Dunn, Cal
Dzubas, Friedel
Eames, John Heagan
Eastman, Gene M
Ecke, Betty Tseng Yu-Ho
Eckert, Lou
Edelheit, Martha
Edwards, Ethel (Mrs Xavier Gonzalez)
Egeli, Peter Even
Eguchi, Yasu
Eisenberg, Sonja Miriam
Eldredge, Stuart Edson
Eliason, Shirley (Shirley Eliason Haupt)
Ellis, Edwin Charles
Ellis, Richard
Engel, Michael Martin, II
Engelson, Carol
Engeran, Whitney John, Jr
Engle, Chet
Enman, Tom Kenneth
Eppink, Norman R
Erdle, Rob
Ericson, Ernest
Ernst, James Arnold
Eshoo, Robert
Eshraw, Ra
Estes, Richard
Etter, Howard Lee
Evett, Kenneth Warnock
Eyre, Ivan
Fabion, John
Fagg, Kenneth (Stanley)
Fainter, Robert A
Farnham, Emily
Feigin, Marsha
Fein, B R
Fein, Stanley
Feininger, T Lux
Feldman, Hilda (Mrs Neville S Dickinson)
Ferguson, Edward Robert
Feriola, James Philip
Fett, William F
Fillerup, Mel
Finson, Hildred A
Fiore, Joseph A
Firfires, Nicholas Samuel
Fish, George A
Flax, Serene
Fleckenstein, Opal R
Flecker, Maurice Nathan
Fluek, Toby
Fohr, Jenny
Fon, Jade
Fontanez, Carmelo
Ford, Ruth Vansickle
Forman, Kenneth Warner
Forsyth, Constance
Fosburgh, James Whitney
Foshag, Merle
Fousek, Frank Daniel
Franco, Robert John
Fransioli, Thomas Adrian
Frater, Hal
Freed, William
Freifeld, Eric
Freilich, Ann
Frerichs, Ruth Colcord
Freund, Harry Louis
Friedensohn, Elias
Froman, Ramon Mitchell
Fromberg, LaVerne Ray
Fruhauf, Aline
Fry, Guy
Fuchs, Mary Tharsilla
Fuller, Sue
Fussiner, Howard
Gage, Harry (Lawrence)
Gale, William Henry
Gammon, Juanita-La Verne
Garel, Leo
Garnsey, Clarke Henderson
Garzon-Blanco, Armando
Gasser, Henry Martin
Gatrell, Marion Thompson
Gatrell, Robert Morris
Gaul, Arrah Lee
Gawboy, Carl
Geis, Milton Arthur
Gelber, Samuel
Geller, Esther (Esther Geller Shapero)
Genders, Richard Atherstone
Gentry (Augustus Calahan, Jr)
Gerard, Paula (Mrs Herbert Renison)
Gerardia, Helen
Gerhold, William Henry
Gibson, George
Gilbert, Albert Earl
Gilbert, Clyde Lingle
Giles, Newell Walton, Jr
Ginsburg, Estelle
Girona, Julio
Gliko, Carl Albert
Gobin, Henry (Delano)
Goedicke, Jean
Goetz, Peter Henry
Goff, Lloyd Lozes
Goings, Ralph
Goldberg, Chaim
Goldberg, Joseph Wallace
Golden, Rolland Harve

Good, Leonard
Goodacre, Glenna
Goodman, Brenda Joyce
Goodman, Sidney
Goray, John C
Gordley, Metz Tranbarger
Gordon, Josephine
Gore, Samuel Marshall
Graese, Judy (Judith Ann)
Graham, Walter
Gramatky, Hardie
Granstaff, William Boyd
Grass, Patty Patterson
Graves, Morris
Gray, Gladys
Gray, Jim
Gray, Marie Elise
Greaver, Harry
Greco, Frank
Greeley, Charles Matthew
Green, Edward Anthony
Green, Morris Baldwin
Greenberg, Irwin
Greenbowe, F Douglas
Greer, Walter Marion
Grey, Estelle (Estelle Ashby)
Grimley, Oliver Fetterolf
Grissom, Freda Gill
Grissom, Kenneth Ryland, II
Gross, Earl
Grosse (Carolyn Ann Gawarecki)
Grossman, Morton
Groth, John August
Grotz, Dorothy Rogers
Grove, Edward Ryneal
Guerin, John William
Gumpel, Hugh
Gunning, Eleonore Victoria
Gussow, Alan
Gwathmey, Robert
Haden, Eunice (Barnard)
Haerer, Carol
Halbach, David Allen
Haley, Patience E (Patience E Haley Ghikas)
Hall, Lee
Halvorsen, Ruth Elise
Hamilton, Frank Moss
Hamlett, Dale Edward
Hammett, Polly Horton
Hammond, Natalie Hays
Hammond, Ruth MacKrille
Hampton, John W
Hampton, Phillip Jewel
Hampton, Roy (George LeRoy Hampton)
Hamwi, Richard Alexander
Handville, Robert T
Hanna, Boyd Everett
Hansen, Frances Frakes
Hapke, Paul Frederick
Hardaway, Pearl (Pearl Hardaway Reese)
Hardy, (Clarion) Dewitt
Hardy, Thomas (Austin)
Harmon, Cliff Franklin
Harms, Elizabeth
Harootian, Khoren Der
Harris, Marian D
Harrison, Pat (Broeder)
Hart, Agnes
Hart, Morgan Drake
Hartgen, Vincent Andrew
Ha-So-De (Narcisco Abeyta)
Hastie, Reid
Hatch, John W
Hatfield, Donald Gene
Haworth, B Cogill (Mrs Peter Haworth)
Hawthorne, Jack Gardner
Hayes, Robert T
Hayes, Tua
Haynes, George Edward
Healy, Arthur K D
Hedden-Sellman, Zelda
Heflin, Tom Pat
Hefner, Harry Simon
Heise, Myron Robert
Held, Alma M
Heliker, John Edward
Helioff, Anne Graile (Mrs Benjamin Hirschberg)
Henderson, Jack W
Hennesy, Gerald Craft
Henry, Robert
Henslee, Jack
Herbert, James Arthur
Herpst, Martha Jane
Hertzberg, Rose
Hessing, Valjean McCarty
Higa, Charles Eisho
Highberg, Stephanie Wenner
Hill, Polly Knipp
Hill, Richard Wayne
Hobbie, Lucille
Hofer, Ingrid (Ingeborg)
Hoffman, Elaine Janet
Hoffman, Richard Peter
Hogue, Alexandre
Hoie, Claus
Holden, Raymond James
Holgate, Jeanne
Holmes, David Bryan
Holton, Leonard T
Holtz, Itshak Jack
Hopkinson, Glen Spencer
Hopper, Frank J
Hornaday, Richard Hoyt
Housser, Yvonne McKague
Howell, Claude Flynn
Howell, Douglass (Morse)
Howell, Elizabeth Ann (Mitch)
Howell, Frank
Hoyt, Dorothy (Dorothy Hoyt Dillingham)
Hoyt, Whitney F
Hrdy, Olinka
Hudson, Jacqueline
Hughes, Edward John
Hull, Marie (Atkinson)
Humphrey, S L
Hurd, Peter
Hutchison, Elizabeth S
Iacurto, Francesco
Iannone, Dorothy
Ingraham, Esther Price
Ingram, Jerry Cleman
Irvin, Fred Maddox
Iskowitz, Gershon
Jackson, Billy Morrow
Jackson, Vaughn L
Jackson, Ward
Jacob, Ned
Jacobson, Arthur Robert
Jacquette, Yvonne Helene (Yvonne Helen Burckhardt)
Jagman, Ed
Jaidinger, Judith C (Judith Clarann Szesko)
Jameson, Demetrios George
Jamison, Philip (Duane, Jr)
Janelsins, Veronica
Janschka, Fritz
Jarkowski, Stefania Agnes
Jarvis, Donald
Jarvis, John Brent
Jauss, Anne Marie
Ject-Key, Elsie
Jenkinson, Geoffrey
Jennerjahn, W P
Jennings, Frank Harding
Jensen, John Edward
Jensen, Leo (Vernon)
Jensen, Pat
Jewell, William M
Johansen, Anders Daniel
Johansen, Robert
Johnson, Avery Fischer
Johnson, Buffie
Johnson, Cecile Ryden
Johnson, Homer
Johnson, Pauline B
Jones, Claire (Deann Burtchaell)
Jones, Dan Burne
Jones, Franklin Reed
Jones, Reita
Jonynas, Vytautas K
Jordan, Barbara Schwinn
Jorgensen, Flemming
Josimovich, George
Joyce, Marshall Woodside
Judkins, Sylvia
Jung, Kwan Yee
Jung, Yee Wah
Kaep, Louis Joseph
Kagy, Sheffield Harold
Kaiser, Charles James
Kaiser, Vitus J
Kamen, Gloria
Kamys, Walter
Kan, Diana
Kanemitsu, Matsumi
Kao, Ruth (Yu-Hsin) Lee
Kass, Ray
Katz, Leo
Katz, Theodore (Harry)
Kawa, Florence Kathryn
Kaye, George
Keeling, Henry Cornelious
Keena, Janet Laybourn
Kelley, Ramon
Kelpe, Paul
Kermes, Constantine John
Kerr, Kenneth A
Kerstetter, Barbara Ann
Kerswill, J W Roy
Kessler, Edna Leventhal
Kessler, Shirley
Kester, Lenard
Keyser, Robert Gifford
Kijanka, Stanley Joseph
Kimbrough, (Sara) Dodge
Kimura, Sueko M
King, William Alfred
Kinghan, Charles Ross
Kingman, Dong M
Kirkland, Vance Hall
Kiskadden, Robert Morgan
Klebe, Gene (Charles Eugene)
Kleiman, Alan
Klein, Beatrice T
Klein, Medard
Kline, Harriet
Klonis, Stewart
Klopfenstein, Philip Arthur
Kloss, Gene (Alice Geneva Glasier)
Knaub, Raymond L
Knee, Gina (Mrs Alexander Brook)
Knerr, Sallie Frost
Knobler, Lois Jean
Knowles, Dorothy Elsie (Dorothy Elsie Perehudoff)
Knudson, Robert LeRoy
Kobayashi, Katsumi Peter
Kolin, Sacha
Kolliker, William Augustin
Konopka, Joseph
Koons, Darell J
Korow, Elinore Maria
Kortheuer, Dayrell
Kotala, Stanislaw Waclaw
Kouba, Leslie Carl
Kovner, Saul
Kramer, James
Kramer, Marjorie Anne
Kranking, Margaret Graham
Kratz, Mildred Sands
Krause, LaVerne Erickson
Krigstein, Bernard
Kuczun, Ann-Marie
Kupferman, Lawrence
Kushner, Dorothy Browdy
Kushner-Weiner, Anita May
Kwiecinski, Chester Martin
Laessig, Robert
Lafon, Dee J
Laguna, Muriel
Lahey, Richard (Francis)
La Hotan, Robert L
Laine, Lenore
La Malfa, James Thomas
Landau, Jacob
Landers, Bertha
Landfield, Ronnie (Ronald T)
Lang, Margo Terzian
Lanyon, Ellen
La Pierre, Thomas
Lapointe, Frank
Larmer, Oscar Vance
Lasuchin, Michael
Latham, Catherine Doris
Lauffer, Alice A
Lavoy, Walter Joseph
Law, C Anthony
Law, Pauline Elizabeth
Lawrence, Jacob
Lawrence, James A
Laycox, (William) Jack
Lebkicher, Anne Ross
Lecky, Susan
Le Clair, Charles
Lee, Amy Freeman
Lee, Briant Hamor
Lee, Dora Fugh
Lee, Margaret F
Leeds, Annette
Lee-Smith, Hughie
Leet, Richard Eugene
Leff, Rita
Lefranc, Margaret (Margaret Lefranc Schoonover)
Lehrer, Leonard
Leitman, Samuel
Leland, Whitney Edward
Lem, Richard Douglas
Lenney, Annie
Leonard, Leon Lank, Sr
Lerman, Ora
Lerner Levine, Marion
Lesher, Marie Palmisano
Levering, Robert K
Levine, David
Levine, Reeva (Anna) Miller
Lewin, Keith Kerton
Lewis, Nat Brush
Lewis, Ronald Walter
Lewis, William Arthur
Lewis, William R
Lewton, Val Edwin
Lieberman, Meyer Frank
Ligare, David H
Linder, Stasia
Lindmark, Arne
Lindner, Ernest
Lindner, Richard
Lissim, Simon
Livingston, Charlotte (Mrs Francis Vendeveer Kughler)
Livingston, Sidnee
Livingston, Virginia (Mrs Hudson Warren Budd)
Loew, Michael
Loney, Doris Howard
Long, Walter Kinscella
Lopina, Louise Carol
Lougheed, Robert Elmer
Loughlin, John Leo
Loveless, Jim
Low, Joseph
Lowe, Joe Hing
Luitjens, Helen Anita
Lumbers, James Richard
Lund, Jane
Lunge, Jeffrey (Roy)
Lutz, Dan S
Lux, Gladys Marie
Luz, Virginia
Lyford, Cabot
Lynch, Mary Britten
Lyon, Hayes Paxton
MacGillis, Robert Donald
MacKendrick, Lilian
MacKenzie, Hugh Seaforth

PAINTER (cont)

MacNutt, Glenn Gordon
Madden, Betty I
Madura, Jack Joseph
Magafan, Ethel
Mah, Peter
Makarenko, Zachary Philipp
Malsch, Ellen L
Mandel, Howard
Mangione, Patricia Anthony
Mapes, Doris Williamson
Margolies, Ethel Polacheck
Margules, Gabriele Ella
Marin, Augusto
Marinsky, Harry
Marriott, William Allen
Marsh, David Foster
Marshall, Bruce
Marshall, Robert Leroy
Martell, Barbara Bentley
Martin, Alexander Toedt
Martin, Charles E
Martin, Fletcher
Martin, Keith Morrow
Martin, Margaret M
Martin, Ron
Martinez, Ernesto Pedregon
Martino, Antonio P
Martino, Giovanni
Martone, William Robert
Martyl (Martyl Schweig Langsdorf)
Marzano, Albert
Mason, Harold Dean
Matson, Greta (Greta Matson Khouri)
Matthews, Gene
Mau, Hui-Chi
Mawicke, Tran
Maxwell, John
Mayer, Bena Frank
Mayer, Rosemary
Maynard, William
McAdoo, Donald Eldridge
McAninch, Beth
McBride, James Joseph
McBryde, Sarah Elva
McCarthy, Doris Jean
McChristy, Quentin L
McCloskey, Eunice LonCoske
McCormick, Harry
McCosh, David J
McCoy, Wirth Vaughan
McCullough, Joseph
McGee, Olivia Jackson
McGee, William Douglas
McGough, Charles E
McGrew, Bruce Elwin
McInerney, Gene Joseph
McIver, John Kolb
McKeeby, Byron Gordon
McKesson, Malcolm Forbes
McKie, Todd Stoddard
McKinin, Lawrence
McLean, Roddy (Verneda Rodriguez)
McMillan, Constance
McNary, Oscar L
McNear, Everett C
McQuillan, Frances C
Megargee, Lawrence Anthony (Laurie)
Meigs, John Liggett
Melikian, Mary
Meltzer, Robert Hiram
Mendelowitz, Daniel Marcus
Mendenhall, Jack
Meng, Wendy
Mermin, Mildred (Shire)
Merrick, James Kirk
Merrill, Ross M
Meserole, Vera Stromsted
Messersmith, Fred Lawrence
Metson, Graham
Metz, Frank Robert
Metz, Gerry Michael
Meyers, Dale (Mrs Mario Cooper)
Michod, Susan A
Middleman, Raoul F
Miezajs, Dainis
Milette, Clemence M
Mill, Eleanor
Miller, Vel
Mina-Mora, Dorise Olson
Mina-Mora, Raul Jose
Minnick, Esther Tress
Mion, Pierre Riccardo
Miotke, Anne E
Mitchell, Fred
Mitra, Gopal C
Mochizuki, Betty Ayako
Moglia, Luigi (John)
Mohn, Cheri (Ann)
Moller, Hans
Momaday, Al
Momiyama, Nanae
Monaghan, Eileen (Mrs Frederic Whitaker)
Montgomery, Claude
Moon, Marc
Moore, Ina May
Moore, John J
Moore, Michael Shannon
Moore, Robert Eric
Morgan, Gladys B
Morgan, Norma Gloria
Morningstern, Harry V
Morrison, Doris
Morrison, Fritzi Mohrenstecher
Morrison, Keith Anthony
Mortensen, Gordon Louis
Morton, Richard H
Moseley, Ralph Sessions
Moses, Forrest (Lee), (Jr)
Moss, Joel C
Mould, Lola Frowde
Moy, May (Wong)
Moyers, Wm
Muccioli, Anna Maria
Munoz, Rie (Marie Angelina Muroz)
Murray, Albert (Ketcham)
Murray, Floretta May
Murraygreen, Ryan
Myers, Malcolm Haynie
Nagano, Paul Tatsumi
Nagler, Edith Kroger
Nakamura, Kazuo
Nakatani, Carlos
Nathan, Helmuth Max
Nay, Mary Spencer
Naylor, Alice Stephenson
Nechis, Barbara (Friedman)
Neddeau, Donald Frederick Price
Neff, John A
Nelson, Harry William
Nelson, Mary Carroll
Nepote, Alexander
Nestor, Lulu B
Newman, Elias
Newman, John Beatty
Newport, Esther
Nicholas, Thomas Andrew
Nichols, Alice W
Niemann, Edmund E
Nirvanno, Comet (Vincent Romano)
Nobili, Louise
Nordstrand, Nathalie Johnson
Norton, Mary Joyce
Norwood, Malcolm Mark
Novotny, Elmer Ladislaw
Nuala (Elsa De Brun)
Nuki (Daniel Millsaps)
O'Brien, Marjorie (Marjorie O'Brien Rapaport)
O'Connell, Ann Brown
O'Dell, Erin (Anne)
Oehler, Helen Gapen
Oloffson, Werner Olaf
Olsen, Ernest Moran
Olson, Joseph Olaf
O'Neill, John Patton
Onley, Toni
Order, Trudy
Ordonez, Efren
Osborn, Robert
Osby, Larissa Geiss
Osyczka, Bohdan Danny
Owens, Mary (Mary Louis Schnore)
Pace, Margaret Bosshardt
Pace, Stephen S
Pachner, William
Packer, Clair Lange
Page, Bill
Pajaud, William Etienne
Palmer, Mabel (Evelyn)
Papo, Iso
Parke, Walter Simpson
Parker, Robert Andrew
Parks, James Dallas
Parra, Thomas (Garcia)
Parry, Marian (Marian Parry Feld)
Parton, Nike
Patch, Peggie (Margaret Thompson Williamson)
Patterson, Patricia
Patterson, William Joseph
Paulley, David Gordon
Payson, Dale Constance
Peace, Bernie (Kinzel)
Pearson, Henry C
Peck, James Edward
Pellew, John Clifford
Pels, Albert
Pen, Rudolph
Pena, Amado Maurilio, Jr
Perine, Robert Heath
Perrin, C Robert
Perry, Kathryn Powers
Peter, George
Peters, Carl W
Peterson, A E S
Petrie, Ferdinand Ralph
Pettet, William
Phillips, Gordon Dale
Phillips, Matt
Phillips, Melita Ahl
Pickens, Vinton Liddell
Pickford, Rollin, Jr
Pierce, Delilah W
Pierce, Diane (Diane Pierce Huxtable)
Pigott, Marjorie
Pinckney, Stanley
Pinto, Biagio
Pitcher, John Charles
Pitz, Molly Wood
Pleissner, Ogden Minton
Poduska, T F
Pollaro, Paul
Pollock, Merlin F
Polsky, Cynthia
Poole, Richard Elliott
Poor, Anne
Pope, Richard Coraine
Porter, Albert Wright
Porter, Elmer Johnson
Porter, J Erwin
Post, George (Booth)
Potvin, Daniel
Pounian, Albert Kachouni
Powell, Leslie (Joseph)
Pozzatti, Rudy O
Pratt, Frances (Frances Elizabeth Usui)
Pratt, Mary Frances
Preissler, Audrey
Prestopino, Gregorio
Preuss, Roger
Pribble, Easton
Price, Rosalie Pettus
Pringle, Burt Evins
Pross, Lester Fred
Punia, Constance Edith
Quick, Birney MacNabb
Quinn, Noel Joseph
Quirk, Thomas Charles, Jr
Rabinovitch, William Avrum
Rabkin, Leo
Raffael, Judith K
Raffel, Alvin Robert
Rainey, John Watts
Ramanauskas, Dalia Irena
Ramos, Melvin John
Ramos-Prida, Fernando
Ramstead, Edward Oliver, Jr
Rankin, Don
Rapp, Lois
Rasmussen, Keith Eric
Rath, Hildegard
Rave, Georgia
Rawlinson, Jonlane Frederick
Ray, Deborah
Rayen, James Wilson
Rayner, Ada (Ada Rayner Hensche)
Reale, Nicholas Albert
Redstone, Louis Gordon
Reese, William Foster
Reichert, Donald O
Reid, Charles
Reid, Robert Dennis
Reiff, Robert Frank
Reindorf, Samuel
Reinhart, Margaret Emily
Reinsel, Walter N
Reisman, Philip
Renner, Eric
Reynolds, Ralph William
Reynolds, Robert
Rhoads, Eugenia Eckford
Riley, Art (Arthur Irwin)
Rising, Dorothy Milne
Robb, Charles (Charles Robert Bush)
Roberts, Clyde Harry
Roberts, Thomas (Kieth)
Roberts, William Griffith
Robertson, D Hall
Robinson, Mary Ann
Robinson, Robert Doke
Rodriguez, Joe Bastida
Rogers, John
Roller, Marion Bender
Rollins, Jo Lutz
Rollman-Shay, Ed & Charlotte
Romeling, W B
Ronald, William
Rosenhouse, Irwin Jacob
Rosenthal, Seymour Joseph
Rosofsky, Seymour
Ross, Alexander
Ross, Janice Koenig
Rossman, Ruth Scharff
Rothschild, Judith
Rowan, Frances Physioc
Rowe, Charles Alfred
Rozzi, (James A)
Ruble, Ronald L
Ruellan, Andree
Ruffing, Anne Elizabeth
Rush, Andrew
Ruthven, John Aldrich
Ryerson, Margery Austen
Sachse, Janice R
Safford, Ruth Perkins
Salamone, Gladys L
Salemme, Antonio
Salemme, Martha
Salt, John
Salter, John Randall
Sanders, Joop A
Sanderson, Charles Howard
Sandol, Maynard
Sarsony, Robert
Sassone, Marco
Saunders, Aulus Ward
Savage, Roger
Savas, Jo-Ann (Mrs George T Savas)
Sawada, Ikune
Sawai, Noboru
Sawyer, Helen (Helen Sawyer Farnsworth)

Saxon, Charles David
Sazegar, Morteza
Scalise, Nicholas Peter
Schabacker, Betty Barchet
Schaefer, Carl Fellman
Schary, Saul
Scheu, Leonard
Schiller, Beatrice
Schimmel, William Berry
Schlemm, Betty Lou
Schloss, Edith
Schmalz, Carl (Nelson, Jr)
Schnurr-Colflesh, E
Schoener, Jason
Schreiber, Eileen Sher
Schreyer, Greta L
Schueler, Jon R
Schuler, Melvin Albert
Schultz, Harold A
Schulz, Ken
Schuster, Cita Fletcher (Sarah E)
Schwab, Eloisa (Mrs A H Rodriguez)
Schwabacher, Ethel K
Schwacha, George
Schwalb, Susan
Schwarz, Gladys
Scott, Jonathan
Scott, Walter
Seabourn, Bert Dail
Selchow, Roger Hoffman
Selwitz, Ruth F
Serwazi, Albert B
Setterberg, Carl Georg
Shaddle, Alice
Shadrach, Jean H
Shapiro, Frank D
Shapiro, Irving
Sharpe, David Flemming
Shatter, Susan Louise
Sheehan, Evelyn
Sheehe, Lillian Carolyn
Sheets, Millard Owen
Sheppard, John Craig
Sherker, Michael Z
Shields, Alan J
Shook, Georg
Shooter, Tom
Shore, Mary
Shores, (James) Franklin
Shubin, Morris Jack
Shuck, Kenneth Menaugh
Shutt, Ken
Sideris, Alexander
Sievan, Maurice
Simon, Howard
Simper, Frederick
Simpkins, Henry John
Singer, Arthur B
Sisson, Laurence P
Skalagard, Hans
Sklar, Dorothy
Sleigh, Sylvia
Slider, Dorla Dean
Sloan, Robert Smullyan
Smart, Wini
Smith, Dolph
Smith, John Bertie
Smith, Oliver
Smith, Paul Roland
Smith, R Harmer
Smith, Robert Alan
Smith, Susan Carlton
Smongeski, Joseph Leon
Smyth, Ed
Snow, Cynthia Reeves
Snyder, James Wilbert (Wilb)
Snyder, Seymour
Snyder, Toni Goessler
Snyder, William B
Solberg, Morten Edward
Soloway, Reta
Soltesz, Frank Joseph
Sommers, John Sherman
Sorby, J Richard
Sorge, Walter
Soroka, Margery
Souza, Paul Marciel
Soviak, Harry
Sowers, Miriam R
Spaventa, George
Speers, Teryl Townsend
Spink, Frank Henry, Jr
Spongberg, Grace
Sproul, Ann Stephenson
Stack, Frank Huntington
Stallwitz, Carolyn
Stamper, Willson Young
Starrs, Mildred
Steele, Benjamin Charles
Stegman, Patricia (Patricia Stegman Snyder)
Stein, Harve
Stein, Walter
Steinhouse, Tobie (Thelma)
Stemelos, Electra Georgia Mousmoules
Stevens, Edward John, Jr
Stevens, Marjorie
Stevens, Richard Clive
Stevens, Walter Hollis
Stevens, William Ansel, Sr
Stewart, Arthur
Stewart, Jarvis Anthony
Stewart, John P
Stewart, William
Sticker, Robert Edward
Stoltenberg, Donald Hugo
Stone, John Lewis, Jr
Strawbridge, Edward R
Strickland, Allen
Strisik, Paul
Strother, Virginia Vaughn
Stull, Jean Himrod
Sublett, Carl C
Sudlow, Robert N
Sugimoto, Henry Y
Summer, (Emily) Eugenia
Summers, Robert
Sundberg, Wilda (Regelman)
Surrey, Philip Henry
Suter, Sherwood Eugene
Sutherland, Sandy
Sutton, Patricia
Swanson, Ray V
Swartz, Beth Ames
Sway, Albert
Sweney, Fred
Swenson, Anne
Swinton, George
Szesko, Lenore Rundle
Tabuena, Romeo Villalva
Tait, Katharine Lamb
Takashima, Shizuye Violet
Tarin, Gilberto A
Taulbee, Dan J
Taylor, Gage
Taylor, Grace Martin
Taylor, John (Williams)
Taylor, Sandra Ortiz
Teague, Donald
Teichman, Sabina
Tejeda, Carlos
Terenzio, Anthony
Thelin, Valfred P
Thiery, Thomas Allen
Thollander, Earl
Thomas, Alma Woodsey
Thompson, Ernest Thorne
Thompson, Kenneth Webster
Thompson, Malcolm Barton
Thompson, Robert Charles
Thomson, William David
Tiffany, Marguerite Bristol
Tillim, Sidney
Timmas, Osvald
Timmins, William Frederick
Tinning, George Campbell
Toigo, Daniel Joseph
Toledo, Francisco
Tomlinson, Florence Kidder
Toschik, Larry
Trachtman, Arnold S
Trank, Lynn Edgar
Trauerman, Margy Ann
Treaster, Richard A
Triplett, Margaret L
Trivigno, Pat
Tse, Stephen
Tsutakawa, George
Tucker, James Ewing
Tucker, Peri
Turner, Arthur Charles
Turner, Bruce Backman
Turner, (Charles) Arthur
Turner, Theodore Roy
Tyson, Mary (Mrs Kenneth Thompson)
Uchima, Ansei
Uhrman, Celia
Uhrman, Esther
Underwood, Evelyn Notman
Unwin, Nora Spicer
Uttech, Thomas Martin
Valenstein, Alice
Vallee, Jack (Land)
Vallee, William Oscar
Van Buren, Helen Rae
Van Der Voort, Amanda Venelia
Van Oordt, Peter
Van Suchtelen, Adrian
Van Veen, Stuyvesant
Vargo, John
Vigil, Veloy Joseph
Vincent, Tom
Vo-Dinh, Mai
Vogel, Donald
Voorhees, Donald Edward
Voos, William John
Vorhees, D Lawrey
Vorwerk, E Charlsie
Wagoner, Robert B
Walker, James Adams
Walker, Sandra Radcliffe
Wallace, Soni
Walsh, John Stanley
Walsh, Patricia Ruth
Wands, Alfred James
Wang, Chi-Chien
Wang, Yinpao
Ward, William Edward
Warder, William
Wasser, Paula Kloster
Wasserman, Albert
Waterhouse, Russell Rutledge
Waterston, Harry Clement
Watford, Frances Mizelle
Watia, Tarmo
Webb, Frank (Francis H Webb)
Weber, Idelle
Webster, Larry
Weeber, Gretchen
Weekes, Shirley Marie
Weidenaar, Reynold Henry
Weinbaum, Jean
Weiss, Anton
Weiss, Lee (Elyse C Weiss)
Wellington, Duke
Wells, Mac
Wentworth, Murray Jackson
Werner-Vaughn, Salle
West, Clifford Bateman
West, E Gordon
Westermann, Horace Clifford
Wheeler, Mark
White, Doris A
White, Ralph
White, Roger Lee
Whitehill, Florence (Fitch)
Whiteside, William Albert, II
Wilbert, Robert John
Wilcox, Gordon Cumnock
Wilkinson, Kirk Cook
Williams, Raymond Lester
Williamson, Jason H
Willson, Robert
Wilson, Nicholas Jon
Winter, Lumen Martin
Wise, Geneva H (Holcomb)
Wolins, Joseph
Wong, Ching
Wong, Frederick
Wood, Jim (James Reid Wood)
Wood, Robert E
Woodruff, Hale A
Woodson, Shirley Ann
Woodward, Cleveland Landon
Woof, Maija (Maija Gegeris Zack Peeples)
Wostrel, Nancy J
Wray, Margaret
Wright, Catharine Morris
Wright, Harold David
Wyckoff, Sylvia Spencer
Wyeth, Andrew Newell
Wyeth, James Browning
Yarbrough, Leila Kepert
Yasko, Caryl Anne
Yater, George David
Yoakum, Delmer J
Youkeles, Anne
Young, Doug Y H
Young, Marjorie Ward
Young, Robert John
Younglove, Ruth Ann (Mrs Benjamin Rhees Loxley)
Zacha, George William
Zimmerman, William Harold
Zisla, Harold
Zivic, William Thomas
Zoretich, George Stephen
Zornes, James Milford
Zucker, Jacques
Zuckerberg, Stanley M

PATRON

Akston, Joseph James
Alsdorf, James W
Altschul, Arthur G
Amsden, Floyd T
Bass, John
Becker, Martin Earle
Beren, Stanley O
Berg, Phil
Berman, Muriel Mallin
Berman, Philip I
Bernstein, Joseph
Bickford, George Percival
Block, Huntington Turner
Blos, May (Elizabeth)
Browne, Robert M
Burrows, Selig S
Chapman, Mrs Gilbert W
Childers, Betty Bivins
Clowes, Allen Whitehill
Cohen, Wilfred P
Cooley, William, Jr
Crawford, John McAllister, Jr
Dalton, Harry L
D'Amico, Augustine A
Daniels, David M
Davidson, Ian J
Davidson, Suzette Morton
Davis, Mr & Mrs Walter
Dreitzer, Albert J
Dunnington, Mrs Walter Grey
Eckstein, Joanna
Eiteljorg, Harrison
Elowitch, Robert Jason
Erdelac, Joseph Mark
Evans, Nancy
Field, Lyman
Finch, Ruth Woodward
Fitch, George Hopper
Freeman, Gertrude
Garbaty, Marie Louise
Gilbert, Arthur
Goldberger, Mr & Mrs Edward
Goldsmith, C Gerald

PATRON (cont)
Gollin, Mr & Mrs Joshua A
Goodman, Benjamin
Gottlieb, Abe
Greenwald, Charles D
Grey, Mrs Benjamin Edwards
Gross, Mr & Mrs Merrill Jay
Grundy, John Owen
Guggenheim, Peggy
Gumberts, William A
Gussman, Herbert
Hage, Raymond Joseph
Halseth, Elmer Johann
Harris, Leon A, Jr
Harrison, Joseph Robert, Jr
Hartford, Huntington
Headley, Sherman Knight
Heinz, Mr & Mrs Henry J, II
Hilles, Susan Morse
Holcombe, R Gordon, Jr
Holt, Margaret McConnell
Hooker, Mrs R Wolcott
Huntington, John W
Irwin, George M
Isaacs, Carole Schaffer
Johnson, Ruth Carter
Kaplan, Alice Manheim
Katz, Joseph M
Kincade, Arthur Warren
King, Ethel May
Klein, Esther M
Knox, Seymour H
Kreeger, David Lloyd
LaDow, Jesse
Lansdowne, James Fenwick
Larkin, John E, Jr
Laugesen, Madelyn A
Lederer, Kurt
Linsky, Mr & Mrs Jack
List, Vera G
Lloyd, Mrs H Gates
Ludington, Wright S
Marcus, Betty
Marks, Mr & Mrs Cedric H
May, Morton David
McDonough, John Joseph
Meadows, Algur H
Melamed, Abraham
Miller, Mrs Robert Watt
Moe, Richard D
Murray, William Colman
Navas, Elizabeth S
Neuberger, Roy R
Neustadter, Edward L
Niemeyer, Arnold Matthew
Ochs, Robert David
Palmer, Fred Loren
Parkinson, Elizabeth Bliss
Penney, Charles Rand
Pilavin, Selma F
Pizitz, Silvia
Pleasants, Frederick R
Polan, Lincoln M
Pratt, Dallas
Pulitzer, Mr & Mrs Joseph, Jr
Rauch, John G
Rautbord, Dorothy H
Ravel, Dana B
Redstone, Louis Gordon
Reiner, Mr & Mrs Jules
Richmond, Frederick W
Roby, Sara (Mary Barnes)
Rockefeller, John Davison, III
Rockefeller, Nelson Aldrich
Roebling, Mary G
Rosenwald, Lessing Julius
Ruskin, Lewis J
Samuels, John Stockwell, 3d
Schoen, Mr & Mrs Arthur Boyer
Schooler, Lee
Schramm, James Siegmund
Schumsky, Felicie Roberta
Schwartz, Eugene M
Selig, Mr & Mrs Manfred
Semans, James Hustead
Seymour, Rachel
Shapiro, Daisy Viertel
Sheldon, Olga N (Mrs A B Sheldon)
Siden, Harriet Field
Smart, Mary-Leigh
Smith, Mrs Bertram
Smith, Justin V
Solinger, David M
Sonnenschein, Hugo
Sosnowitz, Henry Abram
Speiser, Stuart M
Stachelberg, Mrs Charles G
Stamats, Peter Owen
Steiner, Julia Bourne
Stern, H Peter
Stralem, Donald S
Taft, Frances Prindle
Tobin, Robert L B
Turner, Joseph
Ullman, Mrs George W
Ulrich, Edwin Abel
Walter, May E
Walter, Paul F
Weiner, Ted
Weinstein, Mr & Mrs Joseph
Winokur, James L
Woods, Sarah Ladd
Zeisler, Richard Spiro
Zlotnick, Diana Shirley

PHOTOGRAPHER

Adams, Ansel Easton
Adams, Robert Hickman
Adler, Billy (Telethon)
Alexander, Robert Seymour
Alinder, James Gilbert
Allen, (Harvey) Harold
Alpert, George
Amft, Robert
Anderson, William
Arcuri, Frank J
Astman, Barbara Anne
Avedon, Richard
Avison, David
Bailey, Oscar
Bakaty, Mike
Baldessari, John Anthony
Baltz, Lewis
Barnett, Ed Willis
Barrow, Thomas Francis
Barschel, Hans J
Bell, Evelyn Behnan
Beny, Roloff
Berman, Fred J
Beydler, Gary Earl
Bhalla, Hans
Bierk, David Charles
Bishop, Barbara Lee
Block, Joyce
Blos, Peter W
Borglum, James Lincoln de la Mothe
Boyd, Donald Edgar
Brown, Rhett Delford (Harriett Gurney Brown)
Burchard, Peter Duncan
Burchfield, Jerry Lee
Burckhardt, Rudy
Cadge, William Fleming
Callahan, Harry
Capa, Cornell
Caponigro, Paul
Carr-Harris, Ian Redford
Chambers, John
Channing, Susan Rose
Chesley, Paul Alexander
Childers, Malcolm Graeme
Cohen, Joan Lebold
Cohen, Lynne G
Coke, F Van Deren
Comes, Marcella
Connor, Linda Stevens
Cooper, Ron
Corpron, Carlotta Mae
Crane, Barbara Bachmann
Crane, Michael Patrick
Crawford, Ralston
Crouse, John L (Jay)
Crouton, Francois (Francois LaFortune)
Curran, Darryl Joseph
Davies, Theodore Peter
Davis, Ben H
Davis, George
Davis, Philip Charles
Deal, Joe
Dean, Nicholas Brice
Defeo, Jay
Delano, Jack
deLory, Peter
Diamond, Paul
Dibbets, Jan
Dickson, Jennifer Joan
DiPerna, Frank Paul
Divola, John Manford, Jr
Doll, Donald Arthur
Dunn, Cal
Eckersley, Thomas Cyril
Edelson, Mary Beth
Edge, Douglas Benjamin
Edwards, Ellender Morgan
Edwards, James F
Eide, John
Eisenberg, Sonja Miriam
Ellison, Nancy
Endsley, Fred Starr
Enos, Chris
Estabrook, Reed
Faller, Marion
Faurer, Louis
Fenical, Marlin E
Fichter, Robert
Finch, Ruth Woodward
Fink, Laurence B
Fink, Louis R
Finn, David
Fisher, Elaine
Flach, Victor H
Fleisher, Pat
Flick, Robert
Folsom, Karl Leroy
Ford, Charles Henri
Frazer, James Nisbet, Jr
Freed, Hermine
Friedman, Benno
Fuller, John Charles
Furman, Aaron & Joyce
Gagliani, Oliver
Garnett, William Ashford
Gefter, Judith Michelman
Genders, Richard Atherstone
Gibson, Ralph H
Gillingwater, Denis Claude
Gilpin, Laura
Glasgow, Lukman
Glassman, Joel A
G'Miglio (Gloria Miglionico)
Golden, Eunice
Gooch, Donald Burnette
Gore, Tom
Grady, Ruby McLain
Graham, Daniel H
Greaves, Fielding Lewis
Gutmann, John
Haar, Francis
Hahn, Betty
Halberstadt, Ernst
Hallman, Gary Lee
Hammer, Alfred Emil
Hannibal, Joseph Harry
Harrison, Helen Mayer
Harsley, Alex
Hayes, Robert T
Heath, David Martin
Hein, Max
Heinecken, Robert Friedli
Henderson, Lester Kierstead
Henderson, Victor (Lance)
Hendricks, Barkley Leonnard
Henning, Paul Harvey
Hernandez, Anthony Louis
Hesse, Don
Heywood, J Carl
Higa, (Yoshiharu)
Hill, John Conner
Hill, Richard Wayne
Hilton, Eric G
Hodgson, Trevor
Hofer, Evelyn
Hoffman, Richard Peter
Holliday, Betty
Holmes, Reginald
Hough, Richard
Howard, David
Howell, Raymond
Huff, Howard Lee
Hunter, Debora
Hutchinson, Peter Arthur
Huth, Marta
Iwamasa, Ken
Jachna, Joseph David
Jacobshagen, N Keith, II
James, Christopher P
Jansen, Angela Bing
Jansen, Catherine Sandra
Jay, Bill
Jennings, Thomas
Jensen, Gary
Johnson, James Ralph
Johnson, Selina (Tetzlaff)
Johnston, Robert Harold
Jones, Ben
Jones, Elizabeth
Jones, Harold Henry
Kalischer, Clemens
Kaminisky, Jack Allan
Karsh, Yousuf
Katsiff, Bruce
Kindermann, Helmmo
Kirby, Kent Bruce
Klindt, Steven
Klosty, James Michael
Knight, Thomas Lincoln, Jr
Koga, Mary
Kornmayer, J Gary (John)
Kowal, Dennis J
Kriensky, (Morris E)
Krims, Leslie Robert
Kropf, Joan R
Kumler, Kipton (Cornelius)
Lacy, Suzanne
La Malfa, James Thomas
Landreau, Anthony Norman
Landry, Richard Miles
Land-Weber, Ellen E
LaPena, Frank Raymond
Lapointe, Frank
Laposky, Ben Francis
Larson, William G
Lawrence, James A
Lazarus, Marvin P
Lee, Russell
Leeber, Sharon Corgan
Lerner, Abe
Lerner, Nathan Bernard
Levit, Herschel
Levy, David Corcos
Lewis, Stanley
Liberman, Alexander
Lipton, Barbara B
Lipzin, Janis Crystal
Lonidier, Fred Spencer
Lothrop, Kristin Curtis
Lotterman, Hal
Maddox, Jerald Curtis
Madsen, Viggo Holm
Maldre, Mati
Mann, Vaughan (Vaughan Grayson)
Mansaram, Panchal
Marchese, Lamar Vincent
Margolies, John
Mark, Enid (Epstein)

Martmer, William P
McCall, Anthony
McCaslin, Walter Wright
McDarrah, Fred William
McMillan, Jerry Edward
Meilach, Dona Z
Menthe, Melissa
Mercer, John Douglas
Mesaros, Ron
Metzker, Ray K
Meyer, Ursula
Michals, Duane
Mirano, Virgil Marcus
Monroe, Robert
Monthan, Guy
Moore, Michael Shannon
Moore, Peter
Moore, Robert James
Morath, Inge (Inge Morath Miller)
Morgan, Barbara Brooks
Morrison, Boone M
Moulton, Rosalind Kimball
Murray, Joan
Musgrave, Shirley H
Myers, Richard Lewis
Namuth, Hans
Nathans, Rhoda R
Newman, Arnold
Nickel, Jim H
Niese, Henry Ernst
Noggle, Anne
Norfleet, Barbara Pugh
Norman, Dorothy (S)
Nowytski, Sviatoslav (Slavko)
Oakes, John Warren
O'Connell, Edward E
Ohman, Richard Michael
Oloffson, Werner Olaf
Olsen, Ernest Moran
Orkin, Ruth (Mrs Morris Engel)
Pace, Margaret Bosshardt
Padula, Fred David
Palmgren, Donald Gene
Papageorge, Tod
Parker, Ann (Ann Parker Neal)
Partridge, Roi
Penn, Irving
Petrochuk, Konstantin
Phillips, Bertrand D
Phillips, Donna-Lee
Pierce, James Smith
Pollack, Peter
Porter, Eliot Furness
Power, Mark
Prekop, Martin Dennis
Puchalski, Gregory John
Rachel, Vaughan
Ranalli, Daniel
Reeves, John Alexander
Reider, David H
Reitzenstein, Reinhard
Renner, Eric
Resnick, Marcia Aylene
Rhyne, Charles Sylvanus
Riley, Art (Arthur Irwin)
Riss, Murray
Rosenthal, Gloria M
Rosenthal, John W
Rubinstein, Susan R
Ruscha, Edward Joseph
Sahlstrand, James Michael
Salmoiraghi, Frank
Salter, Richard Mackintire
Sarff, Walter
Savage, Naomi
Schietinger, James Frederick
Schley, Evander Duer (Van)
Schmid, Richard Alan
Schulze, John H
Schwartz, Sing-Si
Segalove, Ilene Judy
Sekula, Allan
Semak, Michael
Seyffert, Richard Leopold
Siegel, Adrian
Sigrin, Michael E
Sinsabaugh, Art
Sister Adele
Sklar-Weinstein, Arlene (Joyce)
Slavin, Neal
Smith, Henry Holmes
Smith, Keith A
Smyth, Ed
Sommer, Frederick
Sonneman, Eve
Stallwitz, Carolyn
Stark, Ron
Stephany, Jaromir
Stephens, Curtis
Stuler, Jack
Swigart, Lynn S
Szabo, Stephen Lee
Tavenner, Patricia (Pat)
Taylor, Harry George
Teske, Edumnd Rudolph
Thomas, Lew
Thurston, Jacqueline Beverly
Tice, George Andrew
Tilley, Lewis Lee
Torbert Stephanie Birch
Toth, Carl Wayne
Traub, Charles H
Triester, Kenneth
Truax, Karen
Twardowicz, Stanley Jan
Uelsmann, Jerry
Ullrich-Zuckerman, B
Upton, John David
Uttech, Thomas Martin
Vanco, John Leroy
Vazan, William Joseph
Wade, Robert Schrope
Wall, Ralph Alan
Wang, Samuel
Warren, Julianne Busset Baker
Webb, Spider
Webster, Larry
Weege, William
Wegman, William
Weiss, John Joseph
Werner, Donald (Lewis)
Wessel, Henry, Jr
Wexler, Jerome LeRoy
White, Amos, IV
Widmer, Gwen Ellen
Wiedenhoeft, Renate
Wiest, Kay Van Elmendorf
Winningham, Geoff
Winogrand, Garry
Witteman, Alisa Wells
Wolf, Jack Clifford
Woodson, Doris
Wyrick, Charles Lloyd, Jr (Pete)
Yanosky, Tom
Zucker, Bob
Zulpo-Dane, Bill

PRINTMAKER

All Media

Abany, Albert Charles
Achepohl, Keith Anden
Adams, Glenn Nelson
Adelman, Dorothy (Lee) McClintock
Adler, Myril
Ahn, Don C
Alicea, Jose
Allan, William George
Allen, Patricia (Patricia Allen Bott)
Amen, Irving
Anaya, Stephen Raul
Anderson, Lennart
Anderson, Robert Raymond
Andrew, David Neville
Andrews, Michael Frank
Andrews, Sybil (Sybil Andrews Morgan)
Andrus, James Roman
Apel, Barbara Jean
Appel, Keith Kenneth
Armstrong, John Albert
Aronson, Irene Hilde
Asher, Lila Oliver
Austin, Pat
Auth, Robert R
Bachinski, Walter Joseph
Bahm, Henry
Baker, Jill Withrow
Barnet, Will
Barooshian, Martin
Batchelor, Anthony John
Beal, Jack
Beall, Dennis Ray
Beaumont, Mona M
Becker, Helmut Julius
Bell, Evelyn Behnan
Bengtz, Ture
Beny, Roloff
Bernard, David Edwin
Berneche, Jerry Douglas
Bernstein, Judith
Blackburn, Morris (Atkinson)
Blair, Robert Noel
Blaustein, Alfred H
Bodnar, Peter
Bogarin, Rafael
Bookatz, Samuel
Borochoff, (Ida) Sloan
Boughton, William Harrison
Bowman, Dorothy (Louise)
Boyd, James Henderson
Boyd, John David
Boyd, Lakin
Boynton, James W
Brandt, Rexford Elson
Breverman, Harvey
Briansky, Rita Prezament
Brice, William
Brodsky, Judith Kapstein
Broner, Robert
Brooks, Wendell T
Brown, Hilton Edward
Brulc, Lillian G
Brunkus, Richard Allen
Bultman, Fritz
Bushman, David Franklin
Cain, James Frederick, Jr
Calapai, Letterio
Cale, Robert Allan
Callner, Richard
Camarata, Martin L
Campbell, Richard Horton
Cardoso, Anthony
Casarella, Edmond
Cassara, Frank
Chesney, Lee R, Jr
Chesney, Lee Roy, III
Chester, Charlotte Wanetta
Childers, Malcolm Graeme
Christensen, Val Alan
Cimbalo, Robert W
Citron, Minna Wright
Coelho, Luiz Carlos
Coker, Carl David
Conn, David Edward
Connett, Dee M
Conrad, George
Consuegra, Hugo
Coochsiwukioma, DH (Del Honanie)
Cook, Howard Norton
Coughlin, Jack
Crispo, Dick
Crossgrove, Roger Lynn
Curry, Noble Wilbur
Cyril, R
Daily, Evelynne B
Daly, Kathleen (Kathleen Daly Pepper)
Davidson, Robert William
Davis, Alonzo Joseph
Davis, Douglas Matthew
Davis, Ronald Wendel
Day, Worden
Dehner, Dorothy
de Martelly, John Stockton
Demartis, James J
DeMatties, Nick Frank
de Miskey, Julian
Denes, Agnes C
Dergalis, George
Dhaemers, Robert August
Dickinson, David Charles
Dienes, Sari
Dirube, Rolando Lopez
Dodworth, Allen Stevens
Donneson, Seena
Dozier, Otis
Drake, James
Dreskin-Haig, Jeanet Elizabeth
Drew, Joan
Drewes, Werner
Duback, Charles S
Duncan, Richard Hurley
Eckstein, Ruth
Eitel, Cliffe Dean
Elliott, Bruce Roger
England, Paul Grady
Enriquez, Gaspar
Epting, Marion Austin
Everts, Connor
Fehl, Philipp P
Feigin, Marsha
Feld, Augusta
Fels, C P
Fendell, Jonas J
Fichter, Herbert Francis
Fine, Ruth Eileen
Floethe, Richard
Foose, Robert James
Foote, Howard Reed
Fornas, Leander
Forsberg, Jim
Fournier, Alexander Paul
Frances, Harriette Anton
Frasconi, Antonio
Freed, David
Freimark, Robert (Matthew)
Fricano, Tom S
Fuchs, Mary Tharsilla
Garcia, Danny
Garhart, Martin J
Garrett, Alan Thomas
Gerard, Paula (Mrs Herbert Renison)
Gersovitz, Sarah Valerie
Gettinger, Edmond Walter
Gilkey, Gordon Waverly
Gilling, Lucille
Gilmartin, F Thomas
Ginzel, Roland
Giorgi, Vita
Goddard, Vivian
Goell, Abby Jane
Goertz, Augustus Frederick
Goldberg, Chaim
Golden, Libby
Gomez-Quiroz, Juan Manuel
Gorelick, Shirley
Gorman, William D
Gramberg, Liliana
Graziano, Florence V Mercolino
Green, Martin Leonard
Greenbaum, Marty
Greenwood, William James
Greer, John Sydney
Grippe, Peter J
Guiffreda, Mauro Francis
Hadzi, Dimitri
Hannibal, Joseph Harry
Hari, Kenneth
Held, Philip
Helfond, Riva
Heller, Jules
Herfindahl, Lloyd Manford
Herman, Susan L
Heywood, J Carl
Hood, Gary Allen
Hood, (Thomas) Richard
Horn, Bruce

PRINTMAKER (cont)
Horton, Jan E
Huggins, Victor, (Jr)
Hunter, Robert Howard
Hutton, Dorothy Wackerman
Ihle, John Livingston
Inukai, Kyohei
Irizarry, Carlos
Jackson, Herb
Jacobs, Peter Alan
Jameson, Demetrios George
Jansen, Angela Bing
Jerviss, Joy
Johnson, Donald Ray
Johnson, Lois Marlene
Jones, Amy (Amy Jones Frisbie)
Jones, Edward Powis
Jones, Frederick George
Jones, Herb (Leon Herbert Jones, Jr)
Jones, James Edward
Jones, Marvin Harold
Jonynas, Vytautas K
Ju, I-Hsiung
Kaericher, John Conrad
Kainen, Jacob
Kappel, R Rose (Mrs Irving Gould)
Kassoy, Bernard
Katz, Alex
Katz, Hilda (Hilda Weber)
Katz, Leo
Keane, Lucina Mabel
Keener, Anna Elizabeth
Kenda, Juanita Echeverria
Kenny, Thomas Henry
Kenojuak (Kenojuak Ashevak)
Kessler, Edna Leventhal
Kimura, William Yusaburo
Kirby, Kent Bruce
Kjargaard, John Ingvard
Knerr, Sallie Frost
Knigin, Michael Jay
Koch, Virginia Greenleaf
Kohlhepp, Norman
Kohn, William Roth
Komodore, Bill
Koppelman, Chaim
Kowalke, Ronald Leroy
Krause, LaVerne Erickson
Kressley, Margaret Hyatt
Krug, Harry Elno
Lacroix, Richard
Lafon, Dee J
Lai, Waihang
Landon, Edward August
Lang, J T
Lansdon, Gay Brandt
La Pierre, Thomas
Larkin, Eugene
Larsen, Patrick Heffner
Lasansky, Mauricio L
Lasuchin, Michael
Latham, Barbara
Law, Carol L
Lea, Stanley E
Leathers, Winston Lyle
Leech, Merle Eugene
Leff, Rita
Lehman, Irving
Leiber, Gerson August
Lekakis, Michael Nicholas
Levee, John H
Levin, Morton D
Lidov, Arthur Herschel
Lieber, France
Limont, Naomi Charles
Lionni, Leo
Little, John
Lock, Charles L
Longo, Vincent
Lorber, Stephen Neil
Loring, Clarice
Loring, John
Loro, Anthony Pivotto
Lowe, Marvin
Madsen, Viggo Holm
Magafan, Ethel
Maltzman, Stanley
Manilla, Tess (Tess Manilla Weiner)
Margulies, Joseph
Marin, Kathryn Garrison
Mark, Enid (Epstein)
Martin, Bernice Fenwick
Martin, Doris-Marie Constable
Matheson, Donald Roy
Mattern, Penny Greig
Maurice, Alfred Paul
Maxwell, William C
Maynard, Valerie
Mayorga, Gabriel Humberto
Mazzocca, Gus (Augustus Nicholas Mazzocca)
McCarthy, Denis
McCarty, Lorraine Chambers
McCloy, William Ashby
McCormick, Harry
McCray, Dorothy M
McGarrell, James
McGee, Winston Eugene
McGough, Charles E
McIvor, John Wilfred
McKeeby, Byron Gordon
McKennis, Gail
McKie, Todd Stoddard
McKnight, Eline
McLean, James Albert
McNamara, Raymond Edmund
McSheehy, Cornelia Marie
McWhinnie, Harold James
Meeker, Dean Jackson
Mejer, Robert Lee
Mellon, James
Meltzer, Doris
Mendelson, Haim
Menihan, John Conway
Merkin, Richard Marshall
Mesibov, Hugh
Messeguer, Villoro Benito
Meyer, Frank Hildbridge
Milette, Clemence M
Miller, Barbara Darlene
Miller, Lee Anne
Miller, Leon Gordon
Mills, Lev Timothy
Mitchell, Clifford
Miyamoto, Wayne Akira
Motherwell, Robert
Moy, Seong
Mueller, Henrietta Waters
Murata, Hiroshi
Myers, Malcolm Haynie
Naegle, Stephen Howard
Nama, George Allen
Nardone, Vincent Joseph
Narotzky, Norman David
Nathan, Helmuth Max
Natkin, Robert
Nawrocki, Thomas Dennis
Negri, Rocco Antonio
Nemec, Nancy
Nesbitt, Lowell (Blair)
Neustadt, Barbara (Barbara Meyer)
Newman, Libby
Nichols, Ward H
Noe, Jerry Lee
Nulf, Frank Allen
Oi, Motoi
Olds, Elizabeth
Olitski, Jules
Olugebefola, Ademola
Ortman, George Earl
Page, John Henry, Jr
Paone, Peter
Parker, Ann (Ann Parker Neal)
Patchett, Daniel Claude
Paterson, Anthony R
Patnode, J Scott
Patterson, William Joseph
Paul, Ken (Hugh)
Payne, John D
Pehap, Erich K
Penkoff, Ronald Peter
Peterdi, Gabor F
Picken, George
Pierce, Danny P
Pierce, J Michael
Polonsky, Arthur
Ponce de Leon, Michael
Porter, (Edwin) David
Porter, Liliana
Portmann, Frieda Bertha Anne
Pozzatti, Rudy O
Prentice, David Ramage
Pride, Joy
Putterman, Florence Grace
Racz, Andre
Ragland, Jack Whitney
Rakovan, Lawrence Francis
Refregier, Anton
Reichek, Jesse
Reif, Rubin
Rice, Philip Somerset
Richards, Walter DuBois
Ridlon, James A
Riess, Lore
Ritchie, William
Roberts, Donald
Robinson, Grove
Robinson, Sally W
Rogalski, Walter
Rogers, Charles B
Rollman-Shay, Ed & Charlotte
Romano, Clare Camille
Rose, Herman
Rosenblum, Sadie Skoletsky
Rosenhouse, Irwin Jacob
Ross, Conrad Harold
Ross, John T
Rossi, Barbara
Rotholz, Rina
Rozman, Joseph John
Ruffo, Joseph Martin
Ruscha, Edward Joseph
Rush, Andrew
Rutherford, Erica
Sabatini, Raphael
Saff, Donald Jay
Saltzman, Marvin
Saret, Alan Daniel
Sarsony, Robert
Sarvis, Alva Taylor
Satty, Wilfried
Sauls, Frederick Inabinette
Saunders, J Boyd
Savelli, Angelo
Scanga, Italo
Schafer, Alice Pauline
Schaffer, Rose
Schein, Eugenie
Schnackenberg, Roy
Scholder, Fritz
Schorgl, Thomas Barry
Schrut, Sherry
Schutz, Estelle
Schwartz, Aubrey E
Schwieger, C Robert
Seace, Barry William
Seawell, Thomas Robert
Seidler, Doris
Seltzer, Phyllis
Sexauer, Donald Richard
Shapiro, David
Sharpe, David Flemming
Shead, S Ray
Shelton, Robert Lee
Sheppard, Luvon
Sherman, Sarai
Sherman, Z Charlotte
Shields, Alan J
Shoulberg, Harry
Shuff, Lily (Lillian Shir)
Siebner, Herbert (Vom Siebenstein)
Siegel, Irene
Simon, Jewel Woodard
Singleton, Robert Ellison
Slavin, Arlene
Smith, Gordon
Smith, Moishe
Smith, William Arthur
Snow, John
Solman, Joseph
Sommerburg, Miriam
Sparks, John Edwin
Sperakis, Nicholas George
Spruce, Everett Franklin
Spruyt, E Lee
Stack, Frank Huntington
Stasack, Edward Armen
Stasik, Andrew J
Steg, J L
Stevenson, Branson Graves
Stewart, John P
Stewart, Norman (William)
Stratton, Dorothy (Mrs William A King)
Stussy, Jan
Summ, Helmut
Swensen, Mary Jeanette Hamilton (Jean)
Swift, Dick
Sykes, (William) Maltby
Szarama, Judith Layne
Takal, Peter
Talleur, John J
Taylor, Harry George
Taylor, John (Williams)
Thomas, Steffen Wolfgang
Thompson, Donald Roy
Thompson, Ernest Thorne
Threlkeld, Dale
Tilley, Lewis Lee
Toney, Anthony
Toulis, Vasilios (Apostolos)
Trank, Lynn Edgar
Trosky, Helene Roth
Tubis, Seymour
Turner, Janet E
Tyler, Kenneth Eugene
Tyler, Valton
Unwin, Nora Spicer
Upton, Richard Thomas
Vaccarino, Robin
Valier, Biron (Frank)
Vaness, Margaret Helen
Van Vliet, Claire
Veljkovic, Andrev
Viera, Ricardo
Viesulas, Romas
Volpe, Robert
Walker, Herbert Brooks
Walters, Sylvia Solochek
Weber, John Pitman
Webster, Stokely
Weedman, Kenneth Russell
Weege, William
Weller, John Sidney
Wells, James Lesesne
Whipple, Barbara (Mrs Grant Heilman)
Whitesell, John D
Will, John A
Williams, Walter (Henry)
Witham, Vernon Clint
Witold-k (Kaczanowski)
Witt, John
Witt, Nancy Camden
Witteman, Alisa Wells
Wolfe, Mildred Nungester
Wujcik, Theo
Yochim, Louise Dunn
Young, Charles Alexander
Young, Robert John
Zelt, Martha
Ziemann, Richard Claude
Zimiles, Murray
Zwick, Rosemary G

Etching

Abeles, Sigmund
Abramowicz, Janet

Altman, Harold
Anderson, Gunnar Donald
Arnold, Paul Beaver
Asmar, Alice
Atirnomis (Rita Simon)
Autry, Carolyn (Carolyn Autry Elloian)
Baney, Vera
Baranoff, Mort
Barrett, Barbara
Barth, Charles John
Bass, Joel
Bate, Norman Arthur
Baumbach, Harold
Bayefsky, Aba
Beament, Tib (Thomas Harold)
Benney, Robert
Benson, S Patricia (McMahon)
Ben-Zion
Berdich, Vera
Berman, Vivian
Bettinson, Brenda
Birmelin, August Robert
Bishop, Barbara Lee
Bishop, Isabel (Mrs Harold G Wolff)
Blackwood, David (Lloyd)
Bleifeld, Stanley
Blumberg, Ron
Boxer, Stanley (Robert)
Boylan, John Lewis
Braley, Jean Duffield
Brecher, Samuel
Breiger, Elaine
Brendel, Bettina
Broomfield, Adolphus George
Browne, Vivian E
Bumbeck, David A
Bunn, Cecine Cole
Cadmus, Paul
Calderon, Juan
Cassill, Herbert Carroll
Cataldo, John William
Cawein, Kathrin
Chafetz, Sidney
Chinni, Peter Anthony
Chodkowski, Henry, Jr
Christensen, Ted
Cohoe, Grey
Coleman, Michael
Colescott, Warrington W
Conn, David Edward
Consuegra, Hugo
Cornell, Thomas Browne
Cortese, Don F
Corzas, Francisco
Crumbo, Woody
Crump, Walter Moore
Csoka, Stephen
Curtis, Mary Cranfill
Daskaloff, Gyorgy
Davis, Wayne Lambert
De Armond, Dale B
De Groat, George Hugh
Delson, Elizabeth
Dennis, Cherre Nixon
Dickinson, David Charles
Dickson, Jennifer Joan
Dillon, Mildred (Murphy)
Dreskin-Haig, Jeanet Elizabeth
Driesbach, David Fraiser
Dugmore, Edward
Duncan, (Eleanore) Klari
Durieux, Caroline Wogan
Eames, John Heagan
Edmondson, Leonard
Edmunds, Allan Logan
Egleson, Jim (James Downey)
Ellingson, William John
Engelson, Carol
Engle, George Richard
Esler, John Kenneth
Etchison, Bruce
Fausett, (William) Dean
Feigin, Marsha
Feldhaus, Paul A
Field, Philip Sidney
Folsom, Karl Leroy
Forester, Russell
Forsyth, Constance
Fousek, Frank Daniel
Fowler, Mel
Francis, Madison Ke, Jr
Fredrick, Eugene Wallace
Freeman, Robert Lee
Fried, Theodore
Fuller, Sue
Furr, Jim
Gaines, Alan Jay
Gardner, Robert Earl
Garey, Pat
Gecse, Helene
Geerlings, Gerald Kenneth
Gehr, Mary (Mary Ray)
Gelb, Jan
Genders, Richard Atherstone
Gentry (Augustus Calahan, Jr)
Gibson, James D
Golbin, Andree
Goldsmith, Elsa M
Gonzalez-Tornero, Sergio
Goodman, Sidney
Gorsline, Douglas Warner
Greaver, Hanne
Greaver, Harry
Grissom, Eugene Edward
Grupp, Carl Alf
Hammond, Gale Thomas
Hanes, James (Albert)
Hannah, John Junior
Harrison, Tony
Hatch, W A S
Heise, Myron Robert
Hendershot, J L
Herfield, Phyllis Anne
Hickins, Walter H
Hicks, Leon Nathaniel
Hildreth, Joseph Alan
Hill, Polly Knipp
Himmelfarb, John David
Hoie, Claus
Holmes, David Bryan
Hurwitz, Sidney J
Isaak, Nicholas, Jr
Isham, Sheila Eaton
Itchkawich, David Michael
Jacob, Ned
Jacques, Michael Louis
Jansen, Angela Bing
Johanson, George E
Johnsen, May Anne
Johnston, Thomas Alix
Johnston, Ynez
Jones, John Paul
Judd, Donald Clarence
Kakas, Christopher
Kaminisky, Jack Allan
Kaplan, Jerome Eugene
Kappel, Philip
Kasten, Karl Albert
Kaulitz, Garry Charles
Kerslake, Kenneth Alvin
Kim, Bongtae
King, Clinton Blair
Kipniss, Robert
Kirk, Michael
Klabunde, Charles Spencer
Kline, Harriet
Klitgaard, Georgina
Kloss, Gene (Alice Geneva Glasier)
Knee, Gina (Mrs Alexander Brook)
Knipschild, Robert
Kolliker, William Augustin
Konrad, Adolf Ferdinand
Kovatch, Jak Gene
Kraner, Florian G
Krauser, Joel
Kumm, Marguerite Elizabeth
Kupferman, Lawrence
Lack, Richard Frederick
Lambert, Eddie
Lanyon, Ellen
Larson, Philip Seely
Leaf, Ruth
Ledyard, Walter William
Levine, Martin
Lew, Weyman Michael
Lewicki, James
Lindquist, Evan
Lipinsky de Orlov, Lino S
Locke, Charles Wheeler
Loewer, Henry Peter
Lucioni, Luigi
Lukasiewicz, Ronald Joseph
Lytle, Richard
Mackay, Donald Cameron
MacKenzie, Hugh Seaforth
Maestro, Giulio Marcello
Malone, Robert R
Manarey, Thelma Alberta
Mann, Katinka
Manning, Jo
Margulies, Joseph
Martin, Langton
Marx, Robert Ernst
Mason, Harold Dean
Massey, Robert Joseph
Masurovsky, Gregory
Matthews, Wanda Miller
Maxwell, Robert Edwin
Mayes, Steven Lee
McBryde, Sarah Elva
McVicker, J Jay
Menses, Jan
Midgette, Willard Franklin
Mills, Agnes
Milton, Peter Winslow
Mitchell, James E
Mitchell, John Blair
Mitra, Gopal C
Mogensen, Paul
Montgomery, Claude
Morgan, Norma Gloria
Morrow, Terry
Moskowitz, Shirley (Mrs Jacob W Gruber)
Myers, Frances
Nakatani, Carlos
Nakazato, Hitoshi
Navrat, Den (Dennis Edward Navrat)
Neiman, LeRoy
Nelson, Robert Allen
Nichols, Francis N, II
O'Brien, Marjorie (Marjorie O'Brien Rapaport)
Ocvirk, Otto G
Okamura, Arthur
Okoshi, Eugenia Sumiye
Opie, John Mart
Oubre, Hayward Louis
Pace, Stephen S
Paredes, Limon Mariano
Parke, Walter Simpson
Partridge, Roi
Passuntino, Peter Zaccaria
Pate, Lee
Pepper, Beverly
Perlmutter, Merle
Perret, Nell Foster
Petersen, Roland Conrad
Petrie, Sylvia Spencer
Pickhardt, Carl
Pinto, Angelo Raphael
Pitcher, John Charles
Pletcher, Gerry
Pogue, Stephanie Elaine
Priest, Hartwell Wyse
Pufahl, John K
Pusey, Mavis
Quandt, Elizabeth (Elizabeth Quandt Barr)
Quat, Helen S
Rabkin, Leo
Rasmussen, Keith Eric
Rebbeck, Lester James, Jr
Redd, Richard James
Reddy, Krishna N
Reed, Doel
Reed, Jesse Floyd
Reid, (William) Richard
Reisman, Philip
Reynolds, Robert
Richards, Jeanne Herron
Rivard, J Bernard
Roberds, Gene Allen
Rogers, P J
Rose, Roslyn
Rosenquit, Bernard
Rosofsky, Seymour
Ross, Conrad Harold
Royce, Richard Benjamin
Ruble, Ronald L
Ruellan, Andree
Ruggles, Joanne Beaule
Russell, Philip C
Ryerson, Margery Austen
Sahlstrand, Margaret Ahrens
St Tamara
Sawai, Noboru
Schaefer, Ronald H
Schary, Emanuel
Schiff, Lonny
Schmid, Richard Alan
Scholder, Laurence
Schonwalter, Jean Frances
Schwedler, Wm A
Scott, Campbell
Semmel, Joan
Shipley, Roger Douglas
Shokler, Harry
Siberell, Anne Hicks
Silver, Pat
Simel, Elaine
Sjolseth, Minn Solveig
Sloane, Phyllis Lester
Smigocki, Stephen Vincent
Smith, Donald C
Smith, Donald Eugene
Smith, Keith A
Smith, R Harmer
Smith, Vincent D
Snyder, Toni Goessler
Sokolowski, Linda Robinson
Solomon, Bernard Alan
Sorge, Walter
Spagnolo, Kathleen Mary
Sparks, John Edwin
Spitz, Barbara S
Staven, Leland Carroll
Stegman, Patricia (Patricia Stegman Snyder)
Steinhouse, Tobie (Thelma)
Steward, Donn Horatio
Strickland, Thomas J
Stussy, Jan
Summy, Anne Tunis
Sussman, Arthur
Sway, Albert
Tahedl, Ernestine
Talaba, L (Linda Talaba Cummens)
Talbot, Jonathan
Tejeda, Carlos
Teller, Jane (Simon)
Tennyson, Merle Berry
Tevis, Gary Lee
Thompson, Phyllis
Tift, Mary Louise
Todd, Michael Cullen
Tomchuk, Marjorie
Travers, Gwyneth Mabel
Trlak, Roger
Tschacbasov, Nahum
Unger, Mary Ann
Van Hoesen, Beth (Mrs Mark Adams)
Van Vranken, Rose (Rose Van Vranken Hickey)
Verner, Elizabeth O'Neill
Vogel, Donald
Waisler, Lee
Wall, Sue

PRINTMAKER (cont)
Washburn, Stan
Weare, Shane
Weber, Idelle
Webster, Larry
Weidenaar, Reynold Henry
Weingarten, Hilde (Kevess)
Weisberg, Ruth Ellen
Werth, Kurt
Whyte, Raymond A
Wicks, Eugene Claude
Wilson, John
Winters, John L
Wright, Frank
Wunderman, Jan (Liljan Darcourt Wunderman)
Wynn, Donald James
Yanosky, Tom
Yarbrough, Leila Kepert
Yeh, Carol
Yudin, Carol
Zavel (Zavel Silber)
Zeitlin, Harriet Brooks
Zevon, Irene
Zoellner, Richard C
Zonia, Dhimitri
Zugor, Sandor

Engraving

Bate, Norman Arthur
Bejar, Feliciano
Benson, S Patricia (McMahon)
Berdich, Vera
Bishop, Isabel (Mrs Harold G Wolff)
Bleifeld, Stanley
Braley, Jean Duffield
Brody, Arthur William
Brussel-Smith, Bernard
Bumbeck, David A
Cassill, Herbert Carroll
Chappell, Berkley Warner
Cook, August Charles
Cuevas, Jose Luis
De Marco, Jean Antoine
De Pol, John
Driesbach, David Fraiser
Elloian, Peter
Feldhaus, Paul A
Fredrick, Eugene Wallace
Fumagalli, Barbara Merrill
Grissom, Eugene Edward
Hanna, Boyd Everett
Harrison, Tony
Hicks, Leon Nathaniel
Hill, Polly Knipp
Jaidinger, Judith C (Judith Clarann Szesko)
Johanson, George E
Kakas, Christopher
Kerslake, Kenneth Alvin
Klabunde, Charles Spencer
Landeck, Armin
Laventhol, Hank
Lazzari, Pietro
Leaf, Ruth
Leighton, Clare
Levine, Martin
Lindquist, Evan
Lipman-Wulf, Peter
Manning, Jo
Marsh, Anne Steele
Martin, Langton
Matthews, Wanda Miller
McCoy, Ann
McGinnis, Christine
Midgette, Willard Franklin
Milton, Peter Winslow
Mitchell, John Blair
Morgan, Norma Gloria
Moser, Barry
Myers, Virginia Anne
Nichols, Francis N, II
O'Connell, George D
Ocvirk, Otto G
Pickens, Alton
Pufahl, John K
Ranes, Chris
Redd, Richard James
Reddy, Krishna N
Reibel, Bertram
Richards, Jeanne Herron
Roberds, Gene Allen
Rogers, P J
Rose, Roslyn
Ross, Conrad Harold
Russell, Philip C
Scott, Campbell
Smith, Donald C
Solomon, Bernard Alan
Spitz, Barbara S
Steinhouse, Tobie (Thelma)
Steward, Donn Horatio
Summy, Anne Tunis
Szesko, Lenore Rundle
Talbot, Jonathan
Tevis, Gary Lee
Toral, Maria Teresa
Tschacbasov, Nahum
Van Hoesen, Beth (Mrs Mark Adams)
Waisler, Lee
Ych, Carol
Zeitlin, Harriet Brooks
Zoellner, Richard C

Lithography

Abeles, Sigmund
Adams, Clinton
Altman, Harold
Aquino, Edmundo
Arcilesi, Vincent J
Ascher, Mary
Baber, Alice
Baeder, John
Baldwin, John
Ballou, Anne MacDougall
Baranoff, Mort
Bates, Maxwell Bennett
Baumbach, Harold
Beament, Tib (Thomas Harold)
Bechtle, Robert Alan
Bennett, Don Bemco
Berg, Thomas
Berman, Steven M
Berman, Vivian
Billmyer, John Edward
Block, Amanda Roth
Bookbinder, Jack
Boyd, John David
Boylan, John Lewis
Bransby, Eric James
Brendel, Bettina
Brooks, James
Brown, Marvin Prentiss
Browne, Vivian E
Browning, Colleen
Brussel-Smith, Bernard
Bunker, George
Burkert, Robert Randall
Butler, James D
Byard, Carole Marie
Cadmus, Paul
Catlett, Elizabeth
Chu, Gene
Clutz, William
Colescott, Warrington W
Copeland, Lila
Cortright, Steven M
Corzas, Francisco
Crawford, Ralston
Crutchfield, William Richard
Csoka, Stephen
Cuevas, Jose Luis
Curry, Noble Wilbur
Daskaloff, Gyorgy
D'Aulaire, Ingri (Mortenson) Parin
Davidson, Herbert Laurence
De Armond, Dale B
Dehn, Virginia
Dennis, Cherre Nixon
Dike, Philip Latimer
Doyle, John Lawrence
Dreskin-Haig, Jeanet Elizabeth
Driesbach, David Fraiser
Durieux, Caroline Wogan
Eagerton, Robert Pierce
Edmunds, Allan Logan
Eichenberg, Fritz
Ellingson, William John
Ernst, Jimmy
Etchison, Bruce
Faiers, Edward Spencer (Ted)
Farm, Gerald E
Farnsworth, Jerry
Feldhaus, Paul A
Filmus, Tully
Florsheim, Richard A
Forsyth, Constance
Fortess, Karl E
Foster, April
Fousek, Frank Daniel
Frances, Harriette Anton
Fruhauf, Aline
Furr, Jim
Gabin, George Joseph
Gagnon, Charles Eugene
Gardner, Robert Earl
Geerlings, Gerald Kenneth
George, Raymond Ellis
Gerzso, Gunther
Giampaoli, James Francis
Gliko, Carl Albert
Goedicke, Jean
Gold, Leah
Goldsmith, Elsa M
Goodman, Sidney
Gorsline, Douglas Warner
Gourevitch, Jacqueline
Granstaff, William Boyd
Greaver, Hanne
Greaver, Harry
Green, Edward Anthony
Groell, Theophil
Grosch, Laura
Grupp, Carl Alf
Guiffreda, Mauro Francis
Gwathmey, Robert
Hack, Howard Edwin
Haessle, Jean-Marie Georges
Hagan, (Robert) Frederick
Halbrooks, Darryl Wayne
Harrison, Pat (Broeder)
Hatch, W A S
Hayes, Robert T
Hebald, Milton Elting
Hedrick, Wally Bill
Heflin, Tom Pat
Hendershot, J L
Hibel, Edna
Higgins, Dick
High, Timothy Griffin
Hildreth, Joseph Alan
Himmelfarb, John David
Hirsch, Gilah Yelin
Hobbie, Lucille
Hollander, Gino F
Holtz, Itshak Jack
Hook, Walter
Horn, Bruce
Hrdy, Olinka
Hultberg, John Phillip
Hunkler, Dennis Francis
Hunter, Mel
Ida, Shoichi
Imana, Jorge Garron
Ingram, Jerry Cleman
Isham, Sheila Eaton
Iwamasa, Ken
Jacobson, Arthur Robert
Jameson, Demetrios George
Janzen, Loren Gene
Jennings, Thomas
Jimenez, Luis Alfonso, Jr
Johnston, Ynez
Kaplan, Jerome Eugene
Kelley, Donald William
Kelly, James
Kenny, Lisa A
Kermes, Constantine John
Kilian, Austin Farland
Kingman, Dong M
Kipniss, Robert
Kitta, George Edward
Kniffin, Ralph Gus
Knobler, Nathan
Ko, Anthony
Konrad, Adolf Ferdinand
Kovatch, Jak Gene
Krebs, Rockne
Landau, Jacob
Lanyon, Ellen
Lapointe, Frank
Laub-Novak, Karen
Lauffer, Alice A
Lazzari, Pietro
Lecoque
Ledyard, Walter William
Leepa, Allen
Lehrer, Leonard
Levine, Martin
Locke, Charles Wheeler
Locker, Thomas
Long, Walter Kinscella
Longley, Bernique
Lowney, Bruce Stark
Lund, Jane
Machetanz, Fred
Majeski, Thomas H
Margulies, Joseph
Markow, Jack
Marshall, James Duard
Martyl (Martyl Schweig Langsdorf)
Mason, Harold Dean
Masurovsky, Gregory
McCallum, Corrie (Mrs William Halsey)
McCormick, Harry
McCoy, Ann
McGinnis, Christine
Melville, Grevis Whitaker
Menses, Jan
Mercier, Monique
Merida, Carlos
Mittleman, Ann
Miyasaki, George Joji
Morehouse, William Paul
Morrow, Terry
Mosca, August
Muench, John
Munoz, Rie (Marie Angelina Muroz)
Nakazato, Hitoshi
Naminha, Dan
Nathan, Helmuth Max
Nelson, Robert Allen
Nevelson, Mike
Nichols, Francis N, II
Noble, John A
O'Connell, George D
O'Connor, Thom
O'Hara, (James) Frederick
Pajaud, William Etienne
Parfenoff, Michael S
Passuntino, Peter Zaccaria
Pate, Lee
Pen, Rudolph
Perlmutter, Jack
Petersen, Will
Petheo, Bela Francis
Pettet, William
Pickhardt, Carl
Pratt, Mary Frances
Preuss, Roger
Priest, Hartwell Wyse
Puccinelli, Raimondo
Quick, Birney MacNabb
Rasmussen, Keith Eric

Rayen, James Wilson
Richards, Jeanne Herron
Robinson, Charlotte
Rode, Meredith Eagon
Rodman, Ruth M
Rohm, Robert
Rosenthal, Seymour Joseph
Rosofsky, Seymour
Roszak, Theodore
Rubenstein, Lewis W
Ruble, Ronald L
Rudquist, Jerry Jacob
Ruellan, Andree
Ryerson, Margery Austen
Salt, John
Saltonstall, Elizabeth
Samburg, Grace (Blanche)
Sargent, Richard
Sawyer, Helen (Helen Sawyer Farnsworth)
Schary, Emanuel
Schary, Susan
Scheu, Leonard
Schreyer, Greta L
Schuselka, Elfi
Schwartz, Carl E
Schwartz, William S
Scott, John Tarrell
Seckel, Paul Bernhard
Secunda, (Holland) Arthur
Serra-Badue, Daniel
Shapiro, David
Sharp, Anne
Simson, Bevlyn A
Sivard, Robert Paul
Sjolseth, Minn Solveig
Sloan, Jeanette Pasin
Smith, Lawrence Beall
Smyth, David Richard
Snidow, Gordon E
Sokole, Miron
Solodkin, Judith
Somers, H
Sommers, John Sherman
Sparks, John Edwin
Sprang, Elizabeth Lewis
Spruce, Everett Franklin
Stegman, Patricia (Patricia Stegman Snyder)
Stoianovich, Marcelle
Strickland, Thomas J
Surrey, Philip Henry
Swensen, Mary Jeanette Hamilton (Jean)
Swirnoff, Lois
Taggart, William John
Tarin, Gilberto A
Teller, Jane (Simon)
Thom, Robert Alan
Tooker, George
Ulbricht, John
Urban, Reva
Vega, Edward
Vigil, Veloy Joseph
Vogel, Donald
Vogl, Don George
Waldman, Paul
Watson, Robert
Wayne, June
Weiler, Melody M
Weisberg, Ruth Ellen
Werth, Kurt
Westermann, Horace Clifford
Westlund, Harry E
Wheeler, Cleora Clark
Whidden, Conni (Constance)
Whitaker, William
Whyte, Raymond A
Wilson, Nicholas Jon
Woehrman, Ralph
Wolfe, Robert, Jr
Yust, David E
Zirker, Joseph
Zucker, Jacques
Zver, James M

Mezzotint

Alexander, Peter
Benson, S Patricia (McMahon)
Berdich, Vera
Brody, Arthur William
Hanes, James (Albert)
Harrison, Tony
Higgins, Dick
Leaf, Ruth
Pusey, Mavis
Quaytman, Harvey
Sahlstrand, Margaret Ahrens
Smith, Donald C
Woehrman, Ralph

Miscellaneous Media

Abrams, Jane Eldora
Alps, Glen Earl
Anderson, William
Anderson, William Thomas
Angulo, Chappie
Appleman, David Earl
Bacon, Peggy
Barry, Anne Meredith
Barsch, Wulf Erich
Barth, Charles John
Becker, Bettie (Bettie Geraldine Wathall)
Belfiore, Gerardo
Bell, Alistair Macready
Bell, Peter Alan
Benedict, Nan M
Bennett, Don Bemco
Benz, Lee R
Berlin, Beatrice Winn
Berman, Vivian
Binning, Robin
Bittner, Hans Oskar
Blumenthal, Fritz
Borne, Mortimer
Brown, Catharine Homan
Brulc, Dennis
Burkert, Robert Randall
Byars, Donna
Caiserman-Roth, Ghitta
Cameron, Brooke Bulovsky
Camins, Jacques Joseph
Cederstrom, John Andrew
Childers, Richard Robin
Clerk, Pierre
Clifton, Michelle Gamm
Clymer, Albert Anderson
Coelho, Luiz Carlos
Coiner, Charles Toucey
Colverson, Ian
Creech, Franklin Underwood
Crittenden, John William Neil
Crump, Walter Moore
Curran, Darryl Joseph
Davila, Carlos
Davis, J Ray
DeLamonica, Roberto
Deming, David Lawson
Deshaies, Arthur
Duff, Ann MacIntosh
Dugmore, Edward
Durieux, Caroline Wogan
Eckmair, Frank C
Ellis, Robert Carroll
Elwell, Chip
Ettling, Ruth (Droitcour)
Evans, Henry
Evans, Richard
Fay, Joe
Ferguson, Edward Robert
Fohr, Jenny
Foster, April
Foster, Barbara Lynn
Fraze, Denny T
Freeman, Mark
French, Ray H
Fuerst, Shirley Miller
Gantz, Ann Cushing
Gantz, Jeanne A
Garcia, Ofelia
Gaucher, Yves
Gelb, Jan
Geller, Esther (Esther Geller Shapero)
George, Raymond Ellis
Gerardia, Helen
Getty, Nilda Fernandez
Gifford, J Nebraska
Goldstein, Milton
Golinkin, Joseph Webster
Haas, Richard John
Habergritz, George Joseph
Hack, Howard Edwin
Hahn, Betty
Hamilton, John
High, Freida
Hildebrand, June Mary Ann
Hildebrandt, William Albert
Hillman, Arthur Stanley
Hoare, Tyler James
Howard, David
Hughes, Donald N
Hunkler, Dennis Francis
Hurtig, Martin Russell
Hushlak, Gerald Marshall
Ingram, Judith
Jacquette, Yvonne Helene (Yvonne Helen Burckhardt)
Janzen, Loren Gene
Johnson, Joyce
Johnston, Robert Porter
Jones, Theodore Joseph
Jorgensen, Flemming
Kaplan, Stanley
Kasten, Karl Albert
Kemenyffy, Susan B Hale
Kemp, Paul Zane
Kenny, Lisa A
Kerkovius, Ruth
Kerslake, Kenneth Alvin
Kimura, Riisaburo
Kinnaird, Richard William
Kitaj, R B
Kohn, Misch
Koons, Darell J
Kramolc, Theodore Maria
Kreneck, Lynwood
Kuchar, Kathleen Ann
Kushner, Dorothy Browdy
La More, Chet Harmon
Lasansky, Leonardo da Iowa
Law, Carol L
Lent, Blair
Lewis, Stanley
Limont, Naomi Charles
Littleton, Harvey K
Low, Joseph
Lukosius, Richard Benedict
Luray, J (J Luray Schaffner)
Maitin, Samuel (Calman)
Margo, Boris
Marozzi, Eli Raphael
Massey, Charles Wesley, Jr
Matteson, Ira
McClelland, Jeanne C
McGovern, Robert F
McMillen, Michael Chalmers
Michaels, Glen
Mitchell, Dow Penrose
Mitchell, Jeffrey Malcolm
Montague, James L
Moore, Robert James
Myers, Virginia Anne
Nardin, Mario
Neal, (Minor) Avon
Neals, Otto
Nelson, Harry William
Nemec, Nancy
Neustein, Joshua
Noordhoek, Harry Cecil
Norris, (Robert) Ben
O'Connell, Edward E
O'Hara, (James) Frederick
Ortlieb, Robert Eugene
Parry, Marian (Marian Parry Feld)
Partridge, David Gerry
Paschke, Edward F (Ed)
Penney, James
Perkins, A Alan
Petrie, Sylvia Spencer
Philbrick, Margaret Elder
Pohl, Louis G
Potter, (George) Kenneth
Price, Kenneth
Renouf, Edda
Richardson, James Lewis
Rodman, Ruth M
Roman, Shirley
Rowan, Dennis Michael
Sanderson, Charles Howard
Sankowsky, Itzhak
Schieferdecker, Ivan E
Schloss, Arleen P (Arleen P Kelly)
Sherwood, A (Frances Ann Crane)
Siberell, Anne Hicks
Sidenius, W Christian
Sonenberg, Jack
Sparks, John Edwin
Spero, Nancy
Stanforth, Melvin Sidney
Stapp, Ray Veryl
Swartzman, Roslyn
Taylor, Harry George
Taylor, Sandra Ortiz
Thompson, Phyllis
Thrall, Arthur
Tomchuk, Marjorie
Tooker, George
Torbert Stephanie Birch
Turner, (Charles) Arthur
Van Suchtelen, Adrian
Venor, Robert George
Verzyl, Kenneth H
Vian, Orfeo
Wall, Ralph Alan
Weingarten, Hilde (Kevess)
Winkler, Maria Paula
Woehrman, Ralph
Yarbrough, Leila Kepert
Youkeles, Anne
Younglove, Ruth Ann (Mrs Benjamin Rhees Loxley)
Yudin, Carol
Zirker, Joseph

Serigraphy, Silkscreen

Adams, Glenn Nelson
Adler, Lee
Ahlgren, Roy B
Alford, Gloria K
Anderson, Ivan Delos
Angeloch, Robert (Henry)
Aquino, Edmundo
Arnold, Florence M
Ascher, Mary
Auvil, Kenneth William
Avakian, John
Bach, Dirk
Baker, Eugene Ames
Ballou, Anne MacDougall
Banks, Anne Johnson
Barry, Anne Meredith
Bates, Betsey
Baumbach, Harold
Benz, Lee R
Berlyn, Sheldon
Berman, Ariane R
Berman, Vivian
Berry, William David
Betancourt, R Arenas
Biberman, Edward
Bieler, Ted Andre
Bierk, David Charles
Bishop, Barbara Lee
Block, Amanda Roth
Bothwell, Dorr

PRINTMAKER (cont)

Boughton, William Harrison
Bradford, Howard
Brandt, Frederick Robert
Brod, Stanford
Brooks, James
Burkert, Robert Randall
Cady, Dennis Vern
Caples, Barbara Barrett
Cardoso, Anthony
Carron, Maudee Lilyan
Carter, Clarence Holbrook
Chernow, Ann
Chieffo, Clifford Toby
Chinni, Peter Anthony
Christensen, Ronald Julius
Christensen, Ted
Christ-Janer, Arland F
Clark, John Dewitt
Colescott, Warrington W
Colville, Alexander
Condeso, Orlando
Conrad, Nancy R
Crumbo, Woody
Curran, Darryl Joseph
Curtis, Mary Cranfill
Danby, Ken
Davies, Theodore Peter
Dean, Nicholas Brice
De Armond, Dale B
Dieringer, Ernest A
Dike, Philip Latimer
Dillon, Mildred (Murphy)
Dmytruk, Ihor
Dorst, Claire V
Drew, Joan
Drutz, June
Duff, Ann MacIntosh
Durham, William
Eades, Luis Eric
Eden, F Brown
Edmunds, Allan Logan
Edwards, Ellender Morgan
Ellingson, William John
Engle, Barbara Jean
Engle, George Richard
Ernst, Jimmy
Estes, Richard
Federe, Marion
Felter, James Warren
Forman, Kenneth Warner
Foulger, Richard F
Francis, Madison Ke, Jr
Fransioli, Thomas Adrian
Friedeberg, Pedro
Fukui, Nobu
Gardner, Andrew Bradford
Gardner, Susan Ross
Garwood, Audrey
Gatrell, Marion Thompson
Gatrell, Robert Morris
Gerardia, Helen
Gerzso, Gunther
Gill, Gene
Goodnow, Frank A
Goreleigh, Rex
Govan, Francis Hawks
Greenleaf, Esther (Hargrave)
Gurr, Lena
Haessle, Jean-Marie Georges
Hanna, Paul Dean, Jr
Hannah, John Junior
Hein, Max
Hicken, Philip Burnham
Hickins, Walter H
Higgins, Dick
Hildebrand, June Mary Ann
Hillman, Arthur Stanley
Hobbs, Robert Dean
Hoffmann, Arnold, Jr
Homar, Lorenzo
Hotvedt, Kris J
Hurtubise, Jacques
Izuka, Kunio
Johnson, Lois Marlene
Jones, Ben
Jones, Frederick George
Jorgensen, Flemming
Kaminisky, Jack Allan
Katayama, Toshihiro
Kaulitz, Garry Charles
Kipp, Orval
Kirk, Michael
Kirkwood, Larry Thomas
Kirsten-Daiensai, Richard Charles
Klein, Beatrice T
Knowles, Alison
Kohn, William Roth
Kreneck, Lynwood
Krug, Harry Elno
Kuczun, Ann-Marie
Kupferman, Lawrence
Lagorio, Irene R
Lambert, Eddie
Landon, Edward August
Lee, Margaret F
Leeper, Doris Marie
Le Roy, Harold M
Levy, Hilda
Lew, Weyman Michael
Lieberman, Meyer Frank
Lipzin, Janis Crystal
Locker, Thomas
Lukasiewicz, Ronald Joseph
Mahmoud, Ben
Malone, Robert R
Mandziuk, Michael Dennis
Mann, Vaughan (Vaughan Grayson)
Mansaram, Panchal
Maradiaga, Ralph
Marchese, Patricia Davis
Marcus, Marcia
Mari (Mari M Eagerton)
Marriott, William Allen
Martin, Fletcher
Mayes, Steven Lee
McElroy, Jacquelyn Ann
McLean, Roddy (Verneda Rodriguez)
McVicker, J Jay
Meader, Jonathan Grant (Ascian)
Merida, Carlos
Mesches, Arnold
Micheli, Julio
Miller, Nancy
Miller, Richard Kidwell
Mills, Agnes
Munoz, Rie (Marie Angelina Muroz)
Murphy, Gladys Wilkins
Murray, John Michael
Myers, Jack Fredrick
Nakazato, Hitoshi
Navrat, Den(Dennis Edward Navrat)
Neiman, LeRoy
Nind, Jean
O'Connell, Edward E
Okamura, Arthur
Oldham, Berton Jepsen
Parker, Samuel Murray
Pascal, David
Pattee, Rowena
Payor, Eugene
Peace, Bernie (Kinzel)
Pearson, John
Pena, Amado Maurilio, Jr
Perlman, Raymond
Pinto, Biagio
Poleskie, Stephen Francis
Pond, Clayton
Pope, Mary Ann Irwin
Pratt, Mary Frances
Prestopino, Gregorio
Priest, Hartwell Wyse
Priest, T
Prohaska, Ray
Pusey, Mavis
Quat, Helen S
Ragland, Jack Whitney
Reibel, Bertram
Reid, (William) Richard
Robbins, Hulda D
Robinson, Charlotte
Rose, Roslyn
Ross, Fred (Joseph)
Rothschild, Judith
Rozzi, (James A)
Ruggles, Joanne Beaule
Rugolo, Lawrence
Saalburg, Allen Russel
Sachse, Janice R
Sassone, Marco
Sato, Masaaki
Savage, Roger
Schein, Eugenie
Schepis, Anthony Joseph
Schlump, John Otto
Schmalz, Carl (Nelson, Jr)
Schuselka, Elfi
Schwartz, Carl E
Schwedler, Wm A
Schwieger, C Robert
Seawell, Thomas Robert
Secunda, (Holland) Arthur
Selwitz, Ruth F
Sharp, Anne
Shimomura, Roger Yutaka
Shipley, Roger Douglas
Shokler, Harry
Shoulberg, Harry
Simson, Bevlyn A
Sjolseth, Minn Solveig
Sklar-Weinstein, Arlene (Joyce)
Slettehaugh, Thomas Chester
Sloane, Phyllis Lester
Smith, Henry Holmes
Smith, Robert Alan
Somers, H
Spagnolo, Kathleen Mary
Spongberg, Grace
Spurgin, John Edwin
Stallwitz, Carolyn
Statman, Jan B
Stevens, May
Stomps, Walter E, Jr
Stovall, Luther McKinley (Lou)
Street, John Michael
Strider, Marjorie Virginia
Stroud, Peter Anthony
Sundberg, Carl Gustave
Surrey, Philip Henry
Sznajderman, Marius S
Talaba, L (Linda Talaba Cummens)
Ten Eyck, Catryna (Catryna Ten Eyck Seymour)
Tennyson, Merle Berry
Thomas, John
Thompson, Phyllis
Thomson, William David
Thwaites, Charles Winstanley
Tift, Mary Louise
Tousignant, Claude
Twitty, James (Watson)
Vaccaro, Patrick Frank (Patt Vaccaro)
Van Riper, Peter
Vaux, Richard
Vian, Orfeo
Vincent, Tom
Voelker, John
Volkin, Hilda Appel
Von Gunten, Roger
Wagner, G Noble
Wald, Sylvia
Walker, James Adams
Walker, Joy
Wang, Samuel
Wasserman, Burton
Watson, Robert
Weiler, Melody M
Westlund, Harry E
White, Doris A
Winter, Gerald Glen
Winter, Roger
Wood, Robert E
Yoakum, Delmer J
Youkeles, Anne
Yust, David E
Zacha, George William
Zucker, Murray Harvey
Zver, James M

Woodcut

Abbe, Elfriede Martha
Allman, Margo
Arnold, Paul Beaver
Aronson, Sanda
Ashby, Carl
Barry, Anne Meredith
Barth, Charles John
Bell, Alistair Macready
Berger, Jason
Berman, Ariane R
Billmyer, John Edward
Boylan, John Lewis
Bragar, Philip Frank
Brender a Brandis, Gerard William
Brody, Arthur William
Bunn, Cecine Cole
Cano, Margarita
Cassill, Herbert Carroll
Chafetz, Sidney
Chodkowski, Henry, Jr
Conover, Robert Fremont
Currie, Bruce
D'Amato, Janet Potter
Dance, Robert Bartlett
Darr, William Humiston
Davies, Theodore Peter
De Armond, Dale B
Dillon, Mildred (Murphy)
Dimondstein, Morton
Domjan, Joseph (also Spiri)
Drake, James
Drewes, Werner
Eckmair, Frank C
Eden, F Brown
Eichenberg, Fritz
Eliason, Shirley (Shirley Eliason Haupt)
Ente, Lily
Ettling, Ruth (Droitcour)
Federe, Marion
Ferro, Walter
Fowler, Mel
Fried, Theodore
Fruhauf, Aline
Gains, Jacob
Gary, Jan (Mrs William D Gorman)
Gaul, Arrah Lee
George, Thomas
Gold, Leah
Goldstein, Daniel Joshua
Gurr, Lena
Hanna, Boyd Everett
Hanna, Paul Dean, Jr
Harmon, Cliff Franklin
Hedman, Teri Jo
High, Freida
Hillsmith, Fannie
Hnizdovsky, Jacques
Hobbie, Lucille
Hodgell, Robert Overman
Homar, Lorenzo
Hotvedt, Kris J
Humble, Douglas
Hurwitz, Sidney J
Hyde, Laurence
Inman, Pauline Winchester
Jacobson, Ursula Mercedes
Jaidinger, Judith C (Judith Clarann Szesko)
Johnston, Ynez
Judd, Donald Clarence
Kaplan, Jerome Eugene
Karp, Richard Gordon
Kasten, Karl Albert
Kemble, Richard

Kermes, Constantine John
Kerstetter, Barbara Ann
Kinigstein, Jonah
Kleiman, Alan
Koster, Marjory Jean
Kumm, Marguerite Elizabeth
Landau, Jacob
Leaf, Ruth
Leff, Juliette
Levy, Hilda
Lipman-Wulf, Peter
Lourie, Herbert S
Macdonnell, Cameron
Marshall, James Duard
Martin, Roger
McAdoo, Donald Eldridge
McBryde, Sarah Elva
McCallum, Corrie (Mrs William Halsey)
McClelland, Jeanne C
McLarty, William James (Jack)
Messick, Ben (Newton)
Mirko (Wolodymyr Walter Pylyshenko)
Mitra, Gopal C
Mogensen, Paul
Mora, Francisco
Morrison, Robert Clifton
Mortensen, Gordon Louis
Moser, Barry
Nevelson, Mike
Norton, Mary Joyce
Offner, Elliot
O'Hara, (James) Frederick
Okoshi, Eugenia Sumiye
Ortlieb, Robert Eugene
Pace, Stephen S
Parton, Nike
Perez, Vincent
Peterson, A E S
Pinto, Angelo Raphael
Pletcher, Gerry
Pohl, Louis G
Poucher, Elizabeth Morris
Prekop, Martin Dennis
Quest, Charles Francis
Reindorf, Samuel
Richards, Jeanne Herron
Rogers, P J
Rosenquit, Bernard
Rowan, Frances Physioc
Satorsky, Cyril
Sawai, Noboru
Schanker, Louis
Scharff, Constance Kramer
Schein, Eugenie
Schiller, Beatrice
Scott, Campbell
Shokler, Harry
Shuff, Lily (Lillian Shir)
Siberell, Anne Hicks
Skelley, Robert Charles
Slater, Van E
Smith, Ben
Solodkin, Judith
Solomon, Bernard Alan
Stell, H Kenyon
Stoltenberg, Donald Hugo
Summers, Carol
Sznajderman, Marius S
Taylor, Grace Martin
Thompson, Robert Charles
Tomchuk, Marjorie
Travers, Gwyneth Mabel
Uchima, Ansei
Vian, Orfeo
Vo-Dinh, Mai
Waitzkin, Stella
Walters, Sylvia Solochek
Washington, James W, Jr
Waters, Herbert (Ogden)
Werth, Kurt
Westermann, Horace Clifford
Winters, John L
Yeh, Carol
Zavel (Zavel Silber)
Zevon, Irene
Zweerts, Arnold

PUBLISHER

Abrams, Harry N
Anbinder, Paul
Barton, John Murray
Becker, Martin Earle
Bendig, William Charles
Bergling, Virginia Catherine (Mrs Stephen J Kozazcki)
Bernard, Felix S
Califano, Edward Christopher
Cloud, Jack L
Cornell, Thomas Browne
Davidson, Suzette Morton
deAK, Edit
De Grazia, Ettore Ted
Dorn, Peter Klaus
Eagerton, Robert Pierce
English, John Arbogast
Esterow, Milton
Fanning, Robbie
Fedele, Frank D
Feinman, Stephen E
Goldman, Louis & Sondra
Goodman, Marian
Gordon, Martin
Haber, William
Hamady, Walter Samuel
Heath, David C
Howard, David
Iolas, Alexander
Isaacs, Avrom
Lanou, Tobie E
Lewin, Mr & Mrs Robert L
Loeffler, Carl Eugene
Love, Richard Henry
MacDonald, Colin Somerled
Marrozzini, Luigi
McCann, Cecile Nelken
McGilvery, Laurence
Mercer, John Douglas
Moos, Walter A
Morton, Robert Alan
Newman, Louis
Offin, Charles Z
Petersen, Will
Prakapas, Eugene Joseph
Redstone, Louis Gordon
Ring, Edward Alfred
Rosenberg, Alex Jacob
Rosenthal, John W
Saff, Donald Jay
Schapiro, Miriam
Schlosberg, Carl Martin
Schumsky, Felicie Roberta
Seraphin, Joseph Anthony
Shark, Herman R
Smith, Ross Ransom Williams
Solomon, Richard H
Solway, Carl E
Steward, Donn Horatio
Szoke, John
Thom, Robert Alan
Tomchuk, Marjorie
Tyler, Kenneth Eugene
Walton, Donald William
Wheeler, Mark
Wing, Robin Stewart

RESTORER

see also **Conservator**

Bailey, James Arlington, Jr
Beardsley, Barbara H
Bernstein, Gerald
Brownett, Thelma Denyer
Cederstrom, John Andrew
Craig, Martin
Czimbalmos, Szabo Kalman
Dunn, Nate
Fitzgerald, Edmond James
Ghikas, Panos George
Gonzalez, Jose Luis
Heberling, Glen Austin
Jakstas, Alfred John
Johnson, Kenn Elmer
Kemoha (George W Patrick Patterson)
Knowlton, Daniel Gibson
Lamanna, Carmen
Lebedev, Vladimir
Leisher, William Rodger
Lysun, Gregory
MacDonald, Gayle Coleman
Mohr, Pauline Catherine
Moonier, Syliva
Morse, Mitchell Ian
Pablo (Paul Burgess Edwards)
Rabin, Bernard
Richard, Jack
Schiff, Lonny
Silberfeld, Kay
Sisti, Anthony J (Tony)
Stacks, William Leon
Stein, Harve
Stoner, Joyce Hill
Texidor, Fernando
Zarand, Julius John

SCULPTOR

All Media

Aarons, Anita
Aarons, George
Abbe, Elfriede Martha
Abbott, Dorothy I
Acconci, Vito
Acton, Arlo C
Adams, Katherine Langhorne
Adler, Billy (Telethon)
Agopoff, Agop Minass
Agostinelli, Mario
Agostini, Peter
Ahlskog, Sirkka
Aidlin, Jerome
Ajay, Abe
Alaupovic, Alexandra V
Albrecht, Mary Dickson
Albright, Malvin Marr
Allen, Tom, Jr
Allman, Margo
Allumbaugh, James
Ambrose, Charles Edward
Anargyros, Spero
Anderson, Gordon
Anderson, Jeremy Radcliffe
Andre, Carl
Andrews, Michael Frank
Anthony, Lawrence Kenneth
Appel, Eric A
Archambault, Louis
Archie, James Lee
Arcuri, Frank J
Arman
Aronson, Boris
Artschwager, Richard Ernst
Asher, Elise
Ayaso, Manuel
Aycock, Alice
Bachinski, Walter Joseph
Bakanowsky, Louis J
Baldwin, John
Baldwin, Russell W
Balsley, John Gerald
Band, Max
Barbarossa, Theodore C
Barr, Roger Terry
Barrett, Bill
Baskin, Leonard
Bates, Gladys Edgerly
Bayer, Herbert
Bayer, Jeffrey Joshua
Beckley, Bill
Beeler, Joe (Neil)
Beer, Kenneth John
Beling, Helen
Bell, Larry Stuart
Benglis, Lynda
Benno, Benjamin G
Benton, Fletcher
Ben-Zion
Berlant, Tony
Bernstein, Sylvia
Besner, J Jacques
Bieler, Ted Andre
Bladen, Ronald
Blai, Boris
Blair, Robert Noel
Blazeje, Zbigniew
Bleifeld, Stanley
Bodo, Sandor
Bodolai, Joseph Stephen
Bolotowsky, Ilya
Bonevardi, Marcelo
Bookatz, Samuel
Borgatta, Isabel Case
Borglum, James Lincoln de la Mothe
Borne, Mortimer
Bornstein, Eli
Bott, H J
Boulton, Joseph L
Bouras, Harry D
Boyd, James Henderson
Breer, Robert C
Breschi, Karen Lee
Bright, Barney
Brink, Guido Peter
Brock, Robert W
Brody, Myron Roy
Brookins, Jacob Boden
Brose, Morris
Brown, Joseph
Browne, Tom Martin
Brulc, Lillian G
Brun, Thomas
Buba, Joy Flinsch
Buckner, Paul Eugene
Buczak, Brian Elliot
Burchess, Arnold
Burden, Chris
Burgess, David Lowry
Burnett, Patricia Hill
Burnham, Lee
Burr, Horace
Bush, Beverly
Bushman, David Franklin
Bussabarger, Robert Franklin
Butterbaugh, Robert Clyde
Caglioti, Victor
Calfee, William Howard
Cantini, Virgil D
Cantor, Robert Lloyd
Cardoso, Anthony
Cariola, Robert J
Carl, Joan
Carr, Sally Swan
Carstenson, Cecil C
Carter, Dean
Carter, Granville W
Casarella, Edmond
Cascieri, Arcangelo
Caver, William Ralph
Cecere, Gaetano
Chamberlain, John Angus
Chase, Doris (Totten)
Chavez, Edward Arcenio
Chinni, Peter Anthony
Christo (Javacheff)
Chryssa, (Vardea)
Cimbalo, Robert W
Ciuca, Eugen
Clements, Robert Donald
Clover, James B
Coe, Matchett Herring

SCULPTOR (cont)
Cohen, Adele
Coker, Carl David
Collins, Jim
Conaway, Gerald
Coochsiwukioma, DH (Del Honanie)
Cook, Robert Howard
Cooper, Ron
Coppola, Andrew
Coronel, Pedro
Corwin, Sophia M
Coughtry, John Graham
Cox, Ernest Lee
Craig, Martin
Crawford, William H
Crawley, Wesley V
Cremean, Robert
Crist, William Gary
Crotto, Paul
Crutchfield, William Richard
Cyril, R
Daly, Norman
Danhausen, Eldon
Daoust, Sylvia
Darricarrere, Roger Dominique
Davis, Alonzo Joseph
Day, Worden
Deaton, Charles
de Garthe, William Edward
Degen, Paul
Dehner, Dorothy
DeLap, Tony
De Larios, Dora
DeLauro, Joseph Nicola
de la Vega, Enrique Miguel
de Lesseps, Tauni
Delford Brown, Robert
Delihas, Neva C
de Lisio, Michael
DeLonga, Leonard Anthony
De Lue, Donald
De Marco, Jean Antoine
Demartis, James J
Deming, David Lawson
de Miskey, Julian
De Nike, Michael Nicholas
De Niro, Robert
De Pedery-Hunt, Dora
Dergalis, George
Dern, F Carl
De Weldon, Felix George Weihs
Dhaemers, Robert August
Dienes, Sari
DiGiusto, Gerald N
Dill, Guy Girard
Dill, Laddie John
Dimondstein, Morton
Dine, James
Dioda, Adolph T
Diodato, Baldo
Dirube, Rolando Lopez
Di Suvero, Mark
Domareki, Joseph Theodore
Donati, Enrico
Donhauser, Paul Stefan
Donneson, Seena
Downey, Juan
Doyle, Thomas J
Drew, Joan
Drumm, Don
Dryfoos, Nancy
Dubin, Ralph
Duff, John Ewing
Dunwiddie, Charlotte
Edelson, Mary Beth
Efrat, Benni
Elder, Muldoon
Eliscu, Frank
Elkins, (E) Lane
Elsky, Herb
England, Paul Grady
Epler, Venetia
Etrog, Sorel
Evjen, Rudolph Berndt
Facci, Domenico (Aurelio)
Falk, Gathie
Favro, Murray
FeBland, Harriet
Felguerez, Manuel
Ferguson, Frank Wayne
Ferguson, Kathleen Elizabeth
Fernie, John Chipman
Ferrari, Virginio Luig
Fine, Jud
Fiore, Rosario Russell
Fischer, John J
Flakey Rose Hip (Glenn Alun Lewis)
Fogel, Seymour
Forakis, Peter
Fox, Terry Alan
Frank, Mary
Franklin, Charlotte White
Fraughton, Edward James
Fredericks, Marshall Maynard
Freeland, William Lee
Friedman, Alan
Frishmuth, Harriet Whitney
Fuchs, Mary Tharsilla
Fugate-Wilcox, Terry
Fuller, Emily (Emily Fuller Kingston)
Fumagalli, Orazio
Gabriel, Robert A
Gach, George
Gage, Frances M
Gagnon, Charles Eugene
Gallo, Enzo D
Gallo, Frank
Garrett, Alan Thomas
Gasparro, Frank
Gates, Harry Irving
Gebhardt, Harold
Gebhardt, Peter Martin
Gebhardt, Roland
Geissbuhler, Arnold
Geran, Joseph, Jr
Gianakos, Cristos
Giannotti, John J
Gibran, Kahlil George
Gikas, Christopher
Gill, James (Francis)
Gill, Sue May
Glasco, Joseph M
Goeritz, Mathias
Goldberg, Chaim
Goldstein, Jack
Golubic, Theodore
Gonzalez, Xavier
Goo, Benjamin
Goto, Joseph
Granlund, Paul Theodore
Graves, Bradford
Gray, Jim
Green, George Thurman
Greene-Mercier, Marie Zoe
Greenleaf, Kenneth Lee
Greer, John Sydney
Gressel, Michael L
Grieger, (Walter) Scott
Grippe, Peter J
Gross, Chaim
Gross, Charles Merrill
Gross, Irene (Irene Gross Berzon)
Grossman, Nancy
Grosvenor, Robert
Grove, Edward Ryneal
Grove, Jean Donner
Gruppe, Karl Heinrich
Gurria, Angela
Haacke, Hans Christoph
Haas, Helen (Helen Haas de Langley)
Haber, Ira Joel
Hadzi, Dimitri
Haley, John Charles
Halkin, Theodore
Hamouda, Amy
Hancock, Walker (Kirtland)
Hansen, James Lee
Haozous, Robert L
Harmon, Lily
Harrington, William Charles
Harris, Julian Hoke
Harris, Paul
Harvey, (William) Andre
Hatfield, Donald Gene
Hauser, Alonzo
Hayden, Michael
Hebert, Julien
Herard, Marvin T
Heric, John F
Hesketh
Higgins, (George) Edward
Hilton, Eric G
Hinman, Charles B
Hirsch, Willard Newman
Hobbs, (Carl) Fredric
Hobson, Katherine Thayer
Holbrook, Elizabeth Bradford
Holen, Norman Dean
Holmes, Ruth Atkinson
Holschuh, (George) Fred
Holt, Charlotte Sinclair
Holt, Nancy Louise
Hood, Ethel Painter
Horn, Milton
Horwitt, Will
House, James Charles, Jr
Hovell, Joseph
Hovsepian, Leon
Howard, Cecil Ray
Howard, Robert Boardman
Hubbard, Robert
Hudson, Robert H
Hunter, Leonard LeGrande, III
Hutchins, Maude Phelps McVeigh
Icaza (Francisco de Icaza)
Ikeda, Masuo
Ipsen, Kent Forrest
Ireland, Patrick (Brian O'Doherty)
Ispanky, Laszlo
Italiano, Joan Nylen
Izuka, Kunio
Jackson, Hazel Brill
Jackson, Sarah
Jacobs, David (Theodore)
Jacobson, Ursula Mercedes
Jacobsson, Sten Wilhelm John
Jacquard (Jerald Wayne Jackard)
Janowsky, Bela
Jansen, Catherine Sandra
Jensen, Leo (Vernon)
Johanson, Patricia (Maureen)
Johnson, Cletus Merlin
Johnson, Daniel LaRue
Johnston, William Edward
Jones, Ben
Jones, Edward Powis
Jones, Jerry
Jonynas, Vytautas K
Kaish, Luise
Kalinowski, Eugene M
Kallem, Herbert
Kaltenbach, Stephen James
Kane, Margaret Brassler
Kaplan, Muriel Sheerr
Karpel, Eli
Kassoy, Bernard
Kasuba, Aleksandra
Kaufman, Mico
Kaz, Nathaniel
Kearl, Stanley Brandon
Kelly, Ellsworth
Kennedy, James Edward
Kestenbaum, Lothar J
Kim, Bongtae
King, William Dickey
Kirschenbaum, Bernard Edwin
Kiselewski, Joseph
Kissel, William Thorn, Jr
Kittelson, John Henry
Kleiman, Alan
Klein, Sandor C
Kleinholz, Frank
Klotz-Reilly, Suzanne Ruth
Knapp, Sadie Magnet
Knapp, Tom
Knobler, Nathan
Kober, Alfred John
Koch, Edwin E
Koebbeman, Skip
Koepnick, Robert Charles
Koni, Nicolaus
Kopmanis, Augusts A
Kos, Paul Joseph
Kowal, Dennis J
Kowalski, Dennis Allen
Kratina, K George
Krebs, Rockne
Kreznar, Richard J
Krugman, Irene
Kujundzic, Zeljko D
Kurhajec, Joseph A
Kuvshinoff, Bertha Horne
Kuvshinoff, Nicolai
Lafon, Dee J
Lagunes, Maria (Maria Lagunes Hernandez)
Lane, Marion Jean Arrons
La Noue, Terence David
Larsen, Patrick Heffner
Lauck, Anthony Joseph
Lavatelli, Carla
Lawrence, Howard Ray
Lawton, James L
Lay, Patricia Anne
Leech, Merle Eugene
Leeper, Doris Marie
Lehman, Irving
Lekakis, Michael Nicholas
Lesher, Marie Palmisano
Leventhal, Ruth Lee
Levine, Les
Levinson, Mon
Levitan, Israel (Jack)
Le Witt, Sol
Liberi, Dante
Liberman, Alexander
Lichtenstein, Roy
Lijn, Liliane
Liles, Raeford Bailey
Lintault, Roger Paul
Lionni, Leo
Lipman-Wulf, Peter
Lipofsky, Marvin B
Lipton, Seymour
Little, John
Livesay, Thomas Andrew
Lochrie, Elizabeth Davey
Logan, Juan Leon
Lo Medico, Thomas Gaetano
London, Jeff
Lopez, Rhoda Le Blanc
Lorcini, Gino
Lorenzani, Arthur Emanuele
Loring, Clarice
Lothrop, Kristin Curtis
Love, Jim
Lucchesi, Bruno
Luisi, Jerry
Lux, Gwen (Gwen Lux Creighton)
Lye, Len
MacLean-Smith, Elizabeth
Macomber, Allison
Magnan, Oscar Gustav
Makarenko, Zachary Philipp
Malicoat, Philip Cecil
Malinowski, Jerome Joseph
Mallary, Robert
Mallory, Ronald
Manca, Albino
Mankowski, Bruno
Manuella, Frank R
Margulies, Isidore
Marisol, Escobar
Markle, Sam
Martin, Knox
Martin, William Henry (Bill)
Matta-Clark, Gordon
Matteson, Ira
Matthews, Harriett

Maynard, Valerie
Mazzone, Domenico
McCarthy, Denis
McCracken, Philip
McDonnell, Joseph Anthony
McElcheran, William Hodd
McIlvain, Douglas Lee
McMillen, Michael Chalmers
McVey, William M
McWhorter, Elsie Jean
Meizner, Paula
Mellor, George Edward
Messeguer, Villoro Benito
Meyer, Fred (Robert)
Milder, Jay
Miller, Leon Gordon
Miller, Richard McDermott
Minisci, Brenda (Eileen)
Mintich, Mary Ringelberg
Miralda, Antoni
Miss, Mary
Mitcham, Georgia Whitman
Mitchell, Henry (Weber)
Mockers, Michel M
Molinari, Guido
Monaghan, William Scott
Montana, Pietro
Moore, E Bruce
Morgan, Helen Bosart
Morris, Hilda
Morris, Robert
Moss, Joe (Francis)
Mueller, Henrietta Waters
Mundt, Ernest Karl
Murphy, Hass
Myers, Forrest Warden
Myers, Legh
Naegle, Stephen Howard
Nakian, Reuben
Nama, George Allen
Nash, Katherine E
Naylor, John Geoffrey
Neijna, Barbara
Nelson, Carey Boone
Neubert, George Walter
Nevelson, Mike
Nickford, Juan
Nicodemus, Chester Roland
Nivola, Constantino
Noe, Jerry Lee
Noguchi, Isamu
Nong
Norvell, Patsy
Ocvirk, Otto G
Offner, Elliot
Oppenheim, Dennis A
Ortiz, Ralph
Ortlieb, Robert Eugene
Ortman, George Earl
Orze, Joseph John
Ostuni, Peter W
Osze, Andrew E
Oubre, Hayward Louis
Outterbridge, John Wilfred
Paradise, Phil (Herschel)
Parella, Albert Lucian
Parks, Christopher Cropper
Parton, Ralf
Paterson, Anthony R
Patterson, Curtis Ray
Paulson, Alan
Payne, John D
Pearson, James Eugene
Peck, Judith
Pekar, Ronald Walter
Pershing, Louise
Piccolo, Thomas Frank
Pierce, Danny P
Pierce, James Smith
Pinardi, Enrico Vittorio
Pineda, Marianna (Marianna Pineda Tovish)
Pollack, Reginald Murray
Pomeroy, James Calwell, Jr
Ponce de Leon, Michael
Popinsky, Arnold Dave
Porter, (Edwin) David
Portmann, Frieda Bertha Anne
Posey, Leslie Thomas
Potts, Don
Prince, Richard Edmund
Pruitt, Lynn
Puccinelli, Raimondo
Quinn, Brian Grant
Rabinowitch, David
Rabinowitch, Royden Leslie
Randall, (Lillian) Paula
Randell, Richard K
Ratkai, George
Rebeck, Steven Augustus
Reiback, Earl M
Reichek, Jesse
Relis, Sandy
Remsing, (Joseph) Gary
Renick, Charles Cooley
Reynolds, Nancy Du Pont
Rhodes, James Melvin
Richardson, Gretchen (Mrs Ronald Freelander)
Richenburg, Robert Bartlett
Richter, Hank
Ridlon, James A
Risley, John Hollister
Roberts, Gilroy
Rockburne, Dorothea
Rocklin, Raymond
Romano, Umberto Roberto
Romans, Van Anthony
Rosati, James
Roseberg, Carl Andersson
Rosenblatt, Adolph
Rosenblum, Sadie Skoletsky
Ross, Douglas Allan
Rosse, Maryvonne
Roster, Fred Howard
Roszak, Theodore
Rotan, Walter
Roussel, Claude Patrice
Rudy, Charles
Rush, Jon N
Rust, Edwin C
Ryden, Kenneth Glenn
Sabatini, Raphael
Sakaoka, Yasue
Salemme, Antonio
Samaras, Lucas
Samstag, Gordon
Samuels, Gerald
Sankowsky, Itzhak
Sato, Tadashi
Savelli, Angelo
Saxe, Henry
Scanga, Italo
Scarpitta, Salvatore
Schlemowitz, Abram
Schmidt, Arnold Alfred
Schmidt, Julius
Schmutzhart, Berthold Josef
Schmutzhart, Slaithong Chengtrakul
Schulthess, Amalia
Schuselka, Elfi
Schwalbach, Mary Jo
Schwartz, William S
Schweiss, Ruth Keller
Scuris, Stephanie
Searles, Stephen
Segal, George
Seletz, Emil
Seley, Jason
Seplowin, Charles Joseph
Serra, Richard
Serra, Rudy
Shaw, Elsie Babbitt
Shaw, Richard Blake
Shead, S Ray
Sherbell, Rhoda
Shore, Richard Paul
Sider, Deno
Silver, Thomas C
Simkin, Phillips M
Simon, Herbert Bernheimer
Simon, Sidney
Simoni, John Peter
Sims, Agnes
Sinnard, Elaine (Janice)
Sirena (Contessa Antonia Mastrocristino Fanara)
Sister Thomasita (Mary Thomasita Fessler)
Smith, Bradford Leaman
Smith, Gord
Smith, Leon Polk
Smith, Thelma deGoede
Smith, Tony
Smyth, David Richard
Snow, John
Snyder, Kim Lawrence
Soffer, Sasson
Soleri, Paolo
Sommerburg, Miriam
Squier, Jack Leslie
Squires, Norma-Jean
Stark, George King
Stein, Ronald Jay
Stelzer, Michael Norman
Sterne, Dahli
Stevanov, Zoran
Stewart, Albert T
Stewart, Charles Carl
Stiegelmeyer, Norman Earl
Stoloff, Irma
Storm, Larue
Strawn, Melvin Nicholas
Streett, Tylden Westcott
Strider, Marjorie Virginia
Struppeck, Jules
Stussy, Maxine Kim
Suarez, Magdalena Frimkess
Sufi (Ahmad Antung)
Sugarman, George
Svenson, John Edward
Tait, Cornelia Damian
Tajiri, Shinkichi
Talbot, William (H M)
Tania (Schreiber-Milicevic)
Tanner, Warren
Tascona, Antonio Tony
Tatti, Benedict Michael
Tauch, Waldine Amanda
Terrell, Allen Townsend
Terris, Albert
Tewi, Thea
Thomas, Steffen Wolfgang
Thompson, Richard Craig
Thornhill, Anna
Tobias, Abraham Joel
Tobias, Robert Paul
Toledo, Francisco
Tolgesy, Victor
Torffield, Marvin
Trakas, George
Trakis, Louis
Triester, Kenneth
Trova, Ernest Tino
Tsai, Hsiao Hsia
Tubis, Seymour
Turner, James Thomas, Sr
Turner, Ralph James
Ullberg, J Kent
Unger, Mary Ann
Urban, Reva
Utescher, Gerd
Valinski, Dennis John
Vandenberge, Peter Willem
Van Loen, Alfred
Van Roijen, Hildegarde Graham
Van Vranken, Rose (Rose Van Vranken Hickey)
Van Winkle, Lester G
Van Wolf, Henry
Varga, Ferenc
Vargas, Rudolph
Vazan, William Joseph
Vega, Edward
Vierthaler, Arthur A
Viner, Frank Lincoln
Vodicka, Ruth Kessler
von Meyer, Michael
Von Schlegell, David
Voulkos, Peter
Wahling, B Jon
Waldman, Paul
Walker, Herbert Brooks
Walter, Valerie Harrisse
Wardy, Frederick
Wasey, Jane
Watts, Robert M
Webster, Stokely
Wedin, Winslow Elliott
Weedman, Kenneth Russell
Weill, Erna
Wein, Albert W
Weiner, Lawrence Charles
Weinrib, David
Weiss, Harvey
Welch, Roger
Wells, Charles Arthur, Jr
Werner, Nat
Weschler, Anita
Westcoast, Wanda
Weyhe, Arthur
Wheeler, Orson Shorey
White, Robert (Winthrop)
Widstrom, Edward Frederick
Wille, O Louis
Willer, Jim
Williams, Roger
Williams, Warner
Willis, Jay Steward
Wilmarth, Christopher Mallory
Wilson, Edward N
Wimberley, Frank Walden
Wingate, Arline (Hollander)
Winkel, Nina
Winsor, V Jacqueline
Witham, Vernon Clint
Witold-k (Kaczanowski)
Wolfe, Ann (Ann Wolfe Graubard)
Woodham, Derrick James
Woods, Gurdon Grant
Woody, (Thomas) Howard
Worth, Peter John
Wu, Linda Yee Chau
Yanish, Elizabeth
Yokoi, Rita
Young, Joseph Louis
Zach, Jan
Zajac, Jack
Zammitt, Norman
Zavel (Zavel Silber)
Zelenak, Edward John
Ziegler, Jacqueline (Jacqueline Chalat-Ziegler)
Zimmerman, Elyn
Zucker, Barbara M
Zucker, Murray Harvey
Zwick, Rosemary G

Clay

Abeles, Sigmund
Acosta, Manuel Gregorio
Aidlin, Jerome
Allen, Margo (Mrs Harry Shaw)
Anderson, James P
Angelo, Domenick Michael
Anthonisen, George Rioch
Antonovici, Constantin
Arneson, Robert Carston
Aronson, Sanda
Asher, Lila Oliver
Baldwin, Richard Wood
Barton, Georgie Read
Beerman, Miriam H
Bolmgren, Donna Hollen
Bova, Joe
Breschi, Karen Lee
Brown, Bruce Robert
Brown, Catharine Homan
Bryant, Olen L
Bubb, Nancy (Jane)

SCULPTOR (cont)

Bugbee, Joan Scott
Burroughs, John Coleman
Burt, Clyde Edwin
Bussabarger, Robert Franklin
Campbell, Dorothy Bostwick
Canfield, Jane (White)
Cantrell, Jim
Caplan, Jerry L
Chalke, John
Chandler, Elisabeth Gordon
Chappelle, Jerry Leon
Chavez, Joseph Arnold
Chicago, Judy
Cindric, Michael Anthony
Cohen, Michael S
Conover, Claude
Conrad, John W
Cooper, Lucille Baldwin
Cooper, Phillis
Cornell, David E
Corso, Patrick
Cossitt, Franklin D
Cronbach, Robert M
Crume, Gregg
Daley, William P
d'Andrea, Albert Philip
Dean, Abner
Dombek, Blanche M
Drummond, (I G)
Earl, Jack Eugene
Eino (Eino Antti Romppanen)
Elsner, Larry Edward
Engelson, Carol
Eyre, Ivan
Facci, Domenico (Aurelio)
Faden, Lawrence Steven
Fafard, Joe (Joseph Yvon)
Fasano, Clara
Fellows, Fred
Fenci, Renzo
Ferreira, (Armando) Thomas
Fichter, Herbert Francis
Finke, Leonda Froelich
Finson, Hildred A
Frazier, Le Roy Dyyon
Free, John D
Fuller, Mary (Mary Fuller McChesney)
Funk, Verne J
Furman, David Stephen
Garver, Jack
Gaylord, Frank Chalfant
Geber, Hana
Gernhardt, Henry Kendall
Getz, Dorothy
Giambertone, Paul
Gilhooly, David James, III
Glasgow, Lukman
Glasson, Lloyd
Glover, Robert Leon
Goff, Thomas Jefferson
Gould, Stephen
Goulet, Lorrie (Lorrie J De Creeft)
Grasso, Doris (Ten-Eyck)
Graziano, Florence V Mercolino
Grey, Estelle (Estelle Ashby)
Grigor, Margaret Christian
Gross, Alice (Alice Gross Fish)
Gruppe, Karl Heinrich
Grygutis, Barbara
Halko, Joe
Halpern, Lea
Hardy, Robert
Harmon, Eloise (Norstad)
Harvey, (William) Andre
Ha-So-De (Narcisco Abeyta)
Hay, Dick
Hayes, David Vincent
Hayward, Peter
Higa, Charles Eisho
Hill, Jim
Hodgell, Robert Overman
Hoffman, Edward Fenno, III
Hofsted, Jolyon Gene
Hollingworth, Keith William
Hood, Dorothy
Hopkinson, Glen Spencer
Iacurto, Francesco
Jacobson, Yolande (Mrs J Craig Sheppard)
Jencks, Penelope
Jolley, Geraldine H (Jerry)
Jones, Amy (Amy Jones Frisbie)
Judson, Sylvia Shaw
Kaiser, Diane
Kassoy, Hortense
Kelsey, Muriel Chamberlin
Kemenyffy, Steven
Kenny, Lisa A
Kepalas (Elena Kepalaite)
Key-Oberg, Ellen Burke
Kissel, William Thorn, Jr
Knowlton, Grace Farrar
Konzal, Joseph
Koss, Gene H
Kottler, Howard William
Laird, E Ruth
Larsen, D Dane
Lawrence, Les
Lecoque
Lee, Dora Fugh
Lehman, Mark Ammon
Leonard, Leon Lank, Sr
Lerman, Ora
Levine, Marilyn Anne
Lewis, Don
Lopez, Michael John
Ludwig, Eva
Lupori, Peter John
MacClintock, Dorcas
Marak, Louis Bernard
Margoulies, Berta (Berta Margoulies O'Hare)
Marinsky, Harry
Mason, John
Massaro, Karen Thuesen
Mayorga, Gabriel Humberto
McCabe, Lawrence
McCoon, Betty Jean
McIlvain, Douglas Lee
McIntosh, Harrison Edward
McVey, Leza
Melchert, James Frederick
Mignosa, Santo
Miller, Donald Richard
Miller, H McRae
Mirabal, Miguel Enrique
Moise, William Sidney
Moquin, Richard Attilio
Morgan, Arthur C
Morgan, Frances Mallory
Morrison, Art Jens
Moss, Joel C
Mount, Pauline Ward
Muccioli, Anna Maria
Mueller, Trude
Muir, Emily Lansingh
Murray, Richard Deibel
Myers, Legh
Natzler, Otto
Newmark, Marilyn (Marilyn Newmark Meiselman)
Nicholas, Donna Lee
Nickerson, Ruth (Ruth Nickerson Greacen)
Nigrosh, Leon Isaac
Olitski, Jules
Oliveira, V'Lou
Olsen, Frederick L
Ortmayer, Constance
Pardington, Ralph Arthur
Pearson, Clifton
Peeler, Richard
Pickens, Alton
Plavcan, Joseph Michael
Popinsky, Arnold Dave
Poucher, Elizabeth Morris
Prange, Sally Bowen
Quest, Charles Francis
Rakovan, Lawrence Francis
Randall, Theodore A
Rapp, Ebba (Ebba Rapp McLauchlan)
Raul Esparza S (Raul Esparza Sanchez)
Redd Ekks (Robert Norman Rasmussen)
Redinger, Walter Fred
Rice, James William, Jr
Richard, Betti
Rippon, Ruth Margaret
Rippon, Tom Michael
Robinson, Margot (Margot Steigman)
Rockwell, Peter Barstow
Rodrigue, George G
Roller, Marion Bender
Roloff, John Scott
Romano, Salvatore Michael
Rosenthal, Rachel
Sage, Bill B
St Maur, Kirk (Kirk Seymour McReynolds)
Sanderson, Raymond Phillips
Schary, Susan
Schietinger, James Frederick
Schlanger, Jeff
Schulz, William Gallagher
Scriver, Robert Macfie (Bob)
Shannonhouse, Sandra Lynne
Sherman, Z Charlotte
Shrady, Frederick C
Silverman, David Frederick
Simon, Jewel Woodard
Simonds, Charles Frederick
Skinner, Elsa Kells
Small, Amy Gans
Smith, Cecil Alden
Smith, Emily Guthrie
Smith, John Ivor
Soldner, Paul Edmund
Soriano, Juan
Spaventa, George
Squires, Gerald Leopold
Stephenson, John H
Stewart, Lizbeth McNett
Stone, Willard
Stull, Robert J
Stussy, Maxine Kim
Swanson, J N
Takemoto, Henry Tadaaki
Tamburine, Jean
Taylor, Frederick Bourchier
Taylor, Rosemary
Teichman, Sabina
Tornheim, Norman
Townsend, Storm D
Unterseher, Chris Christian
Urso, Richard Carl
Van Aalten, Jacques
Vance, George Wayne
Vandenberge, Peter Willem
Van Wert, Gordon Franklin
Visco, Anthony Salvatore
Von Neumann, Robert A
Wallace, Elizabeth S
Warashina, M Patricia
Watson, Halen Richter
Weinstein, Florence
Westervelt, Robert F
Will, Mary Shannon
Williams, Gerald
Williams, Wayne Francis
Wilson, Warren Bingham
Winter, Thelma Frazier
Worth, Karen
Yiannes, (Iordanidis)
Yochim, Louise Dunn
Zakin, Mikhail
Zevon, Irene
Ziegler, Laura

Metal, Cast

Abbott, Dorothy I
Abdell, Douglas
Adams, Alice
Aidlin, Jerome
Albert, Calvin
Allen, Margo (Mrs Harry Shaw)
Allwell, Stephen S
Amateis, Edmond Romulus
Anderson, James P
Angelo, Domenick Michael
Anthonisen, George Rioch
Antonovici, Constantin
Aronson, David
Asawa, Ruth (Ruth Asawa Lanier)
Baker, George
Barrett, Bill
Bartlett, Donald Loring
Baz, Marysole Worner
Beasley, Bruce
Behl, Wolfgang
Belshe, Mirella Monti
Bentov, Mirtala
Bermudez, Jose Ygnacio
Berry, William David
Biederman, Charles (Karel Joseph)
Binning, Robin
Bisgyer, Barbara G (Barbara G Cohn)
Black, David Evans
Blair, Helen (Helen Blair Crosbie)
Block, Adolph
Boghosian, Varujan
Bogucki (Edwin Arnold Bogucki)
Boiger, Peter
Bolinsky, Joseph Abraham
Born, James E
Boyce, Richard
Breitenbach, William John
Britton, Edgar
Bronson, Clark Everice
Brown, Bruce Robert
Brumer, Shulamith
Bugbee, Joan Scott
Bultman, Fritz
Burnham, Lee
Burns, Sid
Burns, Stan
Burroughs, John Coleman
Burton, Gloria
Buscaglia, Jose
Cabrera, Geles
Canfield, Jane (White)
Caparn, Rhys (Rhys Caparn Steel)
Carlyle, Julian (Julian Carlyle Wells)
Carr, Sally Swan
Casanova, Aldo John
Cataldo, John William
Catchi (Catherine O Childs)
Catlett, Elizabeth
Chaffee, John W
Chandler, Elisabeth Gordon
Chase, Allan (Seamans)
Chase-Riboud, Barbara Dewayne
Clague, John Rogers
Clark, John Dewitt
Cleary, Fritz
Clipsham, Jacqueline Ann
Collier, Ric
Cook, Robert Howard
Coughlin, Jack
Cronbach, Robert M
Dagys, Jacob
Daley, William P
Davidson, Allan Albert
Davidson, Robert William
Davis, David Ensos
De Bellis, Hannibal
de Gerenday, Laci Anthony
DeWit, Floyd Tennison
Diska
Dombek, Blanche M
Driesbach, David Fraiser
Drumm, Don
Duca, Alfred Milton
Duhme, H Richard, Jr
Du Pen, Everett George

Egri, Ted
Eino (Eino Antti Romppanen)
Elder, David Morton
Elmo, James
Emery, Lin (Lin Emery Braselman)
Ente, Lily
Escobedo, Augusto Ortega
Eversley, Frederick John
Fares, William O
Fasano, Clara
FeBland, Harriet
Feldman, Bella Tabak
Fenci, Renzo
Fenton, Beatrice
Filipovic, Augustin
Filipowski, Richard E
Filkosky, Josefa
Finke, Leonda Froelich
Finkelstein, Max
Fix, John Robert
Florio, Sal Erseny
Forrestall, Thomas De Vany
Forrester, Charles Howard
Francis, Madison Ke, Jr
Free, John D
French, Jared
Friscia, Albert Joseph
Fuhrman, Esther
Gach, George
Gagnon, Charles Eugene
Geber, Hana
Getz, Dorothy
Giambertone, Paul
Gibbs, Craig Stevens
Gibbs, Tom
Giusti, George
Glasson, Lloyd
Glickman, Maurice
Goff, Thomas Jefferson
Goodacre, Glenna
Gore, Samuel Marshall
Graese, Judy (Judith Ann)
Graham, Walter
Grausman, Philip
Gray, Cleve
Green, David Oliver
Greenamyer, George Mossman
Greenwood, Paul Anthony
Gross, Alice (Alice Gross Fish)
Groth, Bruno
Gruppe, Karl Heinrich
Guerriero, Henry Edward
Guite, Suzanne
Gussow, Roy
Haber, Leonard
Hale, Nathan Cabot
Hanbury, Una
Hansen, James Lee
Hara, Teruo
Hardin, Adlai S
Harman, Jack Kenneth
Harootian, Khoren Der
Harrison, Carole
Harvey, (William) Andre
Haskin, Donald Marcus
Hayden, Frank
Hayes, David Vincent
Hayward, Peter
Hebald, Milton Elting
Henry, John Raymond
Herr, Richard Joseph
Hoffman, Edward Fenno, III
Horne, (Arthur Edward) Cleeve
Hostetler, David
Houser, Allan C
Howell, Elizabeth Ann (Mitch)
Humes, Ralph H
Hunt, Richard Howard
Huntington, Jim
Iselin, Lewis
Jackson, Harry Andrew
Jackson, Sarah
Jacobson, Yolande (Mrs J Craig Sheppard)
Johnston, Richard M
Johnston, Robert Porter
Jones, Amy (Amy Jones Frisbie)
Jones, (Charles) Dexter (Weatherbee), III
Jones, Elizabeth
Jones, Jacobine
Jordan, Jack
Judson, Sylvia Shaw
Kammerer, Herbert Lewis
Karesh, Ann Bamberger
Karpel, Eli
Kassoy, Hortense
Katz, Eunice
Kearl, Stanley Brandon
Kearney, John (W)
Kearns, James Joseph
Kelsey, Muriel Chamberlin
Kepalas (Elena Kepalaite)
Khendry, Janak Kumar
Kimmelman, Harold
Kipp, Lyman
Kirsten-Daiensai, Richard Charles
Kissel, William Thorn, Jr
Kittelson, John Henry
Kline, Alma
Kober, Alfred John
Koebbeman, Skip
Kohlhepp, Norman
Konzal, Joseph
Koochin, William
Koras, George
Kramer, Reuben
Krentzin, Earl
Kruger, Louise
Kyriakos, Aleko
La Malfa, James Thomas
Landis, Lily
Langland, Harold Reed
Lantz, Michael F
Laslo, Patricia Louise
Lawton, James L
Leach, Frederick Darwin
Lehman, Mark Ammon
Lekberg, Barbara Hult
Lewis, Jackson Pittman
Linn, Steven Allen
Lipman, Stan
Lippold, Richard
Lipton, Sondra (Sahlman)
Logan, David George
Logan, Gene Adams
Longley, Bernique
Lubbers, Leland Eugene
Ludtke, Lawrence Monroe
Luisi, Jerry
Lyford, Cabot
Mack, Rodger Allen
Mahlke, Ernest D
Manton, Jock (Archimedes Aristides Giacomantonio)
Margoulies, Berta (Berta Margoulies O'Hare)
Marinsky, Harry
Marks, George B
Mavroudis, Demetrios
Mayhew, Elza
McCabe, Lawrence
McClure, Thomas F
McCoon, Betty Jean
McGeoch, Lillian Jean
Medrich, Libby E
Meyer, Seymour W
Meyer, Ursula
Micale, Albert
Miller, Donald Richard
Miller, Richard McDermott
Miller, Vel
Mol, Leo
Morgan, Arthur C
Morgan, Frank James
Morin, Thomas Edward
Mount, Pauline Ward
Moyers, Wm
Mueller, Trude
Muno, Richard Carl
Namingha, Dan
Naranjo, Michael Alfred
Nardin, Mario
Nelson, Carey Boone
Nesbitt, Lowell (Blair)
Newman, (John) Christopher
Newmark, Marilyn (Marilyn Newmark Meiselman)
Nickerson, Ruth (Ruth Nickerson Greacen)
Nierman, Leonardo M
Niizuma, Minoru
Noordhoek, Harry Cecil
Norton, Ann
Notaro, Anthony
Oesterle, Leonhard Freidrich
O'Hanlon, Richard E
Ohe, Katie (Minna)
Ordonez, Efren
Ortmayer, Constance
Ottiano, John William
Owen, Bill
Padovano, Anthony John
Paeff, Bashka (Bashka Paeff Waxman)
Paris, Harold Persico
Parks, Eric Vernon
Parsons, David Goode
Peabody, Amelia
Pederson, Molly Fay
Perless, Robert
Pickens, Alton
Polland, Donald Jack
Popescu, Cara
Portanova, Joseph Domenico
Price, Michael Benjamin
Proctor, Gifford MacGregor
Pruitt, A Kelly
Rachelski, Florian W
Ralston, James Kenneth
Rapp, Ebba (Ebba Rapp McLauchlan)
Recanati, Dina
Recchia, Richard (Henry)
Reed, Hal
Rice, Anthony Hopkins
Rich, Frances L
Richard, Betti
Rippey, Clayton
Rishell, Robert Clifford
Rockwell, Peter Barstow
Rodrigue, George G
Rogers, John H
Rosenthal, Tony (Bernard)
Rozzi, (James A)
Rubin, Donald Vincent
Rubins, David Kresz
Ryden, Kenneth Glenn
St Maur, Kirk (Kirk Seymour McReynolds)
Saito, Seiji
Sanderson, Raymond Phillips
Sauls, Frederick Inabinette
Savoy, Chyrl Lenore
Schlam, Murray J
Schnier, Jacques
Schnittmann, Sascha S
Schon, Nancy Quint
Schreck, Michael Henry
Schultz, Roger d
Schulz, William Gallagher
Schweitzer, Gertrude
Scott, John Tarrell
Shapiro, Joel (Elias)
Sheppard, Joseph Sherly
Sherbell, Rhoda
Sherman, Z Charlotte
Sherry, William Grant
Shrady, Frederick C
Silverman, Sherley C
Simon, Helene
Simpson, Tommy Hall
Sinaiko, Arlie
Sing Hoo (Sing Hoo Yuen)
Slivka, David
Smith, George W
Smith, John Ivor
Smith, Joseph Anthony
Smith, Kent Alvin
Snidow, Gordon E
Soriano, Juan
Spampinato, Clemente
Spaventa, George
Speed, (Ulysses) Grant
Sprague, Nancy Kunzman
Steiner, Michael
Stephen, Francis B
Stone, Willard
Storm, Mark (Kennedy)
Summers, Robert
Sunderland, Nita Kathleen
Suttman, Paul
Swanson, J N
Swarz, Sahl
Talaba, L (Linda Talaba Cummens)
Taylor, Frederick Bourchier
Taylor, Joseph Richard
Taylor, Marie
Taylor, Rod Allen
Taysom, Wayne Pendelton
Terken, John
Thompson, Joanne
Thompson, William Joseph
Townsend, Storm D
Trudeau, Yves
Turano, Don
Turner, Raymond
Umana, Alfonso
Van Aalten, Jacques
Vielehr, William Ralph
Visco, Anthony Salvatore
Vollmer, Ruth
Von Neumann, Robert A
Vrana, Albert S
Waddell, John Henry
Wagoner, Robert B
Walch, John Leo
Walter, Valerie Harrisse
Walton, Marion (Marion Walton Putnam)
Warren, Melvin Charles
Weaver, John Barney
Weems, Katharine Lane
Weiner, Egon
Weinman, Robert Alexander
Westervelt, Robert F
White, Bruce Hilding
Whitley, Philip Waff
Wiedenhoeft-Wesler, Anita Kae
Williams, Chester Lee
Williams, Wayne Francis
Woell, J Fred
Worth, Karen
Worthen, William Marshall
Wright, G Alan
Zacha, George William
Zivic, William Thomas
Zuniga, Francisco

Metal, Precious

Ahvakana, Ulaaq (Lawrence Reynold Ahvakana)
Aird, Neil Carrick
Andrews, Oliver
Bennett, Jamie
Blodgett, Peter
Boggs, Mayo Mac
Busch, Julia M
Chase-Riboud, Barbara Dewayne
Christensen, Hans-Jorgen Thorvald
Filipowski, Richard E
Geber, Hana
Gironda, R
Herschler, David
Hu, Mary Lee
Jones, Elizabeth
Kearl, Stanley Brandon
Kearney, John (W)
Krentzin, Earl
Logan, David George

SCULPTOR (cont)
Long, Frank Weathers
Manhold, John Henry
Norman, Emile
Perless, Robert
Pinto, James
Polland, Donald Jack
Prestini, James Libero
Rubin, Donald Vincent
Russin, Robert I
Safer, John
Scherr, Mary Ann
Shecter, Pearl S
Sheng, Shao Fang
Stephen, Francis B
Thomas, Robert Chester
Tovish, Harold
Waddell, Eugene
Watson, Lynda
Wiedenhoeft-Wesler, Anita Kae
Worth, Karen

Metal, Welded

Abdell, Douglas
Aidlin, Jerome
Alps, Glen Earl
Anderson, David Paul
Andrews, Oliver
Angelo, Domenick Michael
Appel, Karel
Archambault, Louis
Asawa, Ruth (Ruth Asawa Lanier)
Aschenbach, (Walter) Paul
Bailey, Clark T
Baldwin, Harold Fletcher
Balossi, John
Barger, Raymond Granville
Barr, David John
Barrett, Bill
Beal, Mack
Beasley, Bruce
Behl, Wolfgang
Bentham, Douglas Wayne
Benton, Suzanne E
Bermudez, Jose Ygnacio
Bertoia, Harry
Betancourt, R Arenas
Bigger, Michael Dinsmore
Bisgyer, Barbara G (Barbara G Cohn)
Black, David Evans
Bolomey, Roger Henry
Booth, Laurence Ogden
Bottini, David M
Bowie, William
Braitstein, Marcel
Buchanan, Sidney Arnold
Buchman, James Wallace
Burt, David Sill
Burton, Gloria
Cabrera, Geles
Carlberg, Norman Kenneth
Carlyle, Julian (Julian Carlyle Wells)
Carron, Maudee Lilyan
Cervantes, Pedro
Chaffee, John W
Clague, John Rogers
Clark, Nancy Kissel
Clymer, Albert Anderson
Cody, John (Alexis)
Corwin, Sophia M
Cossitt, Franklin D
Cronbach, Robert M
Crouch, Ned Philbrick
Crovello, William George
Davis, David Ensos
De Rivera, Jose
DeWit, Floyd Tennison
Domareki, Joseph Theodore
Egri, Ted
Eldredge, Mary Agnes
Eloul, Kosso
Elsner, Larry Edward
Emery, Lin (Lin Emery Braselman)
Eversley, Frederick John
Ferber, Herbert
Filipowski, Richard E
Finkelstein, Max
Fisher, James Donald
Forrestall, Thomas De Vany
Frazier, Le Roy Dyyon
Frazier, Paul D
French, Ray H
Giambertone, Paul
Gibbs, Craig Stevens
Gibbs, Tom
Ginnever, Charles
Gironda, R
Gold, Debra Lynn
Goldfarb, Roz
Goodelman, Aaron J
Grady, Ruby McLain
Greenamyer, George Mossman
Grey, Estelle (Estelle Ashby)
Groth, Bruno
Gussow, Roy
Hale, Nathan Cabot
Hall, Michael David
Hardy, Thomas (Austin)
Harrison, Carole
Harvey, (William) Andre
Haskin, Donald Marcus
Hatchett, Duayne
Hay, Ike
Hayes, David Vincent
Hedrick, Wally Bill
Helman, Phoebe
Henry, John Raymond
Herschler, David
Hicks, Harold Jon (Jack)
Holvey, Samuel Boyer
Houskeeper, Barbara
Howard, Robert A
Hunt, Richard Howard
Ihara, Michio
Indiana, Robert
Inukai, Kyohei
Jennings, Francis
Jensen, Hank
Johnston, Richard M
Jolley, George B
Kagy, Sheffield Harold
Kammerer, Herbert Lewis
Kangas, Gene
Kapsalis, Thomas Harry
Katzen, Lila (Pell)
Kearney, John (W)
Kelly, Lee
Kemble, Richard
Kepalas (Elena Kepalaite)
Kimmelman, Harold
Kington, Louis Brent
Kipp, Lyman
Knowlton, Grace Farrar
Koni, Nicolaus
Konzal, Joseph
Krust, Walter
Kussoy, Bernice (Helen)
La Malfa, James Thomas
La More, Chet Harmon
Larson, Philip Seely
Lawton, James L
Leeber, Sharon Corgan
Lekberg, Barbara Hult
Lipman, Stan
Logan, David George
Logan, Gene Adams
Lowe, J Michael
Lubbers, Leland Eugene
Lupori, Peter John
Mahlke, Ernest D
Maki, Robert Richard
Mark, Phyllis
Markusen, Thomas Roy
Martin, William Barriss, II
McCabe, Lawrence
McCloy, William Ashby
McClure, Thomas F
McManus, James William
McVicker, J Jay
Meadmore, Clement L
Meizner, Paula
Meyer, Ursula
Milonadis, Konstantin
Murray, Robert (Gray)
Neijna, Barbara
Nevelson, Louise
Newman, (John) Christopher
Nugent, John Cullen
Ohe, Katie (Minna)
Oleksiw, Michael Nicholas, II
Olitski, Jules
Padovano, Anthony John
Paley, Albert Raymond
Parks, Eric Vernon
Pascual, Manolo
Pearson, Louis O
Peart, Jerry Linn
Pepper, Beverly
Perless, Robert
Perlman, Joel Leonard
Perry, Charles O
Perry, Frank
Popescu, Cara
Quinn, Brian Grant
Ragland, Bob
Rakovan, Lawrence Francis
Ray, Robert Arthur
Reber, Mick
Reed, Paul Allen
Reginato, Peter
Renk, Merry
Rennels, Frederic M
Renouf, Edward Pechmann
Rhoden, John W
Rice, Anthony Hopkins
Rich, Frances L
Rickey, George W
Riegel, Michael Byron
Riveron, Enrique
Romano, Salvatore Michael
Rush, Jon N
Ryden, Kenneth Glenn
Salomon, Lawrence
Schlam, Murray J
Schneider, Noel
Schreiber, Martin
Scriver, Robert Macfie (Bob)
Sellers, William Freeman
Seyfried, John Louis
Seyle, Robert Harley
Shapshak, Rene
Shaw, Elsie Babbitt
Shaw, Ernest Carl
Sherry, William Grant
Sherwood, A (Frances Ann Crane)
Shimoda, Osamu
Shostak, Edwin Bennett
Silverman, Sherley C
Simon, Herbert Bernheimer
Simpson, Tommy Hall
Sinnard, Elaine (Janice)
Slater, Gary Lee
Slusky, Joseph
Small, Amy Gans
Smith, George W
Snelson, Kenneth D
Sprague, Nancy Kunzman
Stankiewicz, Richard Peter
Stein, Walter
Steiner, Michael
Stephenson, John H
Stern, Jan Peter
Strautmanis, Edvins
Streeter, Tal
Sturman, Eugene
Swarz, Sahl
Taira, Frank
Tardo, (Manuel) Rodulfo
Tatro, Ronald Edward
Taysom, Wayne Pendelton
Todd, Michael Cullen
Trudeau, Yves
Tsai, Wen-Ying
Tsutakawa, George
Tucker, William G
Tyson, Rae Julian
Udinotti, Agnese
Urban, Mychajlo Raphael
Urry, Steven
Vaccarino, Robin
Van de Bovenkamp, Hans
Van Wert, Gordon Franklin
Ventimiglia, John Thomas
Vollmer, Ruth
Wagner, G Noble
Walburg, Gerald
Wall, Brian
Warsinske, Norman George, Jr
Weinman, Robert Alexander
Weiss, Anton
White, Bruce Hilding
White, Roger Lee
Whitley, Philip Waff
Williams, Todd
Williams, Wayne Francis
Winter, Clark
Witkin, Isaac
Witt, Nancy Camden
Woitena, Ben S
Wojcik, Gary Thomas
Wolfe, James
Woodham, Jean
Worthen, William Marshall
Zaidenberg, Arthur
Zeidenbergs, Olafs
Ziegler, Laura

Miscellaneous Media

Abish, Cecile
Abramowicz, Janet
Adams, Alice
Albert, Calvin
Alhilali, Neda
Amateis, Edmond Romulus
Anker, Suzanne C
Antonakos, Stephen
Applebroog, Ida H
Ascott, Roy
Askin, Walter Miller
Aycock, Alice
Bakaty, Mike
Banerjee (bimal)
Barger, Raymond Granville
Barnes, Carroll
Battenberg, John
Batuz
Bauermeister, Mary Hilde Ruth
Bell, Larry Stuart
Belshe, Mirella Monti
Benoit, Jean
Berge, Henry
Beydler, Gary Earl
Billeci, Andre George
Binford, Julien
Blake, John Clemens
Bochner, Mel
Bolinger, Truman
Bonet, Jordi
Bontecou, Lee
Booth, Laurence Ogden
Bourgeois, Louise
Boussard, Dana
Bowles, Thomas Andrew, III
Boyd, Donald Edgar
Braitstein, Marcel
Brams, Joan
Bramson, Phyllis Halperin
Breder, Hans Dieter
Breinin, Raymond
Breschi, Karen Lee
Breslin, Wynn
Brewster, Michael
Brown, Larry K
Brown, Marvin Prentiss
Bubb, Nancy (Jane)

Bucher, George Robert
Buckley, Mary L (Mrs Joseph M Parriott)
Bunch, Clarence
Bundy, Stephen Allen
Bunn, Kenneth Rodney
Burgues, Irving Carl
Burnham, Lee
Burton, Scott
Busa, Peter
Byars, Donna
Cable, Maxine Roth
Cadle, Ray Kenneth
Caglioti, Victor
Campbell, Kenneth
Campoli, Cosmo
Campus, Peter
Caparn, Rhys (Rhys Caparn Steel)
Card, Greg S
Carlyle, Julian (Julian Carlyle Wells)
Casey, John Joseph
Cathers, James O
Cavanaugh, John W
Cederstrom, John Andrew
Cheatham, Frank Reagan
Childers, Richard Robin
Cho, David
Christo (Javacheff)
Cicansky, Victor
Clark, Jon Frederic
Clerk, Pierre
Clifton, Michelle Gamm
Cochran, Dewees (Dewees Cochran Helbeck)
Cook, Richard Lee
Cooper, Lucille Baldwin
Corse, Mary Ann
Costigan, Constance Christian
Creech, Franklin Underwood
Creecy, Herbert Lee, Jr
Cronin, Robert (Lawrence)
Cunningham, J
Dailey, Daniel Owen
Daphnis, Nassos
Daphnis-Avlon, Helen
Darton, Christopher
Daugherty, Marshall Harrison
Daugherty, Michael F
Day, John
Decker, Lindsey
DeLuigi, Janice Cecilia
De Maria, Walter
Dey, Kris
Di Meo, Dominick
Drewelowe, Eve
Duhme, H Richard, Jr
Eagleboy, Wayne
East, N S, Jr
Edge, Douglas Benjamin
Elder, David Morton
Eliscu, Frank
Eloul, Kosso
Estern, Neil
Evans, Robert Graves
Fabion, John
Fahlen, Charles
Faiers, Edward Spencer (Ted)
Fairbanks, Avard
Falkenstein, Claire
Feigenbaum, Harriet (Mrs Neil Chamberlain)
Feldman, Bella Tabak
Fendell, Jonas J
Fender, Tom Mac
Ferreira, (Armando) Thomas
Ferrer, Rafael
Fink, Ray (Raymond Russell)
Fish, Robert (Robert James Field)
Flavin, Dan
Floeter, Kent
Fohr, Jenny
Follett, Jean Frances
Fontanini, Clare
Ford, John Charles
Formigoni, Maurie Monihon
Forst, Miles
Francis, Jean Thickens
Francis, Madison Ke, Jr
Fredman, Faiya R
Freeman, Phyllis (Therese)
Frey, Viola
Friedberg, Ray E
Friedeberg, Pedro
Friedman, Kenneth Scott
Friscia, Albert Joseph
Frudakis, Evangelos William
Fuge, Paul H
Fuhrman, Esther
Fuller, Emily (Emily Fuller Kingston)
Fuller, Mary (Mary Fuller McChesney)
Galen, Elaine
Gellis, Sandy L
Gellman, Beah (Mrs William C McNulty)
Gentile, Gloria Irene
Gianakos, Cristos
Gianakos, Steve
Gillingwater, Denis Claude
Glaser, David
Goldstein, Daniel Joshua
Gonzalez, Jose Luis
Goodridge, Lawrence Wayne
Gordin, Sidney
Gordon, John S
Gore, Samuel Marshall
Gorski, Daniel Alexander
Graham, Robert
Grant, James
Graves, Nancy Stevenson
Gray, Cleve
Graysmith, Robert
Greco, Anthony Joseph
Green, Tom
Greenbaum, Dorothea Schwarcz
Greer, John Sydney
Gregory, Angela
Grossen, Francoise
Gruppe, Karl Heinrich
Gunderson, Barry L
Gutkin, Peter
Hacklin, Allan Dave
Hague, Raoul
Halpern, Lea
Hammond, Harmony
Hampton, Lucille Charlotte
Hamrol, Lloyd
Handler, Audrey
Hanson, Duane
Hanson, Lawrence
Hanson, Philip Holton
Hare, David
Harkavy, Minna
Harris, Margo Liebes
Harrison, Carole
Hartwig, Cleo
Harvey, Dermot
Harvey, Donald Gilbert
Havis, C Kenneth
Hay, George Austin
Healy, Anne Laura
Helman, Phoebe
Hendricks, Donald Teves
Henselmann, Caspar
Herr, Richard Joseph
Hershman, Lynn Lester
Hess, Emil John
Hickins, Walter H
Hicks, Harold Jon (Jack)
Hicks, Sheila
Hillsmith, Fannie
Hoare, Tyler James
Hobbs, Joe Ferrell
Hoffman, Edward Fenno, III
Hook, Walter
Hooks, Earl J
Howard, Linda
Hsiao, Chin
Huchthausen, David Richard
Huebler, Douglas
Hunt, Kari
Hurst, Ralph N
Hurtig, Martin Russell
Ida, Shoichi
Inukai, Kyohei
Ipcar, Dahlov
Jackson, William Davis
Jacobs, Harold
Jansen, Catherine Sandra
Johnson, Joyce
Jolley, Geraldine H (Jerry)
Jones, Anthony
Jones, David Lee
Jones, Howard William
Jules, Mervin
Kangas, Gene
Kasak, Nikolai (Kazak)
Kawecki, Jean Mary
Kearns, James Joseph
Kelley, Donald William
Kessler, Alan
Kinnaird, Richard William
Kipp, Lyman
Kirk, Jerome
Kisch, Gloria
Koebbeman, Skip
Kolin, Sacha
Korman, Barbara
Kos, Paul Joseph
Koss, Gene H
Kramer, Reuben
Kuehn, Edmund Karl
Kuehn, Gary
Kusama, Yayoi
Kushner, Robert Ellis
Kwartler, Alexander
Labino, Dominick
Landsman, Stanley
Lang, Rodger Alan
Lassaw, Ibram
Lathrop, Gertrude K
Lawrence, Jaye A
Leaf, June
Leax, Ronald Allen
Lennie, Beatrice E C
Leon, Dennis
Lepper, Robert Lewis
Lerman, Doris (Harriet)
Lewis, John Conard
Lewis, Mary
Lidov, Arthur Herschel
Lindgren, Charlotte
Littleton, Harvey K
Lloyd, Gary Marchal
Lloyd, Tom
Lothrop, Kristin Curtis
Lubbers, Leland Eugene
Lutze
Macdonnell, Cameron
Madsen, Loren Wakefield
Malone, James William
Mann, Katinka
Marcheschi, (Louis) Cork
Margo, Boris
Mari (Mari M Eagerton)
Marioni, Tom
Mark, Phyllis
Markle, Jack M
Markowski, Eugene David
Marozzi, Eli Raphael
Martin, Doris-Marie Constable
Martinelli, Ezio
Marx, Nicki D
Marzollo, Claudio
Matta-Clark, Gordon
Mattiello, Roberto
Mayer, Rosemary
McCracken, John Harvey
McElroy, Nancy Lynn
McGowin, Ed
McManus, James William
McMillan, Jerry Edward
Meneeley, Edward
Metyko, Michael Joseph
Metzger, Evelyn Borchard
Meyer, Seymour W
Michaels, Glen
Michelson-Bagley, Henrietta
Midener, Walter
Miles, Jeanne Patterson
Miller, Nancy
Millonzi, Victor
Mills, Agnes
Mills, Lev Timothy
Miralda, Antoni
Mitchell, Jeffrey Malcolm
Moquin, Richard Attilio
Morehouse, William Paul
Morrison, Art Jens
Mount, Pauline Ward
Mueller, Trude
Mullen, Philip Edward
Mullican, Lee
Nardone, Vincent Joseph
Nauman, Bruce
Neri, Manuel
Nirvanno, Comet (Vincent Romano)
Okulick, John A
Oldenburg, Claes Thure
Omwake, Leon, Jr
Ordonez, Efren
O'Shea, Terrençe Patrick
Ossorio, Alfonso A
Ostrowitz, Judith Maura
Pacileo, Dolores Margaret
Padovano, Anthony John
Parks, Charles Cropper
Parton, Nike
Partridge, David Gerry
Pascual, Manolo
Passuntino, Peter Zaccaria
Pattison, Abbott
Peabody, Amelia
Pearson, John
Peiperl, Adam
Pennuto, James William
Pfeifer, Bodo
Phillips, Gordon Dale
Phillips, Melita Ahl
Picard, Lil
Piene, Otto
Platus, Libby
Polk, Frank Fredrick
Potter, (George) Kenneth
Potts, Don
Prekop, Martin Dennis
Prent, Mark
Price, Kenneth
Pulido, Guillermo Aguilar
Puryear, Martin
Quisgard, Liz Whitney
Rabkin, Leo
Raciti, Cherie
Ray, Robert (Donald)
Rees, Joseph F
Reibel, Bertram
Reitzenstein, Reinhard
Rennick, Dan
Riley, Gerald Patrick
Ringgold, Faith
Rivoli, Mario
Robles, Julian
Rohm, Robert
Rose, Thomas Albert
Rosen-Queralt, Jann
Ross, Charles
Ross, Douglas Allan
Rothschild, Amalie (Rosenfeld)
Rowan, C Patrick
Rowe, Reginald M
Royce, Richard Benjamin
Rutsch, Alexander
Saari, Peter H
Saarinen, Lilian
Saltzman, William
Sandback, Frederick Lane
Sapien, Darryl Rudolph
Saxe, Henry
Scala, Joseph (A)
Schanker, Louis

SCULPTOR (cont)

Schloss, Arleen P (Arleen P Kelly)
Schmidt, Randall Bernard
Schreckengost, Viktor
Schuler, Melvin Albert
Schuselka, Elfi
Selchow, Roger Hoffman
Seyler, David W
Shaddle, Alice
Shaw, Donald Edward
Shimoda, Osamu
Simon, Helene
Sinaiko, Arlie
Sisti, Anthony J (Tony)
Slavit, Ann L
Smith, Lawson Wentworth
Smith, Susan Carlton
Sonenberg, Jack
Sproat, Christopher Townsend
Squires, Norma-Jean
Staffel, Rudolf Harry
Steele, Emily
Stern, Gerd Jacob
Stiegelmeyer, Norman Earl
Streeter, Tal
Stuart, Michelle
Sturman, Eugene
Swartzman, Roslyn
Talaba, L (Linda Talaba Cummens)
Tasgal-Kliegman, Gerda
Tatschl, John
Taylor, Michael (Leach)
Thek, Paul
Thiele, Robert Ransom
Thorne, Gordon (Kit)
Thornhill, Anna
Tobias, Julius
Tousignant, Claude
Townley, Hugh
Trudeau, Yves
Tsai, Wen-Ying
Tucker, William G
Turoff, Muriel Pargh
Turrell, James Archie
Tyson, Rae Julian
Ubertalli, Hector
Umlauf, Charles
Urquhart, Tony
Urso, Richard Carl
Uthco, T R (John Emil Hillding)
Valentine, DeWain
Van Tongeren, Harold (Herk)
Viner, Frank Lincoln
Visco, Anthony Salvatore
Vodicka, Ruth Kessler
Von Huene, Stephan R
Waddell, John Henry
Wade, Robert Schrope
Wagner, Gordon Parsons
Wald, Sylvia
Wallace, Elizabeth S
Weinbaum, Jean
Weinberg, Elbert
Weinrib, David
Weinstein, Florence
Westermann, Horace Clifford
Westfall, Carol D
Whiten, Colette
Wilke, Hannah
Willenbecher, John
Willson, Robert
Wilson, Helen J
Wilson, May
Wiper, Thomas William
Wood, Harry Emsley, Jr
Wyse, Alexander John
Yuristy, Russell Michael
Zeidenbergs, Olafs
Zimmerman, Elyn

Plastic

Adamy, George E
Alexander, Peter
Alford, Gloria K
Amino, Leo
Angelo, Domenick Michael
Arnautoff, Jacob Victor
Asher, Elise
Bakaty, Mike
Balance, Jerrald Clark
Banks, Anne Johnson
Bartlett, Donald Loring
Bayer, Jeffrey Joshua
Beasley, Bruce
Bejar, Feliciano
Black, David Evans
Booth, Laurence Ogden
Bourgeois, Louise
Breed, Charles Ayars
Bunch, Clarence
Burt, David Sill
Butchkes, Sydney
Bynum, E Anderson (Esther Pearl)
Carlberg, Norman Kenneth
Castoro, Rosemarie
Covington, Harrison Wall
DeAndrea, John Louis
Dignac, Geny (Eugenia M Bermudez)
Drake, James
Elsky, Herb
Emery, Lin (Lin Emery Braselman)
Eversley, Frederick John
Fafard, Joe (Joseph Yvon)
Fagg, Kenneth (Stanley)
FeBland, Harriet
Filkosky, Josefa
Finke, Leonda Froelich
Fisher, James Donald
Franco, Robert John
Fredman, Faiya R
Fuerst, Shirley Miller
Fuhrman, Esther
Fuller, Sue
Gaylord, Frank Chalfant
Ginsburg, Estelle
Goldfarb, Roz
Green, David Oliver
Greenwood, Paul Anthony
Gruber, Aaronel De Roy
Guerriero, Henry Edward
Guy, James M
Hanson, Duane
Harrison, Carole
Hatgil, Paul
Hausman, Fred S
Hay, Ike
Hendler, Raymond
Herr, Richard Joseph
Holvey, Samuel Boyer
Houskeeper, Barbara
Howard, Robert A
Howard, Robert Boardman
Jackson, Sarah
Jimenez, Luis Alfonso, Jr
Judd, Donald Clarence
Katzen, Lila (Pell)
Kauffman, Robert Craig
Kern, Arthur (Edward)
Knowlton, Grace Farrar
Kober, Alfred John
Koblick, Freda
Koscielny, Margaret
Kostyniuk, Ronald P
Kotin, Albert
Krebs, Rockne
Kyriakos, Aleko
Lamis, Leroy
Landis, Lily
Levee, John H
Manship, John Paul
Massin, Eugene Max
Mayorga, Gabriel Humberto
McCullough, David William
McManus, James William
Medrich, Libby E
Miles, Jeanne Patterson
Morgan, Frank James
Oleksiw, Michael Nicholas, II
Paris, Harold Persico
Peiperl, Adam
Prent, Mark
Pruitt, Lynn
Rankine, V V
Redinger, Walter Fred
Reimann, William P
Rodriguez, Oscar
Rose, Thomas Albert
Roukes, Nicholas M
Salzman, Rick
Sarnoff, Lolo
Schlanger, Jeff
Schnier, Jacques
Schonberger, Fred
Schuller, Grete
Seyfried, John Louis
Shute, Roberta E
Shutt, Ken
Smith, John Ivor
Sonnenberg, Frances
Staprans, Raimonds
Stein, Walter
Stone, Sylvia
Taysom, Wayne Pendelton
Truitt, Anne (Dean)
Udvardy, John Warren
Van Buren, Richard
Vasa (Vasa Velizar Mihich)
Vollmer, Ruth
Waitzkin, Stella
Watson, Lynda
Weedman, Kenneth Russell
Whitaker, Irwin A
White, Norman Triplett
Whitney, Maynard Merle
Woods, Ted
Zeidenbergs, Olafs

Stone

Abbatecola (Oronzo)
Abbott, Dorothy I
Ahvakana, Ulaaq (Lawrence Reynold Ahvakana)
Amateis, Edmond Romulus
Anderson, James P
Anderson, William
Anker, Suzanne C
Antonovici, Constantin
Armstrong, Jane Botsford
Aschenbach, (Walter) Paul
Aycock, Alice
Bailey, Richard H
Barger, Raymond Granville
Batista, Tomas
Batuz
Baz, Marysole Worner
Beal, Mack
Behl, Wolfgang
Bender, Beverly Sterl
Betancourt, R Arenas
Binford, Julien
Binning, Robin
Bisgyer, Barbara G (Barbara G Cohn)
Boiger, Peter
Bolinsky, Joseph Abraham
Borgatta, Isabel Case
Borgatta, Robert Edward
Bourgeois, Louise
Boxer, Stanley (Robert)
Boyce, Richard
Brumer, Shulamith
Buchman, James Wallace
Cabrera, Geles
Canfield, Jane (White)
Caparn, Rhys (Rhys Caparn Steel)
Caponi, Anthony
Carl, Joan
Carlberg, Norman Kenneth
Carr, Sally Swan
Carter, Dudley Christopher
Casanova, Aldo John
Catchi (Catherine O Childs)
Catlett, Elizabeth
Cave, Leonard Edward
Cesar, Gaston Gonzalez
Chavez, Joseph Arnold
Clark, John Dewitt
Cody, John (Alexis)
Conlon, James Edward
Crovello, William George
Davidson, Allan Albert
Davis, David Ensos
De Coux, Janet
De Creeft, Jose
Diska
Driesbach, Walter Clark, Jr
Du Pen, Everett George
Egri, Ted
Eino (Eino Antti Romppanen)
Eldredge, Mary Agnes
Ente, Lily
Escobedo, Augusto Ortega
Facci, Domenico (Aurelio)
Florio, Sal Erseny
Fontanini, Clare
French, Jared
Gaylord, Frank Chalfant
Geist, Sidney
Glickman, Maurice
Gonzales, Carlotta (Mrs Richard Lahey)
Goo, Benjamin
Goodelman, Aaron J
Goulet, Lorrie (Lorrie J De Creeft)
Grausman, Philip
Green, David Oliver
Grimley, Oliver Fetterolf
Gross, Alice (Alice Gross Fish)
Guite, Suzanne
Hamrol, Lloyd
Hanbury, Una
Harootian, Khoren Der
Hauser, Alonzo
Hilts, Alvin
Hoffman, Edward Fenno, III
Hoover, John Jay
Houser, Allan C
Howard, Robert Boardman
Jones, Jacobine
Judson, Sylvia Shaw
Kammerer, Herbert Lewis
Kassoy, Hortense
Kawecki, Jean Mary
Kelsey, Muriel Chamberlin
Kenojuak (Kenojuak Ashevak)
Key-Oberg, Ellen Burke
Kline, Alma
Koochin, William
Kyriakos, Aleko
Laird, E Ruth
Landis, Lily
Lantz, Michael F
Lavatelli, Carla
Ledyard, Walter William
Lewis, Jackson Pittman
Lewis, Mary
Lewis, Stanley
Lipton, Sondra (Sahlman)
Lyford, Cabot
Mack, Rodger Allen
Malicoat, Philip Cecil
Manton, Jock (Archimedes Aristides Giacomantonio)
Margoulies, Berta (Berta Margoulies O'Hare)
Meizner, Paula
Miller, Donald Richard
Model, Elisabeth D
Morgan, Arthur C
Morgan, Frances Mallory
Morgan, Frank James
Muccioli, Anna Maria

Myers, Legh
Namingha, Dan
Neals, Otto
Nickerson, Ruth (Ruth Nickerson Greacen)
Nierman, Leonardo M
Noordhoek, Harry Cecil
Norton, Ann
Oesterle, Leonhard Friedrich
O'Hanlon, Richard E
Ortmayer, Constance
Parton, Ralf
Peabody, Amelia
Peeler, Richard
Perry, Frank
Phillips, Melita Ahl
Plamondon, Marius Gerald
Popescu, Cara
Post, Anne B
Poucher, Elizabeth Morris
Prince, Arnold
Quinn, Brian Grant
Rabinovitch, William Avrum
Rachelski, Florian W
Reddy, Krishna N
Regat, Jean Jacques
Regat, Mary E
Reynolds, Richard (Henry)
Rhoden, John W
Richard, Betti
Richardson, Gretchen (Mrs Ronald Freelander)
Ridley, Gregory D, Jr
Robinson, Margot (Margot Steigman)
Rockwell, Peter Barstow
Romano, Salvatore Michael
Rubins, David Kresz
St Maur, Kirk (Kirk Seymour McReynolds)
Saito, Seiji
Salerno, Charles
Salter, John Randall
Schnier, Jacques
Schnittmann, Sascha S
Schreck, Michael Henry
Schuler, Melvin Albert
Schuller, Grete
Shapshak, Rene
Shaw, Ernest Carl
Simon, Bernard
Simon, Helene
Simon, Jewel Woodard
Sing Hoo (Sing Hoo Yuen)
Sisler, Rebecca
Slivka, David
Small, Amy Gans
Smith, Lawrence Beall
Sonnenberg, Frances
Spampinato, Clemente
Sponenburgh, Mark
Stark, Shirley
Stone, Willard
Sunderland, Nita Kathleen
Suttman, Paul
Taylor, Frederick Bourchier
Taylor, Joseph Richard
Taylor, Marie
Taylor, Rod Allen
Tewi, Thea
Thomas, Robert Chester
Thompson, William Joseph
Umana, Alfonso
Van Wert, Gordon Franklin
Walter, Valerie Harrisse
Walton, Marion (Marion Walton Putnam)
Warneke, Heinz
Washington, James W, Jr
Weaver, John Barney
Weinman, Robert Alexander
Wells, Charles Arthur, Jr
White, Bruce Hilding
Woods, Ted
Worth, Karen
Wright, G Alan
Young, Milton
Ziolkowski, Korczak
Zuniga, Francisco

Wood

Abbatecola (Oronzo)
Abbe, Elfriede Martha
Adams, Alice
Ahvakana, Ulaaq (Lawrence Reynold Ahvakana)
Amateis, Edmond Romulus
Anderson, John S
Anderson, William
Antonovici, Constantin
Appel, Karel
Athena
Aycock, Alice
Azara, Nancy J
Baird, Roger Lee
Baldwin, Harold Fletcher
Baney, Ralph Ramoutar
Barger, Raymond Granville
Barr, David John
Batista, Tomas
Bauermeister, Mary Hilde Ruth
Beal, Mack
Beall, Joanna
Behl, Wolfgang
Bender, Beverly Sterl
Benson, Martha J
Bernard, David Edwin
Blanc, Peter (William Peters Blanc)
Boiger, Peter
Bolinsky, Joseph Abraham
Bolomey, Roger Henry
Borgatta, Isabel Case
Borne, Mortimer
Bostelle, Thomas (Theodore)
Bourgeois, Louise
Boxer, Stanley (Robert)
Bragar, Philip Frank
Breitenbach, William John
Brown, Bruce Robert
Bryant, Olen L
Bueno, Jose (Joe Goode)
Bunch, Clarence
Canfield, Jane (White)
Carlberg, Norman Kenneth
Carr, Sally Swan
Carr-Harris, Ian Redford
Carter, Dudley Christopher
Casanova, Aldo John
Castle, Wendell Keith
Catlett, Elizabeth
Catusco, Louis
Cave, Leonard Edward
Cho, David
Clark, G Fletcher
Clark, John Dewitt
Colby, Victor E
Collier, Ric
Conlon, James Edward
Cook, Robert Howard
Crouch, Ned Philbrick
Crume, Gregg
Dagys, Jacob
Dal Fabbro, Mario
David, Dianne
Davis, David Ensos
De Coux, Janet
De Forest, Roy Dean
de Gerenday, Laci Anthony
Diska
Dombek, Blanche M
Drewelowe, Eve
Driesbach, Walter Clark, Jr
Du Pen, Everett George
Dworzan, George R
Egri, Ted
Eino (Eino Antti Romppanen)
Eldredge, Mary Agnes
Elmo, James
Elsner, Larry Edward
Ente, Lily
Eyre, Ivan
Facci, Domenico (Aurelio)
Finke, Leonda Froelich
Follett, Jean Frances
Fontanini, Clare
Foote, Howard Reed
Ford, Charles Henri
Frank, Charles William
Freeman, Robert Lee
Friedensohn, Elias
Friedman, Alan
Geist, Sidney
Gilhooly, David James, III
Ginsburg, Estelle
Glickman, Maurice
Goo, Benjamin
Goodelman, Aaron J
Goulet, Lorrie (Lorrie J De Creeft)
Graham, Richard Marston
Green, David Oliver
Grigor, Margaret Christian
Grimley, Oliver Fetterolf
Gross, Alice (Alice Gross Fish)
Groth, Bruno
Guite, Suzanne
Haber, Leonard
Hagan, James Garrison
Halko, Joe
Hamrol, Lloyd
Hardin, Adlai S
Harootian, Khoren Der
Hayden, Frank
Hebald, Milton Elting
Helman, Phoebe
Henkle, James Lee
Hicks, Harold Jon (Jack)
Hilts, Alvin
Hogbin, Stephen James
Hoover, John Jay
Hoptner, Richard
Hostetler, David
Houser, Allan C
Howard, Robert Boardman
Hueter, James Warren
Huntington, Jim
Hurst, Ralph N
Jacobson, Yolande (Mrs J Craig Sheppard)
Jaffe, Nora
Jensen, Hank
Johnston, William Edward
Jones, Herb (Leon Herbert Jones, Jr)
Jones, Theodore Joseph
Jones, W Louis
Jordan, Jack
Judd, Donald Clarence
Kagy, Sheffield Harold
Kahane, Anne
Karesh, Ann Bamberger
Kassoy, Hortense
Kelsey, Muriel Chamberlin
Key-Oberg, Ellen Burke
Kittelson, John Henry
Kline, Alma
Komodore, Bill
Koni, Nicolaus
Konzal, Joseph
Koochin, William
Kostyniuk, Ronald P
Kruger, Louise
Krugman, Irene
Kyriakos, Aleko
Larsen, D Dane
Lavatelli, Carla
Leax, Ronald Allen
Ledyard, Walter William
Lewis, Mary
Linn, Steven Allen
Lipton, Sondra (Sahlman)
Logan, Gene Adams
Long, C Chee
Long, Hubert
Ludwig, Eva
Lupori, Peter John
Lyford, Cabot
Mack, Rodger Allen
Mahlke, Ernest D
Maki, Robert Richard
Mangum, William (Goodson)
Margoulies, Berta (Berta Margoulies O'Hare)
Mark, Phyllis
Martin, William Barriss, II
Martino, Eva E
Mavroudis, Demetrios
McCabe, Lawrence
McCracken, John Harvey
McGovern, Robert F
McIlvain, Douglas Lee
McKesson, Malcolm Forbes
McKoy, Victor Grainger
McManus, James William
Michelson-Bagley, Henrietta
Milette, Clemence M
Model, Elisabeth D
Morgan, Arthur C
Morgan, Frances Mallory
Morgan, Frank James
Moskowitz, Shirley (Mrs Jacob W Gruber)
Mueller, Trude
Muno, Richard Carl
Murray, Richard Deibel
Murraygreen, Ryan
Myers, Legh
Neals, Otto
Nevelson, Louise
Nickel, Jim H
Niemann, Edmund E
Norman, Emile
Norton, Ann
Notaro, Anthony
Olson, Gary Spangler
Ortmayer, Constance
Ostrowitz, Judith Maura
Pardington, Ralph Arthur
Parker, Nancy Winslow
Parsons, Betty Bierne
Parsons, David Goode
Peeler, Richard
Perless, Robert
Posey, Leslie Thomas
Post, Anne B
Poucher, Elizabeth Morris
Prince, Arnold
Pruitt, Lynn
Puryear, Martin
Quinn, Brian Grant
Rachelski, Florian W
Racine, Albert Batiste
Rebbeck, Lester James, Jr
Reber, Mick
Reddy, Krishna N
Regat, Jean Jacques
Regat, Mary E
Reimann, William P
Reynolds, Richard (Henry)
Rice, Anthony Hopkins
Richard, Betti
Ridley, Gregory D, Jr
Robinson, Margot (Margot Steigman)
Rodriguez, Oscar
Rogers, John H
Rothschild, Lincoln
Rowe, Reginald M
Sacklarian, Stephen
Saito, Seiji
Saltzman, William
Sanderson, Raymond Phillips
Savoy, Chyrl Lenore
Schlanger, Jeff
Schmeckebier, Laurence E
Schneider, Noel
Schnier, Jacques
Schuler, Melvin Albert
Schwidder, Ernst Carl
Scott, Arden
Scott, Campbell
Sellers, William Freeman

SCULPTOR (cont)
Seyle, Robert Harley
Shapshak, Rene
Shostak, Edwin Bennett
Shutt, Ken
Sieg, Robert Lawrence
Simon, Bernard
Simpson, Tommy Hall
Sinaiko, Arlie
Sing Hoo (Sing Hoo Yuen)
Sisler, Rebecca
Slivka, David
Small, Amy Gans
Smith, Alfred James, Jr
Smith, Kent Alvin
Smith, Lawson Wentworth
Sonenberg, Jack
Sponenburgh, Mark
Steig, William
Stone, Willard
Storm, Howard
Strautmanis, Edvins
Sunderland, Nita Kathleen
Tatschl, John
Taylor, Joseph Richard
Taylor, Marie
Teller, Jane (Simon)
Thomas, Robert Chester
Thompson, William Joseph
Tolgesy, Victor
Torffield, Marvin
Tornheim, Norman
Townley, Hugh
Townsend, John F
Truitt, Anne (Dean)
Tsutakawa, George
Tucker, William G
Turano, Don
Turner, James Thomas, Sr
Turner, Raymond
Udvardy, John Warren
Urban, Mychajlo Raphael
Urquhart, Tony
Urso, Richard Carl
Vargas, Rudolph
Vass, Gene
Von Neumann, Robert A
Vrana, Albert S
Walter, Valerie Harrisse
Walton, Marion (Marion Walton Putnam)
Warner, Jo
Weaver, John Barney
Weinman, Robert Alexander
Weiss, Anton
Whiten, Colette
Whitney, Maynard Merle
Williams, Todd
Williams, Wayne Francis
Wilson, Warren Bingham
Yoshimura, Fumio
Young, Milton
Yuristy, Russell Michael
Zeidenbergs, Olafs
Zoellner, Richard C

SERIGRAPHER

see also **Printmaker**

Abdalla, Nick
Albrecht, Mary Dickson
Andrade, Edna Wright
Askin, Walter Miller
Auvil, Kenneth William
Azuma, Norio
Bach, Dirk
Baker, Eugene Ames
Dash, Harvey Dwight
Delgado-Guitart, Jose
Eden, F Brown
Folsom, Karl Leroy
Gersovitz, Sarah Valerie
Golden, Libby
Hee, Hon-Chew
Hein, Max
Hickman, David Coleman
High, Timothy Griffin
Jensen, Marit
Kirk, Michael
Knerr, Sallie Frost
Magnan, Oscar Gustav
Mandziuk, Michael Dennis
Marder, Dorie
Miller, Nancy
Myers, Jack Fredrick
Ocejo (Jose Garcia)
Pope, Richard Coraine
Ranson, Nancy Sussman
Rosenthal, Gloria M
Sloane, Phyllis Lester
Somers, H
Stevens, Nelson L
Stewart, Norman (William)
Stone, Gwen
Stovall, Luther McKinley (Lou)
Vaux, Richard
Walker, Joy
Waterman, Donald Calvin

SILVERSMITH

Aird, Neil Carrick
Allen, Constance Olleen Webb
Baird, Roger Lee
Bambas, Thomas Reese
Betteridge, Lois Etherington
Bowling, Jack
Christensen, Hans-Jorgen Thorvald
Croft, Michael Flynt
Crozier, William K, Jr
DiPasquale, Dominic Theodore
Dockstader, Frederick J
Eikerman, Alma
Engle, Barbara Jean
Fix, John Robert
Freund, Will Frederick
Hageman, Charles Lee
Ha-So-De (Narcisco Abeyta)
Helzer, Richard Brian
Jensen, Claud
Johnson, Donald Marvin
Kington, Louis Brent
Knapp, Tom
Krentzin, Earl
LaPlantz, David
Lechtzin, Stanley
Marshall, John Carl
Monongye, Preston Lee
Neumann, William A
Nichols, Eleanor Cary
Orr, Veronica Marie (Veronica Marie Ingram)
Piccolo, Thomas Frank
Pulos, Arthur Jon
Roysher, Hudson (Brisbine)
Satterfield, John Edward
Schlup, Elaine Smitha
Seppa, Heikki Markus
Sider, Deno
Skelly, Barbara Jean
Snyder, Toni Goessler
Taira, Frank
Thompson, Ernest Thorne, Jr
van Duinwyk, George Paul
Van Wert, Gordon Franklin
Van Wolf, Henry
Walker, Mary Carolyn
Wardle, Alfred Hill
Watson, Lynda
Wegner, Nadene R

STAINED GLASS ARTIST

Adams, Mark
Altabe, Joan Berg
Amen, Irving
Ascher, Mary
Bacigalupa, Andrea
Beaman, Richard Bancroft
Bengtz, Ture
Cariola, Robert J
Celender, Donald Dennis
Clark, Nancy Kissel
Cowley, Edward P
Cox, Allyn
Darricarrere, Roger Dominique
Dufour, Paul Arthur
Epler, Venetia
Fields, Fredrica H
Fogel, Seymour
Gikas, Christopher
Gold, Leah
Heaton, Maurice
Huntington, Daphne
Jameikis, Brone Aleksandra
Jonynas, Vytautas K
Jungwirth, Irene Gayas (I Gayas Jungwirth)
Karawina, Erica (Mrs Sideny C Hsiao)
Katz, Eunice
Kester, Lenard
Knapp, Tom
Korjus, Veronica Maria Elisabeth
Landau, Jacob
Leighton, Clare
Loy, John Sheridan
Maas, Arnold (Marcolino)
McGlauchlin, Tom
Miller, Eva-Hamlin
Miller, Leon Gordon
Mueller, M Gerardine
Mullen, Buell
Nuala (Elsa De Brun)
Olson, Joseph Olaf
Paone, Peter
Porter, Priscilla Manning
Posner, Richard Perry
Potvin, Daniel
Raffael, Judith K
Reynolds, Joseph Gardiner
Rhodes, James Melvin
Schneider, Noel
Simon, Ellen R
Skinner, Orin Ensign
Smith, Oliver
Tahedl, Ernestine
Tait, Katharine Lamb
Tatschl, John
Terry, Duncan Niles
Willet, Henry Lee
Wolfe, Lynn Robert
Wolff, Richard Evans

TAPESTRY ARTIST

Adams, Mark
Ahlskog, Sirkka
Akston, Joseph James
Ames, Arthur Forbes
Aquino, Edmundo
Askild, Anita (Anita Askild Feinstein)
Asmar, Alice
Bassler, James W
Bayer, Herbert
Bejar, Feliciano
Bobrowicz, Yvonne P
Boussard, Dana
Boyd, Karen White
Brooks, Lois Ziff
Brown, Rhett Delford (Harriett Gurney Brown)
Callner, Richard
Carewe, Sylvia
Clerk, Pierre
Dey, Kris
Domjan, Joseph (also Spiri)
Dyer, Carolyn Price
Easterwood, Henry Lewis
Edvi Illes, Emma
Fassett, Kaffe Havrah
Fischer, Mildred (Gertrude)
Freimark, Robert (Matthew)
Funk, Charlotte M
Gregor, Helen Frances
Hemenway, Nancy (Mrs Robert D Barton)
Hicks, Sheila
Higgins, Mary Lou
Hill, John Conner
Hobbs, (Carl) Fredric
Jaworska, Tamara
Kaye, David Haigh
Kusama, Tetsuo
Lavatelli, Carla
Lindgren, Charlotte
Maldjian, Vartavar B
Maltby, Hazel Farrow
Mercier, Monique
Michaels, Glen
Morrison, Bee (Berenice G)
Notarbartolo, Albert
Palau, Marta
Pendleton, Mary Caroline
Pinckney, Stanley
Platus, Libby
Porter, (Edwin) David
Replinger, Dot (Dorothy Thiele)
Roberson, William
Roda (Rhoda Lillian Sablow)
Rosen-Queralt, Jann
Rothschild, Amalie (Rosenfeld)
Rousseau-Vermette, Mariette
Soffer, Sasson
Tasgal-Kliegman, Gerda
Todd, Louise (Louise Todd Cope)
Wallace, Lysbeth (Mai)
Ward, Evelyn Svec
Wayne, June
West, Virginia M
Wilson, Helen J
Wyngaard, Susan Elizabeth

VIDEO ARTIST

Accurso, Anthony Salvatore
Antin, Eleanor
Askevold, David
Baldessari, John Anthony
Barron, Ros
Breder, Hans Dieter
Byrne, James Richard
Cameron, Eric
Campbell, Colin Keith
Campus, Peter
Clancy, Patrick
Crouton, Francois (Francois LaFortune)
Davis, Ben H
Davis, Douglas Matthew
De Monte, Claudia
Dickinson, Eleanor Creekmore
Dupuy, Jean
Edwards, James F
Endsley, Fred Starr
Favro, Murray
Fernie, John Chipman
Forst, Miles
Freed, Hermine
Fried, Howard Lee
Fuge, Paul H

Glassman, Joel A
Graham, Daniel H
Gusella, Ernest
Hamouda, Amy
Harding, Noel Robert
Hayden, Michael
Hendricks, David Charles
Holton, Leonard T
Hompson, Davi Det (David Elbridge Thompson)
Hunt, Kari
Iimura, Taka
Jonas, Joan
Jones, Howard William
Karwelis, Donald Charles
Kataoka, Mits
Korot, Beryl
Kos, Paul Joseph
Kubota, Shigeko
Landry, Richard Miles
Laposky, Ben Francis
Levine, Les
Lijn, Liliane
Lindquist, Evan
Lloyd, Tom
Loeffler, Carl Eugene
Lotterman, Hal
Mann, Andy
Margolies, John
McCafferty, Jay David
McCullough, David William
Muntadas, Antonio
Oppenheim, Dennis A
Paik, Nam June
Pekar, Ronald Walter
Ritchie, William
Rosler, Martha Rose
Ross, David Anthony
Rumsey, David MacIver
Salzman, Rick
Sapien, Darryl Rudolph
Sasaki, Tomiyo
Satty, Wilfried
Saxon, Charles David
Schiff, Jean
Schley, Evander Duer (Van)
Schneider, Ira
Seace, Barry William
Segalove, Ilene Judy
Sekula, Allan
Sharp, Willoughby
Smith, Barbara Turner
Sonnier, Keith
Stahl, Ben (Albert)
Steele, Lisa
Sturgeon, John Floyd
Sussman, Arthur
Van Riper, Peter
Van Schley (Evander Duer Van Schley)
Wegman, William
Welch, Roger
Wiegand, Robert
Willis, Jay Steward
Young, Robert John
Zack, David

WEAVER

Alhilali, Neda
Askild, Anita (Anita Askild Feinstein)
Bakke, Karen Lee
Bassler, James W
Beauchemin, Micheline
Bobrowicz, Yvonne P
Bolley, Irma S
Boyd, Karen White
Buranabunpot, Pornpilai
Caver, William Ralph
Dey, Kris
Dyer, Carolyn Price
Elliott, Lillian
Fender, Tom Mac
Funk, Charlotte M
Gregor, Helen Frances
Hallman, H Theodore, Jr
Himler, Ronald Norbert
Hoffmann, Lilly Elisabeth
Jess (Jess Collins)
Johnson, Ivan Earl
Kelly, Isaac Perry
Kennedy, Leta Marietta
Korot, Beryl
Lafaye, Nell Murray
Landreau, Anthony Norman
Larsen, Jack Lenor
Lindgren, Charlotte
Maldjian, Vartavar B
Maltby, Hazel Farrow
Matson, Elina
McElroy, Nancy Lynn
McVey, Leza
Merchant, Pat (Jean)
Meredith, Dorothy Laverne
Miller, Barbara Darlene
Morrison, Bee (Berenice G)
Pardington, Joyce Elizabeth
Pendleton, Mary Caroline
Plath, Iona
Platus, Libby
Regensteiner, Else (Friedsam)
Replinger, Dot (Dorothy Thiele)
Roberson, William
Schira, Cynthia Jones
Schuman, Robert Conrad
Sekimachi, Kay
Seyler, David W
Shaw, Courtney Ann
Smith, Sherry
Tawney, Lenore
Tiffany, Marguerite Bristol
Todd, Louise (Louise Todd Cope)
Trentham, Gary Lynn
Van Leunen, Alice Louise
Vasquez J, Alberto
Wahling, B Jon
Wallace, Lysbeth (Mai)
Ward, Evelyn Svec
Warner, Lucy Ann
West, Virginia M
Westfall, Carol D
Williams, Benjamin Forrest
Wilson, Helen J
Windeknecht, Margaret Brake
Wyngaard, Susan Elizabeth
Younglove, Ruth Ann (Mrs Benjamin Rhees Loxley)

WRITER

Aach, Herb
Ablow, Joseph
Adams, Clinton
Ahl, Henry C
Airola, Paavo
Akston, Joseph James
Albright, Thomas
Alexenberg, Melvin (Menahem)
Alf, Martha Joanne
Aliki (Aliki Brandenberg)
Alper, M Victor
Amaya, Mario Anthony
Ames, Lee Judah
Amoss, Berthe
Anderson, Donald Myers
Anderson, Doug
Andrews, Michael Frank
Antin, David A
Armstrong, Jane Botsford
Arnason, H Harvard
Arnheim, Rudolf
Arnosky, James Edward
Artz, Frederick B
Ascott, Roy
Askew, Pamela
Atirnomis (Rita Simon)
Auer, James Matthew
Bach, Otto Karl
Bacon, Peggy
Baer, Jo
Baigts, Juan
Bailey, Walter Alexander
Baird, Joseph Armstrong, Jr
Ballinger, Louise Bowen
Balmaceda, Margarita S
Banta, Melissa Wiekser
Banz, George
Barbour, Arthur J
Barker, Walter William
Barnett, Ed Willis
Barrio, Raymond
Barrio-Garay, Jose Luis
Barr-Sharrar, Beryl
Bartle, Dorothy Budd
Bartlett, Jennifer Losch
Barton, Phyllis Grace
Barzun, Jacques
Bass, Ruth Gilbert
Bates, Kenneth Francis
Battcock, Gregory
Baur, John I H
Beam, Philip Conway
Bearden, Romare Howard
Bearman, Jane Ruth
Beatty, Frances Fielding Lewis
Beck, Doreen
Becker, Martin Earle
Beery, Eugene Brian
Bender, Bill
Benedikt, Michael
Benson, Gertrude Ackerman
Benton, Suzanne E
Berge, Carol
Berkman, Aaron
Bessemer, Auriel
Betancourt, R Arenas
Bevlin, Marjorie Elliott
Biederman, Charles (Karel Joseph)
Bier, Justus
Biggers, John Thomas
Bishop, Robert Charles
Bochner, Mel
Boros, Billi (Mrs Philip Bisaccio)
Botkin, Henry
Bowman, Bruce
Boyle, Richard J
Brandt, Rexford Elson
Brommer, Gerald F
Bronson, A A (Michael Wayne Tims)
Brooks, Frank Leonard
Brown, Joseph
Brown, Robert K
Brown, William Ferdinand, II
Brumbaugh, Thomas Brendle
Bruner, Louise Katherine (Mrs Paul Orr)
Burch, Claire R
Burgart, Herbert Joseph
Burgess, Joseph James, Jr
Burnett, Calvin
Burnett, Patricia Hill
Burnham, Jack Wesley
Bush-Brown, Albert
Calas, Nicolas
Calle, Paul
Campbell, Dorothy Bostwick
Campbell, (James) Lawrence
Campbell, Vivian (Vivian Campbell Stoll)
Capp, Al
Case, Elizabeth
Caswell, Helen Rayburn
Cate, Phillip Dennis
Chamberlain, Betty
Chapin, Louis (Le Bourgeois)
Chappell, Warren
Chase, Alice Elizabeth
Cheney, Sheldon
Chernow, Burt
Chicago, Judy
Chieffo, Clifford Toby
Chow Chian-Chiu
Chow Leung Chen-Ying
Clemens, Paul
Cochran, George McKee
Coffelt, Beth
Cohen, Joan Lebold
Cohoe, Grey
Coiner, Charles Toucey
Cole, Bruce
Cole, Harold David
Cole, Sylvan, Jr
Collier, Graham (Alan Graham-Collier)
Collins, Christiane C
Collins, George R
Colorado, Charlotte
Colt, Priscilla C
Congdon, William (Grosvenor)
Conrad, John W
Cook, Gladys Emerson
Cooney, Barbara (Mrs Charles Talbot Porter)
Corbin, George Allen
Cordy-Collins, Alana (Alana Kathleen Cordy-Collins Riesland)
Cossitt, Franklin D
Cowles, Fleur
Cox, Richard William
Crane, Roy (Campbell)
Craven, Wayne
Criquette (Ruth DuBarry Montague)
Crite, Allan Rohan
Cutler, Grayce E
Dal Fabbro, Mario
D'Amato, Janet Potter
Damaz, Paul F
Dame, Lawrence
Dane, William Jerald
Danikian, Caron Le Brun
D'Aulaire, Ingri (Mortenson) Parin
Davidson, Abraham A
Davidson, Morris
Daviee, Jerry Michael
Davis, George
Davis, James Wesley
Dawdy, Doris Ostrander
Dawley, Joseph William
Dean, Abner
Deats, Margaret (Margaret Deats Bott)
de Borhegyi, Suzanne Sims
De Grazia, Ettore Ted
De Jong, Gerrit, Jr
de Kolb, Eric
de Kooning, Elaine Marie Catherine
Delaney, Joseph
De Nike, Michael Nicholas
Dentzel, Carl Schaefer
de Paola, Tomie
De Ruth, Jan
DeShazo, Edith Kind
De Tolnay, Charles
Dibble, George
Donohoe, Victoria
Dowden, Anne Ophelia Todd
Dunbar, Jill H
Duvoisin, Roger
Dwight, Edward Harold
Dyer, Carolyn Price
Ehresmann, Julia Moore
Ellis, Richard
Emerson, Walter Caruth
Emmerich, Andre
England, Paul Grady
Eshraw, Ra
Ets, Marie Hall
Evans, Bruce Haselton
Evans, Paul Fredric
Ewald, Elin Lake
Fanning, Robbie

WRITER (cont)
Farian, Babette S
Farnham, Alexander
Farnham, Emily
Farnsworth, Jerry
Farrell, Patric
Faul, Roberta Heller
Fax, Elton Clay
Feiffer, Jules
Feigen, Richard L
Feininger, T Lux
Fels, C P
Ferguson, Kathleen Elizabeth
Fern, Alan Maxwell
Fernie, John Chipman
Fifield, Mary
Finck, Furman J
Fine, Jud
Fine, Ruth Eileen
Finkelstein, Louis
Fisher Joel A
Fisher, Leonard Everett
Flach, Victor H
Flavin, Dan
Flexner, James Thomas
Forge, Andrew Murray
Forrest, James Taylor
Fosburgh, James Whitney
Foster, Stephen C
Franck, Frederick S
Frank, Charles William
Fredericksen, Burton Baum
Freed, Hermine
Freeman, Margaret B
Freeman, Phyllis (Therese)
Frick, Robert Oliver
Friedman, B H
Friend, David
Frinta, Mojmir Svatopluk
Fuller, Mary (Mary Fuller McChesney)
Fuller, R Buckminster
Fussiner, Howard
Gale, Peggy
Garber, Susan R
Garchik, Morton Lloyd
Garman, Ed
Garrard, Mary DuBose
Garver, Thomas H
Gary, Dorothy Hales
Gasser, Henry Martin
Gear, Josephine
Gefter, Judith Michelman
Geisel, Theodor Seuss (Dr Seuss)
Genauer, Emily
Ghent, Henri
Gibson, Walter Samuel
Gilkey, Gordon Waverly
Gilpin, Laura
Giraudier, Antonio
Gladstone, M J
Glaser, David
Glasgow, Vaughn Leslie
Glauber, Robert H
Glickman, Maurice
Glimcher, Arnold B
Glueck, Grace (Helen)
Goddard, Donald
Godsey, Glenn
Goetzl, Thomas Maxwell
Goldsmith, Barbara
Goldstein, Nathan
Gonzales, Shirley
Goodrich, Lloyd
Goossen, Eugene Coons
Gordon, John
Gordon, Leah Shanks
Gordon, Violet
Gramatky, Hardie
Gray, Don
Greaves, Fielding Lewis
Greenbaum, Marty
Greenberg, Clement
Gregg, Richard Nelson
Griffin, Rachael S
Grigsby, Jefferson Eugene, Jr
Gross, Earl
Grosser, Maurice
Grove, Richard
Groves, Naomi Jackson
Grundy, John Owen
Gundersheimer, Herman (Samuel)
Gussow, Alan
Gysin, Brion
Haber, Ira Joel
Hackenbroch, Yvonne Alix
Hall, Carl Alvin
Hall, Julie Ann
Halvorsen, Ruth Elise
Hames, Carl Martin
Hammond, Leslie King
Hammond, Ruth MacKrille
Hanks, David Allen
Hanna, Katherine
Hansen, Harold John
Harsley, Alex
Haskins, John Franklin
Hastie, Reid
Hawkins, Myrtle H
Hay-Messick, Velma
Held, Julius S
Heller, Jules
Henrickson, Paul Robert
Herman, Alan David
Herring, Jan(et Mantel)
Hess, Thomas B
Hinkhouse, Forest Melick
Hirsch, Richard Teller
Hirschfeld, Albert
Hoff, (Syd)
Hogue, Alexandre
Holden, Donald
Hollister, Paul
Homer, William Innes
Hoover, F Herbert
Hopkins, Peter
Horn, Milton
Horn, Stuart Alan
Hornung, Clarence Pearson
Howell, Elizabeth Ann (Mitch)
Howland, Richard Hubbard
Hudson, Ralph Magee
Hugo, Joan (Dowey)
Hunt, David Curtis
Hunt, Kari
Hunter, Graham
Hurd, Peter
Hutchinson, Peter Arthur
Hyde, Laurence
Immerwahr, Sara Anderson
Ipcar, Dahlov
Ireland, Patrick (Brian O'Doherty)
Irving, Donald J
Isaacson, Philip Marshal
Ivey, James Burnett
Jackson, Suzanne Fitzallen
Jacobs, Jay
Jacobsen, Michael A
Janis, Sidney
Jauss, Anne Marie
Jellico, John Anthony
Jennings, Jan
Jensen, Dean N
Jensen, Gary
Johnson, Fridolf Lester
Johnson, James Ralph
Johnson, Lincoln Fernando
Johnson, Pauline B
Johnson, Una E
Jones, Elizabeth Orton
Jones, Franklin Reed
Judson, Sylvia Shaw
Kappel, Philip
Katz, Hilda (Hilda Weber)
Katz, Leo
Kaufman, Edgar, Jr
Kaupelis, Robert John
Kay, Reed
Kaye, George
Kayser, Stephen S
Keats, Ezra Jack
Keith, Eros
Kenda, Juanita Echeverria
Kenny, Bettie Ilene Cruts (BIK)
Kent, Jack
Kessler, Leonard H
Key, Donald D
Killam, Walt
Kind, Joshua B
King, William Alfred
Klebe, Gene (Charles Eugene)
Klosty, James Michael
Knox, Katharine McCook
Koch, Robert
Kouwenhoven, John A
Kovinick, Philip Peter
Kowal, Dennis J
Kozloff, Max
Kramer, Burton
Kramer, Jack N
Kriensky, (Morris E)
Kubler, George Alexander
Kultermann, Udo
Kurdian, Haroutiun Harry
Kusama, Yayoi
Labino, Dominick
Labrie, Rose
Laird, Mary (Mary Laird Hamady)
Lane, Alvin Seymour
Lane, Marion Jean Arrons
Langner, Nola
Laning, Edward
Lariar, Lawrence
Larsen, Jack Lenor
Larson, Jane (Warren)
Lash, Kenneth
Lathrop, Dorothy P
Laub-Novak, Karen
Lauck, Anthony Joseph
Laury, Jean Ray (Jean Ray Bitters)
Lea, Tom
Lee, Amy Freeman
Lefebvre d'Argence, Rene-Yvon
Leighton, Clare
Leon, Dennis
Lerman, Leo
Levy, Julien
Lewis, Don
Lewis, Donald Sykes, Jr
Lewis, Phillip Harold
Lewison, Florence (Mrs Maurice Glickman)
Lewton, Jean Louise
Libby, William C
Liberman, Alexander
Libhart, Myles Laroy
Lieb, Vered (Vered Shapiro-Lieb)
Lijn, Liliane
Lindsay, Kenneth C
Lionni, Leo
Lipman, Jean
Lippard, Lucy Rowland
Little, Nina Fletcher
Loewer, Henry Peter
Logan, Frederick Manning
Long, Glenn Alan
Longaker, Jon Dasu
Longstreet, Stephen
Loran, Erle
Lorber, Richard
Love, Frances Taylor
Love, Richard Henry
Ludman, Joan Hurwitz
Lunde, Karl Roy
Lynes, Russell
Mabie, Don Edward
Macaualy, David Alexander
MacDonald, Colin Somerled
MacDonald, William L
Madigan, Mary Jean Smith
Mainardi, Patricia M
Mann, Vaughan (Vaughan Grayson)
Manning, Reg (West)
Markow, Jack
Marks, Claude
Marozzi, Eli Raphael
Mason, Lauris Lapidos
Mattil, Edward L
Mauldin, Bill
Maxwell, John
Mayer, Ralph
Mayer, Rosemary
Mayor, Alpheus Hyatt
McCaslin, Walter Wright
McCloskey, Eunice LonCoske
McCloskey, Robert
McCormick, Jo Mary (Jo Mary McCormick-Sakurai)
McDarrah, Fred William
McFee, June King
McLanathan, Richard B K
Medoff, Eve
Meigs, John Liggett
Meilach, Dona Z
Meixner, Mary Louise
Mendelowitz, Daniel Marcus
Mendoza, David C
Merkel, Jayne (Silverstein)
Merritt, Francis Sumner
Metzger, Robert Paul
Meyer, Susan E
Michael, Gary
Millard, Charles Warren, III
Miller, Donald
Miller, George
Miller, H McRae
Mitchell, James E
Moise, William Sidney
Montequin, Francois-Auguste de
Moreton, Russell
Morgan, Charles H
Morgan, Theodora
Morgan, William
Morley, Grace L McCann
Morris, George North
Morris, Jack Austin, Jr
Morrison, Art Jens
Morrison, Boone M
Morrison C L
Morse, A Reynolds
Morse, John D
Morton, Robert Alan
Moser, Charlotte
Moulton, Susan Gene
Movalli, Charles Joseph
Muehsam, Gerd
Muensterberger, Werner
Muller, Jerome Kenneth
Musick, Archie L
Myers, John B
Nagano, Paul Tatsumi
Nardone, Vincent Joseph
Neal, (Minor) Avon
Nelson, Mary Carroll
Nemser, Cindy
Ness, (Albert) Kenneth
Ness, Evaline (Mrs Arnold A Bayard)
Newhall, Beaumont
Newman, Elias
Newman, Ralph Albert
Newsom, Barbara Ylvisaker
Nichols, Dale William
Nordness, Lee
Norman, Dorothy (S)
Norris, Andrea Spaulding
Nossal, Audrey Jean
Notarbartolo, Albert
Nuki (Daniel Millsaps)
O'Connor, Francis Valentine
O'Connor, Harold Thomas
O'Gorman, James Francis
Olpin, Robert Spencer
Orenstein, Gloria Feman
Ostendorf, (Arthur) Lloyd, Jr
Packer, Clair Lange
Papageorge, Tod
Paris, Jeanne C
Parish, Betty Waldo
Parker, John William
Parkhurst, Charles
Parnall, Peter
Pearlman, Etta S

Peladeau, Marius Beaudoin
Pendergraft, Norman Elveis
Pendleton, Mary Caroline
Perine, Robert Heath
Perret, George Albert
Perry, Regenia Alfreda
Petersen, Will
Phillips, Donna-Lee
Phillips, Gifford
Pike, John
Pilsk, Adele Inez
Plagens, Peter
Plath, Iona
Plaut, James S
Pollack, Peter
Pollack, Reginald Murray
Porter, Eliot Furness
Prescott, Kenneth Wade
Preuss, Roger
Pride, Joy
Purser, Stuart Robert
Quinn, Raymond John
Quinsac, Annie-Paule
Rachel, Vaughan
Rainey, Froelich Gladstone
Raleigh, Henry Patrick
Raskins, Ellen
Ratcliff, Carter
Raven, Arlene
Reed, Michael Arthur
Reed, Walt Arnold
Reep, Edward Arnold
Regensteiner, Else (Friedsam)
Reid, Charles
Rembski, Stanislav
Rensch, Roslyn (Roslyn Maria Erbes)
Rey, H A
Rice, Harold Randolph
Rice, James William, Jr
Richardson, Brenda
Richardson, Edgar Preston
Richman, Robert M
Rinhart, George R
Rising, Dorothy Milne
Robbin, Anthony Stuart
Robbins, Eugenia S
Robins, Corinne
Robinson, Charles K
Rodman, Selden
Rogers, Charles B
Romeu, Joost A
Rose, Barbara E
Rosenberg, Charles Michael
Rosenberg, Harold
Rosenberg, Jakob
Ross, David Anthony
Rothschild, Lincoln
Roukes, Nicholas M
Salemme, Lucia (Autorino)
Sanders, Andrew Dominick
Saphire, Lawrence M
Savitt, Sam
Sawyer, Alan R
Sawyer, Helen (Helen Sawyer Farnsworth)
Schlemm, Betty Lou
Schmidt, Harvey Lester
Schnessel, S Michael
Schwalb, Susan
Schwartz, Barbara Ann
Schwartz, Marvin D
Schwartz, Therese
Schwarz, Myrtle Cooper
Scully, Vincent
Segy, Ladislas
Seligmann, Herbert J
Selvig, Forrest Hall
Sendak, Maurice Bernard
Shadbolt, Jack Leonard
Shapley, Fern Rusk
Sherman, Claire Richter
Sherman, Lenore (Walton)
Silverman, Ronald H
Simon, Leonard Ronald
Simoni, John Peter
Singer, Esther Forman
Sipiora, Leonard Paul
Skelton, Robin
Skolle, John
Slate, Joseph Frank
Slatkes, Leonard Joseph
Slettehaugh, Thomas Chester
Sloane, Eric
Sloane, Joseph Curtis
Smith, Barbara Turner
Smith, Ralph Alexander
Smith, William Arthur
Smyth, Ed
Snodgrass, Jeanne Owens (Mrs M Eugene King)
Snow, Lee Erlin
Soby, James Thrall
Soleri, Paolo
Soloway, Reta
Sommer, Frank H
Sorel, Edward
Sovary, Lilly
Sowers, Miriam R
Spaeth, Eloise O'Mara
Spector, Naomi
Spencer, Eleanor Patterson
Spencer, Harold Edwin
Spink, Frank Henry, Jr
Stacy, Donald L
Stahl, Ben (Albert)
Starks, Elliott Roland
Statman, Jan B
Stein, Roger Breed
Steiner, Paul
Stephens, William Blakely
Stevens, Elisabeth Goss
Stevens, May
Stewart, John Lincoln
Stofflet, Mary
Stoloff, Carolyn
Stucki, Margaret Elizabeth
Sward, Robert S
Swarzenski, Hanns Peter Theophil
Swinton, George
Sylvester, Lucille
Sylvestre, Guy
Takal, Peter
Tam, Reuben
Tarshis, Jerome
Taubes, Frederic
Taylor, John Frank Adams
Taylor, Robert
Thomas, Helen (Doane)
Thomas, Lew
Thompson, F Raymond (Ray)
Thorndike, Charles Jesse (Chuck)
Tice, George Andrew
Tillenius, Clarence (Ingwall)
Tillim, Sidney
Tomkins, Calvin
Toney, Anthony
Toschik, Larry
Town, Harold Barling
Tracy, (Lois) Bartlett
Tripp, Wallace Whitney
Trosky, Helene Roth
Tselos, Dimitri Theodore
Tucker, Peri
Tucker, William G
Tudor, Tasha
Turano, Jane Van Norman
Turner, Norman Huntington
Uhrman, Celia
Van Arsdale, Dorothy Thayer
Van Dommelen, David B
Van Wyk, Helen
Vermeule, Cornelius Clarkson, III
Verner, Elizabeth O'Neill
Von Wiegand, Charmion
Walsh, John Stanley
Walton, Donald William
Wands, Alfred James
Wang, Yinpao
Ward, Lynd (Kendall)
Warner, Harry Backer, Jr
Wasserman, Burton
Watson, Aldren Auld
Watson, Robert
Watson, Wendy
Weber, John Pitman
Wechter, Vivienne Thaul
Weil, Lisl
Weil, Stephen Edward
Weinhardt, Carl Joseph, Jr
Weisgard, Leonard Joseph
Weismann, Donald Leroy
Weiss, Peg
Weitzmann, Kurt
West, Virginia M
Wexler, Jerome LeRoy
Whitney, Edgar Albert
Wiener, Louise Weingarten
Wight, Frederick S
Willer, Jim
Willig, Nancy Tobin
Wilson, William S, III
Winchester, Alice
Wines, James N
Wingate, Adina (R)
Winokur, James L
Winter, H Edward
Withers, Josephine
Wofford, Philip
Wolf, Jack Clifford
Wood, Harry Emsley, Jr
Wright, Barton Allen
Wright, Catharine Morris
Wyrick, Charles Lloyd, Jr (Pete)
Young, Mahonri S
Zaidenberg, Arthur
Zimiles, Murray
Zornes, James Milford
Zucker, Barbara M

Necrology

Cumulative 1953-1978

ABBATE, PAUL S Sculptor (1884-1972)
ABBELL, SAMUEL Art Patron (1925-1969)
ABBOT, EDITH Painter (-1964)
ABBOTT, JOHN EVANS Library Director (-1952)
ABEL, MYER Lithographer, Painter
ACKERMANN, JOHN JOSEPH Painter, Designer (-1950)
ADAMS, MARGARET BOROUGHS Painter (-1965)
ADAMS, (MOULTON) LEE Painter, Illustrator (1922-1971)
ADEN, ALONZO J Museum Director (-1963)
ADLOW, DOROTHY Critic (-1964)
AGA-OGLU, MEHMET Educator, Lecturer, Writer (-1948)
AIKEN, CHARLES Painter (-1965)
ALAN, JAY Cartoonist (-1965)
ALBERS, JOSEF Painter, Printmaker (1888-1976)
ALBRIGHT, HENRY J Educator, Painter (-1951)
ALDER, MARY ANN Painter, Art Restorer (-1952)
ALEXANDER, CHRISTINE Curator (1893-1975)
ALFSEN, JOHN MARTIN Painter (-1972)
ALLEN, ARTHUR D Painter, Lithographer (-1949)
ALLEN, CHARLES CURTIS Painter, Educator (-1950)
ALLEN, JANE MENGEL (MRS ARTHUR) Painter (-1952)
ALLEN, JUNIUS Painter (-1962)
ALLEN, MARY STOCKBRIDGE Painter, Sculptor (-1949)
ALSTON, CHARLES HENRY Painter, Educator (1907-1977)
ANDERSEN, ANDREAS STORRS Educator, Painter (1908-1974)
ANDERSON, CARL THOMAS Cartoonist, Illustrator (-1948)
ANSBACHER, JESSIE Painter (-1964)
ARCHIPENKO, ALEXANDER Sculptor (1887-1964)
ARLT, WILLIAM H Designer, Teacher, Painter
ARNO, PETER Cartoonist (-1968)
ARTIS, WILLIAM ELLISWORTH Educator, Ceramist (1914-1977)
ARTZYBASHEFF, BORIS Illustrator (-1965)
ASHTON, ETHEL V Artist (-1975)
ASHTON, MAY STANHOPE (MALONE) Artist (1878-1976)
ATHERTON, J CARLTON Craftsman (-1964)
ATHERTON, JOHN Painter, Illustrator (-1952)
ATKINS, ALBERT H Sculptor, Painter (-1951)
AUERBACH-LEVY, WILLIAM Etcher
AULT, GEORGE COPELAND Painter (-1948)
AVERY, MILTON Painter (1893-1965)
AVERY, RALPH HILLYER Painter, Illustrator (1906-1976)
AVINOFF, ANDREY Painter, Illustrator (-1948)
AYERS, HESTER MERWIN Portrait Painter (1902-1975)
BACH, RICHARD F Educator (-1968)
BAIN, LILIAN PHERNE Painter, Etcher
BAIZERMAN, SAUL Sculptor (1898-1957)
BAKER, CHARLES EDWIN Art Historian, Writer (1902-1971)
BALDWIN, HARRY, II Painter
BALDWIN, MURIEL FRANCES Art Librarian
BARBER, JOHN Painter (1898-1965)
BARBER, MURIEL V Painter (-1971)
BARKER, ALBERT WINSLOW Lithographer, Teacher (-1947)
BARKER, VIRGIL Writer Critic (-1964)
BARNETT, HERBERT P Educator, Painter (1910-1972)
BARNEY, MAGINAL WRIGHT Craftsman (-1966)
BARRETT, H STANFORD Painter, Educator (1909-1970)
BARRETT, THOMAS WEEKS Painter, Designer (-1947)
BASS, JOHANNA (MRS JOHN) Collector, Patron (-1970)
BATCHELOR, CLARENCE DANIEL Cartoonist (-1977)
BATES, KENNETH Painter (1895-1973)
BAUMGARTNER, WARREN W Illustrator (-1963)
BAYLINSON, A S Painter, Teacher (-1950)
BAYLOS, ZELMA U Painter, Sculptor
BAZIOTES, WILLIAM Painter (1912-1963)
BEAL, REYNOLDS Painter, Etcher (-1951)
BEALL, LESTER THOMAS Illustrator, Designer (1903-1969)
BEAR, DONALD Museum Director (-1952)
BECKER, NAOMI Sculptor (-1974)
BEETZ, CARL HUGO Painter, Instructor (1911-1974)
BEGG, JOHN ALFRED Designer, Sculptor (1903-1974)
BEIL, CHARLES A Sculptor (-1976)
BELCHER, HILDA Painter (-1963)
BELKNAP, MORRIS B Painter (-1952)
BELLINGER, LOUISA Curator (-1968)
BELLMER, HANS Painter, Graphic Artist & Sculptor (1902-1975)
BELMONT, IRA JEAN Painter
BEMELMANS, LUDWIG Painter (-1963)
BEMIS, WALDO EDMUND Designer, Illustrator (-1951)
BENDA, W T Designer, Illustrator (-1948)
BENESCH, OTTO Art Historian (-1964)
BENSON, EMANUEL M Art Administrator, Art Dealer (1904-1971)
BENSON, FRANK W Painter, Etcher (-1951)
BENSON, JOHN P Painter (-1947)
BENTON, MARGARET PEAKE Painter (-1975)
BENTON, THOMAS HART Painter, Writer (1889-1975)
BENTZ, JOHN Painter (-1950)
BERHARD, MRS RICHARD J Collector
BERMAN, EUGENE Painter, Designer (1899-1972)
BERNEY, BERTRAM S Painter
BERNINGHAUS, OSCAR E Painter, Designer (-1952)
BERRYMAN, CLIFFORD KENNEDY Cartoonist, Illustrator (-1949)
BETTS, LOUIS Painter (-1961)
BIDDLE, GEORGE Painter, Sculptor (1885-1973)
BIDWELL, WATSON Painter
BIEBEL, FRANKLIN M Museum Director
BIEBER, MARGARETE Art Historian (1880-1978)
BILOTTI, SALVATORE F Sculptor (-1953)
BINNING, BERTRAM CHARLES Painter (1909-1976)
BIRCHANSKY, LEO Painter, Cartoonist (-1949)
BISGARD, JAMES DEWEY Collector, Patron (1898-1975)
BISHOP, RICHARD EVETT Printmaker (1897-1975)
BLACK, ELEANOR SIMMS (MRS ROBERT M) Painter (-1949)
BLACK, WENDELL H Educator (1919-1972)
BLAIR, STREETER Painter (-1966)

BLAKE, LEO B Illustrator (1887-1976)
BLANCH, ARNOLD Painter (-1968)
BLISS, MRS ROBERT WOODS Collector (-1969)
BLOCH, ALBERT Painter (1882-1961)
BLOCH, JULIUS Painter (-1966)
BLODGETT, EDMUND WALTON Painter
BLOEDEL, LAWRENCE HOTCHKISS Collector (1902-1976)
BLOWER, DAVID HARRISON Painter (1901-1976)
BLUMBERG, YULI Painter (-1964)
BOARDMAN, NELL Painter (-1968)
BOBLETER, LOWELL STANLEY Educator, Painter (1902-1973)
BOESCHENSTEIN, BERNICE (MRS C K) Painter (-1951)
BOHNERT, HERBERT Portrait Painter (-1967)
BONNEY, THERESE Photographer (1895-1978)
BONNYCASTLE, MURRAY C Painter
BOORAEM, HENDRIK Painter (-1951)
BORDUAS, PAUL EMILE Painter (-1960)
BORGHI, GUIDO RINALDO Painter (1903-1971)
BORN, WOLFGANG Historian, Writer
BORSTEIN, YETTA Painter (-1968)
BOSWELL, PEYTON, JR Writer, Editor (-1950)
BOTTIS, HUGH P Printmaker (-1964)
BOUCHE, LOUIS Painter (-1969)
BOUCHE, RENE Portrait Painter (-1963)
BOURDELL, PIERRE VAN PARYS Sculptor (-1966)
BOWDOIN, HARRIETTE Painter
BOWER, ALEXANDER Museum Director (-1952)
BOWLES, JANET PAYNE Craftsman (-1948)
BOYD, E Art Administrator, Writer (1903-1974)
BOYD, RUTHERFORD Painter, Designer (-1951)
BOYER, RALPH LUDWIG Painter, Etcher (-1952)
BOYKO, FRED Painter, Teacher (-1951)
BRAIDER, DONALD Art Writer (-1977)
BRANDON, WARREN EUGENE Painter (1916-1977)
BRANNER, ROBERT Art Historian (1927-1973)
BRAZEAU, WENDELL (PHILLIPS) Painter (1910-1974)
BREGER, DAVE (DAVID) Cartoonist (1908-1970)
BRENDEL, OTTO J Art Historian (1901-1973)
BREWER, BESSIE MARSH Etcher, Lithographer (-1952)
BREWINGTON, MARION VERNON Art Historian, Writer (1902-1974)
BRIGGS, AUSTIN Illustrator, Collector
BRIGGS, BERTA N Painter, Writer (1884-1976)
BRINLEY, DANIEL PUTNAM Painter (-1963)
BRITTAIN, MILLER G Painter (-1968)
BRODIE, GANDY Painter, Designer (1924-1975)
BROUILLETTE, GILBERT T Art Dealer, Consultant-Research
BROWN, CARLYLE Painter (-1964)
BROWN, MARGARET Writer (-1952)
BROWN, RICHARD M Portrait Painter (-1964)
BROWNING, G WESLEY Painter (-1951)
BRUNDAGE, AVERY Collector (-1975)
BUCK, RICHARD D Conservator (1903-1977)
BUFF, CONRAD Printmaker, Illustrator (1886-1975)
BULLIET, C J Art Critic (-1952)
BULLOCK, WYNN Photographer (1902-1975)
BURCHFIELD, CHARLES Painter (1893-1967)
BURLIN, PAUL Painter (-1969)
BURLIUK, DAVID Painter (1882-1967)
BURNSIDE, CAMERON Painter, Teacher (-1952)
BUSH, ELLA SHEPART Painter
BUSH, JACK Painter (1909-1977)
CADORIN, ETTORE Sculptor (-1952)
CAHAN, SAMUEL G Artist (-1974)
CALDER, ALEXANDER Sculptor (1898-1976)
CALLERY, MARY Sculptor (1903-1977)
CALVERT, JENNIE C (MRS FINLEY H) Painter
CAMPBELL, EDMUND S Painter, Architect (-1950)
CAMPBELL, ORLAND Portrait Painter (1890-1972)
CAMPBELL, WILLIAM PATRICK Art Historian, Curator (1914-1976)
CANDELL, VICTOR Painter, Educator (1903-1977)
CARLES, ARTHUR B Painter (1882-1952)
CARMACK, PAUL R Cartoonist (1895-1977)
CARRILLO, LILIA Painter (1929-1974)
CASTLE, MRS ALFRED L Art Patron (1886-1970)
CAVALLITO, ALBINO Sculptor (1905-1966)
CHAMBERLAIN, SAMUEL Printmaker, Writer (1895-1975)
CHANDOR, DOUGLAS Portrait Painter (-1953)
CHANIN, ABRAHAM L Lecturer
CHAPELLIER, GEORGE Art Dealer, Collector (1890-1978)
CHAPELLIER, ROBERT Art Dealer (-1974)
CHAPIN, FRANCIS Painter (-1965)
CHAPMAN, CHARLES SHEPARD Painter (-1962)
CHARLES, CLAYTON (HENRY) Sculptor, Educator (1913-)
CHASE, EDWARD Portrait Painter (-1965)
CHASE, GEORGE H Educator, Writer (-1952)
CHASE, JOSEPH CUMMINGS Portrait Painter (-1965)
CHATTERTON, CLARENCE KERR Painter (1880-1973)
CHEFFETZ, ASA Engraver (-1965)
CHERNEY, MARVIN Painter (-1966)
CHIAPELLA, EDWARD EMILE Painter (-1951)
CHOATE, NATHANIEL Sculptor (-1965)
CHOUINARD, MRS NELBERT Educator (-1969)
CHRIST-JANER, ALBERT WILLIAM Painter, Printmaker (1910-1973)
CHRISTOPHER, WILLIAM R Painter (1924-1973)
CHRISTY, HOWARD CHANDLER Painter (-1952)
CHURCH, FREDERIC E Painter
CIAMPAGLIA, CARLO Mural Painter (1891-1975)
CLARK, ALLAN Sculptor (-1950)
CLARK, ALSON SKINNER Painter, Lithographer (-1949)
CLARK, ANTHONY MORRIS Curator, Collector (1923-1976)
CLEAR, CHARLES V Museum Consultant
CLEAVES, MURIEL MATTOCK (MRS H) Illustrator, Painter (-1947)
CLELAND, THOMAS MAITLAND Illustrator (-1964)
COATES, ROBERT M Writer, Art Critic (1897-)
COE, LLOYD Painter, Illustrator (1899-1977)
COE, ROLAND Cartoonist
COFFEY, MABEL Painter, Etcher
COLBY, HOMER WAYLAND Illustrator, Etcher (-1950)
COLEMAN, RALPH P Painter (-1968)
COLETTI, JOSEPH ARTHUR Sculptor, Writer (1898-1973)
COLLINS, KREIGH Illustrator (1908-1974)
COLLINS, ROY H Illustrator (-1949)
CONE, MARVIN Painter (-1964)
CONNAWAY, JAY HALL Painter (1893-1970)
CONNER, JOHN RAMSEY Painter (-1952)
CONSTABLE, WILLIAM GEORGE Art Historian, Writer (1887-1976)
COOK, WALTER WILLIAM SPENCER Educator (-1962)
COOKE, HEREWARD LESTER Art Historian, Painter (1916-1973)
COOKE, KATHLEEN MCKEITH Painter, Sculptor (1908-1978)
COOMARASWAMY, ANANDA K Museum Curator (-1947)
COOPER, FRED G Cartoonist (-1962)
CORBETT, EDWARD M Educator, Painter (1919-1971)
CORBETT, GAIL SHERMAN (MRS HARVEY WILEY CORBETT) Sculptor (-1952)
CORBINO, JOHN Painter (-1964)
CORCOS, LUCILLE Painter, Illustrator (1908-1973)
CORNELL, JOSEPH Sculptor (1903-1972)
COSGRAVE, J O'HARA, II Illustrator (-1968)
COSLA, O K Collector
COSTIGAN, JOHN EDWARD Painter (1888-1972)
COTTON, LILLIAN Painter (-1962)
COURTICE, RODY KENNY Painter (-1973)
COVERT, JOHN Painter (1882-1960)
COWAN, WOODSON MESSICK Cartoonist, Painter (1886-1977)
COWDREY, MARY BARTLETT Art Historian, Art Critic (1910-1974)
COX, J HALLEY Painter, Educator
COZE-DABIJA, PAUL Painter, Writer (1903-1975)
CRAMPTON, ROLLIN Painter (-1970)
CRANDELL, BRADSHAW Painter (-1966)
CRASKE, LEONARD Sculptor, Lithographer (-1950)
CRATZ, BENJIMIN ARTHUR Painter, Cartoonist
CRAVATH, GLENN Cartoonist (-1964)
CRESPI, PACHITA Painter (1900-1971)

CRESSON, MARGARET Sculptor, Writer (1889-1973)
CRISS, FRANCIS H Painter (1901-1973)
CROCKWELL, DOUGLAS Commercial Artist (-1968)
CROUGHTON, AMY H Critic (-1951)
CRUMP, KATHLEEN (WHEELER) Sculptor (1884-1977)
CRUMP, W LESLIE Painter (-1962)
CUMING, BEATRICE Painter (1903-1975)
CUNNINGHAM, BENJAMIN FRAZIER Painter, Educator (1904-1975)
CUNNINGHAM, IMOGEN Photographer (1883-1976)
CUNNINGHAM, MARION Serigrapher, Lithographer
CUPRIEN, FRANK W Painter (-1948)
CURRIER, CYRUS BATES Painter, Designer
CUSUMANO, STEFANO Painter, Educator (1912-1975)
DAHL, FRANCIS W Cartoonist (1907-1973)
DAINGERFIELD, MARJORIE JAY Sculptor (-1977)
DALE, BENJAMIN MORAN Illustrator (-1951)
DANIEL, LEWIS C Painter, Illustrator (-1952)
DARIUS, DENYLL (DENNIS MITCHELL) Painter (1942-1976)
DATUS, JAY Painter, Art Administrator (1914-1974)
DATZ, A MARK Painter
DAUGHERTY, JAMES HENRY Painter, Writer (1898-1974)
DAVEY, RANDALL Painter (-1964)
DAVIDSON, JO Sculptor (-1952)
DAVIS, ESTHER M Sculptor, Painter (1893-1974)
DAVIS, JAMES Abstract Artist (-1974)
DAVIS, PHIL Cartoonist (-1964)
DAVIS, STUART Painter (1894-1964)
DEAN, ERNEST WILFRID Painter
DE BORHEGYI, STEPHEN Museum Director, Writer (1921-1969)
DECKER, JOHN Painter
DE ERDELY, FRANCIS Painter, Educator (1904-1959)
DEFRANCESCO, ITALO I Educator (-1967)
DE FRANCISCI, ANTHONY Sculptor (-1964)
DEHN, ADOLF Graphic Artist (-1968)
DEINES, E HUBERT Engraver (-1967)
DEKNATEL, FREDERICK BROCKWAY Art Historian, Educator (1905-1973)
DEL CASTILLO, MARY VIRGINIA Painter
DE MANCE, HENRI Painter (-1948)
DE MENIL, JOHN Collector (1904-1973)
DEMETRIOS, GEORGE Sculptor (-1974)
DENSLOW, DOROTHEA HENRIETTA Sculptor (1900-1971)
DE PREY, JUAN Painter (-1962)
DERUJINSKY, GLEB W Sculptor, Craftsman (1888-1975)
DESSAR, LOUIS PAUL Painter (-1952)
DE TORE, JOHN E Painter (1902-1975)
DEVREE, HOWARD Critic (-1966)
DIBONA, ANTHONY Sculptor, Lithographer
DICKERSON, WILLIAM JUDSON Painter
DILLER, BURGOYNE Painter (1906-1965)
DIMAN, HOMER Painter (1914-1974)
DIRKS, RUDOLPH Cartoonist (-1968)
DIXON, FRANCIS S Painter (-1967)
DISMUKES, MARY ETHEL Painter (-1952)
DOBBS, ELLA VICTORIA Educator (-1952)
DOBKIN, ALEXANDER Painter (1908-1975)
DOI, ISAMI Painter
DONAHEY, JAMES HARRISON Cartoonist
DONATO, GIUSEPPE Sculptor (-1965)
DOUGLAS, ROBERT LANGTON Critic (-1951)
DOVE, ARTHUR GARFIELD Painter (1880-1946)
DOWLING, ROBERT W Patron
DRABKIN, STELLA Painter, Designer (1906-1976)
DREIER, KATHERINE S Painter, Lecturer (-1952)
DRUMMOND, ARTHUR A Painter, Illustrator (1891-)
DUBLE, LU Sculptor (1896-1970)
DUFFY, EDMUND Cartoonist (-1962)
DU MOND, FRANK V Painter (-1951)
DUNN, ALAN (CANTWELL) Cartoonist, Writer (1900-1974)
DUNN, HARVEY T Illustrator, Painter (-1952)
DUPONT, HENRY F Museum Curator (-1969)
EASBY, DUDLEY T, JR Art Administrator, Art Historian (1905-1973)
EASTMAN, WILLIAM JOSEPH Painter (-1950)
EASTON, FRANK LORENCE Painter
EATON, ALLEN HENDERSHOTT Writer (-1962)
ECKE, GUSTAV Museum Curator (-1971)
EDWARDS, GEORGE WHARTON Painter, Illustrator (-1950)
EDWARDS, ROBERT Painter, Engraver (-1948)
EGAS, CAMILO Educator (-1962)
EGE, OTTO F Educator, Writer (-1951)
EHRMAN, FREDERICK L Collector (1906-1973)
ELDER, ARTHUR JOHN Painter, Etcher
ELDLITZ, DOROTH MEIGS Patron, Photographer (1891-1976)
ELISOFON, ELIOT Painter, Photographer (1911-1973)
ELLERHUSEN, FLORENCE COONEY Painter (-1950)
ELLIS, CARL EUGENE Art Administrator, Instructor (1932-1977)
ELLIS, JOSEPH BAILEY Educator, Sculptor
EMIL, ALLAN D Collector, Patron (1898-)
EMMET, LYDIA FIELD Painter (-1952)
ENGEL, HARRY Painter (1901-1970)
ENGEL, MICHAEL M Art Publicist (-1969)
ENO, JAMES LORNE Painter, Teacher (-1952)
EPSTEIN, ETHEL S Collector
ERLANGER, ELIZABETH N Painter, Lecturer (1901-1975)
ERNST, MAX Painter, Sculptor (1891-1976)
ERSKINE, HAROLD PERRY Sculptor (-1951)
ESHERICK, WHARTON Sculptor, Designer (1887-1970)
EVANS, DONALD Painter (1946-1977)
EVERETT, MARY O (MRS H G) Painter (-1948)
EVERGOOD, PHILIP Painter, Graphic Artist (1901-1973)
EVERINGHAM, MILLARD Painter, Etcher
FABRI, RALPH Painter, Writer (1894-1975)
FAHLSTROM, OYVIND Painter (1928-1976)
FARR, FRED Sculptor (1914-1973)
FARRELL, KATHERINE L Painter, Etcher
FAULKNER, BARRY Painter
FAULKNER, KADY B Painter, Educator (1901-1977)
FAULKNER, RAY N Educator, Writer (1906-1975)
FAUSETT, LYNN Painter (1894-1977)
FAWCETT, ROBERT Illustrator (-1967)
FEELEY, PAUL Painter (1913-1966)
FEIGIN, DOROTHY Painter (-1969)
FENTON, JOHN NATHANIEL Painter, Etcher (1912-1977)
FERNALD, HELEN ELIZABETH Educator (-1964)
FERRARI, FEBO Sculptor
FERREN, JOHN Painter (1905-1970)
FIELDS, MITCHELL Sculptor (-1966)
FIENE, ERNEST Painter (-1965)
FIERO, EMILIE L Sculptor (1889-1974)
FILTZER, HYMAN Sculptor, Restorer (1901-1967)
FINLEY, DAVID EDWARD Art Administrator (1890-1977)
FINLEY, MARY L Painter (-1964)
FISHER, REGINALD Writer (-1966)
FISKE, GERTRUDE Painter (-1961)
FITE, HARVEY Sculptor (1903-1976)
FITZGERALD, J EDWARD Photographer (1923-1977)
FITZSIMMONS, JAMES JOSEPH Painter, Architect (1908-)
FLANAGAN, JOHN Sculptor (-1952)
FLEISCHMANN, ADOLF R Painter (-1969)
FLEISCHMANN, JULIUS Collector
FLIEGEL, LESLIE Painter (-1968)
FLOCH, JOSEPH Painter (1895-1977)
FLORY, ARTHUR L Graphic Artist, Painter (1914-1972)
FOOTE, JOHN, JR Painter (-1968)
FOOTE, WILL HOWE Painter (-1965)
FORBES, EDWARD W Museum Director (-1969)
FORCE, JULIANA R Museum Director (-1948)
FORD, ELEANOR CLAY Patron (1896-1976)
FOSTER, JAMES W, SR Museum Director
FOSTER, KENNETH E Museum Director (-1964)
FOURNIER, ALEXIS JEAN Painter (-1948)
FOX, MILTON S Painter (1904-1971)
FRANKFURTER, DR ALFRED Art Editor (-1965)
FRANKLE, PHILIP Painter (-1968)
FRANKLIN, CLARENCE Collector (-1967)
FRASER, LAURA G Sculptor (-1966)
FRASER, MALCOLM Painter (-1949)

FRAZIER, KENNETH Painter (-1949)
FREED, ERNEST BRADFIELD Printmaker, Painter
FREEMAN, DON Author & Illustrator of Children's Books (1909-1978)
FREEMAN, JANE Portrait Painter (-1963)
FREILICH, MICHAEL L Art Dealer, Collector (1912-1975)
FREY, ERWIN F Sculptor (-1967)
FRIEDLAENDER, WALTER Art Historian (-1966)
FRIEDLANDER, ISAC Engraver (-1968)
FROELICH, PAUL Painter
FROMBERG, GERALD Educator, Filmmaker (1925-)
FUERSTENBURG, PAUL W Commercial Artist (-1953)
FULLER, RICHARD EUGENE Museum Director (1897-1976)
FULTON, CYRUS JAMES Painter (-1949)
GABO, NAUM Sculptor (1890-1977)
GAILIS, JANIS Painter (1909-1975)
GALLATIN, ALBERT EUGENE Painter (1882-1952)
GALOS, BEN Painter (-1963)
GALVAN, JESUS GUERRERO Painter
GANNAM, JOHN Painter (-1965)
GARBATY, EUGENE L Collector (-1966)
GARTH, JOHN Painter (1894-1971)
GATCH, LEE Painter (-1968)
GAYNE, CLIFTON ALEXANDER, JR Educator (1912-1971)
GEARHART, MAY Etcher
GEE, YUN Painter (-1963)
GEESEY, TITUS CORNELIUS Collector, Patron (1893-1969)
GEIGER, ELIZABETH DE CHAMISSO Sculptor
GERTH, RUTH Illustrator (-1952)
GETTY, J PAUL Collector, Writer (1892-1976)
GIAMBRUNI, TIO Sculptor (1925-1971)
GIBBERD, ERIC WATERS Painter (1897-1972)
GILCHRIST, AGNES ADDISON Art & Architectural Historian (1907-1976)
GILL, FREDERICK JAMES Painter, Instructor (1906-1974)
GILRIN, THEODORE H Painter (-1967)
GLARNER, FRITZ Painter (1899-1972)
GLINES, ELLEN (MRS WALTER A) Painter (-1951)
GLINSKY, VINCENT Sculptor, Educator (1895-1975)
GOLDBERG, ELIAS Painter (1887-1978)
GOLDIN, AMY Art Critic (1926-1978)
GOLDSMITH, MORTON RALPH Collector, Patron (1882-1971)
GOLDWATER, ROBERT Art Historian (1907-1973)
GORHAM, SIDNEY Painter (-1947)
GOSS, JOHN Illustrator
GOTTLIEB, ADOLPH Painter (1903-1974)
GRAHAM, JOHN D Painter (1881-1961)
GRANT, GORDON HOPE Etcher (-1962)
GRAVES, MAITLAND Writer, Painter (1902-)
GRAY, HAROLD Cartoonist (-1968)
GRAY, JABEZ Painter (-1950)
GRAY, WELLINGTON BURBANK Educator, Designer (1919-1977)
GRAYSON, CLIFFORD PREVOST Painter (-1951)
GREACEN, EDMUND Painter (-1949)
GREATHOUSE, WALSER S Museum Director (-1966)
GRECO, ROBERT Painter (-1965)
GREEN, BERNARD Painter (-1951)
GREENE, ELMER WESTLEY Painter (-1964)
GREENE, J BARRY Painter (-1966)
GREENE, VERNON VAN ATTA Cartoonist (-1965)
GREEN-FIELD, ALBERT Art Publicist
GREENLEAF, RAY Illustrator (-1950)
GREENWOOD, MARION Painter, Lithographer (1909-1970)
GREGORY, WAYLANDE Sculptor, Designer (1905-1971)
GRIER, HARRY DOBSON MILLER Museum Director (1914-1972)
GRIESSLER, FRANZ ANTON Painter (1897-1974)
GRIGAUT, PAUL L Museum Curator (-1969)
GRIMES, FRANCES Sculptor (-1963)
GRINAGER, ALEXANDER Painter (-1949)
GRODENSKY, SAMUEL Painter (1894-1974)
GROPPER, WILLIAM Painter, Lithographer (1897-)
GROSZ, GEORGE Painter (1893-1959)
GROTELL, MAIJA Ceramist, Educator (1899-1973)
GROVES, HANNAH CUTIER Painter, Etcher (-1952)
GRUBB, PAT PINCOMBE Painter, Writer (1922-1977)
GRUENTHER, SUE CORY (MRS RUDOLPH) Painter (-1948)
GRUGER, FREDERICK Illustrator (-1953)
GRUMMANN, PAUL H Museum Director (-1950)
GUGGENHEIM, HARRY FRANK Collector, Publisher, Writer (1890-1971)
GUGGENHEIMER, RICHARD HENRY Painter, Writer (1906-1977)
GUSTAVSON, LEALAND Illustrator (-1966)
GUTE, HERBERT JACOB Painter, Educator (1907-1977)
HADER, ELMER (STANLEY) Illustrator, Writer (1889-1973)
HAGGIN, BEN ALI Painter, Designer (-1951)
HALE, LILLIAN WESTCOTT Painter (-1963)
HAMMER, VICTOR KARL Painter (-1967)
HAMPTON, BILL Painter (1925-1977)
HAND, MOLLY WILLIAMS Teacher, Painter (-1951)
HANDFORTH, THOMAS Lithographer (-1948)
HANLEY, T EDWARD Collector (-1969)
HANNA, THOMAS KING Painter (-1951)
HARE, MICHAEL MEREDITH Scholar (-1968)
HARER, FREDERICK W Painter, Sculptor (-1949)
HARPER, GEORGE COBURN Etcher (-1962)
HARRIS, MARGIE COLEMAN Painter
HARSANYI, CHARLES Painter (1905-1973)
HART, JOHN FRANCIS Cartoonist, Engraver
HARTL, LEON Painter (1889-)
HARTMANN, GEORG THEO Painter, Etcher (1894-1976)
HARTWELL, GEORGE KENNETH Lithographer (-1949)
HARVEY, JAMES V Painter (-1965)
HASKELL, WILLIAM H Educator (-1952)
HASWELL, ERNEST BRUCE Sculptor (1889-1965)
HATHAWAY, CALVIN S Curator (-1974)
HATHAWAY, LOVERING Painter (-1949)
HATLO, JAMES Cartoonist (-1963)
HAUSCHKA, CAROLA SPAETH Painter (-1948)
HAUSMANN, MARIANNE PISKO Painter
HAVENS, MURRY P Designer
HAWLEY, MARGARET FOOTE Portrait Painter (-1963)
HAYES, WILLIAM CHRISTOPHER Museum Curator (-1963)
HECHT, ZOLTAN Painter (-1968)
HEERAMANECK, NASILI M Collector, Patron, Art Dealer (1902-1971)
HEINTZELMAN, ARTHUR W Etcher (-1965)
HELLER, MAXWELL L Painter (-1963)
HELM, JOHN F, JR Educator, Painter (1900-1972)
HELWIG, ARTHUR LOUIS Painter, Instructor (-1976)
HENRICKSEN, RALF CHRISTIAN Educator, Painter (1907-1975)
HERING, HARRY Painter (-1967)
HERING, HENRY Sculptor (-1949)
HERRINGTON, ARTHUR W Collector, Patron
HERRINGTON, NELL RAY Collector, Patron
HERTER, ALBERT Painter (-1950)
HERVES, MADELINE Painter (-1969)
HESSE, EVA Sculptor (1936-1972)
HEUERMANN, MAGDA Painter
HEYL, BERNARD CHAPMAN Scholar
HIBBARD, ALDRO THOMPSON Painter (1886-1972)
HIGGINS, VICTOR Painter (-1949)
HILER, HILAIRE Painter (-1966)
HILL, GEORGE SNOW Painter (-1969)
HILL, HOMER Illustrator
HILL, (JAMES) JEROME Painter (1905-)
HILLMAN, ALEX L Collector (-1968)
HILLS, LAURA COOMBS Painter (-1952)
HINTON, CHARLES LOUIS Painter (-1950)
HIRSCH, STEFAN Educator (-1964)
HOCKADAY, HUGH Painter (-1968)
HOEHN, HARRY Painter, Printmaker (1918-1974)
HOFFMAN, ARNOLD Painter (-1966)
HOFFMAN, MALVINA Sculptor (-1966)
HOFMANN, HANS Painter, Educator (1880-1966)
HOLCOMB, ALICE (MCCAFFERY) Painter (1906-1977)

HOLCOMBE, BLANCHE KEATON Painter, Educator (1912-)
HOLGATE, EDWIN HEADLEY Painter (1892-1977)
HOLLAND, JANICE Illustrator (-1962)
HOLLOWAY, H MAXSON Museum Director (-1966)
HOLMGREN, R JOHN Illustrator (-1963)
HOLTY, CARL ROBERT Painter, Writer (1900-1973)
HOOD, GEORGE W Painter (-1949)
HOOVER, MARIE LOUISE (ROCHON) Artist (1895-1976)
HOPKINSON, CHARLES Painter (-1962)
HOPPER, EDWARD Painter (1882-1967)
HOPPER, JO N Painter (-1968)
HORD, DONAL Sculptor (-1966)
HORNYANSKY, NICHOLAS Etcher (1896-1965)
HOVANNES, JOHN Painter (1900-1973)
HOWLAND, EDITH Sculptor (-1949)
HOWLAND, GARTH Educator, Painter (-1950)
HUBBARD, CHARLES D Painter (-1951)
HUBBELL, HENRY SALEM Painter (-1949)
HUMPHREY, JACK WELDON Painter (-1967)
HUNT, WAYNE WOLF ROBE (KEWA-TSE SHE) Silversmith, Painter (1905-1977)
HUNTINGTON, A MONTGOMERY Designer (-1967)
HUNTINGTON, ANNA V HYATT Sculptor (-1973)
HUNTLEY, VICTORIA HUTSON Lithographer (1900-1971)
HURLEY, EDWARD TIMOTHY Etcher, Painter (-1950)
HUTCHISON, MARY ELIZABETH Painter (1906-1970)
HUTTON, HUGH MCMILLEN Cartoonist (1897-1976)
INGLE, TOM Painter, Lecturer (1920-1973)
IPSEN, ERNEST L Portrait Painter (-1951)
IRVIN, REA Painter (1881-1972)
ITTLESON, HENRY, JR Collector (1900-1973)
ISAACS, BETTY LEWIS Sculptor (1894-1971)
IVES, NORMAN S Painter, Printmaker, Graphic Designer (1924-1978)
JACK, RICHARD Painter (-1952)
JACKSON, ALEXANDER YOUNG Painter (1882-1974)
JACKSON, HENRY ALDEN Textile Designer (-1952)
JACKSON, JOHN EDWIN Painter, Designer
JACKSON, MARTHA Gallery Director (-1969)
JAFFE, WILLIAM B Collector (-1972)
JANICKI, HAZEL (MRS WILLIAM SCHOCK) Painter, Instructor (1918-1976)
JANSSEN, HANS Educator, Museum Curator
JARRELL, RANDALL Critic, Poet (-1965)
JECT-KEY, DAVID Painter
JEFFERYS, CHARLES WILLIAM Illustrator (-1951)
JENKINS, BURRIS Cartoonist (-1966)
JENKINS, PAUL RIPLEY Sculptor, Painter (1940-1974)
JENNEWEIN, C PAUL Sculptor (1890-1978)
JOHANSEN, JOHN C Portrait Painter
JOHN, GRACE SPAULDING Painter, Writer (1890-1972)
JOHNSON, BEN Painter (1902-1967)
JOHNSON, BRUCE Museum Director (1949-1976)
JOHNSON, CONTENT Portrait Painter (-1949)
JOHNSON, CROCKETT Painter, Writer (1906-1976)
JONES, JOSEPH JOHN (JOE) Painter (-1963)
JONES, MURRAY Painter
JONSON, JON Sculptor (-1947)
JORDAN, LENA E Painter
JORN, ASGER Painter, Writer (1914-1973)
JUDSON, ALICE Painter (-1948)
JUNGWIRTH, LEONARD D Sculptor (-1964)
JUNKIN, MARION MONTAGUE Painter, Educator (1905-1977)
KACHERGIS, GEORGE JOSEPH Painter, Educator (1917-1974)
KANAGA, CONSEULO Photographer (1894-1978)
KANTACK, WALTER W Industrial Artist (-1953)
KANTOR, MORRIS Painter (1896-1974)
KARFIOL, BERNARD Painter (-1952)
KARP, LEON Painter (-1951)
KATZ, (ALEXANDER) RAYMOND Painter (-1974)
KATZ, SIDNEY L Architect (1915-1978)
KATZENBACH, WILLIAM E Designer, Lecturer (1904-1975)
KATZENELLENBOGEN, ADOLF Educator (-1964)
KATZENSTEIN, IRVING Painter
KATZMANN, HERBERT Painter
KAYN, HILDE Painter (-1950)
KECK, CHARLES Sculptor (-1951)
KEFAUVER, NANCY Advisor on Fine Arts (-1967)
KELLER, HENRY G Painter, Etcher (-1949)
KENDERDINE, AUGUSTUS FREDERICK Painter (-1947)
KENNEDY, JANET ROBSON Painter, Illustrator (1902-1974)
KENT, FRANK WARD Painter (1912-1977)
KENT, NORMAN Engraver, Book Designer (1903-1972)
KENT, ROCKWELL Painter (1882-1971)
KERKAM, EARL Painter (-1965)
KERR, E COE Art Dealer (1914-1973)
KEYES, BERNARD M Painter (1898-1973)
KHOURI, ALFRED Painter (-1962)
KIESLER, FREDERICK J Architect (-1966)
KILGORE, RUPERT Educator (1910-1971)
KILHAM, WALTER H Painter, Architect (-1948)
KILPATRICK, ADA AURILLA Painter (-1951)
KILPATRICK, ELLEN PERKINS Painter (-1951)
KIMAK, GEORGE Painter (1921-1972)
KING, FRANK Cartoonist (-1969)
KING, HAMILTON Illustrator (-1952)
KING, MABEL DEBRA Painter (-1950)
KING, PAUL Painter (-1947)
KINGMAN, EUGENE Painter, Art Administrator (1909-1975)
KIRK, FRANK C Painter (-1963)
KIRKBRIDE, EARLE R Painter (-1968)
KLETT, WALTER CHARLES Illustrator (-1966)
KLINE, FRANZ Painter (1910-1962)
KLINKER, ORPHA Etcher (-1964)
KNATHS, (OTTO) KARL Painter (1891-1971)
KNIGHT, TACK (BENJAMIN THACKSTON) Cartoonist (1895-1976)
KOCH, BERTHA COUCH Painter (1899-1975)
KOHLER, ROSE Sculptor, Painter (-1947)
KOHLHEPP, DOROTHY IRENE Painter (-1964)
KOHN, GABRIEL Sculptor (1910-1975)
KOOPMAN, JOHN R Painter (-1949)
KOPMAN, BENJAMIN Painter (-1965)
KOPPE, RICHARD Painter, Educator (1916-)
KOSA, EMIL J, JR Painter (-1968)
KREINDLER, DORIS BARSKY Painter, Lithographer (1901-1974)
KREIS, HENRY Sculptor (-1963)
KROLL, LEON Painter, Lithographer (1884-1974)
KRONBERG, LOUIS Painter
KUHLER, OTTO AUGUST Etcher, Painter (1894-1977)
KUHN, WALT Painter (-1949)
KUNIYOSHI, YASUO Painter (1893-1953)
KUNTZ, ROGER EDWARD Painter, Sculptor (1926-1975)
KURZ, GERTRUDE ALICE Craftsman (-1951)
LAGATTA, JOHN Illustrator (-1976)
LAKE, FREDERIC Art Dealer
LAMONT, FRANCES Sculptor (-1975)
LANDACRE, PAUL Engraver (-1963)
LANGE, DOROTHEA Photographer (-1965)
LANGLAIS, BERNARD Sculptor, Painter (1921-1977)
LANGSNER, JULES Art Writer (-1967)
LANGSTON, MILDRED J Art Dealer, Collector (1902-1976)
LARKIN, OLIVER Educator (1896-1970)
LARKIN, WILLIAM Painter, Printmaker (1902-1969)
LASSEN, BEN Painter (-1968)
LAUGHLIN, ALICE D Printer (-1952)
LAUGHLIN, THOMAS Painter, Publisher (-1965)
LAUNOIS, JOHN RENE Photographer
LAURENT, ROBERT Sculptor, Collector (1890-1970)
LAURITZ, PAUL Painter (1889-1975)
LAVANOUX, MAURICE Art Editor (-1974)
LAWRENCE, HELEN HUMPHREYS Painter
LAWRIE, LEE Sculptor (-1963)
LAYTON, GLORIA (MRS HARRY GEWISS) Painter (1914-)
LEAF, MUNRO Illustrator of Children's Books (1906-1977)
LEAKE, GERALD Painter (-1975)
LEBRUN, RICO (FEDERICO) Painter (-1964)
LEDGERWOOD, ELLA RAY Painter (-1951)
LEE, GEORGE J Art Administrator, Photographer (1919-1976)

LEECH, HILTON Painter, Instructor (-1969)
LEHMAN, ROBERT Collector (-1969)
LEIGHTON, A C Painter (-1965)
LEITH-ROSS, HARRY Painter
LENSKI, LOIS Writer, Illustrator (1893-)
LENSON, MICHAEL Painter (1903-1971)
LENTINE, JOHN Painter
LEONID (LEONID BERMAN) Painter (1896-1976)
LE PRINCE, GABRIELLA Ceramist (-1953)
LEVI, CARLO Painter, Writer
LEVY, BEATRICE S Painter (1892-1974)
LEVY, FLORENCE N Writer, Editor (-1947)
LEWITIN, LANDES Painter (-1966)
LEYENDECKER, JOSEPH C Painter (-1951)
LIBERTE, JEAN Painter (-1965)
LICHTENSTEIN, SARA Art Historian (1929-)
LIEBES, DOROTHY (MRS RELMAN MORIN) Textile Designer (1899-1972)
LILIENFIELD, KARL Scholar (-1966)
LINTOTT, EDWARD BARNARD Painter (-1951)
LIPCHITZ, JACQUES Sculptor (1891-1973)
LIPPERT, LEON Painter
LISTON, MRS FLORENCE CARY Portraitist (-1964)
LITAKER, THOMAS (FRANKLIN) Painter (1906-1976)
LOCKWOOD, WARD Painter (-1963)
LOGAN, MAURICE Painter, Illustrator (1886-1977)
LOGGIE, HELEN A Printmaker, Painter (-1976)
LONG, STANLEY M Painter (1892-1972)
LONGACRE, LYDIA E Miniature Painter (-1951)
LONGACRE, MARGARET GRUEN Printmaker, Lecturer (1910-1976)
LORIMER, AMY MCCLELLAN Painter
LOSCH, TILLY Painter (1904-1975)
LOUIS, MORRIS Painter (1912-1963)
LOVET-LORSKI, BORIS Sculptor (1894-1973)
LOW, SANFORD Museum Director, Painter (-1964)
LOWE, EMILY Painter (-1966)
LOZOWICK, LOUIS Painter, Printmaker (1892-1973)
LUKE, ALEXANDRA Painter (1901-)
LUNDBORG, FLORENCE Painter (-1949)
LUNDIE, EDWIN HUGH Architect (1886-1972)
LYMAN, JOHN Painter (-1967)
LYTTON, BART Collector (-1969)
MACAGY, DOUGLAS GUERNSEY Art Administrator
MACAGY, JERMAYNE Educator
MACDONALD, HERBERT Painter (1898-1972)
MACDONALD-WRIGHT, STANTON Painter (1890-1973)
MACGILVARY, NORWOOD Painter, Educator
MACHLIN, SHELDON M Sculptor, Printmaker (1918-1975)
MACKEOWN, IDA C Portrait Painter (-1952)
MACLANE, JEAN Painter (-1964)
MACLEOD, PEGI NICHOL Painter, Teacher
MAGAFAN, JENNE Painter, Lithographer
MALDARELLI, ORONZIO Sculptor (-1963)
MALRAUX, ANDRE Writer (1901-1976)
MANN, MARGERY (MARGERY MANN VASEY) Photographer, Curator (1919-1977)
MAN RAY Artists, Photographer (1890-1976)
MANSHIP, PAUL Sculptor (1885-1966)
MARANS, MOISSAYE Sculptor, Instructor (1902-1977)
MARANTZ, IRVING Painter (1912-1972)
MARCUS, EDWARD S Collector (1910-1977)
MARGULES, DEHIRSH Painter (-1965)
MARIN, JOHN Painter (1870-1953)
MARKUS, HENRY A Collector
MARSH, REGINALD Painter (1898-1954)
MARYAN, MARYAN S Painter (1927-1977)
MASON, ALICE TRUMBULL Painter (1904-1971)
MASON, ROY MARTELL Painter (1886-1972)
MAST, GERALD Painter (1908-1971)
MATTERN, KARL Painter (-1969)
MATTISON, DONALD MANGUS Painter (1905-1975)
MATTSON, HENRY (ELIS) Painter (1887-1971)
MATULKA, JAN Painter (1890-1972)
MAUNSBACH, GEORGE ERIC Painter
MAXON, JOHN Museum Director (1916-1977)
MCBRIDE, HENRY Critic (-1962)
MCCARTHY, JUSTIN Painter (1892-)
MCCAUSLAND, ELIZABETH Writer (-1965)
MCCURRY, HARR ORR Museum Director (-1964)
MCFEE, HENRY LEE Painter (-1953)
MCGILL, HAROLD A Cartoonist (-1952)
MCGLYNN, THOMAS Sculptor (1906-)
MCHUGH, JAMES FRANCIS Collector (-1968)
MCKEE, FRANCES BARRETT Illustrator (1909-1975)
MCKENDRY, JOHN Curator
MCKENZIE, VINNORMA SHAW Painter (-1952)
MCLAUGHLIN, DONAL Architect (1875-1978)
MCMAHON, A PHILIP Writer, Educator
MCMEIN, NEYSA Painter, Designer
MCMULLEN, E ORMOND Painter
MCMURTRIE, EDITH Painter
MCNETT, WILLIAM BROWN Illustrator (-1968)
MCNULTY, WILLIAM CHARLES Painter (-1963)
MCPHARLIN, PAUL Writer, Illustrator (-1948)
MEANS, ELLIOTT Painter
MECHLIN, LEILA Critic, Writer
MECKLEM, AUSTIN MERRILL Painter (-1951)
MEISS, MILLARD Art Historian, Writer (1904-1975)
MEISSNER, LEO J Painter, Engraver (1895-1977)
MELCARTH, EDWARD Painter, Sculptor
MELVIN, GRACE WILSON Painter, Illustrator (-1977)
MENCONI, RALPH JOSEPH Sculptor (1915-1972)
MERYMAN, HOPE Artist, Illustrator (-1975)
MESS, GEORGE JO Painter (-1962)
MEYERS, ROBERT WILLIAM Illustrator (1919-1970)
MIELZINER, JO Designer, Lecturer (1901-1976)
MIES VAN DER ROHE, LUDWIG Architect (1886-1969)
MILHOUS, KATHERINE Illustrator, Writer (1894-1977)
MILLER, BARSE Painter, Educator (1924-1973)
MILLER, KENNETH HAYES Painter, Teacher (1876-1952)
MILLMAN, EDWARD Painter (1907-1964)
MINER, DOROTHY EUGENIA Museum Curator, Art Historian (1904-1973)
MINNEGERODE, CUTHBERT POWELL Museum Director (-1951)
MITCHELL, BRUCE HANDISIDE Painter (-1963)
MITCHELL, GLEN Painter (1894-1972)
MITCHELL, THOMAS W Painter
MOCHI, UGO Sculptor (1894-1977)
MOCHON, DONALD Graphic Artists, Educator (1916-)
MOE, HENRY ALLEN Art Administrator (1894-1975)
MOFFETT, ROSS E Painter
MOLARSKY, MAURICE Painter, Teacher (-1950)
MONTANA, BOB Cartoonist (1920-1975)
MONTGOMERY, CHARLES FRANKLIN Art Administrator, Educator (1910-1978)
MOON, CARL Illustrator (-1948)
MORDVINOFF, NICOLAS, Painter, Illustrator (1911-1973)
MORE, HERMON Museum Director (-1968)
MORGAN, WALLACE Illustrator (-1948)
MORISSET, GERARD Educator (1898-1970)
MORRIS, DUDLEY Painter (-1966)
MORRIS, GEORGE L K Painter, Sculptor (1905-1975)
MORSE, GLENN TILLEY Painter (-1950)
MORTON, REE Sculptor, Environmental Artist, Painter (1936-1977)
MOSBY, WILLIAM HARRY Painter (-1964)
MOSE, CARL C Sculptor, Lecturer (-1973)
MOSELSIO, SIMON Sculptor
MOSER, FRANK H Painter (-1964)
MOSES, FORREST KING Painter (1893-1974)
MOTT-SMITH, MAY Medalist, Painter (-1952)
MUIR, WILLIAM HORACE Sculptor (-1965)
MULLER, JAN Painter (1922-1958)
MUNDY, ETHEL FRANCES Sculptor
MUNDY, LOUISE EASTERDAY Painter (-1952)
MUNOWITZ, KEN Illustrator of Children's Books (1936-1978)
MUNRO, THOMAS Art Scholar (1897-1974)
MURCH, WALTER Painter (-1967)
MURPHY, ROWLEY WALTER Painter, Designer (1891-1975)
MUSGROVE, A J Museum Director

MYRICK, KATHERINE S Painter
NAGEL, STINA Painter (-1969)
NAHA, RAYMOND Painter (-1975)
NAILOR, GERALD LLOYDE Painter, Illustrator (-1952)
NAKAMIZO, FUJI Painter
NASON, GERTRUDE Painter
NASON, THOMAS W Engraver (1889-1971)
NATZLER, GERTRUD Ceramic Craftsman (-1971)
NEBEL, BERTHOLD Sculptor
NEFF, JOSEPH Collector (-1969)
NEILSON, KATHARINE B Art Historian (1902-1977)
NEILSON, RAYMOND P R Painter (-1964)
NELSON, GEORGE LAURENCE Painter (1887-1978)
NEMEROV, DAVID Painter (-1963)
NESBERT, VINCENT Miniature Painter (-1976)
NESEMANN, ENNO Painter (-1949)
NEUMEYER, ALFRED Art Historian (1901-1973)
NEUTRA, RICHARD Architect (1892-1970)
NEWBERRY, CLARE TURLAY Illustrator (1903-1970)
NEWBERRY, JOHN S Museum Curator (-1964)
NEWMAN, BARNETT Painter (1905-1970)
NICHOLS, HOBART Painter (-1962)
NICHOLS, SPENCER B Painter (-1950)
NITZSCHE, ELSA KOENIG Portrait Painter (-1952)
NODEL, SOL Illuminator, Designer (1912-1976)
NORBURY, LOUISE H Painter (-1952)
NOYES, ELIOT Architect, Designer (1910-1977)
NUGENT, ARTHUR WILLIAM Cartoonist, Illustrator (1891-1975)
OCHIKUBO, TETSUO Painter, Designer (1923-1975)
OCHTMAN, DOROTHY (MRS W A DEL MAR) Painter (1892-1971)
OERI, GEORGINE Critic (-1968)
OGDEN, RALPH E Collector, Patron (-1974)
OGG, OSCAR Designer, Writer (1908-1971)
O'HARA, ELIOT Painter (1890-1969)
OLMER, HENRY Sculptor (-1950)
OLSEN, HERB Painter, Writer (1905-1973)
OPDYCKE, LEONARD Educator (1895-1977)
ORME, LYDIA GARDNER Painter (-1963)
OZENFANT, AMEDEE Painter (-1966)
PACH, MAGDA F Painter (-1950)
PAGES, JEAN Illustrator, Muralist (1907-1977)
PAGET-FREDERICKS, J ROUS-MARTEN Illustrator (-1963)
PAINE, ROBERT T Museum Curator (-1965)
PALMER, ALLEN INGELS Painter (-1950)
PAPASHVILY, GEORGE Sculptor, Writer (1898-1978)
PARDI, JUSTIN A Painter (-1951)
PARKER, THOMAS Former Art Federation Director (-1967)
PARRISH, MAXFIELD Painter (-1966)
PARSONS, ERNESTINE Painter (-1967)
PARSONS, LLOYD HOLMAN Painter (-1968)
PATRICK, RANSOM R Educator (1906-1971)
PAUL, BORIS DUPONT Painter (1901-)
PEARLMAN, HENRY Collector (1895-1974)
PEARSON, JOSEPH T, JR Painter (-1951)
PECK, EDWARD Director University Galleries (-1970)
PEETS, ORVILLE Painter (-1968)
PEIRCE, WALDO Painter (1884-)
PENA, TONITA Painter
PEPPER, CHARLES HOVEY Painter (-1950)
PEREIRA, I RICE Painter (1901-1971)
PERKINS, MABLE H Collector (1880-1974)
PERKINS, PHILIP R Painter (-1968)
PERKINS-RIPLEY, LUCY FAIRFIELD Painter
PERLS, FRANK (RICHARD) Art Dealer, Collector (1910-1975)
PERRETT, GALEN J Painter (-1949)
PETERS, FRANCIS C Painter (1902-1977)
PETERSON, JANE Painter
PETERSON, JOHN P Craftsman (-1949)
PETREMONT, CLARICE M Painter (-1949)
PEYTON, BERTHA MENZLER Painter
PFISTER, JEAN JACQUES Painter (-1949)
PHILBRICK, OTIS Painter, Printmaker (1888-1973)
PHILLIPS, DOROTHY W Art Administrator, Writer (1906-1977)
PHILLIPS, DUNCAN Museum Director
PHILLIPS, J CAMPBELL Painter (-1949)
PICCIRILLI, FURIO Sculptor (-1949)
PIERCE, GARY Painter (-1969)
PITTMAN, HOBSON Painter (1900-1972)
PITZ, HENRY CLARENCE Painter, Writer (1895-1976)
PLATE, WALTER Painter, Educator (1925-1972)
PLATT, ELEANOR Sculptor
PLUNGUIAN, GINA Painter (-1962)
POLKES, ALAN H Collector, Patron (1931-)
POLLACK, LOUIS Art Dealer (1921-1970)
POLLACK, VIRGINIA MORRIS Sculptor
POLLOCK, JACKSON Painter (1912-1956)
POLLOCK, JAMES ARLIN Painter (-1949)
POND, DANA Painter (-1962)
POND, WILLI BAZE (MRS CHARLES E) Painter (-1947)
POOLE, EARL LINCOLN Illustrator, Art Administrator (1891-1972)
POOR, HENRY VARNUM Painter (1888-1970)
PORAY, STAN P Painter, Designer (-1948)
PORTER, FAIRFIELD Painter, Lecturer (1907-1975)
PORTNOFF, ALEXANDER Sculptor (-1949)
POTTER, WILLIAM J Painter (-1964)
POUSETTE-DART, NATHANIEL Painter (-1965)
POWELL, DOANE Craftsman (-1951)
POWELL, LYDIA BOND Art Administrator, Consultant (1892-1978)
POWERS, MARILYN Painter (1925-1976)
PRATT, DUDLEY Sculptor (1897-1975)
PRATT, ELIZABETH SOUTHWICK Painter (-1964)
PRENDERGAST, CHARLES E Painter (-1948)
PRESSER, JOSEF Painter (-1967)
PREZZI, WILMA M Painter
PRICE, CHESTER B Illustrator (-1962)
PRICE, CLAYTON S Painter (1874-1950)
PRICE, FREDERIC NEWLIN Museum Director (-1963)
PRICE, MARGARET E Illustrator, Painter
PRICE, NORMAN MILLS Illustrator (-1951)
PRIEST, ALAN Museum Curator (-1968)
PRINCE, WILLIAM MEADE Illustrator (-1951)
PRIOR, HARRIS KING Art Administrator, Educator (1911-1975)
PROCTOR, A PHIMISTER Sculptor (-1950)
PUSHMAN, HOVSEP Painter (-1966)
PUTNAM, BRENDA Sculptor (-1975)
QUANDT, RUSSELL JEROME Museum Art Restorer (1919-1970)
QUATTROCCHI, EDMONDO Sculptor (-1966)
QUINN, ROBERT HAYES Illustrator (-1962)
QUIRK, FRANCIS JOSEPH Painter, Museum Director (1907-1974)
QUIRT, WALTER Painter, Educator (1902-1968)
QUISTGAARD, JOHAN WALDEMAR DE REHLING Portrait Painter (-1962)
RAAB, ADA DENNETT (MRS S V) Painter (-1950)
RAINVILLE, PAUL Museum Director (-1952)
RANEY, SUZANNE BRYANT Printmaker (-1967)
RATTNER, ABRAHAM Painter (1895-1978)
RAVENSCROFT, ELLEN Painter
RAVESON, SHERMAN HAROLD Painter, Writer (-1974)
RAY, RUTH (MRS JOHN REGINALD GRAHAM) Painter (1919-1977)
READ, HELEN APPLETON Art Historian, Art Critic (1887-1974)
REBAY, HILLA Painter (-1967)
REDER, BERNARD Sculptor (-1963)
REDFIELD, EDWARD W Painter (-1965)
REEVES, J MASON Painter (1898-1973)
REGENSBURG, SOPHY P Painter, Collector (1885-1974)
REGESTER, CHARLOTTE Painter
REID, GEORGE AGNEW Painter (-1947)
REINDEL, WILLIAM GEORGE Painter (-1948)
REINHARDT, AD F Painter (1913-1967)
REISE, BARBARA Art Critic (-1978)
RENIER, JOSEPH EMILE Sculptor (-1966)
REYNARD, GRANT T Painter (-1967)

RIBA, PAUL F Painter (1912-1977)
RICH, DANIEL CATTON Art Administrator, Lecturer (1904-1976)
RICHTER, GISELA MARIE AUGUSTA Museum Curator, Writer (1882-1972)
RICHTER, HANS Artist, Filmmaker (1888-1976)
RIDABOCK, RAY (BUDD) Painter, Instructor (1904-1970)
RIGGS, ROBERT Lithographer (1896-1970)
RINGIUS, CARL Painter (-1950)
RIPLEY, ALDEN LASSELL Painter (-1969)
RIPLEY, ROBERT Illustrator
RITMAN, LOUIS Painter (-1963)
RITSCHEL, WILLIAM Painter (-1949)
RIU, VICTOR Sculptor (1887-1974)
ROBERTS, MORTON Painter (-1964)
ROBERTSON, SARAH M Painter (-1948)
ROBINSON, BOARDMAN Painter, Teacher (-1952)
ROBUS, HUGO Sculptor (-1964)
ROCKEFELLER, WINTHROP Collector
ROGERS, MEYRIC REYNOLD Museum Curator (1893-1972)
ROHLAND, PAUL Painter, Serigrapher
ROJANKOVSKY, FEODOR STEPANOVICH Illustrator (1891-1970)
ROMANS, CHARLES JOHN Painter (1891-1973)
RONNEBECK, ARNOLD H Sculptor (-1947)
ROOD, JOHN Sculptor, Painter (1906-1974)
ROOT, MRS EDWARD W Collector
RORIMER, JAMES J Museum Director
ROSE, BILLY Collector (-1966)
ROSE, HANNA TOBY Art Administrator (1909-1976)
ROSE, IVER Painter (1899-1972)
ROSELAND, HARRY HERMAN Painter (-1950)
ROSEN, CHARLES Painter, Illustrator (-1950)
ROSENBERG, SAEMY Art Dealer
ROSENBERG, SAMUEL Painter (1896-1972)
ROSENTHAL, DAVID Painter, Etcher (-1949)
ROSENTHAL, DORIS Painter, Lithographer
ROSIN, HARRY Sculptor, Educator (-1973)
ROSS, ALVIN Painter, Educator (1920-1975)
ROSS, C CHANDLER Portrait Painter (-1952)
ROSS, LOUIS Mural Painter (-1963)
ROTHKO, MARK Painter (1903-1970)
ROTHSCHILD, HERBERT Art Collector (1892-1976)
ROTIER, PETER Painter
ROUSSEAU, THEODORE, JR Museum Curator (1912-1974)
ROWAN, EDWARD BEATTY Painter (-1946)
ROWE, CORINNE Painter (-1965)
ROWE, GUY Painter (-1969)
ROWLAND, BENJAMIN, JR Educator (1904-1972)
RUBEL, C ADRIAN Collector (1904-1978)
RUSSELL, BRUCE ALEXANDER Cartoonist (-1963)
RUSSELL, HELEN CROCKER Collector
RUSSELL, MORGAN Painter (1886-1953)
RUSSOLI, FRANCO Art Critic (1923-1977)
RYDER, CHAUNCEY FOSTER Painter (-1949)
RYLAND, ROBERT KNIGHT Painter (-1951)
SAARINEN, EERO Architect, Designer (1910-1961)
SACHS, JAMES H Collector, Patron (1907-1971)
SACHS, PAUL J Educator (-1965)
SAGE, KAY (TANGUY) Painter
SAHLER, HELEN GERTRUDE Painter (-1950)
SALTER, GEORGE Book Designer (-1967)
SALVATORE, VICTOR Sculptor (-1965)
SAMPLE, PAUL Painter (1896-1974)
SANDER, LUDWIG Painter (1906-1975)
SARDEAU, HELENE Sculptor (-1968)
SARKIS (SARKIS SARKISIAN) Painter (1909-1977)
SAUGSTAD, OLAF Craftsman, Teacher (-1950)
SAUNDERS, CLARA ROSMAN Painter, Teacher (-1951)
SAWYER, PHILIP AYER Painter (-1949)
SCARAVAGLIONE, CONCETTA MARIA Sculptor (-1975)
SCHINDLER, R M Architect (1887-1953)
SCHMEIDLER, BLANCHE J Painter
SCHMITZ, CARL LUDWIG Sculptor (-1967)
SCHNAKENBERG, HENRY Painter (1892-1970)
SCHOLLE, HARDINGE Museum Director (-1969)
SCHRACK, JOSEPH EARL Painter (-1973)
SCHREIBER, GEORGES Painter (1904-1977)
SCHREIVER, GEORGE AUGUST Curator, Art Historian (-1977)
SCHROEDER, ERIC Museum Curator, Writer
SCHUSTER, CARL Art Historian, Art Writer (1904-)
SCHUTZ, ANTON Etcher, Writer (1894-1977)
SCHWARTZ, MANFRED Painter (1909-1970)
SCHWARTZMAN, DANIEL Architect (1909-1977)
SCHWARZ, FRANK HENRY Painter (-1951)
SCHWARZ, HEINRICH Museum Curator, Educator (1894-1974)
SCOTT, BERTHA Portrait Painter (-1965)
SEAVER, ESTHER Educator (-1965)
SEIBEL, FRED O Cartoonist (-1968)
SEITZ, WILLIAM CHAPIN Educator, Art Historian (1914-1974)
SELDIS, HENRY J Art Critic (1925-1978)
SELIGMANN, KURT Painter, Printmaker (1900-1962)
SENNHAUSER, JOHN Painter, Designer (-1978)
SERGER, FREDERICK B Painter (-1965)
SESSLER, ALFRED Painter (-1963)
SEXTON, EMILY STRYKER Painter (-1948)
SEYMOUR, CHARLES, JR Art Historian, Curator (1912-1977)
SHAFER, BURR Cartoonist (-1965)
SHAFER, MARGUERITE (PHILLIPS) NEUHAUSER Artist (1888-1976)
SHAHN, BEN Painter (1898-1969)
SHAVER, JAMES ROBERT Painter (-1949)
SHAW, CHARLES GREEN Painter, Writer (1892-1974)
SHEELER, CHARLES Painter (1883-1965)
SHEFFER, GLEN C Painter, Illustrator (-1948)
SHEFFERS, PETER WINTHROP Painter (-1949)
SHEPLER, DWIGHT (CLARK) Painter, Writer (1905-)
SHERMAN, JOHN K(URTZ) Critic (1898-)
SHERWOOD, ROSINA EMMET Painter (-1948)
SHERWOOD, WILLIAM ANDERSON Painter, Etcher (-1951)
SHINN, EVERETT Painter (1876-1953)
SHOENFELT, JOSEPH FRANKLIN Painter (-1968)
SHOPE, IRVIN (SHORTY) Painter (1900-1977)
SHOPEN, KENNETH Painter (-1967)
SHRYOCK, BURNETT HENRY, SR Painter (1904-1971)
SHULL, JAMES MARION Painter
SIEGL, THEODOR Conservator, Lecturer (-1976)
SILVA, WILLIAM POSEY Painter (-1948)
SILVERCRUYS, SUZANNE (MRS EDWARD FORD STEVENSON) Sculptor, Lecturer (-1973)
SILVERMAN, MEL Painter (-1966)
SIMMONS, WILLIAM Etcher (-1949)
SIMONET, SEBASTIAN Illustrator, Painter (-1948)
SIMONS, LOUISE BEDELL Painter (1912-1977)
SIPORIN, MITCHELL Painter, Educator (1910-1976)
SIQUEIROS, DAVID ALFARO Painter (1896-1974)
SKEGGS, DAVID POTTER Designer, Painter (1924-1973)
SKILES, CHARLES Cartoonist (-1969)
SKINAS, JOHN CONSTANTINE Painter (-1966)
SKLAR, GEORGE Animal Painter (-1968)
SKOOGFORS, OLAF Silversmith (-1975)
SLATER, FRANK Portrait Painter (-1965)
SLATKIN, CHARLES E Art Dealer (1908-1977)
SLICK, JAMES NELSON Painter, Sculptor (1901-1975)
SLOAN, JOHN Painter, Teacher
SLOBODKIN, LOUIS Sculptor, Illustrator (1903-1975)
SMALLEY, JANET Illustrator
SMITH, ALBERT DELMONT Portrait Painter (-1962)
SMITH, BARBARA NEFF Patron (1908-1977)
SMITH, DAVID Sculptor (1906-1965)
SMITH, JUDSON Painter (-1962)
SMITH, LAWRENCE M C Collector, Patron (1902-1975)
SMITH, ROBERT C Educator (1912-1975)
SMITH, W HARRY Painter, Etcher (-1951)
SMITH, WALT ALLEN Sculptor, Designer (1910-1971)
SMITHSON, ROBERT I Sculptor, Lecturer (1938-1974)
SMOLIN, NAT Sculptor, Painter (-1950)
SNELGROVE, GORDON WILLIAM Educator
SOGLOW, OTTO Cartoonist (1900-1975)

SOLES, WILLIAM Sculptor (-1967)
SONED, WARREN Painter (-1966)
SOPHER, AARON Painter, Illustrator (1905-1972)
SOPHER, BERNHARD D Sculptor (-1949)
SORENSEN, JOHN HJELMHOF Cartoonist (-1969)
SOROKIN, DAVIS Art Dealer, Painter (1908-1977)
SOYER, MOSES Painter (1899-1974)
SOZIO, ARMANDO Painter (-1966)
SPAETH, OTTO Collector (-1966)
SPEICHER, EUGENE Painter (-1962)
SPENCER, HUGH Illustrator, Photographer (1887-1975)
SPENCER, LEONTINE G Painter (-1964)
SPENCER, NILES Painter (1893-1952)
SPRAGUE-SMITH, ISABELLE DWIGHT (MRS CHARLES) (1861-1951)
SPRAYREGEN, MORRIS Collector
SPRINCHORN, CARL Painter (1887-1971)
SPRINGWEILER, ERWIN FREDERICK Sculptor (1896-1968)
SPRUANCE, BENTON Lithographer (-1967)
SQUIRE, ALLAN TAFT Designer
STARK, JACK GAGE Painter (-1950)
STARKWEATHER, WILLIAM Painter (-1969)
STECHOW, WOLFGANG Art Historian (1896-1975)
STEDMAN, WILFRED HENRY Sculptor (-1950)
STEENE, WILLIAM Painter (-1965)
STEINBERG, MRS MILTON (EDITH) Art Director (1910-1970)
STEINITZ, KATE TRAUMAN Writer, Art Historian
STEPPAT, LEO LUDWIG Sculptor, Educator (-1964)
STERN, HAROLD PHILLIP Museum Director, Writer (1922-1977)
STERRETT, CLIFF Cartoonist (-1964)
STEVENS, LAWRENCE TENNY Sculptor (1896-1972)
STEVENSON, BEULAH Painter (-1965)
STILWELL, WILBUR MOORE Educator, Writer (1908-1974)
STITES, RAYMOND SOMMERS Art Historian, Writer (1899-1974)
STONE, ANNA B Painter
STONE, BEATRICE Sculptor (-1962)
STONEHILL, MARY (MRS GEORGE) Painter (-1951)
STOOPS, HERBERT Illustrator (-1948)
STORRS, JOHN Sculptor (1885-1956)
STRUNK, HERBERT JULIAN Sculptor
STYLES, GEORGE WILLIAM Painter (-1949)
SUMMERS, DUDLEY GLOYNE Painter, Illustrator (1892-1975)
SUSSMAN, RICHARD N Painter, Graphic Artist (1908-1971)
SWAN, BRADFORD F Art Critic, Painter (1907-1976)
SWANN, ERWIN Collector, Patron (1906-1973)
SWARTBURG, B ROBERT Architect (1895-1975)
SWAZO, (PATRICK SWAZO HINDS) Painter, Illustrator (1924-1974)
SWINDELL, BERTHA Painter (-1951)
SWINNERTON, EDNA HUESTIS Miniature Painter (-1964)
SWINNERTON, JAMES Cartoonist, Painter (1875-1974)
SZANTO, LOUIS P Painter (-1965)
SZYK, ARTHUR Illustrator (-1951)
TAKIS, NICHOLAS Painter (-1965)
TANGUY, YVES Painter (1900-1955)
TAYLOR, EMILY (MRS J MADISON TAYLOR) Miniature Painter (-1952)
TEE-VAN, HELEN DAMROSCH Painter, Illustrator (1893-1976)
TEFFT, CHARLES EUGENE Sculptor
TENGGREN, GUSTAV ADOLF Painter (1896-1970)
TEPPER, NATALIE ARRAS Painter (-1950)
THAL, SAMUEL Etcher
THOMPSON, BOB Painter (-1966)
THOMPSON, LESLIE P Painter (-1963)
THOMPSON, WALTER WHITCOMB Painter (-1948)
THORP, EARL NORWELL Sculptor (-1951)
TISCHLER, VICTOR Painter, Lithographer (-1951)
TISHMAN, JACK A Collector (-1966)
TOBEY, MARK Painter (1890-1976)
TOBIAS, THOMAS J Collector, Museum Trustee (1906-1970)
TOMLIN, BRADLEY WALKER Painter (1899-1953)
TOPCHEVSKY, MORRIS Painter, Etcher
TOPPING, JAMES Painter (-1949)
TORRES, HORACIO Painter (1924-1976)
TOWNSEND, LEE Painter (-1965)
TRAPHAGEN, ETHEL Designer (-1963)
TRAVIS, KATHRYNE HAIL Painter (1894-1972)
TRIFON, HARRIETTE Painter, Sculptor
TROCHE, E GUNTER Museum Director (1909-1971)
TUDOR, ROSAMOND Painter, Etcher (-1949)
TUNIS, EDWIN Writer, Illustrator (1897-1973)
TUPPER, ALEXANDER GARFIELD Painter
TURNBULL, GRACE HILL Sculptor, Painter (1880-1976)
TURNBULL, JAMES B Painter (1909-1976)
TURNER, HARRIET FRENCH Painter (-1967)
UHLER, RUTH PERSHING Painter
ULREICH, NURA WOODSON Painter (-1950)
UNDERWOOD, ELISABETH (KENDALL) Artist (1896-1976)
VAGIS, POLYGNOTIS Sculptor (-1965)
VAIL, LAURENCE Collagist (-1968)
VAN DER ROHE, LUDWIG M Architect (-1969)
VAN DRESSER, WILLIAM Portrait Painter (-1950)
VAN ROSEN, ROBERT E Industrial Designer (-1966)
VAN SOELEN, THEODORE Painter (-1964)
VARLEY, FREDERICK H Painter (-1969)
VASILIEFF, NICHOLAS Painter (1892-1970)
VAWTER, MARY H MURRAY Painter
VELSEY, SETH M Sculptor (-1967)
VILLON, VLADIMAR Exhibition Director (1905-1976)
VOGEL, EDWIN CHESTER Collector (-1973)
VON DER LANCKEN, FRANK Painter (-1950)
VON FUEHRER, OTTMAR F Painter (-1967)
VON JOST, ALEXANDER Painter (-1968)
VON WICHT, JOHN Painter, Graphic Designer (1888-1970)
VORIS, MARK Educator, Painter (1907-1974)
VOSE, ROBERT C Art Dealer (-1965)
VUILLEMENOT, FRED A Designer, Sculptor (-1952)
WADDELL, RICHARD H Art Dealer (-1974)
WALDRON, JAMES MACKEILAR Painter (1909-1974)
WALKER, EVERETT Educator (-1968)
WALKER, HENRY BABCOCK, JR Collector (-1966)
WALKER, HERSCHEL CAREY Collector
WALKER, HUDSON D Collector, Art Administrator (1907-1976)
WALKOWITZ, ABRAHAM Painter (1880-1965)
WALTER, WILLIAM F Artist (1904-1977)
WALTMANN, HARRY FRANKLIN Painter (-1951)
WARING, LAURA WHEELER Portrait Painter (-1949)
WARNER, EVERETT LONGLEY Painter (-1963)
WARREN, MRS GEORGE HENRY Collector (1897-1976)
WASHBURN, CADWALLADER Painter (-1965)
WATKINS, FRANKLIN CHENAULT Painter (1894-1972)
WATSON, HILDEGARDE LASELL Artist, Patron (-1976)
WATTS, DOROTHY BURT (TROUT) Artist (1892-1977)
WAUGH, COULTON Painter, Writer (1896-1973)
WAUGH, SIDNEY Sculptor (-1963)
WEBER, HUGO Painter (1918-1971)
WEBER, MAX Painter, Sculptor (1881-1961)
WEBSTER, H T Cartoonist (-1952)
WECHSIER, HERMAN J Art Consultant, Writer (1904-1976)
WEDOW, RUDY Sculptor (-1965)
WEEKS, LEO ROSCO Painter, Illustrator (1903-1977)
WEHR, PAUL ADAM Illustrator, Designer (1914-1973)
WEINBERGER, DR MARTIN Educator, Scholar (-1965)
WEINGAERTNER, HANS Painter (1896-1970)
WEINMAN, ADOLPH ALEXANDER Sculptor (-1952)
WEISBECKER, CLEMENT Painter
WEISEL, DEBORAH DELP Painter (-1951)
WEISSBUCH, OSCAR Painter (-1948)
WELCH, LIVINGSTON Sculptor, Painter (1901-1976)
WENGENROTH, STOW Lithographer (1906-1978)
WENLEY, ARCHIBALD GIBSON Museum Director (-1962)
WERTHEIM, MRS MAURICE Collector (-1974)

WESCOTT, PAUL Painter (1904-1970)
WEST, PENNERTON Painter (-1965)
WESTON, HAROLD Painter (1894-1972)
WHARTON, JAMES PEARCE Educator (-1963)
WHITE, EUGENE B Painter (-1966)
WHITE, MINOR Photographer (1908-1976)
WHITE, WALTER L Painter
WHITNEY, CHARLES E Interior Designer, Publisher (1903-1977)
WIEGHARDT, PAUL Painter, Educator (1897-1969)
WIENER, GEORGE Art Dealer
WIGGINS, GUY Painter (-1962)
WILCOX, LUCIA Painter
WILDENSTEIN, FELIX Gallery Director (-1952)
WILDENSTEIN, GEORGES Art Editor (-1963)
WILDMAN, CAROLINE LAX Painter (-1949)
WILES, IRVING R Portrait Painter (-1948)
WILFORD, LORAN Painter, Educator (1892-1972)
WILFRED, THOMAS Sculptor (1889-1968)
WILKINSON, JOHN Painter (1913-1973)
WILLIAMS, EDWARD K Painter
WILLIAMS, HERMANN WARNER, JR Art Administrator, Writer (1908-1975)
WILLIAMS, JULIA TOCHIE Painter (-1948)
WILLIAMS, KEITH SHAW Painter, Etcher (-1951)
WILLIAMS, WHEELER Sculptor (1897-1972)
WILLIAMSON, CLARA MCDONALD Painter (-1976)
WILSON, HELEN Sculptor (-1974)
WILSON, ORME Patron (-1966)
WILSON, SOL Painter (1896-1974)
WINGERT, PAUL STOVER Writer, Art Historian (1900-1974)
WINSTANLEY, JOHN BREYFOGLE Painter (-1947)
WINTER, EZRA Painter (-1949)
WISA, LOUIS, SR Cartoonist (-1953)
WISE, LOUISE WATERMAN (MRS STEPHEN S) Painter (-1947)
WITTENBORN, GEORGE Collector, Art Dealer (1905-1974)
WOLFF, ROBERT JAY Painter, Writer (1905-1978)
WOLFSON, SIDNEY Painter, Sculptor (1911-1973)
WOLLE, MURIEL SIBELL Painter, Writer (1898-1977)
WOODWARD, STANLEY Painter (1890-1970)
WOOLF, SAMUEL J Painter (-1948)
WORCESTER, EVA Painter (1892-1970)
WORTHAM, HAROLD Painter, Art Consultant (1909-1974)
WRIGHT, GEORGE HAND Etcher, Painter (-1951)
WRIGHT, RUSSEL Designer, Sculptor (1904-1976)
WURTZBURGER, JANET E C Collector, Patron (1908-)
XCERON, JEAN Painter (1890-1967)
YEE, CHIANG Painter, Calligrapher (1903-1977)
YERBYSMITH, ERNEST ALFRED Sculptor (-1952)
YORK, ROBERT Cartoonist (1919-1975)
YOST, FRED Painter (-1968)
YOUNG, CHARLES MORRIS Painter (-1964)
YOUNG, CHIC (MURAT BERNARD YOUNG) Cartoonist (1901-)
ZACKS, SAMUEL JACOB Collector, Patron (1904-1970)
ZEIGLER, LEE WOODWARD Illustrator (-1952)
ZERBE, KARL Painter, Educator (1903-1972)
ZIGROSSER, CARL Writer (1891-1975)
ZILZER, GYULA Printmaker, Painter (1898-1969)
ZIMMER, FRITZ Sculptor
ZIMMERMAN, FREDERICK A Painter, Instructor (1886-1974)
ZIROLI, ANGELO GERARDO Sculptor (-1948)
ZOGBAUM, WILFRID Painter (-1965)
ZORACH, MARGUERITE Painter (-1968)
ZORACH, WILLIAM Sculptor (1887-1966)
ZUEHLKE, CLARENCE EDGAR Painter (-1963)